PRESENTED TO:

BY:

ON:

CSB **Student** Study Bible

CSB **Student** Study Bible

CSB Student Study Bible
Copyright © 2021 by Holman Bible Publishers
Nashville, Tennessee. All Rights Reserved.

Christian Standard Bible® Copyright © 2017 by Holman Bible Publishers.
Christian Standard Bible® and CSB® are federally registered trademarks of Holman Bible Publishers.
CSB Text Edition: 2020

The interior of the *CSB Student Study Bible* was designed and typeset by 2K/DENMARK, using Bible Serif created by 2K/DENMARK, Højbjerg, Denmark. Proofreading was provided by Peachtree Publishing Services, Peachtree City, Georgia.

Binding	ISBN
Slate Hardcover	978-1-0877-4754-5
Deep Coral Hardcover	978-1-0877-5028-6
Emerald LeatherTouch	978-1-0877-5030-9
Ginger LeatherTouch	978-1-0877-5031-6
Brown LeatherTouch	978-1-0877-5029-3
Brown LeatherTouch Indexed	978-1-0877-5033-0
Navy LeatherTouch	978-1-0877-5032-3
Navy LeatherTouch Indexed	978-1-0877-5034-7

Printed in China
1 2 3 4 5 — 24 23 22 21
RRD

▼ Table of Contents

▼ Books of the Bible

Old Testament

New Testament

◥ CSB Student Study Bible Features

99 Essential Christian Truths

99 Key Scripture Memory Verses

◥ Introduction to
the CSB Student Study Bible

Christians have long affirmed the belief that God is there and he is not silent. The Bible not only testifies to the objective truth that God exists, but it also reveals God's nature, character, and purpose in creating humanity. Unlike other written works—whether modern or ancient—the Bible is unique in this respect. Yes, the Scriptures of the Old and New Testaments contain vital historical information supported by modern archaeology, as well as biographical details on some of the most fascinating individuals throughout history. However, the Bible isn't merely a historical or biographical record, nor is it simply a collection of sixty-six books spread across centuries of ancient history. First and foremost, the Bible is God's authoritative means of revealing his character and purposes to us. Through the Bible, we gain answers to the most fundamental questions about our existence: Where did we come from? Why are we here? What is the cause of the brokenness we see around us? How can everything be made right? The Bible provides answers to all these questions and more by telling a unified, true story that applies to all peoples in all places at all times. It is the grand narrative of humanity's existence, and the hero of that true story is the same hero we need today—Jesus!

Since the Bible is essential in knowing God personally, it is essential to know how to navigate the Bible's books and genres so that we may interpret and understand it correctly. The good news is that one doesn't require a specialized theological degree to do this. Thankfully, helpful resources exist to enable readers to understand Scripture. The *CSB Student Study Bible* is one such resource representing the work of scholars and teachers who have devoted their lives to living and teaching the truths of God's Word.

The goal of each tool in this study Bible—whether study notes, articles, book introductions, maps, illustrations, or charts—is to help bring the text of Scripture to light for you. Of course, these study tools are subservient to the text, designed to keep the focus on Scripture. In the end, our hope is that this study Bible equips students to engage God's Word on a deep level. Our prayer is that students will see how all the events and stories of Scripture connect and point to the Rescuer, Jesus (Lk 24:13–35); that they will see the glory of God in the face of Jesus (2Co 4:6); and that they themselves will experience the type of life change and transformation that could only be the result of encountering Jesus through his Word. In short, we pray the study tools in this Bible will draw you deeper into the inspired Word of God that continues to speak to us today. May all who use this Bible hear the voice of Jesus and faithfully follow him as King!

Andy McLean
General Editor

◢ Features
of the CSB Student Study Bible

The CSB was undertaken as a translation that strongly supports Bible study. In the *CSB Student Study Bible*, the Scripture is primary. All features and tools are designed to help you understand the Scripture and be transformed by it.

1 Study notes provide historical, cultural, linguistic, and biblical information that enhances your understanding of a given passage. Words in bold are directly from the Scripture text.

2 Introductions give overviews of biblical books by providing information on circumstances of writing including author and background, message and purpose, contribution to the Bible, structure, and an outline.

3 Articles give in-depth coverage to major biblical/theological issues.

4 Character profiles discuss biblical figures, their role in the biblical storyline, and how you can learn from them.

5 Maps illuminate the Bible text by showing its geographical context.

6 Charts organize information in a way that enables the reader to grasp important connections quickly.

7 Knowing your faith Q&A consider significant objections to Christianity and offer reliable answers to strengthen your faith.

8 Essential truths provide brief discussions of important teachings of the Christian faith.

9 Illustrations recreate architectural structures that were part of the landscape in which the Bible was written. Being able to visualize these structures provides a context in which to read and study passages of Scripture.

10 Timelines place the book in a chronological framework of biblical events.

1 Samuel Timeline

1350–1150 BC

DEBORAH 1360?–1300?
GIDEON 1250?–1175?
The Olmec civilization flourishes in Central America, establishing a foundation for subsequent civilizations in the Americas. **1200**
The process of iron smelting is developed in Armenia. **1200–1000**
World's first recorded labor strike, Thebes, Egypt **1170**

1150–1000 BC

JEPHTHAH 1250?–1175?
RUTH 1175?–1125?
Events in Ruth **1140?**
Botanical gardens are developed by Assyrians during the reign of Tiglath-pileser I. **1114–976**
Events in 1 Samuel **1105?–1010**
Saul is anointed king. **1050**
David becomes king of Judah. **1010**
Events in 2 Samuel **1010–970**
Events in 1 Chronicles **1010–970**
David becomes king over all Israel. **1003**

forefather's family, so that none in your family will reach old age. **32** You will see distress in the place of worship, in spite of all that is good in

If he calls you, say, 'Speak, LORD, for your servant is listening.' " So Samuel went and lay down in his place.

^2:20 DSS; MT reads *he* ^2:27 Lit *the house of your father* ^2:28 Lit *selected him* ^2:33 Lit *grief to your eyes* ^2:33 DSS, LXX read *die by the sword of men* ^2:33 Lit *die men* ^3:4 DSS, LXX read *called, "Samuel! Samuel!"*

2:21 The LORD paid attention to Hannah's need is literally "Yahweh visited Hannah." The same Hebrew expression occurs in reference to Abraham's wife Sarah when she conceived Isaac, another child of promise (Gn 21:1). Hannah is abundantly blessed, but her **three sons and two daughters** are nonetheless contrasted with **the boy Samuel**, who **grew up in the presence of the LORD**.
2:23–25 The words **since the LORD intended to kill them** reveal that much like Pharaoh in Moses's day (Ex 4:21; 5:2; 7:13), the persistent unbelief of Hophni and Phinehas led to God's giving them over to judgment.

2:26 The phrase **grew in stature and in favor with the LORD and with people** is strikingly similar to the description of Jesus as a child (Lk 2:52).
2:29 Eli is held responsible for his sons' actions. **Despise** is literally "kick at." **You have honored your sons more than me** rebukes Eli on the basis of the first commandment and the command to love the Lord with all one's heart, soul, and strength.
2:34 As the chief sinners, **Hophni and Phinehas** would be the first to **die**—and would do so **on the same day**.
2:35 Some suggest Samuel is intended by the phrase **a faithful priest**, but Samuel

did not have a **lasting dynasty** (8:1–5). The term may denote the priestly line of Zadok, who eventually succeeded Eli's line (1Kg 2:27), or any and all priests who followed the Lord faithfully. **My anointed one** designates the line of David, for whom God also built a lasting dynasty (2Sm 7:11–16).
3:1 Prophetic visions were not widespread because of the general corruption of the time.
3:2–3 The **lamp of God** was to burn from evening until morning (Ex 27:21), so the wording suggests a time just before dawn.
3:9 Eli's suggested words to Samuel, **Speak, LORD, for your servant is listening**, provide

---

① **Study notes**

▼ Introduction to
1 Samuel

Circumstances of Writing
Early tradition suggests 1 and 2 Samuel were originally one book. Some scholars believe Samuel was largely responsible for the material up to 1 Samuel 25 and that the prophets Nathan and Gad gave significant input to the rest (based on 1Ch 29:29). This proposal, however, must remain speculative, because the books name no authors. First Samuel 27:6 suggests the book was not completed until perhaps a few generations after the division of the kingdom around 930 BC.
After Israel's conquest of the land during the days of Joshua, Israel entered a time of apostasy. The book of Judges describes recurrences of a cycle with predictable phases. First, the people sinned against the Lord and fell into idolatry. Second, the Lord raised up an adversary to afflict them and turn them back to him. Third, the people cried out to the Lord in repentance. Fourth, the Lord brought deliverance for them through a judge whom he raised up. The book of Judges' famous verse, "In those days there was no king in Israel; everyone did whatever seemed right to him" (21:25), aptly describes the period. The book of 1 Samuel picks up the historical record toward the end of those stormy days.

Contribution to the Bible
The books of 1 and 2 Samuel describe Israel's transition from a loosely organized tribal league under God (a theocracy) to centralized leadership under a king who answered to God (a monarchy). Samuel's life and ministry

greatly shaped this period of restructuring as he consistently pointed people back to God.
Saul's rule highlighted the dangers to which the Israelites fell victim as they clamored for a king to lead them. Samuel's warnings fell on deaf ears (1Sm 8:10–20) because God's people were intent on becoming like the nations around them. In the end, they got exactly what they asked for, but they paid a terrible price. Saul's life stands as a warning to trust God's timing for life's provisions.
David's rule testified to the amazing works the Lord could and would do through a life yielded to him. Israel's second king seemed quite aware of God's blessing on his life and displayed a tender heart toward the things of God (1Sm 5:12; 7:1–2; 22:1–51; 23:1–7). Later generations would receive blessing because of David's life (1s 37:35). God's special covenant with David (1Sm 7:1–29) found its ultimate fulfillment in Jesus, the son of David (Lk 1:32–33). The consequences of David's sin with Bathsheba, however, stand as a warning to all who experience sin's attraction. God holds his children accountable for their actions, and even forgiven sin can have terrible consequences.

Structure
The first seven chapters of 1 Samuel describe Samuel's birth, call, and initial ministry among the Israelites. Chapter 8 is a major turning point as the people ask for a king to rule them "the same as all the other nations have" (v. 5). Chapters 9–12 then describe Saul's selection—at God's direction, yet not his perfect will for the time (12:16–18).

First Samuel 13–31 describes Saul's victories and failures. Saul was a king with great physical stature and military skill (14:47–52), but his heart was not one with the Lord (13:14). His unwillingness to obey the Lord's commands ultimately outweighed his accomplishments, and

chapters 16–31 describe his reign's downward spiral. During this time, God raised up David and was preparing him for the day he would succeed Saul—a fact Saul gradually realized (15:28; 24:20–21; 28:17).

Outline
i. Samuel's Ministry (1:1–12:25)
    A. Samuel's birth and youth (1:1–3:21)
    B. The ark narrative (4:1–7:17)
    C. The people ask for a king (8:1–12:25)
ii. Saul's Reign (13:1–31:13)
    A. Saul's battles with the Philistines (13:1–14:52)
    B. Saul's failure against the Amalekites (15:1–35)
    C. David's selection as Saul's successor (16:1–23)
    D. David's victory over Goliath (17:1–58)
    E. David's struggles with Saul (18:1–26:25)
    F. Saul's reign ends (27:1–31:13)

---

② **Introductions**

1000–970 BC

SAMSON 1120?–1060?
SAMUEL 1105–1025
SAUL 1080–1010
DAVID 1050–970
Iron technology advances throughout India. **1000**
The Chinese store ice for use in refrigeration. **1000**
Oats are cultivated in central Europe. **1000**
David conquers Jerusalem. **1000?**
David moves the ark of the covenant
    to Jerusalem. **1000?**
Absalom's revolt **975?**
Solomon becomes king. **970**

970–900 BC

Solomon begins construction of the
    temple in Jerusalem. **966**
The temple is dedicated. **959**
Ascendancy of Neo-Assyrian Empire **950**
The kingdom divides. **931?**
Israel: the northern kingdom **931–722**
Judah: the southern kingdom **931–586**
Etruscans emigrate from Lydia to Italy as
    a result of an extended famine. **900**

3 Articles

▼ The Uniqueness of the Genesis Creation Story

by Kenneth A. Mathews

While there are many similarities between parts of Genesis and ancient Near Eastern (ANE) myths, there are also fundamental differences. These are seen especially in the significantly different views of the Creator and creation. Five features in particular distinguish the biblical creation account and perspective. The biblical teaching is so theologically distinctive from that

Creation out of Nothing

In Genesis the Creator by inherent authority as Sovereign Lord spoke creation into a functional, well-ordered existence. There was no eternal precreated matter, such as was believed in the ancient myths. Genesis says God spoke all things into origination. This does not mean he uttered words that possessed inherent magical powers. Rather, the irrevo-

---

of living beings (1:20,24,30; 9:12,15–16). Nevertheless, humans are considered to be in a class by themselves since they alone are made in God's image.

2:14 The **Tigris** and **Euphrates** rivers, as well as **Assyria**, probably correspond to geographical features associated with modern Iraq.

stated especially forcefully in the original language, with a two-verb construction, "dying you shall die" (**you will certainly die**). Although Adam and Eve did not die

4 Character profiles

Character profile:
Adam

Of all the men in the Bible, only two knew what it was like to have a personal, untainted, unobstructed relationship with God himself. One was Jesus, the Son of God. The other was Adam.

Adam experienced life in Eden—a name that's become synonymous with paradise, and for good reason. Eden was God's showcase. On display in this garden paradise was nature in perfect harmony, as the Creator intended. Genesis 2:9 says God filled the garden with trees that were "pleasing in appearance and good for food." Imagine the beauty, the wonder, the divine artistry that Adam enjoyed.

God gave Adam the responsibility of working the garden and caring for it. But this was not a burdensome task. Though the nature of work changed later as part of the curse (see Gn 3:17–19), we may assume that Adam derived deep satisfaction and a sense of fulfillment from his work in the garden.

Only Adam could explain what it was like to live on earth with only God himself and the animals as companions. Only Adam could describe the experience of waking from a deep slumber to find his female counterpart—his perfect companion and complement—next to him.

Adam enjoyed God's company, and God enjoyed his. Adam experienced a clean conscience. He knew what it was like to be naked and unashamed. Such was life in Eden.

Ultimately, though, Eden was not enough for Adam. God charged him, "You must not eat from the tree of the knowledge

of good and evil" (2:17), but this proved to be too restrictive for Adam. He gave in to temptation. Along with his wife, he disobeyed God and ate of the fruit. And everything changed in an instant.

Genesis 3:7 describe the consequences of their actions. "The eyes of both of them were opened, and they knew they were naked." They experienced guilt and shame for the first time.

Then when God came to walk in the garden at the time of the evening breeze, Adam didn't join him. Instead, he hid from his Creator.

The punishment for Adam's sin altered the human experience. Among other things, the work that had once brought pleasure and fulfillment would become difficult and painful. And with the ideal of Eden corrupted, Adam and Eve were evicted from the garden. For the rest of their lives they were forced to make their way in an inhospitable world.

More devastating than all of that, though, was the transformation Adam experienced in his relationship with God. Guilt and shame eroded the innocence that had once marked Adam's life. Bitterness and hard-heartedness followed until the ideals of Eden were nothing but a memory. Intimacy was lost.

The good news is that God took the steps that humankind could not take to restore the relationship ruined by Adam's disobedience. In his unfathomable grace, God sent his Son to pay the penalty for Adam's sin—and for the sins of Adam's descendants. Jesus's death and resurrection enable believers to stand before God and to have a personal, intimate relationship with him. Sin and disobedience don't get the final word in our relationship with God—not as long as his grace is available to us.

Hebrew text describes **70 men** literally "with him" (sg.), suggesting some minor textual confusion. Probably the original text read

enough priests to carry the gold and silver donated to the temple (vv. 24–30) and that the **Levites** were needed for this task.

8:17 The distinguished entourage was sent to ask **Iddo** for Levites to join the exiles in their return to the land. Their request was

5 Maps

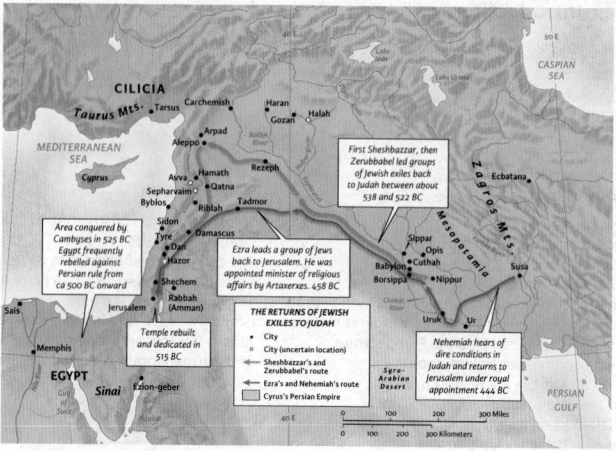

6 Charts

◥ The LORD Will Provide

	SUBJECT TO DEATH	THE SUBSTITUTE	THE REASON
Genesis 22	Isaac—Abraham's "only son" *(Gn 22:2)*	A Ram	Abraham named that place "The LORD Will Provide," so today it is said, "It will be provided on the LORD's mountain" *(Gn 22:14)*.
			The blood on the houses of the Israelites would be

...rering. This law protected vulnerable female slaves who did not have the social power and economic clout that free men had.

...entrails. **Witchcraft** involved interpreting natural phenomena such as clouds or stars, or communicating with the spirits of the dead.

...was also a custom that denoted belonging to a pagan cult, or it was done to ward off spirits of the dead.

7 Knowing your faith Q&A

Q&A: Is "right and wrong" evidence for the existence of God?

by Dave Sterrett

Have you ever been in a situation in which you knew what you were about to do was wrong? Each of us has acted in ways that we knew were not right. In these moments, we knew right from wrong because a universal moral law is written on our hearts. Some people deny the existence of this law. They say morality (a standard of right and wrong) is created by individuals or cultures. While it is true that moral codes differ from one culture to the next, the differences are minor. The deep principles (prohibitions against murder, theft, lying, etc., and positive values of honesty, fidelity, and courage) are universal.

Still, people resist this truth. If someone you know says all morality is relative, try asking him if lying is wrong for all people. He may think it's no big deal to lie to others when it benefits him, but as soon as he finds that someone has lied to *him*, he is sure to be angry. Why? Because deep down he knows lying is wrong. The moral law says so.

The existence of this law points to God's existence. After all, if there is a law written on all human hearts, there must be a law writer. Hence, the moral argument for God's existence is based on the evidence of an absolute moral law that

in turn gives us reason to believe in the existence of a moral law giver (God). After all, these universal laws cannot be the creation of sinful humans, all of whom belong to a specific time and place. Since the law transcends time, place, and culture, the giver of the law must transcend these conditions.

Dr. Martin Luther King Jr. appealed to the God-given universal moral law to explain the evil of racism:

I'm here to say to you this morning that some things are right and some things are wrong. Eternally so, absolutely so. It's wrong to hate. It always has been wrong and it always will be wrong! It's wrong in America, it's wrong in Germany, it's wrong in Russia, it's wrong in China. It was wrong in 2000 BC, and it's wrong in AD 1954. It always has been wrong...Some things in this universe are absolute. The God of the universe has made it so. And so long as we adopt this relative attitude toward right and wrong, we're revolting against the very laws of God himself ("Rediscovering Lost Values," a speech delivered in Detroit, February 28, 1954).

Dr. King got it right. Morality is from God, and a revolt against morality is a revolt against God. By asking the right questions, we can prompt our non-Christian friends to admit that there is a universal standard of right and wrong. Through their admission of the moral law, we can point them to the God of the Bible, the one whose own character is the foundation of the moral law.

8 Essential truths

4:3 Anointed priest refers to the high priest (6:22; 21:10; Ex 29:7). The traditional translation **sin offering** is better understood as "purification offering" since it involved the ritual removal of impurities and provided forgiveness.

The instructions for the sin offering (4:1–5:13) consisted of two parts: the general instructions (4:1–35) and the appendix naming special circumstances (5:1–13). The

the remorseful sinner not only to receive forgiveness but to have the assurance of acceptance with God. For this reason, the ritual included the application of blood to the sanctuary furnishings, not to the person (4:5–7,16–18,25,30,34).

The sin offering varied according to the progressive degrees of responsibility: the high priest (Lv 4:3–12), the congregation collectively (vv. 13–21), the ruler (vv. 22–26), and the individual layperson (vv. 27–35). The underlying principle is that although all sin is contaminating, the sins of leadership (priest, king) and the congregation have greater impact than those of the individual transgressor. The variation in the cost of the sacrifice and the placement of blood on the sanctuary furnishings reflected this same principle.

4:5 This was the only offering that required the high priest to bring the blood into the tent of meeting.

4:6 Seven indicates the thoroughness of the purging; this number occurs also in the accounts of the ordination rite (8:11), purification of lepers (14:7), the Day of Atonement

curtain inside the tent canopy. Aaron lit this each morning and evening (Ex 30:7–8). Only priests could offer the incense (2Ch 26:18). The altar symbolized intercessory prayer (Ps 141:2; Rv 5:8; 8:3–4).

The four **horns**, one protruding from each of the altar's four corners (Ex 30:1–6; 38:2), conveyed the power of a formidable animal (Dt 33:17) and thus the efficacy (strength, e.g., 1Sm 2:10; Am 3:14) of the altar's purpose. The disposal of the remaining blood **at the base of the** (courtyard's) **altar**, around which a trench probably ran (1Kg 18:32), occurred only for the sin offering of the five offerings detailed in Lv 1–7 and also during the special ordination rites of Aaron's priesthood (9:9; Ex 29:12).

4:8–12 A distinguishing feature of the sin offering was that the bull's remaining parts were taken **to a ceremonially clean place outside the camp** where they were burned.

4:13–14 The word **errs** (Hb *shegag*) refers to unintended transgressions (cp. v. 2). This sort of sin escaped **notice** (Hb *'alam*), hidden

#06 99 Essential Christian Truths

GOD IS MERCIFUL

Mercy refers to God's compassion and is often expressed in God withholding punishment for sin (Eph 2:4–5; Ti 3:5). Both mercy and grace are undeserved; humanity can do nothing to earn them from God. If one could, then mercy and grace would no longer be God's free gift.

⑨ Illustrations

309

Typical Israelite Home of the Iron Age
ca 1300 BC–ca 600 BC

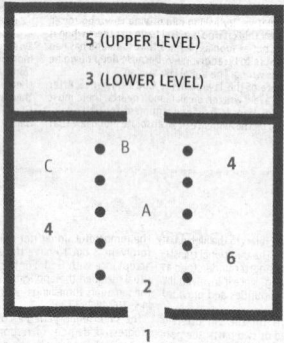

1. ENTRANCE
2. CENTRAL COURTYARD
   A. Fire pit
   B. Cistern
3. LIVING QUARTERS ("LONG ROOM")
4. STORAGE/WORKSHOP/KITCHEN
5. ROOFTOP (EXTRA AREA FOR EATING, WORKING,
   AND SLEEPING DURING WARM WEATHER)
   C. Roller – for recompacting clay roof following
   rain. Man shown is patching roof.
6. ANIMAL PEN

```
           5 (UPPER LEVEL)
           3 (LOWER LEVEL)

        • B
   C    •        •      4
        •        •
        •    A   •
   4    •        •
        •        •      6
        •        •
             2
             1
```

Israelite four-room house. Some interpreters believe Jephthah lived in a four-room house that was common in Israel during the Iron Age. Many such houses had a room for the family's animals. If Jephthah lived in such a house, his vow (11:30) may have been based on the assumption that one of his animals would be the first to greet him when he returned from victory over the Ammonites. For a different view, see the note at 11:29-33.

Introduction to the Christian Standard Bible®

The Bible is God's revelation to humanity. It is our only source for completely reliable information about God, what happens when we die, and where history is headed. The Bible reveals these things because it is God's inspired Word, inerrant in the original manuscripts. Bible translation brings God's Word from the ancient languages (Hebrew, Greek, and Aramaic) into today's world. In dependence on God's Spirit to accomplish this sacred task, the CSB Translation Oversight Committee and Holman Bible Publishers present the Christian Standard Bible.

Textual Base of the CSB

The textual base for the New Testament (NT) is the Nestle-Aland *Novum Testamentum Graece*, 28th edition, and the United Bible Societies' *Greek New Testament*, 5th corrected edition. The text for the Old Testament (OT) is the *Biblia Hebraica Stuttgartensia*, 4th edition.

Where there are significant differences among Hebrew, Aramaic, or Greek manuscripts, the translators follow what they believe is the original reading and indicate the main alternative(s) in footnotes. The CSB uses the traditional verse divisions found in most Protestant Bibles.

Goals of This Translation

- Provide English-speaking people worldwide with an accurate translation in contemporary English.
- Provide an accurate translation for personal study, sermon preparation, private devotions, and memorization.
- Provide a text that is clear and understandable, suitable for public reading, and shareable so that all may access its life-giving message.
- Affirm the authority of Scripture and champion its absolute truth against skeptical viewpoints.

Translation Philosophy of the Christian Standard Bible

Most discussions of Bible translations speak of two opposite approaches: formal equivalence and dynamic equivalence. This terminology is meaningful, but Bible translations cannot be neatly sorted into these two categories. There is room for another category of translation philosophy that capitalizes on the strengths of the other two.

1. Formal Equivalence:

Often called "word-for-word" (or "literal") translation, the principle of formal equivalence seeks as nearly as possible to preserve the structure of the original language. It seeks to represent each word of the original text with an exact equivalent word in the translation so that the reader can see word for word what the original human author wrote. The merits of this approach include its consistency with the conviction that the Holy Spirit did inspire the very words of Scripture in the original manuscripts. It also provides the English Bible student some access to the structure of the text in the original language. Formal equivalence can achieve accuracy to the degree that English has an exact equivalent for each word and that the grammatical patterns of the original language can be reproduced in understandable English. However, it can sometimes result in awkward, if not incomprehensible, English or in a misunderstanding of the author's intent. The literal rendering of ancient idioms is especially difficult.

2. Dynamic or Functional Equivalence:

Often called "thought-for-thought" translation, the principle of dynamic equivalence rejects as misguided the attempt to preserve the structure of the original language. It proceeds by extracting the meaning of a text from its form and then translating that meaning so that it makes the same impact on modern readers that the ancient text made on its original readers. Strengths of this approach include a high degree of clarity and readability, especially in places where the original is difficult to render word for word. It also acknowledges that accurate and effective translation may require interpretation. However, the meaning of a text cannot always be neatly separated from its form, nor can it always be precisely determined. A biblical author may have intended multiple meanings, but these may be lost with the elimination of normal structures. In striving for readability, dynamic equivalence also sometimes overlooks and loses some of the less prominent elements of meaning. Furthermore, lack of formal correspondence to the original makes it difficult to verify accuracy and thus can affect the usefulness of the translation for in-depth Bible study.

3. Optimal Equivalence:

In practice, translations are seldom if ever purely formal or dynamic but favor one theory of Bible translation or the other to varying degrees. Optimal equivalence as a translation philosophy recognizes that form cannot always be neatly separated from meaning and should not be changed unless comprehension demands it. The primary goal of translation is to convey the sense of the original with as much clarity as the original text and the translation language permit. Optimal equivalence appreciates the goals of formal equivalence but also recognizes its limitations.

Optimal equivalence starts with an exhaustive analysis of the text at every level (word, phrase, clause, sentence, discourse) in the original language to determine its original meaning and intention (or purpose). Then, relying on the latest and best language tools and experts, the nearest corresponding semantic and linguistic equivalents are used to convey as much of the information and intention of the original text with as much clarity and readability as possible. This process assures the maximum transfer of both the words and the thoughts contained in the original.

The CSB uses optimal equivalence as its translation philosophy. In the many places throughout the Bible where a word-for-word rendering is understandable, a literal translation is used. When a word-for-word rendering might obscure the meaning for a modern audience, a more dynamic translation is used. The Christian Standard Bible places equal value on fidelity to the original and readability for a modern audience, resulting in a translation that achieves both goals.

The Gender Language Use in Bible Translation

The goal of the translators of the Christian Standard Bible has not been to promote a cultural ideology but to translate the Bible faithfully. Recognizing modern usage of English, the CSB regularly translates the plural of the Greek word ανθρωπος ("man") as "people" instead of "men," and occasionally the singular as "one," "someone," or "everyone," when the supporting pronouns in the original languages validate such a translation. While the CSB avoids using "he" or "him" unnecessarily, the translation does not restructure sentences to avoid them when they are in the text.

History of the CSB

After several years of preliminary development, Holman Bible Publishers, the oldest Bible publisher in North America, assembled an international, interdenominational team of one hundred scholars, editors, stylists, and proofreaders, all of whom were committed to biblical inerrancy. Outside consultants and reviewers contributed valuable suggestions from their areas of expertise. Working from the original languages, an executive team of translators edited, polished, and reviewed the final manuscript, which was first published as the Holman Christian Standard Bible (HCSB) in 2004.

A standing committee was also formed to maintain the HCSB translation and look for ways to improve readability without compromising accuracy. As with the original translation team, the committee that prepared this revision of the HCSB, renamed the Christian Standard Bible, is international and interdenominational, comprising evangelical scholars who honor the inspiration and authority of God's written Word.

Traditional Features Found in the CSB

In keeping with a long line of Bible publications, the CSB has retained a number of features found in traditional Bibles:

1. Traditional theological vocabulary (for example, *justification, sanctification, redemption*) has been retained since such terms have no other translation equivalent that adequately communicates their exact meaning.
2. Traditional spellings of names and places found in most Bibles have been used to make the CSB compatible with most Bible study tools.
3. Some editions of the CSB will print the words of Christ in red letters to help readers easily locate the spoken words of the Lord Jesus Christ.
4. Descriptive headings, printed above each section of Scripture, help readers quickly identify the contents of that section.
5. OT passages quoted in the NT are indicated. In the CSB, they are set in boldface type.

How the Names of God Are Translated

The Christian Standard Bible consistently translates the Hebrew names for God as follows:

Hebrew original:	CSB English:
Elohim	God
YHWH (Yahweh)	LORD
Adonai	Lord
Adonai Yahweh	Lord GOD
Yahweh Sabaoth	LORD of Armies
El Shaddai	God Almighty

Footnotes

Footnotes are used to show readers how the original biblical language has been understood in the CSB.

1. Old Testament (OT) Textual Footnotes

OT textual notes show important differences among Hebrew (Hb) manuscripts and ancient OT versions, such as the Septuagint and the

Vulgate. See the list of abbreviations on page XVIII for a list of other ancient versions used.

Some OT textual notes (like NT textual notes) give only an alternate textual reading. However, other OT textual notes also give the support for the reading chosen by the editors as well as for the alternate textual reading. For example, the CSB text of Psalm 12:7 reads,

> You, LORD, will guard us;
> you will protect us^A from this
> generation forever.

The textual footnote for this verse reads,

> ^A12:7 Some Hb mss, LXX; other Hb mss read *him*

The textual note in this example means that there are two different readings found in the Hebrew manuscripts: some manuscripts read *us* and others read *him*. The CSB translators chose the reading *us*, which is also found in the Septuagint (LXX), and placed the other Hebrew reading *him* in the footnote.

Two other kinds of OT textual notes are:

Alt Hb tradition reads ___	a variation given by scribes in the Hebrew manuscript tradition (known as *Kethiv/ Qere* and *Tiqqune Sopherim* readings)
Hb uncertain	when it is unclear what the original Hebrew text was

2. New Testament (NT) Textual Footnotes

NT textual notes indicate significant differences among Greek manuscripts (mss) and are normally indicated in one of three ways:

> Other mss read ___
> Other mss add ___
> Other mss omit ___

In the NT, some textual footnotes that use the word "add" or "omit" also have square brackets before and after the corresponding verses in the biblical text. Examples of this use of square brackets are Mark 16:9–20 and John 7:53–8:11.

3. Other Kinds of Footnotes

Lit ___	a more literal rendering in English of the Hebrew, Aramaic, or Greek text
Or ___	an alternate or less likely English translation of the same Hebrew, Aramaic, or Greek text
=	an abbreviation for "it means" or "it is equivalent to"
Hb, Aramaic, Gk	the actual Hebrew, Aramaic, or Greek word is given using equivalent English letters
Hb obscure	the existing Hebrew text is especially difficult to translate
emend(ed) to ___	the original Hebrew text is so difficult to translate that competent scholars have conjectured or inferred a restoration of the original text based on the context, probable root meanings of the words, and uses in comparative languages

In some editions of the CSB, additional footnotes clarify the meaning of certain biblical texts or explain biblical history, persons, customs, places, activities, and measurements. Cross references are given for parallel passages or passages with similar wording, and in the NT, for passages quoted from the OT.

◤ Abbreviations in CSB Bibles

AD	In the year of our Lord
BC	before Christ
c.	century
ca	circa
chap(s).	chapter(s)
cp.	compare
DSS	Dead Sea Scrolls
e.g.	for example
Eng	English
etc.	et cetera
Gk	Greek
Hb	Hebrew
i.e.	that is
Lat	Latin
lit	literal(ly)
LXX	Septuagint—an ancient translation of the Old Testament into Greek
MT	Masoretic Text
NT	New Testament
ms(s)	manuscript(s)
OT	Old Testament
pl.	plural
Ps(s)	Psalm(s)
Sam	Samaritan Pentateuch
sg.	singular
Sym	Symmachus
Syr	Syriac
Tg	Targum
Theod	Theodotian
v. / vv.	verse, verses
Vg	Vulgate—an ancient translation of the Bible into Latin
vol(s).	volume(s)

How to Read and Study the Bible

George H. Guthrie

The Bible is unique among the books of the world. Its "release date" is centuries old, yet it still dominates the best-seller lists, confronting moderns with messages as fresh as today's news headlines. At times the Bible is so crystal clear that a child can understand it, yet its difficulties can humble the most learned of scholars. Diverse in theme and literary genres, it conveys a unified story, a message that climaxes in the person and work of Jesus Christ. It was delivered through human writers, yet it truly is God's Word. The Bible can seem as familiar as a walk next door or as foreign as a distant country.

Hearing God in the pages of the Bible takes time and effort; spiritual listening is a skill that we continue to develop all of our lives. Hearing someone well can be challenging when we move across cultural lines, and, in fact, reading the Bible is very much a cross-cultural conversation, since God gave his Word in places, times, and circumstances far removed from our own.

Why Spend Time in the Bible?

Perhaps your past has been marked by starts and stops in reading the Bible, and you are wondering whether you have the discipline to engage the Bible consistently. Well, join the club. Most of us have struggled with the discipline of Bible reading and study. Is it worth giving consistent Bible reading and study another try, or a first try? Most believers know intuitively that it is.

This is *God's* Word. The God who spoke the world into being has spoken his truth about life through the Bible so that we might know what he intends for this world and how we might live for his fame. He calls us to be people who are countercultural in how we approach life. Thus, the Bible serves as the foundation for understanding who we are and what we should be doing in this world. Here are several suggestions that you can start applying daily.

Begin with the Heart

In the parable of the seeds and soils (Mk 4:3–20) Jesus used a word picture to describe the different levels of receptivity people have toward God's Word. He tells of a farmer broadcasting seed along the edge of a field. Some seeds fall on the hard-packed path beside the field; some fall on rocky ground that has little topsoil; some

fall in the weeds; and some fall in fertile soil that offers a good environment for growth. The various places they fall provide images of the human heart as it is confronted with God's Word.

Some people have hearts that are hard packed, like a frequented footpath. God's Word does not get through to these hearts. Others have shallow hearts that seem open to God's Word. The Word comes and they respond, but the moment things get tough, the pressures of life override the principles of God's Word and the spiritual life withers. A third type of person engages God's Word at a deeper level, but worries and desire for worldly things squeeze out the Word, choking it from the person's life. Finally, there are those who receive the Word with a heart like a well-tilled field. This is the picture of a person fully receptive to God's Word, and God's Word brings exponential growth to their spiritual life.

Which pattern of response describes the condition of your heart today? Perhaps you have never committed to following Christ as Lord of your life. I encourage you to talk to a Christian or a minister whom you trust and ask them about following Christ as Lord. A person who is not a Christ-follower cannot engage spiritual truth in a way that is life changing (see 1 Cor 2:14), so this would be the beginning place for you. Turn to Christ, asking him to bring his good news to life in you.

Or perhaps you have committed your life to follow Christ, but your heart is not very receptive to God's Word at this time. You may be plagued by a heart that is consumed with worry or material things. Sin and self-absorption can eat the heart out of your Bible study. Begin your path back to a healthy relationship with God by crying out to him right now, asking him to forgive you for your hard-heartedness, expressing your desire to hear and live his Word.

Motivations

Once our hearts are receptive to the Word, we can hear the motivations offered us in Scripture. Among other motives, we read the Bible . . .

to experience consistent joy (Ps 119:111)

to sort out our thoughts and motivations (Heb 4:12)

to guard ourselves from sin and error (Eph 6:11–17; 1Pt 2:1–2)

to know God in a personal relationship (1Co 1:21; Gl 4:8–9; 1Tm 4:16)

to know truth and think clearly about what God says is valuable (2Pt 1:21)

to be built up as a community with other believers (Ac 20:32; Eph 4:14–16)

to reject conformity to the world as we renew our minds (Rm 12:1–2; 1Pt 2:1–2)

to experience God's freedom, grace, peace, and hope (Jn 8:32; Rm 15:4; 2Pt 1:2)

to live well for God, expressing our love for him (Jn 14:23–24; Rm 12:2; 1Th 4:1–8)

to minister to Christ-followers and to those who have yet to respond to the gospel, experiencing God's approval for work well done (Jos 1:8; 2Tm 2:15; 3:16–17)

Twelve Practical Suggestions for Reading Well

We want to approach our reading of the Bible in a way that will lead to a fulfilling, faithful, and fruitful pattern of life. Below are a dozen suggestions to make your Bible reading more effective and fulfilling.

1. Read the Bible prayerfully: Engaging the Bible regularly is a spiritual exercise, and you need spiritual power and discernment to do it well. As you begin your Bible reading, ask God for a receptive and disciplined heart. Ask him to speak to you through the Word and to use the passages you read to give you thoughts and words you can use as you pray to God.

2. Read expectantly and joyfully: As you pray over your Bible reading, also read it expecting to hear from God, being joyful and thankful for what you find in the Scriptures. Allow the "music" of the Word to give you joy in your walk with God.

3. Meditate on what you are reading: To meditate means to mentally "chew" on what we are reading, to think about what the passage means as well as its implications for belief and practice. Just as food chewed and swallowed too quickly gives indigestion, so we will not be able to digest our Bible readings unless we slow down and consider the "food" we find there.

4. Read for transformation: The Bible is not meant merely to inform—it is meant to transform us in accordance with God's truth (Rm

12:1–2). Therefore, read with expectation that you will hear from the Lord. Be thinking about ways to apply God's truth to your life as you read.

5. Read with perseverance: Commit yourself to being consistent for the next ten to twelve weeks, which is about how long it takes to form a long-term habit. As you are faithful with your Bible reading and begin to see it make a difference in your life, you will begin to hunger for your time in the Word.

6. Be realistic about the goals you set; have a good plan: If you take just twenty to thirty minutes per day, you can read through the whole Bible in a year. In just ten to fifteen minutes per day, you can read through the whole Bible in two years. The key is not volume but consistency and a clear plan.

7. Set aside a consistent time and place to read and study the Bible: Make it a time and place that guards you from distractions and allows you to be consistent, missing no more than a handful of times per month. When you do miss a day, just pick back up the next day.

8. Read with a few good tools at hand: Along with this study Bible, have a good Bible dictionary on hand. These typically provide outlines and message summaries of each book of the Bible, plus quick entries on theological, historical, and cultural elements.

9. Read with a pen in hand: Underline key passages and make notes in the margins as you read. If you prefer a keyboard to an ink pen, store your notes on your computer.

10. Read in light of the immediate context: Not only do we need the "big picture" of the Bible's overarching story, we also need the "little picture" of the immediate context. So read with an awareness of where you are in the development of a particular book.

11. Do your Bible reading and study as part of a community: It helps if you have family or friends who also are reading the Bible, for they can encourage you and discuss the Bible with you. Become part of a community of Christians, a church, so you can have a place to celebrate what you are learning, to pose questions that come up in your study, and to use your spiritual gifts in ministering to others.

12. Read in light of the overarching story of the Bible: Reading the Bible is much more meaningful if you read it in light of its overarching story. As you read, notice great interwoven themes such as how creation in Genesis 1–2 relates to creation themes in Psalm 8, Isaiah 65:17–25, John 1, Romans 8:19-22, and Revelation 21. Read book introductions in your study Bible, noting where each book fits in the overall development of God's story.

▼ The Old Testament

Introduction to the Pentateuch

by Daniel I. Block

The first five books of the Old Testament, sometimes called "the books of Moses," are also called the Pentateuch. The expression Pentateuch derives from two Greek words *penta*, "five," and *teuchos*, "vessel, container." Jewish canons label these books collectively as the Torah, which means "teaching, instruction." In English Bibles these first five books are commonly called "Law." This designation is misleading. Large portions are not law at all; they are actually inspiring narratives.

The Structure and Contents of the Pentateuch

The Pentateuch is one continuous narrative. For example, the first verb in Leviticus 1:1 ("And he called") lacks a subject, which must be supplied from the last verse of Exodus. Because of the physical limitations of scrolls, it was necessary, probably from the outset, to divide the narrative into five segments more easily manageable on leather or vellum scrolls. This division dates at least to the second century BC in the Septuagint, the Greek translation of the OT. The partitioning creates the unfortunate impression that these are distinct compositions to be interpreted separately. This is wrong. The story that begins in Genesis 1:1 climaxes with the making of the covenant at Sinai and ends with Moses's theological exposition of the covenant in Deuteronomy.

The Plot of the Pentateuch

The pivotal event of the Pentateuch is God's revelation of himself at Sinai in Exodus. The patriarchal narratives in Genesis look forward to Sinai. In Genesis 12:2 God promises Abraham that he would be a blessing to the whole world. Later God explains that this would involve being the recipient of the divine revelation (cp. Dt 4:5–8), being a kingdom of priests, a holy nation, a special treasure "out of all the peoples, although the whole earth is mine" (Ex 19:5–6). At Sinai the God of Abraham, Isaac, and Jacob formally became the God of Israel, binding Abraham's descendants to him by confirming the eternal covenant (Ex 31:16–17; Lv 24:8; cp. Jdg 2:1). Finally, Sinai is anticipated in Genesis 26:5, where the Lord recognizes that Abraham "listened to me and kept my mandate, my commands, my statutes, and my

instructions." The expressions echo the Sinai revelation; apparently Abraham fulfilled the requirements of the Sinai covenant without the benefit of the Sinai revelation.

The narratives describing Israel's journey from Sinai to the plains of Moab are told against the backdrop of the Lord's covenant with Israel and Israel's promise to do all that the Lord had told them. Numbers 28:6 explicitly refers to the Sinai revelation. But the book of Deuteronomy, virtually in its entirety, represents Moses's exposition of the Sinai covenant. However, the primary character is not human; this is a record of God's relationship with those he created in his own image, whom he elected, redeemed, and commissioned to be his agents on the earth.

The Themes of the Pentateuch

The theological themes developed in the Pentateuch are virtually innumerable. These represent the theological skeleton of the narratives: God as Creator (Gn 1–2); God as Judge of sinful humanity, who spared Noah (Gn 3:1–11:26); God as the one who elected his agents of blessing the world, entered into covenant relationship with them, and promised to give the land of Canaan to their descendants as an eternal possession (Gn 11:37–50:26); God as one who redeemed his people from slavery (Ex 1:1–15:21); God as one who accompanied his people during their desert travels, providing for their physical needs and punishing the faithless (Ex 15:22–17:7; 18:1–27; Nm 10:11–20:29); God as one who entered into covenant relationship with and revealed his will comprehensively to Israel at Sinai (Ex 19:1–Nm 10:10); God as one who fights for Israel against their enemies (Ex 17:8–16; Nm 22:1–25:18); God as one who will give Israel their land and promises to be with them after the death of Moses (Nm 26:1–Dt 34:12).

The Date and Authorship of the Pentateuch

Although Jewish and Christian traditions almost unanimously recognize Moses as author of the Pentateuch, few issues relating to the OT now are debated as hotly. From the middle of the nineteenth century AD, most critical scholars have rejected Moses having a significant role in the origin of the Pentateuch. The questioning began early with doubts whether Moses recorded his own death and burial (Dt 34), or knew of a place in northern Israel called Dan (Gn 14:14; cp. Jos 19:47; Jdg 18:28b–29), or referred to the conquest of Canaan as past (Dt 2:12).

Thus, scholars developed an alternative explanation for the origins of the Pentateuch known as the Documentary Hypothesis. According to the classical form of the theory, the Pentateuch is the product of a long and complex literary evolution, specifically incorporating at least four major literary strands composed independently over several centuries and not combined in the present form until the time of Ezra (fifth century BC). These sources are identified as J, E, D, and P.

The bewildering variety of theories fosters little confidence in critical scholarship. However, the fact remains that nowhere does the Pentateuch specifically name its author. As was common in the ancient Semitic world, it is anonymous. On the other hand, the internal evidence suggests that Moses kept a record of Israel's experiences in the desert (Ex 17:14; 24:4,7; 34:27; Nm 33:1–2; Dt 31:9,11).

Furthermore, many statements in the OT credit the Pentateuch to Moses (e.g., Jos 1:8; 8:31–32; 1Kg 2:3; 2Kg 14:6; Ezr 6:18; Neh 13:1; Dn 9:11–13; Mal 4:4), and the NT identifies the Torah very closely with him (Mt 19:8; Jn 5:46–47; 7:19; Ac 3:22; Rm 10:5). Moreover, many features within the text point to an early date for its composition, such as an extensive familiarity with Egyptian geography and words.

Moses very well could have written most of the Pentateuch himself. Having been raised in the court of Pharaoh, Moses's own literary qualifications for writing should not be dismissed. Of course, it is unlikely that Moses wrote all the Pentateuch as we have it. It is doubtful he wrote the account of his death in Deuteronomy 34. Frequently the text provides explanatory notes updating facts for a later audience (e.g., Gn 36:1; Dt 2:10–12). In addition, Moses could have used a scribe or secretary.

There is no reason to doubt that Moses wrote down the speeches he delivered (Dt 31:9–13) or that when he came down from Mount Sinai he arranged for the transcription of the revelation he had received on the mountain, if he did not write it all himself. It is equally plausible that he authorized the written composition of many of the stories and family records of the patriarchs that had been transmitted orally or in rudimentary written form. Just as the pieces of the tabernacle were constructed and woven by skilled craftsmen and finally assembled by Moses (Ex 35–40), so literary craftsmen may have composed some bits and pieces of the Pentateuch and submitted them to Moses, who then approved them. When exactly the pieces were put together in their present form we may only speculate. The Pentateuch is fundamentally and substantially Mosaic, and later Israelites accepted it as bearing the full force of his authority.

◤ Introduction to
Genesis

Circumstances of Writing

Since pre-Christian times, authorship of the Torah, the first five books of the Bible, has been attributed to Moses, an enormously influential Israelite leader from the second millennium BC with an aristocratic Egyptian background. Even though Genesis is technically anonymous, both the Old and New Testaments unanimously recognize Moses as the Torah's author (Jos 8:35; 2Ch 23:18; Neh 8:1; Mk 12:19,26; Lk 2:22; Rm 10:5; Heb 10:28). At the same time, evidence in Genesis suggests that minor editorial changes dating to ancient times have been inserted into the text. Examples include the mention of "Dan" (14:14), a city that was not named until the days of the judges (Jdg 18:29), and the use of a phrase that assumed the existence of Israelite kings (Gn 36:31).

The Torah (Hebrew for "law") was seen as one unit until at least the second century BC. Sometime prior to the birth of Christ, the Torah was divided into five separate books, later referred to as the Pentateuch (lit "five vessels"). Genesis, the first book of the Torah, provides both the universal history of humankind and the patriarchal history of the nation of Israel. The first section (chaps. 1–11) is a general history commonly called the "primeval history," showing how all humanity descended from one couple and became sinners. The second section (chaps. 12–50) is a more specific history commonly referred to as the "patriarchal history," focusing on the covenant God made with Abraham and his descendants: Isaac, Jacob, and Jacob's twelve sons. Genesis unfolds God's plan to bless and redeem humanity through Abraham's descendants. The book concludes with the events that led to the Israelites being in the land of Egypt.

Contribution to the Bible

Genesis lays the groundwork for everything else we read and experience in Scripture. Through Genesis we understand where we came from, how we got in the fallen state we are in, and the beginnings of God's gracious work on our behalf. Genesis unfolds God's original purpose for humanity.

Genesis provides the foundation from which we understand God's covenant with Israel that was established with the giving of the Law. For the Israelite community, the stories of the origins of humanity, sin, and the covenant relationship with God helped them understand why God gave them the Law.

Structure

Genesis is chiefly a narrative. From a narrative standpoint, God is the only true hero of the Bible, and the book of Genesis has the distinct privilege of introducing him. God is the first subject of a verb in the

---

2200 BC	2000 BC
Earliest pottery in South America **2200**	Contraceptives are developed in Egypt. **2000**
ABRAHAM 2166–1991	Chinese create first zoo, Park of Intelligence. **2000**
11th Dynasty of Egypt **2134–1991**	Babylonians and Egyptians divide days into
3rd Dynasty of Ur **2113–2006**	hours, minutes, and seconds. **2000**
JOB 2100?–1900?	Mesopotamians learn to solve
Construction of Ziggurat at Ur in Sumer **2100**	quadratic equations. **2000**
Abraham moves from Haran to Canaan. **2091**	Code of medical ethics, Mesopotamia **2000**
Destruction of Sodom and Gomorrah **2085**	Courier systems of communication are
God's covenant with Abraham **2081?**	developed in both China and Egypt. **2000**
Ishmael born **2080?**	12th Dynasty of Egypt **1991–1786**
ISAAC 2066–1886	JOSEPH 1915–1805
JACOB 2006–1859	

Genesis Timeline

book and is mentioned more frequently than any other character in the Bible. The content of the first eleven chapters is distinct from the patriarchal stories in chapters 12–50. The primary literary device is the catchphrase "these are the family records." The phrase is broader in meaning than simply "generation" and refers more to a narrative account.

This was a common practice in ancient Near Eastern writings. This phrase also serves as a link between the key person in the previous narrative and the one anticipated in the next section. Genesis could be described as historical genealogy, which ties together creation and human history in one continuum.

Outline

I. Creation of Heaven and Earth (1:1–2:3)
II. The Human Family In and Outside the Garden (2:4–4:26)
III. Adam's Family Line (5:1–6:8)
IV. Noah and His Family (6:9–9:29)
V. The Nations and the Tower of Babel (10:1–11:26)
VI. Father Abraham (11:27–25:11)
VII. Ishmael's Family Line (25:12–18)
VIII. Isaac's Family: Jacob and Esau (25:19–35:29)
IX. Esau's Family (36:18)
X. Esau, Father of the Edomites (36:9–37:1)
XI. Jacob's Family: Joseph and His Brothers (37:2–50:26)

Key verses in Genesis

1:1   In the beginning God created the heavens and the earth.
1:27 So God created man in his own image; he created him in the image of God; he created them male and female.
1:31 God saw all that he had made, and it was very good indeed. Evening came and then morning: the sixth day.

1900 BC

Benjamin is born; Rachel dies. **1900**
Potter's wheel is introduced to Crete. **1900**
Use of the sail in the Aegean **1900**
Egyptian town of El Lahun gives evidence of town planning with streets at right angles. **1900**
Mesopotamian mathematicians discover what later came to be called the Pythagorean theorem. **1900**
Joseph sold into Egypt **1898**
Khnumhotep II, an architect of Pharaoh Amenemhet II, develops encryption. **1900**

1800 BC

Musical theory, Mesopotamia **1800**
Multiplication tables, Mesopotamia **1800**
Babylonians develop catalog of stars and planets. **1800**
Book of the Dead, Egypt **1800**
Horses are introduced in Egypt. **1800**
Wooden plows, Scandinavia **1800**

The Creation

1 In the beginning God created the heavens and the earth.[A] ²Now the earth was formless and empty, darkness covered the surface of the watery depths, and the Spirit of God was hovering over the surface of the waters. ³Then God said, "Let there be light," and there was light. ⁴God saw that the light was good, and God separated the light from the darkness. ⁵God called the light "day," and the darkness he called "night." There was an evening, and there was a morning: one day.

⁶Then God said, "Let there be an expanse between the waters, separating water from water." ⁷So God made the expanse and separated the water under the expanse from the water above the expanse. And it was so. ⁸God called the expanse "sky."[B] Evening came and then morning: the second day.

⁹Then God said, "Let the water under the sky be gathered into one place, and let the dry land appear." And it was so. ¹⁰God called the dry land "earth," and the gathering of the water he called "seas." And God saw that it was good. ¹¹Then God said, "Let the earth produce vegetation: seed-bearing plants and fruit trees on the earth bearing fruit with seed in it according to their kinds." And it was so. ¹²The earth produced vegetation: seed-bearing plants according to their kinds and trees bearing fruit with seed in it according to their kinds. And God saw that it was good. ¹³Evening came and then morning: the third day.

¹⁴Then God said, "Let there be lights in the expanse of the sky to separate the day from the night. They will serve as signs for seasons[C] and for days and years. ¹⁵They will be lights in the expanse of the sky to provide light on the earth." And it was so. ¹⁶God made the two great lights — the greater light to rule over the day and the lesser light to rule over the night — as well as the stars. ¹⁷God placed them in the expanse of the sky to provide light on the earth, ¹⁸to rule the day and the night, and to separate light from darkness. And God saw that it was good. ¹⁹Evening came and then morning: the fourth day.

[A]1:1 Or *created the universe*   [B]1:8 Or *"heavens."*   [C]1:14 Or *for the appointed times*

1:1 This opening verse of the Bible, seven words in the Hebrew, establishes seven key truths upon which the rest of the Bible is based.

First, God exists. The essential first step in pleasing God is acknowledging his existence (Heb 11:6). Second, God existed before there was a universe and will exist after the universe perishes (Heb 1:10–12). Third, God is the main character in the Bible. He is the subject of the first verb in the Bible (in fact, he is the subject of more verbs than any other character) and performs a wider variety of activities than any other being in the Bible. Fourth, as Creator, God has done what no human could ever do; in its active form the Hebrew verb *bara'*, meaning "to create," never has a human subject. Thus *bara'* signifies a work that is uniquely God's. Fifth, God is mysterious; though this particular Hebrew word for God is plural, the verb form of which "God" is the subject is singular. This is perhaps a subtle allusion to God's Trinitarian nature: He is three divine persons in one divine essence.

Sixth, God is the Creator of heaven and earth. He does not just modify preexisting matter but calls matter into being out of nothing (Ps 33:6,9; Heb 11:3). Seventh, God is not dependent on the universe, but the universe is totally dependent on God (Heb 1:3).

1:2 In an effort to explain the origins of evil and/or find biblical evidence for an old earth, some Bible scholars have suggested that the verb **was** should be translated as "became." They believe a time gap, possibly a vast one, exists between the first two verses of the Bible. This allows interpreters to suggest that the early earth was **formless and empty** because Satan's rebellion marred God's good creation. However, the construction of this sentence in the original Hebrew favors the traditional translation ("was" rather than "became").

The sense of v. 2 is that God created the earth "formless and empty" as an unfinished and unfilled state. **Watery depths**, a single word in Hebrew, suggests an original state of creation that was shapeless as liquid water. The Hebrew verb translated **was hovering**, used also in Dt 32:11, suggests that the Spirit of God was watching over his creation just as a bird watches over its young.

1:4 Another basic truth of the Bible is that **God saw**; this means he is fully aware of his creation. The term **good**, used here for the first of seven times in this chapter to evaluate God's creative work, can be used to express both high quality and moral excellence. The physical universe is a good place because God made it. God found satisfaction in his labor. This is the first instance where God separated the twin realms of light and darkness, day and night.

1:5 In ancient Israel, the act of naming an object, place, or person indicated that you held control over it (35:10; 41:45; Nm 32:42; Dt 3:14; Jos 19:47; 2Kg 23:34; 24:17). When God named the light and the darkness, he asserted his lordship and control over all of time. **There was an evening.** In ancient Israelite and modern Jewish tradition, sundown is the transition point from one day to the next. Scholars differ over the meaning of "day" in the phrases "one day … the second day," etc. Some argue for twenty-four-hour periods, but other options are possible, especially since (1) there was at first no sun by which to distinguish twenty-four-hour periods, (2) "day" means the period of daylight in 1:5a, and (3) "day" refers to the whole creation period in 2:4 ("at the time" is lit "on the day"). Consequently, some scholars understand the "days" of creation as extended periods of uncertain length or as a rhetorical device by which the account of creation is structured.

1:7 God's second act of separation was to divide atmospheric water from terrestrial water. Thus he began the process of giving form to the material world. The clause **it was so**, found six times in this chapter, emphasizes God's absolute power over creation.

1:8 Sky can refer to the earth's atmospheric envelope (v. 20), outer space (v. 15), or "heaven," the spiritual realm where God lives (Ps 11:4).

1:9 God's third and final act of separation created oceans and continents.

1:10 In his third and final act of naming, God demonstrated his authority over all of the earth.

1:11–13 In preparation for the introduction of animal and human life, God provided an abundant supply of food. The consistent biblical teaching is that "like begets like" (Lk 6:44; Jms 3:12); Gn 1:11–12 establishes that principle for plant life. While five of the six days contain at least one act of creation evaluated as **good**, only the third and sixth days have this statement more than once.

1:14–15 The events of day four complement those of day one, filling the day and night with finished forms of light. The various **lights**, or "light-giving objects," were worshiped as gods in the cultures that surrounded ancient Israel. In Genesis, however, the sun, moon, and stars are portrayed as servants of God that would fulfill three roles: separating the newly created realms of **day** and **night**; marking time so that those who worshiped the Creator could keep their festivals in each of the **seasons** (cp. Lv 23:4,44); and providing **light on the earth**.

#01   99 Essential Christian Truths

THE GOODNESS OF CREATION

In Genesis 1, God repeatedly affirmed that all of his creation was good, even "very good" (v. 31). It is good, in God's judgment, because he created it for a purpose that it fulfilled—to reflect and display the good character of the Creator. Therefore, sin and evil should not be seen as a foundational part of the creation but rather as a corruption of it. While the creation has been marred and distorted as a result of sin, it is still good in the hands of God and serves his purpose of proclaiming his glory in the world. God's people should affirm and seek to preserve the goodness of God's creation (Gn 2:15).

The Uniqueness of the Genesis Creation Story

by Kenneth A. Mathews

While there are many similarities between parts of Genesis and ancient Near Eastern (ANE) myths, there are also fundamental differences. These are seen especially in the significantly different views of the Creator and creation. Five features in particular distinguish the biblical creation account and perspective. The biblical teaching is so theologically distinctive from that of Israel's ANE neighbors that it is best explained as the result of divine revelation, not the imagination of the biblical author.

The Identity of God

The basic identity of God as revealed in Genesis is distinct from all other ANE conceptions. The Lord God did not have an origin and did not have a female counterpart. God simply always existed. The concept of fertility was a common explanation among the ancients for how the world was created. It was believed that gods and goddesses joined in sexual union and thus produced the world, just as man and woman can come together to create a child. Israel's God, however, was revealed to be asexual, neither male nor female. According to other ANE religions, the world (or parts of it, like the sun) was a divine "Thou," whereas in Genesis the world was revealed to be an "it," a nonsupernatural reality brought into existence by a supernatural God.

No Rival Gods

While polytheistic views dominated the ANE, Genesis reveals that God has no divine rivals. A common explanation for creation among the ancients was that an epic battle had raged between creator gods and anticreation deities. Ultimately, the creator god overcame the anticreation forces/gods, in some cases using the slain bodies of their enemies to make the stuff of the world. In Genesis there is no rival opposing the Creator. All creation obeyed the voice of God, as expressed in the recurring phrase, "And it was so" (1:7,9,11,15,24).

Creation out of Nothing

In Genesis the Creator by inherent authority as Sovereign Lord spoke creation into a functional, well-ordered existence. There was no eternal precreated matter, such as was believed in the ancient myths. Genesis says God spoke all things into origination. This does not mean he uttered words that possessed inherent magical powers. Rather, the irrevocable power of God's words was grounded in the authority of God himself. Unlike the nature deities whose existence was limited to the world system, God existed before creation and above creation. Also, creation was not the emanation of divine person or power. It was separate from him, a new reality subject to his will.

The Value of Humanity

In Genesis the Creator bestowed special value on humanity. Human beings in the ANE view were not indispensable to the operation of the world, whereas in Genesis they are essential as its chief caretakers. The Lord blessed humanity, assigning man and woman the responsibility to propagate and to rule over the earth (1:26–28). ANE myths explained the purpose of humanity as servants who met the servile interests of the gods. The Bible elevates the person and role of humans who were "crowned . . . with glory and honor" (Ps 8:5), made in the divine image. God prepared the resplendent garden of Eden for humanity, giving humanity meaningful work and purpose (Gn 2:8–18).

The Sabbath

In Genesis the Creator provides the seventh day as a holy day of rest and celebration (2:1–3), which was later memorialized in Israel's Sabbath (Ex 20:8–11). The Sabbath was unique to Israel, not tied to the movement of the stars, such as in the ancient preoccupation with astrology. The Lord was revealed as Master of the material universe *and* of time. All creation was invited to join in the knowledge of God and in the worship of him as Creator and Sustainer of all things.

²⁰ Then God said, "Let the water swarm with^ living creatures, and let birds fly above the earth across the expanse of the sky." ²¹ So God created the large sea-creatures and every living creature that moves and swarms in the water, according to their kinds. He also created every winged creature according to its kind. And God saw that it was good. ²² God blessed them: "Be fruitful, multiply, and fill the waters of the seas, and let the birds multiply on the earth." ²³ Evening came and then morning: the fifth day.

²⁴ Then God said, "Let the earth produce living creatures according to their kinds: livestock, creatures that crawl, and the wildlife of the earth according to their kinds." And it was so. ²⁵ So God made the wildlife of the earth according to their kinds, the livestock according to their kinds, and all the creatures that crawl on the ground according to their kinds. And God saw that it was good.

²⁶ Then God said, "Let us make man^B in^C our image, according to our likeness. They will rule the fish of the sea, the birds of the sky, the livestock, the whole earth, and the creatures that crawl^D on the earth."

²⁷   So God created man in his own image;
       he created him in the image of God;
       he created them male and female.

²⁸ God blessed them, and God said to them, "Be fruitful, multiply, fill the earth, and subdue it. Rule the fish of the sea, the birds of the sky, and every creature that crawls on the earth." ²⁹ God also said, "Look, I have given you every seed-bearing plant on the surface of the entire earth and every tree whose fruit contains seed. This will be food for you, ³⁰ for all the wildlife of the earth, for every bird of the sky, and for every creature that crawls on the earth — everything having the breath of life in it — I have given^E every green plant for food." And it was so. ³¹ God saw all that he had made, and it was very good indeed. Evening came and then morning: the sixth day.

2 So the heavens and the earth and everything in them were completed. ² On the seventh^F day God had completed his work that he had done, and he rested^G on the seventh day from all his work that he had done. ³ God blessed the seventh day and declared it holy, for on it he rested from all his work of creation.

Man and Woman in the Garden

⁴ These are the records of the heavens and the earth, concerning their creation. At the time^H that the LORD God made the earth and the heavens, ⁵ no shrub of the field had yet grown on the land,^I and no plant of the field had yet

---

^1:20 Lit with swarms of   ^B1:26 Or human beings; Hb 'adam, also in v. 27   ^C1:26 Or as   ^D1:26 Or scurry   ^E1:30 I have given added for clarity   ^F2:2 Sam, LXX, Syr read sixth   ^G2:2 Or ceased, also in v. 3   ^H2:4 Lit creation on the day   ^I2:5 Or earth

---

1:20 The fifth day's events complement those of day two, filling the newly formed heavenly domains above and the watery regions below.
1:21 The reuse of the verb **created** (Hb bara', cp. v. 1) emphasizes God's authority over **the large sea-creatures**.
1:22–23 The first of three blessings God pronounced in the creation narrative occurred when **God blessed** the water animals and birds.
1:24–25 The term **living creatures** in vv. 20 and 24 is the same as is translated "living being" in 2:7. The sixth day is for creating land creatures, including people. The three groups of animals are domesticated livestock, crawlers, and wild animals.
1:26 God's use of plural pronouns (**us . . . our . . . our**) to refer to himself has raised many questions (3:22; 11:7; Is 6:8). At least five different suggestions have been put forward to explain them: they may be references to (1) the Trinity; (2) God and his angels; (3) God and creation; (4) God's majesty as expressed by a literary device known as the "plural of majesty"; or (5) a polytheistic view of God. Since the Bible teaches elsewhere that there is only one God (Dt 6:4; Mk 12:29; 1Co 8:4), the fifth option is not tenable.
The two Hebrew words translated as **image** and **likeness** are often understood as having the same meaning. But some interpreters suggest that "image" refers to the ability to reason, with "likeness" referring to the spiritual dimension. What exactly is the "image" of God? Since the Bible teaches that God is Spirit (Jn 4:24), many commentators believe it refers to the nonmaterial aspects of a person—our moral sensibilities, intellectual

abilities, will, and emotions. Based on God's commands in Gn 1:28, others have suggested that it consists of the role humans are to play on earth—their rulership over the planet and its resources, and secondarily the physical, mental, and spiritual abilities that enable them to fulfill that role.
1:27 The creation of humanity is the crowning event of chap. 1, as shown by the fact that **created** is repeated three times. The verb created (Hb bara') is the same one used in v. 1, referring to a kind of creative activity that only God can do. The term **man** (Hb 'adam) is used elsewhere in the Hebrew Bible to refer to humanity in general, not just males (7:21); all people, both male and female, are created **in the image of God** (cp. Jms 3:9). It should not be concluded that God is both male and female.
1:28 In this the longest of the five blessings found in the account of creation, **God** gave humanity five different commands. Implicit in the first three commands is God's blessing on the institutions of marriage and the family. The final two commands, to **subdue** the earth and **rule** the animal kingdom, express God's blessing on the use of the planet's renewable and nonrenewable natural resources.
1:29–30 The repeated use of Hebrew kol, "all, every, entire," in vv. 29–30 shows that the point is to emphasize God's abundant and generous provision for all his creatures, rather than to specify what they were or were not supposed to eat.
1:31 This is the seventh, final, and most elaborate use of the word **good** in the account of the seven days of creation in that it adds **very** to good.

2:1 This verse serves as a complement to 1:1. Together, the two set the first six days of creation apart from the sacred seventh day.
2:2 This is the first use of the number seven in the Bible, a number that will play an especially significant role in the religious and social life of ancient Israel (4:15; 7:2–4,10; 21:28–31; 29:18–20). On the seventh day God rested, thus setting an example for people—who are made in his image—to follow (Ex 20:8–11; Dt 5:12–14). Though God rested **from all his work that he had done**, this is not to say that God has abandoned the universe. In the NT Jesus affirmed that God is still at work in the world, even on the Sabbath (Jn 5:16–17). Also, God's "rest" does not imply that he was tired. It literally means "cease" and implies only that his creative work was complete.
2:3 This is the only instance during the creation process when God **blessed** a unit of time. The term **holy** is applied in the Bible to something set aside for service to God.
2:4 The Hebrew word toledoth, translated here as **records**, is used eleven times in the book of Genesis to introduce new units of material (5:1; 6:9; 10:1; 11:10,27; 25:12,19; 36:1,9; 37:2). Here it introduces a detailed elaboration of some key aspects of the creation account that opens the book of Genesis (1:1–2:3). Special emphasis is placed on the events of day six. Verse 4 includes the first use of God's personal name, rendered in English as **the LORD**, the most commonly used noun in the OT. The Hebrew spelling is transliterated as "YHWH," hence, "Yahweh."
2:5 The **shrub of the field** and the **plant of the field** are not the same as the vegetation

sprouted, for the LORD God had not made it rain on the land, and there was no man to work the ground. **6** But mist would come up from the earth and water all the ground. **7** Then the LORD God formed the man out of the dust from the ground and breathed the breath of life into his nostrils, and the man became a living being.

8 The LORD God planted a garden in Eden, in the east, and there he placed the man he had formed. **9** The LORD God caused to grow out of the ground every tree pleasing in appearance and good for food, including the tree of life in the middle of the garden, as well as the tree of the knowledge of good and evil.

10 A river went^A out from Eden to water the garden. From there it divided and became the source of four rivers.^B **11** The name of the first is Pishon, which flows through the entire land of Havilah,^c where there is gold. **12** Gold from that land is pure;^D bdellium^E and onyx^F are also there. **13** The name of the second river is Gihon, which flows through the entire land of Cush. **14** The name of the third river is Tigris, which runs east of Assyria. And the fourth river is the Euphrates.

15 The LORD God took the man and placed him in the garden of Eden to work it and watch over it. **16** And the LORD God commanded the man, "You are free to eat from any tree of the garden, **17** but you must not eat from the tree of the knowledge of good and evil, for on the day you eat from it, you will certainly

---

^A**2:10** Or *goes* ^B**2:10** Lit *became four heads* ^C**2:11** Or *of the Havilah* ^D**2:12** Lit *good* ^E**2:12** A yellowish, transparent gum resin ^F**2:12** Identity of this precious stone uncertain

---

described in Gn 1:11–12 but are the plants that will make up the garden of Eden.
2:7 The Hebrew verb translated here as **formed** is used elsewhere in the Bible to describe the potter's profession (Jr 18:4; Zch 11:13); God acts here as the divine potter, skillfully fashioning **man out of the dust from the ground**. But the Bible makes it very clear that people are more than just material beings. It was only when God **breathed** into the man's **nostrils** the **breath of life** that Adam became alive. When God breathed into him, Adam and all later humans became a unique mix of the physical and the spiritual. The Hebrew phrase translated as **living being** is used elsewhere in Genesis to describe other types of living beings (1:20,24,30; 9:12,15–16). Nevertheless, humans are considered to be in a class by themselves since they alone are made in God's image.

2:8 The location of **Eden** is unknown; suggestions include Armenia, Iraq, Africa, and Arabia. The Hebrew word *'eden* literally means "pleasantness."
2:9 God's concern for beauty is seen in the fact that the trees he caused to grow were **pleasing in appearance**.
2:11 The location of the **Pishon** river is unknown. A land known as **Havilah** existed in the region of the Arabian peninsula at a later point in time (1Sm 15:7), but the preflood land may have represented a different locale.
2:13 The locations of the **Gihon** river and **Cush** are unknown. A later Cush was located in the region of modern Ethiopia and Sudan (Est 1:1).
2:14 The **Tigris** and **Euphrates** rivers, as well as **Assyria**, probably correspond to geographical features associated with modern Iraq.

2:15 As a being created in God's image, Adam, like God, was to be a worker. Without the taint of sin, **work** was an undiluted blessing. The verb translated here as "work" literally means "serve." Adam's second task in the garden was to **watch over it**. The verb is used elsewhere to refer to the action of God toward his people (Ps 121:3–4) or the work of a military guard (Sg 5:7).
2:17 The only limit God placed on Adam was eating **from the tree of the knowledge of good and evil**, which apparently imparted divine wisdom (3:22). Eating the forbidden fruit represented Adam's rejection of God as the source of divine wisdom and his choice to pursue wisdom apart from God. The penalty for disobedience was stated especially forcefully in the original language, with a two-verb construction, "dying you shall die" (**you will certainly die**). Although Adam and Eve did not die

---

Character profile:
Adam

Of all the men in the Bible, only two knew what it was like to have a personal, untainted, unobstructed relationship with God himself. One was Jesus, the Son of God. The other was Adam.

Adam experienced life in Eden—a name that's become synonymous with *paradise*, and for good reason. Eden was God's showcase. On display in this garden paradise was nature in perfect harmony, as the Creator intended. Genesis 2:9 says God filled the garden with trees that were "pleasing in appearance and good for food." Imagine the beauty, the wonder, the divine artistry that Adam enjoyed.

God gave Adam the responsibility of working the garden and caring for it. But this was not a burdensome task. Though the nature of work changed later as part of the curse (see Gn 3:17–19), we may assume that Adam derived deep satisfaction and a sense of fulfillment from his work in the garden.

Only Adam could explain what it was like to live on earth with only God himself and the animals as companions. Only Adam could describe the experience of waking from a deep slumber to find his female counterpart—his perfect companion and complement—next to him.

Adam enjoyed God's company, and God enjoyed his. Adam experienced a clean conscience. He knew what it was like to be naked and unashamed. Such was life in Eden.

Ultimately, though, Eden was not enough for Adam. God charged him, "You must not eat from the tree of the knowledge of good and evil" (2:17), but this proved to be too restrictive for Adam. He gave in to temptation. Along with his wife, he disobeyed God and ate of the fruit. And everything changed in an instant.

Genesis 3:7 describe the consequences of their actions. "The eyes of both of them were opened, and they knew they were naked." They experienced guilt and shame for the first time.

Then when God came to walk in the garden at the time of the evening breeze, Adam didn't join him. Instead, he hid from his Creator.

The punishment for Adam's sin altered the human experience. Among other things, the work that had once brought pleasure and fulfillment would become difficult and painful. And with the ideal of Eden corrupted, Adam and Eve were evicted from the garden. For the rest of their lives they were forced to make their way in an inhospitable world.

More devastating than all of that, though, was the transformation Adam experienced in his relationship with God. Guilt and shame eroded the innocence that had once marked Adam's life. Bitterness and hard-heartedness followed until the ideals of Eden were nothing but a memory. Intimacy was lost.

The good news is that God took the steps that humankind could not take to restore the relationship ruined by Adam's disobedience. In his unfathomable grace, God sent his Son to pay the penalty for Adam's sin—and for the sins of Adam's descendants. Jesus's death and resurrection enable believers to stand before God and to have a personal, intimate relationship with him. Sin and disobedience don't get the final word in our relationship with God—not as long as his grace is available to us.

die." **¹⁸** Then the LORD God said, "It is not good for the man to be alone. I will make a helper corresponding to him." **¹⁹** The LORD God formed out of the ground every wild animal and every bird of the sky, and brought each to the man to see what he would call it. And whatever the man called a living creature, that was its name. **²⁰** The man gave names to all the livestock, to the birds of the sky, and to every wild animal; but for the man^A no helper was found corresponding to him. **²¹** So the LORD God caused a deep sleep to come over the man, and he slept. God took one of his ribs and closed the flesh at that place. **²²** Then the LORD God made the rib he had taken from the man into a woman and brought her to the man. **²³** And the man said:

> This one, at last, is bone of my bone
> and flesh of my flesh;
> this one will be called "woman,"
> for she was taken from man.

²⁴ This is why a man leaves his father and mother and bonds with his wife, and they become one flesh. **²⁵** Both the man and his wife were naked, yet felt no shame.

The Temptation and the Fall

3 Now the serpent was the most cunning of all the wild animals that the LORD God had made. He said to the woman, "Did God really say, 'You can't eat from any tree in the garden'?" **²** The woman said to the serpent, "We may eat the fruit from the trees in the garden. **³** But about the fruit of the tree in the middle of the garden, God said, 'You must not eat it or touch it, or you will die.'"

⁴ "No! You will certainly not die," the serpent said to the woman. **⁵** "In fact, God knows that when^B you eat it your eyes will be opened and you will be like God, knowing good and evil." **⁶** The woman saw that the tree was good for food and delightful to look at, and that it was desirable for obtaining wisdom. So she took some of its fruit and ate it; she also gave some to her husband, who was with her, and he ate it. **⁷** Then the eyes of both of them were opened, and they knew they were naked; so they sewed fig leaves together and made coverings for themselves.

Sin's Consequences

⁸ Then the man and his wife heard the sound of the LORD God walking in the garden at the time of the evening breeze,^C and they hid from the LORD God among the trees of the garden. **⁹** So the LORD God called out to the man and said to him, "Where are you?"

¹⁰ And he said, "I heard you^D in the garden, and I was afraid because I was naked, so I hid."

¹¹ Then he asked, "Who told you that you were naked? Did you eat from the tree that I commanded you not to eat from?"

¹² The man replied, "The woman you gave to be with me — she gave me some fruit from the tree, and I ate."

¹³ So the LORD God asked the woman, "What have you done?"

And the woman said, "The serpent deceived me, and I ate."

¹⁴ So the LORD God said to the serpent:

> Because you have done this,
> you are cursed more than any livestock
> and more than any wild animal.
> You will move on your belly

---

^A **2:20** Or *for Adam*   ^B **3:5** Lit *on the day*   ^C **3:8** Lit *at the wind of the day*   ^D **3:10** Lit *the sound of you*

---

physically **on the day** they ate the fruit, they died spiritually.
2:18 God declared that Adam's being alone is **not good**. God created the man with a need to relate to one **corresponding to him**, and now God will meet that need.
2:19 Like man, animals were **formed out of the ground**, but they received neither the breath of life from God (v. 7) nor the image of God. By giving names to the animals, Adam showed that he ruled the animals and that he perceived the nature of each animal.
2:21 Because **God took one of his ribs** to use as his raw material, the woman would correspond perfectly—though not identically—to Adam. Like Adam, the woman possessed God's image.
2:22–23 Adam's first recorded words express his delight with God's handiwork and his recognition of the unique suitability of God's last recorded act in the creation accounts. As with no other work of divine craftsmanship, this one was singularly suited for the man, being **bone of** his **bone** and **flesh of** his **flesh**. Adam viewed her as his equal. The Hebrew term *'ishshah*, **woman**, identifies her as the feminine complement to *'ish*, the **man**.
2:24 God's timeless design for marriage is declared here. The **one flesh** relationship certainly involves sexual union, but also includes

a husband and wife coming together in spiritual, mental, and emotional harmony.
2:25 Because the devastating effects of sin had not yet ravaged nature or humanity, there was no need for clothing.
3:1 Though we know the **serpent** was an instrument of Satan (Rm 16:20; Rv 12:9; 20:2), it was just a created being. Its description as **cunning** suggests it offered a wisdom not based on the fear of God.
3:2–3 The woman's claim that God said, **You must not . . . touch** the tree, **or you will die**, goes beyond anything recorded in God's instructions to Adam. Therefore it seems that Adam had given his wife an additional command beyond what God said, or else Eve herself exaggerated the command as Satan tempted her to view God as selfish and overly restrictive.
3:4–5 The serpent boldly contradicted what she had reported to be God's command. He then skillfully lied (Jn 8:44) by distorting God's word (Mt 4:6), implying that God had prohibited people from eating the fruit only to keep them from becoming as knowledgeable as he.
3:6 Since the woman did not die when she touched the fruit—in contradiction to what she had thought God said (v. 3.)—she **ate it**. Though Adam **was with her** at the time, he did nothing to stop her.

3:7–8 As the serpent had indicated, **the eyes of both of them were opened, and they knew**, but instead of producing godlike power, the knowledge brought only a sense of human inadequacy, fear, and shame.
3:9 God took the initiative in reaching out to sinful humanity. The all-knowing God asked Adam, **Where are you?** for Adam's benefit, to encourage Adam to face his sin.
3:11 Through the use of two direct questions God brought Adam to accountability for his sin.
3:12 Adam answered neither of God's questions; instead, he sought to shift the blame for his sin first to **the woman**, and then to God.
3:13 The woman passed the blame to **the serpent** and admitted that prior to eating, she was **deceived** (1Tm 2:14).
3:14 Though accountability began with God's confrontation of Adam, judgment began with the **serpent**. Because of the serpent's key role (being used of Satan) in bringing sin into the human experience, it would be permanently consigned to the position of ultimate shame, under the foot.
3:15 This verse is known in Christendom as the *protoevangelium*, or "first good news," because it is the first foretelling of the gospel of Jesus Christ. Using an emphatic Hebrew construction, God announced here that a

and eat dust all the days of your life.
¹⁵ I will put hostility between you
    and the woman,
    and between your offspring
    and her offspring.ᴬ
He will strike your head,
    and you will strike his heel.

¹⁶ He said to the woman:
I will intensify your labor pains;
    you will bear children with painful effort.
Your desire will be for your husband,
    yet he will rule over you.

¹⁷ And he said to the man, "Because you listened to your wife and ate from the tree about which I commanded you, 'Do not eat from it':
The ground is cursed because of you.
You will eat from it by means of
    painful laborᴮ
all the days of your life.

¹⁸ It will produce thorns and thistles
    for you,
    and you will eat the plants of the field.
¹⁹ You will eat breadᶜ by the sweat
    of your brow
until you return to the ground,
    since you were taken from it.
For you are dust,
    and you will return to dust."

²⁰ The man named his wife Eveᴰ because she was the mother of all the living. ²¹ The LORD God made clothing from skins for the man and his wife, and he clothed them.
²² The LORD God said, "Since the man has become like one of us, knowing good and evil, he must not reach out, take from the tree of life, eat, and live forever." ²³ So the LORD God sent him away from the garden of Eden to work the ground from which he was taken. ²⁴ He drove the man out and stationed the cherubim and

ᴬ3:15 Lit *your seed and her seed* ᴮ3:17 Lit *it through pain* ᶜ3:19 Or *food* ᴰ3:20 Lit *Living,* or *Life*

male descendant—**He**—would someday deal the serpent (meaning Satan) a fatal blow. The NT writers understood Jesus Christ to have fulfilled this prophecy (Heb 2:14; 1Jn 3:8). The assertion that the snake would only strike his opponent's **heel** (as opposed to **head**) suggests that the devil will be defeated in the ensuing struggle (Rv 2:2,7–10). **3:16** Even though the woman had been deceived into eating the forbidden fruit, she was still held accountable for her act. Two penalties were imposed; both struck at the heart of a woman's roles in life. More than would have been the case had sin not entered creation, bearing children would add to the sum of **painful effort** in the universe (God said he would **intensify**, not originate, woman's **labor pains**). Marriage would also be marred; though the woman's

desire would be for her **husband**, sin would mar God's plan for marriage and create tormenting inequality and subjugation. **3:17** Adam's relationship with the ground would now be damaged by sin. **All the days** of his life he would experience **painful labor** (cp. the woman's labor pains, v. 16) as he worked to bring forth the fruit of the earth. Because of sin, all creation is **cursed** and longs for its day of deliverance (Rm 8:19–22). **3:18** Prior to the first couple's sins God is only recorded as having put trees in the garden (2:8–9); now there would also be **thorns and thistles**. **3:19** The simple plucking of fruit in order to **eat** food (lit "**bread**") would now be replaced by backbreaking labor and **the sweat of** the **brow**. Working daily in the soil, Adam would be continually reminded that he was **dust** and that he would **return to dust**.

3:20 The new name Adam gave his wife emphasizes the woman's life-giving role that counteracts the curse of sin, which is death. **3:21** By making **clothing from skins**, the **LORD God** graciously provided for humanity's need in a way superior to what Adam and Eve had done with fig leaves. In the NT, the apostle Paul spoke of a day when God would clothe his people with immortality (1Co 15:53–54; 2Co 5:4), thus providing the complete undoing of the curse of humanity's sin. **3:22** Because of sin, people now knew **good and evil** experientially. Expulsion was at the same time an act of mercy. Banning the humans from the **tree of life** allowed for their redemption rather than for them to live a life of perpetual sin in an unredeemed condition. **3:24** Following their sin, the first couple went **east**, a direction associated with departure

Character profile:
Eve

When God made humans "in his own image" (Gn 1:27), he created Adam first. A few verses later we read, "Then the LORD God said, 'It is not good for the man to be alone. I will make a helper corresponding to him'" (2:18).

When we read that God called Eve Adam's "helper," we are reminded that the Old Testament speaks of God himself as the helper of his people (Dt 33:7; Pss 33:20; 70:5; 115:9–11; 146:5). Thus, her role was essential. Eve was God's very tangible way of saying, "Adam, you need help."

The idea that Eve would be a helper "corresponding to" Adam means that she would perfectly complement him. She would supply strengths he lacked, and vice versa. Ultimately, Eve would be the "very good" solution (Gn 1:31) to Adam's "not good" solitary existence.

And so it was. God crafted this wonderful human being to help and to complement Adam. As the first human female and wife, Eve experienced wonders in life none of us can fathom: glorious face-to-face walks and talks with God, marriage as it was meant to be, creation in all its piercing beauty and none of its brokenness.

How long did this perfect bliss last? However long it was, Eve had it. Then, inexplicably, she gave in to temptation. She believed Satan's lie: God can't be trusted; God isn't enough. Yet she doesn't bear the blame alone. The Bible makes it clear

that Adam "was with her" (3:6). For incomprehensible reasons he stood by passively, saying and doing nothing as the devil questioned God's words.

The tragic result was exactly what God had warned: death. They experienced immediate spiritual death and would eventually experience physical death. It was the catastrophic end to a harmonious relationship with God, with others, and with creation itself. Gone were virtues like vulnerability, trust, and selflessness.

Expulsion from Eden followed, meaning a loss of access to God and to the tree of life. Adam and Eve could only look back over their shoulders at paradise and wonder what might have been. Post-Eden, Eve became a mom to children. At one point, she faced the parental nightmare of having one son murder another son.

How tragic that this special woman, "the mother of all the living" (3:20), also played a prominent role in bringing death into the world. In a sense, Eve's life prefigures every life. Each is special, made in God's image. But each is also marked by doubt and disobedience, marred by the tragedy of sin—and utterly dependent on the one who alone can reverse the curse (see 3:15).

Let us learn from Eve's beautiful yet tragic experience. Life works best when we cling to God's Word. We have an enemy who uses deceit to destroy (see Jn 8:44; 1Pt 5:8). Though we will continually be subjected to a chorus of competing voices, we can be assured that God loves us and is completely worthy of our trust.

the flaming, whirling sword east of the garden of Eden to guard the way to the tree of life.

Cain Murders Abel

4 The man was intimate with his wife Eve, and she conceived and gave birth to Cain. She said, "I have had a male child with the Lord's help."^A ² She also gave birth to his brother Abel. Now Abel became a shepherd of flocks, but Cain worked the ground. ³ In the course of time Cain presented some of the land's produce as an offering to the Lord. ⁴ And Abel also presented an offering — some of the firstborn of his flock and their fat portions. The Lord had regard for Abel and his offering, ⁵ but he did not have regard for Cain and his offering. Cain was furious, and he looked despondent. ⁶ Then the Lord said to Cain, "Why are you furious? And why do you look despondent? ⁷ If you do what is right, won't you be accepted? But if you do not do what is right, sin is crouching at the door. Its desire is for you, but you must rule over it."

⁸ Cain said to his brother Abel, "Let's go out to the field."^B And while they were in the field, Cain attacked his brother Abel and killed him. ⁹ Then the Lord said to Cain, "Where is your brother Abel?"

"I don't know," he replied. "Am I my brother's guardian?"

¹⁰ Then he said, "What have you done? Your brother's blood cries out to me from the ground! ¹¹ So now you are cursed, alienated from the ground that opened its mouth to receive your brother's blood you have shed.^C ¹² If you work the ground, it will never again give you its yield. You will be a restless wanderer on the earth."

¹³ But Cain answered the Lord, "My punishment^D is too great to bear! ¹⁴ Since you are banishing me today from the face of the earth, and I must hide from your presence and become a restless wanderer on the earth, whoever finds me will kill me."

¹⁵ Then the Lord replied to him, "In that case,^E whoever kills Cain will suffer vengeance seven times over." And he placed a mark on Cain so that whoever found him would not kill him. ¹⁶ Then Cain went out from the Lord's presence and lived in the land of Nod,^F east of Eden.

The Line of Cain

¹⁷ Cain was intimate with his wife, and she conceived and gave birth to Enoch. Then Cain became the builder of a city, and he named the city Enoch after his son. ¹⁸ Irad was born to Enoch, Irad fathered Mehujael, Mehujael fathered Methushael, and Methushael fathered Lamech. ¹⁹ Lamech took two wives for himself,

---

^A 4:1 Lit *the Lord* ^B 4:8 Sam, LXX, Syr, Vg; MT omits *"Let's go out to the field."* ^C 4:11 Lit *blood from your hand* ^D 4:13 Or *sin* ^E 4:15 LXX, Syr, Vg read *"Not so!"* ^F 4:16 Lit *Wandering*

---

from God in numerous biblical examples. Other instances of eastward movement in Genesis include Cain's journeys after judgment (4:16), humanity's migration toward Babylon (11:2), and the migration of Keturah's sons (25:6). **Cherubim** are used as an artistic motif in the tabernacle (Ex 25:18–22; 26:1) and are also mentioned in Ezk 10 and 11.
4:1 Adam and Eve now begin to fulfill God's original command to them, to "be fruitful" and "multiply" (1:28). **Eve**, whose name means "life," now becomes the life-giver. Eve knew that the child was more than the result of her and her husband's love; he came into being **with the Lord's help**. A wordplay in the Hebrew suggests that the name **Cain** (*qayin*) came from the verb **had** (*qaniti*) in Eve's comment, **I have** "*had*" **a male child**.
4:2 The name **Abel** means "breath"; the term is used elsewhere in the OT to refer to that which passes away quickly and is insubstantial (Ps 62:10; Ec 1:2).
4:3 Cain's sacrifice marks the first mention of **an offering to the Lord** in the Bible. The Hebrew term used here suggests a freewill gift given to an authority.
4:4–5 Ironically, the first recorded offering given to God was also the first one rejected by him. Since grain offerings were authorized in the law of Moses, the fact that Cain's offering was of vegetation rather than an animal is not why God **did not have regard** for it. Cain's **furious** reaction suggests that the offering was rejected because of sin in his heart, not the nature of his offering.
4:8 In a move that demonstrates premeditation, Cain led Abel **to the field** and **attacked** him in a place where there were no

human witnesses. Cain's killing of his brother brought about the first death of a human.
4:9 God's use of questions with guilty sinners continues here (v. 6; cp. 3:9–13). By claiming he did not know where his brother was, Cain added lying to his sin of murder. God once made Adam a guardian (Hb *shamar*) in the garden (2:15). Cain now asked if he was to be his **brother's guardian** (Hb *shamar*). The Bible's answer to Cain's question is yes (Lv 19:18; Mt 22:39; Gl 5:14).
4:10 Unlike his father Adam (3:12), Cain never confessed his guilt, even though God directly confronted him with his sin. Though Abel never spoke in the preceding narrative, his **blood** now cried out **from the ground**.
4:11 God's judgment began with a curse whose wording in the Hebrew parallels the curse placed on the snake. This is particularly fitting since both were liars and murderers (Jn 8:44).
4:12 Cain's punishment destroyed his livelihood as a farmer and turned him into a **restless wanderer**.
4:13 Cain's response has several possible English renderings. The CSB—which reflects the unrepentant attitude Cain showed earlier—expresses Cain's anguish, but no remorse. The Septuagint and Martin Luther translated it as, "My sin is too great to be forgiven," while early rabbis took it as a question: "Is my sin too great to forgive?" In view of Cain's previous and later actions, the CSB's translation seems best.
4:14 Just as his father Adam had been driven out (Hb *garash*) of the garden, Cain noted that God was **banishing** (Hb *garash*) him **from the face of the earth**. Since he would **hide** (or possibly, "be hidden") from God's

protective **presence**, he feared that other descendants of Adam and Eve (5:4) would **kill** him to avenge Abel's murder.
4:15 True to his compassionate and forgiving nature (Ex 34:6–7), God made two provisions for Cain to protect him despite his sin.
4:16 Cain's departure **from the Lord's presence** was both physical and spiritual (Jnh 1:3,10). *Nod* means "wandering." The **land of Nod** is never mentioned again in the Bible. Perhaps the phrase simply referred to any location in which Cain resided. The notation that Cain departed to live **east of Eden** identifies him with other sinners who also moved east (see note at 3:24).
4:17 The parallel tracks of Adam's and Cain's lives—sin, judgment by God, banishment, and eastward movement—continue with the notation that after these things **Cain was intimate with his wife** (cp. v. 1). In spite of his grave sin, Cain still fulfilled the divine command to be fruitful and multiply (1:28). The city of **Enoch** is not mentioned elsewhere in the Bible, and its location is unknown.
Cain's genealogy in vv. 17–24 has similarities with Seth's genealogy (5:3–32). Two of the names in both lines are identical (Enoch, Lamech) and others are similar (Cain/Kenan; Methushael/Methuselah). In addition, the seventh member of both genealogies (Cain's Lamech, Seth's Enoch) are given special emphasis, and both conclude with a person who has three named sons. Notable differences exist as well: Seth's genealogy is longer and contains life span details, but it omits any mention of occupations or wives' names.
4:19 More details are provided in this genealogical section for **Lamech**, the seventh

one named Adah and the other named Zillah. [20] Adah bore Jabal; he was the first[A] of the nomadic herdsmen. [21] His brother was named Jubal; he was the first[A] of all who play the lyre and the flute. [22] Zillah bore Tubal-cain, who made all kinds of bronze and iron tools. Tubal-cain's sister was Naamah.

[23] Lamech said to his wives:

Adah and Zillah, hear my voice;
wives of Lamech, pay attention
     to my words.
For I killed a man for wounding me,
a young man for striking me.
[24]   If Cain is to be avenged
     seven times over,
then for Lamech it will be
     seventy-seven times!

[25] Adam was intimate with his wife again, and she gave birth to a son and named him Seth, for she said, "God has given[B] me another offspring[C] in place of Abel, since Cain killed him." [26] A son was born to Seth also, and he named him Enosh. At that time people began to call on the name of the LORD.

The Line of Seth

5 This is the document containing the family[D] records of Adam.[E] On the day that God created man,[F] he made him in the likeness of God; [2] he created them male and female. When they were created, he blessed them and called them mankind.[G]

[3] Adam was 130 years old when he fathered a son in his likeness, according to his image, and named him Seth. [4] Adam lived 800 years after he fathered Seth, and he fathered other sons and daughters. [5] So Adam's life lasted 930 years; then he died.

[6] Seth was 105 years old when he fathered Enosh. [7] Seth lived 807 years after he fathered Enosh, and he fathered other sons and daughters. [8] So Seth's life lasted 912 years; then he died.

[9] Enosh was 90 years old when he fathered Kenan. [10] Enosh lived 815 years after he fathered Kenan, and he fathered other sons and daughters. [11] So Enosh's life lasted 905 years; then he died.

[12] Kenan was 70 years old when he fathered Mahalalel. [13] Kenan lived 840 years after he

---

[A]4:20,21 Lit father   [B]4:25 The Hb word for given sounds like the name "Seth."   [C]4:25 Lit seed   [D]5:1 Lit written family
[E]5:1 Or mankind   [F]5:1 Or Adam, human beings   [G]5:2 Hb 'adam

---

member of Adam's line through Cain, than for any other. His three named sons made crucial contributions to human culture. By taking **two wives for himself** Lamech became the first polygamist, a violation of God's intentions for marriage (2:22; Mk 10:6–8).
4:20 Jabal brought about key advances in the profession of **the nomadic herdsmen**—those who cared for sheep, goats, and cattle (Hb *miqneh*). This represents an advance beyond what Abel had done since he is only known to have tended sheep and goats (v. 2; Hb *tso'n*).
4:21 Jubal advanced civilization in the area of the musical arts, playing a key role in developing two of the most important musical instruments of the ancient world, **the lyre and the flute**.
4:22 Tubal-cain's metallurgical advances in creating **bronze** (made by combining copper and tin) and smelting **iron** would prove crucial for crafting **tools** and weapons.
4:23 Lamech's so-called "Song of the Sword," the longest recorded speech by a human to this point in the Bible (twenty-one Hebrew words), represents the dark climax of the Cainite genealogy. His level of retaliation against **a man** and **a young man** goes far beyond the biblical limits (Ex 21:23–25), and his boast of killing for vengeance foreshadows the conditions that led to the flood in Noah's day (Gn 6:11).
4:25 The name **Seth** (Hb *sheth*) is a word-play on the verb translated **has given** (Hb *shath*). Once again (v. 1), Eve recognized God as the ultimate source of her offspring. This family line that ultimately produced Jesus is traceable through Seth (Lk 3:38).
4:26 The name **Enosh**, like the name Adam, means "humanity." In a very real sense Enosh's birth marks a new and brighter beginning for humanity, as **people began to call on the name of the LORD**, "Yahweh." Yahweh is God's personal name (Ex 3:15).

5:1 This is the second of eleven (Hb) *tole-doth* sections in Genesis (2:4; 6:9; 10:1; 11:10,27; 25:12,19; 36:1,9; 37:2). The Hebrew term *tole-doth* ("family records") refers to "those who were given birth." Each section contains genealogical information and/or accounts regarding the descendants of the people or things named in the section title.
Only the Sethite genealogy is called the **family records of Adam**, even though Cain's descendants are equally related. The reason for this is undoubtedly the contrasting descendants within the brothers' genealogies; only offspring in Seth's line are noted as being righteous.
5:2 Key themes of chap. 1 are repeated and extended in the Sethite genealogy: (1) God created both **male** and **female**, thus making it possible for humanity to fulfill the divine mandate to create offspring; (2) people, though made in God's image, are not God; **they were created**; (3) humanity has been specially **blessed** by God; and (4) humanity is under God's authority, as demonstrated by the fact that God assigned them the name **mankind**.
5:4 The phrase **fathered other sons and daughters** is repeated nine times in the Sethite genealogy, but it never occurs in the Cainite genealogy. The clear implication is that the line of Seth more faithfully fulfilled God's command to be fruitful and multiply (1:28).
5:5 Only three individuals are said to have lived longer than Adam's **930 years**. They are Noah (950), Jared (962), and Methuselah (969). The notation that **he died** emphasizes the solemn truth of God's curse following Adam's sin (3:19).
5:6–31 The name **Kenan** (Hb *qeynan*) is closely linked to Cain (Hb *qayin*), and may mean "metalworker."
The name **Mahalalel** may mean "one who praises God."

The name **Enoch** means "dedication." **Enoch**, as the seventh member of the Sethite genealogy, is given special emphasis. The name **Methuselah** may mean either "man of the spear" or "man of Shelah."
Enoch's life stands in stark contrast to Lamech, the seventh member of Cain's line. Whereas Lamech was notorious for his immorality and violence, **Enoch walked with God.** The phrase "walked with God" suggests living a life consistent with God's will as well as experiencing fellowship with him.
The description of Enoch's life differs from the others in two remarkable ways: (1) His righteousness is highlighted through the double notation that **Enoch walked with God**. (2) The description of the end of his life is mysterious: **he was not there because God took him**. The NT confirms the meaning of this phrase: "Enoch was taken away, and so he did not experience death" (Heb 11:5). Enoch's experience, like Elijah's later (2Kg 2:11), anticipates an experience reserved for Christians living at the end of time (1Co 15:51–55; 1Th 4:17). Methuselah's **969 years** marks him as the oldest person in the Bible.
The **Lamech** of the Sethite genealogy (v. 28) stands in sharp contrast to the Lamech of the Cainite genealogy. Both Lamechs are the only individuals in their respective genealogies to have quotations attributed to them, but Cain's Lamech spoke of murder and vengeance (4:23–24), while the Lamech in this chapter spoke words of hope and deliverance. The name **Noah** means "rest/relief." Prophetically, Lamech declared that the son born to him would live up to his name: he would **bring . . . relief** to humanity **from the agonizing labor** that had resulted from Adam's sin. The Hebrew verb "relief" is more commonly translated "comfort."
A final point of comparison between the Cainite and Sethite Lamechs is the use of sevens. The first Lamech mentioned Cain's

fathered Mahalalel, and he fathered other sons and daughters. [14] So Kenan's life lasted 910 years; then he died.

[15] Mahalalel was 65 years old when he fathered Jared. [16] Mahalalel lived 830 years after he fathered Jared, and he fathered other sons and daughters. [17] So Mahalalel's life lasted 895 years; then he died.

[18] Jared was 162 years old when he fathered Enoch. [19] Jared lived 800 years after he fathered Enoch, and he fathered other sons and daughters. [20] So Jared's life lasted 962 years; then he died.

[21] Enoch was 65 years old when he fathered Methuselah. [22] And after he fathered Methuselah, Enoch walked with God 300 years and fathered other sons and daughters. [23] So Enoch's life lasted 365 years. [24] Enoch walked with God; then he was not there because God took him.

[25] Methuselah was 187 years old when he fathered Lamech. [26] Methuselah lived 782 years after he fathered Lamech, and he fathered other sons and daughters. [27] So Methuselah's life lasted 969 years; then he died.

[28] Lamech was 182 years old when he fathered a son. [29] And he named him Noah,[A] saying, "This one will bring us relief from the agonizing labor of our hands, caused by the ground the LORD has cursed." [30] Lamech lived 595 years after he fathered Noah, and he fathered other sons and daughters. [31] So Lamech's life lasted 777 years; then he died.

[32] Noah was 500 years old, and he fathered Shem, Ham, and Japheth.

Sons of God and Daughters of Mankind

6 When mankind began to multiply on the earth and daughters were born to them, [2] the sons of God saw that the daughters of mankind were beautiful, and they took any they chose as wives for themselves. [3] And the LORD said, "My Spirit will not remain[B] with[C] mankind forever, because they are corrupt.[D] Their days will be 120 years." [4] The Nephilim[E] were on the earth both in those days and afterward, when the sons of God came to the daughters of mankind, who bore children to them. They were the powerful men of old, the famous men.

Judgment Decreed

[5] When the LORD saw that human wickedness was widespread on the earth and that every inclination of the human mind was nothing but

---

[A]5:29 In Hb, the name *Noah* sounds like "bring us relief." [B]6:3 Or *strive* [C]6:3 Or *in* [D]6:3 Lit *flesh* [E]6:4 Possibly means "fallen ones"; traditionally, "giants"; Nm 13:31–33

---

sevenfold curse and pronounced a 77-fold curse on anyone who would bring death to him, while Seth's Lamech lived **777 years** before death came to him.
5:32 The mention of **Noah** at the end of the Sethite genealogy serves as both a conclusion to this section of Genesis and a subtle introduction of the central human character in its next major section.
6:1–4 This brief portion of Genesis is one of the most controversial sections of the entire Bible. Major disagreements surround each of these verses. Careful study of the Hebrew text does not end the debates; if anything, it only sharpens them. The controversies are listed below.
6:2 Using language that parallels the sequence leading to humanity's first sin in the garden (3:6), the **sons of God** first **saw** something that they thought was good, and then **took** what they desired **for themselves**.
Controversy (cp. Jdg 14:1–2) surrounds the phrase "the sons of God." Three different basic

positions have been staked out regarding the identity of these "sons." They have been understood as heavenly beings (an ancient Jewish position, still accepted by many today), as kings or men of high social status, and as men from the godly family line of Seth.
Favoring their identity as heavenly beings—likely angels—is the fact that elsewhere in the OT the phrase "sons of God" refers only to heavenly creatures (Jb 1:6; 2:1; 38:7) and that the NT refers to fallen angels (2Pt 2:4; Jd 6). Those who accept this view hold that the sin that prompted God's anger in this passage was a violation of Gn 2:24, brought about by sexual relations between human and angelic beings, resulting in the creation of the Nephilim. But this view has its difficulties. For instance, Jesus indicated that angels do not marry (Mt 22:30) and Paul used the phrase "sons of God" to refer to godly people, not angels (Gl 3:26).
The view that the "sons of God" are kings or aristocrats is supported by the fact that *Elohim*, the common Hebrew word for "God," is sometimes applied to persons who have great social power (Ps 82:6–7; Jn 10:34–35). Advocates of this position say that the "daughters of mankind" were people of lower social status. Thus the passage is thought to indicate possible abuse of lower class women by licentious men of privilege. Interpreters who take this view do not necessarily connect the Nephilim with these marriages.
The third position is the most popular view among evangelical Christians. It assumes that the "sons of God" were descendants of godly Seth, while the "daughters of mankind" were descendants of ungodly Cain.
6:3 The meaning of this verse is one of the most disputed in the Bible: Is it about God shortening humanity's life spans, or about God setting a time for the universal flood? There is

no general agreement as to its meaning, so the various Bible translations reflect translators' differing viewpoints. Accordingly, disagreement exists among translators regarding the reference to **Spirit**; some understand the Hebrew word to refer to the animating force present in living beings—thus rendering it "spirit" (KJV)—while many others, such as the CSB, understand it to refer to the Holy Spirit. Closely related to this issue is the appropriate translation of the phrase rendered in the CSB as **remain with**. Significant variations include "abide in" (ESV) and "contend with" (NIV). Complicating the issue still further is the Hebrew word *basar*, which is normally translated "flesh" (KJV) but which can be taken figuratively to refer to that which is **corrupt**.
6:4 Two major questions arise in this verse: who are the **Nephilim** and what if anything is the connection of the Nephilim to the **sons of God** and the **daughters of mankind**? The word *Nephilim* is actually a transliteration—not a translation—of the Hebrew word; translated, it means "fallen ones," a phrase that could mean morally or physically degraded individuals, or possibly angels who fell from heaven (Is 14:12).
In spite of its literal meaning, many versions (e.g., KJV, NLT) have followed the Septuagint in translating it as "giants," a guess seemingly based on the mention of Nephilim in Nm 13:33. This proposal appears unlikely, however, since no Nephilim would have survived the flood (Gn 7:22–23) and thus could not have lived during the post-flood events narrated in Numbers. Further, the Nephilim are never mentioned as one of the groups to be wiped out by the Israelites when they entered Canaan. Their mention in Nm 13 probably came from the lips of a fear-crazed spy who misinterpreted what he had seen in Canaan.

evil all the time, ⁶ the LORD regretted that he had made man on the earth, and he was deeply grieved. ⁷ Then the LORD said, "I will wipe mankind, whom I created, off the face of the earth, together with the animals, creatures that crawl, and birds of the sky — for I regret that I made them." ⁸ Noah, however, found favor with the LORD.

God Warns Noah

⁹ These are the family records of Noah. Noah was a righteous man, blameless among his contemporaries; Noah walked with God. ¹⁰ And Noah fathered three sons: Shem, Ham, and Japheth.

¹¹ Now the earth was corrupt in God's sight, and the earth was filled with wickedness.ᴬ ¹² God saw how corrupt the earth was, for every creature had corrupted its way on the earth. ¹³ Then God said to Noah, "I have decided to put an end to every creature, for the earth is filled with wickedness because of them; therefore I am going to destroy them along with the earth.

¹⁴ "Make yourself an ark of gopherᴮ wood. Make rooms in the ark, and cover it with pitch inside and outside. ¹⁵ This is how you are to make it: The ark will be 450 feet long, 75 feet wide, and 45 feet high.ᶜ ¹⁶ You are to make a roof,ᴰ finishing the sides of the ark to within eighteen inchesᴱ of the roof. You are to put a door in the side of the ark. Make it with lower, middle, and upper decks.

¹⁷ "Understand that I am bringing a flood — floodwaters on the earth to destroy every creature under heaven with the breath of life in it. Everything on earth will perish. ¹⁸ But I will establish my covenant with you, and you will enter the ark with your sons, your wife, and your sons' wives. ¹⁹ You are also to bring into the ark two of all the living creatures, male and female, to keep them alive with you. ²⁰ Two of everything — from the birds according to their kinds, from the livestock according to their kinds, and from the animals that crawl on the ground according to their kinds — will come to you so that you can keep them alive. ²¹ Take with you every kind of food that is eaten; gather it as food for you and for them." ²² And Noah did this. He did everything that God had commanded him.

Entering the Ark

7 Then the LORD said to Noah, "Enter the ark, you and all your household, for I have seen that you alone are righteous before me in this generation. ² You are to take with you seven pairs, a male and its female, of all the clean animals, and two of the animals that are not clean, a male and its female, ³ and seven pairs, male and female, of the birds of the sky — in order to keep offspring alive throughout the earth. ⁴ Seven days from now I will make it rain on the earth forty days and forty nights, and every

---

ᴬ6:11 Or *injustice*, also in v. 13　ᴮ6:14 Unknown species of tree; perhaps pine or cypress　ᶜ6:15 Or *300 cubits long, 50 cubits wide, and 30 cubits high*　ᴰ6:16 Or *window*, or *hatch*; Hb uncertain　ᴱ6:16 Lit *to a cubit*

Were the Nephilim products of the marriages between the sons of God and the daughters of mankind (v. 2)? Possibly, but in the Hebrew text there is no explicit connection between them.
6:5 God, who alone can observe both people's outward actions (Jb 34:21) and their thoughts (1Sm 16:7), **saw** what was visible—**that human wickedness was widespread**—and what was invisible—**that every inclination of the human mind was nothing but evil all the time**. The word translated "mind" is literally "heart," reflecting the ancient conception that this organ was the seat of the intellect, emotion, and will.
6:6 For the first time in the Bible, **the LORD regretted** something **that he had made**. However, his regret did not stem from something he had done wrong, but rather from what humanity was doing wrong.
6:8 This contrast to the rest of humanity anticipates Noah's contrasting destiny. The word **favor** means undeserved blessing given by a powerful being to one who is less powerful.
6:9–10 The family records of Noah is the third of eleven (Hb) *toledoth* sections in Genesis (2:4; 5:1; 10:1; 11:10,27; 25:12,19; 36:1,9; 37:2).
6:11–12 Within these two verses three different forms of the verb **corrupt** are used to describe what humanity had done to itself and the world in Noah's day. The Hebrew word translated "corrupt" means "to bring to ruin, to destroy."
6:14 Because of God's grace (v. 8) and Noah's relationship with God (v. 9), Noah and

his family would be saved in an **ark**, along with the land and animals. The Hebrew term translated "ark" is used only in the Noah account and the story of Moses's early childhood (Ex 2:3); as used in the Bible it refers to a watertight vessel used to preserve human life from impending disaster. **Gopher** is the transliteration of a Hebrew word whose meaning is unknown; gopher wood may be pine or cypress or something extinct.
6:15 Noah was **to make** the ark rectangular and barge-like in shape, six times longer than it was wide, and ten times longer than it was high. In the Hebrew text the measurements are expressed as "cubits", a cubit being the length from a person's elbow to the end of the fully extended middle finger—about eighteen inches. The **450**-foot length made the ark the largest ship known to be constructed in ancient times. The ark was to contain an unspecified number of rooms—literally, "nests"— and was to have two layers of pitch, (that is, asphalt or bitumen) painted over the boards.
6:16 The Hebrew word translated **roof** can also be translated "window" or "hatch." If the term means "roof," then the text probably indicates that it was to extend **eighteen inches** over the sides of the boat. If the term means "window," then it refers to an eighteen-inch high gap separating the four sides of the boat from its roof.
6:17 Only after he commanded Noah to make the ark did God tell him why it was to be built: God was **bringing a flood**—a term used only in connection with the massive, all-destroying flood in Noah's day. **Everything on earth**

will perish. The biblical language here and elsewhere in Gn 6–8 most naturally indicates that Noah's flood covered the entire globe. The apostle Peter seems to affirm this (2Pt 2:5; 3:6). Some evangelicals conclude that Noah's flood covered only that portion of the earth that was inhabited by humans.
6:18 The term **covenant** refers to a binding, formal agreement between two parties—a sort of treaty, pact, or contract.
6:19 Noah was **to bring into the ark** one **male** and one **female of all the living creatures**. Representatives of all vulnerable species were to be preserved.
6:22 An undetermined amount of time had passed between this verse and the previous verses in this chapter. Certainly the construction of the ark would have been a lengthy endeavor.
7:1 Following the ark's completion, **the LORD** gave **Noah** the order to begin the complex process of boarding the craft. Because of Noah's **righteous** walk with God he and his **household** would be saved.
7:2–3 While one male and one female of every species of air and land animal were to be taken aboard the ark, **all the clean animals**—both those of the land and among the **birds of the sky**—were to have **seven pairs** of males and females onboard. The concept of clean animals is explained elsewhere in the Torah (Lv 11:1–46); essentially, these were animals that were fit for human consumption and could be offered as sacrifices to God.
7:4 The advance warning God gave Noah here about the onset of rain was necessary,

living thing I have made I will wipe off the face of the earth." ⁵ And Noah did everything that the LORD commanded him.

⁶ Noah was six hundred years old when the flood came and water covered the earth. ⁷ So Noah, his sons, his wife, and his sons' wives entered the ark because of the floodwaters. ⁸ From the animals that are clean, and from the animals that are not clean, and from the birds and every creature that crawls on the ground, ⁹ two of each, male and female, came to Noah and entered the ark, just as God had commanded him. ¹⁰ Seven days later the flood-waters came on the earth.

The Flood

¹¹ In the six hundredth year of Noah's life, in the second month, on the seventeenth day of the month, on that day all the sources of the vast watery depths burst open, the flood-gates of the sky were opened, ¹² and the rain fell on the earth forty days and forty nights. ¹³ On that same day Noah and his three sons, Shem, Ham, and Japheth, entered the ark, along with Noah's wife and his three sons' wives. ¹⁴ They entered it with all the wild-life according to their kinds, all livestock according to their kinds, all the creatures that crawl on the earth according to their kinds, every flying creature — all the birds and every winged creature — according to their kinds. ¹⁵ Two of every creature that has the breath of life in it came to Noah and entered the ark. ¹⁶ Those that entered, male and fe-male of every creature, entered just as God had commanded him. Then the LORD shut him in.

¹⁷ The flood continued for forty days on the earth; the water increased and lifted up the ark so that it rose above the earth. ¹⁸ The water surged and increased greatly on the earth, and the ark floated on the surface of the water. ¹⁹ Then the water surged even higher on the earth, and all the high mountains under the whole sky were covered. ²⁰ The mountains were covered as the water surged above them more than twenty feet.^ ²¹ Every creature per-ished — those that crawl on the earth, birds, livestock, wildlife, and those that swarm on the earth, as well as all mankind. ²² Every-thing with the breath of the spirit of life in its nostrils — everything on dry land died. ²³ He wiped out every living thing that was on the face of the earth, from mankind to livestock, to creatures that crawl, to the birds of the sky, and they were wiped off the earth. Only Noah was left, and those that were with him in the ark. ²⁴ And the water surged on the earth 150 days.

The Flood Recedes

8 God remembered Noah, as well as all the wildlife and all the livestock that were with him in the ark. God caused a wind to pass over the earth, and the water began to subside. ² The sources of the watery depths and the floodgates of the sky were closed, and the rain from the sky stopped. ³ The water steadi-ly receded from the earth, and by the end of 150 days the water had decreased significant-ly. ⁴ The ark came to rest in the seventh month, on the seventeenth day of the month, on the mountains of Ararat.

⁵ The water continued to recede until the tenth month; in the tenth month, on the first day of the month, the tops of the mountains were visible. ⁶ After forty days Noah opened the window of the ark that he had made, ⁷ and he sent out a raven. It went back and forth until the water had dried up from the

^7:20 Lit *surged 15 cubits*

for it almost certainly would have taken **seven days** to finish loading, securing, and tending to the dietary needs of all the wild animals onboard the three-level barge-like structure.

The number *forty* played a significant role throughout the OT: Isaac and Esau were for-ty when they married (25:20; 26:34), Moses was on Mount Sinai forty days and nights receiving the law from God (Ex 24:18; 34:28; Dt 9:11,18,25), Israel spent forty years in the wilderness following their disobedience (Nm 32:13), the Philistines oppressed Israel for forty years (Jdg 13:1), and several judges and kings ruled over Israel for forty years (Othniel, Jdg 3:11; Deborah, Jdg 5:31; Gideon, Jdg 8:28; Eli, 1Sm 4:8; David, 2Sm 5:4; Solo-mon, 1Kg 11:42; Joash, 2Kg 12:1; Saul, Ac 13:21). **7:6–10** Noah's age at the onset of the flood—**six hundred years old**—will be used to indicate the duration of the flood (8:13). No other human after Noah will be said to live to this age. **7:11** Water came from two different sourc-es—one below and one above. Exactly what is meant by **all the sources of the vast watery**

depths is unknown; the phrase appears to re-fer to a massive outflow of pressurized water from underground sources that **burst** out of the ground with devastating effect. **7:16 Shut him in**—The author gave no details to explain how God performed the supernatural act of shutting Noah in. **7:17–20 More than twenty feet** is literally fifteen cubits, which is about 22½ feet. **7:24** Though the text does not explicitly say so, the total of 150 days seems to include the forty days of rain. The Hebrew word trans-lated as **surged** emphasizes the power of the waters. **8:1 Remembered** does not suggest that God had ever forgotten about Noah; when used of God, "remember" suggests the ini-tiation of a miraculous, saving act of God. Using language that reflects God's initial act of creating the universe (Gn 1:2), **God caused** (Hb) *ruach*—"Spirit" or **wind**—to pass over the waters of **the earth**. Immediately **the water began to subside**. **8:2** Following the 150 days of ever-surging waters, a turnabout occurred: all **the sources** of water (from above and below) **stopped**

and the water began to subside. The initial downpour ended after forty days and nights (7:12), so presumably the rains that are said to have ceased in the present verse were only sporadic showers. **8:3** Just as the flood had increased upon the earth for 150 days, so it **steadily receded from the earth** for **150 days**, until the levels had decreased significantly. **8:4** Exactly five months after the flood had begun (7:11), **the ark came to rest . . . on the mountains of Ararat**—modern Turkey or Armenia. **8:5–6** This is the only mention of a **window** (Hb *hallon*) in the ark. **8:7** Rabbis have suggested that Noah first **sent out a raven**, a ritually unclean bird, because it was expendable. The fact that it **went back and forth** from the ark means that it could find no suitable habitat. **8:8** Perhaps simultaneous with the release of the raven or soon thereafter, Noah **sent out a dove**. Since the dove ate seed and in-sects, it would provide a useful indication of **whether the water on the earth's surface had gone down**.

Salvation
Through Judgment

JUDGMENT	THE EVENT	THE MEANS	SALVATION
The Wicked	The Flood (Gn 6–9)	Floodwater	Noah and His Family
The Egyptians	The Exodus (Ex 1–15)	The Plagues and the Red Sea	The Israelites
Judah and Jerusalem	The Exile (2Ch 36)	The Babylonians	The Remnant
Sinners/Jesus Christ	The Cross (Rm 5)	God's Wrath on Our Substitute	Believers in Christ
God's Enemies	The Final Judgment (2Th 1)	God's Wrath and Hell	God's People

earth. **8** Then he sent out a dove to see whether the water on the earth's surface had gone down, **9** but the dove found no resting place for its foot. It returned to him in the ark because water covered the surface of the whole earth. He reached out and brought it into the ark to himself. **10** So Noah waited seven more days and sent out the dove from the ark again. **11** When the dove came to him at evening, there was a plucked olive leaf in its beak. So Noah knew that the water on the earth's surface had gone down. **12** After he had waited another seven days, he sent out the dove, but it did not return to him again. **13** In the six hundred first year,^A in the first month, on the first day of the month, the water that had covered the earth was dried up. Then Noah removed the ark's cover and saw that the surface of the ground was drying. **14** By the twenty-seventh day of the second month, the earth was dry.

The LORD's Promise

15 Then God spoke to Noah, **16** "Come out of the ark, you, your wife, your sons, and your sons' wives with you. **17** Bring out all the living creatures that are with you — birds, livestock, those that crawl on the earth — and they will spread over the earth and be fruitful and multiply on the earth." **18** So Noah, along with his sons, his wife, and his sons' wives, came out. **19** All the animals, all the creatures that crawl, and all the flying creatures — everything that moves on the earth — came out of the ark by their families.

20 Then Noah built an altar to the LORD. He took some of every kind of clean animal and every kind of clean bird and offered burnt offerings on the altar. **21** When the LORD smelled the pleasing aroma, he said to himself, "I will never again curse the ground because of human beings, even though the inclination of the human heart is evil from youth onward. And I will never again strike down every living thing as I have done.

^A 8:13 = of Noah's life

8:9 Though the ark was now resting on Ararat (v. 4) and mountaintops were visible (v. 5), the waters had not yet receded enough for the dove to find a **resting place for its foot**.
8:10–11 When the dove returned to Noah from its second foray with an **olive leaf**, this confirmed that the lower elevations (where olive trees grow) were now above water.
8:12 When Noah sent the dove out a third time and it **did not return**, it was clear that

life-sustaining conditions now existed at the earth's more temperate, lower elevations.
8:13–14 On Noah's six hundred first birthday he **removed the ark's cover** and confirmed what the dove had indicated—that the plains beneath the mountain range were **drying**. Some fifty-seven days later, **the earth was dry**.
8:20 Noah's first act following his departure from the ark was to worship God by giving a burnt offering. Since **every kind of clean animal** and **bird**—that is, one of every mammal

that chewed the cud and possessed split hoofs, as well as one representative of every kind of bird that did not eat carrion—was offered.
8:21 Using anthropomorphic language—words that describe God's actions in human terms—the text notes that **the LORD smelled the pleasing aroma**. The phrase means that God accepted God's sacrifice. Following Noah's sacrifice the Lord made a solemn promise **never again** to **curse the ground** as he had done following Adam's

22 As long as the earth endures,
    seedtime and harvest, cold and heat,
    summer and winter, and day and night
    will not cease."

God's Covenant with Noah

9 God blessed Noah and his sons and said to them, "Be fruitful and multiply and fill the earth. **2** The fear and terror of you will be in every living creature on the earth, every bird of the sky, every creature that crawls on the ground, and all the fish of the sea. They are placed under your authority. **3** Every creature that lives and moves will be food for you; as I gave the green plants, I have given you everything. **4** However, you must not eat meat with its lifeblood in it. **5** And I will require a penalty for your lifeblood;^ I will require it from any animal and from any human; if someone murders a fellow human, I will require that person's life.

6   Whoever sheds human blood,
        by humans his blood will be shed,
        for God made humans in his image.

7 But you, be fruitful and multiply; spread out over the earth and multiply on it."

8 Then God said to Noah and his sons with him, **9** "Understand that I am establishing my covenant with you and your descendants after you, **10** and with every living creature that is with you — birds, livestock, and all wildlife of the earth that are with you — all the animals of the earth that came out of the ark. **11** I establish my covenant with you that never again will every creature be wiped out by floodwaters; there will never again be a flood to destroy the earth." **12** And God said, "This is the sign of the covenant I am making between me and you and every living creature with you, a covenant for all future generations: **13** I have placed my bow in the clouds, and it will be a sign of the covenant between me and the earth. **14** Whenever I form clouds over the earth and the bow appears in the clouds, **15** I will remember my covenant between me and you and all the living creatures: water will never again become a flood to destroy every creature. **16** The bow will be in the clouds, and I will look at it and remember the permanent covenant between God and all the living creatures on earth." **17** God said to Noah, "This is the sign of the covenant that I have established between me and every creature on earth."

Prophecies about Noah's Family

18 Noah's sons who came out of the ark were Shem, Ham, and Japheth. Ham was the father of Canaan. **19** These three were Noah's sons, and from them the whole earth was populated. **20** Noah, as a man of the soil, began by planting^B a vineyard. **21** He drank some of the wine, became drunk, and uncovered himself inside his tent. **22** Ham, the father of Canaan, saw his father naked and told his two brothers outside. **23** Then Shem and Japheth took a cloak and placed it over both their shoulders, and walking backward, they covered their father's nakedness. Their faces were turned away, and they did not see their father naked.

24 When Noah awoke from his drinking and learned what his youngest son had done to him, **25** he said:

    Canaan is cursed.
    He will be the lowest of slaves
        to his brothers.

---

^9:5 Lit *And your blood belonging to your life I will seek*   ^9:20 Or *Noah began to be a farmer and planted*

---

sin (Gn 3:17; 5:29). Almost with a sense of resignation, God noted that **the inclination of the human heart is evil from youth** onward (Ps 14:1; Rm 3:9,23). The flood did not significantly change the human heart (cp. Gn 6:5). Yet in spite of humanity's sinful nature, God's grace and love would prevail: He would **never again** destroy all life as he had done in Noah's day.
9:1–2 This blessing fortifies the parallels between Noah and Adam (1:28), as both blessings began with the command to **be fruitful and multiply and fill the earth.** However, in Noah's day the blessing is altered. Mankind is still to take dominion over creation (1:28), but due to the presence of sin, the harmony that existed in the garden of Eden had ended; now animals were filled with **the fear and terror** of humans.
9:3 The phrase referring to animal food sources can be translated literally as "every creeping/gliding animal" and would normally be understood to refer to smaller animals on land or sea, but it is usually understood here to mean **every creature** that **moves.** Israelites would later be limited to eating only clean animals (Lv 11).
9:4 God required Noah and his offspring to drain the **lifeblood** from any animal before eating it. This guideline would be expanded

and clarified in Israel's Sinai law code (Lv 7:26–27; 17:10–14; 19:26; Dt 12:16,24; 15:23). To avoid offending Jewish Christians, first-century Gentile Christians were also encouraged not to eat blood (Ac 15:20,29).
9:5–6 Because **God made humans in his image,** the taking of a human life by either an animal or another person was not treated like the death of an animal. **Any animal** and **any human** who killed a human was to have its own **blood . . . shed . . . by humans** as a just punishment.
9:7 God's blessing of humanity in Noah's day begins (v. 1) and ends with the command to **be fruitful and multiply.**
9:8–11 These verses are the formal conclusion of the covenant first mentioned in 6:18. This portion of the Noahic covenant unconditionally promises that **there will never again be a flood** of the same destructive scale as Noah's flood.
9:12–17 Accompanying the covenant was a visible confirmation of the agreement between God **and the earth** that would continue **for all future generations:** God's **bow in the clouds** represented his promise that he would **never again** send **a flood to destroy every creature.** This covenant is one of three in the Bible that were accompanied by a sign; the other signs were

circumcision (Gn 17:11) and the Sabbath (Ex 31:16–17).
9:21 After sin entered the world, shattering innocence, nakedness was associated with shame (cp. 2:25; 3:10). In this case Noah brought the shame on himself through his sinful drunkenness. A minimum of two years likely elapsed between vv. 20 and 21 since grapevines must grow that long before they can produce grapes.
9:22 Noah "uncovered himself," and Ham **saw** Noah **naked.** This passage does not say that Ham "uncovered the nakedness of Noah," which would be a euphemism for perverted sexual activity (Lv 18:6–19). In this case, Ham dishonored his father and thus sinned (Ex 20:12; Dt 5:16) in two ways: First, he dishonored his father by staring at his nakedness (Hab 2:15). Second, he increased both his sin and his father's shame by reporting his father's condition to others.
9:23 **Shem** and **Japheth** demonstrated their nobler natures by reacting to their father's condition far differently from Ham. First, they did not look upon their father's shameful condition. Second, **they covered their father's nakedness,** thus ending his shame.
9:24–27 When Noah **learned what his youngest son had done,** he placed the curse on Ham's son, **Canaan,** who would

²⁶ He also said:
Blessed be the LORD, the God of Shem;
Let Canaan beᴬ Shem's slave.
²⁷ Let God extend Japheth;ᴮ
let Japheth dwell in the tents of Shem;
let Canaan be Shem's slave.

²⁸ Now Noah lived 350 years after the flood. ²⁹ So Noah's life lasted 950 years; then he died.

The Table of Nations

10 These are the family records of Noah's sons, Shem, Ham, and Japheth. They also had sons after the flood.

² Japheth's sons: Gomer, Magog, Madai, Javan, Tubal, Meshech, and Tiras. ³ Gomer's sons: Ashkenaz, Riphath, and Togarmah.

⁴ And Javan's sons: Elishah, Tarshish, Kittim, and Dodanim.ᶜ ⁵ From these descendants, the peoples of the coasts and islands spread out into their lands according to their clans in their nations, each with its own language.

⁶ Ham's sons: Cush, Mizraim, Put, and Canaan. ⁷ Cush's sons: Seba, Havilah, Sabtah, Raamah, and Sabteca. And Raamah's sons: Sheba and Dedan.

⁸ Cush fathered Nimrod, who began to be powerful in the land. ⁹ He was a powerful hunter in the sight of the LORD. That is why it is said, "Like Nimrod, a powerful hunter in the sight of the LORD." ¹⁰ His kingdom started with Babylon, Erech,ᴰ Accad,ᴱ and Calneh,ᶠ in the land of Shinar.ᴳ ¹¹ From that land he went to Assyria and built Nineveh, Rehoboth-ir, Calah,

ᴬ**9:26** As a wish or prayer; others interpret the verbs in vv. 26–27 as prophecy: *Canaan will be . . .*   ᴮ**9:27** In Hb, the name *Japheth* sounds like the word "extend."   ᶜ**10:4** Some Hb mss, LXX read *Rodanim*; 1Ch 1:7   ᴰ**10:10** Or *Uruk*   ᴱ**10:10** Or *Akkad*   ᶠ**10:10** Or *and all of them*   ᴳ**10:10** Or *in Babylonia*

be the lowest of slaves to his brothers, that is, the slave of the descendants of Shem and Japheth. This curse on Canaan had prophetic implications. In later centuries the Canaanites, the descendants of Canaan, were pressed into slavery by the Israelites (Jos 17:13; Jdg 1:28–35; 1Kg 9:20–21). This curse does not refer to the descendants of Ham who settled in Africa. **9:28–29** Noah's **950 years** mark him as the third-oldest human in biblical history, behind Methuselah (969 years) and Jared (962 years). **10:1 The family records of Noah's sons** is the fourth of eleven (Hb) *toledoth* sections in Genesis (2:4; 5:1; 6:9; 11:10,27; 25:12,19; 36:1,9; 37:2). The purpose of this section is twofold: to show that Noah's sons fulfilled the command to be fruitful, multiply, and spread out over the earth (9:7), and to distinguish the "unchosen" lines of

Noah's descendants (the Japhethites and Hamites) from the line that would be both the recipient and the agent of God's special blessing to the rest of humanity (the Shemites). Genesis 10:1–32 lists a total of seventy descendants in the family lines of **Shem, Ham**, and **Japheth**. This is labeled a list of clans, languages, nations, and lands (vv. 5,20,31; cp. Rv 14:6). Thus some of the names refer to the regions where that person's descendants settled; some refer to people groups. **10:2–5** Fourteen of **Japheth's** descendants are listed here. **Peoples of the coasts and islands** refers to people living in areas reachable by ship, especially in the Mediterranean basin. The fact that **each** group had **its own language** suggests that this listing refers to the situation after the Tower of Babylon event (11:1–9).

10:6–7 Thirty of **Ham's** descendants are included in this list. The geographic or ethnic identifications of most of the names have been lost in history, but they are associated with regions in Africa and Arabia. **Mizraim** is the Hebrew word for Egypt. **Havilah** probably refers to a different geographic region than the Havilah of 2:11. Two different persons by the name of **Sheba** are listed in Genesis genealogies (v. 28; 25:3); **Dedan** is also found in 25:3. It is best to understand each of these as different persons, and the founders of different people groups. **10:8–12** **Nimrod . . . began to be powerful in the land**, that is, he was successful as an aggressive empire builder. Nimrod's origins are from Cush, that is, Africa; his empire was Asian, stretching across the Tigris-Euphrates river basin. The order of place names suggests that Nimrod's empire expanded from

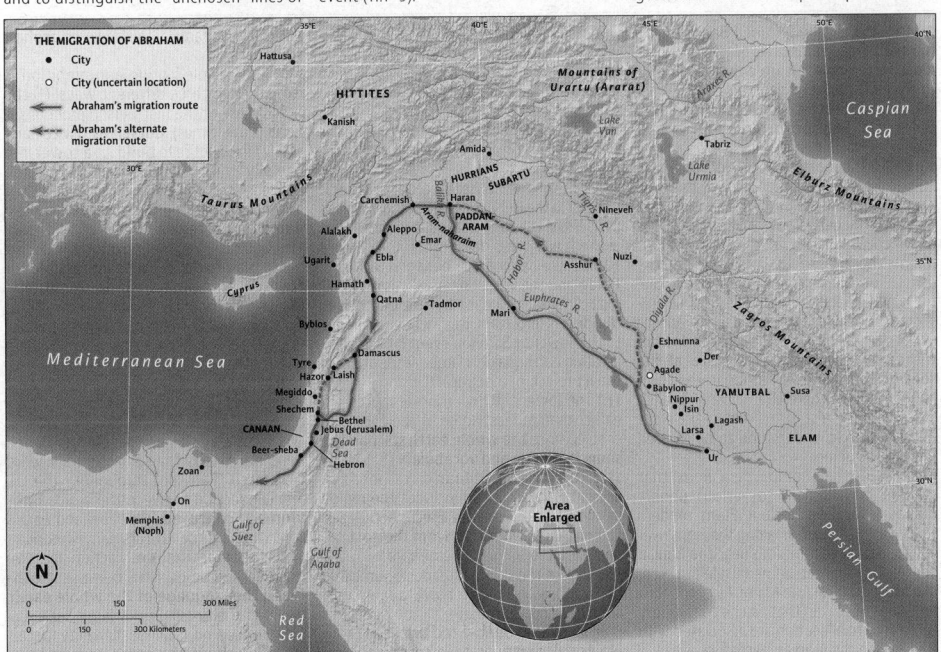

THE MIGRATION OF ABRAHAM
- City
- ○ City (uncertain location)
- ← Abraham's migration route
- ←- Abraham's alternate migration route

¹² and Resen, between Nineveh and the great city Calah.

¹³ Mizraim^A fathered the people of Lud, Anam, Lehab, Naphtuh, ¹⁴ Pathrus, Casluh (the Philistines came from them), and Caphtor.

¹⁵ Canaan fathered Sidon his firstborn and Heth, ¹⁶ as well as the Jebusites, the Amorites, the Girgashites, ¹⁷ the Hivites, the Arkites, the Sinites, ¹⁸ the Arvadites, the Zemarites, and the Hamathites. Afterward the Canaanite clans scattered. ¹⁹ The Canaanite border went from Sidon going toward Gerar as far as Gaza, and going toward Sodom, Gomorrah, Admah, and Zeboiim as far as Lasha.

²⁰ These are Ham's sons by their clans, according to their languages, in their lands and their nations.

²¹ And Shem, Japheth's older brother, also had sons. Shem was the father of all the sons of Eber. ²² Shem's sons were Elam, Asshur, Arpachshad, Lud, and Aram. ²³ Aram's sons: Uz, Hul, Gether, and Mash. ²⁴ Arpachshad fathered^B Shelah, and Shelah fathered Eber. ²⁵ Eber had two sons. One was named Peleg,^c for during his days the earth was divided; his brother was named Joktan. ²⁶ And Joktan fathered Almodad, Sheleph, Hazarmaveth, Jerah, ²⁷ Hadoram, Uzal, Diklah, ²⁸ Obal, Abimael, Sheba, ²⁹ Ophir, Havilah, and Jobab. All these were Joktan's sons. ³⁰ Their settlements extended from Mesha to Sephar, the eastern hill country.

³¹ These are Shem's sons by their clans, according to their languages, in their lands and their nations.

³² These are the clans of Noah's sons, according to their family records, in their nations. The nations on earth spread out from these after the flood.

The Tower of Babylon

11 The whole earth had the same language and vocabulary. ² As people migrated from the east,^D they found a valley in the land of Shinar and settled there. ³ They said to each other, "Come, let's make oven-fired bricks." (They used brick for stone and asphalt for mortar.) ⁴ And they said, "Come, let's build ourselves a city and a tower with its top in the sky. Let's make a name for ourselves; otherwise, we will be scattered throughout the earth."

⁵ Then the LORD came down to look over the city and the tower that the humans^E were building. ⁶ The LORD said, "If they have begun to do this as one people all having the same language, then nothing they plan to do will be impossible for them. ⁷ Come, let's go down there and confuse their language so that they will not understand one another's speech." ⁸ So from there the LORD scattered them throughout the earth, and they stopped building the city. ⁹ Therefore it is called Babylon,^F,^G for there the LORD confused the language of the whole earth, and from there the LORD scattered them throughout the earth.

^A 10:13 = Egypt   ^B 10:24 LXX reads *fathered Cainan, and Cainan fathered*; Gn 11:12–13; Lk 3:35–36   ^c 10:25 = Division   ^D 11:2 Or *migrated eastward*   ^E 11:5 Or *the descendants of Adam*   ^F 11:9 Hb *Babel*   ^G 11:9 In Hb, the name for "Babylon," *babel* sounds like the word for "confuse," *balal*.

---

south to north, and included **Babylon** and **Nineveh**, the capital cities of two of Israel's most formidable future enemies. **Shinar** corresponds to the ancient regions of Sumer and **Accad**; **Erech** to ancient Uruk; **Calah** to Nimrod; **Rehoboth-ir** may be ancient Asshur.

10:15–20 The most complex portion of the Hamite list is the **Canaan** branch, with eleven named descendants or people groups.

10:21–31 The genealogy of **Shem**, portions of which will be repeated in 11:10–17, represents the "chosen" line of Noah's descendants. From Shem's line will come Abraham, the Israelites, and ultimately Jesus. This presentation includes the "unchosen" branches of Shem's lineage, especially that of **Joktan** with his thirteen sons. The mention of **all the sons of Eber** brings attention to the point in Shem's line where the "chosen" branch splits from the rest of the family. The word *Hebrew* is often understood to be derived from Eber's name.

Names in the Shemite genealogy that scholars have linked to various people groups or locations include **Elam**, modern southwest Iran; **Asshur**, along the Tigris river in Iraq; **Aram**, eastern Iraq near the Iranian border; **Uz**, the Arabian peninsula or Edom; and **Mash**, central Asia Minor. All of the thirteen sons of Joktan that can be confidently connected to a location are associated with locations in the Arabian peninsula.

The name **Ophir** may not be connected with the Ophir mentioned elsewhere in Scripture (1Kg 9:28; Jb 22:24; Ps 45:9) since the latter name appears to be a distant location, possibly in Africa or India. Joktan's **Havilah** should not be equated with Cush's Havilah, though the two share the same name.

10:21 The phrase **Japheth's older brother** is difficult in the Hebrew: several other versions (KJV, NKJV, NIV) understand it to mean that Japheth was the older brother.

10:25 A wordplay exists between the name **Peleg** and the verbal phrase "was divided." Exactly what is meant by **the earth was divided** is uncertain. It may be a reference to the Tower of Babylon event (11:9), a devastating earthquake, a large Mesopotamian canal project, or a political division.

11:1 The Tower of Babylon incident occurred earlier than at least some of the events of chap. 10 since **the whole earth** still **had the same language and vocabulary** (10:5,20,31).

11:2 The land of Shinar corresponds to ancient Babylonia and includes the region of the cities of Babylon, Erech, Accad, and Calneh (10:10). **Migrated from the east** can be translated "migrated eastward."

11:3 Unlike the original readers' homeland of Israel, with its extensive quantity of limestone building material, the people of Babylonia used **oven-fired bricks**. Archaeological excavations have confirmed that

ancient inhabitants of the land used **asphalt for mortar**.

11:4 The people's pride and ambition is expressed in three different ways: (1) the fivefold use of the first-person pronouns—**Let's** (three times), **ourselves** (twice), and **we**; (2) their desire to **build . . . a tower** into **the sky**, thus giving them access to "the heavens," the domain of God; and (3) their attempt at self-glorification—**let's make a name for ourselves**.

11:6 God's concern that **nothing** the people might **plan to do** would **be impossible for them** does not express a divine fear that humans might someday become as powerful as God. Rather, it conveys dismay that people, unchecked, would undertake extraordinary deeds of evil and defiance.

11:8 What the people did not want, to be "scattered" (v. 4), was what happened after all.

11:9 Most English versions refer to "Babel" here, but this is the same Hebrew word translated "Babylon" throughout the OT. The connection between the words **Babylon** and **confused** (Hb *babel* and *balal*) constitute another of the many wordplays in this chapter. The Lord's action had two positive outcomes: first, because it **confused the language of the whole earth**, it ended the possibility of large-scale evil ventures; second, it caused humanity to scatter **throughout the earth**, thus bringing

From Shem to Abram

¹⁰ These are the family records of Shem. Shem lived 100 years and fathered Arpachshad two years after the flood. ¹¹ After he fathered Arpachshad, Shem lived 500 years and fathered other sons and daughters. ¹² Arpachshad lived 35 years^A and fathered Shelah. ¹³ After he fathered Shelah, Arpachshad lived 403 years and fathered other sons and daughters. ¹⁴ Shelah lived 30 years and fathered Eber. ¹⁵ After he fathered Eber, Shelah lived 403 years and fathered other sons and daughters. ¹⁶ Eber lived 34 years and fathered Peleg. ¹⁷ After he fathered Peleg, Eber lived 430 years and fathered other sons and daughters. ¹⁸ Peleg lived 30 years and fathered Reu. ¹⁹ After he fathered Reu, Peleg lived 209 years and fathered other sons and daughters. ²⁰ Reu lived 32 years and fathered Serug. ²¹ After he fathered Serug, Reu lived 207 years and fathered other sons and daughters. ²² Serug lived 30 years and fathered Nahor. ²³ After he fathered Nahor, Serug lived 200 years and fathered other sons and daughters. ²⁴ Nahor lived 29 years and fathered Terah. ²⁵ After he fathered Terah, Nahor lived 119 years and fathered other sons and daughters. ²⁶ Terah lived 70 years and fathered Abram, Nahor, and Haran.

²⁷ These are the family records of Terah. Terah fathered Abram, Nahor, and Haran, and Haran fathered Lot. ²⁸ Haran died in his native land, in Ur of the Chaldeans, during his father Terah's lifetime. ²⁹ Abram and Nahor took wives: Abram's wife was named Sarai, and Nahor's wife was named Milcah. She was the daughter of Haran, the father of both Milcah and Iscah. ³⁰ Sarai was unable to conceive; she did not have a child.

³¹ Terah took his son Abram, his grandson Lot (Haran's son), and his daughter-in-law Sarai, his son Abram's wife, and they set out together from Ur of the Chaldeans to go to the land of Canaan. But when they came to Haran, they settled there. ³² Terah lived 205 years and died in Haran.

The Call of Abram

12 The LORD said to Abram:
Go from your land,
your relatives,
and your father's house
to the land that I will show you.
² I will make you into a great nation,
I will bless you,
I will make your name great,
and you will be a blessing.
³ I will bless those who bless you,
I will curse anyone who treats you
with contempt,
and all the peoples on earth
will be blessed^B through you.^C

⁴ So Abram went, as the LORD had told him, and Lot went with him. Abram was seventy-five years old when he left Haran. ⁵ He took his wife, Sarai, his nephew Lot, all the possessions they had accumulated, and the people they had acquired in Haran, and they set out for the land of Canaan. When they came to the land of Canaan, ⁶ Abram passed through the land to the site of Shechem, at the oak of Moreh. (At that time the Canaanites were in the land.) ⁷ The LORD appeared to Abram and said, "To your offspring^D I will give this land." So he built an altar there to

^A **11:12–13** LXX reads *years and fathered Cainan.* ¹³*After he fathered Cainan, Arpachshad lived 430 years and fathered other sons and daughters, and he died. Cainan lived 130 years and fathered Shelah. After he fathered Shelah, Cainan lived 330 years and fathered other sons and daughters, and he died;* Gn 10:24; Lk 3:35–36 ^B **12:3** Or *will find blessing* ^C **12:3** Or *will bless themselves by you* ^D **12:7** Lit *seed*

people into compliance with God's command to fill the earth (9:1).

11:10–26 The family records of Shem constitute the fifth of eleven (Hb) *toledoth* sections in Genesis (2:4; 5:1; 6:9; 10:1; 11:27; 25:12,19; 36:1,9; 37:2). Whereas the previous *toledoth* section ("the family records of Noah's sons," 10:1–11:9) presented Noah's "unchosen" descendants, this one traces the "chosen" offspring.

This genealogical table, which partially repeats information provided in 10:21–25, connects Noah's son Shem to Abram/Abraham. Though this list contains fewer names (12 vs. 26) than the genealogy in chap. 10, it traces out more generations (10 vs. 6) and includes chronological data as well. Whereas chap. 5 stretches from Adam to Noah (the preflood world), this table connects Seth to Abram/Abraham (the postflood world).
11:12 Departing from the Hebrew text, both Lk 3:35–36 and the Septuagint version of this verse indicate that Arpachshad's actual son was Cainan. Because the inspired NT author confirms the Septuagint's reading, Cainan should be accepted as Arpachshad's son. Thus it is best to accept

Arpachshad as Shelah's father in an indirect sense, and to view the Hebrew version here as a stylized genealogy shaped for thematic purposes.
11:17 Eber lived a total of 464 years. This distinguishes him as the longest living person in the Bible who was born after the flood.
11:27–30 The family records of Terah is the sixth of eleven (Hb) *toledoth* sections in Genesis (2:4; 5:1; 6:9; 10:1; 11:10; 25:12,19; 36:1,9; 37:2). In the Hebrew, the spelling of the personal name **Haran** differs from the place name *Haran* (*charan;* v. 31).
Nahor's wife . . . Milcah eventually produced eight sons (22:20–23); her most famous son, Bethuel, became the father-in-law of Abraham's son Isaac (25:20).

In contrast to Milcah, **Sarai** (later called Sarah) **was unable to conceive.** This painful fact is emphasized by the biblical writer restating the fact: **she did not have a child.** God's provision of an heir for Abraham in spite of Sarah's barrenness is a major theme in the narratives that follow (15:2–4; 17:15–21; 21:10).
11:31–32 Until Terah's death Abram was under the authority of his father.

12:1–3 According to Ac 7:2, **the LORD** spoke **to Abram** while he was still in Mesopotamia (Gn 11:31). God gave Abram a one-verb command with four aspects to it. Abram was to **go from** (1) his **land,** (2) his **relatives,** and (3) his **father's house,** (4) **to a land** chosen by God. Saying **I will** five times, God unilaterally promised Abram progeny, prominence, and protection.
12:4 Having migrated with his father's household from Ur (11:31), Abram stayed an uncertain amount of time in Haran.
12:5 Abram was apparently his nephew Lot's protector since Lot's father had died in Ur (11:28). The group's journey to **Canaan** was about 450 miles.
12:6 Shechem is in north central Israel on the slope of Mount Ebal. The **Canaanites** were a distinct cultural group (Gn 15:21), but the term *Canaanite* is also an umbrella term for many different people groups who were living in the region, including the Hethites, Amorites, Perizzites, Girgashites, Hivites, and Jebusites.
12:7 This is the first of three times Scripture indicates that the Lord physically **appeared to Abram** (cp. 17:1; 18:1). The Lord's promise

the LORD who had appeared to him. ⁸ From there he moved on to the hill country east of Bethel and pitched his tent, with Bethel on the west and Ai on the east. He built an altar to the LORD there, and he called on the name of the LORD. ⁹ Then Abram journeyed by stages to the Negev.

Abram in Egypt

¹⁰ There was a famine in the land, so Abram went down to Egypt to stay there for a while because the famine in the land was severe. ¹¹ When he was about to enter Egypt, he said to his wife, Sarai, "Look, I know what a beautiful woman you are. ¹² When the Egyptians see you, they will say, 'This is his wife.' They will kill me but let you live. ¹³ Please say you're my sister so it will go well for me because of you, and my life will be spared on your account." ¹⁴ When Abram entered Egypt, the Egyptians saw that the woman was very beautiful. ¹⁵ Pharaoh's officials saw her and praised her to Pharaoh, so the woman was taken to Pharaoh's household. ¹⁶ He treated Abram well because of her, and Abram acquired flocks and herds, male and female donkeys, male and female slaves, and camels.

¹⁷ But the LORD struck Pharaoh and his household with severe plagues because of Abram's wife, Sarai. ¹⁸ So Pharaoh sent for Abram and said, "What have you done to me? Why didn't you tell me she was your wife? ¹⁹ Why did you say, 'She's my sister,' so that I took her as my wife? Now, here is your wife. Take her and go!" ²⁰ Then Pharaoh gave his men orders about him, and they sent him away with his wife and all he had.

Abram and Lot Separate

13 Abram went up from Egypt to the Negev — he, his wife, and all he had, and Lot with him. ² Abram was very rich in livestock, silver, and gold. ³ He went by stages from the Negev to Bethel, to the place between Bethel and Ai where his tent had formerly been, ⁴ to the site where he had built the altar. And Abram called on the name of the LORD there.

⁵ Now Lot, who was traveling with Abram, also had flocks, herds, and tents. ⁶ But the land was unable to support them as long as they stayed together, for they had so many possessions that they could not stay together, ⁷ and there was quarreling between the herdsmen of Abram's livestock and the herdsmen of Lot's livestock. (At that time the Canaanites and the Perizzites were living in the land.)

⁸ So Abram said to Lot, "Please, let's not have quarreling between you and me, or between your herdsmen and my herdsmen, since we are relatives. ⁹ Isn't the whole land before you? Separate from me: if you go to the left, I will go to the right; if you go to the right, I will go to the left."

¹⁰ Lot looked out and saw that the entire plainᴬ of the Jordan as far as Zoar was well watered everywhere like the LORD's garden and the land of Egypt. (This was before the LORD destroyed Sodom and Gomorrah.) ¹¹ So Lot chose the entire plain of the Jordan for himself. Then Lot journeyed eastward, and they separated from each other. ¹² Abram lived in the land of Canaan, but Lot lived in the cities on the plain and set up his tent near Sodom. ¹³ (Now the men of Sodom were evil, sinning immenselyᴮ against the LORD.)

ᴬ13:10 Lit *circle*; i.e., probably the large round plain where the Jordan River empties into the Dead Sea, also in v. 11
ᴮ13:13 Lit *evil and sinful*

---

to **give** the **land** of Canaan to Abram's **off-spring** is the single most repeated affirmation in the Torah. At least thirty-seven references are made to it in the books of Moses. The altar Abram built at Shechem is the first of four he is said to have built; others were set up between Bethel and Ai (v. 8), at Hebron (13:18), and at Mount Moriah (22:9).
12:8 Bethel, modern Beitin, was about twenty miles south of Shechem. This **altar** is the second of the four that Abram built in the land of Canaan (v. 7). When Abram **called on the name of the LORD** here, he identified himself as a true member of the godly line of Seth (4:26). This is the first of three occasions on which Abram is said to do this (13:4; 21:3).
12:9 The **Negev** is the semidesert region west and south of the Dead Sea and about fifty miles south of Bethel.
12:10 Canaan relied heavily on rainfall for its drinking water and crops. When there was no rain **there was a famine**. To avoid the famine, **Abram went down to Egypt**, the location with the best water supply.
12:11 Even though **Sarai** was at least sixty-five years old at this time (Sarai was ten years younger than Abram [17:17], and he was at least seventy-five [v. 4]), she was still

considered **beautiful**. Her desirability was due in part to the fact that she was the most powerful woman in a wealthy clan.
12:12–13 By telling his wife to **say** that she was his **sister**, Abram was technically asking her to be truthful since Sarai was his half sister (20:12).
12:14–15 Since Abram's group had many people and animals, they had to be given special permission to live and trade in Egypt. Important economic and political contracts in the ancient world were sometimes finalized by the weaker party giving a woman to the leader of the stronger party. The woman would then become part of the leader's harem.
12:17 This act foreshadowed what God would do in Moses's day to bring the Israelites out of Egypt again (Ex 12:29), to take them to the promised land.
12:18 Pharaoh connected the plagues with Sarai's entrance into his harem. An investigation revealed that he had been tricked into marrying a woman who was the **wife** of another man.
13:1 Having been forced to go out **from Egypt**, Abram returned **to the Negev**, the last place he had lived in the promised land (12:9) before his departure to Africa.

13:2–3 Abram moved northward **to Bethel**, an area of Canaan with greater rainfall—and thus more vegetation—than **the Negev**. This move was probably necessary in order to feed the large flocks of Abram and his nephew Lot.
13:4 For the first time since he left Canaan for Egypt, **Abram called on the name of the LORD**.
13:5–6 Especially during the dry summer months, **the land** around Bethel and Ai was too dry for such a large number of flocks and people. To remain in the area, Abram and Lot would have to separate.
13:9 Abram realized the only way to end the dispute was for them to **separate**. As senior member and head of the clan, he should have been the one to select the region where he would live. But Abram graciously handed the choice over to Lot, allowing his nephew to lay claim to the most desirable spot in **the whole land**.
13:11 Lot's journey **eastward** has some troubling implications. Other situations in the early chapters of Genesis in which the "east" is mentioned as a destination include those of Adam and Eve following their sin in Eden (3:24), Cain following his judgment (4:16), and sinful humanity prior to the Tower of Babylon incident (11:2).

¹⁴ After Lot had separated from him, the LORD said to Abram, "Look from the place where you are. Look north and south, east and west, ¹⁵ for I will give you and your offspring^A forever all the land that you see. ¹⁶ I will make your offspring like the dust of the earth, so that if anyone could count the dust of the earth, then your offspring could be counted. ¹⁷ Get up and walk around the land, through its length and width, for I will give it to you."

¹⁸ So Abram moved his tent and went to live near the oaks of Mamre at Hebron, where he built an altar to the LORD.

Abram Rescues Lot

14 In those days King Amraphel of Shinar, King Arioch of Ellasar, King Chedorlaomer of Elam, and King Tidal of Goiim^B ² waged war against King Bera of Sodom, King Birsha of Gomorrah, King Shinab of Admah, and King Shemeber of Zeboiim, as well as the king of Bela (that is, Zoar). ³ All of these came as allies to the Siddim Valley (that is, the Dead Sea). ⁴ They were subject to Chedorlaomer for twelve years, but in the thirteenth year they rebelled. ⁵ In the fourteenth year Chedorlaomer and the kings who were with him came and defeated the Rephaim in Ashteroth-karnaim, the Zuzim in Ham, the Emim in Shaveh-kiriathaim, ⁶ and the Horites in the mountains of Seir, as far as El-paran by the wilderness. ⁷ Then they came back to invade En-mishpat (that is, Kadesh), and they defeated the whole territory of the Amalekites, as well as the Amorites who lived in Hazazon-tamar.

⁸ Then the king of Sodom, the king of Gomorrah, the king of Admah, the king of Zeboiim, and the king of Bela (that is, Zoar) went out and lined up for battle in the Siddim Valley ⁹ against King Chedorlaomer of Elam, King Tidal of Goiim, King Amraphel of Shinar, and King Arioch of Ellasar — four kings against five. ¹⁰ Now the Siddim Valley contained many asphalt pits, and as the kings of Sodom and Gomorrah fled, some fell into them,^C but the rest fled to the mountains. ¹¹ The four kings took all the goods of Sodom and Gomorrah and all their food and went on. ¹² They also took Abram's nephew Lot and his possessions, for he was living in Sodom, and they went on.

¹³ One of the survivors came and told Abram the Hebrew, who lived near the oaks belonging to Mamre the Amorite, the brother of Eshcol and the brother of Aner. They were bound by a treaty with Abram. ¹⁴ When Abram heard that his relative had been taken prisoner, he assembled^D his 318 trained men, born in his household, and they went in pursuit as far as Dan. ¹⁵ And he and his servants deployed against them by night, defeated them, and pursued them as far as Hobah to the north of Damascus. ¹⁶ He brought back all the goods and also his relative Lot and his goods, as well as the women and the other people.

Melchizedek's Blessing

¹⁷ After Abram returned from defeating Chedorlaomer and the kings who were with him, the king of Sodom went out to meet him in the Shaveh Valley (that is, the King's Valley). ¹⁸ Melchizedek, king of Salem,^E brought out bread and wine; he was a priest to God Most High. ¹⁹ He blessed him and said:

> Abram is blessed by God Most High,
> Creator^F of heaven and earth,

---

^A13:15 Lit seed ^B14:1 Or nations ^C14:10 Sam, LXX; MT reads fell there ^D14:14 Sam; MT reads poured out ^E14:18 = Jerusalem ^F14:19 Or Possessor

---

13:14–15 In spite of Abram's commitment to Lot, the Lord himself would give Abram all the land that he could see in every direction. Lot's offspring would not be left landless, however. His sons—Moab and Ben-ammi (19:37–38)—would become the founders of Moab and Ammon, nations east of the land promised to Abram.
13:16 Since Abram was more than seventy-five years old and still childless at the time the Lord spoke these words, this divine pledge was particularly amazing.
13:17–18 Perhaps as a test of Abram's faith, the Lord issued two commands. With them came a reaffirmation of the promise first uttered when Abram arrived in the promised land (12:7). Abram went to live near the oaks of Mamre, a site about two miles north of Hebron. Hebron became the primary residence of Abram and, later, his son Isaac (18:1; 23:2; 35:27; 37:14).
14:1 The prosperity of the lower Jordan River Valley attracted not only Lot, but it also got the attention of four Asian kings hundreds of miles to the north and east. Chedorlaomer = the Elamite name Kutir + a deity name; Arioch = the name Arriwuk/ Arriyuk found at Mari; Tidal = the Hittite

name Tudkhalia. The name Amraphel seems to be a Semitic name. Shinar (Babylonia) is in modern Iraq; Elam is in modern southwest Iran; Ellasar and Goiim are unknown locations.
14:2 The north Asian kings probably waged war against the peoples of the southern Jordan Valley in order to control a trade route (the King's Highway in the area of modern Jordan) as well as the food supply.
14:3 The Siddim Valley is mentioned in the Bible only in this narrative.
14:4 For twelve years the five kings of the southern Jordan Valley were subject to (lit "served") Chedorlaomer; that is, they sent a portion of their annual income to him.
14:5–7 Chedorlaomer could not mount an immediate military response to the regional rebellion. But having assembled a coalition of kings by the following spring, he led the troops southward down the King's Highway to subjugate the rebellious city-states. Among those conquered were Ashteroth-karnaim (modern Tell Ashtarah in Syria), Ham . . . Shaveh-kiriathaim (probably near the ancient Moabite city of Kiriathaim, Jr 48:1), and El-paran (in ancient Edom). He then went to En-mishpat . . . Kadesh in the

northern Sinai desert and Hazazon-tamar (En-gedi, 2Ch 20:2).
14:8–10 The battlefield, with its many asphalt pits, proved to be more dangerous than the enemy.
14:11–13 One of the survivors (lit "the escapee") came to Abram's camp, some seventeen miles west of the Dead Sea.
14:14 When the survivor informed Abram that Lot had been taken prisoner, the elderly clan leader hastily assembled his 318 trained men—his adult male slaves—and headed 120 miles north as far as Dan in pursuit of his nephew's captors.
14:17 The king of Sodom, who apparently survived his fall into the asphalt pit (v. 10), met Abram's triumphant group in the Shaveh Valley, probably located just east of Jerusalem.
14:18 Melchizedek, whose name means "king of righteousness" (Heb 7:2), held two titles: he was king of Salem (lit "King of Peace")—"Salem" being another name for nearby Jerusalem—and priest to God Most High. Abram considered Melchizedek, who is the first person in the Bible to be called a priest, to be a priest of Yahweh, since he equated the title "God Most High" with the

²⁰ and blessed be God Most High
who has handed over your enemies
    to you.
And Abram gave him a tenth of everything.
²¹ Then the king of Sodom said to Abram, "Give me the people, but take the possessions for yourself."
²² But Abram said to the king of Sodom, "I have raised my hand in an oath to the LORD, God Most High, Creator of heaven and earth, ²³ that I will not take a thread or sandal strap or anything that belongs to you, so you can never say, 'I made Abram rich.' ²⁴ I will take nothing except what the servants have eaten. But as for the share of the men who came with me — Aner, Eshcol, and Mamre — they can take their share."

The Abrahamic Covenant

15 After these events, the word of the LORD came to Abram in a vision:
Do not be afraid, Abram.
I am your shield;
your reward will be very great.

² But Abram said, "Lord GOD, what can you give me, since I am childless and the heir of my house is Eliezer of Damascus?"ᴬ ³ Abram continued, "Look, you have given me no offspring, so a slave born inᴮ my house will be my heir."
⁴ Now the word of the LORD came to him: "This one will not be your heir; instead, one who comes from your own bodyᶜ will be your heir." ⁵ He took him outside and said, "Look at the sky and count the stars, if you are able to count them." Then he said to him, "Your offspring will be that numerous."
⁶ Abram believed the LORD, and he credited it to him as righteousness.
⁷ He also said to him, "I am the LORD who brought you from Ur of the Chaldeans to give you this land to possess."
⁸ But he said, "Lord GOD, how can I know that I will possess it?"
⁹ He said to him, "Bring me a three-year-old cow, a three-year-old female goat, a three-year-old ram, a turtledove, and a young pigeon."
¹⁰ So he brought all these to him, cut them in half, and laid the pieces opposite each other, but he did not cut the birds in half. ¹¹ Birds of prey came down on the carcasses, but Abram drove them away. ¹² As the sun was setting, a deep sleep came over Abram, and suddenly great terror and darkness descended on him.
¹³ Then the LORD said to Abram, "Know this for certain: Your offspring will be resident aliens for four hundred years in a land that does not belong to them and will be enslaved and oppressed.ᴰ ¹⁴ However, I will judge the nation they serve, and afterward they will go out with many possessions. ¹⁵ But you will go to your ancestors in peace and be buried at a good old age. ¹⁶ In the fourth generation they will return here, for the iniquity of the Amorites has not yet reached its full measure."ᴱ
¹⁷ When the sun had set and it was dark, a smoking fire pot and a flaming torch appeared and passed between the divided animals. ¹⁸ On that day the LORD made a covenant

---

ᴬ15:2 Hb obscure   ᴮ15:3 Lit *a son of*   ᶜ15:4 Lit *loins*   ᴰ15:13 Lit *will serve them and they will oppress them*   ᴱ15:16 Lit *Amorites is not yet complete*

LORD" (v. 22). The writer of Hebrews drew significant parallels between Melchizedek and Jesus Christ (Heb 5:6; 7:1–28).
14:20 In a construction that paralleled his blessing to Abram, Melchizedek also **blessed** (gave praise to) **God Most High** because of the saving acts he had performed. The first recorded act of tithing took place here as Abram gave the priest **a tenth** of the booty he had acquired from the Mesopotamian kings. Abram's tithe anticipates Israel's tithe to God (Lv 27:30–32; Nm 18:21–30; Mt 23:23).
14:21 The **king of Sodom** then ordered Abram to hand over the liberated captives, including citizens of the king's city. As payment for his military efforts, however, the king gave Abram the recaptured **possessions**, a term that can refer to livestock as well as objects.
14:22–24 With Melchizedek king of Salem, who worshiped God, Abram was cooperative (vv. 18–20); but when the Canaanite king of Sodom told him to take the possessions, he refused. Abram would not let the king diminish God's glory by taking credit for Abram's prosperity.
15:1 The only other patriarch who is said to have received a vision was Jacob (Gn 46:2). The content of Abram's vision included a command (**Do not be afraid**), an assurance (**I am your shield**), and a promise (**your reward will be very great**). Though Abram

turned down a reward from the king of Sodom, the Lord would reward him richly.
15:2–3 Neither God's protection nor his reward seemed important to elderly Abram since all his goods would go to **Eliezer of Damascus . . . slave born in** his **house**. Abram made seven references to himself (in the Hb) in the space of twenty-two Hebrew words and twice utters the complaint that he was **childless**.
15:4–5 Ignoring Abram's apparent lack of gratitude, **the LORD** gave Abram one of the great promises of the Bible; the elderly patriarch would produce an heir . . . from his own body. God then made the breathtaking promise that Abram's **offspring** would **be** as **numerous** as **the stars**.
15:6 Old and childless, **Abram believed the LORD**; that is, he affirmed that God is dependable. God **credited it to him as righteousness**, that is, he judged or accounted that Abram measured up to the standard, conformed to the norm. Abram's faith and God's gracious response to it served as a paradigm of the Christian experience in three different NT books (Rm 4:3; Gl 3:6; Jms 2:23).
15:7 For the third time in Abram's life (12:1; 13:14–17) **the LORD** addressed the issue of land.
15:9 God provided assurance in the form of a solemn commitment ceremony. The **cow . . . female goat**, and **ram** were mammals later authorized for sacrifice in the law

of Moses; however, this is the only time that three-year-olds—specimens in the prime of their lives—were used. The ceremony here differs from other sacred rituals in the OT involving animals in that no animal parts were burned.
15:10–11 In an act unparalleled in the OT, Abram **cut** the animals **in half, and laid the pieces opposite each other**, creating a clear central lane flanked by the carcass portions.
15:12 Abram's **deep sleep** (Hb *tardemah*) recalls the one Adam experienced when the Lord created Eve (2:21).
15:13–16 Here **the LORD** revealed **to Abram** an outline of the events of Gn 46 through Ex 13.
15:17 Both elements symbolized essential aspects of God; the smoke perhaps representing divine inscrutability, and the flame God's power. Typically, both covenant partners would walk between the pieces, but here God was unilaterally obligating himself to fulfill his promise.
An alternate interpretation is that the animal parts represented the Israelites, Abram's future descendants, and God hereby promised to be among them.
15:18–21 The covenant with Abram was expressed in 12:1–3 and ceremonially confirmed here. The list of ten different people groups here is the longest list of Canaan's inhabitants in the Torah. This is the only list

with Abram, saying, "I give this land to your offspring, from the Brook of Egypt to the great river, the Euphrates River: [19] the land of the Kenites, Kenizzites, Kadmonites, [20] Hethites, Perizzites, Rephaim, [21] Amorites, Canaanites, Girgashites, and Jebusites."

Hagar and Ishmael

16 Abram's wife, Sarai, had not borne any children for him, but she owned an Egyptian slave named Hagar. [2] Sarai said to Abram, "Since the LORD has prevented me from bearing children, go to my slave; perhaps through her I can build a family." And Abram agreed to what Sarai said. [3] So Abram's wife, Sarai, took Hagar, her Egyptian slave, and gave her to her husband, Abram, as a wife for him. This happened after Abram had lived in the land of Canaan ten years. [4] He slept with[A] Hagar, and she became pregnant. When she saw that she was pregnant, her mistress became contemptible to her. [5] Then Sarai said to Abram, "You are responsible for my suffering![B] I put my slave in your arms,[C] and when she saw that she was pregnant, I became contemptible to her. May the LORD judge between me and you."

[6] Abram replied to Sarai, "Here, your slave is in your power; do whatever you want with her." Then Sarai mistreated her so much that she ran away from her.

[7] The angel of the LORD found her by a spring in the wilderness, the spring on the way to Shur. [8] He said, "Hagar, slave of Sarai, where have you come from and where are you going?"

She replied, "I'm running away from my mistress Sarai."

[9] The angel of the LORD said to her, "Go back to your mistress and submit to her authority." [10] The angel of the LORD said to her, "I will greatly multiply your offspring, and they will be too many to count."

[11] The angel of the LORD said to her, "You have conceived and will have a son. You will name him Ishmael,[D] for the LORD has heard your cry of affliction. [12] This man will be like a wild donkey. His hand will be against everyone, and everyone's hand will be against him; he will settle near all his relatives."

[13] So she named the LORD who spoke to her: "You are El-roi,"[E] for she said, "In this place, have I actually seen the one who sees me?"[F] [14] That is why the well is called Beer-lahai-roi.[G] It is between Kadesh and Bered.

[15] So Hagar gave birth to Abram's son, and Abram named his son (whom Hagar bore) Ishmael. [16] Abram was eighty-six years old when Hagar bore Ishmael to him.

Covenant Circumcision

17 When Abram was ninety-nine years old, the LORD appeared to him, saying, "I am God Almighty. Live[H] in my presence and be blameless. [2] I will set up my covenant between me and you, and I will multiply you greatly."

[3] Then Abram fell facedown and God spoke with him: [4] "As for me, here is my covenant with you: You will become the father of many nations. [5] Your name will no longer be Abram;[I] your name will be Abraham,[J] for I will make you the father of many nations. [6] I will make you extremely fruitful and will make nations and kings come from you. [7] I will confirm my covenant that is between me and you and your

[A]16:4 Lit *He came to*   [B]16:5 Or *"May my suffering be on you!*   [C]16:5 Lit *bosom*   [D]16:11 = God Hears   [E]16:13 = God Sees Me   [F]16:13 Hb obscure   [G]16:14 = Well of the Living One Who Sees Me   [H]17:1 Or *Walk*   [I]17:5 = The Father Is Exalted   [J]17:5 = Father of a Multitude

to include the **Kenites, Kenizzites,** and **Kadmonites**; the Kenites and Kenizzites were probably groups living in the Negev that coexisted peacefully with the Israelites (Nm 32:12; Jdg 1:16). Perhaps the Kadmonites were the same as the Qedemites, a desert-dwelling enemy of Israel (Jdg 6:33). The **Hethites** were descendants of Heth, son of Canaan (Gn 10:15).
16:2–3 Sarai faced a dilemma. On the one hand, **the LORD** had **prevented** her—Abram's only wife—**from bearing children**. On the other hand, the Lord promised that her husband would become a father. To "fix" the problem, she ordered her husband to **go to** her **slave** and try to **build a family** through her. **Abram**, now eighty-five, **agreed**. Sarai likely intended to use **Hagar** as a surrogate mother, and then adopt the child as her own.
16:5 Sarai, whose inadequacies were highlighted with Hagar's pregnancy, now found her own **suffering** unbearable. In one sense Abram had caused the pregnancy, thus he was **responsible** for Sarai's **slave** girl looking down on her. Sarai called on **the LORD** to hold Abram accountable for her humiliation and pain.

16:7–8 Hagar could run away from Sarai, but not from **the angel of the LORD**. He **found her** at a **spring** on a road leading **to Shur** and Egypt, where she might have been able to get assistance from passing caravans. Hagar, like many runaways, could say where she was from, but ignored the question of where she was going.
16:9–10 The angel of the LORD directed Hagar to **go back** and **submit** to Sarai. The true source of Hagar's problems was her own bad attitude, not her owner. By obeying the angel's divine guidance, she and her **offspring** would receive a tremendous blessing. God's promise to **multiply** her descendants both paralleled and enhanced the promise given to Abram (15:5).
16:11–12 This is the final and longest of three consecutive speeches by **the angel** to Hagar. Hagar is told that she **will have a son**, the more prestigious gender of offspring for a woman in the ancient Near East to bear. Then she is directed to **name** her son **Ishmael** ("God Hears"), in recognition of the fact that **the LORD . . . heard** her **cry of affliction**. In the climactic final quatrain, character and destiny are presented: the boy will live outside of cultured society like **a wild donkey**.

16:13–14 In wonder-filled recognition of God's intervention in her life, Hagar gave **the LORD** the title **El-roi** (or "The God Who Sees Me"). She is thus the only person in the Bible who is said to have renamed Yahweh.
16:15–16 The fact that **Abram**, the eighty-six-year-old clan leader, **named his son . . . Ishmael** indicates that he allowed the young slave girl to tell him her story, and he believed it.
17:1 Thirteen years after Ishmael's birth, **the LORD appeared to** Abram for the second time (12:7). In contrast to Hagar naming the Lord (16:13), here the Lord gives himself a name: *El Shaddai*, the meaning of which is unknown, though it is translated as **God Almighty**, based on a tradition going back more than two thousand years. In commanding Abram to **live in my presence and be blameless**, God told Abram to live like Enoch and Noah (Gn 5:24; 6:9).
17:2 As Abram obeyed the Lord, God promised him two things: first, he would **set up** his **covenant** with Abram and second, God would **multiply** the patriarch **greatly**.
17:4–8 This section contains the fullest presentation of God's covenant with Abram. Eight different aspects of the covenant are

future offspring throughout their generations. It is a permanent covenant to be your God and the God of your offspring after you. **8** And to you and your future offspring^A I will give the land where you are residing — all the land of Canaan — as a permanent possession, and I will be their God."

9 God also said to Abraham, "As for you, you and your offspring after you throughout their generations are to keep my covenant. **10** This is my covenant between me and you and your offspring after you, which you are to keep: Every one of your males must be circumcised. **11** You must circumcise the flesh of your foreskin to serve as a sign of the covenant between me and you.^B **12** Throughout your generations, every male among you is to be circumcised at eight days old — every male born in your household or purchased from any foreigner and not your offspring. **13** Whether born in your household or purchased, he must be circumcised. My covenant will be marked in your flesh as a permanent covenant. **14** If any male is not circumcised in the flesh of his foreskin, that man will be cut off from his people; he has broken my covenant."

15 God said to Abraham, "As for your wife Sarai, do not call her Sarai, for Sarah^C will be her name. **16** I will bless her; indeed, I will give you a son by her. I will bless her, and she will produce nations; kings of peoples will come from her."

17 Abraham fell facedown. Then he laughed and said to himself, "Can a child be born to a hundred-year-old man? Can Sarah, a ninety-year-old woman, give birth?" **18** So Abraham said to God, "If only Ishmael were acceptable^D to you!"

19 But God said, "No. Your wife Sarah will bear you a son, and you will name him Isaac.^E I will confirm my covenant with him as a permanent covenant for his future offspring. **20** As for Ishmael, I have heard you. I will certainly bless him; I will make him fruitful and will multiply

him greatly. He will father twelve tribal leaders, and I will make him into a great nation. **21** But I will confirm my covenant with Isaac, whom Sarah will bear to you at this time next year." **22** When he finished talking with him, God withdrew^F from Abraham.

23 So Abraham took his son Ishmael and those born in his household or purchased — every male among the members of Abraham's household — and he circumcised the flesh of their foreskin on that very day, just as God had said to him. **24** Abraham was ninety-nine years old when the flesh of his foreskin was circumcised, **25** and his son Ishmael was thirteen years old when the flesh of his foreskin was circumcised. **26** On that very day Abraham and his son Ishmael were circumcised. **27** And all the men of his household — whether born in his household or purchased from a foreigner — were circumcised with him.

Abraham's Three Visitors

18 The LORD appeared to Abraham at the oaks of Mamre while he was sitting at the entrance of his tent during the heat of the day. **2** He looked up, and he saw three men standing near him. When he saw them, he ran from the entrance of the tent to meet them, bowed to the ground, **3** and said, "My lord, if I have found favor with you, please do not go on past your servant. **4** Let a little water be brought, that you may wash your feet and rest yourselves under the tree. **5** I will bring a bit of bread so that you may strengthen yourselves. This is why you have passed your servant's way. Later, you can continue on."

"Yes," they replied, "do as you have said."

6 So Abraham hurried into the tent and said to Sarah, "Quick! Knead three measures^G of fine flour and make bread."^H **7** Abraham ran to the herd and got a tender, choice calf. He gave it to a young man, who hurried to prepare it. **8** Then

---

^A**17:8** Lit *seed*   ^B**17:11** *You* in v. 11 is pl.   ^C**17:15** = Princess   ^D**17:18** Lit *alive*   ^E**17:19** = He Laughs   ^F**17:22** Lit *went up,* or *ascended*   ^G**18:6** Lit *three seahs*; about 21 quarts   ^H**18:6** A round, thin, unleavened bread

---

presented in these verses. Most of these promises are not new, but nowhere else are they put together in one place. The new aspect is where God changed the patriarch's name, thus indicating his authority over him: instead of **Abram** ("Exalted Father"), his new name would be **Abraham** ("Father of a Multitude").

17:9–14 God now placed one final covenant-related demand on **Abraham** and his **offspring**: circumcision. This surgical removal of the **foreskin** of the penis was typically done with a razor-sharp flint knife (Jos 5:2–3). On newborns it was performed when the boy was **eight days old**; no form of female circumcision was authorized. So vital was the acceptance of the sign on the body that anyone who lacked it was to be **cut off from his people** because he had **broken** the **covenant**.

17:15–16 The Lord decreed that Abraham's **wife Sarai** was now to receive the name **Sarah** ("Princess," which is an alternate form of Sarai). This "princess" would be given the privilege of producing **nations; kings of peoples** would **come from her**. During the OT period at least four nations came from Sarah's womb: Israel, Judah, Edom, and the Amalekites. Over Israel and Judah collectively a total of forty-one kings reigned. Sarah is the only woman in the OT whom the Lord specifically indicated he would **bless**.

17:17–22 Undaunted by Abraham's well-intended suggestion regarding Ishmael, God reaffirmed that **Sarah** would **bear** him **a son** who, appropriately, would be named **Isaac**—"He Laughs." With Isaac God would confirm **a permanent covenant.** Lesser promises were made for **Ishmael.** Though no covenant would be established with him, God would **bless** Ishmael. No kings were

promised in Ishmael's lineage, but from him would come **twelve tribal leaders** (25:13–16), and his offspring would become **a great nation**.

17:23–27 Promptly after the Lord ascended, Abraham **circumcised** himself and all the males in his **household**.

18:1 For the third time in Abraham's life **the LORD appeared** to him (12:7; 17:1). **Mamre**, near Hebron, was Abraham's preferred abode in Canaan (13:18; 14:13). This divine encounter must have taken place within three months after the events of the previous chapter.

18:2–8 Abraham is presented as the ideal host. He sees **three men**—actually God and two angels (19:1)—to whom he eagerly extended greeting and showed proper respect by calling them "my lord" (Hb *adonai*, a term that can refer to God) and bowing to **the ground**. Then he provided water, rest, and a feast that included **bread** baked from

Abraham took curds^A and milk, as well as the calf that he had prepared, and set them before the men. He served^B them as they ate under the tree.

Sarah Laughs

⁹ "Where is your wife Sarah?" they asked him.

"There, in the tent," he answered.

¹⁰ The LORD said, "I will certainly come back to you in about a year's time, and your wife Sarah will have a son!" Now Sarah was listening at the entrance of the tent behind him. ¹¹ Abraham and Sarah were old and getting on in years.^C Sarah had passed the age of childbearing. ¹² So she laughed to herself: "After I am worn out and my lord is old, will I have delight?" ¹³ But the LORD asked Abraham, "Why did Sarah laugh, saying, 'Can I really have a baby when I'm old?'¹⁴ Is anything impossible for the LORD? At the appointed time I will come back to you, and in about a year she will have a son."¹⁵ Sarah denied it. "I did not laugh," she said, because she was afraid.

But he replied, "No, you did laugh."

Abraham's Plea for Sodom

¹⁶ The men got up from there and looked out over Sodom, and Abraham was walking with them to see them off. ¹⁷ Then the LORD said, "Should I hide what I am about to do from Abraham? ¹⁸ Abraham is to become a great and powerful nation, and all the nations of the earth will be blessed through him. ¹⁹ For I have chosen^D him so that he will command his children and his house after him to keep the way of the LORD by doing what is right and just. This is how the LORD will fulfill to Abraham what he promised him." ²⁰ Then the LORD said, "The outcry against Sodom and Gomorrah is immense, and their sin is extremely serious. ²¹ I will go down to see if what they have done justifies the cry that has come up to me. If not, I will find out."

²² The men turned from there and went toward Sodom while Abraham remained standing before the LORD.^E ²³ Abraham stepped forward and said, "Will you really sweep away the righteous with the wicked? ²⁴ What if there are fifty righteous people in the city?

---

^A18:8 Or *butter* ^B18:8 Lit *was standing by* ^C18:11 Lit *days* ^D18:19 Lit *known* ^E18:22 Alt Hb tradition reads *while the LORD remained standing before Abraham*

---

twenty-one quarts of **flour** and a **tender, choice calf.**
18:16–19 The Lord and the two angels—she learned that Abram wanted her for a wife (see Gn referred to here as **the men** because of their manlike appearance—headed in the direction of **Sodom**, Lot's home since 13:12. **Abraham,** the ideal host, accompanied them to see them off. **The LORD** did not want to **hide** from him what he intended to do to the place where his nephew lived. God gave two reasons for revealing his plans

to the patriarch: the fact that Abraham had been chosen **to become a great . . . nation** through whom **all the nations of the earth will be blessed,** and the fact that God had "known" (CSB, **chosen**—that is, had a personal relationship with) Abraham to establish a people who would **keep the way of the LORD. 18:20–21** The Lord would investigate **Sodom and Gomorrah** for two reasons: **the outcry** coming from their victims was

immense, and the cities' sin was **extremely serious.** According to Ezk 16:49–50, the sins of Sodom and Gomorrah included self-centered pride, neglect of the poor and needy, and doing unnamed detestable things. According to Gn 19:5–9, one of the detestable acts was attempted homosexual gang rape. **18:22–32** This passage is one of the three greatest illustrations of petitionary prayer in the OT (cp. Ex 32:11–14; Am 7:1–6).

Character profile:
Sarah

The Bible doesn't reveal how Sarah (Sarai) reacted when she learned that Abram wanted her for a wife (see Gn 11:29). We're also not told how she handled the fact that she was unable to bear children (see 11:30). We don't know Sarah's response the day her husband said God had called them to move south and west to Canaan (see 12:1–5).

What did a sixty-five-year-old, infertile woman think of God's promise that she would give birth to a great nation? Was she confused? Depressed? To her credit, she gathered up her belongings, and hand in hand with her husband they set out (see 12:6–9).

How about Abram's attempt to protect himself in Egypt by passing her off as his sister (see 12:10–20)? How did Sarah respond to that? When he had to arm his servants and embark on a dangerous mission to rescue their nephew Lot, who had gotten caught up in a tribal war (see 14:1–24), did Sarah worry, cry, panic, or pray?

There's so much we don't know about Sarah's thoughts and feelings concerning the upheaval in their lives. Only in a couple of instances do we get a glimpse into Sarah's heart.

One of these came more than a decade after God's promise of a child to Abraham. Sarah suggested a plan: "Since the LORD has prevented me from bearing children, go to my slave; perhaps through her I can build a family" (16:2). Abraham signed off on the idea. The result was a boy, Ishmael.

Immediately Sarah was the polar opposite of happy. The sight of that gloating Hagar holding a cooing baby ripped her soul in two. Sarah lashed out at her husband. She turned bitter and mean (see 16:5–16).

After another thirteen long years passed, we once again see the raw reaction of Sarah when three visitors showed up (see 18:1–15). Only when she heard one of the visitors speak her name did she begin to listen in on their conversation. That's when the eighty-nine-year-old Sarah heard the speaker say that she would become a mother within the year. The thought was too crazy, too unthinkable, too outlandish. Sarah started to laugh in amused disbelief. And, when the Lord asked Abraham why Sarah would doubt the word of God, she got flustered and tried to deny her reaction. But the Lord wasn't buying it.

At long last, when the child of the promise finally arrived a year later, Sarah's response was genuine laughter (see 21:6). In fact, these two elderly, new parents decided to name the boy Isaac, which means "he laughs."

If you are facing a grim situation, reflect on the story of Sarah. At the height of her hopelessness, Sarah was on the receiving end of perhaps the best rhetorical question in the Bible. As she struggled against doubt and cynicism, she was asked, "Is anything impossible for the LORD?" (18:14).

The answer is, of course, no. Nothing is impossible for God. Lots of things are difficult for us to endure, but nothing is too hard for God. It's this one truth that can produce laughter even when nothing else can.

Will you really sweep it away instead of sparing the place for the sake of the fifty righteous people who are in it? ²⁵ You could not possibly do such a thing: to kill the righteous with the wicked, treating the righteous and the wicked alike. You could not possibly do that! Won't the Judge of the whole earth do what is just? "

²⁶ The LORD said, "If I find fifty righteous people in the city of Sodom, I will spare the whole place for their sake."

²⁷ Then Abraham answered, "Since I have ventured to speak to my lord — even though I am dust and ashes — ²⁸ suppose the fifty righteous lack five. Will you destroy the whole city for lack of five?"

He replied, "I will not destroy it if I find forty-five there."

²⁹ Then he spoke to him again, "Suppose forty are found there?"

He answered, "I will not do it on account of forty."

³⁰ Then he said, "Let my lord not be angry, and I will speak further. Suppose thirty are found there?"

He answered, "I will not do it if I find thirty there."

³¹ Then he said, "Since I have ventured to speak to my lord, suppose twenty are found there?"

He replied, "I will not destroy it on account of twenty."

³² Then he said, "Let my lord not be angry, and I will speak one more time. Suppose ten are found there?"

He answered, "I will not destroy it on account of ten." ³³ When the LORD had finished speaking with Abraham, he departed, and Abraham returned to his place.

The Destruction of Sodom and Gomorrah

19 The two angels entered Sodom in the evening as Lot was sitting in Sodom's gateway. When Lot saw them, he got up to meet them. He bowed with his face to the ground ² and said, "My lords, turn aside to your servant's house, wash your feet, and spend the night. Then you can get up early and go on your way."

"No," they said. "We would rather spend the night in the square." ³ But he urged them so strongly that they followed him and went into his house. He prepared a feast and baked unleavened bread for them, and they ate.

⁴ Before they went to bed, the men of the city of Sodom, both young and old, the whole population, surrounded the house. ⁵ They called out to Lot and said, "Where are the men who came to you tonight? Send them out to us so we can have sex with them!"

⁶ Lot went out to them at the entrance and shut the door behind him. ⁷ He said, "Don't do this evil, my brothers. ⁸ Look, I've got two daughters who haven't been intimate with a man. I'll bring them out to you, and you can do whatever you wantᴬ to them. However, don't do anything to these men, because they have come under the protection of my roof."

⁹ "Get out of the way!" they said, adding, "This one came here as an alien, but he's acting like a judge! Now we'll do more harm to you than to them." They put pressure on Lot and came up to break down the door. ¹⁰ But the angelsᴮ reached out, brought Lot into the house with them, and shut the door. ¹¹ They struck the men who were at the entrance of the house, both young and old, with blindnessᶜ so that they were unable to find the entrance.

¹² Then the angels said to Lot, "Do you have anyone else here: a son-in-law, your sons and daughters, or anyone else in the city who belongs to you? Get them out of this place, ¹³ for we are about to destroy this place because the outcry against its people is so great before the LORD, that the LORD has sent us to destroy it."

¹⁴ So Lot went out and spoke to his sons-in-law, who were going to marry his daughters. "Get up," he said. "Get out of this place, for the LORD is about to destroy the city!" But his sons-in-law thought he was joking.

¹⁵ At daybreak the angels urged Lot on: "Get up! Take your wife and your two daughters who are here, or you will be swept away in the punishmentᴰ of the city." ¹⁶ But he hesitated. Because of the LORD's compassion for him, the men grabbed his hand, his wife's hand, and the hands of his two daughters. They brought him out and left him outside the city.

¹⁷ As soon as the angels got them outside, one of themᴱ said, "Run for your lives! Don't look back and don't stop anywhere on the plain!

ᴬ**19:8** Lit *do what is good in your eyes*   ᴮ**19:10** Lit *men,* also in v. 12   ᶜ**19:11** Or *a blinding light*   ᴰ**19:15** Or *iniquity,* or *guilt*
ᴱ**19:17** LXX, Syr, Vg read *outside, they*

19:1–3 Lot's position at the **gateway** may indicate that he was accorded a spot of honor with the elders of the city (Pr 31:23). Like Abraham in Gn 18, Lot also played the role of gracious host to divine beings in human form, though in a lesser way. Whereas Abraham "ran" to greet his guests and prepared a lavish meal, by contrast Lot only **got up to meet them**, preparing a **feast** that consisted only of **unleavened bread**.
19:6–8 Ancient Asian hospitality customs made Lot responsible for his visitors'

safety while **under the protection of** his **roof**—no matter what the cost. Accordingly, he put himself at risk by facing the mob and warning them that their intentions were **evil**. Failing in his appeal to their higher moral instincts, Lot then put his family at risk, offering up his **two** virgin **daughters** to satisfy the rabble's sexual desires.
19:9–11 Enraged because Lot had declared homosexual rape to be evil, the mob condemned him for **acting like a judge**.

19:15–22 Lot and his family apparently disbelieved the angels' warnings as well, because the next morning they were still in **the city**. The family was literally saved **because of the LORD's compassion** as the angels **grabbed** the **hands of** each family member. Like Abraham (18:23–32), Lot negotiated a deal with God to save his life. As with Abraham, God graciously granted the **request** and spared a wicked village for the sake of the righteous people in it. Prior to this time **Zoar** (lit "Small") was named Bela (14:2).

Run to the mountains, or you will be swept away!" **¹⁸** But Lot said to them, "No, my lords^ — please. **¹⁹** Your servant has indeed found favor with you, and you have shown me great kindness by saving my life. But I can't run to the mountains; the disaster will overtake me, and I will die. **²⁰** Look, this town is close enough for me to flee to. It is a small place. Please let me run to it — it's only a small place, isn't it? — so that I can survive." **²¹** And he said to him, "All right,^ I'll grant your request^ about this matter too and will not demolish the town you mentioned. **²²** Hurry up! Run to it, for I cannot do anything until you get there." Therefore the name of the city is Zoar.^

²³ The sun had risen over the land when Lot reached Zoar. **²⁴** Then out of the sky the LORD rained on Sodom and Gomorrah burning sulfur from the LORD. **²⁵** He demolished these cities, the entire plain, all the inhabitants of the cities, and whatever grew on the ground. **²⁶** But Lot's wife looked back and became a pillar of salt.

²⁷ Early in the morning Abraham went to the place where he had stood before the LORD. **²⁸** He looked down toward Sodom and Gomorrah and all the land of the plain, and he saw that smoke was going up from the land like the smoke of a furnace. **²⁹** So it was, when God destroyed the cities of the plain, he remembered Abraham and brought Lot out of the middle of the upheaval when he demolished the cities where Lot had lived.

The Origin of Moab and Ammon

³⁰ Lot departed from Zoar and lived in the mountains along with his two daughters, because he was afraid to live in Zoar. Instead, he and his two daughters lived in a cave. **³¹** Then the firstborn said to the younger, "Our father is old, and there is no man in the land to sleep with us as is the custom of all the land. **³²** Come, let's get our father to drink wine so that we can sleep with him and preserve our father's line." **³³** So they got their father to drink wine that night, and the firstborn came and slept with her father; he did not know when she lay down or when she got up.

³⁴ The next day the firstborn said to the younger, "Look, I slept with my father last night. Let's get him to drink wine again tonight so you can go sleep with him and we can preserve our father's line." **³⁵** That night they again got their father to drink wine, and the younger went and slept with him; he did not know when she lay down or when she got up.

³⁶ So both of Lot's daughters became pregnant by their father. **³⁷** The firstborn gave birth to a son and named him Moab.^ He is the father of the Moabites of today. **³⁸** The younger also gave birth to a son, and she named him Ben-ammi.^ He is the father of the Ammonites of today.

Sarah Rescued from Abimelech

20 From there Abraham traveled to the region of the Negev and settled between Kadesh and Shur. While he was staying in Gerar, **²** Abraham said about his wife Sarah, "She is my sister." So King Abimelech of Gerar had Sarah brought to him.

³ But God came to Abimelech in a dream by night and said to him, "You are about to die because of the woman you have taken, for she is a married woman."^

⁴ Now Abimelech had not approached her, so he said, "Lord, would you destroy a nation even though it is innocent? **⁵** Didn't he himself say to me, 'She is my sister'? And she herself said, 'He is my brother.' I did this with a clear conscience^ and clean^ hands."

⁶ Then God said to him in the dream, "Yes, I know that you did this with a clear conscience.^ I have also kept you from sinning against me. Therefore I have not let you touch her. **⁷** Now return the man's wife, for he is a prophet, and he will pray for you and you will live. But if you do not return her, know that you will certainly die, you and all who are yours."

⁸ Early in the morning Abimelech got up, called all his servants together, and personally^ told them all these things, and the men were terrified.

---

^19:18 Or *my Lord*, or *my lord* ^19:21 Or *"Look!* ^19:21 Lit *I will lift up your face* ^19:22 In Hb, the name *Zoar* is related to "small" in v. 20; its previous name was "Bela"; Gn 14:2. ^19:37 = From My Father ^19:38 = Son of My People ^20:3 Lit *is possessed by a husband* ^20:5 Lit *with integrity of my heart* ^20:5 Lit *cleanness of my* ^20:6 Lit *with integrity of your heart* ^20:8 Lit *in their ears*

19:23–25 The LORD rained . . . burning sulfur (lit "sulfur and fire"). No natural explanation (e.g., volcano) is suggested, only a supernatural one: it came **from the LORD.** Perhaps the asphalt pits (14:10) were ignited, adding to the destruction.
19:27–29 The destruction was so complete that thick **smoke** like that of a **furnace** was still billowing up twenty-four hours later.
20:1–2 Abraham traveled from Mamre to **Gerar,** a Philistine settlement west of the Dead Sea **between Kadesh and Shur,** perhaps to get farther away from the devastated

area where Sodom had been. Then, less than three months after God had promised that Sarah would bear Abraham a son (18:10), the patriarch gave his wife to **Abimelech!** Abraham had previously told pharaoh that his wife was his **sister** (12:12–15); later his son would try the same trick (26:7).
20:3–8 God in his mercy intervened to keep Sarah from being destroyed by Abraham's foolish act. In addition to warning **Abimelech** that Sarah was **married,** the Lord had also created a health crisis in his household, causing all the other women to become

temporarily sterile (v. 18). Because Abimelech had acted **with a clear conscience and clean hands**—despite accepting Sarah into his harem—God would not **destroy** Gerar's governmental leadership and thus undermine the **nation.**
Abraham is the first person to be called a **prophet** in the OT, though Enoch, who lived before him, is called a prophet in the NT (Jd 14). As Abraham's intercession with God had saved Lot's life (Gn 18:23–32; 19:29), so now his prayer for Abimelech would save his life.

⁹ Then Abimelech called Abraham in and said to him, "What have you done to us? How did I sin against you that you have brought such enormous guilt on me and on my kingdom? You have done things to me that should never be done." ¹⁰ Abimelech also asked Abraham, "What made you do this?"

¹¹ Abraham replied, "I thought, 'There is absolutely no fear of God in this place. They will kill me because of my wife.' ¹² Besides, she really is my sister, the daughter of my father though not the daughter of my mother, and she became my wife. ¹³ So when God had me wander from my father's house, I said to her: Show your loyalty to me wherever we go and say about me, 'He's my brother.'"

¹⁴ Then Abimelech took flocks and herds and male and female slaves, gave them to Abraham, and returned his wife Sarah to him. ¹⁵ Abimelech said, "Look, my land is before you. Settle wherever you want."ᴬ ¹⁶ And he said to Sarah, "Look, I am giving your brother one thousand pieces of silver. It is a verification of your honorᴮ to all who are with you. You are fully vindicated."

¹⁷ Then Abraham prayed to God, and God healed Abimelech, his wife, and his female slaves so that they could bear children, ¹⁸ for the LORD had completely closed all the wombs in Abimelech's household on account of Sarah, Abraham's wife.

The Birth of Isaac

21 The LORD came to Sarah as he had said, and the LORD did for Sarah what he had promised. ² Sarah became pregnant and bore a son to Abraham in his old age, at the appointed time God had told him. ³ Abraham named his son who was born to him — the one Sarah bore to him — Isaac. ⁴ When his son Isaac was eight days old, Abraham circumcised him, as God had commanded him. ⁵ Abraham was a hundred years old when his son Isaac was born to him.

⁶ Sarah said, "God has made me laugh, and everyone who hears will laugh with me."ᶜ ⁷ She also said, "Who would have told Abraham that Sarah would nurse children? Yet I have borne a son for himᴰ in his old age."

Hagar and Ishmael Sent Away

⁸ The child grew and was weaned, and Abraham held a great feast on the day Isaac was weaned. ⁹ But Sarah saw the son mocking — the one Hagar the Egyptian had borne to Abraham. ¹⁰ So she said to Abraham, "Drive out this slave with her son, for the son of this slave will not be a coheir with my son Isaac!"

¹¹ This was very distressing toᴱ Abraham because of his son. ¹² But God said to Abraham, "Do not be distressedᶠ about the boy and about your slave. Whatever Sarah says to you, listen to her, because your offspring will be traced through Isaac, ¹³ and I will also make a nation of the slave's son because he is your offspring."

¹⁴ Early in the morning Abraham got up, took bread and a waterskin, put them on Hagar's shoulders, and sent her and the boy away. She left and wandered in the Wilderness of Beer-sheba. ¹⁵ When the water in the skin was gone, she left the boy under one of the bushes ¹⁶ and went and sat at a distance, about a bowshot away, for she said, "I can't bear to watch the boy die!" While she sat at a distance, sheᴳ wept loudly.

¹⁷ God heard the boy crying, and theᴴ angel of God called to Hagar from heaven and said to her, "What's wrong, Hagar? Don't be afraid, for God has heard the boy crying from the place where he is. ¹⁸ Get up, help the boy up, and grasp his hand, for I will make him a great nation." ¹⁹ Then God opened her eyes, and she saw a well. So she went and filled the waterskin and gave the boy a drink. ²⁰ God was with the boy, and he grew; he settled in the wilderness and became an archer. ²¹ He settled in the Wilderness of Paran, and his mother got a wife for him from the land of Egypt.

ᴬ20:15 Lit Settle in the good in your eyes ᴮ20:16 Lit a covering of the eyes ᶜ21:6 Isaac = He Laughs; Gn 17:19 ᴰ21:7 Sam, Tg Jonathan; MT omits him ᴱ21:11 Lit was very bad in the eyes of ᶠ21:12 Lit "Let it not be bad in your eyes ᴳ21:16 LXX reads the boy ᴴ21:17 Or an

20:9–18 Abimelech comes off appearing to be Abraham's moral superior. He is penitent and also generous. A **verification of your honor** in v. 16 is literally "a covering of the eyes." According to John Wenham, "the gift makes one blind to what has happened."

21:5 Though **Abraham was a hundred years old** at Isaac's birth, at least four preflood patriarchs had fathered children when they were older than he (5:6,18,25,28).

21:6–7 The name Isaac means "He Laughs." His birth turned his parents' doubting laughter (17:7; 18:12) into obedience and joy.

21:8–10 The Bible does not indicate Isaac's age when he **was weaned**. In some cultures children receive nourishment from their mother into their fifth year. When the day came for Isaac to be weaned, **Abraham held**

a **great feast** to assist the child psychologically in taking this step. During the party, however, Ishmael was **mocking** Isaac. **Drive out** (Hb garash) is the same term used to describe the expulsions of Adam and Cain following their sins (3:24; 4:14).

21:11–13 It was **very distressing to Abraham** (lit "it was very bad in Abraham's eyes") to expel his firstborn son from the household. However, God's guidance and comforting assurances enabled Abraham to do the wise thing.

21:14–19 Abraham's love and concern for Hagar and Ishmael are reflected in his diligence—getting up **early** and giving them provisions. The banished pair wandered in **the Wilderness of Beer-sheba**, an area some twenty miles west of the southern end of the Dead Sea. When Hagar and

Ishmael ran out of water, Ishmael almost died, perhaps of heatstroke. Overwhelmed with grief, Hagar placed him in the shadow of **one of the bushes** and then went about **a bowshot away**—just far enough to avoid hearing **the boy** as he lay dying. Though Hagar may not have known that where there is large vegetation in a desert there is also a high water table, **God opened her eyes** to the fact that **a well** was nearby.

21:20–21 Honoring his promises to Abraham (v. 13; 17:20) and Hagar (21:18), God protected Ishmael, who eventually settled in the **Wilderness of Paran**, west of the Gulf of Aqaba in the northern Sinai Desert. Hagar, who was herself an Egyptian (16:3), got her son an Egyptian wife. Ishmael would produce twelve sons (25:13–15).

Abraham's Covenant with Abimelech

²² At that time Abimelech, accompanied by Phicol the commander of his army, said to Abraham, "God is with you in everything you do. ²³ Swear to me by God here and now, that you will not break an agreement with me or with my children and descendants. As I have been loyal to you, so you will be loyal to me and to the country where you are a resident alien."

²⁴ And Abraham said, "I swear it." ²⁵ But Abraham complained to Abimelech because of the well that Abimelech's servants had seized. ²⁶ Abimelech replied, "I don't know who did this thing. You didn't report anything to me, so I hadn't heard about it until today."

²⁷ Abraham took flocks and herds and gave them to Abimelech, and the two of them made a covenant. ²⁸ Abraham separated seven ewe lambs from the flock. ²⁹ And Abimelech said to Abraham, "Why have you separated these seven ewe lambs?"

³⁰ He replied, "You are to accept the seven ewe lambs from me so that this act^A will serve as my witness that I dug this well." ³¹ Therefore that place was called Beer-sheba^B because it was there that the two of them swore an oath. ³² After they had made a covenant at Beer-sheba, Abimelech and Phicol, the commander of his army, left and returned to the land of the Philistines.

³³ Abraham planted a tamarisk tree in Beer-sheba, and there he called on the name of the Lᴏʀᴅ, the Everlasting God. ³⁴ And Abraham lived as an alien in the land of the Philistines for many days.

The Sacrifice of Isaac

22 After these things God tested Abraham and said to him, "Abraham!"

"Here I am," he answered.

² "Take your son," he said, "your only son Isaac, whom you love, go to the land of Moriah, and offer him there as a burnt offering on one of the mountains I will tell you about."

³ So Abraham got up early in the morning, saddled his donkey, and took with him two of his young men and his son Isaac. He split wood for a burnt offering and set out to go to the place God had told him about. ⁴ On the third day Abraham looked up and saw the place in the distance. ⁵ Then Abraham said to his young men, "Stay here with the donkey. The boy and I will go over there to worship; then we'll come back to you." ⁶ Abraham took the wood for the burnt offering and laid it on his son Isaac. In his hand he took the fire and the knife, and the two of them walked on together.

⁷ Then Isaac spoke to his father Abraham and said, "My father."

And he replied, "Here I am, my son."

Isaac said, "The fire and the wood are here, but where is the lamb for the burnt offering?"

⁸ Abraham answered, "God himself will provide^C the lamb for the burnt offering, my son." Then the two of them walked on together.

⁹ When they arrived at the place that God had told him about, Abraham built the altar there and arranged the wood. He bound his son Isaac^D and placed him on the altar on top of the wood. ¹⁰ Then Abraham reached out and took the knife to slaughter his son.

¹¹ But the angel of the Lᴏʀᴅ called to him from heaven and said, "Abraham, Abraham!"

He replied, "Here I am."

¹² Then he said, "Do not lay a hand on the boy or do anything to him. For now I know that you fear God, since you have not withheld your only son from me." ¹³ Abraham looked up and saw a ram^E caught in the thicket by its horns. So Abraham went and took the ram and offered

---

^A 21:30 Lit *that it*   ^B 21:31 = Well of the Oath, or Seven Wells   ^C 22:8 Lit *see*   ^D 22:9 Or *Isaac hand and foot*   ^E 22:13 Some Hb mss, Sam, LXX, Syr, Tg; other Hb mss read *saw behind him a ram*

21:22–24 Fearing that Abraham, who had hundreds of trained fighters in his camp (14:14), might mount a successful attack on Gerar, **Abimelech** and his military commander Phicol asked Abraham to **swear** that he would never **break an agreement** of peace with their community. Abraham calmed their fears by making an oath of peace.
21:25–32 Having relieved their worries about war, the patriarch then expressed his own concerns about water rights. Though Abimelech's group had wronged the patriarch, Abraham gave **flocks and herds** to Abimelech as part of a formal **covenant**. This gift, reminiscent of Abimelech's gift to Abraham earlier (20:14), was probably used in part for the animal sacrifices offered up when a covenant was established. Abimelech's acceptance of the additional gift of **seven ewe lambs** obligated him to recognize that the **well** that Abraham's men had **dug** would not be seized. The name **Beer-sheba** is a wordplay, meaning both "well of oath" and "well of seven."

21:33–34 In recognition of God's good gifts, including a son who would carry the bloodline forward into the future, **Abraham planted a tamarisk tree**, a tree with many branches and small leaves. It likely grew to a height of twenty to thirty feet. He also worshiped **the Lᴏʀᴅ as the Everlasting God** (Hb *'el 'olam*) in recognition of the perpetuity of God's promises to Abraham.
22:1–2 Abraham's ultimate test of obedience to God is described in 22:1–19, a section known in the Hebrew tradition as the *Akedah* (lit "the binding," v. 9). The Hebrew verb *nis-sah*, translated as **tested**, means "to prove the quality of," not "to entice to do wrong." God used this event to affirm the sterling character of Abraham's faith by giving him the incredibly difficult task of sacrificing his son Isaac in **the land of Moriah**, i.e., the Jerusalem area (2Ch 3:1). With this command God was asking Abraham to demonstrate that he was as committed to the Lord God as pagans were to their gods. God refers to Isaac as Abraham's **only son** because Isaac is the son of the promise.

22:3–4 Confirmation of Abraham's amazing trust in God is found first in the fact that he was up before sunrise (**early in the morning**) the next day to begin the journey. Traveling from Beer-sheba, it was not until **the third day** that Abraham reached the Jerusalem area.
22:5–8 Evidence that Abraham believed God could raise Isaac from the dead (Heb 11:17–18) is found in his comment, **we'll come back**. Ignorant of God's command and surprised that his father would forget the most important element in an animal sacrifice, Isaac asked Abraham where **the lamb** (Hb *seh* also means "sheep") was. Abraham's faith-filled response was that **God himself** would **provide the lamb** ("sheep").
22:11–12 Abraham's willingness to sacrifice Isaac foreshadows in a small way God's sacrifice of his only Son, Jesus.
22:13–14 Exactly as Abraham had predicted (v. 8), God had miraculously provided a sheep—and the most prized variety, **a ram**. To memorialize the event Abraham named that place **The Lᴏʀᴅ Will Provide**.

it as a burnt offering in place of his son. ¹⁴ And Abraham named that place The LORD Will Provide,ᴬ so today it is said, "It will be provided ᴮ on the LORD's mountain."

¹⁵ Then the angel of the LORD called to Abraham a second time from heaven ¹⁶ and said, "By myself I have sworn," this is the LORD's declaration: "Because you have done this thing and have not withheld your only son, ¹⁷ I will indeed bless you and make your offspring as numerous as the stars of the sky and the sand on the seashore. Your offspring will possess the city gates of theirᶜ enemies. ¹⁸ And all the nations of the earth will be blessed ᴰ by your offspring because you have obeyed my command."

¹⁹ Abraham went back to his young men, and they got up and went together to Beer-sheba. And Abraham settled in Beer-sheba.

Rebekah's Family

²⁰ Now after these things Abraham was told, "Milcah also has borne sons to your brother Nahor: ²¹ Uz his firstborn, his brother Buz, Kemuel the father of Aram, ²² Chesed, Hazo, Pildash, Jidlaph, and Bethuel." ²³ And Bethuel fathered Rebekah. Milcah bore these eight to Nahor, Abraham's brother. ²⁴ His concubine, whose name was Reumah, also bore Tebah, Gaham, Tahash, and Maacah.

Sarah's Burial

23 Now Sarah lived 127 years; these were all the years of her life. ² Sarah died in Kiriath-arba (that is, Hebron) in the land of Canaan, and Abraham went in to mourn for Sarah and to weep for her.

³ When Abraham got up from beside his dead wife, he spoke to the Hethites: ⁴ "I am an alien residing among you. Give me burial property among you so that I can bury my dead."ᴱ

⁵ The Hethites replied to Abraham,ᶠ ⁶ "Listen to us, my lord. You are a prince of Godᴳ among

us. Bury your dead in our finest burial place."ᴴ None of us will withhold from you his burial place for burying your dead."

⁷ Then Abraham rose and bowed down to the Hethites, the people of the land. ⁸ He said to them, "If you are willing for me to bury my dead, listen to me and ask Ephron son of Zohar on my behalf ⁹ to give me the cave of Machpelah that belongs to him; it is at the end of his field. Let him give it to me in your presence, for the full price, as burial property."

¹⁰ Ephron was sitting among the Hethites. So in the hearingᴵ of all the Hethites who came to the gate of his city, Ephron the Hethite answered Abraham: ¹¹ "No, my lord. Listen to me. I give you the field, and I give you the cave that is in it. I give it to you in the sightᴶ of my people. Bury your dead."

¹² Abraham bowed down to the people of the land ¹³ and said to Ephron in the hearing of the people of the land, "Listen to me, if you please. Let me pay the price of the field. Accept it from me, and let me bury my dead there."

¹⁴ Ephron answered Abraham and said to him, ¹⁵ "My lord, listen to me. Land worth four hundred shekels of silver — what is that between you and me? Bury your dead."

¹⁶ Abraham agreed with Ephron, and Abraham weighed out to Ephron the silver that he had agreed to in the hearing of the Hethites: four hundred standard shekelsᴷ of silver. ¹⁷ So Ephron's field at Machpelah near Mamre — the field with its cave and all the trees anywhere within the boundaries of the field — became ¹⁸ Abraham's possession in the sight of all the Hethites who came to the gate of his city. ¹⁹ After this, Abraham buried his wife Sarah in the cave of the field at Machpelah near Mamre (that is, Hebron) in the land of Canaan. ²⁰ The field with its cave passed from the Hethites to Abraham as burial property.

ᴬ 22:14 = Yahweh-yireh　ᴮ 22:14 Or "He will be seen　ᶜ 22:17 Lit his　ᴰ 22:18 Or will consider themselves blessed, or will find blessing　ᴱ 23:4 Lit dead from before me　ᶠ 23:5 Lit Abraham, saying to him　ᴳ 23:6 Or a mighty prince　ᴴ 23:6 Or finest graves　ᴵ 23:10 Lit ears, also in vv. 13,16　ᴶ 23:11 Lit in the eyes of the sons　ᴷ 23:16 Lit 400 shekels passing to the merchant

22:15–18 As the angel (meaning "messenger") of the LORD who had the Lord's authority, the divine emissary delivered a second message (v. 12), this one in the first person. Because Abraham had passed the "priorities test" by obeying God and not withholding his only son, the Lord would indeed bless him with offspring, victory, land, and goodwill. Since there is nothing greater, God swears by himself (cp. Ex 32:13; Is 45:23; Jr 22:5; 49:13).

22:20–24 Genesis next presents the offspring of Abraham's brother Nahor through his wife Milcah and his concubine Reumah. This brief section prepares the reader for the events of chap. 24 by introducing Bethuel and identifying him as the father of Rebekah, Isaac's future wife.

23:1–2 Indicative of Sarah's importance is the fact that she is the only woman in the

Bible whose age at the time of her death is reported. Kiriath-arba ("City of Four") was the name for the city later known as Hebron. 23:3–6 Though God had promised this land to Abraham, and Abraham had lived there over sixty years, he still owned no land in Canaan, so he had to obtain burial property from the Hethites to bury Sarah (on Hethites, see note at 15:18–21). Like the Philistines earlier (21:22), the Hethites recognized that Abraham was a prince of God among them. 23:7–11 In the market square at the gate of Kiriath-arba, Abraham showed his respect for the Hethites, placing his head at the level of their feet. The patriarch played the role of one who was unworthy to speak to the landowner whose property he desired. Accordingly, he asked the Hethites to ask Ephron on his behalf for the right to purchase the cave of Machpelah. Though Abraham was a skilled

bargainer (18:23–32), he offered to pay the full price for the property. Matching Abraham's decorum, Ephron the Hethite spoke directly to Abraham and offered to give him not only the cave, but also the field. 23:12–18 With both parties in agreement, Abraham bowed again respectfully and repeated his willingness to pay the full price of the field—even though he did not yet know how much that would be. Four hundred shekels of silver—perhaps the price of eight healthy adult male slaves (Lv 27:3)—may or may not have been a reasonable valuation. Either way, Abraham agreed to the price. 23:19–20 Following the successful negotiations, Abraham buried his wife Sarah in the cave . . . at Machpelah. Others who would be buried there included Abraham, Isaac, Rebekah, Leah, and Jacob (49:31; 50:13).

The LORD Will Provide

	SUBJECT TO DEATH	THE SUBSTITUTE	THE REASON
Genesis 22	Isaac—Abraham's "only son" *(Gn 22:2)*	A Ram	Abraham named that place The LORD Will Provide, so today it is said, It will be provided on the LORD's mountain *(Gn 22:14)*.
Exodus 12–13 *(The Passover)*	The Firstborn Sons of Israel	An Unblemished Lamb or Goat	The blood on the houses of the Israelites would be a sign to distinguish them; when God saw the blood, he would pass over them *(Ex 12:13)*.
Leviticus 16 *(The Day of Atonement)*	The People of Israel	Animals, Including a Ram	On this day, atonement was made for the Israelites to cleanse them from all their sins so they could be clean before the Lord *(Lv 16:30)*.
Revelation 5	Sinners	Jesus—"the Lamb of God" *(Jn 1:29)*	Jesus, the Lamb, was slaughtered in order to redeem people for God by his blood—people from every tribe, language, people, and nation *(Rv 5:9)*.

A Wife for Isaac

24 Abraham was now old, getting on in years,^A and the LORD had blessed him in everything. ² Abraham said to his servant, the elder of his household who managed all he owned, "Place your hand under my thigh, ³ and I will have you swear by the LORD, God of heaven and God of earth, that you will not take a wife for my son from the daughters of the Canaanites among whom I live, ⁴ but will go to my land and my family to take a wife for my son Isaac."

⁵ The servant said to him, "Suppose the woman is unwilling to follow me to this land? Should I have your son go back to the land you came from?"

⁶ Abraham answered him, "Make sure that you don't take my son back there. ⁷ The LORD, the God of heaven, who took me from my father's house and from my native land, who spoke to me and swore to me, 'I will give this land to your offspring'^B — he will send his angel before you, and you can take a wife for my son from there. ⁸ If the woman is unwilling to follow you, then you are free from this oath to me, but don't let my son go back there." ⁹ So the servant placed his hand under his master Abraham's thigh and swore an oath to him concerning this matter.

¹⁰ The servant took ten of his master's camels, and with all kinds of his master's goods in hand, he went to Aram-naharaim, to Nahor's town. ¹¹ At evening, the time when women went out to draw water, he made the camels kneel beside a well outside the town.

¹² "LORD, God of my master Abraham," he prayed, "make this happen for me today, and show kindness to my master Abraham. ¹³ I am standing here at the spring where the daughters of the men of the town are coming out to draw water. ¹⁴ Let the girl to whom I say, 'Please lower your water jug so that I may drink,' and who responds, 'Drink, and I'll water your camels also' — let her be the one you have appointed for your servant Isaac. By this I will know that you have shown kindness to my master."

¹⁵ Before he had finished speaking, there was Rebekah — daughter of Bethuel son of Milcah, the wife of Abraham's brother Nahor — coming with a jug on her shoulder. ¹⁶ Now the girl was very beautiful, a virgin — no man had been intimate with her. She went down to the spring, filled her jug, and came up. ¹⁷ Then the servant ran to meet her and said, "Please let me have a little water from your jug."

¹⁸ She replied, "Drink, my lord." She quickly lowered her jug to her hand and gave him a drink. ¹⁹ When she had finished giving him a drink, she said, "I'll also draw water for your camels until they have had enough to drink."^C ²⁰ She quickly emptied her jug into the trough and hurried to the well again to draw water. She drew water for all his camels ²¹ while the man silently watched her to see whether or not the LORD had made his journey a success.

²² As the camels finished drinking, the man took a gold ring weighing half a shekel, and for her wrists two bracelets weighing ten shekels of gold. ²³ "Whose daughter are you?" he asked. "Please tell me, is there room in your father's house for us to spend the night?"

²⁴ She answered him, "I am the daughter of Bethuel son of Milcah, whom she bore to Nahor." ²⁵ She also said to him, "We have plenty of straw and feed and a place to spend the night."

²⁶ Then the man knelt low, worshiped the LORD, ²⁷ and said, "Blessed be the LORD, the God of my master Abraham, who has not withheld his kindness and faithfulness from my master. As for me, the LORD has led me on the journey to the house of my master's relatives."

²⁸ The girl ran and told her mother's household about these things. ²⁹ Now Rebekah had a brother named Laban, and Laban ran out to the man at the spring. ³⁰ As soon as he had seen the ring and the bracelets on his sister's wrists, and when he had heard his sister Rebekah's words — "The man said this to me!" — he went to the man. He was standing there by the camels at the spring. ³¹ Laban said, "Come, you who are blessed by the LORD. Why are you standing out here?

---

^A 24:1 Lit *days* ^B 24:7 Lit *seed* ^C 24:19 Lit *they are finished drinking*

24:1–9 Abraham, now 140 years of age, had been **blessed** by the **LORD** in **everything**, but one thing was missing—a worthy wife for his forty-year-old son to ensure the continuance of the covenant line. Abraham did not want Isaac to marry a woman **from the daughters of the Canaanites**. Instead, she must come from his relatives hundreds of miles away in northwest Mesopotamia. Abraham himself was too old to make the journey back, so he summoned his most trusted **servant**, perhaps Eliezer (15:2), to fulfill the task. Finding the right wife for Isaac required divine help, so Abraham had his servant take an oath **by the LORD, God of heaven and God of earth**, and also to **place** his **hand under** Abraham's **thigh**,

the bodily zone associated with Abraham's posterity. **24:10–11** The chief **servant** and several other slaves (v. 32) took **goods** reflective of Abraham's wealth, which could be used to pay the bride-price for Isaac's wife. The journey from Beer-sheba to **Aram-naharaim**—located somewhere in northwest Mesopotamia—could have taken a couple of weeks. **Nahor's town** could mean that "Nahor" was the name of the village or that it was Nahor's hometown. "Nahor" was the name of Abraham's brother and grandfather (11:25–26), thus suggesting that this village was populated by Abraham's relatives. **24:12–14** A thirsty camel can drink as much as thirty gallons of water in fifteen minutes.

Since ten camels accompanied the servant (v. 10), it is possible that the young woman would have had to draw three hundred gallons of water (equal to 2,500 lbs.) from the spring to pass the servant's test. **24:23–27** The servant received the best possible answers to two questions: Rebekah was indeed **the daughter** of Abraham's nephew **Bethuel**, and the men and their camels could **spend the night** with her family. Overwhelmed with gratitude, the servant **knelt low, worshiped the LORD**, and praised him for his acts of **kindness** (Hb *chesed*; "covenant loyalty") **and faithfulness**. **24:28–33** The level of hospitality provided by Rebekah and her family rivals the hospitality Abraham showed his visitors in 18:3–8.

I have prepared the house and a place for the camels." ³² So the man came to the house, and the camels were unloaded. Straw and feed were given to the camels, and water was brought to wash his feet and the feet of the men with him. ³³ A meal was set before him, but he said, "I will not eat until I have said what I have to say."

So Laban said, "Please speak."

³⁴ "I am Abraham's servant," he said. ³⁵ "The Lord has greatly blessed my master, and he has become rich. He has given him flocks and herds, silver and gold, male and female slaves, and camels and donkeys. ³⁶ Sarah, my master's wife, bore a son to my master in her ^A old age, and he has given him everything he owns. ³⁷ My master put me under this oath: 'You will not take a wife for my son from the daughters of the Canaanites in whose land I live ³⁸ but will go to my father's family and to my clan to take a wife for my son.' ³⁹ But I said to my master, 'Suppose the woman will not come back with me?' ⁴⁰ He said to me, 'The Lord before whom I have walked will send his angel with you and make your journey a success, and you will take a wife for my son from my clan and from my father's family. ⁴¹ Then you will be free from my oath if you go to my family and they do not give her to you — you will be free from my oath.'

⁴² "Today when I came to the spring, I prayed: Lord, God of my master Abraham, if only you will make my journey successful! ⁴³ I am standing here at a spring. Let the young woman ^B who comes out to draw water, and I say to her, 'Please let me drink a little water from your jug,' ⁴⁴ and who responds to me, 'Drink, and I'll draw water for your camels also' — let her be the woman the Lord has appointed for my master's son.

⁴⁵ "Before I had finished praying silently, there was Rebekah coming with her jug on her shoulder, and she went down to the spring and drew water. So I said to her, 'Please let me have a drink.' ⁴⁶ She quickly lowered her jug from her shoulder and said, 'Drink, and I'll water your camels also.' So I drank, and she also watered the camels. ⁴⁷ Then I asked her, 'Whose daughter are you?' She responded, 'The daughter of Bethuel son of Nahor, whom Milcah bore to him.' So I put the ring on her nose

and the bracelets on her wrists. ⁴⁸ Then I knelt low, worshiped the Lord, and blessed the Lord, the God of my master Abraham, who guided me on the right way to take the granddaughter of my master's brother for his son. ⁴⁹ Now, if you are going to show kindness and faithfulness to my master, tell me; if not, tell me, and I will go elsewhere." ^C

⁵⁰ Laban and Bethuel answered, "This is from the Lord; we have no choice in the matter. ^D ⁵¹ Rebekah is here in front of you. Take her and go, and let her be a wife for your master's son, just as the Lord has spoken."

⁵² When Abraham's servant heard their words, he bowed to the ground before the Lord. ⁵³ Then he brought out objects of silver and gold, and garments, and gave them to Rebekah. He also gave precious gifts to her brother and her mother. ⁵⁴ Then he and the men with him ate and drank and spent the night.

When they got up in the morning, he said, "Send me to my master."

⁵⁵ But her brother and mother said, "Let the girl stay with us for about ten days. Then she ^E can go."

⁵⁶ But he responded to them, "Do not delay me, since the Lord has made my journey a success. Send me away so that I may go to my master."

⁵⁷ So they said, "Let's call the girl and ask her opinion." ^F

⁵⁸ They called Rebekah and said to her, "Will you go with this man?"

She replied, "I will go." ⁵⁹ So they sent away their sister Rebekah with the one who had nursed and raised her, ^G and Abraham's servant and his men.

⁶⁰ They blessed Rebekah, saying to her:

Our sister, may you become
thousands upon ten thousands.
May your offspring possess
the city gates of their ^H enemies.

⁶¹ Then Rebekah and her female servants got up, mounted the camels, and followed the man. So the servant took Rebekah and left.

⁶² Now Isaac was returning from Beer-lahai-roi, ^I for he was living in the Negev region. ⁶³ In the early evening Isaac went out to walk ^J in the field, and looking up he saw camels coming.

---

^A 24:36 Sam, LXX read his   ^B 24:43 Or the virgin   ^C 24:49 Lit go to the right or to the left   ^D 24:50 Lit we cannot say to you anything bad or good   ^E 24:55 Or you   ^F 24:57 Lit mouth   ^G 24:59 Lit with her wet nurse; Gn 35:8   ^H 24:60 Lit his   ^I 24:62 = A Well of the Living One Who Sees Me   ^J 24:63 Or pray, or meditate; Hb obscure

---

24:34–49 In the longest recorded speech by a slave in the OT (238 words in the Hebrew), **Abraham's servant** recounted in detail three relevant matters: how **the Lord** greatly blessed Abraham, why a young woman was needed from Bethuel's **family**, and how God had revealed that he had **appointed** Rebekah for his **master's son**. **24:50–53** When **Laban and Bethuel**—the ruling adult males in the clan—were

presented with evidence that **the Lord** had **spoken** and had selected Rebekah for Isaac, they released her to **be a wife** for Abraham's **son**. As the bride-price the servant then presented **gifts** to **Rebekah . . . her brother and her mother**. **24:54–61** As a wedding gift the family gave Rebekah **the one who had nursed** her, a beloved slave named Deborah (35:8) who attended to her for many years.

24:62–66 After a journey of hundreds of miles on camelback, the caravan returned to Isaac's home. Rebekah **saw Isaac** for the first time on the day she married him. As was apparently the custom on the wedding day, Rebekah **covered herself** with a veil before meeting her husband. Before presenting Rebekah to Isaac, Abraham's servant told **everything he had done** and what God had done for him.

⁶⁴ Rebekah looked up, and when she saw Isaac, she got down from her camel ⁶⁵ and asked the servant, "Who is that man in the field coming to meet us?"

The servant answered, "It is my master." So she took her veil and covered herself. ⁶⁶ Then the servant told Isaac everything he had done.

⁶⁷ And Isaac brought her into the tent of his mother Sarah and took Rebekah to be his wife. Isaac loved her, and he was comforted after his mother's death.

Abraham's Other Wife and Sons

25 Abraham had taken^A another wife, whose name was Keturah, ² and she bore him Zimran, Jokshan, Medan, Midian, Ishbak, and Shuah. ³ Jokshan fathered Sheba and Dedan. Dedan's sons were the Asshurim, Letushim, and Leummim. ⁴ And Midian's sons were Ephah, Epher, Hanoch, Abida, and Eldaah. All these were sons of Keturah. ⁵ Abraham gave everything he owned to Isaac. ⁶ But Abraham gave gifts to the sons of his concubines, and while he was still alive he sent them eastward, away from his son Isaac, to the land of the East.

Abraham's Death

⁷ This is the length of Abraham's life:⁸ 175 years. ⁸ He took his last breath and died at a good old age, old and contented,ᶜ and he was gathered to his people. ⁹ His sons Isaac and Ishmael buried him in the cave of Machpelah near Mamre, in the field of Ephron son of Zohar the Hethite. ¹⁰ This was the field that Abraham bought from the Hethites. Abraham was buried there with his wife Sarah. ¹¹ After Abraham's death,

God blessed his son Isaac, who lived near Beer-lahai-roi.

Ishmael's Family Records

¹² These are the family records of Abraham's son Ishmael, whom Hagar the Egyptian, Sarah's slave, bore to Abraham. ¹³ These are the names of Ishmael's sons; their names according to the family records are Nebaioth, Ishmael's firstborn, then Kedar, Adbeel, Mibsam, ¹⁴ Mishma, Dumah, Massa, ¹⁵ Hadad, Tema, Jetur, Naphish, and Kedemah. ¹⁶ These are Ishmael's sons, and these are their names by their settlements and encampments: twelve leadersᴰ of their clans.ᴱ ¹⁷ This is the lengthᶠ of Ishmael's life: 137 years. He took his last breath and died, and was gathered to his people. ¹⁸ And theyᴳ settled from Havilah to Shur, which is opposite Egypt as you go toward Asshur.ᴴ Heᴵ stayed nearᴶ all his relatives.

The Birth of Jacob and Esau

¹⁹ These are the family records of Isaac son of Abraham. Abraham fathered Isaac. ²⁰ Isaac was forty years old when he took as his wife Rebekah daughter of Bethuel the Aramean from Paddan-aram and sister of Laban the Aramean. ²¹ Isaac prayed to the Lord on behalf of his wife because she was childless. The Lord was receptive to his prayer, and his wife Rebekah conceived. ²² But the children inside her struggled with each other, and she said, "Why is this happening to me?"ᴷ So she went to inquire of the Lord. ²³ And the Lord said to her:

Two nations are in your womb;
two peoples will come from you
    and be separated.

^25:1 Or *Abraham took*   ^B 25:7 Lit *And these are the days of the years of the life of Abraham that he lived*   ^C 25:8 Sam, LXX, Syr read *full of days*   ^D 25:16 Or *chieftains*   ^E 25:16 Or *peoples*   ^F 25:17 Lit *And these are the years*   ^G 25:18 LXX, Vg read *he*   ^H 25:18 Or *Assyria*   ^I 25:18 = Ishmael and his descendants   ^J 25:18 Or *He settled down alongside of*   ^K 25:22 Lit *said, "If thus, why this I?"*

24:67 As part of the marital ritual, Isaac brought Rebekah **into** what had been his mother Sarah's **tent**. This would now become her home, which marked her as the clan matriarch, the most powerful woman in the

group. There Isaac and Rebekah consummated the marriage. Having waited forty years to marry, **Isaac loved** his wife deeply, and was finally **comforted after his mother's death**, which had occurred three years earlier (17:17; 23:1; 25:20).

25:1–4 Probably after Sarah's death **Abraham** took **another wife** with concubine status, **Keturah**. In partial fulfillment of God's promise that he would have descendants as numerous as the stars (15:5; 22:17), aged Abraham fathered six additional sons.

25:5–6 Keturah, like Hagar, was a concubine; she and her sons had less status than Sarah and Isaac. Accordingly, Abraham only **gave** **gifts** to Keturah's sons, while he gave Isaac **everything he owned**. Because God had given the land of Canaan only to Isaac's descendants, Abraham sent Keturah's sons **eastward** to the Arabian Peninsula.

25:7–11 Abraham lived some thirty-seven years after Sarah's death and died at the age of **175**. The patriarch's two oldest sons **Isaac** (now seventy-five; see 21:5) and **Ishmael** (now eighty-nine; see 16:16) took the responsibility of burying their father.

25:12–18 The family records of Abraham's son Ishmael, the seventh of the eleven

(Hb) *toledoth* sections of Genesis (see note at 5:1), complement the family records of Abraham's son Isaac (25:19). The lesser status of Ishmael's family line compared to Isaac's is reflected in the section's relatively small size (7 vs. 364 verses) and the notation that Ishmael's mother **Hagar** was the **slave** of Isaac's mother Sarah.

Ishmael fathered twelve sons, all of whom became **leaders of their clans**. Their **settlements and encampments** stretched **from** **Havilah to Shur**—the region between the modern Suez canal and the Wadi el-Arish. Later their settlements, the best known of which was **Kedar**, would extend into the northwest Arabian Peninsula; these would be involved in incense trade. During his **137 years**, Ishmael would also father two daughters, Mahalath and Basemath (28:9; 36:3).

25:19 The family records of Isaac son of Abraham, the eighth of the eleven (Hb) *toledoth* sections in Genesis (see note at 5:1), extend from 25:19 through 35:29.

25:20–26 Esau was prophesied to be the ancestor of a nation, the Edomites, who would generally be ruled by Israel, the nation descended from Jacob. According to Mal

One people will be stronger
    than the other,
and the older will serve the younger.

²⁴ When her time came to give birth, there were indeed twins in her womb. ²⁵ The first one came out red-looking,ᴬ covered with hairᴮ like a fur coat, and they named him Esau. ²⁶ After this, his brother came out grasping Esau's heel with his hand. So he was named Jacob.ᶜ Isaac was sixty years old when they were born.

Esau Sells His Birthright

²⁷ When the boys grew up, Esau became an expert hunter, an outdoorsman,ᴰ but Jacob was a quiet man who stayed at home.ᴱ ²⁸ Isaac loved Esau because he had a taste for wild game, but Rebekah loved Jacob.

²⁹ Once when Jacob was cooking a stew, Esau came in from the field exhausted. ³⁰ He said to Jacob, "Let me eat some of that red stuff, because I'm exhausted." That is why he was also named Edom.ᶠ

³¹ Jacob replied, "First sell me your birthright."

³² "Look," said Esau, "I'm about to die, so what good is a birthright to me?"

³³ Jacob said, "Swear to me first." So he swore to Jacob and sold his birthright to him. ³⁴ Then Jacob gave bread and lentil stew to Esau; he ate, drank, got up, and went away. So Esau despised his birthright.

The Promise Reaffirmed to Isaac

26 There was another famine in the land in addition to the one that had occurred in Abraham's time. And Isaac went to Abimelech, king of the Philistines, at Gerar. ² The LORD appeared to him and said, "Do not go down to Egypt. Live in the land that I tell you about; ³ stay in this land as an alien, and I will be with you and bless you. For I will give all these lands to you and your offspring, and I will confirm the oath that I swore to your father Abraham. ⁴ I will make your offspring as numerous as the stars of the sky, I will give your offspring all these lands, and all the nations of the earth will be blessedᴳ by your offspring, ⁵ because Abraham listened to me and kept my mandate, my commands, my statutes, and my instructions." ⁶ So Isaac settled in Gerar.

Isaac's Deception

⁷ When the men of the place asked about his wife, he said, "She is my sister," for he was afraid to say "my wife," thinking, "The men of the place will kill me on account of Rebekah, for she is a beautiful woman." ⁸ When Isaac had been there for some time, Abimelech king of the Philistines looked down from the window and was surprised to seeᴴ Isaac caressing his wife Rebekah.

⁹ Abimelech sent for Isaac and said, "So she is really your wife! How could you say, 'She is my sister'?"

Isaac answered him, "Because I thought I might die on account of her."

¹⁰ Then Abimelech said, "What have you done to us? One of the people could easily have slept with your wife, and you would have brought guilt on us." ¹¹ So Abimelech warned all the people, "Whoever harms this man or his wife will certainly be put to death."

Conflicts over Wells

¹² Isaac sowed seed in that land, and in that year he reapedᴵ a hundred times what was sown. The LORD blessed him, ¹³ and the man became rich and kept getting richer until he was very wealthy. ¹⁴ He had flocks of sheep, herds of cattle, and many slaves, and the Philistines were envious of him. ¹⁵ Philistines stopped up all the wells that his father's servants had dug in the days of his father Abraham, filling them with

---

ᴬ**25:25** In Hb, *red-looking* sounds like "Edom"; Gn 32:3.   ᴮ**25:25** In Hb, *hair* sounds like "Seir"; Gn 32:3.   ᶜ**25:26** = He Grasps the Heel   ᴰ**25:27** Lit *a man of the field*   ᴱ**25:27** Lit *man living in tents*   ᶠ**25:30** = Red   ᴳ**26:4** Or *will consider themselves blessed*   ᴴ**26:8** Or *and he looked and behold*—   ᴵ**26:12** Lit *found*

1:2–3, quoted in Rm 9:13, the prophecy also meant that God chose Jacob to inherit the Abrahamic promise.
25:27–28 The differences between Esau and Jacob, already apparent at birth, became more pronounced as **the boys grew up**. Esau was a rough-and-tumble **hunter** and **outdoorsman** (lit "man of rural regions"); Jacob was quiet and **stayed at home** (lit "dweller in tents"). The differences between the boys highlighted a division between the parents: **Isaac**, something of an outdoorsman himself (24:63), **loved** his rugged son **Esau**, while **Rebekah loved** her more domestic son **Jacob**, even teaching him how to cook.
25:29–34 Esau's impatient, appetite-driven life contrasted sharply with Jacob's shrewd, calculating character. Esau willingly traded his **birthright**—the right of the firstborn son to a double portion (or perhaps two-thirds of the inheritance (Dt 21:17)—for the

chance to **eat some . . . red stuff**. Because of his fateful decision, Esau picked up the alternate name **Edom** ("Red"), which would be carried by the people group stemming from him (32:3). And because Jacob had made him **swear** to **sell** his birthright, the decision could not be undone.
26:1–6 Isaac and his clan experienced the second recorded famine of the Bible (12:10). To avoid the effects of the famine, Isaac sought refuge in the region where his father had once lived (20:1). The **Abimelech** mentioned here may or may not be the same one with whom Abraham negotiated a treaty (21:27). The name may have been given to each succeeding king within a dynastic family.
26:7–11 Isaac would have had to negotiate with the Philistines to enjoy certain privileges among them. As a result he might have to provide a wife for someone's harem. If the

person asked for Rebekah (and she was, after all, the most important female in the clan and **a beautiful woman**), Isaac might be killed if he refused. Thus Isaac, like Abraham before him (12:13; 20:2), told outsiders that his wife was his sister. Isaac's lie was uncovered when he was caught **caressing** (lit "laughing/playing with") **Rebekah. Abimelech**, as the supreme authority in the region, **sent for Isaac** and demanded an explanation. Isaac patterned his defense after his father's (20:11); he feared he **might die on account of** his wife.
26:12–22 Because the **LORD blessed him**, Isaac enjoyed amazing success as a farmer, achieving the highest level of agricultural productivity recorded in the Bible (cp. Mt 13:8). The Philistines viewed Isaac as a rich foreigner with a reputation for trickery, and they wanted him off their land. Isaac complied, moving to the nearby **Gerar Valley**,

dirt. [16] And Abimelech said to Isaac, "Leave us, for you are much too powerful for us."[A]

[17] So Isaac left there, camped in the Gerar Valley, and lived there. [18] Isaac reopened the wells that had been dug in the days of his father Abraham and that the Philistines had stopped up after Abraham died. He gave them the same names his father had given them. [19] Then Isaac's servants dug in the valley and found a well of spring[B] water there. [20] But the herdsmen of Gerar quarreled with Isaac's herdsmen and said, "The water is ours!" So he named the well Esek[C] because they argued with him. [21] Then they dug another well and quarreled over that one also, so he named it Sitnah.[D] [22] He moved from there and dug another, and they did not quarrel over it. He named it Rehoboth[E] and said, "For now the LORD has made space for us, and we will be fruitful in the land."

The LORD Appears to Isaac

[23] From there he went up to Beer-sheba, [24] and the LORD appeared to him that night and said, "I am the God of your father Abraham. Do not be afraid, for I am with you. I will bless you and multiply your offspring because of my servant Abraham." [25] So he built an altar there, called on the name of the LORD, and pitched his tent there. Isaac's servants also dug a well there.

Covenant with Abimelech

[26] Now Abimelech came to him from Gerar with Ahuzzath his adviser and Phicol the commander of his army. [27] Isaac said to them, "Why have you come to me? You hated me and sent me away from you." [28] They replied, "We have clearly seen how the LORD has been with you. We think there should be an oath between two parties — between us and you. Let us make a covenant with you: [29] You will not harm us, just as we have not harmed you but have done only what was good

to you, sending you away in peace. You are now blessed by the LORD." [30] So he prepared a banquet for them, and they ate and drank. [31] They got up early in the morning and swore an oath to each other.[F] Isaac sent them on their way, and they left him in peace. [32] On that same day Isaac's servants came to tell him about the well they had dug, saying to him, "We have found water!" [33] He called it Sheba.[G] Therefore the name of the city is still Beer-sheba[H] today.

Esau's Wives

[34] When Esau was forty years old, he took as his wives Judith daughter of Beeri the Hethite, and Basemath daughter of Elon the Hethite. [35] They made life bitter[I] for Isaac and Rebekah.

The Stolen Blessing

27 When Isaac was old and his eyes were so weak that he could not see, he called his older son Esau and said to him, "My son."

And he answered, "Here I am."

[2] He said, "Look, I am old and do not know the day of my death. [3] So now take your hunting gear, your quiver and bow, and go out in the field to hunt some game for me. [4] Then make me a delicious meal that I love and bring it to me to eat, so that I can bless you before I die."

[5] Now Rebekah was listening to what Isaac said to his son Esau. So while Esau went to the field to hunt some game to bring in, [6] Rebekah said to her son Jacob, "Listen! I heard your father talking with your brother Esau. He said, [7] 'Bring me game and make a delicious meal for me to eat so that I can bless you in the LORD's presence before I die.' [8] Now, my son, listen to me and do what I tell you. [9] Go to the flock and bring me two choice young goats, and I will make them into a delicious meal for your father — the kind he loves. [10] Then take it to your father to eat so that he may bless you before he dies."

[A]26:16 Or *are more numerous than we are*   [B]26:19 Lit *living*   [C]26:20 = Argument   [D]26:21 = Hostility   [E]26:22 = Open Spaces
[F]26:31 Lit *swore, each man to his brother*   [G]26:33 Or *Shibah*   [H]26:33 = Well of the Oath   [I]26:35 Lit *And they became bitterness of spirit*

---

reopening old wells that had been filled with dirt and having his slaves dig three new ones to accommodate his increased herds and flocks without threatening the Philistines. However, as in the days of Abraham (Gn 21:25) the contentious Philistines claimed the rights to the first two wells, giving rise to the names **Esek** (Argument) and **Sitnah** (Hostility). When at last the Philistines **did not quarrel** over a well, Isaac rejoiced and **named** the well Rehoboth (Open Spaces). **26:23–25** Isaac's clan moved about twenty-five miles southeast to **Beer-sheba**, where his father had once lived (21:31). There **the LORD appeared** to Isaac and reassured him at a time when the Philistines were making trouble. Isaac was the third patriarch to build an altar (besides Noah, 8:20; and Abraham, 12:7–8; 13:18; 22:9).

26:30–33 Isaac's preparation of a **banquet** signified his acceptance of the treaty, which became official the next day when the parties swore an oath of non-aggression. That same day Isaac's slaves reported success in digging a fifth well, this one named **Sheba** (Hb *shiva'h*; "Seven"), similar to the Hebrew word for "oath" (*shevua'*) and confirming Abraham's name for Beer-sheba (21:31). **26:34–35** Esau married at the same age his father had (25:20). His marriages to two pagan Hethites, **Judith** ("Praise") and **Basemath** ("Balsam/Spice"), expressed more of his undisciplined nature (see note at 25:27–28). Esau's wives **made life bitter for Isaac and Rebekah**, most likely by being contentious about Jacob's favored status. **27:1–4** Isaac was now no less than a hundred years old (see 25:26; 26:34). Though

he would live to 180 (35:28) — at the very least twenty years beyond this point (31:38) — Isaac may have been sick, since his vision was obviously poor and he was so concerned to bless **his older son Esau** before he died. The blessing given by a clan patriarch to his heir was of great significance since it formally conferred the right to rule over the clan following the patriarch's death. **27:5–17** After learning of Isaac's intentions for Esau, Rebekah came up with a scheme to overturn the plans. Perhaps she did it because she remembered the decades-old prophecy about Jacob dominating his older brother (25:23).

With this the Bible paints a picture of a troubled family: Rebekah using **her son** (not "their son") to destroy her husband's plans,

11 Jacob answered Rebekah his mother, "Look, my brother Esau is a hairy man, but I am a man with smooth skin. **12** Suppose my father touches me. Then I will be revealed to him as a deceiver and bring a curse rather than a blessing on myself."

13 His mother said to him, "Your curse be on me, my son. Just obey me and go get them for me."

14 So he went and got the goats and brought them to his mother, and his mother made the delicious food his father loved. **15** Then Rebekah took the best clothes of her older son Esau, which were in the house, and had her younger son Jacob wear them. **16** She put the skins of the young goats on his hands and the smooth part of his neck. **17** Then she handed the delicious food and the bread she had made to her son Jacob.

18 When he came to his father, he said, "My father."

And he answered, "Here I am. Who are you, my son?"

19 Jacob replied to his father, "I am Esau, your firstborn. I have done as you told me. Please sit up and eat some of my game so that you may bless me."

20 But Isaac said to his son, "How did you ever find it so quickly, my son?"

He replied, "Because the LORD your God made it happen for me."

21 Then Isaac said to Jacob, "Please come closer so I can touch you, my son. Are you really my son Esau or not?"

22 So Jacob came closer to his father Isaac. When he touched him, he said, "The voice is the voice of Jacob, but the hands are the hands of Esau." **23** He did not recognize him, because his hands were hairy like those of his brother Esau; so he blessed him. **24** Again he asked, "Are you really my son Esau?"

And he replied, "I am."

25 Then he said, "Bring it closer to me, and let me eat some of my son's game so that I can bless you." Jacob brought it closer to him, and he ate; he brought him wine, and he drank.

26 Then his father Isaac said to him, "Please come closer and kiss me, my son." **27** So he came closer and kissed him. When Isaac smelled^A his clothes, he blessed him and said:

Ah, the smell of my son
is like the smell of a field
that the LORD has blessed.
28 May God give to you —
from the dew of the sky
and from the richness of the land —
an abundance of grain and new wine.
29 May peoples serve you
and nations bow in worship to you.
Be master over your relatives;
may your mother's sons bow in worship
to you.
Those who curse you will be cursed,
and those who bless you will be blessed.

30 As soon as Isaac had finished blessing Jacob and Jacob had left the presence of his father Isaac, his brother Esau arrived from his hunting. **31** He had also made some delicious food and brought it to his father. He said to his father, "Let my father get up and eat some of his son's game, so that you may bless me."

32 But his father Isaac said to him, "Who are you?"

He answered, "I am Esau your firstborn son."

33 Isaac began to tremble uncontrollably. "Who was it then," he said, "who hunted game and brought it to me? I ate it all before you came in, and I blessed him. Indeed, he will be blessed!"

34 When Esau heard his father's words, he cried out with a loud and bitter cry and said to his father, "Bless me too, my father!"

35 But he replied, "Your brother came deceitfully and took your blessing."

36 So he said, "Isn't he rightly named Jacob?^B For he has cheated me twice now. He took my birthright, and look, now he has taken my blessing." Then he asked, "Haven't you saved a blessing for me?"

37 But Isaac answered Esau, "Look, I have made him a master over you, have given him all of his relatives as his servants, and have sustained him with grain and new wine. What then can I do for you, my son?"

38 Esau said to his father, "Do you have only one blessing, my father? Bless me too, my father!" And Esau wept loudly.^C

39 His father Isaac answered him,

Look, your dwelling place will be
away from the richness of the land,

---

^A**27:27** Lit *smelled the smell of*   ^B**27:36** = He Grasps the Heel   ^C**27:38** Lit *Esau lifted up his voice and wept*

---

and Jacob agreeing to lie to his father and cheat his brother.

27:18–27a Isaac was blind, but he could still use his other senses in addition to his reasoning. To overcome this, Jacob used at least five different things to deceive his father: goatskins to make his **hands** seem rough and **hairy** (v. 23), the cooked goat his mother prepared (v. 25), his brother's **clothes** in order to smell like Esau (v. 27), alcohol to impair his father's judgment (v. 25), and blatant lies (vv. 19,20,24). He even blasphemously credited **the LORD your God** with helping him.

Jacob's craftiness paid off since his father **blessed** him.

27:27b–29 Isaac's blessing included four elements: agricultural prosperity (v. 28)—even as he had done for Isaac (26:12); international respect and success (27:29); a command directing Jacob to **be master over** the entire clan; and the transference of the protective provision of cursing and blessing that God had once given Jacob's grandfather Abraham (12:3).

27:30–38 Esau complained that Jacob had now **cheated** him **twice**, first gaining the

double portion of inheritance (25:31–33), and now the clan's headship. **Jacob** (Hb *ya'aqov*), whose name sounds similar to words meaning "deceitfulness" (Hb *'aqevah*) and "to supplant/replace" (Hb *'aqav*), had lived up to his name. Having lost every desirable blessing, Esau begged his father to find some way to **bless** him, **too**.

27:39–40 Isaac's response to Esau was much shorter than Jacob's blessing (21 vs. 34 Hebrew words), and was more of an "anti-blessing." Creating an ironic wordplay with phrases from Jacob's blessing (v. 28), Isaac

away from the dew of the sky above.
40 You will live by your sword,
and you will serve your brother.
But when you rebel,^A
you will break his yoke from your neck.

Esau's Anger

41 Esau held a grudge against Jacob because of the blessing his father had given him. And Esau determined in his heart, "The days of mourning for my father are approaching; then I will kill my brother Jacob."

42 When the words of her older son Esau were reported to Rebekah, she summoned her younger son Jacob and said to him, "Listen, your brother Esau is consoling himself by planning to kill you. **43** So now, my son, listen to me. Flee at once to my brother Laban in Haran, **44** and stay with him for a few days until your brother's anger subsides — **45** until your brother's rage turns away from you and he forgets what you have done to him. Then I will send for you and bring you back from there. Why should I lose you both in one day?"

46 So Rebekah said to Isaac, "I'm sick of my life because of these Hethite girls. If Jacob marries someone from around here,^B like these Hethite girls, what good is my life?"

Jacob's Departure

28 So Isaac summoned Jacob, blessed him, and commanded him, "Do not marry a Canaanite girl. **2** Go at once to Paddan-aram, to the house of Bethuel, your mother's father. Marry one of the daughters of Laban, your mother's brother. **3** May God Almighty bless you and make you fruitful and multiply you so that you become an assembly of peoples. **4** May God give you and your offspring the blessing of Abraham so that you may possess the land where you live as a foreigner, the land God gave to Abraham." **5** So Isaac sent Jacob to Paddan-aram, to Laban son of Bethuel the Aramean, the brother of Rebekah, the mother of Jacob and Esau.

6 Esau noticed that Isaac blessed Jacob and sent him to Paddan-aram to get a wife there. When he blessed him, Isaac commanded Jacob, "Do not marry a Canaanite girl." **7** And Jacob listened to his father and mother and went to Paddan-aram. **8** Esau realized that his father Isaac disapproved of the Canaanite women, **9** so Esau went to Ishmael and married, in addition to his other wives, Mahalath daughter of Ishmael, Abraham's son. She was the sister of Nebaioth.

Jacob at Bethel

10 Jacob left Beer-sheba and went toward Haran. **11** He reached a certain place and spent the night there because the sun had set. He took one of the stones from the place, put it there at his head, and lay down in that place. **12** And he dreamed: A stairway was set on the ground with its top reaching the sky, and God's angels were going up and down on it. **13** The LORD was standing there beside him,^C saying, "I am the LORD, the God of your father Abraham and the God of Isaac. I will give you and your offspring the land on which you are lying. **14** Your offspring will be like the dust of the earth, and you will spread out toward the west, the east, the north, and the south. All the peoples on earth will be blessed through you and your offspring. **15** Look, I am with you and will watch over you wherever you go. I will bring you back to this land, for I will not leave you until I have done what I have promised you."

16 When Jacob awoke from his sleep, he said, "Surely the LORD is in this place, and I did not know it." **17** He was afraid and said, "What an awesome place this is! This is none other than the house of God. This is the gate of heaven."

18 Early in the morning Jacob took the stone that was near his head and set it up as a marker. He poured oil on top of it **19** and named the place Bethel,^D though previously the city was named Luz. **20** Then Jacob made a vow: "If God will be with me and watch over me during this

---

^A 27:40 Hb obscure ^B 27:46 Lit *someone like these daughters of the land* ^C 28:13 Or *there above it* ^D 28:19 = House of God

---

stated that Esau would live **away from the richness of the land** and **from the dew of the sky**. Jacob would "be master" (v. 29), but Esau would **serve**. Living a life of violence by the sword, Esau's only consolation was that he would someday **break** Jacob's **yoke from** his **neck**.

27:41–46 For a second time in this chapter, Rebekah intervened to change Jacob's destiny. Her latest plan was for Jacob to **stay with** his uncle **Laban in Haran**—hundreds of miles away—until Esau's **anger** subsided. The **few days**, however, turned out to be more than twenty years (31:38).

28:1–2 As with Abraham in the previous generation, Isaac was concerned that his youngest son not **marry a Canaanite girl** (lit "daughters of Canaan"; cp. 24:3).

28:3–5 Before Jacob's departure Isaac extended to him two major covenant blessings:

offspring and **land**. The blessing of being **fruitful** was previously given to Adam (1:28), Noah and his sons (9:1,7), Abraham (17:6), and Ishmael (17:20). Isaac invoked it using the name *El Shaddai* (**God Almighty**), a name first revealed to Abraham (17:1; see note there). The second blessing was possession of **the land God gave to Abraham**, a blessing that only God could give.

28:6–9 When **Esau noticed** that **his father Isaac disapproved** of the two **Canaanite women** he had married (26:34), he added to them, taking his cousin **Mahalath daughter of Ishmael** as a third wife. Mahalath was also known as Basemath (36:3). Mahalath's brother **Nebaioth** was Ishmael's firstborn son (1Ch 1:29).

28:10–15 Jacob started northward on the approximately five-hundred-mile journey to **Haran**. At the end of one of his first days he

stopped in central Palestine and camped outdoors. That night God appeared to him. Perhaps the **stairway** (a better translation than "ladder") **he dreamed** of was a supernatural version of humanity's Tower of Babylon (11:4), with **God's angels**—and not sinful humans—using it to commute from heaven to earth. In the dream **the LORD** transferred to Jacob all the essential elements of the promises given originally to Abraham and Isaac.

28:16–19 No other person in the OT is recorded as anointing a sacred stone; Jacob would do it twice (35:14). Jacob renamed the site **Bethel** ("House of God"), a name that would be retained throughout Israelite history (Jdg 1:23; Neh 11:31).

28:20–22 Jacob is the only patriarch to make **a vow**. Years later Jacob would confess that God had indeed kept the terms of his promises (35:3).

journey I'm making, if he provides me with food to eat and clothing to wear, ²¹ and if I return safely to my father's family, then the LORD will be my God. ²² This stone that I have set up as a marker will be God's house, and I will give to you a tenth of all that you give me."

Jacob Meets Rachel

29 Jacob resumed his journey^A and went to the eastern country.^B ² He looked and saw a well in a field. Three flocks of sheep were lying there beside it because the sheep were watered from this well. But a large stone covered the opening of the well. ³ The shepherds would roll the stone from the opening of the well and water the sheep when all the flocks^C were gathered there. Then they would return the stone to its place over the well's opening. ⁴ Jacob asked the men at the well, "My brothers! Where are you from?"

"We're from Haran," they answered.

⁵ "Do you know Laban, Nahor's grandson?" Jacob asked them.

They answered, "We know him."

⁶ "Is he well?" Jacob asked.

"Yes," they said, "and here is his daughter Rachel, coming with his sheep."

⁷ Then Jacob said, "Look, it is still broad daylight. It's not time for the animals to be gathered. Water the flock, then go out and let them graze."

⁸ But they replied, "We can't until all the flocks have been gathered and the stone is rolled from the well's opening. Then we will water the sheep."

⁹ While he was still speaking with them, Rachel came with her father's sheep, for she was a shepherdess. ¹⁰ As soon as Jacob saw his uncle Laban's daughter Rachel with his sheep,^D he went up and rolled the stone from the opening and watered his uncle Laban's sheep. ¹¹ Then Jacob kissed Rachel and wept loudly.^E ¹² He told Rachel that he was her father's relative, Rebekah's son. She ran and told her father.

Jacob Deceived

¹³ When Laban heard the news about his sister's son Jacob, he ran to meet him, hugged him, and kissed him. Then he took him to his house, and Jacob told him all that had happened. ¹⁴ Laban said to him, "Yes, you are my own flesh and blood."^F

After Jacob had stayed with him a month, ¹⁵ Laban said to him, "Just because you're my relative, should you work for me for nothing? Tell me what your wages should be."

¹⁶ Now Laban had two daughters: the older was named Leah, and the younger was named Rachel. ¹⁷ Leah had tender eyes, but Rachel was shapely and beautiful. ¹⁸ Jacob loved Rachel, so he answered Laban, "I'll work for you seven years for your younger daughter Rachel."

¹⁹ Laban replied, "Better that I give her to you than to some other man. Stay with me." ²⁰ So Jacob worked seven years for Rachel, and they seemed like only a few days to him because of his love for her.

²¹ Then Jacob said to Laban, "Since my time is complete, give me my wife, so I can sleep with^G her." ²² So Laban invited all the men of the place and sponsored a feast. ²³ That evening, Laban took his daughter Leah and gave her to Jacob, and he slept with her. ²⁴ And Laban gave his slave Zilpah to his daughter Leah as her slave.

²⁵ When morning came, there was Leah! So he said to Laban, "What have you done to me? Wasn't it for Rachel that I worked for you? Why have you deceived me?"

²⁶ Laban answered, "It is not the custom in our country to give the younger daughter in marriage before the firstborn. ²⁷ Complete this week of wedding celebration, and we will also give you this younger one in return for working yet another seven years for me."

²⁸ And Jacob did just that. He finished the week of celebration, and Laban gave him his daughter Rachel as his wife. ²⁹ And Laban gave his slave Bilhah to his daughter Rachel as her slave. ³⁰ Jacob slept with Rachel also, and indeed, he loved Rachel more than Leah. And he worked for Laban another seven years.

Jacob's Sons

³¹ When the LORD saw that Leah was neglected, he opened her womb; but Rachel was unable to conceive. ³² Leah conceived, gave birth

---

^29:1 Lit Jacob picked up his feet ^B 29:1 Lit the land of the children of the east ^C 29:3 Sam, some LXX mss read flocks and the shepherds ^D 29:10 Lit with the sheep of Laban his mother's brother ^E 29:11 Lit and he lifted his voice and wept ^F 29:14 Lit my bone and my flesh ^G 29:21 Lit can go to

29:7–12 Jacob's actions contrasted sharply with those of the local shepherds. Inspired by the appearance of Rachel, Jacob rolled the heavy stone from the well's opening all by himself. His act of watering his uncle Laban's sheep is reminiscent of his mother's act of watering Abraham's camels years earlier (24:20). Rachel is the first shepherdess of the Bible (cp. Ex 2:16); the task of shepherding flocks was usually given to men. The first mention in the Bible of a man kissing a woman occurs in Gn 29:11; such actions were not normally performed in public. 29:13–20 In the ancient Near East, a male kissing another male in greeting signified acceptance of and respect for the other person (27:27; 45:15; Ex 18:7; 1Sm 10:1). Laban called Jacob my own flesh and blood and gave him the right to stay in the home permanently. It was agreed that Jacob would work for seven years for the right to marry Rachel. 29:21–24 Jacob, now almost fifty years old (25:24–26; 26:34–35; 27:46) after working for Laban seven years, informed Laban that it was time for him to sleep with Rachel. Arranging a week-long wedding feast, Laban proceeded to cheat the family member who had cheated other people in the past (27:12–25,36). Instead of the expected younger daughter Rachel, Laban gave Leah to Jacob. In the darkness of the evening and with his bride concealed behind a veil (24:65), Jacob did not realize she wasn't the one. Accordingly, he slept with Leah. 29:31–35 In a society where a woman's prestige depended almost entirely on her success in bearing sons, the Lord gave Leah four sons before she temporarily (31:17) stopped having children. Three themes

to a son, and named him Reuben,^A^ for she said, "The LORD has seen my affliction; surely my husband will love me now."

^33^ She conceived again, gave birth to a son, and said, "The LORD heard that I am neglected and has given me this son also." So she named him Simeon.^B^

^34^ She conceived again, gave birth to a son, and said, "At last, my husband will become attached to me because I have borne three sons for him." Therefore he was named Levi.^C^

^35^ And she conceived again, gave birth to a son, and said, "This time I will praise the LORD." Therefore she named him Judah.^D^ Then Leah stopped having children.

30 When Rachel saw that she was not bearing Jacob any children, she envied her sister. "Give me sons, or I will die!" she said to Jacob.

^2^ Jacob became angry with Rachel and said, "Am I in the place of God? He has withheld offspring^E^ from you!"

^3^ Then she said, "Here is my maid Bilhah. Go sleep with her, and she'll bear children for me^F^ so that through her I too can build a family." ^4^ So Rachel gave her slave Bilhah to Jacob as a wife, and he slept with her. ^5^ Bilhah conceived and bore Jacob a son. ^6^ Rachel said, "God has vindicated me; yes, he has heard me and given me a son," so she named him Dan.^G^

^7^ Rachel's slave Bilhah conceived again and bore Jacob a second son. ^8^ Rachel said, "In my wrestlings with God,^H^ I have wrestled with my sister and won," and she named him Naphtali.^I^

^9^ When Leah saw that she had stopped having children, she took her slave Zilpah and gave her to Jacob as a wife. ^10^ Leah's slave Zilpah bore Jacob a son. ^11^ Then Leah said, "What good fortune!"^J^ and she named him Gad.^K^

^12^ When Leah's slave Zilpah bore Jacob a second son, ^13^ Leah said, "I am happy that the women call me happy," so she named him Asher.^L^

^14^ Reuben went out during the wheat harvest and found some mandrakes in the field. When he brought them to his mother Leah, Rachel asked, "Please give me some of your son's mandrakes."

^15^ But Leah replied to her, "Isn't it enough that you have taken my husband? Now you also want to take my son's mandrakes?"

"Well then," Rachel said, "he can sleep with you tonight in exchange for your son's mandrakes."

^16^ When Jacob came in from the field that evening, Leah went out to meet him and said, "You must come with me, for I have hired you with my son's mandrakes." So Jacob slept with her that night.

^17^ God listened to Leah, and she conceived and bore Jacob a fifth son. ^18^ Leah said, "God has rewarded me for giving my slave to my husband," and she named him Issachar.^M^

^19^ Then Leah conceived again and bore Jacob a sixth son. ^20^ "God has given me a good gift," Leah said. "This time my husband will honor me because I have borne six sons for him," and she named him Zebulun.^N^ ^21^ Later, Leah bore a daughter and named her Dinah.

^22^ Then God remembered Rachel. He listened to her and opened her womb. ^23^ She conceived and bore a son, and she said, "God has taken away my disgrace." ^24^ She named him Joseph^O^ and said, "May the LORD add another son to me."

Jacob's Flocks Multiply

^25^ After Rachel gave birth to Joseph, Jacob said to Laban, "Send me on my way so that I can return to my homeland. ^26^ Give me my wives and my children that I have worked for, and let me go. You know how hard I have worked for you."

---

^A^ **29:32** = See, a Son; in Hb, the name *Reuben* sounds like "has seen my affliction." ^B^ **29:33** In Hb, the name *Simeon* sounds like "has heard." ^C^ **29:34** In Hb, the name *Levi* sounds like "attached to." ^D^ **29:35** In Hb, the name *Judah* sounds like "praise." ^E^ **30:2** Lit *the fruit of the womb* ^F^ **30:3** Lit *bear on my knees* ^G^ **30:6** In Hb, the name *Dan* sounds like "has vindicated," or "has judged." ^H^ **30:8** Or *"With mighty wrestlings* ^I^ **30:8** In Hb, the name *Naphtali* sounds like "my wrestling." ^J^ **30:11** Alt Hb tradition, LXX, Vg read *"Good fortune has come!"* ^K^ **30:11** = Good Fortune ^L^ **30:13** = Happy ^M^ **30:18** In Hb, the name *Issachar* sounds like "reward." ^N^ **30:20** In Hb, the name *Zebulun* sounds like "honored." ^O^ **30:24** = He Adds

---

are present in Leah's remarks: her conviction that God provided these children in response to her **affliction** and **neglected** condition, her hope that the births would cause her **husband** to **love** her, and her **praise** to the **LORD** for what he had done.

30:1–8 Rachel's extreme unhappiness created serious tensions in the marriage. Jacob reminded her that it was God, not he, who had **withheld offspring** (lit "fruit of a womb") from her. Partial relief came through the practice of surrogate motherhood as Rachel gave Jacob her **maid Bilhah** so she could **bear children** "upon [Rachel's] knees" **for me**. The phrase suggests that the adoption process involved placing the newborn child on the adopting mother's knees (50:23).

30:9–13 Leah, who had once used her fertility to try to win her husband's love, now resorted to the desperate act of giving **her slave** to **Jacob as a** surrogate **wife** to produce additional sons. Leah signaled their adoption by being the one who named them. **30:14–21** During the late springtime **harvest**, Leah's oldest son Reuben found some wild **mandrakes**. A plant possessing tuberous roots resembling human torsos, the mandrake was thought to enhance one's sexual powers and fertility. Leah, still lonely and desperate for her husband's affection, bartered some of the mandrakes with Jacob's favorite wife Rachel for the right to sleep with Jacob for a night. Because **God listened to Leah**—and not because of the mandrakes—**she conceived and bore** a fifth

son, **Issachar**. When Leah **bore Jacob a sixth son . . . Zebulun**—her last—she gave **God** the credit. Jacob's only named daughter, **Dinah**, would play a tragic role in chap. 34. **30:22–24** For the third time in Genesis **God** is said to have **remembered** someone (cp. 8:1; 19:21), an event that always indicates the onset of a beneficial act by God. In this case he gave Rachel her firstborn **son . . . Joseph**, whose name (Hb *yoseph*) is actually a verb that expressed Rachel's prayerful hopes— "May he [**the LORD**] add" another son. **30:25–36** Jacob, now with a dozen children and four wives but very little else, demanded release from his responsibilities in Laban's household so he could return to his **homeland**, where he would be the head of a wealthy clan. Laban's wealth had

²⁷ But Laban said to him, "If I have found favor with you, stay. I have learned by divination that the Lord has blessed me because of you." ²⁸ Then Laban said, "Name your wages, and I will pay them."

²⁹ So Jacob said to him, "You know how I have served you and how your herds have fared with me. ³⁰ For you had very little before I came, but now your wealth has increased. The Lord has blessed you because of me. And now, when will I also do something for my own family?"

³¹ Laban asked, "What should I give you?"

And Jacob said, "You don't need to give me anything. If you do this one thing for me, I will continue to shepherd and keep your flock. ³² Let me go through all your sheep today and remove every sheep that is speckled or spotted, every dark-colored sheep among the lambs, and the spotted and speckled among the female goats. Such will be my wages. ³³ In the future when you come to check on my wages, my honesty will testify for me. If I have any female goats that are not speckled or spotted, or any lambs that are not black, they will be considered stolen."

³⁴ "Good," said Laban. "Let it be as you have said."

³⁵ That day Laban removed the streaked and spotted male goats and all the speckled and spotted female goats — every one that had any white on it — and every dark-colored one among the lambs, and he placed his sons in charge of them. ³⁶ He put a three-day journey between himself and Jacob. Jacob, meanwhile, was shepherding the rest of Laban's flock.

³⁷ Jacob then took branches of fresh poplar, almond, and plane wood, and peeled the bark, exposing white stripes on the branches. ³⁸ He set the peeled branches in the troughs in front of the sheep — in the water channels where the sheep came to drink. And the sheep bred when they came to drink. ³⁹ The flocks bred in front of the branches and bore streaked, speckled, and spotted young. ⁴⁰ Jacob separated the

lambs and made the flocks face the streaked sheep and the completely dark sheep in Laban's flocks. Then he set his own stock apart and didn't put them with Laban's sheep. ⁴¹ Whenever the stronger of the flock were breeding, Jacob placed the branches in the troughs, in full view of the flocks, and they would breed in front of the branches. ⁴² As for the weaklings of the flocks, he did not put out the branches. So it turned out that the weak sheep belonged to Laban and the stronger ones to Jacob. ⁴³ And the man became very rich.ᴬ He had many flocks, female and male slaves, and camels and donkeys.

Jacob Separates from Laban

31 Now Jacob heard what Laban's sons were saying: "Jacob has taken all that was our father's and has built this wealth from what belonged to our father." ² And Jacob saw from Laban's face that his attitude toward him was not the same as before.

³ The Lord said to him, "Go back to the land of your ancestors and to your family, and I will be with you."

⁴ Jacob had Rachel and Leah called to the field where his flocks were. ⁵ He said to them, "I can see from your father's face that his attitude toward me is not the same as before, but the God of my father has been with me. ⁶ You know that with all my strength I have served your father ⁷ and that he has cheated me and changed my wages ten times. But God has not let him harm me. ⁸ If he said, 'The spotted sheep will be your wages,' then all the sheep were born spotted. If he said, 'The streaked sheep will be your wages,' then all the sheep were born streaked. ⁹ God has taken away your father's herds and given them to me.

¹⁰ "When the flocks were breeding, I saw in a dream that the streaked, spotted, and speckled males were mating with the females. ¹¹ In that dream the angel of God said to me, 'Jacob!' and I said, 'Here I am.' ¹² And he said, 'Look up

---

ᴬ **30:43** Lit *The man spread out very much, very much*

---

increased because **the Lord** had **blessed** him through Jacob, just as the Lord had promised (28:14). Laban, who had **learned by** the abominable practice of **divination** (Lv 19:26) that God had **blessed** him **because of** Jacob, realized the great advantages of keeping Jacob around, so he offered to **pay** Jacob whatever **wages** his son-in-law would **name**.

Jacob asked for two things: the right to **continue to shepherd** Laban's **flock**, and all of Laban's sheep and goats that had rare and unusual markings. Laban readily agreed to the terms and virtually assured Jacob's financial failure by removing from the flocks every animal that possessed the traits Jacob had specified. To guarantee that Jacob could not use them, he drove them **a three-day journey**—forty to fifty miles—away and put **his** own **sons in charge of them**.

30:37–43 Jacob began a six-year effort (31:41) to increase his wealth at Laban's expense. During that time he used at least three different techniques to make the flocks produce sheep and goats he could keep: (1) he separated the strong animals from the weak, using only the strong ones for his breeding purposes; (2) he **set . . . peeled branches . . . in the water channels** where the sheep bred; and (3) he **made the flocks face the streaked . . . and . . . completely dark sheep in Laban's flocks**. Though the latter two practices have no scientific value, God himself (31:7–8,42) and the angel of God (31:11–12) caused Jacob to become **very rich**.

31:1–3 Jacob's overwhelming success created deep resentment in **Laban's sons**; their father's loss meant less inheritance for them. It also changed Laban's **attitude** to the point where Jacob no longer felt welcome. As the

situation deteriorated, **the Lord** gave Jacob a command and a promise: he was to return to his clan and to the land promised to his grandfather (12:7).

31:4–16 Jacob presented Rachel and Leah with three reasons for making a major move away from the only home they had ever known to a land they had never seen: (1) their father Laban had an unfavorable **attitude toward** Jacob; (2) Laban was unethical in business, having **cheated** Jacob and **changed** his **wages ten times**—almost every time a new generation of sheep and goats was born (there would have been about fourteen breeding cycles for sheep in six years); and (3) most important of all, the God who had **taken** their **father's herds and given them** to Jacob had now ordered him to **return to** his **native land . . . Rachel and Leah** were agreeable to the idea since

and see: all the males that are mating with the flocks are streaked, spotted, and speckled, for I have seen all that Laban has been doing to you. ¹³ I am the God of Bethel, where you poured oil on the stone marker and made a solemn vow to me. Get up, leave this land, and return to your native land.' "

¹⁴ Then Rachel and Leah answered him, "Do we have any portion or inheritance in our father's family? ¹⁵ Are we not regarded by him as outsiders? For he has sold us and has certainly spent our purchase price. ¹⁶ In fact, all the wealth that God has taken away from our father belongs to us and to our children. So do whatever God has said to you."

¹⁷ So Jacob got up and put his children and wives on the camels. ¹⁸ He took all the livestock and possessions he had acquired in Paddan-aram, and he drove his herds to go to the land of Canaan, to his father Isaac. ¹⁹ When Laban had gone to shear his sheep, Rachel stole her father's household idols. ²⁰ And Jacob deceived ᴬ Laban the Aramean, not telling him that he was fleeing. ²¹ He fled with all his possessions, crossed the Euphrates, and headed for ᴮ the hill country of Gilead.

Laban Overtakes Jacob

²² On the third day Laban was told that Jacob had fled. ²³ So he took his relatives with him, pursued Jacob for seven days, and overtook him in the hill country of Gilead. ²⁴ But God came to Laban the Aramean in a dream at night. "Watch yourself! " God warned him. "Don't say anything to Jacob, either good or bad."

²⁵ When Laban overtook Jacob, Jacob had pitched his tent in the hill country, and Laban and his relatives also pitched their tents in the hill country of Gilead. ²⁶ Laban said to Jacob, "What have you done? You have deceived me and taken my daughters away like prisoners of war! ²⁷ Why did you secretly flee from me, deceive me, and not tell me? I would have sent you away with joy and singing, with tambourines and lyres, ²⁸ but you didn't even let me kiss my grandchildren and my daughters. You have

acted foolishly. ²⁹ I could do you great harm, but last night the God of your father said to me, 'Watch yourself! Don't say anything to Jacob, either good or bad.' ³⁰ Now you have gone off because you long for your father's family — but why have you stolen my gods? "

³¹ Jacob answered, "I was afraid, for I thought you would take your daughters from me by force. ³² If you find your gods with anyone here, he will not live! Before our relatives, point out anything that is yours and take it." Jacob did not know that Rachel had stolen the idols.

³³ So Laban went into Jacob's tent, Leah's tent, and the tents of the two concubines, ᶜ but he found nothing. When he left Leah's tent, he went into Rachel's tent. ³⁴ Now Rachel had taken Laban's household idols, put them in the saddlebag of the camel, and sat on them. Laban searched the whole tent but found nothing. ³⁵ She said to her father, "Don't be angry, my lord, that I cannot stand up in your presence; I am having my period." So Laban searched, but could not find the household idols.

Jacob's Covenant with Laban

³⁶ Then Jacob became incensed and brought charges against Laban. "What is my crime? " he said to Laban. "What is my sin, that you have pursued me? ³⁷ You've searched all my possessions! Have you found anything of yours? ᴰ Put it here before my relatives and yours, and let them decide between the two of us. ³⁸ I've been with you these twenty years. Your ewes and female goats have not miscarried, and I have not eaten the rams from your flock. ³⁹ I did not bring you any of the flock torn by wild beasts; I myself bore the loss. You demanded payment from me for what was stolen by day or by night. ⁴⁰ There I was — the heat consumed me by day and the frost by night, and sleep fled from my eyes. ⁴¹ For twenty years in your household I served you — fourteen years for your two daughters and six years for your flocks — and you have changed my wages ten times! ⁴² If the God of my father, the God of Abraham, the Fear of Isaac, had not been with me, certainly now you would have sent me off empty-handed. But

ᴬ31:20 Lit And he stole the heart of　ᴮ31:21 Lit and set his face to　ᶜ31:33 Lit servants　ᴰ31:37 Lit What have you found from all of the possessions of your house?

their father had treated them like "foreigners" (**outsiders**).
31:17–21 Though he had left twenty years earlier alone and with no possessions, Jacob now returned with a family and an abundance of property. Even as Jacob "stole the heart of" (**deceived**) Laban by leaving secretly, his wife **Rachel** had also stolen **her father's household idols** (Hb *teraphim*). The group **crossed the Euphrates** in what is now Syria, then **headed** south for **Gilead** (part of modern Jordan).
31:22–30 Learning of Jacob's secret departure, Laban gathered a posse and set out to catch the group. Laban intended to harm

Jacob, probably because he believed Jacob had **stolen** his household **gods**, but **the God of** Jacob's **father** kept the promise of protection made twenty years earlier (28:15) and **warned** Laban **in a dream** not to harm Jacob.
31:31–35 Ignorant of what his favorite wife Rachel had done, Jacob promised death for the person possessing Laban's household **gods**. As shrewd and deceptive as her father Laban, Rachel prevented him from checking the saddlebags by claiming she was **having** her monthly **period**. During that phase of a woman's monthly cycle, anything she sat on became ceremonially

unclean and was not to be touched by others (Lv 15:26).
31:36–43 Jacob unleashed a torrent of pent-up anger at **Laban**, noting seven ways in which he had helped his father-in-law and labored selflessly on his behalf. Then Jacob confessed that Yahweh, **the God of** his grandfather **Abraham**, alternately known as **the Fear of Isaac** (vv. 42 and 53 are the only use of this term in the Bible), was Jacob's **affliction**, protected him from financial ruin, and **issued** a **verdict** on his behalf. In response, Laban expressed his disgust by insisting that **everything** Jacob had was rightfully his.

God has seen my affliction and my hard work,^ and he issued his verdict last night."

43 Then Laban answered Jacob, "The daughters are my daughters; the children, my children; and the flocks, my flocks! Everything you see is mine! But what can I do today for these daughters of mine or for the children they have borne? **44** Come now, let's make a covenant, you and I. Let it be a witness between the two of us."

45 So Jacob picked out a stone and set it up as a marker. **46** Then Jacob said to his relatives, "Gather stones." And they took stones and made a mound, then ate there by the mound. **47** Laban named the mound Jegar-sahadutha, but Jacob named it Galeed.^

48 Then Laban said, "This mound is a witness between you and me today." Therefore the place was called Galeed **49** and also Mizpah,^ for he said, "May the LORD watch between you and me when we are out of each other's sight. **50** If you mistreat my daughters or take other wives, though no one is with us, understand that God will be a witness between you and me." **51** Laban also said to Jacob, "Look at this mound and the marker I have set up between you and me. **52** This mound is a witness and the marker is a witness that I will not pass beyond this mound to you, and you will not pass beyond this mound and this marker to do me harm. **53** The God of Abraham, and the gods of Nahor — the gods of their father^ — will judge between us." And Jacob swore by the Fear of his father Isaac. **54** Then Jacob offered a sacrifice on the mountain and invited his relatives to eat a meal. So they ate a meal and spent the night on the mountain. **55** Laban got up early in the morning, kissed his grandchildren and daughters, and blessed them. Then Laban left to return home.

Preparing to Meet Esau

32 Jacob went on his way, and God's angels met him. **2** When he saw them, Jacob said, "This is God's camp." So he called that place Mahanaim.^

3 Jacob sent messengers ahead of him to his brother Esau in the land of Seir, the territory of Edom. **4** He commanded them, "You are to say to my lord Esau, 'This is what your servant Jacob says. I have been staying with Laban and have been delayed until now. **5** I have oxen, donkeys, flocks, and male and female slaves. I have sent this message to inform my lord, in order to seek your favor.'"

6 When the messengers returned to Jacob, they said, "We went to your brother Esau; he is coming to meet you — and he has four hundred men with him." **7** Jacob was greatly afraid and distressed; he divided the people with him into two camps, along with the flocks, herds, and camels. **8** He thought, "If Esau comes to one camp and attacks it, the remaining one can escape."

9 Then Jacob said, "God of my father Abraham and God of my father Isaac, the LORD who said to me, 'Go back to your land and to your family, and I will cause you to prosper,' **10** I am unworthy of all the kindness and faithfulness you have shown your servant. Indeed, I crossed over the Jordan with my staff, and now I have become two camps. **11** Please rescue me from my brother Esau, for I am afraid of him; otherwise, he may come and attack me, the mothers, and their children. **12** You have said, 'I will cause you to prosper, and I will make your offspring like the sand of the sea, too numerous to be counted.'"

13 He spent the night there and took part of what he had brought with him as a gift for his brother Esau: **14** two hundred female goats, twenty male goats, two hundred ewes, twenty rams, **15** thirty milk camels with their young, forty cows, ten bulls, twenty female donkeys, and ten male donkeys. **16** He entrusted them to his slaves as separate herds and said to them, "Go on ahead of me, and leave some distance between the herds."

17 And he told the first one, "When my brother Esau meets you and asks, 'Who do you belong to? Where are you going? And whose animals are these ahead of you?' **18** then tell him, 'They belong to your servant Jacob. They are a gift sent to my lord Esau. And look, he is behind us.'"

19 He also told the second one, the third, and everyone who was walking behind the animals, "Say the same thing to Esau when you find him. **20** You are also to say, 'Look, your servant Jacob is right behind us.'" For he thought, "I want to appease Esau with the gift that is going ahead of me. After that, I can face him, and perhaps he will forgive me."

---

^**31:42** Lit *and the work of my hands* ^**31:47** *Jegar-sahadutha* is Aramaic, and *Galeed* is Hb; both names = Mound of Witness ^**31:49** = Watchtower ^**31:53** Two Hb mss, LXX omit *the gods of their father* ^**32:2** = Two Camps

31:44–55 To end the dispute, Laban proposed that he and Jacob **make a covenant** that would bring peace and a separation between the Israelite (Jacob's) and the Aramean (Laban's) branches of the Terah clan. **32:1–2** For the second time while on a journey, Jacob saw **God's angels** (cp. 28:12). As before, he named the place where he encountered them. In this case he called it **Mahanaim**, "Two Camps," probably in recognition of the fact that both people and angels were at the same location. **32:3–12** Remembering Esau's death threats from twenty years earlier (27:41–42), Jacob now made a special effort to gain Esau's favor with the assistance of messengers. The first prong of his strategy was verbal: Jacob had the messengers call Esau **lord** and himself **your servant**, thus honoring Esau's position as firstborn. Jacob also made sure he was the first to initiate contact between the brothers, **in order to seek** Esau's **favor**.

To prepare for the coming confrontation with his brother, Jacob did two things: first, **he divided** his group in two so at least some of his people could **escape** if necessary; second, he offered a prayer with three elements: an admission that he was **unworthy of** the many blessings God had given him, a prayer

²¹ So the gift was sent on ahead of him while he remained in the camp that night. ²² During the night Jacob got up and took his two wives, his two slave women, and his eleven sons, and crossed the ford of Jabbok. ²³ He took them and sent them across the stream, along with all his possessions.

Jacob Wrestles with God

²⁴ Jacob was left alone, and a man wrestled with him until daybreak. ²⁵ When the man saw that he could not defeat him, he struck Jacob's hip socket as they wrestled and dislocated his hip. ²⁶ Then he said to Jacob, "Let me go, for it is daybreak."

But Jacob said, "I will not let you go unless you bless me."

²⁷ "What is your name?" the man asked.

"Jacob," he replied.

²⁸ "Your name will no longer be Jacob," he said. "It will be Israelᴬ because you have struggled with God and with men and have prevailed."

²⁹ Then Jacob asked him, "Please tell me your name."

But he answered, "Why do you ask my name?" And he blessed him there.

³⁰ Jacob then named the place Peniel,ᴮ "For I have seen God face to face," he said, "yet my life has been spared." ³¹ The sun shone on him as he passed by Penuelᶜ — limping because of his hip. ³² That is why, still today, the Israelites don't eat the thigh muscle that is at the hip socket: because he struck Jacob's hip socket at the thigh muscle.ᴰ

Jacob Meets Esau

33 Now Jacob looked up and saw Esau coming toward him with four hundred men. So he divided the children among Leah, Rachel, and the two slave women. ² He put the slaves and their children first, Leah and her children next, and Rachel and Joseph last. ³ He himself went on ahead and bowed to the ground seven times until he approached his brother.

⁴ But Esau ran to meet him, hugged him, threw his arms around him, and kissed him. Then they wept. ⁵ When Esau looked up and

---

ᴬ**32:28** In Hb, the name *Israel* sounds like "he struggled (with) God."   ᴮ**32:30** = Face of God   ᶜ**32:31** Variant of *Peniel*   ᴰ**32:32** Or *tendon*

---

for **rescue**, and a reminder of God's promises to **prosper** and multiply Jacob.

32:22–23 As a final measure of self-protection that **night**, Jacob put one more barrier between himself and Esau, moving his family and possessions across the **Jabbok**, a westward-flowing tributary emptying into the Jordan River fifteen miles north of the Dead Sea.

32:24–30 Now Jacob experienced his third and final encounter with God while on a journey (cp. v. 1; 27:12–15). **A man**, understood by later Israelites to be God or an angel possessing the authority of God (Hs 12:3–4), **wrestled with** the elderly patriarch **until daybreak**. The fight ended when the divine being **dislocated** Jacob's **hip**. Jacob, injured but still unwilling to release his grip on the being, demanded that he **bless** him. Asserting his authority over Jacob, the man changed Jacob's name to **Israel** (Hb *yisra'el*), linking the name with the fact that the patriarch had **struggled** (Hb *sarah*) **with God** (Hb *'el*), as well as **with men**, and had **prevailed**.

Jacob was the third person to be renamed by God, joining Abraham and Sarah (17:5,15). The renamed man now renamed the place **Peniel**—or "**Penuel**"—literally "the face of God."

33:1–3 Following his transforming encounter with God, Jacob went from hiding behind his wives and children (32:22–23) to boldly taking the lead in protecting his family. In a display of respect unparalleled in the Bible, Jacob **bowed** down to Esau **seven times** as he approached.

33:4–11 The once-estranged brothers **hugged** . . . **kissed**, and **wept** together in gracious reunion. Esau, who had three wives and five sons (36:2–5), inquired about Jacob's family. Each of the mothers approached Esau with **their children** and respectfully **bowed down**. The fact that **Joseph** was the only named son in the group and was mentioned ahead of his mother foreshadows his leading role in later narratives.

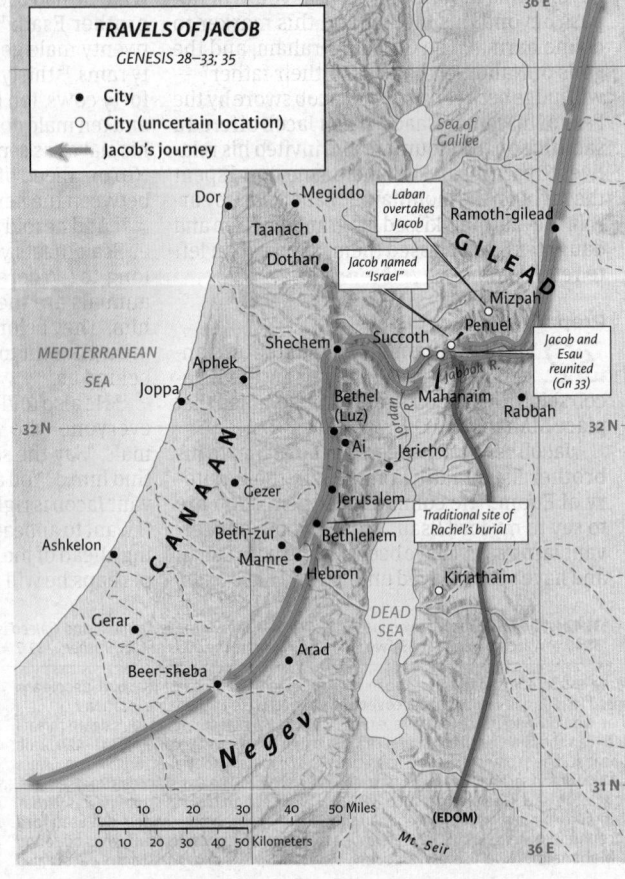

TRAVELS OF JACOB
GENESIS 28–33; 35

- ● City
- ○ City (uncertain location)
- ◀ Jacob's journey

saw the women and children, he asked, "Who are these with you?"

He answered, "The children God has graciously given your servant." [6] Then the slaves and their children approached him and bowed down. [7] Leah and her children also approached and bowed down, and then Joseph and Rachel approached and bowed down.

[8] So Esau said, "What do you mean by this whole procession[A] I met?"

"To find favor with you, my lord," he answered.

[9] "I have enough, my brother," Esau replied. "Keep what you have."

[10] But Jacob said, "No, please! If I have found favor with you, take this gift from me. For indeed, I have seen your face, and it is like seeing God's face, since you have accepted me. [11] Please take my present that was brought to you, because God has been gracious to me and I have everything I need." So Jacob urged him until he accepted.

[12] Then Esau said, "Let's move on, and I'll go ahead of you."

[13] Jacob replied, "My lord knows that the children are weak, and I have nursing flocks and herds. If they are driven hard for one day, the whole herd will die. [14] Let my lord go ahead of his servant. I will continue on slowly, at a pace suited to the livestock and the children, until I come to my lord at Seir."

[15] Esau said, "Let me leave some of my people with you."

But he replied, "Why do that? Please indulge me,[B] my lord."

[16] That day Esau started on his way back to Seir, [17] but Jacob went to Succoth. He built a house for himself and shelters for his livestock; that is why the place was called Succoth.[C] [18] After Jacob came from Paddan-aram, he arrived safely at Shechem in the land of Canaan and camped in front of the city. [19] He purchased a section of the field where he had pitched his tent from the sons of Hamor, Shechem's father, for a hundred pieces of silver.[D] [20] And he set up an altar there and called it God, the God of Israel.[E]

Dinah Defiled

34 Leah's daughter Dinah, whom Leah bore to Jacob, went out to see some of the young women of the area. [2] When Shechem — son of Hamor the Hivite, who was the region's chieftain — saw her, he took her and raped her. [3] He became infatuated with Jacob's daughter Dinah. He loved the young girl and spoke tenderly to her.[F] [4] "Get me this girl as a wife," he told his father.

[5] Jacob heard that Shechem had defiled his daughter Dinah, but since his sons were with his livestock in the field, he remained silent until they returned. [6] Meanwhile, Shechem's father Hamor came to speak with Jacob. [7] Jacob's sons returned from the field when they heard about the incident. They were deeply grieved and very angry, for Shechem had committed an outrage against Israel by raping Jacob's daughter, and such a thing should not be done.

[8] Hamor said to Jacob's sons, "My son Shechem has his heart set on your[G] daughter. Please give her to him as a wife. [9] Intermarry with us; give your daughters to us, and take our daughters for yourselves. [10] Live with us. The land is before you. Settle here, move about, and acquire property in it."

[11] Then Shechem said to Dinah's father and brothers, "Grant me this favor,[H] and I'll give you whatever you say. [12] Demand of me a high compensation[I] and gift; I'll give you whatever you ask me. Just give the girl to be my wife!"

[13] But Jacob's sons answered Shechem and his father Hamor deceitfully because he had defiled their sister Dinah. [14] "We cannot do this thing," they said to them. "Giving our sister to an uncircumcised man is a disgrace to us. [15] We will agree with you only on this condition: if

---

[A] 33:8 Lit *camp*   [B] 33:15 Lit *May I find favor in your eyes*   [C] 33:17 = Stalls or Huts   [D] 33:19 Lit *100 qesitahs*; the value of this currency is unknown   [E] 33:20 = El-Elohe-Israel   [F] 34:3 Lit *spoke to her heart*   [G] 34:8 The Hb word for *your* is pl, showing that Hamor is speaking to Jacob and his sons.   [H] 34:11 Lit *"May I find favor in your eyes*   [I] 34:12 Or *bride-price*, or *betrothal present*

Though Esau encouraged Jacob to keep what animals he had earlier sent ahead, Jacob insisted that Esau **take** the **gift** as a confirmation that the younger brother had **found favor with** him.
33:12–15 To compensate Jacob for his generous gift, Esau offered to provide companionship ("let us go"; **let's move on**), leadership (**I'll go ahead**), and—with the assistance of his four hundred men—protection to Jacob's group for the remainder of the journey. Jacob respectfully declined the offer, calling his brother **my lord**, but suggesting that he needed to travel alone. Jacob's mention of following Esau to **Seir** might have been a mere social convention or another example of Jacob's intentional obfuscation. Jacob may have eventually traveled to Seir on his way to Shechem. In

any event, the brothers agreed not to live in the same region (36:6–7).
33:16–17 Esau went south **to Seir**, a forested mountainous region east of the Dead Sea, while Jacob's group traveled a few miles north to settle at **Succoth** (Hb for "Temporary Shelters"), named for the temporary facilities Jacob constructed **for his livestock**. The Bible does not indicate that Jacob and Esau met again until they buried their father many years later (35:29).
33:18–20 Jacob's journey ended when he **arrived safely at Shechem**, where his grandfather Abraham had first lived when he entered Canaan (12:6). Jacob intended to live permanently in the land promised to him by God (28:13), so he **purchased a section** of land in front of Shechem from **the sons of Hamor**, including his son Shechem, whose

name matched the city's name. The price of **a hundred pieces of silver** represents an unknown quantity. Like Abraham and Isaac before him (12:8; 13:18; 22:9; 26:25), Jacob also **set up an altar**, naming it *El-Elohe-Israel*, **God, the God of Israel**.
34:1–7 Shechem, one of the previous owners of the property on which Dinah now lived, **saw her**, forcefully **took her**, and then **raped** ("humbled") **her**. The fact that **he loved her**, **spoke tenderly to her**, and even ordered his father to **get** that **girl** for him to take **as a wife** suggests that Shechem was following Hivite customs in his treatment of Dinah, though what he did **should not be done** in Israelite society.
34:13–18 In an outrageous misuse of the sacred rite of circumcision (Gn 17:9–14), **Jacob's sons** stated that they could only **give** their

all your males are circumcised as we are. ¹⁶ Then we will give you our daughters, take your daughters for ourselves, live with you, and become one people. ¹⁷ But if you will not listen to us and be circumcised, then we will take our daughter and go."

¹⁸ Their words seemed good to Hamor and his son Shechem. ¹⁹ The young man did not delay doing this, because he was delighted with Jacob's daughter. Now he was the most important in all his father's family. ²⁰ So Hamor and his son Shechem went to the gate of their city and spoke to the men of their city.

²¹ "These men are peaceful toward us," they said. "Let them live in our land and move about in it, for indeed, the region is large enough for them. Let's take their daughters as our wives and give our daughters to them. ²² But the men will agree to live with us and be one people only on this condition: if all our men are circumcised as they are. ²³ Won't their livestock, their possessions, and all their animals become ours? Only let's agree with them, and they will live with us."

²⁴ All the men who had come to the city gates listened to Hamor and his son Shechem, and all those men were circumcised. ²⁵ On the third day, when they were still in pain, two of Jacob's sons, Simeon and Levi, Dinah's brothers, took their swords, went into the unsuspecting city, and killed every male. ²⁶ They killed Hamor and his son Shechem with their swords, took Dinah from Shechem's house, and went away. ²⁷ Jacob's sons came to the slaughter and plundered the city because their sister had been defiled. ²⁸ They took their flocks, herds, donkeys, and whatever was in the city and in the field. ²⁹ They captured all their possessions, dependents, and wives and plundered everything in the houses.

³⁰ Then Jacob said to Simeon and Levi, "You have brought trouble on me, making me odious to the inhabitants of the land, the Canaanites and the Perizzites. We are few in number; if they unite against me and attack me, I and my household will be destroyed." ³¹ But they answered, "Should he treat our sister like a prostitute?"

Return to Bethel

35 God said to Jacob, "Get up! Go to Bethel and settle there. Build an altar there to the God who appeared to you when you fled from your brother Esau."

² So Jacob said to his family and all who were with him, "Get rid of the foreign gods that are among you. Purify yourselves and change your clothes. ³ We must get up and go to Bethel. I will build an altar there to the God who answered me in my day of distress. He has been with me everywhere I have gone."

⁴ Then they gave Jacob all their foreign gods and their earrings, and Jacob hid them under the oak near Shechem. ⁵ When they set out, a terror from God came over the cities around them, and they did not pursue Jacob's sons. ⁶ So Jacob and all who were with him came to Luz (that is, Bethel) in the land of Canaan. ⁷ Jacob built an altar there and called the place El-bethel^A because it was there that God had revealed himself to him when he was fleeing from his brother.

⁸ Deborah, the one who had nursed and raised Rebekah,^B died and was buried under the oak south of Bethel. So Jacob named it Allon-bacuth.^C

^A^35:7 = God of Bethel   ^B^35:8 Lit *Deborah, Rebekah's wet nurse*; Gn 24:59   ^C^35:8 = Oak of Weeping

daughters—and their sister Dinah—away in marriage to men who had been **circumcised**. **34:19–24** As the future prince over the region, Shechem had great influence over the citizens of the village bearing his name. Meeting with the men at **the gate of their city**, where people gathered to share news and consider proposals, Shechem and Hamor provided the men with four reasons to establish a treaty with Jacob's sons, ratifying it with circumcision. **34:25–29** While the men of Shechem **were still in pain**, immobilized and recovering from the removal of their foreskins with flint knives, they were murdered by **Simeon and Levi**, two of Jacob's four sons who had the same mother (Leah) as Dinah. After killing **Shechem**, they took Dinah from his house. When Jacob's other adult sons learned of it, they **plundered the city**, using the excuse that **their sister had been defiled**. The Hivite **dependents** and **wives** they stole would possibly have been sold to slave traders (37:27–28). **34:30–31** Upon learning of the outrageous actions of **Simeon and Levi**, Jacob condemned them. Their deeds had not only

brought death to the Hivites, they had **brought trouble on** their father as well. Jacob's reputation for being a man of peace (v. 21) had now been destroyed. Simeon and Levi would later be cursed by their father (49:5–7) because of their horrific crime. **35:1–5** In Jacob's time of trouble **God** called **Jacob** back **to Bethel**, the spot where he had first met God. There Jacob was to **build** a more formal **altar** to **God** than the marker he had left there twenty years earlier (28:22). God's command in Gn 35:1 represents the only time in Genesis that he ordered an altar be built. The patriarch ordered **his family and all who were with him** to prepare themselves for an encounter with the living God.

This preparation involved three things: first, getting **rid of the foreign gods** among them. Laban's household idols (31:19) as well as possible Hivite idols acquired in the raid on Shechem (34:29) were among the items that Jacob buried **under the oak near Shechem**. Second, the people were to **purify** themselves, a command that normally involved washing the body and clothing (Ex 19:10; 30:19–21; Lv 16:26), as well as avoidance of sexual contact since seminal emissions

created temporary ritual uncleanness (Lv 15:16–18). Third, they were to **change** their **clothes** (Lv 6:10–11). **35:6–8** At **Bethel**, known to the Canaanites as **Luz**, Jacob built **El-bethel** (God of Bethel), his second named altar (33:20). Bethel's nurse **Deborah** (see 24:59 and note at 24:54–61), a woman who probably was like a beloved second mother to Jacob, **died** at Bethel. Her death, along with Isaac's in v. 28, marked the passing of a generation. **35:9–15** God's final recorded words to Jacob came as he spoke to him for the second time (cp. v. 1) since the patriarch returned from **Paddan-aram**. In this proclamation the Lord revealed himself as **God Almighty** (Hb *El Shaddai*), a name for God revealed first to Abraham (17:1; see note there) and later known to Isaac (28:3). The twenty-six Hebrew words in God's speech reaffirm promises previously made to Jacob (cp. 28:13).

At the same time God **blessed** Jacob with words that enlarged previously given promises. For the first time also it is stated that **kings** and **an assembly of nations** would come from the patriarch. After the revelatory words, **God** "went up" (**withdrew**) from the

⁹ God appeared to Jacob again after he returned from Paddan-aram, and he blessed him. ¹⁰ God said to him, "Your name is Jacob; you will no longer be named Jacob, but your name will be Israel." So he named him Israel. ¹¹ God also said to him, "I am God Almighty. Be fruitful and multiply. A nation, indeed an assembly of nations, will come from you, and kings will descend from you.ᴬ ¹² I will give to you the land that I gave to Abraham and Isaac. And I will give the land to your future descendants." ¹³ Then God withdrewᴮ from him at the place where he had spoken to him.

¹⁴ Jacob set up a marker at the place where he had spoken to him — a stone marker. He poured a drink offering on it and poured oil on it. ¹⁵ Jacob named the place where God had spoken with him Bethel.

Rachel's Death

¹⁶ They set out from Bethel. When they were still some distance from Ephrath, Rachel began to give birth, and her labor was difficult. ¹⁷ During her difficult labor, the midwife said to her, "Don't be afraid, for you have another son." ¹⁸ With her last breath — for she was dying — she named him Ben-oni,ᶜ but his father called him Benjamin.ᴰ ¹⁹ So Rachel died and was buried on the way to Ephrath (that is, Bethlehem). ²⁰ Jacob set up a marker on her grave; it is the marker at Rachel's grave still today.

Israel's Sons

²¹ Israel set out again and pitched his tent beyond the Tower of Eder.ᴱ ²² While Israel was living in that region, Reuben went in and slept with his father's concubine Bilhah, and Israel heard about it.

Jacob had twelve sons:
²³   Leah's sons were Reuben
        (Jacob's firstborn),
        Simeon, Levi, Judah,
        Issachar, and Zebulun.

²⁴   Rachel's sons were
        Joseph and Benjamin.
²⁵   The sons of Rachel's slave Bilhah
        were Dan and Naphtali.
²⁶   The sons of Leah's slave Zilpah
        were Gad and Asher.
These are the sons of Jacob, who were born to him in Paddan-aram.

Isaac's Death

²⁷ Jacob came to his father Isaac at Mamre in Kiriath-arba (that is, Hebron), where Abraham and Isaac had stayed. ²⁸ Isaac lived 180 years. ²⁹ He took his last breath and died, and was gathered to his people, old and full of days. His sons Esau and Jacob buried him.

Esau's Family

36 These are the family records of Esau (that is, Edom). ² Esau took his wives from the Canaanite women: Adah daughter of Elon the Hethite, Oholibamah daughter of Anah and granddaughterᶠ of Zibeon the Hivite, ³ and Basemath daughter of Ishmael and sister of Nebaioth. ⁴ Adah bore Eliphaz to Esau, Basemath bore Reuel, ⁵ and Oholibamah bore Jeush, Jalam, and Korah. These were Esau's sons, who were born to him in the land of Canaan.

⁶ Esau took his wives, sons, daughters, and all the people of his household, as well as his herds, all his livestock, and all the property he had acquired in Canaan; he went to a land away from his brother Jacob. ⁷ For their possessions were too many for them to live together, and because of their herds, the land where they stayed could not support them. ⁸ So Esau (that is, Edom) lived in the mountains of Seir.

⁹ These are the family records of Esau, father of the Edomites in the mountains of Seir.
¹⁰   These are the names of Esau's sons:
        Eliphaz son of Esau's wife Adah,
        and Reuel son of Esau's wife Basemath.

ᴬ35:11 Lit *will come from your loins*   ᴮ35:13 Lit *went up*   ᶜ35:18 = Son of My Sorrow   ᴰ35:18 = Son of the Right Hand
ᴱ35:21 Or *beyond Migdal-eder*   ᶠ36:2 Sam, LXX read *Anah son*

place. To memorialize the event and bring closure to his vow to make Yahweh his God (28:21), Jacob set up **a stone marker**, pouring **a drink offering on it** (2Sm 23:16) and **oil**. **35:16–20** While Jacob's clan was making a fifteen-mile journey to **Ephrath, Rachel**—now pregnant with her second child—**began to give birth**. As her **son** was being born she apparently began hemorrhaging. Before she died **she named** her son **Ben-oni**, meaning "son of my sorrow." However, to make sure that his wife's dying gift to him would be properly remembered, Jacob renamed the child **Benjamin**, meaning "right-hand son," the most honored son. Jacob also **set up a marker** at Rachel's burial site in the Bethlehem area. **35:21–22** The disgusting character of another of Jacob's sons—this time his firstborn **Reuben**—was revealed **beyond the Tower of**

Eder, a spot probably situated southwest of Bethlehem. Reuben **slept** with **Bilhah**, the mother of his half brothers Dan and Naphtali. By doing this Reuben was asserting his right to take his father's place as leader of the group (2Sm 12:8,11; 16:21–22). His father learned of it and later cursed Reuben because of it (Gn 49:3–4). **35:27–29** Jacob moved his family to stay with **his father Isaac**, who was living near the family burial cave at **Mamre** in the vicinity of **Hebron**. Isaac would live for many more years, dying at the age of **180** and being buried by **Esau and Jacob** in the family cave of Machpelah (49:31). **36:1–8 The family records of Esau**, the ninth and shortest of the eleven (Hb) *toledoth* sections in Genesis (see note at 5:1), consists only of 36:1–8. This section complements the *toledoth* section of vv. 9–43,

which also contains family records of Esau, in that this emphasizes the "Canaan" portion of Esau's life. Esau, whose nickname was **Edom** (cp. 25:30), moved his family and property to Edom, whose primary feature is **the mountains of Seir**. **36:9 The family records of Esau, father of the Edomites**, the tenth of the (Hb) *toledoth* sections in Genesis (see note at 5:1), consists of 36:9–43. This section, which repeats the genealogical information of vv. 1–5, differs from the previous *toledoth* unit in that it provides five major subsections that focus on historical and genealogical details relevant to Edom. **36:10–14** These verses contain the first of five subsections found in the second Esau (Hb) *toledoth*, and it expands on vv. 4–5. This section supplements previous materials with a listing of six sons born to Adah's son

11 The sons of Eliphaz were Teman, Omar, Zepho, Gatam, and Kenaz.

12 Timna, a concubine of Esau's son Eliphaz, bore Amalek to Eliphaz. These are the sons of Esau's wife Adah.

13 These are Reuel's sons: Nahath, Zerah, Shammah, and Mizzah. These are the sons of Esau's wife Basemath.

14 These are the sons of Esau's wife Oholibamah daughter of Anah and granddaughter[A] of Zibeon: She bore Jeush, Jalam, and Korah to Edom.

15 These are the chiefs among Esau's sons: the sons of Eliphaz, Esau's firstborn: chief Teman, chief Omar, chief Zepho, chief Kenaz,

16 chief Korah,[B] chief Gatam, and chief Amalek. These are the chiefs descended from Eliphaz in the land of Edom. These are the sons of Adah.

17 These are the sons of Reuel, Esau's son: chief Nahath, chief Zerah, chief Shammah, and chief Mizzah. These are the chiefs descended from Reuel in the land of Edom. These are the sons of Esau's wife Basemath.

18 These are the sons of Esau's wife Oholibamah: chief Jeush, chief Jalam, and chief Korah. These are the chiefs descended from Esau's wife Oholibamah daughter of Anah.

19 These are the sons of Esau (that is, Edom), and these are their chiefs.

Seir's Family

20 These are the sons of Seir the Horite, the inhabitants of the land:

21 Lotan, Shobal, Zibeon, Anah, Dishon, Ezer, and Dishan. These are the chiefs among the Horites, the sons of Seir, in the land of Edom.

22 The sons of Lotan were Hori and Heman. Timna was Lotan's sister.

23 These are Shobal's sons: Alvan, Manahath, Ebal, Shepho, and Onam.

24 These are Zibeon's sons: Aiah and Anah. This was the Anah who found the hot springs[C] in the wilderness while he was pasturing the donkeys of his father Zibeon.

25 These are the children of Anah: Dishon and Oholibamah daughter of Anah.

26 These are Dishon's sons: Hemdan, Eshban, Ithran, and Cheran.

27 These are Ezer's sons: Bilhan, Zaavan, and Akan.

28 These are Dishan's sons: Uz and Aran.

29 These are the chiefs among the Horites: chief Lotan, chief Shobal, chief Zibeon, chief Anah,

30 chief Dishon, chief Ezer, and chief Dishan. These are the chiefs among the Horites, clan by clan,[D] in the land of Seir.

Rulers of Edom

31 These are the kings who reigned in the land of Edom before any king reigned over the Israelites:

32 Bela son of Beor reigned in Edom; the name of his city was Dinhabah.

33 When Bela died, Jobab son of Zerah from Bozrah reigned in his place.

34 When Jobab died, Husham from the land of the Temanites reigned in his place.

35 When Husham died, Hadad son of Bedad reigned in his place. He defeated Midian in the field of Moab; the name of his city was Avith.

36 When Hadad died, Samlah from Masrekah reigned in his place.

37 When Samlah died, Shaul from Rehoboth on the Euphrates River reigned in his place.

[A]36:14 Sam, LXX read Anah son [B]36:16 Sam omits Korah [C]36:24 Syr, Vg; Tg reads the mules; Hb obscure [D]36:30 Lit Horites, for their chiefs

---

Eliphaz and four sons descending from Basemath's son Reuel . . . Teman ("South") is the namesake of an important region in southern Edom (Jr 49:20; Ob 9) associated with wisdom (Jr 49:7). Timna was the daughter of Seir the Horite (vv. 20–22); thus, her son Amalek provides an important genealogical link between the Edomites and the Horites.

36:15–19 The second of the four Esau-related subsections contains the chiefs among Esau's sons, listing all of Esau's sons and grandsons in vv. 10–14, but adding a seventh son, Korah, to the listing of Eliphaz's sons. The term translated as "chiefs" (Hb 'alluph) refers to the leader of a familial unit or of a geographical region.

36:20–30 The third subsection of the second Esau (Hb) toledoth comprises the sons and chiefs of Seir the Horite, the father of Eliphaz's concubine Timna.

36:31–39 The fourth subsection of the second Esau (Hb) toledoth lists eight consecutive kings who reigned in the land of Edom prior to the days of King Saul, i.e.,

³⁸ When Shaul died, Baal-hanan son of Achbor reigned in his place. ³⁹ When Baal-hanan son of Achbor died, Hadar^A reigned in his place. His city was Pau, and his wife's name was Mehetabel daughter of Matred daughter of Me-zahab.

⁴⁰ These are the names of Esau's chiefs, according to their families and their localities, by their names: chief Timna, chief Alvah, chief Jetheth, ⁴¹ chief Oholibamah, chief Elah, chief Pinon, ⁴² chief Kenaz, chief Teman, chief Mibzar, ⁴³ chief Magdiel, and chief Iram. These are Edom's chiefs, according to their settlements in the land they possessed. Esau^B was father of the Edomites.

Joseph's Dreams

37 Jacob lived in the land where his father had stayed, the land of Canaan. ² These are the family records of Jacob.

At seventeen years of age, Joseph tended sheep with his brothers. The young man was working with the sons of Bilhah and Zilpah, his father's wives, and he brought a bad report about them to their father. ³ Now Israel loved Joseph more than his other sons because Joseph was a son born to him in his old age, and he made a long-sleeved robe^C for him. ⁴ When his brothers saw that their father loved him more than all his brothers, they hated him and could not bring themselves to speak peaceably to him.

⁵ Then Joseph had a dream. When he told it to his brothers, they hated him even more. ⁶ He said to them, "Listen to this dream I had: ⁷ There we were, binding sheaves of grain in the field. Suddenly my sheaf stood up, and your sheaves gathered around it and bowed down to my sheaf."

⁸ "Are you really going to reign over us?" his brothers asked him. "Are you really going to rule us?" So they hated him even more because of his dream and what he had said. ⁹ Then he had another dream and told it to his brothers. "Look," he said, "I had another dream, and this time the sun, moon, and eleven stars were bowing down to me." ¹⁰ He told his father and brothers, and his father rebuked him. "What kind of dream is this that you have had?" he said. "Am I and your mother and your brothers really going to come and bow down to the ground before you?" ¹¹ His brothers were jealous of him, but his father kept the matter in mind.

Joseph Sold into Slavery

¹² His brothers had gone to pasture their father's flocks at Shechem. ¹³ Israel said to Joseph, "Your brothers, you know, are pasturing the flocks at Shechem. Get ready. I'm sending you to them."

"I'm ready," Joseph replied.

¹⁴ Then Israel said to him, "Go and see how your brothers and the flocks are doing, and bring word back to me." So he sent him from the Hebron Valley, and he went to Shechem.

¹⁵ A man found him there, wandering in the field, and asked him, "What are you looking for?"

¹⁶ "I'm looking for my brothers," Joseph said. "Can you tell me where they are pasturing their flocks?"

¹⁷ "They've moved on from here," the man said. "I heard them say, 'Let's go to Dothan.'" So Joseph set out after his brothers and found them at Dothan.

¹⁸ They saw him in the distance, and before he had reached them, they plotted to kill him. ¹⁹ They said to one another, "Oh, look, here comes that dream expert!^D ²⁰ So now, come on, let's kill him and throw him into one of the pits.^E We can say that a vicious animal ate him. Then we'll see what becomes of his dreams!" ²¹ When Reuben heard this, he tried to save him from them.^F He said, "Let's not take his life."

^A36:39 Many Hb mss, Sam, Syr read *Hadad*   ^B36:43 Lit *He Esau*   ^C37:3 Or *an ornate robe*; see 2Sm 13:18,19   ^D37:19 Lit *comes the lord of the dreams*   ^E37:20 Or *cisterns*   ^F37:21 Lit *their hands*

before 1050 BC. Its inclusion demonstrates the fulfillment of God's promise to Abraham (17:6). **36:40–43** The fifth and final subsection of the second Esau (Hb) *toledoth* consists of a list of eleven of **Esau's chiefs** who ruled over various portions of the land of Edom. This list appears in abbreviated form in 1Ch 1:51b–54. **37:1** In contrast to Esau, who left the land promised to Abraham's descendants, **Jacob** remained in **the land of Canaan**. **37:2–4 The family records of Jacob**, which extend through the end of the book, constitute the eleventh and last of the (Hb) *toledoth* sections in Genesis (see note at 5:1). The account begins with a description

of seventeen-year-old **Joseph**, the central human figure in this section. These opening verses continue the troubled portrait of Jacob's sons begun in chap. 35, as **the sons of Bilhah and Zilpah**—Dan, Naphtali, Gad, and Asher—misbehaved. Jacob's unequal treatment of his sons (cp. 25:28) aroused great jealousy, so Joseph's brothers **hated** him. The **long-sleeved robe** probably marked Joseph as Jacob's chosen successor for clan leadership. **37:5–11** Like his father Jacob (28:12–15; 31:10–13), **Joseph** received two dreams from God during his lifetime. Both portrayed Joseph gaining a position of supremacy in his family, though the symbols differed greatly. The first

dream used an agricultural image (v. 7). The second, more important and wider in scope than the first, was astronomical (vv. 9–10). **37:12–17 Joseph**, who had earlier given a bad report about his older brothers, was once again called upon to report how they were doing. Joseph traveled about fifty miles north **to Shechem**. Learning that his brothers had moved on, he finally found them at **Dothan**, some fifteen miles farther north. **37:18–24** Joseph's older brothers, all of whom hated him and were violent men (34:27–29) or even murderers (34:25–26), immediately **plotted to kill him**, calling him "the lord of the dreams" (**that dream expert**). Being skilled at deception as well

²²Reuben also said to them, "Don't shed blood. Throw him into this pit in the wilderness, but don't lay a hand on him" — intending to rescue him from them and return him to his father. ²³When Joseph came to his brothers, they stripped off Joseph's robe, the long-sleeved robe that he had on. ²⁴Then they took him and threw him into the pit. The pit was empty, without water. ²⁵They sat down to eat a meal, and when they looked up, there was a caravan of Ishmaelites coming from Gilead. Their camels were carrying aromatic gum, balsam, and resin, going down to Egypt. ²⁶Judah said to his brothers, "What do we gain if we kill our brother and cover up his blood? ²⁷Come on, let's sell him to the Ishmaelites and not lay a hand on him, for he is our brother, our own flesh," and his brothers agreed. ²⁸When Midianite traders passed by, his brothers pulled Joseph out of the pit and sold him for twenty pieces of silver to the Ishmaelites, who took Joseph to Egypt.

²⁹When Reuben returned to the pit and saw that Joseph was not there, he tore his clothes. ³⁰He went back to his brothers and said, "The boy is gone! What am I going to do?"^A ³¹So they took Joseph's robe, slaughtered a male goat, and dipped the robe in its blood. ³²They sent the long-sleeved robe to their father and said, "We found this. Examine it. Is it your son's robe or not?"

³³His father recognized it. "It is my son's robe," he said. "A vicious animal has devoured him. Joseph has been torn to pieces!" ³⁴Then Jacob tore his clothes, put sackcloth around his waist, and mourned for his son many days. ³⁵All his sons and daughters tried to comfort him, but he refused to be comforted. "No," he said. "I will go down to Sheol to my son, mourning." And his father wept for him.

³⁶Meanwhile, the Midianites sold Joseph in Egypt to Potiphar, an officer of Pharaoh and the captain of the guards.

Judah and Tamar

38 At that time Judah left his brothers and settled near an Adullamite named Hirah. ²There Judah saw the daughter of a Canaanite named Shua; he took her as a wife and slept with her. ³She conceived and gave birth to a son, and he named him Er. ⁴She conceived again, gave birth to a son, and named him Onan. ⁵She gave birth to another son and named him Shelah. It was at Chezib that^B,C she gave birth to him.

⁶Judah got a wife for Er, his firstborn, and her name was Tamar. ⁷Now Er, Judah's firstborn, was evil in the LORD's sight, and the LORD put him to death. ⁸Then Judah said to Onan, "Sleep with your brother's wife. Perform your duty as her brother-in-law and produce offspring for your brother." ⁹But Onan knew that the offspring would not be his, so whenever he slept with his brother's wife, he released his semen on the ground so that he would not produce offspring for his brother. ¹⁰What he did was evil in the LORD's sight, so he put him to death also.

¹¹Then Judah said to his daughter-in-law Tamar, "Remain a widow in your father's house until my son Shelah grows up." For he thought, "He might die too, like his brothers." So Tamar went to live in her father's house.

¹²After a long time^D Judah's wife, the daughter of Shua, died. When Judah had finished mourning, he and his friend Hirah the Adullamite went up to Timnah to his sheepshearers. ¹³Tamar was told, "Your father-in-law is going up to Timnah to shear his sheep." ¹⁴So she took off her widow's clothes, veiled her face, covered herself, and sat at the entrance to Enaim, which is on the way to Timnah. For she saw that, though Shelah had grown up, she had not been given to him as a wife. ¹⁵When Judah saw her, he thought she was a prostitute, for she had covered her face.

---

^A37:30 Lit And I, where am I going?   ^B38:5 LXX reads She was at Chezib when   ^C38:5 Or He was at Chezib when   ^D38:12 Lit And there were many days, and

---

(34:13), the brothers also concocted the lie that **a vicious animal ate him**. They **threw him into** a dry cistern designed to store water for the flocks. **Reuben** objected to fratricide.

37:25–28 The fact that Joseph's brothers **sat down to eat a meal** soon after they disposed of him reveals how brazenly sinful they were. Judah convinced seven of his brothers that it was more profitable to sell Joseph as a slave than to kill him. According to 42:21, Joseph pleaded with his brothers, but to no avail. They sold him for **twenty pieces of silver**, the standard price for a teenage male slave (Lv 27:5). **Midianite** is another designation for Ishmaelites in this narrative.

37:29–35 Reuben had not been present when his brothers decided to sell Joseph. He was shocked and dismayed when he discovered what had happened. In a traditional ancient Near Eastern show of grief, he **tore his clothes** (cp. v. 34).

Jacob naturally concluded that **a vicious animal** had **torn** Joseph **to pieces**. Thus when confronted with this evidence, **he refused to be comforted**, expressing instead the desire to **go down to Sheol**—the traditional term for the place of the dead—to be with his **son**.

38:1–5 Continuing the dark picture of Jacob's sons begun in chap. 34, Judah rejected the covenant family's marriage tradition (24:3; 28:1) and took **the daughter of a Canaanite . . . as a wife**. The couple conceived three sons, **Er** ("Watchful"), **Onan** ("Strength/Vigorous"), and **Shelah** ("Drawn Out [from the Womb]"). **38:6–11** In keeping with ancient Near Eastern tradition, **Judah got a wife for** his son Er (24:2–4; Ex 2:21; Jdg 4:1–3). The absence of any ethnic identification for Er's wife **Tamar** ("Palm Tree") may mean she was not

a Canaanite. Er died before fathering any children, and ancient Near Eastern custom required the childless widow's **brother-in-law** to marry her and **produce offspring** who would be counted as the deceased male's heir (Dt 25:5–6).

Onan, however, realized **that the offspring would not be his**, so he took a course of action to prevent conception—probably *coitus interruptus*. Onan's motive **was evil in the LORD's sight**, and so God killed him also. With two sons having died while married to Tamar, Judah feared that Shelah might die too if he fulfilled the responsibility to his sister-in-law. Consequently Judah sent her away **to live in her father's house**, with the deceptive excuse that Shelah was not old enough.

38:12–19 Even after **Shelah had grown up** and was eligible for marriage, Tamar remained a widow. In the meantime, **Judah's**

¹⁶ He went over to her and said, "Come, let me sleep with you," for he did not know that she was his daughter-in-law.

She said, "What will you give me for sleeping with me?"

¹⁷ "I will send you a young goat from my flock," he replied.

But she said, "Only if you leave something with me until you send it."

¹⁸ "What should I give you?" he asked.

She answered, "Your signet ring, your cord, and the staff in your hand." So he gave them to her and slept with her, and she became pregnant by him. ¹⁹ She got up and left, then removed her veil and put her widow's clothes back on.

²⁰ When Judah sent the young goat by his friend the Adullamite in order to get back the items he had left with the woman, he could not find her. ²¹ He asked the men of the place, "Where is the cult prostitute who was beside the road at Enaim?"

"There has been no cult prostitute here," they answered.

²² So the Adullamite returned to Judah, saying, "I couldn't find her, and besides, the men of the place said, 'There has been no cult prostitute here.'"

²³ Judah replied, "Let her keep the items for herself; otherwise we will become a laughingstock. After all, I did send this young goat, but you couldn't find her."

²⁴ About three months later Judah was told, "Your daughter-in-law, Tamar, has been acting like a prostitute, and now she is pregnant."

"Bring her out," Judah said, "and let her be burned to death!"

²⁵ As she was being brought out, she sent her father-in-law this message: "I am pregnant by the man to whom these items belong." And she added, "Examine them. Whose signet ring, cord, and staff are these?"

²⁶ Judah recognized them and said, "She is more in the right^A than I, since I did not give her to my son Shelah." And he did not know her intimately again.

²⁷ When the time came for her to give birth, there were twins in her womb. ²⁸ As she was giving birth, one of them put out his hand, and the midwife took it and tied a scarlet thread around it, announcing, "This one came out first." ²⁹ But then he pulled his hand back, out came his brother, and she said, "What a breakout you have made for yourself!" So he was named Perez.^B ³⁰ Then his brother, who had the scarlet thread tied to his hand, came out, and was named Zerah.^C

Joseph in Potiphar's House

39 Now Joseph had been taken to Egypt. An Egyptian named Potiphar, an officer of Pharaoh and the captain of the guards, bought him from the Ishmaelites who had brought him there. ² The LORD was with Joseph, and he became a successful man, serving^D in the household of his Egyptian master. ³ When his master saw that the LORD was with him and that the LORD made everything he did successful, ⁴ Joseph found favor with his master and became his personal attendant. Potiphar also put him in charge of his household and placed all that he owned under his authority.^E ⁵ From the time that he put him in charge of his household and of all that he owned, the LORD blessed the Egyptian's house because of Joseph. The LORD's blessing was on all that he owned, in his house and in his fields. ⁶ He left all that he owned under Joseph's authority;^F he did not concern himself with anything except the food he ate.

---

^A**38:26** Or *more righteous* ^B**38:29** = Breaking Out ^C**38:30** = Brightness of Sunrise; perhaps related to the scarlet thread ^D**39:2** Lit *and he was* ^E**39:4** Lit *owned in his hand* ^F**39:6** Lit *owned in Joseph's hand*

---

wife had **died**. In order to get Judah to fulfill his family's obligation to produce an heir for Er and remove the stigma of her childlessness, Tamar apparently took advantage of her father-in-law's immoral character. She **took off her widow's clothes** (signs of mourning), **veiled her face**, positioned herself alone by **Enaim** ("Two Springs") where she knew Judah would pass, and played the role of a roadside cult prostitute.

Judah did not recognize her and so propositioned her. As proof of his willingness to pay once he had money in hand, Judah had to give Tamar his "cylinder seal" (**signet ring**), among other items. Having achieved her objective by getting pregnant, Tamar returned home and **put her widow's clothes back on** for the time being.

38:20–23 Keeping his promise, **Judah sent** Hirah (v. 1) to the supposed prostitute with a young goat to get back his possessions. When Hirah **returned to Judah** without recovering Judah's possessions, Judah recognized he had been outwitted by her since

his credentials represented his honor and were thus more valuable than a young goat. He attempted to minimize the humiliation by giving up on the search and thus telling no one else what had happened.

38:24–26 Three months after the fateful encounter Judah was informed that his **daughter-in-law** was **pregnant**. Since she had an obligation to remain chaste and available for marriage to Shelah, Shelah's father ordered that she be **burned to death**. Before she could be executed, however, Tamar informed her would-be executioners that she was **pregnant by the man** whose "cylinder seal" (**signet ring**) she possessed. Confronted by indisputable evidence of his responsibility for Tamar's pregnancy, Judah admitted that **she was more** . . . **right** than he; he had wronged her by denying her the right to marry his **son Shelah**.

38:27–30 Six months later it was discovered that Tamar was carrying **twins in her womb**; the language mirrors that of Jacob

and Esau's birth (25:24). The birth was a complicated one, as one of the babies stuck **his hand**—not his head, as is normal—out the birth canal. The child **pulled his hand back** inside the mother.

As it turned out, **his brother** actually came out first, earning himself not only the rights of the firstborn but also the name **Perez** ("Bursting Forth/Breach"). **His brother**, born belatedly with the **scarlet thread** still **tied to his hand**, received the name **Zerah** ("Dawning/Shining"). Perez would later be mentioned as an ancestor of both David (Ru 4:12,18) and Jesus (Mt 1:3).

39:1 This verse, which retraces details presented in 37:36, returns the storyline to **Joseph**.

39:2–6 God's active presence in Joseph's life made him **successful**. Potiphar noticed the teenage Hebrew slave's remarkable effectiveness, and as a result Joseph not only **found favor** with him, but was put in charge of Potiphar's entire **household** as well.

Now Joseph was well-built and handsome. [7] After some time his master's wife looked longingly at Joseph and said, "Sleep with me." [8] But he refused. "Look," he said to his master's wife, "with me here my master does not concern himself with anything in his house, and he has put all that he owns under my authority.[A] [9] No one in this house is greater than I am. He has withheld nothing from me except you, because you are his wife. So how could I do this immense evil, and how could I sin against God?"

[10] Although she spoke to Joseph day after day, he refused to go to bed with her.[B] [11] Now one day he went into the house to do his work, and none of the household servants were there.[C] [12] She grabbed him by his garment and said, "Sleep with me!" But leaving his garment in her hand, he escaped and ran outside. [13] When she saw that he had left his garment with her and had run outside, [14] she called her household servants. "Look," she said to them, "my husband brought a Hebrew man to make fools of us. He came to me so he could sleep with me, and I screamed as loud as I could. [15] When he heard me screaming for help,[D] he left his garment beside me and ran outside."

[16] She put Joseph's garment beside her until his master came home. [17] Then she told him the same story: "The Hebrew slave you brought to us came to make a fool of me, [18] but when I screamed for help,[E] he left his garment beside me and ran outside."

[19] When his master heard the story his wife told him — "These are the things your slave did to me" — he was furious [20] and had him thrown into prison, where the king's prisoners were confined. So Joseph was there in prison.

Joseph in Prison

[21] But the LORD was with Joseph and extended kindness to him. He granted him favor with the prison warden. [22] The warden put all the prisoners who were in the prison under Joseph's authority,[F] and he was responsible for everything that was done there. [23] The warden did not bother with anything under Joseph's authority,[G] because the LORD was with him, and the LORD made everything that he did successful.

Joseph Interprets Two Prisoners' Dreams

40 After this, the king of Egypt's cupbearer and baker offended their master, the king of Egypt. [2] Pharaoh was angry with his two officers, the chief cupbearer and chief baker, [3] and put them in custody in the house of the captain of the guards in the prison where Joseph was confined. [4] The captain of the guards assigned Joseph to them as their personal attendant, and they were in custody for some time.[H]

[5] The king of Egypt's cupbearer and baker, who were confined in the prison, each had a dream. Both had a dream on the same night, and each dream had its own meaning. [6] When Joseph came to them in the morning, he saw that they looked distraught. [7] So he asked Pharaoh's officers who were in custody with him in his master's house, "Why do you look so sad today?"

[8] "We had dreams," they said to him, "but there is no one to interpret them."

Then Joseph said to them, "Don't interpretations belong to God? Tell me your dreams."

[9] So the chief cupbearer told his dream to Joseph: "In my dream there was a vine in front of me. [10] On the vine were three branches. As soon as it budded, its blossoms came out and

---

^**39:8** Lit *owns in my hand*   ^B**39:10** Lit *he did not listen to her to lie beside her, to be with her*   ^C**39:11** Lit *there in the house*
^D**39:15** Lit *he heard that I raised my voice and I screamed*   ^E**39:18** Lit *I raised my voice and screamed*   ^F**39:22** Lit *prison in the hand of Joseph*   ^G**39:23** Lit *anything in his hand*   ^H**40:4** Lit *custody days*

39:7–10 In contrast to his brother Judah, Joseph refused the advances of his master's wife. To commit adultery would have been an **immense evil** and a **sin against God** (cp. Ex 20:14). Potiphar's wife persisted, telling Joseph **day after day** to "lie beside her" (**go to bed with her**).
39:11–15 When the subtle approach failed to seduce Joseph, Potiphar's wife resorted to a more direct method. Finding—or perhaps creating—a situation where **none of the household servants** were in the house, she grabbed Joseph **by his garment** and ordered him to **sleep with her**. In a courageous display of godly self-control, Joseph resisted, **escaped and ran outside** ... **leaving his garment in her hand**. Potiphar's wife then lied to **her household servants**, perhaps playing upon the other slaves' jealousy that had been inflamed when Potiphar placed the Hebrew young man over them as their boss. The presence of Joseph's **garment** seemed like circumstantial evidence for her false claim.

39:16–20 When Potiphar's wife repeated the story to her husband, she framed the lie in a way that placed the blame squarely on him. Her story made Potiphar **furious**. Without investigating the truth of her claims, Potiphar declared Joseph guilty. But instead of killing him, he **had him thrown into prison** (lit "the round house").
39:21–23 **The LORD was with Joseph** in prison. God, who is rich in "faithful love" (**kindness**; Hb *chesed*; see Ex 34:7), demonstrated his love by granting Joseph **favor with the prison warden**. For the third time in his life (cp. v. 4; Gn 37:14), Joseph was given authority over his peers—in this case, **all the prisoners who were in the prison**. Mirroring Potiphar's level of confidence in Joseph, the warden did not "see anything in his hand" (**bother with anything under Joseph's authority**) because **the LORD** caused everything Joseph did to be **successful** (Hb *matsliach*; cp. Ps 1:3 "prospers").
40:1–4 After Joseph had been imprisoned for a number of years and was now

twenty-eight years old (41:1,46), Pharaoh "became furious" (**was angry**; Hb *qatsaph*) with two high-ranking officials (Hb *saris*), **the chief cupbearer and the chief baker**. Joseph, as a young Hebrew slave, was assigned **as their personal attendant**. The officials stayed in prison for "days" (**some time**).
40:5–8 During their confinement the royal cupbearer and baker **both had a dream on the same night**—the third and fourth non-Israelites to have dreams with divinely inspired meanings (cp. Abimelech, 20:3; Laban, 31:24). When they awoke the men were **distraught** (lit their "faces were bad") because there was no professional Egyptian dream interpreter present. Joseph told them that accurate **interpretations belong to God**. And since the Lord was with Joseph even in prison (39:2,21,23), the men were directed to tell their dreams to him.
40:9–15 The chief cupbearer, who was an adviser and security officer for Pharaoh, was the first to tell **his dream to Joseph**.

its clusters ripened into grapes. [11] Pharaoh's cup was in my hand, and I took the grapes, squeezed them into Pharaoh's cup, and placed the cup in Pharaoh's hand."

[12] "This is its interpretation," Joseph said to him. "The three branches are three days. [13] In just three days Pharaoh will lift up your head and restore you to your position. You will put Pharaoh's cup in his hand the way you used to when you were his cupbearer. [14] But when all goes well for you, remember that I was with you. Please show kindness to me by mentioning me to Pharaoh, and get me out of this prison. [15] For I was kidnapped from the land of the Hebrews, and even here I have done nothing that they should put me in the dungeon." [A]

[16] When the chief baker saw that the interpretation was positive, he said to Joseph, "I also had a dream. Three baskets of white bread were on my head. [17] In the top basket were all sorts of baked goods for Pharaoh, but the birds were eating them out of the basket on my head."

[18] "This is its interpretation," Joseph replied. "The three baskets are three days. [19] In just three days Pharaoh will lift up your head — from off you — and hang you on a tree. [B] Then the birds will eat the flesh from your body." [C]

[20] On the third day, which was Pharaoh's birthday, he gave a feast for all his servants. He elevated [D] the chief cupbearer and the chief baker among his servants. [21] Pharaoh restored the chief cupbearer to his position as cupbearer, and he placed the cup in Pharaoh's hand. [22] But Pharaoh hanged [E] the chief baker, just as Joseph had explained to them. [23] Yet the chief cupbearer did not remember Joseph; he forgot him.

Joseph Interprets Pharaoh's Dreams

41 At the end of two years Pharaoh had a dream: He was standing beside the Nile, [2] when seven healthy-looking, well-fed cows came up from the Nile and began to graze among the reeds. [3] After them, seven other cows, sickly and thin, came up from the Nile and stood beside those cows along the bank of

the Nile. [4] The sickly, thin cows ate the healthy, well-fed cows. Then Pharaoh woke up. [5] He fell asleep and dreamed a second time: Seven heads of grain, plump and good, came up on one stalk. [6] After them, seven heads of grain, thin and scorched by the east wind, sprouted up. [7] The thin heads of grain swallowed up the seven plump, full ones. Then Pharaoh woke up, and it was only a dream.

[8] When morning came, he was troubled, so he summoned all the magicians of Egypt and all its wise men. Pharaoh told them his dreams, but no one could interpret them for him.

[9] Then the chief cupbearer said to Pharaoh, "Today I remember my faults. [10] Pharaoh was angry with his servants, and he put me and the chief baker in the custody of the captain of the guards. [11] He and I had dreams on the same night; each dream had its own meaning. [12] Now a young Hebrew, a slave of the captain of the guards, was with us there. We told him our dreams, he interpreted our dreams for us, and each had its own interpretation. [13] It turned out just the way he interpreted them to us: I was restored to my position, and the other man was hanged."

[14] Then Pharaoh sent for Joseph, and they quickly brought him from the dungeon. [A] He shaved, changed his clothes, and went to Pharaoh.

[15] Pharaoh said to Joseph, "I have had a dream, and no one can interpret it. But I have heard it said about you that you can hear a dream and interpret it."

[16] "I am not able to," Joseph answered Pharaoh. "It is God who will give Pharaoh a favorable answer." [F]

[17] So Pharaoh said to Joseph, "In my dream I was standing on the bank of the Nile, [18] when seven well-fed, healthy-looking cows came up from the Nile and grazed among the reeds. [19] After them, seven other cows — weak, very sickly, and thin — came up. I've never seen such sickly ones as these in all the land of Egypt. [20] Then the thin, sickly cows ate the first seven well-fed cows. [21] When they had devoured them, you could not tell that they had

---

[A] 40:15; 41:14 Or pit, or cistern   [B] 40:19 Or and impale you on a pole   [C] 40:19 Lit eat your flesh from upon you   [D] 40:20 Lit He lifted up the head of   [E] 40:22 Or impaled   [F] 41:16 Or "God will answer Pharaoh with peace of mind."

Confident that the interpretation was accurate, Joseph pleaded for the cupbearer to **remember** him, mention him to Pharaoh, and arrange to get him out of prison. However, the cupbearer forgot about Joseph's request (v. 23).

40:16–19 Heartened by Joseph's positive interpretation of the cupbearer's dream, the **chief baker** shared his **dream**. This time the meaning was a dark one: Pharaoh would decapitate the chief baker and hang him on a tree (or possibly "impale" him "on wood"). The birds eating white bread symbolized the birds that would eat the baker's body.

41:1–7 Pharaoh, the most powerful man in the world of his day, was also the Egyptian who received dreams from God that were far-reaching in their implications. His two dreams, both on the same night, had essentially identical plots, though the images were different. Both had fourteen items, seven **healthy** and seven **thin** and **sickly**. In both dreams the seven healthy things appeared first, only to be consumed by the afflicted ones.

41:8–14 These dreams clearly indicated trouble, but exactly what trouble was the question. To unravel the mystery, Pharaoh **summoned all the** court **magicians**, who

would have received instruction from ancient Egyptian scrolls of dream interpretation. Pharaoh also summoned all of Egypt's **wise men** to assist in the critical task of discerning the dreams' meanings. However, **no one could interpret** the dreams satisfactorily.

The crisis caused **the chief cupbearer** to remember how Joseph had accurately interpreted two mysterious dreams two years earlier. Desperate for insight into his own dreams, Pharaoh immediately **sent for Joseph**. Prior to entering the royal court he had to be **shaved**—probably both his beard and scalp—and he put on **clothes** made of linen, as was appropriate for the Egyptian court.

devoured them; their appearance was as bad as it had been before. Then I woke up. [22] In my dream I also saw seven heads of grain, full and good, coming up on one stalk. [23] After them, seven heads of grain — withered, thin, and scorched by the east wind — sprouted up. [24] The thin heads of grain swallowed the seven good ones. I told this to the magicians, but no one can tell me what it means."

[25] Then Joseph said to Pharaoh, "Pharaoh's dreams mean the same thing. God has revealed to Pharaoh what he is about to do. [26] The seven good cows are seven years, and the seven good heads are seven years. The dreams mean the same thing. [27] The seven thin, sickly cows that came up after them are seven years, and the seven worthless heads of grain scorched by the east wind are seven years of famine.

[28] "It is just as I told Pharaoh: God has shown Pharaoh what he is about to do. [29] Seven years of great abundance are coming throughout the land of Egypt. [30] After them, seven years of famine will take place, and all the abundance in the land of Egypt will be forgotten. The famine will devastate the land. [31] The abundance in the land will not be remembered because

of the famine that follows it, for the famine will be very severe. [32] Since the dream was given twice to Pharaoh, it means that the matter has been determined by God, and he will carry it out soon.

[33] "So now, let Pharaoh look for a discerning and wise man and set him over the land of Egypt. [34] Let Pharaoh do this: Let him appoint overseers over the land and take a fifth of the harvest of the land of Egypt during the seven years of abundance. [35] Let them gather all the excess food during these good years that are coming. Under Pharaoh's authority, store the grain in the cities, so they may preserve it as food. [36] The food will be a reserve for the land during the seven years of famine that will take place in the land of Egypt. Then the country will not be wiped out by the famine."

Joseph Exalted

[37] The proposal pleased Pharaoh and all his servants, [38] and he said to them, "Can we find anyone like this, a man who has God's spirit^A in him?" [39] So Pharaoh said to Joseph, "Since God has made all this known to you, there is no one as discerning and wise as you are. [40] You

^A 41:38 Or *the spirit of the gods*, or *a god's spirit*

41:25–32 Joseph prefaced his interpretation with three important insights: first, Pharaoh actually had only one dream (lit "Pharaoh's dream is one"), though it **was given twice** using different symbols. Second, the dream's source was the one true **God** (lit "the God"). Third, it revealed what God was **about to do**.

41:33–36 Joseph advised Pharaoh to take specific steps in preparation for the upcoming fourteen-year cycle of events in order to create a food reserve for the **seven years of famine**.

41:37–46 Joseph's insight into the dream, along with his ability to devise such a prudent plan, convinced Pharaoh that Joseph had **God's spirit in him**. Pharaoh gave Joseph the Egyptian name **Zaphenath-pa-neah** ("Then God Said, 'Let Him Live'") and a wife of high social status. **Asenath** ("She Who Belongs to the Goddess Neith") was the **daughter** of **Potiphera**, a **priest at On** (Heliopolis), the prestigious religious center of solar worship in ancient Egypt. Joseph was

Character profile:
Joseph

Joseph's ten older brothers hated him because their father loved him more than he loved the rest of his children. He lavished attention and gifts on Joseph while the rest of his sons burned with envy.

In this dysfunctional family context, Joseph recounted his dreams in which his entire family bowed down to him. Of course, that made his brothers even angrier.

So one day they got rid of him. They sold Joseph to slave traders who were traveling to Egypt and then made their father think he'd been killed by a wild animal. In Egypt the slave traders sold Joseph to a government official named Potiphar. And Joseph was faced with the prospect of being a lowly servant in a foreign land for the rest of his life.

Joseph didn't curl up into a ball of self-pity. Instead, he worked hard to become the best servant in Potiphar's household. And Potiphar took notice. He recognized Joseph's skills and potential—not to mention the way Joseph's God seemed to bless everything he did—and he put Joseph in charge of his entire household.

That's when Potiphar's wife started taking a romantic interest in Joseph. Unfortunately, when Joseph rebuffed her advances, she accused him of attempted rape. Joseph was thrown into prison.

Joseph truly understood what it feels like to hit rock bottom. He had no one to help him, no hope for release. So what did he do? He worked hard to become a model prisoner. And before long, the warden put him in charge of everything that went on inside the prison.

When Pharaoh's cupbearer and baker were thrown into prison, Joseph befriended them and interpreted their dreams using his God-given skills. Three days later Joseph's predictions came true. When the cupbearer was released from prison, Joseph asked him to put in a good word with Pharaoh. But the cupbearer forgot all about Joseph for two years—until Pharaoh himself had a couple of disturbing dreams.

When no one else could interpret the dreams, the cupbearer finally remembered and suggested Joseph. Pharaoh sent for him immediately. Many people would have wilted under such scrutiny, but not Joseph. Joseph trusted his God.

With confidence he told Pharaoh that his dream meant that there would be seven years of abundance for Egypt followed by seven years of famine. Furthermore, he advised Pharaoh to appoint a wise leader to oversee preparations for the famine. In response Pharaoh gave the job to Joseph, making him second-in-command over all of Egypt.

When the famine hit, people from across the region came to Egypt to buy food. Among them were Joseph's brothers. They didn't recognize Joseph as their sibling, but they did recognize him as the Egyptian official who could save their lives. So they bowed down to him—just like in his dream.

Joseph could have exacted a dark revenge on his brothers for what they'd done to him so many years earlier. Instead, he chose to see God's hand in his circumstances. He recognized that he was in a position to save his family—not to mention Egypt and the surrounding nations—from the famine precisely because of what God had done in his life.

Joseph had no reason for hope in Egypt. Yet he didn't give in to despair, anger, or self-pity. He put his hope in God—who sovereignly sent him to Egypt to preserve life (Gn 45:5).

will be over my house, and all my people will obey your commands.^A Only I, as king,^B will be greater than you." ⁴¹ Pharaoh also said to Joseph, "See, I am placing you over all the land of Egypt." ⁴² Pharaoh removed his signet ring from his hand and put it on Joseph's hand, clothed him with fine linen garments, and placed a gold chain around his neck. ⁴³ He had Joseph ride in his second chariot, and servants called out before him, "Make way!"^C So he placed him over all the land of Egypt. ⁴⁴ Pharaoh said to Joseph, "I am Pharaoh and no one will be able to raise his hand or foot in all the land of Egypt without your permission." ⁴⁵ Pharaoh gave Joseph the name Zaphenath-paneah and gave him a wife, Asenath daughter of Potiphera, priest at On.^D And Joseph went throughout^E the land of Egypt.

Joseph's Administration

⁴⁶ Joseph was thirty years old when he entered the service of Pharaoh king of Egypt. Joseph left Pharaoh's presence and traveled throughout the land of Egypt.

⁴⁷ During the seven years of abundance the land produced outstanding harvests. ⁴⁸ Joseph gathered all the excess food in the land of Egypt during the seven years and put it in the cities. He put the food in every city from the fields around it. ⁴⁹ So Joseph stored up grain in such abundance — like the sand of the sea — that he stopped measuring it because it was beyond measure.

⁵⁰ Two sons were born to Joseph before the years of famine arrived. Asenath daughter of Potiphera, priest at On, bore them to him. ⁵¹ Joseph named the firstborn Manasseh^F and said, "God has made me forget all my hardship and my whole family." ⁵² And the second son he named Ephraim^G and said, "God has made me fruitful in the land of my affliction."

⁵³ Then the seven years of abundance in the land of Egypt came to an end, ⁵⁴ and the seven years of famine began, just as Joseph had said. There was famine in every land, but in the whole land of Egypt there was food. ⁵⁵ When the whole land of Egypt was stricken with famine, the people cried out to Pharaoh for food. Pharaoh told all Egypt, "Go to Joseph and do whatever he tells

you." ⁵⁶ Now the famine had spread across the whole region, so Joseph opened all the storehouses and sold grain to the Egyptians, for the famine was severe in the land of Egypt. ⁵⁷ Every land came to Joseph in Egypt to buy grain, for the famine was severe in every land.

Joseph's Brothers in Egypt

42 When Jacob learned that there was grain in Egypt, he said to his sons, "Why do you keep looking at each other? ² Listen," he went on, "I have heard there is grain in Egypt. Go down there and buy some for us so that we will live and not die." ³ So ten of Joseph's brothers went down to buy grain from Egypt. ⁴ But Jacob did not send Joseph's brother Benjamin with his brothers, for he thought, "Something might happen to him."

⁵ The sons of Israel were among those who came to buy grain, for the famine was in the land of Canaan. ⁶ Joseph was in charge of the country; he sold grain to all its people. His brothers came and bowed down before him with their faces to the ground. ⁷ When Joseph saw his brothers, he recognized them, but he treated them like strangers and spoke harshly to them.

"Where do you come from?" he asked.

"From the land of Canaan to buy food," they replied.

⁸ Although Joseph recognized his brothers, they did not recognize him. ⁹ Joseph remembered his dreams about them and said to them, "You are spies. You have come to see the weakness^H of the land."

¹⁰ "No, my lord. Your servants have come to buy food," they said. ¹¹ "We are all sons of one man. We are honest; your servants are not spies."

¹² "No," he said to them. "You have come to see the weakness of the land."

¹³ But they replied, "We, your servants, were twelve brothers, the sons of one man in the land of Canaan. The youngest is now^I with our father, and one is no longer living."

¹⁴ Then Joseph said to them, "I have spoken:^J 'You are spies!' ¹⁵ This is how you will be tested:

^A 41:40 Lit *will kiss your mouth*   ^B 41:40 Lit *Only the throne I*   ^C 41:43 Or *"Kneel!"*   ^D 41:45 Or *Heliopolis*, also in v. 50   ^E 41:45 Or *Joseph gained authority over*   ^F 41:51 In Hb, the name *Manasseh* sounds like the verb "forget."   ^G 41:52 In Hb, the name *Ephraim* sounds like the word for "fruitful."   ^H 42:9 Lit *nakedness*, also in v. 12   ^I 42:13 Or *today*, also in v. 32   ^J 42:14 Lit *"That which I spoke to you saying:*

now **thirty years old**. He who had spent years in prison now went **throughout the land of Egypt** overseeing a project that would save the lives of untold thousands. **41:47–52** In addition to giving blessing on the harvests, God blessed Joseph's personal life with two sons. Manasseh's name reflected the fact that **God** had helped Joseph **forget** his **hardship** both in Egypt and in his **whole family**. Ephraim's name confessed that **God** had **made** Joseph **fruitful** in a land where he had once been treated as a despised felon.

42:1–5 News of Egypt's willingness to sell **grain** to outsiders reached Jacob. Jacob sent ten of Joseph's brothers out to do the family's work, but he spared a son of his beloved late wife Rachel (Benjamin). Jacob's sons joined a stream of others who came to Egypt **to buy grain**. **42:6–13** When Joseph's older **brothers . . . bowed down before him with their faces to the ground**, they fulfilled Joseph's prophetic dreams (37:7,9). Joseph had not seen his brothers for twenty years, yet **he recognized them** immediately. But

the brothers did not recognize him; as a top Egyptian official Joseph had no hair on his head, wore eye makeup and expensive clothing, and spoke fluent Egyptian.

Joseph devised a test to see if they had changed during the past two decades: he accused them of being **spies** sent to identify **the weakness of the land** (lit "the nakedness of the land"). **42:14–20** As part of his test Joseph threatened to keep nine of the brothers imprisoned, letting one return to Canaan and come back with their **youngest brother** Benjamin.

As surely as Pharaoh lives, you will not leave this place unless your youngest brother comes here. ¹⁶ Send one from among you to get your brother. The rest of you will be imprisoned so that your words can be tested to see if they are true. If they are not, then as surely as Pharaoh lives, you are spies!" ¹⁷ So Joseph imprisoned them together for three days.

¹⁸ On the third day Joseph said to them, "I fear God — do this and you will live. ¹⁹ If you are honest, let one of you^A be confined to the guardhouse, while the rest of you go and take grain to relieve the hunger of your households. ²⁰ Bring your youngest brother to me so that your words can be confirmed; then you won't die." And they consented to this.

²¹ Then they said to each other, "Obviously, we are being punished for what we did to our brother. We saw his deep distress when he pleaded with us, but we would not listen. That is why this trouble has come to us."

²² But Reuben replied, "Didn't I tell you not to harm the boy? But you wouldn't listen. Now we must account for his blood!"^B

²³ They did not realize that Joseph understood them, since there was an interpreter between them. ²⁴ He turned away from them and wept. When he turned back and spoke to them, he took Simeon from them and had him bound before their eyes. ²⁵ Joseph then gave orders to fill their containers with grain, return each man's silver to his sack, and give them provisions for their journey. This order was carried out. ²⁶ They loaded the grain on their donkeys and left there.

The Brothers Return Home

²⁷ At the place where they lodged for the night, one of them opened his sack to get feed for his donkey, and he saw his silver there at the top of his bag. ²⁸ He said to his brothers, "My silver has been returned! It's here in my bag." Their

hearts sank. Trembling, they turned to one another and said, "What has God done to us?"

²⁹ When they reached their father Jacob in the land of Canaan, they told him all that had happened to them: ³⁰ "The man who is the lord of the country spoke harshly to us and accused us of spying on the country. ³¹ But we told him, 'We are honest and not spies. ³² We were twelve brothers, sons of the same^C father. One is no longer living, and the youngest is now with our father in the land of Canaan.' ³³ The man who is the lord of the country said to us, 'This is how I will know if you are honest: Leave one brother with me, take food to relieve the hunger of your households, and go. ³⁴ Bring back your youngest brother to me, and I will know that you are not spies but honest men. I will then give your brother back to you, and you can trade in the country.'"

³⁵ As they began emptying their sacks, there in each man's sack was his bag of silver! When they and their father saw their bags of silver, they were afraid.

³⁶ Their father Jacob said to them, "It's me that you make childless. Joseph is gone, and Simeon is gone. Now you want to take Benjamin. Everything happens to me!"

³⁷ Then Reuben said to his father, "You can kill my two sons if I don't bring him back to you. Put him in my care,^D and I will return him to you."

³⁸ But Jacob answered, "My son will not go down with you, for his brother is dead and he alone is left. If anything happens to him on your journey, you will bring my gray hairs down to Sheol in sorrow."

Decision to Return to Egypt

43 Now the famine in the land was severe. ² When they had used up the grain they had brought back from Egypt, their father said to them, "Go back and buy us a little food."

^42:19 Lit your brothers   ^42:22 Lit Even his blood is being sought!   ^42:32 Lit of our   ^42:37 Lit hand

To give all ten of them a small taste of what they had made him experience, Joseph had them **imprisoned** for **three days**. After their initial "shock probation" Joseph softened his initial conditions, requiring that only **one** of them **be confined to the guardhouse** while the rest returned to Jacob. Before leaving, however, **they consented** to bring Benjamin back to Egypt.

42:21–26 The brothers' harsh treatment in Egypt made it plain to them that they were **being punished** for what they had done to their **brother** twenty years earlier. **Reuben**, eldest of the group and the one who had kept Joseph from being killed by his brothers (37:22), interpreted the current events as a divine accounting for Joseph's **blood**, i.e., his death.

Joseph, whose heart—but not his outward appearance—had been softened toward his brothers by Reuben's comments, understood the words the brothers spoke in Hebrew,

turned away from his brothers, **and wept**. After dismissing his brothers Joseph compassionately provided them not only with **grain** for the family, but returned **each man's silver to his sack** and gave them food for **their journey**. Joseph's act of kindness was probably also meant to test the brothers' character; if they were honest, they would return the money.

42:27–35 Joseph's brothers felt their hearts "depart" (**sank**) when they received this money from him. Worried that they would be pursued as criminals, they trembled in fear of what **God had done to** them. Upon their return home Jacob was greeted by only nine men. The matter worsened when he was told that the brothers were **accused** of **spying**, and the clan could get Simeon back and **trade** for additional food in Egypt only if the men brought back their **youngest brother** Benjamin. Everyone became even more afraid when they found **bags of silver**

in **each man's sack**; now all nine brothers could be imprisoned as thieves if they ever returned to Egypt.

42:36–38 Reduced to despair by his sons' report, Jacob responded by saying, **Everything happens to me!** Jacob's adamant refusal to let Benjamin **go down** with his brothers to Egypt was understandable but irrational, since it meant that the entire clan would die of starvation. **Reuben** now stepped forward to save the clan. He countered his father's fears of losing Benjamin by offering to experience the loss of two of his four sons (Ex 6:14) if anything happened to Benjamin in a return trip to Egypt. If Benjamin died, Reuben would experience a proportionately worse fate than his father. However, Reuben's argument had no effect on Jacob; if Jacob's son should die, it would not make him feel better to kill two of his grandchildren as well.

43:1–10 Two years into **the famine** (cp. 45:6), Jacob's family **had used up the**

³ But Judah said to him, "The man specifically warned us, 'You will not see me again unless your brother is with you.' ⁴ If you will send our brother with us, we will go down and buy food for you. ⁵ But if you will not send him, we will not go, for the man said to us, 'You will not see me again unless your brother is with you.'"

⁶ "Why have you caused me so much trouble?" Israel asked. "Why did you tell the man that you had another brother?"

⁷ They answered, "The man kept asking about us and our family: 'Is your father still alive? Do you have another brother?' And we answered him accordingly. How could we know that he would say, 'Bring your brother here'?"

⁸ Then Judah said to his father Israel, "Send the boy with me. We will be on our way so that we may live and not die — neither we, nor you, nor our dependents. ⁹ I will be responsible for him. You can hold me personally accountable!^ If I do not bring him back to you and set him before you, I will be guilty before you forever. ¹⁰ If we had not delayed, we could have come back twice by now."

¹¹ Then their father Israel said to them, "If it must be so, then do this: Put some of the best products of the land in your packs and take them down to the man as a gift — a little balsam and a little honey, aromatic gum and resin, pistachios and almonds. ¹² Take twice as much silver with you. Return the silver that was returned to you in the top of your bags. Perhaps it was a mistake. ¹³ Take your brother also, and go back at once to the man. ¹⁴ May God Almighty cause the man to be merciful to you so that he will release your other brother and Benjamin to you. As for me, if I am deprived of my sons, then I am deprived."

The Return to Egypt

¹⁵ The men took this gift, double the amount of silver, and Benjamin. They immediately went down to Egypt and stood before Joseph.

¹⁶ When Joseph saw Benjamin with them, he said to his steward, "Take the men to my house. Slaughter an animal and prepare it, for they will eat with me at noon." ¹⁷ The man did as Joseph had said and brought them to Joseph's house.

¹⁸ But the men were afraid because they were taken to Joseph's house. They said, "We have been brought here because of the silver that was returned in our bags the first time. They intend to overpower us, seize us, make us slaves, and take our donkeys." ¹⁹ So they approached Joseph's steward^B and spoke to him at the doorway of the house.

²⁰ They said, "My lord, we really did come down here the first time only to buy food. ²¹ When we came to the place where we lodged for the night and opened our bags of grain, each one's silver was at the top of his bag! It was the full amount of our silver, and we have brought it back with us. ²² We have brought additional silver with us to buy food. We don't know who put our silver in the bags."

²³ Then the steward said, "May you be well. Don't be afraid. Your God and the God of your father must have put treasure in your bags. I received your silver." Then he brought Simeon out to them. ²⁴ The steward brought the men into Joseph's house, gave them water to wash their feet, and got feed for their donkeys. ²⁵ Since the men had heard that they were going to eat a meal there, they prepared their gift for Joseph's arrival at noon. ²⁶ When Joseph came home, they brought him the gift they had carried into the house, and they bowed to the ground before him.

²⁷ He asked if they were well, and he said, "How is your elderly father that you told me about? Is he still alive?"

²⁸ They answered, "Your servant our father is well. He is still alive." And they knelt low and paid homage to him.

²⁹ When he looked up and saw his brother Benjamin, his mother's son, he asked, "Is this your youngest brother that you told me about?" Then he said, "May God be gracious to you, my son." ³⁰ Joseph hurried out because he was overcome with emotion for his brother, and he was about to weep. He went into an inner room and wept there. ³¹ Then he washed

---

^43:9 Lit can seek him from my hand   ^B43:19 Lit approached the one who was over the house

grain purchased by the brothers in Egypt. Jacob, as clan head, ordered nine of his sons to go back to Egypt and buy more food. Judah, Jacob's fourth-born but still the most trusted of his older sons (34:30; 35:22), reminded his father that he must send Benjamin to Egypt in order for the family to buy food. Judah finally convinced his father to let his sons go by using two things. First, his father's own words: they must go so that we may live and not die (cp. 42:2), and second, his willingness to have Jacob hold him personally accountable for Benjamin's well-being.

43:11–14 Jacob realized he had to send Benjamin to Egypt, but to increase the likelihood that his beloved son of Rachel would return safely, he directed his sons to give the Egyptian some of the best products associated with the land of Canaan. Likely hoping that his sons had not actually stolen the money, Jacob had them return the original money, taking twice as much silver as before. Finally, they were to travel with their brother Benjamin, accompanied by a prayer that God Almighty would secure the release of Simeon and Benjamin.

43:25–28 Learning that they were to eat the noon meal—the first meal of the day—with Joseph, the brothers prepared the food gift (v. 11) and then humbly presented it to Joseph (cp. 37:7,9). Then the powerful Egyptian asked them about their elderly father, eliciting a polite response and a second bowing to the ground.

43:29–31 Joseph confirmed the identity of his brother Benjamin, his mother's only other son and therefore his only full brother. Joseph's blessing on Benjamin in the name of God was the first time Joseph blessed one of his brothers. The sight of Benjamin overwhelmed him. To retain his dignity he quickly went into an inner room and wept there. The fact that as an Egyptian official he was wearing eye makeup was probably in part why he washed his face before returning to the room.

his face and came out. Regaining his composure, he said, "Serve the meal."

³² They served him by himself, his brothers by themselves, and the Egyptians who were eating with him by themselves, because Egyptians could not eat with Hebrews, since that is detestable to them. ³³ They were seated before him in order by age, from the firstborn to the youngest. The men looked at each other in astonishment. ³⁴ Portions were served to them from Joseph's table, and Benjamin's portion was five times larger than any of theirs. They drank and became drunk with Joseph.

Joseph's Final Test

44 Joseph commanded his steward, "Fill the men's bags with as much food as they can carry, and put each one's silver at the top of his bag. ² Put my cup, the silver one, at the top of the youngest one's bag, along with the silver for his grain." So he did as Joseph told him.

³ At morning light, the men were sent off with their donkeys. ⁴ They had not gone very far from the city when Joseph said to his steward, "Get up. Pursue the men, and when you overtake them, say to them, 'Why have you repaid evil for good? ⁵ Isn't this the cup that my master drinks from and uses for divination? What you have done is wrong!'"

⁶ When he overtook them, he said these words to them. ⁷ They said to him, "Why does my lord say these things? Your servants could not possibly do such a thing. ⁸ We even brought back to you from the land of Canaan the silver we found at the top of our bags. How could we steal silver or gold from your master's house? ⁹ If it is found with one of us, your servants, he must die, and the rest of us will become my lord's slaves."

¹⁰ The steward replied, "What you have said is right, but only the one who is found to have it will be my slave, and the rest of you will be blameless."

¹¹ So each one quickly lowered his sack to the ground and opened it. ¹² The steward searched, beginning with the oldest and ending with the youngest, and the cup was found in Benjamin's sack. ¹³ Then they tore their clothes, and each one loaded his donkey and returned to the city.

¹⁴ When Judah and his brothers reached Joseph's house, he was still there. They fell to the ground before him. ¹⁵ "What have you done?" Joseph said to them. "Didn't you know that a man like me could uncover the truth by divination?"

¹⁶ "What can we say to my lord?" Judah replied. "How can we plead? How can we justify ourselves? God has exposed your servants' iniquity. We are now my lord's slaves — both we and the one in whose possession the cup was found."

¹⁷ Then Joseph said, "I swear that I will not do this. The man in whose possession the cup was found will be my slave. The rest of you can go in peace to your father."

Judah's Plea for Benjamin

¹⁸ But Judah approached him and said, "My lord, please let your servant speak personally to my lord. Do not be angry with your servant, for you are like Pharaoh. ¹⁹ My lord asked his servants, 'Do you have a father or a brother?' ²⁰ and we answered my lord, 'We have an elderly father and a younger brother, the child of his old age. The boy's brother is dead. He is the only one of his mother's sons left, and his father loves him.' ²¹ Then you said to your servants, 'Bring him to me so that I can see him.' ²² But we said to my lord, 'The boy cannot leave his father. If he were to leave, his father would die.' ²³ Then you said to your servants, 'If your younger brother does not come down with you, you will not see me again.'

²⁴ "This is what happened when we went back to your servant my father: We reported to him the words of my lord. ²⁵ But our father said, 'Go again, and buy us a little food.' ²⁶ We

---

43:32–34 Because of racial and cultural prejudice, the meal was served at two different tables. Food was first brought to Joseph and the rest of **the Egyptians**, who ate at one table, then portions were brought to the table of the Hebrews. As an indication of respect for seniority among these non-Egyptians, the brothers were seated **from the firstborn to the youngest**—a fact that created **astonishment** among them since it would have required a detailed knowledge of the family. Perhaps as a further test of the brothers, **Benjamin's portion was five times larger than any of** the other brothers'. Joseph may have made sure they **became drunk** to loosen the brothers' self-restraint; if they harbored any jealousy or hatred toward Benjamin, Rachel's son, it would be more likely to show.

44:1–2 Joseph secretly put in place the ultimate test of his older brothers, ordering the steward to put Joseph's ceremonial silver cup . . . **at the top** of Benjamin's bag. By watching the other brothers' response to Benjamin's trouble, Joseph would be able to observe firsthand the other brothers' true character.

44:3–13 Joseph then ordered **his steward** to **overtake** the small caravan. Armed with a scripted accusation regarding the ceremonial **cup**, the steward confronted the group. Joseph mentions **divination** as part of the ploy to make the brothers think this is a very valuable cup.

The brothers responded with disbelief and disavowal to the steward's accusation. Quickly mounting a defense, they first provided evidence of their honesty: they had **brought back . . . the silver** found in their **bags** after the first journey. Next they proposed a harsh punishment for any of their number caught with the cup—**he must die**. Finally, they offered the remaining ten of their group as lifelong **slaves**.

Rejecting their excessive offer, the steward indicated that only the guilty party would become his slave. Though the steward gave the innocent brothers permission to return home, they all **returned to the city** in a show of solidarity with Benjamin.

44:14–17 Jacob's most trusted son, Judah, spoke for the group. Bowing **to the ground before** Joseph (cp. 37:7,9), Judah confessed that **God** had **exposed** the men's **iniquity**—a reference to the sins against Joseph more than twenty years earlier (37:18–28). Second, Judah maintained the group's solidarity by indicating that all the brothers, not just Benjamin, would become **my lord's slaves**. Joseph's immediate rejection of the offer would have added more tension to the situation.

44:18–29 Judah's speech, the longest in the Bible by any of Jacob's sons (218 Hebrew words), marks the turning point in the relationship between Joseph and his brothers.

told him, 'We cannot go down unless our younger brother goes with us. If our younger brother isn't with us, we cannot see the man.' ²⁷ Your servant my father said to us, 'You know that my wife bore me two sons. ²⁸ One is gone from me — I said he must have been torn to pieces — and I have never seen him again. ²⁹ If you also take this one from me and anything happens to him, you will bring my gray hairs down to Sheol in sorrow.'

³⁰ "So if I come to your servant my father and the boy is not with us — his life is wrapped up with the boy's life — ³¹ when he sees that the boy is not with us, he will die. Then your servants will have brought the gray hairs of your servant our father down to Sheol in sorrow. ³² Your servant became accountable to my father for the boy, saying, 'If I do not return him to you, I will always bear the guilt for sinning against you, my father.' ³³ Now please let your servant remain here as my lord's slave, in place of the boy. Let him go back with his brothers. ³⁴ For how can I go back to my father without the boy? I could not bear to see the grief that would overwhelm my father."

Joseph Reveals His Identity

45 Joseph could no longer keep his composure in front of all his attendants,ᴬ so he called out, "Send everyone away from me!" No one was with him when he revealed his identity to his brothers. ² But he wept so loudly that the Egyptians heard it, and also Pharaoh's household heard it. ³ Joseph said to his brothers, "I am Joseph! Is my father still living?" But they could not answer him because they were terrified in his presence.

⁴ Then Joseph said to his brothers, "Please, come near me," and they came near. "I am Joseph, your brother," he said, "the one you sold into Egypt. ⁵ And now don't be grieved or angry with yourselves for selling me here, because God sent me ahead of you to preserve life. ⁶ For the famine has been in the land these two years, and there will be five more years without plowing or harvesting. ⁷ God sent me ahead of you to establish you as a remnant within the land and to keep you alive by a great deliverance.ᴮ ⁸ Therefore it was not you who sent me here, but God. He has made me a father to Pharaoh, lord of his entire household, and ruler over all the land of Egypt.

⁹ "Return quickly to my father and say to him, 'This is what your son Joseph says: "God has made me lord of all Egypt. Come down to me without delay. ¹⁰ You can settle in the land of Goshen and be near me — you, your children, and your grandchildren, your flocks, your herds, and all you have. ¹¹ There I will sustain you, for there will be five more years of famine. Otherwise, you, your household, and everything you have will become destitute."' ¹² Look! Your eyes and the eyes of my brother Benjamin can see that I'mᶜ the one speaking to you. ¹³ Tell my father about all my glory in Egypt and about all you have seen. And bring my father here quickly."

¹⁴ Then Joseph threw his arms around his brother Benjamin and wept, and Benjamin wept on his shoulder. ¹⁵ Joseph kissed each of his brothers as he wept,ᴰ and afterward his brothers talked with him.

The Return for Jacob

¹⁶ When the news reached Pharaoh's palace, "Joseph's brothers have come," Pharaoh and his servants were pleased. ¹⁷ Pharaoh said to Joseph, "Tell your brothers, 'Do this: Load your animals and go on back to the land of Canaan. ¹⁸ Get your father and your families, and come

ᴬ45:1 Lit all those standing about him   ᴮ45:7 Or keep alive for you many survivors   ᶜ45:12 Lit that my mouth is   ᴰ45:15 Lit brothers, and he wept over them

In a display of great humility, Judah referred to Joseph on eight occasions as **my lord**, and on twelve occasions referred to himself and members of his clan as **your servants**. After a representation of three contentious conversations—one that the brothers had had with Joseph (vv. 19–23; 42:13–20) and two involving Jacob (vv. 25–29; 42:38; 43:2–7)—Judah said that his father would die of grief if anything happened to Benjamin.
44:30–34 Judah had voluntarily made himself **accountable** to his **father** for the well-being of Benjamin, Rachel's only other son besides Joseph (43:8–9). Now Benjamin, like his older brother Joseph, was on the verge of being made a slave in Egypt. Knowing that he would always **bear the guilt for sinning against** his **father** if Benjamin did not return home, Judah volunteered to **remain** in Egypt as Joseph's **slave**.
45:1–4 Joseph was overwhelmed by Judah's words. Not wishing to lose his dignity before his Egyptian attendants, he ordered everyone but his brothers out of the room. Joseph then released more than twenty years of pent-up emotions, weeping **so loudly that the Egyptians** outside the room **heard it**. Joseph's revelation of his true identity—undoubtedly spoken in Hebrew, not Egyptian—so **terrified** his brothers that they could not **answer** his question about his father's well-being. Violating protocol, Joseph ordered the brothers to **come near** to him so he could speak to them more intimately, this time explicitly identifying himself.
45:5–8 These verses stand as the theological high point of the account of Joseph's life (chaps. 37–50) and one of the most eloquent affirmations in the Bible regarding God's sovereignty in human events. With amazing spiritual maturity Joseph confessed that God had worked beyond the foul intentions of his older brothers to accomplish two vital things: **to preserve life** through Joseph's leadership leading up to and during the seven-year famine, and **to establish** Israel **as a remnant** "on the earth" (**within the land**). Three times Joseph affirmed that it was **God**—not his brothers—who had sent him to Egypt. Therefore the brothers did not need to **be grieved or angry** with themselves. Indeed, God had made Joseph **a father**—a top-level adviser—**to Pharaoh**, and a **ruler over all the land of Egypt.**
45:9–15 Joseph, who had once presented a plan to Pharaoh to save Egypt, now offered a plan to his brothers to save Israel's clan by moving them to Egypt to live in **Goshen** during the five more years of famine that were to come. Goshen was a region in the eastern portion of Egypt's Nile Delta and was also known as "the land of Rameses" (47:11).
45:16–20 Affirming the commands Joseph had given, Pharaoh told him to have his brothers load their animals with food, **go on back** to Jacob in **Canaan**, and then return with their families. New to the set of instructions was Pharaoh's provision of **wagons from the land of Egypt** to transport the weaker members of the clan down to Egypt, the promise that Joseph's family could live in **the best of the land of Egypt**, and that they would be permitted to **eat from the richness** ("the fat") **of the land.**

back to me. I will give you the best of the land of Egypt, and you can eat from the richness of the land.' ¹⁹ You are also commanded to tell them, 'Do this: Take wagons from the land of Egypt for your dependents and your wives and bring your father here. ²⁰ Do not be concerned about your belongings, for the best of all the land of Egypt is yours.' "

²¹ The sons of Israel did this. Joseph gave them wagons as Pharaoh had commanded, and he gave them provisions for the journey. ²² He gave each of the brothers changes of clothes, but he gave Benjamin three hundred pieces of silver and five changes of clothes. ²³ He sent his father the following: ten donkeys carrying the best products of Egypt and ten female donkeys carrying grain, food, and provisions for his father on the journey. ²⁴ So Joseph sent his brothers on their way, and as they were leaving, he said to them, "Don't argueᴬ on the way."

²⁵ So they went up from Egypt and came to their father Jacob in the land of Canaan. ²⁶ They said, "Joseph is still alive, and he is ruler over all the land of Egypt!" Jacob was stunned,ᴮ for he did not believe them. ²⁷ But when they told Jacob all that Joseph had said to them, and when he saw the wagons that Joseph had sent to transport him, the spirit of their father Jacob revived.

²⁸ Then Israel said, "Enough! My son Joseph is still alive. I will go to see him before I die."

Jacob Leaves for Egypt

46 Israel set out with all that he had and came to Beer-sheba, and he offered sacrifices to the God of his father Isaac. ² That night God spoke to Israel in a vision: "Jacob, Jacob!" he said.

And Jacob replied, "Here I am."

³ God said, "I am God, the God of your father. Do not be afraid to go down to Egypt, for I will make you into a great nation there. ⁴ I will go down with you to Egypt, and I will also bring you back. Joseph will close your eyes when you die."ᶜ

⁵ Jacob left Beer-sheba. The sons of Israel took their father Jacob in the wagons Pharaoh had sent to carry him, along with their

dependents and their wives. ⁶ They also took their cattle and possessions they had acquired in the land of Canaan. Then Jacob and all his offspring with him came to Egypt. ⁷ His sons and grandsons, his daughters and granddaughters, indeed all his offspring, he brought with him to Egypt.

Jacob's Family

⁸ These are the names of the sons of Israel who came to Egypt — Jacob and his sons:
Jacob's firstborn: Reuben.
⁹ Reuben's sons: Hanoch, Pallu, Hezron, and Carmi.
¹⁰ Simeon's sons: Jemuel, Jamin, Ohad, Jachin, Zohar, and Shaul, the son of a Canaanite woman.
¹¹ Levi's sons: Gershon, Kohath, and Merari.
¹² Judah's sons: Er, Onan, Shelah, Perez, and Zerah; but Er and Onan died in the land of Canaan.
The sons of Perez were Hezron and Hamul.
¹³ Issachar's sons: Tola, Puvah,ᴰ Jashub,ᴱ and Shimron.
¹⁴ Zebulun's sons: Sered, Elon, and Jahleel.
¹⁵ These were Leah's sons born to Jacob in Paddan-aram, as well as his daughter Dinah. The total number of persons:ᶠ thirty-three.
¹⁶ Gad's sons: Ziphion, Haggi, Shuni, Ezbon, Eri, Arodi, and Areli.
¹⁷ Asher's sons: Imnah, Ishvah, Ishvi, Beriah, and their sister Serah.
Beriah's sons were Heber and Malchiel.
¹⁸ These were the sons of Zilpah — whom Laban gave to his daughter Leah — that she bore to Jacob: sixteen persons.
¹⁹ The sons of Jacob's wife Rachel: Joseph and Benjamin.
²⁰ Manasseh and Ephraim were born to Joseph in the land of Egypt. They were born to him by Asenath daughter of Potiphera, a priest at On.ᴳ
²¹ Benjamin's sons: Bela, Becher, Ashbel, Gera, Naaman, Ehi, Rosh, Muppim, Huppim, and Ard.

ᴬ45:24 Or be anxious ᴮ45:26 Lit Jacob's heart was numb ᶜ46:4 Lit will put his hand on your eyes ᴰ46:13 Sam, Syr read Puah; 1Ch 7:1 ᴱ46:13 Sam, LXX; MT reads Iob ᶠ46:15 Lit All persons his sons and his daughters: ᴳ46:20 Or Heliopolis

45:21–24 The translation of Joseph's final command (Don't argue) is uncertain and may also mean "Don't fear" or "Don't take undue risks."
45:25–28 Jacob experienced a storm of emotion when the group returned from Egypt. Initially he experienced relief, as all eleven brothers came back to him. His "heart went numb" (was stunned) when he was told that Joseph was still alive and he realized his other sons had maintained a deception for twenty years.
46:1–4 Jacob, referred to here by his covenant name Israel, had God speak to him in a vision. Calling the elderly patriarch's name twice—a practice in the Bible reserved for special revelatory moments (cp. 22:1; Ex 3:4)—God, the God of Jacob's father made four important remarks to Jacob. First, he commanded Jacob not to be afraid to go down to Egypt because he would go down with him. Second, God affirmed the generations-old promise to make Abraham's family line—represented through Jacob—a great nation, even in Egypt. Third, he promised to
bring Israel's descendants back. Finally, God promised that Jacob's beloved son Joseph would close the patriarch's eyes—i.e., be present at Jacob's death.
46:8–27 Not counting Jacob or his four wives, the list of those who came to Egypt contains the names of seventy-one people descended from Jacob/Israel. Ac 7:14, reflecting the Septuagint, states seventy-five people went to Egypt; this number includes five more of Joseph's descendants: three grandsons and two great-grandsons (Nm 26:29,35–36).

Family Tree of
Abraham

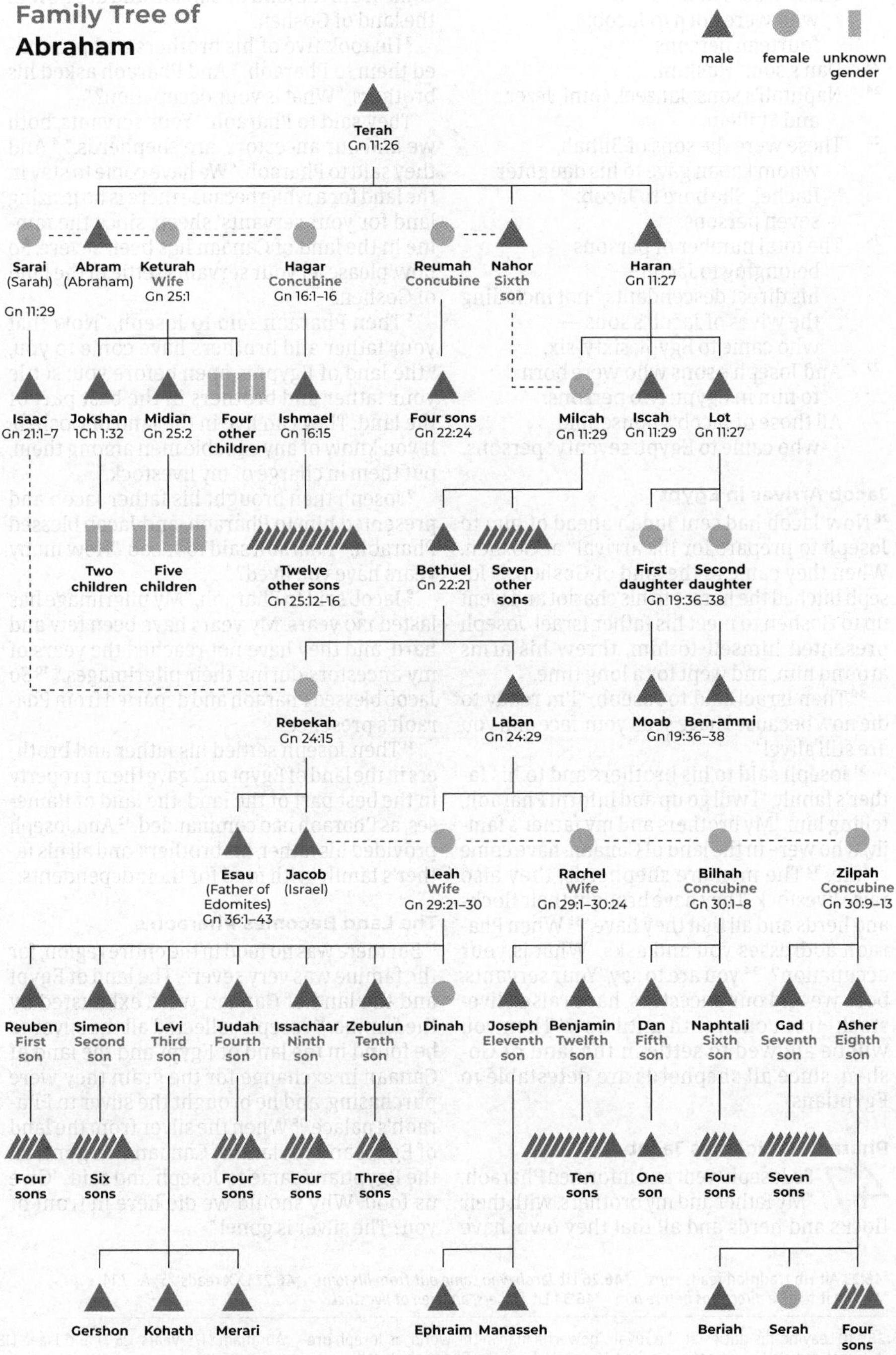

△ male   ● female   ▮ unknown gender

Terah
Gn 11:26

● **Sarai** (Sarah)
Gn 11:29

△ **Abram** (Abraham)

● **Keturah** Wife
Gn 25:1

● **Hagar** Concubine
Gn 16:1–16

● **Reumah** Concubine

△ **Nahor** Sixth son

△ **Haran**
Gn 11:27

△ **Isaac**
Gn 21:1–7

△ **Jokshan**
1Ch 1:32

△ **Midian**
Gn 25:2

▮▮▮▮ **Four other children**

△ **Ishmael**
Gn 16:15

△ **Four sons**
Gn 22:24

● **Milcah**
Gn 11:29

● **Iscah**
Gn 11:29

△ **Lot**
Gn 11:27

▮▮ **Two children**

▮▮▮▮▮ **Five children**

///// **Twelve other sons**
Gn 25:12–16

△ **Bethuel**
Gn 22:21

///// **Seven other sons**

● **First daughter**

● **Second daughter**
Gn 19:36–38

● **Rebekah**
Gn 24:15

△ **Laban**
Gn 24:29

△ **Moab**
Gn 19:36–38

△ **Ben-ammi**

△ **Esau** (Father of Edomites)
Gn 36:1–43

△ **Jacob** (Israel)

● **Leah** Wife
Gn 29:21–30

● **Rachel** Wife
Gn 29:1–30:24

● **Bilhah** Concubine
Gn 30:1–8

● **Zilpah** Concubine
Gn 30:9–13

△ **Reuben** First son

△ **Simeon** Second son

△ **Levi** Third son

△ **Judah** Fourth son

△ **Issachaar** Ninth son

△ **Zebulun** Tenth son

● **Dinah**

△ **Joseph** Eleventh son

△ **Benjamin** Twelfth son

△ **Dan** Fifth son

△ **Naphtali** Sixth son

△ **Gad** Seventh son

△ **Asher** Eighth son

/// **Four sons**

/// **Six sons**

/// **Four sons**

/// **Four sons**

/// **Three sons**

///// **Ten sons**

△ **One son**

/// **Four sons**

///// **Seven sons**

△ **Gershon**

△ **Kohath**

△ **Merari**

△ **Ephraim**

△ **Manasseh**

△ **Beriah**

● **Serah**

/// **Four sons**

²² These were Rachel's sons
who were born to Jacob:
fourteen persons.
²³ Dan's son:^A Hushim.
²⁴ Naphtali's sons: Jahzeel, Guni, Jezer,
and Shillem.
²⁵ These were the sons of Bilhah,
whom Laban gave to his daughter
Rachel. She bore to Jacob:
seven persons.
²⁶ The total number of persons
belonging to Jacob —
his direct descendants,^B not including
the wives of Jacob's sons —
who came to Egypt: sixty-six.
²⁷ And Joseph's sons who were born
to him in Egypt: two persons.
All those of Jacob's household
who came to Egypt: seventy^C persons.

Jacob Arrives in Egypt

²⁸ Now Jacob had sent Judah ahead of him to Joseph to prepare for his arrival^D at Goshen. When they came to the land of Goshen, ²⁹ Joseph hitched the horses to his chariot and went up to Goshen to meet his father Israel. Joseph presented himself to him, threw his arms around him, and wept for a long time.
³⁰ Then Israel said to Joseph, "I'm ready to die now because I have seen your face and you are still alive!"
³¹ Joseph said to his brothers and to his father's family, "I will go up and inform Pharaoh, telling him, 'My brothers and my father's family, who were in the land of Canaan, have come to me. ³² The men are shepherds; they also raise livestock. They have brought their flocks and herds and all that they have.' ³³ When Pharaoh addresses you and asks, 'What is your occupation?' ³⁴ you are to say, 'Your servants, both we and our ancestors, have raised livestock^E from our youth until now.' Then you will be allowed to settle in the land of Goshen, since all shepherds are detestable to Egyptians."

Pharaoh Welcomes Jacob

47 So Joseph went and informed Pharaoh: "My father and my brothers, with their flocks and herds and all that they own, have

come from the land of Canaan and are now in the land of Goshen." ² He took five of his brothers and presented them to Pharaoh. ³ And Pharaoh asked his brothers, "What is your occupation?"
They said to Pharaoh, "Your servants, both we and our ancestors, are shepherds." ⁴ And they said to Pharaoh, "We have come to stay in the land for a while because there is no grazing land for your servants' sheep, since the famine in the land of Canaan has been severe. So now, please let your servants settle in the land of Goshen." ⁵ Then Pharaoh said to Joseph, "Now that your father and brothers have come to you, ⁶ the land of Egypt is open before you; settle your father and brothers in the best part of the land. They can live in the land of Goshen. If you know of any capable men among them, put them in charge of my livestock." ⁷ Joseph then brought his father Jacob and presented him to Pharaoh, and Jacob blessed Pharaoh. ⁸ Pharaoh said to Jacob, "How many years have you lived?"
⁹ Jacob said to Pharaoh, "My pilgrimage has lasted 130 years. My years have been few and hard, and they have not reached the years of my ancestors during their pilgrimages." ¹⁰ So Jacob blessed Pharaoh and departed from Pharaoh's presence.
¹¹ Then Joseph settled his father and brothers in the land of Egypt and gave them property in the best part of the land, the land of Rameses, as Pharaoh had commanded. ¹² And Joseph provided his father, his brothers, and all his father's family with food for their dependents.

The Land Becomes Pharaoh's

¹³ But there was no food in the entire region, for the famine was very severe. The land of Egypt and the land of Canaan were exhausted by the famine. ¹⁴ Joseph collected all the silver to be found in the land of Egypt and the land of Canaan in exchange for the grain they were purchasing, and he brought the silver to Pharaoh's palace. ¹⁵ When the silver from the land of Egypt and the land of Canaan was gone, all the Egyptians came to Joseph and said, "Give us food. Why should we die here in front of you? The silver is gone!"

^A46:23 Alt Hb tradition reads *sons:*   ^B46:26 Lit *Jacob who came out from his loins*   ^C46:27 LXX reads *75*; Ac 7:14
^D46:28 Lit *to give directions before him*   ^E46:34 Lit *fathers, are men of livestock*

46:28–30 Leaving his duties at the royal court, Joseph traveled by chariot to **Goshen to meet his father Israel**. The meeting was satisfying to both parties, as Joseph at last threw his arms around his father, hugged him, **and wept for a long time**. Jacob would live an additional seventeen years in Egypt (47:28).
47:7–10 The climax of the family's visit to the royal courts of Egypt was the introduction of the clan patriarch to the most powerful man in the world, as Joseph **presented** Jacob **to Pharaoh**. Jacob's initial (v. 7) and concluding (v. 10) blessings of Pharaoh fulfilled earlier prophecies (28:14; cp. 12:3; 18:18; 22:18). In the brief ceremonial meeting Pharaoh asked Jacob one question: **How many years have you lived?** Jacob's response of **130 years** marks him as one of the oldest men in post-flood history. He would live to age 147 (v. 28), but was surpassed by the years of his **ancestors** Abraham (175 years; 25:7) and Isaac (180 years; 35:28).
47:11–12 The land of Rameses is an alternate name for the land of Goshen and may be the result of a later scribe updating the place names.
47:13–17 As the famine progressed, the region's inhabitants spent all their money. Joseph therefore authorized a barter system to trade **livestock** for food.

[16] But Joseph said, "Give me your livestock. Since the silver is gone, I will give you food in exchange for your livestock." [17] So they brought their livestock to Joseph, and he gave them food in exchange for the horses, the flocks of sheep, the herds of cattle, and the donkeys. That year he provided them with food in exchange for all their livestock.

[18] When that year was over, they came the next year and said to him, "We cannot hide from our lord that the silver is gone and that all our livestock belongs to our lord. There is nothing left for our lord except our bodies and our land. [19] Why should we die here in front of you — both us and our land? Buy us and our land in exchange for food. Then we with our land will become Pharaoh's slaves. Give us seed so that we can live and not die, and so that the land won't become desolate."

[20] In this way, Joseph acquired all the land in Egypt for Pharaoh, because every Egyptian sold his field since the famine was so severe for them. The land became Pharaoh's, [21] and Joseph made the people servants[A] from one end of Egypt to the other. [22] The only land he did not acquire belonged to the priests, for they had an allowance from Pharaoh. They ate from their allowance that Pharaoh gave them; therefore they did not sell their land.

[23] Joseph said to the people, "Understand today that I have acquired you and your land for Pharaoh. Here is seed for you. Sow it in the land. [24] At harvest, you are to give a fifth of it to Pharaoh, and four-fifths will be yours as seed for the field and as food for yourselves, your households, and your dependents."

[25] "You have saved our lives," they said. "We have found favor with our lord and will be Pharaoh's slaves." [26] So Joseph made it a law, still in effect today in the land of Egypt, that a fifth of the produce belongs to Pharaoh. Only the priests' land does not belong to Pharaoh.

Israel Settles in Goshen

[27] Israel settled in the land of Egypt, in the region of Goshen. They acquired property in it and became fruitful and very numerous. [28] Now Jacob lived in the land of Egypt 17 years, and his life span was 147 years. [29] When the time approached for him to die, he called his son Joseph and said to him, "If I have found favor with you, put your hand under my thigh and promise me that you will deal with me in kindness and faithfulness. Do not bury me in Egypt. [30] When I rest with my ancestors, carry me away from Egypt and bury me in their burial place."

Joseph answered, "I will do what you have asked."

[31] And Jacob said, "Swear to me." So Joseph swore to him. Then Israel bowed in thanks at the head of his bed.[B]

Jacob Blesses Ephraim and Manasseh

48 Some time after this, Joseph was told, "Your father is weaker." So he set out with his two sons, Manasseh and Ephraim. [2] When Jacob was told, "Your son Joseph has come to you," Israel summoned his strength and sat up in bed.

[3] Jacob said to Joseph, "God Almighty appeared to me at Luz in the land of Canaan and blessed me. [4] He said to me, 'I will make you fruitful and numerous; I will make many nations come from you, and I will give this land as a permanent possession to your future descendants.' [5] Your two sons born to you in the land of Egypt before I came to you in Egypt are now mine. Ephraim and Manasseh belong to me just as Reuben and Simeon do. [6] Children born to you after them will be yours and will be recorded under the names of their brothers with regard to their inheritance. [7] When I was returning from Paddan, to my sorrow Rachel died along the way, some distance from Ephrath in the land of Canaan. I buried her there along the way to Ephrath" (that is, Bethlehem).

[A] 47:21 Sam, LXX; MT reads and he moved the people to the cities   [B] 47:31 Or Israel worshiped while leaning on the top of his staff

---

47:18–22 Consistent with cultures throughout Asia and Africa at that time, the Egyptians asked their government to **buy** them as slaves once all their resources were exhausted. Such slavery was often temporary and might be terminated when the debt was paid (Dt 15:12).

Joseph accepted their offer. Members of the Egyptian priesthood were exempted from the land contract since the land was **an allowance from Pharaoh**. The Hebrew text, unlike the Septuagint, suggests that Joseph took the additional step of relocating "the people to the cities" during the famine; if the Hebrew text represents the accurate reading, perhaps Joseph adopted this policy in order to make the food distribution program more efficient.

47:23–26 Though the citizens gave up ownership of their land, Joseph permitted them to continue working their old fields. They were required to **give a fifth** of their produce **to Pharaoh**. Egypt's citizens gratefully accepted Joseph's program. Joseph's policies produced such a stable society that they remained **in effect** hundreds of years later in the days of the biblical writer.

47:27 While the Egyptians were losing their possessions, land, and freedom because of the famine, the clan of **Israel**/Jacob prospered.

47:28–31 As Jacob's death approached, he called for **his son Joseph** (cp. 46:4) and made him swear a solemn oath while his **hand** was **under** Jacob's **thigh**, an act that expressed great trust and accompanied only the most

serious requests (cp. 24:2–4). Jacob asked that his son not bury him in Egypt, but rather that he be buried in the promised land **with** his **ancestors . . . in their burial place** near Hebron in the cave at Machpelah (23:19; 25:9; 35:27–29; 50:13).

48:1–7 Joseph, accompanied by his two eldest sons, visited Jacob again. Summoning his strength on this last day of his life, Jacob **sat up in bed** and spoke with Joseph of how **God Almighty** (El Shaddai; see note at 17:1) gave a second revelation to him at Bethel, more than fifty years earlier (35:9–12). Ephraim and Manasseh would receive the blessings of the first-and second-born, instead of **Reuben and Simeon**, who had previously dishonored Jacob (Gn 34:25–30).

⁸ When Israel saw Joseph's sons, he said, "Who are these?"

⁹ And Joseph said to his father, "They are my sons God has given me here." So Israel said, "Bring them to me and I will bless them." ¹⁰ Now his eyesight was poor because of old age; he could hardly[A] see. Joseph brought them to him, and he kissed and embraced them. ¹¹ Israel said to Joseph, "I never expected to see your face again, but now God has even let me see your offspring." ¹² Then Joseph took them from his father's knees and bowed with his face to the ground.

Ephraim's Greater Blessing

¹³ Then Joseph took them both — with his right hand Ephraim toward Israel's left, and with his left hand Manasseh toward Israel's right — and brought them to Israel. ¹⁴ But Israel stretched out his right hand and put it on the head of Ephraim, the younger, and crossing his hands, put his left on Manasseh's head, although Manasseh was the firstborn. ¹⁵ Then he blessed Joseph and said:

The God before whom my fathers
   Abraham and Isaac walked,
the God who has been my shepherd
   all my life to this day,
¹⁶ the angel who has redeemed me
   from all harm —
may he bless these boys.
And may they be called by my name
and the names of my fathers Abraham
   and Isaac,
and may they grow to be numerous
   within the land.

¹⁷ When Joseph saw that his father had placed his right hand on Ephraim's head, he thought it was a mistake[B] and took his father's hand to move it from Ephraim's head to Manasseh's. ¹⁸ Joseph said to his father, "Not that way, my father! This one is the firstborn. Put your right hand on his head."

¹⁹ But his father refused and said, "I know, my son, I know! He too will become a tribe,[C] and he too will be great; nevertheless, his younger brother will be greater than he, and his offspring will become a populous nation."[D] ²⁰ So he blessed them that day, putting Ephraim before Manasseh when he said, "The nation Israel will invoke blessings by you, saying, 'May God make you like Ephraim and Manasseh.'"

²¹ Israel said to Joseph, "Look, I am about to die, but God will be with you and will bring you back to the land of your fathers. ²² Over and above what I am giving your brothers, I am giving you the one mountain slope[E] that I took from the Amorites with my sword and bow."

Jacob's Last Words

49 Then Jacob called his sons and said, "Gather around, and I will tell you what will happen to you in the days to come.[F]
² Come together and listen, sons of Jacob; listen to your father Israel:

³ Reuben, you are my firstborn,
   my strength and the firstfruits
   of my virility,
excelling in prominence,
   excelling in power.
⁴ Turbulent as water, you will not excel,
because you got into your father's bed
and you defiled it — he[G] got
   into my bed.

⁵ Simeon and Levi are brothers;
   their knives are vicious weapons.
⁶ May I never enter their council;
may I never join their assembly.
For in their anger they kill men,
and on a whim they hamstring oxen.
⁷ Their anger is cursed, for it is strong,

A 48:10 Lit he was not able to   B 48:17 Or he was displeased; lit head, it was bad in his eyes   C 48:19 Lit people   D 48:19 Or a multitude of nations; lit a fullness of nations   E 48:22 Or Shechem, Joseph's burial place; lit one shoulder   F 49:1 Or in the last days   G 49:4 LXX, Syr, Tg read you

48:9–12 Jacob used his last measure of strength to **bless** his sons, beginning with the two newly adopted ones. Before blessing them, Jacob **kissed and embraced them** (cp. 27:26–27).
48:13–16 Joseph presented **Ephraim** (at his **right hand** side) and **Manasseh** (at his **left hand** side) to Jacob in hopes that Jacob would reach out with his right hand and confer the greater blessing to the elder son, Manasseh, who was standing to Joseph's left. But Jacob crossed his arms and put his **right hand . . . on the head of Ephraim**, the younger, thus symbolically conferring the greater blessing on him. Jacob then **blessed Joseph**, but because his two hands were on Joseph's sons, it was they who received the blessing. Calling on the God of his fathers **Abraham and Isaac**, who had been his **shepherd** (cp. Pss 23:1; 80:1; Ezk 34:11–12; Jn 10:11) all his life, Jacob's requests

on behalf of Ephraim and Manasseh included that they would be called by the names of Jacob, **Abraham and Isaac**, that is, that they would identify with God's covenant people, not with Egyptian culture and religion.
48:17–20 Frustrated because it seemed that his nearly blind father had made a mistake, Joseph **took his father's hand to move it from Ephraim's head.** Emboldened by prophetic insight, however, Jacob refused to move his hands because by God's own hand Ephraim's blessings were ordained to exceed Manasseh's. Manasseh would become a **tribe**, but **his younger brother** Ephraim would become something more—a **populous nation.** In later Israelite history, prophets often referred to the entire northern kingdom of Israel as Ephraim (Is 7:5; Jr 31:20; Ezk 37:16; Hs 5:13; Zch 10:7).
49:3–27 Jacob's prophetic words to his twelve sons were delivered in three units:

those delivered to (1) the sons of Leah (vv. 3–15); (2) the sons of the concubines Bilhah and Zilpah (vv. 16–21); and (3) the sons of Rachel (vv. 22–27).
49:3–4 As the oldest son in a Semitic family **Reuben** was poised to lead the clan when his father died. However, Reuben lost his rights as firstborn because he had intimate relations with Jacob's wife Bilhah (35:22).
49:5–7 **Simeon** and **Levi** are grouped together because **in their anger** they conspired together to **kill the men** of Shechem, even hamstringing the **oxen** after seizing them (34:25–29). Their out-of-control anger at Dinah's rape (34:2) cost them the full measure of their inheritance. Historically, Simeon's land allotment was shared with Judah (Jos 19:9), and the Levites were never given a region to call their own; they had to live in specified cities within the territories of the other tribes (Jos 14:3–4).

◤ Seeing Jesus in Genesis

▼ Old Testament	▼ New Testament
THE FIRST ADAM: Brought Death *(Gn 3)*	**THE SECOND ADAM:** Brought Life *(Rm 5)*
The Protevangelium: The Promise of Deliverance from the Serpent *(Gn 3:15)*	**The Fulfillment:** Jesus Destroys the Works of the Devil *(1Jn 3:8)*
Abel's Blood: Cries Out for Justice *(Gn 4)*	**Jesus's Blood:** Proclaims Forgiveness *(Heb 12:24)*
The Flood: Ark Rescues Noah's Family *(Gn 6–8)*	**Baptism:** Christ's Resurrection Rescues Us *(1Pt 3:20–21)*
The Promise to Abraham: Seed and Blessing to the World *(Gn 12)*	**The Fulfillment in Jesus:** The Seed and Salvation from Sin to the World *(Gl 3)*
The Almost Sacrifice of Isaac: "The LORD Will Provide" *(Gn 22)*	**The Crucifixion of Jesus:** "The Lamb of God" *(Jn 1:29)*
Jacob's Stairway *(or Ladder)*: The Promise of God's Presence *(Gn 28)*	**Jesus Is the Stairway *(or Ladder)*:** The Fullness of God's Presence *(Jn 1:51)*
Joseph Suffered: According to God's Plan *(Gn 50:20)*	**Jesus Suffered:** According to God's Plan *(Ac 2:23)*
Joseph Forgave: His Brothers *(Gn 45)*	**Jesus Forgives:** Sinners *(Lk 23:34)*
Joseph Saved: People from Famine *(Gn 45)*	**Jesus Saves:** People from Sin *(Ac 2:36–41)*

and their fury, for it is cruel!
I will disperse them throughout Jacob
and scatter them throughout Israel.

8 Judah, your brothers will praise you.
Your hand will be on the necks
of your enemies;
your father's sons will bow down to you.
9 Judah is a young lion —
my son, you return from the kill.
He crouches; he lies down like a lion
or a lioness — who dares to rouse him?
10 The scepter will not depart from Judah
or the staff from between his feet
until he whose right it is comes^A
and the obedience of the peoples
belongs to him.
11 He ties his donkey to a vine,
and the colt of his donkey
to the choice vine.
He washes his clothes in wine
and his robes in the blood of grapes.
12 His eyes are darker than wine,
and his teeth are whiter than milk.

13 Zebulun will live by the seashore
and will be a harbor for ships,
and his territory will be next to Sidon.

14 Issachar is a strong donkey
lying down between the saddlebags.^B
15 He saw that his resting place was good
and that the land was pleasant,
so he leaned his shoulder to bear a load
and became a forced laborer.

16 Dan will judge his people
as one of the tribes of Israel.
17 Dan will be a snake by the road,

a viper beside the path,
that bites the horse's heels
so that its rider falls backward.

18 I wait for your salvation, LORD.

19 Gad will be attacked by raiders,
but he will attack their heels.

20 Asher's^C food will be rich,
and he will produce royal delicacies.

21 Naphtali is a doe set free
that bears beautiful fawns.

22 Joseph is a fruitful vine,
a fruitful vine beside a spring;
its branches^D climb over the wall.^E
23 The archers attacked him,
shot at him, and were hostile
toward him.
24 Yet his bow remained steady,
and his strong arms were made agile
by the hands of the Mighty One of Jacob,
by the name of^F the Shepherd, the Rock
of Israel,
25 by the God of your father
who helps you,
and by the Almighty who blesses you
with blessings of the heavens above,
blessings of the deep that lies below,
and blessings of the breasts
and the womb.
26 The blessings of your father excel
the blessings of my ancestors^G
and^H the bounty of the ancient hills.^E
May they rest on the head of Joseph,
on the brow of the prince
of his brothers.

^A49:10 Or until tribute comes to him, or until Shiloh comes, or until he comes to Shiloh   ^B49:14 Or sheep pens
^C49:19–20 LXX, Syr, Vg; MT reads their heel. ²⁰From Asher   ^D49:22 Lit daughters   ^E49:22,26 Hb obscure   ^F49:24 Syr, Tg; MT
reads Jacob, from there   ^G49:26 Or of the mountains   ^H49:26 Lit to

49:8–12 Judah, Jacob's fourth-born son, received the second-longest of the blessings, behind Joseph's (55 vs. 61 Hebrew words). The scepter and staff—symbols of kingship in ancient Israel—foretold the establishment of the Davidic dynasty as Israel's kings (2Sm 7:8–16). The he and him of v. 10b have been understood for thousands of years as messianic references (Ezk 21:27) and, for Christians, a prophecy of Jesus's coming.
49:13 Though the territorial allotment of Zebulun, Jacob's tenth-born son, was landlocked (Jos 19:10–16), Jacob's mention of a harbor for ships may refer to the prosperity of the sea trade associated with the Mediterranean coastal city of Sidon. Alternatively, Jacob may have referred to Zebulun's territorial division that was later mentioned in Ezk 48:26.
49:14–15 Jacob's ninth-born son Issachar was prophetically compared to a strong donkey situated between two saddlebags. Though the descendants of Issachar would live in a land that was pleasant (Jos 19:17–22), they would be compelled to do

the work of a forced laborer—probably a reference to the oppression this tribe suffered at the hands of their own leaders and foreign invaders.
49:16–18 Jacob used a wordplay to describe the key positive action associated with his fifth-born son: Dan will judge (Hb dan yadin; "the judging one will judge")—a possible prophetic reference to Samson's work (Jdg 15:20). Dan was compared to a snake, the enemy of humanity in the garden of Eden. The comparison is to an animal with venom so poisonous that it could kill horses. This contrast between images foreshadows the checkered history of the tribe of Dan. Though Samson led Israel for twenty years, the Danites also played a leading role in encouraging idolatry in Israel (Jdg 18:14–27; 1Kg 12:28–30).
49:19 Gad, Jacob's seventh-born son, was once associated with good fortune (30:11). However, in an involved wordplay (Hb gad gedud yegudennu) Jacob prophesied that Gad would be attacked by raiders, a reference to the tribe's vulnerability based on

the location of its land allotment east of the Jordan River. But Jacob praised the tenacity of the Gadites because they would not give up but rather attack the heels of their oppressors.
49:20 Asher, Jacob's eighth-born, was prophetically foreseen to enjoy prosperity that, associated with its coastal land allotment, would produce royal delicacies supporting Israel's prosperity.
49:21 Jacob's sixth-born son, Naphtali, whose descendants would live just west of the Sea of Galilee, was foreseen to produce a people who would be free and populous, like a doe that bears beautiful fawns.
49:22–26 Jacob's longest blessing (sixty-one Hebrew words) was associated with Joseph, Rachel's firstborn son (his eleventh son). This section contains the largest number and variety of references to God (five: Mighty One of Jacob . . . Shepherd . . . Rock of Israel . . . God of your father . . . Almighty) and the greatest number of references to "blessing" (six: one verb, five nouns). Joseph alone is termed the prince of his brothers

²⁷ Benjamin is a wolf; he tears his prey.
  In the morning he devours the prey,
  and in the evening he divides
     the plunder."

²⁸ These are the tribes of Israel, twelve in all, and this is what their father said to them. He blessed them, and he blessed each one with a suitable blessing.

Jacob's Burial Instructions

²⁹ Then he commanded them, "I am about to be gathered to my people. Bury me with my ancestors in the cave in the field of Ephron the Hethite. ³⁰ The cave is in the field of Machpelah near Mamre, in the land of Canaan. This is the field Abraham purchased from Ephron the Hethite as burial property. ³¹ Abraham and his wife Sarah are buried there, Isaac and his wife Rebekah are buried there, and I buried Leah there. ³² The field and the cave in it were purchased from the Hethites." ³³ When Jacob had finished giving charges to his sons, he drew his feet into the bed, took his last breath, and was gathered to his people.

Jacob's Burial

50 Then Joseph, leaning over his father's face, wept and kissed him. ² He commanded his servants who were physicians to embalm his father. So they embalmed Israel. ³ They took forty days to complete this, for embalming takes that long, and the Egyptians mourned for him seventy days.

⁴ When the days of mourning were over, Joseph said to Pharaoh's household, "If I have found favor with you, please tell Pharaoh that ⁵ my father made me take an oath, saying, 'I am about to die. You must bury me there in the tomb that I made for myself in the land of Canaan.' Now let me go and bury my father. Then I will return."

⁶ So Pharaoh said, "Go and bury your father in keeping with your oath."

⁷ Then Joseph went to bury his father, and all Pharaoh's servants, the elders of his household, and all the elders of the land of Egypt went with him, ⁸ along with all Joseph's family, his brothers, and his father's family. Only their dependents, their flocks, and their herds were left in the land of Goshen. ⁹ Horses and chariots went up with him; it was a very impressive procession. ¹⁰ When they reached the threshing floor of Atad, which is across the Jordan, they lamented and wept loudly, and Joseph mourned seven days for his father. ¹¹ When the Canaanite inhabitants of the land saw the mourning at the threshing floor of Atad, they said, "This is a solemn mourning on the part of the Egyptians." Therefore the place is named Abel-mizraim.ᴬ It is across the Jordan.

¹² So Jacob's sons did for him what he had commanded them. ¹³ They carried him to the land of Canaan and buried him in the cave at Machpelah in the field near Mamre, which Abraham had purchased as burial property from Ephron the Hethite. ¹⁴ After Joseph buried his father, he returned to Egypt with his brothers and all who had gone with him to bury his father.

Joseph's Kindness

¹⁵ When Joseph's brothers saw that their father was dead, they said to one another, "If Joseph is holding a grudge against us, he will certainly repay us for all the suffering we caused him." ¹⁶ So they sent this message to Joseph, "Before he died your father gave a command: ¹⁷ 'Say this to Joseph: Please forgive your

---

ᴬ 50:11 = Mourning of Egypt

---

and is the one who uniquely receives from God **blessings of the heavens above,** **blessings of the deep,** and **blessings of** numerous offspring.
49:27 Jacob's final prophetic blessing was reserved for his last-born son **Benjamin.** Metaphorically compared to a **wolf,** Jacob identified him as one who **tears** and **devours** prey and **divides the plunder.** Benjamin's descendants were thus characterized as dangerous fighters, but also as ones who would provide benefits for others. Benjamin was the fifth of the sons to be prophetically compared to an animal (also Judah: lion; Issachar: donkey; Dan: snake; Naphtali: deer).
49:29–33 The dying patriarch emphasized two matters in his final words: where he was to be buried, and with whom he was to be buried. Jacob asked to be buried with his grandparents **Abraham and his wife Sarah,** his parents **Isaac and his wife Rebekah,** and his first wife **Leah.** Jacob, who had spent seventeen years in Egypt (47:28), outlived the famine by approximately twelve years.

50:1–3 The usual Hebrew custom was to practice same-day burial without embalming; however, embalming was necessary to prepare Jacob's body for the journey to Canaan. Egyptian embalming, which **took forty days to complete,** was normally a religious practice performed by priests to prepare the person for the afterlife; the fact that Joseph used physicians rather than priests to perform the task may suggest that he had rejected Egyptian afterlife beliefs and wished to avoid giving a different impression.
The **seventy days** of mourning probably reflected Egyptian customs associated with the deaths of particularly important individuals; normal Hebrew mourning periods were either seven days (1Sm 31:13) or thirty days (one lunar cycle; Dt 34:8).
50:4–9 As a sign of Pharaoh's continuing gratitude for Joseph's work, he permitted **all** his **servants, the elders of his household, and all the elders of the land of Egypt**—a considerable number of high-ranking Egyptian politicians—to accompany all the adult members of the clan of Jacob on the journey

to Canaan. **Horses and chariots,** prestigious transportation used only by members of the Egyptian aristocracy, were part of **a very impressive procession** to Canaan.
50:10–14 The group camped at the open, level **threshing floor of Atad** and went through a Hebrew mourning ritual. The presence of a large number of Egyptians publicly displaying solemn mourning so impressed the local **Canaanite inhabitants** that they renamed the place **Abel-mizraim** ("The Meadow of Egypt"), a wordplay on a Semitic word for "weeping" (*ebel*). Proceeding westward to the cave at Machpelah two miles north of Hebron, **Joseph buried his father,** thus fulfilling what his father had commanded Joseph and his brothers to do.
50:15–21 Despite having lived under Joseph's provision and protection for many years, and despite knowing that Joseph had named one son Manasseh ("God has made me forget all my hardship in my father's house"), the brothers still doubted that Joseph had forgiven them. With Jacob now dead, Joseph's older brothers feared for their lives

brothers' transgression and their sin — the suffering they caused you.' Therefore, please forgive the transgression of the servants of the God of your father." Joseph wept when their message came to him. [18] His brothers also came to him, bowed down before him, and said, "We are your slaves!"

[19] But Joseph said to them, "Don't be afraid. Am I in the place of God? [20] You planned evil against me; God planned it for good to bring about the present result — the survival of many people. [21] Therefore don't be afraid. I will take care of you and your children." And he comforted them and spoke kindly to them.^A

Joseph's Death

[22] Joseph and his father's family remained in Egypt. Joseph lived 110 years. [23] He saw Ephraim's sons to the third generation; the sons of Manasseh's son Machir were recognized by^B,C Joseph.

[24] Joseph said to his brothers, "I am about to die, but God will certainly come to your aid and bring you up from this land to the land he swore to give to Abraham, Isaac, and Jacob." [25] So Joseph made the sons of Israel take an oath: "When God comes to your aid, you are to carry my bones up from here."

[26] Joseph died at the age of 110. They embalmed him and placed him in a coffin in Egypt.

^A **50:21** Lit *spoke to their hearts* ^B **50:23** Lit *were born on the knees of* ^C **50:23** Referring to a ritual of adoption or of legitimation; Gn 30:3

and hoped that saying their father called for forgiveness **before he died** would protect them from Joseph's wrath. They were so afraid of Joseph that they did not dare at first to come to him personally; instead, they only **sent** a **message** entreating him to **forgive** his **brothers'** "rebellion" (**transgression**) and **sin**, especially since they were "slaves" (**servants**) **of the God of your father**—that is, they worshiped the same God that Joseph did. Perhaps the reason the brothers came to Joseph was that they heard he had **wept** when he received their message. To maximize their chances of survival they **bowed down before him** (cp. 37:7,9) and offered themselves as his personal **slaves**.

Joseph refused their offer. They were slaves of God, not of him, and he would not put himself **in the place of God** to make them

his slaves. He admitted that his older brothers **planned evil against** him, but with great spiritual insight he also confessed that **God planned it for good to bring about . . . the survival of many people.** Far from being embittered, Joseph was emboldened to take care of the very ones who had tried to kill him, along with their **children**. He **spoke kindly to them** (lit "spoke upon their heart"; cp. Is 40:2) and **comforted them.**

50:22–23 God's blessing on Joseph's life is apparent as he **lived 110 years**, 93 of them in Egypt and 80 of them as a ruler there. He lived to see **the third generation** of descendants through **Ephraim**, a phrase that could refer either to great-grandsons or great-great-grandsons. A further sign of God's blessing was the fact that Gilead (Nm 26:29) and other great-grandsons by Machir son of Manasseh^were born on the knees of

Joseph," that is, they were ritually adopted by him (Gn 30:3; Ru 4:16).

50:24–26 As **Joseph** was **about to die,** some fifty-four years after his father Jacob's death, he called **his brothers** to him for one last time and gave them two prophetic promises. First, that God would **certainly come to** the **aid** of their descendants. Second, that God would indeed bring their descendants up from Egypt **to the land he swore to give to Abraham, Isaac, and Jacob** (12:7; 13:15,17; 15:7,18; 24:7; 26:3; 28:13).

After **Joseph died,** he was **embalmed**—one of only two persons in the Bible said to have been embalmed (also Jacob; see v. 2 and note at vv. 1–3). His preserved body was then **placed . . . in a coffin,** awaiting a future day when it was to be carried by Moses and the Israelites to the promised land (Ex 13:19; Jos 24:32).

◥ Introduction to Exodus

Circumstances of Writing

The book of Exodus does not state who its author was. It does refer to occasions when Moses made a written record of events that took place and what God had said (17:14; 24:4,7; 34:27–28). The book also contains references to preserving and passing on information. Along with the other four books of the Pentateuch, it has long been considered to be primarily the work of Moses. Moses could have written Exodus at any time during a forty-year time span: after the Israelites finished constructing and dedicating the tabernacle at Mount Sinai, at the start of their second year after leaving Egypt (1445 BC), or before his death in the land of Moab (ca 1406 BC).

Exodus picks up where the Genesis narrative ended, with the death of Joseph around 1805 BC. It quickly moves us forward almost three hundred years to a time when the circumstances of Jacob's descendants had changed in Egypt. The Israelites were serving as slaves during Egypt's Eighteenth Dynasty, probably under the pharaohs Thutmose and Amenhotep II. The Hebrew slaves experienced a miraculous deliverance by God's hand through his servant-leader Moses. The Israelite slavery ended in 1446 BC. The book of Exodus records the events surrounding the exodus from Egypt and the Israelites' first year in the wilderness, including the giving of the law.

The date of the exodus is disputed, but biblical evidence favors 1446 BC. First Kings 6:1 states that the exodus occurred 480 years before Solomon's fourth year as king, established by biblical data combined with Assyrian chronology to be 966 BC. In Judges 11:26, Jephthah said that Israel had been living in regions of Palestine for three hundred years. Jephthah lived around 1100 BC, thus dating the end of the wilderness journey to around 1400 BC.

Contribution to the Bible

Exodus provides the high point of redemptive history in the Old Testament. Many patterns and concepts from Exodus receive attention, further development, and fulfillment elsewhere in Scripture, especially in the past, present, and future work of the Lord Jesus. These include rescue from oppression, provision of sustenance, God's faithfulness to his promises, the self-revelation of God, knowledge of God resulting from his actions, the presence of God, God's glory, efforts required to preserve the knowledge of God, a new identity for people that is based on God's actions, provision for worship, provision for life in community, connection between the reputation of God and his relationship with a group of people, obedience and rebellion, intercession, and gracious forgiveness.

Structure

Exodus is considered a part of the Law, but it is more historical narrative than law. The book is structured around the life and travels of Moses. Sandwiched between the narratives of chapters 1–18 and 32–40 are the establishment of the covenant (chaps. 19–24) and the laws related to the tabernacle and priesthood.

Exodus Timeline

3000–1750 BC

Edwin Smith Surgical Papyrus dating to **1550** is the earliest known surgical treatise; it is a copy of a much older Egyptian document attributed to Imhotep, architect, high priest, and physician of the Old Kingdom. **3000–2500**
Jacob's family settles in Egypt. **1876**
Jacob dies. **1859**
Joseph dies. **1805**
Hammurabi develops the first legal code in Mesopotamia. **1792–1750**

1700 BC

Body armor is used in China. **1700**
Minoans develop a system for running water. **1700**
Underground ice houses, Kingdom of Mari, northwest Iraq **1700**
Cookbook, Mesopotamia **1700**
Linear A script comes into use on Crete. **1700**
Egyptians show proficiency in geometry including a formula for calculating the volume of a truncated pyramid. Sources: The Moscow Papyrus and the Rhind Papyrus. **1700**

Outline

I. Oppression of God's People in Egypt (1:1–11:10)
  A. Egyptian slavery (1:1–22)
  B. Preparation of the deliverer (2:1–4:31)
  C. Struggles with the oppressor (5:1–11:10)
II. Deliverance of God's People from Egypt (12:1–14:31)
  A. Redemption by blood (12:1–51)
  B. Redemption by divine miracles (13:1–14:31)
III. Education of God's People in the Wilderness (15:1–18:27)
  A. Israel's song of victory (15:1–21)
  B. Testing and trials (15:22–17:16)
  C. Shared leadership under Moses (18:1–27)
IV. Consecration of God's People at Sinai (19:1–34:35)
  A. Acceptance of the law (19:1–31:18)
  B. Breaking of the law (32:1–35)
  C. Restoration of the law (33:1–34:35)
V. Worship of God's People in the Tabernacle (35:1–40:38)
  A. Gifts and workmen for the tabernacle (35:1–35)
  B. Construction and furnishings of the tabernacle (36:1–39:43)
  C. Filling of the tabernacle with God's glory (40:1–38)

Key verses in Exodus

20:12 Honor your father and your mother so that you may have a long life in the land that the LORD your God is giving you.

24:7 He then took the covenant scroll and read it aloud to the people. They responded, "We will do and obey all that the LORD has commanded."

1650–1600 BC ———————————— **1445 BC** ————————————————————▶

Hyksos rule Egypt. **1630–1543**
Volcanic island of Thera (Santorini) erupts with massive environmental consequences felt as far as the British Isles and North America. **1600**
Chocolate originates in northern Honduras. **1600**
Children's swings invented, Crete **1600**
Linear B script comes into use on Crete. **1600**
War chariots are used in Egypt. **1600**

MOSES 1526–1406
Egyptians develop effective pharmaceutical compounds. **1500**
JOSHUA 1490?–1380?
Moses flees to Midian. **1487**
Moses is commissioned. **1447**
The ten plagues begin. **1446**
The Passover is instituted. **1446**
Exodus and defeat of Pharaoh at the Red Sea **1446**
God's covenant with Israel at Sinai **1446**
Tabernacle is built and dedicated. **1445**

Israel Oppressed in Egypt

1 These are the names of the sons of Israel who came to Egypt with Jacob; each came with his family:

² Reuben, Simeon, Levi, and Judah;
³ Issachar, Zebulun, and Benjamin;
⁴ Dan and Naphtali; Gad and Asher.

⁵ The total number of Jacob's descendants^A was seventy;^B Joseph was already in Egypt.

⁶ Joseph and all his brothers and all that generation eventually died. ⁷ But the Israelites were fruitful, increased rapidly, multiplied, and became extremely numerous so that the land was filled with them.

⁸ A new king, who did not know about Joseph, came to power in Egypt. ⁹ He said to his people, "Look, the Israelite people are more numerous and powerful than we are. ¹⁰ Come, let's deal shrewdly with them; otherwise they will multiply further, and when war breaks out, they will join our enemies, fight against us, and leave the country." ¹¹ So the Egyptians assigned taskmasters over the Israelites to oppress them with forced labor. They built Pithom and Rameses as supply cities for Pharaoh. ¹² But the more they oppressed them, the more they multiplied and spread so that the Egyptians came to dread^C the Israelites. ¹³ They worked the Israelites ruthlessly ¹⁴ and made their lives bitter with difficult labor in brick and mortar and in all kinds of fieldwork. They ruthlessly imposed all this work on them.

¹⁵ The king of Egypt said to the Hebrew midwives — the first, whose name was Shiphrah, and the second, whose name was Puah — ¹⁶ "When you help the Hebrew women give birth, observe them as they deliver. If the child is a son, kill him, but if it's a daughter, she may live." ¹⁷ The midwives, however, feared God and did not do as the king of Egypt had told them; they let the boys live. ¹⁸ So the king of Egypt summoned the midwives and asked them, "Why have you done this and let the boys live?"

¹⁹ The midwives said to Pharaoh, "The Hebrew women are not like the Egyptian women, for they are vigorous and give birth before the midwife can get to them."

²⁰ So God was good to the midwives, and the people multiplied and became very numerous. ²¹ Since the midwives feared God, he gave them families. ²² Pharaoh then commanded all his people, "You must throw every son born to the Hebrews into the Nile, but let every daughter live."

Moses's Birth and Adoption

2 Now a man from the family of Levi married a Levite woman. ² The woman became pregnant and gave birth to a son; when she saw that he was beautiful,^D she hid him for three

---

^A 1:5 Lit of people issuing from Jacob's loins   ^B 1:5 LXX, DSS read 75; Gn 46:27; Ac 7:14   ^C 1:12 Or Egyptians loathed
^D 2:2 Or healthy

1:1–7 These verses summarize Gn 37–50, which describe in full how Jacob's family arrived in Egypt, the welcome they received, and the deaths of **Jacob** and **Joseph**.
1:5 Two other Scripture passages also say that the number who went to Egypt was **seventy** (Gn 46:27; Dt 10:22). The Septuagint (at Gn 46:27 and Ex 1:5 but not Dt 10:22), two Qumran manuscripts of Exodus, and Ac 7:14 all mention seventy-five. The Septuagint of Gn 46:20 lists five sons and grandsons of Ephraim and Manasseh. These go unmentioned in the Hebrew text

and therefore account for the different totals.
1:7 Verses 7, 12, and 20 use several terms to talk about the multiplication of the Israelites. These terms also appear repeatedly in God's creation and flood mandates (Gn 1:20–22,28; 9:1,7) and in promises he made to the patriarchs (Gn 17:2,6,20; 18:18; 26:4,24; 28:14; 35:11).
1:8–22 These unsuccessful attempts to **deal shrewdly** with the Israelites seem to escalate in desperation and decline in shrewdness.
1:8 One plausible explanation of Egyptian and Israelite connections contends that Joseph came to Egypt when the native Egyptian Twelfth Dynasty ruled in the Middle Kingdom era. Years later, Semitic resident aliens known as "Hyksos" took over much of Egypt until the time of Kamose, who reasserted Egyptian rule. The **new king** is not named in Exodus, nor is any other Egyptian king, but perhaps he was a Hyksos ruler without concern for the rights granted to the Israelites by an earlier regime. Another suggestion is that the "new king" was Ahmose, who followed his brother Kamose as ruler, reigned about twenty-five years, completed the restoration of Egyptian rule, and founded Dynasty Eighteen and the New Kingdom era, a period when Egypt exerted a powerful presence in the ancient Near East. Any Eighteenth Dynasty king might have been wary of the Israelites if he associated them with resident aliens such as the ousted Hyksos. So when it says this king **did not know about Joseph**, it means he felt no obligation to honor an

agreement entered into by the previous administration.
1:9 This is the first time **the Israelite people** are called a "people." They came to Egypt as an extended family, but now Pharaoh compared their numbers with his own.
1:11 Pithom is probably Tel el-Retaba. **Rameses** is probably Qantir or Avaris. Both were located in the eastern Nile delta near the Wadi Tumilat. These were **supply cities** probably in the sense that they stood ready to supply arms, food, and fortifications for troops.
1:13–14 Five forms of the same Hebrew word are translated here with forms of "work" or "labor." (A different word for **labor** is in v. 11.) The repetition drives home what the Egyptians were doing. Elsewhere forms of the word translated **bitter** describe situations of severe hardship and loss (Ru 1:13,20; 1Sm 30:6; 2Kg 4:27; Is 22:4).
1:15 In this book that takes a profound interest in identities, ironically the king is nameless, but the **midwives** who honored God are named.
1:16 Observe them as they deliver is literally "look at the stones," meaning check the genitals. The orders are clear; the midwives must kill Israelite sons and let the daughters live.
2:2 The combination of **saw** and **beautiful** in Ex 2 echoes the theme of Gn 1. Hebrews 11:23 refers to hiding this child as an exercise of faith by his parents.
2:3 Asphalt and pitch made the basket waterproof; even full-sized boats could be similarly sealed (Is 18:2).

#04 99 Essential Christian Truths

GOD IS JUST

God establishes standards for his moral creatures that are in accordance with his righteousness, and his moral creatures will be judged according to those righteous standards (Lv 11:44–45; Rm 2:5–11; 2Co 5:10). It would be an injustice if God were not to uphold his righteousness, for such a failure would require God to violate his own righteous character. Since humanity has sinned by failing to live up to God's righteous standards, God has taken it upon himself to make provision by being both just and the justifier of those who place their faith in Christ (Rm 3:25–26).

months. ³But when she could no longer hide him, she got a papyrus basket for him and coated it with asphalt and pitch. She placed the child in it and set it among the reeds by the bank of the Nile. ⁴Then his sister stood at a distance in order to see what would happen to him.

⁵Pharaoh's daughter went down to bathe at the Nile while her servant girls walked along the riverbank. She saw the basket among the reeds, sent her slave girl, took it, ⁶opened it, and saw him, the child — and there he was, a little boy, crying. She felt sorry for him and said, "This is one of the Hebrew boys."

⁷Then his sister said to Pharaoh's daughter, "Should I go and call a Hebrew woman who is nursing to nurse the boy for you?"

⁸"Go," Pharaoh's daughter told her. So the girl went and called the boy's mother. ⁹Then Pharaoh's daughter said to her, "Take this child and nurse him for me, and I will pay your wages." So the woman took the boy and nursed him. ¹⁰When the child grew older, she brought him to Pharaoh's daughter, and he became her son. She named him Moses,ᴬ "Because," she said, "I drew him out of the water."

Moses in Midian

¹¹Years later,ᴮ after Moses had grown up, he went out to his own peopleᶜ and observed their forced labor. He saw an Egyptian striking a Hebrew, one of his people. ¹²Looking all around and seeing no one, he struck the Egyptian dead and hid him in the sand. ¹³The next day he went out and saw two Hebrews fighting. He asked the one in the wrong, "Why are you attacking your neighbor?"ᴰ

¹⁴"Who made you a commander and judge over us?" the man replied. "Are you planning to kill me as you killed the Egyptian?"

Then Moses became afraid and thought, "What I did is certainly known."

¹⁵When Pharaoh heard about this, he tried to kill Moses. But Moses fled from Pharaoh and went to live in the land of Midian, and sat down by a well.

¹⁶Now the priest of Midian had seven daughters. They came to draw water and filled the troughs to water their father's flock. ¹⁷Then some shepherds arrived and drove them away, but Moses came to their rescue and watered their flock. ¹⁸When they returned to their father Reuel,ᴱ he asked, "Why have you come back so quickly today?"

¹⁹They answered, "An Egyptian rescued us from the shepherds. He even drew water for us and watered the flock."

²⁰"So where is he?" he asked his daughters. "Why then did you leave the man behind? Invite him to eat dinner."

²¹Moses agreed to stay with the man, and he gave his daughter Zipporah to Moses in marriage. ²²She gave birth to a son whom he named Gershom,ᶠ for he said, "I have been a resident alien in a foreign land."

²³After a long time, the king of Egypt died. The Israelites groaned because of their difficult labor, they cried out, and their cry for help because of the difficult labor ascended to God. ²⁴God heard their groaning, and God remembered his covenant with Abraham, with Isaac, and with Jacob. ²⁵God saw the Israelites, and God knew.

ᴬ2:10 The name *Moses* sounds like "drawing out" in Hb and "born" in Egyptian.   ᴮ2:11 Lit *And it was in those days*   ᶜ2:11 Lit *his brothers*   ᴰ2:13 Or *fellow Hebrew*   ᴱ2:18 Jethro's clan or last name was Reuel; Ex 3:1.   ᶠ2:22 In Hb the name *Gershom* sounds like the phrase "a stranger there."

2:7–9 At this time, children were nursed for three or four years before being weaned. 2:10 During the New Kingdom era, Egypt would bring foreign boys to court to train them for service in Egyptian territories. Moses's name had significance for both Egyptian and Hebrew hearers. In an Egyptian name like *Thutmose, mose* is related to an Egyptian verb meaning "bear, produce, bring forth" and a noun meaning "child," while Thut/ Thoth was a god; so "Thutmose" and similar names celebrated a connection between the birth of a child and an Egyptian god. The name calls to mind a verb meaning "draw out" (2Sm 22:17; Ps 18:16), which to Hebrew readers must have sounded appropriate for the person who led the Israelites out of Egypt. 2:11–12 Despite having lived with privileges for nearly forty years in Pharaoh's palace, Moses identified with the Israelites as **his own people**. Moses's caution indicates that his action was deliberate. **Struck** translates the same root word as "striking" (v. 11) and "attacking" (v. 13). In other words, the Egyptian was striking a Hebrew man, a Hebrew man struck another Hebrew, and Moses struck the Egyptian but with a different

outcome. **Hid** translates a word used sometimes in contexts involving burying something (Gn 35:4; Jos 2:6; 7:21); it is different from the word used in vv. 2 and 3 about Moses's mother hiding him. 2:15 The **land of Midian** included territory in modern Saudi Arabia, on the east of the Gulf of Aqaba. When he **sat down by a well** as a newcomer, Moses positioned himself to meet people, as had Abraham's servant when he met Rebekah, and as Jacob had done when he met Rachel (Gn 24:11–14; 29:1–6). 2:16 The **priest of Midian**, the father of **seven daughters**, was called Reuel (v. 18; Nm 10:29), Hobab (Jdg 4:11), and most often Jethro (Ex 3:1; 4:18; 18:1–12). Midianites were descendants of Abraham through his wife Keturah (Gn 25:1–2). Because of this connection, perhaps Jethro led others in worship of the God of Abraham and Isaac, as did Melchizedek (Gn 14:18–20). The Midianites as a whole seem to have been nomadic desert dwellers who were later enemies of Israel (Gn 37:28,36; Nm 22:4,7; 25:1–18; 31:1–20; Jos 13:21; Jdg 6–8; 9:17; Ps 83:9; Is 9:4; 10:26; 60:6). 2:17–19 Again Moses came to the defense of someone. He rescued several shepherd girls from what seems to have been a common

annoyance, and they thought he was **an Egyptian**. 2:20–22 The name **Gershom** reflected Moses's status as an alien in both Egypt and Midian. 2:23–25 The word for **groaning** describes a man with broken arms in Ezk 30:24. Four different words for the Israelite outcry and four words for God's response combine to make a weighty statement of desperation and response. The formality is enhanced in Hebrew by the unusual repetition of the word **God** as the subject of each verb in vv. 24–25, which also underscores God's superiority and sovereignty: **God heard** . . . **God remembered** . . . **God saw** . . . **and God knew**. God's remembering is more than mental awareness; it implies action in keeping with his covenant promises (Gn 8:1; 19:29; 30:22; Lv 26:42–45; Pss 105:8; 106:44–46; Jr 14:21; Am 1:9).

"Knew" (1:8; 5:2; 6:3,7; 7:5; 16:12; 18:11), like "remember," typically involves more than awareness of information. Here it carries the thought of having regard for something or someone and of exercising personal concern (Pss 31:7; 37:18; 144:3; Hs 13:4). Because God knew their situation and took action, the

Moses and the Burning Bush

3 Meanwhile, Moses was shepherding the flock of his father-in-law Jethro,^A the priest of Midian. He led the flock to the far side of the wilderness and came to Horeb,^B the mountain of God. ² Then the angel of the LORD appeared to him in a flame of fire within a bush. As Moses looked, he saw that the bush was on fire but was not consumed. ³ So Moses thought, "I must go over and look at this remarkable sight. Why isn't the bush burning up?"

⁴ When the LORD saw that he had gone over to look, God called out to him from the bush, "Moses, Moses!"

"Here I am," he answered.

⁵ "Do not come closer," he said. "Remove the sandals from your feet, for the place where you are standing is holy ground." ⁶ Then he continued, "I am the God of your father,^C the God of Abraham, the God of Isaac, and the God of Jacob." Moses hid his face because he was afraid to look at God.

⁷ Then the LORD said, "I have observed the misery of my people in Egypt, and have heard them crying out because of their oppressors. I know about their sufferings, ⁸ and I have come down to rescue them from the power of the Egyptians and to bring them from that land to a good and spacious land, a land flowing with milk and honey — the territory of the Canaanites, Hethites, Amorites, Perizzites, Hivites, and Jebusites. ⁹ So because the Israelites' cry for help has come to me, and I have also seen the way the Egyptians are oppressing them, ¹⁰ therefore, go. I am sending you to

Pharaoh so that you may lead my people, the Israelites, out of Egypt."

¹¹ But Moses asked God, "Who am I that I should go to Pharaoh and that I should bring the Israelites out of Egypt?"

¹² He answered, "I will certainly be with you, and this will be the sign to you that I am the one who sent you: when you bring the people out of Egypt, you will all worship^D God at this mountain."

¹³ Then Moses asked God, "If I go to the Israelites and say to them, 'The God of your ancestors has sent me to you,' and they ask me, 'What is his name?' what should I tell them?"

¹⁴ God replied to Moses, "I AM WHO I AM.^E This is what you are to say to the Israelites: I AM has sent me to you." ¹⁵ God also said to Moses, "Say this to the Israelites: The LORD, the God of your ancestors, the God of Abraham, the God of Isaac, and the God of Jacob, has sent me to you. This is my name forever; this is how I am to be remembered in every generation.

¹⁶ "Go and assemble the elders of Israel and say to them: The LORD, the God of your ancestors, the God of Abraham, Isaac, and Jacob, has appeared to me and said: I have paid close attention to you and to what has been done to you in Egypt. ¹⁷ And I have promised you that I will bring you up from the misery of Egypt to the land of the Canaanites, Hethites, Amorites, Perizzites, Hivites, and Jebusites — a land flowing with milk and honey. ¹⁸ They will listen to what you say. Then you, along with the elders of Israel, must go to the king of Egypt and say to him: The LORD, the God of the Hebrews, has

---

Israelites and others would come to know him in a new way.

3:1 Many ancient gods were associated with a **mountain** where they were believed to live. The Lord was by no means limited to this mountain.

3:2–3 The **angel of the LORD** was active in Genesis to inform, rebuke, protect, and provide guidance and success (Gn 16:7–11; 21:17; 22:11,15; 24:7,40; 31:11). The account in Ex 3 describes the following conversation as directly between the Lord and Moses, without concern for how the event occurred. **Fire** is frequently associated with special displays of God's presence (Ex 13:21–22; 19:18; 40:38; Dt 4:11–24,33–36; Jdg 6:21; 13:20; 1Kg 18:24,38; 2Ch 7:1–3; Pss 18:8,12–13; 50:3; 97:1–5; Is 66:15–16; Dn 7:9).

3:4–6 This place was holy, not because of any quality intrinsic to it, but because of God's presence and activity there. To stay at a distance and remove footwear was then and is now in many cultures a sign of respect and humility. The Lord's self-identification, which began, **I am the God of your father**, connected this event with the past both by naming the patriarchs and by the wording of the statement (Gn 15:7; 17:1; 26:24; 28:13; 31:13; 35:11; 46:3). It also had the ring of a formal pronouncement like a king (Gn 41:44).

3:7 The emphatic construction rendered **have observed** could also be rendered "have carefully watched." The **misery** and **sufferings** of God's people never escape his notice or his concern.

3:8 The word for **honey** may also describe a sweet syrup made from boiling dates, grapes, and other fruit.

3:11–12 The Lord's promise to Moses, **I will certainly be with you**, depends for its value on who the Lord is; it matters that he is present because he is willing and able to act. This promise gave Moses grounds for authority that were missing earlier (2:11–15) and continues the important theme of God's personal involvement in the lives of his people. To **worship God** with all the Israelites at the **mountain** where God and Moses were speaking would be a sign for Moses because he would be able to look back and know that this worship was possible only because of what the Lord had done (Ex 18:1–12; 24:1–11).

3:13–15 God's statement is worded with a finality that sometimes appears at the end of a conversation, typically to put an end to debate without volunteering information.

The statements containing **I AM** use the same Hebrew verb that God's promise, "I will certainly be with you," does in v. 12 (and also 4:12,15). The wordplay with the verb makes it

especially prominent and recalls the promise, as if to remind Moses, "The one who promises to be with you is the one who sends you." Since Hebrew verbs gather much of their temporal meaning from their contexts, the same form can indicate present or future or both at once, depending on the situation. Here the promises in 3:12; 4:12,15 are oriented to the future; so though "will" is appropriate in English, it does not exclude God's presence with Moses at the time they were speaking. Nor does the English present tense "am" in 3:14 exclude the future.

3:16 When the present translation uses the word **LORD** (with large and small capital letters), it is representing the Hebrew name that can also be transliterated "Yahweh." The name *Yahweh* is connected etymologically with the Hebrew verb "to be" that appears so prominently in vv. 12 and 14. Yahweh was no stranger. He was the God of their **ancestors**: Abraham, Isaac, and Jacob. Four hundred years in Egypt had not annulled the promises made to them and their offspring (2:24).

3:18 A three-day trip . . . so that we may sacrifice was a reasonable request, since other slave groups in Egypt received permission for similar journeys to worship their gods.

met with us. Now please let us go on a three-day trip into the wilderness so that we may sacrifice to the Lord our God. ¹⁹ "However, I know that the king of Egypt will not allow you to go, even under force from a strong hand. ²⁰ But when I stretch out my hand and strike Egypt with all my miracles that I will perform in it, after that, he will let you go. ²¹ And I will give these people such favor with the Egyptians that when you go, you will not go empty-handed. ²² Each woman will ask her neighbor and any woman staying in her house for silver and gold jewelry, and clothing, and you will put them on your sons and daughters. So you will plunder the Egyptians."

Miraculous Signs for Moses

4 Moses answered, "What if they won't believe me and will not obey me but say, 'The Lord did not appear to you'?"

² The Lord asked him, "What is that in your hand?"

"A staff," he replied.

³ "Throw it on the ground," he said. So Moses threw it on the ground, it became a snake, and he ran from it. ⁴ The Lord told Moses, "Stretch out your hand and grab it by the tail." So he stretched out his hand and caught it, and it became a staff in his hand. ⁵ "This will take place," he continued, "so that they will believe that the Lord, the God of their ancestors, the God of Abraham, the God of Isaac, and the God of Jacob, has appeared to you."

⁶ In addition the Lord said to him, "Put your hand inside your cloak." So he put his hand inside his cloak, and when he took it out, his hand was diseased, resembling snow.ᴬ ⁷ "Put your hand back inside your cloak," he said. So he put his hand back inside his cloak, and when he took it out, it had again become like the rest of his skin. ⁸ "If they will not believe you and will not respond to the evidence of the first sign, they may believe the evidence of the second sign. ⁹ And if they don't believe even these two signs or listen to what you say, take some water from the Nile and pour it on the dry ground. The water you take from the Nile will become blood on the ground."

¹⁰ But Moses replied to the Lord, "Please, Lord, I have never been eloquent — either in the past or recently or since you have been speaking to your servant — because my mouth and my tongue are sluggish."ᴮ

¹¹ The Lord said to him, "Who placed a mouth on humans? Who makes a person mute or deaf, seeing or blind? Is it not I, the Lord? ¹² Now go! I will help you speakᶜ and I will teach you what to say."

¹³ Moses said, "Please, Lord, send someone else."ᴰ

¹⁴ Then the Lord's anger burned against Moses, and he said, "Isn't Aaron the Levite your brother? I know that he can speak well. And also, he is on his way now to meet you. He will rejoice when he sees you. ¹⁵ You will speak with him and tell him what to say. I will help both you and him to speakᴱ and will teach you both what to do. ¹⁶ He will speak to the people for you. He will serve as a mouth for you, and you will serve as God to him. ¹⁷ And take this staff in your hand that you will perform the signs with."

Moses's Return to Egypt

¹⁸ Then Moses went back to his father-in-law, Jethro, and said to him, "Please let me return to my relatives in Egypt and see if they are still living."

Jethro said to Moses, "Go in peace."

ᴬ4:6 A reference to whiteness or flakiness of the skin ᴮ4:10 Lit *heavy of mouth and heavy of tongue* ᶜ4:12 Lit *will be with your mouth* ᴰ4:13 Lit *send by the hand of whom you will send* ᴱ4:15 Lit *will be with your mouth and with his mouth*

3:19–20 Here God showed his full knowledge of people's character and thinking processes by predicting that Pharaoh would remain stubborn, thus also anticipating the "hardness of heart" theme that recurs in the plague stories (see 4:21–23 and note there). The two clauses **when I stretch out my hand** and **he will let you go** both use a form of the same Hebrew verb, making tight connection between cause and effect. When God's hand goes to work, the Israelites will go out of Egypt. The contest would be between the **strong hand** of the Lord and the "power [lit "hand"] of the Egyptians" as personified by Pharaoh (v. 8). **3:21–22** Gifts of **silver** and **gold** would fulfill what the Lord had told Abram (Gn 15:14), repeating the pattern of Abram's own departure from Egypt with wealth that had been handed to him (Gn 12:16,20; cp. Gn 20:14,16). **4:1–9** These three signs the Lord gave Moses pertain to areas of common human vulnerability—attack by other creatures, illness, and the need for water—all of which are under the sovereign power of the Lord.

4:2–4 Moses ordinarily would have used his **staff** to defend himself and his flock from snakes; now his staff **became a snake.** As Moses reached out, the tail would have been closest to him. **4:6–7** Traditionally and in many translations, Moses's disease has been called "leprosy," though the Hebrew term used here covers a variety of severe afflictions (Lv 13–14; Nm 12:10; Dt 24:8–9; 2Kg 5; 2Ch 26:19–21). **4:10–12** Moses's next objection that his **mouth** and **tongue** were **sluggish** returned to the problem of his personal identity and unsuitability (2:14; 3:11), as if God were dependent on him. God's answer returned attention to who he is and what he would do. **4:10** Moses began by saying he was not **eloquent** (lit "I am not a man of words"). Ironically, Moses used twenty-one Hebrew words arranged in somewhat complicated expressions to say that he could not speak well. He used a figure of speech referring to his mouth and tongue as "heavy" (lit "I am heavy of mouth and heavy of tongue"). The word for "heavy" also describes ears that do

not hear (Is 6:10; 59:1; Zch 7:11) and eyes that do not see (Gn 48:10). **4:11** The Lord answered by arguing from the greater to the lesser, implying that the Creator of all can deal with the problem of one. **4:13** Moses had offered many excuses not to do what God instructed—he was not adequate or prepared for the task (3:11), he wouldn't know what to say to the Israelites or how to answer their questions (3:13), the Israelites might not believe God sent him (4:1), and he was not eloquent enough (4:10). But here he finally gets to the heart of the issue: he just didn't want to do what God said. The irony of calling him **Lord** was not lost on Moses. God was right to be angry with him. **4:14–17** The working relationship that the Lord described for Aaron and Moses was analogous to that of a prophet with God. Aaron would serve as Moses's spokesman or messenger, and Moses would be like God for Aaron in telling him what to say to the people.

¹⁹ Now in Midian the LORD told Moses, "Return to Egypt, for all the men who wanted to kill you are dead." ²⁰ So Moses took his wife and sons, put them on a donkey, and returned to the land of Egypt. And Moses took God's staff in his hand.

²¹ The LORD instructed Moses, "When you go back to Egypt, make sure you do before Pharaoh all the wonders that I have put within your power. But I will harden his heartᴬ so that he won't let the people go. ²² And you will say to Pharaoh: This is what the LORD says: Israel is my firstborn son. ²³ I told you: Let my son go so that he may worship me, but you refused to let him go. Look, I am about to kill your firstborn son!"

²⁴ On the trip, at an overnight campsite, it happened that the LORD confronted him and intended to put him to death. ²⁵ So Zipporah took a flint, cut off her son's foreskin, threw it at Moses's feet, and said, "You are a bridegroom of blood to me!" ²⁶ So he let him alone. At that time she said, "You are a bridegroom of blood," referring to the circumcision.

Reunion of Moses and Aaron

²⁷ Now the LORD had said to Aaron, "Go and meet Moses in the wilderness." So he went and met him at the mountain of God and kissed him. ²⁸ Moses told Aaron everything the LORD had sent him to say, and about all the signs he had commanded him to do. ²⁹ Then Moses and Aaron went and assembled all the elders of the Israelites. ³⁰ Aaron repeated everything the LORD had said to Moses and performed the signs before the people. ³¹ The people believed, and when they heard that the LORD had paid attention to them and that he had seen their misery, they knelt low and worshiped.

Moses Confronts Pharaoh

5 Later, Moses and Aaron went in and said to Pharaoh, "This is what the LORD, the God of Israel, says: Let my people go, so that they may hold a festival for me in the wilderness."

² But Pharaoh responded, "Who is the LORD that I should obey him by letting Israel go? I don't knowᴮ the LORD, and besides, I will not let Israel go."

³ They answered, "The God of the Hebrews has met with us. Please let us go on a three-day trip into the wilderness so that we may sacrifice to the LORD our God, or else he may strike us with plague or sword."

⁴ The king of Egypt said to them, "Moses and Aaron, why are you causing the people to neglect their work? Get to your labor!" ⁵ Pharaoh also said, "Look, the people of the land are so numerous, and you would stop them from their labor."

Further Oppression of Israel

⁶ That day Pharaoh commanded the overseers of the people as well as their foremen, ⁷ "Don't continue to supply the people with straw for making bricks, as before. They must go and gather straw for themselves. ⁸ But require the same quota of bricks from them as they were

---

ᴬ4:21 Or will make him stubborn   ᴮ5:2 Or recognize

4:20 This is the first mention of Moses's two **sons.** Gershom was named in 2:22. The name of the second was "Eliezer" (18:3).
4:21–23 God informed Moses here not of what he was to say initially to Pharaoh but of the final result. In order to free the Lord's **firstborn son,** Pharaoh's **firstborn son** would have to die (11:4–8).
  When he presented the matter as a formal declaration (**This is what the LORD says**), God framed the message as a demand from a king to an underling. In the language of ancient treaties and letters, when a king declared that someone was his son, respect for the superior rank and authority of the "father" was called for. The Lord was claiming that he, and not Pharaoh, had authority over Israel. The Lord was also demanding that Pharaoh show proper respect to the Lord by treating his "son" with respect. Everyone understood that failure to comply would call for severe penalties.
  Such a demand to submit to the Lord would go entirely against the grain of Egyptian culture and beliefs about Pharaoh as a deity and the only king—inferior to no one.
  Exodus uses three different Hebrew words for **harden** to describe what the Lord and Pharaoh himself did to his heart. The word here is especially associated with strength. Depending on the context, it could have a positive meaning (courage, steadfastness, Pss 27:14; 31:24) or a negative meaning (stubbornness, obstinacy, Ezk 2:4). When the Lord

hardened hearts, it was a matter of executing judgment against confirmed rebels. It meant that Pharaoh would not listen and obey but would demonstrate that he deserved God's judgment.
  The hardening of Pharaoh's heart was especially appropriate as an attack on Egyptian beliefs. Egyptians valued a "hard heart," since it was needed after death during judgment to testify on behalf of the dead individual rather than to admit wrongdoing. This terminology was also used to describe the ideal person in public life, who because of his "hard heart" would always appear firm and unshaken. When Pharaoh's heart becomes hard in Exodus, however, he is not cool and in command, and the truth about his character becomes known.
4:24–26 Perhaps the statement that the Lord **intended to put him to death** expressed how the circumstances appeared to Moses and Zipporah. It was apparent to Zipporah what had to be done, and nothing is said about what would have happened if she had failed to act. **Circumcision** on the eighth day had been commanded of Abraham as the sign of God's covenant (Gn 17:1–14; 21:4). Moses's failure to circumcise his son shows that Moses had not been acting like a member of the covenant community, a serious offense. If Moses was to speak for Abraham's God, who was in the process of keeping his covenant promises, Moses needed to observe the sign of that covenant.

When Zipporah said, **You are a bridegroom of blood to me!** she may have meant that her action of bloodshed saved her husband's life, or that the ceremonial act effectively made her a close relative.
5:2 Pharaoh intended his question as an insult, not as a request for information (like the question asked about Moses's identity and authority in 2:14). Proverbs 30:9 describes the question "Who is the LORD?" as that of a self-satisfied person who is denying God's providence. Pharaoh's assertion **I don't know the LORD** continues the insult and makes no admission of ignorance. Pharaoh would have believed the answer to his rhetorical question to be "The LORD is certainly no one that I need to recognize or obey." Pharaoh was rejecting the Lord's position of superiority. A right knowledge of and respect for the identity of the Lord is central to the issue of whether or not to obey him (cp. Jn 8:48–55); the events recorded in the book of Exodus answer Pharaoh's question about who the Lord is for the benefit of the Israelites (Ex 6:7), the Egyptians (7:5), onlookers (18:11; Jos 2:8–11; Jdg 2:2–11; 1Sm 4:7–8; 6:6), and subsequent readers (Ps 105; Is 63:7–14), providing ample grounds for obedience.
5:4–18 Obedience does not always bring immediate blessing. The Israelites accuse Moses and Aaron of being the cause of their increased workload.

making before; do not reduce it. For they are slackers — that is why they are crying out, 'Let us go and sacrifice to our God.' ⁹ Impose heavier work on the men. Then they will be occupied with it and not pay attention to deceptive words."

¹⁰ So the overseers and foremen of the people went out and said to them, "This is what Pharaoh says: 'I am not giving you straw. ¹¹ Go get straw yourselves wherever you can find it, but there will be no reduction at all in your workload.'" ¹² So the people scattered throughout the land of Egypt to gather stubble for straw. ¹³ The overseers insisted, "Finish your assigned work each day, just as you did when straw was provided." ¹⁴ Then the Israelite foremen, whom Pharaoh's slave drivers had set over the people, were beaten and asked, "Why haven't you finished making your prescribed number of bricks yesterday or today, as you did before?"

¹⁵ So the Israelite foremen went in and cried for help to Pharaoh: "Why are you treating your servants this way? ¹⁶ No straw has been given to your servants, yet they say to us, 'Make bricks!' Look, your servants are being beaten, but it is your own people who are at fault."

¹⁷ But he said, "You are slackers. Slackers! That is why you are saying, 'Let us go sacrifice to the LORD.' ¹⁸ Now get to work. No straw will be given to you, but you must produce the same quantity of bricks."

¹⁹ The Israelite foremen saw that they were in trouble when they were told, "You cannot reduce your daily quota of bricks." ²⁰ When they left Pharaoh, they confronted Moses and Aaron, who stood waiting to meet them.

²¹ "May the LORD take note of you and judge," they said to them, "because you have made us reek to Pharaoh and his officials — putting a sword in their hand to kill us!"

²² So Moses went back to the LORD and asked, "Lord, why have you caused trouble for this people? And why did you ever send me? ²³ Ever since I went in to Pharaoh to speak in your name he has caused trouble for this people, and you haven't rescued your people at all."

6 But the LORD replied to Moses, "Now you will see what I will do to Pharaoh: because of a strong hand he will let them go, and because of a strong hand he will drive them from his land."

God Promises Freedom

² Then God spoke to Moses, telling him, "I am the LORD. ³ I appeared to Abraham, Isaac, and Jacob as God Almighty, but I was not known to them by my name 'the LORD.'^A ⁴ I also established my covenant with them to give them the land of Canaan, the land they lived in as aliens. ⁵ Furthermore, I have heard the groaning of the Israelites, whom the Egyptians are forcing to work as slaves, and I have remembered my covenant.

⁶ "Therefore tell the Israelites: I am the LORD, and I will bring you out from the forced labor of the Egyptians and rescue you from slavery to them. I will redeem you with an outstretched

---

^6:3 LORD (in small capitals) stands for the personal name of God, which in Hb is *Yahweh*. There is a long tradition of substituting "LORD" for "Yahweh" out of reverence.

5:19 Repeated mention of the **daily quota** (lit "the requirement/amount of a day in its day") from 5:13 helps convey the oppressiveness of the situation: the Egyptians made demands and kept account of what the Israelites did every day.
5:21 Earlier when Moses intervened in a fight between Israelites, one of them challenged his right to act as a **judge** and accused Moses of intending to kill him (2:14). Now the foremen called on the Lord to judge Moses. They were not expecting freedom at this point. Their hopes for restoring the status quo had just been crushed, so much so that they considered Moses responsible for their impending death. They believed Moses had made the Israelites so offensive to the Egyptians (**you have made us reek**) that they would want to kill the Israelites.
5:22–23 The foremen hoped to gain favor with Pharaoh by blaming others for the trouble. They still saw their welfare as under his control. When he spoke to the Lord, Moses boldly blamed both the Lord and Pharaoh (**you caused trouble** and **he has caused trouble**) for worsening conditions and asserted that the Lord had done nothing to rescue his people.
6:1 The Hebrew wording does not include a pronoun to specify that the **strong hand** must be that of the Lord rather than Pharaoh, but this theme has been mentioned in 3:19–20.

6:2–3 A variety of attempts have been made to derive English renderings other than (or more precise than) **God Almighty** for the Hebrew name *El Shaddai*, based on proposed etymological connections with words in Hebrew or in other Semitic languages. But as with many names, usage provides the best insights into its significance. The rendering of *Shaddai* as "Almighty" is traceable to Greek translations done before the time of Christ *(pantokrator)* and to the Vulgate *(Omnipotens)*. Meanwhile, the word *El* is associated with a Hebrew word for strength, and forms of it appear widely in ancient Semitic languages to refer to deity.
El is a generic word for deity—a classifying word—while *Yahweh* ("**the LORD**") is a personal name. Because this name is used in Genesis, even frequently in quoted speech (Gn 9:26; 15:2,7–8; 16:5; 18:4; 19:13–14; 21:33; 22:14,17; 24:27–56; 26:28–29; 27:20,27; 28:13), scholars have debated about what is meant when in Ex 6:3 God says, **I was not known to them by my name 'the LORD'** —referring to Abraham, Isaac, and Jacob. Since the name "the LORD" was well known by the time Genesis was written, some have proposed its usage in Genesis is anachronistic but compatible with common literary practice. Or it may be that Ex 6:3 is not indicating that the name "the LORD" was previously unknown among the Israelites but rather that now the

Israelites would see the truth of the name's meaning displayed before them. They would come to know by experience the LORD as their covenant-keeping God.
It is also possible to translate God's words as "Did I not reveal my name 'the LORD'?" (cp. 2Sm 23:5; Ps 105:28). This rendering would relieve the present difficulty, but few translations have thought it the most accurate rendering.
For God to recall to Moses the name *El Shaddai*, a deeply meaningful name from the experiences of the patriarchs, while also referring to himself as the LORD, is part of emphasizing the continuity between God's promises to the patriarchs and what he was doing for Israel through Moses.
6:4–5 I have remembered is a way of saying that he was about to act in accordance with his covenant with the ancestors (Pss 98:1–3; 109:14–16; 115:12; Jr 14:21; Am 1:9).
6:6–8 God's message for the Israelites put emphasis at the beginning, middle, and end on his identity: **I am the LORD**. Freeing Israel from Egypt would be part of a permanent relationship between the Lord and the Israelites. By what God did, the Israelites would come to **know** from experience who he is, and their own identity as his people would be established and displayed.
6:6 The references to **forced labor** in vv. 6 and 7 translate the same Hebrew word that

arm and great acts of judgment. ⁷ I will take you as my people, and I will be your God. You will know that I am the LORD your God, who brought you out from the forced labor of the Egyptians. ⁸ I will bring you to the land that I swore^ to give to Abraham, Isaac, and Jacob, and I will give it to you as a possession. I am the LORD." ⁹ Moses told this to the Israelites, but they did not listen to him because of their broken spirit and hard labor.
¹⁰ Then the LORD spoke to Moses, ¹¹ "Go and tell Pharaoh king of Egypt to let the Israelites go from his land."
¹² But Moses said in the LORD's presence, "If the Israelites will not listen to me, then how will Pharaoh listen to me, since I am such a poor speaker?"⁸ ¹³ Then the LORD spoke to Moses and Aaron and gave them commands concerning both the Israelites and Pharaoh king of Egypt to bring the Israelites out of the land of Egypt.

Genealogy of Moses and Aaron
¹⁴ These are the heads of their fathers' families:
The sons of Reuben, the firstborn of Israel:
Hanoch and Pallu, Hezron and Carmi.
These are the clans of Reuben.

¹⁵ The sons of Simeon:
Jemuel, Jamin, Ohad, Jachin, Zohar, and Shaul, the son of a Canaanite woman.
These are the clans of Simeon.

¹⁶ These are the names of the sons of Levi according to their family records;
Gershon, Kohath, and Merari.
Levi lived 137 years.
¹⁷ The sons of Gershon:
Libni and Shimei, by their clans.
¹⁸ The sons of Kohath:
Amram, Izhar, Hebron, and Uzziel.
Kohath lived 133 years.
¹⁹ The sons of Merari:
Mahli and Mushi.

These are the clans of the Levites according to their family records.

²⁰ Amram married his father's sister Jochebed,
and she bore him Aaron and Moses.
Amram lived 137 years.
²¹ The sons of Izhar:
Korah, Nepheg, and Zichri.
²² The sons of Uzziel:
Mishael, Elzaphan, and Sithri.
²³ Aaron married Elisheba,
daughter of Amminadab and sister of Nahshon.
She bore him Nadab and Abihu, Eleazar and Ithamar.
²⁴ The sons of Korah:
Assir, Elkanah, and Abiasaph.
These are the clans of the Korahites.
²⁵ Aaron's son Eleazar married one of the daughters of Putiel,
and she bore him Phinehas.
These are the heads of the Levite families by their clans.

²⁶ It was this Aaron and Moses whom the LORD told, "Bring the Israelites out of the land of Egypt according to their military divisions." ²⁷ Moses and Aaron were the ones who spoke to Pharaoh king of Egypt in order to bring the Israelites out of Egypt.

Moses and Aaron before Pharaoh
²⁸ On the day the LORD spoke to Moses in the land of Egypt, ²⁹ he said to him, "I am the LORD; tell Pharaoh king of Egypt everything I am telling you."
³⁰ But Moses replied in the LORD's presence, "Since I am such a poor speaker, how will Pharaoh listen to me?"
7 The LORD answered Moses, "See, I have made you like God to Pharaoh, and Aaron your brother will be your prophet. ² You must say whatever I command you; then Aaron your brother must declare it to Pharaoh so that he will let the Israelites go from his land.

was heard twice when Pharaoh complained that Moses and Aaron were stopping the Israelites "from their labor" (5:5) and told them to get back to their "labor" (5:4); it is also used at the start of the oppression (1:11; cp. 2:11).
The promise **I will redeem you** uses a legal term that pictures the Lord's action as that of a close relative who protects a family member or recovers property that belongs to someone in the extended family (Lv 25; 27; Dt 19; Jr 32:6–15). Boaz did this for Naomi and Ruth (Ru 3:2,9–13; 4:1–17). Such things were a matter of special interest to the Lord, who gained the reputation as Redeemer supreme (Pr 23:10–11; Is 41:14; 44:6; Jr 31:9–11). For the Lord to speak of himself

as redeeming the Israelites by means of his **outstretched arm** clarified the nature of the conflict with Pharaoh.
In a later prophecy about the future defeat of Egypt, Pharaoh's arms are broken (Ezk 30:20–26). The Lord's **great acts of judgment** (cp. Ex 7:4) would include action taken against the gods of Egypt (12:12; Nm 33:4).
6:10–12 Moses's self-deprecating **I am such a poor speaker** is (lit) "I am uncircumcised of lips." The term uncircumcised is used elsewhere of ears that could not listen (Jr 6:10) as well as being a derogatory description of the enemies of Israel (Jdg 14:3; 15:18; 1Sm 14:6; Jr 9:26; Ezk 28:10).
6:13–7:6 This genealogy interrupts the conversation between the Lord and Moses

and creates suspense by forcing readers to wait for the answer that Moses presumably received immediately. In answer to questions raised in chaps. 2–6 about the identity and abilities of Moses, it supplies a formal identification of Moses and Aaron that 6:13,26–27 and 7:6 make even more formal.
6:16–25 This family would be important to the institution of worship at the tabernacle in the wilderness, since Aaron and his sons and finally one line of his sons (Nm 25:1–18) would be designated as priests. Moses's sons are not mentioned.
6:26 According to their military divisions uses a military term to speak of the Israelites leaving in an orderly fashion.

³ But I will harden Pharaoh's heart and multiply my signs and wonders in the land of Egypt. ⁴ Pharaoh will not listen to you, but I will put my hand into Egypt and bring the military divisions of my people the Israelites out of the land of Egypt by great acts of judgment. ⁵ The Egyptians will know that I am the LORD when I stretch out my hand against Egypt and bring out the Israelites from among them."

⁶ So Moses and Aaron did this; they did just as the LORD commanded them. ⁷ Moses was eighty years old and Aaron eighty-three when they spoke to Pharaoh.

⁸ The LORD said to Moses and Aaron, ⁹ "When Pharaoh tells you, 'Perform a miracle,' tell Aaron, 'Take your staff and throw it down before Pharaoh. It will become a serpent.'" ¹⁰ So Moses and Aaron went in to Pharaoh and did just as the LORD had commanded. Aaron threw down his staff before Pharaoh and his officials, and it became a serpent. ¹¹ But then Pharaoh called the wise men and sorcerers — the magicians of Egypt, and they also did the same thing by their occult practices. ¹² Each one threw down his staff, and it became a serpent. But Aaron's staff swallowed their staffs. ¹³ However, Pharaoh's heart was hard, and he did not listen to them, as the LORD had said.

The First Plague: Water Turned to Blood

¹⁴ Then the LORD said to Moses, "Pharaoh's heart is hard: He refuses to let the people go. ¹⁵ Go to Pharaoh in the morning. When you see him walking out to the water, stand ready to meet him by the bank of the Nile. Take in your hand the staff that turned into a snake. ¹⁶ Tell him: The LORD, the God of the Hebrews, has sent me to tell you: Let my people go, so that they may worship^ me in the wilderness. But so far you have not listened. ¹⁷ This is what the LORD says: Here is how you will know that I am the LORD. Watch. I am about to strike the water in the Nile with the staff in my hand, and it will turn to blood. ¹⁸ The fish in the Nile will

^7:16 Or serve; Ex 4:23

7:3–5 God promised to harden Pharaoh's heart (cp. 4:21), this time using a word that also describes the oppression that Pharaoh inflicted on the Israelites. Pharaoh had made their slavery "difficult" or "hard" (1:14; 6:9; Dt 26:6), and in return, his heart would become "hard." This way it would be clear that when the Israelites left Egypt it was not because of the persuasiveness of Moses or the wise leadership of Pharaoh. Earlier the Lord had said that as a result of his actions, the Israelites would know him as the Lord their God (Ex 6:7). Now he said that also the Egyptians will know that I am the LORD by the way he would bring the Israelites out of Egypt. To Pharaoh and the Egyptians the acts God was about to perform would be great acts of judgment; to the Israelites, they would be signs and wonders.

7:7 Moses's life divides into three periods: the first forty years were spent in Egypt, the second forty in Midian, and the final forty leading God's people through the wilderness. Moses died at age 120 (Dt 34:7), and Aaron died at 123 (Nm 33:39).

7:8–13 Miracle in v. 9 represents the singular form of the same word translated "wonders" in vv. 10 and 12 is a different Hebrew word than in 4:3. But seeing this wonder did Pharaoh no good, since he did not respond with faith and obedience (Heb 3:13–4:6). A staff (sometimes called a scepter) as a symbol of power and authority was recognized across cultures (Ps 110:2; Is 10:5,24; 14:5; Ezk 19:10–14). Both staffs and serpents were prominent in Egyptian art. The kings of Egypt are also pictured wearing crowns that display a menacing cobra as a symbol of protection for the king and danger for his enemies, so that all would respect his commands.

7:9 The term translated serpent here and in vv. 10 and 12 is a different Hebrew than in 4:3. Since it is sometimes used to refer to large water creatures (Is 27:1; Ezk 29:3; 32:2), its appearance here may emphasize the size and frightening effect of the snakes in the contest.

7:11–12 Pharaoh summoned the wise men and sorcerers. These men used occult practices to demonstrate their power and that

of Pharaoh by duplicating what Moses and Aaron did when they simply obeyed the Lord (cp. 1Kg 18:25–39). Israel was unique among ancient Near Eastern cultures in that all forms of occult activity were outlawed because the people of God were to trust him and his provisions for their security (Lv 19:26–31; Dt 18:9–14; 2Kg 21:1–12; Is 8:13–22; 47:9–15).

7:13 This verse uses the word for hard associated with strength and firmness (as in 4:21) to describe Pharaoh's heart.

7:14–11:10 The ten plagues described in this section are in three groups of three plagues each, plus one last climactic plague—the death of the firstborn. Each plague that has an announcement comes with the same command: Let my people go, so that they may worship me (v. 16; 8:1,20; 9:1,13; 10:3). The exception is the tenth plague. There Moses informed Pharaoh that after this last plague, Pharaoh's own people would come to Moses to beg the Israelites to leave Egypt (11:8).

In each group of plagues, Moses brings the announcement of the first one to Pharaoh when meeting him "in the morning" (7:15; cp. 8:20; 9:13). The second plague of each group is announced in Pharaoh's palace, when Moses "went in to Pharaoh" (10:3; cp. 8:1; 9:1). After each of the nine plagues comes a notice about the condition of Pharaoh's heart (7:22–23; 8:15,19,32; 9:7,12,35; 10:20,27).

The plagues involved natural elements and events that were familiar to Egyptians—water, frogs, insects, east and west winds, storms, diseases, darkness—but they were not merely natural. The Lord, to and through Moses and Aaron, foretold the timing, intensity, and extent of the plagues, which set them apart from mere natural disasters. The Lord also announced the purpose of the plagues, explaining that they were intended to reveal his identity, to make him known to a wide audience (6:1,7; 7:5,17; 8:10,22; 9:14–16,29; 10:2; 11:7). Note the gradual increase in seriousness and the gradual defeat of the magicians (7:12; 8:18–19; 9:11).

Attempts have been made to identify each of the plagues as an attack on one of

the many Egyptian gods. Such equivalence is not required, however, for the events to show the futility of Egyptian beliefs, the powerlessness of Egyptian deities, and the necessity of allegiance to the Lord.

7:14 The word hard (lit "heavy") represents a Hebrew figure of speech. In English to have a "heavy heart" typically means to be troubled or sad. But the Hebrew term for "heavy" could describe a mouth and tongue that did not speak well (4:10), eyes that did not see (Gn 48:10), or ears that did not hear (Is 6:10; 59:1; Zch 7:11). In both Egyptian and Hebrew, the heart (like the mind)—as the center of mental, emotional, and volitional activity—was supposed to listen and respond appropriately. Pharaoh was failing to respond as he ought.

Pharaoh's "heavy" heart registered another problem, because according to Egyptian beliefs, gods would weigh a person's heart after death to determine his destiny in the afterlife. If it was heavy by comparison with a feather, a symbol for wisdom, then a fierce god stood by to devour the individual. Elsewhere in the OT, iniquity is spoken of as heavy and as making the heart heavy (Gn 18:20; Ps 38:4; Is 1:4; 24:20), and the Lord is the one who weighs hearts, which makes him the ultimate Judge of all, including Pharaoh and other kings (1Sm 2:3; Pr 16:2; 21:2; 24:12; Dn 5:25–28).

7:15–18 Suggestions about why Pharaoh was expected to go out in the morning to the river (8:20) include the possibility of a worship ritual, something about his personal habits, or to measure the river's depth and reach during its flood stage. It is unclear whether the river became actual blood, or whether it was so polluted that the word "blood" would best describe how it looked. The Hebrew word is related to the word for the color red and is sometimes used to describe something that had the appearance of blood but was not literal blood (Gn 49:11; Dt 32:14; 2Kg 3:22; Jl 2:31). Either way, it caused the fish to die, the water to stink, and people to need something else to drink. Pharaoh had used

die, the river will stink, and the Egyptians will be unable to drink water from it."

¹⁹ So the Lᴏʀᴅ said to Moses, "Tell Aaron: Take your staff and stretch out your hand over the waters of Egypt — over their rivers, canals, ponds, and all their water reservoirs — and they will become blood. There will be blood throughout the land of Egypt, even in wooden and stone containers."

²⁰ Moses and Aaron did just as the Lᴏʀᴅ had commanded; in the sight of Pharaoh and his officials, he raised the staff and struck the water in the Nile, and all the water in the Nile was turned to blood. ²¹ The fish in the Nile died, and the river smelled so bad the Egyptians could not drink water from it. There was blood throughout the land of Egypt.

²² But the magicians of Egypt did the same thing by their occult practices. So Pharaoh's heart was hard, and he would not listen to them, as the Lᴏʀᴅ had said. ²³ Pharaoh turned around, went into his palace, and didn't take even this to heart. ²⁴ All the Egyptians dug around the Nile for water to drink because they could not drink the water from the river. ²⁵ Seven days passed after the Lᴏʀᴅ struck the Nile.

The Second Plague: Frogs

8 Then the Lᴏʀᴅ said to Moses, "Go in to Pharaoh and tell him: This is what the Lᴏʀᴅ says: Let my people go, so that they may worship me. ² But if you refuse to let them go, then I will plague all your territory with frogs. ³ The Nile will swarm with frogs; they will come up and go into your palace, into your bedroom and on your bed, into the houses of your officials and your people, and into your ovens and kneading bowls. ⁴ The frogs will come up on you, your people, and all your officials."

⁵ The Lᴏʀᴅ then said to Moses, "Tell Aaron: Stretch out your hand with your staff over the rivers, canals, and ponds, and cause the frogs to come up onto the land of Egypt." ⁶ When Aaron stretched out his hand over the waters of Egypt, the frogs came up and covered the land of Egypt. ⁷ But the magicians did the same thing by their occult practices and brought frogs up onto the land of Egypt.

⁸ Pharaoh summoned Moses and Aaron and said, "Appeal to the Lᴏʀᴅ to remove the frogs from me and my people. Then I will let the people go and they can sacrifice to the Lᴏʀᴅ."

⁹ Moses said to Pharaoh, "You may have the honor of choosing. When should I appeal on behalf of you, your officials, and your people, that the frogs be taken away from you and your houses, and remain only in the Nile?"

¹⁰ "Tomorrow," he answered.

Moses replied, "As you have said, so that you may know there is no one like the Lᴏʀᴅ our God, ¹¹ the frogs will go away from you, your houses, your officials, and your people. The frogs will remain only in the Nile." ¹² After Moses and Aaron went out from Pharaoh, Moses cried out to the Lᴏʀᴅ for help concerning the frogs that he had brought against Pharaoh. ¹³ The Lᴏʀᴅ did as Moses had said: the frogs in the houses, courtyards, and fields died. ¹⁴ They piled them in countless heaps, and there was a terrible odor in the land. ¹⁵ But when Pharaoh saw there was relief, he hardened his heart and would not listen to them, as the Lᴏʀᴅ had said.

The Third Plague: Gnats

¹⁶ Then the Lᴏʀᴅ said to Moses, "Tell Aaron: Stretch out your staff and strike the dust of the land, and it will become gnatsᴬ throughout the land of Egypt." ¹⁷ And they did this. Aaron stretched out his hand with his staff, and when

ᴬ8:16 Perhaps sand fleas or mosquitoes

the Nile to bring death to Israelite babies, but now it would be a source of death rather than life for Egyptians.
7:19-21 The Israelite foremen had complained that Moses had made them reek to Pharaoh (same Hb verb as in v. 18; 5:21),

but now there was something that truly stank—**the Nile**.
7:22 The magicians were able to duplicate on a small scale by simple trickery the changing of the water's appearance. The magicians were unable to undo the plague on the Egyptians' water supply. So the magicians only made matters worse!
8:1-7 The second plague of frogs is described here. The magicians are again able to produce a few frogs but unable to remove the hordes of them. So again, the magicians only made matters worse.
8:8 The wording of Pharaoh's request shows that he understood what had happened and what he ought to do.
8:9-14 The opportunity for Pharaoh to choose the time would show that the end of the plague was under the Lord's control. Unless Pharaoh's answer, **Tomorrow**, was idiomatic for "immediately," or "as soon as possible," his **choosing** postponed the end of the plague until the next day. The response to Moses's prayer pointed to the Lord's incomparability; he could start and stop this plague at will.

8:15 This is the first instance of Pharaoh making his heart "heavy" himself (cp. 7:14), but it is matched by the notice in 7:23 that he failed to "take . . . to heart" the first plague. References to Pharaoh's hardening his own heart, in the sense of making it "heavy" and so inoperative, also include 8:32; 9:34.
8:16-19 Researchers have debated about exactly what kind of troublesome insects these were: **gnats**, fleas, mosquitoes, or ticks. Pharaoh's magicians could not duplicate a miracle that involved creating animate life from inanimate **dust**. Only God can do that (Gn 2:7). So they declared, **This is the finger of God** (cp. 31:18; Dt 9:10; Ps 8:3). Yet, by their description, this disaster required the action of *just* a finger of God who had said he would put his hand into Egypt. After the magicians' admission, Goshen began to be excluded from the plagues beginning with the fourth, making it irrefutable that the God of the Hebrews was responsible since he spared his own people.

#05 **99 Essential Christian Truths**

AUTHORITY OF SCRIPTURE

Since the Bible is the inspired Word from God, his special revelation to humanity, the Bible is the ultimate standard of authority for the Christian. Because it is truthful in everything that it teaches, Scripture is humanity's source for wisdom, instructing us on how to live life to the glory of God. Submitting to the authority of Scripture means that we are to believe and obey God by believing and obeying his Word.

te83

Exodus 9:9

he struck the dust of the land, gnats were on people and animals. All the dust of the land became gnats throughout the land of Egypt. [18] The magicians tried to produce gnats using their occult practices, but they could not. The gnats remained on people and animals.

[19] "This is the finger of God," the magicians said to Pharaoh. But Pharaoh's heart was hard, and he would not listen to them, as the LORD had said.

The Fourth Plague: Swarms of Flies

[20] The LORD said to Moses, "Get up early in the morning and present yourself to Pharaoh when you see him going out to the water. Tell him: This is what the LORD says: Let my people go, so that they may worship[A] me. [21] But if you will not let my people go, then I will send swarms of flies[B] against you, your officials, your people, and your houses. The Egyptians' houses will swarm with flies, and so will the land where they live.[C] [22] But on that day I will give special treatment to the land of Goshen, where my people are living; no flies will be there. This way you will know that I, the LORD, am in the land. [23] I will make a distinction[D] between my people and your people. This sign will take place tomorrow."

[24] And the LORD did this. Thick swarms of flies went into Pharaoh's palace and his officials' houses. Throughout Egypt the land was ruined because of the swarms of flies. [25] Then Pharaoh summoned Moses and Aaron and said, "Go sacrifice to your God within the country."

[26] But Moses said, "It would not be right[E] to do that, because what we will sacrifice to the LORD our God is detestable to the Egyptians. If we sacrifice what the Egyptians detest in front of them, won't they stone us? [27] We must go a distance of three days into the wilderness and sacrifice to the LORD our God as he instructs us."

[28] Pharaoh responded, "I will let you go and sacrifice to the LORD your God in the wilderness, but don't go very far. Make an appeal for me."

[29] "As soon as I leave you," Moses said, "I will appeal to the LORD, and tomorrow the swarms of flies will depart from Pharaoh, his officials, and his people. But Pharaoh must not act deceptively again by refusing to let the people go and sacrifice to the LORD." [30] Then Moses left Pharaoh's presence and appealed to the LORD. [31] The LORD did as Moses had said: He removed the swarms of flies from Pharaoh, his officials, and his people; not one was left. [32] But Pharaoh hardened his heart this time also and did not let the people go.

The Fifth Plague: Death of Livestock

9 Then the LORD said to Moses, "Go in to Pharaoh and say to him: This is what the LORD, the God of the Hebrews, says: Let my people go, so that they may worship me. [2] But if you refuse to let them go and keep holding them, [3] then the LORD's hand will bring a severe plague against your livestock in the field — the horses, donkeys, camels, herds, and flocks. [4] But the LORD will make a distinction between the livestock of Israel and the livestock of Egypt, so that nothing of all that the Israelites own will die." [5] And the LORD set a time, saying, "Tomorrow the LORD will do this thing in the land." [6] The LORD did this the next day. All the Egyptian livestock died, but none among the Israelite livestock died. [7] Pharaoh sent messengers who saw that not a single one of the Israelite livestock was dead. But Pharaoh's heart was hard, and he did not let the people go.

The Sixth Plague: Boils

[8] Then the LORD said to Moses and Aaron, "Take handfuls of furnace soot, and Moses is to throw it toward heaven in the sight of Pharaoh. [9] It will become fine dust over the entire land of

---

[A]8:20 Or serve [B]8:21 Or insects [C]8:21 Lit are [D]8:23 LXX, Syr, Vg; MT reads will place redemption [E]8:26 Or allowable

8:22–23 During the fourth plague and others to follow, the Lord would distinguish his people from Pharaoh's people in order to give knowledge of his sovereign presence. Goshen was in northeastern Egypt, possibly near Wadi Tumilat, and had excellent pasture for sheep and goats (Gn 45:10; 46:34; 47:4,6). 8:24–28 The rare word translated swarms of flies does not specify a particular insect and may indicate a mixture. Pharaoh's stipulations in vv. 25 and 28 show that he still thought he was in charge and could assert his authority. His don't go very far uses an emphatic construction and the kind of negative command that only someone of superior status could issue. The word Moses used for detest is the same one that Gn 43:32 and 46:34 use to talk about the Egyptians' refusal to eat with Joseph's Hebrew brothers, that is, the Egyptian scorn for shepherds. Pharaoh would let the Israelites go and sacrifice in the wilderness, but his quick

command—make an appeal for me—just two words in Hebrew, shows what he was primarily interested in. 8:29 Jacob used the word translated here act deceptively to describe how Laban had cheated him when he kept changing Jacob's pay (Gn 31:7). 9:1–2 The phrase holding them uses a form of the same verb that 4:4 uses where Moses "caught" the snake. To speak of Pharaoh holding on to the Israelites fits scenes in Egyptian art that depict the king as a warrior with one hand grasping a captive by the hair and the other holding a club ready to strike him. 9:3 Plague five is in keeping with the Lord's earlier announcements that he would put his hand into Egypt and extend his hand against Egypt (3:20; 7:4–5). 9:4–7 Again a distinction was made; no Israelite livestock died, which Pharaoh knew both from the plague announcement and

from checking afterward, but he did not benefit from the information he gathered. Verse 7 highlights Pharaoh's contradictory behavior by using two forms of the Hebrew word for "send"; he sent to find out about Israelite livestock but would not send the Israelites out of Egypt. Later events (vv. 19–25) indicate that all the Egyptian livestock is meant to be taken as (1) an intentional hyperbole or general statement, with exceptions being minor enough not to matter, or (2) that it refers to most of the varieties mentioned in v. 3, or (3) that animals not "in the field" (v. 3) were spared, or (4) that enough time passed for Egyptians to acquire more animals. 9:8 Furnace soot may have been readily available from brick kilns, which would have offered a measure of poetic justice. 9:9 Festering boils and specifically Egyptian boils were infamous enough to be included among the covenant curses in Dt 28:27,35.

Egypt. It will become festering boils on people and animals throughout the land of Egypt." [10] So they took furnace soot and stood before Pharaoh. Moses threw it toward heaven, and it became festering boils on people and animals. [11] The magicians could not stand before Moses because of the boils, for the boils were on the magicians as well as on all the Egyptians. [12] But the LORD hardened Pharaoh's heart and he did not listen to them, as the LORD had told Moses.

The Seventh Plague: Hail

[13] Then the LORD said to Moses, "Get up early in the morning and present yourself to Pharaoh. Tell him: This is what the LORD, the God of the Hebrews says: Let my people go, so that they may worship me. [14] For this time I am about to send all my plagues against you,[A] your officials, and your people. Then you will know there is no one like me on the whole earth. [15] By now I could have stretched out my hand and struck you and your people with a plague, and you would have been obliterated from the earth. [16] However, I have let you live for this purpose: to show you my power and to make my name known on the whole earth. [17] You are still acting arrogantly against[B] my people by not letting them go. [18] Tomorrow at this time I will rain down the worst hail that has ever occurred in Egypt from the day it was founded until now. [19] Therefore give orders to bring your livestock and all that you have in the field into shelters. Every person and animal that is in the field and not brought inside will die when the hail falls on them." [20] Those among Pharaoh's officials who feared the word of the LORD made their servants and livestock flee to shelters, [21] but those who didn't take to heart the LORD's word left their servants and livestock in the field.

[22] Then the LORD said to Moses, "Stretch out your hand toward heaven and let there be hail throughout the land of Egypt — on people and animals and every plant of the field in the land of Egypt." [23] So Moses stretched out his staff toward heaven, and the LORD sent thunder and

hail. Lightning struck the land, and the LORD rained hail on the land of Egypt. [24] The hail, with lightning flashing through it, was so severe that nothing like it had occurred in the land of Egypt since it had become a nation. [25] Throughout the land of Egypt, the hail struck down everything in the field, both people and animals. The hail beat down every plant of the field and shattered every tree in the field. [26] The only place it didn't hail was in the land of Goshen, where the Israelites were.

[27] Pharaoh sent for Moses and Aaron. "I have sinned this time," he said to them. "The LORD is the righteous one, and I and my people are the guilty ones. [28] Make an appeal to the LORD. There has been enough of God's thunder and hail. I will let you go; you don't need to stay any longer."

[29] Moses said to him, "When I have left the city, I will spread out my hands to the LORD. The thunder will cease, and there will be no more hail, so that you may know the earth[C] belongs to the LORD. [30] But as for you and your officials, I know that you still do not fear the LORD God." [31] The flax and the barley were destroyed because the barley was ripe[D] and the flax was budding, [32] but the wheat and the spelt were not destroyed since they are later crops.[E]

[33] Moses left Pharaoh and the city, and spread out his hands to the LORD. Then the thunder and hail ceased, and rain no longer poured down on the land. [34] When Pharaoh saw that the rain, hail, and thunder had ceased, he sinned again and hardened his heart, he and his officials. [35] So Pharaoh's heart was hard, and he did not let the Israelites go, as the LORD had said through Moses.

The Eighth Plague: Locusts

10 Then the LORD said to Moses, "Go to Pharaoh, for I have hardened his heart and the hearts of his officials so that I may do these miraculous signs of mine among them,[F] [2] and so that you may tell[G] your son and grandson how severely I dealt with the Egyptians and

---

[A]9:14 Lit *plagues to your heart*   [B]9:17 Or *still obstructing*   [C]9:29 Or *land*   [D]9:31 Lit *was ears of grain*   [E]9:32 Lit *are late*
[F]10:1 Lit *mine in his midst*   [G]10:2 Lit *tell in the ears of*

9:10–11 Moses and Aaron **stood before Pharaoh**, but **the magicians could not stand before Moses**. This turnabout of wording enhances the status of Moses by putting him in the position of "holding court." The magicians were finished and are not mentioned again in Exodus.
9:12 This is the first *instance* in which **the LORD hardened Pharaoh's heart**. Earlier notices have mentioned his heart's condition (7:13,22; 8:19) or recorded that Pharaoh did the hardening (8:15,32), although the first *reference* to the Lord's hardening Pharaoh's heart is in 4:21.
9:13–17 The Lord could easily have destroyed Pharaoh and his people without plagues or the hardening of Pharaoh's heart (cp. Dn 2:20–21), but these events were designed

to show the Lord's incomparability (**there is no one like me on the whole earth**). Thus God now made for himself the claim that Moses made for him earlier (8:10).
9:18–19 Previous plagues did not include direct commands about how to avoid damage.
9:27–28 When Pharaoh said, **I have sinned**, he may have been admitting to being merely "at fault," or "in the wrong," using the word translated "sinned" in a way similar to its use in 5:16.
9:29 Spreading **out . . . hands** was a gesture associated with prayer and a sign of need and dependence (1Kg 8:22,38,54; Jr 4:31). The seventh plague added significance to the Lord's name by showing his ownership of and sovereignty over the entire earth, not just a portion as with many pagan gods.

9:31–32 The description of the crops when the seventh plague hit indicates that people might have held out hope for a good harvest, but the locusts of the eighth plague would soon devour resources.
9:33–34 Here the word for **sinned** gets its full force and perhaps a touch of irony (cp. v. 27; 5:16).
9:34–10:1 These verses contain three references to the hardening of Pharaoh's heart following the plague of hail. The first reference names Pharaoh as the agent (**he . . . hardened his heart**), and it says that his officials did the same. The second names no agent and simply describes the condition (**Pharaoh's heart was hard**). The third names the Lord as the agent (**I have hardened his heart and the hearts of his**

performed miraculous signs among them, and you will know that I am the Lord."

³ So Moses and Aaron went in to Pharaoh and told him, "This is what the Lord, the God of the Hebrews, says: How long will you refuse to humble yourself before me? Let my people go, that they may worship me. ⁴ But if you refuse to let my people go, then tomorrow I will bring locusts into your territory. ⁵ They will cover the surface of the land so that no one will be able to see the land. They will eat the remainder left to you that escaped the hail; they will eat every tree you have growing in the fields. ⁶ They will fill your houses, all your officials' houses, and the houses of all the Egyptians — something your fathers and grandfathers never saw since the time they occupied the land until today." Then he turned and left Pharaoh's presence.

⁷ Pharaoh's officials asked him, "How long must this man be a snare to us? Let the men go, so that they may worship the Lord their God. Don't you realize yet that Egypt is devastated?"

⁸ So Moses and Aaron were brought back to Pharaoh. "Go, worship the Lord your God," Pharaoh said. "But exactly who will be going?"

⁹ Moses replied, "We will go with our young and with our old; we will go with our sons and with our daughters, with our flocks and with our herds because we must hold the Lord's festival."

¹⁰ He said to them, "The Lord would have to be with you if I would ever let you and your families go! Look out — you're heading for trouble. ¹¹ No, go — just able-bodied men — worship the Lord, since that's what you want." And they were driven from Pharaoh's presence.

¹² The Lord then said to Moses, "Stretch out your hand over the land of Egypt, and the locusts will come up over it and eat every plant in the land, everything that the hail left." ¹³ So Moses stretched out his staff over the land of Egypt, and the Lord sent an east wind over the land all that day and through the night. By

morning the east wind had brought in the locusts. ¹⁴ The locusts went up over the entire land of Egypt and settled on the whole territory of Egypt. Never before had there been such a large number of locusts, and there never will be again. ¹⁵ They covered the surface of the whole land so that the land was black, and they consumed all the plants on the ground and all the fruit on the trees that the hail had left. Nothing green was left on the trees or the plants in the field throughout the land of Egypt.

¹⁶ Pharaoh urgently sent for Moses and Aaron and said, "I have sinned against the Lord your God and against you. ¹⁷ Please forgive my sin once more and make an appeal to the Lord your God, so that he will just take this death away from me." ¹⁸ Moses left Pharaoh's presence and appealed to the Lord. ¹⁹ Then the Lord changed the wind to a strong westᴬ wind, and it carried off the locusts and blew them into the Red Sea. Not a single locust was left in all the territory of Egypt. ²⁰ But the Lord hardened Pharaoh's heart, and he did not let the Israelites go.

The Ninth Plague: Darkness

²¹ Then the Lord said to Moses, "Stretch out your hand toward heaven, and there will be darkness over the land of Egypt, a darkness that can be felt." ²² So Moses stretched out his hand toward heaven, and there was thick darkness throughout the land of Egypt for three days. ²³ One person could not see another, and for three days they did not move from where they were. Yet all the Israelites had light where they lived.

²⁴ Pharaoh summoned Moses and said, "Go, worship the Lord. Even your families may go with you; only your flocks and herds must stay behind."

²⁵ Moses responded, "You must also let us haveᴮ sacrifices and burnt offerings to prepare for the Lord our God. ²⁶ Even our livestock must go with us; not a hoof will be left behind

ᴬ10:19 Lit *sea*   ᴮ10:25 Lit *also give in our hand*

officials). The first (9:34) and third (10:1) use the same verb.
10:3–7 This is the first time Moses and Aaron deliver the plague announcement and then leave, showing the Lord's control of events and revealing to readers what will happen.
10:8–11 In an attempt to forestall the plague of locusts, Moses and Aaron were brought back to Pharaoh, who immediately began an argument over who should go. Moses's list included everyone and everything they owned, since the entire nation belonged to the Lord. **You're heading for trouble** translates a terse phrase with no verb, literally, "evil [is] opposite your face." The word translated "trouble" often refers to calamity or disaster; so it may be that Pharaoh referred to the trouble that the Israelites would experience if they continued to annoy him with talk of leaving—"Look out, you are

about to be in trouble from me; it's right in front of you!" Or he may have been saying that what they were contemplating was bad, evil from his point of view.
10:16–20 Pharaoh's hurry to call Moses and Aaron back, his longer confession, and his request for relief from the plague show its impact on him. Unlike before, in the aftermath of this plague, Moses said nothing to Pharaoh.
10:19 The Hebrew name for **the Red Sea**, *yam suph*, is used here for the first time. It is also applied to what is now called the Gulf of Aqaba or Gulf of Eilat, the branch of the Red Sea that extends east of the Sinai Peninsula and west of the Arabian Peninsula (1Kg 9:26). The translation "Reed Sea" or "Sea of Reeds" that is sometimes suggested recognizes that the word *suph* means "reed" or "reeds," as in Ex 2:3,5 and Is 19:6. The name

"Red Sea" reflects ancient Greek usage, which included the Gulf of Suez, the Gulf of Aqaba, the Arabian Sea, and the Persian Gulf under the Greek equivalent of "Red Sea" (*eruthra thalassey*).
10:21–23 Darkness seems appropriate as an attack on the Egyptian king, since Pharaoh was believed to be the son of Egypt's chief god, the sun god *Re*. Pharaoh had refused to allow a three-day journey for the Israelites, and now, ironically, Pharaoh's people were surrounded by darkness and unable to go anywhere for **three days**, while the Lord's people had **light** for their activities.
10:25–27 Sacrifices and burnt offerings were practiced before the Mosaic law (Gn 8:20). The word for **worship** is *'abad*, which also means "serve." Moses would much rather serve the Lord than Pharaoh.

◥ The Plagues

THE PLAGUE (OR EVENT)	EGYPT'S FALSE GODS*	SATAN'S COUNTERFEIT
Aaron's Staff Became a Serpent (Ex 7:8–13)	Wadjet (the snake goddess)	Magicians' staffs became serpents, but swallowed by Aaron's staff
Nile River to Blood (7:14–25)	Hapi (the god of the Nile flood)	Magicians also turned water to blood
Frogs (8:1–15)	Heqet (the frog goddess)	Magicians also summoned frogs
Gnats (8:16–19)	Geb (the earth god)	Magicians unable to duplicate plague
Flies (8:20–32)	Kheprer (the resurrection god, depicted as a beetle)	–
Death of Livestock (9:1–7)	Apis (the chief bull god)	–
Boils (9:8–12)	Sekhmet (the patron goddess of physicians)	Magicians affected by boils, unable to stand
Hail (9:13–35)	Nut (the sky goddess)	–
Locusts (10:1–20)	Min (the patron god of crops)	–
Darkness (10:21–29)	Amon-Re (the sun god) and the Pharaoh (the son of Re)	–
Death of the Firstborn (11:4–12:42)	All the gods of Egypt, including Pharaoh's son (12:12,29–30)	–
The Crossing of the Red Sea (13:17–14:31)	Pharaoh and the Egyptian army	Pharaoh's army swallowed by the waters of the Red Sea

PHARAOH'S HEART	"I AM THE LORD"	ISRAEL'S PROTECTION
Pharaoh's heart hardened	–	–
Pharaoh's heart hardened	"You will know that I am the LORD" (7:17)	All the Egyptians dug for water
Pharaoh hardened his heart	"There is no one like the LORD our God" (8:10)	Frogs only invaded Egyptian homes
Pharaoh's heart hardened	Magicians said, "This is the finger of God" (8:19)	–
Pharaoh hardened his heart	"You will know that I, the LORD, am in the land" (8:22)	No flies in Goshen, where the Israelites lived
Pharaoh's heart was hardened	–	None of the Israelites' livestock died
The LORD hardened Pharaoh's heart	–	Boils only on the Egyptians
Pharaoh hardened his heart	"The earth belongs to the LORD" (9:29)	No hail in Goshen, where the Israelites lived
The LORD hardened Pharaoh's heart	"You will know that I am the LORD" (10:2)	Locusts only invaded Egyptian homes
The LORD hardened Pharaoh's heart	–	All the Israelites had light where they lived
The LORD hardened Pharaoh's heart	"I am the LORD" (12:12)	God passed over the Israelites' houses marked with blood
The LORD hardened Pharaoh's heart	"The Egyptians will know that I am the LORD" (14:4)	The Israelites walked through the sea on dry ground

*The Egyptian gods listed here are false gods being confronted by the plagues.

because we will take some of them to worship the LORD our God. We will not know what we will use to worship the LORD until we get there." ²⁷ But the LORD hardened Pharaoh's heart, and he was unwilling to let them go. ²⁸ Pharaoh said to him, "Leave me! Make sure you never see my face again, for on the day you see my face, you will die."

²⁹ "As you have said," Moses replied, "I will never see your face again."

The Tenth Plague: Death of the Firstborn

11 The LORD said[A] to Moses, "I will bring one more plague on Pharaoh and on Egypt. After that, he will let you go from here. When he lets you go,[B] he will drive you out of here. ² Now announce to the people that both men and women should ask their neighbors for silver and gold items." ³ The LORD gave[C] the people favor with the Egyptians. In addition, Moses himself was very highly regarded[D] in the land of Egypt by[E] Pharaoh's officials and the people.

⁴ So Moses said, "This is what the LORD says: About midnight I will go throughout Egypt, ⁵ and every firstborn male in the land of Egypt will die, from the firstborn of Pharaoh who sits on his throne to the firstborn of the servant girl who is at the grindstones, as well as every firstborn of the livestock. ⁶ Then there will be a great cry of anguish through all the land of Egypt such as never was before or ever will be again. ⁷ But against all the Israelites, whether people or animals, not even a dog will snarl,[F] so that you may know that the LORD makes a distinction between Egypt and Israel. ⁸ All these officials of yours will come down to me and bow before me, saying: Get out, you and all the people who follow you.[G] After that, I will get out." And he went out from Pharaoh's presence fiercely angry.

⁹ The LORD said to Moses, "Pharaoh will not listen to you, so that my wonders may be multiplied in the land of Egypt." ¹⁰ Moses and Aaron did all these wonders before Pharaoh, but the LORD hardened Pharaoh's heart, and he would not let the Israelites go out of his land.

Instructions for the Passover

12 The LORD said to Moses and Aaron in the land of Egypt, ² "This month is to be the beginning of months for you; it is the first month of your year. ³ Tell the whole community of Israel that on the tenth day of this month they must each select an animal of the flock according to their fathers' families, one animal per family. ⁴ If the household is too small for a whole animal, that person and the neighbor nearest his house are to select one based on the combined number of people; you should apportion the animal according to what each will eat. ⁵ You must have an unblemished animal, a year-old male; you may take it from either the sheep or the goats. ⁶ You are to keep it until the fourteenth day of this month; then the whole assembly of the community of Israel will slaughter the animals at twilight. ⁷ They must take some of the blood and put it on the two doorposts and the lintel of the houses where they eat them. ⁸ They are to eat the meat that night; they should eat it, roasted over the fire along with unleavened bread and bitter herbs. ⁹ Do not eat any of it raw or cooked in boiling[H] water, but only roasted over fire — its head as well as its legs and inner organs. ¹⁰ You must not leave any of it until morning; any part of it left until morning you must burn. ¹¹ Here is how you must eat it: You must be dressed for travel,[I] your sandals on your feet, and your staff in your hand. You are to eat it in a hurry; it is the LORD's Passover.

[A] 11:1 Or had said   [B] 11:1 Or go, it will be finished —   [C] 11:3 Or had given   [D] 11:3 Lit was very great   [E] 11:3 Or in the eyes of   [F] 11:7 Lit point its tongue   [G] 11:8 Lit people at your feet   [H] 12:9 Or or boiled at all in   [I] 12:11 Lit must have your waist girded

---

10:28–29 Make sure you never see my face again has to do with initiating a formal appearance before Pharaoh, not a casual sighting (cp. 23:17; 34:23; 2Sm 14:23–33). Moses did see Pharaoh again secretly (Ex 12:31). Moses's words in v. 29 may also mean "I will not keep seeing you" rather than **I will never see your face again.** The angry exchange between Pharaoh and Moses shows that they agreed on one thing—that Moses's series of announcements and demands was finished. There would be no more bargaining. For Pharaoh to threaten to kill the messenger of the Lord shows that he still disrespected them both.

11:1–3 The notice that **the LORD gave the people favor with the Egyptians** and that **Moses himself was very highly regarded** by them summarizes opinions that were unexpected and different from those of Pharaoh. He was not shaping the Egyptians' opinions to the degree that a king would like to do.

11:2–5 The instructions to request **silver** and **gold** and the announcement that the

firstborn of **Egypt** would die return to matters that the Lord had told Moses about much earlier (3:19–22; 4:21–23).

11:6 A great cry of anguish corresponds to the cry of the oppressed Israelites in 3:7,9.

11:8 Moses's anger is unusual, since during the cycle of plagues nothing is said about his feelings. Moses expressed anger on behalf of the Lord. The notice of anger contributes to recognizing that Moses, although he knew about the hardening of Pharaoh's heart, considered him accountable for his actions.

12:1–13:16 Chapters 12–13 are arranged topically in a way that intersperses long sections of instruction with short sections that describe events taking place. With earlier plagues, the report of the plague follows immediately after its announcement. Not so with the tenth. Instructions to Moses and Aaron and then to the Israelites about how to observe **the LORD's Passover** (12:11) postpone the report of the plague's enactment (12:29–42). The report of the exodus (12:29–42) is followed by further instructions for future celebrations (12:43–49) and a short

summary of the first Passover observance and the exodus (12:50–51).

Another section of instructions for the future follows. It involves dedication of the firstborn and observing the Festival of Unleavened Bread (13:1–16) before the account returns to the unfolding events of the exodus (13:17–14:31).

12:2 Because of what the Lord was about to do in the current month, the Israelites were to consider it the first month of their year (**the beginning of months**). Its Canaanite name was *Abib* and its Babylonian name was *Nisan* (13:4). This lunar month overlaps with portions of the solar months of March and April.

12:3 To **select an animal of the flock** four days in advance would give opportunity to observe it for defects.

12:11–14 The declarations **it is the LORD's Passover** and **I am the LORD** reinforce the truth that what was happening centered on God's identity and his self-revelatory actions (6:2–8,29; 7:5,17, etc.). In this instance he exercised his ability and right to **execute judgments against all the gods of Egypt.**

¹² "I will pass through the land of Egypt on that night and strike every firstborn male in the land of Egypt, both people and animals. I am the LORD; I will execute judgments against all the gods of Egypt. ¹³ The blood on the houses where you are staying will be a distinguishing mark for you; when I see the blood, I will pass over you. No plague will be among you to destroy you when I strike the land of Egypt.

¹⁴ "This day is to be a memorial for you, and you must celebrate it as a festival to the LORD. You are to celebrate it throughout your generations as a permanent statute. ¹⁵ You must eat unleavened bread for seven days. On the first day you must remove yeast from your houses. Whoever eats what is leavened from the first day through the seventh day must be cut off from Israel. ¹⁶ You are to hold a sacred assembly on the first day and another sacred assembly on the seventh day. No work may be done on those days except for preparing what people need to eat — you may do only that.

¹⁷ "You are to observe the Festival of Unleavened Bread because on this very day I brought your military divisions out of the land of Egypt. You must observe this day throughout your generations as a permanent statute. ¹⁸ You are to eat unleavened bread in the first month, from the evening of the fourteenth day of the month until the evening of the twenty-first day. ¹⁹ Yeast must not be found in your houses for seven days. If anyone eats something leavened, that person, whether a resident alien or native of the land, must be cut off from the community of Israel. ²⁰ Do not eat anything leavened; eat unleavened bread in all your homes."ᴬ

²¹ Then Moses summoned all the elders of Israel and said to them, "Go, select an animal from the flock according to your families, and slaughter the Passover animal. ²² Take a cluster of hyssop, dip it in the blood that is in the basin, and brush the lintel and the two doorposts with some of the blood in the basin. None of you may go out the door of his house until morning. ²³ When the LORD passes through to strike Egypt and sees the blood on the lintel and the two doorposts, he will pass over the door and not let the destroyer enter your houses to strike you.

²⁴ "Keep this command permanently as a statute for you and your descendants. ²⁵ When you enter the land that the LORD will give you as he promised, you are to observe this ceremony. ²⁶ When your children ask you, 'What does this ceremony mean to you?' ²⁷ you are to reply, 'It is the Passover sacrifice to the LORD, for he passed over the houses of the Israelites in Egypt when he struck the Egyptians, and he spared our homes.'" So the people knelt low and worshiped. ²⁸ Then the Israelites went and did this; they did just as the LORD had commanded Moses and Aaron.

The Exodus

²⁹ Now at midnight the LORD struck every firstborn male in the land of Egypt, from the firstborn of Pharaoh who sat on his throne to the firstborn of the prisoner who was in the dungeon, and every firstborn of the livestock. ³⁰ During the night Pharaoh got up, he along with all his officials and all the Egyptians, and there was a loud wailing throughout Egypt because there wasn't a house without someone dead. ³¹ He summoned Moses and Aaron during the night and said, "Get out immediately from among my people, both you and the Israelites, and go, worship the LORD as you have said. ³² Take even your flocks and your herds as you asked and leave, and also bless me."

³³ Now the Egyptians pressured the people in order to send them quickly out of the country, for they said, "We're all going to die!" ³⁴ So the people took their dough before it was leavened, with their kneading bowls wrapped up in their clothes on their shoulders.

³⁵ The Israelites acted on Moses's word and asked the Egyptians for silver and gold items and for clothing. ³⁶ And the LORD gave the people such favor with the Egyptians that they gave them what they requested. In this way they plundered the Egyptians.

³⁷ The Israelites traveled from Rameses to Succoth, about six hundred thousand able-bodied

12:15–20 Eating **unleavened bread** would remind the Israelites of their rapid departure from Egypt that did not allow time for a leavening agent to make the bread rise (v. 39). **12:21–22** The instructions were summarized for the elders, who would pass the instructions on to the rest of the Israelites. Hyssop would be used in cleansing rituals (Lv 14:4,6,49,51–52; Nm 19:6,18; Ps 51:7; Heb 9:19). **12:23** The descriptions of the death of the firstborn say nothing more about **the destroyer**, nor do they indicate how the humans or animals died. The Lord's sovereign activity was the issue, and he presented himself as bringing about the deaths. He also referred to the plague as destroying (v. 13), in an expression that uses a Hebrew word

closely related to the one here translated "destroyer." **12:29–30 The prisoner who was in the dungeon** was a person opposite Pharaoh in social standing. Mention of both extremes encompassed all people in between. **12:31–32** Pharaoh had one last encounter with **Moses and Aaron**. He had declared that Moses would die if they met again, but he could not keep that resolve. Instead, he capitulated and gave unconditional release of all the Israelites to go and worship, but he himself made no mention of worshiping the Lord (cp. 2Kg 5:17–18). **12:33–34 We're all going to die!** is the last recorded statement to Moses by ordinary Egyptians. It uses just two words in Hebrew

and assesses the situation without any pretense, the expectation being that all the Egyptians were about to die if the Israelites stayed any longer in Egypt. **12:35–36** These verses describe what the statements in 3:21–22 and 11:2–3 had looked toward. **12:37 Rameses** and **Succoth** are thought to have been in eastern Egypt (1:11), with Succoth east of Rameses in an area that the ancient Egyptians called Tjeku. This was at the eastern end of the Wadi Tumilat and contained fortifications because the area was a trade route with access to the Sinai Peninsula. The large number of people who left Egypt contrasts with the small number who had entered it (1:1–5). The census of

men on foot, besides their families. ³⁸ A mixed crowd also went up with them, along with a huge number of livestock, both flocks and herds. ³⁹ The people baked the dough they had brought out of Egypt into unleavened loaves, since it had no yeast; for when they were driven out of Egypt, they could not delay and had not prepared provisions for themselves.

⁴⁰ The time that the Israelites lived in Egypt^A was 430 years. ⁴¹ At the end of 430 years, on that same day, all the LORD's military divisions went out from the land of Egypt. ⁴² It was a night of vigil in honor of the LORD, because he would bring them out of the land of Egypt. This same night is in honor of the LORD, a night vigil for all the Israelites throughout their generations.

Passover Instruction

⁴³ The LORD said to Moses and Aaron, "This is the statute of the Passover: no foreigner may eat it. ⁴⁴ But any slave a man has purchased may eat it, after you have circumcised him. ⁴⁵ A temporary resident or hired worker may not eat the Passover. ⁴⁶ It is to be eaten in one house. You may not take any of the meat outside the house, and you may not break any of its bones. ⁴⁷ The whole community of Israel must celebrate^B it. ⁴⁸ If an alien resides among you and wants to observe the LORD's Passover, every male in his household must be circumcised, and then he may participate;^C he will become like a native of the land. But no uncircumcised person may eat it. ⁴⁹ The same law will apply to both the native and the alien who resides among you."

⁵⁰ Then all the Israelites did this; they did just as the LORD had commanded Moses and Aaron. ⁵¹ On that same day the LORD brought the Israelites out of the land of Egypt according to their military divisions.

13 The LORD spoke to Moses: ² "Consecrate every firstborn male to me, the firstborn from every womb among the Israelites, both man and domestic animal; it is mine."

³ Then Moses said to the people, "Remember this day when you came out of Egypt, out of the place of slavery, for the LORD brought you out of here by the strength of his hand. Nothing leavened may be eaten. ⁴ Today, in the month of Abib,^D you are going out. ⁵ When the LORD brings you into the land of the Canaanites, Hethites, Amorites, Hivites, and Jebusites,^E which he swore to your ancestors that he would give you, a land flowing with milk and honey, you must carry out this ceremony in this month. ⁶ For seven days you must eat unleavened bread, and on the seventh day there is to be a festival to the LORD. ⁷ Unleavened bread is to be eaten for those seven days. Nothing leavened may be found among you, and no yeast may be found among you in all your territory. ⁸ On that day explain to your son, 'This is because of what the LORD did for me when I came out of Egypt.' ⁹ Let it serve as a sign for you on your hand and as a reminder on your forehead,^F so that the LORD's instruction may be in your mouth; for the LORD brought you out of Egypt with a strong hand. ¹⁰ Keep this statute at its appointed time from year to year.

¹¹ "When the LORD brings you into the land of the Canaanites, as he swore to you and your ancestors, and gives it to you, ¹² you are to present to the LORD every firstborn male of the womb. All firstborn offspring of the livestock you own that are males will be the LORD's. ¹³ You must redeem every firstborn of a donkey with a flock animal, but if you do not redeem it, break its

---

^A 12:40 LXX, Sam add *and in Canaan*   ^B 12:47 Lit *do*   ^C 12:48 Lit *may come near to do it*   ^D 13:4 March–April; called Nisan in the post-exilic period; Neh 2:1; Est 3:7   ^E 13:5 DSS, Sam, LXX, Syr add *Girgashites* and *Perizzites*; Jos 3:10   ^F 13:9 Lit *reminder between your eyes*

---

about six hundred thousand able-bodied men implies a total population of more than two million.
12:38 The **mixed crowd** may have included other laborers who saw an opportunity to escape from Egyptian servitude, but who had not necessarily come to faith in the Lord (Nm 11:4).
12:40–41 Starting from 966 BC, when Solomon began to build the Lord's temple, and adding 480 years (1Kg 6:1) yields 1446 BC for the date of the exodus. Adding **430 years** to that brings Jacob to Egypt in 1876 BC, during the Egyptian Middle Kingdom era.
12:43–49 Passover was a family event for those who belonged to the covenant community of Israel, to whom circumcision was the sign of the covenant that God was in the process of fulfilling (2:24; Gn 17:9–13). The restriction against breaking the **bones** of the lamb foreshadows Jesus, the true Passover Lamb (Jn 19:33–36; cp. Ps 34:20).
13:1–16 In addition to having the Passover Feast and Festival of Unleavened Bread, the Israelites would memorialize what the Lord had

done for them when they set apart, or consecrated, the firstborn males of both humans and animals. In future years the Israelites were to reenact certain events of the exodus. They would eat a meal like their last one in Egypt, and they would eat unleavened bread, as they had done in the early days of their journey out of Egypt (12:39). Because the Lord had distinguished and redeemed Israel, his firstborn, they would redeem their firstborn sons (4:22–23; 6:6; 15:13; 22:29–31; 34:18–20; Dt 7:8; 9:26).
13:2 The significance of Israel's firstborn sons and animals was tied to what the Lord had done and said rather than to anything special about them.
13:3 The theme of God's strong **hand** comes up repeatedly in instructions about the celebration (vv. 9,14,16; cp. 32:11) and uses forms of the Hebrew word for "strong" or "strength" that describe the hardening of Pharaoh's heart by strengthening his resolve and making him more firmly determined (7:13,22; 8:19; 9:35; 10:22,27; 11:10; 14:4,8,17).
13:5 On the groups in Canaan that the Israelites would drive out, see Dt 7:1.

13:9 That the LORD's instruction may be in your mouth emphasizes that the Israelites would accept, meditate on, and do what the Lord prescribed (Dt 30:14; Jos 1:8; Ps 1:2; Is 59:21). The effect of what the Lord had done should be as great as if it all were displayed on each person's **hand** (easy for the person to see) and **forehead** (easy for others to see). When that was the case, the individual would readily speak of what the Lord had said, meditate on it, and act accordingly (Pss 50:16; 119:46–48; Mal 2:7).
13:12 The command **you are to present to the LORD** uses a verb that refers elsewhere to transferring property (Gn 32:16; Nm 27:7–8; 2Sm 3:10; Is 45:14). It is not normally used to describe offerings to the Lord. Its use in Ex 13:12 ("pass something over to"/"convey over to") recalls its use in describing the actions of the Lord, who "passed through" Egypt (12:12,23). What he had done must shape what his people would do.
13:13 Redemption brought an animal or person back into its original or ordinary use (Lv 25:23–28). Donkeys could not be sacrificed,

neck. However, you must redeem every first-born among your sons.

¹⁴ "In the future, when your son asks you, 'What does this mean?' say to him, 'By the strength of his hand the LORD brought us out of Egypt, out of the place of slavery. ¹⁵ When Pharaoh stubbornly refused to let us go, the LORD killed every firstborn male in the land of Egypt, both the firstborn of humans and the firstborn of livestock. That is why I sacrifice to the LORD all the firstborn of the womb that are males, but I redeem all the firstborn of my sons.' ¹⁶ So let it be a sign on your hand and a symbol^ on your forehead, for the LORD brought us out of Egypt by the strength of his hand."

The Route of the Exodus

¹⁷ When Pharaoh let the people go, God did not lead them along the road to the land of the Philistines, even though it was nearby; for God said, "The people will change their minds and return to Egypt if they face war." ¹⁸ So he led the people around toward the Red Sea along the road of the wilderness. And the Israelites left the land of Egypt in battle formation.

¹⁹ Moses took the bones of Joseph with him, because Joseph had made the Israelites swear a solemn oath, saying, "God will certainly come to your aid; then you must take my bones with you from this place."

²⁰ They set out from Succoth and camped at Etham on the edge of the wilderness. ²¹ The LORD went ahead of them in a pillar of cloud to lead them on their way during the day and in a pillar of fire to give them light at night, so that they could travel day or night. ²² The pillar of cloud by day and the pillar of fire by night never left its place in front of the people.

14 Then the LORD spoke to Moses: ² "Tell the Israelites to turn back and camp in front of Pi-hahiroth, between Migdol and the sea; you must camp in front of Baal-zephon, facing it by the sea. ³ Pharaoh will say of the Israelites: They are wandering around the land in confusion; the wilderness has boxed them in. ⁴ I will harden Pharaoh's heart so that he will pursue them. Then I will receive glory by means of Pharaoh and all his army, and the Egyptians will know that I am the LORD." So the Israelites did this.

The Egyptian Pursuit

⁵ When the king of Egypt was told that the people had fled, Pharaoh and his officials changed their minds about the people and said, "What have we done? We have released Israel from serving us." ⁶ So he got his chariot ready and took his troops⁸ with him; ⁷ he took six hundred of the best chariots and all the rest of the chariots of Egypt, with officers in each one. ⁸ The LORD hardened the heart of Pharaoh king of Egypt, and he pursued the Israelites, who were going out defiantly.ᶜ ⁹ The Egyptians — all Pharaoh's horses and chariots, his horsemen,ᴰ and his army — chased after them and caught up with them as they camped by the sea beside Pi-hahiroth, in front of Baal-zephon.

¹⁰ As Pharaoh approached, the Israelites looked up and there were the Egyptians coming after them! The Israelites were terrified and cried out to the LORD for help. ¹¹ They said to Moses, "Is it because there are no graves in Egypt that you have taken us away to die in

---

^13:16 Or *phylactery* ⁸14:6 Lit *people* ᶜ14:8 Lit *with a raised hand* ᴰ14:9 Or *chariot drivers*

---

so the **firstborn of a donkey** should be redeemed for normal use by giving a sheep or goat in its place. A human firstborn must be redeemed (Nm 18:15–16). The Lord's requirement of redemption for a human firstborn contrasted with the practices of pagan worshipers who killed children in rituals designed to curry favor with their gods.
13:17 The Lord could have taken his people safely on any route he wished. The choice of route here and the comment on it offer insight into the thinking of both the Lord and the Israelites. The Lord knew the Israelites better than Pharaoh, who considered them a military threat (1:10).
This choice of route displays who the Lord is. As a result of it, the Israelites would watch the Lord fight for them (14:13–14). They would experience his care and his willingness to work in spite of their frailties (Ps 103:13–14). The **Philistines** came to the western coast of the Mediterranean from islands in the Aegean Sea and would later be frequent foes of Israel.
13:18 The road of the wilderness would take Israel east into the Sinai Peninsula, to the Wilderness of Shur (15:22; cp. 1Sm 15:7). "Wilderness" describes uninhabited areas with varying amounts of water and

pasturage, depending on the area and the time of year. The description of the Israelites leaving **in battle formation** uses a rare word (Jos 1:14; 4:12; "troops" in Jdg 7:11).
13:19 God was doing exactly what **Joseph** had said he would do (3:16; 4:31; Gn 50:24–25).
13:20–22 The Lord signified his presence with the Israelites by means of a **pillar of cloud** and a **pillar of fire**. Even other peoples heard about it (Nm 14:14).
14:1–2 The Lord led the Israelites to where they could be trapped between the sea and the Egyptian army. The name **Pi-hahiroth** may mean "mouth of the canal." The remnants of an ancient canal have been found east of Wadi Tumilat, a route into the Sinai Peninsula. **Migdol** means "tower" or "watchtower." **Baal-zephon**, "Lord of the North," incorporates the name of a Canaanite god important to seafarers.
14:4 The Hebrew word translated **glory** (related to the idea of being heavy) is related to one of the words describing Pharaoh's "hardened" heart (8:15,32; 9:7,34; 10:1). The Lord would receive glory from Pharaoh's refusal to give glory.
14:5 The Israelites' actions appeared to evidence fear, which fit the Egyptian opinion of them better than the triumph described in

v. 8. The word translated **fled** indicates they had cleared out entirely, as did Moses after killing the Egyptian (2:15). It is typically used of people who were emigrating in order to escape the reach of a powerful person (Gn 16:6,8; 31:21–22; 1Sm 19:12,18; 21:10; 27:4; 1Kg 11:17,23,40). The Egyptians began to focus on their loss—**we have released Israel from serving us**—plus the change in the situation of the Israelites.
14:6–7 To people on foot, **chariots** and horses would have seemed as terrifying as armored tanks (see v. 10 and note there). Egypt took pride in its chariots, portraying them in art meant to display Egyptian power.
14:10 Verses 5–9 provided a panoramic perspective. The perspective switches here to that of the Israelites, using a word that older translations render "and behold," which Hebrew authors could use to make a rapid switch in perspective and give readers a momentary share in the experience of someone in the story. When the Egyptian army suddenly appeared, the Israelites' eyes became wide with terror: **there were the Egyptians**!
14:11–12 Terror turned Israelite elation and triumph into sarcasm and accusation. They considered Moses responsible for their

the wilderness? What have you done to us by bringing us out of Egypt? [12] Isn't this what we told you in Egypt: Leave us alone so that we may serve the Egyptians? It would have been better for us to serve the Egyptians than to die in the wilderness."

[13] But Moses said to the people, "Don't be afraid. Stand firm and see the LORD's salvation that he will accomplish for you today; for the Egyptians you see today, you will never see again. [14] The LORD will fight for you, and you must be quiet."

Escape through the Red Sea

[15] The LORD said to Moses, "Why are you crying out to me? Tell the Israelites to break camp. [16] As for you, lift up your staff, stretch out your hand over the sea, and divide it so that the Israelites can go through the sea on dry ground. [17] As for me, I am going to harden the hearts of the Egyptians so that they will go in after them, and I will receive glory by means of Pharaoh, all his army, and his chariots and horsemen. [18] The Egyptians will know that I am the LORD when I receive glory through Pharaoh, his chariots, and his horsemen."

[19] Then the angel of God, who was going in front of the Israelite forces, moved and went behind them. The pillar of cloud moved from in front of them and stood behind them. [20] It came between the Egyptian and Israelite forces. There was cloud and darkness, it lit up the night, and neither group came near the other all night long. [21] Then Moses stretched out his hand over the sea. The LORD drove the sea back with a powerful east wind all that night and turned the sea into dry land. So the waters were divided, [22] and the Israelites went through the sea on dry ground, with the waters like a wall to them on their right and their left.

[23] The Egyptians set out in pursuit — all Pharaoh's horses, his chariots, and his horsemen — and went into the sea after them. [24] During the morning watch, the LORD looked down at the Egyptian forces from the pillar of fire and cloud, and threw the Egyptian forces into confusion. [25] He caused their chariot wheels to swerve[A,B] and made them drive[C] with difficulty. "Let's get away from Israel," the Egyptians said, "because the LORD is fighting for them against Egypt!"

[26] Then the LORD said to Moses, "Stretch out your hand over the sea so that the water may come back on the Egyptians, on their chariots and horsemen." [27] So Moses stretched out his hand over the sea, and at daybreak the sea returned to its normal depth. While the Egyptians were trying to escape from it, the LORD threw them into the sea. [28] The water came back and covered the chariots and horsemen, plus the entire army of Pharaoh that had gone after them into the sea. Not even one of them survived. [29] But the Israelites had walked through the sea on dry ground, with the waters like a wall to them on their right and their left. [30] That day the LORD saved Israel from the power of the Egyptians, and Israel saw the Egyptians dead on the seashore. [31] When Israel saw the great power that the LORD used against the Egyptians, the people feared the LORD and believed in him and in his servant Moses.

Israel's Song

15 Then Moses and the Israelites sang this song to the LORD. They said:

I will sing to the LORD,
    for he is highly exalted;
he has thrown the horse

[A]14:25 Sam, LXX, Syr read *He bound their chariot wheels* [B]14:25 Or *fall off* [C]14:25 Or *and they drove them*

---

impending doom, and themselves helpless victims. Their assessment gave no thought to any third option besides death or servitude in Egypt. By not considering the Lord's involvement, the Israelites resembled faithless Pharaoh.
14:13–14 The command **Don't be afraid**, given as a word from the Lord to his people or an affirmation of confidence before battle, has many parallels (Nm 21:34; Dt 1:21,29; 3:2,22; Jos 8:1; 10:8,25; 2Ch 20:15,17; 32:7; Neh 4:14). Moses gave no defense of himself but focused instead on what the Lord would accomplish. The words **salvation** (here and Ex 15:2; Hb *yeshu'ah*) and "saved" (14:30) mark the instructions for the encounter with Egyptian forces, its summary, and its celebration. An earlier pharaoh was afraid that the Israelites might fight against Egypt (1:10), but something greater happened—the Lord fought for Israel and against Egypt (14:14,25).
14:15–18 The Lord informs Moses and all Israel how he is going to deliver them from this impossible situation. **The Egyptians will know that I am the LORD** occurs here for the third time (7:5; 14:4).

14:19–20 The **angel of God** and the **pillar of cloud** may have looked familiar to Moses, for he saw the angel and the fire when God commissioned him to return to Egypt (3:2; Nm 20:16; Dt 31:15). Besides showing the way to go, day or night, the pillar of cloud prevented a clash between the **Egyptian and Israelite forces**.
14:22 The **waters like a wall** on both sides forced the Egyptians to follow straight ahead and protected the Israelites from a flanking attack.
14:24–25 The night hours were divided into three "watches." **The morning watch** or end of the night was roughly 2:00–6:00 a.m. The Lord observed the Egyptians from his superior vantage point (cp. Dt 26:15; Pss 14:2; 53:2; 85:11; 102:19). With his accurate reconnaissance, God threw the Egyptians **into confusion**. This is a weapon he used on a number of occasions (23:27; Jos 10:10; 1Sm 5:9,11; 7:10; cp. 2Kg 7:6–7). Now the Lord, rather than the Israelites, was the one who fought against Egypt, and the Egyptians themselves announced the fact.
14:29–31 These verses summarize the completeness of the Lord's victory by using many

terms that the speakers have used earlier, mostly in the near context. Instead of dying (vv. 11–12), the Israelites **saw the Egyptians dead** . . . **The LORD saved Israel from the power** [lit "hand"] **of the Egyptians** (cp. 3:8; 18:10; Dt 7:8; 2Kg 17:7). The assertion that **Israel saw the great power** [lit "hand"] **that the LORD used** continues the theme of the Lord's action as an exercise of his hand (Ex 3:20; 7:4–5; 9:3,15; 13:3,9,14,16) in contest with the hand of Pharaoh and the Egyptians, and it uses the verb that Moses used in 14:13 (cp. vv. 5,11). **The people feared the LORD**, and this is what Pharaoh had failed to do (1:17,21; 9:20–21,30). The mention of Moses as the Lord's **servant** accords Moses the highest of titles in the hierarchy of the Lord's society and is the one by which Moses was called many times (Nm 12:7–8; Dt 34:5; Jos 1:1,7,13,15; cp. Gn 26:24; 2Sm 3:18; Is 41:8; Rm 1:1; Rv 19:10).
15:1–18 The introduction of this song conveys a change of atmosphere and highlights the importance of the occasion. While the prose account speaks *about* the Lord, the song speaks *to* the Lord and is more personal. Since Moses had complained about being inarticulate, it is something of a surprise as

and its rider into the sea.
² The LORD is my strength and my song;^A
he has become my salvation.
This is my God, and I will praise him,
my father's God, and I will exalt him.
³ The LORD is a warrior;
the LORD is his name.

⁴ He threw Pharaoh's chariots
and his army into the sea;
the elite of his officers
were drowned in the Red Sea.
⁵ The floods covered them;
they sank to the depths like a stone.
⁶ LORD, your right hand is glorious
in power.
LORD, your right hand shattered
the enemy.
⁷ You overthrew your adversaries
by your great majesty.
You unleashed your burning wrath;
it consumed them like stubble.
⁸ The water heaped up at the blast
from your nostrils;
the currents stood firm like a dam.
The watery depths congealed
in the heart of the sea.

⁹ The enemy said:
"I will pursue, I will overtake,
I will divide the spoil.
My desire will be gratified
at their expense.
I will draw my sword;
my hand will destroy^B them."
¹⁰ But you blew with your breath,
and the sea covered them.
They sank like lead
in the mighty waters.

¹¹ LORD, who is like you among the gods?
Who is like you, glorious in holiness,
revered with praises,
performing wonders?
¹² You stretched out your right hand,
and the earth swallowed them.
¹³ With your faithful love,
you will lead the people
you have redeemed;
you will guide them
to your holy dwelling
with your strength.

¹⁴ When the peoples hear,
they will shudder;

^A15:2 Or *might*   ^B15:9 Or *conquer*

---

well. Other poetic reflections on the exodus include Pss 77; 78; 105; 106; Is 63:7–14.
15:2–3 This is my God affirms the Lord's objective that the Israelites would know him as their God (6:7). **My father's God** ties this event to the covenant relationship between the Lord and the patriarchs (2:24; 3:6).
15:7 Stubble recalls how the Egyptians had troubled the Israelites over obtaining straw

for bricks, forcing them to scrabble about for "stubble" (5:12). Now the Egyptians had been reduced to stubble.
15:12 The earth swallowed them is a poetic way of saying that they died (Pss 63:9; 71:20; Pr 1:12; Jnh 2:6).
15:13 The word translated **faithful love** refers to displays of loyalty and kind provisions of help between family members or friends,

often in situations where the needy party would have no legal right to the assistance (20:6; 34:6–7 contain the other uses of the word in Exodus; cp. Ru 1:8; 2:20; 3:10; 1Sm 20:8; 2Sm 9:1).
15:14–16 The nations are listed in the order Israel would encounter them during the exodus: first the people of **Philistia**, then those in **Edom** (descended from Esau), **Moab**

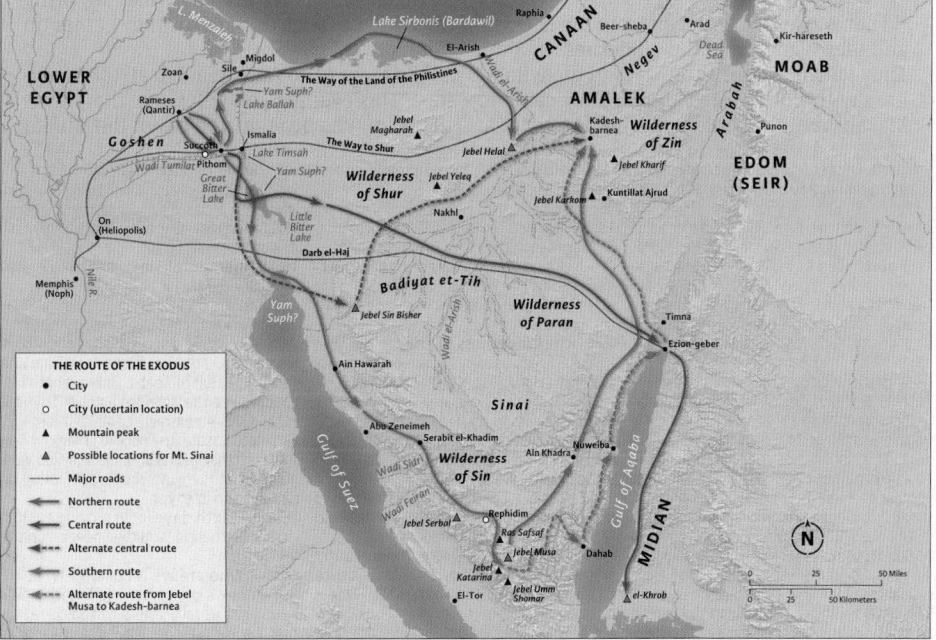

anguish will seize the inhabitants
of Philistia.
15 Then the chiefs of Edom will be
terrified;
trembling will seize the leaders
of Moab;
all the inhabitants of Canaan will panic;
16 terror and dread will fall on them.
They will be as still^A as a stone
because of your powerful arm
until your people pass by, LORD,
until the people whom you purchased^B
pass by.

17 You will bring them in and plant them
on the mountain of your possession;
LORD, you have prepared the place
for your dwelling;
Lord,^c your hands have established
the sanctuary.
18 The LORD will reign forever and ever!

19 When Pharaoh's horses with his chariots and horsemen went into the sea, the LORD brought the water of the sea back over them. But the Israelites walked through the sea on dry ground. 20 Then the prophetess Miriam, Aaron's sister, took a tambourine in her hand, and all the women came out following her with tambourines and dancing. 21 Miriam sang to them:

Sing to the LORD,
for he is highly exalted;
he has thrown the horse
and its rider into the sea.

Water Provided

22 Then Moses led Israel on from the Red Sea, and they went out to the Wilderness of Shur. They journeyed for three days in the wilderness without finding water. 23 They came to Marah, but they could not drink the water at Marah because it was bitter — that is why it was named Marah.^D 24 The people grumbled to Moses, "What are we going to drink?" 25 So he cried out to the LORD, and the LORD showed him a tree. When he threw it into the water, the water became drinkable.

The LORD made a statute and ordinance for them at Marah, and he tested them there. 26 He said, "If you will carefully obey the LORD your God, do what is right in his sight, pay attention to his commands, and keep all his statutes, I will not inflict any illnesses on you that I inflicted on the Egyptians. For I am the LORD who heals you." 27 Then they came to Elim, where there were twelve springs and seventy date palms, and they camped there by the water.

Manna and Quail Provided

16 The entire Israelite community departed from Elim and came to the Wilderness of Sin, which is between Elim and Sinai, on the fifteenth day of the second month after they had left the land of Egypt. 2 The entire Israelite community grumbled against Moses and Aaron in the wilderness. 3 The Israelites said to them, "If only we had died by the LORD's hand in the land of Egypt, when we sat by pots of meat and ate all the bread we wanted. Instead, you brought us into this wilderness to make this whole assembly die of hunger!"

4 Then the LORD said to Moses, "I am going to rain bread from heaven for you. The people are to go out each day and gather enough for that day. This way I will test them to see whether or not they will follow my instructions. 5 On the sixth day, when they prepare what they bring in, it will be twice as much as they gather on other days."^E

6 So Moses and Aaron said to all the Israelites, "This evening you will know that it was the LORD who brought you out of the land of

---

^A15:16 Or silent   ^B15:16 Or created   ^c15:17 Some Hb mss, DSS, Sam, Tg read LORD   ^D15:23 = Bitter or Bitterness   ^E16:5 Lit as gathering day to day

---

(descended from Lot), and **Canaan** (descended from Ham's son Canaan). The idea that God **purchased** or redeemed Israel is also found elsewhere (see Ps 74:2; Is 11:11, where "recover" translates the same verb). The verb is often used of buying a slave (Gn 39:1; Ex 21:2) or land (Gn 47:20; 2Sm 24:21).
15:20 Moses and Aaron were already familiar with the work of prophets and prophecy (4:14–16; 6:30–7:2). Their sister **Miriam** shared in the work (6:20; Nm 12:1–15; 26:59; cp. Jdg 4:4; 2Kg 22:12–20; Neh 6:14; Is 8:3; Ezk 13; Jl 2:28–29).
15:21 The last lines of the song repeat the first, except that the first is a declaration of resolve to praise and the last is a command, an exhortation to praise. The song was sung antiphonally (cp. Ps 136).
15:22–17:16 In this section, the primary conflict is no longer the Lord and Moses versus Pharaoh and the Egyptians, but the Lord and Moses versus the Israelites, who still tended to look back to Egypt for provision (13:17; 17:3).

15:22–27 The account of water provided at **Marah** introduces themes prominent in the accounts of Israel's time in the wilderness: grumbling, testing, and the need for attention and obedience to the Lord's commands.
15:22 The **Wilderness of Shur**, in the Sinai Peninsula, has been mentioned in connection with Hagar (Gn 16:7–14) and Abraham (Gn 20:1).
15:24 The word translated **grumbled** signals a hostile question and is used mostly to describe the Israelites' rebellious complaining (chaps. 15–17; Nm 14–17).
15:25–26 The word translated **tested** is used once before in the Pentateuch when the Lord tested Abraham by commanding him to sacrifice Isaac (Gn 22:1–2). The changing of bitter water recalls when God did the opposite in Egypt's water (Ex 7:17–24; cp. 23:25). There is no naturalistic or herbal explanation of how **a tree** made the water drinkable.

15:27 Elim may be modern Wadi Gharandel, in western Sinai, Egypt.
16:1 Wilderness of Sin uses a transliterated Hebrew word that may be a shortened form of **Sinai**. The traditional site of Mount Sinai, *Jebel Musa* in Arabic, is in the southern Sinai Peninsula. Other proposed sites for Mount Sinai are in central and northern Sinai and east of the Gulf of Aqaba. Only a month had passed since the Israelites had left Egypt.
16:2–3 This time Israel's complaint is longer and more hostile. The people's memory was short and their hearts ungrateful. If God were going to let them die, they would rather he had done so in Egypt.
16:5 The **sixth day** would provide enough that no gathering would be needed on the seventh day.
16:6–8 Who are we is literally, "What are we?" Moses's use of the interrogative pronoun that usually refers to things rather than people presents himself and Aaron as

Egypt, ⁷ and in the morning you will see the LORD's glory because he has heard your complaints about him. For who are we that you complain about us?" ⁸ Moses continued, "The LORD will give you meat to eat this evening and all the bread you want in the morning, for he has heard the complaints that you are raising against him. Who are we? Your complaints are not against us but against the LORD."

⁹ Then Moses told Aaron, "Say to the entire Israelite community, 'Come before the LORD, for he has heard your complaints.'" ¹⁰ As Aaron was speaking to the entire Israelite community, they turned toward the wilderness, and there in a cloud the LORD's glory appeared. ¹¹ The LORD spoke to Moses, ¹² "I have heard the complaints of the Israelites. Tell them: At twilight you will eat meat, and in the morning you will eat bread until you are full. Then you will know that I am the LORD your God."

¹³ So at evening quail came and covered the camp. In the morning there was a layer of dew all around the camp. ¹⁴ When the layer of dew evaporated, there were fine flakes on the desert surface, as fine as frost on the ground. ¹⁵ When the Israelites saw it, they asked one another, "What is it?" because they didn't know what it was.

Moses told them, "It is the bread the LORD has given you to eat. ¹⁶ This is what the LORD has commanded: 'Gather as much of it as each person needs to eat. You may take two quartsᴬ per individual, according to the number of people each of you has in his tent.'"

¹⁷ So the Israelites did this. Some gathered a lot, some a little. ¹⁸ When they measured it by quarts,ᴮ the person who gathered a lot had no surplus, and the person who gathered a little had no shortage. Each gathered as much as he needed to eat. ¹⁹ Moses said to them, "No one is to let any of it remain until morning." ²⁰ But they didn't listen to Moses; some people left part of it until morning, and it bred worms and stank. Therefore Moses was angry with them.

²¹ They gathered it every morning. Each gathered as much as he needed to eat, but when the sun grew hot, it melted. ²² On the sixth day they gathered twice as much food, four quartsᶜ apiece, and all the leaders of the community came and reported this to Moses. ²³ He told them, "This is what the LORD has said: 'Tomorrow is a day of complete rest, a holy Sabbath to the LORD. Bake what you want to bake, and boil what you want to boil, and set aside everything left over to be kept until morning.'"

²⁴ So they set it aside until morning as Moses commanded, and it didn't stink or have maggots in it. ²⁵ "Eat it today," Moses said, "because today is a Sabbath to the LORD. Today you won't find any in the field. ²⁶ For six days you will gather it, but on the seventh day, the Sabbath, there will be none."

²⁷ Yet on the seventh day some of the people went out to gather, but they did not find any. ²⁸ Then the LORD said to Moses, "How long will youᴰ refuse to keep my commands and instructions? ²⁹ Understand that the LORD has given you the Sabbath; therefore on the sixth day he will give you two days' worth of bread. Each of you stay where you are; no one is to leave his place on the seventh day." ³⁰ So the people rested on the seventh day.

³¹ The house of Israel named the substance manna.ᴱ It resembled coriander seed, was white, and tasted like wafers made with honey. ³² Moses said, "This is what the LORD has commanded: 'Two quartsᶠ of it are to be preserved throughout your generations, so that they may see the bread I fed you in the wilderness when I brought you out of the land of Egypt.'"

³³ Moses told Aaron, "Take a container and put two quartsᴳ of manna in it. Then place it before the LORD to be preserved throughout your generations." ³⁴ As the LORD commanded Moses, Aaron placed it before the testimony to be preserved.

³⁵ The Israelites ate manna for forty years, until they came to an inhabited land. They ate manna until they reached the border of the land of Canaan. ³⁶ (They used a measure called an omer, which held two quarts.ᴴ)

ᴬ16:16 Lit *an omer* ᴮ16:18 Lit *by an omer* ᶜ16:22 Lit *two omers* ᴰ16:28 The Hb word for *you* is pl, referring to the whole nation. ᴱ16:31 = what?; Ex 16:15 ᶠ16:32 Lit *'A full omer* ᴳ16:33 Lit *a full omer* ᴴ16:36 Lit *(The omer is a tenth of an ephah.)*

---

unimportant in the situation. Their grumbling against Moses and Aaron was in fact a complaint against the Lord.
16:9–10 Like its English rendering, the Hebrew word for **glory** refers to God's excellence on display, often in action, as here. It can also refer to the recognition of that excellence, as when someone is said "to give glory."
16:11–15 When quail migrate between Europe and Africa, they fly over northern Sinai, and need to rest after flying over the Mediterranean Sea.
16:21–26 Sabbath is an anglicized form of the Hebrew word *shabbath*, associated with

a verb meaning "cease, stop, rest" (v. 30; 5:5; 31:12–17; Gn 8:22).
16:27–28 The rhetorical question expresses the Lord's displeasure and returns to the theme of testing for obedience (v. 4; 15:25–26). The Israelites' refusal to keep the Lord's commands puts them in the company of Pharaoh, who refused to humble himself (4:23; 7:14; 10:3; cp. Dt 8:16).
16:31–36 The name **manna** is the anglicized form of the Hebrew word *man* (interrogative "What?"), which partially echoes the question in v. 15 (Hb *man hu'*), "What is it?" No naturally occurring substance matches the description, constancy, and duration of

manna well enough to account for it. The **testimony** is a shortened form of "the ark of the testimony," the box that would later contain the Ten Commandments and would testify about the covenant the Lord had given Israel (25:16,21; 26:33; 30:36; 31:18; Nm 17:1–10). The construction of the ark is described in Ex 37:1–9, so it was not built until after 16:33–34. God continued sending the manna until the day after the Israelites first ate food grown in their new land (Jos 5:12).
16:36 The measure of **an omer** (Hb *'omer*) appears only in Ex 16. It is explained as a tenth of an ephah (Hb *'eyphah*). Apparently the ephah remained in use longer than the omer.

Water from the Rock

17 The entire Israelite community left the Wilderness of Sin, moving from one place to the next according to the Lord's command. They camped at Rephidim, but there was no water for the people to drink. ² So the people complained to Moses, "Give us water to drink."

"Why are you complaining to me?" Moses replied to them. "Why are you testing the Lord?"

³ But the people thirsted there for water and grumbled against Moses. They said, "Why did you ever bring us up from Egypt to kill us and our children and our livestock with thirst?"

⁴ Then Moses cried out to the Lord, "What should I do with these people? In a little while they will stone me!"

⁵ The Lord answered Moses, "Go on ahead of the people and take some of the elders of Israel with you. Take the staff you struck the Nile with in your hand and go. ⁶ I am going to stand there in front of you on the rock at Horeb; when you hit the rock, water will come out of it and the people will drink." Moses did this in the sight of the elders of Israel. ⁷ He named the place Massah^A and Meribah^B because the Israelites complained, and because they tested the Lord, saying, "Is the Lord among us or not?"

The Amalekites Attack

⁸ At Rephidim, Amalek^c came and fought against Israel. ⁹ Moses said to Joshua, "Select some men for us and go fight against Amalek. Tomorrow I will stand on the hilltop with God's staff in my hand."

¹⁰ Joshua did as Moses had told him, and fought against Amalek, while Moses, Aaron,

and Hur went up to the top of the hill. ¹¹ While Moses held up his hand,^D Israel prevailed, but whenever he put his hand^D down, Amalek prevailed. ¹² When Moses's hands grew heavy, they took a stone and put it under him, and he sat down on it. Then Aaron and Hur supported his hands, one on one side and one on the other so that his hands remained steady until the sun went down. ¹³ So Joshua defeated Amalek and his army^E with the sword.

¹⁴ The Lord then said to Moses, "Write this down on a scroll as a reminder and recite it to Joshua: I will completely blot out the memory of Amalek under heaven."

¹⁵ And Moses built an altar and named it, "The Lord Is My Banner."^F ¹⁶ He said, "Indeed, my hand is lifted up toward^G the Lord's throne. The Lord will be at war with Amalek from generation to generation."

Jethro's Visit

18 Moses's father-in-law, Jethro, the priest of Midian, heard about everything that God had done for Moses and for God's people Israel when the Lord brought Israel out of Egypt.

² Now Jethro, Moses's father-in-law, had taken in Zipporah, Moses's wife, after he had sent her back, ³ along with her two sons, one of whom was named Gershom^H (because Moses had said, "I have been a resident alien in a foreign land") ⁴ and the other Eliezer (because he had said, "The God of my father was my helper and rescued me from Pharaoh's sword").^I

⁵ Moses's father-in-law, Jethro, along with Moses's wife and sons, came to him in the wilderness where he was camped at the mountain

---

^A 17:7 = Testing ^B 17:7 = Quarreling ^C 17:8 A seminomadic people descended from *Amalek*, a grandson of Esau; Gn 36:12 ^D 17:11 Sam, LXX, Syr, Tg, Vg read *hands* ^E 17:13 Or *people* ^F 17:15 = *Yahweh-nissi* ^G 17:16 Or *hand was on*, or *hand was against*; Hb obscure ^H 18:3 In Hb the name *Gershom* sounds like the phrase "a stranger there." ^I 18:4 = My God Is Help

---

17:1–7 At Rephidim the Israelites complained about lack of water, but again the core issue was their mistrust of the Lord. The level of their hostility continued to increase.
17:2–3 The verb translated **complained** here and in v. 7 has not been used before in Exodus. It and a closely related noun describe disputes like the one between Jacob and Laban (Gn 31:36). Later in Exodus they describe interpersonal conflict that might lead to blows between two men (Ex 21:18) or to formal legal proceedings (23:2; cp. Dt 17:8; 25:1). By continuing to accuse Moses, the Israelites were **testing the Lord**.
17:5 The instruction to **take some of the elders** fits the thought that the Israelite "complaining" had become a quasi-official legal case.
17:6 Moses pointed back to this and similar events in Dt 8:15. The apostle Paul considered **the rock** here to be a significant sign pointing to Christ (1Co 10:4). The Lord is referred to in the OT as "the Rock" (Dt 32:4,15,18,30; 1Sm 2:2). God could also bring fire out of rock (Jdg 6:21).
17:7 To remind everyone of conduct to be avoided in light of God's presence and provision, Moses renamed the place. The name

Massah is closely related to the verb translated "tested," and the name **Meribah** is cognate to the verb translated **complained** (see Ps 95:8–9). So the new name was something like "*Testing and Complaint*" or "*Quarrelsome Trial*." The Israelites' question expressed their impatience with what they considered unsatisfactory performance.
17:8 Deuteronomy 25:18 describes how **Amalek** preyed on the weakest among the Israelites. Amalekites troubled Israel intermittently for many years (Nm 14:40–45; Jdg 3:12–13; 6:3–6; 7:12; 10:12; 1Sm 14:47–48; 15:1–33; 27:8; 30:1–18; 2Sm 1:1–16; 1Ch 4:43).
17:9–11 Raising the **staff** in this case likely symbolized God's exercise of power (v. 11; 7:20; 14:16,21,26–27). **Joshua** would go on to serve Moses and succeed him as leader of the Israelites (24:13; Nm 27:18–23; Jos 1:1–9). **Hur** is best known for his part in this event and for Moses trusting him to help the Israelites when Moses was away (24:14).
17:12–13 The weakness of Moses showed that he was not the source of the victory.
17:14–15 The **scroll** could be a kind of diary from which Moses would write the book of Exodus. When Moses called the altar *Yahweh*

Nissi (**The Lord Is My Banner**), the sort of "banner" that he referred to was commonly hoisted high on a pole as a rallying point or signal. The image asserts Moses's intention to orient his life and actions according to the Lord's direction.
18:1–27 The events in this chapter mark a turning point in the book of Exodus. The first half looks back at what had happened and describes responses to it, while the second half looks ahead by showing the need for the Israelites to be organized to conduct life with one another as a nation.
18:1–2 Earlier mentions of **Jethro** and **Zipporah** are in 2:18–21; 3:1; 4:18–26. Nothing is said about when or why Moses had sent his family to stay with Jethro.
18:3–4 **Gershom** was introduced in 2:22. He was no longer an alien in Egypt or a fugitive in Midian. **Eliezer** is mentioned here for the first time, perhaps because now his name has even more to commemorate, since the Lord had repeatedly helped Moses and had rescued him from two pharaohs who wanted to kill him.
18:5 Moses was back at the place where the Lord had first spoken to him from the burning bush (3:1–4).

of God. **⁶** He sent word to Moses, "I, your father-in-law Jethro, am coming to you with your wife and her two sons."

⁷ So Moses went out to meet his father-in-law, bowed down, and then kissed him. They asked each other how they had been^A and went into the tent. **⁸** Moses recounted to his father-in-law all that the Lord had done to Pharaoh and the Egyptians for Israel's sake, all the hardships that confronted them on the way, and how the Lord rescued them.

⁹ Jethro rejoiced over all the good things the Lord had done for Israel when he rescued them from the power of the Egyptians. **¹⁰** "Blessed be the Lord," Jethro exclaimed, "who rescued you from the power of Egypt and from the power of Pharaoh. He has rescued the people from under the power of Egypt! **¹¹** Now I know that the Lord is greater than all gods, because he did wonders when the Egyptians acted arrogantly against Israel."^B

¹² Then Jethro, Moses's father-in-law, brought a burnt offering and sacrifices to God, and Aaron came with all the elders of Israel to eat a meal with Moses's father-in-law in God's presence.

¹³ The next day Moses sat down to judge the people, and they stood around Moses from morning until evening. **¹⁴** When Moses's father-in-law saw everything he was doing for them he asked, "What is this you're doing for the people? Why are you alone sitting as judge, while all the people stand around you from morning until evening?"

¹⁵ Moses replied to his father-in-law, "Because the people come to me to inquire of God. **¹⁶** Whenever they have a dispute, it comes to me, and I make a decision between one man and another. I teach them God's statutes and laws."

¹⁷ "What you're doing is not good," Moses's father-in-law said to him. **¹⁸** "You will certainly wear out both yourself and these people who are with you, because the task is too heavy for you. You can't do it alone. **¹⁹** Now listen to me; I will give you some advice, and God be with you. You be the one to represent the people before God and bring their cases to him. **²⁰** Instruct them about the statutes and laws, and teach them the way to live and what they must do. **²¹** But you should select from all the people able men, God-fearing, trustworthy, and hating dishonest profit. Place them over the people as commanders of thousands, hundreds, fifties, and tens. **²²** They should judge the people at all times. Then they can bring you every major case but judge every minor case themselves. In this way you will lighten your load,^C and they will bear it with you. **²³** If you do this, and God so directs you, you will be able to endure, and also all these people will be able to go home satisfied."^D

²⁴ Moses listened to his father-in-law and did everything he said. **²⁵** So Moses chose able men from all Israel and made them leaders over the people as commanders of thousands, hundreds, fifties, and tens. **²⁶** They judged the people at all times; they would bring the hard cases to Moses, but they would judge every minor case themselves.

²⁷ Moses let his father-in-law go, and he journeyed to his own land.

Israel at Sinai

19 In the third month from the very day the Israelites left the land of Egypt, they came to the Sinai Wilderness. **²** They traveled from Rephidim, came to the Sinai Wilderness, and camped in the wilderness. Israel camped there in front of the mountain.

³ Moses went up the mountain to God, and the Lord called to him from the mountain: "This is what you must say to the house of Jacob

---

^A**18:7** Lit *other about well-being* ^B**18:11** Hb obscure ^C**18:22** Lit *lighten from on you* ^D**18:23** Lit *go to their place in peace*

18:6–9 These details present **Jethro** and **Moses** as men of rank and dignity. All this shows who Moses had become and portrays Jethro as a person qualified to offer advice. **18:10–11** The references to rescue from the **power of Egypt** continue the use of "hand" in Hebrew as a prominent means by which power is displayed. The breadth of the word translated **know** could mean that Jethro was previously unconvinced of the Lord's superiority, or that he was simply declaring a new awareness from experience. Either way, he was convinced and glad to say so. **18:12** A **burnt offering** was consumed by fire, and parts of **sacrifices** were burned, but most was roasted and eaten by people present to worship and celebrate (Lv 1:2–17; 3:1–17; 7:11–18). **18:21–22** The word translated **commanders** is the plural of the one in 2:14. It is used repeatedly in 18:21,25 (lit "commanders of thousands, commanders of hundreds," etc.). This tends to strengthen the tie with the question about Moses's status in 2:14.

Jethro's list of qualifications for leadership requires qualities of character, belief, and behavior rather than age, wealth, or family position (Dt 1:13,16–17; 2Ch 19:6–7,9–10). **18:23–27** The verb rendered **endure** can also mean "stand." It repeats the Hebrew verb for "stand/endure" from the descriptions in vv. 13 and 14 of the people standing around Moses waiting for him to hear their cases. If Moses followed Jethro's advice, the people would not have to "stand around" so much and Moses would be able to "stand" the work. **19:1–24:11** This section describes events surrounding the making of the covenant between the Lord and Israel, using practices and terms familiar in the culture. Such treaties contained: (1) formal self-identification of the more powerful ruler; (2) a review of the history between the parties as grounds for issuing and accepting the covenant; (3) the requirement of loyalty to the suzerain (king); (4) stipulations regulating future conduct of the vassal; (5) positive and negative consequences for obedience or disobedience;

and (6) instructions for copying, storing, and publicly reading the covenant.

The Mosaic covenant with its laws was given to people who had expressed belief in the Lord (14:31)—people already rescued from Egypt. Its purpose was not to provide a means for people to initiate or merit a relationship with the Lord. Rather, the covenant was a means of communicating what Israel should do as a people who already belonged to him.

Israel's laws came from their God with the recognition that people who claimed the Lord as God should resemble him in their dealings.

19:1–2 The **Sinai Wilderness** is the setting for the rest of Exodus, all of Leviticus, and Nm 1:1–10:10. They would be there about eleven months. **19:3** One purpose for Moses making three trips **up the mountain** and back (vv. 3,7–8,14,20,25) was to clarify visually the unique role and privileges he was granted. The people needed to acknowledge his authority

and explain to the Israelites: ⁴ 'You have seen what I did to the Egyptians and how I carried you on eagles' wings and brought you to myself. ⁵ Now if you will carefully listen to me and keep my covenant, you will be my own possession out of all the peoples, although the whole earth is mine, ⁶ and you will be my kingdom of priests and my holy nation.' These are the words that you are to say to the Israelites."

⁷ After Moses came back, he summoned the elders of the people and set before them all these words that the LORD had commanded him. ⁸ Then all the people responded together, "We will do all that the LORD has spoken." So Moses brought the people's words back to the LORD.

⁹ The LORD said to Moses, "I am going to come to you in a dense cloud, so that the people will hear when I speak with you and will always believe you." Moses reported the people's words to the LORD, ¹⁰ and the LORD told Moses, "Go to the people and consecrate them today and tomorrow. They must wash their clothes ¹¹ and be prepared by the third day, for on the third day the LORD will come down on Mount Sinai in the sight of all the people. ¹² Put boundaries for the people all around the mountain and say: Be careful that you don't go up on the mountain or touch its base. Anyone who touches the mountain must be put to death. ¹³ No hand may touch him;ᴬ instead he will be stoned or shot with arrows and not live, whether animal or human. When the ram's horn sounds a long blast, they may go up the mountain."

¹⁴ Then Moses came down from the mountain to the people and consecrated them, and they washed their clothes. ¹⁵ He said to the people, "Be prepared by the third day. Do not have sexual relations with women."

¹⁶ On the third day, when morning came, there was thunder and lightning, a thick cloud on the mountain, and a very loud blast from a ram's horn, so that all the people in the camp shuddered. ¹⁷ Then Moses brought the people out of the camp to meet God, and they stood at the foot of the mountain. ¹⁸ Mount Sinai was completely enveloped in smoke because the LORD came down on it in fire. Its smoke went up like the smoke of a furnace, and the whole mountain shook violently. ¹⁹ As the sound of the ram's horn grew louder and louder, Moses spoke and God answered him in the thunder.

²⁰ The LORD came down on Mount Sinai at the top of the mountain. Then the LORD summoned Moses to the top of the mountain, and he went up. ²¹ The LORD directed Moses, "Go down and warn the people not to break through to see the LORD; otherwise many of them will die. ²² Even the priests who come near the LORD must consecrate themselves, or the LORD will break out in anger against them."

²³ Moses responded to the LORD, "The people cannot come up Mount Sinai, since you warned us: Put a boundary around the mountain and consecrate it." ²⁴ And the LORD replied to him, "Go down and come back with Aaron. But the priests and the people must not break through to come up to the LORD, or he will break out in anger against them." ²⁵ So Moses went down to the people and told them.

The Ten Commandments

20 Then God spoke all these words: ² I am the LORD your God, who brought you out of the land of Egypt, out of the place of slavery.

ᴬ 19:13 Or it

---

as God's representative and the importance of his message.

19:5 The Lord wanted Israel to be known by what he had done as well as by what they would do. **My own possession** uses a word that is sometimes translated "treasure." David used to speak of his "personal treasures of gold and silver" that he had set aside for building the Lord's temple (1Ch 29:3).

19:6 The ideas of priesthood and holiness go together, since special requirements marked priests as set apart for special service that benefited others (Lv 21). The tasks of priests included helping people offer sacrifices to God, according to the need or condition of the person (Lv 1–7). Priests acted as judges, both in matters of ritual purity and in civil controversies (Lv 13–14; Dt 17:9; 21:5), and they taught God's law (Lv 10:11; Mal 2:7–9). These tasks pointed to the work of Israel among the nations. Now all who believe in Christ are a royal priesthood and a holy nation (1Pt 2:9).

19:7–8 Moses explained the covenant to the elders, who apparently explained it to all the people, who accepted it unanimously.

19:9–25 The preparations for a meeting between the Lord and the Israelites continue

the extended metaphor that compares the Lord to a great king issuing a covenant to his vassal. For as long as the Lord visited Mount Sinai, it was holy ground, an extension of his royal court. Approaching the mountain required a royal summons. It was not a casual meeting of equals.

19:10 The requirements to be purified and to wear clean **clothes** involved everyone in the preparation.

19:12 Refusal to observe **boundaries** was a sign of disrespect. Those who violated the warning would die.

19:15 Abstaining from sex would prevent contact with semen, which caused ritual uncleanness (Lv 15:16–18).

19:18 **Like the smoke of a furnace** uses the word for "furnace" that also appears in 9:8,10. Its only other use is to describe the source of the smoke compared with what came from the ruins of Sodom and Gomorrah (Gn 19:28). The **whole mountain shook violently** uses the same Hebrew verb as the statement that "all the people in the camp shuddered" (v. 16).

19:21 Moses's warning **not . . . to see the LORD** on penalty of death shows God's concern to protect the Israelites and to reveal to them his awesome, personal reality.

20:1–17 Hebrew has two forms of negative command. One is used for specific, immediate situations, and the other, used here, is for general prohibitions. The idea is "Don't ever . . ." It is used by a superior to an inferior but not the reverse. The eight negative commands and two positive commands (vv. 8,12) became known as the Ten Commandments (lit "the ten words"; 34:28; Dt 4:13; 10:4), or the Decalogue (from Gk for "ten words," *deka + logoi*). They provide basic principles that laid the foundation for the other rules and regulations for ancient Israel.

These were the commands written on the stone tablets and stored in the ark of the covenant to be kept in the most holy part of the tabernacle (34:28; Dt 4:13; 10:10–11; 10:4–5). The importance of these commandments is further indicated by their repetition in Dt 5:6–21 and elsewhere (Mt 19:18; Mk 10:19; Lk 18:20). The first four commands (Ex 20:2–11) focus on loyalty to the Lord, while the last six (vv. 12–17) focus on dealings between humans.

20:1–2 To start with self-identification, as **the LORD** does here, was normal for a covenant document sent from a king and for royal proclamations and inscriptions.

The Ten Commandments

First	No Other Gods (Ex 20:3)	The Israelites needed to understand that God was to be the exclusive recipient of their worship.	
Second	No Idols (20:4–6)	God is to be worshiped as he is, not as an image of what people can create.	The first and greatest commandment: Love the Lord your God with all your heart, soul, and mind (Mt 22:37–38; see Dt 6:5).
Third	Don't Misuse the Lord's Name (20:7)	God's name was to be revered, not used flippantly.	
Fourth	Remember the Sabbath (20:8–11)	The people were to set aside one day of the week—the Sabbath—as an act of devotion and worship to God.	
Fifth	Honor Your Father and Mother (20:12)	If we love our parents, we will give them the honor they are due.	
Sixth	Do Not Murder (20:13)	If we love our neighbor, we will not seek to harm or kill them.	
Seventh	Do Not Commit Adultery (20:14)	If we love our neighbor, we will not seek an adulterous relationship with someone else.	The second greatest commandment: Love your neighbor as yourself (Mt 22:39; see Lv 19:18,34).
Eighth	Do Not Steal (20:15)	If we love our neighbor, we will respect what God has given them.	
Ninth	Do Not Give False Testimony (20:16)	If we love our neighbor, we will not lie about them to get them in trouble or to take advantage of them.	
Tenth	Do Not Covet (20:17)	If we love our neighbor, we will not be envious of their relationships or their property.	

³ Do not have other gods besides me.
⁴ Do not make an idol for yourself, whether in the shape of anything in the heavens above or on the earth below or in the waters under the earth. ⁵ Do not bow in worship to them, and do not serve them; for I, the LORD your God, am a jealous God, bringing the consequences of the fathers' iniquity on the children to the third and fourth generations of those who hate me, ⁶ but showing faithful love to a thousand generations of those who love me and keep my commands.
⁷ Do not misuse the name of the LORD your God, because the LORD will not leave anyone unpunished who misuses his name.
⁸ Remember the Sabbath day, to keep it holy: ⁹ You are to labor six days and do all your work, ¹⁰ but the seventh day is a Sabbath to the LORD your God. You must not do any work — you, your son or daughter, your male or female servant, your livestock, or the resident alien who is within your city gates. ¹¹ For the LORD made the heavens and the earth, the sea, and everything in them in six days; then he rested on the seventh day. Therefore the LORD blessed the Sabbath day and declared it holy.

¹² Honor your father and your mother so that you may have a long life in the land that the LORD your God is giving you.
¹³ Do not murder.
¹⁴ Do not commit adultery.
¹⁵ Do not steal.
¹⁶ Do not give false testimony against your neighbor.
¹⁷ Do not covet your neighbor's house. Do not covet your neighbor's wife, his male or female servant, his ox or donkey, or anything that belongs to your neighbor.

The People's Reaction

¹⁸ All the people witnessed[A] the thunder and lightning, the sound of the ram's horn, and the mountain surrounded by smoke. When the people saw it[B] they trembled and stood at a distance. ¹⁹ "You speak to us, and we will listen," they said to Moses, "but don't let God speak to us, or we will die."
²⁰ Moses responded to the people, "Don't be afraid, for God has come to test you, so that you will fear him and will not[C] sin." ²¹ And the people remained standing at a distance as Moses approached the total darkness where God was.

Moses Receives Additional Laws

²² Then the LORD told Moses, "This is what you are to say to the Israelites: You have seen that I have spoken to you from heaven. ²³ Do not

---

Delivering the Israelites had become part of his identity, what people should think of when his name was mentioned. In Israel, lawbreaking was first of all an offense against the Lord, not just a disruption of order or an offense against other people.
20:3–6 Not to make an **idol** ran counter to every instinct of ancient Near Eastern cultures, but to do so is an affront to **a jealous God**. If the Israelites made idols to worship, it would be an act of hatred, disloyalty, and repudiation. When the Lord made himself known to the Israelites, they did not see any form (Dt 4:10–20).
Bringing the consequences of the fathers' iniquity on the children did not mean that a son would be sentenced for his father's crime (Dt 24:16), or that individual standing with God was determined by the behavior of one's parents (Jr 31:29–30; Ezk 18:1–32). It did mean the excuse, "They don't know any better; it's how they were raised," does not work with God. Yet the Lord's **faithful love** would far exceed his judgment (**to a thousand generations**; Lv 26:39–45; Is 65:6–7; Jr 11:9–12; 32:17–19; Dn 9:8–16).
20:7 In ancient times misusing **the name of the LORD** could have meant failing to fulfill a sworn oath or making an oath with the intention of deceiving someone. Those who swore an oath in the Lord's name called on him to bring punishment if they did not keep the promise or tell the truth (Gn 24:3; Lv 19:12; Jos 2:12). To swear by the Lord's name was an affirmation of allegiance to him that required appropriate action (Jos 23:6–8). By

extension, this command would also apply when a person attached the Lord's name to an activity contrary to his character or will, resulting in certain punishment (cp. Ps 50:16–23; Jr 14:14–16). In a sense, misusing the Lord's name misrepresented his character, purposes, and actions revealed to the people of Israel and amounted to lying about who God is.
20:8–11 The **Sabbath** would serve as a reminder of the Mosaic or Sinai covenant. In Exodus it comes up for discussion again in 23:12; 31:12–17; 35:1–3. Verses 8 and 11 use forms of the same Hebrew verb qadash, "keep/declare holy," to speak of consecrating the Sabbath. The Lord had set this day apart (**declared it holy**), so the Israelites should treat it as such. The list in v. 10 makes the Sabbath command particularly directed to adults who had children and were wealthy enough to own servants and livestock. If it applied to these people—the ones with the most influence in a community—it would apply to everyone. Here the Sabbath is linked to God's resting on the seventh day from his creative work (Gn 2:3), whereas in Dt 5:12–15 it is linked to Israel's redemption from Egypt.
20:12 A stubborn and rebellious son who refused other discipline could be taken before the elders for judgment (Dt 21:18–21; cp. Lv 19:3). **Long life** may refer to the tenure of the nation in the land. Failure to honor parents was one of the sins that Ezekiel listed in a description of the people of Jerusalem before the city was destroyed (Ezk 22:7; cp. Mc 7:6). Paul also mentioned the promise associated

with this command in the context of the church community (Eph 6:1–3; cp. Mk 7:9–13).
20:13 The word translated **murder** is not a general word for "killing," and it is not used for killing animals or for killing humans in war or legal execution.
20:14 Adultery includes sex between a married person and anyone other than their spouse. It is referred to as unfaithfulness or betrayal.
20:15 This commandment assumes the legitimacy of personal property. It includes kidnapping as well as taking other things without permission.
20:16 Honesty is required in the case of a charge against one's **neighbor**. Implied in this law is the requirement for honesty in all one's affairs.
20:17 This command addresses the inner life, the source of wrong actions including murder, adultery, and stealing (Jms 1:14–15). Coveting reflects greed, which is idolatry (Eph 5:5; Col 3:5).
20:18–21 In the same breath Moses told the people not to fear (**Don't be afraid**) but to fear (lit "so that the fear of him will be before your face"). They should not fear that God might capriciously exterminate them. Nevertheless, the purpose of the frightening display is that they might recognize God's power, his presence, and his holiness and be motivated to avoid **sin** and consequent judgment.
20:22–23:19 This section includes laws that were similar to those of other ancient cultures—which we know from ancient

make gods of silver to rival me; do not make gods of gold for yourselves. ²⁴ "Make an earthen altar for me, and sacrifice on it your burnt offerings and fellowship offerings, your flocks and herds. I will come to you and bless you in every place where I cause my name to be remembered. ²⁵ If you make a stone altar for me, do not build it out of cut stones. If you use your chisel on it, you will defile it. ²⁶ Do not go up to my altar on steps, so that your nakedness is not exposed on it.

21 "These are the ordinances that you are to set before them:

Laws about Slaves

² "When you buy a Hebrew slave, he is to serve for six years; then in the seventh he is to leave as a free man^A without paying anything. ³ If he arrives alone, he is to leave alone; if he arrives with^B a wife, his wife is to leave with him. ⁴ If his master gives him a wife and she bears him sons or daughters, the wife and her children belong to her master, and the man must leave alone.

⁵ "But if the slave declares, 'I love my master, my wife, and my children; I do not want to leave as a free man,' ⁶ his master is to bring him to the judges^C and then bring him to the door or doorpost. His master will pierce his ear with an awl, and he will serve his master for life.

⁷ "When a man sells his daughter as a concubine,^D she is not to leave as the male slaves do. ⁸ If she is displeasing to her master, who chose her for himself, then he must let her be redeemed. He has no right to sell her to foreigners because he has acted treacherously toward her. ⁹ Or if he chooses her for his son, he must deal with her according to the customary treatment of daughters. ¹⁰ If he takes an additional wife, he must not reduce the food, clothing, or marital rights of the first wife.

¹¹ And if he does not do these three things for her, she may leave free of charge, without any payment.^E

Laws about Personal Injury

¹² "Whoever strikes a person so that he dies must be put to death. ¹³ But if he did not intend any harm,^F and yet God allowed it to happen, I will appoint a place for you where he may flee. ¹⁴ If a person schemes and willfully^G acts against his neighbor to murder him, you must take him from my altar to be put to death.

¹⁵ "Whoever strikes his father or his mother must be put to death.

¹⁶ "Whoever kidnaps a person must be put to death, whether he sells him or the person is found in his possession.

¹⁷ "Whoever curses his father or his mother must be put to death.

¹⁸ "When men quarrel and one strikes the other with a stone or his fist, and the injured man does not die but is confined to bed, ¹⁹ if he can later get up and walk around outside leaning on his staff, then the one who struck him will be exempt from punishment. Nevertheless, he must pay for his lost work time^H and provide for his complete recovery.

²⁰ "When a man strikes his male or female slave with a rod, and the slave dies under his abuse,^I the owner must be punished.^J ²¹ However, if the slave can stand up after a day or two, the owner should not be punished^K because he is his owner's property.^L

²² "When men get in a fight and hit a pregnant woman so that her children are born prematurely but there is no injury, the one who hit her must be fined as the woman's husband demands from him, and he must pay according to judicial assessment. ²³ If there is an injury, then you must give life for life, ²⁴ eye for eye, tooth

---

^A21:2 Lit to go forth   ^B21:3 Lit he is the husband of   ^C21:6 Or to God; that is, to his sanctuary or court   ^D21:7 Or servant   ^E21:11 She doesn't have to pay any redemption price.   ^F21:13 Lit he was not lying in wait   ^G21:14 Or maliciously   ^H21:19 Lit his inactivity   ^I21:20 Lit hand   ^J21:20 Or must suffer vengeance   ^K21:21 Or not suffer vengeance   ^L21:21 Lit silver

---

documents—put into a context of motivation based on the Lord's actions, character, requirements, and oversight.
20:24–26 Mention of places where the Lord would come and bless the Israelites provided a reminder that, unlike pagan gods, the Lord must not be considered limited to Mount Sinai or any other locality.
21:1–6 These rules for Hebrew slaves applied to both males and females, according to Dt 15:12–17 (cp. Ex 21:20,26–27,32; Jr 34:13–16). An Israelite might choose to go into slavery to pay restitution for theft, to repay another debt, or to obtain food and shelter in hard times. On penalty of death, Ex 21:16 rules out kidnapping and forcing an Israelite into slavery. And while the life of slaves might be difficult, there were penalties for mistreatment (vv. 20–21,26–27) and slaves who ran away were not to be returned to their masters (Dt 23:15–16).
21:7–11 These verses deal with the status and rights of a woman who had been sold

with the expectation of becoming a second-class wife, somewhat like Hagar, Bilhah, and Zilpah, who bore children for Abraham and Jacob.
21:12–13 Verse 13 applies to manslaughter. **I will appoint a place** refers to cities of refuge controlled by Levites.
21:14 You must take him from my altar pictures the murderer as having come to the sanctuary for protection. But even the Lord's altar provided no asylum for a person who planned a murder (cp. 1Kg 1:50–53; 2:28–34).
21:15 This law covers cases in which someone attacks one's parent with the intent of doing bodily harm.
21:16 Under this statement, what Joseph's brothers did to him (Gn 37:27–28) was a death-penalty offense.
21:17 The nature of the **curses** is unclear (cp. Lv 20:9; Pr 20:20).
21:20–21 If a slave died from being beaten, the death would be avenged by death (vv. 12–14). If the slave lived but sustained

permanent injury, the slave would go free (vv. 26–27). A later death might be from another cause than the owner's action, so the owner should not die. **Because he is his owner's property** adopts a pragmatic stance and assumes that the owner had shown regard for potential monetary loss and had not intended to kill or permanently injure the slave.
21:22–25 A fine was to be assessed for a blow that caused premature delivery. The only other uses of the word translated "injury" here occur in Gn 42:4,38, where the harm that Jacob feared was that Benjamin might die. The series that begins with **life for life** seems to have been a formula that might be repeated partly or in full, even in situations like blasphemy, where physical harm was not an issue (Lv 24:17–21; Dt 19:16–21). The formula called for proportionate punishment rather than a process of escalating violence between individuals or families (in contrast to the attitude of Lamech in Gn 4:23–24).

A Biblical View of Crime and Punishment

by Hunter Baker

Today we most often use the terms *jail* and *prison* to describe the places where criminals are sent once they are convicted of crimes, but the name *penitentiary* is also commonly used. One need not be a language scholar to discern the root of *penitentiary*, which is penitent. In its adjectival form, *penitent* is used to denote a strong sense of regret. Taken as a noun, a penitent is a person who seeks forgiveness from God. The founding of penitentiaries, beginning in the eighteenth century with John Howard in England, expressed the Christian hope that criminals could repent, find forgiveness from God and people, and return to the community as citizens who contribute to the common good.

The Bible's influence on approaches to crime and punishment preceded the rehabilitation movement of the eighteenth century. The Hebrew Scriptures (the Old Testament) tell us that God chose a people (the Hebrews) and set them apart from all other peoples by giving them regulations for running a just society.

Although it is sometimes argued that ancient codes from Hammurabi or the Hittites provided inspiration for the laws set forth in the Old Testament, Jewish scholars point to important distinctions that show the uniqueness and greater justice of the laws given by God. They argue that the Hammurabi code is more brutal and primitive than the laws of Israel. The Hittite code, which was compensation based, also falls short of the standards expressed in the law as given by God in the Old Testament. According to the Hittite approach, someone charged with an offense as serious as murder could be bought off with enough cash. In contrast, Exodus 21:23–25, with its eye-for-an-eye reasoning, is more proportionate to the offense and is thus more just.

The Hebrew law codes reveal a great desire for true justice rather than a rush to judgment. One example is Deuteronomy's rule requiring two eyewitnesses to be in agreement in order to establish evidence of a crime (Dt 17:6; 19:15). This means no one would be executed without the evidence of more than one witness. The laws of the United States offer less protection than this. Similar to the instructions in Deuteronomy, Matthew 18:16 indicates that one should take witnesses along when attempting to resolve a dispute. Such advice demonstrates a concern with establishing truth in a reliable fashion, drawing on the perspectives of multiple persons. In both Testaments great care is taken to be certain of the truth of an offense, and emphasis is placed on the strong connection between the punishment, the offender, and the severity of the offense.

Three Schools of Thought

In contemporary thinking about crime and punishment, there are at least three major schools of thought regarding how to deal with lawbreaking. Theorists often speak and write in terms of retribution, utilitarianism, and rehabilitation.

Retribution

Retribution-based thinking is at odds with the more social-scientific thrust of much of today's thinking about punishment. It is seen as crude, vengeance based, and perhaps barbaric. Many of the punishments in the Old Testament are perceived in this light. Nevertheless, others have argued convincingly that retributive approaches are anything but crude and cruel. Rather, the choice of retribution attributes dignity to both the victim and the offender. Retribution vindicates the rights of the victim because it recognizes that something important has been violated and punishment must follow the violation. At the same time, retribution assigns respect to the offender as well because punishing the offender indicates that God and society had real expectations for better decision making and behavior. In essence, people who transgress have not lived up to God's standard (or society's) and thus must be reminded that we respect them enough to punish the wrongdoing.

Utilitarianism

Utilitarian theories of crime and punishment focus less on the rights of individuals and more on the scientific control of populations. For example, a utilitarian might say that we should come up with laws that reduce social friction between citizens rather than continuing to enforce laws that lead to conflict. The danger of the utilitarian approach is that it is mostly concerned with social regulation. For example, let us imagine that a series of murders have been committed. In the utilitarian view, it would be nearly as good to convince the public that the murderer has been caught and punished (even if that weren't true), as it would be to actually catch the villain. Perception would count nearly as much as reality. It might even be better to pin the crime on an innocent party, if it could be done convincingly, than to let the public go on thinking a murderer is on the loose.

Rehabilitation

As mentioned above, rehabilitation theories were originally motivated by Christian thinking about crime and punishment. The Christian view tended to support retribution-based consequences while adding a component of rehabilitation. Forgiveness does not necessarily wipe out the penalty, but it does pave the way for full acceptance back into the social body once punishment and rehabilitation are complete. During the twentieth century, however, thinking about rehabilitation went through a transformation, dropping the idea of a "penitent" person paying a debt and seeking forgiveness. Rehabilitation approaches came to view crime as a result of broad, structural social injustices that produce marginalized

victims of the system who perpetuate injustices by engaging in social pathologies such as stealing. While there is some value to thinking about social systems in this way, the effect can be to undermine the moral dimension of crime and the recognition that the offender has personally done wrong against others and should repent of sin.

Not everyone has appreciated these developments. Anger at progressive penal policies has led to the creation of victims' rights movements. Among other things, these movements have sought to make society and the judicial system aware of the harm victims suffer when they perceive that the wrongs perpetrated against them have gone unpunished or inadequately punished.

Christians remain highly active in prison ministry today, though often with less official influence in the penal system than they once had. Prison Fellowship, founded by Charles Colson after his imprisonment following the Watergate scandal, has led the way in sharing the good news of redemption through Jesus Christ with prisoners. After many years of effective ministry to prisoners and their families, Prison Fellowship gained the ability to participate in some institutions by hosting special Christian cellblocks and offering seminary programs in others. Early evidence indicates that their ministry reduces recidivism among those released. Whatever good government may achieve through attempts to address the social causes of crime—and we must not dismiss these—crime remains a manifestation of a spiritual problem that must be addressed. The true rehabilitator and vindicator of injustices is Jesus Christ, the Son of God, and we must point both victims and criminals to his gospel.

for tooth, hand for hand, foot for foot, [25] burn for burn, bruise for bruise, wound for wound. [26] "When a man strikes the eye of his male or female slave and destroys it, he must let the slave go free in compensation for his eye. [27] If he knocks out the tooth of his male or female slave, he must let the slave go free in compensation for his tooth.

[28] "When an ox[A] gores a man or a woman to death, the ox must be stoned, and its meat may not be eaten, but the ox's owner is innocent. [29] However, if the ox was in the habit of goring, and its owner has been warned yet does not restrain it, and it kills a man or a woman, the ox must be stoned, and its owner must also be put to death. [30] If instead a ransom is demanded of him, he can pay a redemption price for his life in the full amount demanded from him. [31] If it gores a son or a daughter, he is to be dealt with according to this same law. [32] If the ox gores a male or female slave, he must give thirty shekels of silver[B] to the slave's master, and the ox must be stoned.

[33] "When a man uncovers a pit or digs a pit, and does not cover it, and an ox or a donkey falls into it, [34] the owner of the pit must give compensation; he must pay to its owner, but the dead animal will become his.

[35] "When a man's ox injures his neighbor's ox and it dies, they must sell the live ox and divide its proceeds; they must also divide the dead animal. [36] If, however, it is known that the ox was in the habit of goring, yet its owner has not restrained it, he must compensate fully, ox for ox; the dead animal will become his.

Laws about Theft

22 "When a man steals an ox or a sheep and butchers it or sells it, he must repay five cattle for the ox or four sheep for the sheep. [2] If a thief is caught in the act of breaking in, and he is beaten to death, no one is guilty of bloodshed. [3] But if this happens after sunrise, the householder is guilty of bloodshed. A thief must make full restitution. If he is unable, he is to be sold because of his theft. [4] If what was stolen — whether ox, donkey, or sheep — is

actually found alive in his possession, he must repay double.

Laws about Crop Protection

[5] "When a man lets a field or vineyard be grazed in, and then allows his animals to go and graze in someone else's field, he must repay[C] with the best of his own field or vineyard.

[6] "When a fire gets out of control, spreads to thornbushes, and consumes stacks of cut grain, standing grain, or a field, the one who started the fire must make full restitution for what was burned.

Laws about Personal Property

[7] "When a man gives his neighbor valuables[D] or goods to keep, but they are stolen from that person's house, the thief, if caught, must repay double. [8] If the thief is not caught, the owner of the house must present himself to the judges[E] to determine[F] whether or not he has taken his neighbor's property. [9] In any case of wrongdoing involving an ox, a donkey, a sheep, a garment, or anything else lost, and someone claims, 'That's mine,'[G] the case between the two parties is to come before the judges.[H] The one the judges condemn[I] must repay double to his neighbor.

[10] "When a man gives his neighbor a donkey, an ox, a sheep, or any other animal to care for, but it dies, is injured, or is stolen, while no one is watching, [11] there must be an oath before the LORD between the two of them to determine whether or not he has taken his neighbor's property. Its owner must accept the oath, and the other man does not have to make restitution. [12] But if, in fact, the animal was stolen from his custody, he must make restitution to its owner. [13] If it was actually torn apart by a wild animal, he is to bring it as evidence; he does not have to make restitution for the torn carcass.

[14] "When a man borrows an animal from his neighbor, and it is injured or dies while its owner is not there with it, the man must make full restitution. [15] If its owner is there with it, the man does not have to make restitution. If

---

^A 21:28 Or *a bull*, or *a steer*　^B 21:32 About one pound of silver　^C 22:5 LXX adds *from his field according to its produce. But if someone lets his animals graze an entire field, he must repay*; DSS, Sam also support this reading.　^D 22:7 Lit *silver*　^E 22:8 Or *to God*　^F 22:8 LXX, Tg, Vg read *swear*　^G 22:9 Lit *That is it*　^H 22:9 Or *before God*　^I 22:9 Or *one whom God condemns*

21:26–27 Laws protecting slaves are not found in other ancient Near Eastern law collections.
21:28–32 Stoning was a form of public execution and not the ordinary way to slaughter an animal (Dt 13:10; 17:5; Jos 7:25; 1Kg 1:13). If the owner's negligence caused the death, he too must die or pay a ransom for his life. The possibility of a ransom implies that the owner was less directly responsible for the person's death than in cases of murder (Ex 21:12,20,23; Nm 35:31). In case a child died, the stipulation that the negligent owner was **to be dealt with**

according to this same law treated the lives of children as valuable and protected the negligent owner's child.
21:33–36 Unlike the death of a human, the death of an **ox** was a monetary matter. When the matter was unforeseeable, the owners of both oxen bore the loss equally.
22:1–4 The difference in responses to burglary at different times rests on the concern that the owners' lives might be at stake, especially if the break-in took place at night. During the day they could recognize the thief and know whether or not this was a dangerous intruder (cp. Jr

2:26,34–35). Even the life of a thief was valued; he could not be sold as a slave or be killed in revenge.
22:5–6 This covers the necessity for restitution in cases of negligence causing the loss of crops.
22:7–9 In these verses, **the judges** translates the Hebrew word *elohim*, which usually refers to "God" or to "gods." Here it refers to superiors in the society, or judges. The noun translated **wrongdoing** and its related verb are used in both political and private situations in which a breach of trust, violation of an agreement, disloyalty, or treachery was

it was rented, the loss is covered by^A its rental price.

Laws about Seduction

¹⁶ "If a man seduces a virgin who is not engaged, and he sleeps with her, he must certainly pay the bridal price for her to be his wife. ¹⁷ If her father absolutely refuses to give her to him, he must pay an amount in silver equal to the bridal price for virgins.

Capital Offenses

¹⁸ "Do not allow a sorceress to live.

¹⁹ "Whoever has sexual intercourse with an animal must be put to death.

²⁰ "Whoever sacrifices to any gods, except the LORD alone, is to be set apart for destruction.

Laws Protecting the Vulnerable

²¹ "You must not exploit a resident alien or oppress him, since you were resident aliens in the land of Egypt. ²² "You must not mistreat any widow or fatherless child. ²³ If you do mistreat them, they will no doubt cry to me, and I will certainly hear their cry. ²⁴ My anger will burn, and I will kill you with the sword; then your wives will be widows and your children fatherless.

²⁵ "If you lend silver to my people, to the poor person among you, you must not be like a creditor to him; you must not charge him interest.

²⁶ "If you ever take your neighbor's cloak as collateral, return it to him before sunset. ²⁷ For it is his only covering; it is the clothing for his body.^B What will he sleep in? And if he cries out to me, I will listen because I am gracious.

Respect for God

²⁸ "You must not blaspheme God^C or curse a leader among your people.

²⁹ "You must not hold back offerings from your harvest or your vats. Give me the firstborn of your sons. ³⁰ Do the same with your cattle and your flock. Let them stay with their mothers for seven days, but on the eighth day you are to give them to me.

³¹ "Be my holy people. You must not eat the meat of a mauled animal found in the field; throw it to the dogs.

Laws about Honesty and Justice

23 "You must not spread a false report. Do not join^D the wicked to be a malicious witness.

² "You must not follow a crowd in wrongdoing. Do not testify in a lawsuit and go along with a crowd to pervert justice. ³ Do not show favoritism to a poor person in his lawsuit.

⁴ "If you come across your enemy's stray ox or donkey, you must return it to him.

⁵ "If you see the donkey of someone who hates you lying helpless under its load, and you want to refrain from helping it, you must help with it.^E

⁶ "You must not deny justice to a poor person among you in his lawsuit. ⁷ Stay far away from a false accusation. Do not kill the innocent and the just, because I will not justify the guilty. ⁸ You must not take a bribe, for a bribe blinds the clear-sighted and corrupts the words^F of the righteous. ⁹ You must not oppress a resident alien; you yourselves know how it feels to be a resident alien because you were resident aliens in the land of Egypt.

Sabbaths and Festivals

¹⁰ "Sow your land for six years and gather its produce. ¹¹ But during the seventh year you are to let it rest and leave it uncultivated, so that the poor among your people may eat from it and the wild animals may consume what they

---

^A 22:15 Lit *rented, it comes with* ^B 22:27 Lit *skin* ^C 22:28 Or *judges* ^D 23:1 Lit *join hands with* ^E 23:5 Or *load, you must refrain from leaving it to him; you must set it free with him* ^F 23:8 Or *and subverts the cause*

involved (23:21; Gn 31:36; 50:17; 1Kg 12:19; 2Kg 1:1; Pr 28:24; Is 1:2).

22:16–17 The verb rendered **seduces** expresses the idea of persuading or enticing someone, often used negatively in the case of a gullible individual (Jdg 14:15; 16:5; Pr 1:10; 16:29). "Makes a fool of" would be another possible translation. Payment of a **bridal price** to the girl's father was a widely established ancient custom. The payment eventually should become her possession (Gn 31:14–15; 34:12). If a man had sexual intercourse with a woman to whom he was not engaged, he was required to pay the bridal price and marry her.

22:18 This prohibition represents one of several that outlawed all forms of occult activity (Lv 19:26–31; Dt 18:9–14). The three violations in Ex 22:18–20 would be more of a temptation once the Israelites reached the land of Canaan (23:32–33; Lv 18:1–5,23–30; 20:15–27; Dt 18:14–15).

22:19 The prohibition on sex with animals is not only because it was a sexual deviation

but because of its associations with animal cults.

22:21–27 The word translated **oppress** in v. 21 and 23:9 is used in 3:9 to describe what prompted the Israelites to call out for help. They needed to avoid putting themselves in the position of the Egyptians. The mention of the collateral consisting of a garment needed for warmth at night shows that the loan involved helping a poverty-stricken person survive. No luxury or business venture is in view.

22:28 Respect for God displayed in behavior toward others. Respect for a **leader** is included, perhaps in both halves of the verse, if the Hebrew word *elohim* has the same reference to "judges" that it seems to have in vv. 8–9.

22:29–30 Offerings and the firstborn of humans and animals belonged to God. Only the firstborn of animals suitable for sacrificing were actually sacrificed. Others were redeemed for a price.

23:1–9 These verses touch on every economic status or personal feeling that might

tempt someone to treat another unjustly. Favoritism either to the poor or to the rich is ruled out (Lv 19:15). Even in private matters involving the need of an enemy, an Israelite must not only return straying livestock but also render aid on the spot (Lv 19:15–18; Mt 5:43–48; Rm 12:17–21).

23:6–9 As in 22:21–26, the Israelites must remember who they were and what it was like as resident aliens, and they must consider who the Lord is in his support of justice. The warning in 23:7 not to execute an innocent person comes with a reason: **because I will not justify the guilty.** This may refer to God ultimately bringing to justice a guilty person who might slip through the court when judges take care not to execute an innocent person. Or it may refer to God bringing to justice any witness or judge who contributes to the execution of an innocent person.

23:10–11 The Lord's provision for his people from year to year would be like his provision of manna from day to day; there would be

leave. Do the same with your vineyard and your olive grove.

[12] "Do your work for six days but rest on the seventh day so that your ox and your donkey may rest, and the son of your female slave as well as the resident alien may be refreshed.

[13] "Pay strict attention to everything I have said to you. You must not invoke the names of other gods; they must not be heard on your lips.^A

[14] "Celebrate a festival in my honor three times a year. [15] Observe the Festival of Unleavened Bread. As I commanded you, you are to eat unleavened bread for seven days at the appointed time in the month of Abib,^B because you came out of Egypt in that month. No one is to appear before me empty-handed. [16] Also observe the Festival of Harvest^C with the firstfruits of your produce from what you sow in the field, and observe the Festival of Ingathering^D at the end of the year, when you gather your produce^E from the field. [17] Three times a year all your males are to appear before the Lord GOD.

[18] "You must not offer the blood of my sacrifices with anything leavened. The fat of my festival offering must not remain until morning.

[19] "Bring the best of the firstfruits of your land to the house of the LORD your God.

"You must not boil a young goat in its mother's milk.

Promises and Warnings

[20] "I am going to send an angel before you to protect you on the way and bring you to the place I have prepared. [21] Be attentive to him and listen to him. Do not defy him, because he will not forgive your acts of rebellion, for my name is in him. [22] But if you will carefully obey him and do everything I say, then I will be an enemy to your enemies and a foe to your foes. [23] For my angel will go before you and bring you to the land of the Amorites, Hethites, Perizzites, Canaanites, Hivites, and Jebusites, and I will wipe them out. [24] Do not bow in worship to their gods, and do not serve them. Do not imitate their practices. Instead, demolish them^F and smash their sacred pillars to pieces. [25] Serve the LORD your God, and he^G will bless your bread and your water. I will remove illnesses from you. [26] No woman will miscarry or be childless in your land. I will give you the full number of your days.

[27] "I will cause the people ahead of you to feel terror^H and will throw into confusion all the nations you come to. I will make all your enemies turn their backs to you in retreat.^I [28] I will send hornets^J in front of you, and they will drive the Hivites, Canaanites, and Hethites away from you. [29] I will not drive them out ahead of you in a single year; otherwise, the land would become desolate, and wild animals would multiply against you. [30] I will drive them out little by little ahead of you until you have become numerous^K and take possession of the land. [31] I will set your borders from the Red Sea to the Mediterranean Sea,^L and from the wilderness to the Euphrates River.^M For I will place the inhabitants of the land under your control, and you will drive them out ahead of you. [32] You

---

^A 23:13 Lit *mouth*   ^B 23:15 March–April; called Nisan in the post-exilic period; Neh 2:1; Est 3:7   ^C 23:16 The *Festival of Harvest* is called Festival of Weeks elsewhere; Ex 34:22. In the NT it is called Pentecost; Ac 2:1.   ^D 23:16 The *Festival of Ingathering* is called Festival of Shelters elsewhere; Lv 23:34–36.   ^E 23:16 Lit *labors*   ^F 23:24 Probably the idols   ^G 23:25 LXX, Vg read *I* ^H 23:27 Lit *will send terror of me ahead of you*   ^I 23:27 Or *I will give your enemies to you by the neck*   ^J 23:28 Or *send panic* ^K 23:30 Lit *fruitful*   ^L 23:31 Lit *the Sea of the Philistines*   ^M 23:31 Lit *the River*

---

sufficient left over for the seventh day and for the **seventh year** so that everyone could eat without constant labor.
23:12 The two animals and two sorts of people here are illustrative and not an exhaustive list of who would **rest** and **be refreshed** (cp. 20:10).
23:13 This verse does not mean an Israelite must never pronounce the name of a false god, since the names of some pagan gods are included in Scripture. Rather, it is a prohibition against calling on any other god for guidance, help, thanksgiving, or praise.
23:14–17 The **Festival of Unleavened Bread** took place near the start of the barley harvest; the **Festival of Harvest** took place at the time of the wheat harvest; and the **Festival of Ingathering** celebrated the completion of all the harvesting, including grapes and olives. Bringing **firstfruits**, the first items harvested, expressed gratitude for the harvest as coming from the Lord and faith that he would supply the remainder of the harvest (Dt 26:1–11). The name **Lord GOD** emphasizes his sovereignty and could also be rendered "the Sovereign [or "Master"], Yahweh." In the ancient Near East, the appearance of **all your males** would demonstrate the loyalty

or rebellion of those with potential for military service.
23:18–19 Based on 34:25, the sacrifice and **festival offering** is the Passover lamb, which was sacrificed, roasted, and eaten on the eve of the week of the Festival of Unleavened Bread. All leaven was to be dispensed with before the Passover lamb was offered (Dt 16:2–4). The fat and anything else left from the Passover lamb was to be burned (Ex 12:10). The prohibition about boiling **a young goat in its mother's milk** is repeated in 34:26 and Dt 14:21. It may have been connected with the Festival of Ingathering, since goats gave birth around that time, or it may have referred to a pagan custom of unknown significance.
23:20–23 The Lord's sending of **an angel** (cp. 13:21; 14:19) continues the picture of Israel's relationship with the Lord as that of a vassal with a suzerain. The vassal must understand that the envoy came with the king's authority behind him (**my name is in him**).
23:26 The Lord referred to provision and preservation of life at both ends of the spectrum—for infants and the elderly—having already spoken about what was needed in between (vv. 22,25). He was concerned about all aspects of life.

23:27–30 The Lord may have intended to use a plague of hornets to **drive . . . out** the groups living in the land (Dt 7:20; Jos 24:12). It may also be a figure of speech referring to the image of people running away from a place as if chased by swarming hornets (cp. Dt 1:44; Ps 118:12; Is 7:18–19).
I will cause the people ahead of you to feel terror is literally, "My terror I will send before you." God may be interpreted as either the source or the object of the terror. In the events that followed, both took place: the Lord caused fear/confusion and was also the object of fear as his reputation spread. Rahab's report in Jos 2:9 of what was happening among people in Canaan uses the same rare word for "terror" as does Ex 15:16.
23:30–31 I will drive them out and **you will drive them out** assume the involvement of both divine and human effort. **Borders from the Red Sea** refers to the portion of the Red Sea known as the Gulf of Aqaba (cp. 1Kg 9:26). **The Mediterranean Sea**, as it is called now, is in Hebrew literally "the sea of the Philistines," since they lived along the coast (cp. 13:17).
23:32–33 It will be a snare for you uses the word that 10:7 used to express what Pharaoh's men thought about Moses as they

must not make a covenant with them or their gods. ³³ They must not remain in your land, or else they will make you sin against me. If you serve their gods, it will be a snare for you."

The Covenant Ceremony

24 Then he said to Moses, "Go up to the LORD, you and Aaron, Nadab, and Abihu, and seventy of Israel's elders, and bow in worship at a distance. ² Moses alone is to approach the LORD, but the others are not to approach, and the people are not to go up with him."

³ Moses came and told the people all the commands of the LORD and all the ordinances. Then all the people responded with a single voice, "We will do everything that the LORD has commanded." ⁴ And Moses wrote down all the words of the LORD. He rose early the next morning and set up an altar and twelve pillars for the twelve tribes of Israel at the base of the mountain. ⁵ Then he sent out young Israelite men, and they offered burnt offerings and sacrificed bulls as fellowship offerings to the LORD. ⁶ Moses took half the blood and set it in basins; the other half of the blood he splattered on the altar. ⁷ He then took the covenant scroll and read it aloud to the people. They responded, "We will do and obey all that the LORD has commanded."

⁸ Moses took the blood, splattered it on the people, and said, "This is the blood of the covenant that the LORD has made with you concerning all these words."

⁹ Then Moses went up with Aaron, Nadab, and Abihu, and seventy of Israel's elders, ¹⁰ and they saw the God of Israel. Beneath his feet was something like a pavement made of lapis lazuli,

as clear as the sky itself. ¹¹ God did not harm^A the Israelite nobles; they saw him, and they ate and drank.

¹² The LORD said to Moses, "Come up to me on the mountain and stay there so that I may give you the stone tablets with the law and commandments I have written for their instruction."

¹³ So Moses arose with his assistant Joshua and went up the mountain of God. ¹⁴ He told the elders, "Wait here for us until we return to you. Aaron and Hur are here with you. Whoever has a dispute should go to them." ¹⁵ When Moses went up the mountain, the cloud covered it. ¹⁶ The glory of the LORD settled on Mount Sinai, and the cloud covered it for six days. On the seventh day he called to Moses from the cloud. ¹⁷ The appearance of the LORD's glory to the Israelites was like a consuming fire on the mountaintop. ¹⁸ Moses entered the cloud as he went up the mountain, and he remained on the mountain forty days and forty nights.

Offerings to Build the Tabernacle

25 The LORD spoke to Moses: ² "Tell the Israelites to take an offering for me. You are to take my offering from everyone who is willing to give. ³ This is the offering you are to receive from them: gold, silver, and bronze; ⁴ blue, purple, and scarlet yarn; fine linen and goat hair; ⁵ ram skins dyed red and fine leather;^B acacia wood; ⁶ oil for the light; spices for the anointing oil and for the fragrant incense; ⁷ and onyx^C along with other gemstones for mounting on the ephod and breastpiece.^D

⁸ "They are to make a sanctuary for me so that I may dwell among them. ⁹ You must make

---

^A 24:11 Lit *not stretch out his hand against*   ^B 25:5 Hb obscure   ^C 25:7 Or *carnelian*   ^D 25:7 Traditionally, *breastplate*

---

surveyed the damage caused by the plagues. Snares were naturally associated with death (1Sm 18:21; Ps 18:5; Pr 13:14; 14:27; 18:7). Idolatry as a snare to the Israelites pictured serious trouble, not a minor inconvenience (Ex 34:12; Dt 7:16; Jos 23:13; Jdg 2:3; Ps 106:36).
24:1–2 The ceremonies in chap. 24 are the climax of preparations and instructions in chaps. 19–23. To **bow in worship at a distance** fits ancient customs that called for bowing in full-length prostration at various points when approaching a person to whom one showed great respect (Gn 33:3).
24:3 All the commands may refer specifically to the Ten Commandments (20:1–17), and **the ordinances** to additional commands given in 20:22–23:33.
24:4 The **twelve pillars** represented the people as silent witnesses to their participation and agreement.
24:5–8 Burnt offerings were burned entirely, except for the animal hides, and they showed total dedication to the Lord. **Fellowship offerings** were primarily cooked and eaten by the worshipers, symbolizing that the people and the Lord, who had invited them, were at peace with one another. The shedding of blood when making a covenant reminded everyone of the covenant's seriousness and the penalties for breaking it (Jr

34:18–20). The sprinkling of blood marked the altar and the people as associated with the covenant sacrifices. And because this covenant was with God, the shed blood was also a provision for atonement and forgiveness, life for life (Lv 4:13–20; 17:1–16; Heb 9:13–22).
In addition to telling the people what the Lord commanded (v. 3), Moses read aloud **the covenant scroll** before he sprinkled them with blood, so they knew exactly what responsibilities they were agreeing to fulfill.
24:9–11 The description of what Moses and the Israelite leaders saw when they approached **the God of Israel** must employ comparisons. It was **something like a pavement made of lapis lazuli,** and it had a clarity like that of **the sky.** It was similar to, but beyond anything people knew of (likewise in v. 17). The description is further limited in that it offers the point of view of someone face down and able to see only what was **beneath his feet.** The mention that **God did not harm the Israelite nobles** (lit "stretch out his hand") reflects ancient customs that gave kings the ability to call for a subject's removal or death with just a hand gesture.
24:16–18 The LORD's glory had appeared previously only in Ex 16:10. **Six days** may allude to creation or reflect how long it took Moses and Joshua to climb the mountain.

Presumably Joshua stayed outside the cloud. **Forty days** signified a long time (see note at Gn 7:4).
25:1–31:17 These chapters contain instructions for the tabernacle and its furnishings and the clothing for priests that the Israelites were to make. Much of the information is repeated in chaps. 35–40, which report the tabernacle's construction.
25:1 The statement **The LORD spoke to Moses** divides chaps. 25–31 into seven unequal segments, ending with instructions about the Sabbath, as if to show a connection between creation and this new building where God would meet with humans (25:1; 30:11,17,22,34; 31:1,12; cp. Rv 21:1–3).
25:2 This offering would be the result of internal compulsion and not external—as with taxes or public pressure. The willingness of the people extended so far that the workmen had more than enough materials (36:3–7).
25:3–6 Most of these items were part of the plunder the Israelites received from the Egyptians (cp. Ex 3:22; 11:2–3).
25:7 The **ephod and breastpiece** are described more fully in chap. 28, along with other priestly garments.
25:8 The word translated **dwell** is rendered "settled" in the statement that "the glory of

it according to all that I show you — the pattern of the tabernacle as well as the pattern of all its furnishings.

The Ark

¹⁰ "They are to make an ark of acacia wood, forty-five inches long, twenty-seven inches wide, and twenty-seven inches high.^A ¹¹ Overlay it with pure gold; overlay it both inside and out. Also make a gold molding all around it. ¹² Cast four gold rings for it and place them on its four feet, two rings on one side and two rings on the other side. ¹³ Make poles of acacia wood and overlay them with gold. ¹⁴ Insert the poles into the rings on the sides of the ark in order to carry the ark with them. ¹⁵ The poles are to remain in the rings of the ark; they must not be removed from it. ¹⁶ Put the tablets of^B the testimony that I will give you into the ark. ¹⁷ Make a mercy seat of pure gold, forty-five inches long and twenty-seven inches wide.^C ¹⁸ Make two cherubim of gold; make them of hammered work at the two ends of the mercy seat. ¹⁹ Make

one cherub at one end and one cherub at the other end. At its two ends, make the cherubim of one piece with the mercy seat. ²⁰ The cherubim are to have wings spread out above, covering the mercy seat with their wings, and are to face one another. The faces of the cherubim should be toward the mercy seat. ²¹ Set the mercy seat on top of the ark and put the tablets of the testimony that I will give you into the ark. ²² I will meet with you there above the mercy seat, between the two cherubim that are over the ark of the testimony; I will speak with you from there about all that I command you regarding the Israelites.

The Table

²³ "You are to construct a table of acacia wood, thirty-six inches long, eighteen inches wide, and twenty-seven inches high.^D ²⁴ Overlay it with pure gold and make a gold molding all around it. ²⁵ Make a three-inch^E frame all around it and make a gold molding for it all around its frame. ²⁶ Make four gold rings for

^A 25:10 Lit *two and a half cubits its length, one and a half cubits its width, and one and a half cubits its height* ^B 25:16 *the tablets of* supplied for clarity, also in v. 21 ^C 25:17 Lit *two and a half cubits its length, one and a half cubits its width* ^D 25:23 Lit *two cubits its length, one cubit its width, and one and a half cubits its height* ^E 25:25 Lit *Make it a handbreadth*

the LORD settled on Mount Sinai" in 24:16. It is closely associated with the word *shekinah*, used in postbiblical discussions of the Lord's presence. By commissioning the building of the tabernacle, a portable worship center, the Lord showed that he intended to live among the Israelites more closely than when meeting with them on Mount Sinai.
25:10–22 The **ark**, a rectangular wooden box covered inside and out with gold, sat in the most sacred area in the tabernacle. It symbolized the Lord's presence with the Israelites in at least three ways: (1) It was a repository for the stone tablets given to Moses, which were a witness, or **testimony** to the requirements the Israelites had agreed to. (2) On the annual Day of

Atonement, the high priest sprinkled blood on the **mercy seat**, the ark's cover, in keeping with the Lord's provision for dealing with the sins of the people (Lv 16:13–15,29–34). (3) The ark was also where the Lord met with Moses and spoke with him (Nm 7:89). This was in keeping with his earlier assurance of his presence with Moses (Ex 3:11–12; 4:11–15).
25:10 Many measurements for the tabernacle and its furnishings used a unit called *ammah* in Hebrew, traditionally rendered "cubit." The Hebrew word also meant "forearm," and an *ammah* measured from the tip of a man's fingers to his elbow, roughly eighteen inches. The CSB makes the conversions United States customary units.

25:14 Repeatedly the tabernacle and its furnishings are described as having **rings** on them (25:26; 27:4; 30:4). This emphasizes the portable nature of this center of worship. God will be on the move and so will be his people—ready to go at any time.
25:18 The cover of the ark was to be decorated with two **cherubim**. Elsewhere the Lord is spoken of as enthroned above the cherubim, so that the ark was his footstool (1Sm 4:4; 2Sm 6:2; 2Kg 19:15; Pss 99:1,5; 132:7). "Cherubim" is the plural for "cherub," and both are anglicized Hebrew words. Winged beings of this sort were commissioned "to guard the way to the tree of life" (Gn 3:24), and they were described by the prophet Ezekiel, who saw them transporting God's throne (Ezk 10).
25:23–29 Generally thought to be for the Bread of the Presence, the table was also **for pouring drink offerings**. To present drink offerings, a priest would pour out a

Reconstruction of the ark of the covenant, drawn in Egyptian style, reflects the influence of 400 years of bondage in Egypt. The mysterious origin of the ark is seen by contrasting the two accounts of how it was made in the Pentateuch. The more elaborate account of the manufacture and ornamentation of the ark by the craftsman Bezalel appears in Ex 25:10–22; 31:2,7; 35:30–35; 37:1–9. It was planned during Moses's first sojourn on Sinai and built after the tabernacle specifications had been communicated and completed. The other account is found in Dt 10:1–5. After the sin of the golden calf and the breaking of the original Decalogue tablets, Moses made a plain box of acacia wood as a container to receive the new tablets of the law. A very ancient poem, the "Song of the Ark" in Nm 10:35–36, sheds some light on the function of the ark in the wanderings in the wilderness.

it, and attach the rings to the four corners at its four legs. [27] The rings should be next to the frame as holders for the poles to carry the table. [28] Make the poles of acacia wood and overlay them with gold, and the table can be carried by them. [29] You are also to make its plates and cups, as well as its pitchers and bowls for pouring drink offerings. Make them out of pure gold. [30] Put the Bread of the Presence on the table before me at all times.

The Lampstand

[31] "You are to make a lampstand out of pure, hammered gold. It is to be made of one piece: its base and shaft, its ornamental cups, and its buds[A] and petals. [32] Six branches are to extend from its sides, three branches of the lampstand from one side and three branches of the lampstand from the other side. [33] There are to be three cups shaped like almond blossoms, each with a bud and petals, on one branch, and three cups shaped like almond blossoms, each with a bud and petals, on the next branch. It is to be this way for the six branches that extend from the lampstand. [34] There are to be four cups shaped like almond blossoms on the lampstand shaft along with its buds and petals. [35] For the six branches that extend from the lampstand, a bud must be under the first pair of branches from it, a bud under the second pair of branches from it, and a bud under the third pair of branches from it. [36] Their buds and branches are to be of one piece.[B] All of it is to be a single hammered piece of pure gold. [37] "Make its seven lamps, and set them up so that they illuminate the area in front of it. [38] Its snuffers and firepans must be of pure gold. [39] The lampstand[C] with all these utensils is to be made from seventy-five pounds[D] of pure gold. [40] Be careful to make them according to the pattern you have been shown on the mountain.

The Tabernacle

26 "You are to construct the tabernacle itself with ten curtains. You must make them of finely spun linen, and blue, purple, and scarlet yarn, with a design of cherubim worked into them. [2] Each curtain should be forty-two feet[E] long and six feet[F] wide; all the curtains are to have the same measurements. [3] Five of the curtains should be joined together, and the other five curtains joined together. [4] Make loops of blue yarn on the edge of the last curtain in the first set, and do the same on the edge of the outermost curtain in the second set. [5] Make fifty loops on the one curtain and make fifty loops on the edge of the curtain in the second set, so that the loops line up together. [6] Also make fifty gold clasps and join the curtains together with the clasps, so that the tabernacle may be a single unit.

[7] "You are to make curtains of goat hair for a tent over the tabernacle; make eleven of these curtains. [8] Each curtain should be forty-five feet[G] long and six feet wide. All eleven curtains are to have the same measurements. [9] Join five of the curtains by themselves, and the other six curtains by themselves. Then fold the sixth curtain double at the front of the tent. [10] Make fifty loops on the edge of one curtain, the outermost in the first set, and make fifty loops on the edge of the corresponding curtain of the second set. [11] Make fifty bronze clasps; put the clasps through the loops and join the tent together so that it is a single unit. [12] As for the flap that remains from the tent curtains, the leftover half curtain is to hang over the back of the tabernacle. [13] What remains along the length of the tent curtains — a half yard[H] on one side and a half yard on the other side — should hang over the sides of the tabernacle on either side to cover it. [14] Make a covering for the tent from ram skins dyed red and a covering of fine leather[I] on top of that.

[15] "You are to make upright supports[J] of acacia wood for the tabernacle. [16] Each support is to be fifteen feet[K] long and twenty-seven inches[L] wide. [17] Each support will have two tenons for joining. Do the same for all the supports of the tabernacle. [18] Make the supports for the tabernacle as follows: twenty supports for the south side, [19] and make forty silver bases under the twenty supports, two bases under the first support for its two tenons, and two bases under the next support for its two tenons; [20] twenty supports for the second side of the tabernacle, the north side, [21] along with their forty silver bases, two bases under the first

---

A 25:31 = the outer covering of a flower **B 25:36** Lit *piece with it* **C 25:39** Lit *lt* **D 25:39** Lit *a talent* **E 26:2** Lit *28 cubits*
F 26:2 Lit *four cubits*, also in v. 8 **G 26:8** Lit *30 cubits* **H 26:13** Lit *the cubit* **I 26:14** Hb obscure **J 26:15** Or *frames*, or *beams*
K 26:16 Lit *10 cubits* **L 26:16** Lit *a cubit and a half*

---

liquid—wine, for example—to be burned along with certain animal sacrifices (29:40–41; Lv 23:9–13).
25:30 The **Bread of the Presence** consisted of twelve loaves made with fine flour and arranged in two rows on the gold-covered table located just outside the most holy area of the tabernacle (Lv 24:5–9). This bread was for the Israelite priests to eat as a symbolic provision from the Lord's table.
25:31–40 The highly decorated **lampstand** (Hb *menorah*) resembled the almond tree,

noted for its early blossoming. The Hebrew word for "almond" is associated with a verb that means "watch over" or "keep watch," so that almond blossoms seem an appropriate decoration for an item that enhanced visibility. Aaron's staff was made of almond wood (Nm 17:8). In Jr 1:11–12 it is a symbol of God watching over his word to accomplish his purpose.
26:1–14 The tabernacle proper was made with four layers; the first of **finely spun linen**, the second of woven **goat hair**, the third of leather made from **ram skins dyed red**, and the

fourth another kind of leather whose source is uncertain. The word used for it appears also in Ezk 16:10 to describe material for special sandals. The Hebrew word translated **fine leather** (also in 25:5; 35:7) might be borrowed from an Egyptian term. The Hebrew word also sounds similar to an Arabic word for a marine mammal, probably the manatee or dugong.
26:15–30 The tabernacle would be oriented with its open side to the east, its short wall on the west, and its long walls on the north and south.

support and two bases under each support; [22] and make six supports for the west side of the tabernacle. [23] Make two additional supports for the two back corners of the tabernacle. [24] They are to be paired at the bottom, and joined together[A] at the top in a single ring. So it should be for both of them; they will serve as the two corners. [25] There are to be eight supports with their silver bases: sixteen bases; two bases under the first support and two bases under each support.

[26] "You are to make five crossbars of acacia wood for the supports on one side of the tabernacle, [27] five crossbars for the supports on the other side of the tabernacle, and five crossbars for the supports on the back side of the tabernacle on the west. [28] The central crossbar is to run through the middle of the supports from one end to the other. [29] Then overlay the supports with gold, and make their rings of gold as the holders for the crossbars. Also overlay the crossbars with gold. [30] You are to set up the tabernacle according to the plan for it that you have been shown on the mountain.

[31] "You are to make a curtain of blue, purple, and scarlet yarn, and finely spun linen with a design of cherubim worked into it. [32] Hang it on four gold-plated pillars of acacia wood that have gold hooks and that stand on four silver bases. [33] Hang the curtain under the clasps[B] and bring the ark of the testimony there behind the curtain, so the curtain will make a separation for you between the holy place and the most holy place. [34] Put the mercy seat on the ark of the testimony in the most holy place. [35] Place the table outside the curtain and the lampstand on the south side of the tabernacle, opposite the table; put the table on the north side.

[36] "For the entrance to the tent you are to make a screen embroidered[C] with blue, purple, and scarlet yarn, and finely spun linen. [37] Make five pillars of acacia wood for the screen and overlay them with gold; their hooks are to be gold, and you are to cast five bronze bases for them.

[A]26:24 Lit and together they are to be complete [B]26:33 The clasps that join the ten curtains of the tabernacle; Ex 26:6 [C]26:36 Or woven

---

26:31–35 The curtain (Hb paroketh) is a term used only of this drapery that divides the two halves of the tabernacle proper. The outer room, the holy place, would contain the table and the lampstand described in chap. 25. The inner room, the most holy place, would contain the ark and its cover, the mercy seat.

26:36–37 The entrance to the holy place, on the east side of the tabernacle, would have a woven linen screen of the same fine material as the veil, but with no mention of the cherubim design.

Reconstruction of the tabernacle and its court (26:1–35). The tabernacle was always set up to face east, so this view is from the northeast.

The Altar of Burnt Offering

27 "You are to construct the altar of acacia wood. The altar must be square, 7½ feet long, and 7½ feet wide;ᴬ it must be 4½ feet high.ᴮ ² Make horns for it on its four corners; the horns are to be of one piece.ᶜ Overlay it with bronze. ³ Make its pots for removing ashes, and its shovels, basins, meat forks, and firepans; make all its utensils of bronze. ⁴ Construct a grate for it of bronze mesh, and make four bronze rings on the mesh at its four corners. ⁵ Set it below, under the altar's ledge,ᴰ so that the mesh comes halfway upᴱ the altar. ⁶ Then make poles for the altar, poles of acacia wood, and overlay them with bronze. ⁷ The poles are to be inserted into the rings so that the poles are on two sides of the altar when it is carried. ⁸ Construct the altar with boards so that it is hollow. They are to make it just as it was shown to you on the mountain.

The Courtyard

⁹ "You are to make the courtyard for the tabernacle. Make hangings for the south side of the courtyard out of finely spun linen, 150 feetᶠ long on that side ¹⁰ including twenty posts and twenty bronze bases, with silver hooks and silver bandsᴳ for the posts. ¹¹ And so make hangings 150 feet long for the north side, including twenty posts and their twenty bronze bases, with silver hooks and silver bands for the posts. ¹² For the width of the courtyard, make hangings 75 feetᴴ long for the west side, including their ten posts and their ten bases. ¹³ And for the width of the courtyard on the east side toward the sunrise, 75 feet, ¹⁴ make hangings 22½ feetᴵ long for one side of the gate, including their three posts and their three bases. ¹⁵ And make hangings 22½ feet long for the other side, including three posts and their three bases. ¹⁶ The gate of the courtyard is to have a 30-footᴶ screen

embroideredᴷ with blue, purple, and scarlet yarn, and finely spun linen. It is to have four posts and their four bases. ¹⁷ "All the posts around the courtyard are to be banded with silver and have silver hooks and bronze bases. ¹⁸ The courtyard is to be 150 feet long, 75 feet wide at each end, and 7½ feet high,ᴸ all of it made of finely spun linen. The bases of the posts are to be bronze. ¹⁹ All the utensils of the tabernacle for every use and all its tent pegs as well as all the tent pegs of the courtyard are to be made of bronze.

The Lampstand Oil

²⁰ "You are to command the Israelites to bring you pure oil from crushed olives for the light, in order to keep the lamp burning regularly. ²¹ In the tent of meeting outside the curtain that is in front of the testimony, Aaron and his sons are to tend the lamp from evening until morning before the LORD. This is to be a permanent statute for the Israelites throughout their generations.

The Priestly Garments

28 "Have your brother Aaron, with his sons, come to you from the Israelites to serve me as priest — Aaron, his sons Nadab and Abihu, Eleazar and Ithamar. ² Make holy garments for your brother Aaron, for glory and beauty. ³ You are to instruct all the skilled artisans,ᴹ whom I have filled with a spirit of wisdom, to make Aaron's garments for consecrating him to serve me as priest. ⁴ These are the garments that they must make: a breastpiece, an ephod, a robe, a specially woven tunic,ᴺ a turban, and a sash. They are to make holy garments for your brother Aaron and his sons so that they may serve me as priests. ⁵ They should useᴼ gold; blue, purple, and scarlet yarn; and fine linen.

ᴬ27:1 Lit *five cubits in length and five cubits in width*   ᴮ27:1 Lit *wide; and its height three cubits*   ᶜ27:2 Lit *piece with it*   ᴰ27:5 Perhaps a *ledge* around the altar on which the priests could stand; Lv 9:22   ᴱ27:5 Or *altar's rim, so that the grid comes halfway down*   ᶠ27:9 Lit *100 cubits*, also in v. 11   ᴳ27:10 Or *connecting rods*, also in v. 11   ᴴ27:12 Lit *50 cubits*, also in v. 13   ᴵ27:14 Lit *15 cubits*, also in v. 15   ᴶ27:16 Lit *20-cubit*   ᴷ27:16 Or *woven*   ᴸ27:18 Lit *be 100 by the cubit, and the width 50 by 50, and the height five cubits*   ᴹ28:3 Lit *all wise of heart*   ᴺ28:4 Hb obscure   ᴼ28:5 Lit *receive*

27:1 The **altar** (also called "the bronze altar"; see 38:30; 39:39) would sit outside the sanctuary or tabernacle proper in the middle of the courtyard square in front of the holy place. It was massive in size; a person of average height standing beside it would barely be able to look over it.
27:2 The incense altar would also have horns (30:1–2), which may have been symbols of strength. Blood was put on the horns of both the altar of burnt offering and the incense altar (Ex 29:12; 30:10; Lv 4:7,18,25,30,34; 8:15; 9:9; 16:18). A person seeking refuge in hope of avoiding death would grasp the horns on the altar for burnt offerings (1Kg 1:50–51; 2:28).
27:9–19 The **courtyard for the tabernacle** would be enclosed by a fence 7 ½ feet high made with linen cloth hung from posts at

7 ½-foot intervals. Like the tabernacle proper, it would open to the east.
27:20–21 This variety of **pure oil from crushed olives** (crushed and pressed rather than ground in a mill) would give bright light with little smoke. Mention of **Aaron and his sons**, who would **tend the lamp**, prepares for the start of a lengthy section (chaps. 28–29) that describes preparations for their service. The tabernacle is called **the tent of meeting** in view of the Lord's intention to meet with his people there (25:22; 29:42–43; 30:6,36).
28:1–2 The **holy garments** of Aaron and his sons marked them as the Lord's priests. The phrase **for glory and beauty** indicates that the priestly garments were much more than utilitarian. They resembled other elements of the tabernacle complex, which featured fine

fabrics, colorful designs, precious metals, and specialized workmanship, as appropriate for honoring the Lord, who would reside there. **Nadab and Abihu** accompanied their father and the Israelite elders who were privileged to take part in the covenant ceremony on Mount Sinai (24:1–11). Their sudden deaths are recorded in Lv 10:1–7. **Eleazar** followed Aaron as high priest (Nm 20:28). **Ithamar** directed the Levites, who made an inventory of materials used in constructing the tabernacle (Ex 38:21).
28:3–5 The men and women who would make the priestly **garments** would use abilities that God gave them. These people were "wise of heart" and were **filled with a spirit of wisdom**. Wisdom in this case would display itself in both willingness and skill to do the needed work.

Plate of pure gold
with inscription:
"HOLY TO THE LORD."
Ex 28:36

Turban or mitre
Ex 28:36–38

The shoulder straps for
the breastplate capped
with two onyx stones
bearing the names of
Israel's twelve sons, six on
each, in order of their birth
Ex 28:9–10

Twelve gemstones,
each bearing a name of
one of the twelve tribes
Ex 28:17–21

Sash
Ex 28:4,39,40

Ephod, woven and
reflecting the colors of
the sanctuary
Ex 28:5–15,31

Fringe composed of
alternating pomegranates
and gold bells; the pomegranates
are woven from blue, purple,
and scarlet yarn
Ex 28:33–35

Artist's rendition of the high priest's garments (28:1–38)

The Ephod

⁶ "They are to make the ephod of finely spun linen embroidered^A with gold, and with blue, purple, and scarlet yarn. ⁷ It must have two shoulder pieces attached to its two edges so that it can be joined together. ⁸ The artistically woven waistband that is on the ephod^B must be of one piece,^C according to the same workmanship of gold, of blue, purple, and scarlet yarn, and of finely spun linen.

⁹ "Take two onyx stones and engrave on them the names of Israel's sons: ¹⁰ six of their names on the first stone and the remaining six names on the second stone, in the order of their birth. ¹¹ Engrave the two stones with the names of Israel's sons as a gem cutter engraves a seal. Mount them, surrounded with gold filigree settings. ¹² Fasten both stones on the shoulder pieces of the ephod as memorial stones for the Israelites. Aaron will carry their names on his two shoulders before the LORD as a reminder. ¹³ Fashion gold filigree settings ¹⁴ and two chains of pure gold; you will make them of braided cord work, and attach the cord chains to the settings.

The Breastpiece

¹⁵ "You are to make an embroidered breastpiece for making decisions.^D Make it with the same workmanship as the ephod; make it of gold, of blue, purple, and scarlet yarn, and of finely spun linen. ¹⁶ It must be square and folded double, nine inches long and nine inches wide.^E ¹⁷ Place a setting of gemstones^F on it, four rows of stones:

The first row should be
a row of carnelian, topaz, and emerald;^G
¹⁸   the second row,
a turquoise,^H a lapis lazuli,
and a diamond;^I
¹⁹   the third row,
a jacinth,^J an agate, and an amethyst;
²⁰   and the fourth row,
a beryl, an onyx, and a jasper.
They should be adorned with gold filigree in their settings. ²¹ The twelve stones are to

correspond to the names of Israel's sons. Each stone must be engraved like a seal, with one of the names of the twelve tribes.

²² "You are to make braided chains^K of pure gold cord work for the breastpiece. ²³ Fashion two gold rings for the breastpiece and attach them to its two corners. ²⁴ Then attach the two gold cords to the two gold rings at the corners of the breastpiece. ²⁵ Attach the other ends of the two cords to the two filigree settings, and in this way attach them to the ephod's shoulder pieces in the front. ²⁶ Make two other gold rings and put them at the two other corners of the breastpiece on the edge that is next to the inner border of the ephod. ²⁷ Make two more gold rings and attach them to the bottom of the ephod's two shoulder pieces on its front, close to its seam,^L and above the ephod's woven waistband. ²⁸ The artisans are to tie the breastpiece from its rings to the rings of the ephod with a cord of blue yarn, so that the breastpiece is above the ephod's waistband and does not come loose from the ephod.

²⁹ "Whenever he enters the sanctuary, Aaron is to carry the names of Israel's sons over his heart on the breastpiece for decisions, as a continual reminder before the LORD. ³⁰ Place the Urim and Thummim in the breastpiece for decisions, so that they will also be over Aaron's heart whenever he comes before the LORD. Aaron will continually carry the means of decisions for the Israelites over his heart before the LORD.

The Robe

³¹ "You are to make the robe of the ephod entirely of blue yarn. ³² There should be an opening at its top in the center of it. Around the opening, there should be a woven collar with an opening like that of body armor^J so that it does not tear. ³³ Make pomegranates of blue, purple, and scarlet yarn on its lower hem and all around it. Put gold bells between them all the way around, ³⁴ so that gold bells and pomegranates alternate around the lower hem of the robe. ³⁵ The robe will be worn by Aaron

---

^A 28:6 Or woven ^B 28:8 Lit waistband of its ephod, which is on it ^C 28:8 Lit piece with the ephod ^D 28:15 Used for determining God's will; Nm 27:21 ^E 28:16 Lit a span its length and a span its width ^F 28:17 Many of these stones cannot be identified with certainty. ^G 28:17 Or beryl ^H 28:18 Or malachite, or garnet ^I 28:18 Hb obscure; LXX, Vg read jasper ^J 28:19,32 Hb obscure ^K 28:22 The same chains mentioned in v. 14 ^L 28:27 The place where the shoulder pieces join the front of the ephod

---

28:6–8 The word **ephod** is a transliterated Hebrew word referring to a vestlike garment worn by the high priest.
28:9–14 A **seal** would stamp a distinctive impression into wax or clay, or leave an identifying pattern of ink and act like a signature (cp. Gn 38:18; 1Kg 21:8; Jr 22:24). Exodus 28:12 does not specify who should be reminded by the stones or for what purpose.
28:15–30 The breastpiece was **folded double**, it seems, to create a pocket or pouch for storing **the Urim and Thummim.**

28:29 The high priest represented the Israelites, as symbolized by the double display of the names of each tribe on the two stones on the ephod (v. 11) and also by the name on each of the twelve stones on his **breastpiece.**
28:30 Little is known about what the words **Urim and Thummim** meant (the Hebrew words are transliterated rather than translated), or how these objects worked. One suggested meaning is that "Urim" had to do with "light" and "Thummim" with "completion, perfection." Another possibility is that

they are associated with words that mean "curse" and "innocence." Their use included receiving direction from the Lord for decisions (Nm 27:18–21; 1Sm 28:5–6). The high priest to carry into the presence of the Lord both the names of the tribes and items used in rendering decisions presupposed the Lord's sovereignty in these quests for guidance.
28:31–34 The colors, precious stones, fine materials and specialized workmanship, and certainly the bells that went into making the priest's clothing contributed to marking the

whenever he ministers, and its sound will be heard when he enters the sanctuary before the LORD and when he exits, so that he does not die.

The Turban

36 "You are to make a pure gold medallion and engrave it, like the engraving of a seal: HOLY TO THE LORD. **37** Fasten it to a cord of blue yarn so it can be placed on the turban; the medallion is to be on the front of the turban. **38** It will be on Aaron's forehead so that Aaron may bear the guilt connected with the holy offerings that the Israelites consecrate as all their holy gifts. It is always to be on his forehead, so that they may find acceptance with the LORD.

Other Priestly Garments

39 "You are to weave the tunic from fine linen, make a turban of fine linen, and make an embroidered sash. **40** Make tunics, sashes, and headbands for Aaron's sons to give them glory and beauty. **41** Put these on your brother Aaron and his sons; then anoint, ordain,[A] and consecrate them, so that they may serve me as priests. **42** Make them linen undergarments to cover their naked bodies; they must extend from the waist to the thighs. **43** These must be worn by Aaron and his sons whenever they enter the tent of meeting or approach the altar to minister in the sanctuary area, so that they do not incur guilt and die. This is to be a permanent statute for Aaron and for his future descendants.

Instructions about Consecration

29 "This is what you are to do for them to consecrate them to serve me as priests. Take a young bull and two unblemished rams, **2** with unleavened bread, unleavened cakes mixed with oil, and unleavened wafers coated with oil. Make them out of fine wheat flour, **3** put them in a basket, and bring them in the basket, along with the bull and two rams. **4** Bring Aaron and his sons to the entrance to the tent of meeting and wash them with water. **5** Then take the garments and clothe Aaron with the tunic, the robe for the ephod, the ephod itself, and the breastpiece; fasten the ephod on him with its woven waistband. **6** Put the turban on his head and place the holy diadem on the turban. **7** Take the anointing oil, pour it on his head, and anoint him. **8** You must also bring his sons and clothe them with tunics. **9** Tie the sashes on Aaron and his sons and fasten headbands on them. The priesthood is to be theirs by a permanent statute. This is the way you will ordain Aaron and[B] his sons.

10 "You are to bring the bull to the front of the tent of meeting, and Aaron and his sons must lay their hands on the bull's head. **11** Slaughter the bull before the LORD at the entrance to the tent of meeting. **12** Take some of the bull's blood and apply it to the horns of the altar with your finger; then pour out all the rest of the blood at the base of the altar. **13** Take all the fat that covers the entrails, the fatty lobe of the liver, and the two kidneys with the fat on them, and burn them on the altar. **14** But burn the bull's flesh, its hide, and its waste outside the camp; it is a sin offering.

15 "Take one ram, and Aaron and his sons are to lay their hands on the ram's head. **16** You are to slaughter the ram, take its blood, and splatter it on all sides of the altar. **17** Cut the ram into pieces. Wash its entrails and legs, and place them with its head and its pieces on the altar. **18** Then burn the whole ram on the altar; it is a burnt offering to the LORD. It is a pleasing aroma, a food offering to the LORD.

19 "You are to take the second ram, and Aaron and his sons must lay their hands on the ram's head. **20** Slaughter the ram, take some of its blood, and put it on Aaron's right earlobe, on his sons' right earlobes, on the thumbs of

---

---

high priest and drawing attention to his work and movements.
28:35 To wear the specified clothing would show that the priest recognized the sanctity of the holy place because of God's presence.
28:36–37 The phrase HOLY TO THE LORD indicated ownership—"belonging to." The priest was marked as someone devoted to the Lord for service, representing the Israelites, who were likewise to be holy (19:5–6; 22:31; Lv 11:44–45). The same words are used to describe the Sabbath in Ex 31:15 (cp. Ezr 8:28; Jr 2:2–3; Zch 14:20–21).
28:38 In place of and as representatives of the rest of the Israelites, Aaron and his sons were responsible to care for the tabernacle and present offerings there (Nm 17:12–18:7). The high priest would **bear the guilt** (or suffer the consequences) associated with failure to observe the requirements of holiness (cp. v. 43).
28:39–40 Aaron's sons refers to other priests besides the high priest. They were

not to wear robes but only **tunics, sashes, and headbands** plus a **turban**.
29:4–9 Leviticus 8 describes the ceremony enacted in the tabernacle.
29:6 Holy diadem is another term for the engraved gold plate described in 28:36–37 (cp. 39:30).
29:7 Instructions for making the fragrant **anointing oil** appear in 30:22–25.
29:10 Aaron and his sons would associate themselves with the bull by putting their hands on it, transferring their guilt to receive atonement and forgiveness as the bull was offered up (Lv 4:4,15,24,29,33). The bull would be sacrificed as a substitute for the people; they must do likewise with two rams (Ex 29:15,19; cp. Lv 16:21; Nm 8:10; 27:18–23).
29:11–13 The use of **blood** reflects its significance as essential to life and to God's provision of a substitute whose life was lost on behalf of the worshiper (Lv 17:11). Certain portions of the animal's **fat** were to be burned as a way of offering what was

best to the Lord. While the blood symbolized life, the fat symbolized abundance and was characteristic of an animal that had been well fed and cared for; it was considered the finest part (Gn 4:4; 45:18, "richness"; Ezk 34:3). The **kidneys** were associated with the inner life of a person, along with the heart (Pss 7:10; 73:21; Jr 17:10; 20:12).
29:14 The various kinds of **sin offering** and their circumstances are described in Lv 4:1–5:13. Sometimes called a purification offering, its purpose was to atone for sin or ceremonial uncleanness in order to restore communion. Most of the animal had to be burned **outside the camp** (cp. Heb 13:11–12).
29:15–18 The first ram was given as a **burnt offering.** It went up in smoke as a gift in tribute to God by means of fire, making it **a food offering.** That it would make **a pleasing aroma** signified God's acceptance of the offering and the worshiper (Lv 1).
29:19–21 No reason is given for placing **blood** on the **right earlobes . . . thumbs,**

their right hands, and on the big toes of their right feet. Splatter the remaining blood on all sides of the altar. ²¹ Take some of the blood that is on the altar and some of the anointing oil, and sprinkle them on Aaron and his garments, as well as on his sons and their garments. So he and his garments will be holy, as well as his sons and their garments.

²² "Take the fat from the ram, the fat tail, the fat covering the entrails, the fatty lobe of the liver, the two kidneys and the fat on them, and the right thigh (since this is a ram for ordination^); ²³ take one loaf of bread, one cake of bread made with oil, and one wafer from the basket of unleavened bread that is before the LORD; ²⁴ and put all of them in the hands of Aaron and his^B sons and present them as a presentation offering before the LORD. ²⁵ Take them from their hands and burn them on the altar on top of the burnt offering, as a pleasing aroma before the LORD; it is a food offering to the LORD.

²⁶ "Take the breast from the ram of Aaron's ordination and present it as a presentation offering before the LORD; it is to be your portion. ²⁷ Consecrate for Aaron and his sons the breast of the presentation offering that is presented and the thigh of the contribution that is lifted up from the ram of ordination. ²⁸ This will belong to Aaron and his sons as a regular portion from the Israelites, for it is a contribution. It will be the Israelites' contribution from their fellowship sacrifices, their contribution to the LORD.

²⁹ "The holy garments that belong to Aaron are to belong to his sons after him, so that they can be anointed and ordained^C in them. ³⁰ Any priest who is one of his sons and who succeeds him and enters the tent of meeting to minister in the sanctuary must wear them for seven days.

³¹ "You are to take the ram of ordination and boil its flesh in a holy place. ³² Aaron and his sons are to eat the meat of the ram and the bread that is in the basket at the entrance to the tent of meeting. ³³ They must eat those things

by which atonement was made at the time of their ordination^D and consecration. An unauthorized person must not eat them, for these things are holy. ³⁴ If any of the meat of ordination or any of the bread is left until morning, burn what is left over. It must not be eaten because it is holy.

³⁵ "This is what you are to do for Aaron and his sons based on all I have commanded you. Take seven days to ordain them. ³⁶ Sacrifice a bull as a sin offering each day for atonement. Purify^E the altar when you make atonement for it, and anoint it in order to consecrate it. ³⁷ For seven days you must make atonement for the altar and consecrate it. The altar will be especially holy. Whatever touches the altar will be consecrated.

³⁸ "This is what you are to offer regularly on the altar every day: two year-old lambs. ³⁹ In the morning offer one lamb, and at twilight offer the other lamb. ⁴⁰ With the first lamb offer two quarts^F of fine flour mixed with one quart^G of oil from crushed olives, and a drink offering of one quart of wine. ⁴¹ You are to offer the second lamb at twilight. Offer a grain offering and a drink offering with it, like the one in the morning, as a pleasing aroma, a food offering to the LORD. ⁴² This will be a regular burnt offering throughout your generations at the entrance to the tent of meeting before the LORD, where I will meet you^H to speak with you. ⁴³ I will also meet with the Israelites there, and that place will be consecrated by my glory. ⁴⁴ I will consecrate the tent of meeting and the altar; I will also consecrate Aaron and his sons to serve me as priests. ⁴⁵ I will dwell among the Israelites and be their God. ⁴⁶ And they will know that I am the LORD their God, who brought them out of the land of Egypt, so that I might dwell among them. I am the LORD their God.

The Incense Altar

30 "You are to make an altar for the burning of incense; make it of acacia wood. ² It must be square, eighteen inches long and eighteen inches wide;^I it must be

---

^A 29:22 The priest would normally receive the right thigh to be eaten, but here it is burned; Lv 7:32-34. ^B 29:24 Lit in the hands of his ^C 29:29 Lit him for anointing in them and for filling their hand ^D 29:33 Lit made to fill their hand ^E 29:36 Or Make a sin offering on ^F 29:40 Lit offer a tenth ^G 29:40 Lit a fourth of a hin ^H 29:42 = Moses ^I 30:2 Lit one cubit its length and one cubit its width

---

and **toes**, though it may have symbolized totality (see note at Lv 8:22-30).
29:22-25 The sacrifice of the second **ram** is one of the "fellowship sacrifices" (Lv 3; 7:11-21). It celebrated communion with God with ceremonies including a shared meal. The ram's designation as **a ram for ordination** explains why the **right thigh** was to be burned rather than eaten, as was normal for fellowship sacrifices. The words *ordination* and *ordain* reflect the idiomatic Hebrew expression that reads literally, "to fill the hand of someone." By placing items in the hands of Aaron and his sons and then

presenting and burning the items, Moses would act out the filling of the hands of the new priests. It would become their work to present to the Lord the offerings that the Israelites would bring.
29:26-28 It is to be your portion specifies that this time Moses would receive **the breast** because he was the officiating priest. On later occasions it would go to Aaron or his sons (Lv 7:34-36).
29:29-30 Priestly garments were passed on to the next generation.
29:31-35 Instructions for eating the ordination ram are followed by a summary of the

seven-day ordination (v. 35). The number **seven** symbolized the completeness of the process (cp. Lv 8:33-36).
29:38-42 After the instructions for the seven-day consecration of Aaron and his sons and of the altar in vv. 1-37, instructions for regular sacrifices to be offered on normal days are presented.
29:43-46 The most important consecrations would be accomplished not by the Israelites but by the Lord.
30:1-5 Incense is a picture of prayer (Ps 141:2; Rv 5:8; 8:3-4).

thirty-six inches high.^A Its horns must be of one piece with it. ³ Overlay its top, all around its sides, and its horns with pure gold; make a gold molding all around it. ⁴ Make two gold rings for it under the molding on two of its sides; put these on opposite sides of it to be holders for the poles to carry it with. ⁵ Make the poles of acacia wood and overlay them with gold.

⁶ "You are to place the altar in front of the curtain by the ark of the testimony — in front of the mercy seat that is over the testimony — where I will meet with you. ⁷ Aaron must burn fragrant incense on it; he must burn it every morning when he tends the lamps. ⁸ When Aaron sets up the lamps at twilight, he must burn incense. There is to be an incense offering before the LORD throughout your generations. ⁹ You must not offer unauthorized incense on it, or a burnt or grain offering; you are not to pour a drink offering on it.

¹⁰ "Once a year Aaron is to perform the atonement ceremony for the altar. Throughout your generations he is to perform the atonement ceremony for⁸ it once a year, with the blood of the sin offering for atonement on the horns. The altar is especially holy to the LORD."

The Atonement Money

¹¹ The LORD spoke to Moses: ¹² "When you take a census of the Israelites to register them, each of the men must pay a ransom for his life to the LORD as they are registered. Then no plague will come on them as they are registered. ¹³ Everyone who is registered must pay half a shekel^c according to the sanctuary shekel (twenty gerahs to the shekel). This half shekel is a contribution to the LORD. ¹⁴ Each man who is registered, twenty years old or more, must give this contribution to the LORD. ¹⁵ The wealthy may not give more and the poor may not give less than half a shekel when giving the contribution to the LORD to atone for^D your lives. ¹⁶ Take the atonement price^E from the Israelites and use it for the service of the tent of meeting. It will serve as a reminder for the Israelites before the LORD to atone for your lives."

The Bronze Basin

¹⁷ The LORD spoke to Moses: ¹⁸ "Make a bronze basin for washing and a bronze stand for it. Set it between the tent of meeting and the altar, and put water in it. ¹⁹ Aaron and his sons must wash their hands and feet from the basin. ²⁰ Whenever they enter the tent of meeting or approach the altar to minister by burning a food offering to the LORD, they must wash with water so that they will not die. ²¹ They must wash their hands and feet so that they will not die; this is to be a permanent statute for them, for Aaron and his descendants throughout their generations."

The Anointing Oil

²² The LORD spoke to Moses: ²³ "Take for yourself the finest spices: 12 ½ pounds^F of liquid myrrh, half as much (6 ¼ pounds^G) of fragrant cinnamon, 6 ¼ pounds of fragrant cane, ²⁴ 12 ½ pounds of cassia (by the sanctuary shekel), and a gallon^H of olive oil. ²⁵ Prepare from these a holy anointing oil, a scented blend, the work of a perfumer; it will be holy anointing oil. ²⁶ "With it you are to anoint the tent of meeting, the ark of the testimony, ²⁷ the table with all its utensils, the lampstand with its utensils, the altar of incense, ²⁸ the altar of burnt offering with all its utensils, and the basin with its stand. ²⁹ Consecrate them and they will be especially holy. Whatever touches them will be consecrated. ³⁰ Anoint Aaron and his sons and consecrate them to serve me as priests.

³¹ "Tell the Israelites: This will be my holy anointing oil throughout your generations. ³² It must not be used for ordinary anointing on a person's body, and you must not make anything like it using its formula. It is holy, and it must be holy to you. ³³ Anyone who blends something like it or puts some of it on an unauthorized person must be cut off from his people."

The Sacred Incense

³⁴ The LORD said to Moses, "Take fragrant spices: stacte, onycha, and galbanum; the spices and pure frankincense are to be in equal measures. ³⁵ Prepare expertly blended incense from these; it is to be seasoned with salt, pure and

^A30:2 Lit wide; and two cubits its height   ^B30:10 Or on   ^c30:13 A shekel is about two-fifths of an ounce of silver   ^D30:15 Or to ransom, also in v. 16   ^E30:16 Lit the silver of the atonement   ^F30:23 Lit 500 (shekels), also in v. 24   ^G30:23 Lit 250 (shekels)   ^H30:24 Lit a hin

30:10 To perform the atonement ceremony involved putting blood on the horns of the incense altar on the Day of Atonement (Lv 16:16–20).
30:11–16 The motive for taking a census was typically military (Nm 1:2–3,20–45; Jdg 20:2,15–17). The need to pay a ransom, also called a contribution, of half a shekel each in order to avert a plague reminded everyone that the nation as a whole and its citizens belonged to the Lord. Their preservation depended ultimately on him, not their

military strength, wealth, or poverty (12:13; 15:26; 17:8–16; Nm 8:19).
30:13 At the time of Moses, a shekel was a measure of weight. Measuring according to the sanctuary may mean that this weight was different from the one commonly used in scales (Gn 23:16) or that the sanctuary was the center for a system of standardizing weights.
30:22–38 The oil and incense for the tabernacle required costly ingredients and expert knowledge to compound them properly.

Myrrh came from the sap of a tree found in Arabia and Ethiopia. Cinnamon came from the bark of a tree grown in Ceylon and Malaysia. Cassia may have come from a type of tree bark. Stacte is a transliterated Greek term used for different varieties of tree and plant sap. Onycha, based on an Arabic word, may have come from a type of mollusk. Galbanum came from the sap of a plant grown in Afghanistan and Persia. Frankincense also came from sap and could be imported from Arabia or Ethiopia.

holy. ³⁶ Grind some of it into a fine powder and put some in front of the testimony in the tent of meeting, where I will meet with you. It must be especially holy to you. ³⁷ As for the incense you are making, you must not make any for yourselves using its formula. It is to be regarded by you as holy — belonging to the Lord. ³⁸ Anyone who makes something like it to smell its fragrance must be cut off from his people."

God's Provision of the Skilled Workers

31 The Lord also spoke to Moses: ² "Look, I have appointed by name Bezalel son of Uri, son of Hur, of the tribe of Judah. ³ I have filled him with God's Spirit, with wisdom, understanding, and ability in every craft ⁴ to design artistic works in gold, silver, and bronze, ⁵ to cut gemstones for mounting, and to carve wood for work in every craft. ⁶ I have also selected Oholiabᴬ son of Ahisamach, of the tribe of Dan, to be with him. I have put wisdom in the heart of every skilled artisanᴮ in order to make all that I have commanded you: ⁷ the tent of meeting, the ark of the testimony, the mercy seat that is on top of it, and all the other furnishings of the tent — ⁸ the table with its utensils, the pure gold lampstand with all its utensils, the altar of incense, ⁹ the altar of burnt offering with all its utensils, the basin with its stand — ¹⁰ the specially wovenᶜ garments, both the holy garments for the priest Aaron and the garments for his sons to serve as priests, ¹¹ the anointing oil, and the fragrant incense for the sanctuary. They must make them according to all that I have commanded you."

Observing the Sabbath

¹² The Lord said to Moses, ¹³ "Tell the Israelites: You must observe my Sabbaths, for it is a sign between me and you throughout your generations, so that you will know that I am the Lord who consecrates you. ¹⁴ Observe the Sabbath, for it is holy to you. Whoever profanes it must be put to death. If anyone does work on it, that person must be cut off from his people. ¹⁵ Work

may be done for six days, but on the seventh day there must be a Sabbath of complete rest, holy to the Lord. Anyone who does work on the Sabbath day must be put to death. ¹⁶ The Israelites must observe the Sabbath, celebrating it throughout their generations as a permanent covenant. ¹⁷ It is a sign forever between me and the Israelites, for in six days the Lord made the heavens and the earth, but on the seventh day he rested and was refreshed."

The Two Stone Tablets

¹⁸ When he finished speaking with Moses on Mount Sinai, he gave him the two tablets of the testimony, stone tablets inscribed by the finger of God.

The Gold Calf

32 When the people saw that Moses delayed in coming down from the mountain, they gathered around Aaron and said to him, "Come, make godsᴰ for us who will go before us because this Moses, the man who brought us up from the land of Egypt — we don't know what has happened to him!"

² Aaron replied to them, "Take off the gold rings that are on the ears of your wives, your sons, and your daughters and bring them to me." ³ So all the people took off the gold rings that were on their ears and brought them to Aaron. ⁴ He took the gold from them, fashioned it with an engraving tool, and made it into an image of a calf.

Then they said, "Israel, these are your gods,ᴱ who brought you up from the land of Egypt!" ⁵ When Aaron saw this, he built an altar in front of it and made an announcement: "There will be a festival to the Lord tomorrow." ⁶ Early the next morning they arose, offered burnt offerings, and presented fellowship offerings. The people sat down to eat and drink, and got up to party.

⁷ The Lord spoke to Moses: "Go down at once! For your people you brought up from the land of Egypt have acted corruptly. ⁸ They

---

ᴬ31:6 LXX, Syr read *Eliab* ᴮ31:6 Lit *everyone wise of heart* ᶜ31:10 Hb obscure ᴰ32:1 Or *make a god*, also in v. 23 ᴱ32:4 Or *"Israel, this is your god* or *"Israel, this is your God*, also in v. 8

31:1–11 The Israelites would construct the tabernacle and its furnishings by using a wide variety of skills that the Lord had supplied to the builders. Like other matters in Exodus, these abilities to make beautiful objects involved the person's "heart." **Every skilled artisan** is more literally "everyone wise of heart." The Lord provided what people needed to make things that would be valuable to him and to other people. A fuller description appears in Ex 35:4–36:7. **31:12–13** Here again action leads to knowledge, but this time it is what the Israelites must do—**observe my Sabbaths**—that will lead to knowing the identity of the Lord and of themselves. The term translated **consecrates you** can also be translated "sets you apart" or "sanctifies you." The Israelites were

to have a unique identity, distinct from other nations and closely associated with the Lord. **31:14–15 Whoever profanes** the Sabbath by working in is in willful rebellion against the Lord. **31:16–17** To **observe the Sabbath** would be **a sign forever** of the covenant between the Lord and the Israelites, reminding them of the Lord's provision as the one who had **made the heavens and the earth** and as the one who had made Israel a new nation (16:24–30; 20:8–11). **32:1 When the people saw that Moses delayed in coming down** presents the situation from the viewpoint of the people. Their way of speaking about **this Moses, the man who brought us up from . . . Egypt**, gives insight into their ungrateful attitude. What

they said was insulting to Moses and also to the Lord, since it ignored his involvement. It matched their earlier complaints (14:11–12; 16:2–3,6–8; 17:3). The assumption seems to be that Moses (not to mention Joshua) had abandoned them. **32:2–6** To worship a calf fit well with both Egyptian and Canaanite practices, in which the calf was a symbol of strength and fertility. **32:6** Mixing genuine worship with pagan elements degenerates into depravity. The Hebrew word translated **party** can mean joking (Gn 19:14), mocking (Gn 21:9), or amorous amusement (Gn 26:28). **32:7–8** The word translated **acted corruptly** indicates total ruin, as in 8:24 (cp. Gn 6:12–13; 19:13; Jr 12:10; 13:7). The word

have quickly turned from the way I commanded them; they have made for themselves an image of a calf. They have bowed down to it, sacrificed to it, and said, 'Israel, these are your gods, who brought you up from the land of Egypt.'" ⁹ The LORD also said to Moses, "I have seen this people, and they are indeed a stiff-necked people. ¹⁰ Now leave me alone, so that my anger can burn against them and I can destroy them. Then I will make you into a great nation."

¹¹ But Moses sought the favor of the LORD his God: "LORD, why does your anger burn against your people you brought out of the land of Egypt with great power and a strong hand? ¹² Why should the Egyptians say, 'He brought them out with an evil intent to kill them in the mountains and eliminate them from the face of the earth'? Turn from your fierce anger and relent concerning this disaster planned for your people. ¹³ Remember your servants Abraham, Isaac, and Israel — you swore to them by yourself and declared, 'I will make your offspring as numerous as the stars of the sky and will give your offspring all this land that I have promised, and they will inherit it forever.'" ¹⁴ So the LORD relented concerning the disaster he had said he would bring on his people.

¹⁵ Then Moses turned and went down the mountain with the two tablets of the testimony in his hands. They were inscribed on both sides — inscribed front and back. ¹⁶ The tablets were the work of God, and the writing was God's writing, engraved on the tablets.

¹⁷ When Joshua heard the sound of the people as they shouted, he said to Moses, "There is a sound of war in the camp."

¹⁸ But Moses replied,

It's not the sound of a victory cry
and not the sound of a cry of defeat;
I hear the sound of singing!

¹⁹ As he approached the camp and saw the calf and the dancing, Moses became enraged and threw the tablets out of his hands, smashing them at the base of the mountain. ²⁰ He took the calf they had made, burned it up, and ground it to powder. He scattered the powder over the surface of the water and forced the Israelites to drink the water.

²¹ Then Moses asked Aaron, "What did these people do to you that you have led them into such a grave sin?"

²² "Don't be enraged, my lord," Aaron replied. "You yourself know that the people are intent on evil. ²³ They said to me, 'Make gods for us who will go before us because this Moses, the man who brought us up from the land of Egypt — we don't know what has happened to him!' ²⁴ So I said to them, 'Whoever has gold, take it off,' and they gave it to me. When I threw it into the fire, out came this calf!"

²⁵ Moses saw that the people were out of control, for Aaron had let them get out of control, making them a laughingstock to their enemies.ᴬ ²⁶ And Moses stood at the camp's entrance and said, "Whoever is for the LORD, come to me." And all the Levites gathered around him. ²⁷ He told them, "This is what the LORD, the God of Israel, says, 'Every man fasten his sword to his side; go back and forth through the camp from entrance to entrance, and each of you kill his brother, his friend, and his neighbor.'" ²⁸ The Levites did as Moses commanded, and about three thousand men fell dead that day among the people. ²⁹ Afterward Moses said, "Today you have been dedicatedᴮ to the LORD, since each man went against his son and his brother. Therefore you have brought a blessing on yourselves today."

³⁰ The following day Moses said to the people, "You have committed a grave sin. Now I will go up to the LORD; perhaps I will be able to atone for your sin."

³¹ So Moses returned to the LORD and said, "Oh, these people have committed a grave sin; they have made a god of gold for themselves. ³² Now if you would only forgive their sin. But

---

ᴬ32:25 Hb obscure　ᴮ32:29 Text emended; MT reads *Today dedicate yourselves*; LXX, Vg read *Today you have dedicated yourselves*

---

corrupt describes something irrevocably spoiled in such a way that it is no longer of any use.
32:9–14 That the Lord told Moses about the situation and did not immediately destroy the Israelites left the door open for Moses to pray for them and for the Lord to relent (unlike Jr 15:1). Moses uses the Lord's own words to persuade him to have mercy on his people. This displayed the depth of the victory that the Lord had won in Moses's heart.
32:11–12 The same terms describe the anger of both the Lord and Moses (vv. 10–11,19,22). Moses agreed with the Lord's assessment that the Israelites were stubbornly rebellious ("stiff-necked," v. 9; 33:3,5; 34:9) and called what they had done "grave sin" (v. 31).
32:15–16 This lengthy description of the **two tablets** reinforces their importance and

underscores the statement Moses made by smashing them.
32:17–18 No one had told **Joshua** what was happening in the Israelite **camp**. His concerned but erroneous explanation conveyed how bad things had gotten.
32:19 Moses's breaking of the tablets was an important symbolic act. Violation of a covenant is routinely described in the ancient Semitic world as "breaking" of the covenant.
32:20 Drinking **water** containing the ground-up golden **calf** meant that whatever was left of the calf would become nothing but human waste.
32:21–22 This attempt to deflect blame shows that Aaron knew that making the calf was wrong.
32:23–24 Aaron's account minimizes his participation by leaving out much of what

he did (see v. 4) and by describing the calf as a surprise.
32:25–29 The Levites must have killed known leaders of the rebellion but not all of the participants, since later events show that not all guilty parties died at this point. The **Levites** who were **for the LORD** were of the tribe of Aaron, the leader of the rebellion, and of Moses, the one who was putting an end to it.
32:30–33 By requesting to die if the people died, Moses identified himself with them and refused to be the start of a "great nation" to replace them (v. 10). Moses expressed willingness to be removed from **the book** God has **written**. This image of God's record of those who are his is found in both the OT and the NT.

if not, please erase me from the book you have written." ³³ The LORD replied to Moses, "Whoever has sinned against me I will erase from my book. ³⁴ Now go, lead the people to the place I told you about; see, my angel will go before you. But on the day I settle accounts, I will hold them accountable for their sin." ³⁵ And the LORD inflicted a plague on the people for what they did with the calf Aaron had made.

The Tent Outside the Camp

33 The LORD spoke to Moses: "Go up from here, you and the people you brought up from the land of Egypt, to the land I promised to Abraham, Isaac, and Jacob, saying: I will give it to your offspring. ² I will send an angel ahead of you and will drive out the Canaanites, Amorites, Hethites, Perizzites,^A Hivites, and Jebusites. ³ Go up to a land flowing with milk and honey. But I will not go up with you because you are a stiff-necked people; otherwise, I might destroy you on the way." ⁴ When the people heard this bad news, they mourned and didn't put on their jewelry. ⁵ For the LORD said to Moses, "Tell the Israelites: You are a stiff-necked people. If I went up with you for a single moment, I would destroy you. Now take off your jewelry, and I will decide what to do with you." ⁶ So the Israelites remained stripped of their jewelry from Mount Horeb onward.

⁷ Now Moses took a tent and pitched it outside the camp, at a distance from the camp; he called it the tent of meeting. Anyone who wanted to consult the LORD would go to the tent of meeting that was outside the camp. ⁸ Whenever Moses went out to the tent, all the people would stand up, each one at the door of his tent, and they would watch Moses until he entered the tent. ⁹ When Moses entered the tent, the pillar of cloud would come down and remain at the entrance to the tent, and the LORD would speak with Moses. ¹⁰ As all the people saw the pillar of cloud remaining at the entrance to the tent, they would stand up, then bow in worship, each one at the door of his tent. ¹¹ The LORD would speak with Moses face to face, just as a man speaks with his friend, then Moses would return to the camp. His assistant, the young man Joshua son of Nun, would not leave the inside of the tent.

The LORD's Glory

¹² Moses said to the LORD, "Look, you have told me, 'Lead this people up,' but you have not let me know whom you will send with me. You said, 'I know you by name, and you have also found favor with me.' ¹³ Now if I have indeed found favor with you, please teach me your ways, and I will know you, so that I may find favor with you. Now consider that this nation is your people."

¹⁴ And he replied, "My presence will go with you, and I will give you rest."

¹⁵ "If your presence does not go," Moses responded to him, "don't make us go up from here. ¹⁶ How will it be known that I and your people have found favor with you unless you go with us? I and your people will be distinguished by this from all the other people on the face of the earth."

¹⁷ The LORD answered Moses, "I will do this very thing you have asked, for you have found favor with me, and I know you by name."

¹⁸ Then Moses said, "Please, let me see your glory."

¹⁹ He said, "I will cause all my goodness to pass in front of you, and I will proclaim the name 'the LORD' before you. I will be gracious to whom I will be gracious, and I will have compassion on whom I will have compassion." ²⁰ But he added, "You cannot see my face, for humans cannot see me and live." ²¹ The LORD said, "Here is a place near me. You are to stand on the rock, ²² and when my glory passes by, I

---

^A33:2 Sam, LXX add *Girgashites*

32:35 The **plague** was only a taste of God's wrath.
33:1–5 The Lord said that he would not go among the Israelites. This amounted to saying that there would be no use for the tabernacle to be built, since it was intended as the dwelling of the Lord among his people (29:45–46). Earlier the Israelites had questioned whether the Lord was among them (17:7), and now he assured them that he would not be.
33:6 The verb translated **stripped** recalls 3:22 and 12:36, which use a form of the same Hebrew verb to speak of the Egyptians being "plundered" when they gave gold and silver items to the Israelites. The disobedience of the Israelites made them like the Egyptians in worship and now in the loss of their ornaments.
33:7–11 The tent **outside the camp** contrasts with the splendid tabernacle that had

been intended for the middle of the camp. At the same time, the tent's location kept open the possibility of further consideration on all sides without immediate danger to the Israelites. The description of the close access that Moses enjoyed provides a background for his further requests. Moses, more than anyone else, knew what the Israelites were in danger of losing.
33:14 The phrase **I will give you rest** may be short for "rest from your enemies." It probably refers to security for the Israelites in their new land (Dt 3:20; 12:9–10; 25:19; Jos 1:13,15; 21:44; 22:4; 23:1; 2Sm 7:1,11). This continues the presentation of the Lord as the one who gave his people rest, both from danger and from labor (Ex 16:21–30; 20:8–11; 23:10–12), by his presence and provision (Mt 11:28–29; 28:20; Heb 13:5).
33:17 The agreement—**I will do this very thing you have asked**—was a display of the

Lord's **favor**, or grace, already extended to Moses, who was interceding for the Israelites on that basis rather than on the basis of their merits (vv. 12–13,16; cp. Dt 7:7; 9:4–6).
33:18–19 The Lord's words about grace and compassion would have been encouraging in view of his earlier words, "On the day I settle accounts, I will hold them accountable for their sin" (32:34).
33:20–23 Scripture often speaks of the potential danger of an encounter with God (3:6; 24:9–11; Gn 28:12–17; 32:30; Nm 17:12–13; Jdg 6:22–24; 13:22; Pss 76:7; 103:3; Is 2:10; 6:1–7; cp. Jn 1:18; 14:8–9; 1Tm 6:16). The description of the Lord's provision for Moses presents Moses as so small and the Lord as so great that protecting Moses would be like the action of a man who could cover a little opening with his hand while walking past it. Of the Hebrew words for **hand**, the one used here

will put you in the crevice of the rock and cover you with my hand until I have passed by. ²³ Then I will take my hand away, and you will see my back, but my face will not be seen."

New Stone Tablets

34 The LORD said to Moses, "Cut two stone tablets like the first ones, and I will write on them the words that were on the first tablets, which you broke. ² Be prepared by morning. Come up Mount Sinai in the morning and stand before me on the mountaintop. ³ No one may go up with you; in fact, no one should be seen anywhere on the mountain. Even the flocks and herds are not to graze in front of that mountain."

⁴ Moses cut two stone tablets like the first ones. He got up early in the morning, and taking the two stone tablets in his hand, he climbed Mount Sinai, just as the LORD had commanded him.

⁵ The LORD came down in a cloud, stood with him there, and proclaimed his name, "the LORD." ⁶ The LORD passed in front of him and proclaimed:

The LORD — the LORD is a compassionate and gracious God, slow to anger and abounding in faithful love and truth, ⁷ maintaining faithful love to a thousand generations, forgiving iniquity, rebellion, and sin. But he will not leave the guilty unpunished, bringing the consequences of the fathers' iniquity on the children and grandchildren to the third and fourth generation.

⁸ Moses immediately knelt low on the ground and worshiped. ⁹ Then he said, "My Lord, if I have indeed found favor with you, my Lord, please go with us (even though this is a stiff-necked people), forgive our iniquity and our sin, and accept us as your own possession."

Covenant Obligations

¹⁰ And the LORD responded, "Look, I am making a covenant. In the presence of all your people I will perform wonders that have never been doneᴬ in the whole earth or in any nation. All the people you live among will see the LORD's work, for what I am doing with you is awe-inspiring. ¹¹ Observe what I command you today. I am going to drive out before you the Amorites, Canaanites, Hethites, Perizzites, Hivites,ᴮ and Jebusites. ¹² Be careful not to make a treaty with the inhabitants of the land that you are going to enter; otherwise, they will become a snare among you. ¹³ Instead, you must tear down their altars, smash their sacred pillars, and chop down their Asherah poles. ¹⁴ Because the LORD is jealous for his reputation, you are never to bow down to another god.ᶜ He is a jealous God.

¹⁵ "Do not make a treaty with the inhabitants of the land, or else when they prostitute themselves with their gods and sacrifice to their gods, they will invite you, and you will eat their sacrifices. ¹⁶ Then you will take some of their daughters as brides for your sons. Their daughters will prostitute themselves with their gods and cause your sons to prostitute themselves with their gods.

¹⁷ "Do not make cast images of gods for yourselves.

¹⁸ "Observe the Festival of Unleavened Bread. You are to eat unleavened bread for seven days at the appointed time in the month of Abib,ᴰ as I commanded you, for you came out of Egypt in the month of Abib.

¹⁹ "The firstborn male from every womb belongs to me, including all your maleᴱ,ᶠ livestock, the firstborn of cattle or sheep. ²⁰ You may redeem the firstborn of a donkey with a sheep, but if you do not redeem it, break its neck. You must redeem all the firstborn of your sons. No one is to appear before me empty-handed.

²¹ "You are to labor six days but you must rest on the seventh day; you must even rest during plowing and harvesting times.

²² "Observe the Festival of Weeks with the firstfruits of the wheat harvest, and the Festival of Ingatheringᴳ at the turn of the agricultural year. ²³ Three times a year all your males

ᴬ**34:10** Lit *created* ᴮ**34:11** DSS, Sam, LXX add *Girgashites* ᶜ**34:14** Or *the LORD — his name is Jealous* or *the LORD, being jealous by nature* ᴰ**34:18** March–April; called Nisan in the post-exilic period; Neh 2:1; Est 3:7 ᴱ**34:19** LXX, Theod, Vg, Tg read *males* ᶠ**34:19** Hb obscure ᴳ**34:22** The *Festival of Ingathering* is called Festival of Shelters elsewhere; Lv 23:34–36.

refers to the palm of the hand (Ex 3:20; 5:21). The contrast between seeing God's **face** and his **back** is figurative for full and partial revelation.
34:1–4 Writing new tablets signified that God had forgiven Israel and had reinstated his covenant with them.
34:5–7 Rather than providing a new visual description (in contrast with chaps. 3; 13–14; 19–20; 24), the account of the Lord's display of his glory this time offers his list of a series of invisible qualities. The Lord has the capacity to be **compassionate and gracious**, to be **slow to anger**, and to forgive, in addition to exacting punishment (cp. Nm 14:18; Neh

9:17; Pss 86:15; 103:6–14; 145:8; Jl 2:13–14; Jnh 4:2; Nah 1:3).
34:8–9 Nowhere in Moses's prayers for the Israelites did he point to their repentance or promise any improvement; their future would depend on the Lord's ongoing *favor*, forgiveness, and faithfulness.
34:10–13 As v. 10 makes clear, **I am making a covenant** does not mean this is a new covenant. God is reinstating the original covenant. The verses essentially are a summary of Ex 23:20–33.
34:14 The phrase translated **the LORD is jealous** is (lit) "The LORD jealous his name." It reflects the close connection between traits

of character and the concept of name or reputation. It can also be rendered, "The LORD's name is Jealous" or "The LORD is jealous for his name." It is a forceful assertion that the Lord zealously protects the integrity of his relationships (cp. 20:5; Dt 4:24; 5:9; 6:15; Jos 24:19; Nah 1:2).
34:15–17 The derogatory way of referring to pagan worship and to the Israelites' possible participation in it shows that it was wrong for both (Nm 25:1–13).
34:18–28 These verses reemphasize the laws previously given (23:14–19) with a sampling of instructions.

are to appear before the Lord God, the God of Israel. ²⁴ For I will drive out nations before you and enlarge your territory. No one will covet your land when you go up three times a year to appear before the Lord your God.

²⁵ "Do not present^ the blood for my sacrifice with anything leavened. The sacrifice of the Passover Festival must not remain until morning.

²⁶ "Bring the best firstfruits of your land to the house of the Lord your God.

"You must not boil a young goat in its mother's milk."

²⁷ The Lord also said to Moses, "Write down these words, for I have made a covenant with you and with Israel based on these words."

²⁸ Moses was there with the Lord forty days and forty nights; he did not eat food or drink water. He wrote the Ten Commandments, the words of the covenant, on the tablets.

Moses's Radiant Face

²⁹ As Moses descended from Mount Sinai — with the two tablets of the testimony in his hands as he descended the mountain — he did not realize that the skin of his face shone as a result of his speaking with the Lord.^B ³⁰ When Aaron and all the Israelites saw Moses, the skin of his face shone! They were afraid to come near him. ³¹ But Moses called out to them, so Aaron and all the leaders of the community returned to him, and Moses spoke to them. ³² Afterward all the Israelites came near, and he commanded them to do everything the Lord had told him on Mount Sinai. ³³ When Moses had finished speaking with them, he put a veil over his face. ³⁴ But whenever Moses went before the Lord to speak with him, he would remove the veil until he came out. After he came out, he would tell the Israelites what he had been commanded, ³⁵ and the Israelites would see that Moses's face^C was radiant. Then Moses would put the veil over his face again until he went to speak with the Lord.

The Sabbath Command

35 Moses assembled the entire Israelite community and said to them, "These are the things that the Lord has commanded you to do: ² For six days work is to be done, but on the seventh day you are to have a holy day, a Sabbath of complete rest to the Lord. Anyone who does work on it must be executed.

³ Do not light a fire in any of your homes on the Sabbath day."

Building the Tabernacle

⁴ Then Moses said to the entire Israelite community, "This is what the Lord has commanded: ⁵ Take up an offering among you for the Lord. Let everyone whose heart is willing bring this as the Lord's offering: gold, silver, and bronze; ⁶ blue, purple, and scarlet yarn; fine linen and goat hair; ⁷ ram skins dyed red and fine leather;^D acacia wood; ⁸ oil for the light; spices for the anointing oil and for the fragrant incense; ⁹ and onyx with gemstones to mount on the ephod and breastpiece.

¹⁰ "Let all the skilled artisans^E among you come and make everything that the Lord has commanded: ¹¹ the tabernacle — its tent and covering, its clasps and supports, its crossbars, its pillars and bases; ¹² the ark with its poles, the mercy seat, and the curtain for the screen; ¹³ the table with its poles, all its utensils, and the Bread of the Presence; ¹⁴ the lampstand for light with its utensils and lamps as well as the oil for the light; ¹⁵ the altar of incense with its poles; the anointing oil and the fragrant incense; the entryway screen for the entrance to the tabernacle; ¹⁶ the altar of burnt offering with its bronze grate, its poles, and all its utensils; the basin with its stand; ¹⁷ the hangings of the courtyard, its posts and bases, and the screen for the gate of the courtyard; ¹⁸ the tent pegs for the tabernacle and the tent pegs for the courtyard, along with their ropes; ¹⁹ and the specially woven^D garments for ministering in the sanctuary — the holy garments for the priest Aaron and the garments for his sons to serve as priests."

²⁰ Then the entire Israelite community left Moses's presence. ²¹ Everyone whose heart was moved and whose spirit prompted him came and brought an offering to the Lord for the work on the tent of meeting, for all its services, and for the holy garments. ²² Both men and women came; all who had willing hearts brought brooches, earrings, rings, necklaces, and all kinds of gold jewelry — everyone who presented a presentation offering of gold to the Lord. ²³ Everyone who possessed blue, purple, or scarlet yarn, fine linen or goat hair, ram skins dyed red or fine leather,^D brought them. ²⁴ Everyone making an offering of silver or bronze brought it as a contribution to the

^A 34:25 Lit slaughter ^B 34:29 Lit with him ^C 34:35 Lit see Moses's face, that the skin of his face ^D 35:7,19,23 Hb obscure ^E 35:10 Lit the wise of heart

34:28 This is the second time Moses spent **forty days** and nights on the mountain. It would only have taken a day or so to write what God spoke. His prolonged fast was an earnest (and successful) appeal for God's grace in the face of Israel's rebellion. **He wrote** probably refers to God (v. 1).

34:29–35 The shining (**Moses's face was radiant**) and the veil demonstrate the success of Moses's intercession; the Lord had agreed to go with the Israelites in such a gracious way that they could safely see his glory among them, despite their stiff-necked frailty (cp. 2Co 3:13–14).

35:4–36:7 This section describes the preparation of materials and workers needed to build the tabernacle. The people who brought the prized and costly materials contributed them willingly (35:5,21–22,29; 36:2–3,5). They also worked willingly (35:26; 36:2), using God-given skills in design, execution, and teaching (35:30–36:2).

LORD. Everyone who possessed acacia wood useful for any task in the work brought it. [25] Every skilled^A woman spun yarn with her hands and brought it: blue, purple, and scarlet yarn, and fine linen. [26] And all the women whose hearts were moved spun the goat hair by virtue of their skill. [27] The leaders brought onyx and gemstones to mount on the ephod and breastpiece, [28] as well as the spice and oil for the light, for the anointing oil, and for the fragrant incense. [29] So the Israelites brought a freewill offering to the LORD, all the men and women whose hearts prompted them to bring something for all the work that the LORD, through Moses, had commanded to be done.

Bezalel and Oholiab

[30] Moses then said to the Israelites, "Look, the LORD has appointed by name Bezalel son of Uri, son of Hur, of the tribe of Judah. [31] He has filled him with God's Spirit, with wisdom, understanding, and ability in every kind of craft [32] to design artistic works in gold, silver, and bronze, [33] to cut gemstones for mounting, and to carve wood for work in every kind of artistic craft. [34] He has also given^B both him and Oholiab son of Ahisamach, of the tribe of Dan, the ability to teach others. [35] He has filled them with skill^C to do all the work of a gem cutter; a designer; an embroiderer^D in blue, purple, and scarlet yarn and fine linen; and a weaver. They can do every kind of craft and design artistic

36 designs. [1] Bezalel, Oholiab, and all the skilled^E people are to work based on everything the LORD has commanded. The LORD has given them wisdom and understanding to know how to do all the work of constructing the sanctuary."

[2] So Moses summoned Bezalel, Oholiab, and every skilled person in whose heart the LORD had placed wisdom, all whose hearts moved them, to come to the work and do it. [3] They took from Moses's presence all the contributions that the Israelites had brought for the task of making the sanctuary. Meanwhile, the people continued to bring freewill offerings morning after morning. [4] Then all the artisans who were doing all the work for the sanctuary came one by one from the work they were doing [5] and said to Moses, "The people are bringing more than is needed

for the construction of the work the LORD commanded to be done."

[6] After Moses gave an order, they sent a proclamation throughout the camp: "Let no man or woman make anything else as an offering for the sanctuary." So the people stopped. [7] The materials were sufficient for them to do all the work. There was more than enough.

Building the Tabernacle

[8] All the skilled artisans^F among those doing the work made the tabernacle with ten curtains. Bezalel made them of finely spun linen, as well as blue, purple, and scarlet yarn, with a design of cherubim worked into them. [9] Each curtain was forty-two feet^G long and six feet^H wide; all the curtains had the same measurements. [10] He joined five of the curtains to each other, and the other five curtains he joined to each other. [11] He made loops of blue yarn on the edge of the last curtain in the first set and did the same on the edge of the outermost curtain in the second set. [12] He made fifty loops on the one curtain and fifty loops on the edge of the curtain in the second set, so that the loops lined up with each other. [13] He also made fifty gold clasps and joined the curtains to each other, so that the tabernacle became a single unit. [14] He made curtains of goat hair for a tent over the tabernacle; he made eleven of them. [15] Each curtain was forty-five feet^I long and six feet wide. All eleven curtains had the same measurements. [16] He joined five of the curtains together, and the other six together. [17] He made fifty loops on the edge of the outermost curtain in the first set and fifty loops on the edge of the corresponding curtain in the second set. [18] He made fifty bronze clasps to join the tent together as a single unit. [19] He also made a covering for the tent from ram skins dyed red and a covering of fine leather^J on top of it.

[20] He made upright supports^K of acacia wood for the tabernacle. [21] Each support was fifteen feet^L long and twenty-seven inches^M wide. [22] Each support had two tenons for joining one to another. He did the same for all the supports of the tabernacle. [23] He made supports for the tabernacle as follows: He made twenty for the south side, [24] and he made forty silver bases to put under the twenty supports, two bases under the first support for its two tenons, and two bases under each of the following supports

---

^A35:25 Lit *wise of heart*   ^B35:34 Lit *also put in his heart*   ^C35:35 Lit *with wisdom of heart*   ^D35:35 Or *weaver*   ^E36:1 Lit *wise of heart, also in v. 2*   ^F36:8 Lit *the wise of heart*   ^G36:9 Lit *28 cubits*   ^H36:9 Lit *four cubits, also in v. 15*   ^I36:15 Lit *30 cubits*   ^J36:19 Hb obscure   ^K36:20 Or *made frames*   ^L36:21 Lit *10 cubits*   ^M36:21 Lit *a cubit and a half*

35:31 Because the Lord had called Bezalel and **filled him with God's Spirit**, he would be able to do with excellence what the Lord had commanded (Nm 11:17; Dt 34:9; Jdg 3:10; 6:14–16,34).
35:34–36:1 The **ability to teach others** attributed to Bezalel and Oholiab is described as both a matter of the "heart" and a work

of God in them. The idiomatic Hebrew expression says, "And he has put in his heart to teach," referring first to Bezalel, who is mentioned before Oholiab. Moses added that the Lord had **filled them with skill**. He further described Bezalel, Oholiab, and the other workers—all those who were "wise/skillful of heart"—as people "in whom the Lord has put

wisdom/skill and understanding." This is why they would **know how to do all the work of constructing the sanctuary**.
36:1–2 The **heart**, or inner core, of a person was spoken of as central to both willingness and skillfulness to do **work** in service to the Lord, even as it was spoken of as central to Pharaoh's rebellion.

for their two tenons. ²⁵ For the second side of the tabernacle, the north side, he made twenty supports, ²⁶ with their forty silver bases, two bases under the first support and two bases under each of the following ones. ²⁷ And for the back of the tabernacle, on the west side, he made six supports. ²⁸ He also made two additional supports for the two back corners of the tabernacle. ²⁹ They were paired at the bottom and joined together^A at the^B top in a single ring. This is what he did with both of them for the two corners. ³⁰ So there were eight supports with their sixteen silver bases, two bases under each one.

³¹ He made five crossbars of acacia wood for the supports on one side of the tabernacle, ³² five crossbars for the supports on the other side of the tabernacle, and five crossbars for those at the back of the tabernacle on the west. ³³ He made the central crossbar run through the middle of the supports from one end to the other. ³⁴ He overlaid them with gold and made their rings out of gold as holders for the crossbars. He also overlaid the crossbars with gold.

³⁵ Then he made the curtain with blue, purple, and scarlet yarn, and finely spun linen. He made it with a design of cherubim worked into it. ³⁶ He made four pillars of acacia wood for it and overlaid them with gold; their hooks were of gold. And he cast four silver bases for the pillars.

³⁷ He made a screen embroidered^C with blue, purple, and scarlet yarn, and finely spun linen for the entrance to the tent, ³⁸ together with its five pillars and their hooks. He overlaid the tops of the pillars and their bands with gold, but their five bases were bronze.

Making the Ark

37 Bezalel made the ark of acacia wood, forty-five inches long, twenty-seven inches wide, and twenty-seven inches high.^D ² He overlaid it with pure gold inside and out and made a gold molding all around it. ³ He cast four gold rings for it, for its four feet, two rings on one side and two rings on the other side. ⁴ He made poles of acacia wood and overlaid them with gold. ⁵ He inserted the poles into the rings on the sides of the ark for carrying the ark.

⁶ He made a mercy seat of pure gold, forty-five inches long and twenty-seven inches wide.^E ⁷ He made two cherubim of gold; he made them of hammered work at the two ends of the mercy seat, ⁸ one cherub at one end and one cherub at the other end. At each end, he made a cherub of one piece with the mercy seat. ⁹ They had wings spread out. They faced

each other and covered the mercy seat with their wings. The faces of the cherubim were looking toward the mercy seat.

Making the Table

¹⁰ He constructed the table of acacia wood, thirty-six inches long, eighteen inches wide, and twenty-seven inches high.^F ¹¹ He overlaid it with pure gold and made a gold molding all around it. ¹² He made a three-inch^G frame all around it and made a gold molding all around its frame. ¹³ He cast four gold rings for it and attached the rings to the four corners at its four legs. ¹⁴ The rings were next to the frame as holders for the poles to carry the table. ¹⁵ He made the poles for carrying the table from acacia wood and overlaid them with gold. ¹⁶ He also made the utensils that would be on the table out of pure gold: its plates and cups, as well as its bowls and pitchers for pouring drink offerings.

Making the Lampstand

¹⁷ Then he made the lampstand out of pure hammered gold. He made it all of one piece: its base and shaft, its ornamental cups, and its buds and petals. ¹⁸ Six branches extended from its sides, three branches of the lampstand from one side and three branches of the lampstand from the other side. ¹⁹ There were three cups shaped like almond blossoms, each with a bud and petals, on one branch, and three cups shaped like almond blossoms, each with a bud and petals, on the next branch. It was this way for the six branches that extended from the lampstand. ²⁰ There were four cups shaped like almond blossoms on the lampstand shaft along with its buds and petals. ²¹ For the six branches that extended from it, a bud was under the first pair of branches from it, a bud under the second pair of branches from it, and a bud under the third pair of branches from it. ²² Their buds and branches were of one piece with it. All of it was a single hammered piece of pure gold. ²³ He also made its seven lamps, snuffers, and firepans of pure gold. ²⁴ He made it and all its utensils of seventy-five pounds^H of pure gold.

Making the Altar of Incense

²⁵ He made the altar of incense out of acacia wood. It was square, eighteen inches long and eighteen inches wide; it was thirty-six inches high.^I Its horns were of one piece with it. ²⁶ He overlaid it, its top, all around its sides, and its horns with pure gold. Then he made a gold molding all around it. ²⁷ He made two gold rings for it under the molding on two of

---

^A 36:29 Lit and together they are to be complete ^B 36:29 Lit its ^C 36:37 Or woven ^D 37:1 Lit two and a half cubits its length, one and a half cubits its width, and one and a half cubits its height ^E 37:6 Lit two and a half cubits its length and one and a half cubits its width ^F 37:10 Lit two cubits its length, one cubit its width, and one and a half cubits its height ^G 37:12 Lit a handbreadth ^H 37:24 Lit a talent ^I 37:25 Lit a cubit its length, a cubit its width, and two cubits its height

its sides; he put these on opposite sides of it to be holders for the poles to carry it with. **28** He made the poles of acacia wood and overlaid them with gold.

29 He also made the holy anointing oil and the pure, fragrant, and expertly blended incense.

Making the Altar of Burnt Offering

38 Bezalel constructed the altar of burnt offering from acacia wood. It was square, 7½ feet long and 7½ feet wide,^A^ and was 4½ feet^B^ high. **2** He made horns for it on its four corners; the horns were of one piece with it. Then he overlaid it with bronze. **3** He made all the altar's utensils: the pots, shovels, basins, meat forks, and firepans; he made all its utensils of bronze. **4** He constructed for the altar a grate of bronze mesh under its ledge,^C^ halfway up from the bottom. **5** He cast four rings at the four corners of the bronze grate as holders for the poles. **6** He made the poles of acacia wood and overlaid them with bronze. **7** Then he inserted the poles into the rings on the sides of the altar in order to carry it with them. He constructed the altar with boards so that it was hollow.

Making the Bronze Basin

8 He made the bronze basin and its stand from the bronze mirrors of the women who served at the entrance to the tent of meeting.

Making the Courtyard

9 Then he made the courtyard. The hangings on the south side of the courtyard were of finely spun linen, 150 feet^D^ long, **10** including their twenty posts and their twenty bronze bases, with silver hooks and silver bands^E^ for the posts. **11** The hangings on the north side were also 150 feet long, including their twenty posts and twenty bronze bases. The hooks and bands of the posts were silver. **12** The hangings on the west side were 75 feet^F^ long, including their ten posts and their ten bases, with silver hooks and silver bands for the posts. **13** And for the east side toward the sunrise, 75 feet long, **14** the hangings on one side of the gate were 22½ feet,^G^ including their three posts and their three bases. **15** It was the same for the other side of the courtyard gate. The hangings were 22½ feet,

including their three posts and their three bases. **16** All the hangings around the courtyard were of finely spun linen. **17** The bases for the posts were bronze; the hooks and bands of the posts were silver; and the plating for the tops of the posts was silver. All the posts of the courtyard were banded with silver.

18 The screen for the gate of the courtyard was made of finely spun linen, expertly embroidered^H^ with blue, purple, and scarlet yarn. It was 30 feet^I^ long, and like the hangings of the courtyard, 7½ feet^J^ high.^K^ **19** It had four posts with their four bronze bases. Their hooks were silver, and their top plating and their bands were silver. **20** All the tent pegs for the tabernacle and for the surrounding courtyard were bronze.

Inventory of Materials

21 This is the inventory for the tabernacle, the tabernacle of the testimony, that was recorded at Moses's command. It was the work of the Levites under the direction of^L^ Ithamar son of Aaron the priest. **22** Bezalel son of Uri, son of Hur, of the tribe of Judah, made everything that the LORD commanded Moses. **23** With him was Oholiab son of Ahisamach, of the tribe of Dan, a gem cutter, a designer, and an embroiderer with blue, purple, and scarlet yarn, and fine linen.

24 All the gold of the presentation offering that was used for the project in all the work on the sanctuary, was 2,193 pounds,^M^ according to the sanctuary shekel. **25** The silver from those of the community who were registered was 7,544 pounds,^N^ according to the sanctuary shekel — **26** one-fifth of an ounce^O^ per man, that is, half a shekel according to the sanctuary shekel, from everyone twenty years old or more who had crossed over to the registered group, 603,550 men. **27** There were 7,500 pounds^P^ of silver used to cast the bases of the sanctuary and the bases of the curtain — one hundred bases from 7,500 pounds, 75 pounds^Q^ for each base. **28** With the remaining 44 pounds^R^ he made the hooks for the posts, overlaid their tops, and supplied bands for them.

29 The bronze of the presentation offering totaled 5,310 pounds.^S^ **30** He made with it the bases for the entrance to the tent of meeting, the bronze altar and its bronze grate, all the utensils

^A^**38:1** Lit *five cubits its length and five cubits its width* ^B^**38:1** Lit *three cubits* ^C^**38:4** Or *rim* ^D^**38:9** Lit *100 cubits*, also in v. 11 ^E^**38:10** Or *connecting rods*, also in vv. 11,17,19,28 ^F^**38:12** Lit *50 cubits*, also in v. 13 ^G^**38:14** Lit *15 cubits*, also in v. 15 ^H^**38:18** Or *woven* ^I^**38:18** Lit *20 cubits* ^J^**38:18** Lit *five cubits* ^K^**38:18** Lit *high in width* ^L^**38:21** Lit *Levites by the hand of* ^M^**38:24** Lit *29 talents and 730 shekels* ^N^**38:25** Lit *100 talents and 1,775 shekels* ^O^**38:26** Lit *a beka* ^P^**38:27** Lit *100 talents* ^Q^**38:27** Lit *one talent* ^R^**38:28** Lit *1,775* (shekels) ^S^**38:29** Lit *70 talents and 2,400 shekels*

38:8 Since the instructions for the tabernacle do not refer to **the women who served at the entrance to the tent of meeting**, little is known about them beyond this mention (cp. 1Sm 2:22–25). The Hebrew verb that describes their service is somewhat rare; a related noun and this verb also describe service by Levites at the tabernacle (Nm 4:23; 8:24). Its connections with military service give it overtones of organization and service in the sense of being "on duty" (cp. 2Kg 25:19). **38:21 The inventory** was appropriate even when supplies were plentiful. It promoted order, showed concern for conservation rather than waste or theft, and let people know what had been accomplished with their offerings. **38:26** Each man moved from one group to another when he had paid his **half a shekel** (30:11–16).

for the altar, [31] the bases for the surrounding courtyard, the bases for the gate of the courtyard, all the tent pegs for the tabernacle, and all the tent pegs for the surrounding courtyard.

Making the Priestly Garments

39 They made specially woven[A] garments for ministry in the sanctuary, and the holy garments for Aaron from the blue, purple, and scarlet yarn, just as the LORD had commanded Moses.

Making the Ephod

[2] Bezalel made the ephod of gold, of blue, purple, and scarlet yarn, and of finely spun linen. [3] They hammered out thin sheets of gold, and he[B] cut threads from them to interweave with the blue, purple, and scarlet yarn, and the fine linen in a skillful design. [4] They made shoulder pieces for attaching it; it was joined together at its two edges. [5] The artistically woven waistband that was on the ephod was of one piece with the ephod, according to the same workmanship of gold, of blue, purple, and scarlet yarn, and of finely spun linen, just as the LORD had commanded Moses.

[6] Then they mounted the onyx stones surrounded with gold filigree settings, engraved with the names of Israel's sons as a gem cutter engraves a seal. [7] He fastened them on the shoulder pieces of the ephod as memorial stones for the Israelites, just as the LORD had commanded Moses.

Making the Breastpiece

[8] He also made the embroidered[C] breastpiece with the same workmanship as the ephod of gold, of blue, purple, and scarlet yarn, and of finely spun linen. [9] They made the breastpiece square and folded double, nine inches long and nine inches wide.[D] [10] They mounted four rows of gemstones[E] on it.

The first row was
a row of carnelian, topaz, and emerald;[F]
[11] the second row,
a turquoise,[G] a lapis lazuli, and a diamond;[H]
[12] the third row,
a jacinth,[A] an agate, and an amethyst;
[13] and the fourth row,
a beryl, an onyx, and a jasper.
They were surrounded with gold filigree in their settings.

[14] The twelve stones corresponded to the names of Israel's sons. Each stone was engraved like a seal with one of the names of the twelve tribes.

[15] They made braided chains of pure gold cord for the breastpiece. [16] They also fashioned two gold filigree settings and two gold rings and attached the two rings to its two corners. [17] Then they attached the two gold cords to the two gold rings on the corners of the breastpiece. [18] They attached the other ends of the two cords to the two filigree settings, and in this way they attached them to the ephod's shoulder pieces in front. [19] They made two other gold rings and put them at the two other corners of the breastpiece on the edge that is next to the inner border of the ephod. [20] They made two more gold rings and attached them to the bottom of the ephod's two shoulder pieces on its front, close to its seam,[I] above the ephod's woven waistband. [21] Then they tied the breastpiece from its rings to the rings of the ephod with a cord of blue yarn, so that the breastpiece was above the ephod's waistband and did not come loose from the ephod. They did just as the LORD had commanded Moses.

Making the Robe

[22] They made the woven robe of the ephod entirely of blue yarn. [23] There was an opening in the center of the robe like that of body armor[A] with a collar around the opening so that it would not tear. [24] They made pomegranates of finely spun blue, purple, and scarlet yarn[J] on the lower hem of the robe. [25] They made bells of pure gold and attached the bells between the pomegranates, all around the hem of the robe between the pomegranates, [26] a bell and a pomegranate alternating all around the lower hem of the robe[K] to be worn for ministry. They made it just as the LORD had commanded Moses.

The Other Priestly Garments

[27] They made the tunics of fine woven linen for Aaron and his sons. [28] They made the turban and the ornate headbands[L] of fine linen, the linen undergarments of finely spun linen, [29] and the sash of finely spun linen expertly embroidered with blue, purple, and scarlet yarn. They did just as the LORD had commanded Moses.

Making the Holy Diadem

[30] They made a medallion, the holy diadem, out of pure gold and wrote on it an inscription like the engraving on a seal: HOLY TO THE LORD. [31] They attached a cord of blue yarn to it

[A]39:1,12,23 Hb obscure   [B]39:3 Sam, Syr, Tg read they   [C]39:8 Or woven   [D]39:9 Lit a span its length and a span its width
[E]39:10 Many of these stones cannot be identified with certainty.   [F]39:10 Or beryl   [G]39:11 Or malachite, or garnet
[H]39:11 Hb uncertain; LXX, Vg read jasper   [I]39:20 The place where the shoulder pieces join the front of the ephod
[J]39:24 Sam, LXX, Vg add and linen   [K]39:26 Lit bell and pomegranate, bell and pomegranate, on the hem of the robe around
[L]39:28 Lit and the headdresses of headbands

39:30–31 As the final item in the record of construction, the inscription of the high priest's headdress serves as a kind of finishing label for everything the artisans had made, all marked as belonging to the Lord.

in order to mount it on the turban, just as the Lord had commanded Moses.

Moses's Inspection of the Tabernacle

³² So all the work for the tabernacle, the tent of meeting, was finished. The Israelites did everything just as the Lord had commanded Moses. ³³ They brought the tabernacle to Moses: the tent with all its furnishings, its clasps, its supports, its crossbars, and its pillars and bases; ³⁴ the covering of ram skins dyed red and the covering of fine leather;^A the curtain for the screen; ³⁵ the ark of the testimony with its poles and the mercy seat; ³⁶ the table, all its utensils, and the Bread of the Presence; ³⁷ the pure gold lampstand, with its lamps arranged and all its utensils, as well as the oil for the light; ³⁸ the gold altar; the anointing oil; the fragrant incense; the screen for the entrance to the tent; ³⁹ the bronze altar with its bronze grate, its poles, and all its utensils; the basin with its stand; ⁴⁰ the hangings of the courtyard, its posts and bases, the screen for the gate of the courtyard, its ropes and tent pegs, and all the furnishings for the service of the tabernacle, the tent of meeting; ⁴¹ and the specially woven^A garments for ministering in the sanctuary, the holy garments for the priest Aaron and the garments for his sons to serve as priests. ⁴² The Israelites had done all the work according to everything the Lord had commanded Moses. ⁴³ Moses inspected all the work they had accomplished. They had done just as the Lord commanded. Then Moses blessed them.

Setting Up the Tabernacle

40 The Lord spoke to Moses: ² "You are to set up the tabernacle, the tent of meeting, on the first day of the first month.^B ³ Put the ark of the testimony there and screen off the ark with the curtain. ⁴ Then bring in the table and lay out its arrangement; also bring in the lampstand and set up its lamps. ⁵ Place the gold altar for incense in front of the ark of the testimony. Put up the screen for the entrance to the tabernacle. ⁶ Position the altar of burnt offering in front of the entrance to the tabernacle, the tent of meeting. ⁷ Place the basin between the tent of meeting and the altar, and put water in it. ⁸ Assemble the surrounding

courtyard and hang the screen for the gate of the courtyard.

⁹ "Take the anointing oil and anoint the tabernacle and everything in it; consecrate it along with all its furnishings so that it will be holy. ¹⁰ Anoint the altar of burnt offering and all its utensils; consecrate the altar so that it will be especially holy. ¹¹ Anoint the basin and its stand and consecrate it.

¹² "Then bring Aaron and his sons to the entrance to the tent of meeting and wash them with water. ¹³ Clothe Aaron with the holy garments, anoint him, and consecrate him, so that he can serve me as a priest. ¹⁴ Have his sons come forward and clothe them in tunics. ¹⁵ Anoint them just as you anointed their father, so that they may also serve me as priests. Their anointing will serve to inaugurate a permanent priesthood for them throughout their generations."

¹⁶ Moses did everything just as the Lord had commanded him. ¹⁷ The tabernacle was set up in the first month of the second year, on the first day of the month.^C ¹⁸ Moses set up the tabernacle: He laid its bases, positioned its supports, inserted its crossbars, and set up its pillars. ¹⁹ Then he spread the tent over the tabernacle and put the covering of the tent on top of it, just as the Lord had commanded Moses.

²⁰ Moses took the testimony and placed it in the ark, and attached the poles to the ark. He set the mercy seat on top of the ark. ²¹ He brought the ark into the tabernacle, put up the curtain for the screen, and screened off the ark of the testimony, just as the Lord had commanded him.

²² Moses placed the table in the tent of meeting on the north side of the tabernacle, outside the curtain. ²³ He arranged the bread on it before the Lord, just as the Lord had commanded him. ²⁴ He put the lampstand in the tent of meeting opposite the table on the south side of the tabernacle ²⁵ and set up the lamps before the Lord, just as the Lord had commanded him.

²⁶ Moses installed the gold altar in the tent of meeting, in front of the curtain, ²⁷ and burned fragrant incense on it, just as the Lord had commanded him. ²⁸ He put up the screen at the entrance to the tabernacle. ²⁹ He placed the

---

^A39:34,41 Hb obscure   ^B40:2 Lit on the day of the first month, on the first of the month   ^C40:17 DSS, Sam, LXX add of their coming out of Egypt

---

39:32-43 The text repeatedly states that the Israelites did everything just as God had commanded them (vv. 32,42,43; see note at 40:16-33).
39:38 The **gold altar** was the altar for incense (30:1-5).
39:39 The **bronze altar** was the altar for burnt offerings (27:1-6).
40:1-2 The first day of the first month, in other words New Year's day, was appropriate for inaugurating use of the new

structure. Since the Israelites had left Egypt at the middle of the first month of the year (12:1-11), the tabernacle was to be erected two weeks before the first anniversary of their exodus, at the start of the month that marked the beginning of their second year of freedom (40:17), and nine months after their arrival at Mount Sinai (19:1).
40:12-15 A full description of installing Aaron and his sons as priests appears in Lv 8-9.

40:16-33 Moses complied with the Lord's instructions. The phrase **just as the Lord had commanded Moses/him** occurs eight times here. The perfect obedience of Israel and Moses in chaps. 39 and 40 is a momentary high point, in contrast with what went on earlier (chap. 32) and what will happen later (e.g., Nm 14).
40:17 The first month of the second year refers to the start of the Israelites' second year after they had left Egypt.

Seeing Jesus in Exodus

▼ Old Testament	▼ New Testament
THE LORD, GOD: "I AM" *(Ex 3:14–15)*	**JESUS:** "I am" *(Jn 8:58)*
Moses: A Mediator *(Ex 32:11–14)*	**Jesus:** The One Mediator *(1Tm 2:5–6)*
Moses: A Prophet *(Dt 18:18–19)*	**Jesus:** The Prophet *(Ac 3:22–26)*
Israel, God's Firstborn Son: Called Out of Egypt *(Ex 4:22–23)*	**Christ, God's Firstborn Son:** The Fulfillment *(Mt 2:15)*
The Passover Lamb: Protection from the Plague *(Ex 12)*	**Christ, Our Passover Lamb:** Purification from Sin *(1Co 5:7–8)*
Manna: Bread from Heaven *(Ex 16)*	**Jesus:** The Bread of Life *(Jn 6)*
The Rock in the Wilderness: Struck to Satisfy the People's Thirst *(Ex 17)*	**Jesus:** The Rock Struck for Our Salvation *(1Co 10:4)*
The Law: Given through Moses *(Ex 20–24)*	**Grace and Truth:** Come through Jesus Christ *(Jn 1:17)*
The Tabernacle: God's Temporary Dwelling Place with Israel *(Ex 40)*	**Jesus:** The Word Became Flesh and Dwelt among Us *(Jn 1:14)*
Balaam's Blessing: A Star from Jacob; a Scepter from Israel *(Nm 24:17)*	**Jesus's Birth:** Born King of the Jews, Heralded by a Star *(Mt 2:2)*
The Law's Curse: Anyone Hung on a Tree Is under God's Curse *(Dt 21:22–23)*	**The Gospel's Blessing:** Christ Became a Curse for Us to Redeem Us *(Gl 3:13–14)*

altar of burnt offering at the entrance to the tabernacle, the tent of meeting, and offered the burnt offering and the grain offering on it, just as the LORD had commanded him.

³⁰ He set the basin between the tent of meeting and the altar and put water in it for washing. ³¹ Moses, Aaron, and his sons washed their hands and feet from it. ³² They washed whenever they came to the tent of meeting and approached the altar, just as the LORD had commanded Moses.

³³ Next Moses set up the surrounding courtyard for the tabernacle and the altar and hung a screen for the gate of the courtyard. So Moses finished the work.

The LORD's Glory

³⁴ The cloud covered the tent of meeting, and the glory of the LORD filled the tabernacle. ³⁵ Moses was unable to enter the tent of meeting because the cloud rested on it, and the glory of the LORD filled the tabernacle.

³⁶ The Israelites set out whenever the cloud was taken up from the tabernacle throughout all the stages of their journey. ³⁷ If the cloud was not taken up, they did not set out until the day it was taken up. ³⁸ For the cloud of the LORD was over the tabernacle by day, and there was a fire inside the cloud by night, visible to the entire house of Israel throughout all the stages of their journey.

40:34–35 This visible display, in the form of a **cloud**, showed that the Lord was consecrating the tabernacle by his presence, as he had promised (25:8; 29:44–46). The Lord was revealing himself to his redeemed people at this meeting place (1Kg 8:10–11,56–60; 9:3; Mt 17:1–8; Mk 9:2–8; Lk 9:28–36; Jn 1:14,18; 2Co 3:18; 4:6; Eph 1:17–18; Rv 21:3).

▼ Introduction to Leviticus

Circumstances of Writing

Although the book of Leviticus is technically anonymous, the evidence from the Bible and from Jewish and Christian traditions attributes it to the lawgiver, Moses (see 18:5 with Rm 10:5). Moses was the chief recipient of God's revelation in the book of Leviticus (1:1; 4:1). Elsewhere, Moses is said to have written down revelation that he received (Ex 24:4; 34:28; Mk 10:4–5; 12:19; Jn 1:45; 5:46). The author of Leviticus was someone well acquainted with the events in the book, and he was knowledgeable of the Sinai Wilderness, making him most likely a firsthand witness.

About one year passed from the time Israel arrived at Sinai until they departed (Ex 19:1; Nm 10:11). During that time, Moses received the covenant from the Lord, erected the tabernacle (Ex 40:17), and received all the instructions in Leviticus and in the early chapters of Numbers. This block of material is the continuous narrative extending from Exodus 19 through Leviticus to Numbers 10:11. Since these events occurred in just one year and yet received the largest amount of space in the books from Exodus through Deuteronomy, Moses showed the special importance of the Sinai revelation to the writing of the Pentateuch. The repeated expression "The LORD spoke to Moses" throughout Leviticus leaves no doubt that its instructions were of divine origin, not the creation of Moses (Lv 1:1; 27:1).

Contribution to the Bible

Leviticus is often neglected because Christians have misunderstood its message and purpose. This was not true of Jesus, who designated "love your neighbor as yourself" (19:18) as the second-greatest commandment (Mt 22:39). The apostle Paul considered these words the summation of the Mosaic commandments (Rm 13:9; Gl 5:14; see Jms 2:8). The writer of Hebrews relied on the images of Leviticus in describing the person and role of Jesus Christ: sacrifice, the priesthood, and the Day of Atonement (4:14–10:18). Studying Leviticus gives us a deeper devotion to Jesus Christ, a stronger worship of God, and a better understanding of daily Christian living.

Structure

Leviticus is primarily a collection of laws, with a little historical narrative. The laws contained in Leviticus can be divided into two groups. First are the commands, or apodictic law. These are both positive commands ("You must . . .") and negative commands ("You must not . . ."). The second type of law is casuistic law. These are case laws using an example of what to do if such-and-such happened ("If a man . . ."). Some scholars seek to divide the laws further into civil laws, moral laws, and ceremonial laws, but there is no evidence that the Israelites made such a distinction.

Leviticus Timeline

1750–1500 BC

Hyksos rule Egypt **1630–1543**
Eighteenth Dynasty of Egypt **1570–1303** (includes Thutmose and Amenhotep; traditionally the pharaohs of oppression)
The New Kingdom begins in Egypt. **1540**
The god Osiris is represented in Egyptian tombs as a symbol of resurrection in the world to come. **1540**

1500–1450 BC

AARON **1529–1409?**
Egyptians find a way to create lubricants that last and do not burn off. **1500**
Clay tablet map of the Babylonian city of Nippur **1500**
Battle of Megiddo between Egyptian forces of Pharaoh Thutmose III and a Kadesh alliance, reestablishing Egyptian hegemony in the Levant **1479**
Queen Makare Hatshepsut, daughter of Thutmose I, reigned in Egypt during a period of peace and prosperity. **1479–1457**

Outline

Key verse in Leviticus

22:31 You are to keep my commands and do them; I am the LORD.

1450–1405 BC	1405–1300 BC
The exodus and defeat of Pharaoh at the Red Sea **1446**	Musical notation, Ugarit **1400**
The Passover is instituted. **1446**	Water clocks were invented. **1400**
God's covenant at Sinai **1446**	The Amarna letters were diplomatic
The tabernacle is built and dedicated. **1445**	correspondence between administrators in
Events in Leviticus **1445**	Egypt's New Kingdom and their representatives
Exploration of Canaan by twelve spies **1445**	in Canaan and other states of the ancient Near
JOSHUA 1409?–1380	East. They were written on clay tablets. **1345**

The Burnt Offering

1 Then the Lord summoned Moses and spoke to him from the tent of meeting: ² "Speak to the Israelites and tell them: When any of you brings an offering to the Lord from the livestock, you may bring your offering from the herd or the flock.

³ "If his offering is a burnt offering from the herd, he is to bring an unblemished male. He will bring it to the entrance to the tent of meeting so that he^A may be accepted by the Lord. ⁴ He is to lay his hand on the head of the burnt offering so it can be accepted on his behalf to make atonement for him. ⁵ He is to slaughter the bull before the Lord; Aaron's sons the priests are to present the blood and splatter it on all sides of the altar that is at the entrance to the tent of meeting. ⁶ Then he is to skin the burnt offering and cut it into pieces.^B ⁷ The sons of Aaron the priest will prepare a fire on the altar and arrange wood on the fire. ⁸ Aaron's sons the priests are to arrange the pieces, the head, and the fat on top of the burning wood on the altar. ⁹ The offerer is to wash its entrails and legs with water. Then the priest will burn all of it on the altar as a burnt offering, a food offering, a pleasing aroma to the Lord.

¹⁰ "But if his offering for a burnt offering is from the flock, from sheep or goats, he is to present an unblemished male. ¹¹ He will slaughter it on the north side of the altar before the Lord. Aaron's sons the priests will splatter its blood against the altar on all sides. ¹² He will cut the animal into pieces with its head and its fat, and the priest will arrange them on top of the burning wood on the altar. ¹³ But he is to wash the entrails and legs with water. The priest will then present all of it and burn it on the altar; it is a burnt offering, a food offering, a pleasing aroma to the Lord.

¹⁴ "If his offering to the Lord is a burnt offering of birds, he is to present his offering from the turtledoves or young pigeons.^C ¹⁵ Then the priest is to bring it to the altar, and will twist off its head and burn it on the altar; its blood should be drained at the side of the altar. ¹⁶ He will remove its digestive tract,^D cutting off the tail feathers, and throw it on the east side of the altar at the place for ashes. ¹⁷ He will tear it open by its wings without dividing the bird. Then the priest is to burn it on the altar on top of the burning wood. It is a burnt offering, a food offering, a pleasing aroma to the Lord.

The Grain Offering

2 "When anyone presents a grain offering as an offering to the Lord, it is to consist of fine flour. He is to pour olive oil on it, put frankincense on it, ² and bring it to Aaron's sons the priests. The priest will take a handful of fine flour and oil from it, along with all its frankincense, and will burn this memorial portion of it on the altar, a food offering, a pleasing aroma to the Lord. ³ But the rest of the grain offering will belong to Aaron and his sons; it is the holiest part of the food offerings to the Lord.

⁴ "When you present a grain offering baked in an oven, it is to be made of fine flour, either unleavened cakes mixed with oil or unleavened wafers coated with oil. ⁵ If your offering is a grain offering prepared on a griddle, it is to be unleavened bread made of fine flour mixed with oil. ⁶ Break it into pieces and pour oil on it; it is a grain offering. ⁷ If your offering is a grain offering prepared in a pan, it is to be made of fine flour with oil. ⁸ When you bring to the Lord the grain offering made in any of these ways, it is to be presented to the priest, and he will take it to the altar. ⁹ The priest will remove the memorial portion^E from the grain offering and burn

---

^A 1:3 Or *it*   ^B 1:6 Lit *its pieces*, also in v. 12   ^C 1:14 Or *or pigeons*   ^D 1:16 Or *its crop*, or *its crissum*   ^E 2:9 Lit *portion of it*

1:1 The **tent of meeting** refers to the tabernacle tent erected under Moses's supervision at Sinai (Ex 40), not the temporary tent used only for communication (Ex 33:7). The period from the building of the structure to the departure from Sinai was about forty-eight days (Ex 40:2; Nm 10:11), which included all the events of Leviticus and the preparations for departure in Nm 1:1–10:10. **1:3** The **burnt offering** (Hb *'olah*) is the first of the five regular offerings: burnt, grain, fellowship, sin, and guilt. The first three offerings were voluntary gifts, and the last two were required. The burnt offering was for the general (nonspecific) sinfulness of the offerer. The term *'olah* means "an ascending" (Hb *'alah*; "to ascend"), referring probably to the rising smoke of the burning carcass. The burnt offering was also known as the "whole burnt offering" because it was totally consumed on the altar (v. 9), except the hide (7:8), expressing the person's total dedication to God. Since it was so commonly associated with the altar of sacrifice, the altar itself was sometimes called "the altar of burnt offering" (4:7).

He . . . he refers to the layperson, not the priests, who are identified as "Aaron's sons" (vv. 5,7,11). **He may be accepted** can also be translated "it will be accepted," indicating the animal, not the offerer. "Accepted" (Hb *ratson*) means divine favor, indicating that the person received forgiveness (v. 4). **1:4** By laying **his hand on the head**, the layperson symbolically transferred guilt or identified with the fate of the victim (16:21). The result was **to make atonement** (Hb *kapper*), which meant appeasement (propitiation) with God (Gn 32:20) by removing (expiation) sin and impurities (Day of Atonement, Lv 16:30; 23:28; "atoning sacrifice," Rm 3:25; Heb 9:25). **1:5** The offerer himself slit the bull's throat (2Kg 10:7; Talmud), and the priest splattered the **blood . . . on all sides of the altar**. **1:6** The skinning provided the gift of the hide for the priest (7:8). **1:9 Pleasing aroma** is a frequent expression meaning the Lord accepted the gift (vv. 13,17; Gn 8:21; Ex 29:18). The Greek translation of the phrase is used of the sacrifice of Christ in Eph 5:2 and of Christian giving in Php 4:18.

1:10–13 Sheep were the most common burnt offering. The **north side of the altar** was especially for the flock (also sin offering, 4:24,29,33), perhaps because less space was needed for them than cattle, which were slaughtered "before the Lord," that is, on the larger east side facing the entrance to the tent of meeting (1:5). **1:14** Mary offered birds at Jesus's birth for her purification (Lk 2:22–24). **2:1** By the **grain offering** (or cereal offering) the worshiper acknowledged God as the source of provision and prosperity. This could be offered in raw, cooked, ground (into flour), and baked forms. Typically, it accompanied animal offerings (Lv 7:12–13; 14:20; Nm 28:4–15), but it could be presented independently (Lv 5:11; 7:12–14). **Frankincense**, a white resin of pleasant fragrance, was widely valued in the ancient world (Mt 2:11). Tabernacle worship required its pure form in the incense for anointing (Ex 30:34) and the bread loaves (Lv 24:7). **2:2** The **memorial portion**, given to God, was a representative handful of the treated flour and all of the frankincense (v. 16).

it on the altar, a food offering, a pleasing aroma to the LORD. [10] But the rest of the grain offering will belong to Aaron and his sons; it is the holiest part of the food offerings to the LORD. [11] "No grain offering that you present to the LORD is to be made with yeast, for you are not to burn[A] any yeast or honey as a food offering to the LORD. [12] You may present them to the LORD as an offering of firstfruits, but they are not to be offered on the altar as a pleasing aroma. [13] You are to season each of your grain offerings with salt; you must not omit from your grain offering the salt of the covenant with your God. You are to present salt with each of your offerings. [14] "If you present a grain offering of firstfruits to the LORD, you are to present fresh heads of grain, crushed kernels, roasted on the fire, for your grain offering of firstfruits. [15] You are to put oil and frankincense on it; it is a grain offering. [16] The priest will then burn some of its crushed kernels and oil with all its frankincense as a food offering to the LORD.

The Fellowship Offering

3 "If his offering is a fellowship sacrifice, and he is presenting an animal from the herd, whether male or female, he is to present one without blemish before the LORD. [2] He is to lay his hand on the head of his offering and slaughter it at the entrance to the tent of meeting. Then Aaron's sons the priests will splatter the blood on all sides of the altar. [3] He will present part of the fellowship sacrifice as a food offering to the LORD: the fat surrounding the entrails, all the fat that is on the entrails, [4] and the two kidneys with the fat on them at the loins; he will also remove the fatty lobe of the liver with the kidneys. [5] Aaron's sons will burn it on the altar along with the burnt offering that is on the burning wood, a food offering, a pleasing aroma to the LORD.

[6] "If his offering as a fellowship sacrifice to the LORD is from the flock, he is to present a male or female without blemish. [7] If he is presenting a lamb for his offering, he is to present it before the LORD. [8] He must lay his hand on the head of his offering, then slaughter it before the tent of meeting. Aaron's sons will splatter its blood on all sides of the altar. [9] He will then present part of the fellowship sacrifice as a food offering to the LORD consisting of its fat and the entire fat tail, which he is to remove close to the backbone. He will also remove the fat surrounding the entrails, all the

---

[A] 2:11 Some Hb mss, Sam, LXX, Tg read *present*

2:11–12 Yeast had a corrupting influence and thus could symbolize evil (Mk 8:15; 1Co 5:8). Perhaps **honey** was prohibited because it was used in pagan rites. **2:13–14** Yeast and honey could be offered as **firstfruits** although not burned on the altar (23:17). Firstfruits, the first portion of the harvest, were viewed as the choice part that belonged to God as the source of all blessing. The permanent quality of **salt** indicates the eternality of the relationship between the Lord and his people (Nm 18:19). **Fresh heads** describes the first ripening

sheaves, indicating the best produce (Ex 23:19). **3:1–2** The three kinds of **fellowship sacrifice** were thanksgiving, vow, and freewill (7:11–21). The fellowship offering signified communion between the worshiper and God (9:18,21; 23:19; Nm 6:18) because it was the only sacrifice in which the worshiper ate the shared meal with the priests (Lv 7:31–35). **3:3–5** The rationale for restricting the **fat** is not stated, except that the fat was the prerogative of God (Is 43:24; Ezk 44:7). The fat was considered the best part of

an animal (Gn 4:4; 45:18; Is 34:6) and was associated with robust power (2Sm 1:22; Is 10:27). Fat was especially associated with the fellowship offering (1Kg 8:64; 2Ch 7:7). Figuratively, the **kidneys** conveyed a person's feelings and inner thoughts (often parallels "heart," Ps 73:1), and both the **liver** and kidneys were vital to physical life (Jb 16:13; Pr 7:23). **3:6–10** The **entire fat tail** refers to the broad-tail sheep whose tail was reputed to be a heavy fat organ weighing from five to fifteen pounds (*Herodotus*).

SACRIFICIAL SYSTEM

NAME	REFERENCE	ELEMENTS	SIGNIFICANCE
Burnt Offering	Lv 1; 6:8–13	Bull, ram, male goat, male dove, or young pigeon without blemish. (Always male animals, but species of animal varied according to individual's economic status.)	Voluntary. Signifies propitiation for sin and complete surrender, devotion, and commitment to God.
Grain Offering Also called Meal, or Tribute, Offering	Lv 2; 6:14–23	Flour, bread, or grain made with olive oil and salt (always unleavened); or incense.	Voluntary. Signifies thanksgiving for firstfruits.
Fellowship Offering Also called Peace Offering: includes (1) Thank Offering, (2) Vow Offering, and (3) Freewill Offering	(1) Lv 3; 7:11–36; 22:17-30; 27	Any animal without blemish. (Species of animal varied according to individual's economic status.) (1) Can be grain offering.	Voluntary. Symbolizes fellowship with God. (1) Signifies thankfulness for a specific blessing; (2) offers a ritual expression of a vow; and (3) symbolizes general thankfulness (to be brought to one of three required religious services).
Sin Offering	Lv 4:1–5:13; 6:24-30; 12:6–8	Male or female animal without blemish—as follows: bull for high priest on congregation; male goat for king; female goat or lamb for common person; dove or pigeon for slightly poor; tenth of an ephah of flour for the very poor.	Mandatory. Made by one who had sinned unintentionally or was unclean in order to attain purification.
Guilt Offering	Lv 5:14–6:7; 7:1–6; 14:12–18	Ram or lamb without blemish	Mandatory. Made by a person who had either deprived another of his rights or had desecrated something holy. Made by lepers for purification.

fat on the entrails, ¹⁰ the two kidneys with the fat on them at the loins, and the fatty lobe of the liver above the kidneys. ¹¹ Then the priest will burn the food on the altar, as a food offering to the LORD.

¹² "If his offering is a goat, he is to present it before the LORD. ¹³ He must lay his hand on its head and slaughter it before the tent of meeting. Aaron's sons will splatter^A its blood on all sides of the altar. ¹⁴ He will present part of his offering as a food offering to the LORD: the fat surrounding the entrails, all the fat that is on the entrails, ¹⁵ and the two kidneys with the fat on them at the loins; he will also remove the fatty lobe of the liver with the kidneys. ¹⁶ Then the priest will burn the food on the altar, as a food offering for a pleasing aroma.^B

"All fat belongs to the LORD. ¹⁷ This is a permanent statute throughout your generations, wherever you live: you must not eat any fat or any blood."

The Sin Offering

4 Then the LORD spoke to Moses: ² "Tell the Israelites: When someone sins unintentionally against any of the LORD's commands and does anything prohibited by them —

³ "If the anointed priest sins, bringing guilt on the people, he is to present to the LORD a young, unblemished bull as a sin^C offering for the sin he has committed. ⁴ He is to bring the bull to the entrance to the tent of meeting before the LORD, lay his hand on the bull's head, and slaughter it before the LORD. ⁵ The anointed priest will then take some of the bull's blood and bring it into the tent of meeting. ⁶ The priest is to dip his finger in the blood and sprinkle some of it seven times before the LORD in front of the curtain of the sanctuary. ⁷ The priest is to apply some of the blood to the horns of the altar of fragrant incense that is before the LORD in the tent of meeting. He must pour out the rest of the bull's blood at the base of the altar of burnt offering that is at the entrance to the tent of meeting. ⁸ He is to remove all the fat from the bull of the sin offering: the fat surrounding the entrails, all the fat that is on the entrails, ⁹ and the two kidneys with the fat on them at the loins. He will also remove the fatty lobe of the liver with the kidneys, ¹⁰ just as the fat is removed from the ox of the fellowship sacrifice. The priest is to burn them on the altar of burnt offering. ¹¹ But the hide of the bull and all its flesh, with its head and legs, and its entrails and waste — ¹² all the rest of the bull — he must bring to a ceremonially clean place outside the camp to the ash heap, and must burn it on a wood fire. It is to be burned at the ash heap.

¹³ "Now if the whole community of Israel errs, and the matter escapes the notice of the assembly, so that they violate any of the LORD's commands and incur guilt by doing what is prohibited, ¹⁴ then the assembly must present a young bull as a sin offering. They are to bring it before the tent of meeting when the sin they have committed in regard to the command becomes known. ¹⁵ The elders of the community

---

^A 3:13 Or dash   ^B 3:16 Sam, LXX add to the LORD   ^C 4:3 Or purification

3:16b–17 Belongs to the LORD applies to the **fat** that was removed from a sacrifice at the altar (Ezk 44:7) and not necessarily the fat of animals for the common table.
4:1–2 Sins committed **unintentionally** (Hb *shegagah*) are inadvertent transgressions committed through ignorance or neglect, not premeditated, defiant sins.
4:3 Anointed priest refers to the high priest (6:22; 21:10; Ex 29:7). The traditional translation **sin offering** is better understood as "purification offering" since it involved the ritual removal of impurities and provided forgiveness.
The instructions for the sin offering (4:1–5:13) consisted of two parts: the general instructions (4:1–35) and the appendix naming special circumstances (5:1–13). The

#06 **99 Essential Christian Truths**

GOD IS MERCIFUL

Mercy refers to God's compassion and is often expressed in God withholding punishment for sin (Eph 2:4–5; Ti 3:5). Both mercy and grace are undeserved; humanity can do nothing to earn them from God. If one could, then mercy and grace would no longer be God's free gift.

sin offering addressed the consequences of sin, which always rendered the sanctuary and its furnishings unclean and impaired the relationship between the worshiper and God. This made it unacceptable for the worshiper to access the sanctuary and receive God's forgiveness. The sin offering removed the corrupting effects of sin, which permitted the remorseful sinner not only to receive forgiveness but to have the assurance of acceptance with God. For this reason, the ritual included the application of blood to the sanctuary furnishings, not to the person (4:5–7,16–18,25,30,34).
The sin offering varied according to the progressive degrees of responsibility: the high priest (Lv 4:3–12), the congregation collectively (vv. 13–21), the ruler (vv. 22–26), and the individual layperson (vv. 27–35). The underlying principle is that although all sin is contaminating, the sins of leadership (priest, king) and the congregation have greater impact than those of the individual transgressor. The variation in the cost of the sacrifice and the placement of blood on the sanctuary furnishings reflected this same principle.
4:5 This was the only offering that required the high priest to bring the blood into the tent of meeting.
4:6 **Seven** indicates the thoroughness of the purging; this number occurs also in the accounts of the ordination rite (8:11), purification of lepers (14:7), the Day of Atonement

(16:14,19), and the ceremony of the red heifer (Nm 19:4). The **curtain** (Hb *paroketh*) separated the holy place from the most holy place inside the tent canopy (Ex 26:33).
4:7 The priest **is to apply** (Hb *natan*) the blood by smearing rather than sprinkling (Hb *nazah*) it; the **altar of fragrant incense** refers to the golden altar before the dividing curtain inside the tent canopy. Aaron lit this each morning and evening (Ex 30:7–8). Only priests could offer the incense (2Ch 26:18). The altar symbolized intercessory prayer (Ps 141:2; Rv 5:8; 8:3–4).
The four **horns**, one protruding from each of the altar's four corners (Ex 30:1–6; 38:2), conveyed the power of a formidable animal (Dt 33:17) and thus the efficacy (strength, e.g., 1Sm 2:10; Am 3:14) of the altar's purpose. The disposal of the remaining blood **at the base of the** (courtyard's) **altar**, around which a trench probably ran (1Kg 18:32), occurred only for the sin offering of the five offerings detailed in Lv 1–7 and also during the special ordination rites of Aaron's priesthood (9:9; Ex 29:12).
4:8–12 A distinguishing feature of the sin offering was that the bull's remaining parts were taken **to a ceremonially clean place outside the camp** where they were burned.
4:13–14 The word **errs** (Hb *shegag*) refers to unintended transgressions (cp. v. 2). This sort of sin escaped **notice** (Hb *'alam*), hidden

are to lay their hands on the bull's head before the LORD and it is to be slaughtered before the LORD. ¹⁶ The anointed priest will bring some of the bull's blood into the tent of meeting. ¹⁷ The priest is to dip his finger in the blood and sprinkle it seven times before the LORD in front of the curtain. ¹⁸ He is to apply some of the blood to the horns of the altar that is before the LORD in the tent of meeting. He will pour out the rest of the blood at the base of the altar of burnt offering that is at the entrance to the tent of meeting. ¹⁹ He is to remove all the fat from it and burn it on the altar. ²⁰ He is to offer this bull just as he did with the bull in the sin offering; he will offer it the same way. So the priest will make atonement on their behalf, and they will be forgiven. ²¹ Then he will bring the bull outside the camp and burn it just as he burned the first bull. It is the sin offering for the assembly. ²² "When a leader^A sins and unintentionally violates any of the commands of the LORD his God by doing what is prohibited, and incurs guilt, ²³ or someone informs him about the sin he has committed, he is to bring an unblemished male goat as his offering. ²⁴ He is to lay his hand on the head of the goat and slaughter it at the place where the burnt offering is slaughtered before the LORD. It is a sin offering. ²⁵ Then the priest is to take some of the blood from the sin offering with his finger and apply it to the horns of the altar of burnt offering. The rest of its blood he is to pour out at the base of the altar of burnt offering. ²⁶ He must burn all its fat on the altar, like the fat of the fellowship sacrifice. In this way the priest will make atonement on his behalf for that person's sin, and he will be forgiven.

²⁷ "Now if any of the common people^B sins unintentionally by violating one of the LORD's commands, does what is prohibited, and incurs guilt, ²⁸ or if someone informs him about the sin he has committed, then he is to bring an unblemished female goat as his offering for the sin that he has committed. ²⁹ He is to lay his hand on the head of the sin offering and slaughter it at the place of the burnt offering.

³⁰ Then the priest is to take some of its blood with his finger and apply it to the horns of the altar of burnt offering. He is to pour out the rest of its blood at the base of the altar. ³¹ He is to remove all its fat just as the fat is removed from the fellowship sacrifice. The priest is to burn it on the altar as a pleasing aroma to the LORD. In this way the priest will make atonement on his behalf, and he will be forgiven.

³² "Or if the offering that he brings as a sin offering is a lamb, he is to bring an unblemished female. ³³ He is to lay his hand on the head of the sin offering and slaughter it as a sin offering at the place where the burnt offering is slaughtered. ³⁴ Then the priest is to take some of the blood of the sin offering with his finger and apply it to the horns of the altar of burnt offering. He is to pour out the rest of its blood at the base of the altar. ³⁵ He is to remove all its fat just as the fat of the lamb is removed from the fellowship sacrifice. The priest will burn it on the altar along with the food offerings to the LORD. In this way the priest will make atonement on his behalf for the sin he has committed, and he will be forgiven.

Cases Requiring Sin Offerings

5 "When someone sins in any of these ways: If he has seen, heard, or known about something he has witnessed, and did not respond to a public call to testify, he will bear his iniquity.

² Or if someone touches anything unclean — a carcass of an unclean wild animal, or unclean livestock, or an unclean swarming creature — without being aware of it, he is unclean and incurs guilt. ³ Or if he touches human uncleanness — any uncleanness by which one can become defiled — without being aware of it, but later recognizes it, he incurs guilt. ⁴ Or if someone swears rashly to do what is good or evil — concerning anything a person may speak rashly in an oath — without being aware of it, but later recognizes it, he incurs guilt in such an instance.

---

^A4:22 Or *ruler*   ^B4:27 Lit *the people of the land*

---

at the time of the trespass, but was perceived later.
4:20–21 This is the first occurrence in Leviticus of the word **forgiven** (Hb *salach*; cp. vv. 26,31,35; 5:10,13,16,18; 6:7; 19:22); the Hebrew passive form of the verb implies that it is God alone who can forgive sin.
4:22–23 A **leader** (Hb *nasi'*) was a ruler over a tribe (Gn 25:16; Ex 34:31).
4:24 The burnt offering was **slaughtered** north of the altar (see note at 1:10–13). The declaration that it **is a sin offering** was a reminder that this rite should not be confused with the burnt offering.
4:25 The blood remained outside the tent and was applied to the courtyard's **altar of burnt offering** for its purgation (Ex 29:38–42).

4:26 The phrase **he will be forgiven** only occurs with the sin offering and the restitution offering.
4:27–35 The individual was permitted to offer a female goat or female sheep.
4:27 Common people renders (lit) "people of the land," meaning anyone who was not the high priest or an official.
5:1–13 The remaining instructions for the sin offering provide four case examples (vv. 1–4) and the ritual procedure required (vv. 5–6), including special directives for the poor (vv. 5–13).
5:1–4 The four cases involve those who failed to testify in court (v. 1); those who became unclean through contact with an unclean animal (v. 2) or an unclean person (v. 3); and those who uttered an oath rashly

(v. 4). The first and fourth of these cases of sin pertained to an oath, and the second and third cases regarded ceremonial uncleanness.
5:1 A **public call to testify** (lit "voice of an oath") indicates a judicial matter in which formal testimony is requested of those who have knowledge to contribute to a court proceeding.
5:2 The possibility of touching an unclean creature was always a threat (11:24–28,35–40). For the **unclean swarming creature**, see the specifics in chap. 11.
5:4 Rashly (Hb *bata'*) describes hurtful, hastily spoken words (Ps 106:33; Pr 12:18); here it indicates a careless **oath**, made regardless of whether it was virtuous or not. Typically, an unfulfilled oath included a divine punishment.

⁵ If someone incurs guilt in one of these cases, he is to confess he has committed that sin. ⁶ He must bring his penalty for guilt for the sin he has committed to the LORD: a female lamb or goat from the flock as a sin offering. In this way the priest will make atonement on his behalf for his sin.

⁷ "But if he cannot afford an animal from the flock, then he may bring to the LORD two turtledoves or two young pigeons as penalty for guilt for his sin — one as a sin offering and the other as a burnt offering. ⁸ He is to bring them to the priest, who will first present the one for the sin offering. He is to twist its head at the back of the neck without severing it. ⁹ Then he will sprinkle some of the blood of the sin offering on the side of the altar, while the rest of the blood is to be drained out at the base of the altar; it is a sin offering. ¹⁰ He will prepare the second bird as a burnt offering according to the regulation. In this way the priest will make atonement on his behalf for the sin he has committed, and he will be forgiven.

¹¹ "But if he cannot afford two turtledoves or two young pigeons, he may bring two quartsᴬ of fine flourᴮ as an offering for his sin. He must not put olive oil or frankincense on it, for it is a sin offering. ¹² He is to bring it to the priest, who will take a handful from it as its memorial portion and burn it on the altar along with the food offerings to the LORD; it is a sin offering. ¹³ In this way the priest will make atonement on his behalf concerning the sin he has committed in any of these cases, and he will be forgiven. The rest will belong to the priest, like the grain offering."

The Guilt Offering

¹⁴ Then the LORD spoke to Moses: ¹⁵ "If someone offends by sinning unintentionally in regard to any of the LORD's holy things,ᶜ he must bring his penalty for guilt to the LORD: an unblemished ram from the flock (based on your assessment of its value in silver shekels, according to the sanctuary shekel) as a guilt offering. ¹⁶ He is to make restitution for his sin regarding any holy thing, adding a fifth of its value to it, and give it to the priest. Then the priest will make atonement on his behalf with the ram of the guilt offering, and he will be forgiven.

¹⁷ "If someone sins and without knowing it violates any of the LORD's commands concerning anything prohibited, he is guilty, and he will bear his iniquity. ¹⁸ He must bring an unblemished ram from the flock according to your assessment of its value as a guilt offering to the priest. Then the priest will make atonement on his behalf for the error he has committed unintentionally, and he will be forgiven. ¹⁹ It is a guilt offering; he is indeed guilty before the LORD."

6 The LORD spoke to Moses: ² "When someone sins and offends the LORD by deceiving his neighbor in regard to a deposit, a security,ᴰ or a robbery; or defrauds his neighbor; ³ or finds something lost and lies about it; or swears falsely about any of the sinful things a person may do — ⁴ once he has sinned and acknowledged his guilt — he must return what he stole or defrauded, or the deposit entrusted to him, or the lost item he found, ⁵ or anything else about which he swore falsely. He will make full restitution for it and add a fifth of its value to it. He is to pay it to its owner on the day he acknowledges his guilt. ⁶ Then he is to bring his guilt offering to the LORD: an unblemished ram from the flock according to your assessment of its value as a guilt offering to the priest. ⁷ In this way the priest will make atonement on his behalf before the LORD, and he will be forgiven for anything he may have done to incur guilt."

ᴬ5:11 Lit one-tenth of an ephah   ᴮ5:11 Lit flour as a sin offering   ᶜ5:15 Things dedicated to the LORD   ᴰ6:2 Or an investment

5:5–6 Two measures were required of the offender for any of these four crimes. The root word for confess (Hb yadah) can also mean to "praise aloud" (Ps 7:17), indicating that confession involved declaring one's sin publicly (Lv 16:21; 26:40; Nm 5:6–7; 1Jn 1:9). The penalty for guilt (Hb 'asham) was an animal offering. The word can also mean "guilt" (4:13; 5:16,18,19). It is called the "guilt offering" (or "restitution" offering; traditionally "trespass" offering) in 5:14–6:7. 5:8 Two birds were necessary since the regular sin offering required two acts (4:6–10): (1) the disposal of the blood, and (2) the burning of its internal organs and fat. The sin offering granted cleansing and acceptance with God, which was necessary before the burnt offering (indicating devotion) was appropriate. 5:11 Oil and incense that characterized the grain offering were omitted from the sin offering since these elements signified the joy of worship. The amount of flour was small enough that the very poor could afford it. 5:14–6:7 The penalty for guilt or guilt offering (5:15), sometimes translated "trespass"

offering, remedied the sins of defrauding God's "holy things" (5:14–19) or defrauding a person, which involved offending the Lord through a false oath (6:1–7). This offering addressed the damage of depriving someone of his rightful due; thus, monetary reparations were required.

The offering involved an assessment by the priest of the damages plus a surcharge payment of 20 percent. The restitution ritual varied for compensating damages against God and against a person. 5:15 The term offends (Hb ma'al) means "acts treacherously," which can describe sacrilege against God (Jos 7:1) or betrayal of another person (Nm 5:6). The guilt offering included additional steps. The offender had to pay for the damages, as evaluated by the priest (27:12), according to the standard sanctuary shekel (27:3), with an additional 20 percent charge (5:16). 5:17 The second case was a transgression in which the person had desecrated something holy without knowing it. This distinguished the guilt offering from the sin offering, which

described an offender who later came to realize his crime (4:2,22,27). 6:1 The third case was a breach of trust that involved the misappropriation of another person's property. Since it most likely involved an oath in the Lord's name, the crime also ultimately offended the Lord. If the defrauded person was dead and a relative could not be repaid, then the priest as the representative of God received the compensation (Nm 5:5–10). 6:2–3 Six examples are listed: the illegal withholding of another's property received through (1) a deposit given for safekeeping, (2) an investment made in a business, (3) theft, (4) property falsely acquired through defrauding a neighbor, (5) keeping lost property, and (6) swearing against a neighbor falsely. 6:7 The Suffering Servant, our Lord Jesus Christ, was the ultimate "guilt offering" (Is 53:10) that provided full forgiveness. 6:8–7:38 The previous descriptions of the five offerings were addressed primarily to everyday Israelites, but these regulations are directed primarily to the priests.

The Burnt Offering

8 The LORD spoke to Moses: **9** "Command Aaron and his sons: This is the law of the burnt offering; the burnt offering itself must remain on the altar's hearth all night until morning, while the fire of the altar is kept burning on it. **10** The priest is to put on his linen robe and linen undergarments.^A He is to remove the ashes of the burnt offering the fire has consumed on the altar, and place them beside the altar. **11** Then he will take off his garments, put on other clothes, and bring the ashes outside the camp to a ceremonially clean place. **12** The fire on the altar is to be kept burning; it must not go out. Every morning the priest will burn wood on the fire. He is to arrange the burnt offering on the fire and burn the fat portions from the fellowship offerings on it. **13** Fire must be kept burning on the altar continually; it must not go out.

The Grain Offering

14 "Now this is the law of the grain offering: Aaron's sons will present it before the LORD in front of the altar. **15** The priest is to remove a handful of fine flour and olive oil from the grain offering, with all the frankincense that is on the offering, and burn its memorial portion on the altar as a pleasing aroma to the LORD. **16** Aaron and his sons may eat the rest of it. It is to be eaten in the form of unleavened bread in a holy place; they are to eat it in the courtyard of the tent of meeting. **17** It must not be baked with yeast; I have assigned it as their portion from my food offerings. It is especially holy, like the sin offering and the guilt offering. **18** Any male among Aaron's descendants may eat it. It is a permanent portion^B throughout your generations from the food offerings to the LORD. Anything that touches the offerings will become holy."

19 The LORD spoke to Moses: **20** "This is the offering that Aaron and his sons are to present to the LORD on the day that he is anointed: two quarts^C of fine flour as a regular grain offering,

half of it in the morning and half in the evening. **21** It is to be prepared with oil on a griddle; you are to bring it well-kneaded. You are to present it as a grain offering of baked pieces,^D a pleasing aroma to the LORD. **22** The priest, who is one of Aaron's sons and will be anointed to take his place, is to prepare it. It must be completely burned as a permanent portion for the LORD. **23** Every grain offering for a priest will be a whole burnt offering; it is not to be eaten."

The Sin Offering

24 The LORD spoke to Moses: **25** "Tell Aaron and his sons: This is the law of the sin offering. The sin offering is most holy and must be slaughtered before the LORD at the place where the burnt offering is slaughtered. **26** The priest who offers it as a sin offering will eat it. It is to be eaten in a holy place, in the courtyard of the tent of meeting. **27** Anything that touches its flesh will become holy, and if any of its blood spatters on a garment, then you must wash that garment^E in a holy place. **28** A clay pot in which the sin offering is boiled is to be broken; if it is boiled in a bronze vessel, it is to be scoured and rinsed with water. **29** Any male among the priests may eat it; it is especially holy. **30** But no sin offering may be eaten if its blood has been brought into the tent of meeting to make atonement in the holy place; it must be burned.

The Guilt Offering

7 "Now this is the law of the guilt^F offering; it is especially holy. **2** The guilt offering is to be slaughtered at the place where the burnt offering is slaughtered, and the priest is to splatter its blood on all sides of the altar. **3** The offerer is to present all the fat from it: the fat tail, the fat surrounding the entrails,^G **4** and the two kidneys with the fat on them at the loins; he will also remove the fatty lobe of the liver with the kidneys. **5** The priest will burn them on the altar as a food offering to the LORD; it is

---

^A **6:10** Lit *undergarments on his flesh*   ^B **6:18** Or *statute*   ^C **6:20** Lit *a tenth of an ephah*   ^D **6:21** Hb obscure   ^E **6:27** Lit *wash what it spattered on*   ^F **7:1** Or *restitution*   ^G **7:3** LXX, Sam add *and all the fat that is on the entrails*; Lv 3:3,9,14; 4:8

6:9 The daily **burnt offering** (Ex 29:42–43; Nm 28:3,6,10), known as the *tamid* ("continually," Lv 6:13) offering, provided for the roasting of the meat **all night until morning**; the phrase **kept burning** describes the perpetual flame on the altar (vv. 12–13). The eternal flame came from the Lord (see note at 9:24), indicating perpetual cleansing and intercession.
6:10–11 Special holy garments were required of the priest (Ex 28:42–43) when handling the **ashes** in the sacred courtyard.
6:14–23 This passage probably describes the layperson's private grain offering, although it may refer to the daily grain offering of Israel presented by the priest that accompanied the daily burnt offering.
6:16–17 Only the priests were qualified to eat the remainder of the sacrifice, which they consumed in the **courtyard** (2:11).

6:17 Especially holy (Hb *qodesh qadashim*) refers to the offerings from which the priests received their sustenance (vv. 25–26; 2:3; 7:1,6; Nm 18:8–10); therefore, these sacrifices could only be consumed in the sanctuary courtyard.
6:22–23 The successor to Aaron as high priest would make the offering at the altar. The burning of the entire offering indicated that the priest could not benefit from the offering made for himself; this was a perpetual reminder to the priest and congregation that he must be dedicated totally to the Lord.
6:24–30 The purpose of this segment was to protect the holiness of the offering and to warn those who might desecrate the meat through unlawful consumption.
6:28 Since a **clay pot** used in this sacrifice was made of porous material that absorbed

the animal's blood, it could not be used again, but a **bronze** pot could be **scoured and rinsed with water**.
6:30 The exception to the priestly consumption of the offering was that a priest could not benefit from a sin offering given for himself. When the priest took the blood inside the sacred tent, or **the holy place**, that was the sin offering to atone for the sins of the priest and the congregation (cp. 4:5,16). The carcass was therefore **burned** on the ash heap (4:12,21).
7:2 The blood splattered **on all sides of the altar** was also part of the rituals for the burnt and fellowship offerings (1:11; 3:2,8,13) but not the sin offering (see note at 6:25).
7:8 The gift of the **hide** to the officiating **priest** of the burnt offering is new information, not mentioned in chap. 1; the skin of the sin offering was burned (4:11).

a guilt offering. ⁶ Any male among the priests may eat it. It is to be eaten in a holy place; it is especially holy.

⁷ "The guilt offering is like the sin offering; the law is the same for both. It belongs to the priest who makes atonement with it. ⁸ As for the priest who presents someone's burnt offering, the hide of the burnt offering he has presented belongs to him; it is the priest's. ⁹ Any grain offering that is baked in an oven or prepared in a pan or on a griddle belongs to the priest who presents it; it is his. ¹⁰ But any grain offering, whether dry or mixed with oil, belongs equally to all of Aaron's sons.

The Fellowship Sacrifice

¹¹ "Now this is the law of the fellowship sacrifice that someone may present to the Lord: ¹² If he presents it for thanksgiving, in addition to the thanksgiving sacrifice, he is to present unleavened cakes mixed with olive oil, unleavened wafers coated with oil, and well-kneaded cakes of fine flour mixed with oil. ¹³ He is to present as his offering cakes of leavened bread with his thanksgiving sacrifice of fellowship. ¹⁴ From the cakes he is to present one portion of each offering as a contribution to the Lord. It will belong to the priest who splatters the blood of the fellowship offering; it is his. ¹⁵ The meat of his thanksgiving sacrifice of fellowship must be eaten on the day he offers it; he may not leave any of it until morning.

¹⁶ "If the sacrifice he offers is a vow or a freewill offering, it is to be eaten on the day he presents his sacrifice, and what is left over may be eaten on the next day. ¹⁷ But what remains of the sacrificial meat by the third day must be burned. ¹⁸ If any of the meat of his fellowship

sacrifice is eaten on the third day, it will not be accepted. It will not be credited to the one who presents it; it is repulsive. The person who eats any of it will bear his iniquity.^A

¹⁹ "Meat that touches anything unclean must not be eaten; it is to be burned. Everyone who is clean may eat any other meat. ²⁰ But the one who eats meat from the Lord's fellowship sacrifice while he is unclean, that person must be cut off from his people. ²¹ If someone touches anything unclean, whether human uncleanness, an unclean animal, or any unclean, abhorrent^B creature, and eats meat from the Lord's fellowship sacrifice, that person is to be cut off from his people."

Fat and Blood Prohibited

²² The Lord spoke to Moses: ²³ "Tell the Israelites: You are not to eat any fat of an ox, a sheep, or a goat. ²⁴ The fat of an animal that dies naturally or is mauled by wild beasts^C may be used for any other purpose, but you must not eat it. ²⁵ If anyone eats animal fat from a food offering presented to the Lord, the person who eats it is to be cut off from his people. ²⁶ Wherever you live, you must not eat the blood of any bird or animal. ²⁷ Whoever eats any blood is to be cut off from his people."

The Portion for the Priests

²⁸ The Lord spoke to Moses: ²⁹ "Tell the Israelites: The one who presents a fellowship sacrifice to the Lord is to bring an offering to the Lord from his sacrifice. ³⁰ His own hands will bring the food offerings to the Lord. He will bring the fat together with the breast. The breast is to be presented as a presentation offering before the Lord. ³¹ The priest is to burn the fat on the altar, but the breast belongs to

---

^A7:18 Or *will bear his guilt* ^B7:21 Some Hb mss, Sam, Syr, Tg read *swarming* ^C7:24 Lit *fat of a carcass or the fat of a mauled beast*

7:9–10 The officiating priest received his due, but provision of **grain** was designated for all the priests, whether officiated at offerings or not. This included priests with physical defects (2:3; 6:18,29; 22:21–22).
7:11–21 Three subtypes made up the **fellowship sacrifice**: thanksgiving (vv. 12–15), vow, and freewill offerings (vv. 16–18). Since the fellowship offering was voluntary and it was shared with family and guests, the offering demonstrated the generosity of the giver, who made his offering as an expression of praise.
7:12–13 Thanksgiving (Hb *todah*) offerings were typically associated with a song of joy (Neh 12:27; Pss 42:14; 50:14; 69:30; 100:1; 116:17). This was the Israelite's response to answered prayer and a proclamation to others of God's goodness; the worshiper in similar fashion was generous toward others by sharing his meal with guests. A grain offering of three bread products accompanied the thanksgiving animal (chap. 3). One of the cakes had to be made of yeast (**leavened bread**), a departure from the typical practice. The inclusion of yeast

was appropriate since this sacrifice was an offering of joy.
7:14 Contribution (Hb *terumah*), traditionally known as the "heave offering," was not necessarily lifted up in the ritual. It is related to the word "to remove" (Hb *herim*), which describes a dedicatory portion that was set aside especially for the Lord (2:9; 6:15).
7:16–17 The **vow** offering was a grateful response to the completion of a vow, and the **freewill offering** was a general expression of joyful thanksgiving by the worshiper. The freewill gift was often given in conjunction with the establishment of community worship (Ex 35:29; Nm 29:39; 1Ch 29:6; Ezr 2:68). The psalmist depicted them as offerings of praise (Pss 54:6; 119:108).
7:20–21 If the person who ate this sacrifice was ceremonially unclean, he was **cut off**, which meant either excommunicated from worship (22:3) or premature death by the intervention of God (17:4). First Corinthians 11:27–32 contains a similar warning against those who took the Lord's Supper unworthily.

7:24 Animal **fat** that came from a source other than a sacrifice could be used for household purposes (e.g., oil), but the blood from an animal could never be consumed (3:16–17; 17:13).
7:28–36 After detailing the procedure about the laity and the disposal of the bread and meat, the passage focuses on the portions of the fellowship offering presented to the Lord—that which belonged to the priests.
7:30–31 His own hands refers to the individual layperson, emphasizing that the gift came voluntarily from the owner. Since the **fat** belonged to the Lord, it must be burned up, and the **breast** was given to the priests collectively, symbolizing that the sacrifice had been accepted by the Lord. The expression **presented as a presentation offering**, traditionally known as the "wave offering," describes the (Hb) *tenuphah* offering (v. 34; 8:27; 9:21; 10:14–15; Ex 29:24; 35:22). Rather than waving the offering, the worshiper presented it as a dedicatory gift ("elevation offering") to the Lord. This symbolized the transfer of the gift portion from the owner's possession.

Aaron and his sons. ³² You are to give the right thigh to the priest as a contribution from your fellowship sacrifices. ³³ The son of Aaron who presents the blood of the fellowship offering and the fat will have the right thigh as a portion. ³⁴ I have taken from the Israelites the breast of the presentation offering and the thigh of the contribution from their fellowship sacrifices, and have assigned them to the priest Aaron and to his sons as a permanent portionᴬ from the Israelites."

³⁵ This is the portion from the food offerings to the Lᴏʀᴅ for Aaron and his sons since the day they were presented to serve the Lᴏʀᴅ as priests. ³⁶ The Lᴏʀᴅ commanded this to be given to them by the Israelites on the day he anointed them. It is a permanent portion throughout their generations.

³⁷ This is the law for the burnt offering, the grain offering, the sin offering, the guilt offering, the ordination offering, and the fellowship sacrifice, ³⁸ which the Lᴏʀᴅ commanded Moses on Mount Sinai on the day he commanded the Israelites to present their offerings to the Lᴏʀᴅ in the Wilderness of Sinai.

Ordination of Aaron and His Sons

8 The Lᴏʀᴅ spoke to Moses: ² "Take Aaron, his sons with him, the garments, the anointing oil, the bull of the sinᴮ offering, the two rams, and the basket of unleavened bread, ³ and assemble the whole community at the entrance to the tent of meeting." ⁴ So Moses did as the Lᴏʀᴅ commanded him, and the community assembled at the entrance to the tent of meeting. ⁵ Moses said to them, "This is what the Lᴏʀᴅ has commanded to be done."

⁶ Then Moses presented Aaron and his sons and washed them with water. ⁷ He put the tunic on Aaron, wrapped the sash around him, clothed him with the robe, and put the ephod on him. He put the woven band of the ephod around him and fastened it to him. ⁸ Then he put the breastpiece on him and placed the Urim and Thummim into the breastpiece. ⁹ He also put the turban on his head and placed the gold medallion, the holy diadem, on the front of the turban, as the Lᴏʀᴅ had commanded Moses.

¹⁰ Then Moses took the anointing oil and anointed the tabernacle and everything in it to consecrate them. ¹¹ He sprinkled some of the oil on the altar seven times, anointing the altar with all its utensils, and the basin with its stand, to consecrate them. ¹² He poured some of the anointing oil on Aaron's head and anointed and consecrated him. ¹³ Then Moses presented Aaron's sons, clothed them with tunics, wrapped sashes around them, and fastened headbands on them, as the Lᴏʀᴅ had commanded Moses.

¹⁴ Then he brought the bull near for the sin offering, and Aaron and his sons laid their hands on the head of the bull for the sin offering. ¹⁵ Then Moses slaughtered it,ᶜ took the blood, and applied it with his finger to the horns of the altar on all sides, purifying the altar. He poured out the blood at the base of the altar and consecrated it so that atonement can be made on it.ᴰ ¹⁶ Moses took all the fat that was on the entrails, the fatty lobe of the liver, and the two kidneys with their fat, and he burned them on the altar. ¹⁷ He burned the bull with its hide, flesh, and waste outside the camp, as the Lᴏʀᴅ had commanded Moses.

¹⁸ Then he presented the ram for the burnt offering, and Aaron and his sons laid their hands on the head of the ram. ¹⁹ Moses slaughtered it andᴱ splattered the blood on all sides of the altar. ²⁰ Moses cut the ram into pieces and burned the head, the pieces, and the fat, ²¹ but he washed the entrails and legs with water. He then burned the entire ram on the altar. It was a burnt offering for a pleasing aroma, a food offering to the Lᴏʀᴅ as he had commanded Moses.

²² Next he presented the second ram, the ram of ordination, and Aaron and his sons laid their hands on the head of the ram. ²³ Moses slaughtered it,ᶠ took some of its blood, and put it on Aaron's right earlobe, on the thumb of his right hand, and on the big toe of his right foot. ²⁴ Moses also presented Aaron's sons and put some of the blood on their right earlobes, on the thumbs of their right hands, and on the big toes of their right feet. Then Moses splattered the blood on all sides of the altar. ²⁵ He took the

---

ᴬ7:34 Or *statute*, also in v. 36   ᴮ8:2 Or *purification*   ᶜ8:14–15 Or *offering, and he slaughtered it.* ¹⁵*Then Moses*   ᴰ8:15 Or *it by making atonement for it*   ᴱ8:18–19 Or *ram,* ¹⁹*and he slaughtered it. Moses*   ᶠ8:22–23 Or *ram,* ²³*and he slaughtered it. Moses*

7:32–33 The officiating priest received the **right thigh** (cp. Nm 18:18–19) as a **contribution** (Hb *terumah;* see note at v. 14). The breast and thigh were meaty portions that provided a regular stipend for the priestly families, showing the generosity of the Lord. **8:1–2 Take Aaron** begins the installation service that was prescribed in Ex 29. Just as Aaron was a mediator for the nation, Israel was to function as priest to the nations (Ex 19:5–6). **8:3–5** The service was a public installation to assure the community of the legitimacy of the Aaronic priesthood.

8:6 Aaron underwent a ceremonial washing to show the moral purity required of priests (1Pt 3:21). **8:7–9** The outfitting of the priests in sacred garments gave them "glory and beauty" in the eyes of the congregation (Ex 28:2,40). **8:10–13 All its utensils** refers to the items that enabled the carrying out of the offerings, such as forks, firepans, and the tabernacle furniture (Ex 27:3). **8:14–17** The priests made **atonement** for their own sins before they could mediate for the people. The death of an animal was necessary, but this could not take away the

sins of the people (Heb 5:3; 9:22; 10:4). The death of Jesus Christ alone achieved complete atonement (2Co 5:21; Col 1:20). The high priest Jesus had no need to make atonement for his own sins since he was without sin (Heb 4:15; 5:9–10; 7:26–27; 10:11–12). **8:22–30** The application of the blood from the **ram of ordination** to the priests' extremities symbolized the total cleansing of the priests. The ear indicated hearing the confessions of the people, the hand represented the touching and handling of the offerings, and the foot represented the holy courtyard and tent in which they served.

fat — the fat tail, all the fat that was on the entrails, the fatty lobe of the liver, and the two kidneys with their fat — as well as the right thigh. ²⁶ From the basket of unleavened bread that was before the LORD he took one cake of unleavened bread, one cake of bread made with oil, and one wafer, and placed them on the fat portions and the right thigh. ²⁷ He put all these in the hands of Aaron and his sons and presented them before the LORD as a presentation offering. ²⁸ Then Moses took them from their hands and burned them on the altar with the burnt offering. This was an ordination offering for a pleasing aroma, a food offering to the LORD. ²⁹ He also took the breast and presented it before the LORD as a presentation offering; it was Moses's portion of the ordination ram as the LORD had commanded him.

³⁰ Then Moses took some of the anointing oil and some of the blood that was on the altar and sprinkled them on Aaron and his garments, as well as on his sons and their garments. In this way he consecrated Aaron and his garments, as well as his sons and their garments.

³¹ Moses said to Aaron and his sons, "Boil the meat at the entrance to the tent of meeting and eat it there with the bread that is in the basket for the ordination offering as I commanded:^A Aaron and his sons are to eat it. ³² Burn up what remains of the meat and bread. ³³ Do not go outside the entrance to the tent of meeting for seven days, until the time your days of ordination are completed, because it will take seven days to ordain you.^B ³⁴ The LORD commanded what has been done today in order to make atonement for you. ³⁵ You must remain at the entrance to the tent of meeting day and night for seven days and keep the LORD's charge so that you will not die, for this is what I was commanded." ³⁶ So Aaron and his sons did everything the LORD had commanded through Moses.

The Priestly Ministry Inaugurated

9 On the eighth day Moses summoned Aaron, his sons, and the elders of Israel. ² He said to Aaron, "Take a young bull for a sin^C

offering and a ram for a burnt offering, both without blemish, and present them before the LORD. ³ And tell the Israelites:^D Take a male goat for a sin offering; a calf and a lamb, male yearlings without blemish, for a burnt offering; ⁴ an ox and a ram for a fellowship offering to sacrifice before the LORD; and a grain offering mixed with oil. For today the LORD is going to appear to you."

⁵ They brought what Moses had commanded to the front of the tent of meeting, and the whole community came forward and stood before the LORD. ⁶ Moses said, "This is what the LORD commanded you to do, that the glory of the LORD may appear to you." ⁷ Then Moses said to Aaron, "Approach the altar and sacrifice your sin offering and your burnt offering; make atonement for yourself and the people.^E Sacrifice the people's offering and make atonement for them, as the LORD commanded."

⁸ So Aaron approached the altar and slaughtered the calf as a sin offering for himself. ⁹ Aaron's sons brought the blood to him, and he dipped his finger in the blood and applied it to the horns of the altar. He poured out the blood at the base of the altar. ¹⁰ He burned the fat, the kidneys, and the fatty lobe of the liver from the sin offering on the altar, as the LORD had commanded Moses. ¹¹ He burned the flesh and the hide outside the camp.

¹² Then he slaughtered the burnt offering. Aaron's sons brought him the blood, and he splattered it on all sides of the altar. ¹³ They brought him the burnt offering piece by piece, along with the head, and he burned them on the altar. ¹⁴ He washed the entrails and the legs and burned them with the burnt offering on the altar.

¹⁵ Aaron presented the people's offering. He took the male goat for the people's sin offering, slaughtered it, and made a sin offering with it as he did before. ¹⁶ He presented the burnt offering and sacrificed it according to the regulation. ¹⁷ Next he presented the grain offering,

---

^A 8:31 LXX, Syr, Tg read was commanded; Ex 29:31-32   ^B 8:33 Lit because he will fill your hands for seven days   ^C 9:2 Or purification   ^D 9:3 Sam, LXX read elders of Israel   ^E 9:7 LXX reads and your household

---

8:30 The Hebrew term for **consecrated** (*qaddesh*) refers to select persons, places, or things that were designated exclusively for the Lord's service (Ex 29:21; Heb 10:22). **8:31–32** The **ordination** meal was also public and was consumed by the priests to indicate the divine approval of their offerings and to symbolize their fellowship with the Lord. **8:33–36** The number **seven** symbolized the completion of the ritual's purpose. Since the ordination rite was about consecration, the priests could not leave the sacred grounds during the ordination week. **9:1–24** Verses 6 and 23 are the only ones in Leviticus that include the word **glory**. The call to worship (vv. 1–6) was followed by the ritual cleansing of the priests (vv. 7–14) and

of the people (vv. 15–21). The conclusion was the act of worship (vv. 22–24). **9:1** On the **eighth day** after the seven days of ordination (8:33; Ex 29:35), the divine call to worship began a new creative act. All the events of this first communal service occurred on this one day. **9:2** Aaron and his sons had to present a **sin offering** (4:1–5:13) and a **burnt offering** (1:3–17), although they had undergone seven days of consecration. This demonstrated their constant need for atonement before they officiated as mediators. **9:3–5** Four of the five offerings described in chaps. 1–7 were called for; the exception, the guilt offering, involved restitution and was a private, individual ceremony. The word

appear (Hb *ra'ah*) occurs three times (vv. 4,6,23); the "appearance" was a visible manifestation of the presence of the Lord. This theophany, an outward manifestation of the invisible God, involved a light or fire (Ex 3:2). The fiery presence of the Lord was an echo of God's coming to Moses at Sinai (Ex 19:18), making the portable tent another "Sinai." **9:8–11** When Aaron went **outside the camp**, this was the first time he had left the sanctuary since his seven-day ordination. The incineration of the sacrificial animal demonstrated that the officiating priest could not benefit from the offering made for his own sins (8:17). **9:15–16** By offering a **male goat** in accordance with the **regulation** of the sin offering

took a handful of it, and burned it on the altar in addition to the morning burnt offering. [18] Finally, he slaughtered the ox and the ram as the people's fellowship sacrifice. Aaron's sons brought him the blood, and he splattered it on all sides of the altar. [19] They also brought the fat portions from the ox and the ram — the fat tail, the fat surrounding the entrails, the kidneys, and the fatty lobe of the liver — [20] and placed these on the breasts. Aaron burned the fat portions on the altar, [21] but he presented the breasts and the right thigh as a presentation offering before the LORD, as Moses had commanded.[A]

[22] Aaron lifted up his hands toward the people and blessed them. He came down after sacrificing the sin offering, the burnt offering, and the fellowship offering. [23] Moses and Aaron then entered the tent of meeting. When they came out, they blessed the people, and the glory of the LORD appeared to all the people. [24] Fire came from the LORD and consumed the burnt offering and the fat portions on the altar. And when all the people saw it, they shouted and fell facedown.

Nadab and Abihu

10 Aaron's sons Nadab and Abihu each took his own firepan, put fire in it, placed incense on it, and presented unauthorized fire before the LORD, which he had not commanded them to do. [2] Then fire came from the LORD and consumed them, and they died

before the LORD. [3] Moses said to Aaron, "This is what the LORD has spoken:

I will demonstrate my holiness[B]
to those who are near me,
and I will reveal my glory[C]
before all the people."

And Aaron remained silent.

[4] Moses summoned Mishael and Elzaphan, sons of Aaron's uncle Uzziel, and said to them, "Come here and carry your relatives away from the front of the sanctuary to a place outside the camp." [5] So they came forward and carried them in their tunics outside the camp, as Moses had said.

[6] Then Moses said to Aaron and his sons Eleazar and Ithamar, "Do not let your hair hang loose and do not tear your clothes, or else you will die, and the LORD will become angry with the whole community. However, your brothers, the whole house of Israel, may weep over the fire that the LORD caused. [7] You must not go outside the entrance to the tent of meeting or you will die, for the LORD's anointing oil is on you." So they did as Moses said.

Regulations for Priests

[8] The LORD spoke to Aaron: [9] "You and your sons are not to drink wine or beer when you enter the tent of meeting, or else you will die; this is a permanent statute throughout your generations. [10] You must distinguish between the holy and the common, and the clean and the

[A]9:21 Some Hb mss, LXX, Sam read as the LORD commanded Moses   [B]10:3 Or will be treated as holy   [C]10:3 Or will be glorified

for a leader, both the elders, and by proxy, the entire community were represented by the animal (4:22–23).
9:17–21 The priests continued to represent the entire community by carrying out the **grain** and **fellowship** offerings that were typically offered by an individual Israelite.
9:22 When Aaron **lifted up his hands**, it showed that he invoked the Lord (1Kg 8:22; Ps 28:2).
9:23 The entrance into **the tent** by Moses and Aaron confirmed the legitimacy of the newly ordained Aaron, who would enter the holy place every day from then on (Ex 29:42–44; 30:7–8).
9:24 The fiery blast probably came out of the tent from the most holy place and incinerated the remains of the smoldering offerings. The response of the people exhibited their joy and humility (cp. 2Ch 7:1–3). **Shouted** (Hb *ranan*) means to give a ringing cry aloud (Jr 31:7), and **fell facedown** (Hb *naphal*) also describes later reactions to the fiery demonstrations of the Lord (Jdg 13:20; 2Ch 7:3; cp. Nm 16:22; 20:6; Mt 17:6).
10:1 Nadab was the firstborn of Aaron, and presumably **Abihu** was his second born (Ex 6:23). The location **before the LORD** may refer to the bronze altar in the courtyard (1:5) or inside the tent in the holy place (4:4). The word **unauthorized** (Hb *zarah*) translates the adjective "strange, foreign," meaning that the fire came from some place other than the altar of the sanctuary (16:12; Nm 16:46). The

crime of Aaron's sons was not the incense (Ex 30:9) but the fire that came from some place other than the legitimate source.
10:2 The phrase **fire came from the LORD and consumed** is the same Hebrew expression as that in 9:24 (cp. Nm 16:35) in which the fire that consumed the offerings on the altar came from the Lord himself (the most holy place).
10:3 God's immediate lethal response displayed his **holiness to those who are near me**, the officiating priests. The incident especially illustrates the failure of the priests to distinguish between the "holy" and the "common" (v. 10).
10:4–5 Mishael and **Elzaphan** were cousins of Aaron and Moses (Ex 6:16–22), making them Levites—and thus responsible for the purity of the sanctuary—but not priests. They could remove the bodies of Nadab and Abihu without offending God (Nm 3:5–10; 18:2–6).
10:6 Eleazar and **Ithamar** (Ex 28:1) replaced their deceased brothers (Nm 3:4), and Eleazar later succeeded Aaron as high priest (Dt 10:6). Eleazar's descendant Zadok ultimately displaced the priestly family of Abiathar, a descendant of Ithamar (1Kg 2:27,35). Disheveled **hair** and torn **clothes** (Gn 37:34) were part of mourning rites (Lv 13:45; 21:10). By desecrating the holy sanctuary through mourning, the priests risked death and bringing guilt on the **whole community**. If the priests compromised the holiness of God

and were disqualified to make atonement, the community would not be protected from divine wrath. Although Aaron and his sons could not mourn, the community (**brothers**) could fulfill their obligation.
10:7 Priests bearing holy **anointing oil** (cp. 8:12) would defile themselves if they left the holy precinct for mourning rites during the time of their consecration (21:10–12).
10:8 Only here in Leviticus does Aaron alone receive a direct word from the Lord (cp. Ex 4:27; Nm 18:1,8). God usually addressed Aaron and Moses as a team (Lv 13:1).
10:9 During their performance of priestly functions, the priests were not allowed to drink **wine or beer** so they would be clear-headed in making judgments and carrying out their duties in the sanctuary (v. 10).
10:10 The assignment for the priests was cultic—distinguishing between the holy and the ordinary—and pedagogical—instructing the congregation in cultic matters (Ezk 22:26). **Distinguish** (from Hb *badal*; "to separate, divide") meant differentiating the distinctive from the commonplace, such as edible animals from prohibited animals (11:47; 20:25). The **holy** (Hb *qodesh*) versus the **common** (Hb *chol*) refers to anything or anyone that was dedicated to the Lord and his service as opposed to that which was for normal use. **Clean** (Hb *tahor*) and **unclean** (Hb *tame'*) refer to matters pertaining to the physical existence of the people, especially foods (chap. 11; Dt 14) and persons (Lv 12–15; Nm 5:2–4).

unclean, [11] and teach the Israelites all the statutes that the LORD has given to them through Moses."

[12] Moses spoke to Aaron and his remaining sons, Eleazar and Ithamar: "Take the grain offering that is left over from the food offerings to the LORD, and eat it prepared without yeast beside the altar, because it is especially holy. [13] You must eat it in a holy place because it is your portion[A] and your sons' from the food offerings to the LORD, for this is what I was commanded. [14] But you and your sons and your daughters may eat the breast of the presentation offering and the thigh of the contribution in any ceremonially clean place, because these portions have been assigned to you and your children from the Israelites' fellowship sacrifices. [15] They are to bring the thigh of the contribution and the breast of the presentation offering, together with the food offerings of the fat portions, to present as a presentation offering before the LORD. It will belong permanently to you and your children, as the LORD commanded."

[16] Then Moses inquired carefully about the male goat of the sin offering, but it had already been burned up. He was angry with Eleazar and Ithamar, Aaron's surviving sons, and asked, [17] "Why didn't you eat the sin offering in the sanctuary area? For it is especially holy, and he has assigned it to you to take away the guilt of the community and make atonement for them before the LORD. [18] Since its blood was not brought inside the sanctuary, you should have eaten it in the sanctuary area, as I commanded."

[19] But Aaron replied to Moses, "See, today they presented their sin offering and their burnt offering before the LORD. Since these things have happened to me, if I had eaten the sin offering today, would it have been acceptable in the LORD's sight?" [20] When Moses heard this, it was acceptable to him.[B]

Clean and Unclean Land Animals

11 The LORD spoke to Moses and Aaron: [2] "Tell the Israelites: You may eat all these kinds of land animals. [3] You may eat any animal with divided hooves and that chews the cud. [4] But among the ones that chew the cud or have divided hooves you are not to eat these:

camels, though they chew the cud, do not have divided hooves — they are unclean for you;
[5] hyraxes, though they chew the cud, do not have hooves — they are unclean for you;
[6] hares, though they chew the cud, do not have hooves — they are unclean for you;
[7] pigs, though they have divided hooves, do not chew the cud — they are unclean for you.
[8] Do not eat any of their meat or touch their carcasses — they are unclean for you.

Clean and Unclean Aquatic Animals

[9] "This is what you may eat from all that is in the water: You may eat everything in the water that has fins and scales, whether in the seas or streams. [10] But these are to be abhorrent to you: everything in the seas or streams that does not have fins and scales among all the swarming things and other living creatures in the water. [11] They are to remain abhorrent to you; you must not eat any of their meat, and you must abhor their carcasses. [12] Everything in the water that does not have fins and scales will be abhorrent to you.

Unclean Birds

[13] "You are to abhor these birds. They must not be eaten because they are abhorrent:
eagles,[C] bearded vultures,
Egyptian vultures,[D] [14] kites,[E]
any kind of falcon,[F]

[A]10:13 Or statute   [B]10:20 Lit acceptable in his sight   [C]11:13 Or griffon-vultures   [D]11:13 Or ospreys, or bearded vultures
[E]11:14 Or hawks   [F]11:14 Or buzzards, or hawks

10:11 The term **teach** (Hb yarah) means "to instruct," but it can also mean "to determine" (14:57). The instruction was intended to enable the people to discern the proper conduct in cultic matters and everyday activities. The Levites in general and the priests in particular were to direct the people in the ways commanded by the Lord (Dt 17:9–11; 33:10; Ezk 44:23–24).
10:16–18 Moses complained that Aaron's sons had failed to eat the consecration portions of the **sin offering** as prescribed by the Lord. By their failure to perform the proper ritual ceremony, the guilt of the community remained. The Hebrew phrase translated **inquired carefully** (darosh darash) reflects the urgency of Moses's concern for proper observance.
10:19 Aaron had to determine whether the desecration by Nadab and Abihu made the **sin offering** portions inappropriate for

priestly consumption. Rather than run the risk of defiling the sanctuary further, Aaron chose to burn up the entire goat.
10:20 A wordplay on **acceptable** (Hb yatav), which describes the divine approval in v. 19, also describes Moses's acceptance of the explanation; Moses accepted the determination of Aaron according to v. 10.
11:1–47 This chapter includes two separate listings of clean and unclean creatures (vv. 1–23; vv. 41–45); the identity of many of the animals is uncertain. If the food laws were observed by the Israelites, the holiness of God would extend from the sanctuary to their homes, ensuring his continued presence. Although there may have been some hygienic benefit derived from keeping the food laws, the prohibited creatures were not consistently unhealthy for human consumption. More likely, these laws reflected the distinctive kinds at creation (Gn 1:26) and

thereby taught the Israelites that there was an ordained pattern of conformity.
The food laws that once separated the Israelites and the nations are not binding on modern believers (Ac 10:11–16; Col 2:16).
11:1 The Lord included **Aaron** as the recipient of the purity instructions (chaps. 11–15) since they were primarily a priestly responsibility (10:10–11; 13:1; 14:33; 15:1).
11:3 Some mammals are "ruminants," from Latin ruminare, "to chew again." Such animals have four stomachs and regurgitate into the mouth the fermented food in the first stomach to chew it again. Ruminants include cattle, goats, giraffes, yaks, deer, antelope, and some in the kangaroo family.
11:9–12 The unacceptable sea creatures were designated **abhorrent** (Hb sheqets) three times (vv. 10–12).
11:13–19 These birds may have been outlawed because they are scavengers.

¹⁵ every kind of raven, ¹⁶ ostriches,^A short-eared owls, gulls,^B any kind of hawk, ¹⁷ little^c owls, cormorants,^D long-eared owls,^E ¹⁸ barn^F owls, eagle owls,^G ospreys, ¹⁹ storks,^H any kind of heron,^I hoopoes, and bats.

Clean and Unclean Flying Insects

²⁰ "All winged insects that walk on all fours are to be abhorrent to you. ²¹ But you may eat these kinds of all the winged insects that walk on all fours: those that have jointed legs above their feet for hopping on the ground. ²² You may eat these:

any kind of locust, katydid, cricket, and grasshopper.

²³ All other winged insects that have four feet are to be abhorrent to you.

Purification after Touching Dead Animals

²⁴ "These will make you unclean. Whoever touches their carcasses will be unclean until evening, ²⁵ and whoever carries any of their carcasses is to wash his clothes and will be unclean until evening. ²⁶ All animals that have hooves but do not have a divided hoof and do not chew the cud are unclean for you. Whoever touches them becomes unclean. ²⁷ All the four-footed animals that walk on their paws are unclean for you. Whoever touches their carcasses will be unclean until evening, ²⁸ and anyone who carries their carcasses is to wash his clothes and will be unclean until evening. They are unclean for you.

²⁹ "These creatures that swarm on the ground are unclean for you:

weasels,^J mice, any kind of large lizard,^K ³⁰ geckos, monitor lizards,^L common lizards,^M skinks,^N and chameleons.^O

³¹ These are unclean for you among all the swarming creatures. Whoever touches them when they are dead will be unclean until

evening. ³² When any one of them dies and falls on anything it becomes unclean — any item of wood, clothing, leather, sackcloth, or any implement used for work. It is to be rinsed with water and will remain unclean until evening; then it will be clean. ³³ If any of them falls into any clay pot, everything in it will become unclean; you are to break it. ³⁴ Any edible food coming into contact with that unclean water will become unclean, and any drinkable liquid in any container will become unclean. ³⁵ Anything one of their carcasses falls on will become unclean. If it is an oven or stove, it is to be smashed; it is unclean and will remain unclean for you. ³⁶ A spring or cistern containing water will remain clean, but someone who touches a carcass in it will become unclean. ³⁷ If one of their carcasses falls on any seed that is to be sown, it is clean; ³⁸ but if water has been put on the seed and one of their carcasses falls on it, it is unclean for you.

³⁹ "If one of the animals that you use for food dies, anyone who touches its carcass will be unclean until evening. ⁴⁰ Anyone who eats some of its carcass is to wash his clothes and will be unclean until evening. Anyone who carries its carcass must wash his clothes and will be unclean until evening.

Unclean Swarming Creatures

⁴¹ "All the creatures that swarm on the earth are abhorrent; they must not be eaten. ⁴² Do not eat any of the creatures that swarm on the earth, anything that moves on its belly or walks on all fours or on many feet,^P for they are abhorrent. ⁴³ Do not become contaminated by any creature that swarms; do not become unclean or defiled by them. ⁴⁴ For I am the LORD your God, so you must consecrate yourselves and be holy because I am holy. Do not defile yourselves by any swarming creature that crawls on the ground. ⁴⁵ For I am the LORD, who brought you up from the land of Egypt to be your God, so you must be holy because I am holy.

⁴⁶ "This is the law concerning animals, birds, all living creatures that move in the water, and all creatures that swarm on the ground, ⁴⁷ in

---

^A11:16 Or *eagle owls*   ^B11:16 Or *long-eared owls*   ^C11:17 Or *tawny*   ^D11:17 Or *pelicans*   ^E11:17 Or *ibis*   ^F11:18 Or *little*   ^G11:18 Or *pelicans*, or *horned owls*   ^H11:19 Or *herons*   ^I11:19 Or *cormorants*, or *hawks*   ^J11:29 Or *mole rats*, or *rats*   ^K11:29 Or *of thorntailed*, or *dabb lizard*, or *of crocodile*   ^L11:30 Or *spotted lizards*, or *chameleons*   ^M11:30 Or *geckos*, or *newts*, or *salamanders*   ^N11:30 Or *sand lizards*, or *newts*, or *snails*   ^O11:30 Or *salamanders*, or *moles*   ^P11:42 Lit *fours, to anything multiplying pairs of feet*

11:24–25 Defilement occurred by touching **carcasses** or by transporting them. When transporting them, the clothing of the person was defiled by contact and required laundering. All corpses conveyed uncleanness through touch (22:4; Nm 5:2). For consecrated persons, just being in the presence of a dead body resulted in defilement (Lv 21:11; Nm 6:6; Hg 2:13). The duration of uncleanness stretched until sunset, which concluded a day (Dt 22:26; Jos 8:29).

11:27 Four-footed animals that walked on **paws** (lit "palms"), such as dogs and cats, were considered unclean. **11:29–38 Carcasses** of creatures that **swarm on the ground** (such as insects) conveyed defilement through direct contact or indirectly to persons who handled inanimate things which had already come into contact with the dead creatures. Since a **clay pot** absorbed the liquid polluted by a carcass, it must be thrown away; food or drink touched secondarily by the contaminated water in the

pot was unclean. Two exceptions pertained to water: the water of a reservoir from which a carcass was retrieved remained clean, probably because of the ritual significance of water for purification; and **seed** already germinated by **water** was **unclean**. **11:39–40 Animals** that had been killed by wild animals or that had died by natural means—that is, not slaughtered for food— could be eaten, but they still conveyed uncleanness (17:15; they were prohibited for a priest, 22:8).

order to distinguish between the unclean and the clean, between the animals that may be eaten and those that may not be eaten."

Purification after Childbirth

12 The LORD spoke to Moses: [2] "Tell the Israelites: When a woman becomes pregnant and gives birth to a male child, she will be unclean seven days, as she is during the days of her menstrual impurity. [3] The flesh of his foreskin must be circumcised on the eighth day. [4] She will continue in purification from her bleeding for thirty-three days. She must not touch any holy thing or go into the sanctuary until completing her days of purification. [5] But if she gives birth to a female child, she will be unclean for two weeks as she is during her menstrual impurity. She will continue in purification from her bleeding for sixty-six days.

[6] "When her days of purification are complete, whether for a son or daughter, she is to bring to the priest at the entrance to the tent of meeting a year-old male lamb for a burnt offering, and a young pigeon or a turtledove for a sin[A] offering. [7] He will present them before the LORD and make atonement on her behalf; she will be clean from her discharge of blood. This is the law for a woman giving birth, whether to a male or female. [8] But if she doesn't have sufficient means[B] for a sheep, she may take two turtledoves or two young pigeons, one for a burnt offering and the other for a sin offering. Then the priest will make atonement on her behalf, and she will be clean."

Skin Diseases

13 The LORD spoke to Moses and Aaron: [2] "When a person has a swelling,[c] scab,[D] or spot on the skin of his body, and it may be a serious disease on the skin of his body, he is to be brought to the priest Aaron or to one of his sons, the priests. [3] The priest will examine the sore on the skin of his body. If the hair in the sore has turned white and the sore appears to be deeper than the skin of his body, it is in fact a serious skin disease. After the priest examines him, he must pronounce him unclean. [4] But if the spot on the skin of his body is white and does not appear to be deeper than the skin, and the hair in it has not turned white, the priest will quarantine the stricken person for seven days. [5] The priest will then reexamine him on the seventh day. If he sees that the sore remains unchanged and has not spread on the skin, the priest will quarantine him for another seven days. [6] The priest will examine him again on the seventh day. If the sore has faded and has not spread on the skin, the priest is to pronounce him clean; it is a scab. The person is to wash his clothes and will become clean. [7] But if the scab spreads further on his skin after he has presented himself to the priest for his cleansing, he is to present himself again to the priest. [8] The priest will examine him, and if the scab has spread on the skin, then the priest must pronounce him unclean; he has a serious skin disease.

[9] "When a case of serious skin disease may have developed on a person, he is to be brought to the priest. [10] The priest will examine him. If there is a white swelling on the skin that has turned the hair white, and there is a patch of raw flesh in the swelling, [11] it is a chronic serious disease on the skin of his body, and the priest must pronounce him unclean. He need not quarantine him, for he is unclean. [12] But if the skin disease breaks out all over the skin so that it covers all the skin of the stricken person from his head to his feet so far as the priest can see, [13] the priest will look, and if the skin disease has covered his entire body, he is to pronounce the stricken person clean. Since

---

[A] 12:6 Or *purification*, also in v. 8   [B] 12:8 Lit *if her hand cannot obtain what is sufficient*   [C] 13:2 Or *discoloration*   [D] 13:2 Or *rash*, or *eruption*

12:1–8 The newborn child of a mother was not impure, since the male child was circumcised on the eighth day while the mother was in isolation. That circumcision was a part of her duty showed the mother's valued contribution to the community. She was the vehicle of God's blessing of children within Israel's covenant with God (Gn 17). Children were considered a gift from God; the woman was not ritually defiled when she was pregnant. The impurity resulted from blood and fluids that are a part of the birth process (Lv 12:4–5,7). Men also underwent separation and ritual reintegration due to bodily discharges (15:2–18).
12:2 Although the text does not say that anyone who came into contact with a woman after childbirth became unclean, the parallel instructions about menstruation and any other discharge of blood made this explicit (15:25–30). Her domestic duties would defile the home and members of her family through touch.

12:5 The rationale for doubling the period of isolation for the birth of a **female child** was not a matter of gender bias since the purification rite was the same for the male child. Possibly the circumstance of bearing a future mother doubled the period of time.
12:6–7 The **sin offering** is better understood as a "purification offering," since no sin was committed by the mother or child. The mother was in a state of ritual uncleanness because of the **discharge of blood**.
13:2 The Hebrew word for "skin disease" (*tsara'ath*) was translated into the Greek as *lepra* and transliterated as such into Latin. Thus most English translations render the word as "leprosy." The Hebrew word, however, is a generic term that refers to changes in the surface of the human skin and is best translated as **a serious disease on the skin**; it can also indicate fungus or mildew (v. 47; 14:34). During the postexilic period, rabbis identified seventy-two types of skin disease.

13:3–8 Two different types of problems are described here. One can be classified as minor because the disorder was not severe and the isolation was not long, but in the second type, the infinitive absolute in v. 7 indicates that the infection had spread drastically. The ritual period of **seven days** is predominant in Leviticus (8:33; 12:2; 14:8; 15:13,28, 23:6; 25:4). The number *seven* and its derivatives occur 176 times in Leviticus. It symbolizes fullness, perfection, or completion. Later rabbis suggested that the person being isolated was banished outside the camp or city, while others suggested that it was in special quarters, as in the case of King Uzziah (1Kg 15:5; 2Ch 26:21).
13:9,11,15 The **chronic serious disease on the skin** involved the presence of raw flesh rendering a person unclean. The Hebrew word *tsara'ath* appears thirty-five times in the OT, but only six times outside of Leviticus (Dt 24:8; 2Kg 5:3,6–7,27; 2Ch 26:19). A person is pronounced **unclean** seven times in chap. 13 (vv. 11,15,36,44,46,51,55).

he has turned totally white, he is clean. ¹⁴ But whenever raw flesh appears on him, he will be unclean. ¹⁵ When the priest examines the raw flesh, he must pronounce him unclean. Raw flesh is unclean; this is a serious skin disease. ¹⁶ But if the raw flesh changesᴬ andᴮ turns white, he is to go to the priest. ¹⁷ The priest will examine him, and if the sore has turned white, the priest must pronounce the stricken person clean; he is clean.

¹⁸ "When a boil appears on the skin of someone's body and it heals, ¹⁹ and a white swelling or a reddish-white spot develops where the boil was, the person is to present himself to the priest. ²⁰ The priest will make an examination, and if the spot seems to be beneath the skin and the hair in it has turned white, the priest must pronounce him unclean; it is a case of serious skin disease that has broken out in the boil. ²¹ But when the priest examines it, if there is no white hair in it, and it is not beneath the skin but is faded, the priest will quarantine him seven days. ²² If it spreads further on the skin, the priest must pronounce him unclean; it is in fact a disease. ²³ But if the spot remains where it is and does not spread, it is only the scar from the boil. The priest is to pronounce him clean.

²⁴ "When there is a burn on the skin of one's body produced by fire, and the patch made raw by the burn becomes reddish-white or white, ²⁵ the priest is to examine it. If the hair in the spot has turned white and the spot appears to be deeper than the skin, it is a serious skin disease that has broken out in the burn. The priest must pronounce him unclean; it is a serious skin disease. ²⁶ But when the priest examines it, if there is no white hair in the spot and it is not beneath the skin but is faded, the priest will quarantine him seven days. ²⁷ The priest will reexamine him on the seventh day. If it has spread further on the skin, the priest must pronounce him unclean; it is in fact a case of serious skin disease. ²⁸ But if the spot has remained where it was and has not spread on the skin but is faded, it is the swelling from the burn. The priest is to pronounce him clean, for it is only the scar from the burn.

²⁹ "When a man or woman has a condition on the head or chin, ³⁰ the priest is to examine the condition. If it appears to be deeper than the skin, and the hair in it is yellow and sparse, the priest must pronounce the person unclean. It is a scaly outbreak, a serious skin disease of the head or chin. ³¹ When the priest examines the scaly condition, if it does not appear to be deeper than the skin, and there is no black hair in it, the priest will quarantine the person with the scaly condition for seven days. ³² The priest will reexamine the condition on the seventh day. If the scaly outbreak has not spread and there is no yellow hair in it and it does not appear to be deeper than the skin, ³³ the person is to shave himself but not shave the scaly area. Then the priest will quarantine the person who has the scaly outbreak for another seven days. ³⁴ The priest will examine the scaly outbreak on the seventh day, and if it has not spread on the skin and does not appear to be deeper than the skin, the priest is to pronounce the person clean. He is to wash his clothes, and he will be clean. ³⁵ But if the scaly outbreak spreads further on the skin after his cleansing, ³⁶ the priest is to examine the person. If the scaly outbreak has spread on the skin, the priest does not need to look for yellow hair; the person is unclean. ³⁷ But if as far as he can see, the scaly outbreak remains unchanged and black hair has grown in it, then it has healed; he is clean. The priest is to pronounce the person clean.

³⁸ "When a man or a woman has white spots on the skin of the body, ³⁹ the priest is to make an examination. If the spots on the skin of the body are dull white, it is only a rashᶜ that has broken out on the skin; the person is clean.

⁴⁰ "If a man loses the hair of his head, he is bald, but he is clean. ⁴¹ Or if he loses the hair at his hairline, he is bald on his forehead, but he is clean. ⁴² But if there is a reddish-white condition on the bald head or forehead, it is a serious skin disease breaking out on his head or forehead. ⁴³ The priest is to examine him, and if the swelling of the condition on his bald head or forehead is reddish-white, like the appearance of a serious skin disease on his body, ⁴⁴ the man is afflicted with a serious skin disease; he is unclean. The priest must pronounce him unclean; the infection is on his head.

⁴⁵ "The person who has a case of serious skin disease is to have his clothes torn and his hair hanging loose, and he must cover his mouth and cry out, 'Unclean, unclean!' ⁴⁶ He will remain unclean as long as he has the disease; he is unclean. He must live alone in a place outside the camp.

Contaminated Fabrics

⁴⁷ "If a fabric is contaminated with mildew — in wool or linen fabric, ⁴⁸ in the warp or weft of

ᴬ13:16 Or recedes ᴮ13:16 Or flesh again ᶜ13:39 Hb obscure

13:30 The term scaly outbreak appears only in this pericope of the Bible (vv. 30–37; 14:54). It refers to a skin disease that appeared on a person's head or chin. 13:45–46 The person rendered unclean was relegated to life outside the community until healed. The torn . . . clothes were a sign of mourning, while the crying out was a warning to those who were ceremonially clean. This practice was still observed during Jesus's time, when ten men with serious skin diseases stood at a distance from the community and were asked by Jesus to show themselves to the priest after he had healed them (Lk 17:11–14). 13:47–59 As with contagious skin diseases, so also with mildew or fungus; no spreadable contamination of fabric or leather was permitted to undermine the ceremonial cleanliness of the community.

linen or wool, or in leather or anything made of leather — ⁴⁹ and if the contamination is green or red in the fabric, the leather, the warp, the weft, or any leather article, it is a mildew contamination and is to be shown to the priest. ⁵⁰ The priest is to examine the contamination and quarantine the contaminated fabric for seven days. ⁵¹ The priest is to reexamine the contamination on the seventh day. If it has spread in the fabric, the warp, the weft, or the leather, regardless of how it is used, the contamination is harmful mildew; it is unclean. ⁵² He is to burn the fabric, the warp or weft in wool or linen, or any leather article, which is contaminated. Since it is harmful mildew it must be burned.

⁵³ "When the priest examines it, if the contamination has not spread in the fabric, the warp or weft, or any leather article, ⁵⁴ the priest is to order whatever is contaminated to be washed and quarantined for another seven days. ⁵⁵ After it has been washed, the priest is to reexamine the contamination. If the appearance of the contaminated article has not changed, it is unclean. Even though the contamination has not spread, you must burn the fabric. It is a fungus^A on the front or back of the fabric.

⁵⁶ "If the priest examines it, and the contamination has faded after it has been washed, he is to cut the contaminated section out of the fabric, the leather, or the warp or weft. ⁵⁷ But if it reappears in the fabric, the warp or weft, or any leather article, it has broken out again. You must burn whatever is contaminated. ⁵⁸ But if the contamination disappears from the fabric, the warp or weft, or any leather article, which have been washed, it is to be washed again, and it will be clean.

⁵⁹ "This is the law concerning a mildew contamination in wool or linen fabric, warp or weft, or any leather article, in order to pronounce it clean or unclean."

Cleansing of Skin Diseases

14 The LORD spoke to Moses: ² "This is the law concerning the person afflicted with a skin disease on the day of his cleansing.

He is to be brought to the priest, ³ who will go outside the camp and examine him. If the skin disease has disappeared from the afflicted person,^B ⁴ the priest will order that two live clean birds, cedar wood, scarlet yarn, and hyssop be brought for the one who is to be cleansed. ⁵ Then the priest will order that one of the birds be slaughtered over fresh water in a clay pot. ⁶ He is to take the live bird together with the cedar wood, scarlet yarn, and hyssop, and dip them all into the blood of the bird that was slaughtered over the fresh water. ⁷ He will then sprinkle the blood seven times on the one who is to be cleansed from the skin disease. He is to pronounce him clean and release the live bird over the open countryside. ⁸ The one who is to be cleansed must wash his clothes, shave off all his hair, and bathe with water; he is clean. Afterward he may enter the camp, but he must remain outside his tent for seven days. ⁹ He is to shave off all his hair again on the seventh day: his head, his beard, his eyebrows, and the rest of his hair. He is to wash his clothes and bathe himself with water; he is clean.

¹⁰ "On the eighth day he must take two unblemished male lambs, an unblemished year-old ewe lamb, a grain offering of six quarts^C of fine flour mixed with olive oil, and one-third of a quart^D of olive oil. ¹¹ The priest who performs the cleansing will place the person who is to be cleansed, together with these offerings, before the LORD at the entrance to the tent of meeting. ¹² The priest is to take one male lamb and present it as a guilt offering, along with the one-third quart of olive oil, and he will present them as a presentation offering before the LORD. ¹³ He is to slaughter the male lamb at the place in the sanctuary area where the sin offering and burnt offering are slaughtered, for like the sin offering, the guilt offering belongs to the priest; it is especially holy. ¹⁴ The priest is to take some of the blood from the guilt offering and put it on the lobe of the right ear of the one to be cleansed, on the thumb of his right hand, and on the big toe of his right foot. ¹⁵ Then the priest will take some of the one-third quart of olive oil and pour it into his left palm. ¹⁶ The priest will dip his right finger into

---

^A13:55 Hb obscure   ^B14:3 Lit *the person afflicted with skin disease*   ^C14:10 Lit *three-tenths*; probably three-tenths of an ephah   ^D14:10 Lit *one log*, also in vv. 12,15,21,24

14:1–32 God, in his grace, provided for the restoration of the person rendered unclean by a skin disease. The priests did not cure the disease and helped with the religious rituals subsequent to a person's healing. Chapter 14 points to the grace of God, who made provision for the people affected by a skin disease to return to the community of the faithful. **14:3** The examination of the person afflicted with a skin disease had to be done **outside the camp** in case the disease had not healed completely. People or things rendered unclean had to be taken outside the camp—a

place where ashes were dumped (4:12,21; 6:11; 8:17; 9:11; 16:27), corpses were buried (10:4–5), illegitimate sacrifices were offered (17:3), blasphemers were executed (24:14,23), and people with skin diseases were banished. **14:4** Although the person was healed, he had to go through a cleansing ritual that involved animal sacrifice. The **scarlet yarn** was a woolen yarn colored with a crimson-scarlet dye made from the kermes or cochineal scale insects. The plant known as **hyssop** had a good absorbing quality, was abundant in Israel, and was associated with purification (Ps 51:7).

14:11–13 A **guilt offering** was necessary because the person afflicted was absent from the community and was separated from God by not being allowed in the **sanctuary**. This offering was unique in that it was the only blood sacrifice in which the entire animal had to undergo the presentation rite (see note at 7:30–31). Because the blood of the lamb was crucial for this offering, a person could not commute this sacrifice with money (1Pt 1:19–20). **14:14** The placing of blood on the healed person's extremities symbolized that his entire being—his **ear** . . . **hand**, and **foot**—must be consecrated to God.

the oil in his left palm and sprinkle some of the oil with his finger seven times before the LORD. [17] From the oil remaining in his palm the priest will put some on the lobe of the right ear of the one to be cleansed, on the thumb of his right hand, and on the big toe of his right foot, on top of the blood of the guilt offering. [18] What is left of the oil in the priest's palm he is to put on the head of the one to be cleansed. In this way the priest will make atonement for him before the LORD. [19] The priest is to sacrifice the sin offering and make atonement for the one to be cleansed from his uncleanness. Afterward he will slaughter the burnt offering. [20] The priest is to offer the burnt offering and the grain offering on the altar. The priest will make atonement for him, and he will be clean.

[21] "But if he is poor and cannot afford these, he is to take one male lamb for a guilt offering to be presented in order to make atonement for him, along with two quarts[A] of fine flour mixed with olive oil for a grain offering, one-third of a quart of olive oil, [22] and two turtledoves or two young pigeons, whatever he can afford, one to be a sin offering and the other a burnt offering. [23] On the eighth day he is to bring these things for his cleansing to the priest at the entrance to the tent of meeting before the LORD. [24] The priest will take the male lamb for the guilt offering and the one-third quart of olive oil, and present them as a presentation offering before the LORD. [25] After he slaughters the male lamb for the guilt offering, the priest is to take some of the blood of the guilt offering and put it on the right earlobe of the one to be cleansed, on the thumb of his right hand, and on the big toe of his right foot. [26] Then the priest will pour some of the oil into his left palm. [27] With his right finger the priest will sprinkle some of the oil in his left palm seven times before the LORD. [28] The priest will also put some of the oil in his palm on the right earlobe of the one to be cleansed, on the thumb of his right hand, and on the big toe of his right foot, on the same place as the blood of the guilt offering. [29] What is left of the oil in the priest's palm he is to put on the head of the one to be cleansed to make atonement for him before the LORD. [30] He is to then sacrifice one type of what he can afford, either the turtledoves or young pigeons, [31] one as a sin offering and the other as a burnt offering, sacrificing what he can afford together with the grain offering. In this way the priest

will make atonement before the LORD for the one to be cleansed. [32] This is the law for someone who has[B] a skin disease and cannot afford the cost of his cleansing."

Cleansing of Contaminated Objects

[33] The LORD spoke to Moses and Aaron: [34] "When you enter the land of Canaan that I am giving you as a possession, and I place a mildew contamination in a house in the land you possess,[C] [35] the owner of the house is to come and tell the priest: Something like a contamination has appeared[D] in my house. [36] The priest must order them to clear the house before he enters to examine the contamination, so that nothing in the house becomes unclean. Afterward the priest will come to examine the house. [37] He will examine it, and if the contamination in the walls of the house consists of green or red indentations[E] that appear to be beneath the surface of the wall, [38] the priest is to go outside the house to its doorway and quarantine the house for seven days. [39] The priest is to return on the seventh day and examine it. If the contamination has spread on the walls of the house, [40] the priest must order that the stones with the contamination be pulled out and thrown into an unclean place outside the city. [41] He is to have the inside of the house completely scraped, and have the plaster[F] that is scraped off dumped in an unclean place outside the city. [42] Then they are to take different stones to replace the former ones and take additional plaster to replaster the house.

[43] "If the contamination reappears in the house after the stones have been pulled out, and after the house has been scraped and replastered, [44] the priest is to come and examine it. If the contamination has spread in the house, it is harmful mildew; the house is unclean. [45] It must be torn down with its stones, its beams, and all its plaster, and taken outside the city to an unclean place. [46] Whoever enters the house during any of the days the priest quarantines it will be unclean until evening. [47] Whoever lies down in the house is to wash his clothes, and whoever eats in it is to wash his clothes.

[48] "But when the priest comes and examines it, if the contamination has not spread in the house after it was replastered, he is to pronounce the house clean because the contamination has disappeared.[G] [49] He is to take two birds, cedar wood, scarlet yarn, and hyssop to

[A]14:21 Lit him, and one-tenth; probably one-tenth of an ephah   [B]14:32 Lit someone on whom there is   [C]14:34 Lit land of your possession   [D]14:35 Lit appeared to me   [E]14:37 Or eruptions; Hb obscure   [F]14:41 Lit dust, also in v. 42   [G]14:48 Lit healed

14:18–20 The priest must also bring a **burnt offering** in order to **make atonement** for the person who had been healed. The verb translated "make atonement" can mean "to wipe away," "to purge," "to purify," or "to atone for." As a result, the healed person would be

pronounced **clean** and thus forgiven, ready to enter God's presence with confidence. **14:33–53** As with mildew in fabric in 13:47– 59, **mildew** in a **house** would compromise the ceremonial cleanness of the community and therefore was not allowed. Because it

could spread, it was thoroughly eradicated (vv. 43–45). The ceremony for purifying a building with mildew was similar to that for a person with a skin disease, except that there was no guilt offering or sin offering for the building since it only had to be declared

purify the house, **50** and he is to slaughter one of the birds over a clay pot containing fresh water. **51** He will take the cedar wood, the hyssop, the scarlet yarn, and the live bird, dip them in the blood of the slaughtered bird and the fresh water, and sprinkle the house seven times. **52** He will purify the house with the blood of the bird, the fresh water, the live bird, the cedar wood, the hyssop, and the scarlet yarn. **53** Then he is to release the live bird into the open countryside outside the city. In this way he will make atonement for the house, and it will be clean.

54 "This is the law for any skin disease or mildew, for a scaly outbreak, **55** for mildew in clothing or on a house, **56** and for a swelling, scab, or spot, **57** to determine when something is unclean or clean. This is the law regarding skin disease and mildew."

Bodily Discharges

15 The LORD spoke to Moses and Aaron: **2** "Speak to the Israelites and tell them: When any man has a discharge from his member, he is unclean. **3** This is uncleanness of his discharge: Whether his member secretes the discharge or retains it, he is unclean. All the days that his member secretes or retains anything because of his discharge,^ he is unclean. **4** Any bed the man with the discharge lies on will be unclean, and any furniture he sits on will be unclean. **5** Anyone who touches his bed is to wash his clothes and bathe with water, and he will remain unclean until evening. **6** Whoever sits on furniture that the man with the discharge was sitting on is to wash his clothes and bathe with water, and he will remain unclean until evening. **7** Whoever touches the body⁸ of the man with a discharge is to wash his clothes and bathe with water, and he will remain unclean until evening. **8** If the man with the discharge spits on anyone who is clean, he is to wash his clothes and bathe with water, and he will remain unclean until evening. **9** Any saddle the man with the discharge rides on will be unclean. **10** Whoever touches anything that was under him will be unclean until evening, and whoever carries such things is to wash his clothes and bathe with water, and he will

remain unclean until evening. **11** If the man with the discharge touches anyone without first rinsing his hands in water, the person who was touched is to wash his clothes and bathe with water, and he will remain unclean until evening. **12** Any clay pot that the man with the discharge touches must be broken, while any wooden utensil is to be rinsed with water.

13 "When the man with the discharge has been cured of it, he is to count seven days for his cleansing, wash his clothes, and bathe his body in fresh water; he will be clean. **14** He must take two turtledoves or two young pigeons on the eighth day, come before the LORD at the entrance to the tent of meeting, and give them to the priest. **15** The priest is to sacrifice them, one as a sin offering and the other as a burnt offering. In this way the priest will make atonement for him before the LORD because of his discharge.

16 "When a man has an emission of semen, he is to bathe himself completely with water, and he will remain unclean until evening. **17** Any clothing or leather on which there is an emission of semen is to be washed with water, and it will remain unclean until evening. **18** If a man sleeps with a woman and has an emission of semen, both of them are to bathe with water, and they will remain unclean until evening.

19 "When a woman has a discharge, and it consists of blood from her body, she will be unclean because of her menstruation for seven days. Everyone who touches her will be unclean until evening. **20** Anything she lies on during her menstruation will become unclean, and anything she sits on will become unclean. **21** Everyone who touches her bed is to wash his clothes and bathe with water, and he will remain unclean until evening. **22** Everyone who touches any furniture she was sitting on is to wash his clothes and bathe with water, and he will remain unclean until evening. **23** If discharge is on the bed or the furniture she was sitting on, when he touches it he will be unclean until evening. **24** If a man sleeps with her, and blood from her menstruation gets on him, he will be unclean for seven days, and every bed he lies on will become unclean.

---

^**15:3** DSS, Sam, LXX; MT omits *he is unclean. All the days that his member secretes or retains anything because of his discharge* ⁸**15:7** Or *member*, also in v. 13

---

clean; it did not have to be prepared for communion with God.
15:1–3 The word **member** here is a euphemism for the male genitalia. The word **discharge** occurs only in Leviticus. It probably refers to some chronic infection in men. The adjective **unclean** is used twenty-five times in Leviticus, and it can refer to either an ethical or a religious impurity.
15:8 Spitting was a gesture of extreme contempt, and it pointed not just to the outside uncleanness but to the man's wicked heart.

15:14–15 The **sin offering** removed the impurity, while the **burnt offering** restored the man to the Israelite community. The animals needed for these offerings are the least costly, **two turtledoves or two young pigeons** (1:14; 5:11; 12:8; 14:22,30; Lk 2:24).
15:16–18 The phrase **emission of semen** can refer to a nocturnal ejaculation (vv. 16–17) as well as ejaculation in sexual intercourse (v. 18). This passage does not suggest that God considered sex sinful. Rather, God gave laws to ensure that sex must not be part of the sanctuary rites. These laws were a

clear contrast with the ancient Near Eastern religions that portrayed gods and goddesses engaging in sexual relations and their followers imitating them as part of pagan temple worship.
15:19 The word **body** here (the same as "member" in vv. 1–3) is a euphemism for the female genitalia.
15:20 The idea that **menstruation** rendered a woman unclean was a common conception throughout the ancient Near East. Both the Egyptians and the Persians thought of menstruation as cultic uncleanness.

²⁵ "When a woman has a discharge of her blood for many days, though it is not the time of her menstruation, or if she has a discharge beyond her period, she will be unclean all the days of her unclean discharge, as she is during the days of her menstruation. ²⁶ Any bed she lies on during the days of her discharge will be like her bed during menstrual impurity; any furniture she sits on will be unclean as in her menstrual period. ²⁷ Everyone who touches them will be unclean; he must wash his clothes and bathe with water, and he will remain unclean until evening. ²⁸ When she is cured of her discharge, she is to count seven days, and after that she will be clean. ²⁹ On the eighth day she must take two turtledoves or two young pigeons and bring them to the priest at the entrance to the tent of meeting. ³⁰ The priest is to sacrifice one as a sin offering and the other as a burnt offering. In this way the priest will make atonement for her before the LORD because of her unclean discharge. ³¹ "You must keep the Israelites from their uncleanness, so that they do not die by defiling my tabernacle that is among them. ³² This is the law for someone with a discharge: a man who has an emission of semen, becoming unclean by it; ³³ a woman who is in her menstrual period; anyone who has a discharge, whether male or female; and a man who sleeps with a woman who is unclean."

The Day of Atonement

16 The LORD spoke to Moses after the death of two of Aaron's sons when they approached the presence of ^ the LORD and died. ² The LORD said to Moses, "Tell your brother Aaron that he may not come whenever he wants into the holy place behind the curtain in front of the mercy seat on the ark or else he will die, because I appear in the cloud above the mercy seat. ³ "Aaron is to enter the most holy place in this way: with a young bull for a sin offering and a ram for a burnt offering. ⁴ He is to wear a holy linen tunic, and linen undergarments are to

be on his body. He is to tie a linen sash around him and wrap his head with a linen turban. These are holy garments; he must bathe his body with water before he wears them. ⁵ He is to take from the Israelite community two male goats for a sin offering and one ram for a burnt offering.

⁶ "Aaron will present the bull for his sin offering and make atonement for himself and his household. ⁷ Next he will take the two goats and place them before the LORD at the entrance to the tent of meeting. ⁸ After Aaron casts lots for the two goats, one lot for the LORD and the other for an uninhabitable place, ᴮ,ᶜ ⁹ he is to present the goat chosen by lot for the LORD and sacrifice it as a sin offering. ¹⁰ But the goat chosen by lot for an uninhabitable place is to be presented alive before the LORD to make atonement with it by sending it into the wilderness for an uninhabitable place.

¹¹ "When Aaron presents the bull for his sin offering and makes atonement for himself and his household, he will slaughter the bull for his sin offering. ¹² Then he is to take a firepan full of blazing coals from the altar before the LORD and two handfuls of finely ground fragrant incense, and bring them inside the curtain. ¹³ He is to put the incense on the fire before the LORD, so that the cloud of incense covers the mercy seat that is over the testimony, or else he will die. ¹⁴ He is to take some of the bull's blood and sprinkle it with his finger against the east side of the mercy seat; then he will sprinkle some of the blood with his finger before the mercy seat seven times.

¹⁵ "When he slaughters the male goat for the people's sin offering and brings its blood inside the curtain, he will do the same with its blood as he did with the bull's blood: He is to sprinkle it against the mercy seat and in front of it. ¹⁶ He will make atonement for the most holy place in this way for all their sins because of the Israelites' impurities and rebellious acts. He will do the same for the tent of meeting that remains among them, because it is surrounded by their impurities. ¹⁷ No one may be in the tent of meeting from the time he enters to make atonement

---

^16:1 LXX, Tg, Syr, Vg read *they brought strange fire before*; Nm 3:4   ᴮ16:8 Lit *for Azazel*, also in vv. 10 (2x),26
ᶜ16:8 Traditionally "for the scapegoat"; perhaps a term that means "for the goat that departs," or "for removal," or "for a rough, difficult place," or "for a goat-demon"; Hb obscure, also in vv. 10,26

15:25 This **discharge** refers to a chronic condition that is not related to menstruation. **15:31** The verb **keep** comes from the Hebrew root *nazar*, which means "to refrain," "to be a Nazirite." Here it conveys the idea that the Israelites were to refrain from being unclean so they could enter God's sanctuary. **Defiling** the sanctuary was grounds for the death penalty. **16:1–34** In his mercy and grace, God provided the Day of Atonement as a sacred time in which the high priest cleansed the sanctuary and made atonement for the sins of the people. **16:2** The **holy place** refers to the holy of holies (vv. 16–17,20,23,27,33). The **mercy seat**

was the place of atonement and was made of a solid gold slab that covered the ark of the covenant. The **cloud** is not the cloud of smoke from the incense; it is the divine cloud representing God's presence that descended on the tabernacle as a sign that Israel was to make camp (Ex 40:34–35) and that rested on the ark when God spoke to Moses (Ex 25:22; Nm 7:89). **16:4** The high priest wore the **garments** of an ordinary priest, indicating that he must be humble, free of all pretense. The high priest would **bathe** his body twice (vv. 4, 26), and he would wash his hands and feet each time he entered the tabernacle or officiated at the altar (v. 24; Ex 30:19).

16:7–10 Three different interpretations have been proposed for the meaning of *azazel* (**an uninhabitable place**), a word that occurs only in chap. 16. The LXX translates it as "the one carrying away evil," from which we got the term *scapegoat*. The second view was developed by later rabbis who suggested that *azazel* means "a rough and difficult place" and that it represented the goat's destination. The third view suggests that the word is the name of a demon that inhabited the desert. Later Jewish interpreters identified *azazel* with Azael, whom legend identified as the leader of the fallen angels. **16:17–19** Only here and in 8:15 is the altar said to be **set . . . apart** or sanctified.

in the most holy place until he leaves after he has made atonement for himself, his household, and the whole assembly of Israel. **18** Then he will go out to the altar that is before the LORD and make atonement for it. He is to take some of the bull's blood and some of the goat's blood and put it on the horns on all sides of the altar. **19** He is to sprinkle some of the blood on it with his finger seven times to cleanse and set it apart from the Israelites' impurities.

20 "When he has finished making atonement for the most holy place, the tent of meeting, and the altar, he is to present the live male goat. **21** Aaron will lay both his hands on the head of the live goat and confess over it all the Israelites' iniquities and rebellious acts — all their sins. He is to put them on the goat's head and send it away into the wilderness by the man appointed for the task.^A **22** The goat will carry all their iniquities into a desolate land, and the man will release it there.

23 "Then Aaron is to enter the tent of meeting, take off the linen garments he wore when he entered the most holy place, and leave them there. **24** He will bathe his body with water in a holy place and put on his clothes. Then he must go out and sacrifice his burnt offering and the people's burnt offering; he will make atonement for himself and for the people. **25** He is to burn the fat of the sin offering on the altar. **26** The man who released the goat for an uninhabitable place is to wash his clothes and bathe his body with water; afterward he may reenter the camp. **27** The bull for the sin offering and the goat for the sin offering, whose blood was brought into the most holy place to make atonement, must be brought outside the camp and their hide, flesh, and waste burned. **28** The one who burns them is to wash his clothes and bathe himself with water; afterward he may reenter the camp.

29 "This is to be a permanent statute for you: In the seventh month, on the tenth day of the month you are to practice self-denial and do no work, both the native and the alien who resides among you. **30** Atonement will be made for you on this day to cleanse you, and you will be clean from all your sins before the LORD. **31** It is a Sabbath of complete rest for you, and you must practice self-denial; it is a permanent statute. **32** The priest who is anointed and ordained^B to serve as high priest in place of his father will make atonement. He will put on the linen garments, the holy garments, **33** and make atonement for the most holy place. He will make atonement for the tent of meeting and the altar and will make atonement for the priests and all the people of the assembly. **34** This is to be a permanent statute for you, to make atonement for the Israelites once a year because of all their sins." And all this was done as the LORD commanded Moses.

Forbidden Sacrifices

17 The LORD spoke to Moses: **2** "Speak to Aaron, his sons, and all the Israelites and tell them: This is what the LORD has commanded: **3** Anyone from the house of Israel who slaughters an ox, sheep, or goat in the camp, or slaughters it outside the camp, **4** instead of bringing it to the entrance to the tent of meeting to present it as an offering to the LORD before his tabernacle — that person will be considered guilty.^C He has shed blood and is to be cut off from his people. **5** This is so the Israelites will bring to the LORD the sacrifices they have been offering in the open country. They are to bring them to the priest at the entrance to the tent of meeting and offer them as fellowship sacrifices to the LORD. **6** The priest will then splatter the blood on the LORD's altar at the entrance to the tent of meeting and burn the fat as a pleasing aroma to the LORD. **7** They must no longer offer their sacrifices to the goat-demons that they have prostituted themselves with. This will be a permanent statute for them throughout their generations.

8 "Say to them: Anyone from the house of Israel or from the aliens who reside among them who offers a burnt offering or a sacrifice **9** but

---

^A **16:21** Lit *wilderness in the hand of a ready man*   ^B **16:32** Lit *and will fill his hand*   ^C **17:4** Lit *tabernacle — blood will be charged against that person*

Scholars differ on whether this is the incense altar or the main altar, but the latter is more likely.

16:20–28 The second phase of purification occurred through the removal of the scapegoat. The author of Hebrews drew a parallel to this ritual when he affirmed that Christ offered himself as a sin offering once and for all (Heb 10:10). Jesus is also compared to the scapegoat because he also "suffered outside the gate, so that he might sanctify the people by his own blood" (Heb 13:12). The fact that Jesus took our sins upon himself is also affirmed in Is 53:5–6; 2Co 5:21; Gl 3:13; 1Pt 2:24. From a symbolic perspective, when Jesus died on the cross, the curtain that divided the holy of holies from the holy place was torn from top to bottom (Mt 27:51; Mk 15:38; Lk

23:45), signaling access to God by all people through Christ's atoning act on our behalf.

16:29 The Day of Atonement (Hb *yom kippur*) was an annual ceremony held on the tenth day of Tishri (September/October). Self-denial is usually associated with fasting and prayer (Is 58:3,5).

17:1–16 This chapter introduces what is known as the Holiness Code (Lv 17–26), laws that call the people to live holy lives before a holy God.

17:1–6 Slaughters is a technical term for all sacrificial slaughter (1:5; 3:8; 4:29,33; 7:2). It does not refer to the killing of animals in general. This was not a command prohibiting nonsacrificial slaughter or hunting (Dt 12:20–25). The seriousness of the offense can be seen in the phrase **be cut off**, an expression

that always refers to the death penalty when used in the context of punishment (vv. 9,10,14; 7:20–21,25,27; 18:29; 19:8; 20:3; 22:3).

17:7–9 In their wilderness wandering, the Israelites resorted to worshiping **goat-demons**, which could refer to demons in the form of goats that haunted the wilderness (Is 13:21; 34:14). Unfaithfulness toward the Lord was often depicted as prostitution, so the reference here does not suggest that the Israelites were worshiping Canaanite fertility gods (Jr 2–3; Ezk 16; 23; Hs 1–3). God in his grace also included resident **aliens** who lived among the covenant people; they had to observe the commandment not to worship other gods (vv. 8,10,12–13,15). The expression **burnt offering or a sacrifice** (Nm 15:3; Dt 12:6; 1Sm 15:22; 2Kg 5:17; Is 43:23) is a figure

does not bring it to the entrance to the tent of meeting to sacrifice it to the LORD, that person is to be cut off from his people.

Eating Blood and Carcasses Prohibited

¹⁰ "Anyone from the house of Israel or from the aliens who reside among them who eats any blood, I will turn^ against that person who eats blood and cut him off from his people. ¹¹ For the life of a creature is in the blood, and I have appointed it to you to make atonement on the altar for⁸ your lives, since it is the lifeblood that makes atonement. ¹² Therefore I say to the Israelites: None of you and no alien who resides among you may eat blood.

¹³ "Any Israelite or alien residing among them, who hunts down a wild animal or bird that may be eaten must drain its blood and cover it with dirt. ¹⁴ Since the life of every creature is its blood, I have told the Israelites: You are not to eat the blood of any creature, because the life of every creature is its blood; whoever eats it must be cut off.

¹⁵ "Every person, whether the native or the resident alien, who eats an animal that died a natural death or was mauled by wild beasts is to wash his clothes and bathe with water, and he will remain unclean until evening; then he will be clean. ¹⁶ But if he does not wash his clothes and bathe himself, he will bear his iniquity."

Prohibited Pagan Practices

18 The LORD spoke to Moses: ² "Speak to the Israelites and tell them: I am the LORD your God. ³ Do not follow the practices of the land of Egypt, where you used to live, or follow the practices of the land of Canaan, where I am bringing you. You must not follow their customs. ⁴ You are to practice my ordinances and you are to keep my statutes by following them; I am the LORD your God. ⁵ Keep my statutes and ordinances; a person will live if he does them. I am the LORD.

⁶ "You are not to come near any close relative^c for sexual intercourse; I am the LORD. ⁷ You are not to violate the intimacy that belongs to your father and mother.^D She is your mother; you must not have sexual intercourse with her. ⁸ You are not to have sex with your father's wife; she is your father's family. ⁹ You are not to have sexual intercourse with your sister, either your father's daughter or your mother's, whether born at home or born elsewhere. You are not to have sex with her. ¹⁰ You are not to have sexual intercourse with your son's daughter or your daughter's daughter, for they are your family.^E ¹¹ You are not to have sexual intercourse with your father's wife's daughter, who is adopted by^f your father; she is your sister. ¹² You are not to have sexual intercourse with your father's sister; she is your father's close relative. ¹³ You are not to have sexual intercourse with your mother's sister, for she is your mother's close relative. ¹⁴ You are not to violate the intimacy that belongs to^G your father's brother by approaching his wife to have sexual intercourse; she is your aunt. ¹⁵ You are not to have sexual intercourse with your daughter-in-law. She is your son's wife; you are not to have sex with her. ¹⁶ You are not to have sexual intercourse with your brother's wife; she is your brother's family. ¹⁷ You are not to have sexual intercourse with a woman and

---

^17:10 Lit *will set my face* ⁸17:11 Or *to ransom* ^18:6 Lit *any flesh of his flesh* ^18:7 Lit *Do not uncover your father's nakedness and your mother's nakedness* ^18:10 Lit *because they are your nakedness* ^18:11 Lit *daughter, a relative of* ^18:14 Lit *Do not uncover the nakedness of*

---

of speech called a *merism*, and it points to all sacrifices. The law's intent was to ban all sacrifices offered to any god other than Yahweh.
17:10 The prohibition against eating **blood** pertains to both sacrificial and nonsacrificial animals and is mentioned in other parts of the Torah (3:17; 7:26–27; Gn 9:4; Dt 12:16,23–25). The expression **I will turn against** is literally "I will set my face against." It points to God's decision not just to oppose those who disobey the law, but also to destroy those who committed such lawlessness (20:3; 26:17; Ezk 14:8; 15:7).
17:11–14 The concept that **the life is in the blood** goes back to creation (Gn 2:7; 7:22). Here the Lord gave a rationale for the law—that the blood is the life, and God has designed the blood for **atonement**. Not eating blood would profane something that God had sanctified or set apart for the sanctuary. Not eating blood was one of the requirements the Jerusalem Council placed on the Gentiles (Ac 15:29).
18:1–3 Egypt was known for its licentiousness and for condoning intrafamilial practices such as father-daughter, brother-sister,

aunt-nephew, and uncle-niece marriages. **Canaan** was identified with homosexuality (Gn 19:5–8) and bestiality. Seven times Israel is warned not to behave like those living in Canaan (Lv 18:3,24,26–27,29–30). Six times the expression **I am the LORD** appears in chap. 18 as the motive for observing the law (vv. 2,4,5,6,21,30). The formula "I am the LORD your God" appears frequently in the context of God's redeeming Israel from Egypt (v.2; 19:34,36; 23:43; 25:38,55; 26:13; Ex 6:7; Nm 15:41). In this context, the formula shows that these statutes were God's commandments and not human conventions.
18:4–5 Ordinances and **statutes** together encompass the whole divine law. The instruction is emphasized by being repeated in v. 5.
18:6 The expression **close relative** (lit "flesh of his flesh") designates all close blood relatives, such as father, mother, brother, sister, son, daughter, and grandchild (vv. 12–13; 20:19; 21:2–3). Sexual intercourse with **any** close relative—even those who are not specifically mentioned in the list—is prohibited.
18:7 This prohibition is repeated because of the possibility of double incest—with the **father** and with the **mother**.

18:8 Your father's wife would include a stepmother or another wife or concubine in a polygamous marriage.
18:9–11 Marriage with one's half **sister** (Gn 20:12) was not prohibited before the Mosaic covenant at Sinai. Brother-sister marriages were commonplace in Egypt, Phoenicia, and pre-Islamic Arabia.
18:12–14 While sexual intercourse between aunts and nephews was forbidden, unions between uncles and nieces were permitted (Jos 15:17; Jdg 1:13).
18:15 The prohibition of a sexual relationship with one's **daughter-in-law** extends to a person who is divorced or widowed, even though this practice was common in the ancient Near East.
18:16 John the Baptist used this law to rebuke Herod for marrying his **brother's** wife (Mt 14:4; Mk 6:18). This law was in effect only if the brother was alive. If the brother died, the law of levirate marriage, which was instituted in Dt 25:5–9, would go into effect.
18:17 Orgies involving a woman and her daughter were classified as **depraved**, a legal term that was also used for incest (20:14), rape (Jdg 20:6), and prostitution (Lv 19:29; Ezk

her daughter. You are not to marry her son's daughter or her daughter's daughter and have sex with her. They are close relatives; it is depraved. **¹⁸** You are not to marry a woman as a rival to her sister and have sexual intercourse with her during her sister's lifetime.

¹⁹ "You are not to approach a woman during her menstrual impurity to have sexual intercourse with her. **²⁰** You are not to have sexual intercourse with^A your neighbor's wife, defiling yourself with her.

²¹ "You are not to sacrifice any of your children in the fire^B to Molech. Do not profane the name of your God; I am the LORD. **²²** You are not to sleep with a man as with a woman; it is detestable. **²³** You are not to have sexual intercourse with^C any animal, defiling yourself with it; a woman is not to present herself to an animal to mate with it; it is a perversion.

²⁴ "Do not defile yourselves by any of these practices, for the nations I am driving out before you have defiled themselves by all these things. **²⁵** The land has become defiled, so I am punishing it for its iniquity, and the land will vomit out its inhabitants. **²⁶** But you are to keep my statutes and ordinances. You must not commit any of these detestable acts — not the native or the alien who resides among you. **²⁷** For the people who were in the land prior to you have committed all these detestable acts, and the land has become defiled. **²⁸** If you defile the land, it will vomit you out as it has vomited out the nations that were before you. **²⁹** Any person who does any of these detestable practices is to be cut off from his people. **³⁰** You must keep my instruction to not do any of the detestable customs that were practiced before you, so that you do not defile yourselves by them; I am the LORD your God."

Laws of Holiness

19 The LORD spoke to Moses: **²** "Speak to the entire Israelite community and tell them: Be holy because I, the LORD your God, am holy.

³ "Each of you is to respect his mother and father. You are to keep my Sabbaths; I am the LORD your God. **⁴** Do not turn to worthless idols or make cast images of gods for yourselves; I am the LORD your God.

⁵ "When you offer a fellowship sacrifice to the LORD, sacrifice it so that you may be accepted. **⁶** It is to be eaten on the day you sacrifice it or on the next day, but what remains on the third day must be burned. **⁷** If any is eaten on the third day, it is a repulsive thing; it will not be accepted. **⁸** Anyone who eats it will bear his iniquity, for he has profaned what is holy to the LORD. That person is to be cut off from his people.

⁹ "When you reap the harvest of your land, you are not to reap to the very edge of your field or gather the gleanings of your harvest. **¹⁰** Do not strip your vineyard bare or gather its fallen grapes. Leave them for the poor and the resident alien; I am the LORD your God.

¹¹ "Do not steal. Do not act deceptively or lie to one another. **¹²** Do not swear falsely by my name, profaning the name of your God; I am the LORD.

¹³ "Do not oppress your neighbor or rob him. The wages due a hired worker must not remain with you until morning. **¹⁴** Do not curse the deaf or put a stumbling block in front of the blind, but you are to fear your God; I am the LORD.

¹⁵ "Do not act unjustly when deciding a case. Do not be partial to the poor or give preference to the rich; judge your neighbor fairly. **¹⁶** Do not go about spreading slander among

---

^A**18:20** Lit *to give your emission of semen to*   ^B**18:21** Lit *to make any of your children pass through the fire*   ^C**18:23** Lit *to give your emission to*

16:27). Orgies of any type were prohibited and were seen as paganistic, profane acts.
18:18 A man was not to marry two sisters, as in the case of Jacob.
18:19 Refraining from sex during a woman's **menstrual impurity** was meant to keep the other person ceremonially clean (15:19–24).
18:20 This prohibition restates the seventh of the Ten Commandments (Ex 20:14; Dt 5:18), and it refers to sexual intercourse with a married or engaged person.
18:21 Child sacrifice practiced as worship of **Molech** was common among the Canaanites. The name "Molech" appears five times in Leviticus (v. 21; 20:2,3,4,5), and it refers to the god of the Ammonites. Human sacrifice was practiced in Israel only by corrupt rulers (1Kg 11:7; 2Kg 23:10; Jr 32:35). The literal expression *pass through the fire* indicates that the child was probably burned to honor Molech in a pagan ritual. This practice was labeled as **profane** by God.
18:22 Homosexuality is clearly prohibited throughout the Bible (20:13; Rm 1:27; 1Co 6:9). The Sodomites were destroyed because of

their sodomy (Gn 19:5), and the men of Gibeah were destroyed following their homosexual rampage (Jdg 19:22). Homosexuality is called **detestable** because it is against God's order of creation and against his laws pertaining to the covenant community. The word occurs 116 times in the OT in contexts addressing idolatry, magic, transvestism, and defective sacrifice.
18:23 Just like homosexuality, bestiality is prohibited in the Bible under all circumstances. This act was classified as **a perversion**, a violation of the divine order.
18:24–30 The punishment for these **detestable acts** was the death penalty. When the covenant community profaned God's name by following pagan practices, it was not just a mistake, it was a grave **iniquity**, an abomination, and something that defiled the community. The fact that the laws of chap. 18 begin and end with the statement **I am the LORD your God** shows the seriousness of these laws.
19:1–37 All commandments from the Decalogue are reasserted here.

19:2 This is the only time when God tells Moses to speak directly to the **entire Israelite community**. The imperative **be holy** (11:44; 20:7,26) and the reason for the people's holiness—**because I, the LORD your God, am holy**—are the main message of this chapter as well as the theme of the entire book of Leviticus.
19:3 The placement of the **mother** before the **father** is unusual in the male-oriented Israelite society.
19:9–10 God in his grace made provision for **the poor and the resident alien**. Boaz obeyed this commandment when Ruth was allowed to glean after the reapers (Ru 2:8–9).
19:14 The command against abusing the **deaf** and **the blind** can be applied concerning any handicapped or disadvantaged people. The imperative **you are to fear your God** serves as the rationale for the law because, unlike the deaf and the blind, God can see and hear everything.
19:15 The law against acting **unjustly** is directed not at judges (Dt 1:16; 16:18) but at the people in general, since any Israelite

your people; do not jeopardize[A] your neighbor's life; I am the LORD. [17] "Do not harbor hatred against your brother.[B] Rebuke your neighbor directly, and you will not incur guilt because of him. [18] Do not take revenge or bear a grudge against members of your community, but love your neighbor as yourself; I am the LORD. [19] "You are to keep my statutes. Do not crossbreed two different kinds of your livestock, sow your fields with two kinds of seed, or put on a garment made of two kinds of material. [20] "If a man has sexual intercourse with a woman who is a slave designated for another man, but she has not been redeemed or given her freedom, there must be punishment.[C] They are not to be put to death, because she had not been freed. [21] However, he must bring a ram as his guilt[D] offering to the LORD at the entrance to the tent of meeting. [22] The priest will make atonement on his behalf before the LORD with

the ram of the guilt offering for the sin he has committed, and he will be forgiven for the sin he committed. [23] "When you come into the land and plant any kind of tree for food, you are to consider the fruit forbidden.[E] It will be forbidden to you for three years; it is not to be eaten. [24] In the fourth year all its fruit is to be consecrated as a praise offering to the LORD. [25] But in the fifth year you may eat its fruit. In this way its yield will increase for you; I am the LORD your God. [26] "You are not to eat anything with blood in it.[F] You are not to practice divination or witchcraft. [27] You are not to cut off the hair at the sides of your head or mar the edge of your beard. [28] You are not to make gashes on your bodies for the dead or put tattoo marks on yourselves; I am the LORD. [29] "Do not debase[G] your daughter by making her a prostitute, or the land will be prostituted

[A]19:16 Lit not stand against　[B]19:17 Or your fellow Israelite　[C]19:20 Or compensation　[D]19:21 Or restitution　[E]19:23 Lit uncircumcised　[F]19:26 Or anything over its blood　[G]19:29 Lit profane

could be a juror and stand in judgment of his **neighbor** (Ru 4).
19:17 One way to show love for a **neighbor** is to **rebuke** him when he does wrong.
19:18 The importance of the command to **love your neighbor as yourself** was affirmed by Jesus and the apostle Paul; it also shows continuity between the OT and the NT (Mt 22:39–40; Rm 13:9).
19:20–22 Having **sexual intercourse with a woman who is a slave** was a sin, and this is why a **guilt offering** had to be made, though the death penalty was not required. The man alone was guilty since the female slave was not required to bring the guilt offering. This law protected vulnerable female slaves who did not have the social power and economic clout that free men had.

19:23–25 The prohibition from eating the **fruit** of a newly planted fruit **tree** may have had to do with the fact that the fruit did not taste good in the first **three years**. Because the firstfruits belonged to God (Nm 18:12–17), the fruit of the fourth year was **consecrated** to God as **a praise offering** to which the covenant community recognized that God was the one who gave them the good things the earth produced. Following this law would result in an **increase** of production.
19:26 Divination involved trying to determine the future by such devices as casting lots, using arrows, or looking at liquids or entrails. **Witchcraft** involved interpreting natural phenomena such as clouds or stars, or communicating with the spirits of the dead.

Both of these practices were common in the ancient Near East.
19:27 In Israel **hair** was the sign of a person's strength and beauty. The **beard** was a symbol of manhood. To **mar the edge of** the beard may have been a pagan practice that Israel was forbidden to emulate. In later Israelite culture, shaving was considered disgraceful (2Sm 10:4–5; Is 7:20).
19:28 The pagan custom of gashing the body as a sign of mourning was prohibited (Dt 14:1; Jr 16:6; 41:5; 47:5; 48:37). This is what the pagan priests of Baal did in the contest with Elijah on Mount Carmel (1Kg 18:28). Painting one's body (**tattoo marks**) was also a custom that denoted belonging to a pagan cult, or it was done to ward off spirits of the dead.

Q&A: Is "right and wrong" evidence for the existence of God?

by Dave Sterrett

Have you ever been in a situation in which you knew what you were about to do was wrong? Each of us has acted in ways that we knew were not right. In these moments, we knew right from wrong because a universal moral law is written on our hearts. Some people deny the existence of this law. They say morality (a standard of right and wrong) is created by individuals or cultures. While it is true that moral codes differ from one culture to the next, the differences are minor. The deep principles (prohibitions against murder, theft, lying, etc., and positive values of honesty, fidelity, and courage) are universal.

Still, people resist this truth. If someone you know says all morality is relative, try asking him if lying is wrong for all people. He may think it's no big deal to lie to others when it benefits him, but as soon as he finds that someone has lied to *him*, he is sure to be angry. Why? Because deep down he knows lying is wrong. The moral law says so.

The existence of this law points to God's existence. After all, if there is a law written on all human hearts, there must be a law writer. Hence, the moral argument for God's existence is based on the evidence of an absolute moral law that

in turn gives us reason to believe in the existence of a moral law giver (God). After all, these universal laws cannot be the creation of sinful humans, all of whom belong to a specific time and place. Since the law transcends time, place, and culture, the giver of the law must transcend these conditions.

Dr. Martin Luther King Jr. appealed to the God-given universal moral law to explain the evil of racism:

> I'm here to say to you this morning that some things are right and some things are wrong. Eternally so, absolutely so. It's wrong to hate. It always has been wrong and it always will be wrong! It's wrong in America, it's wrong in Germany, it's wrong in Russia, it's wrong in China. It was wrong in 2000 BC, and it's wrong in AD 1954. It always has been wrong . . . Some things in this universe are absolute. The God of the universe has made it so. And so long as we adopt this relative attitude toward right and wrong, we're revolting against the very laws of God himself ("Rediscovering Lost Values," a speech delivered in Detroit, February 28, 1954).

Dr. King got it right. Morality is from God, and a revolt against morality is a revolt against God. By asking the right questions, we can prompt our non-Christian friends to admit that there is a universal standard of right and wrong. Through their admission of the moral law, we can point them to the God of the Bible, the one whose own character is the foundation of the moral law.

and filled with depravity. [30] Keep my Sabbaths and revere my sanctuary; I am the LORD. [31] "Do not turn to mediums^A or consult spiritists,^B or you will be defiled by them; I am the LORD your God. [32] "You are to rise in the presence of the elderly and honor the old. Fear your God; I am the LORD. [33] "When an alien resides with you in your land, you must not oppress him. [34] You will regard the alien who resides with you as the native-born among you. You are to love him as yourself, for you were aliens in the land of Egypt; I am the LORD your God. [35] "Do not be unfair in measurements of length, weight, or volume. [36] You are to have honest balances, honest weights, an honest dry measure,^c and an honest liquid measure;^D I am the LORD your God, who brought you out of the land of Egypt. [37] Keep all my statutes and all my ordinances and do them; I am the LORD."

Molech Worship and Spiritism

20 The LORD spoke to Moses: [2] "Say to the Israelites: Any Israelite or alien residing in Israel who gives any of his children to Molech must be put to death; the people of the country are to stone him. [3] I will turn^E against that man and cut him off from his people, because he gave his offspring to Molech, defiling my sanctuary and profaning my holy name. [4] But if the people of the country look the other way when that man^F gives any of his children to Molech, and do not put him to death, [5] then I will turn against that man and his family, and cut off from their people both him and all who follow^G him in prostituting themselves with Molech.

[6] "Whoever turns to mediums^A or spiritists^B and prostitutes himself with them, I will turn against that person and cut him off from his people. [7] Consecrate yourselves and be holy, for I am the LORD your God. [8] Keep my statutes and do them; I am the LORD who sets you apart.

Family and Sexual Offenses

[9] "If anyone curses his father or mother, he must be put to death. He has cursed his father or mother; his death is his own fault.^H [10] "If a man commits adultery with a married woman — if he commits adultery with his neighbor's wife — both the adulterer and the adulteress must be put to death. [11] If a man sleeps with his father's wife, he has violated the intimacy that belongs to his father.^I Both of them must be put to death; their death is their own fault.^J [12] If a man sleeps with his daughter-in-law, both of them must be put to death. They have acted perversely; their death is their own fault. [13] If a man sleeps with a man as with a woman, they have both committed a detestable act. They must be put to death; their death is their own fault. [14] If a man marries^K a woman and her mother, it is depraved. Both he and they must be burned, so that there will be no depravity among you. [15] If a man has sexual intercourse with^L an animal, he must be put to death; you are also to kill the animal. [16] If a woman approaches any animal and mates with it, you are to kill the woman and the animal. They must be put to death; their death is their own fault. [17] If a man marries his sister, whether his father's daughter or his mother's daughter, and they have sexual relations,^M it is a disgrace. They are to be cut off publicly from their people. He has had sexual intercourse with his sister; he will bear his iniquity. [18] If a man sleeps with a menstruating woman and has sexual intercourse with her, he has exposed the source of her flow, and she has uncovered the source of her blood. Both of them are to be cut off from their people. [19] You must not have sexual intercourse with your mother's sister or your father's sister, for it is exposing one's own blood relative; both people will bear their iniquity. [20] If a man sleeps with his aunt, he has violated the intimacy that belongs to his uncle;^N they will bear their guilt and die childless. [21] If a man marries his brother's wife, it is impurity. He has violated the intimacy that belongs to his brother;^O they will be childless.

Holiness in the Land

22 "You are to keep all my statutes and all my ordinances, and do them, so that the land where I am bringing you to live will not vomit you out. **23** You must not follow the statutes of the nations I am driving out before you, for they did all these things, and I abhorred them. **24** And I promised you: You will inherit their land, since I will give it to you to possess, a land flowing with milk and honey. I am the LORD your God who set you apart from the peoples. **25** Therefore you are to distinguish the clean animal from the unclean one, and the unclean bird from the clean one. Do not become contaminated by any land animal, bird, or whatever crawls on the ground; I have set these apart as unclean for you. **26** You are to be holy to me because I, the LORD, am holy, and I have set you apart from the nations to be mine.

27 "A man or a woman who is[A] a medium or a spiritist must be put to death. They are to be stoned; their death is their own fault."

The Holiness of the Priests

21 The LORD said to Moses, "Speak to Aaron's sons, the priests, and tell them: A priest is not to make himself ceremonially unclean for a dead person among his relatives, **2** except for his immediate family: his mother, father, son, daughter, or brother. **3** He may make himself unclean for his unmarried virgin sister in his immediate family. **4** He is not to make himself unclean for those related to him by marriage[B] and so defile himself.

5 "Priests may not make bald spots on their heads, shave the edge of their beards, or make gashes on their bodies. **6** They are to be holy to their God and not profane the name of their God. For they present the food offerings to the LORD, the food of their God, and they must be holy. **7** They are not to marry a woman defiled by prostitution.[C] They are not to marry one divorced by her husband, for the priest is holy to his God. **8** You are to consider him holy since he presents the food of your God. He will be holy to you because I, the LORD who sets you apart, am holy. **9** If a priest's daughter defiles herself by promiscuity,[D] she defiles her father; she must be burned to death.

10 "The priest who is highest among his brothers, who has had the anointing oil poured on his head and has been ordained[E] to wear the clothes, must not dishevel his hair[F] or tear his clothes. **11** He must not go near any dead person or make himself unclean even for his father or mother. **12** He must not leave the sanctuary or he will desecrate the sanctuary of his God, for the consecration of the anointing oil of his God is on him; I am the LORD. **13** "He is to marry a woman who is a virgin. **14** He is not to marry a widow, a divorced woman, or one defiled by prostitution. He is to marry a virgin from his own people, **15** so that he does not corrupt his bloodline[G] among his people, for I am the LORD who sets him apart."

Physical Defects and Priests

16 The LORD spoke to Moses: **17** "Tell Aaron: None of your descendants throughout your generations who has a physical defect is to come near to present the food of his God. **18** No man who has any defect is to come near: no man who is blind, lame, facially disfigured, or deformed; **19** no man who has a broken foot or hand, **20** or who is a hunchback or a dwarf,[H] or who has an eye defect, a festering rash, scabs, or a crushed testicle. **21** No descendant of the priest Aaron who has a defect is to come near to present the food offerings to the LORD. He has a defect and is not to come near to present the food of his God. **22** He may eat the food of his God from what is especially holy as well as from what is holy. **23** But because he has a defect, he must not go near the curtain or approach the altar. He is not to desecrate my holy places, for I am the LORD who sets them apart." **24** Moses said this to Aaron and his sons and to all the Israelites.

Priests and Their Food

22 The LORD spoke to Moses: **2** "Tell Aaron and his sons to deal respectfully with the holy offerings of the Israelites that they have consecrated to me, so they do not profane my holy name; I am the LORD. **3** Say to them: If any man from any of your descendants

---

[A] **20:27** Lit is in them   [B] **21:4** Lit unclean a husband among his people   [C] **21:7** Or a prostitute, or a defiled woman   [D] **21:9** Or prostitution   [E] **21:10** Lit and one has filled his hand   [F] **21:10** Or not uncover his head   [G] **21:15** Lit not profane his seed   [H] **21:20** Or or emaciated

---

21:1–24 The standard of holiness was set higher for the priests. While all Israelites were part of the "holy nation" (Ex 19:5–6), the leaders were held to a higher standard in matters such as mourning, marriage, and family. **21:4–5** Since contact with the dead defiled a person (Nm 19:11–22), **priests** could not even bury their wives for burial because they were not blood relatives. The priest was also forbidden to follow the mourning laws of the Canaanites, who would mutilate their **bodies** to show their sorrow and pain as well as to venerate the dead.

21:7 In the ancient Near East, there were two types of prostitutes. Common prostitutes were sexually loose and were paid for their services. Cult prostitutes, on the other hand, committed sexual acts as worship to pagan gods. Although a priest could marry a widow, the high priest could not (v. 14). Perhaps this was to ensure the legitimacy of his offspring to inherit the high priesthood. **21:16–23** A **priest** in Israel had to be in good physical condition and without **physical defect**. While the text lists twelve blemishes

that would prevent a person from serving as a priest, later rabbis expanded the list of blemishes to 142. **22:1–33** Since the priests led in corporate worship, they had to be ceremonially pure (vv. 1–16). The sacrifices they brought also had to be unblemished in order to be acceptable to the Lord (vv. 17–33). **22:1–3** Serving while unclean carried the most severe penalty short of execution, being permanently barred from temple service.

throughout your generations is in a state of uncleanness yet approaches the holy offerings that the Israelites consecrate to the LORD, that person will be cut off from my presence; I am the LORD. [4] No man of Aaron's descendants who has a skin disease[A] or a discharge is to eat from the holy offerings until he is clean. Whoever touches anything made unclean by a dead person or by a man who has an emission of semen, [5] or whoever touches any swarming creature that makes him unclean or any person who makes him unclean — whatever his uncleanness — [6] the man who touches any of these will remain unclean until evening and is not to eat from the holy offerings unless he has bathed his body with water. [7] When the sun has set, he will become clean, and then he may eat from the holy offerings, for that is his food. [8] He must not eat an animal that died naturally or was mauled by wild beasts,[8] making himself unclean by it; I am the LORD. [9] They must keep my instruction, or they will be guilty and die because they profane it; I am the LORD who sets them apart.

[10] "No one outside a priest's family[c] is to eat the holy offering. A foreigner staying with a priest or a hired worker is not to eat the holy offering. [11] But if a priest purchases someone with his own silver, that person may eat it, and those born in his house may eat his food. [12] If the priest's daughter is married to a man outside a priest's family,[D] she is not to eat from the holy contributions.[E] [13] But if the priest's daughter becomes widowed or divorced, has no children, and returns to her father's house as in her youth, she may share her father's food. But no outsider may share it. [14] If anyone eats a holy offering in error, he is to add a fifth to its value and give the holy offering to the priest. [15] The priests must not profane the holy offerings the Israelites give to the LORD [16] by letting the people eat their holy offerings and having them bear the penalty of restitution. For I am the LORD who sets them apart."

Acceptable Sacrifices

[17] The LORD spoke to Moses: [18] "Speak to Aaron, his sons, and all the Israelites and tell them: Any man of the house of Israel or of the resident aliens in Israel who presents his offering — whether they present payment of vows or freewill gifts to the LORD as burnt offerings — [19] must offer an unblemished male from the cattle, sheep, or goats in order for you to be accepted. [20] You are not to present anything that has a defect, because it will not be accepted on your behalf.

[21] "When a man presents a fellowship sacrifice to the LORD to fulfill a vow or as a freewill offering from the herd or flock, it has to be unblemished to be acceptable; there must be no defect in it. [22] You are not to present any animal to the LORD that is blind, injured, maimed, or has a running sore, festering rash, or scabs; you may not put any of them on the altar as a food offering to the LORD. [23] You may sacrifice as a freewill offering any animal from the herd or flock that has an elongated or stunted limb, but it is not acceptable as a vow offering. [24] You are not to present to the LORD anything that has bruised, crushed, torn, or severed testicles; you must not sacrifice them in your land. [25] Neither you nor[F] a foreigner are to present food to your God from any of these animals. They will not be accepted for you because they are deformed and have a defect."

[26] The LORD spoke to Moses: [27] "When an ox, sheep, or goat is born, it is to remain with[G] its mother for seven days; from the eighth day on, it will be acceptable as an offering, a food offering to the LORD. [28] But you are not to slaughter an animal from the herd or flock on the same day as its young. [29] When you offer a thanksgiving sacrifice to the LORD, offer it so that you may be accepted. [30] It is to be eaten on the same day. Do not let any of it remain until morning; I am the LORD.

[31] "You are to keep my commands and do them; I am the LORD. [32] You must not profane my holy name; I must be treated as holy among the Israelites. I am the LORD who sets you apart, [33] the one who brought you out of the land of Egypt to be your God; I am the LORD."

Holy Days

23 The LORD spoke to Moses: [2] "Speak to the Israelites and tell them: These are my appointed times, the times of the LORD that you will proclaim as sacred assemblies.

[A]22:4 Or has leprosy or scale disease [B]22:8 Lit eat a carcass or a mauled beast [C]22:10 Lit "No stranger [D]22:12 Lit to a stranger [E]22:12 Lit the contribution of holy offerings [F]22:25 Lit nor from the hand of [G]22:27 Lit under

22:4–5 The impurities that rendered a priest unclean are listed in descending order of severity.
22:8 This law is more strict for the priest than for the common people (cp. 17:15–16).
22:10–11 This law was consistent with the instruction given to Abraham to circumcise purchased slaves (Gn 17:12–13), thus making them part of the covenant community.
22:17–20 These instructions cover burnt offerings.

22:19 The word unblemished comes from a term that means "to be complete, perfect." It conveys the idea that sacrifices must be without flaw.
22:21–24 These instructions cover fellowship offerings.
23:1–44 God set aside a sacred period that included festivals and holy days to give the covenant community rest from everyday life. These special days would also help them remember his acts of creation, deliverance, protection, and provision.

23:1–2 The expression sacred assemblies occurs eleven times in chap. 23 (vv. 2,3, 4,7,8,21,24,27,35,36,37) and seven times elsewhere in the Torah (Ex 12:16; Nm 28:18,25,26; 29:1,7,12). A sacred assembly was a time during which the people were to lay aside their usual work to focus on the worship of the Lord. The eight days that designated sacred assemblies were the first and seventh days of Unleavened Bread (Lv 23:7–8), the Festival of Weeks (v. 21), the first day of the seventh month (v. 24), the Day of Atonement

³ "Work may be done for six days, but on the seventh day there is to be a Sabbath of complete rest, a sacred assembly. You are not to do any work; it is a Sabbath to the LORD wherever you live. ⁴ "These are the LORD's appointed times, the sacred assemblies you are to proclaim at their appointed times. ⁵ The Passover to the LORD comes in the first month, at twilight on the fourteenth day of the month. ⁶ The Festival of Unleavened Bread to the LORD is on the fifteenth day of the same month. For seven days you must eat unleavened bread. ⁷ On the first day you are to hold a sacred assembly; you are not to do any daily work. ⁸ You are to present a food offering to the LORD for seven days. On the seventh day there will be a sacred assembly; do not do any daily work."

⁹ The LORD spoke to Moses: ¹⁰ "Speak to the Israelites and tell them: When you enter the land I am giving you and reap its harvest,ᴬ you are to bring the first sheaf of your harvest to the priest. ¹¹ He will present the sheaf before the LORD so that you may be accepted; the priest is to present it on the day after the Sabbath. ¹² On the day you present the sheaf, you are to offer a year-old male lambᴮ without blemish as a burnt offering to the LORD. ¹³ Its grain offering is to be four quartsᶜ of fine flour mixed with oil as a food offering to the LORD, a pleasing aroma, and its drink offering will be one quartᴰ of wine. ¹⁴ You must not eat bread, roasted grain, or any new grainᴱ until this very day, and until you have brought the offering to your God. This is to be a permanent statute throughout your generations wherever you live.

¹⁵ "You are to count sevenᶠ complete weeksᴳ starting from the day after the Sabbath, the day you brought the sheaf of the presentation

ᴬ 23:10 = the barley harvest   ᴮ 23:12 Or *a male lamb in its first year*   ᶜ 23:13 Lit *two-tenths of an ephah*, also in v. 17   ᴰ 23:13 Lit *one-fourth of a hin*   ᴱ 23:14 Grain or bread from the new harvest   ᶠ 23:14 Lit *count; they will be seven*   ᴳ 23:15 Or *Sabbaths*

(v. 27), the first and eighth days of Shelters (vv. 35–36), and the Sabbath.

23:3 The **Sabbath** is the only holy day commanded in the Ten Commandments (Ex 20:8–11) and the only commandment grounded in creation (Ex 20:11). Examples of **work** mentioned in the Torah are plowing and reaping (Ex 34:21), kindling fire (35:3), and gathering wood (Nm 15:32–36). Work that was prohibited elsewhere in the OT includes trade (Am 8:5) and carrying burdens (Jr 17:21–27). The Hebrew verb *shavath* means "to rest" or "to cease," and it is the root on which the word "Sabbath" was formed. Jesus affirmed that he is "Lord of the Sabbath" (Mt 12:8) and that "it is lawful to do what is good on the Sabbath" (Mt 12:12). The book of Hebrews also speaks of a spiritual rest into which the community of faith enters through Jesus Christ (Heb 3–4).

23:4–5 The Passover was celebrated in the first month, Abib (later called Nisan; March–April). Further instructions about Passover

were given in Ex 12, before the Israelites were delivered by God's mighty hand. It was during the Passover Festival that Jesus was crucified, signaling that he was the unblemished lamb sacrificed for all humanity (Is 53:5–6; 1Co 5:7; Heb 8–10; 1Pt 1:18–19).

23:6–8 The Festival of Unleavened Bread began on the fifteenth day of Abib and was a reminder of the haste with which the Hebrews left Egypt (Ex 12). The word *festival* designates the event as a pilgrimage, and it could not be celebrated at home. The unleavened bread was usually in the form of small round wafers baked from new grain without leaven (Lv 2:4). Over time, leaven came to signify corruption. Thus, the festival was intended to remind the covenant community that they were supposed to purge corruption as they celebrated redemption (1Co 5:8).

23:9–14 The Festival of Weeks, or Harvest, occurred during the week of Unleavened Bread and was both commemorative and

prophetic. During this feast the Israelites were to show their gratitude to God for his provision. The community of faith was to acknowledge God's provision by giving him the **first** of their income. The waving of the **sheaf** was to be an outward sign of an inward attitude; therefore, it was accompanied by the bringing of sacrifices. The people could only eat from the fruit of the land after they acknowledged God as its source.

23:15–22 The word *Pentecost* comes from the Greek. It means "fiftieth," and it concluded the period of **seven weeks** that began during Passover. Originally the Festival of Weeks was for the wheat harvest (Ex 34:22), but later it was tied with the events on Sinai. During this feast the Jews were supposed to show gratitude for God's provisions by bringing gifts (Lv 23:15–17), times for worship (vv. 18–21), and by making provision for the **poor**. The Jews were celebrating this pilgrimage feast when the

JEWISH FEASTS AND FESTIVALS

NAME	MONTH: DATE	REFERENCE	SIGNIFICANCE
Passover	Nisan (Mar./Apr.): 14	Ex 12:2–20; Lv 23:5	Commemorates God's deliverance of Israel out of Egypt.
Festival of Unleavened Bread	Nisan (Mar./Apr.): 15–21	Lv 23:6–8	Commemorates God's deliverance of Israel out of Egypt. Includes a Day of Firstfruits for the barley harvest.
Festival of Weeks, or Harvest (Pentecost)	Sivan (May/June): 6 (seven weeks after Passover)	Ex 23:16; 34:22; Lv 23:15–21	Commemorates the giving of the law at Mount Sinai. Includes a Day of Firstfruits for the wheat harvest.
Festival of Trumpets (Rosh Hashanah)	Tishri (Sept./Oct.): 1	Lv 23:23–25; Nm 29:1–6	Day of the blowing of the trumpets to signal the beginning of the civil new year.
Day of Atonement (Yom Kippur)	Tishri (Sept./Oct.): 10	Lv 23:26–33; Ex 30:10	On this day the high priest makes atonement for the nation's sin. Also a day of fasting.
Festival of Shelters, or Tabernacles (Sukkot)	Tishri (Sept./Oct.): 15–21	Lv 23:33–43; Nm 29:12–39; Dt 16:13	Commemorates the forty years of wilderness wandering.
Festival of Dedication, or Festival of Lights (Hanukkah)	Kislev (Nov./Dec.): 25–Tebeth (Dec./Jan.) 2 or 3	Jn 10:22	Commemorates the purification of the temple by Judas Maccabaeus in 164 BC.
Festival of Purim, or Esther	Adar (Feb./Mar.): 14	Est 9	Commemorates the deliverance of the Jewish people in the days of Esther.

offering. **16** You are to count fifty days until the day after the seventh Sabbath and then present an offering of new grain to the LORD. **17** Bring two loaves of bread from your settlements as a presentation offering, each of them made from four quarts of fine flour, baked with yeast, as firstfruits to the LORD. **18** You are to present with the bread seven unblemished male lambs a year old, one young bull, and two rams. They will be a burnt offering to the LORD, with their grain offerings and drink offerings, a food offering, a pleasing aroma to the LORD. **19** You are also to prepare one male goat as a sin offering, and two male lambs a year old as a fellowship sacrifice. **20** The priest will present the lambs with the bread of firstfruits as a presentation offering before the LORD; the bread and the two lambs will be holy to the LORD for the priest. **21** On that same day you are to make a proclamation and hold a sacred assembly. You are not to do any daily work. This is to be a permanent statute wherever you live throughout your generations. **22** When you reap the harvest of your land, you are not to reap all the way to the edge of your field or gather the gleanings of your harvest. Leave them for the poor and the resident alien; I am the LORD your God."

23 The LORD spoke to Moses: **24** "Tell the Israelites: In the seventh month, on the first day of the month, you are to have a day of complete rest, commemoration, and trumpet blasts — a sacred assembly. **25** You must not do any daily work, but you must present a food offering to the LORD."

26 The LORD again spoke to Moses: **27** "The tenth day of this seventh month is the Day of Atonement. You are to hold a sacred assembly and practice self-denial; you are to present a food offering to the LORD. **28** On this particular day you are not to do any work, for it is a Day of Atonement to make atonement for yourselves before the LORD your God. **29** If any person does not practice self-denial on this particular day, he is to be cut off from his people. **30** I will destroy among his people anyone who does any work on this same day. **31** You are not to do any work. This is a permanent statute throughout your generations wherever you live. **32** It will be a Sabbath of complete rest for you, and you must practice self-denial. You are to observe

your Sabbath from the evening of the ninth day of the month until the following evening."

33 The LORD spoke to Moses: **34** "Tell the Israelites: The Festival of Shelters^A to the LORD begins on the fifteenth day of this seventh month and continues for seven days. **35** There is to be a sacred assembly on the first day; you are not to do any daily work. **36** You are to present a food offering to the LORD for seven days. On the eighth day you are to hold a sacred assembly and present a food offering to the LORD. It is a solemn assembly; you are not to do any daily work.

37 "These are the LORD's appointed times that you are to proclaim as sacred assemblies for presenting food offerings to the LORD, burnt offerings and grain offerings, sacrifices and drink offerings, each on its designated day. **38** These are in addition to the offerings for the LORD's Sabbaths, your gifts, all your vow offerings, and all your freewill offerings that you give to the LORD.

39 "You are to celebrate the LORD's festival on the fifteenth day of the seventh month for seven days after you have gathered the produce of the land. There will be complete rest on the first day and complete rest on the eighth day. **40** On the first day you are to take the product of majestic trees — palm fronds, boughs of leafy trees, and willows of the brook — and rejoice before the LORD your God for seven days. **41** You are to celebrate it as a festival to the LORD seven days each year. This is a permanent statute for you throughout your generations; celebrate it in the seventh month. **42** You are to live in shelters for seven days. All the native-born of Israel must live in shelters, **43** so that your generations may know that I made the Israelites live in shelters when I brought them out of the land of Egypt; I am the LORD your God." **44** So Moses declared the LORD's appointed times to the Israelites.

Tabernacle Oil and Bread

24 The LORD spoke to Moses: **2** "Command the Israelites to bring you pure oil from crushed olives for the light, in order to keep the lamp burning regularly. **3** Aaron is to tend it continually from evening until morning before the LORD outside the curtain of the testimony in the tent of meeting. This is

---

^**23:34** Or *Tabernacles*, or *Booths*

Holy Spirit came upon those gathered in Jerusalem (Ac 2).
23:23–25 What later became known as the Festival of Trumpets was observed in the seventh month of Tishri, when the Israelites celebrated the end of the harvest. During the postexilic time, this day became the Jewish New Year (Rosh Hashanah).
23:26–32 The **Day of Atonement** was to be celebrated during the tenth day of Tishri. Details on the celebration of this day are outlined in chap. 16. In contrast to the other feasts, this was to be a day of fasting

in which the people exercised **self-denial** and expressed remorse over personal and corporate sin.
23:33–36 The Festival of Shelters or Tabernacles began on Tishri 15. It was primarily a thanksgiving festival showing gratitude for God's provision (Ex 34:22) and closing out the agricultural year. The shelters (Hb *succoth*) were also a reminder that the Israelites lived in tents during the forty-year journey from Egypt to the promised land (Lv 23:42–43). Jesus went to Jerusalem to celebrate this festival (Jn 7:1–15 and possibly Jn 5:1).

23:39–43 These verses cover additional instructions for the Festival of Shelters. This is the only festival where the Israelites are commanded to **rejoice before the LORD** (v. 40; cp. Dt 12:10–12; Php 4:4).
24:1–4 The **lampstand** was the seven-branched menorah that lighted the holy place of the tabernacle (Ex 25:31–40). The light represented the presence of God with his people. Jesus's affirmation that he was the light of the world was a polemic against those who put their faith in a menorah that only the symbol of a greater reality (Jn 8:12; 9:5).

a permanent statute throughout your generations. [4] He must continually tend the lamps on the pure gold lampstand in the LORD's presence.

[5] "Take fine flour and bake it into twelve loaves; each loaf is to be made with four quarts.[A] [6] Arrange them in two rows, six to a row, on the pure gold table before the LORD. [7] Place pure frankincense near each row, so that it may serve as a memorial portion for the bread and a food offering to the LORD. [8] The bread is to be set out before the LORD every Sabbath day as a permanent covenant obligation on the part of the Israelites. [9] It belongs to Aaron and his sons, who are to eat it in a holy place, for it is the holiest portion for him from the food offerings to the LORD; this is a permanent rule."

A Case of Blasphemy

[10] Now the son of an Israelite mother and an Egyptian father was[B] among the Israelites. A fight broke out in the camp between the Israelite woman's son and an Israelite man. [11] Her son cursed and blasphemed the Name, and they brought him to Moses. (His mother's name was Shelomith, a daughter of Dibri of the tribe of Dan.) [12] They put him in custody until the LORD's decision could be made clear to them.

[13] Then the LORD spoke to Moses: [14] "Bring the one who has cursed to the outside of the camp and have all who heard him lay their hands on his head; then have the whole community stone him. [15] And tell the Israelites: If anyone curses his God, he will bear the consequences of his sin. [16] Whoever blasphemes the name of the LORD must be put to death; the whole community is to stone him. If he blasphemes the Name, he is to be put to death, whether the resident alien or the native.

[17] "If a man kills anyone, he must be put to death. [18] Whoever kills an animal is to make restitution for it, life for life. [19] If any man inflicts a permanent injury on his neighbor, whatever he has done is to be done to him: [20] fracture for fracture, eye for eye, tooth for tooth. Whatever injury he inflicted on the person, the same is to be inflicted on him. [21] Whoever kills an animal is to make restitution for it, but whoever kills a person is to be put to death. [22] You are to have the same law for the resident alien and the native, because I am the LORD your God."

[23] After Moses spoke to the Israelites, they brought the one who had cursed to the outside of the camp and stoned him. So the Israelites did as the LORD had commanded Moses.

Sabbath Years and Jubilee

25 The LORD spoke to Moses on Mount Sinai: [2] "Speak to the Israelites and tell them: When you enter the land I am giving you, the land will observe a Sabbath to the LORD. [3] You may sow your field for six years, and you may prune your vineyard and gather its produce for six years. [4] But there will be a Sabbath of complete rest for the land in the seventh year, a Sabbath to the LORD: you are not to sow your field or prune your vineyard. [5] You are not to reap what grows by itself from your crop, or harvest the grapes of your untended vines. It is to be a year of complete rest for the land. [6] Whatever the land produces during the Sabbath year can be food for you — for yourself, your male or female slave, and the hired worker or alien who resides with you. [7] All of its growth may serve as food for your livestock and the wild animals in your land.

[8] "You are to count seven sabbatical years, seven times seven years, so that the time period of the seven sabbatical years amounts to forty-nine. [9] Then you are to sound a ram's horn loudly in the seventh month, on the tenth day of the month; you will sound it throughout your land on the Day of Atonement. [10] You are to consecrate the fiftieth year and proclaim freedom in the land for all its inhabitants. It will be your Jubilee, when each of you is to return to his property and each of you to his clan. [11] The fiftieth year will be your Jubilee; you are not to sow, reap what grows by itself, or harvest its untended vines. [12] It is to be holy to you

---

[A]24:5 Lit *two-tenths of an ephah*   [B]24:10 Lit *went out*

24:5–9 The **twelve loaves** of bread were called "the Bread of the Presence" (Ex 25:30). They were a constant reminder of God's provision for the Israelites every day and especially during the wilderness period. The twelve loaves represented the twelve tribes of Israel, pointing to the totality of God's provision. Jesus affirmed that he was the bread of life (Jn 6:33,35,48,51), satisfying the spiritual hunger of humanity.
24:13–16 The punishment for blasphemy was the **death** penalty by stoning, a punishment used also for those who worshiped Molech (20:2).
24:17–22 The **eye for eye, tooth for tooth** (v. 20) principle was a figurative way of

pointing to God's justice and showed that the punishment should fit the crime. The principle of punishing an offender with the same injury that he had inflicted is called (Lat) *lex talionis*. Quoting this verse, Jesus raised the bar in his teaching on turning the other cheek (Mt 5:38–42)—that is, offering of forgiveness instead of retribution.
24:23 This is the last of twelve places in Leviticus where some form of the phrase **as the LORD had commanded** is used. It is found twenty-three times in Numbers.
25:1–7 These verses give instructions concerning what is called the sabbatical year.
25:4 The expression **a Sabbath of complete rest** occurs only with the sabbatical year, the Sabbath (23:3), and the Day of Atonement

(23:32). These are the only times in which abstinence from all work was prescribed.
25:8–22 These verses concern the Jubilee year. In addition to the regulations related to the Sabbath year, debts were to be canceled and properties returned to their original owners.
25:8 The number seven is sacred, so the expression **seven times seven years** points to a most sacred time which ushered in the Year of Jubilee. Failure to obey this law was one factor leading to Israel's exile (26:34–35,43; 2Ch 36:21).
25:10 Israel was asked to **consecrate** or sanctify only the Sabbath (Ex 20:8,11; Dt 5:12; Jr 17:22,24,27; Ezk 20:20; 44:24) and the Year of Jubilee. The verb "consecrate" may be translated "to sanctify" or "to treat as holy."

because it is the Jubilee; you may only eat its produce directly from the field.

¹³ "In this Year of Jubilee, each of you will return to his property. ¹⁴ If you make a sale to your neighbor or a purchase from him, do not cheat one another. ¹⁵ You are to make the purchase from your neighbor based on the number of years since the last Jubilee. He is to sell to you based on the number of remaining harvest years. ¹⁶ You are to increase its price in proportion to a greater amount of years, and decrease its price in proportion to a lesser amount of years, because what he is selling to you is a number of harvests. ¹⁷ You are not to cheat one another, but fear your God, for I am the LORD your God.

¹⁸ "You are to keep my statutes and ordinances and carefully observe them, so that you may live securely in the land. ¹⁹ Then the land will yield its fruit, so that you can eat, be satisfied, and live securely in the land. ²⁰ If you wonder, 'What will we eat in the seventh year if we don't sow or gather our produce?' ²¹ I will appoint my blessing for you in the sixth year, so that it will produce a crop sufficient for three years. ²² When you sow in the eighth year, you will be eating from the previous harvest. You will be eating this until the ninth year when its harvest comes in.

²³ "The land is not to be permanently sold because it is mine, and you are only aliens and temporary residents on my land.ᴬ ²⁴ You are to allow the redemption of any land you occupy. ²⁵ If your brother becomes destitute and sells part of his property, his nearest relative may come and redeem what his brother has sold. ²⁶ If a man has no family redeemer, but he prospersᴮ and obtains enough to redeem his land, ²⁷ he may calculate the years since its sale, repay the balance to the man he sold it to, and return to his property. ²⁸ But if he cannot obtain enough to repay him, what he sold will remain in the possession of its purchaser until the Year of Jubilee. It is to be released at the Jubilee, so that he may return to his property.

²⁹ "If a man sells a residence in a walled city, his right of redemption will last until a year has passed after its sale; his right of redemption will last a year. ³⁰ If it is not redeemed by the end of a full year, then the house in the walled city is permanently transferred to its purchaser throughout his generations. It is not to be released on the Jubilee. ³¹ But houses in settlements that have no walls around them are to be classified as open fields. The right to redeem such houses stays in effect, and they are to be released at the Jubilee.

³² "Concerning the Levitical cities, the Levites always have the right to redeem houses in the cities they possess. ³³ Whatever property one of the Levites can redeemᶜ — a house sold in a city they possess — is to be released at the Jubilee, because the houses in the Levitical cities are their possession among the Israelites. ³⁴ The open pastureland around their cities may not be sold, for it is their permanent possession.

³⁵ "If your brother becomes destitute and cannot sustain himself amongᴰ you, you are to support him as an alien or temporary resident, so that he can continue to live among you. ³⁶ Do not profit or take interest from him, but fear your God and let your brother live among you. ³⁷ You are not to lend him your silver with interest or sell him your food for profit. ³⁸ I am the LORD your God, who brought you out of the land of Egypt to give you the land of Canaan and to be your God.

³⁹ "If your brother among you becomes destitute and sells himself to you, you must not force him to do slave labor. ⁴⁰ Let him stay with you as a hired worker or temporary resident; he may work for you until the Year of Jubilee. ⁴¹ Then he and his children are to be released from you, and he may return to his clan and his ancestral property. ⁴² They are not to be sold as slaves,ᴱ because they are my servantsᶠ that I brought out of the land of Egypt. ⁴³ You are not to rule over them harshly but fear your God. ⁴⁴ Your male and female slaves are to be from the nations around you; you may purchase male and female slaves. ⁴⁵ You may also purchase them from the aliens residing with you, or from their families living among you — those born in your land. These may become your property. ⁴⁶ You may leave them to your sons after you to inherit as property; you can make them slaves for life. But concerning your brothers, the Israelites, you must not rule over one another harshly.

⁴⁷ "If an alien or temporary resident living among you prospers, but your brother living near him becomes destitute and sells himself to the alien living among you, or to a member of the resident alien's clan, ⁴⁸ he has the right of redemption after he has been sold. One of

---

ᴬ**25:23** Lit *residents with me*   ᴮ**25:26** Lit *but his hand reaches*   ᶜ**25:33** Hb obscure   ᴰ**25:35** Lit *and his hand falters with*
ᴱ**25:42** Lit *sold with a sale of a slave*   ᶠ**25:42** Or *slaves*

25:23–55 These verses concern the family redeemer in relation to the Jubilee year.
25:23 The land refers to the promised land. The notion of God's ownership of the land occurs throughout the OT (Ex 15:17; Pss 10:16; 85:1; Is 14:2,25; Jr 2:7; Ezk 36:5; 38:16; Hs 9:3).
25:25 In order to keep **property** in the family, a well-off **relative**, known as a family redeemer, was allowed to buy it. This law was applied when Ruth was redeemed by Boaz after her closest family redeemer refused to marry her.
25:32–34 Even though the **Levites** were not allotted permanent property in the promised land (Nm 18:23; 26:62), they were provided permanent residences and pastureland.
These consisted of forty-eight towns and their surrounding fields (Nm 35:1–8).
25:39–55 God provided for the poor who had to sell themselves as indentured servants. However, slavery for an Israelite could only be a temporary condition, and the law prohibited harsh treatment and provided for release in the **Year of Jubilee**.

his brothers may redeem him. ⁴⁹ His uncle or cousin may redeem him, or any of his close relatives from his clan may redeem him. If he prospers, he may redeem himself. ⁵⁰ The one who purchased him is to calculate the time from the year he sold himself to him until the Year of Jubilee. The price of his sale will be determined by the number of years. It will be set for him like the daily wages of a hired worker. ⁵¹ If many years are still left, he must pay his redemption price in proportion to them based on his purchase price. ⁵² If only a few years remain until the Year of Jubilee, he will calculate and pay the price of his redemption in proportion to his remaining years. ⁵³ He will stay with him like a man hired year by year. A resident alien is not to rule over him harshly in your sight. ⁵⁴ If he is not redeemed in any of these ways, he and his children are to be released at the Year of Jubilee. ⁵⁵ For the Israelites are my servants. They are my servants that I brought out of the land of Egypt; I am the LORD your God.

Covenant Blessings and Discipline

26 "Do not make worthless idols for yourselves, set up a carved image or sacred pillar for yourselves, or place a sculpted stone in your land to bow down to it, for I am the LORD your God. ² Keep my Sabbaths and revere my sanctuary; I am the LORD.

³ "If you follow my statutes and faithfully observe my commands, ⁴ I will give you rain at the right time, and the land will yield its produce, and the trees of the field will bear their fruit. ⁵ Your threshing will continue until grape harvest, and the grape harvest will continue until sowing time; you will have plenty of food to eat and live securely in your land. ⁶ I will give peace to the land, and you will lie down with nothing to frighten you. I will remove dangerous animals from the land, and no sword will pass through your land. ⁷ You will pursue your enemies, and they will fall before you by the sword. ⁸ Five of you will pursue a hundred, and a hundred of you will pursue ten thousand; your enemies will fall before you by the sword.

⁹ "I will turn to you, make you fruitful and multiply you, and confirm my covenant with you. ¹⁰ You will eat the old grain of the previous year and will clear out the old to make room for the new. ¹¹ I will place my residence^A among you, and I will not reject you. ¹² I will walk among you and be your God, and you will be my people. ¹³ I am the LORD your God, who brought you out of the land of Egypt, so that you would no longer be their slaves. I broke the bars of your yoke and enabled you to live in freedom.^B

¹⁴ "But if you do not obey me and observe all these commands — ¹⁵ if you reject my statutes and despise my ordinances, and do not observe all my commands — and break my covenant, ¹⁶ then I will do this to you: I will bring terror on you — wasting disease and fever that will cause your eyes to fail and your life to ebb away. You will sow your seed in vain because your enemies will eat it. ¹⁷ I will turn^C against you, so that you will be defeated by your enemies. Those who hate you will rule over you, and you will flee even though no one is pursuing you.

¹⁸ "But if after these things you will not obey me, I will proceed to discipline you seven times for your sins. ¹⁹ I will break down your strong pride. I will make your sky like iron and your land like bronze, ²⁰ and your strength will be used up for nothing. Your land will not yield its produce, and the trees of the land will not bear their fruit.

²¹ "If you act with hostility toward me and are unwilling to obey me, I will multiply your plagues seven times for your sins. ²² I will send wild animals against you that will deprive you of your children, ravage your livestock, and reduce your numbers until your roads are deserted.

²³ "If in spite of these things you do not accept my discipline, but act with hostility toward me, ²⁴ then I will act with hostility toward you; I also will strike you seven times for your sins. ²⁵ I will bring a sword against you to execute the vengeance of the covenant. Though you withdraw into your cities, I will

---

^26:11 Or *tabernacle*   ^26:13 Lit *to walk uprightly*   ^26:17 Lit *will set my face*

26:1–2 The verb **keep** refers to the detailed observation of the commandments. The expression **keep my Sabbaths** occurs four times (v. 2; 19:3,30; Ex 31:13), and it is an allusion to the fourth commandment about keeping and sanctifying the Sabbath.
26:3–13 Here is the list of blessings the Lord promises Israel if they keep his law.
26:4 In Hebrew the word **rain** is in the plural. It refers to the two rainy periods that occurred in autumn and spring (Dt 11:14; Jr 5:24; Jl 2:23).
26:8 The one to twenty and one to a hundred proportions point to the miraculous victories over their **enemies** with which God would reward his people if they obeyed his commandments.

26:11 The promise of divine fellowship is rendered by the phrase, **I will place my residence among you**. The "residence" is literally a "tabernacle." This is a direct parallel to Jn 1:14, where John affirmed that Jesus, the Word, became flesh "and dwelt among us," or "tabernacled" among us.
26:13 The **bars of your yoke** were a reminder of the Egyptian bondage from which God delivered the Israelites. Here Israel is pictured as an animal held down by a heavy yoke. Later Jesus invited humanity to take his light yoke and partake of his rest (Mt 11:28–30).
26:14–39 Here is the list of curses that would befall Israel if they failed to keep the Lord's law.
26:14–17 The five sets of curses that begin in v. 14 are presented as punishment for

disobedience of God's **commands . . . statutes . . . ordinances**, and **covenant**. These curses match the five sets of blessings in vv. 3–13. The curses increase in severity with a persistent refusal to repent. The Lord would **turn against** his people only after they defiantly turned against him.
26:18–20 The number **seven** associated with the **discipline** for **sins** is not to be taken literally, but it is used figuratively to mean "many times" or "thoroughly."
26:22 Because the Lord is the God of all creation, he can also sovereignly use **wild animals** to punish his people. The outbreak of wild animals is frequently regarded as punishment for sin (Dt 32:24; 2Kg 2:24; 17:25; Is 13:21–22).

send a pestilence among you, and you will be delivered into enemy hands. ²⁶ When I cut off your supply of bread, ten women will bake your bread in a single oven and ration out your bread by weight, so that you will eat but not be satisfied.

²⁷ "And if in spite of this you do not obey me but act with hostility toward me, ²⁸ I will act with furious hostility toward you; I will also discipline you seven times for your sins. ²⁹ You will eat the flesh of your sons; you will eat the flesh of your daughters. ³⁰ I will destroy your high places, cut down your shrines,^ and heap your lifeless bodies on the lifeless bodies of your idols; I will reject you. ³¹ I will reduce your cities to ruins and devastate your sanctuaries. I will not smell the pleasing aroma of your sacrifices. ³² I also will devastate the land, so that your enemies who come to live there will be appalled by it. ³³ But I will scatter you among the nations, and I will draw a sword to chase after you. So your land will become desolate, and your cities will become ruins.

³⁴ "Then the land will make up for its Sabbath years during the time it lies desolate, while you are in the land of your enemies. At that time the land will rest and make up for its Sabbaths. ³⁵ As long as it lies desolate, it will have the rest it did not have during your Sabbaths when you lived there.

³⁶ "I will put anxiety in the hearts of those of you who survive in the lands of their enemies. The sound of a wind-driven leaf will put them to flight, and they will flee as one flees from a sword, and fall though no one is pursuing them. ³⁷ They will stumble over one another as if fleeing from a sword though no one is pursuing them. You will not be able to stand against your enemies. ³⁸ You will perish among the nations; the land of your enemies will devour you. ³⁹ Those^B who survive in the lands of your enemies will waste away because of their iniquity; they will also waste away because of their ancestors' iniquities along with theirs.

⁴⁰ "But when they confess their iniquity and the iniquity of their ancestors — their unfaithfulness that they practiced against me, and how they acted with hostility toward me, ⁴¹ and I acted with hostility toward them and brought them into the land of their enemies — and when

their uncircumcised hearts are humbled and they make amends for their iniquity, ⁴² then I will remember my covenant with Jacob. I will also remember my covenant with Isaac and my covenant with Abraham, and I will remember the land. ⁴³ For the land abandoned by them will make up for its Sabbaths by lying desolate without the people, while they make amends for their iniquity, because they rejected my ordinances and abhorred my statutes. ⁴⁴ Yet in spite of this, while they are in the land of their enemies, I will not reject or abhor them so as to destroy them and break my covenant with them, since I am the LORD their God. ⁴⁵ For their sake I will remember the covenant with their ancestors, whom I brought out of the land of Egypt in the sight of the nations to be their God; I am the LORD."

⁴⁶ These are the statutes, ordinances, and laws the LORD established between himself and the Israelites through Moses on Mount Sinai.

Funding the Sanctuary

27 The LORD spoke to Moses: ² "Speak to the Israelites and tell them: When someone makes a special vow to the LORD that involves the assessment of people, ³ if the assessment concerns a male from twenty to sixty years old, your assessment is fifty silver shekels measured by the standard sanctuary shekel. ⁴ If the person is a female, your assessment is thirty shekels. ⁵ If the person is from five to twenty years old, your assessment for a male is twenty shekels and for a female ten shekels. ⁶ If the person is from one month to five years old, your assessment for a male is five silver shekels, and for a female your assessment is three shekels of silver. ⁷ If the person is sixty years or more, your assessment is fifteen shekels for a male and ten shekels for a female. ⁸ But if one is too poor to pay the assessment, he is to present the person before the priest and the priest will set a value for him. The priest will set a value for him according to what the one making the vow can afford.

⁹ "If the vow involves one of the animals that may be brought as an offering to the LORD, any of these he gives to the LORD will be holy. ¹⁰ He may not replace it or make a substitution for it, either good for bad, or bad for good. But if he

^26:30 Or *incense altars*   ᴮ26:39 Lit *Those of you*

26:29 This curse was fulfilled during the siege of Samaria, the capital of the northern kingdom (2Kg 6:24–29) and later the siege of Jerusalem (Jr 19:9; Lm 4:10; Ezk 5:10). **26:31** The expression **I will not smell the pleasing aroma of your sacrifices** refers to the fact that God would not accept his people's sacrifices, and thus he was rejecting the people. Sacrifices without obedience are meaningless (1Sm 15:22). **26:33** The Hebrew verb *zarâ*, translated here as **scatter**, can also be translated "winnow." In the mind of the Jews it would trigger the

image of wicked people being blown away like chaff (Ps 1:4). **26:34–35** This curse anticipates Israel's failure to keep the **Sabbath years**. The chronicler fused this verse with Jeremiah's prophecy that the exile would last seventy years (2Ch 36:21; cp. Jr 25:11; 29:10). **26:40–45** These verses explain that restoration would be possible. **26:40–41** The expression **but when** indicates a turning point and involves a note of hope. The promised restoration is contingent upon the people's confession

of **iniquity** and their humility. The verb translated **humbled** is literally "to bring to one's knees." **26:44** The purifying agent will be the exile, not the flood that destroyed the earth during the time of Noah (Gn 6; 9). **27:2–8** People who were dedicated by vow to the Lord's service could be redeemed through a sum of money established by God or the priest. **27:9–13** These instructions concern vows of animals. **Will be holy** means that it becomes the property of the sanctuary.

does substitute one animal for another, both that animal and its substitute will be holy.

11 "If the vow involves any of the unclean animals that may not be brought as an offering to the LORD, the animal must be presented before the priest. **12** The priest will set its value, whether high or low; the price will be set as the priest makes the assessment for you. **13** If the one who brought it decides to redeem it, he must add a fifth to the^ assessed value.

14 "When a man consecrates his house as holy to the LORD, the priest will assess its value, whether high or low. The price will stand just as the priest assesses it. **15** But if the one who consecrated his house redeems it, he must add a fifth to the assessed value, and it will be his.

16 "If a man consecrates to the LORD any part of a field that he possesses, your assessment of value will be proportional to the seed needed to sow it, at the rate of fifty silver shekels for every six bushels^B of barley seed.^C **17** If he consecrates his field during the Year of Jubilee, the price will stand according to your assessment. **18** But if he consecrates his field after the Jubilee, the priest will calculate the price for him in proportion to the years left until the next Year of Jubilee, so that your assessment will be reduced. **19** If the one who consecrated the field decides to redeem it, he must add a fifth to the assessed value, and the field will transfer back to him. **20** But if he does not redeem the field or if he has sold it to another man, it is no longer redeemable. **21** When the field is released in the Jubilee, it will be holy to the LORD like a field permanently set apart; it becomes the priest's property.

22 "If a person consecrates to the LORD a field he has purchased that is not part of his inherited landholding, **23** then the priest will calculate for him the amount of the assessment up to the Year of Jubilee, and the person will pay the assessed value on that day as a holy offering to the LORD. **24** In the Year of Jubilee the field will return to the one he bought it from, the original owner. **25** All your assessed values will be measured by the standard sanctuary shekel,^D twenty gerahs to the shekel.

26 "But no one can consecrate a firstborn of the livestock, whether an animal from the herd or flock, to the LORD, because a firstborn already belongs to the LORD. **27** If it is one of the unclean livestock, it can be ransomed according to your assessment by adding a fifth of its value to it. If it is not redeemed, it can be sold according to your assessment.

28 "Nothing that a man permanently sets apart to the LORD from all he owns, whether a person, an animal, or his inherited landholding, can be sold or redeemed; everything set apart is especially holy to the LORD. **29** No person who has been set apart for destruction is to be ransomed; he must be put to death.

30 "Every tenth of the land's produce, grain from the soil or fruit from the trees, belongs to the LORD; it is holy to the LORD. **31** If a man decides to redeem any part of this tenth, he must add a fifth to its value. **32** Every tenth animal from the herd or flock, which passes under the shepherd's rod, will be holy to the LORD. **33** He is not to inspect whether it is good or bad, and he is not to make a substitution for it. But if he does make a substitution, both the animal and its substitute will be holy; they cannot be redeemed."

34 These are the commands the LORD gave Moses for the Israelites on Mount Sinai.

^**27:13** Lit *your*, also in vv. 15,19,23   ^B**27:16** Lit *for a homer*   ^C**27:16** Or *grain*   ^D**27:25** A *shekel* is about two-fifths of an ounce of silver

27:14-25 This concerns houses (vv. 14-15) or fields (vv. 16-24) that are dedicated to the sanctuary (the meaning of **consecrate**).
27:26-33 These instructions concern exceptions to the previous laws on vows.
27:26-27 No one could **consecrate a firstborn** because he already belonged **to the LORD** (Ex 13:2; 34:19-20).

27:28-29 The penalty for disobeying God's law regarding things **set apart . . . to the LORD** was death.
27:30-33 The tithe is not a human invention but a divine command. The first time the tithe is mentioned in the Bible was when Abram gave a tenth of what he had to Melchizedek (Gn 14:20). The Israelites are told to tithe from their **land's produce** (cp. Dt 14:22-24). During

the monarchy, the tithe was important because it provided the capital necessary for the day-to-day operation of the temple. The giving of the tithe was revived by Nehemiah during the postexilic era since it seems that the practice had been ignored (Neh 13:10-13,37-38). Through the prophet Malachi, God rebuked the people for robbing God by not bringing their tithes to the temple (Mal 3:8-10).

▼ Introduction to Numbers

Circumstances of Writing

Christian scholars have traditionally held that Moses was the author of the Pentateuch, which includes the book of Numbers. As with the other books in the Pentateuch, Numbers is anonymous, but Moses is a central character throughout. Moses kept a journal (33:2), and the phrase "The LORD spoke to Moses" is used thirty-one times. It is possible that a few portions were later added by scribes, such as the reference to Moses's humility (12:3) and the reference to the "Book of the LORD's Wars" (21:14). Moses remains the primary writer.

Numbers continues the historical narrative begun in Exodus. It picks up one month after the close of Exodus (Ex 40:2; Nm 1:1), which is about one year after the Israelites' departure from Egypt. Numbers covers the remaining thirty-nine years of the Israelites' stay in the wilderness, from Sinai to Kadesh, and finally to the plains on the eastern side of the Jordan River.

Contribution to the Bible

Numbers shows us how God responded to the unbelief of the Israelites. There are consequences to our disobedience, but God's grace remains, and his redemptive plan and desire for us will not be stopped. The book of Numbers underscores for us the importance of obedience in the life of a Christian, and Paul reminded us of the value of learning from the way God has worked in the past (Rm 15:4; 1Co 10:6,11).

Structure

Numbers reflects the challenging message of faithfulness. The book consists of seven cycles of material, with the repetition of the following types of material: (1) a statement of the historical setting, (2) reference to the twelve tribes of Israel and their respective leaders, (3) matters related to the priests and Levites, and (4) laws for defining the nature of the faithful community. This book of the Law is primarily narrative with portions of case law interwoven into a vibrant literary fabric.

Numbers Timeline

1600–1525 BC

The Hittites destroy Babylon. **1530**
MOSES 1526–1406
The Hittites develop iron technology. **1500**
Ahmose I, first pharaoh of Egypt's Eighteenth Dynasty, expels the Hyksos from Egypt. **1525**

1500–1450 BC

Glass bottles are first used in Egypt. **1500**
Copper trumpet is developed in Egypt. **1500**
JOSHUA 1490?–1380?
Hatshepsut, female pharaoh in Egypt **1479–1457**
In the first well-documented battle in history, Pharaoh Thutmose III defeats an alliance of enemies at Megiddo. **1469**

Outline

1450–1445 BC

Passover is instituted. **1446**
The exodus and defeat of Pharaoh
  at the Red Sea **1446**
The Ten Commandments are given
  at Mount Sinai. **1446**
Tabernacle is built and dedicated **1445**
Exploration of Canaan by twelve spies **1445**

1445–1375 BC

Events in Leviticus **1445**
Events in Numbers **1445–1407**
Events in Deuteronomy **1406**
Events in Joshua **1406–1380?**
The Egyptians develop a water clock, a container
  into which water dripped at a constant
  rate indicating the amount of time that
  had elapsed by reference to marks on the
  container into which the water flowed. This
  device had an advantage over the sundial
  in being able to tell time at night. **1400**

The Census of Israel

1 The LORD spoke to Moses in the tent of meeting in the Wilderness of Sinai, on the first day of the second month of the second year after Israel's departure from the land of Egypt: ² "Take a census of the entire Israelite community by their clans and their ancestral families,^ counting the names of every male one by one. ³ You and Aaron are to register those who are twenty years old or more by their military divisions — everyone who can serve in Israel's army.⁸ ⁴ A man from each tribe is to be with you, each one the head of his ancestral family.ᶜ ⁵ These are the names of the men who are to assist you:

Elizur son of Shedeur from Reuben;
6   Shelumiel son of Zurishaddai
       from Simeon;
7   Nahshon son of Amminadab
       from Judah;
8   Nethanel son of Zuar from Issachar;
9   Eliab son of Helon from Zebulun;
10   from the sons of Joseph:
       Elishama son of Ammihud
       from Ephraim,
       Gamaliel son of Pedahzur
       from Manasseh;
11   Abidan son of Gideoni from Benjamin;
12   Ahiezer son of Ammishaddai from Dan;
13   Pagiel son of Ochran from Asher;
14   Eliasaph son of Deuelᴰ from Gad;
15   Ahira son of Enan from Naphtali.

¹⁶ These are the men called from the community; they are leaders of their ancestral tribes, the heads of Israel's clans."

¹⁷ So Moses and Aaron took these men who had been designated by name, ¹⁸ and they assembled the whole community on the first day of the second month. They recorded their ancestry by their clans and their ancestral families, counting one by one the names of those twenty years old or more, ¹⁹ just as the LORD commanded Moses. He registered them in the Wilderness of Sinai:

²⁰ The descendants of Reuben, the firstborn of Israel: according to their family records by their clans and their ancestral families, counting one by one the names of every male twenty years or more, everyone who could serve in the army,

²¹ those registered for the tribe of Reuben numbered 46,500.

²² The descendants of Simeon: according to their family records by their clans and their ancestral families, those registered counting one by one the names of every male twenty years old or more, everyone who could serve in the army, ²³ those registered for the tribe of Simeon numbered 59,300.

²⁴ The descendants of Gad: according to their family records by their clans and their ancestral families, counting the names of those twenty years old or more, everyone who could serve in the army, ²⁵ those registered for the tribe of Gad numbered 45,650.

²⁶ The descendants of Judah: according to their family records by their clans and their ancestral families, counting the names of those twenty years old or more, everyone who could serve in the army, ²⁷ those registered for the tribe of Judah numbered 74,600.

²⁸ The descendants of Issachar: according to their family records by their clans and their ancestral families, counting the names of those twenty years old or more, everyone who could serve in the army, ²⁹ those registered for the tribe of Issachar numbered 54,400.

³⁰ The descendants of Zebulun: according to their family records by their clans and their ancestral families, counting the names of those twenty years old or more, everyone who could serve in the army, ³¹ those registered for the tribe of Zebulun numbered 57,400.

³² The descendants of Joseph:

The descendants of Ephraim: according to their family records by their clans and their ancestral families, counting the names of those twenty years old or more,

---

^1:2 Lit *the house of their fathers*, also in vv. 18,20,22,24,26,28,30,32,34,36,38,40,42,45   ᵇ1:3 Lit *everyone going out to war in Israel*   ᶜ1:4 Lit *the house of his fathers*, also in v. 44   ᴰ1:14 LXX, Syr read *Reuel*

1:1 **The LORD spoke to Moses** is a key phrase in the book of Numbers. It is best understood as a statement of divine revelation and instruction. Church tradition from the fourth century AD places Mount Sinai in the south central mountains of the Sinai Peninsula at Jebel Musa ("Mount of Moses"). Other mountains suggested included Jebel Sin Bisher in west central Sinai, and Jebel Helal in northeast Sinai. The **tent of meeting** was the place of divine disclosure that housed the

ark of the covenant and other items used in worship. The mobile shrine (tabernacle) had just been constructed one month before (7:1, Ex 40:17). **First day of the second month** indicates that the first ten chapters of Numbers are not set forth chronologically but theologically. The military conscription census took place two weeks after the Passover described in 9:1–14. 1:5–16 Through **Nahshon** of Judah came the lineage of Boaz, who married Ruth and

fathered the Davidic ancestry (Ru 4:20–22), and hence the messianic line of Jesus Christ (Mt 1:4–16; Lk 3:23–33). Elishama's grandson was Joshua son of Nun, the successor to Moses and leader of the Israelites in the conquest account. 1:20–43 Judah was the largest tribe with 74,600, more than both of the Joseph tribes (Ephraim and Manasseh) combined.

everyone who could serve in the army,
³³ those registered for the tribe of Ephraim
numbered 40,500.

³⁴ The descendants of Manasseh: according to their family records by their clans
and their ancestral families, counting the
names of those twenty years old or more,
everyone who could serve in the army,
³⁵ those registered for the tribe of Manasseh numbered 32,200.

³⁶ The descendants of Benjamin: according to their family records by their clans
and their ancestral families, counting the
names of those twenty years old or more,
everyone who could serve in the army,
³⁷ those registered for the tribe of Benjamin numbered 35,400.

³⁸ The descendants of Dan: according to
their family records by their clans and
their ancestral families, counting the
names of those twenty years old or more,
everyone who could serve in the army,
³⁹ those registered for the tribe of Dan
numbered 62,700.

⁴⁰ The descendants of Asher: according to their family records by their clans
and their ancestral families, counting the
names of those twenty years old or more,
everyone who could serve in the army,
⁴¹ those registered for the tribe of Asher
numbered 41,500.

⁴² The descendants of Naphtali: according to their family records by their clans
and their ancestral families, counting the
names of those twenty years old or more,
everyone who could serve in the army,
⁴³ those registered for the tribe of Naphtali
numbered 53,400.

⁴⁴ These are the men Moses and Aaron registered, with the assistance of the twelve leaders of Israel; each represented his ancestral
family. ⁴⁵ So all the Israelites twenty years old
or more, everyone who could serve in Israel's
army, were registered by their ancestral families. ⁴⁶ All those registered numbered 603,550.

Duties of the Levites

⁴⁷ But the Levites were not registered with
them by their ancestral tribe. ⁴⁸ For the Lᴏʀᴅ
had told Moses, ⁴⁹ "Do not register or take a
census of the tribe of Levi with the other Israelites. ⁵⁰ Appoint the Levites over the tabernacle of the testimony, all its furnishings, and
everything in it. They are to transport the tabernacle and all its articles, take care of it, and
camp around it. ⁵¹ Whenever the tabernacle is
to move, the Levites are to take it down, and
whenever it is to stop at a campsite, the Levites
are to set it up. Any unauthorized person who
comes near it is to be put to death.
⁵² "The Israelites are to camp by their military divisions, each man with his encampment and under his banner. ⁵³ The Levites are
to camp around the tabernacle of the testimony and watch over it, so that no wrath will fall
on the Israelite community." ⁵⁴ The Israelites
did everything just as the Lᴏʀᴅ had commanded Moses.

Organization of the Camps

2 The Lᴏʀᴅ spoke to Moses and Aaron: ² "The
Israelites are to camp under their respective banners beside the flags of their ancestral
families.ᴬ They are to camp around the tent of
meeting at a distance from it:
³ Judah's military divisions will camp on
the east side toward the sunrise under
their banner. The leader of the descendants of Judah is Nahshon son of Amminadab. ⁴ His military division numbers
74,600. ⁵ The tribe of Issachar will camp
next to it. The leader of the Issacharites is Nethanel son of Zuar. ⁶ His military division numbers 54,400. ⁷ The tribe
of Zebulun will be next. The leader of the
Zebulunites is Eliab son of Helon. ⁸ His military division numbers 57,400. ⁹ The total
number in their military divisions who
belong to Judah's encampment is 186,400;
they will move out first.

¹⁰ Reuben's military divisions will camp
on the south side under their banner. The
leader of the Reubenites is Elizur son of
Shedeur. ¹¹ His military division numbers
46,500. ¹² The tribe of Simeon will camp
next to it. The leader of the Simeonites is

ᴬ2:2 Lit *the house of their fathers*, also in v. 32

1:44–46 The total of **603,550** is consistent
with the round number 600,000 in 11:21 and
Ex 12:37. According to the second census
in chap. 26, the total militia prospects decreased by only 1,820 (3 percent) during forty
years in the wilderness.
1:47–53 Based on the Levites' zealous actions in defense of the faith in the golden calf
incident (Ex 32:26–29), this tribe was granted
the privilege of servicing the **tabernacle** and
assisting the Aaronic priests.

2:1–2 The members of each tribe were giv-
en a designated area to pitch their tents
around the tabernacle. The Hebrew terms
degel ("standard") and *'ototh* ("banners,
signs") refer to a flag or placard with an
insignia or color scheme to represent the
given tribe. The Levites served as guardians
to prevent defilement of the sacred space
and to keep anyone from experiencing
God's punishment for coming too close to
the tabernacle.

2:3–31 Judah's military divisions were giv-
en a positional priority, leading the camps of
Issachar and Zebulun on the **east side** of the
camp. The eastern tribes would lead Israel
when they marched. Reuben would lead the
tribes camping south of the tabernacle who
would follow the tribes on the east when they
marched. Next would come the Levites and
the tabernacle itself, followed by the tribes
camped on the west, led by Ephraim. Last
would be Dan and the tribes on the north.

Shelumiel son of Zurishaddai. ¹³ His military division numbers 59,300. ¹⁴ The tribe of Gad will be next. The leader of the Gadites is Eliasaph son of Deuel.ᴬ ¹⁵ His military division numbers 45,650. ¹⁶ The total number in their military divisions who belong to Reuben's encampment is 151,450; they will move out second.

¹⁷ The tent of meeting is to move out with the Levites' camp, which is in the middle of the camps. They are to move out just as they camp, each in his place,ᴮ with their banners.

¹⁸ Ephraim's military divisions will camp on the west side under their banner. The leader of the Ephraimites is Elishama son of Ammihud. ¹⁹ His military division numbers 40,500. ²⁰ The tribe of Manasseh will be next to it. The leader of the Manassites is Gamaliel son of Pedahzur. ²¹ His military division numbers 32,200. ²² The tribe of Benjamin will be next. The leader of the Benjaminites is Abidan son of Gideoni. ²³ His military division numbers 35,400. ²⁴ The total in their military divisions who belong to Ephraim's encampment number 108,100; they will move out third.

²⁵ Dan's military divisions will camp on the north side under their banner. The leader

of the Danites is Ahiezer son of Ammishaddai. ²⁶ His military division numbers 62,700. ²⁷ The tribe of Asher will camp next to it. The leader of the Asherites is Pagiel son of Ochran. ²⁸ His military division numbers 41,500. ²⁹ The tribe of Naphtali will be next. The leader of the Naphtalites is Ahira son of Enan. ³⁰ His military division numbers 53,400. ³¹ The total number who belong to Dan's encampment is 157,600; they are to move out last, with their banners."

³² These are the Israelites registered by their ancestral families. The total number in the camps by their military divisions is 603,550. ³³ But the Levites were not registered among the Israelites, just as the LORD had commanded Moses. ³⁴ The Israelites did everything the LORD commanded Moses; they camped by their banners in this way and moved out the same way, each man by his clan and by his ancestral family.ᶜ

Aaron's Sons and the Levites

3 These are the family records of Aaron and Moses at the time the LORD spoke with Moses on Mount Sinai. ² These are the names of Aaron's sons: Nadab, the firstborn, and Abihu, Eleazar, and Ithamar. ³ These are the names of Aaron's sons, the anointed priests, who were ordained to serve as priests. ⁴ But Nadab and

---

ᴬ2:14 Some Hb mss, Sam, Vg; other Hb mss read *Reuel* ᴮ2:17 Lit *each on his hand* ᶜ2:34 Lit *the house of his fathers*

3:1–3 Within the cultural framework of the ancient Near East, **family records** (Hb *toledoth*, see note at Gn 5:1) served several purposes: (1) to provide historical connection to a pivotal point in the past, (2) to preserve familial community and organization within the larger societal structure, (3) to justify one's position within the societal structure by providing a historical precedent from within one's family line, and (4) to provide future generations with a source of pride. **3:4 Nadab and Abihu** suffered the judgment of death (Lv 10:1–2) by offering an unholy censer of incense (by fire). **Eleazar**

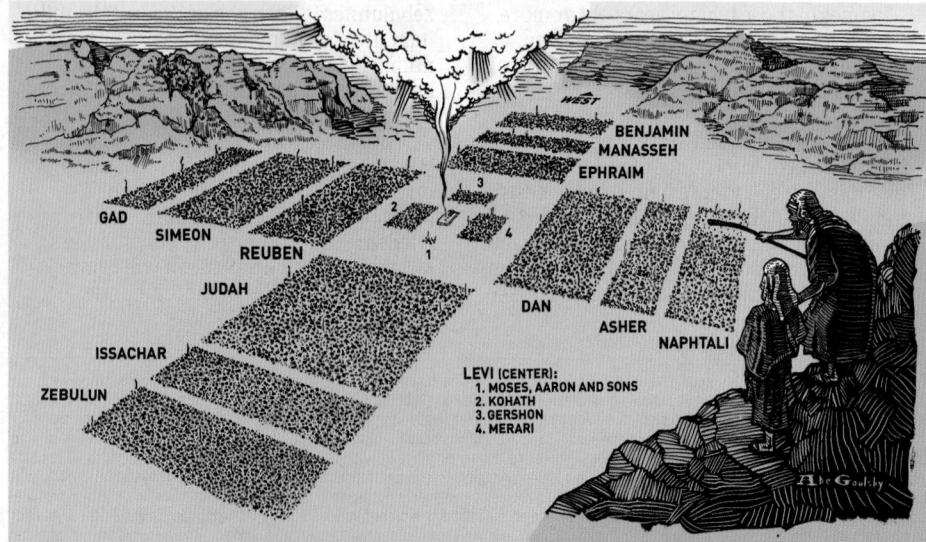

The Lord prescribed a specific arrangement for the Israelites to camp in the wilderness around the tent of meeting (2:1–34).

Abihu died in the Lord's presence when they presented unauthorized fire before the Lord in the Wilderness of Sinai, and they had no sons. So Eleazar and Ithamar served as priests under the direction of Aaron their father.

⁵ The Lord spoke to Moses: ⁶ "Bring the tribe of Levi near and present them to the priest Aaron to assist him. ⁷ They are to perform duties for ᴬ him and the entire community before the tent of meeting by attending to the service of the tabernacle. ⁸ They are to take care of all the furnishings of the tent of meeting and perform duties for the Israelites by attending to the service of the tabernacle. ⁹ Assign the Levites to Aaron and his sons; they have been assigned exclusively to him ᴮ from the Israelites. ¹⁰ You are to appoint Aaron and his sons to carry out their priestly responsibilities, but any unauthorized person who comes near the sanctuary is to be put to death."

¹¹ The Lord spoke to Moses: ¹² "See, I have taken the Levites from the Israelites in place of every firstborn Israelite from the womb. The Levites belong to me, ¹³ because every firstborn belongs to me. At the time I struck down every firstborn in the land of Egypt, I consecrated every firstborn in Israel to myself, both man and animal. They are mine; I am the Lord."

The Levitical Census

¹⁴ The Lord spoke to Moses in the Wilderness of Sinai. ¹⁵ "Register the Levites by their ancestral families ᶜ and their clans. You are to register every male one month old or more." ¹⁶ So Moses registered them in obedience to the Lord as he had been commanded:

¹⁷ These were Levi's sons by name: Gershon, Kohath, and Merari. ¹⁸ These were the names of Gershon's sons by their clans: Libni and Shimei. ¹⁹ Kohath's sons by their clans were Amram, Izhar, Hebron, and Uzziel. ²⁰ Merari's sons by their clans were Mahli and Mushi. These were the Levite clans by their ancestral families.

²¹ The Libnite clan and the Shimeite clan came from Gershon; these were the Gershonite clans. ²² Those registered, counting every male one month old or more, numbered 7,500. ²³ The Gershonite clans camped behind the tabernacle on the west side, ²⁴ and the leader of the Gershonite families ᴰ was Eliasaph son of Lael. ²⁵ The Gershonites' duties at the tent of meeting involved the tabernacle, the tent, its covering, the screen for the entrance to the tent of meeting, ²⁶ the hangings of the courtyard, the screen for the entrance to the courtyard that surrounds the tabernacle and the altar, and the tent ropes — all the work relating to these.

²⁷ The Amramite clan, the Izharite clan, the Hebronite clan, and the Uzzielite clan came from Kohath; these were the Kohathites. ²⁸ Counting every male one month old or more, there were 8,600 ᴱ responsible for the duties of ᶠ the sanctuary. ²⁹ The clans of the Kohathites camped on the south side of the tabernacle, ³⁰ and the leader of the families of the Kohathite clans was Elizaphan son of Uzziel. ³¹ Their duties involved the ark, the table, the lampstand, the altars, the sanctuary utensils that were used with these, and the screen ᴳ — and all the work relating to them. ³² The chief of the Levite leaders was Eleazar son of Aaron the priest; he had oversight of those responsible for the duties of the sanctuary.

³³ The Mahlite clan and the Mushite clan came from Merari; these were the Merarite clans. ³⁴ Those registered, counting every male one month old or more, numbered 6,200. ³⁵ The leader of the families of the Merarite clans was Zuriel son of Abihail; they camped on the north side of the tabernacle. ³⁶ The assigned duties of

---

ᴬ3:7 Or *to guard*, also in v. 8   ᴮ3:9 Some Hb mss, LXX, Sam read *me*; Nm 8:16   ᶜ3:15 Lit *the house of their fathers*, also in v. 20   ᴰ3:24 Lit *a father's house*, also in vv. 30,35   ᴱ3:28 LXX reads *8,300*   ᶠ3:28 Or *for guarding*, also in v. 32   ᴳ3:31 The screen between the most holy place and the holy place; Ex 35:12

---

would succeed his father in the high priest position following Aaron's death in the region of Moab, across the Jordan River from the promised land (20:23–29; 33:38–39).
3:7–9 The duties of the Levites on behalf of the **entire community** included daily maintenance to ensure the ceremonial purity of the sacrificial implements and curtains of the tabernacle furnishings that only they were allowed to touch.
3:11–12 In place of every firstborn of the Israelite families, the Levites served as a substitutionary living sacrifice before God for sacred service on behalf of the people of the other twelve tribes. The firstborn males of the Israelite families were to be presented to God through the agency of the priests (Ex 13:2,11–16; 22:29–30; 34:19–20).

The firstborn were God's sole possession based on the redemption-of-the-firstborn principle.
3:13 The price of the Israelite redemption in the exodus was the death of the **firstborn** of Egypt, from Pharaoh to slave, as well as the firstborn of all Egyptian animals.
3:14–39 The census of the **Levites** was separated from the militia (1:17–46). They were exempt from military service. The census of the militia numbered those twenty years of age and older, but the Levites were counted for the purpose of the firstborn redemption beginning at age **one month**.
3:21–26 The **Gershonite** clan transported the tabernacle and the tent. The **tabernacle** was composed of ten curtains of finely twisted blue, purple, and scarlet linen, each

forty-two feet by six feet, with cherubim symbols woven into them (Ex 26:1–6). The **tent** was made from eleven curtains of goat hair, forty-five feet by six feet, with additional coverings of dyed red ram skins and fine leather (Ex 26:7–14).
3:27–32 The **Kohathite** clan was assigned the tasks of guarding and transporting the sacred tabernacle furnishings, including the **ark** of the covenant. They did not actually handle these items; this was done by the priests, who wrapped the implements and then handed them over to the Kohathites for transport.
3:33–36 The **clan** of **Merari** were the caretakers and transporters of the equipment needed to erect and dismantle the tabernacle.

Merari's descendants involved the tabernacle's supports, crossbars, pillars, bases, all its equipment, and all the work related to these, [37] in addition to the posts of the surrounding courtyard with their bases, tent pegs, and ropes.

[38] Moses, Aaron, and his sons, who performed the duties of[A] the sanctuary as a service on behalf of the Israelites, camped in front of the tabernacle on the east, in front of the tent of meeting toward the sunrise. Any unauthorized person who came near it was to be put to death. [39] The total number of all the Levite males one month old or more that Moses and Aaron[B] registered by their clans at the LORD's command was 22,000.

Redemption of the Firstborn

[40] The LORD told Moses, "Register every firstborn male of the Israelites one month old or more, and list their names. [41] You are to take the Levites for me — I am the LORD — in place of every firstborn among the Israelites, and the Levites' cattle in place of every firstborn among the Israelites' cattle." [42] So Moses registered every firstborn among the Israelites, as the LORD commanded him. [43] The total number of the firstborn males one month old or more listed by name was 22,273.

[44] The LORD spoke to Moses again: [45] "Take the Levites in place of every firstborn among the Israelites, and the Levites' cattle in place of their cattle. The Levites belong to me; I am the LORD. [46] As the redemption price for the 273 firstborn Israelites who outnumber the Levites, [47] collect five shekels for each person, according to the standard sanctuary shekel — twenty gerahs to the shekel.[C] [48] Give the silver to Aaron and his sons as the redemption price for those who are in excess among the Israelites."

[49] So Moses collected the redemption amount from those in excess of the ones redeemed by the Levites. [50] He collected the silver from the firstborn Israelites: 1,365 shekels[D]

measured by the standard sanctuary shekel. [51] He gave the redemption silver to Aaron and his sons in obedience to the LORD, just as the LORD commanded Moses.

Duties of the Kohathites

4 The LORD spoke to Moses and Aaron: [2] "Among the Levites, take a census of the Kohathites by their clans and their ancestral families,[E] [3] men from thirty years old to fifty years old — everyone who is qualified[F] to do work at the tent of meeting.

[4] "The service of the Kohathites at the tent of meeting concerns the most holy objects. [5] Whenever the camp is about to move on, Aaron and his sons are to go in, take down the screening curtain, and cover the ark of the testimony with it. [6] They are to place over this a covering made of fine leather,[G] spread a solid blue cloth on top, and insert its poles.

[7] "They are to spread a blue cloth over the table of the Presence and place the plates and cups on it, as well as the bowls and pitchers for the drink offering. The regular bread offering is to be on it. [8] They are to spread a scarlet cloth over them, cover them with a covering made of fine leather, and insert the poles in the table.

[9] "They are to take a blue cloth and cover the lampstand used for light, with its lamps, snuffers, and firepans, as well as its jars of oil by which they service it. [10] Then they are to place it with all its utensils inside a covering made of fine leather and put them on the carrying frame.

[11] "They are to spread a blue cloth over the gold altar, cover it with a covering made of fine leather, and insert its poles. [12] They are to take all the serving utensils they use in the sanctuary, place them in a blue cloth, cover them with a covering made of fine leather, and put them on a carrying frame.

[13] "They are to remove the ashes from the bronze altar, spread a purple cloth over it, [14] and place all the equipment on it that they use in serving: the firepans, meat forks, shovels, and basins — all the equipment of the altar. They

---

^3:38 Or who guarded   ^3:39 Some Hb mss, Sam, Syr omit and Aaron   ^3:47 A shekel is about two-fifths of an ounce of silver   ^3:50 Over 34 pounds of silver   ^4:2 Lit the house of their fathers, also in vv. 22,29,34,38,40,42,46   ^4:3 Lit everyone entering the service   ^4:6 Hb obscure, also in vv. 8,10,11,12,14,25

3:40–51 The excess number of Israelite males was to be redeemed by five shekels, which amounted to 2.1 ounces of silver according to the twenty-gerah **sanctuary shekel**. The **redemption** price for each man in the Israelite militia was one-half shekel (Ex 30:11–16). These funds provided support for the service of the tent of meeting. Five shekels was the standard **price** of a slave and six months of wages for the average day laborer. **3:43** The census figure of 22,273 presents a practical problem. If there were only that many **firstborn** males, then each firstborn had an average

of twenty-six brothers—an incredible birthrate not substantiated in the Bible or elsewhere. R. B. Allen attempts to solve the problem by contending that the author employed hyperbolic language, exaggerating the actual number of 60,355 by a factor of ten, yielding 603,550. Such tactics were common in ancient literature and were considered a meaningful use of symbolic or sacred numbers (e.g., seven, ten). Another solution is to identify the 22,273 as only those firstborn males who were born during the year and a half between the exodus and the census since the total number of

firstborn among the 603,550 would have been much higher. **4:1–4** The **most holy objects** were the ark of the covenant, the bronze laver, the seven-tiered menorah, and other implements of the tabernacle. **4:3** Levites at this time served from age thirty to fifty (see also vv. 23,30,35,39,43,47). **4:7–8** The twelve loaves, representing the twelve tribes of Israel, were replaced weekly on the Sabbath and were symbolic of God's presence and constant provision for his people (Ex 24:5–9).

are to spread a covering made of fine leather over it and insert its poles.[A]

¹⁵ "Aaron and his sons are to finish covering the holy objects and all their equipment whenever the camp is to move on. The Kohathites will come and carry them, but they are not to touch the holy objects or they will die. These are the transportation duties of the Kohathites regarding the tent of meeting. ¹⁶ "Eleazar, son of Aaron the priest, has oversight of the lamp oil, the fragrant incense, the daily grain offering, and the anointing oil. He has oversight of the entire tabernacle and everything in it, the holy objects and their utensils."[B]

¹⁷ Then the LORD spoke to Moses and Aaron: ¹⁸ "Do not allow the Kohathite tribal clans to be wiped out from the Levites. ¹⁹ Do this for them so that they may live and not die when they come near the most holy objects: Aaron and his sons are to go in and assign each man his task and transportation duty. ²⁰ The Kohathites are not to go in and look at the holy objects as they are covered[C] or they will die."

Duties of the Gershonites

²¹ The LORD spoke to Moses: ²² "Take a census of the Gershonites also, by their ancestral families and their clans. ²³ Register men from thirty years old to fifty years old, everyone who is qualified to perform service, to do work at the tent of meeting. ²⁴ This is the service of the Gershonite clans regarding work and transportation duties: ²⁵ They are to transport the tabernacle curtains, the tent of meeting with its covering and the covering made of fine leather on top of it, the screen for the entrance to the tent of meeting, ²⁶ the hangings of the courtyard, the screen for the entrance at the gate of the courtyard that surrounds the tabernacle and the altar, along with their ropes and all the equipment for their service. They will carry out everything that needs to be done with these items. ²⁷ "All the service of the Gershonites, all their transportation duties and all their other work, is to be done at the command of Aaron and his sons; you are to assign to them all that they are responsible to carry. ²⁸ This is the service of the Gershonite clans at the tent of meeting, and their duties will be under the direction of Ithamar son of Aaron the priest.

Duties of the Merarites

²⁹ "As for the Merarites, you are to register them by their clans and their ancestral families.

³⁰ Register men from thirty years old to fifty years old, everyone who is qualified to do the work of the tent of meeting. ³¹ This is what they are responsible to carry as the whole of their service at the tent of meeting: the supports of the tabernacle, with its crossbars, pillars, and bases, ³² the posts of the surrounding courtyard with their bases, tent pegs, and ropes, including all their equipment and all the work related to them. You are to assign by name the items that they are responsible to carry. ³³ This is the service of the Merarite clans regarding all their work at the tent of meeting, under the direction of Ithamar son of Aaron the priest."

Census of the Levites

³⁴ So Moses, Aaron, and the leaders of the community registered the Kohathites by their clans and their ancestral families, ³⁵ men from thirty years old to fifty years old, everyone who was qualified for work at the tent of meeting. ³⁶ The men registered by their clans numbered 2,750. ³⁷ These were the registered men of the Kohathite clans, everyone who could serve at the tent of meeting. Moses and Aaron registered them at the LORD's command through Moses.

³⁸ The Gershonites were registered by their clans and their ancestral families, ³⁹ men from thirty years old to fifty years old, everyone who was qualified for work at the tent of meeting. ⁴⁰ The men registered by their clans and their ancestral families numbered 2,630. ⁴¹ These were the registered men of the Gershonite clans. At the LORD's command Moses and Aaron registered everyone who could serve at the tent of meeting.

⁴² The men of the Merarite clans were registered by their clans and their ancestral families, ⁴³ those from thirty years old to fifty years old, everyone who was qualified for work at the tent of meeting. ⁴⁴ The men registered by their clans numbered 3,200. ⁴⁵ These were the registered men of the Merarite clans; Moses and Aaron registered them at the LORD's command through Moses.

⁴⁶ Moses, Aaron, and the leaders of Israel registered all the Levites by their clans and their ancestral families, ⁴⁷ from thirty years old to fifty years old, everyone who was qualified to do the work of serving at the tent of meeting and transporting it. ⁴⁸ Their registered men numbered 8,580. ⁴⁹ At the LORD's command they were registered under the direction of Moses, each one according to his work and transportation duty, and his assignment was as the LORD commanded Moses.

ᴬ4:14 Sam, LXX add *They are to take a purple cloth and cover the wash basin and its base. They are to place them in a covering made of fine leather and put them on the carrying frame.* ᴮ4:16 Or *the sanctuary and its furnishings* ᶜ4:20 Or *objects, even long enough to swallow,*

4:17–20 Violation of the Holiness Code, even for the **Kohathites**, was punishable by death. The priests were to carefully supervise the Kohathites lest they violate their instructions and be **wiped out**.

Isolation of the Unclean

5 The LORD instructed Moses, [2] "Command the Israelites to send away anyone from the camp who is afflicted with a skin disease, anyone who has a discharge, or anyone who is defiled because of a corpse. [3] Send away both male or female; send them outside the camp, so that they will not defile their camps where I dwell among them." [4] The Israelites did this, sending them outside the camp. The Israelites did as the LORD instructed Moses.

Compensation for Wrongdoing

[5] The LORD spoke to Moses: [6] "Tell the Israelites: When a man or woman commits any sin against another, that person acts unfaithfully toward the LORD and is guilty. [7] The person is to confess the sin he has committed. He is to pay full compensation, add a fifth of its value to it, and give it to the individual he has wronged. [8] But if that individual has no relative to receive compensation, the compensation goes to the LORD for the priest, along with the atonement ram by which the priest will make atonement for the guilty person. [9] Every holy contribution the Israelites present to the priest will be his. [10] Each one's holy contribution is his to give; what each one gives to the priest will be his."

The Jealousy Ritual

[11] The LORD spoke to Moses: [12] "Speak to the Israelites and tell them: If any man's wife goes astray, is unfaithful to him, [13] and sleeps with another,[A] but it is concealed from her husband, and she is undetected, even though she has defiled herself, since there is no witness against her, and she wasn't caught in the act; [14] and if a feeling of jealousy comes over the husband and he becomes jealous because of his wife who has defiled herself — or if a feeling of jealousy comes over him and he becomes jealous of her though she has not defiled herself — [15] then the man is to bring his wife to the priest. He is also to bring an offering for her of two quarts[B] of barley flour. He is not to pour oil over it or put frankincense on it because it is a grain offering of jealousy, a grain offering for remembrance to draw attention to guilt. [16] "The priest is to bring her forward and have her stand before the LORD. [17] Then the

priest is to take holy water in a clay bowl, take some of the dust from the tabernacle floor, and put it in the water. [18] After the priest has the woman stand before the LORD, he is to let down her hair[C] and place in her hands the grain offering for remembrance, which is the grain offering of jealousy. The priest is to hold the bitter water that brings a curse. [19] The priest will require the woman to take an oath and will say to her, 'If no man has slept with you, if you have not gone astray and become defiled while under your husband's authority, be unaffected by this bitter water that brings a curse. [20] But if you have gone astray while under your husband's authority, if you have defiled yourself and a man other than your husband has slept with you' — [21] at this point the priest will make the woman take the oath with the sworn curse, and he is to say to her — 'May the LORD make you into an object of your people's cursing and swearing when he makes your womb[D] shrivel and your belly swell. [22] May this water that brings a curse enter your stomach, causing your belly to swell and your womb to shrivel.'

"And the woman will reply, 'Amen, Amen.'

[23] "Then the priest is to write these curses on a scroll and wash them off into the bitter water. [24] He will require the woman to drink the bitter water that brings a curse, and it will enter her to cause bitter suffering. [25] The priest is to take the grain offering of jealousy from the woman, present the offering before the LORD, and bring it to the altar. [26] The priest is to take a handful of the grain offering as a memorial portion and burn it on the altar. Afterward, he will require the woman to drink the water. [27] "When he makes her drink the water, if she has defiled herself and been unfaithful to her husband, the water that brings a curse will enter her to cause bitter suffering; her belly will swell, and her womb will shrivel. She will become a curse among her people. [28] But if the woman has not defiled herself and is pure, she will be unaffected and will be able to conceive children.

[29] "This is the law regarding jealousy when a wife goes astray and defiles herself while under her husband's authority, [30] or when a feeling of jealousy comes over a husband and he becomes jealous of his wife. He is to have the

A 5:13 Lit and man lies with her and has an emission of semen   B 5:15 Lit a tenth of an ephah   C 5:18 Or to uncover her head
D 5:21 Lit thigh, also in vv. 22,27

5:1-2 These people were not banished, but sent outside the sacred area so the holy place would not be defiled. The unclean were quarantined on the outer perimeter of the camp. Leviticus 13–14 describes the process of purification by which people could be restored to the camp of the holy. Skin diseases ranged from abscesses or eczema to leprosy. Bodily discharges refer to those emitted by male and female sexual organs (cp. Lv 15). Contact with a dead animal rendered a person impure for a day, but

pollution by contact with a human corpse made him unclean for a week.
5:11-14 Probably no case study in pentateuchal law has so many conditional clauses. If any man's wife was apprehended in the act of adultery, her act was punishable by death along with the adulterous male partner (Lv 20:10). The ritual outlined here put the matter in the hands of God (who sees and knows all) when adultery was suspected but not proven by human witnesses. The woman would not be stoned if the community followed this legislation.

5:18 To let down her hair was a sign of mourning or disgrace (Lv 10:6; 13:45; 21:10).
5:19-22 The extended oath of imprecation took place at the entrance to the sanctuary before God and the priest. The mixture of holy water and dust from the tabernacle floor (v. 16) became either a purification tonic if the woman was innocent or a curse that left her barren for life.
5:23-28 In the solemn ceremony, the woman drank the potion and the results were left to God.

woman stand before the LORD, and the priest will carry out all these instructions for her. [31] The husband will be free of guilt, but that woman will bear her iniquity."

The Nazirite Vow

6 The LORD instructed Moses, [2] "Speak to the Israelites and tell them: When a man or woman makes a special vow, a Nazirite vow, to consecrate himself to the LORD, [3] he is to abstain from wine and beer. He must not drink vinegar made from wine or from beer. He must not drink any grape juice or eat fresh grapes or raisins. [4] He is not to eat anything produced by the grapevine, from seeds to skin, during the period of his consecration.

[5] "You must not cut his hair[A] throughout the time of his vow of consecration. He may be holy until the time is completed during which he consecrates himself to the LORD; he is to let the hair of his head grow long. [6] He must not go near a dead body during the time he consecrates himself to the LORD. [7] He is not to defile himself for his father or mother, or his brother or sister, when they die, while the mark of consecration to his God is on his head. [8] He is holy to the LORD during the time of consecration.

[9] "If someone suddenly dies near him, defiling his consecrated head, he must shave his head on the day of his purification; he is to shave it on the seventh day. [10] On the eighth day he is to bring two turtledoves or two young pigeons to the priest at the entrance to the tent of meeting. [11] The priest is to offer one as a sin offering and the other as a burnt offering to make atonement on behalf of the Nazirite, since he incurred guilt because of the corpse. On that day he is to consecrate his head again. [12] He is to rededicate his time of consecration to the LORD and to bring a year-old male lamb as a guilt offering. But do not count the initial period of consecration because it became defiled.

[13] "This is the law of the Nazirite: On the day his time of consecration is completed, he is to be brought to the entrance to the tent of

meeting. [14] He is to present an offering to the LORD of one unblemished year-old male lamb as a burnt offering, one unblemished year-old female lamb as a sin offering, one unblemished ram as a fellowship offering, [15] along with their grain offerings and drink offerings, and a basket of unleavened cakes made from fine flour mixed with oil, and unleavened wafers coated with oil. [16] The priest is to present these before the LORD and sacrifice the Nazirite's sin offering and burnt offering. [17] He will also offer the ram as a fellowship sacrifice to the LORD, together with the basket of unleavened bread. Then the priest will offer the accompanying grain offering and drink offering. [18] The Nazirite is to shave his consecrated head at the entrance to the tent of meeting, take the hair from his head, and put it on the fire under the fellowship sacrifice. [19] The priest is to take the boiled shoulder from the ram, one unleavened cake from the basket, and one unleavened wafer, and put them into the hands of the Nazirite after he has shaved his consecrated head. [20] The priest is to present them as a presentation offering before the LORD. It is a holy portion for the priest, in addition to the breast of the presentation offering and the thigh of the contribution. After that, the Nazirite may drink wine.

[21] "These are the instructions about the Nazirite who vows his offering to the LORD for his consecration, in addition to whatever else he can afford; he must fulfill whatever vow he makes in keeping with the instructions for his consecration."

The Priestly Blessing

[22] The LORD spoke to Moses: [23] "Tell Aaron and his sons, 'This is how you are to bless the Israelites. You should say to them,

[24] "May the LORD bless you
and protect you;
[25] may the LORD make his face shine
on you
and be gracious to you;

[A] 6:5 Lit *"A razor is not to pass over his head*

6:1 After two chapters of Levitical and priestly instructions (chaps. 3–4), and a series of community purity laws in chap. 5, the Nazirite legislation defines an additional level of service for the laity in the community of faith.
6:2 Unlike the priestly and Levitical service, which was limited to males of a certain age and ancestral heritage, the **Nazirite vow** was a special dedicatory service for the Lord that was open to females. Samson was dedicated as a Nazirite for the purpose of delivering Israel from Philistine oppression (Jdg 13:2–4). The mothers of Samson and Samuel took Nazirite vows during their times of barrenness. **6:3–4** The Nazirite vow involved total restriction from the vineyard and any of its products. **Beer** translates a Hebrew term

traditionally translated "strong drink," derived from the verb *shakar*, "to be drunk." The distillation process, which leads to a higher alcoholic content than can be achieved via mere fermentation, was unknown until the ninth century AD. For this reason the CSB translators reason that "beer" is a more accurate translation since it has a lower alcohol percentage than the "strong drink" that results from distillation. **6:5–6** The uncut **hair** would be an outward symbol to others of the Nazirite dedication. Refraining from coming near the **dead** or participating in the burial ritual would be a reminder to that person's family that he had been totally dedicated to the Lord. **6:7–8** Like the high priest (Lv 21:11), a Nazirite could not go through the normal grief

process if a family member died (cp. Mt 8:21–22). **6:13–21** The concluding ceremony of the **Nazirite** vow involved each of these sacrificial offerings: (1) a **burnt offering** (Hb *'olah*) for consecration, (2) a **sin offering** (Hb *chatta'ath*) for purification, and (3) a **fellowship offering** (Hb *shelomim*) for celebration. **6:23** Blessing was invoking the power of God on behalf of the people of God (**bless the Israelites**). This blessing would bring such things as numerous descendants, a fruitful land, good health, long life, deliverance from danger and oppression, protection from one's enemies, and God's abiding presence. **6:25** The **face** reflected the righteous character of God. **Be gracious to you** evoked God's favor, which was beyond measure.

²⁶   may the LORD look with favor on you^
and give you peace."ᶦ
²⁷ In this way they will pronounce my name
over⁸ the Israelites, and I will bless them."

Offerings from the Leaders

7 On the day Moses finished setting up the
tabernacle, he anointed and consecrated
it and all its furnishings, along with the altar
and all its utensils. After he anointed and consecrated these things, ² the leaders of Israel, the
heads of their ancestral families,ᶜ presented
an offering. They were the tribal leaders who
supervised the registration. ³ They brought as
their offering before the LORD six covered carts
and twelve oxen, a cart from every two leaders
and an ox from each one, and presented them
in front of the tabernacle. ⁴ The LORD said to Moses, ⁵ "Accept these
from them to be used in the work of the tent
of meeting, and give this offering to the Levites,
to each division according to their service."
⁶ So Moses took the carts and oxen and gave
them to the Levites. ⁷ He gave the Gershonites two carts and four oxen corresponding
to their service, ⁸ and gave the Merarites four
carts and eight oxen corresponding to their
service, under the direction of Ithamar son of
Aaron the priest. ⁹ But he did not give any to
the Kohathites, since their responsibility was
service related to the holy objects carried on
their shoulders.
¹⁰ The leaders also presented the dedication gift for the altar when it was anointed.
The leaders presented their offerings in front
of the altar. ¹¹ The LORD told Moses, "Each day
have one leader present his offering for the
dedication of the altar."
¹² The one who presented his offering on
the first day was Nahshon son of Amminadab from the tribe of Judah. ¹³ His offering was one silver dish weighing 3 ¼
poundsᴰ and one silver basin weighing 1 ¾
pounds,ᴱ measured by the standard sanctuary shekel, both of them full of fine flour
mixed with oil for a grain offering; ¹⁴ one
gold bowl weighing four ounces,ᶠ full of
incense; ¹⁵ one young bull, one ram, and
one male lamb a year old, for a burnt offering; ¹⁶ one male goat for a sin offering;
¹⁷ and two bulls, five rams, five male goats,

and five male lambs a year old, for the fellowship sacrifice. This was the offering of
Nahshon son of Amminadab.

¹⁸ On the second day Nethanel son of Zuar,
leader of Issachar, presented an offering.
¹⁹ As his offering, he presented one silver dish weighing 3 ¼ pounds and one silver basin weighing 1 ¾ pounds, measured
by the standard sanctuary shekel, both of
them full of fine flour mixed with oil for a
grain offering; ²⁰ one gold bowl weighing
four ounces, full of incense; ²¹ one young
bull, one ram, and one male lamb a year
old, for a burnt offering; ²² one male goat
for a sin offering; ²³ and two bulls, five
rams, five male goats, and five male lambs
a year old, for the fellowship sacrifice. This
was the offering of Nethanel son of Zuar.

²⁴ On the third day Eliab son of Helon, leader of the Zebulunites, presented an offering. ²⁵ His offering was one silver dish
weighing 3 ¼ pounds and one silver basin weighing 1 ¾ pounds, measured by the
standard sanctuary shekel, both of them
full of fine flour mixed with oil for a grain
offering; ²⁶ one gold bowl weighing four
ounces, full of incense; ²⁷ one young bull,
one ram, and one male lamb a year old, for
a burnt offering; ²⁸ one male goat for a sin
offering; ²⁹ and two bulls, five rams, five
male goats, and five male lambs a year old,
for the fellowship sacrifice. This was the
offering of Eliab son of Helon.

³⁰ On the fourth day Elizur son of Shedeur,
leader of the Reubenites, presented an offering. ³¹ His offering was one silver dish
weighing 3 ¼ pounds and one silver basin weighing 1 ¾ pounds, measured by the
standard sanctuary shekel, both of them
full of fine flour mixed with oil for a grain
offering; ³² one gold bowl weighing four
ounces, full of incense; ³³ one young bull,
one ram, and one male lamb a year old, for
a burnt offering; ³⁴ one male goat for a sin
offering; ³⁵ and two bulls, five rams, five
male goats, and five male lambs a year old,
for the fellowship sacrifice. This was the
offering of Elizur son of Shedeur.

---

^6:26 Lit LORD lift his face to you   ᴮ6:27 Or put my name on   ᶜ7:2 Lit the house of their fathers   ᴰ7:13 Lit dish, 130 its shekel-
weight, also in vv. 19,25,31,37,43,49,55,61,67,73,79   ᴱ7:13 Lit 70 shekels, also in vv. 19,25,31,37,43,49,55,61,67,73,79   ᶠ7:14 Lit 10
(shekels), also in vv. 20,26,32,38,44,50,56,62,68,74,80,86

God's grace would be exemplified when
God brought the second generation into
the promised land after the rejection of that
gift by the generation delivered from Egypt.
**6:26 Look with favor on you and give
you peace** expresses God's grace and beneficence. Favor is the directing of one's full
attention toward the needs and desires of
another person.

6:27 The name of God is a reflection of the
fullness of his character.
7:1 The historical setting of the construction
of the tabernacle (Ex 40:17) is the first day of
the first month of the second year, nearly a
year after the exodus from Egypt.
7:2–11 The presented carts and oxen would
be used to transport the tabernacle and its
furnishings.

7:12–83 Each of the twelve tribal representatives presented the given number of
items for use in the Israelite celebration. The
repetition in this passage highlights the fact
that every tribe participated in the ritual
celebrations and had an equal role in the
religious practices. Only the guilt offering is
not mentioned in this context of consecration and celebration.

36 On the fifth day Shelumiel son of Zurishaddai, leader of the Simeonites, presented an offering. **37** His offering was one silver dish weighing 3¼ pounds and one silver basin weighing 1¾ pounds, measured by the standard sanctuary shekel, both of them full of fine flour mixed with oil for a grain offering; **38** one gold bowl weighing four ounces, full of incense; **39** one young bull, one ram, and one male lamb a year old, for a burnt offering; **40** one male goat for a sin offering; **41** and two bulls, five rams, five male goats, and five male lambs a year old, for the fellowship sacrifice. This was the offering of Shelumiel son of Zurishaddai.

42 On the sixth day Eliasaph son of Deuel,^ leader of the Gadites, presented an offering. **43** His offering was one silver dish weighing 3¼ pounds and one silver basin weighing 1¾ pounds, measured by the standard sanctuary shekel, both of them full of fine flour mixed with oil for a grain offering; **44** one gold bowl weighing four ounces full of incense; **45** one young bull, one ram, and one male lamb a year old, for a burnt offering; **46** one male goat for a sin offering; **47** and two bulls, five rams, five male goats, and five male lambs a year old, for the fellowship sacrifice. This was the offering of Eliasaph son of Deuel.^

48 On the seventh day Elishama son of Ammihud, leader of the Ephraimites, presented an offering. **49** His offering was one silver dish weighing 3¼ pounds and one silver basin weighing 1¾ pounds, measured by the standard sanctuary shekel, both of them full of fine flour mixed with oil for a grain offering; **50** one gold bowl weighing four ounces, full of incense; **51** one young bull, one ram, and one male lamb a year old, for a burnt offering; **52** one male goat for a sin offering; **53** and two bulls, five rams, five male goats, and five male lambs a year old, for the fellowship sacrifice. This was the offering of Elishama son of Ammihud.

54 On the eighth day Gamaliel son of Pedahzur, leader of the Manassites, presented an offering. **55** His offering was one silver dish weighing 3¼ pounds and one silver basin weighing 1¾ pounds, measured by the standard sanctuary shekel, both of them full of fine flour mixed with oil for a grain offering; **56** one gold bowl weighing four ounces, full of incense; **57** one young bull, one ram, and one male

lamb a year old, for a burnt offering; **58** one male goat for a sin offering; **59** and two bulls, five rams, five male goats, and five male lambs a year old, for the fellowship sacrifice. This was the offering of Gamaliel son of Pedahzur.

60 On the ninth day Abidan son of Gideoni, leader of the Benjaminites, presented an offering. **61** His offering was one silver dish weighing 3¼ pounds and one silver basin weighing 1¾ pounds, measured by the standard sanctuary shekel, both of them full of fine flour mixed with oil for a grain offering; **62** one gold bowl weighing four ounces, full of incense; **63** one young bull, one ram, and one male lamb a year old, for a burnt offering; **64** one male goat for a sin offering; **65** and two bulls, five rams, five male goats, and five male lambs a year old, for the fellowship sacrifice. This was the offering of Abidan son of Gideoni.

66 On the tenth day Ahiezer son of Ammishaddai, leader of the Danites, presented an offering. **67** His offering was one silver dish weighing 3¼ pounds and one silver basin weighing 1¾ pounds, measured by the standard sanctuary shekel, both of them full of fine flour mixed with oil for a grain offering; **68** one gold bowl weighing four ounces, full of incense; **69** one young bull, one ram, and one male lamb a year old, for a burnt offering; **70** one male goat for a sin offering; **71** and two bulls, five rams, five male goats, and five male lambs a year old, for the fellowship sacrifice. This was the offering of Ahiezer son of Ammishaddai.

72 On the eleventh day Pagiel son of Ochran, leader of the Asherites, presented an offering. **73** His offering was one silver dish weighing 3¼ pounds and one silver basin weighing 1¾ pounds, measured by the standard sanctuary shekel, both of them full of fine flour mixed with oil for a grain offering; **74** one gold bowl weighing four ounces, full of incense; **75** one young bull, one ram, and one male lamb a year old, for a burnt offering; **76** one male goat for a sin offering; **77** and two bulls, five rams, five male goats, and five male lambs a year old, for the fellowship sacrifice. This was the offering of Pagiel son of Ochran.

78 On the twelfth day Ahira son of Enan, leader of the Naphtalites, presented an offering. **79** His offering was one silver dish weighing 3¼ pounds and one silver basin

---

^7:42,47 LXX, Syr read *Reuel*

weighing 1¾ pounds, measured by the standard sanctuary shekel, both of them full of fine flour mixed with oil for a grain offering; **⁸⁰** one gold bowl weighing four ounces, full of incense; **⁸¹** one young bull, one ram, and one male lamb a year old, for a burnt offering; **⁸²** one male goat for a sin offering; **⁸³** and two bulls, five rams, five male goats, and five male lambs a year old, for the fellowship sacrifice. This was the offering of Ahira son of Enan.

⁸⁴ This was the dedication gift from the leaders of Israel for the altar when it was anointed: twelve silver dishes, twelve silver basins, and twelve gold bowls. **⁸⁵** Each silver dish weighed 3¼ pounds,^ and each basin 1¾ pounds.ᴮ The total weight of the silver articles was 60 poundsᶜ measured by the standard sanctuary shekel. **⁸⁶** The twelve gold bowls full of incense each weighed four ounces measured by the standard sanctuary shekel. The total weight of the gold bowls was 3 pounds.ᴰ **⁸⁷** All the livestock for the burnt offering totaled twelve bulls, twelve rams, and twelve male lambs a year old, with their grain offerings, and twelve male goats for the sin offering. **⁸⁸** All the livestock for the fellowship sacrifice totaled twenty-four bulls, sixty rams, sixty male goats, and sixty male lambs a year old. This was the dedication gift for the altar after it was anointed.

⁸⁹ When Moses entered the tent of meeting to speak with the LORD, he heard the voice speaking to him from above the mercy seat that was on the ark of the testimony, from between the two cherubim. He spoke to him that way.

The Lighting in the Tabernacle

8 The LORD spoke to Moses: **²** "Speak to Aaron and tell him: When you set up the lamps, the seven lamps are to give light in front of the lampstand." **³** So Aaron did this; he set up its lamps to give light in front of the lampstand just as the LORD had commanded Moses. **⁴** This is the way the lampstand was made: it was a hammered work of gold, hammered from its base to its flower petals. The lampstand was made according to the pattern the LORD had shown Moses.

Consecration of the Levites

⁵ The LORD spoke to Moses: **⁶** "Take the Levites from among the Israelites and ceremonially cleanse them. **⁷** Do this to them for their purification: Sprinkle them with the purification water. Have them shave their entire bodies and wash their clothes, and so purify themselves. **⁸** "They are to take a young bull and its grain offering of fine flour mixed with oil, and you are to take a second young bull for a sin offering. **⁹** Bring the Levites before the tent of meeting and assemble the entire Israelite community. **¹⁰** Then present the Levites before the LORD, and have the Israelites lay their hands on them. **¹¹** Aaron is to present the Levites before the LORD as a presentation offering from the Israelites, so that they may perform the LORD's work. **¹²** Next the Levites are to lay their hands on the heads of the bulls. Sacrifice one as a sin offering and the other as a burnt offering to the LORD, to make atonement for the Levites.

¹³ "You are to have the Levites stand before Aaron and his sons, and you are to present them before the LORD as a presentation offering. **¹⁴** In this way you are to separate the Levites from the rest of the Israelites so that the Levites will belong to me. **¹⁵** After that the Levites may come to serve at the tent of meeting, once you have ceremonially cleansed them and presented them as a presentation offering. **¹⁶** For they have been exclusively assigned to me from the Israelites. I have taken them for myself in place of all who come first from the womb, every Israelite firstborn. **¹⁷** For every firstborn among the Israelites is mine, both man and animal. I consecrated them to myself on the day I struck down every firstborn in the land of Egypt. **¹⁸** But I have taken the Levites in place of every firstborn among the Israelites. **¹⁹** From the Israelites, I have given the Levites exclusively to Aaron and his sons to perform the work for the Israelites at the tent of meeting and to make atonement on their behalf, so that no plague will come against the Israelites when they approach the sanctuary."

²⁰ Moses, Aaron, and the entire Israelite community did this to the Levites. The Israelites did everything to them the LORD commanded Moses regarding the Levites. **²¹** The Levites purified themselves and washed their

---

^**7:85** Lit *130* (shekels)   ᴮ**7:85** Lit *70* (shekels)   ᶜ**7:85** Lit *2,400* (shekels)   ᴰ**7:86** Lit *120* (shekels)

7:84–89 This passage fulfills the promise of Ex 25:22. The **tent of meeting**, where Moses had sought revelation from God, had formerly been located outside the camp, but with the tabernacle construction completed, it was placed within the area of the ark of the covenant. Moses could not enter the tent immediately after its construction because of the smoke from the cloud of the Lord that had descended (Ex 40:34–38), but now with the dedication of the tabernacle implements and sacrifices, he could once more seek counsel from God.

8:1–4 The **lampstand**, or menorah, mentioned in 3:31 and 4:9, was a symbol of God's presence and glory.
8:5–7 The **purification** process involved three steps: (1) sprinkling the Levites with special **purification water**, probably taken from the bronze basin in the outer court of the tabernacle; (2) shaving their entire **bodies**, as the Nazirite would do if the vow were broken (6:9,18); and (3) washing their **clothes** (19:8; Lv 16:26,28).
8:8–12 Two **bulls** were sacrificed in the ceremony after the Levites had laid their

hands on the bulls' heads as a symbol of substitutionary identification in the atonement process. The order of **sin offering** and then **burnt offering** follows the delineation in Leviticus, the first for ceremonial purification and the second for consecration.
8:15–19 The **Levites** served as assistants to the Aaronic priests, transporting and maintaining sanctuary structures and implements. They also served as guardians against encroachment upon the holiness of the sanctuary.

clothes; then Aaron presented[A] them before the LORD as a presentation offering. Aaron also made atonement for them to cleanse them ceremonially. [22] After that, the Levites came to do their work at the tent of meeting in the presence of Aaron and his sons. So they did to them as the LORD had commanded Moses concerning the Levites.

[23] The LORD spoke to Moses: [24] "In regard to the Levites: From twenty-five years old or more, a man enters the service in the work at the tent of meeting. [25] But at fifty years old he is to retire from his service in the work and no longer serve. [26] He may assist his brothers to fulfill responsibilities[B] at the tent of meeting, but he must not do the work. This is how you are to deal with the Levites regarding their duties."

The Second Passover

9 In the first month of the second year after their departure from the land of Egypt, the LORD told Moses in the Wilderness of Sinai, [2] "The Israelites are to observe the Passover at its appointed time. [3] You must observe it at its appointed time on the fourteenth day of this month at twilight; you are to observe it according to all its statutes and ordinances." [4] So Moses told the Israelites to observe the Passover, [5] and they observed it in the first month on the fourteenth day at twilight in the Wilderness of Sinai. The Israelites did everything as the LORD had commanded Moses.

[6] But there were some men who were unclean because of a human corpse, so they could not observe the Passover on that day. These men came before Moses and Aaron the same day [7] and said to him, "We are unclean because of a human corpse. Why should we be excluded from presenting the LORD's offering at its appointed time with the other Israelites?"

[8] Moses replied to them, "Wait here until I hear what the LORD commands for you."

[9] Then the LORD spoke to Moses: [10] "Tell the Israelites: When any one of you or your descendants is unclean because of a corpse or is on a distant journey, he may still observe the

Passover to the LORD. [11] Such people are to observe it in the second month, on the fourteenth day at twilight. They are to eat the animal with unleavened bread and bitter herbs; [12] they may not leave any of it until morning or break any of its bones. They must observe the Passover according to all its statutes.

[13] "But the man who is ceremonially clean, is not on a journey, and yet fails to observe the Passover is to be cut off from his people, because he did not present the LORD's offering at its appointed time. That man will bear the consequences of his sin.

[14] "If an alien resides with you and wants to observe the Passover to the LORD, he is to do it according to the Passover statute and its ordinances. You are to apply the same statute to both the resident alien and the native of the land."

Guidance by the Cloud

[15] On the day the tabernacle was set up, the cloud covered the tabernacle, the tent of the testimony, and it appeared like fire above the tabernacle from evening until morning. [16] It remained that way continuously: the cloud would cover it,[C] appearing like fire at night. [17] Whenever the cloud was lifted up above the tent, the Israelites would set out; at the place where the cloud stopped, there the Israelites camped. [18] At the LORD's command the Israelites set out, and at the LORD's command they camped. As long as the cloud stayed over the tabernacle, they camped.

[19] Even when the cloud stayed over the tabernacle many days, the Israelites carried out the LORD's requirement and did not set out. [20] Sometimes the cloud remained over the tabernacle for only a few days. They would camp at the LORD's command and set out at the LORD's command. [21] Sometimes the cloud remained only from evening until morning; when the cloud lifted in the morning, they set out. Or if it remained a day and a night, they moved out when the cloud lifted. [22] Whether it was two days, a month, or longer,[D] the Israelites camped and did not set out as long as the cloud

---

[A] 8:21 Lit waved   [B] 8:26 Or to keep guard   [C] 9:16 LXX, Vg, Syr, Tg read it by day   [D] 9:22 Or a year

---

8:23–26 The addendum to the dedication of the **Levites** cites their retirement age as fifty and their minimum age of service as **twenty-five years**, whereas 4:3 suggests a minimum age of thirty. Some scholars attempt to resolve the inconsistency by suggesting that the Levites may have served a five-year apprenticeship beginning at age twenty-five. Others suggest that the age minimum was raised as a result of the deaths of Nadab and Abihu (Lv 10:1–3).
9:1 In the first month of the second year after the exodus, the Israelites celebrated their second Passover, just two days after the receiving of the tribal offerings (7:12–88), and two weeks before the first military census (1:2–44).

9:8–13 The legislation of vv. 10–13 probably served as the historical precedent for the second month **Passover** in the late eighth century BC, during the reign of King Hezekiah (2Ch 30:1–27), after the king had led the people to destroy pagan worship centers in and around Jerusalem.
9:14 Israelite law gave considerable attention to the status of resident aliens who identified with the Israelite religion. The same law applied to the native Israelite and to the **alien**. Anyone who wanted to identify with the Israelite community of faith and who was willing to submit to the Lord's laws and statutes was permitted to do so.

9:15–16 The chronological sequence returns to that of 7:1 and Ex 40:17, the day when the tabernacle construction was completed—on the first day of the first month of year two. **9:17–23** The poetic structure of v. 17 hints that this section was originally a song that was sung during the wilderness journey. The song's refrain occurs in v. 18. This "Song of the Journey" set the stage for the actual departure from Mount Sinai in 10:11–36. **9:19–22** The periodic movement of God's presence from one campsite to the next varied from a day to several months—perhaps a year or more at Kadesh-barnea after the people refused to enter the promised land (13:25–14:38).

stayed over the tabernacle. But when it was lifted, they set out. ²³ They camped at the LORD's command, and they set out at the LORD's command. They carried out the LORD's requirement according to his command through Moses.

Two Silver Trumpets

10 The LORD spoke to Moses: ² "Make two trumpets of hammered silver to summon the community and have the camps set out. ³ When both are sounded in long blasts, the entire community is to gather before you at the entrance to the tent of meeting. ⁴ However, if one is sounded, only the leaders, the heads of Israel's clans, are to gather before you. ⁵ "When you sound short blasts, the camps pitched on the east are to set out. ⁶ When you sound short blasts a second time, the camps pitched on the south are to set out. Short blasts are to be sounded for them to set out. ⁷ When calling the assembly together, you are to sound long blasts, not short ones. ⁸ The sons of Aaron, the priests, are to sound the trumpets. Your use of these is a permanent statute throughout your generations.

⁹ "When you enter into battle in your land against an adversary who is attacking you, sound short blasts on the trumpets, and you will be remembered before the LORD your God and be saved from your enemies. ¹⁰ You are to sound the trumpets over your burnt offerings and your fellowship sacrifices and on your joyous occasions, your appointed festivals, and the beginning of each of your months. They will serve as a reminder for you before your God: I am the LORD your God."

From Sinai to Paran

¹¹ During the second year, in the second month on the twentieth day of the month, the cloud was lifted up above the tabernacle of the testimony. ¹² The Israelites traveled on from the Wilderness of Sinai, moving from one place to the next until the cloud stopped in the Wilderness of Paran. ¹³ They set out for the first time according to the LORD's command through Moses.

¹⁴ The military divisions of the camp of Judah's descendants with their banner set out first, and Nahshon son of Amminadab was over their divisions. ¹⁵ Nethanel son of Zuar was over the division of the tribe of Issachar's descendants, ¹⁶ and Eliab son of Helon was over the division of the tribe of Zebulun's descendants. ¹⁷ The tabernacle was then taken down, and the Gershonites and the Merarites set out, transporting the tabernacle.

¹⁸ The military divisions of the camp of Reuben with their banner set out, and Elizur son of Shedeur was over their divisions. ¹⁹ Shelumiel son of Zurishaddai was over the division of the tribe of Simeon's descendants, ²⁰ and Eliasaph son of Deuel^A was over the division of the tribe of Gad's descendants. ²¹ The Kohathites then set out, transporting the holy objects; the tabernacle was to be set up before their arrival.

²² Next the military divisions of the camp of Ephraim's descendants with their banner set out, and Elishama son of Ammihud was over their divisions. ²³ Gamaliel son of Pedahzur was over the division of the tribe of Manasseh's descendants, ²⁴ and Abidan son of Gideoni was over the division of the tribe of Benjamin's descendants.

²⁵ The military divisions of the camp of Dan's descendants with their banner set out, serving as rear guard for all the camps, and Ahiezer son of Ammishaddai was over their divisions. ²⁶ Pagiel son of Ochran was over the division of the tribe of Asher's descendants, ²⁷ and Ahira son of Enan was over the division of the tribe of Naphtali's descendants. ²⁸ This was the order of march for the Israelites by their military divisions as they set out.

²⁹ Moses said to Hobab, descendant of Reuel the Midianite and Moses's relative by marriage, "We're setting out for the place the LORD promised, 'I will give it to you.' Come with us, and we will treat you well, for the LORD has promised good things to Israel."

³⁰ But he replied to him, "I don't want to go. Instead, I will go to my own land and my relatives."

---

^10:20 LXX, Syr read *Reuel*

10:1–2 The **two trumpets of hammered silver** were different from the ram's horn (Hb *shofar*). The shofar announced the Day of Atonement (Lv 25:9), and it was used in the march around Jericho at the beginning of the conquest of the promised land (Jos 6:2–21). The distinctive pitch of the silver trumpets summoned the people to march through the wilderness. It was also blown by the priest Phinehas in the battle against Midian (Nm 31:6).
10:11–13 The twentieth of the month was less than a week after the unclean persons were able to celebrate Passover on the fourteenth of the **second month** (cp. 9:8–13). This was also about a month after the weeklong Passover described in 9:1–14 (cp. Ex 13:6).

After they spent eleven months in the Sinai Wilderness, the Lord would now begin to lead the people to his intended destination—the promised land.
10:12 The geographical parameters of this initial movement are the Sinai and Paran deserts. The Israelites camped at Taberah (11:3), Kibroth-hattavah (11:34–35), and Hazeroth (12:16) on their way to the **Wilderness of Paran**. Paran was west of Midian, east of Egypt, extending northward from some point north or northeast of Mount Sinai, northward toward Kadesh-barnea, and eastward to the Arabah.
10:14–28 The orderly departure from Mount Sinai of the priests, Levites, and twelve tribes follows the pattern of the

encampment detailed in 2:1–3:38, with Judah led by **Nahshon** setting out first (v. 14). Order, harmony, and faithfulness marked the beginning of the wilderness journey.
10:29–32 Moses noted twice that **the LORD has promised good things to Israel**, and twice Moses promised Hobab that the goodness would be apportioned to him as well if he would help guide them through the wilderness. Who was this **Hobab** son of **Reuel**? The dual names "Reuel" (Ex 2:18) and "Jethro" (Ex 3:1) in reference to Moses's in-laws are perhaps references to two generations of this Midianite clan, since the Hebrew term can mean "father-in-law," "brother-in-law," or just "in-law." Thus the patriarchal clan leader was probably named "Reuel" (taking "father"

³¹ "Please don't leave us," Moses said, "since you know where we should camp in the wilderness, and you can serve as our eyes. ³² If you come with us, whatever good the LORD does for us we will do for you."

³³ They set out from the mountain of the LORD on a three-day journey with the ark of the LORD's covenant traveling ahead of them for those three days to seek a resting place for them. ³⁴ Meanwhile, the cloud of the LORD was over them by day when they set out from the camp.

³⁵ Whenever the ark set out, Moses would say:

Arise, LORD!
Let your enemies be scattered,
and those who hate you flee
    from your presence.

³⁶ When it came to rest, he would say:
Return, LORD,
to the countless thousands of Israel.

Complaints about Hardship

11 Now the people began complaining openly before ^A^ the LORD about hardship. When the LORD heard, his anger burned, and fire from the LORD blazed among them and consumed the outskirts of the camp. ² Then the people cried out to Moses, and he prayed to the LORD, and the fire died down. ³ So that place was named Taberah, ^B^ because the LORD's fire had blazed among them.

Complaints about Food

⁴ The riffraff ^c^ among them had a strong craving for other food. The Israelites wept again and said, "Who will feed us meat? ⁵ We remember the free fish we ate in Egypt, along with the cucumbers, melons, leeks, onions, and garlic. ⁶ But now our appetite is gone; ^D^ there's nothing to look at but this manna!"

⁷ The manna resembled coriander seed, and its appearance was like that of bdellium. ^E^ ⁸ The people walked around and gathered it. They ground it on a pair of grinding stones or crushed it in a mortar, then boiled it in a cooking pot and shaped it into cakes. It tasted like a pastry cooked with the finest oil. ⁹ When the dew fell on the camp at night, the manna would fall with it.

¹⁰ Moses heard the people, family after family, weeping at the entrance of their tents. The LORD was very angry; Moses was also provoked. ^F^ ¹¹ So Moses asked the LORD, "Why have you brought such trouble on your servant? Why are you angry with me, ^G^ and why do you burden me with all these people? ¹² Did I conceive all these people? Did I give them birth so you should tell me, 'Carry them at your breast, as a nursing mother carries a baby,' to the land that you swore to give their ancestors? ¹³ Where can I get meat to give all these people? For they are weeping to me, 'Give us meat to eat!' ¹⁴ I can't carry all these people by myself. They are too much for me. ¹⁵ If you are going to treat me like this, please kill me right now if I have found favor with you, and don't let me see my misery ^H^ anymore."

Seventy Elders Anointed

¹⁶ The LORD answered Moses, "Bring me seventy men from Israel known to you as elders and officers of the people. Take them to the tent of meeting and have them stand there with you. ¹⁷ Then I will come down and speak with you there. I will take some of the Spirit who is on you and put the Spirit on them. They will help you bear the burden of the people, so that you do not have to bear it by yourself.

---

as "grandfather" which is common in the Hebrew Bible) and the actual father-in-law of Moses was named "Jethro." Others suggest Jethro and Reuel are the same person, since dual names are commonly reflected in Bronze Age texts.

Did Moses show a lack of faith by asking his brother-in-law to serve as a guide in the wilderness? The text does not even hint at this suggestion, since the focus is on the involvement of Hobab as a potential recipient of the covenant blessings of Israel. Hobab would provide valuable support in the desert setting known by the Midianites.

10:33–36 The "Battle Song of the Ark" (vv. 35–36) is preceded by a dual chronological marker about the first stage in the movement of the Lord's cloud. A **three-day journey** would mean a distance of about thirty-five to forty-five miles, based on travel rates mentioned in military annals of the pharaohs of Egypt. On the journey the **cloud**, symbolizing God's presence and leadership (9:15–23), preceded them at a distance though still covering them for protection. **The ark of the LORD's covenant**, the symbolic throne of God in king-to-servant relationship with Israel, led the way for the people. The three-day journey is reminiscent of Moses's request to Pharaoh to allow the Israelites to journey three days into the wilderness to worship the Lord.

11:1–3 These verses establish the complaint pattern of later narratives (chaps. 11–25): (1) complaint, (2) divine punishment, and (3) naming the place after some aspect of the event. Hence, the "fiery" judgment of God led to the place being named **Taberah**, or "blaze."

11:4 The **riffraff** refers to a mixed crowd of Israelites including descendants of Jacob as well as others who had left Egypt in the exodus.

11:5–6 The people's complaint is summarized in the words, **We remember the free fish we ate in Egypt**. This amounted to calling the evil of the Egyptian oppression "good" and God's good provision in the wilderness "evil."

11:7–9 The phrase **the manna resembled coriander seed** is one of the few descriptions of the wilderness diet. Manna's association with coriander seed is probably an indicator of its taste, since the seed was used for flavoring. The comparison of manna to **bdellium** indicates a yellow-white aromatic resin similar to a by-product of the tamarisk tree found in northern Arabia.

11:16 The term for "officers" (Hb *shote-rim*) also denotes scribes, whom R. K. Harrison has suggested were responsible for the writing and collecting of documents that would eventually become the Pentateuch. The **tent of meeting** was the place of revelation and mediation, two aspects of the relationship between God and his people.

11:17 The possession of the **Spirit** of God that had been exclusively on Moses would now be distributed to the seventy elders, giving them

18 "Tell the people: Consecrate yourselves in readiness for tomorrow, and you will eat meat because you wept in the LORD's hearing, 'Who will feed us meat? We were better off in Egypt.' The LORD will give you meat and you will eat. **19** You will eat, not for one day, or two days, or five days, or ten days, or twenty days, **20** but for a whole month — until it comes out of your nostrils and becomes nauseating to you — because you have rejected the LORD who is among you, and wept before him, 'Why did we ever leave Egypt?'"

21 But Moses replied, "I'm in the middle of a people with six hundred thousand foot soldiers, yet you say, 'I will give them meat, and they will eat for a month.' **22** If flocks and herds were slaughtered for them, would they have enough? Or if all the fish in the sea were caught for them, would they have enough?"

23 The LORD answered Moses, "Is the LORD's arm weak?ᴬ Now you will see whether or not what I have promised will happen to you."

24 Moses went out and told the people the words of the LORD. He brought seventy men from the elders of the people and had them stand around the tent. **25** Then the LORD descended in the cloud and spoke to him. He took some of the Spirit who was on Moses and placed the Spirit on the seventy elders. As the Spirit rested on them, they prophesied, but they never did it again. **26** Two men had remained in the camp, one named Eldad and the other Medad; the Spirit rested on them — they were among those listed, but had not gone out to the tent — and they prophesied in the camp. **27** A young man ran and reported to Moses, "Eldad and Medad are prophesying in the camp."

28 Joshua son of Nun, assistant to Moses since his youth,ᴮ responded, "Moses, my lord, stop them!"

29 But Moses asked him, "Are you jealous on my account? If only all the LORD's people were prophets and the LORD would place his Spirit on them!" **30** Then Moses returned to the camp along with the elders of Israel.

Quail in the Camp

31 A wind sent by the LORD came up and blew quail in from the sea; it dropped them all around the camp. They were flying three feetᶜ offᴰ the ground for about a day's journey in every direction. **32** The people were up all that day and night and all the next day gathering the quail — the one who took the least gathered sixty bushelsᴱ — and they spread them out all around the camp.ᶠ

33 While the meat was still between their teeth, before it was chewed, the LORD's anger burned against the people, and the LORD struck them with a very severe plague. **34** So they named that place Kibroth-hattaavah,ᴳ because there they buried the people who had craved the meat.

35 From Kibroth-hattaavah the people moved on to Hazerothᴴ and remained there.

Miriam and Aaron Rebel

12 Miriam and Aaron criticized Moses because of the Cushite woman he married (for he had married a Cushite woman). **2** They said, "Does the LORD speak only through Moses? Does he not also speak through us?" And the LORD heard it. **3** Moses was a very humble man, more so than anyone on the face of the earth.

4 Suddenly the LORD said to Moses, Aaron, and Miriam, "You three come out to the tent of meeting." So the three of them went out. **5** Then the LORD descended in a pillar of cloud, stood at

---

ᴬ**11:23** Lit *the LORD's arm too short* ᴮ**11:28** Or *Moses, from his elite young men* ᶜ**11:31** Lit *two cubits* ᴰ**11:31** Or *They were three feet deep on* ᴱ**11:32** Lit *10 homers* ᶠ**11:32** To dry or cure the meat; 2Sm 17:19; Ezk 26:5,14 ᴳ**11:34** = Graves of Craving ᴴ**11:35** = Settlements; Nm 12:16; 33:16–17

---

a spiritual dimension that would set them apart from the administrative and judicial appointees of Ex 18:25–26. The work of the Spirit of God would enable the elders and officers to carry out the tasks of teaching, judging, and leading the Israelites through the wilderness. **11:18 Consecrate yourselves** refers to the process of purification through the washing of body and clothes to prepare people to receive a theophany—a manifestation of God's presence. **11:19–20** God declared to the Israelites that they would eat . . . **for a whole month**. The supply of quail in Ex 16:13 was in response to a need for food in the first wilderness journey before reaching Mount Sinai. **11:24–25** That God **took some of the Spirit who was on Moses** and placed it on the Israelite elders did not diminish the Spirit that was on Moses. This miracle provided the necessary power and wisdom to those who functioned on behalf of God and under the direction of Moses. **11:26–30** Two elders, **Eldad** and **Medad**, who had not attended the presentation

ceremony, prophesied in the same manner as the other elders, demonstrating that God's Spirit cannot be confined to any space or time. Joshua saw the actions of Eldad and Medad as a challenge to Moses's leadership. Moses is apparently now glad to share his responsibilities. **11:31–32** In a manner similar to the **wind** that blew back the waters of the Red Sea in the exodus event, a divinely driven wind brought a large quantity of **quail** across the camp. The extraordinary quantity of quail was swept in from the sea, probably from the Gulf of Aqaba (Elath) if the wind were from the east, and then northwest toward the encampment of Israel. **11:33** The **severe plague** sent upon the people might have been food poisoning due to the time the quail meat remained in the sun without proper processing and drying. **11:34** The blessing turned to craving, and the craving to disease and death, leading to the naming of the location **Kibroth-hattaavah** ("Graves of Craving").

12:1 The supposed reason for the complaint of **Miriam and Aaron** against Moses was his marriage to a **Cushite woman**, though the real reason was Moses's authority as God's primary spokesman. Explanations for the Cushite identity include: (1) she was Moses's second wife of Cushite origin (Nubian = modern Ethiopian or Sudanese), whom Moses perhaps had married while Zipporah was back in Midian visiting her father Jethro; (2) perhaps Zipporah (a Midianite) had died and Moses had recently remarried; and (3) Zipporah and the Cushite woman are one and the same. **12:2** The terminology and the context suggest that Aaron and Miriam were challenging Moses's prophetic position as the primary recipient of revelation from God. **12:3** This parenthetical statement probably came from the narrator rather than from Moses. It suggests that Moses would have let the challenge go unanswered. **12:4–5** The **pillar of cloud** descended to provide the personal encounter for divine disclosure.

the entrance to the tent, and summoned Aaron and Miriam. When the two of them came forward, **6** he said:

"Listen to what I say:
If there is a prophet among you
    from the LORD,
I make myself known to him
    in a vision;
I speak with him in a dream.
7 Not so with my servant Moses;
he is faithful in^A all my household.
8 I speak with him directly,^B
openly, and not in riddles;
he sees the form of the LORD.
So why were you not afraid to speak against my servant Moses?" **9** The LORD's anger burned against them, and he left.

10 As the cloud moved away from the tent, Miriam's skin suddenly became diseased, resembling snow.^C When Aaron turned toward her, he saw that she was diseased **11** and said to Moses, "My lord, please don't hold against us this sin we have so foolishly committed.

12 Please don't let her be like a dead baby^D whose flesh is half eaten away when he comes out of his mother's womb." **13** Then Moses cried out to the LORD, "God, please heal her!"

14 The LORD answered Moses, "If her father had merely spit in her face, wouldn't she remain in disgrace for seven days? Let her be confined outside the camp for seven days; after that she may be brought back in." **15** So Miriam was confined outside the camp for seven days, and the people did not move on until Miriam was brought back in. **16** After that, the people set out from Hazeroth and camped in the Wilderness of Paran.

Scouting Out Canaan

13 The LORD spoke to Moses: **2** "Send men to scout out the land of Canaan I am giving to the Israelites. Send one man who is a leader among them from each of their ancestral tribes." **3** Moses sent them from the Wilderness of Paran at the LORD's command. All

^A**12:7** Or *is entrusted with*   ^B**12:8** Lit *mouth to mouth*   ^C**12:10** A reference to whiteness or flakiness of the skin   ^D**12:12** Alt Hb tradition reads *baby who comes out of our mother's womb and our flesh is half eaten away.*

12:6–7 Being called **my servant** by the Lord and a **faithful** prophet placed Moses in the category of Abraham (Gn 26:24) and the "servant" in the Servant Songs of Isaiah (Is 42–53).
12:8 God declared of Moses, **I speak with him directly, openly.** The expression denotes the direct method by which the will of God was communicated through the words of Moses, which could legitimately be translated "mouth to mouth," since out of the mouth of a person echoes his character (Mt 12:34).

12:9–13 The description of Miriam's disease as **resembling snow** like a stillborn **baby** suggests a variety of ailments ranging from skin cancer to psoriasis, or perhaps even modern leprosy, Hansen's disease. All of these would render him unclean according to Levitical law (Lv 13–14).
12:14–15 The **seven days** of separation after healing follows the Levitical law consistently, and the purification process described in Lv 14:1–32 is assumed here.
12:16 The Paran Wilderness is a broad area of northeastern Sinai, bordered on the

northeast by the Zin Wilderness within which Kadesh-barnea is located (cp. 33:15–37).
13:1–14:45 The climax to the first cycle of rebellions is the refusal of the people to enter the promised land. The people adopted the majority report of ten of twelve spies—that the inhabitants of the land and their fortified cities were too strong for them to conquer. The rejection of the land was a rejection of God and his blessings.
13:3 The geographical designations in the chapter move from the broader context of the **Wilderness of Paran** to the more

Character profile:
Miriam

Miriam was the sister of Moses. Though she's not named in the famous story of the infant Moses being hidden in a basket, placed in the Nile River, and discovered by Pharaoh's daughter (see Ex 2), she's almost certainly the sister mentioned there.

The first time she is called by name in Scripture is when the children of Israel are celebrating their great deliverance from slavery in Egypt and safe passage through the Red Sea. Miriam is shown playing a prominent role, leading the women in singing (see 15:20–21).

Over time, Miriam and her two brothers became a kind of "executive leadership team," with Moses functioning like the CEO. He was the one handpicked by God to lead the Israelites to freedom and the one who met regularly face-to-face with God (see 33:11). Miriam's other brother, Aaron, acted as Moses's chief communications officer (see 7:1–2). Miriam had the role of "prophetess" (15:20), meaning that, like her brother Moses, she too received revelations directly from the Lord.

One day Aaron and Miriam finally had enough of playing second fiddle to Moses. They were sick of watching Moses get so much glory. When their frustration reached critical mass, they began to criticize their brother (see Nm 12:1–12). "They said, 'Does the LORD speak only through Moses? Does he not also speak through us?' And the LORD heard it" (12:2).

What happened next wasn't pretty. God called a meeting of these three siblings. When they arrived at the tent of meeting,

God called Miriam and Aaron to come forward. He told them in no uncertain terms that Moses was "my servant . . . faithful in all my household" (12:7). By criticizing Moses, they had criticized God.

To underline his anger, God caused Miriam's skin to become white and diseased (thus, she was the true instigator of this challenge to Moses's leadership). But Moses then stepped forward and pleaded with God to restore his sister to health. God agreed, but first he gave Miriam seven days to think about what she'd done (see Nm 12).

What significant life lessons might Miriam have learned from this incident? Do with joy the thing God has called you to do. Be thankful for the opportunity to serve, and don't overstep your bounds. Refuse to compare yourself with others, resist the snare of envy. Miriam isn't mentioned again in the Bible until the time of her death (see 20:1).

If you've ever tried to lead anything—a family, an organization, a project, or a company—you know that leadership is tricky business. Every decision gets questioned and second-guessed. Everyone always seems to have a better idea. It's easy to become critical of those who lead.

God calls us to humbly play the role he's given us instead of focusing on the shortcomings of others, wishing we had someone else's life, or grumbling about another person getting more attention.

If you want to fixate on something, let it be this question: Am I being faithful in my own responsibilities? As Paul wrote, "Who are you to judge another's household servant? Before his own Lord he stands or falls" (Rm 14:4).

JOURNEY OF THE SPIES
NUMBERS 13:1–33; 34:1–12

- ● City
- ○ City (uncertain location)
- ● Oasis
- ▲ Mountain peak
- ← Journey of the twelve spies
-    The promised land

the men were leaders in Israel. [4] These were their names:

Shammua son of Zaccur from the tribe of Reuben;

[5] Shaphat son of Hori from the tribe of Simeon;

[6] Caleb son of Jephunneh from the tribe of Judah;

[7] Igal son of Joseph from the tribe of Issachar;

[8] Hoshea son of Nun from the tribe of Ephraim;

[9] Palti son of Raphu from the tribe of Benjamin;

[10] Gaddiel son of Sodi from the tribe of Zebulun;

[11] Gaddi son of Susi from the tribe of Manasseh (from the tribe of Joseph);

[12] Ammiel son of Gemalli from the tribe of Dan;

[13] Sethur son of Michael from the tribe of Asher;

[14] Nahbi son of Vophsi from the tribe of Naphtali;

[15] Geuel son of Machi from the tribe of Gad.

[16] These were the names of the men Moses sent to scout out the land, and Moses renamed Hoshea son of Nun, Joshua.

[17] When Moses sent them to scout out the land of Canaan, he told them, "Go up this way to the Negev, then go up into the hill country. [18] See what the land is like, and whether the people who live there are strong or weak, few or many. [19] Is the land they live in good or bad? Are the cities they live in encampments or fortifications? [20] Is the land fertile or unproductive? Are there trees in it or not? Be courageous. Bring back some fruit from the land." It was the season for the first ripe grapes.

[21] So they went up and scouted out the land from the Wilderness of Zin[A] as far as Rehob near the entrance to Hamath.[B] [22] They went up through the Negev and came to Hebron, where Ahiman, Sheshai, and Talmai, the descendants of Anak, were living. Hebron was built seven years before Zoan in Egypt. [23] When they came to Eshcol Valley, they cut down a branch with a single cluster of grapes, which was carried on a pole by two men. They also took some pomegranates and figs. [24] That place was called Eshcol[C] Valley because of the cluster of grapes the Israelites cut there. [25] At the end of forty days they returned from scouting out the land.

Report about Canaan

[26] The men went back to Moses, Aaron, and the entire Israelite community in the Wilderness of Paran at Kadesh. They brought back a report for them and the whole community, and they showed them the fruit of the land. [27] They reported to Moses, "We went into the land where you sent us. Indeed it is flowing with milk and honey, and here is some of its fruit. [28] However, the people living in the land are strong, and the cities are large and fortified. We also saw the descendants of Anak there. [29] The Amalekites are living in the land of the Negev; the Hethites, Jebusites, and Amorites live in the hill country; and the Canaanites live by the sea and along the Jordan."

---

^A 13:21 Southern border of the promised land   ^B 13:21 Or *near Lebo-hamath*   ^C 13:24 = Cluster

---

specific citation of Kadesh (-barnea) in the Zin Wilderness (33:36–37), the starting point of their exploration (13:21). The Zin Wilderness is defined by the desert drainage basin of the Nahal Zin, a subsection of the Paran Wilderness. Today the Nahal Zin is viewed as portions of Sinai and the Negev in modern Israel.

13:4–16 The list of these scouts contains a number of unusual names, rarely appearing again in the OT, with the exception of Joshua and Caleb. This gives an indication of the early date of the composition of Numbers.

13:17–20 The parenthetic note about the season of the **first ripe grapes** places the exploration of Canaan in August or early September, several months after the departure from Mount Sinai in early spring.

13:17 The **Negev** in the OT refers to the region south of Hebron, but north of the Zin Wilderness.

13:22 Hebron is said to have been fortified **seven years before Zoan**, which was in the eastern Nile Delta, about a hundred miles northeast of Cairo. The Egyptian name for Zoan is *Dja'net*, which was pronounced by the Greeks as *Tanis*. It is associated with the site known as Tel el-Daba. The names of the three clans descended from **Anak** indicate they were Semitic. They were also known as being "strong and tall" (Dt 9:2).

13:23–24 The Hebrew word *'eshcol* means "a cluster of grapes," and hence **Eshcol Valley** reflects the productivity of the vineyards in the valley, which is located west of Hebron. Ripe **pomegranates and figs** suggest a date of late August or early September for this exploration of Canaan.

13:25 The scouts' **forty days** of exploring the land matches the approximate time it would have taken for the 350- to 400-mile journey on foot, based upon the twelve to fifteen miles per day average.

13:26 The Israelite scouts had departed from the **Paran** Desert area and had worked their way north into the Negev and through what would later be Judah and Israel. The Israelites meanwhile continued their journey to the oasis of **Kadesh**-barnea, presumed to be the area of Quseima, at the headwaters of the wilderness basin of the Nahal Zin.

13:27 The report of the scouts began on the positive side with the demonstration of the fruitfulness of the promised land. **Milk and honey** became the classic description of the abundance of natural flora and fauna of the land of Canaan (Ex 3:8,17; 13:5; 33:3; Lv 20:24; Dt 6:3; 11:9).

13:28–29 The tenor of the report quickly changed to a negative assessment of the possibility of conquering the heavily fortified cities and the numerous inhabitants, which they claimed included giants.

The **Amalekites** were a seminomadic tribe from the region of Edom that ranged throughout the southern Levant, from northern Sinai to the hill country of Samaria.

The **Hethites**, known from the patriarchal period (Gn 23:3–20), were from the central highlands; they originated in eastern Anatolia around the third millennium BC.

The **Jebusites** were a non–Semitic clan who lived in Jerusalem during the middle Bronze through Iron I periods (2000–1000 BC); they remained in control of the city until the time of the Davidic conquests (2Sm 5:6–9). They are unknown outside the Bible.

The Semitic **Amorites** lived in the hill country of the central and southern Levant. The term *Amorite* can refer to a number of inhabitants of areas known today as Syria, Lebanon, Jordan, Israel, and Palestine. It may also refer more specifically to ethnic descendants of Canaan as delineated in Gn 10:16.

The **Canaanites** emerged in the middle Bronze Age (2000–1550 BC) in the southern Levant (Gn 12:6) and continued to be a significant percentage of the population into the late Bronze Age (1550–1200 BC) and Iron I Age (1200–1000 BC).

³⁰ Then Caleb quieted the people in the presence of Moses and said, "Let's go up now and take possession of the land because we can certainly conquer it!"

³¹ But the men who had gone up with him responded, "We can't attack the people because they are stronger than we are!" ³² So they gave a negative report to the Israelites about the land they had scouted: "The land we passed through to explore is one that devours its inhabitants, and all the people we saw in it are men of great size. ³³ We even saw the Nephilim there — the descendants of Anak come from the Nephilim! To ourselves we seemed like grasshoppers, and we must have seemed the same to them."

Israel's Refusal to Enter Canaan

14 Then the whole community broke into loud cries, and the people wept that night. ² All the Israelites complained about Moses and Aaron, and the whole community told them, "If only we had died in the land of Egypt, or if only we had died in this wilderness! ³ Why is the LORD bringing us into this land to die by the sword? Our wives and children will become plunder. Wouldn't it be better for us to go back to Egypt?" ⁴ So they said to one another, "Let's appoint a leader and go back to Egypt."

⁵ Then Moses and Aaron fell facedown in front of the whole assembly of the Israelite community. ⁶ Joshua son of Nun and Caleb son of Jephunneh, who were among those who scouted out the land, tore their clothes ⁷ and said to the entire Israelite community, "The land we passed through and explored is an extremely good land. ⁸ If the LORD is pleased with us, he will bring us into this land, a land flowing with milk and honey, and give it to us. ⁹ Only don't rebel against the LORD, and don't be afraid of the people of the land, for we will devour them. Their protection has been removed

from them, and the LORD is with us. Don't be afraid of them!"

¹⁰ While the whole community threatened to stone them, the glory of the LORD appeared to all the Israelites at the tent of meeting.

God's Judgment of Israel's Rebellion

¹¹ The LORD said to Moses, "How long will these people despise me? How long will they not trust in me despite all the signs I have performed among them? ¹² I will strike them with a plague and destroy them. Then I will make you into a greater and mightier nation than they are."

¹³ But Moses replied to the LORD, "The Egyptians will hear about it, for by your strength you brought up this people from them. ¹⁴ They will tell it to the inhabitants of this land. They have heard that you, LORD, are among these people, how you, LORD, are seen face to face, how your cloud stands over them, and how you go before them in a pillar of cloud by day and in a pillar of fire by night. ¹⁵ If you kill this people with a single blow,[A] the nations that have heard of your fame will declare, ¹⁶ 'Since the LORD wasn't able to bring this people into the land he swore to give them, he has slaughtered them in the wilderness.'

¹⁷ "So now, may my Lord's power be magnified just as you have spoken: ¹⁸ The LORD is slow to anger and abounding in faithful love, forgiving iniquity and rebellion. But he will not leave the guilty unpunished, bringing the consequences of the fathers' iniquity on the children to the third and fourth generation. ¹⁹ Please pardon the iniquity of this people, in keeping with the greatness of your faithful love, just as you have forgiven them from Egypt until now."

²⁰ The LORD responded, "I have pardoned them as you requested. ²¹ Yet as I live and as the whole earth is filled with the LORD's glory,

---

^14:15 Lit people as one man

13:30 Caleb was the first to counter the objections of the majority of the scouts. The name "Caleb" means "dog."
13:33 The reference to the descendants of Anak as **Nephilim** was designed to instill fear in the hearts of the Israelites. The Nephilim, "fallen ones" ("giants" in the LXX), are noted in Gn 6:4 as the offspring of the "sons of God" ("angelic beings" or "divine warriors") and the "daughters of men." The Nephilim were of large stature, but they all would have been destroyed in Noah's flood (Gn 6:11), so it is best to conclude that the frightened spies gave an exaggerated report. **Grasshoppers** were the smallest of edible creatures permitted for Israelite consumption (Lv 11:22).
14:4 The rebellion turned to the rejection of God's chosen and faithful leaders: Moses, Aaron, Caleb, and later Joshua.
14:5–9 Moses and Aaron **fell facedown** in humble submission before God at the entrance to the tabernacle where the people had gathered. At the same time they were

bowing before the rebellious Israelites, propitiating God on their behalf. The faithful scouts Joshua and Caleb **tore their clothes** as a symbol of mourning and disdain for the defiant Israelites and their humiliated leaders. The tearing of one's garments was a gesture of mourning for the dead, for expressing lament over disease or plague, and for introducing a prophetic lament of judgment against an individual or nation.
14:11–12 God threatened to destroy the Israelites and start over with a new people through Moses. This was not the first time God threatened this (Ex 32:10).
14:13–16 Moses intervened on behalf of a rebellious nation with an appeal to God's reputation among the nations (**the Egyptians will hear about it**) and to the power of God to fulfill his promises. God's glory was at stake in this crisis.
14:14 Most translations have **face to face** (lit "eye to eye,"), but neither Israel nor Moses could look upon God's face (Ex 33:11,20–23).

The expression denotes the method by which the will of God was communicated directly through the words of Moses.
14:17–18 Slow to anger describes God's longsuffering character. **Abounding in faithful love** describes God's lovingkindness and covenant loyalty to the descendants of Abraham, Isaac, and Jacob. But in spite of his love, his justice and righteousness would not allow him to **leave the guilty unpunished**.
The phrase **bringing the consequences of the fathers' iniquity on the children** meant that stemming the tide of sinfulness within the family structure often took many generations. God does not cause one's descendants to suffer because of the sins of their fathers (Dt 24:16; Ezk 18), but he does punish children who keep doing the same sorts of sins as their parents.
14:20–23 In refusing to enter the promised land, the older generation had rejected an essential part of their covenant relationship with God that was set forth in the Abrahamic

²² none of the men who have seen my glory and the signs I performed in Egypt and in the wilderness, and have tested me these ten times and did not obey me, ²³ will ever see the land I swore to give their ancestors. None of those who have despised me will see it. ²⁴ But since my servant Caleb has a different spirit and has remained loyal to me, I will bring him into the land where he has gone, and his descendants will inherit it. ²⁵ Since the Amalekites and Canaanites are living in the lowlands,ᴬ turn back tomorrow and head for the wilderness in the direction of the Red Sea."

²⁶ Then the LORD spoke to Moses and Aaron: ²⁷ "How long must I endure this evil community that keeps complaining about me? I have heard the Israelites' complaints that they make against me. ²⁸ Tell them: As I live — this is the LORD's declaration — I will do to you exactly as I heard you say. ²⁹ Your corpses will fall in this wilderness — all of you who were registered in the census, the entire number of you twenty years old or more — because you have complained about me. ³⁰ I swear that none of you will enter the land I promisedᴮ to settle you in, except Caleb son of Jephunneh and Joshua son of Nun. ³¹ I will bring your children whom you said would become plunder into the land you rejected, and they will enjoy it. ³² But as for you, your corpses will fall in this wilderness. ³³ Your children will be shepherds in the wilderness for forty years and bear the penalty for your acts of unfaithfulness until all your corpses lie scattered in the wilderness. ³⁴ You will bear the consequences of your iniquities forty years based on the number of the forty days that you scouted the land, a year for each day.ᶜ You will know my displeasure.ᴰ ³⁵ I, the LORD, have spoken. I swear that I will do this to the entire evil community that has conspired against me. They will come to an end in the wilderness, and there they will die."

³⁶ So the men Moses sent to scout out the land, and who returned and incited the entire community to complain about him by spreading a negative report about the land — ³⁷ those men who spread the negative report about the land were struck down by the LORD. ³⁸ Only Joshua son of Nun and Caleb son of Jephunneh remained alive of those men who went to scout out the land.

Israel Routed

³⁹ When Moses reported these words to all the Israelites, the people were overcome with grief. ⁴⁰ They got up early the next morning and went up the ridge of the hill country, saying, "Let's go to the place the LORD promised, for we were wrong."

⁴¹ But Moses responded, "Why are you going against the LORD's command? It won't succeed. ⁴² Don't go, because the LORD is not among you and you will be defeated by your enemies. ⁴³ The Amalekites and Canaanites are right in front of you, and you will fall by the sword. The LORD won't be with you, since you have turned from following him."

⁴⁴ But they dared to go up the ridge of the hill country, even though the ark of the LORD's covenant and Moses did not leave the camp. ⁴⁵ Then the Amalekites and Canaanites who lived in that part of the hill country came down, attacked them, and routed them as far as Hormah.

Laws about Offerings

15 The LORD instructed Moses, ² "Speak to the Israelites and tell them: When you enter the land I am giving you to settle in, ³ and you make a food offering to the LORD from the herd or flock — either a burnt offering or a sacrifice, to fulfill a vow, or as a freewill offering, or at your appointed festivals — to produce a pleasing aroma for the LORD, ⁴ the one presenting his offering to the LORD is also to present a grain offering of two quartsᴱ of fine flour mixed with a quartᶠ of oil. ⁵ Prepare a quart of wine as a drink offering with the burnt offering or sacrifice of each lamb.

⁶ "If you prepare a grain offering with a ram, it is to be four quartsᴳ of fine flour mixed with a

covenant (Gn 12:1–3,7; 13:14–18; 15:18–21; 17:7–8). God's judgment did not apply to those who were under twenty years old of the generation that left Egypt (Nm 14:29). **14:24 Caleb**, the faithful scout from the tribe of Judah, would join Hoshea (Joshua) of Ephraim as one of only two exceptions to God's judgment against the ten scouts who had issued the majority report (v. 30). **14:25 The wilderness in the direction of the Red Sea** was the line of the trade route that connected to Ezion-geber on the Gulf of Aqaba/Elath from Kadesh-barnea through the Zin Wilderness and the southern Arabah. The Red Sea refers to the eastern arm of the Red Sea known as the Gulf of Aqaba (1Kg 9:26–28).

14:26–28 As I live is the language of the court as the Lord, God of Israel, took an oath on his own honor and announced the verdict against the guilty spies. **14:29–35** A form of talionic justice (judgment equal to the crime, "an eye for an eye") was announced: **forty days** of spying, which led to the negative report, would be matched by **forty years** of wandering, with an effective death sentence on the first generation of Israelite leaders and militia. **14:39–43** Any attempt to launch out in conquest of the land without the Lord's blessing would be futile. Deliberate disobedience to God's command not to attack the Canaanites would meet with resounding defeat.

14:44–45 The city of **Hormah** has been identified tentatively with Tel Masos in the Beer-sheba Valley region. **15:1–41** This chapter consists of three units that address important matters issuing from the rebellious acts in chaps. 11–14: land, sinfulness, and the need to remember God and his revelation. **15:3–13** A **food offering** presented in celebration stands in contrast to the destructive fire of God depicted in 11:1–4. The consecration offering described in Lv 1 in which the entire offering was consumed by fire on the altar is the **burnt offering**. This form of dedication typically followed the sin offering that was given to restore one's relationship with God through atonement

third of a gallon^A of oil. ⁷ Also present a third of a gallon of wine for a drink offering as a pleasing aroma to the LORD.

⁸ "If you prepare a young bull as a burnt offering or as a sacrifice, to fulfill a vow, or as a fellowship offering to the LORD, ⁹ a grain offering of six quarts^B of fine flour mixed with two quarts^C of oil is to be presented with the bull. ¹⁰ Also present two quarts of wine as a drink offering. It is a food offering, a pleasing aroma to the LORD. ¹¹ This is to be done for each ox, ram, lamb, or goat. ¹² This is how you are to prepare each of them, no matter how many.

¹³ "Every Israelite is to prepare these things in this way when he presents a food offering as a pleasing aroma to the LORD. ¹⁴ When an alien resides with you or someone else is among you and wants to prepare a food offering as a pleasing aroma to the LORD, he is to do exactly as you do throughout your generations. ¹⁵ The assembly is to have the same statute for both you and the resident alien as a permanent statute throughout your generations. You and the alien will be alike before the LORD. ¹⁶ The same law and the same ordinance will apply to both you and the alien who resides with you."

¹⁷ The LORD instructed Moses, ¹⁸ "Speak to the Israelites and tell them: After you enter the land where I am bringing you, ¹⁹ you are to offer a contribution to the LORD when you eat from the food of the land. ²⁰ You are to offer a loaf from your first batch of dough as a contribution; offer it just like a contribution from the threshing floor. ²¹ Throughout your generations, you are to give the LORD a contribution from the first batch of your dough.

²² "When you sin unintentionally and do not obey all these commands that the LORD spoke to Moses — ²³ all that the LORD has commanded you through Moses, from the day the LORD issued the commands and onward throughout your generations — ²⁴ and if it was done unintentionally without the community's awareness, the entire community is to prepare one young bull for a burnt offering as a pleasing aroma to the LORD, with its grain offering and drink offering according to the regulation, and one male goat as a sin offering. ²⁵ The priest will then make atonement for the entire Israelite community so that they may be forgiven, for the sin was unintentional. They are to bring their offering, a food offering to the LORD, and their sin offering before the LORD for their unintentional sin. ²⁶ The entire Israelite community and the alien who resides among them will be forgiven, since it happened to all the people unintentionally.

²⁷ "If one person sins unintentionally, he is to present a year-old female goat as a sin offering. ²⁸ The priest will then make atonement before the LORD on behalf of the person who acts in error sinning unintentionally, and when he makes atonement for him, he will be forgiven. ²⁹ You are to have the same law for the person who acts in error, whether he is an Israelite or an alien who resides among you.

³⁰ "But the person who acts defiantly,^D whether native or resident alien, blasphemes the LORD. That person is to be cut off from his people. ³¹ He will certainly be cut off, because he has despised the LORD's word and broken his command; his guilt remains on him."

Sabbath Violation

³² While the Israelites were in the wilderness, they found a man gathering wood on the Sabbath day. ³³ Those who found him gathering wood brought him to Moses, Aaron, and the entire community. ³⁴ They placed him in custody because it had not been decided what should be done to him. ³⁵ Then the LORD told Moses, "The man is to be put to death. The entire community is to stone him outside the camp." ³⁶ So the entire community brought him outside the camp and stoned him to death, as the LORD had commanded Moses.

Tassels for Remembrance

³⁷ The LORD said to Moses, ³⁸ "Speak to the Israelites and tell them that throughout their

^A15:6 Lit a third hin, also in v. 7   ^B15:9 Lit three-tenths (of an ephah)   ^C15:9 Lit a half hin, also in v. 10   ^D15:30 Lit with a high hand

and purification. The **sacrifice, to fulfill a vow** and the **fellowship offering** were forms of communion offering, designed to celebrate the relationship with God among the community of faith. Out of those blessings the people would bring offerings from the produce of the land in celebration of the Lord's goodness and miraculous works in history, commemorated in the appointed festivals: Passover, Pentecost, and Shelters. Numbers 15:1–21 complements Lv 1–3 with details about the amounts and proportions of grain, oil, and wine that were supplements to the normal offerings. **15:14–16** Sacrificial requirements were the same for native Israelites and foreign residents who wanted to identify with the Israelite faith and submit to the authority of the Torah. Faith for Israel was not limited to the descendants of the sons of Jacob. **15:17–21** The **first batch of dough**, a form of firstfruits offering, was dedicated to the Lord in celebration of the abundant produce from the land. Even the mundane daily practice of kneading dough for making bread was to be a time of worship and celebration of God's goodness. **15:22–23** Unintentional sins included matters in which the individual or community acted unknowingly in breaking a legal stipulation or in failing to perform certain ritual requirements. **15:24–29** Leviticus 4:1–5:19 provides several examples of these unintentional sins. **15:30–31** When a person acted **defiantly** in breaking the covenant relationship, that person blasphemed the Lord and defamed his righteous reputation. The penalty was either capital punishment or permanent banishment from the community of faith. **15:32–36** The defiant breaking of the law of God is exemplified by an Israelite who performed work on the **Sabbath**. The Sabbath was a sign of the Mosaic covenant, so the breaking of it would mean the rejection of the covenant relationship with God. Permitting such behavior would be dangerous to the whole people, especially at this critical juncture in Israelite history. **15:37–39** The instructions in this verse were about the outward symbol for reminding the people of their covenant faith—the blue corded **tassels** attached to the **corners of their garments** (Dt 22:12).

generations they are to make tassels for the corners of their garments, and put a blue cord on the tassel at each corner. **39** These will serve as tassels for you to look at, so that you may remember all the LORD's commands and obey them and not prostitute yourselves by following your own heart and your own eyes. **40** This way you will remember and obey all my commands and be holy to your God. **41** I am the LORD your God who brought you out of the land of Egypt to be your God; I am the LORD your God."

Korah Incites Rebellion

16 Now Korah son of Izhar, son of Kohath, son of Levi, with Dathan and Abiram, sons of Eliab, and On son of Peleth, sons of Reuben, took **2** two hundred fifty prominent Israelite men who were leaders of the community and representatives in the assembly, and they rebelled against Moses. **3** They came together against Moses and Aaron and told them, "You have gone too far! Everyone in the entire community is holy, and the LORD is among them. Why then do you exalt yourselves above the LORD's assembly?"

4 When Moses heard this, he fell facedown. **5** Then he said to Korah and all his followers, "Tomorrow morning the LORD will reveal who belongs to him, who is set apart, and the one he will let come near him. He will let the one he chooses come near him. **6** Korah, you and all your followers are to do this: take firepans, and tomorrow **7** place fire in them and put incense on them before the LORD. Then the man the LORD chooses will be the one who is set apart. It is you Levites who have gone too far!"

8 Moses also told Korah, "Now listen, Levites! **9** Isn't it enough for you that the God of Israel has separated you from the Israelite

^16:11 Or *Aaron, what has he done*

community to bring you near to himself, to perform the work at the LORD's tabernacle, and to stand before the community to minister to them? **10** He has brought you near, and all your fellow Levites who are with you, but you are pursuing the priesthood as well. **11** Therefore, it is you and all your followers who have conspired against the LORD! As for Aaron, who is he^ that you should complain about him?"

12 Moses sent for Dathan and Abiram, the sons of Eliab, but they said, "We will not come! **13** Is it not enough that you brought us up from a land flowing with milk and honey to kill us in the wilderness? Do you also have to appoint yourself as ruler over us? **14** Furthermore, you didn't bring us to a land flowing with milk and honey or give us an inheritance of fields and vineyards. Will you gouge out the eyes of these men? We will not come!"

15 Then Moses became angry and said to the LORD, "Don't respect their offering. I have not taken one donkey from them or mistreated a single one of them." **16** So Moses told Korah, "You and all your followers are to appear before the LORD tomorrow — you, they, and Aaron. **17** Each of you is to take his firepan, place incense on it, and present his firepan before the LORD — 250 firepans. You and Aaron are each to present your firepan also."

18 Each man took his firepan, placed fire in it, put incense on it, and stood at the entrance to the tent of meeting along with Moses and Aaron. **19** After Korah assembled the whole community against them at the entrance to the tent of meeting, the glory of the LORD appeared to the whole community. **20** The LORD spoke to Moses and Aaron, **21** "Separate yourselves from this community so I may consume them instantly."

15:41 The declaration **I am the LORD your God** resonates with covenant overtones, calling to mind the initial words of Moses's encounter with God in Ex 6:2–8 and the introduction to the Ten Commandments in Ex 20:2.

16:1–19:22 The second cycle of rebellion focuses on a challenge to the Aaronic priesthood. The insurrection resulted in the deaths of the 250 followers of Korah and an additional 14,700 from the plague that followed. This section warns against violation of the holiness of the sanctuary.

16:1–2 In patriarchal tribal societies in the ancient Near East, the firstborn son often carried the initial words of Moses's religious traditions for the family. This could be why **Dathan and Abiram**, who were from the tribe of **Reuben**, the firstborn of Jacob, decided to join the rebellion. But the leader of the insurrection was **Korah**, a Levite from the Kohathite clan. The Kohathites had been granted responsibilities in 3:27–32; 4:1–20, but Korah wanted a higher status (16:8–10).

16:3 Korah's claim that **everyone in the entire community is holy, and the LORD**

is among them had an element of truth, since God had called Israel to be "my kingdom of priests and my holy nation" (Ex 19:6). But that role was based on Israel's faithful obedience to God's revelation. God had ordained Moses and Aaron's exalted positions; they had not assigned themselves these roles.

16:4–7 The **firepans** were pans or shallow bowls with long handles (Lv 10:1) in which the priests carried hot coals upon which incense was sprinkled. Incense enhanced the sweet-smelling aroma of burning sacrifices that ascended into the heavens. Moses's words **the man the LORD chooses will be the one who is set apart** set the challenge in the court of God to identify and defend the truly faithful servant.

16:8–10 Korah and the Kohathites had a favored status among the three Levite clans in handling the holy things of the tabernacle (3:27–32), but they desired greater glory for themselves.

16:11–14 The rebels claimed Moses had failed to bring the people to a place of rest and abundance. They would not admit that it

was their rebellion that led to the wilderness judgment.

16:20–22 Only the true servants of God—Moses and Aaron—**fell facedown** and, risking their own lives, appealed to his graciousness so the **whole community** might not suffer his **wrath**.

#07 **99 Essential Christian Truths**

GOD IS IMMANENT

When we say that God is immanent, we mean that God is personable and relatable to those made in his image, while remaining completely distinct and unique from all of his creation. God is not a distant deity (as imagined by the deist) who only sits on his heavenly throne with no interaction; instead, he is a personal God who created people in his image to be in personal relationship with him.

²² But Moses and Aaron fell facedown and said, "God, God who gives breath to all,^A when one man sins, will you vent your wrath on the whole community?"

²³ The LORD replied to Moses, ²⁴ "Tell the community: Get away from the dwellings of Korah, Dathan, and Abiram."

²⁵ Moses got up and went to Dathan and Abiram, and the elders of Israel followed him. ²⁶ He warned the community, "Get away now from the tents of these wicked men. Don't touch anything that belongs to them, or you will be swept away because of all their sins." ²⁷ So they got away from the dwellings of Korah, Dathan, and Abiram. Meanwhile, Dathan and Abiram came out and stood at the entrance of their tents with their wives, children, and infants.

²⁸ Then Moses said, "This is how you will know that the LORD sent me to do all these things and that it was not of my own will: ²⁹ If these men die naturally as all people would, and suffer the fate of all, then the LORD has not sent me. ³⁰ But if the LORD brings about something unprecedented, and the ground opens its mouth and swallows them along with all that belongs to them so that they go down alive into Sheol, then you will know that these men have despised the LORD."

³¹ Just as he finished speaking all these words, the ground beneath them split open. ³² The earth opened its mouth and swallowed them and their households, all Korah's people, and all their possessions. ³³ They went down alive into Sheol with all that belonged to them. The earth closed over them, and they vanished from the assembly. ³⁴ At their cries, all the people of Israel who were around them fled because they thought, "The earth may swallow us too!" ³⁵ Fire also came out from the LORD and consumed the 250 men who were presenting the incense.

³⁶ Then the LORD spoke to Moses: ³⁷ "Tell Eleazar son of Aaron the priest to remove the firepans from the burning debris, because they are holy, and scatter the fire far away. ³⁸ As for the firepans of those who sinned at the cost of their own lives, make them into hammered sheets as plating for the altar, for they presented them

before the LORD, and the firepans are holy. They will be a sign to the Israelites."

³⁹ So the priest Eleazar took the bronze firepans that those who were burned had presented, and they were hammered into plating for the altar, ⁴⁰ just as the LORD commanded him through Moses. It was to be a reminder for the Israelites that no unauthorized person outside the lineage of Aaron should approach to offer incense before the LORD and become like Korah and his followers.

⁴¹ The next day the entire Israelite community complained about Moses and Aaron, saying, "You have killed the LORD's people!" ⁴² When the community assembled against them, Moses and Aaron turned toward the tent of meeting, and suddenly the cloud covered it, and the LORD's glory appeared.

⁴³ Moses and Aaron went to the front of the tent of meeting, ⁴⁴ and the LORD said to Moses, ⁴⁵ "Get away from this community so that I may consume them instantly." But they fell facedown.

⁴⁶ Then Moses told Aaron, "Take your firepan, place fire from the altar in it, and add incense. Go quickly to the community and make atonement for them, because wrath has come from the LORD; the plague has begun." ⁴⁷ So Aaron took his firepan as Moses had ordered, ran into the middle of the assembly, and saw that the plague had begun among the people. After he added incense, he made atonement for the people. ⁴⁸ He stood between the dead and the living, and the plague was halted. ⁴⁹ But those who died from the plague numbered 14,700, in addition to those who died because of the Korah incident. ⁵⁰ Aaron then returned to Moses at the entrance to the tent of meeting, since the plague had been halted.

Aaron's Staff Chosen

17 The LORD instructed Moses, ² "Speak to the Israelites and take one staff from them for each ancestral tribe,^B twelve staffs from all the leaders of their tribes.^C Write each man's name on his staff. ³ Write Aaron's name on Levi's staff, because there is to be one staff for the head of each tribe. ⁴ Then place them in the tent of meeting in front of the testimony

---

^A 16:22 Or *God of the spirits of all flesh* ^B 17:2 Lit *father's house* ^C 17:2 Lit *the house of their fathers*, also in vv. 3,6

16:26 The tents, families, and property of the rebellious leaders had effectively been dedicated to destruction (Hb *cherem*), and anyone who touched any of these things would be swallowed up in the devastation. **16:33–35** The grave (**Sheol**) at this point in Israel's history was perceived to be a shadowy, unknowable realm of the dead, the netherworld of both good and evil where a person was gathered among ancestors at death. In this incident the bodies of the leading rebels, their families, and their possessions plummeted into the gaping abyss. A judgmental **fire … consumed the** other 250

insurrectionists. The second census informs us that Korah's fate was the same as that of Dathan and Abiram (26:10). Since Moses pronounced the curse before it happened, no one could mistake the judgment as accidental. **16:41–50** The lesson of the previous day was soon forgotten as **the entire Israelite community complained about Moses and Aaron**, citing them as the reason for the judgment against the rebellious Korah and his conspirators. God's reaction followed the judgment sequence of the previous day with a call for the people to separate themselves

from the insurgents as God's glory descended, lest they be consumed in the judgment. Aaron's act on behalf of the people portrays the concept of propitiatory **atonement** as he literally stood as the mediator between **the dead and the living** to ward off the wrath of God. **17:1–3** The **staff** was the official symbol of the tribal chieftain. One word (Hb *matteh*) means both "tribe" and "staff/scepter," and each carried some signification of tribal identity. In this context the names were inscribed for identification. Aaron's name was inscribed on the staff of the tribe of

where I meet with you. ⁵ The staff of the man I choose will sprout, and I will rid myself of the Israelites' complaints that they have been making about you."

⁶ So Moses spoke to the Israelites, and each of their leaders gave him a staff, one for each of the leaders of their tribes, twelve staffs in all. Aaron's staff was among them. ⁷ Moses placed the staffs before the LORD in the tent of the testimony.

⁸ The next day Moses entered the tent of the testimony and saw that Aaron's staff, representing the house of Levi, had sprouted, formed buds, blossomed, and produced almonds! ⁹ Moses then brought out all the staffs from the LORD's presence to all the Israelites. They saw them, and each man took his own staff. ¹⁰ The LORD told Moses, "Put Aaron's staff back in front of the testimony to be kept as a sign for the rebels, so that you may put an end to their complaints before me, or else they will die." ¹¹ So Moses did as the LORD commanded him.

¹² Then the Israelites declared to Moses, "Look, we're perishing! We're lost; we're all lost! ¹³ Anyone who comes near the LORD's tabernacle will die. Will we all perish?"

Provision for the Priesthood

18 The LORD said to Aaron, "You, your sons, and your ancestral family^A will be responsible for iniquity against the sanctuary. You and your sons will be responsible for iniquity involving your priesthood. ² But also bring your relatives with you from the tribe of Levi, your ancestral tribe, so they may join you and assist you and your sons in front of the tent of the testimony. ³ They are to perform duties for you and for the whole tent. They must not come near the sanctuary equipment or the altar; otherwise, both they and you will die. ⁴ They are to join you and guard the tent of meeting, doing all the work at the tent, but no unauthorized person may come near you.

⁵ "You are to guard the sanctuary and the altar so that wrath may not fall on the Israelites again. ⁶ Look, I have selected your fellow Levites from the Israelites as a gift for you, assigned by the LORD to work at the tent of meeting. ⁷ But you and your sons will carry out your priestly responsibilities for everything concerning the altar and for what is inside the curtain, and you will do that work. I am giving you the work of the priesthood as a gift,^B but an unauthorized person who comes near the sanctuary will be put to death."

Support for the Priests and Levites

⁸ Then the LORD spoke to Aaron, "Look, I have put you in charge of the contributions brought to me. As for all the holy offerings of the Israelites, I have given them to you and your sons as a portion and a permanent statute. ⁹ A portion of the holiest offerings kept from the fire will be yours; every one of their offerings that they give me, whether the grain offering, sin offering, or guilt offering will be most holy for you and your sons. ¹⁰ You are to eat it as a most holy offering.^C Every male may eat it; it is to be holy to you.

¹¹ "The contribution of their gifts also belongs to you. I have given all the Israelites' presentation offerings to you and to your sons and daughters as a permanent statute. Every ceremonially clean person in your house may eat it. ¹² I am giving you all the best of the fresh oil, new wine, and grain, which the Israelites give to the LORD as their firstfruits. ¹³ The firstfruits of all that is in their land, which they bring to the LORD, belong to you. Every clean person in your house may eat them.

¹⁴ "Everything in Israel that is permanently dedicated to the LORD belongs to you. ¹⁵ The firstborn of every living thing, human or animal, presented to the LORD belongs to you. But you must certainly redeem a human firstborn, and redeem the firstborn of an unclean animal. ¹⁶ You will pay the redemption price for a month-old male according to your assessment: five shekels^D of silver by the standard sanctuary shekel, which is twenty gerahs.

^A 18:1 Lit *the house of your father*   ^B 18:7 Or *curtain. So you are to perform the service; a gift of your priesthood I grant*   ^C 18:10 Or *it in a most holy place*   ^D 18:16 A shekel is about two-fifths of an ounce

Levi, since he was the oldest son in his family.

17:8–9 The fourfold statement of the miraculous produce from Aaron's staff (**sprouted, formed buds, blossomed, and produced almonds**) heightened the drama, with God demonstrating the priority of the Aaronic priesthood.

17:10 After Moses showed the other tribal leaders the collection of tribal staffs, they were able to see God's blessing upon Aaron's staff. Then God told Moses to **put Aaron's staff back in front of the testimony to be kept as a sign.** Moses placed the staff in front of the ark of the covenant as a sign against the rebels that

God had indeed chosen the Aaronic line for priestly service.

17:11 Moses the faithful and humble servant of God carried out the Lord's instructions, even though the opposition again had placed a heavy burden on his shoulders.

17:12–13 These verses contain the people's panicked response to the incidents narrated in 16:1–17:11 and furnishes the context for chap. 18. They were convinced that the very presence of the tabernacle amid the tribes of Israel was a danger.

18:1–6 The Aaronic priests were camped in front of the entrance to the tabernacle on the east side of the sanctuary. The three clans of the Levites—Kohathites, Gershonites, and

Merarites—were camped on the other three sides. This arrangement provided a physical and spiritual barrier against violation of the holy place.

18:7 Trespassers and irreverent persons would **be put to death,** so God's wrath might not bring widespread destruction on the nation.

18:8–13 The priests and Levites provisions were gifts of tithes and offerings from the people. Even the priests and Levites were required to tithe their gifts to the Lord (vv. 26–28).

18:14–20 Based on the principle of Ex 11:1–10 and 13:2–16, Israel was redeemed through the firstborn of Egypt, both human and animal.

¹⁷ "However, you must not redeem the first-born of an ox, a sheep, or a goat; they are holy. You are to splatter their blood on the altar and burn their fat as a food offering for a pleasing aroma to the LORD. ¹⁸ But their meat belongs to you. It belongs to you like the breast of the presentation offering and the right thigh.

¹⁹ "I give to you and to your sons and daughters all the holy contributions that the Israelites present to the LORD as a permanent statute. It is a permanent covenant of salt before the LORD for you as well as your offspring."

²⁰ The LORD told Aaron, "You will not have an inheritance in their land; there will be no portion among them for you. I am your portion and your inheritance among the Israelites.

²¹ "Look, I have given the Levites every tenth in Israel as an inheritance in return for the work they do, the work of the tent of meeting. ²² The Israelites must never again come near the tent of meeting, or they will incur guilt and die. ²³ The Levites will do the work of the tent of meeting, and they will bear the consequences of their iniquity. The Levites will not receive an inheritance among the Israelites; this is a permanent statute throughout your generations. ²⁴ For I have given them the tenth that the Israelites present to the LORD as a contribution for their inheritance. That is why I told them that they would not receive an inheritance among the Israelites."

²⁵ The LORD instructed Moses, ²⁶ "Speak to the Levites and tell them: When you receive from the Israelites the tenth that I have given you as your inheritance, you are to present part of it as an offering to the LORD — a tenth of the tenth. ²⁷ Your offering will be credited to you as if it were your grain from the threshing floor or the full harvest from the winepress. ²⁸ You are to present an offering to the LORD from every tenth you receive from the Israelites. Give some of it to the priest Aaron as an offering to the LORD. ²⁹ You must present the entire offering due the LORD from all your gifts. The best part of the tenth is to be consecrated.

³⁰ "Tell them further: Once you have presented the best part of the tenth, and it is credited to you Levites as the produce of the threshing floor or the winepress, ³¹ then you and your household may eat it anywhere. It is your wage in return for your work at the tent of meeting. ³² You will not incur guilt because of it once you have presented the best part of it, but you must not defile the Israelites' holy offerings, so that you will not die."

Purification Ritual

19 The LORD spoke to Moses and Aaron, ² "This is the legal statute that the LORD has commanded: Instruct the Israelites to bring you an unblemished red cow that has no defect and has never been yoked. ³ Give it to the priest Eleazar, and he will have it brought outside the camp and slaughtered in his presence. ⁴ The priest Eleazar is to take some of its blood with his finger and sprinkle it seven times toward the front of the tent of meeting. ⁵ The cow is to be burned in his sight. Its hide, flesh, and blood, are to be burned along with its waste. ⁶ The priest is to take cedar wood, hyssop, and crimson yarn, and throw them onto the fire where the cow is burning. ⁷ Then the priest must wash his clothes and bathe his body in water; after that he may enter the camp, and he will remain ceremonially unclean until evening. ⁸ The one who burned the cow must also wash his clothes and bathe his body in water, and he will remain unclean until evening.

⁹ "A man who is clean is to gather up the cow's ashes and deposit them outside the camp in a ceremonially clean place. The ashes will be kept by the Israelite community for preparing the water to remove impurity; it is a sin offering. ¹⁰ Then the one who gathers up the cow's ashes must wash his clothes, and he will remain unclean until evening. This is a permanent statute for the Israelites and for the alien who resides among them.

¹¹ "The person who touches any human corpse will be unclean for seven days. ¹² He is

---

18:19 Salt was associated with seasoning, preserving, and purifying. It was to accompany all the Levitical offerings, referred to as "the salt of the covenant with your God" (Lv 2:13; Ezr 6:9). It symbolized a permanent relationship with God (2Ch 13:5).
18:21–24 The gift of the **tenth** to the Le-vites was new legislation, whereas much of vv. 1–20 is a review of existing legislation. This highlights the role of the priests and Levites within the community after the threat to their positions in the Korah rebellion.
18:25–32 The Levites in turn were required to present to the Lord **a tenth of the tenth**, and thus participate in the full cycle of blessings. The **best part of the tenth**, the highest quality from the produce of the flocks and fields, was to be presented to the Aaronic priesthood.

19:1–6 The original historical context of the **red cow** ritual was under the auspices of the priesthood of **Eleazar**, while his father Aaron was still alive (his death is cited in 20:22–29). The sprinkling of the blood of the slaughtered cow is consistent with other blood rituals in the Pentateuch (Lv 4:6,17; 8:11; 16:14,19). The **unblemished** cow was entirely red—not spotted or mottled.
Since the cow had never been yoked, it was probably young and strong. Elsewhere it was a bull that was sacrificed as a sin offering for the high priest and his family (Lv 4:3–12; 16:6,11), or on behalf of the entire community (Lv 4:13–21). Thus the female is specified here so there would be no confusion of purification agents or rituals. The cow would also offer the maximum yield of purification ashes so the ritual need not be repeated as often. The redness of the cow reflected the

color of blood, as did the other sacrificial elements burned with the cow.
The plant species translated **hyssop** was probably not the Greek *hussopos*, but marjoram, sage, or thyme, the leaves of which are very absorbent. Other reddish or colored elements in ritual sanctification included cypress wood, roses, red wine, and cedar sap.
19:7–10 The **priest**, the assistant **who burned the cow**, and the **one who** gathered and stored the **ashes**, were each made unclean by touching this purification (sin) offering—the red cow ashes—but this was a lesser state of uncleanness than what was generated by touching a dead body. The ashes alone caused uncleanness, but when mixed with water they became a purifying agent.
19:11–22 Ritual impurity from exposure to the dead required a "sin offering" that was

to purify himself with the water^A on the third day and the seventh day; then he will be clean. But if he does not purify himself on the third and seventh days, he will not be clean. ¹³ Anyone who touches a body of a person who has died, and does not purify himself, defiles the tabernacle of the LORD. That person will be cut off from Israel. He remains unclean because the water for impurity has not been sprinkled on him, and his uncleanness is still on him.

¹⁴ "This is the law when a person dies in a tent: everyone who enters the tent and everyone who is already in the tent will be unclean for seven days, ¹⁵ and any open container without a lid tied on it is unclean. ¹⁶ Anyone in the open field who touches a person who has been killed by the sword or has died, or who even touches a human bone, or a grave, will be unclean for seven days. ¹⁷ For the purification of the unclean person, they are to take some of the ashes of the burnt sin offering, put them in a jar, and add fresh water to them. ¹⁸ A person who is clean is to take hyssop, dip it in the water, and sprinkle the tent, all the furnishings, and the people who were there. He is also to sprinkle the one who touched a bone, a grave, a corpse, or a person who had been killed.

¹⁹ "The one who is clean is to sprinkle the unclean person on the third day and the seventh day. After he purifies the unclean person on the seventh day, the one being purified must wash his clothes and bathe in water, and he will be clean by evening. ²⁰ But a person who is unclean and does not purify himself, that person will be cut off from the assembly because he has defiled the sanctuary of the LORD. The water for impurity has not been sprinkled on him; he is unclean. ²¹ This is a permanent statute for them. The person who sprinkles the water for impurity is to wash his clothes, and whoever

touches the water for impurity will be unclean until evening. ²² Anything the unclean person touches will become unclean, and anyone who touches it will be unclean until evening."

Water from the Rock

20 The entire Israelite community entered the Wilderness of Zin in the first month, and they^B settled in Kadesh. Miriam died and was buried there.

² There was no water for the community, so they assembled against Moses and Aaron. ³ The people quarreled with Moses and said, "If only we had perished when our brothers perished before the LORD. ⁴ Why have you brought the LORD's assembly into this wilderness for us and our livestock to die here? ⁵ Why have you led us up from Egypt to bring us to this evil place? It's not a place of grain, figs, vines, and pomegranates, and there is no water to drink!"

⁶ Then Moses and Aaron went from the presence of the assembly to the doorway of the tent of meeting. They fell facedown, and the glory of the LORD appeared to them. ⁷ The LORD spoke to Moses, ⁸ "Take the staff and assemble the community. You and your brother Aaron are to speak to the rock while they watch, and it will yield its water. You will bring out water for them from the rock and provide drink for the community and their livestock."

⁹ So Moses took the staff from the LORD's presence just as he had commanded him. ¹⁰ Moses and Aaron summoned the assembly in front of the rock, and Moses said to them, "Listen, you rebels! Must we bring water out of this rock for you?" ¹¹ Then Moses raised his hand and struck the rock twice with his staff, so that abundant water gushed out, and the community and their livestock drank.

^A 19:12 Or *ashes*; lit *with it*   ^B 20:1 Lit *the people*

---

actually a purification. Failure to perform the symbolic cleansings on the **third** and **seventh** days resulted in banishment from the community or death. Contamination could result from several situations:(1) being in or entering a tent where someone had just died, (2) contact with the dead in battle or by accidental proximity, or (3) contact with a grave or its remains. The seven-day period of the impurity was the maximum length for persons who had become unclean through a variety of serious diseases. Other forms of impurity, such as contact with the red cow, rendered a person impure only until sundown.

19:13 The severity of the impurity resulting from touching a corpse is evidenced in the ritual washings administered on the third and seventh days, the potential of defiling the sanctuary from a distance if left unpurified, and the potential penalty of (Hb) *karath*—being **cut off from** the community.

19:21 In future generations (**this is a permanent statute for them**) this purification offering and ritual would be a common purification offering, not only because of

the exposure to corpses, but because it was considered acceptable for cleansing other forms of impurity. In his presentation of the person and work of Jesus Christ as superior to OT ceremonies, the writer of the book of Hebrews combined the ritual of the ashes of the red cow with that of the Day of Atonement in demonstrating the once-and-for-all sufficiency of the blood of Christ in cleansing us from all our sins (Heb 9:11–14).

20:1 The **first month**, Abib (Nisan), in the spring of the fortieth year, brought the conclusion of the punishment of Israel in the wilderness. The chapter begins with the death of **Miriam** and concludes with Aaron's death on the first day of the fifth month of the fortieth year after the exodus (33:38–39). This was the month of the deliverance from Egypt, in which the people should have been celebrating the Passover and the Festival of Unleavened Bread in the promised land. Instead they found themselves back at Kadesh after forty years. Miriam's death is recounted briefly.

20:2 The grumbling Israelites were now back where they had first received the scouts'

report assessing the promised land (13:25–26). Their ten-person majority report had produced a rebellious rejection of the land by the Israelites and the forty-year judgment in the wilderness.

20:3–5 The shortage of water led to an insurrection of the Israelites against their leaders. This event recalls the earlier event by the older generation in Ex 17:1–7. Once more the people claimed that it would have been better to **die** in **Egypt** than to suffer such hardship in that barren wilderness. They preferred bondage, oppression, and death in captivity over their miraculous deliverance, freedom, and provision from the Lord.

20:6–8 The **staff** mentioned here was probably the staff of Aaron that had budded, blossomed, and produced almonds to confirm Aaron's priestly authority.

20:9–11 Moses fell into unfaithfulness by unleashing a verbal attack on the rebels and declaring that he and Aaron were about to bring forth water from a rock. Then he **struck the rock twice** instead of speaking to it. God punished Moses by declaring that he would **not bring this assembly into the land**.

¹² But the LORD said to Moses and Aaron, "Because you did not trust me to demonstrate my holiness in the sight of the Israelites, you will not bring this assembly into the land I have given them." ¹³ These are the Waters of Meribah,ᴬ where the Israelites quarreled with the LORD, and he demonstrated his holiness to them.

Edom Denies Passage

¹⁴ Moses sent messengers from Kadesh to the king of Edom, "This is what your brother Israel says, 'You know all the hardships that have overtaken us. ¹⁵ Our ancestors went down to Egypt, and we lived in Egypt many years, but the Egyptians treated us and our ancestors badly. ¹⁶ When we cried out to the LORD, he heard our plea,ᴮ and sent an angel,ᶜ and brought us out of Egypt. Now look, we are in Kadesh, a city on the border of your territory. ¹⁷ Please let us travel through your land. We won't travel through any field or vineyard, or drink any well water. We will travel the King's Highway; we won't turn to the right or the left until we have traveled through your territory.'"

¹⁸ But Edom answered him, "You will not travel through our land, or we will come out and confront you with the sword." ¹⁹ "We will go on the main road," the Israelites replied to them, "and if we or our herds drink your water, we will pay its price. There will be no problem; only let us travel through on foot." ²⁰ Yet Edom insisted, "You may not travel through." And they came out to confront them with a large force of heavily-armed people.ᴰ ²¹ Edom refused to allow Israel to travel through their territory, and Israel turned away from them.

Aaron's Death

²² After they set out from Kadesh, the entire Israelite community came to Mount Hor. ²³ The LORD said to Moses and Aaron at Mount Hor on the border of the land of Edom, ²⁴ "Aaron will be gathered to his people; he will not enter the land I have given the Israelites, because you both rebelled against my command at the Waters of Meribah. ²⁵ Take Aaron and his son Eleazar and bring them up Mount Hor. ²⁶ Remove Aaron's garments and put them on his son Eleazar. Aaron will be gathered to his people and die there."

²⁷ So Moses did as the LORD commanded, and they climbed Mount Hor in the sight of the whole community. ²⁸ After Moses removed Aaron's garments and put them on his son Eleazar, Aaron died there on top of the mountain. Then Moses and Eleazar came down from the mountain. ²⁹ When the whole community saw that Aaron had passed away, the entire house of Israel mourned for him thirty days.

Canaanite King Defeated

21 When the Canaanite king of Arad, who lived in the Negev, heard that Israel was coming on the Atharim road, he fought against Israel and captured some prisoners. ² Then Israel made a vow to the LORD, "If you will hand this people over to us, we will completely destroy their cities." ³ The LORD listened to Israel's request and handed the Canaanites over to them, and Israel completely destroyed them and their cities. So they named the place Hormah.ᴱ

The Bronze Snake

⁴ Then they set out from Mount Hor by way of the Red Sea to bypass the land of Edom, but the people became impatient because of the

---

ᴬ 20:13 = Quarreling   ᴮ 20:16 Lit voice   ᶜ 20:16 Or a messenger   ᴰ 20:20 Lit with numerous people and a strong hand   ᴱ 21:3 = Destruction

---

20:14–17 Moses's message to **the king of Edom** followed classical Hebrew epistolary form and customary protocol of the Bronze and Iron ages.

The mention of the point of origin for the letter at **Kadesh, a city on the border of your territory,** made the king of Edom aware of Israel's immediate need for passage. If this Kadesh is taken to be Kadesh-barnea, and if it lay near the border of Edomite territory, this implies that some of the early tribal Edomites had settled or controlled some areas west of the Arabah. Others believe the phrase means that Israel under Moses was simply approaching the Edomite region. Like Israel, the Edomites did not become a formal state in the modern sense until the Iron II period (1000–550 BC).

Moses's request included specifics about how the Israelites would respect Edomite domain if they would grant passage. The seasonal description indicates spring, when grain fields were at or near harvest time and vine dressing for the summer and fall crops had just begun. Thus, it was important to

assure the Edomites that their crops would not be trampled or scavenged. Water rights also were of great concern. The Israelites would presumably bring their own water supply from Kadesh during their brief passage of perhaps two days through the Edomite highlands.

The King's Highway was a famous trade route connecting Damascus with Arabia, Sinai, and Egypt through the Transjordan tablelands (Golan, Bashan, Gilead, Ammon, Moab, and Edom) and the southern mountains, paralleling the Arabah on the eastern side. Caravans brought highly prized incense, spices, perfumes, precious jewels, and copper from the Sinai and Paran wilderness sources. **20:18–21** The suggestion of payment for safe passage was in keeping with ancient Near Eastern protocol, as tolls or tribute were often exacted from trade caravans. The harsh Edomite answer caused bitter feelings between Israel and Edom for centuries.

20:22 The location of **Mount Hor** depends on the route followed by the Israelites. As with Kadesh (v. 16), Mount Hor was on

the border with Edom, according to 33:37. Suggested mountains have included the traditional Islamic identity of Jebel Nebi Harun ("Mount of the Prophet Aaron") near Petra; Jebel Medra about six miles northeast of Kadesh; 'Imaret el-Khurisheh about eight miles north of Kadesh; or Jebel Madurah about fifteen miles northeast of Kadesh-barnea.

21:1–3 After the death of Aaron, the Israelites set out from Mount Hor to go around Edom along **the Atharim road**. The Atharim was another trade route leading from Kadesh-barnea to Arad along which the fortresses of Bir Hafir, Oboda, and Aroer were built during the Israelite monarchy. Hormah was the scene of the Israelites' defeat forty years earlier (14:45).

21:4 The trade route referred to as the **way of the Red Sea** extended from Elath on the eastern finger of the Red Sea in the Gulf of Aqaba northward through the Arabah to the Dead Sea. Hence the desert route would have the Israelites approaching the northern end of the Arabah from the southwest, and

journey. [5] The people spoke against God and Moses: "Why have you led us up from Egypt to die in the wilderness? There is no bread or water, and we detest this wretched food!" [6] Then the LORD sent poisonous[A] snakes among the people, and they bit them so that many Israelites died.

[7] The people then came to Moses and said, "We have sinned by speaking against the LORD and against you. Intercede with the LORD so that he will take the snakes away from us." And Moses interceded for the people.

[8] Then the LORD said to Moses, "Make a snake image and mount it on a pole. When anyone who is bitten looks at it, he will recover." [9] So Moses made a bronze snake and mounted it on a pole. Whenever someone was bitten, and he looked at the bronze snake, he recovered.

Journey around Moab

[10] The Israelites set out and camped at Oboth. [11] They set out from Oboth and camped at Iye-abarim in the wilderness that borders Moab on the east. [12] From there they went and camped at Zered Valley. [13] They set out from there and camped on the other side of the Arnon River, in the wilderness that extends from the Amorite border, because the Arnon was the Moabite border between Moab and the Amorites. [14] Therefore it is stated in the Book of the LORD's Wars:

Waheb in Suphah
and the ravines of the Arnon,
[15] even the slopes of the ravines
that extend to the site of Ar
and lie along the border of Moab.

[16] From there they went to Beer,[B] the well the LORD told Moses about, "Gather the people so I may give them water." [17] Then Israel sang this song:

Spring up, well — sing to it!
[18] The princes dug the well;
the nobles of the people hollowed it out
with a scepter and with their staffs.

They went from the wilderness to Mattanah, [19] from Mattanah to Nahaliel, from Nahaliel to Bamoth, [20] from Bamoth to the valley in the territory of Moab near the Pisgah highlands that overlook the wasteland.[C]

Amorite Kings Defeated

[21] Israel sent messengers to say to King Sihon of the Amorites, [22] "Let us travel through your land. We won't go into the fields or vineyards. We won't drink any well water. We will travel the King's Highway until we have traveled through your territory." [23] But Sihon would not let Israel travel through his territory. Instead, he gathered his whole army and went out to confront Israel in the wilderness. When he came to Jahaz, he fought against Israel. [24] Israel struck him with the sword and took possession of his land from the Arnon to the Jabbok, but only up to the Ammonite border, because it was fortified.[D] [25] Israel took all the cities and lived in all these Amorite cities, including Heshbon and all its surrounding villages. [26] Heshbon was the city of King Sihon of the Amorites, who had fought against the former king of Moab and had taken control of all his land as far as the Arnon. [27] Therefore the poets[E] say:

[A] 21:6 Lit Burning   [B] 21:16 = Well   [C] 21:20 Or overlook Jeshimon   [D] 21:24 LXX reads because the Ammonite border was Jazer
[E] 21:27 Lit ones who speak proverbs

---

then crossing the Arabah between Tamar and Zalmonah.
21:5 For the seventh time, **the people spoke against God and Moses**. Their words were the same monotonous complaint about food and water.
21:6-7 God's judgment against the people came in the form of **poisonous snakes**, likely the carpet viper (Echis carinatus or E. coleratus).
21:8-9 The Lord directed Moses to **make a snake image and mount it on a pole** as an antidote for those who had been bitten by these snakes. Those who looked at this snake image would be healed—by faith in God's provision, not by faith in the graven serpent. The bronze snake, however, was preserved in Israel for about 700 years, until it was destroyed by King Hezekiah (2Kg 18:4). John's Gospel cited Jesus's use of this imagery as a metaphor for his crucifixion (Jn 3:14–16).
21:10-13 The pattern of the Israelites' journey was from south to north and around the area occupied by the Edomites. They departed from Mount Hor, through Zalmon and Punon, which are not mentioned here but are in Moses's recording of the stages of the journey (33:42). They continued through

Oboth in the upper Arabah, south of the Dead Sea, to **Iye-abarim**, located near the edge of the Moabite region.
21:14-15 The Book of the LORD's Wars was apparently an early source of Israelite documentation of God's victories on behalf of his people. This source is otherwise unknown in the OT. **Waheb in Suphah** is probably south of the Arnon River. The mention of **ravines** is indicative of the **Arnon** River gorge. **Ar of Moab** was a city, probably south of the Arnon River (v. 28; Dt 2:9; Is 15:1).
21:16-20 The epic narrative poem sung by Israel continues the journey motif from this **well** where the Israelites did not complain about a lack of water. They journeyed to the sites of Mattanah ("gift"), Nahaliel ("river of God"), Bamoth ("high places, cultic center"), a valley in the Moabite countryside, and the peak of the **Pisgah** mountains which overlooks **the wasteland**. Translators and commentators alike have faced the problem of whether these are genuine place names or just descriptive terms. Poised on top of Mount Nebo in the Pisgah mountains, Moses would be granted a glimpse of the promised land.

On a clear winter day from the traditional Mount Nebo, one can see where the Jordan River flows into the Dead Sea, the northern end of the Judean Wilderness, and the Jericho oasis.
21:21-22 Moses dispatched diplomatic envoys to **King Sihon of the Amorites** to negotiate rights of passage northward along the King's Highway in the Transjordan highlands and then westward down the hillsides to the shores of the Jordan River. The Amorites were a large ethnic group that formed in upper Mesopotamia near the end of the early Bronze Age, about 2300–2000 BC.
21:23-25 Just as the king of Edom had refused to grant the Israelites passage through his territory, so too **Sihon**, the recent usurper and conqueror of Moab, **would not let Israel travel through his territory**. But his military's attempt to block the advance of Israel was met with a resounding defeat, a victory that would be remembered throughout Israel's history (Dt 2:26–31; Jos 12:2–5; 13:21; Jdg 11:19–21; 1Kg 4:19, Neh 9:22; Jr 48:45).
21:26-31 The Amorite woe oracle song, which the Israelites adapted for singing about their victory over the great conqueror Sihon, denounced the Moabites

Come to Heshbon, let it be rebuilt;
let the city of Sihon be restored.^A
28 For fire came out of Heshbon,
a flame from the city of Sihon.
It consumed Ar of Moab,
the citizens of Arnon's heights.
29 Woe to you, Moab!
You have been destroyed,
people of Chemosh!
He gave up his sons as refugees,
and his daughters into captivity
to Sihon the Amorite king.
30 We threw them down;
Heshbon has been destroyed
as far as Dibon.
We caused desolation as far as Nophah,
which reaches as far as Medeba.

31 So Israel lived in the Amorites' land. 32 After Moses sent spies to Jazer, Israel captured its surrounding villages and drove out the Amorites who were there.

33 Then they turned and went up the road to Bashan, and King Og of Bashan came out against them with his whole army to do battle at Edrei. 34 But the LORD said to Moses, "Do not fear him, for I have handed him over to you along with his whole army and his land. Do to him as you did to King Sihon of the Amorites, who lived in Heshbon." 35 So they struck him, his sons, and his whole army until no one was left,^B and they took possession of his land.

Balak Hires Balaam

22 The Israelites traveled on and camped in the plains of Moab near the Jordan across from Jericho. 2 Now Balak son of Zippor saw all that Israel had done to the Amorites. 3 Moab was terrified of the people because they were numerous, and Moab dreaded the Israelites. 4 So the Moabites said to the elders of Midian, "This horde will devour everything around us like an ox eats up the green plants in the field."

Since Balak son of Zippor was Moab's king at that time, 5 he sent messengers to Balaam son of Beor at Pethor, which is by the Euphrates in the land of his people.^C,D Balak said to him, "Look, a people has come out of Egypt; they cover the surface of the land and are living right across from me. 6 Please come and put a curse on these people for me because they are more powerful than I am. I may be able to defeat them and drive them out of the land, for I know that those you bless are blessed and those you curse are cursed."

7 The elders of Moab and Midian departed with fees for divination in hand. They came to Balaam and reported Balak's words to him. 8 He said to them, "Spend the night here, and I will give you the answer the LORD tells me." So the officials of Moab stayed with Balaam.

9 Then God came to Balaam and asked, "Who are these men with you?"

10 Balaam replied to God, "Balak son of Zippor, king of Moab, sent this message to me: 11 'Look, a people has come out of Egypt, and they cover the surface of the land. Now come and put a curse on them for me. I may be able to fight against them and drive them away.'"

12 Then God said to Balaam, "You are not to go with them. You are not to curse this people, for they are blessed."

13 So Balaam got up the next morning and said to Balak's officials, "Go back to your land, because the LORD has refused to let me go with you."

---

^A21:27 Or firmly founded   ^B21:35 Lit left to him   ^C22:5 Sam, Vg, Syr read of the Ammonites   ^D22:5 Or of the Amawites

---

and their god Chemosh. Portions of this song would be recounted in the prophets' oracles against Moab in the eighth to the sixth centuries BC, including Is 15:1–14 and Jr 48:1–47.

Chemosh was the patron deity of the Moabites. The worship of Chemosh of Moab was brought into Jerusalem in the tenth century BC by King Solomon, who built a temple to Chemosh on the hill opposite that upon which the temple of the Lord was built early in his reign.

21:32 Jazer may have come under Amorite dominion in the expansion of Sihon or Og into the Ammonite region. "Jazer" was both the name of a region (32:1) and its principal city (32:3). The town of Jazer was located in the valley of the Wadi Kefrein, which flows down toward the Jordan River.

21:33–35 The capital for **King Og of Bashan** was located at Ashtaroth, situated on a northern tributary of the Yarmuk River (Dt 1:4). The battle ensued at **Edrei**, generally associated with modern Der'a on the Syrian-Jordanian border, about thirty miles east of the Sea of Galilee. Though no other battles in this campaign are recounted in Numbers, sixty cities from the kingdom of Og of Bashan were subjected to the stipulations of holy war (Dt 3:4–6).

22:1–24:25 This passage contains the account of Balaam, a renowned pagan divination expert, and his oracles of blessing upon Israel. As the very antithesis of the great prophet Moses, this prophet sought Israel's demise at the bidding of the Moabite king Balak. Instead, Balaam was used by God in a manner like Moses to pronounce future divine blessing for Israel.

22:1 The setting of this story for Israel was the eastern side of the Jordan River. The leading characters Balak and Balaam were situated in the hills of Transjordan, overlooking the Israelite encampment from the southeast. The **plains of Moab** was the broad plain between the Transjordan highlands and the Jordan River, extending about ten miles from just north of the Dead Sea.

22:2–4 Balak is called **Moab's king**, meaning he was the head of an emerging tribal confederation like similar groups in Transjordan, such as the Edomites and Ammonites. The Midianites originated in northern Arabia and southern Transjordan. According to Gn 25:1–6, they were descendants of Abraham and his concubine Keturah. A group of Midianite **elders** joined Balak's emissaries in enlisting the services of Balaam to curse Israel.

22:5 Balaam was from the Mesopotamian town of **Pethor**, identified with Pitru, on the Sajur River tributary west of the Euphrates River. The distance from Pethor to Moab would have exceeded 400 miles, making each trip by the emissaries of Balak twenty-five days each way.

22:7–8 Balaam was to be rewarded after fulfilling his cursing of Israel (v. 37; 24:11).

22:9–11 Appearing to **Balaam** in a dreamlike manner, **God** began a dialogue with the pagan diviner.

22:12 God's clear intent was to bless his people as he had promised to do since the call of Abram (Gn 12:1–3).

22:13–21 The attempt at procuring Balaam's service by a second, higher-ranking group of emissaries from Balak was met with a cautious response. The words used in v. 18 indicate that Balaam would become God's spokesman. Balaam should only "do" (Hb 'asah) what God "speaks" (Hb davar, v. 20). These terms are used together throughout the book of Numbers in the context of the faithful following of the Lord's commands

14 The officials of Moab arose, returned to Balak, and reported, "Balaam refused to come with us."

15 Balak sent officials again who were more numerous and higher in rank than the others. **16** They came to Balaam and said to him, "This is what Balak son of Zippor says: 'Let nothing keep you from coming to me, **17** for I will greatly honor you and do whatever you ask me. So please come and put a curse on these people for me!'" **18** But Balaam responded to the servants of Balak, "If Balak were to give me his house full of silver and gold, I could not go against the command of the Lord my God to do anything small or great. **19** Please stay here overnight as the others did, so that I may find out what else the Lord has to tell me."

20 God came to Balaam at night and said to him, "Since these men have come to summon you, get up and go with them, but you must only do what I tell you." **21** When he got up in the morning, Balaam saddled his donkey and went with the officials of Moab.

Balaam's Donkey and the Angel

22 But God was incensed that Balaam was going, and the angel of the Lord took his stand on the path to oppose him. Balaam was riding his donkey, and his two servants were with him. **23** When the donkey saw the angel of the Lord standing on the path with a drawn sword in his hand, she turned off the path and went into the field. So Balaam hit her to return her to the path. **24** Then the angel of the Lord stood in a narrow passage between the vineyards, with a stone wall on either side. **25** The donkey saw the angel of the Lord and pressed herself against the wall, squeezing Balaam's foot against it. So he hit her once again. **26** The angel of the Lord went ahead and stood in a narrow place where there was no room to turn to the right or the left. **27** When the donkey saw the angel of the Lord, she crouched down under Balaam. So he became furious and beat the donkey with his stick. **28** Then the Lord opened the donkey's mouth, and she asked Balaam, "What have I done to you that you have beaten me these three times?"

29 Balaam answered the donkey, "You made me look like a fool. If I had a sword in my hand, I'd kill you now!"

30 But the donkey said, "Am I not the donkey you've ridden all your life until today? Have I ever treated you this way before?"

"No," he replied.

31 Then the Lord opened Balaam's eyes, and he saw the angel of the Lord standing in the path with a drawn sword in his hand. Balaam knelt low and bowed in worship on his face. **32** The angel of the Lord asked him, "Why have you beaten your donkey these three times? Look, I came out to oppose you, because I consider what you are doing to be evil.[A] **33** The donkey saw me and turned away from me these three times. If she had not turned away from me, I would have killed you by now and let her live."

34 Balaam said to the angel of the Lord, "I have sinned, for I did not know that you were standing in the path to confront me. And now, if it is evil in your sight, I will go back."

35 Then the angel of the Lord said to Balaam, "Go with the men, but you are to say only what I tell you." So Balaam went with Balak's officials.

36 When Balak heard that Balaam was coming, he went out to meet him at the Moabite city[B] on the Arnon border at the edge of his territory. **37** Balak asked Balaam, "Did I not send you an urgent summons? Why didn't you come to me? Am I really not able to reward you?"

38 Balaam said to him, "Look, I have come to you, but can I say anything I want? I must speak only the message God puts in my mouth." **39** So Balaam went with Balak, and they came to Kiriath-huzoth.[C] **40** Balak sacrificed cattle, sheep, and goats and sent for Balaam and the officials who were with him.

41 In the morning, Balak took Balaam and brought him to Bamoth-baal.[D] From there he saw the outskirts of the people's camp.

Balaam's Oracles

23 Then Balaam said to Balak, "Build me seven altars here and prepare seven bulls and seven rams for me." **2** So Balak did as Balaam directed, and they offered a bull and a

---

[A] **22:32** Lit *because your way is perverse before me*   [B] **22:36** Or *at Ir-moab*, or *at Ar of Moab*   [C] **22:39** = The City of Streets   [D] **22:41** = The High Places of Baal

---

in the sequence of God speaking and Moses (or others) doing just what the Lord commanded. **22:18** Balaam's reference to **the Lord my God** represents his claim to be a spokesman for Yahweh. The words echo the reality that he had indeed had an encounter with the God of Israel, through which the true God had confronted and revealed himself to the pagan diviner. But his words do not indicate he was a true worshiper of Yahweh. **22:23–27** The words **when the donkey saw the angel of the Lord** are filled with irony, especially when used three times in this context. This renowned "seer of the gods" could

not see what his lowly donkey saw. Furthermore, this donkey was a female, placing the animal in an even lower status when compared to the relative value and usefulness of male donkeys. Balaam beat her into submission, though she was ultimately more submissive to God than was the one whom God was sending to pronounce blessing upon Israel. **22:28–30** Two general interpretations of this event are offered. (1) God literally gave the donkey the power of speech (**the Lord opened the donkey's mouth**), or (2) the donkey's normal braying was heightened to such a degree that it was perceived and interpreted by Balaam in a human manner.

22:36–38 Balaam's repetition of the words of divine instruction—**I must speak only the message God puts in my mouth** (cp. vv. 20,35)—shows that what is about to come from him is divine revelation. **22:39–40 Kiriath-huzoth**, the "city of plazas" as the name translates, may have been a central market area for the city of Ar in Moab. **22:41** Balaam's sacrificial activity began at **Bamoth-baal** ("the high places of Baal"), a cultic center for the worship of the Semitic deity Baal, the champion of creation in the mythology of Ugarit. **23:1–2** The preference for performing seven rituals was widespread in the ancient Near

ram on each altar. ³ Balaam said to Balak, "Stay here by your burnt offering while I am gone. Maybe the LORD will meet with me. I will tell you whatever he reveals to me." So he went to a barren hill.

⁴ God met with him and Balaam said to him, "I have arranged seven altars and offered a bull and a ram on each altar." ⁵ Then the LORD put a message in Balaam's mouth and said, "Return to Balak and say what I tell you."

⁶ So he returned to Balak, who was standing there by his burnt offering with all the officials of Moab.

Balaam's First Oracle

⁷ Balaam proclaimed his poem:
Balak brought me from Aram;
the king of Moab,
from the eastern mountains:
"Come, put a curse on Jacob for me;
come, denounce Israel!"
⁸   How can I curse someone
God has not cursed?
How can I denounce someone the LORD
has not denounced?
⁹   I see them from the top of rocky cliffs,
and I watch them from the hills.
There is a people living alone;
it does not consider itself
among the nations.
¹⁰   Who has counted the dust of Jacob
or numbered even one-fourth of Israel?
Let me die the death of the upright;
let the end of my life be like theirs.

¹¹ "What have you done to me?" Balak asked Balaam. "I brought you to curse my enemies, but look, you have only blessed them!"

¹² He answered, "Shouldn't I say exactly what the LORD puts in my mouth?"

Balaam's Second Oracle

¹³ Then Balak said to him, "Please come with me to another place where you can see them. You will only see the outskirts of their camp; you won't see all of them. From there, put a curse on

them for me." ¹⁴ So Balak took him to Lookout FieldᴬΑ on top of Pisgah, built seven altars, and offered a bull and a ram on each altar.

¹⁵ Balaam said to Balak, "Stay here by your burnt offering while I seek the LORD over there."

¹⁶ The LORD met with Balaam and put a message in his mouth. Then he said, "Return to Balak and say what I tell you."

¹⁷ So he returned to Balak, who was standing there by his burnt offering with the officials of Moab. Balak asked him, "What did the LORD say?"

¹⁸ Balaam proclaimed his poem:
Balak, get up and listen;
son of Zippor, pay attention to what
I say!
¹⁹   God is not a man, that he might lie,
or a son of man, that he might change
his mind.
Does he speak and not act,
or promise and not fulfill?
²⁰   I have indeed received a command
to bless;
since he has blessed,ᴮ I cannot change it.
²¹   He considers no disaster for Jacob;
he sees no trouble for Israel.ᶜ
The LORD their God is with them,
and there is rejoicing over the King
among them.
²²   God brought them out of Egypt;
he is like the horns of a wild ox
for them.ᴰ
²³   There is no magic curse against Jacob
and no divination against Israel.
It will now be said about Jacob
and Israel,
"What great things God has done!"
²⁴   A people rise up like a lioness;
they rouse themselves like a lion.
They will not lie down until they devour
the prey
and drink the blood of the slain.

²⁵ Then Balak told Balaam, "Don't curse them and don't bless them!"

ᴬ23:14 Or to the field of Zophim   ᴮ23:20 Sam, LXX read since I will bless   ᶜ23:21 Or He does not observe sin in Jacob; he does not see wrongdoing in Israel   ᴰ23:22 Or Egypt; they have the horns of a wild ox

---

East, though multiple altars are not mentioned elsewhere in the OT.
23:13–26 From another outpost overlooking the northeastern corner of the Dead Sea and the plains of Moab where Israel was camped, Balaam and Balak repeated the ritual sacrifices of the first encounter. Nothing Balaam could muster could bring any harm to God's people.
23:14 The **Lookout Field on top of Pisgah** was probably so named because of its strategic observation location. Several scholars interpret this location as a known place for observing heavenly omens and making astrological observations.
23:19–20 Unlike the gods of Mesopotamia, who were depicted often as whimsical

and easily manipulated through sorcery and divination, the God of Israel was **not a man, that he might lie** or **change his mind**. Balaam could not change what God had instructed him to proclaim—blessing for Israel, God's chosen people.
23:23 Israel did not need augurs, diviners, or magicians; in fact, these were condemned and prohibited. Augury included reading cloud patterns, bird movements, and other activities in the skies. Divination included extispicy, the ritual slaughter of animals and the reading of their entrails by hepatoscopy (liver dissection) and colonoscopy (viewing of the intestinal lining). Such practices were not the source of Israel's defense, nor could

such powers be used against God's people. The Lord would use Balaam, a pagan diviner, to bless those he had been called to condemn.
23:25–24:9 After two failed attempts, Balak reeled from the words of Balaam and called for the prophet to refrain from pronouncing a blessing on them. Then Balaam and Balak resorted to a third cultic center, in the heights above **Peor**, overlooking Jeshimon, from which they could see **Israel encamped tribe by tribe** (24:2). The sevenfold ritual is repeated again, without resorting to divination as Balaam had previously done. An ecstatic encounter with the Spirit of God ensued, opening Balaam's **eyes** to a vision

²⁶ But Balaam answered him, "Didn't I tell you: Whatever the Lᴏʀᴅ says, I must do?"

Balaam's Third Oracle

²⁷ Again Balak said to Balaam, "Please come. I will take you to another place. Maybe it will be agreeable to God that you can put a curse on them for me there." ²⁸ So Balak took Balaam to the top of Peor, which overlooks the wasteland.ᴬ

²⁹ Balaam told Balak, "Build me seven altars here and prepare seven bulls and seven rams for me." ³⁰ So Balak did as Balaam said and offered a bull and a ram on each altar.

24 Since Balaam saw that it pleased the Lᴏʀᴅ to bless Israel, he did not go to seek omens as on previous occasions, but turnedᴮ toward the wilderness. ² When Balaam looked up and saw Israel encamped tribe by tribe, the Spirit of God came on him, ³ and he proclaimed his poem:

> The oracle of Balaam son of Beor,
> the oracle of the man whose eyes
>   are opened,
> ⁴ the oracle of one who hears the sayings
>   of God,
> who sees a vision from the Almighty,
> who falls into a trance with his eyes
>   uncovered:
> ⁵ How beautiful are your tents, Jacob,
>   your dwellings, Israel.
> ⁶ They stretch out like river valleys,ᶜ
> like gardens beside a stream,
> like aloes the Lᴏʀᴅ has planted,
> like cedars beside the water.
> ⁷ Water will flow from his buckets,
> and his seed will be by abundant water.
> His king will be greater than Agag,
> and his kingdom will be exalted.
> ⁸ God brought him out of Egypt;
> he is likeᴰ the horns of a wild ox
>   for them.
> He will feed on enemy nations
> and gnaw their bones;
> he will strike them with his arrows.
> ⁹ He crouches, he lies down like a lion
> or a lioness — who dares to rouse him?

> Those who bless you will be blessed,
> and those who curse you will be cursed.

¹⁰ Then Balak became furious with Balaam, struck his hands together, and said to him, "I summoned you to put a curse on my enemies, but instead, you have blessed them these three times. ¹¹ Now go to your home! I said I would reward you richly, but look, the Lᴏʀᴅ has denied you a reward."

¹² Balaam answered Balak, "Didn't I previously tell the messengers you sent me: ¹³ If Balak were to give me his house full of silver and gold, I could not go against the Lᴏʀᴅ's command, to do anything good or bad of my own will? I will say whatever the Lᴏʀᴅ says. ¹⁴ Now I am going back to my people, but first, let me warn you what these people will do to your people in the future."

Balaam's Fourth Oracle

¹⁵ Then he proclaimed his poem:

> The oracle of Balaam son of Beor,
> the oracle of the man whose eyes
>   are opened;
> ¹⁶ the oracle of one who hears the sayings
>   of God
> and has knowledge
>   from the Most High,
> who sees a vision from the Almighty,
> who falls into a trance with his
>   eyes uncovered:
> ¹⁷ I see him, but not now;
> I perceive him, but not near.
> A star will come from Jacob,
> and a scepter will arise from Israel.
> He will smash the foreheadᴱ of Moab
> and strike downᶠ all the Shethites.ᴳ
> ¹⁸ Edom will become a possession;
> Seir will become a possession
>   of its enemies,
> but Israel will be triumphant.
> ¹⁹ One who comes from Jacob will rule;
> he will destroy the city's survivors.

²⁰ Then Balaam saw Amalek and proclaimed his poem:

ᴬ**23:28** Or *overlooks Jeshimon*   ᴮ**24:1** Lit *set his face*   ᶜ**24:6** Or *like date palms*   ᴰ**24:8** Or *he has*   ᴱ**24:17** Or *frontiers*   ᶠ**24:17** Sam reads *and the skulls of*; Jr 48:45   ᴳ**24:17** Or *Sethites*

---

of God Almighty. Balaam's utterance forecast the Lord's blessing upon the land with abundance of **water** bringing productivity to the crops, and a powerful kingdom that would surpass that of the forces of **Agag** the Amalekite.

24:10–14 Balak is beside himself with anger, but Balaam reminds him he never promised to curse Israel.

24:15–19 In a visionary encounter similar to that of the third oracle, Balaam uttered predictive prophecy about the distant future of Israel. The **star** and **scepter** are symbols of a glorious and powerful kingdom that would subdue the enemies of Israel, typified

as **Moab** and **Edom**. In the early Israelite monarchy, David fulfilled this prophecy by defeating and subjugating both Moab and Edom (2Sm 8:1–12). Later this passage would be interpreted messianically to refer to a coming glorious king. The model of a just and righteous king was brought to ultimate fulfillment in Jesus's establishment of the kingdom of God.

24:20–24 Three brief oracles about the destiny of other nations conclude the account of Balaam. Their collective theme is that God would subdue all peoples like Moab who opposed his will and his people. The people of **Amalek** would be

subdued under Saul, Samuel, and David. The **Kenites**, a nomadic clan from the eastern Sinai region, would be subdued by their neighbors, the northern Sinai tribe of Asshur (Gn 25:3,18). The Asshurite people, descendants of Abraham and his concubine Keturah, would in turn be conquered by the **Kittim**. "Kittim" is one of the ancient terms for Cyprus (Gn 10:4), derived from its major city Kition (thus Kitionites). In several OT passages, the term was used generically for the islands of the Mediterranean and their inhabitants (Jr 2:10; Dn 11:30), such as the Philistines. They too would see their demise.

Amalek was first among the nations,
but his future is destruction.

²¹ Next he saw the Kenites and proclaimed his poem:
Your dwelling place is enduring;
your nest is set in the cliffs.
²² Kain will be destroyed
when Asshur takes you captive.

²³ Once more he proclaimed his poem:
Ah, who can live when God does this?
²⁴ Ships will come from the coast
of Kittim;
they will carry out raids against Asshur
and Eber,
but they too will come to destruction.
²⁵ Balaam then arose and went back to his homeland, and Balak also went his way.

Israel Worships Baal

25 While Israel was staying in the Acacia Grove,ᴬ the people began to prostitute themselves with the women of Moab. ² The women invited them to the sacrifices for their gods, and the people ate and bowed in worship to their gods. ³ So Israel aligned itself with Baal of Peor, and the LORD's anger burned against Israel. ⁴ The LORD said to Moses, "Take all the leaders of the people and executeᴮ them in broad daylight before the LORD so that his burning anger may turn away from Israel."

⁵ So Moses told Israel's judges, "Kill each of the men who aligned themselves with Baal of Peor."

Phinehas Intervenes

⁶ An Israelite man came bringing a Midianite woman to his relatives in the sight of Moses and the whole Israelite community while they were weeping at the entrance to the tent of meeting. ⁷ When Phinehas son of Eleazar, son of Aaron the priest, saw this, he got up from the assembly, took a spear in his hand, ⁸ followed the Israelite man into the tent,ᶜ and drove it through both the Israelite man and the woman — through her belly. Then the plague on the Israelites was stopped, ⁹ but those who died in the plague numbered twenty-four thousand.

¹⁰ The LORD spoke to Moses, ¹¹ "Phinehas son of Eleazar, son of Aaron the priest, has turned back my wrath from the Israelites because he was zealous among them with my zeal,ᴰ so that I did not destroy the Israelites in my zeal. ¹² Therefore declare: I grant him my covenant of peace. ¹³ It will be a covenant of perpetual priesthood for him and his future descendants, because he was zealous for his God and made atonement for the Israelites."

¹⁴ The name of the slain Israelite man, who was struck dead with the Midianite woman, was Zimri son of Salu, the leader of a Simeonite family.ᴱ ¹⁵ The name of the slain Midianite woman was Cozbi, the daughter of Zur, a tribal head of a family in Midian.

Vengeance against the Midianites

¹⁶ The LORD told Moses, ¹⁷ "Attack the Midianites and strike them dead. ¹⁸ For they attacked you with the treachery that they used against you in the Peor incident. They did the same in the case involving their sister Cozbi, daughter of the Midianite leader who was killed the day the plague came at Peor."

The Second Census

26 After the plague, the LORD said to Moses and Eleazar son of Aaron the priest, ² "Take a census of the entire Israelite community by their ancestral familiesᶠ of those twenty years old or more who can serve in Israel's army."

³ So Moses and the priest Eleazar said to them in the plains of Moab by the Jordan across from Jericho, ⁴ "Take a census of those twenty years old or more, as the LORD had commanded Moses and the Israelites who came out of the land of Egypt."

ᴬ25:1 Or in Shittim ᴮ25:4 Or impale, or hang, or expose; Hb obscure ᶜ25:8 Perhaps a tent shrine or bridal tent ᴰ25:11 Or jealousy ᴱ25:14 Lit a father's house, also in v. 15 ᶠ26:2 Lit the house of their fathers

---

24:25 Balaam began his trek homeward, but as 31:8 suggests, he was killed in the Midianite campaign, having been instrumental in instigating the idolatrous enticement of Israelites in chap. 25.

25:1 The scene moves from the mountains of Moab to the Israelite camp at **Acacia Grove** (see Jos 2:1). **Prostitute themselves with** refers to ritual worship of foreign deities (Ex 34:15–16; Lv 17:7; Dt 31:16; Jdg 2:17).

25:3 This is the first reference in the OT to the god Baal (**Baal of Peor**), who would become the primary competitor to Yahweh for the devotion of the people of Israel.

25:4–5 The Lord instructed Moses, who delegated authority to the righteous **judges** of Israel to **execute** (lit "impale") the leaders of this rebellion immediately to avert any further judgment against the people. The guilty parties were to be executed **before the LORD,** meaning that they were to be rendered unto the Lord to expiate the divine wrath demonstrated in the plague.

25:6–7 **Phinehas son of Eleazar** was Aaron's grandson. He executed a rebellious Israelite who dared to present his Midianite seductress to his family near the entrance of the tabernacle, the place reserved for sacred presentation of offerings to God.

25:8–9 Phinehas, with his executioner's spear in hand, impaled the man and his mistress together, quite possibly while they were beginning to have sexual relations (v. 1). 25:11–13 The zeal of Phinehas in defending the faith was rewarded with a divinely ordained relationship. His descendants would serve continuously as high priests (**covenant of perpetual priesthood**) over the nation of Israel. A **covenant of peace** is also mentioned in Is 54:10; Ezk 34:25; 37:26; and Mal 2:5. The recipients of this covenant were assured of God's presence, protection, and provision in times of trouble.

25:14–15 The people killed by Phinehas were from prominent families, the man being a son of a **Simeonite** leader and the woman being the daughter of **Zur,** a **Midianite** tribal leader.

26:1–2 Verses 1–2 are very similar to God's command in 1:1–2 mandating the first census. 26:3–4 The first census took place at the foot of Mount Sinai in the wilderness, the second at the doorway of the promised land, **in the plains of Moab by the Jordan across from Jericho.**

⁵ Reuben was the firstborn of Israel. Reuben's descendants: the Hanochite clan from Hanoch; the Palluite clan from Pallu; ⁶ the Hezronite clan from Hezron; the Carmite clan from Carmi. ⁷ These were the Reubenite clans, and their registered men numbered 43,730. ⁸ The son of Pallu was Eliab. ⁹ The sons of Eliab were Nemuel, Dathan, and Abiram. (It was Dathan and Abiram, chosen by the community, who fought against Moses and Aaron; they and Korah's followers fought against the LORD. ¹⁰ The earth opened its mouth and swallowed them with Korah, when his followers died and the fire consumed 250 men. They serve as a warning sign. ¹¹ The sons of Korah, however, did not die.)

¹² Simeon's descendants by their clans: the Nemuelite clan from Nemuel; the Jaminite clan from Jamin; the Jachinite clan from Jachin; ¹³ the Zerahite clan from Zerah; the Shaulite clan from Shaul. ¹⁴ These were the Simeonite clans, numbering 22,200 men.

¹⁵ Gad's descendants by their clans: the Zephonite clan from Zephon; the Haggite clan from Haggi; the Shunite clan from Shuni; ¹⁶ the Oznite clan from Ozni; the Erite clan from Eri; ¹⁷ the Arodite clan from Arod; the Arelite clan from Areli. ¹⁸ These were the Gadite clans numbered by their registered men: 40,500.

¹⁹ Judah's sons included Er and Onan, but they died in the land of Canaan. ²⁰ Judah's descendants by their clans: the Shelanite clan from Shelah; the Perezite clan from Perez; the Zerahite clan from Zerah. ²¹ The descendants of Perez: the Hezronite clan from Hezron; the Hamulite clan from Hamul. ²² These were Judah's clans numbered by their registered men: 76,500.

²³ Issachar's descendants by their clans: the Tolaite clan from Tola;

the Punite clan from Puvah;[A] ²⁴ the Jashubite clan from Jashub; the Shimronite clan from Shimron. ²⁵ These were Issachar's clans numbered by their registered men: 64,300.

²⁶ Zebulun's descendants by their clans: the Seredite clan from Sered; the Elonite clan from Elon; the Jahleelite clan from Jahleel. ²⁷ These were the Zebulunite clans numbered by their registered men: 60,500.

²⁸ Joseph's descendants by their clans from Manasseh and Ephraim: ²⁹ Manasseh's descendants: the Machirite clan from Machir. Machir fathered Gilead; the Gileadite clan from Gilead. ³⁰ These were Gilead's descendants: the Iezerite clan from Iezer; the Helekite clan from Helek; ³¹ the Asrielite clan from Asriel; the Shechemite clan from Shechem; ³² the Shemidaite clan from Shemida; the Hepherite clan from Hepher; ³³ Zelophehad son of Hepher had no sons — only daughters. The names of Zelophehad's daughters were Mahlah, Noah, Hoglah, Milcah, and Tirzah. ³⁴ These were Manasseh's clans, numbered by their registered men: 52,700. ³⁵ These were Ephraim's descendants by their clans: the Shuthelahite clan from Shuthelah; the Becherite clan from Becher; the Tahanite clan from Tahan. ³⁶ These were Shuthelah's descendants: the Eranite clan from Eran. ³⁷ These were the Ephraimite clans numbered by their registered men: 32,500. These were Joseph's descendants by their clans.

³⁸ Benjamin's descendants by their clans: the Belaite clan from Bela; the Ashbelite clan from Ashbel; the Ahiramite clan from Ahiram; ³⁹ the Shuphamite clan from Shupham;[B] the Huphamite clan from Hupham. ⁴⁰ Bela's descendants from Ard and Naaman: the Ardite clan from Ard;

[A]26:23 Sam, LXX, Vg, Syr read *Puite clan from Puah*; 1Ch 7:1 [B]26:39 Some Hb mss, Sam, LXX, Syr, Tg, Vg; other Hb mss read *Shephupham*

26:5–51 More than thirty-eight years had passed since the first census.
    The tribes of Simeon (declined by 37,100; 26:12) and Naphtali (declined by 8,000; v. 48) had suffered the greatest losses in their militias during the wilderness era, and the tribe of Simeon would eventually dissipate into Judah within whose territory they were given an allotment. Manasseh (increased by 20,500; v. 29), Asher (increased by 11,900; v. 44), and Issachar (increased by 9,900; v. 23) reaped the

the Naamite clan from Naaman.

41 These were the Benjaminite clans numbered by their registered men: 45,600.

42 These were Dan's descendants by their clans: the Shuhamite clan from Shuham. These were the clans of Dan by their clans.

43 All the Shuhamite clans numbered by their registered men: 64,400.

44 Asher's descendants by their clans: the Imnite clan from Imnah; the Ishvite clan from Ishvi; the Beriite clan from Beriah.

45 From Beriah's descendants: the Heberite clan from Heber; the Malchielite clan from Malchiel.

46 And the name of Asher's daughter was Serah.

47 These were the Asherite clans numbered by their registered men: 53,400.

48 Naphtali's descendants by their clans: the Jahzeelite clan from Jahzeel; the Gunite clan from Guni;

49 the Jezerite clan from Jezer; the Shillemite clan from Shillem.

50 These were the Naphtali clans numbered by their registered men: 45,400.

51 These registered Israelite men numbered 601,730.

52 The LORD spoke to Moses, **53** "The land is to be divided among them as an inheritance based on the number of names. **54** Increase the inheritance for a large tribe and decrease it for a small one. Each is to be given its inheritance according to those who were registered in it. **55** The land is to be divided by lot; they will receive an inheritance according to the names of their ancestral tribes. **56** Each inheritance will be divided by lot among the larger and smaller tribes."

57 These were the Levites registered by their clans:

the Gershonite clan from Gershon; the Kohathite clan from Kohath; the Merarite clan from Merari.

58 These were the Levite family groups: the Libnite clan, the Hebronite clan, the Mahlite clan, the Mushite clan, and the Korahite clan.

Kohath was the ancestor of Amram. **59** The name of Amram's wife was Jochebed, a descendant of Levi, born to Levi in Egypt. She bore to Amram: Aaron, Moses, and their sister Miriam. **60** Nadab, Abihu, Eleazar, and Ithamar were born to Aaron, **61** but Nadab and Abihu died when they presented unauthorized fire before the LORD. **62** Those registered were 23,000, every male one month old or more; they were not registered among the other Israelites, because no inheritance was given to them among the Israelites.

63 These were the ones registered by Moses and the priest Eleazar when they registered the Israelites on the plains of Moab by the Jordan across from Jericho. **64** But among them there was not one of those who had been registered by Moses and the priest Aaron when they registered the Israelites in the Wilderness of Sinai. **65** For the LORD had said to them that they would all die in the wilderness. None of them was left except Caleb son of Jephunneh and Joshua son of Nun.

A Case of Daughters' Inheritance

27 The daughters of Zelophehad approached; Zelophehad was the son of Hepher, son of Gilead, son of Machir, son of Manasseh from the clans of Manasseh, the son of Joseph. These were the names of his daughters: Mahlah, Noah, Hoglah, Milcah, and Tirzah. **2** They stood before Moses, the priest Eleazar, the leaders, and the entire community at the entrance to the tent of meeting and said, **3** "Our father died in the wilderness, but he was not among Korah's followers, who gathered together against the LORD. Instead, he died because of his own sin, and he had no sons. **4** Why should the name of our father be taken away from his clan? Since he had no son, give us property among our father's brothers."

most significant increases. The net decrease from the first census was 1,820 warriors.
26:55 Divided by lot refers to a second principle governing land allocation—providential probability as expressed through a game of chance. The Lord was presumed to oversee the casting of the lots, thereby bringing his decision to pass (Pr 16:33). The casting of lots was a common means of determining the will of God.
26:57–62 In a manner similar to the first census, the second numbering of the Levites

separately from the militia follows the genealogical pattern of vv. 5–52.
26:63–65 The census of the second generation militia concludes with a reminder to the people of the consequences of rebellion.
27:1 Only male descendants were registered by patriarchal lineage in the census. According to levirate law, in a case where a man died without a male heir, a male relative would redeem the land to keep it within the clan. This account is an example of case law development early in Israelite history.

(1) The specific case was presented to the leaders at the entrance of the tabernacle (vv. 1–4). (2) An appeal was made by the leader to divine legislative authority (v. 5). (3) A precedent-setting decision was issued, accompanied by principles derived from the case (vv. 6–11).
27:2–5 The **daughters of Zelophehad** were concerned that their family, lacking a male heir, would be passed over and their patriarchal ancestral name would be forgotten. The daughters of Zelophehad sought status and

⁵ Moses brought their case before the Lord, ⁶ and the Lord answered him, ⁷ "What Zelophehad's daughters say is correct. You are to give them hereditary property among their father's brothers and transfer their father's inheritance to them. ⁸ Tell the Israelites: When a man dies without having a son, transfer his inheritance to his daughter. ⁹ If he has no daughter, give his inheritance to his brothers. ¹⁰ If he has no brothers, give his inheritance to his father's brothers. ¹¹ If his father has no brothers, give his inheritance to the nearest relative of his clan, and he will take possession of it. This is to be a statutory ordinance for the Israelites as the Lord commanded Moses."

Joshua Commissioned to Succeed Moses

¹² Then the Lord said to Moses, "Go up this mountain of the Abarim range^A and see the land that I have given the Israelites. ¹³ After you have seen it, you will also be gathered to your people, as Aaron your brother was. ¹⁴ When the community quarreled in the Wilderness of Zin, both of you rebelled against my command to demonstrate my holiness in their sight at the waters." Those were the Waters of Meribah-kadesh^B in the Wilderness of Zin.

¹⁵ So Moses appealed to the Lord, ¹⁶ "May the Lord, the God who gives breath to all,^C appoint a man over the community ¹⁷ who will go out before them and come back in before them, and who will bring them out and bring them in, so that the Lord's community won't be like sheep without a shepherd."

¹⁸ The Lord replied to Moses, "Take Joshua son of Nun, a man who has the Spirit in him, and lay your hands on him. ¹⁹ Have him stand before the priest Eleazar and the whole community, and commission him in their sight. ²⁰ Confer some of your authority on him so that the entire Israelite community will obey

him. ²¹ He will stand before the priest Eleazar who will consult the Lord for him with the decision of the Urim. He and all the Israelites with him, even the entire community, will go out and come back in at his command."

²² Moses did as the Lord commanded him. He took Joshua, had him stand before the priest Eleazar and the entire community, ²³ laid his hands on him, and commissioned him, as the Lord had spoken through Moses.

Prescribed Offerings

28 The Lord spoke to Moses, ² "Command the Israelites and say to them: Be sure to present to me at its appointed time my offering and my food as my food offering, a pleasing aroma to me. ³ And say to them: This is the food offering you are to present to the Lord:

Daily Offerings

"Each day present two unblemished year-old male lambs as a regular burnt offering. ⁴ Offer one lamb in the morning and the other lamb at twilight, ⁵ along with two quarts^D of fine flour for a grain offering mixed with a quart^E of olive oil from crushed olives. ⁶ It is a regular burnt offering established at Mount Sinai for a pleasing aroma, a food offering to the Lord. ⁷ The drink offering is to be a quart with each lamb. Pour out the offering of beer to the Lord in the sanctuary area. ⁸ Offer the second lamb at twilight, along with the same kind of grain offering and drink offering as in the morning. It is a food offering, a pleasing aroma to the Lord.

Sabbath Offerings

⁹ "On the Sabbath day present two unblemished year-old male lambs, four quarts^F of fine flour mixed with oil as a grain offering, and its drink offering. ¹⁰ It is the burnt offering for

---

^A 27:12 = Mount Nebo; Nm 33:47–48; Dt 32:49; Jr 22:20 ^B 27:14 = Quarreling ^C 27:16 Or *God of the spirits of all flesh* ^D 28:5 Lit *one-tenth of an ephah* ^E 28:5 Lit *a fourth of a hin,* also in v. 7 ^F 28:9 Lit *two-tenths* (of an ephah), also in vv. 12,20,28

---

inheritance rights within the Machirite clan of Manasseh. Later the Machirites received an inheritance in the Gilead region of Transjordan (Nm 32:39–42).

27:6–11 The decision in the case (**what Zelophehad's daughters say is correct**) set forth in the days of Moses in the second millennium BC, and fulfilled by Joshua in the land distribution (Jos 17:3–6), was still in force more than 500 years later.

27:12 The **Abarim range** extended from an area northeast of the Dead Sea and then southward along the western edge of the Moabite plateau in Transjordan. The opportunity for Moses to **see the land** of promise from Dan to Zoar took place at Mount Nebo in the heights of Pisgah (Dt 32:49; 34:1).

27:15–17 Moses's words **the God who gives breath to all** speak of God's sovereignty over all humankind. He is the master of the universe who can thwart even the ways of a pagan diviner like Balaam and accomplish

his desires for his people. Moses, the elder statesman of Israel, appealed to God the way a humble servant would appeal before his master. Moses desired that the newly appointed leader would be just as concerned as he had been for the welfare of the nation. The language of going **out** and coming in has to do with successfully leading the people in battle. The **shepherd** can also be a military metaphor (1Kg 22:17).

27:18–21 The phrase **take Joshua son of Nun, a man who has the Spirit in him** reflects the language of formal appointment. "Take" means to exert authority. Possession of the Holy Spirit in the OT was for the purpose of carrying out the specific tasks to which a person had been appointed by the Lord.

27:22–23 The formal transfer of leadership from Moses to Joshua begins with a statement about Moses faithfully following the Lord's instruction. The ceremony involved the oversight of the high priest **Eleazar** in

the ritual ceremony, accompanied by the laying on of **hands** in symbolic transfer of blessing and authority.

28:3–8 Every day was holy and thus was to be dedicated to the Lord at the entrance of the tabernacle through the rendering of a **burnt offering**, a sacrifice for consecration of the day. Both in the morning and in the evening a **lamb** was sacrificed on behalf of the nation in a substitutionary identification ritual accomplished by the priest placing his hands on the head of the lamb. As the priest recited special blessings, the life blood of the animal was extracted as the animal was slaughtered. Then the blood was poured out to the Lord around the altar. The sacrifice would be accompanied by its appropriate portion of **grain** and **oil**, plus a prescribed amount of **beer** for the **drink offering**—a libation poured over the animal and grain elements as they were roasting on the fire of the sacrificial altar. For "beer" see note at 6:3–4.

every Sabbath, in addition to the regular burnt offering and its drink offering.

Monthly Offerings

¹¹ "At the beginning of each of your months present a burnt offering to the LORD: two young bulls, one ram, seven male lambs a year old — all unblemished — ¹² with six quarts^A of fine flour mixed with oil as a grain offering for each bull, four quarts of fine flour mixed with oil as a grain offering for the ram, ¹³ and two quarts^B of fine flour mixed with oil as a grain offering for each lamb. It is a burnt offering, a pleasing aroma, a food offering to the LORD. ¹⁴ Their drink offerings are to be two quarts^C of wine with each bull, one and a third quarts^D with the ram, and one quart^E with each male lamb. This is the monthly burnt offering for all the months of the year. ¹⁵ And one male goat is to be offered as a sin offering to the LORD, in addition to the regular burnt offering with its drink offering.

Offerings for Passover

¹⁶ "The Passover to the LORD comes in the first month, on the fourteenth day of the month. ¹⁷ On the fifteenth day of this month there will be a festival; unleavened bread is to be eaten for seven days. ¹⁸ On the first day there is to be a sacred assembly; you are not to do any daily work. ¹⁹ Present a food offering, a burnt offering to the LORD: two young bulls, one ram, and seven male lambs a year old. Your animals are to be unblemished. ²⁰ The grain offering with them is to be of fine flour mixed with oil; offer six quarts with each bull and four quarts with the ram. ²¹ Offer two quarts with each of the seven lambs ²² and one male goat for a sin offering to make atonement for yourselves. ²³ Offer these with the morning burnt offering that is part of the regular burnt offering. ²⁴ You are to offer the same food each day for

seven days as a food offering, a pleasing aroma to the LORD. It is to be offered with its drink offering and the regular burnt offering. ²⁵ On the seventh day you are to hold a sacred assembly; you are not to do any daily work.

Offerings for the Festival of Weeks

²⁶ "On the day of firstfruits, you are to hold a sacred assembly when you present an offering of new grain to the LORD at your Festival of Weeks; you are not to do any daily work. ²⁷ Present a burnt offering as a pleasing aroma to the LORD: two young bulls, one ram, and seven male lambs a year old, ²⁸ with their grain offering of fine flour mixed with oil, six quarts with each bull, four quarts with the ram, ²⁹ and two quarts with each of the seven lambs, ³⁰ and one male goat to make atonement for yourselves. ³¹ Offer them with their drink offerings in addition to the regular burnt offering and its grain offering. Your animals are to be unblemished.

Festival of Trumpets Offerings

29 "You are to hold a sacred assembly in the seventh month, on the first day of the month, and you are not to do any daily work. This will be a day of trumpet blasts for you. ² Offer a burnt offering as a pleasing aroma to the LORD: one young bull, one ram, seven male lambs a year old — all unblemished — ³ with their grain offering of fine flour mixed with oil, six quarts^F with the bull, four quarts^G with the ram, ⁴ and two quarts^H with each of the seven male lambs. ⁵ Also offer one male goat as a sin offering to make atonement for yourselves. ⁶ These are in addition to the monthly and regular burnt offerings with their prescribed grain offerings and drink offerings. They are a pleasing aroma, a food offering to the LORD.

---

^A 28:12 Lit *three-tenths* (of an ephah), also in vv. 20,28 ^B 28:13 Lit *one-tenth* (of an ephah), also in vv. 21,29 ^C 28:14 Lit *a half hin* ^D 28:14 Lit *bull, a third hin* ^E 28:14 Lit *a fourth hin* ^F 29:3 Lit *three-tenths* (of an ephah), also in vv. 9,14 ^G 29:3 Lit *two-tenths* (of an ephah), also in vv. 9,14 ^H 29:4 Lit *one-tenth* (of an ephah), also in vv. 10,15

28:11–15 At the **beginning of each of your months** additional burnt offerings of consecration were made, constituting a grand rite through which the nation paid homage to God as its Creator and Sustainer.
28:16–25 According to Ex 12:8, the foundational **Passover** foods were the Passover lamb, unleavened bread, and bitter herbs. These helped the people remember the events that brought about the redemption of Israel from Egypt. Passover **lambs** were offered as communal sacrifices, with portions consumed by both the priests and the offerers in the presence of God in the Israelite camp. **Unleavened bread**, which Deuteronomy calls the "bread of hardship," was consumed in imitation of the original setting. The bitter herbs were a reminder of the bitterness of slavery in Egypt. In this passage some elements are added to the celebration: Sabbath designation (meaning no work) for the first and final days of the

Festival of Unleavened Bread, complete with a **sacred assembly** at the sanctuary; and additional sacrifices equivalent to those offered on the New Moon (two bulls, one ram, and seven lambs, each accompanied by their appropriate grain/oil and libation offerings). The sacrificial list was completed with the offering of a goat for a **sin offering** on behalf of the people.
28:26–31 The first day of the **Festival of Weeks** (Hb *shavuoth*) was called the **day of firstfruits**. It was considered a Sabbath, with burnt and sin offerings essentially the same as the New Moon sacrifices. The firstfruits offering of the new grain harvest was included in the ritual practices for the day when the seven weeks after the first sheaf (Lv 23:10) were completed. Sheaves of new barley and wheat were elevated and waved before the Lord in celebration of the gift of the harvest. These were in addition to the prescribed offering of two loaves of

leavened bread (Lv 23:15–22; Dt 16:3) given in thanksgiving for the abundance of God's blessing. In the NT, the Festival of Weeks is called Pentecost, since the day is the fiftieth day after the first sheaf.
29:1–38 The beginning of the agricultural year, in the **seventh month, on the first day**, was the beginning of the penitential season. The tenth day of the month was considered the holiest day of the year, the Day of Atonement. Five days later the Festival of Shelters began and lasted for a week. In early Israelite history, the seventh month was known as Ethanim, but when the Jews adopted the Babylonian calendar during the exile, the month was called Tishri.
29:1–6 The collective offerings presented on the **day of trumpet blasts** were three bulls, two rams, sixteen male lambs, one and one-half bushels of fine flour, and six gallons each of oil and wine. Traditionally, the first of Tishri was called the "day for

Offerings for the Day of Atonement

7 "You are to hold a sacred assembly on the tenth day of this seventh month and practice self-denial; do not do any work. **8** Present a burnt offering to the Lord, a pleasing aroma: one young bull, one ram, and seven male lambs a year old. All your animals are to be unblemished. **9** Their grain offering is to be of fine flour mixed with oil, six quarts with the bull, four quarts with the ram, **10** and two quarts with each of the seven lambs. **11** Offer one male goat for a sin offering. The regular burnt offering with its grain offering and drink offerings are in addition to the sin offering of atonement.

Offerings for the Festival of Shelters

12 "You are to hold a sacred assembly on the fifteenth day of the seventh month; you do not do any daily work. You are to celebrate a seven-day festival for the Lord. **13** Present a burnt offering, a food offering, a pleasing aroma to the Lord: thirteen young bulls, two rams, and fourteen male lambs a year old. They are to be unblemished. **14** Their grain offering is to be of fine flour mixed with oil, six quarts with each of the thirteen bulls, four quarts with each of the two rams, **15** and two quarts with each of the fourteen lambs. **16** Also offer one male goat as a sin offering. These are in addition to the regular burnt offering with its grain and drink offerings.

17 "On the second day present twelve young bulls, two rams, and fourteen male lambs a year old — all unblemished — **18** with their grain and drink offerings for the bulls, rams, and lambs, in proportion to their number. **19** Also offer one male goat as a sin offering. These are in addition to the regular burnt offering with its grain and drink and their drink offerings.

20 "On the third day present eleven bulls, two rams, fourteen male lambs a year old — all unblemished — **21** with their grain and drink offerings for the bulls, rams, and lambs, in proportion to their number. **22** Also offer one male goat as a sin offering. These are in addition to the regular burnt offering with its grain and drink offerings.

23 "On the fourth day present ten bulls, two rams, fourteen male lambs a year old — all unblemished — **24** with their grain and drink offerings for the bulls, rams, and lambs, in proportion to their number. **25** Also offer one male goat as a sin offering. These are in addition to the regular burnt offering with its grain and drink offerings.

26 "On the fifth day present nine bulls, two rams, fourteen male lambs a year old — all unblemished — **27** with their grain and drink offerings for the bulls, rams, and lambs, in proportion to their number. **28** Also offer one male goat as a sin offering. These are in addition to the regular burnt offering with its grain and drink offerings.

29 "On the sixth day present eight bulls, two rams, fourteen male lambs a year old — all unblemished — **30** with their grain and drink offerings for the bulls, rams, and lambs, in proportion to their number. **31** Also offer one male goat as a sin offering. These are in addition to the regular burnt offering with its grain and drink offerings.

32 "On the seventh day present seven bulls, two rams, and fourteen male lambs a year old — all unblemished — **33** with their grain and drink offerings for the bulls, rams, and lambs, in proportion to their number. **34** Also offer one male goat as a sin offering. These are in addition to the regular burnt offering with its grain and drink offerings.

35 "On the eighth day you are to hold a solemn assembly; you are not to do any daily work. **36** Present a burnt offering, a food offering, a pleasing aroma to the Lord: one bull, one ram, seven male lambs a year old — all unblemished — **37** with their grain and drink offerings for the bulls, rams, and lambs, in proportion to their number. **38** Also offer one male goat as a sin offering. These are in addition to the regular burnt offering with its grain and drink offerings.

39 "Offer these to the Lord at your appointed times in addition to your vow and freewill offerings, whether burnt, grain, drink, or fellowship offerings." **40** So Moses told the Israelites everything the Lord had commanded him.

blowing trumpets" in which the ram's horn (Hb *shophar*) was sounded rather than the silver trumpets of 10:1–10. The sounding of the ram's horn was a call to repentance. The designation of this day as Rosh Hashanah, "the head of the year," was a late postexilic development in emerging Judaism. **29:7–11** The holiest day of the year required a **sacred assembly** of **self-denial**, and Sabbath restrictions against work as described in Lv 23:16–32. A full description of the activities for the Day of Atonement (Hb *yom kippur*) is found in Lv 16:1–34, where the focus is upon the unique purification rituals required. The acts of self-denial included fasting, leading

to the day being called "The Fast" in later Judaism. Other restrictions included any activities that brought comfort and pleasure.

The work of Christ on the cross brought fulfillment to the ritual of the Day of Atonement. Functioning as a high priest of a superior order—of Melchizedek (Heb 7:17–28)—Christ offered himself as a once-for-all, eternal sacrifice (Heb 9:11–28). His work accomplished redemption from sin and cleansed our guilty consciences (Heb 10:19–22). **29:12–38** The longest section of these two chapters is devoted to a description of the daily offerings of the Festival of Shelters (or Tabernacles or Booths; Hb *sukkoth*). The first

day of the festival and the appended eighth day were considered Sabbaths for sacred assembly. The *sukkah* was a hut or tent constructed in imitation of the dwellings of early Israelites during the wilderness period, when God provided what was needed for protection. First called the Festival of Ingathering (Ex 23:16), the celebration commemorated God's provision in the fall harvest of the vegetable crops, the vineyards, and finally the olive orchards. The association of Shelters with the exodus from Egypt provided a continuation of the salvation/redemption/ providence/preservation motifs of Passover, Unleavened Bread, and Pentecost.

Regulations about Vows

30 Moses told the leaders of the Israelite tribes, "This is what the LORD has commanded: ² When a man makes a vow to the LORD or swears an oath to put himself under an obligation, he must not break his word; he must do whatever he has promised.

³ "When a woman in her father's house during her youth makes a vow to the LORD or puts herself under an obligation, ⁴ and her father hears about her vow or the obligation she put herself under, and he says nothing to her, all her vows and every obligation she put herself under are binding. ⁵ But if her father prohibits her on the day he hears about it, none of her vows and none of the obligations she put herself under are binding. The LORD will release her because her father has prohibited her.

⁶ "If a woman marries while her vows or the rash commitment she herself made are binding, ⁷ and her husband hears about it and says nothing to her when he finds out, her vows are binding, and the obligations she put herself under are binding. ⁸ But if her husband prohibits her when he hears about it, he will cancel her vow that is binding or the rash commitment she herself made, and the LORD will release her.

⁹ "Every vow a widow or divorced woman puts herself under is binding on her.

¹⁰ "If a woman in her husband's house has made a vow or put herself under an obligation with an oath, ¹¹ and her husband hears about it, says nothing to her, and does not prohibit her, all her vows are binding, and every obligation she put herself under is binding. ¹² But if her husband cancels them on the day he hears about it, nothing that came from her lips, whether her vows or her obligation, is binding.

Her husband has canceled them, and the LORD will release her. ¹³ Her husband may confirm or cancel any vow or any sworn obligation to deny herself. ¹⁴ If her husband says nothing at all to her from day to day, he confirms all her vows and obligations, which are binding. He has confirmed them because he said nothing to her when he heard about them. ¹⁵ But if he cancels them after he hears about them, he will be responsible for her commitment."ᴬ

¹⁶ These are the statutes that the LORD commanded Moses concerning the relationship between a man and his wife, or between a father and his daughter in his house during her youth.

War with Midian

31 The LORD spoke to Moses, ² "Execute vengeance for the Israelites against the Midianites. After that, you will be gathered to your people."

³ So Moses spoke to the people, "Equip some of your men for war. They will go against Midian to inflict the LORD's vengeance on them. ⁴ Send one thousand men to war from each Israelite tribe." ⁵ So one thousand were recruited from each Israelite tribe out of the thousandsᴮ in Israel — twelve thousand equipped for war. ⁶ Moses sent one thousand from each tribe to war. They went with Phinehas son of Eleazar the priest, in whose care were the holy objects and signal trumpets.

⁷ They waged war against Midian, as the LORD had commanded Moses, and killed every male. ⁸ Along with the others slain by them, they killed the Midianite kings — Evi, Rekem, Zur, Hur, and Reba, the five kings of Midian. They also killed Balaam son of Beor with the

ᴬ30:15 Or *will bear her guilt* ᴮ31:5 Or *clans*

30:1–16 In this section the legal force of vows and oaths is set forth for both men and women. The force of a woman's vows was limited by her male guardian, usually either her father or her husband. If the guardian was passive or assenting, the vows of the woman had the same legal force as a man's vow. The vows of widows and divorced women were also binding. This statute also applied to a woman who was taking a Nazirite vow (6:1–21). 30:1–2 Making vows was voluntary, but any **man** who made a **vow** or swore an **oath** to the Lord was required to fulfill his **obligation**. Vows involved a verbal act of commitment to a task, or to consecration of oneself or property to the Lord. Oral vows were just as binding as formal written documents. To break a vow in which God's name had been evoked was to profane God's name (Lv 27:28–29). Sacrificial offerings were part of the obligation ritual, especially in ancient Israel where oaths were to be made only to God. In the case of the Nazirite vow (Nm 6), the procedure included an oath of abstinence from wine and strong drink, from shaving of the head, and from contamination by a corpse. Jesus cites 30:2 in Mt 5:33.

30:3–5 If **a woman in her father's house during her youth** had made a vow, the patriarchal headship of her father became the controlling factor. A young female lived under her father's authority until she married (usually in the late teenage years), at which time her husband assumed this responsibility (vv. 6–8). 30:9 In the case of a **widow or divorced woman**, she no longer lived under the patriarchal authority of her father or husband, so she had the same status and responsibility as a man with regard to vows. 30:10–15 In the patriarchal society of ancient Israel, vows could be annulled by the **husband** if they were considered detrimental to the woman, to her husband, or to the husband-wife relationship. Special considerations were given to the circumstances under which the wife took a vow, when the husband was apprised of the commitment, and how he responded to the information. 31:1–2 The **Midianites** are an enigmatic people in biblical, historical, and archaeological research. According to Gn 25:1–4, Midian was one of the sons of Abraham through his concubine Keturah. Midianites were allied at times with the Moabites (Gn 36:35; Nm

22:7; 25:6,14–18), the Amalekites (Jdg 6:3; 7:12), and the Ishmaelites (Gn 37:28). The Midianites seem to have been a loosely connected confederation of nomadic and seminomadic tribes with origins in northern Saudi Arabia who traveled the regions of the western Sinai Peninsula, southern Jordan, and the Arabah. 31:3–5 Here **one thousand men . . . from each Israelite tribe** are mustered for battle. Equal participation in the conquest by the tribes parallels their equal contribution of gifts for the tabernacle in chap. 7. 31:6 The model for holy war is presented with the priest **Phinehas** accompanying the twelve thousand-man army into battle. They carried with them the sanctuary vessels for needed purification rituals and the **trumpets** for sounding battle alerts (10:1–10). 31:7–12 The five **Midianite kings** defeated in the campaign are listed in the same order in the battle summary of Jos 13:21, where they are called "princes of Sihon." The nature of the political relationships among the Amorites, Moabites, and Midianites remains nebulous. One of these Midianite leaders, **Zur**, was the father of Cozbi, the Midianite woman who was killed by Phinehas along with her Israelite lover Zimri ben Salu (25:14–18).

sword. ⁹ The Israelites took the Midianite women and their dependents captive, and they plundered all their cattle, flocks, and property. ¹⁰ Then they burned all the cities where the Midianites lived, as well as all their encampments, ¹¹ and took away all the spoils of war and the captives, both people and animals. ¹² They brought the prisoners, animals, and spoils of war to Moses, the priest Eleazar, and the Israelite community at the camp on the plains of Moab by the Jordan across from Jericho.

¹³ Moses, the priest Eleazar, and all the leaders of the community went to meet them outside the camp. ¹⁴ But Moses became furious with the officers, the commanders of thousands and commanders of hundreds, who were returning from the military campaign. ¹⁵ "Have you let every female live?" he asked them. ¹⁶ "Yet they are the ones who, at Balaam's advice, incited the Israelites to unfaithfulness against the LORD in the Peor incident, so that the plague came against the LORD's community. ¹⁷ So now, kill every male among the dependents and kill every woman who has gone to bed with a man, ¹⁸ but keep alive for yourselves all the young females who have not gone to bed with a man. ¹⁹ "You are to remain outside the camp for seven days. All of you and your prisoners who have killed a person or touched the dead are to purify yourselves on the third day and the seventh day. ²⁰ Also purify everything: garments, leather goods, things made of goat hair, and every article of wood."

²¹ Then the priest Eleazar said to the soldiers who had gone to battle, "This is the legal statute the LORD commanded Moses: ²² The gold, silver, bronze, iron, tin, and lead — ²³ everything that can withstand fire — you are to pass through fire, and it will be clean. It must still be purified with the purification water. Anything that cannot withstand fire, pass through the water. ²⁴ On the seventh day wash your clothes, and you will be clean. After that you may enter the camp."

²⁵ The LORD told Moses, ²⁶ "You, the priest Eleazar, and the family heads of the community are to take a count of what was captured, people and animals. ²⁷ Then divide the captives between the troops who went out to war and the entire community. ²⁸ Set aside a tribute for the LORD from what belongs to the fighting men who went out to war: one out of every five hundred people, cattle, donkeys, sheep, and goats.

²⁹ Take the tribute from their half and give it to the priest Eleazar as a contribution to the LORD. ³⁰ From the Israelites' half, take one out of every fifty from the people, cattle, donkeys, sheep, and goats, all the livestock, and give them to the Levites who perform the duties ofᴬ the LORD's tabernacle."

³¹ So Moses and the priest Eleazar did as the LORD commanded Moses. ³² The captives remaining from the plunder the army had taken totaled:

675,000 sheep and goats,
³³ 72,000 cattle,
³⁴ 61,000 donkeys,
³⁵ and 32,000 people, all the females who had not gone to bed with a man.

³⁶ The half portion for those who went out to war numbered:

337,500 sheep and goats,
³⁷ and the tribute to the LORD was 675 from the sheep and goats;
³⁸ from the 36,000 cattle, the tribute to the LORD was 72;
³⁹ from the 30,500 donkeys, the tribute to the LORD was 61;
⁴⁰ and from the 16,000 people, the tribute to the LORD was 32 people.

⁴¹ Moses gave the tribute to the priest Eleazar as a contribution for the LORD, as the LORD had commanded Moses.

⁴² From the Israelites' half, which Moses separated from the men who fought, ⁴³ the community's half was:

337,500 sheep and goats,
⁴⁴ 36,000 cattle,
⁴⁵ 30,500 donkeys,
⁴⁶ and 16,000 people.

⁴⁷ Moses took one out of every fifty, selected from the people and the livestock of the Israelites' half. He gave them to the Levites who perform the duties of the LORD's tabernacle, as the LORD had commanded him.

⁴⁸ The officers who were over the thousands of the army, the commanders of thousands and of hundreds, approached Moses ⁴⁹ and told him, "Your servants have taken a census of the fighting men under our command, and not one of us is missing. ⁵⁰ So we have presented to the LORD an offering of the gold articles each man found — armlets, bracelets, rings, earrings, and necklaces — to make atonement for ourselves before the LORD."

ᴬ31:30 Or who protect

31:13–24 The purpose of holy war was to eradicate impure elements, whether persons or property, from society. This battle followed on the heels of the idolatrous activity of Baal-peor (chap. 25) that began with unholy sexual relations and resulted in the death of thousands of Israelites. It also set the stage for the instructions in 33:50–56 for possessing the promised land by driving out the Canaanites and eradicating the sources of idolatry.

31:26–46 These instructions for the distribution of the spoils of war among the community members set the standard for the coming campaigns in the promised land.

31:48–54 The amount of **gold** offered by Israel's commanders exceeded the minimal requirement of one-half shekel per person by nearly threefold, with the armlets, bracelets, signet rings, earrings, and necklaces totaling 16,750 shekels (6,700 ounces, or nearly 420 **pounds**). The leaders gave sacrificially in the spirit of thanksgiving to God.

⁵¹ Moses and the priest Eleazar received from them all the articles made out of gold. ⁵² All the gold of the contribution they offered to the LORD, from the commanders of thousands and of hundreds, was 420 pounds.^ ⁵³ Each of the soldiers had taken plunder for himself. ⁵⁴ Moses and the priest Eleazar received the gold from the commanders of thousands and of hundreds and brought it into the tent of meeting as a memorial for the Israelites before the LORD.

Transjordan Settlements

32 The Reubenites and Gadites had a very large number of livestock. When they surveyed the lands of Jazer and Gilead, they saw that the region was a good one for livestock. ² So the Gadites and Reubenites came to Moses, the priest Eleazar, and the leaders of the community and said, ³ "The territory of Ataroth, Dibon, Jazer, Nimrah, Heshbon, Elealeh, Sebam,ᴮ Nebo, and Beon, ⁴ which the LORD struck down before the community of Israel, is good land for livestock, and your servants own livestock." ⁵ They said, "If we have found favor with you, let this land be given to your servants as a possession. Don't make us cross the Jordan."

⁶ But Moses asked the Gadites and Reubenites, "Should your brothers go to war while you stay here? ⁷ Why are you discouraging the Israelites from crossing into the land the LORD has given them? ⁸ That's what your ancestors did when I sent them from Kadesh-barnea to see the land. ⁹ After they went up as far as Eshcol Valley and saw the land, they discouraged the Israelites from entering the land the LORD had given them. ¹⁰ So the LORD's anger burned that day, and he swore an oath: ¹¹ 'Because they did not remain loyal to me, none of the men twenty years old or more who came up from Egypt will see the land I swore to give Abraham, Isaac, and Jacob — ¹² none except Caleb son of Jephunneh the Kenizzite and Joshua son of Nun, because they did remain loyal to

the LORD.' ¹³ The LORD's anger burned against Israel, and he made them wander in the wilderness forty years until the whole generation that had done what was evil in the LORD's sight was gone. ¹⁴ And here you, a brood of sinners, stand in your ancestors' place adding even more to the LORD's burning anger against Israel. ¹⁵ If you turn back from following him, he will once again leave this people in the wilderness, and you will destroy all of them."

¹⁶ Then they approached him and said, "We want to build sheep pens here for our livestock and cities for our dependents. ¹⁷ But we will arm ourselves and be ready to go ahead of the Israelites until we have brought them into their place. Meanwhile, our dependents will remain in the fortified cities because of the inhabitants of the land. ¹⁸ We will not return to our homes until each of the Israelites has taken possession of his inheritance. ¹⁹ Yet we will not have an inheritance with them across the Jordan and beyond, because our inheritance will be across the Jordan to the east."

²⁰ Moses replied to them, "If you do this — if you arm yourselves for battle before the LORD, ²¹ and every one of your armed men crosses the Jordan before the LORD until he has driven his enemies from his presence, ²² and the land is subdued before the LORD — afterward you may return and be free from obligation to the LORD and to Israel. And this land will belong to you as a possession before the LORD. ²³ But if you don't do this, you will certainly sin against the LORD; be sure your sin will catch up with you. ²⁴ Build cities for your dependents and pens for your flocks, but do what you have promised."

²⁵ The Gadites and Reubenites answered Moses, "Your servants will do just as my lord commands. ²⁶ Our dependents, wives, livestock, and all our animals will remain here in the cities of Gilead, ²⁷ but your servants are equipped for war before the LORD and will go across to the battle as my lord orders."

---

^31:52 Lit *16,750 shekels* ᴮ32:3 Sam, LXX read *Sibmah* (v. 38); Syr reads *Sebah*

32:1–5 Having journeyed through the arid regions such as Edom and Moab south of the Arnon River, the **Reubenites and Gadites** observed that the region around **Gilead** was more fertile. The several rivers in the region such as the Yarmuk, Jabesh, and Jabbok, along with the numerous springs, would provide an ample water supply for their needs. The cities named were located in the highland plains of Transjordan on the eastern side of the Dead Sea. The request for territorial allocation east of the Jordan River was made in proper protocol: they presented themselves as servants seeking favor before **Moses . . . Eleazar, and the leaders of the community** (cp. 31:13). Their claim was that since the Lord had provided victory over the Amorites and others, and the land could provide ample pasturage for

their **livestock**, they should be allowed to settle there. They added the stipulation that they not be required to **cross the Jordan** River—they did not want to go to war. 32:6–15 Moses called attention to the real reason why these tribes wanted to settle the Transjordan highlands: they were hesitant about going to **war**. This was a potentially treasonous act against God's plan for the nation. The promised land was across the Jordan River to the west (34:12) and not on the eastern side of the river. Moses realized that their request had all the hallmarks of the great rebellion in which Israel had rejected God's gift of the land. Note the words "discouraging" and "discouraged" in 32:7,9. 32:16–19 The Reubenites and Gadites pledged their full support for the conquest

of the land west of the Jordan River—even to the point of leading the way for the remainder of the tribes (**we will arm ourselves and be ready to go**)—if Moses would allow them to take their inheritance in Transjordan and permit them to leave their families in the safekeeping of the local towns. 32:20–24 Moses consented to the request of these tribes under both positive (**if you do this**) and negative (**if you don't do this**) stipulations. The covenant between the Gad-Reuben alliance and the other ten tribes had Moses as the mediator and the Lord as the witness and guarantor of the commitment made by the two groups. 32:25–32 The **Gadites and Reubenites** ratified the agreement as **servants** of Moses, and ultimately of God. All treaty arrangements were ratified in the context of the

[28] So Moses gave orders about them to the priest Eleazar, Joshua son of Nun, and the family heads of the Israelite tribes. [29] Moses told them, "If the Gadites and Reubenites cross the Jordan with you, every man in battle formation before the LORD, and the land is subdued before you, you are to give them the land of Gilead as a possession. [30] But if they don't go across with you in battle formation, they must accept land in Canaan with you."

[31] The Gadites and Reubenites replied, "What the LORD has spoken to your servants is what we will do. [32] We will cross over in battle formation before the LORD into the land of Canaan, but we will keep our hereditary possession across the Jordan."

[33] So Moses gave them — the Gadites, Reubenites, and half the tribe of Manasseh son of Joseph — the kingdom of King Sihon of the Amorites and the kingdom of King Og of Bashan, the land including its cities with the territories surrounding them. [34] The Gadites rebuilt Dibon, Ataroth, Aroer, [35] Atroth-shophan, Jazer, Jogbehah, [36] Beth-nimrah, and Beth-haran as fortified cities, and built sheep pens. [37] The Reubenites rebuilt Heshbon, Elealeh, Kiriathaim, [38] as well as Nebo and Baal-meon (whose names were changed), and Sibmah. They gave names to the cities they rebuilt.

[39] The descendants of Machir son of Manasseh went to Gilead, captured it, and drove out the Amorites who were there. [40] So Moses gave Gilead to the clan of Machir son of Manasseh, and they settled in it. [41] Jair, a descendant of Manasseh, went and captured their villages, which he renamed Jair's Villages.[A] [42] Nobah went and captured Kenath with its surrounding villages and called it Nobah after his own name.

Wilderness Travels Reviewed

33 These were the stages of the Israelites' journey when they went out of the land of Egypt by their military divisions under the leadership of Moses and Aaron. [2] At the LORD's command, Moses wrote down the starting points for the stages of their journey; these are the stages listed by their starting points:

[3] They traveled from Rameses in the first month, on the fifteenth day of the month. On the day after the Passover the Israelites went out defiantly[B] in the sight of all the Egyptians. [4] Meanwhile, the Egyptians were burying every firstborn male the LORD had struck down among them, for the LORD had executed judgment against their gods. [5] The Israelites traveled from Rameses and camped at Succoth.

[6] They traveled from Succoth and camped at Etham, which is on the edge of the wilderness.

[7] They traveled from Etham and turned back to Pi-hahiroth, which faces Baal-zephon, and they camped before Migdol.

[8] They traveled from Pi-hahiroth[C] and crossed through the middle of the sea into the wilderness. They took a three-day journey into the Wilderness of Etham and camped at Marah.

[9] They traveled from Marah and came to Elim. There were twelve springs and seventy date palms at Elim, so they camped there.

[10] They traveled from Elim and camped by the Red Sea.

[11] They traveled from the Red Sea and camped in the Wilderness of Sin.

[12] They traveled from the Wilderness of Sin and camped in Dophkah.

[13] They traveled from Dophkah and camped at Alush.

[14] They traveled from Alush and camped at Rephidim, where there was no water for the people to drink.

[15] They traveled from Rephidim and camped in the Wilderness of Sinai.

A 32:41 Or renamed Havvoth-jair   B 33:3 Lit with a raised hand; Ex 14:8   C 33:8 Some Hb mss, Sam, Syr, Vg; other Hb mss read from before Hahiroth

---

religious assembly and climaxed by rituals overseen by the priests.

32:33–36 The **Gadites** were granted land in the southern part of the territory formerly held by **King Sihon of the Amorites**. Gad shared its northern border with the half-tribe of Manasseh. The cities listed for Gad in the OT suggest that a narrow strip of land in the Jordan River plain, extending from the Jabbok River to the Sea of Galilee, was to be included in the allocation. **Aroer** (modern 'Ara'ir) was located on the King's Highway, just north of the Arnon River. The Gadite cities are described in Jos 13:24–28. The allocation to **half the tribe of Manasseh** was generally to the north of the tribe of Gad, extending from the region of Gilead into Bashan and Golan. **32:37–38** The **Reubenites** were allocated lands and cities south of Gad, especially the

cities of **Heshbon** (the former capital of Sihon's Amorite kingdom), **Elealeh**, **Kiriathaim** . . . **Nebo and Baal-meon**. Additional cities and territories are described in Jos 13:15–23, including Dibon and Aroer, which were located on the highland plateau just north of the Arnon River valley. **32:39–42** The Machirite clan of the tribe of **Manasseh** apparently joined in the quest for Transjordan territory after gaining victory over the **Amorites** in the upper and northern Gilead region. The language here closely parallels that of 21:32 and 33:52–54, the model terminology for the conquest of the land. They were to take control of the given territory, drive out the inhabitants, and destroy all cultic objects of false religion. **33:1–10** The pattern of "they **traveled** / they **camped**" echoes the pattern of the journey

song of 9:18–23, providing continuity in the literary style of these two sections of the book. The first cycle, **from Rameses** to **the Red Sea**, provides the date and setting of the miraculous and historic deliverance of Israel from bondage in Egypt—highlighting the death of the firstborn in Egypt, which provided redemption for the firstborn Israelites (3:13) and victory over the gods of Egypt. **33:11–17** From **the Wilderness of Sin** to **Hazeroth**, Mount Sinai is not mentioned, though the Sinai Wilderness is included. The details of the year-long stay in the vicinity of the mountain of God are found in Ex 19–40 and Nm 1–10. One of the key questions in attempting to locate these sites is the location of Mount Sinai. Through the centuries more than twenty different mountains have been suggested. These include Jebel

¹⁶ They traveled from the Wilderness of Sinai and camped at Kibroth-hattaavah.
¹⁷ They traveled from Kibroth-hattaavah and camped at Hazeroth.
¹⁸ They traveled from Hazeroth and camped at Rithmah.
¹⁹ They traveled from Rithmah and camped at Rimmon-perez.
²⁰ They traveled from Rimmon-perez and camped at Libnah.
²¹ They traveled from Libnah and camped at Rissah.
²² They traveled from Rissah and camped at Kehelathah.
²³ They traveled from Kehelathah and camped at Mount Shepher.
²⁴ They traveled from Mount Shepher and camped at Haradah.
²⁵ They traveled from Haradah and camped at Makheloth.
²⁶ They traveled from Makheloth and camped at Tahath.
²⁷ They traveled from Tahath and camped at Terah.
²⁸ They traveled from Terah and camped at Mithkah.
²⁹ They traveled from Mithkah and camped at Hashmonah.
³⁰ They traveled from Hashmonah and camped at Moseroth.
³¹ They traveled from Moseroth and camped at Bene-jaakan.
³² They traveled from Bene-jaakan and camped at Hor-haggidgad.
³³ They traveled from Hor-haggidgad and camped at Jotbathah.
³⁴ They traveled from Jotbathah and camped at Abronah.
³⁵ They traveled from Abronah and camped at Ezion-geber.
³⁶ They traveled from Ezion-geber and camped in the Wilderness of Zin (that is, Kadesh).

³⁷ They traveled from Kadesh and camped at Mount Hor on the edge of the land of Edom. ³⁸ At the Lord's command, the priest Aaron climbed Mount Hor and died there on the first day of the fifth month in the fortieth year after the Israelites went out of the land of Egypt. ³⁹ Aaron was 123 years old when he died on Mount Hor. ⁴⁰ At that time the Canaanite king of Arad, who lived in the Negev in the land of Canaan, heard the Israelites were coming.
⁴¹ They traveled from Mount Hor and camped at Zalmonah.
⁴² They traveled from Zalmonah and camped at Punon.
⁴³ They traveled from Punon and camped at Oboth.
⁴⁴ They traveled from Oboth and camped at Iye-abarim on the border of Moab.
⁴⁵ They traveled from Iyim^A and camped at Dibon-gad.
⁴⁶ They traveled from Dibon-gad and camped at Almon-diblathaim.
⁴⁷ They traveled from Almon-diblathaim and camped in the Abarim range facing Nebo.
⁴⁸ They traveled from the Abarim range and camped on the plains of Moab by the Jordan across from Jericho.
⁴⁹ They camped by the Jordan from Beth-jeshimoth to the Acacia Meadow^B on the plains of Moab.

Instructions for Occupying Canaan

⁵⁰ The Lord spoke to Moses in the plains of Moab by the Jordan across from Jericho, ⁵¹ "Tell the Israelites: When you cross the Jordan into the land of Canaan, ⁵² you must drive out all the inhabitants of the land before you, destroy all their stone images and cast images, and demolish all their high places. ⁵³ You are to take possession of the land and settle in it because I have given you the land to possess. ⁵⁴ You are

---

^A 33:45 A shortened form of Iye-abarim   ^B 33:49 Or to Abel-shittim

---

Helal in the northeastern Sinai Peninsula near the Way of the Wilderness of Shur (Ex 15:22), Jebel Sin Bisher in the west central region, Jebel Serbal and the traditional Jebel Musa in the southern Sinai region, and Har Karkom in the Paran Wilderness region. Several mountains in northwestern Saudi Arabia have also been proposed, including Jebel el-Lawra, southeast of Aqaba. If the request of Moses before Pharaoh to journey three days into the wilderness to celebrate a festival to the Lord (Ex 8:3) is to be applied to the quest for the mountain's locale, then the sacred summit must be closer to the Egyptian border fortresses than most of the mountains except Jebel Sin Bisher or perhaps another mountain in western Sinai. The clearest statement regarding this part of the itinerary is found in Dt 1:2, which states that the distance from Horeb (= Sinai) to Kadesh-barnea via Ezion-geber

was an eleven-day journey, or about 140 to 150 miles. **33:18–31** None of the sites in the third or fourth cycles can be accurately located. Most of them are unknown to the rest of Scripture, later history, and modern historical geographers. **33:32–41** From **Hor-haggidgad** to **Zalmonah**—the fifth cycle includes the death on **Mount Hor** of the first high priest **Aaron**, who like Moses was prohibited from entering the promised land because of his rebellion "at the Waters of Meribah" (20:11–13,23–29). The reference to the **king of Arad** reminds the reader of the victory over the Canaanite armies (21:1–3) that had once defeated Israel soon after the Israelites refused to enter the promised land (14:39–45). **33:42–49** From **Punon** to **the plains of Moab**—the sites mentioned in the sixth

cycle are in the vicinity of the Arabah south of the Dead Sea and in the Transjordan regions of Edom, Moab, and Ammon. **33:50–56** The seventh and final cycle of victory-march stages would begin from the plains of Moab directly opposite the city of Jericho. This Canaanite city would become the initial victory for the Israelites when they faithfully followed the Lord's commands to march around the city on successive days (Jos 6). **33:52** These idols were representations of the pagan gods, a record of the perception of reality conceived of by a worshiper or craftsman. **Cast images** were molten forms (Hb *massekoth*) of deities from clay or molten metal such as copper or bronze. **High places** translates the Hebrew *bamoth*, referring to a cultic worship center, which may or may not indicate an elevated site or structure. All forms of local idolatrous worship were to be

to receive the land as an inheritance by lot according to your clans. Increase the inheritance for a large clan and decrease it for a small one. Whatever place the lot indicates for someone will be his. You will receive an inheritance according to your ancestral tribes. ⁵⁵ But if you don't drive out the inhabitants of the land before you, those you allow to remain will become barbs for your eyes and thorns for your sides; they will harass you in the land where you will live. ⁵⁶ And what I had planned to do to them, I will do to you."

Boundaries of the Promised Land

34 The LORD spoke to Moses, ² "Command the Israelites and say to them: When you enter the land of Canaan, it will be allotted to you as an inheritanceᴬ with these borders:

³ Your southern side will be from the Wilderness of Zin along the boundary of Edom. Your southern border on the east will begin at the east end of the Dead Sea. ⁴ Your border will turn south of the Scorpions' Ascent,ᴮ proceed to Zin, and end south of Kadesh-barnea. It will go to Hazar-addar and proceed to Azmon. ⁵ The border will turn from Azmon to the Brook of Egypt, where it will end at the Mediterranean Sea.

⁶ Your western border will be the coastline of the Mediterranean Sea; this will be your western border.

⁷ This will be your northern border: From the Mediterranean Sea draw a line to Mount Hor; ⁸ from Mount Hor draw a line to the entrance of Hamath,ᶜ and the border will reach Zedad. ⁹ Then the border will go to Ziphron and end at Hazar-enan. This will be your northern border.

¹⁰ For your eastern border, draw a line from Hazar-enan to Shepham. ¹¹ The border will go down from Shepham to Riblah east of Ain. It will continue down and reach the eastern slope of the Sea of Chinnereth.ᴰ ¹² Then the border will go down to the Jordan and end at the Dead Sea. This will be your land defined by its borders on all sides."

¹³ So Moses commanded the Israelites, "This is the land you are to receive by lot as an inheritance, which the LORD commanded to be given to the nine and a half tribes. ¹⁴ For the tribe of Reuben's descendants and the tribe of Gad's descendants have received their inheritance according to their ancestral families,ᴱ and half the tribe of Manasseh has received its inheritance. ¹⁵ The two and a half tribes have received their inheritance across the Jordan east of Jericho, toward the sunrise."

Leaders for Distributing the Land

¹⁶ The LORD spoke to Moses, ¹⁷ "These are the names of the men who are to distribute the land as an inheritance for you: the priest

---

ᴬ34:2 Lit *inheritance — the land of Canaan* ᴮ34:4 Lit *of Scorpions*; Jos 15:3; Jdg 1:36 ᶜ34:8 Or *to Lebo-hamath*
ᴰ34:11 = the Sea of Galilee; Jos 12:3; 13:27; Lk 5:1 ᴱ34:14 Lit *the house of their fathers*

---

eradicated from the land, lest the Israelites be tempted to adopt them.
33:55–56 The statement of conditional judgment of Israel gives evidence of the literary and thematic unity of the Pentateuch, paralleling the message of judgment in Lv 26:14–33 and Dt 28:15–68. Just as God intended for Israel to displace (disinherit) the Canaanites, so he could drive the Israelites from the promised land if they failed to obey his commands.
34:1–2 The **borders** of the promised land represented the limits of the land of Canaan during the late Bronze Age (1550–1200 BC) and were the ideal setting for the national boundaries.
34:3–5 The **southern side** of the border began with the **Wilderness of Zin**, from which the original scouts returned with their report (13:21). The line extended northeast to the southern end of the **Dead Sea** (Salt Sea), avoiding the Edomite territory on the west side of the Arabah, and then moved westward from the Wilderness of Zin, gradually turning more northwest. The border ran along the edge of Edomite territory in order to avoid any further conflicts with those who had prohibited passage for the Israelites when they moved into Transjordan. The description continues on a general line south of **the Scorpions' Ascent** and on through the south side of **Kadesh-barnea** ('Ain Qedeis or 'Ain el-Qudeirat), and extending toward

the **Brook of Egypt** (modern Wadi el-Arish) just south of Raphia and the Gaza Strip. The border then followed the brook northwest to the **Mediterranean Sea** (**Hazar-addar** and **Azmon** are unknown).
34:6 The **western border** was the natural barrier formed by the "Great Sea," the **Mediterranean**.
34:7–9 The **northern border** reached from the **Mediterranean** toward **Mount Hor**, perhaps today's Jebel Akkar. The **entrance of Hamath** (or Lebo-hamath) is generally identified with modern Lebweh near one of the sources of the Orontes River. Hamath was the northernmost extent of the land surveyed by the twelve Israelite scouts, according to 13:21. It was also the northern boundary of the Israelite kingdom during the monarchy of David and Solomon (1Kg 8:65).
34:10–12 The **eastern border** began with the site of **Hazar-enan**, which has been associated with either the oasis of Qaryatein or modern Hadr in the vicinity of Mount Hermon. The border continued southeast toward **Shepham** (location unknown) and then south toward **Riblah**, then around the east side of **Ain**, and onward to the eastern edge of the Sea of Galilee (**Chinnereth**). The town of Ain ("spring") may be identified with one of the springs that serve as the sources of the Jordan River. The boundary extended to the eastern side of the Huleh (upper Jordan) Valley, descending toward

the Sea of Galilee, including a narrow strip of land on the eastern side of the Jordan up to the lower slopes of the Golan Heights. From the Sea of Galilee the eastern border then followed the **Jordan** River down to the Salt Sea (**Dead Sea**), a distance of about sixty miles, though the river itself meanders back and forth over a distance of more than a hundred miles.
34:13–15 Moses fulfilled the task given to him, and the responsibility to carry out these instructions would fall on Joshua son of Nun, his successor. The distribution of the land **by lot** and according to the relative size of each of the tribes was completed under Joshua (Jos 13–19). This allotment applied to the nine and one-half tribes who lived on the west side of the Jordan River, whereas the other two and one-half tribes had already received their allotment, according to the description in Nm 32:33–42. The borders reflect the ideal territorial limits for the land of Israel as outlined by divine instruction, but this was not fully realized until the time of the united monarchy under David and Solomon (2Sm 8:1–18; 10:1–19; 2Ch 18:1–20:3).
34:16–29 Of the original twelve spies sent to assess the land, only **Caleb** remained as a leader of a tribe for the territorial allotments. With the new leadership responsibilities placed on the shoulders of Joshua, his place as the representative for the tribe of Ephraim was assumed by **Kemuel son of Shiphtan**.

Eleazar and Joshua son of Nun. [18] Take one leader from each tribe to distribute the land. [19] These are the names of the men:

Caleb son of Jephunneh from the tribe of Judah;

[20] Shemuel son of Ammihud from the tribe of Simeon's descendants;

[21] Elidad son of Chislon from the tribe of Benjamin;

[22] Bukki son of Jogli, a leader from the tribe of Dan's descendants;

[23] from the sons of Joseph:

Hanniel son of Ephod, a leader from the tribe of Manasseh's descendants,

[24] Kemuel son of Shiphtan, a leader from the tribe of Ephraim's descendants;

[25] Eli-zaphan son of Parnach, a leader from the tribe of Zebulun's descendants;

[26] Paltiel son of Azzan, a leader from the tribe of Issachar's descendants;

[27] Ahihud son of Shelomi, a leader from the tribe of Asher's descendants;

[28] Pedahel son of Ammihud, a leader from the tribe of Naphtali's descendants."

[29] These are the ones the LORD commanded to distribute the inheritance to the Israelites in the land of Canaan.

Cities for the Levites

35 The LORD again spoke to Moses in the plains of Moab by the Jordan across from Jericho: [2] "Command the Israelites to give cities out of their hereditary property for the Levites to live in and pastureland around the cities. [3] The cities will be for them to live in, and their pasturelands will be for their herds, flocks, and all their other animals. [4] The pasturelands of the cities you are to give the Levites will extend from the city wall five hundred yards[A] on every side. [5] Measure a thousand yards[B] outside the city for the east side, a thousand yards for the south side, a thousand yards for the west side, and a thousand yards for the north side, with the city in the center. This will belong to them as pasturelands for the cities.

[6] "The cities you give the Levites will include six cities of refuge, which you will provide so that the one who kills someone may flee there; in addition to these, give forty-two other cities. [7] The total number of cities you give the Levites will be forty-eight, along with their pasturelands. [8] Of the cities that you give from the Israelites' territory, you should take more from a larger tribe and less from a smaller one. Each tribe is to give some of its cities to the Levites in proportion to the inheritance it receives."

Cities of Refuge

[9] The LORD said to Moses, [10] "Speak to the Israelites and tell them: When you cross the Jordan into the land of Canaan, [11] designate cities to serve as cities of refuge for you, so that a person who kills someone unintentionally may flee there. [12] You will have the cities as a refuge from the avenger, so that the one who kills someone will not die until he stands trial before the assembly. [13] The cities you select will be your six cities of refuge. [14] Select three cities across the Jordan and three cities in the land of Canaan to be cities of refuge. [15] These six cities will serve as a refuge for the Israelites and for the alien or temporary resident among them, so that anyone who kills a person unintentionally may flee there.

[16] "If anyone strikes a person with an iron object and death results, he is a murderer; the murderer must be put to death. [17] If anyone has in his hand a stone capable of causing death and strikes another person and he dies, the murderer must be put to death. [18] If anyone has in his hand a wooden object capable of causing death and strikes another person and he dies, the murderer must be put to death. [19] The avenger of blood himself is to kill the murderer; when he finds him, he is to kill him. [20] Likewise, if anyone in hatred pushes a person or throws an object at him with malicious intent and he dies, [21] or if in hostility he strikes him with his hand and he dies, the one who struck him must be put to death; he is a murderer. The avenger of blood is to kill the murderer when he finds him.

[22] "But if anyone suddenly pushes a person without hostility or throws any object at him without malicious intent [23] or without looking

---

^35:4 Lit *1,000 cubits*   ^35:5 Lit *2,000 cubits*

35:2–5 This special allocation provided lands among the twelve Israelite tribes for the **Levites to live in and pastureland around the cities** for their flocks and herds acquired through the collection of tithes and offerings from the Israelites (18:21–32). From these settlements they and the priests could teach the people the laws of God, a vital concern if the nation was to learn the statutes and precepts of God's law.
35:6–8 Parallel to the encampment of the priests and Levites around the tabernacle during the wilderness journey (chap. 2), the theocratic state organization was such that the Levites provided a visible presence among the twelve tribes to remind them of

the need for holiness and righteousness as the people of God.
35:9–15 The **six cities of refuge** were needed in order to maintain purity and order in the community. The three cities on the eastern side of the Jordan, as well as the three cities later designated on the western side of the Jordan are delineated in Jos 20:7–9: Bezer in the Reubenite territory of southern Transjordan, Ramoth in Gilead in the Gadite highlands, and Golan in the Bashan region. The three cities of refuge on the western side of the Jordan were Kedesh, Shechem, and Hebron.
35:16–21 Those deaths involving deliberate use of lethal weapons or deliberate personal

assaults were considered murder and therefore were not covered under the guidelines of the cities of refuge. Murderers were to be executed by the **avenger of blood**, a designated kinsman to the deceased. The Hebrew word *go'el* here is the same term used of the family redeemer in Ru 2:20; 4:4,6. He was one who redeemed property or persons from another. The avenger of blood was a kinsman who redeemed the life of an individual by taking the life of the murderer.
35:22–29 The promised land was to be a holy land, free from the impurity of shed blood. The six cities of refuge provided a sanctuary to protect the lives of those convicted of manslaughter. It also served

LEVITICAL CITIES AND
CITIES OF REFUGE
NUMBERS 35

● Levitical city
○ Levitical city
   (uncertain location)
■ City of refuge
● Other city
▲ Mountain peak

Sidon
Damascus
Abana River
Mt. Hermon
Pharpar River
Litani River
Rehob
Kedesh
Abdon
Lake Huleh
ASHER
NAPHTALI
EAST MANASSEH
Mishal
Rimmon
Sea of Galilee
Kartan
Nahalal
ZEBULUN
Hammath
Golan
Ashtaroth
Helkath
Daberath
Joknean
Kishion
Tabor
ISSACHAR
Jarmuth
Yarmuk River
Taanach
En-gannim
Ramoth-gilead
Ibleam
WEST MANASSEH
Shechem
Jordan River
Jabbok River
Mahanaim
AMMON
GAD
Gath-rimmon
Yarkon River
EPHRAIM
Kibzaim
Jazer
DAN
Beth-horon
Eltekeh
Gibeon
Gezer
Geba
Mephaath
Aijalon
Almon
Heshbon
Gibbethon
Anathoth
Bezer
Beth-shemesh
Jerusalem
BENJAMIN
Kedemoth
Libnah
Hebron
REUBEN
Gaza
JUDAH
Debir
Juttah
Jahaz
Holon
Eshtemoa
N. Besor
Ashan
Jattir
DEAD SEA
Arnon River
Eastern Desert
MEDITERRANEAN SEA
SIMEON
MOAB
Zered River
31 N
EDOM
Arabah
35 E
36 E
33 N
32 N

0   10   20   30   40 Miles
0 10 20 30 40 Kilometers

drops a stone that could kill a person and he dies, but he was not his enemy and didn't intend to harm him, [24] the assembly is to judge between the person who kills someone and the avenger of blood according to these ordinances. [25] The assembly is to protect the one who kills someone from the avenger of blood. Then the assembly will return him to the city of refuge he fled to, and he must live there until the death of the high priest who was anointed with the holy oil. [26] "If the one who kills someone ever goes outside the border of the city of refuge he fled to, [27] and the avenger of blood finds him outside the border of his city of refuge and kills him, [28] for the one who killed a person was supposed to live in his city of refuge until the death of the high priest. Only after the death of the high priest may the one who has killed a person return to the land he possesses. [29] These instructions will be a statutory ordinance for you throughout your generations wherever you live.

[30] "If anyone kills a person, the murderer is to be put to death based on the word of witnesses. But no one is to be put to death based on the testimony of one witness. [31] You are not to accept a ransom for the life of someone who is guilty of murder; he must be put to death. [32] Neither should you accept a ransom for the person who flees to his city of refuge, allowing him to return and live in the land before the death of the high priest.

[33] "Do not defile the land where you live, for bloodshed defiles the land, and there can be no atonement for the land because of the blood that is shed on it, except by the blood of the person who shed it. [34] Do not make the land unclean where you live and where I dwell; for I, the LORD, reside among the Israelites."

The Inheritance of Zelophehad's Daughters

36 The family heads from the clan of the descendants of Gilead — the son of Machir, son of Manasseh — who were from the clans of the sons of Joseph, approached and addressed Moses and the leaders who were heads of the Israelite families. [2] They said, "The LORD commanded my lord to give the land as an inheritance by lot to the Israelites. My lord was further commanded by the LORD to give our brother Zelophehad's inheritance to his daughters. [3] If they marry any of the men from the other Israelite tribes, their inheritance will be taken away from our fathers' inheritance and added to that of the tribe into which they marry. Therefore, part of our allotted inheritance would be taken away. [4] When the Jubilee comes for the Israelites, their inheritance will be added to that of the tribe into which they marry, and their inheritance will be taken away from the inheritance of our ancestral tribe."

[5] So Moses commanded the Israelites at the word of the LORD, "What the tribe of Joseph's descendants says is right. [6] This is what the LORD has commanded concerning Zelophehad's daughters: They may marry anyone they like provided they marry within a clan of their ancestral tribe. [7] No inheritance belonging to the Israelites is to transfer from tribe to tribe, because each of the Israelites is to retain the inheritance of his ancestral tribe. [8] Any daughter who possesses an inheritance from an Israelite tribe must marry someone from the clan of her ancestral tribe, so that each of the Israelites will possess the inheritance of his fathers. [9] No inheritance is to transfer from one tribe to another, because each of the Israelite tribes is to retain its inheritance."

[10] The daughters of Zelophehad did as the LORD commanded Moses. [11] Mahlah, Tirzah, Hoglah, Milcah, and Noah, the daughters of Zelophehad, married cousins on their father's side. [12] They married men from the clans of the descendants of Manasseh son of Joseph, and their inheritance remained within the tribe of their father's clan.

---

as the place of banishment for offenders. If a person was placed under the protection of a city of refuge but then decided to leave the city, he could be subject to execution by the blood avenger. City elders were responsible for assessing each case to determine the nature and cause of a person's death. Atonement was offered to the person who had committed manslaughter only through the time of the high priest's death. Thus that person was required to remain inside the city until that time. Murderers who sought refuge in these cities were not protected under the law. Capital punishment for willful death cases was to be carried out by the city after the elders had determined that the death penalty was justified.
35:30–34 The final section addresses the issues of the number of witnesses necessary to bring a murder conviction, the prohibition of monetary compensation in lieu of paying the proper penalty for the crime, and the theological basis for maintaining justice in the land in capital cases.
36:1–3 Patriarchal leaders of the Machirites of the tribe of **Manasseh** feared that if the women married outside their clan, the land allotment might go to some other tribe or clan. This would upset the balanced distribution called for in 33:54.
36:4 The Year of **Jubilee** occurred every fifty years (Lv 25:13–55), after seven sabbatical years. During Jubilee, property that had been bought and sold among various tribes or clans reverted to its original tribal owner. This custom maintained the balance of land and wealth distribution among the twelve tribes. The law in Leviticus addressed matters of purchased property, but not that of inherited lands. During the Jubilee Year various debts, such as those of indentured servants, were forgiven and individuals were freed of financial and other obligations in order to rebuild their lives. "Jubilee" is an anglicized word from the Hebrew word *yovel* ("ram's horn"), which was sounded to usher in the year of celebration, redemption, and restoration.
36:5–9 The adjudication of the case came through the Lord's instruction to Moses that would permit the women to marry the person of their choosing **provided they marry within a clan of their ancestral tribe**. Hence, a loophole from the earlier case was closed.
36:10–12 The faithful adherence to the instruction from the Lord is highlighted as **the daughters of Zelophehad did as LORD commanded Moses**. These words remind the reader of the central theme of the book of Numbers—faithfulness to the Lord's instruction.

13 These are the commands and ordinances the LORD commanded the Israelites through Moses in the plains of Moab by the Jordan across from Jericho.

36:13 The conclusion to the book of Numbers summarizes the position of the Israelite nation as it was poised to inherit the promised land. Throughout the book, references to Israel's faithfulness to God have been defined by the phraseology, "[Moses, Israelites, etc.] did just as the LORD had commanded." The laws of Torah and the extensions of case law in various settings of life in the book of Numbers (and the subsequent book of Deuteronomy) must be the foundation of the community of faith as they enter the land of Canaan as the people of God. If they are faithful and obedient, the blessings of the covenant relationship in the inheritance and productivity of the land will be theirs, but if they do not follow the Lord's commands, their lives will be beset by opposition from without—foreign enemy attacks—and from within—plague, civil war, and natural disaster.

◢ Introduction to Deuteronomy

Circumstances of Writing

The book itself asserts that Moses is the principal source and author for the material (1:1), as do subsequent Old Testament texts (Jos 1:7–8; 1Kg 2:3; Ezr 3:2) and New Testament texts (Mt 19:7; Ac 3:22; Rm 10:19). This attribution remained virtually unchallenged until the advent of modern rationalism in the seventeenth and eighteenth centuries, but no arguments advanced by this school of thought have successfully overcome the ancient Mosaic tradition.

The exodus probably occurred in 1446 BC, whereupon Israel set out for Canaan, the inheritance God had promised his people. Because of their rebellious spirit, the Israelites were forced to wander in the desert for forty years (Dt 2:7) until at last they arrived in Moab, just opposite Jericho (32:49). It was there that Moses put pen to parchment to compose this farewell treatise (31:9,24).

Contribution to the Bible

Next to the books of Psalms and Isaiah, the New Testament alludes to Deuteronomy more than any other book in the Old Testament.

This is true not only in terms of the sheer number of instances but especially in the passages where theological truth seems most to be at issue. Jesus and the apostles considered Deuteronomy of paramount importance to their own teaching about God and his dealings with his chosen people and humanity at large. Jesus in his temptation quoted the book of Deuteronomy three times against Satan (Mt 4:4–10).

Structure

The style of the book of Deuteronomy appears as a series of repetitious, reminiscent, and even irregular exhortations, which is fitting for a collection of Moses's sermons preparing the people for their move into the promised land. The style is also reflective of the typical suzerain-vassal treaties, which could contain a preamble, historical prologue, main provisions, blessings and curses, and plans for continuing the covenant relationship. The book of Deuteronomy could be considered the constitution for the nation of Israel once it was established in the promised land.

Deuteronomy Timeline

1550–1500 BC

AARON 1529–1409?
MOSES 1526–1406?
Amenhotep I becomes pharaoh of Egypt. 1525
Glass is invented accidentally in Phoenicia. 1530
Thutmose I becomes pharaoh of Egypt. 1506
Hebrew parents are ordered to throw
    newborn sons into the Nile. 1528

1500–1450 BC

Bronze razors, Scandinavia 1500
Egyptians develop effective pharmaceutical
    compounds. 1500
First tomb in the Valley of the Kings in Egypt 1500
Cinnamon is exported from Kerala to
    the ancient Near East. 1500
Evidence of gold hammered into
    foil in South America 1500
JOSHUA 1490–1380?
Moses flees Egypt. 1487

Outline

Key verses in Deuteronomy

6:5   Love the LORD your God with all your heart, with all your soul, and with all your strength.

6:17   Carefully observe the commands of the LORD your God, the decrees and statutes he has commanded you.

6:18   Do what is right and good in the LORD's sight, so that you may prosper and so that you may enter and possess the good land the LORD your God swore to give your ancestors.

1450–1445 BC

Pictographic writing appears in China. **1450**
Thutmose III erects numerous obelisks in
   Egypt, one of which has mistakenly been
   called "Cleopatra's Needle." The shadow
   of this obelisk was used to calculate
   time, seasons, and solstices. **1450**
Dogs are domesticated in North America. **1450**
Single tube seed drill is developed
   by the Sumerians. **1450**

1445–1375 BC

The exodus and defeat of Pharaoh
   at the Red Sea **1446**
Events in Leviticus **1445**
Events in Numbers **1445–1407**
Events in Deuteronomy **1406**
Miraculous crossing of the Jordan River **1406**

Introduction

1 These are the words Moses spoke to all Israel across the Jordan in the wilderness, in the Arabah opposite Suph,^A between Paran and Tophel, Laban, Hazeroth, and Di-zahab. ² It is an eleven-day journey from Horeb to Kadesh-barnea by way of Mount Seir. ³ In the fortieth year, in the eleventh month, on the first of the month, Moses told the Israelites everything the LORD had commanded him to say to them. ⁴ This was after he had defeated King Sihon of the Amorites, who lived in Heshbon, and King Og of Bashan, who lived in Ashtaroth, at Edrei. ⁵ Across the Jordan in the land of Moab, Moses began to explain this law, saying:

Departure from Horeb

⁶ "The LORD our God spoke to us at Horeb: 'You have stayed at this mountain long enough. ⁷ Resume your journey and go to the hill country of the Amorites and their neighbors in the Arabah, the hill country, the Judean foothills,^B the Negev and the sea coast — to the land of the Canaanites and to Lebanon as far as the great river, the Euphrates River. ⁸ See, I have set the land before you. Enter and take possession of the land the LORD swore to give to your ancestors Abraham, Isaac, and Jacob and their future descendants.'

Leaders for the Tribes

⁹ "I said to you at that time: I can't bear the responsibility for you on my own. ¹⁰ The LORD your God has so multiplied you that today you are as numerous as the stars of the sky. ¹¹ May the LORD, the God of your ancestors, increase you a thousand times more, and bless you as he promised you. ¹² But how can I bear your troubles, burdens, and disputes by myself? ¹³ Appoint for yourselves wise, understanding, and respected men from each of your tribes, and I will make them your leaders.

¹⁴ "You replied to me, 'What you propose to do is good.'

¹⁵ "So I took the leaders of your tribes, wise and respected men, and set them over you as leaders: commanders for thousands, hundreds, fifties, and tens, and officers for your tribes. ¹⁶ I commanded your judges at that time: Hear the cases between your brothers, and judge rightly between a man and his brother or his resident alien. ¹⁷ Do not show partiality when deciding a case; listen to small and great alike. Do not be intimidated by anyone, for judgment belongs to God. Bring me any case too difficult for you, and I will hear it. ¹⁸ At that time I commanded you about all the things you were to do.

Israel's Disobedience at Kadesh-barnea

¹⁹ "We then set out from Horeb and went across all the great and terrible wilderness you saw on the way to the hill country of the Amorites, just as the LORD our God had commanded us. When we reached Kadesh-barnea, ²⁰ I said to you: You have reached the hill country of the Amorites, which the LORD our God is giving us. ²¹ See, the LORD your God has set the land before you. Go up and take possession of it as the LORD, the God of your ancestors, has told you. Do not be afraid or discouraged.

²² "Then all of you approached me and said, 'Let's send men ahead of us, so that they may explore the land for us and bring us back a report about the route we should go up and the cities we will come to.' ²³ The plan seemed good to me, so I selected twelve men from among you, one man for each tribe. ²⁴ They left and went up into the hill country and came to Eshcol Valley, scouting the land. ²⁵ They took some of the fruit from the land in their hands, carried it down to us, and brought us back a report: 'The land the LORD our God is giving us is good.'

²⁶ "But you were not willing to go up. You rebelled against the command of the LORD your God. ²⁷ You grumbled in your tents and said, 'The LORD brought us out of the land of Egypt to hand us over to the Amorites in order to destroy us, because he hates us. ²⁸ Where can we go? Our brothers have made us lose

---

^A1:1 LXX, Tg, Vg read the Red Sea   ^B1:7 Or the Shephelah

1:1 The reference to Moses being **across the Jordan** is from the perspective of one standing in Canaan to the west. The east side of the river was called Transjordan, even by those living there.

1:2–3 Forty years had passed since Israel's exodus from Egypt. Though the journey from **Horeb** (Sinai) to Kadesh-barnea was normally eleven days (v. 2), Israel, because of its sin, had spent forty years on the not-much-longer route from Egypt to Moab (2:7; 8:2,4; Nm 14:33).

1:4 **Sihon** and **Og** were rulers of kingdoms in Transjordan whose defeat permitted Israel to occupy most of the region, which was later settled by the tribes of Reuben, Gad, and part of Manasseh (Nm 32; Jos 22).

1:6–7 **The Amorites and their neighbors** is a way of speaking of all the peoples of

Canaan. **Arabah** more technically describes the Great Rift Valley of the Jordan River and the Dead Sea.

1:15 The adjective **respected** means literally "known." These leaders must have been thoroughly scrutinized and found to be all that they professed to be.

1:17 **Do not show partiality** is a translation of a phrase that can be rendered, "Do not recognize faces." A judge must not be swayed by friendship or high rank.

1:19 **Kadesh-barnea** was Israel's main staging area throughout the forty years of desert sojourn. Known today as 'Ain Qedeis, this large oasis would have been adequate for hundreds of thousands of Hebrews and their animals.

1:22–23 See Nm 13:1–3. Either Moses interpreted a suggestion by the people as a

word from God or he consulted God before agreeing to the plan.

1:24–25 **Eshcol Valley** was in southern Canaan near Hebron. Its name means "bunch of grapes," from the abundance of this fruit that grew there. Canaan had already been called a "land flowing with milk and honey" (6:3; 11:9; 26:9; cp. Nm 13:27), so this display of grapes reinforced the lushness of the land the Lord had bequeathed to his people Israel (Dt 1:25).

1:26–28 The description of the cities of Canaan as **fortified to the heavens** came from spies who were afraid to trust God for victory and therefore exaggerated the difficulties involved. The **Anakim**, named for Anak, a descendant of the founder of Hebron (Jos 21:11), were a gigantic people (Nm 13:33), some of whom moved to Philistia and may

heart,^A saying: The people are larger and taller than we are; the cities are large, fortified to the heavens. We also saw the descendants of the Anakim there.' ²⁹ "So I said to you: Don't be terrified or afraid of them! ³⁰ The Lᴏʀᴅ your God who goes before you will fight for you, just as you saw him do for you in Egypt. ³¹ And you saw in the wilderness how the Lᴏʀᴅ your God carried you as a man carries his son all along the way you traveled until you reached this place. ³² But in spite of this you did not trust the Lᴏʀᴅ your God, ³³ who went before you on the journey to seek out a place for you to camp. He went in the fire by night and in the cloud by day to guide you on the road you were to travel.

³⁴ "When the Lᴏʀᴅ heard your^B words, he grew angry and swore an oath: ³⁵ 'None of these men in this evil generation will see the good land I swore to give your ancestors, ³⁶ except Caleb the son of Jephunneh. He will see it, and I will give him and his descendants the land on which he has set foot, because he remained loyal to the Lᴏʀᴅ.' ³⁷ "The Lᴏʀᴅ was angry with me also because of you and said, 'You will not enter there either. ³⁸ Joshua son of Nun, who attends you, will enter it. Encourage him, for he will enable Israel to inherit it. ³⁹ Your children, who you said would be plunder, your sons who^C don't yet know good from evil, will enter there. I will give them the land, and they will take possession of it. ⁴⁰ But you are to turn back and head for the wilderness by way of the Red Sea.'

⁴¹ "You answered me, 'We have sinned against the Lᴏʀᴅ. We will go up and fight just as the Lᴏʀᴅ our God commanded us.' Then each of you put on his weapons of war and thought it would be easy to go up into the hill country. ⁴² "But the Lᴏʀᴅ said to me, 'Tell them: Don't go up and fight, for I am not with you to keep you from being defeated by your enemies.' ⁴³ So I spoke to you, but you didn't listen. You

rebelled against the Lᴏʀᴅ's command and defiantly went up into the hill country. ⁴⁴ Then the Amorites who lived there came out against you and chased you like a swarm of bees. They routed you from Seir as far as Hormah. ⁴⁵ When you returned, you wept before the Lᴏʀᴅ, but he didn't listen to your requests or pay attention to you. ⁴⁶ For this reason you stayed in Kadesh as long as you did.^D

Journey past Seir

2 "Then we turned back and headed for the wilderness by way of the Red Sea, as the Lᴏʀᴅ had told me, and we traveled around the hill country of Seir for many days. ² The Lᴏʀᴅ then said to me, ³ 'You've been traveling around this hill country long enough; turn north. ⁴ Command the people: You are about to travel through the territory of your brothers, the descendants of Esau, who live in Seir. They will be afraid of you, so be very careful. ⁵ Don't provoke them, for I will not give you any of their land, not even a foot of it,^E because I have given Esau the hill country of Seir as his possession. ⁶ You may purchase food from them, so that you may eat, and buy water from them to drink. ⁷ For the Lᴏʀᴅ your God has blessed you in all the work of your hands. He has watched over your journey through this immense wilderness. The Lᴏʀᴅ your God has been with you these past forty years, and you have lacked nothing.'

Journey past Moab

⁸ "So we bypassed our brothers, the descendants of Esau, who live in Seir. We turned away from the Arabah road and from Elath and Ezion-geber. We traveled along the road to the Wilderness of Moab. ⁹ The Lᴏʀᴅ said to me, 'Show no hostility toward Moab, and do not provoke them to battle, for I will not give you any of their land as a possession, since I have given Ar as a possession to the descendants of Lot.' "

^A1:28 Lit have melted our hearts ^B1:34 Lit the sound of your ^C1:39 Lit who today ^D1:46 Lit Kadesh for many days, according to the days you stayed ^E2:5 Lit land as far as the width of a sole of a foot

have been related to Goliath and other giant Philistines (Jos 11:21–22; cp. 1Ch 20:4–8). **1:34–36** Other exceptions were men under twenty years of age (as well as women) and Joshua, who is included in v. 38. **1:37–38** This curious statement is not Moses's attempt to deflect guilt from himself to the nation. The point was that he as well as the older generation of Israelites would fail to enter the land of promise because all alike were guilty. **1:39** The sons who don't yet know good from evil were not morally deficient but too young to form moral values (Is 7:16; 8:4). They were innocent and therefore not disqualified from entering the land of promise. **1:40–46** Surprisingly, the people thought that another act of disobedience would correct the first. **From Seir as far as Hormah**

refers to an area just south of the Dead Sea and about fifty miles across. Its residents expelled the Israelites because Israel had attempted to penetrate the area despite God's command not to do so (v. 42). **2:1** The **Red Sea** mentioned here is not the body of water at the Gulf of Suez crossed by Israel during the exodus, but another arm of that sea between the Sinai Peninsula and Arabia. **2:2–3** The Israelites had tried to avoid the difficult route through the **hill country** by penetrating Canaan from the south. When that failed they had to go south to the Red Sea, skirt the hill country by hugging the coast, then **turn north** through Edom's interior. **2:4–7** When Israel encountered the Edomites **(the descendants of Esau)**, they did not

attack them because the Lord had **given . . . the hill country of Seir as his possession**. Thus, Israel was not the only people given a promised land (vv. 9,19; cp. Gn 33:16; 36:1–8). **2:8** The **Arabah road** linked the Dead Sea with the Gulf of Aqaba and took its name from the valley that is part of the Great Rift geological fault (1:1). **2:9** The **descendants of Lot** were the Moabites and Ammonites, named for the sons whom Lot fathered by his own daughters following the destruction of Sodom and Gomorrah (Gn 19:30–38). Lot was Abraham's nephew, and it was this kinship that permitted **Moab** and Ammon to be treated with such favor. **Ar** was a city just south of the Arnon Gorge, but the name here is synonymous with all of Moab.

218

¹⁰ The Emim, a great and numerous people as tall as the Anakim, had previously lived there. ¹¹ They were also regarded as Rephaim, like the Anakim, though the Moabites called them Emim. ¹² The Horites had previously lived in Seir, but the descendants of Esau drove them out, destroying them completely^A and settling in their place, just as Israel did in the land of its possession the LORD gave them.

¹³ "The LORD said, 'Now get up and cross the Zered Valley.' So we crossed the Zered Valley. ¹⁴ The time we spent traveling from Kadesh-barnea until we crossed the Zered Valley was thirty-eight years until the entire generation of fighting men had perished from the camp, as the LORD had sworn to them. ¹⁵ Indeed, the LORD's hand was against them, to eliminate them from the camp until they had all perished.

Journey past Ammon

¹⁶ "When all the fighting men had died among the people, ¹⁷ the LORD spoke to me, ¹⁸ 'Today you are going to cross the border of Moab at Ar. ¹⁹ When you get close to the Ammonites, don't show any hostility to them or provoke them, for I will not give you any of the Ammonites' land as a possession; I have given it as a possession to the descendants of Lot.'"

²⁰ This too used to be regarded as the land of the Rephaim. The Rephaim lived there previously, though the Ammonites called them Zamzummim, ²¹ a great and numerous people, tall as the Anakim. The LORD destroyed the Rephaim at the advance of the Ammonites, so that they drove them out and settled in their place. ²² This was just as he had done for the descendants of Esau who lived in Seir, when he destroyed the Horites before them; they drove them out and have lived in their place until now. ²³ The Caphtorim, who came from Caphtor,^B destroyed the Avvites, who lived in villages as far as Gaza, and settled in their place.

Defeat of Sihon the Amorite

²⁴ "The LORD also said, 'Get up, move out, and cross the Arnon Valley. See, I have handed the Amorites' King Sihon of Heshbon and his land over to you. Begin to take possession of it; engage^C him in battle. ²⁵ Today I will begin to put the fear and dread of you on the peoples

everywhere under heaven. They will hear the report about you, tremble, and be in anguish because of you.'

²⁶ "So I sent messengers with an offer of peace to King Sihon of Heshbon from the Wilderness of Kedemoth, saying, ²⁷ 'Let us travel through your land; we will keep strictly to the highway. We will not turn to the right or the left. ²⁸ You can sell us food in exchange for silver so we may eat, and give us water for silver so we may drink. Only let us travel through on foot, ²⁹ just as the descendants of Esau who live in Seir did for us, and the Moabites who live in Ar, until we cross the Jordan into the land the LORD our God is giving us.' ³⁰ But King Sihon of Heshbon would not let us travel through his land, for the LORD your God had made his spirit stubborn and his heart obstinate in order to hand him over to you, as has now taken place.

³¹ "Then the LORD said to me, 'See, I have begun to give Sihon and his land to you. Begin to take possession of it.' ³² So Sihon and his whole army came out against us for battle at Jahaz. ³³ The LORD our God handed him over to us, and we defeated him, his sons, and his whole army. ³⁴ At that time we captured all his cities and completely destroyed the people of every city, including the women and children. We left no survivors. ³⁵ We took only the livestock and the spoil from the cities we captured as plunder for ourselves. ³⁶ There was no city that was inaccessible to^D us, from Aroer on the rim of the Arnon Valley, along with the city in the valley, even as far as Gilead. The LORD our God gave everything to us. ³⁷ But you did not go near the Ammonites' land, all along the bank of the Jabbok River, the cities of the hill country, or any place that the LORD our God had forbidden.

Defeat of Og of Bashan

3 "Then we turned and went up the road to Bashan, and King Og of Bashan came out against us with his whole army to do battle at Edrei. ² But the LORD said to me, 'Do not fear him, for I have handed him over to you along with his whole army and his land. Do to him as you did to King Sihon of the Amorites, who lived in Heshbon.' ³ So the LORD our God also handed over King Og of Bashan and his whole army to us. We struck him until there was no

---

^A 2:12 Lit *them before them* ^B 2:23 Probably Crete ^C 2:24 Or *provoke* ^D 2:36 Or *was too high for*

2:10-11 Verses 10-12 are parenthetical. The **Rephaim** (and **Anakim**) were a giant race associated not only with Moab (as here) but with Bashan (Jos 12:4) and Ammon (Dt 2:20). Their identification as Anakim locates them also in Canaan, particularly in Philistine areas (Jos 11:21-22; 14:12,15; 15:13-14). **2:13** The **Zered Valley**, now known as Wadi el-Hesa, flows from the Edomite hill country into the southeast corner of the Dead Sea.

2:16-19 Ammon, the brother of Moab—born as the result of incest between Lot and his daughters (v. 9)—was the ancestor of the **Ammonites**. **2:23** The **Caphtorim** appear to be equivalent to the earlier Philistines of the patriarchal era (Gn 21:32,34; 26:1,8). They are said to have settled in the vicinity of **Gaza** (Jos 13:3), and elsewhere they are said to have originated in Caphtor, likely on the island of Crete (Jr 47:4; Am 9:7; cp. Gn 10:14).

2:25 This was confirmed when Joshua's spies spoke with Rahab in Jos 2:8-11. **2:30 The LORD** making Sihon's **spirit stubborn and his heart obstinate** is similar to God's hardening of Pharaoh's heart before the exodus (Ex 9:12; 10:1,20)—an act of God that followed Pharaoh's consistent hardening of his own heart (Ex 8:15,32; 9:34). **2:34-35** Sihon's destruction sanctioned by the Lord must be viewed not as a cruel act but as a means of eliminating a hopelessly

survivor left. [4] We captured all his cities at that time. There wasn't a city that we didn't take from them: sixty cities, the entire region of Argob, the kingdom of Og in Bashan. [5] All these were fortified with high walls, gates, and bars, besides a large number of rural villages. [6] We completely destroyed them, as we had done to King Sihon of Heshbon, destroying the men, women, and children of every city. [7] But we took all the livestock and the spoil from the cities as plunder for ourselves.

The Land of the Transjordan Tribes

[8] "At that time we took the land from the two Amorite kings across the Jordan, from the Arnon Valley as far as Mount Hermon, [9] which the Sidonians call Sirion, but the Amorites call Senir, [10] all the cities of the plateau, Gilead, and Bashan as far as Salecah and Edrei, cities of Og's kingdom in Bashan. [11] (Only King Og of Bashan was left of the remnant of the Rephaim. His bed[A] was made of iron. Isn't it in Rabbah of the Ammonites? It is 13 ½ feet long and 6 feet wide by a standard measure.[B])

[12] "At that time we took possession of this land. I gave to the Reubenites and Gadites the area extending from Aroer by the Arnon Valley, and half the hill country of Gilead along with its cities. [13] I gave to half the tribe of Manasseh the rest of Gilead and all Bashan, the kingdom of Og. The entire region of Argob, the whole territory of Bashan, used to be called the land of the Rephaim. [14] Jair, a descendant of Manasseh, took over the entire region of Argob as far as the border of the Geshurites and Maacathites. He called Bashan by his own name, Jair's Villages,[C] as it is today. [15] I gave Gilead to Machir, [16] and I gave to the Reubenites and Gadites the area extending from Gilead to the Arnon Valley (the middle of the valley was the border) and up to the Jabbok River, the border of the Ammonites. [17] The Arabah and Jordan are also borders from Chinnereth[D] as far as the Sea of the Arabah, the Dead Sea, under the slopes of Pisgah on the east.

[18] "I commanded you at that time: The LORD your God has given you this land to possess. All your valiant men will cross over in battle formation ahead of your brothers the Israelites. [19] But your wives, dependents, and livestock — I know that you have a lot of livestock — will remain in the cities I have given you [20] until the LORD gives rest to your brothers as he has to you, and they also take possession of the land the LORD your God is giving them across the Jordan. Then each of you may return to his possession that I have given you.

The Transfer of Israel's Leadership

[21] "I commanded Joshua at that time: Your own eyes have seen everything the LORD your God has done to these two kings. The LORD will do the same to all the kingdoms you are about to enter. [22] Don't be afraid of them, for the LORD your God fights for you.

[23] "At that time I begged the LORD: [24] Lord GOD, you have begun to show your greatness and your strong hand to your servant, for what god is there in heaven or on earth who can perform deeds and mighty acts like yours? [25] Please let me cross over and see the beautiful land on the other side of the Jordan, that good hill country and Lebanon.

[26] "But the LORD was angry with me because of you[E] and would not listen to me. The LORD said to me, 'That's enough! Do not speak to me again about this matter. [27] Go to the top of Pisgah and look to the west, north, south, and east, and see it with your own eyes, for you will not cross the Jordan. [28] But commission Joshua and encourage and strengthen him, for he will cross over ahead of the people and enable them to inherit this land that you will see.' [29] So we stayed in the valley facing Beth-peor.

Call to Obedience

4 "Now, Israel, listen to the statutes and ordinances I am teaching you to follow, so that you may live, enter, and take possession of the land the LORD, the God of your ancestors, is giving you. [2] You must not add anything to what I command you or take anything away from it, so that you may keep the commands of

---

[A] 3:11 Or sarcophagus   [B] 3:11 Lit nine cubits its length and four cubits its width, by a man's cubit   [C] 3:14 Or Havvoth-jair   [D] 3:17 = the Sea of Galilee; Jos 12:3; 13:27; Lk 5:1   [E] 3:26 Or me for your sake

---

unrepentant people who, if left alive, would corrupt the Israelites through intermarriage and religious syncretism (7:1–6).

3:4 The name **Bashan** (cp. v. 1) is a general term for the whole region north of the Yarmuk River, now the border between Jordan and Syria. **Argob** appears to have been the technical name for the political entity in Bashan over which **Og** was ruler.

3:8–10 Mount Hermon, more than 9,000 feet high, is the tallest peak of the Anti-Lebanon range.

3:11 The **bed . . . made of iron** of **Og** may in fact have been his sarcophagus. The Hebrew term describing it (*'eres*) should likely be taken figuratively of Og's resting place in death.

3:12–17 The conquest of the region of **Bashan** and part of **Gilead** was accomplished not by **Manasseh** *per se* but by Manassite clans, namely **Jair** and **Machir** (cp. Nm 32:39–42). Jair seems to have been a descendant of Machir (1Ch 2:21–23). In any case, they were not contemporaneous, suggesting that the conquest took a number of years.

3:25 The beautiful land is literally "the good land." This phrase occurs eight times in Deuteronomy and only twice in the rest of the Bible (cp. Jos 23:16; 1Ch 28:8).

3:27 Pisgah is the name of a summit in the range of hills in Transjordan called Abarim overlooking the Arabah and the Dead Sea. It

lies just north of Mount Nebo, the traditional setting of Moses's vantage point from which he could see the land of Canaan (32:49). Pisgah (now identified as Ras Siyaghah) and Nebo were twin peaks of the same mountain, but it was from Pisgah that the great lawgiver viewed the land he was forbidden to enter (34:1).

4:1 Statutes and ordinances are technical terms referring to elements common to covenant texts. They occur together regularly in Deuteronomy (vv. 5,8,14,45; 5:1,31; 6:1,20; 7:11; 11:1; 12:1) and always to describe the Lord's requirement of his people Israel with whom he had entered into covenant fellowship.

the LORD your God I am giving you. ³ Your eyes have seen what the LORD did at Baal-peor, for the LORD your God destroyed every one of you who followed Baal of Peor. ⁴ But you who have remained faithful^A to the LORD your God are all alive today. ⁵ Look, I have taught you statutes and ordinances as the LORD my God has commanded me, so that you may follow them in the land you are entering to possess. ⁶ Carefully follow them, for this will show your wisdom and understanding in the eyes of the peoples. When they hear about all these statutes, they will say, 'This great nation is indeed a wise and understanding people.' ⁷ For what great nation is there that has a god near to it as the LORD our God is to us whenever we call to him? ⁸ And what great nation has righteous statutes and ordinances like this entire law I set before you today?

⁹ "Only be on your guard and diligently watch yourselves, so that you don't forget the things your eyes have seen and so that they don't slip from your mind^B as long as you live. Teach them to your children and your grandchildren. ¹⁰ The day you stood before the LORD your God at Horeb, the LORD said to me, 'Assemble the people before me, and I will let them hear my words, so that they may learn to fear me all the days they live on the earth and may instruct their children.' ¹¹ You came near and stood at the base of the mountain, a mountain blazing with fire into the heavens and enveloped in a totally black cloud. ¹² Then the LORD spoke to you from the fire. You kept hearing the sound of the words, but didn't see a form; there was only a voice. ¹³ He declared his covenant to you. He commanded you to follow the Ten Commandments, which he wrote on two stone tablets. ¹⁴ At that time the LORD commanded me to teach you statutes and ordinances for you to follow in the land you are about to cross into and possess.

Worshiping the True God

¹⁵ "Diligently watch yourselves — because you did not see any form on the day the LORD spoke to you out of the fire at Horeb — ¹⁶ so you don't act corruptly and make an idol for yourselves in the shape of any figure: a male or female form, ¹⁷ or the form of any animal on the earth, any winged creature that flies in the sky, ¹⁸ any creature that crawls on the ground, or any fish in the waters under the earth. ¹⁹ When you look

^A 4:4 Lit *have held on*   ^B 4:9 Or *don't depart from your heart*

4:3 Baal-peor was the place in Transjordan where Israel was first seduced into the licentious worship of the fertility deity **Baal of Peor** (Nm 25:1–9). As a result the Lord commanded Moses to kill all the men who had participated in this sexually perverse paganism.
4:9–12 Here in v. 10 is the first reference in Deuteronomy to the fear of the Lord as required of God's people. The fear of God can be equated with wisdom, which should be the guiding principle of one's life (Jb 28:28; Ps 111:10; Pr 1:7; Mc 6:9). According to Is 33:6 the fear of the Lord is the key to the divine treasure of "salvation, wisdom, and knowledge."
4:13–14 The **Ten Commandments** were the foundational principles upon which the covenant between the Lord and Israel was based. As with legal texts in general, there must be two copies. Exodus 32:15 points out that each of the **two stone tablets** was inscribed on both sides.
4:19 There is a word here of polemic in the suggestion that it is the Lord who controls his creation for the benefit of humankind. He, and not creation itself, must be revered—no matter how powerful it may appear to be.

Q & A: Is the Old Testament reliable?

by Chad Gross

The Old Testament was originally written in Hebrew (with a few chapters penned in Aramaic). It contains thirty-nine books written from about 1400–400 BC. The scribes who copied and preserved the text were careful and extremely thorough. Effective safeguards were implemented as part of a painstaking process to ensure the accurate transmission of the text. Scribes developed numerical systems to ensure an accurate copy: they counted the number of lines, letters, and words per page of the new copy and then compared it to the original. If differences were present, the copy was destroyed; they had to start over.

One of the strongest confirmations for the reliability of the Old Testament text came with the discovery of the Dead Sea Scrolls in 1947 at Qumran. Until that time, skeptics believed that an older text would be found demonstrating that the text had been significantly altered and corrupted. However, the opposite happened.

For example, an entire manuscript of Isaiah was found dating to approximately 75 BC. When Old Testament scholars compared it with the earliest existing copy of the book of Isaiah known at that time (dating to AD 1008–09), the results were staggering. They concluded ninety-five percent of the text had been copied and passed down accurately over a period of almost 1,100 years! The other five percent—comprised of mere slips of the pen—consisted only of misspelled words and absent letters.

While many skeptics have dismissed the historicity of various Old Testament figures, places, and events, archaeological discoveries continue to vindicate the biblical record and silence its critics. Some of the key biblical figures attested by discoveries include King David, the patriarchs (Abraham, Isaac, and Jacob), King Solomon, and King Nebuchadnezzar.

Key places proven include the cities of Sodom, Gomorrah, Admah, Zoar, and Zeboiim mentioned in Genesis 14. Also discovered was the entire kingdom of the Hethites that was once thought to be mythological and the site of Solomon's temple.

Moreover, ancient finds have authenticated some events recorded in the Old Testament. One example involves the walls discovered at the site of Jericho; there a thick layer of soot indicates the city was destroyed by fire as described in Joshua 6:24. Further discoveries have demonstrated these walls fell outward, which is noteworthy when one considers that attacked city walls fall in the opposite direction. This anomaly would have provided invaders a ramp to easily enter the city—precisely what Joshua 6:20 reports.

Finally, and perhaps most significantly, Jesus clearly believed the Old Testament is historically reliable. Perhaps in anticipation of future skepticism, Jesus affirmed as true many passages that modern day Bible skeptics deny. He affirmed the historicity of Adam and Eve (Mt 19:4), Noah's flood (24:39), and the story of Jonah swallowed by a great fish (12:40).

On the grounds that the Old Testament text has been accurately preserved; that discoveries in archaeology have confirmed many of the people, places, and events recorded in its pages; and that Jesus himself taught the Old Testament as real history, Christians can be confident the Old Testament is indeed historically reliable.

to the heavens and see the sun, moon, and stars — all the stars in the sky — do not be led astray to bow in worship to them and serve them. The LORD your God has provided them for all people everywhere under heaven. [20] But the LORD selected you and brought you out of Egypt's iron furnace to be a people for his inheritance, as you are today.

[21] "The LORD was angry with me on your account. He swore that I would not cross the Jordan and enter the good land the LORD your God is giving you as an inheritance. [22] I won't be crossing the Jordan because I am going to die in this land. But you are about to cross over and take possession of this good land. [23] Be careful not to forget the covenant of the LORD your God that he made with you, and make an idol for yourselves in the shape of anything he has forbidden you. [24] For the LORD your God is a consuming fire, a jealous God.

[25] "When you have children and grandchildren and have been in the land a long time, and if you act corruptly, make an idol in the form of anything, and do what is evil in the sight of the LORD your God, angering him, [26] I call heaven and earth as witnesses against you today that you will quickly perish from the land you are about to cross the Jordan to possess. You will not live long there, but you will certainly be destroyed. [27] The LORD will scatter you among the peoples, and you will be reduced to a few survivors[A] among the nations where the LORD your God will drive you. [28] There you will worship man-made gods of wood and stone, which cannot see, hear, eat, or smell. [29] But from there, you will search for the LORD your God, and you will find him when you seek him with all your heart and all your soul. [30] When you are in distress and all these things have happened to you, in the future you will return to the LORD your God and obey him. [31] He will not leave you, destroy you, or forget the covenant with your ancestors that he swore to them by oath, because the LORD your God is a compassionate God.

[32] "Indeed, ask about the earlier days that preceded you, from the day God created mankind[B] on the earth and from one end of the heavens to the other: Has anything like this great event ever happened, or has anything like it been heard of? [33] Has a people heard God's voice speaking from the fire as you have, and lived? [34] Or has a god attempted to go and take a nation as his own out of another nation, by trials, signs, wonders, and war, by a strong hand and an outstretched arm, by great terrors, as the LORD your God did for you in Egypt before your eyes? [35] You were shown these things so that you would know that the LORD is God; there is no other besides him. [36] He let you hear his voice from heaven to instruct you. He showed you his great fire on earth, and you heard his words from the fire. [37] Because he loved your ancestors, he chose their descendants after them and brought you out of Egypt by his presence and great power, [38] to drive out before you nations greater and stronger than you and to bring you in and give you their land as an inheritance, as is now taking place. [39] Today, recognize and keep in mind that the LORD is God in heaven above and on earth below; there is no other. [40] Keep his statutes and commands, which I am giving you today, so that you and your children after you may prosper and so that you may live long in the land the LORD your God is giving you for all time."

Cities of Refuge

[41] Then Moses set apart three cities across the Jordan to the east. [42] Someone could flee there who committed manslaughter, killing his neighbor accidentally without previously hating him. He could flee to one of these cities and stay alive: [43] Bezer in the wilderness on the plateau land, belonging to the Reubenites; Ramoth in Gilead, belonging to the Gadites; or Golan in Bashan, belonging to the Manassites.

Introduction to the Law

[44] This is the law Moses gave the Israelites. [45] These are the decrees, statutes, and ordinances

---

[A] 4:27 Lit be left few in number   [B] 4:32 Or Adam

4:20 Egypt's description as an **iron furnace** is a metaphor for a smelter or crucible whose function was to melt down metals under such intense heat that all the dross and other impurities were separated from them, leaving them pure and usable (Pr 17:3). The Lord had allowed Israel to suffer in Egypt so they would be better prepared **to be a people for his inheritance** (cp. 1Kg 8:51; Jr 11:4–5; Zch 13:9; Mal 3:3).
4:25–26 This is the first of several such warning passages in the book (see 28:15–68; 29:22–28; 31:16–29). Since humans are not qualified to certify the durability and reliability of God's promises, and since no other gods exist to serve as witnesses, Moses invoked **heaven and earth** to serve that function (30:19; 31:28).

4:29–31 When Israel went into exile they would find the Lord when they sought him **with all** their **heart** and **soul**. Yet the promise is clear that this would happen, because they would in fact return to the Lord **in the future**.
4:32–34 The **event** in view is the whole complex of God's election of Abraham to establish a nation, the deliverance of that nation from Egyptian bondage (v. 34), his gracious act of making covenant with them (v. 33), and his care for them ever since. This event was unique in the history of the world (cp. 32:9; 33:29).
4:35–40 In v. 37 **loved** and **chose** are virtually synonymous. The exodus deliverance was predicated on Israel's prior election by the Lord.

4:41–43 Before Moses's death and the conquest of Canaan, he selected **three cities** as places of refuge for people accused but not convicted of manslaughter (see 19:2–13): one in the territory of Reuben, one in the territory of Gad, and the third in the allotment of Manasseh (4:43).
4:42 Manslaughter is qualified here as the killing of a person **accidentally without previously hating him**. If the accused hated the victim, there might be cause to suspect him of premeditated murder, in which case no refuge could suffice.
4:44–49 The law is literally "the Torah." The term usually refers to the Pentateuch, but here to the full collection of principles and stipulations about to be promulgated by Moses.

Moses proclaimed to them after they came out of Egypt, **46** across the Jordan in the valley facing Beth-peor in the land of King Sihon of the Amorites. He lived in Heshbon, and Moses and the Israelites defeated him after they came out of Egypt. **47** They took possession of his land and the land of Og king of Bashan, the two Amorite kings who were across the Jordan to the east, **48** from Aroer on the rim of the Arnon Valley as far as Mount Sion (that is, Hermon) **49** and all the Arabah on the east side of the Jordan as far as the Dead Sea below the slopes of Pisgah.

The Ten Commandments

5 Moses summoned all Israel and said to them, "Israel, listen to the statutes and ordinances I am proclaiming as you hear them today. Learn and follow them carefully. **2** The LORD our God made a covenant with us at Horeb. **3** He did not make this covenant with our ancestors, but with all of us who are alive here today. **4** The LORD spoke to you face to face from the fire on the mountain. **5** At that time I was standing between the LORD and you to report the word^A of the LORD to you, because you were afraid of the fire and did not go up the mountain. And he said:

6 I am the LORD your God, who brought you out of the land of Egypt, out of the place of slavery.

7 Do not have other gods besides me.

8 Do not make an idol for yourself in the shape of anything in the heavens above or on the earth below or in the waters under the earth. **9** Do not bow in worship to them, and do not serve them, because I, the LORD your God, am a jealous God, bringing the consequences of the fathers' iniquity on the children to the third and fourth generations of those who hate me, **10** but showing faithful love to a thousand generations of those who love me and keep my commands.

11 Do not misuse the name of the LORD your God, because the LORD will not leave anyone unpunished who misuses his name.

12 Be careful to remember the Sabbath day, to keep it holy as the LORD your God has commanded you. **13** You are to labor six days and do all your work, **14** but the seventh day is a Sabbath to the LORD your God. Do not do any work — you, your son or daughter, your male or female slave, your ox or donkey, any of your livestock, or the resident alien who lives within your city gates, so that your male and female slaves may rest as you do.

15 Remember that you were a slave in the land of Egypt, and the LORD your God brought you out of there with a strong hand and an outstretched arm. That is why the LORD your God has commanded you to keep the Sabbath day.

16 Honor your father and your mother, as the LORD your God has commanded you, so that you may live long and so that you may prosper in the land the LORD your God is giving you.

17 Do not murder.

18 Do not commit adultery.

19 Do not steal.

20 Do not give dishonest testimony against your neighbor.

21 Do not covet your neighbor's wife or desire your neighbor's house, his field, his male or female slave, his ox or donkey, or anything that belongs to your neighbor.

^A 5:5 One Hb ms, DSS, Sam, LXX, Syr, Vg read *words*

5:1–3 Though revealed again now in a new, expanded form in Moab, **this covenant** was essentially a restatement of the covenant given forty years earlier. **Ancestors** refers to the patriarchs beginning with Abram with whom God had made a covenant centuries earlier (Gn 12:1–3; 15:1–21; 17:1–21). **5:4–5 Face to face** is a metaphor for "directly" as opposed to through a mediator. Therefore, v. 5 seems to contradict v. 4. The explanation is in vv. 5:22–31. Although Israel heard the Ten Commandments directly from God, the rest of the law was mediated to them by Moses. **5:8** The Hebrew term translated **idol** (*pesel*) means "a carved thing." It could, in this context, refer not just to likenesses of pagan gods but to that of the Lord himself (4:15–16). **5:9–10** To **hate** God in a covenant context means not so much to detest him with strong emotional overtones as it does to reject him as a covenant partner. For Israel to **love** God was to choose him and agree to obey him (6:4–5; Jn 14:15). Conversely, to hate him was to disobey him. **5:11** The Hebrew word behind the term **misuse** bears the literal idea of using **the name of the LORD** in an empty, flippant, or purposeless way. To make light of his name is to denigrate God himself (12:5). **5:12–13** To **remember the Sabbath day** is, literally, to set it apart for a special purpose. The emphasis is not so much on remaining inactive on the Sabbath as it is on making it a time of reflection, praise, worship, and service. **5:14** The **seventh day** calls to mind the seventh day of creation by which time all of God's creation work had been accomplished (Gn 2:1–2). **5:15** To **remember** in Hebrew idiom carries the sense of deep reflection and meditation on the past, particularly with regard to God's mighty acts of love and grace (7:18; 8:2; 9:7; 15:15; Pss 42:4,6; 77:11; 137:6; Is 46:8; 1Co 11:24–25). In the exodus account, the motive for remembering the Sabbath was that God had ceased his creation work on the seventh day (Ex 20:11). In Deuteronomy, Israel was called on to remember a more recent event, God's mightiest work on their behalf—their redemption from cruel bondage. **5:16** The word **honor** translates a verb meaning literally "regard as weighty." It is associated with the notion that important people are "heavyweights," loaded down with glory and honor. Parents were to be considered as such, heavy with responsibility and privilege of which children must be aware and to which they must submit if they are to be obedient and pleasing to God. The opposite is to dishonor parents by considering them to be nobodies. **5:17** Though a generic term for killing is used here, the intent clearly is to speak of premeditated **murder**. Murder is heinous because human beings are created in the image of God and their murder, in effect, is a blow against God himself (Gn 9:5–6). **5:18 Adultery** is described in a number of ancient Near Eastern texts as "the great sin," suggesting that even pagans were aware of its seriousness. **5:20** The ninth commandment is most at home in a legal setting where testimony is required of witnesses or other knowledgeable persons. Since a person accused of a crime could suffer serious penalties or death for his violation of the law, it was essential that the evidence presented be trustworthy (cp. 17:6; 19:15–21). **5:21** To **covet** and to **desire** are essentially the same thing, as is seen in Ex 20:17 where the same Hebrew verb is used of both houses

The People's Response

²² "The LORD spoke these commands in a loud voice to your entire assembly from the fire, cloud, and total darkness on the mountain; he added nothing more. He wrote them on two stone tablets and gave them to me. ²³ All of you approached me with your tribal leaders and elders when you heard the voice from the darkness and while the mountain was blazing with fire. ²⁴ You said, 'Look, the LORD our God has shown us his glory and greatness, and we have heard his voice from the fire. Today we have seen that God speaks with a person, yet he still lives. ²⁵ But now, why should we die? This great fire will consume us and we will die if we hear the voice of the LORD our God any longer. ²⁶ For who out of all humanity has heard the voice of the living God speaking from the fire, as we have, and lived? ²⁷ Go near and listen to everything the LORD our God says. Then you can tell us everything the LORD our God tells you; we will listen and obey.'

²⁸ "The LORD heard your^A words when you spoke to me. He said to me, 'I have heard the words that these people have spoken to you. Everything they have said is right. ²⁹ If only they had such a heart to fear me and keep all my commands always, so that they and their children would prosper forever. ³⁰ Go and tell them: Return to your tents. ³¹ But you stand here with me, and I will tell you every command — the statutes and ordinances — you are to teach them, so that they may follow them in the land I am giving them to possess.'

³² "Be careful to do as the LORD your God has commanded you; you are not to turn aside to the right or the left. ³³ Follow the whole instruction the LORD your God has commanded you,

so that you may live, prosper, and have a long life in the land you will possess.

The Greatest Command

6 "This is the command — the statutes and ordinances — the LORD your God has commanded me to teach you, so that you may follow them in the land you are about to enter and possess. ² Do this so that you may fear the LORD your God all the days of your life by keeping all his statutes and commands I am giving you, your son, and your grandson, and so that you may have a long life. ³ Listen, Israel, and be careful to follow them, so that you may prosper and multiply greatly, because the LORD, the God of your ancestors, has promised you a land flowing with milk and honey.

⁴ "Listen, Israel: The LORD our God, the LORD is one.^B ⁵ Love the LORD your God with all your heart, with all your soul, and with all your strength. ⁶ These words that I am giving you today are to be in your heart. ⁷ Repeat them to your children. Talk about them when you sit in your house and when you walk along the road, when you lie down and when you get up. ⁸ Bind them as a sign on your hand and let them be a symbol^C on your forehead.^D ⁹ Write them on the doorposts of your house and on your city gates.

Remembering God through Obedience

¹⁰ "When the LORD your God brings you into the land he swore to your ancestors Abraham, Isaac, and Jacob that he would give you — a land with large and beautiful cities that you did not build, ¹¹ houses full of every good thing that you did not fill them with, cisterns that you did not dig, and vineyards and olive groves that you did not plant — and when you

---

^A5:28 Lit the sound of your   ^B6:4 Or the LORD is our God; the LORD is one, or The LORD is our God, the LORD alone, or The LORD our God is one LORD   ^C6:8 Or phylactery; Mt 23:5   ^D6:8 Lit symbol between your eyes

---

and wives. Here the same verb occurs for **wife** and a different verb for everything else. A possible explanation is that in the land of Canaan families would live in close quarters where desire for a neighbor's property might be a more glaring temptation.
5:22 The **two stone tablets** reflect the ancient Near Eastern custom of making a copy of the covenant texts for each party. One of these was for the Lord and the other for Israel.
5:32–33 Turn aside to the right or the left alludes to the metaphor of following the Lord's ways (see Dt 1:36; 5:1,31; 13:4; Nm 14:24,43; 32:11–12,15) as opposed to following the ways of the nations (Dt 6:14; 11:28; 13:2).
6:2 The **fear** of the Lord is not a condition of terror or foreboding. Rather, it is a profound reverence for God.
6:3 Milk and honey were products of the comparatively rich soils of Canaan, but are also metaphorical of the best the **land** had to offer from human labor (milk) and nature (honey). The phrase became a cliché that is likely also a merism, a figure of speech intended to include all things

by mentioning two of its parts (11:9; Ex 3:8,17; Nm 13:27).
6:4–5 These two verses are commonly known as the Shema (*shuh MAH*), after the first word of v. 4 in Hebrew. This was considered the greatest commandment; Jesus Christ, when asked which commandment was greatest, cited this passage (Mk 12:28–30). The Shema is divided between a statement asserting the nature of God and one enjoining a certain response to that understanding. He is described as being **one**. Other interpretations are that **the LORD** alone is our God or the Lord our God is one Lord.
6:7 The old adage that "repetition aids learning" is an ancient one as this verse attests. Parents must **repeat** the words of the Shema and the rest of God's instruction to their **children** and not in a hit-or-miss manner. There must be strong intentionality that issues in constant instruction by word and deed **about** devotion to God. By a figure of speech (merism) Moses described the unremitting process of education by speaking in terms of opposites. To **sit** and to **walk** suggest

being at rest and being active, that is, in any situation. To **lie down** and to **get up** naturally call to mind nighttime and daytime, that is, *all the time.*
6:8 Though the command to **bind** the commandments is most likely figurative language, such practices were taken literally as early as the first century BC, and remain part of contemporary conservative Jewish custom when phylacteries are worn.
6:9 The **doorposts** of Israel's houses and their **city gates** must be identified as those dedicated to covenant compliance by the affixing of the law to them as well. Small metal boxes known as (Hb) *mezuzah* are to this day attached to doorways of Jewish homes to signify the commitment of their inhabitants to Judaism. These also contain Scripture portions (vv. 4–9; 11:13–21).
6:10–11 The references here are significant in terms of the nature of Israel's conquest of Canaan. With few exceptions, physical structures and agricultural assets were left intact precisely so Israel could take them over and thus more quickly and easily settle the land (Jos 11:13; 24:13). On the other hand,

eat and are satisfied, [12] be careful not to forget the LORD who brought you out of the land of Egypt, out of the place of slavery. [13] Fear the LORD your God, worship him, and take your oaths in his name. [14] Do not follow other gods, the gods of the peoples around you, [15] for the LORD your God, who is among you, is a jealous God. Otherwise, the LORD your God will become angry with you and obliterate you from the face of the earth. [16] Do not test the LORD your God as you tested him at Massah. [17] Carefully observe the commands of the LORD your God, the decrees and statutes he has commanded you. [18] Do what is right and good in the LORD's sight, so that you may prosper and so that you may enter and possess the good land the LORD your God swore to give your ancestors, [19] by driving out all your enemies before you, as the LORD has said.

[20] "When your son asks you in the future, 'What is the meaning of the decrees, statutes, and ordinances that the LORD our God has commanded you?' [21] tell him, 'We were slaves of Pharaoh in Egypt, but the LORD brought us out of Egypt with a strong hand. [22] Before our eyes the LORD inflicted great and devastating signs and wonders on Egypt, on Pharaoh, and on all his household, [23] but he brought us from there in order to lead us in and give us the land that he swore to our ancestors. [24] The LORD commanded us to follow all these statutes and to fear the LORD our God for our prosperity always and for our preservation, as it is today. [25] Righteousness will be ours if we are careful to follow every one of these commands before the LORD our God, as he has commanded us.'

Israel to Destroy Idolatrous Nations

7 "When the LORD your God brings you into the land you are entering to possess, and he drives out many nations before you — the Hethites, Girgashites, Amorites, Canaanites, Perizzites, Hivites and Jebusites, seven nations more numerous and powerful than you — [2] and when the LORD your God delivers them over to you and you defeat them, you must completely destroy them. Make no treaty with them and show them no mercy. [3] You must not intermarry with them, and you must not give your daughters to their sons or take their daughters for your sons, [4] because they will turn your sons away from me to worship other gods. Then the LORD's anger will burn against you, and he will swiftly destroy you. [5] Instead, this is what you are to do to them: tear down their altars, smash their sacred pillars, cut down their Asherah poles, and burn their carved images. [6] For you are a holy people belonging to the LORD your God. The LORD your God has chosen you to be his own possession out of all the peoples on the face of the earth.

[7] "The LORD had his heart set on you and chose you, not because you were more numerous than all peoples, for you were the fewest of all peoples. [8] But because the LORD loved you and kept the oath he swore to your ancestors, he brought you out with a strong hand and redeemed you from the place of slavery, from the power of Pharaoh king of Egypt. [9] Know that the LORD your God is God, the faithful God who keeps his gracious covenant loyalty for a thousand generations with those who love him and keep his commands. [10] But he directly pays back[A] and destroys those who hate him. He will not hesitate to pay back directly[B] the one who hates him. [11] So keep the command — the statutes and ordinances — that I am giving you to follow today.

[12] "If you listen to and are careful to keep these ordinances, the LORD your God will keep his covenant loyalty with you, as he swore to your ancestors. [13] He will love you, bless you, and multiply you. He will bless your offspring,[C] and the produce of your land — your grain, new wine, and fresh oil — the young of your herds, and the newborn of your flocks, in the

---

[A]7:10 Lit *He pays back to their faces* [B]7:10 Lit *to pay back to their faces* [C]7:13 Lit *bless the fruit of your womb*

the wicked Canaanite populations were to be destroyed.

6:12–15 Here is the third of many warnings in Deuteronomy not to forget the Lord, his acts, or his covenant (4:9,23; 8:11,14,19; 9:7; 25:19). On the Lord's jealousy see 4:24; 5:9; Ex 20:5; 34:14; Jos 24:19; 1Kg 14:22; Ezk 23:24; 39:25; Jl 2:18; Nah 1:2; Zch 1:14; 8:2.

6:16 Massah means "testing" and refers to an episode in Exodus in which Israel, fresh from deliverance from Egypt, demanded that Moses provide them water to drink (Ex 17:1–7).

6:24 The reason for remembering the history of God's dealings with his people was so that future generations might understand them (v. 20) and **fear the LORD**. This would ensure **prosperity** from the Lord as well as their **preservation**.

7:1 The **seven nations** were the inhabitants of Canaan who in some cases had

lived there since the days of Abraham (Gn 12:6; 13:7; 15:21). Their long tenure there had not secured them any claim to the land, however, for in the plan of God Canaan had from ages past been allotted to Abraham and his descendants (Gn 12:1; 13:14–17; 15:18–21). The time had now come to dispossess these people so that Israel, the offspring of Abraham, could take their rightful place.

7:2 Completely destroy translates a Hebrew verb that has the technical meaning of placing someone or something under the ban (*charam*), an aspect of what may be described as "holy war" or "Yahweh war." **7:3–4** Prohibition against intermarriage between Israel and the nations was designed to protect Israel from the **worship** of other gods.

7:5 Sacred pillars, usually of stone, marked places deemed to be holy because of the

appearance there of deity. Sometimes they were erected by God's people (Gn 28:18–22; 35:14; Ex 24:4), but usually they were associated with Baal worship (Ex 23:24; 34:13; 2Kg 18:4; 23:14). **Asherah**, the principal goddess of the Canaanite pantheon, was represented sometimes as a living tree (16:21; Mc 5:14) but most often as a wooden pole (1Kg 14:15,23; 16:33; 2Kg 17:10,16; Is 17:8). Both objects symbolized fertility rites and other rituals of the crudest kind.

7:6 The term **possession** translates a Hebrew noun (*segullah*) that describes an unusually precious treasure. It occurs also in Ex 19:5 upon the Lord's offer of the Mosaic covenant to Israel at Mount Sinai.

7:9 A thousand generations is a term denoting an immeasurable future and not a specific span of time. The point is that God's **covenant loyalty** is boundless and unending.

land he swore to your ancestors that he would give you. [14] You will be blessed above all peoples; there will be no infertile male or female among you or your livestock. [15] The LORD will remove all sickness from you; he will not put on you all the terrible diseases of Egypt that you know about, but he will inflict them on all who hate you. [16] You must destroy all the peoples the LORD your God is delivering over to you and not look on them with pity. Do not worship their gods, for that will be a snare to you.

[17] "If you say to yourself, 'These nations are greater than I; how can I drive them out?' [18] do not be afraid of them. Be sure to remember what the LORD your God did to Pharaoh and all Egypt: [19] the great trials that you saw, the signs and wonders, the strong hand and outstretched arm, by which the LORD your God brought you out. The LORD your God will do the same to all the peoples you fear. [20] The LORD your God will also send hornets against them until all the survivors and those hiding from you perish. [21] Don't be terrified of them, for the LORD your God, a great and awesome God, is among you. [22] The LORD your God will drive out these nations before you little by little. You will not be able to destroy them all at once; otherwise, the wild animals will become too numerous for you. [23] The LORD your God will give them over to you and throw them into great confusion until they are destroyed. [24] He will hand their kings over to you, and you will wipe out their names under heaven. No one will be able to stand against you; you will annihilate them. [25] Burn up the carved images of their gods. Don't covet the silver and gold on the images and take it for yourself, or else you will be ensnared by it, for it is detestable to the LORD your God. [26] Do not bring any detestable thing into your house, or you will be set apart for destruction like it. You are to abhor and detest it utterly because it is set apart for destruction.

Remember the LORD

8 "Carefully follow every command I am giving you today, so that you may live and increase, and may enter and take possession of the land the LORD swore to your ancestors. [2] Remember that the LORD your God led you on the entire journey these forty years in the wilderness, so that he might humble you and test you to know what was in your heart, whether or not you would keep his commands. [3] He humbled you by letting you go hungry; then he gave you manna to eat, which you and your ancestors had not known, so that you might learn that man does not live on bread alone but on every word that comes from the mouth of the LORD. [4] Your clothing did not wear out, and your feet did not swell these forty years. [5] Keep in mind that the LORD your God has been disciplining you just as a man disciplines his son. [6] So keep the commands of the LORD your God by walking in his ways and fearing him. [7] For the LORD your God is bringing you into a good land, a land with streams, springs, and deep water sources, flowing in both valleys and hills; [8] a land of wheat, barley, vines, figs, and pomegranates; a land of olive oil and honey; [9] a land where you will eat food without shortage, where you will lack nothing; a land whose rocks are iron and from whose hills you will mine copper. [10] When you eat and are full, you will bless the LORD your God for the good land he has given you.

[11] "Be careful that you don't forget the LORD your God by failing to keep his commands, ordinances, and statutes that I am giving you today. [12] When you eat and are full, and build beautiful houses to live in, [13] and your herds and flocks grow large, and your silver and gold multiply, and everything else you have increases, [14] be careful that your heart doesn't become proud and you forget the LORD your God who brought you out of the land of Egypt, out of the place of slavery. [15] He led you through the great and terrible wilderness with its poisonous[A]

^8:15 Lit burning

7:17–19 Signs and wonders (words commonly joined in the OT; cp. 4:34; 6:22; 26:8; 29:3; Neh 9:10; Ps 135:9; Dn 6:27) were deeds done by **the LORD** to generate faith in the part of his people and to sustain them in times of doubt, such as the exodus deliverance referred to here (Ex 7:3; 8:23; 10:2; 11:9).
7:20 Hornets is likely a metaphor for military forces (1:44; Is 7:18–19) or other means, natural or otherwise, that **the LORD** would use to drive out the illegal residents of the land.
7:21–23 Awesome is literally "fearsome." The reason not to fear the enemy is that the God in their midst is more fearsome than they are.
7:24 The threat to **wipe out** the **names** of Israel's enemies indicates their utter destruction.
7:25–26 The warning not to **covet** went unheeded by Achan, who, following the

conquest of Jericho, buried stolen silver and gold in his tent (Jos 7:20–23). Because these things had been placed under the ban (Hb *cherem*, cp. Dt 7:2), they should have been turned over as tribute to the Lord. Should any Israelites (like Achan) take such spoils into their houses, the annihilation that often accompanied *cherem* would fall on them. This is the meaning of the phrase **set apart for destruction**.
8:1–2 The **forty**-year **journey** . . . **in the wilderness** was partly a punishment of Israel for her unwillingness to occupy the land at first (Nm 14:26–35), but it also was a time for the Lord to **humble** and **test** his people to determine the quality of their character and their commitment to obedience.
8:3 **Manna** (cp. Ex 16:31) was a bread-like substance that the Lord miraculously

provided his people as a sign of his loving care and, more importantly, of the fact that Israel must recognize its dependence on him. When Jesus was tempted by Satan to turn stones into bread, he cited this text to remind the enemy that physical bread lasts for a little while and has limited value (Mt 4:4). On another occasion he described himself as the bread of life (Jn 6:35).
8:5–6 In biblical imagery, **walking** is a metaphor for pursuing a course of life, while **fearing** suggests a sense of reverence, appreciating the holy and solemn awesomeness of God.
8:11 Forgetting **the LORD** is not simply failing to recall that God exists, but acting as though he does not.
8:12–17 Self-sufficiency has a tendency to turn into pride and forgetfulness in the environment of our sinful natures.

snakes and scorpions, a thirsty land where there was no water. He brought water out of the flint rock for you. [16] He fed you in the wilderness with manna, which your ancestors had not known, in order to humble and test you, so that in the end he might cause you to prosper. [17] You may say to yourself, 'My power and my own ability have gained this wealth for me,' [18] but remember that the LORD your God gives you the power to gain wealth, in order to confirm his covenant he swore to your ancestors, as it is today. [19] If you ever forget the LORD your God and follow other gods to serve them and bow in worship to them, I testify against you today that you will certainly perish. [20] Like the nations the LORD is about to destroy before you, you will perish if you do not obey the LORD your God.

Warning against Self-Righteousness

9 "Listen, Israel: Today you are about to cross the Jordan to enter and drive out nations greater and stronger than you, with large cities fortified to the heavens. [2] The people are strong and tall, the descendants of the Anakim. You know about them and you have heard it said about them, 'Who can stand up to the sons of Anak?' [3] But understand that today the LORD your God will cross over ahead of you as a consuming fire; he will devastate and subdue them before you. You will drive them out and destroy them swiftly, as the LORD has told you. [4] When the LORD your God drives them out before you, do not say to yourself, 'The LORD brought me in to take possession of this land because of my righteousness.' Instead, the LORD will drive out these nations before you because of their wickedness. [5] You are not going to take possession of their land because of your righteousness or your integrity. Instead, the LORD your God will drive out these nations before you because of their wickedness, in order to fulfill the promise he swore to your ancestors Abraham, Isaac, and Jacob. [6] Understand that the LORD your God is not giving you this good land

to possess because of your righteousness, for you are a stiff-necked people.

Israel's Rebellion and Moses's Intercession

[7] "Remember and do not forget how you provoked the LORD your God in the wilderness. You have been rebelling against the LORD from the day you left the land of Egypt until you reached this place. [8] You provoked the LORD at Horeb, and he was angry enough with you to destroy you. [9] When I went up the mountain to receive the stone tablets, the tablets of the covenant the LORD made with you, I stayed on the mountain forty days and forty nights. I did not eat food or drink water. [10] On the day of the assembly the LORD gave me the two stone tablets, inscribed by God's finger. The exact words were on them, which the LORD spoke to you from the fire on the mountain. [11] The LORD gave me the two stone tablets, the tablets of the covenant, at the end of the forty days and forty nights.

[12] "The LORD said to me, 'Get up and go down immediately from here. For your people whom you brought out of Egypt have acted corruptly. They have quickly turned from the way that I commanded them; they have made a cast image for themselves.' [13] The LORD also said to me, 'I have seen this people, and indeed, they are a stiff-necked people. [14] Leave me alone, and I will destroy them and blot out their name under heaven. Then I will make you into a nation stronger and more numerous than they.'

[15] "So I went back down the mountain, while it was blazing with fire, and the two tablets of the covenant were in my hands. [16] I saw how you had sinned against the LORD your God; you had made a calf image for yourselves. You had quickly turned from the way the LORD had commanded for you. [17] So I took hold of the two tablets and threw them from my hands, shattering them before your eyes. [18] I fell down like the first time in the presence of the LORD for forty days and forty nights; I did not eat food or drink water because of all the sin you

8:19–20 The threat that Israel would **perish** cannot mean utter annihilation because the promise God made to the ancestors was that they would endure forever (Gn 17:7; Ps 105:9–10; Jr 33:25–26; Rm 11:25–32). In light of future events, the perishing of Israel was her exile from the land and the cessation of her self-governance, which interrupted the dynasty of David. **9:1** The **nations greater and stronger than** Israel are the seven listed in 7:1, all of which were essentially Canaanite by that time. **9:2** The **Anakim** were a giant people so feared that a proverb arose comparing any difficult situation to that of facing the Anakim. Joshua defeated them later (Jos 11:21–23). **9:3** The depiction of God as **a consuming fire** reflects not only his righteous judgment (4:24; Ex 24:17; Nm 26:10; 2Sm 22:9; Is 30:27,30; 33:14;

Ezk 22:31; Zph 1:18; Heb 12:29) but also his role as a warrior leading his hosts in holy war (Ex 15:6–7; Pss 18:7–15; 21:9; 50:3–5; Rv 1:12–16). **9:6** Israel's possession of the **land** would take place not because of her **righteousness**, for, in fact, she was anything but righteous. She was a **stiff-necked people**, a nation like a stubborn ox that would not submit to the yoke and pull its load. Any good thing that came to her from the Lord—including the conquest of Canaan—issued only from the grace of God. **9:7–9** The provocation **at Horeb** concerned the fabrication of a golden calf by Aaron and many of the people while Moses was receiving the Ten Commandments (Ex 32:1–6). **9:10** The reference to **God's finger** is an anthropomorphism, which is the attribution of human characteristics to God. Since he has no physical body, "God's finger" must

be construed as his direct involvement in the inscription on the **stone tablets**. He ordinarily revealed himself through dreams and visions (Nm 12:6), the more immediate process of inscripturation (the writing of Scripture) here is striking. **9:12** The **cast image** was in the form of a calf, but it likely was not a pagan deity but an attempt to represent the Lord himself. Israel was no doubt familiar with the powerful Apis bull of Egyptian mythology and also with El (also called "Bull"), chief of the Canaanite pantheon. **9:13–14** God made this threat on two different occasions (Ex 32:9–14; Nm 14:12). **9:15–17** Moses's **shattering** of the **tablets** was more than an act of justifiable rage. Just as the commandments now lay in a thousand pieces, so Israel had smashed the covenant seemingly beyond repair.

committed, doing what was evil in the Lord's sight and angering him. ¹⁹ I was afraid of the fierce anger the Lord had directed against you, because he was about to destroy you. But again the Lord listened to me on that occasion. ²⁰ The Lord was angry enough with Aaron to destroy him. But I prayed for Aaron at that time also. ²¹ I took the sinful calf you had made and burned it. I crushed it, thoroughly grinding it to powder as fine as dust, and threw its dust into the stream that came down from the mountain.

²² "You continued to provoke the Lord at Taberah, Massah, and Kibroth-hattaavah. ²³ When the Lord sent you from Kadesh-barnea, he said, 'Go up and possess the land I have given you'; you rebelled against the command of the Lord your God. You did not believe or obey him. ²⁴ You have been rebelling against the Lord ever since I haveᴬ known you.

²⁵ "I fell down in the presence of the Lord forty days and forty nights because the Lord had threatened to destroy you. ²⁶ I prayed to the Lord:

Lord God, do not annihilate your people, your inheritance, whom you redeemed through your greatness and brought out of Egypt with a strong hand. ²⁷ Remember your servants Abraham, Isaac, and Jacob. Disregard this people's stubbornness, and their wickedness and sin. ²⁸ Otherwise, those in the land you brought us from will say, 'Because the Lord wasn't able to bring them into the land he had promised them, and because he hated them, he brought them out to kill them in the wilderness.' ²⁹ But they are your people, your inheritance, whom you brought out by your great power and outstretched arm.

The Covenant Renewed

10 "The Lord said to me at that time, 'Cut two stone tablets like the first ones and come to me on the mountain and make a wooden ark. ² I will write on the tablets the words that were on the first tablets you broke, and you are to place them in the ark.' ³ So I made

an ark of acacia wood, cut two stone tablets like the first ones, and climbed the mountain with the two tablets in my hand. ⁴ Then on the day of the assembly, the Lord wrote on the tablets what had been written previously, the Ten Commandments that he had spoken to you on the mountain from the fire. The Lord gave them to me, ⁵ and I went back down the mountain and placed the tablets in the ark I had made. And they have remained there, as the Lord commanded me."

⁶ The Israelites traveled from Beeroth Bene-jaakanᴮ to Moserah. Aaron died and was buried there, and Eleazar his son became priest in his place. ⁷ They traveled from there to Gudgodah, and from Gudgodah to Jotbathah, a land with flowing streams.

⁸ "At that time the Lord set apart the tribe of Levi to carry the ark of the Lord's covenant, to stand before the Lord to serve him, and to pronounce blessings in his name, as it is today. ⁹ For this reason, Levi does not have a portion or inheritance like his brothers; the Lord is his inheritance, as the Lord your God told him.

¹⁰ "I stayed on the mountain forty days and forty nights like the first time. The Lord also listened to me on this occasion; he agreed not to annihilate you. ¹¹ Then the Lord said to me, 'Get up. Continue your journey ahead of the people, so that they may enter and possess the land I swore to give their ancestors.'

What God Requires

¹² "And now, Israel, what does the Lord your God ask of you except to fear the Lord your God by walking in all his ways, to love him, and to worship the Lord your God with all your heart and all your soul? ¹³ Keep the Lord's commands and statutes I am giving you today, for your own good. ¹⁴ The heavens, indeed the highest heavens, belong to the Lord your God, as does the earth and everything in it. ¹⁵ Yet the Lord had his heart set on your ancestors and loved them. He chose their descendants after them — he chose you out of all the peoples, as it is today. ¹⁶ Therefore, circumcise your hearts

---

ᴬ9:24 Sam, LXX read *since he has*   ᴮ10:6 Or *from the wells of Bene-jaakan,* or *from the wells of the Jaakanites*

9:22–24 The three place names in v. 22 have ominous meanings. **Taberah** (Nm 11:1–3) means "blaze." **Massah** (Ex 17:1–7) means "testing." **Kibroth-hattaavah** (Nm 11:31–34) means "graves of craving." **9:26–27** Moses's prayer that the Lord would **remember** his **servants** rose not out of any fear that he would no longer retain them in his consciousness but out of a desire that he would act to keep his covenant promises to them. "Remember" when in reference to God always carries with it an implicit response or action. **9:29** For Israel to be God's **inheritance** meant that they belonged to him (7:6) and also that he belonged to them, a unique relationship that gave each of them exclusive claims on the other.

10:1–5 God's answer to Moses's prayer was in the form of these instructions. The fact that the new **tablets** had the same **words** as **the first** suggests that Moses was not free to improvise and capture just the essence of their wording. This attention to precise detail lays the foundation for a verbal plenary view of inspiration. God's Word may have come through human instruments, but it was written down without error of the slightest kind (2Tm 3:16–17; 2Pt 1:20–21). **10:6–7** Like the office of king, that of the priesthood was hereditary. **Aaron** and his sons were selected first, as members of the priestly tribe of Levi (Nm 17:3,8). Two of Aaron's four sons died because of an act of sacrilege (Lv 10:1–5). Of his two surviving

sons, **Eleazar** was next in line for the office of chief **priest** (Nm 20:25–26). **10:8–9** All the tribes of Israel except **Levi** received allotments of territory; **the Lord** was Levi's **inheritance**. Levi was to devote itself fully to the service of the Lord, at first in the tabernacle in the wilderness and then in the temple in Jerusalem. **10:16** Circumcision was the sign of the Abrahamic covenant, a rite to be followed by all succeeding generations of the faithful (Gn 17:9–14). Circumcision of the flesh alone could not guarantee a right relationship to the Lord because that relationship was one of faith springing from the heart. Moses therefore commanded Israel, **Circumcise your hearts and don't be stiff-necked any longer**, an and don't be stiff-necked any longer. **17** For the LORD your God is the God of gods and Lord of lords, the great, mighty, and awe-inspiring God, showing no partiality and taking no bribe. **18** He executes justice for the fatherless and the widow, and loves the resident alien, giving him food and clothing. **19** You are also to love the resident alien, since you were resident aliens in the land of Egypt. **20** You are to fear the LORD your God and worship him. Remain faithful^A to him and take oaths in his name. **21** He is your praise and he is your God, who has done for you these great and awe-inspiring works your eyes have seen. **22** Your ancestors went down to Egypt, seventy people in all, and now the LORD your God has made you numerous, like the stars of the sky.

Remember and Obey

11 "Therefore, love the LORD your God and always keep his mandate and his statutes, ordinances, and commands. **2** Understand today that it is not your children who experienced or saw the discipline of the LORD your God:

His greatness, strong hand, and outstretched arm; **3** his signs and the works he did in Egypt to Pharaoh king of Egypt and all his land; **4** what he did to Egypt's army, its horses and chariots, when he made the water of the Red Sea flow over them as they pursued you, and he destroyed them completely;^B **5** what he did to you in the wilderness until you reached this place; **6** and what he did to Dathan and Abiram, the sons of Eliab the Reubenite, when in the middle of the whole Israelite camp the earth opened its mouth and swallowed them, their households, their tents, and every living thing with them.

7 Your own eyes have seen every great work the LORD has done.

8 "Keep every command I am giving you today, so that you may have the strength to cross into and possess the land you are to inherit, **9** and so that you may live long in the land the LORD swore to your ancestors to give them and their descendants, a land flowing with milk and honey. **10** For the land you are entering to possess is not like the land of Egypt, from which you have come, where you sowed your seed and irrigated by hand^C as in a vegetable garden. **11** But the land you are entering to possess is a land of mountains and valleys, watered by rain from the sky. **12** It is a land the LORD your God cares for. He is always watching over it from the beginning to the end of the year.

13 "If you carefully obey my commands I am giving you today, to love the LORD your God and worship him with all your heart and all your soul, **14** I^D will provide rain for your land in the proper time, the autumn and spring rains, and you will harvest your grain, new wine, and fresh oil. **15** I^E will provide grass in your fields for your livestock. You will eat and be satisfied. **16** Be careful that you are not enticed to turn aside, serve, and bow in worship to other gods. **17** Then the LORD's anger will burn against you. He will shut the sky, and there will be no rain; the land will not yield its produce, and you will perish quickly from the good land the LORD is giving you.

18 "Imprint these words of mine on your hearts and minds, bind them as a sign on your hands, and let them be a symbol^F on your foreheads.^G **19** Teach them to your children, talking about them when you sit in your house and when you walk along the road, when you lie down and when you get up. **20** Write them on the doorposts of your house and on your city gates, **21** so that as long as the heavens are above the earth, your days and those of your children may be many in the land the LORD swore to give your ancestors. **22** For if you carefully observe every one of these commands I am giving you to follow — to love the LORD your God, walk

---

^A10:20 Lit Hold on   ^B11:4 Lit to this day   ^C11:10 Lit foot   ^D11:14 DSS, Sam, LXX read he   ^E11:15 DSS, Sam, LXX read He   ^F11:18 Or phylactery; Mt 23:5   ^G11:18 Lit symbol between your eyes; Ex 13:16; Dt 6:8

---

exhortation picked up in the NT as well (Rm 2:25–29; Col 2:8–15).
10:17–19 Those delivered from difficult and oppressive situations should be the first to deal kindly with others in similar circumstances.
11:3–4 The **signs** and **works** are the plagues the Lord inflicted on **Pharaoh** and **Egypt** and the miracle of drowning their armies in the **Red Sea**. Seeing these proofs of God's power and glory should have instilled such a sense of awe in his people that they could not help but love and serve him unreservedly, but that was not the case (9:7–24).
11:5–6 Dathan and **Abiram**, along with Korah the Levite, led a rebellion against Moses and Aaron in the wilderness (Nm 16:1–3). Their sin was more against the Lord than against human authority because they questioned his selection of leaders (Nm 16:8–11).

Their rebellion resulted in their destruction and that of their families and properties.
11:8–12 The description of Canaan is especially meaningful in comparison to **Egypt**, where rain was scarce and agriculture depended on the annual overflow of the Nile River and irrigation **by hand**. The fact that Canaan was **watered by rain from the sky** insinuates that the rain came from God himself so that it was he who did the backbreaking work for them. For "hand" (v. 10) the Hebrew has "foot," which may refer to a primitive foot-operated irrigation pump called shaduf in Arabic.
11:13–15 The rainy season in Israel, or early rains, begins in the **autumn**, while **spring** is the time of the late rains. This provision of the Lord for the land indicated his care in "watching over it from the beginning to the end of the year" (v. 12). So important

was this agricultural cycle that the Israelites celebrated the new year in the fall.
11:16 The warning not **to turn aside, serve, and bow in worship to other gods** must be understood in the context of the agricultural motifs just described. Baal, Asherah, Astarte, and other gods and goddesses were thought to generate and sustain life in soil, livestock, and even humans by their own sexual activity, and they became objects of worship, often through various fertility rites. Moses and the prophets constantly condemned such incursions into paganism (2Kg 17:7–15).
11:18–20 Hearts is a metaphor for the intellect, and **minds** represents the person as a whole being. Together, they are the internalizing of the word of God.
11:21 The phrase **as long as the heavens are above the earth** is a biblical way of expressing the idea of forever.

in all his ways, and remain faithful[A] to him — [23] the LORD will drive out all these nations before you, and you will drive out nations greater and stronger than you are. [24] Every place the sole of your foot treads will be yours. Your territory will extend from the wilderness to Lebanon and from the Euphrates River[B] to the Mediterranean Sea. [25] No one will be able to stand against you; the LORD your God will put fear and dread of you in all the land where you set foot, as he has promised you.

A Blessing and a Curse

[26] "Look, today I set before you a blessing and a curse: [27] there will be a blessing, if you obey the commands of the LORD your God I am giving you today, [28] and a curse, if you do not obey the commands of the LORD your God and you turn aside from the path I command you today by following other gods you have not known. [29] When the LORD your God brings you into the land you are entering to possess, you are to proclaim the blessing at Mount Gerizim and the curse at Mount Ebal. [30] Aren't these mountains across the Jordan, beyond the western road in the land of the Canaanites, who live in the Arabah, opposite Gilgal, near the oaks[c] of Moreh? [31] For you are about to cross the Jordan to enter and take possession of the land the LORD your God is giving you. When you possess it and settle in it, [32] be careful to follow all the statutes and ordinances I set before you today.

The Chosen Place of Worship

12 "Be careful to follow these statutes and ordinances in the land that the LORD, the God of your ancestors, has given you to possess all the days you live on the earth. [2] Destroy completely all the places where the nations that you are driving out worship their gods — on the high mountains, on the hills, and under every green tree. [3] Tear down their altars, smash their sacred pillars, burn their Asherah poles, cut down the carved images of their gods, and wipe out their names from every[D] place. [4] Don't worship the LORD your God this way. [5] Instead, turn to the place the LORD your God chooses from all your tribes to put his name for his dwelling and go there. [6] You are to bring there your burnt offerings and sacrifices, your tenths and personal contributions,[E] your vow offerings and freewill offerings, and the firstborn of your herds and flocks. [7] You will eat there in the presence of the LORD your God and rejoice with your household in everything you do,[F] because the LORD your God has blessed you.

[8] "You are not to do as we are doing here today; everyone is doing whatever seems right in his own sight. [9] Indeed, you have not yet come into the resting place and the inheritance the LORD your God is giving you. [10] When you cross the Jordan and live in the land the LORD your God is giving you to inherit, and he gives you rest from all the enemies around you and you live in security, [11] then the LORD your God will choose the place to have his name dwell. Bring there everything I command you: your burnt offerings, sacrifices, offerings of the tenth, personal contributions,[G] and all your choice offerings you vow to the LORD. [12] You will rejoice before the LORD your God — you, your sons and daughters, your male and female slaves, and the Levite who is within your city gates, since he has no portion or inheritance among you. [13] Be careful not to offer your burnt offerings in all the sacred places you see. [14] You must

[A]11:22 Lit *and hold on*   [B]11:24 Some Hb mss, LXX, Tg, Vg read *the great river, the river Euphrates*   [c]11:30 Sam, LXX, Syr, Aq, Sym read *oak*; Gn 12:6   [D]12:3 Lit *that*   [E]12:6 Lit *and the contributions from your hands*   [F]12:7 Lit *you put your hand to*, also in v. 18   [G]12:11 Lit *tenth, the contributions from your hands*

11:24–25 Every place the sole of your foot treads is a way of describing conquest and occupation of a territory, usually (but not always) by military might. The image occurs in Gn 13:17 where Abraham was told to "walk around the land, through its length and width," a sign that it would become his as a gift from the Lord. God also told Joshua on the eve of the conquest of Canaan, "I have given you every place where the sole of your foot treads" (Jos 1:3).

11:26–28 Blessing and curse were essential elements in ancient Near Eastern covenant or treaty texts. Moses, as covenant mediator, set before the people **a blessing and a curse,** the full texts of which he elaborates later (27:15–28:58).

11:29 Mount Gerizim and **Mount Ebal** were twin peaks overshadowing a wide valley in which ancient Shechem (and modern Nablus) was located. This is where Jacob bought property and dug a well (Gn 33:19–20; Jn 4:6), the very well where Jesus encountered the Samaritan woman and from which she directed his attention to Mount Gerizim, the site of the Samaritan temple (Jn 4:20).

12:2 The **high mountains,** the **hills,** and the **green tree** were sites of pagan worship where the peoples of Canaan built their altars and shrines, though at times they were located even in the valleys (2Kg 23:10; 2Ch 28:3). Groves of trees or even single trees also marked sacred **places** because their luxuriant growth, surrounded by sparse vegetation, symbolized the gods' fertility (1Kg 14:23; 2Kg 16:4; Jr 2:20).

12:3–4 The **sacred pillars** and **Asherah poles** were stone and wooden columns that represented, respectively, Baal and Asherah, the principal Canaanite fertility deities (7:5).

12:5 Israel must seek the Lord at **the place** he **chooses** to **put his name.** In the wilderness this was at various altars (Ex 20:24), but once in the land only one central sanctuary would qualify. At first this was Gilgal, then Shechem, then for many years at Shiloh, and finally Jerusalem, the location of Solomon's temple.

12:6 Tenths and personal contributions are essentially synonymous, the former being a generic term for mandatory gifts to the Lord and the latter a subset of offerings

designated to religious personnel, especially the priests and Levites (Lv 7:32,34). A traditional term for tenths is *tithes.* All such gifts must be given to the Lord at the central sanctuary and then redistributed to meet the needs of those who served him there.

12:8 An individual Israelite doing **whatever seems right in his own sight** does not mean that religious anarchy prevailed as in the days of the judges (Jdg 21:25). In this context it speaks to the lack of a single central sanctuary site in the wilderness.

12:9–11 The first permanent central **place** of worship was Shiloh, in the center of the land (Jr 7:12). The tabernacle remained there nearly three hundred years, from the latter days of Joshua until the early years of the prophet Samuel.

12:13–14 The **sacred places** were pagan shrines as well as local worship centers that at times were perfectly appropriate. The former were taboo under any circumstances (vv. 2–3). The prohibition against the others must be understood as distinguishing between private worship and the corporate worship of all Israel.

offer your burnt offerings only in the place the LORD chooses in one of your tribes, and there you must do everything I command you.

Slaughtering Animals to Eat

15 "But whenever you want, you may slaughter and eat meat within any of your city gates, according to the blessing the LORD your God has given you. Those who are clean or unclean may eat it, as they would a gazelle or deer, **16** but you must not eat the blood; pour it on the ground like water. **17** Within your city gates you may not eat the tenth of your grain, new wine, or fresh oil; the firstborn of your herd or flock; any of your vow offerings that you pledge; your freewill offerings; or your personal contributions.^A **18** You are to eat them in the presence of the LORD your God at the place the LORD your God chooses — you, your son and daughter, your male and female slave, and the Levite who is within your city gates. Rejoice before the LORD your God in everything you do, **19** and be careful not to neglect the Levite, as long as you live in your land.

20 "When the LORD your God enlarges your territory as he has promised you, and you say, 'I want to eat meat' because you have a strong desire to eat meat, you may eat it whenever you want. **21** If the place where the LORD your God chooses to put his name is too far from you, you may slaughter any of your herd or flock he has given you, as I have commanded you, and you may eat it within your city gates whenever you want. **22** Indeed, you may eat it as the gazelle and deer are eaten; both the clean and the unclean may eat it. **23** But don't eat the blood, since the blood is the life, and you must not eat the life with the meat. **24** Do not eat blood; pour it on the ground like water. **25** Do not eat it, so that you and your children after you will prosper, because you will be doing what is right in the LORD's sight.

26 "But you are to take the holy offerings you have and your vow offerings and go to the place the LORD chooses. **27** Present the meat and blood of your burnt offerings on the altar of the LORD your God. The blood of your other sacrifices is to be poured out beside the altar of the LORD your God, but you may eat the meat. **28** Be careful to obey all these things I command you, so that you and your children after you may prosper forever, because you will be doing what is good and right in the sight of the LORD your God.

29 "When the LORD your God annihilates the nations before you, which you are entering to take possession of, and you drive them out and live in their land, **30** be careful not to be ensnared by their ways after they have been destroyed before you. Do not inquire about their gods, asking, 'How did these nations worship their gods? I'll also do the same.' **31** You must not do the same to the LORD your God, because they practice every detestable act, which the LORD hates, for their gods. They even burn their sons and daughters in the fire to their gods. **32** Be careful to do everything I command you; do not add anything to it or take anything away from it.

The False Prophet

13 "If a prophet or someone who has dreams arises among you and proclaims a sign or wonder to you, **2** and that sign or wonder he has promised you comes about, but he says, 'Let's follow other gods,' which you have not known, 'and let's worship them,' **3** do not listen to that prophet's words or to that dreamer. For the LORD your God is testing you to know whether you love the LORD your God with all your heart and all your soul. **4** You must follow the LORD your God and fear him. You must keep his commands and listen to him; you must worship him and remain faithful^B to him. **5** That

^A12:17 Lit *or the contributions from your hands* ^B13:4 Lit *and hold on*

12:15–16 When the community as a whole was not in pilgrimage at the three annual festivals, **slaughter** at a local level for profane purposes was acceptable.
12:20–22 Religious rites could be carried out apart from the central sanctuary, provided certain requirements, such as the proper disposal of the blood, were carried out (vv. 22–25).
12:23–24 Blood must not be eaten because **blood is the life**. Since life is regarded as sacred in the Bible (Gn 9:4; Lv 17:11), blood—the most eloquent metaphor for life itself—was also sacred and therefore could not be consumed. In the NT this requirement was placed on Gentile converts by the Jerusalem Council (Ac 15:20).
12:26–28 Burnt offerings is a generic term for sin and trespass offerings and others required to restore fellowship with God. **Other sacrifices** indicate nonexpiatory or propitiatory sacrifices such as fellowship or peace offerings.
12:31 The unthinkable act of burning **sons and daughters** was associated especially

with the Moabite god, Chemosh, and the Ammonite god, Molech (Lv 18:21; 2Kg 3:27). Worse still, Israel at various times permitted or even authorized human sacrifice (Jr 32:35).
13:1 The person who **arises among you** refers to a fellow Israelite. Being the chosen people did not guarantee that no one would ever violate the covenant.
13:2 The genuineness of prophets and dreamers cannot be determined by their ability to perform a **sign or wonder** (cp. 4:34), but by their commitment to the Lord and their faithfulness in proclaiming his word. The message must validate the works of signs and wonders, and not the reverse. See note at 18:21–22.
13:5 The death sentence for false prophets within Israel reflects the severity of their offense. Acts of treason against human rulers and their governments are commonly capital offenses, how much more when seditious disloyalty is displayed against the King of kings?

prophet or dreamer must be put to death, because he has urged rebellion against the Lord your God who brought you out of the land of Egypt and redeemed you from the place of slavery, to turn you from the way the Lord your God has commanded you to walk. You must purge the evil from you.

Don't Tolerate Idolatry

⁶ "If your brother, the son of your mother,ᴬ or your son or daughter, or the wife you embrace, or your closest friend secretly entices you, saying, 'Let's go and worship other gods' — which neither you nor your ancestors have known, ⁷ any of the gods of the peoples around you, near you or far from you, from one end of the earth to the other — ⁸ do not yield to him or listen to him. Show him no pity,ᴮ and do not spare him or shield him. ⁹ Instead, you must kill him. Your hand is to be the first against him to put him to death, and then the hands of all the people. ¹⁰ Stone him to death for trying to turn you away from the Lord your God who brought you out of the land of Egypt, out of the place of slavery. ¹¹ All Israel will hear and be afraid, and they will no longer do anything evil like this among you.

¹² "If you hear it said about one of your cities the Lord your God is giving you to live in, ¹³ that wicked men have sprung up among you, led the inhabitants of their city astray, and said, 'Let's go and worship other gods,' which you have not known, ¹⁴ you are to inquire, investigate, and interrogate thoroughly. If the report turns out to be true that this detestable act has been done among you, ¹⁵ you must strike down the inhabitants of that city with the sword. Completely destroy everyone in it as well as its livestock with the sword. ¹⁶ You are to gather all its spoil in the middle of the city square and completely burn the city and all its spoil for the Lord your God. The city is to remain a mound of ruins forever; it is not to be rebuilt. ¹⁷ Nothing set apart for destruction is to remain in your hand, so that the Lord will turn from his burning anger and grant you mercy, show

you compassion, and multiply you as he swore to your ancestors. ¹⁸ This will occur if you obey the Lord your God, keeping all his commands I am giving you today, doing what is right in the sight of the Lord your God.

Forbidden Practices

14 "You are sons of the Lord your God; do not cut yourselves or make a bald spot on your headᶜ on behalf of the dead, ² for you are a holy people belonging to the Lord your God. The Lord has chosen you to be his own possession out of all the peoples on the face of the earth.

Clean and Unclean Foods

³ "You must not eat any detestable thing. ⁴ These are the animals you may eat:
    oxen, sheep, goats,
  ⁵   deer, gazelles, roe deer,
      wild goats, ibexes, antelopes,
      and mountain sheep.
⁶ You may eat any animal that has hooves divided in two and chews the cud.ᴰ ⁷ But among the ones that chew the cud or have divided hooves, you are not to eat these:
    camels, hares, and hyraxes,
      though they chew the cud, they do not
      have hooves —
    they are unclean for you;
  ⁸   and pigs, though they have hooves,
      they do not chew the cud —
    they are unclean for you.
Do not eat their meat or touch their carcasses.
⁹ "You may eat everything from the water that has fins and scales, ¹⁰ but you may not eat anything that does not have fins and scales — it is unclean for you.
¹¹ "You may eat every clean bird, ¹² but these are the ones you may not eat:
    eagles, bearded vultures,
    black vultures, ¹³ the kites,
    any kind of falcon,ᴱ
  ¹⁴   every kind of raven, ¹⁵ ostriches,
    short-eared owls, gulls,
    any kind of hawk,

ᴬ13:6 DSS, Sam, LXX read *If the son of your father or the son of your mother* ᴮ13:8 Lit *Your eye must not pity him* ᶜ14:1 Or *forehead* ᴰ14:6 The Hb does not specify chewing the cud, but bringing up partially digested food and swallowing it again. ᴱ14:13 Some Hb mss, Sam, LXX; other Hb mss, Vg read *the falcon, the various kinds of kite*

13:6-8 Loyalty to the Lord outweighs loyalty to any other person, family members included. Jesus made this matter clear when he taught his disciples, "The one who loves a father or mother more than me is not worthy of me" (Mt 10:37).
13:10-11 The deterrent effect of stoning a covenant traitor to death was to make **all Israel . . . afraid** so that they would **no longer do** such **evil**.
13:12-13 Unpunished individual apostasy is likely to spread near and far like a disease. If **wicked men** lead **the inhabitants of their city astray**, other individuals or households will become contaminated.

13:14-16 An Israelite **city** that tolerated apostasy must be burned to the ground like a pagan city (cp. 3:6; 7:2). The point is that rebellion against the Lord is rebellion, no matter its source. Furthermore, a city once destroyed as an effect of the ban was never to be rebuilt. This was true of Jericho (Jos 6:26) and Ai (Jos 8:28).
14:1-2 The Canaanites and other heathen lamented their **dead** in all kinds of physical ways, including pulling out the hair and lacerating the body, perhaps to gain sympathy from the gods and thus a renewed sense of peace and equilibrium

(1Kg 18:28; Jr 47:5; Hs 7:14). Israel, however, must not imitate these pagan practices (Lv 19:27-28).
14:3 A **detestable thing** is anything that the Lord declares to be such, regardless of its nature or character.
14:4-21 This list of clean and unclean animals echoes Lv 11:1-23.
14:7 Camels, hares (similar to rabbits) and hyraxes (similar to badgers) are not technically ruminants, but the way they chew their food makes it appear that they **chew the cud**. In this and other cases the Bible reflects the prescientific custom of describing or classifying things by their everyday

¹⁶ little owls, long-eared owls,
barn owls, ¹⁷ eagle owls,
ospreys, cormorants, ¹⁸ storks,
any kind of heron,
hoopoes, and bats.ᴬ
¹⁹ All winged insects are unclean for you; they may not be eaten. ²⁰ But you may eat every clean flying creature.

²¹ "You are not to eat any carcass; you may give it to a resident alien within your city gates, and he may eat it, or you may sell it to a foreigner. For you are a holy people belonging to the LORD your God. Do not boil a young goat in its mother's milk.

A Tenth for the LORD

²² "Each year you are to set aside a tenth of all the produce grown in your fields. ²³ You are to eat a tenth of your grain, new wine, and fresh oil, and the firstborn of your herd and flock, in the presence of the LORD your God at the place where he chooses to have his name dwell, so that you will always learn to fear the LORD your God. ²⁴ But if the distance is too great for you to carry it, since the place where the LORD your God chooses to put his name is too far away from you and since the LORD your God has blessed you, ²⁵ then exchange it for silver, take the silver in your hand, and go to the place the LORD your God chooses. ²⁶ You may spend the silver on anything you want: cattle, sheep, goats, wine, beer, or anything you desire. You are to feast there in the presence of the LORD your God and rejoice with your family. ²⁷ Do not neglect the Levite within your city gates, since he has no portion or inheritance among you.

²⁸ "At the end of every three years, bring a tenth of all your produce for that year and store it within your city gates. ²⁹ Then the Levite, who has no portion or inheritance among you, the resident alien, the fatherless, and the widow within your city gates may come, eat, and be

satisfied. And the LORD your God will bless you in all the work of your hands that you do.

Debts Canceled

15 "At the end of every seven years you must cancel debts. ² This is how to cancel debt: Every creditorᴮ is to cancel what he has lent his neighbor. He is not to collect anything from his neighbor or brother, because the LORD's release of debts has been proclaimed. ³ You may collect something from a foreigner, but you must forgive whatever your brother owes you.

⁴ "There will be no poor among you, however, because the LORD is certain to bless you in the land the LORD your God is giving you to possess as an inheritance — ⁵ if only you obey the LORD your God and are careful to follow every one of these commands I am giving you today. ⁶ When the LORD your God blesses you as he has promised you, you will lend to many nations but not borrow; you will rule many nations, but they will not rule you.

Lending to the Poor

⁷ "If there is a poor person among you, one of your brothers within any of your city gates in the land the LORD your God is giving you, do not be hardhearted or tightfisted toward your poor brother. ⁸ Instead, you are to open your hand to him and freely loan him enough for whatever need he has. ⁹ Be careful that there isn't this wicked thought in your heart, 'The seventh year, the year of canceling debts, is near,' and you are stingy toward your poor brother and give him nothing. He will cry out to the LORD against you, and you will be guilty. ¹⁰ Give to him, and don't have a stingy heartᶜ when you give, and because of this the LORD your God will bless you in all your work and in everything you do.ᴰ ¹¹ For there will never cease to be poor people in the land; that is why I am commanding you, 'Open your hand

---

ᴬ**14:5–18** The identification of some of these animals is uncertain.   ᴮ**15:2** Lit *owner of a loan of his hand*   ᶜ**15:10** Lit *and let not your heart be grudging*   ᴰ**15:10** Lit *you put your hand to*

---

appearance and not according to exhaustive testing and observation.
14:21 Carcass here means any animal that had died naturally. The reason for the prohibition has to do again with the principle of holiness. God's people were strictly forbidden to come in contact with the dead lest they become ritually impure (Lv 11:24–40). By eating a carcass they would compromise their status as **a holy people belonging to the LORD**.
14:22 Paying the **tenth** is not a practice first instituted in the Mosaic law, but one adopted by that law and mandated as part of the regular worship of the Lord. In the context of the Mosaic covenant, the Lord is viewed as the great King to whom tribute is due (Nm 23:21; 31:28).
14:26 The practice of buying offerings continued into NT times but came to be abused by money changers who bought low and

sold high, turning the sacred precincts of the temple into what Jesus called a "marketplace" (Jn 2:16).
14:28–29 In the absence of a "paid clergy" in ancient Israel, priests and Levites depended on the offerings of the people for their livelihood. Thus, every third year a **tenth of all** the **produce** must be stored up for distribution not only to **the Levite**, but to **the resident alien, the fatherless, and the widow**. The more the people cared for the less fortunate, the more they could expect the blessing of the Lord.
15:1–3 The principle of the Sabbath—that all creation should rest and be rejuvenated on the seventh day—was extended to the seventh year as well. Canceling **debts** on the sabbatical year meant one of the following. (1) The borrower who was unable to pay his debt could walk away free of obligation following the seventh year. (2) Repayment

could not be demanded on the seventh year. On the other hand, a resident alien must pay back his loan entirely.
15:4–5 The declaration that **there will be no poor among you** is neither an unqualified assertion nor a prediction. There *should* be no poor because the Lord would abundantly **bless** them **in the land** he was giving them. Due to sin this ideal was never achieved throughout Israel's history and, indeed, Jesus himself affirmed, "You always have the poor with you" (Mt 26:11; cp. Dt 15:11).
15:6 Rule is talking about financial rather than political dominance.
15:7–11 A **stingy** creditor might be tempted not to lend to his poor brother when **the seventh year** was **near** because he would then have less chance of being repaid (cp. v. 2). Such an ungenerous attitude, however, is a sin against the Lord.

willingly to your poor and needy brother in your land.'

Release of Slaves

[12] "If your fellow Hebrew, a man or woman, is sold to you and serves you six years, you must set him free in the seventh year. [13] When you set him free, do not send him away empty-handed. [14] Give generously to him from your flock, your threshing floor, and your winepress. You are to give him whatever the LORD your God has blessed you with. [15] Remember that you were a slave in the land of Egypt and the LORD your God redeemed you; that is why I am giving you this command today. [16] But if your slave says to you, 'I don't want to leave you,' because he loves you and your family, and is well off with you, [17] take an awl and pierce through his ear into the door, and he will become your slave for life. Also treat your female slave the same way. [18] Do not regard it as a hardship[A] when you set him free, because he worked for you six years — worth twice the wages of a hired worker. Then the LORD your God will bless you in everything you do.

Consecration of Firstborn Animals

[19] "Consecrate to the LORD your God every firstborn male produced by your herd and flock. You are not to put the firstborn of your oxen to work or shear the firstborn of your flock. [20] Each year you and your family are to eat it before the LORD your God in the place the LORD chooses. [21] But if there is a defect in the animal, if it is lame or blind or has any serious defect, you may not sacrifice it to the LORD your God. [22] Eat it within your city gates; both the unclean person and the clean may eat it, as though it were a gazelle or deer. [23] But you

must not eat its blood; pour it on the ground like water.

The Festival of Passover

16 "Set aside the month of Abib[B] and observe the Passover to the LORD your God, because the LORD your God brought you out of Egypt by night in the month of Abib. [2] Sacrifice to the LORD your God a Passover animal from the herd or flock in the place where the LORD chooses to have his name dwell. [3] Do not eat leavened bread with it. For seven days you are to eat unleavened bread with it, the bread of hardship — because you left the land of Egypt in a hurry — so that you may remember for the rest of your life the day you left the land of Egypt. [4] No yeast is to be found anywhere in your territory for seven days, and none of the meat you sacrifice in the evening of the first day is to remain until morning. [5] You are not to sacrifice the Passover animal in any of the towns the LORD your God is giving you. [6] Sacrifice the Passover animal only at the place where the LORD your God chooses to have his name dwell. Do this in the evening as the sun sets at the same time of day you departed from Egypt. [7] You are to cook and eat it in the place the LORD your God chooses, and you are to return to your tents in the morning. [8] Eat unleavened bread for six days. On the seventh day there is to be a solemn assembly to the LORD your God; do not do any work.

The Festival of Weeks

[9] "You are to count seven weeks, counting the weeks from the time the sickle is first put to the standing grain. [10] You are to celebrate the Festival of Weeks to the LORD your God with a freewill offering that you give in proportion to how

---

[A]15:18 Lit Let it not be hard in your sight   [B]16:1 March–April; called Nisan in the post-exilic period; Neh 2:1; Est 3:7

15:12–15 Not only a debtor but a bondservant must also be relieved of encumbrances in the **seventh year**. According to the Mosaic law, a poor person could indenture himself to a more affluent Israelite in order to work off any indebtedness (Ex 21:2–11). Unlike the repayment of a monetary debt, which was canceled after a fixed period (Dt 15:1), a bondservant must work a full **six years** and then be **set . . . free** generously supplied with provisions proportionate to the blessing of the Lord upon the benefactor. Even the Egyptians had done this much for their departed Hebrew slaves (Ex 12:35–36). **15:16–17** Release from bondage was not mandatory for bond slaves. Should they love their masters and find life more pleasant and secure in their relationship with them, they were entitled to stay with them (v. 16). Such a commitment was for a lifetime, however. Once the decision was made, the slave submitted to an ordeal in which the master took **an awl** and pierced **through his ear into the door**, thus indicating the slave's desire to become the master's **slave for life**. Besides testifying publicly by this act that the slave was committing himself

wholly and permanently to his master, the scar he bore would be a reminder to him and others from that time forward that he was no longer his own. **15:18 A hired worker** would normally work for hourly wages, while a bond slave could be called upon day and night. For this reason, their service was **worth twice the wages of a hired worker**. **15:19–20** In gratitude to the Lord for his preservation of their **firstborn** in Egypt (Ex 12:12–13,29), the Israelites must dedicate them to him in lifetime service (Ex 13:2). However, they could be redeemed from this service by the payment of a firstborn sacrificial animal (Ex 13:13–16) and, later, by the substitution of a Levite for each firstborn son of Israel (Nm 3:11–13,40–51). Firstborn animals could therefore not be put to the service of the Israelites, but they belonged to the Lord. **16:1–2 The month of Abib** (meaning "ears of grain"), early in the spring, must be observed as the month when the liberating event of the exodus took place. **Passover**, the festival commemorating the deliverance of Israel from the tenth plague, began on

the fourteenth day of Abib and continued through the twenty-first as the Festival of Unleavened Bread (Ex 12:17–20). **16:3–4** The **bread of hardship** symbolized the duress under which Israel lived as slaves in **Egypt** and also the **hurry** in which they escaped, with the Egyptian army hard on their heels (Ex 12:11,34,39). The people of Israel must eat the unleavened bread as a means of remembering the cost of their redemption. **16:5–6** Whereas **sacrifice** in general was permitted at local sites (Ex 20:24–26), three times a year the community—at least males twenty years and older—had to assemble **at the place where** the LORD chose **to have his name dwell**—the central sanctuary (12:5). **16:7–8** To **cook and eat** the Passover sacrifice not only brought the nation together but it also depicted the Lord as the table host. **16:9–12** The **Festival of Weeks**—known to Judaism as (Hb) *Shabuoth* ("weeks") or *Qatsir* ("harvest") and to Christians as Pentecost—was the second of the great pilgrimage festivals at the central sanctuary. It celebrated the harvest of the ripened grain fifty days after gathering the firstfruits (v. 9).

the LORD your God has blessed you. ¹¹ Rejoice before the LORD your God in the place where he chooses to have his name dwell — you, your son and daughter, your male and female slave, the Levite within your city gates, as well as the resident alien, the fatherless, and the widow among you. ¹² Remember that you were slaves in Egypt; carefully follow these statutes.

The Festival of Shelters

¹³ "You are to celebrate the Festival of Shelters for seven days when you have gathered in everything from your threshing floor and winepress. ¹⁴ Rejoice during your festival — you, your son and daughter, your male and female slave, as well as the Levite, the resident alien, the fatherless, and the widow within your city gates. ¹⁵ You are to hold a seven-day festival for the LORD your God in the place he chooses, because the LORD your God will bless you in all your produce and in all the work of your hands, and you will have abundant joy.

¹⁶ "All your males are to appear three times a year before the LORD your God in the place he chooses: at the Festival of Unleavened Bread, the Festival of Weeks, and the Festival of Shelters. No one is to appear before the LORD empty-handed. ¹⁷ Everyone must appear with a gift suited to his means, according to the blessing the LORD your God has given you.

Appointing Judges and Officials

¹⁸ "Appoint judges and officials for your tribes in all your towns the LORD your God is giving you. They are to judge the people with righteous judgment. ¹⁹ Do not deny justice or show partiality to anyone. Do not accept a bribe, for it blinds the eyes of the wise and twists the words of the righteous. ²⁰ Pursue justice and justice alone, so that you will live and possess the land the LORD your God is giving you.

Forbidden Worship

²¹ "Do not set up an Asherah of any kind of wood next to the altar you will build for the LORD your God, ²² and do not set up a sacred pillar; the LORD your God hates them.

17 "Do not sacrifice to the LORD your God an ox or sheep with a defect or any serious flaw, for that is detestable to the LORD your God.

The Judicial Procedure for Idolatry

² "If a man or woman among you in one of your towns that the LORD your God will give you is discovered doing evil in the sight of the LORD your God and violating his covenant ³ and has gone to serve other gods by bowing in worship to the sun, moon, or all the stars in the sky — which I have forbidden — ⁴ and if you are told or hear about it, then investigate it thoroughly. If the report turns out to be true that this detestable act has been done in Israel, ⁵ you are to bring out to your city gates that man or woman who has done this evil thing and stone them to death. ⁶ The one condemned to die is to be executed on the testimony of two or three witnesses. No one is to be executed on the testimony of a single witness. ⁷ The witnesses' hands are to be the first in putting him to death, and after that, the hands of all the people. You must purge the evil from you.

Difficult Cases

⁸ "If a case is too difficult for you — concerning bloodshed, lawsuits, or assaults — cases disputed at your city gates, then go up to the place the LORD your God chooses. ⁹ You are to go to the Levitical priests and to the judge who presides at that time. Ask, and they will give you a verdict in the case. ¹⁰ You must abide by the verdict they give you at the place the LORD chooses. Be careful to do exactly as they instruct you. ¹¹ You must abide by the instruction they give you and the verdict they announce to you. Do not turn to the right or the left from the decision they declare to you. ¹² The person who acts arrogantly, refusing to listen either to the priest who stands there serving the LORD your God or to the judge, must die. You must purge the evil from Israel. ¹³ Then all the people will hear about it, be afraid, and no longer behave arrogantly.

16:13–15 After the Israelites left Egypt, they lived in temporary shelters for forty years thereafter, underscoring the transient nature of their journey and their dependence on the Lord for sustenance. The Festival of Shelters thus served to remind Israel of its fragile history in the wilderness and to celebrate God's goodness to them in the land and the joy that would result in the crops from the work of their hands.
16:16–17 No one is too poor to give something, and no one is expected to give more than he can.
16:18–20 Righteous judgment is the application of the law so as to conform to a set standard determined either by fiat or precedent. In the covenant law, the standard

is Torah itself, so any judgment is righteous only to the extent that it conforms to Torah, which itself reflects the just and righteous character of the Lord.
16:21–22 The Asherah and sacred pillar were cult objects representing the chief goddess and god (Baal) respectively.
17:1–5 To worship false gods was an act of high treason, punishable by death.
17:6–7 The stoning of an idolater must take place only after adequate testimony by credible witnesses. A single witness might have a personal agenda or might have misread what the accused had done. The two or three witnesses required must back up their charges by being the first in putting the evildoer to death, something they would

not be likely to do if they harbored any questions about his guilt.
17:8–9 The presence of priests and a judge makes clear that there was no separation between the secular and the sacred and that every violation of the law was a violation of the covenant between the Lord and his people. In the theocracy of OT Israel, sin and crime were one and the same.
17:10–13 Inasmuch as the judge and the priest were serving the LORD, their judgment was final. This suggests that the verdict was achieved by both wise assessment of the evidence and divine revelation. The person acting arrogantly against the judgment of the court was in fact acting arrogantly against the Lord and was therefore guilty of a capital offense.

Appointing a King

14 "When you enter the land the LORD your God is giving you, take possession of it, live in it, and say, 'I will set a king over me like all the nations around me,' **15** you are to appoint over you the king the LORD your God chooses. Appoint a king from your brothers. You are not to set a foreigner over you, or one who is not of your people. **16** However, he must not acquire many horses for himself or send the people back to Egypt to acquire many horses, for the LORD has told you, 'You are never to go back that way again.' **17** He must not acquire many wives for himself so that his heart won't go astray. He must not acquire very large amounts of silver and gold for himself. **18** When he is seated on his royal throne, he is to write a copy of this instruction for himself on a scroll in the presence of the Levitical priests. **19** It is to remain with him, and he is to read from it all the days of his life, so that he may learn to fear the LORD his God, to observe all the words of this instruction, and to do these statutes. **20** Then his heart will not be exalted above his countrymen, he will not turn from this command to the right or the left, and he and his sons will continue reigning many years^A in Israel.

Provisions for the Levites

18 "The Levitical priests, the whole tribe of Levi, will have no portion or inheritance with Israel. They will eat the LORD's food offerings; that is their^{B,C} inheritance. **2** Although Levi has no inheritance among his brothers, the LORD is his inheritance, as he promised him. **3** This is the priests' share from the people who offer a sacrifice, whether it is an ox, a sheep, or a goat; the priests are to be given the shoulder, jaws, and stomach. **4** You are to give him the firstfruits of your grain, new wine, and fresh oil, and the first sheared wool of your flock. **5** For the LORD your God has chosen him and his sons from all your tribes to stand and minister in his name from now on.^D **6** When a Levite leaves one of your towns in Israel where he was staying and wants to go to the place the LORD chooses, **7** he may serve in the name of the LORD his God like all his fellow Levites who minister there in the presence of the LORD. **8** They will eat equal portions besides what he has received from the sale of the family estate.^E

Occult Practices versus Prophetic Revelation

9 "When you enter the land the LORD your God is giving you, do not imitate the detestable customs of those nations. **10** No one among you is to sacrifice his son or daughter in the fire,^F practice divination, tell fortunes, interpret omens, practice sorcery, **11** cast spells, consult a medium or a spiritist, or inquire of the dead. **12** Everyone who does these acts is detestable to the LORD, and the LORD your God is driving out the nations before you because of these detestable acts. **13** You must be blameless before the LORD your God. **14** Though these nations you are about to drive out listen to fortune-tellers and diviners, the LORD your God has not permitted you to do this.

15 "The LORD your God will raise up for you a prophet like me from among your own brothers. You must listen to him. **16** This is what you requested from the LORD your God at Horeb on the day of the assembly when you said, 'Let us

^A17:20 Lit *will lengthen days on his kingdom* ^B18:1 LXX; MT reads *his* ^C18:1 Or *his* ^D18:5 Lit *name all the days* ^E18:8 Hb obscure ^F18:10 Lit *to make his son or daughter pass through the fire*

17:14 Israel had lived for more than four hundred years under the Egyptian **king**. Though God himself was now their King, they would want a human king as a means of establishing peace and stability at a time when anarchy might otherwise prevail (cp. Jdg 21:25). The desire for a king would not in itself be wrong because the Lord had promised Abraham and Sarah that they would produce a line of kings (Gn 17:6,16), and Jacob prophesied that a messianic King would spring from the tribe of Judah (Gn 49:10). At stake here were guidelines by which such future rulers must govern themselves and their people. **17:15** A future **king** of Israel must be a man whom the **LORD . . . chooses**, and he must not be a **foreigner**. **17:16–17** Having been chosen, the future ruler of Israel must adhere to certain standards to assure the success of his reign, placing his confidence in the Lord rather than in **many horses** and armaments (Is 31:1; cp. Ps 20:7). He must also not participate in polygamy because it would lead him into idolatry when he tried to satisfy all his wives' religious preferences (cp. Solomon, 1Kg 11:1–3). Finally, he must resist the urge to accumulate riches because these would likely cause him to depend on his own resources rather than on the Lord (Pr 11:28).

17:18 This instruction refers at least to the book of Deuteronomy and possibly to the entire Pentateuch. Having **a copy** and also writing a copy **in the presence of the Levitical priests** would establish the word of God deep within the heart and mind of the king and certify before witnesses that he had made the copy himself. **18:1–5** Part of the promise of the Lord to Abraham was that he and his descendants would inherit a land within which they could discharge their ministry as a people chosen to represent him to the nations (Gn 12:1–3; 13:14–17). However, the **Levitical priests** would have no such **portion or inheritance**. In addition, the Levites would be assigned forty-eight cities throughout the land where they would minister to the local people (v. 6; Nm 35:1–7). The Lord bestowed an **inheritance** among the other tribes but was himself the inheritance of Levi. **18:6–7** Should **a Levite** decide to leave his own town, one of forty-eight set aside for Levites (cp. v. 1), he could **go to the place the LORD chooses**—the central sanctuary (12:5). **18:8** This passage is somewhat obscure but seems to suggest that Levites did own private properties handed down from father to son. These could be sold, but these added

assets should not be used against a Levite to deny him his fair share of the benefits of his office (Nm 5:9–10). **18:9 Detestable customs** refers to anything, especially of a religious nature, that is offensive to the Lord. Israel must not **imitate** these practices that were characteristic of paganism because they had been chosen from among the **nations** to show a better way (Ex 19:5–6; cp. Lv 18:1–5; Dt 7:6). **18:10–11 Divination**, the consulting of natural phenomena such as animal entrails, smoke formations, oil slicks, and the like, was undertaken to determine the plans and purposes of the gods before they happened. A **spiritist** is another way of referring to necromancy, the "science" of inquiring of the dead (1Sm 28:3,9; Is 8:19). **18:12** A major reason for the expulsion and destruction of the Canaanite **nations** is that they practiced **these detestable acts** and were therefore likely to infect God's people with their abominable customs (7:4). **18:13–14 Blameless** refers not to sinless perfection but to the avoidance of all that the Lord detests. **18:15** In stark contrast to the pagan prophets stood the office of the **prophet of the LORD** called and equipped by him alone.

not continue to hear the voice of the LORD our God or see this great fire any longer, so that we will not die!' [17] Then the LORD said to me, 'They have spoken well. [18] I will raise up for them a prophet like you from among their brothers. I will put my words in his mouth, and he will tell them everything I command him. [19] I will hold accountable whoever does not listen to my words that he speaks in my name. [20] But the prophet who presumes to speak a message in my name that I have not commanded him to speak, or who speaks in the name of other gods — that prophet must die.' [21] You may say to yourself, 'How can we recognize a message the LORD has not spoken?' [22] When a prophet speaks in the LORD's name, and the message does not come true or is not fulfilled, that is a message the LORD has not spoken. The prophet has spoken it presumptuously. Do not be afraid of him.

Cities of Refuge

19 "When the LORD your God annihilates the nations whose land he is giving you, so that you drive them out and live in their cities and houses, [2] you are to set apart three cities for yourselves within the land the LORD your God is giving you to possess. [3] You are to determine the distances[A] and divide the land the LORD your God is granting you as an inheritance into three regions, so that anyone who commits manslaughter can flee to these cities.[B]

[4] "Here is the law concerning a case of someone who kills a person and flees there to save his life, having killed his neighbor accidentally without previously hating him: [5] If, for example, he goes into the forest with his neighbor to cut timber, and his hand swings the ax to chop down a tree, but the blade flies off the handle and strikes his neighbor so that he dies, that person may flee to one of these cities and live. [6] Otherwise, the avenger of blood in the heat of his anger[C] might pursue the one who committed manslaughter, overtake him because the distance is great, and strike him dead. Yet he did not deserve to die,[D] since he did not previously hate his neighbor. [7] This is why I am commanding you to set apart three cities for yourselves. [8] If the LORD your God enlarges your territory as he swore to your ancestors, and gives you all the land he promised to give them — [9] provided you keep every one of these commands I am giving you today and follow them, loving the LORD your God and walking in his ways at all times — you are to add three more cities to these three. [10] In this way, innocent blood will not be shed, and you will not become guilty of bloodshed in the land the LORD your God is giving you as an inheritance. [11] But if someone hates his neighbor, lies in ambush for him, attacks him, and strikes him fatally, and flees to one of these cities, [12] the elders of his city are to send for him, take him from there, and hand him over to the avenger of blood and he will die. [13] Do not look on him with pity but purge from Israel the guilt of shedding innocent blood, and you will prosper.

Boundary Markers

[14] "Do not move your neighbor's boundary marker, established at the start in the inheritance you will receive in the land the LORD your God is giving you to possess.

Witnesses in Court

[15] "One witness cannot establish any iniquity or sin against a person, whatever that person has done. A fact must be established by the testimony of two or three witnesses.

[16] "If a malicious witness testifies against someone accusing him of a crime, [17] the two people in the dispute are to stand in the presence of the LORD before the priests and judges in authority at that time. [18] The judges are to make a careful investigation, and if the witness turns out to be a liar who has falsely accused

---

[A]19:3 Or to prepare the roads [B]19:3 Lit flee there [C]19:6 Lit heart [D]19:6 Lit did not have a judgment of death

---

18:16–18 Like Moses, the **prophet** would be an Israelite. He would not conjure up his own message or resort to pagan manipulations but would be a vehicle of divine revelation, speaking only what God put into his mouth (Ex 4:15–16; 7:1–2).
18:19–20 Though this passage has clear messianic overtones (Jn 1:21,25), the admonition about the **prophet**-to-come suggests an order of prophets, primarily the "canonical" prophets, the authors of the various OT Prophetic books.
18:21–22 The question arises as to how to tell a false prophet from a prophet of the Lord. A fundamental test presented here is that any **prophet** whose **message does not come true or is not fulfilled** has **spoken . . . presumptuously**.
19:1–12 This section echoes Ex 21:12–14; Nm 35:9–15 (see note there); Dt 4:41–43 and anticipates Jos 20:1–9.

19:1–3 The Israelites must **set apart three cities** of sanctuary or refuge for persons accused of **manslaughter**. These were to be strategically located so that they would be accessible to anyone anywhere in the land. Three cities had already been allotted east of the Jordan River (4:41–43), and there would be a need for three more in Canaan proper. In the event of population growth, three more cities would be added, making nine in all (19:8–9).
19:6–7 Revenge for murder was not only permitted by the law but fully authorized (Nm 35:16–21). However, it was for malicious murder only and not for accidental homicide as in the present passage.
19:8–10 The establishment of strategically located cities of refuge would allow accused parties to find safety before unwarranted vengeance could be inflicted. They would preclude **bloodshed in the**

land the LORD was giving them. Innocent blood defiled the land so that the land figuratively became hostile toward the guilty person and resisted his attempts to make use of it.
19:13 No pity was to be shown the murderer. Murder was deemed to be an assault on God himself, an ultimate act of insubordination and rebellion (Gn 9:5–6).
19:14 The contextual relevance of this passage can be observed by recognizing that a common cause of hostility between persons is a failure to agree on common boundaries and to respect property rights.
19:15 To help prevent a miscarriage of justice, the law required **the testimony of two or three witnesses** (cp. 17:6–7).
19:16–20 Should **a malicious witness** turn out to be guilty of perjury, he must suffer the fate intended for the accused. Strict enforcement acts as a deterrent.

his brother, [19] you must do to him as he intended to do to his brother. You must purge the evil from you. [20] Then everyone else will hear and be afraid, and they will never again do anything evil like this among you. [21] Do not show pity: life for life, eye for eye, tooth for tooth, hand for hand, and foot for foot.

Rules for War

20 "When you go out to war against your enemies and see horses, chariots, and an army larger than yours, do not be afraid of them, for the LORD your God, who brought you out of the land of Egypt, is with you. [2] When you are about to engage in battle, the priest is to come forward and address the army. [3] He is to say to them, 'Listen, Israel: Today you are about to engage in battle with your enemies. Do not be cowardly. Do not be afraid, alarmed, or terrified because of them. [4] For the LORD your God is the one who goes with you to fight for you against your enemies to give you victory.'

[5] "The officers are to address the army, 'Has any man built a new house and not dedicated it? Let him leave and return home. Otherwise, he may die in battle and another man dedicate it. [6] Has any man planted a vineyard and not begun to enjoy its fruit?[A] Let him leave and return home. Otherwise he may die in battle and another man enjoy its fruit.[B] [7] Has any man become engaged to a woman and not married her? Let him leave and return home. Otherwise he may die in battle and another man marry her.' [8] The officers will continue to address the army and say, 'Is there any man who is afraid or cowardly? Let him leave and return home, so that his brothers won't lose heart as he did.'[C] [9] When the officers have finished addressing the army, they will appoint military commanders to lead it.

[10] "When you approach a city to fight against it, make an offer of peace. [11] If it accepts your offer of peace and opens its gates to you, all the people found in it will become forced laborers

for you and serve you. [12] However, if it does not make peace with you but wages war against you, lay siege to it. [13] When the LORD your God hands it over to you, strike down all its males with the sword. [14] But you may take the women, dependents, animals, and whatever else is in the city — all its spoil — as plunder. You may enjoy the spoil of your enemies that the LORD your God has given you. [15] This is how you are to treat all the cities that are far away from you and are not among the cities of these nations. [16] However, you must not let any living thing survive among the cities of these people the LORD your God is giving you as an inheritance. [17] You must completely destroy them — the Hethite, Amorite, Canaanite, Perizzite, Hivite, and Jebusite — as the LORD your God has commanded you, [18] so that they won't teach you to do all the detestable acts they do for their gods, and you sin against the LORD your God.

[19] "When you lay siege to a city for a long time, fighting against it in order to capture it, do not destroy its trees by putting an ax to them, because you can get food from them. Do not cut them down. Are trees of the field human, to come under siege by you? [20] But you may destroy the trees that you know do not produce food. You may cut them down to build siege works against the city that is waging war against you, until it falls.

Unsolved Murders

21 "If a murder victim is found lying in a field in the land the LORD your God is giving you to possess, and it is not known who killed him, [2] your elders and judges are to come out and measure the distance from the victim to the nearby cities. [3] The elders of the city nearest to the victim are to get a young cow that has not been yoked or used for work. [4] The elders of that city will bring the cow down to a continually flowing stream, to a place not tilled or sown, and they will break its neck there by the stream. [5] Then the priests, the sons of Levi,

---

[A] **20:6** Lit *not put it to use*   [B] **20:6** Lit *man put it to use*   [C] **20:8** Lit *brothers' hearts won't melt like his own*

19:21 This principle is called (Lat) *lex talionis*, the law of retaliation. An example is the case described in vv. 16–19 where a lying witness receives the punishment the accused would have received had he been guilty. There is disagreement as to whether **life for life**, **eye for eye**, and the rest were to be taken literally or whether the principle was simply that the punishment must fit the crime. The latter seems more likely given other biblical laws that indicate that tit for tat was not always followed (Ex 22:21; Nm 35:31).
20:1–4 Reference to the **LORD** as the leader in battle is probably an allusion to the ark of the covenant, the symbol of God's presence with his people, since the priests would have carried it with them (Jos 3:1–4,8,11; 1Sm 4:3; Ps 132:6–10).
20:5–7 Israel had a conscripted army, but there were a number of reasons for

deferment, as listed here. The draft law clearly was not rigid and inflexible but revealed sensitivity to human feelings and needs.
20:8–9 The last reason for deferment affected not just the individual himself but the entire army and is thus separated from the others. Anyone afraid of going to war must be excused because his cowardice would undermine the morale of his fellow soldiers (see Jdg 7:3).
20:10–11 Cities outside the areas promised to Israel as an inheritance (cp. v. 15) may be approached with **an offer of peace**, by which is meant terms of surrender, though other cities could not (v. 16). However, even the cities that surrendered peacefully must be reduced to servitude.
20:12–15 Any city that would not surrender could be plundered and its citizens either killed or taken as prisoners of war.

The treatment accorded these distant cities presupposes some kind of provocation against Israel and not likely a desire for Israelite imperialism.
20:16–18 Every living thing in the **cities of** Israel's **inheritance** must be put under the *cherem* (Hb, "the ban") and utterly destroyed.
20:19–20 Trees which **produce food** must not be **cut . . . down**, or "killed," during a siege because they are "innocent."
21:3–7 The ritual that follows was for absolving the community from the sin of only one of its members. A **cow** that had **not been . . . used for work** suggests purity and vitality. The uncultivated field, like the animal, was full of potential, unlike the victim whose potential had been snuffed out. Next the elders must **break** the cow's **neck** and the priests must **wash their hands**, thus symbolizing their innocence and that of the

will come forward, for the LORD your God has chosen them to serve him and pronounce blessings in his name, and they are to give a ruling in^ every dispute and case of assault. ⁶ All the elders of the city nearest to the victim will wash their hands by the stream over the young cow whose neck has been broken. ⁷ They will declare, 'Our hands did not shed this blood; our eyes did not see it. ⁸ LORD, wipe away the guilt of your people Israel whom you redeemed, and do not hold the shedding of innocent blood against them.' Then the responsibility for bloodshed will be wiped away from them. ⁹ You must purge from yourselves the guilt of shedding innocent blood, for you will be doing what is right in the LORD's sight.

Fair Treatment of Captured Women

¹⁰ "When you go to war against your enemies and the LORD your God hands them over to you and you take some of them prisoner, and ¹¹ if you see a beautiful woman among the captives, desire her, and want to take her as your wife, ¹² you are to bring her into your house. She is to shave her head, trim her nails, ¹³ remove the clothes she was wearing when she was taken prisoner, live in your house, and mourn for her father and mother a full month. After that, you may have sexual relations with her and be her husband, and she will be your wife. ¹⁴ Then if you are not satisfied with her, you are to let her go where she wants, but you must not sell her or treat her as merchandise,ᴮ because you have humiliated her.

The Right of the Firstborn

¹⁵ "If a man has two wives, one loved and the other neglected, and both the loved and the neglected bear him sons, and if the neglected wife has the firstborn son, ¹⁶ when that man gives what he has to his sons as an inheritance, he is not to show favoritism to the son of the loved wife as his firstborn over the firstborn of the neglected wife. ¹⁷ He must acknowledge the firstborn, the son of the neglected wife, by

giving him two shares^C,D of his estate, for he is the firstfruits of his virility; he has the rights of the firstborn.

A Rebellious Son

¹⁸ "If a man has a stubborn and rebellious son who does not obey his father or mother and doesn't listen to them even after they discipline him, ¹⁹ his father and mother are to take hold of him and bring him to the elders of his city, to the gate of his hometown. ²⁰ They will say to the elders of his city, 'This son of ours is stubborn and rebellious; he doesn't obey us. He's a glutton and a drunkard.' ²¹ Then all the men of his city will stone him to death. You must purge the evil from you, and all Israel will hear and be afraid.

Display of Executed People

²² "If anyone is found guilty of an offense deserving the death penalty and is executed, and you hang his body on a tree, ²³ you are not to leave his corpse on the tree overnight but are to bury him that day, for anyone hung on a tree is under God's curse. You must not defile the land the LORD your God is giving you as an inheritance.

Caring for Your Brother's Property

22 "If you see your brother Israelite's ox or sheep straying, do not ignore it; make sure you return it to your brother. ² If your brother does not live near you or you don't know him, you are to bring the animal to your home to remain with you until your brother comes looking for it; then you can return it to him. ³ Do the same for his donkey, his garment, or anything your brother has lost and you have found. You must not ignore it. ⁴ If you see your brother's donkey or ox fallen down on the road, do not ignore it; help him lift it up.

Preserving Natural Distinctions

⁵ "A woman is not to wear male clothing, and a man is not to put on a woman's garment, for

---

^21:5 Lit and according to their mouth will be   ᴮ21:14 Hb obscure   ᶜ21:17 Lit him mouth of two, or two mouthfuls
ᴰ21:17 Or two-thirds

---

community. This was no sin offering since no blood was shed, but it was similar to the rite of breaking the neck of a donkey to be presented as an offering (Ex 13:13), possibly suggesting the fate of the criminal should he ever be apprehended and also of witnesses who failed to come forward.
21:10–14 The fact that female prisoners of war would be taken as wives by Israel does not sanction the practice. The law here was designed to protect the **woman** in such a case. She must be considered as an equal, permitted to display her humiliation by shaving her **head** and trimming her **nails**, and allowed to **mourn for her father and mother a full month**. Only then could her Israelite husband make full claim on her as his **wife**. Further protection was accorded her in the case of divorce.

21:15–17 This law (and perhaps the previous one) regulated the practice of polygamy while, as in the previous example, not endorsing it. Though Israel was the people of God and should have lived out its special relationship reflecting his glory and righteousness, they often failed. The law in some cases was thus designed to insure that an imperfect people were kept within certain moral and social boundaries. The present law mandated that a **firstborn son** of a **neglected wife** must receive **two shares** of the **inheritance** according to what appears to be long-standing custom (Gn 25:31–34; 48:8–22).
21:18–21 Capital punishment for a **rebellious** and drunken **son** may seem unduly harsh, but this behavior was a violation of

the commandment to honor one's **father** and **mother** (cp. 5:16).
21:22–23 A further humiliation attached to capital punishment was hanging the criminal's corpse from a tree (1Sm 31:10; 2Sm 21:5–6). However, to leave the body on display too long would spread **God's curse** beyond the criminal. The body must therefore be buried before sundown, a practice that continued until the time of Jesus (Gl 3:13). See Jn 19:31.
22:5 For a woman **to wear male clothing** and a man **a woman's garment** (cross-dressing or transvestitism) is wrong because, among other things, it violates the principle of separation that God has built into the created order.

Animal Rights

by Erik Clary

Few social issues of our day have become as celebrated as so-called animal rights. Chiefly the concern of philosophers only a few decades ago, the movement now boasts a sizable following of A-list celebrities and passionate converts eager to proclaim the purported evils of meat eating, hide wearing, hunting, and laboratory animal research. The core contention is not that animals used for these purposes ought to be treated compassionately but rather that they should not be used at all. Animal liberation is a moral imperative for animal rights activists.

The Basis for Animal Liberation

Animal liberationists view the dividing line between humans and animals as arbitrary and unjust. In their way of thinking, to bear a right or an interest worthy of protection one must have "moral standing," and they assert that any species that has the capacity to suffer or experience pain ("sentience") qualifies. Many animals (not just humans) appear sentient, so with respect to moral status, animal liberationists proclaim a radical equality wherein, as prominent activist Ingrid Newkirk has stated, "a rat is a pig is a dog is a boy" (quoted by Katie McCabe in "Who Will Live, Who Will Die?" *Washingtonian*, August 1, 1986, p. 115).

The Value of Animals

At the heart of animal rights lies a kernel of truth. Animals are due moral consideration—not because they are sentient but because they are creatures of God and he cares for them. Created by him and for him (Col 1:16), they belong to him (Ps 24:1), and he rejoices in them (104:31). He pronounced them good and blessed them apart from humans (Gn 1:21–22,25); thus, they have value beyond what may be attributed to their utility for human ends. Such value is further seen by God's preservation of every kind of wildlife during the flood (7:14–16) and in his concern for the "many animals" of Nineveh (Jnh 4:11).

That God cares about animals is also evident in his provision for their needs. The psalmist declares, "All eyes look to you, and you give them their food at the proper time. You open your hand and satisfy the desire of every living thing" (Ps 145:15–16). For the herbivore, God "causes grass to grow" (104:14), and to the lion he delivers the prey (104:21). To the bird he gives the tree for shelter and as a stage from which to sing (104:12,16–17), and to the sea creature Leviathan he provides an environment suited to its playful disposition (104:26). God knows the needs of his creatures, and he provides accordingly.

As God values animals and concerns himself with their well-being, he demands that we do the same. Scripture thus declares, "The righteous cares about his animal's health, but even the merciful acts of the wicked are cruel" (Pr 12:10). Tending to the needs of animals only when it aligns with self-interest misses the mark. Instead, care that is morally praiseworthy reflects genuine compassion for the beast, and here again God provides the example for "his compassion rests on all he has made" (Ps 145:9). Obligations extend not just to animals we call our own; God commands that livestock belonging to friend or foe be treated mercifully (Ex 23:4–5; Dt 22:1–4). The ox in the ditch is to be rescued and stray animals taken in and cared for until they can be returned to their owner. In these situations, obligations exist even when human interests are not at stake. Wild animals are due our concern, and Scripture mandates that the feral hen brooding a clutch be left alone (22:6–7) and that fields, vineyards, and groves be regularly fallowed in provision for the beasts that roam (Ex 23:11).

Animals and Human Worth

While affirming the moral value of animals, the Bible provides no support for the claim of their equality with humans. Indeed, it refutes that notion. Like the animals, we have been fashioned from the earth and infused with the breath of life (Gn 1:30; 2:7), but we alone have been made in the image of God (1:26–27) and are rendered creatures of his special concern. Jesus testified to our favored status: "Aren't five sparrows sold for two pennies? Yet not one of them is forgotten in God's sight. Indeed, the hairs of your head are all counted. Don't be afraid; you are worth more than many sparrows" (Lk 12:6–7). By God's accounting, animal life has value, but human life is of greater worth; thus, God demands that it be treated with an elevated measure of respect.

In Scripture, the differential in respect due animal and human life is readily apparent. For example, the passerby encountering the wild hen is permitted to take her chicks, but kidnapping a child is a capital offense (Ex 21:16). Similarly, we may with God's blessing kill and consume animals posing no threat to human life (Gn 9:3; Rm 14:2–3), but on account of our image-bearing status the shedding of innocent human blood is strongly condemned (Gn 9:6; Ex 21:12). Thus, Cain sins greatly in killing Abel (Gn 4:10) and David also in ordering the death of Uriah (2 Sm 11:15–27), but Jesus commits no transgression in directing a great catch of fish or in preparing it for breakfast (Jn 21:1–13). In God's moral order, human life is in a category of its own.

Humans' Dominion as a Blessing

In affirming the unique moral status of humans, Scripture offers to balance animal rights ideology. The biblical proclamation of human headship over creation is a matter of divine purpose and blessing. "God blessed [Adam and Eve], and God said to them, 'Be fruitful, multiply, fill the earth, and subdue it. Rule the fish of the sea, the birds of the sky, and every creature that crawls on the earth'" (Gn 1:28). Frequently, proponents of animal rights read into this dominion mandate a license for animal abuse, as if to subdue and rule can only mean that humans are called to function as merciless tyrants. This is a misrepresentation of the biblical teaching. The dominion mandate was established before humanity's fall into sin and after God had already indicated his intention for the animals to flourish (1:22). In other words, our function as vice-regents over creation comes part and parcel with God's plan to bless all creation.

Under human stewardship the creation is intended to flourish, yet because of the curse wrought by sin, its present condition is one of futility and corruption (Gn 3; Rm 8:20–21). The mandate to rule remains after the fall, but it is not immune to the perverting effects of sin, and (with the Noahic covenant) its provisions were expanded by God to include eating meat (Gn 9:3–4). Dominion can indeed manifest as cruelty in this present age, but as Scripture presents it, the solution lies not in the abdication of human authority, as animal liberationists propose, but in our redemption through Christ. "The creation eagerly waits with anticipation for God's sons to be revealed" in the sure hope that it will be "set free from the bondage to decay into the glorious freedom of God's children" (Rm 8:19–21).

Judged in light of Scripture, the ideological commitments underlying the animal rights movement can be a false morality. Its ethic is a product of a secular philosophy that looks no further than nature for the ground of moral value. True goodness and justice find their source not in the creation but in the Creator in whom "there is absolutely no darkness" (1Jn 1:5). "All his ways are just" (Dt 32:4). God has made humans creatures of special worth. He has assigned us the responsibility to care for his creation and the privilege to employ its resources. In that context we bear a duty toward animals and their welfare.

everyone who does these things is detestable to the LORD your God.

6 "If you come across a bird's nest with chicks or eggs, either in a tree or on the ground along the road, and the mother is sitting on the chicks or eggs, do not take the mother along with the young. **7** You may take the young for yourself, but be sure to let the mother go free, so that you may prosper and live long. **8** If you build a new house, make a railing around your roof, so that you don't bring bloodguilt on your house if someone falls from it. **9** Do not plant your vineyard with two types of seed; otherwise, the entire harvest, both the crop you plant and the produce of the vineyard, will be defiled. **10** Do not plow with an ox and a donkey together. **11** Do not wear clothes made of both wool and linen. **12** Make tassels on the four corners of the outer garment you wear.

Violations of Proper Sexual Conduct

13 "If a man marries a woman, has sexual relations with her, and comes to hate her, **14** and accuses her of shameful conduct, and gives her a bad name, saying, 'I married this woman and was intimate with her, but I didn't find any evidence of her virginity,' **15** the young woman's father and mother will take the evidence of her virginity and bring it to the city elders at the city gate. **16** The young woman's father will say to the elders, 'I gave my daughter to this man as a wife, but he hates her.' **17** He has accused her of shameful conduct, saying, "I didn't find any evidence of your daughter's virginity," but here is the evidence of my daughter's virginity.' They will spread out the cloth before the city elders. **18** Then the elders of that city will take the man and punish him. **19** They will also fine him a hundred silver shekels and give them to the young woman's father, because that man gave an Israelite virgin a bad name. She will remain his wife; he cannot divorce her as long as he lives. **20** But if this accusation is true and no evidence of the young woman's virginity is found, **21** they will bring the woman to the door of her father's house, and the men of her

city will stone her to death. For she has committed an outrage in Israel by being promiscuous while living in her father's house. You must purge the evil from you.

22 "If a man is discovered having sexual relations with another man's wife, both the man who had sex with the woman and the woman must die. You must purge the evil from Israel. **23** If there is a young woman who is a virgin engaged to a man, and another man encounters her in the city and sleeps with her, **24** take the two of them out to the gate of that city and stone them to death — the young woman because she did not cry out in the city and the man because he has violated his neighbor's fiancée. You must purge the evil from you. **25** But if the man encounters an engaged woman in the open country, and he seizes and rapes her, only the man who raped her must die. **26** Do nothing to the young woman, because she is not guilty of an offense deserving death. This case is just like one in which a man attacks his neighbor and murders him. **27** When he found her in the field, the engaged woman cried out, but there was no one to rescue her. **28** If a man encounters a young woman, a virgin who is not engaged, takes hold of her and rapes her, and they are discovered, **29** the man who raped her is to give the young woman's father fifty silver shekels, and she will become his wife because he violated her. He cannot divorce her as long as he lives.

30 "A man is not to marry his father's wife; he must not violate his father's marriage bed.ᴬ

Exclusion and Inclusion

23 "No man whose testicles have been crushed or whose penis has been cut off may enter the LORD's assembly. **2** No one of illegitimate birth may enter the LORD's assembly; none of his descendants, even to the tenth generation, may enter the LORD's assembly. **3** No Ammonite or Moabite may enter the LORD's assembly; none of their descendants, even to the tenth generation, may ever enter the LORD's assembly. **4** This is because they did not meet

---

ᴬ**22:30** Lit *not uncover the edge of his father's garment*; Ru 3:9; Ezk 16:8

22:9 To plant a **vineyard with two types of seed** makes the point even more clearly that the mixture of unlike things is harmful. Similarly, Israel would be defiled if she mingled with the pagan nations (7:3–4).
22:10 To hitch an **ox and a donkey** up as a team was to invite all kinds of difficulty because of their different natures and habits. Paul chose this law to illustrate how Christians must not marry outside the faith (2Co 6:14–18).
22:13–20 Nowhere was purity of life expected more in ancient Israel than in the realm of sex and marriage, not only because of its inherent rightness but because Israel's relationship to the Lord was often described with the metaphor of marriage (Hs 2:2). The breaking of the covenant that secured

marriage was tantamount to divorce brought about by spiritual adultery (Hs 2:3–13). One hundred **shekels** was a considerable amount of money, indicating that damage to the reputation of the girl and her family by false accusations was not to be taken lightly.
22:21–22 The harsh penalty of stoning to death underscores the principle of purity and separation addressed in this section of the book. Israel collectively must be pure before God, with every member of the community responsible for maintaining that holy standard.
22:23–29 If an **engaged . . . virgin** had sex with a man **in the city**, it was presumed that she had done so willingly since no one heard her **cry out** in protest. The community must stone him for adultery and her for

complicity. If the act took place **in the open country**, however, the presumption was that the young woman screamed but **there was no one to rescue her**. She must be exonerated in such a case. The requirement that she **become his wife** (v. 29) assumes the condition that she is willing.
22:30 Father's wife refers to a foster mother.
23:1–8 Entry to **the LORD's assembly** refers to participation in public worship, not membership in the covenant people (see Lv 21:20). Verse 1 probably refers to participation in pagan rituals of self-mutilation. **One of illegitimate birth** refers not to one born out of wedlock but to the offspring of a forbidden, perhaps incestuous, relationship (Lv 18:6–20; 20:10–21). Isaiah 56:3–8 indicates that these

you with food and water on the journey after you came out of Egypt, and because Balaam son of Beor from Pethor in Aram-naharaim was hired to curse you. [5] Yet the LORD your God would not listen to Balaam, but he turned the curse into a blessing for you because the LORD your God loves you. [6] Never pursue their welfare or prosperity as long as you live. [7] Do not despise an Edomite, because he is your brother. Do not despise an Egyptian, because you were a resident alien in his land. [8] The children born to them in the third generation may enter the LORD's assembly.

Cleanliness of the Camp

[9] "When you are encamped against your enemies, be careful to avoid anything offensive. [10] If there is a man among you who is unclean because of a bodily emission during the night, he must go outside the camp; he may not come anywhere inside the camp. [11] When evening approaches, he is to wash with water, and when the sun sets he may come inside the camp. [12] You are to have a place outside the camp and go there to relieve yourself. [13] You are to have a digging tool in your equipment; when you relieve yourself, dig a hole with it and cover up your excrement. [14] For the LORD your God walks throughout your camp to protect you and deliver your enemies to you; so your encampments must be holy. He must not see anything indecent among you or he will turn away from you.

Fugitive Slaves

[15] "Do not return a slave to his master when he has escaped from his master to you. [16] Let him live among you wherever he wants within your city gates. Do not mistreat him.

Cult Prostitution Forbidden

[17] "No Israelite woman is to be a cult prostitute, and no Israelite man is to be a cult prostitute. [18] Do not bring a female prostitute's wages or a male prostitute's[A] earnings into the house of the LORD your God to fulfill any vow, because both are detestable to the LORD your God.

Interest on Loans

[19] "Do not charge your brother interest on silver, food, or anything that can earn interest. [20] You may charge a foreigner interest, but you must not charge your brother Israelite interest, so that the LORD your God may bless you in everything you do[B] in the land you are entering to possess.

Keeping Vows

[21] "If you make a vow to the LORD your God, do not be slow to keep it, because he will require it of you, and it will be counted against you as sin. [22] But if you refrain from making a vow, it will not be counted against you as sin. [23] Be careful to do whatever comes from your lips, because you have freely vowed what you promised to the LORD your God.

Neighbor's Crops

[24] "When you enter your neighbor's vineyard, you may eat as many grapes as you want until you are full, but do not put any in your container. [25] When you enter your neighbor's standing grain, you may pluck heads of grain with your hand, but do not put a sickle to your neighbor's grain.

Marriage and Divorce Laws

24 "If a man marries a woman, but she becomes displeasing to him because he finds something indecent about her, he may write her a divorce certificate, hand it to her, and send her away from his house. [2] If after leaving his house she goes and becomes another man's wife, [3] and the second man hates her, writes her a divorce certificate, hands it to her, and sends her away from his house or if he dies, [4] the first husband who sent her away may not marry her again after she has been defiled, because that would be detestable to the LORD. You must not bring guilt on the land the LORD your God is giving you as an inheritance.

[5] "When a man takes a bride, he must not go out with the army or be liable for any duty. He is free to stay at home for one year, so that he can bring joy to the wife he has married.

[A]23:18 Lit *a dog's* [B]23:20 Lit *you put your hand to*

---

exclusions were not absolute. Even David's ancestor, Ruth, was a converted Moabite.
23:9–14 Anything offensive refers to ritual impurity, not immorality (see 1Sm 21:5).
23:15–16 In the context of holy war and Israel's uniqueness, the **slave** here must have **escaped** from a foreign **master**. Contrary to the ordinary practice of repatriating such persons, Israel must show a superior moral code by letting such a slave **live among you wherever he wants.**
23:17–18 A **cult prostitute** was a man or woman engaged in fertility temple rites. This Canaanite practice was taboo to Israel as was the payment of even an ordinary **prostitute's wages** to fulfill a vow made

to God. He is not honored by illegitimate expressions of worship but only by obedience (1Sm 15:22–23).
23:19–20 Similar laws forbidding charging interest on loans to fellow Israelites may be found in Ex 22:25 and Lv 25:35–37. Such laws were unheard of in the surrounding nations. See also Ps 15:5; Pr 28:8; Ezk 18:8,13,17.
23:24–25 A person who crossed through a **neighbor's vineyard** or **grain** field could harvest as much as he could gather and hold in his hand. To exceed that would be to take advantage of the neighbor's generosity, and it would be a form of theft. Jesus and his disciples practiced this limited gathering on the Sabbath with no criticism from the

Pharisees except that they were violating the Sabbath (Mk 2:23–28).
24:1–4 These verses presuppose that divorce in Israel was permitted, but they leave the circumstances of that permission open. The word for **something indecent** is not explained (though it is also found in v. 15). This led to the Jewish controversy Jesus speaks to in Mt 19:3–9. The point of the verses is that a man may not remarry a woman he has divorced if she has previously remarried (and been widowed or divorced). No reason is given for this prohibition, though perhaps it might have the effect of discouraging a husband from divorcing his wife on a whim. The point

Safeguarding Life

6 "Do not take a pair of grindstones or even the upper millstone as security for a debt, because that is like taking a life as security.

7 "If a man is discovered kidnapping one of his Israelite brothers, whether he treats him as a slave or sells him, the kidnapper must die. You must purge the evil from you.

8 "Be careful with a person who has a case of serious skin disease, following carefully everything the Levitical priests instruct you to do. Be careful to do as I have commanded them. **9** Remember what the LORD your God did to Miriam on the journey after you left Egypt.

Consideration for People in Need

10 "When you make a loan of any kind to your neighbor, do not enter his house to collect what he offers as security. **11** Stand outside while the man you are making the loan to brings the security out to you. **12** If he is a poor man, do not sleep with the garment he has given as security. **13** Be sure to return it^A to him at sunset. Then he will sleep in it and bless you, and this will be counted as righteousness to you before the LORD your God.

14 "Do not oppress a hired worker who is poor and needy, whether one of your Israelite brothers or one of the resident aliens in a town^B in your land. **15** You are to pay him his wages each day before the sun sets, because he is poor and depends on them. Otherwise he will cry out to the LORD against you, and you will be held guilty.

16 "Fathers are not to be put to death for their children, and children are not to be put to death for their fathers; each person will be put to death for his own sin. **17** Do not deny justice to a resident alien or fatherless child, and do not take a widow's garment as security. **18** Remember that you were a slave in Egypt, and the LORD your God redeemed you from there. Therefore I am commanding you to do this.

19 "When you reap the harvest in your field, and you forget a sheaf in the field, do not go back to get it. It is to be left for the resident alien, the fatherless, and the widow, so that the LORD your God may bless you in all the work of your hands. **20** When you knock down the fruit from your olive tree, do not go over the branches again. What remains will be for the resident alien, the fatherless, and the widow. **21** When you gather the grapes of your vineyard, do not glean what is left. What remains will be for the resident alien, the fatherless, and the widow. **22** Remember that you were a slave in the land of Egypt. Therefore I am commanding you to do this.

Fairness and Mercy

25 "If there is a dispute between men, they are to go to court, and the judges will hear their case. They will clear the innocent and condemn the guilty. **2** If the guilty party deserves to be flogged, the judge will make him lie down and be flogged in his presence with the number of lashes appropriate for his crime. **3** He may be flogged with forty lashes, but no more. Otherwise, if he is flogged with more lashes than these, your brother will be degraded in your sight.

4 "Do not muzzle an ox while it treads out grain.

Preserving the Family Line

5 "When brothers live on the same property^C and one of them dies without a son, the wife of the dead man may not marry a stranger outside the family. Her brother-in-law is to take her as his wife, have sexual relations with her, and perform the duty of a brother-in-law for her. **6** The first son she bears will carry on the name of the dead brother, so his name will not be blotted out from Israel. **7** But if the man doesn't want to marry his sister-in-law, she is to go to the elders at the city gate and say, 'My brother-in-law refuses to preserve his brother's name in Israel. He isn't willing to perform the duty of a brother-in-law for me.' **8** The elders of his city will summon him and speak with him. If he persists and says, 'I don't want to marry her,' **9** then his sister-in-law will go up to

---

^A24:13 Lit *return what he has given as security*   ^B24:14 Lit *within the city gates*   ^C25:5 Lit *live together*

of the **divorce certificate** is to prove the woman is free to remarry. She is **defiled** (ritually unclean; v. 4) only with respect to remarrying her first husband. The issue here is not divorce *per se*.
24:6 The poor could not be required to promise as collateral items essential to life and well-being. **A pair of grindstones** for grinding food must not be demanded as **security** because human **life** depended on them. Taking just the **upper millstone** similarly rendered the pair unusable.
24:8–9 The reference to **Miriam** recalls the incident when Aaron and Miriam challenged the God-ordained leadership of Moses. As a result Miriam was struck with a loathsome skin disease (Nm 12:10–12).

24:17–22 The law was designed not just to punish the wicked but also to protect the helpless, **the resident alien, the fatherless, and the widow**. In the absence of governmental welfare programs in ancient Israel, the wealthy took responsibility for the less fortunate. As an example, if a farmer should **forget a sheaf in the field** he must leave it for the poor and landless to gather (cp. vv. 20–21). A famous illustration of this occurred in the story of Boaz and Ruth. Boaz, realizing he was next of kin to the unsuspecting Ruth, purposefully left scatterings of grain in his fields for her (Ru 2:15–18).
25:1–3 Limiting the number of **lashes** addresses the fine balance between justice and

mercy. The first-century practice of inflicting thirty-nine lashes was to ensure that no more than forty would accidentally be applied (2Co 11:24).
25:4 Mercy in the application of the law extended even to the treatment of animals, which were to share the fruits of their labor. Paul applied this principle to paying a fair wage to those engaged in ministry (1Co 9:9–14; cp. 1Tm 5:17–18).
25:5–10 Passing a man's name to future generations was so important that if a man should die without a son, his widow was to attempt to have a son by one of her brothers-in-law. This was called the levirate custom (from Lat *levir*, "brother-in-law"). See Ru 4:1–10.

him in the sight of the elders, remove his sandal from his foot, and spit in his face. Then she will declare, 'This is what is done to a man who will not build up his brother's house.' **10** And his family name in Israel will be 'The house of the man whose sandal was removed.'

11 "If two men are fighting with each other, and the wife of one steps in to rescue her husband from the one striking him, and she puts out her hand and grabs his genitals, **12** you are to cut off her hand. Do not show pity.

Honest Weights and Measures

13 "Do not have differing weights in your bag, one heavy and one light. **14** Do not have differing dry measures in your house, a larger and a smaller. **15** You must have a full and honest weight, a full and honest dry measure, so that you may live long in the land the LORD your God is giving you. **16** For everyone who does such things and acts unfairly is detestable to the LORD your God.

Revenge on the Amalekites

17 "Remember what the Amalekites did to you on the journey after you left Egypt. **18** They met you along the way and attacked all your stragglers from behind when you were tired and weary. They did not fear God. **19** When the LORD your God gives you rest from all the enemies around you in the land the LORD your God is giving you to possess as an inheritance, blot out the memory of Amalek under heaven. Do not forget.

Giving the Firstfruits

26 "When you enter the land the LORD your God is giving you as an inheritance, and you take possession of it and live in it, **2** take some of the first of all the land's produce that you harvest from the land the LORD your God is giving you and put it in a basket. Then go to the place where the LORD your God chooses to have his name dwell. **3** When you come before the priest who is serving at that time, say to him, 'Today I declare to the LORD your^A God that I have entered the land the LORD swore to our ancestors to give us.'

4 "Then the priest will take the basket from you and place it before the altar of the LORD your God. **5** You are to respond by saying in the presence of the LORD your God:

My father was a wandering Aramean. He went down to Egypt with a few people and resided there as an alien. There he became a great, powerful, and populous nation. **6** But the Egyptians mistreated and oppressed us, and forced us to do hard labor. **7** So we called out to the LORD, the God of our ancestors, and the LORD heard our cry and saw our misery, hardship, and oppression. **8** Then the LORD brought us out of Egypt with a strong hand and an outstretched arm, with terrifying power, and with signs and wonders. **9** He led us to this place and gave us this land, a land flowing with milk and honey. **10** I have now brought the first of the land's produce that you, LORD, have given me.

You will then place the container before the LORD your God and bow down to him. **11** You, the Levites, and the resident aliens among you will rejoice in all the good things the LORD your God has given you and your household.

The Tenth in the Third Year

12 "When you have finished paying all the tenth of your produce in the third year, the year of the tenth, you are to give it to the Levites, resident aliens, fatherless children, and widows, so that they may eat in your towns and be satisfied. **13** Then you will say in the presence of the LORD your God:

I have taken the consecrated portion out of my house; I have also given it to the Levites, resident aliens, fatherless children, and widows, according to all the commands you gave me. I have not violated or forgotten your commands. **14** I have not eaten any of it while in mourning, or removed any of it while unclean, or offered any of it for the dead. I have obeyed the LORD my God; I have done all you commanded me. **15** Look down from your holy dwelling, from heaven, and bless your people Israel and the land you have given us as you swore to our ancestors, a land flowing with milk and honey.

Covenant Summary

16 "The LORD your God is commanding you this day to follow these statutes and ordinances. Follow them carefully with all your heart and all your soul. **17** Today you have affirmed that the LORD is your God and that you will walk in his ways, keep his statutes, commands, and ordinances, and obey him. **18** And today the LORD has affirmed that you are his own possession as he promised you, that you are to keep all his commands, **19** that he will elevate you to praise, fame, and glory above all the nations he has made, and that you will be a holy people to the LORD your God as he promised."

^A 26:3 LXX reads *my*

25:11-12 Interpreters differ over the meaning of this passage. One possibility is that the woman who forcefully grabbed her husband's opponent by his **genitals** during a fight was to be punished so severely because her act risked emasculating the assailant to the point that he might be unable to sire children. **26:1-3 The first . . . produce** is most likely a reference to the Festival of Harvest (Gk *Pentecost*), fifty days after the Festival of Passover and Unleavened Bread (cp. Ex 34:26; Lv 23:10). **26:4-11** Like later church creeds, these verses encapsulate Israel's core beliefs in the form of a resumé of God's mighty acts in

The Law Written on Stones

27 Moses and the elders of Israel commanded the people, "Keep every command I am giving you today. [2] When you cross the Jordan into the land the LORD your God is giving you, set up large stones and cover them with plaster. [3] Write all the words of this law on the stones after you cross to enter the land the LORD your God is giving you, a land flowing with milk and honey, as the LORD, the God of your ancestors, has promised you. [4] When you have crossed the Jordan, you are to set up these stones on Mount Ebal, as I am commanding you today, and you are to cover them with plaster. [5] Build an altar of stones there to the LORD your God — do not use any iron tool on them. [6] Use uncut stones to build the altar of the LORD your God and offer burnt offerings to the LORD your God on it. [7] There you are to sacrifice fellowship offerings, eat, and rejoice in the presence of the LORD your God. [8] Write clearly all the words of this law on the plastered stones."

The Covenant Curses

[9] Moses and the Levitical priests spoke to all Israel, "Be silent, Israel, and listen! This day you have become the people of the LORD your God. [10] Obey the LORD your God and follow his commands and statutes I am giving you today." [11] On that day Moses commanded the people, [12] "When you have crossed the Jordan, these tribes will stand on Mount Gerizim to bless the people: Simeon, Levi, Judah, Issachar, Joseph, and Benjamin. [13] And these tribes will stand on Mount Ebal to deliver the curse: Reuben, Gad, Asher, Zebulun, Dan, and Naphtali. [14] The Levites will proclaim in a loud voice to every Israelite:

[15] 'The person who makes a carved idol or cast image, which is detestable to the LORD, the work of a craftsman, and sets it up in secret is cursed.'
And all the people will reply, 'Amen!'

[16] 'The one who dishonors his father or mother is cursed.'
And all the people will say, 'Amen!'
[17] 'The one who moves his neighbor's boundary marker is cursed.'
And all the people will say, 'Amen!'
[18] 'The one who leads a blind person astray on the road is cursed.'
And all the people will say, 'Amen!'
[19] 'The one who denies justice to a resident alien, a fatherless child, or a widow is cursed.'
And all the people will say, 'Amen!'
[20] 'The one who sleeps with his father's wife is cursed, for he has violated his father's marriage bed.'[A]
And all the people will say, 'Amen!'
[21] 'The one who has sexual intercourse with any animal is cursed.'
And all the people will say, 'Amen!'
[22] 'The one who sleeps with his sister, whether his father's daughter or his mother's daughter is cursed.'
And all the people will say, 'Amen!'
[23] 'The one who sleeps with his mother-in-law is cursed.'
And all the people will say, 'Amen!'
[24] 'The one who secretly kills his neighbor is cursed.'
And all the people will say, 'Amen!'
[25] 'The one who accepts a bribe to kill an innocent person is cursed.'
And all the people will say, 'Amen!'
[26] 'Anyone who does not put the words of this law into practice is cursed.'
And all the people will say, 'Amen!'

Blessings for Obedience

28 "Now if you faithfully obey the LORD your God and are careful to follow all his commands I am giving you today, the LORD your God will put you far above all the nations of the earth. [2] All these blessings will come and overtake you, because you obey the LORD your God:

---

^27:20 Lit *has uncovered the edge of his father's garment*; Ru 3:9; Ezk 16:8

---

history on her behalf (cp. Gn 12:1; 13:14–17; Ex 13:11).

27:1–13 Israel received the covenant on the plains of Moab but had to wait until they arrived in Canaan to formalize it by a mass ceremony of commitment. This would include the building of a monument containing the fundamental principles of the relationship, a covenant meal, and a catalog of curses and blessings.

27:1–4,8 All the words of this law probably comprised the Ten Commandments, which were to be written on the plastered stones on Mount Ebal, i.e., in Shechem.

27:5–7 The **burnt offerings** provided a means of dealing with sins and trespasses, thus opening the way to fellowship with the Lord. The fellowship offerings were essential to the making and reaffirmation of the covenant relationship (Ex 24:3–8).

27:9–10 The statement that **this day you have become the people of the LORD your God** does not mean that just now Israel had entered into that relationship for the first time. It represents a renewal of the covenant by which Israel, in a sense, was becoming the people of the Lord all over again.

27:11–13 Referring again to the upcoming covenant renewal conclave at Shechem (v. 4), Moses instructed the people upon their arrival there to divide into two groups by **tribes**, half on **Mount Gerizim** and half on **Mount Ebal**. Like a great antiphonal chorus, the tribes on Mount Gerizim would shout out the blessings and the tribes on Mount Ebal would shout the curses of the covenant commitments in the hearing of the Levites in the valley below (v. 14).

27:20 Father's wife has in mind either one's stepmother or a second wife of one's father

(22:30; cp. Lv 18:7–8; 20:11). The father's own shame was at risk when a son had sexual relations with a woman known so intimately by his father.

27:21 Bestiality—**sexual intercourse** with an **animal**—is not only reprehensible, but it goes against God's creation order in which humankind, made in the image of God, is to rule over all other created beings, not to be on the same level with them.

27:22 The **sister** here is a sibling related through polygamy. A **father's daughter** or a **mother's daughter** would thus be a sister by one's stepmother or stepfather.

27:24–25 Secretly means either outside public view or in a manner totally unexpected by the victim.

27:26 The **law** quoted is the entire book of Deuteronomy and not just this list.

3 You will be blessed in the city
and blessed in the country.
4 Your offspring^ will be blessed,
and your land's produce,
and the offspring of your livestock,
including the young of your herds
and the newborn of your flocks.
5 Your basket and kneading bowl
will be blessed.
6 You will be blessed when you come in
and blessed when you go out.

7 "The LORD will cause the enemies who rise up against you to be defeated before you. They will march out against you from one direction but flee from you in seven directions. 8 The LORD will grant you a blessing on your barns and on everything you do;^ he will bless you in the land the LORD your God is giving you. 9 The LORD will establish you as his holy people, as he swore to you, if you obey the commands of the LORD your God and walk in his ways. 10 Then all the peoples of the earth will see that you bear the LORD's name, and they will stand in awe of you. 11 The LORD will make you prosper abundantly with offspring,^c the offspring of your livestock, and your land's produce in the land the LORD swore to your ancestors to give you. 12 The LORD will open for you his abundant storehouse, the sky, to give your land rain in its season and to bless all the work of your hands. You will lend to many nations, but you will not borrow. 13 The LORD will make you the head and not the tail; you will only move upward and never downward if you listen to the LORD your God's commands I am giving you today and are careful to follow them. 14 Do not turn aside to the right or the left from all the things I am commanding you today, and do not follow other gods to worship them.

Curses for Disobedience

15 "But if you do not obey the LORD your God by carefully following all his commands and statutes I am giving you today, all these curses will come and overtake you:

16 You will be cursed in the city
and cursed in the country.
17 Your basket and kneading bowl
will be cursed.
18 Your offspring will be cursed,
and your land's produce,
the young of your herds,
and the newborn of your flocks.
19 You will be cursed when you come in
and cursed when you go out.

20 The LORD will send against you curses, confusion, and rebuke in everything you do until you are destroyed and quickly perish, because of the wickedness of your actions in abandoning me. 21 The LORD will make pestilence cling to you until he has exterminated you from the land you are entering to possess. 22 The LORD will afflict you with wasting disease, fever, inflammation, burning heat, drought,^D blight, and mildew; these will pursue you until you perish. 23 The sky above you will be bronze, and the earth beneath you iron. 24 The LORD will turn the rain of your land into falling^E dust; it will descend on you from the sky until you are destroyed. 25 The LORD will cause you to be defeated before your enemies. You will march out against them from one direction but flee from them in seven directions. You will be an object of horror to all the kingdoms of the earth. 26 Your corpses will be food for all the birds of the sky and the wild animals of the earth, with no one to scare them away.

27 "The LORD will afflict you with the boils of Egypt, tumors, a festering rash, and scabies, from which you cannot be cured. 28 The LORD will afflict you with madness, blindness, and mental confusion, 29 so that at noon you will grope as a blind person gropes in the dark. You will not be successful in anything you do. You will only be oppressed and robbed continually, and no one will help you. 30 You will become engaged to a woman, but another man will rape her. You will build a house but not live in it. You will plant a vineyard but not enjoy its fruit. 31 Your ox will be slaughtered before your eyes, but you will not eat any of it.

^28:4 Lit The fruit of your womb, also in v. 18　^28:8 Lit you put your hand to, also in v. 20　^28:11 Lit abundantly in the fruit of your womb　^28:22 Or sword　^28:24 Lit powder and

28:3–5 The promise to be blessed in the city and in the country uses a figure of speech called a "merism," in this case indicating blessing with no geographical limitations. Wherever the obedient person went, God's favor would follow.
28:6 To be blessed when you come in and when you go out is another merism (v. 3) suggesting no temporal limitation (cp. 6:7). God would bless the obedient all their lives.
28:9 Here the promise of the Lord to establish Israel does not mean that they had not previously enjoyed that status. They were already his people by virtue of the Abrahamic covenant and its ratification at Sinai (Gn 17:3–8; cp. Ex 19:4–6). The verb translated establish bears the idea of confirming or reaffirming.

28:13 The head determines in which direction the whole animal moves while the tail just follows along. Israel was brought into being as God's channel of blessing and hope to the world, to be the head of all the nations (Jr 31:7). Should they fail, however, they would become the tail (cp. Dt 28:44).
28:15–19 The curses for disobedience were as certain to come as were the blessings for obedience. Note the parallel to vv. 3–6.
28:20–22 Curses is literally "the curse." The only other place "the curse" occurs is in Mal 2:2 and 3:9, a clear echo of Dt 28:20. Confusion also has the definite article and alludes to the confusion which God would send on the Canaanites (7:23). The term translated pestilence refers to

sickness in general and not to a particular disease. Literal disease did, indeed, afflict Israel from time to time (2Sm 24:13; 1Kg 8:37), but the allusion here to expulsion from the land suggests that pestilence is a metaphor or a means for deportation by enemies (Lv 26:25).
28:23–24 The metaphors of a bronze sky and an iron earth underscore the severity of the drought referred to in v. 22 (cp. Lv 26:19). The scene is one of absolute hopelessness.
28:27 Just as the exodus of Israel from Egypt was the sign of God's favor, their covenant failures would initiate a kind of reverse exodus. They would experience the boils of Egypt along with a host of other afflictions reminiscent of the ten plagues.

Your donkey will be taken away from you and not returned to you. Your flock will be given to your enemies, and no one will help you. ³² Your sons and daughters will be given to another people, while your eyes grow weary looking for them every day. But you will be powerless to do anything. ³³ A people you don't know will eat your land's produce and everything you have labored for. You will only be oppressed and crushed continually. ³⁴ You will be driven mad by what you see. ³⁵ The Lᴏʀᴅ will afflict you with painful and incurable boils on your knees and thighs — from the sole of your foot to the top of your head.

³⁶ "The Lᴏʀᴅ will bring you and your king that you have appointed to a nation neither you nor your ancestors have known, and there you will worship other gods, of wood and stone. ³⁷ You will become an object of horror, scorn, and ridicule among all the peoples where the Lᴏʀᴅ will drive you.

³⁸ "You will sow much seed in the field but harvest little, because locusts will devour it. ³⁹ You will plant and cultivate vineyards but not drink the wine or gather the grapes, because worms will eat them. ⁴⁰ You will have olive trees throughout your territory but not moisten your skin with oil, because your olives will drop off. ⁴¹ You will father sons and daughters, but they will not remain yours, because they will be taken prisoner. ⁴² Buzzing insects will take possession of all your trees and your land's produce. ⁴³ The resident alien among you will rise higher and higher above you, while you sink lower and lower. ⁴⁴ He will lend to you, but you won't lend to him. He will be the head, and you will be the tail.

⁴⁵ "All these curses will come, pursue, and overtake you until you are destroyed, since you did not obey the Lᴏʀᴅ your God and keep the commands and statutes he gave you. ⁴⁶ These curses will be a sign and a wonder against you and your descendants forever. ⁴⁷ Because you didn't serve the Lᴏʀᴅ your God with joy and a cheerful heart, even though you had an abundance of everything, ⁴⁸ you will serve your enemies that the Lᴏʀᴅ will send against you, in

famine, thirst, nakedness, and a lack of everything. He will place an iron yoke on your neck until he has destroyed you. ⁴⁹ The Lᴏʀᴅ will bring a nation from far away, from the ends of the earth, to swoop down on you like an eagle, a nation whose language you won't understand, ⁵⁰ a ruthless nation, showing no respect for the old and not sparing the young. ⁵¹ They will eat the offspring of your livestock and your land's produce until you are destroyed. They will leave you no grain, new wine, fresh oil, young of your herds, or newborn of your flocks until they cause you to perish. ⁵² They will besiege you within all your city gates until your high and fortified walls, that you trust in, come down throughout your land. They will besiege you within all your city gates throughout the land the Lᴏʀᴅ your God has given you.

⁵³ "You will eat your offspring,ᴬ the flesh of your sons and daughters the Lᴏʀᴅ your God has given you during the siege and hardship your enemy imposes on you. ⁵⁴ The most sensitive and refined man among you will look grudgingly at his brother, the wife he embraces, and the rest of his children, ⁵⁵ refusing to share with any of them his children's flesh that he will eat because he has nothing left during the siege and hardship your enemy imposes on you in all your towns. ⁵⁶ The most sensitive and refined woman among you, who would not venture to set the sole of her foot on the ground because of her refinement and sensitivity, will begrudge the husband she embraces, her son, and her daughter, ⁵⁷ the afterbirth that comes out from between her legs and the children she bears, because she will secretly eat them for lack of anything else during the siege and hardship your enemy imposes on you within your city gates.

⁵⁸ "If you are not careful to obey all the words of this law, which are written in this scroll, by fearing this glorious and awe-inspiring name — the Lᴏʀᴅ, your God — ⁵⁹ he will bring wondrous plagues on you and your descendants, severe and lasting plagues, and terrible and chronic sicknesses. ⁶⁰ He will afflict you again with all the diseases of Egypt, which

---

ᴬ28:53 Lit eat the fruit of your womb

28:33 Oppression by **a people you don't know** was fulfilled a number of times throughout Israel's history, notably in the days of the judges when foreigners wreaked havoc in Israel and even settled there (Jdg 6:1–6; 8:22).
28:38–40 The order of curses is essentially that of the blessings in vv. 1–14.
28:45–48 These verses serve as an initial conclusion to the curses section. Verse 45 repeats the opening of v. 15. Note the contrasts in vv. 47–48.
28:48 An **iron yoke** speaks metaphorically of bondage so severe that it is inescapable. Prisoners of war wore yokes to secure them against escape and to humiliate

them. Jeremiah described the Babylonian captivity of Judah as one in which the people would bear the yoke of oppression (Jr 27:7–8) until the Lord broke it (Jr 28:14; 30:8; Ezk 34:27).
28:49–52 The **nation from far away** turned out to be Assyria, as is made clear in light of later biblical events and descriptions. Assyria besieged Samaria, Israel's capital city, for three years until the city was forced to surrender (2Kg 17:5).
28:53–57 The siege of Samaria would be so severe that the people would resort to cannibalism. Though the horrific behavior described here does not reference the Assyrian siege, an earlier siege under the

Arameans resulted in precisely these events (2Kg 6:24–31). Jeremiah also predicted that the citizens of Jerusalem would become just as desperate to survive the siege of that city by the Babylonians in his own time (Jr 19:9), and in fact he lived to see it with his own eyes (Lm 4:10; Ezk 5:10).
28:58 Moses reiterated that all the curses he had listed—concluding with cannibalism, the worst of them all—would come to pass if the people of Israel were **not careful to obey all the words of this law**, specifically those **written in this scroll**—the book of Deuteronomy. It was covenant violation, then, that would be the cause of all of Israel's future judgment should she refuse to repent.

you dreaded, and they will cling to you. **⁶¹** The LORD will also afflict you with every sickness and plague not recorded in the book of this law, until you are destroyed. **⁶²** Though you were as numerous as the stars of the sky, you will be left with only a few people, because you did not obey the LORD your God. **⁶³** Just as the LORD was glad to cause you to prosper and to multiply you, so he will also be glad to cause you to perish and to destroy you. You will be ripped out of the land you are entering to possess. **⁶⁴** Then the LORD will scatter you among all peoples from one end of the earth to the other, and there you will worship other gods, of wood and stone, which neither you nor your ancestors have known. **⁶⁵** You will find no peace among those nations, and there will be no resting place for the sole of your foot. There the LORD will give you a trembling heart, failing eyes, and a despondent spirit. **⁶⁶** Your life will hang in doubt before you. You will be in dread night and day, never certain of survival. **⁶⁷** In the morning you will say, 'If only it were evening!' and in the evening you will say, 'If only it were morning!' — because of the dread you will have in your heart and because of what you will see. **⁶⁸** The LORD will take you back in ships to Egypt by a route that I said you would never see again. There you will sell yourselves to your enemies as male and female slaves, but no one will buy you."

Renewing the Covenant

29 These are the words of the covenant that the LORD commanded Moses to make with the Israelites in the land of Moab, in addition to the covenant he had made with them at Horeb. **²** Moses summoned all Israel and said to them, "You have seen with your own eyes everything the LORD did in Egypt to Pharaoh, to all his officials, and to his entire land. **³** You saw with your own eyes the great trials and those great signs and wonders. **⁴** Yet to this day the LORD has

not given you a mind to understand, eyes to see, or ears to hear. **⁵** I led you forty years in the wilderness; your clothes and the sandals on your feet did not wear out; **⁶** you did not eat food or drink wine or beer — so that you might know that I am the LORD your God. **⁷** When you reached this place, King Sihon of Heshbon and King Og of Bashan came out against us in battle, but we defeated them. **⁸** We took their land and gave it as an inheritance to the Reubenites, the Gadites, and half the tribe of Manasseh. **⁹** Therefore, observe the words of this covenant and follow them, so that you will succeed in everything you do.

¹⁰ "All of you are standing today before the LORD your God — your leaders, tribes, elders, officials, all the men of Israel, **¹¹** your dependents, your wives, and the resident aliens in your camps who cut your wood and draw your water — **¹²** so that you may enter into the covenant of the LORD your God, which he is making with you today, so that you may enter into his oath **¹³** and so that he may establish you today as his people and he may be your God as he promised you and as he swore to your ancestors Abraham, Isaac, and Jacob. **¹⁴** I am making this covenant and this oath not only with you, **¹⁵** but also with those who are standing here with us today in the presence of the LORD our God and with those who are not here today.

Abandoning the Covenant

¹⁶ "Indeed, you know how we lived in the land of Egypt and passed through the nations where you traveled. **¹⁷** You saw their abhorrent images and idols made of wood, stone, silver, and gold, which were among them. **¹⁸** Be sure there is no man, woman, clan, or tribe among you today whose heart turns away from the LORD our God to go and worship the gods of those nations. Be sure there is no root among you bearing poisonous and bitter fruit. **¹⁹** When someone hears the words of this oath, he may consider himself exempt,^ thinking, 'I will have peace even

^**29:19** Lit *may consider himself blessed in his heart*

28:63 The Lord will **be glad to cause you to perish** is a rhetorical way of saying that he will not hesitate or have pity on them. **28:65–67** These verses describe Israel's emotional state during their exile. **The sole of your foot** alludes to the former blessing in 11:24 (see Jos 1:3). **28:68** The fact that the Lord would return disobedient Israel **to Egypt** suggests that a reverse of the exodus would take place. Many Israelites did indeed end up in Egypt (Jr 44:11–14,24–30). But the reference to ships and to other deportations (Dt 28:63) leads to the conclusion that Egypt was also a figure of speech—a "synecdoche"—to describe all manner of places of deportation and exile. **29:2–30:20** This section consists of a historical review and might be referred to as an epilogue. It is not strictly part of the covenant document as typically crafted. It provides a summation of God's past dealings with Israel, restates the present occasion of the covenant offer and acceptance, and addresses the options of covenant disobedience and obedience respectively. Finally, it exhorts the assembled throng to covenant commitment. **29:12** Deuteronomy is a **covenant** renewal document founded on the covenant first made at Mount Sinai. The idea that Israel was now about to **enter into the covenant of the LORD** means, then, that they were renewing the covenant commitment their fathers had made nearly forty years earlier, assuming its privileges and responsibilities. **29:13** Once Israel had pledged its covenant fidelity, the Lord would reciprocate by establishing Israel as his **people** and himself as their **God** as **promised** to their forefathers (cp. Gn 17:7; Lv 11:45; 26:12). The verb translated **establish** is a technical term referring to the ratification of an already existing agreement such as this one (8:18; 9:5; Gn 6:18; 9:9; 17:19,21; Ex 6:4). God had not just introduced a new covenant arrangement with this generation, but had also confirmed one made with the patriarchs and their fathers at Sinai. **29:14–15** The covenant was being reaffirmed by the Lord not only with Israelites of that generation (v. 14) but **with those who are standing here**—non-Israelite proselytes who had also embraced the God of Israel (cp. v. 11; Ex 12:38). Beyond that, it was being made **with those who are not here today**—the unborn generations who would also need to affirm their commitment to God (4:9). **29:18** The **root** Moses warns against here no doubt refers to the concept of idolatry that, if allowed to grow in the human mind and heart, would produce the fruit of idolatrous practice. **29:19** The **well-watered land as well as the dry land** is a proverbial statement suggesting that no person who sins willfully against the covenant can expect to escape

though I follow my own stubborn heart.' This will lead to the destruction of the well-watered land as well as the dry land. ²⁰ The LORD will not be willing to forgive him. Instead, his anger and jealousy will burn against that person, and every curse written in this scroll will descend on him. The LORD will blot out his name under heaven, ²¹ and single him out for harm from all the tribes of Israel, according to all the curses of the covenant written in this book of the law.

²² "Future generations of your children who follow you and the foreigner who comes from a distant country will see the plagues of that land and the sicknesses the LORD has inflicted on it. ²³ All its soil will be a burning waste of sulfur and salt, unsown, producing nothing, with no plant growing on it, just like the fall of Sodom and Gomorrah, Admah and Zeboiim, which the LORD demolished in his fierce anger. ²⁴ All the nations will ask, 'Why has the LORD done this to this land? Why this intense outburst of anger?' ²⁵ Then people will answer, 'It is because they abandoned the covenant of the LORD, the God of their ancestors, which he had made with them when he brought them out of the land of Egypt. ²⁶ They began to serve other gods, bowing in worship to gods they had not known — gods that the LORD had not permitted them to worship. ²⁷ Therefore the LORD's anger burned against this land, and he brought every curse written in this book on it. ²⁸ The LORD uprooted them from their land in his anger, rage, and intense wrath, and threw them into another land where they are today.' ²⁹ The hidden things belong to the LORD our God, but the revealed things belong to us and our children forever, so that we may follow all the words of this law.

Returning to the LORD

30 "When all these things happen to you — the blessings and curses I have set before you — and you come to your senses while you are in all the nations where the LORD your God has driven you, ² and you and your children return to the LORD your God and obey him with all your heart and all your soul by doing^A everything I am commanding you today,

³ then he will restore your fortunes,^B have compassion on you, and gather you again from all the peoples where the LORD your God has scattered you. ⁴ Even if your exiles are at the farthest horizon, he will gather you and bring you back from there. ⁵ The LORD your God will bring you into the land your ancestors possessed, and you will take possession of it. He will cause you to prosper and multiply you more than he did your ancestors. ⁶ The LORD your God will circumcise your heart and the hearts of your descendants, and you will love him with all your heart and all your soul so that you will live. ⁷ The LORD your God will put all these curses on your enemies who hate and persecute you. ⁸ Then you will again obey him and follow all his commands I am commanding you today. ⁹ The LORD your God will make you prosper abundantly in all the work of your hands, your offspring,^C the offspring of your livestock, and the produce of your land. Indeed, the LORD will again delight in your prosperity, as he delighted in that of your ancestors, ¹⁰ when you obey the LORD your God by keeping his commands and statutes that are written in this book of the law and return to him with all your heart and all your soul.

Choose Life

¹¹ "This command that I give you today is certainly not too difficult or beyond your reach. ¹² It is not in heaven so that you have to ask, 'Who will go up to heaven, get it for us, and proclaim it to us so that we may follow it?' ¹³ And it is not across the sea so that you have to ask, 'Who will cross the sea, get it for us, and proclaim it to us so that we may follow it?' ¹⁴ But the message is very near you, in your mouth and in your heart, so that you may follow it. ¹⁵ See, today I have set before you life and prosperity, death and adversity. ¹⁶ For^D I am commanding you today to love the LORD your God, to walk in his ways, and to keep his commands, statutes, and ordinances, so that you may live^E and multiply, and the LORD your God may bless you in the land you are entering to possess. ¹⁷ But if your heart turns away and you do not listen and you are led astray to bow in worship to other gods and serve them, ¹⁸ I tell you

---

^A 30:2 Lit soul according to   ^B 30:3 Or will end your captivity   ^C 30:9 Lit hands in the fruit of your womb   ^D 30:16 LXX reads If you obey the commands of the LORD your God that   ^E 30:16 LXX reads ordinances, then you will live

---

the judgment of the Lord, no matter how pious his confessions of faith. **29:22–23** The topic changes here from the individual to the whole community. The viewpoint also changes to that of **future generations** after the curses have been implemented. **29:27–28** The wrath of Yahweh finds its most concentrated expression in verses 22–29, with six nouns for anger used. **30:1–3** The grammatical structure of this passage suggests that Israel's repentance and return to the Lord would be at his

initiative, an act of his grace wherein God's promises and Israel's need to be obedient to the conditions of the covenant would be reconciled—one of the hidden mysteries of the mind of God (29:29). **30:4–5** God said he would bring a nation "from the ends of the earth" against his people (28:49). Now he will gather them from **the farthest horizon.** Verse 4 is quoted in Neh 1:9. See Is 41:9; 43:6; Mk 13:27. **30:6–8** The image of circumcising the **heart** derives from the occasion of Abraham's having been physically circumcised,

along with his household, as a sign of his covenant relationship with the Lord (Gn 17:9–14). Jeremiah also spoke of this mark of covenant reality in terms of spiritual circumcision (Jr 4:4; cp. Jr 31:33; Ezk 36:26), and Paul compared it to the new life and relationship to God to be found in Christ (Rm 2:28–29; Col 2:11). **30:11–14** Paul cited this text with reference to the proximity of the gospel and the ease with which it could be understood and appropriated; like the words of the OT covenant, those of the NT message of salvation

today that you will certainly perish and will not prolong your days in the land you are entering to possess across the Jordan. [19] I call heaven and earth as witnesses against you today that I have set before you life and death, blessing and curse. Choose life so that you and your descendants may live, [20] love the LORD your God, obey him, and remain faithful[A] to him. For he is your life, and he will prolong your days as you live in the land the LORD swore to give to your ancestors Abraham, Isaac, and Jacob."

Joshua Takes Moses's Place

31 Then Moses continued to speak these[B] words to all Israel, [2] saying, "I am now 120 years old; I can no longer act as your leader.[C] The LORD has told me, 'You will not cross the Jordan.' [3] The LORD your God is the one who will cross ahead of you. He will destroy these nations before you, and you will drive them out. Joshua is the one who will cross ahead of you, as the LORD has said. [4] The LORD will deal with them as he did Sihon and Og, the kings of the Amorites, and their land when he destroyed them. [5] The LORD will deliver them over to you, and you must do to them exactly as I have commanded you. [6] Be strong and courageous; don't be terrified or afraid of them. For the LORD your God is the one who will go with you; he will not leave you or abandon you."

[7] Moses then summoned Joshua and said to him in the sight of all Israel, "Be strong and courageous, for you will go with[D] this people into the land the LORD swore to give to their ancestors. You will enable them to take possession of it. [8] The LORD is the one who will go before you. He will be with you; he will not leave you or abandon you. Do not be afraid or discouraged."

[9] Moses wrote down this law and gave it to the priests, the sons of Levi, who carried the ark of the LORD's covenant, and to all the elders of Israel. [10] Moses commanded them, "At the end of every seven years, at the appointed time in the year of debt cancellation, during the Festival of Shelters, [11] when all Israel assembles in the presence of the LORD your God at the place he chooses, you are to read this law aloud

before all Israel. [12] Gather the people — men, women, dependents, and the resident aliens within your city gates — so that they may listen and learn to fear the LORD your God and be careful to follow all the words of this law. [13] Then their children who do not know the law will listen and learn to fear the LORD your God as long as you live in the land you are crossing the Jordan to possess."

[14] The LORD said to Moses, "The time of your death is now approaching. Call Joshua and present yourselves at the tent of meeting so that I may commission him." When Moses and Joshua went and presented themselves at the tent of meeting, [15] the LORD appeared at the tent in a pillar of cloud, and the cloud stood at the entrance to the tent.

[16] The LORD said to Moses, "You are about to rest with your ancestors, and these people will soon prostitute themselves with the foreign gods of the land they are entering. They will abandon me and break the covenant I have made with them. [17] My anger will burn against them on that day; I will abandon them and hide my face from them so that they will become easy prey. Many troubles and afflictions will come to them. On that day they will say, 'Haven't these troubles come to us because our God is no longer with us?' [18] I will certainly hide my face on that day because of all the evil they have done by turning to other gods. [19] Therefore write down this song for yourselves and teach it to the Israelites; have them sing it,[E] so that this song may be a witness for me against the Israelites. [20] When I bring them into the land I swore to give their ancestors, a land flowing with milk and honey, they will eat their fill and prosper.[F] They will turn to other gods and worship them, despising me and breaking my covenant. [21] And when many troubles and afflictions come to them, this song will testify against them, because[G] their descendants will not have forgotten it. For I know what they are prone to do,[H] even before I bring them into the land I swore to give them." [22] So Moses wrote down this song on that day and taught it to the Israelites.

[A]30:20 Lit and hold on [B]31:1 Some Hb mss, DSS, LXX, Syr, Vg read all these [C]31:2 Lit no longer go out or come in [D]31:7 Some Hb mss, Sam, Syr, Vg read you will bring [E]31:19 Lit Israelites; put it in their mouths [F]31:20 Lit be fat [G]31:21 Lit because the mouths of [H]31:21 Or know the plans they are devising

---

are ready at hand and made available to all who will believe (Rm 10:6–10).

30:19 In a setting similar to a courtroom, the Lord summoned witnesses to his offer to Israel of **life and death**. Since these witnesses must be enduring and objective, he called not on humans or even angels, but on **heaven and earth** (cp. 4:26; 31:28; 32:1; Is 1:2; Mc 1:2).

31:1–6 The narrative of Moses's imminent death and the succession of Joshua to leadership is reminiscent of an earlier part of Deuteronomy (3:21–28). It also anticipates

the formal call and commissioning of Joshua following Moses's departure (Jos 1:1–9).

31:7–8 Be strong and courageous is found in vv. 6 and 7, then again in v. 23 and in Jos 1:6–7,9,18; 10:25; 1Ch 22:13; 28:20; 32:7; Pss 27:14; 31:25. **He will not leave you or abandon you** also occurs in 31:6,8; Jos 1:5; 1Ch 28:20.

31:9 This law is clearly the bulk of the book of Deuteronomy, since chaps. 5–28 make up the body of covenant stipulations.

31:10–11 Because there was only one copy of the law at the beginning and in light of the limited literacy of the population of Israel at

large, Israel had to assemble to hear it read at **the end of every seven years . . . during the Festival of Shelters** in the fall of the year at the central sanctuary (12:5,11).

31:16–18 The marriage/**prostitute** metaphor describes the **covenant** relationship between the Lord and Israel (Ezk 16:8; 23:36–39; Hs 2:2–13). The worst sin Israel could commit against him was to acknowledge and worship the **foreign gods** of the pagan nations. Such behavior was a violation of the marriage vows enshrined in the covenant text (27:11–26; Ex 19:8).

²³ The Lord commissioned Joshua son of Nun, "Be strong and courageous, for you will bring the Israelites into the land I swore to them, and I will be with you."

Moses Warns the People

²⁴ When Moses had finished writing down on a scroll every single word of this law, ²⁵ he commanded the Levites who carried the ark of the Lord's covenant, ²⁶ "Take this book of the law and place it beside the ark of the covenant of the Lord your God so that it may remain there as a witness against you. ²⁷ For I know how rebellious and stiff-necked you are. If you are rebelling against the Lord now, while I am still alive, how much more will you rebel after I am dead! ²⁸ Assemble all your tribal elders and officers before me so that I may speak these words directly to them and call heaven and earth as witnesses against them. ²⁹ For I know that after my death you will become completely corrupt and turn from the path I have commanded you. Disaster will come to you in the future, because you will do what is evil in the Lord's sight, angering him with what your hands have made." ³⁰ Then Moses recited aloud every single word of this song to the entire assembly of Israel:

Song of Moses

32 Pay attention, heavens, and I will speak;
listen, earth, to the words
from my mouth.

²   Let my teaching fall like rain
and my word settle like dew,
like gentle rain on new grass
and showers on tender plants.
³   For I will proclaim the Lord's name.
Declare the greatness of our God!
⁴   The Rock — his work is perfect;
all his ways are just.
A faithful God, without bias,
he is righteous and true.

⁵   His people have acted corruptly
toward him;
this is their defect^A — they are not
his children
but a devious
and crooked generation.
⁶   Is this how you repay the Lord,
you foolish and senseless people?
Isn't he your Father and Creator?^B
Didn't he make you and sustain you?
⁷   Remember the days of old;
consider the years of past generations.
Ask your father, and he will tell you,
your elders, and they will teach you.
⁸   When the Most High gave the nations
their inheritance^C
and divided the human race,
he set the boundaries of the peoples
according to the number of the people
of Israel.^D
⁹   But the Lord's portion is his people,
Jacob, his own inheritance.

---

^A 32:5 Or *him; through their fault*; Hb obscure   ^B 32:6 Or *Possessor*   ^C 32:8 Or *Most High divided the nations*   ^D 32:8 One DSS reads *number of the sons of God*; LXX reads *number of the angels of God*

31:20–22 The song of witness was forever a nagging reminder of her lack of gratitude to God. The song is found in 32:1–43.
31:23 Joshua would hear these words again after Moses's death (Jos 1:6–7).
31:24 The statement that **Moses** wrote **every single word of this law** attests to

the ancient tradition of his authorship of the book of Deuteronomy, the "law" clearly intended here.
31:25–26 The stone tablets of the Decalogue had already been placed inside the ark of the covenant (Ex 25:16) and now the **book of the law**—no doubt Deuteronomy—must be housed in the most holy place **beside the ark** (cp. Ex 26:33), which represented the earthly dwelling place of the Lord.
31:28 The Lord now, at the point of covenant renewal, would **call heaven and earth as witnesses against them** (cp. 4:26; 30:19). This is in line with the principle that formal legal matters must be addressed in the presence of at least two witnesses in order for them to be valid (17:6; 19:15).
32:1 Using a figure of speech by which inanimate objects are addressed—"apostrophe"—Moses appealed to the **heavens** and the **earth** to **listen** to the words of his **mouth**—to serve as witnesses to what the Lord was about to say through the song of Moses and to the tacit response of commitment by the nation (31:28).
32:3–4 The epithet **The Rock** describes the Lord as both: (1) a firm and secure foundation upon whom one can build and in whom one can trust for salvation (vv. 15,18,30; Hab 1:12), and (2) a companion who is able to lead one through the trackless deserts of life (1Co 10:4).
32:5 Israel had ruined their relationship with the Lord and no longer acted like his children.

They were a grotesque mockery of what God had created them to be.
32:6 The description of the Lord as **Father** (cp. Ps 2:7; 89:26; Is 63:16; 64:8; Jr 3:19; Mal 1:6) and **Creator** (Gn 14:22; Ec 12:1; Is 27:11; 40:28; 43:15) is rare in the OT, and the two are placed together only here. This combination reminded Israel that he was the God of all creation but also the special Father of his people.
32:7 Moses urged the people to remember bygone days in order to be informed and inspired by them.
32:8 Israel's special place in the redemptive program of the Lord is clear from the fact that when he **gave the nations their inheritance and divided the human race**, he did so with Israel especially in mind. Their size and location were the fixed points according to which **he set the boundaries of the peoples**. The Table of Nations of Gn 10 focuses on Shem and his descendants (vv. 21–31), drawing particular attention to Eber, for whom the Hebrews were named (vv. 21,25; cp. 11:14–26). Abram, the ultimate father of Israel, was an Eberite (Hebrew), thus establishing the connection between Israel and Eber, the central individual of the Table of Nations. Israel's role as the nation chosen out of all the others is a major OT theme (7:6–8; Gn 12:1–3; 15:4–5; 17:3–8; Ex 19:4–6).
32:9 What is only hinted at in v. 8 is clear here: Israel is **the Lord's** chosen **people**.

¹⁰ He found him in a desolate land,
in a barren, howling wilderness;
he surrounded him, cared for him,
and protected him as the pupil
of his eye.

¹¹ He watches over^A his nest like an eagle
and hovers over his young;
he spreads his wings, catches him,
and carries him on his feathers.

¹² The LORD alone led him,
with no help from a foreign god.

¹³ He made him ride on the heights
of the land
and eat the produce of the field.
He nourished him with honey
from the rock
and oil from flinty rock,

¹⁴ curds from the herd and milk
from the flock,
with the fat of lambs,
rams from Bashan, and goats,
with the choicest grains of wheat;
you drank wine from the finest grapes.^B

¹⁵ Then^C Jeshurun^D became fat
and rebelled —
you became fat, bloated, and gorged.
He abandoned the God who made him
and scorned the Rock of his salvation.

¹⁶ They provoked his jealousy
with different gods;
they enraged him
with detestable practices.

¹⁷ They sacrificed to demons, not God,
to gods they had not known,
new gods that had just arrived,
which your ancestors did not fear.

¹⁸ You ignored the Rock
who gave you birth;
you forgot the God who gave birth
to you.

¹⁹ When the LORD saw this,
he despised them,
angered by his sons and daughters.

²⁰ He said, "I will hide my face from them;
I will see what will become of them,
for they are a perverse generation —
unfaithful children.

²¹ They have provoked my jealousy
with what is not a god;^E
they have enraged me
with their worthless idols.
So I will provoke their jealousy
with what is not a people;^F
I will enrage them with a foolish nation.

²² For fire has been kindled because of
my anger
and burns to the depths of Sheol;
it devours the land and its produce,
and scorches the foundations
of the mountains.

²³ "I will pile disasters on them;
I will use up my arrows against them.

²⁴ They will be weak from hunger,
ravaged by pestilence
and bitter plague;
I will unleash on them wild beasts
with fangs,
as well as venomous snakes that slither
in the dust.

²⁵ Outside, the sword will take
their children,
and inside, there will be terror;
the young man and the young woman
will be killed,
the infant and the gray-haired man.

²⁶ "I would have said: I will cut them
to pieces^G
and blot out the memory of them
from mankind,

---

^A**32:11** Or *He stirs up* ^B**32:14** Lit *drank the blood of grapes, fermenting wine* ^C**32:15** DSS, Sam, LXX add *Jacob ate his fill;*
^D**32:15** = Upright One, referring to Israel ^E**32:21** Lit *with no gods* ^F**32:21** Lit *with no people* ^G**32:26** LXX reads *will
scatter them*

32:10–14 Israel's position as the chosen nation is confirmed by the special care the Lord accorded her, especially in the desert journey out of Egypt. Moses described the Lord's watchfulness over Israel as that of an **eagle** protecting his young one in the nest and teaching him to fly. He alone was capable of leading them through the desert until at last they reached the land he had promised to give them (v. 12).

32:15–18 Looking into the future, Moses saw a time when Israel would rebel against the Lord and break the covenant with him. When they became **fat, bloated, and gorged** with all the blessings of the land (cp. vv. 13–14), they would attribute their prosperity to **different gods**, abandoning the **God who made** them and the **Rock** of their **salvation** (cp. 8:11–20). By their idolatry they would provoke God to jealousy (cp. 5:9). This would include their sacrifice **to demons** and **gods they had not known.**

This description of demons provides the theological insight that the pagan gods were in fact fallen angels used by Satan to lead people away from the true God (cp. 1Co 10:20; Rv 9:20). The long history of Israel in the land bears sorrowful testimony to the bleak prospects outlined here by Moses (cp. 2Kg 17:7–17).

32:19–21 Once Israel had lapsed into idolatry described in vv. 15–18, the **LORD** would begin to exert judgment. He threatened to **hide** his **face** from his people, a response reminiscent of his reaction to the worship of the golden calf at Sinai (Ex 32:10,34–35). As in that incident, the sin was rebellion epitomized by the violation of the first two commandments. The NT makes clear that those referred to as **not a people** are the Gentiles whom God would call to himself through the gospel. Paul quoted this text to say it was God's favor to the nations that would finally awaken Israel to their own

disobedience, impelling them to see in Christ their promised Messiah (Rm 10:19–21).

32:22 Sheol refers to the grave, the netherworld, or the place of the departed dead in general. Here it suggests only that there is no place that the burning wrath of God cannot reach.

32:23–25 The instruments of God's wrath are figuratively described as **arrows** (see v. 42; Pss 7:13; 18:14; 38:2; 64:7; Lm 3:12–13; Ezk 5:16; Hab 3:9,11). The inclusiveness of the punishment is described by a series of merisms in v. 25: **outside . . . inside**; **young man . . . young woman**; and **infant . . . gray-haired man**.

32:26–27 The Lord declared that if not for his reputation, he would cut Israel to pieces and **blot out the memory of them from mankind**. To do this, however, would allow the enemy to take credit for Israel's failure and punishment rather than attributing it to the Lord. The threat to blot out their memory

27 if I had not feared provocation
    from the enemy,
  or feared that these foes
    might misunderstand
  and say, 'Our own hand has prevailed;
  it wasn't the LORD who did all this.'"

28 Israel is a nation lacking sense
    with no understanding at all.
29 If only they were wise,
    they would comprehend this;
  they would understand their fate.
30 How could one pursue a thousand,
    or two put ten thousand to flight,
  unless their Rock had sold them,
  unless the LORD had given them up?
31 But their "rock" is not like our Rock,
    as even our enemies concede.
32 For their vine is from the vine of Sodom
  and from the fields of Gomorrah.
  Their grapes are poisonous;
    their clusters are bitter.
33 Their wine is serpents' venom,
    the deadly poison of cobras.

34 "Is it not stored up with me,
    sealed up in my vaults?
35 Vengeance and retribution belong
    to me.^A
  In time their foot will slip,
  for their day of disaster is near,
  and their doom is coming quickly."
36 The LORD will indeed vindicate
    his people
  and have compassion on his servants
  when he sees that their strength is gone

and no one is left — slave or free.^B
37 He will say, "Where are their gods,
    the 'rock' they found refuge in?
38 Who ate the fat of their sacrifices
  and drank the wine
    of their drink offerings?
  Let them rise up and help you;
  let it^C be a shelter for you.
39 See now that I alone am he;
    there is no God but me.
  I bring death and I give life;
  I wound and I heal.
  No one can rescue anyone
    from my power.
40 I raise my hand to heaven and declare:
    As surely as I live forever,
41 when I sharpen my flashing sword,
  and my hand takes hold of judgment,
  I will take vengeance on my adversaries
  and repay those who hate me.
42 I will make my arrows drunk with blood
  while my sword devours flesh —
  the blood of the slain and the captives,
  the heads of the enemy leaders."^D

43 Rejoice, you nations,
    concerning his people,^E
  for he will avenge the blood
    of his servants.^F
  He will take vengeance
    on his adversaries;^G
  he will purify his land and his people.^H

44 Moses came with Joshua^I son of Nun and recited all the words of this song in the presence of the people. 45 After Moses finished

---

^A32:35 MT; LXX, reads *On a day of vengeance I will repay.* ^B32:36 Or *left — even the weak and impaired*; Hb obscure ^C32:38 Sam, LXX, Tg, Vg read *them* ^D32:42 Or *the long-haired heads of the enemy* ^E32:43 LXX reads *Rejoice, you heavens, along with him, and let all the sons of God worship him; rejoice, you nations, with his people, and let all the angels of God strengthen themselves in him*; DSS read *Rejoice, you heavens, along with him, and let all the angels worship him*; Heb 1:6 ^F32:43 DSS, LXX read *sons* ^G32:43 DSS, LXX add *and he will repay those who hate him*; v. 41 ^H32:43 Syr, Tg; DSS, Sam, LXX, Vg read *his people's land* ^I32:44 LXX, Syr, Vg; MT reads *Hoshea*; Nm 13:8,16

---

recalls Ex 32:32 where Moses said that if the Lord would not forgive his wicked people, he would gladly have his name erased from the book God had written.
32:28–33 The subject of these verses is unnamed, leading to some confusion. The CSB is probably correct in supplying **Israel** in v. 28. But others believe the subject is the enemies of God and Israel.
32:30 Moses predicted a time when Israel's sin would be so blatant that they would be delivered over to incredibly powerful armies. Though hyperbole is used to describe the future defeat of Israel by a foreign foe (**one pursue a thousand**), the fact remains that when God no longer fights for his people and, in fact, fights against them, there is no chance of victory.
32:31 In contrast to the previous scenario, when the Lord fights for his people, they are certain to prevail because the "**rock**" on which the pagans rely does not exist and therefore has no real power.
32:32–33 The **vine**, the **grapes**, and the **wine** are the products of the enemies' "rock" (v. 31)—the pagan fertility gods. The

Lord, however, linked these imaginary gods to **Sodom** and **Gomorrah**, the epitome of corruption (Gn 18:20; 19:4–28; Is 1:10; 3:9; Mt 10:15; 11:23–24).
32:34–35 The **vaults** is a figurative image conveying the idea that all judgment originates with God and is stored up until the proper time of its administration. **Vengeance and retribution belong to** God. Only he knows all the facts, and only he is absolutely just and righteous (Rm 12:19; Heb 10:30).
32:36 The other side of vengeance on the wicked is vindication of the righteous. The pledge here is that the Lord will be true to his everlasting covenant promises.
32:37–38 At the same time the Lord rescues them, he will taunt his people by asking where **their gods**, their supposed **rock** of **refuge**, have gone. The prophets also taunted idolaters and the gods they worshiped by sarcastically exposing their nonexistence (Is 40:18–20; 44:6–20; Jr 10:1–10).
32:39 The bottom line is that the Lord **alone** is **God**. Surely this puts an end to speculation about other gods and ought to render foolish

the devotion that people—especially his own people Israel—pay to them.
32:40–42 Using a figure of speech called an "anthropomorphism" the Lord swears by **heaven** is his witness and as surely as he lives forever that he will execute **judgment** and **vengeance** on his **adversaries** and the **heads of the enemy leaders** who hate him. The familiar language of the courtroom is used here so Israel can better understand the legal and forensic nature of God's relationship to them and to the nations at large. A second figure of speech—personification—describes the **sword** of the Lord as it **devours flesh** and his **arrows** that are **drunk with blood**. This gruesome scene reflects the other side of the coin of divine love and grace—holiness and justice.
32:43 When the Lord administers judgment to his adversaries, he will also **avenge** . . . **his servants** who have been abused. By judging his foes and vindicating Israel, the Lord will **purify his land and his people**.
32:44–46 The instruction to the people to **take to heart** all the words of Moses's song and to command their children **to follow**

reciting all these words to all Israel, **46** he said to them, "Take to heart all these words I am giving as a warning to you today, so that you may command your children to follow all the words of this law carefully. **47** For they are not meaningless words to you but they are your life, and by them you will live long in the land you are crossing the Jordan to possess."

Moses's Impending Death

48 On that same day the LORD spoke to Moses, **49** "Go up Mount Nebo in the Abarim range in the land of Moab, across from Jericho, and view the land of Canaan I am giving the Israelites as a possession. **50** Then you will die on the mountain that you go up, and you will be gathered to your people, just as your brother Aaron died on Mount Hor and was gathered to his people. **51** For both of you broke faith with me among the Israelites at the Waters of Meribath-kadesh in the Wilderness of Zin by failing to treat me as holy in their presence. **52** Although from a distance you will view the land that I am giving the Israelites, you will not go there."

Moses's Blessings

33 This is the blessing that Moses, the man of God, gave the Israelites before his death. **2** He said:
The LORD came from Sinai
and appeared to them from Seir;
he shone on them from Mount Paran
and came with ten thousand holy ones,^A
with lightning^B from his right hand^C
for them.

3 Indeed he loves the people.^D
All your^E holy ones are in your hand,
and they assemble^F at your feet.
Each receives your words.
4 Moses gave us instruction,
a possession for the assembly of Jacob.
5 So he became King in Jeshurun^G
when the leaders of the people gathered
with the tribes of Israel.

6 Let Reuben live and not die
though his people become few.
7 He said this about Judah:
LORD, hear Judah's cry and bring him
to his people.
He fights for his cause^H
with his own hands,
but may you be a help against his foes.
8 He said about Levi:
Your Thummim and Urim belong to
your faithful one;^I
you tested him at Massah
and contended with him at the Waters
of Meribah.
9 He said about his father and mother,
"I do not regard them."
He disregarded his brothers
and didn't acknowledge his sons,
for they kept your word
and maintained your covenant.
10 They will teach your ordinances
to Jacob
and your instruction to Israel;
they will set incense before you
and whole burnt offerings on your altar.

^A **33:2** LXX reads *Mount Paran with ten thousands from Kadesh*   ^B **33:2** Or *fiery law*; Hb obscure   ^C **33:2** Or *ones, from his southland to the mountain slopes*   ^D **33:3** Or *peoples*   ^E **33:3** Lit *his*, or *its*   ^F **33:3** Hb obscure   ^G **33:5** = Upright One, referring to Israel, also in v. 26   ^H **33:7** Or *He contends for them*   ^I **33:8** DSS, LXX read *Give to Levi your Thummim, your Urim to your favored one*

all the words of this law (i.e., the book of Deuteronomy) calls to mind the admonitions following the giving of the Ten Commandments (5:32–33) and the Shema (6:4–9). These commands of the Lord must be handed down from one generation to the next. **32:47** Because Israel failed to heed these words of admonition, they were eventually uprooted from the land and forced into exile (2Kg 17:7–17; 2Ch 36:15–19). **32:48–52** The reason Aaron and Moses were unable to enter the land of promise is that they **broke faith** with the Lord. The verb translated "broke faith" has at its core in this context the idea of covenant treachery or disloyalty. Moses should have served as a model of kingdom citizenship in a time of stress, but he failed to do so (Nm 20:1–13). **33:1–29** Though on the surface this seems similar to Jacob's blessing of his sons, they serve different purposes. Jacob's blessing is more predictive, whereas Moses's speech is actually a blessing or prayerful intercession. It comprises an introduction (v. 1), a historical review (vv. 2–5), blessings on individual tribes (vv. 6–25), and a blessing on Israel generally (vv. 26–29). **33:2** The listing of **Sinai** ... **Seir,** and **Mount Paran** is an abbreviated itinerary along

which the Lord had led his people on their journey from Egypt to the land of promise. The **holy ones** are the angelic hosts that make up his heavenly armies (Ps 68:17). **Lightning** (lit "fiery law") might better be understood as synonymous with holy ones and thus rendered "angels." **33:3** Here **holy ones** is a reference to the **people** of Israel. The Lord led them to the land of promise because he loved them—a key indicator of their covenant relationship with him (cp. 7:7–11). **33:4** The term **instruction** translates the Hebrew word *torah*. The point is that Israel out of all the nations had been entrusted with God's covenant blessings (14:2,21; Ex 19:4–6). **33:5 Jeshurun** is a poetic term for Israel (v. 26; 32:15; Is 44:2). Moses's reference to the Lord as **King** in Jeshurun provides a basis for the march of conquest of v. 2. The Lord can exercise such power and glory precisely because he is King (29:10; Ex 19:7–8; 34:31–32). **33:6** Turning to the blessing of the individual tribes, Moses first wished for **Reuben,** the eldest son of Jacob, that he might **live and not die though his people become few.** This partially offsets Jacob's curse against him because of Reuben's sin

involving Jacob's concubine (Gn 49:3–4; cp. Gn 35:22). **33:7 Judah,** contending for himself, is in desperate need of the Lord's help. This help could come directly from the Lord or from Judah's strong bond with **his people,** the other tribes. If this interpretation is correct, it anticipates a rupture of the tribes into the two kingdoms of Israel and Judah. **33:8 Levi,** the head of the priestly tribe, was responsible for spiritual leadership. This included determining God's will for them by casting the sacred lots of **Urim** and **Thummim** (Ex 28:15–30; cp. 1Sm 28:6; Ezr 2:63; Neh 7:65). The testing probably refers to the Lord testing Moses the Levite, since otherwise it was the Lord who was being **tested** by Israel and not the other way around (6:16; Ex 17:7; Nm 20:13,24; Pss 95:8–9; 106:32). **33:9** Levi's statement about **his father and mother** probably refers to the impartial attitude of that tribe in punishing Israel for their worship of the golden calf at Sinai (Ex 32:25–29). Thus Levi **kept** the Lord's **word and maintained** his **covenant.** **33:10** Two other privileges reserved only for the Levites were teaching the Lord's **ordinances** (31:9–13; Lv 10:11) and conducting worship.

¹¹ Lord, bless his possessions,ᴬ
    and accept the work of his hands.
  Break the backᴮ of his adversaries
      and enemies,
    so that they cannot rise again.
¹² He said about Benjamin:
  The Lord's beloved restsᶜ securely
      on him.
  Heᴰ shields him all day long,
    and he rests on his shoulders.ᴱ
¹³ He said about Joseph:
  May his land be blessed by the Lord
    with the dew of heaven's bounty
  and the watery depths that lie beneath;
¹⁴   with the bountiful harvest
      from the sun
    and the abundant yield of the seasons;
¹⁵   with the best products
      of the ancient mountains
    and the bounty of the eternal hills;
¹⁶   with the choice gifts of the land
      and everything in it;
  and with the favor of him
    who appearedᶠ in the burning bush.
  May these rest on the head of Joseph,
    on the brow of the prince
      of his brothers.
¹⁷   His firstborn bull hasᴳ splendor,
    and horns likeᴴ those of a wild ox;
  he gores all the peoples with them
    to the ends of the earth.
  Such are the ten thousands of Ephraim,
  and such are the thousands
      of Manasseh.
¹⁸ He said about Zebulun:
  Rejoice, Zebulun, in your journeys,
  and Issachar, in your tents.

¹⁹ They summon the peoples
      to a mountain;
  there they offer acceptable sacrifices.
  For they draw from the wealth
      of the seas
    and the hidden treasures of the sand.
²⁰ He said about Gad:
  The one who enlarges Gad's territory
    will be blessed.
  He lies down like a lion
    and tears off an arm or even a head.
²¹   He chose the best part for himself,
    because a ruler's portion was assigned
      there for him.
  He came with the leaders of the people;
    he carried out the Lord's justice
    and his ordinances for Israel.
²² He said about Dan:
  Dan is a young lion,
    leaping out of Bashan.
²³ He said about Naphtali:
  Naphtali, enjoying approval,
    full of the Lord's blessing,
    takeᴵ possession to the west and the south.
²⁴ He said about Asher:
  May Asherᴶ be the most blessed
      of the sons;
  may he be the most favored
      among his brothers
    and dip his foot in olive oil.
²⁵   May the bolts of your gate be iron
      and bronze,
    and your strength last as long as you live.
²⁶   There is none like the God of Jeshurun,
    who rides the heavens to your aid,
    the clouds in his majesty.

ᴬ**33:11** Or *abilities*   ᴮ**33:11** Or *waist*   ᶜ**33:12** Or *Let the Lord's beloved rest*   ᴰ**33:12** LXX reads *The Most High*   ᴱ**33:12** Or *and he dwells among his mountain slopes*   ᶠ**33:16** Lit *dwelt*   ᴳ**33:17** Some DSS, Sam, LXX, Syr, Vg read *A firstborn bull — he has*   ᴴ**33:17** Lit *and his horns are*   ᴵ**33:23** Sam, LXX, Syr, Vg, Tg read *he will take*   ᴶ**33:24** = Happy or Blessed; Gn 30:13

33:11 Possessions is literally "his strength" and probably refers to Levi's accomplishments as teacher and cultic mediator. **Break the back** may mean to render impotent, or to otherwise undermine their strength.

33:12 The blessing of **Benjamin** also somewhat offsets the last words of Jacob to his sons when he described Benjamin as a wolf who tore his prey (Gn 49:27). Here Benjamin rests on the Lord's **shoulders** much as a shepherd might carry his helpless lambs (Nm 11:12; Ru 4:16; Is 40:11; Jn 10:7–18).

33:13–17 Moses's desire for **Joseph** (the tribes of **Ephraim** and **Manasseh**, Joseph's sons) was primarily for agricultural (vv. 13–16) and military (v. 17) success. The allusion to **him who appeared in the burning bush** is to place Joseph back at the setting of the covenant God made with Israel and all the promises of his abundant grace associated with it (Ex 3:2–4,16–18).

33:18–19 Zebulun and Issachar are linked together as the last two sons of Jacob's wife Leah (Gn 30:18,20) and as neighboring tribes in the area north of the valley of Jezreel. The **mountain** is probably Mount Tabor, the only prominent mountain in their territory.

The only reference to Tabor as a place of sacrifice occurs in Hs 5:1; by Hosea's time it was regarded as illegitimate. However, in an earlier time Tabor may have been a place of local worship. Zebulun's border extended as far west as the Mediterranean Sea, and thus its people could **draw from the wealth of the seas and . . . the sand**.

33:20–21 Gad had been described by Jacob as a ferocious warrior who, though attacked by others, would strike back with vengeance (Gn 49:19). Moses viewed the tribe of Gad as one that would seek to enlarge its **territory**, and he blessed anyone who could make that happen. Already in Moses's day Gad had chosen the fertile land of the northern Transjordan (Nm 32:1–5). Once there, Gad had carved out the largest territory of all the eastern tribes, gaining **a ruler's portion**.

33:22 Jacob depicted **Dan** as a vicious viper that bites horses' heels, throwing their riders to the ground (Gn 49:16–17). Moses compared him to **a young lion, leaping out of Bashan**. Besides affirming the aggressive nature of Dan, the geographical reference to Bashan suggests that the tribe of Dan's occupation of its far northern territory may

have originated in Bashan. Dan had been allotted a region near Philistine territory which it was unable to occupy and from which it moved north for more suitable prospects (Jos 19:40–48; Jdg 18:1–29).

33:23 Naphtali settled on the western side of the Sea of Galilee. Jacob said of this son that he "is a doe set free that bears beautiful fawns" (Gn 49:21). Because of the fertile and fruitful nature of the lower Galilee region, Naphtali, Moses said, would enjoy divine **approval**. The spiritual blessing may be seen most fully when Messiah came and spent most of his life and ministry in and about the territory allotted Naphtali.

33:24–25 Jacob promised his son **Asher** that his "food will be rich, and he will produce royal delicacies" (Gn 49:20). When Moses prayed, **May Asher be the most blessed of the sons**, he was probably referring also to material blessings, particularly to food supplies. This is clear from the desire of Moses that Asher might **dip his foot in olive oil**. Asher's location on the upper Mediterranean coast, the region of the modern city of Haifa, accounted for its access to products of the sea, but the surrounding hills, including

27 The God of old is your dwelling place,
and underneath are
the everlasting arms.
He drives out the enemy before you
and commands, "Destroy!"
28 So Israel dwells securely;
Jacob lives untroubled[A]
in a land of grain and new wine;
even his skies drip with dew.
29 How happy you are, Israel!
Who is like you,
a people saved by the LORD?
He is the shield that protects you,
the sword you boast in.
Your enemies will cringe before you,
and you will tread on their backs.[B]

Moses's Death

34 Then Moses went up from the plains
of Moab to Mount Nebo, to the top
of Pisgah, which faces Jericho, and the LORD
showed him all the land: Gilead as far as Dan,
2 all of Naphtali, the land of Ephraim and Manasseh, all the land of Judah as far as the Mediterranean[C] Sea, 3 the Negev, and the plain in
the Valley of Jericho, the City of Palms, as far
as Zoar. 4 The LORD then said to him, "This is
the land I promised Abraham, Isaac, and Jacob, 'I will give it to your descendants.' I have
let you see it with your own eyes, but you will
not cross into it."
5 So Moses the servant of the LORD died there
in the land of Moab, according to the LORD's
word. 6 He buried him[D] in the valley in the land
of Moab facing Beth-peor, and no one to this
day knows where his grave is. 7 Moses was one
hundred twenty years old when he died; his
eyes were not weak, and his vitality had not
left him. 8 The Israelites wept for Moses in the
plains of Moab thirty days. Then the days of
weeping and mourning for Moses came to an
end.
9 Joshua son of Nun was filled with the spirit
of wisdom because Moses had laid his hands
on him. So the Israelites obeyed him and did as
the LORD had commanded Moses. 10 No prophet has arisen again in Israel like Moses, whom
the LORD knew face to face. 11 He was unparalleled for all the signs and wonders the LORD
sent him to do against the land of Egypt — to
Pharaoh, to all his officials, and to all his land
— 12 and for all the mighty acts of power and
terrifying deeds that Moses performed in the
sight of all Israel.

[A] **33:28** Text emended; MT reads *Jacob's fountain is alone* [B] **33:29** Or *high places* [C] **34:2** Lit *Western* [D] **34:6** Or *he was buried*

Mount Carmel, also yielded vast quantities of olive oil, as is the case to this very day. To "dip the foot in olive oil" is a figure of speech suggesting a luxurious lifestyle.

33:27–28 The God of history is the God of the present and of the ages to come, giving Israel security and prosperity. The term for **dwelling place** is often used of a wild animal's den or lair (see Jb 37:8; 38:40; Ps 104:22; Sg 4:8; Am 3:4; Nah 2:12).

33:29 In a grand finale, Moses called on **Israel** to recognize **how happy** they were—or ought to be. Of all the nations of the earth, the Lord had **saved** only them in the sense of having called them to be his special possession (7:6; Ex 19:4–6). They enjoyed his protection as their **shield** and **sword**, metaphors descriptive of his power and glory (Gn 15:1; Pss 7:10; 18:2; 28:7).

34:1 The Abarim mountain range, east of the Jordan River just opposite **Jericho**, includes **Mount Nebo** on the western slope of **Pisgah**. From there it is possible on a clear day to view all the land of Canaan, including its northernmost borders at **Gilead** and **Dan**.

34:2 The tribes of **Naphtali** . . . **Ephraim** . . . **Manasseh**, and **Judah** later occupied the central hill country. Their territories and even beyond, as far west **as the Mediterranean Sea**, could be seen from Nebo.

34:3 The rest of the land of Canaan to the south was also visible from Moses's vantage point. The **Negev** is the vast desert area south of Judah extending to the Gulf of Aqaba arm of the Red Sea. The **Valley of Jericho** is another name for the portion of the Great Rift Valley that includes the Dead Sea, the southernmost city of which was **Zoar** (cp. Gn 19:18–26).

34:4 What Moses saw was **the land** God had **promised Abraham, Isaac, and Jacob** hundreds of years earlier as part of the covenant blessing (Gn 12:1; 13:14–17; 15:18–21). Though Moses could see the land with his **own eyes**, he was forbidden access to it because of his sin of dishonoring the Lord in the eyes of the people of Israel (32:51).

34:5–8 **According to the LORD's word** in v. 5 is literally "upon the mouth of Yahweh." It occurs twenty-one times, all but three in the Pentateuch. It is usually translated "at the command of the LORD." The Lord buried Moses just north of Pisgah. The people of Israel rightly viewed him as a mighty champion for the Lord and accorded him all the rites and ceremonies appropriate to the demise of such a leader (v. 8).

34:6 Moses's burial place is unknown today. That was even true "**to this day**," that is, at the time of the final editing of the book of Deuteronomy. Jude referred to the mystery surrounding Moses's burial place, alluding to the dispute of Michael the archangel with the devil about the matter (Jd 9).

34:7 Moses's remarkable **vitality** at the age of **one hundred twenty years** is mentioned to make the point that he died not of "natural" causes but because he had finished the task of leadership to which God had called him.

34:9 **Joshua** had been well schooled to succeed Moses (3:28; 31:7–8; Nm 27:18–21), but all the training in the world was insufficient without his being **filled with the spirit of wisdom** (cp. Nm 11:17,24–30). When it was apparent to the people that Joshua was adequately prepared for leadership, they **obeyed him** . . . **as the LORD had commanded Moses**.

34:10 It is impossible to know when the last words of Deuteronomy were penned, but whoever did so remarked that until his day **no prophet** . . . **like Moses** had **arisen again in Israel**. What set him apart was that he was the only one God communicated with **face to face** (Ex 33:19–23; Nm 12:6–8).

34:11–12 Moses was unique among the prophets also in the number and nature of **the signs and wonders the LORD sent him to do against the land of Egypt** (cp. Ex 4–12). These had the effect of convincing the Egyptians of the mighty **power** of Israel's God (Ex 8:19; 9:27–28;10:16–17). They were also **performed in the sight of all Israel** to persuade the Lord's own people of his mighty power and glory (Ex 14:31).

◥ Introduction to the Historical Books

by Kenneth A. Matthews

The Historical Books in the English Bible are Joshua, Judges, Ruth, 1–2 Samuel, 1–2 Kings, 1–2 Chronicles, Ezra, Nehemiah, and Esther. At first the books of 1–2 Samuel were one book, as were 1–2 Kings, 1–2 Chronicles, and Ezra–Nehemiah. The Septuagint, the ancient Greek translation of the Old Testament, was the first to divide the books. The Latin Vulgate and English versions have continued this practice. (The Hebrew division of these books did not occur until the Middle Ages.)

Our English translators, again following the Septuagint, arrange the Historical Books in a loosely chronological order. This continuous narrative traces the history of Israel from the conquest of Canaan by Joshua (about 1400 BC) to the restoration of the Jews during the Persian period (about 400 BC).

The Hebrew canon arranges the Historical Books differently. The Hebrew canon consists of three divisions: Law, Prophets, and Writings. Joshua, Judges (omitting Ruth), 1–2 Samuel, and 1–2 Kings are in the second division, the Prophets. Within this division, these books are designated as the Former Prophets (the Latter Prophets are Isaiah, Jeremiah, Ezekiel, and the twelve Minor Prophets). The books of 1–2 Chronicles, Ezra, and Nehemiah occur in the Writings as the final four books of the Hebrew canon. There, however, they have a reverse order: Ezra, Nehemiah, and 1–2 Chronicles. The books of Ruth and Esther also appear in the Writings.

The Former Prophets (Joshua, Judges, Samuel, and Kings) continue the narrative of Genesis through Deuteronomy, which tells of Israel's birth and rise as a nation. Deuteronomy concludes with the appointment of Joshua as Moses's successor who eventually led Israel into the land. The books of Joshua through 2 Kings relate the occupation of the land of Canaan, continue with the rise of the Hebrew monarchy, and conclude with the destruction and exile of the nation by the Babylonians.

The heading Former Prophets indicates that the Jewish rabbis did not read these books as histories (in our modern sense). Although written in narrative form, they were prophetic. Like the Latter Prophets, these "histories" declared the word of the Lord. They do not give an exhaustive history or a political account (as modern history writing would do). Rather, they interpret Israel's history from the theological perspective of God's covenant with Israel. As prophetic writings, they present God's evaluation and verdict on the history of Israel.

A telling example of this is Omri, king of Israel (885–874 BC). The Bible's account is brief, and its perspective is that Omri did evil in the Lord's sight—more evil than all who preceded him (1Kg 16:25). But the archaeological evidence indicates that Omri led Israel, the northern kingdom, in becoming a formidable regional power. His name is found in Assyrian annals and the expression "House of Omri" became synonymous with the northern kingdom and remained long after his death.

The Hebrew historians did not differentiate between Israel's political fortunes and its religious life. The narrative in Joshua through 2 Kings shows that Israel's success or failure as a nation was determined by its ongoing relationship with God and its fidelity to the Mosaic covenant (Ex 20–24). In particular, the Former Prophets—especially 1–2 Kings—were influenced by Deuteronomy's understanding of the covenant. This understanding emphasizes covenant loyalty and exclusive worship of God and explains how history is affected by a nation's morality.

A different but complementary perspective on Israel's history is provided in 1–2 Chronicles and Ezra–Nehemiah. First and Second Chronicles document Israel's history from creation to the destruction of Jerusalem. Ezra–Nehemiah continues the account with the return of the exiles from Babylon and the restoration of the religious life of Judah (about 400 BC). Since these books were written during and after the exile when there was no monarchy, they focus on the religious life of restored Israel. Temple worship and observance of the law of Moses are particularly emphasized.

Ruth and Esther, classified as Historical Books in English Bibles, are included among the five Megilloth (scrolls) in the Hebrew canon. These five books—Song of Solomon,

Ruth, Lamentations, Ecclesiastes, and Esther—are related to the five festivals (and fasts) of the Jewish calendar. Ruth, set at the harvest, is read at the Festival of Weeks (Pentecost), which celebrates the spring ingathering (May–June).

Esther's story gives the origins of the Festival of Purim and is read on that occasion (fourteenth and fifteenth of Adar [February–March]). Purim is the only Old Testament festival not legislated by the Mosaic law.

Introduction to Joshua

Circumstances of Writing

The author of the book of Joshua is not identified in the Bible and otherwise remains anonymous. If Joshua himself did not originally compose the book that bears his name, it may be presumed that someone who knew him and his exploits recorded the work. There are numerous references throughout Joshua that suggest a final formation of the book after his lifetime. These include the death of Joshua and descriptions of memorials or names that are said to remain "still . . . today" (4:9; 5:9; 6:25; 7:26; 8:28–29; 10:27; 13:13; 14:14; 15:63; 16:10; 22:17; 23:8).

The accounts in the book of Joshua occur in the period immediately after Moses's death. This was a new generation, not the one that had left Egypt. The story of Joshua is thus set when the nation of Israel first appeared in the land west of the Jordan River—the land that would bear its name. First Kings 6:1 states that the exodus occurred 480 years before Solomon's fourth year as king (966 BC). In Judges 11:26, Jephthah said that Israel had been living in regions of Palestine for 300 years. Jephthah lived around 1100 BC, thus dating the end of the wilderness journey and the beginning of the conquest around 1400 BC.

Contribution to the Bible

Just as Joshua's leadership begins with the death of Moses, so the book of Joshua follows and completes the book of Deuteronomy. Deuteronomy serves as a means by which the new generation of Israelites renewed their covenant with God. The book of Joshua provides the means by which God fulfilled his part of the covenant. God gave them victories, but each victory required a step of faith. God's provision for the people as their leader and guide bore witness to later generations of the divinely willed leadership for Israel, and his gracious gift of the land showed how the people's faithful fulfillment of the covenant could result in abundant blessing.

Structure

The book of Joshua should be seen as a land grant, similar to the land grants and suzerain treaties of the ancient Near East. The suzerain, who was Israel's God, gave to his people the land that they were meant to receive. There are three major parts to the structure of the land grant.

First is a review of the history and events leading up to the gift of the land. This occurs in chapter 1 and its discussion of what has brought Joshua to this point—the death of Moses. Chapters 2–5 detail the preparation for the acquisition of the gift of the land. Chapters 6–12 describe the battles that were fought as background to the receipt of the land. The second section considers the allotment of the territories to the tribes and families of Israel. The many specific names and towns of this part of the text provide a particularity to the gift that affirms it was an authentic fulfillment of God's promise to his people. The third section is a renewal of the covenant. Here the key parts are the stipulations of the covenant that require loyalty to God alone (24:14–15) and the response of the people that they agree to these demands.

1500–1450 BC

New Kingdom in Egypt **1540**
AARON 1529–1409?
MOSES 1526–1406
First alphabet developed in Egypt **1500**
Olmecs settle on the Gulf Coast of Mexico. **1500**
JOSHUA 1490?–1380?
Queen Makare Hatshepsut, daughter of Thutmose I, reigned in Egypt during a period of peace and prosperity. **1449–1457**

1450–1425 BC

Bronze hand mirrors were taken from Egypt by Hebrew women. **1446**
The exodus and defeat of Pharaoh at the Red Sea **1446**
Exploration of Canaan by the twelve spies **1445**

Outline

I. Preparation for the Land (1:1–5:12)
   A. Joshua assumes leadership (1:1–18)
   B. Rahab's faith (2:1–24)
   C. Across the Jordan River (3:1–4:24)
   D. Circumcision and Passover (5:1–12)
II. Victories in the Land (5:13–12:24)
III. Allotment of the Land (13:1–21:45)
IV. Worship of God (22:1–24:33)
   A. Transjordan and the altar of controversy (22:1–34)
   B. Joshua's farewell address (23:1–16)
   C. Israel's covenant at Shechem (24:1–28)
   D. Joshua and his generation die (24:29–33)

Key verses in Joshua

1:9 Haven't I commanded you: be strong and courageous? Do not be afraid or discouraged, for the LORD your God is with you wherever you go.

24:24 So the people said to Joshua, "We will worship the LORD our God and obey him."

1425–1400 BC

Events in Deuteronomy **1406**
Events in Joshua **1406–1380?**
Miraculous crossing of the Jordan River **1406**
Destruction of Jericho **1406**

1400–1375 BC

Warriors from the north, called Achaians
   by Homer, enter Greece to form
   foundations of Greek civilization. **1400**
Multiple cropping within the same
   year is developed in China. **1400**
Phoenicians advance open sea transportation
   with ships powered by oars and navigation
   by reference to the stars. **1400**
Division of the land into twelve allotments **1385?**

Encouragement of Joshua

1 After the death of Moses the LORD's servant, the LORD spoke to Joshua son of Nun, Moses's assistant: [2] "Moses my servant is dead. Now you and all the people prepare to cross over the Jordan to the land I am giving the Israelites. [3] I have given you every place where the sole of your foot treads, just as I promised Moses. [4] Your territory will be from the wilderness and Lebanon to the great river, the Euphrates River — all the land of the Hittites — and west to the Mediterranean Sea. [5] No one will be able to stand against you as long as you live. I will be with you, just as I was with Moses. I will not leave you or abandon you.

[6] "Be strong and courageous, for you will distribute the land I swore to their ancestors to give them as an inheritance. [7] Above all, be strong and very courageous to observe carefully the whole instruction my servant Moses commanded you. Do not turn from it to the right or the left, so that you will have success wherever you go. [8] This book of instruction must not depart from your mouth; you are to meditate on[A] it day and night so that you may carefully observe everything written in it. For then you will prosper and succeed in whatever you do. [9] Haven't I commanded you: be strong and courageous? Do not be afraid or discouraged, for the LORD your God is with you wherever you go."

Joshua Prepares the People

[10] Then Joshua commanded the officers of the people, [11] "Go through the camp and tell the people, 'Get provisions ready for yourselves,

[A]1:8 Or to recite

1:1 The **death of Moses** created a leadership vacuum. Moses's epithet, **LORD's servant**, was first applied at his death (Dt 34:5) as this epithet would first be applied to Joshua at his death (Jos 24:29). Used rarely in the earlier part of the Bible as an evaluation of a person's life, it became more common and was enhanced by Jesus (Jn 15:15), although Paul retained the title (Rm 1:1). **Joshua son of Nun, Moses's assistant**, identifies Joshua as the one who had been with Moses since Ex 17. "Assistant" (cp. Ex 24:13) translates a different term than "servant."
1:4 This **wilderness** is not the land of wandering. The term is used in 8:15,20 and 12:8 to describe the area east of Ai and the "desert" region of Judah in the south. It thus designates the southern part of the promised land. **Lebanon** ("white") refers to the mountains

north of Israel in the modern land of that name. The **land of the Hittites** seems to refer not to the Hittite Empire of modern Turkey but to the Egyptian and later Assyrian usage of this term to describe the region controlled by the Hittites in the western part of modern Syria. These lands and boundaries identify Canaan as it was known both to the Bible (Gn 10:19; Nm 13:17,21–22; 34:3–12) and to Egyptian writers of the second millennium BC.
1:5 This verse forms a hinge, concluding the previous sections of promises and introducing the next section of responsibilities. God's promise of his presence occurs again in 1:9 and thus provides an envelope to 1:6–9. All the responsibilities of these verses depend on God's presence that guarantees the mission's success.
1:6 God's command, **Be strong and courageous**, already spoken by Moses to Israel (Dt

31:6), appears three times here (Jos 1:7,9). The expression is used before great undertakings like David's charge to Solomon to build the temple (1Ch 28:20), King Hezekiah's encouragement to his subjects to withstand the enemy's siege (2Ch 32:7), and Joshua's own charge to Israel to fight (Jos 10:25).
1:7 The **whole instruction** (Hb *torah*) describes God's revelation in the form of the previous books of the law of Moses.
1:10 Joshua assumed leadership of the people. These **officers** were equivalent to "foremen" in Egypt (Ex 5:6–19). The title was used for judges and those with other responsibilities (Dt 1:15–18; 20:5–9). They formed a secular or civil counterpart to the priests.
1:11 The **provisions** and the **three days** recall the previous generation's crossing of the Red Sea where the people had no time

---

Character profile:

Joshua

After Moses's death the Hebrews needed a leader to take them into the promised land—someone who understood the enormity of the task and trusted the Lord. They needed Joshua, one of the twelve spies Moses had sent to scout the land of Canaan.

Ten of the spies warned Moses and the Israelites not to try to conquer the people who occupied the land, who were "giants" living in walled cities (see Jos 13:26–33). Joshua was not one of those faithless ten. He and Caleb urged the Israelites to attack immediately, as God had instructed, because God was on their side.

Unfortunately, the Israelites allowed their fears to get the best of them and refused to enter the land. As a result, they were forced to go back into the wilderness for forty years, until the faithless generation died.

Those four wasted decades in the wilderness had strengthened Joshua's resolve to trust God and to act immediately when an opportunity presented itself. And that made Joshua the kind of leader the Israelites needed.

When the time came for entering the promised land, Joshua embraced his responsibilities—not only as the commander of the people and the army but also as God's representative. He made sure the Israelites followed God's instructions precisely. And with great purposefulness, Joshua led the people across the Jordan River into the land God had promised their ancestors.

The Israelites, once too frightened to step foot in the land, prepared themselves to follow Joshua into battle and fight

for what was theirs. Their first destination was the walled city of Jericho.

God sent the commander of his heavenly army to meet Joshua just outside Jericho. He gave Joshua specific—and unusual—battle instructions. Once a day for six days the Israelites were to march around the perimeter of the city in complete silence. On the seventh day they were to march around it seven times. The seventh time around, seven priests were to blow trumpets and all the people were to shout.

Joshua followed the instructions carefully. When the trumpets sounded and the people shouted, the walls of Jericho collapsed, and the Israelites conquered the city and its inhabitants.

When Israel's early battles ended, Joshua oversaw the distribution of land to the various tribes of Israel. He parceled out real estate according to God's instructions, just as he had done with every other leadership responsibility he'd been given. The Israelites expected nothing less from the man who had led them into the promised land.

In his old age Joshua—and all of Israel—enjoyed a time of peace. Even today, Joshua is recognized as one of the greatest leaders in Jewish history.

Enormous tasks are accomplished—and lasting legacies are built—through individual acts of obedience. Joshua wasn't intimidated by the enormity of his responsibilities. He trusted God to lead him one step at a time.

When problems arose, Joshua addressed them immediately. When a victory was won, he gave praise to God and moved forward. He kept fighting the battles that needed to be fought until he had accomplished everything the Lord had set before him. In so doing he set an example for all Christian leaders.

for within three days you will be crossing the Jordan to go in and take possession of the land the LORD your God is giving you to inherit.' "

¹² Joshua said to the Reubenites, the Gadites, and half the tribe of Manasseh, ¹³ "Remember what Moses the LORD's servant commanded you when he said, 'The LORD your God will give you rest, and he will give you this land.' ¹⁴ Your wives, dependents, and livestock may remain in the land Moses gave you on this side of the Jordan. But your best soldiers must cross over in battle formationᴬ ahead of your brothers and help them ¹⁵ until the LORD gives your brothers rest, as he has given you, and they too possess the land the LORD your God is giving them. You may then return to the land of your inheritance and take possession of what Moses the LORD's servant gave you on the east side of the Jordan."

¹⁶ They answered Joshua, "Everything you have commanded us we will do, and everywhere you send us we will go. ¹⁷ We will obey you, just as we obeyed Moses in everything. Certainly the LORD your God will be with you, as he was with Moses. ¹⁸ Anyone who rebels against your order and does not obey your words in all that you command him, will be put to death. Above all, be strong and courageous!"

Spies Sent to Jericho

2 Joshua son of Nun secretly sent two men as spies from the Acacia Grove,ᴮ saying, "Go and scout the land, especially Jericho." So they left, and they came to the house of a prostitute named Rahab, and stayed there.

² The king of Jericho was told, "Look, some of the Israelite men have come here tonight to investigate the land." ³ Then the king of Jericho sent word to Rahab and said, "Bring out the men who came to you and entered your house, for they came to investigate the entire land."

⁴ But the woman had taken the two men and hidden them. So she said, "Yes, the men did come to me, but I didn't know where they were from. ⁵ At nightfall, when the city gate was about to close, the men went out, and I don't know where they were going. Chase after them quickly, and you can catch up with them!" ⁶ But she had taken them up to the roof and hidden them among the stalks of flax that she had arranged on the roof. ⁷ The men pursued them along the road to the fords of the Jordan, and as soon as they left to pursue them, the city gate was shut.

The Promise to Rahab

⁸ Before the men fell asleep, she went up on the roof ⁹ and said to them, "I know that the LORD has given you this land and that the terror of you has fallen on us, and everyone who lives in the land is panicking because of you.ᶜ ¹⁰ For we have heard how the LORD dried up the water of the Red Sea before you when you came out of Egypt, and what you did to Sihon and Og, the two Amorite kings you completely destroyed across the Jordan. ¹¹ When we heard this, we lost heart, and everyone's courage failedᴰ because of you, for the LORD your God is God in heaven above and on earth below. ¹² Now please swear to me by the LORD that you will also show kindness to my father's family, because I showed kindness to you. Give me a sure signᴱ ¹³ that you will spare the lives of my

ᴬ 1:14 Or over armed ᴮ 2:1 Or from Shittim ᶜ 2:9 Or land panics at your approach ᴰ 2:11 Lit and spirit no longer remained in anyone ᴱ 2:12 Or a sign of truth

for preparation and took unleavened bread (Ex 12–15). This time there will be sufficient time to prepare. The three days may also anticipate the length of time that the spies stayed west of the Jordan River (Jos 2:22). **1:13–15** Joshua quoted Moses's word from Dt 3:18–20. The Lord gave these tribes their land east of the Jordan River on the condition that they would follow their fellow tribes across the Jordan River and fight with them. Joshua emphasized the theme of **rest** and how, by crossing over **ahead of your brothers**, these warriors would be in a position to **help them**. These points emphasized the goal of rest for the land and people (11:23; 14:15) and the importance of all Israel working together to achieve the common goal. **1:16–18** This entire statement takes the form of an oath in which promises are made and a curse is invoked upon any who do not carry out their promises. The affirmation includes three phrases that include the words **everything . . . everywhere**, emphasizing the totality of obedience. The blessing they offered recognized that Joshua had indeed succeeded Moses. **2:1** The term for **spies** comes from the same word as *foot*. These "footers" did not always

work as spies. In 2Sm 15:10 they announced Absalom as king. Thus they could disseminate information as well as gather it. **Acacia Grove** translates Hebrew *Shittim*, probably a site some miles east of the Jordan River opposite Jericho, and Israel's camp since Nm 25:1. The Hebrew root for Joshua's command, **Go**, is identical to **they left**. Such a response indicates the spies' obedience. Nevertheless, they did not look over the land but went directly to Jericho. Rahab was an innkeeper and prostitute. The presence of an inn at Jericho (Lk 10:30–35) may be explained by its location on the north-south and east-west trade routes. Here the spies could learn about the land and also discover anyone who might be sympathetic. **2:4–5** Rahab denied knowledge about the origin and the destination of the spies. Thus she risked her life, but she also lied. Despite this, Heb 11:31 and Jms 2:25 admire her faith. Repeating information about the **city gate** (v. 7) is important because it explains how Rahab's ruse could make sense (the gates were not yet shut when the spies left). This second mention explains why the spies could no longer leave as they had entered. The shut gates represent the defiance of

Jericho, resistant to the movement of God and his people. **2:7** The phrase **the road to the fords of the Jordan** informs the reader of how Rahab's ruse worked. **2:8–11** Rahab's **I know** contrasts with her "I didn't know" in v. 4. There follows a true confession in place of the former deceit. The phrases **terror of you has fallen on us** and **the land is panicking** repeat the same expressions from Ex 15:15–16. Those predictions looked forward to reactions that Rahab described as having been fulfilled. This provides an envelope for the central confession of Rahab in v. 10. Her confession is based on the historic acts of God's redemption of Israel at the Red Sea and against Sihon and Og. **2:12 Show kindness** is a key expression that also appears when Abraham's servant requested from God direction to find a wife for Isaac (Gn 24:12). In the Decalogue God shows kindness to a thousand generations of those who are faithful to him (Ex 20:6). Here as well the concern is for the preservation of Rahab's family and her descendants. The **sure sign** is the spies' oath to protect Rahab's family. **2:13** Rahab did not ask for her own salvation, but for that of her family.

father, mother, brothers, sisters, and all who belong to them, and save us from death."

¹⁴ The men answered her, "We will give our lives for yours. If you don't report our mission, we will show kindness and faithfulness to you when the Lord gives us the land."

¹⁵ Then she let them down by a rope through the window, since she lived in a house that was built into the wall of the city. ¹⁶ "Go to the hill country so that the men pursuing you won't find you," she said to them. "Hide there for three days until they return; afterward, go on your way."

¹⁷ The men said to her, "We will be free from this oath you made us swear, ¹⁸ unless, when we enter the land, you tie this scarlet cord to the window through which you let us down. Bring your father, mother, brothers, and all your father's family into your house. ¹⁹ If anyone goes out the doors of your house, his death will be his own fault, and we will be innocent. But if anyone with you in the house should be harmed, his death will be our fault. ²⁰ And if you report our mission, we are free from the oath you made us swear."

²¹ "Let it be as you say," she replied, and she sent them away. After they had gone, she tied the scarlet cord to the window.

²² So the two men went into the hill country and stayed there three days until the pursuers had returned. They searched all along the way, but did not find them. ²³ Then the men returned, came down from the hill country, and crossed the Jordan. They went to Joshua son of Nun and reported everything that had happened to them. ²⁴ They told Joshua, "The Lord has handed over the entire land to us. Everyone who lives in the land is also panicking because of us."ᴬ

Crossing the Jordan

3 Joshua started early the next morning and left the Acacia Groveᴮ with all the Israelites. They went as far as the Jordan and stayed there before crossing. ² After three days the officers went through the camp ³ and commanded the people, "When you see the ark of the covenant of the Lord your God carried by the Levitical priests, you are to break camp and follow it. ⁴ But keep a distance of about a thousand yardsᶜ between yourselves and the ark. Don't go near it, so that you can see the way to go, for you haven't traveled this way before."

⁵ Joshua told the people, "Consecrate yourselves, because the Lord will do wonders among you tomorrow." ⁶ Then he said to the priests, "Carry the ark of the covenant and go on ahead of the people." So they carried the ark of the covenant and went ahead of them.

⁷ The Lord spoke to Joshua: "Today I will begin to exalt you in the sight of all Israel, so they will know that I will be with you just as I was with Moses. ⁸ Command the priests carrying the ark of the covenant: When you reach the edge of the water,ᴰ stand in the Jordan."

⁹ Then Joshua told the Israelites, "Come closer and listen to the words of the Lord your God." ¹⁰ He said, "You will know that the living God is among you and that he will certainly dispossess before you the Canaanites, Hethites, Hivites, Perizzites, Girgashites, Amorites, and Jebusites ¹¹ when the ark of covenant of the Lord of the whole earth goes ahead of you into the Jordan. ¹² Now choose twelve men from the tribes of Israel, one man

---

ᴬ2:24 Or *land also panics at our approach*   ᴮ3:1 Or *left Shittim*   ᶜ3:4 Lit *2,000 cubits*   ᴰ3:8 Lit *waters of the Jordan*

2:15 The actions described did not occur immediately. How secret would a mission be with the spies on the ground below shouting up to Rahab the negotiations of vv. 17–20? That **she let them down by a rope through the window** is a summary that introduces a more detailed description in vv. 16–21—a common technique in OT accounts.
2:16 The Jordan River was east of Jericho, but the steep hills that ascended from the Jordan Valley were to the west. The spies could hide there among the many caves and nooks.
2:17–20 The **scarlet cord** at the opening of her house with the family gathered inside is clearly symbolic of the Passover and its placement of blood on the door frames of the house in which the family was preserved from death (Ex 12:3–13).
2:24 The spies' report is a summary of what Rahab said, using her words (v. 9). This reiterates the fulfillment of prophecy (Ex 15:15) and the power of God to bring success to Israel.
3:1–4:24 These two chapters outline the ceremony of Israel's crossing of the Jordan River. This was not a casual activity but something specifically commanded by God.
3:1 Acacia Grove is the place where Israel had been since Balaam's failed attempt to

curse them (Nm 22:1; 25:1). This was some miles from the actual place where they crossed the Jordan River. In the south opposite Jericho, this meandering river was at that time surrounded by thickets, so it was not a place suitable for a stay of any length (Jr 12:5).
3:2–5 The **ark of the covenant** was the symbol of the presence of God among his people. The considerable distance of **a thousand yards** may suggest the need to remain away from the presence of God, especially as a miracle was happening. The command to **consecrate yourselves** recalls Ex 19:10–15, where consecration was defined as the washing of clothes and abstaining from sexual relations. This would allow God to work through the people to accomplish his **wonders**—a term that describes the plagues of Egypt in Ex 3:20 and more general acts in Ex 34:10.
3:6 Joshua's first instructions to the priests appear here.
3:7 God's promise of his presence with Joshua accompanied a promise to **exalt** Joshua as a seal on his leadership over Israel.
3:9 This is Joshua's first speech to the Israelites. His concern that they **come closer and**

listen suggests the importance of giving attention to God and his word.
3:10 This Hebrew phrase translated **living God** appears elsewhere only three times in the OT (Pss 42:2; 84:2; Hs 1:10). In Hos 1:10 it is used in the context of the fulfillment of God's promises of an innumerable people who belong to him. In Ps 42:2 and 84:2 it describes the deepest yearnings of the psalmist, who longed for the presence of God and intimacy with him. The concern for the presence of God and his fulfillment of his promises for his people are both present here. The **Canaanites, Hethites, Hivites, Perizzites, Girgashites, Amorites, and Jebusites** describe the pre-Israelite inhabitants of the land. *Canaanites* is a general term referring to those living in the land of Canaan, although it may also describe the indigenous peoples of the land.
3:11 The **Lord of the whole earth** uses a phrase identical to that charged against the spies in 2:3 ("the entire land").
3:12 The **twelve men** introduce a third group in addition to the people who will follow the ark and the priests who will carry it. The purpose of these men is explained in 4:2–3.

for each tribe. [13] When the feet[A] of the priests who carry the ark of the LORD, the Lord of the whole earth, come to rest in the Jordan's water, its water will be cut off. The water flowing downstream will stand up in a mass." [14] When the people broke camp to cross the Jordan, the priests carried the ark of the covenant ahead of the people. [15] Now the Jordan overflows its banks throughout the harvest season. But as soon as the priests carrying the ark reached the Jordan, their feet touched the water at its edge [16] and the water flowing downstream stood still, rising up in a mass that extended as far as[B] Adam, a city next to Zarethan. The water flowing downstream into the Sea of the Arabah — the Dead Sea — was completely cut off, and the people crossed opposite Jericho. [17] The priests carrying the ark of the LORD's covenant stood firmly on dry ground in the middle of the Jordan, while all Israel crossed on dry ground until the entire nation had finished crossing the Jordan.

The Memorial Stones

4 After the entire nation had finished crossing the Jordan, the LORD spoke to Joshua: [2] "Choose twelve men from the people, one man for each tribe, [3] and command them: Take twelve stones from this place in the middle of the Jordan where the priests[C] are standing, carry them with you, and set them down at the place where you spend the night." [4] So Joshua summoned the twelve men he had selected from the Israelites, one man for each tribe, [5] and said to them, "Go across to the ark of the LORD your God in the middle of the Jordan. Each of you lift a stone onto his shoulder, one for each of the Israelite tribes, [6] so that this will be a sign among you. In the future, when your children ask you, 'What do

these stones mean to you?' [7] you should tell them, 'The water of the Jordan was cut off in front of the ark of the LORD's covenant. When it crossed the Jordan, the Jordan's water was cut off.' Therefore these stones will always be a memorial for the Israelites."

[8] The Israelites did just as Joshua had commanded them. The twelve men took stones from the middle of the Jordan, one for each of the Israelite tribes, just as the LORD had told Joshua. They carried them to the camp and set them down there. [9] Joshua also set up twelve stones in the middle[D] of the Jordan where the priests who carried the ark of the covenant were standing. The stones are still there today. [10] The priests carrying the ark continued standing in the middle of the Jordan until everything was completed that the LORD had commanded Joshua to tell the people, in keeping with all that Moses had commanded Joshua. The people hurried across, [11] and after everyone had finished crossing, the priests with the ark of the LORD crossed in the sight of the people. [12] The Reubenites, Gadites, and half the tribe of Manasseh went in battle formation in front of the Israelites, as Moses had instructed them. [13] About forty thousand equipped for war crossed to the plains of Jericho in the LORD's presence.

[14] On that day the LORD exalted Joshua in the sight of all Israel, and they revered him throughout his life, as they had revered Moses. [15] The LORD told Joshua, [16] "Command the priests who carry the ark of the testimony to come up from the Jordan." [17] So Joshua commanded the priests, "Come up from the Jordan." [18] When the priests carrying the ark of the LORD's covenant came up from the middle of the Jordan, and their feet[E] stepped out on solid ground, the water of the

---

[A]3:13 Lit soles of the feet   [B]3:16 Alt Hb tradition reads mass at   [C]4:3 Lit feet of the priests, also in v. 9   [D]4:9 Or Now Joshua set up the twelve stones that had been in the middle   [E]4:18 Lit and the soles of the feet of the priests

---

3:13 The **mass** of the water is the same term as that used of the waters of the Red Sea in Ex 15:8 and Ps 78:13. God would act for his people when they crossed the Jordan River—just as he did with the previous generation at the exodus.
3:14–15 At spring flood, after the winter rains and during the barley harvest, the **Jordan** River could reach a width in excess of a hundred feet and a depth of ten feet.
3:16–17 The town of **Adam** is modern Tell ed-Damiye, about seventeen miles north of Jericho. **Zarethan** may be either three or eleven miles north of Adam, depending on which site it is identified with (Tell Umm Hamid or Tell es-Sa'idiyeh). Taking into account the distance from Adam to the **Dead Sea**, this means that approximately 29 percent of the Jordan Valley was affected.
4:1 The term **had finished** could also be interpreted as "were finishing," meaning the crossing and the events of vv. 1–5 overlapped.
4:2 These are the **twelve men** selected at 3:12.

4:3 The **twelve stones** represent the point of the crossing of the whole nation of Israel, all twelve tribes. This would enable future generations to understand and participate spiritually in the crossing that Joshua and the twelve tribes experienced.
4:6–7 The word translated **sign** occurs only two other times in Joshua (2:12; 24:17). The central focus is that the waters of the Jordan were **cut off** when **the ark of the LORD's covenant**, the presence of God, **crossed the Jordan**.
4:8–9 These verses allow for three readings. First, **Joshua** may have set up a separate pile of **stones** in the **middle of the Jordan**, which was probably visible during the dry season. Second, Joshua commanded **twelve men**, one from each tribe, to take a one hundred-pound stone from the middle of the Jordan and set up the twelve stones **in the camp**. Third, v. 9 might be retrospective—Joshua had set up twelve stones in the middle of the Jordan—and the twelve men subsequently picked up those same stones and **set them down** in the camp.

Still . . . today (lit "to this day") occurs in Joshua twelve times. It signifies the importance of remembering the past.
4:10 The phrase **in keeping with all that Moses had commanded Joshua** seems strange since such instructions about the crossing are unknown to us. The point is simply that Joshua was Moses's successor.
4:11 In the sight of the people is emphasized. Like the memorial, the witness of people was the means of preserving the remarkable event and the ceremony that surrounded it.
4:13 The troops that crossed entered enemy territory, but they also had established a foothold in the promised land when they arrived west of the Jordan River. This **forty thousand** represented the best portion of the Transjordanian fighting force that crossed with their kinsmen. According to Nm 26:7,18,34 the total of these two and a half tribes would have been over a hundred thousand. Perhaps the rest were protecting their land and families.

Jordan resumed its course, flowing over all the banks as before.

19 The people came up from the Jordan on the tenth day of the first month, and camped at Gilgal on the eastern limits of Jericho. **20** Then Joshua set up in Gilgal the twelve stones they had taken from the Jordan, **21** and he said to the Israelites, "In the future, when your children ask their fathers, 'What is the meaning of these stones?' **22** you should tell your children, 'Israel crossed the Jordan on dry ground.' **23** For the LORD your God dried up the water of the Jordan before you until you had crossed over, just as the LORD your God did to the Red Sea, which he dried up before us until we had crossed over. **24** This is so that all the peoples of the earth may know that the LORD's hand is strong, and so that you may always fear the LORD your God."

Circumcision of the Israelites

5 When all the Amorite kings across the Jordan to the west and all the Canaanite kings near the sea heard how the LORD had dried up the water of the Jordan before the Israelites until they had crossed over, they lost heart and their courage failed because of the Israelites.

2 At that time the LORD said to Joshua, "Make flint knives and circumcise the Israelite men again." **3** So Joshua made flint knives and circumcised the Israelite men at Gibeath-haaraloth.^A **4** This is the reason Joshua circumcised them: All the people who came out of Egypt who were males — all the men of war — had died in the wilderness along the way after they had come out of Egypt. **5** Though all the people who came out were circumcised, none of the people born in the wilderness along the way were circumcised after they had come out of Egypt. **6** For the Israelites wandered in the wilderness forty years until all the nation's men of war who came out of Egypt had died

off because they did not obey the LORD. So the LORD vowed never to let them see the land he had sworn to their ancestors to give us, a land flowing with milk and honey. **7** He raised up their sons in their place; it was these Joshua circumcised. They were still uncircumcised, since they had not been circumcised along the way. **8** After the entire nation had been circumcised, they stayed where they were in the camp until they recovered. **9** The LORD then said to Joshua, "Today I have rolled away the disgrace of Egypt from you." Therefore, that place is still called Gilgal^B today.

Food from the Land

10 While the Israelites camped at Gilgal on the plains of Jericho, they observed the Passover on the evening of the fourteenth day of the month. **11** The day after Passover they ate unleavened bread and roasted grain from the produce of the land. **12** And the day after they ate from the produce of the land, the manna ceased. Since there was no more manna for the Israelites, they ate from the crops of the land of Canaan that year.

Commander of the LORD's Army

13 When Joshua was near Jericho, he looked up and saw a man standing in front of him with a drawn sword in his hand. Joshua approached him and asked, "Are you for us or for our enemies?"

14 "Neither," he replied. "I have now come as commander of the LORD's army."

Then Joshua bowed with his face to the ground in homage and asked him, "What does my lord want to say to his servant?"

15 The commander of the LORD's army said to Joshua, "Remove the sandals from your feet, for the place where you are standing is holy." And Joshua did that.

^A 5:3 Or *The Hill of Foreskins*   ^B 5:9 = to roll

The Conquest of Jericho

6 Now Jericho was strongly fortified because of the Israelites — no one leaving or entering. ² The LORD said to Joshua, "Look, I have handed Jericho, its king, and its best soldiers over to you. ³ March around the city with all the men of war, circling the city one time. Do this for six days. ⁴ Have seven priests carry seven ram's-horn trumpets in front of the ark. But on the seventh day, march around the city seven times, while the priests blow the rams' horns. ⁵ When there is a prolonged blast of the horn and you hear its sound, have all the troops give a mighty shout. Then the city wall will collapse, and the troops will advance, each man straight ahead."

⁶ So Joshua son of Nun summoned the priests and said to them, "Take up the ark of the covenant and have seven priests carry seven rams' horns in front of the ark of the LORD." ⁷ He said to the troops, "Move forward, march around the city, and have the armed men go ahead of the ark of the LORD."

⁸ After Joshua had spoken to the troops, seven priests carrying seven rams' horns before the LORD moved forward and blew the rams' horns; the ark of the LORD's covenant followed them. ⁹ While the rams' horns were blowing, the armed men went in front of the priests who blew the rams' horns, and the rear guard went behind the ark. ¹⁰ But Joshua had commanded the troops, "Do not shout or let your voice be heard. Don't let one word come out of your mouth until the time I say, 'Shout!' Then you are to shout." ¹¹ So the ark of the LORD was carried around the city, circling it once. They returned to the camp and spent the night there.ᴬ

¹² Joshua got up early the next morning. The priests took the ark of the LORD, ¹³ and the seven priests carrying seven rams' horns marched in front of the ark of the LORD. While the rams' horns were blowing, the armed men went in front of them, and the rear guard went behind the ark of the LORD. ¹⁴ On the second day they

marched around the city once and returned to the camp. They did this for six days.

¹⁵ Early on the seventh day, they started at dawn and marched around the city seven times in the same way. That was the only day they marched around the city seven times. ¹⁶ After the seventh time, the priests blew the rams' horns, and Joshua said to the troops, "Shout! For the LORD has given you the city. ¹⁷ But the city and everything in it are set apart to the LORD for destruction. Only Rahab the prostitute and everyone with her in the house will live, because she hid the messengers we sent. ¹⁸ But keep yourselves from the things set apart, or you will be set apart for destruction. If youᴮ take any of those things, you will set apart the camp of Israel for destruction and make trouble for it. ¹⁹ For all the silver and gold, and the articles of bronze and iron, are dedicated to the LORD and must go into the LORD's treasury."

²⁰ So the troops shouted, and the rams' horns sounded. When they heard the blast of the ram's horn, the troops gave a great shout, and the wall collapsed. The troops advanced into the city, each man straight ahead, and they captured the city. ²¹ They completely destroyed everything in the city with the sword — every man and woman, both young and old, and every ox, sheep, and donkey.

Rahab and Her Family Spared

²² Joshua said to the two men who had scouted the land, "Go to the prostitute's house and bring the woman out of there, and all who are with her, just as you swore to her." ²³ So the young men who had scouted went in and brought out Rahab and her father, mother, brothers, and all who belonged to her. They brought out her whole family and settled them outside the camp of Israel.

²⁴ They burned the city and everything in it, but they put the silver and gold and the articles of bronze and iron into the treasury of the LORD's house. ²⁵ However, Joshua spared Rahab

---

ᴬ6:11 Lit at the camp   ᴮ6:18 LXX reads you covet and; Jos 7:21

6:1 As the gates of Jericho were shut in 2:7, so here the place is similarly described as **strongly fortified**, literally "very much shut." This describes the physical defense, but it also represents a resistance to the plans of God.
6:3–5 These instructions picture a unique ceremony. The ark symbolized the presence of God. The **ram's-horn trumpets** were used for going to war and for the ark (2Sm 6:15; Jr 4:19). The **mighty shout** was used for victory in war and for announcing the ark's journey (1Sm 4:5; 2Ch 13:15). The command to **march around the city** uses the same verb as appears in Ps 48:12 where a pilgrimage was made around Jerusalem to inspect its defenses. In 2Kg 6:14 the king of Aram surrounded Dothan to capture the prophet Elisha. Here at Jericho the march involved a ceremonial inspection of the fort's defenses to note the

obstinacy of Jericho and to provide an opportunity for those inside to surrender and open the gates.
The emphasis on **seven times** and seven days coincides with the Feast of Unleavened Bread celebrating God's defeat of the enemies of his people. At the first Passover, Israel marched out of Egypt during this feast. In Nm 9–10 the nation marched away from Mount Sinai during this feast. Here they would march into the promised land, and then around and through Jericho, **straight ahead**.
6:15 The **seventh day** was the number of perfection, and it signaled the conclusion of the Feast of Unleavened Bread.
6:16 The **shout** was a war cry.
6:17–25 This account of the destruction of Jericho is interwoven with that of the salvation of Rahab and her household (chap. 2).

6:17 Are set apart to the LORD for destruction is literally "is a devoted thing (*cherem*) to the LORD." Anything thus "devoted" must be either destroyed or placed in God's sanctuary.
6:19 The precious metals were assigned to the Lord's tabernacle treasury because these could not be destroyed by fire.
6:21 The list of people and animals here is not to provide an inventory of who was killed, but to emphasize the obedience of Joshua and the people. Verse 2 may suggest that, with the exception of Rahab and her family, the inhabitants of Jericho were military personnel.
6:25 The salvation of **Rahab** was defined as avoidance of death and as life among the people of God, Israel (Jdg 1:22–26). Rahab's uncleanness and therefore her residence outside the camp (Jos 6:23) was probably only temporary.

the prostitute, her father's family, and all who belonged to her, because she hid the messengers Joshua had sent to spy on Jericho, and she still lives in Israel today.

²⁶ At that time Joshua imposed this curse:

The man who undertakes
the rebuilding of this city, Jericho,
is cursed before the LORD.
He will lay its foundation
at the cost of his firstborn;
he will finish its gates
at the cost of his youngest.

²⁷ And the LORD was with Joshua, and his fame spread throughout the land.

Defeat at Ai

7 The Israelites, however, were unfaithful regarding the things set apart for destruction. Achan son of Carmi, son of Zabdi, son of Zerah, of the tribe of Judah, took some of what was set apart, and the LORD's anger burned against the Israelites.

² Joshua sent men from Jericho to Ai, which is near Beth-aven, east of Bethel, and told them, "Go up and scout the land." So the men went up and scouted Ai.

³ After returning to Joshua they reported to him, "Don't send all the people, but send about two thousand or three thousandᴬ men to attack Ai. Since the people of Ai are so few, don't wear out all our people there." ⁴ So about three thousand menᴮ went up there, but they fled from the men of Ai. ⁵ The men of Ai struck down about thirty-six of them and chased them from

outside the city gate to the quarries,ᶜ striking them down on the descent. As a result, the people lost heart.ᴰ

⁶ Then Joshua tore his clothes and fell facedown to the ground before the ark of the LORD until evening, as did the elders of Israel; they all put dust on their heads. ⁷ "Oh, Lord GOD," Joshua said, "why did you ever bring these people across the Jordan to hand us over to the Amorites for our destruction? If only we had been content to remain on the other side of the Jordan! ⁸ What can I say, Lord, now that Israel has turned its back and run from its enemies? ⁹ When the Canaanites and all who live in the land hear about this, they will surround us and wipe out our name from the earth. Then what will you do about your great name?"

¹⁰ The LORD then said to Joshua, "Stand up! Why have you fallen facedown? ¹¹ Israel has sinned. They have violated my covenant that I appointed for them. They have taken some of what was set apart. They have stolen, deceived, and put those things with their own belongings. ¹² This is why the Israelites cannot stand against their enemies. They will turn their backs and run from their enemies, because they have been set apart for destruction. I will no longer be with you unless you remove from among you what is set apart.

¹³ "Go and consecrate the people. Tell them to consecrate themselves for tomorrow, for this is what the LORD, the God of Israel, says: There are things that are set apart among you, Israel. You will not be able to stand against your enemies

---

ᴬ7:3 Or send two or three military units of   ᴮ7:4 Lit men from the people   ᶜ7:5 Or to Shebarim   ᴰ7:5 Lit people's hearts melted and became like water

---

6:26 The **curse** imposed by Joshua required that no construction take place on the mound of Jericho. It must remain in ruins as a witness to God's judgment upon the site for its resistance to God. The references to **foundation** and **gates** and the warning about the loss of the eldest (**firstborn**) and the **youngest** were fulfilled in 1Kg 16:34 when Hiel of Bethel rebuilt Jericho in the ninth century BC.
6:27 The **fame** of Joshua describes his renown at the victory over Jericho. Joshua's success at Jericho, his first battle, demonstrated that he was a powerful figure to be reckoned with.
7:1 Achan's unfaithfulness (in partaking of **what was set apart**—devoted to destruction at Jericho) resulted in God's anger against the entire nation. The genealogy of five generations, from **Achan** back to **the tribe of Judah**, is the longest in the book of Joshua and emphasizes the connection of Achan with one of the twelve tribes and therefore with the entire tribal nation. As much as Israel benefited by Joshua, it would suffer by Achan (Rm 5:12–21).
7:2 Joshua again sent spies before an assault, as in 2:1. **Ai**, like Jericho, may have been an outpost guarding **Beth-aven . . . Bethel**, and other towns in the central hill country. It lay on the central road from Jericho westward

into the hill country and therefore formed an obstacle to Israel's advance.
7:3 The report of these spies contrasts with that of chap. 2 and resembles that of Nm 13. Instead of confessing the promises and acts of God, these spies focused on the strategic details of what appeared to be an easy target. The **two . . . or three thousand men** may refer to two or three squads, as the same word for "thousand" in Hebrew (*'eleph*) also can mean a squad or company of soldiers. The particular form of the verb **wear out** occurs elsewhere only in Ec 3:10, where it describes a fool who does not know the way to town—an apt comment on Jos 7.
7:4–5 The **thirty-six** who died from the three thousand men or three squads (see note at v. 3) may reflect twelve from each squad and thus prefigure the twelve thousand inhabitants of Ai who would die (8:25). The **quarries** designate some of the steep ravines that break into the eastern hill country as it descends sharply into the Jordan Valley. In 2:11 and 5:1, the Canaanites "lost heart" (lit "their hearts melted"). The accomplishments of Israel and its God. Here the Israelites **lost heart**.
7:6 Joshua's actions were those of one in mourning. Only then was **the ark of the LORD** mentioned. Its absence in the opening part of the chapter signifies the absence of

God's presence and blessing on what happened.
7:7–8 The wish to remain east of the **Jordan** resembles the report of the first spies sent to Canaan in Nm 14:2–4. In Numbers it was a wish for death or a return to Egypt. Contrast God's promise that Israel's enemies would turn their backs and flee in Ex 23:27 with the fact that Israel had now **turned its back** ("the back of its neck") and fled.
7:9 The challenge to God's **great name** recalls Moses's intercession for Israel in the same argument in Nm 14:13–19.
7:10–11 Someone had **taken . . . what was set apart**. This violated the general command of Dt 20:16–18 and the specific command of Jos 6:17. By putting these things **with their own belongings**, they had made it impossible to determine the guilty person without divine guidance.
7:12 Here God suggested that so long as the things devoted for destruction remained in Israel's camp, Israel would be **set apart for destruction**. God would not fight for them or be present with them as he had in 1:5–9.
7:13 For Israel **to consecrate themselves** suggests either that they would examine themselves and their families to learn who was responsible for the sin, or that they would prepare themselves for an encounter with God the next day.

until you remove what is set apart. [14] In the morning, present yourselves tribe by tribe. The tribe the LORD selects is to come forward clan by clan. The clan the LORD selects is to come forward family by family. The family the LORD selects is to come forward man by man. [15] The one who is caught with the things set apart must be burned, along with everything he has, because he has violated the LORD's covenant and committed an outrage in Israel."

Achan Judged

[16] Joshua got up early the next morning. He had Israel come forward tribe by tribe, and the tribe of Judah was selected. [17] He had the clans of Judah come forward, and the Zerahite clan was selected. He had the Zerahite clan come forward by heads of families,[A] and Zabdi was selected. [18] He then had Zabdi's family come forward man by man, and Achan son of Carmi, son of Zabdi, son of Zerah, of the tribe of Judah, was selected.

[19] So Joshua said to Achan, "My son, give glory to the LORD, the God of Israel, and make a confession to him.[B] I urge you, tell me what you have done. Don't hide anything from me." [20] Achan replied to Joshua, "It is true. I have sinned against the LORD, the God of Israel. This is what I did: [21] When I saw among the spoils a beautiful cloak from Babylon,[C] five pounds[D] of silver, and a bar of gold weighing a pound and a quarter,[E] I coveted them and took them. You can see for yourself. They are concealed in the ground inside my tent, with the silver under the cloak." [22] So Joshua sent messengers who ran to the tent, and there was the cloak, concealed in his tent, with the silver underneath. [23] They took the things from inside the tent, brought them to Joshua and all the Israelites, and spread them out in the LORD's presence.

[24] Then Joshua and all Israel with him took Achan son of Zerah, the silver, the cloak, and the bar of gold, his sons and daughters, his ox, donkey, and sheep, his tent, and all that he had, and brought them up to the Valley of Achor. [25] Joshua said, "Why have you brought us trouble? Today the LORD will bring you trouble!" So all Israel stoned them[F] to death. They burned their bodies, threw stones on them, [26] and raised over him a large pile of rocks that remains still today. Then the LORD turned from his burning anger. Therefore that place is called the Valley of Achor[G] still today.

Conquest of Ai

8 The LORD said to Joshua, "Do not be afraid or discouraged. Take all the troops with you and go attack Ai. Look, I have handed over to you the king of Ai, his people, city, and land. [2] Treat Ai and its king as you did Jericho and its king, except that you may plunder its spoil and livestock for yourselves. Set an ambush behind the city."

[3] So Joshua and all the troops set out to attack Ai. Joshua selected thirty thousand of his best soldiers and sent them out at night. [4] He commanded them, "Pay attention. Lie in ambush behind the city, not too far from it, and all of you be ready. [5] Then I and all the people who are with me will approach the city. When they come out against us as they did the first time, we will flee from them. [6] They will come after us until we have drawn them away from the city, for they will say, 'They are fleeing from us as before.' While we are fleeing from them, [7] you are to come out of your ambush and seize the city. The LORD your God will hand it over to you. [8] After taking the city, set it on fire. Follow the LORD's command — see that you do as I have ordered you." [9] So Joshua sent them out, and they went to the ambush site and waited

---

[A]7:17 Lit forward man by man [B]7:19 Or and praise him [C]7:21 Lit Shinar [D]7:21 Lit 200 shekels [E]7:21 Lit 50 shekels [F]7:25 Lit him [G]7:26 Or of Trouble

---

7:14 The tribe . . . clan, and family were the basic elements of Israelite society, which can be understood in terms of a greatly extended family. Each larger group would come before God, and he would select the subgroup of the larger group component.
7:15 The verdict that the guilty one must be burned recalls the burning of the devoted things at Jericho (and the town itself) in 6:24, and it fulfills the command to devote the guilty one to God (Dt 13:15–16).
7:16–18 The text does not describe how each group was selected.
7:20–21 Achan's confession, with the emphasis on what he saw and how it was beautiful, recalls Eve's temptation where she also saw something that was pleasing. Achan coveted them and thus violated the tenth commandment of the Decalogue (Ex 20:17; Dt 5:21). The words of Achan's admission are recorded because this was necessary for the sin to be dealt with.

7:24–26 The destruction of Achan with all his family and possessions contrasts with the salvation of Rahab and all her family in chap. 6. The connection of the family with its representative, for good or for ill, illustrates the key value of the family in the OT.
7:25 The references to trouble involve a wordplay on the name of the Valley of Achor. The same root word is used for this verb and for the name of the valley. The description suggests that first all Israel stoned Achan and his family, and then they burned their corpses, thereby fulfilling the law.
7:26 The large pile of rocks raised over Achan uses the Hebrew word gal, which recalls Gilgal where a pile of rocks had also been raised as a memorial (4:20). God's burning anger appeared at the worship of the gold calf (Ex 32:11–12) and at the sin at Baal-peor (Nm 25:4).
8:1 God's words do not be afraid or discouraged recall his first charge to Joshua, where they set the stage for his promise of presence

and for the miracles that followed (1:9). With all the troops, Israel would again be united (unlike 7:3) and thus their victory was more likely. As with the promise about Jericho (6:2), God's instructions to Joshua began with the promise that victory was already assured.
8:2 As with Jericho (6:21), all the people of Ai were to be destroyed. However, here it was possible for Israel to keep the livestock for their own use. The use of an ambush is a strategy known in the ancient Near East and used more than once in Israel's history (Jdg 9; 20).
8:3 Joshua sent the army out at night so they would not be detected easily.
8:4,9 Given the traditional locations of Ai and Bethel (7:2), there is a ravine between them, west of Ai, in which it would be possible for troops to hide and escape notice from either town.
8:9–13 The positions of Joshua's forces were far from the road from which they would be expected to approach. Coming from

between Bethel and Ai, to the west of Ai. But he spent that night with the troops. **10** Joshua started early the next morning and mobilized them. Then he and the elders of Israel led the people up to Ai. **11** All the troops who were with him went up and approached the city, arriving opposite Ai, and camped to the north of it, with a valley between them and the city. **12** Now Joshua had taken about five thousand men and set them in ambush between Bethel and Ai, to the west of the city. **13** The troops were stationed in this way: the main^ camp to the north of the city and its rear guard to the west of the city. And that night Joshua went into the valley.

14 When the king of Ai saw the Israelites, the men of the city hurried and went out early in the morning so that he and all his people could engage Israel in battle at a suitable place facing the Arabah. But he did not know there was an ambush waiting for him behind the city. **15** Joshua and all Israel pretended to be beaten back by them and fled toward the wilderness. **16** Then all the troops of Ai were summoned to pursue them, and they pursued Joshua and were drawn away from the city. **17** Not a man was left in Ai or Bethel who did not go out after Israel, leaving the city exposed while they pursued Israel.

18 Then the LORD said to Joshua, "Hold out the javelin in your hand toward Ai, for I will hand the city over to you." So Joshua held out his javelin toward it. **19** When he held out his hand, the men in ambush rose quickly from their position. They ran, entered the city, captured it, and immediately set it on fire.

20 The men of Ai turned and looked back, and smoke from the city was rising to the sky! They could not escape in any direction, and the troops who had fled to the wilderness now became the pursuers. **21** When Joshua and all Israel saw that the men in ambush had captured the city and that smoke was rising from it, they turned back and struck down the men of Ai. **22** Then men in ambush came out of the city against them, and the men of Ai were trapped between the Israelite forces, some on one side and some on the other. They struck them down until no survivor or fugitive remained, **23** but they

captured the king of Ai alive and brought him to Joshua.

24 When Israel had finished killing everyone living in Ai who had pursued them into the open country, and when every last one of them had fallen by the sword, all Israel returned to Ai and struck it down with the sword. **25** The total of those who fell that day, both men and women, was twelve thousand — all the people of Ai. **26** Joshua did not draw back his hand that was holding the javelin until all the inhabitants of Ai were completely destroyed. **27** Israel plundered only the cattle and spoil of that city for themselves, according to the LORD's command that he had given Joshua.

28 Joshua burned Ai and left it a permanent ruin, still desolate today. **29** He hung^ the body of the king of Ai on a tree^ until evening, and at sunset Joshua commanded that they take his body down from the tree. They threw it down at the entrance of the city gate and put a large pile of rocks over it, which still remains today.

Renewed Commitment to the Law

30 At that time Joshua built an altar on Mount Ebal to the LORD, the God of Israel, **31** just as Moses the LORD's servant had commanded the Israelites. He built it according to what is written in the book of the law of Moses: an altar of uncut stones on which no iron tool has been used. Then they offered burnt offerings to the LORD and sacrificed fellowship offerings on it. **32** There on the stones, Joshua copied the law of Moses, which he had written in the presence of the Israelites. **33** All Israel — resident alien and citizen alike — with their elders, officers, and judges, stood on either side of the ark of the LORD's covenant facing the Levitical priests who carried it. Half of them were in front of Mount Gerizim and half in front of Mount Ebal, as Moses the LORD's servant had commanded earlier concerning the people of Israel. **34** Afterward, Joshua read aloud all the words of the law — the blessings as well as the curses — according to all that is written in the book of the law. **35** There was not a word of all that Moses had commanded that Joshua did not read before the entire assembly of Israel, including the women, the dependents, and the resident aliens who lived among them.

---

^8:13 Lit *way: all the* ^8:29 Or *impaled* ^8:29 Or *wooden stake*

west of Ai provided an additional element of surprise.
8:14–17 The ruse worked as Ai was emptied of its inhabitants. The attack took place **early in the morning** when the advantage would be with Israel's main force because the rising sun would blind the army of Ai as they pursued Joshua's forces eastward.
8:20–22 As the main body of Israel turned west toward the pursuing army of **Ai**, the warriors of the city were driven back. At that point they saw Ai ablaze and found the ambush moving east **out of the city** and

blocking their retreat. Caught between the two forces and despairing at the destruction of their defenses, they were easily defeated, and their army was destroyed.
8:28 The word **Ai** (pronounced like *eye*) means "ruin." Like Jericho, this defeated city would be a memorial to Israel's victory.
8:30–31 Joshua's construction of **an altar on Mount Ebal**, north of Shechem, was a fulfillment of what **Moses ... had commanded** in Dt 27:5. The **burnt offerings** and **fellowship offerings** were the same offerings required in the first law of the altar in Ex 20:24 and

in instructions for this gathering on Mount Ebal in Dt 27:6–7.
8:32 Joshua's copying of **the law of Moses** was commanded in Dt 27:3. It resembled the actions of the king who had to make his own copy of the law (Dt 17:18).
8:33 In Dt 27:12–13 half of Israel was to stand **in front of Mount Gerizim** and half **in front of Mount Ebal** in order to pronounce the blessings and curses for obeying or disobeying the covenant. This account in Joshua included the **resident alien** as well as the **citizen**; thus, the entire nation and all who

Deception by Gibeon

9 When all the kings heard about Jericho and Ai, those who were west of the Jordan in the hill country, in the Judean foothills,^A and all along the coast of the Mediterranean Sea toward Lebanon — the Hethites, Amorites, Canaanites, Perizzites, Hivites, and Jebusites — ² they formed a unified alliance to fight against Joshua and Israel.

³ When the inhabitants of Gibeon heard what Joshua had done to Jericho and Ai, ⁴ they acted deceptively. They gathered provisions^B and took worn-out sacks on their donkeys and old wineskins, cracked and mended. ⁵ They wore old, patched sandals on their feet and threadbare clothing on their bodies. Their entire provision of bread was dry and crumbly. ⁶ They went to Joshua in the camp at Gilgal and said to him and the men of Israel, "We have come from a distant land. Please make a treaty with us."

⁷ The men of Israel replied to the Hivites, "Perhaps you live among us. How can we make a treaty with you?"

⁸ They said to Joshua, "We are your servants." Then Joshua asked them, "Who are you and where do you come from?"

⁹ They replied to him, "Your servants have come from a faraway land because of the reputation of the LORD your God. For we have heard of his fame, and all that he did in Egypt, ¹⁰ and all that he did to the two Amorite kings beyond the Jordan — King Sihon of Heshbon and King Og of Bashan, who was in Ashtaroth. ¹¹ So our elders and all the inhabitants of our land told us, 'Take provisions with you for the journey; go and meet them and say, "We are your servants. Please make a treaty with us."' ¹² This bread of ours was warm when we took it from our houses as food on the day we left to come to you; but see, it is now dry and crumbly. ¹³ These wineskins were new when we filled them; but see, they are cracked. And these clothes and sandals of ours are worn out from the extremely long journey." ¹⁴ Then the men of Israel took some of their provisions, but did not seek the LORD's decision. ¹⁵ So Joshua established peace with them and made a treaty to let them live, and the leaders of the community swore an oath to them.

Gibeon's Deception Discovered

¹⁶ Three days after making the treaty with them, they heard that the Gibeonites were their neighbors, living among them. ¹⁷ So the Israelites set out and reached the Gibeonite cities on the third day. Now their cities were Gibeon, Chephirah, Beeroth, and Kiriath-jearim. ¹⁸ But the Israelites did not attack them, because the leaders of the community had sworn an oath to them by the LORD, the God of Israel. Then the whole community grumbled against the leaders.

¹⁹ All the leaders answered them, "We have sworn an oath to them by the LORD, the God of Israel, and now we cannot touch them. ²⁰ This is how we will treat them: we will let them live, so that no wrath will fall on us because of the oath we swore to them." ²¹ They also said, "Let them live." So the Gibeonites became woodcutters and water carriers for the whole community, as the leaders had promised them.

²² Joshua summoned the Gibeonites and said to them, "Why did you deceive us by telling us you live far away from us, when in fact you live among us? ²³ Therefore you are cursed and will always be slaves — woodcutters and water carriers for the house of my God."

²⁴ The Gibeonites answered him, "It was clearly communicated to your servants that

---

^A 9:1 Or the Shephelah   ^B 9:4 Some Hb mss, LXX, Syr, Vg; other Hb mss read They went disguised as ambassadors

---

lived with Israel were present and standing around **the ark of the LORD's covenant**.
9:1–2 The phrase **when all the kings heard** is identical to that in 5:1. There the kings heard about God's drying up the Jordan River, and it struck fear in their hearts. In 9:1 the text does not specify what the kings heard, but their reaction is different. Instead of fearing Israel, **they formed a unified alliance** to fight against the nation. What caused this change? It was the defeat of Israel at Ai that gave the Canaanites hope that they could defeat the people of God.
9:3 The **inhabitants of Gibeon** reacted differently, however. They did not seek to destroy Israel but to join it.
9:4–5 Because Israel had been commanded to destroy all peoples in Canaan (Dt 20:16–18), Gibeon wanted it to look like they did not live nearby.
9:6 Gilgal here may be different from the Gilgal of 4:19–20 and 5:9–10. It was probably located in the hill country, perhaps near Mount Ebal. Gibeon was a city north of Jerusalem in the territory of the tribe of Benjamin, a few hours journey by foot. The word for **treaty** (Hb berith) is the same as

that for "covenant"; it recalls the experience of Joshua and the Israelites at Mount Ebal (8:30–35).
9:7 The connection of Gibeon with **the Hivites** implies that this group may have been a recent addition to the region, coming originally from north of Palestine in Syria.
9:8 The self-designation by the Gibeonites as Israel's **servants** implies that they accepted a relationship of a vassal nation to the people of God.
9:9–10 The confession of the Gibeonites most closely resembles that of Rahab in 2:9–11. Their expression of faith in God was based on God's historic acts of redemption toward his people. The Gibeonites mentioned the same acts of redemption as Rahab did—the work of God **in Egypt** and against **Sihon** and **Og**.
9:11 The governance of Gibeon by **elders** rather than a king implies a different form of rule than what was common in Canaan at the time, and this may have been part of the deception.
9:14 The note that Israel **did not seek the LORD's decision**, as well as absence of any mention of Joshua in the initial negotiations, all spell trouble.

9:15 That **Joshua established peace** with the Gibeonites demonstrates his own complicity in the actions. The reference to "peace" and the swearing of **an oath** by **the leaders of the community** bound Israel into a treaty relationship with the Gibeonites that could not be broken.
9:16 The phrase **three days** may suggest a literal three days such as seems to occur in 1:11; 2:16,22, or it may imply an indeterminate period of more than a second day.
9:17 Having discovered the ruse of the Gibeonites, the Israelites set out **on the third day** and reached the Gibeonite cities on that same day. Like Gibeon, **Chephirah, Beeroth, and Kiriath-jearim** lie a few miles north of Jerusalem and are close by one another in the territory that would later be assigned to the tribe of Benjamin.
9:21 Deuteronomy 29:11 implied that aliens living in the land of Israel should fulfill the roles of **woodcutters and water carriers**.
9:24–26 How the Gibeonites knew of God's promise is not known (Ex 32:13; Dt 11:25; 19:8), but Rahab also had such knowledge (Jos 2:9). That the Gibeonites became Israel's **servants** meant that they were responsible to

the LORD your God had commanded his servant Moses to give you all the land and to destroy all the inhabitants of the land before you. We greatly feared for our lives because of you, and that is why we did this. **25** Now we are in your hands. Do to us whatever you think is right." **26** This is what Joshua did to them: he rescued them from the Israelites, and they did not kill them. **27** On that day he made them woodcutters and water carriers — as they are today — for the community and for the LORD's altar at the place he would choose.

The Day the Sun Stood Still

10 Now King Adoni-zedek of Jerusalem heard that Joshua had captured Ai and completely destroyed it, treating Ai and its king as he had Jericho and its king, and that the inhabitants of Gibeon had made peace with Israel and were living among them. **2** So Adoni-zedek and his people were^A greatly alarmed because Gibeon was a large city like one of the royal cities; it was larger than Ai, and all its men were warriors. **3** Therefore King Adoni-zedek of Jerusalem sent word to King Hoham of Hebron, King Piram of Jarmuth, King Japhia of Lachish, and King Debir of Eglon, saying, **4** "Come up and help me. We will attack Gibeon, because they have made peace with Joshua and the Israelites." **5** So the five Amorite kings — the kings of Jerusalem, Hebron, Jarmuth, Lachish, and Eglon — joined forces, advanced with all their armies, besieged Gibeon, and fought against it.

6 Then the men of Gibeon sent word to Joshua in the camp at Gilgal: "Don't give up on your servants. Come quickly and save us! Help us, for all the Amorite kings living in the hill country have joined forces against us." **7** So Joshua and all his troops, including all his best soldiers, came from Gilgal.

8 The LORD said to Joshua, "Do not be afraid of them, for I have handed them over to you. Not one of them will be able to stand against you." **9** So Joshua caught them by surprise, after marching all night from Gilgal. **10** The LORD threw them into confusion before Israel. He defeated them in a great slaughter at Gibeon, chased them through the ascent of Beth-horon, and struck them down as far as Azekah and Makkedah. **11** As they fled before Israel, the LORD threw large hailstones on them from the sky along the descent of Beth-horon all the way to Azekah, and they died. More of them died from the hail than the Israelites killed with the sword.

12 On the day the LORD gave the Amorites over to the Israelites, Joshua spoke to the LORD in the presence of Israel:

"Sun, stand still over Gibeon,
and moon, over the Valley of Aijalon."
13 And the sun stood still
and the moon stopped
until the nation took vengeance
on its enemies.

Isn't this written in the Book of Jashar?^B
So the sun stopped
in the middle of the sky

^A**10:2** One Hb ms, Syr, Vg read *So he was* ^B**10:13** Or *of the Upright*

Israel and that Israel was also responsible for Gibeon. Note Gibeon's appeal to **whatever you think is right** (lit "as is good and as is right in your eyes") is the same appeal Jeremiah uses in Jr 26:14–15. Apparently the animosity between Israel and Gibeon continued into Saul's day (2Sm 21:1–9).
10:1 King Adoni-zedek of Jerusalem was the leader of the key city in the region of the Gibeonites. The name may mean "my lord is righteous." The second element of the name, (Hb) *tsedeq*, also occurs with Melchizedek king of (Jeru-)Salem in Gn 14. Some have suggested here a dynastic name that is used of the leader of Jerusalem in succeeding generations.
10:2 Adoni-zedek had heard about Joshua's victory against Ai, and he and **his people were greatly alarmed**. This suggests that things had returned to what they were in 5:1, where all the Canaanites were fearful of Israel. Gibeon lay immediately north of Jerusalem, dominating the plateau and providing key strategic routes to the coastal plain on the west and to the Jordan Valley on the east. Gibeon's defection threatened Jerusalem's trade and contact with the north as well as the west and east. If all the men of Gibeon were **warriors**, this suggests a warlike town whose sole reason for being was to wage war and collect tribute from defeated enemies. If Gibeon joined Israel's side, it could no longer be counted upon to remain loyal to Jerusalem, thus posing a threat.

10:3 The towns **Hebron . . . Lachish**, and **Eglon** formed a line of towns south of Jerusalem and across the entire Judean hill country and desert. The town of **Jarmuth**, probably identified with modern Tel Yarmut, lay to the east of Jerusalem between the Sorek and Elah Valleys that stretched east-west and formed major access routes between the coastal plain and the area of Jerusalem.
10:4–5 Verse 4 recalls the only Canaanite correspondence between Canaanite kings in the Bible. The need to attack Gibeon was based on their peace treaty with Israel.
10:6 Gibeon's appeal to Joshua and the Israelites was based on their peace treaty of 9:15. This agreement, while requiring Gibeonites to serve Israel, also assumed that Gibeon would be protected from its enemies by the stronger party, Israel. Such was a common arrangement for suzerain-vassal treaties in the ancient Near East.
10:7–43 This section describes the battle by using a series of perspectives. There is often a summary description, such as here in vv. 7–10, followed by more details in the text. The work of God, as Israel's leader in war, is described first (vv. 11–15). Then there is consideration of the leaders of the enemy coalition (vv. 16–27) and details of battles with the towns in the southern coalition (vv. 28–40). Finally, there is a summary and a note on Israel's return to camp.
10:10 As at the victory against Egypt at the exodus (Ex 14:24), God **threw them**

into confusion before Israel. This tactic is characteristic of God's warfare against his enemies. God was responsible for **a great slaughter at Gibeon**. He chased the survivors westward through the pass of **Beth-horon**, the major access route for armies between the plateau of Gibeon and the coastal plain. As they fled westward they would reach **Azekah**, a site not far from Jarmuth, the hometown of one of the enemy armies. The site of **Makkedah** (modern Khirbet el-Qom) was close to Hebron, Lachish, and Eglon. Thus the two places represent the final stand of the enemy armies against Israel's God. Close to their homes, with their backs against the wall, they had nowhere to go.
10:12 Some argue that Joshua in his prayer addressed the **sun** and **moon** as deities. This is unlikely in context because in the three previous communications in the chapter (vv. 4, 6, and 8), the addressee is never named in the message itself, but only in the introduction. The same is true here. Instead of addressing the sun and moon as deities, Joshua addressed God and then was given the authority to command the sun and moon. The pass of Beth-horon leads westward into the **Valley of Aijalon**. It was here that Joshua wished to continue or otherwise to succeed in the battle.
10:13 Here is the confirmation of the preceding verse. Miraculously, the **sun** and **moon** ceased in their course across the sky. This enabled Israel to complete its destruction

and delayed its setting almost a full day. [14] There has been no day like it before or since, when the LORD listened to a man, because the LORD fought for Israel. [15] Then Joshua and all Israel with him returned to the camp at Gilgal.

Execution of the Five Kings

[16] Now the five defeated kings had fled and hidden in the cave at Makkedah. [17] It was reported to Joshua, "The five kings have been found; they are hiding in the cave at Makkedah." [18] Joshua said, "Roll large stones against the mouth of the cave, and station men by it to guard the kings. [19] But as for the rest of you, don't stay there. Pursue your enemies and attack them from behind. Don't let them enter their cities, for the LORD your God has handed them over to you." [20] So Joshua and the Israelites finished inflicting a terrible slaughter on them until they were destroyed, although a few survivors ran away to the fortified cities. [21] The people returned safely to Joshua in the camp at Makkedah. And no one dared to threaten the Israelites.

[22] Then Joshua said, "Open the mouth of the cave, and bring those five kings to me out of there." [23] That is what they did. They brought the five kings of Jerusalem, Hebron, Jarmuth, Lachish, and Eglon to Joshua out of the cave. [24] When they had brought the kings to him, Joshua summoned all the men of Israel and said to the military commanders who had accompanied him, "Come here and put your feet on the necks of these kings." So the commanders came forward and put their feet on their necks. [25] Joshua said to them, "Do not be afraid or discouraged. Be strong and courageous, for the LORD will do this to all the enemies you fight."

[26] After this, Joshua struck them down and executed them. He hung[A] their bodies on five trees[B] and they were there until evening. [27] At sunset Joshua commanded that they be taken down from the trees and thrown into the cave where they had hidden. Then large stones were placed against the mouth of the cave, and the stones are still there today.

Conquest of Southern Cities

[28] On that day Joshua captured Makkedah and struck it down with the sword, including its king. He completely destroyed it[C] and everyone in it, leaving no survivors. So he treated the king of Makkedah as he had the king of Jericho.

[29] Joshua and all Israel with him crossed from Makkedah to Libnah and fought against Libnah. [30] The LORD also handed it and its king over to Israel. He struck it down, putting everyone in it to the sword, and left no survivors in it. He treated Libnah's king as he had the king of Jericho.

[31] From Libnah, Joshua and all Israel with him crossed to Lachish. They laid siege to it and attacked it. [32] The LORD handed Lachish over to Israel, and Joshua captured it on the second day. He struck it down, putting everyone in it to the sword, just as he had done to Libnah. [33] At that time King Horam of Gezer went to help Lachish, but Joshua struck him down along with his people, leaving no survivors.

[34] Then Joshua crossed from Lachish to Eglon and all Israel with him. They laid siege to it and attacked it. [35] On that day they captured it and struck it down, putting everyone in it to the sword. He completely destroyed it that day, just as he had done to Lachish.

[36] Next, Joshua and all Israel with him went up from Eglon to Hebron and attacked it. [37] They captured it and struck down its king, all its villages, and everyone in it with the sword. He left no survivors, just as he had done at Eglon. He completely destroyed Hebron and everyone in it.

[38] Finally, Joshua turned toward Debir and attacked it. And all Israel was with him. [39] He captured it — its king and all its villages. They struck them down with the sword and completely destroyed everyone in it, leaving no survivors. He treated Debir and its king as he had treated Hebron and as he had treated Libnah and its king.

[40] So Joshua conquered the whole region — the hill country, the Negev, the Judean foothills,[D] and the slopes — with all their kings, leaving no survivors. He completely destroyed every living being, as the LORD, the God of

---

[A]10:26 Or *impaled*   [B]10:26 Or *wooden stakes*, also in v. 27   [C]10:28 Some Hb mss read *them*   [D]10:40 Or *the Shephelah*

---

of the enemy. The **Book of Jashar** is also mentioned in 2Sm 1:18, where it introduces David's eulogy for Saul and Jonathan.
10:14 Verses 11–14 summarize how **the LORD fought for Israel**. God's part in the miracle was of primary significance. Had he not fought, Israel would not have won. Because he fought, Israel could not lose and needed only to follow up on the victory. The wording here, **listened to a man** ("to the voice of a man") is used with God as the subject elsewhere only in Nm 21:3 and 1Kg 17:22.
10:17–21 When Joshua learned where the kings were hiding, he put a guard on the cave and ordered the army to continue pursuing

the enemy so they could not escape to their fortified centers. The note that **a few survivors ran away to the fortified cities** anticipates vv. 28–42 and the destruction of the various fortified centers.
10:24 The act of the **military commanders** placing their **feet on the necks of these kings** signified the subjugation of the kings and their rule to the army of Israel (Jr 28:14; 30:8; Ezk 21:29).
10:26–27 Joshua's actions toward the kings duplicate those toward the king of Ai (8:29) with execution, hanging on **trees** until sunset, and then "burial" in a **cave** with a pile of **stones** to mark the site.

10:33 Gezer was not attacked but is mentioned as providing an army to fight against Israel at **Lachish**. The city of Lachish was strategically located. Egyptian inscriptions show that it was probably the base for Egypt's empire in southern Canaan. Its defeat would have been among the most important events of Joshua's entire southern campaign.
10:40 A summary of the victories by region is presented in this verse. The effect is to describe a complete destruction **leaving no survivors**. This is a stylized, hyperbolic statement celebrating the victorious southern campaign. The reality, however, is that many

Israel, had commanded. ⁴¹ Joshua conquered everyone from Kadesh-barnea to Gaza, and all the land of Goshen as far as Gibeon. ⁴² Joshua captured all these kings and their land in one campaign, because the LORD, the God of Israel, fought for Israel. ⁴³ Then Joshua returned with all Israel to the camp at Gilgal.

Conquest of Northern Cities

11 When King Jabin of Hazor heard this news, he sent a message to: King Jobab of Madon, the kings of Shimron and Achshaph, ² and the kings of the north in the hill country, the Arabah south of Chinnereth, the Judean foothills,^ and the Slopes of Dor^B to the west, ³ the Canaanites in the east and west, the Amorites, Hethites, Perizzites, and Jebusites in the hill country, and the Hivites at the foot of Hermon in the land of Mizpah. ⁴ They went out with all their armies — a multitude as numerous as the sand on the seashore — along with a vast number of horses and chariots. ⁵ All these kings joined forces; they came and camped together at the Waters of Merom to attack Israel.

⁶ The LORD said to Joshua, "Do not be afraid of them, for at this time tomorrow I will cause all of them to be killed before Israel. You are to hamstring their horses and burn their chariots." ⁷ So Joshua and all his troops surprised them at the Waters of Merom and attacked

them. ⁸ The LORD handed them over to Israel, and they struck them down, pursuing them as far as greater Sidon and Misrephoth-maim, and to the east as far as the Valley of Mizpeh. They struck them down, leaving no survivors. ⁹ Joshua treated them as the LORD had told him; he hamstrung their horses and burned their chariots.

¹⁰ At that time Joshua turned back, captured Hazor, and struck down its king with the sword, because Hazor had formerly been the leader of all these kingdoms. ¹¹ They struck down everyone in it with the sword, completely destroying them; he left no one alive. Then he burned Hazor.

¹² Joshua captured all these kings and their cities and struck them down with the sword. He completely destroyed them, as Moses the LORD's servant had commanded. ¹³ However, Israel did not burn any of the cities that stood on their mounds except Hazor, which Joshua burned. ¹⁴ The Israelites plundered all the spoils and cattle of these cities for themselves. But they struck down every person with the sword until they had annihilated them, leaving no one alive. ¹⁵ Just as the LORD had commanded his servant Moses, Moses commanded Joshua. That is what Joshua did, leaving nothing undone of all that the LORD had commanded Moses.

^11:2 Or *Shephelah*, also in v. 16   ᴮ11:2 Or *and in Naphoth-dor*

Canaanites did escape, as will be apparent in chap. 13 and in Jdg 1.
10:41 This summary defines all the towns in the south as far north as Gibeon. **Goshen** cannot refer to Egypt but must describe an otherwise unknown region (11:16). In 15:51 the town is associated with a district in the tribe of Judah.
10:42 In one campaign is literally "at one time." Emphasis is on how quickly it was completed because the Lord **fought for Israel**.
10:43 The return of **all Israel to the camp at Gilgal** signaled the end of the campaign and the peace that resulted so Israel could rest.
11:1 The role of **King Jabin of Hazor** as the leader of the towns of the northern region corresponded to that of the king of Jerusalem (10:3) in the south. Situated north of the Sea of Galilee, Hazor was the largest ancient site in Israel. It was the dominant city of the entire land and governed trade to the north where it is mentioned in texts as far away as cities on the Euphrates River. The initial phrase **When King Jabin . . . heard** duplicates those in 5:1 and 9:1 and signals that there will be a battle against Israel. **Madon** is unknown. It may be a variant of Merom, found in vv. 5 and 7.
Shimron (modern Tel Shimron) was located in the foothills near the western end of the Jezreel Valley. It lay at the southern end of Galilee. **Achshaph** (modern Tell Keisan) was situated to the west in the Acco Plain. If Madon/Merom is identified as modern Tel Qarnei Hittin, it lay to the east near the Sea of Galilee. The effect is to identify important sites scattered across the populated areas

around the Sea of Galilee to the north and westward along the Jezreel Valley and over to the Acco Plain and the Mediterranean Sea.
11:2 Chinnereth (modern Tel Kinrot) was a site on the northwest end of the Sea of Galilee. Chinnereth was also the name of the sea at that time, so the southern portion of the area could include both the region around the sea and the Jordan Valley farther south. The **Judean foothills** translates *Shephelah*, a word meaning only "low hills." Although the Bible often uses this term to describe the western foothills of Judah, here it probably refers to the foothills of Samaria, farther north and more in agreement with this description of lands and towns in the north. The **Slopes of Dor** is a translation of "Naphoth Dor," an otherwise unknown name.
11:3 The **Hivites** were previously associated with Gibeon, but here they are found farther north at the foot of Mount Hermon. The **Jebusites**, often associated with Jerusalem, are more generally located in the hill country. Apparently these were people groups who populated more than one location. The reference to **Mizpah** anticipates the Valley of Mizpeh to the east in v. 8. Mizpeh could refer to the southern end of the Beqa'a Valley where the Litani River flows south and then west to Tyre.
11:4 The huge number of the armies suggests a larger force than that of the southern coalition. As with Tyre (v. 1), these towns and cities tended to be more populous than those mentioned in chap. 10. The **horses and chariots** were the most sophisticated technology available in ancient warfare, used to move

archers around the battlefield on a mobile firing platform.
11:5 Although there is a site known as **Merom** in upper Galilee, its location makes it unlikely as a strategic place for a battle. Modern Tel Qarni Hattin near the Horns of Hattin, a site famous for Crusader battles, seems more appropriate as the identification of Merom. It lay in the hills west of the Sea of Galilee and served as a dominating position for trade and armies coming south from Syria and for those coming east from the coast and the Jezreel Plain. The plan of these armies **to attack Israel** suggests that what follows would be a defensive war for Israel.
11:7 Again Joshua used the tactic of surprise (cp. 10:9).
11:8 Greater Sidon lay at the northwestern corner of Israel. **Misrephoth-maim** may have been at the northeastern end of the valley of the Litani River. Thus the attack began south of the Sea of Galilee and went westward and north to Sidon before turning eastward to Misrephoth-maim, where it turned south along the **Valley of Mizpeh**/Mizpah (v. 3). Twice the text records how Israel **struck them down** as if to emphasize the complete success of the mission.
11:10 The size and strategic location of **Hazor** made it the most important city in Palestine throughout the second millennium BC.
11:14 The treatment of these captured towns, in which Israel killed all the people but **plundered all the spoils**, resembles that of Ai (8:2,27). Unlike Jericho, at Ai God allowed his people to keep the plunder. Apparently this practice continued elsewhere in the land.

Seeing Jesus in the Promised Land

▼ Old Testament	▼ New Testament
THE LORD: The Lord of All the Earth *(Jos 3:11,13)*	**JESUS CHRIST IS LORD:** The Confession of Every Tongue *(Php 2:9–11)*
Joshua: Entrusted Himself to God's Exaltation *(Jos 3:7)*	**Jesus:** Entrusted Himself to God's Vindication *(1Pt 2:23)*
Joshua (Hebrew): Name Means "The LORD Is Salvation"	**Jesus (Greek):** Salvation Is Found in No Other Name *(Ac 4:12)*
Joshua: Led His People into a Temporary Rest *(Jos 11:23)*	**Jesus:** Leads His People into an Eternal Rest *(Heb 3–4)*
Rahab: Saved by Faith *(Jos 2; 6; Heb 11:31)*	**Jesus:** The Pioneer and Perfecter of Our Faith *(Heb 12:2)*
The Judges: Saved the People While Still Alive *(Jdg 2:18)*	**Jesus:** Saves His People Forever, Being Raised from the Dead *(Rm 8)*
Gideon's Army of 300: God's Glory Through Weakness *(Jdg 7:2–8)*	**Preach Christ Crucified:** God's Power and Wisdom *(1Co 1:23–24)*
Samson's Death: Vengeance upon His Idolatrous Enemies *(Jdg 16:28–30)*	**Jesus's Death:** Salvation for His Enemies Who Believe *(Rm 5:8–10)*
Boaz: A Kinsman Redeemer, Even for a Moabitess *(Ru 2:20; 4:1–12)*	**Jesus:** The Redeemer Who Gave Himself for All People *(Ti 2:11–14)*
Ruth: Great-Grandmother of David *(Ru 4:17,21–22)*	**Jesus:** The Son of David, the Messiah *(Mt 1)*
Samuel: A Prophet to Whom God Revealed Himself by His Word *(1Sm 3:21)*	**Jesus:** In These Last Days, God Has Spoken to Us by His Son *(Heb 1:2)*

Summary of Conquests

¹⁶ So Joshua took all this land — the hill country, all the Negev, all the land of Goshen, the foothills, the Arabah, and the hill country of Israel with its foothills — ¹⁷ from Mount Halak, which ascends to Seir, as far as Baal-gad in the Valley of Lebanon at the foot of Mount Hermon. He captured all their kings and struck them down, putting them to death. ¹⁸ Joshua waged war with all these kings for a long time. ¹⁹ No city made peace with the Israelites except the Hivites who inhabited Gibeon; all of them were taken in battle. ²⁰ For it was the LORD's intention to harden their hearts, so that they would engage Israel in battle, be completely destroyed without mercy, and be annihilated, just as the LORD had commanded Moses.

²¹ At that time Joshua proceeded to exterminate the Anakim from the hill country — Hebron, Debir, Anab — all the hill country of Judah and of Israel. Joshua completely destroyed them with their cities. ²² No Anakim were left in the land of the Israelites, except for some remaining in Gaza, Gath, and Ashdod.

²³ So Joshua took the entire land, in keeping with all that the LORD had told Moses. Joshua then gave it as an inheritance to Israel according to their tribal allotments. After this, the land had rest from war.

Territory East of the Jordan

12 The Israelites struck down the following kings of the land and took possession of their land beyond the Jordan to the east and from the Arnon River to Mount Hermon, including all the Arabah eastward:

² King Sihon of the Amorites lived in Heshbon. He ruled from Aroer on the rim of the Arnon River, along the middle of the valley, and half of Gilead up to the Jabbok River (the border of the Ammonites), ³ the Arabah east of the Sea of Chinnereth^A to the Sea of Arabah (that is, the Dead Sea), eastward through Beth-jeshimoth and southward^B below the slopes of Pisgah.

⁴ King Og^C of Bashan, of the remnant of the Rephaim, lived in Ashtaroth and Edrei. ⁵ He ruled over Mount Hermon, Salecah, all Bashan up to the Geshurite and Maacathite border, and half of Gilead to the border of King Sihon of Heshbon. ⁶ Moses the LORD's servant and the Israelites struck them down. And Moses the LORD's servant gave their land as an inheritance to the Reubenites, Gadites, and half the tribe of Manasseh.

Territory West of the Jordan

⁷ Joshua and the Israelites struck down the following kings of the land beyond the Jordan to the west, from Baal-gad in the Valley of Lebanon to Mount Halak, which ascends toward Seir (Joshua gave their land as an inheritance to the tribes of Israel according to their allotments: ⁸ the hill country, the Judean foothills,^D the Arabah, the slopes, the wilderness, and the Negev — the lands of the Hethites, Amorites, Canaanites, Perizzites, Hivites, and Jebusites):

⁹ the king of Jericho	one
the king of Ai, which is next to Bethel	one

---

^A12:3 = Galilee   ^B12:3 Or *and from Teman*   ^C12:4 LXX; MT reads *The territory of Og*   ^D12:8 Or *the Shephelah*

11:16 The summary of Israel's battles and victories begins with the regions. Those in the south are followed by those in the north. The **land of Goshen** may refer to the region with the town of that name in 10:41, in Judah (15:51). Perhaps it is a variant for the kingdom of Geshur, north of the Sea of Galilee. However, see note at 13:13.

11:17 The summary turns to the boundaries of the newly acquired land. **Mount Halak** (modern Jebel Halaq) lay midway between Kadesh-barnea and the southern tip of the Dead Sea. It thus defined the southern border with **Seir** (Edom). The precise location of **Baal-gad . . . at the foot of Mount Hermon** is unknown. The **Valley of Lebanon** may refer to the Valley of Mizpeh (v. 8; see note at v. 3), or to both it and the Beqa'a—the entire region between the Lebanon and Anti-Lebanon mountain ranges.

11:18 In contrast to the speed with which the previous campaigns were fought, the northern campaign took **a long time**. Appropriately, chap. 12 lists rulers conquered that are not mentioned in chap. 11.

11:21 The **Anakim** represent legendary warriors (Dt 2:10–11). By the time of Joshua they had lived for hundreds of years in Palestine. The three Anakim in Jos 14:15 may correspond to the three towns mentioned here, perhaps as rulers. **Anab** may refer to the site of 'Unnab ets-Tseghur about fifteen miles southwest of **Hebron**. With **Debir**,

these are all located in southern Palestine. When Joshua **completely destroyed** the three cities, he may have been represented by Caleb (15:14–15).

11:22 The remnants of the **Anakim** in **Gaza, Gath, and Ashdod** anticipate the arrival of the Philistines and the presence of a giant such as Goliath (1Sm 17:4).

11:23 The **inheritance** that Joshua presented to Israel uses a word that occurs in Joshua for the first time, but it will occur dozens of times in the remainder of the book. It serves as a transition from the battles to the division of the inheritance.

12:1–6 A summary review of all the land acquired by Israel begins with the territories east of or **beyond the Jordan**. The summary is given in terms of regions, outlined by towns. The conquest of this region took place while Moses remained alive (Nm 21:21–35).

12:1 The southern part of this section, the **Arnon River**, ran from the tableland of Moab westward into the Dead Sea. To the south was territory that belonged to Moab. To the north was the territory allotted Reuben. Gad and Manasseh received lands farther north that reached upward to the modern Golan Heights and to the base of **Mount Hermon**.

12:2–3 The border of the territory ruled by **Sihon** is given in the form of a series of towns. His capital of **Heshbon** was probably not modern Hesban, which was not occupied at that early period. It may be

identified with another neighboring site that was inhabited (modern Tell Jalul or Tall al-'Umeiri). From the **Arnon River** in the south, the territory of Sihon reached to the **Jabbok River** in the north. **Aroer** (modern 'Ara'ir) and **Beth-jeshimoth** (modern Tell 'Azeimeh) were towns in the area. The **Arabah** was the eastern Jordan Valley extending from the **Sea of Chinnereth** (Sea of Galilee) to the **Sea of the Arabah** (the Dead Sea). The **slopes of Pisgah** represent the descent along the northwestern edge of the plateau of Moab. **Gilead** was apparently bisected by the Jabbok River.

12:4–5 The role of **Og** as the **remnant of the Rephaim** suggests a figure of legendary renown similar to the Anakim of vv. 21–22. The towns of **Ashtaroth** (modern Tell 'Ashtarah) and **Edrei** (modern Der'a) lay near the modern border between northern Jordan and southern Syria. The region of **Bashan** where Og ruled was bordered on the south by the Yarmuk River (the northern border of Sihon's kingdom), on the west by the watercourse Nachal Raqqad, on the north by Mount Hermon, and on the east by Jebel Druze. This makes up the southern modern Hauran. The **Geshurite and Maacathite border** ran along the limits of the kingdoms of Geshur and Maacah east and north of what is now the Sea of Galilee.

12:9–24 The thirty-one **kings** listed cover the entire region, with those in vv. 9–16

[10] the king of Jerusalem	one
the king of Hebron	one
[11] the king of Jarmuth	one
the king of Lachish	one
[12] the king of Eglon	one
the king of Gezer	one
[13] the king of Debir	one
the king of Geder	one
[14] the king of Hormah	one
the king of Arad	one
[15] the king of Libnah	one
the king of Adullam	one
[16] the king of Makkedah	one
the king of Bethel	one
[17] the king of Tappuah	one
the king of Hepher	one
[18] the king of Aphek	one
the king of Lasharon	one
[19] the king of Madon	one
the king of Hazor	one
[20] the king of Shimron-meron	one
the king of Achshaph	one
[21] the king of Taanach	one
the king of Megiddo	one
[22] the king of Kedesh	one
the king of Jokneam in Carmel	one
[23] the king of Dor in Naphath-dor[A]	one
the king of Goiim in Gilgal[B]	one
[24] the king of Tirzah	one

the total number of all kings: thirty-one.

Unconquered Lands

13 Joshua was now old, advanced in age, and the LORD said to him, "You have become old, advanced in age, but a great deal of the land remains to be possessed. [2] This is the land that remains:

All the districts of the Philistines and the Geshurites: [3] from the Shihor east of Egypt to the border of Ekron on the north (considered to be Canaanite territory) — the five Philistine rulers of Gaza, Ashdod, Ashkelon, Gath, and Ekron, as well as the Avvites [4] in the south; all the land of the Canaanites, from Arah of the Sidonians to Aphek and as far as the border of the Amorites; [5] the land of the Gebalites; and all Lebanon east from Baal-gad below Mount Hermon to the entrance of Hamath[c] — [6] all the inhabitants of the hill country from Lebanon to Misrephoth-maim, all the Sidonians.

I will drive them out before the Israelites, only distribute the land as an inheritance for Israel, as I have commanded you. [7] Therefore, divide this land as an inheritance to the nine tribes and half the tribe of Manasseh."

The Inheritance East of the Jordan

[8] With the other half of the tribe of Manasseh, the Reubenites and Gadites had received the inheritance Moses gave them beyond the Jordan to the east, just as Moses the LORD's servant had given them:

[9] From Aroer on the rim of the Arnon Valley, along with the city in the middle of the valley, all the Medeba plateau as far as Dibon, [10] and all the cities of King Sihon of the Amorites, who reigned in Heshbon, to the border of the Ammonites; [11] also Gilead and the territory of the Geshurites and Maacathites, all Mount Hermon, and all Bashan to Salecah — [12] the whole kingdom of Og in Bashan, who reigned in Ashtaroth and Edrei; he was one of the remaining Rephaim.

Moses struck them down and drove them out, [13] but the Israelites did not drive out the

---

[A]12:23 Or *in the Slopes of Dor* [B]12:23 LXX reads *Galilee* [C]13:5 Or *to Lebo-hamath*

including the victories in the south described in chaps. 6–10 and those in vv. 17–24 summarizing the victories in the north as discussed in chap. 11.

13:1–21:45 Although some of the initial descriptions of the allotments consider regions, most of the divisions of the tribal territories in these chapters appear in two forms of literature: boundary descriptions and town lists. The boundary descriptions normally identify themselves by using the term *border* and verbs such as *turn, ascend, descend, curve* and other terms linking one town or natural feature with another along the line of the border.

Town lists also appear in many tribal allotments as towns that belong to a tribe. Sometimes they are subdivided into regions of the tribe. This is true of the lengthiest town list in the allotment—that of Judah in 15:20–63.

13:1 The expression **advanced in age** establishes Joshua was at the end of his active life and military leadership. In 24:29 Joshua died at 110. Here he and Israel transitioned from military activity to allotment of the land. Despite the long list of towns and their

kings who were defeated in chap. 12, the Lord confirmed that **a great deal of the land** remained **to be possessed**.

13:2–7 The regions not yet occupied include areas on the fringes of the promised land. The land of the **Philistines** is described in v. 3. The five towns of the Philistines appear here for the first time. The **Shihor** has been described as the Brook of Egypt (15:4). The word for **rulers** (Hb *seren*) is a term only applied to Philistines. The **Avvites** appear as a people living south of the region of the Philistines (Dt 2:23). The **Geshurites** include those inhabiting the region north and east of the Sea of Galilee.

13:4 Arah is not otherwise known, but the region of the **Sidonians** includes coastal areas at the northern end of the land occupied by the twelve tribes. **Aphek** appeared earlier (12:18). It lay on the coastal plain between Joppa and Dor where the plain narrowed and the hill country (**the border of the Amorites**) reached closest to the Mediterranean Sea.

13:5 The **land of the Gebalites** was Byblos, an important coastal city north of Sidon in modern Lebanon. The **entrance of Hamath**,

sometimes called Lebo-hamath, is the most northern place described. It is identified with modern Lebweh north of the Beqa'a.

13:7 The command to **divide this land** is repeated, emphasizing its importance. The **nine tribes and half the tribe of Manasseh** exclude Reuben, Gad, and the other half of Manasseh, who received an allotment east of the Jordan River.

13:8–33 The territory described in this section is identical to the combined areas controlled by Sihon and Og as described in 12:1–5.

13:9 The text begins in the south along the **Arnon Valley**, the border with Moab. The **Medeba plateau** includes the tableland that rises east of the Dead Sea. **Dibon** is perhaps not modern Tell Dhiban.

13:10 border of the Ammonites lay to the east and north of Israel's inheritance and Sihon's previous kingdom. Its capital was Rabbah, modern day Amman.

13:13 The presence of **Geshur** and **Maacath** as independent entities is attested during the time of David. He married the daughter of Geshur's king and fathered Absalom (2Sm 3:3). The statement that Israel **did not drive out** the Canaanites

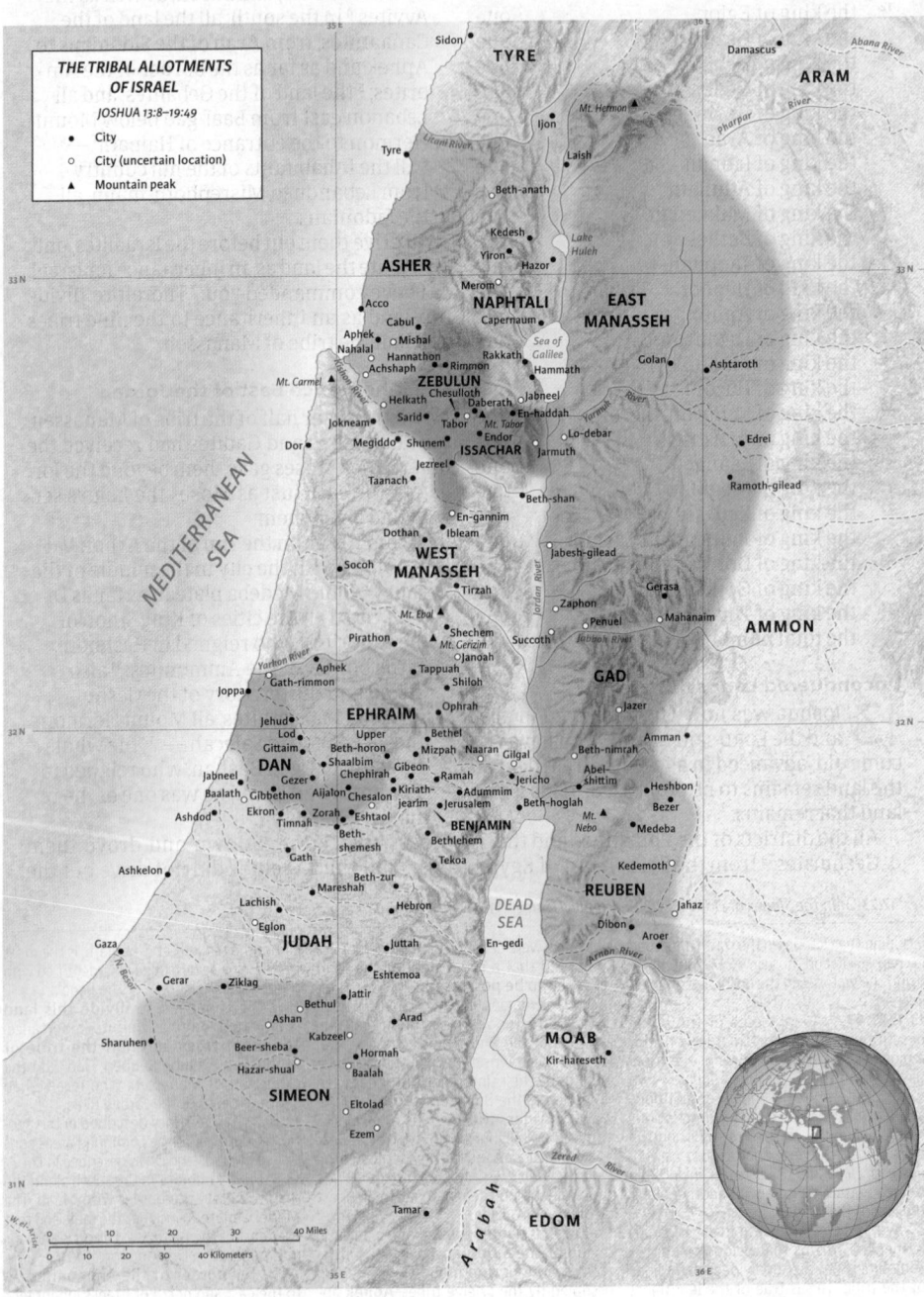

THE TRIBAL ALLOTMENTS
OF ISRAEL

JOSHUA 13:8–19:49

• City
○ City (uncertain location)
▲ Mountain peak

Sidon

TYRE

Damascus

ARAM

Abana River

Ijon

Mt. Hermon ▲

Pharpar River

Tyre

Litani River

Laish

Beth-anath

Kedesh

Lake Huleh

ASHER

Yiron

Hazor

Acco

Merom

NAPHTALI

EAST MANASSEH

Cabul

Capernaum

Aphek

Mishal

Sea of Galilee

Nahalal

Hannathon

Rakkath

Hammath

Golan

Ashtaroth

Achshaph

Rimmon

ZEBULUN

Mt. Carmel ▲

Helkath

Chesulloth

Jabneel

Daberath

En-haddah

Sarid

Tabor

Mt. Tabor

Lo-debar

Edrei

Jokneam

Megiddo

Shunem

Endor

Jarmuth

Ramoth-gilead

Dor

ISSACHAR

Jezreel

Taanach

Beth-shan

En-gannim

Dothan

Ibleam

Jabesh-gilead

WEST MANASSEH

Socoh

Gerasa

Tirzah

Zaphon

Mt. Ebal ▲

Shechem

Penuel

Mahanaim

AMMON

Pirathon

Mt. Gerizim

Succoth

Jabbok River

Janoah

Aphek

Tappuah

GAD

Gath-rimmon

Shiloh

Joppa

EPHRAIM

Ophrah

Jazer

Jehud

Lod

Upper

Bethel

Amman

Gittaim

Beth-horon

Mizpah

Naaran

Gilgal

Beth-nimrah

DAN

Shaalbim

Gibeon

Jericho

Abel-shittim

Jabneel

Gezer

Chephirah

Ramah

Heshbon

Baalath

Gibbethon

Aijalon

Kiriath-jearim

Adummim

Bezer

Ekron

Chesalon

Jerusalem

Beth-hoglah

Ashdod

Zorah

Eshtaol

Mt. Nebo ▲

Medeba

Timnah

Beth-shemesh

BENJAMIN

Bethlehem

Kedemoth

Gath

Tekoa

REUBEN

Ashkelon

Beth-zur

DEAD SEA

Dibon

Jahaz

Lachish

Mareshah

Hebron

Aroer

Gaza

Eglon

JUDAH

Juttah

En-gedi

Arnon River

Gerar

Ziklag

Eshtemoa

Jattir

Ashan

Bethul

Arad

MOAB

Sharuhen

Kabzeel

Kir-hareseth

Beer-sheba

Hormah

Hazar-shual

Baalah

SIMEON

Eltolad

Ezem

Zered River

Tamar

Arabah

EDOM

MEDITERRANEAN SEA

N. Besor

W. el-Arish

Jordan River

0   10   20   30   40 Miles
0   10   20   30   40 Kilometers

33 N

32 N

31 N

35 E

36 E

Geshurites and Maacathites. So Geshur and Maacath still live in Israel today.

¹⁴ He did not, however, give any inheritance to the tribe of Levi. This was their inheritance, just as he had promised: the food offerings made to the Lord, the God of Israel.

Reuben's Inheritance

¹⁵ To the tribe of Reuben's descendants by their clans, Moses gave ¹⁶ this as their territory:

From Aroer on the rim of the Arnon Valley, along with the city in the middle of the valley, the whole plateau as far asᴬ Medeba, ¹⁷ with Heshbon and all its cities on the plateau — Dibon, Bamoth-baal, Beth-baal-meon, ¹⁸ Jahaz, Kedemoth, Mephaath, ¹⁹ Kiriathaim, Sibmah, Zereth-shahar on the hill in the valley, ²⁰ Beth-peor, the slopes of Pisgah, and Beth-jeshimoth — ²¹ all the cities of the plateau, and all the kingdom of King Sihon of the Amorites, who reigned in Heshbon. Moses had killed him and the chiefs of Midian — Evi, Rekem, Zur, Hur, and Reba — the princes of Sihon who lived in the land. ²² Along with those the Israelites put to death, they also killed the diviner, Balaam son of Beor, with the sword.

²³ The border of the Reubenites was the Jordan and its plain. This was the inheritance of the Reubenites by their clans, with the cities and their settlements.

Gad's Inheritance

²⁴ To the tribe of the Gadites by their clans, Moses gave ²⁵ this as their territory:

Jazer and all the cities of Gilead, and half the land of the Ammonites to Aroer, near Rabbah; ²⁶ from Heshbon to Ramath-mizpeh and Betonim, and from Mahanaim to the border of Debir;ᴮ ²⁷ in the valley: Beth-haram, Beth-nimrah, Succoth, and Zaphon — the rest of the kingdom of King Sihon of Heshbon. Their land also included the Jordan and its territory as far as the edge of the Sea of Chinnerethᶜ on the east side of the Jordan.

²⁸ This was the inheritance of the Gadites by their clans, with the cities and their settlements.

East Manasseh's Inheritance

²⁹ And to half the tribe of Manasseh (that is, to half the tribe of Manasseh's descendants by their clans) Moses gave ³⁰ this as their territory:

From Mahanaim through all Bashan — all the kingdom of King Og of Bashan, including all of Jair's Villagesᴰ that are in Bashan — sixty cities. ³¹ But half of Gilead, and Og's royal cities in Bashan — Ashtaroth and Edrei — are for the descendants of Machir son of Manasseh (that is, half the descendants of Machir by their clans).

³² These were the portions Moses gave them on the plains of Moab beyond the Jordan east of Jericho. ³³ But Moses did not give a portion to the tribe of Levi. The Lord, the God of Israel, was their inheritance, just as he had promised them.

Israel's Inheritance in Canaan

14 The Israelites received these portions that the priest Eleazar, Joshua son of Nun, and the family heads of the Israelite tribes gave them in the land of Canaan. ² Their inheritance was by lot as the Lord commanded through Moses for the nine and a half tribes, ³ because Moses had given the inheritance to the two and a half tribes beyond the Jordan. But he gave no inheritance among them to the Levites. ⁴ The descendants of Joseph became two tribes, Manasseh and Ephraim. No portion of the land was given to the Levites except cities to live in, along with pasturelands for their cattle and livestock. ⁵ So the Israelites did as the Lord commanded Moses, and they divided the land.

Caleb's Inheritance

⁶ The descendants of Judah approached Joshua at Gilgal, and Caleb son of Jephunneh the Kenizzite said to him, "You know what the Lord promised Moses the man of God at

---

ᴬ13:16 Some Hb mss read plateau near   ᴮ13:26 Or Lidbir, or Lo-debar   ᶜ13:27 = Galilee   ᴰ13:30 Or all of Havvoth-jair

---

becomes a sad refrain in Joshua and Judges (16:10; 17:13; Jdg 1). **13:14** In accord with Dt 18:1, the **tribe of Levi** received no inheritance of land. **13:15–23** Reuben's allotment also began at Aroer on the rim of the Arnon Valley. It is described through a town list (v v. 17–20). **13:21–22** For the deaths of **Evi, Rekem, Zur, Hur . . . Reba**, and **Balaam son of Beor**, see Nm 31:8. **13:25** With **Rabbah** (modern Amman) as the Ammonite capital, this allotment took over **half the land of the Ammonites**. **13:26** This verse appears to designate towns along the border of Gad located in the higher plateau region inland toward the desert.

13:30 Jair's **Villages** numbered **sixty cities** (here city is a term that can describe a small hamlet). A judge named Jair (Jdg 10:4) had thirty sons who ruled over half of them. **13:31** In 17:1 **Machir son of Manasseh** received **Gilead** and **Bashan** east of the Jordan. The other sons of Manasseh received inheritances west of that river. **13:33** As with the regional summary of vv. 8–14, so the summary of specific allotments ends with a note about the absence of **a portion** for **the tribe of Levi**. **14:1 Eleazar** was the son of Aaron, and his successor as well as the leader of the Levites (Ex 6:23–25; Nm 20:25–28; 26:60; Dt 10:6). He used the Urim (and Thummim) to determine

God's will and to allot the tribal lands (Nm 27:19–22; 34:17). The **land of Canaan** implies that the region east of the Jordan River, allotted in the previous chapter, was not part of Canaan. **14:2** The use of the **lot** for the distribution of the land is explained in Nm 26:55–56; 33:54; 34:13; 36:2. The size of the tribe was also considered (Nm 33:54). The lot was not considered arbitrary but was directed by God (Pr 16:33). **14:6** Judah's relative importance, if only because of its larger size than the other tribes, may give it the right to go first. **Caleb** was one of the two spies, along with **Joshua**, who were sent to spy out the promised

Kadesh-barnea about you and me. ⁷ I was forty years old when Moses the LORD's servant sent me from Kadesh-barnea to scout the land, and I brought back an honest report. ⁸ My brothers who went with me caused the people to lose heart, but I followed the LORD my God completely. ⁹ On that day Moses swore to me, 'The land where you have set foot will be an inheritance for you and your descendants forever, because you have followed the LORD my God completely.'

¹⁰ "As you see, the LORD has kept me alive these forty-five years as he promised, since the LORD spoke this word to Moses while Israel was journeying in the wilderness. Here I am today, eighty-five years old. ¹¹ I am still as strong today as I was the day Moses sent me out. My strength for battle and for daily tasksᴬ is now as it was then. ¹² Now give me this hill country the LORD promised me on that day, because you heard then that the Anakim are there, as well as large fortified cities. Perhaps the LORD will be with me and I will drive them out as the LORD promised."

¹³ Then Joshua blessed Caleb son of Jephunneh and gave him Hebron as an inheritance. ¹⁴ Therefore, Hebron still belongs to Caleb son of Jephunneh the Kenizzite as an inheritance today because he followed the LORD, the God of Israel, completely. ¹⁵ Hebron's name used to be Kiriath-arba; Arba was the greatest man among the Anakim. After this, the land had rest from war.

Judah's Inheritance

15 Now the allotment for the tribe of the descendants of Judah by their clans was in the southernmost region, south to the Wilderness of Zin and over to the border of Edom. ² Their southern border began at the tip of the Dead Sea on the south bayᴮ ³ and went south of the Scorpions' Ascent, proceeded to Zin, ascended to the south of Kadesh-barnea, passed Hezron, ascended to Addar, and turned to Karka. ⁴ It proceeded to Azmon and to the Brook of Egypt and

so the border ended at the Mediterranean Sea. This is yourᶜ southern border.

⁵ Now the eastern border was along the Dead Sea to the mouth of the Jordan.

The border on the north side was from the bay of the sea at the mouth of the Jordan. ⁶ It ascended to Beth-hoglah, proceeded north of Beth-arabah, and ascended to the Stone of Bohan son of Reuben. ⁷ Then the border ascended to Debir from the Valley of Achor, turning north to the Gilgal that is opposite the Ascent of Adummim, which is south of the ravine. The border proceeded to the Waters of En-shemesh and ended at En-rogel. ⁸ From there the border ascended Ben Hinnom Valley to the southern Jebusite slope (that is, Jerusalem) and ascended to the top of the hill that faces Hinnom Valley on the west, at the northern end of Rephaim Valley. ⁹ From the top of the hill the border curved to the spring of the Waters of Nephtoah, went to the cities of Mount Ephron, and then curved to Baalah (that is, Kiriath-jearim). ¹⁰ The border turned westward from Baalah to Mount Seir, went to the northern slope of Mount Jearim (that is, Chesalon), descended to Beth-shemesh, and proceeded to Timnah. ¹¹ Then the border reached to the slope north of Ekron, curved to Shikkeron, proceeded to Mount Baalah, went to Jabneel, and ended at the Mediterranean Sea.

¹² Now the western border was the coastline of the Mediterranean Sea.

This was the boundary of the descendants of Judah around their clans.

Caleb and Othniel

¹³ He gave Caleb son of Jephunneh the following portion among the descendants of Judah based on the LORD's instruction to Joshua: Kiriath-arba (that is, Hebron; Arba was the

---

ᴬ14:11 Lit *for going out and coming in*   ᴮ15:2 Lit *Sea at the tongue that turns southward*   ᶜ15:4 LXX reads *their*

land and returned with a good report (Nm 13–14). Caleb's designation as a **Kenizzite** is otherwise unattested, but it may be related to the name of Caleb's brother, Kenaz (15:17). **14:10** Caleb's reference to **forty-five years** suggests that following the wilderness wanderings of about forty years, the time spent in the battles of chaps. 1–12 amounted to about five years. **14:13–14** When the spies searched the land, they traveled its length. However, the description of their activity focused on Hebron and the nearby Valley of Esh-col (Nm 13:22–24). These were located in the southern hill country of Judah. This would have been among the closest major inland towns in Canaan from their base at Kadesh-barnea. Thus the gift of land to **Caleb** involved the area

of **Hebron** where he had visited and spent more time than anywhere else (Dt 1:36). **14:15** The note about **Hebron's name** recalls the mighty **Anakim** (11:21) who were there, and it anticipates Caleb's defeat of them in 15:14. **Kiriath-arba** is a second and earlier name for Hebron. The first part of the name means "city"; thus, the note suggests the meaning, "city of Arba," where **Arba** is the name of **the greatest man among the Anakim**. This would predate Israel's appearance because none of the Anakim that Caleb fought (15:14) bore this name. The note that **the land had rest from war** indicates success for Caleb. **15:1–12** The account of Caleb in 14:6–15 was a general one in which only one town is mentioned and the occupation of Caleb's

inheritance is summarized. The same is true of the first account of Judah's allotment. It describes the contours of the land in terms of its borders, identified mostly by natural formations. The descriptions move counterclockwise beginning with the southern border. **15:8** The border arches to the south to go around **Jerusalem**, which at the time was populated by the Jebusites and was not part of Israel. **15:13–19** These verses continue the account of 14:6–15. Here the details appear with the names of specific places within Caleb's inheritance and the bequeathing of these to his children. Thus the general part is followed by the specific part. This anticipates the allotment of **Judah**. Joshua 15:1–12 constituted the general places, describing only the

father of Anak). **¹⁴** Caleb drove out from there the three sons of Anak: Sheshai, Ahiman, and Talmai, descendants of Anak. **¹⁵** From there he marched against the inhabitants of Debir, which used to be called Kiriath-sepher, **¹⁶** and Caleb said, "Whoever attacks and captures Kiriath-sepher, I will give my daughter Achsah to him as a wife." **¹⁷** So Othniel son of Caleb's brother, Kenaz, captured it, and Caleb gave his daughter Achsah to him as a wife. **¹⁸** When she arrived, she persuaded Othniel to ask her father for a field. As she got off her donkey, Caleb asked her, "What can I do for you?" **¹⁹** She replied, "Give me a blessing. Since you have given me land in the Negev, give me the springs also." So he gave her the upper and lower springs.

Judah's Cities

²⁰ This was the inheritance of the tribe of the descendants of Judah by their clans.
²¹ These were the outermost cities of the tribe of the descendants of Judah toward the border of Edom in the Negev: Kabzeel, Eder, Jagur, **²²** Kinah, Dimonah, Adadah, **²³** Kedesh, Hazor, Ithnan, **²⁴** Ziph, Telem, Bealoth, **²⁵** Hazor-hadattah, Kerioth-hezron (that is, Hazor), **²⁶** Amam, Shema, Moladah, **²⁷** Hazar-gaddah, Heshmon, Beth-pelet, **²⁸** Hazar-shual, Beer-sheba, Biziothiah, **²⁹** Baalah, Iim, Ezem, **³⁰** Eltolad, Chesil, Hormah, **³¹** Ziklag, Madmannah, Sansannah, **³²** Lebaoth, Shilhim, Ain, and Rimmon — twenty-nine cities in all, with their settlements.

³³ In the Judean foothills:ᴬ Eshtaol, Zorah, Ashnah, **³⁴** Zanoah, En-gannim, Tappuah,ᴮ Enam, **³⁵** Jarmuth, Adullam, Socoh,ᶜ Azekah, **³⁶** Shaaraim, Adithaim, Gederah, and Gederothaim — fourteen cities, with their settlements; **³⁷** Zenan, Hadashah, Migdalgad, **³⁸** Dilan, Mizpeh, Jokthe-el, **³⁹** Lachish, Bozkath, Eglon, **⁴⁰** Cabbon, Lahmam, Chitlish, **⁴¹** Gederoth, Beth-dagon, Naamah, and Makkedah — sixteen cities, with their settlements; **⁴²** Libnah, Ether, Ashan, **⁴³** Iphtah, Ashnah, Nezib, **⁴⁴** Keilah, Achzib, and

Mareshah — nine cities, with their settlements; **⁴⁵** Ekron, with its surrounding villages and settlements; **⁴⁶** from Ekron to the sea, all the cities near Ashdod, with their settlements; **⁴⁷** Ashdod, with its surrounding villages and settlements; Gaza, with its surrounding villages and settlements, to the Brook of Egypt and the coastline of the Mediterranean Sea.

⁴⁸ In the hill country: Shamir, Jattir, Socoh, **⁴⁹** Dannah, Kiriath-sannah (that is, Debir), **⁵⁰** Anab, Eshtemoh, Anim, **⁵¹** Goshen, Holon, and Giloh — eleven cities, with their settlements; **⁵²** Arab, Dumah,ᴰ Eshan, **⁵³** Janim, Beth-tappuah, Aphekah, **⁵⁴** Humtah, Kiriath-arba (that is, Hebron), and Zior — nine cities, with their settlements; **⁵⁵** Maon, Carmel, Ziph, Juttah, **⁵⁶** Jezreel, Jokdeam, Zanoah, **⁵⁷** Kain, Gibeah, and Timnah — ten cities, with their settlements; **⁵⁸** Halhul, Beth-zur, Gedor, **⁵⁹** Maarath, Beth-anoth, and Eltekon — six cities, with their settlements;ᴱ **⁶⁰** Kiriath-baal (that is, Kiriath-jearim), and Rabbah — two cities, with their settlements.

⁶¹ In the wilderness: Beth-arabah, Middin, Secacah, **⁶²** Nibshan, the City of Salt,ᶠ and En-gedi — six cities, with their settlements.
⁶³ But the descendants of Judah could not drive out the Jebusites who lived in Jerusalem. So the Jebusites still live in Jerusalem among the descendants of Judah today.

Joseph's Inheritance

16 The allotment for the descendants of Joseph went from the Jordan at Jericho to the Waters of Jericho on the east, through the wilderness ascending from Jericho into the hill country of Bethel. **²** From Bethel it went to Luz and proceeded to the border of the Archites by Ataroth. **³** It then descended westward to the border of the Japhletites as far as the

---

ᴬ**15:33** Or *the Shephelah*   ᴮ**15:34** Or *En-gannim-tappuah*   ᶜ**15:35** Or *Adullam-socoh*   ᴰ**15:52** Some Hb mss read *Rumah*   ᴱ**15:59** LXX adds *Tekoa, Ephrathah (that is, Bethlehem), Peor, Etam, Culom, Tatam, Sores, Carem, Gallim, Baither, and Manach — eleven cities, with their settlements*   ᶠ**15:62** Or *Ir-hamelach*

---

borders of the land. While vv. 20–63 will deal with the specific places within those borders. Caleb's allotment represents the premier example of all the allotments of Judah. It is so important because it is the allotment of the most faithful Judahite of his generation. It also describes the acquisition of **Hebron**, David's first capital (2Sm 2:1–11).

15:17 The capture of the city of Debir by **Othniel** led to his marriage to Caleb's **daughter**. He and the first judge may be one and the same (Jdg 3:9–11).

15:18–19 The request of Achsah was to increase her dowry and receive a full inheritance that included the necessary water sources for land to be usable in the Judean desert.

15:20–62 This section contains the most detailed town list of any of the allotments. It reflects the large tract of land given to Judah in comparison with the other tribes. The Hebrew text preserves eleven districts: the **Negev** (vv. 21–32); the western **foothills** with towns in the north (vv. 33–36), the south (vv. 37–41), and the center (vv. 42–44); the coastal plain (vv. 45–47); four regions in the **hill country** (vv. 48–51,52–54,55–57,58–59); a fifth hill country region west of Jerusalem (v. 60); and the Judean **wilderness** (vv. 61–62).

16:1–4 These verses describe the southern border of the **Joseph** tribes, that is, the southern boundary of Ephraim.

16:1 The **Jordan at Jericho to the Waters of Jericho** may mean "the Jordan River at Jericho which is also called the Waters of Jericho," or else "the Waters of Jericho" refers to the spring now known as 'Ain es-Sultan.

16:2 The **Archites** are not otherwise known. The Arkites of Gn 10:17 and 1Ch 1:15 are not the same people, as their name is spelled differently in Hebrew. David's friend Hushai, who brought Absalom's plans to ruin, was called an Archite (2Sm 15:32; 16:16; 17:5,14; 1Ch 27:33).

16:3 The **Japhletites** are otherwise unknown. A Japhlet of the tribe of Asher is mentioned in 1Ch 7:32–33.

border of Lower Beth-horon, then to Gezer, and ended at the Mediterranean Sea. [4] So Ephraim and Manasseh, the sons of Joseph, received their inheritance.

Ephraim's Inheritance

[5] This was the territory of the descendants of Ephraim by their clans:

The border of their inheritance went from Ataroth-addar on the east to Upper Beth-horon. [6] In the north the border went westward from Michmethath; it turned eastward from Taanath-shiloh and passed it east of Janoah. [7] From Janoah it descended to Ataroth and Naarah, and then reached Jericho and went to the Jordan. [8] From Tappuah the border went westward along the Brook of Kanah and ended at the Mediterranean Sea.

This was the inheritance of the tribe of the descendants of Ephraim by their clans, together with [9] the cities set apart for the descendants of Ephraim within the inheritance of the descendants of Manasseh — all these cities with their settlements. [10] However, they did not drive out the Canaanites who lived in Gezer. So the Canaanites still live in Ephraim today, but they are forced laborers.

West Manasseh's Inheritance

17 This was the allotment for the tribe of Manasseh as Joseph's firstborn. Gilead and Bashan were given to Machir, the firstborn of Manasseh and the father of Gilead, because he was a man of war. [2] So the allotment was for the rest of Manasseh's descendants by their clans, for the sons of Abiezer, Helek, Asriel, Shechem, Hepher, and Shemida. These are the male descendants of Manasseh son of Joseph, by their clans.

[3] Now Zelophehad son of Hepher, son of Gilead, son of Machir, son of Manasseh, had no sons, only daughters. These are the names of his daughters: Mahlah, Noah, Hoglah, Milcah, and Tirzah. [4] They came before the priest Eleazar, Joshua son of Nun, and the leaders, saying,

"The LORD commanded Moses to give us an inheritance among our male relatives." So they gave them an inheritance among their father's brothers, in keeping with the LORD's instruction. [5] As a result, ten tracts fell to Manasseh, besides the land of Gilead and Bashan, which are beyond the Jordan, [A] [6] because Manasseh's daughters received an inheritance among his sons. The land of Gilead belonged to the rest of Manasseh's sons.

[7] The border of Manasseh went from Asher to Michmethath near Shechem. It then went southward toward the inhabitants of En-tappuah. [8] The region of Tappuah belonged to Manasseh, but Tappuah itself on Manasseh's border belonged to the descendants of Ephraim. [9] From there the border descended to the Brook of Kanah; south of the brook, cities belonged to Ephraim among Manasseh's cities. Manasseh's border was on the north side of the brook and ended at the Mediterranean Sea. [10] Ephraim's territory was to the south and Manasseh's to the north, with the Sea as its border. They reached Asher on the north and Issachar on the east. [11] Within Issachar and Asher, Manasseh had Beth-shean, Ibleam, and the inhabitants of Dor with their surrounding villages; the inhabitants of En-dor, Taanach, and Megiddo — the three cities of [B] Naphath — with their surrounding villages. [12] The descendants of Manasseh could not possess these cities, because the Canaanites were determined to stay in this land. [13] However, when the Israelites grew stronger, they imposed forced labor on the Canaanites but did not drive them out completely.

Joseph's Additional Inheritance

[14] Joseph's descendants said to Joshua, "Why did you give us only one tribal allotment as an inheritance? We have many people, because the LORD has been blessing us greatly."

[15] "If you have so many people," Joshua replied to them, "go to the forest and clear an area for yourselves there in the land of the

---

[A] 17:5 = east of the Jordan River [B] 17:11 LXX, Vg read the third is

16:9 Additional towns located in the territory of **Manasseh** were added to the allotment of **Ephraim**.
16:10 As at the end of Judah's allotment (15:63), so at the end of Ephraim's inheritance, there is a note of towns that were not fully conquered.
17:1 On allotting **Gilead and Bashan** to **Machir**, see 13:29–31. The connection between the Transjordan region and the name of Machir's son, both given as "Gilead," introduces the tendency in Manasseh for town names to follow the names of individuals.
17:2 Several clans in West Manasseh are named in this verse and are also attested as

towns in the southern and western parts of West Manasseh's allotment.
17:3 The five daughters of **Zelophehad** were **Mahlah, Noah, Hoglah, Milcah, and Tirzah**. These were also names of towns in northern and eastern areas of West Manasseh.
17:4–6 Although daughters did not normally inherit land (they received a dowry instead), Moses allowed this special stipulation (Nm 36:1–13) in the absence of any sons. He required only that these women marry within their tribe so the land would not pass out of it.
17:7–13 A border description (vv. 7–9a) is followed by a note about towns of Ephraim

that were in **Manasseh's** territory (v. 9b) and by other tribes and bodies of water that bordered this tribe (vv. 9c–10). The towns of Manasseh that were located within the tribal borders of Issachar and Asher (v. 11) were not occupied for a while because of the strength of the Canaanites (v. 12).
17:14–18 The allocation of additional land was necessary due to the large population among Joseph's descendants who lived in the central hill country of Israel. The **land of the Perizzites and the Rephaim** seems to be identical to the hill country and its forest. The **Canaanites** in the valley had iron chariots, which caused the Ephraimites to doubt their ability to conquer them, but

Perizzites and the Rephaim, because Ephraim's hill country is too small for you."

¹⁶ But the descendants of Joseph said, "The hill country is not enough for us, and all the Canaanites who inhabit the valley area have iron chariots, both at Beth-shean with its surrounding villages and in the Jezreel Valley."

¹⁷ So Joshua replied to Joseph's family (that is, Ephraim and Manasseh), "You have many people and great strength. You will not have just one allotment, ¹⁸ because the hill country will be yours also. It is a forest; clear it and its outlying areas will be yours. You can also drive out the Canaanites, even though they have iron chariots and are strong."

Land Distribution at Shiloh

18 The entire Israelite community assembled at Shiloh and set up the tent of meeting there. The land had been subdued before them, ² but seven tribes among the Israelites were left who had not divided up their inheritance. ³ So Joshua asked the Israelites, "How long will you delay going out to take possession of the land that the LORD, the God of your ancestors, gave you? ⁴ Appoint for yourselves three men from each tribe, and I will send them out. They are to go and survey the land, write a description of it for the purpose of their inheritance, and return to me. ⁵ Then they are to divide it into seven portions. Judah is to remain in its territory in the south and Joseph's family in their territory in the north. ⁶ When you have written a description of the seven portions of land and brought it to me, I will cast lots for you here in the presence of the LORD our God. ⁷ But the Levites among you do not get a portion, because their inheritance is the priesthood of the LORD. Gad, Reuben, and half the tribe of Manasseh have taken their inheritance beyond the Jordan to the east, which Moses the LORD's servant gave them."

⁸ As the men prepared to go, Joshua commanded themᴬ to write down a description of the land, saying, "Go and survey the land, write a description of it, and return to me. I will then cast lots for you here in Shiloh in the presence of the LORD." ⁹ So the men left, went through the land, and described it by towns in a document of seven sections. They returned to Joshua at the camp in Shiloh. ¹⁰ Joshua cast lots for them at Shiloh in the presence of the LORD where he distributed the land to the Israelites according to their divisions.

Benjamin's Inheritance

¹¹ The lot came up for the tribe of Benjamin's descendants by their clans, and their allotted territory lay between Judah's descendants and Joseph's descendants.

¹² Their border on the north side began at the Jordan, ascended to the slope of Jericho on the north, through the hill country westward, and ended at the wilderness around Beth-aven. ¹³ From there the border went toward Luz, to the southern slope of Luz (that is, Bethel); it then went down by Ataroth-addar, over the hill south of Lower Beth-horon.

¹⁴ On the west side, from the hill facing Beth-horon on the south, the border curved, turning southward, and ended at Kiriath-baal (that is, Kiriath-jearim), a city of the descendants of Judah. This was the west side of their border.

¹⁵ The south side began at the edge of Kiriath-jearim, and the border extended westward; it went to the spring at the Waters of Nephtoah. ¹⁶ The border descended to the foot of the hill that faces Ben Hinnom Valley at the northern end of Rephaim Valley. It ran down Hinnom Valley toward the south Jebusite slope and downward to En-rogel. ¹⁷ It curved northward and went to En-shemesh and on to Geliloth, which is opposite the Ascent of Adummim, and continued down to the Stone of Bohan son of Reuben. ¹⁸ Then it went north to the slope opposite the Arabahᴮ and proceeded into the plains.ᶜ ¹⁹ The border continued to the north slope of Beth-hoglah and ended at the northern bay of the Dead Sea, at the southern end of the Jordan. This was the southern border.

²⁰ The Jordan formed the border on the east side.

This was the inheritance of Benjamin's descendants, by their clans, according to its surrounding borders.

Benjamin's Cities

²¹ These were the cities of the tribe of Benjamin's descendants by their clans:

Jericho, Beth-hoglah, Emek-keziz, ²² Beth-arabah, Zemaraim, Bethel, ²³ Avvim, Parah, Ophrah, ²⁴ Chephar-ammoni,

---

ᴬ18:8 Lit the ones going around   ᴮ18:18 LXX reads went northward to Beth-arabah   ᶜ18:18 Or the Arabah

---

Joshua, a man of faith, encouraged them (v. 18; cp. Jdg 1:19; 4:3,13). **18:1-4** This is the first mention of the **tent of meeting** in the book of Joshua. **Shiloh** (modern Khirbet Seilun) lay to the south of Shechem and was situated in the middle of the earliest settlement of Israel in the hill country. It would remain a center for Israel's worship until the time of Samuel (1Sm 1–4). **18:5-7** Mention of the five tribes who had already received their inheritance meant that seven tribes remained. Levi, who did not receive such an inheritance, is again mentioned in anticipation of chap. 21. **18:8-10** The ability of these scouts to **write down a description of the land** meant that they prepared a document that resembled chaps. 18–19 with seven sections, one for each of the remaining tribes. **18:11-28** **Benjamin's** allotment includes a boundary description (vv. 11–20) and a

Ophni, and Geba — twelve cities, with their settlements; [25] Gibeon, Ramah, Beeroth, [26] Mizpeh, Chephirah, Mozah, [27] Rekem, Irpeel, Taralah, [28] Zela, Haeleph, Jebus[A] (that is, Jerusalem), Gibeah, and Kiriath[B] — fourteen cities, with their settlements.

This was the inheritance for Benjamin's descendants by their clans.

Simeon's Inheritance

19 The second lot came out for Simeon, for the tribe of his descendants by their clans, but their inheritance was within the inheritance given to Judah's descendants. [2] Their inheritance included

Beer-sheba (or Sheba), Moladah, [3] Hazar-shual, Balah, Ezem, [4] Eltolad, Bethul, Hormah, [5] Ziklag, Beth-marcaboth, Hazar-susah, [6] Beth-lebaoth, and Sharuhen — thirteen cities, with their settlements; [7] Ain, Rimmon, Ether, and Ashan — four cities, with their settlements; [8] and all the settlements surrounding these cities as far as Baalath-beer (Ramah in the south[C]).

This was the inheritance of the tribe of Simeon's descendants by their clans. [9] The inheritance of Simeon's descendants was within the territory of Judah's descendants, because the share for Judah's descendants was too large. So Simeon's descendants received an inheritance within Judah's portion.

Zebulun's Inheritance

[10] The third lot came up for Zebulun's descendants by their clans.

The territory of their inheritance stretched as far as Sarid; [11] their border went up westward to Maralah, reached Dabbesheth, and met the brook east of Jokneam. [12] From Sarid, it turned due east along the border of Chisloth-tabor, went to Daberath, and went up to Japhia. [13] From there, it went due east to Gath-hepher and to Eth-kazin; it extended to Rimmon, curving around to Neah. [14] The border then circled around Neah on the north to Hannathon and ended at Iphtah-el Valley,

[15] along with Kattath, Nahalal, Shimron, Idalah, and Bethlehem — twelve cities, with their settlements.

[16] This was the inheritance of Zebulun's descendants by their clans, these cities, with their settlements.

Issachar's Inheritance

[17] The fourth lot came out for the tribe of Issachar's descendants by their clans. [18] Their territory went to Jezreel, and included Chesulloth, Shunem, [19] Hapharaim, Shion, Anaharath, [20] Rabbith, Kishion, Ebez, [21] Remeth, En-gannim, En-haddah, and Beth-pazzez. [22] The border reached Tabor, Shahazumah, and Beth-shemesh, and ended at the Jordan — sixteen cities, with their settlements.

[23] This was the inheritance of the tribe of Issachar's descendants by their clans, the cities, with their settlements.

Asher's Inheritance

[24] The fifth lot came out for the tribe of Asher's descendants by their clans. [25] Their boundary included Helkath, Hali, Beten, Achshaph, [26] Allammelech, Amad, and Mishal and reached westward to Carmel and Shihor-libnath. [27] It turned eastward to Beth-dagon, reached Zebulun and Iphtah-el Valley, north toward Beth-emek and Neiel, and went north to Cabul, [28] Ebron, Rehob, Hammon, and Kanah, as far as greater Sidon. [29] The boundary then turned to Ramah as far as the fortified city of Tyre; turned back to Hosah and ended at the Mediterranean Sea, including Mahalab, Achzib,[D] [30] Ummah, Aphek, and Rehob — twenty-two cities, with their settlements. [31] This was the inheritance of the tribe of Asher's descendants by their clans, these cities with their settlements.

Naphtali's Inheritance

[32] The sixth lot came out for Naphtali's descendants by their clans. [33] Their boundary went from Heleph and from the oak in Zaanannim, including

---

town list (vv. 21–28), which took in Jebus/Jerusalem.
19:1–9 The allotment of the tribe of **Simeon** has no boundaries. It is a list of towns (vv. 2–8) located within the southern territory of Judah. This was given to Simeon **because the share for Judah's descendants was too large**. The town list subdivides into an eastern (vv. 2–6) and a western (vv. 7–8) list. This area around the Beer-sheba Valley was already inhabited. Therefore, Simeon's settlement would assist in giving the region an Israelite identity. It would also provide a defense against encroachment by Edomite tribes to the south and east.

19:10–16 The allotment for **Zebulun's descendants** consists of a boundary description, beginning with the southern border (vv. 10–11), moving to the eastern border (vv. 12–13), and concluding with the northern boundary (vv. 14–15). The western border is Asher's eastern border. Zebulun lay in the southwest corner of the hills of Galilee between the Jezreel Valley to the south and the Bet Netofa Valley northward in Galilee.
19:17–23 **Issachar's** allotment preserves a town list that included **sixteen cities** in the Jezreel Valley around Mount **Tabor** and those in the southeastern hills of Galilee.

19:24–31 **Asher's** allotment consists of a boundary list that began in the south (vv. 25–26), turned east along Zebulun (vv. 27–28), and reached north to **greater Sidon** before turning south along the coast (vv. 29–30). **Cabul** and the area around it was later given by Solomon to Hiram king of Tyre in payment for his assistance in constructing the temple of Jerusalem (1Kg 9:11–13).
19:32–39 **Naphtali's** tribe received the largest area among the seven remaining allotments. However, it was perhaps the worst agriculturally, located in upper Galilee where the heights prevented much cultivation. The southern boundary (vv. 33–34) is

Adami-nekeb and Jabneel, as far as Lakkum, and ended at the Jordan. ³⁴ To the west, the boundary turned to Aznoth-tabor and went from there to Hukkok, reaching Zebulun on the south, Asher on the west, and Judah^ at the Jordan on the east. ³⁵ The fortified cities were Ziddim, Zer, Hammath, Rakkath, Chinnereth, ³⁶ Adamah, Ramah, Hazor, ³⁷ Kedesh, Edrei, En-hazor, ³⁸ Iron, Migdal-el, Horem, Beth-anath, and Beth-shemesh — nineteen cities, with their settlements. ³⁹ This was the inheritance of the tribe of Naphtali's descendants by their clans, the cities with their settlements.

Dan's Inheritance

⁴⁰ The seventh lot came out for the tribe of Dan's descendants by their clans. ⁴¹ The territory of their inheritance included Zorah, Eshtaol, Ir-shemesh, ⁴² Shaalabbin, Aijalon, Ithlah, ⁴³ Elon, Timnah, Ekron, ⁴⁴ Eltekeh, Gibbethon, Baalath, ⁴⁵ Jehud, Bene-berak, Gath-rimmon, ⁴⁶ Me-jarkon, and Rakkon, with the territory facing Joppa. ⁴⁷ When the territory of the descendants of Dan slipped out of their control, they went up and fought against Leshem, captured it, and struck it down with the sword. So they took possession of it, lived there, and renamed Leshem after their ancestor Dan. ⁴⁸ This was the inheritance of the tribe of Dan's descendants by their clans, these cities with their settlements.

Joshua's Inheritance

⁴⁹ When they had finished distributing the land into its territories, the Israelites gave Joshua son of Nun an inheritance among them. ⁵⁰ By the LORD's command, they gave him the city Timnath-serah in the hill country of Ephraim, which he requested. He rebuilt the city and lived in it. ⁵¹ These were the portions that the priest Eleazar, Joshua son of Nun, and the family heads

distributed to the Israelite tribes by lot at Shiloh in the LORD's presence at the entrance to the tent of meeting. So they finished dividing up the land.

Cities of Refuge

20 Then the LORD spoke to Joshua, ² "Tell the Israelites: Select your cities of refuge, as I instructed you through Moses, ³ so that a person who kills someone unintentionally or accidentally may flee there. These will be your refuge from the avenger of blood. ⁴ When someone flees to one of these cities, stands at the entrance of the city gate, and states his case before the elders of that city, they are to bring him into the city and give him a place to live among them. ⁵ And if the avenger of blood pursues him, they must not hand the one who committed manslaughter over to him, for he killed his neighbor accidentally and did not hate him beforehand. ⁶ He is to stay in that city until he stands trial before the assembly and until the death of the high priest serving at that time. Then the one who committed manslaughter may return home to his own city from which he fled."

⁷ So they designated Kedesh in the hill country of Naphtali in Galilee, Shechem in the hill country of Ephraim, and Kiriath-arba (that is, Hebron) in the hill country of Judah. ⁸ Across the Jordan east of Jericho, they selected Bezer on the wilderness plateau from Reuben's tribe, Ramoth in Gilead from Gad's tribe, and Golan in Bashan from Manasseh's tribe. ⁹ These are the cities appointed for all the Israelites and the aliens residing among them, so that anyone who kills a person unintentionally may flee there and not die at the hand of the avenger of blood until he stands before the assembly.

Cities of the Levites

21 The Levite family heads approached the priest Eleazar, Joshua son of Nun, and the family heads of the Israelite tribes. ² At Shiloh, in the land of Canaan, they told them, "The

---

supplemented with a town list (vv. 35–38). Its eastern boundaries stretched to the Jordan River and the Sea of Galilee, including the rich and powerful centers of **Chinnereth . . . Kedesh**, and especially **Hazor** (chap. 11).
19:40–48 The territory of the **descendants of Dan** consists of a town list including eastern (vv. 41–44) and western towns (vv. 45–47). Its location alongside the Canaanite and Philistine coastal towns threatened its peace and prosperity. Dan lost part or all of this territory (v. 47) and migrated north to the town of **Leshem** which they captured and renamed **Dan** (Jdg 17–18).
19:49–51 As with Caleb, the other faithful spy of the exodus generation, Joshua received a special allotment in his tribal territory—**Timnath-serah** (modern Khirbet

Tibnah), southwest of Shechem. As Caleb received the first allotment in the promised land (14:6–15), Joshua received the last.
20:1–3 In this chapter some of the land or towns given to Israel are set aside for a specific purpose. On the significance of the **cities of refuge**, see Ex 21:12–14; Nm 35:9–15,22–28; Dt 4:41–43; 19:1–10. These passages indicate that there were to be six towns—three east and three west of the Jordan River. Someone who killed another person **unintentionally or accidentally** could find refuge in one of these towns, avoiding a form of blood vengeance in which the dead person's nearest kin was to seek the death of the killer in order to remove any blood guilt from their family.
20:4–6 The **elders of that city** functioned as the judges who heard all important disputes within the community. The **trial**

before the assembly was presumably a legal trial in his hometown where the killing occurred (Nm 35:22–28). Even if he was acquitted of premeditated murder, he remained in the city of refuge **until the death of the high priest serving at that time.** Presumably the avenger was to accept the high priest's death as a substitute for the guilt incurred by the shedding of innocent blood. The killer was free to return home.
20:8 These cities of refuge located **east** of the **Jordan** River had been designated and named by Moses (Dt 4:41–43).
21:1–2 Eleazar at Shiloh recalls 18:1–10 and the distribution of the tribal allotments. This would be the Levites' allotment.
21:2 The Lord's command **through Moses** about the Levitical cities occurs in Nm 35:1–8, where the towns are not named.

LORD commanded through Moses that we be given cities to live in, with their pasturelands for our livestock." ³ So the Israelites, by the LORD's command, gave the Levites these cities with their pasturelands from their inheritance.
⁴ The lot came out for the Kohathite clans: The Levites who were the descendants of the priest Aaron received thirteen cities by lot from the tribes of Judah, Simeon, and Benjamin. ⁵ The remaining descendants of Kohath received ten cities by lot from the clans of the tribes of Ephraim, Dan, and half the tribe of Manasseh.

⁶ Gershon's descendants received thirteen cities by lot from the clans of the tribes of Issachar, Asher, Naphtali, and half the tribe of Manasseh in Bashan.

⁷ Merari's descendants received twelve cities for their clans from the tribes of Reuben, Gad, and Zebulun.
⁸ The Israelites gave these cities with their pasturelands around them to the Levites by lot, as the LORD had commanded through Moses.

Cities of Aaron's Descendants
⁹ The Israelites gave these cities by name from the tribes of the descendants of Judah and Simeon ¹⁰ to the descendants of Aaron from the Kohathite clans of the Levites, because they received the first lot. ¹¹ They gave them Kiriath-arba (that is, Hebron; Arba was the father of Anak) with its surrounding pasturelands in the hill country of Judah. ¹² But they gave the fields and settlements of the city to Caleb son of Jephunneh as his possession.
¹³ They gave to the descendants of the priest Aaron:
Hebron, the city of refuge for the one who commits manslaughter, with its pasturelands, Libnah with its pasturelands, ¹⁴ Jattir with its pasturelands, Eshtemoa with its pasturelands, ¹⁵ Holon with its pasturelands, Debir with its pasturelands, ¹⁶ Ain with its pasturelands, Juttah with its pasturelands, and Beth-shemesh with its pasturelands — nine cities from these two tribes.

¹⁷ From the tribe of Benjamin they gave:
Gibeon with its pasturelands, Geba with its pasturelands, ¹⁸ Anathoth with its pasturelands, and Almon with its pasturelands

— four cities. ¹⁹ All thirteen cities with their pasturelands were for the priests, the descendants of Aaron.

Cities of Kohath's Other Descendants
²⁰ The allotted cities to the remaining clans of Kohath's descendants, who were Levites, came from the tribe of Ephraim. ²¹ The Israelites gave them:
Shechem, the city of refuge for the one who commits manslaughter, with its pasturelands in the hill country of Ephraim, Gezer with its pasturelands, ²² Kibzaim with its pasturelands, and Beth-horon with its pasturelands — four cities.

²³ From the tribe of Dan they gave:
Elteke with its pasturelands, Gibbethon with its pasturelands, ²⁴ Aijalon with its pasturelands, and Gath-rimmon with its pasturelands — four cities.

²⁵ From half the tribe of Manasseh they gave:
Taanach with its pasturelands and Gath-rimmonᴬ with its pasturelands — two cities.
²⁶ All ten cities with their pasturelands were for the clans of Kohath's other descendants.

Cities of Gershon's Descendants
²⁷ From half the tribe of Manasseh, they gave to the descendants of Gershon, who were one of the Levite clans:
Golan, the city of refuge for the one who commits manslaughter, with its pasturelands in Bashan, and Beeshterah with its pasturelands — two cities.

²⁸ From the tribe of Issachar they gave:
Kishion with its pasturelands, Daberath with its pasturelands, ²⁹ Jarmuth with its pasturelands, and En-gannim with its pasturelands — four cities.

³⁰ From the tribe of Asher they gave:
Mishal with its pasturelands, Abdon with its pasturelands, ³¹ Helkath with its pasturelands, and Rehob with its pasturelands — four cities.

³² From the tribe of Naphtali they gave:
Kedesh in Galilee, the city of refuge for the one who commits manslaughter, with its pasturelands, Hammoth-dor with its

ᴬ21:25 Or Ibleam

21:4 Those Levites who were descendants of the priest Aaron would receive the cities closest to Jerusalem because their responsibilities required them to be close to the temple (Nm 18:1–6). These cities are listed in Jos 21:9–19.
21:5 The descendants of Kohath, second son of Levi (Gn 46:11), received their inheritance in the hill country, at that time the

location of the ark, for which they were responsible in the wilderness (Nm 3:1; 4:15–20; 7:9). These cities are listed in Jos 21:20–26.
21:6 The descendants of Gershon, first son of Levi, had been responsible for the tabernacle's coverings and other textiles (Nm 3:25–26; 4:24–26). They received cities in the northern tribal areas, listed in Jos 21:27–33.

21:7 Merari's descendants, from Levi's third son, guarded the tabernacle and transported its frames (Nm 1:47–53; 3:33–37; 4:29–33). They were given the Transjordanian and Zebulun Levitical cities, listed in Jos 21:34–40.
21:9–42 The forty-eight Levitical cities are listed and subdivided into four groups, with occasional notes. These are further

pasturelands, and Kartan with its pasture-lands — three cities. ³³ All thirteen cities with their pasturelands were for the Gershonites by their clans.

Cities of Merari's Descendants

³⁴ From the tribe of Zebulun, they gave to the clans of the descendants of Merari, who were the remaining Levites:
Jokneam with its pasturelands, Kartah with its pasturelands, ³⁵ Dimnah with its pasturelands, and Nahalal with its pas-turelands — four cities.

³⁶ From the tribe of Reuben they gave: Bezer with its pasturelands, Jahzah^A with its pasturelands, ³⁷ Kedemoth with its pas-turelands, and Mephaath with its pasture-lands — four cities.^B

³⁸ From the tribe of Gad they gave: Ramoth in Gilead, the city of refuge for the one who commits manslaughter, with its pasturelands, Mahanaim with its pasture-lands, ³⁹ Heshbon with its pasturelands, and Jazer with its pasturelands — four cit-ies in all. ⁴⁰ All twelve cities were allotted to the clans of Merari's descendants, the remaining Levite clans.

⁴¹ Within the Israelite possession there were forty-eight cities in all with their pasturelands for the Levites. ⁴² Each of these cities had its own surrounding pasturelands; this was true for all the cities.

The Lord's Promises Fulfilled

⁴³ So the Lord gave Israel all the land he had sworn to give their ancestors, and they took possession of it and settled there. ⁴⁴ The Lord gave them rest on every side according to all he had sworn to their ancestors. None of their en-emies were able to stand against them, for the Lord handed over all their enemies to them. ⁴⁵ None of the good promises the Lord had made to the house of Israel failed. Everything was fulfilled.

Eastern Tribes Return Home

22 Joshua summoned the Reubenites, Gadites, and half the tribe of Manas-seh ² and told them, "You have done everything

Moses the Lord's servant commanded you and have obeyed me in everything I commanded you. ³ You have not deserted your brothers even once this whole time but have carried out the requirement of the command of the Lord your God. ⁴ Now that he has given your brothers rest, just as he promised them, return to your homes in your own land that Moses the Lord's servant gave you across the Jor-dan. ⁵ Only carefully obey the command and instruction that Moses the Lord's servant gave you: to love the Lord your God, walk in all his ways, keep his commands, be loyal to him, and serve him with all your heart and all your soul."

⁶ Joshua blessed them and sent them on their way, and they went to their homes. ⁷ Moses had given territory to half the tribe of Manasseh in Bashan, but Joshua had given territory to the other half,^C with their brothers, on the west side of the Jordan. When Joshua sent them to their homes and blessed them, ⁸ he said, "Re-turn to your homes with great wealth: a huge number of cattle, and silver, gold, bronze, iron, and a large quantity of clothing. Share the spoil of your enemies with your brothers."

Eastern Tribes Build an Altar

⁹ The Reubenites, Gadites, and half the tribe of Manasseh left the Israelites at Shiloh in the land of Canaan to return to their own land of Gilead, which they took possession of accord-ing to the Lord's command through Moses. ¹⁰ When they came to the region of^D the Jordan in the land of Canaan, the Reubenites, Gadites, and half the tribe of Manasseh built a large, im-pressive altar there by the Jordan.

¹¹ Then the Israelites heard it said, "Look, the Reubenites, Gadites, and half the tribe of Ma-nasseh have built an altar on the frontier of the land of Canaan at the region of^E the Jordan, on the Israelite side." ¹² When the Israelites heard this, the entire Israelite community assembled at Shiloh to go to war against them.

Explanation of the Altar

¹³ The Israelites sent Phinehas son of Elea-zar the priest to the Reubenites, Gadites, and half the tribe of Manasseh, in the land of Gil-ead. ¹⁴ They sent ten leaders with him — one family leader for each tribe of Israel. All of them were heads of their ancestral families among the clans of Israel. ¹⁵ They went to the

^A21:36 Or *Jahaz*   ^B21:36–37 Some Hb mss omit these vv.   ^C22:7 Lit *to his half*   ^D22:10 Or *to Geliloth by*   ^E22:11 Or *at Geliloth by*

subdivided by tribes with numerical totals after each grouping.
22:5 Joshua dismissed the Transjordanian tribes with one condition: fully obey God's revealed instruction. To serve God **with all your heart and all your soul** repeats Dt 6:5.
22:9–10 The tribes on the eastern side of the Jordan River **built a large, impressive altar** by the river. The altar that these tribes

constructed is in Hebrew, *mizbeach*, a word that means "slaughter." This is what caused the concern of the other tribes: animal sac-rifice would take place on this altar.
22:11–12 Because the altar was beside the Jordan River and was so large, the ten tribes could probably see it. The rest of Israel as-sembled against the two and a half tribes to war against them from their base **at Shiloh**.

22:13 How much later this took place is not clear, but **Phinehas son of Eleazar the priest** was now the acting priest. He had last appeared in Nm 31:6 where he took articles from the sanctuary into battle.
22:14–19 The ten representatives of the remaining tribes objected because the altar was considered a competitor to the true **altar of the Lord our God**.

Reubenites, Gadites, and half the tribe of Manasseh, in the land of Gilead, and told them, [16] "This is what the LORD's entire community says: 'What is this treachery you have committed today against the God of Israel by turning away from the LORD and building an altar for yourselves, so that you are in rebellion against the LORD today? [17] Wasn't the iniquity of Peor, which brought a plague on the LORD's community, enough for us? We have not cleansed ourselves from it even to this day, [18] and now would you turn away from the LORD? If you rebel against the LORD today, tomorrow he will be angry with the entire community of Israel. [19] But if the land you possess is defiled, cross over to the land the LORD possesses where the LORD's tabernacle stands, and take possession of it among us. But don't rebel against the LORD or against us by building for yourselves an altar other than the altar of the LORD our God. [20] Wasn't Achan son of Zerah unfaithful regarding what was set apart for destruction, bringing wrath on the entire community of Israel? He was not the only one who perished because of his iniquity.'"

[21] The Reubenites, Gadites, and half the tribe of Manasseh answered the heads of the Israelite clans, [22] "The Mighty One, God, the LORD! The Mighty One, God, the LORD![A] He knows, and may Israel also know. Do not spare us today, if it was in rebellion or treachery against the LORD [23] that we have built for ourselves an altar to turn away from him. May the LORD himself hold us accountable if we intended to offer burnt offerings and grain offerings on it, or to sacrifice fellowship offerings on it. [24] We actually did this from a specific concern that in the future your descendants might say to our descendants, 'What relationship do you have with the LORD, the God of Israel? [25] For the LORD has made the Jordan a border between us and you descendants of Reuben and Gad. You have no share in the LORD!' So your descendants may cause our descendants to stop fearing the LORD.

[26] "Therefore we said: Let's take action and build an altar for ourselves, but not for burnt offering or sacrifice. [27] Instead, it is to be a witness between us and you, and between the generations after us, so that we may carry out the worship of the LORD in his presence with our burnt offerings, sacrifices, and fellowship

offerings. Then in the future, your descendants will not be able to say to our descendants, 'You have no share in the LORD!' [28] We thought that if they said this to us or to our generations in the future, we would reply: Look at the replica of the LORD's altar that our ancestors made, not for burnt offering or sacrifice, but as a witness between us and you. [29] We would never ever rebel against the LORD or turn away from him today by building an altar for burnt offering, grain offering, or sacrifice, other than the altar of the LORD our God, which is in front of his tabernacle."

Conflict Resolved

[30] When the priest Phinehas and the community leaders, the heads of Israel's clans who were with him, heard what the descendants of Reuben, Gad, and Manasseh had to say, they were pleased. [31] Phinehas son of Eleazar the priest said to the descendants of Reuben, Gad, and Manasseh, "Today we know that the LORD is among us, because you have not committed this treachery against him. As a result, you have rescued the Israelites from the LORD's power."

[32] Then the priest Phinehas son of Eleazar and the leaders returned from the Reubenites and Gadites in the land of Gilead to the Israelites in the land of Canaan and brought back a report to them. [33] The Israelites were pleased with the report, and they blessed God. They spoke no more about going to war against them to ravage the land where the Reubenites and Gadites lived. [34] So the Reubenites and Gadites named the altar: It[B] is a witness between us that the LORD is God.

Joshua's Farewell Address

23 A long time after the LORD had given Israel rest from all the enemies around them, Joshua was old, advanced in age. [2] So Joshua summoned all Israel, including its elders, leaders, judges, and officers, and said to them, "I am old, advanced in age, [3] and you have seen for yourselves everything the LORD your God did to all these nations on your account, because it was the LORD your God who was fighting for you. [4] See, I have allotted these remaining nations to you as an inheritance for your tribes, including all the nations I have destroyed, from the Jordan westward to the

---

[A] 22:22 Or *The LORD is the God of gods! The LORD is the God of gods!*   [B] 22:34 Some Hb mss, Syr, Tg read *altar Witness because it*

22:17 The **iniquity of Peor** refers to the time when Israel joined Midian in worshiping the Baal or god of the region of Peor, east of the Jordan River, in Nm 25.
22:20 Mention of **Achan son of Zerah** (8:1–29) explains the concern of the ten tribes. They feared that God's judgment for what the Transjordanian tribes had done would also fall on them all.

22:21–28 The two and a half tribes explained they had built the altar as a way to maintain the unity of all the tribes in future generations. Repeatedly the Transjordanian tribes denied any intent to use the altar as a place of sacrifice. The altar bore **witness** that those on both sides of it worshiped the same God at the same tabernacle.

22:30–34 With the conflict resolved, the **altar** was **named** in recognition of the confession of the Transjordanian tribes.
23:1 The note that **Joshua was old** repeats the words from 13:1. Joshua had completed his life's mission.
23:2 Elders, leaders, judges, and officers includes all Israel's leadership at the various levels.

Mediterranean Sea. [5] The LORD your God will force them back on your account and drive them out before you so that you can take possession of their land, as the LORD your God promised you.

[6] "Be very strong and continue obeying all that is written in the book of the law of Moses, so that you do not turn from it to the right or left [7] and so that you do not associate with these nations remaining among you. Do not call on the names of their gods or make an oath to them; do not serve them or bow in worship to them. [8] Instead, be loyal to the LORD your God, as you have been to this day.

[9] "The LORD has driven out great and powerful nations before you, and no one is able to stand against you to this day. [10] One of you routed a thousand because the LORD your God was fighting for you, as he promised.[A] [11] So diligently watch yourselves! Love the LORD your God! [12] If you ever turn away and become loyal to the rest of these nations remaining among you, and if you intermarry or associate with them and they with you, [13] know for certain that the LORD your God will not continue to drive these nations out before you. They will become a snare and a trap for you, a sharp stick[B] for your sides and thorns in your eyes, until you disappear from this good land the LORD your God has given you.

[14] "I am now going the way of the whole earth, and you know with all your heart and all your soul that none of the good promises the LORD your God made to you has failed. Everything was fulfilled for you; not one promise has failed. [15] Since every good thing the LORD your God promised you has come about, so he will bring on you every bad thing until he has annihilated you from this good land the LORD your God has given you. [16] If you break the covenant of the LORD your God, which he commanded you, and go and serve other gods, and bow in worship to them, the LORD's anger will burn against you, and you will quickly

disappear from this good land he has given you."

Review of Israel's History

24 Joshua assembled all the tribes of Israel at Shechem and summoned Israel's elders, leaders, judges, and officers, and they presented themselves before God. [2] Joshua said to all the people, "This is what the LORD, the God of Israel, says: 'Long ago your ancestors, including Terah, the father of Abraham and Nahor, lived beyond the Euphrates River and worshiped other gods. [3] But I took your father Abraham from the region beyond the Euphrates River, led him throughout the land of Canaan, and multiplied his descendants. I gave him Isaac, [4] and to Isaac I gave Jacob and Esau. I gave the hill country of Seir to Esau as a possession.

"'Jacob and his sons, however, went down to Egypt. [5] I sent Moses and Aaron, and I defeated Egypt by what I did within it, and afterward I brought you out. [6] When I brought your ancestors out of Egypt and you reached the Red Sea, the Egyptians pursued your ancestors with chariots and horsemen as far as the sea. [7] Your ancestors cried out to the LORD, so he put darkness between you and the Egyptians, and brought the sea over them, engulfing them. Your own eyes saw what I did to Egypt. After that, you lived in the wilderness a long time.

[8] "'Later, I brought you to the land of the Amorites who lived beyond the Jordan. They fought against you, but I handed them over to you. You possessed their land, and I annihilated them before you. [9] Balak son of Zippor, king of Moab, set out to fight against Israel. He sent for Balaam son of Beor to curse you, [10] but I would not listen to Balaam. Instead, he repeatedly blessed you, and I rescued you from him. [11] "'You then crossed the Jordan and came to Jericho. Jericho's citizens — as well as the Amorites, Perizzites, Canaanites, Hethites, Girgashites, Hivites, and Jebusites — fought against you, but I handed them over to you.

23:6 The requirement for Israel to continue to enjoy success was that they obey promised land. **all that is written in the book of the law of Moses.** This is what Joshua was commanded to do in 1:9–11. His obedience and that of Israel had brought victory. The phrase **turn . . . to the right or left** is also found in 1:7; Dt 2:27; 5:32; 17:11,20; 28:14; 2Kg 22:2; Pr 4:27.

23:11 This warning to **love the LORD your God** is based on Dt 6:4 and is at the heart of Joshua's message.

23:12–13 This warning against association or intermarriage with other nations is repeated in 24:20. Disobedience would result in God withdrawing his strength so that Israel would not fully possess the land. This compromise would lead to a **trap** for Israel and ultimately, in anticipation of the exile centuries later, to the

tribes of Israel disappearing from the promised land.

23:14 The **way of the whole earth** is death, since everything on earth eventually dies (Ec 9:3; Rm 5:12; Heb 9:27).

24:1–27 In this final chapter of the book, Joshua enacted a covenant renewal ceremony with Israel.

24:1 Joshua brought together all the tribes and their leaders to stand before God at **Shechem**, just as he had at Mount Ebal, next to Shechem, in 8:30–35.

24:2b–13 This is the historical review section of the treaty/covenant. Its purpose is to demonstrate God's acts of protection and deliverance toward Israel in the past and to motivate Israel to remain faithful to God in the present.

24:12 **Hornets** were promised in Ex 23:28 and Dt 7:20 as the means by which God

would drive out the inhabitants of the land. God fulfilled his promise.

#10 99 Essential Christian Truths

CHRIST AS KING

God has always been King over his creation, whether in heaven or on earth. Yet some of his creatures in both realms have rebelled against him, leaving destruction in their wake. To restore his broken world, God promised a King who would deliver his people and reclaim all of creation. The promise of a coming King finds its fulfillment in Jesus Christ and looks forward to its consummation when Jesus returns for his bride, the church.

¹² I sent hornets^ ahead of you, and they drove out the two Amorite kings before you. It was not by your sword or bow. ¹³ I gave you a land you did not labor for, and cities you did not build, though you live in them; you are eating from vineyards and olive groves you did not plant.'

The Covenant Renewal

¹⁴ "Therefore, fear the LORD and worship him in sincerity and truth. Get rid of the gods your ancestors worshiped beyond the Euphrates River and in Egypt, and worship the LORD. ¹⁵ But if it doesn't please you to worship the LORD, choose for yourselves today: Which will you worship — the gods your ancestors worshiped beyond the Euphrates River or the gods of the Amorites in whose land you are living? As for me and my family, we will worship the LORD."

¹⁶ The people replied, "We will certainly not abandon the LORD to worship other gods! ¹⁷ For the LORD our God brought us and our ancestors out of the land of Egypt, out of the place of slavery, and performed these great signs before our eyes. He also protected us all along the way we went and among all the peoples whose lands we traveled through. ¹⁸ The LORD drove out before us all the peoples, including the Amorites who lived in the land. We too will worship the LORD, because he is our God."

¹⁹ But Joshua told the people, "You will not be able to worship the LORD, because he is a holy God. He is a jealous God; he will not forgive your transgressions and sins. ²⁰ If you abandon the LORD and worship foreign gods, he will turn against you, harm you, and completely destroy you, after he has been good to you."

²¹ "No!" the people answered Joshua. "We will worship the LORD."

²² Joshua then told the people, "You are witnesses against yourselves that you yourselves have chosen to worship the LORD."

"We are witnesses," they said.

²³ "Then get rid of the foreign gods that are among you and turn your hearts to the LORD, the God of Israel."

²⁴ So the people said to Joshua, "We will worship the LORD our God and obey him."

²⁵ On that day Joshua made a covenant for the people at Shechem and established a statute and ordinance for them. ²⁶ Joshua recorded these things in the book of the law of God; he also took a large stone and set it up there under the oak at the sanctuary of the LORD. ²⁷ And Joshua said to all the people, "You see this stone — it will be a witness against us, for it has heard all the words the LORD said to us, and it will be a witness against you, so that you will not deny your God." ²⁸ Then Joshua sent the people away, each to his own inheritance.

Burial of Three Leaders

²⁹ After these things, the LORD's servant, Joshua son of Nun, died at the age of 110. ³⁰ They buried him in his allotted territory at Timnath-serah, in the hill country of Ephraim north of Mount Gaash. ³¹ Israel worshiped the LORD throughout Joshua's lifetime and during the lifetimes of the elders who outlived Joshua and who had experienced all the works the LORD had done for Israel.

³² Joseph's bones, which the Israelites had brought up from Egypt, were buried at Shechem in the parcel of land Jacob had purchased from the sons of Hamor, Shechem's father, for a hundred pieces of silver.ᴮ It was an inheritance for Joseph's descendants.

³³ And Eleazar son of Aaron died, and they buried him at Gibeah,ᶜ which had been given to his son Phinehas in the hill country of Ephraim.

^24:12 Or sent terror ᴮ24:32 Lit a hundred qesitahs ᶜ24:33 = the Hill

24:13 God's gift of **a land you did not labor for, and cities you did not build** recalls his promise to Israel in Dt 6:10–11.
24:14–15 Joshua does not invite Israel to choose the Lord but repeats Deuteronomy's command to **fear** and to serve/**worship** only the Lord (see Dt 6:13; 10:12,20). Only if they refuse are they faced with a choice: which of the many pagan gods of their **ancestors** or the Amorites/Canaanites to foolishly follow. Joshua refuses to turn from following the Lord.
24:19 After the people promised to worship God alone, Joshua warned them that it would be difficult. The people must not choose lightly or in a moment of good feeling about God, **a holy God**... **a jealous God**.
24:20 If the people chose now for God and changed their minds later, God would **completely destroy** them, just as they did their enemies in lands they now inhabited (2:10). This warning is the closest chap. 24 comes to pronouncing curses.
24:21–22 After Joshua's warning, Israel repeats their pledge to worship the Lord, and Joshua calls them as witnesses of their own word.

24:23–24 Joshua charged Israel to **get rid of the foreign gods that are among you**. The people made their promises, but the report does not indicate that they did away with their gods.
24:25–28 Joshua declared that this covenant would be written **in the book of the law of God**. This suggests that the covenant was preserved in the most sacred and holy place possible. It would never be changed. The **stone** that Joshua erected, like those at the crossing of the Jordan (4:1–7,20–24), would stand as a witness for future generations of all that the people agreed to at this place. Israel might be tempted to change, but the stone would always stand as a reminder to the nation of its commitment to the one true God.
24:29–30 These verses are identical to Jdg 2:9–10, where the story of the judges begins as a continuation of that of Joshua and his generation. Joshua is here called **the Lord's servant**. Just like Moses, who was given this name only at his death, Joshua's honor of receiving it indicates a life of faithfulness (1:1; Dt 34:5). The age of Joseph at

his death was also 110 (Gn 50:22,26).
24:31 Despite some uncertainty about their degree of commitment (v. 23), Israel remained faithful to God during the **lifetime of Joshua** and **the elders** who had experienced God's miracles and guidance. The following generation would be different as Jdg 2:10–13 attests.
24:32 The mention of Joseph is here connected with his **bones** (Gn 50:24–26) and the purchase of the burial place (33:18–20). This ties together the generation that left the promised land with the one that returned and settled there.
24:33 Both **Eleazar son of Aaron** and his **son Phinehas** had been instrumental in the division of the land (14:1; 17:4; 19:51; 21:1; 22:13,30–32). Eleazar represented the religious leadership of the priesthood. He was of Joshua's generation. Phinehas represented the next generation (he would next appear in Jdg 20:28 in a very different context). Unlike Joshua, whose family is not mentioned and who had no successor in leadership, the priestly line was to continue. It would remain a witness of God to his people, the Israelites.

◥ Introduction to Judges

Circumstances of Writing

No author is named in the book of Judges, nor is any indication given of the writer or writers who are responsible for it. The three divisions of the book are on a different footing regarding the sources from which they are drawn. The historical introduction presents a form of the traditional narrative of the conquest of Palestine that is parallel to the book of Joshua. The main portion of the book, comprising the narratives of the judges, appears to be based on oral or written traditions of a local observer.

The period of the Israelite judges lay between the conquest of the promised land under Joshua and the rise of the monarchy with Saul and David. The events described are thus to be dated from the end of the fifteenth century BC to the latter part of the eleventh century BC, a period of around three hundred years. This was a time of social and religious anarchy, characterized by the repeated refrain, "In those days there was no king in Israel; everyone did whatever seemed right to him" (17:6; 18:1; 19:1; 21:25).

We cannot ascertain exactly when the book of Judges was composed. The reference in 18:30 to the fate of Dan at "the time of the exile from the land" suggests a date of final editing after the exile of the northern kingdom by Assyria around 722 BC. Meanwhile, the suggestion that readers could visit the site of Gideon's altar at Ophrah in 6:24 suggests a date prior to the exile of the southern kingdom, Judah, in 586 BC. Its message would have resonated strongly at several points of Israel's history, and it has been argued that it fits well during the dark days of Manasseh (686–642 BC; 2Kg 21:1–18). However, it is not possible to date Judges with precision.

Contribution to the Bible

The book of Judges shows us that the nation of Israel survived the dark days of the judges entirely by the grace of God. In mercy, he sent oppressors as reminders of their rebellion. In mercy, he responded to their cries and raised up deliverers. Judges also illustrates the fundamental problem of the human heart. When God's people forget his saving acts, they go after other gods. Judges also illustrates the link between spiritual commitments and ethical conduct. In the end, the book of Judges illustrates the eternal truth: the Lord will build his kingdom, in spite of our sin and rebellion.

Structure

The book falls into three parts. There is a prologue (1:1–3:6) that deals with the failure of the second generation to press on with the conquest of Canaan. This is followed by a sixfold cycle of sin and salvation (3:7–16:31), which forms the bulk of the book. Finally, there is an appendix (chaps. 17–21) that shows the full effects of total depravity let loose upon the people. This structure demonstrates not only the repetition of patterns of sin and judgment but also the negative progress. The midpoint of the narrative is the linked episode involving Gideon and Abimelech, which serves to highlight further the significance of the issue of kingship.

Judges Timeline

1500–1450 BC

JOSHUA 1490?–1380?
Events in Deuteronomy 1406
Miraculous crossing of the Jordan River 1406
Events in Joshua 1406–1380?
Musical notation, Ugarit 1400
Chopsticks are used in China. 1400

1450–1425 BC

Division of the land into twelve allotments 1385?
DEBORAH 1360?–1300?
Deborah and Barak defeat the Canaanites. 1320?
Pharaoh Horemheb creates a river
 security unit to board and search boats
 suspected of smuggling. 1320
Pharaoh Merneptah (1212–1203) memorializes his
 victories against Libya and Canaan on a granite
 stele, the so-called Merneptah Stele. This is
 the first Egyptian document in which Israel is
 mentioned. The Merneptah Stele was discovered
 in AD 1896 by Flinders Petrie at Thebes.

Outline

I. Prologue (1:1–3:6)
 A. Israel's failure to possess the land (1:1–36)
 B. The pattern of sin, judgment, and restoration (2:1–3:6)
II. The Judges (3:7–16:31)
 A. Othniel (3:7–11)
 B. Ehud (3:12–30)
 C. Shamgar (3:31)
 D. Deborah and Barak (4:1–5:31)
 E. Gideon and Abimelech (6:1–9:57)
 F. Tola and Jair (10:1–5)
 G. Jephthah (10:6–12:7)
 H. Ibzan, Elon, and Abdon (12:8–15)
 I. Samson (13:1–16:31)
III. Epilogue (17:1–21:25)
 A. The religious degeneration of Israel (17:1–18:31)
 B. The moral degeneration of Israel (19:1–21:25)

1425–1400 BC

Events in Judges **1380?–1060?**
JEPHTHAH **1250?–1175?**
RUTH **1225?–1125?**
Gideon defeats the Midianites
  and Amalekites. **1200?**
Invasion of the Sea Peoples **1200?**
The Phoenicians become the world's
  first maritime power. **1200**
The Phoenicians develop warships with
  battering rams on the bow. **1200**
The Egyptians make several attempts
  to connect the Nile River with the
  Red Sea by digging canals. **1200**

1400–1375 BC

Jephthah defeats the Ammonites
  and Philistines. **1170?**
Ramesses III, Egypt's last great pharaoh, dies. **1155**
The Amorite king Nebuchadnezzar I
  captures Babylon. **1124**
SAMSON **1120?–1060?**
Body armor made from rhinoceros hide, China **1100**

Judah's Leadership against the Canaanites

1 After the death of Joshua, the Israelites inquired of the LORD, "Who will be the first to fight for us against the Canaanites?"

[2] The LORD answered, "Judah is to go. I have handed the land over to him."

[3] Judah said to his brother Simeon, "Come with me to my allotted territory, and let's fight against the Canaanites. I will also go with you to your allotted territory." So Simeon went with him.

[4] When Judah attacked, the LORD handed the Canaanites and Perizzites over to them. They struck down ten thousand men in Bezek. [5] They found Adoni-bezek in Bezek, fought against him, and struck down the Canaanites and Perizzites.

[6] When Adoni-bezek fled, they pursued him, caught him, and cut off his thumbs and big toes. [7] Adoni-bezek said, "Seventy kings with their thumbs and big toes cut off used to pick up scraps[A] under my table. God has repaid me for what I have done." They brought him to Jerusalem, and he died there.

[8] The men of Judah fought against Jerusalem, captured it, put it to the sword, and set the city on fire. [9] Afterward, the men of Judah marched down to fight against the Canaanites who were living in the hill country, the Negev, and the Judean foothills.[B] [10] Judah also marched against the Canaanites who were living in Hebron (Hebron was formerly named Kiriath-arba). They struck down Sheshai, Ahiman, and Talmai. [11] From there they marched against the residents of Debir (Debir was formerly named Kiriath-sepher).

[12] Caleb said, "Whoever attacks and captures Kiriath-sepher, I will give my daughter Achsah to him as a wife." [13] So Othniel son of Kenaz, Caleb's youngest brother, captured it, and Caleb gave his daughter Achsah to him as his wife.

[14] When she arrived, she persuaded Othniel to ask her father for a field. As she got off her donkey, Caleb asked her, "What do you want?" [15] She answered him, "Give me a blessing. Since

you have given me land in the Negev, give me springs also." So Caleb gave her both the upper and lower springs.

[16] The descendants of the Kenite, Moses's father-in-law, had gone up with the men of Judah from the City of Palms[C] to the Wilderness of Judah, which was in the Negev of Arad. They went to live among the people.

[17] Judah went with his brother Simeon, struck the Canaanites who were living in Zephath, and completely destroyed the town. So they named the town Hormah. [18] Judah captured Gaza and its territory, Ashkelon and its territory, and Ekron and its territory. [19] The LORD was with Judah and enabled them to take possession of the hill country, but they could not drive out the people who were living in the plain because those people had iron chariots. [20] Judah gave Hebron to Caleb, just as Moses had promised. Then Caleb drove out the three sons of Anak who lived there.

Benjamin's Failure

[21] At the same time the Benjaminites did not drive out the Jebusites who were living in Jerusalem. The Jebusites have lived among the Benjaminites in Jerusalem to this day.

Success of the House of Joseph

[22] The house of Joseph also attacked Bethel, and the LORD was with them. [23] They sent spies to Bethel (the town was formerly named Luz). [24] The spies saw a man coming out of the town and said to him, "Please show us how to get into town, and we will show you kindness." [25] When he showed them the way into the town, they put the town to the sword but released the man and his entire family. [26] Then the man went to the land of the Hittites, built a town, and named it Luz. That is its name still today.

Failure of the Other Tribes

[27] At that time Manasseh failed to take possession of Beth-shean and Taanach and their surrounding villages, or the residents of Dor, Ibleam, and Megiddo and their surrounding

---

^[A]1:7 Lit *toes cut off are gathering* ^[B]1:9 Or *the Shephelah* ^[C]1:16 = Jericho; Dt 34:3; Jdg 3:13; 2Ch 28:15

1:1–2 After the death of Joshua links the book of Judges with the preceding account of the conquest of Canaan in the book of Joshua and sets the agenda for what follows. This is the story of the generations following Joshua's death, who failed to continue the legacy of his faithfulness to the charge Moses gave him. Unlike Moses, Joshua left no successor. So Israel inquired of the Lord, who was the commander-in-chief.
1:3 Judah and **Simeon** covenanted together to fight against the Canaanites, providing a positive example of how the tribes could work together to possess the land.
1:4–7 The victory at **Bezek** is a positive beginning that heightens all the more the tragedy of Israel's subsequent failure.

1:9–11 Verse 9 introduces vv. 10–20 by designating the three regions in which those verses describe fighting. The fighting at Hebron and Debir were in the **hill country**. The **Judean foothills** are often called the Shephelah.
1:12–13 Othniel would later become the first of Israel's judges (3:7–11). Othniel, who was the younger brother or nephew of Caleb, captured **Kiriath-sepher** (Debir), and thereby gained the right to marry Caleb's daughter, **Achsah**. See Jos 15:16–19.
1:16 The descendants of the Kenite were descended from Jethro, the father-in-law of Moses. They also traveled with the Judahites from Jericho (**the City of Palms**). Far from driving out the inhabitants of the land, they **went to live among the people**.

1:17–20 Initial success on the part of Judah and Simeon was followed by jarring failure—they were unable to drive out the people living in the valley because they had **iron chariots**. Iron was a relatively new discovery, and the Canaanites had the technological edge.
1:22–26 The **house of Joseph** (the Ephraimites) had a mixed experience at **Bethel**. The similarities and differences to the assault on Jericho under Joshua are striking (Jos 2; 6).
1:27–33 As the chapter unfolds, conquest is replaced by cohabitation. **Manasseh failed to take possession** of the villages in its territory. Even when the Manassites became stronger than the Canaanites, they failed to drive them out, instead using them as **forced labor**. The same approach was

villages; the Canaanites were determined to stay in this land. **²⁸** When Israel became stronger, they made the Canaanites serve as forced labor but never drove them out completely. **²⁹** At that time Ephraim failed to drive out the Canaanites who were living in Gezer, so the Canaanites have lived among them in Gezer. **³⁰** Zebulun failed to drive out the residents of Kitron or the residents of Nahalol, so the Canaanites lived among them and served as forced labor. **³¹** Asher failed to drive out the residents of Acco or of Sidon, or Ahlab, Achzib, Helbah, Aphik, or Rehob. **³²** The Asherites lived among the Canaanites who were living in the land, because they failed to drive them out. **³³** Naphtali did not drive out the residents of Beth-shemesh or the residents of Beth-anath. They lived among the Canaanites who were living in the land, but the residents of Beth-shemesh and Beth-anath served as their forced labor. **³⁴** The Amorites forced the Danites into the hill country and did not allow them to go down into the valley. **³⁵** The Amorites were determined to stay in Har-heres, Aijalon, and Shaalbim. When the house of Joseph got the upper hand, the Amorites were made to serve as forced labor. **³⁶** The territory of the Amorites extended from the Scorpions' Ascent, that is from Sela upward.

Pattern of Sin and Judgment

2 The angel of the LORD went up from Gilgal to Bochim and said, "I brought you out of Egypt and led you into the land I had promised to your ancestors. I also said: I will never break my covenant with you. **²** You are not to make a covenant with the inhabitants of this land. You are to tear down their altars. But you have not obeyed me. What have you done? **³** Therefore, I now say: I will not drive out these people before you. They will be thorns^A in your sides, and their gods will be a trap for you." **⁴** When the angel of the LORD had spoken these words to all the Israelites, the people wept loudly. **⁵** So they named that place Bochim^B and offered sacrifices there to the LORD.

Joshua's Death

⁶ Previously, when Joshua had sent the people away, the Israelites had gone to take possession of the land, each to his own inheritance. **⁷** The people worshiped the LORD throughout Joshua's lifetime and during the lifetimes of the elders who outlived Joshua. They had seen all the LORD's great works he had done for Israel.

⁸ Joshua son of Nun, the servant of the LORD, died at the age of 110. **⁹** They buried him in the territory of his inheritance, in Timnath-heres, in the hill country of Ephraim, north of Mount Gaash. **¹⁰** That whole generation was also gathered to their ancestors. After them another generation rose up who did not know the LORD or the works he had done for Israel.

¹¹ The Israelites did what was evil in the LORD's sight. They worshiped the Baals **¹²** and abandoned the LORD, the God of their ancestors, who had brought them out of Egypt. They followed other gods from the surrounding peoples and bowed down to them. They angered the LORD, **¹³** for they abandoned him and worshiped Baal and the Ashtoreths.

¹⁴ The LORD's anger burned against Israel, and he handed them over to marauders who raided them. He sold them to the enemies around them, and they could no longer resist their enemies. **¹⁵** Whenever the Israelites went out, the LORD was against them and brought disaster on them, just as he had promised and sworn to them. So they suffered greatly. **¹⁶** The LORD raised up judges, who saved them from the power of their marauders, **¹⁷** but they did not listen to their judges. Instead, they prostituted themselves with other gods, bowing down to them. They quickly turned from the way of their ancestors, who had walked in obedience to the LORD's commands. They did not do as their ancestors did. **¹⁸** Whenever the LORD raised up a judge for the Israelites, the LORD was with him and saved the people from the power of their enemies while the judge was still alive. The LORD was moved to pity whenever they groaned because of those who were oppressing and afflicting them. **¹⁹** Whenever the judge died, the Israelites would act even more corruptly than their ancestors, following other gods to serve them and bow in worship to

---

^A**2:3** Lit *traps* ^B**2:5** Or *Weeping*

1:34–35 The worst situation of all was that of the **Danites**, who were shut up in the hill country by the **Amorites** who **were determined to stay in** their cities. Apparently, the inhabitants of the land were more determined to stay there than God's people were to obey the Lord's command to drive them out.
2:1 The **angel of the LORD** frequently represents God himself.

2:4–5 The **people wept loudly and offered sacrifices**, the outward signs of repentance. They even memorialized their response to the place, **Bochim** ("Weeping"). Yet their actions in the rest of the chapter cast serious doubt on the authenticity of their repentance.
2:11–13 Baal was the Canaanite god of storm and rain, while Ashtoreth (also known as Astarte) was his consort, the goddess of love and fertility. Both of these deities were worshiped under a variety of

local manifestations and were perceived as the key to agricultural success in the land of Canaan.
2:16–19 Because of their distress, the Lord **raised up judges** for Israel, and they saved them from **the power of their marauders**. There is no mention of repentance by the people; the judges were raised up as the result of the Lord's **pity** on their groaning. In relenting from the punishment he had imposed on his people, the Lord showed himself to be "a compassionate and gracious God,

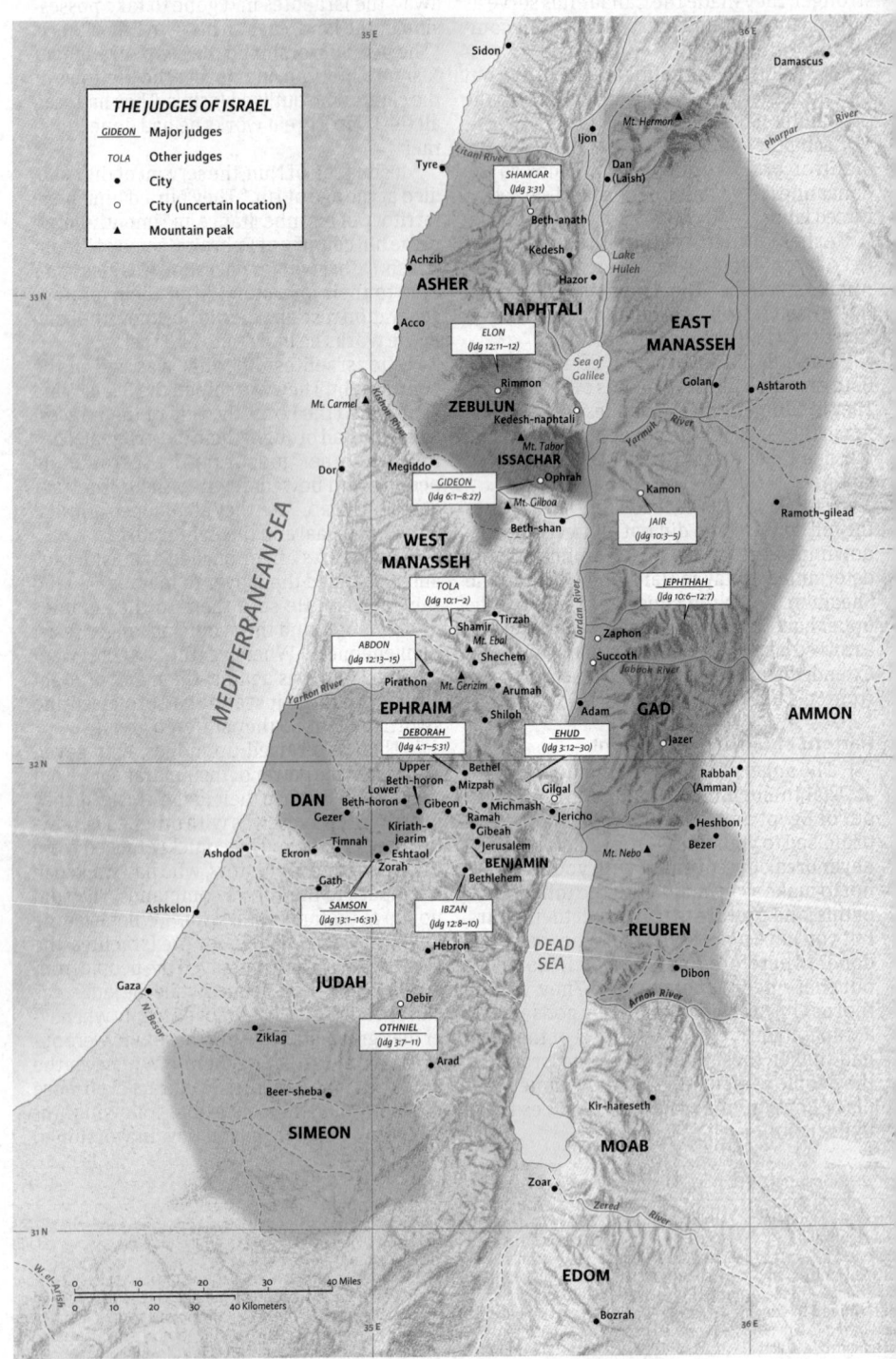

THE JUDGES OF ISRAEL

GIDEON Major judges

TOLA Other judges

• City

○ City (uncertain location)

▲ Mountain peak

them. They did not turn from their evil practices or their obstinate ways.

20 The LORD's anger burned against Israel, and he declared, "Because this nation has violated my covenant that I made with their ancestors and disobeyed me, **21** I will no longer drive out before them any of the nations Joshua left when he died. **22** I did this to test Israel and to see whether or not they would keep the LORD's way by walking in it, as their ancestors had." **23** The LORD left these nations and did not drive them out immediately. He did not hand them over to Joshua.

The LORD Tests Israel

3 These are the nations the LORD left in order to test all those in Israel who had experienced none of the wars in Canaan. **2** This was to teach the future generations of the Israelites how to fight in battle, especially those who had not fought before. **3** These nations included the five rulers of the Philistines and all of the Canaanites, the Sidonians, and the Hivites who lived in the Lebanese mountains from Mount Baal-hermon as far as the entrance to Hamath.^A **4** The LORD left them to test Israel, to determine if they would keep the LORD's commands he had given their ancestors through Moses. **5** But they settled among the Canaanites, Hethites, Amorites, Perizzites, Hivites, and Jebusites. **6** The Israelites took their daughters as wives for themselves, gave their own daughters to their sons, and worshiped their gods.

Othniel, the First Judge

7 The Israelites did what was evil in the LORD's sight; they forgot the LORD their God and worshiped the Baals and the Asherahs. **8** The LORD's anger burned against Israel, and he sold them to King Cushan-rishathaim^B of Aram-naharaim,^c and the Israelites served him eight years. **9** The Israelites cried out to the LORD. So the LORD raised up Othniel son of Kenaz, Caleb's youngest brother, as a deliverer to save the

Israelites. **10** The Spirit of the LORD came on him, and he judged Israel. Othniel went out to battle, and the LORD handed over King Cushan-rishathaim of Aram to him, so that Othniel overpowered him. **11** Then the land had peace for forty years, and Othniel son of Kenaz died.

Ehud

12 The Israelites again did what was evil in the LORD's sight. He gave King Eglon of Moab power over Israel, because they had done what was evil in the LORD's sight. **13** After Eglon convinced the Ammonites and the Amalekites to join forces with him, he attacked and defeated Israel and took possession of the City of Palms.^D **14** The Israelites served King Eglon of Moab eighteen years.

15 Then the Israelites cried out to the LORD, and he raised up Ehud son of Gera, a left-handed Benjaminite,^E as a deliverer for them. The Israelites sent him with the tribute for King Eglon of Moab. **16** Ehud made himself a double-edged sword eighteen inches long.^F He strapped it to his right thigh under his clothes **17** and brought the tribute to King Eglon of Moab, who was an extremely fat man. **18** When Ehud had finished presenting the tribute, he dismissed the people who had carried it. **19** At the carved images near Gilgal he returned and said, "King Eglon, I have a secret message for you." The king said, "Silence!" and all his attendants left him. **20** Then Ehud approached him while he was sitting alone in his upstairs room where it was cool. Ehud said, "I have a message from God for you," and the king stood up from his throne. **21** Ehud reached with his left hand, took the sword from his right thigh, and plunged it into Eglon's belly. **22** Even the handle went in after the blade, and Eglon's fat closed in over it, so that Ehud did not withdraw the sword from his belly. And the waste came out.^G **23** Ehud escaped by way of the porch, closing and locking the doors of the upstairs room behind him.

---

^A 3:3 Or as Lebo-hamath   ^B 3:8 Lit Doubly-Evil   ^c 3:8 = Mesopotamia   ^D 3:13 = Jericho; Dt 34:3; Jdg 1:16; 2Ch 28:15
^E 3:15 = son of the right hand   ^F 3:16 Lit sword a gomed in length   ^G 3:22 Or And Eglon's bowels discharged

---

slow to anger and abounding in faithful love and truth" (Ex 34:6).

2:20–23 It was a mark of the Lord's anger that he no longer referred to Israel as "my people" but as **this nation**.

3:1–6 The list of inhabitants of the land of Canaan in v. 3 encompasses the whole of the promised land: the southwest (**Philistines**), northwest (**Sidonians**), northeast (**Hivites**), and southeast (**Canaanites**).

3:7–11 Here Baal is linked with his more common consort in Canaanite literature, Asherah. Asherah was a fertility goddess often represented in the form of a tree. As a result of Israel's unfaithfulness, the Lord handed them over into the power of an oppressor, **Cushan-rishathaim** ("Cushan the Doubly Evil"). The area of Aram of the Two Rivers (v.

8) was north of Israel in Mesopotamia (Gn 24:10). For an Aramean king to oppress the whole land of Israel as far south as Judea was a mark of his military might. After **eight years** of subjugation, Israel cried out to the Lord, who then raised up and empowered Othniel, who as **Caleb's** nephew (see Jos 15:17) had the credentials to deliver Israel (Jdg 3:9–10). After delivering Israel, Othniel continued to lead them, and Israel was at peace for **forty years**. However, after his death, the cycle of sin and judgment started all over again.

3:12–14 This time the enemy was **King Eglon of Moab**, with the assistance of the **Ammonites** and **Amalekites**. These tribes lived east of Israel, in Transjordan, so the **City of Palms** (Jericho) would have been a natural

base from which to govern their conquered territory. Israel endured **eighteen years** of suffering before they cried out for release.

3:15–17 When Israel cried to the Lord, he again provided a deliverer, **Ehud**, a **left-handed** man. Left-handedness seems to have been relatively common among Benjaminites (20:15), which is ironic since Benjamin means "son of the right hand." The unusual idiom used here (lit "hindered in the right hand") suggests that left-handedness may have been viewed as a defect. Ehud also adopted a different approach to delivering Israel, assassinating the oppressor through deceit and cunning rather than engaging in straightforward battle. Eglon's name means "calf," a feature that resonates with the emphasis throughout the narrative

²⁴ Ehud was gone when Eglon's servants came in. They looked and found the doors of the upstairs room locked and thought he was relieving himself^ in the cool room. ²⁵ The servants waited until they became embarrassed and saw that he had still not opened the doors of the upstairs room. So they took the key and opened the doors — and there was their lord lying dead on the floor!

²⁶ Ehud escaped while the servants waited. He passed the Jordan near the carved images and reached Seirah. ²⁷ After he arrived, he sounded the ram's horn throughout the hill country of Ephraim. The Israelites came down with him from the hill country, and he became their leader. ²⁸ He told them, "Follow me, because the LORD has handed over your enemies, the Moabites, to you." So they followed him, captured the fords of the Jordan leading to Moab, and did not allow anyone to cross over. ²⁹ At that time they struck down about ten thousand Moabites, all stout and able-bodied men. Not one of them escaped. ³⁰ Moab became subject to Israel that day, and the land had peace for eighty years.

Shamgar

³¹ After Ehud, Shamgar son of Anath became judge. He also delivered Israel, striking down six hundred Philistines with a cattle prod.

Deborah and Barak

4 The Israelites again did what was evil in the sight of the LORD after Ehud had died. ² So the LORD sold them to King Jabin of Canaan, who reigned in Hazor. The commander of his army was Sisera who lived in Harosheth

of the Nations.^ ³ Then the Israelites cried out to the LORD, because Jabin had nine hundred iron chariots, and he harshly oppressed them twenty years.

⁴ Deborah, a prophetess and the wife of Lappidoth, was judging Israel at that time. ⁵ She would sit under the palm tree of Deborah between Ramah and Bethel in the hill country of Ephraim, and the Israelites went up to her to settle disputes.

⁶ She summoned Barak son of Abinoam from Kedesh in Naphtali and said to him, "Hasn't the LORD, the God of Israel, commanded you, 'Go, deploy the troops on Mount Tabor, and take with you ten thousand men from the Naphtalites and Zebulunites? ⁷ Then I will lure Sisera commander of Jabin's army, his chariots, and his infantry at the Wadi Kishon to fight against you, and I will hand him over to you.' "

⁸ Barak said to her, "If you will go with me, I will go. But if you will not go with me, I will not go."

⁹ "I will gladly go with you," she said, "but you will receive no honor on the road you are about to take, because the LORD will sell Sisera to a woman." So Deborah got up and went with Barak to Kedesh. ¹⁰ Barak summoned Zebulun and Naphtali to Kedesh; ten thousand men followed him, and Deborah also went with him.

¹¹ Now Heber the Kenite had moved away from the Kenites, the sons of Hobab, Moses's father-in-law, and pitched his tent beside the oak tree of Zaanannim, which was near Kedesh.

¹² It was reported to Sisera that Barak son of Abinoam had gone up Mount Tabor. ¹³ Sisera summoned all his nine hundred iron chariots and all the troops who were with him from

---

^3:24 Lit was covering his feet   ᴮ4:2 Or Harosheth-ha-goiim, also in vv. 13,16

---

on his "fatness." Together with Eglon's name it marked him out as the fattened calf, ripe for slaughter.
3:24–26 The dimwittedness of **Eglon's servants** would have been humorous to the first readers of Judges. The odor might have contributed to the servants' supposition that the king was "occupied." The contents of their master's bowels were indeed being emptied, but not in the manner they imagined.
3:27–30 Ehud then **sounded the ram's horn,** summoning **Ephraim** to holy war against the leaderless **Moabites.** He gave due credit to the Lord's involvement in the battle, and he led his people in a successful assault on the **fords of the Jordan.** This would have cut off the Moabite retreat and separated them from any possible reinforcements. **About ten thousand . . . able-bodied . . . Moabites** may be a way of affirming an overwhelming victory, according to the conventions of ancient literature. The result of the victory was **eighty years** of peace.
3:31 This brief note introduces **Shamgar,** sometimes called a "minor judge," though never explicitly said to judge Israel. His name is extraordinary on two counts: the form "Shamgar" is not that of a normal Hebrew name, and the ascription **son of**

Anath suggests that he was (or had been) a follower of Anath, the Canaanite goddess of war. This foreigner apparently delivered Israel by striking down six hundred Philistines with an oxgoad. The **Philistines,** or Sea Peoples, were not native to Canaan but arrived there in the twelfth to eleventh centuries BC from Anatolia and Crete. From their bases in the coastal plain, the Philistines became an increasing problem for the Israelites as they pressed eastward into the foothills of Israel. A **cattle prod** was a sharp stick up to eight feet long tapering to a sharp point, which may have been tipped with metal (1Sm 13:21).
4:1–3 A new cycle is introduced with the standard formula of Israelite rebellion (cp. 3:7,12). In this instance the enemy was **Jabin,** a Canaanite king from **Hazor,** in the north of Israel. An earlier Jabin had been defeated by Joshua at Hazor about a century earlier (Jos 11:1–15); this suggests that "Jabin" may have been a dynastic name. Hazor was destroyed by Joshua, but as was the case with Jerusalem in Jdg 1:8, the destruction did not prevent some form of reoccupation at a later date. The source of Jabin's strength, humanly speaking, lay in his **nine hundred iron chariots.** These gave him an enormous

technological edge over the Israelites on flat ground.
4:6–7 As God's appointed representative Deborah **summoned Barak** to take the lead in the fighting. She also gave him the Lord's plan of battle, deploying **ten thousand men** of Naphtali and Zebulun on **Mount Tabor,** a strategic location at the northeast corner of the Jezreel Valley. Further, she assured him of the Lord's victory over Israel's enemies.
4:8–10 Although the name **Barak** means "lightning," his response was slow. Deborah agreed to accompany him to **Kedesh** as a sign that the Lord was indeed with him, and he successfully raised an army of **ten thousand men.**
4:11 What seems at first sight to be an irrelevant note introduces the key character in what follows. **Heber the Kenite** was descended from **Moses's father-in-law.** The Kenites were mentioned in 1:16 as settling among the people.
4:12–16 Sisera responded to Barak's movements by summoning his entire force of nine hundred iron chariots to the **Wadi Kishon,** the exact place where the Lord had earlier promised to lure Israel. This was the signal for Israel to prepare for action, a call that significantly came from Deborah rather than Barak.

Harosheth of the Nations to the Wadi Kishon. ¹⁴ Then Deborah said to Barak, "Go! This is the day the LORD has handed Sisera over to you. Hasn't the LORD gone before you?" So Barak came down from Mount Tabor with ten thousand men following him.

¹⁵ The LORD threw Sisera, all his charioteers, and all his army into a panic before Barak's assault. Sisera left his chariot and fled on foot. ¹⁶ Barak pursued the chariots and the army as far as Harosheth of the Nations, and the whole army of Sisera fell by the sword; not a single man was left.

¹⁷ Meanwhile, Sisera had fled on foot to the tent of Jael, the wife of Heber the Kenite, because there was peace between King Jabin of Hazor and the family of Heber the Kenite. ¹⁸ Jael went out to greet Sisera and said to him, "Come in, my lord. Come in with me. Don't be afraid." So he went into her tent, and she covered him with a blanket. ¹⁹ He said to her, "Please give me a little water to drink for I am thirsty." She opened a container of milk, gave him a drink, and covered him again. ²⁰ Then he said to her, "Stand at the entrance to the tent. If a man comes and asks you, 'Is there a man here?' say, 'No.'" ²¹ While he was sleeping from exhaustion, Heber's wife, Jael, took a tent peg, grabbed a hammer, and went silently to Sisera. She hammered the peg into his temple and drove it into the ground, and he died.

²² When Barak arrived in pursuit of Sisera, Jael went out to greet him and said to him, "Come and I will show you the man you are looking for." So he went in with her, and there was Sisera lying dead with a tent peg through his temple!

²³ That day God subdued King Jabin of Canaan before the Israelites. ²⁴ The power of the Israelites continued to increase against King Jabin of Canaan until they destroyed him.

Deborah's Song

5 On that day Deborah and Barak son of Abinoam sang:
² When the leaders lead^A in Israel,
   when the people volunteer,
   blessed be the LORD.
³ Listen, kings! Pay attention, princes!
   I will sing to the LORD;

I will sing praise to the LORD God
   of Israel.
⁴ LORD, when you came from Seir,
   when you marched from the fields
      of Edom,
   the earth trembled,
   the skies poured rain,
   and the clouds poured water.
⁵ The mountains melted
      before the LORD,
   even Sinai,^B before the LORD, the God
      of Israel.

⁶ In the days of Shamgar son of Anath,
   in the days of Jael,
   the main roads were deserted
   because travelers kept to the side roads.
⁷ Villages were deserted,^C
   they were deserted in Israel,
   until I,^D Deborah, arose,
   a mother in Israel.
⁸ Israel chose new gods,
   then there was war in the city gates.
   Not a shield or spear was seen
   among forty thousand in Israel.
⁹ My heart is with the leaders of Israel,
   with the volunteers of the people.
   Blessed be the LORD!
¹⁰ You who ride on white^C donkeys,
   who sit on saddle blankets,
   and who travel on the road,
      give praise!
¹¹ Let them tell the righteous acts
      of the LORD,
   the righteous deeds of his villagers
      in Israel,
   with the voices of the singers
      at the watering places.^C

Then the LORD's people went down
      to the city gates.
¹² "Awake! Awake, Deborah!
   Awake! Awake, sing a song!
   Arise, Barak,
   and take your prisoners,
   son of Abinoam!"
¹³ Then the survivors came down
      to the nobles;
   the LORD's people came down to me^E
      against the warriors.

^A5:2 Or *the locks of hair are loose*   ^B5:5 Or *LORD, this one of Sinai*   ^C5:7,10,11 Hb obscure   ^D5:7 Or *you*   ^E5:13 LXX reads *down for him*

4:17–21 Sisera himself **fled on foot**. Since Heber had allied himself to Jabin, his camp should have been a place of safety for Sisera. However, he had reckoned without **Jael**, Heber's wife. Her approach seemed innocent enough. She **went out to greet Sisera**, welcomed him in with words of peace and safety, and brought him **milk**, like a mother caring for a small child (vv. 19–20). But once Sisera fell asleep, Jael drove a **tent peg** through **his temple . . . into the ground**.

5:1 When God intervenes decisively in the lives of his people, their response is to sing his praise (Ex 15). Here **Deborah and Barak** together led the people in a song of celebration and thanksgiving that focused on the Lord as the central character.
5:4–5 Deborah described the Lord's presence in the battle in the form of a theophany in which the Lord marched out from Mount **Seir** in **Edom**, bringing a mighty rainstorm. This storm not only served the practical function of bogging down Sisera's

chariots and neutralizing his technological edge, but it also depicts the Lord—not Baal—as the true God of the storm who marches out from his mountain home with the clouds and rain. The Lord alone controls the cosmic elements.
5:7–8 Deborah became a **mother in Israel**, a title that not only expresses the respect with which she was viewed as a prophetess, but also highlights her femininity and the absence of a similar male figure as "father" at this time.

¹⁴ Those with their roots in Amalek^A came
      from Ephraim;
   Benjamin came with your people
      after you.
   The leaders came down from Machir,
   and those who carry a marshal's staff
      came from Zebulun.
¹⁵ The princes of Issachar were
      with Deborah;
   Issachar was with Barak;
   they were under his leadership^B
      in the valley.
   There was great searching^C of heart
      among the clans of Reuben.
¹⁶ Why did you sit among the sheep pens^D
      listening to the playing of pipes
      for the flocks?
   There was great searching of heart
      among the clans of Reuben.
¹⁷ Gilead remained beyond the Jordan.
   Dan, why did you linger at the ships?
   Asher remained at the seashore
   and stayed in his harbors.
¹⁸ The people of Zebulun defied death,
   Naphtali also, on the heights
      of the battlefield.

¹⁹ Kings came and fought.
   Then the kings of Canaan fought
   at Taanach by the Waters of Megiddo,

   but they did not plunder the silver.
²⁰ The stars fought from the heavens;
   the stars fought with Sisera
      from their paths.
²¹ The river Kishon swept them away,
   the ancient river, the river Kishon.
   March on, my soul, in strength!
²² The horses' hooves then hammered —
   the galloping, galloping of his^E stallions.
²³ "Curse Meroz," says the angel
      of the LORD,
   "Bitterly curse her inhabitants,
   for they did not come to help the LORD,
   to help the LORD with the warriors."

²⁴ Most blessed of women is Jael,
   the wife of Heber the Kenite;
   she is most blessed among
      tent-dwelling women.
²⁵ He asked for water; she gave him milk.
   She brought him cream
      in a majestic bowl.
²⁶ She reached for a tent peg,
   her right hand,
      for a workman's hammer.
   Then she hammered Sisera —
   she crushed his head;
   she shattered and pierced his temple.
²⁷ He collapsed, he fell, he lay down
      between her feet;

^A5:14 LXX reads in the valley   ^B5:15 Lit they set out as his feet   ^C5:15 Some Hb mss, Syr read There were great resolves
^D5:16 Or the campfires   ^E5:22 = Sisera's

5:19–21 The climax of the song brings into view the battle itself. Defeating Jabin was in effect a defeat for all the **kings of Canaan**. 5:23 **Meroz** cannot be precisely identified. Most likely, they were an Israelite group who had adopted the ways of the Canaanites and remained outside the conflict, thereby earning a **curse** from the **angel of the LORD**. 5:24–27 The curse on Meroz forms a contrast with the blessing on **Jael**, a non-Israelite who came "to help the LORD with the warriors" (v. 23). She is lauded for her resourcefulness and cunning. A comparison to Eglon's fatal encounter with Ehud is invited by a key comparison: Instead of a left-handed assassin, Jael did her work with **her right hand**.

Character profile:

Deborah

By God's grace, this gifted and industrious woman accomplished extraordinary things for her people. Deborah was a prophetess—which means that, like Miriam before her (see Ex 15:20) and Anna after her (see Lk 2:36), she received divine revelation for Israel.

Somewhere along the way Deborah added the job of "judge" to her roles as wife, mother, and prophetess. This was during that lawless, rudderless time in Israel's history between Joshua and Saul, when the nation had no king (see Jdg 17:6)—and even less of a sense of right and wrong.

During her stint as judge, Deborah kept an "office" (literally, a palm tree in the hill country of Ephraim; see 4:5). There she settled disputes among the people. It's safe to assume that juggling all these responsibilities kept Deborah busy. But her shining moment was still to come.

One day, at God's prompting, Deborah called Barak in and commanded him to take ten thousand men and attack the forces of Jabin, which were under the command of General Sisera. Jabin was the Canaanite king who had been a thorn in the side of Israel for more than two decades. Deborah assured Barak that God promised him victory.

Nevertheless, Barak pleaded for her to accompany him to battle. "'I will gladly go with you,' she said, 'but you will receive no honor on the road you are about to take, because the LORD will sell Sisera to a woman.' So Deborah got up and went with Barak to Kedesh" (4:9).

Once the troops were in position, Deborah gave the signal, and Barak led the charge. The ragtag Israelites routed the stronger, battle-tested Canaanites. Sisera fled the battle and hid among the Kenites. As Deborah had prophesied, an Israelite sympathizer, a woman named Jael, took Sisera's life (see 4:17–21).

Following this overwhelming victory, Deborah composed a vivid song (see 5:2–31) to celebrate Israel's great deliverance. The "Song of Deborah" has long been praised for its literary qualities. It is also God-centered, as we would expect from a spiritual leader or prophetess.

Mostly, Deborah's song is humble. It avoids any hint of self-congratulation, beginning with the words, "When the leaders lead in Israel, when the people volunteer, blessed be the LORD" (5:2). In other words, victory is a team effort and ultimately the work of the Lord. Following these events, Israel enjoyed forty years of peace and quiet (see 5:31).

God graces each one of us with unique abilities and opportunities. In certain situations we are called to lead; in other settings we are expected to follow. This much we know: We are all called by God to play a role. We each have a part.

When, like Barak, we doubt the promise of God and shrink back, we miss out on the full experience of being used by God. When, like Deborah, we step forward and bravely exercise our gifts, we may end up having a huge impact. Deborah teaches us to busy ourselves in doing all the things God has given us to do, all for his glory.

he collapsed, he fell between her feet;
where he collapsed, there he fell —
dead.

28 Sisera's mother looked
through the window;
she peered through the lattice,
crying out:
"Why is his chariot so long in coming?
Why don't I hear the hoofbeats
of his horses?"^A
29 Her wisest princesses answer her;
she even answers herself:
30 "Are they not finding and dividing
the spoil —
a girl or two^B for each warrior,
the spoil of colored garments for Sisera,
the spoil of an embroidered garment
or two for my neck?"^C

31 LORD, may all your enemies perish
as Sisera did.^D
But may those who love him
be like the rising of the sun
in its strength.

And the land had peace for forty years.

Midian Oppresses Israel

6 The Israelites did what was evil in the sight
of the LORD. So the LORD handed them over
to Midian seven years, **2** and they oppressed
Israel. Because of Midian, the Israelites made
hiding places for themselves in the mountains,
caves, and strongholds. **3** Whenever the Israelites planted crops, the Midianites, Amalekites,
and the people of the east came and attacked
them. **4** They encamped against them and destroyed the produce of the land, even as far
as Gaza. They left nothing for Israel to eat, as
well as no sheep, ox, or donkey. **5** For the Midianites came with their cattle and their tents
like a great swarm of locusts. They and their

camels were without number, and they entered
the land to lay waste to it. **6** So Israel became
poverty-stricken because of Midian, and the
Israelites cried out to the LORD.
7 When the Israelites cried out to him because of Midian, **8** the LORD sent a prophet to
them. He said to them, "This is what the LORD
God of Israel says: 'I brought you out of Egypt
and out of the place of slavery. **9** I rescued you
from the power of Egypt and the power of all
who oppressed you. I drove them out before
you and gave you their land. **10** I said to you: I
am the LORD your God. Do not fear the gods of
the Amorites whose land you live in. But you
did not obey me.'"

The LORD Calls Gideon

11 The angel of the LORD came, and he sat under
the oak that was in Ophrah, which belonged
to Joash, the Abiezrite. His son Gideon was
threshing wheat in the winepress in order to
hide it from the Midianites. **12** Then the angel of
the LORD appeared to him and said, "The LORD
is with you, valiant warrior."
13 Gideon said to him, "Please, my lord, if the
LORD is with us, why has all this happened?
And where are all his wonders that our ancestors told us about? They said, 'Hasn't the LORD
brought us out of Egypt?' But now the LORD has
abandoned us and handed us over to Midian."
14 The LORD turned to him and said, "Go in the
strength you have and deliver Israel from the
grasp of Midian. I am sending you!"
15 He said to him, "Please, Lord, how can I
deliver Israel? Look, my family is the weakest
in Manasseh, and I am the youngest in my father's family."
16 "But I will be with you," the LORD said to
him. "You will strike Midian down as if it were
one man."
17 Then he said to him, "If I have found favor
with you, give me a sign that you are speaking
with me. **18** Please do not leave this place until

^A5:28 Lit Why have the hoofbeats of his chariots delayed   ^B5:30 Lit a womb or two wombs   ^C5:30 Hb obscure   ^D5:31 Lit
perish in this way

5:28–30 From the bloody murder scene, the song moves poignantly to the image of **Sis-era's mother**, waiting vainly for his return. Her ladies reassured her that what was de-laying her son was just the time involved in **dividing the spoil**. Each soldier would need to select some choice **garments** for them-selves and their ladies, and **a girl or two**, or more literally, a "womb or two," highlighting the sexual and reproductive functions the captive women were expected to provide. **5:31** The final note of the chapter is that **the land had peace** (lit "had rest") for **forty years**. **6:1–6** The second main section of the story of the judges, covering the fourth through the sixth major judges (Gideon, Jephthah, Samson), is introduced with a repetition of the rebellion formula from 3:7. The result was predictable: the Lord handed them over to an oppressor. The **Midianites** were seminomads

who lived in the Sinai Peninsula and western Arabia. They allied themselves with the **Ama-lekites** and the **people of the east** into a loose confederation. These raiders from the east swept across the country seasonally, plundering it like a **great swarm of locusts**. Although they entered the land from the east, they traveled as far as **Gaza** on the western coast, leaving nothing behind them. The Israelites were reduced to an animal-like existence in caves, without any livestock of their own. **6:11–12** The **angel of the LORD**—the Lord's personal representative who spoke with his full authority—appeared to **Gideon** at **Ophrah**, a town probably located in the Jezreel Valley. Gideon's name means "the one who hacks or cuts down," a fitting name for the man whose first task in the Lord's service would be to cut down Baal's altar. Other aspects of Gideon's demeanor

are less promising. In view of the threat of the **Midianites**, he was **threshing wheat** in a **winepress**, a shallow depression in the rock, a safer location than the more exposed threshing floor. Gideon's natural reserve will emerge again as the narrative unfolds, and it is in sharp contrast to the title given to Gideon by the angel—**valiant warrior**. **6:13–16** Gideon's response challenged both aspects of the angel's greeting. First, he cast doubt on the Lord's presence with Israel. The angel of the Lord did not appear to hear Gideon's objection. Instead, he commissioned him to be the mighty warrior that God had named him. This provoked Gideon to chal-lenge this aspect of the angel's greeting as well. Gideon claimed that he was doubly unsuited for this task. **6:17–21** Even with this reassurance, Gide-on was not satisfied. He demanded a **sign**. He prepared an offering the size of which

I return to you. Let me bring my gift and set it before you."

And he said, "I will stay until you return." [19] So Gideon went and prepared a young goat and unleavened bread from a half bushel[A] of flour. He placed the meat in a basket and the broth in a pot. He brought them out and offered them to him under the oak.

[20] The angel of God said to him, "Take the meat with the unleavened bread, put it on this stone, and pour the broth on it." So he did that. [21] The angel of the LORD extended the tip of the staff that was in his hand and touched the meat and the unleavened bread. Fire came up from the rock and consumed the meat and the unleavened bread. Then the angel of the LORD vanished from his sight.

[22] When Gideon realized that he was the angel of the LORD, he said, "Oh no, Lord GOD! I have seen the angel of the LORD face to face!"

[23] But the LORD said to him, "Peace to you. Don't be afraid, for you will not die." [24] So Gideon built an altar to the LORD there and called it The LORD Is Peace.[B] It is still in Ophrah of the Abiezrites today.

Gideon Tears Down a Baal Altar

[25] On that very night the LORD said to him, "Take your father's young bull and a second bull seven years old. Then tear down the altar of Baal that belongs to your father and cut down the Asherah pole beside it. [26] Build a well-constructed altar to the LORD your God on the top of this mound. Take the second bull and offer it as a burnt offering with the wood of the Asherah pole you cut down." [27] So Gideon took ten of his male servants and did as the LORD had told him. But because he was too afraid of his father's family and the men of the city to do it in the daytime, he did it at night.

[28] When the men of the city got up in the morning, they found Baal's altar torn down,

the Asherah pole beside it cut down, and the second bull offered up on the altar that had been built. [29] They said to each other, "Who did this?" After they made a thorough investigation, they said, "Gideon son of Joash did it."

[30] Then the men of the city said to Joash, "Bring out your son. He must die, because he tore down Baal's altar and cut down the Asherah pole beside it."

[31] But Joash said to all who stood against him, "Would you plead Baal's case for him? Would you save him? Whoever pleads his case will be put to death by morning! If he is a god, let him plead his own case because someone tore down his altar." [32] That day Gideon was called Jerubbaal, since Joash said, "Let Baal contend with him," because he tore down his altar.

The Sign of the Fleece

[33] All the Midianites, Amalekites, and people of the east gathered together, crossed over the Jordan, and camped in the Jezreel Valley.

[34] The Spirit of the LORD enveloped[C] Gideon, and he blew the ram's horn and the Abiezrites rallied behind him. [35] He sent messengers throughout all of Manasseh, who rallied behind him. He also sent messengers throughout Asher, Zebulun, and Naphtali, who also came to meet him.

[36] Then Gideon said to God, "If you will deliver Israel by me, as you said, [37] I will put a wool fleece here on the threshing floor. If dew is only on the fleece, and all the ground is dry, I will know that you will deliver Israel by me, as you said." [38] And that is what happened. When he got up early in the morning, he squeezed the fleece and wrung dew out of it, filling a bowl with water.

[39] Gideon then said to God, "Don't be angry with me; let me speak one more time. Please allow me to make one more test with the fleece. Let it remain dry, and the dew be all over the

---

^6:19 Lit *an ephah* ^6:24 = *Yahweh-shalom* ^6:34 Lit *clothed*; 1Ch 12:18; 2Ch 24:20

---

indicates that this was not just human hospitality but an offering to God. When Gideon brought the elements back, the **angel of God** graciously condescended to perform the requested sign.
6:22–24 Realizing the true identity of his visitor, Gideon became convinced he was doomed to die (Ex 33:20). Again, the Lord spoke to reassure him. This time the Lord's message seems to have been heeded by Gideon, who built an altar to the Lord and named it **The LORD is Peace** (Hb *Yahweh Shalom*). This altar erected by Gideon in Ophrah at the beginning of his service contrasts sharply with the ephod idol that he set up there toward the end of his life (8:27).
6:25–27 Before Gideon could take on the Midianites, he first had to confront the idolatry within his own family by tearing down his father's **altar of Baal** and the **Asherah pole** beside it. An Asherah pole was a stylized tree that represented the fertility goddess Asherah, Baal's consort. It was a frequent feature

of Canaanite cult installations. Gideon was to reclaim the area for the Lord by building a new altar to God there, on which he was to offer his father's . . . bull. The **wood of the Asherah pole** would provide fuel for the fire. Gideon did this at once, though it is clear that his earlier timidity had not disappeared. He gathered ten of his father's servants to help him, illustrating a trust in numbers rather than trust in the Lord. He also committed this action **at night** rather than in broad daylight because he **was . . . afraid**, so no one would know who was responsible.
6:28–32 The response of the **men of the city** to Gideon's actions reveals clearly where their loyalties lay. They wanted the sentence of death that ought to have been imposed on idolaters (Dt 13:6–10) carried out on Gideon instead. What is surprising is that Gideon's father, **Joash**, who owned this altar to Baal, defended his son. Gideon acquired another name, **Jerubbaal**, which means "let Baal contend."

6:33–35 Gideon's initial success was soon followed by a greater challenge. Israel's oppressors crossed over the Jordan River for another seasonal pillaging expedition. **The Spirit of the LORD** enveloped (lit "put on") Gideon, empowering him for action to deliver the Lord's people. Remarkably, the men who first had wanted to kill him (v. 30) responded to his call. He also called his whole tribe (**Manasseh**) plus their northern neighbors, who also responded.
6:36–40 The gathering of the tribes should have been sufficient evidence of God's presence with Gideon, but he wanted a sign that God would do what he had promised. He doubted that God would deliver Israel by his strength, even though that was what God had promised. As a result, Gideon put God to the test. In the first test, God did as Gideon asked, but it was not enough; Gideon may have thought that it could have been a fluke. So Gideon, showing his timidity, demanded a second test. Displaying great

ground." **⁴⁰** That night God did as Gideon requested: only the fleece was dry, and dew was all over the ground.

God Selects Gideon's Army

7 Jerubbaal (that is, Gideon) and all the troops who were with him, got up early and camped beside the spring of Harod. The camp of Midian was north of them, below the hill of Moreh, in the valley. **²** The LORD said to Gideon, "You have too many troops for me to hand the Midianites over to them, or else Israel might elevate themselves over me and say,^ 'I saved myself.' **³** Now announce to the troops, 'Whoever is fearful and trembling may turn back and leave Mount Gilead.'" So twenty-two thousand of the troops turned back, but ten thousand remained.

⁴ Then the LORD said to Gideon, "There are still too many troops. Take them down to the water, and I will test them for you there. If I say to you, 'This one can go with you,' he can go. But if I say about anyone, 'This one cannot go with you,' he cannot go." **⁵** So he brought the troops down to the water, and the LORD said to Gideon, "Separate everyone who laps water with his tongue like a dog. Do the same with everyone who kneels to drink." **⁶** The number of those who lapped with their hands to their mouths was three hundred men, and all the rest of the troops knelt to drink water. **⁷** The LORD said to Gideon, "I will deliver you with the three hundred men who lapped and hand the Midianites over to you. But everyone else is to go home." **⁸** So Gideon sent all the Israelites to their tents but kept the three hundred troops, who took the provisions and their rams' horns. The camp of Midian was below him in the valley.

Gideon Spies on the Midianite Camp

⁹ That night the LORD said to him, "Get up and attack the camp, for I have handed it over to

you. **¹⁰** But if you are afraid to attack the camp, go down with Purah your servant. **¹¹** Listen to what they say, and then you will be encouraged to attack the camp." So he went down with Purah his servant to the outpost of the troops⁸ who were in the camp.

¹² Now the Midianites, Amalekites, and all the people of the east had settled down in the valley like a swarm of locusts, and their camels were as innumerable as the sand on the seashore. **¹³** When Gideon arrived, there was a man telling his friend about a dream. He said, "Listen, I had a dream: a loaf of barley bread came tumbling into the Midianite camp, struck a tent, and it fell. The loaf turned the tent upside down so that it collapsed."

¹⁴ His friend answered, "This is nothing less than the sword of Gideon son of Joash, the Israelite. God has handed the entire Midianite camp over to him."

Gideon Attacks the Midianites

¹⁵ When Gideon heard the account of the dream and its interpretation, he bowed in worship. He returned to Israel's camp and said, "Get up, for the LORD has handed the Midianite camp over to you." **¹⁶** Then he divided the three hundred men into three companies and gave each of the men a ram's horn in one hand and an empty pitcher with a torch inside it in the other hand.

¹⁷ "Watch me," he said to them, "and do what I do. When I come to the outpost of the camp, do as I do. **¹⁸** When I and everyone with me blow our rams' horns, you are also to blow your rams' horns all around the camp. Then you will say, 'For the LORD and for Gideon!'"

¹⁹ Gideon and the hundred men who were with him went to the outpost of the camp at the beginning of the middle watch after the sentries had been stationed. They blew their rams' horns and broke the pitchers that were in their hands. **²⁰** The three companies blew their rams'

---

^7:2 Lit *brag against me*   ⁸7:11 Lit *of those who were arranged in companies of 50*

---

patience, the Lord graciously gave him a confirmatory sign.
7:1–3 Gideon's army was strategically camped at the **spring of Harod**, where water supply would not be an issue. The name of this particular spring is "Spring of Trembling," which describes the state of Gideon's army. Yet from the Lord's perspective, there were **too many troops** there. If an army of this size won, even against the innumerable hordes of the Midianites, Israel might be tempted to take credit for the victory. To show that the victory was entirely his, the Lord reduced the size of Gideon's army.
7:4–8 The Lord gave Gideon an additional test to reduce the size of his army further, by taking them **down to the water** to drink. It appears that those chosen scooped water up in their hands and lapped it from there, while those who got down on all fours and drank directly from the river **like a dog** were rejected. The selection process may have been arbitrary, or it may have been designed to

favor those who remained watchful while drinking. Gideon's army now numbered just **three hundred**.
7:9–14 Instead of immediate action, there was further delay while Gideon's continuing fears were addressed. The Lord told Gideon that if he was **afraid** to go against the Midianite camp, he should secretly visit it and **listen** to what the Midianites were saying. Visually nothing had changed since the opening verses of chap. 6. Yet what Gideon heard told a different story—God had given members of the enemy force a dream that was utterly demoralizing.
7:15–16 Eavesdropping on this conversation at last had the desired effect on Gideon. In response, **he bowed in worship**, acknowledging the truth of the Lord's words, now that he had heard them repeated by pagans. He **returned to Israel's camp** and finally delivered to his men the instruction he had received from the Lord in v. 9. Gideon divided his small army into three divisions and

"armed" them with a **ram's horn**, an empty **pitcher**, and a **torch**.
7:19–25 The strategy worked out exactly as planned. The **beginning of the middle watch** would be midnight. Gideon's three groups, spread out surrounding the camp, would sound like a much larger army. The element of surprise, combined with a divinely induced fear, sent the Midianites fleeing for their lives and fighting one another in the confusion. The surviving Midianites fled toward the Jordan River, though the exact locations of the places mentioned in v. 22 are uncertain.
At this point, with victory assured, Gideon called out the men of **Naphtali, Asher, and Manasseh**—presumably the remainder of his original army of thirty thousand—to join in the pursuit. He also called out the men of **Ephraim** to seize the fording places over the **Jordan** to cut off any retreat for the remnant of the Midianites. **Oreb and Zeeb** were Midianite **princes** or military commanders.

horns and shattered their pitchers. They held their torches in their left hands and their rams' horns to blow in their right hands, and they shouted, "A sword for the LORD and for Gideon!" ²¹ Each Israelite took his position around the camp, and the entire Midianite army began to run, and they cried out as they fled. ²² When Gideon's men blew their three hundred rams' horns, the LORD caused the men in the whole army to turn on each other with their swords. They fled to Acacia House^A in the direction of Zererah as far as the border of Abel-meholah near Tabbath. ²³ Then the men of Israel were called from Naphtali, Asher, and Manasseh, and they pursued the Midianites.

The Men of Ephraim Join the Battle

²⁴ Gideon sent messengers throughout the hill country of Ephraim with this message: "Come down to intercept the Midianites and take control of the watercourses ahead of them as far as Beth-barah and the Jordan." So all the men of Ephraim were called out, and they took control of the watercourses as far as Beth-barah and the Jordan. ²⁵ They captured Oreb and Zeeb, the two princes of Midian; they killed Oreb at the rock of Oreb and Zeeb at the winepress of Zeeb, while they were pursuing the Midianites. They brought the heads of Oreb and Zeeb to Gideon across the Jordan.

8 The men of Ephraim said to him, "Why have you done this to us, not calling us when you went to fight against the Midianites?" And they argued with him violently.

² So he said to them, "What have I done now compared to you? Is not the gleaning of Ephraim better than the grape harvest of Abiezer? ³ God handed over to you Oreb and Zeeb, the two princes of Midian. What was I able to do compared to you?" When he said this, their anger against him subsided.

Gideon Pursues the Kings of Midian

⁴ Gideon and the three hundred men came to the Jordan and crossed it. They were exhausted but still in pursuit. ⁵ He said to the men of Succoth, "Please give some loaves of bread to the troops under my command, ^B because they are exhausted, for I am pursuing Zebah and Zalmunna, the kings of Midian."

⁶ But the princes of Succoth asked, "Are Zebah and Zalmunna now in your hands that we should give bread to your army?"

⁷ Gideon replied, "Very well, when the LORD has handed Zebah and Zalmunna over to me, I will tear^C your flesh with thorns and briers from the wilderness!" ⁸ He went from there to Penuel and asked the same thing from them. The men of Penuel answered just as the men of Succoth had answered. ⁹ He also told the men of Penuel, "When I return safely, I will tear down this tower!"

¹⁰ Now Zebah and Zalmunna were in Karkor, and with them was their army of about fifteen thousand men, who were all those left of the entire army of the people of the east. Those who had been killed were one hundred twenty thousand armed men. ¹¹ Gideon traveled on the caravan route^D east of Nobah and Jogbehah and attacked their army while the army felt secure. ¹² Zebah and Zalmunna fled, and he pursued them. He captured these two kings of Midian and routed the entire army.

¹³ Gideon son of Joash returned from the battle by the Ascent of Heres. ¹⁴ He captured a youth from the men of Succoth and interrogated him. The youth wrote down for him the names of the seventy-seven leaders and elders of Succoth. ¹⁵ Then he went to the men of Succoth and said, "Here are Zebah and Zalmunna. You taunted me about them, saying, 'Are Zebah and Zalmunna now in your power that we should give bread to your exhausted men?'" ¹⁶ So he took the elders of the city, and he took some thorns and briers from the wilderness, and he disciplined the men of Succoth with them. ¹⁷ He also tore down the tower of Penuel and killed the men of the city.

¹⁸ He asked Zebah and Zalmunna, "What kind of men did you kill at Tabor?"

"They were like you," they said. "Each resembled the son of a king."

¹⁹ So he said, "They were my brothers, the sons of my mother! As the LORD lives, if you

---

^7:22 Or *Beth-shittah*   ^8:5 Lit *troops at my feet*   ^8:7 Lit *thresh*   ^8:11 Lit *on the route of those who live in tents*

8:1–3 The first complication was a complaint by the Ephraimites that Gideon did not call them out to battle against the Midianites. This is surprising because elsewhere the problem was persuading the tribes to become involved in conflict, not dissuading them. Their complaint shows Gideon's response was a masterpiece of diplomacy. He downplayed his own standing and role in the victory by saying, **Is not the gleaning** (the grapes left behind after the initial harvesting) **of Ephraim better than the grape harvest of Abiezer?** Gideon belonged to the clan of Abiezer. Moreover, the Ephraimites achieved the crowning moment of the victory when God handed over to them Oreb and

Zeeb, the two princes of Midian. This reply defused the Ephraimites' anger.

8:4–9 The Midianite kings, **Zebah and Zalmunna**, escaped across the Jordan River. **Succoth** and **Penuel** were towns in Transjordan under Israelite control. The men of these cities might have been expected to give Gideon aid on his quest, but they refused his appeal for food because they were skeptical of Gideon's ability to thoroughly defeat the Midianites. Gideon threatened revenge on those who failed to assist him.

8:10–12 Gideon finally caught up with Zebah and Zalmunna at **Karkor**, about a hundred miles east of the Dead Sea. A sizeable remnant of their original army of

one hundred thirty-five thousand was with them, numbering around **fifteen thousand men**. Gideon and his force of three hundred caught them by surprise, routed them, and captured Zebah and Zalmunna, the two kings of Midian.

8:13–17 On his return to **Succoth** and **Penuel**, Gideon wasted no time in carrying out his earlier threats.

8:18–21 Gideon then accused the two Midianite kings, **Zebah and Zalmunna**, of atrocities at Mount **Tabor**, not far from his home in the Jezreel Valley. Gideon replied that the men whom the kings slaughtered were his own close relatives. Gideon instructed his son **Jether** to kill the Midianite kings, but

had let them live, I would not kill you." ²⁰ Then he said to Jether, his firstborn, "Get up and kill them." The youth did not draw his sword, for he was afraid because he was still a youth.

²¹ Zebah and Zalmunna said, "Get up and strike us down yourself, for a man is judged by his strength." So Gideon got up, killed Zebah and Zalmunna, and took the crescent ornaments that were on the necks of their camels.

Gideon's Legacy

²² Then the Israelites said to Gideon, "Rule over us, you as well as your sons and your grandsons, for you delivered us from the power of Midian."

²³ But Gideon said to them, "I will not rule over you, and my son will not rule over you; the LORD will rule over you." ²⁴ Then he said to them, "Let me make a request of you: Everyone give me an earring from his plunder." Now the enemy had gold earrings because they were Ishmaelites.

²⁵ They said, "We agree to give them." So they spread out a cloak, and everyone threw an earring from his plunder on it. ²⁶ The weight of the gold earrings he requested was forty-three pounds^A of gold, in addition to the crescent ornaments and ear pendants, the purple garments on the kings of Midian, and the chains on the necks of their camels. ²⁷ Gideon made an ephod from all this and put it in Ophrah, his hometown. Then all Israel prostituted themselves by worshiping it there, and it became a snare to Gideon and his household.

²⁸ So Midian was subdued before the Israelites, and they were no longer a threat. The land had peace for forty years during the days of Gideon. ²⁹ Jerubbaal (that is, Gideon) son of Joash went back to live at his house.

³⁰ Gideon had seventy sons, his own offspring, since he had many wives. ³¹ His concubine who was in Shechem also bore him a son, and he named him Abimelech. ³² Then Gideon

son of Joash died at a good old age and was buried in the tomb of his father Joash in Ophrah of the Abiezrites.

³³ When Gideon died, the Israelites turned and prostituted themselves by worshiping the Baals and made Baal-berith⁸ their god. ³⁴ The Israelites did not remember the LORD their God who had rescued them from the hand of the enemies around them. ³⁵ They did not show kindness to the house of Jerubbaal (that is, Gideon) for all the good he had done for Israel.

Abimelech Becomes King

9 Abimelech son of Jerubbaal went to Shechem and spoke to his uncles and to his mother's whole clan, saying, ² "Please speak in the hearing of all the citizens of Shechem, 'Is it better for you that seventy men, all the sons of Jerubbaal, rule over you or that one man rule over you?' Remember that I am your own flesh and blood."^c

³ His mother's relatives spoke all these words about him in the hearing of all the citizens of Shechem, and they were favorable to Abimelech, for they said, "He is our brother." ⁴ So they gave him seventy pieces of silver from the temple of Baal-berith.⁸ Abimelech used it to hire worthless and reckless men, and they followed him. ⁵ He went to his father's house in Ophrah and killed his seventy brothers, the sons of Jerubbaal, on top of a large stone. But Jotham, the youngest son of Jerubbaal, survived, because he hid. ⁶ Then all the citizens of Shechem and of Beth-millo gathered together and proceeded to make Abimelech king at the oak of the pillar in Shechem.

Jotham's Parable

⁷ When they told Jotham, he climbed to the top of Mount Gerizim, raised his voice, and called to them:

Listen to me, citizens of Shechem,
and may God listen to you:

---

^A 8:26 Lit *1,700 shekels*   ⁸ 8:33; 9:4 Lit *Baal of the Covenant*, or *Lord of the Covenant*   ^c 9:2 Lit *your bone and your flesh*

Jether did not do so because **he was afraid**. Gideon killed Zebah and Zalmunna and took for himself their **crescent** symbols of royalty. **8:22–27** The Israelites recognized the significance of Gideon's behavior. They asked him to **rule over** them as the founder of a dynastic line. Though they carefully avoided the word *king*, it is clear that they were offering Gideon that office. Gideon proceeded to act precisely as a king would. He asked for a royal share of the plunder, **gold earrings** from every man, representing a symbolic token of submission to him. As in Ex 32, where earrings were used in the making of the golden calf, so Gideon used these earrings to manufacture an idol in the form of an **ephod**, a garment worn by the priests and used as a means of determining God's will. The amount of **gold** suggests that the garment included an idolatrous image. The result was spiritually disastrous, ensnaring **all Israel** in prostituting themselves.

8:28–32 Along with supporting idolatry, Gideon married many wives and had **seventy sons**, a family structure forbidden to kings in Dt 17:17. He also intermarried with the local population, taking a concubine from Canaanite **Shechem**, with whom he had a son named **Abimelech**, which literally means "my father is king." Positively, the land **had peace for forty years** during Gideon's lifetime, but from this point on in the Judges narrative, Israel never again attained rest. **8:33–35** After Gideon's death, Israel went from bad to worse and **prostituted themselves** in the worship of the **Baals**. Baal was worshiped in many local manifestations, including **Baal-berith** ("Baal of the Covenant"), who was the patron deity of Shechem. It is ironic that in worshiping a god whose name includes the word for "covenant," Israel forgot the covenant faithfulness of their own God, Yahweh. The place where this Baal was worshiped, Shechem, was where the people

had renewed their covenant with the Lord at the end of the book of Joshua when the people swore never to worship the gods of the land (Jos 24). The irony of Israel's return to Baal worship is heightened by the use of Gideon's other name, **Jerubbaal**, "Let Baal Contend." **9:1–6** Gideon may have formally declined kingship, but Abimelech (whose name means "my father is king") had no such scruples. He went to his mother's family in Shechem, in the center of Israel, and sought the support of **the citizens of Shechem** in a coup that would place him on the throne. Abimelech hired mercenaries to eliminate his rivals, Gideon's other sons. **Beth-millo** may be another way of referring to Shechem's leaders. **9:7–15 Jotham**, the sole son of Gideon to escape the massacre, went to the top of **Mount Gerizim**, which overlooked Shechem. In addition to being a safe place, it was a place with a history. Mount Gerizim and

8 The trees decided
to anoint a king over themselves.
They said to the olive tree,
"Reign over us."
9 But the olive tree said to them,
"Should I stop giving my oil
that people use to honor both God
and men,
and rule^A over the trees?"

10 Then the trees said to the fig tree,
"Come and reign over us."
11 But the fig tree said to them,
"Should I stop giving
my sweetness and my good fruit,
and rule over trees?"

12 Later, the trees said to the grapevine,
"Come and reign over us."
13 But the grapevine said to them,
"Should I stop giving my wine
that cheers both God and man,
and rule over trees?"

14 Finally, all the trees said to the bramble,
"Come and reign over us."
15 The bramble said to the trees,
"If you really are anointing me
as king over you,
come and find refuge in my shade.
But if not,
may fire come out from the bramble
and consume the cedars of Lebanon."

16 "Now if you have acted faithfully and honestly in making Abimelech king, if you have done well by Jerubbaal and his family, and if you have rewarded him appropriately for what he did — **17** for my father fought for you, risked his life, and rescued you from Midian, **18** and now you have attacked my father's family today, killed his seventy sons on top of a large stone, and made Abimelech, the son of his slave woman, king over the citizens of Shechem 'because he is your brother' — **19** so if you have acted faithfully and honestly with Jerubbaal and his house this day, rejoice in Abimelech and may he also rejoice in you. **20** But if not, may fire come from Abimelech and consume the citizens of Shechem and Beth-millo, and may

fire come from the citizens of Shechem and Beth-millo and consume Abimelech." **21** Then Jotham fled, escaping to Beer, and lived there because of his brother Abimelech.

Abimelech's Punishment

22 When Abimelech had ruled over Israel three years, **23** God sent an evil spirit between Abimelech and the citizens of Shechem. They treated Abimelech deceitfully, **24** so that the crime against the seventy sons of Jerubbaal might come to justice and their blood would be avenged on their brother Abimelech, who killed them, and on the citizens of Shechem, who had helped him kill his brothers. **25** The citizens of Shechem rebelled against him by putting men in ambush on the tops of the mountains, and they robbed everyone who passed by them on the road. So this was reported to Abimelech.

26 Gaal son of Ebed came with his brothers and crossed into Shechem, and the citizens of Shechem trusted him. **27** So they went out to the countryside and harvested grapes from their vineyards. They trampled the grapes and held a celebration. Then they went to the house of their god, and as they ate and drank, they cursed Abimelech. **28** Gaal son of Ebed said, "Who is Abimelech and who is Shechem that we should serve him? Isn't he the son of Jerubbaal, and isn't Zebul his officer? You are to serve the men of Hamor, the father of Shechem. Why should we serve Abimelech? **29** If only these people were in my power, I would remove Abimelech." So he said^B to Abimelech, "Gather your army and come out."

30 When Zebul, the ruler of the city, heard the words of Gaal son of Ebed, he was angry. **31** So he secretly sent messengers to Abimelech, saying, "Beware! Gaal son of Ebed and his brothers have come to Shechem and are turning the city against you.^C **32** Now tonight, you and the troops with you, come and wait in ambush in the countryside. **33** Then get up early, and at sunrise attack the city. When he and the troops who are with him come out against you, do to him whatever you can." **34** So Abimelech and all the troops with him got up at night and waited in ambush for Shechem in four units.

^A9:9 Lit *and go to sway*, also in vv. 11,13   ^B9:29 DSS read *They said*; LXX reads *I would say*   ^C9:31 Hb obscure

Mount Ebal were the locations where the people of Israel recited the blessings and curses of the covenant when they had first entered the land (Dt 27:12–13). From the mountain, Jotham proclaimed a *fable*. **9:16–21** Jotham himself provided the interpretation of the fable. Then he invoked a curse that the people would get what they deserve. Jotham then fled, hiding out at a place named **Beer** ("Well"). **9:22–25** Abimelech's reign lasted only **three years**. The translation **evil spirit** does not

necessarily imply demonic activity, since the Hebrew word *ra'ah* can simply mean "bad." The focus is on the fact that God replaced the harmony between Abimelech and the citizens of Shechem with a spirit of distrust and disagreement. As a result, the citizens of Shechem broke faith with Abimelech by ambushing those who passed by on the roads. **9:26–29** Gaal may have been a Shechemite who had gone into exile to escape Abimelech. His return was welcomed by the citizens of Shechem who **harvested grapes**

in order to throw a party for him. The grape harvest was often a time of riotous celebration and drunkenness. On this occasion, after eating and drinking a little too much, the participants **cursed Abimelech**. In a speech whose forthrightness seems emboldened by alcohol, Gaal claimed that if he were king he could do a better job of running Shechem than Abimelech. **9:30–41** Zebul, Abimelech's governor in Shechem, called Gaal's bluff, informing Abimelech of Gaal's insubordination and forcing

³⁵ Gaal son of Ebed went out and stood at the entrance of the city gate. Then Abimelech and the troops who were with him got up from their ambush. ³⁶ When Gaal saw the troops, he said to Zebul, "Look, troops are coming down from the mountaintops!" But Zebul said to him, "The shadows of the mountains look like men to you."

³⁷ Then Gaal spoke again, "Look, troops are coming down from the central part of the land, and one unit is coming from the direction of the Diviners' Oak." ³⁸ Zebul replied, "What do you have to say now? You said, 'Who is Abimelech that we should serve him?' Aren't these the troops you despised? Now go and fight them!"

³⁹ So Gaal went out leading the citizens of Shechem and fought against Abimelech, ⁴⁰ but Abimelech pursued him, and Gaal fled before him. Numerous bodies were strewn as far as the entrance of the city gate. ⁴¹ Abimelech stayed in Arumah, and Zebul drove Gaal and his brothers from Shechem.

⁴² The next day when the people of Shechemᴬ went into the countryside, this was reported to Abimelech. ⁴³ He took the troops, divided them into three companies, and waited in ambush in the countryside. He looked, and the people were coming out of the city, so he arose against them and struck them down. ⁴⁴ Then Abimelech and the units that were with him rushed forward and took their stand at the entrance of the city gate. The other two units rushed against all who were in the countryside and struck them down. ⁴⁵ So Abimelech fought against the city that entire day, captured it, and killed the people who were in it. Then he tore down the city and sowed it with salt.

⁴⁶ When all the citizens of the Tower of Shechem heard, they entered the inner chamberᴮ of the temple of El-berith.ᶜ ⁴⁷ Then it was reported to Abimelech that all the citizens of the Tower of Shechem had gathered. ⁴⁸ So Abimelech and all the troops who were with him went up to Mount Zalmon. Abimelech took his ax in his hand and cut a branch from the trees. He picked up the branch, put it on his

shoulder, and said to the troops who were with him, "Hurry and do what you have seen me do." ⁴⁹ Each of the troops also cut his own branch and followed Abimelech. They put the branches against the inner chamber and set it on fire; about a thousand men and women died, including all the men of the Tower of Shechem.

⁵⁰ Abimelech went to Thebez, camped against it, and captured it. ⁵¹ There was a strong tower inside the city, and all the men, women, and citizens of the city fled there. They locked themselves in and went up to the roof of the tower. ⁵² When Abimelech came to attack the tower, he approached its entrance to set it on fire. ⁵³ But a woman threw the upper portion of a millstone on Abimelech's head and fractured his skull. ⁵⁴ He quickly called his armor-bearer and said to him, "Draw your sword and kill me, or they'll say about me, 'A woman killed him.'" So his armor-bearer ran him through, and he died. ⁵⁵ When the Israelites saw that Abimelech was dead, they all went home.

⁵⁶ In this way, God brought back Abimelech's evil—the evil that Abimelech had done to his father when he killed his seventy brothers. ⁵⁷ God also brought back to the men of Shechem all their evil. So the curse of Jotham son of Jerubbaal came upon them.

Tola and Jair

10 After Abimelech, Tola son of Puah, son of Dodo became judge and began to deliver Israel. He was from Issachar and lived in Shamir in the hill country of Ephraim. ² Tola judged Israel twenty-three years and when he died, was buried in Shamir.

³ After him came Jair the Gileadite, who judged Israel twenty-two years. ⁴ He had thirty sons who rode on thirty donkeys. They had thirty townsᴰ in Gilead, which are still called Jair's Villagesᴱ today. ⁵ When Jair died, he was buried in Kamon.

Israel's Rebellion and Repentance

⁶ Then the Israelites again did what was evil in the sight of the LORD. They worshiped the Baals and the Ashtoreths, the gods of Aram,

---

ᴬ 9:42 of Shechem supplied for clarity   ᴮ 9:46 Or the crypt, or the vault   ᶜ 9:46 = God of the Covenant   ᴰ 10:4 LXX; MT reads donkeys   ᴱ 10:4 Or called Havvoth-jair

---

Gaal to lead **the citizens of Shechem** against Abimelech's army.
9:42–49 Abimelech took excessive revenge against Shechem. He massacred the inhabitants of the city and tore down its buildings. He also scattered **salt** over it. Since salt is a preservative, this act symbolized the eternal and unchanging nature of this destruction. Those who escaped fled to the **temple of El-berith** (Baal-berith, Shechem's god). Rather than waste lives in assaulting this stronghold, Abimelech piled wood around it and burned the occupants alive. The fiery destruction of the citizens of Shechem perfectly matched the imagery of Jotham's fable (vv. 7–15).

9:50–57 Encouraged by his success at Shechem, Abimelech sought to repeat it at **Thebez**, a town not far from Shechem. Instead, he was killed when a **woman** dropped a **millstone** on his head.
10:1–5 After **Abimelech**, there were a pair of minor judges, **Tola** and **Jair**. Both "judged" Israel administratively without being involved in direct conflict. The description of Tola recalls the days of the good judges. However, **Jair the Gileadite** with his **thirty** pampered **sons** suggests multiple wives, while thirty donkeys and towns implies a tendency to accumulate personal wealth. Like Abimelech, there is no mention that they

were raised up by the Lord or empowered for their task by him.
10:6–9 Israel now plumbed the depths of idolatry, serving no fewer than seven false gods. The **Philistines** occupied the coastal plain west of Israel while the **Ammonites** occupied the Transjordanian region to the east. Since the Ammonites were the oppressors in the Jephthah narrative (chap. 11) while the Philistines were the enemy with whom Samson had to deal (chaps. 13–16), this description of spiritual unfaithfulness seems to introduce both of these episodes, which may have been contemporaneous. The Lord's anger with Israel was so great that he afflicted

Sidon, and Moab, and the gods of the Ammonites and the Philistines. They abandoned the LORD and did not worship him. [7] So the LORD's anger burned against Israel, and he sold them to the Philistines and the Ammonites. [8] They shattered and crushed the Israelites that year, and for eighteen years they did the same to all the Israelites who were on the other side of the Jordan in the land of the Amorites in Gilead. [9] The Ammonites also crossed the Jordan to fight against Judah, Benjamin, and the house of Ephraim. Israel was greatly oppressed, [10] so they cried out to the LORD, saying, "We have sinned against you. We have abandoned our God and worshiped the Baals."

[11] The LORD said to the Israelites, "When the Egyptians, Amorites, Ammonites, Philistines, [12] Sidonians, Amalekites, and Maonites[A] oppressed you, and you cried out to me, did I not deliver you from them? [13] But you have abandoned me and worshiped other gods. Therefore, I will not deliver you again. [14] Go and cry out to the gods you have chosen. Let them deliver you whenever you are oppressed."

[15] But the Israelites said, "We have sinned. Deal with us as you see fit; only rescue us today!" [16] So they got rid of the foreign gods among them and worshiped the LORD, and he became weary of Israel's misery.

[17] The Ammonites were called together, and they camped in Gilead. So the Israelites assembled and camped at Mizpah. [18] The rulers[B] of Gilead said to one another, "Which man will begin the fight against the Ammonites? He will be the leader of all the inhabitants of Gilead."

Jephthah Becomes Israel's Leader

11 Jephthah the Gileadite was a valiant warrior, but he was the son of a prostitute, and Gilead was his father. [2] Gilead's wife bore him sons, and when they grew up, they drove Jephthah out and said to him, "You will have no inheritance in our father's family, because you are the son of another woman." [3] So Jephthah fled from his brothers and lived in the land of Tob. Then some worthless men joined Jephthah and went on raids with him.

[4] Some time later, the Ammonites fought against Israel. [5] When the Ammonites made war with Israel, the elders of Gilead went to get Jephthah from the land of Tob. [6] They said to him, "Come, be our commander, and let's fight the Ammonites."

[7] Jephthah replied to the elders of Gilead, "Didn't you hate me and drive me out of my father's family? Why then have you come to me now when you're in trouble?"

[8] They answered Jephthah, "That's true. But now we turn to you. Come with us, fight the Ammonites, and you will become leader of all the inhabitants of Gilead."

[9] So Jephthah said to them, "If you are bringing me back to fight the Ammonites and the LORD gives them to me, I will be your leader."

[10] The elders of Gilead said to Jephthah, "The LORD is our witness if we don't do as you say." [11] So Jephthah went with the elders of Gilead. The people made him their leader and commander, and Jephthah repeated all his terms in the presence of the LORD at Mizpah.

Jephthah Rejects Ammonite Claims

[12] Jephthah sent messengers to the king of the Ammonites, asking, "What do you have against me that you have come to fight me in my land?"

[13] The king of the Ammonites said to Jephthah's messengers, "When Israel came from Egypt, they seized my land from the Arnon to the Jabbok and the Jordan. Now restore it peaceably."

---

^10:12 LXX reads *Midianites*   ^B10:18 Lit *The people, rulers*

---

them with two oppressors at once. The initial focus is on the Ammonites, who for eighteen years oppressed the Israelites living east of the Jordan River in the land of Gilead. The affliction was not limited to the part of Israel closest to the Ammonite homeland. They went further afield, crossing **the Jordan** and fighting against **Judah, Benjamin, and . . . Ephraim**. **10:10–18** When under pressure, Israel **cried out to the LORD**, confessing their sin of abandoning him. Though the Israelites called him **our God**, the Lord refused to accept their claim of a relationship to him. Now he would no longer deliver them. The Lord declared that his patience with Israel's suffering was exhausted. There was no word of any deliverer to come. The only sound was the impending arrival of the Ammonites camping for war in **Gilead**. As a result, instead of seeking a man empowered by the Spirit of God, they sought to motivate someone—anyone—to step forward with the promise of human reward: leadership over **all the inhabitants of Gilead**. This **Mizpah** (v. 17; 11:11,29,34) was

in Transjordan, not on the border between Benjamin and Ephraim (as in 20:1,3; 21:1,5,8). **11:1–3** The candidate that the Gileadites were seeking soon emerged. **Jephthah** is described as a **valiant warrior**. Yet Jephthah was also a social outcast, **the son of a prostitute**. Driven from his home, Jephthah lived the life of a bandit in the land of **Tob**, where he was joined by **worthless men**. This is the same phrase used to describe Abimelech's mercenaries in 9:4. **11:4–6** When the **Ammonites** waged war against Israel, the elders of Gilead invited Jephthah to be their commander. In 10:18 the Gileadites had offered their own citizens the position of leadership (Hb *ro'sh*), which implied long-term leadership over the tribe, but they offered to make Jephthah a military **commander** (Hb *qatsin*), which was a lesser position. **11:7–11** Jephthah was not immediately won over by this appeal. Earlier, the leaders of Gilead had been happy to send him elsewhere; now, in their hour of need, they wanted his help. In response, the **elders of**

Gilead increased their offer to Jephthah, saying they would indeed make him **leader** (Hb *ro'sh*, v. 8). The elders of Gilead made a vow in the Lord's presence and **made him their leader and commander**. The elders and Jephthah both seemed to be using the Lord's name in support of their own interests. **11:12–13** As the new leader, Jephthah acted in king-like fashion, speaking to the king of the Ammonites as an equal and claiming that the land of Gilead was his own personal property (**my land**). The **king of the Ammonites** contested this claim, arguing that the region east of the **Jordan**, from the **Arnon** River in the south to the **Jabbok** River in the north, belonged to him and had been illegally seized **when Israel came from Egypt**. This claim was false. At the time Israel came up from Egypt, the land was occupied by the Amorites, not the Ammonites (Nm 21:21–35). **11:14–22** Negotiations went through another stage, as Jephthah sent more **messengers** to the king. They said that the land of Gilead had never belonged either to **Moab**, Ammon's southern neighbor, or to Ammon.

Typical Israelite Home of the Iron Age

ca 1300 BC–ca 600 BC

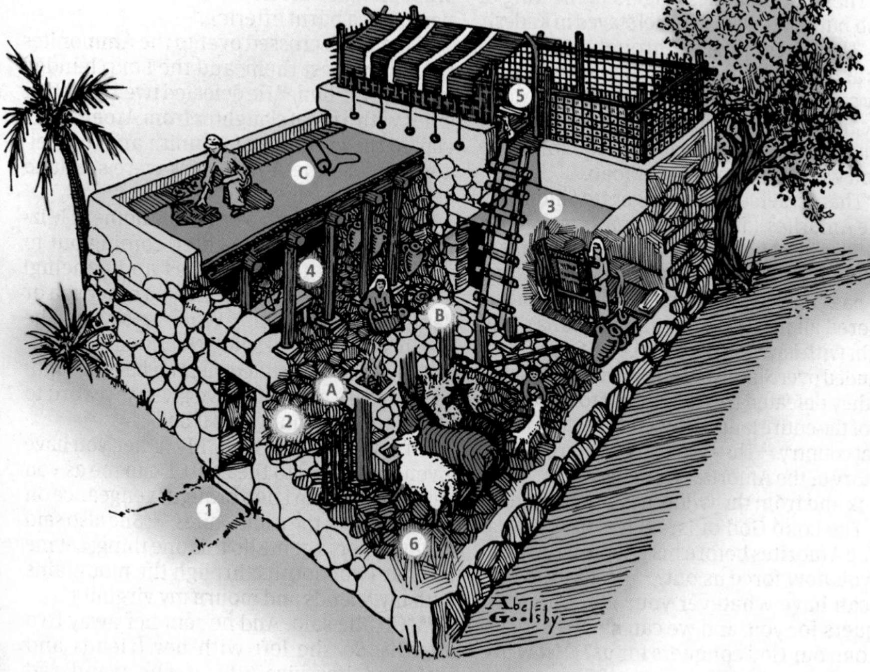
5
C
3
4
B
A
2
1
6
Abel Goolsby

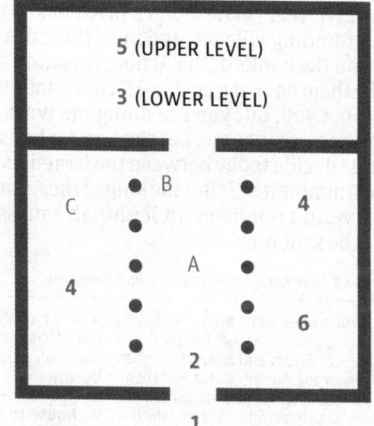

1. **ENTRANCE**
2. **CENTRAL COURTYARD**
   A. Fire pit
   B. Cistern
3. **LIVING QUARTERS** ("LONG ROOM")
4. **STORAGE/WORKSHOP/KITCHEN**
5. **ROOFTOP** (EXTRA AREA FOR EATING, WORKING, AND SLEEPING DURING WARM WEATHER)
   C. Roller – for recompacting clay roof following rain. Man shown is patching roof.
6. **ANIMAL PEN**

5 (UPPER LEVEL)
3 (LOWER LEVEL)
B
C
4
A
4
6
2
1

Israelite four-room house. Some interpreters believe Jephthah lived in a four-room house that was common in Israel during the Iron Age. Many such houses had a room for the family's animals. If Jephthah lived in such a house, his vow (11:30) may have been based on the assumption that one of his animals would be the first to greet him when he returned from victory over the Ammonites. For a different view, see the note at 11:29-33.

¹⁴ Jephthah again sent messengers to the king of the Ammonites ¹⁵ to tell him, "This is what Jephthah says: Israel did not take away the land of Moab or the land of the Ammonites. ¹⁶ But when they came from Egypt, Israel traveled through the wilderness to the Red Sea and came to Kadesh. ¹⁷ Israel sent messengers to the king of Edom, saying, 'Please let us travel through your land,' but the king of Edom would not listen. They also sent messengers to the king of Moab, but he refused. So Israel stayed in Kadesh. ¹⁸ "Then they traveled through the wilderness and around the lands of Edom and Moab. They came to the east side of the land of Moab and camped on the other side of the Arnon but did not enter into the territory of Moab, for the Arnon was the boundary of Moab. ¹⁹ "Then Israel sent messengers to Sihon king of the Amorites, king of Heshbon. Israel said to him, 'Please let us travel through your land to our country,' ²⁰ but Sihon would not trust Israel to pass through his territory. Instead, Sihon gathered all his troops, camped at Jahaz, and fought with Israel. ²¹ Then the LORD God of Israel handed over Sihon and all his troops to Israel, and they defeated them. So Israel took possession of the entire land of the Amorites who lived in that country. ²² They took possession of all the territory of the Amorites from the Arnon to the Jabbok and from the wilderness to the Jordan. ²³ "The LORD God of Israel has now driven out the Amorites before his people Israel, and will you now force us out? ²⁴ Isn't it true that you can have whatever your god Chemosh conquers for you, and we can have whatever the LORD our God conquers for us? ²⁵ Now are you any better than Balak son of Zippor, king of Moab? Did he ever contend with Israel or fight against them? ²⁶ While Israel lived three hundred years in Heshbon and Aroer and their surrounding villages, and in all the cities that are on the banks of the Arnon, why didn't you take them back at that time? ²⁷ I have not sinned against you, but you are doing me wrong by fighting against me. Let the LORD who is the judge decide today between the Israelites and the Ammonites." ²⁸ But the king of the Ammonites would not listen to Jephthah's message that he sent him.

Jephthah's Vow and Sacrifice

²⁹ The Spirit of the LORD came on Jephthah, who traveled through Gilead and Manasseh, and then through Mizpah of Gilead. He crossed over to the Ammonites from Mizpah of Gilead. ³⁰ Jephthah made this vow to the LORD: "If you in fact hand over the Ammonites to me, ³¹ whoever comes out the doors of my house to greet me when I return safely from the Ammonites will belong to the LORD, and I will offer that person as a burnt offering." ³² Jephthah crossed over to the Ammonites to fight against them, and the LORD handed them over to him. ³³ He defeated twenty of their cities with a great slaughter from Aroer all the way to the entrance of Minnith and to Abel-keramim. So the Ammonites were subdued before the Israelites. ³⁴ When Jephthah went to his home in Mizpah, there was his daughter, coming out to meet him with tambourines and dancing! She was his only child; he had no other son or daughter besides her. ³⁵ When he saw her, he tore his clothes and said, "No! Not my daughter! You have devastated me! You have brought great misery on me.ᴬ I have given my word to the LORD and cannot take it back." ³⁶ Then she said to him, "My father, you have given your word to the LORD. Do to me as you have said, for the LORD brought vengeance on your enemies, the Ammonites." ³⁷ She also said to her father, "Let me do this one thing: Let me wander two months through the mountains with my friends and mourn my virginity." ³⁸ "Go," he said. And he sent her away two months. So she left with her friends and mourned her virginity as she wandered through the mountains. ³⁹ At the end of two months, she returned to her father, and he kept the vow he had made about her. And she had never been intimate with a man. Now it became a custom in Israel ⁴⁰ that four days each year the young women of Israel would commemorate the daughter of Jephthah the Gileadite.

Conflict with Ephraim

12 The men of Ephraim were called together and crossed the Jordan to Zaphon. They said to Jephthah, "Why have you

ᴬ11:35 Lit have been among those who trouble me

Rather, when Israel came up out of Egypt, they were careful to respect the territorial boundaries of **Edom** and Moab. But when Sihon king of the Amorites attacked them, they had no choice but to engage him. The Lord then gave Israel Sihon's land, which is the land that the king of the Ammonites had described (vv. 21–22; cp. v. 13).
11:29–33 The Lord gave Jephthah victory over **twenty . . . cities** of the Ammonites, from **Aroer all the way to . . . Minnith and to Abel-keramim**—three towns that defined the traditional border between Israel and Ammon. In between empowerment and

victory, though, there was an intervening episode that undermined Jephthah's triumph. Jephthah sought to ensure the Lord's favor by vowing to sacrifice as a whole burnt offering **whoever** came **out the doors** of his **house to greet** him after he had won his victory.
11:34–35 After the victory, Jephthah's vow came back to haunt him. The one **coming out to meet him** was **his daughter**, with **tambourines and dancing**, the traditional greeting for a returning hero. She was his only daughter, and more importantly, his only child. Jephthah would be left without

progeny. Jephthah **tore his clothes** and mourned her loss.
11:36–40 A few scholars suggest that Jephthah did not kill his daughter but dedicated her to the Lord for her whole life (cp. 1Sm 1:11,24–28). She would remain a virgin, hence the yearly celebration of her willing sacrifice. In this case, Jephthah would still be without progeny. However, the natural sense of the Hebrew—literally "he did to her his vow that he had vowed"—is that he slaughtered her.
12:1–3 In a replay of the explosive situation that Gideon had faced and successfully

crossed over to fight against the Ammonites but didn't call us to go with you? We will burn your house with you in it!"

² Then Jephthah said to them, "My people and I had a bitter conflict with the Ammonites. So I called for you, but you didn't deliver me from their power. ³ When I saw that you weren't going to deliver me, I took my life in my own hands and crossed over to the Ammonites, and the Lᴏʀᴅ handed them over to me. Why then have you come today to fight against me?"

⁴ Then Jephthah gathered all of the men of Gilead. They fought and defeated Ephraim, because Ephraim had said, "You Gileadites are Ephraimite fugitives in the territories of Ephraim and Manasseh." ⁵ The Gileadites captured the fords of the Jordan leading to Ephraim. Whenever a fugitive from Ephraim said, "Let me cross over," the Gileadites asked him, "Are you an Ephraimite?" If he answered, "No," ⁶ they told him, "Please say Shibboleth." If he said, "Sibboleth," because he could not pronounce it correctly, they seized him and executed him at the fords of the Jordan. At that time forty-two thousand from Ephraim died.

⁷ Jephthah judged Israel six years, and when he died, he was buried in one of the cities of Gilead.ᴬ

Ibzan, Elon, and Abdon

⁸ Ibzan, who was from Bethlehem, judged Israel after Jephthah ⁹ and had thirty sons. He gave his thirty daughters in marriage to men outside the tribe and brought back thirty wives for his sons from outside the tribe. Ibzan judged Israel seven years, ¹⁰ and when he died, he was buried in Bethlehem.

¹¹ Elon, who was from Zebulun, judged Israel after Ibzan. He judged Israel ten years, ¹² and when he died, he was buried in Aijalon in the land of Zebulun.

¹³ After Elon, Abdon son of Hillel, who was from Pirathon, judged Israel. ¹⁴ He had forty sons and thirty grandsons, who rode on

seventy donkeys. Abdon judged Israel eight years, ¹⁵ and when he died, he was buried in Pirathon in the land of Ephraim, in the hill country of the Amalekites.

Birth of Samson

13 The Israelites again did what was evil in the Lᴏʀᴅ's sight, so the Lᴏʀᴅ handed them over to the Philistines forty years. ² There was a certain man from Zorah, from the family of Dan, whose name was Manoah; his wife was unable to conceive and had no children. ³ The angel of the Lᴏʀᴅ appeared to the woman and said to her, "Although you are unable to conceive and have no children, you will conceive and give birth to a son. ⁴ Now please be careful not to drink wine or beer, or to eat anything unclean; ⁵ for indeed, you will conceive and give birth to a son. You must never cut his hair,ᴮ because the boy will be a Nazirite to God from birth, and he will begin to save Israel from the power of the Philistines."

⁶ Then the woman went and told her husband, "A man of God came to me. He looked like the awe-inspiring angel of God. I didn't ask him where he came from, and he didn't tell me his name. ⁷ He said to me, 'You will conceive and give birth to a son. Therefore, do not drink wine or beer, and do not eat anything unclean, because the boy will be a Nazirite to God from birth until the day of his death.'"

⁸ Manoah prayed to the Lᴏʀᴅ and said, "Please, Lord, let the man of God you sent come again to us and teach us what we should do for the boy who will be born."

⁹ God listened to Manoah, and the angel of God came again to the woman. She was sitting in the field, and her husband, Manoah, was not with her. ¹⁰ The woman ran quickly to her husband and told him, "The man who came to me the other day has just come back!"

¹¹ So Manoah got up and followed his wife. When he came to the man, he asked, "Are you the man who spoke to my wife?"

"I am," he said.

ᴬ12:7 LXX reads *in his city in Gilead* ᴮ13:5 Lit *And a razor is not to go up on his head*

---

defused in chap. 8, the **men of Ephraim** came out and complained to Jephthah about not being invited to the battle against the Ammonites. They threatened to **burn** his **house** down with him **in it**. Jephthah claimed that he **called** them and they did not come **to deliver** him, whereupon he took his life in his hands and the Lord gave the Ammonites into his hands. Jephthah's claim is not confirmed by the text and may be a convenient fabrication.
12:4–7 Jephthah took action against the Ephraimites because they questioned the legitimacy of Gilead. Jephthah, the illegitimate son who had achieved social acceptability, could not tolerate this insult, so he called out the troops once more—this time against a tribe from his own people. Those who escaped (in a neat twist, the true "Ephraimite

fugitives") and attempted to get back across the **Jordan** River to Ephraim were met at the fords with a test question, **Please say Shibboleth.** The Hebrew word *shibboleth* has no clear meaning, but in the Ephraimite dialect, it was apparently pronounced **Sibboleth.** In view of this kin-group strife that caused **forty-two thousand** deaths, it is not surprising that though **Jephthah judged Israel six years**, there is no mention of the land experiencing any rest during his tenure.
12:8–15 After Jephthah, there were three minor judges, **Ibzan . . . Elon**, and **Abdon**. Ibzan had thirty sons and thirty daughters, while Abdon had forty sons and thirty grandsons. They practiced polygamy and acquired wealth (cp. 8:28–32).
13:1 The story of Samson is introduced with the pattern familiar in the book of

Judges—of doing evil and being handed over to an enemy for a period of time. Based on the coastal plain, the **Philistines** were constantly seeking to expand their territory into the foothills of Israel. They were already a problem for Israel in 3:31, and they continued to be the chief threat to Israel during the time of Samuel and Saul. There is no mention on this occasion of Israel crying out for deliverance, yet the Lord would still send them a deliverer—of a sort.
13:2–7 The name of Samson's father, **Manoah**, means "rest," which is what Israel lacked. A Nazirite made a vow to abstain from **wine** and other alcoholic beverages, to remain separate from corpses and other sources of defilement, and to leave his hair uncut (Nm 6).

▼ The Judges

Throughout the lifetime of Joshua and the elders who outlived him, the Israelites worshiped the Lord. But then a new generation rose up who did not know the Lord or the works he had done for Israel *(Jdg 2:7–10)*.

SIN	JUDGMENT
The Israelites did what was evil in the Lord's sight; they worshiped the Baals and abandoned the Lord *(2:11–13)*.	The Lord's anger burned against Israel, and he gave them over to their enemies around them *(2:14–15)*.
The Israelites did what was evil in the Lord's sight *(3:7)*.	Cushan-rishathaim, king of Mesopotamia, ruled over them eight years *(3:8)*.
The Israelites again did what was evil in the Lord's sight *(3:12a)*.	Eglon, king of Moab, ruled over them eighteen years *(3:12b–14)*.
	Philistines *(3:31)*.
The Israelites again did what was evil in the Lord's sight *(4:1)*.	Jabin, king of Canaan, and Sisera, the commander of his forces, oppressed them twenty years *(4:2–3)*.
The Israelites did what was evil in the Lord's sight *(6:1a)*.	Midian oppressed them seven years *(6:1b–6)*.
The Israelites again did what was evil in the Lord's sight *(10:6)*.	The Philistines and the Ammonites oppressed them eighteen years *(10:7–9)*.
The Israelites again did what was evil in the Lord's sight *(13:1a)*.	The Philistines were over them forty years *(13:1b)*.

DELIVERANCE

When the Israelites cried out, the Lord raised up a judge to save them from their enemies. But when the judge died, the Israelites acted even more corruptly than their fathers had *(2:16–19)*.

Israel cried out to the Lord, and he raised up **Othniel** as a deliverer—the Spirit of the Lord came on him, and he judged Israel. Forty years of peace *(3:9–11)*

Israel cried out to the Lord, and he raised up **Ehud**, a left-handed Benjaminite, as a deliverer. Eighty years of peace *(3:15–30)*.

Shamgar, son of Anath (likely a non-Israelite), delivered Israel *(3:31)*.

Israel cried out to the Lord. **Deborah**, a woman, was judging Israel at that time, and she summoned Barak to fight for them; he was hesitant, so Deborah went with him. In the end, Jael, not Barak, killed Sisera. Forty years of peace *(4:3–5:31)*

Israel cried out to the Lord, and he sent a prophet; then the Lord sent fearful **Gideon** to deliver them. Forty years of peace, though he crafted an ephod, which became an idol for the people and his household *(6:7–8:35)*

Tola arose to deliver Israel; he judged Israel twenty-three years *(10:1–2)*.

Jair judged Israel twenty-two years *(10:3–5)*.

Israel cried out to the Lord, but he said they should cry out to the other gods they had chosen, so they got rid of their idols. The Spirit of the Lord came on **Jephthah**, the son of a prostitute, to fight for them. In keeping a foolish vow, he sacrificed his daughter. He judged Israel six years *(10:10–12:7)*.

Ibzan judged Israel seven years *(12:8–10)*.

Elon judged Israel ten years *(12:11–12)*.

Abdon judged Israel eight years *(12:13–15)*.

The Lord raised up **Samson** to deliver Israel. Though a Nazirite from birth, he often disregarded his vows, and he desired Philistine women. The Spirit of the Lord directed him numerous times until his hair was cut and the Lord left him; then he was captured. He was a more effective judge in his death than he was in his life. He judged Israel twenty years *(13:2–16:31)*.

CHRIST CONNECTION: The judges saved people from the consequences of their sin but could not change the cause of their sin. Jesus is the Savior and Judge who takes upon himself the consequences for our sin and then offers us new hearts that seek his righteousness.

¹² Then Manoah asked, "When your words come true, what will be the boy's responsibilities and work?"

¹³ The angel of the LORD answered Manoah, "Your wife needs to do everything I told her. ¹⁴ She must not eat anything that comes from the grapevine or drink wine or beer. And she must not eat anything unclean. Your wife must do everything I have commanded her."

¹⁵ "Please stay here," Manoah told him, "and we will prepare a young goat for you."

¹⁶ The angel of the LORD said to him, "If I stay, I won't eat your food. But if you want to prepare a burnt offering, offer it to the LORD." (Manoah did not know he was the angel of the LORD.)

¹⁷ Then Manoah said to him, "What is your name, so that we may honor you when your words come true?"

¹⁸ "Why do you ask my name," the angel of the LORD asked him, "since it is beyond understanding?"

¹⁹ Manoah took a young goat and a grain offering and offered them on a rock to the LORD, who did something miraculous^A while Manoah and his wife were watching. ²⁰ When the flame went up from the altar to the sky, the angel of the LORD went up in its flame. When Manoah and his wife saw this, they fell facedown on the ground. ²¹ The angel of the LORD did not appear again to Manoah and his wife. Then Manoah realized that it was the angel of the LORD.

²² "We're certainly going to die," he said to his wife, "because we have seen God!"

²³ But his wife said to him, "If the LORD had intended to kill us, he wouldn't have accepted the burnt offering and the grain offering from us, and he would not have shown us all these things or spoken to us like this."

²⁴ So the woman gave birth to a son and named him Samson. The boy grew, and the LORD blessed him. ²⁵ Then the Spirit of the LORD began to stir him in the Camp of Dan,^B between Zorah and Eshtaol.

Samson's Riddle

14 Samson went down to Timnah and saw a young Philistine woman there. ² He went back and told his father and his mother, "I have seen a young Philistine woman in Timnah. Now get her for me as a wife."

³ But his father and mother said to him, "Can't you find a young woman among your relatives or among any of our people? Must you go to the uncircumcised Philistines for a wife?"

But Samson told his father, "Get her for me. She's the right one for me." ⁴ Now his father and mother did not know this was from the LORD, who wanted the Philistines to provide an opportunity for a confrontation.^C At that time, the Philistines were ruling Israel.

⁵ Samson went down to Timnah with his father and mother and came to the vineyards of Timnah. Suddenly a young lion came roaring at him, ⁶ the Spirit of the LORD came powerfully on him, and he tore the lion apart with his bare hands as he might have torn a young goat. But he did not tell his father or mother what he had done. ⁷ Then he went and spoke to the woman, because she seemed right to Samson.

⁸ After some time, when he returned to marry her, he left the road to see the lion's carcass, and there was a swarm of bees with honey in the carcass. ⁹ He scooped some honey into his hands and ate it as he went along. When he came to his father and mother, he gave some to them and they ate it. But he did not tell them that he had scooped the honey from the lion's carcass.

¹⁰ His father went to visit the woman, and Samson prepared a feast there, as young men were accustomed to do. ¹¹ When the Philistines saw him, they brought thirty men to accompany him.

---

^A 13:19 LXX reads to the LORD, to the one who works wonders   ^B 13:25 Or in Mahaneh-dan   ^C 14:4 for a confrontation supplied for clarity

---

13:24–25 Samson was born as a result of the miraculous intervention of God. As he grew, **the Spirit of the LORD began to stir him.** These elements raise the expectation that he would be used by God to deliver his people powerfully—expectations that would be partially fulfilled but mostly unmet in what followed.

14:1–2 After Samson's empowering by the Spirit in 13:25, his next action was that he wanted to marry a Philistine woman whom he **saw** in Timnah. This city was only six miles west of Zorah, Samson's hometown (13:2), but it was in the hands of the Philistines.

14:3–4 Samson's parents asked him in vain if there were no women among his relatives whom he could marry. Intermarriage with the Philistines was a denial of Samson's calling as a Nazirite. Samson said of the woman he "saw" (v. 1), **She's the right one for me,**

literally, "she is right in my eyes." Yet the Lord would use even Samson's sinful desires to accomplish his purposes. The text literally says **his father and mother did not know** that she **was from the LORD.** This Philistine woman would be the means God would use to stir up Samson to begin a conflict with the Philistines.

14:5–7 On another occasion, Samson was going **down to Timnah** with his parents when a **young lion** rushed at him. This attack happened as he came to the **vineyards of Timnah,** an odd place for a Nazirite to be, since he was required to avoid all contact with grape products. With ease Samson disposed of the lion.

14:8–9 Some time later, as Samson traveled the same road, he turned aside to see the **lion's carcass.** As a Nazirite, he was supposed to remain distant from corpses, yet here he not only went to see the lion's carcass but

also scooped out of it **some honey.** Not only did Samson defile himself, he also defiled his parents by bringing them some of the honey but not informing them of its source. **He gave some to them and they ate it** uses the same vocabulary as when Eve gave Adam the fruit (Gn 3:6).

14:10–13 Having broken his Nazirite vow by deliberately touching the carcass of the lion, Samson then proceeded to despise it further by hosting a drinking party (the Hebrew word translated **feast** comes from the word "to drink") for his new pagan friends. The **thirty men** were probably security forces sent to keep an eye on this imposing foreigner. As the party progressed, Samson proposed a **riddle** that would cost every one of his thirty companions a suit of clothing—an outer garment and a tunic—if they lost and would cost him thirty suits if they were able to solve it before the end of the feast.

12 "Let me tell you a riddle," Samson said to them. "If you can explain it to me during the seven days of the feast and figure it out, I will give you thirty linen garments and thirty changes of clothes. **13** But if you can't explain it to me, you must give me thirty linen garments and thirty changes of clothes."

"Tell us your riddle," they replied.[A] "Let's hear it."

14 So he said to them:

Out of the eater came something to eat,
and out of the strong came something
sweet.

After three days, they were unable to explain the riddle. **15** On the fourth[B] day they said to Samson's wife, "Persuade your husband to explain the riddle to us, or we will burn you and your father's family to death. Did you invite us here to rob us?"

16 So Samson's wife came to him, weeping, and said, "You hate me and don't love me! You told my people the riddle, but haven't explained it to me."

"Look," he said,[C] "I haven't even explained it to my father or mother, so why should I explain it to you?"

17 She wept the whole seven days of the feast, and at last, on the seventh day, he explained it to her, because she had nagged him so much. Then she explained it to her people. **18** On the seventh day, before sunset, the men of the city said to him:

What is sweeter than honey?
What is stronger than a lion?

So he said to them:

If you hadn't plowed with
my young cow,
you wouldn't know my riddle now!

19 The Spirit of the LORD came powerfully on him, and he went down to Ashkelon and killed thirty of their men. He stripped them and gave their clothes to those who had explained the riddle. In a rage, Samson returned to his father's house, **20** and his wife was given to one of the men who had accompanied him.

Samson's Revenge

15 Later on, during the wheat harvest, Samson took a young goat as a gift and visited his wife. "I want to go to my wife in her room," he said. But her father would not let him enter.

2 "I was sure you hated her," her father said, "so I gave her to one of the men who accompanied you. Isn't her younger sister more beautiful than she is? Why not take her instead?"

3 Samson said to them, "This time I will be blameless when I harm the Philistines." **4** So he went out and caught three hundred foxes. He took torches, turned the foxes tail-to-tail, and put a torch between each pair of tails. **5** Then he ignited the torches and released the foxes into the standing grain of the Philistines. He burned the piles of grain and the standing grain as well as the vineyards and olive groves.

6 Then the Philistines asked, "Who did this?" They were told, "It was Samson, the Timnite's son-in-law, because he took Samson's wife and gave her to his companion." So the Philistines went to her and her father and burned them to death.

7 Then Samson told them, "Because you did this, I swear that I won't rest until I have taken vengeance on you." **8** He tore them limb from limb[D] and then went down and stayed in the cave at the rock of Etam.

9 The Philistines went up, camped in Judah, and raided Lehi. **10** So the men of Judah said, "Why have you attacked us?"

They replied, "We have come to tie Samson up and pay him back for what he did to us."

11 Then three thousand men of Judah went to the cave at the rock of Etam, and they asked

---

^A **14:13** Lit replied to him   ^B **14:15** LXX, Syr; MT reads seventh   ^C **14:16** Lit said to her   ^D **15:8** Lit He struck them hip and thigh with a great slaughter

---

14:14–15 Without the interpretive key of Samson's experience with the lion, his riddle was unsolvable.

14:16–17 The woman emotionally blackmailed Samson, claiming that if he would not tell her the answer to his riddle, then he did not love her. Under the pressure of her nagging, Samson relented.

14:18–20 The Philistines' answer not only solved Samson's riddle, but spoke of the current situation at the wedding: though Samson had proved himself stronger than a lion, the sweetness of a woman's love was more powerful still. Samson's response is another miniature poem. As well as a denunciation of their cheating, this reply was also a sharp insult to his Philistine bride. Samson vented his anger by killing thirty suits of clothing necessary to pay his debt. This act was triggered by the **Spirit of the LORD** coming

on him **powerfully**, which shows that his act of personal vengeance was used by the Lord to begin to execute judgment against the Philistines.

15:1–3 Though Samson left Timnah in anger, it was not his intent to call off the wedding. He returned a few weeks later, **during the wheat harvest** in May, with a conventional hospitality gift—**a young goat**—intending to go to his wife's room to consummate the marriage. The father had interpreted Samson's anger as a definitive breach in the relationship, and he had given his daughter to one of the other young men. Nonetheless, he tried to placate Samson by offering him his younger and more attractive daughter. Samson vowed to **harm the Philistines**, thus executing the Lord's purpose in 14:4.

15:4–8 Like Gideon, Samson took on the Lord's enemies with an army of **three hundred**, along with some **torches**. His army

was made up of **foxes** (or perhaps jackals, which were more common in this area) rather than fellow Israelites because Samson always fought alone. He fixed the burning torches to the animals' tails and sent them among the fields that were ready for harvesting, damaging all of the Philistines' major crops at a crucial point in the agricultural cycle. The Philistines retaliated by burning **Samson's wife** and **her father**, fulfilling the threat they had made earlier (14:15). Samson escalated the cycle of violence by slaughtering another batch of Philistines.

15:9–17 The **Philistines** then **camped in Judah**. The Judahites were determined to hand Samson over to the Philistines, as evidence of their good faith submission. Samson, confident in his own strength, was quite content to be handed over. When **the Philistines came to meet him shouting**, Samson seized the **fresh jawbone of a donkey** and promptly

Samson, "Don't you realize that the Philistines rule us? What have you done to us?"

"I have done to them what they did to me," he answered.[A]

[12] They said to him, "We've come to tie you up and hand you over to the Philistines."

Then Samson told them, "Swear to me that you yourselves won't kill me."

[13] "No," they said,[B] "we won't kill you, but we will tie you up securely and hand you over to them." So they tied him up with two new ropes and led him away from the rock.

[14] When he came to Lehi, the Philistines came to meet him shouting. The Spirit of the LORD came powerfully on him, and the ropes that were on his arms and wrists became like burnt flax and fell off. [15] He found a fresh jawbone of a donkey, reached out his hand, took it, and killed a thousand men with it. [16] Then Samson said:

With the jawbone of a donkey
I have piled them in heaps.
With the jawbone of a donkey
I have killed a thousand men.

[17] When he finished speaking, he threw away the jawbone and named that place Jawbone Hill.[C] [18] He became very thirsty and called out to the LORD, "You have accomplished this great victory through your servant. Must I now die of thirst and fall into the hands of the uncircumcised?" [19] So God split a hollow place in the ground at Lehi, and water came out of it. After Samson drank, his strength returned, and he revived. That is why he named it Hakkore Spring,[D] which is still in Lehi today. [20] And he judged Israel twenty years in the days of the Philistines.

Samson and Delilah

16 Samson went to Gaza, where he saw a prostitute and went to bed with her. [2] When the Gazites heard that Samson was there, they surrounded the place and waited in ambush for him all that night at the city gate. They kept quiet all night, saying, "Let's wait until dawn; then we will kill him." [3] But Samson stayed in bed only until midnight. Then he got up, took hold of the doors of the city gate along with the two gateposts, and pulled them out, bar and all. He put them on his shoulders and took them to the top of the mountain overlooking Hebron.

[4] Some time later, he fell in love with a woman named Delilah, who lived in the Sorek Valley. [5] The Philistine leaders went to her and said, "Persuade him to tell you[E] where his great strength comes from, so we can overpower him, tie him up, and make him helpless. Each of us will then give you 1,100 pieces of silver."

[6] So Delilah said to Samson, "Please tell me, where does your great strength come from? How could someone tie you up and make you helpless?"

[7] Samson told her, "If they tie me up with seven fresh bowstrings that have not been dried, I will become weak and be like any other man."

[8] The Philistine leaders brought her seven fresh bowstrings that had not been dried, and she tied him up with them. [9] While the men in ambush were waiting in her room, she called out to him, "Samson, the Philistines are here!"[F] But he snapped the bowstrings as a strand of yarn snaps when it touches fire. The secret of his strength remained unknown.

[10] Then Delilah said to Samson, "You have mocked me and told me lies! Won't you please tell me how you can be tied up?"

[11] He told her, "If they tie me up with new ropes that have never been used, I will become weak and be like any other man."

[12] Delilah took new ropes, tied him up with them, and shouted, "Samson, the Philistines are here!" But while the men in ambush were waiting in her room, he snapped the ropes off his arms like a thread.

[13] Then Delilah said to Samson, "You have mocked me all along and told me lies! Tell me how you can be tied up."

[A]15:11 Lit *answered them* [B]15:13 Lit *said to him* [C]15:17 Hb *Ramath-lehi* [D]15:19 = Spring of the One Who Cried Out [E]16:5 Lit *him and see* [F]16:9 Lit *are on you*, also in vv. 12,14,20

---

dispatched a thousand of the opposition. The word *fresh* emphasizes Samson's neglect of his Nazirite vows—this time by plundering the corpse of an animal for his weapon. Samson's response was to give himself all the glory for the slaughter (cp. Gn 4:23). Samson's song praised himself for making **heaps** (or "a donkey"; the Hebrew words are identical) out of his enemies. He also renamed the location **Jawbone Hill** in honor of his feat.

15:18–19 The parallel between Samson and Israel is highlighted by the echoes of Israel's wilderness experience of Ex 17, where the Lord had made water come out of the rock for his people. Typically, instead of naming the spring that revived him after the Lord, Samson named it after himself, calling it **Hakkore Spring**.

16:1–3 The opening verse parallels 14:1. Samson went to a Philistine town and **saw** a woman. This time he did not want to marry her; he just wanted to sleep with her. **Gaza** was the most distant city of the Philistines from Samson's home. When the Philistines heard that he was there, they surrounded the city and waited for him at the only exit, **the city gate**. Yet such was Samson's enormous strength that the Philistines were unable to trap him. His vast show of strength in uprooting the city gate and carrying it roughly forty miles uphill to the **mountain overlooking Hebron** heightens the irony of his subsequent weakness in the hands of a woman.

16:4–5 Samson's encounter with **Delilah** is the only case where **love** is mentioned.

Once again, his heart was set on a Philistine woman. Delilah's name sounds like the Hebrew word for "night," in keeping with the darkness that was about to descend on Samson. The **Philistine leaders**, the rulers of the five city-states that made up that region (1Sm 6:17–18), sought to persuade Delilah to determine the secret of Samson's strength by promising her an enormous sum of money—1,100 **pieces of silver** from each leader. In comparison, the price of an ordinary slave was thirty pieces of silver (Ex 21:32).

16:6–9 Bowstrings were made from the sinews of animals, so **fresh bowstrings** would come directly from an animal's corpse. Samson displayed a disdain for his Nazirite vow of separation from corpses.

He told her, "If you weave the seven braids on my head into the fabric on a loom — "^A

14 She fastened the braids with a pin and called to him, "Samson, the Philistines are here!" He awoke from his sleep and pulled out the pin, with the loom and the web.

15 "How can you say, 'I love you,'" she told him, "when your heart is not with me? This is the third time you have mocked me and not told me what makes your strength so great!"

16 Because she nagged him day after day and pleaded with him until she wore him out,^B **17** he told her the whole truth and said to her, "My hair has never been cut,^C because I am a Nazirite to God from birth. If I am shaved, my strength will leave me, and I will become weak and be like any other man."

18 When Delilah realized that he had told her the whole truth, she sent this message to the Philistine leaders: "Come one more time, for he has told me the whole truth." The Philistine leaders came to her and brought the silver with them.

19 Then she let him fall asleep on her lap and called a man to shave off the seven braids on his head. In this way, she made him helpless, and his strength left him. **20** Then she cried, "Samson, the Philistines are here!" When he awoke from his sleep, he said, "I will escape as I did before and shake myself free." But he did not know that the Lord had left him.

Samson's Defeat and Death

21 The Philistines seized him and gouged out his eyes. They brought him down to Gaza and bound him with bronze shackles, and he was forced to grind grain in the prison. **22** But his hair began to grow back after it had been shaved.

23 Now the Philistine leaders gathered together to offer a great sacrifice to their god Dagon. They rejoiced and said:

Our god has handed over
our enemy Samson to us.

24 When the people saw him, they praised their god and said:

Our god has handed over to us
our enemy who destroyed our land
and who multiplied our dead.

25 When they were in good spirits,^D they said, "Bring Samson here to entertain us." So they brought Samson from prison, and he entertained them. They had him stand between the pillars.

26 Samson said to the young man who was leading him by the hand, "Lead me where I can feel the pillars supporting the temple, so I can lean against them." **27** The temple was full of men and women; all the leaders of the Philistines were there, and about three thousand men and women were on the roof watching Samson entertain them. **28** He called out to the Lord, "Lord God, please remember me. Strengthen me, God, just once more. With one act of vengeance, let me pay back the Philistines for my two eyes." **29** Samson took hold of the two middle pillars supporting the temple and leaned against them, one on his right hand and the other on his left. **30** Samson said, "Let me die with the Philistines." He pushed with all his might, and the temple fell on the leaders and all the people in it. And those he killed at his death were more than those he had killed in his life. **31** Then his brothers and his father's whole family came down, carried him back, and buried him between Zorah and Eshtaol in the tomb of his father Manoah. So he judged Israel twenty years.

Micah's Priest

17 There was a man from the hill country of Ephraim named Micah. **2** He said to his mother, "The 1,100 pieces of silver taken from

---

^16:13–14 LXX reads *loom and fasten them with a pin into the wall and I will become weak and be like any other man."* **14**And *while he was sleeping, Delilah wove the seven braids on his head into the loom.* ^B16:16 Lit *him and he became short to death* ^C16:17 Lit *A razor has not gone up on my head* ^D16:25 Or *When they were feeling good*

#11 99 Essential Christian Truths

GOD IS OMNIPOTENT

God is all-powerful: There is nothing God cannot do so long as it does not contradict his own nature or law. God has power and authority over the universe he created, from the largest solar system to the smallest particle. Affirming that God is all-powerful does not mean that God can sin— since that would go against his perfect moral nature. As Christians, we rest in the belief that the God who has all power is good, and we gain great comfort by knowing that an all-powerful God is working for our good and joy.

16:15–17 Finally Samson told Delilah **the whole truth** (lit "everything of his heart"), that his strength came from his **Nazirite** vow, symbolized by his uncut hair. In fact, this was the only part of his Nazirite vow that he had not yet broken, and this revelation shows how lightly he took it.

16:18–20 Delilah **realized** that this time she had the secret, so she summoned the Philistine leaders, and **a man** shaved Samson's head. The final statement of v. 20 is a tragic warning to anyone who tries to continue doing the Lord's work when the Lord's power and blessing have **left**.

16:21–22 Samson was carried off to exile in **Gaza**, the city of his earlier exploits in vv. 1–3. His eyes, which had caused so many of his problems, were removed by the Philistines, and his reduced strength was put to work in their service, grinding **grain**. In the midst of his hopeless

situation, there was a ray of hope: **his hair began to grow back**.

16:23–27 The name **Dagon** is related to the word for "grain," which suggests an agricultural role for this deity to which the Philistines also ascribed a role in capturing their tormentor, Samson.

16:28–31 Samson **called out to the Lord**, asking the Lord to **remember** him. In the OT, to "remember" means not simply to think about someone but to act on their behalf. His motivation was still self-centered: he wanted to pay them back for the loss of his eyes. In the process of destroying the building, he fulfilled his destiny: he began "to save Israel from the power of the Philistines" (Jdg 13:5). His body was retrieved to be buried with his family, but his period of leadership achieved no rest for the people.

17:1–21:25 This last section of the book of Judges brings to conclusion two of its central

you, and that I heard you place a curse on — here's the silver. I took it."

Then his mother said, "My son, may you be blessed by the LORD!"

³ He returned the 1,100 pieces of silver to his mother, and his mother said, "I personally consecrate the silver to the LORD for my son's benefit to make a carved image and a silver idol.ᴬ I will give it back to you." ⁴ So he returned the silver to his mother, and she took five pounds of silver and gave it to a silversmith. He made it into a carved image and a silver idol, and it was in Micah's house.

⁵ This man Micah had a shrine, and he made an ephod and household idols, and installed one of his sons to be his priest. ⁶ In those days there was no king in Israel; everyone did whatever seemed right to him.

⁷ There was a young man, a Levite from Bethlehem in Judah, who was staying within the clan of Judah. ⁸ The man left the town of Bethlehem in Judah to stay wherever he could find a place. On his way he came to Micah's home in the hill country of Ephraim.

⁹ "Where do you come from?" Micah asked him.

He answered him, "I am a Levite from Bethlehem in Judah, and I'm going to stay wherever I can find a place."

¹⁰ Micah replied,ᴮ "Stay with me and be my father and priest, and I will give you four ounces of silver a year, along with your clothing and provisions." So the Levite went in ¹¹ and agreed to stay with the man, and the young man became like one of his sons. ¹² Micah consecrated the Levite, and the young man became his priest and lived in Micah's house. ¹³ Then Micah said, "Now I know that the LORD will be good to me, because a Levite has become my priest."

Dan's Invasion and Idolatry

18 In those days, there was no king in Israel, and the Danite tribe was looking for territory to occupy. Up to that time no territory had been captured by them among the tribes of Israel. ² So the Danites sent out five brave men from all their clans, from Zorah and Eshtaol, to scout out the land and explore it. They told them, "Go and explore the land."

They came to the hill country of Ephraim as far as the home of Micah and spent the night there. ³ While they were near Micah's home, they recognized the accent of the young Levite. So they went over to him and asked, "Who brought you here? What are you doing in this place? What is keeping you here?"

⁴ He told them, "This is what Micah has done for me: He has hired me, and I became his priest."

⁵ Then they said to him, "Please inquire of God for us to determine if we will have a successful journey."

⁶ The priest told them, "Go in peace. The LORD is watching over the journey you are going on."

⁷ The five men left and came to Laish. They saw that the people who were there were living securely, in the same way as the Sidonians, quiet and unsuspecting. There was nothing lackingᶜ in the land and no oppressive ruler. They were far from the Sidonians, having no alliance with anyone.ᴰ

⁸ When the men went back to their relatives at Zorah and Eshtaol, their relatives asked them, "What did you find out?"

⁹ They answered, "Come on, let's attack them, for we have seen the land, and it is very good. Why wait? Don't hesitate to go and invade and take possession of the land! ¹⁰ When you get there, you will come to an unsuspecting people and a spacious land, for God has handed it over to you. It is a place where nothing on earth is lacking." ¹¹ Six hundred Danites departed from Zorah and Eshtaol armed with weapons of war. ¹² They went up and camped at Kiriath-jearim in Judah. This is why the place is still called the Camp of Danᴱ today; it is west of Kiriath-jearim. ¹³ From there they traveled to the hill country of Ephraim and arrived at Micah's house.

¹⁴ The five men who had gone to scout out the land of Laish told their brothers, "Did you

---

ᴬ17:3 Or *image and a cast image*, also in v. 4   ᴮ17:10 Lit *replied to him*   ᶜ18:7 Hb obscure   ᴰ18:7 MT; some LXX mss, Sym, Old Lat, Syr read *Aram*   ᴱ18:12 Or *called Mahaneh-dan*

---

threads: idolatrous worship, which comes to a head at Dan (chaps. 17–18), and sexual immorality, which comes to a head with Israel's reenactment of the sin (and fall) of Sodom and Gomorrah (chaps. 19–21).

17:1–4 This section begins with **Micah** ("Who Is Like Yahweh?") confessing to his **mother** that he had stolen from her 1,100 **pieces of silver** (a fortune in that time). She then consecrated this same silver to the Lord to be made into a **carved image**.

17:5–6 Centers of personal devotion like Micah's shrine were outlawed in Dt 12. The ephod is reminiscent of the idol that Gideon constructed at Ophrah (Jdg 8:27). The household idols, or "teraphim," were often associated with divination (Zch 10:2) and were portable objects of veneration throughout

the ancient Near East, although their exact form is unknown. Micah also installed **one of his sons to be his priest**, in opposition to the officially authorized Levitical priesthood. **17:7–8** At this point, a **Levite** arrived, a member of the priestly tribe. He was a **young man**, and therefore he would not have been qualified to serve as a priest in the orthodox worship of the Lord, which began at age thirty (Nm 4:3). He was also from **Bethlehem in Judah**, at the opposite end of Israel from Ephraim. The author does not name the young Levite until 18:30.

17:9–13 Seizing the opportunity to have a priest with a legitimate genealogy, Micah engaged this Levite to be his **father and priest**. "Father" is a title of honor that reflects the role of the priest in communicating

God's law to Israel (Dt 33:10) and thus shaping their behavior. Micah also personally **consecrated** the "priest" to his office (v. 12), emphasizing the Levite's subordinate nature in Micah's household.

18:1–2 During this same period of apostasy, a group of **Danites** were also on the move. Like the Levite in chap. 17, they were not content with the situation assigned them by the Lord and were looking for something better. They had been unable to conquer the rest of the territory allotted to them in Jos 19:40–48 (see Jdg 1:34).

18:5–7 Laish was located in a productive agricultural area at the foot of Mount Hermon. **18:14–21** On the way to their new homeland, the Danites visited the home of Micah. Supported by the **six hundred men armed**

know that there are an ephod, household gods, and a carved image and a silver idol^A in these houses? Now think about what you should do." ¹⁵ So they detoured there and went to the house of the young Levite at the home of Micah and greeted him. ¹⁶ The six hundred Danite men were standing by the entrance of the city gate, armed with their weapons of war. ¹⁷ Then the five men who had gone to scout out the land went in and took the carved image, the ephod, the household idols, and the silver idol,^B while the priest was standing by the entrance of the city gate with the six hundred men armed with weapons of war.

¹⁸ When they entered Micah's house and took the carved image, the ephod, the household idols, and the silver idol, the priest said to them, "What are you doing?"

¹⁹ They told him, "Be quiet. Keep your mouth shut.^C Come with us and be a father and a priest to us. Is it better for you to be a priest for the house of one person or for you to be a priest for a tribe and family in Israel?" ²⁰ So the priest was pleased and took the ephod, household idols, and carved image, and went with the people. ²¹ They prepared to leave, putting their dependents, livestock, and possessions in front of them.

²² After they were some distance from Micah's house, the men who were in the houses near it were mustered and caught up with the Danites. ²³ They called to the Danites, who turned to face them, and said to Micah, "What's the matter with you that you mustered the men?"

²⁴ He said, "You took the gods I had made and the priest, and went away. What do I have left? How can you say to me, 'What's the matter with you?'"

²⁵ The Danites said to him, "Don't raise your voice against us, or angry men will attack you, and you and your family will lose your lives." ²⁶ The Danites went on their way, and Micah turned to go back home, because he saw that they were stronger than he was.

²⁷ After they had taken the gods Micah had made and the priest that belonged to him, they went to Laish, to a quiet and unsuspecting people. They killed them with their swords and burned the city. ²⁸ There was no one to rescue them because it was far from Sidon and they had no alliance with anyone. It was in a valley that belonged to Beth-rehob. They rebuilt the city and lived in it. ²⁹ They named the city Dan, after the name of their ancestor Dan, who was born to Israel. The city was formerly named Laish.

³⁰ The Danites set up the carved image for themselves. Jonathan son of Gershom, son of Moses,^D and his sons were priests for the Danite tribe until the time of the exile from the land. ³¹ So they set up for themselves Micah's carved image that he had made, and it was there as long as the house of God was in Shiloh.

Outrage in Benjamin

19 In those days, when there was no king in Israel, a Levite staying in a remote part of the hill country of Ephraim acquired a woman from Bethlehem in Judah as his concubine. ² But she was unfaithful to^E him and left him for her father's house in Bethlehem in Judah. She was there for four months. ³ Then her husband got up and followed her to speak kindly to her and bring her back. He had his servant with him and a pair of donkeys. So she brought him to her father's house, and when the girl's father saw him, he gladly welcomed him. ⁴ His father-in-law, the girl's father, detained him, and he stayed with him for three days. They ate, drank, and spent the nights there.

⁵ On the fourth day, they got up early in the morning and prepared to go, but the girl's father said to his son-in-law, "Have something to eat to keep up your strength and then you can go." ⁶ So they sat down and the two of them ate and drank together. Then the girl's father said to the man, "Please agree to stay overnight and enjoy yourself." ⁷ The man got up to go, but his father-in-law persuaded him, so he stayed and spent the night there again. ⁸ He got up early in the morning of the fifth day to leave, but the girl's father said to him, "Please keep up your strength." So they waited until late afternoon and the two of them ate. ⁹ The man got up to go with his concubine and his servant,

---

^A18:14 Or *image, the cast image*   ^B18:17 Or *the cast image*, also in v. 18   ^C18:19 Lit *Put your hand on your mouth*
^D18:30 Some Hb mss, LXX, Vg; other Hb mss read *Manasseh*   ^E19:2 LXX reads *was angry with*

---

with weapons of war, the spies went into the house and took the carved image, the ephod, and the household idols. When the young Levite objected, they bribed him to join them, offering him the prospect of being **a father and a priest** to an entire tribe rather than a single family.
18:22–26 The silver Micah stole at the outset was now stolen from him; his mother's curse in 17:2 was fulfilled.
18:27–29 Laish was in a valley that belonged to **Beth-rehob**. They renamed Laish **Dan**, after their ancestor, and established it as the primary center for their idolatrous cult.

Later, Jeroboam would locate one of his two golden calves in Dan, continuing the city's tradition of idolatry (1Kg 12:29).
18:30–31 The idol set up by the **Danites** served as a rival for the true worship of God, which was conducted where the ark was, **in Shiloh**. The Levite, introduced in 17:7, is finally named and is revealed to have an illustrious ancestry. He is **Jonathan**, the grandson of **Moses**.
19:1 The opening line of this chapter anticipates the story's direction. Like the Levite in the last story, this one was **staying** in **the hill country of Ephraim**, and he was

connected to **Bethlehem in Judah** (17:7,9), this time through marriage to a **concubine**, a lower-status wife. The Levite is nameless.
19:2–4 The Levite's concubine was **unfaithful to him**, a broad term that would cover sexual immorality and more general desertion. She left him and returned to her father's house. Finally after **four months**, the Levite went to try to persuade her to go back with him. The girl's father was glad to see him and gave him a warm welcome. As was typical in the ancient Near East, the requirements of hospitality took several days of feasting to fulfill.

when his father-in-law, the girl's father, said to him, "Look, night is coming. Please spend the night. See, the day is almost over. Spend the night here, enjoy yourself, then you can get up early tomorrow for your journey and go home."

¹⁰ But the man was unwilling to spend the night. He got up, departed, and arrived opposite Jebus (that is, Jerusalem). The man had his two saddled donkeys and his concubine with him. ¹¹ When they were near Jebus and the day was almost gone, the servant said to his master, "Please, why not let us stop at this Jebusite city and spend the night here?"

¹² But his master replied to him, "We will not stop at a foreign city where there are no Israelites. Let's move on to Gibeah." ¹³ "Come on," he said,ᴬ "let's try to reach one of these places and spend the night in Gibeah or Ramah." ¹⁴ So they continued on their journey, and the sun set as they neared Gibeah in Benjamin. ¹⁵ They stoppedᴮ to go in and spend the night in Gibeah. The Levite went in and sat down in the city square, but no one took them into their home to spend the night.

¹⁶ In the evening, an old man came in from his work in the field. He was from the hill country of Ephraim, but he was residing in Gibeah where the people were Benjaminites. ¹⁷ When he looked up and saw the traveler in the city square, the old man asked, "Where are you going, and where do you come from?"

¹⁸ He answered him, "We're traveling from Bethlehem in Judah to the remote hill country of Ephraim, where I am from. I went to Bethlehem in Judah, and now I'm going to the house of the LORD.ᶜ No one has taken me into his home, ¹⁹ although there's straw and feed for the donkeys, and I have bread and wine for me, my concubine, and the servantᴰ with us. There is nothing we lack."

²⁰ "Welcome!" said the old man. "I'll take care of everything you need. Only don't spend the night in the square." ²¹ So he brought him to his house and fed the donkeys. Then they washed their feet and ate and drank. ²² While they were enjoying themselves, all of a sudden, wicked men of the city surrounded the house and beat on the door. They said to the old man who was the owner of the house, "Bring out the man who came to your house so we can have sex with him!"

²³ The owner of the house went out and said to them, "Please don't do this evil, my brothers. After all, this man has come into my house. Don't commit this horrible outrage. ²⁴ Here, let me bring out my virgin daughter and the man's concubine now. Abuse them and do whatever you want to them. But don't commit this outrageous thing against this man."

²⁵ But the men would not listen to him, so the man seized his concubine and took her outside to them. They raped her and abused her all night until morning. At daybreak they let her go. ²⁶ Early that morning, the woman made her way back, and as it was getting light, she collapsed at the doorway of the man's house where her master was.

²⁷ When her master got up in the morning, opened the doors of the house, and went out to leave on his journey, there was the woman, his concubine, collapsed near the doorway of the house with her hands on the threshold. ²⁸ "Get up," he told her. "Let's go." But there was no response. So the man put her on his donkey and set out for home.

²⁹ When he entered his house, he picked up a knife, took hold of his concubine, cut her into twelve pieces, limb by limb, and then sent her throughout the territory of Israel. ³⁰ Everyone who saw it said, "Nothing like this has ever happened or has been seen since the day the Israelites came out of the land of Egypt until now.ᴱ Think it over, discuss it, and speak up!"

ᴬ19:13 Lit said to his servant ᴮ19:15 Lit stopped there ᶜ19:18 LXX reads to my house ᴰ19:19 Some Hb mss, Syr, Tg, Vg; other Hb mss read servants ᴱ19:30 LXX reads until now." He commanded the men he sent out, saying, "You will say this to all the men of Israel: Has anything like this happened since the day the Israelites came out of Egypt until this day?

19:10–12 As a result of this profuse hospitality, it was late in the day by the time the Levite and his party got underway. By the time they had arrived at the city of **Jerusalem**, a mere six miles journey from Bethlehem, the day was almost over. The Levite's servant proposed seeking shelter for the night in the city. At this time, Jerusalem was still in the hands of the Jebusites, and the Levite was reluctant to seek hospitality from non-Israelites. The Levite's fear is ironic—the treatment they would experience at the hands of fellow Israelites in Gibeah was to be far worse than anything they could have expected from the Jebusites.
19:13–15 The Levite decided to press on another six miles or so to the Israelite cities of **Gibeah or Ramah**. By the time they reached Gibeah, the sun had already set. They sat down in the **city square** where, according to ancient Near Eastern custom, strangers

might expect to receive hospitality. No offers of hospitality were forthcoming.
19:16–21 Finally, an **old man** came in from his work. Like the Levite, he was **from the hill country of Ephraim** and was merely **residing** in Gibeah, which perhaps explains his greater hospitality. The old man's insistence that they should come to his home and not **spend the night in the square** suggests that he knew things were not as they ought to be in Gibeah. The square, inside the town walls, should have been a safe location.
19:22–24 The echoes of the story of Sodom and Gomorrah in Gn 19 were already present in the preceding verses, in which strangers arrived in the town square in evening and found lodging with one of the town's inhabitants. These echoes now become a virtual reenactment. The scene of peaceful hospitality was shattered by the arrival of **wicked men** (lit "men of Belial,"

or "worthless men"; cp. 9:4). The **old man** appealed to them as his **brothers**, but he characterized their request for sex with his male guest as an offense against hospitality and morality. It would be an **outrage**, a word that characterizes an act that cries out for retributive justice (20:6; Gn 34:7; Dt 22:21). Yet the alternative that the old man proposed is equally abhorrent.
19:25–28 In the morning, the Levite **got up** from his rest and **opened the doors of the house** to leave on his journey, as if nothing had happened the previous night.
19:29–30 The Levite's action of carving up her body as if it were the carcass of an animal and sending the pieces to the twelve tribes of Israel was a call to arms. The similar passage in 1Sm 11:7, where Saul cut up a pair of oxen into twelve parts and distributed them among the tribes, shows that this act included an implied curse. Those who failed

War against Benjamin

20 All the Israelites from Dan to Beer-she-ba and from the land of Gilead came out, and the community assembled as one body before the LORD at Mizpah. ² The leaders of all the people and of all the tribes of Israel presented themselves in the assembly of God's people: four hundred thousand armed foot soldiers. ³ The Benjaminites heard that the Israelites had gone up to Mizpah.

The Israelites asked, "Tell us, how did this evil act happen?"

⁴ The Levite, the husband of the murdered woman, answered, "I went to Gibeah in Benjamin with my concubine to spend the night. ⁵ Citizens of Gibeah came to attack me and surrounded the house at night. They intended to kill me, but they raped my concubine, and she died. ⁶ Then I took my concubine and cut her in pieces, and sent her throughout Israel's territory, because they have committed a wicked outrage in Israel. ⁷ Look, all of you are Israelites. Give your judgment and verdict here and now."

⁸ Then all the people stood united and said, "None of us will go to his tent or return to his house. ⁹ Now this is what we will do to Gibeah: we will attack it. By lot ¹⁰ we will take ten men out of every hundred from all the tribes of Israel, and one hundred out of every thousand, and one thousand out of every ten thousand to get provisions for the troops when they go to Gibeah in Benjamin to punish them for all the outrage they committed in Israel."

¹¹ So all the men of Israel gathered united against the city. ¹² Then the tribes of Israel sent men throughout the tribe of Benjamin, saying, "What is this evil act that has happened among you? ¹³ Hand over the wicked men in Gibeah so we can put them to death and purge evil from Israel." But the Benjaminites would not listen to their fellow Israelites. ¹⁴ Instead, the Benjaminites gathered together from their cities to Gibeah to go out and fight against the Israelites. ¹⁵ On that day the Benjaminites mobilized twenty-six thousand armed men from their cities, besides seven hundred fit young men rallied by the inhabitants of Gibeah. ¹⁶ There were seven hundred fit young men who were left-handed among all these troops; all could sling a stone at a hair and not miss.

¹⁷ The Israelites, apart from Benjamin, mobilized four hundred thousand armed men, every one an experienced warrior. ¹⁸ They set out, went to Bethel, and inquired of God. The Israelites asked, "Who is to go first to fight for us against the Benjaminites?"

And the LORD answered, "Judah will be first."

¹⁹ In the morning, the Israelites set out and camped near Gibeah. ²⁰ The men of Israel went out to fight against Benjamin and took their battle positions against Gibeah. ²¹ The Benjaminites came out of Gibeah and slaughtered twenty-two thousand men of Israel on the field that day. ²² But the Israelite troops rallied and again took their battle positions in the same place where they positioned themselves on the first day. ²³ They went up, wept before the LORD until evening, and inquired of him, "Should we again attack our brothers the Benjaminites?"

And the LORD answered, "Fight against them."

²⁴ On the second day the Israelites advanced against the Benjaminites. ²⁵ That same day the Benjaminites came out from Gibeah to meet them and slaughtered an additional eighteen thousand Israelites on the field; all were armed.

²⁶ The whole Israelite army went to Bethel where they wept and sat before the LORD. They fasted that day until evening and offered burnt offerings and fellowship offerings to the LORD. ²⁷ Then the Israelites inquired of the

---

to respond to the muster could expect to meet a similar fate. Everyone who saw the grisly message agreed that such an outrage demanded a response.

20:1–3 The message conveyed by the carved-up body of the Levite's concubine achieved a remarkable unity among the tribes of Israel. All of the Israelites from the northern border town of **Dan** to the southern border town of **Beer-sheba** came out as one—an achievement that surpassed anything accomplished by the judges raised up by the Lord. Mention of **the land of Gilead** shows that even the Transjordanian tribes responded. A total of **four hundred thousand armed foot soldiers** assembled, a vast army by the standards of the book of Judges. The meeting took place at **Mizpah**, on the border between Benjamin and Ephraim, just north of Jerusalem and only a few miles away from Gibeah. **The Benjaminites**, however, did not take part in this assembly.

20:4–7 The **Levite** presented his own version of the facts to the assembly, carefully leaving out anything that might show him in a bad light. He failed to mention taking his concubine outside, giving her to the men, and then going to bed. Instead, he simply said, **they raped my concubine, and she died.** He termed this act **a wicked outrage** in Israel—a gross sin that demanded a response. All the people therefore determined to take united action against Gibeah.

20:11–17 Before engaging in military action, the Israelites sent messengers among the Benjaminites, appealing to them to hand over the guilty men. The **tribe of Benjamin** was more concerned about tribal solidarity than national solidarity or justice, and so the appeal to put these men to death fell on deaf ears. As a result, instead of Israel against Gibeah, the conflict became Israel against Benjamin. The Benjaminites mobilized their forces for war—**twenty-six thousand armed men**, including seven hundred from Gibeah. This was a significant army, even if outnumbered by the Israelite's **four hundred thousand ... experienced** warriors. There was also a special contingent of seven hundred men who, like the Benjaminite judge Ehud, were **left-handed**, and who were remarkable marksmen, able to hit the smallest of targets with their slings.

20:18–21 The Israelites assembled for war at **Bethel**, northwest of Mizpah, where God had revealed himself to Jacob (Gn 28). There the Israelites inquired of God not about whether they should fight their brothers, but about who should **go first** against the Benjaminites, and the Lord answered **Judah**. Yet when the Israelites went out against the Benjaminites, the Israelites were immediately defeated. The twenty-six thousand Benjaminites **slaughtered twenty-two thousand** Israelites.

20:22–25 In spite of this initial setback, Israel persisted in the conflict. They sought the Lord again and wept before him, as they had in 2:4–5. They asked for confirmation of their course: **Should we again attack our brothers the Benjaminites?** The answer was affirmative, but once again they were defeated by the Benjaminites.

20:26–28 A third time, they went to the Lord. This time, in addition to weeping, they fasted and made **offerings** in recognition that their covenant relationship with God

LORD. In those days, the ark of the covenant of God was there, [28] and Phinehas son of Eleazar, son of Aaron, was serving before it. The Israelites asked, "Should we again fight against our brothers the Benjaminites or should we stop?"

The LORD answered, "Fight, because I will hand them over to you tomorrow." [29] So Israel set up an ambush around Gibeah. [30] On the third day the Israelites fought against the Benjaminites and took their battle positions against Gibeah as before. [31] Then the Benjaminites came out against the troops and were drawn away from the city. They began to attack the troops as before, killing about thirty men of Israel on the highways, one of which goes up to Bethel and the other to Gibeah through the open country. [32] The Benjaminites said, "We are defeating them as before."

But the Israelites said, "Let's flee and draw them away from the city to the highways." [33] So all the men of Israel got up from their places and took their battle positions at Baal-tamar, while the Israelites in ambush charged out of their places west of[A] Geba. [34] Then ten thousand fit young men from all Israel made a frontal assault against Gibeah, and the battle was fierce, but the Benjaminites did not know that disaster was about to strike them. [35] The LORD defeated Benjamin in the presence of Israel, and on that day the Israelites slaughtered 25,100 men of Benjamin; all were armed. [36] Then the Benjaminites realized they had been defeated.

The men of Israel had retreated before Benjamin, because they were confident in the ambush they had set against Gibeah. [37] The men in ambush had rushed quickly against Gibeah; they advanced and put the whole city to the sword. [38] The men of Israel had a prearranged signal with the men in ambush: when they sent up a great cloud of smoke from the city, [39] men of Israel would return to the battle. When Benjamin had begun to strike them down, killing about thirty men of Israel, they said, "They're defeated before us, just as they were in the first battle." [40] But when the column of smoke began to go up from the city, Benjamin looked behind them, and the whole city was going up in smoke.[B] [41] Then the men of Israel returned, and the men of Benjamin were terrified when they realized that disaster had struck them. [42] They retreated before the men of Israel toward the wilderness, but the battle overtook them, and those who came out of the cities[C] slaughtered those between them. [43] They surrounded the Benjaminites, pursued them, and easily overtook them near Gibeah toward the east. [44] There were eighteen thousand men who died from Benjamin; all were warriors. [45] Then Benjamin turned and fled toward the wilderness to Rimmon Rock, and Israel killed five thousand men on the highways. They overtook them at Gidom and struck two thousand more dead.

[46] All the Benjaminites who died that day were twenty-five thousand armed men; all were warriors. [47] But six hundred men escaped into the wilderness to Rimmon Rock and stayed there four months. [48] The men of Israel turned back against the other Benjaminites and killed them with their swords — the entire city, the animals, and everything that remained. They also burned all the cities that remained.

Brides for Benjamin

21 The men of Israel had sworn an oath at Mizpah: "None of us will give his daughter to a Benjaminite in marriage." [2] So the people went to Bethel and sat there before God until evening. They wept loudly and bitterly, [3] and cried out, "Why, LORD God of Israel, has it occurred[D] that one tribe is missing in Israel today?" [4] The next day the people got up early, built an altar there, and offered burnt offerings and fellowship offerings. [5] The Israelites asked, "Who of all the tribes of Israel didn't come to the LORD with the assembly?" For a great oath had been taken that anyone who had not come to the LORD at Mizpah would certainly be put to death.

[6] But the Israelites had compassion on their brothers, the Benjaminites, and said, "Today a

---

[A] 20:33 LXX, Syr, Vg; MT reads places in the plain of, or places in the cave of   [B] 20:40 Lit up to the sky   [C] 20:42 LXX, Vg read city   [D] 21:3 Lit has this occurred in Israel

---

was broken and needed to be restored. They had also apparently brought **the ark** of the Lord from Shiloh, where the tabernacle was at this time, to Bethel, perhaps as a good-luck charm (cp. 1Sm 4). The high priest at this time was **Phinehas**, grandson of Aaron, a detail suggesting that the events described in this chapter took place at an early stage of the period of the judges. The Lord once again responded to their request for guidance, telling Israel that on the next day he would **hand** Benjamin **over to** them. **20:29–35** This time, Israel's strategy was more complex, including a **frontal assault** combined with an **ambush**, a tactic borrowed from the attack on Ai in Jos 8. This

time the casualties were virtually all on the Benjaminite side. **20:36–41** A **great cloud of smoke** signaled the Israelites' success and announced the doom of the Benjaminites. Finally, when it was too late, the Benjaminites **realized that disaster had struck them. 20:42–48** The defeated Benjaminites fled east, toward the wilderness, but there was no escape. Caught between the Israelite army and the troops emerging from Gibeah, Benjamin's army suffered a total of twenty-five thousand casualties (vv. 44–45). A tiny remnant of **six hundred men** escaped and hid at **Rimmon Rock**, where there were many caves in which to hide. Meanwhile,

the Israelite army returned to Benjamin and carried out a war of total destruction against its remaining occupants, human and animal, like those waged against the Canaanite population of the land. The tribe of Benjamin was almost completely destroyed. **21:1–9** Before the battle, all the tribes **had sworn an oath** not to allow their **daughters** to marry a **Benjaminite**. Since the Benjaminite women were wiped out in execution of the holy war and only the six hundred men of Benjamin were left in the wilderness, it seemed that the tribe was destined for extinction. Their solution was to make a scapegoat out of anyone who had failed to show up for the muster at **Mizpah**, when they had

tribe has been cut off from Israel. ⁷ What should we do about wives for the survivors? We've sworn to the Lord not to give them any of our daughters as wives." ⁸ They asked, "Which city among the tribes of Israel didn't come to the Lord at Mizpah?" It turned out that no one from Jabesh-gilead had come to the camp and the assembly. ⁹ For when the roll was called, no men were there from the inhabitants of Jabesh-gilead.

¹⁰ The congregation sent twelve thousand brave warriors there and commanded them, "Go and kill the inhabitants of Jabesh-gilead with the sword, including women and dependents. ¹¹ This is what you should do: Completely destroy every male, as well as every woman who has gone to bed with a man." ¹² They found among the inhabitants of Jabesh-gilead four hundred young virgins, who had not been intimate with a man, and they brought them to the camp at Shiloh in the land of Canaan.

¹³ The whole congregation sent a message of peace to the Benjaminites who were at Rimmon Rock. ¹⁴ Benjamin returned at that time, and Israel gave them the women they had kept alive from Jabesh-gilead. But there were not enough for them.

¹⁵ The people had compassion on Benjamin, because the Lord had made this gap in the tribes of Israel. ¹⁶ The elders of the congregation said, "What should we do about wives for those who are left, since the women of Benjamin have been destroyed?" ¹⁷ They said, "There must be heirs for the survivors of Benjamin, so that a tribe of Israel will not be wiped out. ¹⁸ But we can't give them our daughters as wives." For the Israelites had sworn, "Anyone who gives a wife to a Benjaminite is cursed." ¹⁹ They also said, "Look, there's an annual festival to the Lord in Shiloh, which is north of Bethel, east of the highway that goes up from Bethel to Shechem, and south of Lebonah."

²⁰ Then they commanded the Benjaminites, "Go and hide in the vineyards. ²¹ Watch, and when you see the young women of Shiloh come out to perform the dances, each of you leave the vineyards and catch a wife for yourself from the young women of Shiloh, and go to the land of Benjamin. ²² When their fathers or brothers come to us and protest, we will tell them, 'Show favor to them, since we did not get enough wives for each of them in the battle. You didn't actually give the women to them, soᴬ you are not guilty of breaking your oath.'"

²³ The Benjaminites did this and took the number of women they needed from the dancers they caught. They went back to their own inheritance, rebuilt their cities, and lived in them. ²⁴ At that time, each of the Israelites returned from there to his own tribe and family. Each returned from there to his own inheritance.

²⁵ In those days there was no king in Israel; everyone did whatever seemed right to him.

ᴬ21:22 Lit *at this time*

taken an oath to impose the death penalty on anyone who refused to fight against the Benjaminites.
21:10–12 No reason is given for the failure of **Jabesh-gilead** to send soldiers, nor were the inhabitants given an opportunity to explain themselves. Instead, a force of **twelve thousand brave warriors** was sent to wipe out the men of Jabesh-gilead, along with the married women and male children, while sparing the young virgins, who could provide wives for the remaining six hundred Benjaminites and thus allow the rest of the Israelites to keep their vow not to give their daughters in marriage. This arrangement provided a partial solution to their dilemma.
21:13–14 The four hundred young virgins taken from Jabesh-gilead were not enough to provide wives for the six hundred remaining Benjaminites.
21:19–25 The Israelites proposed a second strategy to provide wives for the Benjaminites, involving the **annual festival to the Lord in Shiloh.** The fact that the Israelites needed detailed directions to find Shiloh suggests that for some time they had not been fulfilling their obligation to appear before the Lord at the tabernacle there three times per year. When the **young women** came out to dance, as would have been typical of such festivals, the Benjaminites would **catch** wives for themselves. This strategy, which resulted in women being taken against their will or the will of their parents, technically absolved the Israelites of breaking their vow not to give their daughters to the Benjaminites. These final chapters of the book give graphic demonstration of the depravity that resulted in Israel from the refusal of the people to recognize the Lord as King.

◤ Introduction to Ruth

Circumstances of Writing

The Talmud attributes the authorship of Ruth to Samuel, but the book itself offers no hint of the identity of its author. We can only speculate about who might have written the book of Ruth, and its provenance and date must be deduced from the internal evidence—language and style, historical allusions, and themes. The family records at the end and the explanation of archaic customs require a date during or later than the reign of King David (1011–971 BC), though it could have been written as late as after the exile, when the issue of the inclusion of Gentiles once again became pressing.

The book of Ruth is set "during the time of the judges" (1:1), a period of social and religious disorder when "everyone did whatever seemed right to him" (Jdg 17:6). Historically, this era bridged the time between the conquest of the land under Joshua and the rise of King David, whose family records form the conclusion of the book. It is not clear exactly when during the time of the judges the book belongs, but it opens with a famine in the land, which may have been the result of Israel's idolatry.

Contribution to the Bible

Ruth's covenantal faithfulness to her mother-in-law, Naomi, and her God provided a model showing that those who were not ethnic Israelites could be incorporated into the people of God through faith. If Moabites who joined themselves to the Lord could be accepted, there was hope for other Gentiles as well (Is 56:3–7). The book also effectively answered questions that may have been raised over the legitimacy of the Davidic line, given his Moabite roots.

Structure

The book of Ruth is a delightful short story with a classical plot that moves from crisis to complication to resolution. The narrator draws the reader into the minds of the characters (successively Naomi, Ruth, and Boaz), inviting us to identify with their personal anxieties and joys and in the end to celebrate the movement from emptiness and frustration to fulfillment and joy.

Outline

I. Scene 1: Moab (1:1–22)
  A. Elimelech's departure (1:1–5)
  B. Naomi's despair (1:6–13)
  C. Ruth's decision (1:14–22)
II. Scene 2: Fields of Bethlehem (2:1–23)
  A. Ruth meets Boaz (2:1–14)
  B. Boaz provides for Ruth and Naomi (2:15–23)
III. Scene 3: Boaz's Threshing Floor (3:1–18)
  A. Boaz's desire to marry Ruth (3:1–11)
  B. Marriage delayed (3:12–18)
IV. Scene 4: City of Bethlehem (4:1–22)
  A. Boaz marries Ruth (4:1–12)
  B. Ruth gives birth to Obed (4:13–15)
  C. Naomi is blessed with a new family (4:16)
  D. Ruth is an ancestor of David (4:17–22)

1200–1100 BC

Gideon defeats the Midianites and Amalekites. **1200?**
Lightning rods are used by the Minoans of Crete. **1200**
Birth of Eli **1157**
Jephthah defeats the Ammonites and Philistines. **1170?**
Events in Ruth **1140?**
SAMSON 1120?–1060?
SAMUEL 1105?–1025?

1100–1000 BC

Samson defeats the Philistines. **1080?**
SAUL 1080-1010
Death of Eli **1070**
Samson destroys the Philistine temple. **1060?**
Philistines capture the ark of the covenant. **1055?**
DAVID 1050–970

Naomi's Family in Moab

1 During the time^ of the judges, there was a famine in the land. A man left Bethlehem in Judah with his wife and two sons to stay in the territory of Moab for a while. ² The man's name was Elimelech, and his wife's name was Naomi. ⁸ The names of his two sons were Mahlon and Chilion. They were Ephrathites from Bethlehem in Judah. They entered the fields of Moab and settled there. ³ Naomi's husband, Elimelech, died, and she was left with her two sons. ⁴ Her sons took Moabite women as their wives: one was named Orpah and the second was named Ruth. After they lived in Moab about ten years, ⁵ both Mahlon and Chilion also died, and the woman was left without her two children and without her husband.

Ruth's Loyalty to Naomi

⁶ She and her daughters-in-law set out to return from the territory of Moab, because she had heard in Moab that the LORD had paid attention to his people's need by providing them food. ⁷ She left the place where she had been living, accompanied by her two daughters-in-law, and traveled along the road leading back to the land of Judah.

⁸ Naomi said to them, "Each of you go back to your mother's home. May the LORD show kindness to you as you have shown to the dead and to me. ⁹ May the LORD grant each of you rest in the house of a new husband." She kissed them, and they wept loudly.

¹⁰ They said to her, "We insist on returning with you to your people."

¹¹ But Naomi replied, "Return home, my daughters. Why do you want to go with me? Am I able to have any more sons who could become your husbands? ¹² Return home, my daughters. Go on, for I am too old to have another husband. Even if I thought there was still hope for me to have a husband tonight and to bear sons, ¹³ would you be willing to wait for them to grow up? Would you restrain yourselves from remarrying?ᶜ No, my daughters, my life is much too bitter for you to share,ᴰ because the LORD's hand has turned against me." ¹⁴ Again they wept loudly, and Orpah kissed her mother-in-law, but Ruth clung to her. ¹⁵ Naomi said, "Look, your sister-in-law has gone back

^1:1 Lit *In the days of the judging*   ᴮ1:2 = Pleasant; also in v. 20   ᶜ1:13 Lit *marrying a man*   ᴰ1:13 Lit *daughters, for more bitter to me than you*

1:1 During the time of the judges identifies the events of this story as taking place during a time when "everyone did whatever seemed right to him" (lit "what was right in his own eyes"), when "there was no king in Israel" (Jdg 21:25). During the time of the judges, **a famine in the land** probably would have been part of God's judgment on his people for their apostasy from him, in pursuing the Baals and Ashtoreths (Jdg 2:11–15). This famine even affected **Bethlehem**, whose Hebrew name means "house of bread." **1:2 Elimelech** means "my God is king." His wife's name, **Naomi**, means "pleasant." The

names of their sons, **Mahlon and Chilion**, seem related to words for sickness and mortality. **1:3–5** Naomi's sons then took **Moabite women** as their wives, contrary to the law that forbade marrying women from nations that served other gods (Dt 7:3–4). Moabite women in particular had a reputation for leading Israelites astray after other gods (Nm 25). **1:6–9** Naomi asked the Lord's blessing upon her daughters-in-law in the form of his **kindness** (Hb *chesed*). This is a covenantal term that combines love and faithfulness, mercy

and grace—all the positive aspects of committed relationship. It is a remarkable request that the Lord's favor should be shown in this way to covenant outsiders like these foreign women. **1:10–14** Ruth **clung to** Naomi—the same Hebrew word used in Gn 2:24 to describe the marriage bond. **1:15–18** The intensity of Naomi's attempts to dissuade her Moabite daughters-in-law from accompanying her back to Bethlehem suggests that she was not completely motivated by concern for their well-being. Their presence would have been a constant

---

Character profile:

Ruth

In the Old Testament book of Ruth, we meet a couple of women who model an extraordinary, highly unlikely relationship. There are a myriad of reasons why these two women never should have come together. They faced the following differences: age, culture, and religion. Naomi was an Israelite; Ruth was a Moabite who likely grew up worshiping the god Chemosh.

Nevertheless, they had been brought together by marriage. Ruth married one of Naomi's two sons. However, by the fifth verse of the book, both women are widows. Life for widows is rough in any culture, but it was especially difficult then. Many ended up begging or turning to prostitution to survive.

Yet with all those strikes against them, Ruth and Naomi forged a close and loving relationship. How?

Mostly what sticks out is Ruth's unusual commitment: "Wherever you go, I will go, and wherever you live, I will live; your people will be my people, and your God will be my God" (Ru 1:16). Here is a woman whose husband had died but who committed herself irrevocably to her Israelite mother-in-law, Israel's people, and Israel's God. It is this kind of head-scratching commitment that can turn potentially bad relationships into blessed ones.

The unselfishness Ruth and Naomi showed in looking out for one other is admirable (see 1:7–14; 2:18). At crucial moments,

each one's greatest concern was not "What do I need or want?" but "What would be best for you?" Such a selfless attitude led to acts of kindness.

In the great story of God, the sparkling behavior of Ruth the Moabite is meant to contrast with the faithlessness of the Israelite people. Ruth is blessed because of her actions. In her new home of Israel she became the wife of Boaz, the great-grandmother of King David, and part of the lineage of Christ. On an interpersonal level, her life shows how it's possible to build relational bridges instead of relational walls.

Think about a difficult relationship in your own life. Maybe you've gotten off to a bad start. Here's the good news: the gospel is all about grace and new beginnings. If you're at fault, own it. Ask for forgiveness. If the person with whom you are trying to relate is a believer, you have every reason to hope for a deeper relationship. The same Holy Spirit indwells you both.

If your difficult relationship is complicated by the fact that the other person is not a follower of Christ, don't despair. Apologize sincerely for any wrong words or actions. Then model what it means to know God. Pray fervently for the Spirit to work.

Difficult relationships work best when both people are committed to Christ, but there can also be movement and growth even if only one of the parties trusts God and determines to do the right thing. Be committed, selfless, and kind like Ruth.

to her people and to her gods. Follow your sister-in-law."

¹⁶ But Ruth replied:

Don't plead with me to abandon you
or to return and not follow you.
For wherever you go, I will go,
and wherever you live, I will live;
your people will be my people,
and your God will be my God.

¹⁷ Where you die, I will die,
and there I will be buried.
May the LORD punish me,
and do so severely,
if anything but death separates you
and me.

¹⁸ When Naomi saw that Ruth was determined to go with her, she stopped talking to her.

¹⁹ The two of them traveled until they came to Bethlehem. When they entered Bethlehem, the whole town was excited about their arrival^A and the local women exclaimed, "Can this be Naomi?"

²⁰ "Don't call me Naomi. Call me Mara,"ᴮ she answered, "for the Almighty has made me very bitter. ²¹ I went away full, but the LORD has brought me back empty. Why do you call me Naomi, since the LORD has opposed^C me, and the Almighty has afflicted me?"

²² So Naomi came back from the territory of Moab with her daughter-in-law Ruth the Moabitess. They arrived in Bethlehem at the beginning of the barley harvest.

Ruth and Boaz Meet

2 Now Naomi had a relative on her husband's side. He was a prominent man of noble character from Elimelech's family. His name was Boaz.

² Ruth the Moabitess asked Naomi, "Will you let me go into the fields and gather fallen grain behind someone with whom I find favor?"

Naomi answered her, "Go ahead, my daughter." ³ So Ruth left and entered the field to gather grain behind the harvesters. She happened to be in the portion of the field belonging to Boaz, who was from Elimelech's family.

⁴ Later, when Boaz arrived from Bethlehem, he said to the harvesters, "The LORD be with you."

"The LORD bless you," they replied.

⁵ Boaz asked his servant who was in charge of the harvesters, "Whose young woman is this?"

⁶ The servant answered, "She is the young Moabite woman who returned with Naomi from the territory of Moab. ⁷ She asked, 'Will you let me gather fallen grain among the bundles behind the harvesters?' She came and has been on her feet since early morning, except that she rested a little in the shelter."ᴰ

⁸ Then Boaz said to Ruth, "Listen, my daughter.ᴱ Don't go and gather grain in another field, and don't leave this one, but stay here close to my female servants. ⁹ See which field they are harvesting, and follow them. Haven't I ordered the young men not to touch you? When you are thirsty, go and drink from the jars the young men have filled."

¹⁰ She fell facedown, bowed to the ground, and said to him, "Why have I found favor with you, so that you notice me, although I am a foreigner?"

¹¹ Boaz answered her, "Everything you have done for your mother-in-law since your husband's death has been fully reported to me: how you left your father and mother and your native land, and how you came to a people you didn't previously know. ¹² May the LORD reward you for what you have done, and may you receive a full reward from the LORD God of Israel, under whose wings you have come for refuge."

¹³ "My lord," she said, "I have found favor with you, for you have comforted and encouraged your servant, although I am not like one of your female servants."

¹⁴ At mealtime Boaz told her, "Come over here and have some bread and dip it in the vinegar sauce." So she sat beside the harvesters,

^1:19 Lit excited because of them ᴮ1:20 = Bitter; see v. 2 ᶜ1:21 LXX, Syr, Vg read has humiliated ᴰ2:7 LXX reads morning, and until evening she has not rested in the field a little; Vg reads morning until now and she did not return to the house; Hb uncertain ᴱ2:8 Lit "Haven't you heard, my daughter?

and embarrassing reminder of her tragic sojourn in Moab. Yet Ruth was not so easily dissuaded. In a crescendo of commitment, she bound herself to **go** with Naomi and to **live** with her. In fact, she would even **die** and **be buried** where Naomi was—the greatest possible commitment in the ancient world. She sealed her commitment with a self-imprecatory oath, taken in the personal name of Naomi's God, **the LORD**, i.e., Yahweh.

1:19–22 Naomi urged the townswomen to rename her **Mara** since the Lord had made her **bitter** rather than "pleasant," which is the meaning of "Naomi." It was at Marah that the Israelites found only bitter water to drink on their way out of Egypt, and so they grumbled against the Lord (Ex 15:23–24).

2:1–3 The practice of gleaning allowed the poor to go through the fields after the harvesters, picking up the grain that was left behind, along with the grain that landowners were required to leave at the edges of their fields (Lv 19:9–10). The phrase translated **man of noble character** could designate Boaz as possessing wealth and property, but it becomes clear as the story unfolds that Boaz is also a man of integrity.

2:4–7 Boaz's noble character was displayed in his care for his workers. Even his greeting to them was in the name of the Lord, and he knew them well enough to recognize a stranger in their midst. His question did not seek Ruth's name but her relationships. **Whose young woman is this?** The servant's answer twice highlighted her foreignness.

2:8–10 Boaz's noble character is again on display in his kind words to Ruth. Gleaning could be dangerous, especially for a young foreign woman; thus, Boaz issued instructions to ensure her safety. He also allowed her to drink the water his **young men** had brought, saving her the lengthy trip to the well. Ruth's response was to prostrate herself as a mark of respect for a social superior.

2:14–16 As an impoverished gleaner, Ruth would normally have had little or nothing to eat while out in the fields. Boaz, however, invited her to eat with him and his harvesters. He went so far as to instruct his harvesters deliberately to leave some grain for her to pick up, an action that went far beyond the demands of the law of Moses.

and he offered her roasted grain. She ate and was satisfied and had some left over.

¹⁵ When she got up to gather grain, Boaz ordered his young men, "Let her even gather grain among the bundles, and don't humiliate her. ¹⁶ Pull out some stalks from the bundles for her and leave them for her to gather. Don't rebuke her." ¹⁷ So Ruth gathered grain in the field until evening. She beat out what she had gathered, and it was about twenty-six quarts^A of barley. ¹⁸ She picked up the grain and went into the town, where her mother-in-law saw what she had gleaned. She brought out what she had left over from her meal and gave it to her.

¹⁹ Her mother-in-law said to her, "Where did you gather barley today, and where did you work? May the LORD bless the man who noticed you."

Ruth told her mother-in-law whom she had worked with and said, "The name of the man I worked with today is Boaz."

²⁰ Then Naomi said to her daughter-in-law, "May the LORD bless him because he has not abandoned his kindness to the living or the dead." Naomi continued, "The man is a close relative. He is one of our family redeemers."

²¹ Ruth the Moabitess said, "He also told me, 'Stay with my young men until they have finished all of my harvest.'"

²² So Naomi said to her daughter-in-law Ruth, "My daughter, it is good for you to work^B with his female servants, so that nothing will happen to you in another field." ²³ Ruth stayed close to Boaz's female servants and gathered grain until the barley and the wheat harvests were finished. And she lived with^C her mother-in-law.

Ruth's Appeal to Boaz

3 Ruth's mother-in-law Naomi said to her, "My daughter, shouldn't I find rest for you, so that you will be taken care of? ² Now isn't Boaz our relative? Haven't you been working with his female servants? This evening he will be winnowing barley on the threshing floor. ³ Wash, put on perfumed oil, and wear your best clothes. Go down to the threshing floor, but don't let the man know you are there until he has finished eating and drinking. ⁴ When he lies down, notice the place where he's lying, go in and uncover his feet, and lie down. Then he will explain to you what you should do."

⁵ So Ruth said to her, "I will do everything you say."^D ⁶ She went down to the threshing floor and did everything her mother-in-law had charged her to do. ⁷ After Boaz ate, drank, and was in good spirits, he went to lie down at the end of the pile of barley, and she came secretly, uncovered his feet, and lay down.

⁸ At midnight, Boaz was startled, turned over, and there lying at his feet was a woman! ⁹ So he asked, "Who are you?"

"I am Ruth, your servant," she replied. "Take me under your wing,^E for you are a family redeemer."

¹⁰ Then he said, "May the LORD bless you, my daughter. You have shown more kindness now than before,^F because you have not pursued younger men, whether rich or poor. ¹¹ Now don't be afraid, my daughter. I will do for you whatever you say,^G since all the people in my town^H know that you are a woman of noble character. ¹² Yes, it is true that I am a family redeemer, but there is a redeemer closer than I am. ¹³ Stay here tonight, and in the morning, if he wants to redeem you, that's good. Let him

---

^2:17 Lit about an ephah ^2:22 Lit go out ^2:23 Some Hb mss, Vg read she returned to ^3:5 Alt Hb tradition reads say to me ^3:9 Or "Spread the edge of your garment"; lit "Spread the wing of your garment"; Ru 2:12 ^3:10 Lit kindness at the last than at the first ^3:11 Some Hb mss, Orig, Syr, Tg, Vg read say to me ^3:11 Lit all the gate of my people

---

2:17-20 The measure of Boaz's generosity and Ruth's hard work is demonstrated in the remarkable quantity of grain that she gathered—an ephah (**about twenty-six quarts**) of barley. This was enough grain to feed a working man for several weeks.

Family redeemers (Hb go'el; v. 20) were relatives obliged to buy back family members from debt-slavery or to redeem their fields if they had to sell them (Lv 25:25–30). The family redeemer would also receive restitution on behalf of a deceased family member or pursue his killer to ensure that justice was served (Nm 5:8; 35:12). He might also raise up a child for the deceased relative in order to maintain the connection between the clan and the relative's hereditary property (Dt 25:5–10), though Boaz had no legal obligation to act in this way.

3:1-3 At the end of the barley harvest, in late May or June, the barley had to be winnowed, tossed into the air with a shovel, allowing the wind to carry away the lighter chaff while the heavier grain fell to the ground. At night, someone would guard the grain against being stolen or eaten by animals.

Apparently, this was Boaz's night to be on duty. Dressing as Naomi instructed would not only enhance Ruth's attractiveness to Boaz but would symbolize an end to her period of mourning for her husband (2Sm 12:20), signaling her willingness to remarry.

3:4-7 Naomi instructed Ruth to go to Boaz when he was asleep and **uncover his feet**, or, more precisely, "uncover the place of his feet." By this act Ruth was inquiring about Boaz's willingness to fulfill the role of family redeemer, to take her as wife and provide for her (see note at 4:5–8). Ruth's action, at Naomi's advice, is ambiguous. The verb uncover is often used in the OT of illicit sexual relations. Thus the word has association with immoral acts, and the threshing floor was notorious as a place of illicit sexual activities. Also, **lie down** often implies sexual activity (Gn 19:33). Further, "**feet**" is used in the OT as a euphemism for male sexual organs (Ex 4:25; Jdg 3:24; 1Sm 24:3; Is 7:20). However, the form of the noun used here is only used one other time, in Dn 10:6, where it clearly refers to the whole of the lower limbs, including the feet, legs, and thighs. On the other hand,

Ruth's actions can be interpreted as a humble petitioner seeking Boaz's protection. She uncovered Boaz's feet to the cold night air so it would arouse him from sleep and she could speak to him privately. This chaste interpretation of all these ambiguities is most likely, as Naomi, Ruth, and Boaz are all consistently portrayed as virtuous and honorable persons.

3:8-9 Ruth responded to Boaz's question about her identity with a clarification of her purpose. She asked him to spread the corner of his robe over her as a symbolic statement of a marriage commitment (Ezk 16:8). The request also involved a wordplay, since **take me under your wing** literally is "spread your wing over me," inviting Boaz to become the answer to his own prayer in 2:12 that she might find refuge under the wings of the Lord.

3:10-11 Boaz's first words, **my daughter**, showed he had not been misled by the potential ambiguity of the situation. He declared himself willing to pay the social and financial costs of welcoming this despised outsider into his family.

redeem you. But if he doesn't want to redeem you, as the LORD lives, I will. Now lie down until morning."

¹⁴ So she lay down at his feet until morning but got up while it was still dark.ᴬ Then Boaz said, "Don't let it be known that aᴮ woman came to the threshing floor." ¹⁵ And he told Ruth, "Bring the shawl you're wearing and hold it out." When she held it out, he shoveled six measures of barley into her shawl, and sheᶜ went into the town.

¹⁶ She went to her mother-in-law, Naomi, who asked her, "What happened,ᴰ my daughter?"

Then Ruth told her everything the man had done for her. ¹⁷ She said, "He gave me these six measures of barley, because he said,ᴱ 'Don't go back to your mother-in-law empty-handed.'"

¹⁸ Naomi said, "My daughter, wait until you find out how things go, for he won't rest unless he resolves this today."

Ruth and Boaz Marry

4 Boaz went to the gate of the town and sat down there. Soon the family redeemer Boaz had spoken about came by. Boaz said, "Come over hereᶠ and sit down." So he went over and sat down. ² Then Boaz took ten men of the town's elders and said, "Sit here." And they sat down. ³ He said to the redeemer, "Naomi, who has returned from the territory of Moab, is selling the portion of the field that belonged to our brother Elimelech. ⁴ I thought I should inform you: Buy it back in the presence of those

seated here and in the presence of the elders of my people. If you want to redeem it, do it. But if you doᴳ not want to redeem it, tell me so that I will know, because there isn't anyone other than you to redeem it, and I am next after you."

"I want to redeem it," he answered.

⁵ Then Boaz said, "On the day you buy the field from Naomi, you will acquireᴴ Ruth the Moabitess, the wife of the deceased man, to perpetuate the man's name on his property."ᴵ

⁶ The redeemer replied, "I can't redeem it myself, or I will ruin my own inheritance. Take my right of redemption, because I can't redeem it."

⁷ At an earlier period in Israel, a man removed his sandal and gave it to the other party in order to make any matter legally binding concerning the right of redemption or the exchange of property. This was the method of legally binding a transaction in Israel.

⁸ So the redeemer removed his sandal and said to Boaz, "Buy back the property yourself."

⁹ Boaz said to the elders and all the people, "You are witnesses today that I am buying from Naomi everything that belonged to Elimelech, Chilion, and Mahlon. ¹⁰ I have also acquired Ruth the Moabitess, Mahlon's widow, as my wife, to perpetuate the deceased man's name on his property, so that his name will not disappear among his relatives or from the gate of his hometown. You are witnesses today."

¹¹ All the people who were at the city gate, including the elders, said, "We are witnesses. May the LORD make the woman who is entering

---

ᴬ3:14 Lit *up before a man could recognize his companion* ᴮ3:14 LXX; MT reads *the* ᶜ3:15 Some Hb mss, Aramaic, Syr, Vg; other Hb mss read *he* ᴰ3:16 Lit *"Who are you* ᴱ3:17 Alt Hb tradition, LXX, Syr, Tg read *said to me* ᶠ4:1 Or *said, "Come here Mr. So-and-so* ᴳ4:4 Some Hb mss, LXX, Syr, Vg; other Hb mss read *if he does* ᴴ4:5 Lit *Naomi and from* ᴵ4:5 Alt Hb tradition reads *Naomi, I will have already acquired from Ruth the Moabitess, the wife of the dead man, the privilege of raising up the name of the dead man on his property*

3:14–15 If it became widely known that Ruth had visited Boaz that night, people would wrongly assume that Boaz had taken Ruth as wife or that they were guilty of sexual impropriety. Boaz was unwilling to preempt his close relative who had first right of refusal to Ruth, so getting Ruth home before daylight kept wrong impressions from being formed. To seal his commitment (and perhaps also to provide Ruth with an excuse for being out so early), Boaz gave her **six measures of barley**.

3:16–18 On Ruth's return, Naomi asked her literally, "Who are you, my daughter?" This is the same question that Boaz asked in 3:8. Was Ruth merely an awkward and embarrassing duty to Naomi, or was she the one who would provide Naomi with an enduring place in the family records of Israel through the provision of a son? The answer depended on what transpired overnight. This was the real nature of Naomi's question, as evidenced by Ruth's answer.

4:1–2 Boaz immediately **went to the gate of the town**, the place where important legal and social matters were transacted in the presence of the town elders. When Boaz summoned the other redeemer, he literally said, "Come over here" (Hb *poloni 'almoni*), a rhyming phrase equivalent to our "Mr.

So-and-So." Boaz gathered a quorum of ten **elders** as official witnesses.

4:3–4 As a widow Naomi could not sell Elimelech's land; however, she could assign someone else the right to use that field until the next Jubilee Year. Rather than have control over the field go (or remain) outside the family, Boaz requested an intervention in the spirit of the family redeemer laws to **buy . . . back** the use of the field. Since "Mr. So-and-So" was the primary relative entitled to **redeem** that property, Boaz was bringing the matter to his attention. If he did not redeem the property, Boaz himself was willing to act.

4:5–8 Along with the financial cost of redeeming the field, there was a social cost. The transaction also included a commitment to marry **Ruth the Moabitess** and thereby to seek **to perpetuate the** dead **man's name on his property**. This is a reference back to the practice of levirate marriage in Dt 25:5–10, by which the brother of a man who died without male offspring was required to marry his widow and raise up a family in name of the dead man. In this case, there was no legal obligation on either "Mr. So-and-So" or on Boaz, yet Boaz asserted a moral obligation to do so. At this, "Mr. So-and-So" backed away from his earlier enthusiasm.

His decision was confirmed by a legal gesture that was archaic even at the time the writing of the book—the removal of a **sandal**, which was given to the other party. **4:9–12** By receiving the sandal, Boaz committed himself to redeem Naomi's property, to marry Ruth, and to perpetuate the names of **Elimelech** and **Mahlon** on their patrimony. The link with **Perez, the son Tamar bore to Judah**, invites a comparison and contrast between Ruth and Tamar,

---

#12 **99 Essential Christian Truths**

PRESERVATION OF SCRIPTURE

God has chosen to reveal himself to humanity through the text of Scripture, having inspired it and directed it to be free from error. God has also acted providentially throughout the course of history to ensure the biblical text is faithfully preserved for future generations. Our belief in the preservation of Scripture is supported by investigating how the canon of Scripture was formed and how manuscripts were faithfully transmitted throughout the centuries.

your house like Rachel and Leah, who together built the house of Israel. May you be powerful in Ephrathah and your name well known in Bethlehem. [12] May your house become like the house of Perez, the son Tamar bore to Judah, because of the offspring the LORD will give you by this young woman."

[13] Boaz took Ruth and she became his wife. He slept with her, and the LORD granted conception to her, and she gave birth to a son. [14] The women said to Naomi, "Blessed be the LORD, who has not left you without a family redeemer today. May his name become well known in Israel. [15] He will renew your life and sustain you in your old age. Indeed, your daughter-in-law, who loves you and is better to you than seven sons, has given birth to him." [16] Naomi took the child, placed him on her lap, and became a mother to him. [17] The neighbor women said, "A son has been born to Naomi," and they named him Obed. He was the father of Jesse, the father of David.

David's Genealogy from Judah's Son

[18] Now these are the family records of Perez:
Perez fathered Hezron,
[19]   Hezron fathered Ram,^A
Ram fathered Amminadab,
[20]   Amminadab fathered Nahshon,
Nahshon fathered Salmon,
[21]   Salmon fathered Boaz,
Boaz fathered Obed,
[22]   Obed fathered Jesse,
and Jesse fathered David.

---

^4:19 LXX reads *Aram*; Mt 1:3–4

---

two foreign women who became part of Judah's genealogy through very different means. Thus Ruth entered the lineage of the Messiah (Mt 1:5).
4:13–17 Although for ten years in Moab, Ruth had been unable to bear a son for Mahlon, through the Lord's direct intervention she immediately conceived and bore a son for Boaz. He was named **Obed**, a short form

of Obadiah, which means "Servant of the LORD." Naomi now had a daughter-in-law whom all recognized as **better to you than seven sons**—an astonishing accolade in the ancient world.
4:18–22 The story concludes with a linear genealogy linking the child, **Obed**, backward and forward. It traces his roots back to **Perez**, the child born in Gn 38 out of the dubious

relationship between Judah and a foreign woman, Tamar. It also traces his progeny on to King **David**. The family records thus show us that the Lord had been pursuing bigger plans than just bringing together two worthy individuals or restoring the emptiness of a Judean widow. Their story formed part of the bigger plan to provide the Redeemer, Christ Jesus, whom Israel needed.

◥ Introduction to 1 Samuel

Circumstances of Writing

Early tradition suggests 1 and 2 Samuel were originally one book. Some scholars believe Samuel was largely responsible for the material up to 1 Samuel 25 and that the prophets Nathan and Gad gave significant input to the rest (based on 1Ch 29:29). This proposal, however, must remain speculative, because the books name no authors. First Samuel 27:6 suggests the book was not completed until perhaps a few generations after the division of the kingdom around 930 BC.

After Israel's conquest of the land during the days of Joshua, Israel entered a time of apostasy. The book of Judges describes recurrences of a cycle with predictable phases. First, the people sinned against the Lord and fell into idolatry. Second, the Lord raised up an adversary to afflict them and turn them back to him. Third, the people cried out to the Lord in repentance. Fourth, the Lord brought deliverance for them through a judge whom he raised up. The book of Judges' famous verse, "In those days there was no king in Israel; everyone did whatever seemed right to him" (21:25), aptly describes the period. The book of 1 Samuel picks up the historical record toward the end of those stormy days.

Contribution to the Bible

The books of 1 and 2 Samuel describe Israel's transition from a loosely organized tribal league under God (a theocracy) to centralized leadership under a king who answered to God (a monarchy). Samuel's life and ministry greatly shaped this period of restructuring as he consistently pointed people back to God.

Saul's rule highlighted the dangers to which the Israelites fell victim as they clamored for a king to lead them. Samuel's warnings fell on deaf ears (1Sm 8:10–20) because God's people were intent on becoming like the nations around them. In the end, they got exactly what they asked for, but they paid a terrible price. Saul's life stands as a warning to trust God's timing for life's provisions.

David's rule testified to the amazing works the Lord could and would do through a life yielded to him. Israel's second king seemed quite aware of God's blessing on his life and displayed a tender heart toward the things of God (2Sm 5:12; 7:1–2; 22:1–51; 23:1–7). Later generations would receive blessing because of David's life (Is 37:35). God's special covenant with David (2Sm 7:1–29) found its ultimate fulfillment in Jesus, the son of David (Lk 1:32–33). The consequences of David's sin with Bathsheba, however, stand as a warning to all who experience sin's attraction. God holds his children accountable for their actions, and even forgiven sin can have terrible consequences.

Structure

The first seven chapters of 1 Samuel describe Samuel's birth, call, and initial ministry among the Israelites. Chapter 8 is a major turning point as the people ask for a king to rule them "the same as all the other nations have" (v. 5). Chapters 9–12 then describe Saul's selection—at God's direction, yet not his perfect will for the time (12:16–18).

First Samuel 13–31 describes Saul's victories and failures. Saul was a king with great physical stature and military skill (14:47–52), but his heart was not one with the Lord (13:14). His unwillingness to obey the Lord's commands ultimately outweighed his accomplishments, and chapters 16–31 describe his reign's downward spiral. During this time, God raised up David and was preparing him for the day he would succeed Saul—a fact Saul gradually realized (15:28; 24:20–21; 28:17).

Outline

I. Samuel's Ministry (1:1–12:25)
    A. Samuel's birth and call (1:1–3:21)
    B. The ark narrative (4:1–7:17)
    C. The people ask for a king (8:1–12:25)

II. Saul's Reign (13:1–31:13)
    A. Saul's battles with the Philistines (13:1–14:52)
    B. Saul's failure against the Amalekites (15:1–35)
    C. David's selection as Saul's successor (16:1–23)
    D. David's victory over Goliath (17:1–58)
    E. David's struggles with Saul (18:1–26:25)
    F. Saul's reign ends (27:1–31:13)

1000–970 BC

SAMSON 1120?–1060?
SAMUEL 1105–1025
SAUL 1080–1010
DAVID 1050–970
Iron technology advances throughout India. **1000**
The Chinese store ice for use in refrigeration. **1000**
Oats are cultivated in central Europe. **1000**
David conquers Jerusalem. **1000?**
David moves the ark of the covenant
   to Jerusalem. **1000?**
Absalom's revolt **975?**
Solomon becomes king. **970**

970–900 BC

Solomon begins construction of the
   temple in Jerusalem. **966**
The temple is dedicated. **959**
Ascendancy of Neo-Assyrian Empire **950**
The kingdom divides. **931?**
Israel: the northern kingdom **931–722**
Judah: the southern kingdom **931–586**
Etruscans emigrate from Lydia to Italy as
   a result of an extended famine. **900**

Hannah's Vow

1 There was a man from Ramathaim-zophim in^ the hill country of Ephraim. His name was Elkanah son of Jeroham, son of Elihu, son of Tohu, son of Zuph, an Ephraimite. ² He had two wives, the first named Hannah and the second Peninnah. Peninnah had children, but Hannah was childless. ³ This man would go up from his town every year to worship and to sacrifice to the LORD of Armies at Shiloh, where Eli's two sons, Hophni and Phinehas, were the LORD's priests.

⁴ Whenever Elkanah offered a sacrifice, he always gave portions of the meat to his wife Peninnah and to each of her sons and daughters. ⁵ But he gave a double⁸ portion to Hannah, for he loved her even though the LORD had kept her from conceiving. ⁶ Her rival would taunt her severely just to provoke her, because the LORD had kept Hannah from conceiving. ⁷ Year after year, when she went up to the LORD's house, her rival taunted her in this way. Hannah would weep and would not eat. ⁸ "Hannah, why are you crying?" her husband, Elkanah, would ask. "Why won't you eat? Why are you troubled? Am I not better to you than ten sons?"

⁹ On one occasion, Hannah got up after they ate and drank at Shiloh.ᶜ The priest Eli was sitting on a chair by the doorpost of the LORD's temple. ¹⁰ Deeply hurt, Hannah prayed to the LORD and wept with many tears. ¹¹ Making a vow, she pleaded, "LORD of Armies, if you will take notice of your servant's affliction, remember and not forget me, and give your servant a son, I will give him to the LORD all the days of his life, and his hair will never be cut."ᴰ

¹² While she continued praying in the LORD's presence, Eli watched her mouth. ¹³ Hannah was praying silently, and though her lips were moving, her voice could not be heard. Eli thought she was drunk ¹⁴ and said to her, "How long are you going to be drunk? Get rid of your wine!"

¹⁵ "No, my lord," Hannah replied. "I am a woman with a broken heart. I haven't had any wine or beer; I've been pouring out my heart before the LORD. ¹⁶ Don't think of me as a wicked woman; I've been praying from the depth of my anguish and resentment."

¹⁷ Eli responded, "Go in peace, and may the God of Israel grant the request you've made of him."

¹⁸ "May your servant find favor with you," she replied. Then Hannah went on her way; she ate and no longer looked despondent.ᴱ

Samuel's Birth and Dedication

¹⁹ The next morning Elkanah and Hannah got up early to worship before the LORD. Afterward, they returned home to Ramah. Then Elkanah was intimate with his wife Hannah, and the LORD remembered her. ²⁰ After some time,ᶠ Hannah conceived and gave birth to a son. She named him Samuel,ᴳ because she said, "I requested him from the LORD."

²¹ When Elkanah and all his household went up to make the annual sacrifice and his vow offering to the LORD, ²² Hannah did not go and explained to her husband, "After the child is weaned, I'll take him to appear in the LORD's presence and to stay there permanently."

²³ Her husband, Elkanah, replied, "Do what you think is best, and stay here until you've weaned him. May the LORD confirm yourᴴ word." So Hannah stayed there and nursed her son until she weaned him. ²⁴ When she had weaned him, she took him with her to Shiloh, as well as a three-year-old bull,ᴵ half a bushelᴶ of flour, and a clay jar of wine. Though the boy was still young,ᴷ she took him to the LORD's house at Shiloh. ²⁵ Then they slaughtered the bull and brought the boy to Eli.

²⁶ "Please, my lord," she said, "as surely as you live, my lord, I am the woman who stood here beside you praying to the LORD. ²⁷ I prayed for this boy, and since the LORD gave me what I

---

^1:1 Or *from Ramathaim, a Zuphite from* ⁸1:5 Or *gave only one*; Hb obscure ᶜ1:9 LXX adds *and presented herself before the LORD* ᴰ1:11 Lit *and no razor will go up on his head* ᴱ1:18 Lit *and her face was not to her again* ᶠ1:20 Lit *In the turning of the days* ᴳ1:20 In Hb, the name *Samuel* sounds like the phrase "requested from God." ᴴ1:23 DSS, LXX, Syr; MT reads *his* ᴵ1:24 DSS, LXX, Syr; MT reads *Shiloh with three bulls* ᴶ1:24 Lit *bull and an ephah* ᴷ1:24 Lit *And the youth was a youth*

1:1 The exact location of **Ramathaim-zophim** is not known, but it is distinct from Ramah, located in the tribal territory of Benjamin (v. 19). It probably designates Elkanah's ancestral home. The name **Elkanah** means "God has acquired." **Ephraimite** denotes Elkanah's place of residence, not his tribal background, which was that of Levi (1Ch 6:25–28).
1:2 The name **Hannah** means "grace." She **was childless**, a condition often viewed with disfavor or even anguish (Gn 16:4–5; 30:1; Lk 1:24–25).
1:3 **Shiloh** was centrally located about thirty miles north of Jerusalem. There Joshua divided the land among the tribes (Jos 18:1–10).
1:4–5 The **double portion** was the amount of the inheritance the firstborn received (Dt

21:17). Here it probably denotes Elkanah's special love for Hannah.
1:9–10 The words **deeply hurt** can be more literally rendered "bitter of soul," using the same Hebrew word that Naomi used (*mara*, Ru 1:20).
1:17 The expression **Go in peace** marks assurance that the request has been granted. This is the only place in the Old Testament that a priest blesses someone.
1:18 The Hebrew word for **favor** with which Hannah replied was a shortened form of her own name.
1:19 **Ramah** lay along the major north-south highway five miles north of Jerusalem in the territory of Benjamin. In the OT, to "remember" means not simply to think about someone but to act on their behalf.

1:20 The name **Samuel** may be a wordplay meaning "Requested from God." A second possibility is the meaning "Heard by God."
1:21 The expression **annual sacrifice** literally means "sacrifice of the days" and probably designates one of the three required festivals—Passover, the Festival of Weeks, or the Festival of Shelters (Dt 16:16).
1:22 Israelite children were **weaned** at around age three.
1:24 The Masoretic Text, overall the most reliable Hebrew manuscript tradition, reads "three bulls." The CSB adopted **three-year-old bull** because of the reference to a single bull in v. 25 and because of the testimony of other early manuscripts. If the Masoretic Text is correct, however, it may be that the one bull constituted Elkanah's sacrifice of

asked him for, ²⁸ I now give the boy to the LORD. For as long as he lives, he is given to the LORD." Then he^ worshiped the LORD there.^B

Hannah's Triumphant Prayer

2 Hannah prayed:

My heart rejoices in the LORD;
  my horn is lifted up by the LORD.
My mouth boasts over my enemies,
  because I rejoice in your salvation.
² There is no one holy like the LORD.
  There is no one besides you!
  And there is no rock like our God.
³ Do not boast so proudly,
  or let arrogant words come out of
    your mouth,
  for the LORD is a God of knowledge,
  and actions are weighed by him.
⁴ The bows of the warriors are broken,
  but the feeble are clothed with strength.
⁵ Those who are full hire themselves out
    for food,
  but those who are starving hunger
    no more.
  The woman who is childless gives birth
    to seven,
  but the woman with many sons
    pines away.
⁶ The LORD brings death and gives life;
  he sends some down to Sheol,
  and he raises others up.
⁷ The LORD brings poverty and gives
    wealth;
  he humbles and he exalts.
⁸ He raises the poor from the dust
  and lifts the needy from the trash heap.
  He seats them with noblemen
  and gives them a throne of honor.^C
  For the foundations of the earth are the
    LORD's;
  he has set the world on them.
⁹ He guards the steps^D
    of his faithful ones,
  but the wicked perish in darkness,

for a person does not prevail by his own
    strength.
¹⁰ Those who oppose the LORD
    will be shattered;^E
  he will thunder in the heavens
    against them.
  The LORD will judge the ends
    of the earth.
  He will give power to his king;
  he will lift up the horn of his anointed.^F

¹¹ Elkanah went home to Ramah, but the boy served the LORD in the presence of the priest Eli.

Eli's Family Judged

¹² Eli's sons were wicked men; they did not respect the LORD ¹³ or the priests' share of the sacrifices from the people. When anyone offered a sacrifice, the priest's servant would come with a three-pronged meat fork while the meat was boiling ¹⁴ and plunge it into the container, kettle, cauldron, or cooking pot. The priest would claim for himself whatever the meat fork brought up. This is the way they treated all the Israelites who came there to Shiloh. ¹⁵ Even before the fat was burned, the priest's servant would come and say to the one who was sacrificing, "Give the priest some meat to roast, because he won't accept boiled meat from you — only raw." ¹⁶ If that person said to him, "The fat must be burned first; then you can take whatever you want for yourself," the servant would reply, "No, I insist that you hand it over right now. If you don't, I'll take it by force!" ¹⁷ So the servants' sin was very severe in the presence of the LORD, because the men treated the LORD's offering with contempt.

¹⁸ Samuel served in the LORD's presence— this mere boy was dressed in the linen ephod. ¹⁹ Each year his mother made him a little robe and took it to him when she went with her husband to offer the annual sacrifice. ²⁰ Eli would bless Elkanah and his wife: "May the LORD give

---

^1:28 DSS read *she*; some Hb mss, Syr, Vg read *they*   ^B1:28 LXX reads *Then she left him there before the LORD*   ^C2:8 DSS, LXX add *He gives the vow of the one who makes a vow and he blesses the years of the just.*   ^D2:9 Lit *feet*   ^E2:10 DSS, LXX read *The LORD shatters those who dispute with him*   ^F2:10 Or *Messiah*

---

thanksgiving for Samuel's birth, while the other two were part of his usual sacrifice, and hence were not mentioned in v. 25.
2:2 The twofold occurrence of **no one** emphasizes God's uniqueness. **Rock** denotes an immovable, jutting cliff, not a mere stone. This word commonly occurs in the Bible to describe God's support and defense of his people (Pss 18:2; 95:1; Is 44:8).
2:6–7 God is sovereign; nothing happens apart from his control.
2:8 The argument of this verse is from the greater to the lesser; if God controls the earth's **foundations**, he controls the status of its citizens.
2:10 The Hebrew word behind **oppose** has a legal connotation; no one has a case against **the LORD**. The mention of God's **king** and **his**

anointed may anticipate the establishment of the kingship in Israel. Some interpreters have suggested that Hannah spoke prophetically of God's everlasting kingdom under the Messiah.
2:11 The term **served** is not used of slaves, and it often denotes a higher level of service (Jos 1:1), including priestly service (Dt 10:8; 1Kg 8:11).
2:12 The phrase **wicked men** means literally "sons of worthlessness." The expression commonly denotes morally corrupt individuals; Hannah used the feminine form of the expression as she implored Eli not to consider her a daughter of worthlessness (1:16).
2:13–14 The priests' **share of the sacrifices** was specifically prescribed in the law of Moses (Lv 7:32–34). A **three-pronged meat**

fork presumably was used to secure more for themselves.
2:15–16 The **fat** was the Lord's portion of the sacrifice (Lv 3:3–5). The text implies Eli's sons were also eating the fat of the sacrificial animals. The warning that **the fat must be burned first**—a warning that went unheeded—indicates the common people had a greater moral conscience than Eli's sons did.
2:17 The Hebrew verb translated **treated . . . with contempt** indicates strong displeasure or disdain.
2:18 Samuel's **linen ephod** was a vest-like garment that priests or the high priest wore (Ex 28:6–13). It contained special embroidery and twelve stones as a visible reminder of Israel's twelve tribes.

you children by this woman in place of the one she^ has given to the LORD." Then they would go home.

²¹ The LORD paid attention to Hannah's need, and she conceived and gave birth to three sons and two daughters. Meanwhile, the boy Samuel grew up in the presence of the LORD.

²² Now Eli was very old. He heard about everything his sons were doing to all Israel and how they were sleeping with the women who served at the entrance to the tent of meeting. ²³ He said to them, "Why are you doing these things? I have heard about your evil actions from all these people. ²⁴ No, my sons, the news I hear the LORD's people spreading is not good. ²⁵ If one person sins against another, God can intercede for him, but if a person sins against the LORD, who can intercede for him?" But they would not listen to their father, since the LORD intended to kill them. ²⁶ By contrast, the boy Samuel grew in stature and in favor with the LORD and with people.

²⁷ A man of God came to Eli and said to him, "This is what the LORD says: 'Didn't I reveal myself to your forefather's family^B when they were in Egypt and belonged to Pharaoh's palace? ²⁸ Out of all the tribes of Israel, I chose your house^c to be my priests, to offer sacrifices on my altar, to burn incense, and to wear an ephod in my presence. I also gave your forefather's family all the Israelite food offerings. ²⁹ Why, then, do all of you despise my sacrifices and offerings that I require at the place of worship? You have honored your sons more than me, by making yourselves fat with the best part of all of the offerings of my people Israel.'

³⁰ "Therefore, this is the declaration of the LORD, the God of Israel: 'I did say that your family and your forefather's family would walk before me forever.' But now,' this is the LORD's declaration, 'no longer! For those who honor me I will honor, but those who despise me will be disgraced. ³¹ Look, the days are coming when I will cut off your strength and the strength of your forefather's family, so that none in your family will reach old age. ³² You will see distress in the place of worship, in spite of all that is good in

Israel, and no one in your family will ever again reach old age. ³³ Any man from your family I do not cut off from my altar will bring grief^D and sadness to you. All your descendants will die violently.^E,^F ³⁴ This will be the sign that will come to you concerning your two sons Hophni and Phinehas: both of them will die on the same day.

³⁵ "Then I will raise up a faithful priest for myself. He will do whatever is in my heart and mind. I will establish a lasting dynasty for him, and he will walk before my anointed one for all time. ³⁶ Anyone who is left in your family will come and bow down to him for a piece of silver or a loaf of bread. He will say: Please appoint me to some priestly office so I can have a piece of bread to eat.'"

Samuel's Call

3 The boy Samuel served the LORD in Eli's presence. In those days the word of the LORD was rare and prophetic visions were not widespread.

² One day Eli, whose eyesight was failing, was lying in his usual place. ³ Before the lamp of God had gone out, Samuel was lying down in the temple of the LORD, where the ark of God was located.

⁴ Then the LORD called Samuel,^G and he answered, "Here I am." ⁵ He ran to Eli and said, "Here I am; you called me."

"I didn't call," Eli replied. "Go back and lie down." So he went and lay down.

⁶ Once again the LORD called, "Samuel!"

Samuel got up, went to Eli, and said, "Here I am; you called me."

"I didn't call, my son," he replied. "Go back and lie down."

⁷ Now Samuel did not yet know the LORD, because the word of the LORD had not yet been revealed to him. ⁸ Once again, for the third time, the LORD called Samuel. He got up, went to Eli, and said, "Here I am; you called me."

Then Eli understood that the LORD was calling the boy. ⁹ He told Samuel, "Go and lie down. If he calls you, say, 'Speak, LORD, for your servant is listening.'" So Samuel went and lay down in his place.

---

^A2:20 DSS; MT reads *he* ^B2:27 Lit *the house of your father* ^C2:28 Lit *selected him* ^D2:33 Lit *grief to your eyes* ^E2:33 DSS, LXX read *die by the sword of men* ^F2:33 Lit *die men* ^G3:4 DSS, LXX read *called, "Samuel! Samuel!"*

2:21 The LORD paid attention to Hannah's need is literally "Yahweh visited Hannah." The same Hebrew expression occurs in reference to Abraham's wife Sarah when she conceived Isaac, another child of promise (Gn 21:1). Hannah is abundantly blessed, but her **three sons and two daughters** are nonetheless contrasted with **the boy Samuel**, who **grew up in the presence of the LORD**.

2:23–25 The words **since the LORD intended to kill them** reveal that much like Pharaoh in Moses's day (Ex 4:21; 5:2; 7:13), the persistent unbelief of Hophni and Phinehas led to God's giving them over to judgment.

2:26 The phrase **grew in stature and in favor with the LORD and with people** is strikingly similar to the description of Jesus as a child (Lk 2:52).

2:29 Eli is held responsible for his sons' actions. **Despise** is literally "kick at." **You have honored your sons more than me** rebukes Eli on the basis of the first commandment and the command to love the Lord with all one's heart, soul, and strength.

2:34 As the chief sinners, **Hophni and Phinehas** would be the first to **die**—and would do so **on the same day**.

2:35 Some suggest Samuel is intended by the phrase **a faithful priest**, but Samuel

did not have a **lasting dynasty** (8:1–5). The term may denote the priestly line of Zadok, who eventually succeeded Eli's line (1Kg 2:27), or any and all priests who followed the Lord faithfully. **My anointed one** designates the line of David, for whom God also built a lasting dynasty (2Sm 7:11–16).

3:1 Prophetic visions were not widespread because of the general corruption of the time.

3:2–3 The **lamp of God** was to burn from evening until morning (Ex 27:21), so the wording suggests a time just before dawn.

3:9 Eli's suggested words to Samuel, **Speak, LORD, for your servant is listening**, provide

¹⁰ The LORD came, stood there, and called as before, "Samuel, Samuel!"

Samuel responded, "Speak, for your servant is listening."

¹¹ The LORD said to Samuel, "I am about to do something in Israel that will cause everyone who hears about it to shudder.ᴬ ¹² On that day I will carry out against Eli everything I said about his family, from beginning to end. ¹³ I told him that I am going to judge his family forever because of the iniquity he knows about: his sons are cursing God,ᴮ and he has not stopped them. ¹⁴ Therefore, I have sworn to Eli's family: The iniquity of Eli's family will never be wiped out by either sacrifice or offering."

¹⁵ Samuel lay down until the morning; then he opened the doors of the LORD's house. He was afraid to tell Eli the vision, ¹⁶ but Eli called him and said, "Samuel, my son."

"Here I am," answered Samuel.

¹⁷ "What was the message he gave you?" Eli asked. "Don't hide it from me. May God punish you and do so severely if you hide anything from me that he told you." ¹⁸ So Samuel told him everything and did not hide anything from him. Eli responded, "He is the LORD. Let him do what he thinks is good."

¹⁹ Samuel grew. The LORD was with him, and he fulfilled everything Samuel prophesied.ᶜ ²⁰ All Israel from Dan to Beer-sheba knew that Samuel was a confirmed prophet of the LORD. ²¹ The LORD continued to appear in Shiloh, because there he revealed himself to Samuel by his word. ¹ And Samuel's words came to all Israel.

The Ark Captured by the Philistines

Israel went out to meet the Philistines in battle andᴰ camped at Ebenezer while the Philistines camped at Aphek. ² The Philistines lined up in battle formation against Israel, and as the battle intensified, Israel was defeated by the Philistines, who struck down about four thousand men on the battlefield.

³ When the troops returned to the camp, the elders of Israel asked, "Why did the LORD defeat us today before the Philistines? Let's bring the ark of the LORD's covenant from Shiloh. Then itᴱ

ᴬ3:11 Lit about it, his two ears will tingle; Hb obscure ᴮ3:13 LXX, Old Lat; MT reads them ᶜ3:19 Lit he let none of his words fall to the ground ᴰ4:1 LXX reads In those days the Philistines gathered together to fight against Israel, and Israel went out to engage them in battle. They ᴱ4:3 Or he

a model prayer for those who seek to follow God's will.
3:10 The twofold **Samuel, Samuel** may indicate urgency, as it did with Abraham on Mount Moriah (Gn 22:11), with Moses at the burning bush (Ex 3:4), or with Saul of Tarsus on the road to Damascus (Ac 9:4).
3:11 The phrase **that will cause everyone who hears about it to shudder** means literally "the two ears of everyone who hears about it will tingle (or ring or quiver)," indicating a response to a horrific report (2Kg 21:12; Jr 19:3).

3:12 **Everything I said about his family** refers to 2:27–36.
3:13 Eli did try to stop **his sons** (2:23–25), but apparently his words came after he had let their abuses continue too long.
3:14 The phrase **wiped out** might be translated "atoned for."
3:20 The cities of **Dan** and **Beer-sheba** essentially marked the northern and southern borders of Israel, respectively, spanning a distance of about 110 miles (2Sm 3:10; 24:2).
4:1 The **Philistines** migrated to the Judean coastline during the twelfth century BC and

began threatening Israel during the days of the judges (chaps. 13–16). The Israelites **camped at Ebenezer** about twenty miles west of Shiloh, while the Philistines **camped at Aphek** across the plain to the west. Israel's enemies had pushed far north from their home along Israel's southern coastline and now threatened the central territory.
4:2–3 The people associated **the ark of the LORD's covenant** (Ex 25:10–22) with God's presence, and they assumed taking the ark into battle would guarantee victory over

Character profile:
Samuel

The circumstances that led to Samuel growing up in the tabernacle and receiving a unique call from God were unusual, even by biblical standards.

His mother, Hannah, had been unable to conceive. To make matters worse, Hannah's husband had another wife who had given birth to several children and incessantly mocked Hannah for her glaring lack of offspring.

Hannah poured her heart out to God in anguish and despair, begging the Lord to give her a son. In exchange, she vowed to give the boy back to God for his service, effectively waiving her right to raise her son.

God answered her desperate plea. Hannah conceived and gave birth to Samuel. True to her vow, Hannah took her son to the tabernacle at Shiloh as soon as he was weaned. She left him in the care of Eli, the elderly high priest, and devoted him to God's service.

One evening, young Samuel was lying down in the tabernacle when he heard a voice call to him. Assuming the voice had been Eli's, he got up and ran to his room, but Eli hadn't called. This happened twice more. The third time, the high priest finally realized what was happening—and whose voice was speaking. He gave Samuel instructions about how to respond to the voice.

When the Lord called again, the boy responded exactly as Eli had instructed him: "Speak, for your servant is listening" (1Sm 3:10). Those six words transformed Samuel's life. In the decades that followed, Samuel served God faithfully—all because of the willingness to serve embodied in his reply to God's call. He approached God with a spirit of humility and obedience. Samuel was content—even eager—to serve God in any capacity.

At that moment, in the quiet of the tabernacle, Samuel couldn't have imagined what God had in store for him. But he soon discovered that God rewards faithful servants with greater and greater responsibilities.

Years later, when Saul was chosen to rule as the first king of Israel, it was Samuel who anointed him (see 10:1). When the time came to choose Saul's successor, it was Samuel who (with God's prompting) informed young David that one day he would be king (see chap. 16). When Samuel died, the entire nation of Israel mourned for him (see 25:1)—a fitting tribute to a humble servant of God.

Samuel's legacy is built on one crucial decision: he submitted completely and unhesitatingly to God's call. He didn't understand it fully. He didn't know where it would lead. But he made obedience the number one priority in his life.

Samuel had the courage to answer God's call, the faith to trust the Lord with his life, and the selflessness to give up his own ambitions and desires for the sake of God's plan. Perhaps that's why God used him in such a powerful way. Anyone looking to be used similarly is well-advised to look to Samuel's example.

will go with us and save us from our enemies." **4** So the people sent men to Shiloh to bring back the ark of the covenant of the LORD of Armies, who is enthroned between the cherubim. Eli's two sons, Hophni and Phinehas, were there with the ark of the covenant of God. **5** When the ark of the covenant of the LORD entered the camp, all the Israelites raised such a loud shout that the ground shook.

6 The Philistines heard the sound of the war cry and asked, "What's this loud shout in the Hebrews' camp?" When the Philistines discovered that the ark of the LORD had entered the camp, **7** they panicked. "A god has entered their camp!" they said. "Woe to us! Nothing like this has happened before. **8** Woe to us! Who will rescue us from these magnificent gods? These are the gods that slaughtered the Egyptians with all kinds of plagues in the wilderness. **9** Show some courage and be men, Philistines! Otherwise, you'll serve the Hebrews just as they served you. Now be men and fight!"

10 So the Philistines fought, and Israel was defeated, and each man fled to his tent. The slaughter was severe — thirty thousand of the Israelite foot soldiers fell. **11** The ark of God was captured, and Eli's two sons, Hophni and Phinehas, died.

Eli's Death and Ichabod's Birth

12 That same day, a Benjaminite man ran from the battle and came to Shiloh. His clothes were torn, and there was dirt on his head. **13** When he arrived, there was Eli sitting on his chair beside the road waiting, because he was anxious about the ark of God. When the man entered the city to give a report, the entire city cried out.

14 Eli heard the outcry and asked, "Why this commotion?" The man quickly came and reported to Eli. **15** At that time Eli was ninety-eight years old, and his eyes didn't move[A] because he couldn't see.

16 The man said to Eli, "I'm the one who came from the battle.[B] I fled from there today."

"What happened, my son?" Eli asked.

17 The messenger answered, "Israel has fled from the Philistines, and also there was a great slaughter among the people. Your two sons, Hophni and Phinehas, are both dead, and the ark of God has been captured." **18** When he mentioned the ark of God, Eli fell backward off the chair by the city gate, and since he was old and heavy, his neck broke and he died. Eli had judged Israel forty years.

19 Eli's daughter-in-law, the wife of Phinehas, was pregnant and about to give birth. When she heard the news about the capture of God's ark and the deaths of her father-in-law and her husband, she collapsed and gave birth because her labor pains came on her. **20** As she was dying,[C] the women taking care of her said, "Don't be afraid. You've given birth to a son!" But she did not respond or pay attention. **21** She named the boy Ichabod,[D] saying, "The glory has departed from Israel," referring to the capture of the ark of God and to the deaths of her father-in-law and her husband. **22** "The glory has departed from Israel," she said, "because the ark of God has been captured."

The Ark in Philistine Hands

5 After the Philistines had captured the ark of God, they took it from Ebenezer to Ashdod, **2** brought it into the temple of Dagon[E] and placed it next to his statue.[F] **3** When the people of Ashdod got up early the next morning, there was Dagon, fallen with his face to the ground before the ark of the LORD. So they took Dagon and returned him to his place. **4** But when they got up early the next morning, there was Dagon, fallen with his face to the ground before the ark of the LORD. This time, Dagon's head and both of his hands were broken off and lying on the threshold. Only Dagon's torso remained.[G] **5** That is why, still today, the priests

---

^A 4:15 Lit *his eyes stood*; 1Kg 14:4 ^B 4:16 LXX reads *camp* ^C 4:20 LXX reads *And in her time of delivery, she was about to die* ^D 4:21 = Where Is Glory? ^E 5:2 A Philistine god of the sea, grain, or storm ^F 5:2 Lit *to Dagon* ^G 5:4 LXX; Hb reads *Only Dagon remained on it*

---

their **enemies**. This is the equivalent of trying to manipulate God through a talisman.
4:4 The phrase **enthroned between the cherubim** is a reference to God's dwelling in the cloud over the mercy seat of the **ark** (Lv 16:2). Ironically, despite their priestly office, **Hophni and Phinehas** were probably the two least worthy individuals to carry the ark.
4:5 The **loud shout** as the **ark . . . entered the camp** further emphasizes the Israelites' incorrect association of God's presence with the ark.
4:6–7 A god has may be translated "God has." Either way, the Philistines feared for their lives.
4:10–11 To flee **to his tent** meant they abandoned the military. According to Ps 78:60–64; Jr 7:12–15 and 26:6, the tabernacle was destroyed at this time and perhaps also the town.

4:12 A **Benjaminite** was a man from the tribal territory of Benjamin to the south. Shiloh was part of Ephraim's territory. **Clothes were torn** and **dirt on his head** were expressions of mourning (2Sm 1:2).
4:13 "Keeping vigil" might be a better translation than **waiting** since Eli was now blind (v. 15). The Hebrew word translated **cried out** always has a negative connotation, as does the related word "outcry" in the next verse.
4:17–18 The messenger saved the worst news until the end—**the ark of God has been captured**. When he heard that, Eli fell over and died.
4:19 Eli's **daughter-in-law, the wife of Phinehas**, had lost three family members—**her father-in-law . . . husband**, and brother-in-law. That news, coupled with the news of the **capture of God's ark**, suddenly brought her **labor pains**.

4:21 Ichabod means "Where Is the Glory?" with the clear implication, as she then said, that **the glory has departed from Israel**.
5:1 The trip **from Ebenezer to Ashdod** was about nineteen miles. Ashdod—along with Ashkelon, Ekron, Gaza, and Gath—was one of Philistia's five major cities.
5:2 Dagon was originally an agricultural and/or storm god of Canaan and Mesopotamia, but the Philistines made him head of their pantheon. Perhaps the Philistines thought they should place the ark **next to his statue** as a symbolic gesture of Dagon's defeat of the Lord in battle.
5:3–4 Dagon's **head and both of his hands were broken off** (lit "cut off"), suggesting Dagon's fall was no accident. The positioning of head and hands **on the threshold** nearby also ruled out an accident.

of Dagon and everyone who enters the temple of Dagon in Ashdod do not step on Dagon's threshold.

⁶ The LORD's hand was heavy on the people of Ashdod. He terrified the people of Ashdod and its territory and afflicted them with tumors.^A,B ⁷ When the people of Ashdod saw what was happening, they said, "The ark of Israel's God must not stay here with us, because his hand is strongly against us and our god Dagon." ⁸ So they called all the Philistine rulers together and asked, "What should we do with the ark of Israel's God?"

"The ark of Israel's God should be moved to Gath," they replied. So they moved the ark of Israel's God. ⁹ After they had moved it, the LORD's hand was against the city of Gath, causing a great panic. He afflicted the people of the city, from the youngest to the oldest, with an outbreak of tumors.

¹⁰ The people of Gath then sent the ark of God to Ekron, but when it got there, the Ekronites cried out, "They've moved the ark of Israel's God to us to kill us and our people!"^C ¹¹ The Ekronites called all the Philistine rulers together. They said, "Send the ark of Israel's God away. Let it return to its place so it won't kill us and our people!"^D For the fear of death pervaded the city; God's hand was oppressing them. ¹² Those who did not die were afflicted with tumors, and the outcry of the city went up to heaven.

The Return of the Ark

6 When the ark of the LORD had been in Philistine territory for seven months, ² the Philistines summoned the priests and the diviners and pleaded, "What should we do with the ark of the LORD? Tell us how we can send it back to its place."

³ They replied, "If you send the ark of Israel's God away, do not send it without an offering. Send back a guilt offering to him, and you will be healed. Then the reason his hand hasn't been removed from you will be revealed."^E

⁴ They asked, "What guilt offering should we send back to him?"

And they answered, "Five gold tumors and five gold mice corresponding to the number of Philistine rulers, since there was one plague for both you^F and your rulers. ⁵ Make images of your tumors and of your mice that are destroying the land. Give glory to Israel's God, and perhaps he will stop oppressing you,^G your gods, and your land. ⁶ Why harden your hearts as the Egyptians and Pharaoh hardened theirs? When he afflicted them, didn't they send Israel away, and Israel left?

⁷ "Now then, prepare one new cart and two milk cows that have never been yoked. Hitch the cows to the cart, but take their calves away and pen them up. ⁸ Take the ark of the LORD, place it on the cart, and put the gold objects that you're sending him as a guilt offering in a box beside the ark. Send it off and let it go its way. ⁹ Then watch: If it goes up the road to its homeland toward Beth-shemesh, it is the LORD who has made this terrible trouble for us. However, if it doesn't, we will know that it was not his hand that punished us — it was just something that happened to us by chance."

¹⁰ The men did this: They took two milk cows, hitched them to the cart, and confined their calves in the pen. ¹¹ Then they put the ark of the LORD on the cart, along with the box containing the gold mice and the images of their tumors. ¹² The cows went straight up the road to Beth-shemesh. They stayed on that one highway, lowing as they went; they never strayed to the right or to the left. The Philistine rulers were walking behind them to the territory of Beth-shemesh.

¹³ The people of Beth-shemesh were harvesting wheat in the valley, and when they looked up and saw the ark, they were overjoyed to see it. ¹⁴ The cart came to the field of Joshua

---

^A5:6 LXX adds *He brought up mice against them, and they swarmed in their ships. Then mice went up into the land and there was a mortal panic in the city.*   ^B5:6 Perhaps bubonic plague   ^C5:10 DSS, LXX read *"Why have you moved . . . people?"*   ^D5:11 DSS, LXX read *"Why don't you return it to . . . people?"*   ^E6:3 DSS, LXX read *healed, and an atonement shall be made for you. Shouldn't his hand be removed from you?"*   ^F6:4 Some Hb mss, LXX; other Hb mss read *them*   ^G6:5 Lit *will lighten the heaviness of his hand from you*

5:6 The Lord now oppressed **the people of Ashdod**, plaguing them as he had plagued the Egyptians (4:8). **Tumors** (Dt 28:27) probably describe symptoms of bubonic plague, a disease spread by rodents (1Sm 6:4). Others believe the term describes boils or hemorrhoids.
5:7–8 Perhaps **Gath**, located more than twenty miles away at the mouth of the Elah Valley, was on friendlier terms with Israel (21:10; 27:3; 2Sm 15:18; 1Kg 2:39), prompting relocation of the **ark**.
5:9 The Philistines' plan failed as God then brought the **tumors** to Gath.
6:1 The allusion to **seven months** dates the battle that resulted in the ark's capture to around late October, since the wheat

harvest (v. 13) typically occurred around late May.
6:3 A **guilt offering** applied to situations where holy things (here the ark) became defiled (Lv 5:15).
6:4 The **five gold tumors** and **five gold mice** do not correspond to the items the law of Moses required for guilt offerings (Lv 5:14–6:7). However, fashioning an offering in the shape of the thing from which a people wanted to be delivered is well attested in the ancient world (Nm 21:6–9).
6:7–8 The Philistines put forth this one final test with a **cart** and two **cows** to make sure the plagues had come from the Lord's hand. Nonetheless, they were certain they needed to **send** the **ark of the LORD** away.

Untrained cows would not normally know how to work together to pull a cart on a road, and they would not normally leave their **calves** behind, so when that happened, they knew it was from God.
6:9 Beth-shemesh lay in the Sorek Valley a short distance from Timnah, which was controlled by the Philistines (Jdg 14:1).
6:10–12 The Philistine rulers followed the cart to **the territory of Beth-shemesh**, which probably marked the beginning of Israelite-controlled land.
6:13 Harvesting **wheat** was typically done around late May. The Festival of Weeks, called *shavu'oth* in Hebrew (Nm 28:26–31; Dt 16:16), marked this time of ingathering and included Pentecost (Lv 23:15–16; Ac 2:1).

of Beth-shemesh and stopped there near a large rock. The people of the city chopped up the cart and offered the cows as a burnt offering to the Lord. **¹⁵** The Levites removed the ark of the Lord, along with the box containing the gold objects, and placed them on the large rock. That day the people of Beth-shemesh offered burnt offerings and made sacrifices to the Lord. **¹⁶** When the five Philistine rulers observed this, they returned to Ekron that same day.

¹⁷ As a guilt offering to the Lord, the Philistines had sent back one gold tumor for each city: Ashdod, Gaza, Ashkelon, Gath, and Ekron. **¹⁸** The number of gold mice also corresponded to the number of Philistine cities of the five rulers, the fortified cities and the outlying villages. The large rock^A on which the ark of the Lord was placed is still in the field of Joshua of Beth-shemesh today.

¹⁹ God struck down the people of Beth-shemesh because they looked inside the ark of the Lord.^B He struck down seventy persons.^C The people mourned because the Lord struck them with a great slaughter. **²⁰** The people of Beth-shemesh asked, "Who is able to stand in the presence of the Lord this holy God? To whom should the ark go from here?"

²¹ They sent messengers to the residents of Kiriath-jearim, saying, "The Philistines have returned the ark of the Lord. Come down and get it."^D

7 So the people of Kiriath-jearim came for the ark of the Lord and took it to Abinadab's house on the hill. They consecrated his son Eleazar to take care of it.

Victory at Mizpah

² Time went by until twenty years had passed since the ark had been taken to Kiriath-jearim.

Then the whole house of Israel longed for the Lord. **³** Samuel told them, "If you are returning to the Lord with all your heart, get rid of the foreign gods and the Ashtoreths that are among you, set your hearts on the Lord, and worship only him. Then he will rescue you from the Philistines." **⁴** So the Israelites removed the Baals and the Ashtoreths and only worshiped the Lord.

⁵ Samuel said, "Gather all Israel at Mizpah, and I will pray to the Lord on your behalf." **⁶** When they gathered at Mizpah, they drew water and poured it out in the Lord's presence. They fasted that day, and there they confessed, "We have sinned against the Lord." And Samuel judged the Israelites at Mizpah.

⁷ When the Philistines heard that the Israelites had gathered at Mizpah, their rulers marched up toward Israel. When the Israelites heard about it, they were afraid because of the Philistines. **⁸** The Israelites said to Samuel, "Don't stop crying out to the Lord our God for us, so that he will save us from the Philistines." **⁹** Then Samuel took a young lamb and offered it as a whole burnt offering to the Lord. He cried out to the Lord on behalf of Israel, and the Lord answered him. **¹⁰** Samuel was offering the burnt offering as the Philistines approached to fight against Israel. The Lord thundered loudly against the Philistines that day and threw them into such confusion that they were defeated by Israel. **¹¹** Then the men of Israel charged out of Mizpah and pursued the Philistines striking them down all the way to a place below Beth-car.

¹² Afterward, Samuel took a stone and set it upright between Mizpah and Shen. He named it Ebenezer,^E explaining, "The Lord has helped us to this point." **¹³** So the Philistines were subdued and^F did not invade Israel's territory

---

^A 6:18 Some Hb mss, LXX, Tg; other Hb mss read *meadow*   ^B 6:19 LXX reads *But the sons of Jeconiah did not rejoice with the men of Beth-shemesh when they saw the ark of the Lord.*   ^C 6:19 Some Hb mss, Josephus; other Hb mss read *70 men, 50,000 men*   ^D 6:21 Lit *and bring it up to you*   ^E 7:12 = Stone of Help   ^F 7:13 LXX reads *The Lord humbled the Philistines and they*

6:15 Beth-shemesh was a city appointed for **the Levites** (Jos 21:16).
6:19 The Masoretic Text reads "seventy men, fifty thousand men," but many manuscripts omit the fifty thousand men, and Beth-shemesh could not have supported such a large population. The reading **seventy persons**, on the other hand, is undisputed. The phrase **looked inside the ark** may also be translated "looked at the ark" in the sense of unholy staring or gazing. The Levites should have covered the ark as soon as possible and treated it more reverently.
6:20 The Philistines had sent the ark away; the citizens of Beth-shemesh now determined to do the same.
6:21 **Kiriath-jearim** was a city in Judah's territory about fifteen miles to the east. Sending the **ark** there instead of to Shiloh suggests the Philistines may have overrun Shiloh after they captured the ark.

7:3 **Samuel** instructed the people to demonstrate the genuineness of their repentant words (the Hb word translated **returning** carries the idea of repentance) with action. **Foreign gods** certainly included Baal, chief of the Canaanite gods and a constant object of worship during Israel's days of compromise (Jdg 2:11; 3:7). **Ashtoreths** were representations of Baal's consort.
7:4 Removal of **the Baals and the Ashtoreths** must have required some time—though certainly not twenty years, the period of spiritual dormancy following the ark's return (v. 2).
7:5 Samuel took an active role in confirming Israel's rededication to God. **Mizpah** was located seven miles north of Jerusalem; during the judges period, the tribes had gathered there for intertribal war against Benjamin (Jdg 20:1). Some interpreters have identified the site with modern Nebi Samwil, approximately five miles northwest of Jerusalem.

7:6 The phrase **Samuel judged the Israelites at Mizpah** shows that he was acting more prominently than he had before.
7:7 The **Philistines heard** of Israel's gathering and appear to have understood it as preparation for war because **their rulers marched up toward Israel**.
7:10 The phrase **as the Philistines approached** suggests urgency; **Samuel** raced to offer the sacrifice as the enemy approached, knowing that God's favor was essential for victory. **The Lord . . . threw them into . . . confusion** as he had done with his enemies in other battles (Ex 14:24; Jos 10:10). That **they were defeated by Israel** highlights the Philistines' rout.
7:11 The exact site of **Beth-car** is unknown; the Israelites probably chased the Philistines back down the ridge route toward Philistine territory (v. 12).
7:12 The location of **Shen** (lit "The Tooth," perhaps referring to some sharp crag or cliff)

again. The Lord's hand was against the Philistines all of Samuel's life. **14** The cities from Ekron to Gath, which they had taken from Israel, were restored; Israel even rescued their surrounding territories from Philistine control. There was also peace between Israel and the Amorites.

15 Samuel judged Israel throughout his life. **16** Every year he would go on a circuit to Bethel, Gilgal, and Mizpah and would judge Israel at all these locations. **17** Then he would return to Ramah because his home was there, he judged Israel there, and he built an altar to the Lord there.

Israel's Demand for a King

8 When Samuel grew old, he appointed his sons as judges over Israel. **2** His firstborn son's name was Joel and his second was Abijah. They were judges in Beer-sheba. **3** However, his sons did not walk in his ways — they turned toward dishonest profit, took bribes, and perverted justice.

4 So all the elders of Israel gathered together and went to Samuel at Ramah. **5** They said to him, "Look, you are old, and your sons do not walk in your ways. Therefore, appoint a king to judge us the same as all the other nations have."

6 When they said, "Give us a king to judge us," Samuel considered their demand wrong, so he prayed to the Lord. **7** But the Lord told him, "Listen to the people and everything they say to you. They have not rejected you; they have rejected me as their king. **8** They are doing the same thing to you that they have done to me,^ since the day I brought them out of Egypt until this day, abandoning me and worshiping other gods. **9** Listen to them, but solemnly warn them and tell them about the customary rights of the king who will reign over them."

10 Samuel told all the Lord's words to the people who were asking him for a king. **11** He said, "These are the rights of the king who will reign over you: He will take your sons and put them to his use in his chariots, on his horses, or running in front of his chariots. **12** He can appoint them for his use as commanders of thousands or commanders of fifties, to plow his ground and reap his harvest, or to make his weapons of war and the equipment for his chariots. **13** He can take your daughters to become perfumers, cooks, and bakers. **14** He can take your best fields, vineyards, and olive orchards and give them to his servants. **15** He can take a tenth of your grain and your vineyards and give them to his officials and servants. **16** He can take your male servants, your female servants, your best cattle,^B and your donkeys and use them for his work. **17** He can take a tenth of your flocks, and you yourselves can become his servants. **18** When that day comes, you will cry out because of the king you've chosen for yourselves, but the Lord won't answer you on that day."

19 The people refused to listen to Samuel. "No!" they said. "We must have a king over us. **20** Then we'll be like all the other nations: our king will judge us, go out before us, and fight our battles."

21 Samuel listened to all the people's words and then repeated them to the Lord. **22** "Listen to them," the Lord told Samuel. "Appoint a king for them."

Then Samuel told the men of Israel, "Each of you, go back to your city."

^8:8 LXX; MT omits *to me*   ^B8:16 LXX; MT reads *young men*

---

is unknown. **Ebenezer** (Hb, "Stone of Help") marks the extent of the Israelite victory and is a different place from the site of Israel's earlier encampment (4:1).
7:14 Such cities as **Ekron** and **Gath** were open to attack because they lay along Israelite-Philistine border territory. **Amorites** probably denotes Canaanite remnant populations in the land.

7:16 The cities of **Bethel, Gilgal, and Mizpah** lay in the territory of Benjamin. Bethel's location is identified with modern Ramallah north of Jerusalem. Gilgal sat in the Jordan Valley near Jericho and was Israel's base camp during the days of Joshua's conquest (Jos 4:19). On Mizpah, see note at 1Sm 7:5.
7:17 The name **Ramah** is preserved in the name *el-Aram*, an Arab village located on the site of ancient Ramah five miles north of Jerusalem. Samuel's establishment of **an altar to the Lord** further suggests Shiloh had been destroyed.
8:1-2 The sons' location in **Beer-sheba** at Israel's southern edge suggests Samuel did not intend to abdicate his role in Ramah just because he had appointed his sons.
8:3 Samuel's sons turned out to be much like Eli's sons (cp. 2:12).
8:4-5 The elders still appreciated Samuel's leadership; in fact, they wanted him to **appoint a king** for Israel. The observation that Samuel was **old** recalls the situation with Eli (2:22). The elders knew they could not count on his leadership much longer. The words **as all the other nations** contradicted God's desire that Israel be distinct (Lv 20:26; Dt

4:6-8), though the law of Moses did allow for the establishment of a king (Dt 17:14-20).
8:9 The words **solemnly warn** could also be translated "strongly testify"; they sound a somber note in the midst of a message of acquiescence. Explaining the **customary rights of the king** denotes a challenge to count the high cost the kingship would bring the people.
8:10-11 On **rights of the king**, see note at v. 9. **Chariots** is actually singular both times, suggesting the duties mentioned in this verse pertain more to the king's personal honor guard.
8:15 The law of Moses commanded tithes to support the priests and Levites, but a king would demand that much or more to meet his desires.
8:17 The king's additional desire for a tenth of the people's **flocks** would impact the shepherds of the land as well as the farmers (v. 15). The heavy burden the people would have to bear to support the monarchy might well leave them feeling like **servants** instead of citizens.
8:19 To listen to could be translated "to obey." The people had heard Samuel's words, but they would not heed them. They were determined to **have a king**.

#13 99 Essential Christian Truths

FAITH

Biblical faith is resting, or trusting, in Christ alone for salvation (Jn 3:16-21). More than being simply a mental agreement of historical facts, genuine faith begins with a recognition and confession of the truth of the gospel (1Jn 4:13-16), followed by a receiving of Christ as Lord and Savior of one's life (Jn 1:10-13). Biblical faith is not blind faith, for it rests on the historical life, death, and resurrection of Jesus Christ.

Saul Anointed King

9 There was a prominent man of Benjamin named Kish son of Abiel, son of Zeror, son of Becorath, son of Aphiah, son of a Benjaminite. [2] He had a son named Saul, an impressive young man. There was no one more impressive among the Israelites than he. He stood a head taller than anyone else.[A]

[3] One day the donkeys of Saul's father Kish wandered off. Kish said to his son Saul, "Take one of the servants with you and go look for the donkeys." [4] Saul and his servant went through the hill country of Ephraim and then through the region of Shalishah, but they didn't find them. They went through the region of Shaalim — nothing. Then they went through the Benjaminite region but still didn't find them.

[5] When they came to the land of Zuph, Saul said to the servant who was with him, "Come on, let's go back, or my father will stop worrying about the donkeys and start worrying about us."

[6] "Look," the servant said, "there's a man of God in this city who is highly respected; everything he says is sure to come true. Let's go there now. Maybe he'll tell us which way we should go."

[7] "Suppose we do go," Saul said to his servant, "what do we take the man? The food from our packs is gone, and there's no gift to take to the man of God. What do we have?"

[8] The servant answered Saul, "Here, I have a little[B] silver. I'll give it to the man of God, and he will tell us which way we should go."

[9] Formerly in Israel, a man who was going to inquire of God would say, "Come, let's go to the seer," for the prophet of today was formerly called the seer.

[10] "Good," Saul replied to his servant. "Come on, let's go." So they went to the city where the man of God was. [11] As they were climbing the hill to the city, they found some young women coming out to draw water and asked, "Is the seer here?"

[12] The women answered, "Yes, he is ahead of you. Hurry, he just now entered the city, because there's a sacrifice for the people at the high place today. [13] As soon as you enter the city, you will find him before he goes to the high place to eat. The people won't eat until he comes because he must bless the sacrifice; after that, the guests can eat. Go up immediately — you can find him now." [14] So they went up toward the city.

Saul and his servant were entering the city when they saw Samuel coming toward them on his way to the high place. [15] Now the day before Saul's arrival, the LORD had informed Samuel, [16] "At this time tomorrow I will send you a man from the land of Benjamin. Anoint him ruler over my people Israel. He will save them from the Philistines because I have seen the affliction of my people, for their cry has come to me." [17] When Samuel saw Saul, the LORD told him, "Here is the man I told you about; he will govern my people."

[18] Saul approached Samuel in the city gate and asked, "Would you please tell me where the seer's house is?"

[19] "I am the seer," Samuel answered.[C] "Go up ahead of me to the high place and eat with me today. When I send you off in the morning, I'll tell you everything that's in your heart. [20] As for the donkeys that wandered away from you three days ago, don't worry about them because they've been found. And who does all Israel desire but you and all your father's family?"

[21] Saul responded, "Am I not a Benjaminite from the smallest of Israel's tribes and isn't

---

[A] 9:2 Lit *From his shoulder and up higher than any of the people*　　[B] 9:8 Lit *a quarter of a shekel* (about a tenth of an ounce)
[C] 9:19 Lit *answered Saul*

9:1 The men in Saul's genealogy are not widely attested or known in Scripture apart from their relationship to Saul. Nonetheless, the careful way the text traces the family tree through five generations suggests Saul came from a **prominent** family in the tribe of Benjamin, Saul's comment in v. 21 notwithstanding.

9:2 As someone who **stood a head taller than anyone else**, Saul looked impressive—seemingly good leadership material according to human perception.

9:4 The **hill country of Ephraim** lay north of Benjamin and boasted fertile ground. **Shalishah** and **Shaalim** were districts northeast of Gibeah.

9:5 **Zuph** lay about five miles north of Gibeah, Saul's hometown.

9:6 The **man of God** was Samuel, though the text does not reveal this until v. 14. Saul's **servant** described him as **highly respected** (lit "honored") and as one whose word consistently proved **true**.

9:7–8 Saul felt it inappropriate to approach **the man of God** without a **gift**. After all,

the prophet's good counsel might result in the discovery of the lost donkeys, leading to his father's financial gain. Or perhaps Saul thought Samuel might expect a reward. At any rate, **the servant** offered his own little piece of **silver** (lit "quarter of a shekel").

9:9 **Seer** (Hb *ro'eh*) describes a person who sees the things of God; **prophet** (Hb *navi'*) means "called one" (i.e., by God). The text clarifies that the term *prophet* eventually replaced *seer*, but the two terms described the same office.

9:10–11 The meeting of the women as they were **coming out to draw water** suggests a late afternoon or early evening time.

9:12 **The women** suggested the men **hurry** because of the impending **sacrifice** that Samuel would oversee. Saul and his servant would want to meet Samuel before the beginning of that ceremony.

9:14 The phrase **entering the city** is literally "coming into the midst of the city." The language may suggest Saul and his servant were already inside the city rather than at the gate (v. 18) when **they saw Samuel coming**.

9:16 Anointing depicted setting someone apart for God's appointed service, especially kings (10:1; 16:13), priests (Lv 4:3), and prophets (1Kg 19:16). The phrases **I have seen the affliction of my people** and **their cry has come to me** recall God's remembrance of Israel in bondage in Egypt, just before he used Moses to free them (Ex 2:25; 3:7).

9:18 **Saul approached Samuel** but did not recognize him, as his question reveals. All Israel knew Samuel was a prophet of the Lord (3:20), but Saul did not even recognize him.

9:19 **Go up ahead of me** was a way of showing honor and respect.

9:20 **Who does all Israel desire but you** may also be translated, "For whom is every desired thing in Israel? Is it not for you?"

9:21 **Smallest of Israel's tribes** well described Benjamin, which occupied a relatively small territory and furthermore faced potential extinction after war with Israel's other tribes in the days of the judges (Jdg 21:1–3). **Least important** also may mean "smallest in size"; this may be the better sense in light of v. 1.

my clan the least important of all the clans of the Benjaminite tribe? So why have you said something like this to me?"

²² Samuel took Saul and his servant, brought them to the banquet hall, and gave them a place at the head of the thirtyᴬ or so men who had been invited. ²³ Then Samuel said to the cook, "Get the portion of meat that I gave you and told you to set aside."

²⁴ The cook picked up the thigh and what was attached to it and set it before Saul. Then Samuel said, "Notice that the reserved piece is set before you. Eat it because it was saved for you for this solemn event at the time I said, 'I've invited the people.'" So Saul ate with Samuel that day. ²⁵ Afterward, they went down from the high place to the city, and Samuel spoke with Saul on the roof.ᴮ

²⁶ They got up early, and just before dawn, Samuel called to Saul on the roof, "Get up, and I'll send you on your way!" Saul got up, and both he and Samuel went outside. ²⁷ As they were going down to the edge of the city, Samuel said to Saul, "Tell the servant to go on ahead of us, but you stay for a while, and I'll reveal the word of God to you." So the servant went on.

10 Samuel took the flask of oil, poured it out on Saul's head, kissed him, and said, "Hasn't the LORD anointed you ruler over his inheritance?ᶜ ² Today when you leave me, you'll find two men at Rachel's Grave at Zelzah in the territory of Benjamin. They will say to you, 'The donkeys you went looking for have been found, and now your father has stopped being concerned about the donkeys and is worried about you, asking: What should I do about my son?'

³ "You will proceed from there until you come to the oak of Tabor. Three men going up to God at Bethel will meet you there, one bringing three goats, one bringing three loaves of bread, and one bringing a clay jar of wine. ⁴ They will ask how you are and give you two loavesᴰ of bread, which you will accept from them.

⁵ "After that you will come to Gibeah of God where there are Philistine garrisons.ᴱ When you arrive at the city, you will meet a group of prophets coming down from the high place prophesying. They will be preceded by harps, tambourines, flutes, and lyres. ⁶ The Spirit of the LORD will come powerfully on you, you will prophesy with them, and you will be transformed. ⁷ When these signs have happened to you, do whatever your circumstances requireᶠ because God is with you. ⁸ Afterward, go ahead of me to Gilgal. I will come to you to offer burnt offerings and to sacrifice fellowship offerings. Wait seven days until I come to you and show you what to do."

⁹ When Saul turned to leave Samuel, God changed his heart,ᴳ and all the signs came about that day. ¹⁰ When Saul and his servant arrived at Gibeah, a group of prophets met him. Then the Spirit of God came powerfully on him, and he prophesied along with them.

¹¹ Everyone who knew him previously and saw him prophesy with the prophets asked each other, "What has happened to the son of Kish? Is Saul also among the prophets?"

¹² Then a man who was from there asked, "And who is their father?"

As a result, "Is Saul also among the prophets?" became a popular saying. ¹³ Then Saul finished prophesying and went to the high place.

¹⁴ Saul's uncle asked him and his servant, "Where did you go?"

"To look for the donkeys," Saul answered. "When we saw they weren't there, we went to Samuel."

¹⁵ "Tell me," Saul's uncle asked, "what did Samuel say to you?"

ᴬ9:22 LXX reads 70 ᴮ9:25 LXX reads city. They prepared a bed for Saul on the roof, and he slept. ᶜ10:1 LXX adds And you will reign over the LORD's people, and you will save them from the hand of their enemies all around. And this is the sign to you that the LORD has anointed you ruler over his inheritance. ᴰ10:4 DSS, LXX read wave offerings ᴱ10:5 Or governors ᶠ10:7 Lit do for yourself whatever your hand finds ᴳ10:9 Lit God turned to him another heart

9:23 At Samuel's direction, the cook had set aside a choice **portion of meat** for a guest whom **Samuel** would designate.
9:24 The Hebrew term behind **thigh** also means "leg," and either way it would constitute a large, choice portion of meat.
9:25 The **roof** was typically flat, and it was a place where people could enjoy cool evening breezes. The subject of conversation is not known. The LXX adds the words "they prepared a bed for Saul on the roof, and he slept," a natural thing for a host to arrange for his guest.
10:1 The act of anointing Saul with **oil** was anticipated in 9:16. The rhetorical question **hasn't the LORD anointed you** implies an affirmative answer.
10:2 Samuel provided Saul a series of signs that would help Saul validate in his own mind that God had indeed chosen him to lead Israel. **Rachel's Grave** seems to have been located near the border of Ephraim. Based on a misunderstanding of Gn 35:19, a Crusader tradition located the tomb near Bethlehem, where a shrine is dedicated to her.
10:3 The site of the **oak of Tabor** is uncertain, except that it was near **Bethel** in Benjamin. **Going up to God** probably is a reference to Bethel as the place where God appeared to Jacob (Gn 28:15).
10:5 **Gibeah of God** (Hb *giv'ath ha-'elohim*) is probably Gibeah, Saul's hometown and eventually his capital city (v. 10). The presence of **Philistine garrisons** meant Israel's enemies were encroaching seriously on Israel's territory. If the Philistines controlled Benjamin, they could cut off Israel's communication between north and south and seriously restrict a major access route to the Mediterranean coast.
10:7 Samuel's words, **do whatever your circumstances require**, indicate that when the **signs** came true, Saul would know what to do.
10:8 **Gilgal** lay in the Jordan Valley near Jericho. It was the site of Israel's base camp during the days of the conquest (Jos 4:19). Later it became a place where illicit sacrifice was offered (Am 4:4; 5:5).
10:9 The words **God changed his heart** demonstrate the beginning of God fulfilling Samuel's prophetic word. The confirmation of **all the signs . . . that day** further emphasize the truth of Samuel's word to Saul.
10:11 The phrase **everyone who knew him previously** describes the citizens of Gibeah, probably Saul's family and friends. Their question, **Is Saul also among the prophets?** reflects their amazement since they had never known him to **prophesy** before.
10:13 The **high place** was the place of worship from which the band of prophets had just come (v. 5).
10:15–16 Saul was reluctant to share Samuel's words **about the matter of kingship** when he first returned home. Perhaps he

¹⁶ Saul told him, "He assured us the donkeys had been found." However, Saul did not tell him what Samuel had said about the matter of kingship.

Saul Received as King

¹⁷ Samuel summoned the people to the LORD at Mizpah ¹⁸ and said to the Israelites, "This is what the LORD, the God of Israel, says: 'I brought Israel out of Egypt, and I rescued you from the power of the Egyptians and all the kingdoms that were oppressing you.' ¹⁹ But today you have rejected your God, who saves you from all your troubles and afflictions. You said to him, 'You^A must set a king over us.' Now therefore present yourselves before the LORD by your tribes and clans."

²⁰ Samuel had all the tribes of Israel come forward, and the tribe of Benjamin was selected. ²¹ Then he had the tribe of Benjamin come forward by its clans, and the Matrite clan was selected.^B Finally, Saul son of Kish was selected. But when they searched for him, they could not find him. ²² They again inquired of the LORD, "Has the man come here yet?"

The LORD replied, "There he is, hidden among the supplies."

²³ They ran and got him from there. When he stood among the people, he stood a head taller than anyone else.^C ²⁴ Samuel said to all the people, "Do you see the one the LORD has chosen? There is no one like him among the entire population." And all the people shouted,^D "Long live the king!"

²⁵ Samuel proclaimed to the people the rights of kingship. He wrote them on a scroll, which he placed in the presence of the LORD. Then Samuel sent all the people home.

²⁶ Saul also went to his home in Gibeah, and brave men whose hearts God had touched went with him. ²⁷ But some wicked men said, "How can this guy save us?" They despised him and did not bring him a gift, but Saul said nothing.^E,^F

Saul's Deliverance of Jabesh-gilead

11 Nahash^G the Ammonite came up and laid siege to Jabesh-gilead. All the men of Jabesh said to him, "Make a treaty with us, and we will serve you."

² Nahash the Ammonite replied, "I'll make one with you on this condition: that I gouge out everyone's right eye and humiliate all Israel."

³ "Don't do anything to us for seven days," the elders of Jabesh said to him, "and let us send messengers throughout the territory of Israel. If no one saves us, we will surrender to you."

⁴ When the messengers came to Gibeah, Saul's hometown, and told the terms to the people, all wept aloud. ⁵ Just then Saul was coming in from the field behind his oxen. "What's the matter with the people? Why are they weeping?" Saul inquired, and they repeated to him the words of the men from Jabesh.

⁶ When Saul heard these words, the Spirit of God suddenly came powerfully on him, and his anger burned furiously. ⁷ He took a team of oxen, cut them in pieces, and sent them

---

^A10:19 Some Hb mss, LXX, Syr, Vg read *You said, 'No, you*   ^B10:21 LXX adds *And he had the Matrite clan come forward, man by man.*   ^C10:23 Lit *people, and he was higher than any of the people from his shoulder and up*   ^D10:24 LXX reads *acknowledged and said*   ^E10:27 DSS add *Nahash king of the Ammonites had been severely oppressing the Gadites and Reubenites. He gouged out the right eye of each of them and brought fear and trembling on Israel. Of the Israelites beyond the Jordan none remained whose right eye Nahash, king of the Ammonites, had not gouged out. But there were seven thousand men who had escaped from the Ammonites and entered Jabesh-gilead.*   ^F10:27 Lit *gift, and he was like a mute person*   ^G11:1 DSS, LXX read *About a month later, Nahash*

---

felt relatives and friends would have a more difficult time believing he would be their new leader.
10:19 Samuel suggested the people's request for **a king** was really a rejection of God's faithful care in favor of a human leader. The law of Moses established the terms for choosing a king (Dt 17:14–20), but Samuel's speech made clear the people had sinned by asking for one at this time in their history.
10:20–21 These verses probably describe the casting of lots.
10:22 Interpreters generally believe the question, **Has the man come here yet?** was a request for Saul's whereabouts. Others suggest the phrase be translated, "Is anyone else here?" **Hidden among the supplies** probably suggests a place at the perimeter. Saul had been hesitant to reveal his destiny to his own uncle (v. 16), and now he appeared slow to accept the responsibility of the kingship.
10:24 At least according to the standards for kingship the nation entertained, Saul seemed like the right choice. The people's enthusiastic, **Long live the king!** signified the instant acceptance Saul received from many.

10:25 The phrase **rights of kingship** recalled Samuel's warning to the people about the cost of having a king (8:11–18). Samuel **wrote them on a scroll** as a lasting testimony or covenant between the people and Saul. Placing the scroll **in the presence of the LORD** meant in the tabernacle (Ex 40:20; Dt 31:26; Jos 24:26), which emphasized God's oversight of the process; he would hold Israel accountable for this decision.
10:26 Saul's hometown, **Gibeah,** then became Israel's capital. **Brave men whose hearts God had touched** were the beginning of Saul's army; the Lord was providing Saul the resources he needed to rule Israel.
10:27 The expression **wicked men** also describes Hophni and Phinehas (2:12). Although the text condemns their attitude, these individuals doubted Saul's abilities—probably because he appeared too timid to accept the kingship (10:22–23). They **did not bring him a gift** as custom dictated when approaching the king. The phrase **Saul said nothing** is literally "Saul was as one deaf," suggesting he chose to pretend his critics' objections had not been voiced. Others would remember the negative comments, however (11:12).

11:1 Nahash the Ammonite controlled Ammon east of Israel beyond the Jordan River. He later may have been on friendlier terms with David than he was with Saul (2Sm 10:1–2), although David controlled his territory (2Sm 8:11–12). **Jabesh-gilead** was located about twenty miles south of the Sea of Galilee and just east of the Jordan River. Thus, Nahash's incursion went deep into Israelite territory. Nonetheless, the city's citizens asked Nahash to offer terms of peace, which might include taxation or tribute paid at designated intervals.
11:2 Nahash's proposal that he **gouge out everyone's right eye** would allow Jabesh-gilead's citizens to see to function for daily tasks, but with their depth perception ruined, they would be at a great disadvantage in combat.
11:6 This was the second such experience for Israel's new king (10:10).
11:7 Saul's **team of oxen** became part of his stern admonition for the Israelites to rally behind their new king against the Ammonites. His strategy worked; the Israelites went out **united** because **the terror of the LORD** came upon them. The mention of

throughout the territory of Israel by messengers who said, "This is what will be done to the ox of anyone who doesn't march behind Saul and Samuel." As a result, the terror of the LORD fell on the people, and they went out united.

⁸ Saul counted them at Bezek. There were three hundred thousandᴬ Israelites and thirty thousandᴮ men from Judah. ⁹ He told the messengers who had come, "Tell this to the men of Jabesh-gilead: 'Deliverance will be yours tomorrow by the time the sun is hot.' " So the messengers told the men of Jabesh, and they rejoiced.

¹⁰ Then the men of Jabesh said to Nahash, "Tomorrow we will come out, and you can do whatever you want to us."

¹¹ The next day Saul organized the troops into three divisions. During the morning watch, they invaded the Ammonite camp and slaughtered them until the heat of the day. There were survivors, but they were so scattered that no two of them were left together.

Saul's Confirmation as King

¹² Afterward, the people said to Samuel, "Who said that Saul should notᶜ reign over us? Give us those men so we can kill them!"

¹³ But Saul ordered, "No one will be executed this day, for today the LORD has provided deliverance in Israel."

¹⁴ Then Samuel said to the people, "Come, let's go to Gilgal, so we can renew the kingship there." ¹⁵ So all the people went to Gilgal, and there in the LORD's presence they made Saul king. There they sacrificed fellowship offerings in the LORD's presence, and Saul and all the men of Israel rejoiced greatly.

Samuel's Final Public Speech

12 Then Samuel said to all Israel, "I have carefully listened to everything you said to me and placed a king over you. ² Now you can see that the king is leading you. As for me, I'm old and gray, and my sons are here with

you. I have led you from my youth until now. ³ Here I am. Bring charges against me before the LORD and his anointed: Whose ox or donkey have I taken? Who have I wronged or mistreated? Who gave me a bribe to overlook something?ᴰ I will return it to you."

⁴ "You haven't wronged us, you haven't mistreated us, and you haven't taken anything from anyone," they responded.

⁵ He said to them, "The LORD is a witness against you, and his anointed is a witness today that you haven't found anything in my hand."

"He is a witness," they said.

⁶ Then Samuel said to the people, "The LORD, who appointed Moses and Aaron and who brought your ancestors up from the land of Egypt, is a witness.ᴱ ⁷ Now present yourselves, so I may confront you before the LORD about all the righteous acts he has done for you and your ancestors.

⁸ "When Jacob went to Egypt,ᶠ your ancestors cried out to the LORD, and he sent them Moses and Aaron, who led your ancestors out of Egypt and settled them in this place. ⁹ But they forgot the LORD their God, so he handed them over to Sisera commander of the army of Hazor, to the Philistines, and to the king of Moab. These enemies fought against them. ¹⁰ Then they cried out to the LORD and said, 'We have sinned, for we abandoned the LORD and worshiped the Baals and the Ashtoreths. Now rescue us from the power of our enemies, and we will serve you.' ¹¹ So the LORD sent Jerubbaal, Barak,ᴳ Jephthah, and Samuel. He rescued you from the power of the enemies around you, and you lived securely. ¹² But when you saw that Nahash king of the Ammonites was coming against you, you said to me, 'No, we must have a king reign over us' — even though the LORD your God is your king.

¹³ "Now here is the king you've chosen, the one you requested. Look, this is the king the LORD has placed over you. ¹⁴ If you fear the LORD, worship and obey him, and if you

---

ᴬ11:8 LXX reads *600,000* ᴮ11:8 DSS, LXX read *70,000* ᶜ11:12 Some Hb mss, LXX; other Hb mss omit *not* ᴰ12:3 LXX reads *bribe or a pair of shoes? Testify against me.* ᴱ12:6 LXX; MT omits *is a witness* ᶠ12:8 LXX reads *"When Jacob and his sons went to Egypt and Egypt humbled them* ᴳ12:11 LXX, Syr; MT reads *Bedan*; Jdg 4:6; Heb 11:32

Saul and Samuel together reflects Samuel's continuing leadership role during the new monarchy.
11:8 Bezek was located in Manasseh west of the Jordan River, about ten miles west of Jabesh-gilead (Jdg 1:4).
11:9 The phrase **the time the sun is hot** refers to noon.
11:10 The **men of Jabesh** now delivered false information to **Nahash**, promising to **come out** (surrender) to him the next day. The information may have given the Ammonite king and his army a false confidence; consequently, they were unprepared for Saul's surprise attack (v. 11).
11:11 Three divisions allowed Saul to attack **the Ammonite camp** from three directions at once. The invasion occurred **during the**

morning watch—just before sunrise, surprising and scattering the Ammonite forces.
11:14 Samuel instructed **the people** to go to **Gilgal** to reconfirm Saul as king, now that he had demonstrated God's hand on him through the victory over Ammon. This time, no doubt remained—Saul was God's choice.
11:15 The people confirmed Saul again as king. **Fellowship offerings** (sometimes translated "peace offerings") were appropriate for occasions of thankfulness (Lv 7:11–15).
12:1 Samuel spoke **to all Israel**, that is, to all who gathered at Gilgal. In light of Israel's **king** now being in place and Samuel's advancing age, God's prophet may have decided this was the time to begin wrapping up his leadership. At the same time, Samuel's speech was powerful, calling Israel

to remember its past failures and to live in light of God's covenant in the days ahead.
12:3 Samuel called the people to bring before God and the new king any complaint about Samuel's lack of integrity. Samuel wished to settle any wrongs publicly, with God and Saul as his witnesses, before all the people.
12:7 Samuel's command **present yourselves** is the same command he gave the people in 10:19, when they gathered to see God's choice for king. This time Samuel wanted to declare to them **all the righteous acts** God had performed in their lives personally and in the lives of their **ancestors**.
12:14–15 To **fear the LORD** includes an attitude of reverence and awe toward God. **Worship** literally means "serve" in this verse.

don't rebel against the LORD's command, then both you and the king who reigns over you will follow the LORD your God. [15] However, if you disobey the LORD and rebel against his command, the LORD's hand will be against you as it was against your ancestors.[A]

[16] "Now, therefore, present yourselves and see this great thing that the LORD will do before your eyes. [17] Isn't the wheat harvest today? I will call on the LORD, and he will send thunder and rain so that you will recognize what an immense evil you committed in the LORD's sight by requesting a king for yourselves." [18] Samuel called on the LORD, and on that day the LORD sent thunder and rain. As a result, all the people greatly feared the LORD and Samuel.

[19] They pleaded with Samuel, "Pray to the LORD your God for your servants so we won't die! For we have added to all our sins the evil of requesting a king for ourselves."

[20] Samuel replied, "Don't be afraid. Even though you have committed all this evil, don't turn away from following the LORD. Instead, worship the LORD with all your heart. [21] Don't turn away to follow worthless[B] things that can't profit or rescue you; they are worthless. [22] The LORD will not abandon his people, because of his great name and because he has determined to make you his own people.

[23] "As for me, I vow that I will not sin against the LORD by ceasing to pray for you. I will teach you the good and right way. [24] Above all, fear the LORD and worship him faithfully with all your heart; consider the great things he has

done for you. [25] However, if you continue to do what is evil, both you and your king will be swept away."

Saul's Failure

13 Saul was thirty years[c] old when he became king, and he reigned forty-two years[D] over Israel.[E] [2] He chose three thousand men from Israel for himself: two thousand were with Saul at Michmash and in Bethel's hill country, and one thousand were with Jonathan in Gibeah of Benjamin. He sent the rest of the troops away, each to his own tent.

[3] Jonathan attacked the Philistine garrison[F] in Gibeah,[G] and the Philistines heard about it. So Saul blew the ram's horn throughout the land saying, "Let the Hebrews hear!"[H] [4] And all Israel heard the news, "Saul has attacked the Philistine garrison, and Israel is now repulsive to the Philistines." Then the troops were summoned to join Saul at Gilgal.

[5] The Philistines also gathered to fight against Israel: three thousand[I] chariots, six thousand horsemen, and troops as numerous as the sand on the seashore. They went up and camped at Michmash, east of Beth-aven.[J]

[6] The men of Israel saw that they were in trouble because the troops were in a difficult situation. They hid in caves, in thickets, among rocks, and in holes and cisterns. [7] Some Hebrews even crossed the Jordan to the land of Gad and Gilead.

Saul, however, was still at Gilgal, and all his troops were gripped with fear. [8] He waited

---

[A]12:15 LXX *against you and against your king*   [B]12:21 LXX reads *away after empty*   [C]13:1 Some LXX mss; MT reads *was one year*   [D]13:1 Text emended; MT reads *two years*   [E]13:1 Some LXX mss omit v. 1   [F]13:3 Or *governor*, also in v. 4   [G]13:3 LXX; MT reads *Geba*   [H]13:3 LXX reads *"The slaves have revolted"*   [I]13:5 One LXX ms, Syr; MT reads *30,000*   [J]13:5 LXX reads *Michmash, opposite Beth-horon to the south*

12:17 The wheat harvest normally occurred around late May, and it was officially marked by the Festival of Weeks (Hb *shavu'oth*; Nm 28:26–31). **Thunder and rain** normally do not come in Israel from about late April to sometime in October. Their coming would function as a sign of **an immense evil** the people had **committed . . . by requesting a king**.
12:18 The Israelites realized the miraculous nature of what was happening and **greatly feared** the Lord and Samuel. Such an amazing sign could only mean they had offended God.
12:19 The people **pleaded with Samuel** because he was clearly God's representative. The words **we have added to all our sins** seem to indicate a certain depth of repentance, to which Samuel responded in the next verse.
12:20 Samuel agreed the people had **committed . . . evil** by asking for a king. The commands, **don't be afraid** and **don't turn away**, emphasize immediacy. The people were afraid and were considering turning away in light of God's judgment. Rather than fear or flight, Samuel instructed, they should **worship** (or "serve") **the LORD** wholeheartedly.
12:21 The command **Don't turn away** is different in structure from the command in

v. 20. Here it emphasizes a general prohibition—"Don't ever turn away." The Hebrew word translated **worthless things** and **worthless** is *tohu* (Gn 1:2, "formless") and here probably designates the worthlessness of following false gods.
12:23 The words **I vow** could also be translated "far be it from me." Samuel's assurance to the people was expressed in the strongest terms. Samuel had been the people's shepherd leader, and **ceasing to pray** on their behalf was sin in his eyes.
13:1 Ancient manuscripts differ on exactly how many years Saul reigned. Based on a comparison of these manuscripts and Ac 13:21, where Paul gives the round number of forty years, **forty-two years** seems the most likely.
13:2 Israel's new king began to establish a standing military presence for his kingdom. In light of the army's larger size mentioned earlier (11:8), the **three thousand men from Israel** may have represented an elite fighting force to protect the king and local interests. **Michmash** lay about four and one-half miles northeast of **Gibeah of Benjamin**, Saul's hometown and new capital. **Bethel's hill country** describes the rugged terrain around the ancient site of Jacob's dream (Gn 28:10–22). **Jonathan** was one of Saul's sons

who would befriend David and become significant later in the narrative (18:1–3; 19:1–3; 20:1–42; 23:16–18).
13:3 The presence of a **Philistine garrison in Gibeah** posed a significant threat to Israel's heartland and to Saul's kingdom. News of the Philistines' defeat at the hands of **Jonathan** quickly reached the coast, and Saul blew the **ram's horn** to alert Israel that a larger battle was certainly coming.
13:5 The **Philistines** responded with **chariots** and **horsemen**. Saul's departure from **Michmash** (vv. 1–4) left the area open for his enemies again.
13:6 The men of Israel . . . were in trouble. The Philistines controlled the high ground—a clear military advantage. Further, their push to Michmash meant they controlled much of the central Benjamin plateau, effectively cutting Israel in half and limiting Saul's access to the coast. Saul's decision to retreat to Gilgal gave his enemies control of this region; the situation was indeed serious.
13:7 Many of Saul's citizens even **crossed the Jordan** River and moved northward **to the land of Gad and Gilead**. They calculated that the Philistines would be content with the territory west of the Jordan River.
13:8 Samuel had told Saul to wait **seven days** at **Gilgal**, at which time he would

seven days for the appointed time that Samuel had set, but Samuel didn't come to Gilgal, and the troops were deserting him. **9** So Saul said, "Bring me the burnt offering and the fellowship offerings." Then he offered the burnt offering.

10 Just as he finished offering the burnt offering, Samuel arrived. So Saul went out to greet him, **11** and Samuel asked, "What have you done?"

Saul answered, "When I saw that the troops were deserting me and you didn't come within the appointed days and the Philistines were gathering at Michmash, **12** I thought, 'The Philistines will now descend on me at Gilgal, and I haven't sought the LORD's favor.' So I forced myself to offer the burnt offering."

13 Samuel said to Saul, "You have been foolish. You have not kept the command the LORD your God gave you. It was at this time that the LORD would have permanently established your reign over Israel, **14** but now your reign will not endure. The LORD has found a man after his own heart,ᴬ and the LORD has appointed him as ruler over his people, because you have not done what the LORD commanded." **15** Then Samuel wentᴮ from Gilgal to Gibeah in Benjamin. Saul registered the troops who were with him, about six hundred men.

16 Saul, his son Jonathan, and the troops who were with them were staying in Geba of Benjamin, and the Philistines were camped at Michmash. **17** Raiding parties went out from the Philistine camp in three divisions. One division headed toward the Ophrah road leading to the land of Shual. **18** The next division headed toward the Beth-horon road, and the last division headed down the border road that looks out over the Zeboim Valley toward the wilderness.

19 No blacksmith could be found in all the land of Israel because the Philistines had said, "Otherwise, the Hebrews will make swords or spears." **20** So all the Israelites went to the Philistines to sharpen their plows, mattocks, axes, and sickles.ᶜ **21** The price was two-thirds of a shekelᴰ for plows and mattocks, and one-third of a shekel for pitchforks and axes, and for putting a point on a cattle prod. **22** So on the day of battle not a sword or spear could be found in the hand of any of the troops who were with Saul and Jonathan; only Saul and his son Jonathan had weapons.

Jonathan's Victory over the Philistines

23 Now a Philistine garrison took control of the pass at Michmash. **14** **1** That same day Saul's son Jonathan said to the attendant who carried his weapons, "Come on, let's cross over to the Philistine garrison on the other side." However, he did not tell his father.

2 Saul was staying under the pomegranate tree in Migron on the outskirts of Gibeah.ᴱ The troops with him numbered about six hundred. **3** Ahijah, who was wearing an ephod, was also there. He was the son of Ahitub, the brother of Ichabod son of Phinehas, son of Eli the LORD's priest at Shiloh. But the troops did not know that Jonathan had left.

4 There were sharp columnsᶠ of rock on both sides of the pass that Jonathan intended to cross to reach the Philistine garrison. One was named Bozez and the other Seneh; **5** one stood to the north in front of Michmash and the other to the south in front of Geba. **6** Jonathan said to the attendant who carried his weapons, "Come on, let's cross over to the garrison of these uncircumcised men. Perhaps the LORD will help us. Nothing can keep the LORD from saving, whether by many or by few."

ᴬ**13:14** Lit *man according to his heart* ᴮ**13:15** LXX reads *Samuel left Gilgal and went on his way, and the rest of the people followed Saul to join the people in his army. They went* ᶜ**13:20** LXX; MT reads *plowshares* ᴰ**13:21** Lit *of a pim*; about one-fourth ounce of silver ᴱ**14:2** LXX reads *on top of the hill* ᶠ**14:4** Lit *There was a tooth*

come and provide further instructions (10:8). Saul, however, looked around and saw the troops were **deserting him** as morale weakened.
13:9 Saul **offered the burnt offering** himself—a task Samuel should have done as Israel's priest.
13:10–11 Samuel's ominous question **What have you done**? recalls God's questions to Eve and to Cain (Gn 3:13; 4:10).
13:12 Saul rightly estimated the seriousness of the Philistine threat. If they reached **Gilgal**, they would control territory from the Mediterranean Sea to the Jordan River. However, **the LORD's favor** did not come through sacrifice but through faithfulness, a fact Samuel would later drive home to Saul (15:22).
13:14 God's purposes would continue for Israel despite Saul's failures because the Lord had **found a man after his own heart**. The phrase **the LORD has appointed him as ruler** indicates how from God's perspective, his work was already moving ahead and was

as good as done, even though David would not become king for several years.
13:15 From **Gilgal to Gibeah** was a distance of about fifteen miles upward—a gain in elevation of about three thousand feet. Meanwhile, only **six hundred men** (cp. v. 2) remained with the king.
13:16 Only about two miles separated Saul's forces from **the Philistines . . . at Michmash**.
13:17–18 Raiding parties secured the access roads to Michmash. The **Ophrah road** ran northwest of Michmash. **Beth-horon** lay to the west, an important ridge route toward the coast. **Zeboim Valley** was located to the east **toward the wilderness** region leading to the Jordan Valley.
13:19 The presence of Philistine-imposed restrictions on metalworking, which limited weapons to those made of wood or stone, shows the extent of their domination in Israel's heartland.
13:22 The phrase **only Saul and his son Jonathan had weapons** paints a dismal picture of Israel's situation.

13:23 Controlling **the pass at Michmash** cut off Israel's advance northward toward that city. A large group of Philistines controlled territory only a few miles from Saul's capital.
14:1 This chapter begins to show a consistent contrast between Saul and **his son Jonathan**. To this point, Saul had largely retreated from the Philistines; but Jonathan courageously decided to challenge them.
14:2 The exact location of the **pomegranate tree in Migron on the outskirts of Gibeah** is unknown. Perhaps Saul's palace had not yet been established. Assuming Saul stationed his **troops** on Gibeah's north side, he was about an hour's march away from the Philistines at Geba.
14:3 Ahijah, a descendant of **Eli**, was present, wearing his priestly **ephod** (Ex 28:4). Thus, God's counsel was available if Saul was willing to ask for it.
14:6–7 With his words, **Nothing can keep the LORD from saving**, Jonathan demonstrated faith beyond that of his father, who

[7] His armor-bearer responded, "Do what is in your heart. Go ahead! I'm completely with you."

[8] "All right," Jonathan replied, "we'll cross over to the men and then let them see us. [9] If they say, 'Wait until we reach you,' then we will stay where we are and not go up to them. [10] But if they say, 'Come on up,' then we'll go up, because the LORD has handed them over to us — that will be our sign."

[11] They let themselves be seen by the Philistine garrison, and the Philistines said, "Look, the Hebrews are coming out of the holes where they've been hiding!" [12] The men of the garrison called to Jonathan and his armor-bearer. "Come on up, and we'll teach you a lesson!" they said.

"Follow me," Jonathan told his armor-bearer, "for the LORD has handed them over to Israel." [13] Jonathan climbed up using his hands and feet, with his armor-bearer behind him. Jonathan cut them down, and his armor-bearer followed and finished them off. [14] In that first assault Jonathan and his armor-bearer struck down about twenty men in a half-acre field.

A Defeat for the Philistines

[15] Terror spread through the Philistine camp and the open fields to all the troops. Even the garrison and the raiding parties were terrified. The earth shook, and terror spread from God.[A] [16] When Saul's watchmen in Gibeah of Benjamin looked, they saw the panicking troops scattering in every direction. [17] So Saul said to the troops with him, "Call the roll and determine who has left us." They called the roll and saw that Jonathan and his armor-bearer were gone.

[18] Saul told Ahijah, "Bring the ark of God," for it was with the Israelites[B] at that time. [19] While Saul spoke to the priest, the panic in the Philistine camp increased in intensity. So Saul said to the priest, "Stop what you're doing."[C]

[20] Saul and all the troops with him assembled and marched to the battle, and there the Philistines were, fighting against each other in great confusion! [21] There were Hebrews from the area who had gone earlier into the camp to join the Philistines, but even they joined the Israelites who were with Saul and Jonathan. [22] When all the Israelite men who had been hiding in the hill country of Ephraim heard that the Philistines were fleeing, they also joined Saul and Jonathan in the battle. [23] So the LORD saved Israel that day.

Saul's Rash Oath

The battle extended beyond Beth-aven, [24] and the men of Israel were worn out that day, for Saul had[D] placed the troops under an oath: "The man who eats food before evening, before I have taken vengeance on my enemies is cursed." So none of the troops tasted any food.

[25] Everyone[E] went into the forest, and there was honey on the ground. [26] When the troops entered the forest, they saw the flow of honey, but none of them ate any of it[F] because they feared the oath. [27] However, Jonathan had not heard his father make the troops swear the oath. He reached out with the end of the staff he was carrying and dipped it into the honeycomb. When he ate the honey,[G] he had renewed energy.[H] [28] Then one of the troops said, "Your father made the troops solemnly swear, 'The man who eats food today is cursed,' and the troops are exhausted."

[A]14:15 Or and a great terror spread   [B]14:18 LXX reads "Bring the ephod." For he wore the ephod before Israel   [C]14:19 Lit "Withdraw your hand"   [D]14:24 LXX adds committed a great act of ignorance and   [E]14:25 Lit All the land   [F]14:26 Lit but there was none who raised his hand to his mouth   [G]14:27 Lit he returned his hand to his mouth   [H]14:27 Lit his eyes became bright

remained at Gibeah with about six hundred men (v. 2).

14:8–10 Jonathan proposed they **cross over** into the Philistines' view and seek a **sign** from **the LORD**. An invitation to **come on up** to the Philistines' location may have indicated they did not have the courage to relinquish the high ground to fight against only two Israelites.

14:11 The phrase **the Hebrews are coming out of the holes where they've been hiding** is probably a sarcastic statement mocking the Israelites' weakened position.

14:13 The two Israelites were vulnerable to Philistine attack as they climbed to the Philistines' position. Probably the overconfident Philistines feared little.

14:14 Jonathan's success in the **first assault** indicated God's hand was with him.

14:15 Terror spread as news of the assault came from the survivors. **Terror . . . from God** came upon them, meaning the Philistines may have feared they had come too far inland and incurred the wrath of the Israelites' God as they had done when they captured the ark (5:6–12).

14:18 Saul apparently intended to inquire of the Lord about what was happening in the Philistine camp by conferring with the priests who carried **the ark of God**.

14:19–20 Stop what you're doing is literally "Withdraw your hand." Saul decided he might lose the opportunity to rout the Philistines if he delayed, and he told the priest to stop inquiring of the Lord. Perhaps the Lord had already revealed his will for Saul through **the panic in the Philistine camp**. Another possibility is that the text reveals yet another example of Saul's refusal to follow the Lord's guidance.

14:21 The Philistines' incursion into Israel had led many **Israelites** to defect to the Philistines, but now the defectors switched back as they sensed the Philistine panic. Their doing so meant the Philistines now found themselves on the battlefield with Israelites of whose allegiance they were unsure. They would not make the mistake of joining forces with any Israelites again (29:2–11).

14:22 The **hill country of Ephraim** lay directly north of the central Benjamin plateau where the **battle** was occurring.

14:23 After giving many details about human participants in the battle, the text gives God, not Saul, credit for the incredible victory.

14:24 Many have questioned the wisdom of Saul's placing his **troops under an oath**. Going into battle did not require abstinence from food; perhaps Saul thought such a vow would secure the Lord's favor. Consequently, however, **the men of Israel were worn out** because they had eaten nothing to sustain them while expending much energy.

14:25–26 The **flow of honey** probably originated from broken nests of wild bees.

14:27 Jonathan **had not heard** the oath and therefore **ate the honey** (lit "put his hand to his mouth") and **had renewed energy** (lit "his eyes brightened").

14:28–30 The Hebrew word behind **trouble** (Hb *'akar*) was used of Achan, the man who kept some of Jericho's spoil for himself and brought trouble to Israel during Joshua's time (Jos 7:25–26). **Jonathan** suggested his **father** the king had likewise hurt Israel's cause.

²⁹ Jonathan replied, "My father has brought trouble to the land. Just look at how I have renewed energy^A because I tasted a little of this honey. ³⁰ How much better if the troops had eaten freely today from the plunder they took from their enemies! Then the slaughter of the Philistines would have been much greater."

³¹ The Israelites struck down the Philistines that day from Michmash all the way to Aijalon. Since the Israelites were completely exhausted, ³² they rushed to the plunder, took sheep, goats, cattle, and calves, slaughtered them on the ground, and ate meat with the blood still in it. ³³ Some reported to Saul, "Look, the troops are sinning against the Lord by eating meat with the blood still in it."

Saul said, "You have been unfaithful. Roll a large stone over here at once." ³⁴ He then said, "Go among the troops and say to them, 'Let each man bring me his ox or his sheep. Do the slaughtering here and then you can eat. Don't sin against the Lord by eating meat with the blood in it.'" So every one of the troops brought his ox that night and slaughtered it there. ³⁵ Then Saul built an altar to the Lord; it was the first time he had built an altar to the Lord.

³⁶ Saul said, "Let's go down after the Philistines tonight and plunder them until morning. Don't let even one remain!"

"Do whatever you want," the troops replied.

But the priest said, "Let's approach God here."

³⁷ So Saul inquired of God, "Should I go after the Philistines? Will you hand them over to Israel?" But God did not answer him that day. ³⁸ Saul said, "All you leaders of the troops, come here. Let's investigate^B how this sin has occurred today. ³⁹ As surely as the Lord lives who saves Israel, even if it is because of my son Jonathan, he must die!" Not one of the troops answered him.

⁴⁰ So he said to all Israel, "You will be on one side, and I and my son Jonathan will be on the other side."

And the troops replied, "Do whatever you want."

⁴¹ So Saul said to the Lord, "God of Israel, why have you not answered your servant today? If the unrighteousness is in me or in my son Jonathan, Lord God of Israel, give Urim; but if the fault is in your people Israel, give Thummim."^C Jonathan and Saul were selected, and the troops were cleared of the charge.

⁴² Then Saul said, "Cast the lot between me and my son Jonathan," and Jonathan was selected. ⁴³ Saul commanded him, "Tell me what you did."

Jonathan told him, "I tasted a little honey with the end of the staff I was carrying. I am ready to die!"

⁴⁴ Saul declared to him, "May God punish me and do so severely if you do not die, Jonathan!"

⁴⁵ But the people said to Saul, "Must Jonathan die? He accomplished such a great deliverance for Israel! No, as the Lord lives, not a hair of his head will fall to the ground, for he worked with God's help today." So the people redeemed Jonathan, and he did not die. ⁴⁶ Then Saul gave up the pursuit of the Philistines, and the Philistines returned to their own territory.

Summary of Saul's Kingship

⁴⁷ When Saul assumed the kingship over Israel, he fought against all his enemies in every direction: against Moab, the Ammonites, Edom, the kings of Zobah, and the Philistines. Wherever he turned, he caused havoc.^D ⁴⁸ He fought bravely, defeated the Amalekites, and rescued Israel from those who plundered them.

^A 14:29 Lit how my eyes became bright ^B 14:38 Lit know and see ^C 14:41 LXX; MT reads said to the Lord, "God of Israel, give us the right decision." ^D 14:47 LXX reads he was victorious

14:31 From Michmash . . . to Aijalon was a distance of about fifteen miles, stretching from one side of the central Benjamin plateau to the other.
14:32 Sheep, goats, cattle, and calves were clean animals according to the Mosaic law (Lv 11:3–8), but the law also prohibited eating meat with the blood still in it (Lv 17:10–14).
14:33–34 To Saul's credit, he acted to prevent people from sinning against the Lord by eating meat with the blood still in it.
14:36 The elevation dropped down over two thousand feet from the central Benjamin plateau to the Philistine coastal cities. Saul suggested the people continue pursuing their enemies through the night and bring complete destruction on them, an idea his army supported. Saul's priest, however, suggested they should approach God before proceeding.
14:38 Saul was convinced that sin was present in the camp and that it was preventing the divine answer.

14:39 Saul swore an oath that the guilty party must die. Not one of his warriors answered him, although many knew who had violated Saul's curse.
14:40 Saul's first step was to determine whether the blame for God's silence lay with his house or with someone in his army.
14:41 Jonathan and Saul were selected shows that Saul now knew one of them was responsible.
14:42 Jonathan was selected, and so Saul now knew his son Jonathan was the cause of God's silence.
14:43 Jonathan had not promised to fast that day, but as he confessed eating, he willingly offered to place himself under his father's oath and suffer the harsh consequences.
14:45 The people insisted Jonathan should not die when God had brought such a great deliverance for Israel through him. Saul had not uttered his original oath with divine authority, and Jonathan had not violated it anyway since he had not heard it. Saul's

rash curse and oath had put him in a difficult situation—either he would have to execute his son, or he would have to go back on his oath. He gave in to the people's wishes and ignored his oath. This whole episode (14:23–46) points to Saul's impulsiveness and lack of discernment.
14:47 Moab lay to Israel's southeast, east of the Dead Sea. The Ammonites were east of the Jordan River to Israel's east and northeast. Edom was located south of the Dead Sea. Zobah was an Aramean city-state in Syria. The verse suggests that at least for a time, Saul secured all Israel's borders.
14:48 The Amalekites were a nomadic group known for their marauding bands (15:2–3; 30:1–2; Ex 17:8–15).
14:49–51 Ishvi is called Abinadab elsewhere (31:2; 1Ch 8:33; 9:39; 10:2). Two other members of Saul's family besides Jonathan would figure prominently in biblical history: Michal (18:20–29; 19:11–17; 25:44; 2Sm 3:13–16; 6:16,20–23) and Abner (2Sm 2:8–9; 3:6–27).

⁴⁹ Saul's sons were Jonathan, Ishvi, and Malchishua. The names of his two daughters were Merab, his firstborn, and Michal, the younger. ⁵⁰ The name of Saul's wife was Ahinoam daughter of Ahimaaz. The name of the commander of his army was Abner son of Saul's uncle Ner. ⁵¹ Saul's father was Kish. Abner's father was Ner son of Abiel.

⁵² The conflict with the Philistines was fierce all of Saul's days, so whenever Saul noticed any strong or valiant man, he enlisted him.

Saul Rejected as King

15 Samuel told Saul, "The LORD sent me to anoint you as king over his people Israel. Now, listen to the words of the LORD. ² This is what the LORD of Armies says: 'I witnessed^A what the Amalekites did to the Israelites when they opposed them along the way as they were coming out of Egypt. ³ Now go and attack the Amalekites and completely destroy everything they have. Do not spare them. Kill men and women, infants and nursing babies, oxen and sheep, camels and donkeys.'"

⁴ Then Saul summoned the troops and counted them at Telaim: two hundred thousand foot soldiers and ten thousand men from Judah. ⁵ Saul came to the city of Amalek and set up an ambush in the wadi. ⁶ He warned the Kenites, "Since you showed kindness to all the Israelites when they came out of Egypt, go on and leave! Get away from the Amalekites, or I'll sweep you away with them." So the Kenites withdrew from the Amalekites.

⁷ Then Saul struck down the Amalekites from Havilah all the way to Shur, which is next to Egypt. ⁸ He captured King Agag of Amalek alive, but he completely destroyed all the rest of the people with the sword. ⁹ Saul and the troops spared Agag, and the best of the sheep, goats, cattle, and choice animals,^B as well as the young rams and the best of everything else. They were not willing to destroy them, but they did destroy all the worthless and unwanted things.

¹⁰ Then the word of the LORD came to Samuel, ¹¹ "I regret that I made Saul king, for he has turned away from following me and has not carried out my instructions." So Samuel became angry and cried out to the LORD all night.

¹² Early in the morning Samuel got up to confront Saul, but it was reported to Samuel, "Saul went to Carmel where he set up a monument for himself. Then he turned around and went down to Gilgal." ¹³ When Samuel came to him, Saul said, "May the LORD bless you. I have carried out the LORD's instructions."

¹⁴ Samuel replied, "Then what is this sound of sheep, goats, and cattle I hear?"

¹⁵ Saul answered, "The troops brought them from the Amalekites and spared the best sheep, goats, and cattle in order to offer a sacrifice to the LORD your God, but the rest we destroyed."

¹⁶ "Stop!" exclaimed Samuel. "Let me tell you what the LORD said to me last night."

"Tell me," he replied.

¹⁷ Samuel continued, "Although you once considered yourself unimportant, haven't you become the leader of the tribes of Israel? The LORD anointed you king over Israel ¹⁸ and then sent you on a mission and said, 'Go and completely destroy the sinful Amalekites. Fight against them until you have annihilated them.' ¹⁹ So why didn't you obey the LORD? Why did

^15:2 LXX reads *I will avenge* ^B15:9 Lit *and the second ones*

14:52 The constancy of the Philistine threat required that Saul maintain the strongest army he could muster, just as Samuel had warned a king would do (8:11).
15:2 Exodus 17:8–16 records Israel's initial victory over Amalek under Joshua's leadership. At that time, God promised to oppose the Amalekites continually.
15:3 The phrase **destroy everything they have** describes the practice of the ban, wherein Israel would destroy everything in a town that had breath, including humans and animals. God had authority over when all life began and ended.
15:4 *Telaim* was probably located in the Negev of Judah (Jos 15:21–24).
15:5 The **city of Amalek** may designate the place the Amalekites were living rather than a city, since the group was nomadic.
15:6 Saul's warning to the **Kenites** was a gracious act prompted by the memory of the Kenites' kindness at the time Israel came out of Egypt (Jdg 1:16; 4:11). The **kindness to all the Israelites** is only mentioned here, but clearly this was part of Israel's memory in a land where people had long memories (2Ch 20:10–11).
15:7 This extensive campaign covered a broad region, from Arabia almost to Egypt's border, whose inhabitants included many descendants of Ishmael (Gn 25:18).
15:9 The Hebrew text emphasizes that **Saul** was the one primarily responsible for sparing **Agag**. The people also **spared . . . the best of everything else**, another violation of God's command (v. 3). Of course, destroying **all the worthless and unwanted things** was no great sacrifice. **Choice animals** is literally "the second ones." Some Jewish commentators proposed that the second born was better than the firstborn. Another possibility is that "the second ones" (Hb *hammishnim*) should be corrected to "the fat ones" (Hb *hammashmannim*).
15:10–11 The verb **regret** with God as its subject occurs only here and in Gn 6:7, where it denotes God's regrets over making humanity and his ultimate decision to bring the great flood. In both cases, people made wrong moral choices, and God's foreknowledge meant he knew what people would do. Nonetheless, it pained him to see the disobedience come to pass. The word translated **turned away** commonly means "repent" when it speaks of turning away from sin, but here it describes Saul's conscious decision to cease **following** the
Lord. **Samuel** was frustrated by Saul's failing kingship, particularly as he remembered he had anointed him (10:1).
15:12 Ironically, **Saul** had gone to **Carmel**, a town about seven miles south of Hebron in Judah's hill country (Jos 15:55), to erect **a monument for himself**. This monument presumably would remind the Carmelites of the peace that came to their region because of Saul's victory over Amalek. **Gilgal** had great historical significance (see notes at 7:16 and 10:8); it lay about fifteen miles east of Gibeah, Saul's capital.
15:14 The **sound of sheep, goats, and cattle** was proof that Saul had failed to execute God's command.
15:15 Saul's reference to **the LORD your God** (not "my God" or "our God") sounds an ominous tone but aptly fits the situation because Saul did not appear to have much of a relationship with the Lord (cp. vv. 21,30). He also tried to blame **the troops** rather than taking responsibility as their commander.
15:16 Stop! The prophet had endured enough of Saul's excuses and interrupted him abruptly, an action most subjects would not dare take with their king.

you rush on the plunder and do what was evil in the LORD's sight?"

²⁰ "But I did obey the LORD!" Saul answered.^ "I went on the mission the LORD gave me: I brought back King Agag of Amalek, and I completely destroyed the Amalekites. ²¹ The troops took sheep, goats, and cattle from the plunder — the best of what was set apart for destruction — to sacrifice to the LORD your God at Gilgal."

²² Then Samuel said:

> Does the LORD take pleasure
> in burnt offerings and sacrifices
> as much as in obeying the LORD?
>
> Look: to obey is better than sacrifice,
> to pay attention is better than the fat
> of rams.
> ²³ For rebellion is like the sin of divination,
> and defiance is like wickedness
> and idolatry.
> Because you have rejected the word
> of the LORD,
> he has rejected you as king.

²⁴ Saul answered Samuel, "I have sinned. I have transgressed the LORD's command and your words. Because I was afraid of the people, I obeyed them. ²⁵ Now therefore, please forgive my sin and return with me so I can worship the LORD."

²⁶ Samuel replied to Saul, "I will not return with you. Because you rejected the word of the LORD, the LORD has rejected you from being king over Israel." ²⁷ When Samuel turned to go, Saul grabbed the corner of his robe, and it tore. ²⁸ Samuel said to him, "The LORD has torn the kingship of Israel away from you today and has given it to your neighbor who is better than you. ²⁹ Furthermore, the Eternal One of Israel

does not lie or change his mind, for he is not man who changes his mind."

³⁰ Saul said, "I have sinned. Please honor me now before the elders of my people and before Israel. Come back with me so I can bow in worship to the LORD your God." ³¹ Then Samuel went back, following Saul, and Saul bowed down to the LORD.

³² Samuel said, "Bring me King Agag of Amalek."

Agag came to him trembling,ᴮ for he thought, "Certainly the bitterness of death has come."ᶜ'ᴰ

³³ Samuel declared:

> As your sword has made women
> childless,
> so your mother will be childless
> among women.

Then he hacked Agag to pieces before the LORD at Gilgal.

³⁴ Samuel went to Ramah, and Saul went up to his home in Gibeah of Saul. ³⁵ Even to the day of his death, Samuel never saw Saul again. Samuel mourned for Saul, and the LORD regretted he had made Saul king over Israel.

Samuel Anoints David

16 The LORD said to Samuel, "How long are you going to mourn for Saul, since I have rejected him as king over Israel? Fill your horn with oil and go. I am sending you to Jesse of Bethlehem because I have selected for myself a king from his sons."

² Samuel asked, "How can I go? Saul will hear about it and kill me!"

The LORD answered, "Take a young cow with you and say, 'I have come to sacrifice to the LORD.' ³ Then invite Jesse to the sacrifice, and I will let you know what you are to do. You are to anoint for me the one I indicate to you."

---

^15:20 Lit *answered Samuel* ᴮ15:32 Hb obscure ᶜ15:32 LXX reads *"Is death bitter in this way?"* ᴰ15:32 Lit *turned*

15:20 Saul's own description of his actions condemned him because he admitted to sparing **Agag** and to putting to death only **the Amalekites** and not their domesticated property as God had commanded (v. 3). 15:21 **Sacrifice . . . at Gilgal** would not substitute for obedience on Saul's part; further, God had already claimed the animals and given orders for their destruction (vv. 2–3). 15:22 Samuel's words **to obey is better than sacrifice** drove home the point that partial obedience of God was really disobedience, and full obedience of God mattered more than any human-concocted alternatives. 15:24 Saul's half-hearted repentance came only after it was too late, since Samuel had already pronounced the Lord's verdict. Saul feared **the people** more than he feared God. 15:27 The words **Saul grabbed the corner** of Samuel's **robe** may suggest that Saul had been kneeling before Samuel. 15:28 The words **has given it to your neighbor** suggest that in God's mind the transfer of power to Israel's new king was

already accomplished, but Samuel would not learn the identity of the next king until chap. 16. 15:30 Saul confessed his sin a second time. 15:31 Saul's persistence paid off as **Samuel went back** and helped the king save face before his troops. 15:32 The Hebrew word behind **trembling** is obscure and may also mean "in bonds" or "confidently." **Certainly the bitterness of death has come** may also be translated "Certainly the bitterness of death has turned aside" and if so, may represent Agag's attempt to keep Samuel from killing him. Context suggests the CSB rendering is correct. 15:33 The prophet, not Saul, now finished God's command. The Hebrew verb translated **hacked . . . to pieces** is *shasaph*, the sound of a whirring sword. 15:34 The two leaders, Samuel and Saul, parted company once and for all, even though their two cities were only two miles apart. 15:35 Technically, Samuel did see Saul again, but it was not a prearranged official visit

(19:24). The words **the LORD regretted he had made Saul king** highlight the seriousness with which God takes the failures of his leaders (2Sm 11:27; 12:7–12; Heb 13:7). 16:1 How much time had passed since the end of chap. 15 is unknown. At any rate, God wanted to move ahead with his plan. The command, **fill your horn with oil**, meant God had someone in mind for Samuel to anoint as king. **Jesse** appears here for the first time in the book. His connection with **Bethlehem** is spelled out in the book of Ruth (Ru 4:17,22). 16:2 Samuel had told Saul that God had rejected his kingship and had chosen another to lead Israel. Consequently, Samuel's travels would be of great interest to Saul. Samuel feared Saul would consider it treason if he anointed another man as king. A **young cow** might be sacrificed in a region where an unsolved murder had occurred (Dt 21:1–9). It is also possible that bringing a **sacrifice to the LORD** merely provided a pretext for Samuel to hide the primary purpose of his journey.

⁴ Samuel did what the LORD directed and went to Bethlehem. When the elders of the town met him, they trembled^A and asked, "Do^B you come in peace?"

⁵ "In peace," he replied. "I've come to sacrifice to the LORD. Consecrate yourselves and come with me to the sacrifice."^C Then he consecrated Jesse and his sons and invited them to the sacrifice. ⁶ When they arrived, Samuel saw Eliab and said, "Certainly the LORD's anointed one is here before him."

⁷ But the LORD said to Samuel, "Do not look at his appearance or his stature because I have rejected him. Humans do not see what the LORD sees,^D for humans see what is visible, but the LORD sees the heart."

⁸ Jesse called Abinadab and presented him to Samuel. "The LORD hasn't chosen this one either," Samuel said. ⁹ Then Jesse presented Shammah, but Samuel said, "The LORD hasn't chosen this one either." ¹⁰ After Jesse presented seven of his sons to him, Samuel told Jesse, "The LORD hasn't chosen any of these." ¹¹ Samuel asked him, "Are these all the sons you have?"

"There is still the youngest," he answered, "but right now he's tending the sheep." Samuel told Jesse, "Send for him. We won't sit down to eat until he gets here." ¹² So Jesse sent for him. He had beautiful eyes and a healthy,^E handsome appearance.

Then the LORD said, "Anoint him, for he is the one." ¹³ So Samuel took the horn of oil and anointed him in the presence of his brothers, and the Spirit of the LORD came powerfully on David from that day forward. Then Samuel set out and went to Ramah.

David in Saul's Court

¹⁴ Now the Spirit of the LORD had left Saul, and an evil spirit sent from the LORD began to torment him, ¹⁵ so Saul's servants said to him, "You see that an evil spirit from God is tormenting you. ¹⁶ Let our lord command your servants here in your presence to look for someone who knows how to play the lyre. Whenever the evil spirit from God comes on you, that person can play the lyre, and you will feel better."

¹⁷ Then Saul commanded his servants, "Find me someone who plays well and bring him to me."

¹⁸ One of the young men answered, "I have seen a son of Jesse of Bethlehem who knows how to play the lyre. He is also a valiant man, a warrior, eloquent, handsome, and the LORD is with him."

¹⁹ Then Saul dispatched messengers to Jesse and said, "Send me your son David, who is with the sheep." ²⁰ So Jesse took a donkey loaded with bread, a wineskin, and one young goat and sent them by his son David to Saul. ²¹ When David came to Saul and entered his service, Saul loved him very much, and David became his armor-bearer. ²² Then Saul sent word to Jesse: "Let David remain in my service, for he has found favor with me." ²³ Whenever the spirit from God came on Saul, David would pick up his lyre and play, and Saul would then be relieved, feel better, and the evil spirit would leave him.

David versus Goliath

17 The Philistines gathered their forces for war at Socoh in Judah and camped between Socoh and Azekah in Ephes-dammim. ² Saul and the men of Israel gathered and camped in the Valley of Elah; then they lined up in battle formation to face the Philistines. ³ The Philistines were standing on one hill, and the Israelites were standing on another hill

---

^A16:4 LXX reads *were astonished*   ^B16:4 DSS, LXX read *"Seer, do*   ^C16:5 LXX reads *and rejoice with me today*   ^D16:7 LXX reads *God does not see as a man sees*   ^E16:12 Or *ruddy*

16:4 The trembling of the **elders of the town** may indicate they feared Saul's wrath if they gave support to Samuel.
16:5 Consecrate means to set oneself apart to God. It involved entering into ritual cleanness. No set "consecration checklist" appears in Scripture, though bathing, putting on clean garments, avoiding contact with a dead body, and suspension of sexual relations are mentioned in various consecration contexts.
16:6 Jesse's son **Eliab** later served in Saul's army (17:13,28); he apparently looked like kingly material to Samuel.
16:8-9 Jesse's sons **Abinadab** and **Shammah** also served in Saul's army (17:13).
16:10-11 The task of **tending the sheep** often fell to **the youngest**.
16:12 The Hebrew word behind **healthy** is related to the word for "red" and may describe either David's reddish-toned hair or skin.
16:13 Despite God's choice of **David** through Samuel, apparently at least Eliab doubted David's heart (17:28). It is also possible that Samuel did not reveal to David's **brothers**

the mission to which God was calling David. The Spirit of the Lord **came powerfully on David** just as he had done with Saul earlier (10:6,10; 11:6), empowering David for God's service.
16:14 The theological difficulty of the expression **evil spirit . . . from the LORD** may be resolved in one of two ways. God may have intended the evil spirit as redemptive—designed to turn Saul to repentance. Or God may have intended the evil spirit as his instrument of judgment against the rebellious king.
16:15-17 Ancient societies believed music had the power to counteract demonic influence. The lyre in particular was believed to have divine power.
16:18 One of the young men of Saul's court apparently knew David well because he described several good qualities beyond David's musical skill. **Warrior** may be anticipatory (suggesting David seemed to have the qualities that would make a good warrior) since it does not seem that at this stage of life David was accustomed to fighting in battle (17:14-15). **The LORD is with him** describes

David's spiritual qualifications, which would prove important as the drama unfolded.
16:19-20 The items **donkey . . . bread . . . wineskin,** and **goat** were either Jesse's gift to **Saul** or a contribution to David's sustenance in the royal court.
16:21-22 David became King Saul's **armor-bearer**, a position that would keep him closer to Saul.
16:23 Being close to Saul also meant David could **pick up his lyre** quickly and play if the king felt troubled.
17:1-2 The heartland of Benjamin and Judah was approachable from the coast through six valleys. The **Philistines** already had come up the Aijalon Valley (13:23). During the days of Samson (Jdg 13-16), they had come up the Sorek Valley. Now they were coming up the **Valley of Elah** and already controlled **Socoh** and **Azekah.** If they got much farther up the valley, they could come up the ridge route into the hill country and threaten Bethlehem, Hebron, and Saul's capital, Gibeah. The situation was desperate for Saul and his army.
17:3 The word translated "valley" in v. 2 designates a broad, flat valley. The word

with a ravine between them. **⁴** Then a champion named Goliath, from Gath, came out from the Philistine camp. He was nine feet, nine inches^A,B tall **⁵** and wore a bronze helmet and bronze scale armor that weighed one hundred twenty-five pounds.^C **⁶** There was bronze armor on his shins, and a bronze javelin was slung between his shoulders. **⁷** His spear shaft was like a weaver's beam, and the iron point of his spear weighed fifteen pounds.^D In addition, a shield-bearer was walking in front of him.

⁸ He stood and shouted to the Israelite battle formations, "Why do you come out to line up in battle formation?" He asked them, "Am I not a Philistine and are you not servants of Saul? Choose one of your men and have him come down against me. **⁹** If he wins in a fight against me and kills me, we will be your servants. But if I win against him and kill him, then you will be our servants and serve us." **¹⁰** Then the Philistine said, "I defy the ranks of Israel today. Send me a man so we can fight each other!" **¹¹** When Saul and all Israel heard these words from the Philistine, they lost their courage and were terrified.

¹² Now David was the son of the Ephrathite from Bethlehem of Judah named Jesse. Jesse had eight sons and during Saul's reign was already an old man. **¹³** Jesse's three oldest sons had followed Saul to the war, and their names were Eliab, the firstborn, Abinadab, the next, and Shammah, the third, **¹⁴** and David was the youngest. The three oldest had followed Saul, **¹⁵** but David kept going back and forth from Saul to tend his father's flock in Bethlehem.

¹⁶ Every morning and evening for forty days the Philistine came forward and took his stand. **¹⁷** One day Jesse had told his son David, "Take this half-bushel^E of roasted grain along with these ten loaves of bread for your brothers and hurry to their camp. **¹⁸** Also take these ten portions of cheese to the field commander.^F Check on the well-being of your brothers and bring a confirmation from them. **¹⁹** They are with Saul and all the men of Israel in the Valley of Elah fighting with the Philistines."

²⁰ So David got up early in the morning, left the flock with someone to keep it, loaded up, and set out as Jesse had charged him.

He arrived at the perimeter of the camp as the army was marching out to its battle formation shouting their battle cry. **²¹** Israel and the Philistines lined up in battle formation facing each other. **²²** David left his supplies in the care of the quartermaster and ran to the battle line. When he arrived, he asked his brothers how they were. **²³** While he was speaking with them, suddenly the champion named Goliath, the Philistine from Gath, came forward from the Philistine battle line and shouted his usual words, which David heard. **²⁴** When all the Israelite men saw Goliath, they retreated from him terrified.

²⁵ Previously, an Israelite man had declared, "Do you see this man who keeps coming out? He comes to defy Israel. The king will make the man who kills him very rich and will give him his daughter. The king will also make the family of that man's father exempt from paying taxes in Israel."

²⁶ David spoke to the men who were standing with him: "What will be done for the man who kills that Philistine and removes this disgrace from Israel? Just who is this uncircumcised Philistine that he should defy the armies of the living God?"

²⁷ The troops told him about the offer, concluding, "That is what will be done for the man who kills him."

---

^A17:4 DSS, LXX read *four cubits and a span*; i.e., six and a half feet   ^B17:4 Lit *was six cubits and a span*   ^C17:5 Lit *5,000 shekels*   ^D17:7 Lit *600 shekels*   ^E17:17 Lit *this ephah*   ^F17:18 Lit *the leader of 1,000*

---

translated **ravine** denotes a narrower, more sharply defined valley or wadi.
17:4 Two other early manuscripts (LXX, DSS) state that Goliath was "six feet, nine inches tall." However, the description of Goliath's combat gear appears to support the larger height of **nine feet, nine inches tall**. At either height, Goliath would have towered over the much smaller Israelites.
17:5–7 The sheer spectacle of Goliath's **armor** and weapons frightened the Israelite army.
17:10 The Hebrew word translated **defy** first came from Goliath's mouth, but it occurs four other times in the account (vv. 25,26,36,45), with the last three emphasizing Goliath's mocking of God's honor.
17:12 The feminine name *Ephrath(ah)* occurs in Judah's genealogical lists, and her son Hur is called Bethlehem's father (1Ch 2:19; 4:4). First Ch 2:13 says seven rather than **eight sons**, but perhaps one died at an early age and therefore was not noted by the Chronicler.
17:13 Eliab . . . Abinadab, and **Shammah** were the three sons of Jesse other than

David mentioned by name in the account of Samuel's anointing of David. If the Philistines made their way up the Valley of Elah, Bethlehem would soon face attack, so these men were defending their own homeland.
17:15 David's primary role was tending his **father's flock in Bethlehem** about fifteen miles east of the battle site, but he **kept going back and forth** to take his brothers food and to update his father on the battle.
17:16 Such a long standoff period as **forty days** would cause problems if it came at a time when fighting men needed to be home working their land.
17:17 Families of soldiers normally provided their sustenance on the battlefields.
17:18 Field commander is literally "commander of the thousand."
17:20 David must have **left** very early in order to have made the fifteen mile journey in time to see **the army . . . marching out**.
17:22–23 Came forward is literally "was going up." The expression may suggest Goliath approached a bit closer than before, actually coming part way up the ravine (v. 3). **David**

heard Goliath's taunts—a subtle turning point in the account.
17:26–27 David's words indicate he had not heard the announcement from Saul's assistant (v. 25). **Uncircumcised** denotes

---

#14 **99 Essential Christian Truths**

GOD IS GRACIOUS

God's nature is to delight in giving unmerited favor to those who are undeserving (Eph 2:8–9). His grace toward sinners is seen most clearly in the salvation he has provided through Christ. Because of sin, humanity is undeserving of salvation—all of us have turned our backs on God, and as a result, we deserve death (Rm 6:23). However, instead of leaving people in their sins, God has demonstrated his graciousness by providing atonement and forgiveness for our sins through the death and resurrection of Jesus (2Co 5:21).

²⁸ David's oldest brother Eliab listened as he spoke to the men, and he became angry with him. "Why did you come down here?" he asked. "Who did you leave those few sheep with in the wilderness? I know your arrogance and your evil heart — you came down to see the battle!"

²⁹ "What have I done now?" protested David. "It was just a question." ³⁰ Then he turned from those beside him to others in front of him and asked about the offer. The people gave him the same answer as before.

³¹ What David said was overheard and reported to Saul, so he had David brought to him. ³² David said to Saul, "Don't let anyone be discouraged by him; your servant will go and fight this Philistine!"

³³ But Saul replied, "You can't go fight this Philistine. You're just a youth, and he's been a warrior since he was young."

³⁴ David answered Saul, "Your servant has been tending his father's sheep. Whenever a lion or a bear came and carried off a lamb from the flock, ³⁵ I went after it, struck it down, and rescued the lamb from its mouth. If it reared up against me, I would grab it by its fur,ᴬ strike it down, and kill it. ³⁶ Your servant has killed lions and bears; this uncircumcised Philistine will be like one of them, for he has defied the armies of the living God." ³⁷ Then David said, "The LORD who rescued me from the paw of the lion and the paw of the bear will rescue me from the hand of this Philistine."

Saul said to David, "Go, and may the LORD be with you."

³⁸ Then Saul had his own military clothes put on David. He put a bronze helmet on David's head and had him put on armor. ³⁹ David strapped his sword on over the military clothes and tried to walk, but he was not used to them.

"I can't walk in these," David said to Saul, "I'm not used to them." So David took them off. ⁴⁰ Instead, he took his staff in his hand and chose five smooth stones from the wadi and put them in the pouch, in his shepherd's bag. Then, with his sling in his hand, he approached the Philistine.

⁴¹ The Philistine came closer and closer to David, with the shield-bearer in front of him. ⁴² When the Philistine looked and saw David, he despised him because he was just a youth, healthyᴮ and handsome. ⁴³ He said to David, "Am I a dog that you come against me with sticks?"ᶜ Then he cursed David by his gods. ⁴⁴ "Come here," the Philistine called to David, "and I'll give your flesh to the birds of the sky and the wild beasts!"

⁴⁵ David said to the Philistine, "You come against me with a sword, spear, and javelin, but I come against you in the name of the LORD of Armies, the God of the ranks of Israel — you have defied him. ⁴⁶ Today, the LORD will hand you over to me. Today, I'll strike you down, remove your head, and give the corpsesᴰ of the Philistine camp to the birds of the sky and the wild creatures of the earth. Then all the world will know that Israel has a God, ⁴⁷ and this whole assembly will know that it is not by sword or by spear that the LORD saves, for the battle is the LORD's. He will hand you over to us."

⁴⁸ When the Philistine started forward to attack him, David ran quickly to the battle line to meet the Philistine. ⁴⁹ David put his hand in the bag, took out a stone, slung it, and hit the Philistine on his forehead. The stone sank into his forehead, and he fell facedown to the ground. ⁵⁰ David defeated the Philistine with a sling and a stone. David overpowered the Philistine and killed him without having a sword. ⁵¹ David ran

---

ᴬ17:35 LXX reads throat; lit beard   ᴮ17:42 Or ruddy   ᶜ17:43 Some LXX mss add and stones?" And David said, "No! Worse than a dog!"   ᴰ17:46 LXX reads give your limbs and the limbs

---

someone outside God's covenant. David saw the threat as not merely political (cp. v. 8) but theological.

17:31 King Saul apparently heard of David's question and interest in the reward for fighting Goliath and summoned the young man.

17:33 Saul rejected David's bold offer because David was just a **youth** and because Goliath had been in training as a warrior from his youth.

17:34–35 Wild animals such as a lion or a bear were always threats to **a lamb from the flock** in Israel at this time, and the shepherd's fighting ability was the lamb's only defense.

17:38–39 Saul brought **his own military clothes** for **David** to wear, a fact that suggests that although he was the youngest, David may not have been smaller than the king. David tried on the **bronze helmet** and other **armor**, but he was not accustomed to wearing them, so he **took them off**. Ironically, it would not be the last time David wore a king's clothes.

17:40 Rather than wearing royal armor, David took the weapons with which he was

most familiar. The **five smooth stones** he chose would have been roughly the size of tennis balls and would fly straighter than jagged stones. As a shepherd, he had likely become proficient with **his sling**, which would also enable him to attack Goliath from a distance instead of in close combat, where the giant would have a big advantage.

17:43 Goliath began his psychological warfare ("trash talk") against David by suggesting the staff David carried was fit only to beat **a dog**. The statement **he cursed David by his gods** further slants the account toward describing a battle between the gods of the Philistines and the God of Israel rather than just a battle between two men.

17:45 David's response to Goliath highlights the contrast in battle strategy. The Philistine relied on his **sword, spear, and javelin,** but David fought **in the name of** (as the representative of and with the authority of) **the LORD of Armies,** who was the God of Israel's military.

17:46 Hand you over to me is literally "shut you into my hand," that is, leave no way of escape. David's reference to the **Philistine**

camp meant the outcome of their personal battle would have implications for the Philistine army. **Birds of the sky and the wild creatures of the earth** mimicked Goliath's mocking taunt (v. 44). David insisted that when victory was his, all the world would know that **Israel** had **a God** mighty enough to rescue in seemingly impossible situations. David's concern was that the nations would also know the power of the Lord.

17:48–49 After a lengthy anticipation of the battle in the narrative, the battle was over almost as soon as it began. The words **fell facedown** describe Goliath falling face-forward. The force of the stone's impact likely rocked him backward initially, but then he either lurched forward again to complete his fall or spun around face first as he continued to fall back (away from David) **to the ground.** Ironically, the same words, "fell facedown," are used to describe showing respect to superiors (20:41; 2Sm 9:6) and worshiping the Lord (Nm 20:6; Jos 7:6), which Goliath had refused to do during his life.

17:51 Goliath was badly wounded but was yet living when David reached him. Unwill-

and stood over him. He grabbed the Philistine's sword, pulled it from its sheath, and used it to kill him. Then he cut off his head. When the Philistines saw that their hero was dead, they fled. ⁵²The men of Israel and Judah rallied, shouting their battle cry, and chased the Philistines to the entrance of the valley and to the gates of Ekron.ᴬ Philistine bodies were strewn all along the Shaaraim road to Gath and Ekron. ⁵³When the Israelites returned from the pursuit of the Philistines, they plundered their camps. ⁵⁴David took Goliath'sᴮ head and brought it to Jerusalem, but he put Goliath's weapons in his own tent.

⁵⁵ᶜ When Saul had seen David going out to confront the Philistine, he asked Abner the commander of the army, "Whose son is this youth, Abner?"

"Your Majesty, as surely as you live, I don't know," Abner replied.

⁵⁶The king said, "Find out whose son this young man is!"

⁵⁷When David returned from killing the Philistine, Abner took him and brought him before Saul with the Philistine's head still in his hand. ⁵⁸Saul said to him, "Whose son are you, young man?"

"The son of your servant Jesse of Bethlehem," David answered.

David's Success

18 When David had finished speaking with Saul, Jonathan was bound to David in close friendship,ᴰ and loved him as much as he loved himself. ²Saul kept David with him

from that day on and did not let him return to his father's house. ³Jonathan made a covenant with David because he loved him as much as himself. ⁴Then Jonathan removed the robe he was wearing and gave it to David, along with his military tunic, his sword, his bow, and his belt.

⁵David marched out with the army and was successful in everything Saul sent him to do. Saul put him in command of the fighting men, which pleased all the people and Saul's servants as well.

⁶As the troops were coming back, when David was returning from killing the Philistine, the women came out from all the cities of Israel to meet King Saul, singing and dancing with tambourines, with shouts of joy, and with three-stringed instruments. ⁷As they danced, the women sang:

> Saul has killed his thousands,
> but David his tens of thousands.

⁸Saul was furious and resented this song. "They credited tens of thousands to David," he complained, "but they only credited me with thousands. What more can he have but the kingdom?" ⁹So Saul watched David jealously from that day forward.

Saul Attempts to Kill David

¹⁰The next day an evil spirit sent from God came powerfully on Saul, and he began to raveᴱ inside the palace. David was playing the lyre as usual, but Saul was holding a spear, ¹¹and he threw it, thinking, "I'll pin David to the wall." But David got away from him twice.

ᴬ**17:52** LXX reads *Ashkelon*   ᴮ**17:54** Lit *the Philistine's*   ᶜ**17:55** LXX omits 1Sm 17:55–18:5   ᴰ**18:1** Lit *the life of Jonathan was bound to the life of David*   ᴱ**18:10** Or *prophesy*

---

to stop short of finishing his task, David used Goliath's own sword to **kill him** and **cut off his head**. Seeing that their official representative in this death match was dead, the Philistines turned and **fled** back down the valley toward Gath.

17:52 Inspired by the Lord's victory through David, Israel's army pursued the Philistines all the way **to the gates of Ekron**, a leading Philistine city (5:1,10) more than ten miles away. **The Shaaraim road** runs north to south right next to Azekah (v. 1); as panic set in, the Philistines tried every avenue possible to escape the Israelites.

17:53–54 Why David took **Goliath's head to Jerusalem** is unclear, since Jerusalem was controlled by the Jebusites at the time. One possibility is that David intended it to frighten the Jebusites and other enemies of Israel. Another is that Jerusalem was a central place where even non-Jebusites could come to divide, barter, and display the spoils of war. A third possibility is that the text was recording what David ultimately did with Goliath's head years later when David conquered Jerusalem (2Sm 5:7), though 17:57 may weigh against this suggestion. The giant's sword ended up at the city of Nob, from which David retrieved it years later (1Sm 21:8–9).

17:55–56 Either Saul's busy schedule, coupled with his torment from the evil spirit

(16:14), resulted in his not recognizing David as his personal lyre player (16:15–23), or Saul knew David but did not know who his father was.

17:57 A comparison of the details of this verse with those of v. 54 does not require the meeting of **Saul** and **David** to have been in Jerusalem, though nothing precludes this possibility.

17:58 Perhaps the king asked for clarification of David's identity so he could reward **Jesse** with tax-exempt status as he had promised to whoever defeated Goliath (v. 25).

18:1 Jonathan was bound to David in close friendship is literally "Jonathan's life was bound together with David's." The same expression occurs in Gn 44:30 in reference to Jacob and his son, Benjamin. Both David and Jonathan were valiant warriors who had taken stands of faith against incredible opposition (1Sm 14:6–14; 17:31–51), so it is not surprising they would become close friends. **As much as he loved himself** could also be translated "as much as he loved his own life." The phrase is repeated in v. 3 and 20:17.

18:4 The covenant between Jonathan and David may have included the giving of special gifts to David, the new warrior hero. David thus secured not only Goliath's sword (17:54), but the **robe** . . . **military tunic** . . . **sword** . . . **bow**, and **belt** of Israel's

prince, showing that God was preparing him for his royal role.

18:5 David enjoyed success with the army wherever **Saul sent him**, so the king made him head of the army. The expression **Saul's servants** probably designate either the king's military officers or his closest advisers.

18:6 The phrase **David was returning from killing the Philistine** probably refers to a later campaign than David's original battle with Goliath because v. 5 mentions David's promotion, implying some passage of time.

18:7 The words **Saul has killed his thousands, but David his tens of thousands** are the only ones preserved from the women's singing. They were not necessarily contrasting Saul's conquests with David's or exalting David over Saul. The Hebrew word translated "but" also may mean "and," and the words for "thousand" and "ten thousand" occur elsewhere as a word pair in poetry (Dt 32:30; Ps 91:7; Mc 6:7). In fact, the women may have intended to praise Saul by what they affirmed about David—the king had made an excellent choice by naming David his commander.

18:8 Whatever the women intended by their song, Saul **resented** what he perceived as their lower assessment of his fighting ability.

18:11 The evil spirit's influence, combined with Saul's jealousy, may have led him to

¹² Saul was afraid of David, because the LORD was with David but had left Saul. ¹³ Therefore, Saul sent David away from him and made him commander over a thousand men. David led the troops ¹⁴ and continued to be successful in all his activities because the LORD was with him. ¹⁵ When Saul observed that David was very successful, he dreaded him. ¹⁶ But all Israel and Judah loved David because he was leading their troops. ¹⁷ Saul told David, "Here is my oldest daughter Merab. I'll give her to you as a wife if you will be a warrior for me and fight the LORD's battles." But Saul was thinking, "I don't need to raise a hand against him; let the hand of the Philistines be against him."

¹⁸ Then David responded, "Who am I, and what is my family or my father's clan in Israel that I should become the king's son-in-law?" ¹⁹ When it was time to give Saul's daughter Merab to David, she was given to Adriel the Meholathite as a wife.

David's Marriage to Michal

²⁰ Now Saul's daughter Michal loved David, and when it was reported to Saul, it pleased him. ²¹ "I'll give her to him," Saul thought. "She'll be a trap for him, and the hand of the Philistines will be against him." So Saul said to David a second time, "You can now be my son-in-law." ²² Saul then ordered his servants, "Speak to David in private and tell him, 'Look, the king is pleased with you, and all his servants love you. Therefore, you should become the king's son-in-law.'" ²³ Saul's servants reported these words directly to David, but he replied, "Is it trivial in your sight to become the king's son-in-law? I am a poor commoner." ²⁴ The servants reported back to Saul, "These are the words David spoke." ²⁵ Then Saul replied, "Say this to David: 'The king desires no other bride-price except a hundred Philistine foreskins, to take revenge on

his enemies.'" Actually, Saul intended to cause David's death at the hands of the Philistines.

²⁶ When the servants reported these terms to David, he was pleased to become the king's son-in-law. Before the wedding day arrived, ²⁷ David and his men went out and killed two hundred ᴬ Philistines. He brought their foreskins and presented them as full payment to the king to become his son-in-law. Then Saul gave his daughter Michal to David as his wife. ²⁸ Saul realized ᴮ that the LORD was with David and that his daughter Michal loved him, ²⁹ and he became even more afraid of David. As a result, Saul was David's enemy from then on.

³⁰ Every time the Philistine commanders came out to fight, David was more successful than all of Saul's officers. So his name became well known.

David Delivered from Saul

19 Saul ordered his son Jonathan and all his servants to kill David. But Saul's son Jonathan liked David very much, ² so he told him, "My father, Saul, intends to kill you. Be on your guard in the morning and hide in a secret place and stay there. ³ I'll go out and stand beside my father in the field where you are and talk to him about you. When I see what he says, I'll tell you."

⁴ Jonathan spoke well of David to his father, Saul. He said to him, "The king should not sin against his servant David. He hasn't sinned against you; in fact, his actions have been a great advantage to you. ⁵ He took his life in his hands when he struck down the Philistine, and the LORD brought about a great victory for all Israel. You saw it and rejoiced, so why would you sin against innocent blood by killing David for no reason?"

⁶ Saul listened to Jonathan's advice and swore an oath: "As surely as the LORD lives, David will not be killed." ⁷ So Jonathan summoned David and told him all these words.

ᴬ**18:27** LXX reads *100* ᴮ**18:28** Lit *saw and knew*

hurl his spear. The allusion to David's twofold escape suggests he remained after Saul's first throw, perhaps intending to reason with the king and help him through his tormented state.
18:13–14 Saul sent David away to military duty to get him out of his presence.
18:16 The fact that **all Israel and Judah loved David** put Saul in a more difficult position, since the people would not understand why Saul removed someone so effective as David.
18:17 Saul tried a new strategy to rid himself of David. He proposed that David marry Saul's **oldest daughter Merab** in exchange for David's increased role as a **warrior**. Saul knew David's chances of death increased the more time he spent in war; perhaps **the Philistines** would kill him and end Saul's problem.

18:19 Merab eventually married and had five sons, all of whom the Gibeonites later put to death to avenge Saul's sin against them (2Sm 21:8–9).
18:20 Michal, another daughter of Saul, **loved David**. The text may imply that Merab, by contrast, had no feelings for David.
18:21–22 Perhaps Saul thought Michal would be a **trap** because she might distract David's attention from his military duties, or that the bride price Saul intended to request (v. 25) would put David in a life-threatening situation. Yet another possibility is that Saul thought Michal would lead David away from the Lord. First Sm 19:13 has been cited to support this, but the context is uncertain.
18:25 To pay the bride price David had to kill **a hundred** Philistines.
18:27 David and his men secured twice the **payment** required—further evidence of

David's desire to please Saul regardless of the risk.
18:28 Through David's friendship with Jonathan (vv. 1–3) and now through his marriage to Michal, he was firmly established as part of the royal family.
19:1–2 Jonathan made sure David knew about Saul's plan. Ironically, Jonathan, as King Saul's oldest son, had the most to gain by David's death.
19:4–5 Jonathan spoke well of David and suggested that his father Saul should spare him for three reasons. First, David was innocent of any sin against Saul. Second, the Lord had used David to bring **a great victory for all Israel**. Third, killing David for no reason would make Saul guilty of shedding **innocent blood**.
19:7–8 It is not clear whether the expression **served him as he did before** denotes

Then Jonathan brought David to Saul, and he served him as he did before.

8 When war broke out again, David went out and fought against the Philistines. He defeated them with such great force that they fled from him.

9 Now an evil spirit sent from the LORD came on Saul as he was sitting in his palace holding a spear. David was playing the lyre, **10** and Saul tried to pin David to the wall with the spear. As the spear struck the wall, David eluded Saul, ran away, and escaped that night. **11** Saul sent agents to David's house to watch for him and kill him in the morning. But his wife Michal warned David, "If you don't escape tonight, you will be dead tomorrow!" **12** So she lowered David from the window, and he fled and escaped. **13** Then Michal took the household idol and put it on the bed, placed some goat hair on its head, and covered it with a garment. **14** When Saul sent agents to seize David, Michal said, "He's sick."

15 Saul sent the agents back to see David and said, "Bring him on his bed so I can kill him." **16** When the agents arrived, to their surprise, the household idol was on the bed with some goat hair on its head.

17 Saul asked Michal, "Why did you deceive me like this? You sent my enemy away, and he has escaped!"

She answered him, "He said to me, 'Let me go! Why should I kill you?'"

18 So David fled and escaped and went to Samuel at Ramah and told him everything Saul had done to him. Then he and Samuel left and stayed at Naioth.

19 When it was reported to Saul that David was at Naioth in Ramah, **20** he sent agents to seize David. However, when they saw the group of prophets prophesying with Samuel leading them, the Spirit of God came on Saul's agents, and they also started prophesying. **21** When they reported to Saul, he sent other agents, and they also began prophesying. So Saul tried again and sent a third group of agents, and even they began prophesying. **22** Then Saul himself went to Ramah. He came to the large cistern at Secu and asked, "Where are Samuel and David?"

"At Naioth in Ramah," someone said.

23 So he went to Naioth in Ramah. The Spirit of God also came on him, and as he walked along, he prophesied until he entered Naioth in Ramah. **24** Saul then removed his clothes and also prophesied before Samuel; he collapsed and lay naked all that day and all that night. That is why they say, "Is Saul also among the prophets?"

Jonathan Protects David

20 David fled from Naioth in Ramah and came to Jonathan and asked, "What have I done? What did I do wrong? How have I sinned against your father so that he wants to take my life?"

2 Jonathan said to him, "No, you won't die. Listen, my father doesn't do anything, great or small, without telling me. So why would he hide this matter from me? This can't be true."

3 But David said, "Your father certainly knows that I have found favor with you. He has said, 'Jonathan must not know of this, or else he will be grieved.'" David also swore, "As surely as the LORD lives and as you yourself live, there is but a step between me and death."

4 Jonathan said to David, "Whatever you say, I will do for you."

5 So David told him, "Look, tomorrow is the New Moon, and I'm supposed to sit down and eat with the king. Instead, let me go, and I'll hide in the countryside for the next two nights.^A **6** If your father misses me at all, say, 'David urgently requested my permission to go quickly to his hometown, Bethlehem, for an annual sacrifice there involving the whole clan.' **7** If he says, 'Good,' then your servant is safe, but if

^**20:5** Lit *countryside until the third night*

David's lyre-playing or leading the military. Perhaps both are intended since both appear in the immediate context (vv. 8–9).
19:10 David eluded Saul . . . and escaped, perhaps because he was more wary after the previous incident (18:10–11). He did not provide the king a second opportunity to strike him down, but fled to his home.
19:11 Michal discovered her father's intentions to murder David and **warned** her husband that delay in fleeing would bring his death.
19:12 Again, a member of Saul's family helped David escape Saul's death sentence.
19:13–14 The **household idol** (Hb *teraphim*) was apparently large enough that it would appear as though David's body lay **on the bed** under a **garment**. Such idols also could be smaller in size (Gn 31:19,34). No explanation is given for why such a thing was in David's house.

19:17 When Saul challenged his daughter **Michal** about her deception, she replied that David had threatened to **kill** her if she did not cooperate. Saul could not prove she was lying since no witnesses were present.
19:18 David fled three miles to **Samuel at Ramah.** The prophet also feared of Saul (16:2), and the two of them went to **Naioth,** perhaps a designation of dwellings for prophets in Ramah (vv. 19,22).
19:19–21 As the king's **agents** encountered a **group of prophets** prophesying with Samuel, God's divine touch overrode their human intentions, and they also started **prophesying.** This also happened with the next two groups that Saul sent (v. 21).
19:23 The **Spirit of God** overruled Saul's intentions just as he had done with the king's agents. The one who sought to kill God's servant now spoke God's praises.

19:24 The proverb, **Is Saul also among the prophets?** (cp. 10:11), once again pointed to actions that were out of character for Saul.
20:1 David **came to Jonathan,** probably at a secret meeting place because Saul's men would have been watching for David around Gibeah.
20:4–5 The **New Moon** refers to a monthly festival (Nm 28:11–15) commemorated by the blowing of trumpets (Nm 10:10). David knew Saul would expect his presence at the meal, but he did not want to risk his life by entering the palace until he knew Saul's intentions.
20:6 Jonathan would tell his father why David was not there if Saul asked about David's absence. The **annual sacrifice** to which Jonathan referred could have been some kind of offering **the whole clan** had determined to offer.

he becomes angry, you will know he has evil intentions. **8** Deal kindly with^A your servant, for you have brought me into a covenant with you before the LORD. If I have done anything wrong, then kill me yourself; why take me to your father?"

9 "No!" Jonathan responded. "If I ever find out my father has evil intentions against you, wouldn't I tell you about it?"

10 So David asked Jonathan, "Who will tell me if your father answers you harshly?"

11 He answered David, "Come on, let's go out to the countryside." So both of them went out to the countryside. **12** "By the LORD, the God of Israel, I will sound out my father by this time tomorrow or the next day. If I find out that he is favorable toward you, will I not send for you and tell you? **13** If my father intends to bring evil on you, may the LORD punish Jonathan and do so severely if I do not tell you and send you away so you may leave safely. May the LORD be with you, just as he was with my father. **14** If I continue to live, show me kindness^B from the LORD, but if I die, **15** don't ever withdraw your kindness from my household — not even when the LORD cuts off every one of David's enemies from the face of the earth." **16** Then Jonathan made a covenant with the house of David, saying, "May the LORD hold David's enemies accountable."^C **17** Jonathan once again swore to David^D in his love for him, because he loved him as he loved himself.

18 Then Jonathan said to him, "Tomorrow is the New Moon; you'll be missed because your seat will be empty. **19** The following day hurry down and go to the place where you hid on the day this incident began and stay beside the rock Ezel. **20** I will shoot three arrows beside it as if I'm aiming at a target. **21** Then I will send a servant and say, 'Go and find the arrows!' Now, if I expressly say to the servant, 'Look, the arrows are on this side of you — get them,' then come, because as the LORD lives, it is safe for you and there is no problem. **22** But if I say this to the youth, 'Look, the arrows are beyond you!' then go, for the LORD is sending

you away. **23** As for the matter you and I have spoken about, the LORD will be a witness^E between you and me forever." **24** So David hid in the countryside.

At the New Moon, the king sat down to eat the meal. **25** He sat at his usual place on the seat by the wall. Jonathan sat facing him^F and Abner took his place beside Saul, but David's place was empty. **26** Saul did not say anything that day because he thought, "Something unexpected has happened; he must be ceremonially unclean — yes, that's it, he is unclean."

27 However, the day after the New Moon, the second day, David's place was still empty, and Saul asked his son Jonathan, "Why didn't Jesse's son come to the meal either yesterday or today?"

28 Jonathan answered, "David asked for my permission to go to Bethlehem. **29** He said, 'Please let me go because our clan is holding a sacrifice in the town, and my brother has told me to be there. So now, if I have found favor with you, let me go so I can see my brothers.' That's why he didn't come to the king's table."

30 Then Saul became angry with Jonathan and shouted, "You son of a perverse and rebellious woman! Don't I know that you are siding with Jesse's son to your own shame and to the disgrace of your mother?^G **31** Every day Jesse's son lives on earth you and your kingship are not secure. Now send for him and bring him to me — he must die!"

32 Jonathan answered his father back, "Why is he to be killed? What has he done?"

33 Then Saul threw his spear at Jonathan to kill him, so he knew that his father was determined to kill David. **34** He got up from the table fiercely angry and did not eat any food that second day of the New Moon, for he was grieved because of his father's shameful behavior toward David.

35 In the morning Jonathan went out to the countryside for the appointed meeting with David. A young servant was with him. **36** He said to the servant, "Run and find the arrows I'm shooting." As the servant ran, Jonathan shot

---

^A**20:8** Or *Show loyalty to*   ^B**20:14** Or *loyalty*, also in v. 15   ^C**20:16** Lit *LORD require it from the hand of David's enemies*   ^D**20:17** LXX; MT reads *Jonathan once again made David swear*   ^E**20:23** LXX; MT omits *a witness*   ^F**20:25** Text emended; MT reads *Jonathan got up*   ^G**20:30** Lit *your mother's nakedness*

20:11 The two men probably went **out to the countryside** so no one would overhear their plan.

20:12–13 Jonathan's words **as he was with my father** suggest he knew the Lord's Spirit had departed from Saul (16:14).

20:14–15 Jonathan asked David never to **withdraw** his **kindness** from his house. Many new kings ordered the death of the former king's family to eliminate contenders for the throne. After Jonathan's death, David honored Jonathan's request (2Sm 9).

20:16 Jonathan now established a **covenant with the house of David**, not with David alone. God himself would hold David's

enemies accountable for their actions against his chosen servant.

20:20–22 Jonathan proposed code language to alert David about Saul's intentions. Calling the **servant** back toward Jonathan to retrieve the three arrows meant that all was **safe**. Telling him to seek the arrows **beyond** him meant David should flee at once.

20:24–25 Saul's **seat by the wall** offered greater security since no one could approach him from behind.

20:26 Saul's assumption that David was **ceremonially unclean** rested on his knowledge of David's faith, which would have prohibited him from partaking of the meal (Lv 7:20–21).

20:27 Saul became suspicious on **the second day**, when uncleanness would not have required David's absence.

20:30 Saul's words, **son of a perverse and rebellious woman**, were an insult to Jonathan by defaming the character of his mother Ahinoam (14:50).

20:31 Saul's reference to **your kingship** reveals that he intended for Jonathan to succeed him, despite Samuel's pronouncement against his house (13:13–14). **Send for him and bring him to me** indicated Saul's belief that Jonathan knew David's whereabouts.

20:33 Saul **threw his spear at Jonathan** because he had sided with the king's enemy.

Seeing Jesus in the Kingdom

▼ Old Testament	▼ New Testament
THE LORD: The King of Glory to Whom Belongs All the Earth *(Ps 24)*	**THE SON OF MAN:** The King of Glory over All the Nations *(Mt 25:31–46)*
Samuel: Grew in Stature and in Favor with the Lord and People *(1Sm 2:26)*	**Jesus:** Grew in Wisdom and Stature and in Favor with God and People *(Lk 2:52)*
Saul: Disobeyed God to Offer Sacrifices to Him *(1Sm 15)*	**Jesus:** Sacrificed Himself in Obedience to God *(Heb 10:5–10)*
David: Unimpressive Appearance, but God's Chosen King *(1Sm 16:6–13)*	**Jesus:** Unimpressive Appearance, but God's Righteous Servant *(Is 52:13–53:12)*
David: Defeated Goliath in the Name of the Lord *(1Sm 17:45)*	**Jesus:** Saves Us from Sin in the Name of the Lord *(Mt 21:9; Rm 10:13)*
Jonathan: Risked His Life for His Friend David *(1Sm 19:4–7; 20:27–34)*	**Jesus:** Laid Down His Life for His Friends *(Jn 15:12–14)*
David's Son: He Would Build a House for God's Name *(2Sm 7:13)*	**The Son of David:** Jesus's Body Is the Sanctuary *(Jn 2:21)*
Solomon: A Son to God, Disciplined for His Sin *(2Sm 7:14; 1Kg 11)*	**The Son of God:** Jesus Knew No Sin but Died for Ours *(1Pt 2:21–25)*
Wisdom: God-Given Insight for Living Well *(Pr 1:1–7)*	**Christ Jesus:** God-Given Wisdom for Our Salvation *(1Co 1:30)*
The Temple: A Place for God's Name *(1Kg 5:5)*	**The True Temple:** A Person—Jesus, the Son of God *(Jn 2:13–22)*
Job: Needed a Mediator Between God and Mankind *(Jb 16:18–22)*	**Jesus:** The One Mediator Between God and Mankind *(1Tm 2:5)*

an arrow beyond him. ³⁷ He came to the location of the arrow that Jonathan had shot, but Jonathan called to him and said, "The arrow is beyond you, isn't it?" ³⁸ Then Jonathan called to him, "Hurry up and don't stop!" Jonathan's servant picked up the arrow and returned to his master. ³⁹ He did not know anything; only Jonathan and David knew the arrangement. ⁴⁰ Then Jonathan gave his equipment to the servant who was with him and said, "Go, take it back to the city."

⁴¹ When the servant had gone, David got up from the south side of the stone Ezel, fell facedown to the ground, and paid homage three times. Then he and Jonathan kissed each other and wept with each other, though David wept more.

⁴² Jonathan then said to David, "Go in the assurance the two of us pledged in the name of the LORD when we said, 'The LORD will be a witness between you and me and between my offspring and your offspring forever.'" Then David left, and Jonathan went into the city.

David Flees to Nob

21 David went to the priest Ahimelech at Nob. Ahimelech was afraid to meet David, so he said to him, "Why are you alone and no one is with you?"

² David answered the priest Ahimelech, "The king gave me a mission, but he told me, 'Don't let anyone know anything about the mission I'm sending you on or what I have ordered you to do.' I have stationed my young men at a certain place. ³ Now what do you have on hand? Give me five loaves of bread or whatever can be found."

⁴ The priest told him, "There is no ordinary bread on hand. However, there is consecrated bread, but the young men may eat it^A only if they have kept themselves from women."

⁵ David answered him, "I swear that women are being kept from us, as always when I go out to battle. The young men's bodies^B are consecrated even on an ordinary mission, so of course their bodies are consecrated today." ⁶ So the priest gave him the consecrated bread, for there was no bread there except the Bread of the Presence that had been removed from the presence of the LORD. When the bread was removed, it had been replaced with warm bread.

⁷ One of Saul's servants, detained before the LORD, was there that day. His name was Doeg the Edomite, chief of Saul's shepherds.

⁸ David said to Ahimelech, "Do you have a spear or sword on hand? I didn't even bring my sword or my weapons since the king's mission was urgent."

⁹ The priest replied, "The sword of Goliath the Philistine, whom you killed in the Valley of Elah, is here, wrapped in a cloth behind the ephod. If you want to take it for yourself, then take it, for there isn't another one here."

"There's none like it!" David said. "Give it to me."

David Flees to Gath

¹⁰ David fled that day from Saul's presence and went to King Achish of Gath. ¹¹ But Achish's servants said to him, "Isn't this David, the king of the land? Don't they sing about him during their dances:

Saul has killed his thousands,
     but David his tens of thousands?"

¹² David took this to heart and became very afraid of King Achish of Gath, ¹³ so he pretended to be insane in their presence. He acted like a madman around them,^C scribbling^D on the doors of the city gate and letting saliva run down his beard.

¹⁴ "Look! You can see the man is crazy," Achish said to his servants. "Why did you bring

---

^A 21:4 DSS; MT omits *may eat it*   ^B 21:5 Lit *vessels*   ^C 21:13 Lit *madman in their hand*   ^D 21:13 LXX reads *drumming*

20:40 Though the coded signal had been sent and Jonathan could have departed, perhaps he could not bear to leave without talking with David first, so he sent the **servant** away. The yearning for a personal farewell led them to abandon the caution afforded them by their system of signals.
20:41 David's position shows the **stone Ezel** probably lay south of Gibeah, so that when Jonathan came out with his servant, they would not immediately see him. David **payed homage** (bowed) **three times** as a sign of his respect and admiration for Jonathan, and they **kissed each other**—a common sign of greeting and farewell among close friends in that culture. They wept because both sensed they might not see each other again.
20:42 Go in the assurance is literally "Go in peace."
21:1 Ahimelech is mentioned for the first time here; some identify him with Ahijah (14:3). **Nob** lay approximately two miles south of Gibeah. Ahimelech was **afraid**,

probably because he had heard of Saul's pursuit of David, a fact that would explain his questioning of David.
21:2 Though David said that the king had given him **a mission**, Saul in fact had not. David did not want to reveal his real circumstances to Ahimelech, lest Saul accuse the priest of aiding a fugitive (22:13).
21:3–4 Consecrated bread, also known as the "Bread of the Presence" (v. 6), came from the tabernacle where twelve loaves representing Israel's twelve tribes were exchanged weekly (Lv 24:5–9). Normally only priests ate this bread, but Ahimelech was willing to share it with ordinary soldiers if they were not ceremonially unclean due to sexual relations (Lv 15:18).
21:5–6 Jesus referred to this account in condemning the religious leaders for their rigid interpretation of the Mosaic law (Mt 12:1–4).
21:7 Perhaps **Doeg the Edomite** was a captive servant of Saul after Saul's campaign against Edom (14:47).

21:8–9 The text does not explain how the sword of Goliath ended up in the tabernacle when David had earlier put it in his own tent (17:54).
21:10 The leading Philistine city, **Gath**, was located at the mouth of the Valley of Elah (17:1). **King Achish** ruled there, seemingly as chief among the Philistine lords (27:2–7; 29:2–4). David probably **fled** from Saul by going westward into the Sorek Valley to Beth-shemesh (6:9,12–13), then along a diagonal highway that connected Judah's valleys to Azekah (17:1). From there he could proceed down the Valley of Elah.
21:12 David became **afraid** when he realized how much the Philistines knew about him.
21:13 In the ancient world, insane people were considered afflicted by the gods and generally left alone. David's letting **saliva run down his beard** brought further disgrace and confirmation of his affliction to Achish (Nm 12:14; Dt 25:9; Jb 17:6; 30:10).

him to me? ¹⁵ Do I have such a shortage of crazy people that you brought this one to act crazy around me? Is this one going to come into my house?"

Saul's Increasing Paranoia

22 So David left Gath and took refuge in the cave of Adullam. When David's brothers and his father's whole family heard, they went down and joined him there. ² In addition, every man who was desperate, in debt, or discontented rallied around him, and he became their leader. About four hundred men were with him.

³ From there David went to Mizpeh of Moab where he said to the king of Moab, "Please let my father and mother stay with you until I know what God will do for me." ⁴ So he left them in the care of the king of Moab, and they stayed with him the whole time David was in the stronghold.

⁵ Then the prophet Gad said to David, "Don't stay in the stronghold. Leave and return to the land of Judah." So David left and went to the forest of Hereth.

⁶ Saul heard that David and his men had been discovered. At that time Saul was in Gibeah, sitting under the tamarisk tree at the high place. His spear was in his hand, and all his servants were standing around him. ⁷ Saul said to his servants, "Listen, men of Benjamin: Is Jesse's son going to give all of you fields and vineyards? Do you think he'll make all of you commanders of thousands and commanders of hundreds? ⁸ That's why all of you have conspired against me! Nobody tells me when my own son makes a covenant with Jesse's son. None of you cares about me or tells me that my son has stirred up my own servant to wait in ambush for me, as is the case today."

⁹ Then Doeg the Edomite, who was in charge of Saul's servants, answered, "I saw Jesse's son come to Ahimelech son of Ahitub at Nob. ¹⁰ Ahimelech inquired of the LORD for him and gave him provisions. He also gave him the sword of Goliath the Philistine."

Slaughter of the Priests

¹¹ The king sent messengers to summon the priest Ahimelech son of Ahitub, and his father's whole family, who were priests in Nob. All of them came to the king. ¹² Then Saul said, "Listen, son of Ahitub!"

"I'm at your service, my lord," he said.

¹³ Saul asked him, "Why did you and Jesse's son conspire against me? You gave him bread and a sword and inquired of God for him, so he could rise up against me and wait in ambush, as is the case today."

¹⁴ Ahimelech replied to the king, "Who among all your servants is as faithful as David? He is the king's son-in-law, captain of your bodyguard, and honored in your house. ¹⁵ Was today the first time I inquired of God for him? Of course not! Please don't let the king make an accusation against your servant or any of my father's family, for your servant didn't have any ideaᴬ about all this."

¹⁶ But the king said, "You will die, Ahimelech — you and your father's whole family!"

¹⁷ Then the king ordered the guards standing by him, "Turn and kill the priests of the LORD because they sided with David. For they knew he was fleeing, but they didn't tell me." But the king's servants would not lift a hand to execute the priests of the LORD.

¹⁸ So the king said to Doeg, "Go and execute the priests!" So Doeg the Edomite went and executed the priests himself. On that day, he killed eighty-five men who wore linen ephods. ¹⁹ He also struck down Nob, the city of the priests, with the sword — both men and women, infants and nursing babies, oxen, donkeys, and sheep.

²⁰ However, one of the sons of Ahimelech son of Ahitub escaped. His name was Abiathar,

---

ᴬ22:15 Lit *didn't know a thing, small or large*

21:14–15 Achish's statement **Do I have . . . a shortage of crazy people** probably was intended sarcastically, though other people with unusual physical features were also associated with Gath (17:4; 2Sm 21:20).
22:1 **Adullam** was located east of Socoh (17:1), approximately ten miles into the Valley of Elah. David's retreat thus moved him back into Saul's territory. Probably David's **brothers and his father's whole family** met him in the **cave** because they feared Saul's reprisal against them.
22:2 Discontentment with the status quo under Saul influenced many people to join forces with David. See 1Ch 12:16–18.
22:3 The exact location of **Mizpeh of Moab** is unknown, though the book of Ruth documents David's ancestral connections there (Ru 4:17–22).
22:4 The **king of Moab** may have been gracious to David because of his ancestral connections (Ru 1:4; 4:17–22) and as a favor to another enemy of Saul. **The stronghold**

probably designates Mizpeh of Moab (v. 3), since the next verse suggests it was not in Judah.
22:5 **Gad** had contact with David at key points in his life (2Sm 24:11–14; 1Ch 29:29). **Land of Judah** probably designates Judah's hill country, since Adullam was also part of Judah.
22:8 The king's words **my son has stirred up my own servant to wait in ambush for me** could not have been further from the truth; Jonathan, though he loved David, would later die fighting alongside his father (31:2).
22:9 **Doeg the Edomite** (21:7) now revealed he had seen David at **Nob**.
22:11–13 Saul's question assumed that Ahimelech was guilty of conspiracy. The king made no attempt to investigate the matter thoroughly.
22:14 Ahimelech's rhetorical question to the king implied no one was **as faithful as David**, a suggestion Saul already had heard

from Jonathan (19:4–5) and did not want to hear again.
22:16 Saul ignored Ahimelech's words and passed the death sentence on the priest's entire household, a decree that further revealed his obsession to kill David.
22:17 Even **the king's servants**—probably his most trusted soldiers—**would not . . . execute the priests** because it was unclear if they were guilty of anything worthy of death.
22:18–19 Though Saul disobeyed God's command to put the Amalekites under the ban (15:9), he effectively puts the Israelite priests at Nob under the ban. The sentence is carried out by a non-Israelite, **Doeg the Edomite.** Eighty-five priests died, along with every other living thing in Nob, because of Saul's misguided wrath.
22:20 **Abiathar** may have caught up with David at Keilah (23:6). He would later serve as priest before David (2Sm 20:25), though he did support Adonijah, David's oldest son,

and he fled to David. [21] Abiathar told David that Saul had killed the priests of the LORD. [22] Then David said to Abiathar, "I knew that Doeg the Edomite was there that day and that he was sure to report to Saul. I myself am responsible for[A] the lives of everyone in your father's family. [23] Stay with me. Don't be afraid, for the one who wants to take my life wants to take your life. You will be safe with me."

Deliverance at Keilah

23 It was reported to David, "Look, the Philistines are fighting against Keilah and raiding the threshing floors."

[2] So David inquired of the LORD: "Should I launch an attack against these Philistines?"

The LORD answered David, "Launch an attack against the Philistines and rescue Keilah."

[3] But David's men said to him, "Look, we're afraid here in Judah; how much more if we go to Keilah against the Philistine forces!"

[4] Once again, David inquired of the LORD, and the LORD answered him, "Go at once to Keilah, for I will hand the Philistines over to you." [5] Then David and his men went to Keilah, fought against the Philistines, drove their livestock away, and inflicted heavy losses on them. So David rescued the inhabitants of Keilah. [6] Abiathar son of Ahimelech fled to David at Keilah, and he brought an ephod with him.

[7] When it was reported to Saul that David had gone to Keilah, he said, "God has handed him over to me, for he has trapped himself by entering a town with barred gates." [8] Then Saul summoned all the troops to go to war at Keilah and besiege David and his men.

[9] When David learned that Saul was plotting evil against him, he said to the priest Abiathar, "Bring the ephod."

[10] Then David said, "LORD God of Israel, your servant has reliable information that Saul intends to come to Keilah and destroy the town

because of me. [11] Will the citizens of Keilah hand me over to him? Will Saul come down as your servant has heard? LORD God of Israel, please tell your servant."

The LORD answered, "He will come down."

[12] Then David asked, "Will the citizens of Keilah hand me and my men over to Saul?"

"They will," the LORD responded.

[13] So David and his men, numbering about six hundred, left Keilah at once and moved from place to place. When it was reported to Saul that David had escaped from Keilah, he called off the expedition. [14] David then stayed in the wilderness strongholds and in the hill country of the Wilderness of Ziph. Saul searched for him every day, but God did not hand David over to him.

A Renewed Covenant

[15] David was in the Wilderness of Ziph in Horesh when he saw that Saul had come out to take his life. [16] Then Saul's son Jonathan came to David in Horesh and encouraged him in his faith[B] in God, [17] saying, "Don't be afraid, for my father Saul will never lay a hand on you. You yourself will be king over Israel, and I'll be your second-in-command. Even my father Saul knows it is true." [18] Then the two of them made a covenant in the LORD's presence. Afterward, David remained in Horesh, while Jonathan went home.

David's Narrow Escape

[19] Some Ziphites came up to Saul at Gibeah and said, "Isn't it true that David is hiding among us in the strongholds in Horesh on the hill of Hachilah south of Jeshimon? [20] So now, whenever the king wants to come down, let him come down. As for us, we will be glad to hand him over to the king."

[21] "May you be blessed by the LORD," replied Saul, "for you have shown concern for me. [22] Go

---

[A]22:22 LXX, Syr, Vg; MT reads *I myself turn in* [B]23:16 Lit *and strengthened his hand*

---

when Adonijah tried to take the throne without David's blessing (1Kg 1:7; 2:26–27).
22:23 David suggested that he and Abiathar could trust each other because they had a common enemy (Saul) from whom they needed to protect themselves. Thus David aligned himself with the priests of the Lord, even as Saul further alienated himself from God.
23:1 Keilah was a town of Judah located about two miles south of Adullam. **Raiding the threshing floors** meant the Philistines were waiting until Keilah's citizens had harvested and threshed their grain; then they stole it from them.
23:2–4 God's instructions to **launch an attack against the Philistines** seemed too dangerous to David's men, who apparently felt that having one enemy, Saul, was risky enough. David's second inquiry confirmed God's command to rescue Keilah. **Go at once** is literally "Arise, go down," indicating David was probably still at the forest of Hereth

(22:5) or even higher into the Judean hill country.
23:5 David and his men **drove their livestock away** either to keep the cattle from eating all the grain on the threshing floors or to keep the **Philistines** from using them to carry off Israelite plunder.
23:7 Saul saw an opportunity to kill David because the town's **barred gates** would prevent his escape.
23:8 Saul's strategy was probably to **besiege** Keilah in the hope that its citizens would hand David over to avoid destruction (v. 12).
23:11–12 Through David's inquiry, the Lord warned him that **the citizens of Keilah** would deliver him **over to Saul**, just as Saul had calculated (v. 8).
23:13 The number of David's sympathizers had grown by 50 percent (22:2). Perhaps Saul **called off the expedition** because he was reluctant to conduct a lengthy military campaign in Judah, David's own tribal territory.

23:14 The **Wilderness of Ziph** (Jos 15:55) was located about four and one-half miles southeast of Hebron, deep in Judah's hill country. **Wilderness strongholds** offered David high vantage points from which his watchmen could detect Saul's approach.
23:15 Horesh means "wooded height," but its exact location is unknown.
23:16 Somehow, perhaps through Saul's intelligence reports, Jonathan knew David's whereabouts. Jonathan **came to David** and **encouraged him in his faith** (lit "strengthened his hand") **in God**.
23:17 Jonathan's words were partly correct because David would indeed be **king over Israel**. Jonathan, despite his humble willingness, would never become David's **second-in-command** because he would die in battle (31:2).
23:19–20 The **Ziphites** informed Saul of David's position in their territory and offered to **hand him over to the king**. Perhaps these Judahites feared Saul might do to them what

and check again. Investigate[A] where he goes[B] and who has seen him there; they tell me he is extremely cunning. [23] Investigate[C] all the places where he hides. Then come back to me with accurate information, and I'll go with you. If it turns out he really is in the region, I'll search for him among all the clans[D] of Judah." [24] So they went to Ziph ahead of Saul.

Now David and his men were in the wilderness near Maon in the Arabah south of Jeshimon, [25] and Saul and his men went to look for him. When David was told about it, he went down to the rock and stayed in the Wilderness of Maon. Saul heard of this and pursued David there.

[26] Saul went along one side of the mountain and David and his men went along the other side. Even though David was hurrying to get away from Saul, Saul and his men were closing in on David and his men to capture them. [27] Then a messenger came to Saul saying, "Come quickly, because the Philistines have raided the land!" [28] So Saul broke off his pursuit of David and went to engage the Philistines. Therefore, that place was named the Rock of Separation. [29] From there David went up and stayed in the strongholds of En-gedi.

David Spares Saul

24 When Saul returned from pursuing the Philistines, he was told, "David is in the wilderness near En-gedi." [2] So Saul took three thousand of Israel's fit young men and went to look for David and his men in front of the Rocks of the Wild Goats. [3] When Saul came to the sheep pens along the road, a cave was there, and he went in to relieve himself.[E] David and his men were staying in the recesses of the cave, [4] so they said to him, "Look, this is the day the LORD told you about: 'I will hand your enemy over to you so you can do to him whatever you desire.'" Then David got up and secretly cut off the corner of Saul's robe.

[5] Afterward, David's conscience bothered[F] him because he had cut off the corner of Saul's robe.[G] [6] He said to his men, "As the LORD is my witness, I would never do such a thing to my lord, the LORD's anointed. I will never lift

my hand against him, since he is the LORD's anointed." [7] With these words David persuaded[H] his men, and he did not let them rise up against Saul.

Then Saul left the cave and went on his way. [8] After that, David got up, went out of the cave, and called to Saul, "My lord the king!" When Saul looked behind him, David knelt low with his face to the ground and paid homage. [9] David said to Saul, "Why do you listen to the words of people who say, 'Look, David intends to harm you'? [10] You can see with your own eyes that the LORD handed you over to me today in the cave. Someone advised me to kill you, but I[I] took pity on you and said: I won't lift my hand against my lord, since he is the LORD's anointed. [11] Look, my father! Look at the corner of your robe in my hand, for I cut it off, but I didn't kill you. Recognize[A] that I've committed no crime or rebellion. I haven't sinned against you even though you are hunting me down to take my life.

[12] "May the LORD judge between me and you, and may the LORD take vengeance on you for me, but my hand will never be against you. [13] As the old proverb says, 'Wickedness comes from wicked people.' My hand will never be against you. [14] Who has the king of Israel come after? What are you chasing after? A dead dog? A single flea? [15] May the LORD be judge and decide between you and me. May he take notice and plead my case and deliver[K] me from you."

[16] When David finished saying these things to him, Saul replied, "Is that your voice, David my son?" Then Saul wept aloud [17] and said to David, "You are more righteous than I, for you have done what is good to me though I have done what is evil to you. [18] You yourself have told me today what good you did for me: when the LORD handed me over to you, you didn't kill me. [19] When a man finds his enemy, does he let him go unharmed?[L] May the LORD repay you with good for what you've done for me today. [20] "Now I know for certain you will be king, and the kingdom of Israel will be established[M] in your hand. [21] Therefore swear to me by the LORD that you will not cut off my descendants or wipe out my name from my father's family."

^23:22; 24:11 Lit Know and see   [B]23:22 Lit watch his place where his foot will be   [C]23:23 Lit See and know   [D]23:23 Or thousands   [E]24:3 Lit to cover his feet   [F]24:5 Lit David's heart struck   [G]24:5 Some Hb mss, LXX, Syr, Vg; other Hb mss omit robe   [H]24:7 Or restrained   [I]24:10 LXX, Syr, Tg; MT reads she or it   [J]24:10 Or my eye   [K]24:15 Lit render a verdict for   [L]24:19 Lit go on a good way   [M]24:20 Or will flourish

he had done at Nob (22:18–19) and what he had considered doing at Keilah (23:7–8).
23:24 David and his men had moved near Maon five miles south. Arabah means a desert or wilderness area with sparse vegetation, yet enough to sustain those accustomed to the life of a shepherd.
23:27–28 Saul's desire to pursue David deep into the Judean wilderness gave the Philistines the opportunity to push into Israel's heartland again. Israel's enemies were capitalizing on Saul's internal troubles.

23:29 Located about fifteen miles northeast of the Wilderness of Maon near the Dead Sea's north-south midpoint, En-gedi provided David's men with shelter and spring water.
24:1 The phrase returned from pursuing the Philistines probably means Saul pushed them back down into their territory and secured Israel's border again.
24:2–3 Two Davidic psalms have as their setting this event when David hid in a cave. His true refuge was in the Lord (Pss 57:1; 142:5–6).

24:13 To illustrate he was not wicked because he had spared Saul's life when he could have killed him, David cited what was probably a well-known saying at the time—Wickedness comes from wicked people (cp. Pr 18:3).
24:14 By comparing himself to a dead dog or a single flea, David suggested that Saul was squandering precious manpower and resources. David was not worth going after since he was a loyal subject.
24:21 Saul asked David not to cut off his descendants or wipe out his name.

²² So David swore to Saul. Then Saul went back home, and David and his men went up to the stronghold.

David, Nabal, and Abigail

25 Samuel died, and all Israel assembled to mourn for him, and they buried him by his home in Ramah. David then went down to the Wilderness of Paran.ᴬ ² A man in Maon had a business in Carmel; he was a very rich man with three thousand sheep and one thousand goats and was shearing his sheep in Carmel. ³ The man's name was Nabal, and his wife's name, Abigail. The woman was intelligent and beautiful, but the man, a Calebite, was harsh and evil in his dealings.

⁴ While David was in the wilderness, he heard that Nabal was shearing sheep, ⁵ so David sent ten young men instructing them, "Go up to Carmel, and when you come to Nabal, greet himᴮ in my name. ⁶ Then say this: 'Long life to you,ᶜ and peace to you, peace to your family, and peace to all that is yours. ⁷ I hear that you are shearing.ᴰ When your shepherds were with us, we did not harass them, and nothing of theirs was missing the whole time they were in Carmel. ⁸ Ask your young men, and they will tell you. So let my young men find favor with you, for we have come on a feastᴱ day. Please give whatever you have on hand to your servants and to your son David.'"

⁹ David's young men went and said all these things to Nabal on David's behalf,ᶠ and they waited.ᴳ ¹⁰ Nabal asked them, "Who is David? Who is Jesse's son? Many slaves these days are running away from their masters. ¹¹ Am I supposed to take my bread, my water, and my meat that I butchered for my shearers and give them to these men? I don't know where they are from."

¹² David's young men retraced their steps. When they returned to him, they reported all these words. ¹³ He said to his men, "All of you, put on your swords!" So each man put on his sword, and David also put on his sword. About four hundred men followed David while two hundred stayed with the supplies.

¹⁴ One of Nabal's young men informed Abigail, Nabal's wife, "Look, David sent messengers from the wilderness to greet our master, but he screamed at them. ¹⁵ The men treated us very well. When we were in the field, we weren't harassed and nothing of ours was missing the whole time we were living among them. ¹⁶ They were a wall around us, both day and night, the entire time we were with them herding the sheep. ¹⁷ Now consider carefullyᴴ what you should do, because there is certain to be trouble for our master and his entire family. He is such a worthless fool nobody can talk to him!"

¹⁸ Abigail hurried, taking two hundred loaves of bread, two clay jars of wine, five butchered sheep, a bushelᴵ of roasted grain, one hundred clusters of raisins, and two hundred cakes of pressed figs, and loaded them on donkeys. ¹⁹ Then she said to her male servants, "Go ahead of me. I will be right behind you." But she did not tell her husband, Nabal.

²⁰ As she rode the donkey down a mountain pass hidden from view, she saw David and his men coming toward her and met them. ²¹ David had just said, "I guarded everything that belonged to this man in the wilderness for nothing. He was not missing anything, yet he paid me back evil for good. ²² May God punish meᴶ and do so severely if I let any of his malesᴷ survive until morning."

²³ When Abigail saw David, she quickly got off the donkey and knelt down with her face to the ground and paid homage to David. ²⁴ She knelt at his feet and said, "The guilt is mine, my lord, but please let your servant speak to you directly. Listen to the words of your servant. ²⁵ My lord should pay no attention to this worthless fool Nabal, for he lives up to his name:ᴸ His name means 'stupid,' and stupidity is all he knows.ᴹ I, your servant, didn't see my lord's young men whom you sent. ²⁶ Now my lord, as surely as the Lᴏʀᴅ lives and as you yourself live— it is the Lᴏʀᴅ who kept you from participating in bloodshed and avenging yourself by your own hand—may your enemies and those who intend to harm my lord be like Nabal. ²⁷ Let this gift your servant has

---

ᴬ25:1 LXX reads to Maon ᴮ25:5 Or Nabal, ask him for peace ᶜ25:6 Lit 'To life ᴰ25:7 Lit you have shearers ᴱ25:8 Lit good ᶠ25:9 Lit name ᴳ25:9 LXX reads and he became arrogant ᴴ25:17 Lit Now know and see ᴵ25:18 Lit sheep, five seahs ᴶ25:22 LXX; MT reads David's enemies ᴷ25:22 Lit of those of his who are urinating against the wall ᴸ25:25 Lit for as is his name is, so he is ᴹ25:25 Lit and foolishness is with him

---

Succeeding kings often did this to eliminate potential rivals or family reprisals (1Kg 15:29; 16:11).
25:1 Samuel's death marked the end of a significant era for **all Israel**. His faithful leadership helped the nation make the transition from theocracy to monarchy. The **Wilderness of Paran** (Gn 21:21; Nm 10:12; 13:3) lay beyond Judah's southern edge.
25:2–3 Maon and **Carmel** were only about a mile apart on the edge of the Judean wilderness. **Nabal**, whose name means "stupid"

(v. 25), was descended from Joshua's friend Caleb (Nm 14:6–9; Jos 14:6–14).
25:4 Shearing sheep was normally a festive occasion (Gn 38:12) since wool was a valuable commodity (2Kg 3:4).
25:5–6 That David **sent ten young men** suggests that he was expecting a considerable amount to be provided.
25:20 Since Abigail descended through **a mountain pass hidden from view**, she may have thought it all the more important to let David know she was coming.

25:21–22 David was so disgusted with Nabal that he did not even mention his name. He referred to him as **this man**, a translation of one Hebrew syllable (zeh). When David expected gratitude and hospitality, he received insults. Consequently, David had vowed to kill all the men in Nabal's household.
25:25–26 Though Abigail referred to her husband as **worthless**, she interceded with David to save his life. She diplomatically suggested she was the Lord's agent in heading

brought to my lord be given to the young men who follow my lord. **²⁸** Please forgive your servant's offense, for the LORD is certain to make a lasting dynasty for my lord because he fights the LORD's battles. Throughout your life, may evil^ not be found in you.

²⁹ "Someone is pursuing you and intends to take your life. My lord's life is tucked safely in the place³ where the LORD your God protects the living, but he is flinging away your enemies' lives like stones from a sling. **³⁰** When the LORD does for my lord all the good he promised you and appoints you ruler over Israel, **³¹** there will not be remorse or a troubled conscience for my lord because of needless bloodshed or my lord's revenge. And when the LORD does good things for my lord, may you remember me your servant."

³² Then David said to Abigail, "Blessed be the LORD God of Israel, who sent you to meet me today! **³³** May your discernment be blessed, and may you be blessed. Today you kept me from participating in bloodshed and

avenging myself by my own hand. **³⁴** Otherwise, as surely as the LORD God of Israel lives, who prevented me from harming you, if you had not come quickly to meet me, Nabal wouldn't have had any males^c left by morning light." **³⁵** Then David accepted what she had brought him and said, "Go home in peace. See, I have heard what you said and have granted your request."

³⁶ Then Abigail went to Nabal, and there he was in his house, holding a feast fit for a king. Nabal's heart was cheerful,ᴰ and he was very drunk, so she didn't say anythingᴱ to him until morning light. **³⁷** In the morning when Nabal sobered up,ᶠ his wife told him about these events. His heart diedᴳ and he became a stone. **³⁸** About ten days later, the LORD struck Nabal dead.

³⁹ When David heard that Nabal was dead, he said, "Blessed be the LORD who championed my cause against Nabal's insults and restrained his servant from doing evil. The LORD brought Nabal's evil deeds back on his own head."

---

^**25:28** Or *trouble* ᴮ**25:29** Lit *bundle* ᶜ**25:34** Lit *had anyone urinating against a wall* ᴰ**25:36** Lit *Nabal's heart was good on him* ᴱ**25:36** Lit *anything at all* ᶠ**25:37** Lit *when the wine had gone out of Nabal* ᴳ**25:37** Lit *Then his heart died within him*

---

off needless **bloodshed**, the act of which might bring guilt on David and serious damage to his reputation in Israel.
25:28 The expression **your servant's offense** refers to Abigail, not to Nabal, and it designates a serious transgression. Again, she took responsibility for Nabal's sin even as she spoke of what she saw as David's future—**a lasting dynasty**. Perhaps Abigail implied **the LORD's battles** should not include a skirmish with Nabal.

25:29 Some interpreters believe the expression **tucked safely in the place** may designate the Book of Life (Php 4:3; Rv 3:5; 22:19), but the expression at least denotes God's sovereign protection of his righteous ones. The imagery of God flinging away David's enemies **like stones from a sling** was well chosen in light of David's famed use of a sling against Goliath (17:49–51).
25:36 Nabal's drunken state showed that he had no idea how much danger he faced

barring Abigail's intervention. The phrase **until morning light** refers to the time by which he and his servants would have been killed (v. 34).
25:37–38 Nabal's **heart died and he became a stone** probably means that he had a seizure and became paralyzed.
25:39 David praised the Lord for two things: (1) intervening for him and (2) protecting him **from doing evil**. In the final analysis, God brought judgment against Nabal.

Character profile:
Abigail

We learn in Scripture that Abigail was "intelligent and beautiful" and married to a wealthy man (1Sm 25:2–3). Yet her life was not as wonderful as it might appear.

Her husband's name was Nabal, which means "fool." Some Bible students think Nabal was simply a nickname, since he is described as one who "was harsh and evil in his dealings" (25:3). With that kind of reputation, it's not hard to imagine that clients and neighbors would pin this label on him. What must it have been like to live with him?

We wouldn't even know about this couple if it weren't for a fateful encounter with David, Israel's famous warrior and king-in-waiting. It unfolded like this: Nabal happened to be shearing some sheep close to where David and his men were camped. When David heard Nabal was in the neighborhood, he sent his men to ask a favor.

David's request went something like this: "Food is scarce out here in the wilderness. Do you think that, in light of the way we've always treated you with respect and even protected your shepherds and flocks, you might be willing to give my hungry men a meal?"

However, Nabal not only scoffed at David's men who delivered the message, but he also heaped insults on them as they departed. In just a few foolish moments, Nabal violated every rule of Middle Eastern hospitality. When David's men reported this humiliating exchange, David was livid: "All of you, put on your swords!" (25:13)

Things would have gotten ugly, but one of Nabal's servants explained to Abigail what had happened. He blurted out the

ugly truth about Nabal (which Abigail no doubt knew all too well): "He is such a worthless fool nobody can talk to him!" (25:17)

The intelligent and now frightened Abigail swung into action. She quickly gathered food for David's men, sent the feast ahead via servants, and then went to see if she could avert a bloodbath.

She intercepted David just in time. Falling humbly at his feet, Abigail acknowledged her husband's arrogance and pleaded for David to show mercy. In effect, she entreated David not to descend to the level of her foolish husband. David's heart was pierced by Abigail's wise warning. He called off his attack, acknowledging that she had kept him from needless bloodshed.

Meanwhile, Abigail returned home to find her obnoxious husband stuffing his face and drunk. Little did he know how close he'd come to meeting his Maker. When Abigail told him the next day what had happened, "his heart died and he became a stone" (25:37)—likely, he had a stroke. Ten days later, he died. After hearing about Nabal's death, David sent one of his men to Abigail to propose marriage.

Abigail reminds us that nobody has it all together. The perfect, ideal life is an imaginary life. It doesn't exist. Even the people who seem to have it all together have struggles and problems. As we ponder Abigail's story, two warnings are in order.

First, be careful about comparing yourself with others and wishing you had someone else's life. You don't really know what goes on in the hearts and homes of other people. Second, be kind. Unless we're like Nabal, we will always look back and regret being harsh. We will never regret showing mercy and compassion toward others.

Then David sent messengers to speak to Abigail about marrying him. **⁴⁰** When David's servants came to Abigail at Carmel, they said to her, "David sent us to bring you to him as a wife."

⁴¹ She stood up, paid homage with her face to the ground, and said, "Here I am, your servant, a slave to wash the feet of my lord's servants." **⁴²** Then Abigail got up quickly, and with her five female servants accompanying her, rode on the donkey following David's messengers. And so she became his wife.

⁴³ David also married Ahinoam of Jezreel, and the two of them became his wives. **⁴⁴** But Saul gave his daughter Michal, David's wife, to Palti son of Laish, who was from Gallim.

David Again Spares Saul

26 Then the Ziphites came to Saul at Gibeah saying, "David is hiding on the hill of Hachilah opposite Jeshimon." **²** So Saul, accompanied by three thousand of the fit young men of Israel, went immediately to the Wilderness of Ziph to search for David there. **³** Saul camped beside the road at the hill of Hachilah opposite Jeshimon. David was living in the wilderness and discovered Saul had come there after him. **⁴** So David sent out spies and knew for certain that Saul had come. **⁵** Immediately, David went to the place where Saul had camped. He saw the place where Saul and Abner son of Ner, the commander of his army, were lying down. Saul was lying inside the inner circle of the camp with the troops camped around him. **⁶** Then David asked Ahimelech the Hethite and Joab's brother Abishai son of Zeruiah, "Who will go with me into the camp to Saul?"

"I'll go with you," answered Abishai.

⁷ That night, David and Abishai came to the troops, and Saul was lying there asleep in the inner circle of the camp with his spear stuck in the ground by his head. Abner and the troops were lying around him. **⁸** Then Abishai said to David, "Today God has delivered your enemy to you. Let me thrust the spear through him

into the ground just once. I won't have to strike him twice!"

⁹ But David said to Abishai, "Don't destroy him, for who can lift a hand against the LORD's anointed and be innocent?" **¹⁰** David added, "As the LORD lives, the LORD will certainly strike him down: either his day will come and he will die, or he will go into battle and perish. **¹¹** However, as the LORD is my witness, I will never lift my hand against the LORD's anointed. Instead, take the spear and the water jug by his head, and let's go."

¹² So David took the spear and the water jug by Saul's head, and they went their way. No one saw them, no one knew, and no one woke up; they all remained asleep because a deep sleep from the LORD came over them. **¹³** David crossed to the other side and stood on top of the mountain at a distance; there was a considerable space between them. **¹⁴** Then David shouted to the troops and to Abner son of Ner, "Aren't you going to answer, Abner?"

"Who are you who calls to the king?" Abner asked.

¹⁵ David called to Abner, "You're a man, aren't you? Who in Israel is your equal? So why didn't you protect your lord the king when one of the people came to destroy him? **¹⁶** What you have done is not good. As the LORD lives, all of you deserve to die^A since you didn't protect your lord, the LORD's anointed. Now look around; where are the king's spear and water jug that were by his head?"

¹⁷ Saul recognized David's voice and asked, "Is that your voice, my son David?"

"It is my voice, my lord and king," David said. **¹⁸** Then he continued, "Why is my lord pursuing his servant? What have I done? What crime have I committed? **¹⁹** Now, may my lord the king please hear the words of his servant: If it is the LORD who has incited you against me, then may he accept an offering. But if it is people, may they be cursed in the presence of the LORD, for today they have banished me from sharing in the inheritance of the LORD, saying, 'Go and

---

^A **26:16** Lit *you are sons of death*

25:42 Marrying Abigail gave David control of a sizable estate in Judah and gained him valuable resources for his cause.

25:43 The biblical text says about **Ahinoam of Jezreel** only that she bore Amnon, David's firstborn (2Sm 3:2). Jezreel probably designates the Judahite city (Jos 15:56), not the more famous city in the Jezreel Valley.

25:44 The text does not clarify whether Saul gave his daughter **Michal**, who was already **David's wife** (18:27), to another man at her request or as punishment for her support of David against her father (19:17).

26:1–5 The **Ziphites came to Saul at Gibeah** with a report that David had returned to his earlier hiding place in Judah. If Saul was on the **hill of Hachilah**, it would mean he had chosen high ground for his camp, which provided him better protection.

David's **place** (v. 5) designates a safe vantage point from which David could see Saul and Abner **inside the inner circle of the camp**. **Abner** was Saul's uncle, the brother of Saul's father.

26:6 **Ahimelech** is described as a **Hethite** (i.e., foreigner), but his name is Hebrew or at least related to Hebrew. **Joab's brother Abishai** is introduced here; he would play an active role in David's kingship (2Sm 10:10; 18:2–3; 23:18). On **Zeruiah**, see note at 2Sm 2:18. **Go** is literally "go down," implying David was at a higher point than Saul and thus at an advantage.

26:11 The **spear** and the **water jug** would provide evidence that again David had been close enough to kill Saul.

26:13–14 The words **on top of the mountain at a distance** means this was a safe

distance from Saul, but it provided good acoustics so David could call **to the king**.

26:15 The phrase **one of the people came to destroy him** may refer to Abishai, who wanted to destroy Saul (v. 8), or hypothetically to **David** himself, who could have destroyed Saul as he stood over him.

26:16–19 David could identify only two sources of Saul's desire to kill him—**the LORD** or the **people**. If the Lord, David wanted Saul to allow him to sacrifice a freewill **offering** to restore the broken fellowship between himself, God, and Saul. But if people had falsely accused him, David called on them to **be cursed**.

26:20 David compared himself to a **single flea** (24:14) or a **partridge** to suggest Saul's pursuit of him was a waste of resources.

worship other gods.' ²⁰ So don't let my blood fall to the ground far from the LORD's presence, for the king of Israel has come out to search for a single flea, like one who pursues a partridge in the mountains."

²¹ Saul responded, "I have sinned. Come back, my son David, I will never harm you again because today you considered my life precious. I have been a fool! I've committed a grave error."

²² David answered, "Here is the king's spear; have one of the young men come over and get it. ²³ The LORD will repay every man for his righteousness and his loyalty. I wasn't willing to lift my hand against the LORD's anointed, even though the LORD handed you over to me today. ²⁴ Just as I considered your life valuable today, so may the LORD consider my life valuable and rescue me from all trouble."

²⁵ Saul said to him, "You are blessed, my son David. You will certainly do great things and will also prevail." Then David went on his way, and Saul returned home.

David Flees to Ziklag

27 David said to himself, "One of these days I'll be swept away by Saul. There is nothing better for me than to escape immediately to the land of the Philistines. Then Saul will give up searching for me everywhere in Israel, and I'll escape from him." ² So David set out with his six hundred men and went over to Achish son of Maoch, the king of Gath. ³ David and his men stayed with Achish in Gath. Each man had his family with him, and David had his two wives: Ahinoam of Jezreel and Abigail of Carmel, Nabal's widow. ⁴ When it was reported to Saul that David had fled to Gath, he no longer searched for him.

⁵ Now David said to Achish, "If I have found favor with you, let me be given a place in one of the outlying towns, so I can live there. Why should your servant live in the royal city with

you?" ⁶ That day Achish gave Ziklag to him, and it still belongs to the kings of Judah today. ⁷ The length of time that David stayed in Philistine territory amounted to a year and four months.

⁸ David and his men went up and raided the Geshurites, the Girzites,ᴬ and the Amalekites. From ancient times they had been the inhabitants of the region through Shur as far as the land of Egypt. ⁹ Whenever David attacked the land, he did not leave a single person alive, either man or woman, but he took flocks, herds, donkeys, camels, and clothing. Then he came back to Achish, ¹⁰ who inquired, "Where did you raid today?"ᴮ

David replied, "The south country of Judah," "The south country of the Jerahmeelites," or "The south country of the Kenites."

¹¹ David did not let a man or woman live to be brought to Gath, for he said, "Or they will inform on us and say, 'This is what David did.'" This was David's custom during the whole time he stayed in the Philistine territory. ¹² So Achish trusted David, thinking, "Since he has made himself repulsive to his people Israel, he will be my servant forever."

Saul and the Medium

28 At that time, the Philistines gathered their military units into one army to fight against Israel. So Achish said to David, "You know, of course, that you and your men must march out in the armyᶜ with me."

² David replied to Achish, "Good, you will find out what your servant can do."

So Achish said to David, "Very well, I will appoint you as my permanent bodyguard."

³ By this time Samuel had died, all Israel had mourned for him and buried him in Ramah, his city, and Saul had removed the mediums and spiritists from the land. ⁴ The Philistines gathered and camped at Shunem. So Saul gathered all Israel, and they camped at Gilboa. ⁵ When

ᴬ27:8 Alt Hb tradition reads Gezerites ᴮ27:10 Some Hb mss, Syr, Tg; LXX, Vg, DSS read "Against whom did you raid today?" ᶜ28:1 DSS, LXX read battle

26:21 Saul's words sounded repentant, but Saul's past actions raised serious doubts in David's mind about their genuineness.
26:25 The two went on their way, having spoken the last words they would ever say to each other.
27:1 David's faith expressed in 26:10 seems to have waned. On the other hand, with the size of David's group (too large to hide), it must have seemed inevitable that Saul would find him in a vulnerable situation and wipe them out.
27:2 David earlier had feared Achish (21:10–15), but now he determined to join him.
27:3–4 Achish granted David and his men refuge in accord with the principle, "The enemy of my enemy is my friend."
27:5 David's request that he receive one of the outlying towns may have helped Achish's reputation with his own people, since some Philistines may have wondered why their king harbored a noted Israelite

warrior in Gath, the royal city. David probably also desired the safety that a little distance from the Philistine capital provided.
27:6 The city of Ziklag was located approximately twenty-five miles southwest of Gath. It originally was allotted to both the tribes of Simeon (Jos 19:5) and Judah (Jos 15:31), but Israel never conquered it. Now Ziklag came under Israelite control without a fight.
27:8 The Geshurites (Jos 13:1–2), the Girzites, and the Amalekites (Ex 17:15–16; Dt 25:17–19) were three non-Israelite groups under God's sentence of judgment. The Girzites occupied territory that overlapped with the promised land.
27:9 David's action against these groups fulfilled God's earlier command to Israel during the days of Joshua to wipe out the land's evil inhabitants (Jos 13:1–7). It also left no witnesses who could relay word to Achish (v. 11).
27:10–11 David's claim to have raided the south country of Judah was technically

correct, and he did fight people in the region of the Jerahmeelites and Kenites, two Judahite clans. Achish thought David meant he had destroyed many Israelites in the process.
27:12 Though Achish trusted David and assumed he would be Achish's servant forever, David was actually eliminating future rivals in Judah's territory.
28:1 Achish's words to David present a serious tension in the narrative. If David's forces were to march with the Philistines, he would end up fighting against his own people.
28:3 The law of Moses prohibited consulting with mediums and spiritists (Lv 19:31; 20:27; Dt 18:10–11), so Saul's effort to rid the land of them was commendable.
28:4 The Philistines camped at Shunem deep into the Jezreel Valley at the foot of Mount Moreh. Saul camped at Gilboa at the valley's southeastern edge, a vantage point from which he could observe the enemy army.

Saul saw the Philistine camp, he was afraid and his heart pounded. [6] He inquired of the LORD, but the LORD did not answer him in dreams or by the Urim or by the prophets. [7] Saul then said to his servants, "Find me a woman who is a medium, so I can go and consult her."

His servants replied, "There is a woman at En-dor who is a medium."

[8] Saul disguised himself by putting on different clothes and set out with two of his men. They came to the woman at night, and Saul said, "Consult a spirit for me. Bring up for me the one I tell you."

[9] But the woman said to him, "You surely know what Saul has done, how he has cut off the mediums and spiritists from the land. Why are you setting a trap for me to get me killed?"

[10] Then Saul swore to her by the LORD: "As surely as the LORD lives, no punishment will come to you[A] from this."

[11] "Who is it that you want me to bring up for you?" the woman asked.

"Bring up Samuel for me," he answered.

[12] When the woman saw Samuel, she screamed, and then she asked Saul, "Why did you deceive me? You are Saul!"

[13] But the king said to her, "Don't be afraid. What do you see?"

"I see a spirit form[B] coming up out of the earth," the woman answered.

[14] Then Saul asked her, "What does he look like?"

"An old man is coming up," she replied. "He's wearing a robe." Then Saul knew that it was Samuel, and he knelt low with his face to the ground and paid homage.

[15] "Why have you disturbed me by bringing me up?" Samuel asked Saul.

"I'm in serious trouble," replied Saul. "The Philistines are fighting against me and God has turned away from me. He doesn't answer me anymore, either through the prophets or in dreams. So I've called on you to tell me what I should do."

[16] Samuel answered, "Since the LORD has turned away from you and has become your enemy, why are you asking me? [17] The LORD has done[C] exactly what he said through me: The LORD has torn the kingship out of your hand and given it to your neighbor David. [18] You did not obey the LORD and did not carry out his burning anger against Amalek; therefore the LORD has done this to you today. [19] The LORD will also hand Israel over to the Philistines along with you. Tomorrow you and your sons will be with me,[D] and the LORD will hand Israel's army over to the Philistines."

[20] Immediately, Saul fell flat on the ground. He was terrified by Samuel's words and was also weak because he had not eaten anything all day and all night. [21] The woman came over to Saul, and she saw that he was terrified and said to him, "Look, your servant has obeyed you. I took my life in my hands and did what you told me to do. [22] Now please listen to your servant. Let me set some food in front of you. Eat and it will give you strength so you can go on your way."

[23] He refused, saying, "I won't eat," but when his servants and the woman urged him, he listened to them. He got up off the ground and sat on the bed.

[24] The woman had a fattened calf at her house, and she quickly slaughtered it. She also took flour, kneaded it, and baked unleavened bread. [25] She served it to Saul and his servants, and they ate. Afterward, they got up and left that night.

Philistines Reject David

29 The Philistines brought all their military units together at Aphek while Israel was camped by the spring in Jezreel. [2] As the Philistine leaders were passing in review with their units of hundreds and thousands,

[A]28:10 Or lives, you will not incur guilt   [B]28:13 Or a god, or a divine being   [C]28:17 Some Hb, some LXX mss, Vg read done to you   [D]28:19 LXX reads sons will fall

28:6 Saul inquired of the LORD for direction. Urim (lit "lights") denoted the device the priest used for discerning God's will (Ex 28:30; Nm 27:21), but Saul may not have had that available to him since Abiathar had taken the ephod to David (1Sm 23:6). The prophets likewise gave Saul no answer, perhaps because Saul had cut himself off from them through his clash with Samuel (15:34–35).
28:7 Desperate to find spiritual guidance of any kind about war with the Philistines, Saul turned to the very avenue he knew was wrong and had tried to destroy. Traveling to En-dor would present some risk since it lay about six miles northeast and two miles beyond the Philistine camp.
28:8 Saul disguised himself to avoid being recognized by Philistines who might be patrolling the valley. Traveling with only two of his men put the king in a high-risk

situation, but they also looked less "official" than a large group.
28:10–13 The king swore that she would suffer no harm—an oath by the very LORD who condemned divination. The text suggests that the spirit of Samuel actually appeared and alluded to events in which Samuel had participated (vv. 15–19); the tone of his speech sounds just like Samuel. Perhaps the woman recognized Saul in the light of Samuel's appearance, or perhaps the king pulled back his hood to look closer at the spirit who appeared before them.
28:17 The spirit of Samuel specifically named Saul's successor as David, whereas before he had only alluded to him (13:14; 15:28).
28:18 The words of Samuel's spirit, You did not obey the LORD, is a reference to 15:1–3,7–9—Saul's miserable failure regarding Amalek, whom God had commanded Saul to destroy.

28:19 The words of Samuel's spirit, you and your sons will be with me, was an unmistakable verdict of death on Saul and his house.
29:1 The text now flashes back to 28:1–2, a time prior to the armies gathering at Shunem and Gilboa (28:4). Aphek was located along the Yarkon River; it marked the site where the Philistines had gathered years earlier to fight Israel during the days of Eli the high priest (4:1). The spring in Jezreel probably refers to a spring in the valley near the town. By camping at Jezreel, Israel gave the Philistines full access to the valley where Philistine chariots would be more effective.
29:2 David and his men joined Achish and the Philistine leaders as they prepared for battle. David's position behind them meant that if he turned traitor, Philistine forces could be trapped between Saul and David (vv. 4–5).

David and his men were passing in review behind them with Achish. ³ Then the Philistine commanders asked, "What are these Hebrews doing here?"

Achish answered the Philistine commanders, "That is David, servant of King Saul of Israel. He has been with me a considerable period of time.^ From the day he defected until today, I've found no fault with him."

⁴ The Philistine commanders, however, were enraged with Achish and told him, "Send that man back and let him return to the place you assigned him. He must not go down with us into battle only to become our adversary during the battle. What better way could he ingratiate himself with his master than with the heads of our men? ⁵ Isn't this the David they sing about during their dances:

Saul has killed his thousands,
but David his tens of thousands?"

⁶ So Achish summoned David and told him, "As the LORD lives, you are an honorable man. I think it is good⁸ to have you fighting⁽ in this unit with me, because I have found no fault in you from the day you came to me until today. But the leaders don't think you are reliable. ⁷ Now go back quietly and you won't be doing anything the Philistine leaders think is wrong."

⁸ "But what have I done?" David replied to Achish. "From the first day I entered your service until today, what have you found against your servant to keep me from going to fight against the enemies of my lord the king?"

⁹ Achish answered David, "I'm convinced that you are as reliable as an angel of God. But the Philistine commanders have said, 'He must not go into battle with us.' ¹⁰ So get up early in the morning, you and your masters' servants who came with you.ᴰ When you've all gotten up early, go as soon as it's light." ¹¹ So David and his men got up early in the morning to return to the land of the Philistines. And the Philistines went up to Jezreel.

David's Defeat of the Amalekites

30 David and his men arrived in Ziklag on the third day. The Amalekites had raided the Negev and attacked and burned Ziklag. ² They also had kidnapped the women and everyone⁵ in it from youngest to oldest. They had killed no one but had carried them off as they went on their way.

³ When David and his men arrived at the town, they found it burned. Their wives, sons, and daughters had been kidnapped. ⁴ David and the troops with him wept loudly until they had no strength left to weep. ⁵ David's two wives, Ahinoam the Jezreelite and Abigail the widow of Nabal the Carmelite, had also been kidnapped. ⁶ David was in an extremely difficult position because the troops talked about stoning him, for they were all very bitter over the loss of their sons and daughters. But David found strength in the LORD his God.

⁷ David said to the priest Abiathar son of Ahimelech, "Bring me the ephod." So Abiathar brought it to him, ⁸ and David asked the LORD, "Should I pursue these raiders? Will I overtake them?"

The LORD replied to him, "Pursue them, for you will certainly overtake them and rescue the people."

⁹ So David and the six hundred men with him went. They came to the Wadi Besor, where some stayed behind. ¹⁰ David and four hundred of the men continued the pursuit, while two hundred stopped because they were too exhausted to cross the Wadi Besor.

¹¹ David's men found an Egyptian in the open country and brought him to David. They gave him some bread to eat and water to drink. ¹² Then they gave him some pressed figs and two clusters of raisins. After he ate he revived,

^29:3 Hb obscure ᴮ29:6 Lit It was good in my eyes ᶜ29:6 Lit you going out and coming in ᴰ29:10 LXX adds and go to the place I appointed you to. Don't take this evil matter to heart, for you are good before me. ᵉ30:2 LXX; MT omits and everyone

29:3 In response to the concerns of the **Philistine commanders**, Achish affirmed David's loyalty to him during the **considerable period of time** (sixteen months, 27:7) that David had served him.
29:4–5 The **Philistine commanders** refused to accept Achish's explanation. If David should become their **adversary** during the battle, they could suffer heavy casualties. They also suspected that David, as one of Saul's former generals, might choose just such a time to **ingratiate himself with his master**. The words **heads of our men** may recall the Goliath episode (17:51), as well as 28:2.
29:8–9 When David spoke of **the enemies of my lord the king** it may have been disintentionally ambiguous. On the surface his king was Achish, but the double meaning may have referred to Saul. The **Philistine commanders** were not convinced of David's loyalty to their cause. **Achish** affirmed his

faith in David, but he felt compelled to follow the counsel of his commanders.
29:10 Achish commanded David to leave **early in the morning** so he would not hinder the Philistine advance northward.
29:11 David's departure providentially prevented him from participating in the battle that would claim Saul's life. Meanwhile, the **Philistines went up to Jezreel** (perhaps a reference to the valley rather than the town), where they would soon engage Saul's army.
30:1 The **Amalekites** whom Saul should have destroyed (15:1–3) had raided the **Negev** (the southern region) and **burned** the city of **Ziklag**.
30:2–5 The Amalekites **kidnapped the women and everyone** in the city. David's **two wives** did not escape the Amalekite attack, so he shared personally in the grief that others experienced.
30:6 The pain the troops felt over the loss of **their sons and daughters** led some to

blame David for their troubles. Nonetheless, David **found strength** (lit "strengthened himself") **in the LORD his God**, a testimony to his faith in difficult times.
30:9 The **Wadi Besor** lay about fifteen miles south of Ziklag.
30:10 A third of David's warriors were **too exhausted** to continue farther because of: (1) their fifty-five-mile journey from Aphek to Ziklag over three days (29:11–30:1), (2) the emotional pain of seeing Ziklag destroyed and their families gone, and (3) the fifteen-mile trek from Ziklag to the **Wadi Besor**.
30:11–14 The **Cherethites** lived along the coast near the Philistines (Ezk 25:16). The **south country of Caleb** denoted the region around Hebron (Jos 14:13–14; 15:13–15). The words **we burned Ziklag** implicated the Egyptian in the battle; at the same time they provided David a potential opportunity.

for he hadn't eaten food or drunk water for three days and three nights.

¹³ Then David said to him, "Who do you belong to? Where are you from?"

"I'm an Egyptian, the slave of an Amalekite man," he said. "My master abandoned me when I got sick three days ago. ¹⁴ We raided the south country of the Cherethites, the territory of Judah, and the south country of Caleb, and we burned Ziklag."

¹⁵ David then asked him, "Will you lead me to these raiders?"

He said, "Swear to me by God that you won't kill me or turn me over to my master, and I will lead you to them."

¹⁶ So he led him, and there were the Amalekites, spread out over the entire area, eating, drinking, and celebrating because of the great amount of plunder they had taken from the land of the Philistines and the land of Judah. ¹⁷ David slaughtered them from twilight until the evening of the next day. None of them escaped, except four hundred young men who got on camels and fled.

¹⁸ David recovered everything the Amalekites had taken; he also rescued his two wives. ¹⁹ Nothing of theirs was missing from the youngest to the oldest, including the sons and daughters, and all the plunder the Amalekites had taken. David got everything back. ²⁰ He took all the flocks and herds, which were driven ahead of the other livestock, and the people shouted, "This is David's plunder!"

²¹ When David came to the two hundred men who had been too exhausted to go with him and had been left at the Wadi Besor, they came out to meet him and to meet the troops with him. When David approached the men, he greeted them, ²² but all the corrupt and worthless men among those who had gone with David argued, "Because they didn't go with us, we will not give any of the plunder we recovered to them except for each man's wife and children. They may take them and go."

²³ But David said, "My brothers, you must not do this with what the LORD has given us. He protected us and handed over to us the raiders who came against us. ²⁴ Who can agree to your proposal? The share of the one who goes into battle is to be the same as the share of the one who remains with the supplies. They will share equally." ²⁵ And it has been so from that day forward. David established this policy^A as a law and an ordinance for Israel and it still continues today.

²⁶ When David came to Ziklag, he sent some of the plunder to his friends, the elders of Judah, saying, "Here is a gift for you from the plunder of the LORD's enemies." ²⁷ He sent gifts^B to those in Bethel, in Ramoth of the Negev, and in Jattir; ²⁸ to those in Aroer, in Siphmoth, and in Eshtemoa; ²⁹ to those in Racal, in the towns of the Jerahmeelites, and in the towns of the Kenites; ³⁰ to those in Hormah, in Bor-ashan, and in Athach; ³¹ to those in all the places where David and his men had roamed.

The Death of Saul and His Sons

31 The Philistines fought against Israel, and Israel's men fled from them and were killed on Mount Gilboa. ² The Philistines pursued Saul and his sons and killed his sons, Jonathan, Abinadab, and Malchishua. ³ When the battle intensified against Saul, the archers found him and severely wounded him.^C ⁴ Then Saul said to his armor-bearer, "Draw your sword and run me through with it, or these uncircumcised men will come and run me through and torture me!" But his armor-bearer

^A 30:25 *this policy* supplied for clarity　^B 30:27 *He sent gifts* supplied for clarity　^C 31:3 LXX reads *and he was wounded under the ribs*

30:16 The language emphasizes how the **Amalekites** were not expecting any kind of retaliation from either the **Philistines** or **Judah**, but they underestimated David's resolve.
30:17 Despite the long journey David and his men had undertaken, they received renewed energy from finding their families alive and from discovering the Amalekites so vulnerable.
30:18–19 The Lord's hand on David's army was evident as David **recovered everything the Amalekites had taken**, including all the people.
30:20 The phrase **all the flocks and herds** designates additional animals not part of the people's assets at Ziklag, since it was called **David's plunder**.
30:22 Normally the victorious soldiers would divide the spoils of the battle. Some of those who had fought did not want to share **any of the plunder** with those who were too tired to proceed past the Wadi Besor.
30:23 David's reply revealed his character. He emphasized that the Lord had **protected**

them and brought the victory. Who could have imagined the rescue of absolutely everything they lost with no loss of life?
30:25 David's decision about the equitable distribution of plunder became **a law and an ordinance** for future generations.
30:27 The exact location of most of the places in Judah mentioned in vv. 27–31 is uncertain. **Ramoth of the Negev** is mentioned in Jos 19:8. **Jattir** was a Levitical city (Jos 21:14), designated for the Levites with its surrounding pasture lands.
30:28 Eshtemoa was also a Levitical city (Jos 21:14).
30:29 The **Jerahmeelites** and **Kenites** lived in the areas where David had fought and destroyed Israel's enemies (27:10).
30:30 Hormah was a place that the Israelites had fought and conquered at least three times (Nm 21:3; Jos 12:14; Jdg 1:17).
30:31 Hebron, Judah's natural capital, lay about nineteen miles south of Jerusalem in the Judean hill country. Hebron was conquered by Caleb during Joshua's time (Jos

14:13–14), and it became both a Levitical city (Jos 21:13) and a city of refuge (Jos 20:7). After Saul's death, the city became David's capital for seven and one-half years (2Sm 5:5).
31:1 The account now shifts to the Jezreel Valley. **Israel's men fled** from the Philistines; that is, Israel lost the battle (4:17).
31:2 Kings and princes normally shielded themselves from the risks associated with the battlefield (2Sm 18:2–4; 21:15–17), but in this battle, **the Philistines** singled out and **pursued Saul and his sons**.
31:3 Archers provided the advantage of inflicting potentially fatal injuries from a distance; raining arrows on Saul's position proved effective.
31:4–6 Saul feared the Philistines would capture him alive and perhaps treat him as they had treated Samson in the judges period (Jdg 16:21). Saul's **armor-bearer**, however, was paralyzed with fear and could not bring himself to obey the king's request (**run me through**). So Saul took his own sword and **fell on it**. On the discrepancy

would not do it because he was terrified. Then Saul took his sword and fell on it. ⁵ When his armor-bearer saw that Saul was dead, he also fell on his own sword and died with him. ⁶ So on that day, Saul died together with his three sons, his armor-bearer, and all his men.

⁷ When the men of Israel on the other side of the valley and on the other side of the Jordan saw that Israel's men had fled and that Saul and his sons were dead, they abandoned the cities and fled. So the Philistines came and settled in them.

⁸ The next day when the Philistines came to strip the slain, they found Saul and his three sons dead on Mount Gilboa. ⁹ They cut off

Saul's head, stripped off his armor, and sent messengers throughout the land of the Philistines to spread the good news in the temples of their idols and among the people. ¹⁰ Then they put his armor in the temple of the Ashtoreths and hung his body on the wall of Beth-shan.

¹¹ When the residents of Jabesh-gilead heard what the Philistines had done to Saul, ¹² all their brave men set out, journeyed all night, and retrieved the body of Saul and the bodies of his sons from the wall of Beth-shan. When they arrived at Jabesh, they burned the bodies there. ¹³ Afterward, they took their bones and buried them under the tamarisk tree in Jabesh and fasted seven days.

---

between these words and 2Sm 1:6–10, see note on 2Sm 1:4–10.

31:8 Part of plundering the enemy involved to **strip the slain** of their valuables. The Philistine victory had been so complete that no Israelites had dared try to rescue the bodies of **Saul and his three sons**.

31:9 First Ch 10:10 notes that Saul's head was placed in the temple of Dagon, perhaps at Ashdod (1Sm 5:1–2), symbolizing Dagon's victory over Israel's king.

31:10 Ashtoreths designated images of the Canaanite goddess Ashtoreth, consort of Baal (7:3–4; 12:10). **Beth-shan** was an Israelite city at the mouth of the valley near the Jordan River, probably abandoned by the Israelites in the wake of the Philistine victory (v. 7).

31:11 Jabesh-gilead was a city east of the Jordan River whose citizens **Saul** rescued from Nahash, king of Ammon (11:1–11).

31:12 Retrieving **the body of Saul and the bodies of his sons** would have been risky

since the Philistines occupied the valley, but Jabesh-gilead's **brave men** did so—probably under cover of darkness. **At Jabesh, they burned the bodies**, not to ashes, but on a funeral pyre to remove the flesh, probably to protect them from further abuse by wild animals. The men had not been able to repay the king for saving them during his life, but they would do what they could now to honor his memory.

Introduction to 2 Samuel

Circumstances of Writing

Early tradition suggests 1 and 2 Samuel were originally one book. Some scholars believe Samuel was largely responsible for the material up to 1 Samuel 25 and that the prophets Nathan and Gad gave significant input to the rest (based on 1Ch 29:29). This proposal, however, must remain speculative, because the books name no authors. First Samuel 27:6 suggests the book was not completed until perhaps a few generations after the division of the kingdom around 930 BC.

After Israel's conquest of the land during the days of Joshua, Israel entered a time of apostasy. The book of Judges describes recurrences of a cycle with predictable phases. First, the people sinned against the Lord and fell into idolatry. Second, the Lord raised up an adversary to afflict them and turn them back to him. Third, the people cried out to the Lord in repentance. Fourth, the Lord brought deliverance for them through a judge whom he raised up. The book of Judges' famous verse, "In those days there was no king in Israel; everyone did whatever seemed right to him" (21:25), aptly describes the period. The book of 1 Samuel picks up the historical record toward the end of those stormy days.

Contribution to the Bible

The books of 1 and 2 Samuel describe Israel's transition from a loosely organized tribal league under God (a theocracy) to centralized leadership under a king who answered to God (a monarchy). Samuel's life and ministry greatly shaped this period of restructuring as he consistently pointed people back to God.

Saul's rule highlighted the dangers to which the Israelites fell victim as they clamored for a king to lead them. Samuel's warnings fell on deaf ears (1Sm 8:10–20) because God's people were intent on becoming like the nations around them. In the end, they got exactly what they asked for, but they paid a terrible price. Saul's life stands as a warning to trust God's timing for life's provisions.

David's rule testified to the amazing works the Lord could and would do through a life yielded to him. Israel's second king seemed quite aware of God's blessing on his life and displayed a tender heart toward the things of God (2Sm 5:12; 7:1–2; 22:1–51; 23:1–7). Later generations would receive blessing because of David's life (Is 37:35). God's special covenant with David (2Sm 7:1–29) found its ultimate fulfillment in Jesus, the son of David (Lk 1:32–33). The consequences of David's sin with Bathsheba, however, stand as a warning to all who experience sin's attraction. God holds his children accountable for their actions, and even forgiven sin can have terrible consequences.

Structure

Second Samuel 1–4 describes the struggle for Israel's throne that began with Saul's death. David was anointed king by the men of Judah (2:4), but Abner anointed Ish-bosheth, Saul's oldest surviving son, as king over Israel (2:8–9). A two-year civil war resulted in Ish-bosheth's death and in David's becoming king over all Israel.

Second Samuel 5–24 presents highlights of David's reign. God established a special covenant with David, promising to establish the

See the introduction to 1 Samuel for the timeline.

throne of his kingdom forever (7:1–29). David's sin with Bathsheba, however, brought disastrous consequences to his reign and became a turning point in 2 Samuel. In the end, David's repentance confirmed his designation as a man after God's heart, but his sin showed that even the king is not above breaking God's laws.

First Samuel 13–31 describes Saul's victories and failures. Saul was a king with great physical stature and military skill (14:47–52), but his heart was not one with the Lord (13:14). His unwillingness to obey the Lord's commands ultimately outweighed his accomplishments, and chapters 16–31 describe his reign's downward spiral. During this time, God raised up David and was preparing him for the day he would succeed Saul—a fact Saul gradually realized (15:28; 24:20–21; 28:17).

Outline

Responses to Saul's Death

1 After the death of Saul, David returned from defeating the Amalekites and stayed at Ziklag two days. ² On the third day a man with torn clothes and dust on his head came from Saul's camp. When he came to David, he fell to the ground and paid homage. ³ David asked him, "Where have you come from?"

He replied to him, "I've escaped from the Israelite camp."

⁴ "What was the outcome? Tell me," David asked him.

"The troops fled from the battle," he answered. "Many of the troops have fallen and are dead. Also, Saul and his son Jonathan are dead."

⁵ David asked the young man who had brought him the report, "How do you know Saul and his son Jonathan are dead?"

⁶ "I happened to be on Mount Gilboa," he replied, "and there was Saul, leaning on his spear. At that very moment the chariots and the cavalry were closing in on him. ⁷ When he turned around and saw me, he called out to me, so I answered: I'm at your service. ⁸ He asked me, 'Who are you?' I told him: I'm an Amalekite. ⁹ Then he begged me, 'Stand over me and kill me, for I'm mortally wounded,ᴬ but my life still lingers.' ¹⁰ So I stood over him and killed him because I knew that after he had fallen he couldn't survive. I took the crown that was on his head and the armband that was on his arm, and I've brought them here to my lord."

¹¹ Then David took hold of his clothes and tore them, and all the men with him did the same. ¹² They mourned, wept, and fasted until the evening for those who died by the sword — for Saul, his son Jonathan, the LORD's people, and the house of Israel.

¹³ David inquired of the young man who had brought him the report, "Where are you from?"

"I'm the son of a resident alien," he said. "I'm an Amalekite."

¹⁴ David questioned him, "How is it that you were not afraid to lift your hand to destroy the LORD's anointed?" ¹⁵ Then David summoned one of his servants and said, "Come here and kill him!" The servant struck him, and he died. ¹⁶ For David had said to the Amalekite, "Your blood is on your own head because your own mouth testified against you by saying, 'I killed the LORD's anointed.'"

¹⁷ David sang the following lament for Saul and his son Jonathan, ¹⁸ and he ordered that the Judahites be taught The Song of the Bow. It is written in the Book of Jashar:ᴮ

19   The splendor of Israel lies slain
            on your heights.
        How the mighty have fallen!
20   Do not tell it in Gath,
        don't announce it in the marketplaces
            of Ashkelon,
        or the daughters of the Philistines
            will rejoice,
        and the daughters of the uncircumcised
            will celebrate.
21   Mountains of Gilboa,
        let no dew or rain be on you,
        or fields of offerings,ᶜ
        for there the shield of the mighty
            was defiled —
        the shield of Saul, no longer anointed
            with oil.
22   Jonathan's bow never retreated,
        Saul's sword never returned unstained,ᴰ
        from the blood of the slain,
        from the fleshᴱ of the mighty.
23   Saul and Jonathan,
        loved and delightful,
        they were not parted in life or in death.
        They were swifter than eagles,
            stronger than lions.
24   Daughters of Israel, weep for Saul,
        who clothed you in scarlet,
            with luxurious things,

ᴬ1:9 LXX reads *for terrible darkness has taken hold of me*   ᴮ1:18 Or *of the Upright*   ᶜ1:21 LXX reads *firstfruits*   ᴰ1:22 Lit *empty*   ᴱ1:22 Lit *fat*

1:1 The historical account of the first kings of Israel continues following the description of **the death of Saul** in 1Sm 31. No doubt David and his men needed some rest, so they **stayed at Ziklag**. In addition, Ziklag needed to be rebuilt (1Sm 30:1).
1:2–3 By **the third day**, Saul had been dead a few days, but David had been occupied elsewhere. **Torn clothes and dust on his head** were signs of mourning, so David immediately knew bad news was forthcoming.
1:4–10 **Mount Gilboa** was the site of the battle, so the messenger's word placed him at the scene. **Saul, leaning on his spear** gives the sense that an eyewitness was speaking. The mention of **chariots and . . . cavalry** was consistent with Philistine warfare, especially in a valley where the chariots had plenty of room to maneuver. Ironically, the man was an **Amalekite**, part of the group Saul had been commanded to destroy (1Sm 15:1–3). Saul's alleged words

could square with the circumstances of 1Sm 31:3–4. With his words **I stood over him and killed him**, the Amalekite claimed responsibility for killing King Saul. Further, the man's possession of Saul's **crown** and **armband** provided proof of the Amalekite's presence at Gilboa and that Saul was dead. Two possibilities exist on harmonizing this verse with 1Sm 31:4. The first is to assume Saul fell on his sword, did not die immediately, and so asked the Amalekite to help bring about a quicker death. The second and more likely is that the Amalekite arrived on the scene after Saul had died but before the Philistines arrived. He saw an opportunity to receive a reward from David, so he took the crown and armband to David and lied about the way Saul died. Perhaps David detected the Amalekite's deceit, which in part would explain his command in v. 15.
1:18 The **Book of Jashar** (or "Book of the Upright") is also mentioned in Jos 10:13. It

has never been discovered, but it appears to have been a collection of some of God's great works among his people.
1:19 **Splendor** also may be translated as "gazelle," describing Saul as a majestic animal. Gazelles often inhabited the **heights**, so the image fits well.
1:20 **Gath** and **Ashkelon** were two leading Philistine cities.
1:21 David called to the **mountains of Gilboa**, the site of Saul's death, to participate in the mourning by lacking **dew** and **rain**, two kinds of moisture much more common in the north where Gilboa was located rather than in the south where David was. The phrase **the shield of Saul, no longer anointed with oil** perhaps indicates the cleaning and polishing of Saul's weapons.
1:24–27 David called Jonathan his **brother** and **friend**. His relationship with Jonathan included a covenant bond of deep mutual respect and loyalty (1Sm 18:1–3; 20:13–17;

who decked your garments
with gold ornaments.

25 How the mighty have fallen in the thick
of battle!
Jonathan lies slain on your heights.

26 I grieve for you, Jonathan, my brother.
You were such a friend to me.
Your love for me was more wondrous
than the love of women.

27 How the mighty have fallen
and the weapons of war have perished!

David, King of Judah

2 Some time later, David inquired of the
LORD: "Should I go to one of the towns of
Judah?"

The LORD answered him, "Go."

Then David asked, "Where should I go?"

"To Hebron," the LORD replied.

2 So David went there with his two wives,
Ahinoam the Jezreelite and Abigail, the widow of Nabal the Carmelite. **3** In addition, David
brought the men who were with him, each one

with his family, and they settled in the towns
near Hebron. **4** Then the men of Judah came,
and there they anointed David king over the
house of Judah. They told David, "It was the
men of Jabesh-gilead who buried Saul."

5 David sent messengers to the men of
Jabesh-gilead and said to them, "The LORD
bless you because you have shown this
kindness to Saul your lord when you buried him. **6** Now, may the LORD show kindness
and faithfulness to you, and I will also show
the same goodness to you because you have
done this deed. **7** Therefore, be strong^A and
valiant, for though Saul your lord is dead,
the house of Judah has anointed me king
over them."

8 Abner son of Ner, commander of Saul's
army, took Saul's son Ish-bosheth^B,^C and moved
him to Mahanaim. **9** He made him king over Gilead, Asher, Jezreel, Ephraim, Benjamin — over
all Israel. **10** Saul's son Ish-bosheth was forty
years old when he became king over Israel;
he reigned for two years. The house of Judah,

---

^A 2:7 Lit *Therefore, strengthen your hands*   ^B 2:8 Some LXX mss read *Ishbaal*; 1Ch 8:33; 9:39   ^C 2:8 = Man of Shame

---

23:16–18). They had much in common and
developed a deep relationship that David
considered **more wondrous than the love
of women**. The text does not suggest that
David had a homosexual relationship with
Jonathan or that David had a poor relationship with his wives. Rather, it speaks to an
unbreakable friendship bond between men.
2:1 Hebron was Judah's natural capital,
located about nineteen miles south of Jerusalem and high in the hill country.
2:2 Ahinoam and **Abigail** remained with
David, though Saul had given Michal, David's
first wife, to another man (1Sm 25:44).

2:4 The **men of Judah** recognized God's hand
on David and anointed him **king over the
house of Judah**—over his own tribe only.
At this time, David heard how the men of
Jabesh-gilead had **buried Saul**. David had
been anointed once before, when he had been
chosen by the Lord (1Sm 16:12–13; cp. 2Sm 5:3).
2:8 Abner, Saul's relative and general, had
survived the battle at Gilboa. **Saul's son Ish-
bosheth** was probably the oldest surviving
son (1Sm 31:2). The exact location of **Mahanaim** is uncertain, but Jos 21:38 designates
it as a Levitical city east of the Jordan River
(Gn 32:2).

2:9 Gilead designated the north-central region of Transjordan. The territory of **Asher**
lay along Israel's northwestern Mediterranean coastline. **Jezreel** probably denotes
the valley rather than the city. **Ephraim**
and **Benjamin** were centrally located with
Ephraim above Benjamin; Benjamin was
Saul's tribe (1Sm 9:1). **All Israel** means everything but Judah in light of v. 4.
2:10 Ish-bosheth's reign of **two years** provides a hint about the length of the period
of transition between Saul's death and
David's assumption of the kingship over
all Israel.

Character profile:

David

D avid is described as a man "after [God's] own heart" (1Sm
13:14). A glimpse into David's life reveals what it takes to
be awarded such a designation.

*First, a person after God's own heart understands God's pow-
er.* David didn't challenge the giant Goliath to prove his own
toughness; he did it to prove God's strength. When this Philistine warrior taunted the Israelite forces and slandered their
God, David expected one of the Israelites to step forward. Instead, he found a group of men too intimidated to do anything.
Since he could see which side actually had the overwhelming
advantage, young David volunteered to face Goliath in God's
power. He declared to the heavily armed Philistine, "You come
against me with a sword, spear, and javelin, but I come against
you in the name of the LORD of Armies, the God of the ranks of
Israel—you have defied him. Today, the LORD will hand you over
to me" (17:45–46). And with one shot he struck down the giant.

*Second, a person after God's own heart acts according to God's
timing.* David had been anointed the future king of Israel when
he was a young man. For years he knew he was destined to
succeed Saul. Yet he never allowed a personal pursuit of the
throne to override God's plans.

David had to flee for his life from Saul. He spent years on
the run, hiding from the king and his men. On more than one
occasion, David had an opportunity to end Saul's life, yet David refused to raise his hand against him because God had not
condoned it. David eventually became king of Israel, but it
happened according to God's timing, not his.

*Third, a person after God's own heart feels personal sin deep-
ly.* David was still a flawed human, capable of horrific sin. On
one occasion when his soldiers were away fighting Israel's
battles, King David took for himself a woman named Bathsheba, the wife of Uriah, one of David's most loyal soldiers.
When Bathsheba became pregnant with David's child, the
king immediately sent for Uriah, reasoning that Uriah would
come home and sleep with his wife and then assume that the
baby was his own.

But Uriah's loyalty to his king got in the way of David's plan.
Uriah refused to sleep with his wife while his fellow soldiers
were still fighting. So David compounded his sin by arranging
for Uriah to be abandoned during battle and killed by Israel's
enemies. Afterwards, David took Bathsheba for his own wife.

But God knew what he had done and sent the prophet Nathan to condemn the king's wickedness. The consequences
included the death of the baby boy and disaster on his family.
David was crushed.

More acute than the grief he felt over his son's death, his
sins against Uriah and Bathsheba, or the humiliation he'd
brought on himself was the devastation he felt over his sins
against God.

In Psalm 51:2–4 David poured out his anguish: "Completely
wash away my guilt and cleanse me from my sin. For I am conscious of my rebellion, and my sin is always before me. Against
you—you alone—I have sinned and done this evil in Your sight."
Those are the words of a man after God's own heart.

Understanding who God is and what he wants from you can
be found through reading his Word and pursuing him in prayer.
By making those things a priority, you can begin to develop a
deeper relationship with God and grow in your loyalty to him.

however, followed David. [11] The length of time that David was king in Hebron over the house of Judah was seven years and six months.

[12] Abner son of Ner and soldiers of Ish-bosheth son of Saul marched out from Mahanaim to Gibeon. [13] So Joab son of Zeruiah and David's soldiers marched out and met them by the pool of Gibeon. The two groups took up positions on opposite sides of the pool.

[14] Then Abner said to Joab, "Let's have the young men get up and compete in front of us."

"Let them get up," Joab replied.

[15] So they got up and were counted off — twelve for Benjamin and Ish-bosheth son of Saul, and twelve from David's soldiers. [16] Then each man grabbed his opponent by the head and thrust his sword into his opponent's side so that they all died together. So this place, which is in Gibeon, is named Field of Blades.^A

[17] The battle that day was extremely fierce, and Abner and the men of Israel were defeated by David's soldiers. [18] The three sons of Zeruiah were there: Joab, Abishai, and Asahel. Asahel was a fast runner, like one of the wild gazelles. [19] He chased Abner and did not turn to the right or the left in his pursuit of him. [20] Abner glanced back and said, "Is that you, Asahel?"

"Yes it is," Asahel replied.

[21] Abner said to him, "Turn to your right or left, seize one of the young soldiers, and take whatever you can get from him." But Asahel would not stop chasing him. [22] Once again, Abner warned Asahel, "Stop chasing me. Why should I strike you to the ground? How could I ever look your brother Joab in the face?"

[23] But Asahel refused to turn away, so Abner hit him in the stomach with the butt of his spear. The spear went through his body, and he fell and died right there. As they all came to the place where Asahel had fallen and died, they stopped, [24] but Joab and Abishai pursued Abner. By sunset, they had gone as far as the hill of Ammah, which is opposite Giah on the way to the wilderness of Gibeon.

[25] The Benjaminites rallied to Abner; they formed a unit and took their stand on top of a hill. [26] Then Abner called out to Joab, "Must the sword devour forever? Don't you realize this will only end in bitterness? How long before you tell the troops to stop pursuing their brothers?"

[27] "As God lives," Joab replied, "if you had not spoken up, the troops wouldn't have stopped pursuing their brothers until morning." [28] Then Joab blew the ram's horn, and all the troops stopped; they no longer pursued Israel or continued to fight. [29] So Abner and his men marched through the Arabah all that night. They crossed the Jordan, marched all morning,^B and arrived at Mahanaim.

[30] When Joab had turned back from pursuing Abner, he gathered all the troops. In addition to Asahel, nineteen of David's soldiers were missing, [31] but they had killed 360 of the Benjaminites and Abner's men. [32] Afterward, they carried Asahel to his father's tomb in Bethlehem and buried him. Then Joab and his men marched all night and reached Hebron at dawn.

Civil War

3 During the long war between the house of Saul and the house of David, David was growing stronger and the house of Saul was becoming weaker.

[2] Sons were born to David in Hebron:

His firstborn was Amnon,
    by Ahinoam the Jezreelite;
[3] his second was Chileab,
    by Abigail, the widow of Nabal
        the Carmelite;
the third was Absalom,
    son of Maacah the daughter
        of King Talmai of Geshur;
[4] the fourth was Adonijah,
    son of Haggith;
the fifth was Shephatiah,
    son of Abital;
[5] the sixth was Ithream,
    by David's wife Eglah.

These were born to David in Hebron.

[6] During the war between the house of Saul and the house of David, Abner kept acquiring more power in the house of Saul. [7] Now

---

^A 2:16 Or Helkath-hazzurim   ^B 2:29 Or marched through the Bithron

---

2:11 After **seven years and six months**, David would move his capital to Jerusalem, where he would reign for thirty-three years (5:5).
2:12 Gibeon lay in the territory of Benjamin about twenty-three miles north of Hebron.
2:13 David's general **Joab** wanted to keep Ish-bosheth's army out of Judah. The **pool of Gibeon** probably denotes a large reservoir near the spring outside the city.
2:18 Zeruiah was David's sister (1Ch 2:16), so **Joab, Abishai, and Asahel** were David's nephews who served in his army.
2:19 Asahel **chased Abner** because he saw an opportunity to strike down the leader of the opposition forces. Both men appear to have been on foot.

2:22 Abner's words, **Stop chasing me,** suggest that **Asahel** was gaining on him. Abner probably was better armed and more experienced in fighting than Asahel.
2:24 The **hill of Ammah** is an unknown site east of Gibeon.
2:27–28 The blowing of a **ram's horn** was a signal to gather the troops—in this case, to stop fighting (18:16; 20:22).
2:29 Abner and **his men** then retreated across the Jordan River and northward about thirty miles to **Mahanaim** (v. 8).
2:30–31 The differences in the number of casualties (**nineteen of David's soldiers** . . . **360 of the Benjaminites and Abner's men**) reveal the overwhelming victory

David's forces achieved and suggest God's favor on David.
2:32 Bethlehem lay approximately ten miles south of the battle site. From there to **Hebron** was another fourteen miles along the highway.
3:2–5 Amnon would prove a tragic figure later (13:1–29). **Absalom** would later die in an attempt to seize his father's throne (15:1–18:33). The reference to his mother as **the daughter of King Talmai of Geshur,** an Aramean city-state near the Sea of Galilee, suggests a marriage alliance between David and Talmai to strengthen David's position in the north. **Adonijah** would later try to assume the throne, but Solomon would succeed David as king (1Kg 1:5–40).

Saul had a concubine whose name was Rizpah daughter of Aiah, and Ish-bosheth questioned Abner, "Why did you sleep with my father's concubine?"

⁸ Abner was very angry about Ish-bosheth's accusation. "Am I a dog's head^A who belongs to Judah?" he asked. "All this time I've been loyal to the family of your father Saul, to his brothers, and to his friends and haven't betrayed you to David, but now you accuse me of wrongdoing with this woman! ⁹ May God punish Abner and do so severely if I don't do for David what the LORD swore to him: ¹⁰ to transfer the kingdom from the house of Saul and establish the throne of David over Israel and Judah from Dan to Beer-sheba." ¹¹ Ish-bosheth did not dare respond to Abner because he was afraid of him.

¹² Abner sent messengers as his representatives to say to David, "Whose land is it? Make your covenant with me, and you can be certain I am on your side to turn all Israel over to you."

¹³ David replied, "Good, I will make a covenant with you. However, there's one thing I require of you: You will not see my face unless you first bring Saul's daughter Michal when you come to see me."

¹⁴ Then David sent messengers to say to Ish-bosheth son of Saul, "Give me back my wife Michal. I was engaged to her for the price of a hundred Philistine foreskins."

¹⁵ So Ish-bosheth sent someone to take her away from her husband, Paltiel son of Laish. ¹⁶ Her husband followed her, weeping all the way to Bahurim. Abner said to him, "Go back." So he went back.

The Assassination of Abner

¹⁷ Abner conferred with the elders of Israel: "In the past you wanted David to be king over you. ¹⁸ Now take action, because the LORD has spoken concerning David: 'Through my servant David I will save my people Israel from the power of the Philistines and the power of all Israel's enemies.'"

¹⁹ Abner also informed the Benjaminites and went to Hebron to inform David about all that was agreed on by Israel and the whole house of Benjamin. ²⁰ When Abner and twenty men came to David at Hebron, David held a banquet for him and his men.

²¹ Abner said to David, "Let me now go and I will gather all Israel to my lord the king. They will make a covenant with you, and you will reign over all you desire." So David dismissed Abner, and he went in peace.

²² Just then David's soldiers and Joab returned from a raid and brought a large amount of plundered goods with them. Abner was not with David in Hebron because David had dismissed him, and he had gone in peace. ²³ When Joab and his whole army arrived, Joab was informed, "Abner son of Ner came to see the king, the king dismissed him, and he went in peace."

²⁴ Joab went to the king and said, "What have you done? Look here, Abner came to you. Why did you dismiss him? Now he's getting away. ²⁵ You know that Abner son of Ner came to deceive you and to find out about your military activities^B and everything you're doing."

²⁶ Then Joab left David and sent messengers after Abner. They brought him back from the well^C of Sirah, but David was unaware of it. ²⁷ When Abner returned to Hebron, Joab pulled him aside to the middle of the city gate, as if to speak to him privately, and there Joab stabbed him in the stomach. So Abner died in revenge for the death of Asahel,^D Joab's brother.

²⁸ David heard about it later and said, "I and my kingdom are forever innocent before the LORD concerning the blood of Abner son of Ner. ²⁹ May it hang over Joab's head and his father's whole family, and may the house of Joab never be without someone who has a discharge or a skin disease, or a man who can only work a spindle,^E or someone who falls by the sword or starves." ³⁰ Joab and his brother Abishai killed Abner because he had put their brother Asahel to death in the battle at Gibeon.

^A 3:8 = a despised person ^B 3:25 Lit your going out and your coming in ^C 3:26 Or cistern ^D 3:27 Lit And he died for the blood of Asahel ^E 3:29 LXX reads who uses a crutch

3:7 Having sexual relations with a woman of the harem was obviously the unique privilege of the king and could have been perceived as an attempt by **Abner** to usurp the kingship (12:8; 16:20–22).
3:9 Ironically, **Abner** was well aware of God's promise to **David**, yet he had been advancing Ish-bosheth's cause.
3:10 The two cities, **Dan** and **Beer-sheba**, essentially marked the northern and southern borders of Israel, respectively, spanning a distance of about 150 miles (24:2; 1Sm 3:20). Abner thus envisioned the entire nation unified under **the throne of David**.
3:12 Abner **sent messengers . . . to David** because he would have wanted to make sure David accepted him.
3:13 **Saul's daughter Michal** was David's first wife (1Sm 18:27) whom Saul took away and gave to Paltiel son of Laish after David became a fugitive (1Sm 25:44). By getting her back, David also would reestablish himself as a legitimate relative and heir to Saul's throne. David had never divorced Michal, so she rightfully belonged with him.
3:14–15 Ish-bosheth's compliance with David's demand further highlights his weakness. Perhaps with Abner having deserted to David's side, Ish-bosheth lacked any real power and was trying to ensure that David did not kill him after becoming king (1Sm 24:20–21).
3:16 Paltiel, Michal's **husband** of several years, was perhaps the one who along with Michal suffered the most through this ordeal.
Bahurim was located near the Benjamin-Judah border. Abner was probably an imposing military man, so when he bluntly told Paltiel to **go back**, Paltiel was intimidated into obeying despite his broken heart.
3:20–21 Abner was ready to coordinate final plans among the northern tribes to **gather all Israel** to David. Once they made a **covenant** ratifying his reign over them, David would control the entire nation.
3:26 The **well of Sirah** was a site about two miles northwest of Hebron.
3:27 Joab **stabbed him** [Abner] **in the stomach** just as Abner had done to **Asahel**, Joab's brother (2:23).
3:30 Perhaps **Abishai** led the delegation that summoned **Abner** back to Hebron, thus serving as Joab's co-conspirator.

³¹ David then ordered Joab and all the people who were with him, "Tear your clothes, put on sackcloth, and mourn over Abner." And King David walked behind the coffin.ᴬ

³² When they buried Abner in Hebron, the king wept aloud at Abner's tomb. All the people wept, ³³ and the king sang a lament for Abner:

Should Abner die as a fool dies?
³⁴   Your hands were not bound,
     your feet not placed in bronze shackles.
     You fell like one who falls victim
        to criminals.

And all the people wept over him even more. ³⁵ Then they came to urge David to eat food while it was still day, but David took an oath: "May God punish me and do so severely if I taste bread or anything else before sunset!" ³⁶ All the people took note of this, and it pleased them. In fact, everything the king did pleased them. ³⁷ On that day all the troops and all Israel were convinced that the king had no part in the killing of Abner son of Ner.

³⁸ Then the king said to his soldiers, "You must know that a great leader has fallen in Israel today. ³⁹ As for me, even though I am the anointed king, I have little power today. These men, the sons of Zeruiah, are too fierce for me. May the LORD repay the evildoer according to his evil!"

The Assassination of Ish-bosheth

4 When Saul's son Ish-bosheth heard that Abner had died in Hebron, he gave up,ᴮ and all Israel was dismayed. ² Saul's son had two men who were leaders of raiding parties: one named Baanah and the other Rechab, sons of Rimmon the Beerothite of the Benjaminites. Beeroth is also considered part of Benjamin, ³ and the Beerothites fled to Gittaim and still reside there as aliens today.

⁴ Saul's son Jonathan had a son whose feet were crippled. He was five years old when the report about Saul and Jonathan came from Jezreel. His nanny picked him up and fled, but as she was hurrying to flee, he fell and became lame. His name was Mephibosheth.

⁵ Rechab and Baanah, the sons of Rimmon the Beerothite, set out and arrived at Ish-bosheth's house during the heat of the day while the king was taking his midday nap. ⁶ They entered the interior of the house as if to get wheat and stabbed him in the stomach. Then Rechab and his brother Baanah escaped. ⁷ They had entered the house while Ish-bosheth was lying on his bed in his bedroom and stabbed and killed him. They removed his head, took it, and traveled by way of the Arabah all night. ⁸ They brought Ish-bosheth's head to David at Hebron and said to the king, "Here's the head of Ish-bosheth son of Saul, your enemy who intended to take your life. Today the LORD has granted vengeance to my lord the king against Saul and his offspring."

⁹ But David answered Rechab and his brother Baanah, sons of Rimmon the Beerothite, "As the LORD lives, the one who has redeemed my life from every distress, ¹⁰ when the person told me, 'Look, Saul is dead,' he thought he was a bearer of good news, but I seized him and put him to death at Ziklag. That was my reward to him for his news! ¹¹ How much more when wicked men kill a righteous man in his own house on his own bed! So now, should I not require his blood from you and purge you from the earth?"

¹² So David gave orders to the young men, and they killed Rechab and Baanah. They cut off their hands and feet and hung their bodies by the pool in Hebron, but they took Ish-bosheth's head and buried it in Abner's tomb in Hebron.

David, King of Israel

5 All the tribes of Israel came to David at Hebron and said, "Here we are, your own flesh and blood.ᶜ ² Even while Saul was king over us, you were the one who led us out to battle and brought us back. The LORD also said to you, 'You will shepherd my people Israel, and you will be ruler over Israel.'"

³ So all the elders of Israel came to the king at Hebron. King David made a covenant with

---

ᴬ3:31 Or *the bier*; lit *the bed*   ᴮ4:1 Lit *his hands dropped*   ᶜ5:1 Lit *your bone and your flesh*

3:31–32 David's public participation in Abner's stately funeral would further distance him from blame for Abner's death. He is also called **King David** for the first time here. Abner's burial in **Hebron** may have been David's way of honoring Abner by treating him as one of David's own tribe members. The king **wept aloud**, something kings did not normally do.

3:33–34 David took his mourning for Abner even further when he **sang a lament**. He alluded to Abner's killers (Joab and Abishai) as **criminals**.

4:1 News of Abner's death reached **Ish-bosheth**, who **gave up** because Ish-bosheth had now lost his strongest general. Probably **all Israel** who had supported him were **dismayed** because they feared reprisal

following a victory by David that now appeared certain.

4:4 Mephibosheth, a **son of Jonathan**, would find favor with David during David's reign (9:1–10).

4:7 Baanah and Rechab beheaded Ish-bosheth because they wanted proof of his death for David. **By way of the Arabah** took them through the Jordan Valley, the quickest and most direct route to Hebron about fifty miles southwest. They hoped they might receive a reward for eliminating David's rival, Saul's son.

4:11 David contrasted the character of Baanah and Rechab with that of Ish-bosheth, whom he called **a righteous man**. The words **in his own house on his own bed** suggested they had committed a cowardly, cold-blooded act (cp. 3:26–30).

4:12 After having the killers executed, David commanded his men to **cut off the hands** that had committed the murder and **feet** that had run to bring the news of the murder to David. **Ish-bosheth's head** was placed in **Abner's tomb in Hebron**, uniting him with family in death but also perhaps subtly identifying him with Judah (3:32).

5:1 Representatives of **all the tribes** then **came to David at Hebron**. They were not his **own flesh and blood** as much as the Judahites were (19:41–43), but they were Israelites just like him. The troops who came to David at Hebron are listed in 1Ch 12:23–40.

5:3 In the LORD's presence (lit "before Yahweh") further confirmed God's blessing over David's reign. This was David's third anointing (cp. 2:4; 1Sm 16:12–13).

them at Hebron in the LORD's presence, and they anointed David king over Israel.

4 David was thirty years old when he began his reign; he reigned forty years. **5** In Hebron he reigned over Judah seven years and six months, and in Jerusalem he reigned thirty-three years over all Israel and Judah.

6 The king and his men marched to Jerusalem against the Jebusites who inhabited the land. The Jebusites had said to David, "You will never get in here. Even the blind and lame can repel you" thinking, "David can't get in here."

7 Yet David did capture the stronghold of Zion, that is, the city of David. **8** He said that day, "Whoever attacks the Jebusites must go through the water shaft to reach the lame and the blind who are despised by David."^A For this reason it is said, "The blind and the lame will never enter the house."^B

9 David took up residence in the stronghold, which he named the city of David. He built it up all the way around from the supporting terraces inward. **10** David became more and more powerful, and the LORD God of Armies was with him. **11** King Hiram of Tyre sent envoys to David; he also sent cedar logs, carpenters, and stonemasons, and they built a palace for David. **12** Then David knew that the LORD had established him as king over Israel and had exalted his kingdom for the sake of his people Israel.

13 After he arrived from Hebron, David took more concubines and wives from Jerusalem, and more sons and daughters were born to him. **14** These are the names of those born to him in Jerusalem: Shammua, Shobab, Nathan, Solomon, **15** Ibhar, Elishua, Nepheg, Japhia, **16** Elishama, Eliada, and Eliphelet.

17 When the Philistines heard that David had been anointed king over Israel, they all went in search of David, but he heard about it and went down to the stronghold. **18** So the

Philistines came and spread out in Rephaim Valley.

19 Then David inquired of the LORD: "Should I attack the Philistines? Will you hand them over to me?"

The LORD replied to David, "Attack, for I will certainly hand the Philistines over to you."

20 So David went to Baal-perazim and defeated them there and said, "Like a bursting flood, the LORD has burst out against my enemies before me." Therefore, he named that place The Lord Bursts Out.^C **21** The Philistines abandoned their idols there, and David and his men carried them off.

22 The Philistines came up again and spread out in Rephaim Valley. **23** So David inquired of the LORD, and he answered, "Do not attack directly, but circle around behind them and come at them opposite the balsam trees. **24** When you hear the sound of marching in the tops of the balsam trees, act decisively, for then the LORD will have gone out ahead of you to strike down the army of the Philistines." **25** So David did exactly as the LORD commanded him, and he struck down the Philistines all the way from Geba to Gezer.

David Moves the Ark

6 David again assembled all the fit young men in Israel: thirty thousand. **2** He and all his troops set out to bring the ark of God from Baale-judah.^D The ark bears the Name, the name of the LORD of Armies who is enthroned between the cherubim. **3** They set the ark of God on a new cart and transported it from Abinadab's house, which was on the hill. Uzzah and Ahio,^E sons of Abinadab, were guiding the cart **4** and brought it with the ark of God from Abinadab's house on the hill. Ahio walked in front of the ark. **5** David and the whole house of Israel were dancing before the LORD with all kinds of fir wood

^A 5:8 Alt Hb tradition, LXX, Tg, Syr read *who despise David* ^B 5:8 Or *temple,* or *palace* ^C 5:20 Or *Baal-perazim*; 2Sm 6:8; 1Ch 13:11 ^D 6:2 = Kiriath-jearim in 1Sm 7:1; 1Ch 13:6; 2Ch 1:4 ^E 6:3 Or *And his brothers*

5:6 The **Jebusites** had held at least a district of Jerusalem since the days of Joshua (Jos 15:63; 1Ch 11:4–9), and they thought their city was invincible.
5:7 **Zion** was a poetic name for Jerusalem; its exact meaning is unknown. The size of Jebusite Jerusalem was only about twelve acres (David subsequently expanded it somewhat), with a population estimated around 1,500. Nonetheless, the city would serve the king well.
5:8 **Water shaft** may designate an almost fifty-foot vertical shaft (today called "Warren's Shaft" after Charles Warren who discovered it) cut through rock from the Gihon Spring, Jerusalem's main water source. David's reference to **the lame and the blind** should be understood as a mocking taunt of the Jebusites who were not, in fact, able to defend their city (cp. v. 6).

5:9 Archaeological excavations have revealed some of David's **supporting terraces** on the city's eastern slope. David's choice of Jerusalem as his capital was a strategic move. It was more centrally located than Hebron, and it was located in Benjamin, the tribe of Saul.
5:11 King Hiram of Tyre, the leader of a wealthy Phoenician port city, sought to placate David through building assistance. He would later partner with David's son, Solomon, in the building of Israel's temple (1Kg 5:1–12).
5:13–16 Of the **sons . . . born to** David in **Jerusalem**, only **Solomon** would later play a role in the biblical account (12:24–25; 1Kg 1:33–40).
5:18 Rephaim Valley lay just southwest of Jerusalem (1Ch 14:13–16).
5:22–25 God added a particular strategy to his encouragement of David to engage the Philistines again. The **sound of marching** in

the **balsam trees** was possibly produced by strong winds that typically would come up in the afternoon combined with an undisclosed act of God. When the Israelites heard this distinct sound, they would know God was marching before them, leading them to victory. David cut off the Philistines' path of retreat, and they had to flee northward down the Aijalon Valley instead of toward **Gezer.**
6:2 Baale-judah was also known as Kiriath-jearim, located in Benjamin. The **ark of God** had been there since Samuel's days (1Sm 7:1).
6:3 The people **set the ark . . . on a new cart** instead of carrying it on poles as the law prescribed (Ex 25:12–15). The people of God did no better than the pagan Philistines had done (1Sm 6:7). This decision would have disastrous consequences (2Sm 6:6–7).

instruments,[A] lyres, harps, tambourines, sistrums,[B] and cymbals. ⁶ When they came to Nacon's threshing floor, Uzzah reached out to the ark of God and took hold of it because the oxen had stumbled. ⁷ Then the LORD's anger burned against Uzzah, and God struck him dead on the spot for his irreverence, and he died there next to the ark of God. ⁸ David was angry because of the LORD's outburst against Uzzah, so he named that place Outburst Against Uzzah,[C] as it is today. ⁹ David feared the LORD that day and said, "How can the ark of the LORD ever come to me?" ¹⁰ So he was not willing to bring the ark of the LORD to the city of David; instead, he diverted it to the house of Obed-edom of Gath. ¹¹ The ark of the LORD remained in his house three months, and the LORD blessed Obed-edom and his whole family.

¹² It was reported to King David, "The LORD has blessed Obed-edom's family and all that belongs to him because of the ark of God." So David went and had the ark of God brought up from Obed-edom's house to the city of David with rejoicing. ¹³ When those carrying the ark of the LORD advanced six steps, he sacrificed an ox and a fattened calf. ¹⁴ David was dancing[D] with all his might before the LORD wearing a linen ephod. ¹⁵ He and the whole house of Israel were bringing up the ark of the LORD with shouts and the sound of the ram's horn. ¹⁶ As the ark of the LORD was entering the city of David, Saul's daughter Michal looked down from the window and saw King David leaping and dancing before the LORD, and she despised him in her heart.

¹⁷ They brought the ark of the LORD and set it in its place inside the tent David had pitched for it. Then David offered burnt offerings and fellowship offerings in the LORD's presence. ¹⁸ When David had finished offering the burnt offering and the fellowship offerings, he blessed the people in the name of the LORD of Armies. ¹⁹ Then he distributed a loaf of bread, a date cake, and a raisin cake to each one in the entire Israelite community, both men and women. Then all the people went home.

²⁰ When David returned home to bless his household, Saul's daughter Michal came out to meet him. "How the king of Israel honored himself today!" she said. "He exposed himself today in the sight of the slave girls of his subjects like a vulgar person would expose himself."

²¹ David replied to Michal, "It was before the LORD who chose me over your father and his whole family to appoint me ruler over the LORD's people Israel. I will dance before the LORD, ²² and I will dishonor myself and humble myself even more.[E,F] However, by the slave girls you spoke about, I will be honored." ²³ And Saul's daughter Michal had no child to the day of her death.

The LORD's Covenant with David

7 When the king had settled into his palace and the LORD had given him rest on every side from all his enemies, ² the king said to the prophet Nathan, "Look, I am living in a cedar house while the ark of God sits inside tent curtains."

³ So Nathan told the king, "Go and do all that is on your mind, for the LORD is with you."

⁴ But that night the word of the LORD came to Nathan: ⁵ "Go to my servant David and say, 'This is what the LORD says: Are you to build me a house to dwell in? ⁶ From the time I brought the Israelites out of Egypt until today I have not dwelt in a house; instead, I have been moving

---

[A]6:5 DSS, LXX read with tuned instruments with strength, with songs; 1Ch 13:8　[B]6:5 = an Egyptian percussion instrument
[C]6:8 Or Perez-uzzah; 2Sm 5:20　[D]6:14 Or whirling　[E]6:22 LXX reads more and I will be humble in your eyes　[F]6:22 Lit more and I will be humble in my own eyes

---

6:6–7 The site of **Nacon's threshing floor** is unknown. **Uzzah** meant well when he tried to steady the ark when the **oxen ... stumbled**, but God **struck him dead** for his irreverence. Good intentions must be coupled with proper reverence when approaching God (cp. Heb 12:29).

6:8 David's anger was perhaps due to Uzzah's carelessness that led to God's anger being displayed. The king had not wanted such a joyous celebration to be marred by death. It is also possible that David's anger was directed at God, for humans often fail to comprehend God's justice.

6:10 The **ark of the LORD** ended up at the house of **Obed-edom** (1Ch 15:16–18). Rather than being from **Gath** (21:19; 1Sm 17:4), Obed-edom may have lived near an olive press or wine press (Hb gath).

6:11 David delayed his plan for **three months**, perhaps to ensure the time of God's wrath had passed (v. 12) or perhaps out of reverent fear (v. 9).

6:12 News of Obed-edom's prosperity convinced David the ark was safe to move carefully now.

6:13 David's sacrifice of **an ox and a fattened calf** after the ark had barely moved probably reveals he still had some concerns about the Lord's anger over the previous incident with Uzzah.

6:14–16 A linen ephod was a fine garment, typically worn by priests or Levites (Ex 28:6; 1Sm 2:18). Although David was **dancing** in worship **before the LORD**, the text does not indicate he actually assumed a priestly role. We should not understand v. 13 as meaning David actually performed the sacrifice, though he certainly was leading his people in worship.

The text states one reason why **Saul's daughter Michal ... saw King David** and **despised him in her heart** is that his actions seemed vulgar to her (cp. v. 20). In addition to this, perhaps she was not sincere in her faith in the Lord (1Sm 19:13), or perhaps she

was angry that David had taken her back from Paltiel (2Sm 3:13–16).

6:17–19 Burnt offerings marked general dedication to God, while **fellowship offerings** were sacrificial meals shared by priests and worshipers.

6:23 Some suggest Michal's childlessness was the result of God's direct judgment, but the text is not clear on this. Her childlessness may have resulted from her and David having no conjugal relations due to the obvious tension in their marriage.

7:2 David's words further revealed his heart for the Lord. It made no sense to him that he had so much and **the ark of God** was housed only by **tent curtains**.

7:3 Nathan is elsewhere called "the prophet Nathan" (1Kg 1:8,10,22–23). He apparently believed he did not need to consult the LORD about whether David should build God a temple, so he gave the king his blessing.

around with a tent as my dwelling. **7** In all my journeys with all the Israelites, have I ever spoken a word to one of the tribal leaders of Israel, whom I commanded to shepherd my people Israel, asking: Why haven't you built me a house of cedar?'

8 "So now this is what you are to say to my servant David: 'This is what the LORD of Armies says: I took you from the pasture, from tending the flock, to be ruler over my people Israel. **9** I have been with you wherever you have gone, and I have destroyed all your enemies before you. I will make a great name for you like that of the greatest on the earth. **10** I will designate a place for my people Israel and plant them, so that they may live there and not be disturbed again. Evildoers will not continue to oppress them as they have done **11** ever since the day I ordered judges to be over my people Israel. I will give you rest from all your enemies.

" 'The LORD declares to you: The LORD himself will make a house for you. **12** When your time comes and you rest with your ancestors, I will raise up after you your descendant, who will come from your body, and I will establish his kingdom. **13** He is the one who will build a house for my name, and I will establish the throne of his kingdom forever. **14** I will be his father, and he will be my son. When he does wrong, I will discipline him with a rod of men and blows from mortals. **15** But my faithful love will never leave him as it did when I removed it from Saul, whom I removed from before you. **16** Your house and kingdom will endure before me^A forever, and your throne will be established forever.' "

17 Nathan reported all these words and this entire vision to David.

David's Prayer of Thanksgiving

18 Then King David went in, sat in the LORD's presence, and said,

Who am I, Lord GOD, and what is my house that you have brought me this far? **19** What you have done so far^B was a little thing to you, Lord GOD, for you have also spoken about your servant's house in the distant future. And this is a revelation^C for mankind, Lord GOD. **20** What more can David say to you? You know your servant, Lord GOD. **21** Because of your word and according to your will, you have revealed all these great things to your servant.

22 This is why you are great, Lord GOD. There is no one like you, and there is no God besides you, as all we have heard confirms. **23** And who is like your people Israel? God came to one nation on earth in order to redeem a people for himself, to make a name for himself, and to perform for them^D great and awesome acts,^E driving out nations and their gods before your people you redeemed for yourself from Egypt. **24** You established your people Israel to be your own people forever, and you, LORD, have become their God.

25 Now, LORD God, fulfill the promise forever that you have made to your servant and his house. Do as you have promised, **26** so that your name will be exalted forever, when it is said, "The LORD of Armies is God over Israel." The house of your servant David will be established before you **27** since you, LORD of Armies, God of Israel, have revealed this to your servant when you said, "I will build a house for you." Therefore, your servant has found the courage to pray this prayer to you. **28** Lord GOD, you are God; your words are true, and you have promised this good thing to your servant. **29** Now, please bless your servant's house so that it will continue before you forever. For you, Lord GOD, have spoken, and with your blessing your servant's house will be blessed forever.

---

^A**7:16** Some Hb mss, LXX, Syr; other Hb mss read *you* ^B**7:19** Lit *Yet this* ^C**7:19** Or *custom*, or *instruction* ^D**7:23** Some Hb mss, Tg, Vg, Syr; other Hb mss read *you* ^E**7:23** LXX; MT reads *acts for your land*

7:9 The expression in Hebrew, "make a great name for" occurs six times in the Old Testament. First Ch 17:8 is parallel to this passage, citizens of Babylon plan to do it for themselves in Gn 11:4, and the Lord has done it for himself in Neh 9:10; Jr 32:20; Dn 9:15. A slightly different Hebrew phrase, "your name will be exalted forever," used in 2Sm 7:26, is also used of Abraham in Gn 12:2, suggesting the similarities between the Abrahamic and Davidic covenants.
7:11 The Lord denied David's desire to build him a house (temple), but he rewarded David's heart by building the king **a house** (dynasty)—composed of David's descendants.
7:13 The phrase **I will establish the throne of his kingdom forever** did not imply that

David's descendants would live forever but that his dynasty and kingdom would.
7:15 God promised David his **faithful love** (Hb *chesed*). This is a rich term, encompassing all that would come to David's line as he belonged to God. On the other hand, the Lord had **removed** such love from **Saul** because of his misguided heart.
7:16–17 Ultimately God's promise to David was fulfilled in the king's most significant descendant, the Lord Jesus Christ, whose **throne** would be **established forever** (Lk 1:32–33).
7:23 God established his covenant with Israel not only **to redeem a people for** himself, but **to make a name for himself** so other peoples could turn to him (Is 45:22).

His **great and awesome acts** included his miracles performed in Egypt and during the journey to the promised land. God's intent was to judge **nations and their gods** who lived in Canaan at the time Israel entered the land.
7:26 David wanted most of all that God's **name** would **be exalted forever** through all he did for David's house. Seeing **the LORD of Armies** receive his proper glory had long been on David's heart (1Sm 17:26,36,45–47).
7:28 David knew God's **words** were **true** (the Hb word rendered "true" is related to the Eng word *amen*). God's truth provided David a foundation for his life, just as it does for all believers (Jn 8:31–32).

David's Victories

8 After this, David defeated the Philistines, subdued them, and took Metheg-ammah^A from Philistine control.^B ^2 He also defeated the Moabites, and after making them lie down on the ground, he measured them off with a cord. He measured every two cord lengths of those to be put to death and one full length of those to be kept alive. So the Moabites became David's subjects and brought tribute.

^3 David also defeated Hadadezer son of Rehob, king of Zobah, when he went to restore his control at the Euphrates River. ^4 David captured seventeen hundred horsemen^C and twenty thousand foot soldiers from him, and he hamstrung all the horses and kept a hundred chariots.^D

^5 When the Arameans of Damascus came to assist King Hadadezer of Zobah, David struck down twenty-two thousand Aramean men. ^6 Then he placed garrisons in Aram of Damascus, and the Arameans became David's subjects and brought tribute. The LORD made David victorious wherever he went.

^7 David took the gold shields of Hadadezer's officers and brought them to Jerusalem. ^8 King David also took huge quantities of bronze from Betah^E and Berothai, Hadadezer's cities.

^9 When King Toi of Hamath heard that David had defeated the entire army of Hadadezer, ^10 he sent his son Joram to King David to greet him and to congratulate him because David had fought against Hadadezer and defeated

him, for Toi and Hadadezer had fought many wars. Joram had items of silver, gold, and bronze with him. ^11 King David also dedicated these to the LORD, along with the silver and gold he had dedicated from all the nations he had subdued — ^12 from Edom,^F Moab, the Ammonites, the Philistines, the Amalekites, and the spoil of Hadadezer son of Rehob, king of Zobah.

^13 David made a reputation for himself when he returned from striking down eighteen thousand Edomites^G in Salt Valley.^H ^14 He placed garrisons throughout Edom, and all the Edomites were subject to David. The LORD made David victorious wherever he went.

^15 So David reigned over all Israel, administering justice and righteousness for all his people.

^16   Joab son of Zeruiah was over the army;
        Jehoshaphat son of Ahilud was
            court historian;
^17   Zadok son of Ahitub and Ahimelech
            son of Abiathar were priests;
        Seraiah was court secretary;
^18   Benaiah son of Jehoiada was over the
            Cherethites and the Pelethites;
        and David's sons were chief officials.^I

David's Kindness to Mephibosheth

9 David asked, "Is there anyone remaining from the family of Saul I can show kindness to for Jonathan's sake?" ^2 There was a servant of Saul's family named Ziba. They

---

^A8:1 Or *took control of the mother city*; Hb obscure   ^B8:1 LXX reads *them, and David took tribute out of the hand of the Philistines*   ^C8:4 LXX, DSS read *1,000 chariots and 7,000 horsemen*   ^D8:4 Or *chariot horses*   ^E8:8 Some LXX mss, Syr read *Tebah*   ^F8:12 Some Hb mss, LXX, Syr; other Hb mss read *Aram*; 1Ch 18:11   ^G8:13 Some Hb mss, LXX, Syr; other Hb mss read *Arameans*; 1Ch 18:12   ^H8:13 = the Dead Sea region   ^I8:18 LXX; MT reads *were priests*; 1Ch 18:17

8:1 The **Philistines** were never again a serious threat to Israel after David **subdued** them. **Metheg-ammah** (lit "bridle of the cubit") is an unknown site. Some suggest the expression is figurative, indicating David took the bridle (the reins of leadership) from his enemies.
8:2 The **Moabites** lived on Israel's southeast border beyond the Dead Sea. David allowed one-third of the defeated army to live; many kings of that time would not have been so merciful. Further, those who remained could then maintain the Moabite economy and thus bring **tribute** (regular tax that subject peoples were required to pay) to David.
8:3 Zobah was one of several Aramean (Syrian) city-states northeast of Israel. Through his conquest of **Hadadezer** and the other Aramean rulers, David gained control as far as the **Euphrates River**.
8:4 David **hamstrung all the horses** of the Arameans probably because chariot horses were not useful for most of Israel's rugged territory. David also affirmed that victory did not depend on horses but on God's will (Ps 20:7; Hos 1:7; cp. Dt 17:16). To hamstring a horse rendered it useless for military purposes.
8:5 Aramean city-states were known to band together against a common enemy.
8:6 Israelite garrisons in **Aram of Damascus** would ensure continued rule over the region. It also guaranteed Israel a profit from controlling major trade routes.

8:7 Gold shields seem to have been a significant part of other kings' public displays as well (1Kg 14:26–27).
8:8 This bronze eventually became the cast-metal reservoir (1Kg 7:23; lit "sea") in Solomon's temple.
8:9 King Toi of Hamath, another Aramean region, sought a treaty with David since David had subdued **Hadadezer**, Toi's enemy (1Sm 27:2–7).
8:12 David's victories are summarized here; his victory over the **Ammonites** is described later (10:1–14; 11:1; 12:26–31). Some manuscripts read "Aram" (Syria) instead of Edom, but Edom is more likely in light of v. 13.
8:13–14 Some early OT manuscripts read **Edomites** while others say "Arameans." The only difference between the two words in Hebrew is one slight variation in a letter. Since **Salt Valley** clearly designates a region by the Dead Sea, "Edomites" is more likely correct (see also v. 14 and Ps 60).
8:15 The phrase **So David reigned over all Israel** indicates that David now controlled not only his own people's territory, but the land of all the surrounding peoples; thus, he had secured his borders. David ruled with **justice and righteousness**, reflecting two aspects of God's character (Is 9:7; Jr 9:24).
8:16 Joab, David's nephew, is well known to the story (2:13–30; 3:22–30). **Jehoshaphat** should not be confused with a descendant

of David by the same name (2Ch 17–20). This Jehoshaphat served as **court historian** (lit "the one causing to remember"), the person who supervised the preservation of important records and who perhaps coordinated the announcement of royal edicts.
8:17 Zadok would serve David throughout his reign (20:25) and also would serve David's son Solomon (1Kg 1:38–39; 2:35). He descended from faithful Eleazar's line (Nm 25:7–13); his followers were known as the Zadokites, a term that became "Sadducees" during Jesus' day (Mt 3:7; 16:1). **Abiathar** son of Ahimelech had escaped from Nob when Saul slaughtered all the priests (1Sm 22:20–21); he probably named his son **Ahimelech** in memory of his own father. **Seraiah** probably assisted Jehoshaphat in his administrative duties.
8:18 Benaiah served Solomon as well as David (1Kg 2:35). The meaning of **Cherethites** and **Pelethites** is uncertain, but many believe the terms designate special units of foreign-born royal bodyguards—perhaps from Crete and Philistia. **Chief officials** is literally "priests"; perhaps **David's sons** served as palace consultants to the priesthood (1Ch 18:17). It is clear David desired a good relationship between his kingship and the priesthood.
9:1–5 David was determined to fulfill his promise regarding **Saul's family**, particularly for **Jonathan's sake** (1Sm 20:14–15; 23:17–18).

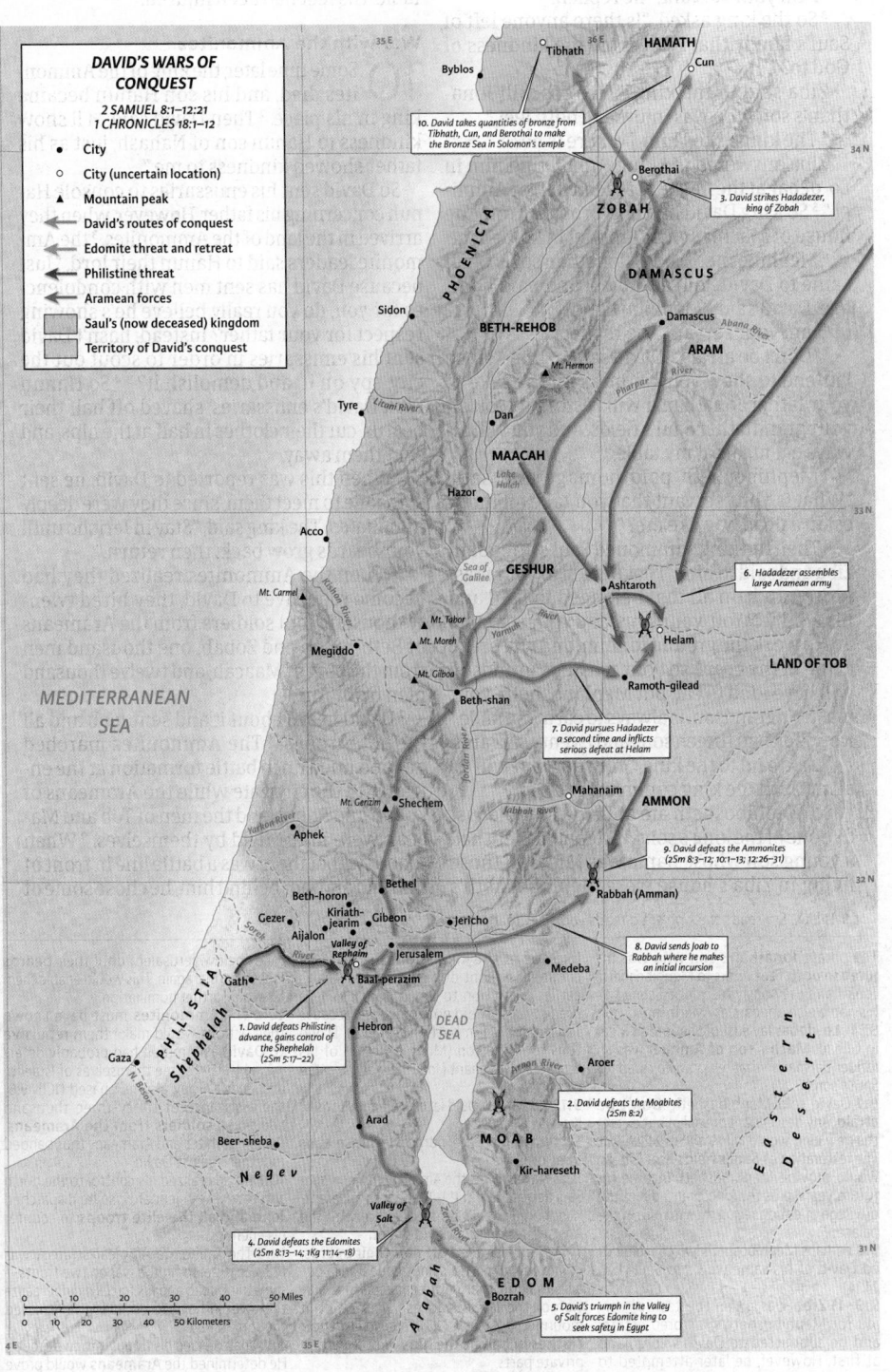

DAVID'S WARS OF CONQUEST

2 SAMUEL 8:1–12:21
1 CHRONICLES 18:1–12

• City
○ City (uncertain location)
▲ Mountain peak
→ David's routes of conquest
→ Edomite threat and retreat
→ Philistine threat
→ Aramean forces
▨ Saul's (now deceased) kingdom
▨ Territory of David's conquest

10. David takes quantities of bronze from Tibhath, Cun, and Berothai to make the Bronze Sea in Solomon's temple

3. David strikes Hadadezer, king of Zobah

6. Hadadezer assembles large Aramean army

7. David pursues Hadadezer a second time and inflicts serious defeat at Helam

9. David defeats the Ammonites (2Sm 8:3–12; 10:1–13; 12:26–31)

8. David sends Joab to Rabbah where he makes an initial incursion

1. David defeats Philistine advance, gains control of the Shephelah (2Sm 5:17–22)

2. David defeats the Moabites (2Sm 8:2)

4. David defeats the Edomites (2Sm 8:13–14; 1Kg 11:14–18)

5. David's triumph in the Valley of Salt forces Edomite king to seek safety in Egypt

HAMATH
Byblos
Tibhath
Cun
Berothai
ZOBAH
DAMASCUS
Damascus
Abana River
ARAM
PHOENICIA
BETH-REHOB
Sidon
Mt. Hermon
Pharpar River
Tyre
Litani River
Dan
MAACAH
Lake Huleh
Hazor
Acco
Sea of Galilee
GESHUR
Ashtaroth
Helam
LAND OF TOB
Mt. Carmel
Kishon River
Mt. Tabor
Mt. Moreh
Megiddo
Mt. Gilboa
Yarmuk River
Ramoth-gilead
Beth-shan
Jordan River
Mt. Gerizim
Shechem
Mahanaim
Jabbok River
AMMON
Aphek
Yarkon River
Bethel
Beth-horon
Rabbah (Amman)
Gezer
Kiriath-jearim
Gibeon
Aijalon
Valley of Rephaim
Jericho
Sorek River
Jerusalem
Gath
Baal-perazim
Medeba
PHILISTIA
Shephelah
Hebron
DEAD SEA
Gaza
N. Besor
Arnon River
Aroer
Arad
Beer-sheba
Eastern Desert
Negev
MOAB
Kir-hareseth
Valley of Salt
Zered River
EDOM
Arabah
Bozrah
MEDITERRANEAN SEA

0   10   20   30   40   50 Miles
0   10   20   30   40   50 Kilometers

summoned him to David, and the king said to him, "Are you Ziba?"

"I am your servant," he replied.

³ So the king asked, "Is there anyone left of Saul's family that I can show the kindness of God to?"

Ziba said to the king, "There is still Jonathan's son who was injured in both feet."

⁴ The king asked him, "Where is he?"

Ziba answered the king, "You'll find him in Lo-debar at the house of Machir son of Ammiel." ⁵ So King David had him brought from the house of Machir son of Ammiel in Lo-debar.

⁶ Mephibosheth son of Jonathan son of Saul came to David, fell facedown, and paid homage. David said, "Mephibosheth!"

"I am your servant," he replied.

⁷ "Don't be afraid," David said to him, "since I intend to show you kindness for the sake of your father Jonathan. I will restore to you all your grandfather Saul's fields, and you will always eat meals at my table."

⁸ Mephibosheth paid homage and said, "What is your servant that you take an interest in a dead dog like me?"

⁹ Then the king summoned Saul's attendant Ziba and said to him, "I have given to your master's grandson all that belonged to Saul and his family. ¹⁰ You, your sons, and your servants are to work the ground for him, and you are to bring in the crops so your master's grandson will have food to eat. But Mephibosheth, your master's grandson, is always to eat at my table." Now Ziba had fifteen sons and twenty servants.

¹¹ Ziba said to the king, "Your servant will do all my lord the king commands."

So Mephibosheth ate at David's^A table just like one of the king's sons. ¹² Mephibosheth had a young son whose name was Mica. All those living in Ziba's house were Mephibosheth's

servants. ¹³ However, Mephibosheth lived in Jerusalem because he always ate at the king's table. His feet had been injured.

War with the Ammonites

10 Some time later, the king of the Ammonites died, and his son Hanun became king in his place. ² Then David said, "I'll show kindness to Hanun son of Nahash, just as his father showed kindness to me."

So David sent his emissaries to console Hanun concerning his father. However, when they arrived in the land of the Ammonites, ³ the Ammonite leaders said to Hanun their lord, "Just because David has sent men with condolences for you, do you really believe he's showing respect for your father? Instead, hasn't David sent his emissaries in order to scout out the city, spy on it, and demolish it?" ⁴ So Hanun took David's emissaries, shaved off half their beards, cut their clothes in half at the hips, and sent them away.

⁵ When this was reported to David, he sent someone to meet them, since they were deeply humiliated. The king said, "Stay in Jericho until your beards grow back; then return."

⁶ When the Ammonites realized they had become repulsive to David, they hired twenty thousand foot soldiers from the Arameans of Beth-rehob and Zobah, one thousand men from the king of Maacah, and twelve thousand men from Tob.

⁷ David heard about it and sent Joab and all the elite troops. ⁸ The Ammonites marched out and lined up in battle formation at the entrance to the city gate while the Arameans of Zobah and Rehob and the men of Tob and Maacah were in the field by themselves. ⁹ When Joab saw that there was a battle line in front of him and another behind him, he chose some of

---

^A 9:11 LXX; Syr reads *the king's*; Vg reads *your*; MT reads *my*

The phrase **Jonathan's son who was injured in both feet** refers to Mephibosheth, Jonathan's previously mentioned son (4:4); his name also appears as "Merib-baal" (1Ch 8:34). **Lo-debar** lay east of the Jordan River in Gilead. **Machir son of Ammiel** was an influential man in that region who cared for Saul's son (17:27).
9:7 David told Mephibosheth, **Don't be afraid**. Any descendant of Saul might expect the new king would kill him (1Sm 24:20–22). The restoration of **Saul's fields** near Gibeah would provide Mephibosheth income for future years, plus the king granted him the privilege of eating regularly with him in the palace.
9:8 Perhaps Mephibosheth's words reminded David of his same words to Saul (1Sm 24:14).
9:9–11 Ziba was given the task of caring for Mephibosheth's restored estate, and he submitted to David's command at first. However, he later attempted to secure the estate for himself and his **fifteen sons** (16:1–4; 19:17,24–30). The phrase **Mephibosheth ate at David's table just**

like one of the king's sons is a touching comment in light of his father Jonathan's earlier prediction to David (1Sm 23:17)—a prediction that did not come true because Jonathan died in battle (1Sm 31:2). David thus took the son (Mephibosheth) of his brother by covenant (Jonathan) and treated him as a son.
9:12–13 Mica would later have four sons of his own (1Ch 8:35).
10:1 Ironically, the name **Hanun** means "gracious."
10:2 Nahash was the Ammonite ruler whom Saul defeated (1Sm 11:1–11). Nahash apparently honored Israel's terms of peace with the Ammonites on into David's reign.
10:4 Hanun **shaved off half their beards**, giving the men a ridiculous appearance but also making them appear to be in violation of the law of Moses (Lv 19:27) or in mourning (Is 15:2; Jr 41:5). He also **cut their clothes in half at the hips**, exposing their private parts.
10:5 David sent a delegation to the **deeply humiliated** men, advising them to **stay in Jericho** in the Jordan Valley about fifteen

miles below Jerusalem until their **beards** looked normal again. This would enable them to avoid further humiliation.
10:6 The **Ammonites** must have known their actions would make them **repulsive to David**, so Ammon had probably determined to try to free themselves of Israelite dominance. They also purchased (1Ch 19:6) the assistance of thirty-three thousand additional **soldiers from the Arameans**. The Ammonites and Arameans thus banded together against David.
10:7 David realized his control to the north and east was in jeopardy, so he dispatched **Joab and all the elite troops** to counter his enemies.
10:8 The Ammonite-Aramean strategy was to force Israel to fight a war on two fronts—something Joab and his forces did not realize they would have to do until they crossed the Jordan River.
10:9 Joab divided his troops into two groups. He determined the **Arameans** would prove the more challenging opponent, so he **chose some** of the **finest young men** to fight them.

Israel's finest young men and lined up in formation to engage the Arameans. **¹⁰** He placed the rest of the forces under the command of his brother Abishai. They lined up in formation to engage the Ammonites.

¹¹ "If the Arameans are too strong for me," Joab said, "then you will be my help. However, if the Ammonites are too strong for you, I'll come to help you. **¹²** Be strong! Let's prove ourselves strong for our people and for the cities of our God. May the LORD's will be done."^A

¹³ Joab and his troops advanced to fight against the Arameans, and they fled before him. **¹⁴** When the Ammonites saw that the Arameans had fled, they too fled before Abishai and entered the city. So Joab withdrew from the attack against the Ammonites and went to Jerusalem.

¹⁵ When the Arameans saw that they had been defeated by Israel, they regrouped. **¹⁶** Hadadezer sent messengers to bring the Arameans who were beyond the Euphrates River, and they came to Helam with Shobach, commander of Hadadezer's army, leading them.

¹⁷ When this was reported to David, he gathered all Israel, crossed the Jordan, and went to Helam. Then the Arameans lined up to engage David in battle and fought against him. **¹⁸** But the Arameans fled before Israel, and David killed seven hundred of their charioteers and forty thousand foot soldiers.^B He also struck down Shobach commander of their army, who died there. **¹⁹** When all the kings who were Hadadezer's subjects saw that they had been defeated by Israel, they made peace with Israel and became their subjects. After this, the Arameans were afraid to ever help the Ammonites again.

David's Adultery with Bathsheba

11 In the spring when kings march out to war, David sent Joab with his officers and all Israel. They destroyed the Ammonites and besieged Rabbah, but David remained in Jerusalem.

² One evening David got up from his bed and strolled around on the roof of the palace. From the roof he saw a woman bathing — a very beautiful woman. **³** So David sent someone to inquire about her, and he said, "Isn't this Bathsheba, daughter of Eliam and wife of Uriah the Hethite?"^c

⁴ David sent messengers to get her, and when she came to him, he slept with her. Now she had just been purifying herself from her uncleanness. Afterward, she returned home. **⁵** The woman conceived and sent word to inform David, "I am pregnant."

⁶ David sent orders to Joab: "Send me Uriah the Hethite." So Joab sent Uriah to David. **⁷** When Uriah came to him, David asked how Joab and the troops were doing and how the war was going. **⁸** Then he said to Uriah, "Go down to your house and wash your feet." So Uriah left the palace, and a gift from the king followed him. **⁹** But Uriah slept at the door of the palace with all his master's servants; he did not go down to his house.

¹⁰ When it was reported to David, "Uriah didn't go home," David questioned Uriah, "Haven't you just come from a journey? Why didn't you go home?"

¹¹ Uriah answered David, "The ark, Israel, and Judah are dwelling in tents, and my master Joab and his soldiers^D are camping in the open field. How can I enter my house to eat and drink and sleep with my wife? As surely as you live and by your life, I will not do this!"

¹² "Stay here today also," David said to Uriah, "and tomorrow I will send you back." So Uriah stayed in Jerusalem that day and the next. **¹³** Then David invited Uriah to eat and drink with him, and David got him drunk. He went out in the evening to lie down on his cot with his master's servants, but he did not go home.

---

^A **10:12** Lit *the* LORD *do what is good in his eyes*   ^B **10:18** Some LXX mss; MT reads *horsemen*; 1Ch 19:18   ^C **11:3** DSS add *Joab's armor-bearer*   ^D **11:11** Lit *servants*

10:10 Joab's **brother Abishai**, another seasoned warrior (2:24; 1Sm 26:6–11), led the second group against the Ammonites. Nonetheless, such a strategy was risky.
10:14 The **Ammonites** knew any hope of victory over Israel was gone when the **Arameans** fled. They **entered the city** of Rabbah (their capital) to defend it from siege. Joab withdrew, content for now to return to Jerusalem.
10:15 The **Arameans** probably feared an Israelite reprisal, so they **regrouped**.
10:16 **Hadadezer**, whom David had earlier subdued (8:3–4), gathered the **Arameans** even from the distant city-states across the **Euphrates River**. They gathered at **Helam** about thirty miles east of the Sea of Galilee.
10:17 David could not ignore this second threat, so he **crossed the Jordan** River to face them. He wanted to keep the battle outside Israelite territory as much as possible.

10:18 Again **the Arameans fled before Israel** (see v. 13). The extent of the victory is indicated by the comment that David **struck down Shobach commander of their army**.
11:1 Spring was an optimal time for **kings to march out to war**. The crops were growing and thus men were not needed as badly to work the fields, and the winter rains were letting up. David's forces under **Joab** had already put down the Ammonite threat (10:14), but David could not leave them unchecked. Israelite forces besieged **Rabbah**, the Ammonite capital. The words **David remained in Jerusalem** do not necessarily suggest David committed sin or folly by doing so. His men may have encouraged him to stay out of the battle (21:15–17), and David had not participated fully in some other battles as well (10:7).
11:2 David saw **a woman bathing** (lit "washing"); the text does not suggest she did so intentionally to lure David into an encounter.

11:3 David discovered the woman's identity—she was **Bathsheba, daughter of Eliam** (one of David's elite warriors; 23:34) and the **wife of Uriah the Hethite** (another of David's elite soldiers, 23:39). Bathsheba also may have been the granddaughter of Ahithophel, one of David's most trusted counselors (2Sm 23:34). At any rate, her married status rendered her off-limits to the king.
11:4 **David . . . slept with her**—meaning he had intercourse with her. The narrative is silent about Bathsheba's feelings about coming to the palace and submitting to the king's wishes.
11:8 The words of the king to Uriah, **wash your feet**, suggested a time of gentle relaxing at Uriah's **house**, where Bathsheba might arrange an intimate evening with her husband to make it appear that he was the baby's father.

Uriah's Death Arranged

14 The next morning David wrote a letter to Joab and sent it with Uriah. **15** In the letter he wrote: Put Uriah at the front of the fiercest fighting, then withdraw from him so that he is struck down and dies.

16 When Joab was besieging the city, he put Uriah in the place where he knew the best enemy soldiers were. **17** Then the men of the city came out and attacked Joab, and some of the men from David's soldiers fell in battle; Uriah the Hethite also died.

18 Joab sent someone to report to David all the details of the battle. **19** He commanded the messenger, "When you've finished telling the king all the details of the battle — **20** if the king's anger gets stirred up and he asks you, 'Why did you get so close to the city to fight? Didn't you realize they would shoot from the top of the wall? **21** At Thebez, who struck Abimelech son of Jerubbesheth?^,^B Didn't a woman drop an upper millstone on him from the top of the wall so that he died? Why did you get so close to the wall?' — then say, 'Your servant Uriah the Hethite is dead also.'" **22** Then the messenger left.

When he arrived, he reported to David all that Joab had sent him to tell. **23** The messenger reported to David, "The men gained the advantage over us and came out against us in the field, but we counterattacked right up to the entrance of the city gate. **24** However, the archers shot down on your servants from the top of the wall, and some of the king's servants died. Your servant Uriah the Hethite is also dead."

25 David told the messenger, "Say this to Joab: 'Don't let this matter upset you because the sword devours all alike. Intensify your fight against the city and demolish it.' Encourage him."

26 When Uriah's wife heard that her husband, Uriah, had died, she mourned for him.^C

27 When the time of mourning ended, David had her brought to his house. She became his wife and bore him a son. However, the LORD considered what David had done to be evil.

Nathan's Parable and David's Repentance

12 So the LORD sent Nathan to David. When he arrived, he said to him:

There were two men in a certain city, one rich and the other poor. **2** The rich man had very large flocks and herds, **3** but the poor man had nothing except one small ewe lamb that he had bought. He raised her, and she grew up with him and with his children. From his meager food she would eat, from his cup she would drink, and in his arms she would sleep. She was like a daughter to him. **4** Now a traveler came to the rich man, but the rich man could not bring himself to take one of his own sheep or cattle to prepare for the traveler who had come to him. Instead, he took the poor man's lamb and prepared it for his guest.^D

5 David was infuriated with the man and said to Nathan, "As the LORD lives, the man who did this deserves to die! **6** Because he has done this thing and shown no pity, he must pay four lambs for that lamb."

7 Nathan replied to David, "You are the man! This is what the LORD God of Israel says: 'I anointed you king over Israel, and I rescued you from Saul. **8** I gave your master's house to you and your master's wives into your arms,^E and I gave you the house of Israel and Judah, and if that was not enough, I would have given you even more. **9** Why then have you despised the LORD's command by doing what I consider^F evil? You struck down Uriah the Hethite with the sword and took his wife as your own wife — you murdered him with the Ammonite's sword. **10** Now therefore, the sword will

---

^11:21 LXX reads *Jerubbaal*   ^B11:21 = Gideon   ^C11:26 Lit *her husband*   ^D12:4 Lit *for the man who had come to him*
^E12:8 Lit *bosom*   ^F12:9 Alt Hb tradition reads *what he considers*

12:1–4 The LORD sent Nathan to David to reveal his message to the king. Nathan had communicated to the king God's incredible promise about David's house (7:8–17). This time, the message would not be as pleasant. Nathan's language emphasizes how the **one small ewe lamb** was more a member of the family than an asset comparable to the rich man's abundant sheep and cattle. The **rich man** did the unthinkable in the name of hospitality.
12:5 David was **infuriated**, a fact that reveals he thought Nathan's words presented a real occurrence in his kingdom. **Deserves to die** is literally "is a son of death."
12:6 David judged that the rich man had responded in an unjust, callous manner. **Four lambs** were the standard restitution for a stolen sheep (Ex 22:1).

12:7 With his powerful words, **You are the man**, the prophet drove home the application of the parable. The parable laid a foundation for what was to come; the words **this is what the LORD God of Israel says** then introduced God's indictment against the wayward king.
12:10–14 Nathan announced a threefold judgment on David: (1) David's **house** would be continuously plagued by violence; (2) David's **wives** would be taken from him and publicly violated; and (3) the child would **die** after birth. The third judgment was fulfilled in v. 18. The second was fulfilled by Absalom in 16:20–22. The first judgment was fulfilled in five parts: (1) between Amnon and Absalom (13:1–39); (2) between Absalom and David (15:1–18:33); (3) between Amasa and Joab (20:8–13); (4) between Adonijah and Solomon (1Kg 1:1–53; 2:13–25); and (5) between

Joab and Solomon (1Kg 2:28–35). David did not get off lightly for his great sins!

never leave your house because you despised me and took the wife of Uriah the Hethite to be your own wife.'

¹¹ "This is what the LORD says, 'I am going to bring disaster on you from your own family: I will take your wives and give them to another^A before your very eyes, and he will sleep with them in broad daylight.^B ¹² You acted in secret, but I will do this before all Israel and in broad daylight.'"^C

¹³ David responded to Nathan, "I have sinned against the LORD."

Then Nathan replied to David, "And the LORD has taken away your sin; you will not die. ¹⁴ However, because you treated^D the LORD with such contempt in this matter, the son born to you will die." ¹⁵ Then Nathan went home.

The Death of Bathsheba's Son

The LORD struck the baby that Uriah's wife had borne to David, and he became deathly ill. ¹⁶ David pleaded with God for the boy. He fasted, went home, and spent the night lying on the ground. ¹⁷ The elders of his house stood beside him to get him up from the ground, but he was unwilling and would not eat anything with them.

¹⁸ On the seventh day the baby died. But David's servants were afraid to tell him the baby was dead. They said, "Look, while the baby was alive, we spoke to him, and he wouldn't listen to us. So how can we tell him the baby is dead? He may do something desperate."

¹⁹ When David saw that his servants were whispering to each other, he guessed that the baby was dead. So he asked his servants, "Is the baby dead?"

"He is dead," they replied.

²⁰ Then David got up from the ground. He washed, anointed himself, changed his clothes, went to the LORD's house, and worshiped. Then he went home and requested something to eat. So they served him food, and he ate.

²¹ His servants asked him, "Why have you done this? While the baby was alive, you fasted and wept, but when he died, you got up and ate food."

²² He answered, "While the baby was alive, I fasted and wept because I thought, 'Who knows? The LORD may be gracious to me and let him live.' ²³ But now that he is dead, why should I fast? Can I bring him back again? I'll go to him, but he will never return to me."

The Birth of Solomon

²⁴ Then David comforted his wife Bathsheba; he went to her and slept with her. She gave birth to a son and named^E him Solomon.^F The LORD loved him, ²⁵ and he sent a message through the prophet Nathan, who named^G him Jedidiah,^H because of the LORD.

Capture of the City of Rabbah

²⁶ Joab fought against Rabbah of the Ammonites and captured the royal fortress. ²⁷ Then Joab sent messengers to David to say, "I have fought against Rabbah and have also captured its water supply. ²⁸ Now therefore, assemble the rest of the troops, lay siege to the city, and capture it. Otherwise I will be the one to capture the city, and it will be named after me." ²⁹ So David assembled all the troops and went to Rabbah; he fought against it and captured it. ³⁰ He took the crown from the head of their king,^I and it was placed on David's head. The crown weighed seventy-five pounds^J of gold, and it had a precious stone in it. In addition, David took away a large quantity of plunder from the city. ³¹ He removed the people who were in the city and put them to work with saws, iron picks, and iron axes, and to labor at brickmaking. He did the same to all the Ammonite cities. Then he and all his troops returned to Jerusalem.

^A**12:11** Or *to your neighbor*   ^B**12:11** Lit *in the eyes of this sun*   ^C**12:12** Lit *and before the sun*   ^D**12:14** Alt Hb tradition, one LXX ms; MT reads *treated the enemies of*; DSS read *treated the word of*   ^E**12:24** Alt Hb tradition reads *he named*   ^F**12:24** In Hb, the name *Solomon* sounds like "peace."   ^G**12:25** Or *prophet to name*   ^H**12:25** = Beloved of the LORD   ^I**12:30** LXX reads *of Milcom*; some emend to *Molech*; 1Kg 11:5,33   ^J**12:30** Lit *a talent*

12:11–12 The words **I will take your wives and give them to another** were fulfilled by David's son Absalom when Absalom tried to usurp the kingship (16:20–22).

12:13 Psalm 51 commemorates this event and expresses David's repentance. Psalm 32 expresses David's joy in being forgiven.

12:14 The language of this verse is difficult and has been rendered different ways. The words **you treated the LORD with . . . contempt** emphasize David's careless treatment of God's commands (v. 9). Other manuscripts read, "You have caused the LORD's enemies to blaspheme," meaning the enemies of God treated him with disdain because they had seen the hypocrisy of his chosen leader. In either case, God's leader had committed a very public sin, a fact that contributed to God's verdict: **the son born to you will die**. God would not allow this

child—a reminder of David's adultery and murder—to live.

12:23 The king's words **I'll go to him, but he will never return to me** may be understood as meaning David would one day join his infant child in heaven. Another possibility is that David was affirming that he would join him one day in death, but the child would never join him in this life again.

12:24 God's grace began anew in the lives of David and his wife Bathsheba. Their next child was Solomon, who would become Israel's next king. Another mark of God's grace was that the LORD loved Solomon.

12:25 Jedidiah, another name for Solomon, means "Beloved of the Lord."

12:26 The account of Joab's battle with the Ammonites that began in 11:1 now resumes. The royal fortress probably designates the part of the city where the palace stood.

12:27 Capturing a city's **water supply** ensured that its defeat was imminent. Cities that anticipated a siege would use extreme measures to guard their water (2Ch 32:3–4,30).

12:28–29 The distance from Jerusalem to Rabbah was about forty miles.

12:30 The placing of the former king's **crown . . . on David's head** symbolized the transfer of power from the Ammonite king to the king of Israel. David also dedicated the plunder to the Lord for the future temple's construction (1Ch 29:2–5).

12:31 David enslaved the captive Ammonite citizens and put them to work with **saws, iron picks, and iron axes, and to labor at brickmaking**. All these tasks were heavy labor. They suggest that David was fortifying key cities and areas throughout his territory.

Amnon Rapes Tamar

13 Some time passed. David's son Absalom had a beautiful sister named Tamar, and David's son Amnon was infatuated with her. [2] Amnon was frustrated to the point of making himself sick over his sister Tamar because she was a virgin, but it seemed impossible to do anything to her. [3] Amnon had a friend named Jonadab, a son of David's brother Shimeah. Jonadab was a very shrewd man, [4] and he asked Amnon, "Why are you, the king's son, so miserable every morning? Won't you tell me?"

Amnon replied, "I'm in love with Tamar, my brother Absalom's sister."

[5] Jonadab said to him, "Lie down on your bed and pretend you're sick. When your father comes to see you, say to him, 'Please let my sister Tamar come and give me something to eat. Let her prepare a meal in my presence so I can watch and eat from her hand.'"

[6] So Amnon lay down and pretended to be sick. When the king came to see him, Amnon said to him, "Please let my sister Tamar come and make a couple of cakes in my presence so I can eat from her hand."

[7] David sent word to Tamar at the palace: "Please go to your brother Amnon's house and prepare a meal for him."

[8] Then Tamar went to his house while Amnon was lying down. She took dough, kneaded it, made cakes in his presence, and baked them. [9] She brought the pan and set it down in front of him, but he refused to eat. Amnon said, "Everyone leave me!" And everyone left him. [10] "Bring the meal to the bedroom," Amnon told Tamar, "so I can eat from your hand." Tamar took the cakes she had made and went to her brother Amnon's bedroom. [11] When she brought them to him to eat, he grabbed her and said,^A "Come sleep with me, my sister!"

[12] "Don't, my brother!" she cried. "Don't disgrace me, for such a thing should never be done in Israel. Don't commit this outrage!

[13] Where could I ever go with my humiliation? And you — you would be like one of the outrageous fools in Israel! Please, speak to the king, for he won't keep me from you." [14] But he refused to listen to her, and because he was stronger than she was, he disgraced her by raping her.

[15] So Amnon hated Tamar with such intensity that the hatred he hated her with was greater than the love he had loved her with. "Get out of here!" he said.

[16] "No," she cried,^B "sending me away is much worse than the great wrong you've already done to me!"

But he refused to listen to her. [17] Instead, he called to the servant who waited on him, "Get this away from me, throw her out, and bolt the door behind her!" [18] Amnon's servant threw her out and bolted the door behind her. Now Tamar was wearing a long-sleeved^C robe, because this is what the king's virgin daughters wore. [19] Tamar put ashes on her head and tore the long-sleeved robe she was wearing. She put her hand on her head and went away crying out.

[20] Her brother Absalom said to her, "Has your brother Amnon been with you? Be quiet for now, my sister. He is your brother. Don't take this thing to heart." So Tamar lived as a desolate woman in the house of her brother Absalom.

Absalom Murders Amnon

[21] When King David heard about all these things, he was furious.^D [22] Absalom didn't say anything to Amnon, either good or bad, because he hated Amnon since he disgraced his sister Tamar.

[23] Two years later, Absalom's sheepshearers were at Baal-hazor near Ephraim, and Absalom invited all the king's sons. [24] Then he went to the king and said, "Your servant has just hired sheepshearers. Will the king and his servants please come with your servant?"

---

^A13:11 Lit *said to her*   ^B13:16 Lit *she said to him*   ^C13:18 Or *ornate*; Gn 37:3   ^D13:21 LXX, DSS add *but he did not grieve the spirit of Amnon his son, for he loved him because he was his firstborn*; 1Kg 1:6

13:1 David had several wives, and he fathered many children by them (3:2–5; 5:13–16). Both **Absalom** and **Tamar** had Maacah as their mother, whereas **Amnon**, David's firstborn son, had Ahinoam as his mother. The words **was infatuated with her** may also be translated as "loved her," but the present translation is better because Amnon's actions toward Tamar show that he never really loved her.

13:2 Amnon was **frustrated** because he wanted **Tamar** for his wife, but he could not marry his half sister (Lv 18:11; 20:17).

13:3 **Jonadab** was Amnon's **friend** and cousin. **Shrewd** is literally "wise," but Jonadab's wisdom was clearly not used for godly means.

13:11 **Sleep with me** is literally "lie with me"—have intercourse.

13:12 Three times Tamar urged her brother not to violate her. Doing **such a thing** was a serious offense in the law of Moses (Dt 22:25–29).

13:13 Tamar also insisted the crime would shame both her and her brother. Tamar then suggested that Amnon **speak to the king** about marrying her first. Her suggestion, however, may have been a means to escape the situation; it is unlikely David would have granted Amnon's request in violation of the Mosaic law (Lv 18:11; 20:17).

13:15 The words **Amnon hated Tamar** show that his feelings toward his half sister had been nothing more than lust (cp. vv. 1,4).

13:16 Amnon's attempt to send Tamar **away** after he had assaulted her was **much worse than** the rape itself since it would ensure that her shame was permanent.

13:17–19 This was a disrespectful way to speak of Amnon's half sister whom he had hoped to marry. Tamar's actions were typical signs of mourning.

13:20 Absalom found Tamar and discovered **Amnon** had raped her. **Be quiet for now** probably meant Absalom wanted Tamar to refrain from revealing what happened until he could think of a way to help her or to take vengeance on Amnon. As a **desolate woman**, Tamar would probably not marry; however, Absalom cared for her in his **house**.

13:21 David was **furious**, but he apparently did nothing.

13:22 Absalom, Tamar's full brother, did not say anything to Amnon, **either good or bad**, choosing instead to wait for an opportunity for revenge.

13:23–25 Two years later was a long time, but **Absalom** had not forgotten Amnon's sin. Sheep-shearing was a time of celebration (1Sm 25:7–8), so Absalom invited **all the king's sons** to Baal-hazor about fourteen miles north of Jerusalem.

²⁵ The king replied to Absalom, "No, my son, we should not all go, or we would be a burden to you." Although Absalom urged him, he wasn't willing to go, though he did bless him. ²⁶ "If not," Absalom said, "please let my brother Amnon go with us."

The king asked him, "Why should he go with you?" ²⁷ But Absalom urged him, so he sent Amnon and all the king's sons.ᴬ

²⁸ Now Absalom commanded his young men, "Watch Amnon until he is in a good mood from the wine. When I order you to strike Amnon, then kill him. Don't be afraid. Am I not the one who has commanded you? Be strong and valiant!" ²⁹ So Absalom's young men did to Amnon just as Absalom had commanded. Then all the rest of the king's sons got up, and each fled on his mule.

³⁰ While they were on the way, a report reached David: "Absalom struck down all the king's sons; not even one of them survived!" ³¹ In response the king stood up, tore his clothes, and lay down on the ground, and all his servants stood by with their clothes torn. ³² But Jonadab, son of David's brother Shimeah, spoke up: "My lord must not think they have killed all the young men, the king's sons, because only Amnon is dead. In fact, Absalom has planned thisᴮ ever since the day Amnon disgraced his sister Tamar. ³³ So now, my lord the king, don't take seriously the report that says all the king's sons are dead. Only Amnon is dead."

³⁴ Meanwhile, Absalom had fled. When the young man who was standing watch looked up, there were many people coming from the road west of him from the side of the mountain.ᶜ ³⁵ Jonadab said to the king, "Look, the king's sons have come! It's exactly like your servant said." ³⁶ Just as he finished speaking,

the king's sons entered and wept loudly. Then the king and all his servants also wept very bitterly. ³⁷ But Absalom fled and went to Talmai son of Ammihud, king of Geshur. And David mourned for his sonᴰ every day.

³⁸ After Absalom had fled to Geshur and had been there three years, ³⁹ King Davidᴱ longed to go to Absalom, for David had finished grieving over Amnon's death.

Absalom Restored to David

14 Joab son of Zeruiah realized that the king's mind was on Absalom. ² So Joab sent someone to Tekoa to bring a wise woman from there. He told her, "Pretend to be in mourning: dress in mourning clothes and don't put on any oil. Act like a woman who has been mourning for the dead for a long time. ³ Go to the king and speak these words to him." Then Joab told her exactly what to say.ᶠ

⁴ When the woman from Tekoa cameᴳ to the king, she fell facedown to the ground, paid homage, and said, "Help me, Your Majesty!"

⁵ "What's the matter?" the king asked her.

"Sadly, I am a widow; my husband died," she said. ⁶ "Your servant had two sons. They were fighting in the field with no one to separate them, and one struck the other and killed him. ⁷ Now the whole clan has risen up against your servant and said, 'Hand over the one who killed his brother so we may put him to death for the life of the brother he murdered. We will eliminate the heir!' They would extinguish my one remaining ember by not preserving my husband's name or posterity on earth."

⁸ The king told the woman, "Go home. I will issue a command on your behalf."

⁹ Then the woman of Tekoa said to the king, "My lord the king, may any blame be on me

---

ᴬ**13:27** LXX adds *And Absalom prepared a feast like a royal feast.* ᴮ**13:32** Lit *In fact, it was established on the mouth of Absalom* ᶜ**13:34** LXX adds *And the watchman came and reported to the king saying, "I see men on the Horonaim road on the side of the mountain."* ᴰ**13:37** Probably Amnon ᴱ**13:39** DSS, LXX, Tg read *David's spirit* ᶠ**14:3** Lit *Joab put the words into her mouth* ᴳ**14:4** Some Hb mss, LXX, Syr, Tg, Vg; other Hb mss read *spoke*

13:28 The narrative shifts suddenly to Baal-hazor. Absalom commanded his **young men** to strike **Amnon**. He reassured them because they probably feared reprisal from David. Absalom commissioned his hit men with words similar to those God spoke to Joshua (Jos 1:9). **13:30–33** Perhaps he who reported to the king that Absalom had **struck down all the king's sons** was one of the first to flee Baal-hazor. Thus he was panicked and lacked full information.

Jonadab clarified that only **Amnon** was dead, and he revealed that **Absalom** had planned Amnon's murder ever since Amnon had **disgraced his sister Tamar**. The text does not reveal how Jonadab knew Absalom's plans; perhaps it was only his theory, or perhaps he had overheard Absalom muttering threats. **13:34–36** **Coming from the road west of him** indicates David's sons had circled around rather than returning directly to Jerusalem.

13:37–38 Talmai was Absalom's maternal grandfather (3:3). He ruled **Geshur**, a small Aramean city-state along the eastern shore of the Sea of Galilee. Since Talmai was Absalom's grandfather and was on friendly terms with David, insisting on Absalom's return would have been politically difficult. Consequently, Absalom stayed **three years** in Geshur. **13:39** David missed **Absalom**, and he had **finished grieving over Amnon's death**. Yet he did not arrange for Absalom's homecoming. David's inaction would lead to further troubles. **14:2–3** **Tekoa** was approximately seven miles southwest of Jerusalem. Perhaps Joab thought Tekoa was far enough away that David would not recognize someone from there. Joab intended the **wise woman** to play a dramatic role that would influence **the king** to bring Absalom back to Jerusalem.

14:4 The clever woman (v. 2) **came to the king** and acted as if she were seeking David's judgment on a matter. **14:5–7** The woman's story recalls that of Cain and Abel (Gn 4:8–16). The woman's **clan** was attempting to execute justice and put her living son to death, fulfilling the role of blood avenger (v. 11; cp. Nm 35:9–29; Dt 19:4–13; Jos 20:1–9). However, if they killed the brother who killed his brother under extreme circumstances, they also would **eliminate the heir** to the woman's estate, and her **husband's** family **name** would come to an end. **14:8** David assured the woman that he would **issue a command** protecting her living son, but the woman's words in vv. 9–11 suggest the matter was not settled in her mind. **14:9** The woman's words suggested she had put David in a difficult position to let a murderer go free, and she asked that **any blame** rest on her and her family.

and my father's family, and may the king and his throne be innocent."

¹⁰ "Whoever speaks to you," the king said, "bring him to me. He will not trouble you again!"

¹¹ She replied, "Please, may the king invoke the LORD your God, so that the avenger of blood will not increase the loss, and they will not eliminate my son!"

"As the LORD lives," he vowed, "not a hair of your son will fall to the ground."

¹² Then the woman said, "Please, may your servant speak a word to my lord the king?"

"Speak," he replied.

¹³ The woman asked, "Why have you devised something similar against the people of God? When the king spoke as he did about this matter, he has pronounced his own guilt. The king has not brought back his own banished one. ¹⁴ We will certainly die and be like water poured out on the ground, which can't be recovered. But God would not take away a life; he would devise plans so that the one banished from him does not remain banished.

¹⁵ "Now therefore, I've come to present this matter to my lord the king because the people have made me afraid. Your servant thought: I must speak to the king. Perhaps the king will grant his servant's request. ¹⁶ The king will surely listen in order to keep his servant from the grasp of this man who would eliminate both me and my son from God's inheritance. ¹⁷ Your servant thought: May the word of my lord the king bring relief, for my lord the king is able to discern the good and the bad like the angel of God. May the LORD your God be with you."

¹⁸ Then the king answered the woman, "I'm going to ask you something; don't conceal it from me!"

"Let my lord the king speak," the woman replied.

¹⁹ The king asked, "Did Joab put you up to^A all this?"

The woman answered. "As you live, my lord the king, no one can turn to the right or left from all my lord the king says. Yes, your servant Joab is the one who gave orders to me; he told your servant exactly what to say.^B ²⁰ Joab your servant has done this to address the issue indirectly,^C but my lord has wisdom like the wisdom of the angel of God, knowing everything on earth."

²¹ Then the king said to Joab, "I hereby grant this request. Go, bring back the young man Absalom."

²² Joab fell with his face to the ground in homage and blessed the king. "Today," Joab said, "your servant knows I have found favor with you, my lord the king, because the king has granted the request of your servant."

²³ So Joab got up, went to Geshur, and brought Absalom to Jerusalem. ²⁴ However, the king added, "He may return to his house, but he may not see my face." So Absalom returned to his house, but he did not see the king.^D

²⁵ No man in all Israel was as handsome and highly praised as Absalom. From the sole of his foot to the top of his head, he did not have a single flaw. ²⁶ When he shaved his head — he shaved it at the end of every year because his hair got so heavy for him that he had to shave it off — he would weigh the hair from his head and it would be five pounds^E according to the royal standard.

²⁷ Three sons were born to Absalom, and a daughter named Tamar, who was a beautiful woman. ²⁸ Absalom resided in Jerusalem two years but never saw the king. ²⁹ Then Absalom sent for Joab in order to send him to the king, but Joab was unwilling to come to him. So he sent again, a second time, but he still would not come. ³⁰ Then Absalom said to his servants, "See, Joab has a field right next to mine, and he

---

^A14:19 Lit *"Is the hand of Joab in* ^B14:19 Lit *he put all these words into the mouth of your servant* ^C14:20 Lit *to go around the face of the matter* ^D14:24 Lit *king's face* ^E14:26 Lit *200 shekels*

14:10 David further assured her that no one would **trouble** her any more.

14:11 The woman persisted, asking David to **invoke** an oath before **the LORD** that her **son** would not die. David vowed that everything would be okay.

14:12 The woman had received her judgment, but she broke protocol and requested a chance to **speak** a further **word** to the king—a request David granted.

14:13 The woman gently but precisely drew a parallel between her situation and David's. Her words **the king . . . has pronounced his own guilt** implied David was unwilling to give himself the same judgment he gave the woman. He was unwilling to restore Absalom, who had murdered Amnon.

14:15–16 The woman acted as though she was returning to the **matter** of her **son** and her **inheritance**.

14:17 The woman's closing words were somewhat ambiguous in their application. Would

the **word of . . . the king bring relief** for her or for David? Her blessing, **May the LORD your God be with you**, may have hinted that just as the king could discern **the good and the bad** for others (19:27; 1Sm 29:9), perhaps with God's help he could discern for himself the wisest thing to do about Absalom.

14:18 David was indeed discerning, and he suspected the woman's collaboration with a member of the royal family.

14:19–20 The woman confessed that **Joab** had used her **to address the issue indirectly**, but David had seen through her presentation.

14:21 Despite David's recognition of Joab's ploy, he asked his nephew to bring **Absalom** from Geshur.

14:22 Joab appeared pleased to have played a part in beginning the reconciliation process between David and Absalom.

14:23–24 Ironically, David gave **Absalom** permission to **return to his house**, but he

would not give Joab an audience. David's "halfway" decision only inflamed the tension between himself and his son.

14:25 The description of Absalom's physical appearance makes him sound like a leader and it prepares the reader for Absalom's coup attempt in chap. 15.

14:26 Five pounds is literally "two hundred shekels." Many manuscripts say "one hundred shekels." Absalom's thick **hair** would have made him appear strong and powerful to many people.

14:27 Absalom had **a daughter named Tamar**. This was his way of honoring his sister.

14:28–30 Both David and **Absalom** lived in Jerusalem, but they did not speak to each other for **two years** as the tension between them mounted. **Absalom** knew if he **set the field** of Joab **on fire**, Joab could no longer avoid talking to him as he had done up to that point.

has barley there. Go and set fire to it!" So Absalom's servants set the field on fire.^A

³¹ Then Joab came to Absalom's house and demanded, "Why did your servants set my field on fire?"

³² "Look," Absalom explained to Joab, "I sent for you and said, 'Come here. I want to send you to the king to ask: Why have I come back from Geshur? I'd be better off if I were still there.' So now, let me see the king. If I am guilty, let him kill me."

³³ Joab went to the king and told him. So David summoned Absalom, who came to the king and paid homage with his face to the ground before him. Then the king kissed Absalom.

Absalom's Revolt

15 After this, Absalom got himself a chariot, horses, and fifty men to run before him. ² He would get up early and stand beside the road leading to the city gate. Whenever anyone had a grievance to bring before the king for settlement, Absalom called out to him and asked, "What city are you from?" If he replied, "Your servant is from one of the tribes of Israel," ³ Absalom said to him, "Look, your claims are good and right, but the king does not have anyone to listen to you." ⁴ He added, "If only someone would appoint me judge in the land. Then anyone who had a grievance or dispute could come to me, and I would make sure he received justice." ⁵ When a person approached to pay homage to him, Absalom reached out his hand, took hold of him, and kissed him. ⁶ Absalom did this to all the Israelites who came to the king for a settlement. So Absalom stole the hearts of the men of Israel.

⁷ When four^B years had passed, Absalom said to the king, "Please let me go to Hebron to fulfill a vow I made to the LORD. ⁸ For your servant made a vow when I lived in Geshur of Aram, saying, 'If the LORD really brings me back to Jerusalem, I will worship the LORD in Hebron.' "^C

⁹ "Go in peace," the king said to him. So he went to Hebron.

¹⁰ Then Absalom sent agents throughout the tribes of Israel with this message: "When you hear the sound of the ram's horn, you are to say, 'Absalom has become king in Hebron!' "

¹¹ Two hundred men from Jerusalem went with Absalom. They had been invited and were going innocently, for they did not know the whole situation. ¹² While he was offering the sacrifices, Absalom sent for David's adviser Ahithophel the Gilonite, from his city of Giloh. So the conspiracy grew strong, and the people supporting Absalom continued to increase.

¹³ Then an informer came to David and reported, "The hearts of the men of Israel are with Absalom."

¹⁴ David said to all the servants with him in Jerusalem, "Get up. We have to flee, or we will not escape from Absalom! Leave quickly, or he will overtake us quickly, heap disaster on us, and strike the city with the edge of the sword."

¹⁵ The king's servants said to the king, "Whatever my lord the king decides, we are your servants." ¹⁶ Then the king set out, and his entire household followed him. But he left behind ten concubines to take care of the palace. ¹⁷ So the king set out, and all the people followed him. They stopped at the last house ¹⁸ while all his servants marched past him. Then all the Cherethites, the Pelethites, and the people of Gath— six hundred men who came with him from there — marched past the king.

¹⁹ The king said to Ittai of Gath, "Why are you also going with us? Go back and stay with the new king since you're both a foreigner and an exile from your homeland. ²⁰ Besides, you only arrived yesterday; should I make you wander around with us today while I go wherever I can? Go back and take your brothers with you. May the LORD show you^D kindness and faithfulness."

^A 14:30 DSS, LXX add *So Joab's servants came to him with their clothes torn and said, "Absalom's servants have set the field on fire!"* ^B 15:7 Some LXX mss, Syr, Vg; other LXX mss, MT read *40* ^C 15:8 Some LXX mss; MT omits *in Hebron* ^D 15:20 LXX; MT omits Lit *May the LORD show you*

14:31–32 **Absalom** asked **Joab** for an audience with David. He suggested it would have been preferable for him to remain in **Geshur**. Absalom wanted his father to decide once and for all how he would handle his murder of Amnon.

14:33 Absalom finally met with his father, David, but this one meeting would not heal a wound that had festered for five years (v. 28; 13:38).

15:1 By gathering chariots, **horses**, and **men**, Absalom took steps to enhance his position in the eyes of the people.

15:2 The **city gate** was the site of the city's important business transactions.

15:7 Some manuscripts read "forty years" instead of **four years** while others read "forty days," but the CSB reading seems most likely.

15:8–9 The law urged prompt fulfillment of a **vow** (Dt 23:21), so the passage of four

years since Absalom's vow (2Sm 15:7) could have raised questions in David's mind. On the other hand, **Hebron**, located nineteen miles south of Jerusalem, was Absalom's birthplace.

15:10 The sound of the **ram's horn** across the land, combined with Absalom's messengers shouting **Absalom has become king in Hebron**, would enable news of Absalom's assuming the throne to spread quickly. Absalom probably hoped he could get to Jerusalem and take power before David could prepare to defend himself. It was in Hebron that David had been proclaimed king over Judah (2:4).

15:11–12 David's adviser **Ahithophel** was one of the king's wisest men, making the **conspiracy** of Absalom even more **strong**.

15:13–14 David summoned his **servants with him in Jerusalem** and insisted they

all needed to **flee** at once. He knew Absalom and his forces would head straight for the capital and attack it if necessary.

15:15–16 David's decision to leave behind **ten concubines** provided the occasion for part of Nathan's judgment oracle to come true (16:20–23).

15:18 On **Cherethites** and **Pelethites**, see note at 8:18. David's influence among the Philistines had gained him the loyalty of **six hundred men** from **Gath**.

15:19 **Ittai of Gath** was **an exile** from Philistia who had cast his lot with David, perhaps during David's flight from Saul (1Sm 18–31).

15:20–22 David excused **Ittai** from accompanying him, but Ittai swore by **the LORD** and **the king** that he would stay with David whether it meant **life or death** for him. David's integrity still garnered respect.

²¹ But in response, Ittai vowed to the king, "As the Lᴏʀᴅ lives and as my lord the king lives, wherever my lord the king is, whether it means life or death, your servant will be there!"

²² "March on," David replied to Ittai. So Ittai of Gath marched past with all his men and the dependents who were with him. ²³ Everyone in the countryside was weeping loudly while all the people were marching out of the city. As the king was crossing the Kidron Valley, all the people were marching past on the road that leads to the wilderness.

²⁴ Zadok was also there, and all the Levites with him were carrying the ark of the covenant of God. They set the ark of God down, and Abiathar offered sacrifices^A until the people had finished marching past. ²⁵ Then the king instructed Zadok, "Return the ark of God to the city. If I find favor with the Lᴏʀᴅ, he will bring me back and allow me to see both it and its^B dwelling place. ²⁶ However, if he should say, 'I do not delight in you,' then here I am — he can do with me whatever pleases him."^C

²⁷ The king also said to the priest Zadok, "Look,^D return to the city in peace and your two sons with you: your son Ahimaaz and Abiathar's son Jonathan. ²⁸ Remember, I'll wait at the fords^E of the wilderness until word comes from you to inform me." ²⁹ So Zadok and Abiathar returned the ark of God to Jerusalem and stayed there.

³⁰ David was climbing the slope of the Mount of Olives, weeping as he ascended. His head was covered, and he was walking barefoot. All of the people with him covered their heads and went up, weeping as they ascended.

³¹ Then someone reported to David, "Ahithophel is among the conspirators with Absalom."

"Lᴏʀᴅ," David pleaded, "please turn the counsel of Ahithophel into foolishness!"

³² When David came to the summit where he used to worship God, Hushai the Archite was there to meet him with his robe torn and dust on his head. ³³ David said to him, "If you go away with me, you'll be a burden to me, ³⁴ but if you return to the city and tell Absalom, 'I will be your servant, Your Majesty! Previously, I was your father's servant, but now I will be your servant,' then you can counteract Ahithophel's counsel for me. ³⁵ Won't the priests Zadok and Abiathar be there with you? Report everything you hear from the palace to the priests Zadok and Abiathar. ³⁶ Take note: their two sons are there with them — Zadok's son Ahimaaz and Abiathar's son Jonathan. Send them to tell me everything you hear." ³⁷ So Hushai, David's personal adviser, entered Jerusalem just as Absalom was entering the city.

Ziba Helps David

16 When David had gone a little beyond the summit,^F Ziba, Mephibosheth's servant, was right there to meet him. He had a pair of saddled donkeys loaded with two hundred loaves of bread, one hundred clusters of raisins, one hundred bunches of summer fruit, and a clay jar of wine. ² The king said to Ziba, "Why do you have these?"

Ziba answered, "The donkeys are for the king's household to ride, the bread and summer fruit are for the young men to eat, and the wine is for those to drink who become exhausted in the wilderness."

³ "Where is your master's grandson?" the king asked.

"Why, he's staying in Jerusalem," Ziba replied to the king, "for he said, 'Today, the house of Israel will restore my grandfather's kingdom to me.'"

⁴ The king said to Ziba, "All that belongs to Mephibosheth is now yours!"

"I bow before you," Ziba said. "May I find favor with you, my lord the king!"

---

^A15:24 Or *Abiathar went up* ^B15:25 Or *his* ^C15:26 Lit *me what is good in his eyes* ^D15:27 LXX; MT reads *"Are you a seer?* ^E15:28 Alt Hb tradition reads *plains* ^F16:1 = Mount of Olives

---

15:23 The **Kidron Valley** skirted Jerusalem's eastern edge, separating the city from the Mount of Olives. Once David and his associates reached the top, they could travel **the road that leads to the wilderness**, most likely the ascent of Adummim that connected Jerusalem with Jericho in the Jordan Valley. **15:24** The **ark of the covenant of God** was probably brought to ensure God's presence and as a mark of David's legitimate right to reign. **Zadok** and **Abiathar** (see note at 8:17) stood by the king who had endorsed their respective ministries and the ministries of the **Levites** (6:12–18). **15:27** David created a spy network that included **Zadok**, Abiathar, and their respective sons **Ahimaaz** and **Jonathan**. **15:28** The **fords of the wilderness** were shallow places where the Jordan River could be crossed. **15:29** Absalom would probably assume David's supporters had fled. He may not have

suspected **Zadok** and **Abiathar** of siding with his father. **15:30** Covering the **head** and **walking barefoot** were signs of deep personal anguish. **15:31** The news that **Ahithophel** had joined the **conspirators with Absalom** was a blow to David's cause. The king's prayer for God to **turn the counsel of Ahithophel into foolishness** was a prayer of great faith because Ahithophel's advice was taken to be like a word from the Lord (16:23). **15:32–35** **Hushai** would end up being the answer to David's prayer (v. 31). Hushai's role was to **counteract Ahithophel's counsel** (no small task in light of 16:23) and to **report everything** to Zadok and Abiathar (see 17:5–16). **15:36** **Ahimaaz** and **Jonathan** would then relay any information they received from their fathers directly to David. **15:37** **Hushai** and **Absalom** arrived in Jerusalem at the same time. The decisive moment

when Absalom had to choose between Hushai's counsel and Ahithophel's counsel is delayed by 16:1–14 and resumes at 16:15. **16:1–2** A **little beyond the summit** on the eastern side of the Mount of Olives, David's delegation could not be seen by Absalom or anyone else in Jerusalem. **Ziba, Mephibosheth's servant**, had earlier arranged for Saul's estate to be restored to his master (9:1–10). Now he brought provisions for David's group, but with a different motive. **16:3** David expressed surprise that Mephibosheth had not come with him and others from his palace. **Ziba** informed David that Mephibosheth was **staying in Jerusalem** because he was hoping to take advantage of the situation to regain Saul's kingdom. **16:4** The truth of Ziba's assertion could not be substantiated, but David, in his turbulent emotional state, decided he believed **Ziba** and rewarded him with Mephibosheth's estate.

David's Enemies

DAVID'S ENEMY	ENEMY'S THREAT	DAVID'S ACTION	GOD'S PROVISION
Lion/Bear	Carried off lambs from David's flock *(1Sm 17:34)*	Killed lions and bears to protect his sheep *(1Sm 17:35–36)*	The Lord rescued David from the paw of the lion and the bear *(1Sm 17:37)*.
Goliath, a Giant	Defied the armies of the living God *(1Sm 17:8–10,26)*	Defeated Goliath with a sling and a stone; with no sword of his own, he struck him down and killed him *(1Sm 17:48–51)*	The Lord handed Goliath over to David *(1Sm 17:45–47)*.
King Saul	Tried to kill David with his spear and his army *(1Sm 18–26)*	Fled from Saul and twice restrained himself from killing Saul, the Lord's anointed *(1Sm 24; 26)*	The Lord delivered David from the hand of Saul *(2Sm 12:7)*.
The Philistines	Searched for King David to kill him *(2Sm 5:17–18)*	Went to war with the Philistines and defeated them *(2Sm 5:20–25)*	The Lord handed the Philistines over to David *(2Sm 5:19,24)*.
David, Himself	Sinned against the Lord by committing adultery and murder *(2Sm 11)*	When confronted by the prophet Nathan, he confessed his sin and repented *(2Sm 12:1–13)*	The Lord took away his sin; he would not die, though his son would and rebellion would come from his own family *(2Sm 12:10–14)*.
Absalom, David's Son	Rebelled against his father to kill him and take the throne *(2Sm 15:1–14)*	Fled Jerusalem, entrusting himself to the Lord's favor or judgment *(2Sm 15:25–26)*	The Lord brought about Absalom's ruin to restore David to the throne *(2Sm 17:14)*.

Shimei Curses David

⁵ When King David got to Bahurim, a man belonging to the family of the house of Saul was just coming out. His name was Shimei son of Gera, and he was yelling curses as he approached. ⁶ He threw stones at David and at all the royalᴬ servants, the people and the warriors on David's right and left. ⁷ Shimei said as he cursed, "Get out, get out, you man of bloodshed, you wicked man! ⁸ The Lᴏʀᴅ has paid you back for all the blood of the house of Saul in whose place you became king, and the Lᴏʀᴅ has handed the kingdom over to your son Absalom. Look, you are in trouble because you're a man of bloodshed!"

⁹ Then Abishai son of Zeruiah said to the king, "Why should this dead dog curse my lord the king? Let me go over and remove his head!"

¹⁰ The king replied, "Sons of Zeruiah, do we agree on anything? He curses me this way because the Lᴏʀᴅᴮ told him, 'Curse David!' Therefore, who can say, 'Why did you do that?'" ¹¹ Then David said to Abishai and all his servants, "Look, my own son, my own flesh and blood,ᶜ intends to take my life — how much more now this Benjaminite! Leave him alone and let him curse me; the Lᴏʀᴅ has told him to. ¹² Perhaps the Lᴏʀᴅ will see my afflictionᴰ and restore goodness to me instead of Shimei's curses today." ¹³ So David and his men proceeded along the road as Shimei was going along the ridge of the hill opposite him. As Shimei went, he cursed David, threw stones at him, and kicked up dust. ¹⁴ Finally, the king and all the people with him arrivedᴱ exhausted, so they rested there.

Absalom's Advisers

¹⁵ Now Absalom and all the Israelites came to Jerusalem. Ahithophel was also with him. ¹⁶ When David's friend Hushai the Archite came to Absalom, Hushai said to Absalom, "Long live the king! Long live the king!"

¹⁷ "Is this your loyalty to your friend?" Absalom asked Hushai. "Why didn't you go with your friend?"

¹⁸ "Not at all," Hushai answered Absalom. "I am on the side of the one that the Lᴏʀᴅ, this people, and all the men of Israel have chosen. I will stay with him. ¹⁹ Furthermore, whom will I serve if not his son? As I served in your father's presence, I will also serve in yours."

²⁰ Then Absalom said to Ahithophel, "Give me your advice. What should we do?"

²¹ Ahithophel replied to Absalom, "Sleep with your father's concubines whom he left to take care of the palace. When all Israel hears that you have become repulsive to your father, everyone with you will be encouraged."ᶠ ²² So they pitched a tent for Absalom on the roof, and he slept with his father's concubines in the sight of all Israel.

²³ Now the advice Ahithophel gave in those days was like someone asking about a word from God — such was the regard that both David and Absalom had for Ahithophel's advice. ¹ Ahithophel said to Absalom, "Let me choose twelve thousand men, and I will set out in pursuit of David tonight. ² I will attack him while he is weary and discouraged,ᴳ throw him into a panic, and all the people with him will scatter. I will strike down only the king ³ and bring all the people back to you. When everyone returns except the man you're looking for, allᴴ the people will be at peace." ⁴ This proposal seemed right to Absalom and all the elders of Israel.

⁵ Then Absalom said, "Summon Hushai the Archite also. Let's hear what he has to say as well."

⁶ So Hushai came to Absalom, and Absalom told him, "Ahithophel offered this proposal. Should we carry out his proposal? If not, what do you say?"

⁷ Hushai replied to Absalom, "The advice Ahithophel has given this time is not good." ⁸ Hushai continued, "You know your father and his men. They are warriors and are desperate like a wild bear robbed of her cubs. Your father is an experienced soldier who won't spend the night with the people. ⁹ He's probably already hiding in one of the cavesᴵ or some other place. If some of our troops fallᴶ first, someone

---

ᴬ16:6 Lit all King David's   ᴮ16:10 Alt Hb tradition reads If he curses, and if the Lᴏʀᴅ   ᶜ16:11 Lit son who came from my belly
ᴰ16:12 Some Hb mss, LXX, Syr, Vg; one Hb tradition reads iniquity; alt Hb tradition reads eyes; another Hb tradition reads
will look with his eye   ᴱ16:14 LXX adds at the Jordan   ᶠ16:21 Lit father, the hands of everyone with you will be strong
ᴳ17:2 Lit and weak of hands   ᴴ17:3 LXX reads to you as a bride returns to her husband. You seek the life of only one man, and
all   ᴵ17:9 Or pits, or ravines   ᴶ17:9 Lit And it will be when a falling on them at

---

16:5 Bahurim was a nearby Benjaminite village. Shimei son of Gera is unknown except for his actions related to Absalom's revolt and David's flight (19:16–23) and his sentence during Solomon's reign (1Kg 2:8–9,36–46). 16:10 Do we agree on anything? is literally "What to me and to you?" It may be rhetorically asking what interests David and Abishai have in common (cp. 19:22; Jdg 11:12; 1Kg 17:18; 2Kg 3:13; 2Ch 35:21; Jn 2:4). This expression reveals David's exasperation with the sons of Zeruiah his sister.

16:16 The account now picks up from 15:37. Hushai and Absalom entered Jerusalem about the same time, and Hushai's greeting, Long live the king, was the beginning of his attempt to convince Absalom he was on his side. 16:18 Hushai's reply was more vague than Absalom realized. David—not Absalom—was the one whom the Lᴏʀᴅ had chosen (1Sm 16:12). 16:20–22 Absalom's lying with his father's concubines would be a visible sign to

everyone that Absalom was taking over the kingdom (including the harem) from David (12:8,11). Sleeping with David's concubines would also sharpen the division between Absalom and his father and encourage others to forsake David and join Absalom. In the sight of all Israel fulfilled God's words to David through the prophet Nathan (12:11). 17:5–6 Hushai probably knew Ahithophel's proposal would succeed. He had to convince Absalom to delay in pressing the attack against David.

is sure to hear and say, 'There's been a slaughter among the people who follow Absalom.' ¹⁰ Then, even a brave man with the heart of a lion will lose heart^A because all Israel knows that your father and the valiant men with him are warriors. ¹¹ Instead, I advise that all Israel from Dan to Beer-sheba — as numerous as the sand by the sea — be gathered to you and that you personally go into battle. ¹² Then we will attack David wherever we find him, and we will descend on him like dew on the ground. Not even one will be left—neither he nor any of the men with him. ¹³ If he retreats to some city, all Israel will bring ropes to that city, and we will drag its stones^B into the valley until not even a pebble can be found there." ¹⁴ Since the LORD had decreed that Ahithophel's good advice be undermined in order to bring about Absalom's ruin, Absalom and all the men of Israel said, "The advice of Hushai the Archite is better than Ahithophel's advice."

David Informed of Absalom's Plans

¹⁵ Hushai then told the priests Zadok and Abiathar, "This is what^C Ahithophel advised Absalom and the elders of Israel, and this is what^D I advised. ¹⁶ Now send someone quickly and tell David, 'Don't spend the night at the wilderness ford,^E but be sure to cross over the Jordan,^F or the king and all the people with him will be devoured.'"

¹⁷ Jonathan and Ahimaaz were staying at En-rogel, where a servant girl would come and pass along information to them. They in turn would go and inform King David, because they dared not be seen entering the city. ¹⁸ However, a young man did see them and informed Absalom. So the two left quickly and came to the house of a man in Bahurim. He had a well in his courtyard, and they climbed down into it. ¹⁹ Then his wife took the cover, placed it over the mouth of the well, and scattered grain on it so nobody would know anything. ²⁰ Absalom's servants came to the woman at the house and asked, "Where are Ahimaaz and Jonathan?"

"They passed by toward the water,"^G the woman replied to them. The men searched but did not find them, so they returned to Jerusalem. ²¹ After they had gone, Ahimaaz and Jonathan climbed out of the well and went and informed King David. They told him, "Get up and immediately ford the river, for Ahithophel has given this advice against you." ²² So David and all the people with him got up and crossed the Jordan. By daybreak, there was no one who had not crossed the Jordan.

²³ When Ahithophel realized that his advice had not been followed, he saddled his donkey and set out for his house in his hometown. He set his house in order and hanged himself. So he died and was buried in his father's tomb.

²⁴ David had arrived at Mahanaim by the time Absalom crossed the Jordan with all the men of Israel. ²⁵ Now Absalom had appointed Amasa over the army in Joab's place. Amasa was the son of a man named Ithra^H the Israelite;^I Ithra had married Abigail daughter of Nahash.^J Abigail was a sister to Zeruiah, Joab's mother. ²⁶ And Israel and Absalom camped in the land of Gilead. ²⁷ When David came to Mahanaim, Shobi son of Nahash from Rabbah of the Ammonites, Machir son of Ammiel from Lo-debar, and Barzillai the Gileadite from Rogelim ²⁸ brought beds, basins,^K and pottery items. They also brought wheat, barley, flour, roasted grain, beans, lentils,^L ²⁹ honey, curds, sheep, goats, and cheese^M from the herd for David and the people with him to eat. They had reasoned, "The people must be hungry, exhausted, and thirsty in the wilderness."

Absalom's Defeat

18 David reviewed his troops and appointed commanders of thousands and of hundreds over them. ² He then sent out the troops, a third under Joab, a third under Joab's brother Abishai son of Zeruiah, and a third under Ittai of Gath. The king said to the troops, "I must also march out with you."

³ "You must not go!" the people pleaded. "If we have to flee, they will not pay any attention

^A17:10 Lit *melt*   ^B17:13 Lit *drag it*   ^C17:15 Lit *"Like this and like this*   ^D17:15 Lit *and like this and like this*   ^E17:16 Some Hb mss; MT reads *plains*   ^F17:16 *the Jordan* supplied for clarity   ^G17:20 Or *brook*; Hb obscure   ^H17:25 Or *Jether*   ^I17:25 Some LXX mss read *Ishmaelite*   ^J17:25 Some LXX mss read *Jesse*   ^K17:28 LXX reads *brought 10 embroidered beds with double coverings, 10 vessels*   ^L17:28 LXX, Syr; MT adds *roasted grain*   ^M17:29 Hb obscure

17:11 From Dan to Beer-sheba was a distance of 110 miles. The two cities basically served as the northern and southern points of Israel, so Hushai was calling for a nationwide muster. Hushai's proposal was much more extensive and time-consuming, giving David and his forces time to regroup.
17:17 En-rogel was a spring in the Kidron Valley about one-fourth of a mile from Jerusalem where the Kidron and Hinnom valleys met.
17:18 Bahurim was the village in Benjamin from which Shimei came (16:5).

17:19 The woman **scattered grain** to make it look like the cover had not been recently disturbed.
17:23 Ahithophel knew that since his **advice had not been followed**, David would regain the throne. And when David was reestablished, Ahithophel would be considered a traitor. Thus he committed suicide.
17:24 Mahanaim was more than thirty miles from Jerusalem. So David and his men may have been about twenty miles from **Absalom** when he **crossed the Jordan**.

17:25 Amasa was another of David's nephews and a cousin of Joab and Abishai (19:13; 20:8–13).
17:28–29 These men of influence knew about David's quick flight from Jerusalem, and they brought him food and supplies. These provisions restored the bodies and spirits of the king's group.
18:1 The phrase **commanders of thousands and of hundreds** shows that David had been able to rally considerable support for his cause.
18:2 Dividing his warriors into thirds would provide David more flexibility in battling Absalom's forces.

to us. Even if half of us die, they will not pay any attention to us because you are worth^A ten thousand of us. Therefore, it is better if you support us from the city."

⁴ "I will do whatever you think is best," the king replied to them. So he stood beside the city gate while all the troops marched out by hundreds and thousands. ⁵ The king commanded Joab, Abishai, and Ittai, "Treat the young man Absalom gently for my sake." All the people heard the king's orders to all the commanders about Absalom.

⁶ Then David's forces marched into the field to engage Israel in battle, which took place in the forest of Ephraim. ⁷ Israel's army was defeated by David's soldiers, and the slaughter there was vast that day — twenty thousand dead. ⁸ The battle spread over the entire area, and that day the forest claimed more people than the sword.

Absalom's Death

⁹ Absalom was riding on his mule when he happened to meet David's soldiers. When the mule went under the tangled branches of a large oak tree, Absalom's head was caught fast in the tree. The mule under him kept going, so he was suspended in midair.^B ¹⁰ One of the men saw him and informed Joab. He said, "I just saw Absalom hanging in an oak tree!"

¹¹ "You just saw him!" Joab exclaimed.^C "Why didn't you strike him to the ground right there? I would have given you ten silver pieces^D and a belt!"

¹² The man replied to Joab, "Even if I had the weight of a thousand pieces of silver^E in my hand, I would not raise my hand against the king's son. For we heard the king command you, Abishai, and Ittai, 'Protect the young man Absalom for me.'^F ¹³ If I had jeopardized my own^G life — and nothing is hidden from the king — you would have abandoned me."

¹⁴ Joab said, "I'm not going to waste time with you!" He then took three spears^H in his hand and thrust them into Absalom's chest. While Absalom was still alive in the oak tree, ¹⁵ ten young men who were Joab's armor-bearers surrounded Absalom, struck him, and killed him. ¹⁶ Joab blew the ram's horn, and the troops broke off their pursuit of Israel because Joab restrained them. ¹⁷ They took Absalom, threw him into a large pit in the forest, and raised up a huge mound of stones over him. And all Israel fled, each to his tent.

¹⁸ When he was alive, Absalom had taken a pillar and raised it up for himself in the King's Valley, since he thought, "I have no son to preserve the memory of my name." So he named the pillar after himself. It is still called Absalom's Monument today.

¹⁹ Ahimaaz son of Zadok said, "Please let me run and tell the king the good news that the LORD has vindicated him by freeing him from his enemies."

²⁰ Joab replied to him, "You are not the man to take good news today. You may do it another day, but today you aren't taking good news, because the king's son is dead." ²¹ Joab then said to a Cushite, "Go tell the king what you have seen." The Cushite bowed to Joab and took off running.

²² However, Ahimaaz son of Zadok persisted and said to Joab, "No matter what, please let me also run behind the Cushite!"

Joab replied, "My son, why do you want to run since you won't get a reward?"^I

²³ "No matter what, I want to run!"

"Then run!" Joab said to him. So Ahimaaz ran by way of the plain and outran the Cushite.

²⁴ David was sitting between the city gates when the watchman went up to the roof of the city gate and over to the wall. The watchman looked out and saw a man running alone. ²⁵ He called out and told the king.

The king said, "If he's alone, he bears good news."

As the first runner came closer, ²⁶ the watchman saw another man running. He called out to the gatekeeper, "Look! Another man is running alone!"

"This one is also bringing good news," said the king.

²⁷ The watchman said, "The way the first man runs looks to me like the way Ahimaaz son of Zadok runs."

---

^A 18:3 Some Hb mss, LXX, Vg; other Hb mss read *because there would now be about* ^B 18:9 Lit *was between heaven and earth* ^C 18:11 Lit *Joab said to the man who told him* ^D 18:11 About four ounces of silver ^E 18:12 About 25 pounds of silver ^F 18:12 Some Hb mss, LXX, Tg, Vg; other Hb mss read *'Protect, whoever, the young man Absalom'*; Hb obscure ^G 18:13 Alt Hb tradition reads *jeopardized his* ^H 18:14 Lit *rods* ^I 18:22 Or *you have no good news?*

18:5 The text makes clear that David gave specific instructions about Absalom's treatment, and it emphasizes that **all the people heard the king's orders**.

18:6 The **forest of Ephraim** lay a few miles northwest of Mahanaim.

18:7–8 David divided his troops into three groups. This allowed him to spread Absalom's forces thinly **over the entire area**, preventing their united stand in the open country where their superior numbers would give them the advantage. A **forest** presented natural obstacles or threats such as wild animals, pits, low branches, and marshes.

18:9–11 Joab learned about Absalom's defenseless position. David's general had once again determined to take matters into his own hands for what he believed to be the king's own good.

18:12 This soldier was not ready to disobey a charge that David had given his general. He also repeated David's charge; the writer is making clear that Joab knew David's command.

18:13 The warriors didn't trust Joab. If they killed Absalom, they thought Joab might let the blame fall on them.

18:18 Absalom had claimed that he had **no son**. Actually, he had three sons (14:27), so they must have preceded him in death.

18:19 Ahimaaz had been David's trusted messenger throughout the ordeal, and now he wished to carry the **good news** of David's victory. He also may have thought he could more gently break the news of Absalom's death to his father than another messenger could.

18:20–22 Joab probably feared the bearer of this news might meet a bad end and considered a Cushite's life less valuable.

18:23 Ahimaaz appears to have taken the longer but easier route and thus **outran the Cushite**.

18:27 David's recognition of **Ahimaaz** brought the king hope that all was well.

"This is a good man; he comes with good news," the king commented.

²⁸ Ahimaaz called out to the king, "All is well," and paid homage to the king with his face to the ground. He continued, "Blessed be the LORD your God! He delivered up the men who rebelled against my lord the king."

²⁹ The king asked, "Is the young man Absalom all right?"

Ahimaaz replied, "When Joab sent the king's servant and your servant, I saw a big disturbance, but I don't know what it was."

³⁰ The king said, "Move aside and stand here." So he stood to one side.

³¹ Just then the Cushite came and said, "May my lord the king hear the good news: The LORD has vindicated you today by freeing you from all who rise against you!"

³² The king asked the Cushite, "Is the young man Absalom all right?"

The Cushite replied, "I wish that the enemies of my lord the king, along with all who rise up against you with evil intent, would become like that young man."

³³ The king was deeply moved and went up to the chamber above the city gate and wept. As he walked, he cried, "My son Absalom! My son, my son Absalom! If only I had died instead of you, Absalom, my son, my son!"

David's Kingdom Restored

19 It was reported to Joab, "The king is weeping. He's mourning over Absalom." ² That day's victory was turned into mourning for all the troops because on that day the troops heard, "The king is grieving over his son." ³ So they returned to the city quietly that day like troops come in when they are humiliated after fleeing in battle. ⁴ But the king covered his face and cried loudly, "My son Absalom! Absalom, my son, my son!"

⁵ Then Joab went into the house to the king and said, "Today you have shamed all your soldiers — those who saved your life as well as your sons, your wives, and your concubines — ⁶ by loving your enemies and hating those who love you! Today you have made it clear that the commanders and soldiers mean nothing to you. In fact, today I know that if Absalom were alive and all of us were dead, it would be fine with you!ᴬ

⁷ "Now get up! Go out and encourageᴮ your soldiers, for I swear by the LORD that if you don't go out, not a man will remain with you tonight. This will be worse for you than all the trouble that has come to you from your youth until now!"

⁸ So the king got up and sat in the city gate, and all the people were told, "Look, the king is sitting in the city gate." Then they all came into the king's presence.

Meanwhile, each Israelite had fled to his tent. ⁹ People throughout all the tribes of Israel were arguing among themselves, saying, "The king rescued us from the grasp of our enemies, and he saved us from the grasp of the Philistines, but now he has fled from the land because of Absalom. ¹⁰ But Absalom, the man we anointed over us, has died in battle. So why do you say nothing about restoring the king?"

¹¹ King David sent word to the priests Zadok and Abiathar: "Say to the elders of Judah, 'Why should you be the last to restore the king to his palace? The talk of all Israel has reached the king at his house. ¹² You are my brothers, my flesh and blood.ᶜ So why should you be the last to restore the king?' ¹³ And tell Amasa, 'Aren't you my flesh and blood?ᴰ May God punish me and do so severely if you don't become commander of my army from now on instead of Joab!'"

¹⁴ So he won overᴱ all the men of Judah, and they unanimously sent word to the king: "Come back, you and all your servants." ¹⁵ Then the king returned. When he arrived at the Jordan, Judah came to Gilgal to meet the king and escort him across the Jordan.

¹⁶ Shimei son of Gera, the Benjaminite from Bahurim, hurried down with the men of Judah

---

ᴬ**19:6** Lit *be right in your eyes* ᴮ**19:7** Lit *speak to the heart of* ᶜ**19:12** Lit *my bone and my flesh* ᴰ**19:13** Lit *my bone and my flesh?* ᴱ**19:14** Lit *he turned the heart of*

18:29–32 David's question revealed the focus of his concern. Ahimaaz, who knew the truth, suddenly found himself at a loss for words. After the Cushite responded essentially as Ahimaaz had (vv. 28,31), David's further inquiry specifically about **Absalom** brought the reply **the king** did not want to hear. The kingdom was David's again, but he had lost another son.
19:1–4 **Joab** returned to Mahanaim from the battle to hear about David's **mourning over Absalom**. Victory was **turned into mourning** because victory had come through Absalom's death. In this bittersweet moment, David's victorious troops **returned to the city** (lit "stole away"), acting as if they had lost the **battle**.
19:5–7 **Joab** recognized the serious public relations problem **the king** would face if he persisted in mourning the traitorous

Absalom. David's soldiers, who had **saved** David and all his family, would feel shame instead of a sense of victory because of the king's mourning. Joab told David to go out and **encourage** his **soldiers**, lest they abandon him. Joab's words in these verses are strong and blunt, but they may have saved David's kingship.
19:8 David returned to the **city gate** where he had reviewed his troops as they headed to battle. It was also at the gate (in Jerusalem) that Absalom had stolen the heart of many of David's subjects when David was supposedly neglecting his duties of administering justice. So his returning to the gate amounted to a "return to normality" (R. P. Gordon).
19:11–12 Apparently because of a lack of response on the people's part, **King David** summoned **Zadok and Abiathar** to begin his

restoration proceedings. He gave the **elders of Judah** first notice—an act of favoritism that would later cause consternation among the other tribes (vv. 41–43).
19:13 David's appointment of **Amasa**, who had headed Absalom's army (17:25), as **commander of** his **army** indicated that David planned to bear no animosity toward those who had sided with Absalom. Amasa was to replace **Joab**—a clear sign that David had heard about Joab's murder of Absalom, but the king felt it would be politically unwise to put Joab to death for killing the person who had conspired for the throne. Amasa was the son of David's half sister Abigail; Joab was a son of David's sister Zeruiah.
19:16 Now that Absalom was dead, the "prophecy" of **Shimei** was clearly false. Moreover, he had cursed the king. He moved quickly to make amends.

to meet King David. ¹⁷ There were a thousand men from Benjamin with him. Ziba, an attendant from the house of Saul, with his fifteen sons and twenty servants also rushed down to the Jordan ahead of the king. ¹⁸ They forded the Jordan to bring the king's household across and do whatever the king desired.ᴬ

When Shimei son of Gera crossed the Jordan, he fell facedown before the king ¹⁹ and said to him, "My lord, don't hold me guilty, and don't remember your servant's wrongdoing on the day my lord the king left Jerusalem. May the king not take it to heart. ²⁰ For your servant knows that I have sinned. But look! Today I am the first one of the entire house of Joseph to come down to meet my lord the king."

²¹ Abishai son of Zeruiah asked, "Shouldn't Shimei be put to death for this, because he cursed the Lᴏʀᴅ's anointed?"

²² David answered, "Sons of Zeruiah, do we agree on anything? Have you become my adversary today? Should any man be killed in Israel today? Am I not aware that today I'm king over Israel?" ²³ So the king said to Shimei, "You will not die." Then the king gave him his oath.

²⁴ Mephibosheth, Saul's grandson, also went down to meet the king. He had not taken care of his feet, trimmed his mustache, or washed his clothes from the day the king left until the day he returned safely. ²⁵ When he came from Jerusalem to meet the king, the king asked him, "Mephibosheth, why didn't you come with me?"

²⁶ "My lord the king," he replied, "my servant Ziba betrayed me. Actually your servant said, 'I'll saddle the donkey for myselfᴮ so that I may ride it and go with the king' — for your servant is lame. ²⁷ Ziba slandered your servant to my lord the king. But my lord the king is like the angel of God, so do whatever you think best.ᶜ ²⁸ For my grandfather's entire family deserves death from my lord the king, but you set your servant among those who eat at your table. So

what further right do I have to keep on making appeals to the king?"

²⁹ The king said to him, "Why keep on speaking about these matters of yours? I hereby declare: you and Ziba are to divide the land."

³⁰ Mephibosheth said to the king, "Instead, since my lord the king has come to his palace safely, let Ziba take it all!"

³¹ Barzillai the Gileadite had come down from Rogelim and accompanied the king to the Jordan River to see him off at the Jordan. ³² Barzillai was a very old man — eighty years old — and since he was a very wealthy man, he had provided for the needs of the king while he stayed in Mahanaim. ³³ The king said to Barzillai, "Cross over with me, and I'll provide for youᴰ at my side in Jerusalem."

³⁴ Barzillai replied to the king, "How many years of my life are left that I should go up to Jerusalem with the king? ³⁵ I'm now eighty years old. Can I discern what is pleasant and what is not? Can your servant taste what he eats or drinks? Can I still hear the voice of male and female singers? Why should your servant be an added burden to my lord the king? ³⁶ Since your servant is only going with the king a little way across the Jordan, why should the king repay me with such a reward? ³⁷ Please let your servant return so that I may die in my own city near the tomb of my father and mother. But here is your servant Chimham; let him cross over with my lord the king. Do for him what seems good to you."ᴱ

³⁸ The king replied, "Chimham will cross over with me, and I will do for him what seems good to you, and whatever you desire from me I will do for you." ³⁹ So all the people crossed the Jordan, and then the king crossed. The king kissed Barzillai and blessed him, and Barzillai returned to his home.

⁴⁰ The king went on to Gilgal, and Chimham went with him. All the troops of Judah and half of Israel's escorted the king. ⁴¹ Suddenly, all the

ᴬ19:18 Lit do what is good in his eyes ᴮ19:26 LXX, Syr, Vg read said to him, 'Saddle the donkey for me ᶜ19:27 Lit do what is good in your eyes ᴰ19:33 LXX reads for your old age ; Ru 4:15 ᴱ19:37 Lit what is good in your eyes, also in v. 38

19:17 Ziba, servant of Mephibosheth, also came to welcome David. He soon would be joined by Mephibosheth, creating an interesting dilemma for David (vv. 24–30).
19:18–20 Shimei confessed that he had sinned. He was trying to atone for his sin by being the first one of the house of Joseph (the northern tribes, Am 5:6) to welcome David back as king.
19:21 Abishai offered for the second time to kill Shimei for his harsh words against the Lᴏʀᴅ's anointed (16:9).
19:23 Shimei would later die when he violated Solomon's edict (1Kg 2:42–46).
19:24 Mephibosheth now met David, showing several signs of having been in mourning from the day the king left.
19:25–26 Mephibosheth contended that Ziba had betrayed (lit "deceived") him and

had not provided him a donkey so Mephibosheth could go with the king.
19:27–28 Mephibosheth asserted his confidence in David's discernment and recognized that he deserved none of David's grace toward him. His final question, what further right do I have to keep on making appeals to the king, anticipated what he hoped would be a favorable ruling.
19:29 David had received Ziba's support as he fled, yet Mephibosheth's testimony seemed credible. David decided on a compromise under which the two of them would divide the land.
19:30 Mephibosheth's expression let Ziba take it all should be understood as a typical Middle Eastern overstatement to honor a ruler, just as his question in v. 28 was an understatement of his own value (cp. 9:8).

19:31–32 Although Rogelim was about fifty miles northeast of David's crossing point, Barzillai, who had provided food and other supplies for the king and his men while he stayed in Mahanaim (17:27–29), accompanied David to the Jordan River.
19:39 Though Barzillai returned to his home after David blessed him, the king did not forget him, later instructing Solomon to continue to show kindness to Barzillai's household (1Kg 2:7). Jeremiah 41:17 mentions Geruth Chimham ("dwelling of Chimham") near Bethlehem—perhaps the fulfillment of David's words.
19:40 Gilgal was Israel's base camp during the days of Joshua's conquest (Jos 4:19).
19:41 Tensions between Judah and the other tribes that were evident earlier in Israel's history (2:10; 3:10; 12:8; 1Sm 11:8; 17:52; 18:16)

men of Israel came to the king. They asked him, "Why did our brothers, the men of Judah, take you away secretly and transport the king and his household across the Jordan, along with all of David's men?"

⁴² All the men of Judah responded to the men of Israel, "Because the king is our relative. Why does this make you angry? Have we ever eaten anything of the king's or been honored at all?"ᴬ

⁴³ The men of Israel answered the men of Judah, "We have ten shares in the king, so we have a greater claim to David than you. Why then do you despise us? Weren't we the first to speak of restoring our king?" But the words of the men of Judah were harsher than those of the men of Israel.

Sheba's Revolt

20 Now a wicked man, a Benjaminite named Sheba son of Bichri, happened to be there. He blew the ram's horn and shouted:

We have no portion in David,
no inheritance in Jesse's son.
Each man to his tent,ᴮ Israel!

² So all the men of Israel deserted David and followed Sheba son of Bichri, but the men of Judah from the Jordan all the way to Jerusalem remained loyal to their king.

³ When David came to his palace in Jerusalem, he took the ten concubines he had left to take care of the palace and placed them under guard. He provided for them, but he was not intimate with them. They were confined until the day of their death, living as widows.

⁴ The king said to Amasa, "Summon the men of Judah to me within three days and be here yourself." ⁵ Amasa went to summon Judah, but he took longer than the time allotted him. ⁶ So David said to Abishai, "Sheba son of Bichri will do more harm to us than Absalom. Take your

lord's soldiers and pursue him, or he will find fortified cities and elude us."ᶜ

⁷ So Joab's men, the Cherethites, the Pelethites, and all the warriors marched out under Abishai's command;ᴰ they left Jerusalem to pursue Sheba son of Bichri. ⁸ They were at the great stone in Gibeon when Amasa joined them. Joab was wearing his uniform and over it was a belt around his waist with a sword in its sheath. As he approached, the sword fell out. ⁹ Joab asked Amasa, "Are you well, my brother?" Then with his right hand Joab grabbed Amasa by the beard to kiss him. ¹⁰ Amasa was not on guard against the sword in Joab's hand, and Joab stabbed him in the stomach with it and spilled his intestines out on the ground. Joab did not stab him again, and Amasa died.

Joab and his brother Abishai pursued Sheba son of Bichri. ¹¹ One of Joab's young men had stood over Amasa saying, "Whoever favors Joab and whoever is for David, follow Joab!" ¹² Now Amasa had been writhing in his blood in the middle of the highway, and the man had seen that all the troops stopped. So he moved Amasa from the highway to the field and threw a garment over him because he realized that all those who encountered Amasa were stopping. ¹³ When he was removed from the highway, all the men passed by and followed Joab to pursue Sheba son of Bichri.

¹⁴ Sheba passed through all the tribes of Israel to Abel of Beth-maacah. All the Beritesᴱ came together and followed him. ¹⁵ Joab's troops came and besieged Sheba in Abel of Beth-maacah. They built a siege ramp against the outer wall of the city. While all the troops with Joab were battering the wall to make it collapse, ¹⁶ a wise woman called out from the city, "Listen! Listen! Please tell Joab to come here and let me speak with him."

¹⁷ When he had come near her, the woman asked, "Are you Joab?"

ᴬ19:42 LXX reads king's or has he given us a gift or granted us a portion ᴮ20:1 Alt Hb tradition reads gods ᶜ20:6 Lit and snatch away our eyes ᴰ20:7 Lit out following him ᴱ20:14 LXX, Vg read Bichrites

now boiled to the surface again as the delegation from **Israel** challenged the king on the protocol for restoring him to Jerusalem. **Take you away secretly** is literally "stole you." The northern tribes also felt they were under-represented in comparison to the leaders from Judah (v. 40).
19:42 The **men of Judah** answered instead of allowing David to do so. They asserted that since David was their **relative** (a closer relative), they had taken the lead in restoring him as king. They insisted, however, that their tribe was not treated with favoritism.
20:1 Sheba son of Bichri is not mentioned outside this account, but he was probably a leader among the **Benjaminite** delegation that escorted David back to Jerusalem. He **blew the ram's horn** and called the people of **Israel** to break off from David (cp. 18:16), citing the more distant relationship.
20:2 In the heat of the moment, following **Sheba** seemed to many people the right thing to do, so the men of **Israel deserted**

David. Meanwhile, the men of **Judah** escorted David **all the way to Jerusalem** to guarantee his safety.
20:3 David compassionately provided for the welfare of the **ten concubines** with whom Absalom had had sex during his coup attempt (16:22). However, **he was not intimate with them** again, perhaps because of Torah considerations (Lv 18:15) but more likely to ensure no confusion arose within the royal line.
20:4–5 Amasa, the new head of David's army (19:13), was commanded to gather the **men of Judah** to crush Sheba's revolt. Time was of the essence, a fact that Amasa apparently did not grasp.
20:6 Abishai was David's next choice to lead the attack against **Sheba**.
20:7 On **Cherethites** and **Pelethites**, see note at 8:18.
20:8 Gibeon, about four miles northwest of Jerusalem, had been the site of Joab's encounter with Abner's forces (2:12–16).

Joab was present, though he was not in charge. His **sword** fell out of its **sheath**, probably a deceptive move by Joab so Amasa would not view him as drawing his weapon.
20:9 Joab grabbed Amasa **by the beard**—reached out and touched his face as he might do before greeting him with a **kiss**.
20:10 The **sword in Joab's hand** did not seem a threat to **Amasa** because it appeared that Joab was merely picking it up after dropping it (v. 8). The first blow clearly a fatal one, though he may not have died at once (cp. v. 12).
20:14 Sheba retreated to the far north; **Abel of Beth-maacah** lay about thirty miles north of the Sea of Galilee.
20:15 Besieging a city generally involved surrounding it, cutting off its food and water supply, building a **siege ramp** to get over the wall, and constructing **battering** rams to break down the city's **wall**.

"I am," he replied.

"Listen to the words of your servant," she said to him.

He answered, "I'm listening."

¹⁸ She said, "In the past they used to say, 'Seek counsel in Abel,' and that's how they settled disputes. ¹⁹ I am one of the peaceful and faithful in Israel, but you're trying to destroy a city that is like a mother in Israel. Why would you devour the LORD's inheritance?"

²⁰ Joab protested: "Never! I would never devour or demolish! ²¹ That is not the case. There is a man named Sheba son of Bichri, from the hill country of Ephraim, who has rebelled against King David. Deliver this one man, and I will withdraw from the city."

The woman replied to Joab, "Watch! His head will be thrown over the wall to you." ²² The woman went to all the people with her wise counsel, and they cut off the head of Sheba son of Bichri and threw it to Joab. So he blew the ram's horn, and they dispersed from the city, each to his own tent. Joab returned to the king in Jerusalem.

²³ Joab commanded the whole army of
  Israel;
Benaiah son of Jehoiada was over the
  Cherethites and Pelethites;
²⁴ Adoramᴬ was over forced labor;
Jehoshaphat son of Ahilud was court
  historian;
²⁵ Sheva was court secretary;
Zadok and Abiathar were priests;
²⁶ and in addition, Ira the Jairite was
  David's priest.

Justice for the Gibeonites

21 During David's reign there was a famine for three successive years, so David inquiredᴮ of the LORD. The LORD answered, "It is due to Saul and to his bloody family, because he killed the Gibeonites."

² The Gibeonites were not Israelites but rather a remnant of the Amorites. The Israelites had taken an oath concerning them, but Saul had tried to kill them in his zeal for the Israelites and Judah. So David summoned the Gibeonites and spoke to them. ³ He asked the Gibeonites, "What should I do for you? How can I make atonement so that you will bring a blessing onᶜ the LORD's inheritance?"

⁴ The Gibeonites said to him, "We are not asking for silver and gold from Saul or his family, and we cannot put anyone to death in Israel."

"Whatever you say, I will do for you," he said.

⁵ They replied to the king, "As for the man who annihilated us and plotted to destroy us so we would not exist within the whole territory of Israel, ⁶ let seven of his male descendants be handed over to us so we may hangᴰ them in the presence of the LORD at Gibeah of Saul, the LORD's chosen."

The king answered, "I will hand them over."

⁷ David spared Mephibosheth, the son of Saul's son Jonathan, because of the oath of the LORD that was between David and Jonathan, Saul's son. ⁸ But the king took Armoni and Mephibosheth, who were the two sons whom Rizpah daughter of Aiah had borne to Saul, and the five sons whom Merabᴱ daughter of Saul had borne to Adriel son of Barzillai the Meholathite ⁹ and handed them over to the Gibeonites. They hangedᶠ them on the hill in the presence of the LORD; the seven of them died together. They were executed in the first days of the harvest at the beginning of the barley harvest.ᴳ

ᴬ20:24 Some Hb mss, LXX, Syr read *Adoniram*; 1Kg 4:6; 5:14 ᴮ21:1 Lit *sought the face of* ᶜ21:3 Lit *will bless* ᴰ21:6 Or *impale*, or *expose* ᴱ21:8 Some Hb mss, LXX, Syr, Tg; other Hb mss read *Michal* ᶠ21:9 Or *impaled*, or *exposed*, also in v. 13 ᴳ21:9 = March–April

---

20:18–19 Abel, a city of long standing within the nation, had a reputation as a place where wisdom often **settled disputes**.
20:23 Joab had become commander of the **whole army of Israel** again, and David may have felt that he should leave well enough alone. After all, Joab had been a factor in reuniting Israel and restoring David's kingdom. Joab's sin, however, was not forgotten, and David later instructed his son Solomon to deal with it when he became king (1Kg 2:5–6).
20:24 Forced labor appears here for the first time; during Solomon's days, only non-Israelites made up this group (1Kg 9:20). On **Jehoshaphat**, see note at 8:16.
20:25 Jehoshaphat was now assisted by **Sheva**, who had apparently replaced Seraiah (8:17) as **court secretary**. Zadok's influence would continue into Solomon's reign (1Kg 2:35), though **Abiathar** would side against Solomon during the transition of power from David to Solomon and suffer banishment from the priesthood (1Kg 1:7; 2:26–27).

20:26 Ira the Jairite, otherwise unknown, was **David's priest**, perhaps assisting him in matters of private worship, but certainly not functioning in place of Torah-prescribed patterns.
21:1 During David's reign is literally "in David's days." The last four chapters of 2 Samuel contain six accounts of matters pertaining to David's life, though not tied chronologically to the rest of the book. It appears the author had additional information he wished to include about David, and he decided this was the best place to put it. In the first account, God used continuing **famine** to prompt David to seek the reason behind this calamity. **The LORD** revealed the answer: **Saul** and **his bloody family** had **killed the Gibeonites**.
21:2 The **Gibeonites** had remained in the land since the days of Joshua. The Israelites **had taken an oath** not to destroy them (Jos 9:3–17); Saul, however, had not honored that oath and had killed many of them.

21:5–6 The Gibeonites asked for the death of **seven** of Saul's **male descendants**. Saul had probably killed many more Gibeonites than this; no doubt the number requested was a symbolic representation of the Gibeonite dead. **Gibeah** was Saul's hometown; since Saul had killed their people at Gibeon, the Gibeonites probably wanted to reciprocate by hanging his descendants in his hometown.
21:7 Even in complying with the Gibeonites request, **David spared Mephibosheth** in accord with his earlier **oath** regarding **Jonathan** (9:1–10; 1Sm 18:3; 20:12–17; 23:18).
21:8 Rizpah was probably the same concubine with whom Abner had sexual relations (3:7). Saul's daughter **Merab** was to have been David's wife but was given to **Adriel** instead (1Sm 18:19). This **Barzillai** is not to be confused with the one who helped David in 19:31–39.
21:9 The beginning of the **barley harvest** was normally during Nisan (March–April), the beginning of the religious year.

The Burial of Saul's Family

¹⁰ Rizpah, Aiah's daughter, took sackcloth and spread it out for herself on the rock from the beginning of the harvest ᴬ until the rain poured down from heaven on the bodies. She kept the birds of the sky from them by day and the wild animals by night.

¹¹ When it was reported to David what Saul's concubine Rizpah daughter of Aiah had done, ¹² he went and got the bones of Saul and his son Jonathan from the citizens of Jabesh-gilead. They had stolen them from the public square of Beth-shan where the Philistines had hung the bodies the day the Philistines killed Saul at Gilboa. ¹³ David had the bones brought from there. They gathered up the bones of Saul's family who had been hanged ¹⁴ and buried the bones of Saul and his son Jonathan at Zela in the land of Benjamin in the tomb of Saul's father Kish. They did everything the king commanded. After this, God was receptive to prayer for the land.

The Philistine Giants

¹⁵ The Philistines again waged war against Israel. David went down with his soldiers, and they fought the Philistines, but David became exhausted. ¹⁶ Then Ishbi-benob, one of the descendants of the giant,ᴮ whose bronze spear weighed about eight pounds ᶜ and who wore new armor, intended to kill David. ¹⁷ But Abishai son of Zeruiah came to his aid, struck the Philistine, and killed him. Then David's men swore to him, "You must never again go out with us to battle. You must not extinguish the lamp of Israel."

¹⁸ After this, there was another battle with the Philistines at Gob. At that time Sibbecai the Hushathite killed Saph, who was one of the descendants of the giant.

¹⁹ Once again there was a battle with the Philistines at Gob, and Elhanan son of Jaare-oregim the Bethlehemite killed ᴰ Goliath of Gath. The shaft of his spear was like a weaver's beam.

²⁰ At Gath there was still another battle. A huge man was there with six fingers on each hand and six toes on each foot — twenty-four in all. He, too, was descended from the giant. ²¹ When he taunted Israel, Jonathan, son of David's brother Shimei, killed him. ²² These four were descended from the giant in Gath and were killed by David and his soldiers.

David's Song of Thanksgiving

22 David spoke the words of this song to the Lᴏʀᴅ on the day the Lᴏʀᴅ rescued him from the grasp of all his enemies and from the grasp of Saul. ² He said:

> The Lᴏʀᴅ is my rock, my fortress,
>   and my deliverer,
> ³ my God,ᴱ my rock where I seek refuge.
>   My shield, the horn of my salvation,
>   my stronghold, my refuge,
>   and my Savior, you save me
>   from violence.
> ⁴ I called to the Lᴏʀᴅ, who is worthy
>   of praise,
>   and I was saved from my enemies.
> ⁵ For the waves of death engulfed me;
>   the torrents of destruction terrified me.
> ⁶ The ropes of Sheol entangled me;
>   the snares of death confronted me.
> ⁷ I called to the Lᴏʀᴅ in my distress;
>   I called to my God.

ᴬ 21:10 = April to October   ᴮ 21:16 Or *Raphah*, also in vv. 18,20,22   ᶜ 21:16 Lit *300* (shekels)   ᴰ 21:19 1Ch 20:5 adds *the brother of*   ᴱ 22:3 LXX, Ps 18:2 read *my God*; MT reads *God of*

21:10 Rizpah performed a tragic act of love for her sons and Merab's sons, protecting their bodies from desecration by **birds** and **wild animals.** The **rain** mentioned normally fell in March and April between the barley and wheat harvest, so the exact length of Rizpah's vigil is unknown.
21:11–13 David heard about what Rizpah had done, and he took action to provide the dead an honored burial. The **bones of Saul and his son Jonathan** (and presumably those of Abinadab and Malchishua, 1Sm 31:2,12–13) were brought from **Jabesh-gilead** back to Benjamin. David also gathered up the bones of **Saul's family.**
21:14 The remains were placed in the family **tomb of Saul's father Kish** (see 1Sm 9:1). The exact location of **Zela** (other than in Benjamin) is unknown (Jos 18:28). **God was receptive to prayer** means that the famine ceased (see v. 1).
21:16 Ishbi-benob is unknown outside this passage, but he may have been **one of the descendants of the giant** (Goliath, 1Sm 17:4), though some scholars understand the Hebrew word translated "giant" *(rapha)* as a proper name ("one of the descendants of

Rapha"). The man **intended to kill David** because killing him would deal Israel a serious blow.
21:17 David's nephew **Abishai** saved the king's life and **struck the Philistine.** As they pondered how close David had come to death, they told him not to participate with them in any more battles, an admonition the king seems to have taken to heart (11:1; 18:2; 20:4,6). Through his leadership David, as the figurative **lamp of Israel**, provided political, military, and spiritual light to the nation.
21:18 Gob ("cistern") may be either identified with or in the close vicinity of Gezer at the mouth of the Aijalon Valley near Philistine territory (1Ch 20:4). On **the giant,** see note at v. 16.
21:19 This verse raises the question of who killed **Goliath of Gath.** First Sm 17:50–51 credits David, but this verse credits **Elhanan.** One interpretation suggests two different Goliaths, though the identical description of Goliath's **spear** being **like a weaver's beam** (cp. 1Sm 17:7) makes this option doubtful. Another explanation is to understand *Elhanan* as David's original name and *David* as David's throne name, but this is not

supported elsewhere in Scripture. By far the most likely explanation is that Elhanan killed not Goliath but Goliath's brother, as 1Ch 20:5 states, and that an early scribe simply miscopied the present verse. Although this verse and 1Ch 20:5 read a bit differently in English, in the Hebrew text only a minor alteration is required to change from one reading to another.
21:20–22 The battle at Gath was against an unnamed **giant** noted by his malformation. **Taunted** is the same word used five times in 1Sm 17.
22:1 On the day is not a reference to a single day, but the general time at which David realized the Lord had given him the kingship and helped him subdue **all his enemies.** The **song** is very similar to Ps 18, but has more emphasis on David's personal worship.
22:2 Rock denotes an immovable, jutting cliff, not a mere stone. This word commonly occurs in the Bible to describe God's support and defense of his people (1Sm 2:2; Pss 18:2; 95:1; Is 44:8).
22:3 Mary also used the expression **horn of my salvation** to describe God's work on her behalf (Lk 1:69).

From his temple he heard my voice,
and my cry for help reached his ears.

8 Then the earth shook and quaked;
the foundations of the heavens[A]
trembled;
they shook because he burned
with anger.

9 Smoke rose from his nostrils,
and consuming fire came
from his mouth;
coals were set ablaze by it.[B]

10 He bent the heavens and came down,
total darkness beneath his feet.

11 He rode on a cherub and flew,
soaring[C] on the wings of the wind.

12 He made darkness a canopy
around him,
a gathering[D] of water and thick clouds.

13 From the radiance of his presence,
blazing coals were ignited.

14 The LORD thundered from heaven;
the Most High made his voice heard.

15 He shot arrows and scattered them;
he hurled lightning bolts
and routed them.

16 The depths of the sea became visible,
the foundations of the world
were exposed
at the rebuke of the LORD,
at the blast of the breath of his nostrils.

17 He reached down from on high
and took hold of me;
he pulled me out of deep water.

18 He rescued me
from my powerful enemy
and from those who hated me,
for they were too strong for me.

19 They confronted me in the day
of my calamity,
but the LORD was my support.

20 He brought me out to a spacious place;
he rescued me because he delighted
in me.

21 The LORD rewarded me
according to my righteousness;
he repaid me
according to the cleanness of my hands.

22 For I have kept the ways of the LORD
and have not turned from my God
to wickedness.

23 Indeed, I let all his ordinances guide me[E]
and have not disregarded his statutes.

24 I was blameless before him

and kept myself from my iniquity.

25 So the LORD repaid me
according to my righteousness,
according to my cleanness[F]
in his sight.

26 With the faithful
you prove yourself faithful,
with the blameless
you prove yourself blameless,

27 with the pure
you prove yourself pure,
but with the crooked
you prove yourself shrewd.

28 You rescue an oppressed people,
but your eyes are set
against the proud—
you humble them.

29 LORD, you are my lamp;
the LORD illuminates my darkness.

30 With you I can attack a barricade,[G]
and with my God I can leap over a wall.

31 God—his way is perfect;
the word of the LORD is pure.
He is a shield to all who take refuge
in him.

32 For who is God besides the LORD?
And who is a rock? Only our God.

33 God is my strong refuge;[H]
he makes my way perfect.[I]

34 He makes my feet like the feet of a deer
and sets me securely on the[J] heights.[K]

35 He trains my hands for war;
my arms can bend a bow of bronze.

36 You have given me the shield
of your salvation;
your help[L] exalts me.

37 You make a spacious place beneath me
for my steps,
and my ankles do not give way.

38 I pursue my enemies and destroy them;
I do not turn back until they are
wiped out.

39 I wipe them out and crush them,
and they do not rise;
they fall beneath my feet.

40 You have clothed me with strength
for battle;
you subdue my adversaries beneath me.

41 You have made my enemies retreat
before me;[M]
I annihilate those who hate me.

42 They look, but there is no one
to save them—

---

^A 22:8 Some Hb mss, Syr, Vg read *mountains*; Ps 18:7   ^B 22:9 Or *him*   ^C 22:11 Some Hb mss; other Hb mss, Syr, Tg read *he was seen*   ^D 22:12 Or *sieve*, or *mass*; Hb obscure   ^E 22:23 Lit *Indeed, all his ordinances have been in front of me*   ^F 22:25 LXX, Syr, Vg read *to the cleanness of my hands*; Ps 18:24   ^G 22:30 Or *a ridge*, or *raiders*   ^H 22:33 DSS, some LXX mss, Syr, Vg read *God clothes me with strength*; Ps 18:32   ^I 22:33 Some LXX mss, Syr; MT reads *he sets free the blameless his way*; Hb obscure   ^J 22:34 LXX; some Hb mss read *my*; other Hb mss read *his*   ^K 22:34 Or *on my high places*   ^L 22:36 LXX reads *humility*; Ps 18:35   ^M 22:41 Lit *you gave me the neck of my enemies*

22:24 Blameless does not mean sinless, but it reflects a deep moral character (Gn 6:9; Ps 119:1).

they look to the LORD, but he does not
    answer them.
⁴³ I pulverize them like dust of the earth;
    I crush them and trample them like mud
    in the streets.

⁴⁴ You have freed me from the feuds
    among my people;
    you have preserved me as head
    of nations;
    a people I had not known serve me.
⁴⁵ Foreigners submit to me cringing;
    as soon as they hear, they obey me.
⁴⁶ Foreigners lose heart
    and come trembling
    from their fortifications.

⁴⁷ The LORD lives — blessed be my rock!
    God, the rock of my salvation, is exalted.
⁴⁸ God — he grants me vengeance
    and casts down peoples under me.
⁴⁹ He frees me from my enemies.
    You exalt me above my adversaries;
    you rescue me from violent men.
⁵⁰ Therefore I will give thanks to you
    among the nations, LORD;
    I will sing praises about your name.
⁵¹ He is a tower of salvation for^A his king;
    he shows loyalty to his anointed,
    to David and his descendants forever.

David's Last Words

23 These are the last words of David:
    The declaration of David son of Jesse,
    the declaration of the man
    raised on high,^B
    the one anointed by the God of Jacob.
    This is the most delightful
    of Israel's songs.
² The Spirit of the LORD spoke through me,
    his word was on my tongue.
³ The God of Israel spoke;
    the Rock of Israel said to me,
    "The one who rules the people
    with justice,

who rules in the fear of God,
⁴ is like the morning light when the sun
    rises
    on a cloudless morning,
    the glisten of rain on sprouting grass."

⁵ Is it not true my house is with God?
    For he has established
    a permanent covenant with me,
    ordered and secured in every detail.
    Will he not bring about
    my whole salvation
    and my every desire?
⁶ But all the wicked are like thorns
    raked aside;
    they can never be picked up by hand.
⁷ The man who touches them
    must be armed with iron and the shaft
    of a spear.
    They will be completely burned up
    on the spot.

Exploits of David's Warriors

⁸ These are the names of David's warriors:
    Josheb-basshebeth the Tahchemonite was
chief of the officers.^C He wielded his spear^D
against eight hundred men that he killed at
one time.
    ⁹ After him, Eleazar son of Dodo son of an
Ahohite was among the three warriors with
David when they defied the Philistines. The men
of Israel retreated in the place they had gathered for battle, ¹⁰ but Eleazar stood his ground
and attacked the Philistines until his hand was
tired and stuck to his sword. The LORD brought
about a great victory that day. Then the troops
came back to him, but only to plunder the dead.
    ¹¹ After him was Shammah son of Agee the
Hararite. The Philistines had assembled in formation where there was a field full of lentils.
The troops fled from the Philistines, ¹² but Shammah took his stand in the middle of the field, defended it, and struck down the Philistines. So the
LORD brought about a great victory.
    ¹³ Three of the thirty leading warriors went
down at harvest time and came to David at the

^A22:51 DSS read *he gives great victory to* ^B23:1 Or *raised up by the high God* ^C23:8 Some Hb mss, LXX read *Three*
^D23:8 Some Hb mss; other Hb mss, LXX read *He was Adino the Eznite*

#16 99 Essential Christian Truths

GOD IS INFINITE

To say that God is infinite means that
there are no boundaries on his qualities
and existence (Jb 11:7–9; Ps 147:5). For
instance, God is infinite when it comes
to space and time, meaning he is not
confined by material space nor is he
restricted by time since he is timeless
(Ps 90:1–2). This also extends to his
knowledge of things as well as his power to do all things according to his will.

23:1–7 Whereas the theme of chap. 22 is the
Lord's great deliverances of David, the theme
of these verses is the Davidic **permanent
covenant**.
23:1 The heading for this chapter, **These
are the last words of David**, is not intended chronologically; other words of
David appear after this section and even
in 1Kg 1:28–35 and 2:1–9. Perhaps the section contains David's last recorded public
statement or testimony to God's work
through his life.
23:3–4 Fear of God denotes a healthy
reverence for his power and majesty; the
book of Proverbs associates such an attitude with wisdom and knowledge (Pr
1:7; 9:10). The Davidic covenant is that one

day Israel would have such a ruler. See Ps
72:1–7; Is 11:1–5.
23:5 My house denotes David's family.
23:8–39 These are the names and accounts
of some of **David's warriors**—his most
valiant soldiers. God blessed David with
exceptional military men. The list includes
the three famous heroes who turned the
tide of events in single combat and the
thirty warriors who served in a special
detachment. There were men from many
different tribes of Israel and even a few
foreigners among the men who rallied to
David.
23:13 The **cave of Adullam** was in the
Valley of Elah (1Sm 17:2) below Bethlehem.
Rephaim Valley lay southwest of Jerusalem.

cave of Adullam, while a company of Philistines was camping in Rephaim Valley. ¹⁴ At that time David was in the stronghold, and a Philistine garrison was at Bethlehem. ¹⁵ David was extremely thirsty^ and said, "If only someone would bring me water to drink from the well at the city gate of Bethlehem!" ¹⁶ So three of the warriors broke through the Philistine camp and drew water from the well at the gate of Bethlehem. They brought it back to David, but he refused to drink it. Instead, he poured it out to the LORD. ¹⁷ David said, "LORD, I would never do such a thing! Is this not the blood of men who risked their lives?" So he refused to drink it. Such were the exploits of the three warriors.

¹⁸ Abishai, Joab's brother and son of Zeruiah, was leader of the Three.^B He wielded his spear against three hundred men and killed them, gaining a reputation among the Three. ¹⁹ Was he not more honored than the Three? He became their commander even though he did not become one of the Three.

²⁰ Benaiah son of Jehoiada was the son of a brave man from Kabzeel, a man of many exploits. Benaiah killed two sons^C of Ariel^D of Moab, and he went down into a pit on a snowy day and killed a lion. ²¹ He also killed an Egyptian, an impressive man. Even though the Egyptian had a spear in his hand, Benaiah went down to him with a staff, snatched the spear out of the Egyptian's hand, and then killed him with his own spear. ²² These were the exploits of Benaiah son of Jehoiada, who had a reputation among the three warriors. ²³ He was the most honored of the Thirty, but he did not become one of the Three. David put him in charge of his bodyguard.

²⁴ Among the Thirty were
    Joab's brother Asahel,
    Elhanan son of Dodo of Bethlehem,
²⁵   Shammah the Harodite,

²⁶   Elika the Harodite,
²⁶   Helez the Paltite,
    Ira son of Ikkesh the Tekoite,
²⁷   Abiezer the Anathothite,
    Mebunnai the Hushathite,
²⁸   Zalmon the Ahohite,
    Maharai the Netophathite,
²⁹   Heleb son of Baanah the Netophathite,
    Ittai son of Ribai from Gibeah
        of the Benjaminites,
³⁰   Benaiah the Pirathonite,
    Hiddai from the wadis of Gaash,^E
³¹   Abi-albon the Arbathite,
    Azmaveth the Barhumite,
³²   Eliahba the Shaalbonite,
    the sons of Jashen,
    Jonathan son of^F ³³ Shammah
        the Hararite,
    Ahiam son of Sharar the Hararite,
³⁴   Eliphelet son of Ahasbai
        son of the Maacathite,
    Eliam son of Ahithophel the Gilonite,
³⁵   Hezro the Carmelite,
    Paarai the Arbite,
³⁶   Igal son of Nathan from Zobah,
    Bani the Gadite,
³⁷   Zelek the Ammonite,
    Naharai the Beerothite,
        the armor-bearer for Joab
        son of Zeruiah,
³⁸   Ira the Ithrite,
    Gareb the Ithrite,
³⁹   and Uriah the Hethite.
There were thirty-seven in all.

David's Military Census

24 The LORD's anger burned against Israel again, and he stirred up David against them to say, "Go, count the people of Israel and Judah."

---

^A 23:15 Lit And David craved   ^B 23:18 Some Hb mss, Syr read the Thirty   ^C 23:20 LXX; MT omits sons   ^D 23:20 Or two warriors   ^E 23:30 Or from Nahale-gaash   ^F 23:32 Some LXX mss; MT omits son of; 1Ch 11:34

23:14 The **stronghold** probably designates the cave in which David was stationed. A **Philistine garrison** occupied **Bethlehem**— perhaps a move designed to draw David out of hiding.
23:16–17 Three of the warriors under David's command took their leader's wish as a challenge and made the twenty-five-mile round-trip journey at the risk of their lives to secure **water from . . . Bethlehem**. Whether the three in this story are the Three in vv. 8–12 or among the Thirty in vv. 24–39 is not certain. David's response revealed the depth to which he was moved by his men's loyalty and bravery. The water from Bethlehem's well was a precious gift because of the sacrifice the men made to get it. Consequently, it was a fitting sacrifice to David's God. David's act turned the water into a drink offering (Gn 35:14; Lv 23:13; Nm 15:7–10; 28:7–15).
23:24 Asahel was a soldier who was killed by Abner during Israel's civil war following Saul's death (2:18–23).

23:25 Harodite may designate a person from the Harod Valley that leads from the Jezreel Valley down to Beth-shan (1Sm 31:10) in the Jordan Valley.
23:26 A **Tekoite** was a person from Tekoa, seven miles south of Jerusalem (Am 1:1).
23:27 Anathoth, located in Benjamin, was later the prophet Jeremiah's hometown (Jr 1:1).
23:29 Gibeah of the Benjaminites was Saul's hometown and capital, a fact that shows David had some following even there.
23:34 According to 11:3, **Eliam** was Bathsheba's father. If this is the same Eliam, then **Ahithophel**, counselor to David and Absalom (15:31; 16:20–23; 17:1–3,23), would be Bathsheba's grandfather.
23:36 Zobah may have been the Aramean city-state that David conquered (8:3–6). **Gadite** probably designates someone from Gad's territory east of the Jordan River.
23:37 David subdued Ammon on his eastern border; at some point **Zelek**, another foreigner, joined David's forces.

23:39 The text intentionally ends with the mention of **Uriah the Hethite**. Uriah was another foreigner among David's mighty men. He gave his life for David under the most evil of circumstances (11:14–17). The fact that **there were thirty-seven** members of the Thirty may be explained in one of two ways: either "Thirty" was a title rather than a specific figure, or the extra men were brought in to replace those who fell in battle.
24:1 The particular sin that brought about God's wrath is not given. First Ch 21:1 credits Satan with enticing David, but no contradiction exists. Both verses are correct; God is able to use even Satan to accomplish his purposes (Jb 1:12; 2:6). Here, God allowed Satan to entice David to **count the people**, an act that, while acceptable under certain circumstances (Ex 30:12), here probably revealed that David was putting trust in his military power rather than in the Lord's protection and guidance. Another possibility is that David failed to instruct his commanders to collect the half-shekel poll tax, bringing on the plague (Ex 30:12–13). In

² So the king said to Joab, the commander of his army, "Go through all the tribes of Israel from Dan to Beer-sheba and register the troops so I can know their number." ³ Joab replied to the king, "May the LORD your God multiply the troops a hundred times more than they are — while my lord the king looks on! But why does my lord the king want to do this?"

⁴ Yet the king's order prevailed over Joab and the commanders of the army. So Joab and the commanders of the army left the king's presence to register the troops of Israel.

⁵ They crossed the Jordan and camped in Aroer, south of the town in the middle of the valley, and then proceeded toward Gad and Jazer. ⁶ They went to Gilead and to the land of the Hittites^A and continued on to Dan-jaan and around to Sidon. ⁷ They went to the fortress of Tyre and all the cities of the Hivites and Canaanites. Afterward, they went to the Negev of Judah at Beer-sheba.

⁸ When they had gone through the whole land, they returned to Jerusalem at the end of nine months and twenty days. ⁹ Joab gave the king the total of the registration of the troops. There were eight hundred thousand valiant armed men^B from Israel and five hundred thousand men from Judah.

¹⁰ David's conscience troubled him after he had taken a census of the troops. He said to the LORD, "I have sinned greatly in what I've done. Now, LORD, because I've been very foolish, please take away your servant's guilt."

David's Punishment

¹¹ When David got up in the morning, the word of the LORD had come to the prophet Gad, David's seer: ¹² "Go and say to David, 'This is what the LORD says: I am offering you three choices. Choose one of them, and I will do it to you.'"

¹³ So Gad went to David, told him the choices, and asked him, "Do you want three^C years of famine to come on your land, to flee from your foes three months while they pursue you, or to have a plague in your land three days? Now, consider carefully^D what answer I should take back to the one who sent me."

¹⁴ David answered Gad, "I have great anxiety. Please, let us fall into the LORD's hands because his mercies are great, but don't let me fall into human hands."

¹⁵ So the LORD sent a plague on Israel from that morning until the appointed time, and from Dan to Beer-sheba seventy thousand men died. ¹⁶ Then the angel extended his hand toward Jerusalem to destroy it, but the LORD relented concerning the destruction and said to the angel who was destroying the people, "Enough, withdraw your hand now!" The angel of the LORD was then at the threshing floor of Araunah^E the Jebusite.

¹⁷ When David saw the angel striking the people, he said to the LORD, "Look, I am the one who has sinned; I am the one^F who has done wrong. But these sheep, what have they done? Please, let your hand be against me and my father's family."

David's Altar

¹⁸ Gad came to David that day and said to him, "Go up and set up an altar to the LORD on the threshing floor of Araunah the Jebusite." ¹⁹ David went up in obedience to Gad's command, just as the LORD had commanded. ²⁰ Araunah looked down and saw the king and his servants coming toward him, so he went out and paid homage to the king with his face to the ground. ²¹ Araunah said, "Why has my lord the king come to his servant?"

David replied, "To buy the threshing floor from you in order to build an altar to the LORD, so the plague on the people may be halted."

^24:6 LXX; MT reads of Tahtim-hodshi; Hb obscure ^24:9 Lit men of valor drawing the sword ^24:13 LXX; MT reads seven; 1Ch 21:12 ^24:13 Lit Now, know and see ^24:16 = Ornan in 1Ch 21:15–28; 2Ch 3:1 ^24:17 LXX reads shepherd

either case, God did not force David to make the wrong decision.
24:2 On **from Dan to Beer-sheba**, see note at 17:11.
24:5 Aroer was the southernmost part of Israel's territory east of the Jordan River. **Gad and Jazer** lay between the Jordan Valley and Ammon.
24:6 Some manuscripts read "Dan, Ijon" instead of **Dan-jaan**, referring to a second city near Dan at Israel's northern border. **Sidon**, a Phoenician city, nonetheless may have had an Israelite garrison there (5:11).
24:7 Tyre was also a Phoenician city. The expression **cities of the Hivites and Canaanites** probably designates areas that David controlled. Joab may have counted the foreign population as well, or merely the Israelite soldiers maintaining order in those regions. The **Negev of Judah at Beer-sheba** completed their counterclockwise loop through the land, and Joab's delegation

probably headed up the patriarchal highway through Hebron and back to Jerusalem with its census numbers.
24:8–9 The numbers given in the parallel passage in 1Ch 21:5 differ significantly, but both authors appear to have rounded their numbers, and the Chronicler may have included Judah's number in Israel's number as well.
24:12–13 David received three **choices** from the Lord through Gad—**famine**, military defeat, or **plague**. The seriousness of these punishments revealed the gravity of David's sin.
24:14 Again, David revealed his heart. He knew **mercies** might come from the Lord, but not from the **human hands** of his enemies.
24:15 Until the appointed time means that it was the third day, though one more act of destruction was planned.
24:16 When **the angel** whom God had sent to bring the plague extended his hand

toward Jerusalem to destroy it, David's thinking proved correct. **The LORD relented** and spared the city. The Jebusites, part of the original Canaanite population during the days of Joshua (Jos 24:11), held Jerusalem until David conquered them (2Sm 5:6–8). **Araunah** apparently had continued to live in the area following David's conquest.
24:17 David asked the Lord, **these sheep, what have they done?** He pleaded with God to strike only him and his family, but sin often has consequences that affect others besides the person who has sinned.
24:18–19 This **altar to the LORD** would mark the point where the plague had stopped.
24:20 Araunah's threshing floor sat above Jerusalem to the north, in the area where Abraham offered Isaac as a sacrifice and where Solomon would later build the temple (2Ch 3:1). Since threshing utilized the wind, threshing floors probably were often in high parts of cities.

²² Araunah said to David, "My lord the king may take whatever he wants^A and offer it. Here are the oxen for a burnt offering and the threshing sledges and ox yokes for the wood. ²³ Your Majesty, Araunah gives everything here to the king." Then he said to the king, "May the LORD your God accept you."

²⁴ The king answered Araunah, "No, I insist on buying it from you for a price, for I will not offer to the LORD my God burnt offerings that cost me nothing." David bought the threshing floor and the oxen for twenty ounces^B of silver. ²⁵ He built an altar to the LORD there and offered burnt offerings and fellowship offerings. Then the LORD was receptive to prayer for the land, and the plague on Israel ended.

---

^A24:22 Lit take what is good in his eyes   ^B24:24 Lit 50 shekels

---

24:22 Araunah made David a generous offer: **My lord the king may take whatever he wants**. Probably his offer was sincere; besides, especially as a foreigner, he was not in a position to bargain with Israel's king. Or Araunah may have anticipated the king would respond with a price (Gn 23:7–16).
24:23 The first sentence of this verse is literally, "All he gives Araunah the king to the king." The first "the king" is usually taken as a vocative, **Your majesty** or "O king." But some have argued that Araunah was the last Jebusite king of Jerusalem (cp. KJV).
24:24 David, however, knew that all genuine sacrifice came at a **price**. To offer to the Lord **burnt offerings that cost . . . nothing** would have been to David a sign of the deepest ingratitude. In light of this, **twenty ounces of silver** was probably more than a fair price.

24:25 Burnt offerings typically signified the general dedication of the worshiper (Lv 1). **Fellowship offerings** involved a meal shared by priest and worshiper, and they could be offered to express thankfulness—in this case thankfulness that **the plague on Israel**, while severe, had not destroyed Jerusalem.

▼ Introduction to 1 Kings

Circumstances of Writing

Scholars cannot identify the authors of any portions of 1 Kings. Traditional guesses such as Samuel and Jeremiah lack evidence, although a prominent worshiper of the Lord like Jeremiah would have been influential in the circles that produced these books. Since the books of 1 and 2 Kings clearly incorporated many earlier documents, the complete authorship would include all writers who contributed to the source documents of this work. At some point, the Holy Spirit worked in the human authors to authenticate the inspired, inerrant books of 1 and 2 Kings. The final stage of composition or compilation had to come after the release of Jehoiachin from Babylonian imprisonment (ca 562 BC). That edition may have added only a postscript to a work completed years earlier, or it may have involved significant additions.

The history recorded in 1 and 2 Kings covers approximately 410 years. First Kings begins around 970 BC with the death of King David; 2 Kings ends around 560 BC with the release of King Jehoiachin from prison. During this time, the nation of Israel split into two kingdoms (930 BC), and both kingdoms went into exile (Israel in 722 BC and Judah in 587 BC).

Contribution to the Bible

For the Bible writers, history could not have existed without God's purposes. This makes all history theological. The books of 1 and 2 Kings interpreted Hebrew history in light of OT covenant theology. The Babylonian exile created the need for this work of historical apologetics. The exiles needed to explain the failure of the religious program established by the sovereign God. In the Deuteronomistic history—Joshua, Judges, 1 and 2 Samuel, and 1 and 2 Kings—this failure was consistently explained as the failures of the people to live up to their part of the covenant.

Structure

The organizing principle of 1 and 2 Kings is not story or narrative. Kings is unique because its basic structural units are the formulaic royal records. Formal openers (1Kg 15:9–10) and closers (15:23–24) usually identify the boundaries of the record of an individual monarch. Then the writer could insert other types of literature before, between, and after the openers and closers: narratives, prayers, descriptions, etc. But the most important element is the evaluation of the ruler's faithfulness to the covenant (15:11–15). All of these materials make up a history of covenant obedience or disobedience.

1 Kings Timeline

1350–1150 BC

DAVID 1010–970
David becomes king of Judah. **1010**
David becomes king over all Israel. **1003**
David conquers Jerusalem. **1000?**
SOLOMON 990–931
Solomon becomes king. **970**
Temple construction begins. **966**
Temple of Solomon is dedicated. **959**
REHOBOAM 941–913
Kingdom divides: Rehoboam, king of southern kingdom; Jeroboam I, king of northern kingdom. **931**

1150–1000 BC

Pharaoh Shoshenq I (Shishak), founder of Egypt's Twenty-second Dynasty, invades Jerusalem and takes treasures from the temple and royal palaces. **926–917**
JEROBOAM 917–909
First temple reform under Asa **897**
Omri makes Samaria his capital. **880**
Elijah's ministry **862–852**
Ben-hadad attacks Samaria. **857**
Elisha's ministry **850?–798?**
Joel's ministry **836–796?**
Second temple reform under Joash **812**

Outline

1000–970 BC

AHAB 874–853
JOASH 835–796
Events in Amos **783–746**
First Olympiad is celebrated in Greece. **776**
The first eclipse of the sun is documented
   in Assyrian annals. **763**
Events in Hosea **750–722?**
Events in Micah **750–686**
Tiglath-pileser's invasions of Israel **745–732**
Isaiah's ministry **742–700**
Syro-Ephraimite War; Aram and
   Israel invade Judah. **735?**

970–900 BC

Samaria falls; northern kingdom is
   taken into exile by Assyrians. **722**
HEZEKIAH 715–686
Third temple reform under Hezekiah **715**
Sennacherib's invasion of Judah **701**
JOSIAH 640–609
Jeremiah's ministry **627–586?**
Fourth temple reform under Josiah **622**
Josiah is killed in battle by Pharaoh Neco. **609**
Nebuchadnezzar's three invasions
   of Judah **605, 597, 586**
Temple of Solomon is destroyed. **586**

David's Last Days

1 Now King David was old and advanced in age. Although they covered him with bedclothes, he could not get warm. [2] So his servants said to him, "Let us[A] search for a young virgin for my lord the king. She is to attend the king and be his caregiver. She is to lie by your side so that my lord the king will get warm." [3] They searched for a beautiful girl throughout the territory of Israel; they found Abishag the Shunammite[B] and brought her to the king. [4] The girl was of unsurpassed beauty, and she became the king's caregiver. She attended to him, but he was not intimate with[C] her.

Adonijah's Bid for Power

[5] Adonijah son of Haggith kept exalting himself, saying, "I will be king!" He prepared chariots, cavalry, and fifty men to run ahead of him.[D] [6] But his father had never once infuriated him by asking, "Why did you do that?" In addition, he was quite handsome and was born after Absalom. [7] He conspired[E] with Joab son of Zeruiah and with the priest Abiathar. They supported Adonijah, [8] but the priest Zadok, Benaiah son of Jehoiada, the prophet Nathan, Shimei, Rei, and David's royal guard[F] did not side with Adonijah.

[9] Adonijah sacrificed sheep, goats, cattle, and fattened cattle near the stone of Zoheleth, which is next to En-rogel. He invited all his royal brothers and all the men of Judah, the servants of the king, [10] but he did not invite the prophet Nathan, Benaiah, the royal guard, or his brother Solomon.

Nathan's and Bathsheba's Appeals

[11] Then Nathan said to Bathsheba, Solomon's mother, "Have you not heard that Adonijah son of Haggith has become king and our lord David does not know it? [12] Now please come and let me advise you. Save your life and the life of your son Solomon. [13] Go, approach King David and say to him, 'My lord the king, did you not swear to your servant: Your son Solomon is to become king after me, and he is the one who is to sit on my throne? So why has Adonijah become king?' [14] At that moment, while you are still there speaking with the king, I'll come in after you and confirm your words."

[15] So Bathsheba went to the king in his bedroom. Since the king was very old, Abishag the Shunammite was attending to him. [16] Bathsheba knelt low and paid homage to the king, and he asked, "What do you want?"

[17] She replied, "My lord, you swore to your servant by the LORD your God, 'Your son Solomon is to become king after me, and he is the one who is to sit on my throne.' [18] Now look, Adonijah has become king. And,[G] my lord the king, you didn't know it. [19] He has lavishly sacrificed oxen, fattened cattle, and sheep. He invited all the king's sons, the priest Abiathar, and Joab the commander of the army, but he did not invite your servant Solomon. [20] Now, my lord the king, the eyes of all Israel are on you to tell them who will sit on the throne of my lord the king after him. [21] Otherwise, when my lord the king rests with his ancestors, I and my son Solomon will be regarded as criminals."

[22] At that moment, while she was still speaking with the king, the prophet Nathan arrived, [23] and it was announced to the king, "The prophet Nathan is here." He came into the king's presence and paid homage to him with his face to the ground.

[24] "My lord the king," Nathan said, "did you say, 'Adonijah is to become king after me, and he is the one who is to sit on my throne'? [25] For today he went down and lavishly sacrificed oxen, fattened cattle, and sheep. He invited all the sons of the king, the commanders of the army, and the priest Abiathar. And look! They're eating and drinking in his presence, and they're saying, 'Long live King Adonijah!' [26] But he did not invite me — me, your servant — or the priest Zadok or Benaiah son of Jehoiada or your servant Solomon. [27] I'm certain my lord the king would not have let this happen

^1:2 Lit them   ^1:3 Shunem was a town in the hill country of Issachar at the foot of Mt. Moreh; Jos 19:17–18.   ^1:4 Lit he did not know   ^1:5 Heralds announcing his procession   ^1:7 Lit His words were   ^1:8 Lit David's warriors   ^1:18 Some Hb mss, LXX, Vg, Syr; other Hb mss read And now

1:2 The strongest Hebrew word for **virgin** (betulah) is used here.
1:3-4 The sole purpose **the girl** served was to provide warmth and care.
1:5-10 In the struggle for Israel's future, Adonijah gathered his supporters and tried to seize the throne. Some of David's loyal followers, such as Joab and Abiathar, joined with Adonijah. Bathsheba and Nathan, supported by some of David's remaining brave warriors and David's loyal Cherethites and the Pelethites, reacted quickly and put an end to the attempted coup. Nathan's warning to Bathsheba to act to save her and Solomon's lives (v. 12) showed the likelihood for violence as a result of this struggle.

1:5 Kept exalting indicates that **Adonijah** had already been proclaiming his future kingship and establishing his entourage for seizing the throne. David had already promised Bathsheba that her son Solomon would be king and had publicly announced to the assembled nation that Solomon was his heir (1Ch 28:5).
1:8 David's royal guard (lit "great men") likely refers to (1) the remnants and/or successors of David's warriors (2Sm 23:8–39); or (2) David's loyal palace guard, the Cherethites and Pelethites.
1:9 Adonijah's great feast amounted to an impromptu coronation, with many of the expected features: a revered setting, a military leader, a priest, pomp, and loyal followers.

1:15-21 Bathsheba raised three issues to arouse David to action: (1) By God's will David had promised the throne to **Solomon**. (2) Adonijah had proclaimed himself king without David's public support or knowledge. (3) She pointed out that she and Solomon would be **regarded as criminals** if David did not act.
1:26-28 Bathsheba had to be called in despite the fact that she was already in the king's bedroom with David when Nathan entered (v. 22). In this case readers should conclude that sometime after v. 22 Bathsheba had temporarily left the king's room, appropriately giving Nathan private audience with his king.

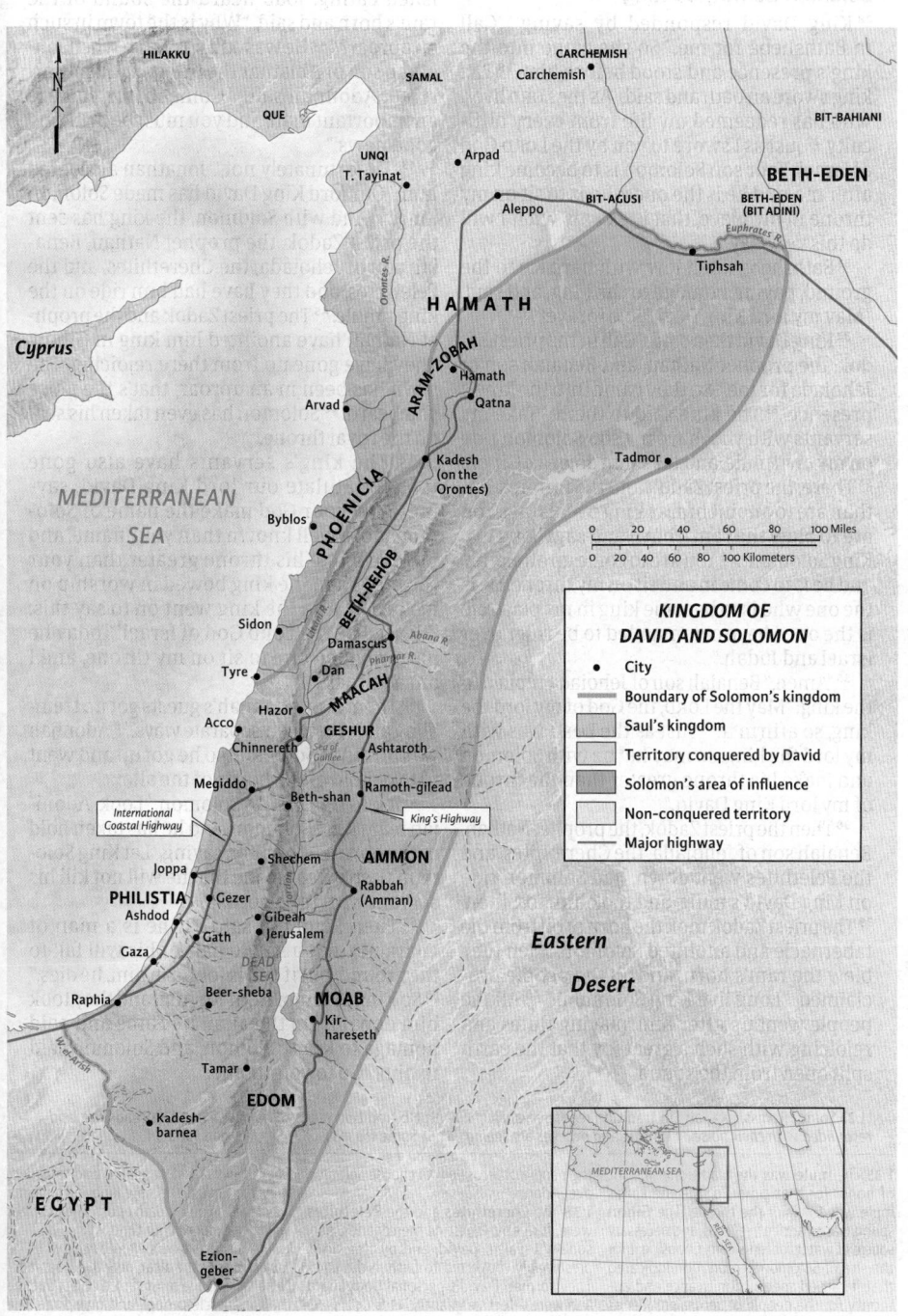

KINGDOM OF DAVID AND SOLOMON

- City
- ━━ Boundary of Solomon's kingdom
- Saul's kingdom
- Territory conquered by David
- Solomon's area of influence
- Non-conquered territory
- ━━ Major highway

without letting your servant^A^ know who will sit on my lord the king's throne after him."

Solomon Confirmed King

28 King David responded by saying, "Call in Bathsheba for me." So she came into the king's presence and stood before him. **29** The king swore an oath and said, "As the LORD lives, who has redeemed my life from every difficulty, **30** just as I swore to you by the LORD God of Israel: Your son Solomon is to become king after me, and he is the one who is to sit on my throne in my place, that is exactly what I will do this very day."

31 Bathsheba knelt low with her face to the ground, paying homage to the king, and said, "May my lord King David live forever!"

32 King David then said, "Call in the priest Zadok, the prophet Nathan, and Benaiah son of Jehoiada for me." So they came into the king's presence. **33** The king said to them, "Take my servants with you, have my son Solomon ride on my own mule, and take him down to Gihon. **34** There, the priest Zadok and the prophet Nathan are to anoint him as king over Israel. You are to blow the ram's horn and say, 'Long live King Solomon!' **35** You are to come up after him, and he is to come in and sit on my throne. He is the one who is to become king in my place; he is the one I have commanded to be ruler over Israel and Judah."

36 "Amen," Benaiah son of Jehoiada replied to the king. "May the LORD, the God of my lord the king, so affirm it. **37** Just as the LORD was with my lord the king, so may he^B^ be with Solomon and make his throne greater than the throne of my lord King David."

38 Then the priest Zadok, the prophet Nathan, Benaiah son of Jehoiada, the Cherethites, and the Pelethites went down, had Solomon ride on King David's mule, and took him to Gihon. **39** The priest Zadok took the horn of oil from the tabernacle and anointed Solomon. Then they blew the ram's horn, and all the people proclaimed, "Long live King Solomon!" **40** All the people went up after him, playing flutes and rejoicing with such a great joy that the earth split open from the sound.^c^

Adonijah Hears of Solomon's Coronation

41 Adonijah and all the invited guests who were with him heard the noise as they finished eating. Joab heard the sound of the ram's horn and said, "Why is the town in such an uproar?" **42** He was still speaking when Jonathan son of Abiathar the priest, suddenly arrived. Adonijah said, "Come in, for you are an important man, and you must be bringing good news."

43 "Unfortunately not," Jonathan answered him. "Our lord King David has made Solomon king. **44** And with Solomon, the king has sent the priest Zadok, the prophet Nathan, Benaiah son of Jehoiada, the Cherethites, and the Pelethites, and they have had him ride on the king's mule. **45** The priest Zadok and the prophet Nathan have anointed him king in Gihon. They have gone up from there rejoicing. The town has been in an uproar; that's the noise you heard. **46** Solomon has even taken his seat on the royal throne.

47 "The king's servants have also gone to congratulate our lord King David, saying, 'May your God make the name of Solomon more well known than your name, and may he make his throne greater than your throne.' Then the king bowed in worship on his bed. **48** And the king went on to say this: 'Blessed be the LORD God of Israel! Today he has provided one to sit on my throne, and I am a witness.'"^D^

49 Then all of Adonijah's guests got up trembling and went their separate ways. **50** Adonijah was afraid of Solomon, so he got up and went to take hold of the horns of the altar.

51 It was reported to Solomon, "Look, Adonijah fears King Solomon, and he has taken hold of the horns of the altar, saying, 'Let King Solomon first^E^ swear to me that he will not kill his servant with the sword.'"

52 Then Solomon said, "If he is a man of character, not a single hair of his will fall to the ground, but if evil is found in him, he dies." **53** So King Solomon sent for him, and they took him down from the altar. He came and paid homage to King Solomon, and Solomon said to him, "Go to your home."

---

^A^**1:27** Some Hb mss, LXX; alt Hb tradition reads *servants* ^B^**1:37** Alt Hb tradition reads *so he will* ^c^**1:40** LXX reads *the land resounded with their noise* ^D^**1:48** Lit *and my eyes are seeing* ^E^**1:51** Some Hb mss, LXX, Syr, Vg read *today*

1:33 The **mule** was the traditional mount of honor for that time. To ride the king's mule was to claim the throne. The **Gihon** spring was an ancient, revered, and necessary source of water for Jerusalem. Choosing it for the site of Solomon's coronation indicated that it carried special significance and authority for the people of Jerusalem just as Adonijah's selection of En-rogel recognized the significance of that site (v. 9).
1:34 The proper religious personnel were to anoint **Solomon**. This was done by the king's command and in the presence of the king's private army. These facts were sufficient for

the people of Jerusalem to choose Solomon over Adonijah.
1:38 The **Cherethites** and the **Pelethites** were, formerly, Philistine mercenaries, personally loyal to David, and by this time, presumably converted to faith in the Lord. They formed David's personal bodyguard and were effective infantry.
1:41 The conflicting coronations were occurring within five hundred yards of each other, the distance between Gihon and En-rogel.
1:47–48 These two speeches were not merely friendly sentiments. First, they represented

David's will. Then, repeated and recorded, they confirmed the new king in the same way that the public oath of office legitimizes an office holder in our time.
1:50 Adonijah's failure was obvious when he took refuge at the **altar**, near the tabernacle. The altar was the most sacred object outside the tabernacle proper, and over time, the **horns** became the most representative part of the altar.
1:51–53 Adonijah was temporarily given pardon.

David's Dying Instructions to Solomon

2 As the time approached for David to die, he ordered his son Solomon, ² "As for me, I am going the way of all of the earth. Be strong and be a man, ³ and keep your obligation to the LORD your God to walk in his ways and to keep his statutes, commands, ordinances, and decrees. This is written in the law of Moses, so that you will have success in everything you do and wherever you turn, ⁴ and so that the LORD will fulfill his promise that he made to me: 'If your sons take care to walk faithfully before me with all their heart and all their soul, you will never fail to have a man on the throne of Israel.'

⁵ "You also know what Joab son of Zeruiah did to me and what he did to the two commanders of Israel's army, Abner son of Ner and Amasa son of Jether. He murdered them in a time of peace to avenge blood shed in war. He spilled that blood on his own waistband and on the sandals of his feet.^A ⁶ Act according to your wisdom, and do not let his gray head descend to Sheol in peace.

⁷ "Show kindness to the sons of Barzillai the Gileadite and let them be among those who eat at your table because they supported me when I fled from your brother Absalom.

⁸ "Keep an eye on Shimei son of Gera, the Benjaminite from Bahurim who is with you. He uttered malicious curses against me the day I went to Mahanaim. But he came down to meet me at the Jordan River, and I swore to him by the LORD, 'I will never kill you with the sword.' ⁹ So don't let him go unpunished, for you are a wise man. You know how to deal with him to bring his gray head down to Sheol with blood."

¹⁰ Then David rested with his ancestors and was buried in the city of David. ¹¹ The length of time David reigned over Israel was forty years: he reigned seven years in Hebron and thirty-three years in Jerusalem. ¹² Solomon sat on the throne of his father David, and his kingship was firmly established.

Adonijah's Foolish Request

¹³ Now Adonijah son of Haggith came to Bathsheba, Solomon's mother. She asked, "Do you come peacefully?"

"Peacefully," he replied, ¹⁴ and then asked, "May I talk with you?"^B

"Go ahead," she answered.

¹⁵ "You know the kingship was mine," he said. "All Israel expected me to be king, but then the kingship was turned over to my brother, for the LORD gave it to him. ¹⁶ So now I have just one request of you; don't turn me down."^C

She said to him, "Go on."

¹⁷ He replied, "Please speak to King Solomon since he won't turn you down. Let him give me Abishag the Shunammite as a wife."

¹⁸ "Very well," Bathsheba replied. "I will speak to the king for you."

¹⁹ So Bathsheba went to King Solomon to speak to him about Adonijah. The king stood up to greet her, bowed to her, sat down on his throne, and had a throne placed for the king's mother. So she sat down at his right hand.

²⁰ Then she said, "I have just one small request of you. Don't turn me down."

"Go ahead and ask, mother," the king replied, "for I won't turn you down."

²¹ So she said, "Let Abishag the Shunammite be given to your brother Adonijah as a wife."

²² King Solomon answered his mother, "Why are you requesting Abishag the Shunammite for Adonijah? Since he is my elder brother, you might as well ask the kingship for him, for the priest Abiathar, and for Joab son of Zeruiah."^D

²³ Then King Solomon took an oath by the LORD: "May God punish me and do so severely if Adonijah has not made this request at the cost of his life. ²⁴ And now, as the LORD lives — the one who established me, seated me on the throne of my father David, and made me a dynasty as

---

^A 2:5 LXX, Old Lat read *on my waistband and . . . my feet*; v. 31   ^B 2:14 Lit *then said, "I have a word for you."*   ^C 2:16 Lit *don't make me turn my face*   ^D 2:22 LXX, Vg, Syr read *kingship for him, and on his side are Abiathar the priest and Joab son of Zeruiah*

2:5–6 David counseled Solomon about some real dangers to the state. David was warning Solomon against tolerance for men whose character made them too dangerous for this new society.

Joab, the double murderer, was the first to be dealt with. His first crime, killing Abner, could have been construed as revenge, although **blood shed in war** was not normally avenged in **peace**. However, the murder of **Amasa** could not be justified. The **blood** on his **waistband** and **sandals** graphically indicated Joab's guilt. Finally, Joab's siding with Adonijah in what could have been a violent civil conflict outweighed any gratitude David owed to Joab for his past faithfulness. **2:7** David counseled **kindness** to the house of **Barzillai**, who supported David in Absalom's rebellion. The Hebrew word translated "kindness" is the usual word for "covenant

faithfulness." For Barzillai, proper covenant faithfulness meant faithfulness to the king. For David, Barzillai's faithfulness deserved reciprocal consideration from the king and his house (17:27–29; 19:31–39). **2:8–9** This counsel implied that **Shimei** still exercised some influence. At the time of David's return, tolerating Shimei may have been beneficial for stabilizing the country. By contrast, Solomon's power was stable enough that Shimei, and any danger he represented, could be suppressed. **2:10–11** This formula statement, **David rested with his ancestors**, provides a narrative transition from David's reign to Solomon's. **2:13–14** This incident is one of many clues (v. 19) that the queen **mother** was a position of great influence. **2:17** One of the customs of the ancient world was for the new king to confirm his

position by taking the wives of the former king (2Sm 16:22). Adonijah must have viewed Solomon as very weak to make this dangerous request. **2:18** It seems unbelievably naive for **Bathsheba** to intercede with Solomon in this request. Or did she see that encouraging Adonijah's foolishness was a good way to make clear to Solomon the threat Adonijah represented? If so, her decision here moved Adonijah a step closer to his demise. **2:19–21** The protocol and ceremony of this scene again pointed to the influence of the queen **mother**. **2:22–25** Solomon's words grouped **Adonijah . . . Abiathar**, and **Joab** together as joint leaders of the failed coup. Adonijah's foolish attempt to extract some advantage from the failure gave Solomon the opportunity to deal with Adonijah and all the plotters.

he promised — I swear Adonijah will be put to death today!" ²⁵ Then King Solomon dispatched Benaiah son of Jehoiada, who struck down Adonijah, and he died.

Abiathar's Banishment

²⁶ The king said to the priest Abiathar, "Go to your fields in Anathoth. Even though you deserve to die, I will not put you to death today, since you carried the ark of the Lord GOD in the presence of my father David and you suffered through all that my father suffered." ²⁷ So Solomon banished Abiathar from being the LORD's priest, and it fulfilled the LORD's prophecy he had spoken at Shiloh against Eli's family.

Joab's Execution

²⁸ The news reached Joab. Since he had supported Adonijah but not Absalom, Joab fled to the LORD's tabernacle and took hold of the horns of the altar.

²⁹ It was reported to King Solomon, "Joab has fled to the LORD's tabernacle and is now beside the altar."

Then Solomon sentᴬ Benaiah son of Jehoiada and told him, "Go and strike him down!"

³⁰ So Benaiah went to the tabernacle and said to Joab, "This is what the king says: 'Come out!'"

But Joab said, "No, for I will die here."

So Benaiah took a message back to the king, "This is what Joab said, and this is how he answered me."

³¹ The king said to him, "Do just as he says. Strike him down and bury him in order to remove from me and from my father's family the blood that Joab shed without just cause. ³² The LORD will bring back his own blood on his head because he struck down two men more righteous and better than he, without my father David's knowledge. With his sword, Joab murdered Abner son of Ner, commander of Israel's army, and Amasa son of Jether, commander of Judah's army. ³³ The responsibility for their deaths will come back to Joab and to his descendantsᴮ forever, but for David, his

descendants, his dynasty, and his throne, there will be peace from the LORD forever."

³⁴ Benaiah son of Jehoiada went up, struck down Joab, and put him to death. He was buried at his house in the wilderness. ³⁵ Then the king appointed Benaiah son of Jehoiada in Joab's place over the army, and he appointed the priest Zadok in Abiathar's place.

Shimei's Banishment and Execution

³⁶ Then the king summoned Shimei and said to him, "Build a house for yourself in Jerusalem and live there, but don't leave there and go anywhere else. ³⁷ On the day you do leave and cross the Kidron Valley, know for sure that you will certainly die. Your blood will be on your own head."

³⁸ Shimei said to the king, "The sentence is fair; your servant will do as my lord the king has spoken." And Shimei lived in Jerusalem for a long time.

³⁹ But then, at the end of three years, two of Shimei's slaves ran away to Achish son of Maacah, king of Gath. Shimei was informed, "Look, your slaves are in Gath." ⁴⁰ So Shimei saddled his donkey and set out to Achish at Gath to search for his slaves. He went and brought them back from Gath.

⁴¹ It was reported to Solomon that Shimei had gone from Jerusalem to Gath and had returned. ⁴² So the king summoned Shimei and said to him, "Didn't I make you swear by the LORD and warn you, saying, 'On the day you leave and go anywhere else, know for sure that you will certainly die'? And you said to me, 'The sentence is fair; I will obey.' ⁴³ So why have you not kept the LORD's oath and the command that I gave you?" ⁴⁴ The king also said, "You yourself know all the evil that you did to my father David. Therefore, the LORD has brought back your evil on your head, ⁴⁵ but King Solomon will be blessed, and David's throne will remain established before the LORD forever."

⁴⁶ Then the king commanded Benaiah son of Jehoiada, and he went out and struck Shimei down, and he died. So the kingdom was established in Solomon's hand.

ᴬ2:29 LXX adds Joab a message: "What is the matter with you, that you have fled to the altar?" And Joab replied, "Because I feared you, I have fled to the Lord." And Solomon the king sent   ᴮ2:33 Lit Their blood will return on the head of Joab and on the head of his seed

---

2:26–27 Abiathar knew that his priestly participation in the abortive coronation was essential to Adonijah's plot; his participation was neither innocent nor casual. Mere banishment was a gentle penalty; death would have been justified. Banishment prevented him from playing an influential role either at the tabernacle or in the Lord's temple yet to be built. Removal of Abiathar from office fulfilled the earlier judgment on **Eli's family** (1Sm 2:30–36). **2:28–29** As the commander of the army, **Joab** could have mobilized the old tribal and clan levies in support of Adonijah. Such

a threat was virtually treasonous, and the treasonous potentialities remained as long as Joab lived. Furthermore, judging Joab for his murders was a necessary step in repudiating the old violent ways—a step that David never took. **2:30–34 Joab** understood perfectly the consequences of his deeds and sought safety at the altar, where **Benaiah** executed the death sentence against him. Joab might have hoped for sanctuary at the altar, but the right of sanctuary only applied to those who committed accidental manslaughter (Ex 21:12–14).

2:35 Benaiah's appointment to **Joab's place over the army** indicated that Joab remained the commander in chief up to his death. **2:36–46** Shimei's situation was the opposite of Abiathar's. **Shimei** was a danger away from **Jerusalem** where he could stir up trouble in distant locales; therefore, Shimei was placed under house arrest in Jerusalem. When Shimei violated his house arrest, possibly thinking Solomon's concern had diminished over the three-year period, he was executed. The **Kidron Valley**, just east of Jerusalem, served as one of the boundaries of Jerusalem.

The Lord Appears to Solomon

3 Solomon made an alliance[A] with Pharaoh king of Egypt by marrying Pharaoh's daughter. Solomon brought her to the city of David until he finished building his palace, the Lord's temple, and the wall surrounding Jerusalem. ² However, the people were sacrificing on the high places, because until that time a temple for the Lord's name had not been built. ³ Solomon loved the Lord by walking in the statutes of his father David, but he also sacrificed and burned incense on the high places.

⁴ The king went to Gibeon to sacrifice there because it was the most famous high place. He offered a thousand burnt offerings on that altar. ⁵ At Gibeon the Lord appeared to Solomon in a dream at night. God said, "Ask. What should I give you?"

⁶ And Solomon replied, "You have shown great and faithful love to your servant, my father David, because he walked before you in faithfulness, righteousness, and integrity.[B] You have continued this great and faithful love for him by giving him a son to sit on his throne, as it is today.

⁷ "Lord my God, you have now made your servant king in my father David's place. Yet I am just a youth with no experience in leadership.[C] ⁸ Your servant is among your people you have chosen, a people too many to be numbered or counted. ⁹ So give your servant a receptive heart to judge your people and to discern between good and evil. For who is able to judge this great people of yours?"

¹⁰ Now it pleased the Lord that Solomon had requested this. ¹¹ So God said to him, "Because you have requested this and did not ask for long life[D] or riches for yourself, or the death[E] of your enemies, but you asked discernment for yourself to administer justice, ¹² I will therefore do what you have asked. I will give you a wise and understanding heart, so that there has never been anyone like you before and never will be again. ¹³ In addition, I will give you what you did not ask for: both riches and honor, so

that no king will be your equal during your entire life. ¹⁴ If you walk in my ways and keep my statutes and commands just as your father David did, I will give you a long life."

¹⁵ Then Solomon woke up and realized it had been a dream. He went to Jerusalem, stood before the ark of the Lord's covenant, and offered burnt offerings and fellowship offerings. Then he held a feast for all his servants.

Solomon's Wisdom

¹⁶ Then two women who were prostitutes came to the king and stood before him. ¹⁷ One woman said, "Please, my lord, this woman and I live in the same house, and I had a baby while she was in the house. ¹⁸ On the third day after I gave birth, she also had a baby and we were alone. No one else[F] was with us in the house; just the two of us were there. ¹⁹ During the night this woman's son died because she lay on him. ²⁰ She got up in the middle of the night and took my son from my side while your servant was asleep. She laid him in her arms, and she put her dead son in my arms. ²¹ When I got up in the morning to nurse my son, I discovered he was dead. That morning, when I looked closely at him I realized that he was not the son I gave birth to."

²² "No," the other woman said. "My son is the living one; your son is the dead one."

The first woman said, "No, your son is the dead one; my son is the living one." So they argued before the king.

²³ The king replied, "This woman says, 'This is my son who is alive, and your son is dead,' but that woman says, 'No, your son is dead, and my son is alive.'" ²⁴ The king continued, "Bring me a sword." So they brought the sword to the king. ²⁵ And the king said, "Cut the living boy in two and give half to one and half to the other."

²⁶ The woman whose son was alive spoke to the king because she felt great compassion[G] for her son. "My lord, give her the living baby," she said, "but please don't have him killed!"

^3:1 Lit Solomon made himself a son-in-law ^3:6 Lit and uprightness of heart with you ^3:7 Lit am a little youth and do not know to go out or come in ^3:11 Lit for many days ^3:11 Lit life ^3:18 Lit No stranger ^3:26 Lit because her compassion grew hot

3:1 Some suggest that brides in political marriages, such as the one between Solomon and **Pharaoh's daughter**, conducted the business that in modern times is conducted by ambassadors. Therefore Solomon's granting his foreign wives and the representatives of their governments the right to worship their own gods while in Israel was, on the human level, a diplomatic courtesy. But the Lord regarded such courtesy toward false gods as apostasy. This was Solomon's first recorded example of conflict between prudent politics and faithfulness to the Lord.

3:2–3a The worship at the **high places**, or hilltop altars, might have been of three sorts: (1) the legal local worship of the Lord before any formal recognition of a national shrine,

(2) the illegal worship of the Lord at such shrines after the recognition of a national shrine, and (3) the syncretistic worship of local Baals at local shrines.

3:5 **Gibeon** was the last of the pre-temple national shrines. It was located about six miles north of Jerusalem. The Hebrews acknowledged its holy status when the tabernacle and the bronze altar were put there.

3:6 **Faithful love** (Hb chesed) almost always refers to covenant faithfulness. David was faithful in his obedience to God; God was, in turn, faithful in giving and keeping his covenant promises to David.

3:7–11 Solomon's prayer marked a major cultural shift in Hebrew life, a shift to peaceful values involving wisdom and skill rather than

military craft. Solomon reflected these new values in asking for a heart that would be **receptive** (to the covenant) in judging the nation. Solomon's request was a request to **discern**.

3:15 Solomon celebrated this oracle with a great sacrificial feast of **fellowship offerings** for his **servants**—perhaps for all the resident palace staff.

3:16–28 **Then** (v. 16) marks the connection to the previous dream that Solomon had. He had asked for the ability to discern so he could judge God's people (v. 9). God answered his prayer (Jms 1:5) and gave more than he asked for. This passage is an example of the use of a God-given discerning mind.

◤ The King of Kings

The Lamb who conquers his enemies—he is called Faithful and True; his name is the Word of God, and he bears the name King of kings and Lord of lords *(Rv 17:14; 19:11–16)*.

SAUL

A head taller than anyone else *(1Sm 9:2; 10:23–24)*.

Son of Kish, of the tribe of Benjamin

Thirty years old when he became king of Israel

Reigned for forty-two years

Died along with his sons in a battle with the Philistines *(1Sm 31:1–13)*

Good	Evil
• The Spirit of God took control of Saul and he prophesied *(1Sm 10:9–10)*. • The Spirit of God took control of Saul, and he defended the Israelites *(11:6–11)*. • Credited the Lord with the victory *(11:13)* • Fought bravely and defeated the enemies of Israel *(14:47–48)*	• Foolishly offered the burnt offering instead of waiting for Samuel *(1Sm 13:3–15)* – His reign would not be permanent but given to another—to a man after God's own heart. • Disobeyed the command to completely destroy the Amalekites *(15:7–31)* – Rejected by the Lord as king, and the Spirit of the Lord left him • Jealous of David and tried to kill him on multiple occasions *(18:8–11; 19:9–10; 24:1–22; 26:1–25)* • Consulted a medium to seek guidance for a battle with the Philistines *(28:1–25)*

Saul exhibited pride, jealousy, and a resistance to submit to the Lord, even when confronted time and again with his sin. The kingdom was torn from him and given to one better than him because he rejected the word of the Lord.

◀ Samuel anoints Saul as king *(1Sm 10:1)*.

DAVID

A man after God's own heart *(1Sm 13:14; 16:7,12)*.

Son of Jesse, of the tribe of Judah

Thirty years old when he became king of Israel

Reigned for forty years

Died in a time of peace with rest from all his enemies *(1Kg 2:10–11)*

Good	Evil
• The Spirit of the Lord took control of David *(1Sm 16:13)*. • Killed Goliath for the glory of the Lord *(17:45–51)* • Victorious in battle against Israel's enemies *(18:5)* • Spared Saul twice because he was the Lord's anointed, entrusting himself to the Lord's plan *(24:1–22; 26:1–25)* • Desired to build God a temple for his name *(2Sm 7:1–7; 1Kg 8:18)* • Showed kindness to Mephibosheth, Jonathan's son *(2Sm 9:1–13)*	• Adultery with Bathsheba and the murder of her husband, Uriah *(2Sm 11:1–27)* • Ordered a census of his fighting men *(24:1–10)*

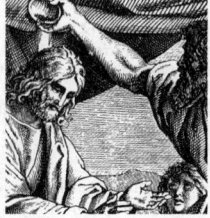

David was ruler over Israel and the shepherd of God's people. The Lord confirmed his covenant with David to build him a house and to establish his throne forever. His son after him would build God's temple, and God would treat him as a son, faithfully loved and disciplined when he did wrong. When David sinned and was confronted, he confessed his guilt and submitted himself to the discipline of the Lord.

◀ David is anointed king at Hebron *(2Sm 5:1–3)*.

SOLOMON

The wisdom of Solomon *(1Kg 3:4–15; 4:29–34)*.

Son of David, of
the tribe of Judah

Reigned for forty years

Died in a time of
unrest from enemies
the Lord raised up
against him
(1Kg 11:41–43)

Good	Evil
• Asked for wisdom from God to lead God's people *(1Kg 3:4–15)* • Built God a temple for his name *(5:1–6:38)* • Displayed his wisdom for the glory of God *(4:29; 5:7; 10:1–9)*	• Had seven hundred wives and three hundred concubines, who turned his heart to worship idols *(1Kg 11:1–8)* – The Lord disciplined him with enemies and took the majority of the kingdom from his son and gave it to his servant *(11:9–40)*.

Solomon received the blessings of the Davidic covenant. His throne was firmly established in wisdom and justice, and he built the Lord's temple as God had said. The wisdom and prosperity of the king and his kingdom were a beacon of light to the nations of the greatness of the Lord. However, he turned to worshiping idols, so the Lord disciplined him and tore the kingdom from his son, though he left him one tribe for the sake of God's promise to David.

◀ Solomon is anointed king at Gihon *(1Kg 1:38–40)*.

JESUS

Son of David,
Son of Abraham
(Mt 1:1)

All authority in heaven
and on earth has been
given to him
(Mt 28:18).

No form, majesty, or beauty that we should desire him *(Is 53:2)*
The Son of David and yet also David's Lord *(Mt 22:41–45)*
Something greater than Solomon is here *(Lk 11:31)*

Jesus is **the true Son of God**, the delight of his Father *(Mt 3:17)*. Through perfect obedience to the Father, even unto death on a cross to save sinners *(Php 2:8)*, Jesus showed himself to be **the true Son of David**, the promised Messiah whose throne would have no end *(Lk 1:30–33)*. He is **the true shepherd** who lays down his life for his sheep *(Jn 10:11–18)*. He is **the true temple** through his resurrection from the dead *(Jn 2:19–22)*. He is **the King of kings** and the Lord of lords *(Rv 19:16)*.

◀ Jesus is crucified as "THE KING OF THE JEWS" *(Jn 19:18–19)*.

But the other one said, "He will not be mine or yours. Cut him in two!"

27 The king responded, "Give the living baby to the first woman, and don't kill him. She is his mother." **28** All Israel heard about the judgment the king had given, and they stood in awe of the king because they saw that God's wisdom was in him to carry out justice.

Solomon's Officials

4 King Solomon reigned over all Israel, **2** and these were his officials:

Azariah son of Zadok, priest;

3 Elihoreph and Ahijah the sons of Shisha, secretaries;

Jehoshaphat son of Ahilud, court historian;

4 Benaiah son of Jehoiada, in charge of the army;

Zadok and Abiathar, priests;

5 Azariah son of Nathan, in charge of the deputies;

Zabud son of Nathan, a priest and adviser to the king;

6 Ahishar, in charge of the palace;

and Adoniram son of Abda, in charge of forced labor.

7 Solomon had twelve deputies for all Israel. They provided food for the king and his household; each one made provision for one month out of the year. **8** These were their names:

Ben-hur, in the hill country of Ephraim;

9 Ben-deker, in Makaz, Shaalbim, Beth-shemesh, and Elon-beth-hanan;

10 Ben-hesed, in Arubboth (he had Socoh and the whole land of Hepher);

11 Ben-abinadab, in all Naphath-dor (Taphath daughter of Solomon was his wife);

12 Baana son of Ahilud, in Taanach, Megiddo, and all Beth-shean which is beside Zarethan below Jezreel, from Beth-shean to Abel-meholah, as far as the other side of Jokmeam;

13 Ben-geber, in Ramoth-gilead (he had the villages of Jair son of Manasseh, which are in Gilead, and he had the region of Argob, which is in Bashan, sixty great cities with walls and bronze bars);

14 Ahinadab son of Iddo, in Mahanaim;

15 Ahimaaz, in Naphtali (he also had married a daughter of Solomon — Basemath);

16 Baana son of Hushai, in Asher and Bealoth;

17 Jehoshaphat son of Paruah, in Issachar;

18 Shimei son of Ela, in Benjamin;

19 Geber son of Uri, in the land of Gilead, the country of King Sihon of the Amorites and of King Og of Bashan.

There was one deputy in the land of Judah.^A

Solomon's Provisions

20 Judah and Israel were as numerous as the sand by the sea; they were eating, drinking, and rejoicing. **21** Solomon ruled all the kingdoms from the Euphrates River to the land of the Philistines and as far as the border of Egypt. They offered tribute and served Solomon all the days of his life.

22 Solomon's provisions for one day were 180 bushels^B of fine flour and 360 bushels^C of meal, **23** ten fattened cattle, twenty range cattle, and

---

^A**4:19** LXX; MT omits *of Judah*   ^B**4:22** Lit *30 cors*   ^C**4:22** Lit *60 cors*

4:2 Azariah, the grandson of **Zadok**, was high priest at a later time in Solomon's rule though not at the very end of his rule (1Ch 6:8–10).

4:3 Secretaries could have been the heads of the royal scribes dealing with day-to-day matters. The **historian** might have been the keeper of the royal archives or chronicles.

4:4 The two competing high priests at the time of Solomon's coronation, **Zadok** and **Abiathar**, are both mentioned, though Abiathar was sent into exile almost immediately.

4:5 Deputies could have been the head officers of the military and bureaucratic forces garrisoned around the country and throughout the empire as well as the officers over forced labor levies (v. 6). Since the word **adviser** literally means "friend," this term probably referred to a close, intimate adviser to the king.

4:6 The official **in charge of the palace** may have administered other properties of the king as well.

4:7 The following verses list the twelve appointed **deputies**, each of whom **provided food** for the royal **household** for one month of the year. These regions were not of equal size and wealth, and Judah is not included;

therefore, this system probably created unfair burdens.

4:8 The **hill country of Ephraim** was roomy, but the settlement and economic development of Ephraim began in earnest only with the Hebrew conquest (see Jos 17:14–18). Therefore the large area assigned to Ben-hur might not have indicated a lighter burden since it might not have been fully productive.

4:9–10 One noted city, **Beth-shemesh**, plus three obscure names could indicate that **Ben-deker** administered a rather small region that likely found it a relatively heavy burden to provide "for the king and his household" (v. 7). The district controlled by **Ben-hesed** was about the same size, but it included some productive coastal plains and the fertile Shephelah region.

4:11 Ben-abinadab was one of two deputies married to daughters of Solomon (see v. 15). His region included some coastal plains but was dominated by southern slopes of the Carmel range.

4:12 The district of **Baana** included several cities on trade routes that opened into the Plain of Esdraelon. For cities of such wealth, making a one-month provision for Solomon was a relatively light burden.

4:13–14 Ben-geber's district in the northern Transjordan, with its **sixty great cities**, was large enough that the financial burden could have been relatively light. A second district around **Mahanaim** would have been relatively small and therefore more heavily burdened. A third in Transjordan (v. 19) is too vaguely defined.

4:15–18 Each of these four districts consisted of the territory of one of Israel's smaller tribes; thus, these were probably heavily burdened.

4:19 In the Hebrew text, **Judah** is not included in this burden. The CSB follows the LXX in including a comment on Judah in this verse, although Judah was not one of the twelve districts.

4:21 The general extent of Solomon's empire included Hebrew tribal territories along with Moab and Edom, most or all of the old Philistine territories (but see 9:16), and most or all of the Aramean kingdoms west of the **Euphrates River** but not the Phoenician coastal cities.

4:22–23 The large quantities provided for Solomon's **provisions for one day** were far more than the expected needs of his palace in Jerusalem. Verses 27–28 hint that these provisions were possibly shared with the

a hundred sheep and goats, besides deer, gazelles, roebucks, and pen-fed poultry,^A 24 for he had dominion over everything west of the Euphrates from Tiphsah to Gaza and over all the kings west of the Euphrates. He had peace on all his surrounding borders. 25 Throughout Solomon's reign, Judah and Israel lived in safety from Dan to Beer-sheba, each person under his own vine and his own fig tree. 26 Solomon had forty thousand^B stalls of horses for his chariots, and twelve thousand horsemen. 27 Each of those deputies for a month in turn provided food for King Solomon and for everyone who came to King Solomon's table. They neglected nothing. 28 Each man brought the barley and the straw for the chariot teams and the other horses to the required place according to his assignment.^C

Solomon's Wisdom and Literary Gifts

29 God gave Solomon wisdom, very great insight, and understanding as vast as the sand on the seashore. 30 Solomon's wisdom was greater than the wisdom of all the people of the East, greater than all the wisdom of Egypt. 31 He was wiser than anyone — wiser than Ethan the Ezrahite, and Heman, Calcol, and Darda, sons of Mahol. His reputation extended to all the surrounding nations. 32 Solomon spoke 3,000 proverbs, and his songs numbered 1,005. 33 He spoke about trees, from the cedar in Lebanon to the hyssop growing out of the wall. He also spoke about animals, birds, reptiles, and fish. 34 Emissaries of all peoples, sent by every king on earth who had heard of his wisdom, came to listen to Solomon's wisdom.

Hiram's Building Materials

5 King Hiram of Tyre sent his emissaries to Solomon when he heard that he had been anointed king in his father's place, for Hiram had always been friends with David.

2 Solomon sent this message to Hiram: 3 "You know my father David was not able to build a temple for the name of the LORD his God. This was because of the warfare all around him until the LORD put his enemies under his feet. 4 The LORD my God has now given me rest on every side; there is no enemy or misfortune. 5 So I plan to build a temple for the name of the LORD my God, according to what the LORD promised my father David: 'I will put your son on your throne in your place, and he will build the temple for my name.'

6 "Therefore, command that cedars from Lebanon be cut down for me. My servants will be with your servants, and I will pay your servants' wages according to whatever you say, for you know that not a man among us knows how to cut timber like the Sidonians."

7 When Hiram heard Solomon's words, he rejoiced greatly and said, "Blessed be the LORD today! He has given David a wise son to be over this great people!" 8 Then Hiram sent a reply to Solomon, saying, "I have heard your message; I will do everything you want regarding the cedar and cypress timber. 9 My servants will bring the logs down from Lebanon to the sea, and I will make them into rafts to go by sea to the place you indicate. I will break them apart there, and you can take them away. You then can meet my needs by providing my household with food."

^A 4:23 Hb obscure ^B 4:26 2Ch 9:25 reads 4,000 stalls ^C 4:28 Lit judgment

military establishment, though the link is unclear.
4:24–25 The north-south range of Solomon's **dominion** indicated here correlates with v. 21 on the north since **Tiphsah** was located on the **Euphrates** River, but in the south, **Gaza** was somewhat north of the Wadi Arish, the traditional border of Egypt. Solomon's control over this large region guaranteed the Israelites a degree of peace and security.
4:26 The writer then presents the major innovation of Solomon's military, a standing army of **chariots**. David did not use chariots. Two factors indicate that Solomon's chariot force was not a native Hebrew force. First, developing a home-grown chariot force was an expensive process involving years of training; hiring mercenaries was quicker. Second, Solomon's chariot armies disappeared in the conflict at Solomon's death, a likely clue that the charioteers returned to their native lands.
Taking the numbers as literal here and using the data from Chronicles, the following situation emerges. There were 1,400 chariots (10:26), an adequate number for a small empire with no competition from the great empires, **twelve thousand** handlers for

horses (probably including both the chariot warriors and the other support personnel for the horses), and facilities for housing and caring for **forty thousand** horses. The figure about the massive number of horses and the facilities for housing them is reasonable if the horses were scattered throughout the empire and in several different facilities, as would make strategic sense. No single facility in ancient times could house forty thousand horses. The Septuagint at 2Ch 9:25 gives a variant figure of four thousand, a reasonable figure for the facilities actually mobilized at any given time.
4:27–28 These verses connect to vv. 7–19 and elaborate on the effective taxation system.
4:29–34 Solomon's extraordinary wisdom is celebrated. Three of the four names listed here also appear in 1Ch 2:6, and a fourth is very close. In harmonizing these two lists, **Mahol** (lit "dance") may represent a professional or guild title, while the Chronicles passage may present actual parentage. These may have been wise men of reputation from a different era. Solomon's reputation for **wisdom** transcended international and chronological boundaries.
5:1 David had traded with Tyre when collecting materials for the Lord's house, the

temple. Solomon also benefited from good relations with **King Hiram of Tyre** in purchasing materials. For Solomon, this cooperation was extended to joint international trade ventures.
5:6 The Israelites, as well as the Egyptians and Assyrians, used both the cedar and cypress lumber of **Lebanon** for their fine buildings.
5:7 Hiram's praise for God probably did not represent real conviction or faith on his part. More likely the Bible writer was paraphrasing Hiram's diplomatic courtesies to express truth about God.
5:8–11 These were the terms of the business arrangements. Solomon bartered **food** for lumber and other products as well. Hiram's men would cut the lumber, bring it to the **sea**, and lash it into **rafts**. Then the rafts were floated south and beached, probably at Joppa, the port nearest Jerusalem. From there they were taken to Jerusalem by the road that passed near Gezer. The amount of grain mentioned here was somewhat more than half the amount of grain collected for Solomon's governmental structure (4:22–23). However, the book of 2 Chronicles adds an equal supply of barley to this amount (2Ch 2:10).

¹⁰ So Hiram provided Solomon with all the cedar and cypress timber he wanted, ¹¹ and Solomon provided Hiram with one hundred twenty thousand bushels^A of wheat as food for his household and one hundred twenty thousand gallons^B of oil from crushed olives. Solomon did this for Hiram year after year.

¹² The LORD gave Solomon wisdom, as he had promised him. There was peace between Hiram and Solomon, and the two of them made a treaty.

Solomon's Workforce

¹³ Then King Solomon drafted forced laborers from all Israel; the labor force numbered thirty thousand men. ¹⁴ He sent ten thousand to Lebanon each month in shifts; one month they were in Lebanon, two months they were at home. Adoniram was in charge of the forced labor. ¹⁵ Solomon had seventy thousand porters and eighty thousand stonecutters in the mountains, ¹⁶ not including his thirty-three hundred^C deputies in charge of the work. They supervised the people doing the work. ¹⁷ The

king commanded them to quarry large, costly stones to lay the foundation of the temple with dressed stones. ¹⁸ So Solomon's builders and Hiram's builders, along with the Gebalites, quarried the stone and prepared the timber and stone for the temple's construction.

Building the Temple

6 Solomon began to build the temple for the LORD in the four hundred eightieth year after the Israelites came out of the land of Egypt, in the fourth year of his reign over Israel, in the month of Ziv, which is the second month.^D ² The temple that King Solomon built for the LORD was ninety feet^E long, thirty feet^F wide, and forty-five feet^G high. ³ The portico in front of the temple sanctuary was thirty feet long extending across the temple's width, and fifteen feet deep^H in front of the temple. ⁴ He also made windows with beveled frames^I for the temple.

⁵ He then built a chambered structure^J along the temple wall, encircling the walls of the temple, that is, the sanctuary and the

^A5:11 Lit 20,000 cors ^B5:11 LXX reads 20,000 baths; MT reads 20 cors ^C5:16 Some LXX mss read 3,600; 2Ch 2:2,18 ^D6:1 April–May ^E6:2 Lit 60 cubits ^F6:2 Lit 20 cubits, also in vv. 3,16,20 ^G6:2 Lit 30 cubits ^H6:3 Lit 10 cubits wide ^I6:4 Hb obscure ^J6:5 Lit built the temple of chamber

5:13–18 These projects were so big that Solomon sent Hebrew **forced laborers** to Phoenicia to help in the work. In this context **thousand** may be a general term with a meaning somewhat like "battalion." The **Gebalites** were the people of ancient Byblos. **6:1** Second Ch 3:2 dates this operation by the precise day in Solomon's reign. By contrast, 1 Kings dates it by its relationship to another great event in covenant history—the exodus from Egypt. The figure of 480 years implies

a fifteenth-century exodus (ca 1440 BC). The month Ziv (Iyyar), the second month of the religious calendar, overlaps with our modern April and May. **6:2–10** These verses give the basic plan for the sanctuary. For comparison, the tabernacle itself (holy place and holy of holies) was forty-five feet long and fifteen feet wide. **6:3** The word **portico** (Hb 'ulam') has two different meanings, translated "hall of pillars" and "canopy with pillars" in 7:6. From

those examples, this portico also might have been a covered hall or entrance with columns, fifteen feet by thirty feet by thirty feet (2Ch 3:4). **6:4** These **windows** pierced the walls above the height of the surrounding rooms (vv. 5–6). **6:5–6** These three levels of storage rooms surrounding the **temple** on the outside are omitted in Chronicles. The lower stories were narrower than the upper stories. The lowest

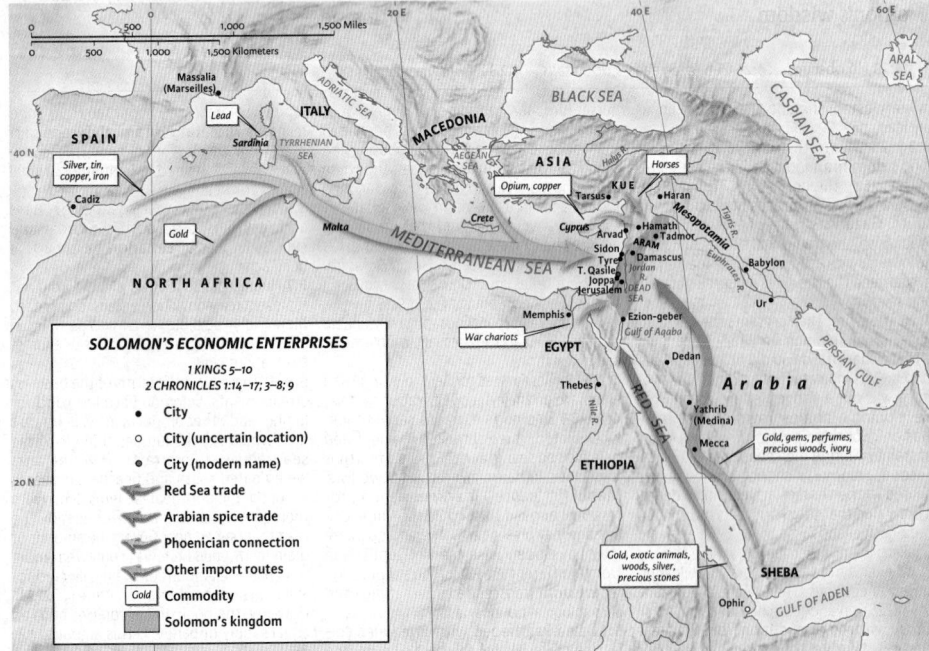

inner sanctuary. And he made side chambers[A] all around. [6] The lowest chamber was 7½ feet[B] wide, the middle was 9 feet[C] wide, and the third was 10½ feet[D] wide. He also provided offset ledges for the temple all around the outside so that nothing would be inserted into the temple walls. [7] The temple's construction used finished stones cut at the quarry so that no hammer, chisel, or any iron tool was heard in the temple while it was being built.

[8] The door for the lowest[E] side chamber was on the right side of the temple. They[F] went up a stairway[G] to the middle chamber, and from the middle to the third. [9] When he finished building the temple, he paneled it with boards and planks of cedar. [10] He built the chambers along the entire temple, joined to the temple with cedar beams; each story was 7½ feet high.

[11] The word of the LORD came to Solomon: [12] "As for this temple you are building — if you walk in my statutes, observe my ordinances, and keep all my commands by walking in them, I will fulfill my promise to you, which I made to your father David. [13] I will dwell among the Israelites and not abandon my people Israel."

[14] When Solomon finished building the temple,[H] [15] he paneled the interior temple walls with cedar boards; from the temple floor to the surface of the ceiling he overlaid the interior with wood. He also overlaid the floor with cypress boards. [16] Then he lined thirty feet of the rear of the temple with cedar boards from the floor to the surface of the ceiling,[I] and he built the interior as an inner sanctuary, the most holy place. [17] The temple, that is, the sanctuary in front of the most holy place,[J] was sixty feet[K] long. [18] The cedar paneling inside the temple was carved with ornamental gourds and flower blossoms. Everything was cedar; not a stone could be seen.

[19] He prepared the inner sanctuary inside the temple to put the ark of the LORD's covenant there. [20] The interior of the sanctuary was thirty feet long, thirty feet wide, and thirty feet high; he overlaid it with pure gold. He also overlaid the cedar altar. [21] Next, Solomon overlaid the interior of the temple with pure gold, and he hung[L] gold chains across the front of the inner sanctuary and overlaid it with gold. [22] So he added the gold overlay to the entire temple until everything was completely finished, including the entire altar that belongs to the inner sanctuary.

[23] In the inner sanctuary he made two cherubim 15 feet[M] high out of olive wood. [24] One wing of the first cherub was 7½ feet long, and the other wing was 7½ feet long. The wingspan was 15 feet from tip to tip. [25] The second cherub also was 15 feet; both cherubim had the same size and shape. [26] The first cherub's height was 15 feet and so was the second cherub's. [27] Then he put the cherubim inside the inner temple. Since their wings were spread out, the first one's wing touched one wall while the second cherub's wing touched the other[N] wall, and in the middle of the temple their wings were touching wing to wing. [28] He also overlaid the cherubim with gold.

[29] He carved all the surrounding temple walls with carved engravings — cherubim, palm trees, and flower blossoms — in the inner and outer sanctuaries. [30] He overlaid the temple floor with gold in both the inner and the outer sanctuaries.

[31] For the entrance of the inner sanctuary, he made olive wood doors. The pillars of the

[A]6:5 Lit made ribs or sides [B]6:6 Lit five cubits, also in vv. 10,24 [C]6:6 Lit six cubits [D]6:6 Lit seven cubits [E]6:8 LXX, Tg; MT reads middle [F]6:8 = People [G]6:8 Hb obscure [H]6:11–14 LXX omits these vv. [I]6:16 LXX; MT omits of the ceiling; 1Kg 6:15 [J]6:17 Lit front of me; Hb obscure [K]6:17 Lit 40 cubits [L]6:21 Lit he caused to pass across [M]6:23 Lit 10 cubits, also in vv. 24,25,26 [N]6:27 Lit the second

ceiling beams pierced the outer **wall** of the storage room at the end away from the temple and rested on a ledge, 1½ feet wide, on the end toward the temple. This ledge was 3 feet from the wall of the temple. The second story beams pierced the same outer wall, but rested on another ledge, 1½ feet wide, that was 1½ feet from the wall. The third story beams pierced the same outer wall but rested on a 1½ foot ledge that touched the wall itself but did not pierce it.
6:7 Cutting the **stones** to exact measure off-site and then putting them in place without further dressing with **iron** tools required great skill.
6:8 The Hebrew language of this verse is obscure. In the LXX it is said that the bottom story was accessed through a door on the **right**, or south, side of the structure. With only one door, access to other stories would have been by an interior doorway and **stairway**, of which we have no exact information. The Hebrew text suggests an external stair or ladder to the second story instead of the outer door mentioned above.

6:9 This verse addresses only the **planks of cedar** and cedar beams that covered the outer surfaces of the temple and surrounding chambers (for the interior surfaces, see vv. 15–22).
6:10 The stories of the outer rooms were 7¼ feet high, apparently including the thickness of the ceilings. Thus the total height of the three stories of outer rooms was just under 22 feet, about half the height of the temple itself.
6:14–15 The interior walls were paneled with cedar, while the flooring was cypress wood, probably Phoenician juniper or some other evergreen.
6:16–17 The **inner sanctuary** of the temple, **the most holy place**, was also paneled with cedar and separated from the rest of the temple by a cedar wall. This produced the common three-part plan: (1) the court, (2) the sanctuary (the holy place), and (3) the inner sanctuary (the most holy place or the holy of holies).
6:18 The interior paneling was carved with **gourds** and **flower blossoms** as well as cherubim and palm trees (v. 29).

6:19–21 The height of the **inner sanctuary** was only **thirty feet**, leaving about fifteen feet between its top and the ceiling of the temple. The stone was completely covered (v. 18). However, the **pure gold** overlay in v. 21 and in 2Ch 3:7 does not necessarily demand that the entire surface was overlaid with gold. This could refer to an aesthetically selective usage of gold overlay.
6:22 Here, in agreement with the LXX, the altar of incense was the **altar that belongs to the inner sanctuary**. This indicated a new location of the altar of incense. In the tabernacle it was in the holy place just outside the veil. Here it was in the inner sanctuary itself (Heb 9:3–4).
6:23–28 If the craftsmanship was typical for the time, the two larger **cherubim** were made of pieces of **olive wood** fastened together, probably glued, then carved, and then covered with **gold**, probably hammered gold foil.
6:30 Even the **floor** was decorated or **overlaid ... with gold**, but probably by a harder gold alloy.

doorposts were five-sided.^A ^32 The two doors were made of olive wood. He carved cherubim, palm trees, and flower blossoms on them and overlaid them with gold, hammering gold over the cherubim and palm trees. ^33 In the same way, he made four-sided^A olive wood doorposts for the sanctuary entrance. ^34 The two doors were made of cypress wood; the first door had two folding sides, and the second door had two folding panels. ^35 He carved cherubim, palm trees, and flower blossoms on them and overlaid them with gold applied evenly over the carving. ^36 He built the inner courtyard with three rows of dressed stone and a row of trimmed cedar beams.

^37 The foundation of the LORD's temple was laid in Solomon's fourth year in the month of Ziv. ^38 In his eleventh year in the month of Bul, which is the eighth month,^B the temple was completed in every detail and according to every specification. So he built it in seven years.

Solomon's Palace Complex

7 Solomon completed his entire palace complex after thirteen years of construction. ^2 He built the House of the Forest of Lebanon. It was one hundred fifty feet^C long, seventy-five feet^D wide, and forty-five feet^E high on four rows of cedar pillars, with cedar beams on top of the pillars. ^3 It was paneled above with cedar at the top of the chambers that rested on forty-five pillars, fifteen per row. ^4 There were three rows of window frames, facing each other^F in three tiers.^G ^5 All the doors and doorposts had rectangular frames, the openings facing each other^H in three tiers. ^6 He made the hall of pillars seventy-five feet long and forty-five feet wide. A portico was in front of the pillars, and a canopy with pillars^A was in front of them. ^7 He made the Hall of the Throne where he would judge — the Hall of Judgment. It was paneled with cedar from the floor to the rafters.^I ^8 Solomon's own palace where he would live, in the other courtyard behind the hall, was of similar construction. And he made a house like this hall for Pharaoh's daughter, his wife.^J

^9 All of these buildings were of costly stones, cut to size and sawed with saws on the inner and outer surfaces, from foundation to coping and from the outside to the great courtyard. ^10 The foundation was made of large, costly stones twelve and fifteen feet^K long. ^11 Above were also costly stones, cut to size, as well as cedar wood. ^12 Around the great courtyard, as well as the inner courtyard of the LORD's temple and the portico of the temple, were three rows of dressed stone and a row of trimmed cedar beams.

^13 King Solomon had Hiram^L brought from Tyre. ^14 He was a widow's son from the tribe of Naphtali, and his father was a man of Tyre, a bronze craftsman. Hiram had great skill, understanding, and knowledge to do every kind of bronze work. So he came to King Solomon and carried out all his work.

---

^A 6:31,33; 7:6 Hb obscure   ^B 6:38 = October–November   ^C 7:2 Lit 100 cubits   ^D 7:2 Lit 50 cubits, also in v. 6   ^E 7:2 Lit 30 cubits, also in vv. 6,23   ^F 7:4 Lit frames, window to window   ^G 7:4 Lit three times; = at 3 different places, also in v. 5   ^H 7:5 Lit frames, opposing window to window   ^I 7:7 Syr, Vg; MT reads floor   ^J 7:8 Lit daughter he had taken   ^K 7:10 Lit ten cubits and eight cubits   ^L 7:13 = Huram in 2Ch 4:11

6:34 This verse could describe each of the sanctuary **doors** as involving two hinged **panels**, perhaps like modern bifold doors.

6:36 The **courtyard** was enclosed by a wall that included **cedar beams**. This technique was often used to bind stone walls together for earthquake protection.

6:37–38 The **temple** was completed in the month of **Bul**, the eighth month of the Canaanite calendar (our modern October–November).

7:1 The word **palace complex** accurately translates the Hebrew word for "house." Solomon took **thirteen years** to build his palace complex in contrast with seven years for building the Lord's house.

7:2–4 If v. 8 describes Solomon's personal dwelling, where he would "live" (or "sit," v. 8), then these verses probably describe a large building dedicated to public business—the structure of **the House of the Forest of Lebanon**.

Understanding this description involves uniting the four rows of **pillars** that held up the central portion of the building (v. 2) with the three rows of pillars associated with three tiers of roof (vv. 3–4). If modeled after Egyptian architecture, these windows were placed in the roof where a change in ceiling height permitted the placing of windows between the columns and between the two different roof levels. The spaces between

two elevations and between the columns of the row left room for a row of windows. The whole row of columns left spaces for a tier of windows.

The three rows of pillars totaling **forty-five pillars, fifteen per row**, would fit in well with the **three rows of window frames**, arranged in **three tiers**. Since the building would normally be symmetrical, with two sets of three tiers facing each other, we may be discussing six tiers of facing windows, three on each side of the high central portion of the king's house. These windows then would be associated with six rows of columns, three on each side of the high central portion. Each tier of windows occupied the elevation between two roof levels of different height.

7:5 This verse seems to describe either three sets of ground level **doors** that faced each other across the width of the building or three matching sets across the front of the building. It is possible that the window **openings** in the doors were in **tiers**.

7:6 This verse uses the Hebrew word translated **portico** (Hb 'ulam) with two different meanings. The first portico, translated **hall of pillars**, could be another covered court with columns. The second is sometimes translated as a "pilastered wall" with a roof or overhang. The CSB communicates roughly the same idea by **canopy with pillars**. This

context clearly indicates that the portico, whatever it was, was covered and may have had pillars.

7:7 The **Hall of the Throne** was another columned entrance or portico. The contextual association with the House of the Forest of Lebanon hints that this hall might have been the public entrance of the larger complex, an appropriate place for the throne where people sought judgment.

7:8 The **palace** in which Solomon **would live** also was another roofed structure with columns and walls paneled with cedar. Solomon's personal dwelling and the **house . . . for Pharaoh's daughter** were the same type of structure.

7:9–11 Since the inner, columnar supports for the roofs have been described, this verse describes the outer walls and perhaps some interior walls of these buildings. These walls were made of fine **stones** finished to measure—**sawed with saws**—on the exposed surfaces. This probably meant sawed to a close approximate shape and then finished smooth by some polishing technique. **Cedar wood** was also used on some upper parts of the walls.

7:13–14 For a devout follower of the Lord, importing the Phoenician **craftsman** named **Hiram** (not to be confused with King Hiram) was more acceptable since his mother was Hebrew.

The Bronze Pillars

¹⁵ He cast two bronze pillars, each 27 feet^A high and 18 feet^B in circumference.^C ¹⁶ He also made two capitals of cast bronze to set on top of the pillars; 7½ feet^D was the height of the first capital, and 7½ feet was also the height of the second capital. ¹⁷ The capitals on top of the pillars had gratings of latticework, wreaths^E made of chainwork — seven for the first capital and seven for the second.

¹⁸ He made the pillars with two encircling rows of pomegranates on the one grating to cover the capital on top; he did the same for the second capital. ¹⁹ And the capitals on top of the pillars in the portico were shaped like lilies, six feet^F high. ²⁰ The capitals on the two pillars were also immediately above the rounded surface next to the grating, and two hundred pomegranates were in rows encircling each^G capital. ²¹ He set up the pillars at the portico of the sanctuary: he set up the right pillar and named it Jachin;^H then he set up the left pillar and named it Boaz.^I ²² The tops of the pillars were shaped like lilies. Then the work of the pillars was completed.

The Basin

²³ He made the cast metal basin,^J 15 feet^K from brim to brim, perfectly round. It was 7½ feet high and 45 feet in circumference. ²⁴ Ornamental gourds encircled it below the brim, ten every half yard,^L completely encircling the basin. The gourds were cast in two rows when the basin was cast. ²⁵ It stood on twelve oxen, three facing north, three facing west, three facing south, and three facing east. The basin was on top of them and all their hindquarters were toward the center. ²⁶ The basin was three inches^M thick, and its rim was fashioned like the brim of a cup or of a lily blossom. It held eleven thousand gallons.^N

The Bronze Water Carts

²⁷ Then he made ten bronze water carts.^O Each water cart was 6 feet long, 6 feet wide, and 4½ feet^P high. ²⁸ This was the design of the carts: They had frames; the frames were between the cross-pieces, ²⁹ and on the frames between the cross-pieces were lions, oxen, and cherubim. On the cross-pieces there was a pedestal above, and below the lions and oxen were wreaths of hanging^Q work. ³⁰ Each cart had four bronze wheels with bronze axles. Underneath the four corners of the basin were cast supports, each next to a wreath. ³¹ And the water cart's opening inside the crown on top was eighteen inches^R wide. The opening was round, made as a pedestal twenty-seven inches^S wide. On it were carvings, but their frames were square, not round. ³² There were four wheels under the frames, and the wheel axles were part of the water cart; each wheel was twenty-seven inches^T tall. ³³ The wheels' design was similar to that of chariot wheels: their axles, rims, spokes, and hubs were all of cast metal. ³⁴ Four supports were at the four corners of each water cart; each support was one piece with the water cart. ³⁵ At the top of the cart was a band nine inches^U high encircling it; also, at the top of the cart, its braces and its frames were one piece with it. ³⁶ He engraved cherubim, lions, and palm trees on the plates of its braces and on its frames, wherever each had space, with encircling wreaths. ³⁷ In this way he made the ten water carts using the same casting, dimensions, and shape for all of them.

Bronze Basins and Other Utensils

³⁸ Then he made ten bronze basins — each basin held 220 gallons^V and each was six feet wide — one basin for each of the ten water carts. ³⁹ He set five water carts on the right

^A7:15 Lit *18 cubits*　^B7:15 Lit *12 cubits*　^C7:15 LXX adds *and the thickness of the pillar was four fingers hollowed and similarly the second pillar*　^D7:16 Lit *five cubits*, also in v. 23　^E7:17 Lit *tassels*　^F7:19 Lit *four cubits*, also in vv. 27,38　^G7:20 Lit *encircling the second*　^H7:21 = He Will Establish　^I7:21 = In Him Is Strength　^J7:23 Lit *sea*　^K7:23 Lit *10 cubits*　^L7:24 Lit *10 per cubit*　^M7:26 Lit *a handbreadth*　^N7:26 Lit *2,000 baths*　^O7:27 Lit *bronze stands*　^P7:27 Lit *three cubits*　^Q7:29 Or *hammered-down*　^R7:31 Lit *a cubit*　^S7:31 Lit *one and a half cubits*　^T7:32 Lit *was one and a half cubits*　^U7:35 Lit *half a cubit*　^V7:38 Lit *40 baths*

7:15–22 The **pillars** were **27 feet** high, with capitals over 7 feet high, for a total of more than 34 feet. **Latticework** and ovoid art covered the structure of the capitals and their ornaments. The shape of the capitals, both for these pillars and for the pillars of the **portico**, was like an open lily blossom. Some have given these pillars a cosmic significance by translating their names as "he established/will establish [from **Jachin**] in strength [from **Boaz**]."
7:23–26 A huge bronze vessel, containing about **eleven thousand gallons**, served as the main **basin** for water used for cleansing. Second Ch 4:6 indicates that this larger reservoir was allotted to priestly cleansing, which might imply that the bronze water carts (1Kg 7:27) were allotted to the Levites.

We are not sure what shape the **ornamental gourds** represented since gourds come in many shapes. Since a cylindrical shape, in contrast to a conical shape, is needed for the stated capacity of the reservoir, the description, **fashioned like . . . a lily blossom**, could refer to only the rim of the reservoir.
7:27–29 The following is one possible understanding of the structure of the **bronze water carts:** They were essentially boxes on wheels for mobility. Each of the four sides had two square panels (**frames**) with carvings. There were carved **cross-pieces** both above and below the panels/frames. Above the top crosspieces were attached supports (**pedestal**), presumably for the basin.

7:31–37 The simplest understanding of v. 31 is that it describes an internal circular structure that, together with the pedestals and the four corner **supports**, supported a bronze basin (v. 38) and held it in place. Real **chariot wheels** were made of wood.
7:38 Then the **bronze basins** were set into the **water carts**. If their shape were more like a cylinder, a depth of slightly more than one foot would give a capacity of roughly 220 gallons. A more conical lily shape would demand a greater depth, possibly as much as three feet. Either could still fit into the cart with the water level about four and one-half feet above the ground.
7:39 The **right side** in descriptions of the Lord's **temple** use is to the south, as if one is standing in the door looking out to the east.

side of the temple and five on the left side. He put the basin near the right side of the temple toward the southeast. **40** Then Hiram made the basins, the shovels, and the sprinkling basins.

Completion of the Bronze Works

So Hiram finished all the work that he was doing for King Solomon on the LORD's temple: **41** two pillars; bowls for the capitals that were on top of the two pillars; the two gratings for covering both bowls of the capitals that were on top of the pillars; **42** the four hundred pomegranates for the two gratings (two rows of pomegranates for each grating covering both capitals' bowls on top of the pillars); **43** the ten water carts; the ten basins on the water carts; **44** the basin; the twelve oxen underneath the basin; **45** and the pots, shovels, and sprinkling basins. All the utensils that Hiram made for King Solomon at the LORD's temple were made of burnished bronze. **46** The king had them cast in clay molds in the Jordan Valley between Succoth and Zarethan. **47** Solomon left all the utensils unweighed because there were so many; the weight of the bronze was not determined.

Completion of the Gold Furnishings

48 Solomon also made all the equipment in the LORD's temple: the gold altar; the gold table that the Bread of the Presence was placed on; **49** the pure gold lampstands in front of the inner sanctuary, five on the right and five on the left; the gold flowers, lamps, and tongs; **50** the pure gold ceremonial bowls, wick trimmers, sprinkling basins, ladles,^A and firepans; and the gold hinges for the doors of the inner temple (that is, the most holy place) and for the doors of the temple sanctuary.

51 So all the work King Solomon did in the LORD's temple was completed. Then Solomon brought in the consecrated things of his father David — the silver, the gold, and the utensils — and put them in the treasuries of the LORD's temple.

Solomon's Dedication of the Temple

8 At that time Solomon assembled the elders of Israel, all the tribal heads and the ancestral leaders of the Israelites before him at Jerusalem in order to bring the ark of the LORD's covenant from the city of David, that is Zion. **2** So all the men of Israel were assembled in the presence of King Solomon in the month of Ethanim, which is the seventh month,^B at the festival.

3 All the elders of Israel came, and the priests picked up the ark. **4** The priests and the Levites brought the ark of the LORD, the tent of meeting, and the holy utensils that were in the tent. **5** King Solomon and the entire congregation of Israel, who had gathered around him and were with him in front of the ark, were sacrificing sheep, goats, and cattle that could not be counted or numbered, because there were so many. **6** The priests brought the ark of the LORD's covenant to its place, into the inner sanctuary of the temple, to the most holy place beneath the wings of the cherubim. **7** For the cherubim were spreading their wings over^C the place of the ark, so that the cherubim covered the ark and its poles from above. **8** The poles were so long that their ends were seen from the holy place in front of the inner sanctuary, but they were not seen from outside the sanctuary; they are still there today. **9** Nothing was in the ark except the two stone tablets that Moses had put there at Horeb,^D where the LORD made a covenant with the Israelites when they came out of the land of Egypt.

10 When the priests came out of the holy place, the cloud filled the LORD's temple, **11** and because of the cloud, the priests were not able to continue ministering, for the glory of the LORD filled the temple.

12 Then Solomon said:

The LORD said that he would dwell
    in total darkness.
13   I have indeed built an exalted temple
        for you,
    a place for your dwelling forever.

14 The king turned around and blessed the entire congregation of Israel while they were standing. **15** He said:

---

^A**7:50** Or *dishes,* or *spoons*; lit *palms*   ^B**8:2** = September–October   ^C**8:7** LXX; MT reads *toward*   ^D**8:9** = Sinai

---

7:40–46 These were generally the new items that had to be made anew for a new context.
7:47 Since **bronze** was a valuable commodity, it is an indication of Solomon's wealth that he did not have to keep track of the amount of bronze used.
8:1–9:9 This dedication was rooted in covenant history. The specific offenses mentioned in Solomon's great prayer reflected the atmosphere, if not the very words, of Lv 26. The prayer also focuses on more recent covenant history, especially the recently chosen dynasty, the dynasty's city, and the new permanent home for God's presence with his people.
8:1 Moving the **ark** from David's private shrine on Mount Zion to the new national temple in **Jerusalem** restored the ark to its role as a national religious symbol.
8:2 The phrase **the men** here refers to people of both genders. This assembly happened in **Ethanim** (aka Tishri, the seventh month, September–October), the month of the great Day of Atonement. The regular **festival** of this month was the Festival of Harvest (Ex 23:16)—Shelters or Tabernacles—that was celebrated about a week after the Day of Atonement.
8:3–4 After the difficult lesson David learned concerning the movement of the ark (2Sm 6:7–8), all the transporting was implemented in the proper manner.
8:8–9 The **poles** had to remain since they could not be removed from the gold rings (Ex 25:15). The note that **they are still there today** means that the author of Kings used sources that were written before the destruction of the Lord's house in 586 BC (see 9:13,21; 10:12; 12:19; 2Kg 2:22; 8:22; 10:27; 14:7; 16:6; 17:23,34,41). Of the three original contents of the **ark**, the sample of manna and Aaron's rod had been lost or decayed so that only the **stone tablets** of the law remained (Ex 16:32–34; Nm 17:10–11). These highlighted the covenant relationship between the Israelites and God.
8:14 Solomon first stood before God speaking for the people. Then he turned from facing God to bless the **entire congregation**.

Blessed be the LORD God of Israel!
He spoke directly to my father David,
and he has fulfilled the promise
   by his power.
He said,
¹⁶ "Since the day I brought
   my people Israel out of Egypt,
I have not chosen a city to build
   a temple in
among any of the tribes of Israel,
so that my name would be there.
But I have chosen David to rule
   my people Israel."
¹⁷ My father David had his heart set
on building a temple for the name
   of the LORD, the God of Israel.
¹⁸ But the LORD said to my father David,
"Since your heart was set on building
   a temple for my name,
you have done well to have this desire.ᴬ
¹⁹ Yet you are not the one to build it;
instead, your son, your own offspring,
will build it for my name."
²⁰ The LORD has fulfilled
   what he promised.
I have taken the place
   of my father David,
and I sit on the throne of Israel,
   as the LORD promised.
I have built the temple for the name
   of the LORD, the God of Israel.
²¹ I have provided a place there for the ark,
where the LORD's covenant is
that he made with our ancestors
when he brought them out of the land
   of Egypt.

Solomon's Prayer

²² Then Solomon stood before the altar of the LORD in front of the entire congregation of Israel and spread out his hands toward heaven. ²³ He said:

LORD God of Israel,
   there is no God like you
in heaven above or on earth below,
who keeps the gracious covenant
with your servants who walk before you
with all their heart.
²⁴ You have kept what you promised
to your servant, my father David.
You spoke directly to him
and you fulfilled your promise
   by your power
as it is today.

²⁵ Therefore, LORD God of Israel,
keep what you promised
to your servant, my father David:
You will never fail to have a man
to sit before me on the throne of Israel,
if only your sons take care to walk
   before me
as you have walked before me.
²⁶ Now LORDᴮ God of Israel,
please confirm what you promised
to your servant, my father David.

²⁷ But will God indeed live on earth?
Even heaven, the highest heaven,
   cannot contain you,
much less this temple I have built.
²⁸ Listenᶜ to your servant's prayer
   and his petition,
LORD my God,
so that you may hear the cry
   and the prayer
that your servant prays
   before you today,
²⁹ so that your eyes may watch over
   this temple night and day,
toward the place where you said,
"My name will be there,"
and so that you may hear the prayer
that your servant prays
   toward this place.
³⁰ Hear the petition of your servant
and your people Israel,
which they pray toward this place.
May you hear in your dwelling place
   in heaven.
May you hear and forgive.

³¹ When a man sins
   against his neighbor
and is forced to take an oath,ᴰ
and he comes to take an oath
before your altar in this temple,
³² may you hear in heaven and act.
May you judge your servants,
condemning the wicked man
   by bringing
what he has done on his own head
and providing justice for the righteous
by rewarding him according to
   his righteousness.

³³ When your people Israel are defeated
   before an enemy,
because they have sinned against you,

ᴬ8:18 Lit well because it was with your heart ᴮ8:26 Some Hb mss, LXX, Syr, Tg, Vg, 2Ch 6:16; other Hb mss omit LORD
ᶜ8:28 Lit Turn ᴰ8:31 Lit and he lifts a curse against him to curse him

8:22 Solomon then turned around again, this time to face God as the representative of the people. At some point (see v. 54), Solomon kneeled with his **hands** held upwards for this prayer.

8:31–32 Here begins a series of seven situations, all but one beginning with **when**, marked by the phrase **may you hear in heaven** (vv. 31–32,33–34,35–36,37–40,41–43,44–45,46–53). **When** uncorroborated testimony must be supported by a solemn

oath, the oath should be taken at this **temple**. In broad terms, God would hear prayer to validate an honest oath and to maintain **justice** and integrity.
8:33–34 God would hear when the Israelites were **defeated** in war. In Solomon's hour of

and they return to you and praise
   your name,
and they pray and plead with you
   for mercy in this temple,
³⁴ may you hear in heaven
and forgive the sin
   of your people Israel.
May you restore them to the land
you gave their ancestors.

³⁵ When the skies are shut and there is
   no rain,
because they have sinned against you,
and they pray toward this place
and praise your name,
and they turn from their sins
because you are afflicting them,
³⁶ may you hear in heaven
and forgive the sin of your servants
and your people Israel,
so that you may teach them to walk on
   the good way.
May you send rain on your land
that you gave your people
   for an inheritance.

³⁷ When there is famine in the land,
when there is pestilence,
when there is blight or mildew, locust
   or grasshopper,
when their enemy besieges them
   in the land and its cities,^A
when there is any plague or illness,
³⁸ every prayer or petition
that any person or that all
   your people Israel may have —
they each know their own affliction^B —
as they spread out their hands
   toward this temple,
³⁹ may you hear in heaven,
   your dwelling place,
and may you forgive, act, and give to
   everyone
according to all their ways,
   since you know each heart,
for you alone know
   every human heart,
⁴⁰ so that they may fear you
all the days they live on the land
you gave our ancestors.

⁴¹ Even for the foreigner who is not
   of your people Israel
but has come from a distant land
because of your name —
⁴² for they will hear of your great name,
strong hand, and outstretched arm,
and will come and pray
   toward this temple —
⁴³ may you hear in heaven,
   your dwelling place,
and do according to all
   the foreigner asks.
Then all peoples of earth will know
   your name,
to fear you as your people Israel do
and to know that this temple I have built
bears your name.

⁴⁴ When your people go out to fight
   against their enemies,^C
wherever you send them,
and they pray to the LORD
in the direction of the city
   you have chosen
and the temple I have built
   for your name,
⁴⁵ may you hear their prayer and petition
   in heaven
and uphold their cause.

⁴⁶ When they sin against you —
for there is no one who does not sin —
and you are angry with them
and hand them over to the enemy,
and their captors deport them
   to the enemy's country —
whether distant or nearby —
⁴⁷ and when they come to their senses^D
in the land where they were deported
and repent and petition you
   in their captors' land:
"We have sinned and done wrong;
we have been wicked,"
⁴⁸ and when they return to you
with all their heart and all their soul
in the land of their enemies
   who took them captive,
and when they pray to you
   in the direction of their land
that you gave their ancestors,

---

^A8:37 Lit *land of its gates*   ^B8:38 Lit *know in his heart of a plague*   ^C8:44 Some Hb mss, some ancient versions, 2Ch 6:34; other Hb mss read *enemy*   ^D8:47 Lit *they return to their heart*

---

greatness, this prayer acknowledged that **sin** could produce defeat.

8:35–50 The following statements about sin, disaster, and restoration are not repetitious, stereotypical formulae. There is much freedom and creativity in composing the statements. Yet certain elements seem to recur. The whole process can involve: (1) sinning; (2) repentance; (3) acknowledgement of truth (either as "confessing" truth, as stating the truth in praise, or as stating the

truth in thanks); (4) prayer; (5) seeking favor; (6) God's hearing; (7) forgiveness; and (8) restoration.

8:37–40 Other natural disasters also were occasions for praying to God. The Lord would hear, forgive, and reward in accordance with **their** (the worshiper's) **ways**. This would result in the **fear** of God among his people. "Fear" is a rich word that includes a multitude of concepts, including formal worship of God, actual fear of God, and reverence for God.

8:41–43 Solomon states the theology of missions that is implicit in God's great works of witness. The **foreigner** should **hear** of God's works and then **pray toward** the **temple** to God. And God would hear that foreigner's prayer. The intended result of OT revelation was the spread of the knowledge of God to **all peoples of earth**.

8:46 Here begins the climactic situation of the seven (vv. 46–53). Solomon here is

the city you have chosen,
and the temple I have built
for your name,
⁴⁹ may you hear in heaven,
your dwelling place,
their prayer and petition and uphold
their cause.
⁵⁰ May you forgive your people
who sinned against you
and all their rebellions^ against you,
and may you grant them compassion
before their captors,
so that they may treat them
compassionately.
⁵¹ For they are your people
and your inheritance;
you brought them out of Egypt,
out of the middle of an iron furnace.
⁵² May your eyes be open
to your servant's petition
and to the petition of your people Israel,
listening to them whenever they call
to you.
⁵³ For you, Lord God, have set them apart
as your inheritance
from all peoples of the earth,
as you spoke
through your servant Moses
when you brought our ancestors
out of Egypt.

Solomon's Blessing

⁵⁴ When Solomon finished praying this entire prayer and petition to the Lord, he got up from kneeling before the altar of the Lord, with his hands spread out toward heaven, ⁵⁵ and he stood and blessed the whole congregation of Israel with a loud voice: ⁵⁶ "Blessed be the Lord! He has given rest to his people Israel according to all he has said. Not one of all the good promises he made through his servant Moses has failed. ⁵⁷ May the Lord our God be with us as he was with our ancestors. May he not abandon us or leave us ⁵⁸ so that he causes us to be devoted⁸ to him, to walk in all his ways, and to keep his commands, statutes, and ordinances, which he commanded our ancestors. ⁵⁹ May my words with which I have made my petition before the Lord be near the Lord our God day and night. May he uphold his servant's cause and the cause of his people Israel, as each

day requires. ⁶⁰ May all the peoples of the earth know that the Lord is God. There is no other! ⁶¹ Be wholeheartedly devoted to the Lord our God to walk in his statutes and to keep his commands, as it is today."

⁶² The king and all Israel with him were offering sacrifices in the Lord's presence. ⁶³ Solomon offered a sacrifice of fellowship offerings to the Lord: twenty-two thousand cattle and one hundred twenty thousand sheep and goats. In this manner the king and all the Israelites dedicated the Lord's temple.

⁶⁴ On the same day, the king consecrated the middle of the courtyard that was in front of the Lord's temple because that was where he offered the burnt offering, the grain offering, and the fat of the fellowship offerings, since the bronze altar before the Lord was too small to accommodate the burnt offerings, the grain offerings, and the fat of the fellowship offerings.

⁶⁵ Solomon and all Israel with him — a great assembly, from the entrance of Hamath^c to the Brook of Egypt — observed the festival at that time in the presence of the Lord our God, seven days, and seven more days — fourteen days.^D ⁶⁶ On the fifteenth day^E he sent the people away. So they blessed the king and went to their homes^f rejoicing and with happy hearts for all the goodness that the Lord had done for his servant David and for his people Israel.

The Lord's Response

9 When Solomon finished building the temple of the Lord, the royal palace, and all that Solomon desired to do, ² the Lord appeared to Solomon a second time just as he had appeared to him at Gibeon. ³ The Lord said to him:

I have heard your prayer and petition you have made before me. I have consecrated this temple you have built, to put⁶ my name there forever; my eyes and my heart will be there at all times.

⁴ As for you, if you walk before me as your father David walked, with a heart of integrity and in what is right, doing everything I have commanded you, and if you keep my statutes and ordinances, ⁵ I will establish your royal throne over Israel forever, as I promised your father David: You will

---

^8:50 Lit *rebellions that they had rebelled*   ⁸8:58 Lit *causes our hearts to be inclined*   ^c8:65 Or *from Lebo-hamath*
^D8:65 Temple dedication lasted seven days, and the Festival of Shelters lasted seven days.   ^e8:66 Lit *the eighth day*
^f8:66 Lit *tents*   ^c9:3 Or *by putting*

---

praying out of Lv 26:40–45 and Dt 30:1–10. **Sin** produces defeat in war and captivity. **8:54–56** Solomon's role as the spiritual intermediary between the people and God continued when Solomon stood, turned to the people, and **blessed** them by announcing, **Blessed be the Lord! 8:62–63** The large number of offerings, especially the **fellowship offerings** eaten

by the worshipers, turned this into a huge, state-funded, national festival. **8:65–66** Extrabiblical documents confirm that the Brook of Egypt was the Wadi Arish or was near this wadi. **9:1–3** At this point, about 946 BC in Solomon's twenty-fifth year, God again **appeared to Solomon** and reaffirmed his holy status of the Lord's **temple**. Though

the human consecrations had occurred, the most important consecration was when God declared the house fit for his residence. Three points were made. God's **name** would dwell there. God's **eyes** would be there, giving attention to the house and in seeing out from it as well. And it would be the center of God's affections, or God's **heart**.

never fail to have a man on the throne of Israel.

⁶ If you or your sons turn away from following me and do not keep my commands — my statutes that I have set before you — and if you go and serve other gods and bow in worship to them, ⁷ I will cut off Israel from the land I gave them, and I will reject^A the temple I have sanctified for my name. Israel will become an object of scorn and ridicule among all the peoples. ⁸ Though this temple is now exalted,^B everyone who passes by will be appalled and will scoff.^C They will say, "Why did the LORD do this to this land and this temple?" ⁹ Then they will say, "Because they abandoned the LORD their God who brought their ancestors out of the land of Egypt. They held on to other gods and bowed in worship to them and served them. Because of this, the LORD brought all this ruin on them."

King Hiram's Twenty Towns

¹⁰ At the end of twenty years, during which Solomon had built the two houses, the LORD's temple and the royal palace — ¹¹ King Hiram of Tyre having supplied him with cedar and cypress logs and gold for his every wish — King Solomon gave Hiram twenty towns in the land of Galilee. ¹² So Hiram went out from Tyre to look over the towns that Solomon had given him, but he was not pleased with them. ¹³ So he said, "What are these towns you've given me, my brother?" So he called them the Land of Cabul,^D as they are still called today. ¹⁴ Now Hiram had sent the king nine thousand pounds^E of gold.

Solomon's Forced Labor

¹⁵ This is the account of the forced labor that King Solomon had imposed to build the LORD's

temple, his own palace, the supporting terraces, the wall of Jerusalem, and Hazor, Megiddo, and Gezer. ¹⁶ Pharaoh king of Egypt had attacked and captured Gezer. He then burned it, killed the Canaanites who lived in the city, and gave it as a dowry to his daughter, Solomon's wife. ¹⁷ Then Solomon rebuilt Gezer, Lower Beth-horon, ¹⁸ Baalath, Tamar^F,G in the Wilderness of Judah, ¹⁹ all the storage cities that belonged to Solomon, the chariot cities, the cavalry cities, and whatever Solomon desired to build in Jerusalem, Lebanon, or anywhere else in the land of his dominion.

²⁰ As for all the peoples who remained of the Amorites, Hethites, Perizzites, Hivites, and Jebusites, who were not Israelites — ²¹ their descendants who remained in the land after them, those whom the Israelites were unable to destroy completely — Solomon imposed forced labor on them; it is still this way today. ²² But Solomon did not consign the Israelites to slavery; they were soldiers, his servants, his commanders, his captains, and commanders of his chariots and his cavalry. ²³ These were the deputies who were over Solomon's work: 550 who supervised the people doing the work.

Solomon's Other Activities

²⁴ Pharaoh's daughter moved from the city of David to the house that Solomon had built for her; he then built the terraces.

²⁵ Three times a year Solomon offered burnt offerings and fellowship offerings on the altar he had built for the LORD, and he burned incense with them in the LORD's presence. So he completed the temple.

²⁶ King Solomon put together a fleet of ships at Ezion-geber, which is near Eloth on the shore of the Red Sea in the land of Edom. ²⁷ With the fleet, Hiram sent his servants, experienced seamen, along with Solomon's servants. ²⁸ They

---

^A 9:7 Lit *send from my presence*   ^B 9:8 Some ancient versions read *temple will become a ruin*   ^C 9:8 Lit *hiss*   ^D 9:13 = Like Nothing   ^E 9:14 Lit *120 talents*   ^F 9:18 Alt Hb traditions, LXX, Syr, Tg, Vg read *Tadmor*; 2Ch 8:4   ^G 9:18 Tamar was a city in southern Judah; Ezk 47:19; 48:28.

9:10–25 The biblical writer then recorded, not in chronological order, several general social and economic policies loosely related to Solomon's building operations.

9:10–14 The scenario here is of two equal rulers haggling over an international business deal. Solomon may have driven a hard bargain with **Hiram**—large amounts of building materials plus **gold**—for some unproductive border villages. Hiram's words **my brother** probably indicated the treaty relationship between the two rulers.

9:15 Solomon's building operations were widespread and significant for politics, for forced labor economics, and for displaying glory and magnificence. First there were the building operations in Jerusalem: the **LORD's temple**, the royal **palace, the supporting terraces**, and **the wall of Jerusalem**. One theory about the supporting terraces, also called the *Millo*, is that they were needed to keep the walls from collapsing into the

unsettled "fill" (Hb *millo*) of an earlier valley that had been filled or partially filled. The next three names—**Hazor, Megiddo, and Gezer**—referred to cities that guarded vulnerable routes of attack in the highland heart of Judah and that were fortified by Solomon, using **forced labor**.

9:16 This verse explains Solomon's control over **Gezer**. Gezer was strategic for Israel, permitting them to control the coastal north-south trade route and one of the approaches from the coast to Jerusalem.

9:17–19 These verses describe more of Solomon's military building operations together with some of the more important names involved. These operations were more extensive and expensive than this brief description indicates. They involved garrison and provision cities for a world-class chariot army. This demanded huge initial expenses, road maintenance, and facilities for feeding and caring for the chariot horses as well as

living quarters for the charioteers and support personnel. Since this text is ambiguous concerning Tamar (in southern Judah) and Tadmor (ancient Palmyra in Aramean territories), we are not positive which location is referred to here.

9:24 Moving **Pharaoh's daughter** out of Jerusalem and so away from the Lord's house can be interpreted in two ways: as an act of piety that removed pagan pollution from the vicinity of the house of the Lord or as an act of respect for the most prestigious of Solomon's political marriages by giving her quarters worthy of her stature.

9:26–10:29 We must recognize Solomon's historical role in world trade as presented in these documents. North-south trade in luxury items was already producing wealth. Southern Arabia, Africa, and points further east were sources of expensive commodities such as gold, ivory, and jewels; esoteric luxury items such as apes and baboons; and spices.

went to Ophir and acquired gold there — sixteen tons[A] — and delivered it to Solomon.

The Queen of Sheba

10 The queen of Sheba heard about Solomon's fame connected with the name of the LORD and came to test him with difficult questions. [2] She came to Jerusalem with a very large entourage, with camels bearing spices, gold in great abundance, and precious stones. She came to Solomon and spoke to him about everything that was on her mind. [3] So Solomon answered all her questions; nothing was too difficult for the king to explain to her. [4] When the queen of Sheba observed all of Solomon's wisdom, the palace he had built, [5] the food at his table, his servants' residence, his attendants' service and their attire, his cupbearers, and the burnt offerings he offered at the LORD's temple, it took her breath away.

[6] She said to the king, "The report I heard in my own country about your words and about your wisdom is true. [7] But I didn't believe the reports until I came and saw with my own eyes. Indeed, I was not even told half. Your wisdom and prosperity far exceed the report I heard. [8] How happy are your men.[B] How happy are these servants of yours, who always stand in your presence hearing your wisdom. [9] Blessed be the LORD your God! He delighted in you and put you on the throne of Israel, because of the LORD's eternal love for Israel. He has made you king to carry out justice and righteousness."

[10] Then she gave the king four and a half tons[C] of gold, a great quantity of spices, and precious stones. Never again did such a quantity of spices arrive as those the queen of Sheba gave to King Solomon.

[11] In addition, Hiram's fleet that carried gold from Ophir brought from Ophir a large quantity of almug[D] wood and precious stones. [12] The king made the almug wood into steps for the LORD's temple and the king's palace and into lyres and harps for the singers. Never before did such almug wood arrive, and the like has not been seen again.

[13] King Solomon gave the queen of Sheba her every desire — whatever she asked — besides what he had given her out of his royal bounty. Then she, along with her servants, returned to her own country.

Solomon's Wealth

[14] The weight of gold that came to Solomon annually was twenty-five tons,[E] [15] besides what came from merchants, traders' merchandise, and all the Arabian kings and governors of the land.

[16] King Solomon made two hundred large shields of hammered gold; fifteen pounds[F] of gold went into each shield. [17] He made three hundred small shields of hammered gold; nearly four pounds[G] of gold went into each shield. The king put them in the House of the Forest of Lebanon.

[18] The king also made a large ivory throne and overlaid it with fine gold. [19] The throne had six steps; there was a rounded top at the back of the throne, armrests on either side of the seat, and two lions standing beside the armrests. [20] Twelve lions were standing there on the six steps, one at each end. Nothing like it had ever been made in any other kingdom.

[21] All of King Solomon's drinking cups were gold, and all the utensils of the House of the Forest of Lebanon were pure gold. There was no silver, since it was considered as nothing in Solomon's time, [22] for the king had ships of Tarshish at sea with Hiram's fleet, and once every three years the ships of Tarshish would arrive bearing gold, silver, ivory, apes, and peacocks.[H]

[A]9:28 Lit *420 talents* [B]10:8 LXX, Syr read *your wives* [C]10:10 Lit *120 talents* [D]10:11 = algum in 2Ch 2:8; 9:10–11 [E]10:14 Lit *666 talents* [F]10:16 Lit *600* (shekels) [G]10:17 Lit *three minas* [H]10:22 Or *baboons*

These goods could move from the region of southern Arabia north. Depending on the security of sea travel, they could come north by ships on the Red Sea, or they could come north by camel caravan on the Red Sea coast of the Arabian Peninsula. If they came by sea, they could move to the Mediterranean Sea either through Egypt, via the famed Wadi Hammamat, or they could move through the region of Palestine. In either case, once the goods reached the Mediterranean Sea, they went to points further west in Phoenicia via ships. At this time violent repercussions of Greek-speaking invaders still hampered sea trade to the north toward the Black Sea.

Solomon's joint sea ventures with Hiram were a way of controlling this trade and channeling it through Hebrew territory so that Solomon, instead of Pharaoh, shared in the wealth of such trade.

9:26–28 These verses indicate that Solomon implemented regular mercantile, seafaring expeditions from **Ezion-geber**. Some believe it is more accurate to speak in terms

of caravan trade from the south rather than seafaring commerce.

10:1–29 This chapter deals with Solomon's wealth, his international reputation, and his trade practices.

10:1 The author begins with **the queen of Sheba** (Sabea in the southwestern corner of Arabia) investigating Solomon's rumored wisdom. Perhaps other political and economic interests motivated her visit as well.

10:2 Since the land routes were more convenient for traveling from southern Arabia, and perhaps because Solomon's fleets had cut her off from sea travel, the queen came with a camel caravan loaded with the luxury goods that made her land wealthy and famous.

10:10 Sheba was famous for spice production and probably also had its own maritime trade with points further east. The **gold** that the queen brought was probably in payment for goods that Solomon was shipping south.

10:11–12 The location of **Ophir** is unknown. **Almug wood** is probably a variety of

aromatic sandalwood or red sandalwood from India.

10:16–17 This **hammered gold** probably utilized a technology in which soft, nearly pure gold was hammered into thin sheets. Then this foil, because of its malleability, could be applied to almost any surface. This kind of fragile decoration was intended for purely ceremonial use. The **large shields** were modeled after the large rectangular shields more useful for heavy infantry lined up in formation in battle. The circular prototypes of the **small shields** were better suited for more mobile, light-armed infantry.

10:19 Lions were a common motif associated with royalty in ancient times. They may here symbolize the king's glory, which ultimately derived from God's glory.

10:21–22 That the mercantile expeditions were undertaken **every three years** indicates that they were far-reaching, perhaps even bypassing the seafaring interests of possible allies such as Sheba. The expeditions also imply the existence of firm alliances with

[23] King Solomon surpassed all the kings of the world in riches and in wisdom. [24] The whole world wanted an audience with Solomon to hear the wisdom that God had put in his heart. [25] Every man would bring his annual tribute: items^A of silver and gold, clothing, weapons,^B spices, and horses and mules.

[26] Solomon accumulated 1,400 chariots and 12,000 horsemen and stationed them in the chariot cities and with the king in Jerusalem. [27] The king made silver as common in Jerusalem as stones, and he made cedar as abundant as sycamore in the Judean foothills. [28] Solomon's horses were imported from Egypt and Kue.^C The king's traders bought them from Kue at the going price. [29] A chariot was imported from Egypt for fifteen pounds^D of silver, and a horse for four pounds.^E In the same way, they exported them to all the kings of the Hittites and to the kings of Aram through their agents.

Solomon's Unfaithfulness to God

11 King Solomon loved many foreign women in addition to Pharaoh's daughter: Moabite, Ammonite, Edomite, Sidonian, and Hittite women [2] from the nations about which the LORD had told the Israelites, "You must not intermarry with them, and they must not intermarry with you, because they will turn your heart away to follow their gods." To these women Solomon was deeply attached^F in love. [3] He had seven hundred wives who were princesses and three hundred who were concubines, and they turned his heart away.

[4] When Solomon was old, his wives turned his heart away to follow other gods. He was not wholeheartedly devoted to the LORD his God, as his father David had been. [5] Solomon followed Ashtoreth, the goddess of the Sidonians, and Milcom, the abhorrent idol of the Ammonites. [6] Solomon did what was evil in

the LORD's sight, and unlike his father David, he did not remain loyal to the LORD.

[7] At that time, Solomon built a high place for Chemosh, the abhorrent idol of Moab, and for Milcom,^G the abhorrent idol of the Ammonites, on the hill across from Jerusalem. [8] He did the same for all his foreign wives, who were burning incense and offering sacrifices to their gods.

[9] The LORD was angry with Solomon, because his heart had turned away from the LORD, the God of Israel, who had appeared to him twice. [10] He had commanded him about this, so that he would not follow other gods, but Solomon did not do what the LORD had commanded.

[11] Then the LORD said to Solomon, "Since you have done this^H and did not keep my covenant and my statutes, which I commanded you, I will tear the kingdom away from you and give it to your servant. [12] However, I will not do it during your lifetime for the sake of your father David; I will tear it out of your son's hand. [13] Yet I will not tear the entire kingdom away from him. I will give one tribe to your son for the sake of my servant David and for the sake of Jerusalem that I chose."

Solomon's Enemies

[14] So the LORD raised up Hadad the Edomite as an enemy against Solomon. He was of the royal family in Edom. [15] Earlier, when David was in Edom, Joab, the commander of the army, had gone to bury the dead and had struck down every male in Edom. [16] For Joab and all Israel had remained there six months, until he had killed every male in Edom. [17] Hadad fled to Egypt, along with some Edomites from his father's servants. At the time Hadad was a small boy. [18] Hadad and his men set out from Midian and went to Paran. They took men with them from Paran and went

---

^A 10:25 Or vessels, or weapons   ^B 10:25 Or fragrant balsam   ^C 10:28 = Cilicia   ^D 10:29 Lit 600 shekels   ^E 10:29 Lit 150 shekels
^F 11:2 Lit Solomon clung   ^G 11:7 Lit Molech   ^H 11:11 Lit "Since this was with you

---

#17 99 Essential Christian Truths

SIN AS IDOLATRY

Sin is not only a physical act of rebellion against God, such as lying or stealing, but it is also a matter of the heart. The physical displays of sin are the fruit of what has been birthed in the heart of a person (Mt 15:10–20). In Scripture, idolatry usually refers to bowing down to a statue made of wood or gold, worshiping created things instead of the Creator. But idolatry can take on more subtle forms: seeking approval, security, power, pleasure, etc. We can diagnose the idolatry of our heart by examining the areas where the desires of our heart have turned into idolatrous demands (Jms 4:1–2).

distant trading partners since the fleets had to have access to friendly harbors during the annual monsoon winds. **Tarshish** was likely in Spain. The Hebrew word translated **peacocks** is difficult to interpret. In light of the close diplomatic and cultural connections between Solomon and Egypt, the word may actually refer to a type of baboon native to Egypt.

10:26 The **12,000 horsemen** probably included the human handlers, trainers, other support personnel for the chariot horses, and the chariot warriors themselves.

10:28–29 An important part of Solomon's trade and commerce was his trade in chariots and chariot **horses**. The best chariots were made in Egypt. One of the major suppliers of horses was a place in northern Egypt known as Mitsri. This indicates that Solomon had established himself as the middleman for much of the north-south arms trade of his day.

11:1–2 David had also married **foreign** wives, but they did not change either his religious

life or that of the nation. Solomon's wives, on the other hand, were known devotees of their national deities. Solomon's Hethite wives had historical ties with the old Hethite aristocracies of the preceding millennium.

11:3 Princesses probably designated his political wives in contrast to his three hundred ordinary harem women, or **concubines**.

11:4–8 Both **Ashtoreth** (Astarte, Ishtar) and **Milcom** (Molech) were international deities worshiped under numerous names in different countries. Milcom/Molech was associated with child sacrifice (2Kg 23:10). **Chemosh**, by contrast, was a god of **Moab**, probably a god of war.

11:14–17 The resentment in **Edom** against **Joab** and **David** for their brutality (2Sm 8:13–14) helped to weaken Solomon years later. **All Israel** refers only to the group under discussion—the soldiers involved in the campaign against Edom.

11:18–22 God used Pharaoh's opportunism to weaken Solomon. **Pharaoh** exploited both

to Egypt, to Pharaoh king of Egypt, who gave Hadad a house, ordered that he be given food, and gave him land. ¹⁹ Pharaoh liked Hadad so much^A that he gave him a wife, the sister of his own wife, Queen Tahpenes. ²⁰ Tahpenes's sister gave birth to Hadad's son Genubath. Tahpenes herself weaned him in Pharaoh's palace, and Genubath lived there along with Pharaoh's sons.

²¹ When Hadad heard in Egypt that David rested with his ancestors and that Joab, the commander of the army, was dead, Hadad said to Pharaoh, "Let me leave, so I may go to my own country."

²² But Pharaoh asked him, "What do you lack here with me for you to want to go back to your own country?"

"Nothing," he replied, "but please let me leave."

²³ God raised up Rezon son of Eliada as an enemy against Solomon. Rezon had fled from his master King Hadadezer of Zobah ²⁴ and gathered men to himself. He became leader of a raiding party when David killed the Zobaites. He^B went to Damascus, lived there, and became king in Damascus. ²⁵ Rezon was Israel's enemy throughout Solomon's reign, adding to the trouble Hadad had caused. He reigned over Aram^C and loathed Israel.

²⁶ Now Solomon's servant, Jeroboam son of Nebat, was an Ephraimite from Zeredah. His widowed mother's name was Zeruah. Jeroboam rebelled against Solomon, ²⁷ and this is the reason he rebelled against the king: Solomon had built the supporting terraces and repaired the opening in the wall of the city of his father David. ²⁸ Now the man Jeroboam was capable, and Solomon noticed the young man because he was getting things done. So he appointed him over the entire labor force of the house of Joseph.

²⁹ During that time, the prophet Ahijah the Shilonite met Jeroboam on the road as Jeroboam came out of Jerusalem. Now Ahijah had wrapped himself with a new cloak, and the two of them were alone in the open field. ³⁰ Then Ahijah took hold of the new cloak he had on, tore it into twelve pieces, ³¹ and said to Jeroboam, "Take ten pieces for yourself, for this is what the LORD God of Israel says: 'I am about to tear the kingdom out of Solomon's hand. I

will give you ten tribes, ³² but one tribe will remain his for the sake of my servant David and for the sake of Jerusalem, the city I chose out of all the tribes of Israel. ³³ For they have abandoned me; they have bowed down to Ashtoreth, the goddess of the Sidonians, to Chemosh, the god of Moab, and to Milcom, the god of the Ammonites. They have not walked in my ways to do what is right in my sight and to carry out my statutes and my judgments as his father David did.

³⁴ "'However, I will not take the whole kingdom from him but will let him be ruler all the days of his life for the sake of my servant David, whom I chose and who kept my commands and my statutes. ³⁵ I will take ten tribes of the kingdom from his son and give them to you. ³⁶ I will give one tribe to his son, so that my servant David will always have a lamp^D before me in Jerusalem, the city I chose for myself to put my name there. ³⁷ I will appoint you, and you will reign as king over all you want, and you will be king over Israel.

³⁸ "'After that, if you obey all I command you, walk in my ways, and do what is right in my sight in order to keep my statutes and my commands as my servant David did, I will be with you. I will build you a lasting dynasty just as I built for David, and I will give you Israel. ³⁹ I will humble David's descendants, because of their unfaithfulness, but not forever.'"^E

⁴⁰ Therefore, Solomon tried to kill Jeroboam, but he fled to Egypt, to King Shishak of Egypt, where he remained until Solomon's death.

Solomon's Death

⁴¹ The rest of the events of Solomon's reign, along with all his accomplishments and his wisdom, are written in the Book of Solomon's Events. ⁴² The length of Solomon's reign in Jerusalem over all Israel totaled forty years. ⁴³ Solomon rested with his ancestors and was buried in the city of his father David. His son Rehoboam became king in his place.

The Kingdom Divided

12 Then Rehoboam went to Shechem, for all Israel had gone to Shechem to make him king. ² When Jeroboam son of Nebat

---

^A 11:19 Lit *Hadad found much favor in Pharaoh's eyes*   ^B 11:24 LXX; Hb reads *They*   ^C 11:25 Some Hb mss, LXX, Syr read *Edom*   ^D 11:36 Or *dominion*   ^E 11:38-39 LXX omits *and I will give . . . but not forever*

Hadad and Jeroboam to undermine Solomon. The presence of foreign threats such as these could explain why Solomon willingly compromised his faith in order to appease his wives. He hoped better relations with his Egyptian wife might prompt Egypt to enact a more favorable foreign policy toward Israel. Even while Solomon lived, control over Edom was weak enough to permit Hadad to return home. An insecure Edom threatened the caravan routes from Eloth (9:26) northward. **11:23-25** With Rezon's rule, **Damascus** became Israel's main enemy in **Aram**.

11:26-28 Jeroboam is introduced as a rebel in an introductory summary of his career under Solomon. **11:29-32** God intervened in governmental affairs through the prophecy of **Ahijah**. The fact that **ten tribes** and **one tribe** does not account for all twelve tribes of Israel should not be taken as problematic. Levi may or may not be counted in such groupings, or Ahijah may have meant that one tribe would remain in addition to Judah. **11:40** Solomon's attempt to **kill Jeroboam** reduced him to the same tyranny as Saul

when Saul tried to kill David. By sheltering Jeroboam, **King Shishak of Egypt** again meddled in Solomon's affairs. **11:41-43 The Book of . . . Events** was probably the official, factual record of the king. This formal close to Solomon's rule was the writer's signal that he was finished with Solomon's era. Now the story moves to Solomon's successor. **12:1-33** There are two reasons for the great attention given here to the northern kings. First, because of the covenant offered to Jeroboam I (11:31,38), it was proper to record

heard about it, he stayed in Egypt, where he had fled from King Solomon's presence. Jeroboam stayed in Egypt.[A] [3] But they summoned him, and Jeroboam and the whole assembly of Israel came and spoke to Rehoboam: [4] "Your father made our yoke harsh. You, therefore, lighten your father's harsh service and the heavy yoke he put on us, and we will serve you."

[5] Rehoboam replied, "Go away for three days and then return to me." So the people left. [6] Then King Rehoboam consulted with the elders who had served his father Solomon when he was alive, asking, "How do you advise me to respond to this people?"

[7] They replied, "Today if you will be a servant to this people and serve them, and if you respond to them by speaking kind words to them, they will be your servants forever."

[8] But he rejected the advice of the elders who had advised him and consulted with the young men who had grown up with him and attended him. [9] He asked them, "What message do you advise that we send back to this people who said to me, 'Lighten the yoke your father put on us'?"

[10] The young men who had grown up with him told him, "This is what you should say to this people who said to you, 'Your father made our yoke heavy, but you, make it lighter on us!' This is what you should tell them: 'My little finger is thicker than my father's waist! [11] Although my father burdened you with a heavy yoke, I will add to your yoke; my father disciplined you with whips, but I will discipline you with barbed whips.'"[B]

[12] So Jeroboam and all the people came to Rehoboam on the third day, as the king had ordered: "Return to me on the third day." [13] Then the king answered the people harshly. He rejected the advice the elders had given him [14] and spoke to them according to the young men's advice: "My father made your yoke heavy, but I will add to your yoke; my father disciplined you with whips, but I will discipline you with barbed whips."

[15] The king did not listen to the people, because this turn of events came from the LORD to carry out his word, which the LORD had spoken through Ahijah the Shilonite to Jeroboam son of Nebat. [16] When all Israel saw that the king had not listened to them, the people answered him:

What portion do we have in David?
We have no inheritance in the son
　of Jesse.
Israel, return to your tents;
David, now look after your own house!

So Israel went to their tents, [17] but Rehoboam reigned over the Israelites living in the cities of Judah.

[18] Then King Rehoboam sent Adoram,[C] who was in charge of forced labor, but all Israel stoned him to death. King Rehoboam managed to get into the chariot and flee to Jerusalem. [19] Israel is still in rebellion against the house of David today.

Rehoboam in Jerusalem

[20] When all Israel heard that Jeroboam had come back, they summoned him to the assembly and made him king over all Israel. No one followed the house of David except the tribe of Judah alone. [21] When Rehoboam arrived in Jerusalem, he mobilized one hundred eighty thousand fit young soldiers from the entire house of Judah and the tribe of Benjamin to fight against the house of Israel to restore the kingdom to Rehoboam son of Solomon. [22] But the word of God came to Shemaiah, the man of God: [23] "Say to Rehoboam son of Solomon, king of Judah, to the whole house of Judah and Benjamin, and to the rest of the people, [24] 'This is what the LORD says: You are not to march up and fight against your brothers, the Israelites. Each of you return home, for this situation is from me.'"

So they listened to the word of the LORD and went back according to the word of the LORD.

Jeroboam's Idolatry

[25] Jeroboam built Shechem in the hill country of Ephraim and lived there. From there he went

---

[A]12:2 LXX, Vg read *Jeroboam returned from Egypt*; 2Ch 10:2　[B]12:11 Lit *with scorpions*, also in v. 14　[C]12:18 LXX reads *Adoniram*; 1Kg 4:6; 5:14

---

the evidence that the northern kings rejected God's covenant. Second, though God knew what the future would bring, Israel did not immediately disappear from the prophetic and historical picture.
12:1 **Shechem** was strategically located on the main road north of Jerusalem near the border of Ephraim and Manasseh; therefore, it was a good location for shadowing Jerusalem on the north and for gathering the traditional northern tribal leaders. The advantages of this location were confirmed when Jeroboam made Shechem his capital. **12:2–4 Jeroboam** was summoned from **Egypt** to speak for the people. After living under Solomon's oppressive policies, they demanded that the economic burdens be lightened.

12:5–7 Apparently **Rehoboam** was not happy about hearing the words **servant** and **serve** applied to him. **12:8–16** Rehoboam's arrogance can be explained only by his presumption that he could demand and receive Solomon's absolute power. Rehoboam's younger (fortyish) companions, who had grown up in Solomon's absolutism, supported him with two proverbial similes and overrode the better counsel of the elders. **12:18–19** Rehoboam's naivete and foolishness were demonstrated by his sending **Adoram** (the same man as Adoniram, 5:14), director of the **forced labor** battalions, to enforce his rule. Adoram represented one of the heavier and more degrading of the

burdens Solomon had placed on the people. The northerners killed him in a particularly insulting way, and Rehoboam barely escaped with his life.
12:20 The statement that **the tribe of Judah alone** followed **David** is a true but rhetorical statement (cp. 11:35–36). It was true that only the tribe of Judah *completely* followed David, but portions of Benjamin, remnants of Simeon, many Levites, and even other northerners who wished to remain true to the covenant dynasty also followed the house of David (2Ch 11:13–17).
12:25 The selection of **Shechem** as the capital should have pleased the northerners, for it was a natural site for conducting intertribal business. Then Jeroboam built or fortified

out and built Penuel. [26] Jeroboam said to himself, "The kingdom might now return to the house of David. [27] If these people regularly go to offer sacrifices in the LORD's temple in Jerusalem, the heart of these people will return to their lord, King Rehoboam of Judah. They will kill me and go back to the king of Judah." [28] So the king sought advice.

Then he made two golden calves, and he said to the people, "Going to Jerusalem is too difficult for you. Israel, here are your gods[A] who brought you up from the land of Egypt." [29] He set up one in Bethel, and put the other in Dan. [30] This led to sin; the people walked in procession before one of the calves all the way to Dan.[B]

[31] Jeroboam also made shrines[C] on the high places and made priests from the ranks of the people who were not Levites. [32] Jeroboam made a festival in the eighth month on the fifteenth day of the month, like the festival in Judah. He offered sacrifices on the altar; he made this offering in Bethel to sacrifice to the calves he had made. He also stationed the priests in Bethel for the high places he had made. [33] He offered sacrifices on[D] the altar he had set up in Bethel on the fifteenth day of the eighth month. He chose this month on his own. He made a festival for the Israelites, offered sacrifices on the altar, and burned incense.

Judgment on Jeroboam

13 A man of God came, however, from Judah to Bethel by the word of the LORD while Jeroboam was standing beside the altar to burn incense. [2] The man of God cried out against the altar by the word of the LORD: "Altar, altar, this is what the LORD says, 'A son will be born to the house of David, named Josiah, and he will sacrifice on you the priests of the high places who are burning incense on you. Human bones will be burned on you.'" [3] He gave a sign that day. He said, "This is the sign that

the LORD has spoken: 'The altar will now be ripped apart, and the ashes that are on it will be poured out.'"

[4] When the king heard the message that the man of God had cried out against the altar at Bethel, Jeroboam stretched out his hand from the altar and said, "Arrest him!" But the hand he stretched out against him withered, and he could not pull it back to himself. [5] The altar was ripped apart, and the ashes poured from the altar, according to the sign that the man of God had given by the word of the LORD.

[6] Then the king responded to the man of God, "Plead for the favor of the LORD your God and pray for me so that my hand may be restored to me." So the man of God pleaded for the favor of the LORD, and the king's hand was restored to him and became as it had been at first.

[7] Then the king declared to the man of God, "Come home with me, refresh yourself, and I'll give you a reward."

[8] But the man of God replied, "If you were to give me half your house, I still wouldn't go with you, and I wouldn't eat food or drink water in this place, [9] for this is what I was commanded by the word of the LORD: 'You must not eat food or drink water or go back the way you came.'" [10] So he went another way; he did not go back by the way he had come to Bethel.

The Old Prophet and the Man of God

[11] Now a certain old prophet was living in Bethel. His son[E] came and told him all the deeds that the man of God had done that day in Bethel. His sons also told their father the words that he had spoken to the king. [12] Then their father asked them, "Which way did he go?" His sons had seen[F] the way taken by the man of God who had come from Judah. [13] Then he said to his sons, "Saddle the donkey for me." So they saddled the donkey for him, and he got on it. [14] He followed the man of God and found him

---

[A]12:28 Or *here is your God*, or *here is your god* [B]12:30 Some LXX mss read *calves to Bethel and the other to Dan* [C]12:31 Lit *a house* [D]12:33 Or *He went up to* [E]13:11 Some Hb mss, LXX, Syr, Vg read *sons* [F]13:12 LXX, Syr, Tg, Vg read *sons showed him*

Penuel, almost directly east across the Jordan rift from Shechem. This gave Jeroboam a fortified foothold on each side of the Jordan River. **12:28** This act was not simply rebellion against David; it was also the rejection of the proper worship of the Lord by the leaders and counselors of Israel who advised Jeroboam. The king then set up a new system of worship for the people to keep them from going to Jerusalem for worship. Jeroboam's words are identical to those of Aaron four hundred years earlier (Ex 32:4). **12:29 Dan** already had a history of illegal, idolatrous worship of the Lord (Jdg 18). The calf shrine in **Bethel** was on the traditional border between Benjamin and Ephraim, barely ten miles north of the national temple in Jerusalem. **12:30–31** Jeroboam also set up other illegal shrines throughout the country, which

he staffed illegally with non-Levites. This dispossessing of the Levites from their assigned duties encouraged their emigration southward. Ironically, God may have used Jeroboam's idolatry to concentrate the Levites where their influence for good would be most effective. **12:32–33** Again, with political astuteness but religious disobedience, **Jeroboam** changed the calendar. He established a festival **like the festival in Judah**, on the fifteenth day of the **eighth month**. This festival apparently replaced the observances in the seventh month, Tishri, which included both the Day of Atonement and the Festival of Ingathering (Ex 23:16; also known as the Festival of Shelters). **13:1** This chapter could be either a dramatic turn in the preceding story or an entirely different event on a later occasion when King Jeroboam officiated at a sacrifice.

13:2–3 This prophecy that **Josiah**, centuries later, would desecrate this altar with the corpses of its **priests** was a powerful statement of God's rejection of this disobedient worship. **13:4–7** God also miraculously punished Jeroboam. The immediate healing of his **hand** as a result of the prophet's intercession should have been another witness to direct Jeroboam into faith and obedience. Jeroboam offered the prophet a **reward** and thus treated God like a bargaining partner. **13:8–10** To **eat food** with Jeroboam might be perceived as withdrawing judgment and endorsing his kingdom (1Sm 15:24–31). **13:11–19** Jeroboam's shallow perception of God's holiness would be matched by **a certain old prophet** who lived in **Bethel**.

sitting under an oak tree. He asked him, "Are you the man of God who came from Judah?"

"I am," he said.

[15] Then he said to him, "Come home with me and eat some food."

[16] But he answered, "I cannot go back with you or accompany you; I will not eat food or drink water with you in this place. [17] For a message came to me by the word of the LORD: 'You must not eat food or drink water there or go back by the way you came.'"

[18] He said to him, "I am also a prophet like you. An angel spoke to me by the word of the LORD: 'Bring him back with you to your house so that he may eat food and drink water.'" The old prophet deceived him, [19] and the man of God went back with him, ate food in his house, and drank water.

[20] While they were sitting at the table, the word of the LORD came to the prophet who had brought him back, [21] and the prophet cried out to the man of God who had come from Judah, "This is what the LORD says: 'Because you rebelled against the LORD's command and did not keep the command that the LORD your God commanded you — [22] but you went back and ate food and drank water in the place that he said to you, "Do not eat food and do not drink water" — your corpse will never reach the grave of your ancestors.'"

[23] So after he had eaten food and after he had drunk, the old prophet saddled the donkey for the prophet he had brought back. [24] When he left,[A] a lion attacked[B] him along the way and killed him. His corpse was thrown on the road, and the donkey was standing beside it; the lion was standing beside the corpse too.

[25] There were men passing by who saw the corpse thrown on the road and the lion standing beside it, and they went and spoke about it in the city where the old prophet lived. [26] When the prophet who had brought him back from his way heard about it, he said, "He is the man of God who disobeyed the LORD's command. The LORD has given him to the lion, and it has mauled and killed him, according to the word of the LORD that he spoke to him."

[27] Then the old prophet instructed his sons, "Saddle the donkey for me." They saddled it, [28] and he went and found the corpse thrown on the road with the donkey and the lion standing beside the corpse. The lion had not eaten the corpse or mauled the donkey. [29] So the prophet lifted the corpse of the man of God and laid it on the donkey and brought it back. The old prophet came into the city to mourn and to bury him. [30] Then he laid the corpse in his own grave, and they mourned over him, "Oh, my brother!"

[31] After he had buried him, he said to his sons, "When I die, bury me in the grave where the man of God is buried; lay my bones beside his bones, [32] for the message that he cried out by the word of the LORD against the altar in Bethel and against all the shrines of the high places in the cities of Samaria is certain to happen."

[33] Even after this, Jeroboam did not repent of his evil way but again made priests for the high places from the ranks of the people. He ordained whoever so desired it, and they became priests of the high places. [34] This was the sin that caused the house of Jeroboam to be cut off and obliterated from the face of the earth.

Disaster on the House of Jeroboam

14 At that time Abijah son of Jeroboam became sick. [2] Jeroboam said to his wife, "Go disguise yourself, so they won't know that you're Jeroboam's wife, and go to Shiloh. The prophet Ahijah is there; it was he who told about me becoming king over this people. [3] Take with you ten loaves of bread, some cakes, and a jar of honey, and go to him. He will tell you what will happen to the boy."

[4] Jeroboam's wife did that: she went to Shiloh and arrived at Ahijah's house. Ahijah could not see; he was blind[c] due to his age. [5] But the LORD had said to Ahijah, "Jeroboam's wife is coming soon to ask you about her son, for he is sick. You are to say such and such to her. When she arrives, she will be disguised."

[6] When Ahijah heard the sound of her feet entering the door, he said, "Come in, wife of Jeroboam! Why are you disguised? I have bad news for you. [7] Go tell Jeroboam, 'This is what the LORD God of Israel says: I raised you up from among the people, appointed you ruler over my people Israel, [8] tore the kingdom away from the house of David, and gave it to you. But you were not like my servant David, who kept my commands and followed me with all his heart, doing only what is right in my sight. [9] You behaved more wickedly than all who were before you. In order to anger me, you have proceeded to make for yourself other gods and cast images, but you have flung me behind your back. [10] Because of all this, I am about to bring disaster on the house of Jeroboam:

I will wipe out all of Jeroboam's males,[D]
both slave and free,[E] in Israel;

---

^[A]13:23–24 LXX reads *donkey, and he turned* ^[24]*and left, and* ^[B]13:24 Lit *met* ^[C]14:4 Lit *see, for his eyes stood*; 1Sm 4:15
^[D]14:10 Lit *eliminate Jeroboam's one who urinates against the wall* ^[E]14:10 Or *males, even the weak and impaired*; Hb obscure

---

I will sweep away the house
　　of Jeroboam
as one sweeps away dung until it is
　　all gone!
[11] Anyone who belongs to Jeroboam
　　and dies in the city,
the dogs will eat,
and anyone who dies in the field,
the birds^A will eat,
for the LORD has spoken!'

[12] "As for you, get up and go to your house. When your feet enter the city, the boy will die. [13] All Israel will mourn for him and bury him. He alone out of Jeroboam's house will be given a proper burial because out of the house of Jeroboam something favorable to the LORD God of Israel was found in him. [14] The LORD will raise up for himself a king over Israel, who will wipe out the house of Jeroboam. This is the day, yes,^B even today! [15] For the LORD will strike Israel so that they will^C shake as a reed shakes in water. He will uproot Israel from this good soil that he gave to their ancestors. He will scatter them beyond the Euphrates because they made their Asherah poles, angering the LORD. [16] He will give up Israel because of Jeroboam's sins that he committed and caused Israel to commit."

[17] Then Jeroboam's wife got up and left and went to Tirzah. As she was crossing the threshold of the house, the boy died. [18] He was buried, and all Israel mourned for him, according to the word of the LORD he had spoken through his servant the prophet Ahijah.

[19] As for the rest of the events of Jeroboam's reign, how he waged war and how he reigned, note that they are written in the Historical Record of Israel's Kings. [20] The length of Jeroboam's reign was twenty-two years. He rested with his ancestors, and his son Nadab became king in his place.

Judah's King Rehoboam

[21] Now Rehoboam, Solomon's son, reigned in Judah. Rehoboam was forty-one years old when he became king; he reigned seventeen years in Jerusalem, the city where the LORD had chosen from all the tribes of Israel to put his name. Rehoboam's mother's name was Naamah the Ammonite.

[22] Judah did what was evil in the LORD's sight. They provoked him to jealous anger more than all that their ancestors had done with the sins they committed. [23] They also built for themselves high places, sacred pillars, and Asherah poles on every high hill and under every green tree; [24] there were even male cult prostitutes in the land. They imitated all the detestable practices of the nations the LORD had dispossessed before the Israelites.

[25] In the fifth year of King Rehoboam, King Shishak of Egypt went to war against Jerusalem. [26] He seized the treasuries of the LORD's temple and the treasuries of the royal palace. He took everything. He took all the gold shields that Solomon had made. [27] King Rehoboam made bronze shields to replace them and committed them into the care of the captains of the guards^D who protected the entrance to the king's palace. [28] Whenever the king entered the LORD's temple, the guards would carry the shields, then they would take them back to the armory.^E

[29] The rest of the events of Rehoboam's reign, along with all his accomplishments, are written about in the Historical Record of Judah's Kings. [30] There was war between Rehoboam and Jeroboam throughout their reigns. [31] Rehoboam rested with his ancestors and was buried with his ancestors in the city of David. His mother's name was Naamah the Ammonite. His son Abijam^F became king in his place.

---

^A14:11 Lit *birds of the sky*　^B14:14 Hb obscure　^C14:15 *so that they will* supplied for clarity　^D14:27 Lit *the runners*　^E14:28 Lit *the chamber of the runners*　^F14:31 = Abijah in 2Ch 13

14:12–13 God had found **something favorable** in Jeroboam's sick son. The Bible does not reveal what the good thing was.

14:14–16 Jeroboam's sin resulted in God's raising up a new king who would destroy Jeroboam's dynasty. This is one of the earliest statements in 1 Kings that defined the place of exile as **beyond the Euphrates**. While the latter part of this prophesy would be almost 190 years in coming, God was preparing Baasha on that very **day** to wipe out Jeroboam's dynasty (15:29).

14:19–20 The record of Jeroboam ends with a conventional closing. The **Historical Records of Israel's Kings** were a written account of all the important royal events, probably compiled by the court secretary (2Sm 8:17). Judah's kings had their records as well (v. 29). These records did not survive; this is not the same as the books of 1 and 2 Chronicles.

14:21–31 Rehoboam, **Solomon's son**, was the first of many kings for whom the Bible gives complete formal data. The typical pattern included (1) a formal beginning; (2) an evaluation of his reign, perhaps including some relevant historical notes; and (3) a formal ending.

14:22–24 This list of wicked deeds is even more degrading than the typical offenses of some northern kings. **Judah** had sunk into degraded paganism. And the responsibility for this degradation is traceable directly to the throne. Judah's failure was Rehoboam's failure. The text notes that these were the vices of the people whom God had helped the Israelites to drive out of the promised land.

14:25 We can see how weak the two Israelite kingdoms had become as a result of the invasion of **Shishak**. A briefly resurgent **Egypt** had a large army, and Pharaoh used this army for a devastating plundering raid into Palestine. These invaders, which Solomon's chariots at their height might have easily driven back, plundered both Judah and Israel—including the prosperous merchant cities that opened into the Plain of Esdraelon. Rehoboam's army was so helpless against Shishak's Libyan soldiers that they could not even protect **Jerusalem** from a siege.

14:26–28 Rehoboam's replacement of the plundered **gold shields** with less valuable **bronze shields** was a fitting symbol of the decline of the nation's glory and wealth. That they were kept ready in the **armory** when not in use, instead of on ceremonial display, speaks of the insecurity of the period.

14:29–31 On Judah's **Historical Record** see note at vv. 19–20. The mention of Rehoboam's mother's **Ammonite** heritage may hint that her pagan influence (15:13) affected her son's character. For the kings of Judah, it was common to list the **mother's name**.

Judah's King Abijam

15 In the eighteenth year of Israel's King Jeroboam son of Nebat, Abijam became king over Judah, [2] and he reigned three years in Jerusalem. His mother's name was Maacah daughter[A] of Abishalom.

[3] Abijam walked in all the sins his father before him had committed, and he was not wholeheartedly devoted to the LORD his God as his ancestor David had been. [4] But for the sake of David, the LORD his God gave him a lamp[B] in Jerusalem by raising up his son after him and by preserving Jerusalem. [5] For David did what was right in the LORD's sight, and he did not turn aside from anything he had commanded him all the days of his life, except in the matter of Uriah the Hethite.

[6] There had been war between Rehoboam and Jeroboam all the days of Rehoboam's life. [7] The rest of the events of Abijam's reign, along with all his accomplishments, are written in the Historical Record of Judah's Kings. There was also war between Abijam and Jeroboam. [8] Abijam rested with his ancestors and was buried in the city of David. His son Asa became king in his place.

Judah's King Asa

[9] In the twentieth year of Israel's King Jeroboam, Asa became king of Judah, [10] and he reigned forty-one years in Jerusalem. His grandmother's[C] name was Maacah daughter of Abishalom.

[11] Asa did what was right in the LORD's sight, as his ancestor David had done. [12] He banished the male cult prostitutes from the land and removed all of the idols that his ancestors had made. [13] He also removed his grandmother[D] Maacah from being queen mother because she had made an obscene image of Asherah. Asa chopped down her obscene image and burned it in the Kidron Valley. [14] The high places were not taken away, but Asa was wholeheartedly devoted to the LORD his entire life. [15] He brought his father's consecrated gifts and his own consecrated gifts into the LORD's temple: silver, gold, and utensils.

[16] There was war between Asa and King Baasha of Israel throughout their reigns. [17] Israel's King Baasha went to war against Judah. He built Ramah in order to keep anyone from leaving or coming to King Asa of Judah. [18] So Asa withdrew all the silver and gold that remained in the treasuries of the LORD's temple and the treasuries of the royal palace and gave it to his servants. Then King Asa sent them to Ben-hadad son of Tabrimmon son of Hezion king of Aram who lived in Damascus, saying, [19] "There is a treaty between me and you, between my father and your father. Look, I have sent you a gift of silver and gold. Go and break your treaty with King Baasha of Israel so that he will withdraw from me."

[20] Ben-hadad listened to King Asa and sent the commanders of his armies against the cities of Israel. He attacked Ijon, Dan, Abel-beth-maacah, all Chinnereth, and the whole land of Naphtali. [21] When Baasha heard about it, he quit building Ramah and stayed in Tirzah. [22] Then King Asa gave a command to everyone

---

[A]15:2 Possibly granddaughter, also in v. 10; 2Ch 13:2   [B]15:4 Or *dominion*   [C]15:10 Lit *mother's*   [D]15:13 Lit *mother*

15:1–2 The only revealing detail in the formal opening for Abijam's ("Abijah" in Chronicles) record was that his mother **Maacah** was from the line of Absalom, or **Abishalom**. This relationship might indicate that Solomon's family had to make some accommodations with the family of Absalom, Solomon's half brother, to maintain rule over Judah (see 2Sm 15–18).
15:3–5 Abijam was bad, like **his father** (14:22–24), with the typical negative comparison with **David**.
15:6 The reference to war between **Rehoboam and Jeroboam** departs from the normal pattern of dealing only with the current king. Other translations follow variant texts that read "Abijam" instead of "Rehoboam." Others consider this to be a scribal error. The CSB translates this statement as a factual flashback reference to Rehoboam's rule.
15:9–24 With King Asa of Judah and Nadab of Israel, two parallel movements began. First, religious revival began under Asa so that God had a reason to restore blessings to the good kings of the south. This revival, led by two good kings, Asa and Jehoshaphat, lasted about sixty years. Then, early in the reign of Asa, the rule of Nadab began a bloody process of civil war and violence, which actually ended with the restoration of Hebrew economic and political power under

Omri and Ahab. These two movements were inseparable because God used the renewed power of the wicked kings of the north to bring renewed blessing, power, and wealth to the good kings of the south. Chapters 15 and 16 trace the revival in the south and the resurgence of political power in the north. Asa's revival is recorded first.
15:9–10 The only unexpected point in Asa's opener is that he was a grandson of **Maacah**, from the line of Absalom, or **Abishalom**; thus, Absalom and Solomon were co-ancestors to the covenant royal line.
15:11–12 Asa, nevertheless, turned out to be a godly king. He was the first king since the division of the kingdom to do **what was right in the LORD's sight.**
15:13 As a **queen mother**, Asa's grand-**mother**, Maacah, was a stumbling block to faith in the Lord. Part of cleansing the kingdom was removing her bad influence.
15:14 For all of the good kings, the **high places** that were **not taken away** were probably illegal shrines for worshiping the Lord away from the Lord's house, not for worshiping pagan gods.
15:15 The **gifts** to the **LORD's temple**, especially the **silver** and **gold**, marked the return of prosperity among the people.
15:16–17 With **Baasha**, whose formal record comes later (15:33–16:7), the border skirmishes became **war.** His offensives involved both

Judah and the Philistine plain. Apparently, Baasha penetrated Benjamite territory and began building a fortress at **Ramah** about six miles north of Jerusalem. This could have cut off all trade on that road. There were two locations named Ramah just north of Jerusalem. The one in the middle of Benjamin would have posed the greater threat. This would have been a serious blow to whatever limited benefit Judah was gaining from north-south trade on the road through Jerusalem. Most of the significant trade bypassed Jerusalem by moving up the coastal plain and then inland through passes that opened into the Plain of Esdraelon. From there the trade moved to points west in Phoenician ships or by land to points northeast of Palestine.
15:18–22 This was such a serious threat that Asa purchased an alliance with the Arameans of **Damascus**. The Chronicler rebukes Asa for not trusting in the Lord instead (2Ch 16:7–10). Now the king of Judah had to pay the Arameans to deliver him from the threat of Israel. The Arameans' response was devastating to Israel. The northern regions were plundered, and **Baasha**, despite a small resurgence of Hebrew strength, had to take refuge in his capital, **Tirzah.** Asa then used the building materials at Ramah to build his own defenses north of Jerusalem at **Geba** and **Mizpah** in Benjamin. Depending on the

without exception in Judah, and they carried away the stones of Ramah and the timbers Baasha had built it with. Then King Asa built Geba of Benjamin and Mizpah with them.

²³ The rest of all the events of Asa's reign, along with all his might, all his accomplishments, and the cities he built, are written in the Historical Record of Judah's Kings. But in his old age he developed a disease in his feet. ²⁴ Then Asa rested with his ancestors and was buried in the city of his ancestor David. His son Jehoshaphat became king in his place.

Israel's King Nadab

²⁵ Nadab son of Jeroboam became king over Israel in the second year of Judah's King Asa; he reigned over Israel two years. ²⁶ Nadab did what was evil in the LORD's sight and walked in the ways of his father and the sin he had caused Israel to commit.

²⁷ Then Baasha son of Ahijah of the house of Issachar conspired against Nadab, and Baasha struck him down at Gibbethon of the Philistines while Nadab and all Israel were besieging Gibbethon. ²⁸ In the third year of Judah's King Asa, Baasha killed Nadab and reigned in his place.

²⁹ When Baasha became king, he struck down the entire house of Jeroboam. He did not leave Jeroboam any survivors but^ destroyed his family according to the word of the LORD he had spoken through his servant Ahijah the Shilonite. ³⁰ This was because Jeroboam had angered^B the LORD God of Israel by the sins he had committed and had caused Israel to commit.

³¹ The rest of the events of Nadab's reign, along with all his accomplishments, are written in the Historical Record of Israel's Kings. ³² There was war between Asa and King Baasha of Israel throughout their reigns.

Israel's King Baasha

³³ In the third year of Judah's King Asa, Baasha son of Ahijah became king over all Israel, and he reigned in Tirzah twenty-four years.

³⁴ He did what was evil in the LORD's sight and walked in the ways of Jeroboam and the sin he had caused Israel to commit.

16 Now the word of the LORD came to Jehu son of Hanani against Baasha: ² "Because I raised you up from the dust and made you ruler over my people Israel, but you have walked in the ways of Jeroboam and have caused my people Israel to sin, angering me with their sins, ³ take note: I will eradicate Baasha and his house, and I will make your house like the house of Jeroboam son of Nebat:

⁴ Anyone who belongs to Baasha and dies
    in the city,
the dogs will eat,
and anyone who is his and dies
    in the field,
the birds^c will eat."

⁵ The rest of the events of Baasha's reign, along with all his accomplishments and might, are written in the Historical Record of Israel's Kings. ⁶ Baasha rested with his ancestors and was buried in Tirzah. His son Elah became king in his place. ⁷ But through the prophet Jehu son of Hanani the word of the LORD also had come against Baasha and against his house because of all the evil he had done in the LORD's sight. His actions angered the LORD, and Baasha's house became like the house of Jeroboam, because he had struck it down.

Israel's King Elah

⁸ In the twenty-sixth year of Judah's King Asa, Elah son of Baasha became king over Israel, and he reigned in Tirzah two years.

⁹ His servant Zimri, commander of half his chariots, conspired against him while Elah was in Tirzah getting drunk in the house of Arza, who was in charge of the household at Tirzah. ¹⁰ In the twenty-seventh year of Judah's King Asa, Zimri went in and struck Elah down, killing him. Then Zimri became king in his place. ¹¹ When he became king, as soon as he was seated on his throne, Zimri struck down the

---

^A15:29 Lit *Jeroboam anyone breathing until he*   ^B15:30 Lit *provoked in the provocation of*   ^c16:4 Lit *birds of the sky*

---

location selected for Ramah, these fortifications would have formed a defense line just north of Ramah or two miles or so south of the other Ramah.
15:23–24 Asa's foot disease is mentioned without comment, but it may be a hint that his enlistment of help from Aram was viewed by God as an expression of lack of faith. This is brought out more clearly in 2Ch 16:7–12.
15:25–16:28 This section chronicles the reign of five kings of Israel: Nadab, Baasha, Elah, Zimri, and Omri.
15:25–26 These two verses follow the typical formula. They tell of the beginning of the rule of **Nadab** over **Israel** and pass the usual negative moral judgment. Jeroboam's example was not only the measure of **evil** for Nadab, but for almost every other king of Israel.

15:27–30 This campaign against **Gibbethon**, just south of Gezer, demonstrated the resurgence of Israel's military strength. **Nadab** died in a battlefield revolution. Baasha, Nadab's killer, fulfilled the prophecy that the **house of Jeroboam** would be exterminated (14:10–11,14).
15:33–34 This introduction reveals nothing distinctive about the rule of **Baasha**. He was the first of three kings whose beginning and length of rule statements are combined into a single sentence.
16:1–4 The preceding condemnation of Baasha's sin (15:34) did not sufficiently communicate his evil, so this judgment from **Jehu** the prophet reinforced that condemnation. If Jehu's father was the **Hanani** who criticized Asa (2Ch 16:7) and Jehu was the Judean chronicler (2Ch 20:34),

then another southern prophet was condemning a northern king (1Kg 13:1). The oracle of judgment was similar to the second half of the judgment on Jeroboam (14:11). Ironically, we learn more about Baasha in Asa's record (15:16–20) than we do from Baasha's record.
16:7 Baasha's wickedness was so great that even after his closing formula, a third condemnation was added, again by **the prophet Jehu**.
16:8–14 Another formal opener introduces **Elah**. The record of the coup that deposed him reveals three facts about Israel's new army: (1) It was a chariot army; the coup leader, **Zimri**, was a chariot officer. (2) Revenues were sufficient to support such an expensive army. (3) The officers of this force were Hebrews who qualified to seize the throne.

entire house of Baasha. He did not leave a single male,^A including his kinsmen and his friends. [12] So Zimri destroyed the entire house of Baasha, according to the word of the LORD he had spoken against Baasha through the prophet Jehu. [13] This happened because of all the sins of Baasha and those of his son Elah, which they committed and caused Israel to commit, angering the LORD God of Israel with their worthless idols.

[14] The rest of the events of Elah's reign, along with all his accomplishments, are written in the Historical Record of Israel's Kings.

Israel's King Zimri

[15] In the twenty-seventh year of Judah's King Asa, Zimri became king for seven days in Tirzah. Now the troops were encamped against Gibbethon of the Philistines. [16] When these troops heard that Zimri had not only conspired but had also struck down the king, then all Israel made Omri, the army commander, king over Israel that very day in the camp. [17] Omri along with all Israel marched up from Gibbethon and besieged Tirzah. [18] When Zimri saw that the city was captured, he entered the citadel of the royal palace and burned it down over himself. He died [19] because of the sin he committed by doing what was evil in the LORD's sight and by walking in the ways of Jeroboam and the sin he caused Israel to commit.

[20] The rest of the events of Zimri's reign, along with the conspiracy that he instigated, are written in the Historical Record of Israel's Kings. [21] At that time the people of Israel were divided: half the people followed Tibni son of Ginath, to make him king, and half followed Omri. [22] However, the people who followed Omri proved stronger than those who followed Tibni son of Ginath. So Tibni died and Omri became king.

Israel's King Omri

[23] In the thirty-first year of Judah's King Asa, Omri became king over Israel, and he reigned twelve years. He reigned six years in Tirzah, [24] then he bought the hill of Samaria from Shemer for 150 pounds^B of silver, and he built up the hill. He named the city he built Samaria^C based on the name Shemer, the owner of the hill.

[25] Omri did what was evil in the LORD's sight; he did more evil than all who were before him. [26] He walked in all the ways of Jeroboam son of Nebat in every respect and continued in his sins that he caused Israel to commit, angering the LORD God of Israel with their worthless idols. [27] The rest of the events of Omri's reign, along with his accomplishments and the might he exercised, are written in the Historical Record of Israel's Kings. [28] Omri rested with his ancestors and was buried in Samaria. His son Ahab became king in his place.

Israel's King Ahab

[29] Ahab son of Omri became king over Israel in the thirty-eighth year of Judah's King Asa; Ahab son of Omri reigned over Israel in Samaria twenty-two years. [30] But Ahab son of Omri did what was evil in the LORD's sight more than all who were before him. [31] Then, as if following the sin of Jeroboam son of Nebat were not enough, he married Jezebel, the daughter of Ethbaal king of the Sidonians, and then proceeded to serve Baal and bow in worship to him. [32] He set up an altar for Baal in the temple of Baal that he had built in Samaria. [33] Ahab also made an Asherah pole. Ahab did more to anger the LORD God of Israel than all the kings of Israel who were before him.

[34] During his reign, Hiel the Bethelite built Jericho. At the cost of Abiram his firstborn,

---

^A16:11 Lit *leave him one who urinates against the wall*   ^B16:24 Lit *for two talents*   ^C16:24 = Belonging to Shemer's Clan

---

Zimri's bloody purge fulfilled the prophecy against **Baasha** (vv. 3–4).
16:15–22 The formal record for **Zimri** begins here. His revolution was formally part of the record of Elah. **Omri**, a capable battlefield commander, led the troops to **Tirzah**, captured the city, and Zimri committed suicide after ruling only **seven days**. Omri then fought a five-year civil war with **Tibni son of Ginath**. When Tibni died, Omri became king.
16:23–28 Omri's power and wealth were partly based on an economic and marriage alliance with Ethbaal of Tyre. At this time, the Phoenicians controlled Mediterranean trade. They had already established colonies as far away as North Africa and Spain. They produced manufactured goods for export throughout the Mediterranean. Omri's military skill and greatness made him a worthy ally for this maritime trade empire. The Phoenician merchants enhanced Hebrew prosperity by cooperating with Israel's trade just as they had cooperated with Solomon.
The greatest impact of Omri's dynasty was in religion. Omri's daughter-in-law was

Jezebel. Jezebel's Baal was not a typical Palestinian Baal. Rather, he was Baal-melkart, the King of the City (Tyre), the patron deity for more than half of the contemporaneous trade wealth of the Mediterranean. Ahab introduced this deity into Israel, creating a spiritual crisis. The next fifty years of Hebrew history and about seventeen chapters of Kings (1Kg 16:23–2Kg 11:3) are devoted to this crisis; it was the occasion for the miraculous ministries of Elijah and Elisha.
16:24 The purchase of a new capital, **Samaria**, was Omri's outstanding achievement.
16:25 Omri followed the pattern of Jeroboam's false cult, which led Israel into false worship. Omri's full, negative impact became clear only with the introduction of Baal-melkart (see note at vv. 23–28) into Israel. Despite his encouragement of idolatry, Omri established the power that restored wealth and empire to the two good kings of Judah.
16:29–22:40 This section focuses on the reign of Ahab. Despite his succumbing to Jezebel's influence, Ahab was a capable warrior. His military career was marked by

amazing highs and lows. At one time he was so firmly under the domination of Ben-hadad of Damascus (chap. 20) that only divine intervention delivered him from destruction, but then Assyrian records reveal that Ahab led the largest contingent of chariots against Assyria at the battle of Qarqar (853 BC), where the regional allies turned back a serious Assyrian invasion.
16:29–30 Ahab's opener makes two points: the date when he became king and how long he ruled. The evaluation reports that Ahab was the worst king Israel had up until that time.
16:31–33 **Ahab** was even worse than Jeroboam. He not only followed Jeroboam's false worship, he, with Jezebel, went beyond Jeroboam in introducing into Israel the worship of Baal-melkart (see note at vv. 23–28). The **altar for Baal** and the **Asherah pole**, the symbol of his female consort, brought this powerful fertility cult to Israel.
16:34 Recording the rebuilding or refortifying of Jericho at this point identified it as a work of Ahab. This in turn illustrated

he laid its foundation, and at the cost of Segub his youngest, he finished its gates, according to the word of the Lord he had spoken through Joshua son of Nun.

Elijah Announces Famine

17 Now Elijah the Tishbite, from the Gilead settlers,[A] said to Ahab, "As the Lord God of Israel lives, in whose presence I stand, there will be no dew or rain during these years except by my command!"

[2] Then the word of the Lord came to him: [3] "Leave here, turn eastward, and hide at the Wadi Cherith where it enters the Jordan. [4] You are to drink from the wadi. I have commanded the ravens to provide for you there."

[5] So he proceeded to do what the Lord commanded. Elijah left and lived at the Wadi Cherith where it enters the Jordan. [6] The ravens kept bringing him bread and meat in the morning and in the evening, and he would drink from the wadi. [7] After a while, the wadi dried up because there had been no rain in the land.

Elijah and the Widow

[8] Then the word of the Lord came to him: [9] "Get up, go to Zarephath that belongs to Sidon and stay there. Look, I have commanded a woman who is a widow to provide for you there." [10] So Elijah got up and went to Zarephath. When he arrived at the city gate, there was a widow gathering wood. Elijah called to her and said, "Please bring me a little water in a cup and let me drink." [11] As she went to get it, he called to her and said, "Please bring me a piece of bread in your hand." [12] But she said, "As the Lord your God lives, I don't have anything baked — only a handful of flour in the jar and a bit of oil in the jug. Just now, I am gathering a couple of sticks in order to go prepare it for myself and my son so we can eat it and die." [13] Then Elijah said to her, "Don't be afraid; go and do as you have said. But first make me

a small loaf from it and bring it out to me. Afterward, you may make some for yourself and your son, [14] for this is what the Lord God of Israel says, 'The flour jar will not become empty and the oil jug will not run dry until the day the Lord sends rain on the surface of the land.'"

[15] So she proceeded to do according to the word of Elijah. Then the woman, Elijah, and her household ate for many days. [16] The flour jar did not become empty, and the oil jug did not run dry, according to the word of the Lord he had spoken through[B] Elijah.

The Widow's Son Raised

[17] After this, the son of the woman who owned the house became ill. His illness got worse until he stopped breathing. [18] She said to Elijah, "Man of God, what do you have against me? Have you come to call attention to my iniquity so that my son is put to death?" [19] But Elijah said to her, "Give me your son." So he took him from her arms, brought him up to the upstairs room where he was staying, and laid him on his own bed. [20] Then he cried out to the Lord and said, "Lord my God, have you also brought tragedy on the widow I am staying with by killing her son?" [21] Then he stretched himself out over the boy three times. He cried out to the Lord and said, "Lord my God, please let this boy's life come into him again!" [22] So the Lord listened to Elijah, and the boy's life came into him again, and he lived. [23] Then Elijah took the boy, brought him down from the upstairs room into the house, and gave him to his mother. Elijah said, "Look, your son is alive." [24] Then the woman said to Elijah, "Now I know you are a man of God and the Lord's word from your mouth is true."

Elijah's Message to Ahab

18 After a long time, the word of the Lord came to Elijah in the third year: "Go and present yourself to Ahab. I will send rain on the

---

^17:1 LXX reads from Tishbe of Gilead   ^17:16 Lit by the hand of

the long reach of Ahab's foreign policy. The deaths of the sons of **Hiel** could have been viewed as either the impact of an effective curse (Jos 6:26) or a human sacrifice to neutralize the curse.
17:1–19:21 This section describes the clash between the prophet Elijah and King Ahab of Israel.
17:1 The CSB suggests that **Elijah** was one of the **settlers** in Gilead. This raises the possibility that he was a non-Hebrew settler, since a Hebrew was typically described in terms of his tribe and family. Elijah's rustic appearance also set him apart as someone different. He was to announce to one of the most powerful kings in the region that God would send a devastating drought against the land.
17:2–3 The location of the **Wadi Cherith** is not clear. Some authorities identify it with the Wadi Qelt that passes just south of

Jericho. Some translations place it east of the Jordan River, apparently taking the words **where it enters the Jordan** (lit "which is facing/before the Jordan") as being equal to "facing the Jordan from the east." If we permit Elijah's move eastward from delivering his oracle in Israel to include a great deal of southeasterly movement, the Wadi Qelt is possible.
17:4–7 God's miraculous provision of food for Elijah, at a time when God had cut off food for the nation, reminded any hearer/reader that God is the true provider of human needs. Unclean carrion birds (**ravens**) brought this food.
17:8–9 Then God sent Elijah to the Phoenician city of **Zarephath**, a Gentile city under Ethbaal's control, for provision and protection. Jesus gave a theologically suitable interpretation of this passage (Lk 4:26–27)—that God sent his messenger

with beneficial signs and wonders to a Gentile.
17:12 In referring to **the Lord your God**, the widow seemed to show she recognized that Elijah represented the Lord, the God of the Hebrews, yet she did not turn him over to Ethbaal, the king of the Phoenicians. Ethbaal was the father-in-law of Ahab, from whom Elijah was hiding. Either that knowledge was insufficient to specifically identify Elijah to Ethbaal, or she deliberately chose not to betray Elijah.
17:17–24 This miracle teaches three lessons: (1) not all illness is the result of sin, (2) God has power over sickness and death, and (3) the purpose of the signs was to produce faith in **the Lord's word**.
18:1–46 This chapter describes one of history's great power encounters between God and evil; it is comparable to the encounter between the Lord and the gods of Egypt

surface of the land." [2] So Elijah went to present himself to Ahab.

The famine was severe in Samaria. [3] Ahab called for Obadiah, who was in charge of the palace. Obadiah was a man who greatly feared the LORD [4] and took a hundred prophets and hid them, fifty men to a cave, and provided them with food and water when Jezebel slaughtered the LORD's prophets. [5] Ahab said to Obadiah, "Go throughout the land to every spring and to every wadi. Perhaps we'll find grass so we can keep the horses and mules alive and not have to destroy any cattle." [6] They divided the land between them in order to cover it. Ahab went one way by himself, and Obadiah went the other way by himself.

[7] While Obadiah was walking along the road, Elijah suddenly met him. When Obadiah recognized him, he fell facedown and said, "Is it you, my lord Elijah?"

[8] "It is I," he replied. "Go tell your lord, 'Elijah is here!'"[A]

[9] But Obadiah said, "What sin have I committed, that you are handing your servant over to Ahab to put me to death? [10] As the LORD your God lives, there is no nation or kingdom where my lord has not sent someone to search for you. When they said, 'He is not here,' he made that kingdom or nation swear they had not found you. [11] Now you say, 'Go tell your lord, "Elijah is here!"' [12] But when I leave you, the Spirit of the LORD may carry you off to some place I don't know. Then when I go report to Ahab and he doesn't find you, he will kill me. But I, your servant, have feared the LORD from my youth. [13] Wasn't it reported to my lord what I did when

---

[A]**18:8** The Hb words translated *'Elijah is here'* also mean *'Look, my God is the LORD'*

---

before the exodus. The prestige of Baal-melkart, with his association with Phoenician prosperity, was comparable to the historic prestige of the gods of Egypt. The power encounter with Egypt freed the Israelites from physical bondage. One might expect that God's confrontation with Baal-melkart freed Israel from spiritual bondage, but it is difficult to find evidence for this. Neither Ahab nor Jezebel repented. The moral life of the northern kingdom was not noticeably influenced. But we cannot know how much worse things would have gone for faith in the Lord without this encounter. Perhaps the seven thousand (19:18) who had not bowed to Baal were encouraged and strengthened, and thus kept the faith.
18:1–2 In **the third year** of the drought, God announced its end. This was an act of

grace since neither Israel nor Israel's rulers had shown any repentance that warranted it.
18:3–5 Since these verses may have changed to a new story, v. 3 could predate the preceding verses. This would permit the translation, "Ahab had called." This scenario should be interpreted in terms of its historical conditions. It told of two high officials initiating a nationwide effort to find the resources to preserve the kingdom's chariot armies. The story's surface simplicity obscures a grave and historically realistic situation. How could they maintain the provisions for the chariot **horses** and baggage **mules** when forage and grazing were exhausted? This situation could have produced Israel's weakness in chariot forces in the first war of chap. 20.

18:6 Both **Ahab** and **Obadiah** were accompanied by soldiers and officials who purchased or confiscated the resources as needed.
18:7–8 The prophet **Elijah** made his approach through **Obadiah** as the latter **was walking along**, probably with his search party. Obadiah's deference to Elijah revealed Elijah's stature.
18:9–10 Obadiah's response made it clear that Elijah's time in Ethbaal's domains was "undercover" since Ahab had initiated a thorough search for the prophet.
18:11–12 Obadiah was true to his name, a true "servant of the Lord," even though he was ostensibly a servant of Ahab.
18:13–14 This verse gives a remarkable view of the religious turmoil in Israel. With the government engaged in a bloody purge of

---

Character profile:
Elijah

As a prophet of God in Israel during the reign of King Ahab and Queen Jezebel, Elijah was an endangered species. The evil royal couple had done everything in their power to rid the nation of God's spokespeople so that their own prophets of the false gods Baal and Asherah could do their work unopposed.

Elijah had a target on his back because he had announced God's judgment on Israel. A devastating drought gripped the land, wreaking havoc on the nation's food and water supply. Missing the point of judgment completely, King Ahab blamed Elijah for the drought (see 1Kg 18:17).

Elijah refused to be cowed. Prompted by God, he challenged the 450 prophets of Baal and the 400 prophets of Asherah to a winner-take-all contest. The rules were simple. Two sacrificial altars would be built: one to the Lord God and one to Baal. The first deity to send fire to accept his sacrifice would be declared the God of Israel.

On the appointed day the prophets of Baal assembled at Mount Carmel to prepare their sacrifice. From morning until noon they called out to Baal, begging and pleading with him to send a fire. They danced to get his attention, shouted louder, and cut themselves, hoping their blood would arouse Baal's interest. "All afternoon they kept on raving until the offering of the evening sacrifice, but there was no sound; no one answered, no one paid attention" (18:29).

The eyes of the nation turned to Elijah, the sole representative of Yahweh, to see if he could accomplish what his

Baal-worshiping opponents could not. Elijah's first step was to repair the altar of the Lord that had been torn down in Israel's rush to embrace the false gods of their neighbors. He used twelve stones to represent the twelve tribes of Israel.

His next step was to dig a trench, deep enough to hold four gallons of water, around the altar holding the sacrifice. Elijah then instructed people to fill four large pots with water and pour them over his sacrifice and altar—three times. The runoff filled the surrounding trench.

He made it practically impossible for anything to ignite his sacrifice. And that was precisely his intent.

Elijah approached his waterlogged altar and prayed for everyone to hear, asking the God of Abraham, Isaac, and Israel, "Answer me so that this people will know that you, the LORD, are God and that you have turned their hearts back" (18:37).

At that moment fire descended from heaven to devour Elijah's offering, along with the wood beneath it, the stones of the altar, and the dirt on which the altar was built. The flames even consumed every drop of water in the trench that surrounded the altar.

The Lord sent an unmistakable message to his people about what he is capable of—and why false gods should be dismissed as worthless. The impact was immediate and profound. "When all the people saw it, they fell facedown and said, 'The LORD, he is God! The LORD, he is God!'" (18:39).

If you represent God and are doing his work, traditional ideas about what is or isn't possible have no relevance. No odds are too high, no opponent is too intimidating, and no obstacle is too extreme to overcome. The more deeply you cling to those truths, the more willing you'll be to take risks in your faith, as Elijah did.

Jezebel slaughtered the LORD's prophets? I hid a hundred of the prophets of the LORD, fifty men to a cave, and I provided them with food and water. ¹⁴ Now you say, 'Go tell your lord, "Elijah is here!"' He will kill me!"

¹⁵ Then Elijah said, "As the LORD of Armies lives, in whose presence I stand, today I will present myself to Ahab."

¹⁶ Obadiah went to meet Ahab and told him. Then Ahab went to meet Elijah. ¹⁷ When Ahab saw Elijah, Ahab said to him, "Is that you, the one ruining Israel?"

¹⁸ He replied, "I have not ruined Israel, but you and your father's family have, because you have abandoned the LORD's commands and followed the Baals. ¹⁹ Now summon all Israel to meet me at Mount Carmel, along with the 450 prophets of Baal and the 400 prophets of Asherah who eat at Jezebel's table."

Elijah at Mount Carmel

²⁰ So Ahab summoned all the Israelites and gathered the prophets at Mount Carmel. ²¹ Then Elijah approached all the people and said, "How long will you waver between two opinions?ᴬ If the LORD is God, follow him. But if Baal, follow him." But the people didn't answer him a word.

²² Then Elijah said to the people, "I am the only remaining prophet of the LORD, but Baal's prophets are 450 men. ²³ Let two bulls be given to us. They are to choose one bull for themselves, cut it in pieces, and place it on the wood but not light the fire. I will prepare the other bull and place it on the wood but not light the fire. ²⁴ Then you call on the name of your god, and I will call on the name of the LORD. The God who answers with fire, he is God."

All the people answered, "That's fine."

²⁵ Then Elijah said to the prophets of Baal, "Since you are so numerous, choose for yourselves one bull and prepare it first. Then call on the name of your god but don't light the fire."

²⁶ So they took the bull that he gave them, prepared it, and called on the name of Baal from morning until noon, saying, "Baal, answer us!" But there was no sound; no one answered. Then they dancedᴮ around the altar they had made.

²⁷ At noon Elijah mocked them. He said, "Shout loudly, for he's a god! Maybe he's thinking it over; maybe he has wandered away;ᶜ or maybe he's on the road. Perhaps he's sleeping and will wake up!" ²⁸ They shouted loudly, and cut themselves with knives and spears, according to their custom, until blood gushed over them. ²⁹ All afternoon they kept on raving until the offering of the evening sacrifice, but there was no sound; no one answered, no one paid attention.

³⁰ Then Elijah said to all the people, "Come near me." So all the people approached him. Then he repaired the LORD's altar that had been torn down: ³¹ Elijah took twelve stones — according to the number of the tribes of the sons of Jacob, to whom the word of the LORD had come, saying, "Israel will be your name" — ³² and he built an altar with the stones in the name of the LORD. Then he made a trench around the altar large enough to hold about four gallons.ᴰ,ᴱ ³³ Next, he arranged the wood, cut up the bull, and placed it on the wood. He said, "Fill four water pots with water and pour it on the offering to be burned and on the wood." ³⁴ Then he said, "A second time!" and they did it a second time. And then he said, "A third time!" and they did it a third time. ³⁵ So the water ran all around the altar; he even filled the trench with water.

³⁶ At the time for offering the evening sacrifice, the prophet Elijah approached the altar and said, "LORD, the God of Abraham, Isaac, and Israel, today let it be known that you are God in Israel and I am your servant, and that at your

---

ᴬ**18:21** Lit *you hobble on two crutches?* ᴮ**18:26** Or *hobbled* ᶜ**18:27** Or *has turned aside*; possibly to relieve himself
ᴰ**18:32** LXX reads *trench containing two measures of seed* ᴱ**18:32** Lit *altar corresponding to a house of two seahs of seed*

---

those who worshiped the Lord, one of the king's chief political officials was protecting the minority religious party.
18:15–17 Despite Ahab's bravery and abilities in many areas, his accusation against Elijah showed that willful sin can blind a person to reality.
18:18–19 Elijah immediately took the conversation to the crucial issue—Ahab's disobedience of God. Then Elijah issued his challenge to set up a carefully planned and publicized power encounter pitting Elijah against the prophets of **Baal** and his consort, **Asherah**. *Asherah* is a generic name for any divine consort of any fertility god, but is also sometimes a title or name for a particular goddess.
18:20–21 From the course of events, we can see that some of the worshipers of Baal really believed in the power of their deity and that many who should have followed the Lord did not have much faith. Therefore, for

many of the observers, this was a genuine open-ended power encounter to discover which deity was stronger.
18:22–25 Elijah proposed the terms of the test: whichever god miraculously ignited and burned his sacrifice would prove to be the true deity who was worthy of the people's allegiance. Since Baal was the storm god, his followers believed he could answer with fire (lightning). But this encounter would show which deity really controlled the weather and provided what the people needed. At the same time, it would show who was a destroyer of Israel, rebellious Ahab or the Lord's prophet Elijah.
18:26 The priests of Baal entered into the contest with great zeal. Their dancing may have imitated the steps of a lame person, since it uses the same Hebrew word as the one describing Mephibosheth (2Sm 4:4). Perhaps they danced this way as a result of their self-inflicted injuries (1Kg 18:28).

18:27 The Hebrew original possibly indicates that Elijah ridiculed Baal for relieving himself. Reducing deities to any level of human behavior is an insult; therefore, any suggestion that Baal was drawn away to perform a creaturely necessity was a poignant blow by Elijah.
18:28–29 The fanatical zeal of the priests of Baal led them to **cut themselves**. Some suggest that this self-inflicted pain may have been aimed at gaining the pity of the other gods so they would release Baal from his mythological death and thus bring rain. If this is true, these Baal worshipers were vicariously suffering pain for their god.
18:33–35 Elijah took steps to avoid any appearance of trickery or fraud. If his God could get a drenching wet sacrifice to burn, he was God indeed.
18:36–39 Elijah's prayer was a powerful statement of the theology of God's great works. Elijah prayed for a miraculous sign

word I have done all these things. ³⁷ Answer me, LORD! Answer me so that this people will know that you, the LORD, are God and that you have turned their hearts back."

³⁸ Then the LORD's fire fell and consumed the burnt offering, the wood, the stones, and the dust, and it licked up the water that was in the trench. ³⁹ When all the people saw it, they fell facedown and said, "The LORD, he is God! The LORD, he is God!"

⁴⁰ Then Elijah ordered them, "Seize the prophets of Baal! Do not let even one of them escape." So they seized them, and Elijah brought them down to the Wadi Kishon and slaughtered them there. ⁴¹ Elijah said to Ahab, "Go up, eat and drink, for there is the sound of a rainstorm."

⁴² So Ahab went to eat and drink, but Elijah went up to the summit of Carmel. He bent down on the ground and put his face between his knees. ⁴³ Then he said to his servant, "Go up and look toward the sea."

So he went up, looked, and said, "There's nothing."

Seven times Elijah said, "Go back."

⁴⁴ On the seventh time, he reported, "There's a cloud as small as a man's hand coming up from the sea."

Then Elijah said, "Go and tell Ahab, 'Get your chariot ready and go down so the rain doesn't stop you.'"

⁴⁵ In a little while, the sky grew dark with clouds and wind, and there was a downpour. So Ahab got in his chariot and went to Jezreel. ⁴⁶ The power of the LORD was on Elijah, and he tucked his mantle under his belt and ran ahead of Ahab to the entrance of Jezreel.

Elijah's Journey to Horeb

19 Ahab told Jezebel everything that Elijah had done and how he had killed all the prophets with the sword. ² So Jezebel sent a messenger to Elijah, saying, "May the gods punish me and do so severely if I don't make your life like the life of one of them by this time tomorrow!"

³ Then Elijah became afraid^A and immediately ran for his life. When he came to Beer-sheba that belonged to Judah, he left his servant there, ⁴ but he went on a day's journey into the wilderness. He sat down under a broom tree and prayed that he might die. He said, "I have had enough! LORD, take my life, for I'm no better than my ancestors." ⁵ Then he lay down and slept under the broom tree.

Suddenly, an angel touched him. The angel told him, "Get up and eat." ⁶ Then he looked, and there at his head was a loaf of bread baked over hot stones, and a jug of water. So he ate and drank and lay down again. ⁷ Then the angel of the LORD returned for a second time and touched him. He said, "Get up and eat, or the journey will be too much for you." ⁸ So he got up, ate, and drank. Then on the strength from that food, he walked forty days and forty nights to Horeb, the mountain of God. ⁹ He entered a cave there and spent the night.

Elijah's Encounter with the LORD

Suddenly, the word of the LORD came to him, and he said to him, "What are you doing here, Elijah?"

¹⁰ He replied, "I have been very zealous for the LORD God of Armies, but the Israelites have abandoned your covenant, torn down your altars, and killed your prophets with the sword. I alone am left, and they are looking for me to take my life."

¹¹ Then he said, "Go out and stand on the mountain in the LORD's presence."

At that moment, the LORD passed by. A great and mighty wind was tearing at the mountains and was shattering cliffs before the LORD, but

---

^A19:3 Some Hb mss, LXX, Syr, Vg; other Hb mss read *He saw*

---

so **this people** would **know that you, the LORD, are God**. The simplicity of Elijah's procedure is impressive. The prophet prayed, and the sacrifice was miraculously burned. **18:40** Elijah executed God's judgment on the false prophets that Moses commanded in Dt 13:5,13–18; 17:2–5. This was the law for the covenant community, God's holy nation. **18:41–46** Two final miraculous events on this day were: (1) the coming of the **rain** as a result of Elijah's prayer, and (2) Elijah's supernatural strength in leaving the scene and passing Ahab's **chariot** before the storm. Typically, the act of preceding the king's chariot could have been a friendly overture. It was an act of honor to the king and an honor to the runner to be permitted to run before the king. But if this was Elijah's intent, it was lost on Ahab and Jezebel. **19:1–21** This chapter presents facts that argue for the truth of both chaps. 18 and 19. The preceding chapter was one of the best examples of a power encounter in the Bible, but chap. 19 demonstrates that

God's miraculous works did not bring about repentance, at least not on a scale broad enough to mention. Understandably, Elijah collapsed into an almost hysterical pessimism about what he took to be the failure of God's purposes. The clear lesson is that while power witness is both biblical and effective, sinful people can still reject the greatest of God's signs (Lk 16:31). So too, faithful disciples are wrong to suppose that they are all alone or that God's purposes have truly failed. **19:1–2** Jezebel's rejection of God's signs and the determined, defiant way in which she later faced death (2Kg 9:30–31) demonstrate her character as a person who did what she wanted, no matter the consequences. Sin breeds this self-destructive heedlessness. **19:3** Elijah's faith may have crumbled due to physical and emotional exhaustion. Although his future still included several tasks, it may be significant that his next task was to choose his successor. **Beer-sheba**, about a hundred miles south of Mount Carmel,

served as a traditional southern boundary for Israelite territory (Jdg 20:1; 2Sm 24:2). **19:4** A **day's journey** would have taken Elijah out of Judean territory and into deeper desert. The **broom tree** under which the prophet sat provided shade, and its roots could be used for heat and food. Elijah was in deep depression. **19:5–8** God's miraculous provision was resumed, this time purely for the prophet. After Elijah **ate** and rested, he returned to the place where the covenant had been given, Mount **Horeb**, or Sinai. There Elijah would have his personal faith renewed by God's presence. **19:9–10** Elijah explained his presence at Sinai by referring to his discouragement. Israel's immediate future, as hindsight shows, gave good reason for despair. Judah was to have one more period of God-given prosperity under the four good kings from Joash to Jotham, but during that time, Israel was to be deported to Assyria. **19:11–13** God first reveals his presence to Elijah in his greatness and power, but he did not speak from that position. The Lord instead

the LORD was not in the wind. After the wind there was an earthquake, but the LORD was not in the earthquake. ¹² After the earthquake there was a fire, but the LORD was not in the fire. And after the fire there was a voice, a soft whisper. ¹³ When Elijah heard it, he wrapped his face in his mantle and went out and stood at the entrance of the cave.

Suddenly, a voice came to him and said, "What are you doing here, Elijah?"

¹⁴ "I have been very zealous for the LORD God of Armies," he replied, "but the Israelites have abandoned your covenant, torn down your altars, and killed your prophets with the sword. I alone am left, and they're looking for me to take my life."

¹⁵ Then the LORD said to him, "Go and return by the way you came to the Wilderness of Damascus. When you arrive, you are to anoint Hazael as king over Aram. ¹⁶ You are to anoint Jehu son of Nimshi as king over Israel and Elisha son of Shaphat from Abel-meholah as prophet in your place. ¹⁷ Then Jehu will put to death whoever escapes the sword of Hazael, and Elisha will put to death whoever escapes the sword of Jehu. ¹⁸ But I will leave seven thousand in Israel — every knee that has not bowed to Baal and every mouth that has not kissed him."

Elisha's Appointment as Elijah's Successor

¹⁹ Elijah left there and found Elisha son of Shaphat as he was plowing. Twelve teams of oxen were in front of him, and he was with the twelfth team. Elijah walked by him and threw his mantle over him. ²⁰ Elisha left the oxen, ran to follow Elijah, and said, "Please let me kiss my father and mother, and then I will follow you."

"Go on back," he replied, "for what have I done to you?"

²¹ So he turned back from following him, took the team of oxen, and slaughtered^A them. With the oxen's wooden yoke and plow, he cooked the meat and gave it to the people,

and they ate. Then he left, followed Elijah, and served him.

Victory over Ben-hadad

20 Now King Ben-hadad of Aram assembled his entire army. Thirty-two kings, along with horses and chariots, were with him. He marched up, besieged Samaria, and fought against it. ² He sent messengers into the city to King Ahab of Israel and said to him, "This is what Ben-hadad says: ³ 'Your silver and your gold are mine! And your best wives and children are mine as well!'"

⁴ Then the king of Israel answered, "Just as you say, my lord the king: I am yours, along with all that I have."

⁵ The messengers then returned and said, "This is what Ben-hadad says: 'I have sent messengers to you, saying, "You are to give me your silver, your gold, your wives, and your children." ⁶ But at this time tomorrow I will send my servants to you,^B and they will search your palace and your servants' houses. They will lay their hands on and take away whatever is precious to you.'"

⁷ Then the king of Israel called for all the elders of the land and said, "Recognize^C that this one is only looking for trouble, for he demanded my wives, my children, my silver, and my gold, and I didn't turn him down."

⁸ All the elders and all the people said to him, "Don't listen or agree."

⁹ So he said to Ben-hadad's messengers, "Say to my lord the king, 'Everything you demanded of your servant the first time, I will do, but this thing I cannot do.'" So the messengers left and took word back to him.

¹⁰ Then Ben-hadad sent messengers to him and said, "May the gods punish me and do so severely if Samaria's dust amounts to a handful for each of the people who follow me."

¹¹ The king of Israel answered, "Say this: 'Don't let the one who puts on his armor boast like the one who takes it off.'"

¹² When Ben-hadad heard this response, while he and the kings were drinking in their

---

^19:21 Or *sacrificed* ^20:6 Lit *take all the delight of your eyes* ^20:7 Lit *"Know and see*

---

spoke to Elijah in **a soft whisper**, showing himself to be a God who communicates via a still, small voice as well as powerful displays. His power is especially present in his word.
19:14 Elijah is given a second audience with God to make his case against Israel.
19:15–16 God's commands first pointed to judgment. Elijah was to anoint **Hazael** as king over Aram, **Jehu** as king of Israel, and **Elisha** as his own successor. God was still controlling events.
19:17 This command indicated the extent of God's judgment—death at the hands of **Hazael**, at the hands of **Jehu**, and even at the hands of **Elisha** through his pronouncements of judgment.
19:18 The second part of God's response gave hope. God still had **seven thousand**

people through whom he could work in the future.
19:19–21 Here we see an advance in agricultural technology—**teams of oxen** being used for deeper, more effective plowing (Pr 14:4). This showed that Elisha's family was quite prosperous. Elisha's capability to celebrate his new calling with sacrifices and feasting for the whole community also indicated his family's prosperity. The **mantle** or robe worn by Elijah was a symbol of his position and of Elisha's succession to that position. Compare Elijah's words to those Jesus spoke to a would-be disciple in Lk 9:62.
20:1–3 This chapter clashes with the general pattern of Israelite strength under the dynasty of Omri. That general political strength and leadership culminated in Ahab's crucial

participation in resisting the Assyrians at the battle of Qarqar. Since both the great drought and the wars with Ben-hadad occurred late in Ahab's rule, this chapter probably describes a brief weakness caused by the drought (17:1) and also sheds light on Ahab's earlier desperate search for provisions for his chariot corps (18:5).
20:4–9 Ahab tried to end the siege by a total surrender to **Ben-hadad's** initial demands, but Ben-hadad then increased his demands so that even a desperate, weakened Ahab resorted to resistance.
20:10 The oath is a boast in the size of Ben-hadad's army and the degree of destruction that would be meted out to Samaria.
20:11 The point of the saying is that a fighter should not count his victories before battle.

quarters,^ he said to his servants, "Take your positions." So they took their positions against the city.

¹³ A prophet approached King Ahab of Israel and said, "This is what the LORD says: 'Do you see this whole huge army? Watch, I am handing it over to you today so that you may know that I am the LORD.'"

¹⁴ Ahab asked, "By whom?"

And the prophet said, "This is what the LORD says: 'By the young men of the provincial leaders.'"

Then he asked, "Who is to start the battle?" He said, "You."

¹⁵ So Ahab mobilized the young men of the provincial leaders, and there were 232. After them he mobilized all the Israelite troops: 7,000. ¹⁶ They marched out at noon while Ben-hadad and the thirty-two kings who were helping him were getting drunk in their quarters. ¹⁷ The young men of the provincial leaders marched out first. Then Ben-hadad sent out scouts, and they reported to him, saying, "Men are marching out of Samaria."

¹⁸ So he said, "If they have marched out in peace, take them alive, and if they have marched out for battle, take them alive."

¹⁹ The young men of the provincial leaders and the army behind them marched out from the city, ²⁰ and each one struck down his opponent. So the Arameans fled and Israel pursued them, but King Ben-hadad of Aram escaped on a horse with the cavalry. ²¹ Then the king of Israel marched out and attacked the cavalry and the chariots. He inflicted a severe slaughter on Aram.

²² The prophet approached the king of Israel and said to him, "Go and strengthen yourself, then consider carefully^B what you should do, for in the spring the king of Aram will attack you."

²³ Now the king of Aram's servants said to him, "Their gods are gods of the hill country. That's why they were stronger than we were. Instead, we should fight with them on the plain; then we will certainly be stronger than they are. ²⁴ Also do this: remove each king from his position and appoint captains in their place. ²⁵ Raise another army for yourself like the army you lost — horse for horse, chariot for chariot — and let's fight with them on the plain; and we will certainly be stronger than they are." The king listened to them and did it.

²⁶ In the spring, Ben-hadad mobilized the Arameans and went up to Aphek to battle Israel. ²⁷ The Israelites mobilized, gathered supplies, and went to fight them. The Israelites camped in front of them like two little flocks of goats, while the Arameans filled the landscape.

²⁸ Then the man of God approached and said to the king of Israel, "This is what the LORD says: 'Because the Arameans have said, "The LORD is a god of the mountains and not a god of the valleys," I will hand over all this whole huge army to you. Then you will know that I am the LORD.'"

²⁹ They camped opposite each other for seven days. On the seventh day, the battle took place, and the Israelites struck down the Arameans — one hundred thousand foot soldiers in one day. ³⁰ The ones who remained fled into the city of Aphek, and the wall fell on those twenty-seven thousand remaining men.

Ben-hadad also fled and went into an inner room in the city. ³¹ His servants said to him, "Consider this: we have heard that the kings of the house of Israel are merciful kings. So let's put sackcloth around our waists and ropes around our heads, and let's go out to the king of Israel. Perhaps he will spare your life."

³² So they dressed with sackcloth around their waists and ropes around their heads, went to the king of Israel, and said, "Your servant Ben-hadad says, 'Please spare my life.'"

So he said, "Is he still alive? He is my brother."

---

^20:12 Lit booths, also in v. 16   ^B20:22 Lit then know and see

20:13–19 Divine revelation gave encouragement and guidance to **Ahab**. Since there is no mention of Israelite chariots, Ahab's chariot army may have been disabled by the drought. A surprise attack by provincial infantry brought victory for Ahab's army. God's intervention helped in the drunken panic that marked the defeat of the Aramean army. The purpose of the divine intervention was that Ahab would recognize God's character. The lesson failed.

20:20 There are two views on the Aramean **cavalry**. One is that cavalry did not appear until later so that the ambiguous Hebrew word in this verse refers to charioteers. The other is that Assyrian records confirm the presence of cavalry in the region's armies at this time but the chariot was still the major strike force. So at this time Ben-hadad could have fled with the cavalry.

20:21 In this verse, **the cavalry and the chariots** are literally "horses and chariots," a combination that at this time would still more likely refer to chariotry. It is reasonable to conclude that much of the Israelite success came from God's blessing on the surprise infantry attack on the unprepared, unharnessed chariots of the Aramean army.

20:22 God granted Ahab another gracious gift in warning him of Ben-hadad's plans.

20:23–25 The Arameans then prepared for battle in the following year, most likely in the spring, the usual time for war (2Sm 11:1). They assumed that their mobile forces would be more effective in the plains instead of the mountains. But the reorganization of the Aramean chariots may have been disastrous. A feudal system in which kings provided the chariots was replaced by one in which central government officials maintained the chariots. In the long range, this was an advantage, but in the short range it may have replaced battle-tested nobility with less-experienced government officials. Their preparations included replacing the lost war machines, **chariot for chariot**.

20:26 The armies mobilized in the plains near **Aphek** in Bashan.

20:28 Here is another divine gift to Ahab, though it is for the sake of the Lord's name.

20:29–30 The account given here is compatible with several days of destruction against **Aphek** by Ahab's pursuing army as well as a house-to-house search for Ben-hadad.

20:31–34 In this quick agreement, made in Ahab's chariot, it is clear that Ben-hadad relinquished claim to some Israelite cities and gave Ahab trading privileges in Aramean territory. From a human point of view, with the need to create an alliance with **Damascus** and anyone else who would join against the Assyrians, Ahab was politically wise and

33 Now the men were looking for a sign of hope, so they quickly picked up on this^A and responded, "Yes, it is your brother Ben-hadad."

Then he said, "Go and bring him."

So Ben-hadad came out to him, and Ahab had him come up into the chariot. **34** Then Ben-hadad said to him, "I restore to you the cities that my father took from your father, and you may set up marketplaces for yourself in Damascus, like my father set up in Samaria."

Ahab responded, "On the basis of this treaty, I release you." So he made a treaty with him and released him.

Ahab Rebuked by the LORD

35 One of the sons of the prophets said to his fellow prophet by the word of the LORD, "Strike me!" But the man refused to strike him. **36** He told him, "Because you did not listen to the LORD, mark my words: When you leave me, a lion will kill you." When he left him, a lion attacked and killed him. **37** The prophet found another man and said to him, "Strike me!" So the man struck him, inflicting a wound. **38** Then the prophet went and waited for the king on the road. He disguised himself with a bandage over his eyes. **39** As the king was passing by, he cried out to the king and said, "Your servant marched out into the middle of the battle. Suddenly, a man turned aside and brought someone to me and said, 'Guard this man! If he is ever missing, it will be your life in place of his life, or you will weigh out seventy-five pounds^B of silver.' **40** But while your servant was busy here and there, he disappeared."

The king of Israel said to him, "That will be your sentence; you yourself have decided it." **41** He quickly removed the bandage from his eyes. The king of Israel recognized that he was one of the prophets. **42** The prophet said to him, "This is what the LORD says: 'Because you released from your hand the man I had set apart for destruction, it will be your life in place of his life and your people in place of his people.'" **43** The king of Israel left for home resentful and angry, and he entered Samaria.

Ahab and Naboth's Vineyard

21 Some time passed after these events. Naboth the Jezreelite had a vineyard; it was in Jezreel next to the palace of King Ahab of Samaria. **2** So Ahab spoke to Naboth, saying, "Give me your vineyard so I can have it for a vegetable garden, since it is right next to my palace. I will give you a better vineyard in its place, or if you prefer, I will give you its value in silver."

3 But Naboth said to Ahab, "As the LORD is my witness, I will never give my ancestors' inheritance to you."

4 So Ahab went to his palace resentful and angry because of what Naboth the Jezreelite had told him. He had said, "I will not give you my ancestors' inheritance." He lay down on his bed, turned his face away, and didn't eat any food.

5 Then his wife Jezebel came to him and said to him, "Why are you so upset that you refuse to eat?"

6 "Because I spoke to Naboth the Jezreelite," he replied. "I told him, 'Give me your vineyard for silver, or if you wish, I will give you a vineyard in its place.' But he said, 'I won't give you my vineyard!'"

7 Then his wife Jezebel said to him, "Now, exercise your royal power over Israel. Get up, eat some food, and be happy. For I will give you the vineyard of Naboth the Jezreelite." **8** So she wrote letters in Ahab's name and sealed them with his seal. She sent the letters to the elders and nobles who lived with Naboth in his city. **9** In the letters, she wrote:

Proclaim a fast and seat Naboth at the head of the people. **10** Then seat two wicked men opposite him and have them testify against him, saying, "You have cursed God and the king!" Then take him out and stone him to death.

11 The men of his city, the elders and nobles who lived in his city, did as Jezebel had sent word to them, just as it was written in the letters she had sent them. **12** They proclaimed a fast and seated Naboth at the head of the people. **13** The two wicked men came in and sat opposite him. Then the wicked men testified

---

^A**20:33** Some Hb mss, alt Hb tradition, LXX; other Hb mss read *they hastened and caught hold; "Is this it?"* ^B**20:39** Lit *a talent*

---

prudent in dealing gently with the defeated Arameans.
20:35–43 However prudent that policy may have been, the prophetic voices, speaking for God, condemned this act of prudent mercy. Once again, prudent politics conflicted with following the Lord. As far as the prophets were concerned, Ben-hadad had been **set apart** to the ban, just like Jericho (Jos 6:18–19), and Ahab had violated that divine ban.
21:1–3 The law had legal provisions that protected the rights of Israelite land-holding families. The land could not be permanently alienated from the family, but it had

to be returned either by redemption or by the free return in the Jubilee Year (Lv 25:10). There were no provisions for the selling or exchanging of land such as that which **Ahab** requested of **Naboth**. Therefore, Naboth refused to sell his **ancestors' inheritance** to the king.
21:4–6 Ahab the mighty warrior pouted because Naboth the farmer had refused his offer. His scruples, as well as his childishness, are somewhat surprising. But his wife had neither.
21:8–12 Jezebel resolved Ahab's unhappiness with a scheme that involved perverting the

law, perjury, and murder. First, she communicated a sense of seriousness by declaring a solemn **fast**. She then arranged for two **wicked men** to bring false accusations against Naboth. She knew Israelite law well enough to know that two witnesses were needed (Dt 17:6). Then she had Naboth accused of verbally abusing **God** and the **king**.
21:13–14 Jezebel's evil scheme had been executed. What is not related here, though it clearly happened, is that Naboth's male heirs were also killed (2Kg 9:25–26). This was necessary since as long as Naboth had surviving heirs, the land belonged to his family.

against Naboth in the presence of the people, saying, "Naboth has cursed God and the king!" So they took him outside the city and stoned him to death with stones. [14] Then they sent word to Jezebel: "Naboth has been stoned to death."

[15] When Jezebel heard that Naboth had been stoned to death, she said to Ahab, "Get up and take possession of the vineyard of Naboth the Jezreelite who refused to give it to you for silver, since Naboth isn't alive, but dead." [16] When Ahab heard that Naboth was dead, he got up to go down to the vineyard of Naboth the Jezreelite to take possession of it.

The Lord's Judgment on Ahab

[17] Then the word of the Lord came to Elijah the Tishbite: [18] "Get up and go to meet King Ahab of Israel, who is in Samaria. He's in Naboth's vineyard, where he has gone to take possession of it. [19] Tell him, 'This is what the Lord says: Have you murdered and also taken possession?' Then tell him, 'This is what the Lord says: In the place where the dogs licked up Naboth's blood, the dogs will also lick up your blood!'"

[20] Ahab said to Elijah, "So, my enemy, you've found me, have you?"

He replied, "I have found you because you devoted yourself to do what is evil in the Lord's sight. [21] This is what the Lord says: [A] I am about to bring disaster on you and will eradicate your descendants:

I will wipe out all of Ahab's males,[B]
    both slave and free,[C] in Israel;

[22] I will make your house like the house of Jeroboam son of Nebat and like the house of Baasha son of Ahijah, because you have angered me and caused Israel to sin.' [23] The Lord also speaks of Jezebel: 'The dogs will eat Jezebel in the plot of land[D] at Jezreel:

[24]   Anyone who belongs to Ahab and dies
    in the city, the dogs will eat,

and anyone who dies in the field,
    the birds[E] will eat.'"

[25] Still, there was no one like Ahab, who devoted himself to do what was evil in the Lord's sight, because his wife Jezebel incited him. [26] He committed the most detestable acts by following idols as the Amorites had, whom the Lord had dispossessed before the Israelites.

[27] When Ahab heard these words, he tore his clothes, put sackcloth over his body, and fasted. He lay down in sackcloth and walked around subdued. [28] Then the word of the Lord came to Elijah the Tishbite: [29] "Have you seen how Ahab has humbled himself before me? I will not bring the disaster during his lifetime, because he has humbled himself before me. I will bring the disaster on his house during his son's lifetime."

Jehoshaphat's Alliance with Ahab

22 There was a lull of three years without war between Aram and Israel. [2] However, in the third year, King Jehoshaphat of Judah went to visit the king of Israel. [3] The king of Israel had said to his servants, "Don't you know that Ramoth-gilead is ours, but we're doing nothing to take it from the king of Aram?" [4] So he asked Jehoshaphat, "Will you go with me to fight Ramoth-gilead?"

Jehoshaphat replied to the king of Israel, "I am as you are, my people as your people, my horses as your horses." [5] But Jehoshaphat said to the king of Israel, "First, please ask what the Lord's will is."

[6] So the king of Israel gathered the prophets, about four hundred men, and asked them, "Should I go against Ramoth-gilead for war or should I refrain?"

They replied, "March up, and the Lord will hand it over to the king."

^A21:21 LXX; MT omits *This is what the Lord says*   ^B21:21 Lit *eliminate Ahab's one who urinates against the wall*   ^C21:21 Or *males, even the weak and impaired*; Hb obscure   ^D21:23 Some Hb mss, Syr, Tg, Vg, 2Kg 9:36; other Hb mss, LXX read *the rampart*   ^E21:24 Lit *birds of the sky*

21:15–16 Ahab's scruples had disappeared. **21:17–18** The prophet Elijah, who had faded into the background for a while, reenters the story. **21:19–24** The curse pronounced on Ahab came in two different statements. The first was expressed in God's words to Elijah and described the way **dogs** would **lick up** Ahab's **blood** in the same place that they licked up Naboth's blood and the blood of his sons. Second, disaster would come on all the **males**, both slave and free (or as some translations suggest, both "weak and incapacitated"), of Ahab's **house**. Dogs and carrion **birds** would devour their corpses. The statement that dogs would lick Ahab's blood in the same place that they licked Naboth's blood did not happen exactly this way. Naboth was killed in Jezreel, and Ahab's chariot was washed out in Samaria (22:38). However, the Bible implies that this prophecy

of Elijah was fulfilled when Joram, Ahab's son, was left for the dogs on Naboth's land in Jezreel (2Kg 9:24–26). On the other hand, v. 19 can also be translated, "Instead of dogs licking up Naboth's blood, dogs will lick up your blood—yes yours!" **21:25–26** Ahab was not excused of responsibility because his evil was influenced by his wife. See Gn 3:17. **21:27–29** In a surprising acceptance of a very shallow repentance (note Ahab's continued rebellion in the next chapter), God pronounced that the prophesied destruction on Ahab's **house** would happen only after Ahab's death. **22:1–3** For parts of **three years** there were no hostilities with Ben-hadad (ca 854–852 BC). During this time a successful defense against Assyria took place at the battle of Qarqar (853 BC). Then, within a year of that success, Ahab decided to retake **Ramoth-gilead**. This city

should have already been returned under the terms of the informal treaty made in Ahab's chariot (see note at 20:31–34). The exact location of this city is disputed, but it had a history of serving as an important administrative center for Israelite holdings in Transjordan. The best explanation for the statement that Jehoshaphat **went to visit the king of Israel** was that he was reporting for duty as a loyal servant—as a vassal of Ahab. **22:4–5** Jehoshaphat's words in these two verses reflect the two different roles he was playing. In v. 4, his words show that he was a faithful vassal of Ahab; but in v. 5, Jehoshaphat, the pious king of Judah, wanted to consult a legitimate prophet of the Lord. **22:6–7** Since these **prophets** came in response to Jehoshaphat's request, one might expect them to be followers of the Lord, but Jehoshaphat had to persist in asking for a real **prophet of the Lord**.

⁷ But Jehoshaphat asked, "Isn't there a prophet of the LORD here anymore? Let's ask him."

⁸ The king of Israel said to Jehoshaphat, "There is still one man who can inquire of the LORD, but I hate him because he never prophesies good about me, but only disaster. He is Micaiah son of Imlah."

"The king shouldn't say that!" Jehoshaphat replied.

⁹ So the king of Israel called an officer and said, "Hurry and get Micaiah son of Imlah!"

¹⁰ Now the king of Israel and King Jehoshaphat of Judah, clothed in royal attire, were each sitting on his own throne. They were on the threshing floor at the entrance to the gate of Samaria, and all the prophets were prophesying in front of them. ¹¹ Then Zedekiah son of Chenaanah made iron horns and said, "This is what the LORD says: 'You will gore the Arameans with these until they are finished off.'" ¹² And all the prophets were prophesying the same: "March up to Ramoth-gilead and succeed, for the LORD will hand it over to the king."

Micaiah's Message of Defeat

¹³ The messenger who went to call Micaiah instructed him, "Look, the words of the prophets are unanimously favorable for the king. So let your words be like theirs, and speak favorably."

¹⁴ But Micaiah said, "As the LORD lives, I will say whatever the LORD says to me."

¹⁵ So he went to the king, and the king asked him, "Micaiah, should we go to Ramoth-gilead for war, or should we refrain?"

Micaiah told him, "March up and succeed. The LORD will hand it over to the king."

¹⁶ But the king said to him, "How many times must I make you swear not to tell me anything but the truth in the name of the LORD?"

¹⁷ So Micaiah said:

I saw all Israel scattered on the hills like sheep without a shepherd.
And the LORD said,

"They have no master;
let everyone return home in peace."

¹⁸ So the king of Israel said to Jehoshaphat, "Didn't I tell you he never prophesies good about me, but only disaster?"

¹⁹ Then Micaiah said, "Therefore, hear the word of the LORD: I saw the LORD sitting on his throne, and the whole heavenly army was standing by him at his right hand and at his left hand. ²⁰ And the LORD said, 'Who will entice Ahab to march up and fall at Ramoth-gilead?' So one was saying this and another was saying that.

²¹ "Then a spirit came forward, stood in the LORD's presence, and said, 'I will entice him.'

²² "The LORD asked him, 'How?'

"He said, 'I will go and become a lying spirit in the mouth of all his prophets.'

"Then he said, 'You will certainly entice him and prevail. Go and do that.'

²³ "You see, the LORD has put a lying spirit into the mouth of all these prophets of yours, and the LORD has pronounced disaster against you."

²⁴ Then Zedekiah son of Chenaanah came up, hit Micaiah on the cheek, and demanded, "Did^A the Spirit of the LORD leave me to speak to you?"

²⁵ Micaiah replied, "You will soon see when you go to hide in an inner chamber on that day."

²⁶ Then the king of Israel ordered, "Take Micaiah and return him to Amon, the governor of the city, and to Joash, the king's son, ²⁷ and say, 'This is what the king says: Put this guy in prison and feed him only a little bread and water^B until I come back safely.'"

²⁸ But Micaiah said, "If you ever return safely, the LORD has not spoken through me." Then he said, "Listen, all you people!"^C

Ahab's Death

²⁹ Then the king of Israel and Judah's King Jehoshaphat went up to Ramoth-gilead. ³⁰ But the king of Israel said to Jehoshaphat, "I will disguise myself and go into battle, but you

---

^A22:24 Lit "Which way did ^B22:27 Lit him on bread of oppression and water of oppression ^C22:28 LXX omits Then he said, "Listen, all you people!"

22:8 Ahab's attitude toward prophets was pragmatic and agnostic, and it was determined by political expediency. He did not care what truth was. Prophets were tools for the king's political purposes.

22:9–10 A scene of competition between Micaiah and the pagan prophets is set up that reminds us of the scene at Mount Carmel—including the number of false prophets (v. 6).

22:11–12 Horns were symbols of power; **iron horns** represented an even more unbreakable and unyielding power, and they gave King Ahab exactly the message he wanted to hear. Ahab's superiority in chariot warfare supported this confidence in Israel's victory.

22:13–14 Expediency was the theme of the advice given to **Micaiah** by the **messenger**

sent by the king, but Micaiah's response was a statement of faithfulness and truth.

22:15–18 Micaiah was so sarcastic that **the king** recognized his irony. He demanded that the prophet tell him **the truth**. Micaiah then gave Ahab a message from the Lord—a vision of **sheep without a shepherd**. This should have recalled the king's role as shepherd, but Ahab rejected this clear warning.

22:19–23 A difficult issue is God's usage of **a lying spirit** to accomplish his purposes. Similarly, God's anger "stirred up" David (2Sm 24:1) to sin by permitting Satan to incite David to sin (1Ch 21:1). Without pretending to answer all the questions about this issue, we can say that God, at the least, permitted a lying spirit to mislead Ahab for a time. Note too that the deceit was given to prophets who were already presenting false witness.

In the end, the true prophet told Ahab the truth—he would die if he went to battle.

22:24–28 The remainder of this scene hardened the hostile positions toward the prophet **Micaiah** that had already been taken by the king.

22:29–30 Some critics find a discrepancy in Ahab's instructions for Jehoshaphat to put on his **royal attire** when he already had it on in v. 10. However, it is reasonable to suggest that Jehoshaphat had changed out of these for the trip to battle at **Ramoth-gilead**. Both kings probably arrived at the site of battle in war armor rather than royal clothes. It might have seemed prudent to the vassal king to accept the strategy that ordered him to go into battle in royal robes, for this would typically draw heat away from Ahab, the superior king.

wear your royal attire." So the king of Israel disguised himself and went into battle.

³¹ Now the king of Aram had ordered his thirty-two chariot commanders, "Do not fight with anyone at all^ except the king of Israel."

³² When the chariot commanders saw Jehoshaphat, they shouted, "He must be the king of Israel!" So they turned to fight against him, but Jehoshaphat cried out. ³³ When the chariot commanders saw that he was not the king of Israel, they turned back from pursuing him.

³⁴ But a man drew his bow without taking special aim and struck the king of Israel through the joints of his armor. So he said to his charioteer, "Turn around and take me out of the battle,ᵇ for I am badly wounded!" ³⁵ The battle raged throughout that day, and the king was propped up in his chariot facing the Arameans. He died that evening, and blood from his wound flowed into the bottom of the chariot. ³⁶ Then the cry rang out in the army as the sun set, declaring:

Each man to his own city,
and each man to his own land!

³⁷ So the king died and was brought to Samaria. They buried the king in Samaria. ³⁸ Then someone washed the chariot at the pool of Samaria. The dogs licked up his blood, and the prostitutes bathed in it, according to the word of the LORD that he had spoken.

³⁹ The rest of the events of Ahab's reign, along with all his accomplishments, including the ivory palace he built, and all the cities he built, are written in the Historical Record of Israel's Kings. ⁴⁰ Ahab rested with his ancestors, and his son Ahaziah became king in his place.

Judah's King Jehoshaphat

⁴¹ Jehoshaphat son of Asa became king over Judah in the fourth year of Israel's King Ahab. ⁴² Jehoshaphat was thirty-five years old when he became king; he reigned twenty-five years in Jerusalem. His mother's name was Azubah daughter of Shilhi. ⁴³ He walked in all the ways of his father Asa; he did not turn away from them but did what was right in the LORD's sight. However, the high places were not taken away;ᶜ the people still sacrificed and burned incense on the high places. ⁴⁴ Jehoshaphat also made peace with the king of Israel.

⁴⁵ The rest of the events of Jehoshaphat's reign, along with the might he exercised and how he waged war, are written in the Historical Record of Judah's Kings. ⁴⁶ He eradicated from the land the rest of the male cult prostitutes who were left from the days of his father Asa. ⁴⁷ There was no king in Edom; a deputy served as king. ⁴⁸ Jehoshaphat made ships of Tarshish to go to Ophir for gold, but they did not go because the ships were wrecked at Ezion-geber. ⁴⁹ At that time, Ahaziah son of Ahab said to Jehoshaphat, "Let my servants go with your servants in the ships," but Jehoshaphat was not willing. ⁵⁰ Jehoshaphat rested with his ancestors and was buried with them in the city of his ancestor David. His son Jehoram became king in his place.

Israel's King Ahaziah

⁵¹ Ahaziah son of Ahab became king over Israel in Samaria in the seventeenth year of Judah's King Jehoshaphat, and he reigned over Israel two years. ⁵² He did what was evil in the LORD's sight. He walked in the ways of his father, in the ways of his mother, and in the ways of Jeroboam son of Nebat, who had caused Israel to sin. ⁵³ He served Baal and bowed in worship to him. He angered the LORD God of Israel just as his father had done.

^22:31 Lit with small or with great   ᵇ22:34 LXX; MT reads camp   ᶜ22:43 LXX, Syr, Vg read he did not remove the high places

22:31–36 If, as the Assyrian report of the battle of Qarqar indicated, Ahab was stronger in chariotry than Ben-hadad, it was poor strategy to meet Ahab in a direct chariot battle. Perhaps concentrating his chariots on Ahab himself was a good alternate strategy for Ben-hadad. Ahab's counter strategy, having Jehoshaphat serve as the bait for such an attack, seemed to neutralize Ben-hadad's tactics. But God accomplished what human cunning could neither bring about nor prevent by ordaining the flight of a randomly shot arrow.
22:37–38 The Bible writers, at this point, were able to live with partial fulfillment of Elijah's prophecy about Ahab's death. One part was fulfilled when the **dogs licked up his blood**, though Ahab did not die at the place the prophecy indicated (see note at 21:19–24). Later, dogs licked up the blood of one of Ahab's sons in Jezreel when Joram's body

was dumped there (2Kg 9:24–26). Possibly this later event marks the complete fulfillment of the prophecy from 1Kg 21:19–24 since a fate pronounced over a father can be representatively fulfilled in his son and since, according to ancient understanding, the blood of a father courses through the veins of his son.
22:39 Ahab's **ivory palace** was probably a palace decorated with paneling containing ivory inlay.
22:41–44 More is said about King **Jehoshaphat** in the record of Ahab than is said about him in his own record. The evaluative part tells us that Jehoshaphat was a good king, but the fact that he made **peace with the king of Israel** may contain a veiled criticism (2Ch 19:1)—particularly since making peace with Israel meant accepting a vassal role to the king of Israel.
22:45–50 Despite Asa's good intentions, his reforms left some work undone. His son

Jehoshaphat had to remove the remaining **male cult prostitutes**. Edom seems to have been controlled by Jehoshaphat through the agency of a deputy. But the most noteworthy event may have been the failed effort to revive the sea trade to Africa for **gold**. After one failed attempt, Jehoshaphat compromised his loyalty to the house of Ahab in refusing to cooperate with **Ahaziah** in another attempt at restoring that trade. We cannot realize the importance of this refusal unless we know that Jehoshaphat was a vassal king to Israel.
22:51–53 The account of **Ahaziah** is contained at the end of 1 Kings and the beginning of 2 Kings. The assessment of his reign is simple: **He did what was evil in the LORD's sight** in that he supported the worship of **Baal** (Baal-melkart; see note at 16:23–28).

◥ Introduction to 2 Kings

Circumstances of Writing

Scholars cannot identify the authors of any portions of 2 Kings. Traditional guesses such as Samuel and Jeremiah lack evidence, although a prominent worshiper of the Lord, such as Jeremiah, would have been influential in the circles that produced these books. Since the books of 1 and 2 Kings clearly incorporated many earlier documents, the complete authorship would include all writers who contributed to the source documents of this work. At some point, the Holy Spirit worked in the human authors to authenticate the inspired, inerrant books of 1 and 2 Kings. The final stage of composition or compilation had to come after the release of Jehoiachin from Babylonian imprisonment (ca 562 BC). That edition may have added only a postscript to a work completed years earlier, or it may have involved significant additions.

The history recorded in 1 and 2 Kings covers approximately 410 years. First Kings begins around 970 BC with the death of King David; 2 Kings ends around 560 BC with the release of King Jehoiachin from prison. During this time, the nation of Israel split into two kingdoms (930 BC), and both kingdoms went into exile (Israel in 722 BC and Judah in 587 BC).

Contribution to the Bible

For the Bible writers, history could not have existed without God's purposes. This makes all history theological. The books of 1 and 2 Kings interpreted Hebrew history in light of Old Testament covenant theology. The Babylonian exile created the need for this work of historical apologetics. The exiles needed to explain the failure of the religious program established by the sovereign God. In the Deuteronomistic history—Joshua, Judges, 1 and 2 Samuel, and 1 and 2 Kings—this failure was consistently explained as the failures of the people to live up to their part of the covenant.

Structure

The organizing principle of 1 and 2 Kings is not story or narrative. Kings is unique because its basic structural units are the formulaic royal records. Formal openers (1Kg 15:9–10) and closers (1Kg 15:23–24) usually identify the boundaries of the record of a particular monarch. Then the writer could insert other types of literature before, between, and after the openers and closers: narratives, prayers, descriptions, etc. But the most important element is the evaluation of the ruler's faithfulness to the covenant (1Kg 15:11–15). All of these materials make up a history of covenant obedience or disobedience.

See the introduction to 1 Kings for the timeline.

Ahaziah's Sickness and Death

1 After Ahab's death, Moab rebelled against Israel. [2] Ahaziah had fallen through the latticed window of his upstairs room in Samaria and was injured. So he sent messengers, instructing them, "Go inquire of Baal-zebub,[A] the god of Ekron, whether I will recover from this injury."

[3] But the angel of the LORD said to Elijah the Tishbite, "Go and meet the messengers of the king of Samaria and say to them, 'Is it because there is no God in Israel that you are going to inquire of Baal-zebub, the god of Ekron? [4] Therefore, this is what the LORD says: You will not get up from your sickbed; you will certainly die.' " Then Elijah left.

[5] The messengers returned to the king, who asked them, "Why have you come back?"

[6] They replied, "A man came to meet us and said, 'Go back to the king who sent you and declare to him, "This is what the LORD says: Is it because there is no God in Israel that you're sending these men to inquire of Baal-zebub, the god of Ekron? Therefore, you will not get up from your sickbed; you will certainly die." ' "

[7] The king asked them, "What sort of man came up to meet you and spoke those words to you?"

[8] They replied, "A hairy man with a leather belt around his waist."

He said, "It's Elijah the Tishbite."

[9] So King Ahaziah sent a captain with his fifty men to Elijah. When the captain went up to him, he was sitting on top of the hill. He announced, "Man of God, the king declares, 'Come down!' "

[10] Elijah responded to the captain, "If I am a man of God, may fire come down from heaven and consume you and your fifty men." Then fire came down from heaven and consumed him and his fifty men.

[11] So the king sent another captain with his fifty men to Elijah. He took in the situation[B] and announced, "Man of God, this is what the king says: 'Come down immediately!' "

[12] Elijah responded, "If I am a man of God, may fire come down from heaven and consume you and your fifty men." So a divine fire[C] came down from heaven and consumed him and his fifty men.

[13] Then the king sent a third captain with his fifty men. The third captain went up and fell on his knees in front of Elijah and begged him, "Man of God, please let my life and the lives of these fifty servants of yours be precious to you. [14] Already fire has come down from heaven and consumed the first two captains with their companies, but this time let my life be precious to you."

[15] The angel of the LORD said to Elijah, "Go down with him. Don't be afraid of him." So he got up and went down with him to the king.

[16] Then Elijah said to King Ahaziah, "This is what the LORD says: 'Because you have sent messengers to inquire of Baal-zebub, the god of Ekron — is it because there is no God in Israel for you to inquire of his will? — you will not get up from your sickbed; you will certainly die.' "

[17] Ahaziah died according to the word of the LORD that Elijah had spoken. Since he had no son, Joram[D] became king in his place. This happened in the second year of Judah's King Jehoram son of Jehoshaphat.[E] [18] The rest of the events of Ahaziah's reign, along with his accomplishments, are written in the Historical Record of Israel's Kings.[F]

Elijah in the Whirlwind

2 The time had come for the LORD to take Elijah up to heaven in a whirlwind. Elijah and Elisha were traveling from Gilgal, [2] and Elijah said to Elisha, "Stay here; the LORD is sending me on to Bethel."

But Elisha replied, "As the LORD lives and as you yourself live, I will not leave you." So they went down to Bethel.

[3] Then the sons of the prophets who were at Bethel came out to Elisha and said, "Do you know that the LORD will take your master away from you today?"

He said, "Yes, I know. Be quiet."

[4] Elijah said to him, "Elisha, stay here; the LORD is sending me to Jericho."

---

^1:2 = Lord of the Flies   ^1:11 Lit He answered   ^1:12 Lit a fire of God   ^1:17 Lit Jehoram; 2Kg 8:16   ^1:17 LXX omits in the second year . . . Jehoshaphat   ^1:18 LXX adds 4 more vv. here similar to 2Kg 3:1–3.

1:1 This brief statement about the Moabite rebellion and the later complete record of that war (3:4–27) brackets data that deals with Ahaziah, Elijah, and Joram. This bracketing indicates that all these materials should be related to the rebellion.
1:2 The first incident thus bracketed is Ahaziah's injury and subsequent query of **Baal-zebub**, "Lord of the Flies." Baal-zebub was the god of **Ekron**, one of the five cities of the Philistine pentapolis. Turning to pagan deities was disloyalty to God.
1:3–8 Elijah condemned King Ahaziah for seeking counsel from a pagan deity. Elijah challenged King Ahaziah on this false

worship. The question, **Is it because there is no God in Israel**, rhetorically highlighted Ahaziah's lack of faith (v. 16). Then Elijah announced that Ahaziah would die.
1:13–15 The **third captain** had learned the lesson of God's power and appealed for mercy.
1:17–18 Ahaziah's record ends with the statements of his death and the succession of his brother, **Joram**.
2:1 The route of travel from northerly **Gilgal**, through Bethel, and then to Jericho showed that this was not the well-known Gilgal near Jericho. The exact location of this Gilgal is unknown.

2:2 In this incident **Elijah** repeatedly urged **Elisha** to remain behind, perhaps to test his determination to be formally recognized as Elijah's successor. Persistence was a key trait of faithful prophets.
2:3 The presence of godly **sons of the prophets** indicated that prophets of the Lord were still tolerated around **Bethel**, despite Bethel's illegal worship. The conversations show that Elijah's impending departure was common knowledge.
2:4–6 Again **Elisha** was urged to remain behind, again he insisted on following, and again the prophets—this time the **prophets** of **Jericho**—declared that Elijah's departure

But Elisha said, "As the Lord lives and as you yourself live, I will not leave you." So they went to Jericho.

⁵ Then the sons of the prophets who were in Jericho came up to Elisha and said, "Do you know that the Lord will take your master away from you today?"

He said, "Yes, I know. Be quiet."

⁶ Elijah said to him, "Stay here; the Lord is sending me to the Jordan."

But Elisha said, "As the Lord lives and as you yourself live, I will not leave you." So the two of them went on.

⁷ Fifty men from the sons of the prophets came and stood observing them at a distance while the two of them stood by the Jordan. ⁸ Elijah took his mantle, rolled it up, and struck the water, which parted to the right and left. Then the two of them crossed over on dry ground. ⁹ When they had crossed over, Elijah said to Elisha, "Tell me what I can do for you before I am taken from you."

So Elisha answered, "Please, let me inherit two shares of your spirit."

¹⁰ Elijah replied, "You have asked for something difficult. If you see me being taken from you, you will have it. If not, you won't."

¹¹ As they continued walking and talking, a chariot of fire with horses of fire suddenly appeared and separated the two of them. Then Elijah went up into heaven in the whirlwind. ¹² As Elisha watched, he kept crying out, "My father, my father, the chariots and horsemen of Israel!"

Elisha Succeeds Elijah

When he could see him no longer, he took hold of his own clothes, tore them in two, ¹³ picked up the mantle that had fallen off Elijah, and went back and stood on the bank of the Jordan. ¹⁴ He took the mantle Elijah had dropped, and he struck the water. "Where is the Lord God of Elijah?" he asked. He struck the water himself, and it parted to the right and the left, and Elisha crossed over.

¹⁵ When the sons of the prophets from Jericho who were observing saw him, they said, "The spirit of Elijah rests on Elisha." They came to meet him and bowed down to the ground in front of him.

¹⁶ Then the sons of the prophets said to Elisha, "Since there are fifty strong men here with your servants, please let them go and search for your master. Maybe the Spirit of the Lord has carried him away and put him on one of the mountains or into one of the valleys."

He answered, "Don't send them."

¹⁷ However, they urged him to the point of embarrassment, so he said, "Send them." They sent fifty men, who looked for three days but did not find him. ¹⁸ When they returned to him in Jericho where he was staying, he said to them, "Didn't I tell you not to go?"

¹⁹ The men of the city said to Elisha, "My lord can see that even though the city's location is good, the water is bad and the land unfruitful."

²⁰ He replied, "Bring me a new bowl and put salt in it."

After they had brought him one, ²¹ Elisha went out to the spring, threw salt in it, and said, "This is what the Lord says: 'I have healed this water. No longer will death or unfruitfulness result from it.' " ²² Therefore, the water still remains healthy today according to the word that Elisha spoke.

²³ From there Elisha went up to Bethel. As he was walking up the path, some small boys came out of the city and jeered at him, chanting, "Go up, baldy! Go up, baldy!" ²⁴ He turned around, looked at them, and cursed them in the name of the Lord. Then two female bears came out of the woods and mauled forty-two of the children. ²⁵ From there Elisha went to Mount Carmel, and then he returned to Samaria.

Israel's King Joram

3 Joram son of Ahab became king over Israel in Samaria during the eighteenth year of Judah's King Jehoshaphat, and he reigned twelve years. ² He did what was evil in the Lord's sight, but not like his father and mother, for he removed the sacred pillar of Baal his father had made. ³ Nevertheless, Joram clung to the sins that Jeroboam son of Nebat had caused Israel to commit. He did not turn away from them.

---

was near. The repetition underscores the importance of these events.

2:7–8 God's power was demonstrated again, in a very historic and traditional way, as **Elijah** miraculously made a path through the **Jordan** River, reminiscent of God opening the Red Sea when his people left Egypt (Ex 14:21–31) and opening the Jordan as Israel prepared to take the promised land (Jos 3:14–17).

2:9–10 The **two shares** was an indicator of the legitimate heir. Elisha's renewed request for that position highlighted the importance of the role and that Elisha was the person to assume the role. Since this role had already been assigned to Elisha, this request was not arrogant. However, despite the fact

that **Elisha** had already been designated as Elijah's heir (1Kg 19:19–21), Elisha must still observe Elijah's departure for this promise to be implemented.

2:12 The words **chariots and horsemen of Israel** would be repeated at Elisha's death (13:14).

2:13–15 Elijah's **mantle** showed that **Elisha** was the legitimate heir to **Elijah**. We should not attribute magic to the mantle. The **sons of the prophets** recognized Elisha's new role with proper deference.

2:16–18 The unsuccessful search for Elijah's body confirmed that a miraculous work of God had occurred.

2:19–22 Elisha confirmed his role as a channel for God's works by performing a

miracle—one that demonstrated the practical benefits of God's great acts.

2:23–24 The word translated as **boys** is often used for mature men (Boaz's "servant," Ru 2:5), but the behavior of the group suggests they were young. In all likelihood the **children** were preteens or young teens. This passage is often overstated as if all the mockers were killed; **mauled** often connotes being wounded rather than killed.

2:25 Elisha lived at **Samaria** under the eyes of the unfaithful kings of Israel.

3:1–3 These formal statements mark the beginning of Joram's record. **Joram** was bad, but not as bad as Ahab and Jezebel. He suppressed Baalism by removing Baal's

Moab's Rebellion against Israel

4 King Mesha of Moab was a sheep breeder. He used to pay the king of Israel one hundred thousand lambs and the wool of one hundred thousand rams, **5** but when Ahab died, the king of Moab rebelled against the king of Israel. **6** So King Joram marched out from Samaria at that time and mobilized all Israel. **7** Then he sent a message to King Jehoshaphat of Judah: "The king of Moab has rebelled against me. Will you go with me to fight against Moab?"

Jehoshaphat said, "I will go. I am as you are, my people as your people, my horses as your horses."

8 He asked, "Which route should we take?"

He replied, "The route of the Wilderness of Edom."

9 So the king of Israel, the king of Judah, and the king of Edom set out. After they had traveled their indirect route for seven days, they had no water for the army or the animals with them. **10** Then the king of Israel said, "Oh no, the LORD has summoned these three kings, only to hand them over to Moab."

11 But Jehoshaphat said, "Isn't there a prophet of the LORD here? Let's inquire of the LORD through him."

One of the servants of the king of Israel answered, "Elisha son of Shaphat, who used to pour water on Elijah's hands, is here."

12 Jehoshaphat affirmed, "The word of the LORD is with him." So the king of Israel and Jehoshaphat and the king of Edom went to him.

13 However, Elisha said to King Joram of Israel, "What do we have in common? Go to the prophets of your father and your mother!"

But the king of Israel replied, "No, because it is the LORD who has summoned these three kings to hand them over to Moab."

14 Elisha responded, "By the life of the LORD of Armies, before whom I stand: If I did not have respect for King Jehoshaphat of Judah, I wouldn't look at you; I would not take notice of you. **15** Now, bring me a musician."

While the musician played, the LORD's hand came on Elisha. **16** Then he said, "This is what the LORD says: 'Dig ditch after ditch in this wadi.' **17** For the LORD says, 'You will not see wind or rain, but the wadi will be filled with water, and you will drink — you and your cattle and your animals.' **18** This is easy in the LORD's sight. He will also hand Moab over to you. **19** Then you will attack every fortified city and every choice city. You will cut down every good tree and stop up every spring. You will ruin every good piece of land with stones."

20 About the time for the grain offering the next morning, water suddenly came from the direction of Edom and filled the land.

21 All Moab had heard that the kings had come up to fight against them. So all who could bear arms, from the youngest to the oldest, were summoned and took their stand at the border. **22** When they got up early in the morning, the sun was shining on the water, and the Moabites saw that the water across from them was red like blood. **23** "This is blood!" they exclaimed. "The kings have crossed swords^A and their men have killed one another. So, to the spoil, Moab!"

24 However, when the Moabites came to Israel's camp, the Israelites attacked them, and they fled from them. So Israel went into the land attacking the Moabites. **25** They would destroy the cities, and each of them would throw a stone to cover every good piece of land. They would stop up every spring and cut down every good tree. This went on until only the buildings of Kir-hareseth were left. Then men with slings surrounded the city and attacked it.

26 When the king of Moab saw that the battle was too fierce for him, he took seven hundred swordsmen with him to try to break through to the king of Edom, but they could not do it. **27** So he took his firstborn son, who was to become king in his place, and offered him as a burnt offering on the city wall. Great wrath was on the Israelites, and they withdrew from him and returned to their land.

The Widow's Oil Multiplied

4 One of the wives of the sons of the prophets cried out to Elisha, "Your servant, my husband, has died. You know that your servant

---

^**3:23** Or *have been laid waste*

sacred pillar, but there were still hundreds of priests of Baal when he died.
3:4–5 The text returns to the Moabite rebellion (1:1). Mentioning this rebellion at 2Kg 1:1 and 3:4–5 puts Ahaziah's unfaithfulness and Elijah's departure clearly in the context of this war.
3:6–7 King Joram **mobilized all Israel** and both of his remaining vassal kings, Jehoshaphat of Judah and the king of Edom (v. 9).
3:8 The choice of the invasion **route** was particularly deliberate. Moab lay directly across the Dead Sea from Judah. Moab was most directly approached from the north. The choice to attack Moab from the south

through **Edom** thus evaded the Moabite strong points and helped to assure Edom's involvement in the campaign.
3:11–12 Once again, **Jehoshaphat** pointed a king of Israel toward seeking counsel from **the LORD** (cp. 1Kg 22:5). Two surprising facts then emerged. The first was that the man of God, **Elisha**, was there. But the familiarity between Elisha and the king's household is even more surprising.
3:13 For a king with as little faith in God as Joram exhibited, it was hubris to say, **it is the LORD who has summoned these three kings**.
3:14–18 God responded only because of the godly **Jehoshaphat**. Elisha's **musician**

provided the setting in which he could attend to God rather than being distracted.
3:25 Then the combined armies devastated Moab, except for the capital city, **Kir-hareseth**, modern Kerak. This devastation was also a blow to the north-south caravan route that passed through Transjordan and particularly through the Moabite capital.
3:26–27 Finally the devastation came to the point at which the **king of Moab** offered his own crown prince and heir as a human sacrifice. The coalition **withdrew**, and Moab remained independent, though thoroughly devastated.
4:1–7:20 Up to this point, the records of conflict between the kings of Israel and the prophets have been incorporated

Elijah and Elisha

ELIJAH ("YAHWEH IS MY GOD")

Prophesied no rain in the land as God's judgment for Ahab's and Israel's idolatry *(1Kg 17:1)*

An example of a righteous man's effective prayer *(Jms 5:17–18)*

Provided food for a Gentile widow and raised her son from the dead *(1Kg 17:8–24)*

A characteristic of Jesus's ministry among Gentiles *(Lk 4:23–26)*

Faced off against 450 prophets of Baal and executed them; prayed for end of the famine *(1Kg 18)*

Fled from Jezebel and experienced the Lord at Horeb in a still, small voice; told to anoint successors for Aram, Israel, and himself *(1Kg 19)*

ELIJAH CALLS ELISHA

Called Elisha as his successor *(1Kg 19:19–21)*

Confronted Ahab over Naboth's vineyard and prophesied judgment on his house *(1Kg 21:17–29)*

Confronted Ahaziah for inquiring of a foreign god; called fire from heaven to destroy Ahaziah's men sent to arrest him *(2Kg 1)*

An example not followed by Jesus *(Lk 9:51–56)*

ELIJAH'S DEPARTURE

Parted the Jordan River with his mantle to cross on dry ground and then taken into heaven in a whirlwind by a chariot and horses of fire *(2Kg 2:8–11)*

Appeared along with Moses at the transfiguration of Christ *(Lk 9:28–36)*

Elijah was foretold to come again as a forerunner of the Messiah; this prophecy was fulfilled in John the Baptist *(Mal 4:5–6; Mt 17:10–13; Lk 1:16–17)*.

ELISHA ("GOD SAVES")

ELISHA'S CALL

Called as Elijah's successor *(1Kg 19:19–21)*

Elisha's response serves as an example of discipleship *(Lk 9:61–62)*.

ELIJAH'S DEPARTURE

Witnessed Elijah's departure and received his mantle; parted the Jordan River to cross on dry ground *(2Kg 2:11–15)*

Gave instructions to a widow of a prophet to pour oil into empty jars in order to pay her debt and provide for her family *(2Kg 4:1–7)*

Rewarded the Shunammite woman with a son for her hospitality; later raised her son from the dead *(2Kg 4:8–37)*

Jesus raised people from the dead *(Lk 7:11–17; Jn 11)*.

Multiplied bread for the people to eat and had some left over *(2Kg 4:42–44)*

Jesus fed five thousand from bread and fish and had some left over *(Jn 6:1–14)*.

Healed Naaman, a Gentile, of leprosy *(2Kg 5:1–19)*

A characteristic of Jesus's ministry among Gentiles; he also healed those with skin diseases *(Lk 4:23–27; 5:12–14)*

Defeated the Arameans sent to capture him, being surrounded by horses and chariots of fire; Arameans blinded and led to the king of Israel *(2Kg 6:8–23)*

Anointed Hazael as king over Aram and Jehu as king over Israel, fulfilling the Lord's word to Elijah at Horeb *(2Kg 8:7–15; 9:1–10)*

Died and was buried; later, a dead Israelite was thrown into Elisha's tomb—he touched Elisha's bones, was revived, and stood up *(2Kg 13:20–21)*

feared the LORD. Now the creditor is coming to take my two children as his slaves."

² Elisha asked her, "What can I do for you? Tell me, what do you have in the house?"

She said, "Your servant has nothing in the house except a jar of oil."

³ Then he said, "Go out and borrow empty containers from all your neighbors. Do not get just a few. ⁴ Then go in and shut the door behind you and your sons, and pour oil into all these containers. Set the full ones to one side."

⁵ So she left.

After she had shut the door behind her and her sons, they kept bringing her containers, and she kept pouring. ⁶ When they were full, she said to her son, "Bring me another container."

But he replied, "There aren't any more." Then the oil stopped.

⁷ She went and told the man of God, and he said, "Go sell the oil and pay your debt; you and your sons can live on the rest."

The Shunammite Woman's Hospitality

⁸ One day Elisha went to Shunem. A prominent woman who lived there persuaded him to eat some food. So whenever he passed by, he stopped there to eat. ⁹ Then she said to her husband, "I know that the one who often passes by here is a holy man of God, ¹⁰ so let's make a small, walled-in upper room and put a bed, a table, a chair, and a lamp there for him. Whenever he comes, he can stay there."

The Shunammite Woman's Son

¹¹ One day he came there and stopped at the upstairs room to lie down. ¹² He ordered his attendant Gehazi, "Call this Shunammite woman." So he called her and she stood before him.

¹³ Then he said to Gehazi, "Say to her, 'Look, you've gone to all this trouble for us. What can we do for you? Can we speak on your behalf to the king or to the commander of the army?'"

She answered, "I am living among my own people."

¹⁴ So he asked, "Then what should be done for her?"

Gehazi answered, "Well, she has no son, and her husband is old."

¹⁵ "Call her," Elisha said. So Gehazi called her, and she stood in the doorway. ¹⁶ Elisha said, "At this time next year you will have a son in your arms."

Then she said, "No, my lord. Man of God, do not lie to your servant."

¹⁷ The woman conceived and gave birth to a son at the same time the following year, as Elisha had promised her.

The Shunammite's Son Raised

¹⁸ The child grew and one day went out to his father and the harvesters. ¹⁹ Suddenly he complained to his father, "My head! My head!"

His father told his servant, "Carry him to his mother." ²⁰ So he picked him up and took him to his mother. The child sat on her lap until noon and then died. ²¹ She went up and laid him on the bed of the man of God, shut him in, and left.

²² She summoned her husband and said, "Please send me one of the servants and one of the donkeys, so I can hurry to the man of God and come back again."

²³ But he said, "Why go to him today? It's not a New Moon or a Sabbath."

She replied, "It's all right."

²⁴ Then she saddled the donkey and said to her servant, "Go fast; don't slow the pace for me unless I tell you." ²⁵ So she came to the man of God at Mount Carmel.

When the man of God saw her at a distance, he said to his attendant Gehazi, "Look, there's the Shunammite woman. ²⁶ Run out to meet her and ask, 'Are you all right? Is your husband all right? Is your son all right?'"

And she answered, "It's all right."

²⁷ When she came up to the man of God at the mountain, she clung to his feet. Gehazi came to push her away, but the man of God said, "Leave her alone — she is in severe anguish, and the LORD has hidden it from me. He hasn't told me."

²⁸ Then she said, "Did I ask my lord for a son? Didn't I say, 'Do not lie to me?'"

²⁹ So Elisha said to Gehazi, "Tuck your mantle under your belt, take my staff with you, and go. If you meet anyone, don't stop to greet him, and if a man greets you, don't answer him. Then place my staff on the boy's face."

---

into the overall chronological structure of these books. In these four chapters the treatment of miracles changes. The writer here recorded miracles separated from the sequential structure of the book. Because of this technique some of the events involve anonymous kings whose chronological place may be unclear. Unless chronological sequence is explicitly indicated, these events should not be taken as chronologically arranged. The normal chronological pattern of 1 and 2 Kings resumes with the record of Jehoram, son of Jehoshaphat (8:16).

4:2–7 A miraculous provision by the man of God, **Elisha**, compensated for the injustice and the failure of the system that God had established but that apostasy had corrupted. **4:8–10** The **man of God** made such an impression that one **prominent** family wished to show special hospitality to him. In a society that had become largely pagan, a display of friendship to the man of God possibly indicated faith in God. **4:14–17** The woman was barren in a society in which barrenness was seen as a curse. **4:18–26** When death entered the home of the **Shunammite** family, there was another

opportunity to show that God could miraculously bless. **4:27** Elisha modeled both sensitivity and a recognition of his own limitations. His words **the LORD has hidden it from me** showed limitation to the knowledge and power God granted him. **4:29–31** When sent to bring healing to the woman's son, **Gehazi** was to be focused on the task. Gehazi's failed attempt to bring healing also revealed the human limitations of the man of God. Elisha had seemed confident that sending Gehazi was sufficient to heal the woman's son.

³⁰ The boy's mother said to Elisha, "As the LORD lives and as you yourself live, I will not leave you." So he got up and followed her. ³¹ Gehazi went ahead of them and placed the staff on the boy's face, but there was no sound or sign of life, so he went back to meet Elisha and told him, "The boy didn't wake up." ³² When Elisha got to the house, he discovered the boy lying dead on his bed. ³³ So he went in, closed the door behind the two of them, and prayed to the LORD. ³⁴ Then he went up and lay on the boy: he put mouth to mouth, eye to eye, hand to hand. While he bent down over him, the boy's flesh became warm. ³⁵ Elisha got up, went into the house, and paced back and forth. Then he went up and bent down over him again. The boy sneezed seven times and opened his eyes. ³⁶ Elisha called Gehazi and said, "Call the Shunammite woman." He called her and she came. Then Elisha said, "Pick up your son." ³⁷ She came, fell at his feet, and bowed to the ground; she picked up her son and left.

The Deadly Stew

³⁸ When Elisha returned to Gilgal, there was a famine in the land. The sons of the prophets were sitting before him. He said to his attendant, "Put on the large pot and make stew for the sons of the prophets." ³⁹ One went out to the field to gather herbs and found a wild vine from which he gathered as many wild gourds as his garment would hold. Then he came back and cut them up into the pot of stew, but they were unaware of what they were.^A ⁴⁰ They served some for the men to eat, but when they ate the stew they cried out, "There's death in the pot, man of God!" And they were unable to eat it. ⁴¹ Then Elisha said, "Get some flour." He threw it into the pot and said, "Serve it for the people to eat." And there was nothing bad in the pot.

The Multiplied Bread

⁴² A man from Baal-shalishah came to the man of God with his sack full of^B twenty loaves of barley bread from the first bread of the harvest. Elisha said, "Give it to the people to eat." ⁴³ But Elisha's attendant asked, "What? Am I to set this before a hundred men?"

"Give it to the people to eat," Elisha said, "for this is what the LORD says: 'They will eat, and they will have some left over.'" ⁴⁴ So he set it before them, and as the LORD had promised, they ate and had some left over.

Naaman's Disease Healed

5 Naaman, commander of the army for the king of Aram, was a man important to his master and highly regarded because through him, the LORD had given victory to Aram. The man was a valiant warrior, but he had a skin disease. ² Aram had gone on raids and brought back from the land of Israel a young girl who served Naaman's wife. ³ She said to her mistress, "If only my master were with the prophet who is in Samaria, he would cure him of his skin disease." ⁴ So Naaman went and told his master what the girl from the land of Israel had said. ⁵ Therefore, the king of Aram said, "Go, and I will send a letter with you to the king of Israel."

So he went and took with him 750 pounds^C of silver, 150 pounds^D of gold, and ten sets of clothing. ⁶ He brought the letter to the king of Israel, and it read:

When this letter comes to you, note that I have sent you my servant Naaman for you to cure him of his skin disease.

⁷ When the king of Israel read the letter, he tore his clothes and asked, "Am I God, killing and giving life, that this man expects me to cure a man of his skin disease? Recognize^E that he is only picking a fight with me." ⁸ When Elisha the man of God heard that the king of Israel had torn his clothes, he sent a message to the king: "Why have you torn your clothes? Have him come to me, and he will know there is a prophet in Israel." ⁹ So Naaman

---

^A 4:39 *of what they were* added for clarity ^B 4:42 Or *with some heads of fresh grain and* ^C 5:5 Lit *10 talents* ^D 5:5 Lit *6,000 shekels* ^E 5:7 Lit *Know and see*

4:32–37 When Elisha arrived, he carried out a more complicated procedure for healing the son. Here Elisha's success was dependent on his prayer **to the LORD**.
4:38 Since the text had earlier placed **Elisha** and the prophets in a northern **Gilgal** near Bethel, this is likely that same northern Gilgal. The prophets' way of life, at least on some occasions, demanded that they forage for their food. Apparently they partly supported themselves by such foraging and partly by gifts from pious Israelites.
4:39–40 While foraging, one of the prophets **gathered** some poisonous **gourds**.
4:41 Elisha neutralized the poison with another miraculous deed. The lesson was that

God's power could protect his people from careless dangers even in a serious famine.
4:42 Another opportunity for a miraculous provision occurred when a supporter brought a gift of **bread** to the prophets. This gift could indicate that the giver had rejected the apostate priesthood of the north since he gave this gift to the faithful prophets of the Lord. The location of **Baal-shalishah** remains uncertain.
4:43–44 This miracle sounds remarkably similar to the feeding of the 5,000 in the NT.
5:1–27 This chapter gives an example of God's miracle-working influence reaching out to the world and impacting a pagan nation, possibly at a time when that nation was a deadly enemy of Israel.

5:1 Though **Naaman** was regarded as a great military leader, we cannot identify the specific **victory** that earned him this respect.
5:2–3 The young Hebrew captive, in an attitude of faith and resigned to the brutality of the age, seemed to have accepted her situation with a positive attitude, while retaining her personal faith in God. She wished that her **master** could experience God's miraculous healing.
5:7 The reaction of the **king of Israel**, particularly his fear that Damascus was seeking a pretext for war, showed that this was a time of weakness for Israel.
5:8–9 These verses give the most explicit statement of the story's intent—that people might **know there** was **a prophet in Israel**.

came with his horses and chariots and stood at the door of Elisha's house.

¹⁰ Then Elisha sent him a messenger, who said, "Go wash seven times in the Jordan and your skin will be restored and you will be clean."

¹¹ But Naaman got angry and left, saying, "I was telling myself: He will surely come out, stand and call on the name of the LORD his God, and wave his hand over the place and cure the skin disease. ¹² Aren't Abana and Pharpar, the rivers of Damascus, better than all the waters of Israel? Couldn't I wash in them and be clean?" So he turned and left in a rage.

¹³ But his servants approached and said to him, "My father, if the prophet had told you to do some great thing, would you not have done it? How much more should you do it when he only tells you, 'Wash and be clean'?" ¹⁴ So Naaman went down and dipped himself in the Jordan seven times, according to the command of the man of God. Then his skin was restored and became like the skin of a small boy, and he was clean.

¹⁵ Then Naaman and his whole company went back to the man of God, stood before him, and declared, "I know there's no God in the whole world except in Israel. Therefore, please accept a gift from your servant."

¹⁶ But Elisha said, "As the LORD lives, in whose presence I stand, I will not accept it." Naaman urged him to accept it, but he refused.

¹⁷ Naaman responded, "If not, please let your servant be given as much soil as a pair of mules can carry, for your servant will no longer offer a burnt offering or a sacrifice to any other god but the LORD. ¹⁸ However, in a particular matter may the LORD pardon your servant: When my master, the king of Aram, goes into the temple of Rimmon to bow in worship while he is leaning on my arm,^A and I have to bow in the temple of Rimmon — when I bow^B in the temple of Rimmon, may the LORD pardon your servant in this matter."

¹⁹ So he said to him, "Go in peace."

Gehazi's Greed Punished

After Naaman had traveled a short distance from Elisha, ²⁰ Gehazi, the attendant of Elisha the man of God, thought, "My master has let this Aramean Naaman off lightly by not accepting from him what he brought. As the LORD lives, I will run after him and get something from him."

²¹ So Gehazi pursued Naaman. When Naaman saw someone running after him, he got down from the chariot to meet him and asked, "Is everything all right?"

²² Gehazi said, "It's all right. My master has sent me to say, 'I have just now discovered that two young men from the sons of the prophets have come to me from the hill country of Ephraim. Please give them seventy-five pounds^c of silver and two sets of clothing.'"

²³ But Naaman insisted, "Please, accept one hundred fifty pounds."^D He urged Gehazi and then packed one hundred fifty pounds of silver in two bags with two sets of clothing. Naaman gave them to two of his attendants who carried them ahead of Gehazi. ²⁴ When Gehazi came to the hill,^E he took the gifts from them and deposited them in the house. Then he dismissed the men, and they left.

²⁵ Gehazi came and stood by his master. "Where did you go, Gehazi?" Elisha asked him.

He replied, "Your servant didn't go anywhere."

²⁶ "And my heart didn't go^F when the man got down from his chariot to meet you," Elisha said. "Is this a time to accept silver and clothing, olive orchards and vineyards, flocks and herds, and male and female slaves? ²⁷ Therefore, Naaman's skin disease will cling to you and your descendants forever." So Gehazi went out from his presence diseased, resembling snow.^G

The Floating Ax Head

6 The sons of the prophets said to Elisha, "Please notice that the place where we live under your supervision^H is too small for us. ² Please let us go to the Jordan where we can

---

^A 5:18 Lit worship, and he leans on my hand   ^B 5:18 LXX, Vg read when he bows himself   ^C 5:22 Lit a talent   ^D 5:23 Lit two talents   ^E 5:24 Or citadel   ^F 5:26 Or "Did not my heart go   ^G 5:27 A reference to whiteness or flakiness of the skin   ^H 6:1 Lit we are living before you

---

5:10–12 The sequence of events recorded here fits best into a time when Elisha's residence was near the **Jordan** River. The **Abana** and **Pharpar** rivers, flowing from the slopes of Mount Hermon and coming to an end in the desert marshes east of **Damascus**, probably were more attractive and cleaner than the ever muddy Jordan.
5:17–19 Elisha's last words to Naaman implied two concessions to Naaman's new faith. (1) As a man of new faith and incomplete understanding, Naaman believed there would be benefit in having **soil** from Israel at hand when he worshiped Israel's God. Elisha cooperated with Naaman's superstitious belief, much as the apostle Paul

encourages mature believers to do with immature believers (Rm 14). (2) A more significant concession was to allow Naaman to participate (seemingly in body only, not mind and heart) in his king's worship of the god **Rimmon**. "Rimmon" could have been a local name for the god Hadd/Hadad or a local manifestation of that god. Elisha's words, **Go in peace**, imply acceptance of Naaman's requests.
5:25–26 Elisha's answer listed some of the pleasures one could expect to gain with money.
5:27 As a leper, Gehazi was no longer fit to serve as Elisha's servant. As is commonly the case in other biblical narratives, we

should not assume chronological order for the events narrated in this passage unless such order is explicitly indicated in the text. Therefore there is no necessary contradiction between the fact that Gehazi is here banished from Elisha and the fact that he is presented as Elisha's servant in 8:1–6. That incident, though recorded later in the book, could have occurred before Naaman's healing.
6:1–4 **Elisha** lived among and worked with the **prophets**. The communities of the prophets were fairly mobile and could relocate whenever their homes or a neighborhood became crowded. To find room, they went to the lower Jor-

each get a log and can build ourselves a place to live there."

"Go," he said.

³ Then one said, "Please come with your servants."

"I'll come," he answered.

⁴ So he went with them, and when they came to the Jordan, they cut down trees. ⁵ As one of them was cutting down a tree, the iron ax head fell into the water, and he cried out, "Oh, my master, it was borrowed!"

⁶ Then the man of God asked, "Where did it fall?"

When he showed him the place, the man of God cut a piece of wood, threw it there, and made the iron float. ⁷ Then he said, "Pick it up." So he reached out and took it.

The Aramean War

⁸ When the king of Aram was waging war against Israel, he conferred with his servants, "My camp will be at such and such a place."

⁹ But the man of God sent word to the king of Israel: "Be careful passing by this place, for the Arameans are going down there." ¹⁰ Consequently, the king of Israel sent word to the place the man of God had told him about. The man of God repeatedly^A warned the king, so the king would be on his guard.

¹¹ The king of Aram was enraged because of this matter, and he called his servants and demanded of them, "Tell me, which one of us is for the king of Israel?"

¹² One of his servants said, "No one, my lord the king. Elisha, the prophet in Israel, tells the king of Israel even the words you speak in your bedroom."

¹³ So the king said, "Go and see where he is, so I can send men to capture him."

When he was told, "Elisha is in Dothan," ¹⁴ he sent horses, chariots, and a massive army there. They went by night and surrounded the city.

¹⁵ When the servant of the man of God got up early and went out, he discovered an army

with horses and chariots surrounding the city. So he asked Elisha, "Oh, my master, what are we to do?"

¹⁶ Elisha said, "Don't be afraid, for those who are with us outnumber those who are with them."

¹⁷ Then Elisha prayed, "LORD, please open his eyes and let him see." So the LORD opened the servant's eyes, and he saw that the mountain was covered with horses and chariots of fire all around Elisha.

¹⁸ When the Arameans came against him, Elisha prayed to the LORD, "Please strike this nation with blindness."^B So he struck them with blindness, according to Elisha's word. ¹⁹ Then Elisha said to them, "This is not the way, and this is not the city. Follow me, and I will take you to the man you're looking for." And he led them to Samaria. ²⁰ When they entered Samaria, Elisha said, "LORD, open these men's eyes and let them see." So the LORD opened their eyes, and they saw that they were in the middle of Samaria.

²¹ When the king of Israel saw them, he said to Elisha, "Should I kill them, should I kill them, my father?"

²² Elisha replied, "Don't kill them. Do you kill those you have captured with your sword or your bow? Set food and water in front of them so they can eat and drink and go to their master."

²³ So he prepared a big feast for them. When they had eaten and drunk, he sent them away, and they went to their master. The Aramean raiders did not come into Israel's land again.

The Siege of Samaria

²⁴ Some time later, King Ben-hadad of Aram brought all his military units together and marched up and laid siege to Samaria. ²⁵ So there was a severe famine in Samaria, and they continued the siege against it until a donkey's head sold for thirty-four ounces^C of silver, and

---

^A 6:10 Lit *not once and not twice* ^B 6:18 Or *a blinding light* ^C 6:25 Lit *for 80*; "shekels" is assumed

---

dan River Valley to one of many places where the well-watered, lower flood plain abounded with thickets, **trees**, and other vegetation and also with pools and eddies of water.

6:8–8:15 This section, almost two chapters long, shows the man of God intervening in politics. Though his people had rejected him, God did not abandon his people to their enemies or to their own rulers. A likely setting for these events was the political weakness under Jehu and his weak successor, Jehoahaz. In contrast with the severity shown to Elisha's greedy servant, God could still show mercy to Elisha's ungodly king. During this time, Elisha could live safely in Samaria, though suffering occasional personal threats (6:32). The man of God helped Israel in two ways: by sharing supernatural knowledge of the

enemy, and by serving as a rallying point and source of prophetic encouragement for Samaria.

6:8–11 Perhaps during an era of border harassment, the man of God regularly revealed the secret plans of the **Arameans** to the **king of Israel**.

6:14–15 The Arameans sent a major expedition to surround **Elisha** in Dothan, about ten miles north of Samaria.

6:21–23 Elisha's prohibition against killing the Arameans carried the implicit message that God had given this victory.

6:24–25 War had come with a devastating siege of **Samaria** and starvation among the people. The siege was so pressing that ceremonially unclean and detestable substances were being sold for exorbitant prices.

a cup[A] of dove's dung[B] sold for two ounces[C] of silver.

²⁶ As the king of Israel was passing by on the wall, a woman cried out to him, "My lord the king, help!"

²⁷ He answered, "If the LORD doesn't help you, where can I get help for you? From the threshing floor or the winepress?" ²⁸ Then the king asked her, "What's the matter?"

She said, "This woman said to me, 'Give up your son, and we will eat him today. Then we will eat my son tomorrow.' ²⁹ So we boiled my son and ate him, and I said to her the next day, 'Give up your son, and we will eat him,' but she has hidden her son."

³⁰ When the king heard the woman's words, he tore his clothes. Then, as he was passing by on the wall, the people saw that there was sackcloth under his clothes next to his skin. ³¹ He announced, "May God punish me and do so severely if the head of Elisha son of Shaphat remains on his shoulders today."

³² Elisha was sitting in his house, and the elders were sitting with him. The king sent a man ahead of him, but before the messenger got to him, Elisha said to the elders, "Do you see how this murderer has sent someone to remove my head? Look, when the messenger comes, shut the door to keep him out. Isn't the sound of his master's feet behind him?"

³³ While Elisha was still speaking with them, the messenger[D] came down to him. Then he said, "This disaster is from the LORD. Why should I wait for the LORD any longer?"

7 Elisha replied, "Hear the word of the LORD! This is what the LORD says: 'About this time tomorrow at Samaria's gate, six quarts[E] of fine flour will sell for a half ounce of silver[F] and twelve quarts[G] of barley will sell for a half ounce of silver.'"

² Then the captain, the king's right-hand man,[H] responded to the man of God, "Look, even if the LORD were to make windows in heaven, could this really happen?"

Elisha announced, "You will in fact see it with your own eyes, but you won't eat any of it."

³ Now four men with a skin disease were at the entrance to the city gate. They said to each other, "Why just sit here until we die? ⁴ If we say, 'Let's go into the city,' we will die there because

the famine is in the city, but if we sit here, we will also die. So now, come on. Let's surrender to the Arameans' camp. If they let us live, we will live; if they kill us, we will die."

⁵ So the diseased men got up at twilight to go to the Arameans' camp. When they came to the camp's edge, they discovered that no one was there, ⁶ for the Lord[I] had caused the Aramean camp to hear the sound of chariots, horses, and a large army. The Arameans had said to each other, "The king of Israel must have hired the kings of the Hittites and the kings of Egypt to attack us." ⁷ So they had gotten up and fled at twilight, abandoning their tents, horses, and donkeys. The camp was intact, and they had fled for their lives.

⁸ When these diseased men came to the edge of the camp, they went into a tent to eat and drink. Then they picked up the silver, gold, and clothing and went off and hid them. They came back and entered another tent, picked things up, and hid them. ⁹ Then they said to each other, "We're not doing what is right. Today is a day of good news. If we are silent and wait until morning light, our punishment will catch up with us. So let's go tell the king's household."

¹⁰ The diseased men came and called to the city's gatekeepers and told them, "We went to the Aramean camp and no one was there — no human sounds. There was nothing but tethered horses and donkeys, and the tents were intact." ¹¹ The gatekeepers called out, and the news was reported to the king's household.

¹² So the king got up in the night and said to his servants, "Let me tell you what the Arameans have done to us. They know we are starving, so they have left the camp to hide in the open country, thinking, 'When they come out of the city, we will take them alive and go into the city.'"

¹³ But one of his servants responded, "Please, let messengers take five of the horses that are left in the city. Their fate is like the entire Israelite community who will die,[J] so let's send them and see."

¹⁴ The messengers took two chariots with horses, and the king sent them after the Aramean army, saying, "Go and see." ¹⁵ So they followed them as far as the Jordan. They saw that the whole way was littered with clothes

A 6:25 Lit a fourth of a kab   B 6:25 Or seedpods, or wild onions   C 6:25 Lit for five; "shekels" is assumed   D 6:33 Some emend to king   E 7:1 Lit a seah, also in vv. 16,18   F 7:1 Lit a shekel, also in vv. 16,18   G 7:1 Lit two seahs, also in vv. 16,18   H 7:2 Lit captain, upon whose hand the king leaned, also in v. 17   I 7:6 Some Hb mss read LORD   J 7:13 Some Hb mss, LXX, Syr, Vg; other Hb mss read left in it. Indeed, they are like the whole multitude of Israel that are left in it; indeed, they are like the whole multitude of Israel who will die.

6:28–29 The king's interview with one of the two women involved in cannibalism illustrated a depth of sin that had been prophesied much earlier (Lv 26:29).
6:30 The **king** was probably sincere in wearing **sackcloth** under his robes. He could honestly say that he felt the people's pain, and he skillfully displayed the evidences of his

grief. He reacted to the woman's pain with great emotion.
6:32 That the **elders** of the idolatrous city held Elisha in high respect is proven by the fact that they were **in his house . . . sitting with him**.
7:1 The story turns to the coming miraculous deliverance. **Elisha** announced that the

next day at that same time, food would be available at bargain prices at the city **gate**.
7:3–4 Since the nation's leaders were such failures, the Lord brought knowledge of deliverance through four outcasts who were quarantined because of their **skin disease**.
7:5–7 The **Hittites** referred to here were the neo-Hittites, remnants of the older Hittite

and equipment the Arameans had thrown off in their haste. The messengers returned and told the king.

¹⁶ Then the people went out and plundered the Aramean camp. It was then that six quarts of fine flour sold for a half ounce of silver and twelve quarts of barley sold for a half ounce of silver, according to the word of the LORD. ¹⁷ The king had appointed the captain, his right-hand man, to be in charge of the city gate, but the people trampled him in the gate. He died, just as the man of God had predicted when the king had come to him. ¹⁸ When the man of God had said to the king, "About this time tomorrow twelve quarts of barley will sell for a half ounce of silver and six quarts of fine flour will sell for a half ounce of silver at Samaria's gate," ¹⁹ this captain had answered the man of God, "Look, even if the LORD were to make windows in heaven, could this really happen?" Elisha had said, "You will in fact see it with your own eyes, but you won't eat any of it." ²⁰ This is what happened to him: the people trampled him in the city gate, and he died.

The Shunammite's Land Restored

8 Elisha said to the woman whose son he had restored to life, "Get ready, you and your household, and go live as a resident alien wherever you can. For the LORD has announced a seven-year famine, and it has already come to the land."

² So the woman got ready and did what the man of God said. She and her household lived as resident aliens in the land of the Philistines for seven years. ³ When the woman returned from the land of the Philistines at the end of seven years, she went to appeal to the king for her house and field. ⁴ The king had been speaking to Gehazi, the attendant of the man of God, saying, "Tell me all the great things Elisha has done." ⁵ While he was telling the king how Elisha restored the dead son to life, the woman whose son he had restored to life came to appeal to

the king for her house and field. So Gehazi said, "My lord the king, this is the woman and this is the son Elisha restored to life."

⁶ When the king asked the woman, she told him the story. So the king appointed a court official for her, saying, "Restore all that was hers, along with all the income from the field from the day she left the country until now."

Aram's King Hazael

⁷ Elisha came to Damascus while King Benhadad of Aram was sick, and the king was told, "The man of God has come here." ⁸ So the king said to Hazael, "Take a gift with you and go meet the man of God. Inquire of the LORD through him, 'Will I recover from this sickness?'"

⁹ Hazael went to meet Elisha, taking with him a gift: forty camel-loads of all the finest products of Damascus. When he came and stood before him, he said, "Your son, King Benhadad of Aram, has sent me to ask you, 'Will I recover from this sickness?'"

¹⁰ Elisha told him, "Go say to him, 'You are sure toᴬ recover.' But the LORD has shown me that he is sure to die." ¹¹ Then he stared steadily at him until he was ashamed.

The man of God wept, ¹² and Hazael asked, "Why is my lord weeping?"

He replied, "Because I know the evil you will do to the people of Israel. You will set their fortresses on fire. You will kill their young men with the sword. You will dash their children to pieces. You will rip open their pregnant women."

¹³ Hazael said, "How could your servant, a mere dog, do such a mighty deed?"

Elisha answered, "The LORD has shown me that you will be king over Aram."

¹⁴ Hazael left Elisha and went to his master, who asked him, "What did Elisha say to you?"

He responded, "He told me you are sure to recover." ¹⁵ The next day Hazael took a heavy cloth, dipped it in water, and spread it over the king's face. Ben-hadad died, and Hazael reigned in his place.

ᴬ8:10 Alt Hb tradition reads *You will not*

Empire from the second millennium BC. In this context, **Egypt** was probably the northern Egypt from which Solomon imported **horses** (1Kg 10:28).

7:16–20 Now all of Elisha's prophecy was fulfilled. These details, particularly those dealing with the death of the **captain**, were repeated in meticulous detail to highlight the fact that God is faithful.

8:1–6 This incident almost certainly occurred at an earlier time and under an earlier king. Because **Gehazi** was serving Elisha and had an audience with the king, it is likely that this event took place before Gehazi became leprous (chap. 5). Though obviously related to the earlier incident of the healing of the Shunammite woman's son (4:32–37), this material may have been recorded here because it also

dealt with issues of government and beneficial rule. This portion deals with justice for a **woman** who had abandoned her **land** in a time of distress and then had difficulty getting her land back. The prophet's influence helped her to get a just settlement of the issue. Though out of chronological order, this account is topically suited for this context.
8:7–15 Earlier (1Kg 19:15–16), God had instructed Elijah to choose his successor and to anoint two kings. Up to this time, only one of those tasks—choosing his successor—had been accomplished. The other two anointings were to be done by Elisha. Apparently, Elisha's designation of these two kings was sufficient to fulfill the Lord's original command to Elijah.
8:9–11 Elisha gave a devious answer to Ben-hadad's request for an oracle. If one

takes Elisha's message as meaning only that Ben-hadad's current illness was not terminal, it was true, but God also used Hazael's visit to Elisha to incite Hazael to commit murder and start a revolution.
8:12–13 Then Elisha shared his prophetic vision that **Hazael** would devastate Israel. This message ended with Elisha stating unambiguously that Hazael would become **king**. In giving that message, God and Elisha either instigated Hazael's treason or encouraged the initiation of a treason that was already planned.
8:14–15 **Hazael** did, in fact, repeat the prophet's words to **Ben-hadad**, but then he proceeded to murder his king and take the throne.

Judah's King Jehoram

¹⁶ In the fifth year of Israel's King Joram son of Ahab, Jehoram^A^ son of Jehoshaphat became king of Judah, replacing his father.^B^ ¹⁷ He was thirty-two years old when he became king, and he reigned eight years in Jerusalem. ¹⁸ He walked in the ways of the kings of Israel, as the house of Ahab had done, for Ahab's daughter was his wife. He did what was evil in the LORD's sight. ¹⁹ For the sake of his servant David, the LORD was unwilling to destroy Judah, since he had promised to give a lamp^C^ to David and his sons forever.

²⁰ During Jehoram's reign, Edom rebelled against Judah's control and appointed their own king. ²¹ So Jehoram crossed over to Zair with all his chariots. Then at night he set out to attack the Edomites who had surrounded him and the chariot commanders, but his troops fled to their tents. ²² So Edom is still in rebellion against Judah's control today. Libnah also rebelled at that time.

²³ The rest of the events of Jehoram's reign, along with all his accomplishments, are written in the Historical Record of Judah's Kings. ²⁴ Jehoram rested with his ancestors and was buried with his ancestors in the city of David, and his son Ahaziah became king in his place.

Judah's King Ahaziah

²⁵ In the twelfth year of Israel's King Joram son of Ahab, Ahaziah son of Jehoram became king of Judah. ²⁶ Ahaziah was twenty-two years old when he became king, and he reigned one year in Jerusalem. His mother's name was Athaliah, granddaughter of Israel's King Omri. ²⁷ He

walked in the ways of the house of Ahab and did what was evil in the LORD's sight like the house of Ahab, for his father had married into^D^ the house of Ahab.

²⁸ Ahaziah went with Joram son of Ahab to fight against King Hazael of Aram in Ramoth-gilead, and the Arameans wounded Joram. ²⁹ So King Joram returned to Jezreel to recover from the wounds that the Arameans had inflicted on him in Ramoth-gilead^E^ when he fought against Aram's King Hazael. Then Judah's King Ahaziah son of Jehoram went down to Jezreel to visit Joram son of Ahab since Joram was ill.

Jehu Anointed as Israel's King

9 The prophet Elisha called one of the sons of the prophets and said, "Tuck your mantle under your belt, take this flask of oil with you, and go to Ramoth-gilead. ² When you get there, look for Jehu son of Jehoshaphat, son of Nimshi. Go in, get him away from his colleagues, and take him to an inner room. ³ Then take the flask of oil, pour it on his head, and say, 'This is what the LORD says: "I anoint you king over Israel."' Open the door and escape. Don't wait."

⁴ So the young prophet^F^ went to Ramoth-gilead. ⁵ When he arrived, the army commanders were sitting there, so he said, "I have a message for you, commander."

Jehu asked, "For which one of us?"

He answered, "For you, commander."

⁶ So Jehu got up and went into the house. The young prophet poured the oil on his head and said, "This is what the LORD God of Israel says: 'I anoint you king over the LORD's people, Israel.'

---

^A^8:16 = The LORD is Exalted   ^B^8:16 Lit *Judah; Jehoshaphat had been king of Judah*   ^C^8:19 Or *dominion*   ^D^8:27 Lit *for he was related by marriage to*   ^E^8:29 Lit *Ramah*   ^F^9:4 Or *the young man, the attendant of the prophet*

8:16 With this record the data is again arranged chronologically. For a parallel account of Joram, see 2Ch 21:4–20.

8:17–18 After the formal opening, the evaluation reports that Joram was a bad king and observes that the corrupting influences of **Ahab** and Jezebel had reached into Judah. **The ways of the kings of Israel** probably refers to the worship of Baal-melkart (see note at 1Kg 16:25). It was unlikely that the good king, Jehoshaphat, anticipated this outcome when he allowed his son Jehoram to enter into a marriage alliance with Ahab. **8:20–21** These verses record the loss of Judah's last pretense to empire.

The brief description of the **night** attack against surrounding **Edomites** could be translated in two ways. The critical sentence could be either "at night he and his chariot officers attacked the surrounding Edomites" or "at night he attacked the surrounding Edomites and their chariot officers." The first option is more likely because, even in decline, Judah was more likely to have a small chariot division than Edom was. Then the next sentence, "The people (**his troops**) **fled to their tents** (homes)," is also ambiguous. "The people" could be the Edomites, who fled so that the rebellion was not crushed, or they could have been Jehoram's chariots,

who went home without subduing the rebellion. This time the second option is more likely. By losing control of Edom, Judah lost control of the caravan routes to the south. Judah also lost Libnah on the border of the former Philistine territory.

8:22 Today refers to the date of the writing of an earlier document that was incorporated into the canonical version of 2 Kings.

8:25–27 The corrupting relationship with the house of Omri and Ahab is highlighted: his mother was from that family. The **ways of . . . Ahab** probably alludes to bringing the worship of Baal-melkart into Judah (see note at 1Kg 16:25).

8:28–29 The notice about the continued conflict with **Hazael** of Damascus informs the reader that Israel, with Judah as an ally, could still contest control of Gilead with Hazael, the new, more aggressive ruler of Damascus. The big step in the decline of Israel's political power would come with Jehu's widespread massacres. There is no notice for the end of Ahaziah's reign since his death is recorded later as part of Jehu's massacres.

9:1–15:12 The theological and moral reason for this coming period of weakness was the sin of the southern kings beginning with Jehoram, son of Jehoshaphat (8:18). But the immediate, political cause was the violence

and destructiveness of Jehu's revolution against the dynasty of Omri. Decline began immediately with Jehu's massacres and continued into the rule of Jehu's son, Jehoahaz. This period of weakness was the most likely setting for several of the miracle events recorded in topical, non-chronological order in the general career of Elisha.

Then, after Elisha's deathbed intervention in politics, Jehoash, grandson of Jehu, led the north in a new round of successful warfare. This culminated in the reign of Jeroboam II, during whose rule the wealth and power of the northern kingdom was greater than it had yet been. In God's providence, this restoration of power came just in time to bring material blessing to the successors of Joash of Judah.

9:1–4 The second anointing of a ruler commanded of Elijah by the Lord occurred when Elisha sent a young **prophet** to anoint **Jehu**, an experienced chariot commander, to be **king** of **Israel**. At that time Jehu was a commander of the chariots struggling with Aram for control of **Ramoth-gilead**. The delicacy of the situation is shown by the command to the young prophet to **escape** immediately.

9:5–10 In the account of Elisha commissioning the young prophet, the message is summarized in six words (v. 3). Here in

⁷ You are to strike down the house of your master Ahab so that I may avenge the blood shed by the hand of Jezebel — the blood of my servants the prophets and of all the servants of the LORD. ⁸ The whole house of Ahab will perish, and I will wipe out all of Ahab's males,^A both slave and free,^B in Israel. ⁹ I will make the house of Ahab like the house of Jeroboam son of Nebat and like the house of Baasha son of Ahijah. ¹⁰ The dogs will eat Jezebel in the plot of land at Jezreel — no one will bury her.'" Then the young prophet opened the door and escaped.

¹¹ When Jehu came out to his master's servants, they asked, "Is everything all right? Why did this crazy person come to you?"

Then he said to them, "You know the sort and their ranting."

¹² But they replied, "That's a lie! Tell us!"

So Jehu said, "He talked to me about this and that and said, 'This is what the LORD says: I anoint you king over Israel.'"

¹³ Each man quickly took his garment and put it under Jehu on the bare steps.^C They blew the ram's horn and proclaimed, "Jehu is king!"

¹⁴ Then Jehu son of Jehoshaphat, son of Nimshi, conspired against Joram. Joram and all Israel had been at Ramoth-gilead on guard against King Hazael of Aram. ¹⁵ But King Joram had returned to Jezreel to recover from the wounds that the Arameans had inflicted on him when he fought against Aram's King Hazael. Jehu said, "If you commanders wish to make me king,^D then don't let anyone escape from the city to go tell about it in Jezreel."

Jehu Kills Joram and Ahaziah

¹⁶ Jehu got into his chariot and went to Jezreel since Joram was laid up there and King Ahaziah of Judah had gone down to visit Joram. ¹⁷ Now the watchman was standing on the tower in Jezreel. He saw Jehu's mob approaching and shouted, "I see a mob!"

Joram responded, "Choose a rider and send him to meet them and have him ask, 'Do you come in peace?'"

¹⁸ So a horseman went to meet Jehu and said, "This is what the king asks: 'Do you come in peace?'"

Jehu replied, "What do you have to do with peace? Fall in behind me."

The watchman reported, "The messenger reached them but hasn't started back."

¹⁹ So he sent out a second horseman, who went to them and said, "This is what the king asks: 'Do you come in peace?'"

Jehu answered, "What do you have to do with peace? Fall in behind me."

²⁰ Again the watchman reported, "He reached them but hasn't started back. Also, the driving is like that of Jehu son of Nimshi — he drives like a madman."

²¹ "Get the chariot ready!" Joram shouted, and they got it ready. Then King Joram of Israel and King Ahaziah of Judah set out, each in his own chariot, and met Jehu at the plot of land of Naboth the Jezreelite. ²² When Joram saw Jehu he asked, "Do you come in peace, Jehu?"

He answered, "What peace can there be as long as there is so much prostitution and sorcery from your mother Jezebel?"

²³ Joram turned around and fled, shouting to Ahaziah, "It's treachery, Ahaziah!"

²⁴ Then Jehu drew his bow and shot Joram between the shoulders. The arrow went through his heart, and he slumped down in his chariot. ²⁵ Jehu said to Bidkar his aide, "Pick him up and throw him on the plot of ground belonging to Naboth the Jezreelite. For remember when you and I were riding side by side behind his father Ahab, and the LORD uttered this pronouncement against him: ²⁶ 'As surely as I saw the blood of Naboth and the blood of his sons yesterday' — this is the LORD's declaration — 'so will I repay you on this plot of land' — this

^A 9:8 Lit wipe out Ahab's one who urinates against a wall   ^B 9:8 Or males, even the weak and impaired; Hb obscure   ^C 9:13 Lit on the bones of the steps   ^D 9:15 Lit "If your desire exists

the account of delivering the message, the six words are expanded to more than a hundred words (in the CSB translation) followed by an urgent departure. This expanded statement repeated the accusation against the **house of** . . . **Ahab** and gave a detailed presentation of the penalty to be exacted.
9:11–13 The evaluation **Jehu** and **his master's servants** gave about the prophet seems confused. At first the prophet was described as **crazy** and **ranting**, but as soon as the group realized that they actually liked the message he had brought, they allowed the prophet's oracle and anointing of Jehu to instigate the revolution that destroyed the house of Ahab. Whatever Jehu's servants may have initially thought of the messenger, they recognized that his actions implied the divine approval of Jehu as king—a conclusion they apparently reached before Jehu himself did.

9:14 The formula used here to designate **Jehu** could be understood as: "Jehu, the son of Jehoshaphat, of the clan of Nimshi." **All Israel** should not be taken as referring literally to "all Israel" but to all Israel involved in conducting the war.
9:15–16 Jehu plotted with his fellow officers to prevent anyone from going to **Jezreel** to warn the king. Then he took a group of soldiers with him to seize the throne.
9:18 The quickness with which the messenger lined up behind **Jehu**, signaling a switch of allegiance, showed that personal loyalty to King Joram was as shallow in Jezreel as it had been in Ramoth-gilead and that Jehu was a persuasive leader.
9:19–20 After a **second** messenger defected to **Jehu**, the lookout thought he could identify the manner of chariot driving as distinctive of Jehu.
9:21 Joram behaved like a man of bravery and character in going to face the danger

himself. **King Ahaziah of Judah** should also be given similar credit for going with him.
9:22 Taken in its literal meaning, the **prostitution** mentioned by **Jehu** probably referred to the temple prostitutes of Baalism associated with the local Baals of Palestine and Jezebel's imported Baalism from Phoenicia. However, it could easily be stretched to apply to the metaphorical religious adultery of worshiping any god other than the Lord. **Sorcery** was also a routine part of pagan cults.
9:23–26 These events happened near the second royal palace, the summer palace, the place where **Naboth** and his sons were murdered through Jezebel's scheming. Jehu, remembering the time when he and **Bidkar**, his **aide**, were witnesses to those murders, enabled the fulfillment of the prophecy by dumping Joram's corpse on Naboth's land. The Hebrew word for "aide," meaning "third," indicates that Bidkar was a third person in addition to the chariot driver and Jehu.

is the LORD's declaration. So now, according to the word of the LORD, pick him up and throw him on the plot of land."

²⁷ When King Ahaziah of Judah saw what was happening, he fled up the road toward Beth-haggan. Jehu pursued him, shouting, "Shoot him too!" So they shot him in his chariot^A at Gur Pass near Ibleam, but he fled to Megiddo and died there. ²⁸ Then his servants carried him to Jerusalem in a chariot and buried him in his ancestors' tomb in the city of David. ²⁹ It was in the eleventh year of Joram son of Ahab that Ahaziah had become king over Judah.

Jehu Kills Jezebel

³⁰ When Jehu came to Jezreel, Jezebel heard about it, so she painted her eyes, fixed her hair,^B and looked down from the window. ³¹ As Jehu entered the city gate, she said, "Do you come in peace, Zimri, killer of your master?"

³² He looked up toward the window and said, "Who is on my side? Who?" Two or three eunuchs looked down at him, ³³ and he said, "Throw her down!" So they threw her down, and some of her blood splattered on the wall and on the horses, and Jehu rode over her.

³⁴ Then he went in, ate and drank, and said, "Take care of this cursed woman and bury her, since she's a king's daughter." ³⁵ But when they went out to bury her, they did not find anything but the skull, the feet, and the hands. ³⁶ So they went back and told him, and he said, "This fulfills the LORD's word that he spoke through his servant Elijah the Tishbite: 'In the plot of land at Jezreel, the dogs will eat Jezebel's flesh. ³⁷ Jezebel's corpse will be like manure on the surface of the ground in the plot of land at Jezreel so that no one will be able to say: This is Jezebel.'"

Jehu Kills the House of Ahab

10 Since Ahab had seventy sons in Samaria, Jehu wrote letters and sent them to Samaria to the rulers of Jezreel, to the elders, and to the guardians of Ahab's sons,^C saying: ² Your master's sons are with you, and you have chariots, horses, a fortified city, and

weaponry, so when this letter arrives ³ select the most qualified^D of your master's sons, set him on his father's throne, and fight for your master's house.

⁴ However, they were terrified and reasoned, "Look, two kings couldn't stand against him; how can we?"

⁵ So the overseer of the palace, the overseer of the city, the elders, and the guardians sent a message to Jehu: "We are your servants, and we will do whatever you tell us. We will not make anyone king. Do whatever you think is right."^E

⁶ Then Jehu wrote them a second letter, saying:

If you are on my side, and if you will obey me, bring me the heads of your master's sons^F at this time tomorrow at Jezreel.

All seventy of the king's sons were being cared for by the city's prominent men. ⁷ When the letter came to them, they took the king's sons and slaughtered all seventy, put their heads in baskets, and sent them to Jehu at Jezreel. ⁸ When the messenger came and told him, "They have brought the heads of the king's sons," the king said, "Pile them in two heaps at the entrance of the city gate until morning."

⁹ The next morning when he went out and stood at the gate, he said to all the people, "You are innocent. It was I who conspired against my master and killed him. But who struck down all these? ¹⁰ Know, then, that not a word the LORD spoke against the house of Ahab will fail, for the LORD has done what he promised through his servant Elijah." ¹¹ So Jehu killed all who remained of the house of Ahab in Jezreel — all his great men, close friends, and priests — leaving him no survivors.

¹² Then he set out and went to Samaria. On the way, while he was at Beth-eked of the Shepherds, ¹³ Jehu met the relatives of King Ahaziah of Judah and asked, "Who are you?"

They answered, "We're Ahaziah's relatives. We've come down to greet the king's sons and the queen mother's sons."

---

^A 9:27 LXX, Syr, Vg; MT omits *So they shot him*   ^B 9:30 Lit *made her head pleasing*   ^C 10:1 LXX; MT reads *of Ahab*   ^D 10:3 Lit *the good and the upright*   ^E 10:5 Lit *Do what is good in your eyes*   ^F 10:6 Lit *heads of the men of the sons of your master*

9:27–29 Judah was a junior ally of the dynasty of Ahab and was also tied to Ahab by marriage and by the cult of Baal. Though he had not been commanded to do so, Jehu may have believed there was no reason to distinguish between purging the land of the house of Ahab and purging it of the related house of David in Jerusalem. Jehu's men pursued and wounded **King Ahaziah** at the ascent into the **Gur Pass near Ibleam**, although some locate this pass close to the pass that led from Taanach south. The wounded Ahaziah was permitted to flee to **Megiddo** where he died. Neither Joram nor Ahaziah are given formal closers to their records since Jehu's massacres rendered such records superfluous.

9:30–37 This report, written by a follower of Yahweh who considered **Jezebel** the incarnation of evil, described the courage and resolve of this idolatress and murderess as she faced death. She tended to her appearance with black eye paint and then boldly faced her killer. Her fate again showed that the loyalty of the people to Ahab was quite shallow. Two or three of Jezebel's eunuched palace slaves, when challenged by Jehu, threw her to her death. Then, while Jehu **ate and drank**, the dogs destroyed the corpse of the Phoenician princess just as was prophesied (1Kg 21:23). **10:1–7** Having many wives and children was seen as one of the prerogatives of power. Ahab's **sons** and grandsons were apparently distributed among the noble families to

relieve the royal treasury and to provide loyal sets of eyes and ears in the homes where they lived. **Jehu** shrewdly offered the great families of **Samaria** a difficult choice—choose a king and fight for him or deliver evidence that they had killed Ahab's sons. By ordinary standards of the day, these male heirs of Ahab were legitimate targets. **10:11** But Jehu went beyond killing the **house of Ahab** and killed Ahab's **great men** (perhaps the great men loyal to Ahab) and all of Ahab's **friends**. In these killings he clearly went beyond God's commands into excessive slaughter. By the standards of that day, the false **priests** were fair targets. **10:12–14** These verses report even more unnecessary slaughter of the southern royal family.

¹⁴ Then Jehu ordered, "Take them alive." So they took them alive and then slaughtered them at the pit of Beth-eked — forty-two men. He didn't spare any of them.

¹⁵ When he left there, he found Jehonadab son of Rechab coming to meet him. He greeted him and then asked, "Is your heart one with mine?"^A

"It is," Jehonadab replied.

Jehu said, "If it is,^B give me your hand."

So he gave him his hand, and Jehu pulled him up into the chariot with him. ¹⁶ Then he said, "Come with me and see my zeal for the LORD!" So he let him ride with him in his chariot. ¹⁷ When Jehu came to Samaria, he struck down all who remained from the house of Ahab in Samaria until he had annihilated his house, according to the word of the LORD spoken to Elijah.

Jehu Kills the Baal Worshipers

¹⁸ Then Jehu brought all the people together and said to them, "Ahab served Baal a little, but Jehu will serve him a lot. ¹⁹ Now, therefore, summon to me all the prophets of Baal, all his servants, and all his priests. None must be missing, for I have a great sacrifice for Baal. Whoever is missing will not live." However, Jehu was acting deceptively in order to destroy the servants of Baal. ²⁰ Jehu commanded, "Consecrate a solemn assembly for Baal." So they called one.

²¹ Then Jehu sent messengers throughout all Israel, and all the servants of Baal^C came; no one failed to come. They entered the temple of Baal, and it was filled from one end to the other. ²² Then he said to the custodian of the wardrobe, "Bring out the garments for all the servants of Baal." So he brought out their garments.

²³ Then Jehu and Jehonadab son of Rechab entered the temple of Baal, and Jehu said to the servants of Baal, "Look carefully to see that there are no servants of the LORD here among you — only servants of Baal." ²⁴ Then they went in to offer sacrifices and burnt offerings.

Now Jehu had stationed eighty men outside, and he warned them, "Whoever allows any of

the men I am placing in your hands to escape will forfeit his life for theirs." ²⁵ When he finished offering the burnt offering, Jehu said to the guards and officers, "Go in and kill them. Don't let anyone out." So they struck them down with the sword. Then the guards and officers threw the bodies out and went into the inner room of the temple of Baal. ²⁶ They brought out the pillar of the temple of Baal and burned it, ²⁷ and they tore down the pillar of Baal. Then they tore down the temple of Baal and made it a latrine — which it still is today.

Evaluation of Jehu's Reign

²⁸ Jehu eliminated Baal worship from Israel, ²⁹ but he did not turn away from the sins that Jeroboam son of Nebat had caused Israel to commit — worshiping the gold calves that were in Bethel and Dan. ³⁰ Nevertheless, the LORD said to Jehu, "Because you have done well in carrying out what is right in my sight and have done to the house of Ahab all that was in my heart, four generations of your sons will sit on the throne of Israel."

³¹ Yet Jehu was not careful to follow the instruction of the LORD God of Israel with all his heart. He did not turn from the sins that Jeroboam had caused Israel to commit.

³² In those days the LORD began to reduce the size of Israel. Hazael defeated the Israelites throughout their territory ³³ from the Jordan eastward: the whole land of Gilead — the Gadites, the Reubenites, and the Manassites — from Aroer which is by the Arnon Valley through Gilead to Bashan.^D

³⁴ The rest of the events of Jehu's reign, along with all his accomplishments and all his might, are written in the Historical Record of Israel's Kings. ³⁵ Jehu rested with his ancestors and was buried in Samaria. His son Jehoahaz became king in his place. ³⁶ The length of Jehu's reign over Israel in Samaria was twenty-eight years.

Athaliah Usurps the Throne

11 When Athaliah, Ahaziah's mother, saw that her son was dead, she proceeded to annihilate all the royal heirs. ² Jehosheba, who

---

^A**10:15** Lit *heart upright like my heart is with your heart*   ^B**10:15** LXX, Syr, Vg; MT reads *mine?"* Jehonadab said, "It is and it is
^C**10:21** LXX adds *— all his priests and all his prophets —*   ^D**10:33** Lit *Arnon Valley and Gilead and Bashan*

0:15–17 Jehu aligned himself with one of the major religiously conservative leaders of the kingdom — **Jehonadab son of Rechab.** **0:18–19** Since these verses describe Ahab's family and there was one great temple of **Baal,** the record deals with Baal-melkart, not some local Palestinian Baal (see note at 1Kg 16:25). Jehu used deception to lure the priests of Baal-melkart to their deaths. **0:24–27 Jehu** killed the priests of **Baal** and polluted their holy site with the corpses of its priests. Then the **temple of Baal** was torn down. They entered the **inner room** — the most holy place of the Baal temple — and

brought out its furnishings for destruction. In almost all the temple architectures known to us, the innermost room, the most holy place, was the private dwelling place of the deity or of the most sacred symbols of the deity. The final and deepest insult to the Baalist holy place was to turn it into a **latrine**. **10:28–31** The major point in the evaluation of Jehu was that he **eliminated** the worship of Baal-melkart (see note at 1Kg 16:25). For this he was promised **four generations** of heirs on the throne of Israel. However, like every other king of Israel, he did not reverse the illegal worship at the calf shrines.

10:32–33 Because of sin in both kingdoms, God used **Hazael,** king of Aram, not only to take away imperial holdings, but also to seize all Hebrew territories east of the **Jordan** River. **11:1–15:38** This section covers the reigns of four good kings: Joash, Amaziah, Azariah, and Jotham. All four of these kings receive some positive appraisal. The first three started well but ended badly. However, their collective piety brought about a third period of prosperity, power, and blessing. While the revival had begun by Joash's twenty-third year (ca 812 BC), the significant resurgence of Israelite

was King Jehoram's daughter and Ahaziah's sister, secretly rescued Joash son of Ahaziah from among the king's sons who were being killed and put him and the one who nursed him in a bedroom. So he was hidden from Athaliah and was not killed. ³ Joash was in hiding with her in the LORD's temple six years while Athaliah reigned over the land.

Athaliah Overthrown

⁴ In the seventh year, Jehoiada sent for the commanders of hundreds, the Carites, and the guards. He had them come to him in the LORD's temple, where he made a covenant with them and put them under oath. He showed them the king's son ⁵ and commanded them, "This is what you are to do: A third of you who come on duty on the Sabbath are to provide protection for the king's palace. ⁶ A third are to be at the Foundation^ Gate and a third at the gate behind the guards. You are to take turns providing protection for the palace.ᴮ

⁷ "Your two divisions that go off duty on the Sabbath are to provide the king protection at the LORD's temple. ⁸ Completely surround the king with weapons in hand. Anyone who approaches the ranks is to be put to death. Be with the king in all his daily tasks."ᶜ

⁹ So the commanders of hundreds did everything the priest Jehoiada commanded. They each brought their men — those coming on duty on the Sabbath and those going off duty — and came to the priest Jehoiada. ¹⁰ The priest gave to the commanders of hundreds King David's spears and shields that were in the LORD's temple. ¹¹ Then the guards stood with their weapons in hand surrounding the king — from the right side of the temple to the left side, by the altar and by the temple.

¹² Jehoiada brought out the king's son, put the crown on him, gave him the testimony,ᴰ

and made him king. They anointed him and clapped their hands and cried, "Long live the king!"

¹³ When Athaliah heard the noise from the guard and the crowd, she went out to the people at the LORD's temple. ¹⁴ She looked, and there was the king standing by the pillar according to the custom. The commanders and the trumpeters were by the king, and all the people of the land were rejoicing and blowing trumpets. Athaliah tore her clothes and screamed "Treason! Treason!"

¹⁵ Then the priest Jehoiada ordered the commanders of hundreds in charge of the army, "Take her out between the ranks, and put to death by the sword anyone who follows her," for the priest had said, "She is not to be put to death in the LORD's temple." ¹⁶ So they arrested her, and she went through the horse entrance to the king's palace, where she was put to death.

Jehoiada's Reforms

¹⁷ Then Jehoiada made a covenant between the LORD, the king, and the people that they would be the LORD's people and another covenant between the king and the people.ᴱ ¹⁸ So all the people of the land went to the temple of Baal and tore it down. They smashed its altars and images to pieces, and they killed Mattan, the priest of Baal, at the altars.

Then Jehoiada the priest appointed guards for the LORD's temple. ¹⁹ He took the commanders of hundreds, the Carites, the guards, and all the people of the land, and they brought the king from the LORD's temple. They entered the king's palace by way of the guards' gate. Joash sat on the throne of the kings. ²⁰ All the people of the land rejoiced, and the city was quiet, for they had put Athaliah to death by the sword in the king's palace.

^11:6 See 2Ch 23:5; MT here reads *Sur* ᴮ11:6 Hb obscure ᶜ11:8 Lit *king when he goes out and when he comes in* ᴰ11:12 Or *him the copy of the covenant*, or *him a diadem*, or *him jewels* ᴱ11:17 Some Gk versions, 2Ch 23:16 omit *and another covenant between the king and the people*

power and wealth began twenty years later with the victories of Jehoash, grandson of Jehu, over the Arameans.
11:1–21 Athaliah was first introduced in 8:26 as Omri's granddaughter and mother of Ahaziah. Three factors enabled her to seize the throne: the respect for the queen mother, the religious and moral corruption of the last two Davidic kings, and the presence of Baal worshipers in Judah. However, there were three weaknesses that could destroy her: Personal loyalty to Athaliah did not extend far from Jerusalem and was weak even there; many Levites remained loyal to Yahweh; and Jehu's massacres halted support for Athaliah from the north. Athaliah murdered all the males of the royal house in an attempt to eliminate legitimate, Davidic competition. Most of those victims were her own descendants.
11:2–3 Jehosheba, sister of Ahaziah and wife of Jehoiada the priest (2Ch 22:11), saved one of Ahaziah's sons and his wet nurse from

the slaughter and hid them in the **LORD's temple**.
11:4 After six years **Jehoiada** the priest devised and implemented a plan for mobilizing the forces loyal to David. The revolutionaries included the **Carites**. Since the name is foreign without any typical Hebrew extensions, they were probably foreign mercenaries.
11:5–9 Jehoiada gathered his forces and executed the palace coup. The Hebrew terms for the Sur gate and the **Foundation Gate** (2Ch 23:5) are so similar that one is almost certainly a textual error for the other. The units involved in these preparations were placed in position for protecting the young Davidic heir.
11:12 Young Joash was enthroned by the conspirators. The best symbol of the royal theology behind the Davidic dynasty was the **testimony**, the king's personal copy of the covenant that was prepared by the Levites (Dt 17:18). However, some see this as

a physical symbol of royal status, perhaps royal armband (2Sm 1:10). The theological proper enthronement also demanded the presence of a high priest and the bestowal of the **crown**.
11:13–14a The word **pillar** may designate a traditional place where the king was publicly recognized or perhaps a traditional place of covenant renewal (23:3). If this portico of the Lord's temple was also a hall of pillars (1Kg 7:6; the words "portico" and "hall" used in this verse can be the same Hebrew word) then this pillar could have been one of the pillars in that area. Otherwise one of the great bronze pillars was intended.
11:14b–16 Athaliah was removed from the sacred precincts and executed. This clearly evidenced her lack of support.
11:18 A natural step in obedience to the covenant was the destruction of **the temple of Baal**. Killing the **priest of Baal** at the altar was an insulting desecration of that altar.

Judah's King Joash

12 ²¹ Joash^A was seven years old when he became king. ¹ In the seventh year of Jehu, Joash became king, and he reigned forty years in Jerusalem. His mother's name was Zibiah; she was from Beer-sheba. ² Throughout the time the priest Jehoiada instructed him, Joash did what was right in the LORD's sight. ³ Yet the high places were not taken away; the people continued sacrificing and burning incense on the high places.

Repairing the Temple

⁴ Then Joash said to the priests, "All the dedicated silver brought to the LORD's temple, census silver, silver from vows, and all silver voluntarily given for the LORD's temple — ⁵ each priest is to take it from his assessor^B and repair whatever damage is found in the temple."^C

⁶ But by the twenty-third year of the reign of King Joash, the priests had not repaired the damage^D to the temple. ⁷ So King Joash called the priest Jehoiada and the other priests and asked, "Why haven't you repaired the temple's damage? Since you haven't, don't take any silver from your assessors; instead, hand it over for the repair of the temple." ⁸ So the priests agreed that they would receive no silver from the people and would not be the ones to repair the temple's damage.

⁹ Then the priest Jehoiada took a chest, bored a hole in its lid, and set it beside the altar on the right side as one enters the LORD's temple; the priests who guarded the threshold put into the chest all the silver that was brought to the LORD's temple. ¹⁰ Whenever they saw there was a large amount of silver in the chest, the king's secretary and the high priest would go bag up and tally the silver found in the LORD's temple. ¹¹ Then they would give the weighed silver to those doing the work — those who oversaw the LORD's temple. They in turn would pay it out to those working on the LORD's temple — the carpenters, the builders, ¹² the masons, and the stonecutters — and would use it to buy timber and quarried stone to repair the damage to the LORD's temple and for all expenses for temple repairs.

¹³ However, no silver bowls, wick trimmers, sprinkling basins, trumpets, or any articles of gold or silver were made for the LORD's temple from the contributions^E brought to the LORD's temple. ¹⁴ Instead, it was given to those doing the work, and they repaired the LORD's temple with it. ¹⁵ No accounting was required from the men who received the silver to pay those doing the work, since they worked with integrity. ¹⁶ The silver from the guilt offering and the sin offering was not brought to the LORD's temple since it belonged to the priests.

Aramean Invasion of Judah

¹⁷ At that time King Hazael of Aram marched up and fought against Gath and captured it. Then he planned to attack Jerusalem. ¹⁸ So King Joash of Judah took all the items consecrated by himself and by his ancestors — Judah's kings Jehoshaphat, Jehoram, and Ahaziah — as well as all the gold found in the treasuries of the LORD's temple and in the king's palace, and he sent them to King Hazael of Aram. Then Hazael withdrew from Jerusalem.

Joash Assassinated

¹⁹ The rest of the events of Joash's reign, along with all his accomplishments, are written in the Historical Record of Judah's Kings. ²⁰ Joash's servants conspired against him and attacked him at Beth-millo on the road that goes down to Silla. ²¹ It was his servants Jozabad^F son of Shimeath and Jehozabad son of Shomer who attacked him. He died and they buried him with

---

^A 11:21 = The LORD Has Bestowed   ^B 12:5 Hb obscure   ^C 12:5 Lit *repair the breach of the temple wherever there is found a breach*   ^D 12:6 Lit *breach* in 2Kg 12:5–12   ^E 12:13 Lit *silver*   ^F 12:21 Some Hb mss, LXX read *Jozacar*; 2Ch 24:26 reads *Zabad*

12:2–3 Joash was a good king as long as Jehoiada **instructed him.** Due to the restrained nature of the condemnation, the **high places,** both here and for the next three kings, were probably not centers for pagan worship; instead, they were likely illegal shrines for worshiping Yahweh outside of Jerusalem. **12:4–5** Joash's own revival activities seem to have begun with renovating the **LORD's temple.** He directed that some of the gifts coming into the temple should be designated for temple refurbishing. The text is not clear about which temple taxes or gifts the king selected from the list given here. This list mentioned **dedicated silver** (lit "silver of the holy things"), **census silver,** possibly from the annual census of males (Ex 30:13–14), and **silver from vows** (voluntary gifts). **12:13–15** The record is positive concerning the overseers, saying they were so honest that **no accounting** was necessary. Yet, at

this point, funds were inadequate for replacing the utensils necessary for the temple worship. Later, funds became available for this purpose (2Ch 24:14). **12:16** This verse clarifies v. 4. **12:17–18** Second Kings omits any record of Joash's late unfaithfulness to the Lord (2Ch 24:17–22). A plundering expedition by **King Hazael of Aram** was judgment for early stages of Joash's unfaithfulness. This campaign demonstrated the collapse of joint Israelite power. Just two decades earlier, when Jehu seized the throne of Israel, Israel was competing with Hazael for Ramoth-gilead on nearly equal terms. Now, Hazael apparently marched freely through the territory of Israel to the coast and then south along the coast to capture **Gath.** With Gath captured and Judah weak, the route to **Jerusalem** was open. Joash sent the treasures of the palace and the **temple** to buy off Hazael.

From Chronicles we learn that after more years of Joash's unfaithfulness, Aram,

likely under Ben-hadad, again invaded Judah, entered Jerusalem (2Ch 17:23), killed many people, and seized still more plunder. Several factual differences distinguish this actual penetration of Jerusalem from Hazael's threat to Jerusalem mentioned above. Though revival formally began with Joash, it was short-lived and shallow. This could explain why the return of prosperity, power, and blessing was delayed until later. **12:19–21** After the formula sentences about the end of **Joash's reign,** the text reports that he died by assassination—a tragedy almost certainly instigated by his idolatry and the plundering of Jerusalem. The assassination occurred at **Beth-millo.** Similarities in root meaning hint that **Silla** might be another word for the ramp or descending highway just southeast of Jerusalem. This possibility could give the meaning "the Beth-millo that goes down parallel to the highway."

his ancestors in the city of David, and his son Amaziah became king in his place.

Israel's King Jehoahaz

13 In the twenty-third year of Judah's King Joash son of Ahaziah, Jehoahaz son of Jehu became king over Israel in Samaria, and he reigned seventeen years. [2] He did what was evil in the LORD's sight and followed the sins that Jeroboam son of Nebat had caused Israel to commit; he did not turn away from them. [3] So the LORD's anger burned against Israel, and he handed them over to King Hazael of Aram and to his son Ben-hadad during their reigns.

[4] Then Jehoahaz sought the LORD's favor, and the LORD heard him, for he saw the oppression the king of Aram inflicted on Israel. [5] Therefore, the LORD gave Israel a deliverer, and they escaped from the power of the Arameans. Then the people of Israel returned to their former way of life,^ [6] but they didn't turn away from the sins that the house of Jeroboam had caused Israel to commit. Jehoahaz continued them, and the Asherah pole also remained standing in Samaria. [7] Jehoahaz did not have an army left, except for fifty horsemen, ten chariots, and ten thousand foot soldiers, because the king of Aram had destroyed them, making them like dust at threshing.

[8] The rest of the events of Jehoahaz's reign, along with all his accomplishments and his might, are written in the Historical Record of Israel's Kings. [9] Jehoahaz rested with his ancestors, and he was buried in Samaria. His son Jehoash^ became king in his place.

Israel's King Jehoash

[10] In the thirty-seventh year of Judah's King Joash, Jehoash son of Jehoahaz became king over Israel in Samaria, and he reigned sixteen years. [11] He did what was evil in the LORD's sight. He did not turn away from all the sins that Jeroboam son of Nebat had caused Israel to commit, but he continued them. [12] The rest of the events of Jehoash's reign, along with all his accomplishments and the power he had to wage war against Judah's King Amaziah, are written in the Historical Record of Israel's Kings. [13] Jehoash rested with his ancestors, and Jeroboam sat on his throne. Jehoash was buried in Samaria with the kings of Israel.

Elisha's Death

[14] When Elisha became sick with the illness from which he died, King Jehoash of Israel went down and wept over him and said, "My father, my father, the chariots and horsemen of Israel!"

[15] Elisha responded, "Get a bow and arrows." So he got a bow and arrows. [16] Then Elisha said to the king of Israel, "Grasp the bow." So the king grasped it, and Elisha put his hands on the king's hands. [17] Elisha said, "Open the east window." So he opened it. Elisha said, "Shoot!" So he shot. Then Elisha said, "The LORD's arrow of victory, yes, the arrow of victory over Aram. You are to strike down the Arameans in Aphek until you have put an end to them." [18] Then Elisha said, "Take the arrows!" So he took them. Then Elisha said to the king of Israel, "Strike the ground!" So he struck the ground three times and stopped. [19] The man of God was angry with him and said, "You should have struck the ground five or six times. Then you would have struck down Aram until you had put an end to them, but now you will strike down Aram only three times." [20] Then Elisha died and was buried.

Now Moabite raiders used to come into the land in the spring of the year. [21] Once, as the Israelites were burying a man, suddenly they saw a raiding party, so they threw the man into Elisha's tomb. When he touched Elisha's bones, the man revived and stood up!

God's Mercy on Israel

[22] King Hazael of Aram oppressed Israel throughout the reign of Jehoahaz, [23] but the LORD was gracious to them, had compassion on them, and turned toward them because of his covenant with Abraham, Isaac, and Jacob.

---

^13:5 Lit *Israel dwelt in their tents as formerly*   ^13:9 Lit *Joash*

13:1 The reign of **Jehoahaz** marked the low point of Hebrew fortunes between the greatness of Ahab and Jehoshaphat and the greatness of Jeroboam II and Azariah. Ironically, conditions became even worse after Joash's tepid revival. The Assyrians were inactive in Aram and Palestine, so Hazael (possibly a second king by this name) had a free hand in plundering both Israel and Judah.
13:2 Jehoahaz's father had destroyed Baalism in Israel (10:18–27), so Israel was more free from Baal than Judah was, but Jehoahaz restored the false worship that **Jeroboam** had instigated.
13:4–7 Historians generally agree that the **deliverer** was a new king of Assyria, Adad-Nirari III, who attacked the west in 805 BC and diverted Aramean power from Israel.

13:6–7 This **Asherah pole** probably represented the fertility consort of one of the historic Palestinian Baals. The numbers—**fifty horsemen, ten chariots, and ten thousand foot soldiers**—showed the dismal military state of Israel.
13:10–13 This negative estimate of **Jehoash** gives no hint of the good relations recorded between Elisha and Jehoash or of Jehoash's successes against Aram. This closer for Jehoash's reign is structurally correct since the normal pattern was to conclude the current record before taking up the next record (Amaziah, 14:1–22). The repetition of this material in 14:15–16 is out of its natural place.
13:14–19 On Jehoash's words to Elisha, see note at 2:12. Elisha's deathbed interview with

Jehoash was appended to Jehoash's official record. Despite the negative judgment against Jehoash, there was mutual affection between the king and Elisha. The prophet presented a symbolic oracle to Jehoash. Elisha designated the **arrows** as symbols of defeat for **Aram**. Then Elisha ordered the king to implement the curse by symbolically striking the **ground**. He then rebuked Jehoash for not striking the ground enough times, perhaps indicative of Jehoash's lack of zeal.
13:20–21 God still had one more miracle to certify his work through **Elisha**. A dead **man** was brought to life because his corpse came into contact with the **bones** of Elisha.

He was not willing to destroy them. Even now he has not banished them from his presence. ²⁴ King Hazael of Aram died, and his son Ben-hadad became king in his place. ²⁵ Then Jehoash son of Jehoahaz took back from Ben-hadad son of Hazael the cities that Hazael had taken in war from Jehoash's father Jehoahaz. Jehoash defeated Ben-hadad three times and recovered the cities of Israel.

Judah's King Amaziah

14 In the second year of Israel's King Jehoash[A] son of Jehoahaz,[B] Amaziah son of Joash became king of Judah. ² He was twenty-five years old when he became king, and he reigned twenty-nine years in Jerusalem. His mother's name was Jehoaddin;[C] she was from Jerusalem. ³ He did what was right in the Lord's sight, but not like his ancestor David. He did everything his father Joash had done. ⁴ Yet the high places were not taken away, and the people continued sacrificing and burning incense on the high places.

⁵ As soon as the kingdom was firmly in his grasp, Amaziah killed his servants who had killed his father the king. ⁶ However, he did not put the children of the killers to death, as it is written in the book of the law of Moses where the Lord commanded, "Fathers are not to be put to death because of children, and children are not to be put to death because of fathers; instead, each one will be put to death for his own sin."

⁷ Amaziah killed ten thousand Edomites in Salt Valley. He took Sela in battle and called it Joktheel, which is still its name today. ⁸ Amaziah then sent messengers to Jehoash son of Jehoahaz, son of Jehu, king of Israel, and challenged him: "Come, let's meet face to face."

⁹ King Jehoash of Israel sent word to King Amaziah of Judah, saying, "The thistle in Lebanon once sent a message to the cedar in Lebanon, saying, 'Give your daughter to my son as a wife.' Then a wild animal in Lebanon passed by and trampled the thistle. ¹⁰ You have indeed defeated Edom, and you have become overconfident.[D] Enjoy your glory and stay at home. Why should you stir up such trouble that you fall — you and Judah with you?"

¹¹ But Amaziah would not listen, so King Jehoash of Israel advanced. He and King Amaziah of Judah met face to face at Beth-shemesh that belonged to Judah. ¹² Judah was routed before Israel, and each man fled to his own tent. ¹³ King Jehoash of Israel captured Judah's King Amaziah son of Joash,[E] son of Ahaziah, at Beth-shemesh. Then Jehoash went to Jerusalem and broke down two hundred yards[F] of Jerusalem's wall from the Ephraim Gate to the Corner Gate. ¹⁴ He took all the gold and silver, all the articles found in the Lord's temple and in the treasuries of the king's palace, and some hostages. Then he returned to Samaria.

Jehoash's Death

¹⁵ The rest of the events of Jehoash's reign, along with his accomplishments, his might, and how he waged war against King Amaziah of Judah, are written in the Historical Record of Israel's Kings. ¹⁶ Jehoash rested with his ancestors, and he was buried in Samaria with the kings of Israel. His son Jeroboam became king in his place.

Amaziah's Death

¹⁷ Judah's King Amaziah son of Joash lived fifteen years after the death of Israel's King Jehoash son of Jehoahaz. ¹⁸ The rest of the events of Amaziah's reign are written in the Historical Record of Judah's Kings. ¹⁹ A conspiracy was formed against him in Jerusalem, and he fled to Lachish. However, men were sent after him to Lachish, and they put him to death there. ²⁰ They carried him back on horses, and he was buried in Jerusalem with his ancestors in city of David.

²¹ Then all the people of Judah took Azariah,[G] who was sixteen years old, and made him king

---

^A14:1 Lit *Joash*, also in vv. 23,27   ^B14:1 Lit *Joahaz*   ^C14:2 Alt Hb tradition, some Hb mss, Syr, Tg, Vg, 2Ch 25:1; other Hb mss, LXX read *Jehoaddin*   ^D14:10 Lit *and your heart has lifted you*   ^E14:13 Lit *Jehoash*   ^F14:13 Lit *400 cubits*   ^G14:21 = Uzziah in 2Ch 26:1

13:24–25 Elisha's dying oracle (vv. 18–21) called for some record of its fulfillment. Thus the record of those victories was appended here, not in the formal record.

14:1–2 The opener for **Amaziah** is ordinary, except that his length of rule, **twenty-nine years**, obscures the fact that for all but the first four years he was co-regent with his son Azariah.

14:3–4 The evaluation of Amaziah notes that the **high places**, again probably for illegal worship of the Lord rather than pagan gods, were not shut down.

14:7 The resurgence of Israelite power actually began with Jehoash and Amaziah. On Judah's part, this involved a successful but brutal reconquest of Edom. The **Salt Valley** is not precisely identified, but it was probably in the Arabah, south of the Dead Sea. **Sela** was the 1,000-foot-high mountain fortress of Edom near Petra.

14:8 Second Kings hints that Amaziah's presumption came from pride and arrogance from his victory over Edom. The Chronicles account attributes Amaziah's presumption to the rejection of God's will and to idolatry (2Ch 25:14,20).

14:9 Some take Jehoash's fable as indicating that **Amaziah** had become upset at Jehoash's rejection of a request for a marriage alliance between Amaziah and Jehoash.

14:10–14 Jehoash did not want war with **Amaziah**, but Amaziah was insistent, and the results were disastrous for **Judah**. The two gates mentioned here indicated that Jehoash tore down the western half of the northern wall of **Jerusalem** and then plundered the city.

14:15–16 This repetition of the formal ending of **Jehoash's reign** seems to be a copyist's error (13:12–13). On the other hand, some interpreters have suggested that the repetition of this data was purposeful and focused the reader's attention on the north where Jehoash was restoring Israelite fortunes.

14:17–18 Note that v. 17 says that Amaziah **lived** rather than "reigned" fifteen years after Jehoash's death.

14:19–21 A long co-regency is necessary to explain the numbers given (15:2). Therefore, the statement **the people of Judah . . . made him** [Azariah] **king** may have been a flashback reference to when the people forced this co-regency on Amaziah in place of his father Amaziah. ²² After Amaziah the king rested with his ancestors, Azariah rebuilt Elath^ and restored it to Judah.

Israel's King Jeroboam

²³ In the fifteenth year of Judah's King Amaziah son of Joash, Jeroboam son of Jehoash became king of Israel in Samaria, and he reigned forty-one years. ²⁴ He did what was evil in the LORD's sight. He did not turn away from all the sins Jeroboam son of Nebat had caused Israel to commit.

²⁵ He restored Israel's border from Lebo-hamath as far as the Sea of the Arabah, according to the word of the LORD, the God of Israel, had spoken through his servant, the prophet Jonah son of Amittai from Gath-hepher. ²⁶ For the LORD saw that the affliction of Israel was very bitter for both slaves and free people.^B There was no one to help Israel. ²⁷ The LORD had not said he would blot out the name of Israel under heaven, so he delivered them by the hand of Jeroboam son of Jehoash.

²⁸ The rest of the events of Jeroboam's reign — along with all his accomplishments, the power he had to wage war, and how he recovered for Israel Damascus and Hamath, which had belonged to Judah^C — are written in the Historical Record of Israel's Kings. ²⁹ Jeroboam rested with his ancestors, the kings of Israel. His son Zechariah became king in his place.

Judah's King Azariah

15 In the twenty-seventh year of Israel's King Jeroboam, Azariah^D son of Amaziah became king of Judah. ² He was sixteen years old when he became king, and he reigned fifty-two years in Jerusalem. His mother's name was Jecoliah; she was from Jerusalem. ³ Azariah did what was right in the LORD's sight just as his father Amaziah had done. ⁴ Yet the high places were not taken away; the people

continued sacrificing and burning incense on the high places.

⁵ The LORD afflicted the king, and he had a serious skin disease until the day of his death. He lived in quarantine,^E while Jotham, the king's son, was over the household governing the people of the land.

⁶ The rest of the events of Azariah's reign, along with all his accomplishments, are written in the Historical Record of Judah's Kings. ⁷ Azariah rested with his ancestors and was buried with his ancestors in the city of David. His son Jotham became king in his place.

Israel's King Zechariah

⁸ In the thirty-eighth year of Judah's King Azariah, Zechariah son of Jeroboam reigned over Israel in Samaria for six months. ⁹ He did what was evil in the LORD's sight as his predecessors had done. He did not turn away from the sins Jeroboam son of Nebat had caused Israel to commit.

¹⁰ Shallum son of Jabesh conspired against Zechariah. He struck him down publicly,^F killed him, and became king in his place. ¹¹ As for the rest of the events of Zechariah's reign, they are written in the Historical Record of Israel's Kings. ¹² The word of the LORD that he spoke to Jehu was, "Four generations of your sons will sit on the throne of Israel," and it was so.

Israel's King Shallum

¹³ In the thirty-ninth year of Judah's King Uzziah,^G Shallum son of Jabesh became king; he reigned in Samaria a full month. ¹⁴ Then Menahem son of Gadi came up from Tirzah to Samaria and struck down Shallum son of Jabesh there. He killed him and became king in his place. ¹⁵ As for the rest of the events of Shallum's reign, along with the conspiracy that he formed, they are written in the Historical Record of Israel's Kings.

---

^14:22 = Eloth in 2Ch 26:2   ^14:26 Hb obscure   ^14:28 Lit *recovered Damascus and for Judah in Israel*; Hb obscure
^15:1 = Uzziah in 2Ch 26:3   ^15:5 Lit *in a house of exemption from duty*   ^15:10 Some LXX mss read *down at Ibleam*;
Hb uncertain   ^15:13 = Azariah, also in vv. 30,32,34

---

because of his political and military bungling (and idolatry as well, according to 2Ch 25:14). It is likely that Amaziah's death, though some years later, also was a result of such dissatisfaction.
14:25 The Bible writer recognized the territorial expansionism of Jeroboam II, whose kingdom fell short of Solomon's northern boundary at Tiphsah on the Euphrates River. Jeroboam II's boundary reached only to Lebo-hamath. In the south, his territory reached to the **Sea of the Arabah**, clearly the Dead Sea since this body of water was under the slopes of Pisgah (Dt 3:17). Only here do we find that **Jonah**, the minor prophet, joined with Elisha in prophesying this restoration of Hebrew power.
15:1–7 Once again, the record of a king—this time Azariah of Judah, also called Uzziah—does not do full justice to his stature, godliness, and significance. He was co-regent for

twenty-five years with Amaziah (792–767 BC). To see his importance, one must consult the fuller records in Isaiah and Chronicles. Including the co-regency with Amaziah, his reign saw the passing of the dynasty of Jehu and the final end of Israel's imperial power. It is particularly significant that one of the best known and most significant prophetic visions in the OT is dated "in the year that King Uzziah died" (Is 6:1). His death truly did mark the end of an era.
15:1–2 The formula data for the beginning of the reign of **Azariah** of **Judah** again could obscure both the co-regency with his father Amaziah (792–767 BC) and the co-regency with his son Jotham (750–740 BC).
15:5–7 Perhaps out of deference to Azariah's generally positive character, the writer omitted the reason for Azariah's **skin disease**. Azariah became arrogant and performed a task that only priests were allowed to do

(2Ch 26:16–19). The situation was so severe that Azariah finished his life in quarantine, and his son **Jotham**, the successor designate, governed the land in day-to-day matters.
15:10–12 The closer of **Zechariah's** rule is not typical. It is the record of a palace revolution. The meaning of **publicly** (Hb *qabal'am*) is uncertain. This sudden revolution, within six months of the death of the great Jeroboam II, showed how quickly both the throne and imperial power declined after his death. But God had kept his promise that four generations of Jehu's sons would rule **Israel** (see 10:30). Jehu's dynasty was the longest of the northern dynasties.
15:13–15 After a brief opener, the record of **Shallum** of Israel moves immediately to Menahem's revolution. Shallum's record ends with the note that his other deeds are recorded elsewhere in writings now lost to history.

Israel's King Menahem

16 At that time, starting from Tirzah, Menahem attacked Tiphsah, all who were in it, and its territory because they wouldn't surrender. He ripped open all the pregnant women.

17 In the thirty-ninth year of Judah's King Azariah, Menahem son of Gadi became king over Israel, and he reigned ten years in Samaria. **18** He did what was evil in the LORD's sight. Throughout his reign, he did not turn away from the sins Jeroboam son of Nebat had caused Israel to commit.

19 King Pul^A of Assyria invaded the land, so Menahem gave Pul seventy-five thousand pounds^B of silver so that Pul would support him to strengthen his grasp on the kingdom. **20** Then Menahem exacted twenty ounces^C of silver from each of the prominent men of Israel to give to the king of Assyria. So the king of Assyria withdrew and did not stay there in the land.

21 The rest of the events of Menahem's reign, along with all his accomplishments, are written in the Historical Record of Israel's Kings. **22** Menahem rested with his ancestors, and his son Pekahiah became king in his place.

Israel's King Pekahiah

23 In the fiftieth year of Judah's King Azariah, Pekahiah son of Menahem became king over Israel in Samaria, and he reigned two years. **24** He did what was evil in the LORD's sight and did not turn away from the sins Jeroboam son of Nebat had caused Israel to commit.

25 Then his officer, Pekah son of Remaliah, conspired against him and struck him down in Samaria at the citadel of the king's palace — with Argob and Arieh.^D There were fifty Gileadite men with Pekah. He killed Pekahiah and became king in his place.

26 As for the rest of the events of Pekahiah's reign, along with all his accomplishments, they are written in the Historical Record of Israel's Kings.

Israel's King Pekah

27 In the fifty-second year of Judah's King Azariah, Pekah son of Remaliah became king over Israel in Samaria, and he reigned twenty years. **28** He did what was evil in the LORD's sight. He did not turn away from the sins Jeroboam son of Nebat had caused Israel to commit.

29 In the days of King Pekah of Israel, King Tiglath-pileser of Assyria came and captured Ijon, Abel-beth-maacah, Janoah, Kedesh, Hazor, Gilead, and Galilee — all the land of Naphtali — and deported the people to Assyria.

30 Then Hoshea son of Elah organized a conspiracy against Pekah son of Remaliah. He attacked him, killed him, and became king in his place in the twentieth year of Jotham son of Uzziah.

31 As for the rest of the events of Pekah's reign, along with all his accomplishments, they are written in the Historical Record of Israel's Kings.

Judah's King Jotham

32 In the second year of Israel's King Pekah son of Remaliah, Jotham son of Uzziah became king of Judah. **33** He was twenty-five years old when he became king, and he reigned sixteen years in Jerusalem. His mother's name was Jerusha daughter of Zadok. **34** He did what was right in the LORD's sight just as his father Uzziah had done. **35** Yet the high places were not taken away; the people continued sacrificing and burning incense on the high places.

^A15:19 = Tiglath-pileser　^B15:19 Lit 1,000 talents　^C15:20 Lit 50 shekels　^D15:25 Hb obscure

15:16 Some historians see a geographical shift in the center of power in this revolution. **Tirzah** had once been the center of power before Omri moved the capital to Samaria. They then saw **Menahem** as returning to an old power base—the people of Tirzah—who apparently were glad to resume a position of prestige and leadership. The location of **Tiphsah** is uncertain. The Tiphsah on the Euphrates River was too distant to be a part of this struggle. Some read this name as "Tappuah" or "Tirzah." This city resisted the revolution, so Menahem destroyed it. Whether because of his power base in Tirzah or because of his terrifying brutality to Tiphsah, he gained enough authority to rule for ten years.

15:19–20 In 743 BC, near the end of Menahem's reign, Tiglath-pileser III (known in the Bible by his throne name *Pulu* or **Pul**) invaded the region. This created a new political situation since **Assyria** was now the enemy to the north and northeast. Thus the major internal struggle for most of the small kingdoms of Palestine and Aram was between the pro-Assyrian party that advocated peace

with Assyria at any price and the anti-Assyrian party that advocated wars for independence at any price. Menahem purchased his throne by taking a pro-Assyrian stance and paying a huge tribute, **seventy-five thousand pounds of silver**. Menahem raised the tribute money by imposing a head tax on the **prominent men** of Israel. This tax alienated the anti-Assyrian parties in Israel.

15:23–26 Pekahiah ruled only two years. The reason for his short reign was the dissatisfaction of the anti-Assyrian party in Israel. The leader of the rebellion was **Pekah**, who became the next king.

15:27–28 The formal opening statements for **Pekah** indicate that he ruled for **twenty years**, a long and successful rule for this period, though his first twelve years were probably as an independent ruler in Gilead. Then he enjoyed eight years (740–732 BC) of rule over Israel until the Assyrians returned.

15:29 Israel had been briefly free from Assyrian invasion because **Assyria** was too busy elsewhere, so **Pekah** broke his treaty with Assyria. But then, in 734 BC, Tiglath-pileser returned, conquered, and annexed large

portions of northern Israel. The area defined by the names in the text includes significant Transjordan Hebrew holdings and regions north of the fertile Plain of Esdraelon. This still left the king of Israel with the fertile heartland of the country and a reasonable hope of local, though not imperial, prosperity. The Hebrews in the annexed territories were **deported** to the east and—though not stated here—the Assyrians brought in new population to resettle the land.

15:30–31 Pekah was then deposed by a revolution led by **Hoshea**. It is not clear whether this was the work of a pro-Assyrian party or of an anti-Assyrian party that penalized Pekah for not being successful enough in his resistance to Assyria. Hoshea later conspired against Assyria.

15:32–35 The clock turns back to two kings of **Judah** who became king during the reign of **Pekah**. Again, Jotham's length-of-rule formula can be confusing. His **sixteen years** apparently did not include the ten years of co-regency with Azariah, nor did they include the three-year co-regency with Ahaz. He was a good king, except he did not close

Jotham built the Upper Gate of the LORD's temple. **36** The rest of the events of Jotham's reign, along with all his accomplishments, are written in the Historical Record of Judah's Kings. **37** In those days the LORD began sending Aram's King Rezin and Pekah son of Remaliah against Judah. **38** Jotham rested with his ancestors and was buried with his ancestors in the city of his ancestor David. His son Ahaz became king in his place.

Judah's King Ahaz

16 In the seventeenth year of Pekah son of Remaliah, Ahaz son of Jotham became king of Judah. **2** Ahaz was twenty years old when he became king, and he reigned sixteen years in Jerusalem. He did not do what was right in the sight of the LORD his God like his ancestor David **3** but walked in the ways of the kings of Israel. He even sacrificed his son in the fire,^A imitating the detestable practices of the nations the LORD had dispossessed before the Israelites. **4** He sacrificed and burned incense on the high places, on the hills, and under every green tree.

5 Then Aram's King Rezin and Israel's King Pekah son of Remaliah came to wage war against Jerusalem. They besieged Ahaz but were not able to conquer him. **6** At that time Aram's King Rezin recovered Elath for Aram and expelled the Judahites from Elath. Then the Arameans came to Elath, and they still live there today.

7 So Ahaz sent messengers to King Tiglath-pileser of Assyria, saying, "I am your servant and your son. March up and save me from the grasp of the king of Aram and of the king of Israel, who are rising up against me." **8** Ahaz also took the silver and gold found in the LORD's temple and in the treasuries of the king's palace and sent them to the king of Assyria as a bribe. **9** So the king of Assyria listened to him and marched up to Damascus and captured it. He deported its people to Kir but put Rezin to death.

Ahaz's Idolatry

10 King Ahaz went to Damascus to meet King Tiglath-pileser of Assyria. When he saw the altar that was in Damascus, King Ahaz sent a model of the altar and complete plans for its construction to the priest Uriah. **11** Uriah built the altar according to all the instructions King Ahaz sent from Damascus. Therefore, by the time King Ahaz came back from Damascus, the priest Uriah had completed it. **12** When the king came back from Damascus, he saw the altar. Then he approached the altar and ascended it.^B **13** He offered his burnt offering and his grain offering, poured out his drink offering, and splattered the blood of his fellowship offerings on the altar. **14** He took the bronze altar that was before the LORD in front of the temple between his altar and the LORD's temple, and put it on the north side of his altar.

15 Then King Ahaz commanded the priest Uriah, "Offer on the great altar the morning burnt offering, the evening grain offering, and the king's burnt offering and his grain offering. Also offer the burnt offering of all the people of the land, their grain offering, and their drink offerings. Splatter on the altar all the blood of the burnt offering and all the blood of sacrifice. The bronze altar will be for me to seek guidance."^C **16** The priest Uriah did everything King Ahaz commanded.

17 Then King Ahaz cut off the frames of the water carts^D and removed the bronze basin from each of them. He took the basin^E from the bronze oxen that were under it and put it on

^A **16:3** Lit *even made his son pass through the fire*   ^B **16:12** Or *and offered on it:*   ^C **16:15** Hb obscure   ^D **16:17** Lit *the stands*
^E **16:17** Lit *sea*

---

down the worship of the Lord at the illegal shrines on the **high places**. He was the last of the four good kings from Joash to Jotham, and he was the only one who did not finish badly. An addition to the Lord's temple was his outstanding achievement.
15:36–38 The closing comments about **Jotham's** reign cast a cloud on the future in referring to the beginning of raids against Judah by **Aram's King Rezin** and **Pekah** of Israel. Historians take this harassment as trying to force Judah into an anti-Assyrian coalition. By some datings, **Ahaz** may have been ruling as co-regent with Jotham during the invasions of Judah described in the next chapter (16:5–6; see Is 7:3–6).
16:1–2a The **seventeenth year of Pekah** (735 BC) would have been the beginning of Ahaz's co-regency with Jotham. Ahaz's sixteen-year official reign began with his sole regency in 731 BC with Jotham's death. The data does not indicate the year in which Ahaz was **twenty years old**.
16:2b–4 Ahaz was the first bad king of Judah in about one hundred years. The phrase

ways of the kings of Israel could refer to paganism in general, particularly the worship of the Baals. Sacrificing **his son in the fire** showed the depths of Ahaz's paganism, although some suggest this was a different offense than sacrificing the son in Baal's fiery arms. The king's **high places** included those for pagan deities. In pagan cults a **green tree** symbolized a goddess's fertility and sometimes represented the goddess consort of the fertility deity at a high place.
16:5–6 These verses understate the military pressure from Israel and **Aram** during Ahaz's reign. Likely, during the co-regency of Jotham and Ahaz (ca 735–732 BC), both Aram and Israel invaded and devastated Judah in turn (2Ch 28:5–6) and then put Jerusalem under siege. The goal was to force Ahaz into an anti-Assyrian alliance or to replace him with a king who would oppose Assyria. Although they seized valuable territory, including the port of **Elath**, they could not conquer Ahaz.
16:7–9 Ahaz then voluntarily submitted to **Assyria**, who would rule Judah as a vassal for the next century.

16:10–11 Ahaz's imported **altar** was the cultic symbol of his submission to Assyria's main god. The priest **Uriah** represented the complicity of some priests and Levites in this religious corruption.
16:12–13 Ahaz entered into his religious responsibilities to Assyria's chief pagan god with diligence, though he also had time for other pagan deities as well (vv. 3–4).
16:14–15a Perhaps at the suggestion of some visiting Assyrian official (cp. v. 18), Ahaz moved the original **bronze altar** of the Lord to a less central place in the temple to give prominence to the altar of the Assyrian god.
16:15b–16 Ahaz, however, remained true to the Lord in one activity. He designated the **bronze altar** of the Lord as the king's private altar where he would seek guidance, presumably from the Lord. The traditional means of guidance was through the sacred lots, the Urim and Thummim, though some suggest that Ahaz used pagan divinations.
16:17 Bronze was a valuable commodity. So, as an accommodating subject, Ahaz stripped bronze off the sacred fittings of the Lord's

a stone pavement. [18] To satisfy the king of Assyria, he removed from the LORD's temple the Sabbath canopy they had built in the palace, and he closed the outer entrance for the king.

Ahaz's Death

[19] The rest of the events of Ahaz's reign, along with his accomplishments, are written in the Historical Record of Judah's Kings. [20] Ahaz rested with his ancestors and was buried with his ancestors in the city of David, and his son Hezekiah became king in his place.

Israel's King Hoshea

17 In the twelfth year of Judah's King Ahaz, Hoshea son of Elah became king over Israel in Samaria, and he reigned nine years. [2] He did what was evil in the LORD's sight, but not like the kings of Israel who preceded him. [3] King Shalmaneser of Assyria attacked him, and Hoshea became his vassal and paid him tribute. [4] But the king of Assyria caught Hoshea in a conspiracy: He had sent envoys to So king of Egypt and had not paid tribute to the king of Assyria as in previous years.[A] Therefore the king of Assyria arrested him and put him in prison. [5] The king of Assyria invaded the whole land, marched up to Samaria, and besieged it for three years.

The Fall of Samaria

[6] In the ninth year of Hoshea, the king of Assyria captured Samaria. He deported the Israelites to Assyria and settled them in Halah, along the Habor (Gozan's river), and in the cities of the Medes.

Why Israel Fell

[7] This disaster happened because the people of Israel sinned against the LORD their God who had brought them out of the land of Egypt from the power of Pharaoh king of Egypt and because they worshiped[B] other gods. [8] They lived according to the customs of the nations that the LORD had dispossessed before the

Israelites and according to what the kings of Israel did. [9] The Israelites secretly did things[C] against the LORD their God that were not right. They built high places in all their towns from watchtower to fortified city. [10] They set up for themselves sacred pillars and Asherah poles on every high hill and under every green tree. [11] They burned incense there on all the high places just like the nations that the LORD had driven out before them had done. They did evil things, angering the LORD. [12] They served idols, although the LORD had told them, "You must not do this." [13] Still, the LORD warned Israel and Judah through every prophet and every seer, saying, "Turn from your evil ways and keep my commands and statutes according to the whole law I commanded your ancestors and sent to you through my servants the prophets."

[14] But they would not listen. Instead they became obstinate like[D] their ancestors who did not believe the LORD their God. [15] They rejected his statutes and his covenant he had made with their ancestors and the warnings he had given them. They followed worthless idols and became worthless themselves, following the surrounding nations the LORD had commanded them not to imitate.

[16] They abandoned all the commands of the LORD their God. They made cast images for themselves, two calves, and an Asherah pole. They bowed in worship to all the stars in the sky and served Baal. [17] They sacrificed their sons and daughters in the fire[E] and practiced divination and interpreted omens. They devoted themselves to do what was evil in the LORD's sight and angered him.

[18] Therefore, the LORD was very angry with Israel, and he removed them from his presence. Only the tribe of Judah remained. [19] Even Judah did not keep the commands of the LORD their God but lived according to the customs Israel had practiced. [20] So the LORD rejected all the descendants of Israel, punished them, and handed them over to plunderers until he had banished them from his presence.

[A]17:4 Lit as year by year   [B]17:7 Lit feared   [C]17:9 Or Israelites spoke words   [D]17:14 Lit they stiffened their neck like the neck of   [E]17:17 Lit They made their sons and daughters pass through the fire

---

house and even sent the bronze from the twelve **oxen** of the bronze **basin** to Assyria as tribute.
17:1–2 The formulaic opener for **Hoshea** reveals that he was not as bad as his predecessors.
17:3–4 Hoshea was appointed king about 732 BC over an Israel greatly reduced by Tiglath-pileser III (15:29). At some point when **Assyria** was distracted elsewhere Hoshea declared his freedom. The identity of **So** among known Egyptian Pharaohs is uncertain. When Hoshea withheld tribute from Assyria, the end came. Tiglath-pileser died before he could return to Samaria, but his son, Shalmaneser V, invaded Israel (725 BC). After a three-year siege, he captured Samaria, imprisoned Hoshea, and deported

the Hebrew population to Assyria (722 BC). Verse 4 seems to indicate that Shalmaneser arrested Hoshea before besieging Samaria. It is unlikely that the city would have resisted after Hoshea's arrest. It is easier to take vv. 4–6 as topically structured. The topic of v. 4 is Hoshea, whom Shalmaneser **arrested** (confined by siege) and then **put . . . in prison** after the siege ended.
17:5–6a Shalmaneser **besieged** the city for three years and then **deported** the population to points north and east of Israel. Sargon II, the next king of Assyria, may have expedited some of the deportations.
17:6b The Assyrians deported the Hebrews to several different areas. **Halah** was in the general area of Gozan. Some were settled along the **Habor** River, a tributary of the

Euphrates that flowed south from the region of Haran and Gozan to the Euphrates. This region was only about four hundred miles northeast of Israel. However, other Israelites were settled in the territory of the **Medes** in mountain country east and northeast of the plains of Babylon and Assyria. These exiles were almost a thousand miles from home.
17:9–10 The Israelites built numerous **high places**, at first **secretly** and then openly. The typical high place installation consisted of (1) a **sacred** stone or **pillars** for the male fertility deity, usually some Baal; and (2) a sacred pole or **green tree** for the female consort of the Baal. The latter often represented the consort goddess or **Asherah**.
17:16–17 Divination focuses more on gaining knowledge by supernatural means while

The Exiles of Israel

by Duane A. Garrett

Two related but distinct concepts that shaped the history of Israel are *exile* and *Diaspora*. The "exile" is the forced removal of the bulk of the population, especially of the skilled and upper-class people, from their homeland to another country.

There were several Jewish exiles. The first was the exile of the Israelites of the northern kingdom (Samaria) carried out by the Assyrians. It occurred in two phases, first in 734 BC under Tiglath-pileser III (2Kg 15:29) and then, climactically, in 722 under Shalmaneser and his successor, Sargon II, when the city of Samaria was destroyed and the northern kingdom ceased to exist (17:5-6).

The next major exile involved the destruction of the southern kingdom (Judah) and the city of Jerusalem. It, too, took place in several phases, all under the Babylonian king Nebuchadnezzar II (Jr 52:28–30), the most terrible of which was in 586 BC (52:29). This was when Solomon's temple was destroyed and the dynasty of David came to an end.

The third major exile of the Jews took place under the Romans and also was in two phases. In AD 70 the Roman general (later emperor) Titus destroyed Jerusalem and Herod's temple. A second Jewish rebellion (called the Bar Kokhba revolt after the name of its Jewish leader) took place under Emperor Hadrian in the years AD 132–136. This was a bloody struggle, and at the end the victorious Romans decreed that no Jew would be allowed to live in Palestine. All of these events involved exile, the forcible deportation of Jews from the Holy Land by their conquerors.

The Diaspora is the scattering of Jews across the world. This process began around the time of the destruction of Samaria and continued in the aftermath of the Babylonian exile. The story of Esther, for example, involves Jews dispersed across the Persian Empire; this dispersion persisted even though the Persians allowed the Jews to return to their traditional homeland.

We know of some specific Jewish enclaves. For example, there was in the fifth century BC a Jewish community in Elephantine (in southern Egypt), and beginning in the third century BC there was another such community in Alexandria (in northern Egypt). The Jewish Diaspora has involved places as diverse as ancient Rome, medieval Spain, Yemen, Iraq, Russia, Germany, and the United States. It continues to this day even though there is now a Jewish homeland in Israel.

The book of Esther also accurately characterizes the experience of Jews in Diaspora. On the one hand, the Jews are a positive contribution to their host countries and are often highly successful, but on the other hand, they are relentlessly and often unjustly persecuted.

Exile and Diaspora are the punishments God imposed on Israel for idolatry and unbelief (Dt 28:64–68; Is 6:11–12; 39:1–7; Jr 6:1–8; 19:1–13; Ezk 5:5–12; Am 8:1–12). Perhaps the primary passage on the subject is Dt 29:24–28: "All the nations will ask, 'Why has the LORD done this to this land. . . .' Then people will answer, 'It is because they abandoned the covenant of the LORD. . . . They began to serve other gods. . . . Therefore the LORD's anger burned. . . . The LORD uprooted them from their land in his anger, rage, and intense wrath, and threw them into another land where they are today.'"

But this is not the whole story. The prophets also claimed that God would restore David's fallen dynasty (Hs 3:5; Am 9:11) and give Israel a new covenant to replace the one they had broken (Jr 31:31–34). And now, while Israel is in disobedience and Diaspora, the Gentiles are brought into the new covenant (Rm 11:25–32). The true end of exile will be when Israel turns to their Messiah, Jesus, mourning over him whom they have pierced (Zch 12:6–14).

Summary of Israel's History

²¹ When the LORD tore Israel from the house of David, Israel made Jeroboam son of Nebat king. Then Jeroboam led Israel away from following the LORD and caused them to commit grave sin. ²² The Israelites persisted in all the sins that Jeroboam committed and did not turn away from them. ²³ Finally, the LORD removed Israel from his presence just as he had declared through all his servants the prophets. So Israel has been exiled to Assyria from their homeland to this very day.

Foreign Refugees in Israel

²⁴ Then the king of Assyria brought people from Babylon, Cuthah, Avva, Hamath, and Sepharvaim and settled them in place of the Israelites in the cities of Samaria. The settlers took possession of Samaria and lived in its cities. ²⁵ When they first lived there, they did not fear the LORD. So the LORD sent lions among them, which killed some of them. ²⁶ The settlers said to the king of Assyria, "The nations that you have deported and placed in the cities of Samaria do not know the requirements of the god of the land. Therefore he has sent lions among them that are killing them because the people don't know the requirements of the god of the land."

²⁷ Then the king of Assyria issued a command: "Send back one of the priests you deported. Have him go and live there so he can teach them the requirements of the god of the land." ²⁸ So one of the priests they had deported came and lived in Bethel, and he began to teach them how they should fear the LORD.

²⁹ But the people of each nation were still making their own gods in the cities where they lived and putting them in the shrines of the high places that the people of Samaria had made. ³⁰ The men of Babylon made Succoth-benoth, the men of Cuth made Nergal, the men of Hamath made Ashima, ³¹ the Avvites made Nibhaz and Tartak, and the Sepharvites burned their

children in the fire to Adrammelech and Anammelech, the gods of Sepharvaim. ³² They feared the LORD, but they also made from their ranks priests for the high places, who were working for them at the shrines of the high places. ³³ They feared the LORD, but they also worshiped their own gods according to the practice of the nations from which they had been deported.

³⁴ They are still observing the former practices to this day. None of them fear the LORD or observe the statutes and ordinances, the law and commandments that the LORD had commanded the descendants of Jacob, whom he had given the name Israel. ³⁵ The LORD made a covenant with Jacob's descendants and commanded them, "Do not fear other gods; do not bow in worship to them; do not serve them; do not sacrifice to them. ³⁶ Instead fear the LORD, who brought you up from the land of Egypt with great power and an outstretched arm. You are to bow down to him, and you are to sacrifice to him. ³⁷ You are to be careful always to observe the statutes, the ordinances, the law, and the commandments he wrote for you; do not fear other gods. ³⁸ Do not forget the covenant that I have made with you. Do not fear other gods, ³⁹ but fear the LORD your God, and he will rescue you from all your enemies."

⁴⁰ However, these nations would not listen but continued observing their former practices. ⁴¹ They feared the LORD but also served their idols. Still today, their children and grandchildren continue doing as their ancestors did.

Judah's King Hezekiah

18 In the third year of Israel's King Hoshea son of Elah, Hezekiah son of Ahaz became king of Judah. ² He was twenty-five years old when he became king, and he reigned twenty-nine years in Jerusalem. His mother's name was Abi^A daughter of Zechariah. ³ He did what was right in the LORD's sight just as his ancestor David had done. ⁴ He removed the

^18:2 = Abijah in 2Ch 29:1

---

omens are the magical giving of knowledge and the exercise of magic power. Such dabbling with supernatural knowledge and power was condemned by Moses (Lv 20:6; Dt 18:10–11).
17:24 The origins of the Assyrian colonists were the following: (1) **Babylon** in lower Mesopotamia; (2) **Cuthah** in lower Mesopotamia just a few miles from Babylon; (3) **Avva**, also known as Ivvah, of unknown location; (4) **Hamath**, north of Damascus somewhere in Aramean territory.
17:25 The word **fear** can carry a range of meanings, from terror to reverential worship of God. It is not easy to know what level of terror or worship the word communicated in this context.
17:26–28 This priest's work may have been the origin of the Samaritan Pentateuch, a rival to the Hebrew Torah.

17:29–34 The result of all these efforts was a group of people with mixed religious beliefs and practices. They **feared** the Lord, while at the same time they still **worshiped their own gods**, and as a result eventually they did not fear the Lord. **Succoth-benoth** was similar to Sarpanitu, one of Marduk's goddess consorts. **Nergal**, the god of pestilence and one of many consorts of Erishkigal—queen of the underworld—had a shrine in **Cuth**. **Ashima** may have appeared also in the phrase "guilt (Hb *ashmath*) of Samaria" (Am 8:14). This deity was probably the same as Ashim Bethel (or Eshem Bethel), who appeared as a fertility consort of Yahweh in the popular, syncretistic religion of the Jewish colony at Elephantine. Two unknown deities of the **Avvites** were **Nibhaz** and **Tartak**. **Adrammelech** and **Anammelech** of **Sepharvaim** cannot be clearly identified, though the fact that children were sacrificed to them tells something about their character. The

general picture is one of typical ancient fertility religion, including major national deities and minor local deities.
18:1–20:21 This section focuses on the reign of Hezekiah of Judah. He was a godly king, but he and his nation paid a terrible price for his godliness when Sennacherib invaded Judah.
18:1–2 The record of King **Hezekiah** of **Judah** opens with the usual formal statements. However, his dates, like Ahaz's dates, present an unusual circumstance. Some point out that the length of Hezekiah's rule is compatible with the **twenty-nine years** of his sole regency (715–686 BC), while the date of the beginning of his rule refers to the beginning of his co-regency with his father, **Ahaz**. This began in the third year of Hoshea of Israel (729 BC).
18:4–7 Hezekiah had one of the longest lists of good qualities of all the good kings. He acted appropriately (v. 4), had the right

high places, shattered the sacred pillars, and cut down the Asherah poles. He broke into pieces the bronze snake that Moses made, for until then the Israelites were burning incense to it. It was called Nehushtan.[A]

[5] Hezekiah relied on the LORD God of Israel; not one of the kings of Judah was like him, either before him or after him. [6] He remained faithful to the LORD and did not turn from following him but kept the commands the LORD had commanded Moses.

[7] The LORD was with him, and wherever he went he prospered. He rebelled against the king of Assyria and did not serve him. [8] He defeated the Philistines as far as Gaza and its borders, from watchtower to fortified city.

Review of Israel's Fall

[9] In the fourth year of King Hezekiah, which was the seventh year of Israel's King Hoshea son of Elah, Assyria's King Shalmaneser marched against Samaria and besieged it. [10] The Assyrians captured it at the end of three years. In the sixth year of Hezekiah, which was the ninth year of Israel's King Hoshea, Samaria was captured. [11] The king of Assyria deported the Israelites to Assyria and put them in Halah, along the Habor (Gozan's river), and in the cities of the Medes, [12] because they did not listen to the LORD their God but violated his covenant — all he had commanded Moses the servant of the LORD. They did not listen, and they did not obey.

Sennacherib's Invasion

[13] In the fourteenth year of King Hezekiah, Assyria's King Sennacherib attacked all the fortified cities of Judah and captured them. [14] So King Hezekiah of Judah sent word to the king of Assyria at Lachish: "I have done wrong; withdraw from me. Whatever you demand from

me, I will pay." The king of Assyria demanded eleven tons[B] of silver and one ton[C] of gold from King Hezekiah of Judah. [15] So Hezekiah gave him all the silver found in the LORD's temple and in the treasuries of the king's palace.

[16] At that time Hezekiah stripped the gold from the doors of the LORD's sanctuary and from the doorposts he had overlaid and gave it to the king of Assyria.

[17] Then the king of Assyria sent the field marshal, the chief of staff, and his royal spokesman, along with a massive army, from Lachish to King Hezekiah at Jerusalem. They advanced and came to Jerusalem, and[D] they took their position by the aqueduct of the upper pool, by the road to the Launderer's Field. [18] They called for the king, but Eliakim son of Hilkiah, who was in charge of the palace, Shebnah the court secretary, and Joah son of Asaph, the court historian, came out to them.

The Royal Spokesman's Speech

[19] Then the royal spokesman said to them, "Tell Hezekiah this is what the great king, the king of Assyria, says: 'What are you relying on?[E] [20] You think mere words are strategy and strength for war. Who are you now relying on so that you have rebelled against me? [21] Now look, you are relying on Egypt, that splintered reed of a staff that will pierce the hand of anyone who grabs it and leans on it. This is what Pharaoh king of Egypt is to all who rely on him. [22] Suppose you say to me, "We rely on the LORD our God." Isn't he the one whose high places and altars Hezekiah has removed, saying to Judah and to Jerusalem, "You must worship at this altar in Jerusalem"?'

[23] "So now, make a bargain with my master the king of Assyria. I'll give you two thousand horses if you're able to supply riders for them! [24] How then can you drive back a single

---

[A]18:4 = A Bronze Thing　[B]18:14 Lit *300 talents*　[C]18:14 Lit *30 talents*　[D]18:17 LXX, Syr, Vg; MT reads *and came and*　[E]18:19 Lit *'What is this trust which you trust*

---

attitude of faith (v. 5), and persisted in doing good (v. 6). Because of his obedience, God prospered him in everything (v. 7). This prosperity included minor political victories (v. 8) and sufficient economic prosperity to finance the building operations and expensive military preparations for war with Assyria (2Ch 32:1–5). The name **Nehushtan** comes from the words for "snake" (*nahash*) and "piece of bronze" (*nechosheth*).

18:8 In 716 BC, Sargon II advanced victoriously to the border of Egypt but did not threaten Judah, perhaps because Ahaz, the faithful Assyrian vassal, was still alive. After Sargon left, Hezekiah had some local military success in subduing the **Philistines**. All of this coincided with military preparations for rebellion and Hezekiah's refusal to send tribute to Sargon of Assyria.

18:9–12 This is a duplicate record of the fall of Israel, the northern kingdom (cp. 17:3–6). It sets an ominous tone for the following

account of the invasion of Judah by Sennacherib of Assyria.

18:13–16 These verses do not describe the depth of the devastation of the invasion by **Assyria**. Assyrian records report that forty-six walled cities were taken, probably in the typically brutal Assyrian fashion. They further claim that 200,150 captives and much plunder were also taken. Scholars have debated whether one or two Assyrian invasions of Judah are described in chap. 18. If there were two, these present verses may describe the first, and the second may be described in the following verses. If there was only one invasion, these verses could give a preliminary summary or preview of the overall campaign, and then some of its details are further described below. Or perhaps there was only one campaign in which Hezekiah surrendered, made peace, and presented a huge tribute to Assyria; but the Assyrians then reneged on that agreement and tried to destroy Hezekiah

and Jerusalem anyway. Some interpreters suggest the following scenario: Hezekiah promised this huge payment; Sennacherib had to leave without receiving it; Hezekiah sent the payment anyway.

18:17–18 Whatever had happened previously, the Assyrians were now threatening **Jerusalem**, the last outpost of orthodox worship of the Lord. The **field marshal** was a high official, next to the king. If the Assyrians followed the Mesopotamian and Persian practice of using foreign eunuchs in high governmental positions, the meaning of the Hebrew word *saris* indicates that the **chief of staff** was associated with those Assyrian officials. The **royal spokesman** was the diplomatic spokesman for Sennacherib. Some have located the **Launderer's Field** near En-rogel on the southern approaches to Jerusalem. Though this Assyrian deputation had asked for King Hezekiah, they received instead three high palace officials. On this invasion see Is 36:1–22.

officer among the least of my master's servants? How can you rely on Egypt for chariots and for horsemen? ²⁵ Now, have I attacked this place to destroy it without the LORD's approval? The LORD said to me, 'Attack this land and destroy it.'"

²⁶ Then Eliakim son of Hilkiah, Shebnah, and Joah said to the royal spokesman, "Please speak to your servants in Aramaic, since we understand it. Don't speak with us in Hebrew^A within earshot of the people on the wall."

²⁷ But the royal spokesman said to them, "Has my master sent me to speak these words only to your master and to you? Hasn't he also sent me to the men who sit on the wall, destined with you to eat their own excrement and drink their own urine?"

²⁸ The royal spokesman stood and called out loudly in Hebrew: "Hear the word of the great king, the king of Assyria. ²⁹ This is what the king says: 'Don't let Hezekiah deceive you; he can't rescue you from my power. ³⁰ Don't let Hezekiah persuade you to rely on the LORD by saying, "Certainly the LORD will rescue us! This city will not be handed over to the king of Assyria."'

³¹ "Don't listen to Hezekiah, for this is what the king of Assyria says: 'Make peace^B with me and surrender to me. Then each of you may eat from his own vine and his own fig tree, and each may drink water from his own cistern ³² until I come and take you away to a land like your own land — a land of grain and new wine, a land of bread and vineyards, a land of olive trees and honey — so that you may live and not die. But don't listen to Hezekiah when he misleads you, saying, "The LORD will rescue us." ³³ Has any of the gods of the nations ever rescued his land from the power of the king of Assyria? ³⁴ Where are the gods of Hamath and Arpad? Where are the gods of Sepharvaim, Hena, and Ivvah?^C Have they rescued Samaria from my power? ³⁵ Who among all the gods of the lands has rescued his land from my power? So will the LORD rescue Jerusalem from my power?'"

³⁶ But the people kept silent; they did not answer him at all, for the king's command was, "Don't answer him." ³⁷ Then Eliakim son of Hilkiah, who was in charge of the palace, Shebna the court secretary, and Joah son of Asaph, the court historian, came to Hezekiah with their clothes torn and reported to him the words of the royal spokesman.

Hezekiah Seeks Isaiah's Counsel

19 When King Hezekiah heard their report, he tore his clothes, covered himself with sackcloth, and went into the LORD's temple. ² He sent Eliakim, who was in charge of the palace, Shebna the court secretary, and the leading priests, who were covered with sackcloth, to the prophet Isaiah son of Amoz. ³ They said to him, "This is what Hezekiah says: 'Today is a day of distress, rebuke, and disgrace, for children have come to the point of birth, but there is no strength to deliver them. ⁴ Perhaps the LORD your God will hear all the words of the royal spokesman, whom his master the king of Assyria sent to mock the living God, and will rebuke him for the words that the LORD your God has heard. Therefore, offer a prayer for the surviving remnant.'"

⁵ So the servants of King Hezekiah went to Isaiah, ⁶ who said to them, "Tell your master, 'The LORD says this: Don't be afraid because of the words you have heard, with which the king of Assyria's attendants have blasphemed me. ⁷ I am about to put a spirit in him, and he will hear a rumor and return to his own land, where I will cause him to fall by the sword.'"

Sennacherib's Departing Threat

⁸ When the royal spokesman heard that the king of Assyria had pulled out of Lachish, he left and found him fighting against Libnah. ⁹ The king had heard concerning King Tirhakah of Cush, "Look, he has set out to fight against you." So he again sent messengers to Hezekiah, saying, ¹⁰ "Say this to King Hezekiah of Judah: 'Don't let your God, on whom you rely, deceive you by promising that Jerusalem

---

^A**18:26** Lit *Judahite*, also in v. 28   ^B**18:31** Lit *a blessing*   ^C**18:34** Some LXX mss, Old Lat read *Sepharvaim? Where are the gods of the land of Samaria?*

18:25 The royal spokesman claimed that the Lord had commissioned Assyria to attack and destroy Judah.
18:26 Aramaic was the standard language for international dealings, but the Assyrian diplomatic corps included **Hebrew** speakers.
18:32b–35 On the nations mentioned here, see 19:12–13 and note at 19:10–13.
18:36–37 The torn clothes were a formal declaration of grief.
19:5–7 After more than a chapter of bad news, these verses describe the first of five steps of good news. The overall theme is that no matter how bad circumstances appeared, God could and would deliver. Isaiah's response was that despite the Assyrian's

arrogance in insulting God, he would give the Assyrian king such a **spirit**—attitude or desire—that he would want to go **to his own land** where he would die.
19:8–9 Since Sennacherib left **Lachish** without returning, Lachish must have fallen about that time. Sennacherib was dealing with **Libnah** when he heard that **Tirhakah** of Egypt was coming. Tirhakah was the last pharaoh of the Cushite dynasty of Egypt. His power consisted of a small group of Egyptian royalty and nobility united with relatively effective Sudanese soldiers. Tirhakah's army was defeated, and Egypt ceased to be a threat.
19:10–13 Rabshakeh again warned **Hezekiah**, and again the message dealt with

overwhelming Assyrian power. The warning was supported by a list of conquered peoples whose gods had not helped them: **Gozan**, on the Habor tributary of the Euphrates River near **Haran**; **Rezeph**, northeast of Hamath on the trade route to the Euphrates; the **Edenites** (sometimes identified with the Aramean kingdom, Bit Adini, conquered by Assyria ca 855 BC), who like **Telassar** are unknown; **Hamath**, almost directly north of Damascus; **Arpad**, near the site of modern Aleppo; **Sepharvaim** and **Hena**, whose locations are unknown; and finally **Ivvah**, probably identical with Avva (17:31), whose gods are named but whose location is unknown. All of these sites were roughly on Assyria's approach route to Palestine.

will not be handed over to the king of Assyria. ¹¹Look, you have heard what the kings of Assyria have done to all the countries: They completely destroyed them. Will you be rescued? ¹²Did the gods of the nations that my predecessors destroyed rescue them — nations such as Gozan, Haran, Rezeph, and the Edenites in Telassar? ¹³Where is the king of Hamath, the king of Arpad, the king of the city of^A Sepharvaim, Hena, or Ivvah?'"

Hezekiah's Prayer

¹⁴Hezekiah took the letter from the messengers' hands, read it, then went up to the Lᴏʀᴅ's temple, and spread it out before the Lᴏʀᴅ. ¹⁵Then Hezekiah prayed before the Lᴏʀᴅ:

Lᴏʀᴅ God of Israel, enthroned between the cherubim, you are God — you alone — of all the kingdoms of the earth. You made the heavens and the earth. ¹⁶Listen closely, Lᴏʀᴅ, and hear; open your eyes, Lᴏʀᴅ, and see. Hear the words that Sennacherib has sent to mock the living God. ¹⁷Lᴏʀᴅ, it is true that the kings of Assyria have devastated the nations and their lands. ¹⁸They have thrown their gods into the fire, for they were not gods but made by human hands — wood and stone. So they have destroyed them. ¹⁹Now, Lᴏʀᴅ our God, please save us from his power so that all the kingdoms of the earth may know that you, Lᴏʀᴅ, are God — you alone.

God's Answer through Isaiah

²⁰Then Isaiah son of Amoz sent a message to Hezekiah: "The Lᴏʀᴅ, the God of Israel says, 'I have heard your prayer to me about King Sennacherib of Assyria.' ²¹This is the word the Lᴏʀᴅ has spoken against him:

Virgin Daughter Zion
despises you and scorns you;
Daughter Jerusalem
shakes her head behind your back.
²²   Who is it you mocked and blasphemed?
Against whom have you raised
    your voice
and lifted your eyes in pride?
Against the Holy One of Israel!
²³   You have mocked the Lord^B through^C
your messengers.

You have said, 'With my many chariots
I have gone up to the heights
    of the mountains,
to the far recesses of Lebanon.
I cut down its tallest cedars,
    its choice cypress trees.
I came to its farthest outpost,
    its densest forest.
²⁴   I dug wells
and drank water in foreign lands.
I dried up all the streams of Egypt
with the soles of my feet.'
²⁵   Have you not heard?
I designed it long ago;
I planned it in days gone by.
I have now brought it to pass,
and you have crushed fortified cities
into piles of rubble.
²⁶   Their inhabitants have
    become powerless,
dismayed, and ashamed.
They are plants of the field,
    tender grass,
grass on the rooftops,
blasted by the east wind.^D
²⁷   But I know your sitting down,
your going out and your coming in,
and your raging against me.
²⁸   Because your raging against me
and your arrogance have reached
    my ears,
I will put my hook in your nose
and my bit in your mouth;
I will make you go back
the way you came.

²⁹"This will be the sign for you: This year you will eat what grows on its own, and in the second year what grows from that. But in the third year sow and reap, plant vineyards and eat their fruit. ³⁰The surviving remnant of the house of Judah will again take root downward and bear fruit upward. ³¹For a remnant will go out from Jerusalem, and survivors, from Mount Zion. The zeal of the Lᴏʀᴅ of Armies will accomplish this.

³²   Therefore, this is what the Lᴏʀᴅ says
about the king of Assyria:

---

^A19:13 Or king of Lair,   ^B19:23 Many mss read Lᴏʀᴅ   ^C19:23 Lit by the hand of   ^D19:26 DSS; MT reads blasted before standing grain; Is 37:27

19:17–19 The second step (see note at vv. 5–7) in the good news was recognizing that the gods conquered by the Assyrians were **not gods**. The gods of those nations were idols made by men.
19:20–24 God presented the third stage of good news (see note at vv. 5–7) by describing the true power structure of the universe.
19:21 First, the tables were turned to just the opposite of the Assyrians' attitudes. In

truth, Jerusalem, or **Daughter Zion**, was in a position to mock the Assyrians.
19:23–24 Then came the most amazing principle of Isaiah's oracle. He admitted that the power of the Assyrian and his conquests were real. These verses use poetic figures of conquest, marching to the **mountains** of **Lebanon** and trampling the waters of many nations.
19:27–28 The Assyrians were in God's hand. This brings us to the fourth point (see note

at vv. 5–7) of good news: God would lead the Assyrians back to their land by his **hook** in their **nose** just as he would handle a stubborn draft animal.
19:29 It would take two years of work and living on volunteer growth (plants arising from stray seeds not planted by man) to restore the land. These words also suggest that the diminished population could survive on volunteer growth for two years.

He will not enter this city,
shoot an arrow here,
come before it with a shield,
or build up a siege ramp against it.
³³ He will go back
the way he came,
and he will not enter this city.
This is the LORD's declaration.
³⁴ I will defend this city and rescue it
for my sake and for the sake of my
servant David."

Defeat and Death of Sennacherib

³⁵ That night the angel of the LORD went out and struck down one hundred eighty-five thousand in the camp of the Assyrians. When the people got up the next morning — there were all the dead bodies! ³⁶ So King Sennacherib of Assyria broke camp and left. He returned home and lived in Nineveh.

³⁷ One day, while he was worshiping in the temple of his god Nisroch, his sons Adrammelech and Sharezer struck him down with the sword and escaped to the land of Ararat. Then his son Esar-haddon became king in his place.

Hezekiah's Illness and Recovery

20 In those days Hezekiah became terminally ill. The prophet Isaiah son of Amoz came and said to him, "This is what the LORD says: 'Set your house in order, for you are about to die; you will not recover.'"

² Then Hezekiah turned his face to the wall and prayed to the LORD, ³ "Please, LORD, remember how I have walked before you faithfully and wholeheartedly and have done what pleases you."ᴬ And Hezekiah wept bitterly.

⁴ Isaiah had not yet gone out of the inner courtyard when the word of the LORD came to him: ⁵ "Go back and tell Hezekiah, the leader of my people, 'This is what the LORD God of your ancestor David says: I have heard your prayer; I have seen your tears. Look, I will heal you. On the third day from now you will go up to the

LORD's temple. ⁶ I will add fifteen years to your life. I will rescue you and this city from the grasp of the king of Assyria. I will defend this city for my sake and for the sake of my servant David.'"

⁷ Then Isaiah said, "Bring a lump of pressed figs." So they brought it and applied it to his infected skin, and he recovered.

⁸ Hezekiah had asked Isaiah, "What is the sign that the LORD will heal me and that I will go up to the LORD's temple on the third day?"

⁹ Isaiah said, "This is the sign to you from the LORD that he will do what he has promised: Should the shadow go ahead ten steps or go back ten steps?"

¹⁰ Then Hezekiah answered, "It's easy for the shadow to lengthen ten steps. No, let the shadow go back ten steps." ¹¹ So the prophet Isaiah called out to the LORD, and he brought the shadowᴮ back the ten steps it had descended on the stairway of Ahaz.ᶜ

Hezekiah's Folly

¹² At that time Merodach-baladanᴰ son of Baladan, king of Babylon, sent letters and a gift to Hezekiah since he heard that he had been sick. ¹³ Hezekiah listened to the letters and showed the envoys his whole treasure house — the silver, the gold, the spices, and the precious oil — and his armory, and everything that was found in his treasuries. There was nothing in his palace and in all his realm that Hezekiah did not show them.

¹⁴ Then the prophet Isaiah came to King Hezekiah and asked him, "Where did these men come from and what did they say to you?"

Hezekiah replied, "They came from a distant country, from Babylon."

¹⁵ Isaiah asked, "What have they seen in your palace?"

Hezekiah answered, "They have seen everything in my palace. There isn't anything in my treasuries that I didn't show them."

¹⁶ Then Isaiah said to Hezekiah, "Hear the word of the LORD: ¹⁷ 'Look, the days are coming

---

ᴬ20:3 Lit *what is good in your eyes* ᴮ20:11 Lit *shadow on the steps* ᶜ20:11 Tg, Vg; DSS read *on the steps of Ahaz's roof chamber*; Is 38:8 ᴰ20:12 Some Hb mss, LXX, Syr, Tg, some Vg mss, Is 39:1; other Hb mss read *Berodach-baladan*

19:35–36 The fifth and final step of good news (see note at vv. 5–7) was that God did send the **Assyrians** home. God miraculously damaged the Assyrian army so severely that they had to leave Judah. This apparently happened after the Assyrians had defeated the invading Egyptian army.
19:37 Sennacherib had claimed that Hezekiah's God could not save him. Hezekiah's God did save him, but Sennacherib's god could not—even in his own temple.
20:1–21 Most of this chapter (vv. 1–19) clearly occurred before Sennacherib's invasion. The major evidence is that Merodach-baladan's significant activities in Babylon occurred before this invasion. In the absence of explicit markers of chronological sequence, episodes in Hebrew narrative are not necessarily chronologically ordered. This chapter develops

two points: (1) Hezekiah was so pious that God granted his prayer for extra years of life, and (2) Hezekiah, in pride, misused those extra years.
20:4–6 God was neither surprised by nor unprepared for Hezekiah's **prayer**. He not only granted what was asked, but he also gave a promise of deliverance from the coming Assyrian invasion. Thus, this event was to strengthen Hezekiah's faith for that ordeal.
20:7 Some have suggested that what unfolded here was a divinely prescribed medical cure, meaning that God knew the treatment with figs would cure Hezekiah. More likely is that was simply a miraculous healing. But in either case, God worked in response to prayer (v. 2).
20:8 An arrogant demand for a **sign** from **the LORD** is sin (Mt 16:1–4), but God might

choose to honor a humble request for a sign (Jdg 6:36–40).
20:9–11 God let **Hezekiah** choose the final nature of the **sign**. Again, the purpose of this exercise was to strengthen Hezekiah's faith for the future.
20:12 This episode with **Babylon** also looked forward to Sennacherib's invasion. This invasion was a response to a worldwide conspiracy against Assyrian power. **Merodach-baladan** wanted to gain Hezekiah's support in such a rebellion.
20:14–15 Hezekiah's brief answer indicated a reluctance to discuss the issue with **Isaiah**, but the prophet continued his questioning until he received an answer from the king that merited comment.
20:16–18 Isaiah's prophecy concerning Hezekiah's wealth and descendants indicated

when everything in your palace and all that your predecessors have stored up until today will be carried off to Babylon; nothing will be left,' says the LORD. [18] 'Some of your descendants — who come from you, whom you father — will be taken away, and they will become eunuchs[A] in the palace of the king of Babylon.'"

[19] Then Hezekiah said to Isaiah, "The word of the LORD that you have spoken is good," for he thought, "Why not, if there will be peace and security during my lifetime?"

Hezekiah's Death

[20] The rest of the events of Hezekiah's reign, along with all his might and how he made the pool and the tunnel and brought water into the city, are written in the Historical Record of Judah's Kings. [21] Hezekiah rested with his ancestors, and his son Manasseh became king in his place.

Judah's King Manasseh

21 Manasseh was twelve years old when he became king, and he reigned fifty-five years in Jerusalem. His mother's name was Hephzibah. [2] He did what was evil in the LORD's sight, imitating the detestable practices of the nations that the LORD had dispossessed before the Israelites. [3] He rebuilt the high places that his father Hezekiah had destroyed and reestablished the altars for Baal. He made an Asherah, as King Ahab of Israel had done; he also bowed in worship to all the stars in the sky and served them. [4] He built altars in the LORD's temple, where the LORD had said, "Jerusalem is where I will put my name." [5] He built altars

to all the stars in the sky in both courtyards of the LORD's temple. [6] He sacrificed his son in the fire,[B] practiced witchcraft and divination, and consulted mediums and spiritists. He did a huge amount of evil in the LORD's sight, angering him.

[7] Manasseh set up the carved image of Asherah, which he made, in the temple that the LORD had spoken about to David and his son Solomon: "I will establish my name forever in this temple and in Jerusalem, which I have chosen out of all the tribes of Israel. [8] I will never again cause the feet of the Israelites to wander from the land I gave to their ancestors if only they will be careful to do all I have commanded them — the whole law that my servant Moses commanded them." [9] But they did not listen; Manasseh caused them to stray so that they did worse evil than the nations the LORD had destroyed before the Israelites.

[10] The LORD said through his servants the prophets, [11] "Since King Manasseh of Judah has committed all these detestable acts — worse evil than the Amorites who preceded him had done — and by means of his idols has also caused Judah to sin, [12] this is what the LORD God of Israel says: 'I am about to bring such a disaster on Jerusalem and Judah that everyone who hears about it will shudder.[C] [13] I will stretch over Jerusalem the measuring line used on Samaria and the mason's level used on the house of Ahab, and I will wipe Jerusalem clean as one wipes a bowl — wiping it and turning it upside down. [14] I will abandon the remnant of my inheritance and hand them over to their enemies. They will become plunder and spoil to all their enemies, [15] because they have done

[A]**20:18** Or *court officials* [B]**21:6** Lit *He made his son pass through the fire* [C]**21:12** Lit *about it, his two ears will tingle*; Hb obscure

---

the king had erred in showing all of Judah's wealth to the Babylonian embassy. The prideful sin may have included using God's blessings as bargaining points in an international political power play. This, then, could be another example of the recurrent conflict between playing a prudent role in international politics and failing to properly trust in the Lord.
20:19 Hezekiah's acceptance of God's punishment could have been either humble acceptance of God's will, or selfish rejoicing because he would experience **peace and security** in his own day.
20:20–21 The story leaps over Sennacherib's invasion to the summary and conclusion of **Hezekiah's reign**. After the comment about the other records of Hezekiah's deeds, this conclusion turns the spotlight on one of Hezekiah's most important provisions for that war—the construction of a reservoir for water for a siege and the **tunnel** that allowed water to come into the city of Jerusalem. The record of Hezekiah then closes with the statements of his death and the succession of his son **Manasseh** to the throne.
21:1–18 These verses cover the fifty-five-year reign of Manasseh, including a co-regency with his father, which left him a sole

regency of about forty-three years. (Some reigns or periods can gain or lose a year both at the beginning and ending due to changing conventions in counting parts of a year.) If Manasseh was twelve when he began his co-regency, then he was twenty-two to twenty-four years old at the beginning of his sole rule. He would have been born before God's grant of fifteen extra years of life to his father Hezekiah.
21:2 We are told Manasseh **did what was evil**, but this statement hardly describes the depths of his apostasy. His wickedness was certainly associated with rejecting Hezekiah's anti-Assyrian policy. Manasseh is listed as a loyal vassal king who supplied troops for Ashurbanipal's expedition against Thebes in Egypt (ca 663 BC, see Nah 3:8). Assyrian vassals were expected to display religious loyalty to Asshur, the chief Assyrian god. Manasseh's acceptance of Assyrian deities evolved even further into a tolerant acceptance of any and all pagan deities.
21:3–6 Manasseh's restored **high places** may have included the illegal shrines of Yahweh, which Hezekiah had suppressed, and those altars devoted to other pagan deities. They included the gods of the skies and heavens. Even worse, he desecrated the Lord's temple by worshiping these deities in

the temple itself. Recent scholars have taken the word **mediums** as referring to a ritual pit for bringing up spirits serviced by the **spiritists** (1Sm 28:7).
21:7a Asherah was originally a tree or a wooden pole that represented any divine consort of the chief fertility god. Since the word here is not associated with any local Baal, it seems to refer to a particular female deity. In setting up this image, Manasseh came close to assigning the Lord another female consort (see comments on Ashima in note at 17:29–34).
21:7b–9 The Lord had ceased his wanderings (2Sm 7:6) to dwell in the temple in **Jerusalem**. The covenant associated with it gave the Hebrews rest from wanderings. The corrupting of this temple would return the Israelites to wandering among the nations.
21:10–14 Just as Manasseh's list of sins is the longest of the kings of **Judah**, the judgment for those sins is one of the longest in the individual records.
21:13 The builder's **measuring** instruments symbolized God's judgment of a corrupt society.
21:15 The people's failure and rebellion dated **from the day their ancestors came out of Egypt**. This implied a more profound failure than the occasional transgressions of kings

what is evil in my sight and have angered me from the day their ancestors came out of Egypt until today.' "

[16] Manasseh also shed so much innocent blood that he filled Jerusalem with it from one end to another. This was in addition to his sin that he caused Judah to commit, so that they did what was evil in the LORD's sight.

Manasseh's Death

[17] The rest of the events of Manasseh's reign, along with all his accomplishments and the sin that he committed, are written in the Historical Record of Judah's Kings. [18] Manasseh rested with his ancestors and was buried in the garden of his own house, the garden of Uzza. His son Amon became king in his place.

Judah's King Amon

[19] Amon was twenty-two years old when he became king, and he reigned two years in Jerusalem. His mother's name was Meshullemeth daughter of Haruz; she was from Jotbah. [20] He did what was evil in the LORD's sight, just as his father Manasseh had done. [21] He walked in all the ways his father had walked; he served the idols his father had served, and he bowed in worship to them. [22] He abandoned the LORD God of his ancestors and did not walk in the ways of the LORD.

[23] Amon's servants conspired against him and put the king to death in his own house. [24] The common people[A] killed all who had conspired against King Amon, and they made his son Josiah king in his place.

[25] The rest of the events of Amon's reign, along with his accomplishments, are written in the Historical Record of Judah's Kings. [26] He was buried in his tomb in the garden of Uzza, and his son Josiah became king in his place.

Judah's King Josiah

22 Josiah was eight years old when he became king, and he reigned thirty-one years in Jerusalem. His mother's name was Jedidah the daughter of Adaiah; she was from

Bozkath. [2] He did what was right in the LORD's sight and walked in all the ways of his ancestor David; he did not turn to the right or the left.

Josiah Repairs the Temple

[3] In the eighteenth year of King Josiah, the king sent the court secretary Shaphan son of Azaliah, son of Meshullam, to the LORD's temple, saying, [4] "Go up to the high priest Hilkiah so that he may total up the silver brought into the LORD's temple — the silver the doorkeepers have collected from the people. [5] It is to be given to those doing the work — those who oversee the LORD's temple. They in turn are to give it to the workmen in the LORD's temple to repair the damage. [6] They are to give it to the carpenters, builders, and masons to buy timber and quarried stone to repair the temple. [7] But no accounting is to be required from them for the silver given to them since they work with integrity."

The Book of the Law Found

[8] The high priest Hilkiah told the court secretary Shaphan, "I have found the book of the law in the LORD's temple," and he gave the book to Shaphan, who read it.

[9] Then the court secretary Shaphan went to the king and reported,[B] "Your servants have emptied out the silver that was found in the temple and have given it to those doing the work — those who oversee the LORD's temple." [10] Then the court secretary Shaphan told the king, "The priest Hilkiah has given me a book," and Shaphan read it in the presence of the king. [11] When the king heard the words of the book of the law, he tore his clothes. [12] Then he commanded the priest Hilkiah, Ahikam son of Shaphan, Achbor son of Micaiah, the court secretary Shaphan, and the king's servant Asaiah, [13] "Go and inquire of the LORD for me, for the people, and for all Judah about the words in this book that has been found. For great is the LORD's wrath that is kindled against us because our ancestors have not obeyed the words

---

[A]21:24 Lit *The people of the land*   [B]22:9 Lit *and returned a word to the king and said*

---

and individuals. There was a deeper, systemic problem that demanded a radically different solution: the new covenant written in their hearts (Jr 31:31–34).
21:16 The Bible gives no more specific data about Manasseh's filling Jerusalem with **innocent blood**, and 2 Kings mentions nothing about Manasseh's captivity, repentance, and building operations (2Ch 33:10–14).
21:17–18 This conclusion to Manasseh's reign highlights **the sin that he committed**.
21:19–22 Manasseh's son **Amon** learned nothing from God's judgment of his father.
21:23–24 Amon was assassinated by his own servants, probably a victim of the internal struggle between the pro-Assyrian and anti-Assyrian parties. The **common**

people (lit "people of the land") emerged as the group that maintained loyalty to David's dynasty.
21:25–26 Appropriately, Amon was buried in the tomb of his father Manasseh.
22:1–23:30 The reign of King Josiah of Judah is covered in these two chapters.
22:1–2 The formal statements are typical for a good king: Josiah **walked in all the ways** of David, and he turned neither **to the right or the left**.
22:3–5 At twenty-six years old, Josiah pushed for the repairing of the temple. There was no argument over whose treasury was involved (see Joash, 12:4–8). The king either already had or then assumed the necessary authority for renovating the temple.

22:6–7 Verse 7 is repeated from 12:15 in the account of Joash's repair of the **temple**.
22:9–10 Shaphan seems not to have appreciated the significance of the discovery of "the book of the law." He leads his report to the king with the report of financial diligence. Then he refers to the book (Deuteronomy?) simply as **a book**.
22:11 Whatever had happened, **the king** had been ignorant of some provisions of the law.
22:12–13 Josiah's heart was tender toward God (v. 19). Just as he had searched for God when he was sixteen years old (2Ch 34:3) and had pushed for rebuilding the temple, now he was equally willing to heed this message of sin, guilt, and judgment. He acknowledged that sin had aroused **the LORD's wrath**.

of this book in order to do everything written about us."

Huldah's Prophecy of Judgment

¹⁴ So the priest Hilkiah, Ahikam, Achbor, Shaphan, and Asaiah went to the prophetess Huldah, wife of Shallum son of Tikvah, son of Harhas, keeper of the wardrobe. She lived in Jerusalem in the Second District. They spoke with her.

¹⁵ She said to them, "This is what the LORD God of Israel says: Say to the man who sent you to me, ¹⁶ 'This is what the LORD says: I am about to bring disaster on this place and on its inhabitants, fulfilling^ all the words of the book that the king of Judah has read, ¹⁷ because they have abandoned me and burned incense to other gods in order to anger me with all the work of their hands. My wrath will be kindled against this place, and it will not be quenched.' ¹⁸ Say this to the king of Judah who sent you to inquire of the LORD: 'This is what the LORD God of Israel says: As for the words that you heard, ¹⁹ because your heart was tender and you humbled yourself before the LORD when you heard what I spoke against this place and against its inhabitants, that they would become a desolation and a curse, and because you have torn your clothes and wept before me, I myself have heard' — this is the LORD's declaration. ²⁰ 'Therefore, I will indeed gather you to your ancestors, and you will be gathered to your grave in peace. Your eyes will not see all the disaster that I am bringing on this place.' "

Then they reported^B to the king.

Covenant Renewal

23 So the king sent messengers, and they gathered all the elders of Judah and Jerusalem to him. ² Then the king went to the LORD's temple with all the men of Judah and all the inhabitants of Jerusalem, as well as the priests and the prophets — all the people from the youngest to the oldest. He read in their hearing all the words of the book of the covenant that had been found in the LORD's temple. ³ Next, the king stood by the pillar^C and made a covenant in the LORD's presence to follow the LORD and to keep his commands, his decrees, and his statutes with all his heart and with all his soul in order to carry out the words of this covenant that were written in this book; all the people agreed to^D the covenant.

Josiah's Reforms

⁴ Then the king commanded the high priest Hilkiah and the priests of the second rank and the doorkeepers to bring out of the LORD's sanctuary all the articles made for Baal, Asherah, and all the stars in the sky. He burned them outside Jerusalem in the fields of the Kidron and carried their ashes to Bethel. ⁵ Then he did away with the idolatrous priests the kings of Judah had appointed to burn incense at the high places in the cities of Judah and in the areas surrounding Jerusalem. They had burned incense to Baal, and to the sun, moon, constellations, and all the stars in the sky. ⁶ He brought out the Asherah pole from the LORD's temple to the Kidron Valley outside Jerusalem. He burned it at the Kidron Valley, beat it to dust, and threw its dust on the graves of the common people.^E ⁷ He also tore down the houses of the male cult prostitutes that were in the LORD's temple, in which the women were weaving tapestries^F for Asherah.

⁸ Then Josiah brought all the priests from the cities of Judah, and he defiled the high places from Geba to Beer-sheba, where the priests had burned incense. He tore down the high places of the city gates at the entrance of the gate of Joshua the governor of the city (on the left at the city gate). ⁹ The priests of the high places, however, did not come up to the altar of the LORD in Jerusalem; instead, they ate unleavened bread with their fellow priests.

¹⁰ He defiled Topheth, which is in Ben Hinnom Valley, so that no one could sacrifice his son or daughter in the fire^G to Molech. ¹¹ He did away with the horses that the kings

---

^A 22:16 fulfilling supplied for clarity   ^B 22:20 Lit returned a word   ^C 23:3 2Ch 34:31 reads platform   ^D 23:3 Lit people took a stand in   ^E 23:6 Lit the sons of the people   ^F 23:7 Or clothing   ^G 23:10 Lit could make his son or daughter pass through the fire

---

22:14 Despite the general false worship that was occurring throughout the land, a true **prophetess** was known and tolerated just as apostate Samaria had tolerated Elisha (6:32). **22:15–17** The message of the prophetess was that the sins of the nation must be judged. **22:18–20** Because of Josiah's grief over the sins of the nation, he was assured that destruction would not come until after his death. **23:1–2** All the purifying works of this chapter began quickly after the discovery of the law since, assuming chronological sequencing, these works culminated in the great Passover remembrance, still in Josiah's eighteenth year (1Kg 22:3; 23:23). **23:3** Perhaps this **pillar** was the same place used by Joash (see notes at 11:13–14a; 1Kg

7:15–22) for a **covenant** renewal. The unclear parallel passage in 2 Chronicles probably identifies this same location by a different object. King Josiah, then, committed himself to obedience to the covenant. **All the people** also committed themselves to the covenant. **23:4** Apparently Josiah's earlier piety had not moved him to a complete rejection of all false gods, but at this point his devotion to the Lord became exclusive, and the cleansing of Judah from false worship began in earnest. **23:5–7** In Judah the orders of **idolatrous priests**, founded and perhaps also funded by earlier kings, were deposed or disbanded rather than being slaughtered as in the north (v. 20). Allowing **male** religious **prostitutes**

in the temple until this point indicated extreme degradation and a surprising tolerance for paganism. **23:8–9** Defiling the **high places** disqualified these altars for further use, at least until they were ritually purified. The **priests of the high places** seemed to have been incorporated into the ranks of the regular priests, although they were not permitted to come to **Jerusalem** to participate in worship. This leniency might indicate that these high places were illegal shrines for Yahweh worship rather than shrines for pagan deities. **23:10 Topheth** was a place of human sacrifice (Jr 7:31), and here it specifies that it honored the god **Molech**. Again, Josiah desecrated a sacred site in order to disable it.

of Judah had dedicated to the sun. They had been at the entrance of the LORD's temple in the precincts by the chamber of Nathan-melech, the eunuch. He also burned the chariots of the sun.

¹² The king tore down the altars that the kings of Judah had made on the roof of Ahaz's upper chamber. He also tore down the altars that Manasseh had made in the two courtyards of the LORD's temple. Then he smashed them^A there and threw their dust into the Kidron Valley. ¹³ The king also defiled the high places that were across from Jerusalem, to the south of the Mount of Destruction, which King Solomon of Israel had built for Ashtoreth, the abhorrent idol of the Sidonians; for Chemosh, the abhorrent idol of Moab; and for Milcom, the detestable idol of the Ammonites. ¹⁴ He broke the sacred pillars into pieces, cut down the Asherah poles, then filled their places with human bones.

¹⁵ He even tore down the altar at Bethel and the high place that had been made by Jeroboam son of Nebat, who caused Israel to sin. He burned the high place, crushed it to dust, and burned the Asherah. ¹⁶ As Josiah turned, he saw the tombs there on the mountain. He sent someone to take the bones out of the tombs, and he burned them on the altar. He defiled it according to the word of the LORD proclaimed by the man of God^B who proclaimed these things. ¹⁷ Then he said, "What is this monument I see?"

The men of the city told him, "It is the tomb of the man of God who came from Judah and proclaimed these things that you have done to the altar at Bethel."

¹⁸ So he said, "Let him rest. Don't let anyone disturb his bones." So they left his bones

undisturbed with the bones of the prophet who came from Samaria.

¹⁹ Josiah also removed all the shrines of the high places that were in the cities of Samaria, which the kings of Israel had made to anger the LORD. Josiah did the same things to them that he had done at Bethel. ²⁰ He slaughtered on the altars all the priests of those high places, and he burned human bones on the altars. Then he returned to Jerusalem.

Passover Observed

²¹ The king commanded all the people, "Observe the Passover of the LORD your God as written in the book of the covenant." ²² No such Passover had ever been observed from the time of the judges who judged Israel through the entire time of the kings of Israel and Judah. ²³ But in the eighteenth year of King Josiah, the LORD's Passover was observed in Jerusalem.

Further Zeal for the LORD

²⁴ In addition, Josiah eradicated the mediums, the spiritists, household idols, images, and all the abhorrent things that were seen in the land of Judah and in Jerusalem. He did this in order to carry out the words of the law that were written in the book that the priest Hilkiah found in the LORD's temple. ²⁵ Before him there was no king like him who turned to the LORD with all his heart and with all his soul and with all his strength according to all the law of Moses, and no one like him arose after him.

²⁶ In spite of all that, the LORD did not turn from the fury of his intense burning anger, which burned against Judah because of all the affronts with which Manasseh had angered him. ²⁷ For the LORD had said, "I will also remove Judah from my presence just as I have

---

^A 23:12 Text emended; MT reads *he ran from*   ^B 23:16 LXX adds *when Jeroboam stood by the altar of the feast. And he turned and raised his eyes to the tomb of the man of God*

23:11 Apparently these **horses** symbolically pulled the **chariots of the sun** across the heavens.
23:12–14 Josiah's program continued with the desecration of every illegal altar or place of worship he could find, even those founded

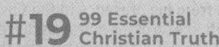

GOD IS OMNIPRESENT

God's omnipresence refers to his presence in all time and all places simultaneously. Because God exists apart from and outside of time and space, he is not limited by their constraints (1Kg 8:27; Ac 17:24). He is present with us wherever we are, and he sees all that occurs; nothing escapes his attention (Pss 33:14; 139:7–10; Is 57:15; Jr 23:23–24; Mt 18:20). God's omnipresence is a deterrent to sin and a source of great comfort and hope for believers.

by **Solomon**. These also were defiled by **human** remains.
23:15–20 It is almost certain that this cleansing of the north took place in the brief period between the fall of Assyrian imperial administration of Samaria and the time when the Egyptians seized control of Judah. It is difficult to tell whether this was political expansionism, religious cleansing, or both. If this cleansing all took place in Josiah's eighteenth year, it could not have been very thorough.
23:15–16 Josiah had to travel only ten miles north to cleanse **Bethel** by destroying its **high place** and desecrating the site with human remains. This fulfilled the prophecy of 1Kg 13:1–2. The gold calf already had been carried off by the Assyrians.
23:17–18 Then Josiah became aware of the **tomb** of the Judean prophet who predicted the deeds Josiah had just done. The prophet's bones were left undisturbed, but Josiah had still desecrated other graves near Bethel. In this context **from Samaria** may indicate only that the prophet was native to Israel, often referred to collectively as "Samaria."

23:19–20 Josiah's reforms took a more brutal turn in the north with a systematic slaughter of the illegal **priests** of the north. Josiah desecrated the altars by killing the priests on their own **altars**.
23:21–23 The events detailed above must have occurred in Josiah's **eighteenth year** before the observance of the **Passover**. The high point of Josiah's reforms was this Passover celebration. The description here does not give adequate reason for this glowing evaluation, but in the Chronicles account (2Ch 35) its importance becomes clear. Chronicles comes close to presenting this Passover as the reestablishment of the guilds and personnel for the ritual life of the Israelites.
23:24 This verse contains a rare mention of the **household idols** in Judah (Jdg 17:5; 18:14–21; 1Sm 19:13).
23:25 Such high praise of Josiah is joined to a quote from Dt 6:5.
23:26–27 Once again, the writer returned to the theme of failure. The national repentance fell far short of what was needed to avoid God's judgment. History shows that the people had not been reached by this revival.

removed Israel. I will reject this city Jerusalem, that I have chosen, and the temple about which I said, 'My name will be there.'"

Josiah's Death
[28] The rest of the events of Josiah's reign, along with all his accomplishments, are written in the Historical Record of Judah's Kings. [29] During his reign, Pharaoh Neco king of Egypt marched up to help the king of Assyria at the Euphrates River. King Josiah went to confront him, and at Megiddo when Neco saw him he killed him. [30] From Megiddo his servants carried his dead body in a chariot, brought him into Jerusalem, and buried him in his own tomb. Then the common people^A took Jehoahaz son of Josiah, anointed him, and made him king in place of his father.

Judah's King Jehoahaz
[31] Jehoahaz was twenty-three years old when he became king, and he reigned three months in Jerusalem. His mother's name was Hamutal daughter of Jeremiah; she was from Libnah. [32] He did what was evil in the LORD's sight just as his ancestors had done. [33] Pharaoh Neco imprisoned him at Riblah in the land of Hamath to keep him from reigning in Jerusalem, and he imposed on the land a fine of seventy-five hundred pounds^B of silver and seventy-five pounds^C of gold.

Judah's King Jehoiakim
[34] Then Pharaoh Neco made Eliakim son of Josiah king in place of his father Josiah and changed Eliakim's name to Jehoiakim. But Neco took Jehoahaz and went to Egypt, and he died there. [35] So Jehoiakim gave the silver and the gold to Pharaoh, but at Pharaoh's command he taxed the land to give it. He exacted the silver and the gold from the common people, each according to his assessment, to give it to Pharaoh Neco.

[36] Jehoiakim was twenty-five years old when he became king, and he reigned eleven years in Jerusalem. His mother's name was Zebidah daughter of Pedaiah; she was from Rumah. [37] He did what was evil in the LORD's sight just as his ancestors had done.

Jehoiakim's Rebellion and Death
24 During Jehoiakim's reign, King Nebuchadnezzar of Babylon attacked. Jehoiakim became his vassal for three years, and then he turned and rebelled against him. [2] The LORD sent Chaldean, Aramean, Moabite, and Ammonite raiders against Jehoiakim. He sent them against Judah to destroy it, according to the word of the LORD he had spoken through his servants the prophets. [3] Indeed, this happened to Judah at the LORD's command to remove them from his presence. It was because of the sins of Manasseh, according to all he had done, [4] and also because of all the innocent blood he had shed. He had filled Jerusalem with innocent blood, and the LORD was not willing to forgive.

[5] The rest of the events of Jehoiakim's reign, along with all his accomplishments, are written in the Historical Record of Judah's Kings. [6] Jehoiakim rested with his ancestors, and his son Jehoiachin became king in his place.

[7] Now the king of Egypt did not march out of his land again, for the king of Babylon took everything that had belonged to the king of Egypt, from the Brook of Egypt to the Euphrates River.

Judah's King Jehoiachin
[8] Jehoiachin was eighteen years old when he became king, and he reigned three months in Jerusalem. His mother's name was Nehushta

---

^A23:30 Lit *the people of the land*, also in v. 35 ^B23:33 Lit *100 talents* ^C23:33 Lit *one talent*

23:28 A formal closer concludes Josiah's reign, except for the following record of his death.
23:29–30 Assyria had earlier suffered major defeats. A coalition of Medes and Babylonians had destroyed Nineveh in 612 BC and captured Haran in 610 BC. **Pharaoh Neco** of Egypt then went north toward the **Euphrates River** to help the Assyrians recapture Haran. Josiah intercepted the Egyptian army near **Megiddo**. He died from wounds he received in this battle. Josiah's accomplishments confirmed his greatness. Though his reforms did not halt God's judgment, his reestablishment of ritual and the religious guilds was essential for the renewal of Israel's religious life after the exile.
23:31–33 The people made Josiah's son **Jehoahaz** (also referred to as Shallum, Jr 22:11–12) king. **Pharaoh Neco imprisoned** Jehoahaz and put Judah under tribute. Neco's victory over Josiah apparently eliminated the Judean army as a significant fighting force.

23:34–35 Jehoahaz's brother **Eliakim**, renamed **Jehoiakim** by Neco, was made king. Renaming a vassal symbolized the ruler's power over the subject king. Jehoiakim sent tribute to Pharaoh. Jehoahaz was a political prisoner in Egypt.
23:36–37 The formal opening statements for **Jehoiakim** identify him as another bad king. The prophet Jeremiah condemned him for social injustice in building a huge palace, while ignoring the poor (Jr 22:13–17).
24:1 The background for this verse was the Babylonian capture of Carchemish (605 BC) that drove Egypt from Syria and Palestine. The object of the Babylonian attack was the Egyptian armies, and Jehoiakim yielded peaceably to **Nebuchadnezzar**. Then, after three years, Jehoiakim rebelled because Egypt temporarily drove the Babylonians northward again (601 BC).
24:2 The Babylonians, as God's instruments, compensated for this setback by encouraging the other local vassals mentioned here to harass **Judah**.

24:3–4 As in the condemnation of Judah at the time of Manasseh (21:15), the writer of 2 Kings took a longer, backward view in accounting for God's judgment on sin. He linked God's judgment and intent to remove the Hebrews **from his presence** to the sins of **Manasseh**. The sin of the times was the continuation of a sinful national character that had already been established and judged.
24:5–6 The Babylonians counterattacked and were soon approaching Jerusalem. **Jehoiakim** died just before or during the Babylonian siege. His rebellion was discredited. The absence of any formal statement about Jehoiakim's burial could confirm Jeremiah's prediction about the shameful circumstances of his death (Jr 22:18–19).
24:7 By this time Egypt had been driven out of Palestine, and all land north of the **Brook of Egypt** (the Wadi Arish) belonged to Babylon.
24:8–9 Jehoiachin was the throne name of Jeconiah (1 Ch 3:16; Jr 24:1), which was shortened to Coniah in Jr 22:24.

daughter of Elnathan; she was from Jerusalem. ⁹ He did what was evil in the LORD's sight just as his father had done.

Deportations to Babylon

¹⁰ At that time the servants of King Nebuchadnezzar of Babylon marched up to Jerusalem, and the city came under siege. ¹¹ King Nebuchadnezzar of Babylon came to the city while his servants were besieging it. ¹² King Jehoiachin of Judah, along with his mother, his servants, his commanders, and his officials,ᴬ surrendered to the king of Babylon.

So the king of Babylon took him captive in the eighth year of his reign. ¹³ He also carried off from there all the treasures of the LORD's temple and the treasures of the king's palace, and he cut into pieces all the gold articles that King Solomon of Israel had made for the LORD's sanctuary, just as the LORD had predicted. ¹⁴ He deported all Jerusalem and all the commanders and all the best soldiers — ten thousand captives including all the craftsmen and metalsmiths. Except for the poorest people of the land, no one remained.

¹⁵ Nebuchadnezzar deported Jehoiachin to Babylon. He took the king's mother, the king's wives, his officials, and the leading men of the land into exile from Jerusalem to Babylon. ¹⁶ The king of Babylon brought captive into Babylon all seven thousand of the best soldiers and one thousand craftsmen and metalsmiths — all strong and fit for war. ¹⁷ And the king of Babylon made Mattaniah, Jehoiachin'sᴮ uncle, king in his place and changed his name to Zedekiah.

Judah's King Zedekiah

¹⁸ Zedekiah was twenty-one years old when he became king, and he reigned eleven years in Jerusalem. His mother's name was Hamutal daughter of Jeremiah; she was from Libnah. ¹⁹ Zedekiah did what was evil in the LORD's sight just as Jehoiakim had done. ²⁰ Because of the LORD's anger, it came to the point in Jerusalem and Judah that he finally banished them from his presence. Then Zedekiah rebelled against the king of Babylon.

Nebuchadnezzar's Siege of Jerusalem

25 In the ninth year of Zedekiah's reign, on the tenth day of the tenth month, King Nebuchadnezzar of Babylon advanced against Jerusalem with his entire army. They laid siege to the city and built a siege wall against it all around. ² The city was under siege until King Zedekiah's eleventh year.

³ By the ninth day of the fourth month the famine was so severe in the city that the common people had no food. ⁴ Then the city was broken into, and all the warriors fled at night by way of the city gate between the two walls near the king's garden, even though the Chaldeans surrounded the city. As the king made his way along the route to the Arabah, ⁵ the Chaldean army pursued him and overtook him in the plains of Jericho. Zedekiah's entire army left him and scattered. ⁶ The Chaldeans seized the king and brought him up to the king of Babylon at Riblah, and they passed sentence on him. ⁷ They slaughtered Zedekiah's sons before his eyes. Finally, the king of Babylon blinded Zedekiah, bound him in bronze chains, and took him to Babylon.

Jerusalem Destroyed

⁸ On the seventh day of the fifth month — which was the nineteenth year of King Nebuchadnezzar of Babylon — Nebuzaradan, the captain of the guards, a servant of the king of Babylon, entered Jerusalem. ⁹ He burned the LORD's temple, the king's palace, and all the houses of Jerusalem; he burned down all the great houses. ¹⁰ The whole Chaldean army with the captain of the guards tore down the walls surrounding Jerusalem. ¹¹ Nebuzaradan,

---

ᴬ24:12 Or eunuchs ᴮ24:17 Lit his

24:10–12 After a brief siege, Jehoiachin and all his high **officials** surrendered to **Nebuchadnezzar** of Babylon. Significantly, the expression **eighth year of his reign** must refer to Nebuchadnezzar's eighth year. This change to a pagan dating of events marked the impending end of Judah. The year was 597 BC.
24:13 The plundering of the city of Jerusalem seemed to be very thorough. It is remarkable that there was still some **gold** from the time of **Solomon** left to be plundered after more than three centuries of foreign plundering. This fulfilled the prophecy to Hezekiah in 20:17.
24:14–16 Everyone except the **poorest** classes of the city were taken into captivity. The able-bodied **soldiers** might have been conscripted into the Babylonian army.
24:17 Mattaniah ("gift of Yahweh") became Zedekiah ("Yahweh is righteous" or "righteousness of Yahweh").

24:18–19 The formal opening statements and evaluation of **Zedekiah** are routine for a wicked, faithless king.
24:20 The grounds for Zedekiah's poor evaluation predated the wickedness of the current king. God was already angry, and judgment was inevitable (vv. 3–4; see 21:15).
25:1 In 588 BC the pharaoh of Egypt led a general rebellion against Babylon that included the Phoenician coast and Transjordanian territories. Just as this rebellion was a coordinated joint rebellion of the region, the resulting Babylonian reprisal was a thorough destruction of the entire region—of non-Israelite territories in Transjordan as well. According to Jr 34:7, it seems that the Babylonians reduced all the other fortifications of Judah before turning to Jerusalem and that their approach at the end came from the southwest, from the Shephelah.
25:2–3 After a **siege** of eighteen months, the **food** supply of Jerusalem failed.

25:4–5 When Jerusalem's wall was breached, the warriors and King Zedekiah fled, probably down the Kidron Valley to the road to **Jericho** and then to the **plains** near Jericho.
25:6–7 **Riblah** was the administrative center for Babylonian control in the region. There, **Zedekiah** was punished. His sons were killed **before his eyes**, thus eliminating the threat of royal heirs to the throne. Zedekiah was **blinded** and taken to prison in **Babylon**. This fulfilled the prophecies that he would see Nebuchadnezzar (Jr 32:4) but would not see Babylon (Ezk 12:11–13).
25:8–10 The end of this historic phase of the Davidic covenant came with the total destruction of everything of significance in **Jerusalem**: literally, the temple, the king's palace, all the houses of Jerusalem, all the great houses, and the defensive wall of Jerusalem.
25:11–12 The **poorest of the land** were unlikely to have skills that could be of use

the captain of the guards, deported the rest of the people who remained in the city, the deserters who had defected to the king of Babylon, and the rest of the population. ¹² But the captain of the guards left some of the poorest of the land to be vinedressers and farmers.

¹³ Now the Chaldeans broke into pieces the bronze pillars of the LORD's temple, the water carts, and the bronze basin,^ which were in the LORD's temple, and carried the bronze to Babylon. ¹⁴ They also took the pots, shovels, wick trimmers, dishes, and all the bronze articles used in the priests' service. ¹⁵ The captain of the guards took away the firepans and sprinkling basins — whatever was gold or silver.

¹⁶ As for the two pillars, the one basin, and the water carts that Solomon had made for the LORD's temple, the weight of the bronze of all these articles was beyond measure. ¹⁷ One pillar was twenty-seven feet⁸ tall and had a bronze capital on top of it. The capital, encircled by a grating and pomegranates of bronze, stood five feet^c high. The second pillar was the same, with its own grating.

¹⁸ The captain of the guards also took away Seraiah the chief priest, Zephaniah the priest of the second rank, and the three doorkeepers. ¹⁹ From the city he took a court official^D who had been appointed over the warriors; five trusted royal aides^E found in the city; the secretary of the commander of the army, who enlisted the people of the land for military duty; and sixty men from the common people^F who were found within the city. ²⁰ Nebuzaradan, the captain of the guards, took them and brought them to the king of Babylon at Riblah. ²¹ The king of Babylon put them to death at Riblah in the land of Hamath. So Judah went into exile from its land.

Gedaliah Made Governor

²² King Nebuchadnezzar of Babylon appointed Gedaliah son of Ahikam, son of Shaphan, over the rest of the people he left in the land of Judah. ²³ When all the commanders of the armies — they and their men — heard that the king of Babylon had appointed Gedaliah, they came to Gedaliah at Mizpah. The commanders included Ishmael son of Nethaniah, Johanan son of Kareah, Seraiah son of Tanhumeth the Netophathite, and Jaazaniah son of the Maacathite — they and their men. ²⁴ Gedaliah swore an oath to them and their men, assuring them, "Don't be afraid of the servants of the Chaldeans. Live in the land and serve the king of Babylon, and it will go well for you."

²⁵ In the seventh month, however, Ishmael son of Nethaniah, son of Elishama, of the royal family, came with ten men and struck down Gedaliah, and he died. Also, they killed the Judeans and the Chaldeans who were with him at Mizpah. ²⁶ Then all the people, from the youngest to the oldest, and the commanders of the army, left and went to Egypt, for they were afraid of the Chaldeans.

Jehoiachin Pardoned

²⁷ On the twenty-seventh day of the twelfth month of the thirty-seventh year of the exile of Judah's King Jehoiachin, in the year Evil-merodach became king of Babylon, he pardoned King Jehoiachin of Judah and released him^G from prison. ²⁸ He spoke kindly to him and set his throne over the thrones of the kings who were with him in Babylon. ²⁹ So Jehoiachin changed his prison clothes, and he dined regularly in the presence of the king of Babylon for the rest of his life. ³⁰ As for his allowance, a regular allowance was given to him by the king, a portion for each day, for the rest of his life.

^25:13 Lit sea   ^B25:17 Lit 18 cubits   ^C25:17 Lit three cubits   ^D25:19 Or eunuch   ^E25:19 Lit five men who look on the king's face   ^F25:19 Lit the people of the land   ^G25:27 and released him supplied for clarity

in Babylon, and so they were left behind to be **farmers**.
25:13–17 The **temple** furnishings were plundered for their scrap-metal value. The list of plundered objects would have read to devout worshipers of the Lord like an obituary list.
25:18–21 Representative leaders of Judah were selected for execution by the Babylonians after being taken to **Riblah**. Of the two, **Seraiah** is otherwise unknown. However, **Zephaniah**, a second-tier leader of the priests, was known for being given the responsibility to root out supposedly false prophets, his major target being Jeremiah (Jr 29:26–29). The Babylonians were probably aware of his anti-Babylonian stance when they executed him. Also, **sixty ... common**

people, probably randomly selected, were also executed.
25:22–25 A more detailed account of these events appears in Jr 40:6–41:9. Here it suffices to note that it was a story of alleged collaboration with the conquerors, wholesale murder by "freedom fighters," and the loss of any hope of civilized life for the Hebrews who remained in Palestine.
25:26 The feared repercussions after the assassination of Gedaliah resulted in a voluntary exodus from Palestine to **Egypt**. Though at the time there was little hope for the future, the Jewish colony at Elephantine would make their mark on history through documents (Elephantine papyri) that have survived to this day, and the Jewish community in Alexandria would

become the intellectual rivals of rabbinic Judaism.
25:27–30 There was one more optimistic development—Jehoiachin's release from prison and his place of honor among the captive kings. The year was 561 BC; Jehoiachin was fifty-five years old. This favor probably resulted partly from his willing surrender to the Babylonians and may have been aimed at creating a better atmosphere for the exiles in Babylon. It may also have aroused hopes for restoration of the Davidic line in the person of Jehoiachin or one of his descendants. At the very least, it signaled a generally favorable Babylonian stance toward the Jewish captives—an optimistic development for God's people in Babylon.

Introduction to 1 Chronicles

Circumstances of Writing

An ancient tradition ascribes the authorship of Chronicles to Ezra. The author must have lived sometime after the return of the Jews to Israel from the Babylonian exile. He also had a strong interest in the reimplementation of the law and the temple, and he must have had access to historical records. All of these criteria suit Ezra, and this identification is corroborated by the fact that the last verses of Chronicles are the first verses of the book of Ezra. However, since the book does not explicitly claim Ezra for its author, in these notes we will refer to him simply as the Chronicler.

The books of 1 and 2 Chronicles include extensive genealogies from the time of Adam and take the reader up to the period of the nation's exile and restoration. First Chronicles gives us the genealogies and focuses on the reign of King David. Second Chronicles focuses on all the kings who followed David up to the exile and restoration. It covers the same time period as 1 and 2 Kings, but 2 Chronicles focuses exclusively on the kings of Judah. The content of the books necessitates that they were written sometime after the return from the exile, perhaps the middle of the fifth century BC.

Contribution to the Bible

Chronicles brings together many dimensions of biblical revelation, such as historical events (as recounted in Genesis through Kings), temple ritual (as prescribed in Leviticus), sin and judgment (as preached by the prophets), and even some psalms. Because a recurring theme is that God will always accept people who return to him no matter how wicked they may have been, it has been called, perhaps a little whimsically, "The Gospel According to Ezra." The books of 1 and 2 Chronicles give us the big picture of Old Testament history, capturing the Davidic covenant in light of Israel's history back to Adam and pointing to the eternal continuation of that covenant through the reign of the Messiah.

Structure

The Hebrew Bible divides its books into three categories: the Law, the Prophets, and the Writings. In this arrangement, the books of Samuel and Kings are counted among the Prophets, whereas Chronicles belongs to the Writings. This classification may be partially due to the fact that Chronicles repeats information, such as the genealogies of Genesis and the histories of the kings of Judah from the books of Samuel and Kings. Still the Chronicler uses this repeated content to support his own point, and he also adds a lot of information that we find in Chronicles alone. He limits his discussion of the various kings almost entirely to those of Judah, the southern kingdom.

1010–970 BC

With the death of Saul, David becomes king of Judah. **1010**
DAVID 1010–970
David becomes king over all Israel. **1003**
David moves the ark of the covenant to Jerusalem. **1000**
God's covenant with David **995**
Solomon becomes Israel's third king. **970**
Construction of the temple begins. **966**
Solomon dedicates the temple. **959**
ASA 911–870

900–825 BC

Notched flute is developed in Peru and Chile. **900**
First temple repair and reform under Asa **897**
Jehoshaphat **872–848**
Jehoram **853–841**
Ahaziah **841**
Etruscans settle in central Italy. **850–800**
Athaliah **841–835**
JOASH 835–796

Outline

I. The Genealogies (1:1–9:44)
   A. Genealogies of the human race (1:1–54)
   B. Genealogies of the twelve tribes (2:1–9:44)
II. The Reign of David (10:1–29:30)
   A. Fall of Saul's house and rise of David (10:1–14:17)
   B. Removal of the ark to Jerusalem (15:1–16:43)
   C. David's desire to build God a house (17:1–27)
   D. David's victories over Israel's enemies (18:1–21:30)
   E. David's preparations for building the temple (22:1–19)
   F. Arrangements for the service of the Levites (23:1–26:32)
   G. David's final days (27:1–29:30)

Key verses in 1 Chronicles

16:8 Give thanks to the LORD; call on his name;
       proclaim his deeds among the peoples.

16:9 Sing to him; sing praise to him;
       tell about all his wondrous works!

825–715 BC	715–600 BC	600–425 BC
Second temple reform under Joash **812**	**HEZEKIAH 715–687**	Babylon under Nebuchadnezzar II becomes the largest city on earth. **600**
Amaziah **796–767**	Third temple reform under Hezekiah **715**	Jehoiachin **598–597**
Uzziah **792–740**	Manasseh **697–643**	**ZEDEKIAH 597–586**
First Olympiad in Greece **776**	Amon **643–641**	The temple in Jerusalem is destroyed under Zedekiah. **586**
Traditional date for the founding of Rome **753**	**JOSIAH 641–609**	Temple of Artemis in Ephesus, third of seven wonders of the ancient world **550**
Jotham **750–732**	Fourth temple reform under Josiah **622**	Statue of Zeus at Olympia, fourth of seven wonders of the ancient world **466–456**
Ahaz **735–716**	Jehoahaz **609**	
	Jehoiakim **609–598**	

From Adam to Abraham

1 Adam, Seth, Enosh,
² Kenan, Mahalalel, Jared,
³ Enoch, Methuselah, Lamech,
⁴ Noah, Noah's sons:ᴬ
Shem, Ham, and Japheth.

⁵ Japheth's sons: Gomer, Magog, Madai, Javan, Tubal, Meshech, and Tiras.
⁶ Gomer's sons: Ashkenaz, Riphath,ᴮ and Togarmah.
⁷ Javan's sons: Elishah, Tarshish, Kittim, and Rodanim.ᶜ

⁸ Ham's sons: Cush, Mizraim,ᴰ Put, and Canaan.
⁹ Cush's sons: Seba, Havilah, Sabta, Raama, and Sabteca.
Raama's sons: Sheba and Dedan.
¹⁰ Cush fathered Nimrod, who was the first to become a great warrior on earth.
¹¹ Mizraim fathered the people of Lud, Anam, Lehab, Naphtuh, ¹² Pathrus, Casluh (the Philistines came from them), and Caphtor.
¹³ Canaan fathered Sidon as his firstborn and Heth, ¹⁴ as well as the Jebusites, Amorites, Girgashites, ¹⁵ Hivites, Arkites, Sinites, ¹⁶ Arvadites, Zemarites, and Hamathites.

¹⁷ Shem's sons: Elam, Asshur, Arpachshad, Lud, Aram, Uz, Hul, Gether, and Meshech.
¹⁸ Arpachshad fathered Shelah, and Shelah fathered Eber. ¹⁹ Two sons were born to Eber. One of them was named Pelegᴱ because the earth was divided during his lifetime, and the name of his brother was Joktan. ²⁰ Joktan fathered Almodad, Sheleph, Hazarmaveth, Jerah, ²¹ Hadoram, Uzal, Diklah, ²² Ebal, Abimael, Sheba, ²³ Ophir, Havilah, and Jobab. All of these were Joktan's sons.

²⁴ Shem, Arpachshad, Shelah,
²⁵ Eber, Peleg, Reu,
²⁶ Serug, Nahor, Terah,
²⁷ and Abram (that is, Abraham).

Abraham's Descendants

²⁸ Abraham's sons: Isaac and Ishmael.

²⁹ These are their family records: Nebaioth, Ishmael's firstborn, Kedar, Adbeel, Mibsam, ³⁰ Mishma, Dumah, Massa, Hadad, Tema, ³¹ Jetur, Naphish, and Kedemah.
These were Ishmael's sons.

³² The sons born to Keturah, Abraham's concubine: Zimran, Jokshan, Medan, Midian, Ishbak, and Shuah.
Jokshan's sons: Sheba and Dedan.
³³ Midian's sons: Ephah, Epher, Hanoch, Abida, and Eldaah.
All of these were Keturah's descendants.

³⁴ Abraham fathered Isaac.
Isaac's sons: Esau and Israel.
³⁵ Esau's sons: Eliphaz, Reuel, Jeush, Jalam, and Korah.
³⁶ Eliphaz's sons: Teman, Omar, Zephi, Gatam, and Kenaz; and by Timna, Amalek.ᶠ
³⁷ Reuel's sons: Nahath, Zerah, Shammah, and Mizzah.

The Edomites

³⁸ Seir's sons: Lotan, Shobal, Zibeon, Anah, Dishon, Ezer, and Dishan.
³⁹ Lotan's sons: Hori and Homam. Timna was Lotan's sister.
⁴⁰ Shobal's sons: Alian, Manahath, Ebal, Shephi, and Onam.
Zibeon's sons: Aiah and Anah.
⁴¹ Anah's son: Dishon.
Dishon's sons: Hamran, Eshban, Ithran, and Cheran.
⁴² Ezer's sons: Bilhan, Zaavan, and Jaakan.
Dishan's sons: Uz and Aran.

ᴬ1:4 LXX; MT omits *Noah's sons* ᴮ1:6 Some Hb mss, LXX, Vg; other Hb mss read *Diphath*; Gn 10:3 ᶜ1:7 Some Hb mss, Syr read *Dodanim*; Gn 10:4 ᴰ1:8 = Egypt ᴱ1:19 = Division ᶠ1:36 LXX; MT reads *and Timna and Amalek*; Gn 36:12

1:1 Even though the Chronicler was specifically writing for the Jews of his day, he began with this brief reminder that all people are creatures who are descended from the first man, **Adam. Seth** represented the ongoing hope after failure (Gn 4:25).
1:2–4 The line of ancient patriarchs moves quickly from Adam to **Noah**. Each of the men in this line had a son comparatively early in life, but he lived for many centuries afterwards. Before going on with the main line of descent, the Chronicler frequently pursued a minor or alternative branch first, such as when he detailed the descendants of **Japheth** and **Ham** before returning to **Shem**.
1:5–7 Japheth's offspring moved to a more northern region than those of his brothers.

1:8–16 Many of **Ham's** sons lent their names to various nations, several of which became the chief opponents of Israel in the promised land.
1:17 Shem's line was the most important one for the Chronicler because it includes Abraham.
1:19 The line of Shem divides with the brothers **Peleg** and **Joktan**. "Peleg" means "division." During his time the episode of the Tower of Babel took place, and the entire human race was divided by the languages they spoke.
1:20–23 Again following a minor branch first, we read of the descendants of **Joktan**.
1:24–27 Here is a quick overview of the links between **Shem** and **Abraham**, based on the descendants of **Peleg**.

1:28 Although **Isaac** is mentioned in this verse, we are still a long way from the line that will eventually lead up to Judah. **Ishmael** and his **sons** come first (vv. 29–31).
1:32–33 After Sarah's death, **Keturah** endowed Abraham with many more sons.
1:34 Again **Isaac** is mentioned, along with Jacob, or **Israel**, but for the moment the Chronicler focuses on **Esau**, again an alternative branch.
1:35–37 We only have this list of names for **Esau's** sons and grandsons, but we know that this clan eventually led to the emergence of several large nations such as Edom.
1:38–42 "Seir" could be a proper name referring to an ancestor of the Edomites. It is also the name of a mountain in Edomite

43 These were the kings who reigned
in the land of Edom
before any king reigned
over the Israelites:
Bela son of Beor.
Bela's town was named Dinhabah.
44 When Bela died, Jobab son of Zerah
from Bozrah reigned in his place.
45 When Jobab died, Husham
from the land of the Temanites
reigned in his place.
46 When Husham died, Hadad
son of Bedad, who defeated Midian
in the territory of Moab, reigned
in his place.
Hadad's town was named Avith.
47 When Hadad died, Samlah
from Masrekah reigned in his place.
48 When Samlah died, Shaul
from Rehoboth on the Euphrates
River reigned in his place.
49 When Shaul died, Baal-hanan
son of Achbor reigned in his place.
50 When Baal-hanan died, Hadad reigned
in his place.
Hadad's city was named Pai, and his
wife's name was Mehetabel
daughter of Matred, daughter
of Me-zahab.
51 Then Hadad died.

Edom's chiefs: Timna, Alvah,^A Jetheth,
52 Oholibamah, Elah, Pinon, 53 Kenaz,
Teman, Mibzar, 54 Magdiel, and Iram.
These were Edom's chiefs.

Israel's Sons

2 These were Israel's sons:
Reuben, Simeon, Levi,
Judah, Issachar, Zebulun,
2 Dan, Joseph, Benjamin,
Naphtali, Gad, and Asher.

Judah's Descendants

3 Judah's sons: Er, Onan, and Shelah. These
three were born to him by Bath-shua the
Canaanite woman. Er, Judah's firstborn,
was evil in the LORD's sight, so he put him
to death. 4 Judah's daughter-in-law Tamar
bore Perez and Zerah to him. Judah had
five sons in all.

5 Perez's sons: Hezron and Hamul.
6 Zerah's sons: Zimri, Ethan, Heman,
Calcol, and Dara^B — five in all.
7 Carmi's son: Achar,^C who brought trouble
on Israel when he was unfaithful by taking
the things set apart for destruction.
8 Ethan's son: Azariah.
9 Hezron's sons, who were born to him:
Jerahmeel, Ram, and Chelubai.^D

10 Ram fathered Amminadab, and
Amminadab fathered Nahshon, a leader of
Judah's descendants.
11 Nahshon fathered Salma, and Salma
fathered Boaz.
12 Boaz fathered Obed, and Obed fathered
Jesse.
13 Jesse fathered Eliab, his firstborn;
Abinadab was born second, Shimea third,
14 Nethanel fourth, Raddai fifth, 15 Ozem
sixth, and David seventh. 16 Their sisters
were Zeruiah and Abigail. Zeruiah's three
sons: Abishai, Joab, and Asahel. 17 Amasa's
mother was Abigail, and his father was
Jether the Ishmaelite.

18 Caleb son of Hezron had children by his
wife Azubah and by Jerioth. These were
Azubah's sons: Jesher, Shobab, and Ar-
don. 19 When Azubah died, Caleb married Ephrath, and she bore Hur to him.
20 Hur fathered Uri, and Uri fathered Bezalel. 21 After this, Hezron slept with the

---

^A1:51 Alt Hb tradition reads *Aliah* ^B2:6 Some Hb mss, LXX, Syr, Tg, Vg read *Darda*; 1Kg 4:31 ^C2:7 = Trouble; Achan in Jos
7:1,16–26 ^D2:9 = Caleb

---

territory. The Edomites lived on the eastern
side of the Jordan River in the vicinity of
the Dead Sea.
1:43–51a Little is known about these
kings . . . in the land of Edom. They apparently lived around the time of the judges
in Israel.
1:51b–54 The chapter concludes with a list of
Edom's chiefs. The book of 1 Chronicles has
now covered several minor lines in contrast
to its major purpose of leading up to the
kings of Judah.
2:1 Now we are ready for the main line of
interest, the descendants of Jacob.
2:3 All three of **Judah's** first sons had a **Canaanite** mother.
2:4 After **Judah's** first two sons were
killed, he had two more sons by his
daughter-in-law **Tamar**, another Canaanite woman, who had disguised herself as a
prostitute (Gn 38). These twins were **Perez**
and **Zerah**.

2:5 Perez continues the main line through
Hezron. Hamul's line is the secondary alternative.
2:6 Zerah's sons constitute another alternative.
2:7 Carmi must be a person of a later generation. He is mentioned only because he
is the father of **Achar**, another bearer of
scandal (aka Achan, Jos 7). Thus, the alternative branch goes: Zerah to Zabdi to Carmi
to Achar.
2:8 Nothing further is known of this Azariah.
2:9 Returning to the main line: Perez had
Hezron (see note at v. 5). Now the line splits
three ways based on **Hezron's** three sons:
Jerahmeel, Ram, and Chelubai. Of these,
Ram's line is the main one, and this time it
gets mentioned first. Chelubai is another
version of the name "Caleb." There are many
different men named Caleb in the list that
follows.

2:10–12 Ram's line of descent connects
through **Boaz** to **Jesse**, the father of David.
2:13–17 In this passage we are given the
names of David's six older brothers and his
two much older sisters **Zeruiah** and **Abigail**.
These two were probably from an earlier
marriage of David's father Jesse since according to 2Sm 17:25, their father was Nahash. So
presumably Jesse married Nahash's widow.
Zeruiah had three sons—**Abishai, Joab, and
Asahel**—who were roughly David's age, and
who would later become leaders in David's
army. Abigail married an **Ishmaelite** named
Jether and gave birth to Amasa, who would
become the leader of Absalom's army against
David. These four were David's half-neph-
ews. Also see the note at 27:18.
2:18–24 We go back to **Hezron**, son of Perez,
who left a sizeable number of descendants—
one of them even after his own death. His
son **Caleb** (called Chelubai in v. 9) also had
a number of sons.

daughter of Machir the father of Gilead. Hezron had married her when he was sixty years old, and she bore Segub to him. ²² Segub fathered Jair, who possessed twenty-three towns in the land of Gilead. ²³ But Geshur and Aram captured^ Jair's Villages^B along with Kenath and its surrounding villages — sixty towns. All these were the descendants of Machir father of Gilead. ²⁴ After Hezron's death in Caleb-ephrathah, his wife Abijah bore^C Ashhur to him. He was the father of Tekoa.

²⁵ The sons of Jerahmeel, Hezron's firstborn: Ram, his firstborn, Oren, Ozem, and Ahijah. ²⁶ Jerahmeel had another wife named Atarah, who was the mother of Onam. ²⁷ The sons of Ram, Jerahmeel's firstborn: Maaz, Jamin, and Eker. ²⁸ Onam's sons: Shammai and Jada. Shammai's sons: Nadab and Abishur. ²⁹ Abishur's wife was named Abihail, who bore Ahban and Molid to him. ³⁰ Nadab's sons: Seled and Appaim. Seled died without children. ³¹ Appaim's son: Ishi. Ishi's son: Sheshan. Sheshan's descendant: Ahlai. ³² The sons of Jada, brother of Shammai: Jether and Jonathan. Jether died without children. ³³ Jonathan's sons: Peleth and Zaza. These were the descendants of Jerahmeel. ³⁴ Sheshan had no sons, only daughters, but he did have an Egyptian servant whose name was Jarha. ³⁵ Sheshan gave his daughter in marriage to his servant Jarha, and she bore Attai to him.

³⁶ Attai fathered Nathan, and Nathan fathered Zabad. ³⁷ Zabad fathered Ephlal, and Ephlal fathered Obed. ³⁸ Obed fathered Jehu, and Jehu fathered Azariah. ³⁹ Azariah fathered Helez, and Helez fathered Elasah. ⁴⁰ Elasah fathered Sismai, and Sismai fathered Shallum. ⁴¹ Shallum fathered Jekamiah, and Jekamiah fathered Elishama.

⁴² The sons of Caleb brother of Jerahmeel: Mesha, his firstborn, fathered Ziph, and Mareshah, his second son,^D fathered Hebron. ⁴³ Hebron's sons: Korah, Tappuah, Rekem, and Shema. ⁴⁴ Shema fathered Raham, who fathered Jorkeam, and Rekem fathered Shammai. ⁴⁵ Shammai's son was Maon, and Maon fathered Beth-zur. ⁴⁶ Caleb's concubine Ephah was the mother of Haran, Moza, and Gazez. Haran fathered Gazez. ⁴⁷ Jahdai's sons: Regem, Jotham, Geshan, Pelet, Ephah, and Shaaph. ⁴⁸ Caleb's concubine Maacah was the mother of Sheber and Tirhanah. ⁴⁹ She was also the mother of Shaaph, Madmannah's father, and of Sheva, the father of Machbenah and Gibea. Caleb's daughter was Achsah. ⁵⁰ These were Caleb's descendants.

The sons of Hur, Ephrathah's firstborn: Shobal fathered Kiriath-jearim; ⁵¹ Salma fathered Bethlehem, and Hareph fathered Beth-gader.

⁵² These were the descendants of Shobal the father of Kiriath-jearim: Haroeh, half of the Manahathites,^E ⁵³ and the families of Kiriath-jearim — the Ithrites, Puthites, Shumathites, and Mishraites. The Zorathites and Eshtaolites descended from these.

⁵⁴ Salma's descendants: Bethlehem, the Netophathites, Atroth-beth-joab, and half of the Manahathites, the Zorites, ⁵⁵ and the families of scribes who lived in Jabez — the Tirathites, Shimeathites, and Sucathites. These are the Kenites who came from Hammath, the father of Rechab's family.

David's Descendants

3 These were David's sons who were born to him in Hebron:
Amnon was the firstborn, by Ahinoam of Jezreel;
Daniel was born second, by Abigail of Carmel;
² Absalom son of Maacah, daughter of King Talmai of Geshur, was third;

2:25–33 The third line of descent coming from Hezron, joining those of Ram and Caleb, is that of **Jerahmeel**. His son **Ram** was the nephew of **Hezron's** brother, Ram. **2:34–35 Sheshan** had been mentioned in v. 31, the sixth generation descendant of Jerahmeel. He did not have a male heir, but a daughter named Ahlai. **Jarha,** his Egyptian servant, provided him with a grandson named **Attai** to carry on the family name. **2:36–41** The list of Jerahmeel's descendants continues from **Attai** onward. **2:42–55** We have already had a list of the descendants of **Caleb** (Chelubai), the son of Perez. This time the descendants mentioned are not individual people but the populations of towns that could trace themselves back to him in direct and indirect ways. **3:1–4** This chapter completes the line of Judah. We find the people who are most important for Chronicles: David and his descendants. **David's sons** are divided into two groups—those born in **Hebron** where David was king for seven years and those who were born in Jerusalem, David's capital for thirty-three years.

Adonijah son of Haggith was fourth;
³ Shephatiah, by Abital, was fifth;
and Ithream, by David's wife Eglah, was
sixth.
⁴ Six sons were born to David in Hebron,
where he reigned seven years and six
months, and he reigned in Jerusalem
thirty-three years.
⁵ These sons were born to him in
Jerusalem:
Shimea, Shobab, Nathan, and Solomon.
These four were born to him by Bath-shua
daughter of Ammiel.
⁶ David's other sons: Ibhar, Elishua,^A
Eliphelet, ⁷ Nogah, Nepheg, Japhia,
⁸ Elishama, Eliada, and Eliphelet — nine
sons.
⁹ These were all David's sons, with their
sister Tamar, in addition to the sons by his
concubines.

Judah's Kings

¹⁰ Solomon's son was Rehoboam;
his son was Abijah, his son Asa,
his son Jehoshaphat, ¹¹ his son
Jehoram,^{B,C}
his son Ahaziah, his son Joash,
¹² his son Amaziah, his son Azariah,
his son Jotham, ¹³ his son Ahaz,
his son Hezekiah, his son Manasseh,
¹⁴ his son Amon, and his son Josiah.
¹⁵ Josiah's sons:
Johanan was the firstborn, Jehoiakim
second,
Zedekiah third, and Shallum fourth.
¹⁶ Jehoiakim's sons:
his sons Jeconiah and Zedekiah.

David's Line after the Exile

¹⁷ The sons of Jeconiah the captive:
his sons Shealtiel, ¹⁸ Malchiram, Pedaiah,
Shenazzar, Jekamiah, Hoshama, and
Nedabiah.
¹⁹ Pedaiah's sons: Zerubbabel and Shimei.
Zerubbabel's sons: Meshullam and
Hananiah, with their sister Shelomith;

²⁰ and five others — Hashubah, Ohel,
Berechiah, Hasadiah, and Jushab-hesed.
²¹ Hananiah's descendants: Pelatiah,
Jeshaiah, and the sons of Rephaiah, Arnan,
Obadiah, and Shecaniah.^D
²² The son^E of Shecaniah: Shemaiah.
Shemaiah's sons: Hattush, Igal, Bariah,
Neariah, and Shaphat — six.
²³ Neariah's sons: Elioenai, Hizkiah, and
Azrikam — three.
²⁴ Elioenai's sons: Hodaviah, Eliashib,
Pelaiah, Akkub, Johanan, Delaiah, and
Anani — seven.

Judah's Descendants

4 Judah's sons: Perez, Hezron, Carmi, Hur,
and Shobal.
² Reaiah son of Shobal fathered Jahath, and
Jahath fathered Ahumai and Lahad.
These were the families of the Zorathites.
³ These were Etam's sons:^F Jezreel, Ishma,
and Idbash, and their sister was named
Hazzelelponi.
⁴ Penuel fathered Gedor, and Ezer fathered
Hushah.
These were the sons of Hur, Ephrathah's
firstborn and the father of Bethlehem:
⁵ Ashhur fathered Tekoa and had two
wives, Helah and Naarah.
⁶ Naarah bore Ahuzzam, Hepher, Temeni,
and Haahashtari to him. These were
Naarah's sons.
⁷ Helah's sons: Zereth, Zohar,^G and Ethnan.
⁸ Koz fathered Anub, Zobebah,^H and the
families of Aharhel son of Harum.

⁹ Jabez^I was more honored than his broth-
ers. His mother named him Jabez and said, "I
gave birth to him in pain."
¹⁰ Jabez called out to the God of Israel, "If
only you would bless me, extend my border,
let your hand be with me, and keep me from
harm, so that I will not experience pain."^J And
God granted his request.
¹¹ Chelub brother of Shuhah fathered
Mehir, who was the father of Eshton.

^A3:6 Lit Elishama; 2Sm 5:15; 1Ch 14:5 ^B3:11 Lit Joram ^C3:11 = The Lᴏʀᴅ is Exalted ^D3:21 LXX reads Jeshaiah, his son
Rephaiah, his son Arnan, his son Obadiah, and his son Shecaniah ^E3:22 LXX; MT reads sons ^F4:3 LXX; MT reads father
^G4:7 Alt Hb tradition reads Izhar ^H4:8 Or Hazzobebah ^I4:9 In Hb, the name Jabez sounds like "he causes pain."
^J4:10 Or not cause any pain

3:5 Bath-shua is more familiar to us as Bathsheba. **Solomon** carried the house of David forward.

3:6–9 These too were born in Jerusalem but not by Bath-shua.

3:10–16 These verses contain a quick overview of most of 2 Chronicles, the line of descendants of David who were kings of Judah.

3:17–24 The line continues after the Babylonian exile, even though there was not an official king of Judah from that point on. These verses help date the book of Chronicles.

3:19 Zerubbabel was the leader of the Jews when they returned from the exile. Under other circumstances, he would have been king. The list ends at a time that is perfectly matched for Ezra to have been the Chronicler.

4:1–23 Having paused to cite David's descendants, the author returns to conclude Judah's kin. The list of names is interrupted by a narrative in vv. 9–10. The descendants of Perez are listed in vv. 1–20, and of Shelah in vv. 21–23. The genealogy is discontinuous and fragmentary and mixes personal names and place names.

4:1 In this verse the word sons refers loosely to "descendants." Skipping several generations, the Chronicler emphasizes certain individuals in **Judah's** line. Adding to **Perez** and **Hezron**, he focuses on **Carmi, Hur, and Shobal.** Carmi may be the same person as the Carmi mentioned in 2:7.

4:4 Hur has already been mentioned in 2:20. As the father of Ephrathah (Bethlehem), he was an important ancestor.

4:5 Ashhur was mentioned earlier as the son who was born to Hezron posthumously.

4:10 Jabez prayed a personal prayer, asking God for his blessing. He wanted more land, he wanted God's **hand** to be with him, and he wanted God to **keep** him **from harm.**

¹² Eshton fathered Beth-rapha, Paseah, and Tehinnah the father of Irnahash. These were the men of Recah.
¹³ Kenaz's sons: Othniel and Seraiah. Othniel's sons: Hathath and Meonothai.^
¹⁴ Meonothai fathered Ophrah, and Seraiah fathered Joab, the ancestor of those in the Craftsmen's Valley,^B for they were craftsmen.
¹⁵ The sons of Caleb son of Jephunneh: Iru, Elah, and Naam. Elah's son: Kenaz.
¹⁶ Jehallelel's sons: Ziph, Ziphah, Tiria, and Asarel.
¹⁷ Ezrah's sons: Jether, Mered, Epher, and Jalon. Mered's wife Bithiah gave birth to Miriam, Shammai, and Ishbah the father of Eshtemoa. ¹⁸ These were the sons of Pharaoh's daughter Bithiah; Mered had married her. His Judean wife gave birth to Jered the father of Gedor, Heber the father of Soco, and Jekuthiel the father of Zanoah.
¹⁹ The sons of Hodiah's wife, the sister of Naham: the father of Keilah the Garmite and the father of Eshtemoa the Maacathite.
²⁰ Shimon's sons: Amnon, Rinnah, Ben-hanan, and Tilon. Ishi's sons: Zoheth and Ben-zoheth.

²¹ The sons of Shelah son of Judah: Er the father of Lecah, Laadah the father of Mareshah, the families of the guild^C of linen workers at Beth-ashbea, ²² Jokim, the men of Cozeba; and Joash and Saraph, who married Moabites^D and returned to Lehem.^E These names are from ancient records. ²³ They were the potters and residents of Netaim and Gederah. They lived there in the service of the king.

Simeon's Descendants

²⁴ Simeon's sons: Nemuel, Jamin, Jarib, Zerah, and Shaul;
²⁵ Shaul's sons: his son Shallum, his son Mibsam, and his son Mishma.
²⁶ Mishma's sons: his son Hammuel, his son Zaccur, and his son Shimei.

²⁷ Shimei had sixteen sons and six daughters, but his brothers did not have many children, so their whole family did not become as numerous as the Judeans. ²⁸ They lived in Beer-sheba, Moladah, Hazar-shual, ²⁹ Bilhah, Ezem, Tolad, ³⁰ Bethuel, Hormah, Ziklag, ³¹ Beth-marcaboth, Hazar-susim, Beth-biri, and Shaaraim. These were their cities until David became king. ³² Their villages were Etam, Ain, Rimmon, Tochen, and Ashan — five cities, ³³ and all their surrounding villages as far as Baal. These were their settlements, and they kept a genealogical record for themselves.

³⁴ Meshobab, Jamlech, Joshah son of Amaziah,
³⁵ Joel, Jehu son of Joshibiah, son of Seraiah, son of Asiel,
³⁶ Elioenai, Jaakobah, Jeshohaiah, Asaiah, Adiel, Jesimiel, Benaiah, ³⁷ and Ziza son of Shiphi, son of Allon, son of Jedaiah, son of Shimri, son of Shemaiah —

³⁸ these mentioned by name were leaders in their families. Their ancestral houses increased greatly. ³⁹ They went to the entrance of Gedor, to the east side of the valley to seek pasture for their flocks. ⁴⁰ They found rich, good pasture, and the land was broad, peaceful, and quiet, for some Hamites had lived there previously.

⁴¹ These who were recorded by name came in the days of King Hezekiah of Judah, attacked the Hamites' tents and the Meunites who were found there, and set them apart for destruction, as they are today. Then they settled in their place because there was pasture for their flocks. ⁴² Now five hundred men from these sons of Simeon went with Pelatiah, Neariah, Rephaiah, and Uzziel, the descendants of Ishi, as their leaders to Mount Seir. ⁴³ They struck down the remnant of the Amalekites who had escaped, and they still live there today.

Reuben's Descendants

5 These were the sons of Reuben the firstborn of Israel. He was the firstborn, but his birthright was given to the sons of Joseph son of Israel, because Reuben defiled his father's bed. He is not listed in the genealogy according

---

^4:13 LXX, Vg; MT omits *and Meonothai* ^4:14 Or *the Ge-harashim* ^4:21 Lit *house* ^4:22 Or *who ruled over Moab*
^4:22 Tg, Vg; MT reads *and Jashubi Lehem*

4:13 Othniel was the first judge (Jdg 2), and he must have been significantly younger than his uncle Caleb.
4:15 This **Caleb** is the spy of Nm 13 who, along with Joshua, trusted God.
4:17–18 Once again a Gentile is part of the line, this time a daughter of a Pharaoh named **Bithiah**.
4:21–23 Shelah was Judah's third son (2:3). His older brothers Er and Onan had been killed and he should have become the husband of Tamar, but Judah prevented this (Gn 38:11–14). Shelah's descendants distinguished themselves as craftsmen.
4:24–37 Because Simeon was violent and cruel, his father Jacob predicted that his tribe would be dispersed in the land (Gn 49:7). At the time of the conquest, the tribe of Simeon received a territory that was adjacent to and intermingled with Judah. The parts that belonged to Simeon alone were mostly desert. As a consequence, Simeon became increasingly absorbed into Judah and Benjamin, and its identity faded. Despite numerous offspring, particularly from **Shimei**, the tribe as a whole remained undistinguished.
4:38–41 Some Simeonites retained their identity into the time of Hezekiah, when they took some fertile land from a group of **Hamites**.
4:42–43 Another group of Simeonites distinguished themselves by an excursion to **Mount Seir** (Edom), where they finally eliminated the **Amalekites** who were hiding out in that area.
5:1–5 The tribes that settled on the eastern side of the Jordan River (**Reuben,**

to birthright. ² Although Judah became strong among his brothers and a ruler came from him, the birthright was given to Joseph.

³ The sons of Reuben, Israel's firstborn: Hanoch, Pallu, Hezron, and Carmi.

⁴ Joel's sons: his son Shemaiah, his son Gog, his son Shimei,

⁵ his son Micah, his son Reaiah, his son Baal, ⁶ and his son Beerah.

Beerah was a leader of the Reubenites, and King Tiglath-pileser^A of Assyria took him into exile. ⁷ His relatives by their families as they are recorded in their family records:

Jeiel the chief, Zechariah,

⁸ and Bela son of Azaz, son of Shema, son of Joel.

They settled in Aroer as far as Nebo and Baal-meon. ⁹ They also settled in the east as far as the edge of the desert that extends to the Euphrates River, because their herds had increased in the land of Gilead. ¹⁰ During Saul's reign they waged war against the Hagrites, who were defeated by their power. And they lived in their tents throughout the region east of Gilead.

Gad's Descendants

¹¹ The sons of Gad lived next to them in the land of Bashan as far as Salecah:

¹² Joel the chief, Shapham the second in command, Janai, and Shaphat in Bashan.

¹³ Their relatives according to their ancestral houses: Michael, Meshullam, Sheba, Jorai, Jacan, Zia, and Eber — seven.

¹⁴ These were the sons of Abihail son of Huri, son of Jaroah, son of Gilead, son of Michael, son of Jeshishai, son of Jahdo, son of Buz.

¹⁵ Ahi son of Abdiel, son of Guni, was head of their ancestral family.^B ¹⁶ They lived in Gilead, in Bashan and its surrounding villages, and throughout the pasturelands of Sharon. ¹⁷ All of them were registered in the genealogies during the reigns of

Judah's King Jotham and Israel's King Jeroboam.

¹⁸ The descendants of Reuben and Gad and half the tribe of Manasseh had 44,760 warriors who could serve in the army — men who carried shield and sword, drew the bow, and were trained for war. ¹⁹ They waged war against the Hagrites, Jetur, Naphish, and Nodab. ²⁰ They received help against these enemies because they cried out to God in battle, and the Hagrites and all their allies were handed over to them. He was receptive to their prayer because they trusted in him. ²¹ They captured the Hagrites' livestock — fifty thousand of their camels, two hundred fifty thousand sheep, and two thousand donkeys — as well as one hundred thousand people. ²² Many of the Hagrites were killed because it was God's battle. And they lived there in the Hagrites' place until the exile.

Half the Tribe of Manasseh

²³ The descendants of half the tribe of Manasseh settled in the land from Bashan to Baal-hermon (that is, Senir or Mount Hermon); they were numerous. ²⁴ These were the heads of their ancestral families: Epher, Ishi, Eliel, Azriel, Jeremiah, Hodaviah, and Jahdiel. They were valiant warriors, famous men, and heads of their ancestral houses. ²⁵ But they were unfaithful to the God of their ancestors. They prostituted themselves with the gods of the nations^C God had destroyed before them. ²⁶ So the God of Israel roused the spirit of King Pul (that is, Tiglath-pileser^A) of Assyria, and he took the Reubenites, Gadites, and half the tribe of Manasseh into exile. He took them to Halah, Habor, Hara, and Gozan's river, where they are until today.

The Levites

6 Levi's sons: Gershom,^D Kohath, and Merari.
² Kohath's sons: Amram, Izhar, Hebron, and Uzziel.

---

^A5:6,26 LXX; MT reads *Tiglath-pileser*   ^B5:15 Lit *the house of their fathers*, also in v. 24   ^C5:25 Lit *the peoples of the land*
^D6:1 In Hb Levi's son's name is spelled "Gershon" here and many other places

---

Gad, and half of Manasseh) asked for this land when Moses and the Israelites first came to the promised land. They received this territory after their men had helped Joshua conquer the land on the river's western side. The tribes are discussed in this chapter, going south to north. Reuben was located by the Dead Sea. He lost his honor as the **firstborn** among the twelve sons of Jacob when he committed incest with Bilhah, one of Reuben's concubines and the mother of two of Reuben's brothers (Gn 35:25).
5:6 A quick and abbreviated genealogy of the tribe of Reuben leads us to **Beerah**, who had the bad fortune of being tribal leader

when **Tiglath-pileser**, king of Assyria, carried the tribe into exile.
5:7–10 Reuben's earlier successes had allowed this tribe to stretch all the way to the **Euphrates River** and to defeat the **Hagrites**. These were the Ishmaelites, the descendants of Hagar.
5:11–17 The tribe of **Gad** was located north of Reuben. The Chronicler's frequent reference to other written documents such as **genealogies** and historical records indicates that biblical writers had at their disposal written sources.
5:23 There was no tribe of Joseph. Instead, Joseph's sons became the ancestors of two separate tribes, Ephraim and **Manasseh**. The

tribe of Manasseh occupied territory on both sides of the Jordan River.
5:24–25 This is the first reference to idolatry in Chronicles.
5:26 Tiglath-pileser was a cruel and vicious king of **Assyria**, but God used him to punish his people for their idolatry.
6:1 We now switch to **Levi's** tribe, the tribe of priests. These are important for the Chronicler because after the exile, the time at which he was writing, reestablishing the proper priesthood was crucial. Anyone who wanted to serve as a priest in the rebuilt temple had to have a clear genealogy within the tribe of Levi (Neh 7:64). Levi had three sons: **Gershom, Kohath, and Merari**. Each

³ Amram's children: Aaron, Moses,
    and Miriam.
Aaron's sons: Nadab, Abihu, Eleazar,
    and Ithamar.
⁴ Eleazar fathered Phinehas;
    Phinehas fathered Abishua;
⁵ Abishua fathered Bukki;
    Bukki fathered Uzzi;
⁶ Uzzi fathered Zerahiah;
    Zerahiah fathered Meraioth;
⁷ Meraioth fathered Amariah;
    Amariah fathered Ahitub;
⁸ Ahitub fathered Zadok;
    Zadok fathered Ahimaaz;
⁹ Ahimaaz fathered Azariah;
    Azariah fathered Johanan;
¹⁰ Johanan fathered Azariah, who served
    as priest in the temple that Solomon
    built in Jerusalem;
¹¹ Azariah fathered Amariah;
    Amariah fathered Ahitub;
¹² Ahitub fathered Zadok;
    Zadok fathered Shallum;
¹³ Shallum fathered Hilkiah;
    Hilkiah fathered Azariah;
¹⁴ Azariah fathered Seraiah;
    and Seraiah fathered Jehozadak.
¹⁵ Jehozadak went into exile when the
    LORD sent Judah and Jerusalem into
    exile at the hands of Nebuchadnezzar.

¹⁶ Levi's sons: Gershom, Kohath,
    and Merari.
¹⁷ These are the names of Gershom's sons:
    Libni and Shimei.
¹⁸ Kohath's sons: Amram, Izhar, Hebron
    and Uzziel.
¹⁹ Merari's sons: Mahli and Mushi.
    These are the Levites' families
    according to their fathers:
²⁰ Of Gershom: his son Libni,
    his son Jahath, his son Zimmah,
²¹ his son Joah, his son Iddo,
    his son Zerah, and his son Jeatherai.
²² Kohath's sons: his son Amminadab,
    his son Korah, his son Assir,
²³ his son Elkanah, his son Ebiasaph,
    his son Assir, ²⁴ his son Tahath,
    his son Uriel, his son Uzziah,
    and his son Shaul.

²⁵ Elkanah's sons: Amasai and Ahimoth,
²⁶ his son Elkanah, his son Zophai,
    his son Nahath, ²⁷ his son Eliab,
    his son Jeroham, and his son Elkanah.
²⁸ Samuel's sons: his firstborn Joel,ᴬ
    and his second son Abijah.
²⁹ Merari's sons: Mahli, his son Libni,
    his son Shimei, his son Uzzah,
³⁰ his son Shimea, his son Haggiah,
    and his son Asaiah.

The Musicians

³¹ These are the men David put in charge of the music in the LORD's temple after the ark came to rest there. ³² They ministered with song in front of the tabernacle, the tent of meeting, until Solomon built the LORD's temple in Jerusalem, and they performed their task according to the regulations given to them. ³³ These are the men who served with their sons.

From the Kohathites: Heman the singer,
    son of Joel, son of Samuel,
³⁴ son of Elkanah, son of Jeroham,
    son of Eliel, son of Toah,
³⁵ son of Zuph, son of Elkanah,
    son of Mahath, son of Amasai,
³⁶ son of Elkanah, son of Joel,
    son of Azariah, son of Zephaniah,
³⁷ son of Tahath, son of Assir,
    son of Ebiasaph, son of Korah,
³⁸ son of Izhar, son of Kohath,
    son of Levi, son of Israel.

³⁹ Heman's relative was Asaph, who stood
    at his right hand:
Asaph son of Berechiah, son of Shimea,
⁴⁰ son of Michael, son of Baaseiah,
    son of Malchijah, ⁴¹ son of Ethni,
    son of Zerah, son of Adaiah,
⁴² son of Ethan, son of Zimmah,
    son of Shimei, ⁴³ son of Jahath,
    son of Gershom, son of Levi.

⁴⁴ On the left, their relatives were
    Merari's sons:
Ethan son of Kishi, son of Abdi,
    son of Malluch, ⁴⁵ son of Hashabiah,
    son of Amaziah, son of Hilkiah,
⁴⁶ son of Amzi, son of Bani,
    son of Shemer, ⁴⁷ son of Mahli,

ᴬ6:28 Some LXX mss, Syr, Arabic; other Hb mss omit *Joel*; 1Sm 8:2

of these three lines performed distinctive duties in the worship of God (Nm 4:1–33). The most crucial line was the one that led to Aaron and, thus, to the priests. This is the line that stemmed from Levi's son Kohath. But not every descendant of Kohath got to be a priest—only those who could trace their lineage back to Aaron. Everyone else went into the larger pool of people who fulfilled general temple duties. **6:3–4** The descendants of **Aaron** who are mentioned here were priests. **Nadab** and

Abihu lost their lives when they violated the sanctity of their duties (Lv 10:1–3), so **Eleazar** became Aaron's true successor, followed by **Phinehas**. **6:5–15** This list of priests is not complete. It does not mention Eli, the priest who raised Samuel (1Sm 1:3). **6:16–21** The second major list in this chapter includes Levites who were not of the priestly line. **6:22–30** We return to **Kohath's** descendants. This list contains four men named

Elkanah. The one mentioned in v. 27 is the father of Samuel since Samuel is mentioned in the next verse. **6:31–32** The Chronicler emphasizes the presence of **music** in the temple; as it was instituted by David and revived in later years. **6:33–47** There are three main musicians: **Heman** (Ps 88), **Asaph** (Pss 50; 73–83), and **Ethan** (also called Jeduthun at times, Ps 89). These three men represent the three branches of the sons of Levi, coming from Kohath, Gershom, and Merari, respectively. Heman was a

son of Mushi, son of Merari,
son of Levi.

Aaron's Descendants

[48] Their relatives, the Levites, were assigned to all the service of the tabernacle, God's temple. [49] But Aaron and his sons did all the work of the most holy place. They presented the offerings on the altar of burnt offerings and on the altar of incense to make atonement for Israel according to all that Moses the servant of God had commanded.
[50] These are Aaron's sons: his son Eleazar, his son Phinehas, his son Abishua,
[51] his son Bukki, his son Uzzi, his son Zerahiah, [52] his son Meraioth, his son Amariah, his son Ahitub,
[53] his son Zadok, and his son Ahimaaz.

The Settlements of the Levites

[54] These were the places assigned to Aaron's descendants from the Kohathite family for their settlements in their territory, because the first lot was for them. [55] They were given Hebron in the land of Judah and its surrounding pasturelands, [56] but the fields and settlements around the city were given to Caleb son of Jephunneh. [57] Aaron's descendants were given:
Hebron (a city of refuge), Libnah and its pasturelands, Jattir, Eshtemoa and its pasturelands, [58] Hilen^ and its pasturelands, Debir and its pasturelands, [59] Ashan and its pasturelands, and Beth-shemesh and its pasturelands. [60] From the tribe of Benjamin they were given Geba and its pasturelands, Alemeth and its pasturelands, and Anathoth and its pasturelands. They had thirteen towns in all among their families.

[61] To the rest of the Kohathites, ten towns from half the tribe of Manasseh were assigned by lot.
[62] The Gershomites were assigned thirteen towns from the tribes of Issachar, Asher, Naphtali, and Manasseh in Bashan according to their families.
[63] The Merarites were assigned by lot twelve towns from the tribes of Reuben, Gad, and Zebulun according to their families. [64] So the Israelites gave these towns and their pasturelands to the Levites. [65] They assigned by lot the towns named above from the tribes of the descendants of Judah, Simeon, and Benjamin.
[66] Some of the families of the Kohathites were given towns from the tribe of Ephraim for their territory:
[67] Shechem (a city of refuge) with its pasturelands in the hill country of Ephraim, Gezer and its pasturelands, [68] Jokmeam and its pasturelands, Beth-horon and its pasturelands, [69] Aijalon and its pasturelands, and Gath-rimmon and its pasturelands. [70] From half the tribe of Manasseh, Aner and its pasturelands, and Bileam and its pasturelands were given to the rest of the families of the Kohathites.

[71] The Gershomites received:
Golan in Bashan and its pasturelands, and Ashtaroth and its pasturelands from the families of half the tribe of Manasseh. [72] From the tribe of Issachar they received Kedesh and its pasturelands, Daberath and its pasturelands, [73] Ramoth and its pasturelands, and Anem and its pasturelands. [74] From the tribe of Asher they received Mashal and its pasturelands, Abdon and its pasturelands, [75] Hukok and its pasturelands, and Rehob and its pasturelands. [76] From the tribe of Naphtali they received Kedesh in Galilee and its pasturelands, Hammon and its pasturelands, and Kiriathaim and its pasturelands.

[77] The rest of the Merarites received:
From the tribe of Zebulun they received Rimmono and its pasturelands and Tabor and its pasturelands. [78] From the tribe of Reuben across the Jordan at Jericho, to the east of the Jordan, they received Bezer in the desert and its pasturelands, Jahzah and its pasturelands, [79] Kedemoth and its pasturelands, and Mephaath and its pasturelands. [80] From the tribe of Gad they received Ramoth in Gilead and its pasturelands, Mahanaim and its pasturelands, [81] Heshbon and its pasturelands, and Jazer and its pasturelands.

Issachar's Descendants

7 Issachar's sons: Tola, Puah, Jashub, and Shimron—four.
[2] Tola's sons: Uzzi, Rephaiah, Jeriel, Jahmai, Ibsam, and Shemuel, the heads of their

---

^**6:58** Some Hb mss, LXX; other Hb mss read *Hilez*

descendant of Kohath, but not through Aaron, so he was not eligible for the priesthood. **6:48–53** Emphasizing the distinction between the descendants of **Aaron** and the other branches derived from Levi, the Chronicler once more lists those who were priests, but states that everyone else was also engaged in the service of the tabernacle. **6:54** The Levites worked in the tabernacle and later the temple, but they did not all live clustered around the sacred location. **6:55–61** The Kohathites got a share of the important city of **Hebron**. The main inheritor of this location was **Caleb**, and it would also serve later for a time as capital city under David's monarchy. **6:62–81** A noticeable feature of this long list is that the Levites were given dwelling space among the eastern tribes of **Manasseh . . . Gad**, and **Reuben**, as well as in the main territory on the west. **7:1–5 Issachar's** tribe is mentioned primarily for the number of soldiers it supplied and its meticulous genealogies.

ancestral families.^A During David's reign, 22,600 descendants of Tola were recorded as valiant warriors in their family records. **3** Uzzi's son: Izrahiah.

Izrahiah's sons: Michael, Obadiah, Joel, Isshiah. All five of them were chiefs. **4** Along with them, they had 36,000 troops for battle according to the family records of their ancestral families, for they had many wives and children. **5** Their tribesmen who were valiant warriors belonging to all the families of Issachar totaled 87,000 in their genealogies.

Benjamin's Descendants

6 Three of Benjamin's sons: Bela, Becher, and Jediael.
7 Bela's sons: Ezbon, Uzzi, Uzziel, Jerimoth, and Iri — five. They were valiant warriors and heads of their ancestral families; 22,034 were listed in their genealogies.
8 Becher's sons: Zemirah, Joash, Eliezer, Elioenai, Omri, Jeremoth, Abijah, Anathoth, and Alemeth; all these were Becher's sons. **9** Their family records were recorded according to the heads of their ancestral families — 20,200 valiant warriors.
10 Jediael's son: Bilhan.
Bilhan's sons: Jeush, Benjamin, Ehud, Chenaanah, Zethan, Tarshish, and Ahishahar. **11** All these sons of Jediael listed by family heads were valiant warriors; there were 17,200 who could serve in the army. **12** Shuppim and Huppim were sons of Ir, and the Hushim were the sons of Aher.

Naphtali's Descendants

13 Naphtali's sons: Jahziel, Guni, Jezer, and Shallum — Bilhah's sons.

Manasseh's Descendants

14 Manasseh's sons through his Aramean concubine: Asriel and Machir the father of Gilead. **15** Machir took wives from Huppim and Shuppim. The name of his sister was Maacah. Another descendant was named Zelophehad, but he had only daughters.

16 Machir's wife Maacah gave birth to a son, and she named him Peresh. His brother was named Sheresh, and his sons were Ulam and Rekem.
17 Ulam's son: Bedan. These were the sons of Gilead son of Machir, son of Manasseh.
18 His sister Hammolecheth gave birth to Ishhod, Abiezer, and Mahlah.
19 Shemida's sons: Ahian, Shechem, Likhi, and Aniam.

Ephraim's Descendants

20   Ephraim's sons: Shuthelah, and
             his son Bered,
         his son Tahath, his son Eleadah,
         his son Tahath, **21** his son Zabad,
         his son Shuthelah, also Ezer, and Elead.

The men of Gath, born in the land, killed them because they went down to raid their cattle. **22** Their father Ephraim mourned a long time, and his relatives^B came to comfort him. **23** He slept with his wife, and she conceived and gave birth to a son. So he named him Beriah, because there had been misfortune in his home.^C **24** His daughter was Sheerah, who built Lower and Upper Beth-horon and Uzzen-sheerah,

25   his son Rephah,^D his son Resheph,
         his son Telah, his son Tahan,
26   his son Ladan, his son Ammihud,
         his son Elishama, **27** his son Nun,
         and his son Joshua.

28 Their holdings and settlements were Bethel and its surrounding villages; Naaran to the east, Gezer and its villages to the west, and Shechem and its villages as far as Ayyah and its villages, **29** and along the borders of the descendants of Manasseh, Beth-shean, Taanach, Megiddo, and Dor with their surrounding villages. The sons of Joseph son of Israel lived in these towns.

Asher's Descendants

30 Asher's sons: Imnah, Ishvah, Ishvi, and Beriah, with their sister Serah.

---

^A **7:2** Lit *the house of their fathers*, also in vv. 4,7,9,40   ^B **7:22** Or *his brothers*   ^C **7:23** In Hb, the name *Beriah* sounds like "in misfortune."   ^D **7:25** Probably Ephraim's son

---

7:6–12 The first of several listings for Benjamin emphasizes the number of soldiers in this tribe. This was the tribe to which Saul, the first king of the Hebrews, belonged.
7:13 Naphtali is mentioned in only one short verse. After the exile there seems to be no large contingent from Naphtali among those who returned to Judah (9:3).
7:14–19 Manasseh's wife was an Aramean, thus another Gentile was included in the lines of descent.

7:15 Zelophehad and his **daughters** made an important contribution to the culture of Israel. In Nm 27:1–6, Zelophehad's five daughters asked Moses to give them their inheritance in the land, and Moses granted their request. This event set a precedent that women could inherit property, something that most surrounding cultures did not allow.
7:20–29 Ephraim was one of the leading tribes, a consistent rival to Judah. When the kingdom split, Ephraim was foremost among

the ten northern tribes so that "Ephraim" is often synonymous with the entire northern kingdom. The deaths of **Ezer** and **Elead** must have happened while the Israelites were in Egypt, so that these men had ventured north to Gaza. Several of the towns inhabited by the Ephraimites, such as **Beth-shean** and **Megiddo**, were important because they were heavily fortified.
7:30–40 Asher's tribe, located in the north on the coast, was of secondary importance.

³¹ Beriah's sons: Heber, and Malchiel, who fathered Birzaith.
³² Heber fathered Japhlet, Shomer, and Hotham, with their sister Shua.
³³ Japhlet's sons: Pasach, Bimhal, and Ashvath. These were Japhlet's sons.
³⁴ Shemer's sons: Ahi, Rohgah, Hubbah, and Aram.
³⁵ His brother Helem's sons: Zophah, Imna, Shelesh, and Amal.
³⁶ Zophah's sons: Suah, Harnepher, Shual, Beri, Imrah, ³⁷ Bezer, Hod, Shamma, Shilshah, Ithran, and Beera.
³⁸ Jether's sons: Jephunneh, Pispa, and Ara.
³⁹ Ulla's sons: Arah, Hanniel, and Rizia.
⁴⁰ All these were Asher's descendants. They were the heads of their ancestral families, chosen men, valiant warriors, and chiefs among the leaders. The number of men listed in their genealogies for military service was 26,000.

Benjamin's Descendants

8 Benjamin fathered Bela, his firstborn; Ashbel was born second, Aharah third, ² Nohah fourth, and Rapha fifth. ³ Bela's sons: Addar, Gera, Abihud,ᴬ ⁴ Abishua, Naaman, Ahoah, ⁵ Gera, Shephuphan, and Huram. ⁶ These were Ehud's sons, who were the heads of the families living in Geba and who were deported to Manahath: ⁷ Naaman, Ahijah, and Gera. Gera deported them and was the father of Uzza and Ahihud.
⁸ Shaharaim had sons in the territory of Moab after he had divorced his wives Hushim and Baara. ⁹ His sons by his wife Hodesh: Jobab, Zibia, Mesha, Malcam, ¹⁰ Jeuz, Sachia, and Mirmah. These were his sons, family heads. ¹¹ He also had sons by Hushim: Abitub and Elpaal. ¹² Elpaal's sons: Eber, Misham, and Shemed who built Ono and Lod and its surrounding villages, ¹³ Beriah and Shema, who were the family heads of Aijalon's residents and who drove out the residents of Gath, ¹⁴ Ahio,ᴮ Shashak, and Jeremoth.

¹⁵ Zebadiah, Arad, Eder, ¹⁶ Michael, Ishpah, and Joha were Beriah's sons.
¹⁷ Zebadiah, Meshullam, Hizki, Heber, ¹⁸ Ishmerai, Izliah, and Jobab were Elpaal's sons.
¹⁹ Jakim, Zichri, Zabdi, ²⁰ Elienai, Zillethai, Eliel, ²¹ Adaiah, Beraiah, and Shimrath were Shimei's sons.
²² Ishpan, Eber, Eliel, ²³ Abdon, Zichri, Hanan, ²⁴ Hananiah, Elam, Anthothijah, ²⁵ Iphdeiah, and Penuel were Shashak's sons.
²⁶ Shamsherai, Shehariah, Athaliah, ²⁷ Jaareshiah, Elijah, and Zichri were Jeroham's sons.
²⁸ These were family heads, chiefs according to their family records; they lived in Jerusalem.

²⁹ Jeielᶜ fathered Gibeon and lived in Gibeon. His wife's name was Maacah. ³⁰ Abdon was his firstborn son, then Zur, Kish, Baal, Nadab, ³¹ Gedor, Ahio, Zecher, ³² and Mikloth who fathered Shimeah. These also lived opposite their relatives in Jerusalem, with their other relatives. ³³ Ner fathered Kish, Kish fathered Saul, and Saul fathered Jonathan, Malchishua, Abinadab, and Esh-baal.ᴰ ³⁴ Jonathan's son was Merib-baal,ᴱ and Merib-baal fathered Micah. ³⁵ Micah's sons: Pithon, Melech, Tarea, and Ahaz. ³⁶ Ahaz fathered Jehoaddah, Jehoaddah fathered Alemeth, Azmaveth, and Zimri, and Zimri fathered Moza. ³⁷ Moza fathered Binea. His son was Raphah, his son Elasah, and his son Azel. ³⁸ Azel had six sons, and these were their names: Azrikam, Bocheru, Ishmael, Sheariah, Obadiah, and Hanan. All these were Azel's sons. ³⁹ His brother Eshek's sons: Ulam was his firstborn, Jeush second, and Eliphelet third. ⁴⁰ Ulam's sons were valiant warriors and archers.ᶠ They had many sons and grandsons — 150 of them. All these were among Benjamin's sons.

ᴬ8:3 Or Gera father of Ehud; Jdg 3:15 ᴮ8:13–14 LXX reads Gath ¹⁴and their brother ᶜ8:29 LXX; MT omits Jeiel; 1Ch 9:35 ᴰ8:33 = Man of Baal ᴱ8:34 = Baal Contends ᶠ8:40 Lit valiant ones who string the bow

However, a descendant of Asher—the prophetess Anna—praised God in the temple for the birth of Jesus.
8:1–40 A second listing for the tribe of Benjamin provides more detail than the first list (7:6–12). This chapter leads up to the tragic end of Saul's kingship (chap. 10). Saul was from Benjamin, but the throne had been promised to Judah (Gn 49:10). Benjamin, the twelfth son of Jacob, had five sons who established their own large clans.
8:1–7 These were the Benjaminites living in Geba.
8:3–6 Gera was the father of Ehud, the left-handed judge who killed Eglon, king of the Amalekites (Jdg 3:15). Abihud in v. 3 should probably be emended to "the father of Ehud."
8:8–12 These were the Benjaminites living in Moab, Ono, and Lod.
8:8–9 Shaharaim had at least three wives: Hushim and Baara—who presumably were Israelites—and Hodesh, who was a Moabite.
8:13–28 These were the Benjaminites living in Aijalon, Gath, and Jerusalem.
8:29–32 These were the Benjaminites living in Gibeon. Jeiel fathered Gibeon may mean that he "founded" Gibeon.
8:33 At this point the Chronicler casually mentions Saul, but without calling any special attention to him. Esh-baal (Ishbosheth) was Saul's son and a younger brother of Jonathan. In 2Sm 2–3 we find Esh-baal attempting to continue Saul's monarchy against David's claim. Joab eliminated virtually the entire clan.
8:34 Merib-baal (Mephibosheth), Jonathan's crippled son, was the only one who escaped the purge.
8:35–40 This completes Saul's genealogy. Verse 40 notes the military skill of this tribe.

After the Exile

9 All Israel was registered in the genealogies that are written in the Book of the Kings of Israel. But Judah was exiled to Babylon because of their unfaithfulness. [2] The first to live in their towns on their own property again were Israelites, priests, Levites, and temple servants.

[3] These people from the descendants of Judah, Benjamin, Ephraim, and Manasseh settled in Jerusalem:

[4] Uthai son of Ammihud, son of Omri, son of Imri, son of Bani, a descendant[A] of Perez son of Judah;

[5] from the Shilonites:

Asaiah the firstborn and his sons;

[6] and from the descendants of Zerah:

Jeuel and their relatives — 690 in all.

[7] The Benjaminites: Sallu son of Meshullam, son of Hodaviah, son of Hassenuah;

[8] Ibneiah son of Jeroham;

Elah son of Uzzi, son of Michri;

Meshullam son of Shephatiah, son of Reuel, son of Ibnijah;

[9] and their relatives according to their family records — 956 in all. All these men were heads of their ancestral families.[B]

[10] The priests: Jedaiah; Jehoiarib; Jachin;

[11] Azariah son of Hilkiah, son of Meshullam, son of Zadok, son of Meraioth, son of Ahitub, the chief official of God's temple;

[12] Adaiah son of Jeroham, son of Pashhur, son of Malchijah;

Maasai son of Adiel, son of Jahzerah, son of Meshullam, son of Meshillemith, son of Immer;

[13] and their relatives, the heads of their ancestral families — 1,760 in all. They were capable men employed in the ministry of God's temple.

[14] The Levites: Shemaiah son of Hasshub, son of Azrikam, son of Hashabiah of the Merarites;

[15] Bakbakkar, Heresh, Galal, and Mattaniah, son of Mica, son of Zichri, son of Asaph;

[16] Obadiah son of Shemaiah, son of Galal, son of Jeduthun;

and Berechiah son of Asa, son of Elkanah who lived in the settlements of the Netophathites.

[17] The gatekeepers: Shallum, Akkub, Talmon, Ahiman, and their relatives. Shallum was their chief; [18] he was previously stationed at the King's Gate on the east side. These were the gatekeepers from the camp of the Levites.

[19] Shallum son of Kore, son of Ebiasaph, son of Korah and his relatives from his ancestral family, the Korahites, were assigned to guard the thresholds of the tent.[C] Their ancestors had been assigned to the LORD's camp as guardians of the entrance. [20] In earlier times Phinehas son of Eleazar had been their leader, and the LORD was with him. [21] Zechariah son of Meshelemiah was the gatekeeper at the entrance to the tent of meeting.

[22] The total number of those chosen to be gatekeepers at the thresholds was 212. They were registered by genealogy in their settlements. David and the seer Samuel had appointed them to their trusted positions. [23] So they and their sons were assigned as guards to the gates of the LORD's temple, which had been the tent-temple. [24] The gatekeepers were on the four sides: east, west, north, and south. [25] Their relatives came from their settlements at fixed times to be with them seven days, [26] but the four chief gatekeepers, who were Levites, were entrusted with the rooms and the treasuries of God's temple. [27] They spent the night in the vicinity of God's temple, because they had guard duty and were in charge of opening it every morning.

[28] Some of them were in charge of the utensils used in worship. They would count them when they brought them in and when they took them out. [29] Others were put in charge of the furnishings and all the utensils of the sanctuary, as well as the fine flour, wine, oil, incense, and spices. [30] Some of the priests' sons

9:1–34 At this point the Chronicler spotlights the postexilic community (see Neh 11:3–19).
9:1 Accurate **genealogies** were essential because so much was dependent on a person's tribal affiliation (Ezr 2:62).
9:2 The decree to return, issued by Cyrus of Persia, directed that they should rebuild the temple (2Ch 36:23). It was natural that most of these people would be directly associated with the temple: **priests, Levites, and temple servants.**
9:3–9 This portion of the list contains the laity among the returning exiles.

9:3 Among those returning to Judah were also some people of the northern tribes, including **Ephraim** and **Manasseh**.
9:7 A large contingent of those returning to Judah were members of the tribe of Benjamin. This tribe had remained loyal to the southern kingdom of Judah.
9:10–13 The list of **priests** is significant. This listing indicates the accurate continuation of the genealogies and shows that the priests must have maintained their knowledge so they could take up their duties as soon as they returned to Judah.

9:14–34 This portion of the list contains the Levites who returned from exile.
9:14–16 This is an introductory genealogy.
9:17–34 This portion of the list contains the gatekeepers.
9:17–18 **Shallum** was a veteran, having been in charge of a gate some forty years earlier before the temple's destruction. Now he led the entire crew of **gatekeepers**.
9:28 The temple priests performed many functions, including many different types of sacrifices, all of which required **utensils**. Trustworthy people were needed to look after the utensils and other equipment.

mixed the spices. [31] A Levite called Mattithiah, the firstborn of Shallum the Korahite, was entrusted with baking the bread.[A] [32] Some of the Kohathites' relatives were responsible for preparing the rows of the Bread of the Presence every Sabbath.

[33] The singers, the heads of the Levite families, stayed in the temple chambers and were exempt from other tasks because they were on duty day and night. [34] These were the heads of the Levite families, chiefs according to their family records; they lived in Jerusalem.

Saul's Family

[35] Jeiel fathered Gibeon and lived in Gibeon. His wife's name was Maacah. [36] Abdon was his firstborn son, then Zur, Kish, Baal, Ner, Nadab, [37] Gedor, Ahio, Zechariah, and Mikloth. [38] Mikloth fathered Shimeam. These also lived opposite their relatives in Jerusalem with their other relatives.

[39] Ner fathered Kish, Kish fathered Saul, and Saul fathered Jonathan, Malchishua, Abinadab, and Esh-baal. [40] Jonathan's son was Merib-baal, and Merib-baal fathered Micah. [41] Micah's sons: Pithon, Melech, Tahrea, and Ahaz.[B] [42] Ahaz fathered Jarah; Jarah fathered Alemeth, Azmaveth, and Zimri; Zimri fathered Moza. [43] Moza fathered Binea. His son was Rephaiah, his son Elasah, and his son Azel. [44] Azel had six sons, and these were their names: Azrikam, Bocheru, Ishmael, Sheariah, Obadiah, and Hanan. These were Azel's sons.

The Death of Saul and His Sons

10 The Philistines fought against Israel, and Israel's men fled from them. Many were killed on Mount Gilboa. [2] The Philistines pursued Saul and his sons and killed his sons Jonathan, Abinadab, and Malchishua. [3] When the battle intensified against Saul, the archers spotted him and severely wounded him. [4] Then Saul said to his armor-bearer,

"Draw your sword and run me through with it, or these uncircumcised men will come and torture me." But his armor-bearer would not do it because he was terrified. Then Saul took his sword and fell on it. [5] When his armor-bearer saw that Saul was dead, he also fell on his own sword and died. [6] So Saul and his three sons died — his whole house died together.

[7] When all the men of Israel in the valley saw that the army had fled and that Saul and his sons were dead, they abandoned their cities and fled. So the Philistines came and settled in them.

[8] The next day when the Philistines came to strip the slain, they found Saul and his sons dead on Mount Gilboa. [9] They stripped Saul, cut off his head, took his armor, and sent messengers throughout the land of the Philistines to spread the good news to their idols and the people. [10] Then they put his armor in the temple of their gods and hung his skull in the temple of Dagon.

[11] When all Jabesh-gilead heard of everything the Philistines had done to Saul, [12] all their brave men set out and retrieved the body of Saul and the bodies of his sons and brought them to Jabesh. They buried their bones under the oak[C] in Jabesh and fasted seven days.

[13] Saul died for his unfaithfulness to the Lord because he did not keep the Lord's word. He even consulted a medium for guidance, [14] but he did not inquire of the Lord. So the Lord put him to death and turned the kingdom over to David son of Jesse.

David's Anointing as King

11 All Israel came together to David at Hebron and said, "Here we are, your own flesh and blood.[D] [2] Even previously when Saul was king, you were leading Israel out to battle and bringing us back. The Lord your God also said to you, 'You will shepherd my people Israel, and you will be ruler over my people Israel.'" [3] So all the elders of Israel came to the king at Hebron. David made a covenant with them at Hebron in the Lord's presence, and they anointed David king over Israel, in keeping with the Lord's word through Samuel.

[A]9:31 Lit *with things prepared in pans* [B]9:41 LXX, Syr, Tg, Vg, Arabic; MT omits *and Ahaz*; 1Ch 8:35 [C]10:12 Or *terebinth*, or *large tree* [D]11:1 Lit *your bone and your flesh*

9:30 A priest could not perform official religious duties until he turned thirty years old. The sons of many priests, while learning their profession, would also be involved in mixing the **spices** used in the sacrificial system.
9:31 This **Shallum** was the veteran gatekeeper (vv. 17–18).
9:33 The **singers** were expected to be ready at a moment's notice whenever a ceremony or sacrifice called for musical accompaniment.
9:35–44 The genealogy of Benjamin in these verses is the same as that in 8:29–38. Here

the genealogy sets up the story of Saul in chap. 10.
10:1 Without going into any of the details leading up to this event, the Chronicler takes us right to the death of Saul and his sons. See 1Sm 31:1–13.
10:6 Not every member of Saul's house **died** at that time, but the family unit, in the sense of Saul's dynasty (**his whole house**), came to a halt.
10:11–12 The inhabitants of **Jabesh-gilead** owed their lives to **Saul** (1Sm 11). Now they risked their lives to protect Saul's body from further desecration.

11:1–2 The Chronicler skips over a lengthy series of events and takes us directly to the time of David's coronation. David was not accepted immediately as king of Israel by everyone. He had opposition from Jonathan's surviving brother Esh-baal, and it took warfare and bloodshed before David emerged as the undisputed victor (2Sm 1–2).
11:3 David's initial coronation took place at **Hebron**, a city from which he ruled for seven years.

David's Capture of Jerusalem

4 David and all Israel marched to Jerusalem (that is, Jebus); the Jebusites who inhabited the land were there. **5** The inhabitants of Jebus said to David, "You will never get in here." Yet David did capture the stronghold of Zion, that is, the city of David.

6 David said, "Whoever is the first to kill a Jebusite will become chief commander." Joab son of Zeruiah went up first, so he became the chief.

7 Then David took up residence in the stronghold; therefore, it was called the city of David. **8** He built up the city all the way around, from the supporting terraces to the surrounding parts, and Joab restored the rest of the city. **9** David steadily grew more powerful, and the LORD of Armies was with him.

Exploits of David's Warriors

10 The following were the chiefs of David's warriors who, together with all Israel, strongly supported him in his reign to make him king according to the LORD's word about Israel. **11** This is the list of David's warriors:

Jashobeam son of Hachmoni was chief of the Thirty;^A he wielded his spear against three hundred and killed them at one time.

12 After him, Eleazar son of Dodo the Ahohite was one of the three warriors. **13** He was with David at Pas-dammim when the Philistines had gathered there for battle. There was a portion of a field full of barley, where the troops had fled from the Philistines. **14** But Eleazar and David^B took their stand in the middle of the field and defended it. They killed the Philistines, and the LORD gave them a great victory.

15 Three of the thirty chief men went down to David, to the rock at the cave of Adullam, while the Philistine army was encamped in Rephaim Valley. **16** At that time David was in the stronghold, and a Philistine garrison was at Bethlehem. **17** David was extremely thirsty^C and said, "If only someone would bring me water to drink from the well at the city gate of Bethlehem!" **18** So the Three broke through the Philistine camp and drew water from the well at the gate of Bethlehem. They brought it back to David, but he refused to drink it. Instead, he poured it out to the LORD. **19** David said, "I would

^A**11:11** Alt Hb tradition reads *Three*　^B**11:14** Lit *But they*　^C**11:17** Lit *And David craved*

11:4–9 The last stronghold of the Canaanites in the promised land was the citadel of **Jebus** at the peak of **Jerusalem**. This was considered virtually impregnable. Despite the defiance declared by the **Jebusites**, David motivated his troops to capture this prize, and his half nephew **Joab** succeeded. He used the water shaft to gain entry into the compound (2Sm 5:8). Joab was rewarded

by being designated **chief commander** of David's army, an office that he had held *de facto* all along. David moved the capital from Hebron to Jerusalem.

11:10–47 The list of **David's** major **warriors** and heroes covers both individual exploits and victories of larger armies. It covers several decades, from the time that David was fleeing Saul until the end of David's

forty-year reign. Not everyone on this list was around all that time. For this reason the list of **the Thirty** (v. 11) actually includes more than thirty people.

11:11–14 Other English Bible versions set apart a special group of "Three" in addition to **the Thirty**, but the manuscripts do not support this distinction. Chronicles mentions only two men

---

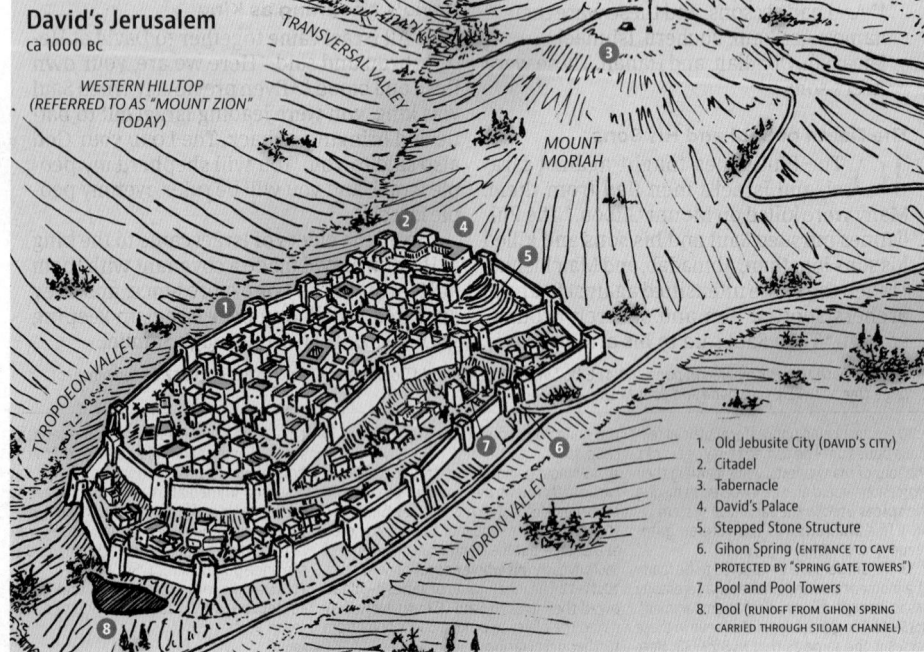

David's Jerusalem
ca 1000 BC

TRANSVERSAL VALLEY

WESTERN HILLTOP
(REFERRED TO AS "MOUNT ZION" TODAY)

MOUNT MORIAH

TYROPOEON VALLEY

KIDRON VALLEY

1. Old Jebusite City (DAVID'S CITY)
2. Citadel
3. Tabernacle
4. David's Palace
5. Stepped Stone Structure
6. Gihon Spring (ENTRANCE TO CAVE PROTECTED BY "SPRING GATE TOWERS")
7. Pool and Pool Towers
8. Pool (RUNOFF FROM GIHON SPRING CARRIED THROUGH SILOAM CHANNEL)

never do such a thing in the presence of my God! How can I drink the blood of these men who risked their lives?" For they brought it at the risk of their lives. So he would not drink it. Such were the exploits of the three warriors.

²⁰ Abishai, Joab's brother, was the leader of the Three.ᴬ He raised his spear against three hundred men and killed them, gaining a reputation among the Three. ²¹ He was more honored than the Three and became their commander even though he did not become one of the Three.

²² Benaiah son of Jehoiada was the son of a brave manᴮ from Kabzeel, a man of many exploits. Benaiah killed two sons of Ariel of Moab,ᶜ and he went down into a pit on a snowy day and killed a lion. ²³ He also killed an Egyptian who was seven and a half feet tall.ᴰ Even though the Egyptian had a spear in his hand like a weaver's beam, Benaiah went down to him with a staff, snatched the spear out of the Egyptian's hand, and then killed him with his own spear. ²⁴ These were the exploits of Benaiah son of Jehoiada, who had a reputation among the three warriors. ²⁵ He was the most honored of the Thirty, but he did not become one of the Three. David put him in charge of his bodyguard.

²⁶ The best soldiers were
  Joab's brother Asahel,
  Elhanan son of Dodo of Bethlehem,
²⁷   Shammoth the Harorite,
  Helez the Pelonite,
²⁸   Ira son of Ikkesh the Tekoite,
  Abiezer the Anathothite,
²⁹   Sibbecai the Hushathite,
  Ilai the Ahohite,
³⁰   Maharai the Netophathite,
  Heled son of Baanah the Netophathite,
³¹   Ithai son of Ribai from Gibeah
    of the Benjaminites,
  Benaiah the Pirathonite,
³²   Hurai from the wadis of Gaash,
  Abiel the Arbathite,
³³   Azmaveth the Baharumite,
  Eliahba the Shaalbonite,
³⁴   the sons ofᴱ Hashem the Gizonite,

  Jonathan son of Shagee the Hararite,
³⁵   Ahiam son of Sachar the Hararite,
  Eliphal son of Ur,
³⁶   Hepher the Mecherathite,
  Ahijah the Pelonite,
³⁷   Hezro the Carmelite,
  Naarai son of Ezbai,
³⁸   Joel the brother of Nathan,
  Mibhar son of Hagri,
³⁹   Zelek the Ammonite,
  Naharai the Beerothite,
    the armor-bearer for Joab
    son of Zeruiah,
⁴⁰   Ira the Ithrite,
  Gareb the Ithrite,
⁴¹   Uriah the Hethite,
  Zabad son of Ahlai,
⁴²   Adina son of Shiza the Reubenite,
    chief of the Reubenites, and thirty
    with him,
⁴³   Hanan son of Maacah,
  Joshaphat the Mithnite,
⁴⁴   Uzzia the Ashterathite,
  Shama and Jeiel the sons of Hotham
    the Aroerite,
⁴⁵   Jediael son of Shimri and his brother
    Joha the Tizite,
⁴⁶   Eliel the Mahavite,
  Jeribai and Joshaviah, the sons
    of Elnaam,
  Ithmah the Moabite,
⁴⁷   Eliel, Obed, and Jaasiel the Mezobaite.

David's First Supporters

12 The following were the men who came to David at Ziklag while he was still banned from the presence of Saul son of Kish. They were among the warriors who helped him in battle. ² They were archers who could use either the right or left hand, both to sling stones and shoot arrows from a bow. They were Saul's relatives from Benjamin:

³ Their chief was Ahiezer son of Shemaah the Gibeathite.
Then there was his brother Joash;
Jeziel and Pelet sons of Azmaveth;
Beracah, Jehu the Anathothite;

ᴬ11:20 Syr reads Thirty   ᴮ11:22 Or was a valiant man   ᶜ11:22 Or He killed two Moabite warriors   ᴰ11:23 Lit who measured five cubits   ᴱ11:34 LXX omits the sons of; 2Sm 23:32

---

in the supposed group of "Three." A parallel list in 2Sm 23 adds a man named Shammah.
11:20–21 It may seem a little confusing that **Abishai**, Joab's brother, was the commander of **the Three** but was not actually one of them. Again, the manuscripts allow for greater flexibility in the translation. He may have been a commander of the "Thirty" (v. 11), but not a part of the most distinguished "Three."
11:22–25 Another commander was **Benaiah**, whom David put in charge of his **bodyguard**. Benaiah's exploits included the killing of a giant. Victories over giants are mentioned several times in Chronicles (see 20:5 and note

there), though the story of David and Goliath occurs only in 1Sm 17.
11:26–47 Best soldiers is literally "those who are mighty in strength."
11:26 Asahel, brother of Joab and Abishai and half nephew of David, was also counted among the "Thirty." But he lost his life early on in the civil war against Esh-baal's supporters (2Sm 2:23).
11:34 Several sets of brothers are included in this list. We do not know how many **sons of Hashem** there were, but pairs of brothers are mentioned in vv. 44–46.
11:42 We see how flexible the designation of the "Thirty" was because **Adina** from Reuben

was a part of this group, together with his own **thirty** supporters.
11:47 Assuming that there were only two sons of Hashem (and not counting Adina's thirty followers), the list adds up to forty-five people.
12:1 This chapter covers a long time span, encompassing the years from David's early days hiding from Saul in the desert to his coronation in Hebron. At the beginning of this chapter, **Saul** was still king. No one would have thought about Esh-baal's attempt to succeed his father because Jonathan was the obvious heir to the throne.
12:2–7 These ambidextrous **archers** and experts with the **sling** were some of Saul's own

⁴ Ishmaiah the Gibeonite, a warrior among the Thirty and a leader over the Thirty; Jeremiah, Jahaziel, Johanan, Jozabad the Gederathite; ⁵ Eluzai, Jerimoth, Bealiah, Shemariah, Shephatiah the Haruphite; ⁶ Elkanah, Isshiah, Azarel, Joezer, and Jashobeam, the Korahites; ⁷ and Joelah and Zebadiah, the sons of Jeroham from Gedor.

⁸ Some Gadites defected to David at his stronghold in the desert. They were valiant warriors, trained for battle, expert with shield and spear. Their faces were like the faces of lions, and they were as swift as gazelles on the mountains.
⁹   Ezer was the chief, Obadiah second, Eliab third,
¹⁰   Mishmannah fourth, Jeremiah fifth,
¹¹   Attai sixth, Eliel seventh,
¹²   Johanan eighth, Elzabad ninth,
¹³   Jeremiah tenth, and Machbannai eleventh.
¹⁴ These Gadites were army commanders; the least of them was a match for a hundred, and the greatest of them for a thousand. ¹⁵ These are the men who crossed the Jordan in the first monthᴬ when it was overflowing all its banks, and put to flight all those in the valleys to the east and to the west.
¹⁶ Other Benjaminites and men from Judah also went to David at the stronghold. ¹⁷ David went out to meet them and said to them, "If you have come in peace to help me, my heart will be united with you, but if you have come to betray me to my enemies even though my hands have done no wrong, may the God of our ancestors look on it and judge."
¹⁸ Then the Spirit envelopedᴮ Amasai, chief of the Thirty, and he said:
We are yours, David,
we are with you, son of Jesse!
Peace, peace to you,
and peace to him who helps you,
for your God helps you.
So David received them and made them leaders of his troops.

¹⁹ Some Manassites defected to David when he went with the Philistines to fight against Saul. However, they did not help the Philistines because the Philistine rulers sent David away after a discussion. They said, "It will be our heads if he defects to his master Saul." ²⁰ When David went to Ziklag, some men from Manasseh defected to him: Adnah, Jozabad, Jediael, Michael, Jozabad, Elihu, and Zillethai, chiefs of thousands in Manasseh. ²¹ They helped David against the raiders, for they were all valiant warriors and commanders in the army. ²² At that time, men came day after day to help David until there was a great army, like an army of God.ᶜ

David's Soldiers in Hebron

²³ The numbers of the armed troops who came to David at Hebron to turn Saul's kingdom over to him, according to the Lᴏʀᴅ's word, were as follows:
²⁴   From the Judahites: 6,800 armed troops bearing shields and spears.
²⁵   From the Simeonites: 7,100 valiant warriors ready for war.
²⁶   From the Levites: 4,600 ²⁷ in addition to Jehoiada, leader of the house of Aaron, with 3,700 men; ²⁸ and Zadok, a young valiant warrior, with 22 commanders from his ancestral family.ᴰ
²⁹   From the Benjaminites, the relatives of Saul: 3,000 (up to that time the majority of the Benjaminites maintained their allegiance to the house of Saul).
³⁰   From the Ephraimites: 20,800 valiant warriors who were famous men in their ancestral families.ᴱ
³¹   From half the tribe of Manasseh: 18,000 designated by name to come and make David king.
³²   From the Issacharites, who understood the times and knew what Israel should do: 200 chiefs with all their relatives under their command.
³³   From Zebulun: 50,000 who could serve in the army, trained for battle

ᴬ12:15 = Nisan (March–April)   ᴮ12:18 Lit clothed; Jdg 6:34; 2Ch 24:20   ᶜ12:22 Or like the ultimate army   ᴰ12:28 Lit the house of his father   ᴱ12:30 Lit the house of their fathers

relatives from **Benjamin** who were already distancing themselves from him. David not only accumulated a sizeable number of supporters, but many of them were excellent warriors. **12:8–15** A group of hardened desert warriors from the tribe of Gad crossed the Jordan River to join David. They had the physical attributes and equipment necessary for being effective soldiers, and they were willing to endure hardship to join the effort. **12:16–18** David was not ready to trust all of these people, particularly those from the tribe of Benjamin. When he warned them of

the dangers of betrayal, **Amasai**, the leader, confirmed his commitment under the inspiration of God. **12:19–22** Men from as far away as Manasseh signed up to support David. **12:23–37** Shifting now to the time of David's coronation at **Hebron**, an army totaling more than 300,000 gathered to follow David's command. **12:26–28** Not only did the **Levites** allow themselves to be conscripted, but even **Zadok**—soon to assume duty as high priest—let himself be counted.

12:29–30 The **Benjaminites** finally pledged their support to David. This was a great change of heart for them. At this point the entire tribe of Benjamin became loyal to David, though the number of their soldiers at **3,000** was still the smallest of the tribes. **12:32** The Chronicler specifically mentions the tribe of Issachar. He declares that they **understood the times**, showing their conviction that David should be made king over all Israel. A total of **200 chiefs** would have been in charge of a large number of soldiers.

with all kinds of weapons of war, with one purpose to help David.^A

34 From Naphtali: 1,000 commanders accompanied by 37,000 men with shield and spear.

35 From the Danites: 28,600 trained for battle.

36 From Asher: 40,000 who could serve in the army, trained for battle.

37 From across the Jordan — from the Reubenites, Gadites, and half the tribe of Manasseh: 120,000 men equipped with all the military weapons of war.

38 All these warriors, lined up in battle formation, came to Hebron wholeheartedly determined to make David king over all Israel. All the rest of Israel was also of one mind to make David king. **39** They spent three days there eating and drinking with David, for their relatives had provided for them. **40** In addition, their neighbors from as far away as Issachar, Zebulun, and Naphtali came and brought food on donkeys, camels, mules, and oxen — abundant provisions of flour, fig cakes, raisins, wine and oil, herds, and flocks. Indeed, there was joy in Israel.

David and the Ark

13 David consulted with all his leaders, the commanders of hundreds and of thousands. **2** Then he said to the whole assembly of Israel, "If it seems good to you, and if this is from the LORD our God, let's spread out and send the message to the rest of our relatives in all the districts of Israel, including the priests and Levites in their cities with pasturelands, that they should gather together with us. **3** Then let's bring back the ark of our God, for we did not inquire of him^B in Saul's days." **4** Since the proposal seemed right to all the people, the whole assembly agreed to do it.

5 So David assembled all Israel, from the Shihor of Egypt to the entrance of Hamath,^C to bring the ark of God from Kiriath-jearim. **6** David and all Israel went to Baalah (that is, Kiriath-jearim that belongs to Judah) to take from there the ark of God, which bears the name of the LORD who is enthroned between the cherubim. **7** At Abinadab's house they set the ark of God on a new cart. Uzzah and Ahio^D were guiding the cart. **8** David and all Israel were dancing with all their might before God with songs and with lyres, harps, tambourines, cymbals, and trumpets. **9** When they came to Chidon's threshing floor, Uzzah reached out to hold the ark because the oxen had stumbled. **10** Then the LORD's anger burned against Uzzah, and he struck him dead because he had reached out to the ark. So he died there in the presence of God.

11 David was angry because of the LORD's outburst against Uzzah, so he named that place Outburst Against Uzzah,^E as it is still named today. **12** David feared God that day and said, "How can I ever bring the ark of God to me?" **13** So David did not bring the ark of God home^F to the city of David; instead, he diverted it to the house of Obed-edom of Gath. **14** The ark of God remained with Obed-edom's family in his house for three months, and the LORD blessed his family and all that he had.

God's Blessing on David

14 King Hiram of Tyre sent envoys to David, along with cedar logs, stonemasons, and carpenters to build a palace for him. **2** Then David knew that the LORD had established him as king over Israel and that his kingdom had been exalted for the sake of his people Israel.

3 David took more wives in Jerusalem, and he became the father of more sons and daughters. **4** These are the names of the children born

^A12:33 LXX; MT omits *David*   ^B13:3 Or *did not seek it*   ^C13:5 Or *to Lebo-hamath*   ^D13:7 Or *And his brothers*   ^E13:11 Or *Perez-uzzah*   ^F13:13 Lit *to himself*

12:37 The enrollment of tribes from the eastern side of the Jordan River—**Reubenites, Gadites, and half the tribe of Manasseh**—underscores the unity of this army.
12:38–40 These warriors were official representatives of their tribes. The times were not yet prosperous, so David could not feed all of them. They brought their own food, **provided** by relatives; others sent caravans of provisions from as far away as the most northern tribes.
13:5–8 At this point the **ark** was at **Kiriath-jearim**, a town north of Jerusalem. It had rested there for several decades after it had been returned by the Philistines. Seventy men of the town of Beth-shemesh had been killed when they looked inside it (1Sm 6:19). Since that time the ark had been largely ignored. Abinadab, the owner of the property on which the ark had settled, had prospered because of its presence (1Sm 7:1). In their eagerness to move the ark to Jerusalem, David's officials made sure that the procession was as grandiose as possible. They got a **new cart**, the best of oxen, and undoubtedly two of the most experienced oxen drivers in the area. With much pomp and circumstance, accompanied by an impressive band, the procession set out in high spirits.
13:10 Good intentions aside, **Uzzah** was violating the sacredness of the **ark** by touching an object that the Lord had declared untouchable. Lest there be any doubt about it, the Chronicler insists that it was the Lord who struck Uzzah dead.
13:13–14 While David pondered what to do, **the ark of God** was parked at the home of **Obed-edom**. Obed-edom's family—just as Abinadab's in Kiriath-jearim had—enjoyed special blessings from the Lord because they were hosting the ark.
14:1 King Hiram of Tyre is a consistent presence throughout the reigns of David and Solomon.
14:3–7 The Chronicler lists further **wives** whom David acquired after his capital was

#20 **99 Essential Christian Truths**

SIN AND DEATH

The ultimate consequence for sin is death—physical death, spiritual death, and eternal death (Rm 6:23). God was clear to Adam and Eve in the garden of Eden that if they ate from the tree of the knowledge of good and evil, they would surely die (Gn 2:17). The type of death that would result from the fall in the garden of Eden wasn't only physical death but spiritual death as well, the separation of a person from God. Spiritual death continues in a permanent state when someone dies apart from the reconciling work of Christ, who defeated death through his own death on the cross and subsequent resurrection.

to him in Jerusalem: Shammua, Shobab, Nathan, Solomon, **5** Ibhar, Elishua, Elpelet, **6** Nogah, Nepheg, Japhia, **7** Elishama, Beeliada, and Eliphelet.

8 When the Philistines heard that David had been anointed king over all Israel, they all went in search of David; when David heard of this, he went out to face them. **9** Now the Philistines had come and raided in Rephaim Valley, **10** so David inquired of God, "Should I attack the Philistines? Will you hand them over to me?"

The LORD replied, "Attack, and I will hand them over to you."

11 So the Israelites went up to Baal-perazim, and David defeated the Philistines there. Then David said, "Like a bursting flood, God has used me to burst out against my enemies." Therefore, they named that place The Lord Bursts Out.^A **12** The Philistines abandoned their idols there, and David ordered that they be burned in the fire.

13 Once again the Philistines raided in the valley. **14** So David again inquired of God, and God answered him, "Do not pursue them directly. Circle around them and attack them opposite the balsam trees. **15** When you hear the sound of marching in the tops of the balsam trees, then go out to battle, for God will have gone out ahead of you to strike down the army of the Philistines." **16** So David did as God commanded him, and they struck down the Philistine army from Gibeon to Gezer. **17** Then David's fame spread throughout the lands, and the LORD caused all the nations to be terrified of him.

The Ark Comes to Jerusalem

15 David built houses for himself in the city of David, and he prepared a place for the ark of God and pitched a tent for it. **2** Then David said, "No one but the Levites may carry the ark of God, because the LORD has chosen them to carry the ark of the LORD and to minister before him forever."

3 David assembled all Israel at Jerusalem to bring the ark of the LORD to the place he had prepared for it. **4** Then he gathered together the descendants of Aaron and the Levites:

5 From the Kohathites, Uriel the leader and 120 of his relatives; **6** from the Merarites, Asaiah the leader and 220 of his relatives; **7** from the Gershomites,^B Joel the leader and 130 of his relatives; **8** from the Elizaphanites, Shemaiah the leader and 200 of his relatives; **9** from the Hebronites, Eliel the leader and 80 of his relatives; **10** from the Uzzielites, Amminadab the leader and 112 of his relatives.

11 David summoned the priests Zadok and Abiathar and the Levites Uriel, Asaiah, Joel, Shemaiah, Eliel, and Amminadab. **12** He said to them, "You are the heads of the Levite families. You and your relatives must consecrate yourselves so that you may bring the ark of the LORD God of Israel to the place I have prepared for it. **13** For the LORD our God burst out in anger against us because you Levites were not with us the first time, for we didn't inquire of him about the proper procedures." **14** So the priests and the Levites consecrated themselves to bring up the ark of the LORD God of Israel. **15** Then the Levites carried the ark of God the way Moses had commanded according to the word of the LORD: on their shoulders with the poles.

16 Then David told the leaders of the Levites to appoint their relatives as singers and to have them raise their voices with joy accompanied by musical instruments — harps, lyres, and cymbals. **17** So the Levites appointed Heman son of Joel; from his relatives, Asaph son of Berechiah; and from their relatives the Merarites, Ethan son of Kushaiah. **18** With them were their relatives second in rank: Zechariah, Jaaziel,^C Shemiramoth, Jehiel, Unni, Eliab, Benaiah, Maaseiah, Mattithiah, Eliphelehu, Mikneiah, and the gatekeepers Obed-edom and Jeiel. **19** The singers Heman, Asaph, and Ethan were to sound the bronze cymbals; **20** Zechariah, Aziel, Shemiramoth, Jehiel, Unni, Eliab, Maaseiah, and Benaiah were to play harps according to *Alamoth*^D **21** and Mattithiah, Eliphelehu, Mikneiah, Obed-edom, Jeiel, and Azaziah were to lead the music with lyres according to the *Sheminith.*

14:11 Or *Baal-perazim* **B15:7** = Gershonites **C15:18** Some Hb mss, LXX; other Hb mss read *Zechariah son and Jaaziel* **D15:20** This may refer to a high pitch, perhaps a tune sung by soprano voices; the Hb word means "young women"; Ps 46 title

---

moved to **Jerusalem**. First Chronicles does not recount his adulterous affair with Bathsheba, and Bathsheba is not invoked by name here, though she had been mentioned earlier (3:5), and her children are included in this list.
14:9 Rephaim Valley, just south of Jerusalem, was a natural path up to the capital city, but it was also an easy place for an army to get locked in.
14:13–16 The **Philistines** must have thought that attacking through the same **valley** was the last thing anyone would expect, but if they were caught again they would be ready. This time the Lord commanded David to use a different strategy—to come from behind. God would give David a signal when it was

time to attack. By following God's orders exactly, he eliminated the threat of the Philistines for a long time to come.
15:1–10 Three months elapsed between the time of David's first attempt to move the **ark** and this renewed effort. The king prepared **a tent** in **Jerusalem** as its official resting place. He followed the instructions given to him by the **Levites** on how the ark should be carried. Numbers 4:15 states that the ark should be carried only by Levites, and only by two long poles inserted through rings in the ark. These poles should rest on the shoulders of the transporting Levites (1Ch 14:15).
15:11–15 The last-minute council of the leaders among the **Levites** and **priests**

included two priests, **Zadok and Abiathar.** The official tabernacle stood at Gibeon, with Zadok working as priest there, even though the ark had not been there for about a hundred years. Because David had no regular access to the tabernacle during Saul's reign, a Kohathite named Abiathar had become David's personal friend and priest (1Sm 22).
15:16–22 David also put the **Levites** in charge of the music, playing various **musical instruments.** The three main musicians— **Heman, Asaph, and Ethan**—took charge. Among the secondary musicians were **Obededom,** the last host of the ark, who would soon become one of the official gatekeepers.

²² Chenaniah, the leader of the Levites in music, was to direct the music because he was skillful. ²³ Berechiah and Elkanah were to be gatekeepers for the ark. ²⁴ The priests, Shebaniah, Joshaphat, Nethanel, Amasai, Zechariah, Benaiah, and Eliezer, were to blow trumpets before the ark of God. Obed-edom and Jehiah were also to be gatekeepers for the ark.

²⁵ David, the elders of Israel, and the commanders of thousands went with rejoicing to bring the ark of the covenant of the LORD from the house of Obed-edom. ²⁶ Because God helped the Levites who were carrying the ark of the covenant of the LORD, with God's help, they sacrificed seven bulls and seven rams.

²⁷ Now David was dressed in a robe of fine linen, as were all the Levites who were carrying the ark, as well as the singers and Chenaniah, the music leader of the singers. David also wore a linen ephod. ²⁸ So all Israel brought up the ark of the covenant of the LORD with shouts, the sound of the ram's horn, trumpets, and cymbals, and the playing of harps and lyres. ²⁹ As the ark of the covenant of the LORD was entering the city of David, Saul's daughter Michal looked down from the window and saw King David leaping^A and dancing, and she despised him in her heart.

16 They brought the ark of God and placed it inside the tent David had pitched for it. Then they offered burnt offerings and fellowship offerings in God's presence. ² When David had finished offering the burnt offerings and the fellowship offerings, he blessed the people in the name of the LORD. ³ Then he distributed to each and every Israelite, both men and women, a loaf of bread, a date cake, and a raisin cake.

⁴ David appointed some of the Levites to be ministers before the ark of the LORD, to celebrate the LORD God of Israel, and to give thanks and praise to him. ⁵ Asaph was the chief and Zechariah was second to him. Jeiel, Shemiramoth, Jehiel, Mattithiah, Eliab, Benaiah, Obed-edom, and Jeiel played the harps and lyres, while Asaph sounded the cymbals ⁶ and the priests Benaiah and Jahaziel blew the trumpets regularly before the ark of the covenant of God.

David's Psalm of Thanksgiving

⁷ On that day David decreed for the first time that thanks be given to the LORD by Asaph and his relatives:

⁸   Give thanks to the LORD; call on
         his name;
     proclaim his deeds among the peoples.
⁹   Sing to him; sing praise to him;
     tell about all his wondrous works!
¹⁰   Boast in his holy name;
     let the hearts of those who seek the
         LORD rejoice.
¹¹   Seek the LORD and his strength;
     seek his face always.
¹²   Remember the wondrous works
         he has done,
     his wonders, and the judgments
         he has pronounced,^B
¹³   you offspring of Israel his servant,
     Jacob's descendants
         — his chosen ones.

¹⁴   He is the LORD our God;
     his judgments govern the whole earth.
¹⁵   Remember his covenant forever —
     the promise he ordained for a thousand
         generations,
¹⁶   the covenant he made with Abraham,
     swore^C to Isaac,
¹⁷   and confirmed to Jacob as a decree,
     and to Israel as a permanent covenant:
¹⁸   "I will give the land of Canaan to you
     as your inherited portion."

¹⁹   When they^D were few in number,
     very few indeed, and resident aliens
         in Canaan
²⁰   wandering from nation to nation
     and from one kingdom to another,
²¹   he allowed no one to oppress them;
     he rebuked kings on their behalf:
²²   "Do not touch my anointed ones
     or harm my prophets."

²³   Let the whole earth sing to the LORD.
     Proclaim his salvation from day to day.

---

^A15:29 Or *whirling*   ^B16:12 Lit *judgments of his mouth*   ^C16:16 Lit *and his oath*   ^D16:19 One Hb ms, LXX, Vg; other Hb mss read *you*

15:23–24 The list flows on, from those who were a part of the procession to the organization that would be implemented after the **ark** arrived in Jerusalem. **Berechiah** ... **Elkanah** ... **Obed-edom**, and **Jehiah** would become gatekeepers, and permanent trumpet players would also be designated. **15:27–29** When **Michal**, David's first wife, saw the king dancing before the ark in public (v. 25), she **despised him in her heart**. This moment finalized their estrangement. Of all David's wives, Michal never bore him any children. **16:1** This **tent** was a special place for the ark where priests could offer sacrifices. The company offered **burnt offerings**, signifying total commitment to the Lord, and **fellowship**

offerings, indicating the covenant between God and his people. **16:4–6** The site of the **ark** was not the main place for worship, which continued to be the tabernacle in Gibeon. As a symbol of the presence of God in their midst, the ark needed to be surrounded by people who praised the Lord. David appointed permanent musicians for this task. This group included **Asaph** on the cymbals, a string ensemble featuring **Obed-edom**, and the trumpeting priests **Benaiah** and **Jahaziel**. **16:7** David instructed **Asaph** to lead in thanksgiving songs, and he composed a psalm for the occasion. It had three parts that were later incorporated into the book of Psalms. Verses 8–22 constitute Ps 105:1–15;

vv. 23–33 are Ps 96:1–13; and vv. 34–36 are Ps 106:1,47–48. The entire psalm as represented in 1 Chronicles comprises four segments exhorting the people to praise God, interspersed with three segments describing God's faithfulness, glory, and creatorship. **16:8–13** The first exhortation to **praise** is a call to remember what God had done and to **proclaim his deeds**. **16:14–22** The first intermediate segment of David's psalm is a reminder of God's **covenant** with **Abraham** and how God had kept the covenant by bringing his people into the promised land. **16:23–24** These verses repeat Israel's obligation to praise God. They add the dimension that this praise should be done **among the**

24 Declare his glory among the nations,
   his wondrous works among all peoples.

25 For the LORD is great and highly praised;
   he is feared above all gods.

26 For all the gods of the peoples are
      worthless idols,
   but the LORD made the heavens.

27 Splendor and majesty are before him;
   strength and joy are in his place.

28 Ascribe to the LORD, families
      of the peoples,
   ascribe to the LORD glory and strength.

29 Ascribe to the LORD the glory
      of his name;
   bring an offering and come before him.
   Worship the LORD
      in the splendor of his holiness;

30 let the whole earth tremble before him.

   The world is firmly established;
   it cannot be shaken.

31 Let the heavens be glad and the earth
      rejoice,
   and let them say among the nations,
      "The LORD reigns!"

32 Let the sea and all that fills it resound;
   let the fields and everything in them
      exult.

33 Then the trees of the forest will shout
      for joy before the LORD,
   for he is coming to judge the earth.

34 Give thanks to the LORD, for he is good;
   his faithful love endures forever.

35 And say, "Save us, God of our salvation;
   gather us and rescue us from
      the nations
   so that we may give thanks to
      your holy name
   and rejoice in your praise.

36 Blessed be the LORD God of Israel
   from everlasting to everlasting."
Then all the people said, "Amen" and "Praise
the LORD."

37 So David left Asaph and his relatives there
before the ark of the LORD's covenant to minister regularly before the ark according to the
daily requirements. 38 He assigned Obed-edom

and his^A sixty-eight relatives. Obed-edom son
of Jeduthun and Hosah were to be gatekeepers. 39 David left the priest Zadok and his fellow priests before the tabernacle of the LORD
at the high place in Gibeon 40 to offer burnt offerings regularly, morning and evening, to the
LORD on the altar of burnt offerings and to do
everything that was written in the law of the
LORD, which he had commanded Israel to keep.
41 With them were Heman, Jeduthun, and the
rest who were chosen and designated by name
to give thanks to the LORD — for his faithful
love endures forever. 42 Heman and Jeduthun
had with them trumpets and cymbals to play
and musical instruments of God. Jeduthun's
sons were at the city gate.

43 Then all the people went home, and David
returned home to bless his household.

The LORD's Covenant with David

17 When David had settled into his palace,
he said to the prophet Nathan, "Look! I
am living in a cedar house while the ark of the
LORD's covenant is under tent curtains."
2 So Nathan told David, "Do all that is on your
mind, for God is with you."

3 But that night the word of God came to Nathan: 4 "Go to David my servant and say, 'This
is what the LORD says: You are not the one to
build me a house to dwell in. 5 From the time I
brought Israel out of Egypt until today I have
not dwelt in a house; instead, I have moved
from one tent site to another, and from one
tabernacle location to another.^B 6 In all my journeys throughout Israel, have I ever spoken a
word to even one of the judges of Israel, whom
I commanded to shepherd my people, asking:
Why haven't you built me a house of cedar?'

7 "So now this is what you are to say to my
servant David: 'This is what the LORD of Armies
says: I took you from the pasture, from tending
the flock, to be ruler over my people Israel. 8 I
have been with you wherever you have gone,
and I have destroyed all your enemies before
you. I will make a name for you like that of the
greatest on the earth. 9 I will designate a place
for my people Israel and plant them, so that
they may live there and not be disturbed again.
Evildoers will not continue to oppress them as

---

^A16:38 LXX, Syr, Vg; Hb reads *their*   ^B17:5 Lit *I was from tent to tent and from tabernacle*

---

nations. The people who had not directly
experienced God's guidance would learn
about it from the Israelites.
16:25–27 This second segment describes the
difference between God and **idols**. Because
idols are man-made they do not have the
power and **majesty** of **the LORD**.
16:28–30a This exhortation to praise connects praising God with worshiping him with
offerings. Just as praise of God is connected
with his works, praise from the worshiper is
connected with active service.
16:30b–33 In this segment of the psalm, the
power of God is recognized by the firmness

of the **world**, the witness of the **heavens**,
the proclamation of the **sea**, and the shouts
of joy of the **trees**. The created order gives
testimony to the Creator's glory.
16:34–36 The fourth and final exhortation to
praise combines another reminder of God's
glory with the need to rely on the Lord for
salvation.
16:37–42 The Chronicler once more focuses
on the service at the **ark** in Jerusalem and
the service at the tabernacle in **Gibeon**.
The ambiguity caused by having two sacred sites shows that a temple that unified
worship was badly needed. **Zadok**, with

the assistance of the musicians **Heman** and
Jeduthun (Ethan), continued the sacrifices
that were commanded by the law at the tabernacle. Just as David had instituted a more
consistent regimen surrounding the ark, he
ordered similar provisions for the tabernacle.
17:1–2 Both David and **the prophet Nathan**
were committed to the idea of building a
temple.
17:3–15 David would not be allowed to build
this **house**, or temple, for God **to dwell in**,
but God would give the king a far greater
promise. The Lord declared that he would
build David's **house**—a dynasty, a succession

they have done [10] ever since the day I ordered judges to be over my people Israel. I will also subdue all your enemies.

"'Furthermore, I declare to you that the LORD himself will build a house for you. [11] When your time comes to be with your ancestors, I will raise up after you your descendant, who is one of your own sons, and I will establish his kingdom. [12] He is the one who will build a house for me, and I will establish his throne forever. [13] I will be his father, and he will be my son. I will not remove my faithful love from him as I removed it from the one who was before you. [14] I will appoint him over my house and my kingdom forever, and his throne will be established forever.'"

[15] Nathan reported all these words and this entire vision to David.

David's Prayer of Thanksgiving

[16] Then King David went in, sat in the LORD's presence, and said,

Who am I, LORD God, and what is my house that you have brought me this far? [17] This was a little thing to you,[A] God, for you have spoken about your servant's house in the distant future. You regard me as a man of distinction,[B] LORD God. [18] What more can David say to you for honoring your servant? You know your servant. [19] LORD, you have done this whole great thing, making known all these great promises for the sake of your servant and according to your will. [20] LORD, there is no one like you, and there is no God besides you, as all we have heard confirms. [21] And who is like your people Israel? God, you came to one nation on earth to redeem a people for yourself, to make a name for yourself through great and awesome works by driving out nations before your people you redeemed from Egypt. [22] You made your people Israel your own people forever, and you, LORD, have become their God.

[23] Now, LORD, let the word that you have spoken concerning your servant and his house be confirmed forever, and do as you have promised. [24] Let your name be confirmed and magnified forever in the saying, "The LORD of Armies, the God of Israel, is God over Israel." May the house of your servant David be established before you. [25] Since you, my God, have revealed to[C] your servant that you will build him a house, your servant has found courage to pray in your presence. [26] LORD, you indeed are God, and you have promised this good thing to your servant. [27] So now, you have been pleased to bless your servant's house that it may continue before you forever. For you, LORD, have blessed it, and it is blessed forever.

David's Military Campaigns

18 After this, David defeated the Philistines, subdued them, and took Gath and its surrounding villages from Philistine control. [2] He also defeated the Moabites, and they became David's subjects and brought tribute.

[3] David also defeated King Hadadezer of Zobah at Hamath when he went to establish his control at the Euphrates River. [4] David captured one thousand chariots, seven thousand horsemen, and twenty thousand foot soldiers from him, hamstrung all the horses, and kept a hundred chariots.[D]

[5] When the Arameans of Damascus came to assist King Hadadezer of Zobah, David struck down twenty-two thousand Aramean men. [6] Then he placed garrisons[E] in Aram of Damascus, and the Arameans became David's subjects and brought tribute. The LORD made David victorious wherever he went.

[7] David took the gold shields carried by Hadadezer's officers and brought them to Jerusalem. [8] From Tibhath and Cun, Hadadezer's cities, David also took huge quantities of bronze, from which Solomon made the bronze basin,[F] the pillars, and the bronze articles.

[9] When King Tou of Hamath heard that David had defeated the entire army of King Hadadezer of Zobah, [10] he sent his son Hadoram to

---

^17:17 Lit *thing in your eyes* ^B17:17 Hb obscure ^C17:25 Lit *have uncovered the ear of* ^D18:4 Or *chariot horses* ^E18:6 Some Hb mss, LXX, Vg; other Hb mss omit *garrisons*; 2Sm 8:6 ^F18:8 Lit *sea*

of kings that would last many generations (vv. 10–12).

17:23–26 There were three important points in this last half of David's prayer. First, he showed submission to what the Lord had planned for him. Second, he showed God that what he desired was whatever God wanted for him. Third, David tells us that it is never wrong to express our thoughts and desires to the Lord.

18:1 This chapter summarizes a number of military victories by David and the spoils that he collected. He defeated the **Philistines**, this time not by repelling their attack, but by taking control of one of their five principal cities and its **surrounding villages**.

18:2 The same thing happened with the **Moabites**. Conquered by David, they contributed to his growing treasury.

18:3 The Arameans were a confederation of various kingdoms east of the Jordan River, ranging all the way from Damascus to the banks of the Euphrates River. **Hadadezer of Zobah** ruled over one of the most easterly regions. By taking over his territory at the Euphrates and by controlling Philistine territory to the south, David fulfilled the promise God had given to Abraham—that his descendants would eventually occupy the land all the way from the Euphrates River to the Brook of Egypt (Gn 15:8). **18:4** The cutting of the tendons (**hamstrung**) of thousands of **horses** was a

standard method of crippling an enemy force. Without their horses, the soldiers were rendered immobile.

18:5–8 The **Arameans of Damascus** attempted to come to the rescue of **Hadadezer**, but this move led them into subjection by David. The **bronze** objects mentioned here would be put to use by Solomon later on.

18:9–10 King Tou of Hamath decided that diplomacy was a better option than warfare. Because he had been at odds with **Hadadezer**, he considered the enemy of his enemy to be his ally, but he still needed to pay a tribute of numerous objects of precious metal.

King David to greet him and to congratulate him because David had fought against Hadadezer and defeated him, for Tou and Hadadezer had fought many wars. Hadoram brought all kinds of gold, silver, and bronze items. ¹¹ King David also dedicated these to the LORD, along with the silver and gold he had carried off from all the nations — from Edom, Moab, the Ammonites, the Philistines, and the Amalekites.

¹² Abishai son of Zeruiah struck down eighteen thousand Edomites in the Salt Valley. ¹³ He put garrisons in Edom, and all the Edomites were subject to David. The LORD made David victorious wherever he went.

¹⁴ So David reigned over all Israel, administering justice and righteousness for all his people.

¹⁵ Joab son of Zeruiah was over the army;
Jehoshaphat son of Ahilud was
    court historian;
¹⁶ Zadok son of Ahitub and Ahimelech^
    son of Abiathar were priests;
Shavsha was court secretary;
¹⁷ Benaiah son of Jehoiada was over the
    Cherethites and the Pelethites;
and David's sons were the chief officials
    at the king's side.

War with the Ammonites

19 Some time later, King Nahash of the Ammonites died, and his son became king in his place. ² Then David said, "I'll show kindness to Hanun son of Nahash, because his father showed kindness to me."

So David sent messengers to console him concerning his father. However, when David's emissaries arrived in the land of the Ammonites to console him, ³ the Ammonite leaders said to Hanun, "Just because David has sent men with condolences for you, do you really believe he's showing respect for your father? Instead, haven't his emissaries come in order to scout out, overthrow, and spy on the land?" ⁴ So Hanun took David's emissaries, shaved them, cut their clothes in half at the hips, and sent them away.

⁵ It was reported to David about his men, so he sent messengers to meet them, since the men were deeply humiliated. The king said, "Stay in Jericho until your beards grow back; then return."

⁶ When the Ammonites realized they had made themselves repulsive to David, Hanun and the Ammonites sent thirty-eight tons⁸ of silver to hire chariots and horsemen from Aram-naharaim, Aram-maacah, and Zobah. ⁷ They hired thirty-two thousand chariots and the king of Maacah with his army, who came and camped near Medeba. The Ammonites also came together from their cities for the battle.

⁸ David heard about this and sent Joab and all the elite troops. ⁹ The Ammonites marched out and lined up in battle formation at the entrance of the city while the kings who had come were in the field by themselves. ¹⁰ When Joab saw that there was a battle line in front of him and another behind him, he chose some of Israel's finest young men^c and lined up in formation to engage the Arameans. ¹¹ He placed the rest of the forces under the command of his brother Abishai. They lined up in formation to engage the Ammonites.

¹² "If the Arameans are too strong for me," Joab said, "then you'll be my help. However, if the Ammonites are too strong for you, I'll help you. ¹³ Be strong! Let's prove ourselves strong for our people and for the cities of our God. May the LORD's will be done."^D

¹⁴ Joab and the people with him approached the Arameans for battle, and they fled before him. ¹⁵ When the Ammonites saw that the Arameans had fled, they likewise fled before Joab's brother Abishai and entered the city. Then Joab went to Jerusalem.

^18:16 Some Hb mss, LXX, Syr, Vg; other Hb mss read *Abimelech*; 2Sm 8:17 ^B19:6 Lit *1,000 talents* ^C19:10 Lit *Israel's choice ones* ^D19:13 Lit *the LORD do what is good in his eyes*

18:11 David did not add all of these things to his personal wealth, but he placed them into a treasury that was **dedicated . . . to the LORD**. Later on, much of it would go into the building of the temple.
18:12–13 **Abishai** was Joab's brother and a general in his army. Abishai represented David in a campaign against the **Edomites**, and **eighteen thousand** enemy warriors were killed. Even though Abishai was the leader of the battle, David was the king, so this section reiterates David's unbroken record of victories.
18:15–16 A quick overview of the most important people surrounding David starts with **Joab**, still his commander in chief. **Jehoshaphat**, the **court historian**, and **Shavsha**, the **court secretary**, kept records of what happened in the palace. There were still two high priests, **Zadok** and **Ahimelech** (who replaced his father Abiathar), because there were still two main places of worship.

18:17 The **Cherethites** and the **Pelethites**, who reported to **Benaiah**, apparently were Philistine groups who were loyal to David and who may have been his bodyguards (see 11:24–25).
19:1–2 **King Nahash of the Ammonites** was a consistent presence in the time of Saul and David. It was he who had first given Saul the occasion to rise to the responsibilities of being king of Israel. He had besieged the town of Jabesh-gilead and agreed to a truce with the citizens of this village on the condition that he could gouge out each person's eye (1Sm 11:2). This threat had enabled Saul to rally the Israelites in a united war against the Ammonites, in which he roundly defeated them. The Bible does not disclose the details of the occasion when Nahash had treated David kindly, but when Nahash died, David sent a delegation to the new king **Hanun** to express his condolences.

19:8–9 David delegated the responsibility for taking on the Ammonites to **Joab** as his commander in chief. By the time Joab arrived on the field and took stock of the situation, he found himself wedged between the **Ammonites**, who had their backs protected by the walls of the town of Medeba, and their Aramean allies on the other side. Israel's defeat seemed inevitable.
19:10–13 Joab decided to have his army fight on two fronts at the same time. He took command of one front against the **Arameans** and let his brother **Abishai** lead the other front against the **Ammonites**. They pledged that if either one ran into trouble, the other would come to his aid.
19:14–15 Apparently the **Arameans** had not expected this aggressive response from Joab and his brother. When they saw the Israelite army advancing, they turned and fled. This was enough for the **Ammonites** to lose heart as well. When they saw the Arameans

[16] When the Arameans realized that they had been defeated by Israel, they sent messengers to summon the Arameans who were beyond the Euphrates River. They were led by Shophach, the commander of Hadadezer's army. [17] When this was reported to David, he gathered all Israel and crossed the Jordan. He came up to the Arameans and lined up against them. When David lined up to engage them, they fought against him. [18] But the Arameans fled before Israel, and David killed seven thousand of their charioteers and forty thousand foot soldiers. He also killed Shophach, commander of the army. [19] When Hadadezer's subjects saw that they had been defeated by Israel, they made peace with David and became his subjects. After this, the Arameans were never willing to help the Ammonites again.

Capture of the City of Rabbah

20 In the spring[A] when kings march out to war, Joab led the army and destroyed the Ammonites' land. He came to Rabbah and besieged it, but David remained in Jerusalem. Joab attacked Rabbah and demolished it. [2] Then David took the crown from the head of their king,[B,C] and it was placed on David's head. He found that the crown weighed seventy-five pounds[D] of gold, and there was a precious stone in it. In addition, David took away a large quantity of plunder from the city. [3] He brought out the people who were in it and put them to work with saws,[E] iron picks, and axes.[F] David

did the same to all the Ammonite cities. Then he and all his troops returned to Jerusalem.

The Philistine Giants

[4] After this, a war broke out with the Philistines at Gezer. At that time Sibbecai the Hushathite killed Sippai, a descendant of the Rephaim,[G] and the Philistines were subdued. [5] Once again there was a battle with the Philistines, and Elhanan son of Jair killed Lahmi the brother of Goliath of Gath. The shaft of his spear was like a weaver's beam. [6] There was still another battle at Gath where there was a man of extraordinary stature with six fingers on each hand and six toes on each foot — twenty-four in all. He, too, was descended from the giant.[H] [7] When he taunted Israel, Jonathan son of David's brother Shimei killed him. [8] These were the descendants of the giant in Gath killed by David and his soldiers.

David's Military Census

21 Satan[I] rose up against Israel and incited David to count the people of Israel. [2] So David said to Joab and the commanders of the troops, "Go and count Israel from Beer-sheba to Dan and bring a report to me so I can know their number." [3] Joab replied, "May the LORD multiply the number of his people a hundred times over! My lord the king, aren't they all my lord's servants? Why does my lord want to do this? Why should he bring guilt on Israel?"

[A]20:1 Lit *At the time of the return of the year*   [B]20:2 LXX, Vg read *of Milcom*   [C]20:2 = Molech; 1Kg 11:5,7   [D]20:2 Lit *a talent*
[E]20:3 Text emended; MT reads *and sawed them with the saw*; 2Sm 12:31   [F]20:3 Text emended; MT reads *saws*; 2Sm 12:31
[G]20:4 Or *the Rephaites*   [H]20:6 Or *Raphah*, also in v. 8   [I]21:1 Or *An adversary*; Jb 1:6; Zch 3:1–2

---

fleeing, they barricaded themselves behind the walls of Medeba.
19:16 Now it was the Arameans' turn to make an error in judgment. Even though they had already been defeated once by David, they decided to take advantage of the situation and turn back on David's forces. While Joab returned victoriously to Jerusalem (v. 15), the **Arameans** made another alliance, this time with their kinsman all the way on the eastern side of the **Euphrates River**, in order to take revenge against David.
19:17–18 This time David himself took charge of the Israelite army. With an even greater force this time, he defeated the combined Aramean army.
19:19 Being defeated by David was nothing new to Hadadezer (see 18:3). Twice now, this king's attempts to establish superiority among the **Arameans** had been thwarted by David. Regardless of their king's ambitions, his subjects had seen enough. They submitted to David—and blamed it all on the **Ammonites**.
20:1 The ideal time to **march out to war** in ancient times was **the spring** because the ground is not too wet or muddy, and the weather is not too cold or hot for soldiers to exert themselves. In addition, for food the army could plunder crops growing in the invaded territory. **Joab**, once again in command, crossed into the territory of Ammon to finish the job started the previous year when the Ammonites had retreated.

He traveled to the town of **Rabbah** and laid siege to this capital of the Ammonites. David did not accompany his troops, but he remained in Jerusalem. This is the time when David had his affair with Bathsheba, and this is the military campaign in which he sent her husband, Uriah, to his death (2Sm 11:2–12:25). The Chronicler omits this entire episode.
20:2–3 After Joab had destroyed the city, David was crowned with the Ammonites' **crown**. His men carried away anything of value.
20:4 Further conflict with the **Philistines** was inevitable. The occasions mentioned here may have happened over a longer period of time; they are brought together here by the Chronicler to report on the various Philistine giants. The first giant mentioned was **Sippai**, referred to as a **descendant of the Rephaim**. The Hebrew word *rephaim* refers to a race of giants, of whom we know nothing more than that they were larger than normal men. Apparently the *rephaim* had left a genetic heritage, even though the last pure member of their race was Og, king of Bashan, whose bed was 13 feet long and 6 feet wide (Dt 3:11). Sippai's killer was **Sibbecai the Hushathite**.
20:5 Goliath had a brother named **Lahmi**, who may have been as tall as Goliath (1Sm 17:4). He was killed by **Elhanan son of Jair**, who is not mentioned anywhere else in the Bible.
20:6–7 Another giant, whose name is not given, copied Goliath by taunting Israel. In

addition to his extraordinary stature, he had an extra digit on each **hand** and **foot**. This time the killing of a giant remained in David's family when his nephew **Jonathan** took care of the matter.
20:8 The elimination of giants is an important aspect of how David finally took possession of the entire promised land.
21:1 Satan is not mentioned often in the OT. When he does appear, he is the adversary of someone beloved by God (Jb 1:6; 2:7; Zch 3:1–2). The parallel passage in 2 Samuel makes it clear that Satan would not have been able to cause trouble for **David** if God had not let him (2Sm 24:1). The census itself was not an infraction of God's law (Nm 1:2; 26:2). David succumbed to the sin of pride. He also violated rules that God had given for carrying out a legitimate census. The law stipulated that each man who was counted had to donate a half-shekel to the temple treasury (Ex 30:11–16). God had decreed that a census taken without these provisions would be punished by a plague.
21:2 David placed **Joab** in charge of this project, reinforcing the idea that the purpose of the census was to evaluate military capability. The expression **from Beer-sheba to Dan** signifies the entire country from south to north.
21:3 Joab knew that what David was proposing would bring harm to everyone, so he objected strongly.

⁴ Yet the king's order prevailed over Joab. So Joab left and traveled throughout Israel and then returned to Jerusalem. ⁵ Joab gave the total troop registration to David. In all Israel there were one million one hundred thousand armed men^A and in Judah itself four hundred seventy thousand armed men. ⁶ But he did not include Levi and Benjamin in the count because the king's command was detestable to him. ⁷ This command was also evil in God's sight, so he afflicted Israel.

⁸ David said to God, "I have sinned greatly because I have done this thing. Now, please take away your servant's guilt, for I've been very foolish."

David's Punishment

⁹ Then the LORD instructed Gad, David's seer, ¹⁰ "Go and say to David, 'This is what the LORD says: I am offering you three choices. Choose one of them for yourself, and I will do it to you.'"

¹¹ So Gad went to David and said to him, "This is what the LORD says: 'Take your choice: ¹² three years of famine, or three months of devastation by your foes with the sword of your enemy overtaking you, or three days of the sword of the LORD — a plague on the land, the angel of the LORD bringing destruction to the whole territory of Israel.' Now decide what answer I should take back to the one who sent me."

¹³ David answered Gad, "I'm in anguish. Please, let me fall into the LORD's hands because his mercies are very great, but don't let me fall into human hands."

¹⁴ So the LORD sent a plague on Israel, and seventy thousand Israelite men died. ¹⁵ Then God sent an angel to Jerusalem to destroy it, but when the angel was about to destroy the city,^B the LORD looked, relented concerning the destruction, and said to the angel who was destroying the people, "Enough, withdraw your hand now!" The angel of the LORD was then standing at the threshing floor of Ornan^C the Jebusite.

¹⁶ When David looked up and saw the angel of the LORD standing between earth and heaven, with his drawn sword in his hand stretched out over Jerusalem, David and the elders, covered in sackcloth, fell facedown. ¹⁷ David said to God, "Wasn't I the one who gave the order to count the people? I am the one who has sinned and acted very wickedly. But these sheep, what have they done? LORD my God, please let your hand be against me and against my father's family, but don't let the plague be against your people."

David's Altar

¹⁸ So the angel of the LORD ordered Gad to tell David to go and set up an altar to the LORD on the threshing floor of Ornan the Jebusite. ¹⁹ David went up at Gad's command spoken in the name of the LORD.

²⁰ Ornan was threshing wheat when he turned and saw the angel. His four sons, who were with him, hid. ²¹ David came to Ornan, and when Ornan looked and saw David, he left the threshing floor and bowed to David with his face to the ground.

²² Then David said to Ornan, "Give me this threshing-floor plot so that I may build an altar to the LORD on it. Give it to me for the full price, so the plague on the people may be stopped."

²³ Ornan said to David, "Take it! My lord the king may do whatever he wants.^D See, I give the oxen for the burnt offerings, the threshing

---

^A 21:5 Lit men drawing the sword   ^B 21:15 Lit but as he was destroying   ^C 21:15–28 = Araunah in 2Sm 24:16–24   ^D 21:23 Lit do what is good in his eyes

---

21:4–5 The number that **Joab** came up with was astounding—over one million **armed men** from **all Israel** (probably including both the northern and southern tribes) and (or including) close to half a million from Judah.

#21 99 Essential Christian Truths

SIN AS SELFISHNESS

When we sin, we are acting out of a selfish attitude and mindset that assumes our action will lead us to more happiness than if we were to obey God. Because sin is manifested in our tendency to be "curved inward" toward self, it is the opposite of love. Love looks outwardly to place others before oneself, operating from the mindset that others are more important (Php 2:3). While sin selfishly seeks personal gratification and happiness, love works for the joy of others in the hope of making others happy in God.

This is one of the cases in which the numbers in Chronicles are different than those in Samuel, where eight hundred thousand are from Israel and five hundred thousand are from Judah (2Sm 24:9). The difference may be a matter of textual transmission, or the two authors may be counting different units from Israel.

21:6 Joab refused to include the tribes of **Levi** and **Benjamin**. Perhaps he did not want God's judgment to fall on the tribe of priests or the tribe in whose territory the tabernacle stood.

21:7 Exactly as God had foretold in Ex 30:12, he punished this illegitimate census with a plague.

21:9–13 Gad and Nathan were the two prophets associated with David. Both of them had the unpleasant duty of announcing divine punishment on the king they served (2Sm 12:7). Gad presented David with three options for punishment: (1) **three years of famine**, (2) **three months of devastation** by his enemies, or (3) **three days of . . . plague on the land**. David chose the plague, reasoning that it most directly

involved the hand of God and therefore had the most potential for mercy.

21:14 David had wanted to know how many **men** he had at his disposal. By divine retribution he wound up with **seventy-thousand** fewer than he had before the census was taken.

21:15–17 The spread of the **plague** is attributed to an **angel** from God (2Ch 32:21). The angel was about to inflict the plague on Jerusalem. He was fully visible, hovering above the **threshing floor of Ornan**. David and the elders of Israel saw the angel floating in a menacing posture with his **sword . . . stretched out**. David pleaded with God to spare the innocent people and let him suffer God's punishment. Ornan is a variant for "Araunah" (2Sm 24:18).

21:18–24 Ornan and his **four sons** received two shocks: they saw the hovering angel, and the king himself showed up on their property. David asked Ornan to sell him this location at its **full price**—without receiving a king's discount—because he was afraid the Lord might not stop the plague if he did not pay the full amount.

sledges for the wood, and the wheat for the grain offering — I give it all."

²⁴ King David answered Ornan, "No, I insist on paying the full price, for I will not take for the Lord what belongs to you or offer burnt offerings that cost me nothing."

²⁵ So David gave Ornan fifteen pounds of gold^A for the plot. ²⁶ He built an altar to the Lord there and offered burnt offerings and fellowship offerings. He called on the Lord, and he answered him with fire from heaven on the altar of burnt offering.

²⁷ Then the Lord spoke to the angel, and he put his sword back into its sheath. ²⁸ At that time, David offered sacrifices there when he saw that the Lord answered him at the threshing floor of Ornan the Jebusite. ²⁹ The tabernacle of the Lord, which Moses made in the wilderness, and the altar of burnt offering were at the high place in Gibeon, ³⁰ but David could not go before it to inquire of God, because he was terrified of the sword of the Lord's angel. ¹ Then David said, "This is **22** the house of the Lord God, and this is the altar of burnt offering for Israel."

David's Preparations for the Temple

² So David gave orders to gather the resident aliens that were in the land of Israel, and he appointed stonecutters to cut finished stones for building God's house. ³ David supplied a great deal of iron to make the nails for the doors of the gates and for the fittings, together with an immeasurable quantity of bronze, ⁴ and innumerable cedar logs because the Sidonians and Tyrians had brought a large quantity of cedar logs to David. ⁵ David said, "My son Solomon is young and inexperienced, and the house that is to be built for the Lord must be exceedingly great and famous and glorious in all the lands. Therefore, I will make provision for it." So David made lavish preparations for it before his death.

⁶ Then he summoned his son Solomon and charged him to build a house for the Lord God of Israel. ⁷ "My son," David said to Solomon, "It was in my heart to build a house for the name of the Lord my God, ⁸ but the word of the Lord came to me: 'You have shed much blood and waged great wars. You are not to build a house for my name because you have shed so much blood on the ground before me. ⁹ But a son will be born to you; he will be a man of rest. I will give him rest from all his surrounding enemies, for his name will be Solomon,^B and I will give peace and quiet to Israel during his reign. ¹⁰ He is the one who will build a house for my name. He will be my son, and I will be his father. I will establish the throne of his kingdom over Israel forever.'

¹¹ "Now, my son, may the Lord be with you, and may you succeed in building the house of the Lord your God, as he said about you. ¹² Above all, may the Lord give you insight and understanding when he puts you in charge of Israel so that you may keep the law of the Lord your God. ¹³ Then you will succeed if you carefully follow the statutes and ordinances the Lord commanded Moses for Israel. Be strong and courageous. Don't be afraid or discouraged.

¹⁴ "Notice I have taken great pains to provide for the house of the Lord — 3,775 tons of gold, 37,750 tons of silver,^C and bronze and iron that can't be weighed because there is so much of it. I have also provided timber and stone, but you will need to add more to them. ¹⁵ You also have many workers: stonecutters, masons, carpenters, and people skilled in every kind of work ¹⁶ in gold, silver, bronze, and iron — beyond number. Now begin the work, and may the Lord be with you."

¹⁷ Then David ordered all the leaders of Israel to help his son Solomon: ¹⁸ "The Lord your God is with you, isn't he? And hasn't he given you rest on every side? For he has handed the land's inhabitants over to me, and the land has been subdued before the Lord and his people. ¹⁹ Now determine in your mind and heart to seek the Lord your God. Get started building the Lord God's sanctuary so that you may bring the ark of the Lord's covenant and the holy articles of God to the temple that is to be built for the name of the Lord."

The Divisions of the Levites

23 When David was old and full of days, he installed his son Solomon as king over Israel. ² Then he gathered all the leaders

---

^A 21:25 Lit *600 shekels of gold by weight*   ^B 22:9 In Hb, the name *Solomon* sounds like "peace."   ^C 22:14 Lit *100,000 talents of gold and 1,000,000 talents of silver*

21:25 The price for the plot of land mentioned here is **fifteen pounds of gold**, while in 2Sm 24:24 it is said to have been twenty ounces of silver. This difference can be explained if David purchased the properties in simultaneous but distinct transactions. Perhaps the silver was the price for the threshing floor while the gold purchased the surrounding property. Ornan may very naturally have priced these items apart from one another. **21:28–30** At the end of this episode, the basic arrangement of sacred locations changed. The ark was still in Jerusalem, and

the **tabernacle** continued in **Gibeon**, but from here on, David no longer used the tabernacle. He performed his sacrifices on this **threshing floor**. Perhaps he was afraid the angel might come back if he left this site. **22:1** Since the threshing floor of Ornan had become the place where David worshiped the Lord, he declared that on this exact site the temple would be built. This temporary **altar** would mark the location of the permanent altar. **22:5** This is the first time we learn that **Solomon** would succeed David and build the temple.

22:6–10 In a private conversation, David gave instructions to **Solomon** about the building of the temple. David's personal history of warfare and **shed . . . blood** disqualified him from being the temple builder. On the other hand, Solomon would enjoy **peace** and **rest**. His name meant "Man of Peace." He would be allowed to build the temple. **23:1** David intended for **Solomon** to be **king** after him. He had made this known to Solomon and to his advisers. Now he acted on this declaration and officially made Solomon co-regent along with him. Despite David's

of Israel, the priests, and the Levites. ³ The Levites thirty years old or more were counted; the total number of men was thirty-eight thousand by headcount. ⁴ "Of these," David said, "twenty-four thousand are to be in charge of the work on the LORD's temple, six thousand are to be officers and judges, ⁵ four thousand are to be gatekeepers, and four thousand are to praise the LORD with the instruments that I have made for worship."

⁶ Then David divided them into divisions according to Levi's sons: Gershom,ᴬ Kohath, and Merari.

⁷ The Gershonites: Ladan and Shimei.

⁸ Ladan's sons: Jehiel was the first, then Zetham, and Joel — three.

⁹ Shimei's sons: Shelomoth, Haziel, and Haran — three. Those were the heads of the families of Ladan.

¹⁰ Shimei's sons: Jahath, Zizah,ᴮ Jeush, and Beriah. Those were Shimei's sons — four.

¹¹ Jahath was the first and Zizah was the second; however, Jeush and Beriah did not have many sons, so they became one familyᶜ and received a single assignment.

¹² Kohath's sons: Amram, Izhar, Hebron, and Uzziel — four.

¹³ Amram's sons: Aaron and Moses. Aaron, along with his descendants, was set apart forever to consecrate the most holy things, to burn incense in the presence of the LORD, to minister to him, and to pronounce blessings in his name forever. ¹⁴ As for Moses the man of God, his sons were named among the tribe of Levi.

¹⁵ Moses's sons: Gershom and Eliezer.

¹⁶ Gershom's sons: Shebuel was first.

¹⁷ Eliezer's sons were Rehabiah, first; Eliezer did not have any other sons, but Rehabiah's sons were very numerous.

¹⁸ Izhar's sons: Shelomith was first.

¹⁹ Hebron's sons: Jeriah was first, Amariah second, Jahaziel third, and Jekameam fourth.

²⁰ Uzziel's sons: Micah was first, and Isshiah second.

²¹ Merari's sons: Mahli and Mushi. Mahli's sons: Eleazar and Kish.

²² Eleazar died having no sons, only daughters. Their cousins, the sons of Kish, married them.

²³ Mushi's sons: Mahli, Eder, and Jeremoth — three.

²⁴ These were the descendants of Levi by their ancestral familiesᴰ — the family heads, according to their registration by name in the headcount — twenty years old or more, who worked in the service of the LORD's temple. ²⁵ For David said, "The LORD God of Israel has given rest to his people, and he has come to stay in Jerusalem forever. ²⁶ Also, the Levites no longer need to carry the tabernacle or any of the equipment for its service" — ²⁷ for according to the last words of David, the Levites twenty years old or more were to be counted — ²⁸ "but their duty will be to assist the descendants of Aaron with the service of the LORD's temple, being responsible for the courts and the chambers, the purification of all the holy things, and the work of the service of God's temple — ²⁹ as well as the rows of the Bread of the Presence, the fine flour for the grain offering, the wafers of unleavened bread, the baking,ᴱ the mixing, and all measurements of volume and length. ³⁰ They are also to stand every morning to give thanks and praise to the LORD, and likewise in the evening. ³¹ Whenever burnt offerings are offered to the LORD on the Sabbaths, New

ᴬ23:6 Lit *Gershon*   ᴮ23:10 LXX, Vg; MT reads *Zina*   ᶜ23:11 Lit *a father's house*   ᴰ23:24 Lit *the house of their fathers*
ᴱ23:29 Lit *the griddle*

public acclaim of Solomon, there would be vigorous dispute of this decision (1Kg 1–2). David reiterated his will on the matter several times (1Kg 1:38–39). Also see 1Ch 29:22.
23:2–3 David called a meeting of the country's **leaders** and the **priests** and **Levites**. The first part of this chapter is directed to those Levites **thirty years old** or older who would be ready to step into their roles as soon as the temple was built. Later on (v. 24) the minimum age is lowered to twenty years old. This lower number would include those who would have been in training and were not yet eligible for actual service, but who needed to be listed in their applicable categories. A total of **thirty-eight thousand** men were ready to get to work. With that many people, everyone would be able to lead a normal life at home for most of the year and be required to spend just a short time in Jerusalem pursuing temple duties.
23:4–5 The Levites were divided along several lines. The largest number (**twenty-four thousand**) consisted of those who were actually doing temple work. Six thousand

men were given the job of prescreening individuals and their potential sacrifices to make sure that neither the persons nor what they brought as offerings were unclean, and that everything proceeded in accordance with the law. The **four thousand** . . . **gatekeepers** were the guards. In keeping with David's vision for worship in the future, a large corps of musicians (**four thousand**) would be available.
23:6 Having established the broad, professional divisions, the same large group also was allocated into the three lines of descent from Levi's sons: **Gershom, Kohath, and Merari**.
23:7–8 The Chronicler assumes his usual method with genealogies in following a specific line and then backtracking.
23:9 This Shimei must have been a fourth son of **Ladan**, named after his uncle, whose descendants are named according to his three sons. Ladan was also called "Libni" (6:17).
23:11 Jeush and Beriah were counted as one because they **did not have many sons**.

23:12 Kohath's clan included the priestly line of Aaron.
23:13–14 For the Chronicler, the descendants of **Aaron** were far more important at this point than those of **Moses**.
23:15–20 The Chronicler lists the involvement of Moses's sons Gershom and Eliezer. See Ex 18:2–4.
23:21–23 The line of **Eleazar** continued by virtue of his daughters marrying the **sons of Kish**. In 24:29 we learn that one of Kish's sons was Jerahmeel. The other supplementary information from 24:26–27 is that Merari had a third son, Jaaziah, who also had three sons.
23:26–29 There was no longer any reason for the **tabernacle** to be carried. Those Levites who had this as their main duty would receive new assignments. The matter of moving the ark would not come up again until hundreds of years later (2Ch 35:2).
23:30–31 The Chronicler again emphasizes David's institution of regular temple music. The musicians must perform on a daily basis as well as at the major sacrifices and on special occasions.

Moons, and appointed festivals, they are to offer them regularly in the LORD's presence according to the number prescribed for them. [32] They are to carry out their responsibilities for the tent of meeting, for the holy place, and for their relatives, the descendants of Aaron, in the service of the LORD's temple."

The Divisions of the Priests

24 The divisions of the descendants of Aaron were as follows: Aaron's sons were Nadab, Abihu, Eleazar, and Ithamar. [2] But Nadab and Abihu died before their father, and they had no sons, so Eleazar and Ithamar served as priests. [3] Together with Zadok from the descendants of Eleazar and Ahimelech from the descendants of Ithamar, David divided them according to the assigned duties of their service. [4] Since more leaders were found among Eleazar's descendants than Ithamar's, they were divided accordingly: sixteen heads of ancestral families[A] were from Eleazar's descendants, and eight heads of ancestral families were from Ithamar's. [5] They were assigned by lot, for there were officers of the sanctuary and officers of God among both Eleazar's and Ithamar's descendants.

[6] The secretary, Shemaiah son of Nethanel, a Levite, recorded them in the presence of the king and the officers, the priest Zadok, Ahimelech son of Abiathar, and the heads of families of the priests and the Levites. One ancestral family[B] was taken for Eleazar, and then one for Ithamar.

[7] The first lot fell to Jehoiarib, the second to Jedaiah,
[8] the third to Harim, the fourth to Seorim,
[9] the fifth to Malchijah, the sixth to Mijamin,
[10] the seventh to Hakkoz, the eighth to Abijah,
[11] the ninth to Jeshua, the tenth to Shecaniah,
[12] the eleventh to Eliashib, the twelfth to Jakim,
[13] the thirteenth to Huppah, the fourteenth to Jeshebeab,
[14] the fifteenth to Bilgah, the sixteenth to Immer,
[15] the seventeenth to Hezir, the eighteenth to Happizzez,
[16] the nineteenth to Pethahiah, the twentieth to Jehezkel,
[17] the twenty-first to Jachin, the twenty-second to Gamul,
[18] the twenty-third to Delaiah, and the twenty-fourth to Maaziah.

[19] These had their assigned duties for service when they entered the LORD's temple, according to their regulations, which they received from their ancestor Aaron, as the LORD God of Israel had commanded him.

The Rest of the Levites

[20] As for the rest of Levi's sons:
from Amram's sons: Shubael;
from Shubael's sons: Jehdeiah.
[21] From Rehabiah:
from Rehabiah's sons: Isshiah was the first.
[22] From the Izharites: Shelomoth;
from Shelomoth's sons: Jahath.
[23] Hebron's[C] sons:
Jeriah the first, Amariah the second, Jahaziel the third, and Jekameam the fourth.
[24] From Uzziel's sons: Micah;
from Micah's sons: Shamir.
[25] Micah's brother: Isshiah;
from Isshiah's sons: Zechariah.
[26] Merari's sons: Mahli and Mushi,
and from his sons, Jaaziah his son.[D]
[27] Merari's sons, by his son Jaaziah:[E]
Shoham, Zaccur, and Ibri.
[28] From Mahli: Eleazar, who had no sons.
[29] From Kish, from Kish's sons:
Jerahmeel.
[30] Mushi's sons: Mahli, Eder, and Jerimoth.

Those were the descendants of the Levites according to their ancestral families.[F] [31] They also cast lots the same way as their relatives the descendants of Aaron did in the presence of King David, Zadok, Ahimelech, and the heads of the families of the priests and Levites — the family heads and their younger brothers alike.

[A]24:4 Lit *house of fathers*　[B]24:6 Lit *father's house*　[C]24:23 Some Hb mss, some LXX mss; other Hb mss omit *Hebron's*; 1Ch 23:19　[D]24:26 Or *Mushi; Jaaziah's sons: Beno.*　[E]24:27 Or *sons, Jaaziah: Beno,*　[F]24:30 Lit *the house of their fathers*

24:1 Among all the **divisions** established at this time, the most important one was for the priests, who were divided into twenty-four segments. These twenty-four groupings were based on **Aaron's** two surviving sons, **Eleazar** and **Ithamar**.

24:3 Two men were serving as high priest during the time of David: **Zadok** who officiated at the tabernacle, and **Ahimelech** who was in charge of the ark in Jerusalem. Ahimelech was the son of Abiathar and grandson of the Ahimelech who was slaughtered at the tabernacle by King Saul's troops. Both men had a legitimate claim to the priesthood, representing the lines of Eleazar and Ithamar, respectively, so both of their descendants were included in this list.

24:4–5 Since **Eleazar's** descendants outnumbered **Ithamar's** by a ratio of two to one, it made sense that of the twenty-four divisions, Eleazar should get **sixteen** shifts, and Ithamar only **eight**.

24:6 An official **secretary** kept a record, and there were overseers from both family lines as well as dignitaries who did not have a vested interest in how this matter was handled.

24:20–31 The other Levites were also divided into twenty-four groups, though it is not easy to identify exactly twenty-four names in this list. The ancestral names of these twenty-four groups cover several generations, so their origin is uneven.

The Levitical Musicians

25 David and the officers of the army also set apart some of the sons of Asaph, Heman, and Jeduthun, who were to prophesy accompanied by lyres, harps, and cymbals. This is the list of the men who performed their service:

[2] From Asaph's sons:

Zaccur, Joseph, Nethaniah, and Asarelah, sons of Asaph, under Asaph's authority, who prophesied under the authority of the king. [3] From Jeduthun: Jeduthun's sons: Gedaliah, Zeri, Jeshaiah, Shimei,[A] Hashabiah, and Mattithiah — six — under the authority of their father Jeduthun, prophesying to the accompaniment of lyres, giving thanks and praise to the Lord. [4] From Heman: Heman's sons: Bukkiah, Mattaniah, Uzziel, Shebuel, Jerimoth, Hananiah, Hanani, Eliathah, Giddalti, Romamti-ezer, Joshbekashah, Mallothi, Hothir, and Mahazioth. [5] All these sons of Heman, the king's seer, were given by the promises of God to exalt him,[B] for God had given Heman fourteen sons and three daughters.

[6] All these men were under their own fathers' authority for the music in the Lord's temple, with cymbals, harps, and lyres for the service of God's temple. Asaph, Jeduthun, and Heman were under the king's authority. [7] They numbered 288 together with their relatives who were all trained and skillful in music for the Lord. [8] They cast lots for their duties, young and old alike, teacher as well as pupil.

[9] The first lot for Asaph fell to Joseph, his sons, and his relatives — 12[C]
to Gedaliah the second: him, his relatives, and his sons — 12
[10] the third to Zaccur, his sons, and his relatives — 12
[11] the fourth to Izri,[D] his sons, and his relatives — 12
[12] the fifth to Nethaniah, his sons, and his relatives — 12
[13] the sixth to Bukkiah, his sons, and his relatives — 12
[14] the seventh to Jesarelah, his sons, and his relatives — 12
[15] the eighth to Jeshaiah, his sons, and his relatives — 12
[16] the ninth to Mattaniah, his sons, and his relatives — 12
[17] the tenth to Shimei, his sons, and his relatives — 12
[18] the eleventh to Azarel,[E] his sons, and his relatives — 12
[19] the twelfth to Hashabiah, his sons, and his relatives — 12
[20] the thirteenth to Shubael, his sons, and his relatives — 12
[21] the fourteenth to Mattithiah, his sons, and his relatives — 12
[22] the fifteenth to Jeremoth, his sons, and his relatives — 12
[23] the sixteenth to Hananiah, his sons, and his relatives — 12
[24] the seventeenth to Joshbekashah, his sons, and his relatives — 12
[25] the eighteenth to Hanani, his sons, and his relatives — 12
[26] the nineteenth to Mallothi, his sons, and his relatives — 12
[27] the twentieth to Eliathah, his sons, and his relatives — 12
[28] the twenty-first to Hothir, his sons, and his relatives — 12
[29] the twenty-second to Giddalti, his sons, and his relatives — 12
[30] the twenty-third to Mahazioth, his sons, and his relatives — 12
[31] and the twenty-fourth to Romamti-ezer, his sons, and his relatives — 12.

The Levitical Gatekeepers

26 The following were the divisions of the gatekeepers:

From the Korahites: Meshelemiah son of Kore, one of the sons of Asaph. [2] Meshelemiah had sons:

Zechariah the firstborn, Jediael the second,
Zebadiah the third, Jathniel the fourth,
[3] Elam the fifth, Jehohanan the sixth,
and Eliehoenai the seventh.
[4] Obed-edom also had sons:

[A]25:3 One Hb ms, LXX; other Hb mss omit *Shimei* [B]25:5 Lit *by the words of God to lift a horn* [C]25:9 LXX; MT lacks *his sons, and his relatives — 12* [D]25:11 Variant of Zeri [E]25:18 Variant of Uzziel

---

25:1 David was a man of music. He placed the **sons of Asaph, Heman, and Jeduthun** (also known as Ethan) in charge of the music for the future temple. The Chronicler associates the musical ministry with prophecy.
25:2–5 This time the numbers work out smoothly. **Asaph** had four sons, **Jeduthun** had six, and **Heman** had fourteen. Thus there were twenty-four natural divisions, and it turned out that the larger number of their relatives came to 288, thus creating twenty-four divisions of exactly twelve each.

Lots were drawn to draft these Levites into their groups.
25:6–31 These 288 musicians were the leaders, who had a total of four thousand men to draw on (23:5). The men of the twenty-four divisions reported to the twelve sons of the three head musicians, and they in turn took their directions directly from the king. For most other temple functions, the high priest was the final authority, but since the order of music was primarily David's innovation, he did not relinquish control over this part of the ministry.

26:1–3 The following list of **gatekeepers** is limited to the two Levitical clans of Kohath and Merari. Since Asaph the musician belonged to the clan of Gershom (6:39–43), the **Asaph** mentioned here is a different person. Possibly "Asaph" here should read "Ebiasaph" instead, as it does in the LXX. Compare also "Ebiasaph" at 9:19.
26:4–8 Obed-edom was a gatekeeper by profession, though he joined the musicians during the transport of the ark to Jerusalem (15:21). Now that plans were being set up

Shemaiah the firstborn, Jehozabad the second,
Joah the third, Sachar the fourth,
Nethanel the fifth, ⁵ Ammiel the sixth, Issachar the seventh, and Peullethai the eighth,
for God blessed him.
⁶ Also, to his son Shemaiah were born sons who ruled their ancestral families^A because they were strong, capable men. ⁷ Shemaiah's sons: Othni, Rephael, Obed, and Elzabad; his relatives Elihu and Semachiah were also capable men. ⁸ All of these were among the sons of Obed-edom with their sons and relatives; they were capable men with strength for the work — sixty-two from Obed-edom. ⁹ Meshelemiah also had sons and relatives who were capable men — eighteen. ¹⁰ Hosah, from the Merarites, also had sons: Shimri the first (although he was not the firstborn, his father had appointed him as the first), ¹¹ Hilkiah the second, Tebaliah the third, and Zechariah the fourth. The sons and relatives of Hosah were thirteen in all.

¹² These divisions of the gatekeepers, under their leading men, had duties for ministering in the LORD's temple, just as their relatives did. ¹³ They cast lots for each temple gate according to their ancestral families, young and old alike. ¹⁴ The lot for the east gate fell to Shelemiah.^B They also cast lots for his son Zechariah, an insightful counselor, and his lot came out for the north gate. ¹⁵ Obed-edom's was the south gate, and his sons' lot was for the storehouses; ¹⁶ it was the west gate and the gate of Shallecheth on the ascending highway for Shuppim and Hosah.

There were guards stationed at every watch. ¹⁷ There were six Levites each day^C on the east, four each day on the north, four each day on the south, and two pair at the storehouses. ¹⁸ As for the court on the west, there were four at the highway and two at the court. ¹⁹ Those were the

divisions of the gatekeepers from the descendants of the Korahites and Merarites.

The Levitical Treasurers and Other Officials

²⁰ From the Levites, Ahijah was in charge of the treasuries of God's temple and the treasuries of what had been dedicated. ²¹ From the sons of Ladan, who were the descendants of the Gershonites through Ladan and were the family heads belonging to Ladan the Gershonite: Jehieli. ²² The sons of Jehieli, Zetham and his brother Joel, were in charge of the treasuries of the LORD's temple.

²³ From the Amramites, the Izharites, the Hebronites, and the Uzzielites: ²⁴ Shebuel, a descendant of Moses's son Gershom, was the officer in charge of the treasuries. ²⁵ His relatives through Eliezer: his son Rehabiah, his son Jeshaiah, his son Joram, his son Zichri, and his son Shelomith.^D ²⁶ This Shelomith and his relatives were in charge of all the treasuries of what had been dedicated by King David, by the family heads who were the commanders of thousands and of hundreds, and by the army commanders. ²⁷ They dedicated part of the plunder from their battles for the repair of the LORD's temple. ²⁸ All that the seer Samuel, Saul son of Kish, Abner son of Ner, and Joab son of Zeruiah had dedicated, along with everything else that had been dedicated, were in the care of Shelomith and his relatives.

²⁹ From the Izrahites: Chenaniah and his sons had duties outside the temple^E as officers and judges over Israel. ³⁰ From the Hebronites: Hashabiah and his relatives, 1,700 capable men, had assigned duties in Israel west of the Jordan for all the work of the LORD and for the service of the king. ³¹ From the Hebronites: Jerijah was the head of the Hebronites, according to the family records of his ancestors. A search was made in the fortieth year of David's reign and strong, capable men were found among them at Jazer in Gilead. ³² There were among Jerijah's relatives 2,700 capable men who were family heads. King David appointed them over

---

^A26:6 Lit the house of their fathers, also in v. 13　^B26:14 Variant of Meshelemiah　^C26:17 LXX; MT omits each day　^D26:25 Or Shelomoth, also in vv. 26,28　^E26:29 the temple added for clarity

---

for permanent duties, he figured prominently among the guards, coming uniquely equipped with a clan of **sixty-two** family members. **Shemaiah**, his son, is a different person than Shemaiah the secretary whose father was Nethanel (24:6).
26:9 The sons of Obed-edom are embedded in the discussion of **Meshelemiah**.
26:10–11 Certain Merarites also served as gatekeepers.
26:12 The Chronicler emphasizes that the service these **gatekeepers** performed was just as significant as the duties of those who led in worship.
26:13 Rather than dividing the gatekeepers into twenty-four shifts, their assignments

were based on which gates they were assigned to guard.
26:14–15 Both son and father were placed in command of their own gates. This was true for **Shelemiah** and his son **Zechariah**, as well as for Obed-edom and **his** sons.
26:16 The **Shalleceth** was the **gate** designated for disposal of refuse and materials left over from animal sacrifices.
26:17–19 Guard duty was not limited to the gates of the temple. Obviously the **storehouses** needed protection, and guards were also installed outside the temple grounds, specifically on the road leading to the temple.
26:20–22 The gatekeepers came primarily from the clans of Merari and Kohath. The

Gershonites were assigned to watch over the **treasuries** of the temple. This included guarding temple resources from theft or vandalism, as well as accounting for them and keeping them stored. **Ahijah** supervised this work. The treasuries included long-term deposits, as well as the funds needed for day-to-day operation of the temple.
26:29 One other group of Levites needed to be organized. These were the **officers and judges** who would enforce the divine law in Israel.
26:30–32 Only at the very end of his reign was David able to provide a suitable teacher for the tribes on the eastern side of the

the Reubenites, the Gadites, and half the tribe of Manasseh as overseers in every matter relating to God and the king.

David's Secular Officials

27 This is the list of the Israelites, the family heads, the commanders of thousands and the commanders of hundreds, and their officers who served the king in every matter to do with the divisions that were on rotated military duty each month throughout^A the year. There were 24,000 in each division:

² Jashobeam son of Zabdiel was in charge of the first division, for the first month; 24,000 were in his division. ³ He was a descendant of Perez and chief of all the army commanders for the first month.

⁴ Dodai the Ahohite was in charge of the division for the second month, and Mikloth was the leader; 24,000 were in his division.

⁵ The third army commander, as chief for the third month, was Benaiah son of the priest Jehoiada; 24,000 were in his division. ⁶ This Benaiah was a mighty man among the Thirty and over the Thirty, and his son Ammizabad was in charge⁸ of his division.

⁷ The fourth commander, for the fourth month, was Joab's brother Asahel, and his son Zebadiah was commander after him; 24,000 were in his division.

⁸ The fifth, for the fifth month, was the commander Shamhuth the Izrahite; 24,000 were in his division.

⁹ The sixth, for the sixth month, was Ira son of Ikkesh the Tekoite; 24,000 were in his division.

¹⁰ The seventh, for the seventh month, was Helez the Pelonite from the descendants of Ephraim; 24,000 were in his division.

¹¹ The eighth, for the eighth month, was Sibbecai the Hushathite, a Zerahite; 24,000 were in his division.

¹² The ninth, for the ninth month, was Abiezer the Anathothite, a Benjaminite; 24,000 were in his division.

¹³ The tenth, for the tenth month, was Maharai the Netophathite, a Zerahite; 24,000 were in his division.

¹⁴ The eleventh, for the eleventh month, was Benaiah the Pirathonite from the descendants of Ephraim; 24,000 were in his division.

¹⁵ The twelfth, for the twelfth month, was Heldai the Netophathite, of Othniel's family;^C 24,000 were in his division.

¹⁶ The following were in charge of the tribes of Israel:
For the Reubenites, Eliezer son of Zichri was the chief official;
for the Simeonites, Shephatiah son of Maacah;
¹⁷ for the Levites, Hashabiah son of Kemuel; for Aaron, Zadok;
¹⁸ for Judah, Elihu, one of David's brothers; for Issachar, Omri son of Michael;
¹⁹ for Zebulun, Ishmaiah son of Obadiah; for Naphtali, Jerimoth son of Azriel;
²⁰ for the Ephraimites, Hoshea son of Azaziah;
for half the tribe of Manasseh, Joel son of Pedaiah;
²¹ for half the tribe of Manasseh in Gilead, Iddo son of Zechariah;
for Benjamin, Jaasiel son of Abner;
²² for Dan, Azarel son of Jeroham.
Those were the leaders of the tribes of Israel.

²³ David didn't count the men aged twenty or under, for the LORD had said he would make Israel as numerous as the stars of the sky. ²⁴ Joab son of Zeruiah began to count them, but he didn't complete it. There was wrath against Israel because of this census, and the number was not entered in the Historical Record^D of King David.

---

^A 27:1 Lit *that came in and went out month by month for all months of* ^B 27:6 LXX; MT omits *in charge* ^C 27:15 Lit *belonging to Othniel* ^D 27:24 LXX; MT reads *the number of the Historical Record*

Jordan River—**Reubenites . . . Gadites, and half . . . of Manasseh**.

27:1 As to the secular officials and the army, the most important category of classification here is that there were twelve **divisions** composed of **24,000** soldiers **each**. Each of those units was on duty for one **month** out of the year during times of peace. During times of war, obviously everyone would be mobilized. Many of the names here appear in the list of the "Thirty" in chap. 11.

27:2–3 As a descendant of **Perez . . . Jashobeam** belonged to the expanded clan within Judah to which David was linked.

27:4 This is an instance with two names, where **Mikloth** may have reported to

Dodai at first, and then may have replaced him later.

27:5–6 We have seen **Benaiah** several times already. He was the most honored of the Thirty (11:22), and he was in charge of the Philistine mercenaries (18:17). Here we see him commanding one of the twelve units of **24,000** as well. His own son **Ammizabad** was second in command to him.

27:7 Asahel was killed during the civil war between David and Esh-baal (2Sm 2:23). So for all practical purposes, the command of this unit belonged to **Zebadiah** the entire time.

27:11 Sibbecai is familiar because he killed one of the Philistine giants (19:4).

27:16 This verse begins a list of those who were **in charge** of each tribe. Gad and Asher

are left out, perhaps because they were governed by the leaders of another tribe. The number of men on the list comes to twelve because each of the two halves of Manasseh is represented separately (vv. 20–21) and Levi has two representatives (v. 17).

27:17 One person was in charge of the tribe of Levi at large, but the descendants of **Aaron**—the priests—were represented separately by **Zadok**.

27:18 Elihu was one of **David's brothers**. He is not listed among David's six brothers in 2:13–15. This could mean that this name is a variation on Eliab, David's older brother, or that this is a seventh brother who is not mentioned earlier by the Chronicler. This

²⁵ Azmaveth son of Adiel was in charge of the king's storehouses.

Jonathan son of Uzziah was in charge of the storehouses in the country, in the cities, in the villages, and in the fortresses. ²⁶ Ezri son of Chelub was in charge of those who worked in the fields tilling the soil. ²⁷ Shimei the Ramathite was in charge of the vineyards.

Zabdi the Shiphmite was in charge of the produce of the vineyards for the wine cellars. ²⁸ Baal-hanan the Gederite was in charge of the olive and sycamore trees in the Judean foothills.ᴬ

Joash was in charge of the stores of olive oil. ²⁹ Shitrai the Sharonite was in charge of the herds that grazed in Sharon, while Shaphat son of Adlai was in charge of the herds in the valleys. ³⁰ Obil the Ishmaelite was in charge of the camels.

Jehdeiah the Meronothite was in charge of the donkeys. ³¹ Jaziz the Hagrite was in charge of the flocks.

All these were officials in charge of King David's property.

³² David's uncle Jonathan was a counselor; he was a man of understanding and a scribe. Jehiel son of Hachmoni attendedᴮ the king's sons. ³³ Ahithophel was the king's counselor. Hushai the Archite was the king's friend. ³⁴ After Ahithophel came Jehoiada son of Benaiah, then Abiathar. Joab was the commander of the king's army.

David Commissions Solomon to Build the Temple

28 David assembled all the leaders of Israel in Jerusalem: the leaders of the tribes, the leaders of the divisions in the king's service, the commanders of thousands and the commanders of hundreds, and the officials in charge of all the property and cattle of the king and his sons, along with the court officials, the fighting men, and all the best soldiers. ² Then King David rose to his feet and said, "Listen to me, my brothers and my people. It was in my heart to build a house as a resting place for the ark of the LORD's covenant and as a footstool for our God. I had made preparations to build, ³ but God said to me, 'You are not to build a house for my name because you are a man of war and have shed blood.'

⁴ "Yet the LORD God of Israel chose me out of all my father's family to be king over Israel forever. For he chose Judah as leader, and from the house of Judah, my father's family, and from my father's sons, he was pleased to make me king over all Israel. ⁵ And out of all my sons — for the LORD has given me many sons — he has chosen my son Solomon to sit on the throne of the LORD's kingdom over Israel. ⁶ He said to me, 'Your son Solomon is the one who is to build my house and my courts, for I have chosen him to be my son, and I will be his father.' ⁷ I will establish his kingdom forever if he perseveres in keeping my commands and my ordinances as he is doing today.'

⁸ "So now in the sight of all Israel, the assembly of the LORD, and in the hearing of our God, observe and follow all the commands of the LORD your God so that you may possess this good land and leave it as an inheritance to your descendants forever.

⁹ "As for you, Solomon my son, know the God of your father, and serve him wholeheartedly and with a willing mind, for the LORD searches every heart and understands the intention of every thought. If you seek him, he will be found by you, but if you abandon him, he will reject you forever. ¹⁰ Realize now that the LORD has chosen you to build a house for the sanctuary. Be strong, and do it."

¹¹ Then David gave his son Solomon the plans for the portico of the temple and its buildings, treasuries, upstairs rooms, inner rooms, and a room for the mercy seat. ¹² The plans contained

---

ᴬ 27:28 Or *the Shephelah*   ᴮ 27:32 Lit *was with*

---

second interpretation makes sense because 1Sm 16:10 refers to seven brothers of David. **27:25–33** These verses tell us about David's cabinet. **Azmaveth** was secretary of the treasury. Under him overseeing the various treasury locations around the nation was **Jonathan son of Uzziah**. There were also cabinet posts for the oversight of agriculture and herding.

27:32 This verse describes the inner circle of David's advisers, though again this is not a permanent group. **Jonathan**, despite these accolades, makes his only appearance in the record at this point. **Jehiel**, who tended David's sons, must have had great skill at diplomacy and conflict resolution.

27:33 Ahithophel was so wise that his advice was considered almost like hearing from

God himself (2Sm 16:23). Unfortunately, none of this wisdom prevented him from joining Absalom's rebellion and ending his life with suicide (2Sm 17:23). **Hushai** helped David by infiltrating Absalom's inner circle and frustrating Ahithophel's advice (2Sm 17:14). **27:34** Although this passage does not mention Ahithophel's death, it is implied by mentioning his successors. First came **Jehoiada son of Benaiah** (not to be confused with the hero Benaiah son of Jehoiada); then came **Abiathar**, who may have been either the priest who was David's friend during the king's time in the wilderness, or his grandson. **28:1** For the Chronicler, the questions of who would be the next king and who would build the temple are synonymous. David called another meeting of **all the leaders of**

Israel (the first meeting occurred in chap. 22) in which he reiterated his answer to both questions.

28:2 This is the last speech by David. **28:3** David disclosed to the people what he had already told Solomon—the reason he could not build the temple (22:8).

28:9 David turned to Solomon and exhorted him to single-minded devotion to the Lord. David directed Solomon's commitment not just to the law, but to the Lord. The covenant that God had made with David about the continuation of his house on the throne did not overrule Solomon's obligation to walk with the Lord.

28:11–19 David made a public display of handing Solomon the information that is recorded in the previous six chapters.

everything he had in mind^A for the courts of the Lord's house, all the surrounding chambers, the treasuries of God's house, and the treasuries for what is dedicated. [13] Also included were plans for the divisions of the priests and the Levites; all the work of service in the Lord's house; all the articles of service of the Lord's house; [14] the weight of gold for all the articles for every kind of service; the weight of all the silver articles for every kind of service; [15] the weight of the gold lampstands and their gold lamps, including the weight of each lampstand and its lamps; the weight of each silver lampstand and its lamps, according to the service of each lampstand; [16] the weight of gold for each table for the rows of the Bread of the Presence and the silver for the silver tables; [17] the pure gold for the forks, sprinkling basins, and pitchers; the weight of each gold dish; the weight of each silver bowl; [18] the weight of refined gold for the altar of incense; and the plans for the chariot of^B the gold cherubim that spread out their wings and cover the ark of the Lord's covenant.

[19] David concluded, "By the Lord's hand on me, he enabled me to understand everything in writing, all the details of the plan."^C

[20] Then David said to his son Solomon, "Be strong and courageous, and do the work. Don't be afraid or discouraged, for the Lord God, my God, is with you. He won't leave you or abandon you until all the work for the service of the Lord's house is finished. [21] Here are the divisions of the priests and the Levites for all the service of God's house. Every willing person of any skill will be at your disposal for the work, and the leaders and all the people are at your every command."

Contributions for Building the Temple

29 Then King David said to all the assembly, "My son Solomon — God has chosen him alone — is young and inexperienced. The task is great because the building will not be built for a human but for the Lord God. [2] So to the best of my ability I've made provision for the house of my God: gold for the gold articles, silver for the silver, bronze for the bronze, iron for the iron, and wood for the wood, as well as onyx, stones for mounting,^D antimony,^E stones of various colors, all kinds of precious stones,

and a great quantity of marble. [3] Moreover, because of my delight in the house of my God, I now give my personal treasures of gold and silver for the house of my God over and above all that I've provided for the holy house: [4] 100 tons^F of gold (gold of Ophir) and 250 tons^G of refined silver for overlaying the walls of the buildings, [5] the gold for the gold work and the silver for the silver, for all the work to be done by the craftsmen. Now who will volunteer to consecrate himself to the Lord today?"

[6] Then the leaders of the households, the leaders of the tribes of Israel, the commanders of thousands and of hundreds, and the officials in charge of the king's work gave willingly. [7] For the service of God's house they gave 185 tons^H of gold and 10,000 gold coins,^I 375 tons^J of silver, 675 tons^K of bronze, and 4,000 tons^L of iron. [8] Whoever had precious stones gave them to the treasury of the Lord's house under the care of Jehiel the Gershonite. [9] Then the people rejoiced because of their leaders' willingness to give, for they had given to the Lord wholeheartedly. King David also rejoiced greatly.

David's Prayer

[10] Then David blessed the Lord in the sight of all the assembly. David said,

May you be blessed, Lord God of our father Israel, from eternity to eternity. [11] Yours, Lord, is the greatness and the power and the glory and the splendor and the majesty, for everything in the heavens and on earth belongs to you. Yours, Lord, is the kingdom, and you are exalted as head over all. [12] Riches and honor come from you, and you are the ruler of everything. Power and might are in your hand, and it is in your hand to make great and to give strength to all. [13] Now therefore, our God, we give you thanks and praise your glorious name.

[14] But who am I, and who are my people, that we should be able to give as generously as this? For everything comes from you, and we have given you only what comes from your own hand.^M [15] For we are aliens and temporary residents in your presence as were all our ancestors. Our days on earth are like a shadow, without hope. [16] Lord our God, all this wealth that we've provided for

---

^A **28:12** Or *he received from the Spirit*   ^B **28:18** Or *chariot, that is* ; Ps 18:10; Ezk 1:5,15   ^C **28:19** Hb obscure   ^D **29:2** Or *mosaic*
^E **29:2** In Hb, the word *antimony* is similar to "turquoise"; Ex 28:18.   ^F **29:4** Lit *3,000 talents*   ^G **29:4** Lit *7,000 talents*
^H **29:7** Lit *5,000 talents*   ^I **29:7** Or *drachmas,* or *darics*   ^J **29:7** Lit *10,000 talents*   ^K **29:7** Lit *18,000 talents*   ^L **29:7** Lit *100,000 talents*   ^M **29:14** Lit *and from your hand we have given you*

29:1 Turning again to the assembled people, David drew attention to Solomon's youth and lack of experience in the face of the immensity of the task.
29:2 Since in v. 3 David refers to giving his own wealth, the donations mentioned in this verse must be a part of the spoils of war that David had collected.

29:3–4 After serving as king for forty years, David had accumulated quite a large personal treasure, out of which he made a large contribution, including **100 tons of gold**.
29:10 David's lengthy prayer began by focusing on God.
29:14–17 As David continued to focus on God, he acknowledged some important

truths. It is not possible to **give** anything to God because God owns everything. David also declared that it is not possible to deceive God. He knows exactly who is giving **willingly** out of true devotion to him and who is giving just to be seen by others. The key is a **heart** that wants to please God.

building you a house for your holy name comes from your hand; everything belongs to you. **¹⁷** I know, my God, that you test the heart and that you are pleased with what is right. I have willingly given all these things with an upright heart, and now I have seen your people who are present^A here giving joyfully and^B willingly to you. **¹⁸** LORD God of Abraham, Isaac, and Israel, our ancestors, keep this desire forever in the thoughts of the hearts of your people, and confirm their hearts toward you. **¹⁹** Give my son Solomon an undivided heart to keep and to carry out all your commands, your decrees, and your statutes, and to build the building for which I have made provision.

²⁰ Then David said to the whole assembly, "Blessed be the LORD your God." So the whole assembly praised the LORD God of their ancestors. They knelt low and paid homage to the LORD and the king.

²¹ The following day they offered sacrifices to the LORD and burnt offerings to the LORD: a thousand bulls, a thousand rams, and a thousand lambs, along with their drink offerings, and sacrifices in abundance for all Israel. **²²** They ate and drank with great joy in the LORD's presence that day.

The Enthronement of Solomon

Then, for a second time, they made David's son Solomon king; they anointed him^C as the LORD's ruler, and Zadok as the priest. **²³** Solomon sat on the LORD's throne as king in place of his father David. He prospered, and all Israel obeyed him. **²⁴** All the leaders and the mighty men, and all of King David's sons as well, pledged their allegiance to King Solomon. **²⁵** The LORD highly exalted Solomon in the sight of all Israel and bestowed on him such royal majesty as had not been bestowed on any king over Israel before him.

A Summary of David's Life

²⁶ David son of Jesse was king over all Israel. **²⁷** The length of his reign over Israel was forty years; he reigned in Hebron for seven years and in Jerusalem for thirty-three. **²⁸** He died at a good old age, full of days, riches, and honor, and his son Solomon became king in his place. **²⁹** As for the events of King David's reign, from beginning to end, note that they are written in the Events of the Seer Samuel, the Events of the Prophet Nathan, and the Events of the Seer Gad, **³⁰** along with all his reign, his might, and the incidents that affected him and Israel and all the kingdoms of the surrounding lands.

---

^A29:17 Lit *found*   ^B29:17 Or *now with joy I've seen your people who are present here giving*   ^C29:22 LXX, Tg, Vg; MT omits *him*

29:20–22 After sacrifices and a feast, David **made . . . Solomon king** for **a second time**. Commentators are divided on the reference to a first coronation and how to interpret 23:1, which states that David installed Solomon as king. Some interpreters see this verse as a general summary of the events that are amplified in this chapter, but this mention of a second coronation could be an understated reference to the turmoil we read about in 1Kg 1. This turmoil resulted in David declaring Solomon to be king as an emergency measure in opposition to Adonijah's bid for the throne. In either case, the transfer of power from David to Solomon proceeded smoothly, and he was acclaimed by all Israel. **29:26–30** These verses summarize David's **reign** and give an assessment of his success. His **good old age** was seventy (2Sm 5:4). The Chronicler also mentions several additional sources of information about David. These ancient books are likely lost, but they could be reflected in our books of 1 and 2 Samuel, which record the ministry of **Samuel . . . Nathan**, and **Gad** during the reign of David (1Sm 16:13; 2Sm 12:1; 24:11).

◥ Introduction to 2 Chronicles

Circumstances of Writing

An ancient tradition ascribes the authorship of Chronicles to Ezra. The author must have lived sometime after the return of the Jews to Israel from the Babylonian exile. He also had a strong interest in the reimplementation of the law and the temple, and he must have had access to historical records. All of these criteria suit Ezra, and this identification is corroborated by the fact that the last verses of Chronicles are the first verses of the book of Ezra. However, since the book does not explicitly claim Ezra for its author, in these notes we will refer to him simply as the Chronicler.

The books of 1 and 2 Chronicles include extensive genealogies from the time of Adam and take the reader up to the period of the nation's exile and restoration. Second Chronicles focuses on all the kings who followed David up to the exile and restoration. It covers the same time period as 1 and 2 Kings, but 2 Chronicles focuses exclusively on the kings of Judah. The content of the books necessitates that they were written sometime after the return from the exile, perhaps the middle of the fifth century BC.

Contribution to the Bible

Chronicles brings together many dimensions of biblical revelation, such as historical events (as recounted in Genesis through Kings), temple ritual (as prescribed in Leviticus), sin and judgment (as preached by the prophets), and even some psalms. Because a recurring theme is that God will always accept people who return to him no matter how wicked they may have been, it has been called, perhaps a little whimsically, "The Gospel According to Ezra." The books of 1 and 2 Chronicles give us the big picture of Old Testament history, capturing the Davidic covenant in light of Israel's history back to Adam and pointing to the eternal continuation of that covenant through the reign of the Messiah.

Structure

The Hebrew Bible divides its books into three categories: the Law, the Prophets, and the Writings. In this arrangement, the books of Samuel and Kings are counted among the Prophets, whereas Chronicles belongs to the Writings. This classification may be partially due to the fact that Chronicles repeats information, such as the genealogies of Genesis and the histories of the kings of Judah from the books of Samuel and Kings. Still the Chronicler uses this repeated content to support his own point, and he also adds a lot of information that we find in Chronicles alone. He limits his discussion of the various kings almost entirely to those of Judah, the southern kingdom.

See the introduction to 1 Chronicles for the timeline.

Solomon's Request for Wisdom

1 Solomon son of David strengthened his hold on his kingdom. The LORD his God was with him and highly exalted him. ² Then Solomon spoke to all Israel, to the commanders of thousands and of hundreds, to the judges, and to every leader in all Israel — the family heads. ³ Solomon and the whole assembly with him went to the high place that was in Gibeon because God's tent of meeting, which the LORD's servant Moses had made in the wilderness, was there. ⁴ Now David had brought the ark of God from Kiriath-jearim to the place^A he had set up for it, because he had pitched a tent for it in Jerusalem, ⁵ but he put^B the bronze altar, which Bezalel son of Uri, son of Hur, had made, in front of the LORD's tabernacle. Solomon and the assembly inquired of him^c there. ⁶ Solomon offered sacrifices there in the LORD's presence on the bronze altar at the tent of meeting; he offered a thousand burnt offerings on it.

⁷ That night God appeared to Solomon and said to him, "Ask. What should I give you?"

⁸ And Solomon said to God, "You have shown great and faithful love to my father David, and you have made me king in his place. ⁹ LORD God, let your promise to my father David now come true. For you have made me king over a people as numerous as the dust of the earth. ¹⁰ Now grant me wisdom and knowledge so that I may lead these people, for who can judge this great people of yours?"

¹¹ God said to Solomon, "Since this was in your heart, and you have not requested riches, wealth, or glory, or for the life of those who hate you, and you have not even requested long life, but you have requested for yourself wisdom and knowledge that you may judge my people over whom I have made you king, ¹² wisdom and knowledge are given to you. I will also give you riches, wealth, and glory, unlike what was given to the kings who were before you, or will be given to those after you." ¹³ So Solomon went to Jerusalem from^D the high place that was in Gibeon in front of the tent of meeting, and he reigned over Israel.

Solomon's Horses and Wealth

¹⁴ Solomon accumulated 1,400 chariots and 12,000 horsemen, which he stationed in the chariot cities and with the king in Jerusalem. ¹⁵ The king made silver and gold as common in Jerusalem as stones, and he made cedar as abundant as sycamore in the Judean foothills. ¹⁶ Solomon's horses came from Egypt and Kue.^E The king's traders would get them from Kue at the going price. ¹⁷ A chariot could be imported from Egypt for fifteen pounds^F of silver and a horse for nearly four pounds.^G In the same way, they exported them to all the kings of the Hittites and to the kings of Aram through their agents.

Solomon's Letter to Hiram

2 Solomon decided to build a temple for the name of the LORD and a royal palace for himself, ² so he assigned 70,000 men as porters, 80,000 men as stonecutters in the mountains, and 3,600 as supervisors over them.

³ Then Solomon sent word to King Hiram^H of Tyre:

Do for me what you did for my father David. You sent him cedars to build him a house to live in. ⁴ Now I am building a temple for the name of the LORD my God in order to dedicate it to him for burning fragrant incense before him, for displaying the rows of the Bread of the Presence continuously, and for sacrificing burnt offerings for the morning and the evening, the

---

^A1:4 Vg; MT omits *the place*   ^B1:5 Some Hb mss, Tg, Syr; other Hb mss, LXX, Vg read *but there was*   ^c1:5 Or *it*   ^D1:13 LXX, Vg; MT reads *to*   ^E1:16 = Cilicia   ^F1:17 Lit *600 shekels*   ^G1:17 Lit *150 shekels*   ^H2:3 Some Hb mss, LXX, Syr, Vg; other Hb mss read *Huram*; 2Sm 5:11; 1Kg 5:1–2

1:1 At one point 1 and 2 Chronicles were bound together as one scroll, but here we come to a meaningful breaking point. The Chronicler starts afresh with his story, beginning by reviewing a number of details in the process.

1:2 We are not given the text of Solomon's inauguration address, but the fact that he gave one shows his acumen as a leader. As he set out to celebrate his new reign, he made sure that representatives from the entire kingdom were involved in the celebration.

1:3–5 The Chronicler reminds us of the ambivalent situation regarding the sacred sites in Israel. The tabernacle, the central place of worship, was still in **Gibeon**. This included the altar made by **Bezalel** in the time of Moses (Ex 38:1–3). The **bronze altar** was actually a wooden altar covered with a bronze grate.

1:6 All of Solomon's sacrifices were **burnt offerings**, meaning that all the animals were consumed by fire.

1:7–10 In response to an open invitation from God (v. 7), Solomon asked for **wisdom**. Solomon was only about twenty years old. He had shown himself capable in asserting his leadership in eliminating Adonijah, his rival, and in uniting the priesthood in the person of Zadok (1Kg 1–2).

1:11–12 God was pleased with Solomon's request, and added a bonus—**riches, wealth, and glory**.

1:13 Solomon honored the holy site that he was about to dismantle.

1:14 This is the first of two listings of Solomon's wealth (9:13–28). A total of **1,400 chariots and 12,000 horsemen** was an extremely large resource. Pharaoh, in pursuing the Israelites at the exodus, had 600 chariots (Ex 14:7) and Sisera of Hazor had 900 (Jdg 4:3).

1:16–17 Solomon invested heavily in **horses** and chariots as a basis for increasing his own wealth. He bought horses from **Egypt** and **Kue**, a region in Turkey, and then sold them to the **Hittites** and the Arameans. Although these items are mentioned here as representative of Solomon's material success, they were also a violation of God's ordinance. The law stated that a future king should not acquire horses from Egypt or accumulate large amounts of silver (Dt 17:16–17).

2:2 In vv. 17–18, where the same list is repeated, we learn that the workers conscripted by Solomon were aliens living in Israel. At this time, Solomon did not force any Israelites to work on his building projects (10:4). The first part of the project was to construct the walls out of large blocks of stone. These stones were quarried in **the mountains**. By shaping this work off-site, the laborers had more space to work on-site, plus they reduced the weight of each block to its minimum, making transportation easier.

2:3 Despite all the materials that David had accumulated, Solomon needed more, particularly cedar wood. So he consulted his father's old trading partner, **King Hiram of Tyre**.

Sabbaths and the New Moons, and the appointed festivals of the Lord our God. This is ordained for Israel permanently. [5] The temple that I am building will be great, for our God is greater than any of the gods. [6] But who is able to build a temple for him, since even heaven and the highest heaven cannot contain him? Who am I then that I should build a temple for him except as a place to burn incense before him? [7] Therefore, send me an artisan who is skilled in engraving to work with gold, silver, bronze, and iron, and with purple, crimson, and blue yarn. He will work with the artisans who are with me in Judah and Jerusalem, appointed by my father David. [8] Also, send me cedar, cypress, and algum[A] logs from Lebanon, for I know that your servants know how to cut the trees of Lebanon. Note that my servants will be with your servants [9] to prepare logs for me in abundance because the temple I am building will be great and wondrous. [10] I will give your servants, the woodcutters who cut the trees, one hundred twenty thousand bushels[B] of wheat flour, one hundred twenty thousand bushels of barley, one hundred twenty thousand gallons[C] of wine, and one hundred twenty thousand gallons of oil.

Hiram's Reply

[11] Then King Hiram of Tyre wrote a letter[D] and sent it to Solomon:

Because the Lord loves his people, he set you over them as king.

[12] Hiram also said:

Blessed be the Lord God of Israel, who made the heavens and the earth! He gave King David a wise son with insight and understanding, who will build a temple for

the Lord and a royal palace for himself. [13] I have now sent Huram-abi,[E] a skillful man who has understanding. [14] He is the son of a woman from the daughters of Dan. His father is a man of Tyre. He knows how to work with gold, silver, bronze, iron, stone, and wood, with purple, blue, crimson yarn, and fine linen. He knows how to do all kinds of engraving and to execute any design that may be given him. I have sent him to be with your artisans and the artisans of my lord, your father David. [15] Now, let my lord send the wheat, barley, oil, and wine to his servants as promised. [16] We will cut logs from Lebanon, as many as you need, and bring them to you as rafts by sea to Joppa. You can then take them up to Jerusalem.

Solomon's Workforce

[17] Solomon took a census of all the resident alien men in the land of Israel, after the census that his father David had conducted, and the total was 153,600. [18] Solomon made 70,000 of them porters, 80,000 stonecutters in the mountains, and 3,600 supervisors to make the people work.

Building the Temple

3 Then Solomon began to build the Lord's temple in Jerusalem on Mount Moriah where the Lord[F] had appeared to his father David, at the site David had prepared on the threshing floor of Ornan[G] the Jebusite. [2] He began to build on the second day of the second month in the fourth year of his reign. [3] These are Solomon's foundations[H] for building God's temple: the length[I] was ninety feet,[J] and the width thirty feet.[K] [4] The portico, which was across the front extending across the width of the temple, was thirty feet wide; its height

---

[A]2:8 = almug in 1Kg 10:11–12   [B]2:10 Lit 20,000 cors   [C]2:10 Lit 20,000 baths   [D]2:11 Lit Tyre said in writing   [E]2:13 Lit Huram my father   [F]3:1 LXX; Tg reads the angel of the Lord; MT reads he   [G]3:1 = Araunah in 2Sm 24:16–24   [H]3:3 Tg reads The measurements which Solomon decreed   [I]3:3 Lit length — cubits in the former measure —   [J]3:3 Lit 60 cubits   [K]3:3 Lit 20 cubits, also in vv. 4,8,11,13

2:7 Solomon asked Hiram for a craftsman who could work with precious metals as well as **bronze** and **iron**. In addition, he should be able to work with dyed textiles. The color **purple**, considered the color of royalty, was one of the chief exports of the Phoenicians. Solomon specified that this craftsman would be in charge of laborers who had been appointed by David. Solomon did not want Hiram to send a large labor force that might pose a military threat.

2:8–9 Not only did the Phoenicians have ready access to the wood that Solomon asked for, but they had more experience than the Israelites in working with it. Solomon sent Israelite **servants** to help with the labor and perhaps to assure the quality of the **logs**.

2:10 Tyre excelled in trade, but largely depended on other nations for food (Ac 12:20).

2:11–12 Hiram's praise of **the Lord** should not be taken to mean that he was a true follower of God.

2:13–14 Hiram proposed to send Solomon a man named **Huram-abi**. Son of an Israelite mother and a Tyrian father, Huram-abi was competent in all the skills specified by Solomon and presumably understood Israelite religion. Solomon was in ultimate control of the building project, and Huram-abi, the Phoenician, was next in charge. A number of Israelite supervisors oversaw the large force of non-Israelites and their foremen.

2:15 This verse mentions the price Solomon was paying for Hiram's help.

2:16 The Phoenicians were among the early pioneers of seafaring. They were willing to risk the dangerous but efficient method of shipping logs as **rafts** along the Mediterranean coast. Then they would be transported overland to **Jerusalem**.

3:1 Mount Moriah was the place God had designated after David saw an angel and a plague was averted (1Ch 21).

3:2 Solomon began the actual building of the temple early in the **fourth year of his reign**. This means he had not waited long after his coronation to start gathering building materials.

3:3–4 The outline of the **temple** was a rectangle, **thirty feet** by **ninety feet**. Its entryway was a thirty-foot tall portal that covered the entire width of the building. The most holy place, or holy of holies, was a thirty-foot cube that constituted the far end, leaving a room thirty feet wide and sixty feet long as the holy place. This seems small, considering the crowds that would visit the temple, but sacrifices would be offered in the courtyard outside the temple. Only priests would enter the holy place, and then only twice a day—in the morning and

was thirty feet;[A] he overlaid its inner surface with pure gold. [5] The larger room[B] he paneled with cypress wood, overlaid with fine gold, and decorated with palm trees and chains. [6] He adorned the temple with precious stones for beauty, and the gold was the gold of Parvaim. [7] He overlaid the temple — the beams, the thresholds, its walls and doors — with gold, and he carved cherubim on the walls.

The Most Holy Place

[8] Then he made the most holy place; its length corresponded to the width of the temple, 30 feet, and its width was 30 feet. He overlaid it with forty-five thousand pounds[C] of fine gold. [9] The weight of the nails was twenty ounces[D] of gold, and he overlaid the ceiling with gold.

[10] He made two cherubim of sculptured work, for the most holy place, and he overlaid them with gold. [11] The overall length of the wings of the cherubim was 30 feet: the wing of one was 7½ feet,[E] touching the wall of the room; its other wing was 7½ feet, touching the wing of the other cherub. [12] The wing of the other[F] cherub was 7½ feet, touching the wall of the room; its other wing was 7½ feet, reaching the wing of the other cherub. [13] The wingspan of these cherubim was 30 feet. They stood on their feet and faced the larger room.[G]

[14] He made the curtain of blue, purple, and crimson yarn and fine linen, and he wove cherubim into it.

The Bronze Pillars

[15] In front of the temple he made two pillars, each 27 feet[H] high. The capital on top of each was 7½ feet high. [16] He had made chainwork in the inner sanctuary and also put it on top of the pillars. He made a hundred pomegranates and fastened them into the chainwork. [17] Then he set up the pillars in front of the sanctuary,

one on the right and one on the left. He named the one on the right Jachin[I] and the one on the left Boaz.[J]

The Altar and Basins

4 He made a bronze altar 30 feet[K] long, 30 feet wide, and 15 feet[L] high.

[2] Then he made the cast metal basin,[M] 15 feet from brim to brim, perfectly round. It was 7½ feet[N] high and 45 feet[O] in circumference. [3] The likeness of oxen[P] was below it, completely encircling it, ten every half yard,[Q] completely surrounding the basin. The oxen were cast in two rows when the basin was cast. [4] It stood on twelve oxen, three facing north, three facing west, three facing south, and three facing east. The basin was on top of them and all their hindquarters were toward the center. [5] The basin was three inches[R] thick, and its rim was fashioned like the brim of a cup or a lily blossom. It could hold eleven thousand gallons.[S]

[6] He made ten basins for washing and he put five on the right and five on the left. The parts of the burnt offering were rinsed in them, but the basin was used by the priests for washing.

The Lampstands, Tables, and Courts

[7] He made the ten gold lampstands according to their specifications and put them in the sanctuary, five on the right and five on the left. [8] He made ten tables and placed them in the sanctuary, five on the right and five on the left. He also made a hundred gold bowls.

[9] He made the courtyard of the priests and the large court, and doors for the court. He overlaid the doors with bronze. [10] He put the basin on the right side, toward the southeast. [11] Then Huram[T] made the pots, the shovels, and the bowls.

[A]3:4 LXX, Syr; MT reads *120 cubits* [B]3:5 Lit *The house* [C]3:8 Lit *600 talents* [D]3:9 Lit *50 shekels* [E]3:11 Lit *five cubits*, also in vv. 12,15 [F]3:12 Syr, Vg; MT reads *the one* [G]3:13 Lit *the house* [H]3:15 Syr reads *18 cubits* (27 feet); Hb reads *35 cubits* (52 ½ feet) [I]3:17 = He Will Establish [J]3:17 = Strength Is in Him [K]4:1 Lit *20 cubits* [L]4:1 Lit *10 cubits*, also in v. 2 [M]4:2 Lit *sea* [N]4:2 Lit *five cubits* [O]4:2 Lit *30 cubits* [P]4:3 = gourds in 1Kg 7:24 [Q]4:3 Lit *10 per cubit* [R]4:5 Lit *a handbreadth* [S]4:5 Text emended; MT reads *3,000 baths* in 1Kg 7:26 [T]4:11 = Hiram in 1Kg 7:13,40,45

---

in the evening—and only the high priest could enter the most holy place, only once a year.

3:5 The decorations of the holy place included **palm trees**. The use of botanical motifs went back to the tabernacle (Ex 37:20).

3:6–7 The location of **Parvaim** is unknown. Suggestions include Farwa in Yemen or el-Farwein in northeast Arabia.

3:8–9 The **most holy place** was covered with **gold**. Gold is very heavy, but it is also soft. The easiest way to achieve the gold on the **ceiling** would have been to apply it to the ceiling beams before they were put in place. The golden **nails** must have had an iron core, or they could not have sustained hammer blows or held their place given gold's softness.

3:10–13 On the back wall of the most holy place were **two cherubim**, each with two

wings 7½ **feet** long, adding up to **30 feet** in width, the exact width of the wall.

3:14 The **curtain** became the highest expression of Phoenician art, with its fabric of many colors, including **blue, purple, and crimson**.

3:15–17 The design of the **temple** followed that of the tabernacle, though the temple was constructed from more permanent materials. Solomon did add two new structures—**two pillars** that were taller than the portico. Each of these pillars had a highly ornate capital, featuring a pomegranate motif. **Pomegranates** were a part of the decorative theme woven into the garments worn by priests (Ex 28:33), so the pomegranate decorations symbolized the priestly function connected to the temple. The names of the pillars, **Jachin** and **Boaz**, signified faith in God, meaning "he will establish" and "strength is in him."

4:1 The various fixtures that Solomon installed in the temple complex were outside the building in the courtyard. The most dominant item was the **bronze altar**, which shared its dimensions with the most holy place, **30 feet** by **30 feet**. Because of its height (**15 feet**), it had a number of steps that priests had to climb to perform sacrifices.

4:2–4 The water **basin** was half the width of the altar in diameter. Here is where priests washed their hands and feet before performing their duties (Ex 30:18–21). Since this large basin was 7½ **feet high**, there must have been steps all around it to give the priests access to the water.

4:5 The rim of the large basin was apparently flared.

4:6 The large **basin** was reserved for the priests, but **ten** smaller **basins** were

Completion of the Bronze Furnishings

So Huram finished doing the work that he was doing for King Solomon in God's temple: [12] two pillars; the bowls and the capitals on top of the two pillars; the two gratings for covering both bowls of the capitals that were on top of the pillars; [13] the four hundred pomegranates for the two gratings (two rows of pomegranates for each grating covering both capitals' bowls on top of the pillars). [14] He also made the water carts[A] and the basins on the water carts. [15] The one basin and the twelve oxen underneath it, [16] the pots, the shovels, the forks, and all their utensils — Huram-abi[B] made them for King Solomon for the LORD's temple. All these were made of polished bronze. [17] The king had them cast in clay molds in the Jordan Valley between Succoth and Zeredah. [18] Solomon made all these utensils in such great abundance that the weight of the bronze was not determined.

Completion of the Gold Furnishings

[19] Solomon also made all the equipment in God's temple: the gold altar; the tables on which to put the Bread of the Presence; [20] the lampstands and their lamps of pure gold to burn in front of the inner sanctuary according to specifications; [21] the flowers, lamps, and gold tongs — of purest gold; [22] the wick trimmers, sprinkling basins, ladles,[C] and firepans — of purest gold; and the entryway to the temple, its inner doors to the most holy place, and the doors of the temple sanctuary — of gold.

5 So all the work Solomon did for the LORD's temple was completed. Then Solomon brought the consecrated things of his father David — the silver, the gold, and all the utensils — and put them in the treasuries of God's temple.

Preparations for the Temple Dedication

[2] At that time Solomon assembled at Jerusalem the elders of Israel — all the tribal heads, the ancestral chiefs of the Israelites — in order to bring the ark of the covenant of the LORD up from the city of David, that is, Zion. [3] So all the men of Israel were assembled in the king's presence at the festival; this was in the seventh month.[D]

[4] All the elders of Israel came, and the Levites picked up the ark. [5] They brought up the ark, the tent of meeting, and the holy utensils that were in the tent. The priests and the Levites brought them up. [6] King Solomon and the entire congregation of Israel who had gathered around him were in front of the ark sacrificing sheep, goats, and cattle that could not be counted or numbered because they were so many. [7] The priests brought the ark of the LORD's covenant to its place, into the inner sanctuary of the temple, to the most holy place, beneath the wings of the cherubim. [8] And the cherubim spread their wings over the place of the ark so that the cherubim formed a cover above the ark and its poles. [9] The poles were so long that their ends were seen from the holy place[E] in front of the inner sanctuary, but they were not seen from outside; they are still there today. [10] Nothing was in the ark except the two tablets that Moses had put in it at Horeb,[F] where the LORD had made a covenant with the Israelites when they came out of Egypt.

[11] Now all the priests who were present had consecrated themselves regardless of their divisions. When the priests came out of the holy place, [12] the Levitical singers dressed in fine linen and carrying cymbals, harps, and lyres were standing east of the altar, and with them were 120 priests blowing trumpets. The Levitical singers were descendants of Asaph, Heman, and Jeduthun and their sons and relatives. [13] The trumpeters and singers joined together to praise and thank the LORD with one voice. They raised their voices, accompanied

---

[A] 4:14 Lit *the stands*   [B] 4:16 Lit *Huram my father*   [C] 4:22 Or *dishes,* or *spoons*; lit *palms*   [D] 5:3 = Tishri (September–October)   [E] 5:9 Some Hb mss, LXX; other Hb mss read *the ark*; 1Kg 8:8   [F] 5:10 = Sinai

---

provided in which to wash the sacrificial animals.

4:17–18 The technique for making items out of bronze involved making clay **molds**, then filling them with hot molten metal, and removing the clay after the metal had cooled. This process required a lot of water. It was easier to create these items next to the Jordan River and transport them up to Jerusalem than to try to make them on site where water was not abundant.

4:19–22 Most of the furnishings inside the temple were also made of gold. This **altar** was intended for the twice-daily burning of incense, not for animal sacrifice. Even though there was a curtain in front of the most holy place, there were also sets of golden doors in front of it and at the entrance to the actual temple building.

5:2 The temple would serve as the only place of worship for all twelve tribes (Dt 12:14). Therefore, it was appropriate for Solomon

to have representatives of all the tribes present for the dedication ceremony. The most important aspect of this celebration was moving the **ark of the covenant** from the tent where David had stored it into the temple.

5:3 Solomon arranged for the temple dedication to occur during the **festival** (probably the Festival of Shelters). All Israelite men were supposed to be in Jerusalem for this celebration, now that a central sanctuary had been built (Ex 23:17; Lv 23:39–43). A large crowd of worshipers would thus take ownership of the temple right from the start.

5:4–6 This procession of the **ark** covered only a small distance, since it was moved from one part of Jerusalem to another. Simultaneously, a much longer procession carried the entire tabernacle (**tent of meeting**) from Gibeon up to Jerusalem, where it became integrated into the temple structure. The ark was carried by the proper people, the

Levites, and in the proper manner, as they threaded two poles through grommets on the ark and then hoisted it on their shoulders.

5:7–9 Once the **ark** was in its proper place, it was situated in such a way that the **cherubim** (3:10–13) created the impression of guarding the ark with their wings. The poles were too long to be confined to the most holy place, so they jutted out into the temple. In the day the Chronicler wrote these words, the ark was no longer in the temple, but the poles were, presumably as a symbol of the missing ark.

5:10 By this time only the **two tablets** with the commandments were in the ark, but at one time it contained two other objects—a pot of manna and Aaron's rod that had sprouted miraculously (Heb 9:4).

5:12–13 The descendants of the three chief musicians—**Asaph, Heman, and Jeduthun**—who had been divided between the tent of the ark in Jerusalem and

by trumpets, cymbals, and musical instruments, in praise to the LORD:

For he is good;
his faithful love endures forever.

The temple, the LORD's temple, was filled with a cloud. [14] And because of the cloud, the priests were not able to continue ministering, for the glory of the LORD filled God's temple.

Solomon's Dedication of the Temple

6 Then Solomon said:
The LORD said he would dwell
in total darkness,
[2] but I have built an exalted temple
for you,
a place for your dwelling forever.

[3] Then the king turned and blessed the entire congregation of Israel while they were standing. [4] He said:

Blessed be the LORD God of Israel!
He spoke directly to my father David,
and he has fulfilled the promise
by his power.
He said,
[5] "Since the day I brought
my people Israel
out of the land of Egypt,
I have not chosen a city to build
a temple in
among any of the tribes of Israel,
so that my name would be there,
and I have not chosen a man
to be ruler over my people Israel.
[6] But I have chosen Jerusalem
so that my name will be there,
and I have chosen David
to be over my people Israel."

[7] My father David had his heart set
on building a temple for the name
of the LORD, the God of Israel.
[8] However, the LORD said
to my father David,
"Since it was your desire to build
a temple for my name,
you have done well to have this desire.
[9] Yet, you are not the one to build
the temple,
but your son, your own offspring,
will build the temple for my name."
[10] So the LORD has fulfilled
what he promised.
I have taken the place of my father David

and I sit on the throne of Israel, as the LORD promised.
I have built the temple for the name
of the LORD, the God of Israel.
[11] I have put the ark there,
where the LORD's covenant is
that he made with the Israelites.

Solomon's Prayer

[12] Then Solomon stood before the altar of the LORD in front of the entire congregation of Israel and spread out his hands. [13] For Solomon had made a bronze platform 7 ½ feet[A] long, 7 ½ feet wide, and 4 ½ feet[B] high and put it in the court. He stood on it, knelt down in front of the entire congregation of Israel, and spread out his hands toward heaven. [14] He said:

LORD God of Israel,
there is no God like you
in heaven or on earth,
who keeps his gracious covenant
with your servants who walk
before you
with all their heart.
[15] You have kept what you promised
to your servant, my father David.
You spoke directly to him,
and you fulfilled your promise
by your power,
as it is today.
[16] Therefore, LORD God of Israel,
keep what you promised
to your servant, my father David:
"You will never fail to have a man
to sit before me on the throne of Israel,
if only your sons take care to walk
in my Law
as you have walked before me."
[17] Now, LORD God of Israel,
please confirm
what you promised
to your servant David.

[18] But will God indeed live on earth
with humans?
Even heaven, the highest heaven,
cannot contain you,
much less this temple I have built.
[19] Listen[C] to your servant's prayer
and his petition,
LORD my God,
so that you may hear the cry
and the prayer
that your servant prays before you,

[A]6:13 Lit *five cubits*   [B]6:13 Lit *three cubits*   [C]6:19 Lit *Turn*

---

the tabernacle in Gibeon were now reunited. Together with their clans, they started to make music.
5:14 God approved of what the people had done, and he displayed his approval by revealing his **glory** through a cloud that **filled** the **temple**.

6:3–11 As the **entire congregation** rose to receive Solomon's blessings, he repeated the familiar story that led up to this point.
6:14–17 Solomon thanked God that the first half of what the Lord had **promised** had taken place: the temple had been built, and the son of David was on the throne. Then

he petitioned God to keep the second part of the promise: the perpetual dynasty of David's descendants as long as they remain faithful.
6:18–20 Solomon recognized that God was not confined to the **temple**.

²⁰ so that your eyes watch over
 this temple
day and night,
toward the place where you said
you would put your name;
and so that you may hear the prayer
your servant prays toward this place.

²¹ Hear the petitions of your servant
and your people Israel,
which they pray toward this place.
May you hear in your dwelling place
 in heaven.
May you hear and forgive.

²² If a man sins against his neighbor
and is forced to take an oath^A
and he comes to take an oath
before your altar in this temple,

²³ may you hear in heaven and act.
May you judge your servants,
condemning the wicked man
 by bringing
what he has done on his own head
and providing justice
 for the righteous
by rewarding him according to
 his righteousness.

²⁴ If your people Israel are defeated
 before an enemy,
because they have sinned against you,
and they return to you and praise
 your name,
and they pray and plead for mercy
before you in this temple,

²⁵ may you hear in heaven
and forgive the sin of your people Israel.
May you restore them to the land
you gave them and their ancestors.

²⁶ When the skies are shut and there is
 no rain
because they have sinned against you,
and they pray toward this place
and praise your name,
and they turn from their sins
because you are afflicting^B them,

²⁷ may you hear in heaven
and forgive the sin of your servants
and your people Israel,

so that you may teach them
 the good way
they should walk in.
May you send rain on your land
that you gave your people
 for an inheritance.

²⁸ When there is famine in the land,
when there is pestilence,
when there is blight or mildew, locust
 or grasshopper,
when their enemies besiege them
in the land and its cities,^{C,D}
when there is any plague or illness,

²⁹ every prayer or petition
that any person or that
 all your people Israel
 may have —
they each know their own affliction^E
 and suffering —
as they spread out their hands
 toward this temple,

³⁰ may you hear in heaven,
 your dwelling place,
and may you forgive
 and give to everyone^F
according to all their ways,
 since you know each heart,
for you alone know the human heart,

³¹ so that they may fear you
and walk in your ways
all the days they live on the land
you gave our ancestors.

³² Even for the foreigner who is not of
 your people Israel
but has come from a distant land
because of your great name
and your strong hand
 and outstretched arm:
when he comes and prays
 toward this temple,

³³ may you hear in heaven in your
 dwelling place,
and do all the foreigner asks you.
Then all the peoples of the earth
 will know your name,
to fear you as your people Israel do
and know that this temple I have built
bears your name.

---

^A6:22 Lit *and he lifts a curse against him to curse him*   ^B6:26 LXX, Vg; MT reads *answering* ; 1Kg 8:35   ^C6:28 Lit *land of its gates*   ^D6:28 Lit *if his* (Israel's) *enemies besiege him in the land of his gates* ; Jos 2:7; Jdg 16:2–3   ^E6:29 Lit *plague*   ^F6:30 Lit *give for the man*

6:21–39 There would be some needs for which the people would pray by directing themselves to the temple, and Solomon asked the Lord to listen and to respond.
6:22–23 The first scenario involved a man who had done wrong and who needed to clear his name or to bring about the end of his punishment by taking **an oath** in the temple. Solomon did not ask that a guilty person would be set free, but that justice would be done.

6:24–25 The second scenario involved the Israelites turning away from God and as a consequence being **defeated before an enemy**. Solomon asked that when the people came to their senses and prayed in the temple, God would **forgive** their sins and give them back the land they had lost.
6:26–27 The third scenario implied that a drought in the land had been caused by the Israelites' turning away from the Lord.

6:28–31 The fourth scenario included a number of disasters. Solomon petitioned God to listen to the prayers by people in the temple, but he stipulated that the prayers must be sincere because God knew **the human heart**.
6:32–33 In the fifth scenario, Solomon made his request on behalf of every **foreigner** who might come to the temple to seek God. His prayer was that these foreigners would find their petitions answered, so Yahweh's

³⁴ When your people go out
    to fight against their enemies,
    wherever you send them,
    and they pray to you
    in the direction of this city
    you have chosen
    and the temple that I have built
    for your name,
³⁵ may you hear their prayer and petition
    in heaven
    and uphold their cause.

³⁶ When they sin against you —
    for there is no one who does not sin —
    and you are angry with them
    and hand them over to the enemy,
    and their captors deport them
    to a distant or nearby country,
³⁷ and when they come to their senses
    in the land where they were deported
    and repent and petition you
    in their captors' land,
    saying, "We have sinned and done wrong;
    we have been wicked,"
³⁸ and when they return to you with all
    their mind and all their heart
    in the land of their captivity
    where they were taken captive,
    and when they pray in the direction
    of their land
    that you gave their ancestors,
    and the city you have chosen,
    and toward the temple I have built
    for your name,
³⁹ may you hear their prayer and petitions
    in heaven,
    your dwelling place,
    and uphold their cause.ᴬ
    May you forgive your people
    who sinned against you.

⁴⁰ Now, my God,
    please let your eyes be open
    and your ears attentive
    to the prayer of this place.
⁴¹ Now therefore:

    Arise, Lord God, come
    to your resting place,

you and your powerful ark.
    May your priests, Lord God, be clothed
    with salvation,
    and may your faithful people rejoice
    in goodness.
⁴² Lord God, do not reject
    your anointed one;ᴮ
    remember your servant David's acts of
    faithful love.

The Dedication Ceremonies

7 When Solomon finished praying, fire descended from heaven and consumed the burnt offering and the sacrifices, and the glory of the Lord filled the temple. ² The priests were not able to enter the Lord's temple because the glory of the Lord filled the temple of the Lord. ³ All the Israelites were watching when the fire descended and the glory of the Lord came on the temple. They bowed down on the pavement with their faces to the ground. They worshiped and praised the Lord:

For he is good,
    for his faithful love endures forever.

⁴ The king and all the people were offering sacrifices in the Lord's presence. ⁵ King Solomon offered a sacrifice of twenty-two thousand cattle and one hundred twenty thousand sheep and goats. In this manner the king and all the people dedicated God's temple. ⁶ The priests and the Levites were standing at their stations. The Levites had the musical instruments of the Lord, which King David had made to give thanks to the Lord — "for his faithful love endures forever" — when he offered praise with them. Across from the Levites, the priests were blowing trumpets, and all the people were standing. ⁷ Since the bronze altar that Solomon had made could not accommodate the burnt offering, the grain offering, and the fat of the fellowship offerings, Solomon first consecrated the middle of the courtyard that was in front of the Lord's temple and then offered the burnt offerings and the fat of the fellowship offerings there.

⁸ So Solomon and all Israel with him — a very great assembly, from the entrance to Hamathᶜ to the Brook of Egypt — observed the

---

ᴬ6:39 Lit and do their judgment, or justice   ᴮ6:42 Some Hb mss, LXX; other Hb mss read ones; Ps 132:10   ᶜ7:8 Or from Lebo-hamath

---

name would be glorified among those who lived far away.
6:34–35 In the sixth scenario, Solomon asked God for strength in battle.
6:36–39 The seventh and last scenario concerned the exile: The nation might be deported into a **distant . . . country**. This possibility had already been mentioned by Moses (Dt 28:33). Solomon asked that once the people repented and started to pray in the direction of the temple that the Lord would **forgive** them and bring them back to their own land.

7:1–2 Fire had **descended** from heaven once before on an offering at precisely the same spot where the temple stood—on David's sacrifice on the threshing floor of Ornan (1Ch 21:25). This dramatic occurrence showed that God approved of what Solomon and the people had done. The **glory of the Lord** was a cloud and a light so bright that no one could stand in its presence (Ezk 1:28; 10:4).
7:4–6 The sacrifice of this many animals required rigorous organization. The **priests** had specific tasks at their designated area and the offerings were made virtually

assembly-line style, while the musicians took turns providing background music, just as David had envisioned.
7:7 Sacrifices were supposed to be made on the altar of the temple, but it was not large enough to accommodate them all. Solomon **consecrated** the **courtyard** for this occasion, and the animals were sacrificed right there on the ground.
7:8–9 Since the dedication of the temple also coincided with the **festival** (Festival of Shelters), many people were in Jerusalem for the celebration of this feast. **Hamath** is

festival at that time for seven days. ⁹ On the eighth day^A they held a solemn assembly, for the dedication of the altar lasted seven days and the festival seven days. ¹⁰ On the twenty-third day of the seventh month he sent the people home,^B rejoicing and with happy hearts for the goodness the LORD had done for David, for Solomon, and for his people Israel.

¹¹ So Solomon finished the LORD's temple and the royal palace. Everything that had entered Solomon's heart to do for the LORD's temple and for his own palace succeeded.

The LORD's Response

¹² Then the LORD appeared to Solomon at night and said to him:

I have heard your prayer and have chosen this place for myself as a temple of sacrifice. ¹³ If I shut the sky so there is no rain, or if I command the grasshopper to consume the land, or if I send pestilence on my people, ¹⁴ and my people, who bear my name, humble themselves, pray and seek my face, and turn from their evil ways, then I will hear from heaven, forgive their sin, and heal their land. ¹⁵ My eyes will now be open and my ears attentive to prayer from this place. ¹⁶ And I have now chosen and consecrated this temple so that my name may be there forever; my eyes and my heart will be there at all times.

¹⁷ As for you, if you walk before me as your father David walked, doing everything I have commanded you, and if you keep my statutes and ordinances, ¹⁸ I will establish your royal throne, as I promised your father David: You will never fail to have a man ruling in Israel.

¹⁹ However, if you turn away and abandon my statutes and my commands that I have set before you and if you go and serve other gods and bow in worship to them, ²⁰ then I will uproot Israel from the soil that I gave them, and this temple that I have sanctified for my name I will banish from my presence; I will make it an object of scorn and ridicule among all the peoples. ²¹ As for this temple, which was exalted, everyone who passes by will be appalled and will say, "Why did the LORD do this to this land and this temple?" ²² Then they will say, "Because they abandoned the LORD God of their ancestors who brought them out of the land of Egypt. They clung to other gods and bowed in worship to them and served them. Because of this, he brought all this ruin on them."

Solomon's Later Building Projects

8 At the end of twenty years during which Solomon had built the LORD's temple and his own palace — ² Solomon had rebuilt the cities Hiram^C gave him and settled Israelites there — ³ Solomon went to Hamath-zobah and seized it. ⁴ He built Tadmor in the wilderness along with all the storage cities that he built in Hamath. ⁵ He built Upper Beth-horon and Lower Beth-horon — fortified cities with walls, gates, and bars — ⁶ Baalath, all the storage cities that belonged to Solomon, all the chariot cities, the cavalry cities, and everything Solomon desired to build in Jerusalem, Lebanon, or anywhere else in the land of his dominion.

⁷ As for all the peoples who remained of the Hethites, Amorites, Perizzites, Hivites, and

---

^A **7:9** = the day after the festival, or the 15th day   ^B **7:10** Lit *people to their tents*   ^C **8:2** = the king of Tyre

in the far north and the **Brook of Egypt** is the southern border of Israel.
7:10 Finally after three weeks, Solomon declared the festivities over and sent everyone **home**. This expression, literally "to their tents," does not mean that most Israelites were still living in tents rather than houses. This was a familiar figure of speech (10:16). In addition, during the celebration of the Festival of Shelters, many people put up temporary shelters, or booths, to represent Israel's period of wandering in the wilderness.
7:11 The Chronicler conflates the completion of the **temple** and of Solomon's **royal palace** into one brief sentence. The total time for building the temple, followed by the palace, was twenty years (1Kg 6:38–7:1).
7:12 Ten years earlier, Solomon had begun his reign by visiting the tabernacle at Gibeon (1:7). Just as the Lord had done at Gibeon, he **appeared to Solomon at night**. This time God confirmed everything for which Solomon had prayed.
7:13–16 This promise presupposes a very specific context. It was given to God's **people, who bear** his **name**, and it is a part of

God's answer to Solomon's prayer. It refers to times when the Israelites have become faithless to God and are enduring the consequences, whether it was a famine, an invasion, or even the deportation to another country. To be **humble . . . pray . . . seek** God, and **turn** from sin are four aspects of one attitude: repentance. If Israel would repent, he would **forgive** them and **heal** their spiritual relationship with him associated with the promised **land**.
8:1 The building of the **temple** took seven years, and Solomon's palace took another thirteen, making a total of **twenty years** (see 1Kg 6:38–7:1).
8:2 A partial payment from Solomon to **Hiram** for the building materials he provided consisted of twenty **cities** (villages by modern standards) to add to Hiram's kingdom (1Kg 9:10–14). These locations would have been of use to Hiram only if they were affluent enough to pay taxes or could serve as military defenses. When Hiram went to visit his new acquisitions, he discovered they were worthless little hamlets, so he gave them back to the king of Judah. Solomon was willing to invest

in these locations by having them **rebuilt** and resettled.
8:3 In contrast to his father David, Solomon undertook few military campaigns. One exception was his seizure of **Hamath-zobah**. This city was on the edge of Palestine, a natural destination for caravans crossing the desert between Mesopotamia and Lebanon.
8:4 Now all Solomon needed to do to take control of the trade across the Aramean Desert was to claim an oasis located halfway along the caravan route. **Tadmor** was such a location. By establishing it along with Hamath, Solomon dominated all the trade to and from Mesopotamia.
8:5–6 Solomon continued with his nationwide building program by fortifying the route leading up to Jerusalem. The cities of **Lower** and **Upper Beth-horon** were garrisons intended to keep invaders from reaching the capital city.
8:7–9 The last of the Canaanites now made up Solomon's slave force (**forced labor**) for his construction projects. **Israelites** were not supposed to become slaves. However, they did have to work for Solomon, and his requirements grew increasingly strenuous.

SOLOMON'S TEMPLE, EXTERIOR VIEW (LOOKING WEST)

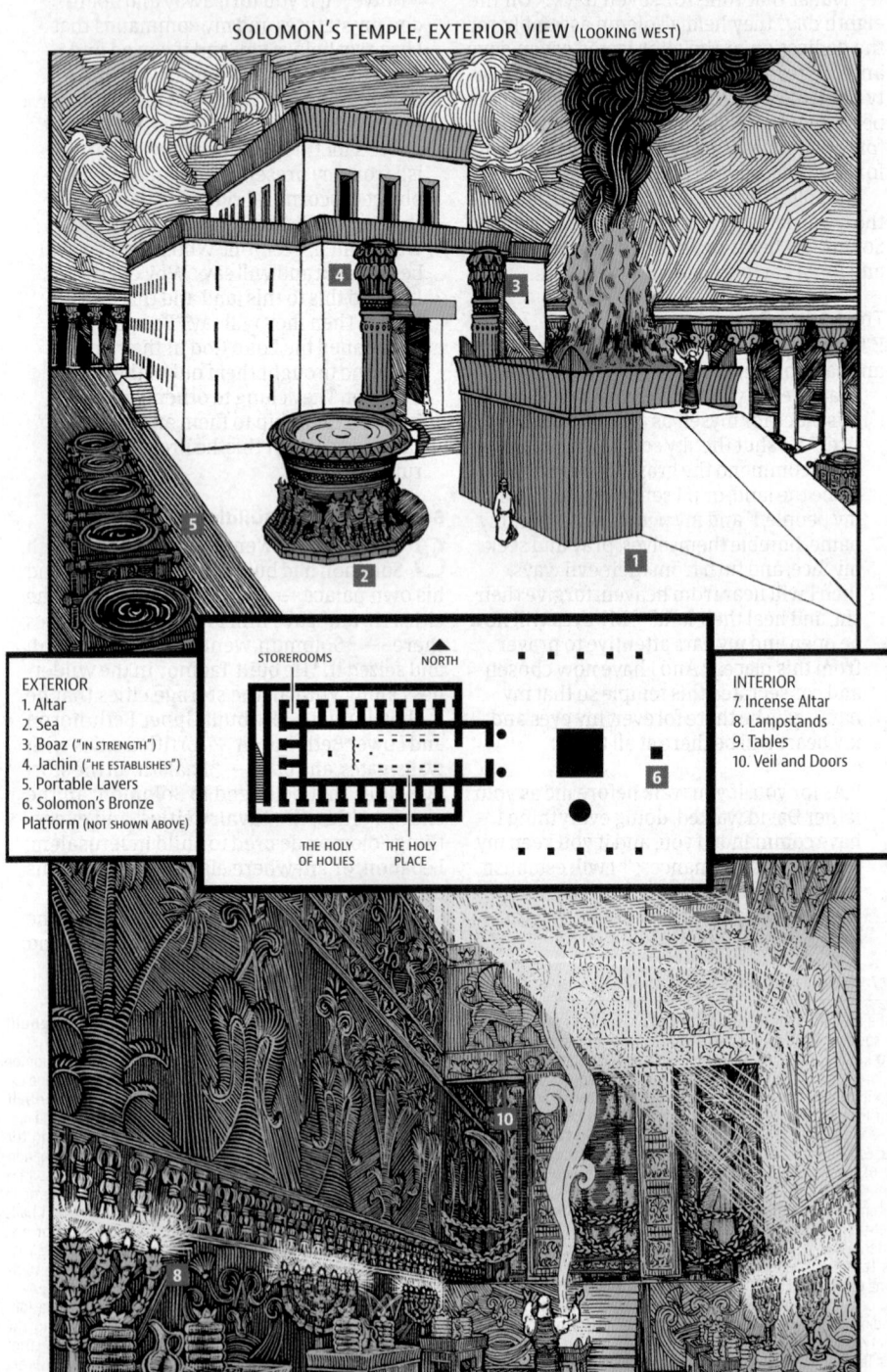

EXTERIOR
1. Altar
2. Sea
3. Boaz ("IN STRENGTH")
4. Jachin ("HE ESTABLISHES")
5. Portable Lavers
6. Solomon's Bronze
Platform (NOT SHOWN ABOVE)

STOREROOMS

NORTH

THE HOLY
OF HOLIES

THE HOLY
PLACE

INTERIOR
7. Incense Altar
8. Lampstands
9. Tables
10. Veil and Doors

SOLOMON'S TEMPLE, INTERIOR VIEW (LOOKING WEST)

Jebusites, who were not from Israel — [8] their descendants who remained in the land after them, those the Israelites had not completely destroyed — Solomon imposed forced labor on them; it is this way today. [9] But Solomon did not consign the Israelites to be slaves for his work; they were soldiers, commanders of his captains, and commanders of his chariots and his cavalry. [10] These were King Solomon's deputies: 250 who supervised the people.

[11] Solomon brought the daughter of Pharaoh from the city of David to the house he had built for her, for he said, "My wife must not live in the house^ of King David of Israel because the places the ark of the LORD has come into are holy."

Public Worship Established at the Temple

[12] At that time Solomon offered burnt offerings to the LORD on the LORD's altar he had made in front of the portico. [13] He followed the daily requirement for offerings according to the commandment of Moses for Sabbaths, New Moons, and the three annual appointed festivals: the Festival of Unleavened Bread, the Festival of Weeks, and the Festival of Shelters. [14] According to the ordinances of his father David, he appointed the divisions of the priests over their service, of the Levites over their responsibilities to offer praise and to minister before the priests following the daily requirement, and of the gatekeepers by their divisions with respect to each temple gate, for this had been the command of David, the man of God. [15] They did not turn aside from the king's command regarding the priests and the Levites concerning any matter or concerning the treasuries. [16] All of Solomon's work was carried out from the day the foundation was laid for the LORD's temple until it was finished. So the LORD's temple was completed.

Solomon's Fleet

[17] At that time Solomon went to Ezion-geber and to Eloth on the seashore in the land of Edom. [18] So Hiram^B sent ships to him by his servants along with crews of experienced seamen. They went with Solomon's servants to Ophir, took from there seventeen tons^C of gold, and delivered it to King Solomon.

The Queen of Sheba

9 The queen of Sheba heard of Solomon's fame, so she came to test Solomon with difficult questions at Jerusalem with a very large entourage, with camels bearing spices, gold in abundance, and precious stones. She came to Solomon and spoke with him about everything that was on her mind. [2] So Solomon answered all her questions; nothing was too difficult for Solomon to explain to her. [3] When the queen of Sheba observed Solomon's wisdom, the palace he had built, [4] the food at his table, his servants' residence, his attendants' service and their attire, his cupbearers and their attire, and the burnt offerings he offered at the LORD's temple, it took her breath away.

[5] She said to the king, "The report I heard in my own country about your words and about your wisdom is true. [6] But I didn't believe their reports until I came and saw with my own eyes. Indeed, I was not even told half of your great wisdom! You far exceed the report I heard. [7] How happy are your men.^D How happy are these servants of yours, who always stand in your presence hearing your wisdom. [8] Blessed be the LORD your God! He delighted in you and put you on his throne as king for the LORD your God. Because your God loved Israel enough to establish them forever, he has set you over them as king to carry out justice and righteousness."

[9] Then she gave the king four and a half tons^E of gold, a great quantity of spices, and precious stones. There never were such spices as those the queen of Sheba gave to King Solomon. [10] In addition, Hiram's servants and Solomon's servants who brought gold from

---

^A 8:11 LXX reads *city*   ^B 8:18 Lit *Huram*   ^C 8:18 Lit *450 talents*   ^D 9:7 LXX, Old Lat read *wives*; 1Kg 10:8   ^E 9:9 Lit *120 talents*

8:10 Israelites served as supervisors of the labor force.
8:11 In contrast to the record of 1 Kings, the Chronicler does not dwell on Solomon's shortcomings or his many marriages. He does mention Solomon's **wife** who was the **daughter of Pharaoh**, though only to emphasize that, out of respect for the holiness of the **ark** and the facilities that David had erected, Solomon moved his Egyptian wife to quarters outside Jerusalem. In 1Kg 11:6 we learn that Solomon even went so far as to participate in pagan sacrifices in order to please his wives.
8:17–18 The cities of **Ezion-geber** and **Eloth** were located at the southernmost end of Israel on the shore of the Red Sea. These locations made it possible for Solomon to carry on trade with the people on the Arabian Peninsula and possibly beyond. But Solomon had no ships, and the Israelites knew nothing

about sailing. On the other hand, King **Hiram** was the ruler of a seafaring people who were busy carrying on trade throughout the Mediterranean Sea, but if the Phoenicians wanted to establish trade relations with Arabia, they had to sail all the way through the Mediterranean down the west coast of Africa, around the Cape of Good Hope and back up north all the way along the east coast of Africa to Arabia. In short, Solomon had convenient harbors but no ships, while Hiram had ships but no convenient harbor. They were able to work together and haul in huge amounts of **gold**. The location of **Ophir** is unknown. Solomon considered the gold his personal property, so it was stored in his palace (9:15). The people eventually revolted against the king's practices when they declared, "What portion do we have in David? We have no inheritance in the son of Jesse" (10:16). The hard labor imposed by Solomon might have

been more acceptable if it had resulted in nationwide economic benefits.
9:1 Sheba is identical with the ancient kingdom of Saba, located in what is today Yemen at the southern tip of the Arabian Peninsula. This was a thriving kingdom, strategically located between the more distant parts of Asia and the Middle East, thus able to profit from the trade between the two areas. The **queen** of Sheba had heard many stories about this king who was noted for his wealth and wisdom. She made this long, arduous journey to meet Solomon face to face, to learn his secrets of statecraft, and presumably to be on the right side of any potential conflict. She attempted to impress this king who had more wealth than he could ever use by bringing him even more riches.
9:10–11 Algum, more commonly called almug, was one of several types of sandalwood

Ophir also brought algum wood and precious stones. [11] The king made the algum wood into walkways for the LORD's temple and for the king's palace and into lyres and harps for the singers. Never before had anything like them been seen in the land of Judah.

[12] King Solomon gave the queen of Sheba her every desire, whatever she asked — far more than she had brought the king. Then she, along with her servants, returned to her own country.

Solomon's Wealth

[13] The weight of gold that came to Solomon annually was twenty-five tons,[A] [14] besides what was brought by the merchants and traders. All the Arabian kings and governors of the land also brought gold and silver to Solomon.

[15] King Solomon made two hundred large shields of hammered gold; 15 pounds[B] of hammered gold went into each shield. [16] He made three hundred small shields of hammered gold; 7 ½ pounds[C] of gold went into each shield. The king put them in the House of the Forest of Lebanon.

[17] The king also made a large ivory throne and overlaid it with pure gold. [18] The throne had six steps; there was a footstool covered in gold for the throne, armrests on either side of the seat, and two lions standing beside the armrests. [19] Twelve lions were standing there on the six steps, one at each end. Nothing like it had ever been made in any other kingdom.

[20] All of King Solomon's drinking cups were gold, and all the utensils of the House of the Forest of Lebanon were pure gold. There was no silver, since it was considered as nothing in Solomon's time, [21] for the king's ships kept going to Tarshish with Hiram's servants, and once every three years the ships of Tarshish would arrive bearing gold, silver, ivory, apes, and peacocks.[D]

[22] King Solomon surpassed all the kings of the world in riches and wisdom. [23] All the kings of the world wanted an audience with Solomon to hear the wisdom God had put in his heart. [24] Each of them would bring his own gift — items[E] of silver and gold, clothing, weapons,[F,G] spices, and horses and mules — as an annual tribute.

[25] Solomon had four thousand stalls for horses and chariots, and twelve thousand horsemen. He stationed them in the chariot cities and with the king in Jerusalem. [26] He ruled over all the kings from the Euphrates River to the land of the Philistines and as far as the border of Egypt. [27] The king made silver as common in Jerusalem as stones, and he made cedar as abundant as sycamore in the Judean foothills. [28] They were bringing horses for Solomon from Egypt and from all the countries.

Solomon's Death

[29] The remaining events of Solomon's reign, from beginning to end, are written in the Events of the Prophet Nathan, the Prophecy of Ahijah the Shilonite, and the Visions of the Seer Iddo concerning Jeroboam son of Nebat. [30] Solomon reigned in Jerusalem over all Israel for forty years. [31] Solomon rested with his ancestors and was buried in the city of his father David. His son Rehoboam became king in his place.

The Kingdom Divided

10 Then Rehoboam went to Shechem, for all Israel had gone to Shechem to make him king. [2] When Jeroboam son of Nebat heard about it — for he was in Egypt where he had fled from King Solomon's presence — Jeroboam returned from Egypt. [3] So they summoned him. Then Jeroboam and all Israel came and spoke to Rehoboam: [4] "Your father made our yoke harsh. Therefore, lighten your father's harsh service and the heavy yoke he put on us, and we will serve you."

[A] 9:13 Lit 666 talents   [B] 9:15 Lit 600 (shekels)   [C] 9:16 Lit 300 (shekels)   [D] 9:21 Or baboons   [E] 9:24 Or vessels, or weapons
[F] 9:24 LXX reads resin   [G] 9:24 Or fragrant balsam

---

known for its fragrance. Solomon incorporated this wood into **walkways** for the temple and into musical instruments.

9:13–16 Solomon hoarded the accumulating amount of **gold** and devised an ingenious method of storing it by molding it into **shields** that covered the walls of his palace. People could admire it, but he had quick access to it if he needed it.

9:17–21 The Chronicler sees Solomon's wealth and his splendor as evidence of God's blessing (1:12). His acquisitions included ornate furniture and exotic animals, most coming to him as profit from his partnership with Hiram.

9:22–24 Some of Solomon's **wisdom** has been preserved for us in the books of Proverbs and Ecclesiastes.

9:29–31 If we compare Solomon's final notice with David's, we see that Solomon's obituary carries neither praise nor condemnation.

10:1 Throughout the rest of 2 Chronicles some of the kings have similar names. Some of these kings appear under different names in 1 and 2 Kings. So whenever a king is mentioned for the first time from this point on, we will give a quick summary of his identity.

Rehoboam: First king of Judah; son of Solomon; the king under whom the united kingdom split into the north (Israel) and the south (Judah). There seemed to be little question about Rehoboam's readiness for the kingship at forty-one years old, so **all Israel** went to **Shechem** for his coronation.

10:2 Jeroboam: First king of Israel (where Israel refers only to the northern kingdom); leader in the revolt of the ten northern tribes against Rehoboam; instituted official idol worship in the north. Jeroboam, from the tribe of Ephraim, at one time had been the leader of Solomon's labor force in Jerusalem (1Kg 11:26–40). One day when he was outside the city walls, the prophet Ahijah approached him and told him that he would be king over the ten northern tribes (1Kg 11:29). Realizing that he had been officially designated as a future traitor and that Solomon could execute him, Jeroboam fled to Egypt and remained there for the rest of Solomon's reign. As soon as Jeroboam heard about the impending coronation of Rehoboam, he made his way back from exile in Egypt to join the assembly.

10:3–4 Jeroboam's talent for leadership was known to the people, who immediately appointed him to be their spokesman and to convey to **Rehoboam** their desire for a reduction in forced labor.

⁵ Rehoboam replied, "Return to me in three days." So the people left.

⁶ Then King Rehoboam consulted with the elders who had attended his father Solomon when he was alive, asking, "How do you advise me to respond to this people?"

⁷ They replied, "If you will be kind to this people and please them by speaking kind words to them, they will be your servants forever."

⁸ But he rejected the advice of the elders who had advised him, and he consulted with the young men who had grown up with him, the ones attending him. ⁹ He asked them, "What message do you advise we send back to this people who said to me, 'Lighten the yoke your father put on us'?"

¹⁰ Then the young men who had grown up with him told him, "This is what you should say to the people who said to you, 'Your father made our yoke heavy, but you, make it lighter on us!' This is what you should say to them: 'My little finger is thicker than my father's waist! ¹¹ Now therefore, my father burdened you with a heavy yoke, but I will add to your yoke; my father disciplined you with whips, but I, with barbed whips.'"ᴬ

¹² So Jeroboam and all the people came to Rehoboam on the third day, just as the king had ordered, saying, "Return to me on the third day." ¹³ Then the king answered them harshly. King Rehoboam rejected the elders' advice ¹⁴ and spoke to them according to the young men's advice, saying, "My father made your yoke heavy,ᴮ but I will add to it; my father disciplined you with whips, but I, with barbed whips."

¹⁵ The king did not listen to the people because the turn of events came from God, in order that the LORD might carry out his word that he had spoken through Ahijah the Shilonite to Jeroboam son of Nebat.

¹⁶ When all Israel sawᶜ that the king had not listened to them, the people answered the king:

What portion do we have in David?
We have no inheritance in the son of Jesse.

Israel, each to your tent;
David, look after your own house now!
So all Israel went to their tents. ¹⁷ But as for the Israelites living in the cities of Judah, Rehoboam reigned over them.

¹⁸ Then King Rehoboam sent Hadoram,ᴰ who was in charge of the forced labor, but the Israelites stoned him to death. However, King Rehoboam managed to get into his chariot to flee to Jerusalem. ¹⁹ Israel is in rebellion against the house of David until today.

Rehoboam in Jerusalem

11 When Rehoboam arrived in Jerusalem, he mobilized the house of Judah and Benjamin — one hundred eighty thousand fit young soldiers — to fight against Israel to restore the reign to Rehoboam. ² But the word of the LORD came to Shemaiah, the man of God: ³ "Say to Rehoboam son of Solomon, king of Judah, to all Israel in Judah and Benjamin, and to the rest of the people, ⁴ 'This is what the LORD says: You are not to march up and fight against your brothers. Each of you return home, for this incident has come from me.'"

So they listened to what the LORD said and turned back from going against Jeroboam.

Judah's King Rehoboam

⁵ Rehoboam stayed in Jerusalem, and he fortified citiesᴱ in Judah. ⁶ He built up Bethlehem, Etam, Tekoa, ⁷ Beth-zur, Soco, Adullam, ⁸ Gath, Mareshah, Ziph, ⁹ Adoraim, Lachish, Azekah, ¹⁰ Zorah, Aijalon, and Hebron, which are fortified cities in Judah and in Benjamin. ¹¹ He strengthened their fortifications and put

---

10:5–7 Rehoboam was unable to decide how to respond to this simple request. First he went to the older counselors, those who had served alongside Solomon, and asked them what he should do.

10:8–10 Rehoboam did not like the advice of the **elders**, so he consulted his peers, who are identified as **young men** (a comparative term, since they were roughly the same age as Rehoboam—in their forties). These younger men coached their befuddled ruler into repeating an absurd saying that would have alienated even a person who had meant to support Rehoboam.

10:11 The CSB correctly translates the word that is literally "scorpions" as **barbed whips**—a common instrument of discipline in the ancient Near East.

10:16 When the people (**all Israel**) realized that Rehoboam was not willing to listen to their reasonable request, they turned their backs on him and went home.

10:17 Rehoboam did not lose all his territory, but his kingdom was restricted to the tribe of **Judah**. Technically, this region also encompassed the area of Simeon, but this tribe had been assimilated into Judah over the centuries (though not entirely, see 1Ch 4:41). The tribe of Benjamin, once the fiercest opponent of the house of David, was now also fully integrated into Judah.

10:18–19 Still at Shechem, Rehoboam thought he could force the rebellious people to submit to him. He assigned **Hadoram**, his minister of labor, to call the Israelites back to their duty. The people of the northern tribes expressed their dissatisfaction with rocks and killed their would-be supervisor. Rehoboam managed to escape, but the kingdom was split for good.

11:2–4 Since God had brought about the split of the kingdom as a punishment, he informed **Rehoboam** through a prophet named **Shemaiah** that the king should give

up any thought of invading and restoring the northern tribes. This was not the time for a civil war; the people of **Judah and Benjamin** needed to go home and settle in under the new conditions.

11:5–12 Instead of carrying out an invasion, **Rehoboam** assumed a defensive posture and **fortified cities** throughout the territory of **Judah and Benjamin**. Solomon had created large fortifications all over his kingdom, but many of those installations now belonged to the northern kingdom. Rehoboam needed to establish a smaller circle around Jerusalem. Cities that previously had not been that important, such as **Bethlehem**, now became crucial defensive posts. Not only did Rehoboam see to it that they were physically reinforced, but also that each of those places had a leader, a supply of **food, oil, and wine**, and **large shields and spears**.

leaders in them with supplies of food, oil, and wine. ¹² He also put large shields and spears in each and every city to make them very strong. So Judah and Benjamin were his.

¹³ The priests and Levites from all their regions throughout Israel took their stand with Rehoboam, ¹⁴ for the Levites left their pasturelands and their possessions and went to Judah and Jerusalem, because Jeroboam and his sons refused to let them serve as priests of the LORD. ¹⁵ Jeroboam appointed his own priests for the high places, the goat-demons, and the golden calves he had made. ¹⁶ Those from every tribe of Israel who had determined in their hearts to seek the LORD their God followed the Levites to Jerusalem to sacrifice to the LORD, the God of their ancestors. ¹⁷ So they strengthened the kingdom of Judah and supported Rehoboam son of Solomon for three years, because they walked in the ways of David and Solomon for three years.

¹⁸ Rehoboam married Mahalath, daughter of David's son Jerimoth and of Abihail daughter of Jesse's son Eliab. ¹⁹ She bore sons to him: Jeush, Shemariah, and Zaham. ²⁰ After her, he married Maacah daughterᴬ of Absalom. She bore Abijah, Attai, Ziza, and Shelomith to him. ²¹ Rehoboam loved Maacah daughter of Absalom more than all his wives and concubines. He acquired eighteen wives and sixty concubines and was the father of twenty-eight sons and sixty daughters.

²² Rehoboam appointed Abijah son of Maacah as chief, leader among his brothers, intending to make him king. ²³ Rehoboam also showed discernment by dispersing some of his sons to all the regions of Judah and Benjamin and to all the fortified cities. He gave them plenty of provisions and sought many wives for them.

Shishak's Invasion

12 When Rehoboam had established his sovereignty and royal power, he abandoned the law of the LORD — he and all Israel with him. ² Because they were unfaithful to the LORD, in the fifth year of King Rehoboam, King Shishak of Egypt went to war against Jerusalem ³ with 1,200 chariots, 60,000 cavalrymen, and countless people who came with him from Egypt — Libyans, Sukkiim, and Cushites. ⁴ He captured the fortified cities of Judah and came as far as Jerusalem.

⁵ Then the prophet Shemaiah went to Rehoboam and the leaders of Judah who were gathered at Jerusalem because of Shishak. He said to them, "This is what the LORD says: You have abandoned me; therefore, I have abandoned you to Shishak."

⁶ So the leaders of Israel and the king humbled themselves and said, "The LORD is righteous."

⁷ When the LORD saw that they had humbled themselves, the LORD's message came to Shemaiah: "They have humbled themselves; I will not destroy them but will grant them a little deliverance. My wrath will not be poured out on Jerusalem through Shishak. ⁸ However, they will become his servants so that they may recognize the difference between serving me and serving the kingdoms of other lands."

⁹ So King Shishak of Egypt went to war against Jerusalem. He seized the treasuries of the LORD's temple and the treasuries of the royal palace. He took everything. He took the gold shields that Solomon had made. ¹⁰ King Rehoboam made bronze shields to replace them and committed them into the care of the captains of the guardsᴮ who protected the entrance to the king's palace. ¹¹ Whenever the king entered the LORD's temple, the guards would

---

ᴬ**11:20** Possibly *granddaughter*, also in v. 21; 2Ch 13:2   ᴮ**12:10** Lit *the runners*

11:13–16 Meanwhile, **Jeroboam** in the north was faced with a serious problem of his own. The mindset of the people over whom he was supposed to rule made it almost impossible for him to be an effective king. He had broken away from Rehoboam and Jerusalem, but the temple was in **Jerusalem**, and the **priests** and **Levites** were still loyal to the temple. Jeroboam did not permit priests of the Jerusalem-bound religion to officiate in his new territory. Under Jeroboam's direction, the new kingdom of the north was rooted in idolatry right from the beginning. Jeroboam replaced the worship of God with the worship of **goat-demons** and two **golden calves**, one in the northern section of his kingdom at Dan, and the other in the south close to the border with Judah at Bethel. He also installed a new priesthood of those who were willing to serve these idols rather than the Lord.
11:17 During the first **three years**, both kingdoms looked inward to strengthen themselves. The south rallied around the temple and the service of the Lord, while

the north focused on the cult of idolatry instigated by Jeroboam.
11:18–21 Rehoboam had **eighteen wives**, many of them from within his wider circle of blood relations. **Mahalath** was his half cousin, **Abihail** was his great aunt, unless some intervening generations have not been mentioned. His favorite wife, **Maacah** (also called Micaiah), was probably Absalom's granddaughter by his son or son-in-law Uriel (13:2). She would become influential in leading the people into idolatry.
11:22–23 Having spent the first forty-one years of his life in limbo, Rehoboam made sure that his **sons** had a meaningful purpose. He put them in charge of many of the newly **fortified cities** and provided them with numerous **wives**.
12:1 All Israel in this context refers to residents of the kingdom of Judah, since the northern kingdom had already adopted Jeroboam's idolatry as the new state religion.
12:2–3 No sooner had Rehoboam fallen away into idolatry than **Shishak**, the new pharaoh of **Egypt**, mobilized his forces for

an invasion of Judah (as well as Israel, as documented in his own records). Now there was a new family of rulers in Egypt, headed up by Shishak, known to history as Shoshenq I (or Sheshonk). Shishak was a Libyan. He was able to take control of the Egyptians as well as the adjoining people such as **Libyans, Sukkiim** [a nation related to the Libyans], **and Cushites**.
12:5–6 When **the prophet Shemaiah** (11:2) explained to King **Rehoboam** that his sin was the cause of this invasion, he and the people repented.
12:9 Shishak's army arrived in **Jerusalem** and helped themselves to all the treasures that David and Solomon had collected. The **gold shields**, so conveniently stored on the walls of Solomon's palace, became easy objects for the Egyptian army to carry off (see note at 9:13–16). Yet just as Shemaiah had predicted, Shishak did not destroy Jerusalem.
12:10–11 Having lost the gold shields, Rehoboam replaced them with **bronze shields**.

carry the shields and take them back to the armory.^A ^12 When Rehoboam humbled himself, the LORD's anger turned away from him, and he did not destroy him completely. Besides that, conditions were good in Judah.

Rehoboam's Last Days

^13 King Rehoboam established his royal power in Jerusalem. Rehoboam was forty-one years old when he became king, and he reigned seventeen years in Jerusalem, the city the LORD had chosen from all the tribes of Israel to put his name. Rehoboam's mother's name was Naamah the Ammonite. ^14 Rehoboam did what was evil, because he did not determine in his heart to seek the LORD.

^15 The events of Rehoboam's reign, from beginning to end, are written in the Events of the Prophet Shemaiah and of the Seer Iddo concerning genealogies. There was war between Rehoboam and Jeroboam throughout their reigns. ^16 Rehoboam rested with his ancestors and was buried in the city of David. His son Abijah^B became king in his place.

Judah's King Abijah

13 In the eighteenth year of Israel's King Jeroboam, Abijah^B became king over Judah, ^2 and he reigned three years in Jerusalem. His mother's name was Micaiah^C daughter of Uriel; she was from Gibeah.

There was war between Abijah and Jeroboam. ^3 Abijah set his army of warriors in order with four hundred thousand fit young men. Jeroboam arranged his mighty army of eight hundred thousand fit young men in battle formation against him. ^4 Then Abijah stood on Mount Zemaraim, which is in the hill country of Ephraim, and said, "Jeroboam and all Israel, hear me. ^5 Don't you know that the LORD God of Israel gave the kingship over Israel to David and his descendants forever by a covenant of salt? ^6 But Jeroboam son of Nebat, a servant of Solomon son of David, rose up and rebelled

against his lord. ^7 Then worthless and wicked men gathered around him to resist Rehoboam son of Solomon when Rehoboam was young, inexperienced, and unable to assert himself against them.

^8 "And now you are saying you can assert yourselves against the LORD's kingdom, which is in the hand of one of David's sons. You are a vast number and have with you the golden calves that Jeroboam made for you as gods.^D ^9 Didn't you banish the priests of the LORD, the descendants of Aaron and the Levites, and make your own priests like the peoples of other lands do? Whoever comes to ordain himself with a young bull and seven rams may become a priest of what are not gods.

^10 "But as for us, the LORD is our God. We have not abandoned him; the priests ministering to the LORD are descendants of Aaron, and the Levites serve at their tasks. ^11 They offer a burnt offering and fragrant incense to the LORD every morning and every evening, and they set the rows of the Bread of the Presence on the ceremonially clean table. They light the lamps of the gold lampstand every evening. We are carrying out the requirements of the LORD our God, while you have abandoned him. ^12 Look, God and his priests are with us at our head. The trumpets are ready to sound the charge against you. Israelites, don't fight against the LORD God of your ancestors, for you will not succeed."

^13 Now Jeroboam had sent an ambush around to advance from behind them. So they were in front of Judah, and the ambush was behind them. ^14 Judah turned and discovered that the battle was in front of them and behind them, so they cried out to the LORD. Then the priests blew the trumpets, ^15 and the men of Judah raised the battle cry. When the men of Judah raised the battle cry, God routed Jeroboam and all Israel before Abijah and Judah. ^16 So the Israelites fled before Judah, and God handed them over to them. ^17 Then Abijah and his people struck them with a mighty blow,

---

^A 12:11 Lit *the chamber of the runners*   ^B 12:16; 13:1 = Abijam in 1Kg 14:31–15:8   ^C 13:2 LXX, Syr, Arabic read *Maacah*; 1Kg 15:2; 2Ch 11:22   ^D 13:8 Or *God*; 1Kg 12:28

---

and five hundred thousand fit young men of Israel were killed. [18] The Israelites were subdued at that time. The Judahites succeeded because they depended on the LORD, the God of their ancestors.

[19] Abijah pursued Jeroboam and captured some cities from him: Bethel, Jeshanah, and Ephron,^ along with their surrounding villages. [20] Jeroboam no longer retained his power^B during Abijah's reign; ultimately, the LORD struck him and he died.

[21] However, Abijah grew strong, acquired fourteen wives, and fathered twenty-two sons and sixteen daughters. [22] The rest of the events of Abijah's reign, along with his ways and his sayings, are written in the Writing of the Prophet Iddo. [1] Abijah rested with his ancestors and was buried in the city of David. His son Asa became king in his place. During his reign the land experienced peace for ten years.

Judah's King Asa

[2] Asa did what was good and right in the sight of the LORD his God. [3] He removed the pagan altars and the high places. He shattered their sacred pillars and chopped down their Asherah poles. [4] He told the people of Judah to seek the LORD God of their ancestors and to carry out the instruction and the commands. [5] He also removed the high places and the shrines^C from all the cities of Judah, and the kingdom experienced peace under him.

[6] Because the land experienced peace, Asa built fortified cities in Judah. No one made war with him in those days because the LORD gave him rest. [7] So he said to the people of Judah, "Let's build these cities and surround them with walls and towers, with doors and bars. The land is still ours because we sought the LORD our God. We sought him and he gave us rest on every side." So they built and succeeded.

The Cushite Invasion

[8] Asa had an army of three hundred thousand from Judah bearing large shields and spears, and two hundred eighty thousand from Benjamin bearing regular shields and drawing the bow. All these were valiant warriors. [9] Then Zerah the Cushite came against them with an army of one million men and three hundred^D chariots. They came as far as Mareshah. [10] So Asa marched out against him and lined up in battle formation in Zephathah Valley at Mareshah.

[11] Then Asa cried out to the LORD his God, "LORD, there is no one besides you to help the mighty and those without strength. Help us, LORD our God, for we depend on you, and in your name we have come against this large army. LORD, you are our God. Do not let a mere mortal hinder you."

[12] So the LORD routed the Cushites before Asa and before Judah, and the Cushites fled. [13] Then Asa and the people who were with him pursued them as far as Gerar. The Cushites fell until they had no survivors, for they were crushed before the LORD and his army. So the people of Judah carried off a great supply of loot. [14] Then they attacked all the cities around Gerar because the terror of the LORD was on them. They also plundered all the cities, since there was a great deal of plunder in them. [15] They also attacked the tents of the herdsmen and captured many sheep and camels. Then they returned to Jerusalem.

Revival under Asa

15 The Spirit of God came on Azariah son of Oded. [2] So he went out to meet Asa and said to him, "Asa and all Judah and Benjamin,

---

^13:19 Alt Hb tradition reads *Ephrain*   ^B13:20 Lit *He did not restrain the power of Jeroboam*   ^C14:5 Or *incense altars*
^D14:9 Syr, Arabic read *30,000*

Judah **cried out**, fought with desperation, and God took it from there. They killed more than half of Jeroboam's army, but the Chronicler makes it clear that it was **the LORD** who was responsible for the victory.

13:19–20 Abijah and his army not only routed **Jeroboam**, but they also captured the town of **Bethel**—the southern sanctuary for Jeroboam's golden calves. For Jeroboam, this was the beginning of the end. God judged him severely, and after **he died**, his son Nadab was assassinated after only two years on the throne (1Kg 13–14; 15:25–28).

13:22 The **Writing of the Prophet Iddo** is not known to us.

14:1 In light of the single event of Abijah's life that the Chronicler highlights, Abijah received a neutral death notice. He was buried on Mount Zion in the vicinity of David's tomb. The line of succession passed on to his son Asa.

   Asa: Third king of Judah; son of Abijah; devoted to God, but closed himself off from God at the end of his life. The years given for

the kings' reigns make it clear that at times there was some overlap, when the father had already elevated his son as coregent with him. Thus, the **ten years** of peace could include the latter years of Abijah's reign and the first years of Asa's reign.

14:2–3 Asa receives high praise from the Chronicler. He **removed** all the objects of idol worship and exhorted the people to obey God. **High places** were places of worship to various gods. Many, but not all, were **pagan**. **Asherah poles** were dedicated to the Canaanite goddess Asherah. The Canaanites believed that Asherah was the wife of the high god El and the mother of the main god Baal. She was a goddess of sexuality, and worshiping her by venerating sacred poles was supposed to produce fertility for crops and animals.

14:6–7 Encouraged by the time of **peace**, Asa set about redoing the fortifications throughout the land.

14:8–10 Asa's army was even larger than that of Abijah; the four hundred thousand warriors had grown to five hundred eighty

thousand. Unfortunately, this huge number still put him at a disadvantage when **Zerah the Cushite** (an Ethiopian) came calling with an army of **one million men and three hundred chariots**. Instead of concealing himself behind his newly built fortifications, Asa and his smaller army marched out to confront Zerah in the vicinity of **Mareshah**, a town in western Judah.

14:11 Asa knew the odds were against him, but he had evidently learned from his father's success against Jeroboam's army. He **cried out to the LORD** for help. The battle believed the outcome of the battle would not be determined by **a mere mortal**.

14:13–15 Zerah and his huge army had advanced this far because they had received support from the people of **Gerar** and the cattle-raising nomads in the vicinity. Thus, the army of Judah plundered **all the cities** around Gerar.

15:1–2 Azariah son of Oded came with a message of encouragement for **Asa** to continue his devotion to the Lord.

hear me. The LORD is with you when you are with him. If you seek him, he will be found by you, but if you abandon him, he will abandon you. [3] For many years Israel has been without the true God, without a teaching priest, and without instruction, [4] but when they turned to the LORD God of Israel in their distress and sought him, he was found by them. [5] In those times there was no peace for those who went about their daily activities because the residents of the lands had many conflicts. [6] Nation was crushed by nation and city by city, for God troubled them with every possible distress. [7] But as for you, be strong; don't give up,[A] for your work has a reward."

[8] When Asa heard these words and the prophecy of Azariah son of Oded the prophet, he took courage and removed the abhorrent idols from the whole land of Judah and Benjamin and from the cities he had captured in the hill country of Ephraim. He renovated the altar of the LORD that was in front of the portico of the LORD's temple. [9] Then he gathered all Judah and Benjamin, as well as those from the tribes of Ephraim, Manasseh, and Simeon who were residing among them, for they had defected to him from Israel in great numbers when they saw that the LORD his God was with him. [10] They were gathered in Jerusalem in the third month of the fifteenth year of Asa's reign. [11] At that time they sacrificed to the LORD seven hundred cattle and seven thousand sheep and goats from all the plunder they had brought. [12] Then they entered into a covenant to seek the LORD God of their ancestors with all their heart and all their soul. [13] Whoever would not seek the LORD God of Israel would be put to death, young or old,[B] man or woman. [14] They took an oath to the LORD in a loud voice, with shouting, with trumpets, and with rams' horns.

[15] All Judah rejoiced over the oath, for they had sworn it wholeheartedly. They had sought him with all sincerity, and he was found by them. So the LORD gave them rest on every side. [16] King Asa also removed Maacah, his grandmother,[C] from being queen mother because she had made an obscene image of Asherah. Asa chopped down her obscene image, then crushed it and burned it in the Kidron Valley. [17] The high places were not taken away from Israel; nevertheless, Asa was wholeheartedly devoted his entire life.[D] [18] He brought his father's consecrated gifts and his own consecrated gifts into God's temple: silver, gold, and utensils.

[19] There was no war until the thirty-fifth year of Asa's reign.

Asa's Treaty with Aram

16 In the thirty-sixth year of Asa, Israel's King Baasha went to war against Judah. He built Ramah in order to keep anyone from leaving or coming to King Asa of Judah. [2] So Asa brought out the silver and gold from the treasuries of the LORD's temple and the royal palace and sent it to Aram's King Ben-hadad, who lived in Damascus, saying, [3] "There's a treaty between me and you, between my father and your father. Look, I have sent you silver and gold. Go break your treaty with Israel's King Baasha so that he will withdraw from me."

[4] Ben-hadad listened to King Asa and sent the commanders of his armies to the cities of Israel. They attacked Ijon, Dan, Abel-maim,[E] and all the storage cities[F] of Naphtali. [5] When Baasha heard about it, he quit building Ramah and stopped his work. [6] Then King Asa brought all Judah, and they carried away the stones of Ramah and the timbers Baasha had

---

[A]15:7 Lit don't let your hands drop　[B]15:13 Or insignificant or great　[C]15:16 Lit mother; 1Kg 15:2; 2Ch 11:22　[D]15:17 Lit wholehearted all his days　[E]16:4 Abel-beth-maacah in 1Kg 15:20　[F]16:4 = all Chinnereth in 1Kg 15:20

15:8 It is not clear when this event occurred. It is possible that this passage is an elaboration of the introduction to Asa in 14:2, but we cannot rule out that Asa had not completely followed through on his earlier attempts at reform and that Azariah's message led him to become more aggressive in his purge of idolatry.

15:9–11 The people responded favorably to Asa's reforms, including further defections from the north. They held a major feast of sacrifice in the temple, which the king had renovated (15:8). The animals that were **sacrificed** came from the **plunder** of Asa's earlier victory (14:13–15).

15:12–15 Everyone took an oath of allegiance to the Lord, and they did so joyfully and voluntarily. This oath included an automatic death penalty for anyone who would **not seek the LORD**. The Lord rewarded their zeal and genuine repentance with **rest** (Dt 4:29; 1Sm 7:3).

15:16 One of the important acts of Asa was that he removed from power **Maacah**, his grandmother, because she was a supporter of idol worship.

15:17 This verse illustrates the difference between **high places** that were pagan sites and those that were used for worship of the Lord (see note at 14:2–3). The high places that Asa did not remove were dedicated to the true God.

16:1 Baasha: Third king of Israel; began his own dynasty; defeated by Asa of Judah. In the northern kingdom, Jeroboam's son Nadab had been replaced by Baasha, who decided to go to war against the southern kingdom. The first step in his strategy was to block access to Jerusalem by fortifying the town of **Ramah**. Baasha had also formed an alliance with Ben-hadad, king of Aram in Damascus. This meant that once Asa was cut off from the outside world, it would be an easy thing to capture Jerusalem.

16:2–6 Asa emptied the **treasuries** of the temple and bribed **Ben-hadad** of **Damascus** to break his treaty with Baasha of Israel. The king of Damascus not only complied

built it with. Then he built Geba and Mizpah with them.

Hanani's Rebuke of Asa

⁷ At that time, the seer Hanani came to King Asa of Judah and said to him, "Because you depended on the king of Aram and have not depended on the LORD your God, the army of the king of Aram has escaped from you. ⁸ Were not the Cushites and Libyans a vast army with many chariots and horsemen? When you depended on the LORD, he handed them over to you. ⁹ For the eyes of the LORD roam throughout the earth to show himself strong for those who are wholeheartedly devoted to him. You have been foolish in this matter. Therefore, you will have wars from now on." ¹⁰ Asa was enraged with the seer and put him in prison^A because of his anger over this. And Asa mistreated some of the people at that time.

Asa's Death

¹¹ Note that the events of Asa's reign, from beginning to end, are written in the Book of the Kings of Judah and Israel. ¹² In the thirty-ninth year of his reign, Asa developed a disease in his feet, and his disease became increasingly severe. Yet even in his disease he didn't seek the LORD but only the physicians. ¹³ Asa rested with his ancestors; he died in the forty-first year of his reign. ¹⁴ He was buried in his own tomb that he had made for himself in the city of David. They laid him out in a coffin that was full of spices and various mixtures of prepared ointments; then they made a great fire in his honor.

Judah's King Jehoshaphat

17 His son Jehoshaphat became king in his place and strengthened himself against Israel. ² He stationed troops in every fortified city of Judah and set garrisons in the land of Judah and in the cities of Ephraim that his father Asa had captured.

³ Now the LORD was with Jehoshaphat because he walked in the former ways of his ancestor David. ⁸ He did not seek the Baals ⁴ but sought the God of his father and walked by his commands, not according to the practices of Israel. ⁵ So the LORD established the kingdom in his hand. Then all Judah brought him tribute, and he had riches and honor in abundance. ⁶ He took great pride in the LORD's ways, and he again removed the high places and Asherah poles from Judah.

Jehoshaphat's Educational Plan

⁷ In the third year of his reign, Jehoshaphat sent his officials — Ben-hail,^C Obadiah, Zechariah, Nethanel, and Micaiah — to teach in the cities of Judah. ⁸ The Levites with them were Shemaiah, Nethaniah, Zebadiah,^D Asahel, Shemiramoth, Jehonathan, Adonijah, Tobijah, and Tob-adonijah; the priests, Elishama and Jehoram, were with these Levites. ⁹ They taught throughout Judah, having the book of the LORD's instruction with them. They went throughout the towns of Judah and taught the people.

¹⁰ The terror of the LORD was on all the kingdoms of the lands that surrounded Judah, so they didn't fight against Jehoshaphat. ¹¹ Some of the Philistines also brought gifts and silver as tribute to Jehoshaphat, and the Arabs brought him flocks: 7,700 rams and 7,700 male goats.

Jehoshaphat's Military Might

¹² Jehoshaphat grew stronger and stronger. He built fortresses and storage cities in Judah ¹³ and carried out great works in the towns of Judah. He had fighting men, valiant warriors, in Jerusalem. ¹⁴ These are their numbers according to their ancestral families.^E For Judah, the commanders of thousands:

> Adnah the commander and three hundred thousand valiant warriors with him;

---

^A**16:10** Lit *the house of stocks* ^B**17:3** Some Hb mss, LXX omit *David* ^C**17:7** = Son of Power ^D**17:8** Some Hb mss, Syr, Tg, Arabic read *Zechariah* ^E**17:14** Lit *the house of their fathers*

---

willingly, but even sent his soldiers into Israel to compensate themselves for the plunder they missed by not attacking Jerusalem. Asa was able to destroy Baasha's blockade and assert his dominance over his northern border area again.
16:7–9 Rather than reaping praise for his diplomatic achievement, Asa was rebuked for his actions by **Hanani**. This prophet reminded the king that God wanted Asa to depend on him and not on his own cleverness or on help from pagans. After Asa defeated the superior forces of the **Cushites and Libyans** he should have known that God rewards devotion with deliverance.
16:10 This was more than Asa could handle. His ego had been bruised, so he put the prophet Hanani **in prison** and abused other people. He had forgotten his earlier

assertion that a mere mortal could not hinder God (14:11).
16:11–12 The glorious reign of Asa, who had acted for God so effectively, came to a sour end. When he developed a serious **disease in his feet**, he avoided turning to the Lord and sought healing by **physicians** instead.
16:13–14 Nevertheless, Asa received a glorious burial. The **great fire** was a tribute of honor from the people (see 21:19).
17:1 Jehoshaphat: Fourth king of Judah; son of Asa; thoroughly devoted to God, but made disastrous alliances with Ahab and Ahaziah of Israel.
17:3–6 Jehoshaphat was one of the outstanding kings of Judah. He stood for all the things that should characterize a king of Judah. Since his father Asa had lost his grip on the kingdom in his later years, Jehoshaphat

had to purge the land of **high places and Asherah poles**.
17:7–9 An important part of David's original plan in assigning duties to the Levites was a contingent of teachers throughout the country (1Ch 26:29–32), but this proved impossible once the kingdom was divided. **Jehoshaphat** revived this idea and designated certain **Levites** as itinerant teachers. They carried copies of the law and instructed everyone in Judah how to live as God's people.
17:14–18 There was another increase in the size of the army of Judah. Rehoboam's army had numbered 180,000 (11:1); Abijah had 400,000 soldiers (13:3); Asa's army numbered 580,000 (14:8). The grand total for Jehoshaphat's army was 1,160,000 **valiant warriors**.

¹⁵ next to him, Jehohanan the commander and two hundred eighty thousand with him;

¹⁶ next to him, Amasiah son of Zichri, the volunteer of the LORD, and two hundred thousand valiant warriors with him;

¹⁷ from Benjamin, Eliada, a valiant warrior, and two hundred thousand with him armed with bow and shield;

¹⁸ next to him, Jehozabad and one hundred eighty thousand with him equipped for war.

¹⁹ These were the ones who served the king, besides those he stationed in the fortified cities throughout all Judah.

Jehoshaphat's Alliance with Ahab

18 Now Jehoshaphat had riches and honor in abundance, and he made an alliance with Ahab through marriage.ᴬ ² Then after some years, he went down to visit Ahab in Samaria. Ahab slaughtered many sheep, goats, and cattle for him and for the people who were with him, and he persuaded him to attack Ramoth-gilead, ³ for Israel's King Ahab asked Judah's King Jehoshaphat, "Will you go with me to Ramoth-gilead?"

He replied to him, "I am as you are, my people as your people; we will be with you in the battle." ⁴ But Jehoshaphat said to the king of Israel, "First, please ask what the LORD's will is."

⁵ So the king of Israel gathered the prophets, four hundred men, and asked them, "Should we go to Ramoth-gilead for war or should I refrain?"

They replied, "March up, and God will hand it over to the king."

⁶ But Jehoshaphat asked, "Isn't there a prophet of the LORD here anymore? Let's ask him."

⁷ The king of Israel said to Jehoshaphat, "There is still one man who can inquire of the LORD, but I hate him because he never prophesies good about me, but only disaster. He is Micaiah son of Imlah."

"The king shouldn't say that," Jehoshaphat replied.

⁸ So the king of Israel called an officer and said, "Hurry and get Micaiah son of Imlah!"

⁹ Now the king of Israel and King Jehoshaphat of Judah, clothed in royal attire, were each sitting on his own throne. They were sitting on the threshing floor at the entrance to Samaria's gate, and all the prophets were prophesying in front of them. ¹⁰ Then Zedekiah son of Chenaanah made iron horns and said, "This is what the LORD says: You will gore the Arameans with these until they are finished off." ¹¹ And all the prophets were prophesying the same, saying, "March up to Ramoth-gilead and succeed, for the LORD will hand it over to the king."

Micaiah's Message of Defeat

¹² The messenger who went to call Micaiah instructed him, "Look, the words of the prophets are unanimously favorable for the king. So let your words be like theirs, and speak favorably."

¹³ But Micaiah said, "As the LORD lives, I will say whatever my God says."ᴮ

¹⁴ So he went to the king, and the king asked him, "Micaiah, should we go to Ramoth-gilead for war, or should Iᶜ refrain?"

Micaiah said, "March up and succeed, for they will be handed over to you."

¹⁵ But the king said to him, "How many times must I make you swear not to tell me anything but the truth in the name of the LORD?"

¹⁶ So Micaiah said:

I saw all Israel scattered on the hills
like sheep without a shepherd.
And the LORD said,
"They have no master;
let each return home in peace."

¹⁷ So the king of Israel said to Jehoshaphat, "Didn't I tell you he never prophesies good about me, but only disaster?"

¹⁸ Then Micaiah said, "Therefore, hear the word of the LORD. I saw the LORD sitting on his throne, and the whole heavenly army

---

ᴬ18:1 Lit *made himself a son-in-law to Ahab*; 1Kg 3:1; Ezr 9:14   ᴮ18:13 LXX, Vg add *to me*; 1Kg 22:14   ᶜ18:14 LXX reads *we*; 1Kg 22:15

18:1 Ahab: Sixth king of Israel, son of Omri; made Baal worship the state religion of the northern kingdom (1Kg 16:31); formed an alliance with Jehoshaphat of Judah. Jehoshaphat contracted a marriage between his son Jehoram and Athaliah, daughter of Ahab and Jezebel.

18:3–4 At Ahab's initiative, **Jehoshaphat** agreed to combine their armies to fight the Arameans. As an afterthought, Jehoshaphat asked that they consult the Lord on whether this was really **the LORD's will**.

18:5 Ahab had **four hundred men** on his payroll. These **prophets**, who were servants of Baal, were well-schooled in declaring whatever King Ahab wanted to hear, so they encouraged him to go ahead with his plans.

18:6 Conferring with false prophets was not what Jehoshaphat had in mind, so he asked if **a prophet of the LORD** was available. This was an astounding request because prophets of Yahweh were not welcome at the court of Ahab and Jezebel.

18:7–8 It was Ahab's insolent **I hate him** to which Jehoshaphat objected.

18:9–10 Word had come to the prophets of Baal that what the king of Judah wanted to hear was the word of the Lord. One of their leaders, **Zedekiah**, decided to add a visual touch to his prophecy. He decorated himself with a symbol of Baal, a set of **iron horns**, and began to act out the Lord's supposed prediction of Ahab's success in battle.

18:12–13 The court messenger wanted to avoid controversy and did not want to

offend the king, so he encouraged Micaiah to go along with the crowd. As a true prophet, **Micaiah** knew he must speak the message God gave him (Nm 22:18; 2Co 2:17; Gl 1:10; 1Th 2:4).

18:14–15 There may have been a sarcastic tone in Micaiah's first statement, because Ahab detected that it was not the truth.

18:16–17 Putting sarcasm aside, Micaiah stated that he saw **all Israel** scattered on the hills **like sheep without a shepherd**, implying that Ahab would be killed in the battle. Ahab said that this was precisely what he had come to expect from Micaiah.

18:18–24 Micaiah also stated that Ahab's court **prophets** were the instruments of a **spirit** sent by God with the specific intention of leading Ahab into destruction with

was standing at his right hand and at his left hand. ¹⁹ And the LORD said, 'Who will entice King Ahab of Israel to march up and fall at Ramoth-gilead?' So one was saying this and another was saying that.

²⁰ "Then a spirit came forward, stood before the LORD, and said, 'I will entice him.'

"The LORD asked him, 'How?'

²¹ "So he said, 'I will go and become a lying spirit in the mouth of all his prophets.'

"Then he said, 'You will entice him and also prevail. Go and do that.'

²² "Now, you see, the LORD has put a lying spirit into the mouth ofᴬ these prophets of yours, and the LORD has pronounced disaster against you."

²³ Then Zedekiah son of Chenaanah came up, hit Micaiah on the cheek, and demanded, "Which way did the spirit from the LORD leave me to speak to you?"

²⁴ Micaiah replied, "You will soon see when you go to hide in an inner chamber on that day."

²⁵ Then the king of Israel ordered, "Take Micaiah and return him to Amon, the governor of the city, and to Joash, the king's son, ²⁶ and say, 'This is what the king says: Put this guy in prison and feed him only a little bread and waterᴮ until I come back safely.'"

²⁷ But Micaiah said, "If you ever return safely, the LORD has not spoken through me." Then he said, "Listen, all you people!"

Ahab's Death

²⁸ Then the king of Israel and Judah's King Jehoshaphat went up to Ramoth-gilead. ²⁹ But the king of Israel said to Jehoshaphat, "I will disguise myself and go into battle, but you wear your royal attire." So the king of Israel disguised himself, and they went into battle.

³⁰ Now the king of Aram had ordered his chariot commanders, "Do not fight with anyone at allᶜ except the king of Israel."

³¹ When the chariot commanders saw Jehoshaphat, they shouted, "He must be the king of

Israel!" So they turned to attack him, but Jehoshaphat cried out and the LORD helped him. God drew them away from him. ³² When the chariot commanders saw that he was not the king of Israel, they turned back from pursuing him.

³³ But a man drew his bow without taking special aim and struck the king of Israel through the joints of his armor. So he said to the charioteer, "Turn around and take me out of the battle,ᴰ for I am badly wounded!" ³⁴ The battle raged throughout that day, and the king of Israel propped himself up in his chariot facing the Arameans until evening. Then he died at sunset.

Jehu's Rebuke of Jehoshaphat

19 King Jehoshaphat of Judah returned to his home in Jerusalem in peace. ² Then Jehu son of the seer Hanani went out to confront himᴱ and said to King Jehoshaphat, "Do you help the wicked and love those who hate the LORD? Because of this, the LORD's wrath is on you. ³ However, some good is found in you, for you have eradicated the Asherah poles from the land and have determined in your heart to seek God."

Jehoshaphat's Reforms

⁴ Jehoshaphat lived in Jerusalem, and once again he went out among the people from Beer-sheba to the hill country of Ephraim and brought them back to the LORD, the God of their ancestors. ⁵ He appointed judges in all the fortified cities of the land of Judah, city by city. ⁶ Then he said to the judges, "Consider what you are doing, for you do not judge for a man, but for the LORD, who is with you in the matter of judgment. ⁷ And now, may the terror of the LORD be on you. Watch what you do, for there is no injustice or partiality or taking bribes with the LORD our God."

⁸ Jehoshaphat also appointed in Jerusalem some of the Levites and priests and some

a lie. **Zedekiah** questioned Micaiah's divine authority by slapping him and accusing him of infringing on Zedekiah's right to speak for the Lord. Micaiah replied that the matter would be settled on the day that Zedekiah, confronted by the defeat of Ahab's army, would try to protect himself by hiding in a toilet.
18:25–27 Ahab's safe return would prove Micaiah a false prophet and a traitor deserving death. Micaiah publicly announced he would submit to the test of a true prophet: whether his prediction came to pass (Dt 18:21–22).
18:28–29 Ahab, knowing that the Arameans wanted to kill him, made it look like Jehoshaphat was the only king on the battlefield. His superstition may have led him to think that a disguise could avert what was prophesied.
18:30–32 The Arameans did, in fact, have orders to single out Ahab. Since **Jehoshaphat**

was the only visible king, they focused on him and almost killed him. Jehoshaphat **cried out** to **the LORD**. God graciously caused the Arameans to back off by letting the Aramean **chariot commanders** recognize that Jehoshaphat was not Ahab, their intended target.
18:33–34 One lone Aramean archer shot a random arrow. The Hebrew could also be taken to mean that he "simply" shot or that he was merely doing what a good soldier should do. This arrow not only hit Ahab but penetrated **through the joints of his armor**, something even the best archer was unlikely to achieve on purpose. When Ahab **died at sunset**, Micaiah, the prophet of the Lord, had been vindicated, and Zedekiah, the prophet of Baal, had been repudiated.
19:1–3 Jehoshaphat was able to return safely to Jerusalem where he had to face God's

evaluation of what he had done. Just as Asa, his father, had been greeted by the prophet Hanani, now **Jehu son of . . . Hanani** scolded Jehoshaphat, king of Judah. It was wrong for Jehoshaphat to team up with a king who was not a worshiper of Yahweh. But because Jehoshaphat was a good king who had gone further than any other in purging the land of idolatry, he would not have to face serious judgment as his father did.
19:5–7 In appointing regional **judges**, Jehoshaphat reminded them of two things: that God would be watching them, and that God was the model for impartiality. Jehoshaphat was not merely pragmatic in his governing but led the country in spiritual matters as well.
19:8–11 Jehoshaphat also carried out judicial reform in **Jerusalem**. Some of these judges were **Levites and priests** and thus were

of the Israelite family heads for deciding the LORD's will and for settling disputes of the residents of^A Jerusalem. ⁹ He commanded them, saying, "In the fear of the LORD, with integrity, and wholeheartedly, you are to do the following: ¹⁰ For every dispute that comes to you from your brothers who dwell in their cities — whether it regards differences of bloodguilt, law, commandment, statutes, or judgments — you are to warn them, so they will not incur guilt before the LORD and wrath will not come on you and your brothers. Do this, and you will not incur guilt.

¹¹ "Note that Amariah, the chief priest, is over you in all matters related to the LORD, and Zebadiah son of Ishmael, the ruler of the house of Judah, in all matters related to the king, and the Levites are officers in your presence. Be strong; may the LORD be with those who do what is good."

War against Eastern Enemies

20 After this, the Moabites and Ammonites, together with some of the Meunites,^B came to fight against Jehoshaphat. ² People came and told Jehoshaphat, "A vast number from beyond the Dead Sea and from Edom^C has come to fight against you; they are already in Hazazon-tamar" (that is, En-gedi). ³ Jehoshaphat was afraid, and he resolved to seek the LORD. Then he proclaimed a fast for all Judah, ⁴ who gathered to seek the LORD. They even came from all the cities of Judah to seek him.

Jehoshaphat's Prayer

⁵ Then Jehoshaphat stood in the assembly of Judah and Jerusalem in the LORD's temple before the new courtyard. ⁶ He said:

LORD, God of our ancestors, are you not the God who is in heaven, and do you not rule over all the kingdoms of the nations? Power and might are in your hand, and no one can stand against you. ⁷ Are you not our God who drove out the inhabitants of this land before your people Israel and who gave it forever to the descendants of Abraham your friend? ⁸ They have lived in the land and have built you a sanctuary in it for your name and have said, ⁹ "If disaster comes on us — sword or judgment, pestilence or

famine — we will stand before this temple and before you, for your name is in this temple. We will cry out to you because of our distress, and you will hear and deliver."

¹⁰ Now here are the Ammonites, Moabites, and the inhabitants of Mount Seir. You did not let Israel invade them when Israel came out of the land of Egypt, but Israel turned away from them and did not destroy them. ¹¹ Look how they repay us by coming to drive us out of your possession that you gave us as an inheritance. ¹² Our God, will you not judge them? For we are powerless before this vast number that comes to fight against us. We do not know what to do, but we look to you.^D

God's Answer

¹³ All Judah was standing before the LORD with their dependents, their wives, and their children. ¹⁴ In the middle of the congregation, the Spirit of the LORD came on Jahaziel (son of Zechariah, son of Benaiah, son of Jeiel, son of Mattaniah, a Levite from Asaph's descendants), ¹⁵ and he said, "Listen carefully, all Judah and you inhabitants of Jerusalem, and King Jehoshaphat. This is what the LORD says: 'Do not be afraid or discouraged because of this vast number, for the battle is not yours, but God's. ¹⁶ Tomorrow, go down against them. You will see them coming up the Ascent of Ziz, and you will find them at the end of the valley facing the Wilderness of Jeruel. ¹⁷ You do not have to fight this battle. Position yourselves, stand still, and see the salvation of the LORD. He is with you, Judah and Jerusalem. Do not be afraid or discouraged. Tomorrow, go out to face them, for the LORD is with you.'"

¹⁸ Then Jehoshaphat knelt low with his face to the ground, and all Judah and the inhabitants of Jerusalem fell down before the LORD to worship him. ¹⁹ Then the Levites from the sons of the Kohathites and the Korahites stood up to praise the LORD God of Israel shouting loudly.

Victory and Plunder

²⁰ In the morning they got up early and went out to the wilderness of Tekoa. As they were about to go out, Jehoshaphat stood and said, "Hear me, Judah and you inhabitants of Jerusalem. Believe in the LORD your God, and you

---

^A19:8 LXX, Vg; MT reads *disputes and they returned to*   ^B20:1 LXX; MT reads *Ammonites*; 2Ch 26:7   ^C20:2 Some Hb mss, Old Lat; other Hb mss read *Aram*   ^D20:12 Lit *but on you our eyes*

---

accountable only to the Lord. Their supervisor was not the king but **Amariah**, the high priest. They would serve as an appeals court for the regional judges. **Zebadiah . . . the ruler of the house of Judah**, along with the Levites, was to be the final authority in cases that involved the king himself. **20:1** With the northern kingdom of Israel occupied in war against the Arameans, the countries east of the Jordan River and the

Dead Sea decided to invade Judah. The **Meunites** were also referred to as the Edomites. **20:2** By the time the word of this invasion got to Jehoshaphat, the army had come as far as **En-gedi**, about fifty miles from Jerusalem on the west shore of the Dead Sea. **20:5–9** In a public prayer in front of the **temple**, Jehoshaphat reaffirmed Solomon's prayer and God's response to it. This was

precisely one of the scenarios that Solomon had envisioned (6:34): the kingdom being invaded by a foreign power. On behalf of all the people, Jehoshaphat pleaded with the Lord for deliverance. **20:13–17** God caused a priest to prophesy. **Jahaziel**, who came from a distinguished line of Levites reaching all the way back to Asaph—one of David's main musicians—conveyed God's approval to Jehoshaphat.

will be established; believe in his prophets, and you will succeed." ²¹ Then he consulted with the people and appointed some to sing for the LORD and some to praise the splendor of his holiness. When they went out in front of the armed forces, they kept singing:^

Give thanks to the LORD,
for his faithful love endures forever.

²² The moment they began their shouts and praises, the LORD set an ambush against the Ammonites, Moabites, and the inhabitants of Mount Seir who came to fight against Judah, and they were defeated. ²³ The Ammonites and Moabites turned against the inhabitants of Mount Seir and completely annihilated them. When they had finished with the inhabitants of Seir, they helped destroy each other.

²⁴ When Judah came to a place overlooking the wilderness, they looked for the large army, but there were only corpses lying on the ground; nobody had escaped. ²⁵ Then Jehoshaphat and his people went to gather the plunder. They found among them⁸ an abundance of goods on the bodiesⁿ and valuable items. So they stripped them until nobody could carry any more. They were gathering the plunder for three days because there was so much. ²⁶ They assembled in the Valley of Beracah⁰ on the fourth day, for there they blessed the LORD. Therefore, that place is still called the Valley of Beracah today.

²⁷ Then all the men of Judah and Jerusalem turned back with Jehoshaphat their leader, returning joyfully to Jerusalem, for the LORD enabled them to rejoice over their enemies. ²⁸ So they came into Jerusalem to the LORD's temple with harps, lyres, and trumpets.

²⁹ The terror of God was on all the kingdoms of the lands when they heard that the LORD had fought against the enemies of Israel. ³⁰ Then Jehoshaphat's kingdom was quiet, for his God gave him rest on every side.

Summary of Jehoshaphat's Reign

³¹ Jehoshaphat became king over Judah. He was thirty-five years old when he became king, and

he reigned twenty-five years in Jerusalem. His mother's name was Azubah daughter of Shilhi. ³² He walked in the ways of Asa his father; he did not turn away from it but did what was right in the LORD's sight. ³³ However, the high places were not taken away; the people had not yet set their hearts on the God of their ancestors.

³⁴ The rest of the events of Jehoshaphat's reign from beginning to end are written in the Events of Jehu son of Hanani, which is recorded in the Book of Israel's Kings.

Jehoshaphat's Fleet of Ships

³⁵ After this, Judah's King Jehoshaphat made an alliance with Israel's King Ahaziah, who was guilty of wrongdoing. ³⁶ Jehoshaphat formed an alliance with him to make ships to go to Tarshish, and they made the ships in Ezion-geber. ³⁷ Then Eliezer son of Dodavahu of Mareshah prophesied against Jehoshaphat, saying, "Because you formed an alliance with Ahaziah, the LORD has broken up what you have made." So the ships were wrecked and were not able to go to Tarshish.

Jehoram Becomes King over Judah

21 Jehoshaphat rested with his ancestors and was buried with his ancestors in the city of David. His son Jehoram⁵ became king in his place. ² He had brothers, sons of Jehoshaphat: Azariah, Jehiel, Zechariah, Azariah, Michael, and Shephatiah; all these were the sons of King Jehoshaphat of Judah.⁶ ³ Their father had given them many gifts of silver, gold, and valuable things, along with fortified cities in Judah, but he gave the kingdom to Jehoram because he was the firstborn. ⁴ When Jehoram had established himself over his father's kingdom, he strengthened his position by killing with the sword all his brothers as well as some of the princes of Israel.

Judah's King Jehoram

⁵ Jehoram was thirty-two years old when he became king, and he reigned eight years in

---

^20:21 Lit *saying*   ⁸20:25 LXX reads *found cattle*   ⁿ20:25 Some Hb mss, Old Lat, Vg read *goods, garments*
⁰20:26 = Blessing   ⁵21:1 = Joram   ⁶21:2 Some Hb mss, LXX, Syr, Vg, Arabic; other Hb mss read *Israel*

20:21 The next day, as the army set out to march toward En-gedi, one refrain kept coming up: **Give thanks to the LORD, for his faithful love endures forever** (cp. Ps 136). This is the same chorus that was the theme song during the transport of the ark to Jerusalem (1Ch 16:34) and at the dedication of the Lord's house (2Ch 5:13; 7:3,6).
20:22–23 There were three separate armies that did not know one another. Suddenly, these armies heard what they took to be shouting—which was actually praising. In their God-ordained confusion they destroyed **each other**.
20:24–26 Thus, this site was called the "Valley of Praise" or "Valley of Blessing."

20:31 Jehoshaphat's twenty-five years included a three-year coregency with Asa his father.
20:35–37 Jehoshaphat again tied himself to the northern kingdom by making a contract with **King Ahaziah** to build **ships**, which they would then send to **Tarshish** (possibly Spain). The best place to construct these ships appeared to be **Ezion-geber**, at the very tip of the Red Sea, not the Mediterranean coast. Once again, God did not allow Jehoshaphat to get away with such compromise. He sent a prophet named **Eliezer** to condemn Jehoshaphat's sin. As punishment, a storm came up and all the ships were destroyed.

Ahaziah: Seventh king of Israel, son of Ahab and Jezebel.
21:1 Jehoram: Fifth king of Judah; son of Jehoshaphat; promoted Baal worship; brought calamity on Judah.
21:2–6 Jehoshaphat may have thought that by having his son **Jehoram** marry the daughter of Ahab and Jezebel (v. 6), Jehoram might eventually become ruler of a kingdom that was once again united, and thus perhaps return all Israel to the worship of God and obedience to the law. But rather than being a new David, Jehoram became the personification of Ahab in Judah. Together with Athaliah, his wife, Jehoram began to refashion the kingdom of Judah so it would

Jerusalem. ⁶ He walked in the ways of the kings of Israel, as the house of Ahab had done, for Ahab's daughter was his wife. He did what was evil in the LORD's sight, ⁷ but for the sake of the covenant the LORD had made with David, he was unwilling to destroy the house of David since the LORD had promised to give a lampᴬ to David and to his sons forever.

⁸ During Jehoram's reign, Edom rebelled against Judah's control and appointed their own king. ⁹ So Jehoram crossed into Edom with his commanders and all his chariots. Then at night he set out to attack the Edomites who had surrounded him and the chariot commanders. ¹⁰ And now Edom is still in rebellion against Judah's control today. Libnah also rebelled at that time against his control because he had abandoned the LORD, the God of his ancestors. ¹¹ Jehoram also built high places in the hillsᴮ of Judah, and he caused the inhabitants of Jerusalem to prostitute themselves, and he led Judah astray.

Elijah's Letter to Jehoram

¹² Then a letter came to Jehoram from the prophet Elijah, saying:

This is what the LORD, the God of your ancestor David says: "Because you have not walked in the ways of your father Jehoshaphat or in the ways of King Asa of Judah ¹³ but have walked in the ways of the kings of Israel, have caused Judah and the inhabitants of Jerusalem to prostitute themselves like the house of Ahab prostituted itself, and also have killed your brothers, your father's family, who were better than you, ¹⁴ the LORD is now about to strike your

people, your sons, your wives, and all your possessions with a horrible affliction. ¹⁵ You yourself will be struck with many illnesses, including a disease of the intestines, until your intestines come out day after day because of the disease."

Jehoram's Last Days

¹⁶ The LORD roused the spirit of the Philistines and the Arabs who lived near the Cushites to attack Jehoram. ¹⁷ So they went to war against Judah and invaded it. They carried off all the possessions found in the king's palace and also his sons and wives; not a son was left to him except Jehoahaz,ᶜ his youngest son. ¹⁸ After all these things, the LORD afflicted him in his intestines with an incurable disease. ¹⁹ This continued day after day until two full years passed. Then his intestines came out because of his disease, and he died from severeᴰ illnesses. But his people did not hold a fire in his honor like the fire in honor of his predecessors. ²⁰ Jehoram was thirty-two years old when he became king; he reigned eight years in Jerusalem. He died to no one's regretᴱ and was buried in the city of David but not in the tombs of the kings.

Judah's King Ahaziah

22 Then the inhabitants of Jerusalem made Ahaziah, his youngest son, king in his place, because the troops that had come with the Arabs to the camp had killed all the older sons.ᶠ So Ahaziah son of Jehoram became king of Judah. ² Ahaziah was twenty-twoᴳ years old when he became king, and he reigned one

ᴬ21:7 Or *dominion* ᴮ21:11 Some Hb mss, LXX, Vg read *cities* ᶜ21:17 LXX, Syr, Tg read *Ahaziah* ᴰ21:19 Lit *evil* ᴱ21:20 Lit *He walked in no desirability* ᶠ22:1 Lit *the former ones* ᴳ22:2 Some LXX mss, Syr; MT reads *42*; 2Kg 8:26

look just like the northern kingdom, where Baal was supreme and assassination was the preferred method of changing government. As soon as Jehoram had full grasp of the southern kingdom, he proceeded to kill all his brothers and anyone else who might have some claim on the throne.
21:8–9 The **Edomites** had suffered defeat during the time of Jehoram's father, Jehoshaphat. When they realized that Jehoram was not worshiping the same powerful God as Jehoshaphat had done (see v. 10; cp. 20:29), they declared their independence from Judah and reestablished their own government. Jehoram set out to attack the insurgent Edomites, crossing into their territory with bulky chariots and a large force, but God was not on his side. He quickly found himself surrounded.
21:10 The report that **Edom is still in rebellion . . . today** shows that Jehoram's mission was unsuccessful. Also, the town of **Libnah** in Judah rebelled against Jehoram. The citizens of this town refused to follow Jehoram because he had abandoned **the LORD, the God of his ancestors**. Not everyone turned a blind eye to the disaster into which Jehoram was taking his country.

21:11 The statement that Jehoram **caused the inhabitants of Jerusalem to prostitute themselves** can be both literal and symbolic. In a symbolic sense, the people were committing spiritual adultery; in the literal sense, many of the pagan practices involved sexual lewdness.
21:12–15 Since Jehoram was Ahab's son-in-law, it is not surprising that **the prophet Elijah**—Ahab's long-standing opponent—chastised Jehoram for the same behavior for which he had rebuked Ahab. Elijah's **letter** mentioned the many sins that Jehoram had committed, including idolatry and fratricide, and promised a swift and harsh punishment. Just as Jehoram eliminated his brothers, now Jehoram's household would be eliminated.
21:16–17 The **Philistines** and their Arab neighbors took back the tribute and everything else in the **king's palace**. They killed all of Jehoram's **sons** except **Jehoahaz** (who is subsequently called Ahaziah) and all his **wives** except Athaliah, the one who shared responsibility for this catastrophe.
21:18–20 Just as Elijah had predicted, Jehoram contracted a horrible disease **in his intestines** from which he eventually died. None of his subjects mourned his departure.

He was not accorded a ceremonial **fire of honor**, and he was not buried alongside other kings of Judah.
22:1 Ahaziah: Sixth king of Judah; son of Jehoram and Athaliah; killed when Jehu annihilated the house of Ahab. Despite the people's dissatisfaction with Jehoram, when he died they acclaimed his son Ahaziah as the next king.
In order to make sense out of the events in this section, one must recognize the duplication of the names of the kings in the southern and northern kingdoms. In the northern kingdom of Israel, Ahab had two sons, Ahaziah and Jehoram. When Ahab died, his son Ahaziah succeeded him, and he in turn was succeeded by his brother, Jehoram (aka Joram). In the southern kingdom of Judah, Jehoshaphat was succeeded by his son Jehoram, and his successor was his son (and Jehoshaphat's grandson), Ahaziah (aka Jehoahaz). Thus, the successions in the north were: Ahab, Ahaziah, Jehoram; in the south the successions were: Jehoshaphat, Jehoram, Ahaziah.
22:2–4 Ahaziah of Judah was just as evil as his father Jehoram. His mother **Athaliah** received a large share of the blame

year in Jerusalem. His mother's name was Athaliah, granddaughter[A] of Omri.

[3] He walked in the ways of the house of Ahab, for his mother gave him evil advice. [4] So he did what was evil in the LORD's sight like the house of Ahab, for they were his advisers after the death of his father, to his destruction. [5] He also followed their advice and went with Joram[B] son of Israel's King Ahab to fight against King Hazael of Aram, in Ramoth-gilead. The Arameans[C] wounded Joram, [6] so he returned to Jezreel to recover from the wounds they inflicted on him in Ramoth-gilead[D] when he fought against King Hazael of Aram. Then Judah's King Ahaziah[E] son of Jehoram went down to Jezreel to visit Joram son of Ahab since Joram was ill.

[7] Ahaziah's downfall came from God when he went to Joram. When Ahaziah arrived, he went out with Joram to meet Jehu son of Nimshi, whom the LORD had anointed to destroy the house of Ahab. [8] So when Jehu executed judgment on the house of Ahab, he found the rulers of Judah and the sons of Ahaziah's brothers who were serving Ahaziah, and he killed them. [9] Then Jehu looked for Ahaziah, and Jehu's soldiers captured him (he was hiding in Samaria). So they brought Ahaziah to Jehu, and they killed him. The soldiers buried him, for they said, "He is the grandson of Jehoshaphat who sought the LORD with all his heart." So no one from the house of Ahaziah had the strength to rule the kingdom.

Athaliah Usurps the Throne

[10] When Athaliah, Ahaziah's mother, saw that her son was dead, she proceeded to annihilate all the royal heirs[F] of the house of Judah. [11] Jehoshabeath,[G] the king's daughter, rescued Joash son of Ahaziah from the king's sons who were being killed and put him and the one who nursed him in a bedroom. Now Jehoshabeath was the daughter of King Jehoram and the wife

of the priest Jehoiada. Since she was Ahaziah's sister, she hid Joash from Athaliah so that she did not kill him. [12] He was hiding with them in God's temple for six years while Athaliah reigned over the land.

Athaliah Overthrown

23 Then, in the seventh year, Jehoiada summoned his courage and took the commanders of hundreds into a covenant with him: Azariah son of Jeroham, Ishmael son of Jehohanan, Azariah son of Obed, Maaseiah son of Adaiah, and Elishaphat son of Zichri. [2] They made a circuit throughout Judah. They gathered the Levites from all the cities of Judah and the family heads of Israel, and they came to Jerusalem.

[3] Then the whole assembly made a covenant with the king in God's temple. Jehoiada said to them, "Here is the king's son! He will reign, just as the LORD promised concerning David's sons. [4] This is what you are to do: a third of you, priests and Levites who are coming on duty on the Sabbath, are to be gatekeepers. [5] A third are to be at the king's palace, and a third are to be at the Foundation Gate, and all the troops will be in the courtyards of the LORD's temple. [6] No one is to enter the LORD's temple but the priests and those Levites who serve; they may enter because they are holy, but all the people are to obey the requirement of the LORD. [7] The Levites are to completely surround the king with weapons in hand. Anyone who enters the temple is to be put to death. Accompany the king in all his daily tasks."[H]

[8] So the commanders of hundreds did everything the priest Jehoiada commanded. They each brought their men — those coming on duty on the Sabbath and those going off duty on the Sabbath — for the priest Jehoiada did not release the divisions. [9] The priest Jehoiada gave to the commanders of hundreds

---

^A 22:2 Lit *daughter*   ^B 22:5 = Jehoram   ^C 22:5 Lit *Rammites*   ^D 22:6 Lit *in Ramah*   ^E 22:6 Some Hb mss, LXX, Syr, Vg; other Hb mss read *Azariah*   ^F 22:10 Lit *seed*   ^G 22:11 = Jehosheba; 2Kg 11:2   ^H 23:7 Lit *king when he comes in and when he goes out*

---

by misleading him. Because of the family connection to the house of Ahab, Ahaziah received **advice** from his relatives in the northern kingdom. Ahaziah followed the practices of the northern kingdom, including idolatry and violence.

22:5–6 Just as Jehoshaphat had gone with Ahab of Israel to **Ramoth-gilead** to fight against the Arameans, so **Ahaziah** of Judah went along with Joram of Israel to the same place for the same purpose. The result was almost identical. Joram was seriously wounded.

Joram (also called Jehoram): Eighth king of Israel, son of Ahab, brother of Ahaziah; killed by Jehu after he and Ahaziah of Judah fought against Hazael of Aram; last king of the house of Ahab in Israel.

22:7–9 God had appointed **Jehu** to put an end to the dynasty of Ahab and to become king himself (2Kg 9:1–10). Jehu went too far in eliminating Judah's King Ahaziah, thus

setting up the situation where Athaliah almost eliminated the line of David when she seized the Davidic throne (2Ch 22:10–12).

22:10 Athaliah: Usurper of the throne of Judah; daughter of Jezebel and Ahab; wife of Jehoram; executed in Jehoiada's plot to reinstall Joash as king. Who would fill the vacant throne of Judah? Athaliah, **Ahaziah's mother,** leaped at the chance and made herself queen of Judah. She had no legitimate claim to the throne because she was not descended from David. She followed her husband's earlier practice and killed anyone who had a claim to the throne, even her own grandchildren.

22:11–12 There was one heir whom Athaliah was not able to eliminate. **Joash** was a baby, having been born about the time of Ahaziah's accession. Ahaziah's sister **Jehoshabeath** and her husband **Jehoiada** the high priest raised Joash in seclusion in the **temple** for **six years.**

23:1–3 Jehoiada waited patiently for six years before he carried out his plan to overthrow Athaliah. Jehoiada did not act rashly, but he made sure he had the military leaders on his side as well as the **Levites** and the prominent families.

23:4–7 Jehoiada made it appear as though the **priests and Levites** were carrying on with their usual duties, with the normal one-third of the total work force serving in the temple. At the same time, the other Levites were in the immediate vicinity, half of them at the nearby **king's palace** and half at one of the major gates. The armed troops were in the **courtyards,** but Jehoiada insisted that the sanctity of the temple not be violated. The presence of the military would assure that nothing happened to young Joash.

23:8–10 The **temple** contained an arsenal of weapons that had been stored there since the time of David. Thus, the soldiers were able to walk into the temple precinct

King David's spears, shields, and quivers[A] that were in God's temple. [10] Then he stationed all the troops with their weapons in hand surrounding the king — from the right side of the temple to the left side, by the altar and by the temple.

[11] They brought out the king's son, put the crown on him, gave him the testimony, and made him king. Jehoiada and his sons anointed him and cried, "Long live the king!"

[12] When Athaliah heard the noise from the troops, the guards, and those praising the king, she went to the troops in the LORD's temple. [13] As she looked, there was the king standing by his pillar[B] at the entrance. The commanders and the trumpeters were by the king, and all the people of the land were rejoicing and blowing trumpets while the singers with musical instruments were leading the praise. Athaliah tore her clothes and screamed, "Treason! Treason!"

[14] Then the priest Jehoiada sent out the commanders of hundreds, those in charge of the army, saying, "Take her out between the ranks, and put anyone who follows her to death by the sword," for the priest had said, "Don't put her to death in the LORD's temple." [15] So they arrested her, and she went by the entrance of the Horse Gate to the king's palace, where they put her to death.

Jehoiada's Reforms

[16] Then Jehoiada made a covenant between himself, the king, and the people that they would be the LORD's people. [17] So all the people went to the temple of Baal and tore it down. They smashed its altars and images and killed Mattan, the priest of Baal, at the altars.

[18] Then Jehoiada put the oversight of the LORD's temple into the hands of the Levitical priests, whom David had appointed over the LORD's temple, to offer burnt offerings to the LORD as it is written in the law of Moses, with rejoicing and song ordained by[C] David. [19] He stationed gatekeepers at the gates of the LORD's temple so that nothing unclean could enter for any reason. [20] Then he took with him the commanders of hundreds, the nobles, the governors of the people, and all the people of the land and brought the king down from the LORD's temple. They entered the king's palace through the Upper Gate and seated the king on the throne of the kingdom. [21] All the people of the land rejoiced, and the city was quiet, for they had put Athaliah to death by the sword.

Judah's King Joash

24 Joash was seven years old when he became king, and he reigned forty years in Jerusalem. His mother's name was Zibiah; she was from Beer-sheba. [2] Throughout the time of the priest Jehoiada, Joash did what was right in the LORD's sight. [3] Jehoiada acquired two wives for him, and he was the father of sons and daughters.

Repairing the Temple

[4] Afterward, Joash took it to heart to renovate the LORD's temple. [5] So he gathered the priests and Levites and said, "Go out to the cities of Judah and collect silver from all Israel to repair the temple of your God as needed year by year, and do it quickly."

However, the Levites did not hurry. [6] So the king called Jehoiada the high priest and said, "Why haven't you required the Levites to bring from Judah and Jerusalem the tax imposed by the LORD's servant Moses and the assembly of Israel for the tent of the testimony? [7] For the sons of that wicked Athaliah broke into the LORD's temple and even used the sacred things of the LORD's temple for the Baals."

[8] At the king's command a chest was made and placed outside the gate of the LORD's temple. [9] Then a proclamation was issued in Judah and Jerusalem that the tax God's servant Moses imposed on Israel in the wilderness be brought to the LORD. [10] All the leaders and all the people rejoiced, brought the tax, and put it in the chest until it was full. [11] Whenever the chest was brought by the Levites to the king's overseers, and when they saw that there was

---

[A]23:9 Or *spears and large and small shields*   [B]23:13 LXX reads *post*   [C]23:18 Lit *song on the hands of*

---

unarmed, but they received weapons as soon as they entered.
23:11 Then they brought in Joash and began to acclaim the child as king. The **testimony** may have been a copy of the Torah, perhaps Deuteronomy, but it may also have been a copy of the agreement that Jehoiada had made with all the leaders acknowledging Joash as the rightful king.
23:12–13 The **pillar** was apparently where coronations traditionally took place (Jdg 9:6; 2Kg 11:14; 23:3). Athaliah probably would not have recognized little Joash, so she concluded that someone was committing **treason**.
23:16–17 Jehoiada would speak for the child **king** while he was too young to make decisions. On behalf of the king, he and **the**

people agreed to return to the Lord. They went to **the temple of Baal**, the main center of worship during the time of Jehoram, Ahaziah, and Athaliah. They destroyed the building, the **altars**, the idols, and the priest of Baal, **Mattan**.
23:20–21 Jehoiada and his co-conspirators escorted young Joash to the royal **palace** and placed him on the **throne**. The word **quiet** is the same word used in Judges when the nation was at peace, with no threats (Jdg 3:11; cp. Jb 3:26; Is 32:17; Jr 30:10).
24:1–3 Joash: Seventh king of Judah; son of Ahaziah; installed while still a boy by Jehoiada when he dethroned Athaliah; obeyed God as long as Jehoiada was alive, but turned to evil as soon as Jehoiada died.

24:4 Upon reaching adulthood, Joash decided it was time for **the LORD's temple** to be repaired and renovated. It had been largely ignored for many years.
24:5 Joash commissioned the **Levites** to travel throughout the kingdom of Judah and to **collect silver** for this renovation.
24:6–7 Jehoiada, as **high priest**, was supervisor of the **Levites**. Joash called him to account for the lack of speed by those who reported to him.
24:8–11 Jehoiada did not send the Levites from town to town to collect the money. Instead, he sent them out to require the people to come to Jerusalem and deposit money in a **chest** that Joash had placed at the **gate** of the temple. This plan worked.

a large amount of silver, the king's secretary and the high priest's deputy came and emptied the chest, picked it up, and returned it to its place. They did this daily and gathered the silver in abundance. [12] Then the king and Jehoiada gave it to those in charge of the labor on the LORD's temple, who were hiring stonecutters and carpenters to renovate the LORD's temple, also blacksmiths and coppersmiths to repair the LORD's temple.

[13] The workmen did their work, and through them the repairs progressed. They restored God's temple to its specifications and reinforced it. [14] When they finished, they presented the rest of the silver to the king and Jehoiada, who made articles for the LORD's temple with it — articles for ministry and for making burnt offerings, and ladles[A] and articles of gold and silver. They regularly offered burnt offerings in the LORD's temple throughout Jehoiada's life.

Joash's Apostasy

[15] Jehoiada died when he was old and full of days; he was 130 years old at his death. [16] He was buried in the city of David with the kings because he had done what was good in Israel with respect to God and his temple.

[17] However, after Jehoiada died, the rulers of Judah came and paid homage to the king. Then the king listened to them, [18] and they abandoned the temple of the LORD, the God of their ancestors, and served the Asherah poles and the idols. So there was wrath against Judah and Jerusalem for this guilt of theirs. [19] Nevertheless, he sent them prophets to bring them back to the LORD; they admonished them, but the people would not listen.

[20] The Spirit of God enveloped[B] Zechariah son of Jehoiada the priest. He stood above the people and said to them, "This is what God says, 'Why are you transgressing the LORD's commands so that you do not prosper? Because you have abandoned the LORD, he has abandoned you.'" [21] But they conspired against him and stoned him at the king's command in the courtyard of the LORD's temple. [22] King Joash didn't remember the kindness that Zechariah's father Jehoiada had extended to him, but killed his son. While he was dying, he said, "May the LORD see and demand an account."

Aramean Invasion of Judah

[23] At the turn of the year, an Aramean army attacked Joash. They entered Judah and Jerusalem and destroyed all the leaders of the people among them and sent all the plunder to the king of Damascus. [24] Although the Aramean army came with only a few men, the LORD handed over a vast army to them because the people of Judah had abandoned the LORD, the God of their ancestors. So they executed judgment on Joash.

Joash Assassinated

[25] When the Arameans saw that Joash had many wounds, they left him. His servants conspired against him, and killed him on his bed, because he had shed the blood of the sons of the priest Jehoiada. So he died, and they buried him in the city of David, but they did not bury him in the tombs of the kings.

[26] Those who conspired against him were Zabad, son of the Ammonite woman Shimeath, and Jehozabad, son of the Moabite woman Shimrith.[C] [27] The accounts concerning his sons, the many divine pronouncements about him, and the restoration of God's temple are recorded in the Writing of the Book of the Kings. His son Amaziah became king in his place.

Judah's King Amaziah

25 Amaziah became king when he was twenty-five years old, and he reigned twenty-nine years in Jerusalem. His mother's name was Jehoaddan; she was from Jerusalem. [2] He did what was right in the LORD's sight but not wholeheartedly.

[3] As soon as the kingdom was firmly in his grasp,[D] he executed his servants who had killed his father the king. [4] However, he did not put

---

[A] 24:14 Or *dishes*, or *spoons*; lit *palms*   [B] 24:20 Lit *clothed*   [C] 24:26 = Shomer in 2Kg 12:21   [D] 25:3 LXX, Syr; MT reads *was strong on him*; 1Kg 14:4

24:12–13 The money collected went exactly where it was needed—to the **workmen** who were carrying out the renovation.
24:14 When all the construction work was done and the workers had been paid, there was enough money left over to replace the temple utensils so sacrificial rituals could be carried out efficiently and with dignity.
24:15–16 Jehoiada the high priest, Joash's adviser, died at the age of **130 years**. He was buried with honor normally accorded only to kings.
24:17–18 The people who won Joash's confidence had authority in various parts of Judah. Like Rehoboam, Joash followed bad advice (10:8). They persuaded the king to abandon the Lord and to return to the

idolatry that Joash along with **Jehoiada** had attempted to root out.
24:19 God did not give up on Joash but conveyed his will by way of **prophets**. Yet the king continued to support and encourage false worship.
24:20–22 Jehoiada's son **Zechariah** made a speech confronting the people with their idolatry. The king enlisted a number of functionaries who stoned Zechariah to death in the **courtyard** of the **temple**. To this day, the tomb of Zechariah can be seen outside Jerusalem in the Kidron Valley. It was this Zechariah to whom Jesus referred when he accused the leaders of his day of hypocrisy (Lk 11:47–51).
24:23–24 With a weak and confused King **Joash** on the throne, and absent the Lord's

protection, the Arameans were able to conquer Jerusalem with a small force and carry off valuables again.
24:25 The **Arameans** despised Joash so much that they left him to die after he was severely wounded. **His servants** took advantage of the situation and killed him as he was lying defenseless **on his bed**. Joash was buried unceremoniously outside the usual location for the **tombs of the kings**.
24:26 The two servants who assassinated Joash were Gentiles, sons of an **Ammonite woman** and a **Moabite woman**, respectively.
25:1–4 Amaziah: Ninth king of Judah, son of Joash; turned from God to idol worship. Amaziah **executed** the two men who had killed his father, but he did not follow the

their children to death, because — as it is written in the Law, in the book of Moses, where the LORD commanded — "Fathers are not to die because of children, and children are not to die because of fathers, but each one will die for his own sin."

Amaziah's Campaign against Edom

⁵ Then Amaziah gathered Judah and assembled them according to ancestral families,^ according to commanders of thousands, and according to commanders of hundreds. He numbered those twenty years old or more for all Judah and Benjamin. He found there to be three hundred thousand fit young men who could serve in the army, bearing spear and shield. ⁶ Then for 7,500 pounds^B of silver he hired one hundred thousand valiant warriors from Israel.

⁷ However, a man of God came to him and said, "King, do not let Israel's army go with you, for the LORD is not with Israel — all the Ephraimites. ⁸ But if you go with them, do it! Be strong for battle! But God will make you stumble before the enemy, for God has the power to help or to make one stumble."

⁹ Then Amaziah said to the man of God, "What should I do about the 7,500 pounds of silver I gave to Israel's division?"

The man of God replied, "The LORD is able to give you much more than this."

¹⁰ So Amaziah released the division that came to him from Ephraim to go home. But they got very angry with Judah and returned home in a fierce rage.

¹¹ Amaziah strengthened his position and led his people to the Salt Valley. He struck down ten thousand Seirites,^C ¹² and the Judahites captured ten thousand alive. They took them to the top of a cliff where they threw them off, and all of them were dashed to pieces.

¹³ As for the men of the division that Amaziah sent back so they would not go with him into battle, they raided the cities of Judah from Samaria to Beth-horon, struck down three thousand of their people, and took a great deal of plunder.

¹⁴ After Amaziah came from the attack on the Edomites, he brought the gods of the Seirites and set them up as his gods. He worshiped before them and burned incense to them. ¹⁵ So the LORD's anger was against Amaziah, and he sent a prophet to him, who said, "Why have you sought a people's gods that could not rescue their own people from you?"

¹⁶ While he was still speaking to him, the king asked, "Have we made you the king's counselor? Stop, why should you lose your life?"

So the prophet stopped, but he said, "I know that God intends to destroy you, because you have done this and have not listened to my advice."

Amaziah's War with Israel's King Jehoash

¹⁷ King Amaziah of Judah took counsel and sent word to Jehoash^D son of Jehoahaz, son of Jehu, king of Israel, and challenged him: "Come, let's meet face to face."

¹⁸ King Jehoash of Israel sent word to King Amaziah of Judah, saying, "The thistle in Lebanon sent a message to the cedar in Lebanon, saying, 'Give your daughter to my son as a wife.' Then a wild animal in Lebanon passed by and trampled the thistle. ¹⁹ You have said, 'Look, I^E have defeated Edom,' and you have become overconfident^F that you will get glory. Now stay at home. Why stir up such trouble so that you fall and Judah with you?"

---

^25:5 Lit *house of fathers*   ^25:6 Lit *100 talents*, also in v. 9   ^25:11 = Edomites, also in v. 14   ^25:17 Lit *Joash*   ^25:19 Some LXX mss, Old Lat, Tg, Vg; MT reads *you*   ^25:19 Lit *and your heart has lifted you*

---

usual practice of executing an entire family (22:10; 2Kg 10:11), killing only the men and **not . . . their children** (Dt 24:16).
25:5–6 The nation of Edom had rebelled against Judah's control during the reign of Jehoram (21:8). Now **Amaziah** decided to bring the Edomites back in line, and he assembled an army for this purpose. The army that Amaziah put together was the smallest since the division of the kingdom. Amaziah could only conscript **three hundred thousand** soldiers. He felt that this was not enough, so he hired **one hundred thousand** mercenaries from the northern kingdom of Israel. Once again a king of Judah allied himself with armed forces from **Israel**, though this time he did it in his own cause and at the hefty cost of **7,500 pounds of silver**, paid in advance.
25:7–10 A prophet appeared on the scene to issue a warning from God to the king. He told **Amaziah** that if he took the northern soldiers on his venture, he would ensure defeat. Amaziah was flabbergasted that all the Lord expected him to waste all that silver. Before they returned **home**, the mercenaries

attacked a number of cities of Judah. They helped themselves to plunder to compensate for what they had missed by not participating in the war against Edom (v. 13).
25:11–12 As promised, Amaziah's expedition against Edom was a success. The army of Judah killed **ten thousand** Edomites in battle and then executed another **ten thousand** prisoners of war.
25:13 It is hard to understand how northern troops could plunder cities of Judah starting **from Samaria**. Perhaps "Samaria" is another name for Migron in Judah. Another possibility is that the troops were released immediately after mustering in Samaria, and they worked their way south from there into Judah. **Beth-horon** is northwest of Jerusalem.
25:14–15 Amaziah's next action is virtually unfathomable. **Amaziah** had just won over the **Edomites**, and he did so after he had fulfilled God's ultimatum when the prophet assured him of victory on that basis. But incredibly, Amaziah took the **gods** of the people whom he had defeated and started to worship them.

25:16 When God sent another **prophet** to rebuke the king, Amaziah reacted defensively and threatened to kill the prophet (cp. 32:25–26), but the prophet managed to get in the last word and told Amaziah his destruction was assured.
25:17 Jehoash: Twelfth king of Israel; **son of Jehoahaz**; defeated Amaziah of Judah in response to Amaziah's challenge. Once again, it is essential to keep track of the names of the kings because of the duplication of names in the northern and southern kingdoms. Jehoahaz of Israel was the son of Jehu, who had killed Ahab and made himself king of Israel. Jehoash was Jehoahaz's son. Jehoash was the king of Israel contemporary with **Amaziah of Judah**. When Amaziah had returned home after his campaign against Edom and had learned of the damage done by the mercenaries from the north, he called for a showdown with Jehoash.
25:18–20 Amaziah had acquired an inflated sense of his military prowess, so when **Jehoash** tried to talk him out of going to war, Amaziah persisted with his plan to invade the northern kingdom.

20 But Amaziah would not listen, for this turn of events was from God in order to hand them over to their enemies because they went after the gods of Edom. **21** So King Jehoash of Israel advanced. He and King Amaziah of Judah met face to face at Beth-shemesh that belonged to Judah. **22** Judah was routed before Israel, and each man fled to his own tent. **23** King Jehoash of Israel captured Judah's King Amaziah son of Joash, son of Jehoahaz,^A at Beth-shemesh. Then Jehoash took him to Jerusalem and broke down two hundred yards^B of Jerusalem's wall from the Ephraim Gate to the Corner Gate.^C **24** He took all the gold, silver, all the utensils that were found with Obed-edom in God's temple, the treasures of the king's palace, and the hostages. Then he returned to Samaria.

Amaziah's Death

25 Judah's King Amaziah son of Joash lived fifteen years after the death of Israel's King Jehoash son of Jehoahaz. **26** The rest of the events of Amaziah's reign, from beginning to end, are written in the Book of the Kings of Judah and Israel. **27** From the time Amaziah turned from following the LORD, a conspiracy was formed against him in Jerusalem, and he fled to Lachish. However, men were sent after him to Lachish, and they put him to death there. **28** They carried him back on horses and buried him with his ancestors in the city of Judah.^D

Judah's King Uzziah

26 All the people of Judah took Uzziah,^E who was sixteen years old, and made him king in place of his father Amaziah. **2** After Amaziah the king rested with his ancestors, Uzziah rebuilt Eloth^F and restored it to Judah. **3** Uzziah was sixteen years old when he became king, and he reigned fifty-two years in Jerusalem. His mother's name was Jecoliah; she was from Jerusalem. **4** He did what was right in the LORD's sight just as his father Amaziah had done. **5** He sought God throughout the lifetime of Zechariah, the teacher of the fear^G of God. During the time that he sought the LORD, God gave him success.

Uzziah's Exploits

6 Uzziah went out to wage war against the Philistines, and he tore down the wall of Gath, the wall of Jabneh, and the wall of Ashdod. Then he built cities in the vicinity of Ashdod and among the Philistines. **7** God helped him against the Philistines, the Arabs that live in Gur-baal, and the Meunites. **8** The Ammonites^H paid tribute to Uzziah, and his fame spread as far as the entrance of Egypt, for God made him very powerful. **9** Uzziah built towers in Jerusalem at the Corner Gate, the Valley Gate, and the corner buttress, and he fortified them. **10** Since he had many cattle both in the Judean foothills^I and the plain, he built towers in the desert and dug many wells. And since he was a lover of the soil, he had farmers and vinedressers in the hills and in the fertile lands.^J **11** Uzziah had an army equipped for combat that went out to war by division according to their assignments, as recorded by Jeiel the court secretary and Maaseiah the officer under the authority of Hananiah, one of the king's commanders. **12** The total number of family heads was 2,600 valiant warriors.

^A **25:23** = Ahaziah in 2Kg 14:13   ^B **25:23** Lit *400 cubits*   ^C **25:23** Some Hb mss; other Hb mss read *to Happoneh*   ^D **25:28** Some Hb mss read *city of David*   ^E **26:1** = Azariah in 2Kg 14:21   ^F **26:2** LXX, Syr, Vg read *Elath*   ^G **26:5** Some Hb mss, LXX, Syr, Tg, Arabic; other Hb mss, Vg read *visions*   ^H **26:8** LXX reads *Meunites*   ^I **26:10** Or *the Shephelah*   ^J **26:10** Or *in Carmel*

25:21–24 When **Jehoash** realized that **Amaziah** was not going to let up, he marched with his army into Judah, and Amaziah got the opportunity for the military confrontation that he wanted. Jehoash decimated the army of Judah and captured Amaziah. The **Jehoahaz** referred to here (v. 23) is Amaziah's grandfather, usually called Ahaziah who, again, is not identical with the northern king of the same name. Jehoash used Amaziah as a hostage to allow him to head straight to Jerusalem, where he destroyed **two hundred yards** of the city **wall** and then plundered all the valuables from the palace and the temple, as well as taking **hostages**. **Obed-edom** stems from the name of the Levite who played in the musical ensemble when the ark was moved, and who was made a guard of one of the gates of God's house while his sons were put in charge of the storehouse (1Ch 26:15). Apparently from that time on the gatekeepers were called "Obed-edom" in honor of this man, and thus it was by this name that the Chronicler referred to them as he described Jehoash's plundering. **25:25–28** Amaziah continued as king for many years, but just as his father **Joash** had done, he lost the confidence of his people.

Eventually, because of an assassination plot against him, he had to flee Jerusalem and seek safety in the citadel of **Lachish**, thirty miles southwest of Jerusalem. His pursuers caught up with him there and killed him. At least he was accorded a proper burial in the royal tombs in Jerusalem. **26:1 Uzziah**: Tenth king of Judah; called Azariah in 2Kg 15; son of Amaziah; devoted to God, but was struck with a serious skin disease when he attempted to burn incense to God in the temple. When Uzziah became king of Judah at age **sixteen**, it was probably as a coregent during the time when his father **Amaziah** was held captive by King Jehoash of Israel, and then later when Amaziah was fleeing for his life from his assassins. Uzziah learned the lessons that his predecessor had refused to accept and became a godly and righteous king. His long reign of fifty-two years, though limited by coregency for the first part and his being in seclusion with a disease in the second part, was generally a time of peace and prosperity in the land. **26:2** One of the first things **Uzziah** did was to rebuild the seaport of **Eloth**, at the northern tip of the Red Sea. This meant that Judah was once again a player among the major

powers and had access to the Mediterranean Sea and the Red Sea. **26:5** This **Zechariah**, not the son of Jehoiada (24:20) or the prophet who has a book of the Bible named after him, fulfilled in some ways the same role for Uzziah as Jehoiada had done for Joash (24:2). When Zechariah died, Uzziah also weakened in his commitment to the Lord. **26:6–10** The **Philistines** appeared again during the time of Jehoshaphat when they presented tribute to the king in Jerusalem, and then again during the reign of Ahaziah when they invaded Jerusalem and carried off much treasure. Now Uzziah reasserted Judah's dominance over the Philistines by capturing their cities and destroying their walls. Uzziah was also able to bring back into line certain **Arabs**, the **Meunites** (Edomites), and the **Ammonites**. He not only fortified strategic corners in **Jerusalem**, but he also established settlements in the country, laying claim to the land not by military occupation but by agricultural development. **26:11–15** Uzziah had a different philosophy about the **army** than his predecessors. Instead of drastically increasing the size of his army, he organized them into more flexible

¹³ Under their authority was an army of 307,500 equipped for combat, a powerful force to help the king against the enemy. ¹⁴ Uzziah provided the entire army with shields, spears, helmets, armor, bows, and slingstones. ¹⁵ He made skillfully designed devices in Jerusalem to shoot arrows and catapult large stones for use on the towers and on the corners. So his fame spread even to distant places, for he was wondrously helped until he became strong.

Uzziah's Disease

¹⁶ But when he became strong, he grew arrogant, and it led to his own destruction. He acted unfaithfully against the LORD his God by going into the LORD's sanctuary to burn incense on the incense altar. ¹⁷ The priest Azariah, along with eighty brave priests of the LORD, went in after him. ¹⁸ They took their stand against King Uzziah and said, "Uzziah, you have no right to offer incense to the LORD — only the consecrated priests, the descendants of Aaron, have the right to offer incense. Leave the sanctuary, for you have acted unfaithfully! You will not receive honor from the LORD God."

¹⁹ Uzziah, with a firepan in his hand to offer incense, was enraged. But when he became enraged with the priests, in the presence of the priests in the LORD's temple beside the altar of incense, a skin disease broke out on his forehead. ²⁰ Then Azariah the chief priest and all the priests turned to him and saw that he was diseased on his forehead. They rushed him out of there. He himself also hurried to get out because the LORD had afflicted him. ²¹ So King Uzziah was diseased to the time of his death. He lived in quarantineᴬ with a serious skin disease and was excluded from access to the LORD's temple, while his son Jotham was over the king's household governing the people of the land.

²² Now the prophet Isaiah son of Amoz wrote about the rest of the events of Uzziah's reign, from beginning to end. ²³ Uzziah rested with his ancestors, and he was buried with his ancestors in the burial ground of the kings' cemetery, for they said, "He has a skin disease." His son Jotham became king in his place.

Judah's King Jotham

27 Jotham was twenty-five years old when he became king, and he reigned sixteen years in Jerusalem. His mother's name was Jerushah daughter of Zadok. ² He did what was right in the LORD's sight just as his father Uzziah had done. In addition, he didn't enter the LORD's sanctuary, but the people still behaved corruptly.

³ Jotham built the Upper Gate of the LORD's temple, and he built extensively on the wall of Ophel. ⁴ He also built cities in the hill country of Judah and fortresses and towers in the forests. ⁵ He waged war against the king of the Ammonites. He overpowered the Ammonites, and that year they gave him 7,500 poundsᴮ of silver, 60,000 bushelsᶜ of wheat, and 60,000 bushels of barley. They paid him the same in the second and third years. ⁶ So Jotham strengthened his position because he did not waver in obeyingᴰ the LORD his God.

⁷ As for the rest of the events of Jotham's reign, along with all his wars and his ways, note that they are written in the Book of the Kings of Israel and Judah. ⁸ He was twenty-five years old when he became king, and he reigned sixteen years in Jerusalem. ⁹ Jotham rested with his ancestors and was buried in the city of David. His son Ahaz became king in his place.

Judah's King Ahaz

28 Ahaz was twenty years old when he became king, and he reigned sixteen years in Jerusalem. He did not do what was right in the LORD's sight like his ancestor David, ² for he walked in the ways of the kings of Israel and made cast images of the Baals. ³ He burned incense in Ben Hinnom Valley and burned his children inᴱ the fire, imitating the detestable practices of the nations the LORD

ᴬ26:21 Lit *in a house of exemption from duty* ᴮ27:5 Lit *100 talents* ᶜ27:5 Lit *10,000 cors* ᴰ27:6 Lit *he established his ways before* ᴱ28:3 LXX, Syr, Tg read *and passed his children through*

---

divisions, and he made sure they had effective weapons. As a result, he became well-known and **strong**.
26:16 Although Uzziah did not commit idolatry, he still overstepped his royal authority by assuming a role that God had denied to any person who was not a descendant of Aaron of the tribe of Levi. He went into the holy place and burned **incense**, something that only a priest was allowed to do.
26:17–18 Azariah, a priest, and **eighty** of his colleagues confronted the king and told him that what he was about to do was wrong.
26:19–21 Uzziah already had the incense **firepan** in his hand. Rather than listen to the priests, he became furious and continued. Immediately God punished him by having a **skin disease** break out **on his forehead**. The king dropped what he was doing and

allowed himself to be led out of the **temple** into seclusion for the rest of his life. Though he was still officially the king, **his son Jotham** was placed in charge of the day-to-day duties of king.
26:22 This refers to a writing of the prophet **Isaiah** that we do not have, but see Is 6:1.
26:23 Uzziah received a proper royal burial, though his tomb may have been separated from those of the previous kings because of the unclean condition caused by his skin disease.
27:1 Jotham: Eleventh king of Judah; son of Uzziah; devoted to God but not influential. Much of his time on the throne overlapped with the time that his father, Uzziah, was king.
27:2 The Chronicler gives Jotham a good report card for his personal faith. However,

Jotham did not attempt to purify the land of idolatry or encourage the people to return to God.
27:3 Jotham took advantage of the peace that he inherited to reinforce the **wall** of Jerusalem and to carry out improvements on the **LORD's temple**.
27:4 Jotham apparently coreigned with his father Uzziah from 750 to 740 BC, the year Uzziah died.
27:5–6 Jotham continued his father's policy of controlling the **Ammonites** and carried out a successful military excursion against them. This garnered him a large amount of **silver** and grain for several years.
28:1–4 Ahaz: Eleventh king of Judah; son of Jotham; confirmed idol worshiper; submitted voluntarily to Assyria. When Ahaz ascended the throne, the people and their king had

had dispossessed before the Israelites. **4** He sacrificed and burned incense on the high places, on the hills, and under every green tree.

5 So the LORD his God handed Ahaz over to the king of Aram. He attacked him and took many captives to Damascus.

Ahaz was also handed over to the king of Israel, who struck him with great force: **6** Pekah son of Remaliah killed one hundred twenty thousand in Judah in one day — all brave men — because they had abandoned the LORD God of their ancestors. **7** An Ephraimite warrior named Zichri killed the king's son Maaseiah, Azrikam governor of the palace, and Elkanah who was second to the king. **8** Then the Israelites took two hundred thousand captives from their brothers — women, sons, and daughters. They also took a great deal of plunder from them and brought it to Samaria.

9 A prophet of the LORD named Oded was there. He went out to meet the army that came to Samaria and said to them, "Look, the LORD God of your ancestors handed them over to you because of his wrath against Judah, but you slaughtered them in a rage that has reached heaven. **10** Now you plan to reduce the people of Judah and Jerusalem, male and female, to slavery. Are you not also guilty before the LORD your God? **11** Listen to me and return the captives you took from your brothers, for the LORD's burning anger is on you."

12 So some men who were leaders of the Ephraimites — Azariah son of Jehohanan, Berechiah son of Meshillemoth, Jehizkiah son of Shallum, and Amasa son of Hadlai — stood in opposition to those coming from the war. **13** They said to them, "You must not bring the captives here, for you plan to bring guilt on us from the LORD to add to our sins and our guilt. For we have much guilt, and burning anger is on Israel."

14 The army left the captives and the plunder in the presence of the officers and the congregation. **15** Then the men who were designated by name took charge of the captives and provided clothes for their naked ones from the plunder. They clothed them, gave them sandals, food and drink, dressed their wounds, and provided donkeys for all the feeble. The Israelites brought them to Jericho, the City of Palms, among their brothers. Then they returned to Samaria.

16 At that time King Ahaz asked the king of Assyria for help. **17** The Edomites came again, attacked Judah, and took captives. **18** The Philistines also raided the cities of the Judean foothills[A] and the Negev of Judah. They captured and occupied Beth-shemesh, Aijalon, and Gederoth, as well as Soco, Timnah, and Gimzo with their surrounding villages. **19** For the LORD humbled Judah because of King Ahaz of Judah,[B] who threw off restraint in Judah and was unfaithful to the LORD. **20** Then King Tiglath-pileser[C] of Assyria came against Ahaz; he oppressed him and did not give him support. **21** Although Ahaz plundered the LORD's temple and the palace of the king and of the rulers and gave the plunder to the king of Assyria, it did not help him.

22 At the time of his distress, King Ahaz himself became more unfaithful to the LORD. **23** He sacrificed to the gods of Damascus which had defeated him; he said, "Since the gods of the kings of Aram are helping them, I will sacrifice to them so that they will help me." But they were the downfall of him and of all Israel. **24** Then Ahaz gathered up the utensils of God's temple, cut them into pieces, shut the doors of the LORD's temple, and made himself altars on every street corner in Jerusalem. **25** He made high places in every city of Judah to offer incense to other gods, and he angered the LORD, the God of his ancestors.

A **28:18** Or the Shephelah   B **28:19** Some Hb mss; other Hb mss read Israel   C **28:20** Text emended; MT reads Tilgath-pilneser; 1Ch 5:6,26

---

become confirmed idol worshipers. Ahaz took the worship **of the Baals** to the point of burning his own **children** as an offering to Baal.
28:5–8 Pekah: Eighteenth and next-to-last king of Israel; scored a major victory over Judah, but released all of his prisoners in response to God's command. Ahaz of Judah had forsaken the Lord so he was defeated by the **king** of **Damascus**, who carried away a number of hostages. Furthermore, Pekah, king of the northern kingdom of Israel, also defeated Ahaz of Judah. Out of Judah's army, **one hundred twenty thousand** were killed. This probably meant that Ahaz was left with less than half of his original army. Additionally, Ahaz lost his **son**, his chief of staff, and his prime minister. Pekah's army also took a huge number of people as hostages and transported them to the capital city of Samaria in Israel. **28:9–11** Once again a prophet appeared—this time a man named **Oded**, who lived in

Samaria. He confronted the returning victorious army with some basic facts about God's divine law. Their slaughter of their fellow Hebrews was not acceptable. Israelites were never to enslave other Israelites, but this is what Pekah was planning to do. **28:12–15** Some leaders of the northern kingdom realized the seriousness of the mistake they were about to make. The army of Israel abandoned the hostages, and some other people were put in charge of making sure they returned to Judah. These captives were given **food** and **clothes**, and some even received **donkeys** on which they could ride back as far as Jericho (**the City of Palms**), where they were left. **28:16–21** Ahaz of Judah found himself under increasing pressure. The nation had already been defeated by Aram and the northern kingdom; now the **Edomites** and the **Philistines** returned to do damage. But

rather than turning to the Lord for help, Ahaz tried to solve his problems by asking **King Tiglath-pileser of Assyria** to protect him. He offered the Assyrian king all his possessions and everything that belonged to the **temple**. Tiglath-pileser did defeat Damascus (which he had planned to do anyway). Then he marched to Jerusalem and helped himself to more property. **28:22–23** Ahaz decided to pursue still another solution. Since the Arameans had defeated him earlier, the king concluded that the **gods of Damascus** must be strong, so he worshiped them. **28:24–25** Ahaz seemed to become angry at God. His solution for dealing with these ineffective false gods was to empty the **temple** of the true God, **shut** its **doors**, and continue to proliferate idolatrous worship sites. The prophet Isaiah had specifically warned Ahaz against making this unreliable alliance with the Assyrians (Is 7–8).

Ahaz's Death

[26] As for the rest of his deeds and all his ways, from beginning to end, they are written in the Book of the Kings of Judah and Israel. [27] Ahaz rested with his ancestors and was buried in the city, in Jerusalem, but they did not bring him into the tombs of the kings of Israel. His son Hezekiah became king in his place.

Judah's King Hezekiah

29 Hezekiah was twenty-five years old when he became king, and he reigned twenty-nine years in Jerusalem. His mother's name was Abijah[A] daughter of Zechariah. [2] He did what was right in the LORD's sight just as his ancestor David had done.

[3] In the first year of his reign, in the first month, he opened the doors of the LORD's temple and repaired them. [4] Then he brought in the priests and Levites and gathered them in the eastern public square. [5] He said to them, "Hear me, Levites. Consecrate yourselves now and consecrate the temple of the LORD, the God of your ancestors. Remove everything impure from the holy place. [6] For our ancestors were unfaithful and did what is evil in the sight of the LORD our God. They abandoned him, turned their faces away from the LORD's dwelling place, and turned their backs on him.[B] [7] They also closed the doors of the portico, extinguished the lamps, did not burn incense, and did not offer burnt offerings in the holy place of the God of Israel. [8] Therefore, the wrath of the LORD was on Judah and Jerusalem, and he made them an object of terror, horror, and mockery,[C] as you see with your own eyes. [9] Our fathers fell by the sword, and our sons, our daughters, and our wives are in captivity because of this. [10] It is in my heart now to make a covenant with the LORD, the God of Israel so that his burning anger may turn away from us. [11] My sons, don't be negligent now, for the LORD has chosen you to stand in his presence, to serve him, and to be his ministers and burners of incense."

Cleansing the Temple

[12] Then the Levites stood up:

Mahath son of Amasai and Joel son of Azariah from the Kohathites;

Kish son of Abdi and Azariah son of Jehallelel from the Merarites;

Joah son of Zimmah and Eden son of Joah from the Gershonites;

[13] Shimri and Jeuel from the Elizaphanites;

Zechariah and Mattaniah from the Asaphites;

[14] Jehiel[D] and Shimei from the Hemanites; Shemaiah and Uzziel from the Jeduthunites.

[15] They gathered their brothers together, consecrated themselves, and went according to the king's command by the words of the LORD to cleanse the LORD's temple.

[16] The priests went to the entrance of the LORD's temple to cleanse it. They took all the unclean things they found in the LORD's sanctuary to the courtyard of the LORD's temple. Then the Levites received them and took them outside to the Kidron Valley. [17] They began the consecration on the first day of the first month, and on the eighth day of the month they came to the portico of the LORD's temple. They consecrated the LORD's temple for eight days, and on the sixteenth day of the first month they finished.

[18] Then they went inside to King Hezekiah and said, "We have cleansed the whole temple of the LORD, the altar of burnt offering and all its utensils, and the table for the rows of the Bread of the Presence and all its utensils. [19] We have set up and consecrated all the utensils that King Ahaz rejected during his reign when he became unfaithful. They are in front of the altar of the LORD."

Renewal of Temple Worship

[20] King Hezekiah got up early, gathered the city officials, and went to the LORD's temple. [21] They brought seven bulls, seven rams, seven lambs, and seven male goats as a sin offering for the kingdom, for the sanctuary, and for Judah. Then he told the descendants of Aaron, the priests, to offer them on the altar of the LORD. [22] So they slaughtered the bulls, and the priests received the blood and splattered it on the altar. They slaughtered the rams and splattered the blood on the altar. They slaughtered the lambs and splattered the blood on

---

29:1-2 Hezekiah: Twelfth king of Judah; son of Ahaz; devoted to God; protected miraculously from Sennacherib of Assyria. Just as it looked as if things were so bad they could never be set right again, Hezekiah became king and led Judah in returning to God. With the highest compliment the Chronicler could pay a king, he compared Hezekiah to **David** because of his pursuit of righteousness. **29:3** Soon after becoming king, Hezekiah **opened the doors** of the **temple** again and undid the damage that Ahaz had caused.

29:15-19 Before the **priests** could do anything in the **temple**, they first had to **cleanse** themselves so they would be in a state of spiritual and ritual purity; otherwise, they would contaminate the temple as they were trying to purify it. Once they had taken care of this, they could remove all the things that did not belong there, particularly whatever was associated with idolatry. The **Kidron Valley** was used as a garbage dump where trash was burned (15:16; cp. 2Kg 23:4,6). They worked methodically by

starting at the gate and moving toward the holy place and the most holy place. When they were finished, they reported on their work to the king. **29:20-24 Hezekiah** began the services in the temple with a **sin offering**, the type of sacrifice that was intended to atone for unwitting violations of the law (Lv 4:3-34). There were **seven** of each animal as a symbol of completeness. He and the priests followed the rules as given by God to Moses.

the altar. [23] Then they brought the goats for the sin offering right into the presence of the king and the congregation, who laid their hands on them. [24] The priests slaughtered the goats and put their blood on the altar for a sin offering, to make atonement for all Israel, for the king said that the burnt offering and sin offering were for all Israel.

[25] Hezekiah stationed the Levites in the LORD's temple with cymbals, harps, and lyres according to the command of David, Gad the king's seer, and the prophet Nathan. For the command was from the LORD through his prophets. [26] The Levites stood with the instruments of David, and the priests with the trumpets.

[27] Then Hezekiah ordered that the burnt offering be offered on the altar. When the burnt offerings began, the song of the LORD and the trumpets began, accompanied by the instruments of King David of Israel. [28] The whole assembly was worshiping, singing the song, and blowing the trumpets — all this continued until the burnt offering was completed. [29] When the burnt offerings were completed, the king and all those present with him bowed down and worshiped. [30] Then King Hezekiah and the officials told the Levites to sing praise to the LORD in the words of David and of the seer Asaph. So they sang praises with rejoicing and knelt low and worshiped.

[31] Hezekiah concluded, "Now you are consecrated[A] to the LORD. Come near and bring sacrifices and thanksgiving offerings to the LORD's temple." So the congregation brought sacrifices and thanksgiving offerings, and all those with willing hearts brought burnt offerings. [32] The number of burnt offerings the congregation brought was seventy bulls, one hundred rams, and two hundred lambs; all these were for a burnt offering to the LORD. [33] Six hundred bulls and three thousand sheep and goats were consecrated.

[34] However, since there were not enough priests, they weren't able to skin all the burnt offerings, so their Levite brothers helped them until the work was finished and until the priests consecrated themselves. For the Levites were more conscientious[B] to consecrate

themselves than the priests were. [35] Furthermore, the burnt offerings were abundant, along with the fat of the fellowship offerings and with the drink offerings for the burnt offering.

So the service of the LORD's temple was established. [36] Then Hezekiah and all the people rejoiced over how God had prepared the people, for it had come about suddenly.

Celebration of the Passover

30 Then Hezekiah sent word throughout all Israel and Judah, and he also wrote letters to Ephraim and Manasseh to come to the LORD's temple in Jerusalem to observe the Passover of the LORD, the God of Israel. [2] For the king and his officials and the entire congregation in Jerusalem decided to observe the Passover of the LORD in the second month, [3] because they were not able to observe it at the appropriate time. Not enough of the priests had consecrated themselves, and the people hadn't been gathered together in Jerusalem. [4] The proposal pleased the king and the congregation, [5] so they affirmed the proposal and spread the message throughout all Israel, from Beer-sheba to Dan, to come to observe the Passover of the LORD, the God of Israel in Jerusalem, for they hadn't observed it often,[C] as prescribed.[D]

[6] So the couriers went throughout Israel and Judah with letters from the hand of the king and his officials, and according to the king's command, saying, "Israelites, return to the LORD, the God of Abraham, Isaac, and Israel so that he may return to those of you who remain, who have escaped the grasp of the kings of Assyria. [7] Don't be like your ancestors and your brothers who were unfaithful to the LORD, the God of their ancestors so that he made them an object of horror as you yourselves see. [8] Don't become obstinate[E] now like your ancestors did. Give your allegiance[F] to the LORD, and come to his sanctuary that he has consecrated forever. Serve the LORD your God so that he may turn his burning anger away from you, [9] for when you return to the LORD, your brothers and your sons will receive mercy in the presence of their captors and will return to this land. For the LORD your God is gracious and

---

^29:31 Lit *Now you have filled your hands*   ^29:34 Lit *upright of heart*; Ps 32:11; 64:10   ^30:5 Or *in great numbers*   ^30:5 Lit *often, according to what is written*   ^30:8 Lit *Don't stiffen your neck*   ^30:8 Lit *hand*

29:27–29 Next to be offered were **burnt offerings**, the sacrifice that expressed a person's total devotion to the Lord (Lv 1:1–17). As soon as the offering began, the musicians joined in.

29:30 These songs of **praise** by **David** and **Asaph** might have been the same as some of our psalms.

29:31–33 Now that the temple and the priests were ready, Hezekiah called for a sacrificial feast by the priests and the public.

29:34–35 Killing and sacrificing these animals was hard work. **Not enough priests**

were in a state of purity to be able to get it all done. **Levites**, who did not have priestly privileges, were called upon to do everything short of actually offering the sacrifices on the altar. They were able to assist by slaughtering and skinning animals.

30:1 The Assyrians had conquered Israel, so there was no longer any Israelite king to enforce separation from Judah. This enabled Hezekiah to invite everyone—citizens of **Judah** and **Israel** alike—to come to Jerusalem and participate in the **Passover** he was planning.

30:2–5 The **Passover** was **prescribed** to be observed the first month every year, but that did not allow enough time for preparations, so the Passover observance was postponed until **the second month**. The law had a provision that it could be held a month later if necessary (Nm 9:9–11). **Beer-sheba to Dan** encompasses all of Judah and Israel.

30:6–12 The invitation to people from the northern kingdom met with mixed results. Some **mocked** the messengers and declined the invitation, but a few people decided to make the trip to **Jerusalem** for the Passover

merciful; he will not turn his face away from you if you return to him."

[10] The couriers traveled from city to city in the land of Ephraim and Manasseh as far as Zebulun, but the inhabitants[A] laughed at them and mocked them. [11] But some from Asher, Manasseh, and Zebulun humbled themselves and came to Jerusalem. [12] Also, the power of God was at work in Judah to unite them[B] to carry out the command of the king and his officials by the word of the LORD.

[13] A very large assembly of people was gathered in Jerusalem to observe the Festival of Unleavened Bread in the second month. [14] They proceeded to take away the altars that were in Jerusalem, and they took away the incense altars and threw them into the Kidron Valley. [15] They slaughtered the Passover lamb on the fourteenth day of the second month. The priests and Levites were ashamed, and they consecrated themselves and brought burnt offerings to the LORD's temple. [16] They stood at their prescribed posts, according to the law of Moses, the man of God. The priests splattered the blood received from the Levites, [17] for there were many in the assembly who had not consecrated themselves, and so the Levites were in charge of slaughtering the Passover lambs for every unclean person to consecrate the lambs to the LORD. [18] A large number of the people — many from Ephraim, Manasseh, Issachar, and Zebulun — were ritually unclean, yet they had eaten the Passover contrary to what was written. But Hezekiah had interceded for them, saying, "May the good LORD provide atonement on behalf of [19] whoever sets his whole heart on seeking God, the LORD, the God of his ancestors, even though not according to the purification rules of the sanctuary." [20] So the LORD heard Hezekiah and healed the people. [21] The Israelites who were present in Jerusalem observed the Festival of Unleavened Bread seven days with great joy, and the Levites and the priests praised the LORD day after day with loud instruments. [22] Then Hezekiah encouraged[C] all the Levites who performed skillfully before the LORD. They ate at the appointed festival for seven days, sacrificing fellowship offerings and giving thanks to the LORD, the God of their ancestors.

[23] The whole congregation decided to observe seven more days, so they observed seven days with joy, [24] for King Hezekiah of Judah contributed one thousand bulls and seven thousand sheep for the congregation. Also, the officials contributed one thousand bulls and ten thousand sheep for the congregation, and many priests consecrated themselves. [25] Then the whole assembly of Judah with the priests and Levites, the whole assembly that came from Israel, the resident aliens who came from the land of Israel, and those who were living in Judah, rejoiced. [26] There was great rejoicing in Jerusalem, for nothing like this was known since the days of Solomon son of David, the king of Israel. [27] Then the priests and the Levites stood to bless the people, and God heard them, and their prayer came into his holy dwelling place in heaven.

Removal of Idolatry

31 When all this was completed, all Israel who had attended went out to the cities of Judah and broke up the sacred pillars, chopped down the Asherah poles, and tore down the high places and altars throughout Judah and Benjamin, as well as in Ephraim and Manasseh, to the last one.[D] Then all the Israelites returned to their cities, each to his own possession.

Offerings for Levites

[2] Hezekiah reestablished the divisions of the priests and Levites for the burnt offerings and fellowship offerings, for ministry, for giving thanks, and for praise in the gates of the camp of the LORD, each division corresponding to his service among the priests and Levites. [3] The king contributed[E] from his own possessions for the regular morning and evening burnt offerings, the burnt offerings of the Sabbaths, of the New Moons, and of the appointed feasts, as written in the law of the LORD. [4] He told the

---

^A 30:10 Lit *but they*   ^B 30:12 Lit *to give them one heart*   ^C 30:22 Lit *spoke to the heart of*   ^D 31:1 Lit *Manasseh, until finishing*
^E 31:3 Lit *The king's portion*

30:13–14 The **Kidron Valley** was where garbage was dumped and burned.
30:18–20 Many people from the north did not realize that before they were allowed to eat the **Passover** lamb or the unleavened bread, they had to go through personal **purification**. When King Hezekiah prayed for the people who had accidentally contaminated the feast, God did not hold it against them; the occasion remained joyous.
30:23–24 Hezekiah and a number of his officials **contributed** numerous animals to be offered as sacrifices. This eased the economic burden on some members of the **congregation** and also contributed to the **joy** of

the celebration, so by popular acclaim it was extended for another week.
30:25 Even **the resident aliens**—some of the people who had just been resettled into the former northern kingdom by the Assyrian conquerors—came to Jerusalem and took part in the celebration.
31:1 After this lengthy Passover feast, the people demonstrated their renewed devotion by going throughout the area to destroy all the idols, pagan **altars**, and **Asherah poles**. They even went into the territory of the former northern kingdom—referred to as **Ephraim and Manasseh**—to carry out this purge.

31:2–3 When **Hezekiah** had finished establishing the priestly rotation, going back to the instructions laid down by David, a practical problem needed to be solved. Who would supply the animals for the sacrifices every morning and evening until this became a routine practice, with the people providing these sacrifices? The king himself contributed the sacrificial animals during this interim period.
31:4–10 Another problem was how to support the **priests and Levites** who had returned to **Jerusalem** to officiate in the temple on a regular basis. David's work schedule was based on the concept

people who lived in Jerusalem to give a contribution for the priests and Levites so that they could devote their energy to the law of the LORD. ⁵ When the word spread, the Israelites gave liberally of the best of the grain, new wine, fresh oil, honey, and of all the produce of the field, and they brought in an abundance, a tenth of everything. ⁶ As for the Israelites and Judahites who lived in the cities of Judah, they also brought a tenth of the herds and flocks, and a tenth of the dedicated things that were consecrated to the LORD their God. They gathered them into large piles. ⁷ In the third month they began building up the piles, and they finished in the seventh month. ⁸ When Hezekiah and his officials came and viewed the piles, they blessed the LORD and his people Israel.

⁹ Hezekiah asked the priests and Levites about the piles. ¹⁰ The chief priest Azariah, of the household of Zadok, answered him, "Since they began bringing the offering to the LORD's temple, we have been eating and are satisfied and there is plenty left over because the LORD has blessed his people; this abundance is what is left over."

¹¹ Hezekiah told them to prepare chambers in the LORD's temple, and they prepared them. ¹² The offering, the tenth, and the dedicated things were brought faithfully. Conaniah the Levite was the officer in charge of them, and his brother Shimei was second. ¹³ Jehiel, Azaziah, Nahath, Asahel, Jerimoth, Jozabad, Eliel, Ismachiah, Mahath, and Benaiah were deputies under the authority of Conaniah and his brother Shimei by appointment of King Hezekiah and of Azariah the chief official of God's temple.

¹⁴ Kore son of Imnah the Levite, the keeper of the East Gate, was over the freewill offerings to God to distribute the contribution to the LORD and the consecrated things. ¹⁵ Eden, Miniamin, Jeshua, Shemaiah, Amariah, and Shecaniah in the cities of the priests were to distribute it faithfully under his authority to their brothers by divisions, whether large or small. ¹⁶ In addition, they distributed it to males registered by genealogy three^A years old and above; to all who would enter the LORD's temple for their daily duty, for their service in their

responsibilities according to their divisions. ¹⁷ They distributed also to those recorded by genealogy of the priests by their ancestral families^B and the Levites twenty years old and above, by their responsibilities in their divisions; ¹⁸ to those registered by genealogy — with all their dependents, wives, sons, and daughters — of the whole assembly (for they had faithfully consecrated themselves as holy); ¹⁹ and to the descendants of Aaron, the priests, in the common fields of their cities, in each and every city. There were men who were registered by name to distribute a portion to every male among the priests and to every Levite recorded by genealogy.

²⁰ Hezekiah did this throughout all Judah. He did what was good and upright and true before the LORD his God. ²¹ He was diligent in every deed that he began in the service of God's temple, in the instruction and the commands, in order to seek his God, and he prospered.

Sennacherib's Invasion

32 After Hezekiah's faithful deeds, King Sennacherib of Assyria came and entered Judah. He laid siege to the fortified cities and intended^C to break into them. ² Hezekiah saw that Sennacherib had come and that he planned^D war on Jerusalem, ³ so he consulted with his officials and his warriors about stopping up the water of the springs that were outside the city, and they helped him. ⁴ Many people gathered and stopped up all the springs and the stream that flowed through the land; they said, "Why should the kings of Assyria come and find abundant water?" ⁵ Then Hezekiah strengthened his position by rebuilding the entire broken-down wall and heightening the towers and the other outside wall. He repaired the supporting terraces of the city of David, and made an abundance of weapons and shields.

⁶ He set military commanders over the people and gathered the people in the square of the city gate. Then he encouraged them,^E saying, ⁷ "Be strong and courageous! Don't be afraid or discouraged before the king of Assyria or before the large army that is with him, for there are more with us than with him. ⁸ He has only

---

^A 31:16 Or 30; 1Ch 23:3   ^B 31:17 Lit by the house of their fathers   ^C 32:1 Lit said to himself   ^D 32:2 Lit that his face was for
^E 32:6 Lit he spoke to their hearts

---

that most of these people would live in various parts of the kingdom, support themselves, and spend only one month a year in Jerusalem on temple duty. Hezekiah implemented a regular **contribution** from all the people for the priests and Levites so they would be able to work in the temple without having to worry about supporting themselves. Upon Hezekiah's order, everyone contributed to this fund, providing a tithe of all their crops and livestock. This effort included people from both Israel and Judah.

32:1 Hezekiah's faith in God was put to the test when **King Sennacherib of Assyria** invaded **Judah**. Before attacking Jerusalem, Sennacherib intended to demolish all the cities of Judah and make off with whatever plunder he could seize. This invasion was in 701 BC. See also Is 36–37.
32:2–5 Sennacherib's strategy gave Hezekiah a chance to prepare for the impending siege of the capital city. In addition to rebuilding and strengthening the city **wall**, he made sure the Assyrians would not have access to the region's water supply. He closed

off all external access to the **water of the springs... outside the city** and built a tunnel that permitted his own people to get to the water (v. 30). The 1,777-foot-long tunnel brought water from the Gihon spring to the Pool of Siloam (Jn 9:7). Working from each end, two teams tunneled through solid rock toward each other until they met. In AD 1880 the six-line Siloam Inscription was discovered in the tunnel. It tells of the meeting of the two teams.
32:6–8 Hezekiah organized his army thoroughly. Then he called the people together

human strength,[A] but we have the LORD our God to help us and to fight our battles." So the people relied on the words of King Hezekiah of Judah.

Sennacherib's Servant's Speech

[9] After this, while King Sennacherib of Assyria with all his armed forces besieged[B] Lachish, he sent his servants to Jerusalem against King Hezekiah of Judah and against all those of Judah who were in Jerusalem, [10] "This is what King Sennacherib of Assyria says: 'What are you relying on that you remain in Jerusalem under siege? [11] Isn't Hezekiah misleading you to give you over to death by famine and thirst when he says, "The LORD our God will keep us from the grasp of the king of Assyria"? [12] Didn't Hezekiah himself remove his high places and his altars and say to Judah and Jerusalem, "You must worship before one altar, and you must burn incense on it"?

[13] "'Don't you know what I and my predecessors have done to all the peoples of the lands? Have any of the national gods of the lands been able to rescue their land from my power? [14] Who among all the gods of these nations that my predecessors completely destroyed was able to rescue his people from my power, that your God should be able to deliver you from my power? [15] So now, don't let Hezekiah deceive you, and don't let him mislead you like this. Don't believe him, for no god of any nation or kingdom has been able to rescue his people from my power or the power of my predecessors. How much less will your God rescue you from my power!'"

[16] His servants said more against the LORD God and against his servant Hezekiah. [17] He also wrote letters to mock the LORD, the God of Israel, saying against him:

Just like the national gods of the lands that did not rescue their people from my power, so Hezekiah's God will not rescue his people from my power.

[18] Then they called out loudly in Hebrew[C] to the people of Jerusalem, who were on the wall, to frighten and discourage them in order that he might capture the city. [19] They spoke against the God of Jerusalem like they had spoken against the gods of the peoples of the earth, which were made by human hands.

Deliverance from Sennacherib

[20] King Hezekiah and the prophet Isaiah son of Amoz prayed about this and cried out to heaven, [21] and the LORD sent an angel who annihilated every valiant warrior, leader, and commander in the camp of the king of Assyria. So the king of Assyria returned in disgrace to his land. He went to the temple of his god, and there some of his own children struck him down with the sword.

[22] So the LORD saved Hezekiah and the inhabitants of Jerusalem from the power of King Sennacherib of Assyria and from the power of all others. He gave them rest[D] on every side. [23] Many were bringing an offering to the LORD to Jerusalem and valuable gifts to King Hezekiah of Judah, and he was exalted in the eyes of all the nations after that.

Hezekiah's Illness and Pride

[24] In those days Hezekiah became sick to the point of death, so he prayed to the LORD, who spoke to him and gave him a miraculous sign. [25] However, because his heart was proud, Hezekiah didn't respond according to the benefit that had come to him. So there was wrath on him, Judah, and Jerusalem. [26] Then Hezekiah humbled himself for the pride of his heart — he and the inhabitants of Jerusalem — so the LORD's wrath didn't come on them during Hezekiah's lifetime.

Hezekiah's Wealth and Works

[27] Hezekiah had abundant riches and glory, and he made himself treasuries for silver, gold,

---

[A]32:8 Lit With him an arm of flesh   [B]32:9 Lit with his dominion was against   [C]32:18 Lit Judahite   [D]32:22 Lit He led them; Ps 23:2

---

and reminded them that Assyria was no match for the **strength** of **the LORD**.

32:9–12 Sennacherib's propaganda minister came to **Jerusalem** and addressed the people from outside the city walls. This spokesman brought up a clever argument based on his own perceptions. He taunted the people and asked how they could expect help from a God whose worship sites had just been eliminated by the king who was now asking them to trust in that God. It seemed to the Assyrian that Hezekiah had acted against his own deity and his own country. But of course what Hezekiah had actually done was to remove the illegitimate worship sites and restore centralized worship at the temple in Jerusalem as God had ordained it.

32:16–19 Additional representatives of Assyria joined in to ridicule the notion that

the people of Jerusalem could expect help from God. Some of the Assyrians were even able to speak directly **in Hebrew to the people**, more effectively conveying their propaganda about the superiority of the Assyrian gods.

32:20–22 The parallel passages of this event (2Kg 18; Is 36–37) provide a lengthier description of the verbal exchanges as well as more detailed information about the events surrounding this siege. For the Chronicler, the crucial thing was that Hezekiah, who received encouragement from the prophet **Isaiah**, trusted in God and received a miraculous reward. An Assyrian army of 185,000 gathered around Jerusalem, but the Lord went to work on behalf of his anointed. In one night the entire army was **annihilated**, and **Sennacherib** was forced

to withdraw and return to his homeland where he was eventually assassinated by his own sons.

32:24 Again, 2 Chronicles provides a shorter version of this event than the reports in 2 Kings and Isaiah. Hezekiah became **sick to the point of death**, but God heard his plea and gave him fifteen more years of life. The Lord provided confirmation of this promise by the **miraculous sign** of having a shadow cast by the sun move in a counterclockwise direction (2Kg 20:1–11).

32:25–26 The **pride** for which Hezekiah was rebuked occurred when he received visitors from Babylon and showed them all his treasures (v. 31; 2Kg 20:12–19). The king did not react defensively when he was corrected on this point (cp. 2Ch 25:16), but **humbled himself** before God and became obedient.

precious stones, spices, shields, and every desirable item. ²⁸ He made warehouses for the harvest of grain, new wine, and fresh oil, and stalls for all kinds of cattle, and pens for flocks. ²⁹ He made cities for himself, and he acquired vast numbers of flocks and herds, for God gave him abundant possessions.

³⁰ This same Hezekiah blocked the upper outlet of the water from the Gihon Spring and channeled it smoothly downward and westward to the city of David. Hezekiah succeeded in everything he did. ³¹ When the ambassadors of Babylon's rulers were sent^A to him to inquire about the miraculous sign that happened in the land, God left him to test him and discover what was in his heart.

Hezekiah's Death

³² As for the rest of the events of Hezekiah's reign and his deeds of faithful love, note that they are written in the Visions of the Prophet Isaiah son of Amoz, and in the Book of the Kings of Judah and Israel. ³³ Hezekiah rested with his ancestors and was buried on the ascent to the tombs of David's descendants. All Judah and the inhabitants of Jerusalem paid him honor at his death. His son Manasseh became king in his place.

Judah's King Manasseh

33 Manasseh was twelve years old when he became king, and he reigned fifty-five years in Jerusalem. ² He did what was evil in the LORD's sight, imitating the detestable practices of the nations that the LORD had dispossessed before the Israelites. ³ He rebuilt the high places that his father Hezekiah had torn down and reestablished the altars for the Baals. He made Asherah poles, and he bowed in worship to all the stars in the sky and served them. ⁴ He built altars in the LORD's temple, where the LORD had said, "Jerusalem is where my name will remain forever." ⁵ He built altars to all the stars in the sky in both courtyards of the LORD's temple. ⁶ He passed his sons through the fire in Ben Hinnom Valley. He practiced witchcraft, divination, and sorcery, and consulted

mediums and spiritists. He did a huge amount of evil in the LORD's sight, angering him.

⁷ Manasseh set up a carved image of the idol, which he had made, in God's temple that God had spoken about to David and his son Solomon: "I will establish my name forever⁸ in this temple and in Jerusalem, which I have chosen out of all the tribes of Israel. ⁸ I will never again remove the feet of the Israelites from the land where I stationed your^c ancestors, if only they will be careful to do all I have commanded them through Moses — all the law, statutes, and judgments." ⁹ So Manasseh caused Judah and the inhabitants of Jerusalem to stray so that they did worse evil than the nations the LORD had destroyed before the Israelites.

Manasseh's Repentance

¹⁰ The LORD spoke to Manasseh and his people, but they didn't listen. ¹¹ So he brought against them the military commanders of the king of Assyria. They captured Manasseh with hooks, bound him with bronze shackles, and took him to Babylon. ¹² When he was in distress, he sought the favor of the LORD his God and earnestly humbled himself before the God of his ancestors. ¹³ He prayed to him, and the LORD was receptive to his prayer. He granted his request and brought him back to Jerusalem, to his kingdom. So Manasseh came to know that the LORD is God.

¹⁴ After this, he built the outer wall of the city of David from west of Gihon in the valley to the entrance of the Fish Gate; he brought it around Ophel, and he heightened it considerably. He also placed military commanders in all the fortified cities of Judah.

¹⁵ He removed the foreign gods and the idol from the LORD's temple, along with all the altars that he had built on the mountain of the LORD's temple and in Jerusalem, and he threw them outside the city. ¹⁶ He built^D the altar of the LORD and offered fellowship and thanksgiving sacrifices on it. Then he told Judah to serve the LORD, the God of Israel. ¹⁷ However, the people still sacrificed at the high places, but only to the LORD their God.

---

^A32:31 LXX, Tg, Vg; MT reads *of Babylon sent*   ^B33:7 LXX, Syr, Tg, Vg; 2Kg 21:7; MT reads *name for Elom*   ^C33:8 LXX, Syr, Vg read *land I gave to their*; 2Kg 21:8   ^D33:16 Some Hb mss, Syr, Tg, Arabic; other Hb mss, LXX, Vg read *restored*

32:32–33 Hezekiah received a good evaluation by the Chronicler, and he was mourned by **all Judah**. He was buried with **honor** among the former kings of Judah. **The Visions of the Prophet Isaiah** probably refers to a lost history written by the prophet (cp. 26:22).

33:1–6 Since **Manasseh** was only **twelve years old** when he came to the throne, he would not have been alive at the time of the miraculous victory over the Assyrians. Furthermore, much of his early life was during the time when Hezekiah's pride stood in the way of full devotion to the Lord, thus setting a negative example for Manasseh. Manasseh

reigned for **fifty-five years**. This king not only undid everything good that Hezekiah had done, but he brought the entire kingdom to a new low in idolatry and disobedience. He **rebuilt** all the sites for idol worship; he burned his **sons** as pagan sacrifices; he immersed himself in the occult; and ultimately he brought the entire nation down with him. **33:1 Manasseh**: Thirteenth king of Judah; son of Hezekiah; extreme idol worshiper. **33:7–10** Manasseh even brought idols into the **temple**. The summary statement that **they did worse evil than the nations the LORD had destroyed before the Israelites** is a horrifying assessment.

33:11–13 Manasseh was captured and carried off to **Babylon** by the **king of Assyria**. The parallel passage in 2Kg 21 does not mention this exile and humiliation, nor does it say that he repented and returned to the Lord. It was a sincere repentance that God honored, so Manasseh was able to return to **Jerusalem** and take up his duties as king once again. **33:14–17** Manasseh attempted to undo all the damage he had caused. He repaired the destruction that had been wrought by the Assyrian invasion; he purified the temple; he removed the idols; he reinstituted regular sacrifices; and he instructed the people to **serve the LORD**.

Manasseh's Death

[18] The rest of the events of Manasseh's reign, along with his prayer to his God and the words of the seers who spoke to him in the name of the LORD, the God of Israel, are written in the Events of Israel's Kings. [19] His prayer and how God was receptive to his prayer, and all his sin and unfaithfulness and the sites where he built high places and set up Asherah poles and carved images before he humbled himself, they are written in the Events of Hozai. [20] Manasseh rested with his ancestors, and he was buried in his own house. His son Amon became king in his place.

Judah's King Amon

[21] Amon was twenty-two years old when he became king, and he reigned two years in Jerusalem. [22] He did what was evil in the LORD's sight, just as his father Manasseh had done. Amon sacrificed to all the carved images that his father Manasseh had made, and he served them. [23] But he did not humble himself before the LORD like his father Manasseh humbled himself; instead, Amon increased his guilt.

[24] So his servants conspired against him and put him to death in his own house. [25] The common people[A] killed all who had conspired against King Amon, and they made his son Josiah king in his place.

Judah's King Josiah

34 Josiah was eight years old when he became king, and he reigned thirty-one years in Jerusalem. [2] He did what was right in the LORD's sight and walked in the ways of his ancestor David; he did not turn aside to the right or the left.

Josiah's Reform

[3] In the eighth year of his reign, while he was still a youth, Josiah began to seek the God of his ancestor David, and in the twelfth year he began to cleanse Judah and Jerusalem of the high places, the Asherah poles, the carved images, and the cast images. [4] Then in his presence the altars of the Baals were torn down, and he chopped down the shrines[B] that were above them. He shattered the Asherah poles, the carved images, and the cast images, crushed them to dust, and scattered them over the graves of those who had sacrificed to them. [5] He burned the bones of the priests on their altars. So he cleansed Judah and Jerusalem. [6] He did the same in the cities of Manasseh, Ephraim, and Simeon, and as far as Naphtali and on their surrounding mountain shrines.[C] [7] He tore down the altars, and he smashed the Asherah poles and the carved images to powder. He chopped down all the shrines throughout the land of Israel and returned to Jerusalem.

Josiah's Repair of the Temple

[8] In the eighteenth year of his reign, in order to cleanse the land and the temple, Josiah sent Shaphan son of Azaliah, along with Maaseiah the governor of the city and the court historian Joah son of Joahaz, to repair the temple of the LORD his God.

[9] So they went to the high priest Hilkiah and gave him the silver brought into God's temple. The Levites and the doorkeepers had collected it from Manasseh, Ephraim, and from the entire remnant of Israel, and from all Judah, Benjamin, and the inhabitants of Jerusalem. [10] They gave it to those doing the work — those who oversaw the LORD's temple. They gave it to the workmen who were working in the LORD's temple, to repair and restore the temple; [11] they gave it to the carpenters and builders and also used it to buy quarried stone and timbers — for joining and making beams — for the buildings that Judah's kings had destroyed.

[12] The men were doing the work with integrity. Their overseers were Jahath and Obadiah, Levites from the Merarites, and Zechariah and Meshullam from the Kohathites as supervisors. The Levites were all skilled with musical instruments. [13] They were also over the porters and were supervising all those doing the work task by task. Some of the Levites were secretaries, officers, and gatekeepers.

---

^A 33:25 Lit The people of the land   ^B 34:4 Lit incense altars, also in v. 7   ^C 34:6 One Hb tradition reads Naphtali with their swords; alt Hb tradition, Syr, Vg read Naphtali, the ruins all around; Hb obscure

---

33:18–20 Manasseh's death notice includes references to the sources for the events that are related in 2 Kings as well as for this particular record of his repentance. He was not **buried** in the area reserved for kings but was laid to rest in **his own house**.

33:21–24 Amon: Fourteenth king of Judah; son of Manasseh; idol worshiper; assassinated by his officials. Whatever repentance or reform Manasseh attempted did not carry over to his son and successor, Amon. He picked up where his father had left off before his repentance, going back into idolatry. But with Amon there was no

midlife repentance. His servants assassinated him after he had reigned for **two years**. The people were probably outraged by the assassination, so they had Amon's assassins **killed**.

34:1 Josiah: Fifteenth king of Judah; son of Amon; became king as a boy; carried out a thorough reform. Josiah came to the throne when he was only **eight years old**.

34:3–5 When Josiah was sixteen years old **(in the eighth year of his reign)**, he decided to become a worshiper of God. Four years later he began to assert his will by removing the various idols from the land and abolishing all pagan places of worship.

He desecrated the **graves** of past idolaters and defiled the pagan **shrines**.

34:9–11 Josiah had sent emissaries to collect **silver** for the repair of God's house. This money was allocated to **the high priest Hilkiah**. He distributed it among the contractors, who gave it to the **workmen**, who passed it on to those who were providing the raw materials.

34:12–13 Some **Levites** were placed in supervisory positions as overseers while others carried out clerical tasks for the construction project. The Chronicler also pointed out that some Levites apparently contributed to the effort by playing their **musical instruments**.

The Recovery of the Book of the Law

¹⁴ When they brought out the silver that had been deposited in the LORD's temple, the priest Hilkiah found the book of the law of the LORD written by the hand of Moses. ¹⁵ Consequently, Hilkiah told the court secretary Shaphan, "I have found the book of the law in the LORD's temple," and he gave the book to Shaphan.

¹⁶ Shaphan took the book to the king, and also reported, "Your servants are doing all that was placed in their hands. ¹⁷ They have emptied out the silver that was found in the LORD's temple and have given it to the overseers and to those doing the work." ¹⁸ Then the court secretary Shaphan told the king, "The priest Hilkiah gave me a book," and Shaphan read from it in the presence of the king.

¹⁹ When the king heard the words of the law, he tore his clothes. ²⁰ Then he commanded Hilkiah, Ahikam son of Shaphan, Abdon son of Micah, the court secretary Shaphan, and the king's servant Asaiah, ²¹ "Go and inquire of the LORD for me and for those remaining in Israel and Judah, concerning the words of the book that was found. For great is the LORD's wrath that is poured out on us because our ancestors have not kept the word of the LORD in order to do everything written in this book."

Huldah's Prophecy of Judgment

²² So Hilkiah and those the king had designated^A went to the prophetess Huldah, the wife of Shallum son of Tokhath, son of Hasrah, keeper of the wardrobe. She lived in Jerusalem in the Second District. They spoke with her about this.

²³ She said to them, "This is what the LORD God of Israel says: Say to the man who sent you to me, ²⁴ 'This is what the LORD says: I am about to bring disaster on this place and on its inhabitants, fulfilling^B all the curses written in the book that they read in the presence of the king of Judah, ²⁵ because they have abandoned me and burned incense to other gods so as to

anger me with all the works of their hands. My wrath will be poured out on this place, and it will not be quenched.' ²⁶ Say this to the king of Judah who sent you to inquire of the LORD: 'This is what the LORD God of Israel says: As for the words that you heard, ²⁷ because your heart was tender and you humbled yourself before God when you heard his words against this place and against its inhabitants, and because you humbled yourself before me, and you tore your clothes and wept before me, I myself have heard' — this is the LORD's declaration. ²⁸ 'I will indeed gather you to your ancestors, and you will be gathered to your grave in peace. Your eyes will not see all the disaster that I am bringing on this place and on its inhabitants.'"

Then they reported to the king.

Affirmation of the Covenant by Josiah and the People

²⁹ So the king sent messengers and gathered all the elders of Judah and Jerusalem. ³⁰ The king went up to the LORD's temple with all the men of Judah and the inhabitants of Jerusalem, as well as the priests and the Levites — all the people from the oldest to the youngest. He read in their hearing all the words of the book of the covenant that had been found in the LORD's temple. ³¹ Then the king stood at his post and made a covenant in the LORD's presence to follow the LORD and to keep his commands, his decrees, and his statutes with all his heart and with all his soul in order to carry out the words of the covenant written in this book. ³² He had all those present in Jerusalem and Benjamin agree^C to it. So all the inhabitants of Jerusalem carried out the covenant of God, the God of their ancestors.

³³ So Josiah removed everything that was detestable from all the lands belonging to the Israelites, and he required all who were present in Israel to serve the LORD their God. Throughout his reign they did not turn aside from following the LORD, the God of their ancestors.

^A 34:22 LXX; MT omits *designated*   ^B 34:24 *fulfilling* supplied for clarity   ^C 34:32 Lit *take a stand*.

34:14–15 The **book of the law** that **Hilkiah** found may have been one or more scrolls containing the entire Pentateuch—the books of Moses from Genesis through Deuteronomy. The book is more commonly thought to be the book of Deuteronomy. **34:16–17** Shaphan apparently did not realize the importance of the discovered **book**, since he left the report of it until after he covered the general progress of the work. **34:18–21** When **Shaphan**, the king's secretary, started to read what was in the book, the king was overcome with dread because he knew that Judah had **not kept the word of the LORD** for a long time and severe punishment was likely imminent. Josiah wanted specific guidance from **the LORD** about what he should do. **34:22** **Hilkiah** and other royal officials consulted a **prophetess** named **Huldah** to

determine God's perspective on the situation. As is normal in Chronicles, Huldah's genealogy is given. **34:26–28** Because of Josiah's attitude of repentance and his willingness to obey God, the calamity would not happen until after his death. **34:29–32** King Josiah called a major convocation. Leaders and Levites as well as all the common people of Jerusalem came and heard the public reading of Scripture. The king publicly made a personal **covenant** with God that he would **follow the LORD**, and he compelled the crowd to follow him in this commitment. **35:1** The revival started by the king turned into a massive celebration of the **Passover** (see note at 30:1). In contrast to the Passover under Hezekiah's reforms, Josiah was able to celebrate this festival on its normal

Josiah's Passover Observance

35 Josiah observed the LORD's Passover and slaughtered the Passover lambs on the fourteenth day of the first month. ² He appointed the priests to their responsibilities and encouraged them to serve in the LORD's temple. ³ He said to the Levites who taught all Israel the holy things of the LORD, "Put the holy ark in the temple built by Solomon son of David king of Israel. Since you do not have to carry it on your shoulders, now serve the LORD your God and his people Israel.

⁴ "Organize your ancestral families^A by your divisions according to the written instruction of King David of Israel and that of his son Solomon. ⁵ Serve in the holy place by the groupings of the ancestral families^B for your brothers, the lay people,^c and according to the division of the Levites by family. ⁶ Slaughter the Passover lambs, consecrate yourselves, and make preparations for your brothers to carry out the word of the LORD through Moses."

⁷ Then Josiah donated thirty thousand sheep, lambs, and young goats, plus three thousand cattle from his own possessions, for the Passover sacrifices for all the lay people who were present. ⁸ His officials also donated willingly for the people, the priests, and the Levites. Hilkiah, Zechariah, and Jehiel, chief officials of God's temple, gave twenty-six hundred Passover sacrifices and three hundred cattle for the priests. ⁹ Conaniah and his brothers Shemaiah and Nethanel, and Hashabiah, Jeiel, and Jozabad, officers of the Levites, donated five thousand Passover sacrifices for the Levites, plus five hundred cattle.

¹⁰ So the service was established; the priests stood at their posts and the Levites in their divisions according to the king's command. ¹¹ Then they slaughtered the Passover lambs, and while the Levites were skinning the animals, the priests splattered the blood^D they had been given.^E ¹² They removed the burnt offerings so that they might be given to the groupings of the ancestral families^F of the lay people to offer to the LORD, according to what is written in the book of Moses; they did the same with the cattle. ¹³ They roasted the Passover lambs with fire according to regulation. They boiled the holy sacrifices in pots, kettles, and bowls; and they quickly brought them to the lay people. ¹⁴ Afterward, they made preparations for themselves and for the priests, since the priests, the descendants of Aaron, were busy offering up burnt offerings and fat until night. So the Levites made preparations for themselves and for the priests, the descendants of Aaron.

¹⁵ The singers, the descendants of Asaph, were at their stations according to the command of David, Asaph, Heman, and Jeduthun the king's seer. Also, the gatekeepers were at each temple gate. None of them left their tasks because their Levite brothers had made preparations for them.

¹⁶ So all the service of the LORD was established that day for observing the Passover and for offering burnt offerings on the altar of the LORD, according to the command of King Josiah. ¹⁷ The Israelites who were present in Judah also observed the Passover at that time and the Festival of Unleavened Bread for seven days. ¹⁸ No Passover had been observed like it in Israel since the days of the prophet Samuel. None of the kings of Israel ever observed a Passover like the one that Josiah observed with the priests, the Levites, all Judah, the Israelites who were present in Judah, and the inhabitants of Jerusalem. ¹⁹ In the eighteenth year of Josiah's reign, this Passover was observed.

Josiah's Last Deeds and Death

²⁰ After all this that Josiah had prepared for the temple, King Neco of Egypt marched up to fight at Carchemish by the Euphrates, and Josiah went out to confront him. ²¹ But Neco sent messengers to him, saying, "What is the issue

---

^A 35:4 Lit *the house of your fathers*   ^B 35:5 Lit *the house of the fathers*   ^c 35:5 Lit *the sons of the people,* also in vv. 7,12,13
^D 35:11 LXX, Vg, Tg; MT omits *blood*   ^E 35:11 Lit *splattered from their hand*   ^F 35:12 Lit *house of fathers*

---

day—during **the first month** (see note at 30:2–5).

35:2 This verse begins the account of the preparation for the Passover (vv. 2–9), which would have preceded v. 1.

35:3 This verse is the last time the **ark** of the covenant is mentioned in the OT. Josiah's explanation to the Levites that they no longer needed to carry the ark on their **shoulders** reflects the fact that they learned about this practice when they read the newly discovered book of the law (Ex 25:14; 1Ch 15:15), and they may have been holding it on their shoulders ever since. The other possibility is that Manasseh had made the Levites remove the ark when he desecrated the temple and made them carry it in procession on special occasions. Josiah reassured them that the ark would once

again have a proper, permanent resting place in the **temple**.

35:7–9 Theoretically all families celebrating the Passover should have brought their own sacrificial animals, but the economics of the day made this impossible. Thus the king and his **officials**, including the high priest **Hilkiah** and **the Levites**, supplied a large number of animals for this purpose.

35:10–14 The Levites **made preparations** so that, even while they continued working, they and the **priests** received portions of the feast along with those given to the **lay people**.

35:15 Josiah also implemented David's musical procedures, with the musicians from the lines of **Asaph, Heman, and Jeduthun** contributing to the celebration. **Gatekeepers** were stationed at the temple to ensure ritual purity and physical protection. As with

themselves and the priests, Levites made sure that the gatekeepers on duty enjoyed their share of the feast.

35:16–17 That day refers back to v. 1, which these verses continue.

35:18–19 The Chronicler declared that this was the greatest Passover celebration since the kingship was first established in **the days of . . . Samuel**.

35:20 The three superpowers of that time—Assyria, Babylonia, and Egypt—were about to fight for world supremacy. Egypt and Assyria had formed an alliance against the Babylonians. **Neco**, the pharaoh of Egypt, had assembled a large army and was heading to **Carchemish** in Mesopotamia to join the fight against Babylon.

35:21 Pharaoh **Neco** of Egypt was not an enemy of **Judah**. He had no intention of

between you and me, king of Judah? I have not come against you today[A] but I am fighting another dynasty.[B] God told me to hurry. Stop opposing God who is with me; don't make him destroy you!" [22] But Josiah did not turn away from him; instead, in order to fight with him he disguised himself.[C] He did not listen to Neco's words from the mouth of God, but went to the Valley of Megiddo to fight. [23] The archers shot King Josiah, and he said to his servants, "Take me away, for I am severely wounded!" [24] So his servants took him out of the war chariot, carried him in his second chariot, and brought him to Jerusalem. Then he died, and they buried him in the tomb of his ancestors. All Judah and Jerusalem mourned for Josiah. [25] Jeremiah chanted a dirge over Josiah, and all the male and female singers still speak of Josiah in their dirges today. They established them as a statute for Israel, and indeed they are written in the Dirges. [26] The rest of the events of Josiah's reign, along with his deeds of faithful love according to what is written in the law of the LORD, [27] and his words, from beginning to end, are written in the Book of the Kings of Israel and Judah.

Judah's King Jehoahaz

36 Then the common people[D] took Jehoahaz son of Josiah and made him king in Jerusalem in place of his father.

[2] Jehoahaz[E] was twenty-three years old when he became king, and he reigned three months in Jerusalem. [3] The king of Egypt deposed him in Jerusalem and fined the land seventy-five hundred pounds[F] of silver and seventy-five pounds[G] of gold.

Judah's King Jehoiakim

[4] Then King Neco of Egypt made Jehoahaz's brother Eliakim king over Judah and Jerusalem and changed Eliakim's name to Jehoiakim. But Neco took his brother Jehoahaz and brought him to Egypt.

[5] Jehoiakim was twenty-five years old when he became king, and he reigned eleven years in Jerusalem. He did what was evil in the sight of the LORD his God. [6] Now King Nebuchadnezzar of Babylon attacked him and bound him in bronze shackles to take him to Babylon. [7] Also Nebuchadnezzar took some of the articles of the LORD's temple to Babylon and put them in his temple in Babylon.

[8] The rest of the deeds of Jehoiakim, the detestable actions he committed, and what was found against him, are written in the Book of Israel's Kings. His son Jehoiachin became king in his place.

Judah's King Jehoiachin

[9] Jehoiachin was eighteen[H] years old when he became king, and he reigned three months and ten days in Jerusalem. He did what was evil in the LORD's sight. [10] In the spring[I] Nebuchadnezzar sent for him and brought him to Babylon along with the valuable articles of the LORD's temple. Then he made Jehoiachin's brother Zedekiah king over Judah and Jerusalem.

Judah's King Zedekiah

[11] Zedekiah was twenty-one years old when he became king, and he reigned eleven years in Jerusalem. [12] He did what was evil in the sight of the LORD his God and did not humble himself before the prophet Jeremiah at the LORD's command. [13] He also rebelled against King Nebuchadnezzar who had made him swear

---

[A]35:21 LXX, Syr, Tg, Vg; MT reads *Not against you, you today*   [B]35:21 Lit *house*   [C]35:22 LXX reads *he was determined*   [D]36:1 Lit *the people of the land*   [E]36:2 = Joahaz, also in v. 4   [F]36:3 Lit *100 talents*   [G]36:3 Lit *one talent*   [H]36:9 Some Hb mss, LXX; 2Kg 24:8; other Hb mss read *eight*   [I]36:10 Lit *At the return of the year*

---

conquering Judah. Nevertheless, Josiah marched out to meet the Egyptian army in battle. Ominously, the Chronicler does not say that Josiah inquired of God whether he should fight. Josiah's death at Megiddo occurred in 609 BC.

35:22–24 Josiah confronted Neco on the large plain of **Megiddo**. To protect himself from any personal revenge by Neco, **he disguised himself**. But the king was mortally wounded by an arrow. He was transported to **Jerusalem** where he died. It is ironic that Josiah, one of the best kings of Judah, was killed in a manner remarkably similar to Ahab, perhaps the worst king of Israel (18:29–34).
35:25–27 The Dirges does not refer to the canonical book of Lamentations.
36:1 Jehoahaz: Sixteenth king of Judah; son of Josiah; deposed and deported by Pharaoh Neco. The Chronicler states that the **common people** of Judah made Jehoahaz their next king.
36:2–3 Babylon won the battle of Carchemish (605 BC), reducing the power of both

Assyria and Egypt. Thus, when Neco returned through Judah, he tried to make sure that the new king would not cause trouble as Josiah had done. He **deposed** Jehoahaz after he had reigned for only **three months**. According to 2Kg 23:32, Jehoahaz was about to perpetuate the same evil as some of the earlier kings. It was no loss to the kingdom that Neco carried him off into exile and replaced him with his brother Eliakim (2Ch 36:4; cp. Jr 22:10–12).
36:4 Jehoiakim: Seventeenth king of Judah; son of Josiah; installed by Pharaoh Neco of Egypt; pursued evil. Neco placed **Eliakim** on the throne. He changed his name to **Jehoiakim.** Either version means "God raises up," an ironic name for this godless king.
36:5–8 Jehoiakim was an **evil** king, committing idolatry and opposing the word from God that came to him by the prophet Jeremiah (Jr 36:10–26). He was eventually carried off by **Nebuchadnezzar** to **Babylon** in 605 BC, along with a number of young men from leading families in Jerusalem. This was the first of three deportations, the one in

which Daniel and his friends were relocated to Babylon (Dn 1:1–3).
36:9–10 Jehoiachin: Eighteenth and next-to-last king of Judah; son of Jehoiakim; deposed and deported by Nebuchadnezzar. Jehoiachin wound up having just ten days longer (**three months and ten days**) on the throne than Jehoahaz, but this was sufficient time for him to further aggravate **Nebuchadnezzar.** The king of Babylon returned to Jerusalem, collected more treasures, and carried a group back to Babylon into exile in 597 BC. This was the second deportation, which included the prophet Ezekiel (Ezk 1:1). The next king, Zedekiah, is called his **brother;** this should be interpreted as "kinsman" in this case. Zedekiah, Jehoahaz, and Eliakim/Jehoiakim were all sons of Josiah (v. 1; Jr 36:1; 37:1); Jehoiachin was Jehoiakim's son, making Zedekiah Jehoiachin's uncle.
36:11–14 Zedekiah: Nineteenth and last king of Judah; son of Josiah; uncle of Jehoiachin; refused to submit to **Nebuchadnezzar** and witnessed the destruction of Jerusalem.

allegiance by God. He became obstinate^ and hardened his heart against returning to the Lord, the God of Israel. [14] All the leaders of the priests and the people multiplied their unfaithful deeds, imitating all the detestable practices of the nations, and they defiled the Lord's temple that he had consecrated in Jerusalem.

The Destruction of Jerusalem

[15] But the Lord, the God of their ancestors sent word against them by the hand of his messengers, sending them time and time again, for he had compassion on his people and on his dwelling place. [16] But they kept ridiculing God's messengers, despising his words, and scoffing at his prophets, until the Lord's wrath was so stirred up against his people that there was no remedy. [17] So he brought up against them the king of the Chaldeans, who killed their fit young men with the sword in the house of their sanctuary. He had no pity on young men or young women, elderly or aged; he handed them all over to him. [18] He took everything to Babylon — all the articles of God's temple, large and small, the treasures of the Lord's temple, and the treasures of the king and his

officials. [19] Then the Chaldeans burned God's temple. They tore down Jerusalem's wall, burned all its palaces, and destroyed all its valuable articles.

[20] He deported those who escaped from the sword to Babylon, and they became servants to him and his sons until the rise of the Persian^B kingdom. [21] This fulfilled the word of the Lord through Jeremiah, and the land enjoyed its Sabbath rest all the days of the desolation until seventy years were fulfilled.

The Decree of Cyrus

[22] In the first year of King Cyrus of Persia, in order to fulfill the word of the Lord spoken through^C Jeremiah, the Lord roused the spirit of King Cyrus of Persia to issue a proclamation throughout his entire kingdom and also to put it in writing:

[23] This is what King Cyrus of Persia says: The Lord, the God of the heavens, has given me all the kingdoms of the earth and has appointed me to build him a temple at Jerusalem in Judah. Any of his people among you may go up, and may the Lord his God be with him.

---

^36:13 Lit *He stiffened his neck*   ^36:20 LXX reads *Median*   ^36:22 Lit *Lord by the mouth of*

36:18–20 Four punishments are exacted against rebellious Judah: (1) all the valuable **articles** in the **temple** were taken to Babylon, (2) God's temple and all its palaces were burned down, (3) **Jerusalem's wall** was torn down, and (4) the remaining population was **deported** to Babylon.

36:21 The book of Jeremiah records his prophecy that due to Judah's wickedness, the Babylonians would conquer Judah and deport its inhabitants.

36:22–23 This story was not yet over. The Babylonians were eventually conquered by **King Cyrus of Persia**. Cyrus decreed that all the foreign gods in Babylon and

Persia should be transported back to their places of origin and that the people who worshiped them should return and build new temples for these deities. The Jews correctly saw Cyrus as God's instrument in issuing this command. The decree to release the Jews was made in 539 BC. See also Ezr 1:1–4.

◄ Introduction to Ezra

Circumstances of Writing

Ezra and Nehemiah are anonymous. Ancient Jewish sources usually credit Ezra as the author of Ezra-Nehemiah. More likely Ezra-Nehemiah was written by the "Chronicler," the person (or persons) responsible for 1 and 2 Chronicles. Not only is Ezra-Nehemiah linked to Chronicles at its introduction (Ezr 1:1–2 = 2Ch 36:22–23), but it also shares many similarities in language, terminology, themes, and perspective.

It is probably safe to assume that Ezra-Nehemiah was written soon after the conclusion of Nehemiah's ministry. Most likely the book was written no later than 400 BC.

In Ezra-Nehemiah, it is clear that Ezra came to Jerusalem first, probably in 458 BC, and that Nehemiah followed him thirteen years later, probably in 445 BC. Nehemiah made no mention of Ezra, his ministry, or his reforms. Ezra and Nehemiah appear together in only two texts (Neh 8:9; 12:36). The two events in which Ezra and Nehemiah were together were significant. In Nehemiah 8, the context is the reading of the law to the people; in Nehemiah 12, the two joyous processions walking around the city walls in the dedication ceremony include Ezra (v. 36) and Nehemiah (v. 38).

Contribution to the Bible

The events that occurred in Ezra and Nehemiah, the rebuilt temple, the stabilizing of Jerusalem, and the Jewish community that developed, all played key roles in the life and ministry of Jesus recorded in the Gospels. The rebuilt temple may have paled in comparison to the temple that Solomon built, but it would serve the Jews for centuries until Christ removed the need for a physical temple.

Structure

Ezra was written in two related but distinct languages—Hebrew and Aramaic. The Hebrew sections generally reflect the style of the postexilic era with some evidence of the impact of Aramaic on the language. Aramaic, a Semitic language similar to Hebrew, occurs in two sections in the book of Ezra (4:8–6:18; 7:12–26). During the Persian period (ca 540–330 BC), Aramaic was the official language of diplomacy and commerce.

Ezra is similar to Samuel and Kings, and especially Chronicles, in that many sources were used in its composition. These include two major types of sources. Much of Ezra consists of material from the Ezra Memoir. The Ezra Memoir, written mostly in the first person, includes Ezra 7–10, along with Nehemiah 8 and probably chapter 9; embedded in this memoir are lists and records from other sources used by Ezra. Ezra also contains many lists, genealogies, inventories, letters, and census records throughout the book. For a community attempting to reestablish itself after the disaster of 586 BC and the subsequent exile to Babylon, this material was crucial in reordering its life together.

Ezra Timeline

615–590 BC

Neco II of Egypt commissions Phoenician sailors to be the first to sail around the continent of Africa. **615–595**

Nebuchadnezzar's three invasions of Judah **605, 597, 586**

Events in Obadiah **605–586?**

Daniel is among those taken from Jerusalem to Babylon. **605**

Events in Ezekiel **593–571**

590–560 BC

Athens has two years with no archon (ruler), hence the term *anarchy*. **589**

Temple of Solomon is destroyed. **586**

Cyrus, founder of the Persian Empire, is born. **581**

Aesop, slave of Xanthus of Samos, is credited with collecting and creating fables. They were probably committed to writing at a later time. **570**

Nebuchadnezzar II's successor, Evil-merodach, releases Judah's King Jehoiachin, who had been a prisoner for 36 years. **561**

560–530 BC

Battle of Thymbra between Cyrus the Great and Croesus, commander of the Lydian army **546**

Daniel interprets the handwriting on the wall for Belshazzar. Cyrus captures Babylon without resistance. **539**

Cyrus's decree allows the return of Jews from exile. **538**

Events in Ezra **538–457**

Second temple construction under Zerubbabel's and Joshua's leadership **536–515**

Outline

530–500 BC

Cambyses, son of Cyrus **530–522**

Aeschylus, Greek tragedian (**525–456**), many of whose plays dealt with the Persian invasion of Greece, participated in the Greek victories at Marathon and Salamis

Darius I or Darius the Great **521–486**

Events in Haggai **520**

Events in Zechariah **520–518**

Second temple dedicated **515**

500–480 BC

Greeks develop instruments for surveying. **500**

Sugar cane cultivated in India **500**

Greeks, outnumbered almost five to one, defeat Persians in Battle of Marathon through superior military intelligence and strategy, forestalling Persian expansion into Europe. **490**

Events in Esther **486–465**

Greek victory over Persians in Battle of Salamis, **480**, and Plain of Plataea, **479**, thwarted Persian expansion into Europe

480–445 BC

Xerxes I, Ahasuerus, husband of Esther **486–465**

Esther's reign **479–465?**

Esther saves the Jews within the Persian Empire. **474?**

Ezra goes to Jerusalem. **458**

Nehemiah, cupbearer to Artaxerxes, learns of the disrepair of Jerusalem's walls and leads an effort that restores the walls. **445**

The Decree of Cyrus

1 In the first year of King Cyrus of Persia, in order to fulfill the word of the Lord spoken through Jeremiah, the Lord roused the spirit of King Cyrus to issue a proclamation throughout his entire kingdom and to put it in writing: ² This is what King Cyrus of Persia says:

"The Lord, the God of the heavens, has given me all the kingdoms of the earth and has appointed me to build him a house at Jerusalem in Judah. ³ Any of his people among you, may his God be with him, and may he go to Jerusalem in Judah and build the house of the Lord, the God of Israel, the God who is in Jerusalem. ⁴ Let every survivor, wherever he resides, be assisted by the men of that region with silver, gold, goods, and livestock, along with a freewill offering for the house of God in Jerusalem."

Return from Exile

⁵ So the family heads of Judah and Benjamin, along with the priests and Levites — everyone whose spirit God had roused — prepared to go up and rebuild the Lord's house in Jerusalem. ⁶ All their neighbors supported them^A with silver articles, gold, goods, livestock, and valuables, in addition to all that was given as a freewill offering. ⁷ King Cyrus also brought out the articles of the Lord's house that Nebuchadnezzar had taken from Jerusalem and had placed in the house of his gods. ⁸ King Cyrus of Persia had them brought out under the

supervision of Mithredath the treasurer, who counted them out to Sheshbazzar the prince of Judah. ⁹ This was the inventory:

30 gold basins, 1,000 silver basins,
29 silver knives, ¹⁰ 30 gold bowls,
410 various^B silver bowls,
and 1,000 other articles.

¹¹ The gold and silver articles totaled 5,400. Sheshbazzar brought all of them when the exiles went up from Babylon to Jerusalem.

The Exiles Who Returned

2 These now are the people of the province who came from those captive exiles King Nebuchadnezzar of Babylon^C had deported to Babylon. They returned to Jerusalem and Judah, each to his own town. ² They came with Zerubbabel, Jeshua, Nehemiah, Seraiah, Reelaiah, Mordecai, Bilshan, Mispar, Bigvai, Rehum, and Baanah.

The number of the Israelite men included^D

³	Parosh's descendants	2,172
⁴	Shephatiah's descendants	372
⁵	Arah's descendants	775
⁶	Pahath-moab's descendants:	
	Jeshua's and Joab's descendants	2,812
⁷	Elam's descendants	1,254
⁸	Zattu's descendants	945
⁹	Zaccai's descendants	760
¹⁰	Bani's descendants	642
¹¹	Bebai's descendants	623
¹²	Azgad's descendants	1,222
¹³	Adonikam's descendants	666
¹⁴	Bigvai's descendants	2,056

---

^A 1:6 Lit strengthened their hands   ^B 1:10 Or similar   ^C 2:1 Nebuchadnezzar reigned 605–562 BC   ^D 2:2 Lit the men of the people of Israel

---

1:1 The **first year of King Cyrus** refers to the first year of his rule over Babylonia (538 BC) and not the first year of his reign in Persia that began in 559 BC and continued until 530 BC. **Spoken through Jeremiah** may allude to Jeremiah's prophecy of the seventy years of captivity (Jr 29:10–14). More likely it is a reference to Jr 51:11. The same vocabulary occurs here in Ezr 1:1.
1:2–3 The "proclamation" (v. 1), often referred to as the "Decree of Cyrus," reflects Cyrus's policy to allow the exiles to return to their homeland. The decree, from the closing words of 2 Chronicles (36:23), appears in two versions in the book of Ezra: here in Hebrew, reflecting a strong Jewish perspective, and in 6:3–5 written in Aramaic (the language of diplomacy in the Persian Empire), which appears to be an official court memorandum.
1:4 It is not clear whether the **men of that region** refers to Jewish men or the entire population.
1:5 The kingdom of Judah, conquered by the Babylonians in 586 BC, consisted primarily of the region of **Judah and Benjamin**; thus, the exiles who returned represented three tribal groups: Judah, Benjamin, and Levi (**the priests and Levites**).
1:7 The **articles . . . that Nebuchadnezzar had taken** when the Babylonians sacked the temple were not only extremely valuable but were of priceless spiritual worth to the returning exiles. Though plundered from the temple that Solomon built, they would again

be used in worship in the second temple and would be an additional link to the worshiping community that existed before the great catastrophe of 586 BC.
1:8 Both the name and title of **Mithredath** are Persian. This is the first mention of the enigmatic **Sheshbazzar** (vv. 8,11; 5:14,16). His name is Babylonian ("May Shamash [the sun god] protect the father"). His title, **prince of Judah**, occurs nowhere else in the OT.
1:9–10 The variation in English translations of this passage reflects the difficulty in determining the exact identity of the items mentioned.
1:11 The figure of **5,400** is more than twice the total of the figures given in vv. 9–10. Possibly the items mentioned in the inventory (vv. 9–10) were only a portion of the material returned to Sheshbazzar. A textual corruption, more commonly occurring in lists of numbers, may also account for the disparity.
2:1 The list of returnees probably reflects not the return from Babylon led by Sheshbazzar, but multiple waves of exiles over several decades. While it is possible that **the people of the province** refers to the region in Babylon where the exiles had lived, it more likely refers to the province of Judah to which they returned. Each returnee came back to **his own town**, emphasizing the continuity between the preexilic nation and the postexilic nation.
2:2 The names of the Jewish leaders who returned reflect the history of their

nation. One name is Persian (**Bigvai**) while three others are Babylonian (**Zerubbabel . . . Mordecai**, and **Bilshan**). Zerubbabel probably served as the second governor of Yehud (Judah) after Sheshbazzar. As a grandson of King Jehoiachin, he was a crucial link with the Davidic dynasty. In the biblical books from the postexilic era, Zerubbabel is nearly always mentioned along with **Jeshua**, a grandson of Jozadak, Israel's last high priest before the destruction of the temple in 586 BC. Thus Zerubbabel and Jeshua together link the reborn community in Yehud with the royal and priestly lines of preexilic Israel.
Nehemiah in this verse does not refer to the central figure in the book of Nehemiah, who arrived in Jerusalem almost eighty years later. Another person named Nehemiah is also mentioned in Neh 3:16, referring to a ruler over the region of Bethzur. Neither does the name Mordecai refer to the Mordecai in the book of Esther, who appeared a half century after the Mordecai in Ezr 2.
2:3–60 These lists appear to be based on the nearly identical version in Neh 7:8–60. The primary purpose of these lists was to ensure that those who returned to Judah were authentic Israelites.
2:3–35 The first list consists of Israelite laymen. In vv. 3–20 they are listed by the names of their family patriarchs and in vv. 21–35 according to locality of origin.

567

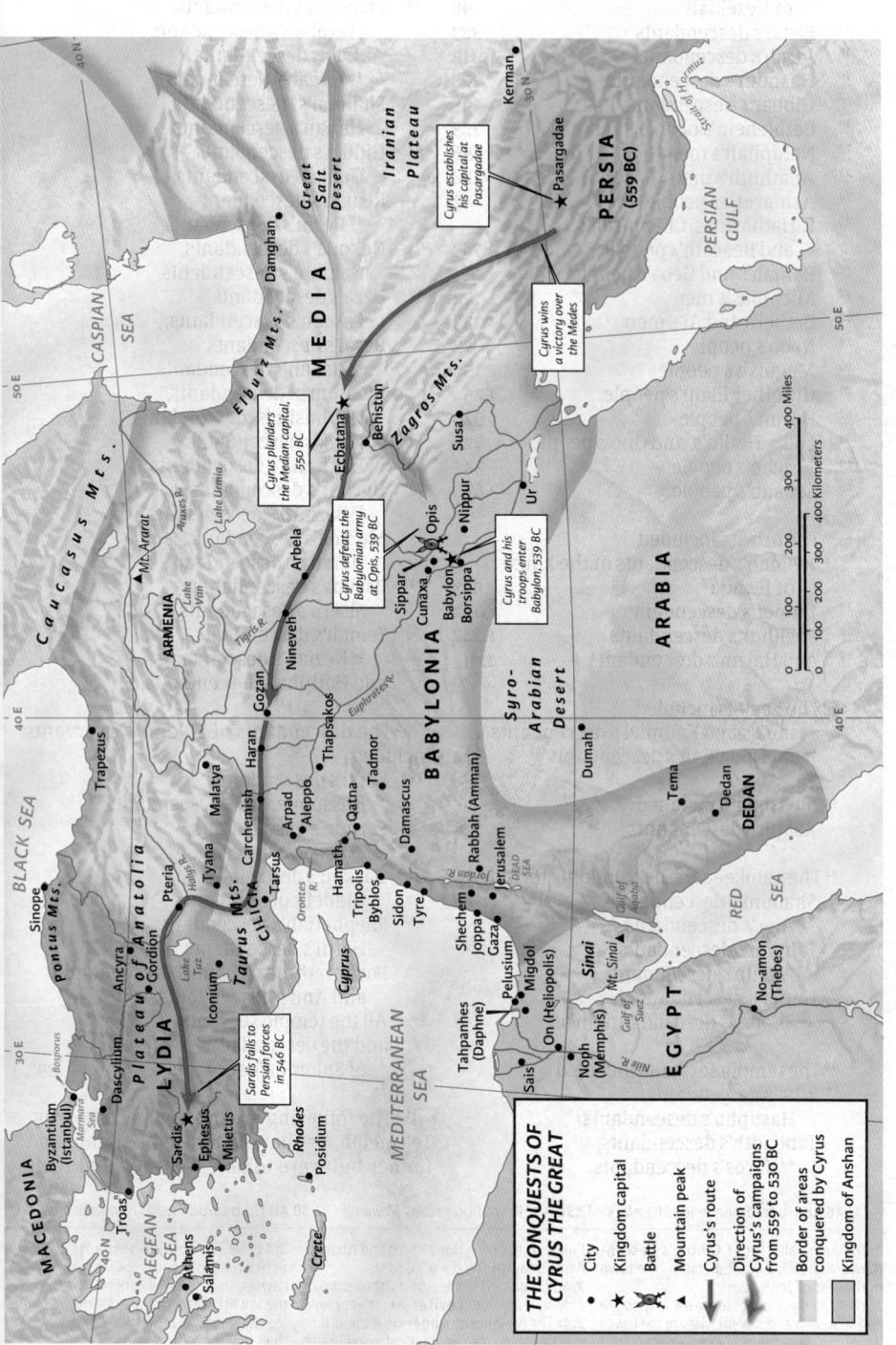

THE CONQUESTS OF CYRUS THE GREAT

- City
- ★ Kingdom capital
- ⚔ Battle
- ▲ Mountain peak
- → Cyrus's route
- → Direction of Cyrus's campaigns from 559 to 530 BC
- Border of areas conquered by Cyrus
- Kingdom of Anshan

Cyrus establishes his capital at Pasargadae

Cyrus wins a victory over the Medes

Cyrus plunders the Median capital, 550 BC

Cyrus defeats the Babylonian army at Opis, 539 BC

Cyrus and his troops enter Babylon, 539 BC

Sardis falls to Persian forces in 546 BC

PERSIA (559 BC)

MEDIA

BABYLONIA

ARABIA

EGYPT

LYDIA

15	Adin's descendants	454	
16	Ater's descendants:		
	of Hezekiah	98	
17	Bezai's descendants	323	
18	Jorah's descendants	112	
19	Hashum's descendants	223	
20	Gibbar's descendants	95	
21	Bethlehem's people	123	
22	Netophah's men	56	
23	Anathoth's men	128	
24	Azmaveth's people	42	
25	Kiriatharim's, Chephirah's,		
	and Beeroth's people	743	
26	Ramah's and Geba's people	621	
27	Michmas's men	122	
28	Bethel's and Ai's men	223	
29	Nebo's people	52	
30	Magbish's people	156	
31	the other Elam's people	1,254	
32	Harim's people	320	
33	Lod's, Hadid's, and Ono's people	725	
34	Jericho's people	345	
35	Senaah's people	3,630	

36 The priests included
Jedaiah's descendants of the house
of Jeshua 973
37 Immer's descendants 1,052
38 Pashhur's descendants 1,247
39 and Harim's descendants 1,017

40 The Levites included
Jeshua's and Kadmiel's descendants
from Hodaviah's descendants 74

41 The singers included
Asaph's descendants 128

42 The gatekeepers' descendants included
Shallum's descendants,
Ater's descendants,
Talmon's descendants,
Akkub's descendants,
Hatita's descendants,
Shobai's descendants, in all 139

43 The temple servants included
Ziha's descendants,
Hasupha's descendants,
Tabbaoth's descendants,
44 Keros's descendants,

Siaha's descendants,
Padon's descendants,
45 Lebanah's descendants,
Hagabah's descendants,
Akkub's descendants,
46 Hagab's descendants,
Shalmai's^ descendants,
Hanan's descendants,
47 Giddel's descendants,
Gahar's descendants,
Reaiah's descendants,
48 Rezin's descendants,
Nekoda's descendants,
Gazzam's descendants,
49 Uzza's descendants,
Paseah's descendants,
Besai's descendants,
50 Asnah's descendants,
Meunim's⁸ descendants,
Nephusim's^c descendants,
51 Bakbuk's descendants,
Hakupha's descendants,
Harhur's descendants,
52 Bazluth's descendants,
Mehida's descendants,
Harsha's descendants,
53 Barkos's descendants,
Sisera's descendants,
Temah's descendants,
54 Neziah's descendants,
and Hatipha's descendants.

55 The descendants of Solomon's servants
included
Sotai's descendants,
Hassophereth's descendants,
Peruda's descendants,
56 Jaalah's descendants,
Darkon's descendants,
Giddel's descendants,
57 Shephatiah's descendants,
Hattil's descendants,
Pochereth-hazzebaim's descendants,
and Ami's descendants.
58 All the temple servants
and the descendants
of Solomon's servants 392.

59 The following are those who came from
Tel-melah, Tel-harsha, Cherub, Addan, and
Immer but were unable to prove that their

---

^**2:46** Alt Hb tradition reads *Shamlai's* ⁸**2:50** Alt Hb tradition reads *Meinim's* ^c**2:50** Alt Hb tradition reads *Nephisim's*

2:20 The parallel list of **Gibbar's descendants** (Neh 7:25) reads "Gibeon('s)," the town northwest of Jerusalem.
2:21–35 All these places are in the immediate area surrounding Jerusalem. Many of the towns were from the tribal area of Benjamin, north of Jerusalem. The only towns mentioned south of Jerusalem are Bethlehem and Netophah.
2:36–39 Priests make up about 10 percent of the returnees. Other priests returned later, because 8:2 mentions priestly families of

Phinehas (Ex 6:23; Nm 25:1–11) and Ithamar, Aaron's fourth son (Ex 6:23).
2:40 Compared to the priests, the return of only seventy-four **Levites** seems very low.
2:41 The presence of **singers** was important in establishing the continuity of worship as it existed before the exile. Perhaps "musicians" better fits the context.
2:42 The gatekeeper's position was established by King David (1Ch 9:18–27) and was regarded as part of the tribe of Levi (1Ch 6).

2:43–58 The **temple servants** were the fifth group of temple personnel (priests, Levites, singers, gatekeepers), and they had the lowest status. A majority of the names are either foreign or are nicknames, reflecting their lowly status.
2:59–63 The final groups are of questionable status: three clans of laymen who could not verify their genealogy (vv. 59–60) and three clans of priestly families who could not prove their priestly lineage (vv. 61–64). Because the

ancestral families^A and their lineage were Israelite:

60 Delaiah's descendants,
Tobiah's descendants,
Nekoda's descendants   652
61 and from the descendants of the priests: the descendants of Hobaiah, the descendants of Hakkoz, the descendants of Barzillai — who had taken a wife from the daughters of Barzillai the Gileadite and who bore their name. **62** These searched for their entries in the genealogical records, but they could not be found, so they were disqualified from the priesthood. **63** The governor ordered them not to eat the most holy things until there was a priest who could consult the Urim and Thummim.

64   The whole combined assembly numbered   42,360
65   not including their 7,337 male and female servants, and their 200 male and female singers.
66   They had 736 horses, 245 mules,
67   435 camels, and 6,720 donkeys.

Gifts for the Work

68 After they arrived at the LORD's house in Jerusalem, some of the family heads gave freewill offerings for the house of God in order to have it rebuilt on its original site. **69** Based on what they could give, they gave 61,000 gold coins,^B 6,250 pounds^C of silver, and 100 priestly garments to the treasury for the project. **70** The priests, Levites, singers, gatekeepers, temple servants, and some of the people settled in their towns, and the rest of Israel settled in their towns.

Sacrifice Restored

3 When the seventh month arrived, and the Israelites were in their towns, the people gathered as one in Jerusalem. **2** Jeshua son of Jozadak and his brothers the priests along with Zerubbabel son of Shealtiel and his brothers began to build the altar of Israel's God in order to offer burnt offerings on it, as it is written in the law of Moses, the man of God. **3** They set up the altar on its foundation and offered burnt offerings for the morning and evening on it to the LORD even though they feared the surrounding peoples. **4** They celebrated the Festival of Shelters as prescribed, and offered burnt offerings each day, based on the number specified by ordinance for each festival day. **5** After that, they offered the regular burnt offering and the offerings for the beginning of each month^D and for all the LORD's appointed holy occasions, as well as the freewill offerings brought to^E the LORD. **6** On the first day of the seventh month they began to offer burnt offerings to the LORD, even though the foundation of the LORD's temple had not yet been laid. **7** They gave money to the stonecutters and artisans, and gave food, drink, and oil to the people of Sidon and Tyre, so they would bring cedar wood from Lebanon to Joppa by sea, according to the authorization given them by King Cyrus of Persia.

Rebuilding the Temple

8 In the second month of the second year after they arrived at God's house in Jerusalem, Zerubbabel son of Shealtiel, Jeshua son of

---

^A**2:59** Lit *that the house of their fathers* ^B**2:69** Or *drachmas*, or *darics* ^C**2:69** Lit *5,000 minas* ^D**3:5** Lit *for the new moons* ^E**3:5** Lit *well as those of everyone making a freewill offering to*

---

purity of the priesthood and the temple was at stake, priests who could not prove their lineage were disqualified from their posts. The term **governor** probably refers to Zerubbabel, although some scholars prefer Sheshbazzar. **2:64–65** The sum of the returnees in the above list is only 29,818; probably the discrepancy reflects the number of women who also returned. While some commentators regard the presence of only 12,542 women as unlikely, it may suggest that most of those who returned were unattached, single men. The **42,360** returnees did not include the slaves who were regarded as property. The **singers** listed here were entertainers employed by wealthy families. **2:66–67** Since **horses** were more expensive than **donkeys**, it is not surprising that far more donkeys (6,720) than horses (736) were involved in the return to the land. **2:68–70** Some of the people gave **freewill offerings** for the reconstruction of the temple. These **coins** (Hb *darkemonim*) probably refer to the Greek drachma. **3:1–13** Neither Haggai nor Zechariah, who prophesied about the temple during this time, ever mentioned an early attempt to lay the foundation of the temple in the time of Cyrus as described in this chapter. They only recounted the laying of the foundation and the building of the temple during the

time of Darius, with the completion of the temple in 515 BC. The chronological indicators in the passage (vv. 6,8; 4:5,24; 5:1–2) attest to a short-lived attempt to rebuild in the time of Cyrus (3:1–4:3) followed by a second, ultimately successful attempt during the time of Darius (chaps. 5–6). **3:1–2 The seventh month** was September–October 537 BC. Taking the lead in reviving the proper sacrificial system was **Jeshua son of Jozadak** (see note at 2:2). In the book of Haggai he is always referred to as "Joshua," an alternative spelling, and nearly always called the "high priest," though never in Ezra-Nehemiah. Those returning to the promised land built their altar the same way, with uncut stones that no iron tool had touched (cp. Dt 27:5–6). **3:3** The morning and evening **burnt offerings** were the basic daily sacrifices in which the entire lamb was burned up. The term **surrounding peoples** (lit "the people of the lands") often has a pejorative sense. Here it probably refers to those with no desire to see a reconstituted Jewish population in the land. **3:4** The seventh month was also the time for the celebration of the **Festival of Shelters** (also referred to as "Tabernacles," or by its Hb name *Succoth*, a harvest festival in which Israel remembered their sojourn in the

wilderness and God's provision. The sacrifices during the seven-day festival were offered in accordance with the law of Moses as written in Nm 29:12–38. **3:5** The mention of **regular burnt offering** is to show how the normal daily sacrificial schedule of offerings, as compared to the burnt offering at the dedication of the altar (v. 3), was reestablished. **Offerings for the beginning of each month** translates a single Hebrew word meaning "new moons." New moon celebrations were prescribed in the Mosaic law (Nm 28:11–15). **3:6** The **first day of the seventh month** would most likely have been September 17, 538 BC. **3:7** As soon as the sacrificial system was in place, the next order of business was the acquisition of building material. Payment was made to the **people of Sidon and Tyre** who cut down the famous cedars of Lebanon and floated the logs down the coast to Joppa, just south of present-day Tel-Aviv, for transit overland to Jerusalem. While **stonecutters** were also hired, they were not as numerous as Solomon's 80,000 who worked on the first temple (2Ch 2:18) since some of the stones from the rubble of the first temple could be reused. **3:8–9** During the seven months preceding the **second month of the second year**,

Jozadak, and the rest of their brothers, including the priests, the Levites, and all who had returned to Jerusalem from the captivity, began to build. They appointed the Levites who were twenty years old or more to supervise the work on the LORD's house. ⁹ Jeshua with his sons and brothers, Kadmiel with his sons, and the sons of Judah^A and of Henadad, with their sons and brothers, the Levites, joined together to supervise those working on the house of God.

Temple Foundation Completed

¹⁰ When the builders had laid the foundation of the LORD's temple, the priests, dressed in their robes and holding trumpets, and the Levites descended from Asaph, holding cymbals, took their positions to praise the LORD, as King David of Israel had instructed. ¹¹ They sang with praise and thanksgiving to the LORD: "For he is good; his faithful love to Israel endures forever." Then all the people gave a great shout of praise to the LORD because the foundation of the LORD's house had been laid.

¹² But many of the older priests, Levites, and family heads, who had seen the first temple, wept loudly when they saw the foundation of this temple, but many others shouted joyfully. ¹³ The people could not distinguish the sound of the joyful shouting from that of the ᴮ weeping, because the people were shouting so loudly. And the sound was heard far away.

Opposition to Rebuilding the Temple

4 When the enemies of Judah and Benjamin heard that the returned exiles^C were building a temple for the LORD, the God of Israel, ² they approached Zerubbabel and the family heads and said to them, "Let us build with you, for we also worship your God and have been sacrificing to him^D since the time King Esarhaddon of Assyria brought us here."

³ But Zerubbabel, Jeshua, and the other heads of Israel's families answered them, "You may have no part with us in building a house for our God, since we alone will build it for the LORD, the God of Israel, as King Cyrus, the king of Persia has commanded us." ⁴ Then the people who were already in the land^E discouraged^F the people of Judah and made them afraid to build. ⁵ They also bribed officials to act against them to frustrate their plans throughout the reign of King Cyrus of Persia and until the reign of King Darius of Persia.

Opposition to Rebuilding the City

⁶ At the beginning of the reign of Ahasuerus, the people who were already in the land wrote an accusation against the residents of Judah and Jerusalem. ⁷ During the time of King Artaxerxes of Persia, Bishlam, Mithredath, Tabeel and the rest of his colleagues wrote to King Artaxerxes. The letter was written in Aramaic and translated.^G

⁸ Rehum the chief deputy and Shimshai the scribe wrote a letter to King Artaxerxes concerning Jerusalem as follows:

^A 3:9 Or *Hodaviah*; Neh 7:43; 1 Esdras 5:58   ᴮ 3:13 Lit *the people*   ^C 4:1 Lit *the sons of the exile*   ^D 4:2 Alt Hb tradition reads *have not been sacrificing*   ^E 4:4 Lit *people of the land*, also in v. 6   ^F 4:4 Lit *weakened the hands of*   ^G 4:7 Ezr 4:8–6:18 is written in Aramaic.

---

enough of the temple site had been cleared that work on the foundation could begin. **Zerubbabel** and **Jeshua** the priest led laymen as well as priests and Levites in the joint effort. In 5:16 Sheshbazzar is mentioned as official governor, maybe he was credited with this event even though Zerubbabel carried on most of the work and would later succeed Sheshbazzar as governor.
3:11 The Levites' antiphonal refrain, **"For he is good; his faithful love to Israel endures forever,"** is found in slightly varying forms in the Psalms (100:4–5; 106:1; 107:1; 118:1; 136:1).
3:12–13 The episode described here is not the same event as described in Hg 2:1–5, which occurred almost twenty years later when the building of the temple finally resumed. Here the author prepares the way for Ezr 4 with the opposition of enemies. Not only did the Lord's people hear the sound but so did their adversaries, who tried to thwart their plans.
4:1–2 The author's description of those who offered to help with the construction as **enemies** shows that their offer was not what it seemed. Their identity is clarified in that they had been **brought . . . here** by **King Esar-haddon of Assyria.**
The claim of these enemies that they also worshiped **your God** was probably true. The problem was that they worshiped the God of Israel along with the false gods of

their homeland (2Kg 17:3–22). If **Zerubbabel** allowed these people to help in the construction, it would be impossible to prevent them from worshiping there as well. Zerubbabel and the other returnees knew well the terrible price their nation had paid for their syncretistic practices and could never allow such a practice again.
4:4–5 These verses highlight one aspect of the opposition from the **people who were already in the land** (lit "the peoples of the land," see note at 3:3): **they . . . bribed officials to act against them** (lit "they hired counselors against them").
4:6–23 This unusual passage has confused and challenged interpreters. It is bracketed by statements (vv. 4–5,24) describing the cessation of building until the time of Darius. Chapter 5 continues with the renewed work in building the temple during the time of Darius. Yet in 4:6–23 the events described take place during the reigns of Ahasuerus (Xerxes) and Artaxerxes, successive kings in Darius's dynasty. Some critical scholars have charged that the author of Ezra-Nehemiah was chronologically confused. Such an assertion is unwarranted and unnecessary when one realizes that the author is not writing a chronological but a thematic account.
4:6 While earlier scholars identified **Ahasuerus** with various individuals, nearly all today identify him as Xerxes (486–465 BC), the son

of Darius. Ahasuerus (Xerxes) is mentioned nowhere else in the OT except for the book of Esther where he plays a central role.
4:7 Another letter was written to thwart the plans of the returned exiles, this time to **Artaxerxes**, who took the throne following the death of his father Xerxes. His reign lasted over forty years (465–425 BC). The ministry of Ezra and Nehemiah occurred during his reign, as well as that of the last writing prophet, Malachi. The Persian name **Mithredath** suggests he may have been a Persian official. The Hebrew name **Tabeel** ("God is Good") finds its equivalent in the Aramaic name *Tobiah*, but it is unlikely the Tabeel mentioned in this verse is Tobiah, the Ammonite official who opposed Nehemiah (Neh 2:10,19).
4:8–6:18 With this verse begins the first of two sections written not in Hebrew but in Aramaic (4:8–6:18; 7:12–26). The Aramaic sections in the OT (here and in Dn 2:4–7:28) are written in "Official Aramaic" (or "Royal Aramaic"), a standardized language of government and diplomacy used throughout the Persian Empire. By the time of Jesus, Aramaic was the "mother tongue" of the Jewish people in Palestine.
4:8 The title **chief deputy** is literally "master of orders," a high-ranking official. Some scholars translate his title as "chancellor" or "high commissioner."

⁹ From Rehum^ the chief deputy, Shimshai the scribe, and the rest of their colleagues — the judges and magistrates^B from Tripolis, Persia, Erech, Babylon, Susa (that is, the people of Elam),^C ¹⁰ and the rest of the peoples whom the great and illustrious Ashurbanipal^D deported and settled in the cities of Samaria and the region west of the Euphrates River. ¹¹ This is the text of the letter they sent to him:

To King Artaxerxes from your servants, the men from the region west of the Euphrates River:

¹² Let it be known to the king that the Jews who came from you have returned to us at Jerusalem. They are rebuilding that rebellious and evil city, finishing its walls, and repairing its foundations. ¹³ Let it now be known to the king that if that city is rebuilt and its walls are finished, they will not pay tribute, duty, or land tax, and the royal revenue^C will suffer. ¹⁴ Since we have taken an oath of loyalty to the king,^E and it is not right for us to witness his dishonor, we have sent to inform the king ¹⁵ that a search should be made in your predecessors' record books. In these record books you will discover and verify that the city is a rebellious city, harmful to kings and provinces. There have been revolts in it since ancient times. That is why this city was destroyed. ¹⁶ We advise the king that if this city is rebuilt and its walls are finished, you will not have any possession west of the Euphrates.

Artaxerxes's Reply

¹⁷ The king sent a reply to his chief deputy Rehum, Shimshai the scribe, and the rest of their colleagues living in Samaria and elsewhere in the region west of the Euphrates River:

Greetings.

¹⁸ The letter you sent us has been translated and read^F in my presence. ¹⁹ I issued a decree and a search was conducted. It was discovered that this city has had uprisings against kings since ancient times, and there have been rebellions and revolts in it. ²⁰ Powerful kings have also ruled over Jerusalem and exercised authority over the whole region west of the Euphrates River, and tribute, duty, and land tax were paid to them. ²¹ Therefore, issue an order for these men to stop, so that this city will not be rebuilt until a further decree has been pronounced by me. ²² See that you not neglect this matter. Otherwise, the damage will increase and the royal interests^G will suffer.

²³ As soon as the text of King Artaxerxes's letter was read to Rehum, Shimshai the scribe, and their colleagues, they immediately went to the Jews in Jerusalem and forcibly stopped them.

Rebuilding of the Temple Resumed

²⁴ Now the construction of God's house in Jerusalem had stopped and remained at a standstill until the second year of the reign of King Darius of Persia. ¹ But when the prophets Haggai and Zechariah son of Iddo prophesied to the Jews who were in Judah and

---

^4:9 Lit *Then Rehum*   ^4:9 Or *ambassadors*   ^4:9,13 Aramaic obscure   ^4:10 Lit *Osnappar*   ^4:14 Lit *have eaten the salt of the palace*   ^4:18 Or *been read clearly*   ^4:22 Lit *the kings*

4:9–10 The difficult Aramaic in v. 9b prohibits certainty in translation. After the mention of **judges and magistrates**, it is not clear whether the next two terms refer to other officials or other locations. **Erech, Babylon,** and **Susa** are the homelands from which their forefathers had been deported by **Ashurbanipal** (a rendering borrowed from extrabiblical sources; the Hb text calls him *Osnappar*), who followed Esar-haddon (see vv. 1–2) as king of Assyria (668–627 BC). **4:11** The authors of the letter specified their residences as **the region west of the Euphrates River** (lit "Beyond [the] River"), which became the standard administrative and political designation for the vast area from the Euphrates River to the Mediterranean Sea. This region is also referred to as the "Trans-Euphrates." **4:12** This is the first occurrence of the word **Jews** in Ezra-Nehemiah. "Jew" (Aramaic *yehuday*; Hb *yehudi*) was derived from the word "Judah" (Hb *yehudah*). During the postexilic era the term became the standard designation of the entire religious community of Israel, whether located in the land of Israel or elsewhere. **4:13** Xerxes's battles with the Greeks were a financial drain on the empire. Later,

Artaxerxes's suppression of the revolt in Egypt was an additional financial burden. Rehum knew that Artaxerxes could not afford the loss of **tribute, duty, or land tax**. **4:14–17 We have taken an oath of loyalty to the king** translates an obscure Aramaic phrase (lit "We have salted the salt of the king"). On the suspicion that a scribal error has altered the original sentence, some scholars note that a minor change of the Aramaic verb would yield a more understandable rendering: "We have eaten the salt of the king." In the OT there are several references that associate salt with a covenant (Lv 2:13; Nm 18:19; 2Ch 13:5), suggesting that salt, a valuable commodity in the ancient world, was used in the ritual of making a covenant. In a letter (Ezr 4:11–16) marked by exaggeration aimed at inciting suppression of the Jews, the concluding warning (v. 16) reached its crescendo: failure to stop the Jews from rebuilding would cause Artaxerxes to lose "Beyond the River"—the region **west of the Euphrates** River. **4:18–19** Due to the efficiency of the Persian administration, letters would have traveled between Samaria and the Persian king in about a week. **4:20 Powerful kings** may be a reference to foreign kings, such as Assyrian and

Babylonian kings who once controlled the **region west of the Euphrates River** and collected **tribute**. However, the context gives no indication of a change in subject. This most naturally suggests that Israelite kings were these "powerful kings." If this is correct, it is possibly another aspect of exaggerating the threat posed by the Jews and Jerusalem. **4:21–22 Until a further decree has been pronounced by me** was a providential loophole. Such a decree was issued in about 446 BC. **4:23** Literally this text reads, "they made them cease by force and might." This must have been a painful and humiliating experience for the Jewish people. **4:24** The verse begins with an Aramaic preposition, *be'dayin*, that is usually translated "then," which suggests that v. 24 temporally follows v. 23. But vv. 6–23 form a parenthesis in which letters written to the Persian kings illustrate opposition to the Jews. Thus v. 5 and v. 24 serve as parallel bookends that bracket the lengthy parenthesis of vv. 6–23. **5:1–6:22** After the thematic presentation of local opposition in chap. 4, the author returns to the situation in Darius's day when construction was resumed and completed (chaps. 5–6).

Jerusalem, in the name of the God of Israel who was over them, [2] Zerubbabel son of Shealtiel and Jeshua son of Jozadak began to rebuild God's house in Jerusalem. The prophets of God were with them, helping them.

[3] At that time Tattenai the governor of the region west of the Euphrates River, Shethar-bozenai, and their colleagues came to the Jews and asked, "Who gave you the order to rebuild this temple and finish this structure?"[A] [4] They also asked them, "What are the names of the workers[B] who are constructing this building?" [5] But God was watching[C] over the Jewish elders. These men wouldn't stop them until a report was sent to Darius, so that they could receive written instructions about this matter.

The Letter to Darius

[6] This is the text of the letter that Tattenai the governor of the region west of the Euphrates River, Shethar-bozenai, and their colleagues, the officials in the region, sent to King Darius. [7] They sent him a report, written as follows:

To King Darius:

All greetings.

[8] Let it be known to the king that we went to the house of the great God in the province of Judah. It is being built with cut[D] stones, and its beams are being set in the walls. This work is being done diligently and succeeding through the people's efforts. [9] So we questioned the elders and asked, "Who gave you the order to rebuild this temple and finish this structure?" [10] We also asked them for their names, so that we could write down the names of their leaders for your information.

[11] This is the reply they gave us:

We are the servants of the God of the heavens and earth, and we are rebuilding the temple that was built many years ago, which a great king of Israel built and finished. [12] But since our ancestors angered the God of the heavens, he handed them over to King Nebuchadnezzar of Babylon, the Chaldean, who destroyed this temple and deported the people to Babylon. [13] However, in the first year of King Cyrus of Babylon, he issued a decree to rebuild the house of God. [14] He also took from the temple in Babylon the gold and silver articles of God's house that Nebuchadnezzar had taken from the temple in Jerusalem and carried them to the temple in Babylon. He released them from the temple in Babylon to a man named Sheshbazzar, the governor by the appointment of King Cyrus. [15] Cyrus told him, "Take these articles, put them in the temple in Jerusalem, and let the house of God be rebuilt on its original site." [16] Then this same Sheshbazzar came and laid the foundation of God's

---

[A]5:3 Or *finish its furnishings*, also in v. 9   [B]5:4 One Aramaic ms, LXX, Syr; MT reads *Then we told them exactly what the names of the men were*   [C]5:5 Lit *But the eye of their God was*   [D]5:8 Or *huge*

5:1 The impetus for a renewed attempt at construction began when **Haggai** and **Zechariah** brought their prophetic oracles to the Jews. In this present verse Zechariah is said to be the **son of Iddo** while in Zch 1:1 he is the "son of Berechiah, son of Iddo." This is no contradiction. The term *son* (Aramaic *bar*) and its Hebrew equivalent (*ben*) can refer to a descendant such as "grandson." Thus Zch 1:1 and Ezr 5:1 are both correct.
5:2 Haggai and Zechariah also pointed to **Zerubbabel** and **Jeshua** the priest as those

#24 **99 Essential Christian Truths**

GOD IS UNCHANGING

God's being and attributes, along with the ethical commitments he has given, cannot change. This means, among other things, that God is committed to being God and that he is the same yesterday, today, and forever. God's unchanging nature is good news for Christians, for it guarantees that he does not change his mind or go back on his promises. Christians can find assurance and peace of mind in knowing that the God who brought them out of darkness into his marvelous light is the God who will carry them through into eternity.

who led the people (2:2; 3:2,8; 4:3) in the renewed construction. **Helping them** did not imply manual labor but encouragement and moral support for those doing the work.
5:3–5 Tattenai is called **governor** of "Beyond the River," the Trans-Euphrates region, even though he probably served as "sub-governor" under Ushtanu, a new governor appointed by Darius in 520 BC, the year when construction on the temple resumed. Zerubbabel is also called "governor" (Hb *pechah*, Hg 1:14; 2:2,21), although he answered to Tattenai and was responsible solely for the region of *Yehud* (Judah).
Tattenai's question about the source of the **order** may have been a genuine concern for the legal authorization of the construction. The word **structure** translates an Aramaic term that could refer to wood used in the furnishings or, more probably, to the wood used in the construction of the walls (v. 8) and the roof. While Tattenai wanted to confirm the legality of the construction, he did not forbid it while waiting for **written instructions**.
5:5 The phrase **God was watching** is literally "the eye of their God was on" the elders. This verse contains the first mention of the **Jewish elders** in the postexilic era. In the Persian period, real power was in the hands of the Persian-appointed authorities, while the elders more often were called together to witness important events and judicial decisions.

5:7 All greetings means literally "all peace."
5:9–10 These verses testify to the accuracy of the information given in narrative in vv. 3–4.
5:11 While the title "God of heaven" is used twelve times in Ezra-Nehemiah, this is the only use of the title **God of the heavens and earth** in the Bible. Solomon's name is not used here, only an oblique reference to **a great king of Israel**.
5:12 The phrase **our ancestors angered the God of the heavens** makes clear that the cause of their nation's destruction and exile was their forefathers' failure to keep the covenant (2Ch 36:15–21; Neh 1:5–11; 9:5–37; Jr 4–6).
5:13 Although **Cyrus** was king of Persia, he also referred to himself as "King of Babylon" after he conquered Babylon in 539 BC. Here the central claim of the Jewish leaders is put forth: Cyrus **issued a decree to rebuild the house of God**. This decree, if found, would verify their right to rebuild the temple.
5:16 The Jewish elders' claim that **Sheshbazzar . . . laid the foundation of God's house** has been the subject of debate (see note at 3:8–9). The claim that it had **been under construction from that time until now** is also difficult since both Haggai and Zechariah, as well as Ezra (4:5,23), say that construction had ceased for nearly twenty years. The claim about ceaseless building appears to be a prevarication on the part of the Jewish elders, borne out of fear that

house in Jerusalem. It has been under construction from that time until now, but it has not been completed.

[17] So if it pleases the king, let a search of the royal archives[A] in Babylon be conducted to see if it is true that a decree was issued by King Cyrus to rebuild the house of God in Jerusalem. Let the king's decision regarding this matter be sent to us.

Darius's Search

6 King Darius gave the order, and they searched in the library of Babylon in the archives.[B] [2] But it was in the fortress of Ecbatana in the province of Media that a scroll was found with this record written on it: [3] In the first year of King Cyrus, he issued a decree concerning the house of God in Jerusalem:

Let the house be rebuilt as a place for offering sacrifices, and let its original foundations be retained.[C] Its height is to be ninety feet[D] and its width ninety feet, [4] with three layers of cut[E] stones and one of timber. The cost is to be paid from the royal treasury.[F] [5] The gold and silver articles of God's house that Nebuchadnezzar took from the temple in Jerusalem and carried to Babylon must also be returned. They are to be brought to the temple in Jerusalem where they belong[G] and put into the house of God.

Darius's Decree

[6] Therefore, you must stay away from that place, Tattenai governor of the region west of the Euphrates River, Shethar-bozenai, and your[H] colleagues, the officials in the region. [7] Leave the construction of the house of God alone. Let the governor and

elders of the Jews rebuild this house of God on its original site.

[8] I hereby issue a decree concerning what you are to do, so that the elders of the Jews can rebuild the house of God:

The cost is to be paid in full to these men out of the royal revenues from the taxes of the region west of the Euphrates River, so that the work will not stop. [9] Whatever is needed — young bulls, rams, and lambs for burnt offerings to the God of the heavens, or wheat, salt, wine, and oil, as requested by the priests in Jerusalem — let it be given to them every day without fail, [10] so that they can offer sacrifices of pleasing aroma to the God of the heavens and pray for the life of the king and his sons.

[11] I also issue a decree concerning any man who interferes with this directive:

Let a beam be torn from his house and raised up; he will be impaled on it, and his house will be made into a garbage dump because of this offense. [12] May the God who caused his name to dwell there overthrow any king or people who dares[I] to harm or interfere with this house of God in Jerusalem. I, Darius, have issued the decree. Let it be carried out diligently.

[13] Then Tattenai governor of the region west of the Euphrates River, Shethar-bozenai, and their colleagues diligently carried out what King Darius had decreed. [14] So the Jewish elders continued successfully with the building under the prophesying of Haggai the prophet and Zechariah son of Iddo. They finished the building according to the command of the God of

---

[A]5:17 Lit *treasure house*   [B]6:1 Lit *Babylon where the treasures were stored*   [C]6:3 Lit *be brought forth*   [D]6:3 Lit *60 cubits*
[E]6:4 Or *huge*   [F]6:4 Lit *the king's house*   [G]6:5 Lit *Jerusalem, to its place,*   [H]6:6 Lit *their*   [I]6:12 Lit *who stretches out its hand*

---

any mention of a long halt of construction would weaken their case that their rebuilding efforts were sanctioned.
5:17 Tattenai suggested that a search be undertaken of **the royal archives** (lit "treasure house") **in Babylon** for Cyrus's decree allowing the Jewish exiles to return to their homeland. The record of the decree in fact was found in the Persian summer capital of Ecbatana (6:2). It appears that neither Sheshbazzar nor Zerubbabel had an official copy, since none was shown to their early opponents (4:1–5) or to Tattenai.
6:1–5 The first version of the Decree of Cyrus (1:2–4) was written in Hebrew and reflected a strong Jewish perspective. The second version given here, in Aramaic, explicitly decreed that funding for the temple would be **paid from the royal treasury**.
6:3 The phrase **let its original foundations be retained** translates a difficult and uncertain Aramaic phrase. Other translations assume the text is corrupted and change

the term *foundations* (Aramaic *'ushohe*) to *fire-offerings* (Aramaic *'eshohe*), thus reading "and where the fire-offerings are brought."
The dimensions of the temple listed here are problematic. Only its width and height are mentioned, suggesting a cube that would be far larger than Solomon's glorious temple. The text in Ezr 6:3 might reflect an ancient scribal error.
6:4 The construction technique of **three layers of cut stones and one of timber** was based on the construction of Solomon's temple (1Kg 6:36). This translation reflects a slight change of the Aramaic text from "new (Aramaic *chadath*) timber" to "one (Aramaic *chad*) of timber." Unseasoned wood would not be used for such important construction.
6:6–7 Just as God was watching over his people (5:5) while they waited for Darius's decision, so his care for them was seen in Darius's decision that prohibited **Tattenai** and the other Persian officials from hindering the **construction** of the temple.

6:8–10 Darius's decree not only provided funds for reconstruction but for the daily sacrificial offerings as well.
6:11–12 The unusual terms in this Aramaic phrase (**raised up; he will be impaled on it**) have led some to translate it as "he will be set upon it (the beam) and struck," that is, *flogged*. However, *impaled* is probably correct. The Greek historian Herodotus claimed that Darius impaled three thousand rebellious Babylonians when he recaptured the city.
6:13–15 Tattenai and his Persian colleagues knew how dangerous it was to disobey the king of Persia. The construction of the temple was done according to the decrees of **Cyrus, Darius, and King Artaxerxes of Persia**. The mention of Artaxerxes is odd since he became king a half century after the temple was completed. Chapters 1–6 were probably the last chapters of Ezra-Nehemiah to be written. The author of this section, well aware both of Artaxerxes's opposition

Israel and the decrees of Cyrus, Darius, and King Artaxerxes of Persia. ¹⁵ This house was completed on the third day of the month of Adar in the sixth year of the reign of King Darius.

Temple Dedication and the Passover

¹⁶ Then the Israelites, including the priests, the Levites, and the rest of the exiles, celebrated the dedication of the house of God with joy. ¹⁷ For the dedication of God's house they offered one hundred bulls, two hundred rams, and four hundred lambs, as well as twelve male goats as a sin offering for all Israel — one for each Israelite tribe. ¹⁸ They also appointed the priests by their divisions and the Levites by their groups to the service of God in Jerusalem, according to what is written in the book of Moses.

¹⁹ The exiles observed the Passover on the fourteenth day of the first month. ²⁰ All of the priests and Levites were ceremonially clean, because they had purified themselves. They killed the Passover lamb for themselves, their priestly brothers, and all the exiles. ²¹ The Israelites who had returned from exile ate it, together with all who had separated themselves from the uncleanness of the Gentiles of the land^A in order to worship the LORD, the God of Israel. ²² They observed the Festival of Unleavened Bread for seven days with joy, because the LORD had made them joyful, having changed the Assyrian king's attitude toward them, so that he supported them^B in the work on the house of the God of Israel.

Ezra's Arrival

7 After these events, during the reign of King Artaxerxes of Persia, Ezra — Seraiah's son, Azariah's son,

Hilkiah's son, ² Shallum's son, Zadok's son, Ahitub's son, ³ Amariah's son, Azariah's son, Meraioth's son, ⁴ Zerahiah's son, Uzzi's son, Bukki's son, ⁵ Abishua's son, Phinehas's son, Eleazar's son, the chief priest Aaron's son ⁶ — came up from Babylon. He was a scribe skilled in the law of Moses, which the LORD, the God of Israel, had given. The king had granted him everything he requested because the hand of the LORD his God was on him. ⁷ Some of the Israelites, priests, Levites, singers, gatekeepers, and temple servants accompanied him to Jerusalem in the seventh year of King Artaxerxes.

⁸ Ezra^C came to Jerusalem in the fifth month, during the seventh year of the king. ⁹ He began the journey from Babylon on the first day of the first month and arrived in Jerusalem on the first day of the fifth month since the gracious hand of his God was on him. ¹⁰ Now Ezra had determined in his heart to study the law of the LORD, obey it, and teach its statutes and ordinances in Israel.

Letter from Artaxerxes

¹¹ This is the text of the letter King Artaxerxes gave to Ezra the priest and scribe, an expert in matters of the LORD's commands and statutes for Israel:^D

¹² Artaxerxes, king of kings, to Ezra the priest, an expert in the law of the God of the heavens:

Greetings.

¹³ I issue a decree that any of the Israelites in my kingdom, including their priests and

---

^A 6:21 Lit land to them   ^B 6:22 Lit strengthened their hands   ^C 7:8 LXX, Syr, Vg read They   ^D 7:11 Ezr 7:12–26 is written in Aramaic.

(4:6–22) and his support (7:11–26), included Artaxerxes in the list of those whose decrees involved the construction of the temple, even though his support came long after the events described in 6:13–15. Construction was most likely completed on March 12, 515 BC.
6:19–20 The author had used Aramaic from 4:8 through 6:18 since he was working with official Persian correspondence written in Aramaic. With that correspondence completed, he returned to Hebrew. The new temple allowed the full implementation of the sacrificial system that existed before the disaster of 586 BC when the first temple was destroyed. This celebration of **Passover** (Hb *pesach*)—probably April 21, 515 BC—would have been a momentous occasion for God's people to remember their forefathers' deliverance from Egypt as well as their own deliverance from exile.
6:21 The OT law allowed even resident aliens to celebrate Passover (Ex 12:48–49) as long as they were circumcised. Those **who had separated themselves** at least included proselytes. Likely it also included Israelites who had never been exiled but had remained

in the land and continued to worship the God of Israel.
6:22 The **Festival of Unleavened Bread** began the day after Passover (Ex 12:14–20). The reference to King Darius of Persia as the **Assyrian** king seems unusual since the Assyrian Empire had collapsed more than a century earlier, but just as the Babylonians saw themselves as the successors of the Assyrians, so the Persian kings regarded themselves as the successors of the Assyrians and the Babylonians.
7:1–10:44 The second major part of Ezra consists primarily of the Ezra Memoir, which tells of the ministry of Ezra the scribe in bringing spiritual renewal to the Jewish people. The final verses of chap. 6 take place in April 515 BC while the opening verses of chap. 7 begin with Ezra's journey to Jerusalem in 458 BC, a gap of over fifty years. This section is written in Hebrew, except for the copy of Artaxerxes's letter (7:12–26) in Aramaic.
7:1–5 Ezra's name is a short form of the common Hebrew name *Azariah*, meaning "Yahweh Has Helped." The genealogy given for Ezra is representative and not complete, as a comparison with 1Ch 6:3–15 demonstrates.

It is enough to show that Ezra's pedigree is impeccable.
7:6 Ezra was **a scribe** (Hb *sopher*), which in this context means more than reading, writing, and keeping records; it identifies a Torah expert who could read and interpret the law.
7:7 Those returning to the land with Ezra are listed in the same order as in the return under Zerubbabel and Jeshua almost eighty years before (2:2–53).
7:8–9 Ezra's journey toward Jerusalem probably began on April 8, 458 BC, but 8:15–31 tells of an immediate delay when it was discovered that no Levites were present. After a fourteen-week, nine hundred mile pilgrimage, they probably arrived in Jerusalem on August 4, 458 BC.
7:11–28 Ezra came to Jerusalem bearing a letter from King Artaxerxes authorizing him and everyone who wanted to join with him to go to Jerusalem (v. 13).
7:11 This verse, written in Hebrew, provides an introduction to Artaxerxes's **letter** that was written in Aramaic (vv. 12–26).
7:12 Artaxerxes used the common royal Persian title **king of kings**, used in the NT in reference to God (1Tm 6:15; Rv 19:16).

Levites, who want to go to Jerusalem, may go with you. ¹⁴ You are sent by the king and his seven counselors to evaluate Judah and Jerusalem according to the law of your God, which is in your possession. ¹⁵ You are also to bring the silver and gold the king and his counselors have willingly given to the God of Israel, whose dwelling is in Jerusalem, ¹⁶ and all the silver and gold you receive throughout the province of Babylon, together with the freewill offerings given by the people and the priests to the house of their God in Jerusalem. ¹⁷ Then you are to be diligent to buy with this money bulls, rams, and lambs, along with their grain and drink offerings, and offer them on the altar at the house of your God in Jerusalem. ¹⁸ You may do whatever seems best to you and your brothers with the rest of the silver and gold, according to the will of your God. ¹⁹ Deliver to the God of Jerusalem all the articles given to you for the service of the house of your God. ²⁰ You may use the royal treasury ᴬ to pay for anything else needed for the house of your God.

²¹ I, King Artaxerxes, issue a decree to all the treasurers in the region west of the Euphrates River:

Whatever Ezra the priest, an expert in the law of the God of the heavens, asks of you must be provided in full, ²² up to 7,500 pounds ᴮ of silver, 500 bushels ᶜ of wheat, 550 gallons ᴰ of wine, 550 gallons of oil, and salt without limit. ᴱ ²³ Whatever is commanded by the God of the heavens must be done diligently for the house of the God of the heavens, so that wrath will not fall on the realm of the king and his sons. ²⁴ Be advised that you do not have authority

to impose tribute, duty, and land tax on any priests, Levites, singers, doorkeepers, temple servants, or other servants of this house of God.

²⁵ And you, Ezra, according to ᶠ God's wisdom that you possess, appoint magistrates and judges to judge all the people in the region west of the Euphrates who know the laws of your God and to teach anyone who does not know them. ²⁶ Anyone who does not keep the law of your God and the law of the king, let the appropriate judgment be executed against him, whether death, banishment, confiscation of property, or imprisonment.

²⁷ Blessed be the LORD, the God of our ancestors, who has put it into the king's mind to glorify the house of the LORD in Jerusalem, ²⁸ and who has shown favor to me before the king, his counselors, and all his powerful officers. So I took courage because I was strengthened by the hand of the LORD my God, ᴳ and I gathered Israelite leaders to return with me.

Those Returning with Ezra

8 These are the family heads and the genealogical records of those who returned with me from Babylon during the reign of King Artaxerxes:

²   Gershom, from Phinehas's descendants;
     Daniel, from Ithamar's descendants;
     Hattush, from David's descendants,
³   who was of Shecaniah's descendants;
     Zechariah, from Parosh's descendants,
     and 150 men ᴴ with him
       who were registered by genealogy;
⁴   Eliehoenai son of Zerahiah
     from Pahath-moab's descendants,
     and 200 men with him;
⁵   Shecaniah ᴵ son of Jahaziel

ᴬ 7:20 Lit *the king's house*   ᴮ 7:22 Lit *100 talents*   ᶜ 7:22 Lit *100 cors*   ᴰ 7:22 Lit *100 baths*   ᴱ 7:22 Lit *without instruction*
ᶠ 7:25 Lit *to your*   ᴳ 7:28 Lit *because the hand of the LORD my God was on me*   ᴴ 8:3 Or *males*; also in vv. 4–14   ᴵ 8:5 LXX,
1 Esdras 8:32; MT reads *the descendants of Shecaniah*

7:13–14 The Greek historian Herodotus described the practice of a Persian king having seven trusted counselors. Esther 1:13–14 names Xerxes's seven trusted advisers and states that they had personal access to the king.
7:15–17 Funds for Ezra's journey to **Jerusalem** and the purchase of sacrificial animals there came from the royal treasury and from gifts gathered from the Jewish exiles in Babylon.
7:19 It is not clear what the royal **articles** were. In 5:14 the same term is used to describe the gold and silver articles looted from the temple by Nebuchadnezzar in 586 BC and returned by King Cyrus (1:7).
7:20 Amazingly, the king gave Ezra a "blank check."
7:21–22 The provisions that Ezra was entitled to were used daily in the sacrifices at the temple. The quantities listed here would be

sufficient for approximately two years. The **7,500 pounds** (lit "a hundred talents") **of silver** seems out of proportion to the other items. The entire annual tax for the "Beyond the River" region was 350 talents. A textual corruption, common when scribes were copying numbers, may explain the seemingly implausible amount of silver.
7:24 Persian texts and Greek writings about Persian practice confirm that exemption from taxes was granted to temples and the sacred personnel who served there.
7:25 The charge given to **Ezra** here is not clear. He was to **appoint magistrates and judges**, but it is not certain how their roles related to those of the regular Persian judges and officials. Probably these judges and magistrates dealt only with cases specific to the OT law.
7:26 Those who refused to keep **the law** were subject to typical Persian punishments.

7:27–28 With the completion of the official letter written in Aramaic (vv. 12–26), the author reverts to Hebrew. Here in v. 27 begin the first words of Ezra in the Ezra Memoir.
8:1–14 Almost eighty years before Ezra came to Jerusalem, Zerubbabel and Jeshua led the first return of the Babylonian exiles to the land of their forefathers (chap. 2). The list of returnees at that time (2:2–61) numbered more than 40,000 men (2:64) while the list here involves only about 1,500 men.
8:2a Gershom and **Daniel** represented the two branches of the Aaronic priesthood. Gershom traced his ancestry through Phinehas (Ex 6:25), the son of Eleazar, son of Aaron. Ezra himself was from this priestly lineage.
8:2b–3 Hattush's royal lineage from King David would certainly have been important to the postexilic community in Jerusalem. First Chronicles 3:19–22 gives his genealogy

from Zattu's descendants,
and 300 men with him;
6 Ebed son of Jonathan
from Adin's descendants,
and 50 men with him;
7 Jeshaiah son of Athaliah
from Elam's descendants,
and 70 men with him;
8 Zebadiah son of Michael
from Shephatiah's descendants,
and 80 men with him;
9 Obadiah son of Jehiel
from Joab's descendants,
and 218 men with him;
10 Shelomith[A] son of Josiphiah
from Bani's descendants,
and 160 men with him;
11 Zechariah son of Bebai
from Bebai's descendants,
and 28 men with him;
12 Johanan son of Hakkatan
from Azgad's descendants,
and 110 men with him;
13 these are the last ones,
from Adonikam's descendants,
and their names are

Eliphelet, Jeuel, and Shemaiah,
and 60 men with them;
14 Uthai and Zaccur[B]
from Bigvai's descendants,
and 70 men with them.

15 I gathered them at the river[c] that flows to Ahava, and we camped there for three days. I searched among the people and priests, but found no Levites there. 16 Then I summoned the leaders: Eliezer, Ariel, Shemaiah, Elnathan, Jarib, Elnathan, Nathan, Zechariah, and Meshullam, as well as the teachers Joiarib and Elnathan. 17 I sent them to Iddo, the leader at Casiphia, with a message for[D] him and his brothers, the temple servants at Casiphia, that they should bring us ministers for the house of our God. 18 Since the gracious hand of our God was on us, they brought us Sherebiah — a man of insight from the descendants of Mahli, a descendant of Levi son of Israel — along with his sons and brothers, 18 men, 19 plus Hashabiah, along with Jeshaiah, from the descendants of Merari, and his brothers and their sons, 20 men. 20 There were also 220 of the temple servants, who had been appointed by David and

---

^8:10 Some LXX mss, 1 Esdras 8:36; MT reads *the descendants of Shelomith* ᴮ8:14 Alt Hb tradition, some LXX mss read *Zabud* ᶜ8:15 Or *canal* ᴰ8:17 Lit *Casiphia, and I put in their mouth the words to speak to*

---

as: Zerubbabel/Hananiah/Shecaniah/Shemaiah/Hattush.
8:14 Mentioning two names (**Uthai and Zaccur**) for a family leader is unusual. The Hebrew text describes **70 men** literally "with him" (sg.), suggesting some minor textual confusion. Probably the original text read

"Uthai *son of* Zaccur," a reading supported by the apocryphal 1 Esdras 8:40.
8:15 The term for **river** can mean either "river" or "canal." It appears there were not enough priests to carry the gold and silver donated to the temple (vv. 24–30) and that the **Levites** were needed for this task.

8:16 The list of **leaders** and **teachers** is unusual in that it mentions three individuals named **Elnathan** who are not differentiated by a genealogical description.
8:17 The distinguished entourage was sent to ask **Iddo** for Levites to join the exiles in their return to the land. Their request was

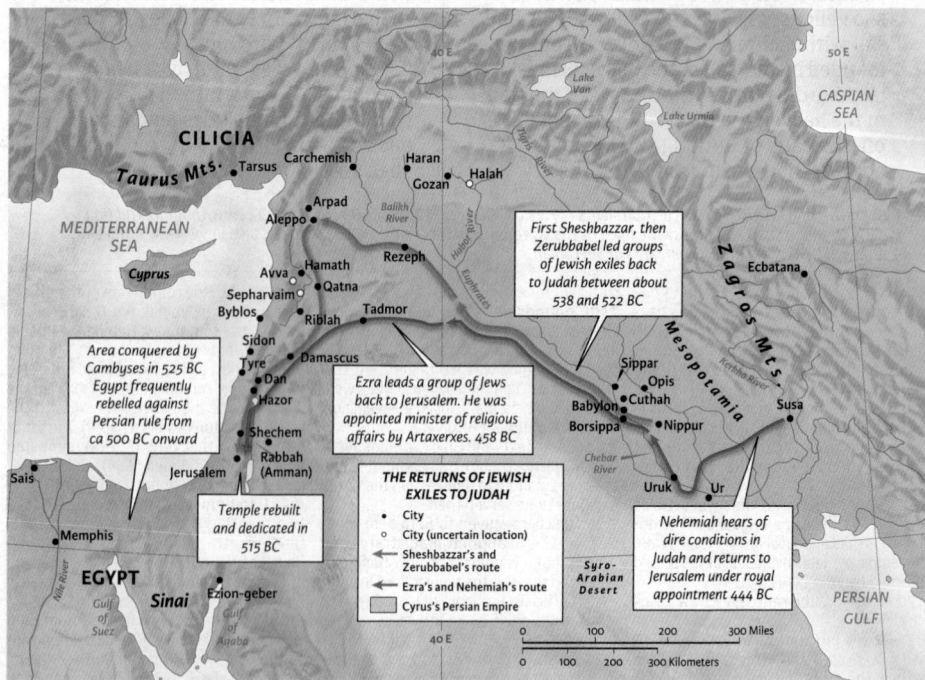

Map labels:
40 E   50 E
CASPIAN SEA
Lake Van
Lake Urmia
CILICIA
Taurus Mts.
Tarsus   Carchemish   Haran   Gozan   Halah
Arpad
Balikh River
Tigris River
MEDITERRANEAN SEA
Aleppo
Rezeph
Cyprus
Avva   Hamath   Qatna
Sepharvaim
Byblos   Riblah   Tadmor
Euphrates
Ecbatana
Zagros Mts.
Habor River
Sidon
Tyre   Dan   Damascus
Hazor
Mesopotamia
Sippar
Opis
Babylon   Cuthah
Borsippa   Nippur
Susa
Kerkha River
Shechem
Rabbah (Amman)
Jerusalem
Chebar River
Uruk   Ur
Sais
Memphis
EGYPT
Sinai
Ezion-geber
Gulf of Suez
Gulf of Aqaba
Syro-Arabian Desert
PERSIAN GULF

First Sheshbazzar, then Zerubbabel led groups of Jewish exiles back to Judah between about 538 and 522 BC

Area conquered by Cambyses in 525 BC Egypt frequently rebelled against Persian rule from ca 500 BC onward

Ezra leads a group of Jews back to Jerusalem. He was appointed minister of religious affairs by Artaxerxes. 458 BC

Nehemiah hears of dire conditions in Judah and returns to Jerusalem under royal appointment 444 BC

Temple rebuilt and dedicated in 515 BC

THE RETURNS OF JEWISH EXILES TO JUDAH
• City
○ City (uncertain location)
← Sheshbazzar's and Zerubbabel's route
← Ezra's and Nehemiah's route
▢ Cyrus's Persian Empire

40 E
0   100   200   300 Miles
0   100   200   300 Kilometers

the leaders for the work of the Levites. All were identified by name.

Preparing to Return

²¹ I proclaimed a fast by the Ahava River,^ so that we might humble ourselves before our God and ask him for a safe journey for us, our dependents, and all our possessions. ²² I did this because I was ashamed to ask the king for infantry and cavalry to protect us from enemies during the journey, since we had told him, "The hand of our God is gracious to all who seek him, but his fierce anger is against all who abandon him." ²³ So we fasted and pleaded with our God about this, and he was receptive to our prayer.

²⁴ I selected twelve of the leading priests, along with Sherebiah, Hashabiah, and ten of their brothers. ²⁵ I weighed out to them the silver, the gold, and the articles — the contribution for the house of our God that the king, his counselors, his leaders, and all the Israelites who were present had offered. ²⁶ I weighed out to them 24 tons⁸ of silver, silver articles weighing 7,500 pounds,ᶜ 7,500 pounds of gold, ²⁷ twenty gold bowls worth a thousand gold coins,ᴰ and two articles of fine gleaming bronze, as valuable as gold. ²⁸ Then I said to them, "You are holy to the LORD, and the articles are holy. The silver and gold are a freewill offering to the LORD God of your ancestors. ²⁹ Guard them carefully until you weigh them out in the chambers of the LORD's house before the leading priests, Levites, and heads of the Israelite families in Jerusalem." ³⁰ So the priests and Levites took charge of the silver, the gold, and the articles that had been weighed out, to bring them to the house of our God in Jerusalem.

Arrival in Jerusalem

³¹ We set out from the Ahava River on the twelfth day of the first month to go to Jerusalem. We were strengthened by our God,ᴱ and he kept us from the grasp of the enemy and from ambush along the way. ³² So we arrived at Jerusalem and rested there for three days. ³³ On the fourth day the silver, the gold, and the articles were weighed out in the house of our God into the care of the priest Meremoth son of Uriah. Eleazar son of Phinehas was with him. The Levites Jozabad son of Jeshua and Noadiah son of Binnui were also with them. ³⁴ Everything was verified by number and weight, and the total weight was recorded at that time.

³⁵ The exiles who had returned from the captivity offered burnt offerings to the God of Israel: twelve bulls for all Israel, ninety-six rams, and seventy-seven lambs, along with twelve male goats as a sin offering. All this was a burnt offering for the LORD. ³⁶ They also delivered the king's edicts to the royal satraps and governors of the region west of the Euphrates, so that they would support the people and the house of God.

Israel's Intermarriage

9 After these things had been done, the leaders approached me and said, "The people of Israel, the priests, and the Levites have not separated themselves from the surrounding peoples whose detestable practices are like those of the Canaanites, Hethites, Perizzites, Jebusites, Ammonites, Moabites, Egyptians, and Amorites. ² Indeed, the Israelite menᶠ have taken some of their daughters as wives for themselves and their sons, so that the holy seed has become mixed with the surrounding peoples. The leadersᴳ and officials have taken the lead in this unfaithfulness!" ³ When I heard this report, I tore my tunic and robe, pulled out some of the hair from my head and beard, and sat down devastated.

Ezra's Confession

⁴ Everyone who trembled at the words of the God of Israel gathered around me, because of the unfaithfulness of the exiles, while I sat devastated until the evening offering. ⁵ At the evening offering, I got up from my time of humiliation, with my tunic and robe torn. Then I

---

^8:21 Or *Canal*, also in v. 31   ⁸8:26 Lit *650 talents*   ᶜ8:26 Lit *100 talents*   ᴰ8:27 Or *1,000 drachmas,* or *1,000 darics*   ᴱ8:31 Lit *The hand of our God was on us*   ᶠ9:2 Lit *they*   ᴳ9:2 Lit *hand of the leaders*

---

significant, asking people to leave their homes and family on short notice for a difficult nine-hundred-mile journey.
8:21 The term **dependents** refers to those unable to walk on the journey, such as the elderly, the infirm, and young children.
8:24–25 Ezra appointed twelve **priests** and twelve Levites to bring their treasure to Jerusalem, both the gifts from those joining Ezra on the journey and those given by King Artaxerxes and his officials.
8:26–27 24 tons is literally "650 talents." The amount seems excessive. Some would suggest a textual error has occurred, and "talents" should be "minas."
8:31 The actual departure for Jerusalem took place **on the twelfth day of the**

first month, not the first day of the first month (probably April 8, 458 BC) as originally planned because of the need to find Levites to join the returnees (vv. 15–20).
8:32–34 Meremoth is probably the same person mentioned in Neh 3:4, where he is referred to as "Meremoth son of Uriah, son of Hakkoz" (also Neh 3:21). Here in v. 34 Ezra notes that **everything was verified by number and weight**. Because Ezra came to Jerusalem bearing huge financial gifts from the king, he would need to provide verification to Artaxerxes that these gifts arrived at the temple.
8:35–36 The first-person narrative by Ezra is interrupted by these two verses in which the author or editor describes the response of the returnees to God's goodness.

9:1 Ezra had not long returned from delivering the king's edicts (8:36) when some leaders presented him with a genuine threat to the postexilic Jewish community—intermarriage between Jews and pagans. The extent of the problem is shown in that all three major groups of the community were involved—the laity (**the people of Israel**) as well as **priests** and **Levites**.
9:2 The situation was made even worse because the **leaders and officials** had **taken the lead in this unfaithfulness**. The issue was not racial but religious.
9:4–5 Ezra got up from his **time of humiliation**, a term that probably implies a penitential act in this context.

fell on my knees and spread out my hands to the LORD my God. **6** And I said:

My God, I am ashamed and embarrassed to lift my face toward you, my God, because our iniquities are higher than our heads and our guilt is as high as the heavens. **7** Our guilt has been terrible from the days of our ancestors until the present. Because of our iniquities we have been handed over, along with our kings and priests, to the surrounding kings, and to the sword, captivity, plundering, and open shame, as it is today. **8** But now, for a brief moment, grace has come from the LORD our God to preserve a remnant for us and give us a stake in his holy place. Even in our slavery, God has given us a little relief and light to our eyes. **9** Though we are slaves, our God has not abandoned us in our slavery. He has extended grace to us in the presence of the Persian kings, giving us relief, so that we can rebuild the house of our God and repair its ruins, to give us a wall in Judah and Jerusalem.

10 Now, our God, what can we say in light of^A this? For we have abandoned the commands **11** you gave through your servants the prophets, saying, "The land you are entering to possess is an impure land. The surrounding peoples have filled it from end to end with their uncleanness by their impurity and detestable practices. **12** So do not give your daughters to their sons in marriage or take their daughters for your sons. Never pursue their welfare or prosperity, so that you will be strong, eat the good things of the land, and leave it as an inheritance to your sons forever." **13** After all that has happened to us because of our evil deeds and terrible guilt — though you, our God, have punished us less than our iniquities deserve and have allowed us to survive^B — **14** should we break your commands again and intermarry with the peoples who commit these detestable practices? Wouldn't you become so angry with us that you would destroy us, leaving neither remnant nor survivor? **15** LORD God of Israel, you are righteous, for we survive as a remnant today. Here we are before you with our guilt, though no one can stand in your presence because of this.

Sending Away Foreign Wives

10 While Ezra prayed and confessed, weeping and falling facedown before the house of God, an extremely large assembly of Israelite men, women, and children gathered around him. The people also wept bitterly. **2** Then Shecaniah son of Jehiel, an Elamite, responded to Ezra, "We have been unfaithful to our God by marrying foreign women from the surrounding peoples, but there is still hope for Israel in spite of this. **3** Therefore, let's make a covenant before our God to send away all the foreign wives and their children, according to the counsel of my lord and of those who tremble at the command of our God. Let it be done according to the law. **4** Get up, for this matter is your responsibility, and we support you. Be strong and take action!"

5 Then Ezra got up and made the leading priests, Levites, and all Israel take an oath to do what had been said; so they took the oath. **6** Ezra then went from the house of God and walked to the chamber of Jehohanan son of Eliashib, where he spent the night.^C He did not eat food or drink water, because he was mourning over the unfaithfulness of the exiles.

7 They circulated a proclamation throughout Judah and Jerusalem that all the exiles should gather at Jerusalem. **8** Whoever did not come within three days would forfeit all his possessions,^D according to the decision of the leaders and elders, and would be excluded from the assembly of the exiles.

9 So all the men of Judah and Benjamin gathered in Jerusalem within the three days. On the twentieth day of the ninth month, all the people sat in the square at the house of God, trembling because of this matter and because of the heavy rain. **10** Then the priest Ezra stood up and said to them, "You have been unfaithful by marrying foreign women, adding to Israel's guilt. **11** Therefore, make a confession to the LORD, the God of your ancestors, and do his will. Separate yourselves from the surrounding peoples and your foreign wives."

^A9:10 Lit say after ^B9:13 Lit and gave us a remnant like this ^C10:6 1 Esdras 9:2, Syr; MT, Vg read he went ^D10:8 Lit would set apart all his possessions for destruction

9:6–7 Ezra began his prayer with his own shame and embarrassment but quickly shifted to a corporate confession of the nation's sins.
9:8–9 The term rendered **stake** literally is "peg," a metaphor for the idea of permanence (Is 33:20) and stability (Is 22:23–25). That the postexilic community existed and had a temple was a sign of God's undeserved mercy.
9:13–15 Ezra warned God's people that to intermarry with pagans once again could lead God to **destroy** them all. God had been

merciful before when they sinned in this way because they survived as **a remnant today**, but they should not presume upon his grace. They needed to repent, specifically in the necessary but heartbreaking task of sending away their foreign wives and children (chap. 10).
10:2–4 Shecaniah's radical solution of sending away **the foreign wives and their children** was not an expression of ethnic prejudice but an act to insure the survival of God's covenant people (9:14). The translation here follows most modern translations in

reading "my lord" (Hb 'adoni) rather than the Masoretic Text "LORD" (Hb 'adonay). The context suggests that Shecaniah was referring to Ezra and not to God.
10:7–8 The three-day notice was sufficient time to notify the entire populace and for them to travel to **Jerusalem**.
10:9 The threats for noncompliance with the proclamation had their desired effect. **All the men of Judah and Benjamin** met on the **twentieth day of the ninth month**—December 458 BC.

¹²Then all the assembly responded loudly, "Yes, we will do as you say! ¹³But there are many people, and it is the rainy season. We don't have the stamina to stay out in the open. This isn't something that can be done in a day or two, for we have rebelled terribly in this matter. ¹⁴Let our leaders represent the entire assembly. Then let all those in our towns who have married foreign women come at appointed times, together with the elders and judges of each town, in order to avert the fierce anger of our God concerning^A this matter." ¹⁵Only Jonathan son of Asahel and Jahzeiah son of Tikvah opposed this, with Meshullam and Shabbethai the Levite supporting them.

¹⁶The exiles did what had been proposed. The priest Ezra selected men^B who were family heads, all identified by name, to represent^C their ancestral families.^D They convened on the first day of the tenth month to investigate the matter, ¹⁷and by the first day of the first month they had dealt with all the men who had married foreign women.

Those Married to Foreign Wives

¹⁸The following were found to have married foreign women from the descendants of the priests:

from the descendants of Jeshua son of Jozadak and his brothers: Maaseiah, Eliezer, Jarib, and Gedaliah. ¹⁹They pledged^E to send their wives away, and being guilty, they offered a ram from the flock for their guilt;

²⁰ Hanani and Zebadiah from Immer's descendants;

²¹ Maaseiah, Elijah, Shemaiah, Jehiel, and Uzziah from Harim's descendants;

²² Elioenai, Maaseiah, Ishmael, Nethanel, Jozabad, and Elasah from Pashhur's descendants.

²³The Levites:
Jozabad, Shimei, Kelaiah (that is Kelita), Pethahiah, Judah, and Eliezer.

²⁴The singers:
Eliashib.
The gatekeepers:
Shallum, Telem, and Uri.

²⁵The Israelites:
Parosh's descendants: Ramiah, Izziah, Malchijah, Mijamin, Eleazar, Malchijah,^F and Benaiah;

²⁶ Elam's descendants: Mattaniah, Zechariah, Jehiel, Abdi, Jeremoth, and Elijah;

²⁷ Zattu's descendants: Elioenai, Eliashib, Mattaniah, Jeremoth, Zabad, and Aziza;

²⁸ Bebai's descendants: Jehohanan, Hananiah, Zabbai, and Athlai;

²⁹ Bani's descendants: Meshullam, Malluch, Adaiah, Jashub, Sheal, and Jeremoth;

³⁰ Pahath-moab's descendants: Adna, Chelal, Benaiah, Maaseiah, Mattaniah, Bezalel, Binnui, and Manasseh;

³¹ Harim's descendants: Eliezer, Isshijah, Malchijah, Shemaiah, Shimeon, ³²Benjamin, Malluch, and Shemariah;

³³ Hashum's descendants: Mattenai, Mattattah, Zabad, Eliphelet, Jeremai, Manasseh, and Shimei;

³⁴Bani's descendants: Maadai, Amram, Uel, ³⁵Benaiah, Bedeiah, Cheluhi, ³⁶Vaniah, Meremoth, Eliashib, ³⁷Mattaniah, Mattenai, Jaasu, ³⁸Bani, Binnui, Shimei, ³⁹Shelemiah, Nathan, Adaiah, ⁴⁰Machnadebai, Shashai, Sharai, ⁴¹Azarel, Shelemiah, Shemariah, ⁴²Shallum, Amariah, and Joseph;

⁴³ Nebo's descendants: Jeiel, Mattithiah, Zabad, Zebina, Jaddai, Joel, and Benaiah.

⁴⁴ All of these had married foreign women, and some of the wives had given birth to children.

^A10:14 Some Hb mss, LXX, Vg; other Hb mss read *until*   ^B10:16 1 Esdras 9:16, Syr; MT, Vg read *priest and men were selected*   ^C10:16 Lit *name, for*   ^D10:16 Lit *the house of their fathers*   ^E10:19 Lit *gave their hand*   ^F10:25 Some LXX mss, 1 Esdras 9:26 read *Hashabiah*

10:12–15 It is significant that the people asked that individual cases of foreign marriage be handled by **leaders** and not by priests who would seem to be the most likely ones to deal with these decisions. Since many priests were some of the worst offenders (vv. 18–22; 9:1), this disqualified them in the eyes of the people, who preferred to have respected family leaders (10:16) deal with this issue.
10:16–17 The **family heads** selected by **Ezra** probably met from December 29, 458 to March 27, 457 BC.
10:18–44 The list of offenders, which concludes the book of Ezra, reflects a "top down" progression that begins with the high priest's own family (vv. 18–19). Only 113 people were identified as involved in the sin of intermarriage. A number of suggestions have been offered for the surprising

brevity of the list, among them: (1) only a partial list has been preserved, (2) only those found guilty of the charge of intermarriage are listed, and (3) only those who were found guilty and followed through by putting away their foreign wives and children are listed. Ezra's ministry did not end the problem of intermarriage, for about thirty years later Nehemiah confronted it once again (Neh 13:23–29).
10:18–19 The first four offenders were of the priestly family of Jedaiah (2:36). These priests vowed to put away their foreign wives and offered **a ram from the flock for their guilt**.
10:20–22 Offenders from the three other priestly families (Immer, Pashhur, and Harim) represented in the return (2:37–39) are listed.
10:34 The second mention (v. 29) of the family name *Bani* is unusual since family names

were usually unique and served as identifiers for their descendants. Some scholars suggest that the text originally read "Bigvai," a person mentioned in the return (2:14) and later in 8:14. The name **Uel** does not occur anywhere else in the OT. A variant of "Uel" is *Joel*.
10:40 The name **Machnadebai** is probably not a Hebrew name and is found nowhere else in the OT. Its position in the verse may suggest that it originally designated a family group, possibly "Zaccai's descendants" (2:9).
10:44 The abrupt ending of the book of Ezra, with no summations or conclusions, is attributable to the fact that Ezra was originally joined with Nehemiah. This was not originally a closing to a book, but merely a closing to the section on Ezra's early ministry.

▼ Introduction to Nehemiah

Circumstances of Writing

Ezra and Nehemiah are anonymous. Ancient Jewish sources usually credit Ezra as the author of Ezra-Nehemiah. More likely Ezra-Nehemiah was written by the "Chronicler," the person (or persons) responsible for 1 and 2 Chronicles. Not only is Ezra-Nehemiah linked to Chronicles at its introduction (Ezr 1:1–2 = 2Ch 36:22–23), it also shares many similarities in language, terminology, themes, and perspective.

It is probably safe to assume that Ezra-Nehemiah was written soon after the conclusion of Nehemiah's ministry. Most likely the book was written no later than 400 BC.

In Ezra-Nehemiah, it is clear that Ezra came to Jerusalem first, probably in 458 BC, and that Nehemiah followed him thirteen years later, probably in 445 BC. Nehemiah made no mention of Ezra, his ministry, or his reforms. Ezra and Nehemiah appear together in only two texts (Neh 8:9; 12:36). The two events in which Ezra and Nehemiah were together were significant. In Nehemiah 8, the context is the reading of the law to the people; in Nehemiah 12, the two joyous processions walking around the city walls in the dedication ceremony include Ezra (v. 36) and Nehemiah (v. 38).

Contribution to the Bible

The events that occurred in Ezra and Nehemiah, the rebuilt temple, the stabilizing of Jerusalem, and the Jewish community that developed, all played key roles in the life and ministry of Jesus recorded in the Gospels. The rebuilt temple may have paled in comparison to the temple that Solomon built, but it would serve the Jews for centuries until Christ removed the need for a physical temple.

Structure

Nehemiah is similar to Samuel and Kings, and especially Chronicles, in that many sources were used in its composition. These include two major types of sources. Much of Nehemiah consists of material from the Nehemiah Memoir. The composition of the Nehemiah Memoir is regarded as including Nehemiah 1–7 as well as 11–13. But here also Nehemiah incorporated lists and records in his memoir. Nehemiah also contains many lists, genealogies, inventories, letters, and census records throughout the book. For a community attempting to reestablish itself after the disaster of 586 BC and the subsequent exile to Babylon, this material was crucial in reordering its life together.

See the introduction to Ezra for the timeline.

Outline

1 The words of Nehemiah son of Hacaliah:

News from Jerusalem

During the month of Chislev in the twentieth year, when I was in the fortress city of Susa, ² Hanani, one of my brothers, arrived with men from Judah, and I questioned them about Jerusalem and the Jewish remnant that had survived the exile. ³ They said to me, "The remnant in the province, who survived the exile, are in great trouble and disgrace. Jerusalem's wall has been broken down, and its gates have been burned."

Nehemiah's Prayer

⁴ When I heard these words, I sat down and wept. I mourned for a number of days, fasting and praying before the God of the heavens. ⁵ I said,

LORD, the God of the heavens, the great and awe-inspiring God who keeps his gracious covenant with those who love him and keep his commands, ⁶ let your eyes be open and your ears be attentive to hear your servant's prayer that I now pray to you day and night for your servants, the Israelites. I confess the sins^ we have committed against you. Both I and my father's family have sinned. ⁷ We have acted corruptly toward you and have not kept the commands, statutes, and ordinances you gave your servant Moses. ⁸ Please remember what you commanded your servant Moses: "If you are unfaithful, I will scatter you among the peoples. ⁹ But if you return to me and carefully observe my commands, even though your exiles were banished to the farthest horizon,ᴮ I will gather them from there and bring them to the place where I chose to have my name dwell." ¹⁰ They are your servants and your people. You redeemed them by your great power and strong hand.

^1:6 Lit sins of the Israelites   ᴮ1:9 Lit skies

1:1 In both the Hebrew and the Greek OT, the books of Ezra and Nehemiah were originally a single book. Nehemiah, whose name means "Yahweh has comforted," is identified as **son of Hacaliah**, to distinguish him from other people named Nehemiah (3:16; 7:7; Ezr 2:2) in the same era.

The text does not identify **the twentieth year**, but the context from Neh 2:1 identifies it as the twentieth year of King Artaxerxes of Persia (445 BC). The mention of the month of **Chislev** is difficult because 2:1 describes a later event occurring in the month of Nisan, also in the twentieth year. Chislev was parallel to our late November to early December, while Nisan was in the spring. Since Nehemiah served in the royal Persian

court, it is possible that he used the official regnal calendar in which the year began in the month a king came to power. In such a calendar Nisan could follow Chislev. **Susa**, in southwestern Iran, became the capital of Persia during the time of Darius. Later kings such as Xerxes and Artaxerxes used it as their winter palace.

1:2 Hanani is described by Nehemiah as **one of my brothers**. While this could be used loosely to refer to his Jewish companions, it probably means his literal brother due to the mention of Hanani in 7.2.

1:5–11 Nehemiah's prayer is shorter than Ezra's (Ezr 9:6–15).

1:5–7 Addressing God as **LORD, the God of the heavens** is not common in the OT, but it does occur several other times (Gn 24:7; 2Ch

36:23; Jnh 1:9). Like Ezra (Ezr 9:6), Nehemiah also identified with the sin of his people confessing that **both I and my father's family have sinned**.

1:8–9 Nehemiah alluded to Moses's warning (Dt 4:27; 28:64) that God would **scatter** Israel **among the peoples** if they were unfaithful to the covenant, and then he summarized God's promise through Moses (Dt 30:1–5) that repentance would bring restoration (Neh 1:9). Repentance is described as **return to me**, using the primary OT term (Hb *shuv*) for repentance that depicts a turning from sin toward God.

1:11 Nehemiah faced the daunting task of asking Artaxerxes to reverse his previous proclamation (Ezr 4:23) stopping all construction in Jerusalem. The **cupbearer** was

Character profile:
Ezra and Nehemiah

One of the hallmarks of God's relationship with the people of Israel was patience. He led them to the promised land despite their constant whining and complaining. He gave them the human monarchy they desired when they rejected him as king. He tempered his punishment when they turned their backs on him to pursue false gods.

But the Israelites were a hard-hearted bunch. They ignored God's prophets and shrugged off his dire warnings until it was too late. When God's judgment came, it came hard. In 722 BC he allowed the northern kingdom of Israel to fall to the Assyrians. In 586 BC the southern kingdom of Judah fell to the Babylonians.

The Babylonians laid waste to the capital city of Jerusalem, leaving no structure undamaged. They destroyed Solomon's temple as well as the walls that surrounded and protected the city. For decades Jerusalem lay in ruins, a testament to God's judgment, while many of its citizens were held captive in Babylon (and later in Persia).

In captivity many Israelites repented and begged God to restore them to their land. God answered their prayers by softening the hearts of their captors. Around 536 BC a group of Jewish exiles received permission from Cyrus, the king of Persia, to return to Jerusalem to rebuild the temple. Around 458 BC a priest named Ezra approached the Persian king, Darius, to request permission to lead a second

wave of Jewish exiles back to Jerusalem. Darius agreed to Ezra's request.

Around 444 BC a Jewish man serving as a royal cupbearer, Nehemiah, received word that the returnees were in grave danger because the walls of Jerusalem were still in ruins. The news devastated Nehemiah, who immediately turned to God in fasting and prayer. King Artaxerxes of Persia gave him permission—and provisions—to lead another group of exiles back to Jerusalem to rebuild the city's walls.

Nehemiah's mission represented an enormous step in the reestablishing of Israel's national identity. It's little surprise, then, that he faced heavy opposition to his plan. The surrounding nations of Canaan were not eager to see Israel's return to prominence. The proposed wall would give Jerusalem protection from attack and restore some of its military viability. It was in the national interest of the surrounding peoples to keep Jerusalem vulnerable.

Rumors of impending attacks did little to disrupt Nehemiah's construction schedule, though. Occasionally builders worked with a tool in one hand and a weapon in the other. Yet Nehemiah persevered and the construction continued. In fifty-four days the walls were completed.

No situation is beyond the Lord's control, and no task is too difficult for him. If he can cause pagan rulers and other unlikely allies to assist the Israelites in restoring their homeland, he can produce all kinds of unexpected blessings in the lives of his people. The key to discovering what God is capable of is to be active in your faith, step outside your comfort zone, and step forward to address the needs of others.

[11] Please, Lord, let your ear be attentive to the prayer of your servant and to that of your servants who delight to revere your name. Give your servant success today, and grant him compassion in the presence of this man." [A]

At the time, I was the king's cupbearer.

Nehemiah Sent to Jerusalem

2 During the month of Nisan in the twentieth year of King Artaxerxes, when wine was set before him, I took the wine and gave it to the king. I had never been sad in his presence, [2] so the king said to me, "Why do you look so sad, when you aren't sick? This is nothing but sadness of heart."

I was overwhelmed with fear [3] and replied to the king, "May the king live forever! Why should I [B] not be sad when the city where my ancestors are buried lies in ruins and its gates have been destroyed by fire?"

[4] Then the king asked me, "What is your request?"

So I prayed to the God of the heavens [5] and answered the king, "If it pleases the king, and if your servant has found favor with you, send me to Judah and to the city where my ancestors are buried, [C] so that I may rebuild it."

[6] The king, with the queen seated beside him, asked me, "How long will your journey take, and when will you return?" So I gave him a definite time, and it pleased the king to send me.

[7] I also said to the king, "If it pleases the king, let me have letters written to the governors of the region west of the Euphrates River, so that they will grant me safe passage until I reach Judah. [8] And let me have a letter written to Asaph, keeper of the king's forest, so that he will give me timber to rebuild the gates of the temple's fortress, the city wall, and the home where I will live." [D] The king granted my requests, for the gracious hand of my God was on me.

---

^1:11 = the king   [B]2:3 Lit *my face*   [C]2:5 Lit *city, the house of the graves of my fathers,*   [D]2:8 Lit *enter*

---

not only responsible for choosing appropriate wines for the king, but he tasted them himself to ensure they were not poisoned. **2:1–3** It is not clear why Nehemiah waited nearly four months (the year was 445 BC) to bring his request to King Artaxerxes (see note at 1:1 for the **month of Nisan**). It is possible that the king spent the winter in Babylon rather than in Susa. It is also possible that Nehemiah waited for the *tukta*, a Persian feast in which the king would often grant the requests of his supplicants. Nehemiah's

explanation for his sadness was carefully expressed. He did not mention Jerusalem by name, since it may have carried negative connotations from the past (Ezr 4:12), but he referred to it as **the city where my ancestors are buried**. **2:6** The word **queen** here is a rare term (Hb *shegal*) that occurs only here and in Ps 45:9. Both ancient and modern commentators suggest that this term identified this woman as a concubine or a sexual favorite of the king. This is suggested because the

term derives from a verb (Hb *shagal*) that often indicates illicit sexual activity. **2:7–8** Nehemiah needed not only time away from Artaxerxes's court but also official royal documents for the **governors . . . west of the Euphrates River** (lit "Beyond the River") who were opposed to any building in Jerusalem (v. 10). His request for timber for the **gates of the temple's fortress** probably refers to a military structure north of the temple that provided protection for the temple

---

THE RETURN FROM EXILE

PHASE	DATE	SCRIPTURE REFERENCE	JEWISH LEADER	PERSIAN RULER	EXTENT OF THE RETURN	EVENTS OF THE RETURN
First	538 BC	Ezra 1–6	Zerubbabel Jeshua	Cyrus	(1) Anyone who wanted to return should go. (2) The temple in Jerusalem was to be rebuilt. (3) Royal treasure provided funding of the temple rebuilding. (4) Gold and silver worship articles taken from temple by Nebuchadnezzar were returned.	(1) Burnt offerings were made. (2) The Festival of Shelters was celebrated. (3) The rebuilding of the temple was begun. (4) Persian ruler ordered rebuilding to be ceased. (5) Darius, King of Persia, ordered rebuilding to be resumed in 520 BC. (6) Temple was completed and dedicated in 516 BC.
Second	458 BC	Ezra 7–10	Ezra	Artaxerxes Longimanus	(1) Anyone who wanted to return could go. (2) Royal treasury provided funding. (3) Jewish civil magistrates and judges were allowed.	Men of Israel intermarried with foreign women.
Third	444 BC	Nehemiah 1–13	Nehemiah	Artaxerxes Longimanus	Rebuilding of Jerusalem was allowed.	(1) Rebuilding of wall of Jerusalem was opposed by Sanballat the Horonite, Tobiah the Ammonite and Geshem the Arab. (2) Rebuilding of wall was completed in fifty-two days. (3) Walls were dedicated. (4) Ezra read the book of the law to the people. (5) Nehemiah initiated reforms.

⁹ I went to the governors of the region west of the Euphrates and gave them the king's letters. The king had also sent officers of the infantry and cavalry with me. ¹⁰ When Sanballat the Horonite and Tobiah the Ammonite official heard that someone had come to pursue the prosperity of the Israelites, they were greatly displeased.

Preparing to Rebuild the Walls

¹¹ After I arrived in Jerusalem and had been there three days, ¹² I got up at night and took a few men with me. I didn't tell anyone what my God had laid on my heart to do for Jerusalem. The only animal I took^ was the one I was riding. ¹³ I went out at night through the Valley Gate toward the Serpent's⁸ Well and the Dung Gate, and I inspected the walls of Jerusalem that had been broken down and its gates that had been destroyed by fire. ¹⁴ I went on to the Fountain Gate and the King's Pool, but farther down it became too narrow for my animal to go through. ¹⁵ So I went up at night by way of the valley and inspected the wall. Then heading back, I entered through the Valley Gate and returned. ¹⁶ The officials did not know where I had gone or what I was doing, for I had not yet told the Jews, priests, nobles, officials, or the rest of those who would be doing the work. ¹⁷ So I said to them, "You see the trouble we are in. Jerusalem lies in ruins and its gates have been burned. Come, let's rebuild Jerusalem's wall, so that we will no longer be a disgrace." ¹⁸ I told them how the gracious hand of my God had been on me, and what the king had said to me.

They said, "Let's start rebuilding," and their hands were strengthened⁽ to do this good work.

¹⁹ When Sanballat the Horonite, Tobiah the Ammonite official, and Geshem the Arab heard about this, they mocked and despised us, and said, "What is this you're doing? Are you rebelling against the king?"

²⁰ I gave them this reply, "The God of the heavens is the one who will grant us success. We, his servants, will start building, but you have no share, right, or historic claim in Jerusalem."

Rebuilding the Walls

3 The high priest Eliashib and his fellow priests began rebuilding the Sheep Gate. They dedicated it and installed its doors. After building the wall to the Tower of the Hundred and the Tower of Hananel, they dedicated it. ² The men of Jericho built next to Eliashib, and next to them Zaccur son of Imri built.

Fish Gate

³ The sons of Hassenaah built the Fish Gate. They built it with beams and installed its doors, bolts, and bars. ⁴ Next to them Meremoth son of Uriah, son of Hakkoz, made repairs. Beside them Meshullam son of Berechiah, son of Meshezabel, made repairs. Next to them Zadok son of Baana made repairs. ⁵ Beside them the Tekoites made repairs, but their nobles did not lift a finger to help⁰ their supervisors.

^2:12 Lit animal with me ⁸2:13 Or Dragon's ⁽2:18 Lit they put their hands ⁰3:5 Lit not bring their neck to the work of

and its worshipers, and probably included the two towers mentioned in 3:1.
2:9 Some have criticized Nehemiah for accepting military protection, which Ezra refused (Ezr 8:22–23). Nehemiah's decision did not reflect a lack of faith on his part, but rather his trust that this was part of God's provision for him.
2:10 This verse introduces opposition as a recurring theme throughout the book and mentions two of Nehemiah's three primary opponents. **Sanballat**, whose name is Babylonian (sin-uballat, "the god Sin has given life"), may have descended from a family displaced by the Assyrians and resettled in the region of Samaria (2Kg 17:24–33). He may have worshiped Yahweh, since his children Shelemiah and Delaiah both have names compounded with the divine name. Sanballat likely was serving already as governor of Samaria, the hill country region north of Judah. The description of Sanballat as **the Horonite** probably refers to his origin from either Upper or Lower Beth-horon northwest of Jerusalem (Jos 18:13). Some scholars contend that **Tobiah** was a high official working for Sanballat and that his description as **the Ammonite** reflects his ancestry. Others maintain that Tobiah was from a Jewish family living east of the Jordan River in the Ammonite region

and that Tobiah was the governor of this province. Clearly both Sanballat and Tobiah were committed to thwarting Nehemiah's plans.
2:11 Ezra also rested **three days** when he arrived in Jerusalem (Ezr 8:32).
2:13–15 Nehemiah's description of his inspection of the city in this passage, along with the more detailed account of rebuilding in chap. 3, provides the best written information for reconstructing the dimensions of Jerusalem in the fifth century BC. Nehemiah's inspection tour began on the western side of Jerusalem and proceeded counterclockwise around the city.
2:13 Nehemiah and his men headed south from the **Valley Gate** toward the **Serpent's Well**, which could be translated as "Dragon's Well" or as "Serpent's/Dragon's Eye." Nehemiah continued south to the **Dung Gate** at the lower tip of the city. This gate led to the Valley of Hinnom where garbage was dumped and burned.
2:14 Nehemiah followed the ruins of the wall north to the **Fountain Gate and the King's Pool** (probably the same place as the "Pool of Shelah" mentioned in 3:15). With the ruined walls on his left and the steep Kidron Valley on his right, his way was blocked and he dismounted. This area of rubble, still visible today, is fifteen feet thick in some places.

2:16 While some assume the **officials** here were Persian officials, it probably refers to the various leaders mentioned among the **Jews, priests, nobles**, and officials.
2:19 Nehemiah's third primary opponent appears in this verse: **Geshem the Arab**. Arabs are mentioned in the Bible from the ninth century BC on. Geshem's vast domain stretched from the Negev south of Judah all the way to Lower Egypt. Together with Sanballat and Tobiah, he **mocked** Nehemiah and his followers, even accusing them of sedition against their Persian overlord.
3:1–32 With the conclusion of chap. 2, the first-person narrative of Nehemiah ends and does not resume until 4:1. Chapter 3, possibly written by someone other than Nehemiah, is a third-person account of the completion of the construction and installation of the doors.
3:1 Only here in this chapter is the dedication of the gate or the walls mentioned, a significant event because **the high priest Eliashib** led it.
3:4–5 In vv. 1–3 the workers are described as "building" the wall and gates while in most of the chapter the builders **made repairs**. This may suggest that the wall in the northern section near the Sheep Gate was so devastated that they had to start from scratch.

Old Gate, Broad Wall, and Tower of the Ovens

⁶ Joiada son of Paseah and Meshullam son of Besodeiah repaired the Old^A Gate. They built it with beams and installed its doors, bolts, and bars. ⁷ Next to them the repairs were done by Melatiah the Gibeonite, Jadon the Meronothite, and the men of Gibeon and Mizpah, who were under the authority⁸ of the governor of the region west of the Euphrates River. ⁸ After him Uzziel son of Harhaiah, the goldsmith, made repairs, and next to him Hananiah son of the perfumer made repairs. They restored Jerusalem as far as the Broad Wall.

⁹ Next to them Rephaiah son of Hur, ruler of half the district of Jerusalem, made repairs. ¹⁰ After them Jedaiah son of Harumaph made repairs across from his house. Next to him Hattush the son of Hashabneiah made repairs. ¹¹ Malchijah son of Harim and Hasshub son of Pahath-moab made repairs to another section, as well as to the Tower of the Ovens. ¹² Beside him Shallum son of Hallohesh, ruler of half the district of Jerusalem, made repairs — he and his daughters.

Valley Gate, Dung Gate, and Fountain Gate

¹³ Hanun and the inhabitants of Zanoah repaired the Valley Gate. They rebuilt it and installed its doors, bolts, and bars, and repaired five hundred yards^C of the wall to the Dung Gate. ¹⁴ Malchijah son of Rechab, ruler of district of Beth-haccherem, repaired the Dung Gate. He rebuilt it and installed its doors, bolts, and bars.

¹⁵ Shallun^D son of Col-hozeh, ruler of the district of Mizpah, repaired the Fountain Gate. He rebuilt it and roofed it. Then he installed its doors, bolts, and bars. He also made repairs to the wall of the Pool of Shelah near the king's garden, as far as the stairs that descend from the city of David.

¹⁶ After him Nehemiah son of Azbuk, ruler of half the district of Beth-zur, made repairs up to a point opposite the tombs of David, as far as the artificial pool and the House of the Warriors. ¹⁷ Next to him the Levites made repairs under Rehum son of Bani. Beside him Hashabiah, ruler of half the district of Keilah,

---

^A 3:6 Or *Jeshanah*   ^B 3:7 Or *Mizpah, the seat*   ^C 3:13 Lit *1,000 cubits*   ^D 3:15 Some Hb mss, Syr read *Shallum*

3:6 The mention of **the Old Gate** is problematic. The Hebrew text reads "the Jeshanah Gate," an unlikely name since the gate leading to Jeshanah (2Ch 13:19) should be on the north wall. This translation, like most others, reads the word not as a proper name but as an adjective meaning "old." Another option is to understand it as the Mishnah Gate or the "Second Gate" that led to the second district of the city mentioned in 2Kg 22:14.

3:8 The word **restored** normally means "to abandon." Most translations assume this verse and 4:2 use a rare verb meaning "to restore." It is not clear why the author would depart from his normal term for "restore." Thus, some scholars and translations read this phrase as "they *abandoned* Jerusalem," that is, they did not attempt to follow the eighth-century walls but left out the western hill section of the city. **3:12** The work crew of **Shallum son of Hallohesh** was unique. Possibly he had no sons,

but his family still joined in the work through the labor of **his daughters**. **3:15** This verse details reconstruction of the southeast corner of the city. The **Pool of Shelah** is probably the same as the King's Pool (2:14). **3:16** The text continues to describe construction from south to north along the eastern side of the city. The fact that the descriptions are not of gates and prominent places along the wall but locations within the city may

---

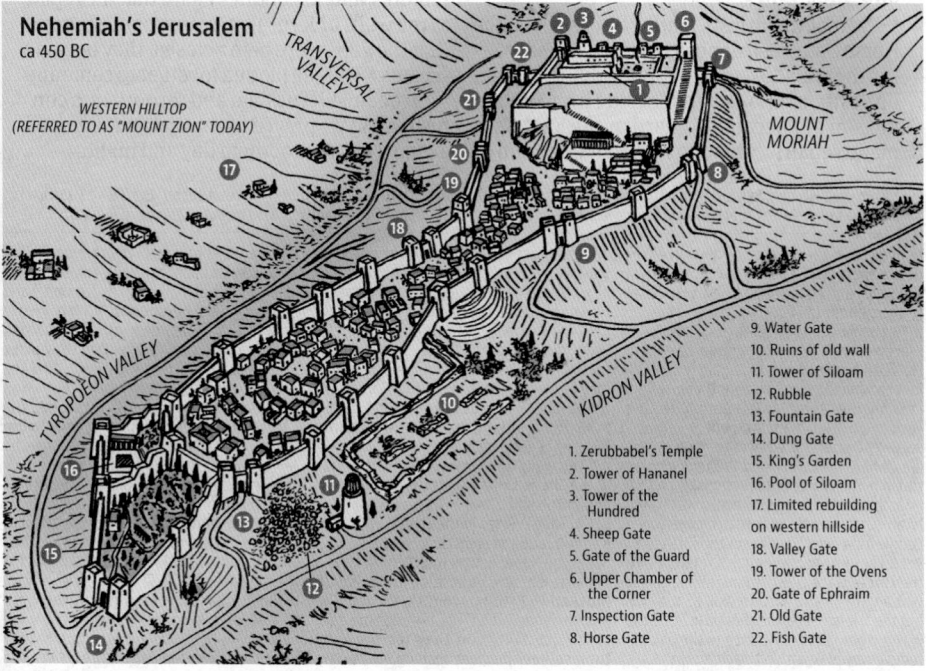

Nehemiah's Jerusalem
ca 450 BC

TRANSVERSAL VALLEY

WESTERN HILLTOP
(REFERRED TO AS "MOUNT ZION" TODAY)

MOUNT MORIAH

TYROPOEON VALLEY

KIDRON VALLEY

1. Zerubbabel's Temple
2. Tower of Hananel
3. Tower of the Hundred
4. Sheep Gate
5. Gate of the Guard
6. Upper Chamber of the Corner
7. Inspection Gate
8. Horse Gate

9. Water Gate
10. Ruins of old wall
11. Tower of Siloam
12. Rubble
13. Fountain Gate
14. Dung Gate
15. King's Garden
16. Pool of Siloam
17. Limited rebuilding on western hillside
18. Valley Gate
19. Tower of the Ovens
20. Gate of Ephraim
21. Old Gate
22. Fish Gate

made repairs for his district. [18] After him their fellow Levites made repairs under Binnui[A] son of Henadad, ruler of half the district of Keilah. [19] Next to him Ezer son of Jeshua, ruler of Mizpah, made repairs to another section opposite the ascent to the armory at the Angle.

The Angle, Water Gate, and Tower on Ophel

[20] After him Baruch son of Zabbai[B] diligently repaired another section, from the Angle to the door of the house of the high priest Eliashib. [21] Beside him Meremoth son of Uriah, son of Hakkoz, made repairs to another section, from the door of Eliashib's house to the end of his house. [22] And next to him the priests from the surrounding area made repairs.

[23] After them Benjamin and Hasshub made repairs opposite their house. Beside them Azariah son of Maaseiah, son of Ananiah, made repairs beside his house. [24] After him Binnui son of Henadad made repairs to another section, from the house of Azariah to the Angle and the corner. [25] Palal son of Uzai made repairs opposite the Angle and tower that juts out from the king's upper palace,[C] by the courtyard of the guard. Beside him Pedaiah son of Parosh [26] and the temple servants living on Ophel made repairs opposite the Water Gate toward the east and the tower that juts out. [27] Next to him the Tekoites made repairs to another section from a point opposite the great tower that juts out, as far as the wall of Ophel.

Horse Gate, Inspection Gate, and Sheep Gate

[28] Each of the priests made repairs above the Horse Gate, each opposite his own house. [29] After them Zadok son of Immer made repairs opposite his house. And beside him Shemaiah son of Shecaniah, guard of the East Gate, made repairs. [30] Next to him Hananiah son of Shelemiah and Hanun the sixth son of Zalaph made repairs to another section.

After them Meshullam son of Berechiah made repairs opposite his room. [31] Next to him Malchijah, one of the goldsmiths, made repairs to the house of the temple servants and the merchants, opposite the Inspection[D] Gate, and as far as the upstairs room on the corner. [32] The goldsmiths and merchants made repairs between the upstairs room on the corner and the Sheep Gate.

Progress in Spite of Opposition

4 When Sanballat heard that we were rebuilding the wall, he became furious. He mocked the Jews [2] before his colleagues and the powerful men[E] of Samaria and said, "What are these pathetic Jews doing? Can they restore it by themselves? Will they offer sacrifices? Will they ever finish it? Can they bring these burnt stones back to life from the mounds of rubble?" [3] Then Tobiah the Ammonite, who was beside him, said, "Indeed, even if a fox climbed up what they are building, he would break down their stone wall!"

[4] Listen, our God, for we are despised. Make their insults return on their own heads and let them be taken as plunder to a land of captivity. [5] Do not cover their guilt or let their sin be erased from your sight, because they have angered[F] the builders.

[6] So we rebuilt the wall until the entire wall was joined together up to half its height, for the people had the will to keep working.

[7] When Sanballat, Tobiah, and the Arabs, Ammonites, and Ashdodites heard that the repair to the walls of Jerusalem was progressing and that the gaps were being closed, they became furious. [8] They all plotted together to come and fight against Jerusalem and throw it into confusion. [9] So we prayed to our God and stationed a guard because of them day and night.

[A]3:18 Some Hb mss, Syr, LXX; Neh 3:24; other Hb mss, Vg read *Bavvai*   [B]3:20 Alt Hb tradition, Vg read *Zaccai*; Ezr 2:9   [C]3:25 Or *and the upper tower that juts out from the palace*   [D]3:31 Or *Muster*   [E]4:2 Or *the army*   [F]4:5 Or *provoked you in front of*

---

be indirect evidence that Nehemiah abandoned the eighth-century wall lower down the valley and established a new wall closer to the summit (2:14).
3:19 The **Angle** may refer to a prominent place where the wall changed direction. However, the term appears again (vv. 24–25) in what would seem to be another location. Possibly the "Angle" was a natural feature such as a hillside or escarpment.
3:26–27 Ophel is used here to describe the area where the palace and the temple were situated. The **Water Gate** presumably provided access to the spring of Gihon. It was by the "Water Gate" that Nehemiah later gathered the people for a public reading of the Torah (8:1).
3:28 The prophet Jeremiah's reference to the **Horse Gate** (Jr 31:40) might suggest it was a gate on the eastern wall of the city, but the "Horse Gate" mentioned in 2Ch 23:15 was the gate at the entrance to the palace/temple complex within the city.

3:29 The **East Gate** was not in the outer city wall but led into the temple complex (Ezk 40:6). **Shemaiah** repaired the section of the wall near where he served.
3:31 The **Inspection Gate** (or the "Muster Gate" or the "Parade Gate") was probably on the northeast corner of the city wall. It may be identical to the Benjamin Gate where the prophet Jeremiah was arrested (Jr 37:13).
3:32 The **goldsmiths and merchants** "closed the loop" as they worked on repairing the walls up to where the work began at the **Sheep Gate** (v. 1) at the northeastern end of the city.
4:1–6 These verses in the Hebrew Bible are a continuation of chap. 3 (3:33–38).
4:1–3 The Nehemiah Memoir resumes again with the renewed opposition of **Sanballat**. **Mocked** is a strong word that means "to jeer, to deride." The first of his derisive rhetorical questions, **Can they restore it by themselves?** involves reading a rare (and

debated) Hebrew verb. Another possibility is to accept a minor textual change (from Hb *lahem*, "to them," to *le'lohim*, "to God") and understand the question as, "Will they leave it all to God?" The meaning of the second question is also not certain: **Will they offer sacrifices?** Perhaps the sense was that the Jews would offer enough sacrifices to God to persuade him to help them rebuild the city. The jest regarding bringing **back to life** the **burnt stones** was a recognition that the Jewish people had no time to quarry new stones but had to make do with the rubble left over from the destruction of 586 BC.
4:7–9 After **Sanballat** and his allies failed to discourage Nehemiah and the people, they virtually surrounded Jerusalem. Sanballat led the force from Samaria, north of Jerusalem, while **Tobiah** and the **Ammonites** were east of Jerusalem. The **Arabs**, probably led by Geshem (2:19), were south/southeast of Jerusalem, with the **Ashdodites**, from the

¹⁰ In Judah, it was said:^A
> The strength of the laborer fails,
> since there is so much rubble.
> We will never be able
> to rebuild the wall.

¹¹ And our enemies said, "They won't realize it^B until we're among them and can kill them and stop the work." ¹² When the Jews who lived nearby arrived, they said to us time and again,^C "Everywhere you turn, they attack^D us." ¹³ So I stationed people behind the lowest sections of the wall, at the vulnerable areas. I stationed them by families with their swords, spears, and bows. ¹⁴ After I made an inspection, I stood up and said to the nobles, the officials, and the rest of the people, "Don't be afraid of them. Remember the great and awe-inspiring Lord, and fight for your countrymen, your sons and daughters, your wives and homes."

Sword and Trowel

¹⁵ When our enemies heard that we knew their scheme and that God had frustrated it, every one of us returned to his own work on the wall. ¹⁶ From that day on, half of my men did the work while the other half held spears, shields, bows, and armor. The officers supported all the people of Judah, ¹⁷ who were rebuilding the wall. The laborers who carried the loads worked with one hand and held a weapon with the other. ¹⁸ Each of the builders had his sword strapped around his waist while he was building, and the one who sounded the ram's horn was beside me. ¹⁹ Then I said to the nobles, the officials, and the rest of the people, "The work is enormous and spread out, and we

are separated far from one another along the wall. ²⁰ Wherever you hear the sound of the ram's horn, rally to us there. Our God will fight for us!" ²¹ So we continued the work, while half of the men were holding spears from daybreak until the stars came out. ²² At that time, I also said to the people, "Let everyone and his servant spend the night inside Jerusalem, so that they can stand guard by night and work by day." ²³ And I, my brothers, my servants, and the men of the guard with me never took off our clothes. Each carried his weapon, even when washing.^E

Social Injustice

5 There was a widespread outcry from the people and their wives against their Jewish countrymen. ² Some were saying, "We, our sons, and our daughters are numerous. Let us get grain so that we can eat and live." ³ Others were saying, "We are mortgaging our fields, vineyards, and homes to get grain during the famine." ⁴ Still others were saying, "We have borrowed money to pay the king's tax on our fields and vineyards. ⁵ We and our children are just like our countrymen and their children, yet we are subjecting our sons and daughters to slavery. Some of our daughters are already enslaved, but we are powerless^F because our fields and vineyards belong to others."

⁶ I became extremely angry when I heard their outcry and these complaints. ⁷ After seriously considering the matter, I accused the nobles and officials, saying to them, "Each of you is charging his countrymen interest." So I called a large assembly against them ⁸ and said, "We have done our best to buy back our Jewish

---

^A4:10 Lit *Judah said*   ^B4:11 Lit *won't know or see*   ^C4:12 Lit *us 10 times*   ^D4:12 Or *again from every place, "You must return to*   ^E4:23 Lit *Each his weapon the water*   ^F5:5 Lit *but there is not the power in our hand*

---

former region of Philistia, southwest of Jerusalem. The response of those in Jerusalem reflected their trust in God as well as their understanding that faith did not preclude action but demanded it (v. 9).

4:10 Nehemiah's problems were internal as well as external. Whether the slogan in this verse was an oft-repeated jingle or a song sung by the workers, it clearly reflected the discouragement and pessimism within the city.

4:11–12 Another possible translation of the second half of v. 12 is, "they said to us repeatedly from all [their] places, 'You must return to us,'" suggesting that the Jewish people outside Jerusalem were encouraging the workers to leave before the city was attacked.

4:13–14 Nehemiah's skill as a leader is exemplified in these verses. Although enemies surrounded him and the people were discouraged, he took action.

4:15–17 As the work resumed, Nehemiah took precautions against a surprise attack. He divided the group he called **my men** (lit "my youths"), which may have been a militia that supported Nehemiah's role as governor. Half of them joined in the work while the other half were on guard duty.

4:18–22 Because the defenders were spread so thinly around the city, Nehemiah had **the one who sounded the ram's horn** beside him, so they could concentrate forces quickly in case of attack. Having everyone **spend the night inside Jerusalem** not only bolstered the defenses but also kept the discouraged or the fearful from deserting during the night.

4:23 Nehemiah and his military entourage set the example for diligence in the face of danger: [we] **never took off our clothes**.

5:1–19 Nehemiah's effort in rebuilding the walls was a crucial step in securing the safety and prosperity of Jerusalem and Judah, but the need for workers inside Jerusalem made an already bad economic situation even worse for the poor.

5:1 The first group of **people and their wives** complaining were the landless poor, who depended on their husbands' work as day laborers for their daily food.

5:2 They complained that they needed to concern themselves with food rather than with building. "You can't eat walls!"

5:3 The second group consisted of those who were forced to mortgage their property in order to survive. These loans would normally be paid back at harvest time in the fall, but

with the men working in Jerusalem during August and early September, many were facing foreclosure.

5:4 The third group that brought their complaints had **borrowed money to pay the king's tax**. During this period the interest rate for borrowing money to pay taxes was often between forty and fifty percent.

5:5 For all three groups (vv. 2–4) the result was the same: parents were selling their **children** into **slavery**. This was allowed under the OT law (Ex 21:2–11) but with some important qualifications (Lv 25:39–46). Often parents would sell their children before selling their property because the sale of property precluded the possibility of earning the money to buy the children back. The situation was even more critical for **daughters** sold into servitude because their master or his son could pressure them into marriage. Moreover, they were also more susceptible to sexual exploitation.

5:7 The translation of Nehemiah's accusation here assumes the issue was usury: **Each of you is charging his countrymen interest**. But the terms used in this context may suggest instead that the issue was acting as a creditor and seizing the properties of those in default—"pressing claims" or "seizing

countrymen who were sold to foreigners, but now you sell your own countrymen, and we have to buy them back." They remained silent and could not say a word. ⁹ Then I said, "What you are doing isn't right. Shouldn't you walk in the fear of our God and not invite the reproach of our foreign enemies? ¹⁰ Even I, as well as my brothers and my servants, have been lending them money and grain. Please, let's stop charging this interest.^ ¹¹ Return their fields, vineyards, olive groves, and houses to them immediately, along with the percentage⁸ of the money, grain, new wine, and fresh oil that you have been assessing them."

¹² They responded, "We will return these things and require nothing more from them. We will do as you say."

So I summoned the priests and made everyone take an oath to do this. ¹³ I also shook the folds of my robe and said, "May God likewise shake from his house and property everyone who doesn't keep this promise. May he be shaken out and have nothing!"

The whole assembly said, "Amen," and they praised the LORD. Then the people did as they had promised.

Good and Bad Governors

¹⁴ Furthermore, from the day King Artaxerxes appointed me to be their governor in the land of Judah — from the twentieth year until his thirty-second year, twelve years — I and my associates never ate from the food allotted to the governor. ¹⁵ The governors who preceded me had heavily burdened the people, taking from them food and wine as well as a pound^c of silver. Their subordinates also oppressed the people, but because of the fear of God, I didn't do this. ¹⁶ Instead, I devoted myself to the construction of this wall, and all my subordinates were gathered there for the work. We didn't buy any land.

¹⁷ There were 150 Jews and officials, as well as guests from the surrounding nations at my table. ¹⁸ Each^D day, one ox, six choice sheep, and some fowl were prepared for me. An abundance of all kinds of wine was provided every ten days. But I didn't demand the food allotted to the governor, because the burden on the people was so heavy.

¹⁹ Remember me favorably, my God, for all that I have done for this people.

Attempts to Discourage the Builders

6 When Sanballat, Tobiah, Geshem the Arab, and the rest of our enemies heard that I had rebuilt the wall and that no gap was left in it — though at that time I had not installed the doors in the city gates — ² Sanballat and Geshem sent me a message: "Come, let's meet together in the villages of^E the Ono Valley." They were planning to harm me.

³ So I sent messengers to them, saying, "I am doing important work and cannot come down. Why should the work cease while I leave it and go down to you?" ⁴ Four times they sent me the same proposal, and I gave them the same reply.

⁵ Sanballat sent me this same message a fifth time by his aide, who had an open letter in his hand. ⁶ In it was written:

It is reported among the nations — and Geshem^f agrees — that you and the Jews plan to rebel. This is the reason you are building the wall. According to these reports, you are to become their king ⁷ and have even set up the prophets in Jerusalem to proclaim on your behalf, "There is a king in Judah." These rumors will be heard by the king. So come, let's confer together.

⁸ Then I replied to him, "There is nothing to these rumors you are spreading; you are inventing them in your own mind." ⁹ For they

<hr>

^5:10 Or *us forgive these debts* ⁸5:11 Lit *hundred* ^c5:15 Lit *40 shekels* ᴰ5:18 Lit *And that which was prepared each* ᵉ6:2 Or *together at Kephirim in* ^f6:6 Lit *Gashmu*

<hr>

collateral." If this was the case, the actions of the **nobles and officials** were not illegal, but nevertheless unconscionable in light of the dire state of the people.
5:8 Most likely Nehemiah was not referring to buying back slaves while living in Babylonia, but recently having **to buy back** Israelites sold to neighboring nations. The nobles and officials were perpetuating the problem.
5:10 It is unlikely that Nehemiah was confessing sin about these issues.
5:12–13 The officials' agreement to Nehemiah's demands was followed by a solemn **oath**, the seriousness of which was reinforced by Nehemiah's ritual act of shaking the **folds** of his **robe** while reciting a curse on those who failed to **keep** it. The folds of the robe were used as pockets. Nehemiah was comparing his pockets to the rooms of a house and bidding God to evict the disobedient from their houses.

5:14 This is the first mention of Nehemiah's appointment as **governor** of the province. Moreover, his duration as governor is given—probably from 445 to 432 BC. Nehemiah distinguished his governance from his predecessors' in that he declined to eat "the bread of the governor," or **the food allotted to the governor**. Such a refusal was at great personal cost to him, as vv. 17–18 demonstrate.
5:15–16 Nehemiah's assertion that they **didn't buy any land** is significant. Those at the center of power often use their power to get "sweetheart deals" to enrich themselves and their friends, but Nehemiah and his men did not take advantage of their power, especially when desperate people were willing to sell their properties for food.
6:1–19 In chap. 6 the focus returns to construction of the wall and three attempts to thwart it by "intimidating" (see vv. 9,14,19) Nehemiah and the workers.

6:1–4 News that the wall was completed (but not the gates) brought on a new attempt by **Sanballat, Tobiah**, and **Geshem the Arab** to stop construction, this time by focusing on Nehemiah himself. The Ono Valley, on the far northwest corner of Judah, may have been a neutral area between Judah and Samaria. Nehemiah recognized the offer to meet as a trap.
6:5–7 After four rejected invitations, **Sanballat** increased the pressure by trying to blackmail Nehemiah. The **open letter** in the hand of his aide made clear that Sanballat's accusations against Nehemiah were for everyone to read. The letter charged Nehemiah with treason against King Artaxerxes, a charge that Sanballat knew had worked before to stop construction in Jerusalem (Ezr 4:7–16).
6:8–9 Nehemiah was not cowed by their slander. This translation of the end of v. 8, like most English translations, takes Nehemiah's words to be a brief prayer. However,

were all trying to intimidate us, saying, "They will drop their hands from^A the work, and it will never be finished."

But now, my God, strengthen my hands.

Attempts to Intimidate Nehemiah

¹⁰ I went to the house of Shemaiah son of Delaiah, son of Mehetabel, who was restricted to his house. He said:

Let's meet at the house of God,
inside the temple.
Let's shut the temple doors
because they're coming to kill you.
They're coming to kill you tonight!^B

¹¹ But I said, "Should a man like me run away? How can someone like me enter the temple and live? I will not go." ¹² I realized that God had not sent him, because of the prophecy he spoke against me. Tobiah and Sanballat had hired him. ¹³ He was hired, so that I would be intimidated, do as he suggested, sin, and get a bad reputation, in order that they could discredit me.

¹⁴ My God, remember Tobiah and Sanballat for what they have done, and also the prophetess Noadiah and the other prophets who wanted to intimidate me.

The Wall Completed

¹⁵ The wall was completed in fifty-two days, on the twenty-fifth day of the month Elul. ¹⁶ When all our enemies heard this, all the surrounding nations were intimidated and lost their confidence,^C for they realized that this task had been accomplished by our God.

¹⁷ During those days, the nobles of Judah sent many letters to Tobiah, and Tobiah's letters came to them. ¹⁸ For many in Judah were bound by oath to him, since he was a son-in-law of Shecaniah son of Arah, and his son Jehohanan had married the daughter of Meshullam son of Berechiah. ¹⁹ These nobles kept mentioning Tobiah's good deeds to me, and they reported my words to him. And Tobiah sent letters to intimidate me.

The Exiles Return

7 When the wall had been rebuilt and I had the doors installed, the gatekeepers, singers, and Levites were appointed. ² Then I put my brother Hanani in charge of Jerusalem, along with Hananiah, commander of the fortress, because he was a faithful man who feared God more than most. ³ I said to them, "Do not open the gates of Jerusalem until the sun is hot, and let the doors be shut and securely fastened while the guards are on duty. Station the citizens of Jerusalem as guards, some at their posts and some at their homes."

⁴ The city was large and spacious, but there were few people in it, and no houses had been built yet. ⁵ Then my God put it into my mind to assemble the nobles, the officials, and the people to be registered by genealogy. I found the genealogical record of those who came back first, and I found the following written in it:

⁶ These are the people of the province who went up among the captive exiles deported by King Nebuchadnezzar of Babylon. Each of them returned to Jerusalem and Judah, to his own town. ⁷ They came with Zerubbabel, Jeshua, Nehemiah, Azariah, Raamiah, Nahamani, Mordecai, Bilshan, Mispereth, Bigvai, Nehum, and Baanah.

The number of the Israelite men included^D

⁸	Parosh's descendants	2,172
⁹	Shephatiah's descendants	372
¹⁰	Arah's descendants	652
¹¹	Pahath-moab's descendants:	
	Jeshua's and Joab's descendants	2,818
¹²	Elam's descendants	1,254
¹³	Zattu's descendants	845
¹⁴	Zaccai's descendants	760
¹⁵	Binnui's descendants	648
¹⁶	Bebai's descendants	628
¹⁷	Azgad's descendants	2,322
¹⁸	Adonikam's descendants	667
¹⁹	Bigvai's descendants	2,067
²⁰	Adin's descendants	655
²¹	Ater's descendants: of Hezekiah	98

^A 6:9 Or *will give up on* ^B 6:10 Or *by night* ^C 6:16 Lit *and fell greatly in their eyes* ^D 7:7 Lit *the men of the people of Israel*

the phrase **my God** does not actually appear here as it does in the other brief prayers of Nehemiah (v. 14; 5:19; 13:14,22). Also, none of the early ancient versions (Gk, Lat, Syr) understood the closing phrase to be a prayer. With this in mind, a possible translation would be, "So now I increased my efforts."
6:10 Shemaiah ("Yahweh Has Heard") is a common OT name shared by more than twenty different people. Why Shemaiah was **restricted** or restrained is not clear. Shemaiah tried a religious approach to trap Nehemiah, urging him to flee to the temple to save himself from assassination.
6:11–13 Nehemiah saw through this religious ruse intended to intimidate and **discredit** him. Moreover, had he entered the **temple** he could have been executed since by law only the priests could enter the temple (Nm 18:7).

6:14 Nehemiah knew that behind Shemaiah's "prophecy" were **Tobiah** and **Sanballat**, who evidently had persuaded others to do their bidding. **Noadiah** is mentioned only here in the OT.
6:15–16 In spite of myriad problems, the wall was **completed in fifty-two days**. The date of the **twenty-fifth day of the month** of **Elul** probably was October 2, 445 BC.
6:17–19 Verse 17 explains why Nehemiah's enemies were so well informed of conditions within Jerusalem, because the **nobles of Judah sent many letters to Tobiah**. These "nobles" were **bound by oath** to Tobiah through marriage. Those aligned with Tobiah tried to convince Nehemiah of Tobiah's **good deeds**, yet his letters were an attempt to **intimidate** Nehemiah.
7:1–3 Though the **wall had been rebuilt**, the danger was not over. Nehemiah's transfer of the **gatekeepers** from their positions in the

temple to protection of the city is understandable. The mention of the **singers** and **Levites** suggests that Nehemiah needed these well-organized groups to take part in the city's defense. And with Tobiah's associates well entrenched in the city, he needed people he could trust such as **Hanani** and **Hananiah**.
No explanation is given on why the gates should remain closed **until the sun** was **hot**, a time when activity slowed. It may imply "midmorning" rather than early morning, in order to give plenty of time for all the guards to come on duty. Another possibility is to understand the word "until" (Hb '*ad*) as "during," a less common meaning (Jdg 3:26; 2Kg 9:22; Jb 20:5; Jnh 4:2). This reading would suggest that the instruction was *not* to keep the gates open during the "siesta" period of the day, when the guards might become lethargic.

22 Hashum's descendants 328
23 Bezai's descendants 324
24 Hariph's descendants 112
25 Gibeon's^A descendants 95
26 Bethlehem's and Netophah's men 188
27 Anathoth's men 128
28 Beth-azmaveth's men 42
29 Kiriath-jearim's, Chephirah's, and Beeroth's men 743
30 Ramah's and Geba's men 621
31 Michmas's men 122
32 Bethel's and Ai's men 123
33 the other Nebo's men 52
34 the other Elam's people 1,254
35 Harim's people 320
36 Jericho's people 345
37 Lod's, Hadid's, and Ono's people 721
38 Senaah's people 3,930.

39 The priests included
Jedaiah's descendants of the house of Jeshua 973
40 Immer's descendants 1,052
41 Pashhur's descendants 1,247
42 Harim's descendants 1,017.

43 The Levites included
Jeshua's descendants: of Kadmiel
Hodevah's descendants 74.

44 The singers included
Asaph's descendants 148.

45 The gatekeepers included
Shallum's descendants,
Ater's descendants,
Talmon's descendants,
Akkub's descendants,
Hatita's descendants,
Shobai's descendants 138.

46 The temple servants included
Ziha's descendants,
Hasupha's descendants,
Tabbaoth's descendants,
47 Keros's descendants,
Sia's descendants, Padon's descendants,
48 Lebanah's descendants,
Hagabah's descendants,
Shalmai's descendants,
49 Hanan's descendants,
Giddel's descendants,
Gahar's descendants,
50 Reaiah's descendants,
Rezin's descendants,
Nekoda's descendants,
51 Gazzam's descendants,
Uzza's descendants,
Paseah's descendants,

52 Besai's descendants,
Meunim's descendants,
Nephishesim's^B descendants,
53 Bakbuk's descendants,
Hakupha's descendants,
Harhur's descendants,
54 Bazlith's descendants,
Mehida's descendants,
Harsha's descendants,
55 Barkos's descendants,
Sisera's descendants,
Temah's descendants,
56 Neziah's descendants,
Hatipha's descendants.

57 The descendants of Solomon's servants included
Sotai's descendants,
Sophereth's descendants,
Perida's descendants,
58 Jaala's descendants,
Darkon's descendants,
Giddel's descendants,
59 Shephatiah's descendants,
Hattil's descendants,
Pochereth-hazzebaim's descendants,
Amon's descendants.

60 All the temple servants and the descendants of Solomon's servants 392

61 The following are those who came from Tel-melah, Tel-harsha, Cherub, Addon, and Immer, but were unable to prove that their ancestral families^C and their lineage were Israelite:
62 Delaiah's descendants,
Tobiah's descendants,
and Nekoda's descendants 642
63 and from the priests: the descendants of Hobaiah, the descendants of Hakkoz, and the descendants of Barzillai — who had taken a wife from the daughters of Barzillai the Gileadite and who bore their name. 64 These searched for their entries in the genealogical records, but they could not be found, so they were disqualified from the priesthood. 65 The governor ordered them not to eat the most holy things until there was a priest who could consult the Urim and Thummim.
66 The whole combined assembly numbered 42,360
67 not including their 7,337 male and female servants, as well as their 245 male and female singers.
68 They had 736 horses, 245 mules,^D
69 435 camels, and 6,720 donkeys.

^7:25 = Gibbar's in Ezr 2:20 ^B7:52 Alt Hb tradition reads *Nephushesim's* ^C7:61 Lit *the house of their fathers* ^D7:68 Some Hb mss, LXX; Ezr 2:66; other Hb mss omit v. 68

⁷⁰ Some of the family heads contributed to the project. The governor gave 1,000 gold coins,^ 50 bowls, and 530 priestly garments to the treasury. **⁷¹** Some of the family heads gave 20,000 gold coins and 2,200 silver minas to the treasury for the project. **⁷²** The rest of the people gave 20,000 gold coins, 2,000 silver minas, and 67 priestly garments. **⁷³** The priests, Levites, gatekeepers, temple singers, some of the people, temple servants, and all Israel settled in their towns.

Public Reading of the Law

When the seventh month came and the Israelites had settled in their towns, **¹** all the people gathered together at the square in front of the Water Gate. They asked the scribe Ezra to bring the book of the law of Moses that the LORD had given Israel. **²** On the first day of the seventh month, the priest Ezra brought the law before the assembly of men, women, and all who could listen with understanding. **³** While he was facing the square in front of the Water Gate, he read out of it from daybreak until noon before the men, the women, and those who could understand. All the people listened attentively^B to the book of the law. **⁴** The scribe Ezra stood on a high wooden platform made for this purpose. Mattithiah, Shema, Anaiah, Uriah, Hilkiah, and Maaseiah stood beside him on his right; to his left were Pedaiah, Mishael, Malchijah, Hashum, Hash-baddanah, Zechariah, and Meshullam. **⁵** Ezra opened the book in full view of all the people, since he was elevated above

everyone. As he opened it, all the people stood up. **⁶** Ezra blessed the LORD, the great God, and with their hands uplifted all the people said, "Amen, Amen!" Then they knelt low and worshiped the LORD with their faces to the ground.

⁷ Jeshua, Bani, Sherebiah, Jamin, Akkub, Shabbethai, Hodiah, Maaseiah, Kelita, Azariah, Jozabad, Hanan, and Pelaiah, who were Levites,^C explained the law to the people as they stood in their places. **⁸** They read out of the book of the law of God, translating and giving the meaning so that the people could understand what was read. **⁹** Nehemiah the governor, Ezra the priest and scribe, and the Levites who were instructing the people said to all of them, "This day is holy to the LORD your God. Do not mourn or weep." For all the people were weeping as they heard the words of the law. **¹⁰** Then he said to them, "Go and eat what is rich, drink what is sweet, and send portions to those who have nothing prepared, since today is holy to our Lord. Do not grieve, because the joy of the LORD is your strength."^D **¹¹** And the Levites quieted all the people, saying, "Be still, since today is holy. Don't grieve." **¹²** Then all the people began to eat and drink, send portions, and have a great celebration, because they had understood the words that were explained to them.

Festival of Shelters Observed

¹³ On the second day, the family heads of all the people, along with the priests and Levites, assembled before the scribe Ezra to study the words of the law. **¹⁴** They found written in the

---

^7:70 Or drachmas, or darics; also in vv. 71,72   ^8:3 Lit *The ears of all the people listened*   ^8:7 Vg, 1 Esdras 9:48; MT reads *Pelaiah and the Levites*   ^8:10 Or stronghold

---

7:73b–10:39 The narrative about the repopulating of Jerusalem breaks off in 7:73a and does not resume until 11:1. Thus chaps. 8–10 seem to be a parenthetical break that was actually part of the Ezra Memoir and originally stood chronologically between Ezr 8 and 9. Many scholars argue that this narrative was moved to its present position to link the ministries of Ezra and Nehemiah.

While it is likely that Ezr 8 (and probably Ezr 9) is part of the Ezra Memoir, this does not necessarily mean that the material has been displaced. While biblical writers sometimes present their material thematically and not chronologically (Ezr 4:6–24; Luke), there are no compelling reasons why Ezra could not be present for this reading of the law (Ezr 8) during the time of Nehemiah.
7:73b–8:2 Verse 73b is awkward. The final phrase (**the Israelites had settled in their towns**) is so similar to v. 73a (**all Israel settled in their towns**) that possibly a copyist mistakenly repeated the phrase. The **seventh month** (Tishri) was an important time in the Jewish calendar during which several events occurred. These events included the New Year, the Day of Atonement, and the Festival of Booths. Every seven years at the Festival of Booths the Law was to be read to the people (Dt 31:10–12). Those who are able to **listen with understanding** include children of a certain age (cp. 10:28; Ezr 10:1).

8:3 It is not stated why Ezra chose to have this assembly and reading of the law at the **Water Gate** rather than at the temple. Exactly what made up the **book of the law** has been the subject of intense discussion. Probably Ezra read the legal sections of a Pentateuch that was virtually identical to what we have today. It does not say that he read it in its entirety, but that **he read out of it**.
8:4 Little is known about the men who stood on **his right** and **his left**.
8:5 The phrase **Ezra opened the book** is a little anachronistic since the book (codex) did not appear until the Christian era. Literally the phrase is "Ezra unrolled the scroll."
8:7 Many of the thirteen **Levites** who assisted Ezra were involved in the covenant renewal described in the following chapters. Eight of the thirteen took part in the public confession (9:3–5), and nine are listed as signers of the covenant (10:9–13).
8:8 The term **translating** is one of several possibilities in understanding the Hebrew term. This verb's basic meaning is "to separate" or "to distinguish," possibly referring to reading paragraph by paragraph. Another possible rendering is to translate the verb as "to explain, make clear." The CSB translation, which understands the Levites as "translating," is supported by the ancient Jewish tradition that the Levites were reading the

Hebrew text but then providing the people with an Aramaic translation of the passage. The Jewish Talmud (b. Megillah 3a) cites this passage (Neh 8:8) as the source of the Targums, the Aramaic paraphrases of the Hebrew texts.
8:9 This verse is important because it links the ministries of **Nehemiah** and **Ezra**. Here the author clearly attests to a joint ministry of Ezra and Nehemiah, who participated together in the covenant renewal (chaps. 8–10) and took part together in the great procession and dedication of the walls of Jerusalem (12:27–43).

Nehemiah's command (or Ezra's?), **Do not mourn or weep**, seems baffling since the leaders would have been encouraged by the contrition and repentance of the people. However, this dedication of the wall occurred on the "first day of the seventh month" (v. 2) during the New Year celebration. The feast days were to be days of joy (Lv 23:24; Dt 12:12; 16:11), not mourning.
8:10–12 Rather than mourning, the people were commanded to **go and eat what is rich, drink what is sweet**. The term *rich* refers to choice foods appropriate for a celebration. The "sweet" drink mentioned here may have been wine mixed with honey, a popular drink.
8:14–15 The Festival of Shelters is mentioned in four books of **the law** (Ex 23:16;

Biblical Interpretation

by George H. Guthrie

Rightly understanding the Bible is foundational for building a Christian worldview. God gave us his Word that we might view appropriately God's world, God himself, and God's purposes for us. He wants us to think well and live well (Dt 6:4–9; Mt 7:24), but we cannot think or live what we do not understand. Thus, sound biblical interpretation is foundational for anyone who wants to live under the lordship of Christ. In 2 Timothy 2:15 we read, "Be diligent to present yourself to God as one approved, a worker who doesn't need to be ashamed, correctly teaching the word of truth." This means that sound interpretation is laudable, that misinterpretation is possible, and that interpreters are held accountable.

Biblical Interpretation: A "Conversation"

Think of biblical interpretation as playing part in a conversation, for in the Bible God communicates with us through human language. John Calvin said that God has talked "baby talk" to us, getting on our level to communicate in a medium we could understand and to which we might respond. When someone speaks to us, we want to listen, understand, and respond to what that person is saying. This integrated paradigm fits well how Scripture speaks about our interaction with God's Word.

"Understanding" stands at the heart of biblical interpretation, but we are not simply after intellectual knowledge. Rather, biblical interpretation should be approached relationally, under the guidance of the Holy Spirit as we cultivate a posture of listening to God, grasping what he wants us to know, and living out his will. In Ezra's day, when the law of God was read before the people, they "listened attentively to the book of the law" (Neh 8:3), the Levites "explained the law to the people . . . translating and giving the meaning so that the people could understand what was read" (8:7–8), and the people responded to the words of the law with mourning and celebration (8:9–12).

We must listen well, for we cannot understand or live what we do not hear. So biblical interpretation begins with a close reading of the text, and it helps to read a text multiple times, perhaps in various translations, to hear or see the contours, the nuances of the particulars in a passage. This means we need to slow down and read carefully. We should also pray, "Open my eyes so that I may contemplate wondrous things from your instruction" (Ps 119:18).

Understanding Words in Context

Once we have begun to hear or see the various aspects of the text, we need sound practices to understand the significance of what we are encountering, and this means we will be working with words. Since God has given us his Word in words, our interpretation will be governed in part by the way words work.

Words are flexible. As we study biblical words (or the words of any language), we find that most words have a range of possible meanings or things they represent. This is called a "semantic range." Thus, an important aspect of biblical interpretation involves getting at the various possible meanings of a word. In English, for instance, the word "hand" has a broad semantic range: the word could refer to "help," "applause," a worker on a ranch, the minute hand on a clock, and about a dozen other actions or items. In Greek, *charis* has a number of different meanings, including "grace," "thanks," "gift," "attractiveness," "charm," or "favor." So interpretation involves seeking to understand, among the various possible meanings of a word at a particular time and place, how an author intended a word to be understood. At Ephesians 2:8 for instance, *charis* should be translated in terms of God's "grace" or "gracious care": "For you are saved by grace through faith, and this is not from yourselves; it is God's gift."

We seek to grasp the appropriate meaning of a word based on how the author uses the word in context. Context refers to circumstances that form the setting for a passage of Scripture by which that passage can be rightly understood. At least four types of context affect our understanding of a text.

1. Historical Context

Historical context refers to events recorded in Scripture or events that form the backdrop for the biblical story. For instance, at 2 Samuel 6 King David, along with thirty thousand warriors, moved the ark of the covenant to Jerusalem. The ark has been placed on a cart; the cart hit a pothole; the ark began to tip over; Uzzah reached out to steady it; and Uzzah was then struck dead by God. Read apart from historical context, this passage may lead someone to understand God as capricious for zapping a person who was just trying to help! Yet one cannot interpret well the death of Uzzah apart from the giving of the law in broader Jewish history. In Numbers 4 we read that God had given specific instructions for the transport of the ark (and other artifacts of the tabernacle), specifically instructing the priests that anyone who touched the ark would die. In short, Uzzah died because David did not carry out the law's clear instructions.

2. Cultural Context

Cultural context has to do with attitudes, patterns of behavior, or expressions of a particular society that affect right understanding of a passage. In Acts 4:1–2 the priests and Sadducees confronted Peter and John because "they were teaching the people and proclaiming in Jesus the resurrection of the dead." Why was that a problem? From the broader culture of the time, we understand that the priests—most of whom were Sadducees—did not believe in resurrection. So, teaching about the resurrection contradicted their teaching and authority. No wonder they were upset.

3. Literary Context

Literary context involves how a word or passage fits and functions in a book or a group of books or in the Bible as a whole. No word works well in isolation. For instance, at the most immediate level of literary context, biblical interpretation involves dynamics of grammar and syntax. At 2 Corinthians 3:3 Paul speaks of the Corinthian church figuratively, saying that they are a letter of recommendation before a watching world: "Christ's letter." The Greek text could be interpreted in various ways. Is Paul saying that the Corinthians are a letter "about Christ" or that they are a letter "of Christ," that is, with Christ as the source or originator of the letter? Based on the immediate context, the latter is probably correct since the broader passage focuses on the "production" of this letter. Good commentaries can help us understand grammar and broader issues of context.

4. Theological Context

Theological context refers to how a word or passage fits in the tapestry of theological themes in the story of the Bible as a whole. For example, when Paul says that Jesus is "our Passover lamb" in 1Corinthians 5:7, we have to read his statement in light of the inauguration of the Passover celebration in Exodus 12, as well as Jesus's death at Passover during the final days of his ministry on earth (Jn 13:1).

The Goal of Interpretation

Biblical interpretation does not end with listening and understanding, for the goal of biblical interpretation has always been responding to Scripture. We are not seeking to master the text but to be mastered by it. As we live faithfully in biblical community, we are part of that extended interpretive community founded by Jesus. He taught us to interpret and live the Scriptures in light of himself, his ministry, his death, and his resurrection (e.g., Lk 24:25–27). We must read the Scriptures under the lordship of Christ, seeking to live out his purposes for us in the world.

law how the LORD had commanded through Moses that the Israelites should dwell in shelters during the festival of the seventh month. ¹⁵ So they proclaimed and spread this news throughout their towns and in Jerusalem, saying, "Go out to the hill country and bring back branches of olive, wild olive, myrtle, palm, and other leafy trees to make shelters, just as it is written." ¹⁶ The people went out, brought back branches, and made shelters for themselves on each of their rooftops and courtyards, the court of the house of God, the square by the Water Gate, and the square by the Ephraim Gate. ¹⁷ The whole community that had returned from exile made shelters and lived in them. The Israelites had not celebrated like this from the days of Joshua son of Nun until that day. And there was tremendous joy. ¹⁸ Ezra^A read out of the book of the law of God every day, from the first day to the last. The Israelites celebrated the festival for seven days, and on the eighth day there was a solemn assembly, according to the ordinance.

National Confession of Sin

9 On the twenty-fourth day of this month the Israelites assembled; they were fasting, wearing sackcloth, and had put dust on their heads. ² Those of Israelite descent separated themselves from all foreigners, and they stood and confessed their sins and the iniquities of their ancestors. ³ While they stood in their places, they read from the book of the law of the LORD their God for a fourth of the day and spent another fourth of the day in confession and worship of the LORD their God. ⁴ Jeshua, Bani, Kadmiel, Shebaniah, Bunni, Sherebiah, Bani, and Chenani stood on the raised platform built for the Levites and cried out loudly to the LORD their God. ⁵ Then the Levites — Jeshua, Kadmiel, Bani,

Hashabneiah, Sherebiah, Hodiah, Shebaniah, and Pethahiah — said, "Stand up. Blessed be the LORD your God from everlasting to everlasting."

Blessed be your glorious name,
and may it be exalted above all blessing
and praise.
⁶ You,^B LORD, are the only God.^C
You created the heavens,
the highest heavens with all their stars,
the earth and all that is on it,
the seas and all that is in them.
You give life to all of them,
and all the stars of heaven worship you.
⁷ You, the LORD,
are the God who chose Abram
and brought him out of Ur
of the Chaldeans,
and changed his name to Abraham.
⁸ You found his heart faithful
in your sight,
and made a covenant with him
to give the land of the Canaanites,
Hethites, Amorites, Perizzites,
Jebusites, and Girgashites —
to give it to his descendants.
You have fulfilled your promise,
for you are righteous.

⁹ You saw the oppression
of our ancestors in Egypt
and heard their cry at the Red Sea.
¹⁰ You performed signs and wonders
against Pharaoh,
all his officials, and all the people
of his land,
for you knew how arrogantly
they treated our ancestors.
You made a name for yourself
that endures to this day.
¹¹ You divided the sea before them,

---

^A 8:18 Some Hb mss, Syr read *They*   ^B 9:6 LXX reads *And Ezra said: You*   ^C 9:6 Lit *are alone*

Lv 23:39–43; Nm 29:12–38; Dt 16:13–15). Also called the Festival of Ingathering, it was an eight-day agricultural festival that began on the fifteenth day of the seventh month, during the grain and grape harvest (Dt 16:13).

Since the celebration of the Festival of Shelters required preparation, the leaders studying the law with Ezra **spread this news throughout their towns and in Jerusalem**. No passage in the OT expressly states the requirement to gather **branches** from **olive** and **myrtle** trees for the construction of **shelters**. This seems to be an explanation and application of the command of Lv 23:40 to gather from "majestic trees—palm fronds, boughs of leafy trees, and willows of the brook."

8:16 Those living in Jerusalem erected their **shelters** (Hb *sukkoth*) **on . . . their rooftops** because most homes had flat roofs. Those who came from outside Jerusalem used whatever space was available, such as **the square by the Water Gate**, where they had read the law two weeks before,

or in **the square by the Ephraim Gate**. The Ephraim Gate is not mentioned in the detailed description of the wall in chap. 3. However, its description in 2Kg 14:13 suggests it was on the north side of the wall. Thus, both locations provided easy access to the temple complex.

8:17 The celebration of the Festival of Shelters was even more significant because the people **had not celebrated like this from the days of Joshua son of Nun until that day**. The phrase *had not celebrated like this* describes the *manner* in which the festival was celebrated. The author of Ezra-Nehemiah described well the experience of the people at the festival: **there was tremendous joy**.

9:1–37 The penitential prayer of chap. 9 is a beautiful confession of God's faithfulness and mercy to his people as well as a confession by the people of their nation's persistent rebellion against God. With the completion of the Festival of Shelters on the twenty-second day of the month, it was now

permissible and appropriate to repent and confess on the twenty-fourth day of the month.

9:1 In the OT era there was a close connection between repentance and mourning.

9:3 Presumably **they** who **stood in their places** were the Israelites who separated themselves from foreigners (v. 2), while **they** who **read from the book of the law** were those mentioned in the following verse (v. 4)—the Levites.

9:4 What they **cried out loudly** was apparently the words of the confession in vv. 5–37.

9:6 The prayer begins with an acknowledgment of the Lord's incomparability. Only the Lord is the true God of creation who gives **life to all** and receives the worship of heavenly beings.

9:7–8 Like **Abram**, many of those taking part in the penitential service had been brought **out of Ur of the Chaldeans** (Babylon).

9:9–11 The description of the exodus from Egypt is recounted with quotes and allusions from Ex 3; 10; 14.

and they crossed through it
　　on dry ground.
You hurled their pursuers
　　into the depths
like a stone into raging water.
¹² You led them with a pillar of cloud
　　　by day,
and with a pillar of fire by night,
to illuminate the way
　　they should go.
¹³ You came down on Mount Sinai,
and spoke to them from heaven.
You gave them impartial ordinances,
　　reliable instructions,
and good statutes and commands.
¹⁴ You revealed your holy Sabbath
　　to them,
and gave them commands, statutes,
　　and instruction
through your servant Moses.
¹⁵ You provided bread from heaven
　　for their hunger;
you brought them water from the rock
　　for their thirst.
You told them to go in and possess
　　the land
you had sworn^A to give them.

¹⁶ But our ancestors acted arrogantly;
they became stiff-necked and did not
　　listen to your commands.
¹⁷ They refused to listen
and did not remember your wonders
you performed among them.
They became stiff-necked
　　and appointed a leader
to return to their slavery in Egypt.^B
But you are a forgiving God,
gracious and compassionate,
slow to anger and abounding
　　in faithful love,
and you did not abandon them.
¹⁸ Even after they had cast an image
　　of a calf
for themselves and said,
"This is your god who brought you
　　out of Egypt,"
and they had committed
　　terrible blasphemies,

¹⁹ you did not abandon them
　　in the wilderness
because of your great compassion.
During the day the pillar of cloud
never turned away from them,
guiding them on their journey.
And during the night the pillar of fire
illuminated the way they should go.
²⁰ You sent your good Spirit
　　to instruct them.
You did not withhold your manna
　　from their mouths,
and you gave them water
　　for their thirst.
²¹ You provided for them in the wilderness
　　forty years,
and they lacked nothing.
Their clothes did not wear out,
and their feet did not swell.

²² You gave them kingdoms and peoples
and established boundaries for them.
They took possession
of the land of King Sihon^C of Heshbon
and of the land of King Og of Bashan.
²³ You multiplied their descendants
like the stars of the sky
and brought them to the land
you told their ancestors to go in
　　and possess.
²⁴ So their descendants went in
　　and possessed the land:
You subdued the Canaanites
　　who inhabited the land
　　before them
and handed their kings
　　and the surrounding peoples over to
　　them,
to do as they pleased with them.
²⁵ They captured fortified cities
　　and fertile land
and took possession of
　　well-supplied houses,
cisterns cut out of rock, vineyards,
olive groves, and fruit trees
　　in abundance.
They ate, were filled,
became prosperous, and delighted
　　in your great goodness.

---

^A9:15 Lit *lifted your hand*　^B9:17 Some Hb mss, LXX; other Hb mss read *in their rebellion*　^C9:22 One Hb ms, LXX; other Hb mss, Vg read *of Sihon, even the land of the king*

9:12–15 The description of the wilderness period (vv. 12–21) begins with a recital of God's care and provisions for his people. Specific mention is made of the law about the **holy Sabbath**, which during the exilic and postexilic era became one of the primary markers of Jewish identity (13:15–22). In v. 10 it was the Egyptians who **arrogantly** mistreated Israel, but now the same verb is used to describe the arrogance of Israel's **ancestors** against God and his commands, in spite of his care and provision. Their rebellion against God (v. 17) was both

deliberate (**they refused to listen**) and non-sensical in their appointment of **a leader** to take them back to their **slavery in Egypt**. **9:18–21** God's mercy was put to the test in the making of the golden **calf** (see Ex 32). Yet even this serious offense was met with mercy. God's presence remained with them in **the pillar of cloud** and **the pillar of fire**, and his provision continued during their entire **forty years** in **the wilderness**. God even sent his **good Spirit to instruct** his people, probably a reference to the seventy elders chosen by Moses (Nm 11:16–17,23–30)

who received some of the Spirit Moses had (Nm 11:25). **9:22–25** The final historical period, the giving of the land (vv. 22–31), is introduced with a synopsis primarily derived from Moses's review of the event in Deuteronomy. The defeats of **Sihon** and **Og** (see Nm 21; Dt 2–3) were crucial victories that secured Transjordan for Israel (Pss 135:11; 136:19–20). All that God had promised he faithfully brought about for his people, who **delighted** in his **great goodness**.

²⁶ But they were disobedient and rebelled
   against you.
They flung your law behind their backs
   and killed your prophets
   who warned them
in order to turn them back to you.
They committed terrible blasphemies.
²⁷ So you handed them over
   to their enemies,
   who oppressed them.
In their time of distress, they cried out
   to you,
and you heard from heaven.
In your abundant compassion
you gave them deliverers,
   who rescued them
   from the power of their enemies.
²⁸ But as soon as they had relief,
they again did what was evil
   in your sight.
So you abandoned them to the power
   of their enemies,
who dominated them.
When they cried out to you again,
you heard from heaven and rescued
   them
many times in your compassion.
²⁹ You warned them to turn back
   to your law,
but they acted arrogantly
and would not obey your commands.
They sinned against your ordinances,
which a person will live by
   if he does them.
They stubbornly resisted,ᴬ
stiffened their necks, and would not
   obey.
³⁰ You were patient with them
   for many years,
and your Spirit warned them
   through your prophets,
but they would not listen.
Therefore, you handed them over
   to the surrounding peoples.
³¹ However, in your abundant compassion,
you did not destroy them or abandon
   them,
for you are a gracious
   and compassionate God.

³² So now, our God — the great, mighty,
   and awe-inspiring God who keeps
   his gracious covenant —
do not view lightly all the hardships
   that have afflicted us,
our kings and leaders,
our priests and prophets,
our ancestors and all your people,
from the days of the Assyrian kings
   until today.
³³ You are righteous concerning all
   that has happened to us,
because you have acted faithfully,
while we have acted wickedly.
³⁴ Our kings, leaders, priests,
   and ancestors
did not obey your law
or listen to your commands
and warnings you gave them.
³⁵ When they were in their kingdom,
with your abundant goodness that
   you gave them,
and in the spacious and fertile land
   you set before them,
they would not serve you or turn
   from their wicked ways.
³⁶ Here we are today,
slaves in the land you gave
   our ancestors
so that they could enjoy its fruit
   and its goodness.
Here we are — slaves in it!
³⁷ Its abundant harvest goes to the kings
you have set over us,
because of our sins.
They rule over our bodies
and our livestock as they please.
We are in great distress.

Israel's Vow of Faithfulness

³⁸ In view of all this, we are making a binding
agreement in writing on a sealed document
containing the names of our leaders, Levites,
and priests.

10 Those whose seals were on the document were
      the governor Nehemiah
         son of Hacaliah, and Zedekiah,

ᴬ9:29 Lit *They gave a stubborn shoulder*

9:26–31 Just as God's faithfulness to his people in the wilderness (vv. 12–15) was rewarded with their rebellion (vv. 16–17), so God's faithfulness in the gift of the land was met with unbelief and unfaithfulness. Verses 27–30 recount the cycle of sin played out repeatedly in the book of Judges. Despite their persistent and repeated failure, God **did not destroy them or abandon them**. **9:32–37** After the long review of Israel's broken promises and rebellion against God, the prayer finally turns from confession to a petition addressed to **our God**, the God who (unlike Israel) **keeps his gracious covenant**.

The only request in this long prayer is that God would take note of their **hardships**. The term *hardships* occurs only rarely in the OT, but it is used to refer to times of great distress or trials, such as the exodus (Ex 18:8) or Jerusalem after its destruction at the hands of the Babylonians (Lm 3:5).

Yet the prayer makes clear (vv. 33–34) that the blame for all their hardships was their own and not God's. God was just. Both the Levites leading the prayer and all who joined in with them confessed their solidarity in sin, because they had **acted wickedly**. The tragic irony was that the land was God's great gift to them—if

they would only keep the covenant. Instead they would lament, **Here we are—slaves in it!** While God's people hoped for his intervention, they ended their prayer by acknowledging the sad reality: **We are in great distress**. **9:38–10:39** In the Hebrew Bible, 9:38 is the first verse of chap. 10, since its subject matter clearly relates to the covenant renewal ceremony that follows. The opening phrase, **In view of all this**, links the covenant renewal with the penitential prayer of chap. 9. **9:38** After their corporate confession of sin, the leaders made **a binding agreement in writing**.

2 Seraiah, Azariah, Jeremiah,
3 Pashhur, Amariah, Malchijah,
4 Hattush, Shebaniah, Malluch,
5 Harim, Meremoth, Obadiah,
6 Daniel, Ginnethon, Baruch,
7 Meshullam, Abijah, Mijamin,
8 Maaziah, Bilgai, and Shemaiah.
These were the priests.

9 The Levites were
Jeshua son of Azaniah,
Binnui of the sons of Henadad, Kadmiel,
10 and their brothers
Shebaniah, Hodiah, Kelita, Pelaiah, Hanan,
11 Mica, Rehob, Hashabiah,
12 Zaccur, Sherebiah, Shebaniah,
13 Hodiah, Bani, and Beninu.

14 The heads of the people were
Parosh, Pahath-moab, Elam, Zattu, Bani,
15 Bunni, Azgad, Bebai,
16 Adonijah, Bigvai, Adin,
17 Ater, Hezekiah, Azzur,
18 Hodiah, Hashum, Bezai,
19 Hariph, Anathoth, Nebai,
20 Magpiash, Meshullam, Hezir,
21 Meshezabel, Zadok, Jaddua,
22 Pelatiah, Hanan, Anaiah,
23 Hoshea, Hananiah, Hasshub,
24 Hallohesh, Pilha, Shobek,
25 Rehum, Hashabnah, Maaseiah,
26 Ahijah, Hanan, Anan,
27 Malluch, Harim, Baanah.

28 The rest of the people — the priests, Levites, gatekeepers, singers, and temple servants, along with their wives, sons, and daughters, everyone who is able to understand and who has separated themselves from the surrounding peoples to obey the law of God — 29 join with

their noble brothers and commit themselves with a sworn oath^A to follow the law of God given through God's servant Moses and to obey carefully all the commands, ordinances, and statutes of the LORD our Lord.

Details of the Vow

30 We will not give our daughters in marriage to the surrounding peoples and will not take their daughters as wives for our sons.

31 When the surrounding peoples bring merchandise or any kind of grain to sell on the Sabbath day, we will not buy from them on the Sabbath or a holy day. We will also leave the land uncultivated in the seventh year and will cancel every debt.

32 We will impose the following commands on ourselves:

To give an eighth of an ounce of silver^B yearly for the service of the house of our God: 33 the bread displayed before the LORD,^C the daily grain offering, the regular burnt offering, the Sabbath and New Moon offerings, the appointed festivals, the holy things, the sin offerings to atone for Israel, and for all the work of the house of our God.

34 We have cast lots among the priests, Levites, and people for the donation of wood by our ancestral families^D at the appointed times each year. They are to bring the wood to our God's house to burn on the altar of the LORD our God, as it is written in the law.

35 We will bring the firstfruits of our land and of every fruit tree to the LORD's house

---

^A10:29 Lit *and enter in a curse and in an oath*   ^B10:32 Lit *give one-third of a shekel*   ^C10:33 Lit *rows of bread*   ^D10:34 Lit *the house of our fathers*

10:2–8 This list is similar to the listing of the priests who "went up with Zerubbabel" (12:1), although it contains some alternative spellings and minor textual corruption. None of the priests alive in Zerubbabel's time would have been present here, suggesting again that these are not the names of living people but the names of the founders of priestly divisions.
10:9–13 The names of **Levites** probably includes both family names (Jeshua, Binnui, and Kadmiel, 12:8; Ezr 3:9) and personal names (Neh 8:7; 9:4).
10:14–27 The list of the **heads of the people** likewise appears to list both family names and individual signers. The first half (vv. 14–19) generally matches the names of the returnees in the list of Ezr 2 and Neh 7; the second half mentions people assigned to rebuild specific sections of the wall in Neh 3.
10:28–29 Once the document was completed, **the rest of the people** had the opportunity to participate in the great event. This **sworn oath** first dealt broadly with obedience to God demonstrated in obedience

to **the law of God given through God's servant Moses**. The particular areas of compliance to the law are then specified in vv. 30–39.
10:30–39 These commands and prohibitions, prescribed in six crucial areas, are not just quotations from throughout the Pentateuch but are an integration and application of the law to the present conditions. What is clear is the presupposition of the absolute authority of law as God's revelation and the presupposition of its applicability to every generation.
10:30 In Ezra's earlier ministry (Ezr 9) the focus was on foreign wives. In this passage the issue is broadened to intermarriage with foreigners in general.
10:31a The law forbade any type of work on the **Sabbath**, but in Nehemiah's time, living in a multicultural situation, the question about buying from non-Israelites on the Sabbath came up. Here the prohibition is extended to the new cultural situation.
10:31b The pledge here is unique in that it brings together two ordinances not originally

combined. The law commanding the **land** to remain fallow on the **seventh year** (Ex 23:10–11) is linked with the remission of all debts on the seventh year (Dt 15:1–6).
10:32–33 In Ex 30:11–16 Moses was commanded to collect a half shekel from every male twenty years old or older. It is not clear why in this passage the temple tax was only a third of a shekel rather than the normal half shekel. Since there was not uniformity between monetary systems, it may be that the shekel in Nehemiah's time was more valuable than in earlier times.
10:34 The OT law commanded that "fire must be kept burning on the altar continually; it must not go out" (Lv 6:13). This required a lot of wood in a country not known for its forests. Thus the priests, Levites, and lay people shared the responsibility for providing wood.
10:35–39 The sixth and final obligation to which the Jews pledged themselves was to give the first and the best to God. This included the **firstfruits** of **every fruit tree**, a specification not found in OT law but a

year by year. ³⁶ We will also bring the first-born of our sons and our livestock, as prescribed by the law, and will bring the firstborn of our herds and flocks to the house of our God, to the priests who serve in our God's house. ³⁷ We will bring a loaf from our first batch of dough to the priests at the storerooms of the house of our God. We will also bring the firstfruits of our grain offerings, of every fruit tree, and of the new wine and fresh oil. A tenth of our land's produce belongs to the Levites, for the Levites are to collect the one-tenth offering in all our agricultural towns. ³⁸ A priest from Aaron's descendants is to accompany the Levites when they collect the tenth, and the Levites are to take a tenth of this offering to the storerooms of the treasury in the house of our God. ³⁹ For the Israelites and the Levites are to bring the contributions of grain, new wine, and fresh oil to the storerooms where the articles of the sanctuary are kept and where the priests who minister are, along with the gatekeepers and singers. We will not neglect the house of our God.

Resettling Jerusalem

11 Now the leaders of the people stayed in Jerusalem, and the rest of the people cast lots for one out of ten to come and live in Jerusalem, the holy city, while the other nine-tenths remained in their towns. ² The people blessed all the men who volunteered to live in Jerusalem.

³ These are the heads of the province who stayed in Jerusalem (but in the villages of Judah each lived on his own property in their towns — the Israelites, priests, Levites, temple servants, and descendants of Solomon's servants — ⁴ while some of the descendants of Judah and Benjamin settled in Jerusalem):

Judah's descendants:

Athaiah son of Uzziah, son of Zechariah, son of Amariah, son of Shephatiah, son of

Mahalalel, of Perez's descendants; ⁵ and Maaseiah son of Baruch, son of Col-hozeh, son of Hazaiah, son of Adaiah, son of Joiarib, son of Zechariah, a descendant of the Shilonite. ⁶ The total number of Perez's descendants, who settled in Jerusalem, was 468 capable men.

⁷ These were Benjamin's descendants:

Sallu son of Meshullam, son of Joed, son of Pedaiah, son of Kolaiah, son of Maaseiah, son of Ithiel, son of Jeshaiah, ⁸ and after him Gabbai and Sallai: 928. ⁹ Joel son of Zichri was the officer over them, and Judah son of Hassenuah was second in command over the city.

¹⁰ The priests:

Jedaiah son of Joiarib, Jachin, and ¹¹ Seraiah son of Hilkiah, son of Meshullam, son of Zadok, son of Meraioth, son of Ahitub, the chief official of God's temple, ¹² and their relatives who did the work at the temple: 822. Adaiah son of Jeroham, son of Pelaliah, son of Amzi, son of Zechariah, son of Pashhur, son of Malchijah ¹³ and his relatives, the heads of families: 242. Amashsai son of Azarel, son of Ahzai, son of Meshillemoth, son of Immer, ¹⁴ and their relatives, capable men: 128. Zabdiel son of Haggedolim, was their chief.

¹⁵ The Levites:

Shemaiah son of Hasshub, son of Azrikam, son of Hashabiah, son of Bunni; ¹⁶ and Shabbethai and Jozabad, from the heads of the Levites, who supervised the work outside the house of God; ¹⁷ Mattaniah son of Mica, son of Zabdi, son of Asaph, the oneᴬ who began the thanksgiving in prayer; Bakbukiah, second among his relatives; and Abda son of Shammua, son of Galal, son of Jeduthun. ¹⁸ All the Levites in the holy city: 284.

^11:17 Lit the head

logical extension of the idea of giving the "firstfruits of [the] land" (Ex 23:19). Just as they brought the firstfruits of the land, so they brought the **firstborn** of their **sons** and **livestock**. Their sons (and the unclean livestock) would be redeemed (Ex 13:13; Lv 27:27) by a monetary payment (or the substitution of a clean animal for an unclean one), while the firstborn of a clean animal was offered **to the priests**. A tenth of the agricultural **produce** was given to the **Levites**, who in turn gave a tenth of the tenth to the temple. To ensure the proper allocation of these gifts and tenths, **a priest from Aaron's descendants** was required to **accompany the Levites** when they accepted these donations (v. 38), a stipulation not found elsewhere in the OT.

11:1–2 Here the author returns to the Nehemiah Memoir and the narrative about the repopulation of Jerusalem first introduced in 7:4–5. Jerusalem was underpopulated and consisted largely of the **leaders of the people**. The solution to the problem was to have a tenth of the population come to **live in Jerusalem**, chosen by the casting of **lots**, a practice common in the OT and even into NT times (Ac 1:26). While this was a burden for those selected, this would not have been the selection of individuals but of families. It is not clear whether the **men who volunteered** were in addition to those chosen by lot.

11:3–21 This list offers many textual challenges—a common phenomenon with names and numbers. The Septuagint (LXX) reflects a much

shorter version of vv. 12–21 than does the Hebrew text. This list is also challenging in that it is clearly related to the list in 1Ch 9:1–17. Both lists (1Ch 9; Neh 11) originated in the postexilic era (1Ch 9:2) and recorded the names of those living in Jerusalem. Both have the same order of presentation: Israelites, priests, Levites, temple servants. Both list many of the same individuals, albeit with slightly different spellings of their names. Yet they differ greatly with each including material not found in the other, and the 1Ch 9 list is longer. A comparison of this list (Neh 11) with 1Ch 9, along with the census lists of Ezr 2 and Neh 7, suggests that this list must be selective and representative. Its purpose was to demonstrate that a representative cross section of the nation was now living in the holy city.

¹⁹ The gatekeepers:

Akkub, Talmon, and their relatives, who guarded the city gates: 172.

²⁰ The rest of Israel, the priests, and the Levites were in all the villages of Judah, each on his own inherited property. ²¹ The temple servants lived on Ophel; Ziha and Gishpa supervised the temple servants.

The Levites and Priests

²² The leader of the Levites in Jerusalem was Uzzi son of Bani, son of Hashabiah, son of Mattaniah, son of Mica, of the descendants of Asaph, who were singers for the service of God's house. ²³ There was, in fact, a command of the king regarding them, and an ordinance regulating the singers' daily tasks. ²⁴ Pethahiah son of Meshezabel, of the descendants of Zerah son of Judah, was the king's agent^A in every matter concerning the people. ²⁵ As for the farming settlements with their fields:

Some of Judah's descendants lived
   in Kiriath-arba
   and Dibon and their surrounding
   villages, and Jekabzeel and
   its settlements;
²⁶   in Jeshua, Moladah, Beth-pelet,
²⁷   Hazar-shual, and Beer-sheba
   and its surrounding villages;
²⁸   in Ziklag and Meconah
   and its surrounding villages;
²⁹   in En-rimmon, Zorah,
   Jarmuth, and
³⁰   Zanoah and Adullam
   with their settlements;

in Lachish with its fields and Azekah
   and its surrounding villages.
So they settled from Beer-sheba
   to Hinnom Valley.

³¹   Benjamin's descendants:
   from Geba,^B Michmash, Aija,
   and Bethel and its surrounding villages,
³²   Anathoth, Nob, Ananiah,
³³   Hazor, Ramah, Gittaim,
³⁴   Hadid, Zeboim, Neballat,
³⁵   Lod, and Ono, in Craftsmen's Valley.
³⁶   Some of the Judean divisions of Levites
   were in Benjamin.

12 These are the priests and Levites who went up with Zerubbabel son of Shealtiel and with Jeshua:
   Seraiah, Jeremiah, Ezra,
²   Amariah, Malluch, Hattush,
³   Shecaniah, Rehum, Meremoth,
⁴   Iddo, Ginnethoi, Abijah,
⁵   Mijamin, Maadiah, Bilgah,
⁶   Shemaiah, Joiarib, Jedaiah,
⁷   Sallu, Amok, Hilkiah, Jedaiah.
These were the heads of the priests and their relatives in the days of Jeshua.

⁸ The Levites:
   Jeshua, Binnui, Kadmiel,
   Sherebiah, Judah, and Mattaniah —
   he and his relatives were in charge
   of the songs of praise.
⁹   Bakbukiah, Unni,^C and their relatives
   stood opposite them in the services.
¹⁰   Jeshua fathered Joiakim,
   Joiakim fathered Eliashib,
   Eliashib fathered Joiada,

^A 11:24 Lit was at the king's hand   ^B 11:31 Or descendants from Geba lived in   ^C 12:9 Alt Hb tradition reads Unno

---

Descendants of the musicians **Asaph** and **Jeduthun** are mentioned, but not of Heman (cp. 1Ch 25:1). This is probably a result of the few Levites who returned from Babylon (Ezr 2:40; 8:15–20).

11:22–24 It is likely that **Uzzi son of Bani** was a great-grandson of **Mattaniah**, who is listed first among the Levites (v. 17). The role of the Levites (v. 23) was regulated by the **command of the king**. While some regard this as a reference to the Persian king, this does not appear likely. The "command of the king" probably refers back to King David's ordering of temple worship (1Ch 23; 25), an identification supported by the reference to David and the Levites in Neh 12:45–46. **Pethahiah son of Meshezabel**, mentioned only here (v. 24) in the Bible, served as the **king's agent**, probably in Judah.

11:25–36 An enigmatic chapter concludes with a puzzling description of the regions of Judah (vv. 25–30) and Benjamin (vv. 31–36). This list of towns and villages is unusual in what it contains as well as in what it omits. Towns that were far beyond the borders of Judah are mentioned, yet towns referred to in Ezra-Nehemiah are not mentioned, including Bethlehem, Mizpah, Gibeon, and

Jericho. In general, the towns listed for Judah were south of Jerusalem, extending all the way into the Negev, while the towns listed for Benjamin were northwest of Jerusalem extending into the Shephelah. While many proposed solutions have been offered for this passage, the most likely is that the list is of those towns that were not destroyed by the Babylonians in the sixth century BC and whose inhabitants remained in the land.

12:1–26 This section of chap. 12 consists of temple personnel in supplementary lists appended to the repopulation list of chap. 11. These lists were representative of the situation a generation after Zerubbabel and Jeshua.

12:1–7 This list appears to enumerate individuals, while the second (vv. 12–21) lists the leaders of the priests. However, it seems some of the names listed in vv. 1–7 must be family names and not the names of individuals.

12:8–9 According to Ezr 2:40, there were only two Levitical families present in the return to the land under Zerubbabel (Jeshua and Kadmiel), numbering only seventy-four people. It is not clear why six families are listed here, especially since **Mattaniah** and **Bakbukiah**

are mentioned as active in Nehemiah's time (v. 25; 11:17). The latter **stood opposite** the others either to offer support or to provide antiphonal music.

12:10–11 These verses list six high priests. The identity of the first and third are clear, with **Jeshua** serving with Zerubbabel in the return to the land (Ezr 2:2) and **Eliashib** serving as high priest during Nehemiah's tenure (3:1,20). However, since there is nearly an eighty-year gap between the first and the third postexilic high priests, it is possible that the list is only representative and not complete, or there may have been times when the office was vacant.

The fourth priest, **Joiada** (also referred to by the longer form of his name, Jehoiada), is mentioned in 13:28 as the son of Eliashib the high priest, although Joiada himself did not yet bear that title. There is no other mention of **Jonathan** during this era. But v. 22 does identify an era by the listing of four priests: Eliashib, Joiada, Johanan, and Jaddua. The last named high priest, **Jaddua**, was mentioned by Josephus, who claimed that Alexander the Great met Jaddua (333 BC). However, since some of Josephus's work is considered legendary, it is probably unwise

¹¹ Joiada fathered Jonathan,
and Jonathan fathered Jaddua.ᴬ

¹² In the days of Joiakim, the heads of the priestly families were

Meraiah	of Seraiah,
Hananiah	of Jeremiah,
¹³ Meshullam	of Ezra,
Jehohanan	of Amariah,
¹⁴ Jonathan	of Malluchi,
Joseph	of Shebaniah,
¹⁵ Adna	of Harim,
Helkai	of Meraioth,
¹⁶ Zechariah	of Iddo,
Meshullam	of Ginnethon,
¹⁷ Zichri	of Abijah,
Piltai	of Moadiah, of Miniamin,
¹⁸ Shammua	of Bilgah,
Jehonathan	of Shemaiah,
¹⁹ Mattenai	of Joiarib,
Uzzi	of Jedaiah,
²⁰ Kallai	of Sallai,
Eber	of Amok,
²¹ Hashabiah	of Hilkiah,
and Nethanel	of Jedaiah.

²² In the days of Eliashib, Joiada, Johanan, and Jaddua, the heads of the families of the Levites and priests were recorded while Darius the Persian ruled. ²³ Levi's descendants, the family heads, were recorded in the Book of the Historical Events during the days of Johanan son of Eliashib. ²⁴ The heads of the Levites — Hashabiah, Sherebiah, and Jeshua son of Kadmiel, along with their relatives opposite them — gave praise and thanks, division by division, as David the man of God had prescribed. ²⁵ This included Mattaniah, Bakbukiah, and Obadiah. Meshullam, Talmon, and Akkub were gatekeepers who guarded the storerooms at the city gates. ²⁶ These served in the days of Joiakim son of Jeshua, son of Jozadak, and in the days of Nehemiah the governor and Ezra the priest and scribe.

Dedication of the Wall

²⁷ At the dedication of the wall of Jerusalem, they sent for the Levites wherever they lived and brought them to Jerusalem to celebrate the joyous dedication with thanksgiving and singing accompanied by cymbals, harps, and lyres. ²⁸ The singers gathered from the region around Jerusalem, from the settlements of the Netophathites, ²⁹ from Beth-gilgal, and from the fields of Geba and Azmaveth, for they had built settlements for themselves around Jerusalem. ³⁰ After the priests and Levites had purified themselves, they purified the people, the city gates, and the wall.

³¹ Then I brought the leaders of Judah up on top of the wall, and I appointed two large processions that gave thanks. One went to the right on the wall, toward the Dung Gate. ³² Hoshaiah and half the leaders of Judah followed, ³³ along with Azariah, Ezra, Meshullam, ³⁴ Judah, Benjamin, Shemaiah, Jeremiah, ³⁵ and some of the priests' sons with trumpets, and Zechariah son of Jonathan, son of Shemaiah, son of Mattaniah, son of Micaiah, son of Zaccur, son of Asaph followed ³⁶ as well as his relatives — Shemaiah, Azarel, Milalai, Gilalai, Maai, Nethanel, Judah, and Hanani, with the musical instruments of David, the man of God. Ezra the scribe went in front of them. ³⁷ At the Fountain Gate they climbed the steps of the city of David on the ascent of the wall and went above the house of David to the Water Gate on the east.

³⁸ The second thanksgiving procession went to the left, and I followed it with half the people along the top of the wall, past the Tower of the Ovens to the Broad Wall, ³⁹ above the Ephraim Gate, and by the Old Gate, the Fish Gate, the Tower of Hananel, and the Tower of the Hundred, to the Sheep Gate. They stopped at the Gate of the Guard. ⁴⁰ The two thanksgiving processions stood in the house of God. So did I and half of the officials accompanying me, ⁴¹ as well as the priests:

ᴬ12:10–11 These men were high priests.

to date Jaddua that late. It is also possible that there were earlier and later high priests with the same name.
12:12–21 The second list of priestly names parallels the earlier one (vv. 1–7), although there is significant variation in the spelling of many names as well as an unexpected omission—Hattush (v. 2). Many of these names appear as signers of the pledge in chap. 10. The final six names are not on the earlier list (vv. 1–7) nor on the list of signatories in chap. 10. Of interest is the mention of **Zechariah of Iddo**, probably a reference to the prophet Zechariah (Ezr 5:1; 6:14; Zch 1:1).
12:22 The identification of **Darius the Persian** is not certain, and all three Persian kings named Darius have been suggested by scholars. Likely, the Darius in this passage is a reference to Darius II Nothus (423–404 BC). **12:27–43** The grand finale of Nehemiah's ministry took place with the joyous

dedication of the rebuilt wall around Jerusalem.
12:30 With the **Levites** and singers (vv. 28–29) present, the mandatory purification procedure could begin. For the priests and Levites (probably the singers as well, assuming they were included among the Levites at this point), this involved washing their clothes and abstaining from sexual intercourse (Ex 19:14–15), bringing special sacrifices (Nm 8:8–12), and being sprinkled with water (Nm 8:7).
12:31–37 The dedicatory procession began with Nehemiah (the text now resumes with the first-person account from the Nehemiah Memoir) bringing the **leaders up on top of the wall**, where they split into two groups. One group **went to the right on the wall**. The procession must have approached the city from the west, probably mounting the wall at the Valley Gate on the west side of

the city. Here they "went to the right"—or south—toward the **Dung Gate**. Archaeological evidence suggests that the top of the wall was about nine feet wide, allowing people to walk two or three abreast. The leader of the procession was **Ezra the scribe**.
12:38–39 The second **procession** left the Valley Gate and **went to the left**, or north, in a clockwise direction, passing the **Fish Gate** (northwest corner of the city) and leaving the wall at the **Sheep Gate** at the north end of the city. From there they traveled to the **Gate of the Guard**, an uncertain location that may be identical with the courtyard of the guard (3:25) or the Inspection Gate (3:31). Presumably either location was near the temple.
12:40–43 The two **processions** met at **the house of God**, the temple. Nehemiah acknowledged **God** as the source of their **great joy**.

Eliakim, Maaseiah, Miniamin,
Micaiah, Elioenai, Zechariah,
and Hananiah, with trumpets;
⁴² and Maaseiah, Shemaiah, Eleazar,
Uzzi, Jehohanan, Malchijah, Elam,
and Ezer.

Then the singers sang, with Jezrahiah as the leader. ⁴³ On that day they offered great sacrifices and rejoiced because God had given them great joy. The women and children also celebrated, and Jerusalem's rejoicing was heard far away.

Support of the Levites' Ministry

⁴⁴ On that same day men were placed in charge of the rooms that housed the supplies, contributions, firstfruits, and tenths. The legally required portions for the priests and Levites were gathered from the village fields, because Judah was grateful to the priests and Levites who were serving. ⁴⁵ They performed the service of their God and the service of purification, along with the singers and gatekeepers, as David and his son Solomon had prescribed. ⁴⁶ For long ago, in the days of David and Asaph, there were heads^A of the singers and songs of praise and thanksgiving to God. ⁴⁷ So in the days of Zerubbabel and Nehemiah, all Israel contributed the daily portions for the singers and gatekeepers. They also set aside daily portions for the Levites, and the Levites set aside daily portions for Aaron's descendants.

Nehemiah's Further Reforms

13 At that time the book of Moses was read publicly to ^B the people. The command was found written in it that no Ammonite or Moabite should ever enter the assembly of God, ² because they did not meet the Israelites with food and water. Instead, they hired Balaam against them to curse them, but our God turned the curse into a blessing. ³ When they heard the law, they separated all those of mixed descent from Israel.

⁴ Now before this, the priest Eliashib had been put in charge of the storerooms of the house of our God. He was a relative^c of Tobiah ⁵ and had prepared a large room for him where they had previously stored the grain offerings, the frankincense, the articles, and the tenths of grain, new wine, and fresh oil prescribed for the Levites, singers, and gatekeepers, along with the contributions for the priests.

⁶ While all this was happening, I was not in Jerusalem, because I had returned to King Artaxerxes of Babylon in the thirty-second year of his reign. It was only later that I asked the king for a leave of absence ⁷ so I could return to Jerusalem. Then I discovered the evil that Eliashib had done on behalf of Tobiah by providing him a room in the courts of God's house. ⁸ I was greatly displeased and threw all of Tobiah's household possessions out of the room. ⁹ I ordered that the rooms be purified, and I had the articles of the house of God restored there, along with the grain offering and frankincense. ¹⁰ I also found out that because the portions for the Levites had not been given, each of the Levites and the singers performing the service had gone back to his own field. ¹¹ Therefore, I rebuked the officials, asking, "Why has the house of God been neglected?" I gathered the Levites and singers together and stationed them at their posts. ¹² Then all Judah brought a tenth of the grain, new wine, and fresh oil into the storehouses. ¹³ I appointed as treasurers over the storehouses the priest

---

^12:46 Alt Hb tradition reads *there was a head*   ^13:1 Lit *read in the ears of*   ^13:4 Or *an associate*

12:44–47 This section is linked to the dedication celebration by the phrase **on that same day**, although the issues mentioned prepare the way for the following chapter. **13:1–3 At that time** designates the era of reform under Nehemiah and not a specific date. During the now customary reading of the **book of Moses**, they read Dt 23:3–6 about the Ammonites and Moabites. The **exclusion** of the Moabites was because of their attempt to block the Israelites on their way to the promised land and their repeated attacks (Jdg 3:13; 10:9–17). All those of **mixed descent** were **separated** from Israel, which probably did not mean deportation or breaking of marriages, but exclusion from the worshiping community. **13:4–5** While some identify **Eliashib** as the high priest (3:1,20–21), this is unlikely. The name "Eliashib" ("God Repays" or "God Leads Back") was common in the postexilic era. Moreover, when Eliashib is identified he is called "the high priest" (3:1,20; 13:28) and never "the priest." Also, the Eliashib in vv. 4–8 was the person responsible for the **storerooms** of the temple, which though a position of responsibility, was hardly a job for the high priest. That a **large room** in the temple complex was now empty of offerings

and available for Tobiah's use points to the problem that Nehemiah dealt with later (vv. 10–13). **13:6–7** With this verse (v. 6) it becomes clear how such a shameful situation could have occurred in the Lord's temple: Nehemiah was in Babylon. In 5:14, Nehemiah's time in Jerusalem was described as from Artaxerxes's "twentieth year until his thirty-second year, twelve years," probably 445–432 BC. Nehemiah stated that it was **only later** that he asked Artaxerxes for a **leave of absence** to return to Jerusalem and deal with the problems that had arisen. The description of his activity suggests that he returned as governor of the province and not just a private citizen. According to the Elephantine Papyri, a governor named Bagohi was active in Jerusalem in 407 BC, thus giving a suggested end date for Nehemiah's second governorship. **13:8–13** Tobiah the Ammonite's profaning of the **rooms** provided by Eliashib meant they had to be **purified** before they were restored to their original function. These rooms were empty during Nehemiah's absence because the people had failed to provide a tenth of their produce. While the priests were provided for by their share of the sacrifices, the people had vowed to give a tenth of

their produce (10:35–39) for the support of the Levites, singers, and gatekeepers. But in Nehemiah's absence, and with heavy Persian taxes, they had failed to keep their promises; the Levites had been forced to return to farming. Nehemiah recalled the Levites and their associates back to the temple and insisted that the people give a tenth. To make sure such a situation would

#25 **99 Essential Christian Truths**

TEMPTATION AND SIN

Temptation is not the equivalent of sin. Temptation can refer to natural and good desires that are twisted and directed toward pleasing of self rather than giving glory to God. Jesus was tempted like we are (Mt 4), and yet he never sinned but faithfully resisted temptation and followed the will of his Father. Knowing our weakness, we are to be on guard against temptation that may lead us to sin (Mt 26:41), and we pray for God to deliver us from the evil one (Mt 6:13).

Shelemiah, the scribe Zadok, and Pedaiah of the Levites, with Hanan son of Zaccur, son of Mattaniah to assist them, because they were considered trustworthy. They were responsible for the distribution to their colleagues.

14 Remember me for this, my God, and don't erase the deeds of faithful love I have done for the house of my God and for its services.

15 At that time I saw people in Judah treading winepresses on the Sabbath. They were also bringing in stores of grain and loading them on donkeys, along with wine, grapes, and figs. All kinds of goods were being brought to Jerusalem on the Sabbath day. So I warned them against selling food on that day. **16** The Tyrians living there were importing fish and all kinds of merchandise and selling them on the Sabbath to the people of Judah in Jerusalem.

17 I rebuked the nobles of Judah and said to them, "What is this evil you are doing — profaning the Sabbath day? **18** Didn't your ancestors do the same, so that our God brought all this disaster on us and on this city? And now you are rekindling his anger against Israel by profaning the Sabbath!"

19 When shadows began to fall on the city gates of Jerusalem just before the Sabbath, I gave orders that the city gates be closed and not opened until after the Sabbath. I posted some of my men at the gates, so that no goods could enter during the Sabbath day. **20** Once or twice the merchants and those who sell all kinds of goods camped outside Jerusalem, **21** but I warned them, "Why are you camping in front of the wall? If you do it again, I'll use force^A against you." After that they did not come again on the Sabbath. **22** Then I instructed the Levites to purify themselves and guard the city gates in order to keep the Sabbath day holy.

Remember me for this also, my God, and look on me with compassion according to the abundance of your faithful love.

23 In those days I also saw Jews who had married women from Ashdod, Ammon, and Moab. **24** Half of their children spoke the language of Ashdod or the language of one of the other peoples but could not speak Hebrew.^B **25** I rebuked them, cursed them, beat some of their men, and pulled out their hair. I forced them to take an oath before God and said, "You must not give your daughters in marriage to their sons or take their daughters as wives for your sons or yourselves! **26** Didn't King Solomon of Israel sin in matters like this? There was not a king like him among many nations. He was loved by his God, and God made him king over all Israel, yet foreign women drew him into sin. **27** Why then should we hear about you doing all this terrible evil and acting unfaithfully against our God by marrying foreign women?" **28** Even one of the sons of Jehoiada, son of the high priest Eliashib, had become a son-in-law to Sanballat the Horonite. So I drove him away from me.

29 Remember them, my God, for defiling the priesthood as well as the covenant of the priesthood and the Levites.

30 So I purified them from everything foreign and assigned specific duties to each of the priests and Levites. **31** I also arranged for the donation of wood at the appointed times and for the firstfruits.

Remember me, my God, with favor.

^A13:21 Lit *again, I will send a hand* ^B13:24 Lit *Judahite*

---

not happen again, Nehemiah appointed four **trustworthy** men who represented the various temple personnel to make an equitable **distribution** of the tenths.
13:14 The first of four brief prayers to God by Nehemiah in this chapter occurs in this verse. He asked the Lord not to **erase** his **deeds of faithful love** (Hb *chesed*). The thought is that in the records of heaven (Ps 69:28; Dn 7:10; 12:1; Mal 3:16) his acts of faithful love would remain and be acknowledged by the Lord.
13:15–16 In 10:31 the people had pledged that they would not buy any merchandise or any kind of grain on the **Sabbath**, but when Nehemiah returned for his second stint as governor, he found they had changed their minds. Moreover, the people were working on the Sabbath as if it were just another day. The **Tyrians** were Phoenician traders whose homeland was the region of Tyre and Sidon.
13:17–18 The word **rebuked** is from a Hebrew term often used in a covenant lawsuit. Nehemiah contended with the nobles of Judah because of their violation of their covenant with God. Even if they were buying only from Gentile traders, their **evil** was clear; they were **profaning the Sabbath day**. Nehemiah reminded the nobles of Judah of the terrible cost of their Sabbath violations in the past (Ezk 20:18–24) that

had brought **this disaster on us and on this city**.
13:19–22 Nehemiah not only "rebuked" the leaders but took action. He closed the **city gates** into Jerusalem during the **Sabbath**. Some merchants tried to get around his orders by setting up shop right outside the walls (v. 20), but he warned them that he would disperse them by **force** if it happened again. Posting his **men** to the city gates was only a temporary measure, so Nehemiah ordered the **Levites to purify themselves** and to **guard the city gates . . . to keep the Sabbath day holy**. While this was an expansion of the Levites' duties, it was certainly in keeping with their overall purpose of maintaining the sanctity of the temple. The second of four brief prayers in this chapter (v. 22b) records Nehemiah's request that God honor his work in restoring the sanctity of the Sabbath and treat him in accordance with his **faithful love** (Hb *chesed*).
13:23–27 Ezra had dealt with the problem of intermarriage with Gentiles about thirty years before (Ezr 10), but the people had reverted to their old ways—to the extent that half of their children spoke **the language of Ashdod** or one of the **other peoples** (lit "the tongue of a people and a people"). Nehemiah's measures to secure the use of Hebrew appear to have had only temporary

success. By the time of Jesus, Aramaic was the common language of the people. Nehemiah's response to this situation (v. 25) seems violent by modern standards, but he reacted strongly because he realized that the sin of intermarriage with Gentiles had been a major cause of the destruction of their nation and their temple.
13:28 To illustrate how serious this problem was, Nehemiah recounted the sad case of a grandson of the high priest **Eliashib** who had married the daughter of **Sanballat the Horonite**, the enemy of Nehemiah and God's people. Once again, Nehemiah's response was swift and decisive. Probably the man left Judah and moved to Samaria where his father-in-law was governor.
13:29 In Nehemiah's third prayer in this chapter, he asked God again to **remember**. However, he did not ask God to remember and bless, but to remember and judge. He asked God to remember **them**, probably referring to Sanballat and those within the priesthood who had defiled the **priesthood** by intermarriage with foreigners.
13:30–31 These final verses of the book of Nehemiah give a brief summary of some of Nehemiah's reforms. The fourth and final prayer of the chapter is also the shortest (just four words in Hebrew): **Remember me, my God, with favor**.

▼ Introduction to Esther

Circumstances of Writing

As in most Old Testament books, the author of the book is unknown. In the Jewish Talmud, it is suggested that the members of the Great Synagogue wrote the book. However, it is hard to imagine this prestigious group of religious scholars writing a book that mentions the Persian king 190 times but never mentions God. Many early writers, Jewish as well as Christian, suggested Mordecai as the author.

Background: The story of Esther is rooted in the historical situation of King Xerxes (Ahasuerus), who ruled as king of Persia from 486 to 465 BC.

Mid-twentieth century critical scholars tended to date the book late, even into the second century BC. However, most now argue for an earlier date. The discovery of the Dead Sea Scrolls in 1947 showed that the Hebrew of Esther was very different from the Hebrew of the first century BC. Also, there are no Greek words in the text of Esther, which would suggest that it was written before Alexander the Great's conquest (ca 333 BC) made Greek the language of the region. Most likely the book was written in the fourth century BC.

The book gives every indication of being a historical narrative. For that reason, the alleged historical anomalies in the text raise problems, for many interpreters, in accepting the historicity of the story. While it is regrettable not to have any extant extrabiblical confirmation of the main characters in the story (Esther, Haman, Mordecai), several points must be considered.

First, there are few extant Persian records for the reign of Xerxes; thus very few historical figures are known from this time. Moreover, the Greek writers, especially Herodotus, were writing their history particularly as it related to the Greeks—not as court historians for the Persians—thus their material is selective and would leave unmentioned many significant figures. Second, the absence of extrabiblical evidence does not mean these people did not exist. Third, while there is no positive extrabiblical confirmation of these individuals, they appear in an account that even ardent critics acknowledge as being remarkably accurate in its description of the Persian era.

Contribution to the Bible

Without ever mentioning God directly, the book of Esther underscores the providence of God. God's promise to give the Jews an eternal ruler remained in place, even in the face of threatened annihilation. Esther shows us that many Jews remained faithful to their God even in exile. They kept their identity as God's people through the synagogues that developed as the centers of the Jewish community wherever Jews settled. The synagogues would later play a significant role as the gospel spread throughout the Roman Empire, for these served as natural starting places for the deliverance of the gospel in the towns visited by the apostles (e.g., Ac 9:20; 17:1–2; 18:19; 19:8).

Esther Timeline

625–600 BC

Nineveh is sacked by the Babylonians and the Medes. The Assyrian Empire collapses. **612**

Nebuchadnezzar's three invasions of Judah **605, 597, 586**

Events in Daniel **605–530**

Prince Nebuchadnezzar of Babylon defeats the Egyptians at the Battle of Carchemish. **605**

Nebuchadnezzar II becomes king of Babylon. **604**

600–550 BC

Jeremiah's Ministry **627–586?**

Events in Obadiah **605–586?**

Events in Ezekiel **593–571**

Lamentations **586**

Temple of Solomon is destroyed. **586**

Nebuchadnezzar dies and is succeeded by Evil-merodach. **562**

Evil-merodach pardons Judah's King Jehoiachin. **561**

550–500 BC

Cyrus the Great defeats King Astyages of Media at Pasargadae. **550**

Cyrus diverts the waters of the Euphrates and launches a surprise attack against the ancient city of Babylon, taking it without a struggle. **539**

Cyrus's decree allows the return of Jews from exile. **538**

Cyrus is killed in a campaign against the Massagetae of central Asia, and his son Cambyses is crowned king of Persia. **530**

Structure

The Hebrew of the Masoretic Text used as the basis for the Christian Standard Bible is a fairly straightforward text. It is written in a form of late biblical Hebrew common to the postexilic era and found in other biblical books of that time, such as Chronicles, Ezra-Nehemiah, and Daniel. Like Ezra-Nehemiah, Esther shows the growing influence of Aramaic in its grammar and vocabulary, as well as the presence of many Persian words.

Outline

500–470 BC

Events in Esther **486–465**
Ahasuerus gives 180-day feast; Vashti is deposed **483**
Esther becomes queen of Persia. **479**
Golden Age of Greek art **477–431**
At Haman's request, a royal decree is issued for the annihilation of the Jews in the Persian Empire. **474**
Esther intercedes with Ahasuerus for her people. **474**
First celebration of Purim **473**

470–430 BC

Events in Malachi **460**
Ezra goes to Jerusalem. **458**
Events in Nehemiah **445–430**
Jerusalem's walls are rebuilt under Nehemiah's leadership. **445**
Athens is defeated by Sparta, second Peloponnesian War **431–404**
Greek philosopher Empedocles speculates that the world is made up of four elements: earth, air, water, and fire. **495–435**

430–400 BC

Greek historian Xenophon is born. **431**
Greek playwright Sophocles writes *Oedipus the King.* **429**
The marble figure of *Nike* is placed in the Temple of Athena. **407**
Thucydides' *History* is finished. **403**

Vashti Angers the King

1 These events took place during the days of Ahasuerus, who ruled 127 provinces from India to Cush. ² In those days King Ahasuerus reigned from his royal throne in the fortress at Susa. ³ He held a feast in the third year of his reign for all his officials and staff, the army of Persia and Media, the nobles, and the officials from the provinces. ⁴ He displayed the glorious wealth of his kingdom and the magnificent splendor of his greatness for a total of 180 days. ⁵ At the end of this time, the king held a week-long banquet in the garden courtyard of the royal palace for all the people, from the greatest to the least, who were present in the fortress of Susa. ⁶ White and blue linen hangings were fastened with fine white and purple linen cords to silver rods on marble^A columns. Gold and silver couches were arranged on a mosaic pavement of red feldspar,^B marble, mother-of-pearl, and precious stones.

⁷ Drinks were served in an array of gold goblets, each with a different design. Royal wine flowed freely, according to the king's bounty. ⁸ The drinking was according to royal decree: "There are no restrictions." The king had ordered every wine steward in his household to serve whatever each person wanted. ⁹ Queen Vashti also gave a feast for the women of King Ahasuerus's palace.

¹⁰ On the seventh day, when the king was feeling good from the wine, Ahasuerus commanded Mehuman, Biztha, Harbona, Bigtha, Abagtha, Zethar, and Carkas — the seven eunuchs who personally served him — ¹¹ to bring Queen Vashti before him with her royal crown. He wanted to show off her beauty to the people and the officials, because she was very beautiful. ¹² But Queen Vashti refused to come at the king's command that was delivered by his eunuchs. The king became furious and his anger burned within him.

The King's Decree

¹³ The king consulted the wise men who understood the times,^C for it was his normal procedure to confer with experts in law and justice. ¹⁴ The most trusted ones^D were Carshena, Shethar, Admatha, Tarshish, Meres, Marsena, and Memucan. They were the seven officials of Persia and Media who had personal access to the king and occupied the highest positions in the kingdom. ¹⁵ The king asked, "According to the law, what should be done with Queen Vashti, since she refused to obey King Ahasuerus's command that was delivered by the eunuchs?"

¹⁶ Memucan said in the presence of the king and his officials, "Queen Vashti has wronged not only the king, but all the officials and the peoples who are in every one of King Ahasuerus's provinces. ¹⁷ For the queen's action will become public knowledge to all the women and cause them to despise their husbands and say, 'King Ahasuerus ordered Queen Vashti brought before him, but she did not come.' ¹⁸ Before this day is over, the noble women of Persia and Media who hear about the queen's act will say the same thing to all the king's officials, resulting in more contempt and fury.

---

^A 1:6 Or *alabaster* ^B 1:6 Or *of porphyry* ^C 1:13 Or *understood propitious times* ^D 1:14 Lit *Those near him*

1:1–2 Ahasuerus is the Hebrew name for King Xerxes, who ruled from 486 to 465 BC; he is mentioned only two other times in the rest of the OT (Ezr 4:6; Dn 9:1). The easternmost border of the vast Persian Empire was the Indus River, now in Pakistan but once part of **India**. The westernmost extent of the empire was to **Cush**, the region south of Egypt called Upper Nubia, which today is part of northern Sudan.

Chapter 1 of Esther is set in the **fortress at Susa**, one of the three capital cities of the Persian Empire along with Ecbatana and Persepolis (some would argue that Babylon was also a capital city). It is located in what is today southwestern Iran. During Xerxes's rule Susa was the usual location of his winter palace.

1:3–4 In the **third year** of Ahasuerus, probably 483 BC, there occurred the first of ten feasts recorded in Esther, which are important structural and thematic markers in the book. The word "feast" is derived from the Hebrew verb *shathah*, meaning "to drink." The **feast** was more of a drinking bout than a meal. It is not clear whether v. 4 suggests that the party itself went on for 180 days, or instead that for a half year after the party there was a royal celebration in which Ahasuerus **displayed the glorious wealth of his kingdom**.

1:5–8 Unlike the first feast, the second **banquet** (or "feast," v. 3) was not for the nobility but for all the citizenry in the **fortress of Susa**. The event is described in great detail (v. 6) to highlight the opulence and wealth of the king. **According to royal decree**, each guest could drink as much as he desired or was capable of drinking since **there are no restrictions**, no restraint.

1:9 The third **feast** was given by **Queen Vashti**. It was only for **the women**. Neither Persian nor Greek records mention a queen named Vashti, but rather identify Amestris as queen during Xerxes's reign. Several prominent OT scholars suggest that "Vashti" may be not a proper name but a title, possibly meaning "the best." Vashti disappears from the story when she is replaced by Esther (2:17).

1:10–12 Most of the references to **eunuchs** in the OT occur in the book of Esther. They held positions of power, such as serving as cupbearer, and could be trusted with the care of the royal wives and concubines. The king's call for **seven** eunuchs could suggest that Queen Vashti was carried to the banquet on a royal litter.

No one was as shocked as King Ahasuerus when Queen Vashti **refused** his royal command. The chronology of this event may give additional insight into the king's anger. If this occurred in "the third year" (v. 3) of Ahasuerus's rule (483 BC), it might coincide with the preparations for war with the Greeks.

Ahasuerus, who needed his soldiers to obey his commands as they went to war, could not even get his own wife to obey him in his own palace!

1:13–14 Some suggest the phrase **who understood the times** refers to astrologers and translate the phrase as "who understood propitious times." More likely the reference to those who "understood the times" is like the usage in 1Ch 12:32. The names of the seven wise men, also called **officials**, are not identifiable with known Persian individuals, but for three of the men (**Meres, Marsena, and Memucan**), Elamite parallels have been found for their names.

1:16–17 Memucan's recommendation (vv. 19–20) was based on his assertion that Queen Vashti's action was not just a personal affront but also a universal affront against **all** the **officials** and the **peoples** who lived in all the **provinces**. Memucan's exaggeration served only to legitimize the poor advice he was about to give the king.

1:18 The syntax of the Hebrew text of v. 18 is difficult because there is no object for the verb **will say**. One simple solution is to assume the loss of a definite article marker before the phrase **who hear**. This would give a translation such as "the noble women of Persia and Media will say *what* they have heard about the queen's act."

¹⁹ "If it meets the king's approval, he should personally issue a royal decree. Let it be recorded in the laws of the Persians and the Medes, so that it cannot be revoked: Vashti is not to enter King Ahasuerus's presence, and her royal position is to be given to another woman who is more worthy than she. ²⁰ The decree the king issues will be heard throughout his vast kingdom, so all women will honor their husbands, from the greatest to the least."

²¹ The king and his counselors approved the proposal, and he followed Memucan's advice. ²² He sent letters to all the royal provinces, to each province in its own script and to each ethnic group in its own language, that every man should be master of his own house and speak in the language of his own people.

The Search for a New Queen

2 Some time later, when King Ahasuerus's rage had cooled down, he remembered Vashti, what she had done, and what was decided against her. ² The king's personal attendants suggested, "Let a search be made for beautiful young virgins for the king. ³ Let the king appoint commissioners in each province of his kingdom, so that they may gather all the beautiful young virgins to the harem at the fortress of Susa. Put them under the supervision of Hegai, the king's eunuch, keeper of the women, and give them the required beauty treatments. ⁴ Then the young woman who pleases the king will become queen instead of Vashti." This suggestion pleased the king, and he did accordingly.

⁵ In the fortress of Susa, there was a Jewish man named Mordecai son of Jair, son of

1:19 The irrevocability of the **laws of the Persians and Medes** is not documented either in Persian or Greek literature, although it is mentioned several times in the OT (8:8; Dn 6:8,12). The consort was always called "Queen Vashti" until this verse; now she is simply **Vashti.**

1:20 This passage is replete with irony and satire. King Ahasuerus, who could not control his own wife, now issues a universal **decree** that **all women** would **honor their husbands**.

1:21–22 The final phrase of the decree is unusual and has engendered much debate: **and speak in the language of his own people**. Some scholars suggest changing the text, while others follow the LXX and simply delete it (NRSV, NLT). Another possibility is to understand the phrase "speak in the language of his own people" as referring to the decree and not to the husband. The issuance of the decree to the entire empire

is ironic because it ensured that everyone in the empire would know about the king's marital struggles, and not just the "noble women" of Susa (v. 18).

2:1 The vague description **some time later** is of little help in determining the time frame in the story. It is clear from v. 16 that Esther did not meet King Ahasuerus until four years after the first events (479–478 BC).

2:5–7 In this important parenthetical flashback, two more main characters in the story are introduced—**Mordecai** and **Esther**. The name "Mordecai" was a common name, a Hebrew form of the Babylonian name Marduka, derived from Marduk, the principle god of Babylon.

Mordecai's genealogy is problematic if it is attempting to link him to **Kish** the father of King Saul (1Sm 9:1). This Kish could hardly have been Mordecai's great-grandfather, since the time gap between the two was

over five hundred years. Either a different Kish is in view, or it could be that the term **son of** means here "descendant of," a common usage in the OT that in this case would indicate that the author is choosing to identify only a handful of Mordecai's line of ancestors.

An additional difficulty is associated with v. 6—he **had been taken into exile from Jerusalem** during the time of Neuchadnezzar. If "he" is Mordecai, this would make him almost 120 years old when Esther was chosen. It is possible to read v. 6 as identifying Kish as the "he" and not Mordecai, which would also lend credence to the theory that a different individual named Kish is intended here, not King Saul's father. Esther is introduced first with her Hebrew name, **Hadassah**, the name of the myrtle tree. Her Gentile name was Esther, derived from the name of the famous goddess Ishtar.

Character profile:
Esther

E sther is the only book in the Bible that never mentions God. Instead, the book reads like a suspenseful novel, full of schemes, plot twists, and intrigue.

When Esther's parents died, her older cousin, Mordecai, adopted her. In Esther 2:7 we learn that Esther was beautiful. And it just so happened that Persia's king, Ahasuerus, was performing a national search for a new queen. When Esther was chosen to become part of the king's harem, Ahasuerus loved her more than all the rest. "He placed the royal crown on her head and made her queen" (2:17).

One day Mordecai overheard some men planning to assasinate the king. He sent word to Queen Esther, and the plot was foiled, the assassins were executed, and the events were recorded in the royal record.

Enter Haman, an insufferable suck-up to the king. Given his high rank, Haman had managed to secure a royal decree requiring people to bow whenever he was present. But Mordecai stubbornly refused. This disrespect enraged Haman. When he learned that Mordecai was a Jew, Haman decided to kill Mordecai, as well as every Jew throughout the Persian kingdom (see 3:6). Clueless to his queen's Jewish heritage, King Ahasuerus went along with Haman's plan. The date of the genocide was set and announced.

Devastated, Mordecai appealed to Esther to approach the king and intercede for her people. Yet, she was reluctant and reminded her cousin that Persian law stated that anyone

initiating an audience with the king was subject to the death penalty.

Mordecai replied, "If you keep silent at this time, relief and deliverance will come to the Jewish people from another place, but you and your father's family will be destroyed. Who knows, perhaps you have come to your royal position for such a time as this" (4:14). With great courage, Esther agreed to stick her neck out, saying, "If I perish, I perish" (4:16).

But she didn't perish. In fact, her story ends with a wonderful divine twist. While Esther planned a banquet to appeal to the king for her people—and while Haman was having gallows built so he could hang Mordecai—King Ahasuerus learned that Mordecai was the one who had previously saved him from assassination.

The king further discovered, however, that Mordecai had never been rewarded for his faithfulness. So, much to Haman's dismay, the king made Haman honor Mordecai. Then, Esther revealed to the king both her Jewish ancestry and Haman's plan to kill her people. In his rage, the king hanged Haman on the very gallows he had built for Mordecai.

How ironic. In a book that doesn't mention God, readers can observe the invisible hand of God orchestrating events to protect his people.

Because of Esther's bravery, the Jews were spared. The Jewish holiday of Purim is still practiced today as a celebration of this victory (see 9:16–32).

God is always at work, accomplishing his plan for individuals and for the world. Unbelievers may speak of coincidence or luck, but the people of God see a gracious heavenly Father who is always at work.

Shimei, son of Kish, a Benjaminite. [6] Kish[A] had been taken into exile from Jerusalem with the other captives when King Nebuchadnezzar of Babylon took King Jeconiah of Judah into exile. [7] Mordecai was the legal guardian of his cousin[B] Hadassah (that is, Esther), because she had no father or mother. The young woman had a beautiful figure and was extremely good-looking. When her father and mother died, Mordecai had adopted her as his own daughter.

[8] When the king's command and edict became public knowledge and when many young women were gathered at the fortress of Susa under Hegai's supervision, Esther was taken to the palace, into the supervision of Hegai, keeper of the women. [9] The young woman pleased him and gained his favor so that he accelerated the process of the beauty treatments and the special diet that she received. He assigned seven hand-picked female servants to her from the palace and transferred her and her servants to the harem's best quarters.

[10] Esther did not reveal her ethnicity or her family background, because Mordecai had ordered her not to make them known. [11] Every day Mordecai took a walk in front of the harem's courtyard to learn how Esther was doing and to see what was happening to her.

[12] During the year before each young woman's turn to go to King Ahasuerus, the harem regulation required her to receive beauty treatments with oil of myrrh for six months and then with perfumes and cosmetics for another six months. [13] When the young woman would go to the king, she was given whatever she requested to take with her from the harem to the palace. [14] She would go in the evening, and in the morning she would return to a second harem under the supervision of the king's eunuch Shaashgaz, keeper of the concubines. She never went to the king again, unless he desired her and summoned her by name.

Esther Becomes Queen

[15] Esther was the daughter of Abihail, the uncle of Mordecai who had adopted her as his own daughter. When her turn came to go to the king, she did not ask for anything except what Hegai, the king's eunuch, keeper of the women, suggested. Esther gained favor in the eyes of everyone who saw her.

[16] She was taken to King Ahasuerus in the palace in the tenth month, the month Tebeth, in the seventh year of his reign. [17] The king loved Esther more than all the other women. She won more favor and approval from him than did any of the other virgins. He placed the royal crown on her head and made her queen in place of Vashti. [18] The king held a great banquet for all his officials and staff. It was Esther's banquet. He freed his provinces from tax payments and gave gifts worthy of the king's bounty.

Mordecai Saves the King

[19] When the virgins were gathered a second time, Mordecai was sitting at the King's Gate. [20] Esther still did not reveal her family background or her ethnicity, as Mordecai had directed. She obeyed Mordecai's orders, as she always had while he raised her.

[21] During those days while Mordecai was sitting at the King's Gate, Bigthan and Teresh, two of the king's eunuchs who guarded the entrance, became infuriated and planned to assassinate[C] King Ahasuerus. [22] When Mordecai learned of the plot, he reported it to Queen Esther, and she told the king on Mordecai's behalf. [23] When the report was investigated and verified, both men were hanged on the gallows.

[A] 2:6 Lit He [B] 2:7 Lit uncle's daughter [C] 2:21 Lit and they sought to stretch out a hand against

---

2:8–9 Esther's chances to become queen increased as she **pleased** Hegai, the eunuch in charge of the potential brides. He also gave her a **special diet**. The Hebrew term used here usually means "portions," often in the sense of delicacies (Neh 8:10,12).

2:10 It is not explicitly stated why Mordecai **ordered** Esther to hide her Jewish background. When Esther finally revealed her ethnicity to King Ahasuerus, he appeared untroubled by it (7:3). Yet clearly some people of that era, especially Haman (3:4–6), hated the Jews.

2:11 The passage does not say that Mordecai obtained news daily or that he talked to Esther directly.

2:12–13 The mention of one-year **beauty treatments** for each **young woman** sounds excessive and indulgent. Each prospect could **take with her** whatever **she requested** when she went to the king, presumably perfumes, jewelry, and clothes.

2:14 The **second harem** would have been separate from the harem in which the women were undergoing their beauty treatments.

2:16–18 Esther's turn to please the king came in what would have been the winter of 479–478 BC. The story gives no hint of moral judgment about the actions of Esther, a young Jewish virgin who gave herself to a pagan, uncircumcised, Persian king.

The vacancy created by the deposing of Vashti was now filled by Esther, whose coronation was celebrated with **a great banquet**. This banquet contrasts with the fateful banquet where Queen Vashti refused to appear (1:12) and foreshadows the banquets yet to come, especially the crucial banquets with Haman (chaps. 5 and 7), and the banquets of rejoicing for the Jewish people in chaps. 8 and 9.

The phrase **freed . . . from tax payments** translates a single Hebrew word *(hanachah)* that occurs only here in the OT. It has the connotation of "causing to rest," possibly indicating a rest from work in commemoration of the queen's coronation.

2:19–20 It may be that the **virgins** of the king's harem (vv. 12–14) were not allowed to be present at "Esther's Banquet" but got together at a different time to celebrate with their friend who was now queen. The mention of **Mordecai** at **the King's Gate** suggests that he was some kind of official in the Persian court. This would help explain why he was living in the fortress at Susa (1:2) and not in the city of Susa, and how he could be within earshot of conspirators who were plotting Ahasuerus's murder. The King's Gate in Susa was a massive monumental structure that measured 131 feet by 92 feet, with a column-like tower on each corner that was 40 feet high.

2:21–23 The story of Esther takes a new turn with Mordecai's discovery of a plot to **assassinate King Ahasuerus**. Mordecai informed the king through **Queen Esther**. In terms of the narrative, this section of the story sets the stage for the delayed honoring of Mordecai at Haman's expense (chaps. 6–7). The seemingly mundane mention of the incident being **recorded in the Historical Record** serves as an important part of the plot, setting up Ahasuerus's later discovery of his failure to honor Mordecai (6:1–3).

This event was recorded in the Historical Record in the king's presence.

Haman's Plan to Kill the Jews

3 After all this took place, King Ahasuerus honored Haman, son of Hammedatha the Agagite. He promoted him in rank and gave him a higher position than all the other officials. ² The entire royal staff at the King's Gate bowed down and paid homage to Haman, because the king had commanded this to be done for him. But Mordecai would not bow down or pay homage. ³ The members of the royal staff at the King's Gate asked Mordecai, "Why are you disobeying the king's command?" ⁴ When they had warned him day after day and he still would not listen to them, they told Haman in order to see if Mordecai's actions would be tolerated, since he had told them he was a Jew.

⁵ When Haman saw that Mordecai was not bowing down or paying him homage, he was filled with rage. ⁶ And when he learned of Mordecai's ethnic identity, it seemed repugnant to Haman to do away withᴬ Mordecai alone. He planned to destroy all of Mordecai's people, the Jews, throughout Ahasuerus's kingdom.

⁷ In the first month, the month of Nisan, in King Ahasuerus's twelfth year, the *pur* — that is, the lot — was cast before Haman for each day in each month, and it fell on the twelfth month, the month Adar. ⁸ Then Haman informed King Ahasuerus, "There is one ethnic group, scattered throughout the peoples in every province of your kingdom, keeping themselves separate. Their laws are different from everyone else's and they do not obey the king's laws. It is not in the king's best interest to tolerate them. ⁹ If the king approves, let an order be drawn up authorizing their destruction, and I will pay 375 tons of silver toᴮ the officials for deposit in the royal treasury."

¹⁰ The king removed his signet ring from his hand and gave it to Haman son of Hammedatha the Agagite, the enemy of the Jews. ¹¹ Then the king told Haman, "The money and people are given to you to do with as you see fit."

¹² The royal scribes were summoned on the thirteenth day of the first month, and the order was written exactly as Haman commanded. It was intended for the royal satraps, the governors of each of the provinces, and officials of each ethnic group and written for each province in its own script and to each ethnic group in its own language. It was written in the name of King Ahasuerus and sealed with the royal signet ring. ¹³ Letters were sent by couriers to each of the royal provinces telling the officials to destroy, kill, and annihilate all the Jewish people — young and old, women and children — and plunder their possessions on a single day, the thirteenth day of Adar, the twelfth month.ᶜ

¹⁴ A copy of the text, issued as law throughout every province, was distributed to all the peoples so that they might get ready for that day. ¹⁵ The couriers left, spurred on by royal command, and the law was issued in the fortress of Susa. The king and Haman sat down to drink, while the city of Susa was in confusion.

Mordecai Appeals to Esther

4 When Mordecai learned all that had occurred, he tore his clothes, put on sackcloth and ashes, went into the middle of the city, and cried loudly and bitterly. ² He went only as far as the King's Gate, since the law prohibited anyone wearing sackcloth from entering the King's Gate. ³ There was great mourning among the Jewish people in every province

---

ᴬ3:6 Lit *to stretch out a hand against*   ᴮ3:9 Lit *will weigh 10,000 silver talents on the hands of*   ᶜ3:13 LXX adds the text of Ahasuerus's letter here.

3:1–6 This section is a critical part of the narrative that introduces the last protagonist in the story (Haman) and the conflict that now dominates the narrative (threat to the Jews). The initial incident that sparked the conflict was Mordecai's refusal to bow to Haman. One of the most plausible explanations for Mordecai's refusal relates to Haman's name: **Haman . . . the Agagite.** Haman was a descendant of Agag (1Sm 15:8–33), the leader of the Amalekites. King Saul's disobedience in sparing King Agag (1Sm 15:8–9) resulted in Samuel's announcement that the Lord had taken the kingdom away from him and by extension his descendants (1Sm 15:27). Possibly this ancient enmity explains Mordecai's refusal to bow to Haman the Agagite.
3:7 The *pur* appears to derive from the Akkadian term *puru* meaning a "lot" or "fate." Presumably Haman wanted his astrologers or diviners to pick the most propitious date to launch his vengeance against Mordecai and his people. The month that was identified

by lot was the month of **Adar** (normally March–April).
3:8–9 Haman cleverly began his presentation to Ahasuerus by starting with the truth (**There is one ethnic group, scattered throughout the peoples**) and ending with a lie (**they do not obey the king's laws**). His offer to give the crown **375 tons of silver** to pay for an empire-wide extermination may have encouraged Ahasuerus, whose coffers had been depleted by the war with the Greeks. Such a gift from Haman would represent over half the annual income of the Persian Empire. Yet it appears that the king may have refused the offer (v. 11), although both Mordecai and Esther assumed the king accepted it (4:7; 7:4).
3:10–11 Haman's request was granted by Ahasuerus, who gave him his **signet ring**, used by the king to put his official wax seal on a state document. With that ring, Haman had the power to carry out his planned extermination. King Ahasuerus never even bothered to ask the identity of the ethnic

group that Haman planned to destroy. **The money . . . given to you** may indicate that the king refused Haman's offer of "375 tons of silver" (v. 9).
3:12–15 The instructions were clear: all **young and old, women and children** were to be destroyed, killed, and annihilated (v. 13). The terrible decree was to be executed eleven months later, on the **thirteenth day of Adar**. The impression is that the people in Susa were not in favor of the decree and did not share Haman's rabid anti-Semitism.
4:1–3 Mordecai's response to the king's edict was typical for his culture (Ezr 9:3; Neh 9:1). All who saw him recognized his grief, especially since he **cried loudly and bitterly** (lit "he cried out a great cry"). The term *to cry out* is often used in the OT to describe a heartbroken howl over injustice (Gn 18:20), personal tragedy (2Sm 13:19), or national tragedy (Ezk 9:8). While Mordecai would not get the king's attention, he did get Esther's (Est 4:4), which was crucial. A law prohibiting a mourner to come into the

where the king's command and edict reached. They fasted, wept, and lamented, and many lay in sackcloth and ashes.

⁴ Esther's female servants and her eunuchs came and reported the news to her, and the queen was overcome with fear. She sent clothes for Mordecai to wear so that he would take off his sackcloth, but he did not accept them. ⁵ Esther summoned Hathach, one of the king's eunuchs who attended her, and dispatched him to Mordecai to learn what he was doing and why.^ ⁶ So Hathach went out to Mordecai in the city square in front of the King's Gate. ⁷ Mordecai told him everything that had happened as well as the exact amount of money Haman had promised to pay the royal treasury for the slaughter of the Jews.

⁸ Mordecai also gave him a copy of the written decree issued in Susa ordering their destruction, so that Hathach might show it to Esther, explain it to her, and command her to approach the king, implore his favor, and plead with him personally for her people. ⁹ Hathach came and repeated Mordecai's response to Esther.

¹⁰ Esther spoke to Hathach and commanded him to tell Mordecai, ¹¹ "All the royal officials and the people of the royal provinces know that one law applies to every man or woman who approaches the king in the inner courtyard and who has not been summoned — the death penalty — unless the king extends the gold scepter, allowing that person to live. I have not been summoned to appear before the king for the last⁸ thirty days." ¹² Esther's response was reported to Mordecai.

¹³ Mordecai told the messenger to reply to Esther, "Don't think that you will escape the fate of all the Jews because you are in the king's palace. ¹⁴ If you keep silent at this time, relief and deliverance will come to the Jewish people from another place, but you and your father's family will be destroyed. Who knows, perhaps you have come to your royal position for such a time as this."

¹⁵ Esther sent this reply to Mordecai: ¹⁶ "Go and assemble all the Jews who can be found in Susa and fast for me. Don't eat or drink for three days, night or day. I and my female servants will also fast in the same way. After that, I will go to the king even if it is against the law. If I perish, I perish." ¹⁷ So Mordecai went and did everything Esther had commanded him.

Esther Approaches the King

5 On the third day, Esther dressed in her royal clothing and stood in the inner courtyard of the palace facing it. The king was sitting on his royal throne in the royal courtroom,ᶜ facing its entrance. ² As soon as the king saw Queen Esther standing in the courtyard, she gained favor with him. The king extended the gold scepter in his hand toward Esther, and she approached and touched the tip of the scepter. ³ "What is it, Queen Esther?" the king asked her. "Whatever you want, even to half the kingdom, will be given to you."

⁴ "If it pleases the king," Esther replied, "may the king and Haman come today to the banquet I have prepared for them."

⁵ The king said, "Hurry, and get Haman so we can do as Esther has requested." So the king and Haman went to the banquet Esther had prepared.

⁶ While drinking theᴰ wine, the king asked Esther, "Whatever you ask will be given to you. Whatever you want, even to half the kingdom, will be done."

⁷ Esther answered, "This is my petition and my request: ⁸ If I have found favor in the eyes of the

---

^4:5 Lit *what is this and why is this*   ᴮ4:11 Lit *king these*   ᶜ5:1 Lit *house*   ᴰ5:6 Lit *During the banquet of*

---

palace is not attested in the ancient sources, but in a similar vein, Nehemiah stated that he had "never been sad" in King Artaxerxes's presence before, and when asked about it by Artaxerxes he "was overwhelmed with fear" (Neh 2:1–2). Mordecai was not alone in his grief. The **Jewish people in that province** wept and **lamented**, and many lay in **sackcloth and ashes**.
4:4–7 The name **Hathach** possibly means "courier."
4:8–9 The courier was told to **explain** the decree. Either **Esther** was illiterate and the decree had to be read to her, or it was written in Persian and had to be translated into Aramaic. Mordecai was certainly aware of the danger he was putting Esther in by telling her to **plead . . . personally** with the king, but their situation was desperate. It is interesting how he emphasized that the Jews were **her people**, the same people he had previously commanded her not to identify with (2:10).
4:10–12 Esther's response to Mordecai through Hathach was to remind him that

to come to the king unbidden was certain **death**. Such a law was understandable in the Persian Empire with its long history of political assassinations (in fact, Ahasuerus was murdered in his own bed less than ten years later). The one exception to this rule was if the king allowed an uninvited person to approach him, signified by his extending **the gold scepter**.
4:13–14 Mordecai's reply to Esther was direct and to the point: Esther had no safe choices. Mordecai's statement that help would come **from another place** if Esther remained quiet is intriguing. The most obvious interpretation is to understand the phrase "another place" as a veiled reference to God, an interpretation supported by the Greek additions to Esther (Alpha Text 5:9), both Aramaic Targums, and Josephus. Others find it more likely that "another place" refers to a human source of deliverance, possibly another well-placed Jewish official similar to Nehemiah, who served Ahasuerus's son (Artaxerxes) as cupbearer.

4:15–16 This **fast** was unusually long, highlighting the severity of the threat to the Jewish people. Esther's last comment to Mordecai in this chapter (**If I perish, I perish**) is not just resigned fatalism but of one facing and coming to grips with a danger.
5:1–2 On the **third day** of the three-day fast, Esther prepared herself for her surprise appearance before the king. She wore not her fasting and mourning clothes but **her royal clothing**, possibly as a reminder to her husband that she was indeed the queen of Persia.
5:3–4 Ahasuerus's offer to Esther, **even to half the kingdom**, was not to be taken literally; it was an exaggeration meant to emphasize the generosity of the king (cp. Mk 6:23). Considering the breadth of the offer, the answer must have been surprising: an invitation for the **king** and **Haman** to come to a **banquet** (Hb *mishteh*) that Esther had prepared. Just as the first banquet in the story ended with the downfall of a queen (chap. 1), so this series of banquets would end with the downfall of the king's second-in-command (chap. 7).

king, and if it pleases the king to grant my petition and perform my request, may the king and Haman come to the banquet I will prepare for them. Tomorrow I will do what the king has asked."

9 That day Haman left full of joy and in good spirits.^A But when Haman saw Mordecai at the King's Gate, and Mordecai didn't rise or tremble in fear at his presence, Haman was filled with rage toward Mordecai. **10** Yet Haman controlled himself and went home. He sent for his friends and his wife Zeresh to join him. **11** Then Haman described for them his glorious wealth and his many sons. He told them all how the king had honored him and promoted him in rank over the other officials and the royal staff. **12** "What's more," Haman added, "Queen Esther invited no one but me to join the king at the banquet she had prepared. I am invited again tomorrow to join her with the king. **13** Still, none of this satisfies me since I see Mordecai the Jew sitting at the King's Gate all the time."

14 His wife Zeresh and all his friends told him, "Have them build a gallows seventy-five feet^B tall. Ask the king in the morning to hang Mordecai on it. Then go to the banquet with the king and enjoy yourself." The advice pleased Haman, so he had the gallows constructed.

Mordecai Honored by the King

6 That night sleep escaped the king, so he ordered the book recording daily events to be brought and read to the king. **2** They found the written report of how Mordecai had informed on Bigthana and Teresh, two of the king's eunuchs who guarded the entrance, when they planned to assassinate King Ahasuerus. **3** The king inquired, "What honor and special recognition have been given to Mordecai for this act?"

The king's personal attendants replied, "Nothing has been done for him."

4 The king asked, "Who is in the court?" Now Haman was just entering the outer court of the palace to ask the king to hang Mordecai on the gallows he had prepared for him.

5 The king's attendants answered him, "Haman is there, standing in the court."

"Have him enter," the king ordered. **6** Haman entered, and the king asked him, "What should be done for the man the king wants to honor?"

Haman thought to himself, "Who is it the king would want to honor more than me?" **7** Haman told the king, "For the man the king wants to honor: **8** Have them bring a royal garment that the king himself has worn and a horse the king himself has ridden, which has a royal crown on its head. **9** Put the garment and the horse under the charge of one of the king's most noble officials. Have them clothe the man the king wants to honor, parade him on the horse through the city square, and call out before him, 'This is what is done for the man the king wants to honor.'"

10 The king told Haman, "Hurry, and do just as you proposed. Take a garment and a horse for Mordecai the Jew, who is sitting at the King's Gate. Do not leave out anything you have suggested."

11 So Haman took the garment and the horse. He clothed Mordecai and paraded him through the city square, calling out before him, "This is what is done for the man the king wants to honor."

12 Then Mordecai returned to the King's Gate, but Haman hurried off for home, mournful and with his head covered. **13** Haman told his wife Zeresh and all his friends everything that had happened. His advisers and his wife Zeresh said to him, "Since Mordecai is Jewish, and you have begun to fall before him, you won't overcome him, because your downfall is certain." **14** While they were still speaking with him, the king's eunuchs arrived and rushed Haman to the banquet Esther had prepared.

Haman Is Executed

7 The king and Haman came to feast^C with Esther the queen. **2** Once again, on the second day while drinking wine, the king asked

---

^A 5:9 Lit *left rejoicing and good of heart*   ^B 5:14 Lit *50 cubits*   ^C 7:1 Lit *drink*

5:9 Haman's **rage** only got worse when he saw that Mordecai not only did not **rise** in his presence but did not even **tremble** in **his presence**. Defying Haman did not even make Mordecai nervous.

5:14 **Zeresh**, along with Haman's **friends**, suggested a plan to publicly murder his enemy, Mordecai.

6:1–3 Verses 1–11 serve as the turning point of Esther's plot. No reason is given for the king's insomnia. The LXX emphasizes the divine cause of his sleeplessness: "The Lord withdrew sleep from the king." Apparently the king believed reading the tedious royal journal of **daily events** might lull him to sleep. Instead, it exposed a glaring royal oversight as mention was made of Mordecai's unrewarded heroism.

6:7–9 Haman did not covet money or power, because he already had both. What he desired was the glory and splendor of royalty, including **royal** robes and a public **parade**.

6:10–11 For Haman, events began to spin out of control. The greatest honor Haman could imagine receiving was bestowed on **Mordecai the Jew**, his enemy whom he had planned to hang that day.

6:12–13 To cover one's head was a sign of mourning (Jr 14:4). While no one had died, Haman was mourning his humiliation. The previous advice of Haman's **wife** and **friends** (5:14), who were presumably his **advisers** (lit "his wise ones," Hb *chakamim*), had been given as they offered a solution to Haman's problem with Mordecai. But now their counsel was ominous: once a person stumbles before a Jew, there is no hope.

6:14 Haman had no time to react to their counsel because he was **rushed** to the **banquet Esther had prepared**. It is significant that this is the fourth mention of Haman "rushing" or "hurrying" in the last two chapters (see vv. 10,12,14; 5:5).

7:1–10 Up to this point two intertwined conflicts have remained unresolved: the

---

#26 **99 Essential Christian Truths**

CALLING

The calling of God to salvation happens in two ways: externally through the proclamation of the gospel and internally through the Holy Spirit working in the heart of the person who hears. Both of these callings are essential, and both work together to bring someone to faith in Christ (2Tm 1:8–10).

Esther, "Queen Esther, whatever you ask will be given to you. Whatever you seek, even to half the kingdom, will be done." [3] Queen Esther answered, "If I have found favor with you, Your Majesty, and if the king is pleased, spare my life; this is my request. And spare my people; this is my desire. [4] For my people and I have been sold to destruction, death, and annihilation. If we had merely been sold as male and female slaves, I would have kept silent. Indeed, the trouble wouldn't be worth burdening the king." [5] King Ahasuerus spoke up and asked Queen Esther, "Who is this, and where is the one who would devise such a scheme?"[A] [6] Esther answered, "The adversary and enemy is this evil Haman."

Haman stood terrified before the king and queen. [7] The king arose in anger and went from where they were drinking wine to the palace garden. [8] Haman remained to beg Queen Esther for his life because he realized the king was planning something terrible for him. [8] Just as the king returned from the palace garden to the banquet hall,[C] Haman was falling on the couch where Esther was reclining. The king exclaimed, "Would he actually violate the queen while I am in the house?" As soon as the statement left the king's mouth, they covered Haman's face.

[9] Harbona, one of the king's eunuchs, said, "There is a gallows seventy-five feet[D] tall at Haman's house that he made for Mordecai, who gave the report that saved[E] the king."

The king said, "Hang him on it." [10] They hanged Haman on the gallows he had prepared for Mordecai. Then the king's anger subsided.

Esther Intervenes for the Jews

8 That same day King Ahasuerus awarded Queen Esther the estate of Haman, the enemy of the Jews. Mordecai entered the king's presence because Esther had revealed her relationship to Mordecai. [2] The king removed his signet ring he had recovered from Haman and gave it to Mordecai, and Esther put him in charge of Haman's estate.

[3] Then Esther addressed the king again. She fell at his feet, wept, and begged him to revoke the evil of Haman the Agagite and his plot he had devised against the Jews. [4] The king extended the gold scepter toward Esther, so she got up and stood before the king.

[5] She said, "If it pleases the king and I have found favor with him, if the matter seems right to the king and I am pleasing in his eyes, let a royal edict be written. Let it revoke the documents the scheming Haman son of Hammedatha the Agagite wrote to destroy the Jews who are in all the king's provinces. [6] For how could I bear to see the disaster that would come on my people? How could I bear to see the destruction of my relatives?"

[7] King Ahasuerus said to Esther the queen and to Mordecai the Jew, "Look, I have given Haman's estate to Esther, and he was hanged on the gallows because he attacked[F] the Jews. [8] Write in the king's name whatever pleases you concerning the Jews, and seal it with the royal signet ring. A document written in the king's name and sealed with the royal signet ring cannot be revoked."

[9] On the twenty-third day of the third month — that is, the month Sivan — the royal scribes were summoned. Everything was written exactly as Mordecai commanded for the Jews, to

primary conflict, the threat of extinction of the Jews because of Haman's royal edict; and the secondary conflict, the personal struggle between Mordecai and Haman. The national threat is not resolved until chap. 9. This short chapter concludes the confrontation between Haman and Mordecai with poetic justice.

7:3–4 Esther's request was direct and to the point: **spare** her **life** and spare her **people**. Esther continued with a carefully nuanced assertion: **For my people and I have been sold**. Esther had not told the king she was Jewish, and she did not identify "her people." But as she continued her plea, the king was given a clue: they had been sold out **to destruction, death, and annihilation**, a direct quote from the edict crafted by Haman and authorized by her husband (3:13).

7:5–6 Both Ahasuerus's questions and Esther's reply reflect the intensity of their emotions.

7:7 For the first time in the book of Esther the king had to make crucial decisions without his counselors. Suddenly he was forced to choose between his prime minister and his

wife. But if he deposed Haman for threatening his wife and her people, would not Haman counter by revealing that the king himself had approved of the plan? While the king struggled with his decisions in the garden, Haman stayed back with Esther **to beg for his life**.

7:8 If the king was still undecided about Haman's fate as he returned from the garden, his decision was made certain as he caught Haman fawning over the queen.

8:1–2 All in the **same day** Haman was forced to honor Mordecai (6:4–11), went to the second banquet and was charged with trying to kill the queen and her people (7:1–8), and was hanged. The theme of reversal continues into chap. 8, as Esther, once threatened by Haman, was **awarded** his **estate**, which elevated her uncle Mordecai. Compare v. 2 with 3:10.

8:3–4 While Esther was certainly pleased with the king's honoring of Mordecai, the larger issue of the death sentence upon her people had not been addressed. Rather than being annoyed at Esther's breach of royal protocol by falling at his feet, the king

extended the gold scepter toward Esther, allowing her to state her request.

8:5–6 Esther prefaced her request with an extended version of the normal deferential statement one would make to a king. The first two phrases were standard (1:19; 5:4; 7:3), but she continued in order to make the king's decision seem like a referendum on his love for her. Esther did not point out the injustice of the decree (which the king had approved), but focused on how it would impact her.

8:7–8 The king's response is ambiguous in the Hebrew Bible. While some commentators think he was positive toward her request, others suggest a tone of exasperation or even irritation. Possibly the Greek (LXX) translation suggests this, as the king reminded her about all he had done for her and added, "What do you yet seek?" Nevertheless, the king gave Esther and Mordecai the opportunity to write a new decree that would counter but not rescind his original order.

8:9 Seventy-eight percent of the words in vv. 9–14 are the same as in 3:12–15. Since the Jewish people were speaking Aramaic, as

the satraps, the governors, and the officials of the 127 provinces from India to Cush. The edict was written for each province in its own script, for each ethnic group in its own language, and to the Jews in their own script and language.

¹⁰ Mordecai wrote in King Ahasuerus's name and sealed the edicts with the royal signet ring. He sent the documents by mounted couriers, who rode fast horses bred in the royal stables. ¹¹ The king's edict gave the Jews in each and every city the right to assemble and defend themselves, to destroy, kill, and annihilate every ethnic and provincial army hostile to them, including women and children, and to take their possessions as spoils of war. ¹² This would take place on a single day throughout all the provinces of King Ahasuerus, on the thirteenth day of the twelfth month, the month Adar. ¹³ A copy of the text, issued as law throughout every province, was distributed to all the peoples so the Jews could be ready to avenge themselves against their enemies on that day. ¹⁴ The couriers rode out in haste on their royal horses at the king's urgent command. The law was also issued in the fortress of Susa.

¹⁵ Mordecai went from the king's presence clothed in royal blue and white, with a great gold crown and a purple robe of fine linen. The city of Susa shouted and rejoiced, ¹⁶ and the Jews celebrated^A with gladness, joy, and honor. ¹⁷ In every province and every city where the king's command and edict reached, gladness and joy took place among the Jews. There was a celebration and a holiday.^B And many of the ethnic groups of the land professed themselves to be Jews because fear of the Jews had overcome them.

Victories of the Jews

9 The king's command and law went into effect on the thirteenth day of the twelfth month, the month Adar. On the day when the Jews' enemies had hoped to overpower them, just the opposite happened. The Jews overpowered those who hated them. ² In each of King Ahasuerus's provinces the Jews assembled in their cities to attack those who intended to harm them.^C Not a single person could withstand them; fear of them fell on every nationality.

³ All the officials of the provinces, the satraps, the governors, and the royal civil administrators^D aided the Jews because they feared Mordecai. ⁴ For Mordecai exercised great power in the palace, and his fame spread throughout the provinces as he became more and more powerful.

⁵ The Jews put all their enemies to the sword, killing and destroying them. They did what they pleased to those who hated them. ⁶ In the fortress of Susa the Jews killed and destroyed five hundred men, ⁷ including Parshandatha, Dalphon, Aspatha, ⁸ Poratha, Adalia, Aridatha, ⁹ Parmashta, Arisai, Aridai, and Vaizatha. ¹⁰ They killed these ten sons of Haman son of Hammedatha, the enemy of the Jews. However, they did not seize^E any plunder.

¹¹ On that day the number of people killed in the fortress of Susa was reported to the king. ¹² The king said to Queen Esther, "In the fortress of Susa the Jews have killed and destroyed five hundred men, including Haman's ten sons. What have they done in the rest of the royal provinces? Whatever you ask will be given to you. Whatever you seek will also be done." ¹³ Esther answered, "If it pleases the king, may the Jews who are in Susa also have tomorrow to carry out today's law, and may the bodies of Haman's ten sons be hung on the gallows." ¹⁴ The king gave the orders for this to be done, so a law was announced in Susa, and they hung the bodies of Haman's ten sons. ¹⁵ The Jews in Susa assembled again on the fourteenth day of the month of Adar and killed

---

^A8:16 Lit *had light*   ^B8:17 Lit *good day*   ^C9:2 Lit *cities to send out a hand against the seekers of their evil*   ^D9:3 Lit *and those who do the king's work*; Est 3:9   ^E9:10 Lit *not put their hands on*, also in vv. 15,16

---

were many in the Persian Empire, the counter-edict that was written **in their own script** must have been written in Hebrew.
8:10 The **edicts** were sealed with the **royal signet ring**, once worn by Haman in order to destroy the Jews, but now worn by Mordecai to save the Jews.
8:11–12 Just as Haman's edict decreed the destruction of the Jews on the thirteenth of Adar (3:12), the Jews now had the legal right to defend themselves that same day.
8:13–14 These verses are a repeat of 3:14–15, showing that this decree reversed the previous one.
8:15–17 Mordecai had once torn his clothes and gone around in "sackcloth and ashes" (4:1); now he wore the **royal blue and white**. Once the city of Susa was "in confusion" (3:15); now the people **shouted and rejoiced**. The Jews had once "fasted, wept, and lamented, and . . . lay in sackcloth and ashes" (4:3); now they **celebrated with**

gladness, joy, and honor. While the Jews had once been in fear of the **ethnic groups** among whom they lived, now some of the ethnic groups were in **fear of the Jews**. The phrase **professed themselves to be Jews** is a single word in Hebrew. Some understand the verb to mean "to become a Jew"—to convert to Judaism; this interpretation is supported by the Greek text (LXX). However, it is more likely that the term means that the people identified themselves with the Jewish people; this meaning may be supported by the Latin Vulgate.
9:2–5 These verses explain how the Jews **overpowered** those who hated them.
9:6–10 Haman's anti-Semitism, and the resentment of those who lost positions of influence when Mordecai replaced Haman, may explain why the Jews in the fortress of **Susa** had to kill **five hundred men**. Haman had taken pride in his **ten sons** (5:11); now they shared his fate.

9:11–15 The **king** seemed unconcerned about the death of **five hundred** of his subjects. After asking for a casualty report from the rest of the kingdom, he offered Esther any additional help she needed (v. 12). Apparently the struggle within the royal fortress was not finished because Esther requested an additional day for the Jews to battle their enemies (v. 13). Her request to hang **the bodies of Haman's ten sons** seems vindictive, but this was a common practice in the Persian period, especially for those who were convicted of insurrection (see Herodotus, *Hist.* 3:125). Moreover, the display of Haman's sons on the gallows would serve as a powerful deterrent to any who might contemplate further attacks against the Jewish people. Again, as in vv. 10 and 16, the text emphasizes that the Jews were not out to pillage and enrich themselves but only sought to defend their lives.

three hundred men in Susa, but they did not seize any plunder.

¹⁶ The rest of the Jews in the royal provinces assembled, defended themselves, and gained relief from their enemies. They killed seventy-five thousandᴬ of those who hated them, but they did not seize any plunder. ¹⁷ They fought on the thirteenth day of the month of Adar and rested on the fourteenth, and it became a day of feasting and rejoicing.

¹⁸ But the Jews in Susa had assembled on the thirteenth and the fourteenth days of the month. They rested on the fifteenth day of the month, and it became a day of feasting and rejoicing. ¹⁹ This explains why the rural Jews who live in villages observe the fourteenth day of the month of Adar as a time of rejoicing and feasting. It is a holiday when they send gifts to one another.

²⁰ Mordecai recorded these events and sent letters to all the Jews in all of King Ahasuerus's provinces, both near and far. ²¹ He ordered them to celebrate the fourteenth and fifteenth days of the month of Adar every year ²² because during those days the Jews gained relief from their enemies. That was the month when their sorrow was turned into rejoicing and their mourning into a holiday. They were to be days of feasting, rejoicing, and of sending gifts to one another and to the poor.

²³ So the Jews agreed to continue the practice they had begun, as Mordecai had written them to do. ²⁴ For Haman son of Hammedatha the Agagite, the enemy of all the Jews, had plotted against the Jews to destroy them. He cast the *pur*—that is, the lot—to crush and destroy them. ²⁵ But when the matter was brought before the king, he commanded by letter that the evil plan Haman had devised against the Jews return on his own head and that he should be hanged with his sons on the gallows. ²⁶ For this reason these days are called Purim, from the word *pur*. Because of all

the instructions in this letter as well as what they had witnessed and what had happened to them, ²⁷ the Jews bound themselves, their descendants, and all who joined with them to a commitment that they would not fail to celebrate these two days each and every year according to the written instructions and according to the time appointed. ²⁸ These days are remembered and celebrated by every generation, family, province, and city, so that these days of Purim will not lose their significance in Jewish lifeᴮ and their memory will not fade from their descendants.

²⁹ Queen Esther, daughter of Abihail, along with Mordecai the Jew, wrote this second letter with full authority to confirm the letter about Purim. ³⁰ He sent letters with assurances of peace and securityᶜ to all the Jews who were in the 127 provinces of the kingdom of Ahasuerus, ³¹ in order to confirm these days of Purim at their proper time just as Mordecai the Jew and Esther the queen had established them and just as they had committed themselves and their descendants to the practices of fasting and lamentation. ³² So Esther's command confirmed these customs of Purim, which were then written into the record.

Mordecai's Fame

10 King Ahasuerus imposed a tax throughout the land even to the farthest shores.ᴰ ² All of his powerful and magnificent accomplishments and the detailed account of Mordecai's great rank with which the king had honored him, have they not been written in the Book of the Historical Events of the Kings of Media and Persia? ³ Mordecai the Jew was second only to King Ahasuerus. He was famous among the Jews and highly esteemed by many of his relatives. He continued to pursue prosperity for his people and to speak for the well-being of all his descendants.

ᴬ9:16 Some LXX mss read *10,107*; other LXX mss read *15,000*   ᴮ9:28 LXX reads *will be celebrated into all times*   ᶜ9:30 Or *of peace and faithfulness*   ᴰ10:1 Or *imposed forced labor on the land and the coasts of the sea*

9:16–17 The death of **seventy-five thousand of those who hated them** seems unusually high, but the text itself is not certain. The Greek text (LXX) lists the number killed as fifteen thousand, while the Alpha Text (Gk) has 10,107. The **fourteenth** day of Adar was not a day of fighting for the Jews in the provinces; instead, they **rested** and proclaimed a holiday.
9:18–19 A **holiday** is literally "a good day."
9:20–22 Mordecai's letter appears to be commanding a two-day celebration for all Jews, an order that seems to conflict with vv. 16–18,31, as well as later Jewish practice.

However, he may have intended whatever day was appropriate for their location—the **fourteenth** in a walled city and the **fifteenth** in an open village—an interpretation probably supported by v. 27.
9:23–28 The days of **Purim** continue to be celebrated, with the first day a day of fasting, and the second a day of feasting and celebrating. Note the book begins with the Persians celebrating and ends with the Jews celebrating.
9:29–32 The meaning of v. 29 is uncertain. The sense is that both Esther and Mordecai confirmed the **authority** of the first letter

(vv. 20–22), as well as placed their authority on the **second letter** (vv. 29–32). That Esther's command was **written into the record** means it became a permanent, official requirement for the Jewish people.
10:1–3 The mention of Ahasuerus imposing **a tax throughout the land** seems out of place. Some interpreters suggest this may be another example of reversal, as the tax relief given to the empire when Ahasuerus married Esther (2:18) was now made up for with the new tax. More likely Mordecai the Jew helped a Gentile king bring prosperity to the crown.

Kings of the Exile

	KING	SIGNIFICANCE	PROCLAMATIONS AND DECREES
BABYLON	**Nebuchadnezzar** *2 Kings 24–25; Daniel 1–4*	The Lord's servant to bring judgment against the people of Judah for their sin *(Jr 25:9)*	• Decree for the execution of all his wise men *(Dn 2:13)* • Proclaimed God is God of gods and Lord of kings and a revealer of mysteries *(Dn 2:47)* • Decree for leaders to worship the king's statue or die in the furnace *(Dn 3:10–11)* • Praised the God of Shadrach, Meshach, and Abednego and decreed honor for him; no other god able to rescue like this *(Dn 3:28–29)* • Praised the Most High God, whose works are true and ways are just and proclaimed his wonders to all the earth *(Dn 4:34–35)*
	Belshazzar *Daniel 5*	The last king of Babylon by the judgment of God *(Dn 5:25–31)*	• Issued a proclamation that Daniel was third ruler in the kingdom *(Dn 5:29)*
MEDO-PERSIA	**Darius the Mede/Cyrus the Persian** *2 Chronicles 36; Ezra 1–4; Daniel 6*	The Lord's shepherd to return the people from exile and rebuild the temple *(Is 44:24–45:7)*	• Decree for the exiles of Judah to return to Jerusalem and rebuild the temple *(Ezr 1:2–4)* • Irrevocable decree that no one petition any god or man except the king for thirty days *(Dn 6:6–9)* • Decree for everyone in the kingdom to tremble in fear before the living God of Daniel, who rescued him from the lions *(Dn 6:26–27)*
	Darius *Ezra 5–6*	The Lord's decree for rebuilding the temple fulfilled through the decree of Darius *(Ezr 6:14)*	• Decree affirming and supporting the rebuilding of the temple of God in Jerusalem *(Ezr 6)*
	Ahasuerus/ Xerxes *Esther*	Made Esther his queen, a position ordained "for such a time as this" *(Est 2:17; 4:14)*	• Irrevocable decree drafted by Haman for the destruction of the Jews *(Est 3:7–15)* • Irrevocable decree drafted by Mordecai for the defense of the Jews *(Est 8:8–14)*
	Artaxerxes *Ezra 4; 7–10; Nehemiah*	The Lord put it into the king's mind to glorify the house of the Lord in Jerusalem *(Ezr 7:27)*	• Decree to stop the rebuilding of Jerusalem until a further decree given *(Ezr 4:17–23)* • Decree permitting Ezra and others to return to Jerusalem and reinstitute the sacrifices and the law of God *(Ezr 7:11–26)* • Permission granted to Nehemiah to go to Jerusalem and rebuild it *(Neh 2:1–8)*

Introduction to the Poetic and Wisdom Literature

by Duane A. Garrett

The Bible is not a manual of religious teachings. It is the Word of God as it has come to us through the experiences of the people of God. It expresses all the emotions of the life of faith, and it deals with many areas of experience that might seem mundane and unspiritual.

This is nowhere more true than in its Poetic and Wisdom literature. The Psalms express every emotion the believer encounters in life—praise and love for God, anger at those who practice violence and deceit, grief and confusion, and appreciation for God's truth. Proverbs not only examines moral issues, but it also helps us deal with the ordinary matters of life, such as indebtedness and work habits. Song of Songs celebrates the joy of love between man and woman. Job and Ecclesiastes make us face our most profound questions and thereby bring us to a more genuine faith in God. In sum, all these books deal with real life.

Traditionally, we speak of Psalms and Song of Songs as being the books of biblical poetry and Job, Proverbs, and Ecclesiastes as books of biblical wisdom. These five books will be the focus of this section. Other Old Testament books, however, share many of the features of poetic and wisdom books. Lamentations is essentially a collection of psalms of lament. Psalms are also found in the prophets (for example, Jnh 2; Hab 3). Ruth, Esther, and Daniel have much more in common with Wisdom literature than the casual reader might realize. Even the New Testament has a few psalms (Lk 1:46–55, 68–79) and proverbs (Ac 20:35; 1Co 15:33).

The five books of Job, Psalms, Proverbs, Ecclesiastes, and Song of Songs still give us the best examples of how we should read biblical hymns, songs, proverbs, and reflections. This in turn allows us to see how wisdom and poetry have affected the rest of the Bible.

Literary Devices of Hebrew Poetry and Wisdom

What gave rise to the wide variety of songs, proverbs, and theological reflections we see in this literature? The Old Testament was not written in a cultural or literary vacuum. Many of the motifs and features of Egyptian, Canaanite, and Mesopotamian literature are found in the OT, especially in the poetic and wisdom passages. Some of the most common are the following.

Parallelism is a device in which one line of poetry is followed by a second that in some way reiterates or reinforces the first. Several types of parallelism are found:

- In *synonymous parallelism* the second line says the same thing in the same word order as the first line; only the vocabulary differs. For example: "A false witness will not go unpunished, / and one who utters lies will not escape" (Pr 19:5).
- In *antithetic parallelism* the second line often reinforces the first by stating the same thought from a negative perspective. For example, "A gentle answer turns away anger, / but a harsh word stirs up wrath" (Pr 15:1).
- With *synthetic parallelism* the second line is not actually parallel to the first, but it reinforces the idea expressed by adding a reason or explanation. For example: "Start a youth out on his way; / even when he grows old he will not depart from it" (Pr 22:6); "Stay away from a foolish person; / you will gain no knowledge from his speech" (Pr 14:7).

In *chiasm* the second line mirrors and thus reinforces the first by reversing the sequence of words or phrases. For example, Proverbs 2:4 in the Hebrew word order reads, "If you look for it [A] as for silver [B] and as for hidden treasure [B'] search for it [A']" (author's translation). The word order of the second line [B'-A'] is the reverse of the first [A-B].

Parallelism and chiasm also occur on a much larger scale. Entire chapters or even entire books can be constructed in parallel or chiastic fashion, in which whole blocks of text parallel one another. In some chiasms there is a central element, X, so it takes the following form: A B X B' A', with X as the key idea or assertion in such a structure.

Other literary patterns are also found:

In an *acrostic poem* each line or section begins with a successive letter of the Hebrew alphabet; the first begins with *aleph* (A), the second with *beth* (B), and so forth. The twenty-two stanzas of Ps 119, the Bible's largest acrostic, have eight verses for each consecutive Hebrew letter.

Rhetorical Devices are also found. The language of biblical poetry and wisdom is meant to make it entertaining and easy to remember. The Hebrew text contains rhyme, alliteration (repetition of initial sounds), and even puns. Simile, a comparison using *like* or *as,* also occurs frequently (Ps 131:2; Pr 25:25). One can also find sarcastic humor (Pr 11:22; 19:24) as well as paradox, a statement contrary to common sense that is nevertheless true (Pr 25:15).

In a society in which multiple copies of a literary document would come at a premium, memorization was the medium in which the document was "published." Most of the literary devices of Hebrew poetry and wisdom served well the memorization of and careful reflection on sacred content.

Varieties of Hebrew Wisdom Literature

In the Bible, "wisdom" broadly falls into three categories. First, there is wisdom in the sense of skills and capabilities. Examples include skill in working with fabric or with metals and jewels (Ex 28:3; 31:1–5; 35:26), in waging war (Is 10:13), and in seamanship (Ps 107:23–27). These texts all describe skills as "wisdom," although this is not always evident in English translation. Wisdom literature says little about this sense of "wisdom," although it does affirm that such skills are valuable (Pr 22:29).

Second, there is wisdom as "prudence," the pursuit of a good and wholesome life. This is the focus of Proverbs, and it arises from the fact that God created us. This includes both moral behavior and the development of skills for interacting within society. Prudence is readily available to all who will receive it. Lady Wisdom stands in the streets, shouting at the top of her lungs, trying to get people to turn to her and embrace her teaching (Pr 1:20–22; 8:1–5).

Third, there is a wisdom that belongs to God alone. It is his hidden counsel, whereby he directs human affairs and achieves his purposes in ways that may seem radically counterintuitive. This wisdom is not accessible to humans. People can come to know it only when God chooses to reveal it. Job 28 describes this wisdom. It is hidden from all, and no amount of effort spent digging into creation can unearth it. In the book of Job, the hero and his three friends try to make sense of what seems inscrutable, that a righteous man should suffer calamitous and apparently final ruin. But Job and the three operate only in the second category of wisdom and have no understanding of God's hidden purposes. This highest type of wisdom is also the focus of 1 Corinthians 1:20–25. Christ crucified, the wisdom of God, is to the human mind incomprehensible; it appears to be folly.

We can succinctly summarize the three books of Wisdom literature as follows. Proverbs teaches the basic principles of wisdom. It addresses the young man on the brink of making decisions that will follow him all his life. It focuses on the second type of wisdom described above. It is "Wisdom 101," the basic rules that everyone should know. It describes unchanging principles for living a wholesome and honorable life, but it does not delve into the complex problems that challenge such principles.

By contrast, Job and Ecclesiastes do address such complex problems. Job contemplates the uneven distribution of suffering and success in the world. How is it, if the basic principles of Proverbs are true, that we see so many examples of immoral people prospering, while others who are better people suffer miserable lives? The book of Job wrestles with this by considering the case of a man whom God afflicted not because of his sin but because of his righteousness.

Ecclesiastes reflects on the brevity and apparent insignificance of human life. Against the certainty of death and the passing of time, it considers all the standard human achievements—wisdom, wealth, and power—to be meaningless.

Both Job and Ecclesiastes ultimately look to the third type of wisdom. Neither book tells us explicitly what God's hidden purpose is, but both assert that even if we remain in the dark about what God is doing, we can still show ourselves wise by fearing him and turning from evil (Jb 28:28; Ec 12:13).

◄ Introduction to
Job

Circumstances of Writing

The author of Job is unknown, but he was a learned man whose knowledge embraced the heavens (Jb 22:12; 38:32–33) and earth (26:7–8; 28:9–11; 37:11,16). His knowledge touched on foreign lands (28:16,19), various products (6:19), and human professions (7:6; 9:26; 18:8–10; 28:1–11). He was familiar with plants (14:7–9) and animals (4:10–11; 38:39–39:30; 40:15–41:34). He was a wise man, familiar with traditional wisdom (6:5–6; 17:5; 28:12,28), but was above all a man of spiritual sensitivity (1:1,5,8; 2:3; 14:14–15; 16:11–21; 19:23–27; 23:10; 34:26–28; 40:1–5; 42:1–6). He was doubtless an Israelite as confirmed by his frequent use of God's covenant name (Yahweh, usually rendered as "the Lord").

The story of Job is set in the patriarchal period. In that era, wealth consisted of the possession of cattle and servants. Like other Old Testament patriarchal family heads, Job performed priestly duties, including offering sacrifices for his family. Like the patriarchs, Job lived to be more than a hundred years old. Geographically, the action took place in the northern Arabian Peninsula, in the land of Uz (1:1), often associated with Edom. Job's three friends also had Edomite or southern associations, as did the young Elihu.

Although Job is set in the patriarchal period, its date of writing is unknown. Jewish tradition places the authorship of Job in the time of Moses.

Contribution to the Bible

The book of Job teaches that suffering comes to everyone, the righteous and unrighteous alike. God does not always keep the righteous from danger or suffering. Ultimately God controls all of life's situations, including limiting the power of Satan. God's comfort and strength are always available to the trusting soul.

Although the book of Job does take note of the problem of suffering, it focuses more on the nature of human conduct before a sovereign and holy God. In harmony with the rest of Scripture, the book teaches that even a consistent practice of religion is insufficient without a genuine heart relationship with God (Dt 6:4–6; Ps 86:11–12; Mt 22:37). The answer to life's problems and goals lies in a proper reverence for him who is perfect in all his being and actions. Man needs not just to confess God but to surrender everything to him. By letting him truly be God in every area of life, a person will find him sufficient.

Structure

The writer was a skilled storyteller, artistically characterizing the distinctions between the protagonist (Job), antagonist (Satan), and literary foils (the three friends and Elihu). The characterization demonstrates that God himself is the ultimate protagonist (or "hero") of the story. Satan was as much challenging God as Job's piety. Although Job's three "comforters" applied traditional wisdom to Job's situation, each did it in a different way. Eliphaz, the rationalist, reasoned with Job (15:17–18); Bildad, the apologist, sought to defend God (25:1–6); and Zophar acted much like a prosecutor (11:1–6). The youthful Elihu served as a mediating influence, to prepare for the divine speeches that followed (33:23–26). The writer constructed a well-developed plot built around dramatic dialogue. The fact that he related the account of Job's test in story form does not mean that Job was not a real person who underwent a real test.

Outline

I. Prologue: The Setting of the Testing of Job (1:1–2:13)
II. Development: Examining Job's Condition (3:1–27:23)
III. Denouement: Explaining Job's Condition (28:1–37:24)
IV. Resolution: Job's Condition and God's Greatness (38:1–42:6)
V. The Scene after the Test (42:7–17)

Key verse in Job

37:14 Listen to this, Job.
Stop and consider God's wonders.

1900–1850 BC

Potter's wheel introduced to Crete **1900**
Egyptian town of El Lahun gives evidence of
  town planning with streets at right angles **1900**
Mesopotamian mathematicians discover
  what later came to be called the
  "Pythagorean theorem." **1900**
Multiplication tables appear in
  Mesopotamia. **1900**
Khnumhotep II, an architect of Pharaoh
  Amenemhet II, develops encryption. **1900**

1850–1100 BC

The Admonition of Ipuwer, Egyptian
  parallel to Job **1850–1600**
MOSES **1826–1406**
Ludlul Bel Nemeqi, Tabu–utul–Bel,
  Babylonian parallel to Job **1700**
JOSHUA **1490?–1380?**
Epic of Keret, Canaanite, extant copy
  1360; Original date unknown
I Will Praise the Lord of Wisdom,
  Mesopotamian **1290**
The Babylonian Theodicy, Mesopotamian **1100**

Job and His Family

1 There was a man in the country of Uz named Job. He was a man of complete integrity, who feared God and turned away from evil. ² He had seven sons and three daughters. ³ His estate included seven thousand sheep and goats, three thousand camels, five hundred yoke of oxen, five hundred female donkeys, and a very large number of servants. Job was the greatest man among all the people of the east.

⁴ His sons used to take turns having banquets at their homes. They would send an invitation to their three sisters to eat and drink with them. ⁵ Whenever a round of banqueting was over, Job would send for his children and purify them, rising early in the morning to offer burnt offerings forᴬ all of them. For Job thought, "Perhaps my children have sinned, having cursed God in their hearts." This was Job's regular practice.

Satan's First Test of Job

⁶ One day the sons of God came to present themselves before the LORD, and Satanᴮ also came with them. ⁷ The LORD asked Satan, "Where have you come from?"

"From roaming through the earth," Satan answered him, "and walking around on it."

⁸ Then the LORD said to Satan, "Have you considered my servant Job? No one else on earth is like him, a man of perfect integrity, who fears God and turns away from evil."

⁹ Satan answered the LORD, "Does Job fear God for nothing? ¹⁰ Haven't you placed a hedge around him, his household, and everything he owns? You have blessed the work of his hands, and his possessions have increased in the land. ¹¹ But stretch out your hand and strike everything he owns, and he will surely curse you to your face."

¹² "Very well," the LORD told Satan, "everything he owns is in your power. However, do not lay a hand on Job himself." So Satan left the LORD's presence.

¹³ One day when Job's sons and daughters were eating and drinking wine in their oldest brother's house, ¹⁴ a messenger came to Job and reported, "While the oxen were plowing and the donkeys grazing nearby, ¹⁵ the

---

ᴬ1:5 Lit for the number of   ᴮ1:6 Or the adversary

1:1 The Hebrew form of Job's name means "Where Is the (Heavenly) Father." The only other use of the name outside this book is in Ezk 14:14,20. **Uz** could name a place east of the Jordan River anywhere from Aram to Edom (Gn 10:22–23; Lm 4:21). Job had **complete integrity** (lit he was "blameless and upright") and walked wisely before the Lord (28:28). This indicates that Job had a consistent spiritual life, not that he was sinless. **1:2–3** Job's impressive family, servants, livestock, and material wealth made him the **greatest man** in **the east**, where "east" could designate any place from Damascus to Arabia and as far east as Persia. **1:4–5** To ensure his family's spiritual purity Job regularly acted as priest. The word **cursed** renders the Hebrew "blessed" (used as a euphemism in this case). Job's wife later used the same word in the same way (2:9). **1:6** The heavenly setting indicates that the **sons of God** are angels (2:1; cp. Pss 29:1; 103:20). **Satan** (the Accuser, cp. Zch 3:1–2) also came to the heavenly council. He always opposes the work of the Lord (Mt 16:23; Rv 12:9) but is limited in his power (Jb 1:12; 2:6). **1:7–8** The Lord's questions suggest that **Satan** came to the meeting uninvited but do not indicate that God was ignorant of Satan's activities. **1:13–15** The **Sabeans** mentioned here were apparently nomads from northern Arabia, not the later wealthy kingdom of south Arabia whose renowned queen Sheba visited King Solomon (1Kg 10:1–13) and whose

---

Character profile:
Job

I f everything good in your life were suddenly taken away, what would you do? Job was a righteous man—someone so above reproach that God held him up to Satan as a model servant. Satan was unimpressed, claiming that Job's faithfulness was a product of the wealth, family, and excellent health that God had blessed him with. If God were to take away those things, Satan challenged, Job would surely curse God.

God agreed to Satan's challenge. He allowed him to bring tragedy and suffering into Job's life. All of Job's flocks—the primary source of his wealth—were stolen or killed. A desert windstorm collapsed the house of his oldest son, where all of Job's children had been celebrating. None of them survived. Next came the theft of his camels and then painful boils on his body.

Job was in agony, emotionally and physically. Yet he maintained a faithful, humble, and obedient attitude toward God. The general consensus, even among those closest to him, was that Job had done something to incur God's wrath. Job's protests of innocence fell on skeptical ears. Three friends—Eliphaz, Bildad, and Zophar—were stunned by what they saw. Job's suffering had made him almost unrecognizable. For seven days the trio sat in silence with Job.

Job broke the vigil by suggesting that it would be preferable never to have been born than to experience the kind of pain and grief he was enduring. Rather than comforting Job, his three companions leveled accusations at him. Eliphaz quickly pointed out that these sorts of things don't happen to innocent people. He believed that Job's suffering was due to sin and urged his friend to repent.

Bildad and Zophar chimed in, instructing Job to be more blameless in his walk with God. But they didn't stop there. Bildad suggested that Job's children had brought their deaths on themselves. Zophar claimed that Job probably deserved even worse punishment for whatever it was he'd done.

Job countered these accusations, insisting once again that he was innocent before God. At the same time, he struggled mightily with his situation, trying to square his suffering with what he knew about God. In the depths of his despair, he posed some difficult questions about God's justice and humankind's inability to grasp his ways.

Through it all, Job managed to hold on to his relationship with the Lord—at times by his fingernails, but he held on just the same. He committed himself to the pursuit of wisdom by fearing God and avoiding wickedness.

When Satan's period of testing was over, God restored Job and blessed him with more sons and daughters. Job walked the path through the valley of darkness and emerged with God's blessing on the other side.

Everyone faces seasons of loss, grief, and suffering. Instead of asking, "Why is this happening to me?" a better response is to ask, "How will I respond?" If you stay close to God when things get dark, you will find opportunities to grow and perhaps even thrive in the midst of your trials. You will also set a powerful example of faith in action for others.

Sabeans swooped down and took them away. They struck down the servants with the sword, and I alone have escaped to tell you!"

¹⁶ He was still speaking when another messenger came and reported, "God's fire fell from heaven. It burned the sheep and the servants and devoured them, and I alone have escaped to tell you!"

¹⁷ That messenger was still speaking when yet another came and reported, "The Chaldeans formed three bands, made a raid on the camels, and took them away. They struck down the servants with the sword, and I alone have escaped to tell you!"

¹⁸ He was still speaking when another messenger came and reported, "Your sons and daughters were eating and drinking wine in their oldest brother's house. ¹⁹ Suddenly a powerful wind swept in from the desert and struck the four corners of the house. It collapsed on the young people so that they died, and I alone have escaped to tell you!"

²⁰ Then Job stood up, tore his robe, and shaved his head. He fell to the ground and worshiped, ²¹ saying:

> Naked I came from my mother's womb,
> and naked I will leave this life.ᴬ
> The Lᴏʀᴅ gives, and the Lᴏʀᴅ
>   takes away.
> Blessed be the name of the Lᴏʀᴅ.

²² Throughout all this Job did not sin or blame God for anything.ᴮ

Satan's Second Test of Job

2 One day the sons of God came again to present themselves before the Lᴏʀᴅ, and Satan also came with them to present himself before the Lᴏʀᴅ. ² The Lᴏʀᴅ asked Satan, "Where have you come from?"

"From roaming through the earth," Satan answered him, "and walking around on it."

³ Then the Lᴏʀᴅ said to Satan, "Have you considered my servant Job? No one else on earth is like him, a man of perfect integrity, who fears God and turns away from evil. He

still retains his integrity, even though you incited me against him, to destroy him for no good reason."

⁴ "Skin for skin!" Satan answered the Lᴏʀᴅ. "A man will give up everything he owns in exchange for his life. ⁵ But stretch out your hand and strike his flesh and bones, and he will surely curse you to your face."

⁶ "Very well," the Lᴏʀᴅ told Satan, "he is in your power; only spare his life." ⁷ So Satan left the Lᴏʀᴅ's presence and infected Job with terrible boils from the soles of his feet to the top of his head. ⁸ Then Job took a piece of broken pottery to scrape himself while he sat among the ashes.

⁹ His wife said to him, "Are you still holding on to your integrity? Curse God and die!"

¹⁰ "You speak as a foolish woman speaks," he told her. "Should we accept only good from God and not adversity?" Throughout all this Job did not sin in what he said.ᶜ

Job's Three Friends

¹¹ Now when Job's three friends — Eliphaz the Temanite, Bildad the Shuhite, and Zophar the Naamathite — heard about all this adversity that had happened to him, each of them came from his home. They met together to go and sympathize with him and comfort him. ¹² When they looked from a distance, they could barely recognize him. They wept aloud, and each man tore his robe and threw dust into the air and on his head. ¹³ Then they sat on the ground with him seven days and nights, but no one spoke a word to him because they saw that his suffering was very intense.

Job's Opening Speech

3 After this, Job began to speak and cursed the day he was born. ² He said:

³   May the day I was born perish,
     and the night that said,
     "A boy is conceived."
⁴   If only that day had turned to darkness!
     May God above not care about it,
     or light shine on it.

ᴬ1:21 Lit will return there; Ps 139:13,15   ᴮ1:22 Lit or ascribe blame to God   ᶜ2:10 Lit sin with his lips

---

people Isaiah prophesied would submit to Israel (Is 45:14).
1:16 God's fire (probably lightning) is normally a divine weapon (2Kg 1:10–14). Ironically, Satan was given permission to use it against God's servants.
1:17 Like the Sabeans, the **Chaldeans** were nomadic raiders. King Nebuchadnezzar II of Babylon was a Chaldean (2Kg 24:1; Dn 1:1).
1:18–19 After the Sabean raid (v. 15), a force of nature completed the attack against Job's family.
1:20 Tearing one's garments (Gn 37:34; 2Ch 34:19) and shaving one's **head** (Am 5:10) were symbolic acts of grief.
1:21–22 Job recognized that ultimately **the Lᴏʀᴅ** determines all things, so he submitted himself to God's sovereign will. Rather than

cursing God as Satan had predicted, Job **blessed** his **name** and did not **blame** God.
2:4–5 Satan's second test suggested that Job was callous and concerned only for himself. The proverbial saying **skin for skin** could indicate Job's willingness to give up all he had, including his family, in order to save his own life or that if the Lord allowed Satan to afflict him bodily, Job would in turn deny the Lord.
2:8 In scraping himself with **broken pottery**, Job may have been trying to get rid of the matter that oozed from his sores (see LXX) and thus alleviate the itching. Job's sitting **among the ashes** symbolized his grief and despondency (2Sm 13:19; Est 4:3). Ash heaps were traditionally located at town dumps.

2:9 Job's wife avoided blasphemy by using a Hebrew euphemism, "bless," for her real intent: **curse**.
2:11 Eliphaz came from Teman, a principal city in Edom (Ezk 25:13; Am 1:12–13). **Bildad** ("Son of Hadad" the storm god) probably came from the tribe of Shuah, descended from Abraham through his second wife Keturah (Gn 25:1–2; 1Ch 1:32). **Zophar** may have been from northern Arabia.
2:12–13 Job's three friends responded to his gruesome appearance with actions symbolic of deep mourning. A seven-day period was observed in times of mourning for the dead (Gn 50:10; 1Sm 31:13). With due propriety Job's friends remained silent, waiting for Job to speak first.

5 May darkness and gloom reclaim it,
and a cloud settle over it.
May what darkens the day terrify it.
6 If only darkness had taken
that night away!
May it not appear^A among the days
of the year
or be listed in the calendar.^B
7 Yes, may that night be barren;
may no joyful shout be heard in it.
8 Let those who curse days
condemn it,
those who are ready
to rouse Leviathan.
9 May its morning stars grow dark.
May it wait for daylight but have none;
may it not see the breaking^C of dawn.
10 For that night did not shut
the doors of my mother's womb,
and hide sorrow from my eyes.

11 Why was I not stillborn;
why didn't I die as I came
from the womb?
12 Why did the knees receive me,
and why were there breasts for me
to nurse?
13 Now I would certainly be lying down
in peace;
I would be asleep.
Then I would be at rest
14 with the kings and counselors
of the earth,
who rebuilt ruined cities for themselves,
15 or with princes who had gold,
who filled their houses with silver.
16 Or why was I not hidden
like a miscarried child,
like infants who never see daylight?
17 There the wicked cease to make trouble,
and there the weary find rest.
18 The captives are completely at rest;
they do not hear a taskmaster's voice.
19 Both small and great are there,
and the slave is set free from his master.

20 Why is light given to one burdened
with grief,
and life to those whose existence
is bitter,
21 who wait for death, but it does not come,
and search for it more than
for hidden treasure,
22 who are filled with much joy
and are glad when they reach the grave?
23 Why is life given to a man whose path
is hidden,
whom God has hedged in?
24 I sigh when food is put before me,^D
and my groans pour out like water.
25 For the thing I feared has overtaken me,
and what I dreaded has happened
to me.
26 I cannot relax or be calm;
I have no rest, for turmoil has come.

FIRST SERIES OF SPEECHES
Eliphaz Speaks

4 Then Eliphaz the Temanite replied:
2 Should anyone try to speak with you
when you are exhausted?
Yet who can keep from speaking?
3 Indeed, you have instructed many
and have strengthened weak hands.
4 Your words have steadied the one
who was stumbling
and braced the knees
that were buckling.
5 But now that this has happened to you,
you have become exhausted.
It strikes you, and you are dismayed.
6 Isn't your piety your confidence,
and the integrity of your life^E
your hope?
7 Consider: Who has perished when he
was innocent?
Where have the honest^F
been destroyed?
8 In my experience,
those who plow injustice
and those who sow trouble reap
the same.
9 They perish at a single blast from God
and come to an end by the breath
of his nostrils.
10 The lion may roar and the fierce
lion growl,
but the teeth of young lions are broken.
11 The strong lion dies if it catches no prey,
and the cubs of the lioness are scattered.

^A 3:6 LXX, Syr, Tg, Vg; MT reads rejoice ^B 3:6 Lit or enter the number of months ^C 3:9 Lit the eyelids ^D 3:24 Or My sighing serves as my food ^E 4:6 Lit ways ^F 4:7 Or the upright, or those with integrity

3:8–10 Leviathan is known from ancient Ugaritic mythology as a sea monster, which the god Baal defeated. Leviathan appears in the OT symbolically in connection with those forces that oppose God (26:12–14; Pss 74:12–14; 104:26; Is 27:1). The mythological allusions in Job (5:7; 7:12; 9:13; 18:13; 38:12) do not indicate scriptural endorsement of pagan theology or mythic zoology but serve as literary allusions. The morning stars were Venus and Mercury.

3:11–12 The knees probably refer to those of his mother either in childbirth (Gn 30:3) or in taking up her child for nursing.
3:13–19 Asleep is used frequently as a metaphor for death in the Bible, especially of the righteous (Jn 11:11–15; 1Co 15:20). Job's words should not be pressed to depict a common condition for all souls in the afterlife.
4:1 Since Job had broken the silence (chap. 3), Eliphaz offered his concerned counsel, filled with various forms of traditional wisdom. Although Eliphaz's counsel contained

truthful observations, they failed to address the reason for Job's condition.
4:3–4 Stumbling and knees…buckling relate as much to the psychological aspects of tragedy as to the physical (Ps 109:24; Ezk 21:7; Nah 2:10).
4:6–9 Eliphaz's advice was meant to be an encouragement and a gentle call for Job's self-reflection, yet it could have implied that Job's children deserved what they got.
4:10–11 The lion is at times symbolic of the wicked (Ps 7:2) or those who rely on self rather than God (Ps 34:10).

¹² A word was brought to me in secret;
my ears caught a whisper of it.
¹³ Among unsettling thoughts
from visions in the night,
when deep sleep comes over men,
¹⁴ fear and trembling came over me
and made all my bones shake.
¹⁵ I felt a draft^A on my face,
and the hair on my body stood up.
¹⁶ A figure stood there,
but I could not recognize
its appearance;
a form loomed before my eyes.
I heard a whispering voice:
¹⁷ "Can a mortal be righteous before God?
Can a man be more pure
than his Maker?"
¹⁸ If God puts no trust in his servants
and he charges his angels
with foolishness,^B
¹⁹ how much more those who dwell
in clay houses,
whose foundation is in the dust,
who are crushed like a moth!
²⁰ They are smashed to pieces from dawn
to dusk;
they perish forever
while no one notices.
²¹ Are their tent cords not pulled up?
They die without wisdom.

5 Call out! Will anyone answer you?
Which of the holy ones will you turn to?
² For anger kills a fool,
and jealousy slays the gullible.
³ I have seen a fool taking root,
but I immediately pronounced a curse
on his home.
⁴ His children are far from safety.
They are crushed at the city gate,
with no one to rescue them.
⁵ The hungry consume his harvest,
even taking it out of the thorns.^C
The thirsty^D pant
for his children's wealth.
⁶ For distress does not grow
out of the soil,

and trouble does not sprout
from the ground.
⁷ But humans are born for trouble
as surely as sparks fly upward.
⁸ However, if I were you, I would appeal
to God
and would present my case to him.
⁹ He does great and unsearchable things,
wonders without number.
¹⁰ He gives rain to the earth
and sends water to the fields.
¹¹ He sets the lowly on high,
and mourners are lifted to safety.
¹² He frustrates the schemes of the crafty
so that they^E achieve no success.
¹³ He traps the wise in their craftiness
so that the plans of the deceptive
are quickly brought to an end.
¹⁴ They encounter darkness by day,
and they grope at noon
as if it were night.
¹⁵ He saves the needy
from their sharp words^F
and from the clutches
of the powerful.
¹⁶ So the poor have hope,
and injustice shuts its mouth.
¹⁷ See how happy is the person whom
God corrects;
so do not reject the discipline
of the Almighty.
¹⁸ For he wounds but he also bandages;
he strikes, but his hands also heal.
¹⁹ He will rescue you from six calamities;
no harm will touch you in seven.
²⁰ In famine he will redeem you
from death,
and in battle, from the power
of the sword.
²¹ You will be safe from slander^G
and not fear destruction when it comes.
²² You will laugh at destruction
and hunger
and not fear the land's wild creatures.
²³ For you will have a covenant
with the stones of the field,

---

^A 4:15 Or a spirit   ^B 4:18 Or error; Hb obscure   ^C 5:5 Hb obscure   ^D 5:5 Aq, Sym, Syr, Vg; MT reads snares   ^E 5:12 Lit their hands
^F 5:15 Lit from the sword of their mouth; Ps 55:21; 59:7   ^G 5:21 Lit be hidden from the whip of the tongue

---

4:12–16 Eliphaz seems to have been awakened out of **deep sleep** to receive a supernatural message. Whether this was a theophany (appearance of God) or an angelic visitation (Dn 2:5) is uncertain. Eliphaz thought his experience had provided him with wisdom to understand one of life's mysteries.
4:18–21 Eliphaz's point here was that because people are not sinless before God, they may expect difficulties in this life, even tragedy and death. People need to acquire godly **wisdom** in order to live properly before God.
5:1 Eliphaz told Job not to expect help from **the holy ones**. The need for a mediator is an important theme in Job (9:33; 16:19–20; 19:25).

5:2–7 The Hebrew word for **sparks** (lit "sons of flame" or "sons of Resheph") may contain an allusion to Resheph, the Canaanite god of pestilence and plague, reinforcing the inevitability of natural disasters.
5:9–16 This is a hymn of praise, possibly used in an ancient worship ceremony.
5:17 The rendering here of **the Almighty** (Hb *Shaddai*) represents a derivation from a verbal root known both in Hebrew and Akkadian indicating overpowering force. Other lexicographers suggest a literal meaning: "Destroyer" or "(God of) Mountain."

5:18 Eliphaz suggested that Job was in need of divine discipline, so he should bear his condition happily (Pr 1:2,7; 3:11–12; 23:12). Then God would bless him again with peace, prosperity, and a large family (Jb 5:18–26). For Eliphaz, as for Job, the evidence of personal piety was seen in God's external blessings.
5:19 The parallel use of **six** and **seven** is an example of a Semitic literary device in which a number and the next higher number are used to indicate indefiniteness.
5:20–26 Eliphaz told Job that the man who walked with God would be blessed with long life, security, peace, many descendants, and vigor even in old age.

and the wild animals will be at peace
with you.

²⁴ You will know that your tent is secure,
and nothing will be missing
when you inspect your home.

²⁵ You will also know that your offspring
will be many
and your descendants like the grass
of the earth.

²⁶ You will approach the grave in full vigor,
as a stack of sheaves is gathered
in its season.

²⁷ We have investigated this, and it is true!
Hear it and understand it for yourself.

Job's Reply to Eliphaz

6 Then Job answered:
² If only my grief could be weighed
and my devastation placed with it
on the scales.

³ For then it would outweigh the sand
of the seas!
That is why my words are rash.

⁴ Surely the arrows of the Almighty
have pierced^A me;
my spirit drinks their poison.
God's terrors are arrayed against me.

⁵ Does a wild donkey bray over fresh grass
or an ox low over its fodder?

⁶ Is bland food eaten without salt?
Is there flavor in an egg white?^B

⁷ I refuse to touch them;
they are like contaminated food.

⁸ If only my request would be granted
and God would provide what I hope for:

⁹ that he would decide to crush me,
to unleash his power and cut me off!

¹⁰ It would still bring me comfort,
and I would leap for joy
in unrelenting pain
that I have not denied^c the words
of the Holy One.

¹¹ What strength do I have, that I should
continue to hope?

What is my future, that I should
be patient?

¹² Is my strength that of stone,
or my flesh made of bronze?

¹³ Since I cannot help myself,
the hope for success has been banished
from me.

¹⁴ A despairing man should receive loyalty
from his friends,^D
even if he abandons the fear
of the Almighty.

¹⁵ My brothers are as treacherous
as a wadi,
as seasonal streams that overflow

¹⁶ and become darkened^E because of ice,
and the snow melts into them.

¹⁷ The wadis evaporate in warm weather;
they disappear from their channels
in hot weather.

¹⁸ Caravans turn away from their routes,
go up into the desert, and perish.

¹⁹ The caravans of Tema look
for these streams.
The traveling merchants of Sheba hope
for them.

²⁰ They are ashamed because they
had been confident of finding water.
When they arrive there,
they are disappointed.

²¹ So this is what you have now become
to me.^F
When you see something dreadful,
you are afraid.

²² Have I ever said, "Give me something"
or "Pay a bribe for me
from your wealth"

²³ or "Deliver me from the enemy's hand"
or "Redeem me from the hand
of the ruthless"?

²⁴ Teach me, and I will be silent.
Help me understand what I did wrong.

²⁵ How painful honest words can be!
But what does your rebuke prove?

²⁶ Do you think that you can disprove
my words

---

^A6:4 Lit *Almighty are in*   ^B6:6 Hb obscure   ^C6:10 Lit *hidden*   ^D6:14 Lit *To the despairing his friend loyalty*   ^E6:16 Or *turbid*
^F6:21 Alt Hb tradition reads *So you have now become nothing*

5:27 Eliphaz exhorted Job to apply the tested and **true** principles Eliphaz had just applied to Job's condition. In so doing Job would understand why God was disciplining him and be able to bear it profitably (v. 17).
6:1–3 The **sand of the seas** is often used as a metaphor for vastness (29:18; cp. Jos 11:4; 1Kg 4:20) or something beyond measure (Gn 22:17; Jdg 7:12; 1Kg 4:29; Hs 1:10).
6:4 God is often portrayed as the divine warrior whose **arrows** shatter the enemy (Dt 32:42; Pss 7:12–13; 18:14; Hab 3:11). God's mighty strength brings terror to the objects of his wrath (Ex 23:27; Is 2:10,19; Jr 49:5). Job felt he was the object of God's personal attack.

6:6–7 The rhetorical question in v. 6 implied a negative answer. Rather than tasteful nourishment to Job's grieving soul, Eliphaz's words were like **contaminated food**.
6:8–10 Contrary to Eliphaz's advice, Job put his **hope** not in his piety (4:6–7) or God's disciplinary action (5:17) but in death (3:11–15; 10:21–22), God's final blow. God's granting of Job's wish to be crushed and **cut . . . off** would relieve his suffering and affirm his innocence.
6:14 Job complained about his treatment by his friends. As their suffering friend, he should receive **loyalty** (or lovingkindness) from them (Pr 14:21).

6:15 Wadi is an Arabian term for an intermittent desert stream.
6:16–18 Like a seasonal stream, Job's "brothers" (v.15) were not dependable. When he really needed them, they were no help.
6:19 The oasis of **Tema** served as a trade center in northwestern Arabia.
6:24–26 The Hebrew word behind **what I did wrong** speaks of unintentional sin. If his friends thought Job had erred, they should tell him honestly but gently, not in a **painful** manner. Job's friends had not yet disproven his claim to innocence; they had only dismissed it.

or that a despairing man's words are
  mere wind?
27 No doubt you would cast lots
  for a fatherless child
  and negotiate a price to sell your friend.

28 But now, please look at me;
  I will not lie to your face.
29 Reconsider; don't be unjust.
  Reconsider; my righteousness is still
  the issue.
30 Is there injustice on my tongue
  or can my palate not taste disaster?

7 Isn't each person consigned
  to forced labor on earth?
  Are not his days like those
  of a hired worker?
2 Like a slave he longs for shade;
  like a hired worker he waits for his pay.
3 So I have been made to inherit months
  of futility,
  and troubled nights have been assigned
  to me.
4 When I lie down I think,
  "When will I get up?"
  But the evening drags on endlessly,
  and I toss and turn until dawn.
5 My flesh is clothed with maggots
  and encrusted with dirt.ᴬ
  My skin forms scabsᴮ and then oozes.

6 My days pass more swiftly
  than a weaver's shuttle;
  they come to an end without hope.
7 Remember that my life is but a breath.
  My eye will never again see
  anything good.
8 The eye of anyone who looks on me
  will no longer see me.
  Your eyes will look for me, but I
  will be gone.
9 As a cloud fades away and vanishes,
  so the one who goes down to Sheol
  will never rise again.
10 He will never return to his house;
  his hometown will no longer
  rememberᶜ him.

11 Therefore I will not restrain
  my mouth.
  I will speak in the anguish of my spirit;
  I will complain in the bitterness
  of my soul.
12 Am I the seaᴰ or a sea monster,
  that you keep me under guard?
13 When I say, "My bed will comfort me,
  and my couch will ease my complaint,"
14 then you frighten me with dreams,
  and terrify me with visions,
15 so that I prefer stranglingᴱ —
  death rather than life in this body.ᶠ
16 I give up! I will not live forever.
  Leave me alone, for my days are
  a breath.ᴳ
17 What is a mere human, that you think
  so highly of him
  and pay so much attention to him?
18 You inspect him every morning,
  and put him to the test every moment.
19 Will you ever look away from me,
  or leave me alone long enough
  to swallow?ᴴ
20 If I have sinned, what have I done to you,
  Watcher of humanity?
  Why have you made me your target,
  so that I have become a burden to you?ᴵ
21 Why not forgive my sin
  and pardon my iniquity?
  For soon I will lie down in the grave.
  You will eagerly seek me, but I
  will be gone.

Bildad Speaks

8 Then Bildad the Shuhite replied:
² How long will you go on saying
  these things?
  Your words are a blast of wind.
3 Does God pervert justice?
  Does the Almighty pervert
  what is right?
4 Since your children sinned against him,
  he gave them over to their rebellion.
5 But if you earnestly seek God
  and ask the Almighty for mercy,
6 if you are pure and upright,

ᴬ7:5 Or and dirty scabs ᴮ7:5 Lit skin hardens ᶜ7:10 Lit know ᴰ7:12 Or the sea god ᴱ7:15 Or suffocation ᶠ7:15 Lit than my bones ᴳ7:16 Or are futile ᴴ7:19 Lit swallow my saliva? ᴵ7:20 Alt Hb tradition, LXX; MT, Vg read myself

---

7:1–2 Job complained that God acted as a harsh master toward humans. The term **forced labor** could be used of military service, but here it involves the institution of service that was demanded of a man for a certain period. Hired hands usually worked for a day's **pay** (Dt 24:14–15). To withhold a person's wages was a miscarriage of justice (Lv 19:13).
7:6 A play on words occurs here. The Hebrew word *tiqwah* can mean both "hope" and "thread." Like a weaver running out of thread, Job's life was moving **swiftly** toward its end, leaving him **without hope**.

7:9–10 In the OT **Sheol** is used both for the grave generally (1Kg 2:6; Pss 16:10; 49:15) and for the final state of the wicked specifically (Ps 49:13–14; Is 14:14–15). At times it reflects a commonly held ancient view of a dismal underworld into which all people passed after death.
7:12 In Canaanite mythology the **sea** god (Yam) and the **sea monster** (Tannin) were defeated by Baal. The allusion in v. 12 compares Job to some primordial adversary on which God is keeping watch. Such mythological allusions appear in the OT about God's victory over and control of the forces

of nature in creation (9:13–14; 26:12–13), at the Red Sea (Ps 74:14–15), and the forces of evil at the end of history (Is 27:1).
7:16 Breath can also designate something worthless or futile (Ec 1:2).
8:1–2 Bildad acted like God's "defense attorney." He charged Job with speaking like an empty windbag.
8:3–4 Bildad's rhetorical question (v. 3) expected a negative answer. God is always righteous in his actions (Dt 32:4). Bildad believed Job's sinning **children** got what they deserved.

then he will move even now
on your behalf
and restore the home where
your righteousness dwells.
7 Then, even if your beginnings
were modest,
your final days will be full of prosperity.

8 For ask the previous generation,
and pay attention to what
their ancestors discovered,
9 since we were born only yesterday
and know nothing.
Our days on earth are but a shadow.
10 Will they not teach you and tell you
and speak from their understanding?
11 Does papyrus grow where there is
no marsh?
Do reeds flourish without water?
12 While still uncut shoots,
they would dry up quicker than
any other plant.
13 Such is the destiny^A of all
who forget God;
the hope of the godless will perish.
14 His source of confidence is fragile;^B
what he trusts in is a spider's web.
15 He leans on his web, but it doesn't
stand firm.
He grabs it, but it does not hold up.
16 He is a well-watered plant
in the sunshine;
his shoots spread out over his garden.
17 His roots are intertwined around a pile
of rocks.
He looks for a home among the stones.
18 If he is uprooted^C from his place,
it will deny knowing him, saying,
"I never saw you."
19 Surely this is the joy of his way of life;
yet others will sprout from the dust.
20 Look, God does not reject a person
of integrity,
and he will not support^D evildoers.
21 He will yet fill your mouth with laughter

and your lips with a shout of joy.
22 Your enemies will be clothed
with shame;
the tent of the wicked will no longer
exist.

Job's Reply to Bildad

9 Then Job answered:
2 Yes, I know what you've said is true,
but how can a person be justified
before God?
3 If one wanted to take him to court,
he could not answer God^E once
in a thousand times.
4 God is wise and all-powerful.
Who has opposed him
and come out unharmed?
5 He removes mountains
without their knowledge,
overturning them in his anger.
6 He shakes the earth from its place
so that its pillars tremble.
7 He commands the sun not to shine
and seals off the stars.
8 He alone stretches out the heavens
and treads on the waves of the sea.^F
9 He makes the stars: the Bear,^G Orion,
the Pleiades, and the constellations^H
of the southern sky.
10 He does great and unsearchable things,
wonders without number.
11 If he passed by me, I wouldn't see him;
if he went by, I wouldn't recognize him.
12 If he snatches something,
who can stop him?
Who can ask him, "What are
you doing?"
13 God does not hold back his anger;
Rahab's assistants cringe in fear
beneath him!
14 How then can I answer him
or choose my arguments against him?
15 Even if I were in the right,
I could not answer.

---

^A 8:13 Lit *Such are the ways* ^B 8:14 Or *cut off*; Hb obscure ^C 8:18 Or *destroyed* ^D 8:20 Lit *grasp the hand of* ^E 9:3 Or *court, God would not answer him* ^F 9:8 Or *and walks on the back of the sea god* ^G 9:9 Or *Aldebaran* ^H 9:9 Or *chambers* ^I 9:12 Or *dissuade*

8:5–7 By implication Bildad suggested that Job had sinned, hence his condition. Because God had spared Job's life, there was yet hope for a change in Job's fortunes. **Home** more strictly denotes pasturage and by extension a dwelling place (5:3,24; see Jr 6:2; Zph 2:6).
8:8–10 Bildad appealed to traditional wisdom. Life is as short as a vanishing **shadow** (14:1–2; Pss 102:11; 109:23; 144:4; Ec 6:12).
8:11–13 As **papyrus** dies without water to nourish it, so the godless will **perish**. To succeed, man needs God, the "water of life."
8:14–15 A man who places his hope in anything but God is like a man who leans against a **spider's web**; it will not hold him up.

8:16–19 The godless are like a vine that appears firmly established among the **rocks**. Yet it is easily **uprooted**, leaving no trace.
8:20–22 Bildad summed up his case: If Job was truly righteous, God would sustain him.
9:1–4 A judicial image occurs throughout chap. 9. Job would like to present his case for innocence **before God** in **court** (vv. 3,16,19,32). As a finite plaintiff his arguments were inadequate (vv. 3–4,14–15,20,32) before an omniscient and omnipotent judge (v. 15). Job needed a mediator to arbitrate his case (vv. 33–35).
9:5–10 Job called on a hymn extolling God's sovereignty as Creator. The imagery is metaphorical and is not to be taken as a cosmology.

9:5–6 Mountains are sometimes portrayed as **pillars** for the sky (26:11).
9:8 The **heavens** could be viewed as a great tent stretched out over the earth (Ps 104:2; Is 40:22). The image of God treading on the **waves of the sea** pictures God as controlling the forces of nature (Mc 1:3) much as a conqueror defeats his foes (Is 63:3; Hab 3:8,15).
9:9 Ancients often identified **stars** and **constellations** as gods and goddesses, used them as navigational guides, and noted their changing positions to mark the seasons.
9:13–14 Job felt that if the forces of nature could not withstand God, how could he hope to win his case before him? Rahab suggests an ancient mythological sea monster. The image is that of God subduing and controlling

I could only beg my Judge for mercy.
16 If I summoned him
    and he answered me,
I do not believe he would
    pay attention to what I said.
17 He batters me with a whirlwind
    and multiplies my wounds
    without cause.
18 He doesn't let me catch my breath
    but fills me with bitter experiences.
19 If it is a matter of strength, look, he is
    the powerful one!
If it is a matter of justice, who can
    summon him?ᴬ
20 Even if I were in the right,
    my own mouth would condemn me;
if I were blameless, my mouth would
    declare me guilty.

21 Though I am blameless,
    I no longer care about myself;
I renounce my life.
22 It is all the same. Therefore I say,
    "He destroys both the blameless
    and the wicked."
23 When catastropheᴮ brings
    sudden death,
he mocks the despair of the innocent.
24 The earthᶜ is handed over to the wicked;
he blindfoldsᴰ its judges.
If it isn't he, then who is it?

25 My days fly by faster than a runner;ᴱ
    they flee without seeing any good.
26 They sweep by like boats made
    of papyrus,
like an eagle swooping down on its prey.
27 If I said, "I will forget my complaint,
    change my expression, and smile,"
28 I would still live in terror of all my pains.
    I know you will not acquit me.
29 Since I will be found guilty,
    why should I struggle in vain?
30 If I wash myself with snow,
    and cleanse my hands with lye,
31 then you dip me in a pit of mud,
    and my own clothes despise me!

32 For he is not a man like me, that I can
    answer him,

that we can take each other to court.
33 There is no mediator between us,
    to lay his hand on both of us.
34 Let him take his rod away from me
    so his terror will no longer frighten me.
35 Then I would speak and not fear him.
    But that is not the case; I am on my own.

10 I am disgusted with my life.
    I will give vent to my complaint
and speak in the bitterness of my soul.
2 I will say to God,
    "Do not declare me guilty!
Let me know why you prosecute me.
3 Is it good for you to oppress,
    to reject the work of your hands,
and favorᶠ the plans of the wicked?
4 Do you have eyes of flesh,
    or do you see as a human sees?
5 Are your days like those of a human,
    or your years like those of a man,
6 that you look for my iniquity
    and search for my sin,
7 even though you know that
    I am not wicked
and that there is no one who can rescue
    from your power?

8 "Your hands shaped me
    and formed me.
Will you now turn and destroy me?
9 Please remember that you formed me
    like clay.
Will you now return me to dust?
10 Did you not pour me out like milk
    and curdle me like cheese?
11 You clothed me with skin and flesh,
    and wove me together with bones
    and tendons.
12 You gave me life and faithful love,
    and your care has guarded my life.

13 "Yet you concealed these thoughts
    in your heart;
I know that this was your hidden plan:ᴳ
14 if I sin, you would notice,ᴴ
    and would not acquit me of my iniquity.
15 If I am wicked, woe to me!
    And even if I am righteous, I cannot
    lift up my head.

ᴬ9:19 LXX; MT reads me ᴮ9:23 Or whip; Hb obscure ᶜ9:24 Or land ᴰ9:24 Lit covers the faces of ᴱ9:25 = a royal messenger ᶠ10:3 Lit shine on ᴳ10:13 Lit was with you ᴴ10:14 Lit notice me

---

the forces of nature (26:12–13; Ps 89:10; Is 51:9–10), a reminder that the Lord alone is truly God and sovereign over all forces that seem to oppose him.
9:21–24 Job felt Eliphaz (5:17–26) and Bildad (8:20) were wrong: God did not distinguish between **the blameless and the wicked**. Since there is only one sovereign God, everything must ultimately trace back to him.
9:30–31 Job suggested Bildad's views about repentance and self-purification were

mistaken; Job felt these acts would be useless. Using **lye** rather than oil for cleansing indicates an extreme measure.
9:32–35 Job sensed the need for an arbitrator to adjudicate between himself and God (16:19–20; 19:25). Job had no angel or Mesopotamian personal god to aid him.
10:1–3 Job's rhetorical question implied a negative response.
10:4–7 Job's rhetorical question amounted to a charge that God was acting from a

human perspective in his investigation of Job. God knew that Job was **not wicked**. Nevertheless, Job viewed God as bringing charges against him just because he could.
10:8–12 The image of **dust** is reminiscent of man's creation in the cycle of life (Gn 2:7; 3:19; Ps 104:14). Like a divine **cheese** maker or weaver, God created Job and nurtured him. Why did he now seek to **destroy** him?

I am filled with shame
and have drunk deeply of^A my affliction.

¹⁶ If I am proud,^B you hunt me like a lion
and again display
your miraculous power against me.

¹⁷ You produce new witnesses^C
against me
and multiply your anger toward me.
Hardships assault me, wave after wave.^D

¹⁸ "Why did you bring me out of
the womb?
I should have died and never been seen.

¹⁹ I wish^E I had never existed
but had been carried from the womb
to the grave.

²⁰ Are my days not few? Stop it!^F
Leave me alone, so that I can smile
a little

²¹ before I go to a land of darkness
and gloom,
never to return.

²² It is a land of blackness
like the deepest darkness,
gloomy and chaotic,
where even the light is
like^G the darkness."

Zophar Speaks

11 Then Zophar the Naamathite replied:
² Should this abundance of words
go unanswered
and such a talker^H be acquitted?

³ Should your babbling put others
to silence,
so that you can keep on ridiculing
with no one to humiliate you?

⁴ You have said, "My teaching is sound,
and I am pure in your sight."

⁵ But if only God would speak
and open his lips against you!

⁶ He would show you the secrets
of wisdom,
for true wisdom has two sides.

Know then that God has chosen
to overlook some of your iniquity.

⁷ Can you fathom the depths of God
or discover the limits of the Almighty?

⁸ They are higher than the heavens —
what can you do?
They are deeper than Sheol — what can
you know?

⁹ Their measure is longer than the earth
and wider than the sea.

¹⁰ If he passes by and throws
someone in prison
or convenes a court, who can stop him?

¹¹ Surely he knows which people
are worthless.
If he sees iniquity, will he not take note
of it?

¹² But a stupid person
will gain understanding
as soon as a wild donkey is born
a human!

¹³ As for you, if you redirect your heart
and spread out your hands to him
in prayer —

¹⁴ if there is iniquity in your hand,
remove it,
and don't allow injustice to dwell
in your tents —

¹⁵ then you will hold your head high,
free from fault.
You will be firmly established
and unafraid.

¹⁶ For you will forget your suffering,
recalling it only as water
that has flowed by.

¹⁷ Your life will be brighter than noonday;
its darkness^I will be like the morning.

¹⁸ You will be confident, because
there is hope.
You will look carefully about
and lie down in safety.

---

^A10:15 Or *and look at*   ^B10:16 Lit *If he lifts up*   ^C10:17 Or *You bring fresh troops*   ^D10:17 Lit *Changes and a host are with me*   ^E10:19 Lit *As if*   ^F10:20 Alt Hb tradition reads *Will he not leave my few days alone?*   ^G10:22 Lit *chaotic, and shines as*   ^H11:2 Lit *a man of lips*   ^I11:17 Text emended; MT reads *noonday; you are dark, you*

10:20–22 Job piled up the images in describing the afterlife as a place of **deepest darkness**. His despairing words reflect a common Mesopotamian understanding about the afterlife but not the biblical view clarified in the NT (1Co 15:51–57).

11:1–3 Zophar began by attacking Job's answers much as a prosecuting attorney would press his case against a defendant. Zophar's rhetorical questions implied negative answers. He called Job a **talker** (lit "a man of lips").

11:4 Zophar misrepresented Job's position like an adversary at law who attacks the implications of another's position rather than its essence. Job had not claimed that his **teaching** was flawless. Rather, he recognized that it lacked patience (6:11) and complete

perspective (7:15,20). Job did not claim that he was sinless (i.e., **pure**), only blameless (9:21; 10:7) and upright (6:29).

11:5–6 Zophar pointed out that wisdom had **two sides**; this probably means the known and the unknown, the seen and the unseen. Only God understood the depths of true **wisdom** and could view things from all perspectives. If only God could see both sides of his situation, he would realize that God's case against him was just. Zophar declared that God had only punished Job for part of his **iniquity**.

11:7–9 Zophar's rhetorical question indicated that Job was not in a position to understand fully all that was happening to him.

11:10–11 Zophar implied that Job had sinned and God certainly knew the facts in Job's case.

11:13–14 Only if Job had a pure **heart** and clean **hands** (Ps 24:4) could he expect God's forgiveness and blessing (Is 1:15–17). To **dwell in your tents** is used metaphorically of sharing in someone's blessings (Ps 9:27) or occupying another's land (Ps 78:55). The tent is also used in the Bible to signify man's earthly body (2Co 5:1).

11:15–16 Zophar believed that confessed sin and a change of lifestyle would restore Job's honor and his position before God and man.

11:17–18 Zophar's encouraging words stood in stark contrast to Job's opening lament (3:4–7), to Eliphaz's observations about the fate of crafty schemers (5:12–14), and to Bildad's warning about evildoers (8:20).

¹⁹ You will lie down with no one to
frighten you,
and many will seek your favor.
²⁰ But the sight of the wicked will fail.
Their way of escape will be cut off,
and their only hope is their last breath.

Job's Reply to Zophar

12 Then Job answered:
² No doubt you are the people,
and wisdom will die with you!
³ But I also have a mind like you;
I am not inferior to you.
Who doesn't know the things you are
talking about?^A

⁴ I am a laughingstock to my^B friends,
by calling on God, who answers me.^C
The righteous and blameless man is
a laughingstock.
⁵ The one who is at ease holds calamity
in contempt
and thinks it is prepared for those
whose feet are slipping.
⁶ The tents of robbers are safe,
and those who trouble God are secure;
God holds them in his hands.^D

⁷ But ask the animals, and they will
instruct you;
ask the birds of the sky, and they will
tell you.
⁸ Or speak to the earth, and it will
instruct you;
let the fish of the sea inform you.
⁹ Which of all these does not know
that the hand of the LORD has done this?
¹⁰ The life of every living thing is
in his hand,
as well as the breath of all humanity.
¹¹ Doesn't the ear test words
as the palate tastes food?
¹² Wisdom is found with the elderly,
and understanding comes
with long life.

¹³ Wisdom and strength belong to God;
counsel and understanding are his.
¹⁴ Whatever he tears down cannot
be rebuilt;
whoever he imprisons cannot
be released.
¹⁵ When he withholds water, everything
dries up,
and when he releases it, it destroys
the land.
¹⁶ True wisdom and power belong to him.
The deceived and the deceiver are his.
¹⁷ He leads counselors away barefoot
and makes judges go mad.
¹⁸ He releases the bonds^E put on by kings
and fastens a belt around their waists.
¹⁹ He leads priests away barefoot
and overthrows established leaders.
²⁰ He deprives trusted advisers of speech
and takes away the elders'
good judgment.
²¹ He pours out contempt on nobles
and disarms^F the strong.
²² He reveals mysteries
from the darkness
and brings the deepest darkness
into the light.
²³ He makes nations great,
then destroys them;
he enlarges nations,
then leads them away.
²⁴ He deprives the world's leaders
of reason,
and makes them wander
in a trackless wasteland.
²⁵ They grope around in darkness
without light;
he makes them stagger like a drunkard.

13 Look, my eyes have seen all this;
my ears have heard and understood it.
² Everything you know, I also know;
I am not inferior to you.
³ Yet I prefer to speak to the Almighty
and argue my case before God.

---

^A12:3 Lit *With whom are not such things as these?* ^B12:4 Lit *his* ^C12:4 Lit *him* ^D12:6 Or *secure; to those who bring their god in their hands* ^E12:18 Text emended; MT reads *discipline* ^F12:21 Lit *and loosens the belt of*

11:19 Zophar assured Job that with restoration his fame and reputation would return. To be "sought out" functions at times idiomatically for the bringing of gifts (see 42:11; Ps 45:12).

11:20 Zophar concluded his speech with a dire warning. Unlike the blessings offered to a repentant sinner that he had just described, the unrepentant **wicked** could expect only suffering. Their prosperity would **fail**, and their only **hope** of relief would be death itself.
12:1–2 Job lashed out sarcastically at all three friends, accusing them of being condescending. Although they claimed the wisdom of the ages, by their simplistic observations of his problem they had misapplied their learning. Acquired knowledge does not guarantee true wisdom.

12:3 Job reminded his friends that he had access to the same body of traditional wisdom that they described. By saying that he had a **mind**, Job implied that, unlike his friends, he weighed the evidence in order to make proper application.
12:5–6 Job's words indicate that Zophar's closing remarks (11:13–19) simply did not fit the facts.
12:11–12 Job's rhetorical question suggested that mere knowledge was insufficient. A person needed to evaluate carefully what he heard. Job had expected to hear better advice from three supposedly wise men (v. 2).
12:16 Job's review of the scope of God's **wisdom and power** includes a stunning but true claim that even **the deceived and the deceiver**, both of whom are presumably

bereft of true knowledge of God and do not willingly submit to him, **are his**.
12:18 It is unclear what **bonds** and **a belt** are intended to convey with regard to **kings**. One possibility is that God easily strips kings of their robes and leads them away. Another is that God can release those whom kings have bound and bind the king instead. A third is that if a king is defeated and bound, God can release him and gird him.
12:19 To be led away **barefoot** pictures defeat, captivity, and exile.
13:1–2 Job made clear that Zophar's remarks about uninformed or stupid men (11:12) did not apply to him!
13:3 Job again (9:3,16,19,32) stated his desire to present his **case before God**. He'd had enough with making his case before finite,

⁴ You use lies like plaster;
  you are all worthless healers.
⁵ If only you would shut up
  and let that be your wisdom!

⁶ Hear now my argument,
  and listen to my defense.^A
⁷ Would you testify unjustly
    on God's behalf
  or speak deceitfully for him?
⁸ Would you show partiality to him
  or argue the case in his defense?
⁹ Would it go well if he examined you?
  Could you deceive him
    as you would deceive a man?
¹⁰ Surely he would rebuke you
  if you secretly showed partiality.
¹¹ Would God's majesty not terrify you?
  Would his dread not fall on you?
¹² Your memorable sayings are proverbs
    of ash;
  your defenses are made of clay.

¹³ Be quiet,^B and I will speak.
  Let whatever comes happen to me.
¹⁴ I will put^C myself at risk^D
  and take my life in my own hands.
¹⁵ Even if he kills me, I will hope in him.^E
  I will still defend my ways
    before him.
¹⁶ Yes, this will result
    in my deliverance,
  for no godless person can appear
    before him.
¹⁷ Pay close attention to my words;
  let my declaration ring in your ears.
¹⁸ Now then, I have prepared my case;
  I know that I am right.
¹⁹ Can anyone indict me?
  If so, I will be silent and die.

²⁰ Only grant these two things to me, God,
  so that I will not have to hide
    from your presence:
²¹ remove your hand from me,
  and do not let your terror frighten me.
²² Then call, and I will answer,
  or I will speak, and you can respond
    to me.
²³ How many iniquities and sins
    have I committed?^F
  Reveal to me my transgression and sin.
²⁴ Why do you hide your face
  and consider me your enemy?
²⁵ Will you frighten a wind-driven leaf?
  Will you chase after dry straw?
²⁶ For you record bitter accusations
    against me
  and make me inherit the iniquities
    of my youth.
²⁷ You put my feet in the stocks
  and stand watch over all my paths,
  setting a limit for the soles^G of my feet.

²⁸ A person wears out
    like something rotten,
  like a moth-eaten garment.

14 Anyone born of woman
   is short of days and full of trouble.
² He blossoms like a flower, then withers;
  he flees like a shadow and does not last.
³ Do you really take notice of one like this?
  Will you bring me into judgment
    against you?^H
⁴ Who can produce something pure
    from what is impure?
  No one!
⁵ Since a person's days are determined
  and the number of his months depends
    on you,

^A13:6 Lit to the claims of my lips ^B13:13 Lit quiet before me ^C13:14 LXX; MT reads Why do I put ^D13:14 Lit I take my flesh in
my teeth ^E13:15 Some Hb mss read I will be without hope ^F13:23 Lit sins are to me ^G13:27 Lit paths. You mark a line around
the roots ^H14:3 LXX, Syr, Vg read him

fallible men. He wanted a formal hearing
before his divine adversary.
13:6 Hear and **listen** are familiar calls to
pay attention to the teacher (Dt 6:4;
Pr 4:1,10; 5:1; 7:24) or poet (Dt 32:1; Jdg 5:3)
has to say.
13:7 Job's rhetorical questions implied that
his friends, by taking God's side against
Job, had twisted traditional wisdom and
applied it **deceitfully**. Surely God could
not be helped by false and unjust testimony.
13:8 The phrase **show partiality** is a translation of a Hebrew idiom, literally, "lift up the
face." This expression has positive and negative connotations depending on the context.
13:12 Instead of ink, a mixture of **ash** and
water was sometimes used to write on a
scroll, but the writing would soon disappear.
13:14 Job suggested that in speaking his
mind plainly he was putting his life **at risk**
(lit "I take my flesh in my teeth"; i.e., "I expose
myself to being consumed"). Yet he was so
confident of his uprightness and integrity

that he would take the chance and defend
himself.
13:15 The Hebrew verb *yachal* can mean either "wait" (29:23) or "hope" (6:11). The CSB
has Job hoping in God (for vindication) even
if God kills him. Alternatively, in the consonantal text (a Hb text that has no vowel
points) the verb is preceded by a particle normally understood as a negative (see textual
footnote), which would have Job observing
that God might kill him, leaving him *without* **hope** (10:20–22). In either rendering, Job
believed that his cause was just and that he
must **defend** the uprightness of his **ways**.
Job felt that he had nothing to lose by this
risky move, because God seemed determined
to find some charge against him in order to
destroy him (9:20–21; 10:4–7).
13:20–21 Job contended that if he were
not oppressed (hence the appeal, **remove
your hand from me**) or terrified (the typical
reaction to being in God's presence; see Ex
20:18–19; Is 6:1), he might be able to state his
case convincingly.

13:24 Idioms involving God's **face** can indicate the Lord's approval or blessing (Nm
6:24–26; 2Ch 30:9) or his disapproval and
judgment (Ps 143:7; Jr 21:10).
13:25 In striking similes Job reminded God
of his frailty as a human. **Dry straw** is often
used metaphorically for something easily
scattered (Ps 83:13; Is 40:23–24; Jr 13:24) or
consumed in God's fiery judgment (Nah
1:10).
13:28 Job again reminded God of the brevity of life (7:6; 9:25; 10:20). As rotting food,
decaying wood, or a **moth-eaten garment**
becomes useless and worthy only of being
destroyed, so Job was wasting away toward
his inevitable end. Although the similes are
phrased with regard to **a person** in general,
Job clearly intended an application to his
specific situation.
14:1–2 Job's similes emphasize that a
person's life passes all too quickly, like a
flower that is soon gone (Ps 103:15–16; Is
5:24; 40:6–8) or like a fleeting **shadow** (8:9;
Ec 6:12).

and since you have set^A limits
   he cannot pass,
6 look away from him and let him rest
   so that he can enjoy his day
      like a hired worker.

7 There is hope for a tree:
   If it is cut down, it will sprout again,
   and its shoots will not die.
8 If its roots grow old in the ground
   and its stump starts to die in the soil,
9 the scent of water makes it thrive
   and produce twigs like a sapling.
10 But a person dies and fades away;
   he breathes his last — where is he?
11 As water disappears from a lake
   and a river becomes parched and dry,
12 so people lie down never to rise again.
   They will not wake up until the heavens
      are no more;
   they will not stir from their sleep.

13 If only you would hide me in Sheol
   and conceal me until your anger passes.
   If only you would appoint a time for me
   and then remember me.
14 When a person dies, will he come back
      to life?
   If so, I would wait all the days
      of my struggle
   until my relief comes.
15 You would call, and I would answer you.
   You would long for the work
      of your hands.
16 For then you would count my steps
   but would not take note of my sin.
17 My rebellion would be sealed up
      in a bag,
   and you would cover over my iniquity.

18 But as a mountain collapses
      and crumbles
   and a rock is dislodged from its place,
19 as water wears away stones
   and torrents wash away the soil
      from the land,
   so you destroy a man's hope.

20 You completely overpower him, and he
      passes on;
   you change his appearance
   and send him away.
21 If his sons receive honor, he does not
      know it;
   if they become insignificant,
   he is unaware of it.
22 He feels only the pain of his own body
   and mourns only for himself.

SECOND SERIES OF SPEECHES
Eliphaz Speaks

15 Then Eliphaz the Temanite replied:
2 Does a wise man answer
   with empty^B counsel
   or fill himself^C with the hot east wind?
3 Should he argue with useless talk
   or with words that serve
      no good purpose?
4 But you even undermine the fear
      of God
   and hinder meditation before him.
5 Your iniquity teaches you what to say,
   and you choose the language
      of the crafty.
6 Your own mouth condemns you, not I;
   your own lips testify against you.

7 Were you the first human ever born,
   or were you brought forth
      before the hills?
8 Do you listen in on the council of God,
   or have a monopoly on wisdom?
9 What do you know that we don't?
   What do you understand that
      is not clear to us?
10 Both the gray-haired and the elderly are
      with us—
   older than your father.
11 Are God's consolations not enough
      for you,
   even the words that deal gently
      with you?
12 Why has your heart misled you,
   and why do your eyes flash
13 as you turn your anger^D against God

---

^A14:5 Lit *set his* ^B15:2 Lit *windy*; Jb 16:3 ^C15:2 Lit *his belly* ^D15:13 Or *spirit*

14:7–12 The **sleep** of death is as permanent as **the heavens** (Dt 11:20–21; Ps 89:28–29). In other contexts this speaks to the fact that earthly life is irrevocably lost upon death, but here Job seemingly expresses that he has no hope of afterlife. **14:13** In his despair Job continues to shift his stance. He now entertains the possibility that death might not end it all. Perhaps in time God's **anger** against him would pass, then he would **remember** Job favorably—that is, act on Job's behalf. This implies Job will have an ongoing existence beyond the grave. By **Sheol** Job referred to the grave (see 7:9–10; 26:5–6). **14:14–15** Job felt that if there was hope of life after death, he could endure his present

struggle (7:1–5). The Hebrew word translated **relief** is used elsewhere to denote a change (Jdg 14:12–13). Job hoped for change to a new life of fellowship and communion with God. This is indicated by his use of the call-answer motif (Jb 13:22; Ps 102:1–2; Is 65:24). **15:1–3** Eliphaz's rhetorical questions suggested a negative answer. Unlike a truly wise man, Job's defense was self-serving and **empty**. Job displayed his passion like a **hot east wind**, or sirocco, which had entered the depths of his belly. **15:4** Eliphaz suggested that Job's intemperate attitude had affected his proper reverence for God. How then could Job claim to

be wise? Wisdom begins with **the fear of God** (see Pr 1:7). **15:5–6** Eliphaz believed that Job's stance against his friends' counsel was dictated by an underlying **iniquity**. In defending himself Job used cunning terms to cover his guilt. Yet Job's words condemned him (9:20). **15:7–10** Eliphaz wanted Job to realize that he had no claim to superior wisdom (12:1–3; 13:1–2). In words bordering on sarcasm, Eliphaz stated that Job had neither priority of birth nor privileged access to the heavenly **council** (1:6; 2:1). Job should understand that time-tested **wisdom**, which had been handed down long before Job's father, was on the side of his friends.

and allow such words to leave
your mouth?

14 What is a mere human, that he
should be pure,
or one born of a woman, that he
should be righteous?

15 If God puts no trust in his holy ones
and the heavens are not pure
in his sight,

16 how much less one who is revolting
and corrupt,
who drinks injustice like water?

17 Listen to me and I will inform you.
I will describe what I have seen,

18 what the wise have declared and
not concealed,
that came from their ancestors,

19 to whom alone the land was given
when no foreigner passed among them.

20 A wicked person writhes in pain
all his days,
throughout the number of
years reserved for the ruthless.

21 Dreadful sounds fill his ears;
when he is at peace, a robber
attacks him.

22 He doesn't believe he will return
from darkness;
he is destined for the sword.

23 He wanders about for food, asking,
"Where is it?"
He knows the day of darkness
is at hand.

24 Trouble and distress terrify him,
overwhelming him like a king prepared
for battle.

25 For he has stretched out his hand
against God
and has arrogantly opposed
the Almighty.

26 He rushes headlong at him
with his thick, studded shields.

27 Though his face is covered with fat^A
and his waistline bulges with it,

28 he will dwell in ruined cities,

in abandoned houses destined
to become piles of rubble.

29 He will no longer be rich; his wealth
will not endure.
His possessions^B will not increase
in the land.

30 He will not escape from the darkness;
flames will wither his shoots,
and by the breath of God's mouth,
he will depart.

31 Let him not put trust
in worthless things, being led astray,
for what he gets in exchange
will prove worthless.

32 It will be accomplished before his time,
and his branch will not flourish.

33 He will be like a vine that drops
its unripe grapes
and like an olive tree that sheds
its blossoms.

34 For the company of the godless
will have no children,
and fire will consume the tents of those
who offer bribes.

35 They conceive trouble and give birth
to evil;
their womb prepares deception.

Job's Reply to Eliphaz

16 Then Job answered:
2 I have heard many things like these.
You are all miserable comforters.

3 Is there no end to your empty^C words?
What provokes you that you
continue testifying?

4 If you were in my place I could also talk
like you.
I could string words together against you
and shake my head at you.

5 Instead, I would encourage you
with my mouth,
and the consolation from my lips
would bring relief.

6 If I speak, my suffering is not relieved,
and if I hold back, does any of it leave
me?

---

^A15:27 Lit with his fat ^B15:29 Text emended; MT reads Their gain ^C16:3 Lit windy; Jb 15:2

15:17–19 Eliphaz appealed to his special grasp of traditional wisdom and wide experience (4:8–9,12–21; 5:3–7,27). His experience and understanding were in harmony with the wisdom that came from the early inhabitants of the land. That was a time of pure knowledge when **no foreigner** was present to bring corrupting influences to bear.
15:20 Job had maintained that God gave no special treatment to the blameless (9:22) but gave control of the earth to the **wicked person** (9:24; 10:3). Eliphaz agreed with Zophar (11:20) that the wicked lived out their few years **in pain**. Neither of these polarized views corresponds with reality.

15:21 Dreadful sounds make the wicked person think someone is about to attack him. **15:26** The term **headlong** (lit "runs at him with the neck") portrays the wicked person as having reckless self-confidence.
15:27–29 Metaphorically, **fat** indicates a person possesses health and wealth (Gn 45:18). It can also carry a negative nuance associated with arrogance (Ps 73:3–7). Both ideas are expressed here.
15:30 As tender shoots **wither** before a scorching sun or a blasting desert wind, so the wicked will lose everything in God's judgment (4:8–9; Is 11:4). **God's mouth** can be used figuratively as the vehicle of his judgment. His **breath** represents the ease

with which his mighty power accomplishes the deed and is a suitable figure for a desert wind.
15:35 Rather than achieving their wicked goals, the godless metaphorically bear children named **trouble . . . evil**, and **deception**. What they did to others would cause their own downfall.
16:1–4 Miserable comforters is literally "comforters (who bring) trouble, harm, or hardship." Shaking the **head** was a gesture of mockery or contempt (2Kg 19:21; Ps 22:7).
16:6–17 Job observed that whether he spoke or said nothing, his suffering remained unaltered (v. 6). He would therefore speak, hoping that God would hear and be sympathetic (vv. 7–17).

⁷ Surely heᴬ has now exhausted me.
 You have devastated my entire family.
⁸ You have shriveled me upᴮ —
 it has become a witness;
 my frailty rises up against me
 and testifies to my face.
⁹ His anger tears at me,
 and he harasses me.
 He gnashes his teeth at me.
 My enemy pierces me with his eyes.
¹⁰ They open their mouths against me
 and strike my cheeks with contempt;
 they join themselves together
 against me.
¹¹ God hands me over to the unjust;ᶜ
 he throws me to the wicked.
¹² I was at ease, but he shattered me;
 he seized me by the scruff of the neck
 and smashed me to pieces.
 He set me up as his target;
¹³ his archersᴰ surround me.
 He pierces my kidneys without mercy
 and pours my bile on the ground.
¹⁴ He breaks through my defenses again
 and again;ᴱ
 he charges at me like a warrior.

¹⁵ I have sewn sackcloth over my skin;
 I have buried my strengthᶠ in the dust.
¹⁶ My face has grown red with weeping,
 and darkness covers my eyes,
¹⁷ although my hands are free
 from violence
 and my prayer is pure.

¹⁸ Earth, do not cover my blood;
 may my cry for help find
 no resting place.
¹⁹ Even now my witness is in heaven,
 and my advocate is in the heights!
²⁰ My friends scoff at me
 as I weep before God.
²¹ I wish that someone might argue
 for a man with God

just as anyoneᴳ would for a friend.
²² For only a few years will pass
 before I go the way of no return.

17

My spirit is broken.
 My days are extinguished.
 A graveyard awaits me.
² Surely mockers surroundᴴ me,
 and my eyes must gaze at their rebellion.

³ Accept my pledge! Put up security
 for me.
 Who else will be my sponsor?ᴵ
⁴ You have closed their minds
 to understanding,
 therefore you will not honor them.
⁵ If a man denounces his friends
 for a price,
 the eyes of his children will fail.

⁶ He has made me an object of scorn
 to the people;
 I have become a man people spit at.ᴶ
⁷ My eyes have grown dim from grief,
 and my whole body has become
 but a shadow.
⁸ The upright are appalled at this,
 and the innocent are roused
 against the godless.
⁹ Yet the righteous person will hold
 to his way,
 and the one whose hands are clean
 will grow stronger.
¹⁰ But come back and try again, all of you.ᴷ
 I will not find a wise man among you.

¹¹ My days have slipped by;
 my plans have been ruined,
 even the things dear to my heart.
¹² They turned night into day
 and made light seem near in the face
 of darkness.
¹³ If I await Sheol as my home,
 spread out my bed in darkness,

ᴬ**16:7** Or *it*   ᴮ**16:8** Or *have seized me*; Hb obscure   ᶜ**16:11** LXX, Vg; MT reads *to a boy*   ᴰ**16:13** Or *arrows*   ᴱ**16:14** Lit *through me, breach on breach*   ᶠ**16:15** Lit *horn*   ᴳ**16:21** Lit *a son of man*   ᴴ**17:2** Lit *are with*   ᴵ**17:3** Or *Who is there that will shake hands with me?*   ᴶ**17:6** Lit *become a spitting to the faces*   ᴷ**17:10** Some Hb mss, LXX, Vg; other Hb mss read *them*

16:7-8 Job switched the form of his verbs from third to second person. Job addressed God as though he were present in the discussions among the four.
16:9 Gnashing of teeth conveys rage or hatred (Ps 37:12; Lm 2:16). Job called God his **enemy**, who so scrutinized him that he seemed to look right through him (7:17–20).
16:12–14 Job reminded his friends of his former state of **ease**. In graphic metaphors Job likened God to a **warrior** in command of a vast army. God had made him the object of his attack (7:20). Eventually an arrow struck Job's vital organ with tragic consequences (6:4). He compared himself to a besieged city whose defenses had been repeatedly assailed and finally penetrated by God's assaults.

16:15 In sorrow and mourning, Job had put on **sackcloth** (2Kg 19:1; Jl 1:13).
16:18 Because Job must surely die soon, he pleaded that his spilled **blood** would not be covered (Gn 37:26). Like the blood of innocent Abel, Job's blood would **cry** out from the ground for justice (Gn 4:10). He asked that his cry for vindication not be forgotten until his blood shed in innocence was avenged (Ezk 24:7–8).
16:21 Job repeated his need of and desire for an arbitrator to represent him before God. Although he longed for an audience with God (13:3) where a fair hearing would vindicate him (13:15–16), he felt inadequate to represent himself (9:2–4,32–33).
17:2 The word for **rebellion** may also be rendered "defiance" or "hostility."

17:4 The CSB translation here suggests that because those who might have helped Job were not capable of **understanding** the issues involved, God would not **honor** anything they might present on Job's behalf. Alternatively, Job might have reminded God that with his case not settled, God would not be honored.
17:5 In this verse Job appears to cite an ancient proverb that a person who was paid to inform on his **friends** endangered his **children**. If Job's friends were attempting to gain favor with God by taking his side against him, it could put their families in jeopardy.
17:6 An object of scorn is literally "for a proverb." That is, Job had become an illustration or object lesson that sin results in suffering.

14 and say to corruption, "You are
　　 my father,"
　 and to the maggot, "My mother"
　　 or "My sister,"
15 where then is my hope?
　 Who can see any hope for me?
16 Will it go down to the gates of Sheol,
　 or will we descend together to the dust?

Bildad Speaks

18 Then Bildad the Shuhite replied:
2 How long until you stop talking?
　 Show some sense, and then we can talk.
3 Why are we regarded as cattle,
　 as stupid in your sight?
4 You who tear yourself in anger^A —
　 should the earth be abandoned
　　 on your account,
　 or a rock be removed from its place?

5 Yes, the light of the wicked
　　 is extinguished;
　 the flame of his fire does not glow.
6 The light in his tent grows dark,
　 and the lamp beside him is put out.
7 His powerful stride is shortened,
　 and his own schemes trip him up.
8 For his own feet lead him into a net,
　 and he strays into its mesh.
9 A trap catches him by the heel;
　 a noose seizes him.
10 A rope lies hidden for him
　　 on the ground,
　 and a snare waits for him
　　 along the path.
11 Terrors frighten him on every side
　 and harass him at every step.
12 His strength is depleted;
　 disaster lies ready for him to stumble.^B
13 Parts of his skin are eaten away;
　 death's firstborn consumes his limbs.

14 He is ripped from the security
　　 of his tent
　 and marched away to the king
　　 of terrors.
15 Nothing he owned remains in his tent.
　 Burning sulfur is scattered
　　 over his home.
16 His roots below dry up,
　 and his branches above wither away.
17 All memory of him perishes
　　 from the earth;
　 he has no name anywhere.^C
18 He is driven from light to darkness
　 and chased from the inhabited world.
19 He has no children or descendants
　　 among his people,
　 no survivor where he used to live.
20 Those in the west are appalled
　　 at his fate,
　 while those in the east tremble
　　 in horror.
21 Indeed, such is the dwelling of the
　　 unjust man,
　 and this is the place of the one
　　 who does not know God.

Job's Reply to Bildad

19 Then Job answered:
2 How long will you torment me
　 and crush me with words?
3 You have humiliated me ten times now,
　 and you mistreat^D me without shame.
4 Even if it is true that I have sinned,
　 my mistake concerns only^E me.
5 If you really want to appear superior
　　 to me
　 and would use my disgrace as evidence
　　 against me,
6 then understand that it is God
　 who has wronged me
　 and caught me in his net.

---

^A 18:4 Lit *He who tears himself in his anger*　^B 18:12 Or *disaster hungers for him*　^C 18:17 Or *name in the streets*　^D 19:3 Hb obscure　^E 19:4 Lit *mistake lives with*

17:13–16 Sheol meant "the grave" (see notes at 7:9–10; 14:13; 26:5–6). In a graphic metaphor, Job pictured the grave as his future home. Job used personification in calling the grave **my father** and **the maggot** that would feed on his body **my mother** or **my sister**. It was as though in the grave Job would enter into a new home housing a new family. **Gates** are often used metaphorically for entrance into the state of death (38:17; Pss 9:13; 107:18).
18:1–2 You in the original text is plural rather than singular. Because Bildad's speech was addressed to Job, the plural serves as a mark of politeness. The second line does not contain an imperative in the Hebrew text. Bildad was expressing a wish.
18:4 Bildad attempted to correct Job's perspective. It was not an angry God who was tearing at Job (12:14; 16:9) but his own **anger** at God. God was not obligated to empty the **earth** or move a **rock** just to satisfy Job's self-serving demands.

18:5–6 Light represents a blessed life lived in accordance with the high standards of God, while darkness symbolizes the opposite (Pr 4:18–19).
18:8–10 Six different words for **trap** are used to depict metaphorically the unanticipated dangers that could ensnare a wicked person.
18:11–13 The dangers that the wicked person encounters bring constant terror, including the prospect of death. **Death's firstborn** means either the plague or the most terrible manner of death.
18:14 Finally the wicked person will lose everything and will be claimed by death, the last enemy (1Co 15:26) and **the king of terrors**. The language is reminiscent of the Canaanite deity Mot (death), whose appetite was insatiable and whose mouth and throat were always open to receive his victims. Death is similarly portrayed in the OT (Is 5:14; Hab 2:5).
18:15 The wicked person's **tent** (home) is destroyed by others. The scattering of **burning**

sulfur over it ensured that it would never be rebuilt and occupied.
18:17–20 Bildad built upon language used by Job in describing public reaction to his condition (17:7–8). **West** and **east** is a merismus (the use of two parts to represent the whole) to designate people everywhere.
19:1–2 Job began his speech by using Bildad's phraseology (18:2): **how long**? Because **words** can **crush**, they should be weighed and used appropriately (Pr 15:1,23; Eph 4:29).
19:3 Rather than being helpful, the words of Job's friends had added to his grief. The number **ten** represents the concept of totality.
19:4 Job admitted that he might have **sinned** unintentionally as all people do (6:24; 7:20). He felt, however, that he had done nothing worthy of such harsh treatment.
19:5–6 Bildad had suggested that a wicked man's lifestyle would lead him into being trapped (18:8–10) and that God does not pervert justice (8:3). On the contrary, Job

⁷ I cry out, "Violence!"
   but get no response;
   I call for help, but there is no justice.
⁸ He has blocked my way so that I cannot
      pass through;
   he has veiled my paths with darkness.
⁹ He has stripped me of my honor
   and removed the crown from my head.
¹⁰ He tears me down on every side so that
      I am ruined.ᴬ
   He uproots my hope like a tree.
¹¹ His anger burns against me,
   and he regards me as one of
      his enemies.
¹² His troops advance together;
   they construct a rampᴮ against me
   and camp around my tent.
¹³ He has removed my brothers from me;
   my acquaintances have abandoned me.
¹⁴ My relatives stop coming by,
   and my close friends have forgotten me.
¹⁵ My house guestsᶜ and female servants
      regard me as a stranger;
   I am a foreigner in their sight.
¹⁶ I call for my servant, but he
      does not answer,
   even if I beg him with my own mouth.
¹⁷ My breath is offensive to my wife,
   and my own familyᴰ finds me repulsive.

¹⁸ Even young boys scorn me.
   When I stand up, they mock me.
¹⁹ All of my best friendsᴱ despise me,
   and those I love have turned against me.
²⁰ My skin and my flesh cling to my bones;
   I have escaped with only the skin
      of my teeth.
²¹ Have mercy on me, my friends,
      have mercy,
   for God's hand has struck me.
²² Why do you persecute me as God does?
   Will you never get enough of my flesh?
²³ I wish that my words were written down,
   that they were recorded on a scroll
²⁴ or were inscribed in stone forever
   by an iron stylus and lead!
²⁵ But I know that my Redeemer lives,ᶠ
   and at the end he will stand on the dust.
²⁶ Even after my skin has been destroyed,ᴳ
   yet I will see God inᴴ my flesh.
²⁷ I will see him myself;
   my eyes will look at him, and not
      as a stranger.ᴵ
   My heart longsᴶ within me.
²⁸ If you say, "How will we pursue him,
   since the root of the problem lies
      with him?"ᴷ

ᴬ19:10 Lit *gone* ᴮ19:12 Lit *they raise up their way* ᶜ19:15 Or *The resident aliens in my household* ᴰ19:17 Lit *and the sons of my belly* ᴱ19:19 Lit *of the men of my council* ᶠ19:25 Or *know my living Redeemer* ᴳ19:26 Lit *skin which they destroyed,* or *skin they destroyed in this way* ᴴ19:26 Or *apart from* ᴵ19:27 Or *not a stranger* ᴶ19:27 Lit *My kidneys grow faint* ᴷ19:28 Some Hb mss, LXX, Vg; other Hb mss read *me*

declared that God had unjustly set out to trap him (7:19–20).

19:7 Job's point is that God is the one responsible for his pain, not some sin(s) he has committed.

19:9–12 Job used several images to describe his situation of being mistreated by God. Finally, Job felt like a besieged city. An army had built a siege **ramp** against him to bring up their battering rams and penetrate his last defenses. He was just a weak human who was more like a **tent** than a mighty city necessitating a strong attack. Contrary to Bildad's description of the lot of the wicked (18:14–15), Job's tent (lifestyle) had been battered undeservedly by God, who wanted to overpower him (14:20). The tent expresses the idea of impermanence (2Co 5:1), the brevity of life (Jb 7:16,21; 9:25–26; 10:20; 14:1–6).

19:15–16 Job's home life was in shambles. His situation had brought the disdain of his **guests and female servants**, and his personal male **servant**. It was as though these relationships had been turned upside down (Pr 30:21–23).

19:17 The phrase **my own family** renders the Hebrew phrase that literally reads, "children of my belly." The word *belly* is a euphemism referring to Job's loins (Ps 132:11; Mc 6:7). But had Job not lost all his children (Jb 1:18–19)? These could be children by one of Job's concubines or slaves, or they could be grandchildren who escaped the earlier destruction and came to live in his house. Alternatively, some interpreters take "my

belly" to refer to Job's mother, hence these "children" would be his blood brothers.

19:18 For children to **mock** an old man was a serious violation of Israelite social norms.

19:19 Picking up the thought from v. 14, Job says that his **best friends** have not only forgotten him but have actively become his enemies.

19:20 In Job's weakness he felt as though his **bones** were clinging to his **skin** and **flesh** (33:21). He is emaciated. The idiom **skin of my teeth** heightens the effect. Job was so weak that he was barely alive.

19:21–22 The Hebrew idiom underlying Job's second question (v. 22) is "to eat the **flesh**." It is used for slander or of levying accusations against someone (Ps 27:2; Dn 3:8; 6:24). Job lamented that by their unkind remarks his friends were consuming his last bastion of defense.

19:23–24 A **scroll** was made of papyrus or leather. Better yet, Job would like his words engraved in **lead** on a **stone** stele. Job's insistence on the carved letters being filled in with lead emphasized his desire for a permanent record of his innocence.

19:25 The Hebrew term **Redeemer** reflects an ancient custom whereby a person's nearest kinsman served as a guarantor of his rights and privileges (Lv 25:23–34,47–54; Dt 19:6–12; Jos 20:2–5; Ru 4:1–17). Although Job had repeatedly described God as his enemy and persecutor (Jb 7:17–21; 16:7–14; 19:7–12), he had also expressed his confidence in God (12:13–16; 13:15–18; 14:14–17; 16:18–20). He said that in the end God was his only hope (17:3).

Job's underlying faith ultimately surfaced, breaking through his dark doubts about God. God was Job's redeemer who alone could serve as a guarantor of his rights and vindicate his cause. If Job were to die, he was confident that the living God would stand on the **dust** of his grave and testify on his behalf.

19:26–27 Job built on his earlier mention of skin and flesh (v. 20). He pointed out the inevitability of what he had come to expect (7:7–10; 10:18,21–22; 14:12; 17:13–16). Although he would lie in the grave (v. 25) with his body decayed, he would personally **see God**. No longer **as a stranger** (one outside of God's household, or an enemy), he would experience renewed fellowship. Job once again entertained the fond hope of personal life after death (14:14–15).

29 then be afraid of the sword,
because wrath brings punishment
by the sword,
so that you may know there is
a judgment.

Zophar Speaks

20 Then Zophar the Naamathite replied:
² This is why my unsettling thoughts
compel me to answer,
because I am upset!ᴬ
³ I have heard a rebuke that insults me,
and my understandingᴮ makes me reply.

⁴ Don't you know that
ever since antiquity,
from the time a human was placed
on earth,
⁵ the joy of the wicked has been brief
and the happiness of the godless
has lasted only a moment?
⁶ Though his arrogance reaches heaven,
and his head touches the clouds,
⁷ he will vanish forever like his own dung.
Those who knowᶜ him will ask,
"Where is he?"
⁸ He will fly away like a dream and never
be found;
he will be chased away like a vision
in the night.
⁹ The eye that saw him will see him
no more,
and his household will no longer see him.
¹⁰ His children will beg fromᴰ the poor,
for his own hands must give back
his wealth.
¹¹ His frame may be full of youthful vigor,
but it will lie down with him in dust.

¹² Though evil tastes sweet in his mouth
and he conceals it under his tongue,
¹³ though he cherishes it and will not
let it go
but keeps it in his mouth,
¹⁴ yet the food in his stomach turns
into cobras' venom inside him.

¹⁵ He swallows wealth but must
vomit it up;
God will force it from his stomach.
¹⁶ He will suck the poison of cobras;
a viper's fangsᴱ will kill him.
¹⁷ He will not enjoy the streams,
the rivers flowing with honey
and curds.
¹⁸ He must return the fruit of his labor
without consuming it;
he doesn't enjoy the profits
from his trading.
¹⁹ For he oppressed and abandoned
the poor;
he seized a house he did not build.
²⁰ Because his appetite is never satisfied,ᶠ
he does not let anything
he desires escape.
²¹ Nothing is left for him to consume;
therefore, his prosperity will not last.
²² At the height of his successᴳ
distress will come to him;
the full weight of miseryᴴ
will crush him.
²³ When he fills his stomach,
God will send his burning anger
against him,
raining it down on him
while he is eating.ᴵ
²⁴ If he flees from an iron weapon,
an arrow from a bronze bow
will pierce him.
²⁵ He pulls it out of his back,
the flashing tip out of his liver.ᴶ
Terrors come over him.
²⁶ Total darkness is reserved
for his treasures.
A fire unfanned by human hands
will consume him;
it will feed on what is left in his tent.
²⁷ The heavens will expose his iniquity,
and the earth will rise up against him.
²⁸ The possessions in his house
will be removed,
flowing away on the day of God's anger.

ᴬ20:2 Lit *because of my feeling within me*   ᴮ20:3 Lit *and a spirit from my understanding*   ᶜ20:7 Lit *have seen*   ᴰ20:10 Or *children must compensate*   ᴱ20:16 Lit *tongue*   ᶠ20:20 Lit *Because he does not know ease in his stomach*   ᴳ20:22 Lit *In the fullness of his excess*   ᴴ20:22 Some Hb mss, LXX, Vg; other Hb mss read *the hand of everyone in misery*   ᴵ20:23 Text emended; MT reads *him, against his flesh*   ᴶ20:25 Or *gallbladder*

20:1–3 Zophar still believed his **understanding** offered insight into Job's problems.
20:4–5 Zophar asserted that the principle of the punishment of the wicked is as old as humanity.
20:11 Zophar was playing on Job's previous words (19:25). No longed-for Redeemer would appear over the **dust** of the wicked person's grave.
20:12–14 Much as a person savors honey under the tongue, the wicked person clings fondly to his ill-gotten gain. But what tastes good in the **mouth** sometimes becomes harmful in the **stomach** (Pr 23:31–32).

20:17 Honey was usually gathered from wild bees in ancient times (Jdg 14:8) rather than apiaries. "Honey" also designated thick date syrup. Together with refreshing **curds** (or fermented milk), honey symbolized an abundance of the best things in life (Ex 3:8; Jl 3:8).
20:20 The second line of v. 20 may also be rendered "from his greed he will not escape."
20:24–25 Referencing the war implements of the day, Zophar described God's arsenal of weapons. It includes a sword made of **iron**, a powerful **bronze bow**, and arrows with metal tips (**flashing tip**). The force of the **arrow** is so great that it pierces the wicked

person's **liver** and goes through to his **back**. In attempting to remove the arrow, he pulls out his internal organs and only adds to his doom. Job had complained that God's arrows had been unleashed against him (16:13) and had pierced him (6:4). Zophar might have been hinting that, like this wicked person, Job was being justly judged.
20:27 Job had maintained that his innocence and integrity were on record in heaven (16:18–19). Zophar hinted that it could be otherwise.
20:28–29 Zophar's final summation is not only a reiteration of his thesis with regard

29 This is the wicked person's lot from God,
the inheritance God ordained for him.

Job's Reply to Zophar

21 Then Job answered:
2 Pay close attention to my words;
let this be the consolation you offer.
3 Bear with me while I speak;
then after I have spoken, you may
continue mocking.

4 As for me, is my complaint
against a human being?
Then why shouldn't I be impatient?
5 Look at me and shudder;
put your hand over your mouth.
6 When I think about it, I am terrified
and my body trembles in horror.
7 Why do the wicked continue to live,
growing old and becoming powerful?
8 Their children are established
while they are still alive,^A
and their descendants, before their eyes.
9 Their homes are secure and free of fear;
no rod from God strikes them.
10 Their bulls breed without fail;
their cows calve and do not miscarry.
11 They let their little ones run
around like lambs;
their children skip about,
12 singing to the tambourine and lyre
and rejoicing at the sound of the flute.
13 They spend^B their days in prosperity
and go down to Sheol in peace.
14 Yet they say to God, "Leave us alone!
We don't want to know your ways.
15 Who is the Almighty, that we
should serve him,
and what will we gain by pleading
with him?"
16 But their prosperity is not
of their own doing.

The counsel of the wicked is far
from me!

17 How often is the lamp of the wicked
put out?
Does disaster^C come on them?
Does he apportion destruction
in his anger?
18 Are they like straw before the wind,
like chaff a storm sweeps away?
19 God reserves a person's punishment
for his children.
Let God repay the person himself,
so that he may know it.
20 Let his own eyes see his demise;
let him drink from the Almighty's wrath!
21 For what does he care about his family
once he is dead,
when the number of his months
has run out?

22 Can anyone teach God knowledge,
since he judges the exalted ones?^D
23 One person dies in excellent health,^E
completely secure^F and at ease.
24 His body is^G well fed,^H
and his bones are full of marrow.^I
25 Yet another person dies
with a bitter soul,
having never tasted prosperity.
26 But they both lie in the dust,
and worms cover them.

27 I know your thoughts very well,
the schemes by which you would
wrong me.
28 For you say, "Where now is
the nobleman's house?"
and "Where are the tents the wicked
lived in?"
29 Have you never consulted
those who travel the roads?

---

^A **21:8** Lit *established before them with them*   ^B **21:13** Alt Hb tradition reads *fully enjoy*   ^C **21:17** Lit *their disaster*
^D **21:22** Probably angels   ^E **21:23** Lit *in bone of his perfection*   ^F **21:23** Text emended; MT reads *health, all at ease*
^G **21:24** Or *His sides are*; Hb obscure   ^H **21:24** Lit *is full of milk*   ^I **21:24** Lit *and the marrow of his bones is watered*

---

to retribution but a declaration that this is indeed God's decreed policy. Rather than leaving an **inheritance** for his heirs, the wicked person will inherit the just judgment that God has **ordained**.
21:1–3 Eliphaz had suggested that he and his friends were offering Job consolation (15:11), but Job contended that Zophar and the others were instead **mocking** him (16:20).
21:4 Job's rhetorical question indicated that his **complaint** was against God (19:4,21–22), not **a human being**. He had grown **impatient** (lit "short of spirit") because he seemingly could not get through to God (7:11–21; 9:33–35; 16:21).
21:5–6 Job invited his friends to take another look at him (2:12; 17:7–8; 18:20). Rather than speaking so glibly, let them gaze at him in silent astonishment (29:9; 40:4; Mc 7:16).
21:7 Job asserted that his friends' statements about the short-lived success of the **wicked**

were wrong (15:20; 18:5–21; 20:5,15–18). The fact is that the wicked often live long, prosperous lives in positions of power (Ec 7:15).
21:8–13 Contrary to his friends' assertions (15:20–30; 18:5–19; 20:21–28), the wicked live out their lives and leave behind **children** who are also successful and prosperous.
21:14–15 As Job viewed it, the wicked succeed, even while rejecting **the Almighty**. They neither serve him nor recognize his lordship (Pss 73:9–12; 94:3).
21:17 Job's rhetorical question implies that despite the **wicked** person's acts of evil and flagrant defiance of God, it does not appear that God disciplines them; thus, Bildad's statements did not hold up (18:5; cp. Ps 73:4–5,12). **Lamp** is used metaphorically as a symbol of a happy life (Ps 18:28). An extinguished lamp refers to an untimely death (2Sm 21:17), often because of the judgment of God (Pr 13:9; 20:20; 24:20).

21:18 Windblown **straw** and **chaff** often symbolize judgment. As Job saw it, the wicked person escapes judgment while he lives. Job's remarks were born of pessimism because of his suffering, and they do not accurately reflect biblical teaching (Ps 1:4; Dn 2:35; Zph 2:1–2).
21:19–20 As Job saw it, God's punishment unfairly passes over the wicked person and lands on the next generation (Dt 24:16; Jr 31:29–30; Ezk 18:2–4). To **drink from the Almighty's wrath** reflects the figure of the cup of God's judgment (Ps 75:8; Is 51:17; Jr 25:15; Ezk 23:31–34).
21:23–26 Job's observations on life pointed to facts that could not be accounted for in the worldview expressed by his friends. As Job saw it, a person's goodness or wickedness had nothing to do with life's fortunes.
21:29–30 Job's questions imply that his friends' doctrine of swift retribution conflicts with facts that anyone who has traveled can

Don't you accept their reports?^A

30 Indeed, the evil person is spared
from the day of disaster,
rescued from the day of wrath.

31 Who would denounce his behavior
to his face?
Who would repay him for what
he has done?

32 He is carried to the grave,
and someone keeps watch over
his tomb.

33 The dirt on his grave is^B sweet to him.
Everyone follows behind him,
and those who go before him are
without number.

34 So how can you offer me
such futile comfort?
Your answers are deceptive.

THIRD SERIES OF SPEECHES
Eliphaz Speaks

22 Then Eliphaz the Temanite replied:
2 Can a man be of any use to God?
Can even a wise man be of use to him?

3 Does it delight the Almighty if you
are righteous?
Does he profit if you perfect
your behavior?

4 Does he correct you and take you
to court
because of your piety?

5 Isn't your wickedness abundant
and aren't your iniquities endless?

6 For you took collateral
from your brothers without cause,
stripping off their clothes
and leaving them naked.

7 You gave no water to the thirsty
and withheld food from the famished,

8 while the land belonged
to a powerful man
and an influential man lived on it.

9 You sent widows away empty-handed,
and the strength of the fatherless
was^C crushed.

10 Therefore snares surround you,
and sudden dread terrifies you,

11 or darkness, so you cannot see,
and a flood of water covers you.

12 Isn't God as high as the heavens?
And look at the highest stars —
how lofty they are!

13 Yet you say, "What does God know?
Can he judge through total darkness?

14 Clouds veil him so that he cannot see,
as he walks on the circle of the sky."

15 Will you continue on the ancient path
that wicked men have walked?

16 They were snatched away
before their time,
and their foundations
were washed away by a river.

17 They were the ones who said to God,
"Leave us alone!"
and "What can the Almighty do to us?"^D

18 But it was he who filled their houses
with good things.
The counsel of the wicked is
far from me!

19 The righteous see this and rejoice;
the innocent mock them, saying,

20 "Surely our opponents are destroyed,
and fire has consumed
what they left behind."

21 Come to terms with God and be at peace;
in this way^E good will come to you.

---

^A 21:29 Lit *signs* ^B 21:33 Lit *The clods of the wadi are* ^C 22:9 LXX, Syr, Vg, Tg read *you have* ^D 22:17 LXX, Syr; MT reads *them* ^E 22:21 Lit *peace; by them*

---

observe. Rather than having their homes destroyed (18:14–15; 20:22), the wicked rich live securely in them.
21:31 Job's friends said that the wicked are on shaky ground and soon fall, but Job observes they are so powerful that no one can touch them.
21:32–33 Job's observation was that the wicked nobleman went to his **grave** with great honor and a large funeral procession (Ec 8:10), which was contrary to Bildad's remarks (Jb 18:17). The image of the **dirt** being **sweet** may indicate that as far as Job could tell, the wicked person's lot was pleasant even in death.
21:34 Job categorically denounced his friends' counsel as failing to provide **comfort** (v. 3; 16:2–3) and being **deceptive** (13:4).
22:1–3 Eliphaz began his speech with a series of rhetorical questions that expected a negative answer.
22:4–5 Previously Eliphaz had told Job that his **piety** would see him through his ordeal (4:6–7) after God's discipline had run its course (5:17–18). Now he accused Job of

wickedness (see vv. 6–9). Later, Job defended himself against these charges (31:16–17).
22:6 Eliphaz charged Job with social crimes. He said Job had taken as **collateral** the outer garments or cloaks of those who were in debt to him. These should have been returned to the person each night as protection against the cool night air (Ex 22:26–27). Job later refuted Eliphaz's charge (31:19–20).
22:7–8 Eliphaz accused Job of insensitivity. Although Job was a **powerful** and **influential man**, his actions showed he was not concerned about the needy. He supplied neither **water** nor **food** to them despite their circumstances (Is 58:7; Mt 10:41–42).
22:9 Eliphaz cited Job for failing to provide for **widows** and orphans. Care of the oppressed served as a standard of common decency and social obligation in the ancient Near East (Dt 14:28–29; 24:17–22; Jms 1:27). The alleviation of their need was of concern to God (Dt 10:17–18; 27:19).
22:10–11 Eliphaz applied Bildad's remarks (18:8–11,18) metaphorically to Job's situation.

Job's misdeeds had so ensnared him that he was overwhelmed like **water** that flooded the soul (27:20; Ps 69:15).
22:12–14 Eliphaz suggested that Job interpreted God's control of the vast universe in the opposite way: God was too distant to see man's actions. Eliphaz misrepresented Job's position, for Job had complained that God scrutinized his actions (Jb 7:12,17–20; 9:17–18; 10:4–8; 13:27). The **total darkness** Job felt was his inability to get through to God (19:7–8).
22:15–16 Eliphaz implied that contrary to Job's observation that the wicked defied God but were seldom punished (Jb 21:15–16), the witness of time confirms that in God's judgment they suffer the loss of everything.
22:17 The defiant ones Job said were permitted to prosper (21:14) were the very ones Eliphaz said died prematurely. Experience shows that neither man was entirely correct.
22:19–20 Eliphaz confirmed Zophar's counsel (20:26–29) that the wicked would lose everything in a fiery end.

²² Receive instruction from his mouth,
and place his sayings in your heart.
²³ If you return to the Almighty, you will
be renewed.
If you banish injustice from your tent
²⁴ and consign your gold to the dust,
the gold of Ophir to the stones
in the wadis,
²⁵ the Almighty will be your gold
and your finest silver.
²⁶ Then you will delight in
the Almighty
and lift up your face to God.
²⁷ You will pray to him, and he will
hear you,
and you will fulfill your vows.
²⁸ When you make a decision, it will be
carried out,ᴬ
and light will shine on your ways.
²⁹ When others are humiliated
and you say, "Lift them up,"
God will save the humble.ᴮ
³⁰ He will even rescue the guilty one,
who will be rescued by the purity
of your hands.

Job's Reply to Eliphaz

23 Then Job answered:
² Today also my complaint is bitter.ᶜ
Hisᴰ hand is heavy
despite my groaning.
³ If only I knew how to find him,
so that I could go to his throne.
⁴ I would plead my case before him
and fill my mouth with arguments.
⁵ I would learn howᴱ he would
answer me;
and understand what he would say
to me.
⁶ Would he prosecute me forcefully?
No, he would certainly pay attention
to me.
⁷ Then an upright man could reason
with him,

and I would escape
from my Judgeᶠ forever.
⁸ If I go east, he is not there,
and if I go west, I cannot perceive him.
⁹ When he is at work to the north,
I cannot see him;
when he turns south, I cannot find him.
¹⁰ Yet he knows the way I have taken;ᴳ
when he has tested me, I will emerge
as pure gold.
¹¹ My feet have followed in his tracks;
I have kept to his way and not
turned aside.
¹² I have not departed from the commands
from his lips;
I have treasuredᴴ the words
from his mouth
more than my daily food.
¹³ But he is unchangeable; who can
oppose him?
He does what he desires.
¹⁴ He will certainly accomplish
what he has decreed for me,
and he has many more things like these
in mind.ᴵ
¹⁵ Therefore I am terrified in his presence;
when I consider this, I am afraid of him.
¹⁶ God has made my heart faint;
the Almighty has terrified me.
¹⁷ Yet I am not destroyedᴶ by the darkness,
by the thick darkness that covers
my face.

24 Why does the Almighty not reserve
times for judgment?
Why do those who know him never see
his days?
² The wicked displace boundary markers.
They steal a flock and provide pasture
for it.
³ They drive away the donkeys owned
by the fatherless

ᴬ22:28 Lit out for you ᴮ22:29 Lit bowed of eyes ᶜ23:2 Syr, Tg, Vg; MT reads rebellion ᴰ23:2 LXX, Syr; MT reads My
ᴱ23:5 Lit the words ᶠ23:7 Or judgment ᴳ23:10 Lit way with me ᴴ23:12 LXX, Vg read treasured in my bosom ᴵ23:14 Lit
these with him ᴶ23:17 Or silenced

22:23–25 The verb **return** connotes turning from self to God with a deliberate choice to abandon sin and godlessness in order to live in submission to God and his standards (Jr 23:5; Ac 2:38). The verb translated **renewed** is literally "be built up." It implies a successful, godly lifestyle. The **gold of Ophir** was highly prized in the ancient Near East (1Kg 9:28), but Job should throw away his precious **gold** and let God be his treasure (Ps 16:5; Is 33:6; Mt 13:44; 19:21; Php 3:7–9; 1Tm 6:6).
22:26–27 Job had complained that he could get no answer from God when he prayed (13:20–24; 19:7–8). Eliphaz restated that when Job had submitted to God's discipline and had been renewed, he would enjoy restored fellowship with God (5:17–26).

22:28 Eliphaz suggested that when Job was restored, his plans would no longer be frustrated. Rather than the darkness he now experienced (vv. 10–11; 19:8), the **light** of God's presence and guidance would **shine** on all he did (Pss 27:1; 56:13; 89:15; 1Jn 1:7).
23:1–2 Job answered Eliphaz with an attempt to justify his attitude.
23:8–9 Job experienced God as highly elusive. He sought God **east** … **west** … **north**, and **south** but could not **perceive him**. At the same time, God was so close Job felt his relentless attacks.
23:10 As dross is removed from **gold** in the crucible, leaving a shining surface, so when God finished dealing with him, Job would appear as a shining example of righteousness (Pr 17:3).

23:11–12 The word translated **daily food** means "portion" (Ex 29:28). A related word means "statute" (Ex 29:9), suggesting that Job had prized God's precepts more than his own natural inclinations (Rm 7:23). The reading found in the Septuagint (LXX) and the Latin Vulgate adds the phrase "in my bosom" after **treasured**. This pictures something close to Job's heart (Ps 119:11).
24:1 Job's observations of society convinced him that God's justice was lacking. Those who kept his standards went unrewarded, and the wicked were not judged for their evil. God should establish **times** for administering justice.
24:2–3 The removal of **boundary markers** was a serious offense (Dt 19:14; Pr 23:10). Confiscation of animals in lieu of a debt

and take the widow's ox as collateral.
⁴ They push the needy off the road;
the poor of the land are forced
into hiding.
⁵ Like wild donkeys in the wilderness,
the poor go out to their task of foraging
for food;
the desert provides nourishment
for their children.
⁶ They gather their fodder in the field
and glean the vineyards of the wicked.
⁷ Without clothing, they spend
the night naked,
having no covering against the cold.
⁸ Drenched by mountain rains,
they huddle against^A the rocks,
shelterless.
⁹ The fatherless infant is snatched
from the breast;
the nursing child of the poor is seized
as collateral.^B
¹⁰ Without clothing,
they wander about naked.
They carry sheaves but go hungry.
¹¹ They crush olives in their presses;^C
they tread the winepresses,
but go thirsty.
¹² From the city, men^D groan;
the mortally wounded cry for help,
yet God pays no attention
to this crime.

¹³ The wicked are those who rebel
against the light.
They do not recognize its ways
or stay on its paths.
¹⁴ The murderer rises at dawn
to kill the poor and needy,
and by night he becomes a thief.
¹⁵ The adulterer's eye watches for twilight,
thinking, "No eye will see me,"
and he covers his face.
¹⁶ In the dark they break^E into houses;
by day they lock themselves in,^F
never experiencing the light.
¹⁷ For the morning is like darkness
to them.
Surely they are familiar with the terrors
of darkness!

¹⁸ They float^G on the surface
of the water.
Their section of the land is cursed,
so that they never go
to their vineyards.
¹⁹ As dry ground and heat snatch away
the melted snow,
so Sheol steals those who have sinned.
²⁰ The womb forgets them;
worms feed on them;
they are remembered no more.
So injustice is broken like a tree.
²¹ They prey on^H the childless woman
who is unable to conceive,
and do not deal kindly with the widow.
²² Yet God drags away^I the mighty
by his power;
when he rises up, they have
no assurance of life.
²³ He gives them a sense of security,
so they can rely on it,
but his eyes watch over their ways.
²⁴ They are exalted for a moment,
then gone;
they are brought low and shrivel up
like everything else.^J
They wither like heads of grain.

²⁵ If this is not true, then who
can prove me a liar
and show that my speech
is worthless?

Bildad Speaks

25 Then Bildad the Shuhite replied:
² Dominion and dread belong to him,
the one who establishes harmony
in his heights.
³ Can his troops be numbered?
Does his light not shine on everyone?
⁴ How can a human be justified
before God?
How can one born of woman
be pure?
⁵ If even the moon does not shine
and the stars are not pure in his sight,
⁶ how much less a human, who is
a maggot,
a son of man,^K who is a worm!

---

^A 24:8 Lit *they embrace* ^B 24:9 Text emended; MT reads *breast; they seize collateral against the poor* ^C 24:11 Lit *olives between their rows* ^D 24:12 One Hb ms, Syr read *the dying* ^E 24:16 Lit *dig* ^F 24:16 Lit *they seal for themselves* ^G 24:18 Lit *are insignificant* ^H 24:21 LXX, Tg read *They harm* ^I 24:22 Or *God prolongs the life of* ^J 24:24 LXX reads *like a mallow plant in the heat* ^K 25:6 Or *a mere mortal*

---

was unforgivable, especially against the **fatherless** and widows. Care of the widow, orphans, and poor is a duty of righteousness (6:27; 22:9; Ps 82:3–4) and a priority to God (Dt 27:17; Ps 68:5).
24:13–17 Evil persons use the cover of darkness to commit foul deeds, including murder, adultery, and theft. These are violations of the sixth, seventh, and eighth commandments. The verb **lock** (lit "seal") indicates that the wicked stay enclosed in their houses like

a person who puts his seal on a document. The **dark** is a friend to evildoers, so **light** terrifies them (Jn 3:20; 1Co 4:5; Eph 5:8–11). **24:25** Although the wicked might die prematurely, they do so without being brought to justice in this life (21:22–34). Job defied his friends to disprove his thesis (17:10).
25:1–2 In the shortest of the speeches by Job's friends, Bildad summed up the friends' position against Job's claims. The might of God, who established **harmony**

in the original creation (Gn 1:31; Ps 104:1–4) and maintained it in mankind (13:11), should inspire **dread** in mankind (13:11).
25:3–6 Bildad asked a series of rhetorical questions implying negative answers. He restated the position of the three friends (4:17; 8:20; 11:14–16; 15:14–16; 22:4) as opposed to Job's claims of innocence and purity (13:18; 16:17; 23:4–7,10–12). If God's heavenly bodies were not **pure**, how could man claim to be (4:18–19; 15:15–16)? Job acknowledged that

Job's Reply to Bildad

26 Then Job answered:
² How you have helped the powerless
and delivered the arm that is weak!
³ How you have counseled the unwise
and abundantly provided insight!
⁴ With whom did you speak these words?
Whose breath came out of your mouth?

⁵ The departed spirits tremble
beneath the waters and all that
inhabit them.
⁶ Sheol is naked before God,
and Abaddon has no covering.
⁷ He stretches the northern skies
over empty space;
he hangs the earth on nothing.
⁸ He wraps up the water in his clouds,
yet the clouds do not burst
beneath its weight.
⁹ He obscures the view of his throne,
spreading his cloud over it.
¹⁰ He laid out the horizon on the surface
of the waters
at the boundary between light
and darkness.
¹¹ The pillars that hold up the sky tremble,
astounded at his rebuke.
¹² By his power he stirred the sea,
and by his understanding
he crushed Rahab.
¹³ By his breath the heavens gained
their beauty;
his hand pierced the fleeing serpent.ᴬ
¹⁴ These are but the fringes of his ways;
how faint is the word we hear of him!
Who can understand
his mighty thunder?

27 Job continued his discourse, saying:
² As God lives, who has deprived me
of justice,
and the Almighty who has
made me bitter,
³ as long as my breath is still in me
and the breath from God remains
in my nostrils,
⁴ my lips will not speak unjustly,
and my tongue will not utter deceit.

⁵ I will never affirm that you are right.
I will maintain my integrityᴮ until I die.
⁶ I will cling to my righteousness
and never let it go.
My conscience will not accuse me
as long as I live!

⁷ May my enemy be like the wicked
and my opponent like the unjust.
⁸ For what hope does
the godless person have when he is
cut off,
when God takes away his life?
⁹ Will God hear his cry
when distress comes on him?
¹⁰ Will he delight in the Almighty?
Will he call on God at all times?
¹¹ I will teach you about God's power.
I will not conceal what the Almighty
has planned.ᶜ
¹² All of you have seen this for yourselves,
why do you keep up this empty talk?

¹³ This is a wicked man's lot from God,
the inheritance the ruthless receive
from the Almighty.
¹⁴ Even if his children increase,
they are destined for the sword;
his descendants will never
have enough food.
¹⁵ Those who survive him will be buried
by the plague,
yet their widows will not weep for them.
¹⁶ Though he piles up silver like dust
and heaps up fine clothing like clay—
¹⁷ he may heap it up, but the righteous
will wear it,
and the innocent will divide up
his silver.
¹⁸ The house he built is
like a moth's cocoon
or a shelter set up by a watchman.
¹⁹ He lies down wealthy, but will do so
no more;
when he opens his eyes, it is gone.
²⁰ Terrors overtake him like a flood;
a storm wind sweeps him away at night.
²¹ An east wind picks him up,
and he is gone;

ᴬ **26:13** = Leviathan   ᴮ **27:5** Lit *will not remove my integrity from me*   ᶜ **27:11** Lit *what is with the Almighty*

his life and man's destiny were tied to maggots and worms (7:5; 17:14; 21:26; 24:20), which speak of man's lowly existence (Ps 22:6) and terminal condition (Is 14:11).
26:1–4 Job replied sarcastically that Bildad had delivered **insight** (or "sound wisdom") to the **unwise** (Job). In truth Bildad had only parroted common knowledge (12:2–3), and his **words** originated with others (4:17–19; 25:4–6).
26:5–6 Job had previously delivered a discourse about God's dominion. Bildad had extolled God's heavenly rule (25:5). Job had added that **Sheol** was open to God's view

(Pr 15:11). Sheol here refers to the place of the wicked **departed spirits**, quartered in the heavenly heights (Ps 48:1–2).
26:7–8 Northern refers to God's dwelling in the heavenly heights (Ps 48:1–2).
26:12–13 God's **power** and wisdom were evident in his control over the primal **sea** with its mighty creatures. The word for **stirred** may also be translated "bring rest to" (Jr 50:34). The reference to God destroying **Rahab** and the **fleeing serpent** counters

ancient cosmologies in which mythical deities conquered chaos at creation. Job underscored the fact that the Lord alone is God and is the controller of everything (9:13–14; Pss 74:13; 89:10).
27:18 House portrays metaphorically the wicked person's life and possessions. A watchman's **shelter** was a temporary structure built during harvest time as a booth from which to guard the fields. After harvest it was allowed to fall into ruin.
27:19–23 Clapping the **hands**, hissing, and shaking the head were common gestures of contempt (Lm 2:15; Nah 3:19; Zph 2:15).

it carries him away from his place.
22 It blasts at him without mercy,
while he flees desperately
from its force.
23 It claps its hands at him
and scoffs at him from its place.

A Hymn to Wisdom

28 Surely there is a mine for silver
and a place where gold is refined.
2 Iron is taken from the ground,
and copper is smelted from ore.
3 A miner puts an end to the darkness;
he probes^ the deepest recesses
for ore in the gloomy darkness.
4 He cuts a shaft far
from human habitation,
in places unknown to those who walk
above ground.
Suspended far away from people,
the miners swing back and forth.
5 Food may come from the earth,
but below the surface the earth
is transformed as by fire.
6 Its rocks are a source of lapis lazuli,
containing flecks of gold.
7 No bird of prey knows that path;
no falcon's eye has seen it.
8 Proud beasts have never walked on it;
no lion has ever prowled over it.
9 The miner uses a flint tool
and turns up ore from the root
of the mountains.
10 He cuts out channels in the rocks,
and his eyes spot every treasure.
11 He dams up the streams from flowing^B
so that he may bring to light
what is hidden.

12 But where can wisdom be found,
and where is understanding located?
13 No one can know its value,^C
since it cannot be found in the land
of the living.
14 The ocean depths say, "It's not in me,"
while the sea declares, "I don't have it."
15 Gold cannot be exchanged for it,
and silver cannot be weighed out
for its price.
16 Wisdom cannot be valued in the gold
of Ophir,
in precious onyx or lapis lazuli.

17 Gold and glass do not compare with it,
and articles of fine gold
cannot be exchanged for it.
18 Coral and quartz are not
worth mentioning.
The price of wisdom is beyond pearls.
19 Topaz from Cush cannot compare
with it,
and it cannot be valued in pure gold.

20 Where then does wisdom come from,
and where is understanding located?
21 It is hidden from the eyes
of every living thing
and concealed from the birds
of the sky.
22 Abaddon and Death say,
"We have heard news of it
with our ears."
23 But God understands the way
to wisdom,
and he knows its location.
24 For he looks to the ends of the earth
and sees everything under the heavens.
25 When God fixed the weight of the wind
and distributed the water by measure,
26 when he established a limit^D
for the rain
and a path for the lightning,
27 he considered wisdom and evaluated it;
he established it and examined it.
28 He said to mankind,
"The fear of the Lord —that is wisdom.
And to turn from evil is understanding."

Job's Final Claim of Innocence

29 Job continued his discourse, saying:
2 If only I could be as in months
gone by,
in the days when God watched over me,
3 when his lamp shone above my head,
and I walked through darkness
by his light!
4 I would be as I was in the days
of my youth
when God's friendship rested
on my tent,
5 when the Almighty was still with me
and my children were around me,
6 when my feet were bathed in curds
and the rock poured out streams of oil
for me!

---

^28:3 Lit probes all ^B28:11 LXX, Vg read He explores the sources of the streams ^C28:13 LXX reads way ^D28:26 Or decree

---

28:3–4 At times men were **suspended** in cages or baskets hung by ropes in order to pick out the minerals at the side of the mineshaft. In some cases they cut horizontal tunnels. In dark places workers illuminated their way with torches.
28:5–6 Sometimes tunnel walls were heated with **fire** and then quickly drenched with water to crack hard stone. The rocks, which were then hauled to the surface, might contain **lapis lazuli** (a dark blue stone), which typically contain **flecks** of **gold**-colored pyrite.
28:15–19 Glass was a valuable commodity in the ancient Near East. **Wisdom** is more valuable than precious metals and gem stones, including the famed **gold of Ophir** (22:23–25) or **topaz from Cush** (Ethiopia). **29:1–3** Job had complained about God's scrutiny (7:17–20; 13:27). Now he recalled previous days when God made him successful. The **lamp** symbolized God's blessings and direction. When it is extinguished, disaster follows (18:6; 21:17).
29:4–6 Job's prior life was filled with God's abundant blessings. **Curds** and **oil** symbolize life's finest pleasures (20:17; Ps 104:15). The **rock** was either the rocky soil where the olive trees grew or the stone press used to extract the oil.

7 When I went out to the city gate
and took my seat in the town square,
8 the young men saw me and withdrew,
while older men stood to their feet.
9 City officials stopped talking
and covered their mouths
with their hands.
10 The noblemen's voices were hushed,
and their tongues stuck to the roof
of their mouths.
11 When they heard me, they blessed me,
and when they saw me, they spoke well
of me.ᴬ
12 For I rescued the poor who cried out
for help,
and the fatherless child who had no one
to support him.
13 The dying blessed me,
and I made the widow's heart rejoice.
14 I clothed myself in righteousness,
and it enveloped me;
my just decisions were like a robe
and a turban.
15 I was eyes to the blind
and feet to the lame.
16 I was a father to the needy,
and I examined the case of the stranger.
17 I shattered the fangs of the unjust
and snatched the prey from his teeth.
18 So I thought, "I will die in my own nest
and multiply my days as the sand.ᴮ
19 My roots will have access to water,
and the dew will rest on my branches
all night.
20 My whole being will be refreshed
within me,
and my bow will be renewed
in my hand."
21 Men listened to me with expectation,
waiting silently for my advice.
22 After a word from me they did not
speak again;
my speech settled on them like dew.
23 They waited for me as for the rain
and opened their mouths as for
spring showers.
24 If I smiled at them, they couldn't
believe it;

they were thrilled atᶜ the light
of my countenance.
25 I directed their course and presided
as chief.
I lived as a king among his troops,
like one who comforts
those who mourn.

30 But now they mock me,
men younger than I am,
whose fathers I would have refused
to put
with my sheep dogs.
2 What use to me was the strength
of their hands?
Their vigor had left them.
3 Emaciated from poverty
and hunger,
they gnawed the dry land,
the desolate wasteland by night.
4 They plucked mallowᴰ
among the shrubs,
and the roots of the broom tree were
their food.
5 They were banished
from human society;
people shouted at them
as if they were thieves.
6 They are living on the slopes
of the wadis,
among the rocks and in holes
in the ground.
7 They bray among the shrubs;
they huddle beneath the thistles.
8 Foolish men, without even a name.
They were forced to leave the land.
9 Now I am mocked by their songs;
I have become an object of scorn
to them.
10 They despise me and keep their distance
from me;
they do not hesitate to spit
in my face.
11 Because God has loosened
myᴱ bowstring and oppressed me,
they have cast off restraint
in my presence.
12 The rabbleᶠ rise up at my right;
they trapᴳ my feet

ᴬ**29:11** Lit *When an ear heard, it called me blessed, and when an eye saw, it testified for me*   ᴮ**29:18** Or *as the phoenix*
ᶜ**29:24** Lit *they did not cast down*   ᴰ**30:4** Or *saltwort*   ᴱ**30:11** Alt Hb tradition, LXX, Vg read *his*   ᶠ**30:12** Hb obscure
ᴳ**30:12** Lit *stretch out*

29:7–10 The **town square** at the **city gate** served as a place for legal (Ru 4:1,11) and judicial decisions, a marketplace (2Kg 7:1), and a general gathering place (Jr 17:19–20). Job's **seat** and the public reaction to his presence indicate prominence and respect.
29:11–13 Contrary to Eliphaz's charges (22:8–9), Job's beneficence toward the needs of the **poor**, orphan, **dying**, and widow earned the admiration of everyone.

29:14–17 In cases where Job served in an official capacity, he demonstrated **righteousness** as he defended the rights of the helpless and rendered their oppressors powerless.
29:18–20 Because of God's blessings and Job's righteousness, Job expected to live a long and healthy life (Dt 4:39–40; 1Kg 3:14). **Sand** symbolizes things too numerous to count (6:3; Gn 22:17; 1Kg 4:29). A **nest** presents a secure image of home and family. The well-watered tree speaks of health and

prosperity as well as Job's righteousness (Pss 1:1–3; 92:12). The **bow** symbolizes strength and virility (Gn 49:24).
30:1–4 Mallow (or saltwort) came from an edible plant that served as food for the poor. The **roots of the broom tree** were usually used to make charcoal rather than **food** (Ps 120:4).
30:9–10 Returning to the topic of v. 1, Job lamented the **songs** the young men created to mock him (Lm 3:14). They also **spit** at him.

and construct their siege ramp[A]
   against me.
¹³ They tear up my path;
   they contribute to my destruction,
   without anyone to help them.
¹⁴ They advance as through
   a gaping breach;
   they keep rolling in through the ruins.
¹⁵ Terrors are turned loose against me;
   they chase my dignity away
     like the wind,
   and my prosperity has passed by
     like a cloud.

¹⁶ Now my life is poured out before me,
   and days of suffering have seized me.
¹⁷ Night pierces my bones,
   but my gnawing pains never rest.
¹⁸ My clothing is distorted
   with great force;
   he chokes me by the neck
   of my garment.[B]
¹⁹ He throws me into the mud,
   and I have become like dust and ashes.

²⁰ I cry out to you for help, but you do not
     answer me;
   when I stand up, you merely look at me.
²¹ You have turned against me
   with cruelty;
   you harass me with your strong hand.
²² You lift me up on the wind and make me
     ride it;
   you scatter me in the storm.
²³ Yes, I know that you will lead me
   to death —
   the place appointed for all who live.

²⁴ Yet no one would stretch out his hand
   against a ruined person[C]
   when he cries out to him for help
   because of his distress.
²⁵ Have I not wept for those
   who have fallen on hard times?
   Has my soul not grieved for the needy?
²⁶ But when I hoped for good, evil came;

when I looked for light, darkness came.
²⁷ I am churning within[D] and cannot rest;
   days of suffering confront me.
²⁸ I walk about blackened, but not
   by the sun.[E]
   I stood in the assembly and cried out
     for help.
²⁹ I have become a brother to jackals
   and a companion of ostriches.
³⁰ My skin blackens and flakes off,[F]
   and my bones burn with fever.
³¹ My lyre is used for mourning
   and my flute for the sound of weeping.

31

I have made a covenant with my eyes.
How then could I look
   at a young woman?[G]
² For what portion would I have
   from God above,
   or what inheritance from the Almighty
     on high?
³ Doesn't disaster come to the unjust
   and misfortune to evildoers?
⁴ Does he not see my ways
   and number all my steps?

⁵ If I have walked in falsehood
   or my foot has rushed to deceit,
⁶ let God weigh me on accurate scales,
   and he will recognize my integrity.

⁷ If my step has turned from the way,
   my heart has followed my eyes,
   or impurity has stained my hands,
⁸ let someone else eat what I have sown,
   and let my crops be uprooted.

⁹ If my heart has gone astray over a
     woman
   or I have lurked at my neighbor's door,
¹⁰ let my own wife grind grain
     for another man,
   and let other men sleep with[H] her.
¹¹ For that would be a disgrace;
   it would be an iniquity
     deserving punishment.

[A]30:12 Lit *and raise up their destructive paths*   [B]30:18 Hb obscure   [C]30:24 Lit *a heap of ruins*   [D]30:27 Lit *My bowels boil*
[E]30:28 Or *walk in sunless gloom*   [F]30:30 Lit *blackens away from me*   [G]31:1 Or *a virgin*   [H]31:10 Lit *men kneel down over*

30:20–23 These verses form a prayer. Job accuses God of **cruelty**; God beats him with a storm, then leads him to **death**, "the meeting-house for all mankind."
30:27–30 Job's suffering was total—physical, spiritual, and emotional. His **churning** insides and **fever** may have been a side-effect of the disease that **blackened** his **skin**. Abandoned by God and his fellow man, he compared his unheeded cries for help to the jackal's woeful howl and the mournful sound of the ostrich (Mc 1:8).
30:31 In bold figures Job portrayed his cries as the sounds of musical instruments. Rather than tunes of joy (21:12; Ps 33:2), praise (Ps 150:4), or comfort (1Sm 16:23), Job's **lyre**

produced only dirge-like tones. His **flute** provided no happy melody (21:12; Mt 11:17), only a mourning **sound** (Mt 9:23).
31:1 Job began the final defense of his purity by declaring that he had never looked at a **young woman** lustfully. The **eyes** were considered the gateway to the inner person. The wandering eye got Samson (Jdg 16:1) and David (2Sm 11:2–3) into serious trouble, and Jesus warned of its dangers (Mt 5:27–30). Job's **covenant** language underscored the seriousness of his purpose and his binding self-limitation.
31:2–4 Job posed three questions, emphasizing God's dealing with him should he violate his covenant not to lust after a young woman. Job would have neither standing

with God nor blessing, and God—who saw all that Job did (7:17–19)—would judge him as an evildoer (18:5–12; 27:13–23).
31:5–6 The metaphor of where one's **foot** walks expresses proper conduct (12:5; 23:11; Pr 4:26–27). The weighing of a man in the **scales** was a test of character (Dn 5:27).
31:7–8 The body parts mentioned here are often used figuratively to express ethical conduct: foot (Ps 17:5), **heart** or mind (Pr 23:19), **eyes** (Ps 101:3), and **hands** (Ps 24:4).
31:9–12 Adultery has dire consequences (Lv 20:10; 2Sm 12:7–10). Illicit sex is likened to a **fire** that burns the person (Pr 6:27–29) to the utmost—all the way to **Abaddon**, the realm of death and destruction (26:6; 28:22).

12 For it is a fire that consumes down
      to Abaddon;
   it would destroy my entire harvest.

13 If I have dismissed the case of my male
      or female servants
   when they made a complaint against me,
14 what could I do when God stands up
      to judge?
   How should I answer him
      when he calls me to account?
15 Did not the one who made me
      in the womb also make them?
   Did not the same God form us both
      in the womb?

16 If I have refused the wishes of the poor
   or let the widow's eyes go blind,
17 if I have eaten my few crumbs alone
      without letting the fatherless
      eat any of it —
18 for from my youth, I raised him
      as his father,
   and since the day I was born^A I guided
      the widow —
19 if I have seen anyone dying for lack
      of clothing
   or a needy person without a cloak,
20 if he^B did not bless me
   while warming himself with the fleece
      from my sheep,
21 if I ever cast my vote^C
      against a fatherless child
   when I saw that I had support
      in the city gate,
22 then let my shoulder blade fall
      from my back,
   and my arm be pulled from its socket.
23 For disaster from God terrifies me,
   and because of his majesty
      I could not do these things.

24 If I placed my confidence in gold
   or called fine gold my trust,

25 if I have rejoiced because my wealth
      is great
   or because my own hand has acquired
      so much,
26 if I have gazed at the sun
      when it was shining
   or at the moon moving in splendor,
27 so that my heart was secretly enticed
   and I threw them a kiss,^D
28 this would also be an iniquity
      deserving punishment,
   for I would have denied God above.

29 Have I rejoiced over
      my enemy's distress,
   or become excited when trouble came
      his way?
30 I have not allowed my mouth to sin
   by asking for his life with a curse.
31 Haven't the members
      of my household said,
   "Who is there who has not had enough
      to eat at Job's table?"
32 No stranger had to spend the night
      on the street,
   for I opened my door to the traveler.
33 Have I covered my transgressions
      as others do^E
   by hiding my iniquity in my heart
34 because I greatly feared the crowds
   and because the contempt of the clans
      terrified me,
   so I grew silent and would not go outside?

35 If only I had someone to hear my case!
   Here is my signature; let the Almighty
      answer me.
   Let my Opponent compose
      his indictment.
36 I would surely carry it on my shoulder
   and wear it like a crown.
37 I would give him an account of all
      my steps;
   I would approach him like a prince.

---

^A31:18 Lit and from my mother's womb   ^B31:20 Lit his loins   ^C31:21 Lit I raise my hand   ^D31:27 Lit and my hand kissed my mouth   ^E31:33 Or as Adam

---

31:16–22 Job offered a long list of if-then statements, calling down a curse on himself if he had failed to do the right thing in any of these cases.
31:16–18 Eliphaz had charged Job with dealing unjustly with the widow, **fatherless**, and **poor** (22:4–9). Job denied such wrongdoing. Even as a young man he had been concerned for the needs of the helpless.
31:19–20 Eliphaz had charged Job with taking the clothes of a debtor as collateral (22:6). Refuting this charge, Job stated that when any person lacked necessary clothing, he supplied it and they blessed him for it. The CSB's **he** (lit "his loins") is a synecdoche where a part refers to the whole body.
31:21 Job denied that he had ever used his official position to take advantage of the

weak, such as the **fatherless**, even though he had the backing of others.
31:24–28 Job offered another list of if-then statements (cp. vv. 16–22), denying that he had sinned in any of these ways (v. 28).
31:24–25 Job disavowed materialistic and greedy desires. Eliphaz's implied criticism was false (22:24–25).
31:26–27 Job had not secretly paid homage to false deities identified with the **sun** or **moon**, as some would do by throwing a **kiss** toward the heavens. Job understood that idolatry and paganism were an abomination to the Lord (Dt 4:19; 17:2–5).
31:29–30 Job had not gloated over an **enemy's** misfortune. This would violate accepted ethical standards (Pr 24:17–18; 25:21–22; Mt 5:43–47).

31:35–37 Job had repeatedly pleaded for a fair hearing before God (13:18–23; 23:2–7) even though he feared such a meeting (9:14–16) and felt the need for an arbitrator (9:32–35; 16:21). Job, nonetheless, felt so confident that his integrity would be vindicated that he signed his affidavit. His **signature** is literally his *tav*, the last letter in the Hebrew alphabet, in the form of an X in ancient Hebrew. The name of the letter means "mark" (Ezk 9:4). Documents were usually sealed with an engraved seal (1Kg 21:8), but when signed by hand, even a literate person used the *tav*. When God presented his **indictment** (7:20), Job would place it proudly on his **shoulder** and approach the Lord as a **prince** wearing a victor's **crown**. Job was certain that he had proven his innocence and righteousness (23:3–7; 27:6).

³⁸ If my land cries out against me
and its furrows join in weeping,
³⁹ if I have consumed its produce
without payment
or shown contempt for its tenants,^A
⁴⁰ then let thorns grow
instead of wheat
and stinkweed instead of barley.

The words of Job are concluded.

Elihu's Angry Response

32 So these three men quit answering Job, because he was righteous in his own eyes. ² Then Elihu son of Barachel the Buzite from the family of Ram became angry. He was angry at Job because he had justified himself rather than God. ³ He was also angry at Job's three friends because they had failed to refute him and yet had condemned him.^B

⁴ Now Elihu had waited to speak to Job because they were all older than he. ⁵ But when he saw that the three men could not answer Job, he became angry.

⁶ So Elihu son of Barachel the Buzite replied:

I am young in years,
while you are old;
therefore I was timid and afraid
to tell you what I know.
⁷ I thought that age should speak
and maturity should teach wisdom.
⁸ But it is the spirit in a person—
the breath from the Almighty—
that gives anyone understanding.
⁹ It is not only the old who are wise
or the elderly who understand
how to judge.
¹⁰ Therefore I say, "Listen to me.
I too will declare what I know."
¹¹ Look, I waited for your conclusions;
I listened to your insights
as you sought for words.
¹² I paid close attention to you.

Yet no one proved Job wrong;
not one of you refuted his arguments.
¹³ So do not claim,
"We have found wisdom;
let God deal with him, not man."
¹⁴ But Job has not directed his argument
to me,
and I will not respond to him
with your arguments.

¹⁵ Job's friends are dismayed and can
no longer answer;
words have left them.
¹⁶ Should I continue to wait now that
they are silent,
now that they stand there
and no longer answer?
¹⁷ I too will answer;^C
yes, I will tell what I know.
¹⁸ For I am full of words,
and my spirit^D compels me to speak.
¹⁹ My heart^E is like unvented wine;
it is about to burst like new wineskins.
²⁰ I must speak so that I can find relief;
I must open my lips and respond.
²¹ I will be partial to no one,
and I will not give anyone
an undeserved title.
²² For I do not know how to give such titles;
otherwise, my Maker would remove me
in an instant.

Elihu Confronts Job

33 But now, Job, pay attention to my speech, and listen to all my words. ² I am going to open my mouth; my tongue will form words on my palate. ³ My words come from my upright heart, and my lips speak with sincerity what they know. ⁴ The Spirit of God has made me,

^A31:39 Lit or caused the breath of its tenants to breathe out   ^B32:3 Alt Hb tradition reads condemned God   ^C32:17 Lit answer my part   ^D32:18 Lit and the spirit of my belly   ^E32:19 Lit belly

31:38–40 Job finished with a final testimony toward his vindication in the form of two more conditional statements and a curse (see vv. 16–22). He had demonstrated his integrity and righteousness toward his fellow man. He had neither overworked his land (see Lv 25:2–7) nor defrauded its tenants (24:10–11). He fortified his declaration with an imprecation involving the failure of his crops (Gn 3:18; Is 5:6).
32:2–3 The names Elihu ("He Is My God") and Barachel ("God Has Blessed") testify to vital faith. The names Elihu and Ram appear in connection with the later family of David (Ru 4:19; 1Ch 27:18). Buz was the brother of Uz and Abraham's nephew (Gn 22:20–21). Job was from the land of Uz (Jb 1:1). Elihu was angry because he perceived that Job had argued for his own righteousness, implying that God was, therefore, unjust (see 40:8),

and because Job's friends had condemned him without getting to the essential issue in his case.
32:4–5 For the fourth time we are told that Elihu was angry.
32:6–10 Elihu's back-to-back speeches are the longest in the book. In fact, "Elihu's speeches are longer than 12 other OT books and 17 of the 27 NT books" (Robert Alden, "Job", New American Commentary). No one answered Elihu. Though he was young, Elihu maintained that wisdom was not the exclusive possession of the old but was available to everyone. Elihu implied that God had so enlightened his spirit that he must speak (Jb 32:17–20).
32:11–12 Elihu prefaced his remarks by noting that he had given due deference to his elders.
32:13–14 Elihu agreed with Job (12:20; 13:12–19; 17:10; 21:34) that the friends had failed to

demonstrate their claim to represent godly instruction (4:12–16) or traditional wisdom (15:17–19). Job would find Elihu a tougher opponent who would not follow the friends' line of argumentation.
32:19–20 Elihu's heart (inner being; lit "belly") was so full that it was about to burst. New wine was normally put into new wineskins, which would expand with the fermentation process (Mt 9:17). If the wineskin was closed off without proper ventilation, it could burst.
32:21–22 Elihu was under divine obligation to speak his mind impartially. The phrase be partial is literally "lift up the face." This idiom is used of showing respect (Gn 32:21) or partiality (Pr 18:5). Elihu would not use flattering speech (Ps 12:1–3; Pr 28:23) by making reference to anyone's title.

and the breath of the Almighty
gives me life.
⁵ Refute me if you can.
Prepare your case against me;
take your stand.
⁶ I am just like you before God;
I was also pinched off
from a piece of clay.
⁷ Fear of me should not terrify you;
no pressure from me should weigh you
down.

⁸ Surely you have spoken in my hearing,
and I have heard these very^A words:
⁹ "I am pure, without transgression;
I am clean and have no iniquity.
¹⁰ But he finds reasons to oppose me;
he regards me as his enemy.
¹¹ He puts my feet in the stocks;
he stands watch over all my paths."

¹² But I tell you that you are wrong
in this matter,
since God is greater than man.
¹³ Why do you take him to court
for not answering anything
a person asks?^B
¹⁴ For God speaks time and again,
but a person may not notice it.
¹⁵ In a dream, a vision in the night,
when deep sleep comes over people
as they slumber on their beds,
¹⁶ he uncovers their ears
and terrifies them^C with warnings,
¹⁷ in order to turn a person
from his actions
and suppress the pride of a person.
¹⁸ God spares his soul from the Pit,
his life from crossing the river of death.^D
¹⁹ A person may be disciplined on his bed
with pain
and constant distress in his bones,
²⁰ so that he detests bread,
and his soul despises his favorite food.

²¹ His flesh wastes away to nothing,^E
and his unseen bones stick out.
²² He draws near to the Pit,
and his life to the executioners.
²³ If there is an angel on his side,
one mediator out of a thousand,
to tell a person what is right for him^F
²⁴ and to be gracious to him and say,
"Spare him from going down to the Pit;
I have found a ransom,"
²⁵ then his flesh will be healthier^G than
in his youth,
and he will return to the days
of his youthful vigor.
²⁶ He will pray to God, and God will delight
in him.
That person will see his face
with a shout of joy,
and God will restore his righteousness
to him.
²⁷ He will look at men and say,
"I have sinned and perverted
what was right;
yet I did not get what I deserved.^H
²⁸ He redeemed my soul from going down
to the Pit,
and I will continue to see the light."
²⁹ God certainly does all these things
two or three times to a person
³⁰ in order to turn him back
from the Pit,
so he may shine with the light of life.
³¹ Pay attention, Job, and listen to me.
Be quiet, and I will speak.
³² But if you have something to say,^I
answer me;
speak, for I would like to justify you.
³³ If not, then listen to me;
be quiet, and I will teach you wisdom.

34

Then Elihu continued,^J saying:
² Hear my words, you wise ones,
and listen to me,
you knowledgeable ones.

^A 33:8 Lit heard a sound of ^B 33:13 Lit court, for he does not answer all his words ^C 33:16 LXX; MT reads and seals ^D 33:18 Or from perishing by the sword ^E 33:21 Lit away from sight ^F 33:23 Or to vouch for a person's uprightness ^G 33:25 Hb obscure ^H 33:27 Lit and the same was not to me ^I 33:32 Lit If there are words ^J 34:1 Lit answered

33:5 Elihu acted like an attorney in a legal proceeding. After he had stated his case, Job was free to try to **refute** him with counter arguments.
33:8–11 Elihu demonstrated that he had listened carefully to Job's claims of being pure and innocent (16:17; 23:7,10–12; 27:5–6), as well as being unjustly oppressed by God (10:6–7; 13:26–27; 19:11; 30:18–19).
33:14–17 Job had complained that God might pass by him without his noting it (9:11) and that God had ignored his requests for him to answer (13:24; 19:7; 30:20). Elihu implied that Job had failed to notice God's speaking to him. Elihu built upon Eliphaz's words about God instructing him in a nighttime visitation (4:12–19). To uncover the ear is to instruct, inform, or reveal (36:15; Ru 4:4; Is 22:14).

33:18 By **the Pit** is meant the grave or the state of death (16:10; 17:14). Just as Israel crossed the Jordan River to enter the promised land, so the image of the **river of death** portrays man's passing from this life into the next. "River" is the preferred rendering of a Hebrew word that also can be translated as "sword."
33:19–22 God may also communicate with a person through the discipline of **pain**. The **distress** may be so aggravating that **a person** loses all desire for food. In his severe pain, Job had expressed the fear that death was near (10:18–22; 16:16,22).
33:23–24 Elihu pointed out that the arbitrator Job had longed for between himself and God (9:33; 16:21) was available to bring a person to repentance. Angels often

served in this capacity (Gn 48:15–16; Ps 34:6–7). God through his mediating angel supplies grace to ransom and deliver the repentant and surrendered person from death (Ex 14:19–20; Jb 17:3; Ps 49:7–9). Alternatively, the word translated **angel** may also be rendered as "messenger" (Jdg 11:13; 1Kg 20:2–10; Mal 2:7). Elihu may have sensed that he was serving as God's messenger to bring about Job's reconciliation with God (Jb 33:6–7).
33:25–28 The result of the angel's work is given here. There will be physical and spiritual restoration, including repentance.
33:31–33 Elihu asked for Job's further **attention** (vv. 1–5) while he developed his teaching. Job should interrupt only if he had something significant to add.

³ Doesn't the ear test words
    as the palate tastes food?
⁴ Let us judge for ourselves what is right;
    let us decide together what is good.
⁵ For Job has declared, "I am righteous,
    yet God has deprived me of justice.
⁶ Would I lie about my case?
    My wound^A is incurable,
    though I am without transgression."
⁷ What man is like Job?
    He drinks derision like water.
⁸ He keeps company with evildoers
    and walks with wicked men.
⁹ For he has said, "A man gains nothing
    when he becomes God's friend."

¹⁰ Therefore listen to me, you men
    of understanding.
    It is impossible for God to do wrong,
    and for the Almighty to act unjustly.
¹¹ For he repays a person according to
    his deeds,
    and he gives him what his conduct
    deserves.^B
¹² Indeed, it is true that God does not
    act wickedly
    and the Almighty does not
    pervert justice.
¹³ Who gave him authority over the earth?
    Who put him in charge of
    the entire world?
¹⁴ If he put his mind to it
    and withdrew the spirit and breath
    he gave,
¹⁵ every living thing would perish together
    and mankind would return to the dust.

¹⁶ If you have understanding, hear this;
    listen to what I have to say.
¹⁷ Could one who hates justice
    govern the world?
    Will you condemn the mighty
    Righteous One,
¹⁸ who says to a king, "Worthless man!"
    and to nobles, "Wicked men!"?
¹⁹ God is not partial to princes

    and does not favor the rich
        over the poor,
    for they are all the work of his hands.
²⁰ They die suddenly in the middle
        of the night;
    people shudder, then pass away.
    Even the mighty are removed
        without effort.

²¹ For his eyes watch over a man's ways,
    and he observes all his steps.
²² There is no darkness, no deep darkness,
    where evildoers can hide.
²³ God does not need to examine
        a person further,
    that one should^C approach him in court.
²⁴ He shatters the mighty
        without an investigation
    and sets others in their place.
²⁵ Therefore, he recognizes their deeds
    and overthrows them by night, and they
        are crushed.
²⁶ In full view of the public,^D
    he strikes them for their wickedness,
²⁷ because they turned aside
        from following him
    and did not understand any of his ways
²⁸ but caused the poor to cry out to him,
    and he heard the outcry of the needy.
²⁹ But when God is silent, who can declare
        him guilty?
    When he hides his face, who can
        see him?
    Yet he watches over both individuals
        and nations,
³⁰ so that godless men should not rule
    or ensnare the people.

³¹ Suppose someone says to God,
    "I have endured my punishment;
    I will no longer act wickedly.
³² Teach me what I cannot see;
    if I have done wrong, I won't do it again."
³³ Should God repay you on your terms
    when you have rejected his?
    You must choose, not I!

---

^A **34:6** Lit *arrow*   ^B **34:11** Lit *and like a path of a man, he causes him to find*   ^C **34:23** Some emend to *God has not appointed a time for man to*   ^D **34:26** Lit *In a place of spectators*

34:3–4 Elihu referred to Job's earlier comments about the ear's ability to **test words** much as the **palate tastes food** (12:11). Elihu was confident that his words would stand up to scrutiny.
34:5–6 Elihu summarized Job's claims, which he was about to refute.
34:7–9 Elihu observed that Job was neither affected by the (justified) **derision** heaped upon him by others, nor was he above deriding others, especially God. In Elihu's opinion, this showed that Job had assumed the stance of an evildoer (see 21:7–15), especially when he complained that being righteous gained a person nothing before God (9:15,29–31).

34:10–12 In returning to his opening issue about God's justice (v. 5; cp. 32:2), Elihu denied Job's claim that God was treating him **unjustly** (27:2). All three friends had repeatedly applied in rigid fashion the doctrine of equal divine retribution: blessings for righteousness, judgment for unrighteousness, each in its proper degree (Jr 25:14; 30:11). Eliphaz had likewise championed that thesis but insisted that God's nature prohibited his wrongdoing (Dt 32:4; Ps 62:12; Jr 9:23–24). Elihu gave the implied answer to Bildad's earlier rhetorical question (Jb 8:2–3). God could not and did not act unrighteously or unjustly (Ps 92:15; Rm 3:5–6).

34:21–23 Elihu built on Job's earlier remarks that God watches everything that men do on earth (7:20; 31:4). There is no place, however dark, where **evildoers** can escape God's view. Job had asked for a court appearance in order to present his case before God (9:32–35; 13:18; 21:3–7; 31:35–37). As the omniscient, all-seeing Judge, he does not need to come to court to **examine** a person's ways.
34:29–30 Job felt that at times the unrighteous seem to have God's provision (12:6), but Elihu declared that such instances are illusions. Although God appears to ignore cases where wickedness prevails, he does see them. God's intervention may appear to be slow in coming, but he will rectify the

So declare what you know.
³⁴ Reasonable men will say to me,
along with the wise men who hear me,
³⁵ "Job speaks without knowledge;
his words are without insight."
³⁶ If only Job were tested to the limit,
because his answers are like those
of wicked men.
³⁷ For he adds rebellion to his sin;
he scornfully claps in our presence,
while multiplying his words
against God.

35

Then Elihu continued, saying:
² Do you think it is just when you say,
"I am righteous before God"?
³ For you ask, "What does it profit you,^A
and what benefit comes to me,
if I do not sin?"
⁴ I will answer you
and your friends with you.
⁵ Look at the heavens and see;
gaze at the clouds high above you.
⁶ If you sin, how does it affect God?
If you multiply your transgressions,
what does it do to him?
⁷ If you are righteous, what do you
give him,
or what does he receive
from your hand?
⁸ Your wickedness affects a person
like yourself,
and your righteousness, a son of man.^B
⁹ People cry out because of
severe oppression;
they shout for help because of
the power of the mighty.
¹⁰ But no one asks, "Where is God
my Maker,
who provides us with songs in the night,

¹¹ who gives us more understanding
than the animals of the earth
and makes us wiser than the birds
of the sky?"
¹² There they cry out,
but he does not answer,
because of the pride of evil people.
¹³ Indeed, God does not listen
to empty cries,
and the Almighty does not take note
of it —
¹⁴ how much less when^C you complain^D
that you do not see him,
that your case is before him
and you are waiting for him.
¹⁵ But now, because God's anger
does not punish
and he does not pay attention
to transgression,^E
¹⁶ Job opens his mouth in vain
and multiplies words
without knowledge.

36

Then Elihu continued, saying:
² Be patient with me a little longer,
and I will inform you,
for there is still more to be said
on God's behalf.
³ I will get my knowledge from a
distant place
and ascribe justice to my Maker.
⁴ Indeed, my words are not false;
one who has complete knowledge is
with you.
⁵ Yes, God is mighty, but he despises
no one;
he understands all things.^F
⁶ He does not keep the wicked alive,
but he gives justice to the oppressed.

^A**35:3** Some emend to *me*   ^B**35:8** Or *a mere mortal*   ^C**35:14** Or *how then can*   ^D**35:14** Lit *say*   ^E**35:15** LXX, Vg; MT reads *folly, or arrogance*; Hb obscure   ^F**36:5** Lit *he is mighty in strength of heart*

situation in accordance with his wise and sovereign disposition of earthly affairs (2Pt 3:8–9).

34:34–35 Job refused to speak, so Elihu declared himself the victor in his exchange with Job.

34:36–37 Elihu alluded to Zophar's initial declaration that God had not punished Job to the full **limit** for his sins (11:4–6). Because he had refused to acknowledge his sins, Job was rebelling against God. Elihu observed that Job had shown contempt for his friends (see Lm 2:15) while condemning God with his speaking (Jb 16:12–17; 30:18–19). This put Job on dangerous ground (Ezk 25:6–7).

35:1–3 In a rhetorical question implying a negative answer, Elihu suggested that Job had established his righteousness apart from God, but Job had made no such assertion. Elihu based his argument on Job's remarks that keeping God's righteous standards appeared to gain mankind nothing (9:22,29–31; 10:1–3,17; 21:4–21; 27:1).

35:4–7 Since God is transcendent and superior to man, neither man's **sin** nor his righteousness can harm or benefit God (7:20; 22:2–3). God's character and glory are not conditioned by man's actions.

35:9–11 The **songs** are the divine gift of music to alleviate painful nights of suffering (Pss 42:8; 77:6). These songs may be those of anticipated deliverance (Ps 30:4–5) or reminders of God's concern for his people in their need (Ps 118:1–7,14,28–29) or praise to God (Pss 96; 98).

35:14 Job had asked God why he did not answer his requests for the opportunity to state his case before him (13:20–24; 23:2–7). Elihu suggested that God's silence (30:20) was not because he was unaware of Job's situation (33:21–23) but was due to Job's self-righteousness and pride in maintaining his innocence (27:2–6; 31:35–37) in the face of God's discipline (34:11–12). Job might be ignoring God's many attempts to communicate with him (33:8–17). He might be missing his opportunities to exercise his God-given

wisdom (35:11) and to consider his Creator's provision for relief in his distress (v. 10).

35:15–16 Elihu ended this discourse on a similar note to his previous speech in which he recounted Job's rebellious tendencies (34:36–37). Because God had not given Job the full punishment that he deserved (11:6), he foolishly babbled on with meaningless prattle.

36:1–4 Elihu claimed to have access to the flawless mind of God. Here he professed **complete knowledge** for himself; in 37:16 he attributed the same to God.

36:5 The phrase **he understands all things** is literally "he is mighty in strength of heart." The Hebrew word for "heart" can refer to the emotions or to the mind (Ps 77:6). Elihu stated categorically that God's great power does not compromise his dealings with mankind. His strength of heart moves him to deal with compassionate firmness of purpose.

36:6 Contrary to Job's insistence that he received no **justice** from God in his suffering (7:19; 9:27–35; 10:20–21; 16:18–22; 19:7;

7 He does not withdraw his gaze
  from the righteous,
but he seats them forever
  with enthroned kings,
  and they are exalted.

8 If people are bound with chains
  and trapped by the cords of affliction,
9 God tells them what they have done
  and how arrogantly
  they have transgressed.
10 He opens their ears to correction
  and tells them to repent from iniquity.
11 If they listen and serve him,
  they will end their days in prosperity
  and their years in happiness.
12 But if they do not listen,
  they will cross the river of death^A
  and die without knowledge.

13 Those who have a godless heart
  harbor anger;
even when God binds them,
  they do not cry for help.
14 They die in their youth;
  their life ends among
  male cult prostitutes.
15 God rescues the afflicted by
  their affliction;
he instructs them by their torment.

16 Indeed, he lured you from the jaws^B
  of distress
to a spacious and unconfined place.
Your table was spread with choice food.
17 Yet now you are obsessed
  with the judgment due the wicked;
judgment and justice have seized you.
18 Be careful that no one lures you
  with riches;^C

do not let a large ransom^D
  lead you astray.
19 Can your wealth^E or all
  your physical exertion
keep you from distress?
20 Do not long for the night
  when nations will disappear
  from their places.
21 Be careful that you do not turn to iniquity,
  for that is why you have been tested
  by^F affliction.

22 Look, God shows himself exalted
  by his power.
Who is a teacher like him?
23 Who has appointed his way for him,
  and who has declared, "You have
  done wrong"?
24 Remember that you should praise
  his work,
which people have sung about.
25 All mankind has seen it;
people have looked at it from a distance.
26 Yes, God is exalted
  beyond our knowledge;
the number of his years
  cannot be counted.
27 For he makes waterdrops evaporate;^G
  they distill the rain into its^H mist,
28 which the clouds pour out
  and shower abundantly on mankind.
29 Can anyone understand how the clouds
  spread out
or how the thunder roars
  from God's pavilion?
30 See how he spreads his lightning
  around him
and covers the depths of the sea.
31 For he judges the nations with these;
  he gives food in abundance.

---

^A36:12 Or *will perish by the sword* ^B36:16 Lit *from a mouth of narrowness* ^C36:18 Or *you into mockery* ^D36:18 Or *bribe*
^E36:19 Or *cry for help* ^F36:21 Or *for you have preferred this to* ^G36:27 Lit *he draws in waterdrops* ^H36:27 Or *his*

30:16–23), Elihu declared that God's justice did extend to the **oppressed** (34:28).
36:7 Job had complained of God's constant scrutiny of him (7:17–20; 10:4–7), yet he had admitted that in times past when God watched over him, he experienced the good life (29:2–6). Elihu pointed out that the all-seeing God always looks to the good of the righteous.
36:8–9 Elihu pointed out that people's good includes their correction. God may allow the righteous to suffer like those **bound with chains** (i.e., like captives of war; see Nah 3:10) in order to keep them from going further along the path to destruction. Apparent injustice may be a disguised good in order that God may bring people's arrogance and sin to their attention.
36:10–12 The uncovered or opened ear symbolizes God's revelation and instruction to mankind (33:16; Is 50:4–5). The sinner's unopened ear indicates rebellion against God (Is 48:8). If a person's **ears** are opened to accept God's **correction**, he will obey God

and serve him faithfully. If the person's ear remains closed in disobedience, he will proceed in ignorance along the road to certain death (33:18).
36:13–14 Elihu pointed out that some people respond to God's chastisement angrily. **Cult prostitutes** were involved in the worship of idols (Dt 23:17; 1Kg 14:22–24; Hs 4:14).
36:15 Rather than being a sign of God's unconcern as Job had reasoned (9:15–16), **affliction** is a mark of God's mercy, keeping one from the deadly path of ignorance (v. 12).
36:16 Elihu turned to Job's speech in which he had contrasted his former life and present situation (chaps. 29–30). Rather than complaining that he was suffering unjustly, Job should recognize that he was experiencing God's means of correction and restoration, as Eliphaz had also argued (5:17–26).
36:20–21 Job should neither wish for death (7:13–16; 10:19–22) nor resign himself to it (17:13–18; 30:20–23). Elihu warned Job that by seeking some alternative method of ending his **affliction**, he was committing **iniquity**.

Rather, Job should learn the reasons for God's discipline in his life.
36:24–25 Rather than finding fault with God, Job should join **all mankind** in singing his **praise** (Pss 48:10; 100:1–2).
36:26–37:13 Elihu followed his own advice and launched into a long hymnlike praise of God. This prayer provides a setting for God's subsequent declarations to Job.
36:26 Elihu began his praise by pointing out that full **knowledge** of God is beyond human comprehension (42:3; Is 40:13–14). Humanity cannot fully appreciate his infinity (Ps 102:27). Job was in no position to criticize such a one, because God's power and wisdom defy human understanding (Is 40:28).
36:27–30 The complexities of the hydrologic cycle are under God's control.
36:31–33 God's control of the forces of nature involves both the sustenance and the judgment of the **nations**. Like a mighty cosmic warrior shooting his arrows (Hab 3:8–13), God propels the **lightning** across the sky (37:3) as an instrument of judgment,

³² He covers his hands with lightning
and commands it to hit its mark.
³³ The^A thunder declares his presence;^B
the cattle also, the approaching storm.

37 My heart pounds at this
and leaps from my chest.^C
² Just listen to his thunderous voice
and the rumbling that comes
from his mouth.
³ He lets it loose beneath the entire sky;
his lightning to the ends of the earth.

⁴ Then there comes a roaring sound;
God thunders with his majestic voice.
He does not restrain the lightning
when his rumbling voice is heard.
⁵ God thunders wondrously
with his voice;
he does great things that
we cannot comprehend.
⁶ For he says to the snow,
"Fall to the earth,"
and the torrential rains,
his mighty torrential rains,
⁷ serve as his sign to all mankind,
so that all men may know his work.
⁸ The wild animals enter their lairs
and stay in their dens.
⁹ The windstorm comes
from its chamber,
and the cold
from the driving north winds.
¹⁰ Ice is formed by the breath of God,
and watery expanses are frozen.
¹¹ He saturates clouds with moisture;
he scatters his lightning through them.
¹² They swirl about,
turning round and round
at his direction,
accomplishing everything
he commands them
over the surface of the inhabited world.

¹³ He causes this to happen
for punishment,
for his land, or for his faithful love.

¹⁴ Listen to this, Job.
Stop and consider God's wonders.
¹⁵ Do you know how God directs
his clouds
or makes their lightning flash?
¹⁶ Do you understand how the clouds float,
those wonderful works of him who has
perfect knowledge?
¹⁷ You whose clothes get hot
when the south wind brings calm
to the land,
¹⁸ can you help God spread out the skies
as hard as a cast metal mirror?
¹⁹ Teach us what we should say to him;
we cannot prepare our case because of
our darkness.
²⁰ Should he be told that I want to speak?
Can a man speak when he is confused?
²¹ Now no one can even look at the sun
after a wind has swept through
and cleared the sky.
²² Out of the north he comes, shrouded
in a golden glow;
awesome majesty surrounds him.
²³ The Almighty — we cannot
reach him —
he is exalted in power!
He will not violate justice and
abundant righteousness,
²⁴ therefore, men fear him.
He does not look favorably on any
who are wise in heart.

The Lord Speaks

38 Then the Lord answered Job from the
whirlwind. He said:
² Who is this who obscures my counsel
with ignorant words?
³ Get ready to answer me like a man;

---

^A**36:33** Lit *His,* or *Its*   ^B**36:33** Lit *thunder announces concerning him* or *it*   ^C**37:1** Lit *from its place*

---

unerringly hitting its **mark** (see Pss 18:14; 144:6). God's power and **presence** are felt by man and beast in the thunderstorm (Ps 77:18). **37:6–8** Both the **snow** (38:22) and **torrential rains** (1Kg 18:45; Ezk 13:11) are under God's control. They testify to his handiwork. Under such conditions even beasts seek shelter from the elements. If winter is in view (as in Jb 37:9–10), Elihu may be noting the process of animal hibernation. **37:9–10** Elihu portrayed as the **breath of God** the chilling winds of winter, transforming the landscape by the power of the Lord and under his direction. **37:14–16** Elihu believed that contemplation of **God's wonders** would give Job insight. **37:19–20** Job had spoken previously of wanting to present his case before the Lord, confident that he was in the right (13:18; 23:4) and would be vindicated (31:35–37). Elihu maintained that no one has the wisdom to

debate God, let alone win. If man cannot understand God's basic activities in the natural world, how can he expect to speak boldly in his presence? **37:21–22** The **north** was linked with God's residence in some cultures of the ancient Near East (Jb 23:9; 26:7; cp. Ps 48:2; Is 14:13–14). **37:24** Elihu's final advice was to **fear** God (Ec 12:13). This is wise, as Job himself had admitted (Jb 28:28). Elihu was from the beginning angry with Job because he believed that Job was self-righteous (Jb 32:2). Although Job feared God, he was playing God in his own life despite his constant acts of piety (1:5; cp. chap. 31). Job had been certain of his righteousness (27:6), but he had failed to recognize God's essential justice and righteousness (32:2; 37:23). Elihu's advice to Job was that he should truly fear (revere) God and turn from his self-centeredness. Then he

would understand both God's power and his moral integrity (42:2–6). Thus Job would find God sufficient for his every trial. **38:1** God's speaking to Job from the **whirlwind** was not from a windstorm such as that which destroyed the house of Job's children (1:18–19) or the winds of judgment (21:18). It was a theophany, a manifestation of God himself (Ezk 1:4; cp. 2Kg 2:11). Job needed to be reminded of who the **Lord** is in order to find him sufficient for his situation. **38:2** God did not impugn Job's integrity, but he did question his knowledge. Job had questioned God's just governance of the world and proposed that he could talk with God as an equal. He was misguided on both counts. **38:3** The Lord addressed Job by challenging him to enter into a dialogue in full possession of his human strength and faculties. The Hebrew word translated **man** often reflects a man in his strength and virility (Jr 30:6). It is

when I question you,
you will inform me.
⁴ Where were you when I established
the earth?
Tell me, if you haveᴬ understanding.
⁵ Who fixed its dimensions?
Certainly you know!
Who stretched a measuring line
across it?
⁶ What supports its foundations?
Or who laid its cornerstone
⁷ while the morning stars sang together
and all the sons of God shouted
for joy?

⁸ Who enclosed the sea behind doors
when it burst from the womb,
⁹ when I made the clouds its garment
and total darkness its blanket,ᴮ
¹⁰ when I determined its boundariesᶜ
and put its bars and doors in place,
¹¹ when I declared, "You may come this far,
but no farther;
your proud waves stop here"?

¹² Have you ever in your life commanded
the morning
or assigned the dawn its place,
¹³ so it may seize the edges of the earth
and shake the wicked out of it?
¹⁴ The earth is changed as clay is by a seal;
its hills stand out like the folds of
a garment.
¹⁵ Lightᴰ is withheld from the wicked,
and the arm raised in violence
is broken.

¹⁶ Have you traveled to the sources
of the sea
or walked in the depths of the oceans?
¹⁷ Have the gates of death been revealed
to you?
Have you seen the gates
of deep darkness?

¹⁸ Have you comprehended the extent
of the earth?
Tell me, if you know all this.

¹⁹ Where is the road to the home of light?
Do you know where darkness lives,
²⁰ so you can lead it back to its border?
Are you familiar with the paths
to its home?
²¹ Don't you know? You were already born;
you have lived so long!ᴱ

²² Have you entered the place
where the snow is stored?
Or have you seen the storehouses
of hail,
²³ which I hold in reserve for times
of trouble,
for the day of warfare and battle?
²⁴ What road leads to the place where light
is dispersed?ᶠ
Where is the source of the east wind
that spreads across the earth?

²⁵ Who cuts a channel for the flooding rain
or clears the way for lightning,
²⁶ to bring rain on an uninhabited land,
on a desert with no human life,ᴳ
²⁷ to satisfy the parched wasteland
and cause the grass to sprout?
²⁸ Does the rain have a father?
Who fathered the drops of dew?
²⁹ Whose womb did the ice come from?
Who gave birth to the frost of heaven
³⁰ when water becomes as hard as stone,ᴴ
and the surface of the watery depths
is frozen?

³¹ Can you fasten the chains
of the Pleiades
or loosen the belt of Orion?
³² Can you bring out the constellationsᴵ
in their season
and lead the Bearᴶ and her cubs?
³³ Do you know the laws of heaven?

ᴬ38:4 Lit know ᴮ38:9 Lit swaddling clothes ᶜ38:10 Lit I broke my statute on it ᴰ38:15 Lit Their light ᴱ38:21 Lit born; the number of your days is great ᶠ38:24 Or where lightning is distributed ᴳ38:26 Lit no man in it ᴴ38:30 Lit water hides itself as the stone ᴵ38:32 Or Mazzaroth; Hb obscure ᴶ38:32 Or lead Aldebaran

used at times of vigorous spiritual strength (Jb 16:21). **Get ready to answer** renders the Hebrew "gird up your loins." The idiom reflects the tucking of one's long garment between the legs and into the belt in preparation for an arduous task such as running (1Kg 18:46) or battle (Is 5:27).
38:4–6 God's first round of questions to Job challenged him to understand something of the Lord's creative power in both the inanimate (vv. 4–38) and animate (38:39–39:30) worlds.
38:7 The stars are personified as being able to sing. Alternatively, the **morning stars** may be a metaphor for the angels, who appear in the parallel line.
38:8–11 The origin of the **sea** is depicted in the imagery of childbirth.

38:16–18 The extent of Job's experiential knowledge is questioned. His limited travels cannot have included going to the hidden springs that lie in the **depths of the oceans**. Job had not seen even the shadow of the **gates of death**, let alone passed through them.
38:19–21 Light and **darkness** are personified, each having a **home** from which they daily emerged and returned. The Lord satirically reminded Job that he had not even been born when God commanded the first light to penetrate the primeval darkness (15:7; Gn 1:2–5).
38:22–23 The imagery of these verses views God as keeping **snow** and **hail** in heavenly storehouses for his use at appropriate times. God could use them as

weapons (Ex 9:18–26; Pss 68:14; 78:47–48; Is 28:2,19).
38:24 God reminded Job that his knowledge did not include the distribution of lightning (see textual footnote; also 36:30,32; 37:3,11,15) or the place where the **east wind** originated. Such a mighty desert wind had swept away Job's family (1:19).
38:31–33 God turned Job's attention to the constellations: **the Pleiades . . . Orion**, and **the Bear**. Job had mentioned them earlier in connection with God's creative activity (9:9). The meaning of the term **constellations** is uncertain and may include the planets (2Kg 23:5). Although Job knew of their existence, he did not understand the **laws** of physics and astronomy and their effect on the earth. God alone exercises dominion over all of this.

Can you impose its^A authority on earth?
³⁴ Can you command^B the clouds
so that a flood of water covers you?
³⁵ Can you send out lightning bolts,
and they go?
Do they report to you, "Here we are"?

³⁶ Who put wisdom in the heart^C
or gave the mind understanding?
³⁷ Who has the wisdom to number
the clouds?
Or who can tilt the water jars of heaven
³⁸ when the dust hardens like cast metal
and the clods of dirt stick together?

³⁹ Can you hunt prey for a lioness
or satisfy the appetite of young lions
⁴⁰ when they crouch in their dens
and lie in wait within their lairs?
⁴¹ Who provides the raven's food
when its young cry out to God
and wander about for lack of food?

39 Do you know when mountain goats
give birth?
Have you watched the deer in labor?
² Can you count the months
they are pregnant^D
so you can know the time
they give birth?
³ They crouch down to give birth
to their young;
they deliver their newborn.^E
⁴ Their offspring are healthy and grow up
in the open field.
They leave and do not return.^F

⁵ Who set the wild donkey free?
Who released the swift donkey
from its harness?
⁶ I made the desert its home,
and the salty wasteland its dwelling.
⁷ It scoffs at the noise of the village

and never hears the shouts of a driver.
⁸ It roams the mountains
for its pastureland,
searching for anything green.
⁹ Would the wild ox be willing
to serve you?
Would it spend the night
by your feeding trough?
¹⁰ Can you hold the wild ox to a furrow
by its harness?
Will it plow the valleys behind you?
¹¹ Can you depend on it because
its strength is great?
Would you leave it to do
your hard work?
¹² Can you trust the wild ox to harvest
your grain
and bring it to your threshing floor?

¹³ The wings of the ostrich flap joyfully,
but are her feathers and plumage
like the stork's?^G
¹⁴ She abandons her eggs on the ground
and lets them be warmed in the sand.
¹⁵ She forgets that a foot may crush them
or that some wild animal
may trample them.
¹⁶ She treats her young harshly, as if
they were not her own,
with no fear that her labor
may have been in vain.
¹⁷ For God has deprived her of wisdom;
he has not endowed her
with understanding.
¹⁸ When she proudly^G spreads her wings,
she laughs at the horse and its rider.

¹⁹ Do you give strength to the horse?
Do you adorn his neck with a mane?^G
²⁰ Do you make him leap like a locust?
His proud snorting fills one with terror.
²¹ He paws^H in the valley and rejoices
in his strength;

---

^A38:33 Or *God's*   ^B38:34 Lit *lift up your voice to*   ^C38:36 Or *the inner self*; Ps 51:6   ^D39:2 Lit *months they fulfill*   ^E39:3 Or *they send away their labor pains*   ^F39:4 Lit *return to them*   ^G39:13,18,19 Hb obscure   ^H39:21 LXX, Syr; MT reads *They dig*

38:36–38 God's questions implied that neither Job nor any human had the **wisdom** to control the weather. In a metaphor the clouds are likened to giant **water jars** (or skins), which are tipped to spill their water on hard, dry soil (see Dt 28:23).
38:39–41 Lions are capable of securing their own prey, but it is God who established the complex relationship of predator and prey. God also cares for the needs of the ravens, scavengers that often feed on the remains of prey. His control of ravens included using them to care for one of his prophets (1Kg 17:4–6). The stately lion and lowly raven serve as a merism, the two extremes (stately and lowly) representing the whole animal world.
39:1–4 The female **mountain goats** (ibex) and **deer** are able to reproduce without human help. God controls the entire process.

39:5–8 God implied that he looks after the **wild donkey** in the **desert**, free from the work and constraints of its domesticated counterpart. There is a theme here: God has placed every animal in a suitable environment. The Hebrew word rendered **scoffs** can mean "laughs" or "plays"; it occurs six times in the divine speeches (vv. 7,18,22; 40:20; 41:5,29).
39:9–12 Only God could control the powerful **wild ox** (probably the aurochs, *Bos primigenius*). Unlike the domesticated ox, the wild ox could not be harnessed to **harvest** man's **grain**. The Assyrian King Sennacherib compared his indomitable courage and strength to that of the wild ox. Its long horns were symbolic of strength (Nm 23:22; 24:8; Dt 33:17).
39:13–18 The depiction of the **ostrich** conforms to popular conception rather

than scientific observation. Because some females shared the same nesting area, one ostrich might look with disdain at another's eggs. Though they are unintelligent, they can outrun horses. Even this strange animal is designed and watched over by God.
39:19–25 The **horse** was particularly prized and possessed by royalty (1Kg 4:26; 10:26–28). The horse's great **strength** and swiftness made it an important part of ancient military forces, especially in pulling war chariots (Ex 15:1; Jdg 5:22; Jr 4:13; Nah 3:2). The leaping ability of locusts as well as their appearance and swift orderly advance when swarming made their comparison with horses a familiar one (Jl 2:4; Rv 9:7). The horse's fearlessness, eagerness, and confidence in the face of battle is personified as his saying "Aha!" (see the textual footnote at Jb 39:25).

he charges into battle.^A

22 He laughs at fear, since he is afraid
    of nothing;
he does not run from the sword.

23 A quiver rattles at his side,
    along with a flashing spear
    and a javelin.

24 He charges ahead^B
    with trembling rage;
he cannot stand still at the sound of the
    ram's horn.

25 When the ram's horn blasts,
    he snorts defiantly.^C
He smells the battle from a distance;
he hears the officers' shouts
    and the battle cry.

26 Does the hawk take flight
    by your understanding
and spread its wings to the south?

27 Does the eagle soar at your command
and make its nest on high?

28 It lives on a cliff where it spends
    the night;
its stronghold is on a rocky crag.

29 From there it searches for prey;
    its eyes penetrate the distance.

30 Its brood gulps down blood,
and where the slain are, it is there.

40

The Lord answered Job:
2 Will the one who contends
    with the Almighty correct him?
Let him who argues with God
    give an answer.^D

3 Then Job answered the Lord:

4 I am so insignificant. How can I
    answer you?
I place my hand over my mouth.

5 I have spoken once, and I will not reply;
twice, but now I can add nothing.

6 Then the Lord answered Job from the
whirlwind:

7 Get ready to answer me like a man;
When I question you, you will inform me.

8 Would you really challenge my justice?
Would you declare me guilty
    to justify yourself?

9 Do you have an arm like God's?
Can you thunder with a voice like his?

10 Adorn yourself with majesty
    and splendor,
and clothe yourself with honor
    and glory.

11 Pour out your raging anger;
look on every proud person
    and humiliate him.

12 Look on every proud person
    and humble him;
trample the wicked where they stand.^E

13 Hide them together in the dust;
imprison them in the grave.^F

14 Then I will confess to you
that your own right hand
    can deliver you.

15 Look at Behemoth,
which I made along with you.

---

^A39:21 Lit *he goes out to meet the weaponry*   ^B39:24 Lit *He swallows the ground*   ^C39:25 Lit *he says, "Aha!"*   ^D40:2 Lit *God respond to it*   ^E40:12 Lit *wicked in their place*   ^F40:13 Lit *together; bind their faces in the hidden place*

39:26–30 God closed this portion of his questioning of Job in the same way he began it. He challenged Job's understanding about the workings of nature (38:4). Job had not taught the **hawk** how to fly or when and where to migrate. The **eagle** did not build its lofty nest in an inaccessible **rocky crag** (Ob 4) at Job's direction. Job did not equip the eagle with keen eyesight.

40:1–2 God questioned Job with a renewed challenge to either answer or make a rebuttal. Otherwise Job must admit that his criticism was groundless. Job had criticized the Lord often in the earlier dialogues (9:14–20; 16:11–12; 21:17–26) and had longed to present his case before God to see how he would answer him (23:2–5; 31:35–37). Job now had that opportunity.

40:3–5 Job's answer was a non-answer. The Hebrew for the phrase **I am so insignificant** is literally "I am light/little." Job did not disclaim his innocence. He had said all he could about his situation. Placing his **hand** over his **mouth** showed Job's reluctance to add anything further.

40:6–7 Job had called on God to answer him (30:20). Now it is the other way around.

40:8 God now came to the heart of the matter. Was Job ready to condemn God, who had demonstrated his loving care for all creatures? Was Job so willing to defend his uprightness and innocence that he would declare God unjust (see 27:2)? Would Job **justify** himself (27:6) rather than see his suffering in the light of God's greater purposes? Job had an attitude problem that must be resolved if his fellowship with God was to be restored (14:15; 19:26–27; 29:2–6).

40:9 The **arm** is used figuratively for strength. God asked Job whether he had sufficient strength to enforce his decision if he were in charge of meting out justice.

40:10 If Job was to be in charge, where were his royal garments and evidence of his authority?

40:11–14 Job had complained that God failed to bring the wicked to justice in this life (21:30–33; 24:1–17), while depriving Job of justice (27:2). Should Job be able to demonstrate his ability to bring the wicked to justice, God would admit Job's sufficiency to care for his own situation. The **right hand** often symbolizes honor, authority, or power (Pss 110:1–2; 118:15–16). By it God lays hold of his enemies and the wicked and brings them to judgment (Ps 21:8–13). If Job was unable to deal similarly with the wicked, he must not accuse God of injustice.

40:15 Some have identified **Behemoth** as a type of mythological beast, such as the bull of heaven in the Mesopotamian *Epic of Gilgamesh* or the ferocious bullock, the Ugaritic goddess that Anat defeated. Allusions to mythological creatures had been made previously (3:8; 7:12; 9:13–14; 26:12–13), but the description here favors a living animal known to Job. The buffalo, a dinosaur, the rhinoceros, and (most often) the hippopotamus

---

#28 **99 Essential Christian Truths**

CREATION OUT OF NOTHING

The Bible teaches that God created the universe—everything both visible and invisible—out of nothing (sometimes expressed in the Latin phrase, "creation *ex nihilo*"). This means that before God created anything, nothing else existed except God himself. God alone is eternal; every created thing has a beginning. Therefore, the eternal God rules over all of his creation and he alone is worthy of worship. Denial of this doctrine has implications for God's sovereignty over and providence in creation. Because God created out of nothing, creation has meaning and purpose and points us to the Creator.

He eats grass like cattle.
16 Look at the strength of his back^A
   and the power in the muscles
      of his belly.
17 He stiffens his tail like a cedar tree;
   the tendons of his thighs are woven
      firmly together.
18 His bones are bronze tubes;
   his limbs are like iron rods.
19 He is the foremost of God's works;
   only his Maker can draw the sword
      against him.
20 The hills yield food for him,
   while all sorts of wild animals
      play there.
21 He lies under the lotus plants,
   hiding in the protection^B
      of marshy reeds.
22 Lotus plants cover him with their shade;
   the willows by the brook surround him.
23 Though the river rages,
      Behemoth is unafraid;
   he remains confident, even if
      the Jordan surges up to his mouth.
24 Can anyone capture him
      while he looks on,^C
   or pierce his nose with snares?

41 Can you pull in Leviathan with a hook
   or tie his tongue down with a rope?
2 Can you put a cord^D through his nose
   or pierce his jaw with a hook?
3 Will he beg you for mercy
   or speak softly to you?
4 Will he make a covenant with you
   so that you can take him
      as a slave forever?
5 Can you play with him like a bird
   or put him on a leash^E for your girls?
6 Will traders bargain for him
   or divide him among the merchants?
7 Can you fill his hide with harpoons
   or his head with fishing spears?
8 Lay a^F hand on him.
   You will remember the battle
   and never repeat it!

9 Any hope of capturing him proves false.
   Does a person not collapse
      at the very sight of him?
10 No one is ferocious enough
      to rouse Leviathan;
   who then can stand against me?
11 Who confronted me, that I
      should repay him?
   Everything under heaven belongs to me.
12 I cannot be silent about his limbs,
   his power, and his graceful proportions.
13 Who can strip off his outer covering?
   Who can penetrate his double layer
      of armor?^G
14 Who can open his jaws,^H
   surrounded by those terrifying teeth?
15 His pride is in his rows of scales,
   closely sealed together.
16 One scale is so close to another^I
   that no air can pass between them.
17 They are joined to one another,
   so closely connected^J they cannot
      be separated.
18 His snorting^K flashes with light,
   while his eyes are like the rays^L of dawn.
19 Flaming torches shoot from his mouth;
   fiery sparks fly out!
20 Smoke billows from his nostrils
   as from a boiling pot or burning reeds.
21 His breath sets coals ablaze,
   and flames pour out of his mouth.
22 Strength resides in his neck,
   and dismay dances before him.
23 The folds of his flesh are joined together,
   solid as metal^M and immovable.
24 His heart is as hard as a rock,
   as hard as a lower millstone!
25 When Leviathan rises, the mighty^N
      are terrified;
   they withdraw because of his thrashing.
26 The sword that reaches him will have
      no effect,
   nor will a spear, dart, or arrow.
27 He regards iron as straw,
   and bronze as rotten wood.

^A40:16 Or waist   ^B40:21 Lit plants, in the hiding place   ^C40:24 Lit capture it in its eyes   ^D41:2 Lit reed   ^E41:5 Lit or bind him
^F41:8 Lit your   ^G41:13 LXX; MT reads double bridle   ^H41:14 Lit open the doors of his face   ^I41:16 Lit One by one they approach
^J41:17 Lit another; they cling together and   ^K41:18 Or sneezing   ^L41:18 Lit eyelids   ^M41:23 Lit together, hard on him
^N41:25 Or the divine beings

have been suggested. The term "behemoth" occurs elsewhere only in Ps 73:22 where the psalmist compared his formerly embittered soul to a brute beast.
40:16–18 The point of comparison between the short tail of the hippopotamus and the **cedar tree** may simply be the fact of their respective hardness. **Tail** could be a euphemism, hence speaking to Behemoth's virility. Readings found in manuscripts of ancient versions (LXX, Vg, Syr) support this possibility.
40:19 Only God would dare to face this creature alone (v. 24). Cattle (Hb *behemah*)

were the first of God's created land animals. Behemoth (pl) would represent the **foremost** of all.
40:23 The **Jordan** may represent any river with a strong current.
40:24 Hunting parties attempted to **pierce** the **nose** of Behemoth to impair his breathing, making him vulnerable to **snares** or hooks.
41:1 Leviathan has been identified by interpreters as a whale, shark, dinosaur, sea monster, and a crocodile. In ancient Egypt the crocodile could symbolize royal power, yet it was a hunted animal.

41:10–11 If Job would not dare to face **Leviathan** single-handedly, how could he hope to confront God, who owned **everything** (including Leviathan), in order to present and win an argument (31:35–37)?
41:18–21 God's portrayal of Leviathan's foaming emergence from water is compared to that of a fire-breathing dragon. Similar creatures are described in Ugaritic mythology depicting Baal's defeat of Yam, the sea god.
41:22–25 Leviathan's **strength** and seemingly impregnable body were exceeded only by his inner courage and fearlessness.

²⁸ No arrow can make him flee;
   slingstones become like stubble to him.
²⁹ A club is regarded as stubble,
   and he laughs at the sound of a javelin.
³⁰ His undersides are jagged potsherds,
   spreading the mud
      like a threshing sledge.
³¹ He makes the depths seethe
      like a cauldron;
   he makes the sea like an ointment jar.
³² He leaves a shining wake behind him;ᴬ
   one would think the deep had gray hair!
³³ He has no equal on earth —
   a creature devoid of fear!
³⁴ He surveys everything that is haughty;
   he is king over all the proud beasts.ᴮ

Job Replies to the LORD

42 Then Job replied to the LORD:
   ² Iᶜ know that you can do anything
   and no plan of yours can be thwarted.
³ You asked, "Who is this who conceals
      my counsel with ignorance?"
   Surely I spoke about things I did not
      understand,
   things too wondrous for me toᴰ know.
⁴ You said, "Listen now, and I will speak.
   When I question you, you will
      inform me."
⁵ I had heard reports about you,
   but now my eyes have seen you.
⁶ Therefore, I reject my words and am
      sorry for them;
   I am dust and ashes.ᴱ,ᶠ

⁷ After the LORD had finished speakingᴳ
to Job, he said to Eliphaz the Temanite, "I am
angry with you and your two friends, for you
have not spoken the truth about me, as my
servant Job has. ⁸ Now take seven bulls and
seven rams, go to my servant Job, and offer
a burnt offering for yourselves. Then my servant Job will pray for you. I will surely accept
his prayer and not deal with you as your folly
deserves. For you have not spoken the truth
about me, as my servant Job has." ⁹ Then Eliphaz the Temanite, Bildad the Shuhite, and
Zophar the Naamathite went and did as the
LORD had told them, and the LORD accepted
Job's prayer.

God Restores Job

¹⁰ After Job had prayed for his friends, the LORD
restored his fortunes and doubled his previous possessions. ¹¹ All his brothers, sisters, and
former acquaintances came to him and dined
with him in his house. They sympathized with
him and comforted him concerning all the adversity the LORD had brought on him. Each one
gave him a piece of silverᴴ and a gold earring.
¹² So the LORD blessed the last part of Job's life
more than the first. He owned fourteen thousand sheep and goats, six thousand camels,
one thousand yoke of oxen, and one thousand
female donkeys. ¹³ He also had seven sons and
three daughters. ¹⁴ He named his first daughter Jemimah, his second Keziah, and his third
Keren-happuch. ¹⁵ No women as beautiful as
Job's daughters could be found in all the land,
and their father granted them an inheritance
with their brothers.
¹⁶ Job lived 140 years after this and saw his
children and their children to the fourth generation. ¹⁷ Then Job died, old and full of days.

ᴬ41:32 Lit *a path* ᴮ41:34 Lit *the children of pride* ᶜ42:2 Alt Hb tradition reads *You* ᴰ42:3 Lit *me, and I did not* ᴱ42:6 LXX
reads *I despise myself and melt; I consider myself dust and ashes* ᶠ42:6 Lit *I reject and I relent, concerning dust and ashes*
ᴳ42:7 Lit *speaking these words* ᴴ42:11 Lit *a qesitah*; the value of this currency is unknown

Leviathan's power and self-assurance made him a fitting symbol of Satan, the fearsome and fallen being whose raging is fully and finally quelled by God in the end (Rv 20:10). **41:30–32** A threshing sledge consisted of two boards whose undersides were embed-ded with sharp stones for crushing grain. When Leviathan dove into the water, he made it foam like ingredients boiled by the perfumer and left a **wake** like **gray hair**. **42:3** Job had questioned the equity and jus-tice of God's dealings (7:20; 21:7–34). God's wise handling of the physical and natural worlds convinced him that though he may have committed no overt sin, he had dabbled in questions beyond his understanding and experience. **42:4–5** Job now understood something of God's justice and wise dealings with the strongest of creatures. Although Job had previously considered himself to be upright, he confessed that he had been influenced by traditional but errant understandings (15:17–19; 16:2). By saying he now saw God, he meant that he had experienced God's presence and understood him better.

42:6 Job was humbled that the Lord of the universe had spoken to him. This went beyond his fondest wish for reestablished fellowship (9:32–35; 19:26–27; 23:3–5; 29:2–6). With genuine contrition he abandoned self in full dependence on God. **42:7** God rebuked **Eliphaz** and his **friends** for their treatment of Job. While defending God, they had attributed false reasons for Job's condition. They did not consider it pos-sible that his suffering was not directly due to sin. They also misrepresented God, as an insensitive enforcer of justice. Elihu, however, was not included in the Lord's rebuke. **42:8–9** The friends had left Job. They must return to him and offer large sacrifices for their transgression so Job could intercede in prayer for them. Job's health apparently had been restored by now. Rather than bearing enmity against his friends, Job graciously prayed for them. **42:10** Job's restoration was complete. The **doubled . . . possessions** (v. 12) reflect God's full acceptance of Job as his own (Dt 21:17; 2Kg 2:9). Not only had Job found God to be sufficient for his every need, but Satan had

been proven wrong. Job did not curse God as Satan had predicted he would (1:11; 2:5) or as his wife had urged him to do (2:9). **42:11** Job's family and friends offered him the comfort they had formerly withheld (12:4; 16:20; 19:14). The **piece of silver** was a unit of silver used in the period covered in some of the earliest biblical accounts (Gn 33:19; Jos 24:32). **42:12–15** The fact that the number of Job's children was not doubled may be meant to indicate that at least the souls of his de-ceased children lived on after death. In a sense, then, his children now numbered twice what they were. Job's fairness toward everyone (29:12–17,21–25) is seen in his concern that his **daughters** would share the **inheritance with their brothers**. **42:16–17** Job's **140 years** may indicate that he was seventy at the time of his testing and may reflect the number of added years that he lived. His epitaph is the same accorded other godly men (Gn 25:8; 1Ch 29:28; 2Ch 24:15). The Septuagint (LXX) adds that Job "will rise again with the ones whom the Lord raises up."

◀ Introduction to Psalms

Circumstances of Writing

Because the book of Psalms is a collection of many different psalms written over a long time, there is not just one author for this collection. By far the most common designation in the titles is "Of David," which may refer to David as the author of those psalms. David's role as a musician in Saul's court (1Sm 16:14–23) as well as his many experiences as a shepherd, a soldier, and a king make him a likely candidate for writing many of these psalms.

The problem is that the mention of his name in the titles consists of an ambiguous Hebrew construction. It is nothing more than a preposition attached to David's name. The preposition could be translated as "written by," "belonging to," "for," or "about." This does nothing more than relate the psalms bearing that title to David in some way but not necessarily naming him as author. The translation "Of David" accurately conveys this same ambiguity.

Other titles include the designations of Solomon (Pss 72; 127), Asaph (Pss 50, 70–83), the sons of Korah (Pss 42; 44–49), Ethan (Ps 89), Heman son of Korah (Ps 88), and Moses (Ps 90). All of these use the same Hebrew preposition that appears with David's name and therefore have the same ambiguity about authorship.

The book of Psalms consists of many different hymns and prayers composed by individuals but used by the community. If one were to take the names in the titles as authors, the date of composition ranges from the time of Moses (fifteenth century BC) to a time following the exile (sixth century BC or later). Some of the titles do contain historical information

that might indicate the setting of the composition, although even this (like the authorship) is ambiguous. They might not refer to the date of composition but to the setting of its contents, being composed sometime after the events had taken place. This is a more likely scenario since some of these psalms describe life-threatening situations, where composing a psalm in the heat of the moment would not have been a top priority. In many cases, these psalms include thanksgiving sections as well, showing that they were written after God had answered the prayers.

Contribution to the Bible

The relationship between God's activities in the lives of his people and their responses to them is the most significant contribution of this book. God never spoke directly in any of the psalms, as he often did in the narratives and prophets. Therefore, they are written from the human perspective as authors work their way through various life situations. The struggle to understand how God's attributes, particularly his sovereignty and goodness, relate to life experiences is a major theme in the collection.

Structure

The book of Psalms is, from first to last, a book of poetry. Hebrew poetry lacks rhyme and regular meter but uses parallelism wherein two (or three) lines are balanced and complete a thought. Some parallelism is synonymous, where the second line echoes the first. Antithetic parallelism uses a contrast between the two segments, and in synthetic parallelism the

---

Psalms Timeline

3000–1600 BC	1600–1500 BC	1500–1300 BC
Hymn to the Creator of the Heavens and the Earth, Ebla **3000–2000**	*Hymn to Ishtar*, Sumero–Akkadian **1600**	The Phoenicians develop a 22-letter alphabet that consisted of consonants only. It was read from right to left and became an important step in the development of the modern Western alphabet. **1600**
Abraham **2166–1991**	*Hymns to Amun*, Egypt **1550–1350**	
Isaac **2066–1866**	Moses **1526–1406**	
Lament for Ur, Sumerian **2000–1500**	Psalm 90, a prayer of Moses, the man of God	Hymn of Amenhotep II, Egypt **1450–1425**
	Book of the Dead, Egyptian texts appear on mummy wrappings **1500**	Ba'al and Anat, Ugarit **1400**
	Rig Veda, a collection of over 1,000 hymns in Sanskrit, the oldest known major work in an Indo–European language **1500**	Events in Judges **1380?–1060?**
		"Hymn to the Sun," Akhenaten **1375–1358**

second segment completes the idea in the first segment.

Another part of the structure of the Psalms is that they are generally grouped together by their titles, such as the Asaph psalms and those of the sons of Korah. Following the close of each of the first four books is a doxology or statement identifying the end of one book and the beginning of another. The psalms containing these statements are known as "seam" psalms because they show the "piecing together" of these psalms to form the collection as it now stands.

Outline

Psalms is unlike most other biblical books since it contains many writings collected and compiled over a period of time and finally organized into its present form. For this reason, it is not possible to outline the book in the standard way. However, there is clearly a structure to the collection. The book is divided into five parts, also known as books. According to Jewish tradition, this fivefold division was based on the arrangement of the Torah (or Pentateuch), the first five books of the Bible. The book divisions are Book 1 (Pss 1–41), Book 2 (Pss 42–72), Book 3 (Pss 73–89), Book 4 (Pss 90–106), and Book 5 (Pss 107–150).

Key verses in Psalms

4:3   Know that the LORD has set apart the faithful for himself;
            the LORD will hear when I call to him.

17:6   I call on you, God, because you will answer me; listen closely to me; hear what I say.

19:14   May the words of my mouth and the meditation of my heart be
            acceptable to you, LORD, my rock and my Redeemer.

46:1   God is our refuge and strength, a helper who is always found in times of trouble.

54:2   God, hear my prayer; listen to the words from my mouth.

56:3   When I am afraid, I will trust in you.

86:10   For you are great and perform wonders; you alone are God.

95:6   Come, let's worship and bow down; let's kneel before the LORD our Maker.

100:2   Serve the LORD with gladness; come before him with joyful songs.

118:24 This is the day the LORD has made; let's rejoice and be glad in it.

119:11 I have treasured your word in my heart so that I may not sin against you.

119:16 I will delight in your statutes; I will not forget your word.

119:34 Help me understand your instruction, and I will obey it and follow it with all my heart.

119:105 Your word is a lamp for my feet and a light on my path.

145:9   The LORD is good to everyone; his compassion rests on all he has made.

1300–900 BC	900–700 BC	700–400 BC
DAVID 1050?–970	Babylonian music makes use	Babylonians invade the
Saul is anointed king. **1050**	of five-tone and seven-	southern kingdom on three
David becomes king	tone scales. **800–700**	occasions. Each time Judeans
over all Israel. **1003**	Fall of Damascus to Tiglath-pileser	are taken to Babylon as
73 Psalms of David, 14	of Assyria **732**	exiles. **605, 597, 586**
of which are tied to	Fall of Samaria to the Assyrians **722**	Cyrus's decree allows return
events in David's life	Assyrians invade Judah but fail	of Jews from exile **538**
Solomon becomes king. **970**	to capture Jerusalem. **701**	Second temple is
Proverbs **970**	Greek poet Hesiod writes	dedicated **516**
Song of Songs **970?**	the *Theogony*, the oldest	Jerusalem's walls are rebuilt. **445**
Ecclesiastes **935?**	surviving account of the origin	Latest of the psalms are
Israel divides into northern	of the Greek gods. **700**	composed, including Psalm
and southern kingdoms. **931**		137. These reflect Israel's
		exile and restoration. **400**

BOOK I (Psalms 1–41)

The Two Ways

1
How happy is the one who does not
  walk in the advice of the wicked
or stand in the pathway with sinners
or sit in the company of mockers!
² Instead, his delight is in the
    LORD's instruction,
  and he meditates on it day and night.
³ He is like a tree planted beside flowing
    streams^A
  that bears its fruit in its season,
  and its leaf does not wither.
  Whatever he does prospers.

⁴ The wicked are not like this;
  instead, they are like chaff that the wind
    blows away.
⁵ Therefore the wicked will not stand up
    in the judgment,
  nor sinners in the assembly
    of the righteous.

⁶ For the LORD watches over the way
    of the righteous,
  but the way of the wicked leads to ruin.

Coronation of the Son

2
Why do the nations rage
  and the peoples plot in vain?
² The kings of the earth take their stand,
  and the rulers conspire together
  against the LORD and his Anointed One:^B

³ "Let's tear off their chains
  and throw their ropes off of us."

⁴ The one enthroned^C
    in heaven laughs;
  the Lord ridicules them.
⁵ Then he speaks to them in his anger
  and terrifies them in his wrath:
⁶ "I have installed my king
  on Zion, my holy mountain."

⁷ I will declare the LORD's decree.
  He said to me, "You are my Son;^D
  today I have become your Father.
⁸ Ask of me,
  and I will make the nations
    your inheritance
  and the ends of the earth
    your possession.
⁹ You will break them
    with an iron scepter;
  you will shatter them like pottery."

¹⁰ So now, kings, be wise;
  receive instruction, you judges
    of the earth.
¹¹ Serve the LORD with reverential awe
  and rejoice with trembling.
¹² Pay homage to^E the Son or he
    will be angry
  and you will perish in your rebellion,^F
    for his anger may ignite
    at any moment.
  All who take refuge in him are happy.

---

^A 1:3 Or *beside irrigation channels*   ^B 2:2 Or *anointed one*   ^C 2:4 Lit *who sits*   ^D 2:7 Or *son*, also in v. 12   ^E 2:12 Lit *Kiss*   ^F 2:12 Lit *perish in the way*

1:1 **Happy** expresses the sense of joy and satisfaction in one's state or circumstances. It often is the result of blessing that comes from trust in and obedience to the Lord (34:8; 40:4; 84:5; 89:15). Though related to God's blessing, it should be distinguished from the Hebrew word that is usually translated "blessed." The three descriptions that follow are expressed in the negative, showing what is *not* characteristic of this **one**. From the structure, it is better to understand these behaviors as parallel rather than progressing from lesser to greater sins.

1:2 The Hebrew word *torah* is sometimes translated as "law," but it is better understood as "teaching" or **instruction**. It is the revelation of God's will for his people rather than a body of legislative material or a collection of judicial decisions. The Lord's instruction is not a burden (Dt 30:11; 1Jn 5:3) but a **delight** for those who trust in him. "Meditating" is an activity closely related to concentrating on something in order to understand it.
1:3 The image of the righteous as flourishing trees is a common metaphor (92:12–14; Jr 17:8). Bearing **fruit** is an extension of the metaphor and refers to the products of the spiritual life in the individual (Pr 12:12; Jn 15:5; Col 1:10).
1:4 The contrast here focuses on the destiny of the two ways rather than on their behavior. **Chaff**, the useless product of threshing, is a contrast to the fruit in the previous verse.
1:5 In this context, **stand up** has the idea of being able to remain (or survive) during the time of **judgment**.
2:1 The question introduced by **why** is rhetorical and expresses surprise at the presumption of **the nations** in light of the reality of God's reign through his co-regent (vv. 6–9). The word **plot** is the same Hebrew word as "meditates" in 1:2, only in this case is used negatively to describe contemplation of plans to be free of God's dominion.

2:2 To **take** a **stand** is often used in military contexts to describe preparation for battle (1Sm 17:16; Jr 46:4). The **kings** and **rulers** are not just two specific groups, but they represent all governing authorities and dignitaries on **the earth** (see Jdg 5:3; Hab 1:10). **Anointed** is translated into Greek as *christos*, and it refers to God's choice and establishment of his King. In this context, the Anointed One is the Davidic king who is ultimately, in the progress of divine revelation, Jesus Christ (Eph 1:20–22).
2:7 **Decree** is used to indicate royal protocol in order to validate the right to rule. This was a particular concern in the ancient world where there was often a conflict following the crowning of a new king.
2:8 The right of sonship includes the right to **inheritance** and **possession** of what belongs to one's father. In this case, it is not limited but extends to **the ends of the earth**, an expression meaning the whole world and everything in it.
2:9 Smashing nations **like pottery** represents the effortless way in which something is annihilated (Is 30:14; Jr 19:11).
2:12 The word **Son** here is a different word from the one used in v. 7. It is an Aramaic word. To **pay homage** is to express obedience. The alternative is to **perish** as a result of God's **anger** that could **ignite** at **any moment**. This psalm ends where Ps 1 began—with the word **happy**.

Confidence in Troubled Times

3 *A psalm of David when he fled from his son Absalom.*

¹ LORD, how my foes increase!
There are many who attack me.
² Many say about me,
"There is no help for him in God."   *Selah*

³ But you, LORD, are a shield around me,
my glory, and the one who lifts up
my head.
⁴ I cry aloud to the LORD,
and he answers me
from his holy mountain.   *Selah*

⁵ I lie down and sleep;
I wake again because the LORD
sustains me.
⁶ I will not be afraid of thousands
of people
who have taken their stand against me
on every side.

⁷ Rise up, LORD!
Save me, my God!
You strike all my enemies
on the cheek;
you break the teeth of the wicked.
⁸ Salvation belongs to the LORD;
may your blessing be
on your people.   *Selah*

A Night Prayer

4 *For the choir director: with stringed instruments. A psalm of David.*

¹ Answer me when I call,
God, who vindicates me.^A
You freed me from affliction;
be gracious to me and hear
my prayer.

² How long, exalted ones,^B will my honor
be insulted?
How long will you love
what is worthless
and pursue a lie?   *Selah*
³ Know that the LORD has set apart
the faithful for himself;
the LORD will hear when I call to him.
⁴ Be angry^C and do not sin;
reflect in your heart while
on your bed and be silent.   *Selah*
⁵ Offer sacrifices in righteousness^D
and trust in the LORD.

⁶ Many are asking, "Who can show us
anything good?"
Let the light of your face shine
on us, LORD.

⁷ You have put more joy in my heart
than they have when their grain
and new wine abound.

---

^A 4:1 Or *God of my righteousness*   ^B 4:2 Lit *long, sons of a man*   ^C 4:4 Or *Tremble*   ^D 4:5 Or *Offer right sacrifices*

Ps 3 title This is one of fourteen psalms (3; 7; 18; 30; 34; 51–52; 54; 56–57; 59; 60; 63; 142) that are linked directly, by virtue of their titles, with specific events in the life of David. Though the titles reference specific events in David's life—in this case the time when **he fled from his son Absalom**—the actual content of these psalms is generalized. For this reason God's people who face the sort of life circumstances discussed in these psalms can identify with the author's words and be blessed. The episode of Absalom's rebellion and David's escape from him is recorded in 2Sm 15–18.
3:2 The meaning of the Hebrew term **Selah** is obscure.
3:3 The image of God as a **shield** is common, especially in the Psalms (18:30; 115:9; 144:2). It represents protection during a time of attack. A more unusual description is identifying God as one's **glory**. The Hebrew word *kavod* (lit "heavy") is often used of a person's reputation or significance, sometimes being translated as "honor." Its use here seems to indicate that the psalmist found his own significance and honor linked to his relationship with the Lord rather than in his own strength.
3:4 The **holy mountain** is Zion, which is the place where God dwelt among his people (Jl 3:17).
3:5–6 To **lie down** and to **sleep** are poetic and tangible ways to describe a state of security. The psalmist was confident that he would **wake again** because it is the Lord himself who sustained (i.e., supported or helped) him. The psalmist's security was

unrelated to his circumstances even though he was surrounded by enemies. Confidence in God's protection does not depend on one's circumstances.
3:7–8 Although the fact that the psalmist was calling out to the Lord is stated in v. 4, it is v. 7 that identifies the content of his plea. The request is rather brief and made up of two imperatives: **rise up** and **save**.
Ps 4 title This is the first psalm in the collection to have musical instructions to the **choir director**. While there is no description of the specific setting of the psalm, its theme and content are similar to Ps 3.
4:1 God, who vindicates me (lit "God of my righteousness/justice") is an appeal to God's justice specifically as it relates to the psalmist's just cause. **Affliction** pictures the idea of being hemmed in or trapped by enemies. In response, God **freed me** (lit "made a broad place for me"). The verb expresses completed action.
4:2 How long is an expression that shows concern about the duration of one's condition and is used in similar contexts in other psalms (79:5; 89:46). The enemies are called **exalted ones**. In Hebrew this is literally "sons of a man" and refers to people of high social status or influence (62:9) and is sometimes contrasted with the poor (49:2).
4:3 Set apart is not the normal expression for "make holy" (Hb *qadash*) but is a word that means "distinguish" or "separate" (Hb *palah*). The Lord makes a clear distinction between the **faithful** (those loyal to him)

and the "exalted ones" in how he relates to each of them (cp. Ex 11:7).
4:4 The Hebrew word translated **be angry** means to "shake" or "tremble" and is sometimes used literally for physical shaking (18:7; 77:18). When used of people it can mean trembling with fear (Ex 15:14; Dt 2:25), quarrelling (Gn 45:24), or a fit of rage (2Kg 19:27–28). It can also refer to provoking God to anger (Jb 12:6). The basic sense of the term when it is not used literally seems to be agitation. The Septuagint (LXX) translates it as "be angry" (from Gk *orgizo*), which is quoted by Paul in Eph 4:26. The idea of anger also works if one assumes that this is a challenge to the angry enemies not to sin. In other words, their anger should not lead to attacks against God's people.
4:5 A further challenge to the enemies is to **offer sacrifices in righteousness**, which means those that are in keeping with God's righteousness that he has prescribed. The final challenge is for these enemies to turn from their ways by trusting **in the LORD**.
4:6 The quotation here seems to be coming from those who were restless and pessimistic about their own situation and fate. This is an example of those within the community of God's people who were not trusting the Lord. The prayer for these people is that God would **let the light of** his **face shine** on the entire community.
4:7–8 The psalmist's own experience is in contrast to the pessimist's view in v. 6.

8 I will both lie down and sleep in peace,
  for you alone, LORD, make me live
    in safety.

The Refuge of the Righteous

5 For the choir director: with the flutes. A psalm
  of David.
¹ Listen to my words, LORD;
  consider my sighing.
² Pay attention to the sound of my cry,
  my King and my God,
  for I pray to you.

³ In the morning, LORD, you hear my voice;
  in the morning I plead my case to you
    and watch expectantly.

⁴ For you are not a God who delights
    in wickedness;
  evil cannot dwell with you.
⁵ The boastful cannot stand in your sight;
  you hate all evildoers.
⁶ You destroy those who tell lies;
  the LORD abhors
    violent and treacherous people.

⁷ But I enter your house
  by the abundance of your faithful love;
  I bow down toward your holy temple
    in reverential awe of you.
⁸ LORD, lead me in your righteousness
  because of my adversaries;
  make your way straight before me.

⁹ For there is nothing reliable in what
    they say;
  destruction is within them;

their throat is an open grave;
  they flatter with their tongues.
¹⁰ Punish them, God;
  let them fall by their own schemes.
  Drive them out because of
    their many crimes,
  for they rebel against you.

¹¹ But let all who take refuge in you rejoice;
  let them shout for joy forever.
  May you shelter them,
  and may those who love your name
    boast about you.
¹² For you, LORD, bless the righteous one;
  you surround him with favor
    like a shield.

A Prayer for Mercy

6 For the choir director: with stringed instruments,
  according to Sheminith. A psalm of David.
¹ LORD, do not rebuke me in your anger;
  do not discipline me in your wrath.
² Be gracious to me, LORD, for I am weak;^A
  heal me, LORD, for my bones
    are shaking;
³ my whole being is shaken with terror.
  And you, LORD — how long?

⁴ Turn, LORD! Rescue me;
  save me because of your faithful love.
⁵ For there is no remembrance of you
    in death;
  who can thank you in Sheol?

⁶ I am weary from my groaning;
  with my tears I dampen my bed
  and drench my couch every night.

^A 6:2 Or sick

5:1–2 God is also addressed as **King** (44:4; 68:24; 74:12; 84:3), indicating confidence in his dominion and his power to answer this prayer.
5:3 In the morning is repeated and indicates the time of the prayer (88:13). **Plead my case** is literally "prepare" or "set in order." It is likely preparing words (Jb 32:14) in a request for vindication.
5:4–5 The term **delights** is the same word as in 1:2, but here it is negated. Not only does God have no desire for **wickedness**, it cannot even exist in his presence. The word **stand** is the same term as in 2:2 describing those who "take their stand" against God. There is no contest between these wicked people and God; they cannot get anywhere near the Lord to attack him.
5:6–7 The combination of **house** and **temple** has led many to assume that this psalm must have been written by someone other than David since Solomon's temple was built after David's time. However, the Hebrew word for "temple" is not only used for Solomon's temple at Shiloh (1Sm 1:9; 3:3), which existed in David's day. God's house is the place where God dwelt among his people (Ps 26:8).
5:8 The connection between the plea for God's guidance and the **adversaries** is that

the situation (i.e., attacks by enemies) calls for not only protection and rescue but also guidance in the midst of the crisis. It is also an affirmation of the intent to remain loyal to the Lord even during the time of danger.
5:9–10 Throat and **tongues** are metaphors for speech. Since there is **nothing reliable in what they say**, all of the enemies' speech is deadly, pictured here as **an open grave**. Since the enemies here were intent on death and destruction, the psalmist asked that God let **their own schemes** bring about their destruction (64:8; 2Sm 15:31).
5:11–12 The emphasis in these verses is on God's protection of those who remain faithful to him. The terms **take refuge in** … **shelter** … **surround**, and **shield** convey this thought. In this context, all these words evoke military ideas. This word for "shield" describes a large piece of flattened metal that was placed in front of a soldier to protect his entire body; they were sometimes called "large shields" (1Kg 10:16).
Ps 6 title The word **Sheminith** is difficult to interpret. The most commonly proposed root meaning is "eight," leading some to identify it with an eight-stringed instrument or an octave (an eight-note scale). In any case, it is part of the musical instructions for this psalm.

6:1 The combination of **rebuke** … **discipline** and **anger** … **wrath** indicates that the psalmist thought there was some sin behind his suffering, although the sin is not specified. The opening to this psalm led the early church fathers to include it as one of the seven penitential psalms (along with 32; 38; 51; 102; 130; 143).
6:2–3 The parallelism between **my bones** and **my whole being** (or "my soul") demonstrates that the suffering was not only physical but also psychological and emotional. The same Hebrew verb—meaning "shaken" when used literally but "terrified" in the figurative sense—is used for both subjects.
6:4–5 The plea has a twofold motivation. First, the appeal for the Lord to act is **because of** his **faithful love** (Hb chesed). This is the covenant loyalty that Yahweh has for his people and is the basis for the psalmist's trust (13:5; 26:3; 136). Second, the psalmist spoke of a loss of praise to the Lord if he was allowed to go to **Sheol** (i.e., to die).
6:6–7 The extent of the psalmist's emotional distress is highlighted in these verses. His crying was so intense that his **bed** was soaked with tears. The second image (**drench my couch**) is hyperbolic and literally reads "make my bed swim." The mention of **enemies** introduces another dimension to the

7 My eyes are swollen from grief;
  they grow old because of all
    my enemies.

8 Depart from me, all evildoers,
  for the LORD has heard the sound
    of my weeping.

9 The LORD has heard my plea for help;
  the LORD accepts my prayer.

10 All my enemies will be ashamed
   and shake with terror;
  they will turn back and suddenly
    be disgraced.

Prayer for Justice

7 A Shiggaion *of David, which he sang to the*
  LORD *concerning the words of Cush,*
a Benjaminite.

1 LORD my God, I seek refuge in you;
  save me from all my pursuers
    and rescue me,

2 or they[A] will tear me like a lion,
  ripping me apart with no one
    to rescue me.

3 LORD my God, if I have done this,
  if there is injustice on my hands,

4 if I have done harm to one at peace
    with me
  or have plundered[B] my adversary
    without cause,

5 may an enemy pursue
    and overtake me;
  may he trample me to the ground
  and leave my honor in the dust.　　*Selah*

6 Rise up, LORD, in your anger;
  lift yourself up against the fury
    of my adversaries;
  awake for me;[C]
  you have ordained a judgment.

7 Let the assembly of peoples gather
    around you;
  take your seat on high over it.

8 The LORD judges the peoples;
  vindicate me, LORD,
  according to my righteousness
    and my integrity.

9 Let the evil of the wicked come
    to an end,
  but establish the righteous.
  The one who examines the thoughts
    and emotions[D]
  is a righteous God.

10 My shield is with God,
  who saves the upright in heart.

11 God is a righteous judge
  and a God who shows his wrath
    every day.

12 If anyone does not repent,
  he will sharpen his sword;
  he has strung his bow and made it ready.

13 He has prepared his deadly weapons;
  he tips his arrows with fire.

14 See, the wicked one is pregnant
    with evil,
  conceives trouble, and gives birth
    to deceit.

15 He dug a pit and hollowed it out
  but fell into the hole he had made.

16 His trouble comes back
    on his own head;
  his own violence comes down on top
    of his head.

17 I will thank the LORD
    for his righteousness;
  I will sing about the name of the LORD
    Most High.

---

^7:2 Lit *he*　^7:4 Or *me and have spared*　^7:6 LXX reads *awake, Lord my God*　^7:9 Lit *examines hearts and kidneys*

suffering: helplessness before enemies because of the psalmist's condition of sickness. **6:8–10** The enemies of v. 7 are further described as **evildoers**. It is likely from the statement in v. 9 that the enemies were taunting the psalmist by saying that God would not deliver him (3:2; 22:7–8; 71:11). Instead of their perception of God's inactivity, these enemies would be shaken with **terror**. The word **shake** is the same Hebrew verb used twice in vv. 2–3 to describe the condition of the psalmist in his suffering. In essence, the prayer ends with a statement of confidence that God will take away his suffering and inflict it upon his enemies.

Ps 7 title The word **Shiggaion** occurs only this one time in the psalm titles, and its meaning is unknown. The identity of **Cush, a Benjaminite** is also uncertain. Scholars have often related the name to one of David's enemies from the tribe of Benjamin: Saul (1Sm 18–31), Shimei (2Sm 16:5–13), or Sheba (2Sm 20).

7:1–2 The use of the word **pursuers** to describe enemies indicates that the psalmist was a hunted man. He compared them collectively to a **lion, ripping . . . apart** its prey. **7:3–5** These verses contain a declaration of innocence in the form of an oath (cp. Jb 31:16–22). The **if** statements are rhetorical, assuming that the psalmist was innocent of those conditions. The consequences are stated in a typical vow formula using the word **may**. This is used to convey the notion of suffering without justifiable cause. **7:6–8** Calling down God's **judgment** on one's enemies is known as imprecation. The call for the Lord to **rise up** was used as a battle cry for Israel when preparing to engage her enemies (Nm 10:35). The judgment that is called for is one that has already been **ordained** (lit "commanded") by God. Some identify the **assembly of peoples** as the divine assembly of angels (82:1); however, "peoples" is most often used of nations and likely represents a

gathering of the nations with Yahweh acting as the Judge. **7:9–11** Protection, pictured as a **shield**, is guaranteed by God's righteousness. The **thoughts and emotions** are literally "hearts and kidneys," imagery used to describe the inner parts of man that are not seen. In this case, they refer to inner thoughts and motives. **7:12–13** The imagery changes from God as a Judge to God as a Warrior. **7:14–16** The terms **pregnant** and **birth** picture the wicked as creating, incubating, and unleashing their **evil** on the world as if their evils were their children (see Jb 15:35; Is 59:4, and Jms 1:15 for similar imagery). The plots of the wicked backfire (Pss 9:15; 35:8; 57:6; 141:10). **7:17 Most High** (Hb *'elyon*) as a title for God first occurs in Gn 14:18–22, but it is also used throughout the OT to emphasize God's sovereignty over all humanity (Dt 32:8; Ps 47:2; Dn 4:17).

God's Glory, Human Dignity

8 *For the choir director: on the* Gittith. *A psalm of David.*

¹ LORD, our Lord,
how magnificent is your name
throughout the earth!

You have covered the heavens
with your majesty.ᴬ
² From the mouths of infants and
nursing babies,
you have established a strongholdᴮ
on account of your adversaries
in order to silence the enemy
and the avenger.

³ When I observe your heavens,
the work of your fingers,
the moon and the stars,
which you set in place,
⁴ what is a human being
that you remember him,
a son of manᶜ that you look after him?
⁵ You made him little less than Godᴰ,ᴱ
and crowned him with glory and honor.
⁶ You made him ruler over the works
of your hands;
you put everything under his feet:
⁷ all the sheep and oxen,
as well as the animals in the wild,
⁸ the birds of the sky,
and the fish of the sea
that pass through the currents of the seas.

⁹ LORD, our Lord,
how magnificent is your name
throughout the earth!

Celebration of God's Justice

9 *For the choir director: according to* Muth-labben. *A psalm of David.*

¹ I will thank the LORD with all my heart;
I will declare all your wondrous works.
² I will rejoice and boast about you;
I will sing about your name, Most High.

³ When my enemies retreat,
they stumble and perish before you.
⁴ For you have upheld my just cause;
you are seated on your throne
as a righteous judge.
⁵ You have rebuked the nations:
You have destroyed the wicked;
you have erased their name forever
and ever.
⁶ The enemy has come to eternal ruin;
you have uprooted the cities,
and the very memory of them
has perished.

⁷ But the LORD sits enthroned forever;
he has established his throne
for judgment.
⁸ And he judges the world
with righteousness;
he executes judgment on the nations
with fairness.
⁹ The LORD is a refuge for the persecuted,
a refuge in times of trouble.
¹⁰ Those who know your name trust in you
because you have not abandoned
those who seek you, LORD.

¹¹ Sing to the LORD, who dwells in Zion;
proclaim his deeds among the nations.

ᴬ8:1 Lit *earth, which has set your splendor upon the heavens*   ᴮ8:2 LXX reads *established praise*   ᶜ8:4 Or *a mere mortal*
ᴰ8:5 LXX reads *angels*   ᴱ8:5 Or *heavenly beings*; Hb *Elohim*

Ps 8 title Some propose that **Gittith** is some kind of musical instrument such as a lyre. The LXX translates it "for the winepress," relating it to a Hebrew root for grapes; in this sense, it could have been a song to be sung during the grape harvest.
8:1 This hymn of praise is more specifically identified as a creation hymn (along with 19:1–6; 33; 104) in its focus on **earth** and **the heavens**, terms describing the whole of creation (Gn 1:1; Ex 20:11; Neh 9:6).
8:2 Even the feeblest of humanity, with their sometimes-inarticulate speech (**mouths**), function as firm testimonies (**a stronghold**) of God's glory and **silence the enemy and the avenger**.
8:3–4 How is it that God would **remember** and **look after** (both words mean "pay attention to and care for") people? This is perplexing in light of the difference between the size and scope of the cosmos and the relative puniness of humanity. The terms "human being" and "son of man" are parallel and are used to describe humankind as a collective whole (146:3; Nm 23:19; Is 51:12).
8:5–8 The answer to the perplexing question in v. 4 is found in these verses, which are essentially a commentary on Gn 1:26–28.

While the perception is that humans are insignificant in the grand scheme of things, the reality is found in God's purpose for creating humanity. The word translated as **God** (Hb *'elohim*) is plural here and could be understood as indicating "gods" or "heavenly beings" instead of its usual sense of a plural of majesty emphasizing God's greatness. Therefore the LXX, which is quoted in Heb 2:7, translates it as "angels." The point is the same in both cases, even if the referent is different: because of their divinely given purpose, humans are functionally closer to God and the angels than to the animals. We have been **made ... ruler over** creation, expressing humanity's function of dominion (Gn 1:26).
8:9 The psalm ends as it began (cp. v. 1).
Ps 9 title The Hebrew word **Muth-labben** could be related to *Alamoth*, which appears in the title of Ps 46. It could be translated as "for the death of a son" in the sense of being used for that occasion. More likely it identifies a specific tune or style of music. Ps 10 does not have a title and is joined to this psalm in the LXX and the Vulgate. Another reason for seeing Pss 9 and 10 as one is that there is an alphabetic acrostic that begins in Ps 9 and is continued in Ps 10. However,

there is a sufficient change that takes place, especially in terms of mood and form (Ps 9 focuses on thanksgiving whereas Ps 10 takes the form of a lament psalm). This seems to argue for them being two distinct psalms.
9:1 With all my heart means "sincerely" (86:12; 111:1; 119:10). **Wondrous works** are unspecified here, but elsewhere the phrase refers to God's acts of creation (136:4), his works in the natural order (Jb 5:9), or the redemptive acts performed on behalf of his people (Ex 3:20).
9:2 The name **Most High** (*'Elyon*) is used twenty-one times in the Psalms.
9:4–6 In this context, the **throne** describes God's judgment (v. 7; 11:4) more than his rule, as it is sometimes used (45:6). Their **name** being **erased** and their **memory** perishing are related phrases; they refer to complete annihilation and the destruction of one's existence (21:10; 83:4; Dt 32:26).
9:9–10 The phrases **know your name**, and **trust in you**, and **seek you** have essentially the same meaning. They describe those who have personal, experiential knowledge of the Lord and who depend on him and look to him in times of need.
9:11 Sing and **proclaim** are parallel commands indicating the responsibility of those

¹² For the one who seeks an accounting
for bloodshed remembers them;
he does not forget the cry
of the oppressed.

¹³ Be gracious to me, LORD;
consider my affliction at the hands
of those who hate me.
Lift me up from the gates of death,
¹⁴ so that I may declare all your praises.
I will rejoice in your salvation
within the gates of Daughter Zion.

¹⁵ The nations have fallen into the pit
they made;
their foot is caught in the net
they have concealed.
¹⁶ The LORD has made himself known;
he has executed justice,
snaring the wicked
by the work of their hands.

Higgaion. Selah

¹⁷ The wicked will return to Sheol —
all the nations that forget God.
¹⁸ For the needy will not always
be forgotten;
the hope of the oppressed^A
will not perish forever.

¹⁹ Rise up, LORD! Do not let
mere humans prevail;
let the nations be judged
in your presence.
²⁰ Put terror in them, LORD;
let the nations know they are
only humans.   *Selah*

Need for God's Justice

10 LORD,^{B,C} why do you stand
so far away?
Why do you hide in times of trouble?
² In arrogance the wicked
relentlessly pursue their victims;
let them be caught in the schemes
they have devised.

³ For the wicked one boasts about
his own cravings;
the one who is greedy curses^D
and despises the LORD.
⁴ In all his scheming,
the wicked person arrogantly thinks,^E
"There's no accountability,
since there's no God."
⁵ His ways are always secure;^F
your lofty judgments have no effect
on him;^G
he scoffs at all his adversaries.
⁶ He says to himself, "I will never
be moved —
from generation to generation I will be
without calamity."
⁷ Cursing, deceit, and violence
fill his mouth;
trouble and malice are
under his tongue.
⁸ He waits in ambush near settlements;
he kills the innocent in secret places.
His eyes are on the lookout
for the helpless;
⁹ he lurks in secret like a lion in a thicket.
He lurks in order to seize a victim;
he seizes a victim and drags him
in his net.
¹⁰ So he is oppressed and beaten down;
helpless people fall because of the
wicked one's strength.
¹¹ He says to himself, "God has forgotten;
he hides his face and will never see."

¹² Rise up, LORD God! Lift up your hand.
Do not forget the oppressed.
¹³ Why has the wicked person
despised God?
He says to himself, "You will not demand
an account."
¹⁴ But you yourself have seen trouble
and grief,
observing it in order to take the matter
into your hands.
The helpless one entrusts himself
to you;

---

^A9:18 Alt Hb tradition reads *humble*   ^B10:1 Some Hb mss, LXX connect Pss 9–10.   ^C10:1 Together Pss 9–10 form a partial acrostic.   ^D10:3 Or *he blesses the greedy*   ^E10:4 Lit *wicked according to the height of his nose*   ^F10:5 Or *prosperous*   ^G10:5 Lit *judgments are away from in front of him*

---

who know God and his works to tell others about him (30:4; 1Ch 16:8; Is 12:4). **9:15–16** The idea of enemies suffering the same fate that they had planned for someone else is found in other psalms (7:15–16; 35:8; 57:6). In this case, the enemies are **the nations** who are being judged by God for their rebellion against his authority (2:1). This is clear from the parallel designation **the wicked** in v. 16. Higgaion comes perhaps from a Hebrew root meaning "murmur." It might refer to the use of quieter instruments. **9:19–20 Rise up** is a martial call for the Lord to act. More specifically, he is asked to **put terror in them**. This is not the "fear of the

LORD" that is characteristic of those who believe in the Lord but the terror of people at the approach of an army (Dt 2:25; 11:25). **10:3–6** The arrogance of **the wicked one** climaxes in a statement denying God's existence. This is not metaphysical atheism, in which there is absolute unbelief in God's existence, but practical atheism, which denies that God pays any attention to what people are doing (14:1; 53:1). The enemy's security rests on his thinking, which is that he can get away with anything **his own cravings** allow. He **will never be moved** (15:5; 16:8; 21:7; 62:2; 112:6) in the sense that no higher being will divert him from doing what he desires.

10:7 Mouth and **tongue** are used for speech, describing the deadly arsenal of the enemy's words (5:9; 140:3). **10:12–15** What is true in Ps 9 is now in conflict with what appears to be happening in Ps 10. God is asked **not** to **forget the oppressed**, but in 9:12,18 he does not forget them. Here the wicked think that God **will not demand an account**, but in 9:12 he clearly does. The tension is between appearance and reality. **Fatherless** is a better rendering than "orphan," since in Hebrew society it was the lack (or loss) of a father that made a person helpless because he was left without property or rights.

you are a helper of the fatherless.

¹⁵ Break the arm of the wicked,
evil person,
until you look for his wickedness,
but it can't be found.

¹⁶ The LORD is King forever and ever;
the nations will perish
from his land.

¹⁷ LORD, you have heard the desire
of the humble;
you will strengthen their hearts.
You will listen carefully,

¹⁸ doing justice for the fatherless
and the oppressed
so that mere humans from the earth
may terrify them no more.

Refuge in the LORD

11 For the choir director. Of David.
I have taken refuge in the LORD.
How can you say to me,
"Escape to the mountains^A
like a bird!

² For look, the wicked string bows;
they put their arrows on bowstrings
to shoot from the shadows
at the upright in heart.

³ When the foundations
are destroyed,
what can the righteous do?"

⁴ The LORD is in his holy temple;
the LORD—his throne is in heaven.
His eyes watch;
his gaze^B examines everyone.^C

⁵ The LORD examines the righteous,
but he hates the wicked
and^D those who love violence.

⁶ Let him rain burning coals^E and sulfur
on the wicked;
let a scorching wind be the portion
in their cup.

⁷ For the LORD is righteous; he loves
righteous deeds.
The upright will see his face.

Oppression by the Wicked

12 For the choir director: according to
Sheminith. A psalm of David.
¹ Help, LORD, for no faithful one remains;
the loyal have disappeared
from the human race.^F

² They lie to one another;
they speak with flattering lips
and deceptive hearts.

³ May the LORD cut off all flattering lips
and the tongue that speaks boastfully.

⁴ They say, "Through our tongues
we have power;
our lips are our own — who can be
our master?"

⁵ "Because of the devastation of the needy
and the groaning of the poor,
I will now rise up," says the LORD.
"I will provide safety for the one
who longs for it."

⁶ The words of the LORD are pure words,
like silver refined in an earthen furnace,
purified seven times.

⁷ You, LORD, will guard us;^G
you will protect us^H
from this generation forever.

⁸ The wicked prowl^I all around,
and what is worthless is exalted
by the human race.

A Plea for Deliverance

13 For the choir director. A psalm of David.
How long, LORD? Will you forget me
forever?
How long will you hide your face from me?

² How long will I store up
anxious concerns^J within me,
agony in my mind every day?
How long will my enemy dominate me?

³ Consider me and answer, LORD my God.
Restore brightness to my eyes;
otherwise, I will sleep in death.

---

^A 11:1 Lit your mountain   ^B 11:4 Lit eyelids   ^C 11:4 Or examines the descendants of Adam   ^D 11:5 Or righteous and the wicked,
and he hates   ^E 11:6 Sym; MT reads rain snares, fire   ^F 12:1 Or the descendants of Adam, also in v. 8   ^G 12:7 Some Hb mss, LXX,
Jer; other Hb mss read them   ^H 12:7 Some Hb mss, LXX; other Hb mss read him   ^I 12:8 Lit walk about   ^J 13:2 Or up counsels

---

11:3 The **foundations** are undefined here but could refer to moral foundations or the principles of justice within society. The activities of the wicked shake the foundations of justice and morality (82:5; Ezk 30:4).
11:4-5 The security of the psalmist rested in the fact that God had not left **his holy temple** (see Mc 1:2; Hab 2:20) and was still on **his throne** (103:19), both of which are **in heaven**. Though the wicked thought that God was not paying any attention to what was happening on earth (10:4; 14:1; 53:1), he was actually watching and examining **everyone** (33:13-14). This included both **the righteous** and **the wicked**.
11:6 The Hebrew text of this verse reads, "Let him rain down traps on the wicked."

This reading might have originated from a connection with v. 1, since the word for "trap" most often describes something used to catch birds (Am 3:5). Another reading is "coals of fire," which only amounts to a slight variation of letters. This seems more likely in light of the parallel with **scorching wind**.
11:7 Seeing God's **face**, a figurative expression, is equivalent to experiencing God's favor or blessing (17:15; Jb 33:26).
Ps 12 title On **Sheminith**, see note at Ps 6 title.
12:6 In contrast to the unreliability of the words of the wicked (vv. 2-4; also 5:9), the Lord's **words** are **pure** like **silver refined**, meaning they are absolutely trustworthy

(18:30; 19:7-10). **Seven times** refers to the fullest sense or the fact that a person cannot exceed this limit (Dn 3:19).
13:1-2 The phrase **how long** is not uncommon in the lament psalms (6:3; 35:17; 74:10; 79:5; 80:4; 94:3); however, it appears more times here (four times) than in any other single text. This highlights the fact that the psalmist had endured his suffering for a long time and was considering that the Lord might have hidden his **face** from him and forgotten him. Both of these descriptions convey the idea of rejection (44:24).
13:3-4 Brightness in the **eyes** represents vitality and is the opposite of one's eyes growing dim during times of grief and

⁴ My enemy will say, "I have triumphed
   over him,"
and my foes will rejoice
   because I am shaken.

⁵ But I have trusted in
   your faithful love;
my heart will rejoice in
   your deliverance.
⁶ I will sing to the LORD
   because he has treated
   me generously.

A Portrait of Sinners

14 *For the choir director. Of David.*
The fool says in his heart,
   "There's no God."
They are corrupt; they do vile deeds.
There is no one who does good.
² The LORD looks down from heaven
   on the human race^A
to see if there is one who is wise,
   one who seeks God.
³ All have turned away;
   all alike have become corrupt.
There is no one who does good,
   not even one.

⁴ Will evildoers never understand?
They consume my people
   as they consume bread;
they do not call on the LORD.

⁵ Then^B they will be filled with dread,
   for God is with those
   who are^C righteous.
⁶ You sinners frustrate the plans
   of the oppressed,
but the LORD is his refuge.

⁷ Oh, that Israel's deliverance would come
   from Zion!
When the LORD restores the fortunes
   of his people,^D
let Jacob rejoice, let Israel be glad.

A Description of the Godly

15 *A psalm of David.*
LORD, who can dwell in your tent?
Who can live on your holy mountain?

² The one who lives blamelessly,
   practices righteousness,
and acknowledges the truth
   in his heart —
³ who does not slander with his tongue,
who does not harm his friend
   or discredit his neighbor,
⁴ who despises the one rejected
   by the LORD^E
but honors those who fear the LORD,
who keeps his word whatever the cost,
⁵ who does not lend his silver at interest
or take a bribe against the innocent —
   the one who does these things
   will never be shaken.

Confidence in the LORD

16 *A Miktam of David.*
Protect me, God, for I take refuge
   in you.
² I^F said to the LORD, "You are my Lord;
I have nothing good besides you."^G
³ As for the holy people who are
   in the land,
they are the noble ones.
All my delight is in them.
⁴ The sorrows of those who take
   another god

^A14:2 Or *the descendants of Adam* ^B14:5 Or *There* ^C14:5 Lit *with the generation of the* ^D14:7 Or *restores his captive people* ^E15:4 Lit *in his eyes the rejected is despised* ^F16:2 Some Hb mss, LXX, Syr, Jer; other Hb mss read *You* ^G16:2 Or *"Lord, my good; there is none besides you."*

---

suffering (6:7; 38:10; Jb 17:7). In this context it is contrasted with **death**. The statement **I am shaken** could refer to dying, but it could also be used to indicate defeat.
13:5–6 Even though the question about the time of God's intervention remained, the psalmist reaffirmed his trust in the Lord's **faithful love**. This is the Hebrew word *chesed*, which is rooted in Yahweh's covenant with his people. The psalmist's trust was not in himself but in the God of the covenant who promised that he would show faithful love to those who love and obey him (Dt 7:9; Neh 1:5; Dn 9:4).
14:1 The statement that **there's no God** affirms practical rather than metaphysical atheism (see note at 10:3–6). The person making this claim is described as **the fool** (Hb *nabal*; 1Sm 25:25). This is not someone who was simple or gullible because it was outside his ability to be otherwise, but someone who was willfully ignorant, closing his mind off from God's wisdom and truth.
14:3 Paul used this verse in a more absolute sense that no one among humankind is righteous since all are **corrupt** (Rm 3:10–12).

14:5–6 Dread is what the wicked bring to God's people (10:18), but the hope is that God will do the same to them (9:20).
14:7 The Hebrew for **restores the fortunes of his people** is difficult. It is literally "turns with a turning his people." The Hebrew word for "turn" can also mean "return," and some understand this to mean the return of captives (perhaps from the exile). Such an event does not seem to fit this context. Here the idea is probably more general and describes God's blessings on his people.
15:1 The phrase **your tent** is parallel to **your holy mountain** and refers to the sanctuary of the Lord.
15:2 Lives blamelessly refers to a life of integrity (18:23; 119:1). The **truth** of God is not just something proclaimed. It must reside in a person's **heart**, which is the mind or the inner person (Dt 6:6; Is 29:13).
Ps 16 title Miktam occurs in the titles of six psalms (16; 56–60). Its meaning is difficult to determine. The Hebrew root from which the form is derived may mean "cover," "secret,"

or "inscribe." It is most likely a musical term, though its precise relationship with music is uncertain.
16:1 The word **protect** can mean to "keep watch over" as a shepherd. God used it in his promise to Jacob at Bethel (Gn 28:15).
16:2 The phrase **nothing good besides you** is literally "my good (is) not above/beyond you" and is difficult in Hebrew. It is most likely related to a similar expression in 73:25 that carries the idea of finding nothing desirable on earth apart from the Lord.
16:3 Holy people (lit "holy ones") and **noble ones** are difficult to identify. Based on a common meaning of "holy ones" as heavenly beings, some have suggested angels. Another suggestion is that these are leaders or rulers because of the designation "noble ones." The phrase **in the land** seems to argue for their identity as mortals. Most likely "holy" and "noble" are used to describe God's people in general.
16:4 Drink offerings of blood could be a reference to human sacrifice (Is 57:5), although it is probably offerings made by

for themselves will multiply;
I will not pour out their drink offerings
of blood,
and I will not speak their names
with my lips.

⁵ LORD, you are my portion^A
and my cup of blessing;
you hold my future.
⁶ The boundary lines have fallen for me
in pleasant places;
indeed, I have a beautiful inheritance.

⁷ I will bless the LORD who counsels me —
even at night when my thoughts
trouble me.^B
⁸ I always let the LORD guide me.^C
Because he is at my right hand,
I will not be shaken.

⁹ Therefore my heart is glad
and my whole being rejoices;
my body also rests securely.
¹⁰ For you will not abandon me to Sheol;
you will not allow your faithful one
to see decay.
¹¹ You reveal the path of life to me;
in your presence is abundant joy;
at your right hand are
eternal pleasures.

A Prayer for Protection

17 *A prayer of David.*
LORD, hear a just cause;
pay attention to my cry;
listen to my prayer —
from lips free of deceit.
² Let my vindication come from you,
for you see what is right.
³ You have tested my heart;
you have examined me at night.
You have tried me and found
nothing evil;

I have determined that my mouth
will not sin.^D
⁴ Concerning what people do:
by the words from your lips
I have avoided the ways of the violent.
⁵ My steps are on your paths;
my feet have not slipped.

⁶ I call on you, God,
because you will answer me;
listen closely to me; hear what I say.
⁷ Display the wonders
of your faithful love,
Savior of all who seek refuge
from those who rebel
against your right hand.^E
⁸ Protect me as the pupil of your eye;
hide me in the shadow of your wings
⁹ from^F the wicked
who treat me violently,^G
my deadly enemies who surround me.

¹⁰ They are uncaring;^H
their mouths speak arrogantly.
¹¹ They advance against me;^I
now they surround me.
They are determined^J
to throw me to the ground.
¹² They are^K like a lion eager to tear,
like a young lion lurking in ambush.

¹³ Rise up, LORD!
Confront him; bring him down.
With your sword, save me
from the wicked.
¹⁴ With your hand, LORD, save me from men,
from men of the world
whose portion is in this life:
You fill their bellies with what you have
in store;
their sons are satisfied,
and they leave their surplus
to their children.

---

^A16:5 Or *allotted portion*   ^B16:7 Or *at night my heart instructs me*   ^C16:8 Lit *I place the LORD in front of me always*
^D17:3 Or *evil; my mouth will not sin*   ^E17:7 Or *love, you who save with your right hand those seeking refuge from adversaries*
^F17:9 Lit *from the presence of*   ^G17:9 Or *who plunder me*   ^H17:10 Lit *have closed up their fat*   ^I17:11 Vg; MT reads *Our steps*
^J17:11 Lit *They set their eyes*   ^K17:12 Lit *He is*

---

those with impure motives who therefore remained guilty of sin (Is 1:15; 66:3).
16:5–6 My portion . . . cup of blessing and **boundary lines . . . inheritance** are terms usually used to describe the land promised to Israel. But the idea that God himself is the true inheritance rather than the land was a promise specifically to Aaron and his sons (Nm 18:20; Dt 10:9). Here the concept is expressed more generally as true for anyone who is among God's people.
16:7 Thoughts is literally "kidneys," which are often used in parallel with "heart" to signify the inner person (26:2; Jr 17:10).
16:8 In legal contexts the person who represented the defense of another was at the **right hand** (109:6). In military contexts the soldier protecting his comrade was at

the right hand; also, it was the location for the sword, the primary weapon used in hand-to-hand combat.
16:9–11 Along with v. 8, these verses are quoted (from the LXX) in the NT and explained as referring to Jesus's resurrection (Ac 2:25–31).
17:7 While **wonders** could be general enough to include works of creation, here it seems to be related to God's intervention in a time of need.
17:8 Both images in v. 8 convey the idea of protection. The **pupil of the eye** is that part of the body that is closely guarded (Dt 32:10; Pr 7:2). The image of being hidden **in the shadow of your wings** portrays God as a mother bird protecting her young (36:7; 57:1).
17:10–12 The Hebrew in v. 10 is literally "they have closed up their fat." Fat represented

prosperity, but such a state of abundance could and often did lead to callousness and rebellion (73:7; Dt 32:15; Jr 5:28). The idea here is that these enemies of God had become **uncaring** toward him and were surrounding the psalmist (both here and in v. 9) to attack a person who was faithful to God. The Hebrew text at the beginning of v. 11 is literally "our steps," which is difficult. **They advance against me** is from the Latin Vulgate, a reading that is more understandable and fits the context.
17:13–14 Rise up probably expresses the military idea of preparing for battle since it is linked with **your sword**. The meaning of **world** here is similar to the use of the Greek *cosmos* in the NT to describe the world system that is against God. These men belong

15 But I will see your face in righteousness;
when I awake, I will be satisfied
with your presence.^A

Praise for Deliverance

18 *For the choir director. Of the servant of the LORD, David, who spoke the words of this song to the LORD on the day the LORD rescued him from the grasp of all his enemies and from the power of Saul. He said:*

1 I love you, LORD, my strength.
2 The LORD is my rock,
my fortress, and my deliverer,
my God, my rock where I seek refuge,
my shield and the horn of my salvation,
my stronghold.
3 I called to the LORD, who is
worthy of praise,
and I was saved from my enemies.

4 The ropes of death were wrapped
around me;
the torrents of destruction terrified me.
5 The ropes of Sheol entangled me;
the snares of death confronted me.
6 I called to the LORD in my distress,
and I cried to my God for help.
From his temple he heard my voice,
and my cry to him reached his ears.

7 Then the earth shook and quaked;
the foundations of the mountains
trembled;
they shook because he burned
with anger.

8 Smoke rose from his nostrils,
and consuming fire came
from his mouth;
coals were set ablaze by it.^B
9 He bent the heavens and came down,
total darkness beneath his feet.
10 He rode on a cherub and flew,
soaring on the wings of the wind.
11 He made darkness his hiding place,
dark storm clouds his canopy
around him.
12 From the radiance of his presence,
his clouds swept onward with hail
and blazing coals.
13 The LORD thundered from^C heaven;
the Most High made his voice heard.^D
14 He shot his arrows and scattered them;
he hurled^E lightning bolts
and routed them.
15 The depths of the sea became visible,
the foundations of the world
were exposed,
at your rebuke, LORD,
at the blast of the breath of your nostrils.

16 He reached down from on high
and took hold of me;
he pulled me out of deep water.
17 He rescued me
from my powerful enemy
and from those who hated me,
for they were too strong for me.
18 They confronted me in the day
of my calamity,
but the LORD was my support.

^A 17:15 Lit *form* ^B 18:8 Or *him* ^C 18:13 Some Hb mss, LXX, Tg, Jer; other Hb mss read *in* ^D 18:13 Some Hb mss read *voice, with hail and blazing coals* ^E 18:14 Or *multiplied*

to the world system, and their inheritance or **portion** was only in **this** earthly **life** (see Ec 9:9).
17:15 Seeing God's **face** is equivalent to receiving blessings from him.
Ps 18 title This title contains more information about its setting than any other psalm. It is linked with the Lord's deliverance of **David . . . from . . . all his enemies and from . . . Saul**. This rescue is not specified or described any further in the title. Neither does its parallel, 2Sm 22, give any detailed information about its precise setting in David's life. However, it is clearly set against the backdrop of a military victory where the Lord fought for David and delivered him from his enemies. Such was the promise for those who obeyed the Lord. He would fight for them and bring them victory (Dt 32:41–42). Elsewhere in the OT, only Moses and Joshua are called **the servant of the LORD** (cp. Ps 36 title).
18:1–2 In no other psalm is there such a large number of metaphors used to convey God's attributes. All of these relate to a military setting where God is seen as the real **strength** behind the person who fights. He also protects the psalmist as a hiding place from the enemy (his **rock . . . fortress**, and **stronghold**). God also protects him by guarding him against the onslaught of

weapons (he is his **shield**) and rescues him from his enemies (he is his **deliverer** and his **salvation**). In keeping with the military imagery in this psalm, the **horn of salvation** may refer to one of the horns of the altar, which represented a place of refuge (1Kg 1:50–51). However, it more likely refers to the horn of a wild animal that gored its enemies (Dt 33:17; Ps 92:10), signifying military strength.
18:4–5 The perception of the inevitability of death is pictured as being entangled in **ropes** and unable to escape (116:3; 119:61). **Torrents** is an image of being overwhelmed with water and in danger of drowning (Jnh 2:3,5). When pieced together, such imagery describes being tangled in ropes while overtaken with a flood of water. There was absolutely no chance to swim away since the psalmist's limbs were bound and unable to move.
18:6 Temple most likely refers to heaven in this context.
18:7–15 These verses describe a theophany where God reveals his power through natural phenomena such as an earthquake (v. 7) and a thunderstorm (vv. 13–14). **Mountains** represent stability within the natural order, so their shaking and trembling describes God's power to bring upheaval to what seemed secure (Jdg 5:5; 1Sm 14:15). **Smoke**

and **consuming fire** combined with God's voice that **thundered from heaven** is reminiscent of the Sinai experience (Ex 24:17; Dt 4:12,24; 9:3). The image of God acting as a warrior who fights for his people and uses the natural elements as his weapons is also connected with Israel's past experiences (Jos 10:11; Jdg 5:4,20). God's riding **on a cherub**—imagery found in creation hymns (19:1; 104:3)—blends the supernatural with the natural. Some interpreters see this section of the psalm as a polemic against Baal, showing that the Lord is the sovereign Lord of creation. Ps 18:15 seems to be connected to the exodus event when **the depths of the sea became visible** because of God's **breath** (see Ex 14:21).
18:16–19 Reaching **down**, taking **hold**, and pulling **out** are anthropomorphic descriptions of God's condescension to rescue the psalmist in his time of need. These terms also allude to the image of a well as the place where one feels trapped during times of distress, connecting the concepts of "drawn up" and rescued (30:3; 40:2; Jr 38:10). The **deep water** is related to the "torrents of destruction" in v. 4 and is identified more specifically as enemies. The **spacious place** is another illustration of being delivered from one's enemies.

19 He brought me out to a spacious place;
   he rescued me because he delighted
      in me.

20 The Lord rewarded me
   according to my righteousness;
   he repaid me
   according to the cleanness of my hands.

21 For I have kept the ways of the Lord
   and have not turned from my God
      to wickedness.

22 Indeed, I let all his ordinances guide me[A]
   and have not disregarded his statutes.

23 I was blameless toward him
   and kept myself from my iniquity.

24 So the Lord repaid me
   according to my righteousness,
   according to the cleanness of my hands
      in his sight.

25 With the faithful
   you prove yourself faithful,
   with the blameless
   you prove yourself blameless,

26 with the pure
   you prove yourself pure,
   but with the crooked
   you prove yourself shrewd.

27 For you rescue an oppressed people,
   but you humble those
      with haughty eyes.

28 Lord, you light my lamp;
   my God illuminates my darkness.

29 With you I can attack a barricade,[B]
   and with my God I can leap over
      a wall.

30 God — his way is perfect;
   the word of the Lord is pure.
   He is a shield to all who take refuge
      in him.

31 For who is God besides the Lord?
   And who is a rock? Only our God.

32 God — he clothes me with strength
   and makes my way perfect.

33 He makes my feet like the feet
      of a deer
   and sets me securely on the heights.[C]

34 He trains my hands for war;
   my arms can bend a bow of bronze.

35 You have given me the shield
      of your salvation;

your right hand upholds me,
and your humility exalts me.

36 You make a spacious place beneath me
      for my steps,
   and my ankles do not give way.

37 I pursue my enemies
      and overtake them;
   I do not turn back until they are
      wiped out.

38 I crush them, and they cannot get up;
   they fall beneath my feet.

39 You have clothed me with strength
      for battle;
   you subdue my adversaries
      beneath me.

40 You have made my enemies retreat
      before me;[D]
   I annihilate those who hate me.

41 They cry for help, but there is no one
      to save them —
   they cry to the Lord, but he does not
      answer them.

42 I pulverize them like dust
      before the wind;
   I trample them[E] like mud in the streets.

43 You have freed me from the feuds
      among the people;
   you have appointed me the head
      of nations;
   a people I had not known serve me.

44 Foreigners submit to me cringing;
   as soon as they hear they obey me.

45 Foreigners lose heart
   and come trembling
      from their fortifications.

46 The Lord lives — blessed be
      my rock!
   The God of my salvation is exalted.

47 God — he grants me vengeance
   and subdues peoples under me.

48 He frees me from my enemies.
   You exalt me above my adversaries;
   you rescue me from violent men.

49 Therefore I will give thanks to you
      among the nations, Lord;
   I will sing praises about your name.

50 He gives great victories to his king;
   he shows loyalty to his anointed,
   to David and his descendants forever.

[A]18:22 Lit *Indeed, all his ordinances have been in front of me* [B]18:29 Or *a ridge*, or *raiders* [C]18:33 Or *on my high places*
[D]18:40 Or *You gave me the necks of my enemies* [E]18:42 Some Hb mss, LXX, Syr, Tg; other Hb mss read *I poured them out*

18:20–24 This declaration of innocence is set off by similar statements in vv. 20 and 24. Righteousness is further clarified as **cleanness of . . . hands**, meaning integrity in his obedience to God's commands. The psalmist was **blameless** in terms of his faithfulness to God (15:2; Dt 18:13).
18:28–29 The psalmist could **leap over a wall**. In other words, he could accomplish the

impossible with God on his side (Mt 19:26; Mk 9:23; Lk 18:27).
18:32–36 The descriptions in these verses are of traits important for warfare. **Strength** is the clothing (1Sm 2:4). **Feet of a deer** represent swiftness (2Sm 1:23; 2:18). God made the psalmist more skillful by training his **hands**. The **bow of bronze** is unusual since bows were not covered with metal. The point

seems to be that it was strengthened and made more effective as a weapon (Jb 20:24). The **shield** is perhaps related to its earlier mention where it was identified with God himself (vv. 2,30).
18:37–42 The shift between first-person and second-person forms in these verses indicates that God is the one who is at work through his warrior. Though God can work

The Witness of Creation and Scripture

19 *For the choir director. A psalm of David.*
The heavens declare the glory of God,
and the expanse proclaims the work
of his hands.

[2] Day after day they pour out speech;
night after night
they communicate knowledge.[A]

[3] There is no speech; there are no words;
their voice is not heard.

[4] Their message[B] has gone out
to the whole earth,
and their words to the ends
of the world.

In the heavens he has pitched a tent
for the sun.

[5] It is like a bridegroom coming from
his home;
it rejoices like an athlete
running a course.

[6] It rises from one end of the heavens
and circles to their other end;
nothing is hidden from its heat.

[7] The instruction of the LORD is perfect,
renewing one's life;
the testimony of the LORD
is trustworthy,
making the inexperienced wise.

[8] The precepts of the LORD are right,
making the heart glad;
the command of the LORD is radiant,
making the eyes light up.

[9] The fear of the LORD is pure,
enduring forever;
the ordinances of the LORD are reliable
and altogether righteous.

[10] They are more desirable than gold —
than an abundance of pure gold;
and sweeter than honey
dripping from a honeycomb.

[11] In addition, your servant is warned
by them,
and in keeping them there is
an abundant reward.

[12] Who perceives his unintentional sins?
Cleanse me from my hidden faults.

[13] Moreover, keep your servant
from willful sins;
do not let them rule me.
Then I will be blameless
and cleansed from blatant rebellion.

[14] May the words of my mouth
and the meditation of my heart
be acceptable to you,
LORD, my rock and my Redeemer.

Deliverance in Battle

20 *For the choir director. A psalm of David.*
May the LORD answer you in a day
of trouble;
may the name of Jacob's God
protect you.

[2] May he send you help
from the sanctuary
and sustain you from Zion.

[3] May he remember all your offerings
and accept your burnt offering.   *Selah*

---

^19:2 Or *Day to day pours out speech, and night to night communicates knowledge*   ^19:4 LXX, Sym, Syr, Vg; MT reads *line*

---

directly, he also uses people as his instruments to accomplish his purposes.
19:1 Although the **heavens** can refer to God's dwelling place, here it is clarified by **expanse**, which is what can be seen from the perspective of those who live on the earth. This is the same Hebrew word as the expanse that separated water from water in Gn 1:6–8. Creation is sometimes personified as a witness to God's work among his people, particularly in the covenant relationship he has with them (Dt 4:26; 30:19; Is 1:2). In this context one specific part of creation is personified as declaring and proclaiming a message. The parallelism between **the glory of God** and **the work of his hands** indicates that the objects of creation are demonstrations (or evidence) of God's glory (50:6; 89:5–8; 97:6; Rm 1:19–20).
19:2–3 Pour out is literally "gush" or "bubble up." This phrase is most often used for springs or fountains of water. The significance of the term here seems to be that **speech** never ceases. The concept is intensified by the doubling of the terms **day** and **night**. The message goes out all the time without ceasing. The paradox is that there is speech in v. 2, but there is **no speech** in v. 3. Although the same Hebrew term ('*omer*) appears in both verses, it is used differently. In the first instance it is equivalent to the message in v. 1; in the second instance

it means **words**. Therefore, it is a message with clearly defined content, but it is not communicated with the words of human language.
19:4–6 While v. 2 says that the message comes at all times, v. 4 adds that it also comes to all places. The word for **world** (Hb *tevel*) is not the usual word for **earth** ('*eretz* in the first line), but it denotes dry land capable of sustaining life (9:8; 24:1)—in other words, the inhabited world. No one can escape the message either in time or in space, and everyone is accountable for the message (Rm 1:20). The focus turns from the more general **heavens** to the most obvious and spectacular object in them: **the sun**. It is also personified and compared to **a** **bridegroom** and **an athlete**. These images are used together to convey the idea of youthful strength.
19:7–9 The shift of subject between vv. 1–6 and vv. 7–14 seems abrupt. However, the common element in both cases is God's revelation of himself and his purposes to mankind. In the first part of the psalm, it is God's creation (general revelation), whereas in the second part, it is the words that God specifically communicated to his people (special revelation). **Renewing one's life** means the restoration of strength or vitality (1Kg 17:22; Lm 1:11). **Making the eyes light up** seems like an unusual idiom, but it makes

a connection between light and truth, or more specifically knowledge and understanding of the truth (119:105,130; Pr 6:23). The **fear of the LORD** is the only subject in this list that involves human response to God's instruction rather than a synonym for it. The concept involves obedience to God with an attitude of humility and reverence.
19:10–11 Gold and **honey** were valuable commodities in the ancient world, but God's words are even more valuable (119:103,127).
19:12–13 Unintentional or **hidden** sins can represent those that occur with or without proper instruction. The question is rhetorical and assumes a negative answer. For this reason, continual cleansing is required for these sins. **Willful sins** are different in that they must be avoided or else they lead to being "cut off" from God and his people (Nm 15:30–31).
19:14 The final plea is that the psalmist's speech and thinking reflect what is **acceptable** to God.
20:1 Day of trouble can refer to any distress (50:15; 77:2; 86:7), but in this case it is a crisis caused by enemies. **Name** appears three times in this psalm (vv. 1,5,7) and is used as a substitute for the Lord (68:4; 145:1–2). The use of **Jacob's** name as a reference to the nation of Israel also emphasizes the personal aspects of God's relationship with his people.

◄ General Revelation

by Bruce Riley Ashford

What is the source of our knowledge of God? The source on which we depend (experience? tradition? society? science? Scripture?) determines the questions we ask and the answers we give. Christians believe that true knowledge of God comes from God's revelation of himself to humanity. When we recognize this self-disclosure and call it *revelation*, we mean at least three things:

- First, God initiates this self-disclosure freely. By his very nature, God communicates.
- Second, God initiates it in order to reveal something about himself.
- Third, he initiates it in order to display his glory and to evoke worship from humanity.

Christians usually divide this revelation into two types: *special* and *general*. In special revelation, God reveals himself through signs and miracles, the words of the prophets and apostles, the person and work of Christ, and the writings of Christian Scripture. This type of revelation is special because it is provided to particular people in specific times and places; it enables them to come to true and saving knowledge of the triune God.

In general revelation, God reveals himself through creation, history, and the moral law he has given to all people everywhere. This type of revelation is general because it is provided to all people of all times, and it provides a basic understanding of God and his moral law. It establishes the facts of God's existence and humanity's moral responsibility but is not sufficient to save fallen humans, who without exception have turned their minds and wills against God. Although general revelation is sufficient to show humans their need to worship and obey the one true God, fallen sinners ultimately reject it and reject him (Rm 1:18–32).

The Fact of General Revelation

The Old Testament contains many passages that speak of the reality of general revelation. Genesis 1–2 teaches that God created humans in his image and likeness. When one looks at humans, one sees an image and likeness of God. Job 38–41 teaches that God has revealed himself through earth and sea, the rising of the sun, snow and hail, wind and rain, frost and ice, the constellations, the animal kingdom, and humans. All aspects of the created order testify to God's existence and character. Job's response to this point was worshipful silence as he recognized that he was very small indeed in comparison to our great God (Jb 40:4–5; 40:15–41:34).

Similarly, Psalm 19:1–4 tells us, "The heavens declare the glory of God, and the expanse proclaims the work of his hands. Day after day they pour out speech; night after night they communicate knowledge. . . . Their message has gone out to the whole earth, and their words to the ends of the world." Stated differently, God's creation testifies clearly enough about him that it can be considered speech and knowledge.

The New Testament likewise articulates God's general revelation. In Acts 17, Paul preaches to a pagan audience on Mars Hill in Athens, Greece. He affirms at least six things that the Athenians could know about God by means of general revelation alone (17:22–31): God is the Creator and Lord of the universe (v. 24), the source of life and everything that is good (v. 25). He is entirely independent and self-sufficient (v. 25). He is the ruler of the nations (v. 26), intelligent (v. 26), close to them (v. 27), and greater than any other possible object of worship (v. 29).

Similarly, in Romans 1:18–25 Paul argues that all humans have a basic knowledge of God. They know that he exists, that he is Creator, and that he is powerful and worthy of worship (vv. 18–21). Humanity is therefore without excuse (v. 20). Nevertheless, humans respond to general revelation by suppressing the truth they know (v. 18), experiencing the corruption of their hearts and minds (v. 21), exchanging truth for a lie (v. 25), and worshiping the creature rather than the Creator (v. 25). In Romans 2:14–16 Paul also makes clear that all people everywhere have an intuitive knowledge of God's moral law.

The Content of General Revelation

These and other biblical passages establish not only the fact of general revelation but

⁴ May he give you what your heart desires
and fulfill your whole purpose.
⁵ Let us shout for joy at your victory
and lift the banner in the name
of our God.
May the LORD fulfill all your requests.

⁶ Now I know that the LORD gives victory
to his anointed;
he will answer him
from his holy heaven
with mighty victories
from his right hand.
⁷ Some take pride in chariots, and others
in horses,
but we take pride in the name of the
LORD our God.
⁸ They collapse and fall,
but we rise and stand firm.
⁹ LORD, give victory to the king!
May heᴬ answer us on the day
that we call.

The King's Victory

21 *For the choir director. A psalm of David.*

LORD, the king finds joy
in your strength.
How greatly he rejoices in your victory!
² You have given him his heart's desire
and have not denied the request
of his lips. *Selah*
³ For you meet him with rich blessings;
you place a crown of pure gold
on his head.
⁴ He asked you for life, and you gave it
to him —
length of days forever and ever.
⁵ His glory is great through your victory;
you confer majesty and splendor on him.
⁶ You give him blessings forever;
you cheer him with joy
in your presence.
⁷ For the king relies on the LORD;
through the faithful love of the Most High
he is not shaken.

ᴬ20:9 Or *LORD, save. May the king*

20:4 The heart's **desires** and **purpose** are related in the sense that God's purposes and his people's desires should be the same. The word *purpose* refers to counsel or plans.
20:5 A **banner** was used in military campaigns to identify members of an army. These banners often included symbols or representations of the national gods who

were fighting for the respective armies. The Lord took on this role with Israel (Ex 15:3; Jos 23:10) and was identified as Israel's banner (Ex 17:15).
20:6 In v. 2 help comes from Zion, but here help comes from **his holy heaven**. Although the Lord dwelt among his people, his real domain from which he ruled was heaven (11:4; Is 66:1).

21:1–2 This is a thanksgiving psalm that expressed thanks to the Lord for giving victory to the king (21:1,7).
21:3 The **crown** is used as a sign of victory over a defeated power (2Sm 12:30).
21:6–7 To be in the **presence** of God is the ultimate **joy** for a person who **relies on the LORD** (16:11).

also its content. Concerning God, general revelation makes clear that he is one (Ac 17:26; Rm 1:20), Creator (Ac 17:25), Sustainer (14:15–16; 17:24–28), and Ruler (Rm 1:26); that he is wise (Ps 104:24), great (Jb 40:15–41:34), powerful (Rm 1:20), intelligent (1:26), immanent and active (Ac 17:24–27), just and good (14:17; Rm 2:14–15). He is worthy of worship (1:25).

Concerning God's law, God has written certain basic moral principles on the human heart. Although the Ten Commandments were crafted for the nation of Israel, the moral principles behind those commandments (Ex 20:1–17) are revealed to all people everywhere through general revelation. We might not see them with perfect clarity or admit that we know them, and we might become confused about them, but we do indeed know them.

The Purpose and Limits of General Revelation

General revelation and special revelation share a common purpose in pointing to the God whom we should worship and adore.

Psalm 19 instructs that general and special revelation have the common purpose of evoking worship and obedience (19:14). Romans 1:18–34 teaches that general revelation makes clear that God exists and ought to be worshiped.

Scripture is equally clear, however, that humanity is immersed with rebellious inclinations, and for this reason it rejects general revelation. In spite of general revelation, people foolishly reject God (Ps 14:1). They suppress the truth about God, exchange it for a lie, and worship the creature rather than the Creator (Rm 1:18–32). Instead of allowing God's creation to evoke worship of him, humans take God's created gifts and make idols of them—idols such as sex, money, power, success, and approval.

Because humans inevitably twist and distort God's general revelation, we need a special revelation from God to help us hear him and submit to him in worship and obedience. This special revelation, which now comes to us in the form of Christian Scripture, is necessary to point us to Jesus Christ—God's ultimate revelation of himself.

8 Your hand will capture all your enemies;
  your right hand will seize
    those who hate you.
9 You will make them burn
  like a fiery furnace when you appear;
  the LORD will engulf them in his wrath,
  and fire will devour them.
10 You will wipe their progeny
   from the earth
   and their offspring from the human race.^A
11 Though they intend to harm^B you
   and devise a wicked plan,
     they will not prevail.
12 Instead, you will put them to flight
   when you ready your bowstrings
     to shoot at them.

13 Be exalted, LORD, in your strength;
   we will sing and praise your might.

From Suffering to Praise

22 For the choir director: according to "The Deer of the Dawn." A psalm of David.

1 My God, my God, why have you
  abandoned me?
  Why are you so far from my deliverance
  and from my words of groaning?
2 My God, I cry by day, but you
  do not answer,
  by night, yet I have no rest.
3 But you are holy,
  enthroned on the praises of Israel.
4 Our ancestors trusted in you;
  they trusted, and you rescued them.
5 They cried to you and were set free;
  they trusted in you
    and were not disgraced.

6 But I am a worm and not a man,
  scorned by mankind and despised
    by people.

7 Everyone who sees me mocks me;
  they sneer^C and shake their heads:
8 "He relies on^D the LORD;
  let him save him;
  let the LORD^E rescue him,
  since he takes pleasure in him."

9 It was you who brought me out
  of the womb,
  making me secure at my mother's breast.
10 I was given over to you at birth;^F
   you have been my God
   from my mother's womb.

11 Don't be far from me, because distress
   is near
   and there's no one to help.

12 Many bulls surround me;
   strong ones of Bashan encircle me.
13 They open their mouths against me —
   lions, mauling and roaring.
14 I am poured out like water,
   and all my bones are disjointed;
   my heart is like wax,
   melting within me.
15 My strength is dried up like baked clay;
   my tongue sticks to the roof
     of my mouth.
   You put me into the dust of death.
16 For dogs have surrounded me;
   a gang of evildoers has closed in on me;
   they pierced^G my hands and my feet.
17 I can count all my bones;
   people^H look and stare at me.
18 They divided my garments
     among themselves,
   and they cast lots for my clothing.

19 But you, LORD, don't be far away.
   My strength, come quickly to help me.

---

^A 21:10 Or the descendants of Adam ^B 21:11 Lit they stretch out harm against ^C 22:7 Lit separate with the lip ^D 22:8 Or Rely on ^E 22:8 Lit let him ^F 22:10 Lit was cast on you from the womb ^G 22:16 Some Hb mss, LXX, Syr; other Hb mss read me; like a lion ^H 22:17 Lit they

---

21:8–10 The Hebrew word for **hand** can mean power or strength, but when used of God it is often a symbol of his judgment (Ex 9:3; Dt 2:15; Jdg 2:15). **Fire** is associated with God's **wrath** (89:46), symbolizing the intensity and destructive power of God's judgment. Being wiped **from the earth** and having no **offspring** show the annihilation of a person or people (Dt 4:26; 2Sm 4:11; Am 9:8).

21:11–12 Put . . . to flight is literally "turn a shoulder." It refers to the enemies turning their back toward their attackers and running away (6:10; 9:3; Ex 23:27).

Ps 22 title The Deer of the Dawn was apparently a known tune of the time.

22:1 This psalm opens with a question about God's rejection, similar to other lament psalms (10:1; 13:1–2). This rejection is represented by the term **abandoned**. Jesus identified with the psalmist (Mt 27:46). When Jesus quoted this first line, he probably was

calling attention to the whole psalm, including the theme of victory at the end.

22:3–5 Enthroned on the praises is unusual, picturing the LORD's dwelling above the cherubim on the ark of the covenant (80:1; 99:1). However, in this instance it is the praise of God's people that is the focus because the Lord is the praise of Israel (Dt 10:21).

22:6–8 Worm expresses humiliation (Jb 25:6; Is 41:14), an idea that is further developed with the scorn of the enemies. Shaking their **heads** was a physical gesture often associated with sneering and mocking.

22:9–10 The phrase **over to you** is in the emphatic position in the Hebrew text, emphasizing that the Lord is the one in whom the psalmist has trusted since birth.

22:11 The words **Don't be far from me** are found in other psalms too (see 35:22; 38:21; 71:12).

22:14–15 The terminology in these verses conveys the notion of being drained of

strength. A **heart** like melting **wax** is similar to the image of "melting hearts" in other contexts where the emotion of fear is so intense that all courage disappears (Dt 20:8; Jos 2:11; 7:5). **Dust of death** implies the nearness and inevitability of death (Jb 7:21; 10:9) and is sometimes linked with Sheol (Jb 17:16).

22:16 The Hebrew text is difficult, reading literally "like a lion my hands and my feet" for **pierced my hands and my feet**. Other manuscript traditions, including the LXX, read the Hebrew ka'ari ("like the lion") as a verb from the Hebrew root krh, meaning either "to bind" or "to dig." Digging could be synonymous with piercing. Christians often adopted this reading and seen it as a prophetic allusion to Christ's crucifixion since NT authors quote so much of this psalm in relation to that event (e.g., Mt 27:46).

22:17–18 Counting **bones** seems to be related to imagery where a person was so emaciated from suffering or brutality that

²⁰ Rescue my life from the sword,
my only life^A from the power
   of these dogs.
²¹ Save me from the lion's mouth,
from the horns of wild oxen.

You answered me!^B
²² I will proclaim your name
   to my brothers and sisters;
I will praise you in the assembly.
²³ You who fear the LORD, praise him!
All you descendants of Jacob,
   honor him!
All you descendants of Israel,
   revere him!
²⁴ For he has not despised or abhorred
the torment of the oppressed.
He did not hide his face from him
but listened when he cried to him
   for help.

²⁵ I will give praise
   in the great assembly
because of you;
I will fulfill my vows
before those who fear you.^C
²⁶ The humble will eat and be satisfied;
those who seek the LORD
   will praise him.
May your hearts live forever!

²⁷ All the ends of the earth will remember
and turn to the LORD.
All the families of the nations
will bow down before you,
²⁸ for kingship belongs to the LORD;
he rules the nations.

²⁹ All who prosper on earth will eat
   and bow down;
all those who go down to the dust
will kneel before him —
   even the one who cannot preserve
   his life.
³⁰ Their descendants will serve him;
the next generation will be told
   about the Lord.
³¹ They will come and declare
   his righteousness;
to a people yet to be born
they will declare what he has done.

The Good Shepherd

23 *A psalm of David.*
The LORD is my shepherd;
I have what I need.
² He lets me lie down in green pastures;
he leads me beside quiet waters.
³ He renews my life;
he leads me along the right paths^D
for his name's sake.
⁴ Even when I go
   through the darkest valley,^E
I fear no danger,
for you are with me;
your rod and your staff
   — they comfort me.

⁵ You prepare a table before me
in the presence of my enemies;
you anoint my head with oil;
my cup overflows.
⁶ Only goodness and faithful love
   will pursue me
all the days of my life,

---

^A**22:20** Lit *my only one*   ^B**22:21** Or *oxen you rescued me*   ^C**22:25** Lit *him*   ^D**23:3** Or *me in paths of righteousness*   ^E**23:4** Or *the valley of the shadow of death*

---

his bones were visible (102:5; Jb 19:20; 33:21). Dividing **garments** is an attested practice in Middle Assyrian laws where a criminal's clothes could be given to the prosecutor or to those carrying out the sentence. It was apparently practiced in other cultures, including Rome in the first century, as evident at the crucifixion of Jesus (Mt 27:35; Jn 19:23). **22:20–21** The psalmist uses imagery from animals to represent enemies. **Dogs** might not seem like a negative image because of their role as pets in modern Western society, but in much of the ancient Near East they were never domesticated and were always wild and ravenous animals. **22:22–24** Verse 22 begins a new major section in this psalm, shifting the focus from petition to thanksgiving. The shift might indicate that the prayer of vv. 1–21 had been answered or that such an answer was anticipated. Thanksgiving was to be offered **in the assembly** to evoke **praise** from the people of God. **22:27–31** The psalm ends by broadening to the most universal purpose of God's kingdom over the earth. Israel's purpose was to be a testimony to other nations so they would **bow down** before the Lord and serve him

(67:2; 72:11,17; 86:9). The growth of the kingdom throughout time is demonstrated in the phrase **a people yet to be born** (future generations). The inclusion of **those who go down to the dust** who would pay homage to the Lord (v. 29) is unusual, since in other psalms it is clear that the dead cannot praise him (6:5; 88:10–12). This is more likely a reference to the final stage of God's kingdom when even the dead are brought back to life to recognize the Lord's authority over all things (Dn 12:2). **23:1** The LORD is often referred to as the **shepherd** of his people, Israel (74:1; 80:1; Is 40:11; Ezk 34:11–16). In the ancient Near East, kings were commonly known as shepherds of their people. **23:2–3 Lets me lie down** is a Hebrew form implying causality, showing that God is the cause of the refreshment. **Right paths** might have a twofold idea. In keeping with the shepherd and sheep image, it can mean safe paths that are free from danger. In the larger context of Wisdom literature it refers to paths of righteousness, though usually that would contrast one path of life with another leading to death. The former idea is probably the primary meaning here.

23:4 Some argue that the Hebrew term *tsalmaweth* is related to an Akkadian word *(tselem)* that means "deep darkness." Others say it comes from two Hebrew words, *tsal* and *moth*, and means "shadow of death." It occurs approximately twenty times in the OT. It is clear that it implies intense darkness that represents extreme danger (Jb 10:21; 28:3; Jr 2:6). "Darkest" fits this specific context, since it is in the **darkest valley** where the greatest danger (such as a predator) lurks. As the psalmist encounters this challenge, he switches from the third person to the second person—he stops talking *about* the Lord and talks *to* the Lord. **23:5** The image shifts from shepherd to friend. The identification of the Lord with a shepherd emphasizes his care and protection, but he is much more than that for a person who is in close fellowship with him. In Jewish society **oil** was a symbol for rejoicing (104:15) and was also used in the welcoming of guests (45:7; 92:10; Lk 7:46). **23:6** The verb **pursue** is commonly used for attackers, but here the Lord's **goodness and faithful love** are personified as the ones who chased the psalmist throughout his life. **As long as I live** represents

and I will dwell in^A the house
of the LORD
as long as I live.^B

The King of Glory

24 *A psalm of David.*
The earth and everything in it,
the world and its inhabitants,
belong to the LORD;
² for he laid its foundation on the seas
and established it on the rivers.

³ Who may ascend the mountain
of the LORD?
Who may stand in his holy place?
⁴ The one who has clean hands
and a pure heart,
who has not appealed to^C what is false,
and who has not sworn deceitfully.
⁵ He will receive blessing
from the LORD,
and righteousness^D from the God
of his salvation.
⁶ Such is the generation of those
who inquire of him,
who seek the face of the God of Jacob.^E
                 Selah

⁷ Lift up your heads, you gates!
Rise up, ancient doors!
Then the King of glory will come in.
⁸ Who is this King of glory?
The LORD, strong and mighty,
the LORD, mighty in battle.
⁹ Lift up your heads, you gates!
Rise up, ancient doors!
Then the King of glory will come in.
¹⁰ Who is he, this King of glory?
The LORD of Armies,
he is the King of glory.   *Selah*

Dependence on the LORD

25 *Of David.*
LORD, I appeal to you.^F
² My God, I trust in you.
Do not let me be disgraced;
do not let my enemies gloat over me.
³ No one who waits for you
will be disgraced;
those who act treacherously
without cause
will be disgraced.

⁴ Make your ways known to me, LORD;
teach me your paths.
⁵ Guide me in your truth and teach me,
for you are the God of my salvation;
I wait for you all day long.
⁶ Remember, LORD, your compassion
and your faithful love,
for they have existed from antiquity.^G
⁷ Do not remember the sins of my youth
or my acts of rebellion;
in keeping with your faithful love,
remember me
because of your goodness, LORD.

⁸ The LORD is good and upright;
therefore he shows sinners the way.
⁹ He leads the humble in what is right
and teaches them his way.
¹⁰ All the LORD's ways show faithful love
and truth
to those who keep his covenant
and decrees.
¹¹ LORD, for the sake of your name,
forgive my iniquity, for it is immense.

¹² Who is this person who fears the LORD?
He will show him the way
he should choose.

---

^A 23:6 LXX, Sym, Syr, Tg, Vg, Jer; MT reads *will return to*   ^B 23:6 Lit LORD *for length of days*; traditionally LORD *forever*
^C 24:4 Lit *not lifted up his soul to*   ^D 24:5 Or *vindication*   ^E 24:6 LXX; some Hb mss, Syr read *seek your face, God of Jacob*;
some Hb mss read *seek your face, Jacob*   ^F 25:1 Or *To you, LORD, I lift up my soul*   ^G 25:6 Or *everlasting*

---

the Hebrew "for the length of days." This
is equivalent to the parallel **all the days
of my life**. Though some translate this
as "forever," it is nowhere else used that
way but always refers to one's earthly life
(91:16; Pr 3:2,16). **Dwell** (Hb *yashav*) is similar
to the word for "return" (Hb *shuv*). In this
verbal form, it differs only in the vowels. It
is possible that the request is to return to
the sanctuary of the Lord throughout one's
life, although the preposition **in** argues for
the idea of "dwell."
24:1–2 World (Hb *tevel*) refers to the inhabited world. According to the ancient Israelite
conception, the earth rested on the waters
(136:6; Ex 20:4); the **seas** and **rivers** are what
was seen of this phenomenon. The **earth** was
set on a firm **foundation**, so it was stable
and secure (104:5; Is 51:13).
24:3–4 Clean hands and **a pure heart** represent innocence and integrity.
24:5 Righteousness can mean "vindication" here.

24:6 Inquire or "seek" means more than
looking for something that is lost or hidden.
It means turning to someone for advice and
help; it is thus synonymous with trust (9:10).
24:7–10 Lift up your heads is a poetic way
of saying "extend your height" in reference
to the gates. Some think that **ancient doors**
refers to the "gate of heaven" (Gn 28:17).
These doors are represented in the earthly
gates of the city of Jerusalem. The **LORD of
Armies** portrays the Lord as Warrior and King
returning from battle (1Sm 17:45).
25:1–3 Disgraced (Hb *bosh*) is used three
times in vv. 2–3. The same Hebrew verb occurs in v. 20. The belief of the psalmist was
that the Lord would not allow his people to
be put to shame because of their faithfulness
to him and the fact that his reputation was
at stake (69:6; 119:31).
25:4–5 Guide and **teach** are essentially
synonymous in this context, and they refer
to the Lord's directing those who are faithful
to him. His **truth** is the guide for their lives

(43:3). The **paths** are similar to "ways" in v.
10 and are connected not only to God's truth
but also to his faithful love.
25:6–7 The juxtaposition of **remember . . . do
not remember**, and **remember** in these verses is significant. The first demonstrates that the
Lord's consciousness of his own attributes is the
motivation for him to act beneficently toward
his people. In contrast to this, the **sins** of the
psalmist must not be remembered, that is, they
must be forgiven (vv. 11,18). Only after this has
taken place could the Lord remember (act on
behalf of) the psalmist (74:2; 106:4; 112:6).
25:8–10 Way and **ways** are probably not the
way of life or conduct of God's people in this
instance, as these terms are commonly used
elsewhere. They are more likely related to vv.
4–5, and they represent the Lord's instruction
of his people in the **truth** (119:15). In this
sense **the LORD's** "ways" are equivalent to
his covenant and decrees.
25:12 God is the subject of **He will show
him the way he should choose**.

¹³ He will live a good life,
   and his descendants will inherit
      the land.ᴬ
¹⁴ The secret counsel of the LORD
   is for those who fear him,
   and he reveals his covenant to them.
¹⁵ My eyes are always on the LORD,
   for he will pull my feet out of the net.

¹⁶ Turn to me and be gracious to me,
   for I am alone and afflicted.
¹⁷ The distresses of my heart increase;ᴮ
   bring me out of my sufferings.
¹⁸ Consider my affliction and trouble,
   and forgive all my sins.
¹⁹ Consider my enemies;
      they are numerous,
   and they hate me violently.
²⁰ Guard me and rescue me;
   do not let me be disgraced,
   for I take refuge in you.
²¹ May integrity and what is right
   watch over me,
   for I wait for you.

²² God, redeem Israel, from all
   its distresses.

Prayer for Vindication

26 *Of David.*
   Vindicate me, LORD,
   because I have lived with integrity
   and have trusted in the LORD
      without wavering.
² Test me, LORD, and try me;
   examine my heart and mind.
³ For your faithful love guides me,ᶜ
   and I live by your truth.

⁴ I do not sit with the worthless
   or associate with hypocrites.
⁵ I hate a crowd of evildoers,
   and I do not sit with the wicked.

⁶ I wash my hands in innocence
   and go around your altar, LORD,
⁷ raising my voice in thanksgiving
   and telling about
      your wondrous works.

⁸ LORD, I love the house where you dwell,
   the place where your glory resides.
⁹ Do not destroy me along with sinners,
   or my life along with men of bloodshed
¹⁰ in whose hands are evil schemes
   and whose right hands are filled
      with bribes.

¹¹ But I live with integrity;
   redeem me and be gracious to me.
¹² My foot stands on level ground;
   I will bless the LORD in the assemblies.

My Stronghold

27 *Of David.*
   The LORD is my light
      and my salvation —
   whom should I fear?
   The LORD is the stronghold of my life —
   whom should I dread?
² When evildoers came against me
      to devour my flesh,
   my foes and my enemies stumbled
      and fell.
³ Though an army deploys against me,
   my heart will not be afraid;
   though a war breaks out against me,
   I will still be confident.

⁴ I have asked one thing from the LORD;
   it is what I desire:
   to dwell in the house of the LORD
   all the days of my life,
   gazing on the beauty of the LORD
   and seeking him in his temple.
⁵ For he will conceal me in his shelter
   in the day of adversity;

ᴬ25:13 Or *earth* ᴮ25:17 Or *Relieve the distresses of my heart* ᶜ26:3 Lit *love is in front of my eyes*

25:14 The Hebrew word *sod* expresses the idea of "confidential," referring either to the material that is **secret** or to a "circle of confidants." Given the parallel in **his covenant**, it seems better to understand this as the content of God's secret **counsel**. God has the right to conceal what he wants (Pr 25:2), but he can also reveal his secret counsel to anyone he chooses. In this case it is revealed to **those who fear him** (trust in him and are faithful to him).
25:15 Eyes are often used in the context of faith in the sense that a person "looks to" the Lord as his source of help (123:2; 141:8).
25:16 A prayer for God to turn (cp. v. 1) means to look favorably upon one.
25:17–19 The Hebrew text of v. 17 is difficult, reading literally "**the distresses of my heart**, they make wide." Although the form for "make wide" usually refers to relief from distress (4:1; 18:36), it can also express

the meaning of "enlarge," which would be a figurative expression for **increase**. This idea is related to numerous enemies who surrounded the psalmist (v. 19).
25:21 Integrity and **what is right** are personified in a similar way as the Lord's attributes were personified in 23:6. These characteristics will protect those who remain in God's will (37:37).
26:1–3 The request for vindication at the beginning sets the tone for this psalm that primarily involves a declaration of innocence.
26:4–5 Evidence of a person's faithfulness toward the Lord is not only in what is done but also in what is avoided, particularly in a person's associations with others. The repeated **do not sit with** in these verses recalls the language from 1:1.
26:6–7 Washing **hands** was part of an oath of purification symbolizing **innocence** (24:4; 73:13; Dt 21:6). Going **around** the **altar** is

more difficult to interpret. The present context suggests being around the altar and making sacrifices to the Lord as part of a person's demonstration of purity and loyalty.
26:12 Level ground is associated with the righteous way in which the Lord leads his people (27:11; 143:10; Is 26:7).
27:1 Light is parallel to salvation, which in this context refers to rescue from danger.
27:4 To **dwell in the house of the LORD** may mean continually returning to the sanctuary for worship. It can also be more general in referring to living one's life in God's presence. In either case, the point is that there is constant fellowship with the Lord throughout one's life (see note at 23:6).
27:5 The words **conceal** and **hide** mean protection when it is the Lord hiding his people. Often the image is connected with a mother bird hiding her young under her wings.

he will hide me under the cover
　　of his tent;
he will set me high on a rock.
6 Then my head will be high
　above my enemies around me;
　I will offer sacrifices in his tent
　　with shouts of joy.
　I will sing and make music to the Lord.

7 Lord, hear my voice when I call;
　be gracious to me and answer me.
8 My heart says this about you:
　"Seek^A his face."
　Lord, I will seek your face.
9 Do not hide your face from me;
　do not turn your servant away in anger.
　You have been my helper;
　do not leave me or abandon me,
　God of my salvation.
10 Even if my father and mother
　　abandon me,
　the Lord cares for me.

11 Because of my adversaries,
　show me your way, Lord,
　and lead me on a level path.
12 Do not give me over to the will
　of my foes,
　for false witnesses rise up against me,
　breathing violence.

13 I am certain that I will see the
　　Lord's goodness
　in the land of the living.
14 Wait for the Lord;
　be strong, and let your heart
　　be courageous.
　Wait for the Lord.

My Strength

28 Of David.
Lord, I call to you;
　my rock, do not be deaf to me.

If you remain silent to me,
I will be like those going down to the Pit.
2 Listen to the sound of my pleading
　when I cry to you for help,
　when I lift up my hands
　toward your holy sanctuary.

3 Do not drag me away with the wicked,
　with the evildoers,
　who speak in friendly ways
　　with their neighbors
　while malice is in their hearts.
4 Repay them according to what
　　they have done —
　according to the evil of their deeds.
　Repay them according to the work
　　of their hands;
　give them back what they deserve.
5 Because they do not consider
　what the Lord has done
　or the work of his hands,
　he will tear them down and not
　　rebuild them.

6 Blessed be the Lord,
　for he has heard the sound
　　of my pleading.
7 The Lord is my strength and my shield;
　my heart trusts in him, and I am helped.
　Therefore my heart celebrates,
　and I give thanks to him with my song.

8 The Lord is the strength of his people;^B
　he is a stronghold of salvation
　　for his anointed.
9 Save your people, bless your possession,
　shepherd them, and carry them forever.

The Voice of the Lord

29 A psalm of David.
Ascribe to the Lord,
　you heavenly beings,^C
ascribe to the Lord glory and strength.

^A 27:8 The command is pl in Hb　^B 28:8 Some Hb mss, LXX, Syr; other Hb mss read *strength for them*　^C 29:1 Or *you sons of gods*, or *you sons of mighty ones*

27:6 Lifting one's **head . . . above** his **enemies** is another way of expressing triumph over those who are defeated (3:3).
27:7–9 **Face** is a key word in these verses, appearing three times. To **seek** God's face is to petition the Lord, most often in the context of worship (2Ch 11:16).
27:10 This verse could also be translated "Because my father and mother have abandoned me."
27:13 The **land of the living** is in contrast to Sheol, the realm of the dead (Ezk 32:27). Being cut off from the land of the living is another way to express being killed (Jr 11:19).
27:14 Waiting **for the Lord** is an abbreviated way to express waiting for an answer to prayer.
28:1 **Deaf** and **silent** are often connected with being "far from" (35:22). These concepts describe God's lack of intervention in a time of need. "Pit" is sometimes parallel

with Sheol, the realm of the dead (30:3; Jb 33:18; Pr 1:12; Is 14:15), so **those going down to the Pit** refers to those who are going to die.
28:2 Lifting up **hands** was a common gesture for prayer. **Sanctuary** is a specific word (Hb *devir*) referring to the innermost part of the sanctuary—the most holy place. This was the place where the ark of the covenant resided, but more importantly it was the location of the mercy seat—the place from which the Lord dispensed mercy on his people (Ex 26:34).
28:3–5 **Repay them** appears twice as a call for retribution on one's enemies; it is also known as an imprecation. The reason for this request for judgment on these **evildoers** is that they did not **consider what the Lord** had **done**. Some think that this refers to God's judgment on the wicked; however, the phrase **work of his hands** is more commonly

used for God's work of creation (19:1; 102:25) or for his work in delivering his people (143:5; Is 60:21). The second of these options seems more likely in this context where there is praise for the Lord's help.
28:6 The shift from petition to thanksgiving is common in lament psalms.
28:8–9 Though **his anointed** can refer to the Davidic king of Israel (18:50; 20:6; 45:7), in this case it is parallel to "his people" and represents the nation as a whole (105:15; Hab 3:13). Israel was also known as the Lord's **possession** (see 135:4; Ex 19:5).
29:1 To **ascribe** something to someone is to acknowledge they have that attribute. **Heavenly beings** is literally "sons of gods." The word for "gods" (Hb *'elim*), although similar to the word for "God" (Hb *'elohim*), is never used of him. It can also refer to people, with the meaning of "the mighty" (Jb 41:25). In this context it is best to understand the

2 Ascribe to the LORD the glory due
    his name;
  worship the LORD
  in the splendor of his holiness.ᴬ

3 The voice of the LORD is
    above the waters.
  The God of glory thunders —
  the LORD, above the vast water,
4 the voice of the LORD in power,
  the voice of the LORD in splendor.
5 The voice of the LORD breaks the cedars;
  the LORD shatters the cedars of Lebanon.
6 He makes Lebanon skip like a calf,
  and Sirion, like a young wild ox.
7 The voice of the LORD flashes
    flames of fire.
8 The voice of the LORD shakes
    the wilderness;
  the LORD shakes the wilderness
    of Kadesh.
9 The voice of the LORD makes the deer
    give birthᴮ
  and strips the woodlands bare.

  In his temple all cry, "Glory!"

10 The LORD sits enthroned over the flood;
   the LORD sits enthroned, King forever.
11 The LORD gives his people strength;
   the LORD blesses his people with peace.

Joy in the Morning

30 A psalm; a dedication song for the house.
    Of David.
1 I will exalt you, LORD,
  because you have lifted me up
  and have not allowed my enemies
  to triumph over me.
2 LORD my God,

I cried to you for help, and you
    healed me.
3 LORD, you brought me up from Sheol;
  you spared me from among those
  going downᶜ to the Pit.

4 Sing to the LORD, you his faithful ones,
  and praise his holy name.
5 For his anger lasts only a moment,
  but his favor, a lifetime.
  Weeping may stay overnight,
  but there is joy in the morning.

6 When I was secure, I said,
  "I will never be shaken."
7 LORD, when you showed your favor,
  you made me stand
    like a strong mountain;
  when you hid your face, I was terrified.
8 LORD, I called to you;
  I sought favor from my Lord:
9 "What gain is there in my death,
  if I go down to the Pit?
  Will the dust praise you?
  Will it proclaim your truth?
10 LORD, listen and be gracious to me;
   LORD, be my helper."

11 You turned my lament into dancing;
   you removed my sackcloth
   and clothed me with gladness,
12 so that I can sing to you and not
     be silent.
   LORD my God, I will praise you forever.

A Plea for Protection

31 For the choir director. A psalm of David.
1 LORD, I seek refuge in you;
  let me never be disgraced.
  Save me by your righteousness.

ᴬ29:2 Or *in holy attire,* or *in holy appearance* ᴮ29:9 Or *the oaks shake* ᶜ30:3 Some Hb mss, LXX, Theod, Orig, Syr; other Hb mss, Aq, Sym, Tg, Jer read *from going down*

term as angelic beings (Ps 89:6). The angels are witnesses of God's creation (Jb 38:7) and are allowed access to God in heaven (Jb 1:6; 2:1). They surround his throne to praise and worship him (Is 6; Ezk 1). It is most appropriate to address them as those who worship the Lord. **29:2** The word for **splendor** can mean "adornment," such as the ornate clothing worn by rulers or dignitaries. In the case of the Lord, he is clothed in his own attributes (93:1), which in this case refers to his **holiness** (96:9; 2Ch 20:21). **29:3–4 Voice** here and through v. 9 is used as the Lord's audible expression of his **power,** comparable to thunder. The description of God's voice **above the vast water** shows his dominion over it (93:3–4; Jr 10:13; 51:16). **29:5–6 Lebanon** was known for its **cedars,** the strongest and most majestic trees in Israel (104:16; Sg 5:15; Is 2:13). **Sirion** refers to Mount Hermon, the tallest mountain in that area (Dt 3:8–9). Together these represent the greatest spectacles of creation in and around Israel.

29:7 Lightning, which accompanies thunder in storms, is called **flames of fire** that flash and come from the Lord's **voice** (18:12–14). **29:8–9** The verb for **shakes** is commonly used to mean "tremble with fear" (96:9; 114:7), so that the picture is of creation itself trembling before the Lord's power. In this psalm **his temple** is heaven (11:4; Mc 1:2). **All** refers to the "heavenly beings" in v. 1. **29:10–11 The flood** continues the image in v. 3. Some interpreters relate it directly to the flood of Noah's time (Gn 6–7), while others see it as the waters at creation (Gn 1:7; Ps 148:4). The point in either case is that the Lord rules over (**sits enthroned**) the most powerful forces in the natural world. **Ps 30 title** If **Of David** means "authored by David," then a dedication song for the house might have been added later to indicate how this psalm was used by the nation of Israel. **30:1–2 Lifted . . . up** is from a Hebrew word (*dlh*) that is most often used to describe drawing water from a well (Ex 2:16,19; Pr 20:5). **30:3 Sheol** in many instances is a synonym for death. To be near Sheol is to be close to

death (88:3), so being **brought . . . up** from Sheol or **spared** from the **Pit** is equivalent to being rescued from death (28:1; 88:4). **30:6–7** Before God allowed the psalmist to suffer, he was so **secure** that he felt he could **never be shaken**. The security apparently became a source of overconfidence even though it was the Lord who **showed** his **favor** and made him **like a strong mountain** (5:12). In other words, the blessing of God gave him a false sense of security. The suffering began when the Lord **hid** his **face**. **30:8** Verse 8 introduces the words of his cry found in vv. 9–10. **30:11–12 Lament** is parallel with **sackcloth,** the clothing used to represent a time of mourning (Gn 37:34; Est 4:3; Ezk 27:31). **Dancing** and being **clothed . . . with gladness** are also related ideas showing the dramatic change after the Lord delivered the psalmist from death. **31:1–4** A number of different Hebrew words are used in these verses for **refuge . . . rock,** and **fortress,** all conveying the sense of the Lord as a source of security and protection

2 Listen closely to me; rescue me quickly.
  Be a rock of refuge for me,
  a mountain fortress to save me.
3 For you are my rock and my fortress;
  you lead and guide me
  for your name's sake.
4 You will free me from the net
  that is secretly set for me,
  for you are my refuge.
5 Into your hand I entrust my spirit;
  you have redeemed me,^A LORD,
    God of truth.

6 I^B hate those who are devoted
    to worthless idols,
  but I trust in the LORD.
7 I will rejoice and be glad
    in your faithful love
  because you have seen my affliction.
  You know the troubles of my soul
8 and have not handed me over
    to the enemy.
  You have set my feet in a spacious place.

9 Be gracious to me, LORD,
  because I am in distress;
  my eyes are worn out
    from frustration —
  my whole being^C as well.
10 Indeed, my life is consumed with grief
  and my years with groaning;
  my strength has failed
  because of my iniquity,^D
  and my bones waste away.
11 I am ridiculed by all my adversaries
  and even by my neighbors.
  I am dreaded by my acquaintances;
  those who see me in the street
    run from me.
12 I am forgotten: gone from memory
  like a dead person
    — like broken pottery.
13 I have heard the gossip of many;
  terror is on every side.
  When they conspired against me,
  they plotted to take my life.

14 But I trust in you, LORD;
  I say, "You are my God."
15 The course of my life is
    in your power;
  rescue me from the power
    of my enemies
  and from my persecutors.
16 Make your face shine on your servant;
  save me by your faithful love.
17 LORD, do not let me be disgraced
    when I call on you.
  Let the wicked be disgraced;
  let them be quiet^E,^F in Sheol.
18 Let lying lips
    that arrogantly speak
      against the righteous
  in proud contempt be silenced.
19 How great is your goodness,
  which you have stored up for those
    who fear you.
  In the presence of everyone^G you
    have acted
  for those who take refuge in you.
20 You hide them in the protection
    of your presence;
  you conceal them in a shelter
  from human schemes,
  from quarrelsome tongues.
21 Blessed be the LORD,
  for he has wondrously shown
    his faithful love to me
  in a city under siege.
22 In my alarm I said,
  "I am cut off from your sight."
  But you heard the sound
    of my pleading
  when I cried to you for help.

23 Love the LORD, all his faithful ones.
  The LORD protects the loyal,
  but fully repays the arrogant.
24 Be strong, and let your heart
    be courageous,
  all you who put your hope
    in the LORD.

---

^A 31:5 Or *spirit. Redeem me*   ^B 31:6 One Hb ms, LXX, Syr, Vg, Jer read *You*   ^C 31:9 Lit *my soul and my belly*   ^D 31:10 LXX, Syr, Sym read *affliction*   ^E 31:17 LXX reads *brought down*   ^F 31:17 Or *them wail*   ^G 31:19 Or *of the descendants of Adam*

(18:1–2). A **net** was metaphorically a malicious plot (35:7; 140:5).
31:5 Spirit could represent the person as a whole or the life-giving force that God gives to each person (Gn 7:22; Is 38:16). **Hand** means possession or control (Jos 7:7). Jesus used these words as he was dying on the cross to describe the release of his own spirit to his Father (Lk 23:46).
31:8 Spacious place conveys the notion of being delivered from surrounding enemies who had someone enclosed without an exit.
31:9–10 Eyes that are **worn out**, most likely from crying (6:7; 88:9; Jb 17:7), and **bones** that **waste away** (see 6:2; 22:14; 102:5) are figurative expressions describing **frustration** and **grief**.

31:11–12 Suffering often results not only in ridicule from enemies but also in abandonment (being **dreaded**) by friends (38:11; 88:18; Jb 16:20; 19:13–19).
31:13 The phrase **terror . . . on every side** occurs frequently in Jeremiah (Jr 6:25; 20:10; 46:5) and is a vivid way to describe being surrounded by enemies.
31:14–15 The request to be in God's **power** instead of the power of one's **enemies** is the central plea in this psalm (v. 5; cp. 2Sm 24:14).
31:16–18 Sheol is "the silence of death" (94:17; 115:17), where the dead are no longer able to communicate with the living. Death is the only thing that will quiet the deception (**lying lips**) of these enemies.

31:21 The psalmist likens his trouble to being in a **city under siege**. Alternately, it could be translated "in a fortified city" and be compared to how the Lord has cared for him.
31:22 Being **cut off** from God's **sight** refers to his rejection that results in separation from him.
31:24 The words **strong** and **courageous** recall the words of God to Joshua and Israel to prepare them for the conquest of the promised land (Dt 31:6–7,23; Jos 1:6–7,9,18).
Ps 32 title Maskil may be derived from a root word meaning "insight." For this reason, some have suggested that psalms with this title deal with wisdom or instruction. The problem is that many of the psalms bearing

The Joy of Forgiveness

32 *Of David. A Maskil.*
How joyful is the one
whose transgression is forgiven,
whose sin is covered!

[2] How joyful is a person whom
the LORD does not charge with iniquity
and in whose spirit is no deceit!

[3] When I kept silent, my bones
became brittle
from my groaning all day long.

[4] For day and night your hand was heavy
on me;
my strength was drained[A]
as in the summer's heat. *Selah*

[5] Then I acknowledged my sin to you
and did not conceal my iniquity.
I said, "I will confess my transgressions
to the LORD,"
and you forgave the guilt
of my sin. *Selah*

[6] Therefore let everyone who is faithful
pray to you immediately.[B]
When great floodwaters come,
they will not reach him.

[7] You are my hiding place;
you protect me from trouble.
You surround me with joyful shouts
of deliverance. *Selah*

[8] I will instruct you and show you the way
to go;
with my eye on you, I will give counsel.

[9] Do not be like a horse or mule,
without understanding,
that must be controlled with bit
and bridle
or else it will not come near you.

[10] Many pains come to the wicked,
but the one who trusts in the LORD
will have faithful love surrounding him.

[11] Be glad in the LORD and rejoice,
you righteous ones;
shout for joy,
all you upright in heart.

Praise to the Creator

33 Rejoice in the LORD,
you righteous ones;
praise from the upright is beautiful.

[2] Praise the LORD with the lyre;
make music to him
with a ten-stringed harp.

[3] Sing a new song to him;
play skillfully on the strings,
with a joyful shout.

[4] For the word of the LORD is right,
and all his work is trustworthy.

[5] He loves righteousness and justice;
the earth is full of the LORD's
unfailing love.

[6] The heavens were made by the word
of the LORD,
and all the stars, by the breath
of his mouth.

A32:4 Hb obscure   B32:6 Lit *you at a time of finding*

---

this title do not have teaching elements (even though this psalm does have them in vv. 8–9). It is also possible to connect the word with the idea of "skill," which is closely tied to the OT concept of "wisdom." In this

sense, the title refers to a "skillful" or an "artistic" psalm.
32:1–2 Four different Hebrew terms are used for **sin** in these verses, highlighting different aspects of sin: (1) *pesha'* (translated **transgression**) has the basic idea of rebellion, (2) *hata'ah* (translated "sin") is a more general term referring to a deliberate offense, (3) *'awon* (translated **iniquity**) has the idea of going astray, and (4) *remiyyah* (translated **deceit**) emphasizes falsehood or even hypocrisy. There are also three different Hebrew verbs associated with the first three of these terms for sin, also showing different aspects of forgiveness: (1) the root *ns'* (translated **forgiven**) is literally "lifted up" and emphasizes the burden of sin being lifted from the person, (2) the root *kasah* (translated **covered**) means to hide or cover something that is offensive, and (3) the root *chashav* (translated **charge**) can mean "reckon" or "regard," but in legal contexts it means to reckon as liable for punishment (impute with guilt).
32:5 In contrast to the suffering in vv. 3–4, the confession of **sin** brings relief because God **forgave the guilt** of sin, which is another way of describing forgiveness. Guilt is not a subjective feeling but liability for punishment in a legal sense. Mere removal of the feelings about sin is clearly not intended, since God brings the conviction. What is needed is forgiveness (vv. 1–2).

32:8–9 This is a wisdom section in the psalm as evidenced by the terms **instruct** and **counsel**.
32:10 This proverb means that although the one who trusts the Lord may find troubles, the Lord's **faithful love** will always be there.
32:11 After the psalmist confessed and experienced forgiveness, he became a conduit for God's praise and called on others to do the same.
33:1–3 This is a typical beginning for a descriptive praise psalm, which has the two main elements: a call to praise (vv. 1–3) and a cause for praise (vv. 4–22). Even though only the **lyre** and **harp** are mentioned, they probably represent all the musical instruments used for worship. A **new song** might be one newly composed for a special occasion, or it might mean a new experience of God's acts through the singing of this psalm.
33:5 Loving **righteousness and justice** means doing acts of righteousness and justice (99:4; Jr 9:24). They are not just abstract attributes but they involve actions, whether directed toward God or his people.
33:6 This verse and what follows specify this psalm as a creation hymn (along with Pss 8 and 104). Even though they refer to different things, **the word of the LORD** here and in v. 4 are related in that they both originate with God. The Lord of creation is the God of revelation. In the biblical text, the God of history

⁷ He gathers the water of the sea
    into a heap;^
he puts the depths into storehouses.
⁸ Let the whole earth fear the Lord;
    let all the inhabitants of the world
        stand in awe of him.
⁹ For he spoke, and it came into being;
    he commanded, and it came
        into existence.

¹⁰ The Lord frustrates the counsel
    of the nations;
he thwarts the plans of the peoples.
¹¹ The counsel of the Lord stands forever,
    the plans of his heart from generation
        to generation.
¹² Happy is the nation whose God
    is the Lord —
the people he has chosen to be
    his own possession!

¹³ The Lord looks down from heaven;
    he observes everyone.
¹⁴ He gazes on all the inhabitants
        of the earth
    from his dwelling place.
¹⁵ He forms the hearts of them all;
    he considers all their works.
¹⁶ A king is not saved by a large army;
    a warrior will not be rescued
        by great strength.
¹⁷ The horse is a false hope for safety;
    it provides no escape by its great power.

¹⁸ But look, the Lord keeps his eye on
        those who fear him —
    those who depend on his faithful love
¹⁹ to rescue them from death
    and to keep them alive in famine.

²⁰ We wait for the Lord;
    he is our help and shield.
²¹ For our hearts rejoice in him
    because we trust in his holy name.

²² May your faithful love rest on us, Lord,
    for we put our hope in you.

The Lord Delivers the Righteous

34 Concerning David, when he pretended to
be insane in the presence of Abimelech,
who drove him out, and he departed.

¹ I will bless the Lord at all times;
    his praise will always be on my lips.
² I will boast in the Lord;
    the humble will hear and be glad.
³ Proclaim the Lord's greatness with me;
    let us exalt his name together.

⁴ I sought the Lord, and he answered me
    and rescued me from all my fears.
⁵ Those who look to him are⁸ radiant
        with joy;
    their faces will never be ashamed.
⁶ This poor man cried, and the Lord
        heard him
    and saved him from all his troubles.
⁷ The angel of the Lord encamps
    around those who fear him,
        and rescues them.

⁸ Taste and see that the Lord is good.
    How happy is the person who
        takes refuge in him!
⁹ You who are his holy ones, fear the Lord,
    for those who fear him lack nothing.
¹⁰ Young lionsᶜ lack food and go hungry,
    but those who seek the Lord
        will not lack any good thing.

¹¹ Come, children, listen to me;
    I will teach you the fear of the Lord.
¹² Who is someone who desires life,
    loving a long life to enjoy what is good?
¹³ Keep your tongue from evil
    and your lips from deceitful speech.
¹⁴ Turn away from evil and do
        what is good;
    seek peace and pursue it.

---

^33:7 LXX, Tg, Syr, Vg, Jer read *sea as in a bottle*   ⁸34:5 Some Hb mss, LXX, Aq, Syr, Jer read *Look to him and be*   ᶜ34:10 LXX, Syr, Vg read *The rich*

---

who interacts with his people is the same God who spoke the world into existence. This brings together the general revelation of creation and the special revelation that God gave to his people.
33:7 Though some interpreters argue that this could describe the exodus event, the immediate context argues for creation.
33:12 The nation . . . he has chosen—Israel—is in contrast to "the nations" in v. 10. The terms *chosen* and **possession** refer to divine election of the nation and its unique relationship to the Lord (Ex 19:5; Dt 7:6).
33:13–15 The omniscience of God is described as his looking down, observing, and gazing on the **inhabitants of the earth**. Even though his **dwelling place** is **heaven**, this does not mean that he is unconcerned with what is happening on

earth. Moreover, he not only knows what is happening but he is actively involved in it. The word **forms** is the same word used in the creation account of God's shaping man from the dust of the earth (Gn 2:7–8). This connects the creative acts of God with his involvement in history.
33:18–19 Eye is in an emphatic position in v. 18. Literally it is "behold the eye," emphasizing God's close watch on his people. The Lord has a concern for his own people that is unique in comparison to the other nations.
Ps 34 title The incident mentioned here is found in 1Sm 21:10–15. It relates David's deliverance from King Achish of Gath.
34:6 Poor in the psalms should not be limited to economic hardship alone.
34:7 The angel of the Lord can also be translated as "messenger of the Lord." In

most contexts there is a distinction between God and this angel.
34:8 Taste can mean "judge" in the sense of determine for oneself (Pr 31:18). **See** most likely carries the same sense in order to reinforce the concept.
34:9–10 God cares for his people more than the rest of his creation (8:5–8). **Lack nothing** also appears in the context of the Lord's role as a shepherd in 23:1.
34:11 The identification of the psalmist's listeners as **children** recalls a common wisdom motif of parents instructing their children (Ex 12:26; Dt 6:6–9) and shows that vv. 11–14 form a wisdom section in this psalm (similar to 32:8–9). Fearing the **Lord** is where wisdom begins (Pr 9:10).
34:12–14 Who is someone who is another way of saying "whoever."

15 The eyes of the LORD are
   on the righteous,
and his ears are open to their cry
   for help.
16 The face of the LORD is set
against those who do what is evil,
to remove^A all memory of them
   from the earth.
17 The righteous^B cry out,
   and the LORD hears,
and rescues them from all
   their troubles.
18 The LORD is near the brokenhearted;
he saves those crushed in spirit.

19 One who is righteous has
   many adversities,
but the LORD rescues him from them all.
20 He protects all his bones;
not one of them is broken.
21 Evil brings death to the wicked,
and those who hate the righteous
   will be punished.
22 The LORD redeems the life
   of his servants,
and all who take refuge in him will not
   be punished.

Prayer for Victory

35 *Of David.*
   Oppose my opponents, LORD;
   fight those who fight me.
2 Take your shields — large and small —
   and come to my aid.
3 Draw the spear and javelin
   against my pursuers,
   and assure me, "I am your deliverance."

4 Let those who intend to take my life
   be disgraced and humiliated;
let those who plan to harm me
   be turned back and ashamed.
5 Let them be like chaff in the wind,
   with the angel of the LORD
   driving them away.
6 Let their way be dark and slippery,
   with the angel of the LORD
   pursuing them.
7 They hid their net for me without cause;

they dug a pit for me without cause.
8 Let ruin come on him unexpectedly,
   and let the net that he hid
   ensnare him;
let him fall into it — to his ruin.

9 Then I will rejoice in the LORD;
I will delight in his deliverance.
10 All my bones will say,
   "LORD, who is like you,
rescuing the poor from one too strong
   for him,
the poor or the needy from one
   who robs him?"

11 Malicious witnesses come forward;
they question me about things
   I do not know.
12 They repay me evil for good,
making me desolate.
13 Yet when they were sick,
my clothing was sackcloth;
I humbled myself with fasting,
and my prayer was genuine.^C
14 I went about mourning as if
   for my friend or brother;
I was bowed down with grief,
like one mourning for a mother.
15 But when I stumbled, they gathered
   in glee;
they gathered against me.
Assailants I did not know
tore at me and did not stop.
16 With godless mockery^D
they gnashed their teeth at me.

17 Lord, how long will you look on?
Rescue me from their ravages;
rescue my precious life
   from the young lions.
18 I will praise you in the great assembly;
I will exalt you among many people.
19 Do not let my deceitful enemies rejoice
   over me;
do not let those who hate me
   without cause
   wink at me maliciously.
20 For they do not speak in friendly ways,
but contrive fraudulent schemes^E

---

^A 34:16 Or *cut off* ^B 34:17 Lit *They* ^C 35:13 Lit *prayer returned to my chest* ^D 35:16 Hb obscure ^E 35:20 Lit *but devise fraudulent words*

34:15 His **ears** being **open** describes his attentiveness to their prayers (18:6; 130:2).
34:16 To **remove** the **memory** of someone **from the earth** is another way to describe annihilation.
34:17–18 **Brokenhearted** and **crushed in spirit** further develop the image of oppression, although the emphasis in these terms is on internal suffering.
34:19–20 Verse 20 was recognized as literally fulfilled by Jesus (Jn 19:36).
35:4–5 Chaff was the waste from threshing. **The angel of the LORD** is sometimes used

in military contexts as the one who fought for Israel.
35:9–10 Bones often represent suffering. In this case they are used for the whole person, but they emphasize that the Lord protects his people from suffering. **Needy** (Hb *'evyon*) is often parallel to **poor** and is used to make the connection between poverty and oppression.
35:15 The **glee** of these people toward the psalmist's troubles also put them in the same category as enemies who triumphed over the afflictions of God's people.

35:16 Gnashing the **teeth** was a sign of anger (37:12; 112:10; Jb 16:9; Lm 2:16), so this **mockery** was more than playful ridicule; it included a "malicious" intent (vv. 11,19).
35:19 Wink at me maliciously is literally "wink the eye." On **those who hate me without cause**, compare Pss 38:19; 69:4. Either 35:19 or 69:4 is quoted in Jn 15:25 as applying to Jesus.
35:20 Live peacefully (lit "quietly") **in the land** is a phrase that occurs only here in the OT, but it describes those who are faithful to the Lord since God promised to give his

against those who live peacefully
    in the land.
21 They open their mouths wide
    against me and say,
    "Aha, aha! We saw it!"ᴬ

22 You saw it, LORD; do not be silent.
    Lord, do not be far from me.
23 Wake up and rise to my defense,
    to my cause, my God and my Lord!
24 Vindicate me, LORD my God,
    in keeping with your righteousness,
    and do not let them rejoice over me.
25 Do not let them say in their hearts,
    "Aha! Just what we wanted."
    Do not let them say,
    "We have swallowed him up!"
26 Let those who rejoice at my misfortune
    be disgraced and humiliated;
    let those who exalt themselves over me
    be clothed with shame and reproach.

27 Let those who want my vindication
    shout for joy and be glad;
    let them continually say,
    "The LORD be exalted.
    He takes pleasure in
    his servant's well-being."
28 And my tongue will proclaim
    your righteousness,
    your praise all day long.

Human Wickedness and God's Love

36 *For the choir director. Of David, the LORD's servant.*

1 An oracle within my heart
    concerning the transgression of the
    wicked person:
    Dread of God has no effect on him.ᴮ
2 For with his flattering opinion
    of himself,
    he does not discover and hate
    his iniquity.

3 The words from his mouth
    are malicious and deceptive;
    he has stopped acting wisely
    and doing good.
4 Even on his bed he makes
    malicious plans.
    He sets himself on a path
    that is not good,
    and he does not reject evil.

5 LORD, your faithful love reaches
    to heaven,
    your faithfulness to the clouds.
6 Your righteousness is
    like the highest mountains,
    your judgments like the deepest sea.
    LORD, you preserve people and animals.
7 How priceless your faithful love is, God!
    People take refuge in the shadow
    of your wings.
8 They are filled from the abundance
    of your house.
    You let them drink from
    your refreshing stream.
9 For the wellspring of life is with you.
    By means of your light we see light.

10 Spread your faithful love over those
    who know you,
    and your righteousness
    over the upright in heart.
11 Do not let the foot of the arrogant
    come near me
    or the hand of the wicked
    drive me away.
12 There! The evildoers have fallen.
    They have been thrown down
    and cannot rise.

Instruction in Wisdom

37 *Of David.*
Do not be agitated by evildoers;
do not envy those who do wrong.

ᴬ**35:21** Lit *Our eyes saw!*   ᴮ**36:1** Lit *There is no dread of God in front of his eyes*

---

people peace in the land when they obeyed him (Lv 26:6). The usual word for "peace" (Hb *shalom*) is actually in the first line and is translated as **friendly ways.**
35:21 Aha is used in contexts involving ridicule. It attempts to shame further those who have suffered some calamity (40:16; 70:4; Ezk 25:3; 26:2; 36:2).
35:22 You saw it is in contrast to "we saw it" in the previous verse. In that case it was the enemies who ridiculed the psalmist because they saw his affliction; here it is the Lord who saw his suffering and was called upon to act on it.
35:24–25 Do not let them rejoice over me is repeated from v. 19. To "swallow" someone is to destroy him so that there is nothing left.
35:26 Shame and reproach are negative attributes that are to be worn (as clothing) by the enemies.

36:1 The Hebrew word *ne'um,* translated here as **oracle,** is used by the prophets in a more formal sense to signify God's official declarations through the prophets to his people (note especially its use in Jeremiah; e.g., 1:8,15,19). Its use here could also refer to an official prophetic oracle against **the wicked.** The difference between this and the prophets is that the message originated within the psalmist's **heart** and not from God's spoken word to him.
36:2 The Hebrew text is difficult here and literally reads, "for it is smooth to him in his own eyes to find his iniquity to hate." The word for "smooth" (Hb *chalaq*) is sometimes used in the context of speech and associated with flattery (12:3; Dn 11:32). This concept makes sense here even though it is not directly related to speech. **Opinion of himself** means in his own estimation; in other words, it is perception and not reality

that prevents this wicked person from hating **his iniquity**.
36:5–6 Heaven and **clouds** illustrate the extent of the Lord's covenant faithfulness as do the extremes of **highest mountains** and **deepest sea.** There is no limit to God's love for his people (Rm 8:35–39) nor any place that is beyond his reach (Ps 139:7–12).
36:7 The imagery **the shadow of your wings** is also found in Pss 17:8; 57:1; 63:7.
36:8 Abundance is literally "oil" and represents blessing (Is 55:2). The imagery of oil and **refreshing stream** bring together the same images as those in Ps 23.
36:9 Wellspring of life is used elsewhere to describe the Lord as the source of life (Jr 2:13; 17:13). **Light** can refer to truth (43:3) or salvation (27:1).
36:11–12 Victory in the ancient world was often represented by the victor's **foot** on the neck of the vanquished (110:1).

² For they wither quickly like grass
and wilt like tender green plants.

³ Trust in the Lord and do what is good;
dwell in the land and live securely.^A
⁴ Take delight in the Lord,
and he will give you your heart's desires.

⁵ Commit your way to the Lord;
trust in him, and he will act,
⁶ making your righteousness shine
like the dawn,
your justice like the noonday.

⁷ Be silent before the Lord and wait
expectantly for him;
do not be agitated by one who prospers
in his way,
by the person who carries out
evil plans.

⁸ Refrain from anger and give up
your rage;
do not be agitated — it can only
bring harm.
⁹ For evildoers will be destroyed,
but those who put their hope
in the Lord
will inherit the land.

¹⁰ A little while, and the wicked person
will be no more;
though you look for him, he will not
be there.
¹¹ But the humble will inherit the land
and will enjoy abundant prosperity.

¹² The wicked person schemes
against the righteous
and gnashes his teeth at him.
¹³ The Lord laughs at him
because he sees that his day is coming.

¹⁴ The wicked have drawn the sword
and strung the^B bow
to bring down the poor and needy
and to slaughter those whose way
is upright.

¹⁵ Their swords will enter
their own hearts,
and their bows will be broken.

¹⁶ The little that the righteous person has
is better
than the abundance
of many wicked people.
¹⁷ For the arms of the wicked
will be broken,
but the Lord supports the righteous.

¹⁸ The Lord watches over the blameless
all their days,
and their inheritance will last forever.
¹⁹ They will not be disgraced in times
of adversity;
they will be satisfied in days of hunger.

²⁰ But the wicked will perish;
the Lord's enemies, like the glory
of the pastures,
will fade away —
they will fade away like smoke.

²¹ The wicked person borrows
and does not repay,
but the righteous one is gracious
and giving.
²² Those who are blessed by the Lord
will inherit the land,
but those cursed by him
will be destroyed.

²³ A person's steps are established
by the Lord,
and he takes pleasure in his way.
²⁴ Though he falls, he will not
be overwhelmed,
because the Lord supports him with
his hand.

²⁵ I have been young and now I am old,
yet I have not seen
the righteous abandoned
or his children begging for bread.
²⁶ He is always generous, always lending,
and his children are a blessing.

---

^A37:3 Or *and cultivate faithfulness*, or *and befriend faithfulness*   ^B37:14 Lit *their*

37:2 To refrain from envying the wicked is easier if we stop to consider their destiny (cp. 73:3,17–20). **Grass** and **tender green plants** are temporary and do not last (103:15; Jb 14:2; Is 40:6; Mt 6:30).
37:5–6 Commit your way to the Lord is literally "Roll your way upon the Lord" and means to rely on him (see 22:8). The images of **shine like the dawn** and **like the noonday** could mean either that the psalmist's vindication (the demonstration of God's **justice** in his life) will be seen by all or that God's justice is as certain as the rising of the sun. **37:8–9** The psalmist's **anger** was apparently caused by the observation that

the wicked were prospering and God had not judged them (v. 1). The prohibition on anger and agitation is repeated, as is the reason—the promise of the destruction of **evildoers**.
37:10 Although from the human perspective God was delaying the execution of his justice, from his perspective it was only **a little while** (Jb 24:24; 2Pt 3:8–9).
37:16 Little is the same word used in v. 10 to describe the time before God dispenses his justice. Here it refers to the quantity of the possessions of **the righteous person** in comparison to the **abundance** (wealth and prosperity) of **many wicked people**.

This is perhaps a play on the word in order to emphasize that what was now the case would change shortly.
37:17 Arms often refer to power (89:10), so breaking one's arm means to render someone powerless (10:15; Jb 38:15; Jr 48:25; Ezk 30:21).
37:20 Pastures recalls the same image as "grass" in v. 2. The word **smoke** conveys the same notion of transience (68:2; 102:3; Is 51:6).
37:23–24 Figuratively, **established** refers to security and stability, and **steps** are related to one's way of life, often represented as a path or road. Therefore, the Lord is the one who brings about a person's stability in life.

²⁷ Turn away from evil, do what is good,
and settle permanently.

²⁸ For the LORD loves justice
and will not abandon his faithful ones.
They are kept safe forever,
but the children of the wicked
will be destroyed.

²⁹ The righteous will inherit the land
and dwell in it permanently.

³⁰ The mouth of the righteous
utters wisdom;
his tongue speaks what is just.

³¹ The instruction of his God is in his heart;
his steps do not falter.

³² The wicked one lies in wait
for the righteous
and intends to kill him;

³³ the LORD will not leave him
in the power of the wicked one
or allow him to be condemned
when he is judged.

³⁴ Wait for the LORD and keep his way,
and he will exalt you to inherit the land.
You will watch when the wicked
are destroyed.

³⁵ I have seen a wicked, violent person
well-rooted,^A like
a flourishing native tree.

³⁶ Then I^B passed by and noticed
he was gone;
I searched for him, but he could not
be found.

³⁷ Watch the blameless and observe
the upright,
for the person of peace will have
a future.^C

³⁸ But transgressors will all be eliminated;
the future of the wicked
will be destroyed.

³⁹ The salvation of the righteous is
from the LORD,
their refuge in a time of distress.

⁴⁰ The LORD helps and delivers them;
he will deliver them from the wicked
and will save them
because they take refuge in him.

Prayer of a Suffering Sinner

38
A psalm of David to bring remembrance.
LORD, do not punish me
in your anger
or discipline me in your wrath.

² For your arrows have sunk into me,
and your hand has pressed down
on me.

³ There is no soundness in my body
because of your indignation;
there is no health^D in my bones
because of my sin.

⁴ For my iniquities have flooded
over my head;
they are a burden too heavy for me
to bear.

⁵ My wounds are foul and festering
because of my foolishness.

⁶ I am bent over and brought very low;
all day long I go around in mourning.

⁷ For my insides are full of
burning pain,
and there is no soundness in my body.

⁸ I am faint and severely crushed;
I groan because of the anguish
of my heart.

⁹ Lord, my every desire is in front of you;
my sighing is not hidden from you.

¹⁰ My heart races, my strength leaves me,
and even the light of my eyes has faded.^E

¹¹ My loved ones and friends stand back
from my affliction,
and my relatives stand at a distance.

¹² Those who intend to kill me set traps,

---

^A**37:35** Hb obscure ^B**37:36** LXX, Syr, Vg, Jer; MT reads *he* ^C**37:37** Or *posterity*, also in v. 38 ^D**38:3** Hb *shalom* ^E**38:10** Or *and the light of my eyes — even that is not with me*

37:30–31 Instruction is the Hebrew word *torah*. The idea of the Lord's instruction being in the **heart** has theological significance in its relation to the new covenant (Jr 31:33; Ezk 36:27). Even before the benefits of that covenant occur, the people of God are known as those "in whose heart is my instruction" (Is 51:7). True devotion of God's people is evident in the heart and not just in outward actions. **37:35 I have seen** is a common expression in Wisdom literature to indicate that what follows is from personal experience (Jb 5:3; Pr 7:6; 24:32; Ec 2:1). A **flourishing . . . tree** is an image generally referring to the righteous, but here the situation is different in that it seems the **wicked** have the stability (**well-rooted**) in life that only the righteous are supposed to have. **37:36** The appearance of stability in v. 35 was an illusion (v. 10).

37:37–38 Future is equivalent to "destiny," "end," or "fate" (73:17; Nm 23:10; Dt 32:29). **37:39–40** The psalm ends with a statement of confidence and certainty, in contrast to the agitation and envy in v. 1. **Ps 38 title** The word **remembrance** may refer to a memorial offering that was a part of the grain offering in Israel (Lv 2:2,9,16; 5:12). A similar title appears in Ps 70. The request for the Lord to remember is another way of asking him to act in a situation. **38:1–2** God's **anger** and **discipline** are often mentioned in lament psalms, indicating the belief that sin is the reason for suffering. The **arrows** picture the Lord as an enemy of the psalmist because of his sin. **38:3–8** The relationship between psychological suffering and physical pain is common in lament psalms. **Bones** seem to

be used most frequently in relation to the image of physical pain. While the language need not be literal, it conveys the idea of intense pain and suffering that is clearly connected to the Lord's discipline. It is significant how many times the phrase **because of** is used in this context. Its objects are **your indignation . . . my sin . . . my foolishness**, and **the anguish of my heart**. These make it clear why the psalmist was suffering. **38:9** The phrase **in front of you** means "in your presence." **38:10 Light** in one's **eyes** is similar to "brightness" and represents vitality. **38:11–12** It is a common experience of a person who is suffering intensely that even **friends** reject him (88:8,18; Jb 19:14–15).

and those who want to harm me
threaten to destroy me;
they plot treachery all day long.

13 I am like a deaf person; I do not hear.
I am like a speechless person
who does not open his mouth.
14 I am like a man who does not hear
and has no arguments in his mouth.
15 For I put my hope in you, LORD;
you will answer me, my Lord, my God.
16 For I said, "Don't let them rejoice
over me —
those who are arrogant toward me
when I stumble."
17 For I am about to fall,
and my pain is constantly with me.
18 So I confess my iniquity;
I am anxious because of my sin.
19 But my enemies are vigorous
and powerful;^A
many hate me for no reason.
20 Those who repay evil for good
attack me for pursuing good.

21 LORD, do not abandon me;
my God, do not be far from me.
22 Hurry to help me,
my Lord, my salvation.

The Fleeting Nature of Life

39 For the choir director, for Jeduthun.
A psalm of David.

1 I said, "I will guard my ways
so that I may not sin with my tongue;
I will guard my mouth with a muzzle
as long as the wicked are
in my presence."
2 I was speechless and quiet;
I kept silent, even from speaking good,
and my pain intensified.
3 My heart grew hot within me;
as I mused, a fire burned.

I spoke with my tongue:
4 "LORD, make me aware of my end
and the number of my days
so that I will know how
short-lived I am.
5 In fact, you have made my days just
inches long,
and my life span is as nothing to you.
Yes, every human being stands as
only a vapor. *Selah*
6 Yes, a person goes about
like a mere shadow.
Indeed, they rush around in vain,
gathering possessions
without knowing who will get them.

7 "Now, Lord, what do I wait for?
My hope is in you.
8 Rescue me from all
my transgressions;
do not make me the taunt of fools.
9 I am speechless; I do not open
my mouth
because of what you have done.
10 Remove your torment from me.
Because of the force of your hand I am
finished.
11 You discipline a person
with punishment for iniquity,
consuming like a moth what is precious
to him;
yes, every human being is only
a vapor. *Selah*

12 "Hear my prayer, LORD,
and listen to my cry for help;
do not be silent at my tears.
For I am here with you as an alien,
a temporary resident like all
my ancestors.
13 Turn your angry gaze from me
so that I may be cheered up
before I die and am gone."

^38:19 Or *numerous*

38:13–14 The psalmist was **speechless** and had **no arguments** (defense) because he knew that God was the one punishing him for his sins. This is much different from the suffering of the innocent where there is a plea for God to act based on his promises to the faithful (Pss 17; 26). In this instance the only thing the Lord will hear is a confession of sin, which is also the only chance for relief from the suffering (32:3–5).
38:17 Fall in this case is not a moral fall—since the psalmist was already in sin—but defeat and perhaps death.
38:18 Iniquity is parallel to **sin** and means a liability for punishment, not just a subjective feeling of guilt.
38:19–22 Once the confession took place, the problem of the enemies still existed. In fact, it probably was more intense since the psalmist was now **pursuing good**, and his enemies were repaying **evil for good**. The

big difference is that God would no longer be against him as well.
Ps 39 title Jeduthun (probably another name for Ethan) also appears in the titles of Pss 62 and 77. According to 1Ch 16:41, he was one of David's chief musicians. If this is not a reference to Jeduthun himself, it may refer to his descendants or a group of musicians using his name (perhaps derived from his own musical style or school).
39:1–2 The reason for the psalmist's silence was to keep from sinning by voicing his protest to God.
39:3 A **heart** growing **hot** is an expression for exasperation (Dt 19:6; Jr 20:9). **Fire** can mean anger, but here it seems to refer to pent-up emotions waiting to escape.
39:4–6 This request for God to **make** the psalmist **aware** that his **days** were **short-lived** shows that he knew his inner feelings must be held in check. **Vapor** is sometimes translated as "breath" (Jb 7:7).

It denotes in its literal sense a small puff of air. Figuratively, it refers to a meaningless existence or futile activities (Ps 94:11; Ec 1:2). When used together with **shadow**, the word emphasizes the fleeting nature of life. The lesson to be learned involves seeing everything as God sees it—from his perspective, rather than from the human perspective.
39:10–11 The most severe suffering from the psalmist's perspective was God's **torment**, which was being used as a corrective measure to bring him to his senses and to help him learn the lesson in vv. 4–6.
39:12 Alien and **temporary resident** are terms for those who were not native inhabitants in the promised land. The use of the words here seems to indicate that the lesson of Ps 39:4–6 about the insignificance and fleeting nature of this earthly life had been learned.

Thanksgiving and a Cry for Help

40 For the choir director. A psalm of David.
I waited patiently for the LORD,
and he turned to me and heard my cry
for help.
2 He brought me up from a desolate^ pit,
out of the muddy clay,
and set my feet on a rock,
making my steps secure.
3 He put a new song in my mouth,
a hymn of praise to our God.
Many will see and fear,
and they will trust in the LORD.

4 How happy is anyone
who has put his trust in the LORD
and has not turned to the proud
or to those who run after lies!
5 LORD my God, you have done
many things —
your wondrous works and your plans
for us;
none can compare with you.
If I were to report and speak of them,
they are more than can be told.

6 You do not delight in sacrifice
and offering;
you open my ears to listen.^B
You do not ask for
a whole burnt offering
or a sin offering.
7 Then I said, "See, I have come;
in the scroll it is written about me.
8 I delight to do your will, my God,
and your instruction is deep
within me."

9 I proclaim righteousness
in the great assembly;
see, I do not keep my mouth closed^c —
as you know, LORD.
10 I did not hide your righteousness
in my heart;
I spoke about your faithfulness
and salvation;

I did not conceal your constant love
and truth
from the great assembly.

11 LORD, you do not^D withhold
your compassion from me.
Your constant love and truth will always
guard me.
12 For troubles without number
have surrounded me;
my iniquities have overtaken me;
I am unable to see.
They are more than the hairs
of my head,
and my courage leaves me.
13 LORD, be pleased to rescue me;
hurry to help me, LORD.

14 Let those who intend to take my life
be disgraced and confounded.
Let those who wish me harm
be turned back and humiliated.
15 Let those who say to me, "Aha, aha!"
be appalled because of their shame.

16 Let all who seek you rejoice and be glad
in you;
let those who love your salvation
continually say,
"The LORD is great!"
17 I am oppressed and needy;
may the Lord think of me.
You are my helper and my deliverer;
my God, do not delay.

Victory in spite of Betrayal

41 For the choir director. A psalm of David.
Happy is one who is considerate
of the poor;
the LORD will save him in a day
of adversity.
2 The LORD will keep him
and preserve him;
he will be blessed in the land.
You will not give him over to the desire
of his enemies.

---

^**40:2** Or watery   ^**40:6** Lit you hollow out ears for me   ^**40:9** Lit not restrain my lips   ^**40:11** Or LORD, do not

---

40:1 Waited patiently shows faithfulness to the Lord in refraining from taking things into one's own hands or going to another source for help.
40:2 Pit can refer to a deep well. Someone trapped in a well would probably sink down in the **muddy clay** and die if someone did not pull him out (Jr 38:6,10). Figuratively the term is related to Sheol, representing death. To be **brought . . . up** means to be rescued from death (30:3).
40:3 The **new song** likely refers to the newness of life after being delivered from death.
40:5 God's **wondrous works** are his saving acts on behalf of his people.
40:6–8 Some interpreters think v. 6 repudiates the act of **sacrifice**, even though God

himself had commanded it. However, the most important issue is **delight** in God's **will**. In other words, acts of sacrifice must be accompanied by cheerful obedience. The phrase **open my ears to listen** (lit "dig/hollow out ears for me") is a symbol of being attentive to the Lord in order to obey him (the opposite of closed or "uncircumcised" ears; see Jr 6:10). This emphasizes the importance of obedience over sacrifice (1Sm 15:22). **See, I have come** is similar to Isaiah's expression, "Here I am" (Is 6:8), showing submission to God's will. Jesus's sacrifice on the cross was the ultimate expression of submission (Heb 10:5–10). The meaning of **the scroll** is unclear. Some suggest it was the book where the deeds of people

were recorded (51:1; 56:8; 87:6; 139:16), but in this context it may refer to God's will (his instruction) in general.
40:11–13 Overtaken is used mostly with enemies as the subject (7:5; Jr 39:5; Lm 1:3), but here it is the psalmist's **iniquities** that have overtaken him.
40:14–15 Aha is an expression often associated with ridicule.
40:16–17 The phrase **oppressed and needy** refers to those who are humble and dependent on the Lord as their only help.
41:1 Poor has the basic idea of "low" in the sense that they are humbled or brought low by their own circumstances or by others. However, the verb **is considerate** might indicate that the idea is economic hardship.

³ The Lᴏʀᴅ will sustain him
    on his sickbed;
    you will heal him on the bed
      where he lies.

⁴ I said, "Lᴏʀᴅ, be gracious to me;
    heal me, for I have sinned against you."
⁵ My enemies speak maliciously
    about me:
    "When will he die and be forgotten?"
⁶ When one of them comes to visit,
    he speaks deceitfully;
    he stores up evil in his heart;
    he goes out and talks.
⁷ All who hate me whisper together
    about me;
    they plan to harm me.
⁸ "Something awful has
    overwhelmed him,ᴬ
    and he won't rise again from where
    he lies!"
⁹ Even my friendᴮ in whom I trusted,
    one who ate my bread,
    has raised his heel against me.

¹⁰ But you, Lᴏʀᴅ, be gracious to me
    and raise me up;
    then I will repay them.
¹¹ By this I know that you delight in me:
    my enemy does not shout in triumph
    over me.
¹² You supported me because of
    my integrity
    and set me in your presence forever.

¹³ Blessed be the Lᴏʀᴅ God of Israel,
    from everlasting to everlasting.
    Amen and amen.

BOOK II (Psalms 42–72)

Longing for God

42 *For the choir director. A* Maskil *of the sons of Korah.*

¹ As a deer longs for flowing streams,
    so I long for you, God.
² I thirst for God, the living God.
    When can I come and appear
      before God?
³ My tears have been my food
    day and night,
    while all day long people say to me,
    "Where is your God?"
⁴ I remember this as I pour out my heart:
    how I walked with many,
    leading the festive procession
      to the house of God,
    with joyful and thankful shouts.

⁵ Why, my soul, are you so dejected?
    Why are you in such turmoil?
    Put your hope in God, for I will
      still praise him,
    my Savior and my God.
⁶ Iᶜ am deeply depressed;
    therefore I remember you from the land
      of Jordan
    and the peaks of Hermon,
    from Mount Mizar.

ᴬ**41:8** Lit *A thing of worthlessness has been poured into him* ᴮ**41:9** Lit *Even a man of my peace* ᶜ**42:5–6** Some Hb mss, LXX, Syr; other Hb mss read *him, the salvation of his presence.* ᴰ**6**My God, I

41:3 Sustain is not quite identical to **heal**. It refers to God's support (v. 12) of someone during a time of adversity, whether it is an illness or some danger (18:35; 20:2; 94:18). Even when there is a delay in God's intervention, there is still his sustaining power that strengthens the person who is suffering. **41:4** Sin is mentioned but not specified or developed (in contrast to Pss 38 and 51). In some cases sin may be assumed, but it is not the main cause of the suffering. Evidence of this is that the psalmist considered himself as having "integrity" (41:12), indicating either that the sin was already confessed or that there was no specific sin involved. The primary issue seems to be physical illness, since there are references to "heal" (v. 3), "sickbed" (v. 3), and "something awful" (v. 8), which is how his enemies described his condition. **41:5–8** The **enemies** are vividly described, with their activities against the psalmist as the focal point. Their intentions were malicious, as demonstrated by their speech and their desire for his demise. To **be forgotten** is equivalent to dying (see 31:12). **Stores up evil** expresses the idea of harvesting it like one does grain. Some think this might be a reference to gossip, which in this case involved evil things said about someone. This idea is reinforced by their whispering about the psalmist (v. 7). Their intention was for him to **die**, so they spoke about his death as if it were a certainty (v. 8).

41:9 In instances of extreme suffering, friends can take on the role of enemies. Indeed there is the adversarial phrase **raised his heel against me**, so there appears to be more than just abandonment in this context. **41:11** The Lord's **delight** in someone is not a mere emotion but involves actions and is equivalent to blessing or showing favor to someone (18:19; 22:8; 35:27). **41:13** This verse marks the close of Book 1 of the Psalms (1–41). It is a doxology including a call to praise followed by a congregational response (**Amen and amen**). There are four psalms (41; 72; 89; 106) that end a book before the beginning of a new one; each has similar material. Such statements were most likely added at the time the Psalms were joined together in their canonical form. **Ps 42 title** On **Maskil**, see note at Ps 32 title. The phrase **sons of Korah** appears in the titles of eleven psalms (42; 44–49; 84–85; 87–88). According to 1Ch 9:17–24 and 26:1–19, the Korahites were the gatekeepers in the temple. In 2Ch 20:19 they stood up in the congregation of Israel and praised the Lord. Most scholars believe they became associated with musicians (perhaps a group of singers) who were involved in the worship of the Lord. Many have argued that although Pss 42 and 43 are separated in the titles in the Hebrew text, they might actually have been composed as one psalm. In the second book, the only other psalms lacking titles are Pss 43 and 71. The strongest evidence for

connecting the two psalms is the occurrence of the same questions and responses in 42:5,11 and 43:5. These verses seem to end each of the sections of the psalms consisting of three strophes or poetic divisions. Psalm 43 would be the third strophe if they were joined as one psalm. **42:1–2** Longing and thirsting picture a prolonged drought where even the animals are dying (Jr 14:1–6; Jl 1:20). **Flowing streams** recalls the blessings of God. What the psalmist desired was to **appear before God** (lit "see the face of God"), which probably refers to receiving God's blessing and favor in his presence (84:7). **42:3** This hyperbolic expression shows the depths of his grief (80:5). **42:4** The **house of God** represents his presence. **42:5** The questions and the response of v. 5 also appear in v. 11 and in 43:5 (perhaps because Ps 43 is part of this psalm; see note at Ps 42 title). The psalmist was speaking to himself (**my soul**) in an attempt to bring comfort and security. In answer to the questions focusing on his depression, he literally commands himself to **hope in God**. This means waiting on God during a time of crisis, trusting that he will answer prayer. There was no reason for his depression if God was his **Savior**. The fact that he repeated this several times shows the difficulty of internalizing this truth. **42:6** The geographical descriptions could refer to the place where the psalmist was

⁷ Deep calls to deep in the roar
of your waterfalls;
all your breakers and your billows
have swept over me.
⁸ The LORD will send his faithful love
by day;
his song will be with me
in the night —
a prayer to the God of my life.

⁹ I will say to God, my rock,
"Why have you forgotten me?
Why must I go about in sorrow
because of the enemy's oppression?"
¹⁰ My adversaries taunt me,
as if crushing my bones,
while all day long they say to me,
"Where is your God?"
¹¹ Why, my soul, are you so dejected?
Why are you in such turmoil?
Put your hope in God, for I will
still praise him,
my Savior and my God.

43 ᴬVindicate me, God, and champion
my cause
against an unfaithful nation;
rescue me from the deceitful
and unjust person.
² For you are the God of my refuge.
Why have you rejected me?
Why must I go about in sorrow
because of the enemy's oppression?

³ Send your light and your truth; let them
lead me.
Let them bring me
to your holy mountain,
to your dwelling place.
⁴ Then I will come to the altar of God,
to God, my greatest joy.
I will praise you with the lyre,
God, my God.

⁵ Why, my soul, are you so dejected?
Why are you in such turmoil?

Put your hope in God, for I will
still praise him,
my Savior and my God.

Israel's Complaint

44 *For the choir director. A Maskil of the
sons of Korah.*
¹ God, we have heard with our ears —
our ancestors have told us —
the work you accomplished
in their days,
in days long ago:
² In order to plant them,
you displaced the nations by your hand;
in order to settle them,
you brought disaster on the peoples.
³ For they did not take the land
by their sword —
their arm did not bring them victory —
but by your right hand, your arm,
and the light of your face,
because you were favorable
toward them.

⁴ You are my King, my God,
who ordainsᴮ victories for Jacob.
⁵ Through you we drive back our foes;
through your name we trample
our enemies.
⁶ For I do not trust in my bow,
and my sword does not
bring me victory.
⁷ But you give us victory over our foes
and let those who hate us be disgraced.
⁸ We boast in God all day long;
we will praise your name forever. *Selah*

⁹ But you have rejected and humiliated us;
you do not march out with our armies.
¹⁰ You make us retreat from the foe,
and those who hate us
have taken plunder for themselves.
¹¹ You hand us over to be eaten like sheep
and scatter us among the nations.
¹² You sell your people for nothing;
you make no profit from selling them.

ᴬPs 43 Many Hb mss connect Pss 42 and 43   ᴮ44:4 LXX, Syr, Aq; MT reads *King, God; ordain*

---

praying since he was distant from the sanctuary, according to v. 3. The **land of Jordan** could refer to the entire Jordan River Valley, but in connection with Mount **Hermon**, which was in the extreme north of Israel, it probably refers to the sources for the river in the mountains of northern Israel. **Mount Mizar** is not as easy to identify, but it was probably part of the same mountain range as Mount Hermon in the north.
42:7 This verse is perhaps related to the Jordan River in v. 6. For similar imagery, see 18:4–5; 29:10–11; 32:6–7.
43:1 Unfaithful nation is parallel to a **deceitful and unjust person**. It is difficult to determine whether these enemies were

Gentiles who were not a part of the Lord's covenant or Israelites who were disloyal to the covenant.
43:2 Rejection by God is a common assumption when one's prayers seem to go unanswered.
43:3–4 The psalmist was requesting guidance in order once again to be in the Lord's presence, represented here by the three descriptions: **your holy mountain . . . your dwelling place**, and **the altar of God**.
Ps 44 title On **Maskil**, see note at Ps 32 title. On **sons of Korah**, see note at Ps 42 title.
44:1–3 The psalm begins with a review of what the Lord has done for Israel. This is similar to the "wondrous works," or God's

saving acts on behalf of his people (9:1; Ex 3:20; 15:11). It is clear from the mention of **ancestors** and **days long ago** that this refers to an early time, specifically the time of conquest and settlement of the promised land.
44:8 Boasting **in God** is in contrast to boasting in one's own power or skill.
44:9–10 This perception is in stark contrast to the Lord's past acts when he fought for his people (v. 5).
44:11 The imagery of **sheep** that were handed over **to be eaten** is similar to v. 22 where they were "slaughtered." God was the shepherd of Israel, but to the psalmist it seemed he was not protecting his sheep but giving them to other **nations** to be killed.

¹³ You make us an object of reproach
    to our neighbors,
a source of mockery and ridicule
    to those around us.
¹⁴ You make us a joke among the nations,
    a laughingstock^A among the peoples.
¹⁵ My disgrace is before me all day long,
    and shame has covered my face,
¹⁶ because of the taunts^B of the scorner
        and reviler,
    because of the enemy and avenger.

¹⁷ All this has happened to us,
    but we have not forgotten you
    or betrayed your covenant.
¹⁸ Our hearts have not turned back;
    our steps have not strayed
        from your path.
¹⁹ But you have crushed us in a haunt
        of jackals
    and have covered us
        with deepest darkness.

²⁰ If we had forgotten the name of our God
    and spread out our hands
        to a foreign god,
²¹ wouldn't God have found this out,
    since he knows the secrets of the heart?
²² Because of you we are being put
        to death all day long;
    we are counted as sheep
        to be slaughtered.

²³ Wake up, LORD! Why are you sleeping?
    Get up! Don't reject us forever!
²⁴ Why do you hide
    and forget our affliction
        and oppression?
²⁵ For we have sunk down to the dust;
    our bodies cling to the ground.
²⁶ Rise up! Help us!
    Redeem us because of your faithful love.

A Royal Wedding Song

45 For the choir director: according to
"The Lilies." A Maskil of the sons of Korah.
A love song.

¹ My heart is moved by a noble theme
    as I recite my verses to the king;
    my tongue is the pen of a skillful writer.
² You are the most handsome of men;^C
    grace flows from your lips.
    Therefore God has blessed you forever.

³ Mighty warrior, strap your sword
        at your side.
    In your majesty and splendor —
⁴ in your splendor ride triumphantly
    in the cause of truth, humility, and justice.
    May your right hand show
        your awe-inspiring acts.
⁵ Your sharpened arrows pierce
        the hearts of the king's enemies;
    the peoples fall under you.

⁶ Your throne, God, is^D forever and ever;
    the scepter of your kingdom is a scepter
        of justice.
⁷ You love righteousness
        and hate wickedness;
    therefore God, your God,
    has anointed you with the oil of joy
        more than your companions.
⁸ Myrrh, aloes, and cassia perfume
        all your garments;
    from ivory palaces harps bring you joy.
⁹ Kings' daughters are
        among your honored women;
    the queen, adorned with gold
        from Ophir,
    stands at your right hand.

¹⁰ Listen, daughter, pay attention
        and consider:

---

^A**44:14** Lit *shaking of the head* ^B**44:16** Lit *voice* ^C**45:2** Or *of the descendants of Adam* ^D**45:6** Or *Your divine throne is,* or *Your throne is God's*

44:13–16 Almost every Hebrew word for **ridicule** is used in these verses. The word for **joke** expresses the idea of a byword or proverbial saying. The **shame** of Israel was so extensive and had lasted so long that **the nations** were using them as the butt of jokes and sayings.
44:17–18 This declaration of innocence expresses the innocence of the nation. The psalmist protested that they had done nothing to deserve this treatment.
44:19 Deepest darkness is the same Hebrew word as that translated "darkest" in 23:4.
44:20 Spreading out **hands** is a gesture used in the context of prayer and worship (88:9; 141:2; 143:6; Ex 9:29,33; Ezr 9:5; Is 1:15).
44:21 The **secrets of the heart** are attitudes and motives.
44:22 This verse is quoted in Rm 8:36.
44:23–26 Wake up calls God to act. **Rise up** is similar, but with military connotations. The **dust** is often used to represent humiliation in

defeat at the hands of an enemy (7:5; 72:9; Is 49:23). It could also refer to humility before the Lord either in worship or in prayer (Dt 9:18; 2Ch 20:18).
Ps 45 title The Lilies was apparently a known tune at the time of composition. On **Maskil**, see note at Ps 32 title. On **sons of Korah**, see note at Ps 42 title. The psalm is further identified as a love song, a description that fits the context of this royal wedding psalm.
45:1–2 It was a common practice in the ancient Near East to compose songs in honor of kings to perpetuate their memory for later generations. Such hyperbolic designations as **most handsome** and **grace flows from your lips** are usually a part of these songs.
45:3–5 While **truth** and **justice** were common traits that were admired by kings and people in the ancient world, **humility** was something more specific to Israel. Kings of the ancient world were rarely humble, seeing humility as a sign of weakness. For a servant of the Lord, this was a characteristic that

signified a close relationship with him (Pr 15:33; 18:12; Zph 2:3).
45:6 A **scepter** symbolized royal dominion. It often was associated with military power. God's **throne** was actually a military weapon. God's **throne** is linked with this king because Israel's king was to function as God's co-regent over his kingdom (2:6–9; 2Sm 7:14; 19:21; 1Ch 28:6).
45:7 The king of Israel was often referred to as God's **anointed**. Oil was a symbol of both **joy** and God's blessing (see 23:5; 36:8).
45:8 The phrase **ivory palaces** does not refer to palaces made completely of ivory but to those having their interior and perhaps furniture covered with ivory (1Kg 22:39; Am 3:15; 6:4).
45:9 Gold from Ophir is synonymous with the finest gold (Jb 28:16; Is 13:12). The exact location of Ophir is uncertain.
45:10–11 To **forget** and then **bow down** represents a change in loyalty from the bride's own people and country to the king whom she was marrying.

Forget your people
and your father's house,

¹¹ and the king will desire your beauty.
Bow down to him, for he is your lord.

¹² The daughter of Tyre,
the wealthy people,
will seek your favor with gifts.

¹³ In her chamber, the royal daughter
is all glorious,
her clothing embroidered with gold.

¹⁴ In colorful garments she is led
to the king;
after her, the virgins, her companions,
are brought to you.

¹⁵ They are led in with gladness
and rejoicing;
they enter the king's palace.

¹⁶ Your sons will succeed your ancestors;
you will make them princes
throughout the land.

¹⁷ I will cause your name
to be remembered for all generations;
therefore the peoples will praise you
forever and ever.

God Our Refuge

46 For the choir director. A song of the sons
of Korah. According to Alamoth.

¹ God is our refuge and strength,
a helper who is always found
in times of trouble.

² Therefore we will not be afraid,
though the earth trembles
and the mountains topple
into the depths of the seas,

³ though its water roars and foams
and the mountains quake
with its turmoil. *Selah*

⁴ There is a river —
its streams delight the city of God,
the holy dwelling place of the Most High.

⁵ God is within her;
she will not be toppled.

God will help her
when the morning dawns.

⁶ Nations rage, kingdoms topple;
the earth melts when he lifts his voice.

⁷ The LORD of Armies is with us;
the God of Jacob is our stronghold. *Selah*

⁸ Come, see the works of the LORD,
who brings devastation on the earth.

⁹ He makes wars cease
throughout the earth.
He shatters bows and cuts spears
to pieces;
he sets wagons ablaze.

¹⁰ "Stop fighting, and know that I am God,
exalted among the nations,
exalted on the earth."

¹¹ The LORD of Armies is with us;
the God of Jacob is our stronghold. *Selah*

God Our King

47 For the choir director. A psalm of the sons
of Korah.

¹ Clap your hands, all you peoples;
shout to God with a jubilant cry.

² For the LORD, the Most High,
is awe-inspiring,
a great King over the whole earth.

³ He subdues peoples under us
and nations under our feet.

⁴ He chooses for us our inheritance —
the pride of Jacob, whom he loves. *Selah*

⁵ God ascends among shouts of joy,
the LORD, with the sound of
a ram's horn.

⁶ Sing praise to God, sing praise;
sing praise to our King, sing praise!

⁷ Sing a song of wisdom,^A
for God is King of the whole earth.

⁸ God reigns over the nations;
God is seated on his holy throne.

⁹ The nobles of the peoples
have assembled
with the people of the God of Abraham.

---

^A47:7 Or *Sing a maskil*

45:12 Tyre, a major trading center on the Mediterranean Sea, was known for its extravagance and wealth.
45:13-15 Virgins and **companions** were essentially maids who accompanied the bride (Est 2:9).
45:16-17 The final wish is for a permanent dynasty for this king that would exalt his **name** (his reputation and fame) beyond that of his **ancestors**.
Ps 46 title On **sons of Korah**, see note at Ps 42 title. **Alamoth** also occurs in 1Ch 15:20 and is used in the same way to designate a song. Suggested renderings include "maidens" (Aquila and Jerome) and "hidden things" (LXX).
46:1 This psalm is the basis for the hymn, "A Mighty Fortress Is Our God."

46:2-3 Trembling **earth** and quaking **mountains** represent unsettling motion in parts of nature that are supposed to be stable.
46:4 The **river** here is difficult to identify precisely. It does not appear to be a literal river in Jerusalem, unless it refers to something like Hezekiah's tunnel. Instead, it seems more likely to refer to God's presence and blessings that fill Jerusalem and flow to other nations (Zch 14:8).
46:8-11 The final command, **stop fighting**, is probably addressed to the nations to stop their hostilities, which were ultimately directed against God (2:10).
Ps 47 title On **sons of Korah**, see note at Ps 42 title.
47:1 The clapping of **hands** is an expression of joy that is used elsewhere to praise a new king (98:8; 2Kg 11:12).

47:2-3 Most High is a title for God expressing his sovereignty over **the whole earth**. **Under** the **feet** is a place of submission.
47:4 Pride of Jacob is parallel to **inheritance** and refers to the promised land (Is 58:14; Am 8:7).
47:5-6 Ascends could refer to God going up into heaven (Gn 17:22; 35:13; Jdg 13:20) or to the ark of the covenant (representing the Lord's presence) being carried up to the temple (2Sm 6:5,16–17). In this psalm it probably expresses the more general idea of the Lord ascending his earthly throne.
47:9 Leaders is literally "shields" and is used to represent those who lead nations, usually kings (84:9; 89:18).

For the leaders[A] of the earth
   belong to God;
he is greatly exalted.

Zion Exalted

48 *A song. A psalm of the sons of Korah.*
The LORD is great and highly praised
in the city of our God.
His holy mountain, [2] rising splendidly,
is the joy of the whole earth.
Mount Zion — the summit of Zaphon —
is the city of the great King.
³ God is known as a stronghold
in its citadels.

⁴ Look! The kings assembled;
   they advanced together.
⁵ They looked and froze with fear;
   they fled in terror.
⁶ Trembling seized them there,
   agony like that of a woman in labor,
⁷ as you wrecked the ships of Tarshish
   with the east wind.

⁸ Just as we heard, so we have seen
   in the city of the LORD of Armies,
   in the city of our God;
God will establish it forever.   *Selah*

⁹ God, within your temple,
   we contemplate your faithful love.
¹⁰ Like your name, God, so your praise
   reaches to the ends of the earth;
   your right hand is filled with justice.
¹¹ Mount Zion is glad.
   Judah's villages[B] rejoice
   because of your judgments.

¹² Go around Zion, encircle it;
   count its towers,
¹³ note its ramparts; tour its citadels
   so that you can tell a future generation:
¹⁴ "This God, our God forever and ever —
   he will always lead us."[C]

Misplaced Trust in Wealth

49 *For the choir director. A psalm of the sons of Korah.*

¹ Hear this, all you peoples;
   listen, all who inhabit the world,
² both low and high,
   rich and poor together.
³ My mouth speaks wisdom;
   my heart's meditation
   brings understanding.
⁴ I turn my ear to a proverb;
   I explain my riddle with a lyre.

⁵ Why should I fear in times of trouble?
   The iniquity of my foes surrounds me.
⁶ They trust in their wealth
   and boast of their abundant riches.
⁷ Yet these cannot redeem a person[D]
   or pay his ransom to God —
⁸ since the price of redeeming him is
      too costly,
   one should forever stop trying[E] —
⁹ so that he may live forever
   and not see the Pit.

¹⁰ For one can see that the wise die;
   the foolish and stupid also pass away.
   Then they leave their wealth to others.
¹¹ Their graves are
      their permanent homes,[F]
   their dwellings from generation
      to generation,
   though they have named estates
      after themselves.
¹² But despite his assets,[G] mankind
      will not last;
   he is like the animals that perish.

¹³ This is the way of those
      who are arrogant,
   and of their followers,
   who approve of their words.[H]   *Selah*
¹⁴ Like sheep they are headed for Sheol;
   Death will shepherd them.

[A]47:9 Lit *shields*   [B]48:11 Lit *daughters*   [C]48:14 Some Hb mss, LXX; other Hb mss read *over death*   [D]49:7 Or *Certainly he cannot redeem himself,* or *Yet he cannot redeem a brother*   [E]49:8 Or *costly, it will cease forever*   [F]49:11 LXX, Syr, Tg; MT reads *Their inner thought is that their houses are eternal*   [G]49:12 Or *honor*   [H]49:13 Lit *and after them with their mouth they were pleased*

Ps 48 title On sons of Korah, see note at Ps 42 title.
48:1–3 Zaphon, a place name, can also be translated as "north."
48:4–5 These verses recall the conquest of Canaan when the Lord caused the people in the land to be terrified of the Israelites (Jos 2:9).
48:7 The destruction of **the ships of Tarshish** may refer to an actual event (1Kg 22:48), or this verse could use Tarshish as a representative of the enemies of God (Ps 72:10).
48:9–11 The **right hand** often represented power and was especially significant in military contexts.
48:12–14 To **encircle** the city sounds like some sort of inspection, but in the context of a psalm and worship, it probably refers to

a thanksgiving procession around the city (Neh 12:27–30).
Ps 49 title On **sons of Korah,** see note at Ps 42 title.
49:1–4 The terms in these verses identify this psalm as a wisdom psalm, providing instruction for those who pay attention.
49:6 Trusting in **wealth** is apparently the main issue in this psalm since this idea is developed in vv. 10–12 and 16–20.
49:7–9 Redeem and **ransom** fit the theme of money and what it can buy. To **see the Pit** is to experience death. The point of 49:8 is that a person cannot buy life, so it is pointless to try. "Ransom" is an especially significant word in light of how it is used in the NT to describe Jesus's payment through his sacrifice (Mt 20:28).

49:10–12 This section as well as vv. 16–20 are similar to the arguments in other Wisdom texts, especially Ecclesiastes, about the futility of wealth: it is left **to others** (39:6; Ec 2:18), **graves** are the **permanent homes** of the wealthy (Ec 12:5), they are **like . . . animals that perish** (Ec 3:19), they will take nothing with them (Jb 27:19; Ps 49:17), and they praise themselves (v. 18; Dt 29:18; Lk 12:19).
49:14 The **sheep** and **shepherd** imagery is used in positive contexts where God shepherds his people; it is used negatively when describing evil leaders who misdirect God's people and lead them into sin (Ezk 34:2–10). Here it is clearly a negative image personifying **Death** as the shepherd of those who trust in their wealth. It leads them into **Sheol,** Death's realm.

The upright will rule over them
　　in the morning,
and their form will waste away
　　in Sheol,^A
far from their lofty abode.
¹⁵ But God will redeem me
　　from the power of Sheol,
　　for he will take me.　　　　　*Selah*

¹⁶ Do not be afraid when a person
　　gets rich,
when the wealth^B
　　of his house increases.
¹⁷ For when he dies, he will take
　　nothing at all;
his wealth will not follow him down.
¹⁸ Though he blesses himself
　　during his lifetime —
and you are acclaimed
　　when you do well for yourself —
¹⁹ he will go to the generation
　　of his ancestors;
they will never see the light.
²⁰ Mankind, with his assets
　　but without understanding,
is like the animals that perish.

God as Judge

50 *A psalm of Asaph.*
The Mighty One, God,^C
the LORD, speaks;
he summons the earth
from the rising of the sun to its setting.
² From Zion, the perfection of beauty,
God appears in radiance.^D
³ Our God is coming; he will not be silent!
Devouring fire precedes him,
and a storm rages around him.
⁴ On high, he summons heaven and earth
in order to judge his people:
⁵ "Gather my faithful ones to me,
those who made a covenant with me
by sacrifice."
⁶ The heavens proclaim
his righteousness,
for God is the Judge.　　　　*Selah*

⁷ "Listen, my people, and I will speak;
I will testify against you, Israel.
I am God, your God.
⁸ I do not rebuke you for your sacrifices
or for your burnt offerings,
which are continually before me.
⁹ I will not take a bull
from your household
or male goats from your pens,
¹⁰ for every animal of the forest is mine,
the cattle on a thousand hills.
¹¹ I know every bird of the mountains,
and the creatures of the field are mine.
¹² If I were hungry, I would not tell you,
for the world and everything in it
is mine.
¹³ Do I eat the flesh of bulls
or drink the blood of goats?
¹⁴ Offer a thanksgiving sacrifice to God,
and pay your vows to the Most High.
¹⁵ Call on me in a day of trouble;
I will rescue you,
and you will honor me."

¹⁶ But God says to the wicked:
"What right do you have to recite
my statutes
and to take my covenant on your lips?
¹⁷ You hate instruction
and fling my words behind you.
¹⁸ When you see a thief,
you make friends with him,
and you associate with adulterers.
¹⁹ You unleash your mouth for evil
and harness your tongue for deceit.
²⁰ You sit, maligning your brother,
slandering your mother's son.
²¹ You have done these things,
and I kept silent;
you thought I was just like you.
But I will rebuke you
and lay out the case before you.^E

²² "Understand this, you who forget God,
or I will tear you apart,
and there will be no one to rescue you.

---

^A 49:14 Hb obscure　^B 49:16 Or *glory*, also in v. 17　^C 50:1 Or *The God of gods*　^D 50:2 Or *God shines forth*　^E 50:21 Lit *lay it out before your eyes*

23 Whoever offers a thanksgiving sacrifice
    honors me,
  and whoever orders his conduct,
  I will show him the salvation of God."

A Prayer for Restoration

51 *For the choir director. A psalm of David, when the prophet Nathan came to him after he had gone to Bathsheba.*

1 Be gracious to me, God,
    according to your faithful love;
  according to your abundant
    compassion,
  blot out my rebellion.
2 Completely wash away my guilt
  and cleanse me from my sin.
3 For I am conscious of my rebellion,
  and my sin is always before me.
4 Against you — you alone
    — I have sinned
  and done this evil in your sight.
  So you are right
    when you pass sentence;
  you are blameless when you judge.
5 Indeed, I was guilty when I was born;
  I was sinful when my mother
    conceived me.

6 Surely you desire integrity
    in the inner self,
  and you teach me wisdom deep within.
7 Purify me with hyssop,
    and I will be clean;
  wash me, and I will be
    whiter than snow.
8 Let me hear joy and gladness;
  let the bones you have crushed rejoice.

9 Turn your face away[A] from my sins
  and blot out all my guilt.

10 God, create a clean heart for me
  and renew a steadfast[B] spirit within me.
11 Do not banish me from your presence
  or take your Holy Spirit from me.
12 Restore the joy of your salvation to me,
  and sustain me by giving me
    a willing spirit.
13 Then I will teach the rebellious
    your ways,
  and sinners will return to you.
14 Save me from the guilt of bloodshed,
    God —
  God of my salvation —
  and my tongue will sing
    of your righteousness.
15 Lord, open my lips,
  and my mouth will declare your praise.
16 You do not want a sacrifice,
    or I would give it;
  you are not pleased
    with a burnt offering.
17 The sacrifice pleasing to God is[C]
    a broken spirit.
  You will not despise a broken
    and humbled heart, God.

18 In your good pleasure, cause Zion
    to prosper;
  build the walls of Jerusalem.
19 Then you will delight
    in righteous sacrifices,
  whole burnt offerings;
  then bulls will be offered on your altar.

^A51:9 Lit *Hide your face* ^B51:10 Or *right* ^C51:17 Lit *The sacrifices of God are*

50:23 Orders his conduct refers to obedience, which is preferable to sacrifice (1Sm 15:22; Ps 40:6–8).
Ps 51 title This psalm has a clearly defined historical setting, which was David's confession of his sins after being confronted by the **prophet Nathan** (2Sm 12:1; the entire background of the sins is in 2Sm 11–12).
51:1–2 Blot out . . . wash away, and **cleanse** are terms for forgiveness, which is David's main plea (see note at 32:1–2 for similar terms). He relied completely on God's mercy, which is evident in the terms **gracious . . . faithful love**, and **abundant compassion**. In David's case, his sins were severe enough that sacrifice was not acceptable (v. 16). According to God's laws, deliberate and premeditated sins such as adultery and murder were referred to as sins of "the high hand" (cp. "defiantly" in Nm 15:30–31). Their punishment was being "cut off" from the community, which in many cases meant death.
51:3 Verses 3–5 include the recognition of sin without specifying the sins. **My rebellion** is in the emphatic position in the Hebrew text, showing that this is the main focus of attention in this confession.
51:4 The statement **against you . . . alone** does not mean that others were not involved

in the effects of the sin, but that even in sinning against others the ultimate affront was against God.
51:5 This verse has prompted a variety of interpretations. Some have interpreted it to mean that marriage and childbearing are a curse; this is untenable in light of the rest of Scripture (127:3; Heb 13:4). Another interpretation is that this refers to a specific sin, perhaps adultery, committed by David's **mother**; but there is no evidence of this in the biblical texts. Others connect this verse with ceremonial uncleanness in childbirth (Lv 12:2,5; 15:18), but this is not the same as sin. Some say David is using rhetorical overstatement to describe his sinfulness. One of the most common interpretations in Christian history is that this verse teaches the doctrine of original sin. While not aiming to strictly identify the origin of human sinfulness with events at biological conception, David recognizes that sin pervades humankind as a universal condition from the very outset of our existence. Sin is everywhere and in everyone, and David confessed that it had been with him since birth.
51:7 The use of **hyssop** can be seen in Ex 12:22 and Nm 19:18.
51:9 Turning away the **face** implies forgiving and forgetting (vv. 1–2).

51:10 The renewal of one's **heart** and **spirit** are common images representing not only forgiveness (vv. 1–2,7–9) but also a change that enables a person to live in obedience to the Lord's commands (1Sm 10:6,9; Jr 32:39; Ezk 36:26).
51:11 Holy Spirit is taken by some to mean the Lord's **presence**. However, in the larger context of the biblical text, it seems to refer to God himself (Is 63:10–14) in the same way that "heart" and "spirit" can refer to people.
51:12 David wanted to experience again the joy of knowing that he was delivered. A **willing spirit** would be the attitude of a heart totally given over to the Lord.
51:13–15 Publicly praising God and teaching others about him was part of the response of God's deliverance in a person's life.
51:18 Some think **build the walls** refers to Nehemiah's time, but this is not necessary if it is used figuratively. It simply refers to strengthening **Zion**, which is where the Lord dwelt among his people (65:1).
51:19 Righteous sacrifices must be connected with vv. 16–17, meaning those offered with the proper motives.

God Judges the Proud

52 *For the choir director. A* Maskil *of David. When Doeg the Edomite went and reported to Saul, telling him, "David went to Ahimelech's house."*

¹ Why boast about evil, you hero!
God's faithful love is constant.
² Like a sharpened razor,
your tongue devises destruction,
working treachery.
³ You love evil instead of good,
lying instead of
speaking truthfully.   *Selah*
⁴ You love any words that destroy,
you treacherous tongue!

⁵ This is why God will bring
you down forever.
He will take you, ripping you out of
your tent;
he will uproot you from the land
of the living.   *Selah*
⁶ The righteous will see and fear,
and they will derisively say
about that hero,ᴬ
⁷ "Here is the man
who would not make God his refuge,
but trusted in the abundance
of his riches,
taking refuge
in his destructive behavior."

⁸ But I am like a flourishing olive tree
in the house of God;
I trust in God's faithful love
forever and ever.
⁹ I will praise you forever for what
you have done.
In the presence of your faithful people,
I will put my hope in your name,
for it is good.

A Portrait of Sinners

53 *For the choir director: on* Mahalath. *A* Maskil *of David.*

¹ The fool says in his heart,
"There's no God."

They are corrupt, and they do vile deeds.
There is no one who does good.
² God looks down from heaven
on the human raceᴮ
to see if there is one who is wise,
one who seeks God.
³ All have turned away;
all alike have become corrupt.
There is no one who does good,
not even one.

⁴ Will evildoers never understand?
They consume my people
as they consume bread;
they do not call on God.
⁵ Then they will be filled with dread —
dread like no other —
because God will scatter
the bones of those who besiege you.
You will put them to shame,
for God has rejected them.

⁶ Oh, that Israel's deliverance would come
from Zion!
When God restores the fortunes
of his people,ᶜ
let Jacob rejoice, let Israel be glad.

Prayer for Deliverance

54 *For the choir director: with stringed instruments. A* Maskil *of David. When the Ziphites went and said to Saul, "Is David not hiding among us?"*

¹ God, save me by your name,
and vindicate me by your might!
² God, hear my prayer;
listen to the words from my mouth.
³ For strangers rise up against me,
and violent men intend to kill me.
They do not let God guide them.ᴰ   *Selah*

⁴ God is my helper;
the Lord is the sustainer of my life.ᴱ
⁵ He will repay my adversaries
for their evil.
Because of your faithfulness,
annihilate them.

ᴬ52:6 Lit *about him* ᴮ53:2 Or *the descendants of Adam* ᶜ53:6 Or *restores his captive people* ᴰ54:3 Lit *They do not set God in front of them* ᴱ54:4 Or *is with those who sustain my life*

Ps 52 title On **Maskil**, see note at Ps 32 title. The historical setting specified in this psalm is when **Doeg the Edomite**, one of Saul's chief herdsmen, informed Saul that David had gone to Ahimelech's house (1Sm 22:9). He had also informed Saul of the help David received from the priests of Nob (1Sm 21:7), so David acknowledged responsibility for the slaughter of eighty-five priests accused of treason against King Saul (1Sm 22:11–23). **52:1** This person was boasting about his sins (10:3). Those who are **faithful** to the Lord boast only in the fact that they know him. **52:2 Razor** symbolizes sharpness that could be used as a weapon of **destruction**. In other contexts, a sharpened **tongue** is a common image for destructive speech (57:4; 64:3; 140:3). **52:4** The word for **destroy** is literally "swallow," picturing destructive speech as devouring others. **52:5 Bring . . . down** is commonly used for judgment on the wicked (147:6; 2Sm 22:48). **Uproot** is the most common description of a wicked person being removed from the Lord's land (Dt 29:28; 2Ch 7:20; Pr 2:22). **Ps 53 title Mahalath** may be related to a Hebrew word meaning "sickness." It is unclear whether it refers to a song tune or a musical form. On **Maskil**, see note at Ps 32 title. **53:1–4** These verses are essentially the same as 14:1–4. **53:5** Scattering **bones** often pictures the dead on the battlefield (141:7; Jr 8:1–2; Ezk 6:5; 37:1–6). **Ps 54 title** The historical setting for this psalm relates to the **Ziphites**, who lived southeast of Hebron and informed Saul of David's hiding place (1Sm 23:19; 26:1). On **Maskil**, see note at Ps 32 title. **54:2–3** The word **strangers** denotes outsiders with regard to the Lord's covenant and people (Is 1:7; 14:1; Eph 2:12). **They do not let God guide them** means that they do not think God's instruction is worthwhile. **54:4–5 Repay** is a term used in contexts describing divine retribution (Dt 32:35).

⁶ I will sacrifice a freewill offering
   to you.
  I will praise your name, LORD,
   because it is good.
⁷ For he has rescued me
   from every trouble,
  and my eye has looked down on
   my enemies.

Betrayal by a Friend

55 For the choir director: with stringed
   instruments. A Maskil of David.

¹ God, listen to my prayer
  and do not hide from my plea for help.
² Pay attention to me and answer me.
  I am restless and in turmoil
   with my complaint,
³ because of the enemy's words,ᴬ
  because of the pressureᴮ of the wicked.
  For they bring down disaster on me
  and harass me in anger.

⁴ My heart shudders within me;
  terrors of death sweep over me.
⁵ Fear and trembling grip me;
  horror has overwhelmed me.
⁶ I said, "If only I had wings like a dove!
  I would fly away and find rest.
⁷ How far away I would flee;
  I would stay in the wilderness.   Selah
⁸ I would hurry to my shelter
  from the raging wind and the storm."

⁹ Lord, confuseᶜ and confound
   their speech,ᴰ
  for I see violence and strife in the city;
¹⁰ day and night they make the rounds
   on its walls.
  Crime and trouble are within it;
¹¹ destruction is inside it;
  oppression and deceit never leave
   its marketplace.

¹² Now it is not an enemy
   who insults me —
  otherwise I could bear it;

it is not a foe who rises up
  against me —
  otherwise I could hide from him.
¹³ But it is you, a man who is my peer,
  my companion and good friend!
¹⁴ We used to have close fellowship;
  we walked with the crowd
   into the house of God.

¹⁵ Let death take them by surprise;
  let them go down to Sheol alive,
  because evil is in their homes
   and within them.
¹⁶ But I call to God,
  and the LORD will save me.
¹⁷ I complain and groan morning, noon,
   and night,
  and he hears my voice.
¹⁸ Though many are against me,
  he will redeem me
   from my battle unharmed.
¹⁹ God, the one enthroned
   from long ago,
  will hear and
   will humiliate them   Selah
  because they do not change
  and do not fear God.

²⁰ My friend acts violently
  against those at peace with him;
  he violates his covenant.
²¹ His buttery words are smooth,
  but war is in his heart.
  His words are softer than oil,
  but they are drawn swords.

²² Cast your burden on the LORD,
  and he will sustain you;
  he will never allow the righteous
   to be shaken.

²³ God, you will bring them down
  to the Pit of destruction;
  men of bloodshed and treachery
  will not live out half their days.
  But I will trust in you.

ᴬ 55:3 Lit *voice*   ᴮ 55:3 Or *threat*, or *oppression*   ᶜ 55:9 Or *destroy*   ᴰ 55:9 Lit *and divide their tongue*

54:6 This is a voluntary and spontaneous **offering** that was not done out of obligation.
Ps 55 title On **Maskil**, see note at Ps 32 title.
55:1-3 Harass is a rare word that expresses the idea of animosity or hatred, often connected with hostility (Gn 49:23; Jb 30:21). This emphasizes malicious intent rather than playful mocking.
55:4-5 Sweep over and **overwhelmed** portray being overtaken by troubles as if by a flood.
55:9-11 These verses recall when God judged those who were building the tower of Babylon by confounding their **speech** (Gn 11:1-9). The terms **city** and **walls** and the description

of the wickedness associated with them are further connections to Babylon.
55:12-14 The shift here is significant in demonstrating that the culprit was not some distant **enemy** but a close **friend**, a worship companion. This "friend" did not merely abandon the psalmist, but actually participated in the malicious **insults**.
55:15 Going **down to Sheol alive** is reminiscent of the fate of those who followed Korah in his rebellion against God (Nm 16:31-33).
55:16-17 The phrase **morning, noon, and night** most likely implies constant prayer rather than specific times of prayer (22:2; 88:1; 119:164; 1Th 5:17).

55:18-19 Enthroned from long ago describes God's eternal rule beginning at creation (29:10; 45:6; Lm 5:19).
55:20 His covenant in this context is not a reference to God's covenant with his people but is used in the more secular sense of a promise or oath made between people. Here it refers to one who violates a friendship because he does not fear God.
55:21 War . . . in his heart relates to the earlier term *harass* (v. 3), which refers to open hostility. The point here is that hostile speech comes from hostile intentions (Mt 12:34; Lk 6:45).
55:22 This verse is quoted in 1Pt 5:7.
55:23 Pit is equivalent to "Sheol" (v. 15) and refers to death.

A Call for God's Protection

56 For the choir director: according to "A Silent Dove Far Away." A Miktam of David. When the Philistines seized him in Gath.

1 Be gracious to me, God, for a man is
  trampling me;
  he fights and oppresses me
  all day long.

2 My adversaries trample me all day,
  for many arrogantly fight against me.[A]

3 When I am afraid,
  I will trust in you.

4 In God, whose word I praise,
  in God I trust; I will not be afraid.
  What can mere mortals do to me?

5 They twist my words all day long;
  all their thoughts against me are evil.

6 They stir up strife,[B] they lurk,
  they watch my steps
  while they wait to take my life.

7 Will they escape in spite of such sin?
  God, bring down the nations in wrath.

8 You yourself have recorded
  my wanderings.[C]
  Put my tears in your bottle.
  Are they not in your book?

9 Then my enemies will retreat on the day
  when I call.
  This I know: God is for me.

10 In God, whose word I praise,
  in the LORD, whose word I praise,

11 in God I trust; I will not be afraid.
  What can mere humans do to me?

12 I am obligated by vows[D] to you, God;
  I will make my thanksgiving sacrifices
  to you.

13 For you rescued me from death,
  even my feet from stumbling,
  to walk before God in the light of life.

Praise for God's Protection

57 For the choir director: "Do Not Destroy." A Miktam of David. When he fled before Saul into the cave.

1 Be gracious to me, God, be gracious
  to me,
  for I take refuge in you.
  I will seek refuge in the shadow
  of your wings
  until danger passes.

2 I call to God Most High,
  to God who fulfills his purpose for me.[E]

3 He reaches down from heaven
  and saves me,
  challenging the one
  who tramples me. Selah
  God sends his faithful love and truth.

4 I am surrounded by lions;
  I lie down among devouring lions —
  people whose teeth are spears
  and arrows,
  whose tongues are sharp swords.

5 God, be exalted above the heavens;
  let your glory be over the whole earth.

6 They prepared a net for my steps;
  I was despondent.
  They dug a pit ahead of me,
  but they fell into it! Selah

7 My heart is confident, God, my heart
  is confident.
  I will sing; I will sing praises.

8 Wake up, my soul!
  Wake up, harp and lyre!
  I will wake up the dawn.

9 I will praise you, Lord,
  among the peoples;
  I will sing praises to you
  among the nations.

10 For your faithful love is as high as
  the heavens;
  your faithfulness reaches the clouds.

11 God, be exalted above the heavens;
  let your glory be over the whole earth.

[A]56:2 Or many fight against me, O exalted one, or many fight against me from the heights   [B]56:6 Or They attack   [C]56:8 Or misery   [D]56:12 Lit On me the vows   [E]57:2 Or who avenges me

---

Ps 56 title A Silent Dove Far Away was probably a known song tune (see note at Ps 22 title). On **Miktam**, see note at Ps 16 title. The historical setting for this psalm is the same as Ps 34 (1Sm 21:10–11; see note at Ps 34 title). **56:1–2 Trampling** appears twice in these verses. There are two meanings for this Hebrew word: (1) "pant" or "long for" (Is 42:14; Jr 2:24) and (2) "crush" or "trample" (Ps 57:3; Am 8:4). Since the first of these is more common, some translations take that as the meaning here. However, the parallel terms **fights** and **oppresses** argue for the second meaning. **56:3–4 Mere mortals** is literally "flesh," which represents man's weakness and mortality (Is 2:22; 31:3; 40:6). This word is often used to contrast man's weakness with God's power (2Ch 32:8).

56:5 Twist expresses the idea of "shape" or "fashion" (Jb 10:8). It portrays these enemies as shaping the psalmist's words into whatever they wanted for their own **evil** purposes. **56:6 Lurk** describes the psalmist's enemies as predatory animals waiting to attack their prey (10:9; 17:12). **56:7** The answer to the question is understood to be no; they will not **escape**. **56:8–9 Tears** probably refers to prayers or, more specifically, laments that involve crying. The **bottle** refers to God's storing of these prayers so he can act on them later. **56:10–11 What can mere humans do to me?** again reminds us of Rm 8:31. **Ps 57 title Do Not Destroy** was probably a known song tune of the time (see note at Ps 22 title). On **Miktam**, see note at Ps 16 title.

There are two possibilities for the historical setting of this psalm, both of which involved David fleeing from Saul and going into a cave (1Sm 22:1; 24:1–3; cp. Ps 142). **57:2 Most High** emphasizes God's sovereignty over the whole earth. **57:5 Glory** carries the idea of "heavy" or "weighty" in the sense of "important." God's glory can either be a physical manifestation, such as that which came down on the ark of the covenant (Ex 40:34–35), or be used to represent his significance, perhaps connected with his reputation or "name" (Pss 29:2; 66:2). In this verse his significance is **over the whole earth**, meaning beyond anything on earth. Verse 11 repeats the same words as v. 5. **57:7–8 My soul** here is literally "my glory" from the same Hebrew word (kavod) as v. 5.

A Cry against Injustice

58 *For the choir director: "Do Not Destroy."*
A Miktam of David.

¹ Do you really speak righteously,
    you mighty ones?ᴬ
  Do you judge people fairly?
² No, you practice injustice in your hearts;
  with your hands you weigh out violence
    in the land.

³ The wicked go astray from the womb;
  liars wander about from birth.
⁴ They have venom like the venom
    of a snake,
  like the deaf cobra that stops up its ears,
⁵ that does not listen to the sound
    of the charmers
  who skillfully weave spells.

⁶ God, knock the teeth out of their mouths;
  LORD, tear out the young lions' fangs.
⁷ May they vanish like water that flows by;
  may they aim their blunted arrows.ᴮ
⁸ Like a slug that moves along in slime,
  like a woman's miscarried child,
  may they not see the sun.

⁹ Before your pots can feel the heat of
    the thorns —
  whether green or burning —
  he will sweep them away.ᶜ
¹⁰ The righteous one will rejoice
    when he sees the retribution;
  he will wash his feet in the blood
    of the wicked.
¹¹ Then people will say,
  "Yes, there is a reward for the righteous!
  There is a God who judges on earth!"

God Our Stronghold

59 *For the choir director: "Do Not Destroy."*
A Miktam of David. When Saul sent
agents to watch the house and kill him.

¹ Rescue me from my enemies, my God;
  protect me from those who rise up
    against me.
² Rescue me from evildoers,
  and save me from men of bloodshed.
³ Because look, LORD, they set an ambush
    for me.
  Powerful men attack me,
  but not because of any sin or rebellion
    of mine.
⁴ For no fault of mine,
  they run and take up a position.
  Awake to help me, and take notice.
⁵ LORD God of Armies, you are the
    God of Israel.
  Rise up to punish all the nations;
  do not show favor
    to any wicked traitors.   *Selah*

⁶ They return at evening, snarling like dogs
  and prowling around the city.
⁷ Look, they spew from their mouths —
  sharp words fromᴰ their lips.
  "For who," they say, "will hear?"
⁸ But you laugh at them, LORD;
  you ridicule all the nations.
⁹ I will keep watch for you, myᴱ strength,
  because God is my stronghold.
¹⁰ My faithful Godᶠ will come to meet me;
  God will let me look down on
    my adversaries.
¹¹ Do not kill them; otherwise, my people
    will forget.

ᴬ**58:1** Or *Can you really speak righteousness in silence?* ᴮ**58:7** Hb obscure ᶜ**58:9** Or *thorns, he will sweep it away, whether raw or cooking* ᴰ**59:7** Lit *swords are on* ᴱ**59:9** Some Hb mss, LXX, Vg, Tg; other Hb mss read *his* ᶠ**59:10** Alt Hb tradition reads *My God in his faithful love*

Here it represents the person but creates an interesting wordplay within the psalm. **Ps 58 title** On **Do Not Destroy**, see note at Ps 22 title. On **Miktam**, see note at Ps 16 title. **58:1** The Hebrew word for **mighty ones** sometimes refers to angelic beings or the gods of the nations, but here it refers to people. The combination of **righteously** (referring to justice) and **judge** shows that they were most likely rulers or judges who were responsible for rendering justice. The designation "mighty ones" is sarcastic since this is how they viewed themselves. **58:2 Injustice in your hearts** contrasts with the fact that they were responsible for judging fairly (v. 1). The "heart" was often used to depict the place of one's motives as well as the human will where decisions were made (1Sm 7:3; 1Kg 8:47–48). **58:3** Speaking of the wicked and liars specifically, the psalmist traces their errant ways to the **womb** and **birth** not in a bid to argue that they are constituted differently from the general population but rather to express the deep-rootedness of their sinfulness. **58:4–5** The comparison of these wicked rulers to a **snake** emphasizes their deadliness (their

venom). The other main point of comparison is stopping up their **ears** and not listening to **charmers**. In the context of judging, it probably refers to not listening to someone's case and therefore not rendering justice fairly. **58:7** The vanishing **water** here may be a reference to a wadi, a seasonal stream that flowed only during the rainy season. The rest of the time it was nothing more than a dry river bed (or valley). **58:8** The image of the **slug** and its **slime** seems to reflect a common perception in the ancient world that the slug was melting away as it moved along. **58:9 Thorns** were often used as fuel to heat food in **pots**. Therefore, this implies the swiftness of God's judgment. **58:10** Seeing **retribution** and washing one's **feet in . . . blood** (spilled blood or death) are parallel concepts. Though the second image is more vivid, the point is the same — the **righteous** will witness God's judgment on these wicked rulers. **Ps 59 title** On **Do Not Destroy**, see note at Ps 22 title. On **Miktam**, see note at Ps 16 title. The "him" in the phrase kill him refers

to David. The background for this setting is found in 1Sm 19:11. **59:1–2 Men of bloodshed** is literally "men of blood." It refers to those who were known for their violence (5:6; 26:9; 55:23), in this case those who desired the death of the psalmist. **59:3–4 No fault of mine** is a statement of innocence, meaning that the psalmist had done nothing to provoke the attacks of his enemies. **59:5 LORD God of Armies** is a military image that describes Yahweh as a warrior who fights for his people. **59:6–7 Dogs** were not domesticated and had a negative connotation in the ancient Near East. They were viewed no differently than other wild and dangerous animals. **Prowling** is also characteristic of wild dogs foraging for food. Note the same image in vv. 14–15. Spewing **from their mouths** perhaps pictures dogs slobbering or foaming at the mouth. **59:10 Look down on** is literally "look on," but the context makes it clear that he will look on them as a victor looks on a vanquished foe. **59:11** Unlike other psalms that call for annihilation of the wicked, this psalm asks that the Lord spare their lives so his **people** will not **forget**.

By your power, make them
　homeless wanderers
and bring them down,
Lord, our shield.
¹² For the sin of their mouths and the
　words of their lips,
let them be caught in their pride.
They utter curses and lies.
¹³ Consume them in fury;
consume them until they are gone.
Then people will know
　throughout^A the earth
that God rules over Jacob. 　　*Selah*

¹⁴ And they return at evening,
　snarling like dogs
and prowling around the city.
¹⁵ They scavenge for food;
they growl if they are not satisfied.

¹⁶ But I will sing of your strength
and will joyfully proclaim
your faithful love in the morning.
For you have been a stronghold for me,
a refuge in my day of trouble.
¹⁷ To you, my strength, I sing praises,
because God is my stronghold —
my faithful God.

Prayer in Difficult Times

60 *For the choir director: according to "The Lily of Testimony." A Miktam of David for teaching. When he fought with Aram-naharaim and Aram-zobah, and Joab returned and struck Edom in Salt Valley, killing twelve thousand.*

¹ God, you have rejected us;
you have broken us down;
you have been angry. Restore us!^B
² You have shaken the land
　and split it open.
Heal its fissures, for it shudders.
³ You have made your people
　suffer hardship;
you have given us wine to drink
that made us stagger.

⁴ You have given a signal flag to those
　who fear you,
so that they can flee
　before the archers.^C 　　*Selah*
⁵ Save with your right hand,
　and answer me,
so that those you love may be rescued.

⁶ God has spoken in his sanctuary:^D
"I will celebrate!
I will divide up Shechem.
I will apportion the Valley of Succoth.
⁷ Gilead is mine, Manasseh is mine,
and Ephraim is my helmet;
Judah is my scepter.
⁸ Moab is my washbasin.
I throw my sandal on Edom;
I shout in triumph over Philistia."

⁹ Who will bring me to the fortified city?
Who will lead me to Edom?
¹⁰ God, haven't you rejected us?
God, you do not march out
　with our armies.
¹¹ Give us aid against the foe,
for human help is worthless.
¹² With God we will perform valiantly;
he will trample our foes.

Security in God

61 *For the choir director: on stringed instruments. Of David.*

¹ God, hear my cry;
pay attention to my prayer.
² I call to you from the ends of the earth
when my heart is without strength.
Lead me to a rock that is high above me,
³ for you have been a refuge for me,
a strong tower in the face of the enemy.
⁴ I will dwell in your tent forever
and take refuge under the shelter
　of your wings. 　　*Selah*

⁵ God, you have heard my vows;
you have given a heritage

^A 59:13 Lit *know to the ends of* 　^B 60:1 Or *Turn back to us* 　^C 60:4 Or *can rally before the archers*, or *can rally because of the truth* 　^D 60:6 Or *has promised by his holy nature*

59:13 The wicked are often pictured as those who **consume** others. In a turn of poetic justice, the Lord consumes them.
59:14–15 This repeats the lament from v. 6.
59:16–17 Praising the Lord **in the morning** is common in the psalms (5:3; 30:5).
Ps 60 title The Lily of Testimony was perhaps a known song tune of the time (see note at Ps 22 title). On **Miktam**, see note at Ps 16 title. The additional term teaching indicates that this psalm had the purpose of instruction, although it is not specifically a wisdom psalm according to its form. The historical setting is quite specific about an incident in David's life. This is found in 1Ch 18:3,12.
60:1 Rejected us . . . broken us . . . restore us indicates that this is a communal lament similar to Ps 44.

60:2 The shaking of the **land** could refer to an actual earthquake, though it can also represent the Lord's power.
60:4 A **signal flag** is probably the same as a "banner," which was used primarily in military campaigns.
60:5 The Lord's **right hand** refers to his power.
60:6–8 The place names in these verses are probably used to represent the whole territory of Canaan, which was owned by the Lord and given to his people. **Shechem** was in the north (forty miles north of Jerusalem). **Succoth** was east of the Jordan River near the Jabbok River. **Gilead** and **Manasseh** were both on the eastern side of the Jordan, together extending from the south (the Arnon River) to the extreme north (the hill

country of **Ephraim**). **Moab . . . Edom**, and **Philistia** were never a permanent part of Israel but represented the outer extremes of Israel's territory to the east, south, and west, respectively. The **helmet** probably represents Ephraim's military strength (Dt 33:17). **Judah** received God's **scepter**, which was the right to rule over his kingdom (Gn 49:10).
61:1–3 The verb translated **without strength** is used with other subjects to describe exhaustion (77:3; 142:3; 143:4; Jnh 2:7).
61:4 Your tent seems to be used in a way similar to "house" or "temple" as a figurative reference to the Lord's presence.
61:5 The **vows** here are most likely those made during a time of petition. They were to be fulfilled by a thank offering.

to those who fear your name.
⁶ Add days to the king's life;
may his years span many generations.
⁷ May he sit enthroned
before God forever.
Appoint faithful love and truth
to guard him.
⁸ Then I will continually sing
of your name,
fulfilling my vows day by day.

Trust in God Alone

62 For the choir director: according to
Jeduthun. A psalm of David.
¹ I am at rest in God alone;
my salvation comes from him.
² He alone is my rock and my salvation,
my stronghold; I will never be shaken.

³ How long will you threaten a man?
Will all of you attack^A
as if he were a leaning wall
or a tottering fence?
⁴ They only plan to bring him down
from his high position.
They take pleasure in lying;
they bless with their mouths,
but they curse inwardly.   *Selah*

⁵ Rest in God alone, my soul,
for my hope comes from him.
⁶ He alone is my rock and my salvation,
my stronghold; I will not be shaken.
⁷ My salvation and glory depend on God,
my strong rock.
My refuge is in God.
⁸ Trust in him at all times, you people;
pour out your hearts before him.
God is our refuge.   *Selah*

⁹ Common people are only a vapor;
important people, an illusion.
Together on a scale,
they weigh less than^B a vapor.

¹⁰ Place no trust in oppression
or false hope in robbery.
If wealth increases,
don't set your heart on it.

¹¹ God has spoken once;
I have heard this twice:
strength belongs to God,
¹² and faithful love belongs to you, Lord.
For you repay each according to
his works.

Praise God Who Satisfies

63 A psalm of David. When he was in the
Wilderness of Judah.
¹ God, you are my God; I eagerly seek you.
I thirst for you;
my body faints for you
in a land that is dry, desolate,
and without water.

² So I gaze on you in the sanctuary
to see your strength and your glory.

³ My lips will glorify you
because your faithful love is better
than life.
⁴ So I will bless you as long as I live;
at your name, I will lift up my hands.
⁵ You satisfy me as with rich food;^C
my mouth will praise you
with joyful lips.

⁶ When I think of you as I lie on my bed,
I meditate on you
during the night watches
⁷ because you are my helper;
I will rejoice in the shadow of your wings.
⁸ I follow close to you;
your right hand holds on to me.

⁹ But those who intend to destroy my life
will go into the depths of the earth.
¹⁰ They will be given over to the power
of the sword;

---

^A **62:3** Some Hb mss read *you be struck down* ^B **62:9** Lit *they go up more than* ^C **63:5** Lit *with fat and fatness*

61:6–7 The request of a long **life** for the king was sometimes used in the context of protection from harm, but in its broader sense it meant the longevity of a dynasty. The promise of being **enthroned . . . forever** and having God's **faithful love** is closely related to the language of the Davidic covenant (2Sm 7:13,15–16). **Ps 62 title** On **Jeduthun**, see note at Ps 39 title. **62:1 Rest** expresses the idea of silence. Here it most likely refers to rest in the sense of waiting on the Lord and feeling secure that he will answer prayer and protect the psalmist. It appears as a command in 62:5. **62:4 High position** indicates that the person being attacked by these enemies was a person of some importance, perhaps a leader. **62:8 Pour out your hearts** is an idiom for opening up to God with all one's requests

(42:4; 102:1; 142:1). It is joined with the idea of **trust** to indicate that through prayer a person can rely on God to meet his needs. **62:9–10 Vapor** represents lack of significance or the fleeting nature of life. It is parallel with **important people**, showing the contrast between human perception and reality. Since vapor literally refers to a small puff of air, the idea of weighing it on **a scale** is absurd. All who think of themselves as prominent weigh **less than a vapor. 62:11 Once . . . twice** is used for emphasis to show that something has been repeated and is therefore significant (Jb 33:14; 40:5). In this case it is a lesson to be learned. **Ps 63 title** The historical setting for this psalm has less detail than other psalms and could refer to David's flight from Saul or from Absalom (1Sm 23:14; 24:2; 2Sm 16:14; 17:2,29).

63:2 Gaze on you in the sanctuary is probably not a theophany but is similar to the idiom "looking to God" for help in the sense of trusting him. **63:3–4** Lifting up **hands** is a gesture for praying. **63:5 Rich food** is a combination of two Hebrew words for "fat," implying being satisfied beyond one's need. Fat represents prosperity in the OT (73:7; Dt 32:15; Jr 5:28). **63:8** The **right hand** represented strength and the place from which the Lord protected and helped his people. **63:9** The **depths of the earth** is another way of describing Sheol or death (86:13; Is 44:23; Ezk 26:20). **63:10** The first line is literally "they will be poured out on the hands of the sword," where "hands" refers to **power**. This is a more intensive way of expressing the idea

they will become a meal for jackals.
11 But the king will rejoice in God;
all who swear by him will boast,
for the mouths of liars will be shut.

Protection from Evildoers

64 *For the choir director. A psalm of David.*
God, hear my voice when I am
in anguish.
Protect my life from the terror
of the enemy.
2 Hide me from the scheming
of wicked people,
from the mob of evildoers,
3 who sharpen their tongues
like swords
and aim bitter words like arrows,
4 shooting from concealed places
at the blameless.
They shoot at him suddenly
and are not afraid.
5 They adopt^A an evil plan;
they talk about hiding traps and say,
"Who will see them?"^B
6 They devise crimes and say,
"We have perfected a secret plan."
The inner man and the heart
are mysterious.

7 But God will shoot them with arrows;
suddenly, they will be wounded.
8 They will be made to stumble;
their own tongues work against them.
All who see them will shake
their heads.
9 Then everyone will fear
and will tell about God's work,
for they will understand
what he has done.

10 The righteous one rejoices
in the LORD
and takes refuge in him;
all those who are upright in heart
will offer praise.

God's Care for the Earth

65 *For the choir director. A psalm of David.
A song.*
1 Praise is rightfully yours,^C
God, in Zion;
vows to you will be fulfilled.
2 All humanity will come to you,
the one who hears prayer.
3 Iniquities overwhelm me;
only you can atone for our rebellions.
4 How happy is the one you choose
and bring near to live in your courts!
We will be satisfied with the goodness
of your house,
the holiness of your temple.^D

5 You answer us in righteousness,
with awe-inspiring works,
God of our salvation,
the hope of all the ends of the earth
and of the distant seas.
6 You establish the mountains
by your power;
you are robed with strength.
7 You silence the roar of the seas,
the roar of their waves,
and the tumult of the nations.
8 Those who live far away are awed
by your signs;
you make east and west shout for joy.

9 You visit the earth
and water it abundantly,
enriching it greatly.
God's stream is filled with water,
for you prepare the earth in this way,
providing people with grain.
10 You soften it with showers and bless
its growth,
soaking its furrows and leveling
its ridges.
11 You crown the year with your goodness;
your carts overflow with plenty.^E
12 The wilderness pastures overflow,
and the hills are robed with joy.

---

^A**64:5** Or *They strengthen themselves with*   ^B**64:5** Or *it*   ^C**65:1** Or *Praise is silence to you,* or *Praise awaits you*   ^D**65:4** Or *house, your holy temple*   ^E**65:11** Lit *your paths drip with fat*

---

of the psalmist's enemies receiving what was coming to them (Jr 18:21; Ezk 35:5).
63:11 Swear by him is a way of saying that the Lord is the only source of security. It is essentially another way of describing a person's trust in God.
64:1–3 Sharpen is often used with **tongues** to describe destructive speech (55:21; 57:4).
64:4 Shooting from concealed places pictures the enemies hiding in ambush and waiting to strike without notice (10:8; 11:2). This was not open conflict but guerrilla warfare.
64:6 The **heart** is **mysterious** in the sense that it is full of concealed wickedness, as revealed in actions (Pr 12:20; Jr 17:9).
64:7 God takes on the role of warrior (7:12), with the picture of him shooting **arrows**

at the psalmist's enemies, even while they were hiding and waiting to **shoot** the innocent (v. 4).
64:8 The phrase **tongues work against them** may be a reference to the enemies' provoking God through their destructive speech. Shaking the head was a gesture often associated with mocking.
65:1 Vows were often used in the context of prayer and were fulfilled with thank-offerings.
65:2 All humanity is literally "all flesh" and refers to the eschatological hope of mankind as a whole trusting in the Lord and coming to him in **prayer** and worship (86:9; Is 2:2–4).
65:3 The Hebrew word for **atone** is difficult to define since its origin is uncertain. The two most likely options are "cover" and "cleanse."

When sin is its object (as here), it is probably another way of describing forgiveness.
65:4 In your courts is equivalent to **house** and **temple**, all of which represent being in the Lord's presence.
65:5–8 The connection between **roar of the seas** and **tumult of the nations** is significant since the nations are often represented by the restless and chaotic sea.
65:9–10 Visit describes God's grace and provision, especially in times of need. Since **water** is the sustainer of life, God's provision of water identifies him as the source and sustainer of life.
65:11–13 Crown the year with your goodness refers to a year "adorned" with blessings.

3

13 The pastures are clothed with flocks
and the valleys covered with grain.
They shout in triumph; indeed, they sing.

Praise for God's Mighty Acts

66 For the choir director. A song. A psalm.
Let the whole earth shout joyfully
to God!

2 Sing about the glory of his name;
make his praise glorious.
3 Say to God, "How awe-inspiring
are your works!
Your enemies will cringe before you
because of your great strength.
4 The whole earth will worship you
and sing praise to you.
They will sing praise to your name." *Selah*

5 Come and see the wonders of God;
his acts for humanity[A]
are awe-inspiring.
6 He turned the sea into dry land,
and they crossed the river on foot.
There we rejoiced in him.
7 He rules forever by his might;
he keeps his eye on the nations.
The rebellious should not
exalt themselves. *Selah*
8 Bless our God, you peoples;
let the sound of his praise be heard.
9 He keeps us alive[B]
and does not allow our feet to slip.

10 For you, God, tested us;
you refined us as silver is refined.
11 You lured us into a trap;
you placed burdens on our backs.
12 You let men ride over our heads;
we went through fire and water,
but you brought us out to abundance.[C]

13 I will enter your house
with burnt offerings;
I will pay you my vows
14 that my lips promised
and my mouth spoke
during my distress.

15 I will offer you fattened sheep
as burnt offerings,
with the fragrant smoke of rams;
I will sacrifice bulls with goats. *Selah*

16 Come and listen, all who fear God,
and I will tell what he has done for me.
17 I cried out to him with my mouth,
and praise was on my tongue.
18 If I had been aware of malice
in my heart,
the Lord would not have listened.
19 However, God has listened;
he has paid attention to the sound
of my prayer.
20 Blessed be God!
He has not turned away my prayer
or turned his faithful love from me.

All Will Praise God

67 For the choir director: with stringed
instruments. A psalm. A song.

1 May God be gracious to us and bless us;
may he make his face shine
upon us *Selah*
2 so that your way may be known on earth,
your salvation among all nations.

3 Let the peoples praise you, God;
let all the peoples praise you.
4 Let the nations rejoice and shout for joy,
for you judge the peoples with fairness
and lead the nations on earth. *Selah*
5 Let the peoples praise you, God,
let all the peoples praise you.

6 The earth has produced its harvest;
God, our God, blesses us.
7 God will bless us,
and all the ends of the earth
will fear him.

God's Majestic Power

68 For the choir director. A psalm of David.
A song.

1 God arises. His enemies scatter,
and those who hate him flee
from his presence.

[A] 66:5 Or *for the descendants of Adam* [B] 66:9 Lit *He sets our soul in life* [C] 66:12 Or *a place of satisfaction*

66:1–4 The whole earth signifies all humankind.
66:5–6 One example of God's "works" (v. 3) is given here: Israel's crossing of the Red Sea when God delivered them from Egypt.
66:7 His eye on the nations means that he pays close attention to what is happening and that he can act at any time.
66:8–9 The image of **feet** not slipping off the path of righteousness is connected with remaining physically and spiritually **alive** (19:10–11; Dt 30:20; Pr 10:30).
66:10 Refining was a process for testing and purification. It can describe the testing of motives and integrity (26:2; Pr 17:3; 27:21).

66:12 Men riding over the **heads** is a description of oppression. **Fire** and **water** are used elsewhere in the context of trials (Is 43:2), but they may also allude to God's pillar of fire and the water of the Red Sea. Since they are transitional from the burdens (Ps 66:11–12) to the blessings (v. 12), it is possible that there is a double meaning here.
66:13–15 These **offerings** represent the fulfillment of **vows** made during a time of prayer. Considering the quantity being offered, it is possible that this represents others who were joining in as a result of God's answer to prayer.
67:3–5 The **praise** of **the nations** accomplishes the goal of bringing the whole world

into the recognition of the Lord's sovereignty (cp. "fear" in v. 7).
67:6 Harvest indicates the exact blessing that is the main point of this psalm. The blessing of one's crops was an outworking of God's covenant with his people as long as they were obedient to him (Dt 28:4).
68:1–2 The image of the Lord as a warrior fighting against the enemies of Israel, who **scatter** at his presence is similar to Ps 18. **Smoke** represents something insignificant that can easily be **blown away**. Melting **wax** recalls the image of Israel's enemies in the conquest of Canaan (Dt 20:8; Jos 2:11; 7:5).

◥ A Biblical View of the Nations

by Jason G. Duesing

The Bible often uses the word *nation* to describe political entities defined by geographic boundaries that have kings or rulers. For example, Deuteronomy 7:1 lists "the Hethites, Girgashites, Amorites, Canaanites, Perizzites, Hivites and Jebusites" as seven nations "more numerous and powerful" than Israel. Additionally, the term *nations* is often used as a collective that describes all groups of people outside of Israel; this large and diverse group is also known by the Latin term *Gentiles* (Ac 10:45). Taking the collective non-Israel use further, *nations* is also used to describe peoples identified by ethnic commonalities such as language or customs. In the covenant God makes with Abraham (Gn 18:18), he indicates "all the nations of the earth" will be blessed through the nation that will descend from Abraham. These people are also described as "families of the earth" (Gn 12:3, KJV) and "all the families of the nations" (Ps 22:27). These phrases reflect a corporate emphasis on non-Israelites in the Bible as opposed to a mere individual focus.

The Nations in the Old Testament

The nations were first created when God broke up a unified and proud human race, all descended from Adam and Eve and then from Noah's family, during their construction of the tower of Babel (Gn 11). Previously having one language, and thus possessing the ability to enforce their will on one another and perfect their rebellion against God, the people were dispersed throughout the earth when God confused their tongues. It was at this time that he gave the people distinct languages so they would be forced to separate from one another and gather together in new communities—each with its own language. Genesis 10 lists Noah's descendants, recognizing the dispersion recorded in the following chapter. It calls the ethnic groups "nations" (10:5).

The nations, both Jewish and Gentile, are central entities in God's plan to display his glory and the work of salvation and judgment. The nation of Israel is called to declare the glory of God among the nations (Ps 96:3), and the psalmist calls on God to "let the nations rejoice and shout for joy" at his work in the world (67:4). God is sovereign over all nations (103:19), and as a part of his covenant plan brought forth from Abraham, God gave Israel to be "a light for the nations" (Is 49:6). God judges all nations (49:24–27) and provides salvation for them (2:2–4).

The Gospel for the Nations

Into the nation of Israel, God sent his Son, Jesus Christ, as Messiah to "suffer and rise from the dead the third day, [that] repentance for forgiveness of sins would be proclaimed in his name to all the nations" (Lk 24:46b–47). After his resurrection and before his ascension to heaven, the Messiah commanded his followers to "make disciples of all nations" (Mt 28:19). This message of salvation first went forth from Jerusalem (Ac 1:8).

It is the commission of Christian churches to continue the task of taking the message of God's plan of salvation (Rm 10:14–15) to those nations who have not heard (15:21). Jesus Christ is the hope of all nations (15:12), and from the nations he will gather his people (Jn 10:16). This message will be proclaimed by his followers "to all nations" until the end of the world (Mt 24:14). At that time the Messiah will return to the earth, and all nations will see God's glory (Is 52:10). They will submit to his rule and reign (Php 2:10–11). People from every nation will worship him (Rv 7:9).

Regardless of ethnicity and culture, there is ultimately no distinction between Jew or Gentile in Christ (Gl 3:28). In him God has made Jew and Gentile "one new man" and "fellow citizens" together (Eph 2:15,19). As the body of Christ is comprised of believers from many nations (Rv 5:9), one's citizenship is permanently in heaven (Php 3:20). This should not discourage temporal patriotism or appropriate stewardship of civic service as earthly citizens of nations; rather, it should serve as a warning against an ethnocentrism that hinders the missionary task. It should show us the folly of racial or ethnic prejudice of any kind. To hold such biases is to position one's self squarely against the revealed will of God, who has created all people and all nations and has offered salvation to everyone.

The story of Jonah illustrates one problem caused when we prioritize one ethnic group

² As smoke is blown away,
   so you blow them away.
   As wax melts before the fire,
   so the wicked are destroyed before God.
³ But the righteous are glad;
   they rejoice before God and celebrate
       with joy.

⁴ Sing to God! Sing praises
       to his name.
   Exalt him who rides on the clouds^A —
   his name is the LORD^B — and celebrate
       before him.
⁵ God in his holy dwelling is
   a father of the fatherless
   and a champion of widows.
⁶ God provides homes for those
       who are deserted.
   He leads out the prisoners
       to prosperity,^C
   but the rebellious live
       in a scorched land.

⁷ God, when you went out
       before your people,
   when you marched
       through the desert,   *Selah*

⁸ the earth trembled and the skies
       poured rain
   before God, the God of Sinai,^D
   before God, the God of Israel.
⁹ You, God, showered abundant rain;
   you revived your inheritance
       when it languished.
¹⁰ Your people settled in it;
   God, you provided for the poor
       by your goodness.

¹¹ The Lord gave the command;
   a great company of women brought
       the good news:
¹² "The kings of the armies flee
       — they flee!"
   She who stays at home divides the spoil.
¹³ While^E you lie among the sheep pens,^F
   the wings of a dove are covered
       with silver,
   and its feathers with glistening gold.
¹⁴ When the Almighty scattered kings
       in the land,
   it snowed on Zalmon.^G

¹⁵ Mount Bashan is
   God's towering mountain;

---

^A **68:4** Or *rides through the desert*   ^B **68:4** Hb *Yah*   ^C **68:6** Or *prisoners with joyous music*; Hb uncertain   ^D **68:8** Or *God, this one of Sinai*   ^E **68:13** Or *If*   ^F **68:13** Or *the campfires*, or *the saddlebags*; Hb obscure   ^G **68:14** Or *Black Mountain*

68:4 That it is **the LORD** who **rides on the clouds** overturns the common mythic imageries of Baal, the storm god of the Canaanites (19:1; 104:3).
68:5–6 Fatherless and **widows** represented the weakest and most vulnerable members of society who were often the most oppressed (94:6). The Lord himself took on the role of their defender (Dt 10:18).

68:7–8 Went out before your people perhaps alludes to the pillars of cloud and fire that led them in the desert (Ex 13:21) or to the ark of the covenant (Nm 10:35; Jos 3:14).
68:13 The image of a **dove** covered with **silver** and **gold** is especially difficult to interpret. Suggestions include prosperity, the glory of the Lord, plunder taken from enemies, and the women of vv. 11–12 dressed in

fine garments that were part of the plunder. Perhaps this last suggestion fits the context best.
68:14 Zalmon as a mountain is only mentioned one other place in the Bible (Jdg 9:48), but it is uncertain how snow relates to it here. It might be a reference to the **scattered kings** being tormented by bad weather from God.

---

over another. When God commanded the Israelite prophet to go to Assyrian Nineveh and "preach against it," Jonah instead boarded a ship and attempted to go to Tarshish (Jnh 1:2–3). So seriously did God take Jonah's disobedience that he sent "a great storm" to threaten the ship and its crew, and he relented only when Jonah was tossed overboard by the reluctant sailors (1:4–15). What was Jonah's motive for shirking God's command? He explains it in a prayer: "I knew that you are a gracious and compassionate God, slow to anger, abounding in faithful love, and one who relents from sending disaster" (4:2). Likely because he despised the military might and strong-arm tendencies of Assyria, Jonah preferred to see God's wrath fall on Nineveh rather than seeing God's mercy extend to its people. This manner of viewing the nations is self-centered and does not reflect awareness

that God is Lord of all peoples and offers them mercy through faith-based repentance.

Allegiance to King Jesus

When one remembers that to God "the nations are like a drop in a bucket" (Is 40:15) and that he has the power both to make them great and to destroy them (Jb 12:23), allegiance to any earthly nation should clearly not supersede allegiance to the Ruler of nations (Ps 22:28). Allegiance to him is our primary and lasting citizenship. Through faith in Christ we are the nation of God, a kingdom drawn from all earthly nations and ethnicities (see Rv 7:9–10). It should be our great joy and high priority to reach both next door and overseas to spread the message of eternal hope in the Son whom God sent to pay our sin debt on the cross and to defeat death in his resurrection.

Mount Bashan is a mountain
of many peaks.
16 Why gaze with envy,
you mountain peaks,
at the mountain God desired
for his abode?
The LORD will dwell there forever!
17 God's chariots are tens of thousands,
thousands and thousands;
the Lord is among them
in the sanctuary^A
as he was at Sinai.
18 You ascended to the heights,
taking away captives;
you received gifts from^B people,
even from the rebellious,
so that the LORD God might dwell there.^C

19 Blessed be the Lord!
Day after day he bears our burdens;
God is our salvation.   Selah
20 Our God is a God of salvation,
and escape from death belongs
to the LORD my Lord.
21 Surely God crushes the heads
of his enemies,
the hairy brow of one who goes on
in his guilty acts.
22 The Lord said, "I will bring them back
from Bashan;
I will bring them back from the depths
of the sea
23 so that your foot may wade^D in blood
and your dogs' tongues may have
their share
from the enemies."
24 People have seen your procession, God,
the procession of my God,
my King, in the sanctuary.
25 Singers lead the way,
with musicians following;
among them are young women
playing tambourines.
26 Bless God in the assemblies;

bless the LORD from the fountain
of Israel.
27 There is Benjamin, the youngest,
leading them,
the rulers of Judah in their assembly,^E
the rulers of Zebulun, the rulers
of Naphtali.

28 Your God has decreed your strength.
Show your strength, God,
you who have acted on our behalf.
29 Because of your temple at Jerusalem,
kings will bring tribute to you.
30 Rebuke the beast in the reeds,
the herd of bulls with the calves
of the peoples.
Trample underfoot those with bars
of silver.^F
Scatter the peoples who take pleasure
in war.
31 Ambassadors will come^G from Egypt;
Cush will stretch out its hands to God.

32 Sing to God, you kingdoms
of the earth;
sing praise to the Lord,   Selah
33 to him who rides in the ancient,
highest heavens.
Look, he thunders
with his powerful voice!
34 Ascribe power to God.
His majesty is over Israel;
his power is among the clouds.
35 God, you are awe-inspiring
in your sanctuaries.
The God of Israel gives power
and strength to his people.
Blessed be God!

A Plea for Rescue

69 For the choir director: according to
"The Lilies." Of David.
1 Save me, God,
for the water has risen to my neck.

---

^A 68:17 Or in holiness, also in v. 24   ^B 68:18 Lit among   ^C 68:18 Or even those rebelling against the LORD God's living there; Hb
obscure   ^D 68:23 LXX, Syr read dip   ^E 68:27 Hb obscure   ^F 68:30 Or peoples, trampling on those who take pleasure in silver,
or peoples, trampling on the bars of silver, or peoples, who trample each other for bars of silver   ^G 68:31 Or They bring red
cloth, or They bring bronze

68:15–16 Mount Bashan probably refers
to the highest mountain in the region
(Mount Hermon). God's choice of the much
smaller Zion made the higher mountains
envious.
68:17 The repetition of **thousands** indicates
that the armies under God's control cannot
be counted.
68:18 This verse is quoted in Eph 4:8. **The
heights** probably refers here to Mount Zion,
where God would **dwell** in triumph. But the
apostle Paul saw a greater ascent in these
words.
68:21 Hairy brow may refer to the ancient
practice of wearing one's hair long as a symbol of power over others during a time of
military campaigns.

68:22–23 Bring them back is probably a
reference to returning with enemies rather than the restoration of Israel, as some
suggest. The enemies are brought to be
executed.
68:27 Benjamin, the **youngest** of Jacob's
sons, is **leading** the procession. One interpretation is that this refers to Benjamin's dominion over the other tribes during Saul's reign,
though it is difficult to say whether this psalm
was written during that time. Another option
is that Benjamin represents Jerusalem since
it was technically in that tribe's territory. The
southern kingdom was often called "Judah and
Benjamin" (2Ch 11:1), and **Zebulun** and **Naphtali** might represent the north (1Ch 12:40). Perhaps the best option is that this procession

mimics an earlier military campaign when
Israel went to war against Sisera (Jdg 5:14).
68:29 Dominion over other peoples was often connected with the bringing of **tribute**
to the dominant power.
68:30 The **beast in the reeds** is perhaps a
reference to Egypt (v. 31; Ezk 32:2), one of the
greatest world powers of that time.
68:32–35 Rides in the . . . heavens along
with the reference to **clouds** recalls the imagery of v. 4.
Ps 69 title On **The Lilies**, see note at Ps
45 title.
69:1–2 The imagery of being trapped in a
well and sinking in **mud** was a common way
to describe life-threatening danger. A **flood**
is also used to represent disaster.

2   I have sunk in deep mud, and there is
        no footing;
    I have come into deep water,
        and a flood sweeps over me.
3   I am weary from my crying;
        my throat is parched.
    My eyes fail, looking for my God.
4   Those who hate me without cause
        are more numerous than the hairs
            of my head;
    my deceitful enemies, who would
            destroy me,
        are powerful.
    Though I did not steal, I must repay.

5   God, you know my foolishness,
        and my guilty acts are not hidden
            from you.
6   Do not let those who put their hope
            in you
        be disgraced because of me,
    Lord GOD of Armies;
    do not let those who seek you
        be humiliated because of me,
    God of Israel.
7   For I have endured insults
        because of you,
    and shame has covered my face.
8   I have become a stranger to my brothers
        and a foreigner to my mother's sons
9   because zeal for your house
        has consumed me,
    and the insults of those who insult you
        have fallen on me.
10 I mourned and fasted,
        but it brought me insults.
11 I wore sackcloth as my clothing,
        and I was a joke to them.
12 Those who sit at the city gate
        talk about me,
    and drunkards make up songs
        about me.
13 But as for me, LORD,
        my prayer to you is for a time of favor.
    In your abundant, faithful love, God,
        answer me with your sure salvation.

14 Rescue me from the miry mud;
        don't let me sink.
    Let me be rescued from those
        who hate me
    and from the deep water.
15 Don't let the floodwaters
        sweep over me
    or the deep swallow me up;
    don't let the Pit close its mouth over me.
16 Answer me, LORD,
        for your faithful love is good.
    In keeping with
        your abundant compassion,
    turn to me.
17 Don't hide your face from your servant,
        for I am in distress.
    Answer me quickly!
18 Come near to me and redeem me;
        ransom me because of my enemies.
19 You know the insults I endure —
        my shame and disgrace.
    You are aware of all my adversaries.
20 Insults have broken my heart,
        and I am in despair.
    I waited for sympathy,
        but there was none;
    for comforters, but found no one.
21 Instead, they gave me gall for my food,
        and for my thirst
    they gave me vinegar to drink.

22 Let their table set before them be
            a snare,
        and let it be a trap for their allies.
23 Let their eyes grow too dim to see,
        and let their hips continually quake.
24 Pour out your rage on them,
        and let your burning anger
            overtake them.
25 Make their fortification desolate;
        may no one live in their tents.
26 For they persecute the one you struck
        and talk about the pain of those
            you wounded.
27 Charge them with crime on top
            of crime;

69:4 This verse is applied to Jesus and quoted in Jn 15:25.

69:6–7 Disgraced and **humiliated because of me** refers not to the psalmist's sins, which were "not hidden" (v. 5), but to his **shame**. The point is that others might lose their faith in the Lord if the suffering of this psalmist is not relieved.

69:8 Stranger refers to an outsider. Alienation by friends and family members was a common experience of those who were suffering.

69:9 It is unclear how the psalmist's **zeal** for God's **house** (the sanctuary or temple) was expressed. Some suggest it refers to the rebuilding of the temple in the postexilic period, but this is not clear. It probably refers to his intense desire to be in the Lord's

presence, especially in the context of worship (27:4; 63:1–2). The **insults** that were intended for the Lord had fallen on the psalmist because of his close connection to God. He was identified with the Lord, and therefore those who were against the Lord were also against him. In the NT, both halves of this verse are applied to Jesus and his humiliation (Jn 2:17; Rm 15:3).

69:13 But as for me contrasts those who insult and make up songs about the psalmist with the psalmist's own humble prayers to God.

69:14–15 The deep and **the Pit** are parallel and represent death, which is personified as something that swallows its victims.

69:17–18 For God to **hide** his **face** implies rejection.

69:21 Gall (essentially poison) and **vinegar** were by no means suitable for quenching **thirst**. These terms are used figuratively here, but in Jesus's suffering they were literal (Mt 27:34,48; Jn 19:28–29).

69:22 The **table set before them** may refer to sacrificial meals rather than ordinary feasts. If that is the case, eating in the Lord's presence would be a "crime" (v. 27), an affront to him, and a practice worthy of his wrath (vv. 23–25).

69:23–25 These requests are imprecations, calling down God's judgment on one's enemies. The request that their **tents** be made empty is a request that the enemies be annihilated.

69:27 Crime implies liability for punishment. The psalmist's enemies were deserving of God's punishment.

do not let them share
in your righteousness.
28 Let them be erased from the book
of life
and not be recorded with the righteous.

29 But as for me — poor and in pain —
let your salvation protect me, God.
30 I will praise God's name with song
and exalt him with thanksgiving.
31 That will please the LORD more than
an ox,
more than a bull with horns and hooves.
32 The humble will see it and rejoice.
You who seek God, take heart!
33 For the LORD listens to the needy
and does not despise
his own who are prisoners.

34 Let heaven and earth praise him,
the seas and everything that moves
in them,
35 for God will save Zion
and build up^A the cities of Judah.
They will live there and possess it.
36 The descendants of his servants
will inherit it,
and those who love his name will live
in it.

A Call for Deliverance

70 For the choir director. Of David. To bring
remembrance.
1 God, hurry to rescue me.
LORD, hurry to help me!

2 Let those who seek to kill me
be disgraced and confounded;
let those who wish me harm
be turned back and humiliated.
3 Let those who say, "Aha, aha!"
retreat because of their shame.

4 Let all who seek you rejoice and be glad
in you;
let those who love your salvation
continually say, "God is great!"
5 I am oppressed and needy;
hurry to me, God.

You are my help and my deliverer;
LORD, do not delay.

God's Help in Old Age

71 LORD, I seek refuge in you;
let me never be disgraced.
2 In your justice, rescue and deliver me;
listen closely to me and save me.
3 Be a rock of refuge for me,
where I can always go.
Give the command to save me,
for you are my rock and fortress.
4 Deliver me, my God, from the power
of the wicked,
from the grasp of the unjust
and oppressive.
5 For you are my hope, Lord GOD,
my confidence from my youth.
6 I have leaned on you from birth;
you took me from my mother's womb.
My praise is always about you.
7 I am like a miraculous sign to many,
and you are my strong refuge.
8 My mouth is full of praise
and honor to you all day long.

9 Don't discard me in my old age.
As my strength fails,
do not abandon me.
10 For my enemies talk about me,
and those who spy on me plot together,
11 saying, "God has abandoned him;
chase him and catch him,
for there is no one to rescue him."
12 God, do not be far from me;
my God, hurry to help me.
13 May my adversaries be disgraced
and destroyed;
may those who intend to harm me
be covered with disgrace
and humiliation.
14 But I will hope continually
and will praise you more and more.
15 My mouth will tell
about your righteousness
and your salvation all day long,
though I cannot sum them up.
16 I come because of the mighty acts
of the Lord GOD;

---

^69:35 Or *and rebuild*

69:28 The **book of life** should be distinguished from the book of remembrance with the prayers of those who suffer and the book with a list of everyone's deeds. It is probably the book where the names of the righteous are listed (Ex 32:32; Dn 12:1; Rv 3:5; 13:8; 17:8; 20:12,15; 21:27). **69:31** The **horns** indicate a **bull** in its prime, and the cloven **hooves** designate a ceremonially acceptable animal. **69:34–35** Creation is personified as a witness of God's workings with his people. Here it voices its **praise** of God's saving work among them.

Ps 70 title On **remembrance**, see note at Ps 38 title. **70:1–5** See notes at 40:14–15,16–17; these verses are the same. **71:1–4 Rock . . . refuge**, and **fortress** convey the idea of the Lord's protection. The requests for **rescue** seem to be not from immediate but rather from prospective danger. **71:5–6** The combination of **youth . . . birth**, and **mother's womb** shows that the psalmist had been loyal to the Lord throughout his life. **71:7–8 Miraculous sign** can refer to an extraordinary display of divine power to terrify

enemies (Ex 7:3; 11:9; Dt 6:22) or an extraordinary sign that points to a future event (1Kg 13:3,5; Is 20:3). Here, the psalmist apparently displays evidence of suffering that **many** observers consider some kind of warning. **71:9 Discard** is a common word for "throw" or "cast." In this context it refers to God abandoning the psalmist (51:11), perhaps because of his loss of **strength**. **71:14–16 Righteousness** and **salvation** are often paired in testimonies of God's **mighty acts** toward his people (40:10; 51:14). Public praise is the responsibility of a person who experiences deliverance by the Lord.

I will proclaim your righteousness,
yours alone.

17 God, you have taught me
from my youth,
and I still proclaim your
wondrous works.
18 Even while I am old and gray,
God, do not abandon me,
while I proclaim your power
to another generation,
your strength to all who are to come.
19 Your righteousness reaches
the heights, God,
you who have done great things;
God, who is like you?
20 You caused me to experience
many troubles and misfortunes,
but you will revive me again.
You will bring me up again,
even from the depths of the earth.
21 You will increase my honor
and comfort me once again.
22 Therefore, I will praise you with a harp
for your faithfulness, my God;
I will sing to you with a lyre,
Holy One of Israel.
23 My lips will shout for joy
when I sing praise to you
because you have redeemed me.
24 Therefore, my tongue will proclaim
your righteousness all day long,
for those who intend to harm me
will be disgraced and confounded.

A Prayer for the King

72 Of Solomon.
God, give your justice to the king
and your righteousness
to the king's son.
2 He will judge your people
with righteousness
and your afflicted ones with justice.
3 May the mountains bring well-being^A
to the people
and the hills, righteousness.
4 May he vindicate the afflicted
among the people,

help the poor,
and crush the oppressor.
5 May they fear you^B while the
sun endures
and as long as the moon,
throughout all generations.
6 May the king be like rain that falls
on the cut grass,
like spring showers that water
the earth.
7 May the righteous^C flourish in his days
and well-being abound
until the moon is no more.
8 May he rule from sea to sea
and from the Euphrates
to the ends of the earth.
9 May desert tribes kneel before him
and his enemies lick the dust.
10 May the kings of Tarshish
and the coasts and islands bring tribute,
the kings of Sheba and Seba offer gifts.
11 Let all kings bow in homage to him,
all nations serve him.
12 For he will rescue the poor who cry out
and the afflicted who have no helper.
13 He will have pity on the poor
and helpless
and save the lives of the poor.
14 He will redeem them from oppression
and violence,
for their lives are^D precious^E in his sight.
15 May he live long!
May gold from Sheba be given to him.
May prayer be offered
for him continually,
and may he be blessed all day long.
16 May there be plenty of grain in the land;
may it wave on the tops
of the mountains.
May its crops be like Lebanon.
May people flourish in the cities
like the grass of the field.
17 May his name endure forever;
as long as the sun shines,

---

^A72:3 Or peace, also in v. 7 ^B72:5 LXX reads May he continue ^C72:7 Some Hb mss, LXX, Syr, Jer read May righteousness
^D72:14 Lit their blood is ^E72:14 Or valuable

71:17–18 The instruction of the Lord in the psalmist's life is passed on to other generations. This was part of his vow to the Lord for delivering him from suffering.
71:19 Reaches the heights means "goes beyond comprehension" (36:5; 57:10).
71:20–21 Depths of the earth means the psalmist was brought up from the very edge of death.
71:22–24 Holy One of Israel is a favorite title for the Lord in the book of Isaiah. Here it links the psalmist who is suffering with the nation of Israel and with the Lord's covenant promises.

Ps 72 title Of Solomon probably functions similarly to "of David." It could mean "authored by," "written for," or even "in the style of."
72:1–4 Justice and **righteousness** are the dominant terms in these verses. They refer to the king's role of dispensing God's justice.
72:5 While the sun endures refers to a long reign or to a long dynasty, similar to the request that the king have a long life.
72:6–7 Rain symbolizes blessing (68:9) and is used here to request that the king's reign be blessed with **well-being**.
72:8–11 This is a list of far distant places. **Tarshish** represents Phoenicia and **Sheba**

represents Arabia. **Seba** could be somewhere in Africa; Josephus identified it with Ethiopia. The summary statement in v. 11 makes the point that these places represent **all kings** and **all nations**.
72:12–14 The poor . . . helpless, and **afflicted** are the downtrodden in society. If a king rendered justice to the poor, his reign would be particularly blessed (Pr 29:14).
72:17–19 Name represents reputation and fame. It is significant that the name of the king and the name of the Lord are intertwined in praise. **Amen and amen** probably form the end of a doxology used to close Book 2 of the Psalms (see note at 41:13).

may his fame increase.
May all nations be blessed by him
and call him blessed.

¹⁸ Blessed be the LORD God, the God
of Israel,
who alone does wonders.
¹⁹ Blessed be his glorious name forever;
the whole earth is filled with his glory.
Amen and amen.
²⁰ The prayers of David son of Jesse
are concluded.

BOOK III (Psalms 73–89)

God's Ways Vindicated

73 A psalm of Asaph.
God is indeed good to Israel,
to the pure in heart.
² But as for me, my feet almost slipped;
my steps nearly went astray.
³ For I envied the arrogant;
I saw the prosperity of the wicked.
⁴ They have an easy time until they die,ᴬ
and their bodies are well fed.ᴮ
⁵ They are not in trouble like others;
they are not afflicted like most people.
⁶ Therefore, pride is their necklace,
and violence covers them
like a garment.
⁷ Their eyes bulge out from fatness;
the imaginations of their hearts
run wild.
⁸ They mock, and they speak maliciously;
they arrogantly threaten oppression.
⁹ They set their mouths against heaven,
and their tongues strut across the earth.
¹⁰ Therefore his people turn to themᶜ
and drink in their overflowing words.ᴰ

¹¹ The wicked say, "How can God know?
Does the Most High know everything?"
¹² Look at them — the wicked!
They are always at ease,
and they increase their wealth.
¹³ Did I purify my heart
and wash my hands in innocence
for nothing?
¹⁴ For I am afflicted all day long
and punished every morning.
¹⁵ If I had decided to say
these things aloud,
I would have betrayed your people.ᴱ
¹⁶ When I tried to understand all this,
it seemed hopelessᶠ
¹⁷ until I entered God's sanctuary.
Then I understood their destiny.
¹⁸ Indeed, you put them
in slippery places;
you make them fall into ruin.
¹⁹ How suddenly they become
a desolation!
They come to an end, swept away
by terrors.
²⁰ Like one waking from a dream,
Lord, when arising, you will despise
their image.
²¹ When I became embittered
and my innermost beingᴳ was wounded,
²² I was stupid and didn't understand;
I was an unthinking animal toward you.
²³ Yet I am always with you;
you hold my right hand.
²⁴ You guide me with your counsel,
and afterward you will take me up
in glory.ᴴ
²⁵ Who do I have in heaven but you?
And I desire nothing on earth but you.

ᴬ73:4 Lit *For there are no pangs to their death* ᴮ73:4 Lit *fat* ᶜ73:10 Lit *turn here* ᴰ73:10 Lit *and waters of fullness are drained by them* ᴱ73:15 Lit *betrayed the generation of your sons* ᶠ73:16 Lit *it was trouble in my eyes* ᴳ73:21 Lit *my kidneys* ᴴ73:24 Or *will receive me with honor*

72:20 These comments were probably added as part of the close of Book 2. This does not mean that everything preceding the comment was from David. It seems to separate the previous psalms from the grouping of Asaph's psalms beginning with Ps 73.
Ps 73 title On **Asaph**, see note at Ps 50 title.
73:4 Easy time and **well fed** refer to prosperity (v. 3). "Well fed" is literally "fat bellies," evidence of having more than a person needs.
73:5 Like most people is an assessment from observation. From the psalmist's own experience, the degree of wickedness and prosperity seem to go together.
73:6 A **necklace** signified status and prominence (Dn 5:29); the wicked wore their **pride** as a status symbol. They also did not bother to hide their malicious **violence**.
73:7 Eyes and **imaginations** are parallel, representing the desires of the wicked in what they saw and thought. "Imagination" (Hb *maskiyyoth*) is also used of idols (Nm

33:52; Ezk 8:12). It has the connotation of "idols of the heart."
73:8 The word for **oppression** also describes fraud and extortion.
73:9 Heaven is a substitute for God himself, so the mocking of the wicked is against God. The image of tongues strutting **across the earth** further emphasizes their brash arrogance.
73:10 His people could refer to those who were connected with these wicked people, but the shift from plural to singular is awkward. If "heaven" in v. 9 represents God, then it is the nearest singular antecedent. In this case the speech of the wicked even leads God's people astray, something this psalmist would not do with his words (v. 15).
73:12 Always at ease means that the wicked did not seem to experience problems (v. 4).
73:13 Washing **hands** was part of an oath of **innocence**.
73:17 The phrase **until I entered . . . then I understood** has caused much speculation

by scholars. Exactly what happened in the **sanctuary**? Suggestions include: the psalmist received an oracle from God, witnessed a theophany, or engaged in ritual acts. It is perhaps best to leave it unanswered and realize the main issue is that the Lord's presence in the sanctuary enlightened the psalmist. This is what became the psalmist's hope later in v. 28 and seems to be reflective of the principle that nearness to the Lord (close fellowship with him) provides a change of perspective.
73:20 The phrase **waking from a dream** could refer to the psalmist's own state before his change of perspective, but it probably refers to God's waking (**arising**, meaning "to act.")
73:23 Holding someone's **right hand** refers to protection (Ps 63:8; Is 41:10,13; 42:6; Jr 31:32).
73:24 Some argue that **take me up in glory** refers to being honored (similar to the image of the "right hand" in v. 23). However, there is no good reason to doubt that this could refer to life after death.

26 My flesh and my heart may fail,
but God is the strength^A of my heart,
my portion forever.

27 Those far from you
will certainly perish;
you destroy all who are
unfaithful to you.

28 But as for me, God's presence is
my good.
I have made the Lord GOD my refuge,
so I can tell about all you do.

Prayer for Israel

74 *A Maskil of Asaph.*
Why have you
rejected us forever, God?
Why does your anger burn
against the sheep of your pasture?

2 Remember your congregation,
which you purchased long ago
and redeemed as the tribe
for your own possession.
Remember Mount Zion
where you dwell.

3 Make your way^B to the perpetual ruins,
to all that the enemy has destroyed
in the sanctuary.

4 Your adversaries roared
in the meeting place
where you met with us.^C
They set up their emblems as signs.

5 It was like men in a thicket of trees,
wielding axes,

6 then smashing all the carvings
with hatchets and picks.

7 They set your sanctuary on fire;
they utterly^D desecrated
the dwelling place of your name.

8 They said in their hearts,
"Let's oppress them relentlessly."

They burned every place
throughout the land
where God met with us.^E

9 There are no signs for us to see.
There is no longer a prophet.
And none of us knows how long
this will last.

10 God, how long will the enemy mock?
Will the foe insult your name forever?

11 Why do you hold back your hand?
Stretch out^F your right hand
and destroy them!

12 God my King is from ancient times,
performing saving acts on the earth.

13 You divided the sea
with your strength;
you smashed the heads
of the sea monsters in the water;

14 you crushed the heads of Leviathan;
you fed him to the creatures
of the desert.

15 You opened up springs and streams;
you dried up ever-flowing rivers.

16 The day is yours, also the night;
you established the moon and the sun.

17 You set all the boundaries of the earth;
you made summer and winter.

18 Remember this: the enemy has mocked
the LORD,
and a foolish people has insulted
your name.

19 Do not give to beasts the life
of your dove;^G
do not forget the lives
of your poor people forever.

20 Consider the covenant,
for the dark places of the land
are full of violence.

---

^A 73:26 Lit *rock*   ^B 74:3 Lit *Lift up your steps*   ^C 74:4 Lit *in your meeting place*   ^D 74:7 Lit *they to the ground*   ^E 74:8 Lit *every meeting place of God in the land*   ^F 74:11 Lit *From your bosom*   ^G 74:19 One Hb ms, LXX, Syr read *life that praises you*

73:26 Flesh and **heart** probably refer to earthly existence, and they reinforce the idea of life after death from v. 24. A **portion** is another way of describing a person's inheritance.

Ps 74 title On **Asaph**, see note at Ps 50 title.

74:3 Perpetual ruins is used elsewhere to describe the annihilation of an enemy (9:6).

74:4 Roared depicts enemies as wild animals who have entered the sanctuary (22:13). **Emblems** are likely related to banners that were used in military campaigns to identify the armies.

74:5–6 The **men** with **axes** portray highly energized destructive activity without thought or concern.

74:8 The allusion to multiple meeting places in **the land** probably does not refer to high places, which had been abolished by Josiah. Rather, it probably includes the various locations in history where the sanctuary had been located—such as Shiloh (Jos 18:1; 1Sm 1:3), Mizpah (Jdg 20:1), Bethel (Gn 12:8; 1Sm 7:16), Gilgal (1Sm 10:8), and now Jerusalem.

74:9 The **signs** the people were apparently looking for were those that would answer their "why" (vv. 1,11) and "how long" (v. 10) questions.

74:11 The **right hand** was the place of the Lord's power.

74:13 Sea monsters (Hb *tanninim*) is used elsewhere for serpents (91:13; Ex 7:10,12; Dt 32:33). It probably refers to the great creatures of the sea that were untamable, but there could also be some connection to Canaanite beliefs. Baal was supposed to have defeated the seas, represented by seven-headed sea monsters; but in response to that mythology, Yahweh is depicted as the one who defeats these creatures by his power.

74:14 Leviathan also appears in other biblical texts (104:26; Jb 3:8; 41; Is 27:1). He represents the most fierce and powerful sea creature. Whether this creature can be linked to a specific animal in the known world is uncertain, although suggestions range from a crocodile to a dinosaur. There certainly is a connection in Canaanite mythology that links this creature with chaos. Therefore, God defeated chaos and **fed him to the creatures of the desert**, which could mean wild beasts.

74:15 Drying up **ever-flowing rivers** could be a reference to God's saving acts at the Red Sea (Ex 14:21–22) or the Jordan River (Jos 3:15–17), the latter of which makes more sense for "rivers." Some have also suggested mythological imagery here, since Baal was supposed to have defeated the rivers by drying them up.

74:17 The **boundaries of the earth** could refer to the boundary between land and sea established at creation (Gn 1:9–10), but it is more likely the regularity of the seasons (Gn 1:14) since it is parallel to **summer and winter**.

74:19 Dove was a term of affection (Sg 6:9). It is used as a designation for Israel here.

74:20 Dark places of the land may be metaphorical for evil, or it could refer to places where enemies hid to attack the unsuspecting.

21 Do not let the oppressed turn away
      in shame;
   let the poor and needy
      praise your name.
22 Rise up, God, champion your cause!
   Remember the insults
      that fools bring against you all day long.
23 Do not forget the clamor
      of your adversaries,
   the tumult of your opponents
      that goes up constantly.

God Judges the Wicked

75 *For the choir director: "Do Not Destroy."*
   A psalm of Asaph. A song.

1 We give thanks to you, God;
   we give thanks to you, for your name
      is near.
   People tell about your wondrous works.

2 "When I choose a time,
   I will judge fairly.
3 When the earth and all
      its inhabitants shake,
   I am the one who steadies its pillars. *Selah*

4 I say to the boastful, 'Do not boast,'
   and to the wicked, 'Do not lift up
      your horn.
5 Do not lift up your horn against heaven[A]
   or speak arrogantly.' "

6 Exaltation does not come
   from the east, the west, or the desert,
7 for God is the Judge:
   He brings down one and exalts another.
8 For there is a cup in the Lord's hand,
   full of wine blended with spices,
      and he pours from it.
   All the wicked of the earth will drink,
   draining it to the dregs.

9 As for me, I will tell about him forever;
   I will sing praise to the God of Jacob.

10 "I will cut off all the horns
      of the wicked,

but the horns of the righteous will be
   lifted up."

God, the Powerful Judge

76 *For the choir director: with stringed*
   instruments. A psalm of Asaph. A song.

1 God is known in Judah;
   his name is great in Israel.
2 His tent is in Salem,
   his dwelling place in Zion.
3 There he shatters the bow's
      flaming arrows,
   the shield, the sword,
      and the weapons of war. *Selah*

4 You are resplendent and majestic
   coming down from the mountains
      of prey.
5 The brave-hearted
      have been plundered;
   they have slipped
      into their final sleep.
   None of the warriors was able to lift
      a hand.
6 At your rebuke, God of Jacob,
   both chariot and horse lay still.

7 And you — you are to be feared.[B]
   When you are angry,
   who can stand before you?
8 From heaven
      you pronounced judgment.
   The earth feared and grew quiet
9 when God rose up to judge
   and to save all the lowly
      of the earth. *Selah*
10 Even human wrath will praise you;
   you will clothe yourself
   with the wrath that remains.[C]

11 Make and keep your vows
      to the Lord your God;
   let all who are around him
      bring tribute
   to the awe-inspiring one.[D]
12 He humbles the spirit of leaders;
   he is feared by the kings of the earth.

[A]75:5 Lit *horn to the height*   [B]76:7 Or *are awe-inspiring*   [C]76:10 Hb obscure   [D]76:11 Or *tribute with awe*

74:21 The words **poor** and **needy** often represent those who are faithful to the Lord. **74:22 Rise up** is used to call God to act. **Ps 75 title** On **Do Not Destroy**, see note at Ps 57 title. On **Asaph**, see note at Ps 50 title. **75:1 Wondrous works** can refer either to God's creative acts or to his saving acts on behalf of his people. **75:2 Choose a time** refers to a "set" or "appointed" time, which in this case is God's time for judging. **75:3** "Shaking" probably refers to earthquakes that were regular occurrences in and around Israel. **75:4 Horn** was a symbol of power, often used in military contexts. Lifting up a horn

is parallel to boasting, probably about one's might. **75:8 Cup** depicts God's judgment (60:3; Is 51:17; Jr 25:15,28; 49:12; 51:7). Since **all the wicked of the earth** are referred to, God's judgment will fall on all humanity. **Ps 76 title** On **Asaph**, see note at Ps 50 title. **76:2 Salem** is a shortened form of Jerusalem. **Zion** also refers to Jerusalem. **His tent** should perhaps be rendered "shelter" in this context. The Hebrew term *sukkah* refers to a hut built from intertwined tree branches. "Shelter" nicely parallels a **dwelling place** protected by thick vegetation. "Shelter" and "dwelling place" figuratively describe the Lord's presence in the temple.

76:3 Flaming arrows, a metaphor for strength, can also mean "lightning bolts." **76:4** The psalmist addressed God directly, using the second person **you**. By calling God **resplendent**, he equated God's presence to "light." **76:6 Jacob** refers to the twelve tribes descended from the patriarch. The **chariot and horse** alludes to the exodus event, a recurrent theme in the psalms of Asaph (Ex 15:1,4). **76:8–9** The Hebrew term *shaqat* never denotes a silence or quietness derived from terror. So this is a reverent fear that stems from a sense of security and comfort as a result of God's correction of injustice and oppression.

Confidence in a Time of Crisis

77 *For the choir director: according to Jeduthun. Of Asaph. A psalm.*

1 I cry aloud to God,
   aloud to God, and he will hear me.
2 I sought the Lord in my day of trouble.
   My hands were continually lifted up
      all night long;
   I refused to be comforted.
3 I think of God; I groan;
   I meditate; my spirit
      becomes weak.   *Selah*

4 You have kept me from closing my eyes;
   I am troubled and cannot speak.
5 I consider days of old,
   years long past.
6 At night I remember my music;
   I meditate in my heart,
      and my spirit ponders.

7 "Will the Lord reject forever
   and never again show favor?
8 Has his faithful love ceased forever?
   Is his promise at an end
      for all generations?
9 Has God forgotten to be gracious?
   Has he in anger
      withheld his compassion?"   *Selah*

10 So I say, "I am grieved
   that the right hand of the Most High
      has changed."ᴬ
11 I will remember the LORD's works;
   yes, I will remember
      your ancient wonders.
12 I will reflect on all you have done
   and meditate on your actions.

13 God, your way is holy.
   What god is great like God?
14 You are the God who works wonders;
   you revealed your strength
      among the peoples.
15 With power you redeemed your people,

the descendants
   of Jacob and Joseph.   *Selah*

16 The water saw you, God.
   The water saw you; it trembled.
   Even the depths shook.
17 The clouds poured down water.
   The storm clouds thundered;
   your arrows flashed back and forth.
18 The sound of your thunder was
      in the whirlwind;
   lightning lit up the world.
   The earth shook and quaked.
19 Your way went through the sea
   and your path through the vast water,
   but your footprints were unseen.
20 You led your people like a flock
   by the hand of Moses and Aaron.

Lessons from Israel's Past

78 *A Maskil of Asaph.*
   My people, hear my instruction;
   listen to the words from my mouth.
2 I will declare wise sayings;
   I will speak mysteries from the past—
3 things we have heard and known
   and that our ancestors
      have passed down to us.
4 We will not hide them
      from their children,
   but will tell a future generation
   the praiseworthy acts of the LORD,
   his might, and the wondrous works
   he has performed.
5 He established a testimony in Jacob
   and set up a law in Israel,
   which he commanded our ancestors
   to teach to their children
6 so that a future generation—
   children yet to be born—might know.
   They were to rise and tell their children
7 so that they might put their confidence
      in God
   and not forget God's works,
   but keep his commands.

ᴬ**77:10** Hb obscure

Ps 77 title On **Jeduthun**, see note at Ps 39 title. On **Asaph**, see note at Ps 50 title.
77:1–3 This psalm begins with a lament, an intense longing to hear from God.
77:7 Typical of Asaph psalms (74:1–2; 80:3–4; 83:1; 88:14), the psalmist characterized God's slow response as rejection and asked how long before the restoration of the Lord's **favor**.
77:8 Faithful love (Hb *chesed*) could be rendered as "covenant love" or "covenant loyalty" in this context. The psalmist hoped an appeal to the Lord's faithful love would persuade God to respond to the crisis.
77:9 Compassion derives from the Hebrew root meaning "womb," suggesting a filial relationship that parallels faithful love in v. 8. A literal rendering of the Hebrew text reads, "has he [God] closed up his womb in anger," a

figurative expression denoting the absence of parental love and concern for offspring.
77:11–12 Your ancient wonders probably refers to the exodus.
77:13 A hymn (vv. 13–20) immediately follows the end of the lament. The rhetorical question **What god is great like God?** often introduces incomparability statements in hymns emphasizing the Lord's sovereignty (18:31; Ex 15:11; 2Sm 22:32; Is 40:18), omnipotence (Ex 15:11; Dt 3:24; Ps 71:19; 89:8), omniscience (Is 44:7), stature (Ps 113:5; Is 40:25), and capacity for forgiveness (Mc 7:18).
77:16–18 Using divine warrior imagery, the psalmist declared that cosmic upheaval accompanies God's presence (18:7–15; 114:3–5; Ex 19:16–19), and creation exults in worship before him. The Lord's **arrows** (v. 17) refer to lightning bolts (29:7; 76:3).

77:20 The psalms of Asaph often use shepherd and **flock** imagery to emphasize the Lord's compassion and care.
Ps 78 title On **Maskil**, see note at Ps 32 title. On **Asaph**, see note at Ps 50 title.
78:2 The psalmist couched the epic psalm in terms of a riddle or paradox, describing Israel's inability to trust God despite God's repeated acts of faithfulness.
78:3–4 These verses give the purpose of the psalm. All the oral traditions of God's wonderful works will be rehearsed in each generation.
78:6–7 Reciting Israel's early history to future generations assures the perpetuation of the account. This would connect generations far removed from the original event to the promises and instructions governing Israel's relationship to God.

8 Then they would not be
   like their ancestors,
 a stubborn and rebellious generation,
 a generation whose heart was not loyal
 and whose spirit was not faithful
    to God.

9 The Ephraimite archers turned back
   on the day of battle.
10 They did not keep God's covenant
   and refused to live by his law.
11 They forgot what he had done,
   the wondrous works
   he had shown them.
12 He worked wonders in the sight of
    their ancestors
 in the land of Egypt, the territory
   of Zoan.
13 He split the sea
   and brought them across;
 the water stood firm like a wall.
14 He led them with a cloud by day
 and with a fiery light
   throughout the night.
15 He split rocks in the wilderness
 and gave them drink as abundant
   as the depths.
16 He brought streams out of the stone
 and made water flow down like rivers.

17 But they continued to sin against him,
 rebelling in the desert
   against the Most High.
18 They deliberately^A tested God,
 demanding the food they craved.
19 They spoke against God, saying,
 "Is God able to provide food
   in the wilderness?
20 Look! He struck the rock and water
   gushed out;
 torrents overflowed.
 But can he also provide bread
 or furnish meat for his people?"
21 Therefore, the Lord heard
   and became furious;
 then fire broke out against Jacob,
 and anger flared up against Israel
22 because they did not believe God
 or rely on his salvation.
23 He gave a command to the clouds above
 and opened the doors of heaven.
24 He rained manna for them to eat;

 he gave them grain from heaven.
25 People^B ate the bread of angels.^C
 He sent them an abundant supply
   of food.
26 He made the east wind blow in the skies
 and drove the south wind by his might.
27 He rained meat on them like dust,
 and winged birds like the sand
   of the seas.
28 He made them fall in the camp,
 all around the tents.
29 The people ate and were
   completely satisfied,
 for he gave them what they craved.
30 Before they had turned from
   what they craved,
 while the food was still in their mouths,
31 God's anger flared up against them,
 and he killed some of their best men.
 He struck down Israel's fit young men.

32 Despite all this, they kept sinning
 and did not believe
   his wondrous works.
33 He made their days end in futility,
 their years in sudden disaster.
34 When he killed some of them,
 the rest began to seek him;
 they repented and searched for God.
35 They remembered that God was
   their rock,
 the Most High God, their Redeemer.
36 But they deceived him
   with their mouths,
 they lied to him with their tongues,
37 their hearts were insincere toward him,
 and they were unfaithful
   to his covenant.
38 Yet he was compassionate;
 he atoned for their iniquity
 and did not destroy them.
 He often turned his anger aside
 and did not unleash^D all his wrath.
39 He remembered that they were
   only flesh,
 a wind that passes and does not return.
40 How often they rebelled against him
 in the wilderness
 and grieved him in the desert.
41 They constantly tested God
 and provoked the Holy One of Israel.

^A78:18 Lit in their heart   ^B78:25 Lit Man   ^C78:25 Lit mighty ones   ^D78:38 Or stir up

78:8 The goal was to educate the children so they did not become another **stubborn and rebellious generation** (66:7; Ex 17:1–7; Is 1:23; 30:1; 65:2).
78:9–10 The sons of Ephraim were well known for their military role as **archers** (Zch 9:13). They broke the **covenant** during the mutiny of the northern tribes.
78:12 **Zoan** was a major Egyptian city that later became its capital (Is 19:11,13; 30:4; Ezk 30:14).

78:13 This verse describes the crossing of the Red Sea (Ex 14:21–22). The waters **stood firm like a wall** (lit "like a heap," 33:7; Ex 15:8; Jos 3:13,16).
78:14 **Cloud** and **light** refer to the pillars of cloud and fire representing the Lord's presence (Ex 14:19–20; 40:36–38).
78:15–16 **Split rocks** and **stone** describe water from the rock at Horeb and Meribah (Ex 17:1–7; Nm 20:7–11).

78:23–25 **Manna** was the basic food that sustained Israel during the wilderness wanderings (Ex 16:4–5).
78:26–31 When Israel murmured against God and desired **meat**, the Lord sent quail (**winged birds**; Nm 11:18–20,31–35). Then God became angry that they had complained about their "hardship" (Nm 11:1) and punished them with a plague.

⁴² They did not remember
  his power shown
    on the day he redeemed them
      from the foe,
⁴³ when he performed
  his miraculous signs in Egypt
    and his wonders in the territory of Zoan.
⁴⁴ He turned their rivers into blood,
  and they could not drink
    from their streams.
⁴⁵ He sent among them swarms of flies,
  which fed on them,
  and frogs, which devastated them.
⁴⁶ He gave their crops to the caterpillar
  and the fruit of their labor to the locust.
⁴⁷ He killed their vines with hail
  and their sycamore fig trees
    with a flood.
⁴⁸ He handed over their livestock to hail
  and their cattle to lightning bolts.
⁴⁹ He sent his burning anger against them:
  fury, indignation, and calamity —
    a band of deadly messengers.ᴬ
⁵⁰ He cleared a path for his anger.
  He did not spare them from death
  but delivered their lives to the plague.
⁵¹ He struck all the firstborn in Egypt,
  the first progeny of the tents of Ham.
⁵² He led his people out like sheep
  and guided them like a flock
    in the wilderness.
⁵³ He led them safely,
  and they were not afraid;
  but the sea covered their enemies.
⁵⁴ He brought them to his holy territory,
  to the mountain
    his right hand acquired.
⁵⁵ He drove out nations before them.
  He apportioned their inheritance by lot
  and settled the tribes of Israel
    in their tents.

⁵⁶ But they rebelliously tested
  the Most High God,
  for they did not keep his decrees.
⁵⁷ They treacherously turned away
  like their ancestors;
  they became warped like a faulty bow.
⁵⁸ They enraged him with their high places
  and provoked his jealousy
    with their carved images.

⁵⁹ God heard and became furious;
  he completely rejected Israel.
⁶⁰ He abandoned the tabernacle at Shiloh,
  the tent where he resided
    among mankind.
⁶¹ He gave up his strength to captivity
  and his splendor to the hand of a foe.
⁶² He surrendered his people to the sword
  because he was enraged with his heritage.
⁶³ Fire consumed his chosen young men,
  and his young women
    had no wedding songs.ᴮ
⁶⁴ His priests fell by the sword,
  and the widows could not lament.

⁶⁵ The Lord awoke as if from sleep,
  like a warrior from the effects of wine.
⁶⁶ He beat back his foes;
  he gave them lasting disgrace.
⁶⁷ He rejected the tent of Joseph
  and did not choose the tribe of Ephraim.
⁶⁸ He chose instead the tribe of Judah,
  Mount Zion, which he loved.
⁶⁹ He built his sanctuary like the heights,
  like the earth that
    he established forever.
⁷⁰ He chose David his servant
  and took him from the sheep pens;
⁷¹ he brought him from tending ewes
  to be shepherd over his people Jacob —
    over Israel, his inheritance.
⁷² He shepherded them with a pure heart
  and guided them with his skillful hands.

Faith amid Confusion

79 *A psalm of Asaph.*
  God, the nations have invaded
    your inheritance,
  desecrated your holy temple,
  and turned Jerusalem into ruins.
² They gave the corpses of your servants
  to the birds of the sky for food,
  the flesh of your faithful ones
  to the beasts of the earth.
³ They poured out their blood
  like water all around Jerusalem,
  and there was no one to bury them.
⁴ We have become an object of reproach
  to our neighbors,
  a source of mockery and ridicule
  to those around us.

ᴬ**78:49** Or *angels*   ᴮ**78:63** Lit *virgins were not praised*

78:44-51 The plagues described in these verses do not follow the sequence in Exodus (Ex 7–11). Egypt suffered **rivers** of **blood** (Ex 7:14–24), **flies** (Ex 8:20–32), **locust** (Ex 10:1–15), **hail** (Ex 9:13–26), and the death of the **firstborn** (Ex 11:1–11). The **tents of Ham** is a name for Egypt (105:23,27; Gn 10:6). **78:54** This **mountain** cannot be Zion since the events at the sanctuary at Shiloh preceded Zion chronologically (v. 60).

78:55 The conquest and settlement of Canaan is recorded in Jos 6–22. **78:56–57** A warped bow is something one runs to in trust but finds is useless in an hour of need. It pictures disloyalty. **78:58** The **high places** were separate sanctuaries and altars constructed for the worship of pagan gods. **78:61 His strength to captivity** is a reference to the capture of the ark by the Philistines (1Sm 4–6).

Ps 79 title On **Asaph**, see note at Ps 50 title. **79:1** The nations **invaded** Jerusalem in 586 BC and **desecrated** the temple. The terms *desecrate* or *defile* in the context of religious ceremony means "to make ceremonially unclean." Verses 1–3 indicate the extensive nature of the devastation since the enemies destroyed Israel's place of worship and harmed the Lord's people. **79:2** Leaving the bodies exposed to the elements where they were consumed by animals signifies humiliation and insult.

⁵ How long, LORD? Will you
    be angry forever?
Will your jealousy keep burning
    like fire?
⁶ Pour out your wrath on the nations
    that don't acknowledge you,
    on the kingdoms that don't call on
      your name,
⁷ for they have devoured Jacob
    and devastated his homeland.
⁸ Do not hold past iniquities^A against us;
    let your compassion come to us quickly,
    for we have become very weak.

⁹ God of our salvation, help us,
    for the glory of your name.
Rescue us and atone for our sins,
    for your name's sake.
¹⁰ Why should the nations ask,
    "Where is their God?"
Before our eyes,
    let vengeance for the shed blood
      of your servants
    be known among the nations.
¹¹ Let the groans of the prisoners reach you;
    according to your great power,
    preserve those condemned to die.

¹² Pay back sevenfold to our neighbors
    the reproach they have hurled at you,
    Lord.
¹³ Then we, your people, the sheep
    of your pasture,
will thank you forever;
    we will declare your praise
    to generation after generation.

A Prayer for Restoration

80 *For the choir director: according to "The Lilies." A testimony of Asaph. A psalm.*

¹ Listen, Shepherd of Israel,
    who leads Joseph like a flock;

    you who sit enthroned
      between the cherubim,
shine ² on Ephraim,
Benjamin, and Manasseh.
Rally your power and come
    to save us.
³ Restore us, God;
    make your face shine on us,
    so that we may be saved.

⁴ LORD God of Armies,
    how long will you be angry
    with your people's prayers?
⁵ You fed them the bread of tears
    and gave them a full measure^B
    of tears to drink.
⁶ You put us at odds
    with our neighbors;
    our enemies mock us.
⁷ Restore us, God of Armies;
    make your face shine on us, so that we
      may be saved.

⁸ You dug up a vine from Egypt;
    you drove out the nations
    and planted it.
⁹ You cleared a place for it;
    it took root and filled the land.
¹⁰ The mountains were covered
    by its shade,
and the mighty cedars^C
    with its branches.
¹¹ It sent out sprouts toward the Sea^D
    and shoots toward the River.^E

¹² Why have you broken down its walls
    so that all who pass by pick its fruit?
¹³ Boars from the forest tear at it
    and creatures of the field feed on it.
¹⁴ Return, God of Armies.
Look down from heaven and see;
    take care of this vine,

---

^A **79:8** Or *hold the sins of past generations* ^B **80:5** Lit *a one-third measure* ^C **80:10** Lit *the cedars of God* ^D **80:11** = the Mediterranean ^E **80:11** = the Euphrates

---

79:5 How long reflects the frustration of the psalmist, who connected the absence or abandonment of God with his failure to respond immediately to the plight of Jerusalem's citizens.
79:6 Kingdoms that don't call on your name is a common idiom distinguishing between the Lord's people and those who opposed him.
79:10 The rhetorical question asked by the nations, **Where is their God?** echoes the response of Israel's enemies to her destruction (42:3; Jl 2:17; Mc 7:10). Calamity and oppression often represent the absence of God's protection. **Vengeance** refers to divine retribution, a privilege belonging to God alone. **Be known among the nations** could be translated "be poured out upon the nations," preserving the wordplay on the Hebrew root *shophek*, "pour out" in vv. 3,6.
79:11 Those condemned to die literally reads "sons of death."

79:12 Pay back sevenfold emphasizes the enduring nature of the vengeance God will inflict upon the nations (Gn 4:15,24; Lv 26:18,21,24).
Ps 80 title On **The Lilies**, see note at Ps 45 title. On **Asaph**, see note at Ps 50 title.
80:1 The imperative form for **listen** is a polite request, as from an inferior to his superior. **Shepherd of Israel** is a metaphor indicating God's intimate relationship with his people as protector and provider (23:1; 121:4). **Joseph** was a name for Israel normally associated with the northern tribes. **Enthroned between the cherubim** refers to the ark of the covenant on which the presence of the Lord resided, emphasizing his kingship (18:10; 97:2; 99:1). **Shine** is meant in the sense that a star rises; it could picture the coming of the Lord in his glory (94:1; Dt 33:2).
80:2 Ephraim, Benjamin, and Manasseh represent the tribes of Israel, settled in

central Palestine. *Benjamin* means "son of the right hand," an allusion to vv. 15,17.
80:4 The psalmist appealed to the **LORD God of Armies**. This evokes divine warrior language, typical imagery in ancient Near Eastern cultures.
80:5 Grief **(the bread of tears)** was the only sustenance for the psalmist in the midst of persecution.
80:7 Repetition of the refrain from v. 3 **(restore us)** forms a natural break in the transition to the second part of the psalm.
80:8 Vine from Egypt alludes to the exodus (Ex 15:17).
80:12–13 Linguistic and contextual similarities between vv. 12–13 and imagery in Is 5:1–7 suggest an intentional allusion to the prophet.
80:14 In a sequential list of actions (**return . . . look down . . . see; take care**), the people's perceived absence of God relates to suffering, captivity, and oppression.

¹⁵ the root^A your right hand planted,
the son^B that you made strong
for yourself.
¹⁶ It was cut down and burned;
they^C perish at the rebuke
of your countenance.
¹⁷ Let your hand be with the man
at your right hand,
with the son of man
you have made strong for yourself.
¹⁸ Then we will not turn away from you;
revive us, and we will call on your name.
¹⁹ Restore us, LORD, God of Armies;
make your face shine on us, so
that we may be saved.

A Call to Obedience

81 For the choir director: on the *Gittith. Of Asaph.*
Sing for joy to God our strength;
shout in triumph to the God of Jacob.
² Lift up a song — play the tambourine,
the melodious lyre, and the harp.
³ Blow the ram's horn on the day of
our feasts^D
during the new moon
and during the full moon.
⁴ For this is a statute for Israel,
an ordinance of the God of Jacob.
⁵ He set it up as a decree for Joseph
when he went throughout^E the land
of Egypt.

I heard an unfamiliar language:
⁶ "I relieved his shoulder
from the burden;
his hands were freed from carrying
the basket.
⁷ You called out in distress,
and I rescued you;

I answered you from the thundercloud.
I tested you at the Waters
of Meribah. *Selah*
⁸ Listen, my people, and I will
admonish you.
Israel, if you would only listen to me!
⁹ There must not be a strange god
among you;
you must not bow down
to a foreign god.
¹⁰ I am the LORD your God,
who brought you up from the land
of Egypt.
Open your mouth wide, and I will fill it.

¹¹ "But my people did not listen to my voice;
Israel did not obey me.
¹² So I gave them over
to their stubborn hearts
to follow their own plans.
¹³ If only my people would listen to me
and Israel would follow my ways,
¹⁴ I would quickly subdue their enemies
and turn my hand against their foes."
¹⁵ Those who hate the LORD
would cower to him;
their doom would last forever.
¹⁶ But he would feed Israel^F
with the best wheat.
"I would satisfy you with honey
from the rock."

A Plea for Righteous Judgment

82 A psalm of Asaph.
God stands in the divine assembly;
he pronounces judgment
among the gods:^G
² "How long will you judge unjustly
and show partiality to the wicked? *Selah*

---

^A80:15 Hb obscure   ^B80:15 Or *shoot*   ^C80:16 Or *may they*   ^D81:3 Lit *feast*   ^E81:5 Or *he gained authority over*   ^F81:16 Lit *him*
^G82:1 Or *the heavenly beings,* or *the earthly rulers;* Hb *elohim*

80:15 The right hand signifies a privileged position or serves as the instrument that executes divine action. **Root** (lit "stem or shoot") occurs only here. If the metaphor is meant to continue, **son** could refer to a scion or shoot; it alludes to the "son of man" in v. 17. **80:16 At the rebuke of your countenance** signifies that sinful people could not survive in the presence of God. **80:17–18 Let your hand be** denotes a request from a subordinate to a superior. The transfer of divine power flows through God's hand and into his agent. The **man at your right hand** is usually a king (110:1; cp. Is 45:1) who received divine appointment and approval. In the NT, Christ is seated at the right hand of God, identical with God in authority, power, and holiness (Heb 1:3). **Ps 81 title** On **Gittith,** see note at Ps 8 title. On **Asaph,** see note at Ps 50 title. **81:1–2 Jacob** is a designation for the twelve tribes of Israel, who all serve one God. **81:3** The assembly blew the **ram's horn** (Hb *shophar*) to herald the beginning of a cultic celebration or before entering into

battle. A **new moon** marked the beginning of festivities, which concluded with the full moon. According to the Hebrew calendar, this time paralleled a series of cultic activities celebrated during two weeks of autumn. **81:4** A feast stipulated by the Torah indicates that the song accompanied one of three great cultic celebrations. **81:5–6** Psalms of Asaph frequently mention **Joseph** as a designation for Israel (50; 73; 83). The song does not refer to the historical person Joseph, but to Israel as Joseph's descendants. The formal establishment of the law occurred long after Joseph's death and only after Israel departed from Egypt. The **unfamiliar language** (lit "a tongue I did not know") does not refer to a divine oracle or prophetic utterance, but to direct communication between God and his people during the exodus. Israel **heard** and understood God. **81:7** Along with v. 6, this verse recollects the exodus and the Lord's faithful response to the suffering of his people. The Lord spoke to Israel **from the thundercloud** (lit "from

hidden thunder") in the desert. The thundercloud evokes the appearance of God in Ex 19. During the sojourn in the wilderness, Rephidim, renamed **Meribah,** was the place where the Israelites tested the Lord's faithfulness and ability to provide water. However, the psalmist depicted the event as one in which the Lord **tested** Israel's faithfulness and dependence on him. **81:8** The Hebrew concept of hearing— *shema*—is the central theme of the psalm. Hearing involves obedience to instruction. Thus, a person does not truly hear God without a response of obedience. **81:10** A formulaic expression **I am the LORD your God** (Ex 6:6–8; Dt 20:1; Jdg 6:13) recollects the revelation of God to Moses (Ex 3:14). **81:16** Two phrases, the **best wheat** and **honey from the rock,** allude to Dt 32:13–14. The passage from Deuteronomy provides the interpretive model for this psalm. **Ps 82 title** On **Asaph,** see note at Ps 50 title. **82:1** The phrase **God stands** indicates sentencing or **judgment** in progress (74:22; 94:2; Is 3:13; 33:10) since judges normally sat (Ex 18:14; Jdg 4:5; Is 28:6). The **divine assembly**

³ Provide justice for the needy
   and the fatherless;
   uphold the rights of the oppressed
   and the destitute.
⁴ Rescue the poor and needy;
   save them from the power of
   the wicked."

⁵ They do not know or understand;
   they wander in darkness.
   All the foundations of the earth
   are shaken.

⁶ I said, "You are gods;
   you are all sons of the Most High.
⁷ However, you will die like humans
   and fall like any other ruler."

⁸ Rise up, God, judge the earth,
   for all the nations belong to you.

Prayer against Enemies

83

A song. A psalm of Asaph.
God, do not keep silent.
Do not be deaf, God; do not be quiet.
² See how your enemies make an uproar;
   those who hate you
   have acted arrogantly.ᴬ
³ They devise clever schemes
   against your people;
   they conspire against
   your treasured ones.
⁴ They say, "Come, let's wipe them out
   as a nation
   so that Israel's name will no longer
   be remembered."
⁵ For they have conspired with one mind;
   they form an allianceᴮ against you —
⁶ the tents of Edom and the Ishmaelites,
   Moab and the Hagrites,
⁷ Gebal, Ammon, and Amalek,
   Philistia with the inhabitants of Tyre.

⁸ Even Assyria has joined them;
   they lend supportᶜ
   to the sons of Lot.ᴰ   *Selah*

⁹ Deal with them as you did with Midian,
   as you did with Sisera
   and Jabin at the Kishon River.
¹⁰ They were destroyed at En-dor;
    they became manure for the ground.
¹¹ Make their nobles like Oreb and Zeeb,
    and all their tribal leaders like Zebah
    and Zalmunna,
¹² who said, "Let's seize God's pastures
    for ourselves."

¹³ Make them like tumbleweed, my God,
    like straw before the wind.
¹⁴ As fire burns a forest,
    as a flame blazes through mountains,
¹⁵ so pursue them with your tempest
    and terrify them with your storm.
¹⁶ Cover their faces with shame
    so that they will seek your name, Lᴏʀᴅ.
¹⁷ Let them be put to shame
    and terrified forever;
    let them perish in disgrace.
¹⁸ May they know that you alone —
    whose name is the Lᴏʀᴅ —
    are the Most High over the whole earth.

Longing for God's House

84

*For the choir director: on the Gittith.
A psalm of the sons of Korah.*
¹ How lovely is your dwelling place,
   Lᴏʀᴅ of Armies.
² I long and yearn
   for the courts of the Lᴏʀᴅ;
   my heart and flesh cry out
   forᴱ the living God.

³ Even a sparrow finds a home,
   and a swallow, a nest for herself

ᴬ**83:2** Lit *have lifted their head*   ᴮ**83:5** Lit *they cut a covenant*   ᶜ**83:8** Lit *they are an arm*   ᴰ**83:8** = Moab and Ammon
ᴱ**84:2** Or *flesh shout for joy to*

---

either refers to heavenly servant beings (103:19) or judges and governors appointed by God as political leaders (Ex 21:6; 22:8; 2Ch 19:5–6).
82:3–4 Here God charges the officials or "gods" with their responsibilities of justice. The quotation marks that end at v. 4 should probably extend through v. 7.
82:6–7 Gods refers to kings (or angels) who failed to perform responsibly and ethically and thus deserved death. The concept finds support in the book of Ezekiel (28:1–19), where the Lord banished his divine servant, the king of Tyre, from his presence to die like a common man. The term *gods* was used of God's vice-regents such as Moses and the kings. Verse 6 is used by Jesus in Jn 10:34.
Ps 83 title On **Asaph**, see note at Ps 50 title.
83:1 A communal lament, this final psalm of Asaph makes three urgent requests of the Lord. Using terms generally attributed

to lifeless, false gods (81:9), the community seeks God's response to the current crisis.
83:4 The rare Hebrew term for **wipe . . . out** denotes complete annihilation, making it as if it had never existed (9:4–6; Ex 23:23; 1Kg 13:34).
83:6–7 While the context implies that all ten enemy nations originated from Lot (v. 9), only **Moab** and **Ammon** descended from him (Gn 19:36–38). The nations listed here divide into two separate groups. The **Ishmaelites** and the **Hagrites** are synonymous with Moab and **Edom**. The remaining nations make up a familiar list of all Israel's fiercest enemies, with the exception of **Gebal**, about which little is known.
83:8 Assyria, as the enemy par excellence, lent **support** (lit "arm"), a term figuratively denoting military resources and strength.
83:9–12 In an extended imprecation, the lament evokes memories of the Lord's intervention in two major victories. **Sisera**

and **Jabin** were defeated by Deborah and Barak (Jdg 4–5), and the nation of **Midi**an—including **Oreb** . . . **Zeeb** . . . **Zebah** and **Zalmunna**—was defeated by Gideon (Jdg 6:1–8:21).
83:16–18 Three Hebrew terms for **shame** in these verses reinforce the extent of the Lord's judgment and his complete humiliation of the oppressors, culminating in the annihilation of hostile peoples. The fate the adversaries sought to inflict on God's people (v. 4) will be exacted on them (see note at 7:14–16). Only then would the nations recognize the Lord as sovereign King.
Ps 84 title On **Gittith**, see note at Ps 8 title. On **sons of Korah**, see note at Ps 42 title.
84:2 The courts refers to the outer precincts of the temple where worshipers gathered.
84:3 How fortunate are the birds who may build their nests above the **altars**. How much more fortunate are the priests who can live at the temple (v. 4).

where she places her young —
near your altars, LORD of Armies,
my King and my God.
⁴ How happy are those who reside
in your house,
who praise you continually.   *Selah*

⁵ Happy are the people whose strength is
in you,
whose hearts are set on pilgrimage.
⁶ As they pass through the Valley of Baca,^A
they make it a source of spring water;
even the autumn rain will cover it
with blessings.^B
⁷ They go from strength to strength;
each appears before God in Zion.

⁸ LORD God of Armies, hear my prayer;
listen, God of Jacob.   *Selah*
⁹ Consider our shield,^C God;
look on the face of your anointed one.

¹⁰ Better a day in your courts
than a thousand anywhere else.
I would rather stand at the threshold
of the house of my God
than live in the tents of wicked people.
¹¹ For the LORD God is a sun and shield.
The LORD grants favor and honor;
he does not withhold the good
from those who live with integrity.
¹² Happy is the person who trusts in you,
LORD of Armies!

Restoration of Favor

85 For the choir director. A psalm of the sons
of Korah.
¹ LORD, you showed favor to your land;
you restored the fortunes of Jacob.^D
² You forgave your people's guilt;
you covered all their sin.   *Selah*
³ You withdrew all your fury;
you turned from your burning anger.

⁴ Return to us, God of our salvation,
and abandon your displeasure
with us.
⁵ Will you be angry with us forever?
Will you prolong your anger for all
generations?
⁶ Will you not revive us again
so that your people may rejoice in you?
⁷ Show us your faithful love, LORD,
and give us your salvation.

⁸ I will listen to what God will say;
surely the LORD will declare peace
to his people, his faithful ones,
and not let them go back
to foolish ways.
⁹ His salvation is very near those who fear
him,
so that glory may dwell in our land.

¹⁰ Faithful love and truth
will join together;
righteousness and peace will embrace.
¹¹ Truth will spring up from the earth,
and righteousness will look
down from heaven.
¹² Also, the LORD will provide
what is good,
and our land will yield its crops.
¹³ Righteousness will go before him
to prepare the way for his steps.

Lament and Petition

86 A prayer of David.
Listen, LORD, and answer me,
for I am poor and needy.
² Protect my life, for I am faithful.
You are my God; save your servant
who trusts in you.
³ Be gracious to me, Lord,
for I call to you all day long.
⁴ Bring joy to your servant's life,
because I appeal to you, Lord.

^A 84:6 Or *Valley of Tears*   ^B 84:6 Or *pools*   ^C 84:9 = the king   ^D 85:1 Or *restored Jacob from captivity*

84:4–5 Whose hearts are set on pilgrimage is literally "the highways are on their hearts." This describes the minds of the godly, their thoughts focused on the ascent to Zion. **84:6–7 The Valley of Baca** derives from the Hebrew term *baka'*, "to weep." The joyful tears of the pilgrims transformed the source of sadness and grief into a spring of blessing, just as the early rains of autumn restored water to the valley. **Ps 85 title** On **sons of Korah**, see note at Ps 42 title. **85:1** The perfect form of the Hebrew verbs, denoting completed action, supports a postexilic date for this psalm that celebrates Jacob's return from Babylonian captivity. The idiomatic expression **restored the fortunes** includes the concept of a release from imprisonment or debt combined with the return of the Lord's people to their homeland (14:7; 53:6; 126:4; Dt 30:3; Jr 29:14; 30:3,18; Am 9:14; Zph 2:7). As a key word of this psalm, the

root *shuv* ("turn," "return," "restore," "revive") occurs five times (vv. 1,3–4,6,8). **85:2** The Hebrew term for **covered**, when combined with the word for **sin**, means "forgave," especially in context with the previous line (32:1). **85:3** The Hebrew root *'avar* ("anger, fury") functions as a wordplay with a second related Hebrew root *'avar*, meaning "pass over, forgive" ("pardon" in Jb 7:21). The Lord has forgiven Israel's sins and **turned** (Hb *shuv*) his anger away from them. **85:4** If God had already forgiven, restored, and showed favor to the exiles, why did the psalmist call on him to do so again? His request acknowledged that God's renewal of his wrath against the people remained a tangible reality. **85:5 To prolong . . . anger for all generations** recalls Ex 34:7, where the Lord promised to punish descendants for the sins of their fathers.

85:6–7 Faithful love (Hb *chesed*, "covenant loyalty") is a cultic term indicating a unique relationship between Yahweh and his people, a relationship built on loyalty by those not obligated to demonstrate that loyalty. **Revive us again** (lit "restore our lives") uses the Hebrew word *shuv*. The Lord restores Israel's fortunes by turning his anger from them, thereby restoring Jacob's vitality. The **salvation** of the Lord results from a demonstration of his covenant loyalty. **85:8 Go back** is the Hebrew word *shuv* (cp. vv. 1,3,6). **85:9–10** Reconciliation is characterized by renewal and the return of peace and prosperity to the **land** (119:151; 145:18; Is 50:8; 55:6; 62:2). **86:1–3** In many individual laments, the psalmist's unceasing prayers (**all day long**) continued until God delivered him. **86:4–5** An appeal to the Lord's kindness, forgiveness, and covenant loyalty (**faithful**

⁵ For you, Lord, are kind and ready
to forgive,
abounding in faithful love to all who call
on you.
⁶ Lᴏʀᴅ, hear my prayer;
listen to my cries for mercy.
⁷ I call on you in the day of my distress,
for you will answer me.

⁸ Lord, there is no one like you
among the gods,
and there are no works like yours.
⁹ All the nations you have made
will come and bow down
before you, Lord,
and will honor your name.
¹⁰ For you are great and perform wonders;
you alone are God.

¹¹ Teach me your way, Lᴏʀᴅ,
and I will live by your truth.
Give me an undivided mind to fear
your name.
¹² I will praise you with all my heart,
Lord my God,
and will honor your name forever.
¹³ For your faithful love for me is great,
and you rescue my life from the depths
of Sheol.

¹⁴ God, arrogant people have attacked me;
a gang of ruthless men intends
to kill me.
They do not let you guide them.ᴬ
¹⁵ But you, Lord, are a compassionate
and gracious God,
slow to anger and abounding
in faithful love and truth.
¹⁶ Turn to me and be gracious to me.
Give your strength to your servant;
save the son of your female servant.
¹⁷ Show me a sign of your goodness;

my enemies will see and be put
to shame
because you, Lᴏʀᴅ, have helped
and comforted me.

Zion, the City of God

87 A psalm of the sons of Korah. A song.
The city he foundedᴮ is
on the holy mountains.
² The Lᴏʀᴅ loves Zion's city gates
more than all the dwellings of Jacob.
³ Glorious things are said about you,
city of God.   *Selah*

⁴ "I will make a record of those
who know me:
Rahab, Babylon, Philistia, Tyre,
and Cush—
each one was born there."
⁵ And it will be said of Zion,
"This one and that one were born
in her."
The Most High himself
will establish her.
⁶ When he registers the peoples,
the Lᴏʀᴅ will record,
"This one was born there."   *Selah*
⁷ Singers and dancersᶜ alike will say,ᴰ
"My whole source of joy isᴱ in you."

A Cry of Desperation

88 A song. A psalm of the sons of Korah. For
the choir director: according to Mahalath
Leannoth. A Maskil of Heman the Ezrahite.
¹ Lᴏʀᴅ, God of my salvation,
I cry out before you day and night.
² May my prayer reach
your presence;
listen to my cry.

³ For I have had enough troubles,
and my life is near Sheol.

ᴬ86:14 Lit *They do not set you in front of them* ᴮ87:1 Lit *His foundation* ᶜ87:7 Or *musicians* ᴰ87:7 Or *As they dance they will sing* ᴱ87:7 Lit *"All my springs are*

love*) is a variation of the formula that occurs again in v. 15.
86:6 Hear requests a respondent who is fully alert. **Cries for mercy** is a supplication, the seeking of divine favor (28:2; 31:22; 130:2; 140:6).
86:13 Sheol refers to the grave, the underworld (Is 14:9; Ezk 31:16), or a place of separation from God (Ps 6:5; Is 38:18) from which there is no praise. Figuratively, mention of Sheol may depict imminent death or the removal of a person from the divine presence (Jnh 2:2).
86:15 The psalmist emphasized the positive attributes of the Lord as **compassionate**, merciful, **slow to anger**, and **abounding** in covenant loyalty and **truth**. Note the absence of the second half of the formula, which describes God's wrathful response to sin (Ex 34:6–7).
86:16–17 Your female servant is figurative for Israel.

Ps 87 title On **sons of Korah**, see note at Ps 42 title.
87:2 Court proceedings, social interaction, and commercial transactions normally took place in the **city gates** (Ru 4:1–2; Jb 29:7–10; Pr 24:7).
87:3 City of God means belonging to God, as a possession.
87:4 The universal outlook of the psalm is evident as the psalmist recounted major powers of Mesopotamia, all once historical enemies of Israel. **Rahab**, the mythical dragon-like chaos monster, represented Egypt (Is 30:7). **Babylon** was known for its oppression while **Philistia** had a reputation for aggression. These, along with the wealthy of **Tyre**, and the Cushites from the Nubian kingdom south of Egypt, would attain the status of naturalized citizens with full privileges though they were born in another country. From an eschatological perspective, these nations would be qualified to participate in

Israel's feasts and Torah instruction since all national distinctions would be eliminated under the Lord's kingship (Is 2:2–4; 49:18–23; 56:3,6–7; Zch 14:16–18).
87:5–7 Despite the inclusion of Gentile nations, the Lord would appoint Israel to a special position of leadership in the eschatological kingdom because of her birthright (Is 60; 62:1–5).
Ps 88 title On **sons of Korah**, see note at Ps 42 title. **Heman the Ezrahite**, a famous wise man during Solomon's reign, served as the king's seer. **According to Mahalath Leannoth** may designate this as a psalm of penitence associated with purification from illness (see note at Ps 53 title).
88:1–2 His prayer **day and night** indicates his need is severe.
88:3 I have had enough troubles means literally "my soul is sated with turmoil." The psalmist described his condition as grave, as his **life** drew near **Sheol**.

⁴ I am counted among those going down
   to the Pit.
   I am like a man without strength,
⁵ abandoned⁴ among the dead.
   I am like the slain lying in the grave,
   whom you no longer remember,
   and who are cut off from your care.ᴮ

⁶ You have put me in the lowest part
   of the Pit,
   in the darkest places, in the depths.
⁷ Your wrath weighs heavily on me;
   you have overwhelmed me with all
      your waves.   *Selah*
⁸ You have distanced my friends from me;
   you have made me repulsive to them.
   I am shut in and cannot go out.
⁹ My eyes are worn out from crying.
   LORD, I cry out to you all day long;
   I spread out my hands to you.

¹⁰ Do you work wonders for the dead?
   Do departed spirits rise up
      to praise you?   *Selah*
¹¹ Will your faithful love be declared
   in the grave,
   your faithfulness in Abaddon?
¹² Will your wonders be known in
   the darkness
   or your righteousness in the land
   of oblivion?

¹³ But I call to you for help, LORD;
   in the morning my prayer meets you.
¹⁴ LORD, why do you reject me?
   Why do you hide your face from me?
¹⁵ From my youth,
   I have been suffering and near death.
   I suffer your horrors; I am desperate.
¹⁶ Your wrath sweeps over me;
   your terrors destroy me.
¹⁷ They surround me like water all day long;
   they close in on me from every side.
¹⁸ You have distanced loved one
   and neighbor from me;
   darkness is my only friend.ᶜ

Perplexity about God's Promises

89 *A Maskil of Ethan the Ezrahite.*
I will sing about the LORD's
   faithful love forever;
   I will proclaim your faithfulness to all
   generations
   with my mouth.
² For I will declare,
   "Faithful love is built up forever;
   you establish your faithfulness
     in the heavens."

³ The LORD said,
   "I have made a covenant
     with my chosen one;
   I have sworn an oath to David my servant:
⁴ 'I will establish your offspring forever
   and build up your throne
     for all generations.'"   *Selah*

⁵ LORD, the heavens praise your wonders —
   your faithfulness also —
   in the assembly of the holy ones.
⁶ For who in the skies can compare
   with the LORD?
   Who among the heavenly beingsᴰ is
   like the LORD?
⁷ God is greatly feared in the council
   of the holy ones,
   more awe-inspiring thanᴱ
   all who surround him.
⁸ LORD God of Armies,
   who is strong like you, LORD?
   Your faithfulness surrounds you.
⁹ You rule the raging sea;
   when its waves surge, you still them.
¹⁰ You crushed Rahab like one who is slain;
   you scattered your enemies
     with your powerful arm.
¹¹ The heavens are yours; the earth also
   is yours.
   The world and everything in it
   — you founded them.
¹² North and south — you created them.
   Tabor and Hermon shout for joy
     at your name.

ᴬ**88:5** Or *set free*   ᴮ**88:5** Or *hand*   ᶜ**88:18** Or *from me, my friends. Oh darkness!*   ᴰ**89:6** Or *the angels,* or *the sons of the mighty*   ᴱ**89:7** Or *ones, revered by*

88:4 The **Pit** is another name for Sheol.
88:6 The **lowest part of the Pit** is often portrayed as the roots of the mountains in the deep sea (Jnh 2:6; Mc 7:19).
88:8 The Hebrew word for **repulsive** often describes unethical practices such as child sacrifice or idolatry ("detestable" in Dt 12:31; 27:15). Those who committed such heinous acts were ceremonially unclean and were ostracized from the community.
88:9 The **hands** being **spread out** implies submission and helplessness.
88:10–12 A series of four rhetorical questions expect negative speeches, typical of disputation speeches. The psalmist asked if God performed miracles on behalf of the

dead in order to receive praise in the **grave**. On the contrary, God blesses the living to receive glory on earth and in heaven. **Departed spirits** could be translated as "shades," a figurative expression for "spirits of the dead" (Jb 26:5; Is 14:9; 26:14,19). **Abaddon**, a place of destruction, is synonymous with Sheol or the Pit (Jb 26:6; 28:22; Pr 15:11).
Ps 89 title Ethan the Ezrahite was a Levitical musician (1Ch 15:17,19). The connections of this psalm with 2Sm 7 and 1Ch 17 are unmistakable.
89:3 I have made a covenant implies obligation and binding responsibility. The **LORD** assumes responsibility while imposing obligations on Israel as part of the covenant.

My chosen one may refer to David, or collectively, to his descendants.
89:5 Heavens could be a metonymy for "heavenly beings."
89:6 Skies refers metaphorically to the heavenly realm (Jb 37:18).
89:8 Armies is military language describing the Lord as warrior.
89:9–10 Rahab, the name for an ancient Near Eastern mythological chaos monster, was associated with the chaotic sea (Jb 26:12; Is 51:9). In contrast with that myth, God created the ocean and continues to demonstrate his sovereignty over it (Ps 74:13–17).
89:12 North and south is a merism, the two extremes referring to everything between

13 You have a mighty arm;
    your hand is powerful;
    your right hand is lifted high.
14 Righteousness and justice are
       the foundation
    of your throne;
    faithful love and truth go before you.
15 Happy are the people who know
       the joyful shout;
    LORD, they walk in the light
       from your face.
16 They rejoice in your name all day long,
    and they are exalted
       by your righteousness.
17 For you are their magnificent strength;
    by your favor our horn is exalted.
18 Surely our shield^A belongs to the LORD,
    our king to the Holy One of Israel.

19 You once spoke in a vision
    to your faithful ones
    and said, "I have granted help
       to a warrior;
    I have exalted one chosen^B
       from the people.
20 I have found David my servant;
    I have anointed him with my sacred oil.
21 My hand will always be with him,
    and my arm will strengthen him.
22 The enemy will not oppress^C him;
    the wicked will not afflict him.
23 I will crush his foes before him
    and strike those who hate him.
24 My faithfulness and love will be
       with him,
    and through my name
    his horn will be exalted.
25 I will extend his power to the sea
    and his right hand to the rivers.
26 He will call to me, 'You are my Father,
    my God, the rock of my salvation.'
27 I will also make him my firstborn,

    greatest of the kings of the earth.
28 I will always preserve my faithful love
       for him,
    and my covenant with him will endure.
29 I will establish his line forever,
    his throne as long as heaven lasts.^D
30 If his sons abandon my instruction
    and do not live by my ordinances,
31 if they dishonor my statutes
    and do not keep my commands,
32 then I will call their rebellion
    to account with the rod,
    their iniquity with blows.
33 But I will not withdraw
    my faithful love from him
    or betray my faithfulness.
34 I will not violate my covenant
    or change what my lips have said.
35 Once and for all
    I have sworn an oath by my holiness;
    I will not lie to David.
36 His offspring will continue forever,
    his throne like the sun before me,
37 like the moon, established forever,
    a faithful witness in the sky."   *Selah*

38 But you have spurned and rejected him;
    you have become enraged
       with your anointed.
39 You have repudiated the covenant
       with your servant;
    you have completely dishonored
       his crown.^E
40 You have broken down all his walls;
    you have reduced his fortified cities
       to ruins.
41 All who pass by plunder him;
    he has become an object of ridicule
       to his neighbors.
42 You have lifted high the right hand
       of his foes;
    you have made all his enemies rejoice.

^A89:18 = the king   ^B89:19 Or *exalted a young man*   ^C89:22 Or *not exact tribute from*   ^D89:29 Lit *as days of heaven*
^E89:39 Lit *have dishonored his crown to the ground*

---

them. The Hebrew word for "create" (*bara'*) is always used of God. **Tabor** and **Hermon** were noteworthy mountains in the north. **89:13** The Lord's right hand is **lifted high** (lit "exalted"), ready to exact judgment. **89:14 Righteousness** and **justice** serve as the platform or pedestal on which the Lord builds his majesty. Combined with **faithful love** and **truth**, the four characteristics summarize the essential attributes of Yahweh. **89:15–17 Horn**, a figurative term for power or strength (75:4), reappears in 89:24, where the Lord raises David's horn through the divine name. **89:18** The **shield** of Israel was their **king**, who with God's help protected and defended the people. **89:19** The **vision** refers to vv. 3 and 4 and the larger context of the oracle of Nathan to David in 2Sm 7:1–17. The **warrior** selected from the people refers to David as the Lord's anointed and divinely empowered warrior.

89:20–38 This passage is similar to 2Sm 7:14–17 and 1Ch 17:3–15, suggesting a conceptual and literary relationship between them. **89:23** The promise in 2Sm 7:10 is here applied to David alone. **89:25** David will act with divine authority, which will extend from the Mediterranean **sea** in the west to the Tigris and Euphrates **rivers** in the east. The **right hand** always denotes the actions of God and his representative with authority and dominion. **89:26 Father** exemplifies the language of adoption. This psalm reached ideal fulfillment in Christ as a descendant of David and as the actual Son of God. **89:27** The father-son relationship in 2Sm 7:14 refers to David's son Solomon, while the idea in this psalm centers on David alone. The **firstborn** son usually received a special blessing from the father and a double inheritance. **Greatest** is the same Hebrew word that describes God as the "Most High" (*elyon*,

87:5; 91:1). While these words fit David, they were fulfilled in Christ. **89:35** Only the Lord can swear **an oath** by his holy nature. Because he is holy, he cannot **lie** (78:36; Is 57:11; Heb 6:18). **89:36–37** The stability of the Davidic throne is as reliable as the course of the **sun** and the **moon** (72:5,17), established forever. The **faithful witness in the sky** could be the moon, God's **throne**, or the Lord himself. **89:38–39** A tone of accusation in a series of charges toward the Lord (vv. 38–45) suggests the psalmist saw his current circumstances as a breach of God's **covenant** agreement. **Repudiated** implies the removal of the Lord's covenant loyalty from his servant. **89:42** In an ironic twist, the Lord had **lifted high** (lit "exalted") the **hand** of David's enemies. In v. 13 the Lord's hand was "lifted high" against Israel's enemies; Israel's horn was "exalted" through God's favor (vv. 16–17); God's anointed was "exalted" from among

⁴³ You have also turned back
   his sharp sword
   and have not let him stand in battle.
⁴⁴ You have made his splendor^A cease
   and have overturned his throne.
⁴⁵ You have shortened the days
   of his youth;
   you have covered him with shame. *Selah*

⁴⁶ How long, Lᴏʀᴅ? Will you hide forever?
   Will your anger keep burning like fire?
⁴⁷ Remember how short my life is.
   Have you created everyone for nothing?
⁴⁸ What courageous person can live and
   never see death?
   Who can save himself from the power
   of Sheol? *Selah*

⁴⁹ Lord, where are the former acts
   of your faithful love
   that you swore to David
   in your faithfulness?
⁵⁰ Remember, Lord, the ridicule
   against your servants —
   in my heart I carry abuse from all
   the peoples —
⁵¹ how your enemies have ridiculed, Lᴏʀᴅ,
   how they have ridiculed every step
   of your anointed.

⁵² Blessed be the Lᴏʀᴅ forever.
   Amen and amen.

BOOK IV (Psalms 90–106)

Eternal God and Mortal Man

90 A prayer of Moses, the man of God.
   Lord, you have been our refuge^B
   in every generation.
² Before the mountains were born,
   before you gave birth to the earth
   and the world,
   from eternity to eternity, you are God.

³ You return mankind to the dust,
   saying, "Return, descendants of Adam."
⁴ For in your sight a thousand years
   are like yesterday that passes by,

like a few hours of the night.
⁵ You end their lives;^C they sleep.
   They are like grass that grows
   in the morning —
⁶ in the morning it sprouts and grows;
   by evening it withers and dries up.

⁷ For we are consumed by your anger;
   we are terrified by your wrath.
⁸ You have set our iniquities before you,
   our secret sins in the light
   of your presence.
⁹ For all our days ebb away
   under your wrath;
   we end our years like a sigh.
¹⁰ Our lives last^D seventy years
   or, if we are strong, eighty years.
   Even the best of them are^E struggle
   and sorrow;
   indeed, they pass quickly and we
   fly away.
¹¹ Who understands the power
   of your anger?
   Your wrath matches the fear that
   is due you.
¹² Teach us to number our days carefully
   so that we may develop wisdom
   in our hearts.^F

¹³ Lᴏʀᴅ — how long?
   Turn and have compassion
   on your servants.
¹⁴ Satisfy us in the morning
   with your faithful love
   so that we may shout with joy
   and be glad all our days.
¹⁵ Make us rejoice for as many days
   as you have humbled us,
   for as many years as
   we have seen adversity.
¹⁶ Let your work be seen by your servants,
   and your splendor by their children.
¹⁷ Let the favor of the Lord our God be
   on us;
   establish for us the work
   of our hands —
   establish the work of our hands!

^A 89:44 Hb obscure ^B 90:1 Some Hb mss, LXX; other Hb mss read *dwelling place* ^C 90:5 Or *You overwhelm them*; Hb obscure ^D 90:10 Lit *The days of our years in them* ^E 90:10 LXX, Tg, Syr, Vg read *Even their span is*; Hb obscure ^F 90:12 Or *develop a heart of wisdom*

the people (v. 19); and the anointed one's horn would be "exalted" (v. 24).
89:43 Not only did the Lord empower David's enemies, but he also removed David's military power.
89:44 Splendor is literally "purity." This cessation of purity connects the political downfall to a state of cultic defilement, eliminating access to God. As the king's crown had been defiled by dust, so the king's **throne** had been **overturned**, reinforcing his humiliation.
Ps 90 title No other psalm is labeled a **prayer of Moses**. The Hebrew preposition may

identify Moses as the author, or it may just suggest the poem reflects a Mosaic perspective.
90:1–2 The nuance of **gave birth** when referring to God always emphasizes his role as Creator and Almighty Father (Col 1:15–17).
90:3 Descendants of Adam could also be translated "sons of man" (8:5). The psalm contrasts humanity's limitations and God's eternality.
90:4 The expression **a thousand years** implies infinity.
90:5–6 Grass is a favorite OT metaphor for mankind's frailty and the brevity of human life (103:15–16; Is 40:6–8; Jms 1:9–11).

90:7–9 Secret sins are transgressions committed discreetly or those unrecognized by the individual (19:13). But God is always aware of humanity's **iniquities** because he is omniscient.
90:10 Seventy or **eighty** years may represent the average lifespan of God's people.
90:13 The Lord "returns" (Hb *shuv*) all living things to dust (v. 3), but the psalmist implored God to **turn** to his people.
90:16–17 Establish . . . **the work of our hands** implies that Israel does have a role in provision, and also makes a direct connection between success and God's providence.

The Protection of the Most High

91 The one who lives under the protection
of the Most High
dwells in the shadow of the Almighty.

² I will say^A concerning the Lord, who is
my refuge and my fortress,
my God in whom I trust:
³ He himself will rescue you
from the bird trap,
from the destructive plague.
⁴ He will cover you with his feathers;
you will take refuge under his wings.
His faithfulness will be
a protective shield.
⁵ You will not fear the terror of the night,
the arrow that flies by day,
⁶ the plague that stalks in darkness,
or the pestilence that ravages at noon.
⁷ Though a thousand fall at your side
and ten thousand at your right hand,
the pestilence will not reach you.
⁸ You will only see it with your eyes
and witness the punishment
of the wicked.

⁹ Because you have made the Lord
— my refuge,
the Most High — your dwelling place,
¹⁰ no harm will come to you;
no plague will come near your tent.
¹¹ For he will give his angels orders
concerning you,
to protect you in all your ways.
¹² They will support you with their hands
so that you will not strike your foot
against a stone.
¹³ You will tread on the lion and the cobra;
you will trample the young lion
and the serpent.

¹⁴ Because he has his heart set on me,
I will deliver him;

I will protect him because he knows
my name.
¹⁵ When he calls out to me,
I will answer him;
I will be with him in trouble.
I will rescue him and give him honor.
¹⁶ I will satisfy him with a long life
and show him my salvation.

God's Love and Faithfulness

92 *A psalm. A song for the Sabbath day.*
It is good to give thanks to the Lord,
to sing praise to your name, Most High,
² to declare your faithful love
in the morning
and your faithfulness at night,
³ with a ten-stringed harp^B
and the music of a lyre.

⁴ For you have made me rejoice, Lord,
by what you have done;
I will shout for joy
because of the works of your hands.
⁵ How magnificent are your works, Lord,
how profound your thoughts!
⁶ A stupid person does not know,
a fool does not understand this:
⁷ though the wicked sprout like grass
and all evildoers flourish,
they will be eternally destroyed.
⁸ But you, Lord, are exalted forever.
⁹ For indeed, Lord, your enemies —
indeed, your enemies will perish;
all evildoers will be scattered.
¹⁰ You have lifted up my horn
like that of a wild ox;
I have been anointed^C with the finest oil.
¹¹ My eyes look at my enemies;
when evildoers rise against me,
my ears hear them.

¹² The righteous thrive like a palm tree
and grow like a cedar tree in Lebanon.

---

^A 91:1–2 LXX, Syr, Jer read ²*Almighty, saying,* or ²*Almighty, he will say*   ^B 92:3 Or *ten-stringed instrument and a harp*
^C 92:10 Syr reads *you have anointed me*

91:1 Under the protection (lit "hiding place") refers to the protection of the sanctuary (27:5; 31:20; 61:4; Jb 40:21). **Shadow** denotes protection or security (121:5; Is 30:2–3; 49:2; 51:16). **The Almighty** is a name for God describing his dual roles as nurturer and protector.

91:4 The imagery of **wings** alludes to the cherubim surrounding the ark of the covenant. The Lord covers the psalmist, shutting him off from danger. "Wings," a figurative term for "cloak," denotes protection (17:8; 36:7; 57:1; 61:4; 63:7; Ru 2:12). Compare Is 40:31 for eagle imagery. Those who seek God's protection will be shielded by his faithfulness.

91:6 The plague includes flood, famine, hail, fire, or anything that threatens livestock and humans. **Pestilence** is often personified as a demon. The psalmist sought safe haven from thieves, wild animals, persecutors,

and sickness—all threats that existed in the **darkness**.

91:9 The Hebrew word for **dwelling place** implies a remote, protected place (71:3; 90:1).
91:11–12 The Lord's **angels** serve as his messengers and agents of his power outside the sanctuary (103:20; Gn 24:7; Heb 1:14). These divine beings have superior power, involving the ability to protect the Lord's people from harm (Gn 19:10–11; 24:40; Is 63:9; Dn 3:28).
91:13 The metaphors of the predatory **lion** and the poisonous **cobra** suggest creatures that stalked their prey or hid in wait.
91:14–16 Those who know God's **name** are in covenant relationship with him. The Lord delivers, protects, answers, honors, satisfies, and reveals his **salvation** through the preservation and blessing of Israel (95:7–11).
92:2–3 Deuteronomy 6 teaches God's people to speak his word day and **night**, reflecting on his covenant **love** and

faithfulness in the presence of the family and the community. The wise person finds delight in meditating on the Torah regularly (1:2). Creation testifies to God's constant care (19:1).

92:5 The term **profound** underscores the unfathomable and mysterious nature of God's thoughts (40:5; 139:17; Is 55:9–10).
92:6 Using wisdom terminology, the psalmist admonished the **stupid** ("uneducated, brutish") **person** and the **fool**. Both fail to sustain a close relationship to God, and they reject the wisdom necessary for right living.
92:10 Being **anointed with . . . oil** can mean consecration for service (Lv 8:10–12), but here it probably refers to an act of hospitality that symbolizes favor (Ps 23:5).
92:12 Lebanon was known for its abundant supply of **cedar** trees used in construction. Trees often refer figuratively to the characteristics of national leaders.

¹³ Planted in the house of the LORD,
they thrive in the courts of our God.
¹⁴ They will still bear fruit in old age,
healthy and green,
¹⁵ to declare, "The LORD is just;
he is my rock,
and there is no unrighteousness
in him."

God's Eternal Reign

93 The LORD reigns! He is robed in majesty;
the LORD is robed,
enveloped in strength.
The world is firmly established;
it cannot be shaken.
² Your throne has been established
from the beginning;ᴬ
you are from eternity.
³ The floods have lifted up, LORD,
the floods have lifted up their voice;
the floods lift up their pounding waves.
⁴ Greater than the roar of a
huge torrent —
the mighty breakers of the sea —
the LORD on high is majestic.

⁵ LORD, your testimonies
are completely reliable;
holiness adorns your house
for all the days to come.

The Just Judge

94 LORD, God of vengeance —
God of vengeance, shine!
² Rise up, Judge of the earth;
repay the proud what they deserve.
³ LORD, how long will the wicked —
how long will the wicked celebrate?

⁴ They pour out arrogant words;
all the evildoers boast.
⁵ LORD, they crush your people;
they oppress your heritage.
⁶ They kill the widow and the resident alien
and murder the fatherless.
⁷ They say, "The LORD doesn't see it.
The God of Jacob doesn't pay attention."

⁸ Pay attention, you stupid people!
Fools, when will you be wise?

⁹ Can the one who shaped the ear
not hear,
the one who formed the eye not see?
¹⁰ The one who instructs nations,
the one who teaches
mankind knowledge —
does he not discipline?
¹¹ The LORD knows the thoughts
of mankind;
they are futile.

¹² LORD, how happy is anyone
you discipline
and teach from your law
¹³ to give him relief from troubled times
until a pit is dug for the wicked.
¹⁴ The LORD will not leave his people
or abandon his heritage,
¹⁵ for the administration of justice will
again be righteous,
and all the upright in heart will followᴮ it.

¹⁶ Who stands up for me against the wicked?
Who takes a stand for me
against evildoers?
¹⁷ If the LORD had not been my helper,
I would soon rest in the silence of death.
¹⁸ If I say, "My foot is slipping,"
your faithful love will support me, LORD.
¹⁹ When I am filled with cares,
your comfort brings me joy.

²⁰ Can a corrupt throne be your ally,
a throne that makes evil laws?
²¹ They band together against the life
of the righteous
and condemn the innocent to death.
²² But the LORD is my refuge;
my God is the rock of my protection.
²³ He will pay them back for their sins
and destroy them for their evil.
The LORD our God will destroy them.

Worship and Warning

95 Come, let's shout joyfully to the LORD,
shout triumphantly to the rock
of our salvation!
² Let's enter his presence
with thanksgiving;
let's shout triumphantly to him in song.

ᴬ93:2 Lit *from then*; ᴮ94:15 Or *heart will support*; lit *heart after*

93:1–2 The first two Hebrew words of this psalm are *Yahweh malak*. This phrase is also found at the beginning of Pss 97 and 99 and in v. 10 of Ps 96. *Malak*, the Hebrew word for **reigns**, is a verb form implying completed action or an established condition. Reference to **the beginning** and **eternity** means the Lord's kingship is timeless.
93:3–4 The psalmist personified primeval forces that threatened creation and then demonstrated the Lord's sovereignty over them.

93:5 God's **testimonies** or decrees are as stable as his throne and the earth (19:8; 25:10; 99:7; 132:12; Dt 4:45; 6:17,20).
94:1 Vengeance ("retribution, vindication") generally describes God's judgment on the nations; rarely does the term apply to Israel.
94:4 To **pour out** speech is figurative for the empty, incessant babbling of the arrogant and deceitful.
94:7–11 These are not atheists but blasphemers. The proud, gloating wicked are also **fools**, as vv. 8–11 point out.

94:14–15 Compare v. 14 with v. 5. If the Lord were to abandon his people, injustice would reign over them forever.
95:1 The **rock of our salvation** is a metaphorical expression denoting security and safety. The Hebrew word for "rock" describes the steadfast character of God (18:1–2,31; 73:26; 92:15; 144:1; Dt 32:15; 2Sm 22:47; Is 44:8).
95:2 To **enter his presence** means to worship God at the temple. The word for **thanksgiving** can also mean "thank offering."

³ For the Lord is a great God,
   a great King above all gods.
⁴ The depths of the earth are in his hand,
   and the mountain peaks are his.
⁵ The sea is his; he made it.
   His hands formed the dry land.

⁶ Come, let's worship and bow down;
   let's kneel before the Lord our Maker.
⁷ For he is our God,
   and we are the people of his pasture,
   the sheep under his care.^

   Today, if you hear his voice:
⁸ Do not harden your hearts as at Meribah,
   as on that day at Massah
   in the wilderness
⁹ where your ancestors tested me;
   they tried me, though they had seen
   what I did.
¹⁰ For forty years I was disgusted
   with that generation;
   I said, "They are a people whose hearts
   go astray;

they do not know my ways."
¹¹ So I swore in my anger,
   "They will not enter my rest."

King of the Earth

96 Sing a new song to the Lord;
   let the whole earth sing to the Lord.
² Sing to the Lord, bless his name;
   proclaim his salvation from day to day.
³ Declare his glory among the nations,
   his wondrous works among all peoples.

⁴ For the Lord is great and is
   highly praised;
   he is feared above all gods.
⁵ For all the gods of the peoples
   are worthless idols,
   but the Lord made the heavens.
⁶ Splendor and majesty are before him;
   strength and beauty are in his sanctuary.

⁷ Ascribe to the Lord, you families
   of the peoples,
   ascribe to the Lord glory and strength.

^95:7 Lit *sheep of his hand*

95:3 The Lord is a great God is an expression prevalent in the psalms that celebrates the Lord's kingship (47:2,7–8; 48:2–3; 96:4; 97:9; 136:2; 149:2). **95:8–11** These verses recall Ex 17:1–7 and Nm 20:2–13. The psalm relies heavily on the covenantal associations and language of the two texts. **95:8–9 Do not harden** warns against the self-reliance of God's people, who followed their own counsel and complained in the wilderness. The names **Meribah** ("contention, controversy") and **Massah** ("test") were given by Moses to the location where God provided water from a rock after the people **tested** God (Ex 17:7; Nm 20:13; Dt 6:16). The Lord tested Israel's faithfulness in the wilderness (Dt 8:2; 33:8). The Hebrew word for "tested" describes the refining of precious metals by smelting (Zch 13:9). **95:11** The concept of **rest** reaches its full development in Heb 4:3–11. **96:1–3** This **new song** was cosmic praise for Yahweh's reign over a universal kingdom comprising all peoples (98:1; 144:9; 149:1; Is 42:10). Mention of the sanctuary (96:6) implies a preexilic origin for this psalm. A threefold repetition of **sing** followed by three imperatives—**bless . . . proclaim**, and **declare**—underscore the purpose of the song: to glorify the Lord's **works** of **salvation**. **96:6** Four descriptive nouns—**splendor . . . majesty . . . strength**, and **beauty**—are personified as divine escorts preceding the Lord's processional entrance into the temple. **96:7–9** These verses represent an expansion of 29:1–2, substituting **families** (lit "tribes,

Q & A: Is beauty evidence for the existence of God?

by John Mark Reynolds

The existence of beauty suggests that God exists and that he is good. Beauty alone is not a sufficient proof for God's existence, but it serves as a confirmation to those whose belief is based on other reasons and experiences.

The harmonious plan of the cosmos allows for variation and freedom for created beings. There is a fundamental pattern and order to creation, but also room for the unexpected within the design plan. Too much regularity would seem stagnant, so thankfully creation shows variability and the capacity to adapt and change. So delightful is the universe that elegant mathematical and scientific theories work better in explaining it than inelegant ones.

These observations suggest that an engineer or artist lies behind the cosmos as its cause and designer. But is our recognition of beauty just a useful natural adaptation? After all, it would be to our advantage to develop a liking for the ecosystem that sustains us. But humans do not just find their local environment pleasing. We also discover that newly explored areas of the cosmos are beautiful.

For instance, when my son first went up in a plane and saw "cloud land," he turned to me with wonder and said, "It's so beautiful." It did not surprise him. Even though the scenery from above the clouds was previously unknown to him, he had learned to expect beauty when he came to new vistas of creation.

Gratuitous beauty, beauty that has no survival value for humankind, exists! Whether we dive to the bottom of the ocean or spy distant corners of space, we find things that are stark, weird, unknown, but beautiful. This superabundance of beauty is a hint that a good and loving God exists.

We do find instances of ugliness, but the ugly is less fundamental than beauty. Ugliness exists as a twisting or disruption of the beautiful created order. Scripture teaches this (Rm 8:20), and it is confirmed in our observations of nature. For instance, every unborn child will grow to beautifully express the divine image (through their talents and attributes) unless their development is somehow aborted by sin.

Viewed with our widest telescopes, the cosmos shows awe-inspiring beauty. This beauty is repeated in the most focused examination of the basic elements of the massive cosmic structure. It is only in the middle range, where we find humans making choices and shaping their world by wrong actions, that the pattern of beauty is twisted and marred. Yet, even there, the staggering ability of humankind to create beauty based on the common image of God within us reminds us that beauty is fundamentally real.

For Christians, existence is good, and goodness is beautiful. As a result, nothing created can be wholly bad or utterly ugly. Even the most shattered part of creation remains part of the beautiful whole, made from the beautiful elements of creation. Parts of creation, especially humans, require redemption. But even the shattered image of God in fallen humans retains enough beauty to remind the keen observer of God.

8 Ascribe to the Lord the glory
   of his name;
bring an offering and enter his courts.
9 Worship the Lord in the splendor
   of his holiness;
let the whole earth tremble before him.

10 Say among the nations,
   "The Lord reigns.
The world is firmly established;
   it cannot be shaken.
He judges the peoples fairly."
11 Let the heavens be glad
   and the earth rejoice;
let the sea and all that fills it resound.
12 Let the fields and everything
   in them celebrate.
Then all the trees of the forest will shout
   for joy
13 before the Lord, for he is coming —
for he is coming to judge the earth.
He will judge the world
   with righteousness
and the peoples with his faithfulness.

The Majestic King

97 The Lord reigns! Let
   the earth rejoice;
let the many coasts and islands be glad.

2 Clouds and total darkness
   surround him;
righteousness and justice are
   the foundation of his throne.
3 Fire goes before him
and burns up his foes on every side.
4 His lightning lights up the world;
the earth sees and trembles.
5 The mountains melt like wax
at the presence of the Lord —
at the presence of the Lord
   of the whole earth.

6 The heavens proclaim
   his righteousness;
all the peoples see his glory.

7 All who serve carved images,
those who boast in worthless idols,
   will be put to shame.
All the gods^A must worship him.

8 Zion hears and is glad,
Judah's villages^B rejoice
because of your judgments, Lord.
9 For you, Lord,
are the Most High over
   the whole earth;
you are exalted above all the gods.

10 You who love the Lord, hate evil!
He protects the lives
   of his faithful ones;
he rescues them from the power of
   the wicked.
11 Light dawns^C,^D for the righteous,
gladness for the upright in heart.
12 Be glad in the Lord,
   you righteous ones,
and give thanks to his holy name.^E

Praise the King

98 A psalm.
Sing a new song to the Lord,
for he has performed wonders;
his right hand and holy arm
have won him victory.

2 The Lord has made his victory known;
he has revealed his righteousness
in the sight of the nations.
3 He has remembered his love
and faithfulness to the house of Israel;
all the ends of the earth
have seen our God's victory.

4 Let the whole earth shout to the Lord;
be jubilant, shout for joy, and sing.
5 Sing to the Lord with the lyre,
with the lyre and melodious song.
6 With trumpets and the blast
   of the ram's horn
shout triumphantly
in the presence of the Lord, our King.

---

^A97:7 LXX, Syr read *All his angels*; Heb 1:6   ^B97:8 Lit *daughters*   ^C97:11 One Hb ms, LXX, some ancient versions read *rises to shine*; Ps 112:4   ^D97:11 Lit *Light is sown*   ^E97:12 Lit *to the memory of his holiness*

---

clans") **of the peoples** for "sons of God," while adding **bring an offering and enter his courts**, and **let the whole earth tremble before him**. The modifications redirect the praise of the Lord from the heavenly realm to the earthly sphere, functioning as a polemic against other deities. To **ascribe** something to someone is to acknowledge they have that attribute.
96:10 With the phrase **the Lord reigns**, the psalmist reinforced Yahweh's dual roles as King and Creator.
96:11–12 The personification of **heavens . . . earth . . . the sea . . . fields**, and **trees** in cosmic praise for the Lord recalls imagery from the prophet Isaiah (Is 44:23; 49:13).

97:1 The **coasts and islands** represent the farthest known habitable places, conveying the scope of the Lord's dominion and praise (Is 20:5–6; 41:1; 42:4,10,12,15).
97:2 Clouds and total darkness recollect the storm imagery on Mount Sinai, where the thick clouds hid God, and from which he spoke. In prophetic texts these Hebrew words usually describe a state of judgment (Is 60:2; Jl 2:2).
97:3–5 Fire combined with **lightning**, earthquakes, and volcanic activity typify the cosmic upheaval experienced at the approach of God (77:16–18; Ex 19:16; Mc 1:3–4).
97:7 The Hebrew word for "worthless gods" always refers to the impotence of **carved**

images and pagan **idols . . . All the gods must worship him** could be translated "all the gods humble themselves before him," conveying the irony of the psalm.
98:1 The Lord's **right hand** and his **holy arm** refer to his immeasurable power. In this psalm, **victory** implies judgment on the nations and salvation for Israel.
98:3 A reference to God's covenantal **faithfulness** combined with the **house of Israel** places this psalm in the preexilic period.
98:4–5 Be jubilant or "break forth" always occurs in combination with **shout for joy** or "ring out" (Is 14:7; 44:23; 49:13; 52:9; 54:1; 55:12).
98:6 The second part of this verse is literally "shout before King Yahweh." The LXX

⁷ Let the sea and all that fills it,
  the world and those who live in it,
    resound.

⁸ Let the rivers clap their hands;
  let the mountains shout together for joy
⁹ before the Lord,
  for he is coming to judge the earth.
  He will judge the world righteously
  and the peoples fairly.

The King Is Holy

99 The Lord reigns! Let
    the peoples tremble.
  He is enthroned between the cherubim.
  Let the earth quake.
² The Lord is great in Zion;
  he is exalted above all the peoples.
³ Let them praise your great
  and awe-inspiring name.
  He is holy.

⁴ The mighty King loves justice.
  You have established fairness;
  you have administered justice
  and righteousness in Jacob.
⁵ Exalt the Lord our God;
  bow in worship at his footstool.
  He is holy.

⁶ Moses and Aaron were among his priests;
  Samuel also was among those calling on
    his name.
  They called to the Lord
  and he answered them.
⁷ He spoke to them in a pillar of cloud;
  they kept his decrees and the statutes
  he gave them.
⁸ Lord our God, you answered them.
  You were a forgiving God to them,
  but an avenger of their sinful actions.

⁹ Exalt the Lord our God;
  bow in worship at his holy mountain,
  for the Lord our God is holy.

Be Thankful

100 *A psalm of thanksgiving.*
    Let the whole earth shout
  triumphantly to the Lord!
² Serve the Lord with gladness;
  come before him with joyful songs.
³ Acknowledge that the Lord is God.
  He made us, and we are his^—
  his people, the sheep of his pasture.
⁴ Enter his gates with thanksgiving
  and his courts with praise.
  Give thanks to him and bless his name.
⁵ For the Lord is good, and his
    faithful love endures forever;
  his faithfulness,
    through all generations.

A Vow of Integrity

101 *A psalm of David.*
    I will sing of faithful love
    and justice;
  I will sing praise to you, Lord.
² I will pay attention to the way
    of integrity.
  When will you come to me?
  I will live with a heart of integrity
    in my house.
³ I will not let anything worthless
    guide me.^B
  I hate the practice of transgression;
  it will not cling to me.
⁴ A devious heart will be far from me;
  I will not be involved with^c evil.

⁵ I will destroy anyone
  who secretly slanders his neighbor;

---

^100:3 Alt Hb tradition, some Hb mss, LXX, Syr, Vg read *and not we ourselves*　^B101:3 Lit *I will not put a worthless thing in front of my eyes*　^c101:4 Lit *not know*

---

rendering, "Shout before the king, O Lord," assumes the poem was performed before a human king, but a reference to an earthly ruler seems out of place in a text that lauds the attributes of the Lord.
98:8 The only other place **mountains shout** is in Isaiah's prophecies (Is 44:23; 49:13).
99:1 The ark of the covenant was regarded as the throne of the invisible Lord, or his footstool (132:7–8; Jr 3:16–17). Because the ark of the covenant was the central symbol of Yahweh's presence with his people Israel, its mysteries remained appropriately veiled within the inner sanctuary of the living God.
99:3 Awe-inspiring (lit "to be feared") denotes both respect and worship. The psalmist declared God's holiness three times (vv. 3,5,9) as in Is 6:3.
99:5 At his footstool associates the Lord's presence with the ark of the covenant (1Ch 28:2) or a central place of worship (Ps 132:7). In the days preceding Solomon's temple, King David instructed the priests to bring the ark, symbolizing the Lord's presence (2Sm 6:12).

Isaiah equated the ark with the sanctuary (Is 60:13), later describing heaven as the Lord's throne and the earth as his footstool (Is 66:1). Enemies become Christ's footstool, showing subjugation (Heb 1:13; 9:5).
99:6 Moses . . . **Aaron**, and **Samuel** served intercessory roles as priests, administering God's justice. They communicated closely with God, obeying his commands.
99:7 The Lord showed his presence to the Israelites in the form of a **pillar of cloud** and fire, from which he communicated his divine will to Israel's leaders during the wilderness experience (Ex 14:19; 16:10; 33:9; 40:36).
99:8 Even after God forgave sins, actions had consequences. The Lord punished Moses and Aaron for their **sinful actions** (Nm 20:12).
100:1–2 Praising the Lord and serving him joyfully were two conditions for entering the sanctuary or presence of God (40:8; 42:2; 43:4; 66:13; 86:9; 118:19–20).
101:1 The king's responsibilities toward his people consisted of **faithful love** (Hb *chesed*, "covenant loyalty") and **justice**, prompting

his promise to live with integrity and to eradicate God's enemies.
101:2 Integrity is a cultic term denoting lack of imperfections or blemishes. It refers to purity of thought or behavior (78:72). Integrity governs private as well as public life (Dt 5:32–33; 6:5–7). The wisdom overtones of this verse establish a connection between wisdom and the royal court.
101:3 The king determined not to let **anything worthless** serve as a standard or compass to **guide** him; the Lord's faithful love and justice would be his touchstone (26:3). **Transgression** is a covenantal term denoting anyone or anything opposed to God and his law. **It will not cling** means the king will not permit evil to remain in his kingdom for any amount of time.
101:4 Saying that a **heart** is **devious** acknowledges humanity's tendency to sin.
101:5–8 These verses focus on the king's promotion of righteousness in the community. The wise ruler rejects slanderers and the **arrogant** but surrounds himself with

I cannot tolerate anyone
with haughty eyes
or an arrogant heart.
⁶ My eyes favor the faithful of the land
so that they may sit down with me.
The one who follows the way
of integrity
may serve me.
⁷ No one who acts deceitfully
will live in my palace;
the one who tells lies
will not be retained here to guide me.ᴬ
⁸ Every morning I will destroy
all the wicked of the land,
wiping out all evildoers
from the LORD's city.

Affliction in light of Eternity

102 *A prayer of a suffering person who is weak and pours out his lament before the LORD.*

¹ LORD, hear my prayer;
let my cry for help come before you.
² Do not hide your face from me
in my day of trouble.
Listen closely to me;
answer me quickly when I call.

³ For my days vanish like smoke,
and my bones burn like a furnace.
⁴ My heart is suffering,
withered like grass;
I even forget to eat my food.
⁵ Because of the sound of my groaning,
my flesh sticks to my bones.
⁶ I am like an eagle owl,
like a little owl among the ruins.
⁷ I stay awake;
I am like a solitary bird on a roof.
⁸ My enemies taunt me all day long;
they ridicule and use my name
as a curse.
⁹ I eat ashes like bread
and mingle my drinks with tears
¹⁰ because of your indignation and wrath;

for you have picked me up
and thrown me aside.
¹¹ My days are like a lengthening shadow,
and I wither away like grass.

¹² But you, LORD, are enthroned forever;
your fame endures to all generations.
¹³ You will rise up and have compassion
on Zion,
for it is time to show favor to her —
the appointed time has come.
¹⁴ For your servants take delight in its stones
and favor its dust.

¹⁵ Then the nations will fear the name
of the LORD,
and all the kings of the earth your glory,
¹⁶ for the LORD will rebuild Zion;
he will appear in his glory.
¹⁷ He will pay attention to the prayer
of the destitute
and will not despise their prayer.

¹⁸ This will be written
for a later generation,
and a people who have not yet
been created will praise the LORD:
¹⁹ He looked down from
his holy heights —
the LORD gazed out from heaven
to earth —
²⁰ to hear a prisoner's groaning,
to set free those condemned to die,ᴮ
²¹ so that they might declare
the name of the LORD in Zion
and his praise in Jerusalem
²² when peoples and kingdoms
are assembled
to serve the LORD.

²³ He has broken myᶜ strength
in midcourse;
he has shortened my days.
²⁴ I say, "My God, do not take me
in the middle of my life!ᴰ

ᴬ101:7 Lit *be established in front of my eyes* ᴮ102:20 Lit *free sons of death* ᶜ102:23 Some Hb mss, LXX read *his* ᴰ102:24 Lit *my days*

---

those who are blameless and **faithful** (Dt 10:8; 17:12; 21:5). The moral standards of the king should be reflected by those who **serve** him; therefore, the ruler will remove from his palace anyone who deceives and **tells lies**. **102:1–2 Do not hide your face** is a figurative expression used by the psalmist, who thought God had forsaken him (10:11; 13:1–2; 69:17). God's face represents the blessing of his presence. **102:3** The **furnace** could be a hearth or brazier (Jr 36:23). **102:4–5** The **heart**, or seat of morale, has been **suffering** as if by disease. **Withered like grass** shows the discouragement of the psalmist. **102:6 A little owl among the ruins** denotes the psalmist's loneliness resulting from ostracism.

102:9–10 The psalmist perceived his circumstances as a direct result of God's casting him out of his presence (Jb 27:21; 30:19,22; Is 64:5). **102:11** A metaphorical expression for imminent death, the phrase **like a lengthening shadow** associates the setting sun with the end of life. **102:12** The psalmist began a new section of the psalm by contrasting the frailty and vulnerability of humanity with the eternal and immutable nature of the Lord. **102:13** The rising of the Lord signifies judgment. **102:14** The value of Zion to her people did not diminish in spite of the Babylonian invasion (Ezk 26:12). **102:15** The return of the Lord has cosmological implications. All the **nations** and

their leaders will recognize and worship the God of Israel (Is 2:1–5; 49:7–23; 60–62; Zch 14). **102:19** When the Lord **looked down** and **gazed** at the earth below, he heard the cries of the exiles, acknowledged the plight of his people, and brought deliverance (Dt 26:15; Is 63:15). Hundreds of years earlier, God had also heard the Israelites in Egypt and looked upon them with great concern (Ex 2:24). **102:20 Those condemned to die** (lit "sons of death") describes the hopelessness of the captives (79:11; 146:7; Is 49:9). **102:22** The assembly of nations for universal worship occurs at the Lord's return to Zion (Is 2:1–5; 66:23–24; Zch 14:16–21).

Your years continue
    through all generations.
25 Long ago you established the earth,
    and the heavens are the work
        of your hands.
26 They will perish, but you will endure;
    all of them will wear out like clothing.
    You will change them like a garment,
    and they will pass away.
27 But you are the same,
    and your years will never end.
28 Your servants' children
    will dwell securely,
    and their offspring will be established
        before you."

The Forgiving God

103 Of David.

My soul, bless the LORD,
and all that is within me, bless
    his holy name.
2 My soul, bless the LORD,
and do not forget all his benefits.

3 He forgives all your iniquity;
he heals all your diseases.
4 He redeems your life from the Pit;
he crowns you with faithful love
    and compassion.
5 He satisfies you[A] with good things;
your youth is renewed like the eagle.

6 The LORD executes acts
    of righteousness
and justice for all the oppressed.
7 He revealed his ways to Moses,
his deeds to the people of Israel.
8 The LORD is compassionate
    and gracious,
slow to anger and abounding
    in faithful love.
9 He will not always accuse us
or be angry forever.
10 He has not dealt with us as
    our sins deserve
or repaid us according to our iniquities.

11 For as high as the heavens are above
    the earth,
so great is his faithful love
toward those who fear him.
12 As far as the east is from the west,
so far has he removed
our transgressions from us.
13 As a father has compassion
    on his children,
so the LORD has compassion on those
    who fear him.
14 For he knows what we are made of,
remembering that we are dust.

15 As for man, his days are like grass —
he blooms like a flower of the field;
16 when the wind passes over it,
    it vanishes,
and its place is no longer known.[B]
17 But from eternity to eternity
the LORD's faithful love is toward
    those who fear him,
and his righteousness
    toward the grandchildren
18 of those who keep his covenant,
who remember to observe
    his precepts.
19 The LORD has established his throne
    in heaven,
and his kingdom rules over all.

20 Bless the LORD,
all his angels of great strength,
who do his word,
obedient to his command.
21 Bless the LORD, all his armies,
his servants who do his will.
22 Bless the LORD, all his works
in all the places where he rules.
My soul, bless the LORD!

God the Creator

104 My soul, bless the LORD!
LORD my God, you are very great;
you are clothed with majesty
    and splendor.

[A]**103:5** Lit *satisfies your ornament*; Hb obscure   [B]**103:16** Lit *place no longer knows it*

102:26–27 The unchanging nature of God extends beyond the course of history. Although the heavens and earth will **wear out like clothing** (Is 50:9; 51:6,8; see Heb 1:10–12), they will undergo transformation at the return of Christ (Rv 21:1).
103:1–2 The threefold repetition of **bless** represents the highest form of worship (Is 6:3). The Hebrew word translated **benefits** means paying back what is deserved (28:4; 94:2; 116:12; 142:7). It most often describes God's divine wrath and retribution toward the enemy (Is 59:18), but here it describes the Lord's blessings enumerated in vv. 3–5.
103:3 Forgives, a cultic expression common in Leviticus and Numbers, finds fuller development in Is 33:24; 43:25, although only Is 55:7 includes the expressed condition of repentance.

103:4–5 The word **redeems** denotes the payment of a ransom price. **Pit** refers to Sheol, the place of the dead. These verses convey a sense of divine providence and peace, so that youthful strength is renewed (lit "renews itself") like an **eagle** (Is 40:31; 57:10).
103:8–9 In this allusion to Ex 34:6–7, the psalmist used the divine formula as the basis on which Israel experienced the Lord's forgiveness.
103:10 While God's holiness demands payment for sin, God's mercy and compassion restrain his discipline. The Hebrew word rendered **repaid** forms a wordplay with v. 2. The Lord's people enjoy his "benefits" because he does not pay them back for their sins.

103:14 The Hebrew word *yetser* (**what we are made of**, "our formation") comes from a verb that denotes the shaping of clay by a craftsman into an acceptable vessel. God's intimate knowledge of his created beings affirms their origin and frailty.
103:17–18 The Hebrew word *yara'* (**fear**) combines obedience and respect with humility before a sovereign God.
103:21 God's **armies** (or "hosts") refer to divine beings who dwell with God and serve him.
104:1–35 This psalm is a companion hymn to Ps 103. It begins with the same words that end that psalm. This psalm alludes to the Noahic covenant and the six days of creation. The psalm is an argument against sun worship.

2 He wraps himself in light as if it were
    a robe,
  spreading out the sky like a canopy,
3 laying the beams of his palace
    on the waters above,
  making the clouds his chariot,
  walking on the wings of the wind,
4 and making the winds his messengers,^A
  flames of fire his servants.

5 He established the earth
    on its foundations;
  it will never be shaken.
6 You covered it with the deep
    as if it were a garment;
  the water stood above the mountains.
7 At your rebuke the water fled;
  at the sound of your thunder
    they hurried away —
8 mountains rose and valleys sank^B —
  to the place you established for them.
9 You set a boundary they cannot cross;
  they will never cover the earth again.

10 He causes the springs to gush
    into the valleys;
  they flow between the mountains.
11 They supply water for every wild beast;
  the wild donkeys quench their thirst.
12 The birds of the sky live
    beside the springs;
  they make their voices heard
    among the foliage.
13 He waters the mountains
    from his palace;
  the earth is satisfied by the fruit
    of your labor.

14 He causes grass to grow for the livestock
  and provides crops for man to cultivate,
  producing food from the earth,
15 wine that makes human hearts glad —
  making his face shine with oil —
  and bread that sustains human hearts.

16 The trees of the LORD flourish,^C
  the cedars of Lebanon that he planted.
17 There the birds make their nests;
  storks make their homes
    in the pine trees.
18 The high mountains are
    for the wild goats;
  the cliffs are a refuge for hyraxes.

19 He made the moon to mark
    the^D festivals;^E
  the sun knows when to set.
20 You bring darkness,
    and it becomes night,
  when all the forest animals stir.
21 The young lions roar for their prey
  and seek their food from God.
22 The sun rises; they go back
  and lie down in their dens.
23 Man goes out to his work
  and to his labor until evening.

24 How countless are
    your works, LORD!
  In wisdom you have made them all;
  the earth is full of your creatures.^F
25 Here is the sea, vast and wide,
  teeming with creatures
    beyond number —
  living things both large and small.
26 There the ships move about,
  and Leviathan, which you formed
    to play there.

27 All of them wait for you
  to give them their food at the right time.
28 When you give it to them,
    they gather it;
  when you open your hand,
    they are satisfied with good things.
29 When you hide your face,
    they are terrified;
  when you take away their breath,
    they die and return to the dust.

^A104:4 Or *angels*   ^B104:7–8 Or *away. They flowed over the mountains and went down valleys*   ^C104:16 Lit *are satisfied*
^D104:19 Lit *moon for*   ^E104:19 Or *the appointed times*   ^F104:24 Lit *possessions*

104:3 The **palace** (or "chamber") refers to God's dwelling place, which contains rain (v. 13; Am 9:6). The Lord rides the clouds (Ps 68:4,17). To walk **on the wings of the wind** refers to God's dominion (18:10).
104:4 The **winds** and rain, controlled by God, are agents of judgment and blessing. **Flames of fire** refers to lightning (29:7; 148:8; see Heb 1:7).
104:5 While vv. 1–4 describe the Lord's sovereignty over natural forces, the emphasis in this verse shifts to the Lord as King over the earth. By divine command, God **established** the earth on its axis. **It will never be shaken** could be rendered as "it will never totter."
104:6–8 God **covered** the earth **with the deep** and **the water stood above the mountains**. The imagery is consistent with

the cosmic flood in Genesis (7:18–20). At God's **rebuke the water fled** like warriors fleeing from battle (114:3–6) and **hurried away** (i.e., in alarm) at the sound of God's voice. The floodwaters receded, uncovering the mountains and redefining the valleys, restoring the earth to its natural state. Just as the Lord established the earth (v. 5), so the mountains and valleys remained in the places God **established for them**.
104:9 As sovereign Creator, God appointed a boundary that the waters could not transcend, so that **they will never cover the earth again** (Is 54:9). This expression recalls the Lord's covenant with Noah, when he promised never to destroy the earth by flood again (Gn 9:11).
104:10–12 The psalmist transformed the destructive role of water into a constructive

role—the provision of water for sustaining the life of his creatures.
104:15 To make a man's **face shine with oil** figuratively describes the abundance of God's provision and the satisfaction of rich foods. **Bread** denotes any type of food.
104:16 Flourish is literally "are satisfied."
104:26 Leviathan (Jb 3:8; Is 27:1) refers to a large sea creature that would **play** in the water.
104:28 The Hebrew word for **satisfied** is a key term in the psalm. The earth is "satisfied" (v. 13), the trees are satisfied ("flourish," v. 16), and all of the earth's inhabitants are "satisfied" (v. 28).
104:29–30 The hiding of God's **face** refers to abandonment. The term **terrified** denotes a state of chaos, and it may also be translated "confused."

30 When you send your breath,^A
they are created,
and you renew the surface
of the ground.

31 May the glory of the LORD
endure forever;
may the LORD rejoice in his works.
32 He looks at the earth, and it trembles;
he touches the mountains,
and they pour out smoke.
33 I will sing to the LORD all my life;
I will sing praise to my God while I live.
34 May my meditation be pleasing to him;
I will rejoice in the LORD.
35 May sinners vanish from the earth
and wicked people be no more.
My soul, bless the LORD!
Hallelujah!

God's Faithfulness to His People

105
Give thanks to the LORD, call on
his name;
proclaim his deeds among the peoples.
2 Sing to him, sing praise to him;
tell about all his wondrous works!
3 Boast in his holy name;
let the hearts of those who seek
the LORD rejoice.
4 Seek the LORD and his strength;
seek his face always.
5 Remember the wondrous works
he has done,
his wonders, and the judgments he
has pronounced,^B
6 you offspring of Abraham his servant,
Jacob's descendants — his chosen ones.

7 He is the LORD our God;
his judgments govern the whole earth.
8 He remembers his covenant forever,
the promise he ordained
for a thousand generations —
9 the covenant he made with Abraham,
swore^C to Isaac,

10 and confirmed to Jacob as a decree
and to Israel as a permanent covenant:
11 "I will give the land of Canaan to you
as your inherited portion."

12 When they were few in number,
very few indeed,
and resident aliens in Canaan,
13 wandering from nation to nation
and from one kingdom to another,
14 he allowed no one to oppress them;
he rebuked kings on their behalf:
15 "Do not touch my anointed ones,
or harm my prophets."

16 He called down famine against the land
and destroyed the entire food supply.
17 He had sent a man ahead of them —
Joseph, who was sold as a slave.
18 They hurt his feet with shackles;
his neck was put in an iron collar.
19 Until the time his prediction came true,
the word of the LORD tested him.
20 The king sent for him and released him;
the ruler of peoples set him free.
21 He made him master of his household,
ruler over all his possessions —
22 binding^D his officials at will
and instructing his elders.

23 Then Israel went to Egypt;
Jacob lived as an alien in the land of Ham.^E
24 The LORD^F made his people very fruitful;
he made them more numerous
than their foes,
25 whose hearts he turned to hate his people
and to deal deceptively
with his servants.
26 He sent Moses his servant,
and Aaron, whom he had chosen.
27 They performed his miraculous signs
among them
and wonders in the land of Ham.
28 He sent darkness, and it became dark —
for did they not defy his commands?

---

^A104:30 Or *Spirit*   ^B105:5 Lit *judgments of his mouth*   ^C105:9 Lit *and his oath*   ^D105:22 LXX, Syr, Vg read *teaching*
^E105:23 = Egypt, also in v. 27   ^F105:24 Lit *He*

104:33–34 This is a vow of praise.
104:35 In the LXX, **Hallelujah!** begins Ps 105; thus, Pss 105–106 each end with the same phrase they begin with—"My soul, bless the LORD!" in 103 and 104, and "Hallelujah!" in 105 and 106. *Hallelujah* is literally "praise Yah." *Yah* is a shortened form of Yahweh. The psalmist was inviting his audience to join him in praising the Lord.
105:1–45 This psalm, an epic poem, resembles Pss 78 and 106 in form and content. Verses 1–15 recur in 1Ch 16:8–22, a song associated with the Davidic procession ushering the ark of the covenant into Jerusalem.
105:3 Boast in denotes continuous praise.
105:4 Strength is figurative for the ark (78:61) that symbolized the Lord's presence and preceded Israel into battle (Jos 6:6–7; 1Sm 4:3).

105:5 God's **judgments** are his ordinances (119:13; Ex 24:3).
105:12–13 The psalmist outlined the birth and growth of the nation of Israel, beginning with the time of the patriarchs, a nomadic people (Gn 12:1; 13:1; 20:1) traveling throughout **Canaan**.
105:14 He rebuked kings refers to the divine protection of Sarah from Pharaoh (Gn 12:17) and Sarah and Rebekah from Abimelech (Gn 20:13; 26:11).
105:15 God's **anointed ones** would include kings, priests, and **prophets**, all of whom received anointing in a dedication ceremony.
105:16 The **famine** in the land of Canaan (Gn 41:53–57) eventually brought Jacob and his sons to Egypt. **The entire food supply** is literally "every staff of bread." The staff could

refer to a rod on which bread, shaped in rings, was hung up to protect it from rodents, or it could be speaking figuratively of bread as the staff of life.
105:23 The designation **Israel** refers to Jacob and his sons (Gn 46). **The land of Ham** is another name for Egypt (78:51; 106:22; Gn 10:6).
105:24 The Hebrew word translated as **more numerous** implies "stronger," with the nuance of physical power.
105:26–27 Moses is called God's servant twelve times in the OT. Aaron was chosen by God to be Moses's prophet (Ex 7:1).
105:28 The psalmist listed the plague of **darkness** out of order because it was the first sign that resulted in Egypt's acknowledgment of the Lord's power (Ex 10:21).

29 He turned their water into blood
and caused their fish to die.
30 Their land was overrun with frogs,
even in their royal chambers.
31 He spoke, and insects came —
gnats throughout their country.
32 He gave them hail for rain,
and lightning throughout their land.
33 He struck their vines and fig trees
and shattered the trees of their territory.
34 He spoke, and locusts came —
young locusts without number.
35 They devoured all the vegetation
in their land
and consumed the produce
of their land.
36 He struck all the firstborn in their land,
all their first progeny.

37 Then he brought Israel out with silver
and gold,
and no one among his tribes stumbled.
38 Egypt was glad when they left,
for the dread of Israel^A had fallen
on them.
39 He spread a cloud as a covering
and gave a fire to light up the night.
40 They asked, and he brought quail
and satisfied them with bread
from heaven.
41 He opened a rock, and water
gushed out;
it flowed like a stream in the desert.
42 For he remembered his holy promise
to Abraham his servant.
43 He brought his people out
with rejoicing,
his chosen ones with shouts of joy.
44 He gave them the lands of the nations,
and they inherited
what other peoples had worked for.

45 All this happened
so that they might keep his statutes
and obey his instructions.
Hallelujah!

Israel's Unfaithfulness to God

106 Hallelujah!
Give thanks to the LORD,
for he is good;
his faithful love endures forever.
2 Who can declare the LORD's mighty acts
or proclaim all the praise due him?
3 How happy are those
who uphold justice,
who practice righteousness at all times.

4 Remember me, LORD,
when you show favor to your people.
Come to me with your salvation
5 so that I may enjoy the prosperity
of your chosen ones,
rejoice in the joy of your nation,
and boast about your heritage.

6 Both we and our ancestors
have sinned;
we have done wrong
and have acted wickedly.
7 Our ancestors in Egypt did not grasp
the significance of
your wondrous works
or remember your many acts
of faithful love;
instead, they rebelled by the sea
— the Red Sea.
8 Yet he saved them for his name's sake,
to make his power known.
9 He rebuked the Red Sea, and it dried up;
he led them through the depths
as through a desert.
10 He saved them from the power
of the adversary;
he redeemed them from the power
of the enemy.
11 Water covered their foes;
not one of them remained.
12 Then they believed his promises
and sang his praise.

13 They soon forgot his works
and would not wait for his counsel.

---

^105:38 Lit them

105:29-36 The psalmist recounted some of the plagues in Egypt that enabled the Lord's people to escape. The plagues were **water into blood** (Ex 7:14–24), **frogs** (Ex 8:5–15), **gnats** (Ex 8:16–19), **hail** (Ex 9:13–35), **locusts** that consumed all the vegetation (Ex 10:1–20), and culminated in the death of **the firstborn** of Egypt (Ex 11:1–10). The firstborn represented the virility and strength of the family. In Egyptian culture, Pharaoh and his firstborn son claimed to have the status of deity. 105:37-38 Verse 37 alludes to Ex 12:35–36, and v. 38 to Ex 12:33. 105:39 The **cloud** and **fire** refer to the pillar of cloud and fire (Ex 13:20–22; 14:19–20; 40:36–37) that guided the Israelites throughout their journey in the wilderness.

105:40-42 The Lord provided **quail** when the Israelites complained about the manna **from heaven** (78:25; Ex 16:4; Nm 11:4–35), and he also gave them **water** from a **rock** (Ex 17:1–7; Nm 20:9–11). God's provision for his people reflects his faithfulness to the covenant first initiated with **Abraham**. 105:43 Israel is called God's **chosen ones** eight times in the OT. 105:44-45 The **lands of the nations** refers to Canaan, which contained wicked peoples long deserving judgment. 106:1-48 The absence of conflict between the northern and southern kingdoms suggests a setting for this psalm during the united monarchy. It consists

of a historical chronology of the exodus and conquest. 106:1 **Hallelujah!** occurs twenty-three times in the OT. It means "praise Yahweh!" The rest of the verse is found also in 107:1; 118:1,29; 136:1; 1Ch 16:34. 106:4-5 This prayer for personal inclusion in God's upcoming saving act is somewhat unusual, although Nehemiah also asks God to **remember me** (Neh 5:19). 106:6 The combining of "we" with "they" turns what would be an indictment into a confession. 106:10 The **adversary** is literally "the one who hated." 106:11-12 Compare these verses with Ex 14:28–15:1.

¹⁴ They were seized with craving
in the wilderness
and tested God in the desert.
¹⁵ He gave them what they asked for,
but sent a wasting disease among them.
¹⁶ In the camp they were envious of Moses
and of Aaron, the LORD's holy one.
¹⁷ The earth opened up
and swallowed Dathan;
it covered the assembly of Abiram.
¹⁸ Fire blazed throughout their assembly;
flames consumed the wicked.

¹⁹ At Horeb they made a calf
and worshiped the cast metal image.
²⁰ They exchanged their glory^A,B
for the image of a grass-eating ox.
²¹ They forgot God their Savior,
who did great things in Egypt,
²² wondrous works in the land of Ham,^C
awe-inspiring acts at the Red Sea.
²³ So he said he would have
destroyed them —
if Moses his chosen one
had not stood before him in the breach
to turn his wrath away
from destroying them.

²⁴ They despised the pleasant land
and did not believe his promise.
²⁵ They grumbled in their tents
and did not listen to the LORD.
²⁶ So he raised his hand against them
with an oath
that he would make them fall
in the desert
²⁷ and would disperse their descendants^D
among the nations,
scattering them throughout the lands.

²⁸ They aligned themselves with Baal
of Peor

and ate sacrifices offered
to lifeless gods.^E
²⁹ They angered the LORD with their deeds,
and a plague broke out against them.
³⁰ But Phinehas stood up and intervened,
and the plague was stopped.
³¹ It was credited to him as righteousness
throughout all generations to come.

³² They angered the LORD at the Waters
of Meribah,
and Moses suffered^F because of them,
³³ for they embittered his spirit,^G
and he spoke rashly with his lips.

³⁴ They did not destroy the peoples
as the LORD had commanded them
³⁵ but mingled with the nations
and adopted their ways.
³⁶ They served their idols,
which became a snare to them.
³⁷ They sacrificed their sons
and daughters to demons.
³⁸ They shed innocent blood —
the blood of their sons and daughters
whom they sacrificed to the idols
of Canaan;
so the land became polluted with blood.
³⁹ They defiled themselves by their actions
and prostituted themselves
by their deeds.

⁴⁰ Therefore the LORD's anger burned
against his people,
and he abhorred his own inheritance.
⁴¹ He handed them over to the nations;
those who hated them ruled over them.
⁴² Their enemies oppressed them,
and they were subdued
under their power.
⁴³ He rescued them many times,
but they continued to rebel deliberately
and were beaten down by their iniquity.

^A106:20 Alt Hb tradition reads his glory, or my glory ^B106:20 = God ^C106:22 = Egypt ^D106:27 Syr; MT reads would make their descendants fall ^E106:28 Lit sacrifices for dead ones ^F106:32 Lit and it was evil for Moses ^G106:33 Some Hb mss, LXX, Syr, Jer; other Hb mss read they rebelled against his Spirit

106:16–18 The Israelites grew envious of Moses and Aaron (Nm 16:1–14,31–39). The Hebrew word often refers to God's righteous jealousy on behalf of his name (Ex 20:5; 34:14; Ezk 39:25). As the LORD's holy one, Aaron served as the first anointed high priest.
106:19–20 Israel replaced God's glory with a manmade image (Ex 32; Dt 9:12). The sin of idolatry is cited in this psalm as the single most significant breach of covenant fidelity.
106:23 Moses stood before God in the breach, mediating on behalf of the wayward people in the wilderness and offering his life to prevent their destruction (105:26; Ex 32:10–11,31). Compare Ps 106:19–23 with Dt 9:8–21.
106:24–27 Rather than following the reports of Joshua and Caleb about the inhabitants

of the land of Canaan, Israel showed a lack of trust and rejected the promised land (78:59,67; Nm 11:20; 14:11). Consequently, Israel's descendants experienced exile and dispersion (Lv 26:33; Dt 4:26–27; 28:64–65; Ezk 20:23). Compare Ps 106:24–27 with Nm 13:25–14:45; Dt 1:21–33.
106:28–31 Israel participated in a fertility cult at Peor in Moab, further endangering their relationship with the Lord. Over twenty-four thousand died from the plague that resulted (Nm 25:1–9). In later Scripture, Baal of Peor symbolizes apostasy (Hs 9:10). Phinehas demonstrated faith by his zeal for God, and God counted it as righteousness to him and to all who follow his example (see Gn 15:6).
106:32–33 The rebellion at Meribah (81:7; 95:8; Ex 17:1–7; Nm 20:2–13) provided the

catalyst for Moses's sin of presumption (Nm 8–13). As a result, he did not enter Canaan.
106:34–38 The Israelites were instructed to annihilate all the inhabitants of the cities they conquered (Ex 34:11; Dt 7:1; 20:16; Jdg 1:21; 2:3), but they failed to do so. Consequently they intermarried with foreigners and adopted many of their idolatrous practices, including infant sacrifice (see Lv 18:21; 2Kg 16:3; 21:6; 23:10). God's faithfulness to his divine promise and covenant was met with infidelity by Israel (Ex 23:32).
106:41–44 The Lord allowed the oppression of Israel by other nations as divine judgment. The goal was discipline and restoration to divine favor (Jdg 2:14; 3:1). The book of Judges recounts the repeated cycle of disobedience, oppression, entreaty, and restoration.

44 When he heard their cry,
he took note of their distress,
45 remembered his covenant with them,
and relented according to
the abundance
of his faithful love.
46 He caused them to be pitied
before all their captors.

47 Save us, LORD our God,
and gather us from the nations,
so that we may give thanks
to your holy name
and rejoice in your praise.

48 Blessed be the LORD God of Israel,
from everlasting to everlasting.
Let all the people say, "Amen!"
Hallelujah!

BOOK V (Psalms 107–150)

Thanksgiving for God's Deliverance

107 Give thanks to the LORD,
for he is good;
his faithful love endures forever.
2 Let the redeemed of the LORD proclaim
that he has redeemed them
from the power of the foe
3 and has gathered them
from the lands —
from the east and the west,
from the north and the south.

4 Some wandered
in the desolate wilderness,
finding no way to a city
where they could live.
5 They were hungry and thirsty;
their spirits failed^A within them.
6 Then they cried out to the LORD
in their trouble;
he rescued them from their distress.
7 He led them by the right path
to go to a city where they could live.
8 Let them give thanks to the LORD
for his faithful love

and his wondrous works for
all humanity.
9 For he has satisfied the thirsty
and filled the hungry with good things.

10 Others sat in darkness and gloom^B —
prisoners in cruel chains —
11 because they rebelled
against God's commands
and despised the counsel
of the Most High.
12 He broke their spirits^C with hard labor;
they stumbled, and there was no one
to help.
13 Then they cried out to the LORD
in their trouble;
he saved them from their distress.
14 He brought them out of darkness
and gloom
and broke their chains apart.
15 Let them give thanks to the LORD
for his faithful love
and his wondrous works for all humanity.
16 For he has broken down
the bronze gates
and cut through the iron bars.

17 Fools suffered affliction
because of their rebellious ways
and their iniquities.
18 They loathed all food
and came near the gates of death.
19 Then they cried out to the LORD
in their trouble;
he saved them from their distress.
20 He sent his word and healed them;
he rescued them from their traps.
21 Let them give thanks to the LORD
for his faithful love
and his wondrous works for
all humanity.
22 Let them offer thanksgiving sacrifices
and announce his works with shouts
of joy.

23 Others went to sea in ships,
conducting trade on the vast water.

^A107:5 Lit their soul fainted   ^B107:10 Or the shadow of death, also in v. 14   ^C107:12 Lit hearts

106:47–48 The psalmist appealed to God's saving acts toward Israel as the grounds for imploring the Lord to **gather** and restore the nation once again (see 1Ch 16:35–36; Is 61:7–14). Every book of the Psalms ends with praise (see note at 41:13).
107:1 Faithful love (Hb *chesed*, "covenant loyalty") is a key word in this psalm, reinforcing Yahweh's unconditional love, the basis on which he intervened on behalf of his people.
107:2 The concept of redemption (Hb *ga'al*, "redeem") relates to blood vengeance exercised by the Lord upon the enemy. The idea is rooted in Levitical law (Nm 35:12,19–27; Dt 19:6–12).

107:3 This verse refers to the return of Israel from exile (Is 42:10–13; 43:5–7).
107:4 While the **wilderness** normally implies the wanderings following the exodus, the context suggests the exiles journeyed through the Syrian-Arabic Desert. The exiles were unable to assimilate into the culture and lifestyle of their captors, anticipating the Lord's rescue at any time.
107:5 Hungry and thirsty is a dual reference to physical hunger and thirst as well as the absence of organized worship and cultic practice (Am 8:11).
107:6 This sentence is repeated in vv. 13,19,28. God's people continually sought the Lord's intervention from adversity and danger.

107:8 This sentence is repeated in vv. 15,21,31. Salvation should result in testimony and praise.
107:15 For all humanity is literally "for the sons of man" (*'adam*).
107:17–18 These verses summarize the fate of those who suffered debilitating illness as a result of their disobedience and guilt.
107:23–32 The OT does not elaborate on the maritime activity of Israel, and commercial seafaring is rarely mentioned (Gn 49:13; 2Ch 9:21; 20:36).
107:23–26 The terminology and rhythm of this section mimic the up-and-down movement of the waves.

²⁴ They saw the LORD's works,
   his wondrous works in the deep.
²⁵ He spoke and raised a stormy wind
   that stirred up the waves of the sea.^A
²⁶ Rising up to the sky, sinking down
      to the depths,
   their courage^B melting away in anguish,
²⁷ they reeled and staggered
      like a drunkard,
   and all their skill was useless.
²⁸ Then they cried out to the LORD
      in their trouble,
   and he brought them
      out of their distress.
²⁹ He stilled the storm to a whisper,
   and the waves of the sea were hushed.
³⁰ They rejoiced when the waves
      grew quiet.
   Then he guided them to the harbor
      they longed for.
³¹ Let them give thanks to the LORD
   for his faithful love
   and his wondrous works for
      all humanity.
³² Let them exalt him in the assembly
      of the people
   and praise him in the council
      of the elders.

³³ He turns rivers into desert,
   springs into thirsty ground,
³⁴ and fruitful land into salty wasteland,
   because of the wickedness
      of its inhabitants.
³⁵ He turns a desert into a pool,
   dry land into springs.
³⁶ He causes the hungry to settle there,
   and they establish a city
      where they can live.
³⁷ They sow fields and plant vineyards
   that yield a fruitful harvest.
³⁸ He blesses them,
      and they multiply greatly;
   he does not let their livestock decrease.

³⁹ When they are diminished
      and are humbled
   by cruel oppression and sorrow,
⁴⁰ he pours contempt on nobles
   and makes them wander
      in a trackless wasteland.

⁴¹ But he lifts the needy out of
      their suffering
   and makes their families multiply
      like flocks.
⁴² The upright see it and rejoice,
   and all injustice shuts its mouth.

⁴³ Let whoever is wise pay attention
      to these things
   and consider the LORD's acts
      of faithful love.

A Plea for Victory

108 A song. A psalm of David.
My heart is confident, God;
   I will sing; I will sing praises
      with the whole of my being.^C
² Wake up, harp and lyre!
   I will wake up the dawn.
³ I will praise you, LORD,
      among the peoples;
   I will sing praises to you
      among the nations.
⁴ For your faithful love is higher
      than the heavens,
   and your faithfulness reaches to
      the clouds.
⁵ God, be exalted above the heavens,
   and let your glory be over
      the whole earth.
⁶ Save with your right hand
      and answer me
   so that those you love may be rescued.

⁷ God has spoken in his sanctuary:^D
   "I will celebrate!
   I will divide up Shechem.
   I will apportion the Valley of Succoth.
⁸ Gilead is mine, Manasseh is mine,
   and Ephraim is my helmet;
   Judah is my scepter.
⁹ Moab is my washbasin;
   I throw my sandal on Edom.
   I shout in triumph over Philistia."

¹⁰ Who will bring me
      to the fortified city?
   Who will lead me to Edom?
¹¹ God, haven't you rejected us?
   God, you do not march out
      with our armies.

---

^A107:25 Lit *of it* ^B107:26 Lit *souls* ^C108:1 Lit *praises, even my glory* ^D108:7 Or *has promised by his holy nature*

107:27 The sailors' actions are compared to those of **a drunkard** (Pr 23:29–35). **Their skill was useless** could be translated "their wisdom was confounded."
107:33–35 Many of those exiled in Babylon became comfortable and were not anxious to return to Judah, so the psalmist, in an effort to encourage native Judeans to return to Jerusalem, reminded them that God could bring about a reversal in natural resources. The **rivers** of Babylon could fail, while

the **desert** areas of Judah could flourish (Is 41:17–18).
107:36–38 The destruction of hunger and homelessness reflects a reversal of vv. 4–5,7. The hungry will become agriculturally independent, producing crops and cattle.
107:39–41 In an ironic twist, those who suffered **oppression**, grief, and misfortune will enjoy prosperity, while those who inflicted misery will be frustrated (7:14–16; Jb 12:21,24).

107:43 The psalm concludes with a wisdom saying centering on Yahweh's covenant loyalty.
108:1–13 This psalm is a combination of 57:7–11 (here, vv. 1–5) and 60:5–12 (here, vv. 6–13).
108:1 The whole of my being is literally "my glory."
108:8 Judah was the location of the king, symbolized by the **scepter**.
108:9 Moab . . . **Edom**, and **Philistia** were three long-standing enemies of Israel. They are symbolically assigned denigrating roles

¹² Give us aid against the foe,
for human help is worthless.
¹³ With God we will perform valiantly;
he will trample our foes.

Prayer against an Enemy

109 *For the choir director. A psalm of David.*

¹ God of my praise, do not be silent.
² For wicked and deceitful mouths open against me;
they speak against me
with lying tongues.
³ They surround me with hateful words
and attack me without cause.
⁴ In return for my love they accuse me,
but I continue to pray.^A
⁵ They repay me evil for good,
and hatred for my love.

⁶ Set a wicked person over him;
let an accuser^B stand at his right hand.
⁷ When he is judged, let him
be found guilty,
and let his prayer be counted as sin.
⁸ Let his days be few;
let another take over his position.
⁹ Let his children be fatherless
and his wife a widow.
¹⁰ Let his children wander as beggars,
searching for food far^C
from their demolished homes.
¹¹ Let a creditor seize all he has;
let strangers plunder what he has
worked for.
¹² Let no one show him kindness,
and let no one be gracious
to his fatherless children.
¹³ Let the line of his descendants
be cut off;
let their name be blotted out
in the next generation.
¹⁴ Let the iniquity of his fathers
be remembered before the LORD,
and do not let his mother's sin
be blotted out.
¹⁵ Let their sins^D always remain
before the LORD,
and let him remove^E all memory of them
from the earth.

¹⁶ For he did not think to show kindness,
but pursued the suffering, needy,
and brokenhearted
in order to put them to death.
¹⁷ He loved cursing — let it fall on him;
he took no delight in blessing —
let it be far from him.
¹⁸ He wore cursing like his coat —
let it enter his body like water
and go into his bones like oil.
¹⁹ Let it be like a robe he wraps
around himself,
like a belt he always wears.
²⁰ Let this be the LORD's payment
to my accusers,
to those who speak evil against me.

²¹ But you, LORD, my Lord,
deal kindly with me
for your name's sake;
because your faithful love is good,
rescue me.
²² For I am suffering and needy;
my heart is wounded within me.
²³ I fade away like a lengthening shadow;
I am shaken off like a locust.
²⁴ My knees are weak from fasting,
and my body is emaciated.^F
²⁵ I have become an object of ridicule
to my accusers;^G
when they see me, they shake
their heads in scorn.

²⁶ Help me, LORD my God;
save me according to your faithful love
²⁷ so they may know that this is your hand
and that you, LORD, have done it.
²⁸ Though they curse, you will bless.
When they rise up, they will be
put to shame,
but your servant will rejoice.
²⁹ My accusers will be clothed
with disgrace;
they will wear their shame like a cloak.
³⁰ I will fervently thank the LORD
with my mouth;
I will praise him in the presence
of many.
³¹ For he stands at the right hand of
the needy

^A109:4 Lit *but I, prayer* ^B109:6 Or *adversary* ^C109:10 LXX reads *beggars, driven far* ^D109:15 Lit *Let them* ^E109:15 Or *cut off* ^F109:24 Lit *denied from fat* ^G109:25 Lit *to them*

109:1-31 This is called an imprecatory psalm, in which the psalmist pronounced curses in relation to the covenant. This plays a significant role in certain psalms (note esp. 7:6–10; 35:8–11; 69:6–7,22–29; 83:9–18).
109:1-2 Lying tongues reflects legal terminology—false testimony (10:4,6–7; 12:3–5; 59:7,12; see Ex 20:16).
109:5-6 The psalmist asked God to **set** (or "appoint") a **wicked person** against his adversary. In some situations the defense attorney stood at the **right hand** of the defendant (v. 31; cp. 16:8). Those who testified for the prosecution also stood in that place (Zch 3:1). In either case, the psalmist wanted an **accuser** (Hb *satan*) there.
109:8-11 After the adversary was tried and convicted, the psalmist called on the Lord to shorten his life. He deserved death because he had inflicted death on others (vv. 16,31). The loss of property and posterity was the worst punishment Israel could imagine, so the psalmist wished poverty and homelessness on the adversary's family.
109:12 Just as the oppressors did not show **kindness** (Hb *chesed*) toward the afflicted, so they deserved no demonstration of covenant loyalty or compassion.
109:23 The weakness of the psalmist is compared to the **lengthening** of his **shadow**, a figurative expression denoting nearness of death (102:11). He also experienced alienation as a result of his sufferings (102:10).

to save him from those who would
condemn him.

The Priestly King

110 *A psalm of David.*
This is the declaration of the LORD
to my Lord:
"Sit at my right hand
until I make your enemies your footstool."
² The LORD will extend
your mighty scepter from Zion.
Rule^A over your surrounding^B enemies.
³ Your people will volunteer
on your day of battle.^C
In holy splendor, from the womb
of the dawn,
the dew of your youth belongs to you.^D
⁴ The LORD has sworn an oath and will not
take it back:
"You are a priest forever
according to the pattern of Melchizedek."

⁵ The Lord is at your right hand;
he will crush kings on the day of his anger.
⁶ He will judge the nations,
heaping up corpses;
he will crush leaders
over the entire world.
⁷ He will drink from the brook by the road;
therefore, he will lift up his head.

Praise for the LORD's Works

111 Hallelujah!^E
I will praise the LORD with all
my heart
in the assembly of the upright
and in the congregation.

² The LORD's works are great,
studied by all who delight in them.
³ All that he does is splendid and majestic;
his righteousness endures forever.
⁴ He has caused his wondrous works
to be remembered.
The LORD is gracious
and compassionate.
⁵ He has provided food for those
who fear him;
he remembers his covenant forever.
⁶ He has shown his people the power
of his works
by giving them the inheritance
of the nations.
⁷ The works of his hands are truth
and justice;
all his instructions are trustworthy.
⁸ They are established forever and ever,
enacted in truth and in uprightness.
⁹ He has sent redemption to his people.
He has ordained his covenant forever.
His name is holy and awe-inspiring.

¹⁰ The fear of the LORD is the beginning
of wisdom;
all who follow his instructions^F have
good insight.
His praise endures forever.

The Traits of the Righteous

112 Hallelujah!^E
Happy is the person who fears
the LORD,
taking great delight in his commands.
² His descendants will be powerful
in the land;

---

^A110:2 One Hb ms, LXX, Tg read *You will rule* ^B110:2 Lit *Rule in the midst of your* ^C110:3 Lit *power* ^D110:3 Hb obscure ^E111:1; 112:1 The lines of this poem form an acrostic. ^F111:10 Lit *follow them*

110:1–7 This is a royal psalm with messianic implications that culminate in the person of Jesus Christ. As a psalm of messianic promise, the poem is the most frequently cited psalm in the NT (Ac 2:34–35; 1Co 15:25; Eph 1:20; Col 3:1; Heb 1:3; 7:17,21; 1Pt 3:22). Although the psalm seems to address the Davidic dynasty, the ideal is never realized except in the Messiah.
110:1 The Lord addresses the Davidic king as his divinely appointed representative. The **right hand** denotes a place of strength, honor, and privilege (45:9). The king as God's co-regent derives his authority from God. The expression **make your enemies your footstool** conveys the idea of being victorious and forcing submission (Jos 10:24).
110:2 To **extend** the **scepter** meant to establish a person's authority and power over the land (45:6).
110:3 This verse is often characterized as the most obscure in the entire book of Psalms. The first line is literally "Your people (will be) freewill offerings in the day of your strength." Some interpreters emend **in holy splendor** (Hb *behade-rey-qodesh*) to "on the holy mountains" *(beharerey-qodesh)*, referring to Zion. **From the womb of the dawn** denotes the young men's eagerness

to do battle for the Lord as soon as the day breaks.
110:4 The reference to **Melchizedek** derives from Gn 14:17–24. The concept of a priestly kingship seems unusual, yet kings served as priests on special occasions or in exceptional circumstances. God promised an eternal dynasty to David (2Sm 7:14–17; see Ps 89:29). Jesus Christ, as a descendant of David and as the Son of God, fulfills the dual roles of king and priest **forever** (Heb 7:17,21).
110:5–6 The **right hand** denotes protection.
110:7 Drinking from **the brook by the road** possibly relates to the rite of drinking from the Gihon Spring as part of an enthronement ceremony (1Kg 1:38), or to pausing to refresh oneself before continuing the pursuit of the vanquished foe (Jdg 8:4).
111:1–10 This psalm is an acrostic, the first letter of each half verse following the order of the Hebrew alphabet (vv. 9 and 10 are three lines each). This psalm provides the theological basis for Ps 112.
111:1 The psalmist praised the Lord both privately and publicly.
111:2 Studied is literally "sought out."
111:3 The words translated **splendid and majestic** occur together six times in the OT. It is literally "splendor and majesty his work."

111:4 Wondrous works usually refers to God's saving acts. He caused them to be **remembered** in the Passover and other feasts.
111:5 Food is from the Hebrew word for "prey" *(tereph)*, possibly implying provision in the wilderness (Ex 16; Nm 11:31–32; Jb 24:5).
111:6 The two lines of v. 6 form the approximate center of the psalm. To give **the inheritance of the nations** reinforces the Lord's gift of land to Israel during the conquest of Canaan. The Lord handed over the heritage inhabited by other nations to his chosen people.
111:9 Redemption denotes the exchange of a payment price for liberation (Dt 7:8; Is 35:10; 50:2; 51:11), and it occurs in this noun form only three other times (Ex 8:23, "distinction"; Ps 130:7; Is 50:2). To refer to God's name as **awe-inspiring** (lit "to be feared") implies a covenantal relationship (68:35; 89:7; 99:3; Ex 34:10; Dt 7:21; 28:58).
111:10 The beginning of wisdom is a wisdom expression (112:1; Jb 28:28; Pr 1:7; 15:33).
112:1–10 This psalm contains wisdom features and vocabulary, and it shares language and acrostic form with Ps 111. It applies the theology expressed there.
112:1 The one who **fears** the Lord honors, trusts, worships, and obeys him.

the generation of the upright
will be blessed.
³ Wealth and riches are in his house,
and his righteousness endures forever.
⁴ Light shines in the darkness
for the upright.
He is gracious, compassionate,
and righteous.
⁵ Good will come to the one
who lends generously
and conducts his business fairly.
⁶ He will never be shaken.
The righteous one will be
remembered forever.
⁷ He will not fear bad news;
his heart is confident,
trusting in the Lord.
⁸ His heart is assured; he will not fear.
In the end he will look in triumph
on his foes.
⁹ He distributes freely to the poor;
his righteousness endures forever.
His horn will be exalted in honor.

¹⁰ The wicked one will see it and be angry;
he will gnash his teeth in despair.
The desire of the wicked leads to ruin.

Praise to the Merciful God

113 Hallelujah!
Give praise, servants of the Lord;
praise the name of the Lord.
² Let the name of the Lord be blessed
both now and forever.
³ From the rising of the sun to its setting,
let the name of the Lord be praised.

⁴ The Lord is exalted above
all the nations,
his glory above the heavens.
⁵ Who is like the Lord our God —

the one enthroned on high,
⁶ who stoops down to look
on the heavens and the earth?
⁷ He raises the poor from the dust
and lifts the needy from the trash heap
⁸ in order to seat them with nobles —
with the nobles of his people.
⁹ He gives the childless woman
a household,
making her the joyful mother of children.
Hallelujah!

God's Deliverance of Israel

114 When Israel came out of Egypt —
the house of Jacob from a people
who spoke a foreign language —
² Judah became his sanctuary,
Israel, his dominion.

³ The sea looked and fled;
the Jordan turned back.
⁴ The mountains skipped like rams,
the hills, like lambs.
⁵ Why was it, sea, that you fled?
Jordan, that you turned back?
⁶ Mountains, that you skipped like rams?
Hills, like lambs?

⁷ Tremble, earth, at the presence
of the Lord,
at the presence of the God of Jacob,
⁸ who turned the rock into a pool,
the flint into a spring.

Glory to God Alone

115 Not to us, Lord, not to us,
but to your name give glory
because of your faithful love, because of
your truth.
² Why should the nations say,
"Where is their God?"

112:2 Descendants (lit "seed") will serve as a conduit of the Lord's strength—not **powerful** in themselves, but through God's blessing.
112:6 Just as the foundations of the world will not be **shaken** (82:5; 96:10; 99:1; 104:5), so nothing will ever make the **righteous** person slip or fall.
112:7 This verse does not promise only good news. It rather recommends trust in the Lord as an antidote to **fear**.
112:8 Trust in the Lord prevents **fear** (vv. 1,7). The **assured . . . heart** conveys the idea of support (111:8).
112:9 The **righteousness** of the generous person **endures**, just as God's instructions (111:8) and praise (111:10) last **forever**. The **horn** is symbolic of power.
112:10 Those who are evil will witness the elevation of the righteous. The term **angry** can be rendered "confused" or "troubled." Those who **desire** anything other than God will ultimately be frustrated.
113:1 This psalm is one of a set of songs recited during Passover. The phrase **servants of the Lord** refers to the priests (134:1; 135:1).

113:3 The travel of the **sun** across the sky is described in 19:4–6 as indicating God's omniscience, and in 72:5,17 it is associated with the longevity of the kingly reign.
113:5 The rhetorical question **who is like the Lord** (cp. Ex 15:11) introduces a hymn praising the Lord. His enthronement **on high** denotes superiority and sovereignty (103:11; Is 7:11; 55:9).
113:6 The word for **stoops down** generally means to "humble or abase" (2:4; 18:16). God lowers himself from above the cosmos to consider his creation (33:13).
113:7 Just as the Lord lowers himself to gaze at his creation, so he **lifts** (lit "raises") the **poor** and **needy** from the **dust** of the street and the **trash heap**, or ash pile—an unsanitary place where rubbish and filth were dumped (Jb 2:8; Lm 4:5).
113:9 Barrenness often resulted in shame since the status of a woman was determined by her ability to bear **children**.
114:1 Israel here refers to the twelve tribes, not just the northern kingdom.
114:2 The reference to **Judah** as a **sanctuary** seems anachronistic since the central

sanctuary was not established until the Davidic kingship, but this could simply mean that Judah was God's metaphorical "holy place." The reference to **Israel** as the Lord's political domain indicates the psalmist had Israel's election as the Lord's people in view.
114:3 The sea looked and fled draws on mythological imagery to describe the parting of the Red Sea (Ex 14:21–22; 15:4–12). The course reversal of the **Jordan** River occurred when Joshua and the people entered Canaan (Jos 3–5). See Ps 66:6 for a similar combination of the Red Sea and Jordan events.
114:4 The **mountains skipped** refers to the shaking of Mount Sinai (Ex 19:16).
114:5–8 Introducing a rhetorical question, the psalmist reflected on the might and majesty of the Lord who caused such phenomena.
115:1–18 This psalm contains a number of lines identical to those in Ps 135.
115:2 The **nations** questioned the presence of Israel's God in light of her dire circumstances. The setting may be exilic, prompting the question, or the question may be a general remark on the absence of any visible manifestation of Israel's God.

3   Our God is in heaven
    and does whatever he pleases.

4   Their idols are silver and gold,
    made by human hands.
5   They have mouths but cannot speak,
    eyes, but cannot see.
6   They have ears but cannot hear,
    noses, but cannot smell.
7   They have hands but cannot feel,
    feet, but cannot walk.
    They cannot make a sound
        with their throats.
8   Those who make them are^ just
        like them,
    as are all who trust in them.

9   Israel,ᴮ trust in the LORD!
    He is their help and shield.
10 House of Aaron, trust in the LORD!
    He is their help and shield.
11 You who fear the LORD,
        trust in the LORD!
    He is their help and shield.
12 The LORD remembers us
        and will bless us.
    He will bless the house of Israel;
    he will bless the house of Aaron;
13 he will bless those who fear
        the LORD —
    small and great alike.

14 May the LORD add to your numbers,
    both yours and your children's.
15 May you be blessed by the LORD,
    the Maker of heaven and earth.
16 The heavens are the LORD's,ᶜ
    but the earth he has given
        to the human race.
17 It is not the dead who praise the LORD,
    nor any of those descending
        into the silence of death.
18 But we will bless the LORD,
    both now and forever.
    Hallelujah!

Thanks to God for Deliverance

116 I love the LORD because he has heard
    my appeal for mercy.
2   Because he has turned his ear to me,
    I will call out to him as long as I live.

3   The ropes of death were wrapped
        around me,
    and the torments of Sheol overcame me;
    I encountered trouble and sorrow.
4   Then I called on the name of the LORD:
    "LORD, save me!"

5   The LORD is gracious and righteous;
    our God is compassionate.
6   The LORD guards the inexperienced;
    I was helpless, and he saved me.
7   Return to your rest, my soul,
    for the LORD has been good to you.
8   For you, LORD, rescued me from death,
    my eyes from tears,
    my feet from stumbling.
9   I will walk before the LORD
    in the land of the living.
10 I believed, even when I said,
    "I am severely oppressed."
11 In my alarm I said,
    "Everyone is a liar."

12 How can I repay the LORD
    for all the good he has done for me?
13 I will take the cup of salvation
    and call on the name of the LORD.
14 I will fulfill my vows to the LORD
    in the presence of all his people.

15 The death of his faithful ones
    is valuable in the LORD's sight.
16 LORD, I am indeed your servant;
    I am your servant, the son
        of your female servant.
    You have loosened my bonds.

17 I will offer you a thanksgiving sacrifice
    and call on the name of the LORD.

---

^115:8 Or *May those who make them become*   ᴮ115:9 Some Hb mss, LXX, Syr read *House of Israel*   ᶜ115:16 Lit *the LORD's heavens*

115:4–8 Compare these verses with 135:15–18. **Idols**, created by humans, are lifeless. The nations' gods are impotent. While the molten images appear to have human characteristics, they are unable to act under their own power. Those who create idols and place their trust in them will be **just like them**—powerless and ineffective.
115:9–13 Verses 12–13 list the consequences of vv. 9–11; Israel trusts God, and God blesses Israel.
115:14 Increased descendants is a sign of the Lord's favor and blessing.
115:15 This expression occurs frequently in poetical texts that herald the Lord's superiority.
115:16 The **human race** is literally "the sons of man (*'adam*)."

115:17–18 Those who have descended into **silence** is a figure for those who are dead—lifeless idols and their makers. Conversely, those who trust in God are alive, and they **bless** his name **forever**.
116:1–19 This psalm shares a number of words and ideas with Jnh 2:2–9, pointing to a literary relationship between these two inspired writings.
116:1 Love here implies love associated with a covenantal relationship.
116:2 When the Lord turns **his ear**, the petitioner is granted his request.
116:5 On **gracious** and **compassionate**, compare 103:8; Ex 34:6–7.
116:6 The Lord **guards the inexperienced**. The Hebrew word for **helpless** means "lowly" or "weak."

116:7 Has been good to can also be translated "has dealt generously with."
116:12 The Hebrew word translated **good** comes from a root that means "payback," here in the good sense of "reward" or "benefit."
116:13–14 Giving someone a **cup** normally denoted forcing something negative on someone, such as "fury" and "staggering" (Is 51:17,22). Here the psalmist received **salvation** from God. Alternatively, it could refer to a libation or drink offering from the psalmist (Ex 29:40–41; Nm 15:5,7; see Mt 26:26–29; 1Co 10:16).
116:15–16 Those in service to the Lord who are threatened with **death** are **valuable** to God, and are thus saved (72:14; Is 43:4). Though they may not escape physical death,

¹⁸ I will fulfill my vows to the LORD
in the presence of all his people,
¹⁹ in the courts of the LORD's house —
within you, Jerusalem.
Hallelujah!

Universal Call to Praise

117 Praise the LORD, all nations!
Glorify him, all peoples!
² For his faithful love to us is great;
the LORD's faithfulness endures forever.
Hallelujah!

Thanksgiving for Victory

118 Give thanks to the LORD,
for he is good;
his faithful love endures forever.
² Let Israel say,
"His faithful love endures forever."
³ Let the house of Aaron say,
"His faithful love endures forever."
⁴ Let those who fear the LORD say,
"His faithful love endures forever."

⁵ I called to the LORD in distress;
the LORD answered me
and put me in a spacious place.ᴬ
⁶ The LORD is for me; I will not be afraid.
What can a mere mortal do to me?
⁷ The LORD is my helper;
therefore, I will look in triumph
on those who hate me.

⁸ It is better to take refuge in the LORD
than to trust in humanity.
⁹ It is better to take refuge in the LORD
than to trust in nobles.

¹⁰ All the nations surrounded me;
in the name of the LORD I destroyed them.
¹¹ They surrounded me, yes,
they surrounded me;

in the name of the LORD
I destroyed them.
¹² They surrounded me like bees;
they were extinguished like a fire
among thorns;
in the name of the LORD
I destroyed them.
¹³ Theyᴮ pushed me hard to make me fall,
but the LORD helped me.
¹⁴ The LORD is my strength and my song;
he has become my salvation.

¹⁵ There are shouts of joy and victory
in the tents of the righteous:
"The LORD's right hand
performs valiantly!
¹⁶ The LORD's right hand is raised.
The LORD's right hand
performs valiantly!"
¹⁷ I will not die, but I will live
and proclaim what the LORD has done.
¹⁸ The LORD disciplined me severely
but did not give me over to death.

¹⁹ Open the gates of righteousness for me;
I will enter through them
and give thanks to the LORD.
²⁰ This is the LORD's gate;
the righteous will enter through it.
²¹ I will give thanks to you
because you have answered me
and have become my salvation.
²² The stone that the builders rejected
has become the cornerstone.
²³ This came from the LORD;
it is wondrous in our sight.
²⁴ This is the day the LORD has made;
let's rejoice and be glad in it.

²⁵ LORD, save us!
LORD, please grant us success!
²⁶ He who comes in the name

ᴬ**118:5** Or *answered me with freedom*   ᴮ**118:13** Lit *You*

---

they will experience eternal life (Mt 10:29–31; Lk 21:16–18; Jn 10:28–29). **116:19** The psalmist intended to fulfill his vow publicly in the temple precincts. In the LXX, **Hallelujah!** begins Ps 117. **117:1 Glorify** occurs only seven other times in the OT. **117:2 Faithful love** denotes the enduring qualities of the Lord's *chesed* (Hb for "covenant loyalty"; 25:10; 57:3,10; 85:10; 89:15). **Hallelujah!** is literally "Praise Yah" (104:35; 105:45; 106:1). **118:1–29** This psalm describes the triumphal entry of the king in terms of humiliation and glory. **118:1 His faithful love endures forever**, a standard liturgical formula, recurs in vv. 2–4 (cp. 100:5; 105:1; 106:1; 136). **118:3 House of Aaron** refers to priests—descendants of the first high priest (135:19; Nm 26:59–60). **118:5 Distress** is a rare term (116:3; Lm 1:3) from a related word that suggests

confinement or restriction. The Lord's remedy is a **spacious place**. **118:7** The term **helper** applies to Eve in Gn 2:18 and frequently describes God and his actions on behalf of people (Ex 18:4; Dt 33:7,29; 1Sm 7:12; Pss 20:2; 115:9–11; 121:2; 124:8; Is 41:10–13). To **look in triumph** is to overcome, as if in war. **118:8–9** The proverbial expressions in these verses are introduced by **better**. This formulaic wisdom saying occurs several times in Proverbs (Pr 15:16–17; 16:32; 19:1,22), while the concept of taking **refuge in the Lord** also enjoys wider usage (61:4; 64:10; 71:1; 141:8; 143:9; 144:2; Dt 32:37; 2Sm 22:3,31; Is 14:32; 57:13). **Nobles** were those who distributed wealth willingly. People should prefer God over common men as well as over those in authority and power. **118:10–12** To act **in the name of the Lord** could mean the king served as the Lord's regent and acted on his behalf, or that the king fought **the nations** while relying on the strength of the Lord (v. 14).

118:15–16 The Lord's **right hand** executes judgment, renders justice, and accomplishes salvation. **Performs valiantly** has a military tone. The raising of the Lord's right hand depicts judgment (89:13; 102:13). **118:19–21** The plural form of **gates** refers to the Eastern Gate of the temple, a gate with two sections (24:7–10). **118:22** The **cornerstone** bears the weight of a building and serves as the standard for orienting and leveling the rest of the structure. The rejected king has been restored to a place of prominence. The imagery of a cornerstone representing the character of the Lord (Zch 4:7) is further developed in the NT (Mt 21:42; Ac 4:11; Eph 2:20–21; 1Pt 2:4–8). **118:23–24** The **day** spoken of here is a feast day. **118:25–29** The last section of the psalm consists of a series of praises to the Lord motivated by the desire of the psalmist for rescue. The Hebrew word *na'*, a particle of entreaty, occurs twice in this verse, emphasizing the

of the LORD is blessed.
From the house of the LORD
we bless you.
27 The LORD is God and has given us light.
Bind the festival sacrifice with cords
to the horns of the altar.
28 You are my God, and I will give
you thanks.
You are my God; I will exalt you.
29 Give thanks to the LORD, for he is good;
his faithful love endures forever.

Delight in God's Word
א Aleph

119 How^A happy are those whose way
is blameless,
who walk according to the LORD's
instruction!
2 Happy are those who keep his decrees
and seek him with all their heart.
3 They do nothing wrong;
they walk in his ways.
4 You have commanded
that your precepts
be diligently kept.
5 If only my ways were committed
to keeping your statutes!
6 Then I would not be ashamed
when I think about all your commands.
7 I will praise you with an upright heart
when I learn your righteous judgments.
8 I will keep your statutes;
never abandon me.

ב Beth
9 How can a young man keep his way
pure?
By keeping your^B word.
10 I have sought you with all my heart;
don't let me wander
from your commands.
11 I have treasured your word in my heart
so that I may not sin against you.
12 LORD, may you be blessed;
teach me your statutes.
13 With my lips I proclaim
all the judgments from your mouth.

14 I rejoice in the way revealed by
your decrees
as much as in all riches.
15 I will meditate on your precepts
and think about your ways.
16 I will delight in your statutes;
I will not forget your word.

ג Gimel
17 Deal generously with your servant
so that I might live;
then I will keep your word.
18 Open my eyes so that I may contemplate
wondrous things from your instruction.
19 I am a resident alien on earth;
do not hide your commands from me.
20 I am continually overcome
with longing for your judgments.
21 You rebuke the arrogant,
the ones under a curse,
who wander from your commands.
22 Take insult and contempt away from me,
for I have kept your decrees.
23 Though princes sit together speaking
against me,
your servant will think
about your statutes;
24 your decrees are my delight
and my counselors.

ד Daleth
25 My life is down in the dust;
give me life through your word.
26 I told you about my life,
and you answered me;
teach me your statutes.
27 Help me understand
the meaning of your precepts
so that I can meditate on your wonders.
28 I am weary^C from grief;
strengthen me through your word.
29 Keep me from the way of deceit
and graciously give me your instruction.
30 I have chosen the way of truth;
I have set your ordinances before me.
31 I cling to your decrees;
LORD, do not put me to shame.

---

^A119:1 The stanzas of this poem form an acrostic. ^B119:9 Or keeping it according to your ^C119:28 Or I weep

desperate pleas of the psalmist. This was part of the expression "Hosanna" (please save) in the triumphal entry (Mt 21:9), where the crowd alluded to vv. 25–26 of this psalm. The phrase **bind the festival sacrifice with cords to the horns of the altar** is unusual since there is no evidence that a sacrifice was ever tied to the altar. However, this concept was fulfilled when Christ was nailed to the cross.
119:1–176 Psalm 119 is an acrostic *par excellence*. The eight-verse sections are arranged according to the order of the Hebrew alphabet. Nearly every verse contains one of eight words for God's revelation: "instruction," "decree," "precept," "statute," "command," "judgment," "promise," and "word."

119:1–8 To be **blameless** derives from the Hebrew word for "perfect, unblemished." The psalmist prayed for total commitment to obedience. His conscience reminded him of his weaknesses (vv. 5–6). The Hebrew word for **upright** (v. 7) means "sincere" or "straight."
119:9–16 A **young man** is one who lacks experience and wisdom. He is easily tempted by worldly desires (Pr 1:8–19; 2:1–22) and enticed away from God. The loyalty of the righteous is maintained by the value they place on God's **word**. To **meditate** is not to empty one's mind, but to fill it with the Torah in order to internalize it.
119:17–24 Deal generously translates the Hebrew word for "recompense" or "benefit."

Contemplate means "consider carefully" ("think about" in v. 15). The psalmist characterized himself as a stranger, a **resident alien** living on God's **earth** and dependent on him. The purpose of **rebuke** is to correct and bring God's people back into relationship with him (Mt 18:15).
119:25–32 The Lord is the source of all life. Only he can rejuvenate those who are bowed down. The psalmist sought clarity, relying on God to help him understand and apply the Torah to his life. The righteous person rejects the way of deceivers (1:6; 16:11; 32:8), and depends on the Lord to keep him on the path of righteousness.

Special Revelation in Scripture

by Mark L. Bailey

General revelation and special revelation are the two ways God has chosen to reveal himself to humanity. These terms have been used to delineate the extent and purpose of revelation. General revelation refers to the general truths that can be known about God through nature. Theologians use the term special revelation in reference to the belief in God's intentional intervention to make his mind and will available that would not be available through general revelation alone. The distinction between general and special revelation has little to do with the source or origin of the revelation since both come from God. Instead, the distinction has to do with the means and goals of revelation.

Special revelation is addressed to humanity with a view to their redemption and ongoing relationship with God. And it is only by special revelation that one can learn how to live a godly life and thereby glorify God. "His divine power has given us everything required for life and godliness through the knowledge of him who called us by his own glory and goodness" (2Pt 1:3). The purpose of special revelation is the redemption of sinners and the magnification of God's glory through both his gracious act of salvation of believers and the just condemnation of those who reject him.

This level of knowledge is not universally available. Rather, it is given by God supernaturally to those who are born again by the Spirit of God (Jn 3:3). Paul says, "'What no eye has seen, no ear has heard, and no human heart has conceived—God has prepared these things for those who love him.' Now God has revealed these things to us by the Spirit, since the Spirit searches everything, even the depths of God" (1Co 2:9–10).

Hebrews 1:1–3 provides a succinct outline of God's special revelation: "Long ago God spoke to the fathers by the prophets at different times and in different ways. In these last days, he has spoken to us by his Son. . . . The Son is the radiance of God's glory and the exact expression of his nature, sustaining all things by his powerful word."

God's special revelation came over the course of time and therefore can be rightfully described as "progressive revelation." Each of these revelations brought a better understanding of God to people. Each biblical writer added to the treasure of knowledge about our Creator. While revelation moved from that which was partial to that which is final, it was never from the imperfect to the perfect. At every point along the way, however, all that had been revealed was fully and equally inspired.

Throughout history, God has used different means to reveal his mind and message to mankind:

Special Manifestation: The Bible records God appearing many times in physical form (Gn 3:8; 18:1; Ex 3:1–4; 34:5–7). Such an appearance is known as a "theophany." Some scholars believe that the "angel of the Lord," a figure prominent in the Hebrew Scriptures, was the Lord Jesus in his preincarnate state (e.g., Gn 16:7–13; 22:15–18; 31:11–13; Jdg 6:11–23). To this may be added the testimony of Paul, who affirmed the actual presence of Christ as a sustaining companion of Israel in the wilderness of Sinai (1Co 10:4).

Direct Communication: Sometimes God spoke to people directly (Gn 2:16), through divinely revealed dreams (Gn 28:12; Nm 12:6; 1Kg 3:5; Dn 2), visions (Gn 15:1; Is 1:1; Ez 8:3–4; Dn 7; Hab 1:1; Zch 1–6; 2Co 12:1–7), or divine announcements out of heaven (1Sm 3; Mt 3:17; 17:5; Jn 12:28).

Miraculous Demonstration: God is also able to interrupt and supersede the laws of nature to make his will or power known, as in the case of the use of the Urim and Thummim (Nm 27:21) or miracles, whether done directly by God—like sending hailstones and making the sun remain still in the sky (Jos 10:11–15)—or accomplished through a prophet like Elijah or Elisha (1Kg 17–18; 2Kg 2:9–14) or through the apostles (Ac 3:1–11).

Personal Incarnation: The ultimate form of special revelation is the person of Jesus Christ. Jesus affirmed, "All things have been entrusted to me by my Father. No one knows the Son except the Father, and no one knows the Father except the Son and anyone to whom the Son desires to reveal him" (Mt 11:27). The special revelation in Jesus came

³² I pursue the way of your commands,
   for you broaden my understanding.ᴬ

ה He

³³ Teach me, LORD, the meaningᴮ
   of your statutes,
   and I will always keep them.ᶜ
³⁴ Help me understand your instruction,
   and I will obey it
   and follow it with all my heart.
³⁵ Help me stay on the path
   of your commands,
   for I take pleasure in it.
³⁶ Turn my heart to your decrees
   and not to dishonest profit.
³⁷ Turn my eyes
   from looking at what is worthless;
   give me life in your ways.ᴰ
³⁸ Confirm what you said to your servant,
   for it produces reverence for you.
³⁹ Turn away the disgrace I dread;
   indeed, your judgments are good.
⁴⁰ How I long for your precepts!
   Give me life through
   your righteousness.

ו Waw

⁴¹ Let your faithful love come to me, LORD,
   your salvation, as you promised.
⁴² Then I can answer the one
   who taunts me,
   for I trust in your word.
⁴³ Never take the word of truth
   from my mouth,
   for I hope in your judgments.
⁴⁴ I will always obey your instruction,
   forever and ever.
⁴⁵ I will walk freely in an open place
   because I study your precepts.
⁴⁶ I will speak of your decrees before kings
   and not be ashamed.
⁴⁷ I delight in your commands,
   which I love.
⁴⁸ I will lift up my hands
   to your commands,
   which I love,
   and will meditate on your statutes.

ז Zayin

⁴⁹ Remember your word to your servant;
   you have given me hope through it.

ᴬ**119:32** Lit *you enlarge my heart* ᴮ**119:33** Lit *way* ᶜ**119:33** Or *will keep it as my reward* ᴰ**119:37** Some Hb mss, Tg read *word*

119:33–40 This section focuses on God's reward for obedience. The pursuit of **dishonest profit** leads to sin, but life is found in the ways of the Lord. On **with all my heart**, compare Dt 6:5.
119:41–48 The psalmist longed for expressions of God's *chesed* (Hb for "covenant loyalty, faithful love") in light of the persecution and hostility against him. He sought God's **salvation** from oppression. The freedom offered the person who walks according to God's word enables him to remain strong through adversity and to maintain his focus on God's decrees. The righteous person is courageous enough to **speak of** the Lord, and he will **not be ashamed** (vv. 6,31,42).
119:49–56 The righteous person is comforted by the Lord's **judgments**, certain that he will execute justice with integrity (v. 52). As the Lord rescued Israel in the past through his miraculous intervention, so the

through his words (Jn 7:16–17), his person (14:7), and his works (5:17–19).

Divine Inspiration: Scripture is the written revelation of God and is the principle way by which God currently reveals himself to humans. As a result, it is the means by which all claims to truth should be evaluated.

The word *inspiration* also calls attention to the process by which the Holy Spirit superintended the production of Scripture. The term refers to that process by which an omnipotent God so guided the human authors of Scripture in the recording of his revelation so that the end product was the Word of God, exactly as God wanted to communicate it in the words of the original manuscripts.

Most evangelical Christians affirm both the infallibility and inerrancy of the Bible because God is its ultimate author. Since the Bible is the inspired Word of God, and because God is incapable of inspiring falsehood, his Word is altogether trustworthy. Psalm 119:160 states, "The entirety of your word is truth, each of your righteous judgments endures forever." If an omnipotent God could take an imperfect person like Mary and incarnate a perfect living Word, Jesus, the Son of God, then that same omnipotent God can take a human author and produce a perfect written Word of God, the Bible, through the process of divine inspiration.

The *process* of inspiration can be seen in 2 Peter 1:20–21: "Above all, you know this: No prophecy of Scripture comes from the prophet's own interpretation, because no prophecy ever came by the will of man; instead, men spoke from God as they were carried along by the Holy Spirit." The *product* of inspiration is best stated in 2 Timothy 3:16–17: "All Scripture is inspired by God and is profitable for teaching, for rebuking, for correcting, for training in righteousness, so that the man of God may be complete, equipped for every good work." Together these passages declare the divine origin of the Bible and its use in equipping us to serve God.

50 This is my comfort in my affliction:
Your promise has given me life.
51 The arrogant constantly ridicule me,
but I do not turn away
from your instruction.
52 Lord, I remember your judgments
from long ago
and find comfort.
53 Fury seizes me because of the wicked
who reject your instruction.
54 Your statutes are the theme of my song
during my earthly life.^
55 Lord, I remember your name
in the night,
and I obey your instruction.
56 This is my practice:
I obey your precepts.

ח *Cheth*

57 The Lord is my portion;^B
I have promised to keep your words.
58 I have sought your favor with all
my heart;
be gracious to me according to
your promise.
59 I thought about my ways
and turned my steps back
to your decrees.
60 I hurried, not hesitating
to keep your commands.
61 Though the ropes of the wicked
were wrapped around me,
I did not forget your instruction.
62 I rise at midnight to thank you
for your righteous judgments.
63 I am a friend to all who fear you,
to those who keep your precepts.
64 Lord, the earth is filled with
your faithful love;
teach me your statutes.

ט *Teth*

65 Lord, you have treated
your servant well,
just as you promised.
66 Teach me good judgment
and discernment,
for I rely on your commands.
67 Before I was afflicted I went astray,
but now I keep your word.
68 You are good, and you do what is good;
teach me your statutes.

69 The arrogant have smeared me
with lies,
but I obey your precepts with all
my heart.
70 Their hearts are hard and insensitive,
but I delight in your instruction.
71 It was good for me to be afflicted
so that I could learn your statutes.
72 Instruction from your lips is better
for me
than thousands of gold
and silver pieces.

י *Yod*

73 Your hands made me
and formed me;
give me understanding
so that I can learn your commands.
74 Those who fear you will see me
and rejoice,
for I put my hope in your word.
75 I know, Lord, that your judgments
are just
and that you have afflicted me fairly.
76 May your faithful love comfort me
as you promised your servant.
77 May your compassion come to me
so that I may live,
for your instruction is my delight.
78 Let the arrogant be put to shame
for slandering me with lies;
I will meditate on your precepts.
79 Let those who fear you,
those who know your decrees,
turn to me.
80 May my heart be blameless
regarding your statutes
so that I will not be put to shame.

כ *Kaph*

81 I long for your salvation;
I put my hope in your word.
82 My eyes grow weary
looking for what you have promised;
I ask, "When will you comfort me?"
83 Though I have become like a wineskin
dried by smoke,
I do not forget your statutes.
84 How many days must
your servant wait?
When will you execute judgment
on my persecutors?

---

^**119:54** Lit *song in the house of my sojourning*   ^B**119:57** Lit *You are my portion,* Lord

---

expectations of the psalmist were based on the testimony of God's works. The psalmist expressed righteous indignation against the **arrogant** and the **wicked** who neglected the instructions of God.
119:57–64 Just as the Levites received no allotment of land during the settlement of Canaan and thus relied on God, so the psalmist depended on God alone for his livelihood. The threat of the **wicked** endangered the

psalmist's life, but he remained focused on God's **righteous judgments**.
119:65–72 The psalmist's past affliction was the direct result of the Lord's discipline. In retrospect, he acknowledged his moral weaknesses (v. 67) and realized God's rebuke served him well (v. 71). The rebellious ones **smeared** him **with lies**. The court language suggests false accusations. The value of God's instructions is beyond measure (19:7–10).

119:73–80 The psalmist did not want to be ashamed, but he prayed that the arrogant would **be put to shame** and reiterated his request to be **blameless**.
119:81–88 This section consists of a lament, in which the psalmist asked **when** the Lord would bring relief. Although near death, he remained loyal to God's precepts, putting his hope in God for life itself (vv. 87–88).

85 The arrogant have dug pits for me;
   they violate your instruction.
86 All your commands are true;
   people persecute me with lies
   — help me!
87 They almost ended my life on earth,
   but I did not abandon your precepts.
88 Give me life in accordance with
      your faithful love,
   and I will obey the decree
      you have spoken.

ל Lamed

89 LORD, your word is forever;
   it is firmly fixed in heaven.
90 Your faithfulness is for all generations;
   you established the earth,
      and it stands firm.
91 Your judgments stand firm today,
   for all things are your servants.
92 If your instruction had not been
      my delight,
   I would have died in my affliction.
93 I will never forget your precepts,
   for you have given me life through them.
94 I am yours; save me,
   for I have studied your precepts.
95 The wicked hope to destroy me,
   but I contemplate your decrees.
96 I have seen a limit to all perfection,
   but your command is without limit.

מ Mem

97 How I love your instruction!
   It is my meditation all day long.
98 Your command makes me wiser
      than my enemies,
   for it is always with me.
99 I have more insight than all my teachers
   because your decrees are
      my meditation.
100 I understand more than the elders
    because I obey your precepts.
101 I have kept my feet from every evil path
    to follow your word.
102 I have not turned from your judgments,
    for you yourself have instructed me.
103 How sweet your word is to my taste —
    sweeter than honey in my mouth.
104 I gain understanding
       from your precepts;
    therefore I hate every false way.

נ Nun

105 Your word is a lamp for my feet
    and a light on my path.
106 I have solemnly sworn
    to keep your righteous judgments.
107 I am severely afflicted;
    LORD, give me life according
       to your word.
108 LORD, please accept
    my freewill offerings of praise,
    and teach me your judgments.
109 My life is constantly in danger,[A]
    yet I do not forget your instruction.
110 The wicked have set a trap for me,
    but I have not wandered
       from your precepts.
111 I have your decrees
    as a heritage forever;
    indeed, they are the joy of my heart.
112 I am resolved to obey your statutes
    to the very end.[B]

ס Samek

113 I hate those who are double-minded,
    but I love your instruction.
114 You are my shelter and my shield;
    I put my hope in your word.
115 Depart from me, you evil ones,
    so that I may obey my God's commands.
116 Sustain me as you promised,
       and I will live;
    do not let me be ashamed of my hope.
117 Sustain me so that I can be safe
    and always be concerned about
       your statutes.
118 You reject all who stray
       from your statutes,
    for their deceit is a lie.
119 You remove all the wicked on earth
    as if they were[C] dross from metal;
    therefore, I love your decrees.
120 I tremble[D] in awe of you;
    I fear your judgments.

ע Ayin

121 I have done what is just and right;
    do not leave me to my oppressors.
122 Guarantee your servant's well-being;
    do not let the arrogant oppress me.
123 My eyes grow weary looking for
       your salvation
    and for your righteous promise.

[A]119:109 Lit in my hand   [B]119:112 Or statutes; the reward is eternal   [C]119:119 Some Hb mss, DSS, LXX, Aq, Sym, Jer read All the wicked of the earth you count as   [D]119:120 Lit My flesh shudders

---

119:89–96 The **word** of God is the central theme of these verses. The Lord's **judgments** that maintain order in the cosmos provide order for human life as well.
119:97–104 Intimate acquaintance with God's **word** results in wise and discerning behavior (Dt 4:5–6; Jr 15:16; Ezk 3:3).
119:105–112 The lighted **path** is not whatever we want it to be, but **righteous**

judgments and God's **precepts**; on such a path there is no **danger** or **trap** but a **heritage** and **joy**. Thus the guidance of the Lord's instruction enabled the psalmist to negotiate right and wrong (19:11–13; Pr 6:23; Jn 8:16).
119:113–120 The upright life surrenders to God's divine instruction for maintaining a relationship with him. The presence of the

wicked and deceitful remains pervasive in this section, suggesting the severe hostility that threatened the psalmist.
119:121–128 The upright are loyal, showing righteous anger toward God's enemies (v. 126; cp. v. 53). The frustration of the psalmist is apparent, as he called on the Lord to intervene.

124 Deal with your servant based on
       your faithful love;
    teach me your statutes.
125 I am your servant;
       give me understanding
    so that I may know your decrees.
126 It is time for the LORD to act,
    for they have violated your instruction.
127 Since I love your commands
    more than gold, even the purest gold,
128 I carefully follow all your precepts
    and hate every false way.

פ Pe

129 Your decrees are wondrous;
    therefore I obey them.
130 The revelation of your words
       brings light
    and gives understanding
       to the inexperienced.
131 I open my mouth and pant
    because I long for your commands.
132 Turn to me and be gracious to me,
    as is your practice toward those
       who love your name.
133 Make my steps steady
       through your promise;
    don't let any sin dominate me.
134 Redeem me from human oppression,
    and I will keep your precepts.
135 Make your face shine on your servant,
    and teach me your statutes.
136 My eyes pour out streams of tears
    because people do not follow
       your instruction.

צ Tsade

137 You are righteous, LORD,
    and your judgments are just.
138 The decrees you issue are righteous
    and altogether trustworthy.
139 My anger overwhelms me
    because my foes forget your words.
140 Your word is completely pure,
    and your servant loves it.
141 I am insignificant and despised,
    but I do not forget your precepts.
142 Your righteousness is
       an everlasting righteousness,
    and your instruction is true.
143 Trouble and distress have overtaken me,
    but your commands are my delight.

144 Your decrees are righteous forever.
    Give me understanding, and I will live.

ק Qoph

145 I call with all my heart;
       answer me, LORD.
    I will obey your statutes.
146 I call to you; save me,
    and I will keep your decrees.
147 I rise before dawn and cry out for help;
    I put my hope in your word.
148 I am awake through each watch
       of the night
    to meditate on your promise.
149 In keeping with your faithful love,
       hear my voice.
    LORD, give me life in keeping with
       your justice.
150 Those who pursue evil plans[A]
       come near;
    they are far from your instruction.
151 You are near, LORD,
    and all your commands are true.
152 Long ago I learned from your decrees
    that you have established them forever.

ר Resh

153 Consider my affliction and rescue me,
    for I have not forgotten
       your instruction.
154 Champion my cause and redeem me;
    give me life as you promised.
155 Salvation is far from the wicked
    because they do not study your statutes.
156 Your compassions are many, LORD;
    give me life according to
       your judgments.
157 My persecutors and foes are many.
    I have not turned from your decrees.
158 I have seen the disloyal and feel disgust
    because they do not keep your word.
159 Consider how I love your precepts;
    LORD, give me life according to
       your faithful love.
160 The entirety of your word is truth,
    each of your righteous judgments
       endures forever.

ש Sin/ ש Shin

161 Princes have persecuted me
       without cause,
    but my heart fears only your word.

---

^A119:150 Some Hb mss, LXX, Sym, Jer read *who maliciously persecute me*

119:129–136 The **revelation** is literally the "door" or "opening" (v. 130). Like a hungry and thirsty animal, the psalmist longed for God's instruction (v. 131). Though sometimes the psalmist expressed righteous indignation at those who did not obey God (vv. 53,126,139,158), here he expressed sorrow (v. 136; cp. Mt 23:37; Lk 19:41; Ac 20:31; Rm 9:2–3; Php 3:18).

119:137–144 The psalmist reinforced God's role as Judge.
119:145–152 The psalmist called on the Lord, seeking his help in overcoming those who devised evil plans against him. He expressed trust and assurance in the Lord's faithfulness. While his enemies were physically **near**, they were spiritually **far** from the **commands** that protected the psalmist because the Lord was **near** (vv. 150–151).

119:153–160 Realizing his utter dependence on God, the psalmist prayed that God would give him **life** (vv. 154,156,159). The psalmist despised the way of the wicked (vv. 155,158; cp. v. 53).
119:161–168 Peace fills the lives of those who trust in God's **instruction**. The goal is not to **obey** God's **precepts** for the sake of obedience, but in order to enjoy abundant life in God's presence (v. 168).

162 I rejoice over your promise
     like one who finds vast treasure.
163 I hate and abhor falsehood,
     but I love your instruction.
164 I praise you seven times a day
     for your righteous judgments.
165 Abundant peace belongs to those
     who love your instruction;
     nothing makes them stumble.
166 Lord, I hope for your salvation
     and carry out your commands.
167 I obey your decrees
     and love them greatly.
168 I obey your precepts and decrees,
     for all my ways are before you.

ת Taw

169 Let my cry reach you, Lord;
     give me understanding according to
         your word.
170 Let my plea reach you;
     rescue me according to your promise.
171 My lips pour out praise,
     for you teach me your statutes.
172 My tongue sings about your promise,
     for all your commands are righteous.
173 May your hand be ready to help me,
     for I have chosen your precepts.
174 I long for your salvation, Lord,
     and your instruction is my delight.
175 Let me live, and I will praise you;
     may your judgments help me.
176 I wander like a lost sheep;
     seek your servant,
     for I do not forget your commands.

A Cry for Truth and Peace

120 A song of ascents.
In my distress I called
to the Lord,
and he answered me.
2 "Lord, rescue me from lying lips
     and a deceitful tongue."

3 What will he give you,
     and what will he do to you,
     you deceitful tongue?
4 A warrior's sharp arrows
     with burning charcoal!^{A}

5 What misery that I have stayed
     in Meshech,^{B}
     that I have lived among the tents
         of Kedar!^{C}
6 I have dwelt too long
     with those who hate peace.
7 I am for peace; but when I speak,
     they are for war.

The Lord Our Protector

121 A song of ascents.
I lift my eyes toward the mountains.
Where will my help come from?
2 My help comes from the Lord,
     the Maker of heaven and earth.

3 He will not allow your foot to slip;
     your Protector will not slumber.
4 Indeed, the Protector of Israel
     does not slumber or sleep.

5 The Lord protects you;
     the Lord is a shelter right by your side.^{D}
6 The sun will not strike you by day
     or the moon by night.

7 The Lord will protect you from all harm;
     he will protect your life.
8 The Lord will protect your coming
         and going
     both now and forever.

A Prayer for Jerusalem

122 A song of ascents. Of David.
I rejoiced with those who said
to me,
"Let's go to the house of the Lord."

---

^{A}**120:4** Lit with coals of the broom bush ^{B}**120:5** = a people far to the north of Palestine ^{C}**120:5** = a nomadic people of the desert to the southeast ^{D}**121:5** Lit is your shelter at your right hand

---

119:169–176 The psalmist concluded the psalm with words of praise, an affirmation of his faithfulness to the Torah, and a final, heartfelt plea for intervention.
Ps 120 title This is the first of fifteen psalms of **ascents** (Pss 120–134). These psalms were designed for pilgrimage processions to celebrate seasonal feasts in Jerusalem. The hymns contain numerous references to Jerusalem or Zion, the temple, Israel, peace, and adversity. The fifteen songs, adapted from ancient hymns heralding the blessings and salvation of Zion, may have been sung on the fifteen steps leading up to the temple.
120:1 From Gn 35:3 the Bible is full of individuals and groups who testify to the Lord's faithfulness. They prayed to the Lord in their **distress** and were heard because he is a God of compassion (see 2Sm 22:7,19; Ps 86:7; Jnh 2:2).

120:2 Metaphorically, **lying lips** and a **deceitful tongue** denote the spread of gossip and baseless rumors (109:2).
120:3–4 Those who spoke lies—possibly while swearing by God that they were not lying—would face severe judgment. **Burning charcoal** is literally "coals of broom," that is, charcoal derived from a hard-stemmed plant called a broom tree (1Kg 19:4–5; Jb 30:4).
120:5–7 **Meshech** was located southeast of the Black Sea. **Kedar** was an eastern plain located at the northern fringe of the Syrian-Arabian Desert. It was normally inhabited by Arab tribes. Together they represent places far and near where Israelites dwelt as aliens.
Ps 121 title On **ascents**, see note at Ps 120 title.
121:1–8 In this psalm the writer exploited the broad semantic range of the Hebrew

verb shamar ("guard, keep, protect, observe") using the term six times (vv. 3,4,5,7[2x],8). In this psalm the CSB consistently translates it as "protect" or "Protector."
121:1 The **mountains** may have seemed like a potential place to hide (11:1), a symbol of God's stability and deliverance (31:2; 125:2; Nah 1:15), or a looming menace (Jnh 2:6). Any of these could prompt the question concerning the source of **help**.
121:2 The Creator is the faithful source of help and blessing (124:8; 134:3; 146:6).
Ps 122 title On **ascents**, see note at Ps 122 title.
122:1–9 Sharing terminology and imagery with Is 2:2–4, this psalm may be an adaptation of that prophetic passage. The focus of the psalm is on the features of the city: house (vv. 1,5,9), gates (v. 2), thrones (v. 5), walls (v. 7), and fortresses (v. 7).

2 Our feet were standing
within your gates, Jerusalem —

3 Jerusalem, built as a city should be,
solidly united,
4 where the tribes, the LORD's tribes,
go up
to give thanks to the name of the LORD.
(This is an ordinance for Israel.)
5 There, thrones for judgment are placed,
thrones of the house of David.

6 Pray for the well-being^A of Jerusalem:
"May those who love you be secure;
7 may there be peace within your walls,
security within your fortresses."
8 Because of my brothers and friends,
I will say, "May peace be in you."^B
9 Because of the house of the LORD
our God,
I will pursue your prosperity.

Looking for God's Favor

123 A song of ascents.
I lift my eyes to you,
the one enthroned in heaven.
2 Like a servant's eyes
on his master's hand,
like a servant girl's eyes
on her mistress's hand,
so our eyes are on the LORD
our God
until he shows us favor.

3 Show us favor, LORD, show us favor,
for we've had more than enough
contempt.
4 We've had more than enough
scorn from the arrogant
and contempt from the proud.

The LORD Is on Our Side

124 A song of ascents. Of David.
If the LORD had not been
on our side —
let Israel say —
2 if the LORD had not been on our side
when people attacked us,
3 then they would have
swallowed us alive
in their burning anger against us.
4 Then the water would have engulfed us;
the torrent would have swept over us;
5 the raging water would have swept
over us.

6 Blessed be the LORD,
who has not let us be ripped apart
by their teeth.
7 We have escaped like a bird
from the hunter's net;
the net is torn, and we have escaped.
8 Our help is in the name of the LORD,
the Maker of heaven and earth.

Israel's Stability

125 A song of ascents.
Those who trust in the LORD are
like Mount Zion.
It cannot be shaken; it remains forever.
2 The mountains surround Jerusalem
and the LORD surrounds his people,
both now and forever.

3 The scepter of the wicked
will not remain
over the land allotted to the righteous,
so that the righteous will not apply
their hands to injustice.
4 Do what is good, LORD, to the good,
to those whose hearts are upright.

^A **122:6** Or *peace* ^B **122:8** = Jerusalem

122:1 On **go to the house of the LORD**, compare Is 2:3; Jr 31:6.
122:2 Standing within the **gates** means entering the Lord's presence.
122:4 The **tribes** are the twelve tribes of Israel. **The LORD's tribes** occurs only here in the Bible. Attendance at the three yearly festivals was mandatory. These were Passover, the Day of Atonement (Yom Kippur), and the Festival of Shelters (Ex 23:14–17; Lv 23; Dt 16).
122:5 The phrase **thrones for judgment** refers to the judicial function of the central sanctuary (Dt 17:8–13; 2Sm 8:15; 15:2–6), while the **thrones of the house of David** refers to kings of Davidic descent. The temple that Solomon built contained a "Hall of the Throne" (1Kg 7:7).
122:6–7 Well-being permits the pursuit of **security** (1Kg 4:20–25; 1Tm 2:1–2).
122:8–9 The pilgrimage to the temple prompted the psalmist to **pursue . . . prosperity** for everyone in the community.
Ps 123 title On **ascents**, see note at Ps 120 title.
123:1 There is humility as well as confidence in this picture of a supplicant before his God.

123:2 A **servant** might watch **his master's hand** intently for a gesture that would signify approval.
123:3–4 The Hebrew term for **contempt** is related to the verb *despise* (31:18; 107:40; Is 37:22).
Ps 124 title On **ascents**, see note at Ps 120 title.
124:1–3 Attacked us is literally "stood up against us" (3:1; 86:14; 92:11). See Rm 8:31: "If God is for us, who is against us?"
124:4–5 Fast-moving **water** and floods would have washed away all evidence of Israel's existence (69:2,15; Is 30:28; 66:12). The Hebrew term translated **raging** is related to a word that means "arrogant" (Dt 17:13; Neh 9:10,29), characterizing the destructive **water** and the oppressive enemy.
124:6 Hostile people are depicted as devouring, unrestrained monsters (79:7; Is 9:12; Jr 51:34).
124:7–8 The mouth of a bird trap (Pr 7:23; Am 3:5) has been **torn** by God and the captured bird has **escaped**, as if from prison. The setting of a fowler's trap suggests

premeditation by the opposition, who lay in wait to capture God's people.
Ps 125 title On **ascents**, see note at Ps 120 title.
125:1 For Israel, **Zion** represented the center of the earth and the place where the Lord dwelt. The Hebrew word *mut* (**shaken**) functions as a wordplay with Hebrew *hammattiym*, "turn aside" (v. 5). Those who trust the Lord will remain stable, while those who depend on evil ways will be turned aside.
125:2 The psalm emphasizes the protection of Zion and her inhabitants as the Lord's chosen nation.
125:3 An unusual expression, **the scepter of the wicked** refers to the authority of evildoers (Ezk 19:11–14), which would not continue to dominate the **land** of **the righteous**. On Judah as the "scepter of righteousness," see Gn 49:10. Those who lived in the land of their inheritance would conduct themselves as God's people, avoiding evil and injustice (Ps 82:2; 107:42).
125:4 The actions and motives of the righteous coincide.

5 But as for those who turn aside
  to crooked ways,
  the LORD will banish them
  with the evildoers.

Peace be with Israel.

Zion's Restoration

126 *A song of ascents.*
When the LORD restored
  the fortunes of Zion,^A
we were like those who dream.
2 Our mouths were filled
  with laughter then,
and our tongues with shouts of joy.
Then they said among the nations,
  "The LORD has done great things
  for them."
3 The LORD had done great things for us;
  we were joyful.

4 Restore our fortunes,^B LORD,
  like watercourses in the Negev.
5 Those who sow in tears
  will reap with shouts of joy.
6 Though one goes along weeping,
  carrying the bag of seed,
he will surely come back with shouts
  of joy,
carrying his sheaves.

The Blessing of the LORD

127 *A song of ascents. Of Solomon.*
Unless the LORD builds a house,
  its builders labor over it in vain;
unless the LORD watches over a city,
  the watchman stays alert in vain.
2 In vain you get up early
  and stay up late,
working hard to have enough food—
  yes, he gives sleep to the one he loves.^C

3 Sons are indeed a heritage
  from the LORD,
offspring, a reward.
4 Like arrows in the hand of a warrior
  are the sons born in one's youth.
5 Happy is the man who has filled
  his quiver with them.
They will never be put to shame
  when they speak with their enemies
  at the city gate.

Blessings for Those Who Fear God

128 *A song of ascents.*
How happy is everyone who fears
  the LORD,
who walks in his ways!
2 You will surely eat
  what your hands have worked for.
You will be happy,
  and it will go well for you.
3 Your wife will be like a fruitful vine
  within your house,
your children, like young olive trees
  around your table.
4 In this very way
  the man who fears the LORD
  will be blessed.

5 May the LORD bless you from Zion,
  so that you will see the prosperity
  of Jerusalem
all the days of your life
6 and will see your children's children!

Peace be with Israel.

Protection of the Oppressed

129 *A song of ascents.*
Since my youth they have often
  attacked me—
let Israel say—

---

^A**126:1** Or *LORD returned those of Zion who had been captives*   ^B**126:4** Or *Return our captives*   ^C**127:2** Or *yes, he gives such things to his loved ones while they sleep*

Ps 126 title On **ascents**, see note at Ps 120 title.
126:1 Restored the fortunes refers to the return of the Babylonian exiles to Jerusalem as an event that had already taken place (84:6; 85:1). The appeal in 126:4 to "restore our fortunes" is difficult since the verb assumes that the action has not yet occurred. While v. 1 refers to the return of Israel, v. 4 may refer to the restoration of prosperity and peace in the land (122:6–7). **Like those who dream** refers to those who eagerly anticipate the future.
126:2–3 God's intervention on Israel's behalf testifies to his omnipotence and superiority (96:3; 113:4; Is 61:9; 66:19; Jr 31:10; Ezk 36:23).
126:4–6 In v. 1 the Lord restores Zion as the political and religious center, but vv. 4–6 focus on the productivity of the land. The **watercourses in the Negev** refer to seasonal streams or wadis, which occasionally blessed the land with a sudden overabundance of water. Along with providing sudden bounty

like a wadi, God also made use of methodical processes and hard labor like agriculture. The person who remains humble before God will **surely** enjoy God's blessings in the land.
Ps 127 title On **ascents**, see note at Ps 120 title.
127:1 No task succeeds apart from God's will. While building a dwelling is the literal meaning here, a **house** could also refer to a household or family, connecting this verse to vv. 3–5.
127:2 Humanity struggles to provide for its needs, **working hard to have enough food** (lit "eating the bread of toil," 80:5; 102:9; Gn 3:17; Is 30:20). The Lord provides rest by blessing the work of the godly.
127:3 While food generally came from hard work, amid the uncertainties of the ancient Near Eastern life, **offspring** came from God (Gn 30:2; Dt 7:14).
127:4–5 The psalmist focused specifically on **sons**, who could continue the family lineage. A full **quiver** of arrows represented prestige and protection. Like **arrows** for a **warrior**,

children were useful in the agricultural society. The man who had many children also enjoyed respect in Near Eastern society.
Ps 128 title On **ascents**, see note at Ps 120 title.
128:1–6 This is a companion psalm to Ps 127. The psalmist affirmed the significance of descendants, revisiting the original promise God made to Abraham in Gn 12:1–3.
128:3 Just as Joseph was described as a **fruitful vine** (Gn 49:22), so a **wife** who is blessed with **children** expands the family. **Olive trees** were known for vitality, strength, productivity, and longevity.
128:5–6 In the ancient Near East, the ultimate earthly blessing would be **prosperity** for one's nation, long life, healthy offspring, and **peace**.
Ps 129 title On **ascents**, see note at Ps 120 title.
129:1–2 Israel **often** suffered affliction from enemies in her early days (106:41–43). On **let Israel say**, compare 118:2–4; 124:1.

2 since my youth they have often
    attacked me,
but they have not prevailed against me.
3 Plowmen plowed over my back;
they made their furrows long.
4 The LORD is righteous;
he has cut the ropes of the wicked.

5 Let all who hate Zion
be driven back in disgrace.
6 Let them be like grass on the rooftops,
which withers before it grows up^A
7 and can't even fill the hands
    of the reaper
or the arms of the one
    who binds sheaves.
8 Then none who pass by will say,
"May the LORD's blessing be on you.
We bless you in the name of the LORD."

Awaiting Redemption

130 A song of ascents.
Out of the depths I call
    to you, LORD!
2 Lord, listen to my voice;
let your ears be attentive
to my cry for help.

3 LORD, if you kept an account
    of iniquities,
Lord, who could stand?
4 But with you there is forgiveness,
so that you may be revered.

5 I wait for the LORD; I wait
and put my hope in his word.
6 I wait for the Lord
more than watchmen
    for the morning —
more than watchmen for the morning.

7 Israel, put your hope in the LORD.
For there is faithful love with the LORD,
and with him is redemption
    in abundance.
8 And he will redeem Israel
from all its iniquities.

A Childlike Spirit

131 A song of ascents. Of David.
LORD, my heart is not proud;
my eyes are not haughty.
I do not get involved with things
too great or too wondrous for me.
2 Instead, I have calmed and quieted my
    soul
like a weaned child with its mother;
my soul is like a weaned child.

3 Israel, put your hope in the LORD,
both now and forever.

David and Zion Chosen

132 A song of ascents.
LORD, remember David
and all the hardships he endured,
2 and how he swore an oath to the LORD,
making a vow to the Mighty One
    of Jacob:
3 "I will not enter my house
or get into my bed,
4 I will not allow my eyes to sleep
or my eyelids to slumber
5 until I find a place for the LORD,
a dwelling for the Mighty One
    of Jacob."

6 We heard of the ark in Ephrathah;^B
we found it in the fields of Jaar.^C
7 Let's go to his dwelling place;
let's worship at his footstool.

^A129:6 Or it can be pulled out   ^B132:6 = Bethlehem   ^C132:6 = Kiriath-jearim

---

129:3 Slaves were often beaten by overseers and owners, creating stripes on their backs (Ex 5:14; Is 50:6; 53:4–6). 129:4 The LORD will prevent the **wicked** from harming his people by eliminating the weapons used to force submission (46:9; Jb 41:26). 129:5–7 The psalmist prayed an imprecation or curse upon those who hated the Lord and his people. Those who oppose the Lord will be like **grass** that sprouts briefly only to become scorched and withered, not living long enough to bear fruit. This is the opposite of 126:6, where the righteous person rejoiced in his harvest. 129:8 Those who hate Zion (v. 5) will suffer God's curse on their harvests. No one who sees them will offer a cheerful greeting (see Ru 2:4). **Ps 130 title** On **ascents**, see note at Ps 120 title. 130:1–2 The most effective prayers are made **out of the depths** of despair and dependence. See 1Sm 1:16. 130:3–4 To keep an account of **iniquities** is literally to "watch over" or "guard" them. All would be lost if God made no provision

to let sins go. The penitent person relies on the mercy and compassion of the Lord to forgive (103:3); otherwise, the Lord would not acknowledge his worship (Ezr 9:15). **Revered** brings out the dual connotation of "fear" and "worship," depicting God's mercy in forgiveness and his judgment of unrighteousness. 130:5–6 **Hope** in adversity anticipates God's response on the basis of **his word** (119:42, 49, 74, 81). 130:7–8 While Israel's **hope** of forgiveness is generated by the Lord's **faithful love** (Hb *chesed*), her **redemption** ("deliverance from an obligation through a payment") depicts the visible result of that forgiveness (Neh 1:10; Is 50:2). **Ps 131 title** On **ascents**, see note at Ps 120 title. 131:1 Humility characterizes the faithful, who depend on the Lord and exalt him. 131:2–3 Israel should adopt the attitude of an infant, depending on **the LORD** for protection and nurture (Mt 18:3). **Ps 132 title** On ascents, see note at Ps 120 title. This royal psalm must have been written after David's time, since it looks back at

King David's plan to build a temple for the ark (vv. 5–8). Also, another anointed king appeals to God's grace in David's name (v. 10). 132:1 The **hardships** David **endured** probably refer to his longing to bring the ark to Jerusalem and his anguish over the incident with Uzzah (2Sm 6:6–8). 132:2 **Mighty One of Jacob** alludes to Israel's heritage in God (Gn 49:24). 132:3–5 David's promise is revisited in vv. 3–5, while vv. 6–8 recall its fulfillment. The Hebrew grammar in these verses shows determination or will, reinforcing David's commitment to bring the ark of the covenant to Jerusalem and install it in a permanent structure. 132:6 The psalmist summarized the history of the installation of the ark in a tabernacle in Jerusalem (1Sm 5–6; 2Sm 6–7). **Ephrathah** was an area near Bethlehem where David received news about the ark. **Jaar**, otherwise known as Kiriath-jearim (1Sm 6:21–7:2), was where the ark was recovered from the Philistines. 132:7 Remembering the ceremonial procession that accompanied the ark to Jerusalem,

⁸ Rise up, LORD, come to
your resting place,
you and your powerful ark.
⁹ May your priests be clothed
with righteousness,
and may your faithful people shout
for joy.
¹⁰ For the sake of your servant David,
do not reject your anointed one.ᴬ

¹¹ The LORD swore an oath to David,
a promise he will not abandon:
"I will set one of your offspringᴮ
on your throne.
¹² If your sons keep my covenant
and my decrees that I will teach them,
their sons will also sit on
your throne forever."

¹³ For the LORD has chosen Zion;
he has desired it for his home:
¹⁴ "This is my resting place forever;
I will make my home here
because I have desired it.
¹⁵ I will abundantly bless its food;
I will satisfy its needy with bread.
¹⁶ I will clothe its priests with salvation,
and its faithful people will shout
for joy.
¹⁷ There I will make a horn grow
for David;
I have prepared a lampᶜ for
my anointed one.
¹⁸ I will clothe his enemies with shame,
but the crown he wearsᴰ
will be glorious."

Living in Harmony

133 *A song of ascents. Of David.*
How delightfully good
when brothers live together
in harmony!
² It is like fine oil on the head,
running down on the beard,
running down Aaron's beard
onto his robes.
³ It is like the dew of Hermonᴱ
falling on the mountains of Zion.
For there the LORD has appointed
the blessing —
life forevermore.

Call to Evening Worship

134 *A song of ascents.*
Now bless the LORD,
all you servants of the LORD
who stand in the LORD's house at night!
² Lift up your hands in the holy place
and bless the LORD!

³ May the LORD,
Maker of heaven and earth,
bless you from Zion.

The LORD Is Great

135 Hallelujah!
Praise the name of the LORD.
Give praise, you servants of the LORD
² who stand in the house of the LORD,
in the courts of the house of our God.
³ Praise the LORD, for the LORD is good;
sing praise to his name,
for it is delightful.

ᴬ**132:10** = the king   ᴮ**132:11** Lit *set the fruit of your belly*   ᶜ**132:17** Or *dominion*   ᴰ**132:18** Lit *but on him his crown*   ᴱ**133:3** The tallest mountain in the region, noted for its abundant precipitation

---

the psalmist appealed to the congregation to enter the temple (1Ch 15–16). **His footstool** is a term referring to the ark.
132:8 Verses 8–10 recur in 2Ch 6:41. The ark denotes the Lord's **resting place** (Nm 10:33–35), serving as a visible representation of God's presence (1Sm 4:4; Is 6:1) and playing a pivotal role in holy conquest (Jos 6:6–7; 1Sm 4:3–8).
132:9 The priests were **clothed with righteousness**, bound to obedience and ethical behavior (v. 16; cp. Is 11:5; 61:10). **Your faithful people** derives from *chesed*, the Hebrew term for "covenant love."
132:10 Reject is literally "turn one's face from" (cp. Ezk 14:6). The **anointed one** is the king.
132:11 Just as David swore an oath to the Lord (v. 2), so **the LORD swore an oath** of fidelity to David (89:35; 110:4). The Lord promised to sustain the Davidic monarchy by keeping one of his **offspring** on the throne (89:3–4,28–29; 2Sm 7).
132:12 Conditionality was always implicit in this promise (89:38–39; 7:14). God's divinely ordained leader was expected to obey his law, serving as a role model to the community.
132:13–15 The designation of **Zion** as the Lord's eternal **resting place** (68:16; 78:68;

87:2) brought a false sense of security to Israel; they wrongly believed the Lord would never allow Jerusalem to be captured or destroyed (Jr 7:3–12; Mc 3:11).
132:16 Just as the priests were expected to exhibit integrity in behavior (v. 9), so they were entrusted with **salvation**. This expressed their responsibility as divine mediators for the spiritual welfare of the people (Ezk 3:18; cp. Mt 16:19; 2Co 5:18–20).
132:17 The **horn** represents victory and salvation. The Hebrew word for **grow** (89:17; 148:14) is sometimes associated with a future Messiah, often figuratively referred to as a "branch" or "sprout" (Jr 23:5; 33:15; Ezk 29:21; Zch 3:8; 6:12). To prepare **a lamp** describes metaphorically the permanence of the dynasty and God's visible presence on the throne (18:28; 2Sm 21:17; 22:29; 1Kg 11:36; Jb 18:6).
132:18 God's priests will display righteousness and salvation (vv. 9,16), but the unrighteous will reflect **shame**. The divinely ordained king will stand out among the nations as the Lord's anointed.
Ps 133 title On **ascents**, see note at Ps 120 title.
133:1 Brothers can denote any fellow Israelite. The psalmist holds up unity as an ideal.
133:2–3 Unity in a society is compared to extravagant blessing of consecrating **oil**

or dewfall on dry ground. **Zion** was the epitome of blessing because **there** God commanded (**appointed**) eternal **life**—possibly alluding to what Christ accomplished in Jerusalem.
Ps 134 title This is the last of the fifteen psalms of **ascents** (see note at Ps 120 title).
134:1 Bless and "praise" are the same word in Hebrew (*brk*). To bless a person is to speak well of him. When people speak well of God, it is praise. When God speaks well of a person, that person is blessed (Gn 24:35; Jb 42:12). After the exile, **servants** designated the faithful community that exemplified an attitude of service (19:11,13; 79:2,10; 86:4,16; 90:13). Congregational singing at the temple often occurred in the evening.
134:3 The "blessing" of the Lord represents divine attention (cp. 128:5; Nm 6:24; Dt 14:29). **Maker of heaven and earth** differentiates Yahweh the Creator from all false gods.
135:1–21 Nearly every verse of this psalm quotes or is quoted by other Scripture, such as Ps 115.
135:2 People stood in the temple to worship (134:1; Neh 9:3), pray (2Ch 20:9), and serve (Dt 10:8; Ezk 44:15).
135:3 The Lord's **name** is his character or reputation (see v. 13).

⁴ For the LORD has chosen Jacob
   for himself,
Israel as his treasured possession.

⁵ For I know that the LORD is great;
our Lord is greater than all gods.
⁶ The LORD does whatever he pleases
in heaven and on earth,
in the seas and all the depths.

⁷ He causes the clouds to rise
   from the ends of the earth.
He makes lightning for the rain
and brings the wind
   from his storehouses.

⁸ He struck down the firstborn of Egypt,
both people and animals.
⁹ He sent signs and wonders
   against you, Egypt,
against Pharaoh and all his officials.
¹⁰ He struck down many nations
and slaughtered mighty kings:
¹¹ Sihon king of the Amorites,
Og king of Bashan,
and all the kings of Canaan.
¹² He gave their land as an inheritance,
an inheritance to his people Israel.

¹³ LORD, your name endures forever,
your reputation, LORD,
through all generations.
¹⁴ For the LORD will vindicate his people
and have compassion on his servants.

¹⁵ The idols of the nations are of silver
   and gold,
made by human hands.
¹⁶ They have mouths but cannot speak,
eyes, but cannot see.
¹⁷ They have ears but cannot hear;
indeed, there is no breath
in their mouths.
¹⁸ Those who make them are just
   like them,
as are all who trust in them.

¹⁹ House of Israel, bless the LORD!
House of Aaron, bless the LORD!
²⁰ House of Levi, bless the LORD!
You who revere the LORD, bless the LORD!
²¹ Blessed be the LORD from Zion;
he dwells in Jerusalem.
Hallelujah!

God's Love Is Eternal

136 Give thanks to the LORD,
   for he is good.
His faithful love endures forever.
² Give thanks to the God of gods.
His faithful love endures forever.
³ Give thanks to the Lord of lords.
His faithful love endures forever.
⁴ He alone does great wonders.
His faithful love endures forever.
⁵ He made the heavens skillfully.
His faithful love endures forever.
⁶ He spread the land on the waters.
His faithful love endures forever.
⁷ He made the great lights:
His faithful love endures forever.
⁸ the sun to rule by day,
His faithful love endures forever.
⁹ the moon and stars to rule by night.
His faithful love endures forever.
¹⁰ He struck the firstborn of the Egyptians
His faithful love endures forever.
¹¹ and brought Israel out from among
   them
His faithful love endures forever.
¹² with a strong hand
and outstretched arm.
His faithful love endures forever.
¹³ He divided the Red Sea
His faithful love endures forever.
¹⁴ and led Israel through,
His faithful love endures forever.
¹⁵ but hurled Pharaoh
and his army into the Red Sea.
His faithful love endures forever.
¹⁶ He led his people in the wilderness.
His faithful love endures forever.

135:4 God's **treasured possession** always referred to Israel (Ex 19:5; Dt 7:6; 14:2; 26:18; Mal 3:17). **135:6** Compare this verse with 115:3. The Lord's decree accomplishes his purposes (Is 55:11). The **depths** (24:2; Ex 20:4) and the **seas** (Is 24:15–16; 42:10) illustrate the Lord's authority over all creation. **135:7** An identical verse occurs in Jr 10:13; 51:16 (cp. Jb 38:22). God controls the weather. The Hebrew word for **storehouses** is also used for a temple treasury or royal storeroom. **135:8–9** Verses 8–12 are similar to Ps 136. The God-ordained death of the **firstborn** in **Egypt** was virtually equivalent to killing their gods, since Pharaoh and his offspring were considered divine. The plagues were Yahweh's polemic against false Egyptian gods. The direct address **against you,**

Egypt could be translated "in the midst of Egypt." **135:10–12 Sihon** and **Og** were kings who denied Israel passage through their lands (Nm 21:33–35; cp. Ps 136:19–20). During the conquest of Canaan, the Lord gave Israel the land that had belonged to these kings. **135:13–14** The enduring character of God's name is based on his salvific work. **135:19–20** Each sector is called upon to bless and acknowledge the Lord as their God, beginning with the nation (**Israel**), the high priest (**Aaron**), the priesthood (**Levi**), and concluding with the community (cp. 115:9–11). **136:1–26** This psalm recollects events from creation to Israel's conquest of Canaan. Each verse concludes with the refrain, **His faithful love endures forever** (cp. 118:1–4), which may have been sung by the congregation in response to the priests.

136:1–3 Compare these verses with 135:3. **136:4** On **wonders**, see 72:18; 75:1; 78:4; 96:3; 98:1; 105:5; 106:7,22; 107:8. **136:5 Skillfully** is literally "through understanding" (78:72; Jb 26:12; Is 44:19; Jr 10:12; 51:15). **136:6–9** The psalmist summarized creation in terms of the separation of **land** and **waters** and the appointment of the **sun** … **moon**, and **stars** to regulate seasons and times (Gn 1:3–8,14–19). Noticeably absent are references to living things. **136:11–15 Strong hand and outstretched arm** always refers to God's power and the deliverance of Israel (Dt 4:34; 5:15; 26:8; Jr 32:21), but especially to Israel's crossing of the Red Sea (Ex 14:2). **136:16** The **wilderness** refers to the forty years of wandering by the Israelites (Dt 8:2; 29:4–5).

¹⁷ He struck down great kings
    His faithful love endures forever.
¹⁸ and slaughtered famous kings —
    His faithful love endures forever.
¹⁹ Sihon king of the Amorites
    His faithful love endures forever.
²⁰ and Og king of Bashan —
    His faithful love endures forever.
²¹ and gave their land as an inheritance,
    His faithful love endures forever.
²² an inheritance to Israel his servant.
    His faithful love endures forever.
²³ He remembered us in our humiliation
    His faithful love endures forever.
²⁴ and rescued us from our foes.
    His faithful love endures forever.
²⁵ He gives food to every creature.
    His faithful love endures forever.
²⁶ Give thanks to the God of heaven!
    His faithful love endures forever.

Lament of the Exiles

137 By the rivers of Babylon —
there we sat down and wept
when we remembered Zion.
² There we hung up our lyres
on the poplar trees,
³ for our captors there asked us
for songs,
and our tormentors, for rejoicing:
"Sing us one of the songs of Zion."

⁴ How can we sing the LORD's song
on foreign soil?
⁵ If I forget you, Jerusalem,
may my right hand forget its skill.
⁶ May my tongue stick to the roof
of my mouth
if I do not remember you,
if I do not exalt Jerusalem
as my greatest joy!

⁷ Remember, LORD,
what the Edomites said
that day^A at Jerusalem:
"Destroy it! Destroy it
down to its foundations!"
⁸ Daughter Babylon,
doomed to destruction,
happy is the one who pays you back
what you have done to us.
⁹ Happy is he who takes your little ones
and dashes them against the rocks.

A Thankful Heart

138 Of David.
I will give you thanks
with all my heart;
I will sing your praise
before the heavenly beings.^B
² I will bow down
toward your holy temple
and give thanks to your name
for your constant love and truth.
You have exalted your name
and your promise above
everything else.^C
³ On the day I called, you answered me;
you increased strength within me.^D

⁴ All the kings on earth
will give you thanks, LORD,
when they hear
what you have promised.^E
⁵ They will sing of the LORD's ways,
for the LORD's glory is great.
⁶ Though the LORD is exalted,
he takes note of the humble;
but he knows the haughty
from a distance.

⁷ If I walk into the thick of danger,
you will preserve my life

---

^A**137:7** The day Jerusalem fell to the Babylonians in 586 BC ^B**138:1** Or *before the gods*, or *before judges*, or *before kings*; Hb *elohim* ^C**138:2** Or *You have exalted your promise above all your name* ^D**138:3** Hb obscure ^E**138:4** Lit *hear the words of your mouth*

136:17–22 Compare this with 135:10–11. These **kings** were **famous** for their military power. On **Sihon** and **Og**, see 135:10–12.
136:23–25 The Lord encouraged the Israelites in the land of Canaan, providing abundant resources for their livelihood (104:14–15,27–28; 145:15–16; 146:7; 147:9).
137:1 The rivers of Babylon were a series of canals running through the southern plain (Ezk 1:1; Dn 8:2). During the exile, the assembled community grieved there.
137:2 The **trees** of Babylon were not the familiar olive and cedar trees of the promised land.
137:3 By asking the community to sing **songs of Zion**, Israel's **captors** were tormenting and mocking them (42:3,10; 79:10).
137:4 The Israelites could not engage in worship since the land of Babylon was unclean and Israel had no temple.
137:5–6 The psalmist took an oath to stay loyal to **Jerusalem**, which represented the

city, the land, and the temple, symbols of God's promise to Israel.
137:7 Remember reflects the theme of the psalm. Israel "remembered" Zion (v. 1), made a pledge to remember Jerusalem (vv. 5–6), and asked the Lord to "remember" Jerusalem's devastation by the Edomites (v. 7). The Edomites descended from Esau, the twin brother of Jacob, and served as Babylon's allies in the destruction of Jerusalem (Ezk 25:12; 36:5). **Destroy it** is literally "strip it down," that is, "raze it."
137:8 Who pays you back what you have done to us reinforces the concept of receiving a punishment equal to the crime (Ex 21:23–25; Mt 5:38–42). God pays back those who reject him (Dt 7:10; 32:35; Is 65:6), and he specifically promised to repay Babylon for their crimes against his people (Jr 51:56).
137:9 This imprecation is startling. Out of the psalmist's intense emotional state, seething with righteous anger, he called for

the execution of just vengeance against the wicked who had perhaps done the described acts (**takes . . . and dashes**) to Israel's **little ones**.
138:2–3 Constant love translates the Hebrew word *chesed*. The fulfillment of God's promises surpasses all previous revelation.
138:4–5 The universal outlook of the psalmist reflects a fairly new understanding for David—that **all the kings on earth** would someday worship Yahweh (22:27–28). Solomon came to know it (72:11; 2Ch 6:33), and it was spoken through the prophets (Is 2:1–4; Rv 21:24).
138:6 From heaven (14:2; 33:13; 34:15; 102:19; 113:5; Is 57:15), God stoops to act on behalf of the downtrodden (**humble**), but he withholds assistance from those who are **haughty** or arrogant.
138:7–8 In light of what the psalmist knows about God, he expresses confidence in the future.

from the anger of my enemies.
You will extend your hand;
your right hand will save me.
⁸ The LORD will fulfill his purpose for me.
LORD, your faithful love
endures forever;
do not abandon the work of your hands.

The All-Knowing, Ever-Present God

139 *For the choir director. A psalm of David.*
LORD, you have searched me
and known me.
² You know when I sit down and when
I stand up;
you understand my thoughts
from far away.
³ You observe my travels and my rest;
you are aware of all my ways.
⁴ Before a word is on my tongue,
you know all about it, LORD.
⁵ You have encircled me;
you have placed your hand on me.
⁶ This wondrous knowledge is
beyond me.
It is lofty; I am unable to reach it.

⁷ Where can I go to escape your Spirit?
Where can I flee from your presence?
⁸ If I go up to heaven, you are there;
if I make my bed in Sheol,
you are there.
⁹ If I fly on the wings of the dawn
and settle down on
the western horizon,ᴬ
¹⁰ even there your hand will lead me;
your right hand will hold on to me.
¹¹ If I say, "Surely the darkness
will hide me,

and the light around me
will be night" —
¹² even the darkness is not dark to you.
The night shines like the day;
darkness and light are alike to you.

¹³ For it was you who created
my inward parts;ᴮ
you knit me together
in my mother's womb.
¹⁴ I will praise you
because I have been remarkably
and wondrously made.ᶜ,ᴰ
Your works are wondrous,
and I know this very well.
¹⁵ My bones were not hidden from you
when I was made in secret,
when I was formed in the depths
of the earth.
¹⁶ Your eyes saw me when I was formless;
all my days were written in your book
and planned
before a single one of them began.

¹⁷ God, how preciousᴱ your thoughts are
to me;
how vast their sum is!
¹⁸ If I counted them,
they would outnumber the grains
of sand;
when I wake up,ᶠ I am still with you.

¹⁹ God, if only you would kill
the wicked —
you bloodthirsty men, stay away
from me —
²⁰ who invoke you deceitfully.
Your enemies swear by you falsely.

ᴬ**139:9** Lit *the end of the sea*   ᴮ**139:13** Lit *my kidneys*   ᶜ**139:14** DSS, some LXX mss, Syr, Jer read *because you are remarkable and wonderful*   ᴰ**139:14** Hb obscure   ᴱ**139:17** Or *difficult*   ᶠ**139:18** Some Hb mss read *I come to an end*

139:1–24 This psalm celebrates the attributes of God.
139:1–4 The Hebrew verbs can be interpreted as timeless truth: "You search me and you know me." God's attributes are not restricted to time. The words **know . . . understand . . . observe**, and **are aware** speak of God's omniscience. The word *observe* comes from a Hebrew root that means "measure." The Hebrew word for **ways** does not necessarily denote literal walking but daily behavior.
139:5 God's omnipresence guarantees protection. The first line is literally "Back and front, you enclosed me." **Your hand on me** denotes absolute control over the psalmist, who was subject to the Lord's loving care and discipline.
139:6 God's attributes of omniscience and omnipresence are beyond human comprehension.
139:7 The psalmist could not remove himself from the realm of God's transcendence, nor could he run from his immanent and personal engagement with him (Jr 23:24; Am 9:2–4; Heb 4:13). The concept is both frightening and comforting.

139:8 The notion of escaping to heaven and hell finds its roots in ancient Near Eastern mythology. The OT acknowledges God's ability to access **Sheol** because he is sovereign (Jb 26:6; Am 9:2), but banishment to the underworld removes a person from God's blessing (Ps 6:5; Ec 9:10).
139:9 Fly on the wings of the dawn is literally "take up the wings of the dawn" (see textual footnote). The LXX renders the phrase, "If I lift my wings to the dawn," reinforcing the concept of flying a long distance to avoid God's presence.
139:10 Yahweh's authority extends beyond the cosmos, and his sovereignty recognizes no limits. Every human is under the power, protection, and authority of God.
139:11 Evildoers cannot conceal their deeds from God (Jb 22:11–14; 34:22).
139:12 Light and **darkness** are artificial distinctions for the Lord; he transcends creation.
139:13 Humankind is the Lord's possession and his creation (Gn 14:19,22; Dt 32:6). **Inward parts** (lit "kidneys") often denote the seat of emotion or affection (16:7; 73:21; Jb 19:27).
139:14 The expression **wondrously made** is a forceful rendering of the text. God's

creation testifies to his power and majesty (Rm 1:20).
139:15 The phrase **depths of the earth** is normally associated with death (63:9; Ezk 26:20), but here it is figurative for the concealment of the womb.
139:16 The concept of the Lord's book that records the existence of all humans reinforces God's sovereignty over life and death (69:28; Ex 32:32–33). The Hebrew is ambiguous about what was written in God's books: **all my days** or something else about my **formless** substance.
139:17 How vast their sum denotes the superiority of God's knowledge in quality and quantity.
139:18 The sum of everything God knows is immeasurable (Is 55:8). **When I wake up** could refer to having pondered God's knowledge all night, or to the resurrection.
139:19–22 The psalmist wished to escape the influence of wicked liars. His zeal for God and righteousness gave him a single-minded determination. Such zeal is commendable (Jn 2:17; 2Co 7:11), but in calmer times it is directed toward love and mercy (Gl 1:14–16; Php 3:6–7).

▼ A Biblical Assessment of Abortion

by Steve W. Lemke

Abortion has been one of the most controversial issues in American culture over the last fifty years. What guidance does the Bible give us about the topic? Although it might seem surprising that an ancient document would address such a contemporary problem, the Bible offers many clear teachings that address abortion from several perspectives.

Who creates life?

Life comes from God. God created humans in his image; therefore, persons are treasured above all creation (Gn 1:26–27; 9:6). God is involved directly and personally in our creation. "The LORD is God. He made us, and we are his—his people, the sheep of his pasture" (Ps 100:3). Psalm 139:13–14 declares, "It was you [God] who created my inward parts; you knit me together in my mother's womb. I will praise you because I have been remarkably and wondrously made."

Elsewhere the Creator is described as breathing life into human beings: "Then the LORD God formed the man out of the dust from the ground and breathed the breath of life into his nostrils, and the man became a living being" (Gn 2:7). Job says, "The Spirit of God has made me, and the breath of the Almighty gives me life" (Jb 33:4). Because God has granted life (10:12), who are we to take life?

Is human life sacred?

The Bible stands strongly for the protection of human life and cries out against the taking of it. Scripture affirms the sanctity of life in numerous places, including Genesis 2:7; Psalms 127:3; 139:13–16a; and Jeremiah 1:4–5. Human life began when God shaped Adam in his own image and breathed into him. "He created them [humankind] male and female" (Gn 1:27). Being made in the image of God, in fact, gives human life its sacredness. The image of God is present when a new life starts in the womb.

The Bible places a strict prohibition against taking human life. The sixth commandment prohibits murder (Ex 20:13). Likewise, after the great flood, God reaffirmed the sacredness of human life and instituted the death penalty for those who take it; this was done to underscore the value of human life (Gn 9:5–6). To take a life at any point following conception is to kill one whom God has made in his own image (1:27; 9:6).

The Old Testament law identifies punishments for actions that cause even an accidental miscarriage or premature birth (Ex 21:22–25). One particular law concerns two men whose fighting leads to a woman being hit accidentally, causing her child to be born early. Whether miscarriage or premature delivery is in view, the inadvertent action is considered a sin to be punished by law. If even an accidental injury were fatal for either the mother or the child, the perpetrator could be liable and executed; this is a harsher penalty than any other form of involuntary manslaughter receives in the Old Testament law.

Is the unborn child a person?

The Bible is clear that life and personhood begin before birth. Unborn infants are shaped by God, known personally by him, and reflect the image of God. Moreover, God has a plan for their lives. Many Scriptures affirm that even as unborn children, humans are shaped by God. Job 31:15 asks, "Did not the one who made me in the womb also make them? Did not the same God form us both in the womb?" In Psalm 22:9 the psalmist says, "It was you [God] who brought me out of the womb, making me secure at my mother's breast." And Psalm 139:14–16 declares, "Your works are wondrous, and I know this very well. My bones were not hidden from you when I was made in secret. . . . Your eyes saw me when I was formless."

The language of Psalm 139 provides a rich resource for a biblical view of unborn children. The author of the psalm refers to himself as an unborn child multiple times, using the personal pronouns "me" and "I." Scripture thus clearly affirms that unborn children have personhood even in utero. Personhood does not change in any fundamental way between conception and birth. Personal identity has an unbroken continuity from the joining of sperm and egg through senior adulthood. The soul that is in the womb originated by the gift of God. That same soul exists outside the womb after birth. Psalm 139 also speaks

²¹ LORD, don't I hate those who hate you,
and detest those who rebel against you?

²² I hate them with extreme hatred;
I consider them my enemies.

²³ Search me, God, and know my heart;
test me and know my concerns.

²⁴ See if there is any offensive^A way in me;
lead me in the everlasting way.

Prayer for Rescue

140

For the choir director. A psalm of David.

¹ Rescue me, LORD, from evil men.
Keep me safe from violent men

² who plan evil in their hearts.
They stir up wars all day long.

³ They make their tongues
as sharp as a snake's bite;
viper's venom is under their lips.   *Selah*

⁴ Protect me, LORD,
from the power of the wicked.
Keep me safe from violent men
who plan to make me stumble.^B

⁵ The proud hide a trap with ropes for me;

they spread a net along the path
and set snares for me.   *Selah*

⁶ I say to the LORD, "You are my God."
Listen, LORD, to my cry for help.

⁷ LORD, my Lord, my strong Savior,
you shield my head on the day of battle.

⁸ LORD, do not grant the desires
of the wicked;
do not let them achieve their goals.
Otherwise, they will
become proud.   *Selah*

⁹ When those who surround me rise up,^C
may the trouble their lips cause
overwhelm them.

¹⁰ Let hot coals fall on them.
Let them be thrown into the fire,
into the abyss, never again to rise.

¹¹ Do not let a slanderer stay in the land.
Let evil relentlessly^D hunt down
a violent man.

¹² I^E know that the LORD upholds
the just cause of the poor,
justice for the needy.

---

^A**139:24** Or *idolatrous*   ^B**140:4** Lit *to trip up my steps*   ^C**140:9** Lit *Head of those who surround me*   ^D**140:11** Hb obscure
^E**140:12** Alt Hb tradition reads *You*

139:23–24 Concluding with an appeal for God to **search me** (cp. v. 1), the psalmist submitted his thoughts and motives (**concerns**) to the Lord's scrutiny. He asked God to reveal any **offensive way** (lit "way of hardship") in him. The Scriptures speak of two opposite ways: that of the upright and that of the wicked (Ps 1; Pr 12:28; Mt 7:13–14).
140:2–3 The metaphor of battle terminology refers to verbal attacks on the psalmist by his enemies. The reference to their **tongues** further supports verbal contention or litigation

(58:5; 64:3; 120:4). Those who oppose God are often characterized as poisonous vipers or snakes (10:7; 55:21; 57:4; cp. Rm 3:13).
140:4 Power is literally "hand," a figurative expression denoting influence or control. **Violent men** were making false accusations and trying to trap the psalmist (v. 1).
140:5 Those who were **proud** believed their plans were beyond discovery. Psalms often describe the deceitful actions of wicked men in terms of traps and **snares** (9:15–16; 10:8–9; 31:4; 57:6; 119:110; 124:7; 141:9).

140:6–8 The psalmist sought the Lord's favorable response to the persecution he faced (28:2; 31:22; 86:6; 130:2).
140:9 The psalmist asked God to bring the lies of his attackers back down on their heads (7:15–16; 40:14–15; Pr 26:27).
140:10–11 Based on Aramaic and Ugaritic usage, the Hebrew word for **abyss** probably means "watery pits."
140:12 The Lord defends the most vulnerable people in society (10:18; 68:5; 146:7–9; Dt 10:18).

---

of God's having an intimate knowledge of the unborn child. Note also the psalmist's recognition that God has a plan for his life (v. 16).

Remarkably, Luke even describes John the Baptist as having the Holy Spirit within him while still in his mother's womb (Lk 1:15b). The affirmation that God has a calling in mind for individual lives, even when those lives are in embryonic or fetal stage, is taught in other Scriptures as well. In Isaiah 49:1 the prophet says, "The LORD called me before I was born. He named me while I was in my mother's womb." In Jeremiah 1:5 God told Jeremiah, "I chose you before I formed you in the womb; I set you apart before you were born. I appointed you a prophet to the nations." The apostle Paul's testimony is similar in Galatians 1:15–17: "When God, who from my mother's womb set me apart and called me by his

grace, was pleased to reveal his Son in me, so that I could preach him among the Gentiles . . . I went." The New Testament makes no clear distinction between the personhood of born or unborn children.

Conclusion

To summarize, the Bible regards unborn infants as fully human individuals who, even in their earliest stages of development, have the potential to achieve that which persons in adulthood might. Though life is a constant process of adjustments, the full person and unique soul formed in the womb remain the same person and soul throughout life. Unborn children have the God-given right to life and should be accorded all the rights normally granted to humans. Christians do well to stand for and protect the lives of the unborn.

13 Surely the righteous will praise
    your name;
  the upright will live in your presence.

Protection from Sin and Sinners

141 A psalm of David.
  LORD, I call on you; hurry to help me.
  Listen to my voice when I call on you.
2 May my prayer be set before you
    as incense,
  the raising of my hands
    as the evening offering.

3 LORD, set up a guard for my mouth;
  keep watch at the door of my lips.
4 Do not let my heart turn to any evil thing
  or perform wicked acts with evildoers.
  Do not let me feast on their delicacies.
5 Let the righteous one strike me —
  it is an act of faithful love;
  let him rebuke me —
  it is oil for my head;
  let me[A] not refuse it.
  Even now my prayer is against
    the evil acts of the wicked.[B]
6 When their rulers[C] will be thrown off
    the sides of a cliff,
  the people[D] will listen to my words,
    for they are pleasing.

7 As when one plows and breaks up
    the soil,
  turning up rocks,
  so our[E] bones have been scattered
    at the mouth of Sheol.

8 But my eyes look to you, LORD, my Lord.
  I seek refuge in you; do not let me die.[F]
9 Protect me from the trap they have set
    for me,

and from the snares of evildoers.
10 Let the wicked fall into their own nets,
  while I pass by safely.

A Cry of Distress

142 A Maskil of David. When he was in the
  cave. A prayer.
1 I cry aloud to the LORD;
  I plead aloud to the LORD for mercy.
2 I pour out my complaint before him;
  I reveal my trouble to him.
3 Although my spirit is weak within me,
  you know my way.

Along this path I travel
  they have hidden a trap for me.
4 Look to the right and see:[G]
  no one stands up for me;
  there is no refuge for me;
  no one cares about me.

5 I cry to you, LORD;
  I say, "You are my shelter,
  my portion in the land of the living."
6 Listen to my cry,
  for I am very weak.
  Rescue me from those who pursue me,
  for they are too strong for me.
7 Free me from prison
  so that I can praise your name.
  The righteous will gather around me
  because you deal generously with me.

A Cry for Help

143 A psalm of David.
  LORD, hear my prayer.
  In your faithfulness listen to my plea,
  and in your righteousness answer me.
2 Do not bring your servant
    into judgment,

[A]141:5 Lit my head [B]141:5 Lit of them [C]141:6 Or judges [D]141:6 Lit cliff, and they [E]141:7 DSS reads my; some LXX mss, Syr read their [F]141:8 Or not pour out my life [G]142:4 DSS, LXX, Syr, Vg, Tg read I look to the right and I see

---

140:13 To **live in your presence** is literally "dwell before you." To stand, walk, or live in God's presence implies a good relationship with God (16:11; 41:12; 56:13; Gn 17:1; 1Kg 2:4; 3:6; 8:23).
141:1–2 Offerings of **incense** were prescribed for both morning and **evening** (Ex 30:7–8; 2Kg 16:15). These represented prayers rising to God in heaven (Neh 13:5,9; Is 1:13; Jr 41:5). The lifting of **hands** was a common practice in worship (28:2; 63:4; 134:2).
141:3 The phrase **door of my lips**, figurative for exercising prudent speech, occurs only here.
141:4 The **delicacies** probably refer metaphorically to illicit sacrificial offerings and pleasurable acts of sin.
141:5 Pouring oil on the head was considered refreshing in that culture (23:5; 45:7; 133:2; Is 61:3; Jms 5:14). Constructive criticism from a **righteous one** is desirable; it would be foolish to **refuse it** (Pr 8:33–36; 15:32). The psalmist remains resolute in his opposition to evil.

141:6 The psalmist will be vindicated. When the wicked rulers are deposed, their followers will come to see that the psalmist has been right.
141:7 The psalmist feels as though his people had been slaughtered and then not provided a proper burial (79:2–4).
141:8 The psalmist affirms his trust in God (2:12; 5:12; 57:1; 64:10; 71:1; 118:8; Is 14:32; 57:13).
141:9–10 While the **evildoers** sought to trap the psalmist, he asked God to cause the **wicked** to **fall** into their own snares (7:16; 9:16; 35:8; 69:22; 106:36; 140:9–11; Pr 26:27).
Ps 142 title On **Maskil**, see note at Ps 32 title. The **cave** referred to here could be Adullam (1Sm 22:1) or En-gedi (1Sm 24:3–4; cp. Ps 57).
142:1–3 Turning to God when in distress showed that David trusted him. David referred to his spirit as **weak**, denoting spiritual or physical collapse (77:3; 143:4).
142:4 An advocate or defender normally stood on a person's **right** (16:8; 109:6; 110:5; 121:5). **No one stands up for me** is literally

"no one recognizes me." **No one cares about me** is literally "no one seeks my soul." The psalmist lacked support.
142:5 A **portion** is another way of describing a person's inheritance.
142:6 In asking God to **listen**, David also wants God to act (55:2).
142:7 Being hunted and having to hide was like being in **prison**. It is appropriate for deliverance to be followed by public **praise**. **You deal generously with me** is literally "you pay back on my behalf," which could have double meaning: God would reward David and punish his false accusers.
143:1–12 In this psalm, David asked God, in his faithful love, to do what he had promised in his covenant.
143:2 Bring your servant into judgment uses legal courtroom terminology typical of a covenant lawsuit (Jb 9:32; 14:3; Ec 11:9). As the psalmist began praying, he became self-conscious of his sinfulness. He acknowledged humanity's weaknesses (**no one . . . is righteous**) as a basis for a positive response

for no one alive is righteous
  in your sight.

3 For the enemy has pursued me,
  crushing me to the ground,
  making me live in darkness
  like those long dead.
4 My spirit is weak within me;
  my heart is overcome with dismay.

5 I remember the days of old;
  I meditate on all you have done;
  I reflect on the work of your hands.
6 I spread out my hands to you;
  I am like parched land
   before you.   *Selah*

7 Answer me quickly, LORD;
  my spirit fails.
  Don't hide your face from me,
  or I will be like those
  going down to the Pit.
8 Let me experience
  your faithful love in the morning,
  for I trust in you.
  Reveal to me the way I should go
  because I appeal to you.
9 Rescue me from my enemies, LORD;
  I come to you for protection.^A
10 Teach me to do your will,
  for you are my God.
  May your gracious Spirit
  lead me on level ground.

11 For your name's sake, LORD,
  let me live.
  In your righteousness deliver me
   from trouble.
12 and in your faithful love
   destroy my enemies.
  Wipe out all those who attack me,
  for I am your servant.

A King's Prayer

144 *Of David.*
Blessed be the LORD, my rock
who trains my hands for battle
and my fingers for warfare.
2 He is my faithful love and my fortress,
  my stronghold and my deliverer.
  He is my shield, and I take refuge in him;
  he subdues my people^B under me.

3 LORD, what is a human that you care
   for him,
  a son of man^C that you think of him?
4 A human is like a breath;
  his days are like a passing shadow.

5 LORD, part your heavens and come down.
  Touch the mountains,
   and they will smoke.
6 Flash your lightning and scatter
   the foe;^D
  shoot your arrows and rout them.
7 Reach down^E from on high;
  rescue me from deep water,
   and set me free
  from the grasp of foreigners
8 whose mouths speak lies,
  whose right hands are deceptive.

9 God, I will sing a new song to you;
  I will play on a ten-stringed harp
   for you —
10 the one who gives victory to kings,
  who frees his servant David
  from the deadly sword.
11 Set me free and rescue me
  from foreigners
  whose mouths speak lies,
  whose right hands are deceptive.

12 Then our sons will be like plants
  nurtured in their youth,

^143:9 One Hb ms, LXX; some Hb mss read *I cover myself to you*   ^144:2 Some Hb mss, DSS, Aq, Syr, Tg, Jer read *subdues peoples*; 2Sm 22:48; Ps 18:47   ^144:3 Or *a mere mortal*   ^144:6 Lit *scatter them*   ^144:7 Lit *down your hands*

from the Lord. The covenant relationship depended on the Lord's willingness to forgive (130:3–4; Jb 4:17; 9:2; 25:4; Rm 3:20; Gl 2:16). **143:3** This verse gives the occasion for the prayer. **143:4** As a result of being pursued, the psalmist was physically and spiritually exhausted (142:3). **143:5–6** The **work** of God's **hands** probably refers to all of his acts of creation and sustenance (8:6; 19:1; 28:5; 102:26; Is 5:12). When David looked back on what God had done in the past, he deeply desired God. **143:7** The **Pit**, like Sheol, meant death or the grave (30:3; 88:3–4; Is 14:11). **143:8** Based on the **faithful love** of the Lord, the psalmist asked for God's guidance in avoiding the traps set by the enemy (142:3). **143:9** This verse gives David's primary prayer. **143:10** In his weakness (v. 2), David recognized he needed God to **teach** him and **lead**

him (cp. "rescue" and "deliver" in vv. 9,11). **Level ground** refers to a path with nothing that would cause one to slip or stumble. **143:11** The foundation for David's prayer is the Lord's character. **143:12** David appealed to God's **faithful love** when asking him to **destroy** his **enemies**. **144:1–15** This psalm has a number of similarities with portions of Pss 8 and 18. Isaiah developed some of these same themes. **144:1** Compare this verse with 18:34. On the Lord as a **rock**, see 18:1–2. **144:2** Compare this verse with 18:2,46–50. **144:3** On **son of man**, see 8:3–4. The emphasis of this verse is on God's concentrated attention on and his intimate knowledge of humanity. **144:4** The life of **a human** is compared to a mere **breath**, reinforcing the fleeting nature of human existence (103:14–15; Is 40:6–8). On **like a passing shadow**, see 102:11.

144:5 Compare this verse with 18:9. The metaphorical imagery is consistent with the language of Ps 18 and descriptions of the divine warrior (Am 9:5). **Mountains** tremble, **smoke** appears, and lightning accompanies the presence of the Lord. **144:6** The Lord scatters **lightning** bolts over the earth, directing them like arrows (18:14; Ezk 5:16; Zch 9:14). **144:7–8 Foreigners** probably refer to those who worship false gods (18:44). **Lies** is literally "emptiness" (see Is 59:4). **Whose right hands are deceptive** refers to those who swore falsely with a raised right hand (Dt 32:40) or while shaking hands (Pr 6:1). **144:9** On **new song**, see 33:1–3. **144:10** David promises to praise the Lord when he answers his prayer for victory. **144:11** See note at vv. 7–8. **144:12** On **sons . . . like plants**, see 80:8,9–11. The OT often refers to God's people in agrarian terms (44:2; Ex 15:17; Is 5:7; Hs 10:1).

our daughters, like corner pillars
that are carved in the palace style.
[13] Our storehouses will be full,
supplying all kinds of produce;
our flocks will increase by thousands
and tens of thousands in
our open fields.
[14] Our cattle will be well fed.[A]
There will be no breach in the walls,
no going into captivity,[B]
and no cry of lament in
our public squares.
[15] Happy are the people with such blessings.
Happy are the people whose God is
the LORD.

Praising God's Greatness

145

A hymn of David.

I[c] exalt you, my God the King,
and bless your name forever and ever.
[2] I will bless you every day;
I will praise your name forever and ever.

[3] The LORD is great and is highly praised;
his greatness is unsearchable.
[4] One generation will declare your works
to the next
and will proclaim your mighty acts.
[5] I[D] will speak of your splendor and
glorious majesty
and[E] your wondrous works.
[6] They will proclaim the power
of your awe-inspiring acts,
and I will declare your greatness.[F]
[7] They will give a testimony
of your great goodness
and will joyfully sing
of your righteousness.

[8] The LORD is gracious
and compassionate,

slow to anger and great
in faithful love.
[9] The LORD is good to everyone;
his compassion rests on all he has made.
[10] All you have made will thank you, LORD;
the[G] faithful will bless you.
[11] They will speak of the glory
of your kingdom
and will declare your might,
[12] informing all people of your mighty acts
and of the glorious splendor
of your[H] kingdom.
[13] Your kingdom is
an everlasting kingdom;
your rule is for all generations.
The LORD is faithful in all his words
and gracious in all his actions.[I]

[14] The LORD helps all who fall;
he raises up all who are oppressed.[J]
[15] All eyes look to you,
and you give them their food at the
proper time.
[16] You open your hand
and satisfy the desire
of every living thing.

[17] The LORD is righteous in all his ways
and faithful in all his acts.
[18] The LORD is near all who call out to him,
all who call out to him with integrity.
[19] He fulfills the desires of those
who fear him;
he hears their cry for help
and saves them.
[20] The LORD guards all those who love him,
but he destroys all the wicked.
[21] My mouth will declare
the LORD's praise;
let every living thing
bless his holy name forever and ever.

[A]144:14 Or *will bear heavy loads*, or *will be pregnant*   [B]144:14 Or *be no plague, no miscarriage*   [C]145:1 The lines of this poem form an acrostic.   [D]145:5 LXX, Syr read *They*   [E]145:5 LXX, Syr read *and they will tell of*   [F]145:6 Alt Hb tradition, Jer read *great deeds*   [G]145:10 Lit *your*   [H]145:12 LXX, Syr, Jer; MT reads *his*   [I]145:13 One Hb ms, DSS, LXX, Syr; other Hb mss omit *The LORD is faithful in all his words and gracious in all his actions.*   [J]145:14 Lit *bowed down*

144:13 David's prayer is not self-centered but carries with it prosperity for his people. **144:14** Some interpreters believe the phrases **breach in the walls** and **going into captivity** look back on Jerusalem's destruction and Judah's exile, proving that this psalm was written after the exile. Others say it is a prophetic warning similar to that in Deuteronomy (Dt 28:52,63–64). **144:15** On **happy**, see 1:1. **145:1–21** This is an acrostic psalm. Each verse begins with a different letter of the Hebrew alphabet, and it has marked similarities with Ps 111. The Masoretic Text has no line beginning with the Hebrew letter *nun*. **145:1–2** The introduction places this psalm with other poems that herald Yahweh as **King** (Pss 47; 93; 96–99). **145:3** Compare this verse with 96:4. God's superiority goes beyond comprehension (cp. 139:6; Is 40:28).

145:4 One generation . . . to the next is literally "generation to generation." The construction resembles "day after day" and "night after night" in 19:2. Both passages emphasize continuous praise of the Lord. **145:5** The Hebrew word for **speak** could be translated "meditate" (77:3,6,12). **145:6** Note the alternation between **they** and **I**. **145:7 They will give a testimony** is literally "they will pour out a memory." **145:8** The language of this verse exemplifies God's covenant love toward his people (103:4; 111:4; Ex 34:6–7). **145:9** God's benevolence extends to all his creatures (Mt 5:45). Often called "common grace," the concept is contrasted with God's particular grace, extended only to his chosen people, believers (Ps 145:18–20; Mt 24:31; Rm 11:5; 2Th 2:13). **145:10–12 All people** will recognize God's sovereignty and dominion.

145:13 This is an acrostic psalm, but in Hebrew one of the letters is missing, which is supplied by the LXX. It is the second half of v. 13 in the CSB. Its deletion was almost certainly accidental. **145:14** The Hebrew term for **helps** suggests sustenance and support (146:8). **145:15** Jesus's prayer, "Give us today our daily bread" (Mt 6:11), could be based on this verse. **145:16** Compare this verse with 104:28. **145:17** This verse is similar to v. 13b. **145:18–19** For those who trust him, God is **near** like a friend and ready to help (cp. 138:6; Is 55:6; Jn 14:14). **145:20** Note the contrast between **those who love him** and **the wicked**. **145:21** The Lord's **name** represents the revelation of his powerful presence and impeccable character (see note at 20:1).

The God of Compassion

146
Hallelujah!
My soul, praise the LORD.
2 I will praise the LORD all my life;
I will sing to my God as long as I live.

3 Do not trust in nobles,
in a son of man,^A who cannot save.
4 When his breath^B leaves him,
he returns to the ground;
on that day his plans die.

5 Happy is the one whose help is the God
of Jacob,
whose hope is in the LORD his God,
6 the Maker of heaven and earth,
the sea and everything in them.
He remains faithful forever,
7 executing justice for the exploited
and giving food to the hungry.
The LORD frees prisoners.
8 The LORD opens the eyes of the blind.
The LORD raises up those
who are oppressed.^C
The LORD loves the righteous.
9 The LORD protects resident aliens
and helps the fatherless and the widow,
but he frustrates the ways
of the wicked.

10 The LORD reigns forever;
Zion, your God reigns
for all generations.
Hallelujah!

God Restores Jerusalem

147
Hallelujah!
How good it is to sing to our God,
for praise is pleasant and lovely.

2 The LORD rebuilds Jerusalem;
he gathers Israel's exiled people.
3 He heals the brokenhearted
and bandages their wounds.
4 He counts the number of the stars;
he gives names to all of them.
5 Our Lord is great, vast in power;
his understanding is infinite.^D
6 The LORD helps the oppressed
but brings the wicked to the ground.

7 Sing to the LORD with thanksgiving;
play the lyre to our God,
8 who covers the sky with clouds,
prepares rain for the earth,
and causes grass to grow on the hills.
9 He provides the animals with their food,
and the young ravens what they cry for.

10 He is not impressed by the strength
of a horse;
he does not value the power
of a warrior.^E
11 The LORD values those who fear him,
those who put their hope
in his faithful love.

12 Exalt the LORD, Jerusalem;
praise your God, Zion!
13 For he strengthens the bars
of your city gates
and blesses your children within you.
14 He endows your territory
with prosperity;^F
he satisfies you with the finest wheat.

15 He sends his command
throughout the earth;
his word runs swiftly.

^A146:3 Or a mere mortal   ^B146:4 Or spirit   ^C146:8 Lit bowed down   ^D147:5 Lit understanding has no number   ^E147:10 Lit the legs of the man   ^F147:14 Or peace

146:1 The last five psalms each begin and end with **Hallelujah!**
146:2 Notice that singing to our God is commended here.
146:3 **Nobles** were the best of men—generous, giving freely (the "willing" in Ex 35:5,22). Such a person could help immensely in this life but could not bestow eternal life (Ps 118:9; cp. Pr 19:6).
146:4 The fleeting nature of life affects everyone, and every man (Hb 'adam in v. 3) eventually returns to the **ground** (Hb 'adamah), reversing creation (Gn 2:7; 3:19). Kings and leaders suffer the same fate (Pss 39:5–6; 90:3–6; 102:11).
146:5 The phrase **God of Jacob** recalls Israel's early history before it became an established nation (20:1; 46:7,11; 84:8; cp. Ex 3:15).
146:6 The formula **Maker of heaven and earth . . . and everything in them** often occurs as a polemic, underscoring the omnipotence of Yahweh and contrasting his power with impotent gods and leaders (96:5; Neh 9:6; Is 37:16; 44:24; 45:18). The LORD's integrity is guaranteed by his holy nature.

146:7–9 The psalmist emphasized God's faithful provision and his role as deliverer (68:6; 82:3–4; Is 42:7). He defends the cause of Israel's most vulnerable citizens. This practice is based in cultic law that was established early in Israel's history (Ex 22:21–22; Dt 24:17).
146:10 The Lord, as Israel's King, will reign **forever**, rendering the help earthly kings cannot provide (cp. vv. 3–4).
147:1 On **Hallelujah!** see note at 146:1.
147:2–3 The restoration and return of Israel to the land is expressed as spiritual and physical healing. Isaiah 61:1 uses some of the same words—**bandages** the **brokenhearted**—which Jesus the Messiah fulfilled (Lk 4:18–21).
147:4–5 While the Lord **counts** (Hb mispar) the **stars** (Is 40:26), humanity is unable to measure (Hb mispar) the Lord's **understanding**.
147:6 God rights wrongs and reverses fortunes (7:14–16; 18:27; 113:8; 1Pt 5:5).
147:7 On **sing to the LORD** and **lyre**, see 33:1–3.
147:8 Three lines trace the progression from **clouds**, to **rain**, to vegetation. The Lord

attends to every aspect of the cosmos, and nothing escapes his attention (72:6; 85:11; 104:14; Is 45:8; 61:11).
147:9 Compare the imagery of this verse with Jb 38:41.
147:10–11 God determines the outcome of any situation, and when he evaluates the participants, **strength** and **power** do not impress him (33:16–17). Rather, he seeks to intervene on behalf of those who **fear** and trust him (2Ch 16:9).
147:12–13 In a clever wordplay, the psalmist described the Lord as strengthening the **bars** (Hb beriychey) of Jerusalem's **gates** and blessing (Hb barak) her **children** (Hb beniyk, "her sons") in her midst (Hb beqirbek). The Lord will restore Judah's protection and offspring.
147:14 The sovereign Lord controls the productivity of the land. His blessing is described in terms of the abundance that Israel will enjoy.
147:15 In a progressive development of the word of God, the Lord **sends** forth **his command**. His spoken "word" accomplishes all that he declares (v. 18; Is 55:10–11).

16 He spreads snow like wool;
  he scatters frost like ashes;
17 he throws his hailstones like crumbs.
  Who can withstand his cold?
18 He sends his word and melts them;
  he unleashes his winds,^A
    and the water flows.

19 He declares his word to Jacob,
  his statutes and judgments to Israel.
20 He has not done this for every nation;
  they do not know his judgments.
  Hallelujah!

Creation's Praise of the LORD

148 Hallelujah!
  Praise the LORD from the heavens;
  praise him in the heights.
2 Praise him, all his angels;
  praise him, all his heavenly armies.
3 Praise him, sun and moon;
  praise him, all you shining stars.
4 Praise him, highest heavens,
  and you waters above the heavens.
5 Let them praise the name of the LORD,
  for he commanded,
    and they were created.
6 He set them in position
    forever and ever;
  he gave an order that will never
    pass away.

7 Praise the LORD from the earth,
  all sea monsters and ocean depths,
8 lightning^B and hail, snow and cloud,
  stormy wind that executes
    his command,
9 mountains and all hills,
  fruit trees and all cedars,
10 wild animals and all cattle,
  creatures that crawl and flying birds,
11 kings of the earth and all peoples,

princes and all judges of the earth,
12 young men as well as young women,
  old and young together.
13 Let them praise the name of the LORD,
  for his name alone is exalted.
  His majesty covers heaven and earth.
14 He has raised up a horn for his people,
  resulting in praise to all
    his faithful ones,
  to the Israelites, the people close to him.
  Hallelujah!

Praise for God's Triumph

149 Hallelujah!
  Sing to the LORD a new song,
  his praise in the assembly
    of the faithful.
2 Let Israel celebrate its Maker;
  let the children of Zion rejoice
    in their King.
3 Let them praise his name with dancing
  and make music to him
    with tambourine and lyre.
4 For the LORD takes pleasure
    in his people;
  he adorns the humble with salvation.
5 Let the faithful celebrate
    in triumphal glory;
  let them shout for joy on their beds.

6 Let the exaltation of God be
    in their mouths^C
  and a double-edged sword
    in their hands,
7 inflicting vengeance on the nations
  and punishment on the peoples,
8 binding their kings with chains
  and their dignitaries with iron shackles,
9 carrying out the judgment
  decreed against them.
This honor is for all his faithful people.
Hallelujah!

---

^A147:18 Or breath   ^B148:8 Or fire   ^C149:6 Lit throat

147:16–17 Compare these verses with Jb 37–38 for God's sovereignty over the weather. Nothing is unaffected by the Lord's **cold**, which permeates creation.
147:18 The psalmist reinforced the association between the Lord's creative word and his spoken **word**. The Hebrew word for **winds** could also be translated "breath."
147:19–20 Describing the Lord's **word** as revelatory, the psalmist alluded to Dt 4:7–8, a text characterizing Israel as unique, with divinely ordained standards to regulate her relationship with God.
148:1 On **Hallelujah!** see note at 146:1. Compare this verse with 19:1; 29:1.
148:2–3 A military term denoting forces, **heavenly armies** often refers to the stars and other heavenly bodies (1Kg 22:19; 2Kg 23:5; Jr 31:35; see 1Sm 17:45).
148:4 Waters above the heavens is figurative for celestial bodies of water, the reservoirs from which God is said to have brought rain (104:3; Gn 1:6–7; 7:11).

148:5 The powerful word of the Lord (33:9) spoke the world into existence (Gn 1): The Hebrew word *bara'* ("create") is only used in reference to God.
148:6 God established creation and set boundaries, exercising sovereign control over the cosmos (104:9; Gn 1:6–10; 9:11; Jb 28:26; 38:8–10).
148:7 The psalmist contrasted the three levels of heaven (vv. 5–6) with three levels of the earth. Even **sea monsters** (Hb *tannin*) are called on to praise God (69:34).
148:8 The elements of nature perform at God's command (103:20; 104:4).
148:9–10 The psalmist hinted at the creation account in these verses, using peculiar expressions typical of Gn 1.
148:11–12 The list of people represents descending social status. All people are united in worship (Rm 10:12; Gl 3:28; Col 3:11). Prophets, priests, and other temple personnel were not mentioned, perhaps because they were the ones who were calling all others to praise God.

148:13 Yahweh's kingly splendor is universal. No other god deserves praise.
148:14 To raise **a horn** signifies strength.
149:1 On **Hallelujah!** see note at 146:1. This introduction **sing . . . a new song** usually denotes dynamic intervention not previously experienced by the writer (33:1–3; 96:1; 98:1; Is 42:10; 61:1). **The faithful** is a designation for Israel.
149:2 The Hebrew for **its Maker** is a plural of majesty (Jb 35:10; Is 54:5). Israel is doubly obligated to honor God since he is both their Creator and their **King**.
149:3 Dancing and **music** were typical modes of worship in the temple (30:11; 87:7; 150:4).
149:4–5 Just as Israel glorified God, so the Lord adorned Israel by saving them and giving them **glory** (Is 60:9; 61:1–3).
149:7–9 God will put the sword (v. 6) in Israel's hand to execute retaliation for wrongdoing (18:47; 58:11; 79:10; 94:1; cp. Est 9:5; Is 13:3; Rm 13:4). Just as God's people were captured and imprisoned, so the Lord will bind kings

Praise the LORD

150 Hallelujah!
Praise God in his sanctuary.
Praise him in his mighty expanse.
² Praise him for his powerful acts;
praise him for his abundant greatness.

³ Praise him with the blast of
a ram's horn;
praise him with harp and lyre.
⁴ Praise him with tambourine and dance;
praise him with strings and flute.
⁵ Praise him with resounding cymbals;
praise him with clashing cymbals.

⁶ Let everything that breathes
praise the LORD.
Hallelujah!

---

with **chains** and **shackles** (Is 45:14). Submission of world powers to God's **people** will bring **honor** to Israel.
150:1 On **Hallelujah!** see note at 146:1. As each of the five books in the Psalms ends with a doxology, the whole book concludes with a psalm of doxology.

150:2 The first half of this verse praises God for his mighty acts, the second half praises him for what he is in himself.
150:3–5 The sophistication of ancient sacred music is clear from the wide range of instruments used for temple worship. All three classifications—wind

instruments, strings, and percussion—are represented.
150:6 It is only logical that everything that has been given the breath of life from the Creator ought to praise him (149:2).

◄ Introduction to Proverbs

Circumstances of Writing

Solomon is credited with the proverbs in chapters 1–29 of the book of Proverbs (1:1; 10:1). There is biblical evidence that Solomon was wise and a collector of wise sayings (1Kg 3:5–14; 4:29–34; 5:7,12; 10:2–3,23–24; 11:41). Chapters 1–24 may have been written down during his reign (970–931 BC). The proverbs in chapters 25–29 were Solomon's proverbs collected by King Hezekiah, who reigned from 716 to 687 BC (25:1). The last two chapters are credited to Agur and Lemuel (30:1; 31:1), about whom nothing else is known. An editor was inspired to collect the proverbs of Solomon, Agur, and Lemuel into the book we now have.

The reign of Solomon represented the peak of prosperity for the nation of Israel. The period saw the greatest extent of the territory, and there was peace and international trade (1Kg 4:20–25; 10:21–29). It is likely Solomon knew about the ancient tradition of wisdom in Egypt (1Kg 3:1), but through inspiration and God's gift he composed even better sayings (1Kg 3:12; 10:6–7,23). Solomon addressed his teaching to his son or sons, but these inspired wise sayings are applicable to all people. The book of Proverbs, like the rest of the Bible, contains stories, teaching, and examples. People should make appropriate application of these truths to their own situations (1Co 10:11).

Contribution to the Bible

The Law and the Prophets teach how to live in spiritual community. Wisdom teaches how to live practically and courteously with one another. The book of Job addresses one main idea: the sovereignty of God with regard to suffering. Ecclesiastes contemplates the meaning of this ephemeral life. Solomon's Song demonstrates romantic love. Proverbs covers the rest of wisdom's topics, from how to conduct business astutely yet fairly, to how to live happily within marriage.

Structure

The book of Proverbs is in the wisdom genre. Wisdom books consist of the intelligent author's observations on the world and the people in it. However, without an inspired godly perspective, the world would be depressing and hopeless, as parts of Job and Ecclesiastes show. Ultimately, biblical wisdom is informed by and founded on faith in God.

The process of observation, contemplation, and inspiration can be seen in Proverbs 24:30–34. After observing the deteriorated condition of "the field of a slacker" and "the vineyard of one lacking sense," Solomon contemplated what he was seeing and was inspired: "I saw, and took it to heart; I looked, and received instruction" (v. 32). He either composed a new proverb or applied a familiar proverb to the situation: "a little sleep, a little slumber, a little folding of the arms to rest, and your poverty will come like a robber, and your need, like a bandit" (vv. 33–34).

Proverbs is written as Hebrew poetry. Hebrew poetry is terse and concise; it uses a lot of imagery, and generally the second line complements or contrasts the thought of the first. Contemplating how the second line relates to the first is a profitable way to meditate on a proverb.

Proverbs Timeline

3000–2200 BC

The Instruction of Prince Hardjedef, Egyptian Old Kingdom **2686–2160**
The Instructions Addressed to Kagemni, Egyptian **2600**
The Instruction of Ptah–Hotep, Egypt's Old Kingdom **2575–2134**
Collections of proverbs found among the royal archives at Ebla **2450–2250**

2200–1700 BC

ABRAHAM 2166–1991
The Royal Instruction of Khety to Merikare, Egyptian **2160**
The Instruction of a Man for His Son, Egyptian Middle Kingdom **2040–1640**
The Instruction of King Amenemhet I for His Son Sesostris I, Egyptian **1925**
Instructions of Shuruppak, Sumerian Proverb Collection **1900–1700**

In chapters 1–9, Solomon used imagery and sustained arguments to teach about the value of wisdom and the seduction of evil. In 22:17–24:34, there are "sayings" made up of several verses each; in chapters 30–31, there are more sayings, including numerical sayings and an alphabetic acrostic in praise of a capable wife. In the rest of the book, each proverb is generally one verse. Some scholars argue that these individual proverbs are carefully arranged in groups and each should be interpreted in the context of its group. Other scholars view the collection as unsystematic and argue that the immediate context seldom has any bearing on interpretation.

In either case, it is important to interpret any single proverb in the context of the book of Proverbs and the Bible as a whole. For example, while 21:14 may seem to encourage bribery, the rest of the book of Proverbs is clearly against it (15:27)—as is the rest of Scripture (Ex 23:8; Ec 7:7).

Outline

I. Solomon's Exhortations and Warnings (1:1–9:18)
   A. Contrast between wisdom and riches (1:1–3:20)
   B. Praise of wisdom, love, and worthy conduct (3:21–4:27)
   C. Warnings against lust, idleness, and deceit (5:1–7:27)
   D. A portrayal of wisdom (8:1–9:18)
II. Solomon's Proverbs (10:1–29:27)
   A. Collected proverbs (10:1–22:16)
   B. Thirty sayings of the wise (22:17–24:22)
   C. More sayings of the wise (24:23–34)
   D. Hezekiah's collection (25:1–29:27)
III. Other Proverbs (30:1–31:31)
   A. Words of Agur (30:1–33)
   B. Words of Lemuel (31:1–9)
   C. Praise of a capable wife (31:10–31)

Key verses in Proverbs

3:5–6 Trust in the LORD with all your heart, and do not rely on your own understanding; in all your ways know him, and he will make your paths straight.

8:33 Listen to instruction and be wise; don't ignore it.

15:1 A gentle answer turns away anger, but a harsh word stirs up wrath.

20:11 Even a young man is known by his actions—by whether his behavior is pure and upright.

22:1 A good name is to be chosen over great wealth; favor is better than silver and gold.

1700–1200 BC

The Phoenicians develop a 22-letter alphabet that consisted of consonants only. It was read from right to left and became an important step in the development of the modern Western alphabet. This was the world's first purely phonetic alphabet. It was based on sounds and not symbolic representations of objects. **1600**

MOSES 1526–1406

The Counsels of Wisdom, Akkadian **1500–1200**

Events in Judges **1380?–1060?**

1200–900 BC

The Instruction of Amenemope, Egypt **1186–1069**

DAVID 1050?–970

Saul anointed king **1050**

David becomes king over all Israel. **1003**

SOLOMON 990?–931

Solomon becomes king. **970**

Proverbs **970**

The Purpose of Proverbs

1 The proverbs of Solomon son of David,
  king of Israel:

2 For learning wisdom and discipline;
  for understanding insightful sayings;

3 for receiving prudent instruction
  in righteousness, justice, and integrity;

4 for teaching shrewdness
    to the inexperienced,^A
  knowledge and discretion
    to a young man —

5 let a wise person listen
    and increase learning,
  and let a discerning person
    obtain guidance —

6 for understanding a proverb
    or a parable,^B
  the words of the wise, and their riddles.

7 The fear of the LORD
    is the beginning of knowledge;
  fools despise wisdom and discipline.

Avoid the Path of the Violent

8 Listen, my son,
    to your father's instruction,
  and don't reject your mother's teaching,

9 for they will be a garland of favor
    on your head
  and pendants^c around your neck.

10 My son, if sinners entice you,
   don't be persuaded.

11 If they say — "Come with us!
   Let's set an ambush and kill someone.^D
   Let's attack some innocent person
     just for fun!^E

12 Let's swallow them alive, like Sheol,
   whole, like those who go down to the Pit.

13 We'll find all kinds of valuable property
   and fill our houses with plunder.

14 Throw in your lot with us,
   and we'll all share the loot"^F —

15 my son, don't travel that road with them
   or set foot on their path,

16 because their feet run toward evil
   and they hurry to shed blood.

17 It is useless to spread a net
   where any bird can see it,

18 but they set an ambush
     to kill themselves;^G
   they attack their own lives.

19 Such are the paths of all who make
     profit dishonestly;
   it takes the lives of those who receive it.^H

Wisdom's Plea

20 Wisdom calls out in the street;
   she makes her voice heard
     in the public squares.

21 She cries out above' the commotion;
   she speaks at the entrance
     of the city gates:

22 "How long, inexperienced ones, will you
     love ignorance?

---

^A1:4 Or *simple*, or *gullible* ^B1:6 Or *an enigma* ^c1:9 Lit *chains* ^D1:11 Lit *Let's ambush for blood* ^E1:11 Lit *person for no reason* ^F1:14 Lit *us; one bag will be for all of us* ^G1:18 Lit *they ambush for their blood* ^H1:19 Lit *takes the life of its masters* '1:21 Lit *at the head of*

1:1 A proverb is a pithy allusion or parable that is rich in truth and meaning. **King of Israel** here refers to Solomon, who was the last king of united Israel (1Kg 1–11).
1:2 Wisdom is having mastery of a subject of knowledge; it encompasses discipline, knowledge, prudence, and other virtues. It is the ability to apply knowledge to overcome any problem in life. Biblical "wisdom," which is a gift from God (2:6), includes morality and the knowledge of God. **Discipline** has to do with warnings about the consequences of errant behavior, or loving correction to those who have failed to heed such warnings. It can involve physical punishment. The Hebrew word is often translated "instruction" (v. 3) because the goal is always edification and education, not just punishment. **Understanding** means internalizing knowledge so that it directs action. **Insightful sayings** are those that reveal truth.
1:3 Prudent instruction is literally "the discipline (see note at v. 2) of prudence." Prudence is skill or cleverness; a talent for insight, observation, or scrutiny; practical wisdom that leads to success. This cleverness is morally guided by **righteousness** (agreement with God's directives), **justice** (restoration of what is right), and **integrity** (what is straight, right, and fair).
1:4 The **inexperienced** are naive people, usually young (7:7), who are still uncommitted. They generally lack shrewdness (8:5) or common sense (9:4,16; 22:3; 27:12). They

have neither chosen wisdom nor become entrenched in folly like the mocker (1:22), but they are willing to believe anything (14:15,18). Those who try to remain uncommitted are condemned because they have not set out on the way of righteousness (1:32; 9:6). They should take warning from those who have chosen the wrong way (19:25; 21:11). The Hebrew word for **shrewdness** always has a positive connotation in the book of Proverbs. **Knowledge** is collected, memorized information. Knowledge is the tool; wisdom is the workman. Without wisdom to apply it, knowledge is ineffective. **Discretion** is the ability to ponder and plan, to think independently. In Proverbs a **young man** is one who is on the verge of maturity; he is making decisions about the course of his life (22:6).
1:6 The words **proverb** and **parable** are synonyms (v. 1). The **words of the wise** refer to sayings that are more than two lines long; two sections are introduced as such (22:17; 24:23; cp. 30:1; 31:1; Ec 9:17; 12:11). A riddle is a proverb that is tricky or difficult to understand (Jdg 14:12; 1Kg 10:1).
1:7 The **fear of the LORD** involves awe, reverence, love, and trust in God. It accompanies knowledge, humility, obedience, and blessing (8:13; 10:27; 14:26–27; 16:6; 19:23; 22:4). This fool (Hb *'ewiyl*) is self-sufficient and detests **wisdom** or any advice or correction.
1:8 Teaching implies a person of authority passing on moral guidelines; in other contexts the same word means "law" (28:4,7,9;

cp. Dt 4:44). The reader should not make too much of the pairing of instruction with the father and teaching with the mother. Splitting them is merely an aspect of Hebrew poetry (Pr 4:3; 6:20; 19:26; 23:22; 30:11,17). Both parents participated in this homeschooling.
1:9 The **garland** and **pendants** were symbols of honor, guidance, and protection.
1:11 Just for fun is literally "for nothing" ("useless" in v. 17; "without cause" in 3:30; 24:28; "for no reason" in 23:29; "undeserved" in 26:2).
1:12–13 Sheol is the grave, and the **Pit** pictures the opening to a grave; both are symbols of death.
1:15 The book of Proverbs frequently warns the reader to avoid the **road**, or way of wickedness and instead choose the way of righteousness (4:13–15).
1:17–18 An animal that sees a **net** has the sense to avoid it, but the wicked who know their lifestyle is self-destructive lack the sense to turn away.
1:20–33 Wisdom is personified as a woman who **calls out** a warning in **public**. Those who reject her guidance will suffer disaster. What she offers is success in practical matters in this life but eternal life as well (3:22).
1:20–21 The **public** square was the marketplace, and the **city** gate was where civic debate and official business were carried out.
1:22 Mockers are obnoxiously obstinate in their folly and unwilling to change. A mocker is suitable only as a negative example for

How long will you mockers
   enjoy mocking
and you fools hate knowledge?
23 If you respond to my warning,^A
   then I will pour out my spirit on you
and teach you my words.
24 Since I called out and you refused,
   extended my hand and no one
     paid attention,
25 since you neglected all my counsel
   and did not accept my correction,
26 I, in turn, will laugh at your calamity.
   I will mock when terror strikes you,
27 when terror strikes you like a storm
   and your calamity comes
     like a whirlwind,
   when trouble and stress overcome you.
28 Then they will call me,
   but I won't answer;
they will search for me, but won't
   find me.
29 Because they hated knowledge,
   didn't choose to fear the LORD,
30 were not interested in my counsel,

and rejected all my correction,
31 they will eat the fruit of their way
   and be glutted with their own schemes.
32 For the apostasy of the inexperienced
   will kill them,
and the complacency of fools
   will destroy them.
33 But whoever listens to me
   will live securely
and be undisturbed by the dread
   of danger."

Wisdom's Worth

2 My son, if you accept my words
   and store up my commands within you,
2 listening closely^B to wisdom
   and directing your heart
     to understanding;
3 furthermore, if you call out to insight
   and lift your voice to understanding,
4 if you seek it like silver
   and search for it like hidden treasure,
5 then you will understand the fear
   of the LORD

---

^A 1:23 Lit *you turn back to my reprimand*   ^B 2:2 Lit *you, stretching out your ear*

---

the inexperienced (19:25; 21:11). Along with being obstinately immoral, he perhaps adds a smug overconfidence that increases his pigheadedness.
1:24-25 Extending the **hand** could be a threatening (Ex 7:5) or a friendly (Is 65:2) gesture; whether invitation or warning, no one responded.
1:26-27 A **calamity** is the sudden onset of severe destruction (Dt 32:35; Jr 48:16). **Terror** is intense fear that causes uncontrollable trembling. The **storm** and **whirlwind** leave

only devastation (10:25; Hs 8:7). The basic idea behind the Hebrew words for **trouble** and **stress** is confinement or being squeezed (24:10).
1:28-29 This Hebrew word for **search** implies eager seeking under stress (Pss 63:1; 78:34; Hs 5:15).
1:32 The Hebrew word for **apostasy** from God (Hs 11:7) can also be translated "unfaithfulness" or "rebellion." **Complacency** is a false sense of security in which some people trust (Ps 30:6; Jr 22:21; Ezk 16:49).

1:33 This Hebrew word translated **securely** generally involves false security if the object of trust is not God (11:28; 28:26). Lady wisdom promises true security because there is a close connection between wisdom and God (2:6).
2:1-22 The first four verses of this chapter are a condition (**if**), followed by two results (**then**) in vv. 5-8 and 9-11. Verses 12-15 and 16-19 describe the benefits of the results—being rescued from the way of evil and from the forbidden woman. Verses 20-22 are the conclusion.

Character profile:
Solomon

Shortly after Bathsheba's son Solomon succeeded his father, David, as king of Israel, God appeared to him in a dream. In it, the Lord made him an unprecedented offer. Anything Solomon requested—wealth, long life, revenge on his enemies—God would grant him.

Solomon replied, "LORD my God, you have now made your servant king in my father David's place. Yet I am just a youth with no experience in leadership. Your servant is among your people you have chosen, a people too numerous to be numbered or counted. So give your servant a receptive heart to judge your people and to discern between good and evil" (1Kg 3:7-9).

God granted Solomon's request by giving him a "wise and understanding heart" (3:12). But that's not all. God was so pleased with Solomon's request that he gave him untold riches and honor as well. On top of his unsurpassed wisdom, Solomon became one of the richest and most renowned people in history. Solomon's prayer and God's response reveal three vital truths about wisdom that still applies today.

First, the selfless pursuit of wisdom pleases God. Solomon asked for wisdom—the ability to discern between good and evil and to judge fairly—not for his own ego but for the sake of God's people. He wanted to be a godly leader.

Second, wisdom is highly valued by other people. When the people of Israel heard about Solomon's wise decisions, "they

stood in awe of the king because they saw that God's wisdom was in him to carry out justice" (3:28). Word of his wisdom spread throughout the surrounding nations as well (see 4:34). Much of the content of Proverbs is attributed to Solomon and his God-given wisdom.

Third, when the pursuit of wisdom is abandoned, bad things happen. With fame and fortune come many temptations. Solomon took more than seven hundred wives and three hundred concubines, many of them from foreign, idol-worshiping nations. Over time their influence turned Solomon's heart away from God. He engaged in idol worship and disobeyed God's commands until God finally tore the kingdom of Israel away from Solomon's son.

The reign that started with such potential and promise turned out to be the beginning of the end of the united kingdom of Israel—all because Solomon abandoned his pursuit of wisdom.

You have the option of pursuing wisdom—which is always the best choice. Wisdom allows you to apply what you know in ways that benefit you and others (and not necessarily in that order). Wisdom helps you understand and apply Scripture, and it allows you to use your God-given gifts in extraordinary ways.

God rewards the pursuit of wisdom. He'll probably not lavish you with wealth and fame as he did Solomon, but he will allow you to experience peace of mind, security, and respect.

Since God is the source of all wisdom, a close relationship with him and his Word is essential in the pursuit of wisdom. The more you understand about what God desires—what pleases and displeases him—the better equipped you'll be to make wise decisions.

and discover the knowledge of God.
⁶ For the LORD gives wisdom;
from his mouth come knowledge
and understanding.
⁷ He stores up success^A for the upright;
He is a shield for those who live
with integrity
⁸ so that he may guard the paths of justice
and protect the way
of his faithful followers.
⁹ Then you will understand
righteousness, justice,
and integrity — every good path.
¹⁰ For wisdom will enter your heart,
and knowledge will delight you.
¹¹ Discretion will watch over you,
and understanding will guard you.
¹² It will rescue you from the way of evil —
from anyone who says perverse things,
¹³ from those who abandon
the right paths
to walk in ways of darkness,
¹⁴ from those who enjoy doing evil
and celebrate perversion,
¹⁵ whose paths are crooked,
and whose ways are devious.
¹⁶ It will rescue you
from a forbidden woman,
from a wayward woman
with her flattering talk,
¹⁷ who abandons the companion
of her youth
and forgets the covenant of her God;
¹⁸ for her house sinks down to death
and her ways to the land
of the departed spirits.
¹⁹ None return who go to her;
none reach the paths of life.
²⁰ So follow the way of the good,
and keep to the paths of the righteous.

²¹ For the upright will inhabit the land,
and those of integrity will remain in it;
²² but the wicked will be cut off
from the land,
and the treacherous ripped out of it.

Trust the LORD

3 My son, don't forget my teaching,
but let your heart keep my commands;
² for they will bring you
many days, a full life,^B and well-being.
³ Never let loyalty and faithfulness
leave you.
Tie them around your neck;
write them on the tablet of your heart.
⁴ Then you will find favor and high regard
with God and people.

⁵ Trust in the LORD with all your heart,
and do not rely on
your own understanding;
⁶ in all your ways know him,
and he will make your paths straight.
⁷ Don't be wise in your own eyes;
fear the LORD and turn away from evil.
⁸ This will be healing for your body^C
and strengthening for your bones.
⁹ Honor the LORD with your possessions
and with the first produce
of your entire harvest;
¹⁰ then your barns will be
completely filled,
and your vats will overflow
with new wine.
¹¹ Do not despise the LORD's instruction,
my son,
and do not loathe his discipline;
¹² for the LORD disciplines the one he loves,
just as a father disciplines the son in
whom he delights.

---

^A 2:7 Or resourcefulness ^B 3:2 Lit days, years of life ^C 3:8 Lit navel

---

2:6 **Wisdom** is not something a man takes but that **the LORD gives** through his words, which in this case Solomon is inspired to speak (2:1).
2:7 As we store up God's commands (v. 1), **he stores up success** as our reward. Success is competence (3:21; 8:14) or sound judgment (18:10). **Upright** means "corresponding to God's ethical instruction." The Hebrew word for **integrity** implies genuineness and reliability; it is also translated "honorable" (10:29) and "honest" (29:10).
2:9–10 Understanding is a further result (**then**, cp. v. 5) of seeking wisdom. A person can live ethically when he has **wisdom** in his **heart**. God's wisdom entering a person and making him **delight** in godly knowledge is regeneration (Jr 31:31–33; Ezk 36:27; 1Co 1:18).
2:12 **Perverse** is literally "turned over" (Jdg 7:13; 2Kg 21:13), making something into something else (Dt 23:5; Is 29:16; Jr 2:21; Am 5:7)—in this case, turning truth into a lie (Jr 23:36).
2:15 **Crooked** is the opposite of "upright" (v. 7); it means "twisted" (11:20) or "distorted" (28:6).

2:16–17 The **forbidden woman** has turned away from her husband (v. 17) and wants to destroy society (5:3,20; 7:5; 22:14). The **wayward woman** has allegiance to a different community and no interest in preserving the community of the faithful (5:20; 6:24; 7:5; 23:27). **Flattering** (lit "smooth") speech always has an agenda that includes the destruction of others (5:3; 7:5,21; 26:28; 28:23; 29:5; Ps 55:21). This warning applies to any person who appeals to base instincts with ulterior motives. **The covenant of her God** (or her covenant with God) is the marriage covenant to which God was witness.
2:18–19 The Hebrew word for **departed spirits** is the same as that of the Rephaim, a Canaanite people (Dt 2:20–21), but in Hebrew poetry it refers to the residents of the grave (Pr 9:18; 21:16; cp. Is 14:9).
2:20–22 Figuratively, to **inhabit the land** means to enjoy God's blessing through a relationship with him (Ps 37:3; Jr 7:5–7). **Treacherous** people are unfaithful in relationships; here they have abandoned commitment to God.

3:1–12 In this section the odd-numbered verses give a command and the even-numbered verses a promised result (the command continues in v. 6a).
3:2 To have **well-being** is to be healthy, free from threat or need, and thus fulfilled, content, prosperous, and at peace in a way that only God can grant (Ps 4:8; 119:165).
3:3–4 **Loyalty** (Hb chesed) and **faithfulness** summarize godliness in contrast to the selfish malice and infidelity of the wicked (14:22; 16:6; 20:28; cp. Mt 22:37–40).
3:5 To **rely on** something—a synonym for "trust"—is to lean on it as if it were a crutch (2Sm 1:6; Jb 8:14–15; Is 50:10).
3:6 To **know** God **in all your ways** is to invite his presence into all daily activities and decisions. **Make your paths straight** (or smooth) means that God will make righteousness attainable.
3:8 **Body** (lit "navel," Sg 7:2) and **bones** stand for the entire person.
3:9–10 **Possessions** is the word for abundant "wealth" (8:18; 10:15; 11:4; 12:27; 13:7,11; 18:11; 19:4,14; 28:8,22; 29:3) or sufficiency (see "enough" in 30:15–16), the stored resources

Wisdom Brings Happiness

¹³ Happy is a man who finds wisdom
   and who acquires understanding,
¹⁴ for she is more profitable than silver,
   and her revenue is better than gold.
¹⁵ She is more precious than jewels;
   nothing you desire can equal her.
¹⁶ Long life^A is in her right hand;
   in her left, riches and honor.
¹⁷ Her ways are pleasant,
   and all her paths, peaceful.
¹⁸ She is a tree of life to those
   who embrace her,
   and those who hold on to her are happy.

¹⁹ The LORD founded the earth by wisdom
   and established the heavens
   by understanding.
²⁰ By his knowledge the watery depths
   broke open,
   and the clouds dripped with dew.

²¹ Maintain sound wisdom and discretion.
   My son, don't lose sight of them.
²² They will be life for you^B
   and adornment^C for your neck.
²³ Then you will go safely on your way;
   your foot will not stumble.
²⁴ When you lie^D down, you will not
   be afraid;
   you will lie down, and your sleep
   will be pleasant.
²⁵ Don't fear sudden danger
   or the ruin of the wicked when it comes,
²⁶ for the LORD will be your confidence^E
   and will keep your foot from a snare.

Treat Others Fairly

²⁷ When it is in your power,^F
   don't withhold good from the one to
   whom it belongs.
²⁸ Don't say to your neighbor, "Go away!
   Come back later.

I'll give it tomorrow" — when it is there
   with you.
²⁹ Don't plan any harm
   against your neighbor,
   for he trusts you and lives near you.
³⁰ Don't accuse anyone without cause,
   when he has done you no harm.
³¹ Don't envy a violent man
   or choose any of his ways;
³² for the devious are detestable
   to the LORD,
   but he is a friend^G to the upright.
³³ The LORD's curse is on the household
   of the wicked,
   but he blesses the home
   of the righteous;
³⁴ He mocks those who mock
   but gives grace to the humble.
³⁵ The wise will inherit honor,
   but he holds up fools to dishonor.^H

A Father's Example

4 Listen, sons, to a father's discipline,
   and pay attention so that
   you may gain understanding,
² for I am giving you good instruction.
   Don't abandon my teaching.
³ When I was a son with my father,
   tender and precious to my mother,
⁴ he taught me and said,
   "Your heart must hold on to my words.
   Keep my commands and live.
⁵ Get wisdom, get understanding;
   don't forget or turn away
   from the words from my mouth.
⁶ Don't abandon wisdom, and she will
   watch over you;
   love her, and she will guard you.
⁷ Wisdom is supreme — so get wisdom.
   And whatever else you get,
   get understanding.
⁸ Cherish her, and she will exalt you;
   if you embrace her, she will honor you.

---

^A 3:16 Lit *Length of days*   ^B 3:22 Or *be your throat*   ^C 3:22 Or *grace*   ^D 3:24 LXX reads *sit*   ^E 3:26 Or *be at your side*   ^F 3:27 Lit *in the power of your hands*   ^G 3:32 Or *confidential counsel*   ^H 3:35 Or *but haughty fools dishonor*, or *but fools exalt dishonor*

---

that are ready for use. The **first produce** was the earliest and best of the crop (Dt 18:4).
3:13–18 This poem praising **wisdom** begins and ends with the word **happy**. To be happy is to discover the good life that the Creator intended (8:32,34; 14:21; 16:20; 20:7; 28:14; Pss 1:1; 32:1; 144:15; Is 30:18).
3:14 This could be the profit gained in trading up to wisdom (4:7) or the subsequent profit made by applying wisdom (8:18–21; 21:20; 24:4).
3:16 The Hebrew word for **honor** is literally "weightiness" ("heavy" in 27:3; "glory" in 22:24); it implies ascribing value or esteem to something or taking it seriously (Ps 50:15; Pr 3:9; Mal 1:6). It is also translated "glory," especially when describing God (Ex 40:34; Ps 96:7; Pr 25:2).
3:18 A **tree of life** is a source provided by God for healing and eternal life (11:30; 13:12; 15:4; cp. Gn 2:9; 3:22; Rv 2:7; 22:2).

3:20 In Palestine **dew** was an important source of moisture.
3:22 Wisdom is the key to **life**—a full life now and eternal life in the future—because it is anchored in the fear of the Lord and it includes practical advice (vv. 2,18; 1:33; 4:13,22–23; 6:23; 8:35; 10:16–17; 11:19; 12:28; 14:27; 16:22; 19:23; 21:21; 22:4; cp. Mk 10:30; 1Tm 4:8).
3:29–30 The mention of one who **lives near you** emphasizes the trust inherent in community. It does not mean that treachery is permissible against distant strangers; it is always wrong (Jdg 18:7,27; 2Sm 3:27; 20:9–10; Ps 55:12–14; Mt 26:14). Bringing accusations without just cause is malicious betrayal of community trust.
3:32 The devious, those who turn aside from what is right, are **detestable** to God, offensive, abhorrent, an abomination; they virtually turn his stomach.

3:33 God's **curse** is the removal of his sustaining presence. A **household** includes all of a person's family, possessions, and property.
3:34 The **humble** (16:19) are those who are poor (14:21; 31:20) not from laziness but because they are exploited or oppressed (15:15; 22:22; 30:14; 31:5,9).
3:35 An inheritance is a permanent possession.
4:3 Being a true **son** implies obedience, not merely being a male child. A **tender** child is delicate as well as teachable. **Precious** means to be treated as if an only child (Jr 6:26; Am 8:10; Zch 12:10).
4:4,6 To **keep . . . commands** is to listen attentively, retain, and obey them; it could also be translated "guard."
4:5–8 Get translates a common Hebrew word for "purchase." There is a great emphasis here that **wisdom** and **understanding** are the most important acquisitions (16:16;

9   She will place a garland of favor
        on your head;
     she will give you a crown of beauty."

Two Ways of Life

10   Listen, my son. Accept my words,
     and you will live many years.
11   I am teaching you the way of wisdom;
     I am guiding you on straight paths.
12   When you walk, your steps will not
        be hindered;
     when you run, you will not stumble.
13   Hold on to instruction; don't let go.
     Guard it, for it is your life.
14   Keep off the path of the wicked;
     don't proceed on the way of evil ones.
15   Avoid it; don't travel on it.
     Turn away from it, and pass it by.
16   For they can't sleep
     unless they have done what is evil;
     they are robbed of sleep
     unless they make someone stumble.
17   They eat the bread of wickedness
     and drink the wine of violence.
18   The path of the righteous is like the light
        of dawn,
     shining brighter and brighter
        until midday.
19   But the way of the wicked is
        like the darkest gloom;
     they don't know what makes
        them stumble.

The Straight Path

20   My son, pay attention to my words;
     listen closely to my sayings.
21   Don't lose sight of them;
     keep them within your heart.
22   For they are life to those who find them,
     and health to one's whole body.
23   Guard your heart above all else,^A
     for it is the source of life.
24   Don't let your mouth speak dishonestly,
     and don't let your lips talk deviously.

25   Let your eyes look forward;
     fix your gaze^B straight ahead.
26   Carefully consider the path^C
        for your feet,
     and all your ways will be established.
27   Don't turn to the right or to the left;
     keep your feet away from evil.

Avoid Seduction

5   My son, pay attention to my wisdom;
     listen closely^D to my understanding
2   so that you may maintain discretion
     and your lips safeguard knowledge.
3   Though the lips of the forbidden woman
        drip honey
     and her words are^E smoother than oil,
4   in the end she's as bitter as wormwood
     and as sharp as a double-edged sword.
5   Her feet go down to death;
     her steps head straight for Sheol.
6   She doesn't consider the path of life;
     she doesn't know that her ways
        are unstable.
7   So now, sons, listen to me,
     and don't turn away from the words
        from my mouth.
8   Keep your way far from her.
     Don't go near the door of her house.
9   Otherwise, you will give up your vitality
        to others
     and your years to someone cruel;
10   strangers will drain your resources,
     and your hard-earned pay will end up
        in a foreigner's house.
11   At the end of your life, you will lament
     when your physical body
        has been consumed,
12   and you will say, "How I hated discipline,
     and how my heart despised correction.
13   I didn't obey my teachers
     or listen closely^F to my instructors.
14   I am on the verge of complete ruin
     before the entire community."

^A4:23 Or heart with all diligence   ^B4:25 Lit eyelids   ^C4:26 Or Clear a path   ^D5:1 Lit wisdom; stretch out your ear   ^E5:3 Lit her palate is   ^F5:13 Lit or turn my ear

18:15; 23:23; cp. 17:16)—literally "in all your purchasing, purchase understanding" (4:7), that is, spend all your assets on understanding. **Supreme** could also mean the beginning (1:7, the first thing to get. A person must stop desiring anything else and **love . . . cherish**, and **embrace** only the one thing—that is part of what it means to give up one's life for something. Paradoxically, the cost is both nothing and everything (Is 55:1; Mt 13:44–46; 16:24; 19:21,27; Lk 5:11,28; Php 3:8).
4:9 The **garland** and **crown** are symbolic of God's grace and favor being visible in one's life.
4:23 Above all else is literally "more than all guarding." To **guard** something is to make sure that it does not get away and that it is safe from attack. In Hebrew the **heart** is the location of knowledge and

also the preconscious source of decisions (27:19; Mt 15:18). Your heart is who you are, the "true you" that directs all your thoughts and emotions. You can educate your heart (Pr 24:32)—consciously form and modify a worldview—after which decisions and actions flow from it (16:9,23; Lk 6:45; Rm 10:10; 2Co 9:7). This education can be worldly, carried out by yourself, or godly, carried out by the Holy Spirit (Pr 2:6; Jr 24:7; Ezk 36:26–27; Ac 16:14; Rm 2:29). The inclination of your heart directs your mortal **life** and determines whether you enter eternal life (3:22).
4:24 While as a rule the heart determines what comes out of the **mouth** (see v. 23), false speech can eventually poison the heart.
4:25–27 The passive voice of **your ways will be established** implies that it is God who does it. "Established" is fixed and firm,

secure, not subject to change or to destruction (12:3; 16:3; 24:3; 25:5). **Right or . . . left** expresses the whole range of evil paths. That is not to say that a middle road, a compromise, is the good way, but that it is important not to leave the only good way.
5:2 To **maintain** and **safeguard** wisdom includes the responsibility to pass it along (Mal 2:7).
5:3–6 Wormwood was a shrub that produced a bitter flavor (Lm 3:15,19).
5:7–8 The Hebrew for **from** in v. 8 is literally "from alongside," implying companionship or attachment with the forbidden woman.
5:9–10 Vitality describes a man in his prime.
5:12–14 How introduces an expression of grief (Gn 44:34). To hate **discipline**, despise **correction**, and not **obey** or **listen** are characteristics of a fool.

Enjoy Marriage

15 Drink water from your own cistern,
   water flowing from your own well.
16 Should your springs flow in the streets,
   streams in the public squares?
17 They should be for you alone
   and not for you to share with strangers.
18 Let your fountain be blessed,
   and take pleasure in the wife
      of your youth.
19 A loving deer, a graceful doe^A —
   let her breasts always satisfy you;
   be lost in her love forever.
20 Why, my son, would you lose yourself
   with a forbidden woman
   or embrace a wayward woman?
21 For a man's ways are before
      the LORD's eyes,
   and he considers all his paths.
22 A wicked man's iniquities will trap him;
   he will become tangled in the ropes
      of his own sin.
23 He will die because there is
      no discipline,
   and be lost because of
      his great stupidity.

Financial Entanglements

6 My son, if you have put up security
   for your neighbor^B
   or entered into an agreement
      with^C a stranger,
2 you have been snared by the words
      of your mouth —
   trapped by the words from your mouth.
3 Do this, then, my son, and free yourself,
   for you have put yourself
      in your neighbor's power:
   Go, humble yourself, and plead
      with your neighbor.

4 Don't give sleep to your eyes
   or slumber to your eyelids.
5 Escape like a gazelle from a hunter,^D
   like a bird from a hunter's trap.^D

Laziness

6 Go to the ant, you slacker!
   Observe its ways and become wise.
7 Without leader, administrator, or ruler,
8 it prepares its provisions in summer;
   it gathers its food during harvest.
9 How long will you stay in bed,
      you slacker?
   When will you get up from your sleep?
10 A little sleep, a little slumber,
   a little folding of the arms to rest,
11 and your poverty will come like
      a robber,
   your need, like a bandit.

The Malicious Man

12 A worthless person, a wicked man
   goes around speaking dishonestly,
13 winking his eyes, signaling with his feet,
   and gesturing with his fingers.
14 He always plots evil with perversity
      in his heart;
   he stirs up trouble.
15 Therefore calamity
      will strike him suddenly;
   he will be shattered instantly,
      beyond recovery.

What the LORD Hates

16 The LORD hates six things;
   in fact, seven are detestable to him:
17 arrogant eyes, a lying tongue,
   hands that shed innocent blood,
18 a heart that plots wicked schemes,
   feet eager to run to evil,

---

^A5:19 Or graceful mountain goat   ^B6:1 Or friend   ^C6:1 Lit or slapped hands for   ^D6:5 Lit hand

---

5:15–19 The many figurative references to **water**—cistern, flowing, well, springs, streams, fountain—are interpreted as one's wife. The allusion is to quenching one's sexual thirst (9:17; Sg 5:1). The father prayed that God would bless his son's wife, with the result that the son would always **take pleasure** in her since something that is blessed is by definition able to **satisfy** (3:33; 22:9). The **wife of your youth** is the first wife (2:17; Is 54:6; Mal 2:14–15). **Loving** implies sexual love (7:18; Hs 8:9). In this context, to **be lost** is to drift unconsciously in pleasure.
5:20 Embrace implies the intimacy of holding on to one's lap or taking into one's arms (6:27; cp. 2Sm 12:8; Mc 7:5).
6:1–2 To **put up security** is "to pledge oneself as a guarantee for another's debts"; if the debtor defaulted, the son was liable to pay or be liable to seizure. **Entered into an agreement** is literally "struck your palm," probably referring to a gesture that made it official (Ru 4:7–8), an ancient equivalent of shaking hands or signing a contract. To risk one's assets and reputation for a **neighbor**

or friend is inadvisable (17:18), much less for a **stranger** (11:15; 20:16; 27:13; cp. 22:26).
6:3 The **son** is in his **neighbor's power** (lit "palm"; see v. 2) because if the neighbor defaults, the son must pay. He should **plead** (lit "assault" his neighbor) incessantly to be released from the security agreement. The word translated **humble yourself** could also be translated "weary yourself."
6:4 Sleep and **slumber** when a person should be working leads to ruin (vv. 9–11).
6:5 This **hunter** is a "fowler" who hunts birds (Ps 91:3; Jr 5:26; Hs 9:8).
6:6 A **slacker** is a lazy person (26:14) who hopes to sustain his life without actually working (20:4; 21:25)—he literally refuses to lift a hand (19:24). He makes excuses not to work (22:13). The slacker has brought his poverty on himself and is not an object of pity.
6:7–8 These verses describe harvester ants that store grain in their nests.
6:9 Asking **how long** generally implies that something bad has been going on for too long (1:22; cp. Ex 10:3; Ps 74:10).
6:10 On **sleep** and **slumber**, see note at v. 4.

6:11 Poverty in this context is destitution brought on oneself (13:18; 28:19). The **robber** is literally a "traveler," perhaps a vagabond or drifter. The **bandit** is literally a "man with a shield," an armed man. His attack is sudden and unexpected.
6:12 The Hebrew word *beliyya'al* (**worthless**) identifies a troublemaker who rebels against all good and godly authority (16:27; 19:28; 2Ch 13:7; Jb 34:18). *Beliy-ya'al* is translated "wicked" in many places (Dt 13:13; Jdg 19:22; 20:13; 1Sm 2:12; 2Sm 20:1). This "worthless" **person** is described in vv. 12–14. "Belial" became a synonym for Satan (2Co 6:15).
6:13 This body language was apparently conspiratorial or deceptive (16:30; Is 58:9). He literally "compresses" his **eyes**, "shuffles" his **feet**, and "throws in" his **fingers**.
6:14 To stir up **trouble** is to spread dissension and strife (6:19; 16:28; Jr 15:10).
6:15 Suddenly implies surprise (24:22; Jos 10:9; Ec 9:12; Is 47:11). **Instantly** further emphasizes the speed of the destruction (Is 29:5–6; 30:13; cp. Jr 4:20).
6:17 Arrogant is literally "raised high." It describes proud people who deny God's

¹⁹ a lying witness who gives false testimony,
and one who stirs up trouble
among brothers.

Warning against Adultery

²⁰ My son, keep your father's command,
and don't reject your mother's teaching.
²¹ Always bind them to your heart;
tie them around your neck.
²² When you walk here and there, they will
guide you;
when you lie down, they will
watch over you;
when you wake up, they will talk to you.
²³ For a command is a lamp,
teaching is a light,
and corrective discipline is the way to life.
²⁴ They will protect you
from an evil woman,^A
from the flattering tongue of
a wayward woman.
²⁵ Don't lust in your heart for her beauty
or let her captivate you
with her eyelashes.
²⁶ For a prostitute's fee is only a loaf
of bread,^B
but the wife of another man^C goes after
a precious life.
²⁷ Can a man embrace fire
and his clothes not be burned?
²⁸ Can a man walk on burning coals
without scorching his feet?
²⁹ So it is with the one who sleeps with
another man's wife;
no one who touches her
will go unpunished.
³⁰ People don't despise the thief if he steals
to satisfy himself when he is hungry.
³¹ Still, if caught, he must pay seven times
as much;
he must give up all the wealth
in his house.

³² The one who commits adultery^D
lacks sense;
whoever does so destroys himself.
³³ He will get a beating^E and dishonor,
and his disgrace will never be removed.
³⁴ For jealousy enrages a husband,
and he will show no mercy
when he takes revenge.
³⁵ He will not be appeased by anything
or be persuaded by lavish bribes.

7 My son, obey my words,
and treasure my commands.
² Keep my commands and live,
and guard my instructions
as you would the pupil of your eye.
³ Tie them to your fingers;
write them on the tablet of your heart.
⁴ Say to wisdom, "You are my sister,"
and call understanding your relative.
⁵ She will keep you
from a forbidden woman,
a wayward woman with
her flattering talk.

A Story of Seduction

⁶ At the window of my house
I looked through my lattice.
⁷ I saw among the inexperienced,^F
I noticed among the youths,
a young man lacking sense.
⁸ Crossing the street near her corner,
he strolled down the road to her house
⁹ at twilight, in the evening,
in the dark of the night.
¹⁰ A woman came to meet him
dressed like a prostitute,
having a hidden agenda.^G
¹¹ She is loud and defiant;
her feet do not stay at home.
¹² Now in the street, now in the squares,
she lurks at every corner.

---

^A**6:24** LXX reads *from a married woman* ^B**6:26** Or *On account of a prostitute, one is left with only a loaf of bread* ^C**6:26** Lit *but a wife of a man* ^D**6:32** Lit *commits adultery with a woman* ^E**6:33** Or *plague* ^F**7:7** Or *simple,* or *gullible,* or *naive* ^G**7:10** Or *prostitute with a guarded heart*

---

authority (21:4; 30:13; cp. 2Kg 19:22; Pss 18:27; 131:1; Is 10:12; 37:23).
6:18 At the center of this list is the wicked **heart**. Cp. 1:16.
6:19 To be a **lying witness** and to give **false testimony** are the same; the two expressions are used for clarity (14:5; 19:5).
6:25 Sexual sin often begins with visual stimulation and eye contact (cp. Jms 1:14–16).
6:26 This verse is very difficult to translate. It may mean that the one who goes to a prostitute will eventually be left with **only a loaf of bread**, or that the one who goes to a prostitute is merely a meal ticket for her. This is not to excuse prostitution (1Co 6:15–20) but to illustrate the terrible penalty of adultery by way of comparison; the adulteress will destroy someone's **life**.
6:27–29 To **go unpunished** is a legal term meaning to be acquitted, declared innocent, pardoned, or released; to be set free from

guilt, liability, or punishment (Ex 21:19; Nm 5:31). To say that someone will not go unpunished is more emphatic than simply saying he will be punished.
6:30–33 A **thief** is guilty of a crime and must pay a severe penalty, but if there are mitigating circumstances he does not totally lose the respect of the community. **Seven times** is not literal here but is an expression that implies he must pay the full penalty, from twice to five times what he stole (Ex 22:1,7,9; cp. Lk 19:8). An adulterer, on the other hand, suffers punishment plus complete, permanent **disgrace**.
6:34–35 While a court can be satisfied when a fine is paid (v. 31), a jealous **husband** can never be satisfied (27:4; cp. Sg 8:6). Verse 35a can be translated, "He will not look favorably on any kind of ransom." The **bribes** are "gifts" with strings attached to subvert justice (17:8,23; 21:14).

7:1–5 This section may connect with 6:20–24 to conclude the speech begun there, or it may introduce 7:6–27. The origin of the Hebrew word translated **pupil** is "little man," the tiny reflection one sees in another person's eye. Because the eye is sensitive yet indispensable, it is closely guarded (Dt 32:10; Zch 2:8). To **write** something on the **heart** is to internalize it so that it directs one's actions (2:1–4; 6:20–24; Jr 17:1; 31:31–34).
7:6 In ancient times a **window** had a **lattice** that let in light and air (Jdg 5:28; 2Kg 1:2; Sg 2:9).
7:8–10 Hidden agenda is literally "a guarded heart." She is cunning.
7:11 The word translated **loud** implies restless movement as well as noise—commotion (1:21); uproar (1Kg 1:41).
7:12 Lurks is literally "ambush" (1:11; 23:28; 24:15; Dt 19:11).

13 She grabs him and kisses him;
she brazenly says^A to him,
14 "I've made fellowship offerings;
today I've fulfilled my vows.
15 So I came out to meet you,
to search for you,
and I've found you.
16 I've spread coverings on my bed —
richly colored linen from Egypt.
17 I've perfumed my bed
with myrrh, aloes, and cinnamon.
18 Come, let's drink deeply of lovemaking
until morning.
Let's feast on each other's love!
19 My husband isn't home;
he went on a long journey.
20 He took a bag of silver with him
and will come home at the time
of the full moon."
21 She seduces him
with her persistent pleading;
she lures with her flattering talk.
22 He follows her impulsively
like an ox going to the slaughter,
like a deer bounding toward a trap^B
23 until an arrow pierces its^C liver,
like a bird darting into a snare —
he doesn't know it will cost him
his life.

24 Now, sons, listen to me,
and pay attention to the words
from my mouth.
25 Don't let your heart turn aside
to her ways;
don't stray onto her paths.
26 For she has brought many
down to death;
her victims are countless.^D
27 Her house is the road to Sheol,
descending to the chambers
of death.

Wisdom's Appeal

8 Doesn't wisdom call out?
Doesn't understanding make her voice
heard?
2 At the heights overlooking the road,
at the crossroads, she takes her stand.
3 Beside the gates leading into the city,
at the main entrance, she cries out:
4 "People, I call out to you;
my cry is to the children of Adam.
5 Learn to be shrewd,
you who are inexperienced;
develop common sense,
you who are foolish.
6 Listen, for I speak of noble things,
and what my lips say is right.
7 For my mouth tells the truth,
and wickedness is detestable to my lips.
8 All the words from my mouth
are righteous;
none of them are deceptive or perverse.
9 All of them are clear to the perceptive,
and right to those
who discover knowledge.
10 Accept my instruction
instead of silver,
and knowledge rather than pure gold.
11 For wisdom is better than jewels,
and nothing desirable can equal it.
12 I, wisdom, share a home
with shrewdness
and have knowledge and discretion.
13 To fear the LORD is to hate evil.
I hate arrogant pride, evil conduct,
and perverse speech.
14 I possess good advice
and sound wisdom;^E
I have understanding and strength.
15 It is by me that kings reign
and rulers enact just law;
16 by me, princes lead,
as do nobles and all righteous judges.^F

^A 7:13 Lit she makes her face strong and says ^B 7:22 Text emended; MT reads like a shackle to the discipline of a fool; Hb obscure ^C 7:23 Or his ^D 7:26 Or and powerful men are all her victims ^E 8:14 Or resourcefulness ^F 8:16 Some Hb mss, LXX read nobles who judge the earth

7:13 To speak **brazenly** is to lie with arrogance (21:29).
7:14–15 She includes religion in her lie. Her flattery includes the lie that she searched specifically for him. In reality she was on the hunt for any vulnerable young man.
7:16–17 She seduces him by describing her **bed** (cp. 31:22) with its luxurious and suggestive perfumes (cp. Sg 4:14).
7:18 **Drink deeply** is the same Hebrew word as "satisfy" in 5:19; she claims to offer what only a wife should give (Sg 5:1). This is not true **love** but lust (2Sm 13:1; Hs 8:9; cp. Sg 6:6–7).
7:19–20 She promises they will not get caught, ignoring the eternal consequences of their sin (v. 23). The length of the husband's business trip is indicated by the amount of money he brought along.
7:21 **Flattering talk** is literally "smoothness of lips." **Lures** implies to forcefully lead astray.
7:23 The **liver** was considered the reservoir of lifeblood.
7:26 **Brought many down to death** and **victims** are military terms.
8:1–3 Wisdom's invitation is very public in broad daylight, her appeal is spiritual not sexual, and her promise is life not death. Wisdom and **understanding** are two names for the same "lady."
8:4 Her appeal to **people** and **the children of Adam** (lit "descendants of Adam") may emphasize her broad appeal (Ps 49:1–2) or the mortality of her audience (2Ch 14:11; Pss 39:5; 90:3; Is 51:12).
8:5 **Common sense** is literally an "understanding heart"—a mind that functions as it should (4:23; cp. 6:32).
8:6 The word translated **noble** might also mean "morally straight" (v. 9).
8:9 Both **clear** and **right** relate to what is straight in front of a person, not twisted, crooked, or off to the side. A **perceptive** person is insightful, intelligent, and discerning (1:5).
8:12–14 The point of **wisdom** sharing **a home** with or possessing the other virtues is that if you find one you find the others. **Arrogant pride** translates two Hebrew words for pride; the first is found in 15:25 and 16:19, the second in 16:18. Pride and arrogance are characteristics of those who refuse to acknowledge God's rule. **Good advice and sound wisdom** imply counsel that brings success (19:20; 20:18; Is 28:29). These kinds of qualities belong to God (Jb 12:13).
8:15–16 **Nobles** are powerful and respected royal courtiers (17:7,26; 19:6; 25:7), the opposite of the boorish fool (Is 32:5,8).
8:17 To **love** and to **search** imply emotional passion and diligence.

¹⁷ I love those who love me,
and those who search for me
find me.
¹⁸ With me are riches and honor,
lasting wealth and righteousness.
¹⁹ My fruit is better than solid gold,
and my harvest than pure silver.
²⁰ I walk in the ways of righteousness,
along the paths of justice,
²¹ giving wealth as an inheritance to those
who love me,
and filling their treasuries.

²² "The LORD acquired^A me
at the beginning of his creation,^B
before his works of long ago.
²³ I was formed^C before ancient times,
from the beginning,
before the earth began.
²⁴ I was born
when there were no watery depths
and no springs filled with water.
²⁵ Before the mountains
were established,
prior to the hills, I was given birth —
²⁶ before he made the land, the fields,
or the first soil on earth.
²⁷ I was there when he established
the heavens,
when he laid out the horizon
on the surface of the ocean,
²⁸ when he placed the skies above,
when the fountains of the ocean
gushed out,
²⁹ when he set a limit for the sea
so that the waters would not violate
his command,
when he laid out the foundations
of the earth.
³⁰ I was a skilled craftsman^D beside him.
I was his^E delight every day,
always rejoicing before him.
³¹ I was rejoicing in his inhabited world,
delighting in the children of Adam.

³² "And now, sons, listen to me;
those who keep my ways are happy.
³³ Listen to instruction and be wise;
don't ignore it.
³⁴ Anyone who listens to me is happy,
watching at my doors every day,
waiting by the posts of my doorway.
³⁵ For the one who finds me finds life
and obtains favor from the LORD,
³⁶ but the one who misses me^F
harms himself;
all who hate me love death."

Wisdom versus Foolishness

9 Wisdom has built her house;
she has carved out her seven pillars.
² She has prepared her meat;
she has mixed her wine;
she has also set her table.
³ She has sent out her female servants;
she calls out from the highest points
of the city:
⁴ "Whoever is inexperienced,
enter here!"
To the one who lacks sense, she says,
⁵ "Come, eat my bread,
and drink the wine I have mixed.
⁶ Leave inexperience behind,
and you will live;
pursue the way of understanding.
⁷ The one who corrects a mocker
will bring abuse on himself;
the one who rebukes the wicked
will get hurt.^G
⁸ Don't rebuke a mocker, or he will
hate you;
rebuke the wise, and he will love you.
⁹ Instruct the wise, and he will be
wiser still;
teach the righteous, and he will
learn more.

¹⁰ "The fear of the LORD is the beginning
of wisdom,

---

^A8:22 Or *possessed*, or *made*   ^B8:22 Lit *way*   ^C8:23 Or *consecrated*   ^D8:30 Or *a confidant*, or *a child*, or *was constantly*   ^E8:30 LXX; MT omits *his*   ^F8:36 Or *who sins against me*   ^G9:7 Lit *man: his blemish*

8:18 Lasting wealth is wealth in this life that does not evaporate (11:7; 13:11; 27:23–24; 28:22), and it includes treasures in heaven as well (Mt 6:20; 1Tm 6:17–18). **8:22–29** This is a figurative way to say that God is its source. Thus true wisdom can only come from him. The concept that God created wisdom also conveys that all God created and all he does are the products of his infinite wisdom. **8:30–31** Wisdom was **beside** God, but only God was the Creator. Wisdom was **rejoicing** in God's creation; it would be sinful to celebrate creation without acknowledging God. Within creation, wisdom's ultimate object of rejoicing and **delighting** is humankind. **8:32–34 And now** draws a logical conclusion from the prior saying. Because wisdom is ancient and was with God in creation and delights

in humanity, she can teach people how to be truly **happy**. **8:35–36** To obtain **favor** is to become someone in whom **the LORD** delights (11:20; 12:2,22; 15:8; 18:22) and whom he blesses. This word for sin literally means "miss the mark" or "fall short" (Is 65:20), an apt contrast to **finds**. Harm refers to violence (Lm 2:6; Ezk 22:26; Zph 3:4) or brutality (Jr 22:3). Rejecting wisdom is self-destructive (Pr 1:18–19,31–32; 2:18–19; 26:6; 29:6,24). **9:1–2** Lady **Wisdom** is preparing a banquet to dedicate her **house** (cp. 1Kg 8:62–66). The **seven pillars**, the number of perfection, suggest that it was a large, durable house. **Mixed ... wine** contained honey or spices (Ps 75:8; Sg 8:2). Symbolically, she is ready to share her enjoyable and beneficial instruction.

9:3 Her . . . servants are sages, teachers, pastors, and parents. **9:4–6 Enter** is literally "turn"; it implies leaving one path in favor of another (3:7; 4:27; 5:7; 11:22; 13:14,19; 14:16,27; 16:6; 22:6). There is no middle road; if he does not choose wisdom, he will end up a mocker (1:22). **9:7–9** The teacher is warned to avoid the unteachable (Mt 7:6). **Abuse** could also be translated "insults" (12:16). Indirectly, this encourages the inexperienced not to become the obstinate, malevolent **mocker** (1:22) or the hostile **wicked** person (2:22), but instead the benevolent **wise** and **righteous** person who continues to **learn more**. The wise never reach the point where they cannot become **wiser still** (1:5; 4:18; 12:1; 13:1; 19:25; 21:11; Mt 13:12).

and the knowledge of the Holy One
    is understanding.
11 For by me your days will be many,
    and years will be added to your life.
12 If you are wise, you are wise
       for your own benefit;
    if you mock, you alone will bear
       the consequences."

13 Folly is a rowdy woman;
    she is gullible and knows nothing.
14 She sits by the doorway of her house,
    on a seat at the highest point of the city,
15 calling to those who pass by,
    who go straight ahead on their paths:
16 "Whoever is inexperienced, enter here!"
    To the one who lacks sense, she says,
17 "Stolen water is sweet,
    and bread eaten secretly is tasty!"
18 But he doesn't know
      that the departed spirits are there,
    that her guests are in the depths
      of Sheol.

A Collection of Solomon's Proverbs

10 Solomon's proverbs:
    A wise son brings joy to his father,
    but a foolish son, heartache
      to his mother.

2 Ill-gotten gains do not profit anyone,
    but righteousness rescues from death.

3 The LORD will not let the righteous
      go hungry,
    but he denies the wicked what they crave.

4 Idle hands make one poor,
    but diligent hands bring riches.

5 The son who gathers during summer
    is prudent;

the son who sleeps during harvest
    is disgraceful.

6 Blessings are on the head
      of the righteous,
    but the mouth of the wicked
      conceals violence.

7 The remembrance of the righteous is
      a blessing,
    but the name of the wicked will rot.

8 A wise heart accepts commands,
    but foolish lips will be destroyed.

9 The one who lives with integrity
      lives securely,
    but whoever perverts his ways will be
      found out.

10 A sly wink of the eye causes grief,
    and foolish lips will be destroyed.

11 The mouth of the righteous is a fountain
      of life,
    but the mouth of the wicked
      conceals violence.

12 Hatred stirs up conflicts,
    but love covers all offenses.

13 Wisdom is found on the lips
      of the discerning,
    but a rod is for the back of the one
      who lacks sense.

14 The wise store up knowledge,
    but the mouth of the fool
      hastens destruction.

15 The wealth of the rich is
      his fortified city;

9:11 These phrases imply both a long **life** and eternal life.
9:14 While wisdom is industrious (vv. 1–3), folly **sits**. Chairs were rare in ancient times. Only kings and honored teachers sat (2Sm 19:8; 1Kg 2:12,19; Est 5:1; Ps 29:10; Mt 5:1; 23:2; Lk 4:20)—so her **seat** (lit "throne") was her pretentious claim of authority to rule or teach.
9:15–16 Folly tempts vulnerable people (Pr 1:11; Mt 23:14–15).
9:17 Lady wisdom offers a feast (vv. 2,5). Folly offers only **water** and **bread**, but her appeal is the attraction that sin has for fallen man (Ps 52:3; Jr 14:10; Mc 3:2; Jn 3:19; 1Pt 4:3).
10:1 Chapters 1–9 contain discourses on wisdom. From here to the end of the book the sayings are—for the most part—individual proverbs.
10:2 Ill-gotten gains are literally "treasures of wickedness," wealth obtained by harming another person.
10:3 This proverb should not be taken as a universal promise that **the righteous** will never go **hungry** in this life. The

10:6 The verb **conceals** is literally "covers." The second half of v. 6 literally means "violence covers the mouth of the wicked." It means his speech is full of violence.
10:7 It was considered a curse to have no one remember you (Ex 17:14) or to fail to pass down your **name** to the next generation (Ps 109:13; cp. Ps 45:17).
10:8 **Commands** are probably moral instructions, which the wise humbly accept and therefore flourish, but the foolish reject and **will be destroyed**.
10:10 A **wink** was apparently some kind of signal used by dishonest people (6:13).
10:13–14 This is a case where two verses clarify each other, though each could stand on its own. The **one who lacks sense** is likely to speak rashly and hasten **destruction**, while **wise** and **discerning** people **store up knowledge** and speak wisely, avoiding public condemnation in this life and eternal destruction as well.
10:15 This is an observation about the way things look from an earthly perspective. The

the poverty of the poor is
their destruction.

16 The reward of the righteous is life;
the wages of the wicked is punishment.

17 The one who follows instruction is
on the path to life,
but the one who rejects correction
goes astray.

18 The one who conceals hatred has
lying lips,
and whoever spreads slander is a fool.

19 When there are many words,
sin is unavoidable,
but the one who controls his lips
is prudent.

20 The tongue of the righteous is
pure silver;
the heart of the wicked is of little value.

21 The lips of the righteous feed many,
but fools die for lack of sense.

22 The Lord's blessing enriches,
and he adds no painful effort to it. ^A

23 As shameful conduct is pleasure for a fool,
so wisdom is for a person
of understanding.

24 What the wicked dreads will come to him,
but what the righteous desire
will be given to them.

25 When the whirlwind passes,
the wicked are no more,
but the righteous are secure forever.

26 Like vinegar to the teeth and smoke
to the eyes,
so the slacker is to the one
who sends him on an errand.

27 The fear of the Lord prolongs life, ^B
but the years of the wicked
are cut short.

28 The hope of the righteous is joy,
but the expectation of the wicked
will perish.

29 The way of the Lord is a stronghold
for the honorable,
but destruction awaits evildoers.

30 The righteous will never
be shaken,
but the wicked will not remain
on the earth.

31 The mouth of the righteous
produces wisdom,
but a perverse tongue will be cut out.

32 The lips of the righteous know
what is appropriate,
but the mouth of the wicked,
only what is perverse.

11 Dishonest scales are detestable
to the Lord,
but an accurate weight is
his delight.

2 When arrogance comes,
disgrace follows,
but with humility comes wisdom.

3 The integrity of the upright
guides them,
but the perversity of the treacherous
destroys them.

4 Wealth is not profitable on a day
of wrath,
but righteousness rescues
from death.

5 The righteousness of the blameless
clears his path,
but the wicked person will fall
because of his wickedness.

6 The righteousness of the upright
rescues them,
but the treacherous are trapped
by their own desires.

---

^A **10:22** Or *and painful effort adds nothing to it* ^B **10:27** Lit *Lord adds to days*

---

next verse teaches long-term and eternal principles about wealth and poverty (11:28; 18:10–11).
10:16 Life should be understood to mean spiritual life. Because of the parallel with life, **punishment** should be understood to include spiritual death.
10:17 To stay on **the path to life**, one must accept correction.
10:18 This verse does not mean a person should display hatred. Rather, the person who has **hatred** concealed within himself inevitably tells lies.

10:20 Tongue is parallel to **heart** because speech reveals the heart.
10:24 This observation on the **wicked** is often valid in this life and always true in eternity.
10:25 This is similar to Jesus's parable of the Two Foundations (Mt 7:24–27).
10:26 Vinegar, or soured wine, had an astringent quality that irritated the **teeth**.
10:32 The Hebrew word translated **what is appropriate** also means "favor, delight" (8:35).
11:1 On **dishonest scales**, see Dt 25:13–16.

11:3 Integrity implies genuineness and reliability. **Perversity** implies subversion and deceit, treachery, and destructiveness.
11:4 Wealth here should be understood to refer to wealth obtained by wickedness.
11:5 To clear a **path** is literally to make it straight, to improve it so it is easy to walk on. A **blameless** person will not grow weary or **fall** on such a path and so will reach his destination.
11:6 Verse 6b is a version of the theme that the wicked are caught by their own malicious schemes.

7 When the wicked person dies,
   his expectation comes to nothing,
   and hope placed in wealth^(A,B) vanishes.

8 The righteous one is rescued
      from trouble;
   in his place, the wicked one goes in.

9 With his mouth the ungodly
      destroys his neighbor,
   but through knowledge the righteous
      are rescued.

10 When the righteous thrive,
      a city rejoices;
   when the wicked die, there is
      joyful shouting.

11 A city is built up by the blessing
      of the upright,
   but it is torn down by the mouth
      of the wicked.

12 Whoever shows contempt
      for his neighbor lacks sense,
   but a person with understanding
      keeps silent.

13 A gossip goes around revealing a secret,
   but a trustworthy person keeps
      a confidence.

14 Without guidance, a people will fall,
   but with many counselors
      there is deliverance.

15 If someone puts up security for a stranger,
      he will suffer for it,
   but the one who hates such agreements
      is protected.

16 A gracious woman gains honor,
   but violent^(C) people gain only riches.

17 A kind man benefits himself,
   but a cruel person brings ruin
      on himself.

18 The wicked person earns
      an empty wage,
   but the one who sows righteousness,
      a true reward.

19 Genuine righteousness leads
      to life,
   but pursuing evil leads to death.

20 Those with twisted minds are detestable
      to the LORD,
   but those with blameless conduct are
      his delight.

21 Be assured^(D) that a wicked person
      will not go unpunished,
   but the offspring of the righteous
      will escape.

22 A beautiful woman who rejects
      good sense
   is like a gold ring in a pig's snout.

23 The desire of the righteous
      turns out well,
   but the hope of the wicked
      leads to wrath.

24 One person gives freely,
      yet gains more;
   another withholds what is right,
      only to become poor.

25 A generous person will be enriched,
   and the one who gives a drink
      of water
   will receive water.

26 People will curse anyone
      who hoards grain,
   but a blessing will come to the one
      who sells it.

27 The one who searches for what is good
      seeks favor,
   but if someone looks for trouble,
      it will come to him.

---

^A 11:7 LXX reads *hope of the ungodly*　^B 11:7 Or *strength*　^C 11:16 Or *ruthless*　^D 11:21 Lit *Hand to hand*

11:7–8 Verse 7 implies that when a righteous person **dies**, his **hope** does not vanish.
11:9 Though the **ungodly** spread slander, the **righteous** are **rescued** through their own **knowledge** and that of their acquaintances. Those who know them realize the slander is untrue.
11:10–11 The **blessing of the upright** probably refers to the blessing God bestows on them.
11:13 A **gossip** spreads slander (Lv 19:16; Jr 6:28; 9:4; Ezk 22:9).
11:15 To guarantee a loan for a stranger may be kind, but it is foolish.
11:16 This proverb teaches that there is something more important than **riches** (cp.

v. 28; 22:1). It is also significant that one **gracious woman** might obtain a greater reward than many **violent people**.
11:17 The **kind man** is one who acts with faithful love (Hb *chesed*). He looks out for others. Conversely, the **cruel person** is merciless and unfaithful, having no concern for others.
11:18 There is a Hebrew pun in this verse. The word for "empty" is *sheger* and the word for "reward" is *seker*.
11:20 This proverb has connections to 10:9; 19:1; and 28:6.
11:21 Be assured is literally "hand to hand." It may mean that it is as sure as a contract solemnized by a handshake (6:1). Righteousness

is so powerful that even the next generation of **the righteous** is likely to **escape** eternal death due to the influence a parent's righteousness has on their offspring (Ex 20:6; cp. Ezk 18).
11:22 The pig was an unclean animal; no amount of adornment could make up for this fundamental defect.
11:24 To give **freely** is literally to "scatter"— to be generous without worrying about where the blessings fall.
11:26 The king of Moab refused to sell grain to the traveling Israelites and came under God's **curse** (Dt 2:26–31), while Joseph sold grain during a famine and was blessed (Gn 41:56; 47:13–20).

²⁸ Anyone trusting in his riches will fall,
but the righteous will flourish
like foliage.

²⁹ The one who brings ruin on his household
will inherit the wind,
and a fool will be a slave
to someone whose heart is wise.

³⁰ The fruit of the righteous is a tree of life,
but a cunning person takes lives.

³¹ If the righteous will be repaid on earth,
how much more the wicked and sinful.

12

Whoever loves discipline
loves knowledge,
but one who hates correction is stupid.

² One who is good obtains favor
from the LORD,
but he condemns a person
who schemes.

³ No one can be made secure
by wickedness,
but the root of the righteous
is immovable.

⁴ A wife of noble character^A is
her husband's crown,
but a wife who causes shame
is like rottenness in his bones.

⁵ The thoughts of the righteous are just,
but guidance from the wicked is deceitful.

⁶ The words of the wicked are
a deadly ambush,
but the speech of the upright
rescues them.

⁷ The wicked are overthrown and perish,
but the house of the righteous
will stand.

⁸ A man is praised for his insight,
but a twisted mind is despised.

⁹ Better to be disregarded, yet have
a servant,
than to act important but have
no food.

¹⁰ The righteous cares about
his animal's health,
but even the merciful acts of the wicked
are cruel.

¹¹ The one who works his land will have
plenty of food,
but whoever chases fantasies
lacks sense.

¹² The wicked desire what evil people
have caught,^B
but the root of the righteous
is productive.

¹³ By rebellious speech an evil person
is trapped,
but a righteous person escapes
from trouble.

¹⁴ A person will be satisfied
with good
by the fruit of his mouth,
and the work of a person's hands
will reward him.

¹⁵ A fool's way is right in his own eyes,
but whoever listens to counsel
is wise.

¹⁶ A fool's displeasure is known at once,
but whoever ignores an insult
is sensible.

¹⁷ Whoever speaks the truth declares
what is right,
but a false witness speaks deceit.

^A12:4 Or *A wife of quality*, or *A wife of good character* ^B12:12 Or *desire a stronghold of evil*

11:29 To **inherit the wind** is to end up with nothing.
11:30 The second part of this verse is difficult. The Hebrew reads literally "the one taking lives is wise." Elsewhere in the Bible the phrase *take a life* is always negative (1:19; 1Sm 24:11; 1Kg 19:10,14; Ps 31:13; Ezk 33:6); it never means "to win a soul." But it does not fit with the rest of Scripture to say that the person who kills people is wise, so there must be another explanation. The CSB interprets *wise* to mean "cunning" in this context: **a cunning person takes lives**. The LXX implies the original Hebrew might have read "violence" (*chamas*) instead of "wise" (*chakam*), thus "violence takes lives."
11:31 **How much more** argues from the lesser to the greater (15:11; 17:7; 19:7,10; 21:27).

This is not to say that the punishment of the **wicked** is more certain than the blessing of the **righteous**. But if God's impartial judgment begins with the righteous, then the **sinful** will not escape (1Pt 4:18).
12:1 The **stupid** person is more like a brutish, irrational animal (Ps 73:22). That he **hates correction** reveals a heart problem more than a head problem.
12:4 This is the same Hebrew phrase as that in the portrayal of the **wife of noble character** in 31:10 and the description of Ruth as "a woman of noble character" (Ru 3:11). **Rottenness** in the **bones** implies loss of joy and strength.
12:8 The Hebrew word for **insight** is related to prudence.
12:9 To have one **servant** signified a modest standard of living in ancient times.

12:10 What the **wicked** person thinks is **merciful** is still **cruel**.
12:11 The opposite of productive **works** is the pursuit of **fantasies** or delusions, such as get-rich-quick schemes, gambling, or idly "waiting for my ship to come in."
12:12 What **the wicked** man desires is literally "the stronghold [or 'net,' snare'] of evil men." That is, he desires what they have obtained by plunder. Verse 12b is literally "but the root of the righteous gives." Some scholars and translations emend the verb to *endures*. CSB renders it **is productive**.
12:17 This is courtroom terminology. The person who **speaks the truth** is the opposite of the **false witness** who has first-hand knowledge but utters lies (6:19; 14:5,25; 19:5,9). To declare **what is right** is to provide the necessary information for a correct verdict, which

¹⁸ There is one who speaks rashly,
   like a piercing sword;
   but the tongue of the wise
      brings healing.

¹⁹ Truthful lips endure forever,
   but a lying tongue, only a moment.

²⁰ Deceit is in the hearts of those
      who plot evil,
   but those who promote peace have joy.

²¹ No disaster overcomes the righteous,
   but the wicked are full of misery.

²² Lying lips are detestable to the LORD,
   but faithful people are his delight.

²³ A shrewd person conceals knowledge,
   but a foolish heart publicizes stupidity.

²⁴ The diligent hand will rule,
   but laziness will lead to forced labor.

²⁵ Anxiety in a person's heart
      weighs it down,
   but a good word cheers it up.

²⁶ A righteous person is careful in dealing
      with his neighbor,ᴬ
   but the ways of the wicked
      lead them astray.

²⁷ A lazy hunter doesn't roast his game,
   but to a diligent person, his wealth
      is precious.

²⁸ There is life in the path of righteousness,
   and in its path there is no death.ᴮ

13 A wise son responds to his
      father's discipline,
   but a mocker doesn't listen to rebuke.

² From the fruit of his mouth,
   a person will enjoy good things,
   but treacherous people have an appetite
      for violence.

³ The one who guards his mouth protects
      his life;
   the one who opens his lips invites
      his own ruin.

⁴ The slacker craves, yet has nothing,
   but the diligent is fully satisfied.

⁵ The righteous hate lying,
   but the wicked bring
      disgust and shame.

⁶ Righteousness guards people
      of integrity,ᶜ
   but wickedness undermines the sinner.

⁷ One person pretends to be rich
      but has nothing;
   another pretends to be poor but has
      abundant wealth.

⁸ Riches are a ransom for a person's life,
   but a poor person hears no threat.

⁹ The light of the righteous
      shines brightly,
   but the lamp of the wicked is put out.

¹⁰ Arrogance leads to nothing but strife,
   but wisdom is gained by those
      who take advice.

¹¹ Wealth obtained by fraud will dwindle,
   but whoever earns it through laborᴰ
      will multiply it.

¹² Hope delayed makes the heart sick,
   but desire fulfilled is a tree of life.

ᴬ12:26 Or *person guides his neighbor* ᴮ12:28 Or *righteousness, but the crooked way leads to death* ᶜ13:6 Lit *guards integrity of way* ᴰ13:11 Lit *whoever gathers upon his hand*

---

could literally save the life of an innocent person (14:25).

12:18 Speaking **rashly**, without thinking, could involve either saying something inconsiderate (Nm 20:10; Ps 106:33) or making reckless vows (Lv 5:4).

12:20 Peace is the opposite of **evil** in the sense that success or welfare is the opposite of disaster (Is 45:7; Jr 29:11).

12:23 The **shrewd** person holds his tongue unless the situation is right. What he has is **knowledge**. The **foolish** person does not restrain himself. What's worse, his speech is pure **stupidity**.

12:26 The **righteous person** literally "spies out" (Nm 13:2) or "investigates" (Ec 7:25) **his neighbor** to make sure he will not mislead him.

12:27 This proverb may also imply that the lazy man does not finish what he started

and **roast** what he has brought home, so it goes to waste; the diligent man takes care of what God has given him.

13:2–4 These three verses play on the Hebrew multipurpose word *nephesh* ("soul, self, appetite, throat, or mouth"). **Treacherous people** will not receive **good things** and in fact have no **appetite** (*nephesh*) for them. Instead, their treachery will backfire as violence (4:17), that is, fierceness, ruthlessness, or malice. In 13:3 the wise man **protects his life** (*nephesh*). In v. 4 *nephesh* as "mouth" is implied. **The slacker . . . has nothing** for his mouth, but the mouth of the **diligent is fully satisfied.**

13:5 Bring disgust is literally "stink" (Gn 34:30; Ex 5:21).

13:6 Undermines is literally "overturns," but it implies being frustrated or subverted (Ex 23:8; Dt 16:19; Jb 12:19) and brought to ruin (Pr 19:3; 21:12; 22:12).

13:8 A rich man can pay a **ransom** to save his earthly **life**. The **poor person** does not have to worry because no robber would typically bother with him.

13:10 Arrogance here contrasts with **those who take advice**, so an arrogant person is viewed as a "know-it-all."

13:11 The Hebrew word for **fraud** here is the word translated "futility" in Ecclesiastes. It is literally "breath" or "vapor," something with no substance. Here it means "ill-gotten" or "rashly" (10:2; 12:11). The same word is used to say that wealth is a "vanishing mist" (21:6) and beauty is "fleeting" (31:30).

13:12 If a person's **hope** is constantly **delayed**, he becomes frustrated and loses **heart**. On **tree of life**, see 3:18; 11:30; 15:4.

¹³ The one who has contempt
    for instruction will pay the penalty,
but the one who respects a command
    will be rewarded.

¹⁴ A wise person's instruction is a fountain
    of life,
turning people away from the snares
    of death.

¹⁵ Good sense wins favor,
but the way of the treacherous
    never changes.^A

¹⁶ Every sensible person
    acts knowledgeably,
but a fool displays his stupidity.

¹⁷ A wicked envoy falls into trouble,
but a trustworthy courier
    brings healing.

¹⁸ Poverty and disgrace come to those
    who ignore discipline,
but the one who accepts correction
    will be honored.

¹⁹ Desire fulfilled is sweet to the taste,
but to turn from evil is detestable
    to fools.

²⁰ The one who walks with the wise
    will become wise,
but a companion of fools
    will suffer harm.

²¹ Disaster pursues sinners,
but good rewards the righteous.

²² A good man leaves an inheritance
    to his^B grandchildren,
but the sinner's wealth is stored up
    for the righteous.

²³ The uncultivated field of the poor yields
    abundant food,
but without justice, it is swept away.

²⁴ The one who will not use the rod hates
    his son,
but the one who loves him disciplines
    him diligently.

²⁵ A righteous person eats
    until he is satisfied,
but the stomach of the wicked
    is empty.

14

Every wise woman builds her house,
but a foolish one tears it down
    with her own hands.

² Whoever lives with integrity
    fears the LORD,
but the one who is devious in his ways
    despises him.

³ The proud speech of a fool brings a rod
    of discipline,^C
but the lips of the wise protect them.

⁴ Where there are no oxen, the
    feeding trough is empty,^D
but an abundant harvest comes through
    the strength of an ox.

⁵ An honest witness does not deceive,
but a dishonest witness utters lies.

⁶ A mocker seeks wisdom
    and doesn't find it,
but knowledge comes easily
    to the perceptive.

⁷ Stay away from a foolish person;
you will gain no knowledge
    from his speech.

---

^A13:15 LXX, Syr, Tg read *treacherous will perish*   ^B13:22 Or *inheritance: his*   ^C14:3 Some emend to *In the mouth of a fool is a rod for his back*   ^D14:4 Or *clean*

13:13 To have **contempt for instruction** is to despise the Lord's word. Such a person is always condemned (Nm 15:31; 2Sm 12:9; 2Ch 36:16; cp. 1Sm 2:17). **Pay the penalty** is literally "pledge collateral to it"; in other words, be in debt to it.
13:14 Note the singular and plural nouns: there is only one **fountain of life**, but there are many **snares of death**.
13:20 Choosing one's friends is a very important matter.
13:21 Rather than saying **sinners** reap **disaster**, this proverb emphatically has disaster chasing them down until it catches them.
13:22 The Hebrew word for **wealth** can stand for "strength" as well. **The sinner's** possessions along with all his capabilities and resources are granted to **the righteous**.
13:23 The **field** that went uncultivated could refer to the marginal lands the poor were forced to live on, or to the fields that were supposed to be left fallow on the Sabbatical Year for the sake of the poor (Ex 23:10–11; Lv 25:1–7). In the latter case, the lack of **justice** was the failure to observe the command (Lv 26:34–35,43; 2Ch 36:21).
13:24 Parents who love their children seek **diligently** to apply the best and most appropriate method of discipline (Heb 12:5–11). In some cases that is the **rod** (22:15; 23:13–14; 29:15), which is appropriate punishment for the fool (10:3; 26:3). Only a parent who **hates** his child would withhold discipline and permit him to remain a fool, knowing that foolishness leads to misery, shame, and ultimately death.
14:1 This **wise woman** is not wisdom personified, as in chaps. 8–9, but a flesh-and-blood woman. Solomon is urging his son (1:8) to look for a wise woman (31:10) to build up a **house** (the word can also mean "household").

Women in turn are encouraged to be the kind who build rather than tear down.
14:3 In the first line the Hebrew is literally "In the mouth of a fool, a rod of pride." In one sense, the **rod** in his mouth is his tongue, which makes **proud speech**. The rod is also a method of **discipline** (13:24), which the **fool** brings upon himself.
14:4 Empty could also be translated "clean" in the sense of "pure." You do not have to worry about having feed on hand and cleaning up after **oxen** if you do not have any, but you also will not have an **abundant harvest**. Sometimes the benefits of an investment outweigh the costs and inconveniences involved.
14:5 A person can tell the quality of testimony by considering the character of the **witness** (cp. 6:19; 27:21).
14:7 The fool's problem is not ignorance but a lack of reverence for the truth.

8 The sensible person's wisdom is
  to consider his way,
but the stupidity of fools deceives them.

9 Fools mock at making reparation,^A
but there is goodwill among the upright.

10 The heart knows its own bitterness,
and no outsider shares in its joy.

11 The house of the wicked
  will be destroyed,
but the tent of the upright will flourish.

12 There is a way that seems right
  to a person,
but its end is the way to death.

13 Even in laughter a heart may be sad,
and joy may end in grief.

14 The disloyal one will get
  what his conduct deserves,
and a good one, what his deeds deserve.

15 The inexperienced one
  believes anything,
but the sensible one watches^B his steps.

16 A wise person is cautious and turns
  from evil,
but a fool is easily angered
  and is careless.^C

17 A quick-tempered person acts foolishly,
and one who schemes is hated.

18 The inexperienced inherit foolishness,
but the sensible are crowned
  with knowledge.

19 The evil bow before those
  who are good,
and the wicked, at the gates
  of the righteous.

20 A poor person is hated even
  by his neighbor,
but there are many who love the rich.

21 The one who despises his neighbor sins,
but whoever shows kindness
  to the poor will be happy.

22 Don't those who plan evil go astray?
But those who plan good find loyalty
  and faithfulness.

23 There is profit in all hard work,
but endless talk^D leads only to poverty.

24 The crown of the wise is their wealth,
but the foolishness of fools
  produces foolishness.

25 A truthful witness rescues lives,
but one who utters lies is deceitful.

26 In the fear of the LORD one has
  strong confidence
and his children have a refuge.

27 The fear of the LORD is a fountain
  of life,
turning people away from the snares
  of death.

28 A large population is a king's splendor,
but a shortage of people is
  a ruler's devastation.

29 A patient person shows great
  understanding,
but a quick-tempered one
  promotes foolishness.

30 A tranquil heart is life to the body,
but jealousy is rottenness to the bones.

31 The one who oppresses the poor person
  insults his Maker,

---

^A**14:9** Or *at guilt offerings*   ^B**14:15** Lit *the prudent understands*   ^C**14:16** Or *and falls*   ^D**14:23** Lit *but word of lips*

14:8 This verse says literally **the stupidity of fools** is deceit. This could mean that they deceive themselves through their own stupidity, or that their stupidity is evident in the deceit they practice on others.
14:10 No one can completely know what another person's **heart** is feeling.
14:13 Sad is literally "in pain." Appearances may be deceptive; the true nature of things is shown by their end.
14:14 A **disloyal** person is literally "one whose heart turned back."
14:15 While the mocker rejects everything, the **inexperienced** person accepts **anything**. The **sensible** person is guided by godly wisdom to "watch" (lit "understand") his own **steps**—to practice discretion.
14:16 The Hebrew word translated **is cautious** is literally "fears." This could imply that **a wise**

person fears the Lord and **turns from evil** (3:7; 16:6). In contrast, the fool's hot temper gets him into trouble. He is **careless** or self-confident because he thinks he is secure, but he is wrong.
14:17 A **quick-tempered person** does bad things impetuously because he does not think first. A schemer does bad things purposely because he is malicious (24:8). Neither thrives. The former squanders his life in foolishness (14:29), and the latter is **hated** and condemned (12:2).
14:19 Judgment took place at the **gates** of cities, suggesting that the righteous person will have a prominent place in the city (31:23) and stand in judgment of the wicked.
14:20 This is not a promise or endorsement; it is an astute observation of human nature.
14:23 **Endless talk** is literally "words of lips"; it could also be translated "mere words" (2Kg

18:20). **Hard work** is labor that is physically or emotionally draining. Outside of the Lord's blessing, it is vain (10:22; Ps 127:1–2). But diligent work (Pr 6:6–11) is better than recklessness (21:5), idleness (10:4), fraud (13:11), or get-rich-quick schemes (28:20).
14:27 This proverb is the same as 13:14 except that **the fear of the LORD** is in place of "a wise person's instruction." The two ideas are nearly interchangeable because wisdom presupposes the fear of the Lord (9:10; 15:33).
14:28 When a **ruler's** followers desert him, he can be devastated or terrified (1Sm 13:11–12; 30:6; 1Kg 12:1–20).
14:29 **Patient** is literally "slow at becoming angry." Outside of Proverbs, the phrase is always used of God in the OT (Ex 34:6; Nm 14:18; Neh 9:17; Pss 86:15; 103:8; 145:8; Is 48:9; Jr 15:15; Jl 2:13; Jnh 4:2; Nah 1:3).

but one who is kind to the needy
    honors him.

32 The wicked one is thrown down
    by his own sin,
but the righteous one has a refuge
    in his death.

33 Wisdom resides in the heart
    of the discerning;
she is known^A even among fools.

34 Righteousness exalts a nation,
but sin is a disgrace to any people.

35 A king favors a prudent servant,
but his anger falls on
    a disgraceful one.

15 A gentle answer turns away anger,
    but a harsh word stirs up wrath.

2 The tongue of the wise
    makes knowledge attractive,
but the mouth of fools
    blurts out foolishness.

3 The eyes of the LORD are everywhere,
observing the wicked and the good.

4 The tongue that heals is a tree of life,
but a devious tongue^B
    breaks the spirit.

5 A fool despises his father's discipline,
but a person who accepts correction
    is sensible.

6 The house of the righteous
    has great wealth,
but trouble accompanies the income
    of the wicked.

7 The lips of the wise
    broadcast knowledge,
but not so the heart of fools.

8 The sacrifice of the wicked is detestable
    to the LORD,
but the prayer of the upright is his delight.

9 The LORD detests the way of the wicked,
but he loves the one
    who pursues righteousness.

10 Discipline is harsh for the one
    who leaves the path;
the one who hates correction will die.

11 Sheol and Abaddon lie open
    before the LORD —
how much more, human hearts.

12 A mocker doesn't love one
    who corrects him;
he will not consult the wise.

13 A joyful heart makes a face cheerful,
but a sad heart produces a broken spirit.

14 A discerning mind seeks knowledge,
but the mouth of fools feeds
    on foolishness.

15 All the days of the oppressed
    are miserable,
but a cheerful heart has
    a continual feast.

16 Better a little with the fear of the LORD
than great treasure with turmoil.

17 Better a meal of vegetables
    where there is love
than a fattened ox with hatred.

^A**14:33** LXX reads *unknown*   ^B**15:4** Lit *but crookedness in it*

14:32 Even while he is dying or after his death (the Hebrew is ambiguous), the **righteous** person looks for and finds refuge in the Lord.
14:33 Wisdom among **fools** is merely **known**; among the **discerning**, she literally "comes to rest."
14:34 While many proverbs promote personal ethics, this proverb takes ethics to a national level.
14:35 Servant of a **king** probably refers to a royal official, not a household slave.
15:1 The Hebrew word used to describe a **gentle answer** describes how a wound is "soothed with oil" (Is 1:6). A soothing answer is not ineffective (Pr 25:15). **Harsh word** is literally "word of pain."
15:4 Heals could also be translated "is tranquil." The author may have intended both meanings. A tranquil tongue heals, and a healing tongue must surely be tranquil (v. 1). Both concepts are also the opposite of fracturing **the spirit**.

15:5 Accepts correction means one listens attentively and obeys (see "keep" at 4:4).
15:6 This Hebrew word for **wealth** includes produce, possessions, and treasures. **Trouble** in Proverbs usually refers to the ruin he brings on himself (v. 27; 11:17,29).
15:10 This verse refers to the **path** of life (v. 24; 5:6; 10:17), the path of the righteous (4:18; 8:20; 12:28), or the right path (3:6). The person who **leaves** the path is the same as **the one who hates correction**; such people are condemned to eternal death (2:11–19).
15:11 Sheol is the grave, and **Abaddon** (Jb 26:6; 28:22; 31:12; Ps 88:11) is the "place of destruction." If God can see into the obscure depths of the grave, **how much more** can he see the recesses of **human hearts**?
15:13 In this proverb, sadness seems to affect a person more deeply than joy since the **heart** is more profound than the **face**.
15:15 The parallelism in this verse suggests that even if a person is **oppressed** and

miserable, if he has a **cheerful heart** he can experience a virtual **continual feast**.
15:16–17 These are typical examples of **better . . . than** proverbs (12:9; 16:8,19; 17:1; 19:1; 27:5,10; 28:6; cp. 3:14; 8:11,19). In each proverb of this type, two categories are considered. Having little or none of one and a lot of the other is compared with the other way around. In 15:16 one category is wealth and the other is a good relationship with God. A little wealth and a very good relationship with God (characterized by **fear**) are better than a lot of wealth and little relationship with God (which brings **turmoil**). In v. 17 one category is lavish food and the other is family **love**. Having no lavish food and a lot of love is better than having the best food and no love.
A **meal** is a daily allowance, like that given a traveler (Jr 40:5). **Vegetables** were the normal, everyday food. A **fattened ox** was a great luxury (Lk 15:23). A fattened ox was kept in a stall and carefully fed, then

18 A hot-tempered person stirs up conflict,
but one slow to anger calms strife.

19 A slacker's way is like a thorny hedge,
but the path of the upright is a highway.

20 A wise son brings joy to his father,
but a foolish man despises his mother.

21 Foolishness brings joy to one
without sense,
but a person with understanding walks
a straight path.

22 Plans fail when there is no counsel,
but with many advisers they succeed.

23 A person takes joy in giving
an answer;[A]
and a timely word — how good that is!

24 For the prudent the path of life
leads upward,
so that he may avoid going down
to Sheol.

25 The Lᴏʀᴅ tears apart the house
of the proud,
but he protects the widow's territory.

26 The Lᴏʀᴅ detests the plans of the one
who is evil,
but pleasant words are pure.

27 The one who profits dishonestly
troubles his household,
but the one who hates bribes will live.

28 The mind of the righteous person thinks
before answering,
but the mouth of the wicked blurts out
evil things.

29 The Lᴏʀᴅ is far from the wicked,
but he hears the prayer of the righteous.

30 Bright eyes cheer the heart;
good news strengthens[B] the bones.

31 One who[C] listens to life-giving rebukes
will be at home among the wise.

32 Anyone who ignores discipline
despises himself,
but whoever listens to correction
acquires good sense.[D]

33 The fear of the Lᴏʀᴅ is what
wisdom teaches,
and humility comes before honor.

16 The reflections of the heart
belong to mankind,
but the answer of the tongue is
from the Lᴏʀᴅ.

2 All a person's ways seem right to him,
but the Lᴏʀᴅ weighs motives.[E]

3 Commit your activities to the Lᴏʀᴅ,
and your plans will be established.

4 The Lᴏʀᴅ has prepared everything
for his purpose —
even the wicked for the day of disaster.

ᴬ**15:23** Lit *in an answer of his mouth*   ᴮ**15:30** Lit *makes fat*   ᶜ**15:31** Lit *An ear that*   ᴰ**15:32** Lit *acquires a heart*   ᴱ**16:2** Lit *spirits*

---

slaughtered in its prime. The result was moist and tender meat, but the profit from the labor of the animal was forfeited.
15:18 The Hebrew word translated **strife** here is also used for a lawsuit or court case (18:17; 22:23; 23:11; 25:9; see Ex 23:2; Hs 4:1), but it often has a nonlegal sense of a dispute or quarrel (Pr 17:1,14; 18:6; 20:3; 26:17,21; 30:33).
15:19 A **hedge** made from thorns was a painful obstacle (Is 5:5; cp. Mc 7:4). A **highway** was an efficient road built up and cleared of obstacles.
15:21 **Foolishness** implies moral waywardness. The person who lacks **sense** actually finds pleasure in sinning (10:23; Heb 11:25). The **person with understanding** knows that even if he does not receive a reward in this life, there is a great reward in heaven (Lk 16:25; Heb 12:2).
15:22 **Counsel** is private, personal advice from intimate friends.
15:23 This Hebrew word for **answer** means the most appropriate and effective thing to say in the given circumstance (v. 1; 16:1).
15:24 The discerning person is on the **path of life** because he trusts in the Lord (3:22; 16:20) and thereby avoids going to **Sheol**.
15:25 The widow represents those who were vulnerable to wicked, greedy people. God

himself **protects the widow's territory** (lit her "boundary") from those who might move the boundary markers (22:28; 23:10).
15:26 **Pure** is "ceremonially clean," acceptable to offer to God.
15:27 God hates bribes because they subvert justice (17:23; cp. 18:5; Dt 16:19; Ps 15:5; Ec 7:7; Is 5:23). Therefore, the person who **hates** bribes agrees with God, and the one who totally agrees with God **will live** (Rm 7:16; 1Co 2:16; 1Tm 6:3).
15:28 The **righteous person thinks**, or ponders or meditates, **before answering** (cp. 18:13). The **wicked**, like the fool (15:2), **blurts out**, or pours out (18:4), what is in his heart. For the wicked it is **evil things**; for the fool it is foolishness (cp. Is 32:6). What comes out of a person's mouth reflects what is inside him (Mt 12:34; 15:18–19; Jms 3:2–12).
15:29 To say that the Lord is **far from** somebody is not a limit on his omnipresence, but refers to losing out on his communion, favor, and help (Gn 3:8,23; Pss 22:12,19; 35:22; 38:21; 71:12).
15:30 The phrase **bright eyes** implies spiritual vitality (29:13; cp. Ezr 9:8; Pss 13:3; 19:8; 38:10). **Bones** represent the inner core, the seat of health (3:8; cp. Jb 20:11; 21:24). To strengthen the bones is literally

to "make them fat," to satiate them. Thus **good news** refreshes and strengthens a person (25:25).
15:31–32 To be **at home** is literally "to spend the night." To ignore or neglect the Lord's counsel and **discipline** is not just harmful (13:18), it is ultimately fatal (1:25,32). To do so is to despise or reject one's very self. To acquire **good sense** is literally to "buy a heart" (19:8; cp. "lacks sense" at 6:32).
15:33 The phrase **what wisdom teaches** probably means "the instruction that results in wisdom." **Humility** and **the fear of the Lᴏʀᴅ** are prerequisites for gaining wisdom and **honor**.
16:1 The Hebrew word translated **reflections** has to do with arranging things in an orderly manner.
16:2 To evaluate or weigh something is to compare it with a standard. If **a person's ways** are not compared to God's standards, they will all **seem right** or pure (20:11; cp. Jb 11:4; 33:9). But **the Lᴏʀᴅ** evaluates the inner **motives** (lit "spirit") of a man (cp. "hearts" in 24:12 and "actions" in 1Sm 2:3).
16:4 **Prepared** could also be translated "created"; either way God is sovereign. A **day of disaster** is literally an "evil day."

5 Everyone with a proud heart is
    detestable to the LORD;
  be assured,^A he will not go unpunished.

6 Iniquity is atoned for by loyalty
    and faithfulness,
  and one turns from evil by the fear
    of the LORD.

7 When a person's ways please the LORD,
  he makes even his enemies to be
    at peace with him.

8 Better a little with righteousness
  than great income with injustice.

9 A person's heart plans his way,
  but the LORD determines his steps.

10 God's verdict is on the lips of a king;^B
  his mouth should not give
    an unfair judgment.

11 Honest balances and scales are
    the LORD's;
  all the weights in the bag are
    his concern.

12 Wicked behavior is detestable to kings,
  since a throne is established
    through righteousness.

13 Righteous lips are a king's delight,
  and he loves one who speaks honestly.

14 A king's fury is a messenger of death,
  but a wise person appeases it.

15 When a king's face lights up, there is life;
  his favor is like a cloud with spring rain.

16 Get wisdom —
  how much better it is than gold!

And get understanding —
  it is preferable to silver.

17 The highway of the upright
    avoids evil;
  the one who guards his way protects
    his life.

18 Pride comes before destruction,
  and an arrogant spirit before a fall.

19 Better to be lowly of spirit
    with the humble^C
  than to divide plunder with the proud.

20 The one who understands a matter
    finds success,
  and the one who trusts in the LORD
    will be happy.

21 Anyone with a wise heart
    is called discerning,
  and pleasant speech^D
    increases learning.

22 Insight is a fountain of life
    for its possessor,
  but the discipline of fools is folly.

23 The heart of a wise person instructs
    his mouth;
  it adds learning to his speech.^E

24 Pleasant words are a honeycomb:
  sweet to the taste^F and health
    to the body.^G

25 There is a way that seems right
    to a person,
  but its end is the way to death.

26 A worker's appetite works for him
  because his hunger^H urges him on.

---

^A16:5 Lit hand to hand ^B16:10 Or A divination is on the lips of a king ^C16:19 Alt Hb tradition reads afflicted ^D16:21 Lit and sweetness of lips ^E16:23 Lit learning upon his lips ^F16:24 Lit throat ^G16:24 Lit bones ^H16:26 Lit mouth

16:5 Proud is literally "high" (cp. 18:12). The same word describes "haughty" eyes (Ps 101:5) or a "proud" spirit (Ec 7:8). All of these imply arrogance, thinking oneself better than anyone, including God.
16:7 The Hebrew is ambiguous whether it is a man or God that transforms **his enemies**.
16:9 This word for **plans** in Proverbs usually involves wicked schemes (v. 30; 24:8; cp. Ps 140:2; Nah 1:9), but it can also refer to good strategies and tactics (Pr 12:5; 16:3; 21:5) or thinking deeply about something (Ps 73:16; 119:59). Even good plans can only be established by the sovereign Lord (Pr 16:3; 19:21).
16:10 God's verdict is literally "divination," which is usually condemned, but the Hebrew word can refer to a **king** seeking God's mind when passing **judgment**.

16:14–15 A king of ancient times held the power of **life** and **death**. Thus unlike a jealous but powerless husband's rage (6:35), a **king's fury** could be appeased (the same Hb word as "atoned" in v. 6). **Spring rain** symbolized life because it gave a boost to the grain and fruit crops before harvest.
16:17 In this Hebrew parallelism, avoiding **evil** is likened to protecting **life**. In other words, engaging in evil is life threatening.
16:18 Here the parallelism is synonymous, and the two lines say nearly the same thing.
16:19 On **better ... than** proverbs, see note at 15:16–17.
16:20 The person who **understands a matter** could also be translated "the one who attends to business" or "the one who pays attention to the way" (Ps 101:2).
16:21 Pleasant speech is literally "sweetness of lips." "Sweetness" is used literally for honey

(24:13; Jdg 14:18; Ps 19:10; Ezk 3:3) and metaphorically for something that is revitalizing or encouraging (Pr 16:24).
16:22 It is possible that the **discipline of fools** is referring to the teaching that fools try to do, which results in mere **folly**; more likely it means that through their own folly fools are disciplined. They reap the punishment of their errant lifestyle (6:33; 14:14,24; 19:3).
16:23 Learning may mean "persuasiveness."
16:24 Pleasant words—morally uplifting speech—are both **sweet** and health-giving.
16:25 This proverb is identical to 14:12. It may have been included twice because it was part of two different collections in Solomon's mind or because it is such a key concept.

27 A worthless person digs up evil,
and his speech is like a scorching fire.

28 A contrary person spreads conflict,
and a gossip separates close friends.

29 A violent person lures his neighbor,
leading him on a path that is not good.

30 The one who narrows his eyes
is planning deceptions;
the one who compresses his lips
brings about evil.

31 Gray hair is a glorious crown;
it is found in the ways of righteousness.

32 Patience is better than power,
and controlling one's emotions,^A
than capturing a city.

33 The lot is cast into the lap,
but its every decision is
from the LORD.

17 Better a dry crust with peace
than a house full of feasting
with strife.

2 A prudent servant will rule over
a disgraceful son
and share an inheritance
among brothers.

3 A crucible for silver, and a smelter
for gold,
and the LORD is the tester of hearts.

4 A wicked person listens to
malicious talk;^B

a liar pays attention to
a destructive tongue.

5 The one who mocks the poor insults
his Maker,
and one who rejoices over calamity
will not go unpunished.

6 Grandchildren are the crown
of the elderly,
and the pride of children is their fathers.

7 Eloquent words are not appropriate
on a fool's lips;
how much worse are lies for a ruler.

8 A bribe seems like a magic stone
to its owner;
wherever he turns, he succeeds.

9 Whoever conceals an offense
promotes love,
but whoever gossips about it
separates friends.

10 A rebuke cuts into
a perceptive person
more than a hundred lashes
into a fool.

11 An evil person desires only rebellion;
a cruel messenger^C will be sent
against him.

12 Better for a person to meet a bear
robbed of her cubs
than a fool in his foolishness.

13 If anyone returns evil for good,
evil will never depart from his house.

---

^A **16:32** Lit *and ruling over one's spirit*   ^B **17:4** Lit *to lips of iniquity*   ^C **17:11** Or *a merciful angel*

16:27 The Hebrew word translated **digs up** could also be translated "purchases" or "cooks up." However he gets it, the **worthless person** is intent on using **evil** destructively.

16:28 A **contrary person** is one who distorts speech, who turns things upside down, who "says perverse things." It may be that he speaks his own lies or that he subverts others' speech by the way he spins it. A **gossip** is someone who grumbles (Dt 1:27; Ps 106:25; Is 29:24) or finds fault but avoids open discussion or confrontation.

16:29 Sinners often want to lure others to join them in sin to excuse their own sinfulness.

16:30 Narrowing one's **eyes** and compressing one's **lips** might refer to subtle nonverbal cues that the wise person should be aware of, or they could refer to gestures made by those **planning deceptions** to signal their accomplices (6:12–14; 10:10).

16:31 The person who stays on the **ways of righteousness** is likely to live to a ripe old age (12:28; 13:6) and attain the respect that elders deserve (Lv 19:32).

16:32 A person who does not let his passions control him is **better than** a powerful military hero who lacks such control.

16:33 The **lot** was a stone the ancient Israelites used to make decisions the same way we might roll dice or flip a coin. The **lap** was a fold or pocket in one's garment. Perhaps the lot was dropped into the pocket for storage, or it was shaken in the pocket, or else the pocket area was where the lot was revealed for its decision.

17:1 On **better . . . than** proverbs, see note at 15:16–17. Bread that is **dry** means either that it is old (Jos 9:5) or that there is no oil or sauce to dip it in (Ru 2:14). **Peace** implies security; **strife** is human conflict. The **feasting** might be an allusion to the fellowship sacrifice which was supposed to make peace between God and the people in the **house**.

17:2 This is probably metaphor or hyperbole. There was no provision in the law for a **servant** to displace a **disgraceful son**, though a "rebellious" son could be stoned (Dt 21:18–21).

17:3 The **crucible** and **smelter** were small clay vessels in which metals were melted at very high temperatures to refine them. To be tested is to be evaluated to see if something is genuine.

17:7 *Nabal*, the Hebrew word used here for the fool, connotes the most irreligious of fools. It is one who curses God (Jb 2:9–10) and denies his existence (Ps 14:1; cp. Is 32:6).

17:8 The **magic stone** is literally "a stone of favor"—a charm that makes people treat others favorably. **Seems like . . . to its owner** is literally "in the eyes of its master." The owner is the one who gives a **bribe**. He only apparently **succeeds** in this life; ultimately bribes are destructive.

17:10 A **hundred lashes** is hyperbole; only forty were allowed by law (Dt 25:3).

17:11 The **cruel messenger** is God's angel of death (16:14; 1Ch 21:15; Ps 78:49).

17:12 The female Aramean brown **bear** had a reputation for fierceness (2Kg 2:24; Lm 3:10) that was intensified if she was **robbed of her cubs** (2Sm 17:8; Hs 13:8).

¹⁴ To start a conflict is to release a flood;
stop the dispute before it breaks out.

¹⁵ Acquitting the guilty and condemning
the just —
both are detestable to the LORD.

¹⁶ Why does a fool have money
in his hand
with no intention of buying wisdom?

¹⁷ A friend loves at all times,
and a brother is born for a difficult time.

¹⁸ One without sense enters
an agreement^A
and puts up security for his friend.

¹⁹ One who loves to offend loves strife;
one who builds a high threshold
invites injury.

²⁰ One with a twisted mind
will not succeed,
and one with deceitful speech will fall
into ruin.

²¹ A man fathers a fool to his own sorrow;
the father of a fool has no joy.

²² A joyful heart is good medicine,
but a broken spirit dries up the bones.

²³ A wicked person secretly takes a bribe
to subvert the course of justice.

²⁴ Wisdom is the focus of the perceptive,
but a fool's eyes roam to the ends
of the earth.

²⁵ A foolish son is grief to his father
and bitterness to the one
who bore him.

²⁶ It is certainly not good to fine
an innocent person
or to beat a noble for his honesty.^B

²⁷ The one who has knowledge restrains
his words,
and one who keeps a cool head^C
is a person of understanding.

²⁸ Even a fool is considered wise
when he keeps silent —
discerning, when he seals his lips.

18 One who isolates himself pursues
selfish desires;
he rebels against all sound wisdom.

² A fool does not delight
in understanding,
but only wants to show off
his opinions.^D

³ When a wicked person comes,
contempt also comes,
and along with dishonor, derision.

⁴ The words of a person's mouth
are deep waters,
a flowing river, a fountain of wisdom.^E

⁵ It is not good to show partiality
to the guilty,
denying an innocent person justice.

⁶ A fool's lips lead to strife,
and his mouth provokes a beating.

⁷ A fool's mouth is his devastation,
and his lips are a trap for his life.

⁸ A gossip's words are like choice food
that goes down
to one's innermost being.^F

^A 18:18 Lit *sense slaps hands* ^B 17:26 Or *noble unfairly* ^C 17:27 Lit *spirit* ^D 18:2 Lit *to uncover his heart* ^E 18:4 Or *waters; a fountain of wisdom is a flowing river* ^F 18:8 Lit *to the chambers of the belly*

17:17 The purpose of a **brother** is to uphold a family member in **a difficult time**. The Hebrew word can be used generally of relatives (Gn 13:8; 29:15; Jdg 14:3). An unlikely but possible interpretation is that a **friend** is better because he **loves at all times**, not just in difficult times.
17:19 It is necessary to step over the **threshold** to enter a house. A **high** threshold would be difficult to step over, possibly causing **injury** to guests. Or a high threshold could indicate someone who arrogantly built his house on a mound or hill above his neighbors. Such a proud person **invites** the Lord's destruction on himself (16:5).
17:21 The first kind of **fool** (Hb *kesiyl*) is immoral, obstinate, and dangerous. The second kind (Hb *nabal*) is sacrilegious.
17:22 Dried-up **bones** represent people who have lost their vitality (Ezk 37:11). The

opposite would be bones saturated with marrow or oil (Jb 21:24; Ps 109:18).
17:24 The **ends of the earth** is a place far from the chosen people of Israel, out where ungodly people are (Dt 13:7; 28:49).
17:26 The **innocent person** is literally "righteous." On **noble**, see note at 8:15-16; on **honesty**, see "upright" in note at 2:7.
17:27-28 There is an implied *a fortiori* argument here: if **even a fool** (Hb *'ewiyl*) **is considered wise when**...**silent**, how much more will an intelligent person be respected for restraint.
18:3 This is probably not teaching that a **wicked person** brings contempt, **dishonor**, and **derision** to others. Instead, society dishonors him.
18:4 This could be saying that good speech can be really **deep** and meaningful—a source of **wisdom**. Or it could mean that typical human speech is often useless (20:5),

but wisdom's **fountain** is a useful, flowing **river**.
18:5 To **show partiality** is literally to "lift the face." It may refer to a superior lifting his own face and looking on an inferior with a smile and a favorable judgment (Nm 6:26; cp. Ps 4:6), or to the inferior who had been bowed and groveling on the ground having his face or head lifted by the superior in vindication (Gn 40:13; Jb 11:15). Besides partiality, it means that the inferior "appeases" the superior (Pr 6:35) and that the superior "accepts" (Jb 42:9) or "grants the request of" the inferior (Gn 19:21; 1Sm 25:35).
18:6-7 **Lips** and **mouth** refer to what the fool says, which causes trouble, escalating from **strife** and a **beating** to **devastation** (or terror) and ultimately to death.
18:8 **Choice food** is readily and greedily swallowed. The **words** go **down** to the hearer's **innermost being** (lit "chamber of

⁹ The one who is lazy in his work
   is brother to a vandal.ᴬ

¹⁰ The name of the Lᴏʀᴅ is a strong tower;
   the righteous run to it
   and are protected.ᴮ

¹¹ The wealth of the rich is
   his fortified city;
   in his imagination it is like a high wall.

¹² Before his downfall a person's heart
   is proud,
   but humility comes before honor.

¹³ The one who gives an answer
   before he listens —
   this is foolishness and disgrace for him.

¹⁴ A person's spirit can endure sickness,
   but who can survive a broken spirit?

¹⁵ The mind of the discerning
   acquires knowledge,
   and the ear of the wise seeks it.

¹⁶ A person's gift opens doorsᶜ for him
   and brings him before the great.

¹⁷ The first to state his case seems right
   until another comes
   and cross-examines him.

¹⁸ Casting the lot ends quarrels
   and separates powerful opponents.

¹⁹ An offended brother is harder to reachᴰ
   than a fortified city,
   and quarrels are like the bars
   of a fortress.

²⁰ From the fruit of a person's mouth
   his stomach is satisfied;

he is filled with the product
   of his lips.

²¹ Death and life are in the power
   of the tongue,
   and those who love it will eat its fruit.

²² A man who finds a wife finds
   a good thing
   and obtains favor from the Lᴏʀᴅ.

²³ The poor person pleads,
   but the rich one answers roughly.

²⁴ One with many friends
   may be harmed,ᴱ
   but there is a friend who stays closer
   than a brother.

19 Better a poor person who lives
   with integrity
   than someone who has deceitful lips
   and is a fool.

² Even zeal is not good
   without knowledge,
   and the one who acts hastilyᶠ sins.

³ A person's own foolishness leads
   him astray,
   yet his heart rages against the Lᴏʀᴅ.

⁴ Wealth attracts many friends,
   but a poor person is separated
   from his friend.

⁵ A false witness will not
   go unpunished,
   and one who utters lies will not escape.

⁶ Many seek a ruler's favor,
   and everyone is a friend of one
   who gives gifts.

ᴬ18:9 Lit *master of destruction*   ᴮ18:10 Lit *raised high*   ᶜ18:16 Lit *gift makes room*   ᴰ18:19 LXX, Syr, Tg, Vg read *is stronger*   ᴱ18:24 Some LXX mss, Syr, Tg, Vg read *friends must be friendly*   ᶠ19:2 Lit *who is hasty with feet*

---

the belly") where they infect his thinking and poison his heart.
18:9 Brother implies solidarity—that he has the same characteristics (Jb 30:29) and supports the same causes (cp. "companion" in Pr 28:24). **Vandal** is literally "master of destruction" (cp. "skilled at destruction" in Ezk 21:31).
18:10–11 These two proverbs illustrate a genuine and an imaginary refuge, respectively. A **strong tower** was a central place in a region or city to which people could **run** when threatened (Jdg 9:51). The Lord's **name** implies his character as the eternal, powerful, faithful, covenant-keeping God (Ex 3:15; 6:6–7; Dt 7:9). The **righteous** people, who call on, rely upon, and have faith in the character of God, will be **protected** (lit "exalted" or lifted up so the enemy cannot reach them). A rich man relies on his **wealth** when he is threatened. To him it seems like a **high** (lit

"exalted") **wall** around a **fortified city** (cp. 10:15), but that is only **in his imagination**. In reality, wealth cannot save (11:28; cp. Jb 31:24–28; 36:18–19; Ps 49; 52:5–7; Mt 16:26; Mk 10:24–25).
18:14 Psychological or spiritual brokenness (15:13) is worse than physical **sickness**.
18:19 Metal **bars** were used to reinforce the doors of a **fortress**. It was nearly impossible to get through in order to reconcile the situation.
18:20 Satisfied and **filled** are the same word in Hebrew. The approach a person takes in his speech will return to him.
18:21 The **tongue** is powerful (Jms 3:1–12). Those who **love** the tongue and **eat its fruit** are those who choose to live or die under its **power**. Prudent speech brings **life** (v. 20; 12:14; 13:2; 21:23), and wicked or excessive speech brings **death** (13:3; Mt 15:18–19).

18:23 To plead is to appeal for mercy or cry for help (Pss 86:6; 116:1; 130:2; 140:6) or present a petition (2Ch 6:21; Dn 9:3,17). The **rich one** thinks his wealth will allow him to get away with answering **roughly** (lit "strong, fierce").
18:24 The first **friends** are neighbors or companions, who may be attracted by money (19:4). The second kind of **friend** is literally "one who loves." Jesus is such a friend to his followers (Jn 15:13–14).
19:1 On **better . . . than** proverbs, see note at 15:16–17.
19:5 On **not go unpunished**, see note at 6:27–29.
19:6 To **seek . . . favor** is literally "to make the face pleasant." It is used when an inferior is petitioning a superior, trying to get him to "smile" at him (Ex 32:11; 1Sm 13:12; Jb 11:19). This is sometimes done through **gifts** or offerings (Ps 45:12), which may degenerate

7 All the brothers of a poor person
 hate him;
how much more do his friends
 keep their distance from him!
He may pursue them with words,
 but they are not there.^A

8 The one who acquires good sense^B
 loves himself;
one who safeguards understanding
 finds success.

9 A false witness will not go unpunished,
 and one who utters lies perishes.

10 Luxury is not appropriate for a fool —
how much less for a slave to rule
 over princes!

11 A person's insight gives him patience,
 and his virtue is to overlook an offense.

12 A king's rage is like the roaring
 of a lion,
but his favor is like dew on the grass.

13 A foolish son is his father's ruin,
 and a wife's nagging is
 an endless dripping.

14 A house and wealth are inherited
 from fathers,
but a prudent wife is from the Lord.

15 Laziness induces deep sleep,
 and a lazy person will go hungry.

16 The one who keeps commands
 preserves himself;
one who disregards^C his ways will die.

17 Kindness to the poor is a loan
 to the Lord,
and he will give a reward to the lender.^D

18 Discipline your son while there is hope;
don't set your heart on being the cause
 of his death.^E

19 A person with intense anger bears
 the penalty;
if you rescue him, you'll have to do
 it again.

20 Listen to counsel
 and receive instruction
so that you may be wise later in life.^F

21 Many plans are in a person's heart,
 but the Lord's decree will prevail.

22 What is desirable in a person is
 his fidelity;
better to be a poor person than a liar.

23 The fear of the Lord leads to life;
one will sleep at night^G without danger.

24 The slacker buries his hand
 in the bowl;
he doesn't even bring it back
 to his mouth!

25 Strike a mocker, and the inexperienced
 learn a lesson;
rebuke the discerning,
 and he gains knowledge.

26 The one who plunders his father
 and evicts his mother
is a disgraceful and shameful son.

27 If you stop listening to correction,
 my son,
you will stray from the words
 of knowledge.

28 A worthless witness mocks justice,
 and a wicked mouth swallows iniquity.

^A19:7 Hb uncertain ^B19:8 Lit acquires a heart ^C19:16 Or despises, or treats lightly ^D19:17 Lit to him ^E19:18 Lit don't lift up your soul to his death ^F19:20 Lit in your end ^G19:23 Lit will spend the night satisfied

into bribery (Pr 15:27). It is better to wait on the Lord (29:26).
19:7 On **how much more**, see note at 11:31.
19:8 If a person **loves himself** (1Sm 20:17; Mt 22:39; Eph 5:29) he should be open to discipline and should listen to correction so he can acquire good sense and ultimately find **success** (lit "good"; cp. 15:32; 16:20). The alternative is to harm oneself and love death (8:36).
19:9 This is identical with 19:5 except there the liar "will not escape" and here he **perishes**, which amounts to the same thing.
19:10 On **how much less**, see note at 11:31. **Not appropriate** means "patently wrong"— not suitable or fitting, threatening to the social order (17:7; 26:1; 30:21).
19:11 Virtue is literally a "beautiful adornment," translated "glory" in 20:29.

19:13 There is an Arabic word related to the Hebrew word for **dripping** that means "a leaky roof." **Nagging** is bitter conflict and discord, strife and dissension, contention and quarreling (21:9,19; 25:24; 27:15; cp. 5:18–19).
19:14 Many things are seen as arising from human activity, but a **prudent wife** (unlike a nagging wife, v. 13) is truly a gift from God (18:22; 31:10).
19:15 In a **deep** sleep, a person is unaware of what is happening around him (Gn 2:21; 1Sm 26:12).
19:16 Keeps and **preserves** both come from the Hebrew word shamar. The **commands** are not just God's commandments, but instruction from any good source. Also, the mention of **his ways** probably does not refer directly to God's ways because God is not mentioned in context. Disregarding one's

own ways has to do with not wanting to watch carefully what one is doing, not taking responsibility—the opposite of making sure that one's ways are God's ways (8:32).
19:17 God takes care of those who care for the **poor** (14:21,31; 22:9; 28:27). The **reward** (lit "repayment") from God is not necessarily money and will not necessarily come in this life.
19:23 The second line reads literally "he will spend the night satisfied, without being visited by evil."
19:27 The Hebrew does not have **if**; instead, it is sarcastic: "**stop listening** . . . in order to stray." To **stray** is to be lost, stagger, or be misled (5:23; 20:1; 28:10; cp. "disregards his ways" in 19:16).
19:28 The meaning of **swallows iniquity** is uncertain. Perhaps the **wicked** person

²⁹ Judgments are prepared for mockers,
and beatings for the backs of fools.

20 Wine is a mocker, beer is a brawler;
whoever goes astray^A
because of them is not wise.

² A king's terrible wrath is
like the roaring of a lion;
anyone who provokes him
endangers himself.

³ Honor belongs to the person who ends
a dispute,
but any fool can get himself
into a quarrel.

⁴ The slacker does not plow
during planting season;^B
at harvest time he looks,^C and there is
nothing.

⁵ Counsel in a person's heart is
deep water;
but a person of understanding
draws it out.

⁶ Many a person proclaims
his own loyalty,
but who can find
a trustworthy person?

⁷ A righteous person acts with integrity;
his children who come after him
will be happy.

⁸ A king sitting on a throne to judge
separates out all evil with his eyes.

⁹ Who can say, "I have kept my heart pure;
I am cleansed from my sin"?

¹⁰ Differing weights
and varying measures^D —
both are detestable to the LORD.

¹¹ Even a young man is known
by his actions —
by whether his behavior is pure
and upright.

¹² The hearing ear and the seeing eye —
the LORD made them both.

¹³ Don't love sleep, or you will
become poor;
open your eyes, and you'll have
enough to eat.

¹⁴ "It's worthless, it's worthless!"
the buyer says,
but after he is on his way, he gloats.

¹⁵ There is gold and a multitude of jewels,
but knowledgeable lips are
a rare treasure.

¹⁶ Take his garment,
for he has put up security for a stranger;
get collateral if it is for foreigners.

¹⁷ Food gained by fraud is sweet
to a person,
but afterward his mouth is full of gravel.

¹⁸ Finalize plans with counsel,
and wage war with sound guidance.

¹⁹ The one who reveals secrets is
a constant gossip;
avoid someone with a big mouth.

²⁰ Whoever curses his father or mother —
his lamp will go out in deep darkness.

²¹ An inheritance gained prematurely
will not be blessed ultimately.

²² Don't say, "I will avenge this evil!"
Wait on the LORD, and he will
rescue you.

---

^A20:1 Or *whoever staggers* ^B20:4 Lit *plow in winter* ^C20:4 Lit *inquires* ^D20:10 Lit *Stone and stone, measure and measure*

considers sin a tasty morsel. Or perhaps the **worthless witness** will be forced to swallow" the consequences of his lies (19:29). **19:29** Judgment is always God's final punishment; it is never meant for correction. **Beatings** are potentially corrective, but **fools** are obstinate and do not change. **20:1** A **brawler** is loud and rowdy (7:11; 9:13). To "go astray" is literally to "wander" into something (19:27) and "get lost" in it (5:19–20,23). **20:2** The last phrase could be literally translated either "he misses (fails to hit) his life" or "he sins against himself"; the essential meaning is the same. **20:3** A wise man might end a dispute by casting lots (18:18) or getting rid of mockers (23:10). Only a fool starts a dispute (17:14). **20:4** The ground has to be plowed to prepare it for **planting**, but the **slacker** avoids work

and does not think ahead (6:6–11). **During** planting **season** is literally "from winter," that is, starting in about November. **He looks** is literally "he asks," that is, he comes to the fields to inquire about his harvest. **20:5** Water in a **deep** well is useful but difficult to draw up. **20:6** Who can find is a rhetorical question that assumes the answer, "no one." **20:8** Separates out pictures throwing grain up in the wind with a winnowing shovel so that the chaff scatters (Ru 3:2; Ps 106:27; Is 30:24; 41:16; Ezk 5:10; cp. Pr 20:26). **20:9** The word for **cleansed** is used for being ritually clean and suitable for temple worship (Nm 8:6). This rhetorical question makes the point that no human is perfect, and no human effort can remove sin (Jb 15:14; 25:4; Rm 3:23; 1Jn 1:8). Only God can

forgive sin and cleanse a person (Is 55:7; Mk 2:5–11; 1Jn 1:7). **20:13** To **become poor** is literally to "be dispossessed" (Jos 3:10), or to be deprived of possessions (Gn 45:11; Zch 9:4; cp. Pr 23:21; 30:9). **20:14** This is a humorous look at bartering, but it also shows that many people are self-idolizing liars. **He gloats** is literally "he praises himself." **20:15** These **jewels** were probably coral (Lm 4:7) or pearls (Jb 28:18). **20:20** To "curse" is literally to "declare inconsequential" or to treat with contempt (Gn 12:3; 1Sm 3:13; 2Sm 16:7). One's **lamp** going **out** is metaphorical for untimely death (13:9; 24:20; 2Sm 21:17; cp. Ex 20:12; Eph 6:2–3). **20:21** This proverb is proved true in the parable of the Lost Son (Lk 15:11–13).

23 Differing weights^A are detestable
to the LORD,
and dishonest scales are unfair.

24 Even a courageous person's steps
are determined by the LORD,
so how can anyone understand
his own way?

25 It is a trap for anyone to dedicate
something rashly
and later to reconsider his vows.

26 A wise king separates out the wicked
and drives the threshing wheel
over them.

27 The LORD's lamp sheds light on
a person's life,^B
searching the innermost parts.^C

28 Loyalty and faithfulness guard a king;
through loyalty he maintains
his throne.

29 The glory of young men is
their strength,
and the splendor of old men is gray hair.

30 Lashes and wounds purge away evil,
and beatings cleanse
the innermost parts.^D

21 A king's heart is like channeled water
in the LORD's hand:
He directs it wherever he chooses.

2 All a person's ways seem right to him,
but the LORD weighs hearts.

3 Doing what is righteous and just
is more acceptable to the LORD
than sacrifice.

4 The lamp that guides the wicked —
haughty eyes and an arrogant heart
— is sin.

5 The plans of the diligent certainly lead
to profit,
but anyone who is reckless
certainly becomes poor.

6 Making a fortune
through a lying tongue
is a vanishing mist,^E a pursuit of death.^F,G

7 The violence of the wicked
sweeps them away
because they refuse to act justly.

8 A guilty one's conduct is crooked,
but the behavior of the innocent
is upright.

9 Better to live on the corner of a roof
than to share a house
with a nagging wife.

10 A wicked person desires evil;
he has no consideration^H
for his neighbor.

11 When a mocker is punished,
the inexperienced become wiser;
when one teaches a wise man,
he acquires knowledge.

12 The Righteous One^I considers the house
of the wicked;
he brings the wicked to ruin.

13 The one who shuts his ears to the cry
of the poor
will himself also call out
and not be answered.

14 A secret gift soothes anger,
and a covert bribe, fierce rage.

15 Justice executed is a joy to the righteous
but a terror to evildoers.

16 The person who strays from the way
of prudence
will come to rest in the assembly of
the departed spirits.

17 The one who loves pleasure
will become poor;

^A20:23 Lit A stone and a stone ^B20:27 Lit breath ^C20:27 Lit the chambers of the belly ^D20:30 Lit beatings the chambers of the belly ^E21:6 Or a breath blown away ^F21:6 Some Hb mss, LXX, Vg read a snare of death ^G21:6 Lit is vanity, ones seeking death ^H21:10 Or favor ^I21:12 Or righteous one

20:26 The process of threshing actually begins with the wheel, which removes the chaff from the grain. Then the chaff is separated by throwing it up in the wind (v. 8). 20:29 Gray hair represents the achievement of honorable old age; few wicked people reach it (10:27; 16:31). 20:30 Corporal punishment, when appropriate, is effective (13:24; 22:15; 23:14). To cleanse is to remove tarnish through rubbing or scouring (Lv 6:28; Jr 46:4).

21:2 Sometimes a man is a poor judge of his own actions because, unlike God, he ignores or justifies his motives (cp. 15:11; 16:2; 17:3; 24:12). 21:4 This Hebrew word for lamp that guides could also be translated "unplowed field of." Just as an unplowed field produces weeds, haughty eyes and an arrogant heart (immodesty and lack of restraint) produce sin. In contrast, a commandment and teaching guide the righteous (6:23).

21:7 "Sweep away" can also mean "drag away" as fish are dragged in a net (Hab 1:15). 21:9 On better . . . than proverbs, see note at 15:16–17. Houses in ancient Israel had flat roofs, and it was possible to build a shelter on them (2Kg 4:10) or to sleep there in the summer (1Sm 9:25–26). Normally, however, the inside of the house was "better." 21:11 He in the second part of this verse could refer to the inexperienced, who first becomes wiser, then acquires knowledge.

Personal Finances

by Timothy D. Dockery

The Bible has much to say about money. The topic of money or wealth is addressed more than seventy times in the New Testament alone. How can a Christian living in the twenty-first century think rightly about finances using principles that were outlined in the first century or earlier? Think about all of the decisions you have made this year that were influenced by how much money you have or lack. Perhaps you chose between coffee at home versus coffee at Starbucks? Maybe you decided between tithing at church or paying off your credit card? It could be that there were days when you just wondered how to buy your next meal. The following offers a quick overview of how the Bible addresses saving money, going into debt, and giving.

To Save or Not to Save?

In Matthew 6:26–29 Jesus says,

> Consider the birds of the sky: They don't sow or reap or gather into barns, yet your heavenly Father feeds them. Aren't you worth more than they? Can any of you add one moment to his lifespan by worrying? And why do you worry about clothes? Observe how the wildflowers of the field grow: They don't labor or spin thread. Yet I tell you that not even Solomon in all his splendor was adorned like one of these.

Earlier in the same chapter Jesus says, "Don't store up for yourselves treasures on earth, where moth and rust destroy and where thieves break in and steal. But store up for yourselves treasures in heaven" (6:19–20).

These verses seem to discourage a Christian from saving money, but several verses in the Bible encourage just that. Proverbs 21:20, for instance, says, "Precious treasure and oil are in the dwelling of a wise person, but a fool consumes them." The wisdom of this advice has been proven many times over, such as when the stock market and other investments lose value quickly. During recessions many people are laid off from jobs they planned to work until retirement. The Bible advocates saving in times of plenty to prepare for times like these.

So, what is a Christian to do? Save as much as possible for tomorrow, or give everything away today and trust in the Lord for future provision? Looking at the verses cited above alone, it might seem that we are given contradictory advice. But, in fact, the Bible advocates balance.

It is wise to save money each paycheck for unexpected future expenses. It is wise to contribute to a retirement account each month, knowing a day may come when we are physically incapable of earning a wage. But it is also important not to hoard all of the money God has given us. When we are saving, we must remember that ultimately God is the provider. Remembering that God provided the money makes it easier to give it back to him through tithing or providing for someone else in need. So, save your money for a rainy day, but don't be afraid to spend it if it rains or to give it away if you see someone else struggling in a downpour.

Should a Christian Ever Have Financial Debt?

According to 2013 statistics from the Federal Reserve, the average American household has about $15,000 in credit card debt, $150,000 in mortgage debt, and $32,000 in outstanding student loans. Many Americans rely on debt to continue their current lifestyle. But debt is a burden that allows past decisions to control our current spending decisions. It can prevent one's ability to be generous. Substantial debt can even hamper your ability to respond to God's call for your vocation. Nevertheless, while the Bible discourages Christians from going into debt, it does not categorically prohibit it.

Going into debt to purchase an item is often a poor use of one's resources. Borrowing money to buy something actually makes that purchase more expensive since you have to pay for the full cost of the item and make interest payments until the debt is paid in full. For example, if you financed a $20,000 car over five years with a ten percent interest rate, it actually costs you $5,500 more than it would have if you'd paid cash. Avoiding debt is one way to do more with the resources God has entrusted to you.

Nevertheless, in the twenty-first-century economy there are situations in which one might have to use debt to purchase a home, pay for education, or pay for a health emergency. You can have debt and still be a good steward so long as you are only borrowing for a need that is manageable to repay. Throughout the Bible, Christians are encouraged to be generous, and we will be more likely to practice generosity if we have avoided entangling ourselves in debt.

How Should a Christian Think about Giving and Tithing?

In the New Testament, the overwhelming expectation with respect to money is generosity. Acts 20:35 admonishes, "In every way I've shown you that it is necessary to help the weak by laboring like this and to remember the words of the Lord Jesus, because he said, 'It is more blessed to give than to receive.'" So, how should a Christian practice tithing and generosity today?

Tithing was strictly required in Old Testament times. All the people of Israel were required to give to the temple ten percent of everything they earned or grew. Several tithes were required that would have made the total giving much higher than the traditional tithe of ten percent (Nm 18; Dt 14).

In contrast, the New Testament does not specify an exact amount or percentage a Christian should give away, but many scholars believe the minimum practice of the Old Testament sets the baseline. We are told to give generously as we are able in keeping with how we prosper (1Co 16:2). While there may not be an exact formula to tell us how to give, the admonishments to generosity are compelling. In Luke 6:30 Jesus tells us, "Give to everyone who asks you, and from someone who takes your things, don't ask for them back." In Luke 3:11 he says, "The one who has two shirts must share with someone who has none, and the one who has food must do the same."

In conclusion, God calls us to be good stewards of the financial assets he blesses us with so that we can seek his wisdom and give generously from what he has given. A Christian can practice that by avoiding debt, saving regularly, and living below his means so he always has something to give. In the end, it is the heart that matters most to God: "Each person should do as he has decided in his heart—not reluctantly or out of compulsion, since God loves a cheerful giver" (2Co 9:7).

whoever loves wine and oil will not
get rich.

¹⁸ The wicked are a ransom
for the righteous,
and the treacherous, for^A^ the upright.

¹⁹ Better to live in a wilderness
than with a nagging
and hot-tempered wife.

²⁰ Precious treasure and oil are
in the dwelling of a wise person,
but a fool consumes them.^B^

²¹ The one who pursues righteousness
and faithful love
will find life, righteousness, and honor.

²² A wise person went up against a city
of warriors
and brought down its secure fortress.

²³ The one who guards his mouth
and tongue
keeps himself out of trouble.

²⁴ The arrogant and proud person,
named "Mocker,"
acts with excessive arrogance.

²⁵ A slacker's craving will kill him
because his hands refuse to work.
²⁶ He is filled with craving^C^ all day long,
but the righteous give and don't
hold back.

²⁷ The sacrifice of a wicked person
is detestable —
how much more so
when he brings it with ulterior motives!

²⁸ A lying witness will perish,
but the one who listens
will speak successfully.

²⁹ A wicked person puts on a bold face,
but the upright one considers his way.

³⁰ No wisdom, no understanding,
and no counsel
will prevail against the LORD.

³¹ A horse is prepared for the day of battle,
but victory comes from the LORD.

22

A good name is to be chosen
over great wealth;
favor is better than silver and gold.

² Rich and poor have this in common:^D^
the LORD makes them all.

³ A sensible person sees danger
and takes cover,
but the inexperienced keep going
and are punished.

⁴ Humility, the fear of the LORD,
results in wealth, honor, and life.

⁵ There are thorns and snares on the way
of the crooked;
the one who guards himself stays
far from them.

⁶ Start a youth out on his way;
even when he grows old he will
not depart from it.

⁷ The rich rule over the poor,
and the borrower is a slave
to the lender.

---

^A^**21:18** Or *in place of*   ^B^**21:20** Lit *it*   ^C^**21:26** Lit *He craves a craving*   ^D^**22:2** Lit *poor meet*

21:17 Wine and **oil** were blessings from God (Dt 7:13; Ps 104:14–15), as was **pleasure** (lit "joy," Ps 21:6), but when God's blessings are pursued without God, they become vices. **21:18** One should not conclude from this proverb that sinners somehow pay the debt of the godly; in fact Christ, the sinless One himself, paid for the sins of all (Ps 49:7–9,15; Gl 3:13; 1Tm 2:6). While this does not explain the means of salvation, it does express the outcome: **the righteous** go free and **the treacherous** will be punished. **21:19** On **nagging . . . wife**, see note at 19:13. A **hot-tempered** person annoys others, causes grief and aggravation, and expresses displeasure (12:16; 17:25; 27:3). **21:20** To "consume" is literally to "gulp down" (1:12; 19:28). The **wise** person accumulates valuable savings but the **fool** spends his income as fast as it is produced. **21:22 Secure fortress** in this verse uses the same two Hebrew words as "strong confidence" in 14:26. However, those who trust in this mighty fortress have unfounded

confidence. A **wise** person can overcome the most formidable obstacles. **21:23** To guard one's **mouth** is the opposite of opening it (13:3). **21:24 Arrogance** is the key to the mocker's character. **21:25–26** The slacker has a selfish **craving** that is unfilled because he is too lazy; he will experience physical and spiritual death. **Righteous** people are generous yet contented (19:24). **21:27** God hates hypocrisy (15:8), but even **more so** (see note at 11:31) when there is a plan to harm others (2Sm 15:7–13; Mt 23:14). **21:28** The person who **listens** could be one who paid attention to the report of a crime so that he could give accurate second-hand testimony, or it could be the accused person who listened to a **lying witness** against him and then gave a good rebuttal. **21:29** To put on a **bold face** is to act brazenly (7:13) or arrogantly (Dn 11:12). **21:30–31 A horse** is an example of human **understanding**—military technology—that

cannot succeed apart from God's will (Pss 20:7; 33:17; Is 31:1; Jr 3:23). **22:1** A person's **name** is his character in life (21:24) and the way he is remembered after death (10:7). **Favor** is respect from people and grace from God, a benefit of wisdom (3:1–4). **22:2** To **have this in common** is literally "meet" or "intersect" (cp. 29:13). There is no class structure in God's eyes (Jb 34:19; Mt 5:45; Rm 10:12; Gl 3:28; Col 3:11). **22:3** The punishment here is literally a "fine" or "penalty" (17:26; 19:19), which implies financial consequences for remaining **inexperienced** (cp. 8:5; 9:6). **22:5** These are large **thorns**—big enough to drag prisoners with (Am 4:2; cp. Jb 5:5). **22:6 Start** is literally to "dedicate" something, such as a building—to have a celebration commemorating the first time it is put to its intended use (Dt 20:5; 1Kg 8:63). Here, the **youth** is consecrated to a life of godly wisdom (4:11). *Youth* typically refers to preteen to late-teen years. The Hebrew

8   The one who sows injustice
        will reap disaster,
    and the rod of his fury will be destroyed.

9   A generous person[A] will be blessed,
    for he shares his food with the poor.

10 Drive out a mocker, and conflict goes too;
    then quarreling and dishonor will cease.

11 The one who loves a pure heart
    and gracious lips — the king is
        his friend.

12 The LORD's eyes keep watch
        over knowledge,
    but he overthrows the words
        of the treacherous.

13 The slacker says, "There's a lion outside!
    I'll be killed in the public square!"

14 The mouth of the forbidden woman is
        a deep pit;
    a man cursed by the LORD will fall into it.

15 Foolishness is bound to the heart
        of a youth;
    a rod of discipline will separate it
        from him.

16 Oppressing the poor to enrich oneself,
    and giving to the rich — both lead
        only to poverty.

Words of the Wise

17 Listen closely,[B] pay attention
        to the words of the wise,
    and apply your mind to my knowledge.
18 For it is pleasing if you keep them
        within you
    and if they are[C] constantly on your lips.
19 I have instructed you today
        — even you —

    so that your confidence may be
        in the LORD.
20 Haven't I written for you thirty sayings[D]
    about counsel and knowledge,
21 in order to teach you true
        and reliable words,
    so that you may give
        a dependable report[E]
    to those who sent you?

22 Don't rob a poor person
        because he is poor,
    and don't crush the oppressed at
        the city gate,
23 for the LORD will champion their cause
    and will plunder those
        who plunder them.

24 Don't make friends
        with an angry person,[F]
    and don't be a companion
        of a hot-tempered one,
25 or you will learn his ways
    and entangle yourself in a snare.

26 Don't be one of those
        who enter agreements,[G]
    who put up security for loans.
27 If you have nothing with which to pay,
    even your bed will be taken
        from under you.

28 Don't move
        an ancient boundary marker
    that your ancestors set up.

29 Do you see a person skilled in his work?
    He will stand in the presence of kings.
    He will not stand in the presence
        of the unknown.

23 When you sit down to dine
        with a ruler,
    consider carefully what[H] is before you,

[A]22:9 Lit *Good of eye*   [B]22:17 Lit *Stretch out your ear*   [C]22:18 Or *you; let them be*, or *you, so that they are*   [D]22:20 Text emended; one Hb tradition reads *you previously*; alt Hb tradition reads *you excellent things*; LXX, Syr, Vg read *you three times*   [E]22:21 Lit *give dependable words*   [F]22:24 Lit *with a master of anger*   [G]22:26 Lit *Don't be among hand slappers*   [H]23:1 Or *who*

---

words translated **on his way** speak of orienting the initiation to fit the challenges of young people. Youth are known for foolishness and lack of discretion or sense (v. 15; 1:4; 7:7); left to themselves, they fall into disgrace (29:15,21). Thus, if a youth is initiated in a manner that is appropriate to his age (1:4; 23:13), it is likely to stick with him. However, this is not a promise, and it does not make the teacher responsible for the student (Ezk 18:20).
22:9 A **generous person** is literally "the good of eye"; the opposite is the "evil eye" of the "stingy" or "greedy" person (23:6; 28:22).
22:13 This is a preposterous excuse.
22:14 The **forbidden woman** lures men with her words (see note at 2:16–17; cp. 7:21;

23:27–28; Jr 18:22). To be **cursed** by God is to experience his indignation (Ezk 22:31).
22:15 Bound means both "tied to" and voluntarily "wrapped up" (Gn 44:30). **Foolishness** is an innate quality that youth cling to (Gn 8:21; Ps 51:5).
22:17–21 This passage introduces a collection of proverbs that runs through 24:22. It is also the first of the **thirty sayings**. On **words of the wise**, see note at 1:6. These sayings were also probably Solomon's (10:1). There are three motivations given for gaining wisdom, two practical and one theological: to be **pleasing**, to have **confidence . . . in the LORD**, and to be dependable when commissioned (v. 21; cp. 10:26; 25:13). **True** words promote justice. **Dependable report**

translates the same Hebrew words as **reliable words**.
22:22–23 The **city gate** was where legal proceedings took place (24:7). God is like the ultimate defense attorney (23:11; Pss 43:1; 119:154; Jr 50:34; Mc 7:9; 1Jn 2:1).
22:26–27 On **security for loans**, see note at 6:1–2.
22:28 On **boundary marker**, see 23:10–11.
22:29 To be **skilled** is to be experienced, learned, efficient, and accurate in one's vocation (Ezr 7:6; Ps 45:1; "quick" in Is 16:5). To **stand** in a ruler's **presence** is to offer oneself to be recognized or commissioned (Ex 8:20; Dt 31:14; Jb 1:6; Zch 6:5).
23:1–3 A **big appetite**, or lack of discipline, might annoy the ruler, which could be fatal

² and put a knife to your throat
   if you have a bigᴬ appetite;
³ don't desire his choice food,
   for that food is deceptive.

⁴ Don't wear yourself out to get rich;
   because you know better, stop!
⁵ As soon as your eyes fly to it,
      it disappears,
   for it makes wings for itself
   and flies like an eagle to the sky.

⁶ Don't eat a stingy person's bread,ᴮ
   and don't desire his choice food,
⁷ for it's like someone calculating
      inwardly.ᶜ
   "Eat and drink," he says to you,
   but his heart is not with you.
⁸ You will vomit the little you've eaten
   and waste your pleasant words.

⁹ Don't speak toᴰ a fool,
   for he will despise the insight
      of your words.

¹⁰ Don't move an ancient boundary marker,
   and don't encroach on the fields
      of the fatherless,
¹¹ for their Redeemer is strong,
   and he will champion their cause
      against you.

¹² Apply yourself to discipline
   and listen to words of knowledge.

¹³ Don't withhold discipline from a youth;
   if you punish him with a rod,
      he will not die.
¹⁴ Punish him with a rod,
   and you will rescue his life from Sheol.

¹⁵ My son, if your heart is wise,
   my heart will indeed rejoice.

¹⁶ My innermost being will celebrate
   when your lips say what is right.

¹⁷ Don't let your heart envy sinners;
   instead, always fear the Lᴏʀᴅ.
¹⁸ For then you will have a future,
   and your hope will not be dashed.

¹⁹ Listen, my son, and be wise;
   keep your mind on the right course.
²⁰ Don't associate with those who drink
      too much wine
   or with those who gorge themselves
      on meat.
²¹ For the drunkard and the glutton
      will become poor,
   and grogginess will clothe them in rags.

²² Listen to your father who gave you life,
   and don't despise your mother
      whenᴱ she is old.
²³ Buy — and do not sell — truth,
   wisdom, instruction,
      and understanding.
²⁴ The father of a righteous son
      will rejoice greatly,
   and one who fathers a wise son
      will delight in him.
²⁵ Let your father and mother have joy,
   and let her who gave birth to you
      rejoice.

²⁶ My son, give me your heart,
   and let your eyes observe my ways.
²⁷ For a prostitute is a deep pit,
   and a wayward woman is a narrow well;
²⁸ indeed, she sets an ambush like a robber
   and increases the number
      of unfaithful people.

²⁹ Who has woe? Who has sorrow?
   Who has conflicts?
   Who has complaints?

ᴬ23:2 Lit you are the master of an ᴮ23:6 Lit eat bread of an evil eye ᶜ23:7 LXX reads it is like someone swallowing a hair in the throat ᴰ23:9 Lit in the ears of ᴱ23:22 Or because

---

(16:14). The admonition to **put a knife to your throat** is hyperbole (Mt 18:9); it calls for total abstinence if restraint is not possible. **Choice food** is the same as the "delicious meal" that caused trouble among Jacob, Isaac, and Esau (Gn 27:4).
23:6–8 A host in ancient times was obligated to offer food and **drink** to any person who visited, but it could be done insincerely. The guest of an insincere host gains nothing: the food is lost and compliments go to **waste**.
23:10–11 Private property was marked off by pillars or cairns and was intended to be kept within a family forever (Lv 25:23–28; Nm 36:7; 1Kg 21:3). Moving a marker amounted to stealing land.
23:13–14 Corporal punishment, properly applied, will actually save a **youth** from death. He will as a rule escape physical death by avoiding dangerous situations and escape

spiritual death (symbolized by **Sheol**) by learning to fear God (19:18).
23:15–16 Innermost being is literally "kidneys" (18:8). It was seen as the seat of the strongest emotions (Ps 73:21).
23:17–18 A future is literally "what comes after."
23:19–21 To **listen** is a prerequisite; to **be wise** and have a disciplined **mind** follow. To **associate** with **the drunkard and the glutton** is to run the risk of becoming like them and sharing their fate (24:21; Jos 23:7; Ps 1:1; 26:4) or of implying approval (1Co 5:11). **Grogginess** is lack of vigilance (Ps 121:3–4; Is 5:27; 56:10).
23:22–25 To say something both positively and negatively—**buy**—**and do not sell**—is a Hebrew method of emphasis (Gn 40:23).
23:26–28 Heart and **eyes** are the key to sexual temptation; both should be given to

the instructor in godly wisdom rather than the **prostitute** (5:1–23; 6:20–7:27; 9:13–18; 22:14; 1Co 6:15–18). **Pit** and **ambush** describe the prostitute's predatory nature (7:21–23; 30:20).
23:29–35 Woe and **sorrow** are exclamations of hopelessness and despair (Is 6:5). The Hebrew behind **red eyes** is unclear; it may mean "bloodshot" or "bleary" (cp. Gn 49:12). **Wine** could be **mixed** with spices (9:2; Sg 8:2; cp. "beer" in Is 5:22). To **go looking** is to "investigate" wine by "sampling." We are called to flee tempting things (1Co 6:18; 10:14; 1Tm 6:11; 2Tm 2:22); not **gaze at** them. **Gleams** is literally "gives its eye," that is, to show luster. **In the end**, like the forbidden woman, wine destroys people (23:26–28). **Absurd** is literally "perverse" (2:12; 8:13; 10:31–32). These are the ramblings of an alcoholic who is physically and mentally out of touch.

Who has wounds for no reason?
Who has red eyes?

³⁰ Those who linger over wine;
those who go looking for mixed wine.

³¹ Don't gaze at wine because it is red,
because it gleams in the cup
and goes down smoothly.

³² In the end it bites like a snake
and stings like a viper.

³³ Your eyes will see strange things,
and you will say absurd things.[A]

³⁴ You'll be like someone sleeping
out at sea
or lying down on the top
of a ship's mast.

³⁵ "They struck me, but[B] I feel no pain!
They beat me, but I didn't know it!
When will I wake up?
I'll look for another drink."

24 Don't envy the evil
or desire to be with them,

² for their hearts plan violence,
and their words stir up trouble.

³ A house is built by wisdom,
and it is established by understanding;

⁴ by knowledge the rooms are filled
with every precious
and beautiful treasure.

⁵ A wise warrior is better
than a strong one,[C]
and a man of knowledge than one
of strength;[D]

⁶ for you should wage war
with sound guidance —
victory comes with many counselors.

⁷ Wisdom is inaccessible to[E] a fool;
he does not open his mouth
at the city gate.

⁸ The one who plots evil
will be called a schemer.

⁹ A foolish scheme is sin,
and a mocker is detestable to people.

¹⁰ If you do nothing in a difficult time,
your strength is limited.

¹¹ Rescue those being taken off to death,
and save those stumbling
toward slaughter.

¹² If you say, "But we didn't know
about this,"
won't he who weighs hearts
consider it?
Won't he who protects your life know?
Won't he repay a person according to
his work?

¹³ Eat honey, my son, for it is good,
and the honeycomb is sweet
to your palate;

¹⁴ realize that wisdom is the same for you.
If you find it, you will have a future,
and your hope will never fade.

¹⁵ Don't set an ambush, you wicked one,
at the camp of the righteous man;
don't destroy his dwelling.

¹⁶ Though a righteous person falls
seven times,
he will get up,
but the wicked will stumble into ruin.

¹⁷ Don't gloat when your enemy falls,
and don't let your heart rejoice
when he stumbles,

¹⁸ or the LORD will see, be displeased,
and turn his wrath away from him.

¹⁹ Don't be agitated by evildoers,
and don't envy the wicked.

²⁰ For the evil have no future;
the lamp of the wicked will be put out.

²¹ My son, fear the LORD, as well as
the king,
and don't associate with rebels,[F]

[A]**23:33** Or *will speak perversities*, or *inverted things*   [B]**23:35** LXX, Syr, Tg, Vg read *me," you will say, "but*   [C]**24:5** LXX, Syr; MT reads *is in strength*   [D]**24:5** LXX, Syr, Tg; MT reads *knowledge exerts strength*   [E]**24:7** Lit *is too high for*   [F]**24:21** Or *those given to change*

24:1–2 This warning is similar to that in 23:17–18. Involvement in **violence** and **trouble** will lead to a person's downfall.
24:3–4 Just as God established the world through **wisdom . . . understanding**, and **knowledge** (3:19–20), so a **house is established** by the same. **Treasure** represents both material and spiritual blessings. Sinners also hope to fill their houses, but their methods are self-destructive (1:13,18).
24:5–6 Verse 5 is difficult to translate; the second line might read, "**a man of knowledge** increases **strength**." In any case, wisdom and **sound guidance** are the keys to success in any situation.
24:7 Important and knowledgeable people oversaw legal and commercial business at

the **city gate** (1:21; 22:22; 31:23; Dt 21:19; Jos 20:4; Ru 4:1; 2Sm 15:2).
24:8–9 What a person is **called** is his reputation (16:21; 21:24), which is difficult to overcome. A **scheme** is a shameful, depraved act (Lv 18:17).
24:10–12 To **do nothing** is literally to go slack. A **difficult time** is literally a "time of restriction." To be **limited** is literally to be "restricted." So to avoid losing **strength**, act. **Death** could be physical or spiritual death or any other misfortune, whether they are **being taken off** by others or they are **stumbling** toward disaster on their own (Ps 82:4; Is 58:6–7). Those who are not on the way of wisdom are on a path to disaster and need to be saved (Pr 10:17; 12:28; 14:12; 15:24). To

deny knowledge and responsibility is futile because God **weighs hearts** (21:12; Ps 44:21). Inactivity is complicity (Ezk 3:17–18). God can withdraw his protection to **repay a person** for his sin.
24:13–14 Wisdom, like **honey**, is beneficial as well as pleasant (16:24; but see 25:16,27). On **future**, see note at 23:17–18.
24:15–16 Seven is the number of completion (6:31; 9:1; 26:16,25; Mt 18:21). If the **righteous person** falls until he is utterly down, maybe even dead, he will still **get up**. Into ruin could also be translated "by means of evil." **24:21–22** God and the king are the **two** who **bring** so much **distress** on evildoers that no one **knows** (cp. Ec 3:21; 6:12; 8:1) its potential magnitude.

²² for destruction will come suddenly
        from them;
    who knows what distress these two
        can bring?

²³ These sayings also
        belong to the wise:

    It is not good to show partiality
        in judgment.
²⁴ Whoever says to the guilty,
        "You are innocent" —
    peoples will curse him, and nations
        will denounce him;
²⁵ but it will go well with those
        who convict the guilty,
    and a generous blessing will come
        to them.

²⁶ He who gives an honest answer
    gives a kiss on the lips.

²⁷ Complete your outdoor work,
        and prepare your field;
    afterward, build your house.

²⁸ Don't testify against your neighbor
        without cause.
    Don't deceive with your lips.
²⁹ Don't say, "I'll do to him what he did
        to me;
    I'll repay the man for what
        he has done."

³⁰ I went by the field of a slacker
    and by the vineyard of one
        lacking sense.
³¹ Thistles had come up everywhere,
    weeds covered the ground,
    and the stone wall was ruined.
³² I saw, and took it to heart;
    I looked, and received instruction:
³³ a little sleep, a little slumber,
    a little folding of the arms to rest,

³⁴ and your poverty will come
        like a robber,
    and your need, like a bandit.

Hezekiah's Collection

25 These too are proverbs of Solomon,
    which the men of King Hezekiah
    of Judah copied.

² It is the glory of God to conceal a matter
    and the glory of kings to investigate
        a matter.
³ As the heavens are high and the earth
        is deep,
    so the hearts of kings cannot
        be investigated.

⁴ Remove impurities from silver,
    and material will be produced^A
        for a silversmith.^B
⁵ Remove the wicked
        from the king's presence,
    and his throne will be established
        in righteousness.

⁶ Don't boast about yourself
        before the king,
    and don't stand in the place of the great;
⁷ for it is better for him to say to you,
        "Come up here!"
    than to demote you in plain view
        of a noble.^C

⁸ Don't take a matter to court hastily.
    Otherwise, what will you do afterward
        if your opponent^D humiliates you?
⁹ Make your case with your opponent
        without revealing another's secret;
¹⁰ otherwise, the one who hears
        will disgrace you,
    and you'll never live it down.^E

¹¹ A word spoken at the right time
    is like gold apples in silver settings.

---

^A25:4 Lit *will come out*; Ex 32:24 ^B25:4 Or *and a vessel will be produced by a silversmith* ^C25:7 Lit *you before a noble whom your eyes see* ^D25:8 Or *neighbor*, also in v. 9 ^E25:10 Lit *and your evil report will not turn back*

24:23–34 These are miscellaneous **sayings** collected by Solomon (10:1) beyond the "thirty" (22:20).
24:23–25 To **show partiality** is literally "to take notice of a face" (28:21; Dt 16:19)—to treat people differently based on their status or position. That the phrase **blessing will come** is in the passive voice implies that the blessing comes from God.
24:26 A **kiss** symbolizes loyal love and solidarity in a family (Gn 33:4; 45:15) or among very close friends (1Sm 20:41). "Honesty" also demonstrates love.
24:27 A young man should first establish his means of income. Besides the structure, to **build a house** could include marrying, having children, and hiring servants (v. 3; 14:1).
24:28–29 To **testify . . . without cause** might be to volunteer to give testimony

without being called and without being an eyewitness.
24:30–34 Elsewhere **thistles** (Is 34:13; Hs 9:6) and **weeds** (Zph 2:9) are symbolic of God's judgment.
25:1 The **proverbs** in chaps. 25–29 were collected by **the men of King Hezekiah** (cp. 1:1; 10:1; 22:17; 24:23), who was a godly king until late in his life (2Kg 18–20).
25:4–5 The **impurities** or dross had to be removed in a crucible (17:3; 27:21) to provide the **silversmith** pure **silver** adequate for making something useful. The people in **the king's presence** are his servants, officials, and advisers. For a **throne to be established** suggests at least uncontested rule, and possibly a dynasty.
25:6–7 Prideful self-promotion is not wise (11:2; 29:23; Rm 12:3). There may have been

a specified order in which the officials were supposed to stand **before the king**; to **stand** in someone else's **place** would be pretentious. It is possible that the last few words (translated **in plain view**) go with the next verse, which means: "That which your eyes have seen, do not be hasty to take to court."
25:8–10 Frivolous litigation and divulging confidences will ruin one's reputation. **You'll never live it down** is literally "a bad report will not return"—that is, the person who disgraces you will not have to eat his words.
25:11–12 These decorative **apples** (or apricots; Sg 2:3,5; 7:8; 8:5) are not just golden in color, but are apparently made of **gold**. They could be spheres set on a tray or images inlaid into it.

¹² A wise correction to a receptive ear
   is like a gold ring or an ornament
      of gold.

¹³ To those who send him,
   a trustworthy envoy
   is like the coolness of snow
      on a harvest day;
   he refreshes the life of his masters.

¹⁴ The one who boasts about a gift
      that does not exist
   is like clouds and wind without rain.

¹⁵ A ruler can be persuaded
      through patience,
   and a gentle tongue can break a bone.

¹⁶ If you find honey, eat only
      what you need;
   otherwise, you'll get sick from it
      and vomit.

¹⁷ Seldom set foot
      in your neighbor's house;
   otherwise, he'll get sick of you
      and hate you.

¹⁸ A person giving false testimony
      against his neighbor
   is like a club, a sword, or a sharp arrow.

¹⁹ Trusting an unreliable person in a
      difficult time
   is like a rotten tooth or a faltering foot.

²⁰ Singing songs to a troubled heart
   is like taking off clothing on a cold day
   or like pouring vinegar on soda.ᴬ

²¹ If your enemy is hungry, give him food
      to eat,
   and if he is thirsty, give him water
      to drink,

²² for you will heap burning coals
      on his head,
   and the LORD will reward you.

²³ The north wind produces rain,
   and a backbiting tongue, angry looks.

²⁴ Better to live on the corner of a roof
   than to share a house
      with a nagging wife.

²⁵ Good news from a distant land
   is like cold water to a parched throat.ᴮ

²⁶ A righteous person who yields
      to the wicked
   is like a muddied spring
      or a polluted well.

²⁷ It is not good to eat too much honey
   or to seek glory after glory.ᶜ

²⁸ A person who does not control
      his temper
   is like a city whose wall is broken down.

26 Like snow in summer and rain
      at harvest,
   honor is inappropriate for a fool.

² Like a flitting sparrow
      or a fluttering swallow,
   an undeserved curse goes nowhere.

³ A whip for the horse, a bridle
      for the donkey,
   and a rod for the backs of fools.

⁴ Don't answer a fool according to
      his foolishness
   or you'll be like him yourself.

⁵ Answer a fool according to
      his foolishness
   or he'll become wise in his own eyes.

⁶ The one who sends a message
      by a fool's hand
   cuts off his own feet
      and drinks violence.

ᴬ**25:20** Lit *natron, or sodium carbonate*   ᴮ**25:25** Or *a weary person*   ᶜ**25:27** Lit *seek their glory, glory*

25:13 Harvest time could be dangerously hot (2Kg 4:18–20). For **snow** to fall at harvest could be disastrous, but the wealthy sometimes had it carried down from the mountains for refreshment.
25:14 Most **rain** in Palestine comes during windy thunderstorms.
25:15 A **bone** is the hardest part of a person; here it represents strong resistance to persuasion.
25:16–17 Too much of a good thing (v. 27; 16:24; 24:13) is bad, so even a good guest should exercise moderation. **Seldom set foot** is literally "make your foot precious (on account of its rarity)" (3:15; 20:15).
25:18 Perjury against a **neighbor** is as devastating as beating him to death with a **club**, or opening him up with a **sword**, or piercing him through the heart with an **arrow**.
25:19 Unreliable is literally "treacherous" (2:22; cp. 20:6).

25:20 Here are some actions that make things worse. Cheery **songs** can make a **troubled** person worse (Ec 3:4; Rm 12:15; but see 1Sm 16:14–16). **Pouring vinegar on soda** makes the vinegar foam; it also neutralizes both and makes them worthless. The word translated "soda" could also be "a deep wound"; pouring vinegar on it would bring suffering with no benefit.
25:21–22 To **heap . . . coals on his head** does not imply vengeance because God does not **reward** vengeance (20:22; Lv 19:18; Rm 12:17–20). Rather, it may refer to the shame an enemy feels when his assaults are met with good deeds.
25:23 In Palestine rain actually comes from the west (1Kg 18:44; Lk 12:54). **North** may suggest the cold wind that accompanies **rain**. Also, "north" comes from a word that means "hidden," which is a pun on **backbiting** (lit "secret"). The second

half is ambiguous in Hebrew and could be reversed: "and angry looks, a backbiting tongue."
25:24 On **nagging wife**, see note at 19:13.
25:27 The second line is difficult. It could mean, "and to investigate matters that are too weighty is not honorable" (cp. vv. 2–3 Ps 131).
26:1–12 The word **fool** (Hb *kesiyl*) occurs in every verse in this section except v. 2.
26:1 Snow in summer and rain at harvest would not only be unusual; they could be catastrophic, destroying the crops and endangering society.
26:4–5 A person should not **answer a fool** by resorting to foolish methods. Yet, someone needs to expose his **foolishness**, ever if he will not listen (23:9).
26:6 To trust a fool as a messenger is as self-destructive as self-mutilation or taking poison (1:19).

7 A proverb in the mouth of a fool
   is like lame legs that hang limp.

8 Giving honor to a fool
   is like binding a stone in a sling.

9 A proverb in the mouth of a fool
   is like a stick with thorns,
   brandished by^A the hand of a drunkard.

10 The one who hires a fool or who hires
      those passing by
   is like an archer who wounds everyone
      indiscriminately.

11 As a dog returns to its vomit,
   so also a fool repeats his foolishness.

12 Do you see a person who is wise
      in his own eyes?
   There is more hope for a fool
      than for him.

13 The slacker says, "There's a lion
      in the road —
   a lion in the public square!"

14 A door turns on its hinges,
   and a slacker, on his bed.

15 The slacker buries his hand in the bowl;
   he is too weary to bring it to his mouth!

16 In his own eyes, a slacker is wiser
   than seven who can answer sensibly.

17 A person who is passing by and
      meddles in a quarrel that's not his
   is like one who grabs a dog by the ears.

18 Like a madman who throws
      flaming darts and deadly arrows,

19 so is the person who deceives
      his neighbor
   and says, "I was only joking!"

20 Without wood, fire goes out;
   without a gossip, conflict dies down.

21 As charcoal for embers and wood for fire,
   so is a quarrelsome person
      for kindling strife.

22 A gossip's words are like choice food
   that goes down to
      one's innermost being.^B

23 Smooth^C lips with an evil heart
   are like glaze on an earthen vessel.

24 A hateful person disguises himself
      with his speech
   and harbors deceit within.

25 When he speaks graciously,
      don't believe him,
   for there are seven detestable things
      in his heart.

26 Though his hatred is concealed
      by deception,
   his evil will be revealed in the assembly.

27 The one who digs a pit will fall into it,
   and whoever rolls a stone —
   it will come back on him.

28 A lying tongue hates those it crushes,
   and a flattering mouth causes ruin.

27 Don't boast about tomorrow,
   for you don't know what a day
      might bring.

2 Let another praise you, and not
      your own mouth —
   a stranger, and not your own lips.

3 A stone is heavy, and sand a burden,
   but aggravation from a fool
      outweighs them both.

4 Fury is cruel, and anger a flood,
   but who can withstand jealousy?

5 Better an open reprimand
   than concealed love.

6 The wounds of a friend are trustworthy,
   but the kisses of an enemy are excessive.

---

^A26:9 Lit *thorn that goes up into*   ^B26:22 Lit *to the chambers of the belly*   ^C26:23 LXX; MT reads *Burning*

26:7 A **lame** person has **legs** but cannot use them.
26:8 A **sling** was a leather strap with a pouch in the middle. A **stone** would be placed in the pouch, then the slinger held both ends of the strap and swung it over his head two or three times. When he let go of one strap, the stone would be released. It would be ridiculous to tie the stone in the pouch. The weapon would be useless, and it could hurt the slinger.
26:9 A **fool** would give a **proverb** a wrong application, causing chaos and destruction, like a belligerent **drunkard** swinging a thorny **stick**.
26:10 The Hebrew here was difficult to understand before scholars discovered that *rav* could mean **archer** (Jb 16:13; Jr 50:29) as well as "great." Hiring a **fool** or someone at random is as harmful to society as a berserk shooter (v. 18; cp. the English idiom "loose cannon").
26:14 This is a sarcastic image of the only "work" a **slacker** does. An ancient hinge

was a hole in the threshold on which the door pivoted.
26:15 In ancient times, food was eaten by hand from a communal dish. The **slacker** does not have the gumption to **bring** food **to his mouth**, which has physical consequences (6:9–11; 20:4; 21:25; cp. 19:15).
26:16 A sensible **answer** implies discernment. **Seven** suggests this is a complete group of counselors (Ezr 7:14).
26:17 **Meddles in** could be translated as "is provoked by" (20:2). Alternatively, it could be the **dog** that **is passing by**, i.e., a stray. Therefore, this could be translated, "One who gets riled up by a quarrel that is not his is like one who grabs a stray dog by the ears." The point is the same.
26:18–19 A liar who calls himself a jester if he gets caught is as dangerous to society as a berserk warrior (v. 10).
26:21 A **quarrelsome person** is a man whose speech stirs up conflict (cp. Jr 15:10).
26:22 On **choice food**, see note at 18:8.

26:23–28 Though vv. 23,27–28 could each stand as independent proverbs, with 24–26 they develop a single theme. The Hebrew *keseph siygiym* ("silver dross"; cp. 25:4) has been emended to *kesaphsagiym* (**glaze**). Silver dross—lead monoxide—was also used as a glaze on pottery, so the point is the same. A flatterer with evil intentions appears nice, but it is an artificial veneer, a pretense. Though a **hateful person disguises himself**, the wise person perceives that his **heart** is detestable. His driving force is **hatred**, the wicked person's passion to destroy anything good and godly. The person who hates will eventually be **revealed** publicly (5:14), and he will suffer the fate he wished on others (Ps 7:15–16; 9:15–16). The last line is ambiguous—the liar seeks the **ruin** of the godly, but he causes his own ruin.
27:1 See Jms 4:13–16.
27:6 **A friend** imparts constructive criticism out of love, but an enemy gives **kisses** (24:26) with deceit in mind.

⁷ A person who is full tramples
　　on a honeycomb,
　but to a hungry person, any bitter thing
　　is sweet.

⁸ Anyone wandering from his home
　is like a bird wandering from its nest.

⁹ Oil and incense bring joy to the heart,
　and the sweetness of a friend is better
　　than self-counsel.ᴬ

¹⁰ Don't abandon your friend
　　or your father's friend,
　and don't go to your brother's house
　　in your time of calamity;
　better a neighbor nearby than a brother
　　far away.

¹¹ Be wise, my son, and bring
　　my heart joy,
　so that I can answer anyone
　　who taunts me.

¹² A sensible person sees danger
　　and takes cover;
　the inexperienced keep going
　　and are punished.

¹³ Take his garment,
　　for he has put up security
　　　for a stranger;
　get collateral if it is for foreigners.ᴮ

¹⁴ If one blesses his neighbor
　　with a loud voice early in the morning,
　it will be counted as a curse to him.

¹⁵ An endless dripping on a rainy day
　　and a nagging wife are alike;
¹⁶ the one who controls her controls
　　the wind
　and grasps oil with his right hand.

¹⁷ Iron sharpens iron,
　and one person sharpens another.ᶜ

¹⁸ Whoever tends a fig tree will eat
　　its fruit,
　and whoever looks after his master
　　will be honored.

¹⁹ As water reflects the face,
　so the heart reflects the person.

²⁰ Sheol and Abaddon are never satisfied,
　and people's eyes are never satisfied.

²¹ As a crucible refines silver,
　　and a smelter refines gold,
　so a person should refine his praise.

²² Though you grind a fool
　　in a mortar with a pestle
　　　along with grain,
　you will not separate his foolishness
　　from him.

²³ Know well the condition of your flock,
　　and pay attention to your herds,
²⁴ for wealth is not forever;
　not even a crown lasts for all time.
²⁵ When hay is removed
　　and new growth appears
　and the grain from the hills
　　is gathered in,
²⁶ lambs will provide your clothing,
　　and goats, the price of a field;
²⁷ there will be enough goat's milk
　　for your food —
　food for your household
　and nourishment for your
　　female servants.

28

²⁸ The wicked flee when no one
　　is pursuing them,
　but the righteous are as bold as a lion.

ᴬ27:9 LXX reads *heart, but the soul is torn up by affliction*　ᴮ27:13 Lit *a foreign woman*　ᶜ27:17 Lit *and a man sharpens his friend's face*

27:9 Being anointed with **oil** and enjoying **incense** were ancient pleasures. The second line could be saying that the **sweetness of a friend** comes from sincere counsel.
27:10 On **better . . . than** proverbs, see note at 15:16–17. Long-term friendships are at times more dependable than blood relations (17:17; 18:24).
27:14 There are two possible interpretations: For someone who is not a morning person, a **loud** greeting **early in the morning** will be annoying. Or, a person who rushes over to shout a blessing is probably insincere, and God will **curse** a hypocrite.
27:19 The **heart** is like a mirror that shows true character (see 4:23).
27:20 **Sheol** and **Abaddon** represent death, which can always take more victims (30:16). **People's eyes** represent their insatiable capacity for lust, envy, and greed (30:15).

27:21 **Praise** here could mean the praise a person receives or the praise he gives. This proverb has several possible meanings. As **a crucible refines silver . . . a person** should evaluate the praise he receives before he accepts it, dismissing flattery and insincerity. If you wonder about the praise a person receives or gives, look to the person; his character will show whether it is genuine. Over time, a person can refine the praise he receives or gives. The Hebrew could also be translated, "and a man according to his praise." That is, a man is tested (17:3) and proven by what kind of praise he receives and how graciously he receives it.
27:22 A **mortar** was a bowl made of fired clay or carved from stone. A **pestle** was a stone or fired-clay rod with a rounded tip. The worker would put a small amount of **grain** (hulled barley, in this case) into the

mortar and pound and **grind** it until it became meal or flour. **Foolishness** taints every molecule of a **fool**.
27:23–27 Just as a farmer cares for his livestock, Solomon here instructed his son the prince to **pay attention** to his people. While **wealth** is fickle (23:4–5) and a dynasty can end, flocks and crops (people and land) are a steady source of sustenance if they are well maintained (24:27). After **hay** was harvested, **new** grass appeared for grazing. Later, **grain** was harvested, which along with the hay, provided feed for livestock. **Lambs** provided wool. Females were kept for breeding and **milk**, while some male **goats** were sold for income that could be reinvested. All people in positions of leadership should be good stewards of their human and material resources.

² When a land is in rebellion, it has
      many rulers,
  but with a discerning
      and knowledgeable person,
      it endures.

³ A destitute leaderᴬ who oppresses
      the poor
  is like a driving rain that leaves no food.

⁴ Those who reject the law
      praise the wicked,
  but those who keep the law pit
      themselves against them.

⁵ The evil do not understand justice,
  but those who seek the Lᴏʀᴅ
      understand everything.

⁶ Better the poor person who lives
      with integrity
  than the rich one who distorts right
      and wrong.ᴮ

⁷ A discerning son keeps the law,
  but a companion of gluttons humiliates
      his father.

⁸ Whoever increases his wealth
      through excessive interest
  collects it for one who is kind
      to the poor.

⁹ Anyone who turns his ear
      away from hearing the law —
  even his prayer is detestable.

¹⁰ The one who leads the upright
       into an evil way
   will fall into his own pit,
   but the blameless will inherit
       what is good.

¹¹ A rich person is wise in his own eyes,
   but a poor one who has discernment
       sees through him.

¹² When the righteous triumph,
   there is great rejoicing,ᶜ
   but when the wicked come
       to power,
   people hide.

¹³ The one who conceals his sins
   will not prosper,
   but whoever confesses
       and renounces them
   will find mercy.

¹⁴ Happy is the one who is always
       reverent,
   but one who hardens his heart falls
       into trouble.

¹⁵ A wicked ruler over
       a helpless people
   is like a roaring lion
       or a charging bear.

¹⁶ A leader who lacks understanding
   is very oppressive,
   but one who hates dishonest profit
   prolongs his life.

¹⁷ Someone burdened by bloodguiltᴰ
   will be a fugitive until death.
   Let no one help him.

¹⁸ The one who lives with integrity
       will be helped,
   but one who distorts right
       and wrongᴱ
   will suddenly fall.

¹⁹ The one who works his land
   will have plenty of food,
   but whoever chases fantasies
   will have his fill of poverty.

²⁰ A faithful person will have
       many blessings,
   but one in a hurry to get rich
   will not go unpunished.

ᴬ28:3 LXX reads *A wicked man*   ᴮ28:6 Lit *who twists two ways*   ᶜ28:12 Lit *glory*   ᴰ28:17 Lit *the blood of a person*   ᴱ28:18 Lit
who is twisted regarding two ways

28:2 The last phrase could also be translated, "right **endures**."
28:3 A hard **rain** at the wrong time could sweep away (Jr 46:15) a crop.
28:4 One's attitude toward God's instruction determines one's attitude toward **the wicked**. Either one loves God's instruction and wages war against wickedness or one hates God's instruction and praises wickedness. There is no middle position.
28:5 To **seek the Lᴏʀᴅ** can mean to consult him for wisdom and knowledge (Ex 33:7; 2Sm 21:1) or to pursue a relationship with him (Dt 4:29; Ps 27:4; Zph 2:3).
28:6 On **better . . . than** proverbs, see note at 15:16–17.

28:8 In this life or in eternity, God will punish those who exploit **the poor** and will reward those who help them.
28:9 To reject God's **law** implies lack of trust, which precludes prayer (1:23–31; Heb 11:6).
28:12 To see the end of the matter, read this verse along with v. 28 and 29:2,16. Under **righteous** leadership there is a public celebration of "glory" or "beauty" (4:9; 15:31; 17:6; 20:29). Under **wicked** leaders, literally "a man is sought."
28:13 It is a good thing to conceal others' **sins** (17:9), but not one's own. To confess and renounce sins is the definition of repentance. The person who finds **mercy** will prosper in the ultimate sense in eternity.
28:14 The Hebrew word for **reverent** usually refers to terror (1:26–27), but in this context

it is synonymous with the fear of the Lord. To have a hard **heart** is to refuse to turn and obey God (Ex 7:3; Ezk 3:7).
28:15 A **wicked ruler** is destructive out of anger (19:12; 20:2).
28:16 **Very oppressive** is literally "much extortion" (Is 33:15).
28:17 **Until death** is literally "to the Pit" (1:12). The innocent should be rescued from death (24:11), but not those guilty of shedding innocent blood (Dt 19:11–13).
28:19 **Have plenty** and **have his fill** translate the same Hebrew word (18:20).
28:20 It is implied that the person **in a hurry to get rich** is willing to use illegal or immoral means. On **not go unpunished**, see note at 6:27–29.

21 It is not good to show partiality —
   yet even a courageous person may sin
      for a piece of bread.

22 A greedy one[A] is in a hurry for wealth;
   he doesn't know that poverty will come
      to him.

23 One who rebukes a person will later find
      more favor
   than one who flatters with his tongue.

24 The one who robs his father
      or mother
   and says, "That's no sin,"
   is a companion to a person
      who destroys.

25 A greedy person stirs up conflict,
   but whoever trusts in the LORD
      will prosper.

26 The one who trusts in himself[B] is
      a fool,
   but one who walks in wisdom
      will be safe.

27 The one who gives to the poor
   will not be in need,
   but one who turns his eyes away[C]
   will receive many curses.

28 When the wicked come to power,
   people hide,
   but when they are destroyed,
   the righteous flourish.

29 One who becomes stiff-necked,
   after many reprimands
   will be shattered instantly —
   beyond recovery.

2 When the righteous flourish,
      the people rejoice,
   but when the wicked rule, people groan.

3 A man who loves wisdom brings joy
      to his father,
   but one who consorts with prostitutes
      destroys his wealth.

4 By justice a king brings stability
      to a land,
   but a person who demands
      "contributions"[D]
   demolishes it.

5 A person who flatters his neighbor
   spreads a net for his feet.

6 An evil person is caught by sin,
   but the righteous one sings
      and rejoices.

7 The righteous person knows the rights[E]
      of the poor,
   but the wicked one does not understand
      these concerns.

8 Mockers inflame a city,
   but the wise turn away anger.

9 If a wise person goes to court
      with a fool,
   there will be ranting and raving
      but no resolution.[F]

10 Bloodthirsty men hate
      an honest person,
   but the upright care about him.[G]

11 A fool gives full vent to his anger,[H]
   but a wise person holds it in check.

[A]28:22 Lit *A man with an evil eye* [B]28:26 Lit *his heart* [C]28:27 Lit *who shuts his eyes* [D]29:4 The Hb word for *contributions* usually refers to offerings in worship. [E]29:7 Lit *justice* [F]29:9 Lit *rest* [G]29:10 Or *person, and seek the life of the upright* [H]29:11 Lit *spirit*

28:21 An unjust judge may eventually give in to small bribes (24:23; Dt 16:19).
28:22 On **in a hurry for wealth**, see notes at vv. 19,20.
28:23 One exception to this is rebuking a mocker (9:7).
28:24 Refusing to call a **sin** a sin **destroys** society. It is sinful to justify stealing money from one's parents (Mt 15:5–6; cp. Pr 20:21; Lk 15:12). A person is known by what kind of companions he has (Ps 1:1; 119:63; Pr 4:14; Jr 15:17).
28:25 **Greedy** is literally "enlarged throat" (Is 5:14) or appetite (Hab 2:5). To **prosper** is literally to "be fat" (15:30). On the benefit of trusting, cp. 16:20; 29:25.
28:26 **Be safe** is literally "escape (judgment)" (19:5, cp. 19:9). This implies the **fool** will perish (1:32) because the object of his trust cannot save him (11:28).
28:27 Generosity results in blessings, not **curses** (22:9; cp. 21:13).

28:28 To **flourish** is to increase in number and power (29:16).
29:1 At the end of God's patient call to obedience comes sudden judgment against the obstinate (2Kg 17:13–14,18; 2Ch 36:16; Neh 9:29–30; Jr 7:2–29; Ac 7:51; 2Pt 3:9–10).
29:2 **People groan** when oppressed (Ex 2:23) or devastated (Lm 1:4,8,11,21).
29:3 This could refer to the father's or the man's **wealth**. Since a father is responsible for a son's debts, and a son hopes for an inheritance, the outcome is the same.
29:4 The Hebrew in the second line could refer to one who **demands** or who gives bribes, either of which subverts justice.
29:5 His **feet** could be the neighbor's or the speaker's own feet (see v. 6; cp. 26:28).
29:6 The first line is literally "In the rebellion of a person of evil [is] a snare." Sin contains the seeds of self-destruction (1:19), but the **righteous** person **rejoices** in security.

29:7 The **rights** refers to a legal decision (Ezr 7:26; Dn 7:22).
29:8 The **wise** encourage peace by their concern for justice and for the well-being of others and by their speech full of truth and grace.
29:9 **Ranting and raving** is literally "shakes (in rage; Jb 39:24) and laughs" (Pr 26:19).
29:10 The second line is difficult to translate (cp. 11:30). It is literally "and the upright ones, they seek his life." Do **bloodthirsty men** seek to kill **the upright**? The phrase *seek his life* almost always means "try to kill," but "upright" is plural and "his life" is singular. Or do the upright seek to take care of the **honest person**? That fits best with the rest of Proverbs, and *seek* can mean to "demand justice" ("require" in 2Sm 4:11).
29:11 The last line is literally "but the wise one, in the end, stills it." This could mean that a **wise person** eventually quiets the fool's ranting (26:5; cp. 29:9).

803

Proverbs 30:3

¹² If a ruler listens to lies,
all his officials will be wicked.

¹³ The poor and the oppressor have this
in common:^A
the LORD gives light to the eyes of both.

¹⁴ A king who judges the poor
with fairness —
his throne will be established forever.

¹⁵ A rod of correction imparts wisdom,
but a youth left to himself^B
is a disgrace to his mother.

¹⁶ When the wicked increase,
rebellion increases,
but the righteous will see
their downfall.

¹⁷ Discipline your child, and it will bring
you peace of mind
and give you delight.

¹⁸ Without revelation^C people run wild,
but one who follows divine instruction
will be happy.

¹⁹ A servant cannot be disciplined by words;
though he understands,
he doesn't respond.

²⁰ Do you see someone who speaks
too soon?
There is more hope for a fool
than for him.

²¹ A servant pampered from his youth
will become arrogant^D later on.

²² An angry person stirs up conflict,
and a hot-tempered one^E
increases rebellion.

²³ A person's pride will humble him,
but a humble spirit will gain honor.

²⁴ To be a thief's partner is
to hate oneself;
he hears the curse but
will not testify.

²⁵ The fear of mankind is a snare,
but the one who trusts in the LORD
is protected.^F

²⁶ Many desire a ruler's favor,
but a person receives justice
from the LORD.

²⁷ An unjust person is detestable
to the righteous,
and one whose way is upright
is detestable to the wicked.

The Words of Agur

30 The words of Agur son of Jakeh.
The pronouncement.^G

The man's oration to Ithiel, to Ithiel
and Ucal:^H

² I am more stupid than
any other person,^I
and I lack a human's ability
to understand.

³ I have not gained wisdom,
and I have no knowledge
of the Holy One.

---

^A29:13 Lit *oppressor meet* ^B29:15 Lit *youth sent away* ^C29:18 Lit *vision* ^D29:21 Hb obscure ^E29:22 Lit *a master of rage* ^F29:25 Lit *raised high* ^G30:1 Or *son of Jakeh from Massa*; Pr 31:1 ^H30:1 Hb uncertain. Sometimes read with different word division as *oration: I am weary, God, I am weary, God, and I am exhausted*, or *oration: I am not God, I am not God, that I should prevail*. LXX reads *My son, fear my words and when you have received them repent. The man says these things to the believers in God, and I pause.* ^I30:2 Lit *I am more stupid than a man*

29:12 A **ruler** who likes to hear **lies** will end up accumulating **wicked** attendants.

29:13 Light to the eyes means life. **The LORD** determines the outcome of both lives.

29:17 Peace of mind means being free from emotional and physical threats (Jb 3:26; Ps 116:7; Is 14:3,7). A wise **child** provides necessities as well as **delight** (Gn 49:20; Lm 4:5).

29:18 Revelation, like instruction, probably refers to the inspired wisdom in Proverbs. True happiness is found within God's plan.

29:19 A foolish **servant** only responds to corporal punishment.

29:20 A **fool** is less likely to get into trouble if he is not one who speaks rashly (18:7; 20:25).

29:21 A **servant**, like any other person, needs to be prepared during **his youth** to fulfill his life's responsibilities (22:6).

29:22 The proverb is similar to 15:18 (see also 22:24). The hothead's resentment causes him to seek a pretext to escalate every difference into a fight. He is ruled by his passions.

29:23 Pride comes from a root that means exaltation, being high, while **humble** means being low. The proud person denies dependence on God and resents submission to God's plans.

29:24 Associating with the wicked is self-destructive (1:19; 24:21–22). In an unsolved case, the legal system would announce a **curse** on the perpetrator and any accomplices (Lv 5:1). If witnesses came forward or the thief turned himself in, they could be exonerated (Jdg 17:2). But God's curse would be on this **partner** if he refused to testify against the thief (Zch 5:3–4; cp. Nm 5:21).

29:25 A **snare** can be fatal (13:14; 14:27; 18:7). **Fear** is literally "sheer terror" (1Sm 14:15; Is 21:4; Dn 10:7). A wise person does not fear mortal man. The only One to fear is **the LORD**, who is able to protect or destroy (18:10; Lk 12:4–5).

29:26 Many try to sway a ruler, but the fact that he might be swayed makes him a less reliable judge than **the LORD** (19:6; cp. 16:10,12).

29:27 To detest an **unjust person** is to agree with God (3:32; 11:1; 12:22; 15:8–9,26; 16:5,12; 17:15; 20:10,23; 21:27; 28:9; Ps 139:21–22; 2Co 6:14–16), but hating the **upright** is wrong (v. 10; Ps 69:4; Mt 10:22; 24:9; Jn 15:18; 17:14; 1Jn 3:13).

30:1 On **Jakeh** and **the pronouncement**, see the textual footnote at v. 1. **Agur**, the author of this chapter (cp. 1:1; 31:1), and **Ithiel and Ucal**, the recipients, are otherwise unknown. These proverbs, though written for specific individuals, have application for all people. An oracle is a message from God (2Kg 9:25; Ezk 12:10; Mal 1:1; cp. Jr 23:33–40). **Oration**, which usually announces a declaration of the Lord (Gn 22:16; 1Sm 2:30; Hg 2:4), is used twice for the "oracle" or "proclamation" of men (Nm 24:3,15; 2Sm 23:1).

30:2–3 Some men claim to have a grasp on God. What Job eventually came to realize (Jb 40:4), Agur reverently states at the beginning: **I have no knowledge of the Holy One.**

⁴ Who has gone up to heaven
and come down?
Who has gathered the wind
in his hands?
Who has bound up the waters
in a cloak?
Who has established all the ends
of the earth?
What is his name,
and what is the name of his son —
if you know?

⁵ Every word of God is pure;ᴬ
he is a shield to those who take refuge
in him.

⁶ Don't add to his words,
or he will rebuke you, and you will be
proved a liar.

⁷ Two things I ask of you;
don't deny them to me before I die:

⁸ Keep falsehood and deceitful words
far from me.
Give me neither poverty nor wealth;
feed me with the food I need.

⁹ Otherwise, I might have too much
and deny you, saying,
"Who is the LORD?"
or I might have nothing and steal,
profaningᴮ the name of my God.

¹⁰ Don't slander a servant to his master
or he will curse you, and you will
become guilty.

¹¹ There is a generation that curses its father
and does not bless its mother.

¹² There is a generation that is pure
in its own eyes,
yet is not washed from its filth.

¹³ There is a generation — how haughty
its eyes

and pretentious its looks.ᶜ

¹⁴ There is a generation whose teeth
are swords,
whose fangs are knives,
devouring the oppressed from the land
and the needy from among mankind.

¹⁵ The leech has two daughters:
"Give, Give!"
Three things are never satisfied;
four never say, "Enough!":

¹⁶ Sheol; a childless womb;
earth, which is never satisfied
with water;
and fire, which never says, "Enough!"

¹⁷ As for the eye that ridicules a father
and despises obedience to a mother,
may ravens of the valley pluck it out
and young vultures eat it.

¹⁸ Three things are too wondrous for me;
four I can't understand:

¹⁹ the way of an eagle in the sky,
the way of a snake on a rock,
the way of a ship at sea,
and the way of a man
with a young woman.

²⁰ This is the way of an adulteress:
she eats and wipes her mouth
and says, "I've done nothing wrong."

²¹ The earth trembles under three things;
it cannot bear up under four:

²² a servant when he becomes king,
a fool when he is stuffed with food,

²³ an unloved woman
when she marries,
and a servant girl when she ousts
her queen.

ᴬ30:5 Lit refined ᴮ30:9 Lit grabbing ᶜ30:13 Lit and its eyelids lifted up

---

30:4 Gathering **wind** and binding **waters** refer to God's control of thunderstorms, which are important for the agricultural cycle. Asking about God's **name** is asking whether the hearer knows his character. **His son** could refer to Israel (Hs 11:1) or to anyone whom God teaches (Dt 8:5; Heb 12:6), but Jesus fulfilled the role perfectly (Mt 2:15; Lk 9:35). **30:5–6** Though only God has access to heaven (v. 4), God's **word** is accessible to all (Dt 30:11–14). Agur does not give reasons that God's word is **pure** and complete; that would make human reason the determination of the value of God's word. **His words** include this inspired word from Agur. We are tempted to **add to** God's Word to make it conform to us, instead of the other way around. **30:7–9** This prayer is comparable to Jesus's model prayer (Mt 6:9–13). Both ask God's protection from temptation; both ask for basic needs to be met (1Tm 6:8; cp. Php 4:12); both are concerned with upholding God's honor. The indulgent person may become a liar and a mocker (Ex 5:2); the destitute

person may become a thief (Pr 6:30). The thief profanes God by implying that God can't provide. **30:10** A **servant** could be a slave or an official. A wronged person can cry out to God and bring guilt on the wrongdoer (Dt 15:9). **30:11–15** A **generation** is a group of people of a certain time with certain characteristics in common. Jesus condemned an evil "generation" of his day (Mt 11:16; 12:39–45; 17:17). **30:12 Filth** is literally "excrement" (Dt 23:13; 2Kg 18:27; Ezk 4:12). It refers figuratively to obvious, detestable sin. **30:13–14** Arrogance leads to exploitation. **30:15–16** The blood-sucking **leech** takes without contributing. Until God restores paradise (Rm 8:19–22; Rv 21:1), **Sheol** and **fire** will always try to destroy, and the **womb** and the soil will always strive to produce (Gn 3:16–17). **30:17** The **eye that ridicules** indicates a haughty person (v. 13). **30:18–20** A **man** is a strong, virile man (20:24), and the **young woman** is of mar-

riageable age, presumably a virgin (Gn 24:43; Is 7:14). If Pr 30:18–19 stand alone, the point might be that the progress of love is as marvelous and mysterious as the motion of the other three items. If v. 20 is connected to the saying, the interpretation is far different. The first three things leave no tracks. The man, like the **adulteress** who **wipes her mouth**, thinks fornication with the young woman leaves no trace. (The adulteress thinks sex is as casual and amoral as a meal.) However, in the end there are consequences (5:4; 14:12). These things are **too wondrous for** Agur (Jb 42:3; Ps 131:1), but God knows (Jr 32:17). **30:21–23** This could be a humorous observation or a serious commentary on the collapse of social order. The **servant** could be an official who seized the kingdom. **Unloved** is literally "hated"; it may refer to a wicked woman who was rightly rejected. All these become destructive when they move into a position they should not be in.

24 Four things on earth are small,
   yet they are extremely wise:
25 ants are not a strong people,
   yet they store up their food
     in the summer;
26 hyraxes are not a mighty people,
   yet they make their homes in the cliffs;
27 locusts have no king,
   yet all of them march in ranks;
28 a lizard^A can be caught in your hands,
   yet it lives in kings' palaces.

29 Three things are stately in their stride;
   four are stately in their walk:
30 a lion, which is mightiest among beasts
   and doesn't retreat before anything;
31 a strutting rooster;^B a goat;
   and a king at the head of his army.^C

32 If you have been foolish
     by exalting yourself
   or if you've been scheming,
   put your hand over your mouth.
33 For the churning of milk
     produces butter,
   and twisting a nose draws blood,
   and stirring up anger produces strife.

The Words of Lemuel

31 The words of King Lemuel,
   a pronouncement^D that his mother
   taught him:

2 What should I say, my son?
   What, son of my womb?
   What, son of my vows?
3 Don't spend your energy on women
   or your efforts on those
     who destroy kings.
4 It is not for kings, Lemuel,
   it is not for kings to drink wine
   or for rulers to desire beer.
5 Otherwise, he will drink,
   forget what is decreed,
   and pervert justice for all
     the oppressed.^E
6 Give beer to one who is dying
   and wine to one whose life is bitter.
7 Let him drink so that he can forget
   his poverty
   and remember his trouble no more.
8 Speak up^F for those who have no voice,^G
   for the justice of all
     who are dispossessed.^H
9 Speak up, judge righteously,
   and defend the cause of the oppressed
     and needy.

In Praise of a Wife of Noble Character

10 Who can find a wife of noble character?^I
   She is far more precious than jewels.^J
11 The heart of her husband trusts in her,
   and he will not lack anything good.
12 She rewards him with good, not evil,
   all the days of her life.

---

^A**30:28** Or *spider*　^B**30:31** Or *a greyhound*　^C**30:31** LXX reads *king addressing his people*　^D**31:1** Or *of Lemuel, king of Massa,* or *of King Lemuel, a burden*　^E**31:5** Lit *sons of affliction*　^F**31:8** Lit *Open your mouth,* also in v. 9　^G**31:8** Lit *who are mute*　^H**31:8** Lit *all the sons of passing away*　^I**31:10** Or *a wife of quality,* or *a capable wife*　^J**31:10** Vv. 10–31 form an acrostic.

30:24–28 A perceptive person can learn from observing God's creation (6:6–8; cp. 24:32). Each of these **small** animals overcomes potentially fatal limitations. **Ants** and **hyraxes** are metaphorically called **people** as if they were a nationality. Ants show forethought. A hyrax (*Procavia syriacus*) is a herbivore the size of a rabbit that lives in herds in cavities among the rocks. Wise men also rely on the Lord as their rock of protection. **Locusts** have unity of purpose, maintaining **ranks** without infighting. The **lizard** (or spider) is vulnerable, yet it can be found in unexpected places.
30:29–31 Stately is literally "good"; that is, they excel in the quality of their **stride**. The **lion** is literally a "hero" (1Sm 17:51). Each of these is supreme in its realm. The phrase that modifies the **king** is obscure.
30:32–33 Putting one's **hand** over one's **mouth** means to immediately stop speaking out of fear (Jdg 18:19; Jb 21:5; 40:4; Mc 7:16). **Churning . . . twisting,** and **stirring up** are all the same word in Hebrew, which has to do with force or pressure and twisting or wringing. The scheming social climber is cautioned that his maneuverings will inevitably bring violence against him.
31:1 This chapter was written by **Lemuel** (cp. 1:1; 30:1). He was not a **king** in Israel, so he was probably a foreign king who converted to the worship of Israel's God (cp. Dn 4:34).
31:2 The Hebrew word for **what** is probably an implicit call to listen (1:8; 4:1) or a rhetorical

question, "What should you do?" Lemuel's mother probably made a vow before his conception (1Sm 1:11).
31:3 Women . . . who destroy kings are either adulteresses (6:26,32; 30:20) or multiple wives (Dt 17:17; 1Kg 11:1–4). David diverted his **energy** to an affair, and it distorted his judgment and ruined his family (2Sm 11–12).
31:4–5 People in positions of authority should avoid **wine** and **beer,** which could affect their judgment (Is 5:22–23; Am 6:6; Eph 5:18; Ti 1:7). Since all persons wear a hat of authority at some point—whether as a parent or a voter in a representative organization—this warning applies to all. The king has a special responsibility to protect **the oppressed** (vv. 8–9; cp. 3:34; 29:4,14).
31:6–7 This is a sarcastic command (cp. 19:27) intended to emphasize that alcohol is not appropriate for kings.
31:8–9 Having **no voice** means being unable to be effective in court and get a fair hearing. The **dispossessed** are literally "vanishing." Each person has a responsibility to help the **needy** (Ps 82:3; Is 1:17).
31:10–31 This poem is an alphabetic acrostic. While Pr 1–9 describe the virtues of the symbolic lady wisdom, this passage celebrates the ideal flesh-and-blood wife. Just as most of the exhortations to the "son" in the rest of Proverbs can be applied to all people of both genders, everyone can learn from the example of this capable wife.

31:10 Noble character (Ru 2:1; 3:11) implies practical competence (v. 29; cp. Gn 47:6), physical strength ("energy" in Pr 31:3; cp. Jdg 3:29), and financial wealth (Pr 13:22; cp. Ps 49:6).
31:11 This is the only case where the Bible commends trusting in anything but God; her husband can trust her because she is godly. **Anything good** is literally "spoil"; it refers to her abundant profits (v. 18).
31:12 Good involves all that is spiritually and physically desirable and beneficial to life.

#32　99 Essential Christian Truths

GOD IS ONE

The Bible affirms that God is one, as seen in Deuteronomy 6:4–9, otherwise known as the *Shema*. In both Old and New Testament times, the advocacy of monotheism (belief in one God) was contrary to the surrounding culture. Although most cultures practiced polytheism (belief in multiple gods) or henotheism (the worship of one god with the belief in multiple gods), the people of God knew, based upon God's self-revelation, that Yahweh, the Lord, is the only one true God.

¹³ She selects wool and flax
 and works with willing hands.
¹⁴ She is like the merchant ships,
 bringing her food from far away.
¹⁵ She rises while it is still night
 and provides food for her household
 and portions^A for her female servants.
¹⁶ She evaluates a field and buys it;
 she plants a vineyard
 with her earnings.^B
¹⁷ She draws on her strength^c
 and reveals that her arms are strong.
¹⁸ She sees that her profits are good,
 and her lamp never goes out at night.
¹⁹ She extends her hands
 to the spinning staff,
 and her hands hold the spindle.
²⁰ Her hands reach^D out to the poor,
 and she extends her hands to the needy.
²¹ She is not afraid for her household
 when it snows,
 for all in her household
 are doubly clothed.^E
²² She makes her own bed coverings;
 her clothing is fine linen and purple.

²³ Her husband is known
 at the city gates,
 where he sits among the elders
 of the land.
²⁴ She makes and sells linen garments;
 she delivers belts^F to the merchants.
²⁵ Strength and honor are her clothing,
 and she can laugh at the time to come.
²⁶ Her mouth speaks wisdom,
 and loving instruction^G is on her tongue.
²⁷ She watches over the activities
 of her household
 and is never idle.^H
²⁸ Her children rise up
 and call her blessed;
 her husband also praises her:
²⁹ "Many women^I have done noble deeds,
 but you surpass them all!"
³⁰ Charm is deceptive and beauty
 is fleeting,
 but a woman who fears the LORD
 will be praised.
³¹ Give her the reward of her labor,^J
 and let her works praise her
 at the city gates.

^A31:15 Or tasks ^B31:16 Or vineyard by her own labors ^C31:17 Lit She wraps strength around her like a belt ^D31:20 Lit Her hand reaches ^E31:21 LXX, Vg; MT reads are dressed in scarlet ^F31:24 Or sashes ^G31:26 Or and the teaching of kindness ^H31:27 Lit and does not eat the bread of idleness ^I31:29 Lit daughters ^J31:31 Lit the fruit of her hands

31:13 Flax fibers were used to make linen (Dt 22:11; Ezk 44:18).
31:14 She could afford imported **food**.
31:15 Food is literally "prey" (Ps 111:5; Mal 3:10), implying diligence, strength, and cunning (Jb 24:5; 38:39).
31:16–17 It requires tremendous **strength** to earn the extra money to buy a **vineyard**, then to clear it of stones, plant the vines, dig a winepress, and build a tower to protect it (Is 5:2).
31:18 The burning **lamp** symbolizes long life and prosperity (20:20).
31:19 The **spinning staff** and **spindle** were used to make thread and to twist it into yarn.
31:20 Her devotion is not only to her family but also to her community.

31:21 If the Masoretic Text reading "dressed in scarlet" is correct, it implies warm wool, since linen does not readily accept dye.
31:22 These **bed coverings** were probably for comfort and decoration (7:16). **Fine linen** may have been imported from Egypt, and **purple** dye came from Phoenicia (Ezk 27:7).
31:23 On **gates**, see note at 24:7. She enabled her husband to sit **among the elders**, a respected local authority.
31:24 She **sells** everything, from the inner **linen garments** that are put on first, to the outer belt or sash.
31:25 She has **strength** like the young and **honor** like the old (20:29).

31:26 Her **instruction** arises out of **wisdom** and love (Hb chesed).
31:27 She is noted for vigilance and diligence. **Is never idle** is literally "does not eat the food of idleness." She is no sluggard.
31:28–31 Here the wife is recognized and rewarded for her character and **works**. Even if all the rare **noble** women were gathered, her **husband** says she would **surpass** them. **Charm** is grace or favor (11:16; 22:1), and **beauty** is outward appearance (6:25; Ezk 16:14); both are temporary. The end **reward** of wisdom depends on its beginning: the fear of the Lord (see 1:7; 9:10; 15:33).

◥ Introduction to Ecclesiastes

Circumstances of Writing

According to Ecclesiastes 1:1 and 1:12, the author of this book was David's son and a king over Israel from Jerusalem. Also, 12:9 speaks of the author as a writer of proverbs, so Solomon appears to be the author. Many scholars believe that Ecclesiastes was written too late in Israel's history for this to be true, and they want to date the book at least five hundred years after Solomon's time (later than 450 BC). However, strong evidence attests that the book does come from the age of Solomon. For instance, it displays a great knowledge of literature from early Mesopotamia and Egypt.

One example is that the book shows an awareness of the "Harper Songs," poetry from Egypt that is much older than the age of Solomon. Ecclesiastes 9:7–9 is similar to that poetry, and it also resembles a portion of the famous *Epic of Gilgamesh* from Mesopotamia. It makes sense that Solomon, who had close contacts with Egypt and whose empire stretched up to the Euphrates River, would know and reflect on such texts. It is doubtful that an anonymous Jew writing five hundred or more years later, when Egyptian and Mesopotamian glory was finished and when Judah was a backwater nation, would have had access to these texts or could have understood them. By contrast, Ecclesiastes shows no similarities to the Greek philosophy that flourished in the fifth century BC and later. All of these conditions point to the traditional view that Solomon authored this book.

Ecclesiastes is Wisdom literature, meaning that it is in the part of the Bible especially concerned with helping readers cope with the practical and philosophical issues of life. It has roots in the Wisdom literature of Egypt and Babylon. Books like Proverbs and Ecclesiastes are the biblical answer to the search for truth. Proverbs is basic wisdom, giving the reader fundamental principles to live by. Ecclesiastes, by contrast, is for a more mature reader. It engages the question of whether death nullifies all purpose and meaning in life.

Contribution to the Bible

Ecclesiastes must be read with care because some of its verses, if read in isolation, seem to contradict other biblical teachings. It seems to deny the afterlife (3:18–22), to warn us against being too righteous (7:16), and to recommend a life of pleasure (10:19). But the real purpose of Ecclesiastes is to force us to take our mortality seriously and thus to consider carefully how we should live. Ecclesiastes knocks away all the façades by which we disguise the fact that life is short and we deny that all our accomplishments will pass away. In this sense, Ecclesiastes anticipates the New Testament teaching that only God's grace, and not excessive zeal, saves us.

Structure

Ecclesiastes does not have the kind of structure we usually look for in a book of the Bible. At first glance it seems to move to and fro among various topics in a way that seems almost incoherent. It has no simple hierarchical outline, and it often jumps rapidly from one topic to the next. But a closer look reveals a structure that alternates between two perspectives: that of human existence apart from God and that of existence lived before God. If Ecclesiastes were music, it would be seen as antiphonal. The resolution of the tensions that permeate Ecclesiastes is found in the affirmation that the most important thing in life is to "fear God and keep his commands" (12:13).

Outline

1800–1500 BC	1500–1200 BC	1200–800 BC
The Admonitions of Ipuwer, Egypt **1600–1400**	Heavy import and export trade, Egypt **1500–1000**	*The Harper's Song for Inherkhway,* Egyptian **1160**
The Satirical Letter of Hori, Egypt **1570–1070**	*Words of Ahiqar,* Egypt **1500–500**	*The Babylonian Theodicy,* Mesopotamian **1100**
Declarations of Innocence from the Egyptian Book of the Dead **1530–1500**	Events in Joshua **1406–1380?**	David becomes king over all Israel. **1003**
MOSES 1526–1406	Events in Judges **1380?–1060?**	Solomon becomes king. **970**
	Epic of Gilgamesh is recorded. **1200**	Proverbs **970**
		Song of Songs **970?**
		Ecclesiastes **935?**

Everything Is Futile

1 The words of the Teacher,[A] son of David, king in Jerusalem.

2 "Absolute futility," says the Teacher.
"Absolute futility. Everything is futile."

3 What does a person gain for all
   his efforts
that he labors at under the sun?

4 A generation goes and a generation
   comes,
but the earth remains forever.

5 The sun rises and the sun sets;
panting, it hurries back to the place
where it rises.

6 Gusting to the south,
turning to the north,
turning, turning, goes the wind,
and the wind returns in its cycles.

7 All the streams flow to the sea,
yet the sea is never full;
to the place where the streams flow,
there they flow again.

8 All things[B] are wearisome,
more than anyone can say.
The eye is not satisfied by seeing
or the ear filled with hearing.

9 What has been is what will be,
and what has been done is
   what will be done;
there is nothing new under the sun.

10 Can one say about anything,
"Look, this is new"?
It has already existed in the ages before us.

11 There is no remembrance of those
   who[C] came before;
and of those who will come after
there will also be no remembrance
by those who follow them.

The Limitations of Wisdom

12 I, the Teacher, have been[D] king over Israel in Jerusalem. 13 I applied my mind to examine and explore through wisdom all that is done under heaven. God has given people[E] this miserable task to keep them occupied. 14 I have seen all the things that are done under the sun and have found everything to be futile, a pursuit of the wind.[F]

15 What is crooked cannot be straightened;
what is lacking cannot be counted.

16 I said to myself, "See, I have amassed wisdom far beyond all those who were over Jerusalem before me, and my mind has thoroughly grasped[G] wisdom and knowledge." 17 I applied my mind to know wisdom and knowledge, madness and folly; I learned that this too is a pursuit of the wind.

18 For with much wisdom is much sorrow;
as knowledge increases, grief increases.

The Emptiness of Pleasure

2 I said to myself, "Go ahead, I will test you with pleasure; enjoy what is good." But it turned out to be futile. 2 I said about laughter, "It is madness," and about pleasure, "What does this accomplish?" 3 I explored with my mind the pull of wine on my body — my mind still guiding me with wisdom — and how to grasp folly, until I could see what is good for people to do under heaven[H] during the few days of their lives.

The Emptiness of Possessions

4 I increased my achievements. I built houses and planted vineyards for myself. 5 I made gardens and parks for myself and planted every kind of fruit tree in them. 6 I constructed

---

^A^1:1 Or of Qoheleth, or of the Leader of the Assembly   ^B^1:8 Or words   ^C^1:11 Or of the things that   ^D^1:12 Or Teacher, was
^E^1:13 Or given the descendants of Adam   ^F^1:14 Or a feeding on wind, or an affliction of spirit ; also in v. 17   ^G^1:16 Or discerned
^H^2:3 Two Hb mss, LXX, Syr read the sun

1:1 The Hebrew word *qoheleth*, here translated as **Teacher**, probably means "assembly leader." It is not the ordinary word for "teacher." It is a rare Hebrew word (found seven times in Ecclesiastes and nowhere else in the Bible), and it could mean "public speaker." This is the author's self-designation throughout the book. For this reason the book of Ecclesiastes is often called "Qoheleth." The words **son of David, king in Jerusalem** could refer to any Davidic king of Judah, but only Solomon was king over all Israel from Jerusalem (v. 12).
1:2 *Hevel*, the Hebrew word for **futile**, basically means "vapor" or "breath," but it comes to mean "vain," "transitory," or "futile." It does not necessarily mean that something is altogether worthless, but it implies that something is at best only of fleeting value. In the context of Ecclesiastes, it means that things done "under the sun" are only of temporary significance and therefore, set against eternity, they have no real value.
1:3–7 The phrase **under the sun** means here on earth; it speaks of the temporal and temporary nature of humanity.

1:8 The phrase **all things are wearisome** could be translated "all words are weary." It refers to our inability to find either meaning or satisfaction in creation.
1:9–10 When Ecclesiastes says that **there is nothing new under the sun**, it means that there is nothing that changes the fundamental facts of the human condition. This does not deny that there are technological innovations or new works of art, literature, and architecture, but these things are all variations on what had already existed; they do not deliver humanity from its bondage to death.
1:11 This verse does not claim that no human is ever remembered in history. The point is that people move on and that fame and glory have no lasting significance.
1:12–18 These verses describe the futility of the quest for knowledge. The claim is not that intellectual pursuits are evil; they are vain and frustrating because no person finds the answers to his fundamental questions by learning.
1:13 The quest for wisdom is here called **this miserable task**, meaning that it is just a hard job.

1:15 This verse is a proverb. **What is crooked cannot be straightened** refers to a problem that cannot be solved. **What is lacking cannot be counted** refers to working with insufficient information. The problem of understanding life is beyond mere humans.
1:18 Instead of answering all our questions and bringing happiness, great learning and **wisdom** only leads to less certainty and more pain.
2:1–2 These verses summarize in advance the whole of vv. 1–11. Solomon looked into finding meaning through riches, and he found it **futile**.
2:3 The word **wine** is literal wine, but it also stands for all the pleasure-giving luxuries of life. **Folly** refers to parties, frivolity, and self-indulgence. When the Teacher said **my mind still guiding me with wisdom**, he meant that he did not give himself over to total dissipation.
2:4–8 The Teacher was rich in every way, having palatial homes, the natural beauty of **vineyards** and **gardens**, abundant and varied food from his herds and estates, riches in the form of livestock and precious metals,

reservoirs for myself from which to irrigate a grove of flourishing trees. ⁷ I acquired male and female servants and had slaves who were born in my house. I also owned livestock — large herds and flocks — more than all who were before me in Jerusalem. ⁸ I also amassed silver and gold for myself, and the treasure of kings and provinces. I gathered male and female singers for myself, and many concubines, the delights of men.ᴬ,ᴮ ⁹ So I became great and surpassed all who were before me in Jerusalem; my wisdom also remained with me. ¹⁰ All that my eyes desired, I did not deny them. I did not refuse myself any pleasure, for I took pleasure in all my struggles. This was my reward for all my struggles. ¹¹ When I considered all that I had accomplishedᶜ and what I had labored to achieve, I found everything to be futile and a pursuit of the wind.ᴰ There was nothing to be gained under the sun.

The Relative Value of Wisdom

¹² Then I turned to consider wisdom, madness, and folly, for what will the king's successorᴱ be like? Heᶠ will do what has already been done. ¹³ And I realized that there is an advantage to wisdom over folly, like the advantage of light over darkness.

¹⁴   The wise person has eyes in his head,
      but the fool walks in darkness.

Yet I also knew that one fate comes to them both. ¹⁵ So I said to myself, "What happens to the fool will also happen to me. Why then have I been overly wise?" And I said to myself that this is also futile. ¹⁶ For, just like the fool, there is no lasting remembrance of the wise, since in the days to come both will be forgotten. How is it that the wise person dies just like the fool? ¹⁷ Therefore, I hated life because the work that was done under the sun was distressing to me. For everything is futile and a pursuit of the wind.

The Emptiness of Work

¹⁸ I hated all my work that I labored at under the sun because I must leave it to the one who comes after me. ¹⁹ And who knows whether he will be wise or a fool? Yet he will take over all my work that I labored at skillfully under the sun. This too is futile. ²⁰ So I began to give myself overᴳ to despair concerning all my work that I had labored at under the sun. ²¹ When there is a person whose work was done with wisdom, knowledge, and skill, and he must give his portion to a person who has not worked for it, this too is futile and a great wrong. ²² For what does a person get with all his work and all his efforts that he labors at under the sun? ²³ For all his days are filled with grief, and his occupation is sorrowful; even at night, his mind does not rest. This too is futile.

²⁴ There is nothing better for a person than to eat, drink, and enjoyᴴ,ᴵ his work. I have seen that even this is from God's hand, ²⁵ because who can eat and who can enjoy lifeᴶ apart from him?ᴷ ²⁶ For to the person who is pleasing in his sight, he gives wisdom, knowledge, and joy; but to the sinner he gives the task of gathering and accumulating in order to give to the one who is pleasing in God's sight. This too is futile and a pursuit of the wind.

The Mystery of Time

3 There is an occasion for everything,
    and a time for every activity
      under heaven:

²   a time to give birth and a time to die;
      a time to plant and a time to uproot;ᴸ
³   a time to kill and a time to heal;
      a time to tear down and a time to build;

ᴬ2:8 LXX, Theod, Syr read *and male cupbearers and female cupbearers*; Aq, Tg, Vg read *a cup and cups*; Hb obscure
ᴮ2:8 Or *many treasures that people delight in* ᶜ2:11 Lit *all my works that my hands had done* ᴰ2:11 Or *a feeding on wind*, or
an affliction of spirit; also in vv. 17,26 ᴱ2:12 Lit *the man who comes after the king* ᶠ2:12 Some Hb mss read *They*
ᴳ2:20 Lit *And I turned to cause my heart* ᴴ2:24 Syr, Tg; MT reads *There is no good in a person who eats and drinks and enjoys*
ᴵ2:24 Lit *and his soul sees good* ᴶ2:25 LXX, Theod, Syr read *can drink* ᴷ2:25 Some Hb mss, LXX, Syr read *me* ᴸ3:2 Lit *uproot
what is planted*

---

and feats of engineering in the form of **res-ervoirs** and aqueducts. He was free of hard labor and was served by an army of **slaves**. He was entertained by **singers**, and his sexual desires were fulfilled by **concubines**.
2:11 Not only did Solomon realize his treasures and accomplishments failed to give him satisfaction, he also understood that none would endure.
2:12 Solomon compared **wisdom, madness, and folly** to see if there was any real value in one way of living over another. The last part of this verse has some extraordinarily difficult Hebrew. Literally it says, "For what is the man who will come after the king whom they already made?" Most interpreters take the king to be Solomon himself and so read the text more or less as the CSB has done. It is possible, however, that "whom they already made" refers to the creation of man in Gn

1:26, where God is referred to in the plural ("Let us make man"). If so, then "the king" is not Solomon but Adam, and the point is that any man (in Hb the word is *'adam*) who comes after Adam must learn to make moral choices involving wisdom and folly. Adam started this when he ate from the tree of the knowledge of good and evil. How can a man who comes after Adam not wrestle with these things?
2:13–15 The Teacher did not deny that wisdom is a good thing. The **fool** will fall into all kinds of troubles because of the poor decisions he makes. On the other hand, wisdom can do nothing to save a person from death, the greatest calamity of all. One person may be prudent and another foolish, but **one fate comes to them both**.
2:18–23 In this section Ecclesiastes returns to the subject of wealth and pleasure. But

unlike vv. 1–11, which focus on the impossibility of finding satisfaction in riches, this text focuses on the absurdity of devoting one's life to acquiring wealth only to leave it all behind to someone else.
2:24–26 The words **there is nothing better for a person than to eat, drink, and enjoy his work** must be understood in context. There are obviously many more things to a good life than just eating, drinking, and enjoying one's work.
3:1–11 These verses, the most famous text in Ecclesiastes, must be read from the context of the fundamental claim of the book: that we are mortals, doomed to perish, and that our work will perish with us. No human work is eternal, and our activities, whether building or tearing down, must change as the situation dictates. We naturally prefer to stay on the positive side of the list, but as

⁴ a time to weep and a time to laugh;
a time to mourn and a time to dance;
⁵ a time to throw stones and a time
to gather stones;
a time to embrace and a time
to avoid embracing;
⁶ a time to search and a time to count
as lost;
a time to keep and a time to throw away;
⁷ a time to tear and a time to sew;
a time to be silent and a time to speak;
⁸ a time to love and a time to hate;
a time for war and a time for peace.

⁹ What does the worker gain from his struggles? ¹⁰ I have seen the task that God has given the children of Adam to keep them occupied. ¹¹ He has made everything appropriate^A in its time. He has also put eternity in their hearts,^B but no one can discover the work God has done from beginning to end. ¹² I know that there is nothing better for them than to rejoice and enjoy the^C good life. ¹³ It is also the gift of God whenever anyone eats, drinks, and enjoys all his efforts. ¹⁴ I know that everything God does will last forever; there is no adding to it or taking from it. God works so that people will be in awe of him. ¹⁵ Whatever is, has already been, and whatever will be, already is. However, God seeks justice for the persecuted.^D

The Mystery of Injustice and Death

¹⁶ I also observed under the sun: there is wickedness at the place of judgment and there is wickedness at the place of righteousness. ¹⁷ I said to myself, "God will judge the righteous

and the wicked, since there is a time for every activity and every work." ¹⁸ I said to myself, "This happens so that God may test the children of Adam and they may see for themselves that they are like animals." ¹⁹ For the fate of the children of Adam and the fate of animals is the same. As one dies, so dies the other; they all have the same breath. People have no advantage over animals since everything is futile. ²⁰ All are going to the same place; all come from dust, and all return to dust. ²¹ Who knows if the spirits of the children of Adam go upward and the spirits of animals go downward to the earth? ²² I have seen that there is nothing better than for a person to enjoy his activities because that is his reward. For who can enable him to see what will happen after he dies?^E

⁴ Again, I observed all the acts of oppression being done under the sun. Look at the tears of those who are oppressed; they have no one to comfort them. Power is with those who oppress them; they have no one to comfort them. ² So I commended the dead, who have already died, more than the living, who are still alive. ³ But better than either of them is the one who has not yet existed, who has not seen the evil activity that is done under the sun.

The Loneliness of Wealth

⁴ I saw that all labor and all skillful work is due to one person's jealousy of another. This too is futile and a pursuit of the wind.^F
⁵ The fool folds his arms
and consumes his own flesh.
⁶ Better one handful with rest

---

^A3:11 Or *beautiful* ^B3:11 Or *has put a sense of past and future into their minds*, or *has placed ignorance in their hearts*
^C3:12 Lit *his* ^D3:15 Lit *God seeks what is pursued* ^E3:22 Lit *after him* ^F4:4 Or *a feeding on wind*, or *an affliction of spirit*;
also in vv. 6,16

---

long as we live in a world of change, conflict, and death, we must accept the fact that we cannot have unchanging bliss. Even so, as v. 11 says, everything is **appropriate in its time**. We must respond appropriately to the seasons of life as they come.
3:5 The meaning of throwing or gathering **stones** is uncertain. It may refer to clearing a field for planting versus building a wall, or spoiling a field (2Kg 3:25) versus clearing it

(Is 5:2). A rabbinical tradition takes it to be a euphemism for participating in or refraining from sexual relations.
3:11 The fact that God **has also put eternity in their hearts** tells us that although we are creatures of time, we are not like the animals, who are fully and exclusively creatures of time.
3:15 The phrase **God seeks justice for the persecuted** is literally "God seeks the pursued" or "God seeks the persecuted." Such a translation suggests that God cares about and seeks out those who are harassed and oppressed. An alternate interpretation is that God is concerned with repeating ("seeks to do") what has occurred in the past ("what was driven away"). The first alternative, as found in the CSB, better anticipates the text on injustice that follows (vv. 16–17).
3:16–17 An absurdity of life is that where there ought to be justice in the law courts, there is often corruption, oppression, and a perversion of justice. Even so, we may take comfort in the fact that God has appointed a final day for judging the world.
3:18–22 These verses are disturbing to Christian readers because they appear to deny the hope of eternal life. What they actually deny is that people *within themselves* have the

power to transcend death. According to the Bible, death is an enemy (1Co 15:26); it is not merely a doorway to a new level of existence. God's people will experience eternal life only because they are known by God and will be raised by his power.
4:1–3 Returning to the topic of **oppression** (see note at 3:16–17), Ecclesiastes asserts that political corruption is terrible precisely because it does not allow common people to do the thing the book recommends—to enjoy their days **under the sun**.
4:3 This verse is "hyperbole," the use of exaggeration for rhetorical effect. Someone who says, "I wish I had never been born," rarely means it literally. When Ecclesiastes declares that **one who has not yet existed** is the most fortunate of all, it is merely saying in an emphatic way that the corruption practiced **under the sun** is a cause for great sorrow.
4:4–8 Ecclesiastes returns to the theme of wealth, describing how foolish it is to spend one's life in the pursuit of riches. First, Solomon declares that people **work** hard not out of love for the task but out of a desire to do better than their peers. Second, a conventional proverb declares that laziness brings on poverty. Against this, v. 6 gives a counter lesson—that it is better to have little with

than two handfuls with effort and a pursuit of the wind.

[7] Again, I saw futility under the sun: [8] There is a person without a companion,[A] without even a son or brother, and though there is no end to all his struggles, his eyes are still not content with riches. "Who am I struggling for," he asks, "and depriving myself of good things?" This too is futile and a miserable task.

[9] Two are better than one because they have a good reward for their efforts. [10] For if either falls, his companion can lift him up; but pity the one who falls without another to lift him up. [11] Also, if two lie down together, they can keep warm; but how can one person alone keep warm? [12] And if someone overpowers one person, two can resist him. A cord of three strands is not easily broken.

[13] Better is a poor but wise youth than an old but foolish king who no longer pays attention to warnings. [14] For he came from prison to be king, even though he was born poor in his kingdom. [15] I saw all the living, who move about under the sun, follow[B] a second youth who succeeds him. [16] There is no limit to all the people who were before them, yet those who come later will not rejoice in him. This too is futile and a pursuit of the wind.

Caution in God's Presence

5 Guard your steps when you go to the house of God. Better to approach in obedience than to offer the sacrifice as fools do, for they ignorantly do wrong. [2] Do not be hasty to speak, and do not be impulsive to make a speech before God. God is in heaven and you are on earth, so let your words be few. [3] Just as dreams accompany much labor, so also a

fool's voice comes with many words. [4] When you make a vow to God, don't delay fulfilling it, because he does not delight in fools. Fulfill what you vow. [5] Better that you do not vow than that you vow and not fulfill it. [6] Do not let your mouth bring guilt on you, and do not say in the presence of the messenger that it was a mistake. Why should God be angry with your words and destroy the work of your hands? [7] For many dreams bring futility; so do many words. Therefore, fear God.

The Realities of Wealth

[8] If you see oppression of the poor and perversion of justice and righteousness in the province, don't be astonished at the situation, because one official protects another official, and higher officials protect them. [9] The profit from the land is taken by all; the king is served by the field.[C]

[10] The one who loves silver is never satisfied with silver, and whoever loves wealth is never satisfied with income. This too is futile. [11] When good things increase, the ones who consume them multiply; what, then, is the profit to the owner, except to gaze at them with his eyes? [12] The sleep of the worker is sweet, whether he eats little or much, but the abundance of the rich permits him no sleep.

[13] There is a sickening tragedy I have seen under the sun: wealth kept by its owner to his harm. [14] That wealth was lost in a bad venture, so when he fathered a son, he was empty-handed. [15] As he came from his mother's womb, so he will go again, naked as he came; he will take nothing for his efforts that he can carry in his hands. [16] This too is a sickening tragedy: exactly as he comes, so he will go. What does the one gain who struggles for the wind? [17] What

---

[A]4:8 Lit *person, but there is not a second,*   [B]4:15 Lit *with*   [C]5:9 Hb obscure

---

peace than to have much with a constant hunger for more.
4:9–12 Friendship is the theme of this section. The advantages of friends are that they help one another get work done, that one friend sustains another when disaster strikes, that they give comfort to one another against the bitterness of life, and that they protect one another from enemies. Interestingly, friendship is one area of life that Ecclesiastes never calls "futile."
4:11–12 These verses do not refer to lying together sexually. It is an image of travelers sleeping outdoors in the desert; they must huddle together to **keep warm**. The fact that v. 12 asserts that **three** are better than **two** makes clear that these are friends, not lovers.
4:13–16 This section illustrates how fleeting political power is. There are two people here. The first person is an old **king**, who in his youth was **poor** but rose to power through skill and perseverance. This king is now **old but foolish**. The second person is a **youth** who, possessing the political skills the old king once had but lost, is now ready and able to usurp him (this is the youth of v. 13, who is called the **second youth** in v. 15). But

even though the second youth is successful for a time and pleases the crowd, he will also eventually get old, lose touch, and be abandoned. Political power and popularity are by nature fleeting.
5:1–7 This passage deals with religious behavior, and it warns that we should not try to impress God. It is in two parallel parts. First, positively, come to the **house of God** in humble **obedience**; negatively, do not try to impress God with big sacrifices and big vows; and then there is a proverb that big **dreams** and **many words** come from an overworked fool. Second, positively, fulfill your **vow**; negatively, do not make a vow you cannot keep; and then a proverb, **many dreams** and **many words** are futile, so it is better to **fear God**. The foundation of these teachings is our mortality: **God is in heaven and you are on earth**. This text calls on us to depend on the grace of God and not on our religious deeds.
5:8–9 Once again, the Teacher looks at political matters. In these verses he tells us not to be surprised by corruption. Layers of governmental bureaucracy are supposed to insure that every official is accountable to

others and is behaving properly, but all these layers of government can make for more layers of corruption.
5:10–6:6 This is a lengthy passage on wealth. It makes the point that a life spent pursuing wealth is futile. Ecclesiastes 5:10–20 gives a series of seven reasons not to devote ourselves to getting rich. First, seeking wealth is an endless quest, because those who want to get rich never feel that they have enough (v. 10). Second, if you get rich, you attract people who care nothing for you but just want your money (v. 11a). Third, once you acquire much money, you cannot do anything with it but look at it (v. 11b). Fourth, working people are not full of anxieties and they **sleep** well; the rich are awake at night worrying about their investments (v. 12). Fifth, wealthy people live in a world of high-stakes financial deals. They can lose their money in bad business deals just when they need the money for their families. In the world of finance, men put their families at risk (vv. 13–14). Sixth, at death you lose it all. You cannot take it with you (vv. 15–16). Seventh, the quest for riches is hard and bitter, and days are spent

is more, he eats in darkness all his days, with much frustration, sickness, and anger.

[18] Here is what I have seen to be good: It is appropriate to eat, drink, and experience good in all the labor one does under the sun during the few days of his life God has given him, because that is his reward. [19] Furthermore, everyone to whom God has given riches and wealth, he has also allowed them to enjoy them, take his reward, and rejoice in his labor. This is a gift of God, [20] for he does not often consider the days of his life because God keeps him occupied with the joy of his heart.

6 Here is a tragedy I have observed under the sun, and it weighs heavily on humanity:[A] [2] God gives a person riches, wealth, and honor so that he lacks nothing of all he desires for himself, but God does not allow him to enjoy them. Instead, a stranger will enjoy them. This is futile and a sickening tragedy. [3] A man may father a hundred children and live many years. No matter how long he lives,[B] if he is not satisfied by good things and does not even have a proper burial, I say that a stillborn child is better off than he. [4] For he comes in futility and he goes in darkness, and his name is shrouded in darkness. [5] Though a stillborn child does not see the sun and is not conscious, it has more rest than he. [6] And if a person lives a thousand years twice, but does not experience happiness, do not both go to the same place?

[7] All of a person's labor is
   for his stomach,[C]
yet the appetite is never satisfied.

[8] What advantage then does the wise person have over the fool? What advantage is there for the poor person who knows how to conduct himself before others? [9] Better what the eyes see than wandering desire. This too is futile and a pursuit of the wind.[D]

[10] Whatever exists was given its name long ago,[E] and it is known what mankind is. But he is not able to contend with the one stronger than he. [11] For when there are many words, they increase futility. What is the advantage for mankind? [12] For who knows what is good for

anyone in life, in the few days of his futile life that he spends like a shadow? Who can tell anyone what will happen after him under the sun?

Wise Sayings

7 A good name is better than
   fine perfume,
and the day of one's death is better than
   the day of one's birth.
[2] It is better to go to a house of mourning
   than to go to a house of feasting,
since that is the end of all mankind,
   and the living should take it to heart.
[3] Grief is better than laughter,
   for when a face is sad, a heart
      may be glad.
[4] The heart of the wise is in a house
      of mourning,
but the heart of fools is in a house
      of pleasure.
[5] It is better to listen to rebuke
      from a wise person
than to listen to the song of fools,
[6] for like the crackling of burning thorns
      under the pot,
so is the laughter of the fool.
This too is futile.
[7] Surely, the practice of extortion turns
      a wise person into a fool,
and a bribe corrupts the mind.
[8] The end of a matter is better
      than its beginning;
a patient spirit is better
      than a proud spirit.
[9] Don't let your spirit rush to be angry,
for anger abides in the heart of fools.
[10] Don't say, "Why were the former days
      better than these?"
since it is not wise of you to ask this.
[11] Wisdom is as good as an inheritance
and an advantage to those who see
      the sun,
[12] because wisdom is protection as silver
      is protection;
but the advantage of knowledge
is that wisdom preserves the life
      of its owner.

[A]6:1 Or *it is common among men* [B]6:3 Lit *how many years* [C]6:7 Lit *mouth* [D]6:9 Or *a feeding on wind*, or *an affliction of spirit* [E]6:10 Lit *name already*

in tedious and vexing work. It is far better to get by with fewer things and less money and be able to enjoy life (vv. 17–20).
6:1–6 A person who has money but who derives no real joy from his privileges is a pitiful wretch. His money serves no purpose but to be passed on to others.
6:3–6 These verses use a **stillborn child** for rhetorical purposes, to make the point that a life without joy, no matter how rich a person may be, is wasted.
6:7–9 This passage contains three proverbs, and it makes the transition from a major discussion of wealth (5:10–6:6) to a major discussion of wisdom and death (6:10–7:4). The

proverbs teach that **appetite** is the thing that drives us, but it **is never satisfied**, that wisdom cannot save us from our appetite or from poverty, and that it is important to be satisfied with what we have.
6:10–7:4 The main point of this passage is given in 6:10: the fundamental truths of life are well **known** and there is nothing to be added. This means that the quest for great knowledge is folly, since no one will find out something that changes the basic truths of life. Thus, a person should not prattle on about supposedly new insights (6:11).
7:5–6 The **song of fools** stands for a life of carefree merrymaking. The image of **thorns**

under the pot indicates that fools are prickly to those who try to deal with them but ultimately are useless, just as thorns are good for nothing but burning.
7:7–9 In these three maxims, the main focus is on how the **wise person** confronts political reality. First, corruption is pervasive and can bring anyone down; one should beware of it. Second, one should not judge by first appearances; those who are winning now may someday come to ruin. One should be **patient** and understand that virtue is proved right in **the end**, and so flee temptations to bribery. Third, abiding **anger** over a current situation in life shows you are a fool.

¹³ Consider the work of God,
for who can straighten out
what he has made crooked?

¹⁴ In the day of prosperity be joyful, but in the day of adversity, consider: God has made the one as well as the other, so that no one can discover anything that will come after him.

Avoiding Extremes

¹⁵ In my futile life^A I have seen everything: someone righteous perishes in spite of his righteousness, and someone wicked lives long in spite of his evil. ¹⁶ Don't be excessively righteous, and don't be overly wise. Why should you destroy yourself? ¹⁷ Don't be excessively wicked, and don't be foolish. Why should you die before your time? ¹⁸ It is good that you grasp the one and do not let the other slip from your hand. For the one who fears God will end up with both of them.

¹⁹   Wisdom makes the wise person
stronger
than ten rulers of a city.
²⁰   There is certainly no one
righteous on the earth
who does good and never sins.

²¹ Don't pay attention^B to everything people say, or you may hear your servant cursing you, ²² for in your heart you know that many times you yourself have cursed others.

What the Teacher Found

²³ I have tested all this by wisdom. I resolved, "I will be wise," but it was beyond me. ²⁴ What exists is beyond reach and very deep. Who can discover it? ²⁵ I turned my thoughts to know, explore, and examine wisdom and an explanation for things, and to know that wickedness is stupidity and folly is madness. ²⁶ And I find more bitter than death the woman who is a trap: her heart a net and her hands chains. The one who pleases God will escape her, but the sinner will be captured by her. ²⁷ "Look," says the Teacher, "I have discovered this by adding

one thing to another to find out the explanation, ²⁸ which my soul continually searches for but does not find: I found one person in a thousand, but none of those was a woman. ²⁹ Only see this: I have discovered that God made people upright, but they pursued many schemes."

Wisdom, Authorities, and Inequities

8 Who is like the wise person, and who knows the interpretation of a matter? A person's wisdom brightens his face, and the sternness of his face is changed.

² Keep^C the king's command because of your oath made before God. ³ Do not be in a hurry; leave his presence, and don't persist in a bad cause, since he will do whatever he wants. ⁴ For the king's word is authoritative, and who can say to him, "What are you doing?" ⁵ The one who keeps a command will not experience anything harmful, and a wise heart knows the right time and procedure. ⁶ For every activity there is a right time and procedure, even though a person's troubles are heavy on him. ⁷ Yet no one knows what will happen because who can tell him what will happen? ⁸ No one has authority over the wind^D to restrain it, and there is no authority over the day of death; no one is discharged during battle, and wickedness will not allow those who practice it to escape. ⁹ All this I have seen, applying my mind to all the work that is done under the sun, at a time when one person has authority over another to his harm.

¹⁰ In such circumstances, I saw the wicked buried. They came and went from the holy place, and they were praised^E in the city where they did those things. This too is futile. ¹¹ Because the sentence against an evil act is not carried out quickly, the heart of people is filled with the desire to commit evil. ¹² Although a sinner does evil a hundred times and prolongs his life, I also know that it will go well with God-fearing people, for they are reverent before him. ¹³ However, it will not go well with the wicked, and they will not lengthen their days like a shadow, for they are not reverent before God.

---

^7:15 Lit *days* ^8:7:21 Lit *Don't give your heart* ^C8:2 Some Hb mss, LXX, Vg, Tg, Syr; other Hb mss read *As for me, keep*
^D8:8 Or *life-breath* ^E8:10 Some Hb mss, LXX, Aq, Theod, Sym; other Hb mss read *forgotten*

7:15–18 These verses seem to say that a little sinning is acceptable. That is not the point; the passage is about an extreme zeal for religious duties that makes life unbearably harsh. In this context, **excessively righteous** refers to being unreasonably demanding on yourself about moral or religious duties. **7:25–29** This passage seems to say that women are more evil than men. However, it needs to be understood in its context; this was a male sage giving advice to other male sages and to men generally. Because Ecclesiastes was originally intended for men (few women were literate), it predominantly reflects the man's point of view. Furthermore,

this text is a reflection on the fall into sin, alluded to in v. 29. The point is that because of sin, the fundamental relationship between male and female, especially husband and wife, is broken (as implied in Gn 3:16). The phrase **none of those was a woman** does not mean that women are intrinsically evil, but that Solomon, as a man, could not find a woman with whom his relationship was without guile, tension, or conflict. He also found that such honest friendships were extremely rare (**I found one person in a thousand**). **8:1–6** A **wise person** respects authority and knows how to approach an authority figure tactfully and at the right moment.

8:9–9:1 This passage focuses on God's governance of the world; it struggles with the question of why evil sometimes seems to triumph. Examples of this include cruel people rising to power (8:9), wicked people being honored in public (8:10), wicked people avoiding punishment (8:11), and good people suffering while the wicked do well (8:14). Against this, Ecclesiastes affirms that God does set things right (8:12–13) and asserts that a person should enjoy life and not always brood over evil (8:15). More than that, we must acknowledge that God alone knows what he is doing and why he does it, and we must be content to let him rule the world (8:16–9:1).

14 There is a futility that is done on the earth: there are righteous people who get what the actions of the wicked deserve, and there are wicked people who get what the actions of the righteous deserve. I say that this too is futile. **15** So I commended enjoyment because there is nothing better for a person under the sun than to eat, drink, and enjoy himself, for this will accompany him in his labor during the days of his life that God gives him under the sun.

16 When I applied my mind to know wisdom and to observe the activity that is done on the earth (even though one's eyes do not close in sleep day or night), **17** I observed all the work of God and concluded that a person is unable to discover the work that is done under the sun. Even though a person labors hard to explore it, he cannot find it; even if a wise person claims to know it, he is unable to discover it.

Enjoy Life Despite Death

9 Indeed, I took all this to heart and explained it all: The righteous, the wise, and their works are in God's hands. People don't know whether to expect love or hate. Everything lies ahead of them. **2** Everything is the same for everyone: There is one fate for the righteous and the wicked, for the good and the bad,^A for the clean and the unclean, for the one who sacrifices and the one who does not sacrifice. As it is for the good, so also it is for the sinner; as it is for the one who takes an oath, so also for the one who fears an oath. **3** This is an evil in all that is done under the sun: there is one fate for everyone. In addition, the hearts of people are full of evil, and madness is in their hearts while they live; after that they go to the dead. **4** But there is hope for whoever is joined^B with all the living, since a live dog is better than a dead lion. **5** For the living know that they will die, but the dead don't know anything. There is no longer a reward for them because the memory of them is forgotten. **6** Their love, their hate, and their envy have already disappeared, and there is no longer a portion for them in all that is done under the sun.

7 Go, eat your bread with pleasure, and drink your wine with a cheerful heart, for God has already accepted your works. **8** Let your clothes be white all the time, and never let oil be lacking on your head. **9** Enjoy life with the wife you love all the days of your fleeting^C life, which has been given to you under the sun, all your fleeting days. For that is your portion in life and in your struggle under the sun. **10** Whatever your hands find to do, do with all your strength, because there is no work, planning, knowledge, or wisdom in Sheol where you are going.

The Limitations of Wisdom

11 Again I saw under the sun that the race is not to the swift, or the battle to the strong, or bread to the wise, or riches to the discerning, or favor to the skillful; rather, time and chance happen to all of them. **12** For certainly no one knows his time: like fish caught in a cruel net or like birds caught in a trap, so people are trapped in an evil time as it suddenly falls on them.

13 I have observed that this also is wisdom under the sun, and it is significant to me: **14** There was a small city with few men in it. A great king came against it, surrounded it, and built large siege works against it. **15** Now a poor wise man was found in the city, and he delivered the city by his wisdom. Yet no one remembered that poor man. **16** And I said, "Wisdom is better than strength, but the wisdom of the poor man is despised, and his words are not heeded."

17 The calm words of the wise are heeded more than the shouts of a ruler over fools.
18 Wisdom is better than weapons of war, but one sinner can destroy much good.

The Burden of Folly

10 Dead flies make a perfumer's oil ferment and stink; so a little folly outweighs wisdom and honor.
2 A wise person's heart goes to the^D right, but a fool's heart to the left.

---

^A9:2 LXX, Aq, Syr, Vg; MT omits *and the bad* ^B9:4 Alt Hb tradition reads *chosen* ^C9:9 Or *futile* ^D10:2 Lit *his*

9:2–6 When Ecclesiastes says **there is one fate for the righteous and the wicked**, it means physical death, not heaven or hell. But people draw the wrong conclusion from this; they assume that since there is nothing they can do to change the fact that death awaits all, they might as well cast away all restraint and live for themselves. **9:7–10** The proper response to death is to treat life as precious. The simple matters of eating and drinking should be done **with a cheerful heart**. Wearing clothes that are **white** and having **oil** on the **head** refer to dressing up, as for a party. The message is that we should treat most days as times of celebration and not of mourning. To **enjoy life with** one's **wife** is to find sexual pleasure in the proper way. **9:10 Sheol** refers to the grave. The point of saying that **no work, planning, knowledge, or wisdom** occurs there is not to deny the possibility of such in the afterlife, but to assert that we have only one opportunity to enjoy this world. **9:11–12** The Teacher asserts that no matter how capable we are, many things are beyond our control. **9:13–10:17** The teachings and proverbs in this section focus on making one's way in the world, and they are especially focused on political life. **9:17–10:1** In this section two contrasting ideas are set against each other. On the one hand, **wisdom** is more effective for governing people than is the brutal exercise of force and violence, described as **shouts** and **weapons of war** (9:17–18a). On the other hand, a single mistake can do a lot of damage and nullify the work of much wisdom (9:18b–10:1). The point of 10:1 is that **dead flies** in a fine ointment make that ointment disgusting. In the same way, one fool can ruin an administration and one mistake can ruin a career. **10:2–3** Folly is usually self-evident. The word **right** in the ancient world meant skillful, and the word **left** connoted ineptness and clumsiness.

3 Even when the fool walks
  along the road, his heart lacks sense,
  and he shows everyone he is a fool.
4 If the ruler's anger rises against you,
  don't leave your post,
  for calmness puts great offenses to rest.

5 There is an evil I have seen under the sun,
an error proceeding from the presence of the
ruler:
6 The fool is appointed to great heights,
  but the rich remain in lowly positions.
7 I have seen slaves on horses,
  but princes walking on the ground
  like slaves.

8 The one who digs a pit may fall into it,
  and the one who breaks through a wall
  may be bitten by a snake.
9 The one who quarries stones
  may be hurt by them;
  the one who splits logs
  may be endangered by them.
10 If the ax is dull, and one does not
  sharpen its edge,
  then one must exert more strength;
  however, the advantage of wisdom is
  that it brings success.
11 If the snake bites before it is charmed,
  then there is no advantage
  for the charmer.^A
12 The words from the mouth
  of a wise person are gracious,
  but the lips of a fool consume him.
13 The beginning of the words
  from his mouth is folly,
  but the end of his speaking
  is evil madness;
14 yet the fool multiplies words.
  No one knows what will happen,

and who can tell anyone
  what will happen after him?
15 The struggles of fools weary them,
  for they don't know how to go
  to the city.
16 Woe to you, land, when your king is
  a youth
  and your princes feast in the morning.
17 Blessed are you, land, when your king is
  a son of nobles
  and your princes feast
  at the proper time —
  for strength and not for drunkenness.
18 Because of laziness the roof caves in,
  and because of negligent hands
  the house leaks.
19 A feast is prepared for laughter,
  and wine makes life happy,
  and money^B is the answer
  for everything.
20 Do not curse the king
  even in your thoughts,
  and do not curse a rich person
  even in your bedroom,
  for a bird of the sky may carry
  the message,
  and a winged creature may report
  the matter.

Invest in Life

11 Send your bread on the surface
  of the water,
  for after many days you may find it.
2 Give a portion to seven or even to eight,
  for you don't know what disaster
  may happen on earth.
3 If the clouds are full, they will pour out
  rain on the earth;
  whether a tree falls to the south
  or the north,

---

^A**10:11** Lit *master of the tongue*   ^B**10:19** Lit *silver*

10:5–7 Sometimes kings and other rulers appoint inept people to high offices but let the competent languish **in lowly positions**. In this context, **slaves** refers to people whose skill and wisdom are so limited they ought to be restricted to doing simple manual labor. **10:8–9** These verses contain two pairs of proverbs that are juxtaposed against each other. Verse 8 describes criminal activity: digging a **pit** refers to setting a trap in order to rob or murder someone, and breaking through a **wall** refers to breaking into a house to plunder it. On the other hand, v. 9 teaches that even honest labor, such as quarrying **stones** or splitting **logs**, can result in severe injury. That is, criminal activity can destroy you, but so can honest work. The Teacher did not intend to discourage honesty but to say we have no guarantee of safety in this life. Even wise behavior can end in disaster. Ultimately, we must trust not in wisdom or in ethical behavior but in God for our security. **10:12–15** The primary service of a counselor was giving advice to a king, and the quality

of his advice marked the counselor as either a sage or a fool. The mark of a foolish counselor is that he says far more than he knows. Since **no one knows what will happen**, the wise counselor limits the amount of advice he gives. It is impossible to speak of the future with any certainty. By contrast, the foolish counselor tries to cover for his lack of knowledge by speaking on and on. **10:16–17** These verses conclude the general discussion of 9:13–10:17 on wisdom in the political world with the remark that few things matter so much in this area as leadership. **10:18–20** These verses contain a series of three proverbs on what makes a safe, pleasant life. First, we must do the work needed to insure that we have the basic comforts that all people desire. Second, we must have some money and pleasure in order to enjoy a good life. In isolation from the rest of the book, this seems to recommend pure hedonism and greed, but this misreads the verse. There are things, such as a good meal, that almost all people enjoy. Money helps us to deal with all kinds of problems (**money** does not literally

solve **everything**, but in fact many of our ordinary problems are financial in nature). Third, we should be careful in dealing with authorities in order to stay out of trouble. **11:1–2** These verses deal with financial investment, not charity. The phrase **bread on the surface of the water** refers to investing in overseas trading ventures (1Kg 9:26–27). The phrase **after many days you may find it** refers to an eventual return on the investment, and the phrase **to seven or even to eight** refers to diversifying one's investments. **11:3–5** These verses expand on the reason that a person must diversify his investments. No one knows what will happen, so it is best to be ready for anything. Verse 3 essentially states that there are some signs that indicate what will happen in the future. Dark **clouds** do not guarantee—but they suggest—that a storm is coming. Certain trends are likely to remain the same. A fallen tree almost certainly will stay where it is. On the other hand, a person can be too concerned with looking for indications of what will happen. Verse 4

the place where the tree falls,
   there it will lie.
4 One who watches the wind will not sow,
  and the one who looks at the clouds
    will not reap.
5 Just as you don't know the path
   of the wind,
  or how bones develop in^A the womb
   of a pregnant woman,
  so also you don't know the work of God
   who makes everything.
6 In the morning sow your seed,
  and at evening do not let
   your hand rest,
  because you don't know
   which will succeed,
  whether one or the other,
  or if both of them will be equally good.
7 Light is sweet,
  and it is pleasing for the eyes to see
   the sun.
8 Indeed, if someone lives many years,
  let him rejoice in them all,
  and let him remember the days
   of darkness, since they will be many.
  All that comes is futile.
9 Rejoice, young person,
   while you are young,
  and let your heart be glad in the days
   of your youth.
  And walk in the ways of your heart
  and in the desire of your eyes;
  but know that for all of these things
   God will bring you to judgment.
10 Remove sorrow from your heart,
  and put away pain from your flesh,

because youth and the prime of life
  are fleeting.

The Twilight of Life

12 So remember your Creator in the days
  of your youth:
  Before the days of adversity come,
  and the years approach
   when you will say,
  "I have no delight in them";
2 before the sun and the light
   are darkened,
  and the moon and the stars,
  and the clouds return after^B the rain;
3 on the day when the guardians
   of the house tremble,
  and the strong men stoop,
  the women who grind grain cease
   because they are few,
  and the ones who watch
   through the windows see dimly,
4 the doors at the street are shut
  while the sound of the mill fades;
  when one rises at the sound of a bird,
  and all the daughters of song grow faint.
5 Also, they are afraid of heights
   and dangers on the road;
  the almond tree blossoms,
  the grasshopper loses its spring,^C
  and the caper berry has no effect;
  for the mere mortal is headed
   to his eternal home,
  and mourners will walk around
   in the street;
6 before the silver cord is snapped,^D
  and the gold bowl is broken,

---

^A11:5 Or *know how the life-breath comes to the bones in*   ^B12:2 Or *with*   ^C12:5 Or *grasshopper is weighed down*, or *grasshopper drags itself along*   ^D12:6 Alt Hb tradition reads *removed*

---

says that people who will not commit until they are absolutely certain of success never do anything. Verse 5 tells us that we know little about the processes that govern the world. Understanding all about the weather or the formation of a fetus is beyond us. Thus, we should not demand infallible information about the future before making any investments.

11:6 A final word of advice on achieving prosperity: work hard in the hopes that at least one of your ventures will **succeed**.

11:7–12:7 Ecclesiastes is primarily concerned with making us understand that we are mortal, that our days are few, that all our works will fade away, and that we should govern our lives accordingly. In this, the last major passage of Ecclesiastes, the book reviews its essential conclusions about how we should spend the time we have. Essentially, the conclusion is twofold: enjoy your days under the sun and fear God.

11:9–10 In these verses two pieces of advice are in tension with each other. The first is that we should enjoy life and the second is that we should fear God. The danger is that some people will try to enjoy life by doing things that are offensive to God. On the other hand, those who have the wrong kind of fear of God believe that anything

that makes people happy must be bad; thus, they deprive themselves of legitimate joys. **12:1–7** Approaches to this passage differ, but it most likely is an extended series of metaphors describing the troubles of old age, culminating in death. The fact that old age is in view is suggested by the details of the metaphors and also by the exhortation in 11:10 to enjoy life while youthful vigor still exists. **12:1** God is called the **Creator** here for two reasons. First, as maker of heaven and earth he is our judge; we must **remember** him in the sense that we live in fear of him and never forget that we are accountable to him for our actions. Second, God as Creator calls us to enjoy life; he made the light, the earth and sky, food and drink, man and woman, and all the other things that in Gn 1 he calls "good." **The days of adversity**, as described in the verses that follow, are the days when a person is feeble and failing.

12:3 The phrase **when the guardians of the house tremble** probably refers to the hands. They are what a person uses to protect himself, and the hands of the elderly are sometimes subject to trembling. The **strong men** who **stoop** refers to the legs and back; these are the largest muscle groups in the body and they become flaccid in old age, leading to bent posture. The **women who grind grain**

are the teeth, because they grind food. In the ancient world, where dental care was nonexistent, even the pharaohs of Egypt lost their teeth if they lived into old age. The teeth are referred to as "women" because typically women in a household did the work of grinding flour for bread. The **ones who watch through the windows** refers to the eyes. Here, however, the language is a metaphor for poor eyesight.

12:4 This verse describes two aspects of the effects of old age on hearing. On the one hand, people no longer hear well, and sounds are muffled and **faint** as if **doors** have been shut. On the other hand, many old people do not sleep well, and even a faint sound awakens them.

12:5 **They are afraid of heights and dangers on the road** reminds us that old people fear falling down and are easy prey for criminals. **Almond tree blossoms** almost certainly refers to white hair. The **grasshopper loses its spring** and **the caper berry has no effect** may refer to impotence; it appears that the caper was regarded as an aphrodisiac. A **mere mortal** going to his **eternal home** with **mourners** walking **in the street** obviously alludes to a funeral. **12:6** The **cord**, the **bowl**, the **jar** . . . **shattered at the spring**, and the **wheel** . . . **bro-**

and the jar is shattered at the spring,
and the wheel is broken into the well;
⁷ and the dust returns to the earth
as it once was,
and the spirit returns to God who gave it.
⁸ "Absolute futility," says the Teacher. "Everything is futile."

The Teacher's Objectives and Conclusion

⁹ In addition to the Teacher being a wise man, he constantly taught the people knowledge; he weighed, explored, and arranged many proverbs. ¹⁰ The Teacher sought to find delightful sayings and write words of truth accurately. ¹¹ The sayings of the wise are like cattle prods, and those from masters of collections are like firmly embedded nails. The sayings are given by one Shepherd.ᴬ

¹² But beyond these, my son, be warned: there is no end to the making of many books, and much study wearies the body. ¹³ When all has been heard, the conclusion of the matter is this: fear God and keep his commands, because this is for allᴮ humanity. ¹⁴ For God will bring every act to judgment, including every hidden thing, whether good or evil.

ᴬ12:11 Or by a shepherd ᴮ12:13 Or is the whole duty of

ken at the well all refer to drawing up water from a well, a spring, or a cistern. Water in the Bible is frequently associated with life. Thus, if these things are broken, death has occurred. Describing these objects as silver and gold implies that life is precious.
12:7 This verse alludes to Gn 2:7; 3:19.
12:8 This verse repeats the theme of the book stated in 1:2. These two verses—1:2 and 12:8—bracket the whole of the book, and it properly ends at this point. What follows, vv. 9–14, is an epilogue.
12:9–14 These verses reveal a few more details about the author's life and give the reader some parting exhortations.

12:11 It is not certain whether embedded nails refers to nails inserted at the ends of cattle prods (1Sm 13:21), or whether this is a different metaphor, describing proverbs as fixed and dependable, like nails driven in a wall. If the latter, it implies that we can hang our lives on these fixed truths.
12:13–14 The meaning of the phrase because this is for all humanity is much debated. The Hebrew literally says, "for this [is] the whole of man." The phrase could mean, as the CSB renders it, that the rule to fear God applies to every person. Alternatively, it could mean obedience to God is the proper role for man in the universe. In other words,

to live in the fear of God is to be truly human. To do otherwise is to lose the essence of our humanity. The conclusion of Ecclesiastes, to fear God, is in keeping with the message of the book—that we are mortal and weak but he is almighty. The advice to fear God trumps everything. The whole of the book has been focused on the brevity of earthly life and on how we should live in light of this reality. But at the end, the book looks beyond this life to the final judgment.

Circumstances of Writing

The Song claims authorship by Solomon in its title (1:1), "The Song of Songs, which is Solomon's." The church has long accepted this at face value, but modern critics raise objections to Solomon as author.

First, critics claim that the title did not originate with the Song but was added later by someone who wanted to attribute the work to the famous Solomon. However, no evidence supports this claim. Moreover, the structure of the book suggests that the title is integral to the book's composition and is thus original. Like other biblical writers, the writer often structured content with attention to certain numbers—three, seven, and ten being some of the most common. Within the Song, for example, the author designed seven sections (see below), a sevenfold praise (4:1–5), twice a tenfold praise (5:10–16; 7:1–5), and a tenfold occurrence of the abstract word for love (2:4–5,7; 3:5; 5:8; 7:6; 8:4,6–7). Apart from the title (1:1), he wove Solomon's name into six other places (1:5; 3:7,9,11; 8:11–12): two in the last section, three in the central, and one in the first. With the inclusion of "Solomon" in the title, the name appears a perfect seven times and is symmetrically balanced within the Song: twice in the first section balanced by twice in the last one, with three in the central. The title is thus as cleverly integrated with the lyrics as possible. It not only conforms to their melodic alliteration and meter, but it completes the sevenfold occurrence of "Solomon" and in a manner that artistically balances it throughout the Song. In fact, the tenfold occurrence of "love" joins the sevenfold appearance of "Solomon" to show the Song's subject and author. Hardly a later addition, the title seems to have been original, constituting its first verse.

Another common objection to Solomon's authorship is the king's well-known possession of seven hundred wives and three hundred concubines (1Kg 11:3). How could a man who lived like that write a song about devotion to one woman? It appears he could do so only because grace touched his heart. In this respect, he foreshadowed other biblical writers who, except for God's grace and calling, were the least qualified to write Scripture. For example, Paul, the great apostle, wrote most eloquently of grace and his unworthiness (see 1Tm 1:12–16). Solomon was a man immersed in power and pleasure, but God opened his eyes to true love. Solomon also authored much of the book of Proverbs. Just as he did not always follow the precepts he recorded there, so too he evidently composed a great love song despite his failure to live in accordance with its ideals.

A compelling historical reason to date the Song as coming from the time of Solomon is its nearest literary parallel—the Egyptian love songs. No one doubts their origin prior to or contemporaneous with the time of Solomon, and the Egyptian love songs are indisputably the Song's closest literary parallels.

Contribution to the Bible

A beautiful love song inspires us like grace, creating within us a desire for its beauty. Like such an enchanting love song, Solomon's Song inspires a pursuit of the love it

3000–2000 BC

Stonehenge construction, phase I **2900**
Stonehenge construction, phase II **2900–2400**
Epic of Gilgamesh oral tradition
  developed from **2700** to **1400**
First libraries in Egypt **2500–2000**
Stonehenge construction, phase III **2400–1600**
ABRAHAM 2166-1991

2000–1800 BC

The Love Poem of a Persistent Woman,
  Old Babylonian **2017–1794**
Dumuzi-Inanna Love Songs, Sumerian **2000**
An Old Akkadian Love Charm **2000**
Love Lyrics of Rim–Sin, Akkadian **1822–1763**

portrays. This romantic delight is not a modern fairytale or fantasy from the past, but reflects God's desire to form within us a pure and devoted love. We discover that there is a bliss in married love that is reflective of the greater love believers experience as the bride of Christ. As this book's imagery informs us of romantic love, it also helps us anticipate the full consummation of our relationship with Christ when he returns for his bride.

Structure

The Song of Songs is a poem whose components form a chiastic structure. A chiasm takes the form:

A
    B
        C
    B´
A´

where A and A´ mirror each other and where the central element, C, conveys the main point of the poem. The author intended to emphasize the central elements of the structure, which are the day and night of the wedding (3:6–5:1). When God inspired Solomon to write this song, he gave divine approval to romantic love.

The Hebrew text makes a distinction between the various speakers through a change in gender and number. The Christian Standard Bible text has added subheadings to clarify when the speakers change.

The design of the Song underscores its central theme: a celebration of the goodness and beauty of romantic love.

Outline

I. Section A: Their Story Begins (1:2–2:7)
II. Section B: Invitation to Enjoy a Spring Day (2:6–17)
III. Section C: Night of Separation Preceding Wedding (3:1–5)
IV. Section D: Wedding Day and Night (3:6–5:1)
V. Section C´: Night of Separation Following Wedding Night (5:2–7:9)
VI. Section B´: Invitation to Enjoy a Spring Day (7:10–8:3)
VII. Section A´: Their Story Complete (8:4–14)

1800–1100 BC

Message of Lundingirra to His Mother,
  Old Babylonian **1800–1600**
Love Lyrics of Nanay and Muati,
  Old Babylonian **1711–1684**
MOSES 1526-1406
Heavy import and export trade, Egypt **1500–1000**
Events in Joshua **1406–1380?**
Events in Judges **1380?–1060?**
Egyptian Love Poetry **1305–1150**

1100–900 BC

Love Lyrics of Nabu and Tasmetu,
  Neo-Assyrian **1180–609**
The Harper's Song for Inherkhway, Egyptian **1160**
David becomes king over all Israel. **1003**
Solomon becomes king. **970**
Proverbs **970**
Song of Songs **970?**
Ecclesiastes **935?**

1

The Song of Songs, which is Solomon's.

Woman

2 Oh, that he would kiss me
   with the kisses of his mouth!
   For your caresses^A are more delightful
      than wine.
3 The fragrance of your perfume
      is intoxicating;
   your name is perfume poured out.
   No wonder young women^B adore you.
4 Take me with you — let's hurry.
   Oh, that the king would bring^C me
      to his chambers.

Young Women

   We will rejoice and be glad in you;
   we will celebrate your caresses
      more than wine.

Woman

   It is only right that they adore you.

5 Daughters of Jerusalem,
   I am dark like the tents of Kedar,
   yet lovely like the curtains of Solomon.
6 Do not stare at me because I am dark,
   for the sun has gazed on me.
   My mother's sons were angry with me;
   they made me take care
      of the vineyards.
   I have not taken care of
      my own vineyard.

7 Tell me, you whom I love:
   Where do you pasture your sheep?
   Where do you let them rest at noon?

Why should I be like one who veils
   herself^D
beside the flocks of your companions?

Man^E

8 If you do not know,
   most beautiful of women,
   follow^F the tracks of the flock,
   and pasture your young goats
   near the shepherds' tents.

9 I compare you, my darling,
   to a^G mare among Pharaoh's chariots.
10 Your cheeks are beautiful with jewelry,
   your neck with its necklace.
11 We will make gold jewelry for you,
   accented with silver.

Woman

12 While the king is on his couch,^H
   my perfume^I releases its fragrance.
13 The one I love is a sachet of myrrh
      to me,
   spending the night between my breasts.
14 The one I love is a cluster
      of henna blossoms to me,
   in the vineyards of En-gedi.

Man

15 How beautiful you are, my darling.
   How very beautiful!
   Your eyes are doves.

Woman

16 How handsome you are, my love.
   How delightful!
   Our bed is verdant;

---

^A1:2 Or *acts of love*   ^B1:3 Or *wonder virgins*   ^C1:4 Or *The king has brought*   ^D1:7 Or *who wanders*   ^E1:8 Some understand the young women to be the speakers in this verse.   ^F1:8 Lit *go out for yourself into*   ^G1:9 Lit *my*   ^H1:12 Or *is at his table*   ^I1:12 Lit *nard*

1:1 Song of Songs means the ultimate song, the finest song. The form of the phrase **which is Solomon's** normally indicates authorship (cp. Pss 72; 127).
1:2 Oh, that he would kiss me with the kisses of his mouth! begins the Song like love often begins: with sudden intensity and excitement. The abrupt beginning artistically weds style to content, signaling to the reader that the Song will move at a quick and entrancing pace. The speaker is unidentified at this point. Later we learn that she is "the Shulammite" (6:13).
1:3 Name (Hb *shem*) and **perfume** (Hb *shemen*) are similar in Hebrew, so the Song presents here the first of its frequent wordplays.
1:5–6 Shulamith explained her darkened appearance as the consequence of her brothers' (**my mother's sons**) assignment to work outside in **vineyards**. We later discover they had leased this vineyard from Solomon (8:10–12).
1:7 A shepherd finds shade for his flock during the heat of the day. So Shulamith could ask **Where do you let them** (the flock) **rest at noon?** implicitly requesting relief in Solomon's protection from the "sun's" heat.

One who veils herself is likely an allusion to Tamar, who disguised herself as a prostitute by donning a veil and then enticed Judah to fulfill his duty to provide for her (Gn 38:14–15). Like Tamar, Shulamith was not what she appeared to be: she was no more a common laborer than Tamar was a prostitute. But unlike Tamar, she did not have to use manipulation since Solomon was willing. So why indeed should Shulamith veil herself to conceal her motives? Later she is likened to a "palm tree," which is *tamar* in Hebrew (Sg 7:7–8).
1:8 Most beautiful of women is a term of address used twice elsewhere by the young women of Jerusalem for Shulamith (5:9; 6:1). **Young goats** is literally "female kids" (used only here in the OT), and it invites a figurative explanation for such an unusual flock. It likely anticipates the praise of Shulamith's long, flowing hair being like a flock of goats descending a mountain (4:1).
1:9 A **mare among Pharaoh's chariots** would stir the chariots' stallions, just as Shulamith would attract the attention of men. **1:10** Archaeological drawings show jewels decorating bridles of horses, so the imagery

of jewels on the **cheeks** and in necklaces likely extends the metaphor of the mare.
1:12 One may also translate **on his couch** as "in his realm," similar to its meaning in 1Kg 6:29; 2Kg 23:5 ("surrounding"), the only other times this phrase appears in the OT.
1:13–14 Spending the night personifies the **sachet of myrrh**, suggesting it was like a pillow a young woman would hold pretending it was her lover. While Solomon was away and about his realm, Shulamith's thoughts about him were as evocative as myrrh. **Henna blossoms** are white or red and fragrant like roses. **En-gedi** was an oasis in the desert. **1:15–2:3** Mutual praise escalates, each building upon the imagery introduced by the other: his praise of her beauty and **eyes** like **doves** (1:15) elicited like praise (1:16a) to which she added additional imagery (1:16b–17); her comparison of herself to a flower (2:1) then elicited like praise (2:2a) from him to which he added additional imagery (2:2b), which she reciprocated (**like an apricot tree**), but also climactically embellished (she delighted **to sit in his shade**, 2:3). Doves were repeatedly shown in the drawings of the day as literal "messengers of love." The

Purpose and Parameters of Sexual Relations

by Christopher Yuan

In a world of infinite shades of gray, ambiguity is elevated as a virtue, and sexual freedom has become the religion of our land. Now, with mere consent as the standard for sexual morality, intercourse is seen by some to be as essential as food and water. Herein lies the deception of today's secular worldview: your sexual desires define you, determine you, and should always delight you. When seen in light of Scripture, however, it becomes clear that the idolatry of sexuality is on a collision course with the gospel.

Before we bemoan the hedonism of modern Western culture, let's not forget that sexual immorality was commonplace in the ancient world. Israel and the early church introduced a new worldview with a unique approach to sexual expression that most likely seemed ridiculous to their pagan neighbors. The ancient Israelites and first-century Christians placed a strong emphasis on sexual purity (sex within marriage) while stressing the existential consequences of sexual immorality (sex outside of marriage). This distinctive paradigm for sexual ethics (which unabashedly celebrates the beauty and virtue of sexual intimacy between a husband and a wife) is grounded in Scripture. Sexual relations in marriage is good (Gn 1:31; 2:24). Sex is God's idea. He created it and blessed it. God created sex as a special and exclusive gift, something to be enjoyed between husband and wife.

In a sexually liberated world, more sex outside of marriage—premarital and extramarital—doesn't celebrate this most intimate act but devalues it. When it is shared with anyone, even with strangers, sex becomes just common and is no longer good. Sexual relations in marriage consummates the two becoming one flesh (Gn 2:24). The biblical concept of one flesh points back to the beginning when God made Eve from one of Adam's ribs (2:21–22) and brought her to him. Adam rejoiced and proclaimed, "This one, at last, is bone of my bone and flesh of my flesh" (2:23). This "one-flesh union" elevates marriage from being a convenient coupling of two people physically attracted to one another into an ontological reality that transcends the material and emotional. God's intent for sexual relations is to be the physical, emotional, and spiritual oneness that only a husband and a wife should share. Sexual relations in marriage help fulfill the creation mandate: "God blessed them, and God said to them, 'Be fruitful, multiply, fill the earth, and subdue it'" (Gn 1:28). The context of this commandment is a divine blessing.

This connection between blessing and offspring can be seen later in the book of Genesis with the establishment of God's covenant with Abraham. In Genesis 12:2 God called Abram to leave the country of his fathers. God promised him, saying, "I will make you into a great nation, I will bless you, I will make your name great, and you will be a blessing." This blessing included offspring in such abundance to be considered a nation, as numerous as the stars in the sky (15:5)! The psalmist writes, "Sons are indeed a heritage from the LORD, offspring, a reward. Like arrows in the hand of a warrior are the sons born in one's youth. Happy is the man who has filled his quiver with them" (Ps 127:3–5). And Proverbs 17:6 states, "Grandchildren are the crown of the elderly, and the pride of children is their fathers."

Sexual relations in marriage is a sign of the marriage covenant. The Hebrew word for covenant occurs 287 times in the Hebrew Bible. These God-initiated covenants were often marked with signs which served to make tangible the intangible reality of a covenant. In Genesis 9 God made a covenant with Noah, his offspring, and all of creation, and the sign of the covenant was the rainbow (vv. 11, 13). One of the signs of the covenant with Abraham was that God gave him a new name. "Your name will no longer be Abram; your name will be Abraham" (Gn 17:5). In addition, God's covenant to give Abraham many offspring and much land (15:18) was marked by the sign of circumcision. "You must circumcise the flesh of your foreskin to serve as a sign of the covenant between me and you" (17:11).

The prophet Malachi calls marriage a covenant: "Because even though the LORD has been a witness between you and the wife of your youth, you have acted treacherously against her. She was your marriage partner and your wife by covenant" (Mal 2:14). And in Genesis 2:24 the "one-flesh" metaphor is covenantal language. "This is why a man leaves his father and mother and bonds with his wife, and they become one flesh." Adam gave a name to Eve as he entered into covenant with her (Gn 2:23). This adds to the significance of a wife taking on her husband's name as they enter into this new covenant in modern times. And this "one-flesh" union of sexual relations in marriage can also be understood as a sign of the marriage covenant.

Sexual relations should not be understood as the prize received after a wedding. Rather, it is the physical sign of the marriage covenant. Each time a husband and a wife engage in sex, it reconfirms the covenant made before God and brothers and sisters in Christ, and it serves as a reminder of that beautiful covenant. Sexual relations in marriage is other-centered. Sexual pleasure is one of the most powerful forces on earth, and the incentivizing nature of it easily turns sex into something self-centered. Pleasure can become an idol, promising more than it can deliver. However, God's Word reminds us that the focus and attention of sexual intimacy must be outward toward our beloved spouse in the context of marriage.

As much as the ancient and modern worlds equate sex with self-gratification, the apostle Paul brought some important clarity. In 1 Corinthians Paul reminds married couples that love for your spouse is the correct focus. "A husband should fulfill his marital duty to his wife, and likewise a wife to her husband. A wife does not have the right over her own body, but her husband does. In the same way, a husband does not have the right over his own body, but his wife does" (7:3–4). Then in Ephesians 5:28–29 Paul makes a similar statement, "In the same way, husbands are to love their wives as their own bodies. He who loves his wife loves himself. For no one ever hates his own flesh but provides and cares for it, just as Christ does for the church." Not only does the wife have authority over her husband's body and the husband over his wife's body, but they also must love each other as their own bodies.

Sexual relations in marriage means surrendering self-determination and pursuing mutual affection, respect, and loyalty. Love "is not self-seeking" (1Co 13:5). Thus, reframing sex in this way affirms the concept of faithfulness in marriage between one man and one woman because it is not possible to belong wholly to more than one person. Adultery is completely out of the question, for my body is not my own to give. Thus, if sexual relations are for marriage only, then God calls us to two specific paths. If you are single, then be sexually abstinent. If you are biblically married, then be faithful to your spouse of the opposite sex. We call this holy sexuality: chastity in singleness and faithfulness in marriage.

¹⁷ the beams of our house are cedars,
and our rafters are cypresses.^A

2 I am a wildflower^B of Sharon,
a lily^C of the valleys.

Man

² Like a lily among thorns,
so is my darling
among the young women.

Woman

³ Like an apricot^D tree among the trees
of the forest,
so is my love among the young men.
I delight to sit in his shade,
and his fruit is sweet to my taste.
⁴ He brought me to the banquet hall,^E
and he looked on me with love.^F
⁵ Sustain me with raisins;
refresh me with apricots,^G
for I am lovesick.
⁶ May his left hand be under my head,
and his right arm embrace me.
⁷ Young women of Jerusalem,
I charge you
by the gazelles and the wild does
of the field,
do not stir up or awaken love
until the appropriate time.^H

⁸ Listen! My love is approaching.
Look! Here he comes,
leaping over the mountains,
bounding over the hills.
⁹ My love is like a gazelle
or a young stag.
See, he is standing behind our wall,

gazing through the windows,
peering through the lattice.
¹⁰ My love calls to me:

Man

Arise, my darling.
Come away, my beautiful one.
¹¹ For now the winter is past;
the rain has ended and gone away.
¹² The blossoms appear in the countryside.
The time of singing^I has come,
and the turtledove's cooing is heard
in our land.
¹³ The fig tree ripens its figs;
the blossoming vines give off
their fragrance.
Arise, my darling.
Come away, my beautiful one.

¹⁴ My dove, in the clefts of the rock,
in the crevices of the cliff,
let me see your face,^J
let me hear your voice;
for your voice is sweet,
and your face is lovely.

Woman^K

¹⁵ Catch the foxes for us —
the little foxes that ruin
the vineyards —
for our vineyards are in bloom.

Woman

¹⁶ My love is mine and I am his;
he feeds among the lilies.
¹⁷ Until the day breaks^L
and the shadows flee,

---

^A1:17 Or *firs*, or *pines*   ^B2:1 Traditionally *rose*   ^C2:1 Or *lotus*   ^D2:3 Or *apple*   ^E2:4 Lit *the house of wine*   ^F2:4 Or *and his banner over me is love*   ^G2:5 Or *apples*   ^H2:7 Lit *until it pleases*   ^I2:12 Or *pruning*   ^J2:14 Or *form*   ^K2:15 The speaker could be the woman, the man, or both.   ^L2:17 Lit *breathes*

---

look of love in lovers' eyes is unmistakable. **Our bed is verdant** (1:16) may also be translated "our resting place is in the branches' foliage," which is perhaps more consistent with the context and other OT usage.
2:1 The Hebrew *shushan* was probably not the **lily** (*Lilium spp.*) but the water lily or lotus flower (*Nymphaea lotus L.*), which the ancient world associated with almost magical, life-giving powers.
2:2–3 The significance of the lotus flower's place **among thorns** is similar to the tree's **shade** and **fruit** in a dangerous forest: both are places of safety surrounded by danger. The implication is that their love was likewise a place of safety in a hostile world. *Fruit* is often a metaphor for speech (Pr 12:14; 13:2; 18:20) that can be described as sweet not only in Proverbs (Pr 16:24), but also in the Song (Sg 5:13,16).
2:4–5 Banquet hall is literally "house of wine," inviting a contrast with the house of nature in 1:17 and the house of wealth in 8:6–7. **He looked on me with love** assumes that the root meaning behind the military banner was the concept of looking. The alternate reading, "His banner over me is love," is supported by

the fact that drawings in the ancient Near East show groups carrying banners with symbols identifying the group. Solomon's love for Shulamith is clear and public. **I am lovesick** affirms the intensity of romantic love.
2:6 Some translate this as a realized fact, "His left hand is." But it is more likely a wish, **may his left hand be**.
2:7 Gazelles (Hb *tseva'oth*) is precisely like "armies" (Hb *tseva'oth*) in "Lord of Armies," and **wild does of the field** (Hb *'ayloth hasadeh*) is similar to *El Shaddai*—two wordplays. The play on the names of God is instructive. Shulamith asked for a promise of patience in love not by the Lord of Armies nor by the Almighty God but by the creatures whose manner modeled romantic ways. Love, as she expresses it here, awakens not in response to the coercive power of an army or the might of God, but to love expressed with the gentle sensitivity of the gazelles or does of the meadow. **Until the appropriate time** (lit "until it pleases") personifies love as their guide.
2:8 Listen! My love is approaching is literally "The voice of my beloved!" *Voice* can also mean "sound," which may be the sense of it here.

2:15 The term **vineyards** refers to Shulamith (1:6; 8:12). **In bloom** anticipates the vineyard's beauty before the harvest, and thus describes the beauty of the two lovers anticipating marriage; **foxes** extends the metaphor to anything harmful to the romance. Perhaps the primary warning is against a "premature harvest" of the fruit Shulamith offered Solomon on the wedding night (4:16). The speaker of **Catch . . . for us** could be Solomon, Shulamith, or both; the ambiguity is likely intentional, suggesting mutual resolve.
2:16 My love is mine and I am his later transforms to "I am my love's and my love is mine" (6:3) and finally to "I am my love's, and his desire is for me" (7:10)—all similar but differing in ways that show a progression in Shulamith's security. First her possession of him was primary, then secondary, then finally omitted completely, as she found security not in her possession of him, but in his devoted love of her. On **lilies**, see note at v. 1. The flower becomes increasingly erotic and evidently associated with tenderness—her breasts, his lips, her abdomen.
2:17 Gazelle or a young stag is identical to the phrase in v. 9 that describes Solomon's

turn around, my love, and be
    like a gazelle
or a young stag
    on the divided mountains.[A]

3 In my bed at night[B]
I sought the one I love;
I sought him, but did not find him.[C]
² I will arise now and go about the city,
    through the streets and the plazas.
I will seek the one I love.
I sought him, but did not find him.
³ The guards who go about the city
    found me.
I asked them, "Have you seen the one
    I love?"
⁴ I had just passed them
    when I found the one I love.
I held on to him and would not
    let him go
until I brought him
    to my mother's house —
to the chamber of the one
    who conceived me.
⁵ Young women of Jerusalem,
    I charge you
by the gazelles and the wild does
    of the field,
do not stir up or awaken love
until the appropriate time.[D]

Narrator

⁶ Who is this coming up
    from the wilderness
like columns of smoke,
scented with myrrh and frankincense
from every fragrant powder
    of the merchant?

⁷ Look! Solomon's bed
surrounded by sixty warriors
from the mighty men of Israel.
⁸ All of them are skilled with swords
and trained in warfare.
Each has his sword at his side
to guard against the terror of the night.

⁹ King Solomon made a carriage
    for himself
with wood from Lebanon.
¹⁰ He made its posts of silver,
    its back[E] of gold,
    and its seat of purple.
Its interior is inlaid with love[F]
by the young women of Jerusalem.
¹¹ Go out, young women of Zion,
and gaze at King Solomon,
wearing the crown his mother placed
    on him
on the day of his wedding —
the day of his heart's rejoicing.

Man

4 How beautiful you are, my darling.
    How very beautiful!
Behind your veil,
    your eyes are doves.
Your hair is like a flock of goats
    streaming down Mount Gilead.
² Your teeth are like a flock
    of newly shorn sheep
coming up from washing,
    each one bearing twins,
    and none has lost its young.[G]
³ Your lips are like a scarlet cord,
    and your mouth[H] is lovely.
Behind your veil,

[A]2:17 Or *the Bether mountains*, or *the mountains of spices*; Hb obscure   [B]3:1 Or *bed night after night*   [C]3:1 LXX adds *I called him, but he did not answer me*   [D]3:5 Lit *until it pleases*   [E]3:10 Or *base*, or *canopy*   [F]3:10 Or *leather*   [G]4:2 Lit *and no one bereaved among them*   [H]4:3 Or *speech*

---

behavior in courtship. Shulamith longed for the same delight on the wedding night. **Divided mountains** (lit "mountains of separation") is a poetic reference to her breasts. In Solomon's answer to this request, he embellished the metaphor as the "mountain of myrrh and hill of frankincense" (4:6; cp. 8:14), adding fragrance to the image. The enjoyment of Shulamith's breasts is again poetically expressed in a later night of lovemaking (7:7–8). So Solomon displayed in the Song what he encouraged in Pr 5:18–19. Until Solomon answered Shulamith's request, the night remained and with it the anxiety of anticipation (3:1–4).
3:1–4 Shulamith and Solomon began the night apart but ended it together, aided by the watchmen of the walls.
3:5 Young women of Jerusalem begins a repetition of the refrain of 2:7 and is a transition to the central section of the wedding day and night (3:6–5:1).
3:6–5:1 These verses feature the songwriter's own words at beginning and end, first celebrating the pageant of the wedding day and then the beauty of the wedding night.

Solomon is more central in the wedding day, his name appearing three times and the pageantry proclaiming his lavish wedding (3:6–11). Shulamith is more central in the wedding night, in praise of her beauty and character (4:1–5:1).
3:6 The word **this** is feminine in Hebrew, perhaps indicating Shulamith was in the procession coming to Solomon. **Coming up from the wilderness** (see 8:5) suggests two complementary allusions: (1) Israel's emergence from the wilderness they had entered after deliverance from Egypt and (2) Adam and Eve's emergence from the wilderness they had entered after disobedience.
3:7–11 This section describes the powerful and magnificent retinue of King Solomon.
4:1–5:1 The wedding night begins with praise of seven aspects of Shulamith (4:1–7), then proceeds to invitation (4:8), lovemaking (4:9–11), and poetic consummation (4:12–5:1).
4:1–7 The praise begins and ends with compliment of the whole person. Within these comprehensive statements Solomon admired Shulamith's eyes, hair, teeth, lips, mouth, neck, and breasts. Between the compliment

of her breasts and the concluding summary compliment is Solomon's answer to Shulamith's request of 2:17.
4:1 Doves were associated with love in the ancient world. Shulamith's eyes were messengers of love to Solomon. **A flock of goats streaming down Mount Gilead** describes her long, flowing hair. The metaphor suggests lively curls and healthy, flowing hair.
4:2 Shulamith's **teeth** were gleaming and white. A festive sheep-shearing may be suggested, too, by **coming up from washing**, occurring after they were shorn, so perhaps Solomon praised her smile as well.
4:3 The prostitute Rahab hung a scarlet cord from her window as a sign to the invading Israelites to protect her home (Jos 2:18). Shulamith's speech, which expressed her character, was her protection. This indicated she belonged to God, just as Rahab's scarlet ribbon indicated she belonged to God and his people. **Your brow** could be translated "your lips." In addition, the word translated **slice** is more precisely rendered "sliced opening," which is consistent with the drawings from this era that show the pomegranate sliced

your brow^A is like a slice
  of pomegranate.
4 Your neck is like the tower of David,
  constructed in layers.
  A thousand shields are hung on it —
  all of them shields of warriors.
5 Your breasts are like two fawns,
  twins of a gazelle, that feed
  among the lilies.
6 Until the day breaks^B
  and the shadows flee,
  I will make my way to the mountain
  of myrrh
  and the hill of frankincense.
7 You are absolutely beautiful, my darling;
  there is no imperfection in you.

8 Come with me from Lebanon,^C my bride;
  come with me from Lebanon!
  Descend from the peak of Amana,
  from the summit of Senir and Hermon,
  from the dens of the lions,
  from the mountains of the leopards.
9 You have captured my heart, my sister,
  my bride.
  You have captured my heart
  with one glance of your eyes,
  with one jewel of your necklace.
10 How delightful your caresses are,
  my sister, my bride.

Your caresses are much better
  than wine,
  and the fragrance of your perfume
  than any balsam.
11 Your lips drip sweetness like
  the honeycomb, my bride.
  Honey and milk are under your tongue.
  The fragrance of your garments is like
  the fragrance of Lebanon.

12 My sister, my bride, you are
  a locked garden —
  a locked garden^D and a sealed spring.
13 Your branches are a paradise^E
  of pomegranates
  with choicest fruits;
  henna with nard,
14 nard and saffron, calamus
  and cinnamon,
  with all the trees of frankincense,
  myrrh and aloes,
  with all the best spices.
15 You are a garden spring,
  a well of flowing water
  streaming from Lebanon.

Woman

16 Awaken, north wind;
  come, south wind.
  Blow on my garden,

---

^A4:3 Or *temple*, or *cheek*, or *lips*　^B4:6 Lit *breathes*　^C4:8 In Hb, the word for *Lebanon* is similar to "frankincense" in Sg 4:6,14,15.　^D4:12 Some Hb mss read *locked fountain*　^E4:13 Or *park*, or *orchard*

---

open but not cut into slices. These compliments are a dazzling array of movement and color. The colors proceed from white doves to black goats to white sheep to red lips and mouth. They also alternate movement: doves flying out, a flock scampering down, shorn sheep scurrying up, lips beckoning in. **4:4** The **neck** expresses the body language of character. If Shulamith's neck was like a military fortress, she had a character that demanded respect. The tower **shields** probably correspond metaphorically to her necklace (v. 9). **4:5** The **lilies**, or lotus flowers (see note at 2:1), suggest the life-giving effect of her breasts. The comparison to **fawns** perhaps suggests Solomon responded as if to playful, baby animals he wanted to hold and caress. **4:7 No imperfection** refers to both inner and outer perfection, so it is an apt summary

of Solomon's praise of Shulamith's beauty and character. **4:8 From the peak . . . from the dens of the lions, from the mountains of the leopards** perhaps are metaphors of the fearful places within Shulamith that she must leave in order to open her heart fully to Solomon. **4:9 My sister, my bride**—a phrase implying a bond as close as that of Adam and Eve—introduces each stage of increasing sexual intimacy: arousal from her presence; delight in her love and fragrance (v. 10); beginning of consummation (v. 12); and the celebration of their union (5:1). **Captured my heart** may also be rendered "made my heart beat faster." **4:10** The phrase translated **your caresses are much better than wine** occurs also in 1:2,4. **Balsam** refers to an aromatic resin that oozes from the balsam tree when cut. It was used to make perfume and beauty treatments. See 1Kg 10:2,10; Est 2:12. **4:11** The phrase **your lips drip sweetness like the honeycomb** is alliterative in Hebrew, suggesting the sound of dripping honey. **Honey and milk** not only describes passionate kisses but likely alludes to the richness of the land that God gave Israel (Ex 3:8,17; Nm 14:8; 16:13–14). Solomon found the same richness in Shulamith and implied she was also a gift from God. **4:12** The phrases **locked garden** and **sealed spring** praise virgin purity in the imagery of a garden paradise and pristine mountain streams (cp. v. 15). **4:13–14** The word **paradise** may mean simply "park" or "orchard," but it may also

allude to the perfection of Eden. The Hebrew rendered **branches** is difficult to translate but not difficult to understand. It refers to all the "extensions" from the garden soil: all the fruits, trees, and spices. It is not the word for "garden," but for all that the garden contains, so it anticipates the entire description in vv. 13–14. **Pomegranates** were symbols of lovemaking and fertility; **henna** had small red and white blossoms; **nard** was famous for its aroma; **saffron** was linked with nard, possibly because the spices were in the saffron's stigmata, which when gathered together resembled a handful of yarn, perhaps providing a delicate metaphor of Shulamith's sexuality. **Calamus** (Hb *qaneh*) **and cinnamon** (Hb *qinnamon*) are alliterative and, like nard and saffron, combine plant (the long, green-ribboned leaves of the calamus that grew in marshes) with fragrance. The **trees of frankincense** continue the movement to the larger, more overwhelming beauty of the garden, perhaps a metaphor for the increasing intensity of the experience. **4:15 Garden spring** joins the metaphors of *garden* and *spring*. Water **from Lebanon** completes the embellishment of spring water with the image of pure, mountain streams. An allusion to Shulamith's sexual response in the metaphor of the waters is consistent with the metaphor of a well in Pr 5:15–18. **4:16** Shulamith resumed both the garden and the spring metaphors. She asked the winds to entice Solomon into the garden with its intoxicating fragrances. **Awaken** is the same word used in the refrain advocating

---

and spread the fragrance of its spices.
Let my love come to his garden
and eat its choicest fruits.

Man

5 I have come to my garden — my sister,
    my bride.
I gather^A my myrrh with my spices.
I eat my honeycomb with my honey.
I drink my wine with my milk.

Narrator

Eat, friends!
Drink, be intoxicated with caresses!^B

Woman

² I was sleeping, but my heart was awake.
A sound! My love was knocking!

Man

Open to me, my sister, my darling,
my dove, my perfect one.
For my head is drenched with dew,
my hair with droplets of the night.

Woman

³ I have taken off my clothing.
How can I put it back on?
I have washed my feet.
How can I get them dirty?
⁴ My love thrust his hand
    through the opening,
and my feelings were stirred for him.
⁵ I rose to open for my love.
My hands dripped with myrrh,
my fingers with flowing myrrh

on the handles of the bolt.
⁶ I opened to my love,
but my love had turned and gone away.
My heart sank^C because he had left.^D
I sought him, but did not find him.
I called him, but he did not answer.
⁷ The guards who go about the city
found me.
They beat and wounded me;
they took my cloak^E from me —
the guardians of the walls.
⁸ Young women of Jerusalem,
    I charge you,
if you find my love,
tell him that I am lovesick.

Young Women

⁹ What makes the one you love better
    than another,
most beautiful of women?
What makes him better than another,
that you would give us this charge?

Woman

¹⁰ My love is fit and strong,^F
notable among ten thousand.
¹¹ His head is purest gold.
His hair is wavy^G
and black as a raven.
¹² His eyes are like doves
beside flowing streams,
washed in milk
and set like jewels.^H
¹³ His cheeks are like beds of spice,
mounds of^I perfume.
His lips are lilies,

---

^A5:1 Lit *pluck*   ^B5:1 Or *Drink your fill, lovers*   ^C5:6 Lit *My soul went out*   ^D5:6 Or *spoken*   ^E5:7 Or *veil*, or *shawl*   ^F5:10 Or *is radiant and ruddy*   ^G5:11 Or *is like palm leaves*; Hb obscure   ^H5:12 Lit *milk sitting in fullness*   ^I5:13 LXX, Vg read *spice, yielding*

---

patient restraint (2:7; 3:5). The songwriter thus reminds the reader that such restraint is no longer needed.
5:1 Solomon celebrated the consummation. The songwriter's words began this section and now conclude it. Since **friends** in the singular was Solomon's customary name for Shulamith (rendered "darling" in 1:9,15; 2:2,10,13; 4:1,7; 6:4) and **caresses** translates a word that, in the singular, was Shulamith's customary name for Solomon (rendered "my love" in 1:16; 2:3,8–9,16–17; 4:16; 5:2,4–6,8–10,16; 6:1–3; 7:9,11; 8:14), an alternative translation is "Eat, O darling companions; drink and drink deeply, O beloveds." In other words, it appears the songwriter addresses the couple by the names they most commonly called each other.
After encouraging the wedding guests at the end of the wedding day (3:11), the song writer blesses the wedding couple at the end of the wedding night (5:1). His authorial perspective is all-knowing and all-present, hinting that he speaks for God.
5:2–7:9 This is the lengthiest section of the Song. This night of relative apathy (5:2a) following the wedding night is structurally opposite the night of anxiety preceding the wedding day.

5:2–8 The contrast with the night before the wedding is apparent. On that earlier night, Shulamith could not sleep because of her anxiety over Solomon's absence; here, sleep comes easily, and she wants continued slumber out of apathy from his presence, as evidenced by Solomon's pleading to **open to me**. In 3:1–4 the watchmen of the walls assisted Shulamith to find him; here, they hinder her, mistaking her for a criminal. In 3:1–4 Shulamith's night ended united with Solomon; here, lengthy anxiety and reconciliation precede the night of reunion.
5:2 Solomon's fourfold terms of endearment, the most of any place in the Song, underscore the contrast of his fervor with her apathetic response.
5:4–5 Many of the terms in these verses have euphemistic possibilities, suggesting a double entendre. She may have been dreaming. **My feelings were stirred** is literally "my insides were agitated."
5:8 Shulamith is no longer apathetic but **lovesick** (lit "faint from love am I"), just as she was in the peak of courtship (2:5).
5:9 This is the first of two questions (v. 9; 6:1) that guide the movement of this section.
5:10–16 This section contains tenfold praise that moves downward from head to feet,

enclosed by comprehensive summary praise in v. 10 and v. 16b. This section is in chiastic balance with the tenfold praise of Shulamith that moves upward from feet to head (7:1–5).
5:10 Fit and strong is literally "radiant and red"; the opposite of a sallow complexion is a ruddy, glowing one, implying fitness and strength. **Among ten thousand** is clearly a ratio emphasizing uniqueness.
5:11 Gold is consistent with the lustrous radiance, and its color and value are paramount in the metaphor. The Hebrew word translated **wavy** may be associated with "palm leaves," a precursor to the palm tree simile of Shulamith in 7:7.
5:12 Eyes . . . like doves is the only identical praise of each by the other (1:15; 4:1). Each had eyes expressing love. Whereas the other aspects of Shulamith's praise are expanded at most by one phrase, this simile is expanded by three: **beside flowing streams, washed in milk and set like jewels** (lit "perched over a pool"). The phrases contribute to imagery of happy, loving eyes.
5:13 The visual metaphors of vv. 11–12 give way to more sensual, aromatic ones in this verse: fragrant spices and perfume describe Solomon's cheeks; liquid **myrrh** drips from his lips. **Lilies** are literally life-giving "lotus

dripping with flowing myrrh.

14 His arms^A^ are rods of gold
set^B^ with beryl.
His body^C^ is an ivory panel
covered with lapis lazuli.

15 His legs are alabaster pillars
set on pedestals of pure gold.
His presence is like Lebanon,
as majestic as the cedars.

16 His mouth is sweetness.
He is absolutely desirable.
This is my love, and this is my friend,
young women of Jerusalem.

Young Women

6 Where has your love gone,
most beautiful of women?
Which way has he^D^ turned?
We will seek him with you.

Woman

2 My love has gone down to his garden,
to beds of spice,
to feed in the gardens
and gather lilies.

3 I am my love's and my love is mine;
he feeds among the lilies.

Man

4 You are as beautiful as Tirzah,
my darling,
lovely as Jerusalem,
awe-inspiring as an army with banners.

5 Turn your eyes away from me,
for they captivate me.
Your hair is like a flock of goats
streaming down from Gilead.

6 Your teeth are like a flock of ewes
coming up from washing,
each one having a twin,
and not one missing.^E^

7 Behind your veil,
your brow^F^ is like a slice
of pomegranate.

8 There are sixty queens
and eighty concubines
and young women^G^ without number.

9 But my dove, my virtuous one, is unique;
she is the favorite of her mother,
perfect to the one who gave her birth.
Women see her and declare
her fortunate;
queens and concubines also,
and they sing her praises:

10 Who is this who shines like the dawn,
as beautiful as the moon,
bright as the sun,
awe-inspiring as an army with banners?

Woman

11 I came down to the walnut grove
to see the blossoms of the valley,
to see if the vines were budding
and the pomegranates blooming.

12 I didn't know what was happening to
me.
I felt like I was
in a chariot with a nobleman.^H^

Young Women

13 Come back, come back, Shulammite!^I^
Come back, come back, that
we may look at you!

---

^A^ 5:14 Lit *hands* ^B^ 5:14 Lit *filled*; Sg 5:2,12 ^C^ 5:14 Lit *abdomen* ^D^ 6:1 Lit *your love* ^E^ 6:6 Lit *and no one bereaved among them* ^F^ 6:7 Or *temple*, or *cheek*, or *lips* ^G^ 6:8 Or *and virgins*; Sg 1:3 ^H^ 6:12 Hb obscure ^I^ 6:13 Or *the perfect one*, or *the peaceable one*

---

flowers" (see note at 2:1). Shulamith praised Solomon's fragrant, intoxicating kisses.
5:14 His arms are literally "his hands," and the **rods of gold** are likely his fingers, a metaphor in praise of Solomon's valued touch. **His body** (lit "his abdomen") is hard and polished like **ivory**, but rippled, as if **covered with lapis lazuli**.
5:15 Alabaster was a valuable mineral normally used for small objects, so its use to create massive **pillars** emphasizes value, just like gold, ivory, or sapphires. "Pillars" imply **legs** of grandeur and strength. The **pedestals of pure gold** of Solomon's feet show gold from head to toe, a visual metaphor for his complete desirability (v. 16).
5:16 Mouth is likely a reference to speech. The affirmation of **love** and friendship intertwined continues the theme begun in 1:9.
6:1 This is the second of two questions (5:9) that guide the movement of this section.
6:2–13 This section first answers the question, showing Shulamith's awareness of Solomon's location, then recounts his affirming praise and the account of their reconciliation.
6:2–3 Lilies are "lotus flowers" (see note at 2:1). **I am my love's** continues the transformation of this refrain (see note at 2:16).

Feeds among the lilies anticipates Solomon's life-giving praise that brings reconciliation.
6:4–10 This section consists of praise designed to reconcile. Although on the wedding night one glance of Shulamith's eyes aroused Solomon (4:9), here Solomon asked that she turn her eyes from him because they captivated (lit "aroused") him. He did not want to express his love physically until they reunited emotionally, which the praise was designed to achieve. He avoided the most erotic of lovemaking praise. He emphasized instead that Shulamith was God's gift for whom his love was unchanged since the wedding night. His comparison of her to the beauty of Israel (6:4,10) implies she was as wonderful a gift to him as the land was to God's people.
Solomon's comparison of Shulamith to **Tirzah** and **Jerusalem** (v. 4), Israel's most prominent cities in the south and the north, appears to be in chiastic balance with the description of her as **beautiful as the moon, bright as the sun**, since both lyrics end with the same phrase: **awe-inspiring as an army with banners**. "An army with banners" may also be translated "bannered hosts" (i.e., "of heaven," which would be "stars," or "of

armies," depending on the context). So Solomon compared Shulamith to the cities and military of Israel, which were like the moon, the sun, and the stars—perhaps recalling the imagery of Israel as the sun, moon, and stars in Joseph's dream (Gn 37:9).
6:11–13 In these verses Shulamith recounted the reconciliation. **If the vines were budding and the pomegranates blooming** is a metaphor expressing their desire to begin a new season of life together (2:17; 7:12). No easy explanation exists for the phrase **in a chariot with a nobleman**, but the implication is that Shulamith had resumed a position of royal prominence. She is here identified as **the Shulammite** for the first time in the Song. We have rendered it throughout the study notes as "Shulamith," the feminine form of Solomon's name. As the feminine form of Solomon, the name shows she and Solomon were "soulmates" who through their hardship and reconciliation had entered into a deeper relationship (8:10). Alternately, rather than a personal or pet name, the word might mean she was from the town of Shulam, which is otherwise unknown, or from Shunem (Jos 19:18; 1Sm 28:4; 2Kg 4:8).

Man

How you gaze at the Shulammite,
　as you look at the dance
　　of the two camps!^A

7 How beautiful are your sandaled feet,
　princess!^B
The curves of your thighs
　are like jewelry,
　the handiwork of a master.
2 Your navel is a rounded bowl;
　it never lacks mixed wine.
Your belly is a mound of wheat
　surrounded by lilies.
3 Your breasts are like two fawns,
　twins of a gazelle.
4 Your neck is like a tower of ivory,
　your eyes like pools in Heshbon
　　by Bath-rabbim's gate.
Your nose is like the tower of Lebanon
　looking toward Damascus.
5 Your head crowns you^C
　like Mount Carmel,

the hair of your head
　like purple cloth —
　a king could be held captive
　　in your tresses.
6 How beautiful you are
　and how pleasant,
my love, with such delights!
7 Your stature is like a palm tree;
　your breasts are clusters
　　of fruit.
8 I said, "I will climb the palm tree
　and take hold of its fruit."
May your breasts be like clusters
　of grapes,
and the fragrance of your breath
　like apricots.
9 Your mouth^D is like fine wine —

Woman

flowing smoothly for my love,
　gliding past my lips and teeth!^E
10 I am my love's,
　and his desire is for me.

---

^A6:13 Or *dance of Mahanaim*　　^B7:1 Lit *daughter of a nobleman,* or *prince*　　^C7:5 Lit *head upon you is*　　^D7:9 Lit *palate*
^E7:9 LXX, Syr, Vg; MT reads *past lips of sleepers*

The **two camps** is *mahanaim* in Hebrew. This was the name of the place where Jacob and Esau's reconciliation took place (Gn 32–33)—an appropriate parallel for the resolution of conflict between husband and wife. **7:1–5** Solomon's tenfold praise of Shulamith from head to toe in this section is in chiastic balance with her tenfold praise of Solomon from toe to head in 5:10–16. This praise also offers interesting comparisons with the lovemaking praise of the wedding night (4:1–7). It is more intimate and lavish—more lavish, in the royal imagery of a **princess** with hair not like a flock descending a mountain but like fine **purple** threads holding **captive** a **king**; more intimate, in praising not only her **breasts** again (more sensually), but her **thighs** (lit "hips"), **navel**, and **belly** (lit "abdomen") for the first time. The praise poetically portrays the greater depth of intimacy that reconciliation and time have achieved. **7:1 Princess** is literally "daughter of a prince" (Hb *bath nadiv*). If this is not a wordplay, it is certainly a link to "a nobleman" (6:12; Hb *'ammi nadiv*). These are the only occurrences of "prince" (Hb *nadiv*) in the Song, and its repetition links the reconciliation section with the lovemaking praise. **Thighs** refer to their upper part, inclusive of the hips, which bear the **curves** that Solomon praised. The **handiwork of a master** (or "of a master craftsman") is another creative way of describing Shulamith as a gift. **7:2** Although some lexical evidence from Arabic suggests the possibility that **navel** is "vulva," the other two occurrences of this word in the OT refer to the body in general (Pr 3:8) and to the umbilical cord (Ezk 16:4). In addition, *navel* is more probable here since it is more like the image of a **rounded bowl** (or "wine chalice") to which it is compared. On the other hand, the image of wine and wheat, coupled with the reference to the "pomegranate" in 8:2 with its wordplay on "drink" and "kiss" (see note at 8:1–2), and the prior wordplays on "caresses" and "mandrakes," and then on "doors" and "opened"

(see note at 7:12–13), suggests that *navel* may be a euphemism for Shulamith's more intimate sexuality. On **surrounded by lilies**, see note at 2:1. Solomon envisioned lotus flowers surrounding the wine and wheat of Shulamith's navel and abdomen that brought delight to him. **7:3** The phrase **breasts are like two fawns** repeats a praise from the wedding night (4:5) but significantly omits "that feed among the lilies." This emphasizes the "feeding" (lit "grazing") among the lotus flowers just implied by their surrounding the wine and wheat of Shulamith's abdomen. Solomon used the metaphor of a palm tree and its fruit to describe his delight in Shulamith's breasts (7:7–8). **7:4** A **tower of ivory** is smooth to the touch, but it has a demeanor that inspires respect (see note at 4:4). **Eyes like pools in Heshbon** perhaps continues the theme of Solomon's eyes like doves "perched over a pool," implying that the pool his dovelike eyes perched over were Shulamith's eyes. They were tranquil waters so that they gave rest by the city gates (**Bath-rabbim**, lit "daughter of many," indicating a busy thoroughfare into the city). The peace and wholeness each found in the other contrasts with the chaos of city crowds. **Nose** is used as the word for anger, arising from its evidence in the flaring of the nostrils; **tower** connotes strength with a military image; **Damascus** was the capital of potential enemies that might violate Israel's borders. Shulamith's anger would flare at anyone who violated her boundaries as well. **7:5 Mount Carmel** has majesty like Shulamith's, giving the capability to bind even the **king** with the power of her **hair** like **purple cloth** (lit "threads" that can bind). The royal imagery of princess and king continues, albeit in irony. The king who stooped to admire the sandaled feet of the princess (v. 1) was bound by her silken hair (v. 5). **7:6–9** If the focus of the wedding night is its beautiful consummation (4:12–5:1), the focus of this later night is the peaceful nurture

their love brings. They fell asleep tasting kisses like wine (see note at 7:9). Sexual intimacy consummates marriage and nurtures it as well. **7:6** The Hebrew underlying **my love, with such delights** is difficult to translate. Linguistic data favors *love* (Hb *'ahavah*) not as a term of address but as an abstract word for "love," as it is in its other nine references in the Song (v. 6; 2:4–5,7; 3:5; 5:8; 8:4,6–7), one of which is in chiastic parallelism with this verse (5:8). So "love" is likely the subject, just as a new subject follows the only other place in the Song where the two Hebrew words rendered **beautiful** appear ("handsome" and "delightful" in 1:16). To paraphrase, Solomon says, "Love flows through your tender affection." This is a beautiful lyric about the heartfelt source of Shulamith's love. **7:7–8** The **fruit** of the **palm tree** transforms from "stalks of dates" (lit "fruit" in v. 8) to **clusters of grapes**, demonstrating first a view from a distance and then the object of Solomon's caresses. "At a distance her breasts seem like clusters of dates on the palm tree. But held close, they are like supple, juicy clusters of grapes" (Craig Glickman). **7:9** The last phrase in this verse could be translated "past the lips of sleepers" (Hb *yeshenim*). This section begins with Shulamith sleeping alone (Hb *yeshenah*, 5:2) and ends with the couple sleeping together. So their kisses—hers as fragrant as apricots and both of theirs as intoxicating as **wine**—lingered on as they drifted peacefully off to sleep. **7:10** This verse repeats the similar refrain where Shulamith affirmed their exclusive bond (see note at 2:16). "Desire" in **his desire is for me** is used only twice elsewhere in the OT: at Gn 3:16, in God's words to Eve describing the consequences of disobedience ("Your desire will be for your husband, yet he will rule over you") and in God's words to Cain describing sin personified as a lion crouching at the door ("Its desire is for you, but you must rule over it," Gn 4:7). So "desire" may connote the desire to rule. This

¹¹ Come, my love,
　　let's go to the field;
　　let's spend the night
　　　among the henna blossoms.ᴬ
¹² Let's go early to the vineyards;
　　let's see if the vine has budded,
　　if the blossom has opened,
　　if the pomegranates are in bloom.
　　There I will give you my caresses.
¹³ The mandrakes give off a fragrance,
　　and at our doors is every delicacy,
　　both new and old.
　　I have treasured them up for you,
　　　my love.

8 If only I could treat you like my brother,ᴮ
　　one who nursed at my mother's breasts,
　　I would find you in public and kiss you,
　　and no one would scorn me.
² I would lead you, I would take you,
　　to the house of my mother
　　　who taught me.ᶜ
　　I would give you spiced wine to drink
　　from the juice of my pomegranate.
³ May his left hand be under my head,
　　and his right arm embrace me.

⁴ Young women of Jerusalem,
　　I charge you,
　　do not stir up or awaken love
　　until the appropriate time.

Young Women

⁵ Who is this coming up
　　from the wilderness,
　　leaning on the one she loves?

Woman

I awakened you under the apricot tree.
There your mother conceived you;
there she conceived and gave you birth.
⁶ Set me as a seal on your heart,
　　as a seal on your arm.
For love is as strong as death;
jealousy is as unrelenting as Sheol.
Love's flames are fiery flames —
an almighty flame!ᴰ
⁷ A huge torrent cannot extinguish love;
rivers cannot sweep it away.
If a man were to give all his wealthᴱ
　　for love,
it would be utterly scorned.

ᴬ**7:11** Or *the villages*　ᴮ**8:1** Lit *Would that you were like a brother to me*　ᶜ**8:2** LXX adds *and into the chamber of the one who bore me*　ᴰ**8:6** Or *the blaze of the* Lᴏʀᴅ　ᴱ**8:7** Lit *all the wealth of his house*

---

verse has been interpreted in at least three ways: (1) now Solomon has a desire (to love or to rule) equal to the desire of Shulamith; (2) now Solomon has a desire to love, but not to dominate; and (3) now Solomon, not Shulamith, has a desire to "rule" in a benevolent sense, perhaps as the sun and moon "rule" (or "govern") the day and night, providing guiding light (Gn 1:18) or as God's "rule" provides loving care for his people (see Pss 22:28; 59:13; 66:7; 89:9). In any case, after a wonderful reconciliation and time of intimacy, Shulamith affirmed her complete security in Solomon's love.
7:11–13 This section contains Shulamith's invitation to enjoy spring. It balances Solomon's earlier invitation to do the same (2:8–14). His invitation concluded with a request to hear her voice (2:14); hers concluded with a request to make love (7:12–13). The Song will conclude on precisely these themes: Solomon's request to hear her voice (8:13) and her request to make love (8:14)—artistically portraying unending seasons of spring in their love.
7:11 The phrase **let's spend the night among the henna blossoms** uses language from 1:13–14 where Shulamith compared Solomon to henna blossoms in En-gedi after comparing him to a pouch of myrrh which spent the night between her breasts. During courtship her thoughts were of him who was like henna blossoms who would "spend the night" with her; now she asked to spend the night with him "among the henna blossoms."
7:12–13 These verses contemplate a new season of spring in their experience. **Caresses** is a wordplay on **mandrakes**, an appropriate name for these plants associated with love and fertility. **Delicacy** is the same word twice rendered "choicest fruits," referring to erotic delicacies of the wedding night (4:13,16). **New** and **old** refer literally to fresh fruit from the harvest and dried fruits from the past. This

refers figuratively to lovemaking "delicacies" that were in part fresh and new and in part familiar and constant. "Old" (Hb *yeshanim*) plays on "of the ones sleeping" (Hb *yeshenim*, v. 9). Since this is the peaceful sleep after lovemaking (see note at v. 9), the poet associates the familiar lovemaking with security and comfort.
The location of delicacies at **our doors** is a play on **has opened** (used of blossoms in v. 12). Both words derived from the same root. "Our doors" is thus a very erotic play on "has opened." Her openings and openness are like the opening of flower blossoms.
8:1–2 In these verses the couple moves inside. On the earlier spring day Solomon's description prepared for his request to see and hear Shulamith. Similarly, now she first wished for a kiss outside with all the innocence of a kiss from a brother, and that prepares for her wish for more intimate kissing in innocence—without scorn—as well. **I would . . . kiss you** is a play on **I would give you . . . to drink**. They would have been identical in the original Hebrew, which did not write the vowels. "I would give you . . . to drink from" could be taken as "I would let you kiss."
Spiced wine . . . from the juice of my pomegranate is a smooth translation, but the literal is more dramatic: "from the wine—the spiced wine—from the sweet wine of my pomegranate." The repetition of "from" reinforces the image of drinking from a container and probably resumes these images: (1) the image of the navel as the chalice of wine (see note at 7:2), (2) the image of drinking her kisses like wine (7:9), and (3) the image of drinking from a mother's breast (8:1). The moisture of Shulamith's mouth was like the sliced opening of a pomegranate on the wedding night; now the moisture of "my pomegranate" is like "spiced wine."
8:3–14 This section concludes the themes introduced in 1:1–2:7 . Refrains similar to the

ones that concluded the first section now begin the last one in chiastic balance. And once again the Song appropriately reintroduces Shulamith's brothers and explains the circumstances introduced in the first section and how the lovers first met.
8:3 This refrain again functions to close the prior section and to introduce the next.
8:4 Caution in love is important, but when the **time** is **appropriate**, do not let its joy pass you by.
8:5–7 All earlier praise was in praise of the lovers. The lyrics of this section, however, praise love itself. The love that pleased to awaken Solomon and Shulamith has a fiery origin in the love of God.
8:5 Who is this coming up from the wilderness begins a new section introduced with words identical to those that begin the wedding procession and with the same complimentary allusions (see 3:6). Solomon and Shulamith have left the wilderness created by Adam and Eve to experience a paradise, and their love is like God's for his people, particularly when after the hardships of the wilderness they emerged trusting and **leaning** on him.
8:6–7 The **seal** is the valuable possession by which all of a person's possessions are identified. **Strong as death** is a stark metaphor, showing that just as death conquers, so does love. But perhaps it implies love has the last word. If death conquers mortality, then love may as well. **Unrelenting as Sheol** extends this image, showing that as the grave pursues all mortals, so love pursues the beloved. **Jealousy** is often attributed to God, who expresses it in fiery concern for those whom he loves (Dt 4:24; 32:21–22). Since its **fiery flames** are the "blaze of the Lᴏʀᴅ" (see textual footnote), it cannot be extinguished. Any improper attempts to attain love are **scorned**.

Brothers

8 Our sister is young;
 she has no breasts.
 What will we do for our sister
 on the day she is spoken for?

9 If she is a wall,
 we will build a silver barricade on her.
 If she is a door,
 we will enclose her with cedar planks.

Woman

10 I am^A a wall
 and my breasts like towers.
 So to him I have become
 like one who finds^B peace.^C

11 Solomon owned a vineyard
 in Baal-hamon.
 He leased the vineyard to tenants.

Each was to bring for his fruit
 one thousand pieces of silver.

12 I have my own vineyard.^D
 The one thousand are for you,
  Solomon,
 but two hundred for those who take
  care of its fruits.

Man

13 You^E who dwell in the gardens,
 companions are listening
  for your voice;
 let me hear you!

Woman

14 Run away with me,^F my love,
 and be like a gazelle
 or a young stag
 on the mountains of spices.

---

^A 8:10 Or *was*   ^B 8:10 Or *brings*   ^C 8:10 In Hb, the word for *peace* sounds similar to Solomon and Shulammite.   ^D 8:12 Lit *My vineyard, which is mine, is before me*; Sg 1:6   ^E 8:13 In Hb, the word for *You* is feminine.   ^F 8:14 Lit *Flee*

8:8–12 This section explains how Shulamith found love properly—by preparing herself for it and by a fortuitous meeting with Solomon in the vineyard.

8:8–9 Shulamith's brothers took responsibility for her care when **she** was **young** and had **no breasts**, promising restrictions if she was promiscuous (**if she is a door**) but rewards if she was responsible (**if she is a wall**) as they prepared for **the day** she was **spoken for**.

8:10 Shulamith affirmed the development of her character (**I am a wall**) and her body (**my breasts like towers**) continuing the imagery of vv. 8–9. Shulamith found **peace** in the eyes of Solomon. It is an appropriate wordplay,

since *Shulamith* and *Shelomoh* (Hb for "Solomon") are feminine and masculine forms of names derived from *shalom* ("peace"). Shulamith found *shalom* with Shelomoh.

8:11–12 These verses describe what happened after Shulamith's brothers leased vineyards from Solomon and placed Shulamith there to work (1:6). Their agreement required them to pay **one thousand pieces of silver** to the owner, Solomon, and allowed them, the caretakers, to keep **two hundred** for themselves. Just as Solomon could do what he wanted with his own literal vineyard, Shulamith was free to do what she pleased with the figurative vineyard of herself (**my . . . vineyard**). Love cannot be

purchased, but it can be given. **Those who take care of its fruits** are the brothers who temporarily cared for the figurative vineyard that was Shulamith (vv. 8–9), just as they cared for Solomon's literal vineyard.

8:13–14 These verses echo the themes of the days in spring (see note at 7:12–13). However, quite remarkably, the themes of spring echoed at the end of the Song show it was Solomon who initiated and longed for communication while it was Shulamith who responded in desire to make love. Not only does this shatter the stereotype and recover the ideal of romantic love, it also reflects the love of God toward us: "We love because he first loved us" (1Jn 4:19).

◤ Introduction to the Prophets

by E. Ray Clendenen

The persistent reader who is unfamiliar with ancient Jewish literature will likely be challenged by the Old Testament prophetic books, since their language and structure are unlike almost anything in modern literature. Even Martin Luther (AD 1483–1546) said that the prophets "have a queer way of talking, like people who, instead of proceeding in an orderly manner, ramble off from one thing to the next, so that you cannot make head or tail of them or see what they are getting at." Nevertheless, with a modern translation and some guidance, a Bible student can have an exciting time encountering afresh the Holy One of Israel in the Prophets.

The Nature of the Prophetic Books

The Prophetic Books are those written by or containing the messages of ancient Israel's "writing prophets" (as opposed to prophets like Elijah and Elisha who left no written prophecies). These writing prophets include Isaiah, Jeremiah, Ezekiel, Daniel, and the twelve Minor Prophets (Hosea, Joel, Amos, Obadiah, Jonah, Micah, Nahum, Habakkuk, Zephaniah, Haggai, Zechariah, Malachi).

The Jews recognized three divisions in their canon of sacred books: Law, Prophets, and Writings. The second division was divided into the "Former Prophets" (Joshua through Kings, excluding Ruth) and the "Latter Prophets" (Isaiah, Jeremiah, Ezekiel, and the twelve Minor Prophets). "Former" and "Latter" refer not to chronology but to their position in the canon.

Daniel was placed in the Writings, presumably because of its unique character (for example, the absence of an opening verse like those found in the other prophetic books) and the fact that Daniel was technically a statesman rather than a divinely appointed mediator (he distinguishes himself from "the prophets" in Dn 9:6, 10; but Jesus acknowledged his possession of a prophetic gift in Mt 24:15).

The "Minor" Prophets are so named not because of their lesser importance but their length. The longest, Hosea, occupies about fourteen pages in an average English Bible, whereas the "Major" Prophets (Isaiah, Jeremiah, Ezekiel, and Daniel) range in size from twenty-four (Daniel) to ninety-seven pages (Jeremiah). Altogether the "Minor" Prophets are about the size of Ezekiel. In spite of having been written at different times as separate books, sometime in the development of the Hebrew canon these twelve books were all bound together on the same scroll and in an order that has generally remained unchanged. Consequently, they came to be known in Jewish tradition as "the Twelve," or "the Book of the Twelve."

The verb *prophesy* occurs for the first time in Numbers 11:25–27, where "prophets" (v. 29) are servants and spokespeople of God who were endowed by the Spirit to confront the people of Israel when they strayed. Sometimes a prophet was called a "man of God" (1Kg 13:1–8) or a "seer" (1Sm 9:9).

The Style of the Prophetic Books

The Prophetic Books may also be characterized by style and function. First, they employ an elevated rhetorical style that often takes the form of poetry. Second, they present their messages as received directly from God (as seen in their opening verses). Third, they use an inventory of literary forms such as lawsuit, lament, woe, and promise. And fourth, because of the common function of the prophets as "enforcers" or "prosecutors" of God's covenant, these books call for behavioral changes on the part of the disobedient covenant people.

The Key to Interpreting the Prophets

This focus on behavioral change explains the prophets' use of messages of indictment, instruction, judgment, and hope or salvation. Indictment messages identified Israel's sins and God's attitude toward them. Instruction told them what they must do about it, and judgment and hope messages motivated the listeners to obey by explaining the consequences of disobedience (judgment) or of repentance and faith (hope). Messages of judgment involve specific applications of the covenant curses found in Leviticus 26 and Deuteronomy 28 (see for example, Jl 1:4–20; Am 4:6–11; Zph 1:13; Hg 1:10–11). They serve, then, as reminders that sin has its consequences.

At least in some cases where judgment is announced with no explicit expression of hope, the possibility of avoiding punishment through repentance may be assumed (e.g., Jr 18:1–12; Jnh 3:4). But even when judgment is decreed as inevitable due to Israel's continued obstinacy, the function is to motivate repentance on the part of those who survive the judgment (cp. Jr 23:20). In these cases, the judgment and salvation oracles combine in a special way to motivate right behavior by a purified remnant. Our historical perspective allows us to recognize that in some cases announcements of future judgment or salvation concerned the distant future, beyond the lifetime of the prophet's immediate audience (e.g., Is 24–25; 40–48; 53; Jr 30–33; Ezk 34:23–24; 36–48; Dn 7–12; Jl 3:14–21; Zch 9:9–17; 12–14; Mal 3:1). But like the assurance of Christ's return for the Christian, this was to have a motivating effect regardless of the time it would occur (e.g., 1Th 4:18; 5:6–11).

Recognizing the vital relationship between words of indictment, instruction, judgment, and hope in the prophets is an important step toward understanding their message. For many the word *prophecy* has only one association: "fulfillment." Students of the prophets often concentrate on the "good news" of prophetic fulfillment to the neglect of the rest of the prophet's message. But it is a misuse of Scripture to listen to only one of the supplementary elements, such as predictive prophecy, without relating it to the central message of the book.

The Prophets and the Covenant

The prophet Joel brings no charges against Israel, and his only message of instruction from God is found in Joel 2:12–13: "Turn to me with all your heart, with fasting, weeping, and mourning. Tear your hearts, not just your clothes, and return to the LORD your God." Joel was relying on Israel's knowledge of the covenant, especially the biblical teaching on repentance, and on their ability to connect his message with that teaching. This strategy, together with the vividness of his imagery of a locust plague, gives Joel's prophecy its unique power.

Typical of the prophets, Joel's message is strongly dependent on Deuteronomy in language, style, and themes. God had announced to Israel through Moses that failure to obey the Lord and follow his law would mean deprivation, barrenness, failure, ruin, loss, disease, drought, defeat, disappointment, frustration, death, sorrow, exile, shame, and locusts (Dt 28:38–42; see also 32:22–27). Strong emphasis is placed on Israel being defeated, devastated, and destroyed by foreign nations and scattered among them (28:64). The specific disobedience in mind is rejection of the Lord for idols and abandoning his covenant (29:18, 25–26; cp. 32:15–18, 21). But compassion, regathering, restoration, and spiritual rebirth are also promised to Israel if from their exile they "return to the LORD your God and obey him with all your heart and all your soul" (30:2).

Joel's message would have triggered this entire script of judgment, repentance, and restoration, making it unnecessary for him to include an explicit citation of Judah's sins. They were guilty of disobeying God's law and abandoning him for other gods. Joel could concentrate, then, on motivating repentance by warning of a coming "day of the LORD" (Jl 1:15; 2:1, 11, 31). The primary goal of the prophets, in fact, was to *persuade*. Their main function is to make us uncomfortable with lives lived apart from the Lord.

THE HEBREW PROPHETS IN HISTORY
(9th–5th CENTURIES BC)

PROPHET	APPROX. DATES (BC)	LOCATION/HOME	BASIC BIBLE PASSAGE	CENTRAL TEACHING	KEY VERSE
Elijah	875–850	Tishbe	1Kg 17:1–2Kg 2:18	Yahweh, not Baal, is God	1Kg 18:21
Micaiah	856	Samaria	1Kg 22; 2Ch 18	Judgment on Ahab; proof of prophecy	1Kg 22:28
Elisha	855–800	Abel Meholah	1Kg 19:15–21; 2Kg 2–9; 13	God's miraculous power	2Kg 5:15
Jonah	786–746	Gath Hepher	2Kg 14:25; Jonah	God's universal concern	Jnh 4:11
Hosea	786–746	Israel	Hosea	God's unquenchable love	Hs 11:8–9
Amos	760–750	Tekoa	Amos	God's call for justice and righteousness	Am 5:24
Isaiah	740–698	Jerusalem	2Kg 19–20; Isaiah	Hope through repentance and suffering	Is 1:18; 53:4–6
Micah	735–710	Moresheth Gath/ Jerusalem	Jr 26:18; Micah	Call for humble mercy and justice	Mc 6:8
Oded	733	Samaria	2Ch 28:9–11	Do not go beyond God's command	2Ch 28:9
Nahum	686–612	Elkosh	Nahum	God's jealousy protects his people	Nah 1:2–3
Zephaniah	640–621	?	Zephaniah	Hope for the humble and righteous	Zph 2:3
Jeremiah	626–584	Anathoth/ Jerusalem	2Ch 36:12; Jeremiah	Faithful prophet points to new covenant	Jr 31:33–34
Huldah (the prophetess)	621	Jerusalem	2Kg 22; 2Ch 34	God's book is accurate	2Kg 22:16
Habakkuk	608–598	?	Habakkuk	God calls for faithfulness	Hab 2:4
Ezekiel	593–571	Babylon	Ezekiel	Future hope for new community of worship	Ezk 37:12–13
Obadiah	580	Jerusalem	Obadiah	Doom on Edom to bring God's kingdom	Ob 21
Joel	539–531	Jerusalem	Joel	Call to repent and experience God's Spirit	Jl 2:28–29
Haggai	520	Jerusalem	Ezr 5:1; 6:14; Haggai	The priority of God's house	Hg 2:8–9
Zechariah	520–514	Jerusalem	Ezr 5:1; 6:14; Zechariah	Faithfulness will lead to God's universal rule	Zch 14:9
Malachi	500–450	Jerusalem	Malachi	Honor God and wait for his righteousness	Mal 4:2

▼ Introduction to Isaiah

Circumstances of Writing

The book of Isaiah presents itself as the writing of one man, Isaiah son of Amoz. The superscription to the book (1:1) dates his prophetic activity as spanning the reigns of four kings of Judah: Uzziah (783–742 BC, Isaiah's call is dated to this king's last year; 6:1); Jotham (742–735 BC); Ahaz (735–716 BC); and Hezekiah (716–686 BC). On Uzziah (also called Azariah), see 2 Kings 15:1–7 and 2 Chronicles 26:1–23. On Jotham, see 2 Kings 15:32–38 and 2 Chronicles 27:1–9. On Ahaz, see 2 Kings 16:1–20 and 2 Chronicles 28:1–27. On Hezekiah, see 2 Kings 18:1–20:21 and 2 Chronicles 29:1–32:33. Not much is known about Isaiah apart from his prophecy.

Isaiah's authorship of the whole book has been vehemently contested in the modern period. Many scholars have argued that the historical Isaiah could not have written chapters 40–66. For those who believe that God knows the future and can reveal it to his servants, it is not problematic that God through Isaiah predicted the rise of Babylon, its victory against Judah, the exile, and the return.

Isaiah 6:1 records that Isaiah received his prophetic call in the last year of Uzziah's reign over Judah (ca 742 BC). Uzziah's reign was a particularly prosperous time in the history of Judah, but storm clouds were on the horizon. Assyria was on the rise again in the person of Tiglath-pileser III (745–727 BC). The Assyrian king threatened to engulf Syria and the northern kingdom of Israel. After the death of Tiglath-pileser, his successors, Shalmaneser and Sargon, defeated the northern kingdom in 722 BC and deported its citizens. This event brought Judah even more under the shadow of that great empire. Isaiah 37:38 suggests that the prophet lived until the death of Sennacherib in 681 BC.

Isaiah's vision extended beyond the eighth century BC, through the rest of the Old Testament period and beyond. The New Testament authors cited Isaiah as finding fulfillment in the great events surrounding Jesus Christ, the Messiah and Suffering Servant.

Contribution to the Bible

It might be argued that without Isaiah, the New Testament could not have been written. There as nowhere else in the Old Testament the message is declared and the stage is set for the Davidic King to bring about a new exodus and establish God's kingdom on earth by means of the sin-bearing Servant.

Structure

The book of Isaiah is a combination of both prose and poetry. The prose is found primarily in chapters 36–39, a section that forms a bridge between the two sections of the book. Isaiah's poetry is rich and varied. He wrote hymns, wisdom poetry, and even poetry that resembles a love song (5:1–7). The richness is seen in Isaiah's vocabulary. He used more than twenty-two hundred different Hebrew words, far more variety than what is found in any other Old Testament book.

Isaiah Timeline

750–725 BC

Death of King Uzziah of Judah **740**
Isaiah's call to be a prophet **740**
Tiglath-pileser III's invasions of Israel **734–732**
Pekah of Israel and Rezin of Damascus form a mutual defense alliance against Assyria and invite Ahaz of Judah to join them. **734**
Ahaz refuses Isaiah's counsel and seeks protection from Assyria by paying tribute to them, creating a heavy financial burden on Judah for years to come. **734**
Alliance between Syria and Israel collapses with the fall of Damascus **(732)** and the fall of Samaria. **722**

725–700 BC

Hezekiah of Judah initiates reforms and shows resistance to Assyria. **715–701**
Hezekiah prepares for war against Assyria, strengthens Jerusalem's defenses, and receives Merodach-baladan's envoys from Babylon. **705–701**
Sennacherib of Assyria defeats the Phoenicians, Philistines, and Egyptians; destroys most cities in Judah; and besieges Jerusalem. **701**
God delivers Jerusalem from the Assyrian forces. **701**

Outline

Key verses in Isaiah

6:8 Then I heard the voice of the Lord asking: Who will I send? Who will go for us? I said: Here I am. Send me.

9:6 For a child will be born for us, a son will be given to us, and the government will be on his shoulders. He will be named Wonderful Counselor, Mighty God, Eternal Father, Prince of Peace.

40:8 The grass withers, the flowers fade, but the word of our God remains forever

45:5 I am the LORD, and there is no other; there is no God but me. I will strengthen you, though you do not know me.

700–600 BC

Manasseh succeeds his father Hezekiah as king of Judah. **687**

Ashurbanipal **(668–631)** rules over a declining Assyrian Empire that experiences revolts **(642)** and contributes to the assassination of Amon of Judah **(641)** and the rise of his son Josiah **(641–609)**.

Josiah killed by the Egyptians at Megiddo **609**

Babylonians defeat Pharaoh Neco of Egypt at Carchemish. **605**

Babylonians attack Jerusalem and take citizens of Judah into exile. **605, 597, 586**

600–500 BC

Cyrus captures Babylon without resistance. **539**

Cyrus issues a decree allowing the Jews to return to Judah. **538**

Work begins on rebuilding the temple in Jerusalem. **536–537**

Renewed work on the temple **520–518**

New temple dedicated **515**

The vision concerning Judah and Jerusalem that Isaiah son of Amoz saw during the reigns[A] of Kings Uzziah, Jotham, Ahaz, and Hezekiah of Judah.

Judah on Trial

2 Listen, heavens,
    and pay attention, earth,
for the LORD has spoken:
"I have raised children[B]
    and brought them up,
but they have rebelled against me.
3 The ox knows its owner,
and the donkey its master's
    feeding trough,
but Israel does not know;
my people do not understand."

4 Oh sinful nation,
people weighed down with iniquity,
brood of evildoers,
depraved children!
They have abandoned the LORD;
they have despised the Holy One of Israel;
they have turned their backs on him.

5 Why do you want more beatings?
Why do you keep on rebelling?
The whole head is hurt,
and the whole heart is sick.
6 From the sole of the foot
    even to the head,
no spot is uninjured —
wounds, welts, and festering sores
not cleansed, bandaged,
or soothed with oil.

7 Your land is desolate,
your cities burned down;
foreigners devour your fields
right in front of you —
a desolation, like a place demolished
    by foreigners.

8 Daughter Zion is abandoned
like a shelter in a vineyard,
like a shack in a cucumber field,
like a besieged city.
9 If the LORD of Armies
had not left us a few survivors,
we would be like Sodom,
we would resemble Gomorrah.

10 Hear the word of the LORD,
you rulers of Sodom!
Listen to the instruction of our God,
you people of Gomorrah!
11 "What are all your sacrifices to me?"
asks the LORD.
"I have had enough of burnt offerings
    and rams
and the fat of well-fed cattle;
I have no desire for the blood of bulls,
lambs, or male goats.
12 When you come to appear before me,
who requires this from you —
this trampling of my courts?
13 Stop bringing useless offerings.
Your incense is detestable to me.
New Moons and Sabbaths,
and the calling of solemn assemblies —
I cannot stand iniquity with a festival.
14 I hate your New Moons
    and prescribed festivals.
They have become a burden to me;
I am tired of putting up with them.
15 When you spread out your hands
    in prayer,
I will refuse to look at you;
even if you offer countless prayers,
I will not listen.
Your hands are covered with blood.

Purification of Jerusalem

16 "Wash yourselves. Cleanse yourselves.
Remove your evil deeds from my sight.
Stop doing evil.

[A]1:1 ca 792–686 BC   [B]1:2 Or *sons*, also in v. 4

1:1 On the historical setting for Isaiah's ministry, see Introduction.
1:2 The opening pronouncement of the book puts Judah on trial. The call goes out to the **heavens** and the **earth** to hear the charges against God's people. God himself describes the rebellion of his people, referring to them as his **children**, underlining the scandal of the betrayal.
1:3 God stood amazed at the stupidity of his people. They were dumber than an ox, even dumber than a **donkey**. The former was smart enough to recognize its owner; the latter might not recognize its **owner**, but it knew where it got its food.
1:4 The opening **Oh** marks the beginning of what is commonly called a "woe oracle." This literary form derives from funeral processions and often signifies the sense that the object of the *Oh*—in this case the **sinful nation** (Judah)—is as good as dead. Isaiah

frequently refers to God as **the Holy One of Israel**. This title emphasizes God's separation from and profound aversion toward sin.
1:5–6 Judah was like a sick man whose injuries stemmed from a beating, perhaps a poetic allusion to Assyrian military threats in 722 BC when the northern kingdom of Israel fell, or perhaps to a later incursion in 701 BC.
1:7–8 Daughter Zion is a personification of Zion, the most holy place in Judah, the mountain where the temple was built. A **shelter in a vineyard** or a **shack in a cucumber field** were both fragile. Without upkeep they would crumble, providing an illuminating analogy for the desolation of Jerusalem.
1:9 God had been gracious. He did not completely destroy his people and make them like **Sodom** and **Gomorrah** (Gn 19). Paul quotes this verse in Rm 9:29.

1:10–15 In these verses God expressed his revulsion at the religious practices of his people.
1:10 Their rulers were like the inhabitants of those depraved cities who denied hospitality to strangers and engaged in perverse sexual acts.
1:13–14 God also commanded that Israel consecrate holy times on a weekly (**Sabbaths**) and yearly (**New Moons** . . . **solemn assemblies** . . . **festivals**) cycle, but they had become loathsome to God because of the hypocrisy of his people.
1:15 This pronouncement has delayed the problem with the people's ritual practice until the last line—their hands were **covered with blood**. That is, they sinned and did not repent but still participated in worship. God did not tolerate such hypocritical behavior.
1:16–17 The pronouncement gives a prescription for change—repent. The metaphor

¹⁷ Learn to do what is good.
Pursue justice.
Correct the oppressor.^A
Defend the rights of the fatherless.
Plead the widow's cause.

¹⁸ "Come, let's settle this,"
says the LORD.
"Though your sins are scarlet,
they will be as white as snow;
though they are crimson red,
they will be like wool.
¹⁹ If you are willing and obedient,
you will eat the good things
of the land.
²⁰ But if you refuse and rebel,
you will be devoured by the sword."
For the mouth of the LORD has spoken.

²¹ The faithful town —
what an adulteress^B she has become!
She was once full of justice.
Righteousness once dwelt in her,
but now, murderers!
²² Your silver has become dross to be
discarded,
your beer^c is diluted with water.
²³ Your rulers are rebels,
friends of thieves.
They all love graft
and chase after bribes.
They do not defend the rights
of the fatherless,
and the widow's case never comes
before them.

²⁴ Therefore the Lord GOD of Armies,
the Mighty One of Israel, declares:
"Ah, I will get even with my foes;
I will take revenge against my enemies.
²⁵ I will turn my hand against you
and will burn away
your dross completely;^D
I will remove all your impurities.

²⁶ I will restore your judges to what they
were at first,
and your advisers to what they were at
the start.
Afterward you will be called
the Righteous City,
a Faithful Town."

²⁷ Zion will be redeemed by justice,
those who repent, by righteousness.
²⁸ At the same time both rebels
and sinners will be broken,
and those who abandon the LORD
will perish.
²⁹ Indeed, they^E will be ashamed
of the sacred trees
you desired,
and you will be embarrassed because of
the garden shrines
you have chosen.
³⁰ For you will become like an oak
whose leaves are withered,
and like a garden without water.
³¹ The strong one will become tinder,
and his work a spark;
both will burn together,
with no one to extinguish the flames.

The City of Peace

2 The vision that Isaiah son of Amoz saw
concerning Judah and Jerusalem:
² In the last days
the mountain of the LORD's house
will be established
at the top of the mountains
and will be raised above the hills.
All nations will stream to it,
³ and many peoples will come and say,
"Come, let's go up to the mountain
of the LORD,
to the house of the God of Jacob.
He will teach us about his ways
so that we may walk in his paths."
For instruction will go out of Zion

^A1:17 Or *Aid the oppressed* ^B1:21 Or *prostitute* ^c1:22 Or *wine* ^D1:25 Lit *dross as with lye* ^E1:29 Some Hb mss; other Hb mss, Tg read *you*

for transformation here is a good washing. Transformation involves a cessation of evil activities as well as the requirement of good deeds. The good deeds are defined as pursuing social justice, particularly resisting oppressors and promoting the interests of the vulnerable (the **fatherless** and the widow). **1:18–20** The Lord presented two options to the people. One was to repent and obey. Now they were blood red as a result of their sin, but repentance would turn them a glorious **white**. The second option was continued rebellion, a course of action that would end with their destruction. **1:21–22** A formerly **faithful town**—Jerusalem—had gone bad. The worship of false gods, idolatry, is often described as a form of adultery. **Dross** and watered-down **beer** are symbols of impurity.

1:24 Therefore marks the transition from indictment (vv. 21–23) to judgment. God will not let the guilty escape their punishment. **1:25–26** The judgment is not just punitive; it purifies. The people started a faithful city (v. 21) and after their cleansing, they will again be a **Faithful Town**. **1:29** One common form of false worship involved **sacred trees** that were probably connected with worship of a Canaanite fertility goddess called Asherah, the mother of Baal. **1:30–31** The pronouncement charged that Judah (**you**) would become like an **oak**. Here the tree image stands for the pride and resistance of God's people. But such apparent strength is undermined by the fact that the tree was not watered and therefore would quickly **burn** when set on fire.

2:1 The repetition of the title here suggests that chap. 1 is the introduction to the book. **2:2–4** This pronouncement is virtually identical to that found in Isaiah's near contemporary, the prophet Micah (Mc 4:1–3). **2:2** The phrase **last days** refers to the future, a time beyond the judgment on the sin of God's people. The **mountain of the LORD's house** is a reference to Zion, where the temple was built. In actuality, Zion was not a physically imposing mountain—indeed, the nearby Mount of Olives was considerably taller—but in terms of spiritual importance, Zion stood above all the other mountains of the world. **2:3** The vision anticipates a day when not only Israel but all the nations will stream toward this **mountain** that represents the presence of God on earth.

and the word of the Lord
    from Jerusalem.
⁴ He will settle disputes
    among the nations
and provide arbitration
    for many peoples.
They will beat their swords into plows
and their spears into pruning knives.
Nation will not take up the sword
    against nation,
and they will never again train for war.

The Day of the Lord

⁵ House of Jacob,
    come and let's walk in the Lord's light.
⁶ For you have abandoned your people,
    the house of Jacob,
because they are full of divination
    from the East
and of fortune-tellers
    like the Philistines.
They are in league^A with foreigners.
⁷ Their^B,C land is full of silver and gold,
and there is no limit to their treasures;
their land is full of horses,
and there is no limit to their chariots.
⁸ Their land is full of worthless idols;
they worship the work of their hands,
what their fingers have made.
⁹ So humanity is brought low,
    and each person is humbled.
Do not forgive them!
¹⁰ Go into the rocks
    and hide in the dust
from the terror of the Lord
    and from his majestic splendor.
¹¹ The pride of mankind^D will be humbled,
    and human loftiness
    will be brought low;
the Lord alone will be exalted on that day.

¹² For a day belonging to the Lord
    of Armies is coming

against all that is proud and lofty,
against all that is lifted up — it will
    be humbled —
¹³ against all the cedars of Lebanon,
    lofty and lifted up,
against all the oaks of Bashan,
¹⁴ against all the high mountains,
against all the lofty hills,
¹⁵ against every high tower,
against every fortified wall,
¹⁶ against every ship of Tarshish,
and against every splendid sea vessel.
¹⁷ The pride of mankind will be brought low,
and human loftiness will be humbled;
the Lord alone will be exalted
    on that day.
¹⁸ The worthless idols
    will vanish completely.

¹⁹ People will go into caves in the rocks
    and holes in the ground,
away from the terror of the Lord
and from his majestic splendor,
when he rises to terrify the earth.
²⁰ On that day people will throw
their worthless idols of silver and gold,
which they made to worship,
to the moles and the bats.
²¹ They will go into the caves of the rocks
and the crevices in the cliffs,
away from the terror of the Lord
and from his majestic splendor,
when he rises to terrify the earth.
²² Put no more trust in a mere human,
who has only the breath in his nostrils.
What is he really worth?

Judah's Leaders Judged

3 Note this: The Lord God of Armies
is about to remove from Jerusalem
    and from Judah
every kind of security:
the entire supply of bread and water,

---

^2:6 Or *They teem,* or *They partner*; Hb obscure   ^B 2:7 Lit *Its*   ^C 2:7 = the house of Jacob   ^D 2:11 Lit *Mankind's proud eyes*

2:4 The **nation** seeking the Lord will experience a great transformation. They will not exert their energies and resources to destruction (**swords . . . spears**), but rather to productive activities (**plows . . . pruning knives**).
2:5 Some scholars believe this call to obey God's way concludes the previous pronouncement. If so, it invites Israel to follow God as the least they can do in anticipation of the fact that the nations will turn to God in the future. However, v. 6 begins with "For," marking the verses that follow as motivation for the repentance of Israel called for in this verse.
2:6 God had removed his presence from his **people** because they had imbibed of the superstitions of their neighbors to the **East** (Edom and Mesopotamia, for instance) and the west (Philistia). In particular, they practiced **divination**. Divination tries to access

the divine realm via rituals, with the aim of foretelling the future and warding off evil. The Torah forbade such practices (Lv 19:26; Dt 18:9–14).
2:7 Deuteronomy 17:14–20 prohibited kings from accumulating precious metals and military assets (**horses** and **chariots**).
2:8 The root of the evil of idolatry is expressed here when the pronouncement states that idols are man-made (**the work of their hands**). Paul reflected this understanding in Rm 1:23.
2:9–10 Do not forgive them is a curious petition. It probably means that Israel's sin cannot just be forgotten but must be punished.
2:11 With the words **the pride of mankind will be humbled**, Isaiah expressed one of the major themes of his book. Through judgment, God cuts down the sinful pretensions of his people.

2:12–18 The prophets often spoke of a coming **day belonging to the Lord** (Jl 1:15; 2:1,11,31; Am 5:18,20; Zph 1:7,14; Zch 14:1). This day is one of judgment of sinners, which means the redemption of God's people. However, God's people in this verse were the object of his anger since they were rebelling against him. **Lebanon** and **Bashan** were well known for their fertile lands and, in particular, their impressive trees. Thus, they are representative of arrogance built on abundance. God's judgment is against all kinds of **pride**.
2:22 The last verse of the pronouncement states an important and pervasive theme in Isaiah connected to the prophet's concern that God's people act with humility. They were not to **trust in a mere human**, but to put their confidence in God.
3:1–3 Since God's people trust in man (2:22) rather than in God, he will remove from them

2 heroes and warriors,
    judges and prophets,
    fortune-tellers and elders,
3 commanders of fifty and dignitaries,
    counselors, cunning magicians,^
    and necromancers.^B
4 "I will make youths their leaders,
    and unstable rulers^C will govern them."
5 The people will oppress one another,
    man against man, neighbor
      against neighbor;
    the young will act arrogantly
      toward the old,
    and the worthless
      toward the honorable.
6 A man will even seize his brother
    in his father's house, saying,
    "You have a cloak — you be our leader!
    This heap of rubble will be
      under your control."
7 On that day he will cry out, saying,
    "I'm not a healer.
    I don't even have food or clothing
      in my house.
    Don't make me the leader
      of the people!"
8 For Jerusalem has stumbled
    and Judah has fallen
    because they have spoken and acted
      against the LORD,
    defying his glorious presence.
9 The look on their faces testifies
      against them,
    and like Sodom, they flaunt their sin;
    they do not conceal it.
    Woe to them,
    for they have brought disaster
      on themselves.
10 Tell the righteous that it will go well
      for them,
    for they will eat the fruit of their labor.
11 Woe to the wicked — it will go badly
      for them,
    for what they have done will be done
      to them.
12 Youths oppress my people,
    and women rule over them.

My people, your leaders mislead you;
    they confuse the direction
      of your paths.

13 The LORD rises to argue the case
    and stands to judge the people.
14 The LORD brings this charge
    against the elders and leaders
      of his people:
    "You have devastated the vineyard.
    The plunder from the poor is
      in your houses.
15 Why do you crush my people
    and grind the faces of the poor?"
    This is the declaration
      of the Lord GOD of Armies.

Jerusalem's Women Judged

16 The LORD also says:
    Because the daughters of Zion
      are haughty,
    walking with heads held high
    and seductive eyes,
    prancing along,
    jingling their ankle bracelets,
17 the Lord will put scabs on the heads
    of the daughters of Zion,
    and the LORD will shave
      their foreheads bare.

18 On that day the Lord will strip their finery: ankle bracelets, headbands, crescents, 19 pendants, bracelets, veils, 20 headdresses, ankle jewelry, sashes, perfume bottles, amulets, 21 signet rings, nose rings, 22 festive robes, capes, cloaks, purses, 23 garments, linen clothes, turbans, and shawls.
24 Instead of perfume there will be a stench;
    instead of a belt, a rope;
    instead of
      beautifully styled hair, baldness;
    instead of fine clothes, sackcloth;
    instead of beauty, branding.^D
25 Your men will fall by the sword,
    your warriors in battle.
26 Then her gates will lament and mourn;
    deserted, she will sit on the ground.

---

^3:3 Or *skilled craftsmen*   ^B3:3 Or *mediums*   ^C3:4 Or *mischief-makers*   ^D3:24 DSS read *shame*

---

every kind of security. While various political, military, and religious leaders are on the list, it begins with the staples of **bread and water**.
3:4–5 With the removal of the leaders in whom the people trust comes the installation of inexperienced **youths** to replace them. The result will be social chaos and oppression.
3:6–7 In the vignette described in these verses, the people are so unwilling and unfit to lead that a **man** will be pressed into a leadership role just because he has a **cloak**. But what would be left for him to lead? Only a **heap of rubble**.

3:8 The initial word **for** probably connects this verse to vv. 1–7. The reason God will remove good government from Israel is that they are spiritually bankrupt.
3:9 Again, God's pronouncement compares Judah to **Sodom** (Gn 19).
3:10–11 But not all people will experience the severe judgment of God. The **righteous** will find reward in a good life, and the **wicked** will suffer. In both cases, they will get what they deserve.
3:13–15 Isaiah returned to the legal language with which the book began (1:2). The leaders were guilty of destroying the **vineyard**, the land of Judah (5:1–7), through their exploitation of the poor.

3:16 The proud **daughters of Zion** stand for the city and the inhabitants of Jerusalem (1:8), not just its female inhabitants.
3:17–24 God will humiliate these proud women who represent the city and inhabitants of Jerusalem. Their physical appearance will be spoiled and their **finery** will be removed. They will end up wearing **sackcloth**, ugly and uncomfortable.
3:25–4:1 War will severely reduce the male population of Jerusalem. There will not be enough **men** to marry all the women. Women without husbands were socially vulnerable. Thus, **seven women** will beg a single man to make them his wives. He will not even need to provide their food

4 On that day seven women
will seize one man, saying,
"We will eat our own bread
and provide our own clothing.
Just let us bear your name.
Take away our disgrace."

Zion's Future Glory

² On that day the Branch^A of the LORD will be beautiful and glorious, and the fruit of the land will be the pride and glory of Israel's survivors. ³ Whoever remains in Zion and whoever is left in Jerusalem will be called holy — all in Jerusalem written in the book of life^B — ⁴ when the Lord has washed away the filth of the daughters of Zion and cleansed the blood-guilt from the heart of Jerusalem by a spirit of judgment and a spirit of burning. ⁵ Then the LORD will create a cloud of smoke by day and a glowing flame of fire by night over the entire site of Mount Zion and over its assemblies. For there will be a canopy over all the glory,^C ⁶ and there will be a shelter for shade from heat by day and a refuge and shelter from storm and rain.

Song of the Vineyard

5 I will sing about the one I love,
a song about my loved one's vineyard:
The one I love had a vineyard
on a very fertile hill.
²   He broke up the soil, cleared it
of stones,
and planted it with the finest vines.
He built a tower in the middle of it
and even dug out a winepress there.
He expected it to yield good grapes,
but it yielded worthless grapes.

³   So now, residents of Jerusalem
and men of Judah,
please judge between me
and my vineyard.
⁴   What more could I have done
for my vineyard
than I did?
Why, when I expected a yield
of good grapes,
did it yield worthless grapes?
⁵   Now I will tell you
what I am about to do
to my vineyard:
I will remove its hedge,
and it will be consumed;
I will tear down its wall,
and it will be trampled.
⁶   I will make it a wasteland.
It will not be pruned or weeded;
thorns and briers will grow up.
I will also give orders to the clouds
that rain should not fall on it.
⁷   For the vineyard of the LORD
of Armies
is the house of Israel,
and the men^D of Judah,
the plant he delighted in.
He expected justice
but saw injustice;
he expected righteousness
but heard cries of despair.

Judah's Sins Denounced

⁸   Woe to those who add house
to house
and join field to field
until there is no more room
and you alone are left in the land.

---

^A 4:2 Or plant   ^B 4:3 Lit Jerusalem recorded for life   ^C 4:5 Or For glory will be a canopy over all   ^D 5:7 Lit man

---

(**bread**) and **clothing** (something mandated even for unloved secondary wives in Ex 21:10–11).

4:2–6 This pronouncement marks a sudden shift from judgment described in the pronouncements of 2:5–4:1 to future salvation.

4:2 That day is a future day, a time that comes after the judgment described in 2:5–4:1. The remnant is here described as **Israel's survivors**. The reference to the **Branch of the LORD** is provocative. After all, the branch has a messianic connotation in Jr 23:5; 33:18; Zch 3:8; 6:12. Many scholars have pointed out that the branch in this verse is parallel with **the fruit of the land** and may indicate the rich abundance that Zion will enjoy in the future. But these two readings may not be mutually exclusive since in Hebrew parallelism the second idea is often not strictly synonymous, but expands the thought of the first idea.

4:3 The remnant will be **holy**. Such implies an obedient lifestyle.

4:4 This verse explicitly states that Zion's blessed future condition will be accomplished through **judgment**.

4:5 After the exodus from Egypt, God guided Israel through the desert by a **cloud** and **flame** (cp. Ex 40:38), which represented God's mysterious and powerful presence with his people. Isaiah used this language to teach that the future remnant will again enjoy an intimate and assuring relationship with God after the judgment.

5:1–7 This poem has been identified as a parable, an allegory, and a love poem. Whatever its precise genre, its message is clear and compelling. It uses imagery to make the point that the people of God deserve the punishment coming their way.

5:1 The loved one in the song turns out to be none other than God himself, and his **vineyard** stands for his people (v. 7).

5:2 The singer continues by describing the labor that went into preparing the vineyard. To create a vineyard was no easy matter. There was a period of a few years that passed from clearing the area of **stones** (pervasive through the hill country of Israel), planting expensive vines, and building a **tower** and a **winepress**. But in spite of all the work, the vineyard produced **worthless grapes**. This signified

that the people of God did not live up to their promise of being an obedient and blessed people who would also bless the nations around them.

5:3–6 In these verses the first-person speaker is God, the owner of the vineyard, demanding an accounting of his grapes, the people of Israel.

5:3–4 When God called on the **residents of Jerusalem to judge** between him and his **vineyard**, he in essence was calling on them to judge themselves.

5:7 The last verse of the poem makes explicit the identification of the **vineyard** as the people of God. It also gives the explanation for their punishment by means of a wordplay. In the land there was **injustice** (Hb mispach) and not **justice** (Hb mishpat), **cries of despair** (Hb tse'aqah) and not **righteousness** (Hb tsedaqah).

5:8–30 The six woes (on "woe," see note at 1:4) that follow illustrate why Israel was so worthless. Judgment pronouncements follow the description of the woes.

5:8 The first **woe** is directed toward those who expanded their real estate holdings. Buying up land was always done at the cost of another person.

⁹ I heard the Lᴏʀᴅ of Armies say:
   Indeed, many houses
      will become desolate,
   grand and lovely ones
      without inhabitants.
¹⁰ For a ten-acreᴬ vineyard will yield
      only six gallons of wine,ᴮ
   and ten bushelsᶜ of seed will yield
      only one bushel of grain.ᴰ

¹¹ Woe to those who rise early
      in the morning
   in pursuit of beer,
   who linger into the evening,
      inflamed by wine.
¹² At their feasts they have lyre, harp,
      tambourine, flute, and wine.
   They do not perceive the Lᴏʀᴅ's actions,
   and they do not see the work
      of his hands.

¹³ Therefore my people will go into exile
   because they lack knowledge;
   herᴱ dignitaries are starving,
   and her masses are parched
      with thirst.
¹⁴ Therefore Sheol enlarges its throat
   and opens wide its enormous jaws,
   and down go Zion's dignitaries,
      her masses,
   her crowds, and those who celebrate
      in her!
¹⁵ Humanity is brought low, each
      person is humbled,
   and haughty eyes are humbled.
¹⁶ But the Lᴏʀᴅ of Armies is exalted
      by his justice,
   and the holy God demonstrates his
      holiness through his righteousness.
¹⁷ Lambs will graze
      as if inᶠ their own pastures,
   and resident aliensᴳ will eat
      among the ruins of the rich.

¹⁸ Woe to those who drag iniquity
      with cords of deceit
   and pull sin along with cart ropes,
¹⁹ to those who say,

"Let him hurry up and do
      his work quickly
so that we can see it!
Let the plan of the Holy One of Israel
      take place
so that we can know it!"
²⁰ Woe to those who call evil good
   and good evil,
who substitute darkness for light
   and light for darkness,
who substitute bitter for sweet
   and sweet for bitter.
²¹ Woe to those who consider themselves
      wise
   and judge themselves clever.ᴴ
²² Woe to those who are heroes
      at drinking wine,
who are champions at pouring beer,
²³ who acquit the guilty for a bribe
   and deprive the innocent of justice.

²⁴ Therefore, as a tongue of fire
      consumes straw
and as dry grass shrivels in the flame,
so their roots will become
   like something rotten
and their blossoms will blow away
   like dust,
for they have rejected
   the instruction of the Lᴏʀᴅ
      of Armies,
and they have despised
   the word of the Holy One of Israel.
²⁵ Therefore the Lᴏʀᴅ's anger burned
      against his people.
He raised his hand against them
   and struck them;
the mountains quaked,
and their corpses were like garbage
   in the streets.
In all this, his anger has not turned
      away,
and his hand is still raised to strike.

²⁶ He raises a signal flag
      for the distant nations
   and whistles for them from the ends
      of the earth.

ᴬ5:10 Lit ten-yoke   ᴮ5:10 Lit one bath   ᶜ5:10 Lit one homer   ᴰ5:10 Lit yield an ephah   ᴱ5:13 Lit its   ᶠ5:17 Syr reads graze in   ᴳ5:17 LXX reads sheep   ᴴ5:21 Lit and clever before their face

5:9–10 While the wealthy intended to grab land to get richer, the result will be the opposite—empty **houses** and poor harvests.
5:11–12 The second **woe** is directed toward those who indulged in excessive drinking of alcoholic beverages (**beer** and **wine**).
5:14 As God's people indulged themselves with drink and food, so **Sheol** will open its large mouth and swallow them. Sheol refers to the grave.
5:15–17 Compare these verses with 2:9,11,17. What marks God as God is his essential justice and righteousness.

5:18–19 The third **woe** begins by picturing people whose sin was so heavy that they ended up pulling it along in a **cart** behind them. Their sin was one of cynicism. With a tone of disbelief, they challenged God to act.
5:20 The fourth **woe** is against those who confused ethical categories. They classified actions as **evil** that God would call **good** and vice versa.
5:21 As with the previous verse, the issue of the fifth **woe** is human autonomy. On being wise in one's own eyes, see Pr 3:7; 26:12; 28:11,26.

5:22–23 The sixth and final **woe** returns to the earlier issue of excessive drinking (**heroes at drinking wine**) and also twisting justice for money.
5:24–25 Two judgment speeches follow (**therefore** introduces vv. 24 and 25) the woes.
5:26–28 God will call for foreign armies to descend on his people. These nations were Assyria and Babylon. Notice that God would signal them with a whistle, and they would immediately respond. This illustrates God's sovereign rule over the nations.

Look — how quickly and swiftly
they come!

27 None of them grows weary or stumbles;
no one slumbers or sleeps.
No belt is loose
and no sandal strap broken.

28 Their arrows are sharpened,
and all their bows strung.
Their horses' hooves are like flint;
their chariot wheels are
like a whirlwind.

29 Their roaring is like a lion's;
they roar like young lions;
they growl and seize their prey
and carry it off,
and no one can rescue it.

30 On that day they will roar over it,
like the roaring of the sea.
When one looks at the land,
there will be darkness and distress;
light will be obscured by clouds.^A

Isaiah's Call and Mission

6 In the year that King Uzziah died, I saw the
Lord seated on a high and lofty throne, and
the hem of his robe filled the temple. 2 Sera-
phim^B were standing above him; they each had
six wings: with two they covered their faces,
with two they covered their feet, and with two
they flew. 3 And one called to another:

Holy, holy, holy is the LORD of Armies;
his glory fills the whole earth.

4 The foundations of the doorways shook at
the sound of their voices, and the temple was
filled with smoke.

5 Then I said:

Woe is me for I am ruined^C
because I am a man of unclean lips
and live among a people of unclean lips,
and because my eyes have seen the King,
the LORD of Armies.

6 Then one of the seraphim flew to me, and
in his hand was a glowing coal that he had

taken from the altar with tongs. 7 He touched
my mouth with it and said:

Now that this has touched your lips,
your iniquity is removed
and your sin is atoned for.

8 Then I heard the voice of the Lord asking:
Who will I send?
Who will go for us?

I said:
Here I am. Send me.

9 And he replied:
Go! Say to these people:
Keep listening, but do not understand;
keep looking, but do not perceive.

10 Make the minds^D of these people dull;
deafen their ears and blind their eyes;
otherwise they might see with their eyes
and hear with their ears,
understand with their minds,
turn back, and be healed.

11 Then I said, "Until when, Lord?" And he
replied:
Until cities lie in ruins
without inhabitants,
houses are without people,
the land is ruined and desolate,

12 and the LORD drives the people far away,
leaving great emptiness in the land.

13 Though a tenth will remain in the land,
it will be burned again.
Like the terebinth or the oak
that leaves a stump when felled,
the holy seed is the stump.

The Message to Ahaz

7 This took place during the reign of Ahaz,
son of Jotham, son of Uzziah king of Judah:
Aram's King Rezin and Israel's King Pekah son
of Remaliah went to fight against Jerusalem,
but they were not able to conquer it.

^5:30 Lit its clouds ^B6:2 = heavenly beings ^C6:5 Or I must be silent ^D6:10 Lit heart

---

5:29 Assyrian royal inscriptions often compare their kings to **lions**.
6:1–13 Isaiah received his commissioning vision in the temple, but in his vision the temple was transformed into the throne room of heaven itself.
6:1 **King Uzziah** (called "Azariah" in 2Kg 15:1) died about 740 BC. He had been a relatively good king, and did "what was right in the LORD's sight" (2Kg 15:3), though he did not remove the high places. God also blessed Uzziah's reign with prosperity and military success. His death, coupled with the rise of Assyria, created great uncertainty in Judah. Note that God is so great that just **the hem of his robe** filled the temple.
6:2 The **seraphim** were angelic creatures of great power and importance. Their name means "burning ones." Covering their eyes shielded them from the brilliance of the

divine glory. Covering their feet (possibly used here as a euphemism) may have been a posture of submission.
6:3 The word **holy** spoken three times is emphatic or superlative and points to God's otherness. His sovereignty is underlined by the fact that his glory filled **the whole earth**.
6:4 The **smoke** was likely incense, which cloaked Isaiah's vision in mystery.
6:5 In the presence of such holiness, Isaiah felt the weight of his own sinfulness.
6:6–7 God prepared Isaiah by cleansing his **lips**, the instrument by which he would execute his prophetic task. He did this symbolically by having one of his seraphim touch the prophet's lips with a burning coal. Fire can purify (Nm 31:22–23), and this burning coal was taken from the altar where sacrifices were offered to atone for **sin** (1Ch 6:49).

6:9–10 Isaiah was a prophet with a message of judgment. Isaiah's message from God would serve only to distance Israel even more from God. These verses are quoted in the NT to explain why Jesus taught in parables (Mt 13:14–15; Mk 4:12; Lk 8:10) and to explain the people's lack of response to the gospel (Jn 12:40; Ac 28:26–27).
6:11–13 From the start Isaiah knew that his message would not lead God's people to repentance. They would experience destruction. Even so, a remnant would survive. This remnant is pictured as a **stump** that is left after a mighty tree falls.
7:1–2 The political situation was tense in Jerusalem. In the early 730s BC the aggressive Assyrian king Tiglath-pileser III was busy on his northern frontier. During this time, **Rezin**, the king of **Aram** with its capital in Damascus, and **Pekah**, the king of Israel (also known

The Worship and Service of God

by David S. Dockery

Worship, though primary in the life of the church, is often elusive and misunderstood, even among Christians. Worship is ascribing worth to God with our voices, our minds, and our hearts. It is the act of bringing glory to God, which, of course, may be and should be applied to all of life. More specifically, though, the word "worship" refers to the act and activity of praising and glorifying God when Christians assemble in a local congregation.

If, as Christians, we are truly concerned with ascribing to God the supreme worth that he alone is worthy to receive, we must be cautious about allowing our worship to be shaped by our own felt needs rather than by Scripture and a healthy appreciation for our Christian heritage. Believers must recognize that worship is the active response to God the Father through the Son. Praise, prayer, preaching, the celebration of ordinances, confession, and giving are all Christ-centered, scripturally informed actions. The focus of the church's worship on the exalted Christ gives a Spirit-enabled depth and content to a gathering. Fitting and acceptable worship, in fact, can only be offered by and through the enabling ministry of the Holy Spirit.

Genuine worship must include the proclamation of the whole counsel of God's Word (Ac 20:27) and the primacy of textually grounded preaching. The gospel message forms the center and shape of worship. With that recognition, worship services need to seek to touch lives while creating worship experiences that simultaneously exalt God and edify his people. Anything less fails to be faithful to the New Testament teaching and the early church's pattern.

When genuine worship takes place, the entire body of Christ is enhanced and built up; moreover, the mission, service, and outreach of local churches are strengthened. The people of God who have worshiped him and who have been mutually strengthened are prepared to enter the world to touch lives, meet needs, counsel hurts, speak to injustices, and both bear witness to and proclaim the saving message of the gospel. Exalting God and serving others are hardly in conflict, especially for Christians who seek to understand and live out the Christian faith in a coherent manner. As a matter of fact, authentic service is built on genuine worship (see Is 6:1–8; Mt 28:16–20) and is focused on the church, the culture, and the world.

The Church

The church was inaugurated at Pentecost (Ac 2) as God's new society (Eph 2:15). It was founded on the finished work of Christ (Jn 19:30) and the baptizing work of the Spirit (1Co 12:13). The church was a mystery (Eph 3:9–11), was prophesied about by Christ (Mt 16:18), and was revealed at the Spirit's coming at Pentecost. The church was built on the foundation of Christ's apostles, with Christ Jesus himself serving as its cornerstone (Eph 2:20–21).

The true church is more than a human organization; it is a visible and tangible expression of the people who are related to Christ. As far as is possible, all Christians should involve and invest themselves in the visible, organized church of Jesus Christ. God gifts his people in the church in order to prepare them for works of service so that they will be strengthened and prepared for faithful living and ministry. The Spirit of God uses gifted leaders in the church to help bring maturity to other Christ followers. They, in turn, will be able to proclaim Christ, admonishing and teaching others with great wisdom and engaging the culture and serving the world through both word and deed (Eph 4:11–13; Col 1:28).

The Culture

Many people today reject the church and the Christian faith, not because they perceive it to be false but because they believe it is superficial or trivial. People are looking for an authentic and integrated way of seeing life that brings coherence to all of life's experiences—some of which are confusing. In many ways, our post-Christian Western culture in general—and American culture in particular—resembles the pre-Christian Athens of Paul's day (see Ac 17), particularly in its focus on the new, the novel, and the world of change. Our culture is similarly enthralled by novelty.

Truth and values in our culture seem to be of minimal concern or consequence. In the address by the apostle Paul in Acts 17 we find a model for how to lovingly and effectively combat such thinking. We learn how to engage culture in meaningful and relevant ways, as well as how to communicate and live this truth in an effective manner in the midst of an incredibly superficial world. The cultural trends that shape much of our society are similarly influenced by the rise of neopaganism and various and diverse forms of spirituality. Thus Paul is an insightful guide who enables thoughtful Christ followers to respond to this changing post-Christian world.

The World

Christians live in a world where English is the new common language in most discussions of globalization. The Spanish language, however, is the most frequently spoken tongue used by Christians around the world. We live in a context that points to the movement of the Christian base toward the Global South. Christ followers in the West, therefore, must be willing to defer to non-Western opinions and ideas whenever our most basic Christian convictions are not at stake. Western wealth and isolation have at times kept us from understanding the real issues of the Majority World and those in the unevangelized belt. Similarly, we must recognize the importance that social justice plays in helping us understand and carry out the mission of God. We need to engage in the serious work that seeks to connect theology, education, justice, and missions together as partners rather than competitors.

Many Christians, particularly younger believers, comprehend the importance of providing homes for the homeless and food for the hungry. They understand that they are to work for justice while simultaneously taking the good news of the gospel to new areas of the world. We must recognize that we now live in a globally connected context, with new faces representing the various contexts and cultures of our larger global family. We must recognize that what brings together Christ's followers is not our homogeneous characteristics but our deep love for Jesus Christ. Our lives are to become an offering of thanks to Jesus. This is best expressed through compassion to the least of these in our world.

Christians should assume a posture of humility, listening to and learning from one another. The current climate of fear that characterizes the world around us will likely create a strong challenge, keeping many people from participating in new opportunities. A love for Jesus Christ and a desire to understand others will help counter this fear, launching exciting global opportunities for the days ahead. We should think not only about international opportunities but intercultural ones as well. The major cities across the United States now look as if the world has moved into these places.

Poverty, homelessness, drug abuse, and violence surround us. Our cities are multiethnic and intercultural. Christians, therefore, must grapple with our own insulation. We have the privilege of locally living out the global implications of our faith, joining with others to forge relevant ties for global service. We thus seek to know and exalt God, to think seriously and coherently about all aspects of life in order to serve others and to take the gospel to the ends of the earth. Let us not shy away from this task. Let us ask the Lord to raise up and develop a new generation of thoughtful, committed, convictional, and courageous Christ followers who will go forth in wisdom, humility, and confidence to serve the church, engage the culture, and disciple the nations for the glory of the triune God.

² When it became known to the house of David that Aram had occupied Ephraim, the heart of Ahaz^A and the hearts of his people trembled like trees of a forest shaking in the wind. ³ The LORD said to Isaiah, "Go out with your son Shear-jashub^B to meet Ahaz at the end of the conduit of the upper pool, by the road to the Launderer's Field. ⁴ Say to him: Calm down and be quiet. Don't be afraid or cowardly because of these two smoldering sticks, the fierce anger of Rezin and Aram, and the son of Remaliah. ⁵ For Aram, along with Ephraim and the son of Remaliah, has plotted harm against you. They say, ⁶ 'Let's go up against Judah, terrorize it, and conquer it for ourselves. Then we can install Tabeel's son as king in it.' "

⁷ This is what the Lord GOD says:
It will not happen; it will not occur.
⁸ The chief city of Aram is Damascus,
the chief of Damascus is Rezin
(within sixty-five years
Ephraim will be too shattered to be
a people),
⁹ the chief city of Ephraim is Samaria,
and the chief of Samaria is the son
of Remaliah.
If you do not stand firm in your faith,
then you will not stand at all.

The Immanuel Prophecy
¹⁰ Then the LORD spoke again to Ahaz: ¹¹ "Ask for a sign from the LORD your God — it can be as deep as Sheol or as high as heaven." ¹² But Ahaz replied, "I will not ask. I will not test the LORD."

¹³ Isaiah said, "Listen, house of David! Is it not enough for you to try the patience of men? Will you also try the patience of my God? ¹⁴ Therefore, the Lord himself will give you^c a sign: See, the virgin will conceive,^D have a son, and name him Immanuel.^E ¹⁵ By the time he learns to reject what is bad and choose what is good, he will be eating curds^F and honey. ¹⁶ For before the boy knows to reject what is bad and choose what is good, the land of the two kings you dread will be abandoned. ¹⁷ The LORD will bring on you, your people, and your father's house such a time as has never been since Ephraim separated from Judah: He will bring the king of Assyria."

¹⁸ On that day
the LORD will whistle to flies
at the farthest streams of the Nile
and to bees in the land of Assyria.
¹⁹ All of them will come and settle
in the steep ravines, in the clefts
of the rocks,
in all the thornbushes, and in all the
water holes.

²⁰ On that day the Lord will use a razor hired from beyond the Euphrates River — the king of Assyria — to shave the hair on your heads, the hair on your legs, and even your beards.
²¹ On that day
a man will raise a young cow
and two sheep,
²² and from the abundant milk they give
he will eat curds,
for every survivor in the land
will eat curds and honey.

^A7:2 Lit *Aram has rested upon Ephraim, his heart*   ^B7:3 = A Remnant Will Return   ^c7:14 In Hb, the word *you* is pl   ^D7:14 Or *virgin is pregnant, will*   ^E7:14 = God With Us   ^F7:15 Or *sour milk*

as **Ephraim**), joined forces to withstand the almost certain Assyrian attack that would follow Tiglath-pileser's victory in the north. Rezin and Pekah wanted Judah to support them, but **Ahaz** wanted nothing to do with the alliance. By this time he might already have paid (or at least was contemplating paying) the Assyrians to rescue him from these kings (2Kg 16:6–9). He probably feared Tiglath-pileser, but he apparently realized the Syro-Ephraimite coalition was a more immediate threat. Isaiah confronted the king with a question: What was the source of his trust: the Lord or the Assyrians?
7:3 The name of Isaiah's son, **Shear-jashub**, means "a remnant will return."
7:5–6 Though no other certain references to Tabeel exist in the Bible or are known outside of it, the political intentions of Rezin and Pekah were clear. They wanted to remove Ahaz from the throne because of his unwillingness to join their coalition, and they intended to install a puppet **king** who would be more easily manipulated.
7:7–8 The reference to **sixty-five years** is puzzling. If this pronouncement is dated to 735 BC or thereabouts, then it would point to approximately 670 BC, but the northern kingdom was soundly defeated by Assyria in 722 BC. Of course, that is "within sixty-five years."

7:10–11 The purpose of **a sign** was to give Ahaz even more reason to have confidence in God rather than Assyria to rescue him from Rezin and Pekah. **Sheol** refers to the underworld.
7:12 From Isaiah's reaction, the reader can discern that Ahaz's reply, which on the surface seems pious, was actually impious.
7:13 The use of **my God** in this verse instead of "your God," as in v. 11, shows that Ahaz's lack of faith was a turning point in his life. Isaiah's reference to him as **house of David** shows also that it would impact the Davidic dynasty, spelling its decline.
7:14 The context indicates that the preliminary fulfillment of this sign must have taken place within a few years of its utterance—the time between a child's conception and his knowing right from wrong (vv. 15–16), traditionally at age twelve. The Hebrew word translated **virgin** means "young woman of marriageable age" and often has the implication of virginity. Thus many scholars feel that the referent is a woman whom Isaiah would marry and, if so, then the birth is mentioned in 8:1–4. This may be the immediate fulfillment of this sign. But its ultimate and more exalted fulfillment is noted in Mt 1:23 as it cites the more specific Greek word found in the Septuagint,

parthenos, which means "virgin." **Immanuel** means "God With Us."
7:15 The first phrase could also be translated, "In order to learn," meaning that hardship will motivate the child to turn to God. The significance of eating **curds and honey** is that the devastation of the land's agriculture (vv. 23–24) will be such that other foods will not be available.
7:16 The Aramean kingdom of Rezin was destroyed in 732 BC. Tiglath-pileser reduced the size of the northern kingdom of Pekah in 733 BC, and the king was assassinated and replaced by Hoshea. Even so, the northern kingdom was totally defeated in 722 BC, about thirteen years after the Immanuel prophecy.
7:17 It was not just Syria and the northern kingdom that would experience Assyrian devastation. Judah would also experience God's punishment. As later events showed, paying Tiglath-pileser to take care of Ahaz's northern problem was not the smartest strategy. From that point on Ahaz paid a heavy tribute as Assyria's vassal (2Kg 16:10–18).
7:18–19 The **flies** (Egypt) and the **bees** (Assyria) will infest (occupy) the land.
7:20 The **razor** is Tiglath-pileser, who will ravage the land of Judah.

²³ And on that day
  every place where there were a
    thousand vines,
  worth a thousand pieces of silver,
  will become thorns and briers.
²⁴ A man will go there with bow
    and arrows
  because the whole land will be thorns
    and briers.
²⁵ You will not go to all the hills
  that were once tilled with a hoe,
  for fear of the thorns and briers.
  Those hills will be places for oxen
    to graze
  and for sheep to trample.

The Coming Assyrian Invasion

8 Then the LORD said to me, "Take a large
piece of parchment^A and write on it with
an ordinary pen:^B Maher-shalal-hash-baz.^C ² I
have appointed^D trustworthy witnesses — the
priest Uriah and Zechariah son of Jeberechiah."
³ I was then intimate with the prophetess,
and she conceived and gave birth to a son.
The LORD said to me, "Name him Maher-shalal-hash-baz, ⁴ for before the boy knows how to
call 'Father,' or 'Mother,' the wealth of Damascus and the spoils of Samaria will be carried
off to the king of Assyria."
⁵ The LORD spoke to me again:
⁶ Because these people rejected
  the slowly flowing water of Shiloah
  and rejoiced with^E Rezin
  and the son of Remaliah,
⁷ the Lord will certainly bring
    against them
  the mighty rushing water
    of the Euphrates River —
  the king of Assyria and all his glory.
  It will overflow its channels
  and spill over all its banks.

⁸ It will pour into Judah,
  flood over it, and sweep through,
  reaching up to the neck;
  and its flooded banks^F
  will fill your entire land, Immanuel!

⁹ Band together,^G peoples,
    and be broken;
  pay attention, all you distant lands;
  prepare for war, and be broken;
  prepare for war, and be broken.
¹⁰ Devise a plan; it will fail.
  Make a prediction; it will not happen.
  For God is with us.^H

The LORD of Armies, the Only Refuge

¹¹ For this is what the LORD said to me with great
power, to keep^I me from going the way of this
people:
¹² Do not call everything a conspiracy
    that these people say is
      a conspiracy.
  Do not fear what they fear;
  do not be terrified.
¹³ You are to regard only the LORD
    of Armies as holy.
  Only he should be feared;
  only he should be held in awe.
¹⁴ He will be a sanctuary;
  but for the two houses of Israel,
  he will be a stone to stumble over
    and a rock to trip over,
  and a trap and a snare to the inhabitants
    of Jerusalem.
¹⁵ Many will stumble over these;
  they will fall and be broken;
  they will be snared and captured.
¹⁶ Bind up the testimony.
  Seal up the instruction
    among my disciples.

---

^A 8:1 Hb obscure   ^B 8:1 Lit *with the pen of a man*   ^C 8:1 = Speeding to the Plunder, Hurrying to the Spoil   ^D 8:2 Vg; MT, one
DSS ms read *I will appoint*; one DSS ms, LXX, Syr, Tg read *Appoint*   ^E 8:6 Or *and rejoiced over*   ^F 8:8 Lit *its outspread wings*
^G 8:9 Or *Raise the war cry*, or *Be shattered*   ^H 8:10 Hb *Immanuel*   ^I 8:11 DSS; MT reads *instruct*

8:1 There is nothing unusual about the use
of **parchment** and **pen** in this verse. Nor
would there be anything unusual if, as some
scholars suggest, the Hebrew here indicates
a clay tablet and a stylus. The significance of
the **large** size of the parchment may simply
be that the writing was prominent and clear.
The name **Maher-shalal-hash-baz** means
"Speeding to the Plunder, Hurrying to the
Spoil," and it signifies the rapid future advance of Assyria.
8:2 The presence of **witnesses** indicates that
the writing of this prophecy had the force
of a legal document. If the prophecy did not
come true, then these two witnesses could
attest to its falsity. If it did come true, they
could proclaim that it was written before,
and not after, the fact. It is possible that
Uriah is mentioned in 2Kg 16:10–18. He was
the high priest during Ahaz's reign who, at
the king's request, modified the altar to
conform to the one in Damascus.

8:3 On **intimate with the prophetess**, see
note at 7:14.
8:5–8 It was good news to Judah that Assyria would defeat Syria and Israel, the two
nations that were allied against it. In this
light, **rejoiced with Rezin** likely refers to
Judah's rejoicing in Rezin's coming defeat.
The pronouncement states that such rejoicing might be premature since the Assyrian
threat would come to its doorstep as well.
8:6 The **water of Shiloah** refers to the small
water channel that carried water from pools
outside Jerusalem into the city. Here it stands
for God himself, contrasting with the raging river mentioned in the next verse. Thus,
Judah's rejection of Shiloah signifies their
rejection of God.
8:7 The **mighty rushing water** of the Eu-
phrates represents the Assyrian king and
thus Assyrian might.
8:8 The waters that represent Assyria will
come up to Judah's **neck**. They will not be

drowned, but they will find themselves paying annual tribute.
8:12 The **conspiracy** may refer to the alliance
between Syria and the northern kingdom of
Israel against Judah or perhaps an inner-Ju-
dean alliance against the pro-Assyrian party
of Ahaz. Whatever the exact alliance in view,
the point was that Isaiah must not be afraid
like the people were.
8:13 There is a difference in the quality of
the two fears described in these verses. The
fear of human beings may be described as
terror (v. 12), while the fear of God is described as **awe**.
8:14 Verse 14 is quoted in Rm 9:33 and 1Pt 2:8.
8:16 The **testimony**, also called the **instruction**, refers to the words of God that
have come to Isaiah. These are to be kept
safely (**bind up . . . seal up**) by Isaiah's
disciples. They will keep the pronouncements of God secure until the events prove
them true.

¹⁷ I will wait for the LORD,
who is hiding his face from the house
of Jacob.
I will wait for him.

¹⁸ Here I am with the children the LORD has given me to be signs and wonders in Israel from the LORD of Armies who dwells on Mount Zion. ¹⁹ When they say to you, "Inquire of the mediums and the spiritists who chirp and mutter," shouldn't a people inquire of their God?^A Should they inquire of the dead on behalf of the living? ²⁰ Go to God's instruction and testimony! If they do not speak according to this word, there will be no dawn for them. ²¹ They will wander through the land, dejected and hungry. When they are famished, they will become enraged, and, looking upward, will curse their king and their God. ²² They will look toward the earth and see only distress, darkness, and the gloom of affliction, and they will be driven into thick darkness.

Birth of the Prince of Peace

9 Nevertheless, the gloom of the distressed land will not be like that of the former times when he humbled the land of Zebulun and the land of Naphtali. But in the future he will bring honor to the way of the sea, to the land east of the Jordan, and to Galilee of the nations.
² The people walking in darkness
have seen a great light;
a light has dawned
on those living in the land of darkness.
³ You have enlarged the nation
and increased its joy.^B
The people have rejoiced before you
as they rejoice at harvest time
and as they rejoice when dividing spoils.
⁴ For you have shattered
their oppressive yoke

and the rod on their shoulders,
the staff of their oppressor,
just as you did on the day of Midian.
⁵ For every trampling boot of battle
and the bloodied garments of war
will be burned as fuel for the fire.
⁶ For a child will be born for us,
a son will be given to us,
and the government will be
on his shoulders.
He will be named
Wonderful Counselor, Mighty God,
Eternal Father, Prince of Peace.
⁷ The dominion will be vast,
and its prosperity will never end.
He will reign on the throne of David
and over his kingdom,
to establish and sustain it
with justice and righteousness
from now on and forever.
The zeal of the LORD of Armies
will accomplish this.

The Hand Raised against Israel

⁸ The Lord sent a message against Jacob;
it came against Israel.
⁹ All the people —
Ephraim and the inhabitants of Samaria
— will know it.
They will say with pride
and arrogance,
¹⁰ "The bricks have fallen,
but we will rebuild with cut stones;
the sycamores have been cut down,
but we will replace them with cedars."
¹¹ The LORD has raised up
Rezin's adversaries against him
and stirred up his enemies.
¹² Aram from the east and Philistia
from the west
have consumed Israel
with open mouths.

^A8:19 Or gods   ^B9:3 Alt Hb tradition reads have not increased joy

In all this, his anger has not turned
away,
and his hand is still raised to strike.

¹³ The people did not turn to him
who struck them;
they did not seek the LORD of Armies.
¹⁴ So the LORD cut off Israel's head and tail,
palm branch and reed in a single day.
¹⁵ The head is the elder, the honored one;
the tail is the prophet, the one teaching
lies.
¹⁶ The leaders of the people mislead them,
and those they mislead
are swallowed up.^A
¹⁷ Therefore the Lord does not rejoice
over^B Israel's young men
and has no compassion
on its fatherless and widows,
for everyone is a godless evildoer,
and every mouth speaks folly.
In all this, his anger has not turned
away,
and his hand is still raised to strike.

¹⁸ For wickedness burns like a fire
that consumes thorns and briers
and kindles the forest thickets
so that they go up in a column of smoke.
¹⁹ The land is scorched
by the wrath of the LORD of Armies,
and the people are like fuel for the fire.
No one has compassion on his brother.
²⁰ They carve meat on the right,
but they are still hungry;
they have eaten on the left,
but they are still not satisfied.
Each one eats the flesh of his arm.
²¹ Manasseh eats Ephraim,
and Ephraim, Manasseh;
together, both are against Judah.
In all this, his anger has not turned
away,
and his hand is still raised to strike.

10 Woe to those enacting
crooked statutes
and writing oppressive laws
² to keep the poor from getting
a fair trial
and to deprive the needy
among my people of justice,
so that widows can be their spoil
and they can plunder the fatherless.
³ What will you do on the day
of punishment
when devastation comes
from far away?
Who will you run to for help?
Where will you leave your wealth?
⁴ There will be nothing to do
except crouch among the prisoners
or fall among the slain.
In all this, his anger has not turned
away,
and his hand is still raised to strike.

Assyria, the Instrument of Wrath

⁵ Woe to Assyria, the rod of my anger —
the staff in their hands is my wrath.
⁶ I will send him against a godless nation;
I will command him to go
against a people destined for my rage,
to take spoils, to plunder,
and to trample them down like clay
in the streets.
⁷ But this is not what he intends;
this is not what he plans.
It is his intent to destroy
and to cut off many nations.
⁸ For he says,
"Aren't all my commanders kings?
⁹ Isn't Calno like Carchemish?
Isn't Hamath like Arpad?
Isn't Samaria like Damascus?^C
¹⁰ As my hand seized the kingdoms of
worthless images,
kingdoms whose idols exceeded
those of Jerusalem and Samaria,

---

^A **9:16** Or *are confused*   ^B **9:17** DSS read *not spare*   ^C **10:9** Cities conquered by Assyria

Note that the last two parts of this verse are repeated in vv. 17,21, as well as 10:4.
9:14 After the first Assyrian incursion into the north (733 BC), Israel continued in its sinful ways. God soon brought a more devastating judgment in 722 BC, ending their independent existence. The expression **head and tail, palm branch and reed** points to a totality (19:15).
9:18–19 Devastation is seen as the natural consequence of wickedness itself (**wickedness burns like a fire**) as well as the result of divine anger (**the land is scorched by the wrath of the LORD of Armies**). Sin breaks up human relationships, even brotherly love.
9:21 Manasseh and **Ephraim** were two large northern tribes whose founding fathers were brothers, the sons of Joseph (Gn 41:50–52; 48:5). Together they turned against **Judah**.
10:1–2 On **woe**, see note at 1:4.

10:4 Verse 4 answers the rhetorical questions of verse 3. With the fourth repetition of the refrain concerning God's **anger** (cp. 9:12,17,21), the section comes to a close. Though punishment has come, God's people still have not repented. More judgment will follow.
10:5 The pronouncement opens with a **woe** against Assyria. On "woe" see note at 1:4 (see also 5:8–30). This woe is directed toward the enemy rather than toward God's people (10:1). Assyria is the tool he will use to bring punishment against Israel and Judah.
10:6 The **godless nation** is ironically not Assyria but Israel. They will become the object of God's anger. The phrase **to take spoils, to plunder** is reminiscent of the name Maher-shalal-hash-baz, "Speeding to the Plunder, Hurrying to the Spoil" (8:1).

10:7 There was a difference between the divine intention and the intention of Assyria. This difference was no obstacle to God's use of Assyria for his purposes, but it did bode poorly for the tool of God's anger. While God's intention was to promote his own glory by punishing his sinful people, Assyria was interested only in imperialistic expansion.
10:8–11 Isaiah quotes the proud words of the Assyrian king.
10:9 These three pairs of cities each begin with the southernmost of the two. Thus, **Calno** (also known as Calneh) was south of Carchemish, **Hamath** was south of Arpad, and **Samaria** was south of Damascus. These cities were paired and listed for geographical and not chronological reasons since **Carchemish** was conquered by the Assyrians in 717 BC, Calno in 738, Hamath in 738 and 720, and **Arpad** in 740.

¹¹ and as I did to Samaria and its worthless images
will I not also do to Jerusalem
and its idols?"

Judgment on Assyria

¹² But when the Lord finishes all his work against Mount Zion and Jerusalem, he will say, "I[A] will punish the king of Assyria for his arrogant acts and the proud look in his eyes." ¹³ For he said:

I have done this by my own strength
and wisdom, for I am clever.
I abolished the borders of nations
and plundered their treasures;
like a mighty warrior, I subjugated
the inhabitants.[B]
¹⁴ My hand has reached out, as if
into a nest,
to seize the wealth of the nations.
Like one gathering abandoned eggs,
I gathered the whole earth.
No wing fluttered;
no beak opened or chirped.

¹⁵ Does an ax exalt itself
above the one who chops with it?
Does a saw magnify itself
above the one who saws with it?
It would be like a rod waving the ones
who lift[C] it!
It would be like a staff lifting the one
who isn't wood!
¹⁶ Therefore the Lord GOD of Armies
will inflict an emaciating disease
on the well-fed of Assyria,
and he will kindle a burning fire
under its glory.
¹⁷ Israel's Light will become a fire,
and its Holy One, a flame.
In one day it will burn and consume
Assyria's thorns and thistles.

¹⁸ He will completely destroy
the glory of its forests and orchards
as a sickness consumes a person.
¹⁹ The remaining trees of its forest
will be so few in number
that a child could count them.

The Remnant Will Return

²⁰ On that day the remnant of Israel and the survivors of the house of Jacob will no longer depend on the one who struck them, but they will faithfully depend on the LORD, the Holy One of Israel.
²¹ The remnant will return, the remnant
of Jacob,
to the Mighty God.
²² Israel, even if your people were
as numerous
as the sand of the sea,
only a remnant of them will return.
Destruction has been decreed;
justice overflows.
²³ For throughout the land
the Lord GOD of Armies
is carrying out a destruction
that was decreed.

²⁴ Therefore, the Lord GOD of Armies says this: "My people who dwell in Zion, do not fear Assyria, though they strike you with a rod and raise their staff over you as the Egyptians did. ²⁵ In just a little while my wrath will be spent and my anger will turn to their destruction." ²⁶ And the LORD of Armies will brandish a whip against him as he did when he struck Midian at the rock of Oreb; and he will raise his staff over the sea as he did in Egypt.

God Will Judge Assyria

²⁷ On that day
his burden will fall from your shoulders,
and his yoke from your neck.

[A]10:12 LXX reads *Jerusalem, he* [B]10:13 Or *I brought down their kings* [C]10:15 Some Hb mss; other Hb mss, Syr, Vg read *the one who lifts*

10:10–11 The comparisons of southern cities to northern ones culminate in a final comparison between **Samaria** in the north and **Jerusalem** in the south: both were practicing idolatry as the Syrian cities did (v. 9). **10:13–14** The boastful quotation from the Assyrian king reflects the type of bombastic language used in contemporary Assyrian royal inscriptions. The image of the Assyrian king stealing **eggs** from an abandoned **nest** emphasizes his cruelty in taking advantage of weaker nations. **10:15** The use of rhetorical questions directed to the king has the function of scolding and embarrassing him in his pretension. Each question has the answer, "Of course not." **10:16–19** The conjunction **therefore** serves as a transition from indictment to judgment. The description of the punishment by **disease** and **fire** could be taken literally, metaphorically, or both.

10:17 The image of God as **Light** both illuminates, so people can see clearly, and also scorches and kills in judgment. **10:21–23** God had promised Abraham that his descendants would be **as numerous as the sand of the sea** (see Gn 22:17; 32:12; 41:49), but because of their punishment, only a **remnant** would survive and even that would be an act of God's grace. Paul quotes vv. 22–23 in Rm 9:27–28. **10:26** Oreb was a Midianite leader who oppressed the Israelites during the period of the judges. He was defeated by the forces of Gideon and executed at a rock that was given his name, the **rock of Oreb** (Jdg 7:24–25). The reference to God's staff in Egypt recalls the crossing of the Red Sea. Moses raised his **staff**, representing God's presence. God caused the sea to divide, allowing the Israelites to escape the Egyptian army (Ex 14:21–31).

10:27 The **yoke** is an image of political domination frequently used by the prophets (14:25; 47:6; 58:6; Jr 27:11; 30:8; Ezk 30:18).

#35 99 Essential Christian Truths

IMPUTATION

When God pardoned sinners at the cross, our sins were imputed, or transferred, to Christ, who became sin on our behalf. In exchange, Christ's righteousness was imputed to us (Rm 5:17; 1Co 1:30). When God the Father looks at those who have trusted in Christ, he does not see their sins but the righteousness of Christ as belonging to them (Rm 4:6).

The yoke will be broken
　because your neck will be too large.[A]

28 Assyria has come to Aiath
and has gone through Migron,
storing their equipment at Michmash.

29 They crossed over at the ford, saying,
"We will spend the night at Geba."
The people of Ramah are trembling;
those at Gibeah of Saul have fled.

30 Cry aloud, daughter of Gallim!
Listen, Laishah!
Anathoth is miserable.

31 Madmenah has fled.
The inhabitants of Gebim
have sought refuge.

32 Today the Assyrians will stand at Nob,
shaking their fists at the mountain
of Daughter Zion,
the hill of Jerusalem.

33 Look, the Lord GOD of Armies
will chop off the branches
with terrifying power,
and the tall trees will be cut down,
the high trees felled.

34 He is clearing the thickets of the forest
with an ax,
and Lebanon with its majesty will fall.

Reign of the Davidic King

11 Then a shoot will grow from the stump
of Jesse,
and a branch from his roots
will bear fruit.

2 The Spirit of the LORD will rest
on him —
a Spirit of wisdom and understanding,
a Spirit of counsel and strength,

a Spirit of knowledge and of the fear
of the LORD.

3 His delight will be in the fear
of the LORD.
He will not judge
by what he sees with his eyes,
he will not execute justice
by what he hears with his ears,

4 but he will judge the poor righteously
and execute justice for the oppressed
of the land.
He will strike the land
with a scepter[B] from his mouth,
and he will kill the wicked
with a command[C] from his lips.

5 Righteousness will be a belt
around his hips;
faithfulness will be a belt
around his waist.

6 The wolf will dwell with the lamb,
and the leopard will lie down
with the goat.
The calf, the young lion, and the fattened
calf will be together,
and a child will lead them.

7 The cow and the bear will graze,
their young ones will lie down together,
and the lion will eat straw like cattle.

8 An infant will play beside the cobra's pit,
and a toddler will put his hand
into a snake's den.

9 They will not harm or destroy each
other
on my entire holy mountain,
for the land will be as full
of the knowledge of the LORD
as the sea is filled with water.

[A]10:27 Lit because of fatness; Hb obscure　[B]11:4 Lit the rod　[C]11:4 Lit with the breath

---

10:28–32 The pronouncement in these verses describes the march of the Assyrian army from the north to the very doorstep of Jerusalem. While some have suggested that this describes an actual attack on Jerusalem, it cannot be equated with the Assyrian advance that took place in 701 BC under Sennacherib because the army took a different route. This leads certain scholars to propose a second, later Assyrian campaign on Judah, but this is doubtful. The route described in these verses is unlikely to be one taken by an actual army since the terrain would be difficult to cross. The best understanding of these verses is as a visionary image of an attack, not a description of an actual attack. The route described is the most direct route "as the crow flies," indicating that not even natural obstacles could slow down the army's advance.
10:28 Aiath is likely identified with Ai (Jos 8), which was about thirty miles north of Jerusalem. But the Hebrew term *Ai* means "ruin" and *Aiath* is plural, "ruins," so the name could be given to a number of different sites. **Migron** refers to the Wadi Swenit, a dry riverbed between **Michmash** and Geba.
10:29 Ramah and **Gibeah** were on the major central hill route north of Jerusalem.

10:30 Gallim . . . Laishah, and **Anathoth** (known as the hometown of the prophet Jeremiah; Jr 1:1) were small towns just north of Jerusalem.
10:31 Madmenah and **Gebim** are still not identified, but they were probably villages just north of Jerusalem.
10:32 Nob is typically associated with modern Mount Scopus, just northeast of Jerusalem. Nob was where David received sustenance and the sword of Goliath as he began his flight from Saul. King Saul repaid the priests at Nob by slaughtering them (1Sm 21:1–9; 22:11–23).
10:33–34 The pronouncement ends with a sudden reversal. Assyria marched on Jerusalem, but the army met with destruction. The Assyrians had been the ax in God's hand against his people (v. 15), but God will wield an ax against them.
11:1 The **stump of Jesse** indicates that the Davidic line has also been cut down, but the tree is yet living. The **shoot** that springs up shows that David's line will have new life. It will be restored and will once again bear fruit. The association of the stump with Jesse rather than David indicates that there is a new beginning here, a going back to origins, and a distancing from the later corrupt kings

of Judah. The continuation of the Davidic line is an indication of the grace of God based on the covenant of kingship with David (2Sm 7:16). The new Davidic dynasty was realized in Jesus Christ.
11:2 The **Spirit of the LORD** will characterize this descendant. The Spirit will fill this leader with **wisdom**: the ability to rule, and **strength**: the power to rule.
11:3 The **fear of the LORD** is the basic characteristic of a wise, godly person (Pr 1:7). The fear described here is not terror but awe. This wise, Spirit-filled person will not judge according to external appearances, but he will cut to the heart of the truth.
11:4 This king will rule with justice and protect the rights of **the poor** and **the oppressed**.
11:5 The term translated **belt** refers to an intimate piece of apparel. The idea is that these two fundamental characteristics of covenant fidelity will be an integral part of the future Davidic king's character.
11:6–9 The future rule is described in Edenic terms where there is no animosity among God's creatures. The **knowledge of the LORD** will permeate this future ideal world.

Israel Regathered

10 On that day the root of Jesse
will stand as a banner for the peoples.
The nations will look to him for
guidance,
and his resting place will be glorious.

11 On that day the Lord will extend his hand
a second time to recover the remnant of his
people who survive — from Assyria, Egypt,
Pathros, Cush, Elam, Shinar, Hamath, and the
coasts and islands of the west.
12 He will lift up a banner for the nations
and gather the dispersed of Israel;
he will collect the scattered of Judah
from the four corners of the earth.
13 Ephraim's envy will cease;
Judah's harassing will end.
Ephraim will no longer be envious
of Judah,
and Judah will not harass Ephraim.
14 But they will swoop down
on the Philistine flank to the west.
Together they will plunder the people
of the east.
They will extend their power over Edom
and Moab,
and the Ammonites will be their subjects.
15 The LORD will divide^(A,B) the Gulf of Suez.^C
He will wave his hand
over the Euphrates
with his mighty wind
and will split it into seven streams,
letting people walk through on foot.
16 There will be a highway for the remnant
of his people
who will survive from Assyria,
as there was for Israel
when they came up from the land
of Egypt.

A Song of Praise

12 On that day you will say:
"I will give thanks to you, LORD,
although you were angry with me.

Your anger has turned away,
and you have comforted me.
2 Indeed, God is my salvation;
I will trust him and not be afraid,
for the LORD, the LORD himself,
is my strength and my song.
He has become my salvation."
3 You will joyfully draw water
from the springs of salvation,
4 and on that day you will say,
"Give thanks to the LORD;
proclaim his name!
Make his works known
among the peoples.
Declare that his name is exalted.
5 Sing to the LORD, for he has done
glorious things.
Let this be known
throughout the earth.
6 Cry out and sing, citizen of Zion,
for the Holy One of Israel is among you
in his greatness."

A Pronouncement against Babylon

13 A pronouncement concerning Babylon
that Isaiah son of Amoz saw:
2 Lift up a banner
on a barren mountain.
Call out to them.
Signal with your hand,
and they will go
through the gates of the nobles.
3 I have commanded
my consecrated ones;
yes, I have called my warriors,
who celebrate my triumph,
to execute my wrath.
4 Listen, a commotion on the mountains,
like that of a mighty people!
Listen, an uproar among the kingdoms,
like nations being gathered together!
The LORD of Armies is mobilizing
an army for war.
5 They are coming from a distant land,
from the farthest horizon —

---

^A 11:15 Text emended; MT reads *destroy*   ^B 11:15 Or *dry up*   ^C 11:15 Lit *the Sea of Egypt*

11:10 The **root of Jesse** is a variant reference to what is called the "stump of Jesse" (see note at v. 1). The root of Jesse is here a **banner**, which refers to a standard around which an army rallied. Here the banner is a rallying point for the regathering of the remnant. **11:11** The list of nations in this verse probably should not be taken as a literal reference as if God's people would return from all of these nations, but from all directions. **Assyria** ... **Elam**, and **Shinar** (Mesopotamia) were to the east; **Egypt**, **Pathros**, and **Cush** were to the south; **Hamath** was to the north; and **the coasts and islands** were to the west. **11:13** The future will bring an end to hostilities and a reunion of God's people. **11:14** A reunited Israel will expand its borders to encompass the small nations to the east: **Edom** ... **Moab**, and Ammon.

11:15–16 Exodus imagery is used to describe the return of the **remnant** from **Assyria**. God will split the **Euphrates** River like he did the Red Sea, but in this case he won't split it into two parts but **seven**. **12:1 On that day** points to a future date. That date is unspecified, but it is a day that will certainly come. **12:3** In a relatively dry land like Israel, **water** and the refreshment it brings was an apt image for **salvation**. The picture of water bubbling up in a spring evokes freshness and abundance. **13:1 Pronouncement** (Hb *massa'*, lit "burden") is a "war oracle." **Babylon** is the object, which is surprising since Babylon was not the major player on the world scene in Isaiah's time. But Babylon will play a major role in the judgment of God's people in Judah. Babylon

represented cultural arrogance and human self-reliance. **13:2** The call to lift a **banner** is a call to rally troops before a battle (5:26; 11:10,12). Even though an actual gate of **the nobles** is unknown, the name evokes ideas of elitism, power, and pride. **13:3 My warriors** might be angelic, but the reference is more likely to human warriors whom God will use for his purposes. **13:4 The LORD of Armies** is God's name that signifies his activity in warfare. The **commotion on the mountains** emanates from God's army that gathers there. **13:5** The **distant land** is not specified, but it may be a reference to the Medes (v. 17) whom God will use (as part of the Persian Empire) to defeat Babylon (**the whole country**).

the Lord and the weapons
of his wrath —
to destroy the whole country.^A

⁶ Wail! For the day of the Lord is near.
It will come as destruction
from the Almighty.
⁷ Therefore everyone's hands
will become weak,
and every man will lose heart.
⁸ They will be horrified;
pain and agony will seize them;
they will be in anguish like a woman
in labor.
They will look at each other,
their faces flushed with fear.
⁹ Look, the day of the Lord is coming —
cruel, with fury and burning anger —
to make the earth a desolation
and to destroy its sinners.
¹⁰ Indeed, the stars of the sky
and its constellations^B
will not give their light.
The sun will be dark when it rises,
and the moon will not shine.
¹¹ I will punish the world for its evil,
and wicked people for their iniquities.
I will put an end to the pride
of the arrogant
and humiliate the insolence of tyrants.
¹² I will make a human more scarce
than fine gold,
and mankind more rare than the gold
of Ophir.
¹³ Therefore I will make
the heavens tremble,
and the earth will shake
from its foundations
at the wrath of the Lord of Armies,
on the day of his burning anger.
¹⁴ Like wandering gazelles
and like sheep without a shepherd,
each one will turn to his own people,
each one will flee to his own land.
¹⁵ Whoever is found will be stabbed,

and whoever is caught will die
by the sword.
¹⁶ Their children will be dashed to pieces
before their eyes;
their houses will be looted,
and their wives raped.
¹⁷ Look! I am stirring up the Medes
against them,
who cannot be bought off with^C silver
and who have no desire for gold.
¹⁸ Their bows will cut young men
to pieces.
They will have no compassion
on offspring;
they will not look with pity on children.

¹⁹ And Babylon, the jewel
of the kingdoms,
the glory of the pride of the Chaldeans,
will be like Sodom and Gomorrah
when God overthrew them.
²⁰ It will never be inhabited
or lived in from generation
to generation;
a nomad will not pitch his tent there,
and shepherds will not let their flocks
rest there.
²¹ But desert creatures will lie down there,
and owls will fill the houses.
Ostriches will dwell there,
and wild goats will leap about.
²² Hyenas will howl in the fortresses,
and jackals, in the luxurious palaces.
Babylon's time is almost up;
her days are almost over.

Israel's Return

14 For the Lord will have compassion on Jacob and will choose Israel again. He will settle them on their own land. The resident alien will join them and be united with the house of Jacob. ² The nations will escort Israel and bring it to its homeland. Then the house of Israel will possess them as male and female slaves in the Lord's land. They will

---

^A 13:5 Or earth   ^B 13:10 Or Orions   ^C 13:17 Lit who have no regard for

---

13:7 Weak **hands** and a melted **heart** refer to physical and psychological reactions to fear. 13:8 Isaiah used the theme of **a woman in labor** as a graphic image of the pain and distress that will result from God's warring activity. 13:9 Here and in v. 6 are the only two references to the **day of the Lord** in Isaiah. 13:10 The incursion of God as warrior causes nature to go into convulsions. On the day of God's judgment, the **sun . . . moon**, and **stars** will go out, plunging the world into darkness (Ezk 32:7; Jl 2:2; 3:1,15; Am 5:18; Mc 3:6; Mt 24:29; Lk 21:25; Rv 8:12). 13:12 God's warring judgment will reduce the population of the earth dramatically. 13:16 Defeated cities endured the horrible atrocities described in this verse. The worst was that their **children** would be killed.

13:17 At last, the attacking army is described as the implacable **Medes**, a people known as early as the ninth century BC. They came from the Zagros Mountains east of the Mesopotamian plain. These warlike people are known in history as Babylon's allies when they defeated Assyria. However, in the sixth century BC they were engulfed by Persia. The combined armies of the Medes and Persians defeated Babylon in 539 BC. 13:19 For the first time **Babylon** is named as the object of God's warring activity. They are described as the **jewel of the kingdoms** in anticipation of the position they will assume after their defeat of Assyria at the end of the seventh century BC. The **Chaldeans** were the leading tribe that produced the leaders (Nabopolassar and Nebuchadnezzar) who led the Babylonian resurgence.

13:20 In 689 BC the Assyrian king Sennacherib "defeated Babylon, tore down its walls, flooded the area, depopulated the city, and made the city into a meadow" (Gary Smith, NAC). The Medes and Persians destroyed Babylon again in 539 BC. 13:21-22 These verses describe animals that lived in ruins and desolate places. **Ostriches** and **owls** were considered unclean (Lv 11:15–16). 14:1-2 A pronouncement anticipating the restoration of God's people appears in the midst of the pronouncement against Babylon. While this seems awkward, Babylon's fall correlates with the rise of a restored Judah. Indeed, this restoration provides the context for the taunt song against Babylon's king in vv. 4–21. 14:2 Power relations will be reversed. Israel had been the slave of the nations; now the nations will serve God's people.

make captives of their captors and will rule over their oppressors.

Downfall of the King of Babylon

³ When the Lord gives you rest from your pain, torment, and the hard labor you were forced to do, ⁴ you will sing this song of contempt about the king of Babylon and say:

How the oppressor has quieted down,
and how the raging^A has become quiet!
⁵ The Lord has broken the staff
of the wicked,
the scepter of the rulers,
⁶ It struck the peoples in anger
with unceasing blows.
It subdued the nations in rage
with relentless persecution.
⁷ The whole earth is calm and at rest;
people shout with a ringing cry.
⁸ Even the cypresses and the cedars
of Lebanon
rejoice over you:
"Since you have been laid low,
no lumberjack has come against us."

⁹ Sheol below is eager to greet
your coming,
stirring up the spirits of the departed
for you —
all the rulers^B of the earth —
making all the kings of the nations
rise from their thrones.
¹⁰ They all respond to you, saying,
"You too have become as weak
as we are;
you have become like us!
¹¹ Your splendor has been brought down
to Sheol,
along with the music of your harps.
Maggots are spread out under you,
and worms cover you."

¹² Shining morning star,^C
how you have fallen from the heavens!
You destroyer of nations,
you have been cut down to the ground.
¹³ You said to yourself,
"I will ascend to the heavens;

I will set up my throne
above the stars of God.
I will sit on the mount
of the gods' assembly,
in the remotest parts of the North.^D
¹⁴ I will ascend above the highest clouds;
I will make myself like the Most High."
¹⁵ But you will be brought down to Sheol,
into the deepest regions of the Pit.

¹⁶ Those who see you will stare at you;
they will look closely at you:
"Is this the man who caused the earth
to tremble,
who shook the kingdoms,
¹⁷ who turned the world into a wilderness,
who destroyed its cities
and would not release the prisoners
to return home?"
¹⁸ All the kings of the nations
lie in splendor, each in his own tomb.
¹⁹ But you are thrown out without a grave,
like a worthless branch,
covered by those slain with the sword
and dumped into a rocky pit
like a trampled corpse.
²⁰ You will not join them in burial,
because you destroyed your land
and slaughtered your own people.
The offspring of evildoers
will never be mentioned again.
²¹ Prepare a place of slaughter for his sons,
because of the iniquity
of their ancestors.
They will never rise up to possess
a land
or fill the surface of the earth
with cities.

²² "I will rise up against them" — this is the declaration of the Lord of Armies — "and I will cut off from Babylon her reputation, remnant, offspring, and posterity" — this is the Lord's declaration. ²³ "I will make her a swampland and a region for herons,^E and I will sweep her away with the broom of destruction." This is the declaration of the Lord of Armies.

---

^A 14:4 DSS; Hb uncertain   ^B 14:9 Lit rams   ^C 14:12 Or Day Star, son of the dawn   ^D 14:13 Or of Zaphon   ^E 14:23 Or hedgehogs; Hb obscure

14:3–4 The following song (vv. 4b–21) has its setting after Israel's return to the land. The song is a **song of contempt** or a taunt song (Hb *mashal*). It was directed toward the **king of Babylon**.
14:5 The **staff** and the **scepter** were held by the king, and they represented his power. The scepter was an ornamented mace used as a weapon, representing the king's fearsome power. The fact that God has broken them indicates his superior power.
14:9 **Sheol** refers to the grave and in some contexts signifies the underworld. In this verse Sheol is personified and pictured as warmly

greeting its new citizen, the Babylonian king. Indeed, Sheol will rouse all the **spirits of the departed** kings to greet the Babylonian king when he arrives in the realm of the dead.
14:11 **Maggots** and **worms** will crawl over the corpse in the grave.
14:12–15 Commentators have often connected this passage to Lk 10:18 and Rv 12:8–9, but the context seems clear that the one fallen from **the heavens** is not Satan (even though the KJV translated **shining morning star** as "Lucifer") but is instead the Babylonian king. If there is a double application, the Bible never indicates as much.

14:12 The **shining morning star** may figuratively refer to a Canaanite deity whose story provides the pattern for this taunting lament for the Babylonian king. But in any case, Venus is the morning "star" that falls so quickly through the sky.
14:18–20 There is even a contrast with other kings, who were buried in fine tombs. This king will not even be given a decent burial but will lie dead on the battlefield, surrounded and even covered by other dead bodies.
14:22–23 Babylon, particularly its most southern part, was a **swampland**.

Assyria Will Be Destroyed

24 The LORD of Armies has sworn:
  As I have purposed, so it will be;
  as I have planned it, so it will happen.
25 I will break Assyria in my land;
  I will tread him down on my mountain.
  Then his yoke will be taken from them,
  and his burden will be removed
    from their shoulders.
26 This is the plan prepared
    for the whole earth,
  and this is the hand stretched out
    against all the nations.
27 The LORD of Armies himself
    has planned it;
  therefore, who can stand in its way?
  It is his hand that is outstretched,
  so who can turn it back?

A Pronouncement against Philistia

28 In the year that King Ahaz died, this pronouncement came:
29 Don't rejoice, all of you in Philistia,
  because the rod of the one
    who struck you is broken.
  For a viper will come from the root^A
    of a snake,
  and from its egg comes a flying serpent.
30 Then the firstborn of the poor will be
    well fed,
  and the impoverished will lie down
    in safety,
  but I will kill your root with hunger,
  and your remnant will be slain.
31 Wail, you gates! Cry out, city!
  Tremble with fear, all Philistia!
  For a cloud of dust is coming
    from the north,
  and there is no one missing from
    the invader's ranks.

32 What answer will be given
    to the messengers from that nation?
  The LORD has founded Zion,
  and his oppressed people find refuge
    in her.

A Pronouncement against Moab

15 A pronouncement concerning Moab:
  Ar in Moab is devastated,
    destroyed in a night.
  Kir in Moab is devastated,
    destroyed in a night.
2 Dibon went up to its temple
    to weep at its high places.
  Moab wails on Nebo and at^B Medeba.
  Every head is shaved;
  every beard is chopped short.
3 In its streets they wear sackcloth;
  on its rooftops and in its public squares
    everyone wails,
  falling down and weeping.
4 Heshbon and Elealeh cry out;
  their voices are heard as far away
    as Jahaz.
  Therefore the soldiers of Moab cry out,
  and they tremble.
5 My heart cries out over Moab,
  whose fugitives flee as far as Zoar,
    to Eglath-shelishiyah;
  they go up the Ascent
    of Luhith weeping;
  they raise a cry of destruction
    on the road to Horonaim.
6 The Waters of Nimrim are desolate;
  the grass is withered, the foliage is gone,
  and the vegetation has vanished.
7 So they carry their wealth
    and belongings
  over the Wadi of the Willows.
8 For their cry echoes

^A 14:29 Or stock ^B 15:2 Or wails over Nebo and over

14:24–27 The pronouncement shifts focus to the northern center of Mesopotamian power, **Assyria**. Assyria was the nation that under Tiglath-pileser III reduced the size of the northern kingdom of Israel in the 730s BC and then in 722 BC, under Shalmaneser, deported its citizens. But God will bring even this strong kingdom to an end. **14:25** The **yoke** was a common metaphor for political servitude (10:27; 47:6; 58:6; Jr 27:11; 30:8; Ezk 30:18). **14:28–32** The pronouncement against **Philistia** is the first in a series of pronouncements against nations that were immediate neighbors of Israel. Philistia occupied part of the promised land in a region west of Jerusalem and on the coast of the Mediterranean Sea. **14:28** The **year that King Ahaz died** is debated. It may have been as early as the 720s BC, but it certainly was not later than 715 BC. **14:29** The broken **rod** may be a reference not to a particular king but to weakness in Assyria. However, the warning is that, though apparently weak, Assyria is not done. From its slumber will come **a flying serpent** against Philistia. Under Sennacherib, Esar-haddon,

and Ashurbanipal, Assyria did experience a major resurgence. **14:31** The **cloud of dust** coming from the north will be none other than the Assyrian army that will destroy Philistia. **14:32** This verse envisions Philistine envoys trying to convince Judah to join them in resisting the Assyrian army. But Judah's trust should be in **Zion**, or God, not foreign alliances. **15:1–16:14** The pronouncement against **Moab** is the second in a series of pronouncements against nations that were immediate neighbors of Israel. Moab was located in Transjordan opposite Jericho and on the east bank of the Dead Sea. Moab's origins go back to the incestuous union between Lot and his daughter (Gn 19:30–38). **15:1 Ar** was a city on the Wadi Arnon in the middle part of Moab, and **Kir** (the same place as Kir-hareseth, 16:7) was further south. **15:2 Nebo** and **Medeba** were two northern Moabite sites east of the northern tip of the Dead Sea. Nebo was further known as the mountain that Moses ascended to catch sight of the promised land before he died (Dt 34:1). **Dibon** was further south about

midway down the coast of the Dead Sea and some twenty miles inland. Its temple was dedicated to Chemosh, the main god of the Moabites. Shaving hair from the **head** and **beard** was an ancient mourning rite. **15:3 Sackcloth** was a rough material, irritating to the skin and worn as part of mourning rites. **15:4 Heshbon and Elealeh** were northeastern cities in Moab. **Jahaz** was further south parallel to Dibon. **15:5** While the location of some of these sites (**Zoar**, for instance) is debated, the fact that others (**Eglath-shelishiyah** and **Horonaim**) are in the south suggests that all the sites mentioned here were in the south. This implies that the destruction was in the northern part of Moab and the refugees fled south. **15:6** The **Waters of Nimrim** may be associated with the Wadi Numeira, continuing the naming of southern Moabite sites. **15:7** The **Wadi of the Willows** may be a reference to the Zered River, the Wadi el-Hesa, which separated Moab from Edom on the south. **15:8** The locations of **Eglaim** and **Beer-elim** are uncertain.

throughout the territory of Moab.
Their wailing reaches Eglaim;
their wailing reaches Beer-elim.
⁹ The Waters of Dibon^A are full of blood,
but I will bring on Dibon even more
than this —
a lion for those who escape from Moab,
and for the survivors in the land.

16 Send lambs to the ruler of the land,
from Sela in the desert
to the mountain of Daughter Zion.
² Like a bird fleeing,
forced from the nest,
the daughters of Moab
will be at the fords of the Arnon.

³ Give us counsel and make a decision.
Shelter us at noonday
with shade that is as dark as night.
Hide the refugees;
do not betray the one who flees.
⁴ Let my refugees stay with you;
be a refuge for Moab^B
from the aggressor.

When the oppressor has gone,
destruction has ended,
and marauders have vanished
from the land,
⁵ a throne will be established in love,
and one will sit on it faithfully^C
in the tent of David,
judging and pursuing what is right,
quick to execute justice.

⁶ We have heard of Moab's pride —
how very proud he is —
his haughtiness, his pride,
his arrogance,
and his empty boasting.
⁷ Therefore let Moab wail;
let every one of them wail for Moab.
You who are completely devastated,
mourn

for the raisin cakes of Kir-hareseth.
⁸ For Heshbon's terraced vineyards
and the grapevines of Sibmah
have withered.
The rulers of the nations
have trampled its choice vines
that reached as far as Jazer
and spread to the desert.
Their shoots spread out
and reached the sea.
⁹ So I join with Jazer
to weep for the vines of Sibmah;
I drench Heshbon and Elealeh
with my tears.
Triumphant shouts have fallen silent^D
over your summer fruit
and your harvest.
¹⁰ Joy and rejoicing have been removed
from the orchard;
no one is singing or shouting for joy
in the vineyards.
No one tramples grapes^E
in the winepresses.
I have put an end to the shouting.
¹¹ Therefore I moan like the sound of a lyre
for Moab,
as does my innermost being
for Kir-heres.
¹² When Moab appears
and tires himself out on the high place
and comes to his sanctuary to pray,
it will do him no good.

¹³ This is the message that the LORD previously announced about Moab. ¹⁴ And now the LORD says, "In three years, as a hired worker counts years, Moab's splendor will become an object of contempt, in spite of a very large population. And those who are left will be few and weak."

A Pronouncement against Damascus

17 A pronouncement concerning Damascus:
Look, Damascus is no longer a city.
It has become a ruined heap.

---

^A15:9 DSS, some LXX mss, Vg; MT reads *Dimon*, twice in this v. ^B16:4 Or *you; Moab — be a refuge for him* ^C16:5 Or *continually* ^D16:9 Or *Battle cries have fallen* ^E16:10 Lit *wine*

15:9 The Hebrew text says the "waters of Dimon," but good textual evidence (as listed in the textual footnote in the CSB) leads to the change of Dimon to **Dibon**. The pronouncement reverts from the south to the midpoint of Moab, but this may be due to the fact that Dibon was the most important city.
16:1–5 The Moabites will turn to Judah (**Zion**) to request refuge.
16:1 Sela (commonly identified as the cliff fortress of Petra) was in Edom, so the Moabite refugees apparently will go that far. Then they will send gifts (**lambs**) to Jerusalem (**Zion**).
16:2 The previous verses place the refugees in Edom, so it is odd that they will now say they are at the **fords of the Arnon** which is in the center of Moab. The metaphor of

the bird pushed from the **nest** presupposes that they were out of their home in Moab.
16:3 The request for **shelter** as well as **shade** is a request for protection, and it implies that Moab will be willing to become a vassal state of Judah.
16:6–12 In response to Moab's request for shelter, the prophet can only lament its destruction.
16:7 Raisins were a delicacy mentioned in Sg 2:5 along with apricots as providing sustenance for lovemaking, though it may not have been an aphrodisiac. Hosea 3:1 suggests that **raisin** cakes were associated with pagan rituals.
16:8–9 Moab was known for its wine production. **Jazer** was in the north on the border with Ammon, and **Sibmah** is of uncertain location.

16:12 His sanctuary refers to the temple of Chemosh, who was no god and therefore could not respond to prayer.
16:13–14 The concluding comment about the Moabite pronouncement declares that it actually had been delivered at an earlier time, but from this moment Moab had only three more years. Most scholars associate this Moabite devastation with the Assyrian king Sargon's campaign against the people of northwest Arabia in approximately 718 BC.
17:1–3 The next **pronouncement** is directed against **Damascus**, an ancient city and capital of Syria. Isaiah 7 describes how Isaiah encouraged Ahaz of Judah to resist the threat of a Syrian-Ephraimite alliance. Assyria under Tiglath-pileser III absorbed Damascus into its growing empire.

² The cities of Aroer are abandoned;
they will be places for flocks.
They will lie down without fear.
³ The fortress disappears from Ephraim,
and a kingdom from Damascus.
The remnant of Aram will be
like the splendor of the Israelites.
This is the declaration of the LORD
of Armies.

Judgment against Israel

⁴ On that day
the splendor of Jacob will fade,
and his healthy body^A
will become emaciated.
⁵ It will be as if a reaper had gathered
standing grain —
his arm harvesting the heads
of grain —
and as if one had gleaned heads
of grain
in Rephaim Valley.
⁶ Only gleanings will be left in Israel,
as if an olive tree had been beaten —
two or three olives at the very top
of the tree,
four or five on its fruitful branches.
This is the declaration of the LORD,
the God of Israel.

⁷ On that day people will look to their Maker and will turn their eyes to the Holy One of Israel. ⁸ They will not look to the altars they made with their hands or to the Asherahs and shrines^B they made with their fingers. ⁹ On that day their strong cities will be
like the abandoned woods
and mountaintops
that were abandoned because of
the Israelites;
there will be desolation.

¹⁰ For you have forgotten the God
of your salvation,
and you have failed to remember
the rock of your strength;
therefore you will plant beautiful plants
and set out cuttings from exotic vines.
¹¹ On the day that you plant,
you will help them to grow,
and in the morning
you will help your seed to sprout,
but the harvest will vanish
on the day of disease
and incurable pain.

Judgment against the Nations

¹² Ah! The roar of many peoples —
they roar like the roaring of the seas.
The raging of the nations —
they rage like the rumble
of rushing water.
¹³ The nations rage like the rumble of a
huge torrent.
He rebukes them, and they flee far away,
driven before the wind like chaff
on the hills
and like tumbleweeds before a gale.
¹⁴ In the evening — sudden terror!
Before morning — it is gone!
This is the fate of those who plunder us
and the lot of those who ravage us.

The LORD's Message to Cush

18 Woe to the land
of buzzing insect wings^C
beyond the rivers of Cush,
² which sends envoys by sea,
in reed vessels over the water.

Go, swift messengers,
to a nation tall and smooth-skinned,
to a people feared far and near,

---

^A 17:4 Lit *and the fat of his flesh* ^B 17:8 Or *incense altars* ^C 18:1 Or *of sailing ships*

17:2 The best known **cities of Aroer** were in Moab, but it seems odd that they are mentioned in the middle of a pronouncement against Damascus. Perhaps these are a different set of cities or perhaps, as some have suggested, the text should be emended to say "its cities are deserted forever." **17:4 On that day** (vv. 7,9) points to a future but unspecified period. The first image of the destruction of Israel is a diseased **body**. **17:5** A second image of destruction is a **reaper** picking grain. **Rephaim Valley** was southwest of Jerusalem. The meaning of its name is ominous: "Valley of the Departed." **17:6** The third image of destruction concerns the harvesting of an **olive tree**. It was shaken, and the fallen olives were eaten. But this image also shows that, though the devastation will be extensive, it will not be total. A remnant, represented by **olives** that stayed attached to the tree, will survive. **17:7-8 On that day** (v. 4) points to a time beyond the judgment. Indeed, the judgment of God will cause the remnant to turn from

false worship to the worship of the true God who created them. Asherah was a Canaanite goddess of love and war. The plural form (**Asherahs**) signifies that the reference is to wooden poles or trees associated with her worship. **17:9 On that day** signals the future time of judgment again (see v. 4). The destruction will turn cities into **abandoned woods and mountaintops**. **17:10-11 To remember** God involves more than a mental activity; it implies obeying and worshiping him. To forget him points to Israel's disobedience. Isaiah spoke of Israel's bad end by using a plant analogy. **17:12** The opening exclamation **Ah!** is the same word earlier translated as "Oh" (see 1:4). It begins a pronouncement that has the form of a funeral dirge. The nations' agitation is compared to the pounding of waves. **Rushing water** is often an image of social and religious chaos (Pss 18:16; 29:3; 32:6). **17:13** Though the **nations rage**, God's rebuke will quiet them by driving them away

(Pss 2; 48). **Chaff** was light and wind blew it away, so God's rebuke will blow away the tumultuous nations. **17:14** God's judgment comes quickly, in a single day (**in the evening . . . before morning**). The victim of the nations (God's people) speaks here in the first person (**us**). **18:1-7** The statement about **Cush** is not called a pronouncement as the previous chapters have specified, but the opening word **Woe** signals a type of judgment speech (see notes at 1:4; 17:12). The land of Cush was south of Egypt, on the upper (southern) portion of the Nile River, roughly identical to modern Ethiopia. **18:1** The best explanation for the reputation of the region beyond the rivers of Cush as being a **land of buzzing insect wings** is that it was renowned for its bugs. **18:2** Cush sent envoys on **reed vessels**, typical of Egypt and Cush, down the Nile River toward Judah. Then follows a command to go to a nation described as having **tall and smooth-skinned** inhabitants who

a powerful nation
  with a strange language,^A
  whose land is divided by rivers.
³ All you inhabitants of the world
  and you who live on the earth,
  when a banner is raised
  on the mountains, look!
  When a ram's horn sounds, listen!

⁴ For the LORD said to me:
  I will quietly look out from my place,
  like shimmering heat in sunshine,
  like a rain cloud in harvest heat.
⁵ For before the harvest,
  when the blossoming is over
  and the blossom becomes
  a ripening grape,
  he will cut off the shoots
  with a pruning knife,
  and tear away and remove
  the branches.
⁶ They will all be left for the birds of prey
  on the hills
  and for the wild animals of the land.
  The birds of prey will spend the summer
  feeding on them,
  and all the wild animals the winter.

⁷ At that time a gift will be brought to the
LORD of Armies from ᴮ a people tall and smooth-
skinned, a people feared far and near, a powerful nation with a strange language, whose land
is divided by rivers — to Mount Zion, the place
of the name of the LORD of Armies.

A Pronouncement against Egypt

19 A pronouncement concerning Egypt:
  Look, the LORD rides on a swift cloud
  and is coming to Egypt.
  Egypt's worthless idols will tremble
  before him,
  and Egypt will lose heart.
² I will provoke Egyptians
  against Egyptians;
  each will fight against his brother
  and each against his friend,

city against city,
  kingdom against kingdom.
³ Egypt's spirit will be disturbed within it,
  and I will frustrate its plans.
  Then they will inquire of
  worthless idols, ghosts,
  mediums, and spiritists.
⁴ I will hand over Egypt to harsh masters,
  and a strong king will rule it.
  This is the declaration
  of the Lord GOD of Armies.

⁵ The water of the sea will dry up,
  and the river will be parched and dry.
⁶ The channels will stink;
  they will dwindle, and Egypt's canals
  will be parched.
  Reed and rush will wilt.
⁷ The reeds by the Nile, by the mouth
  of the river,
  and all the cultivated areas of the Nile
  will wither, blow away, and vanish.
⁸ Then the fishermen will mourn.
  All those who cast hooks into the Nile
  will lament,
  and those who spread nets on the water
  will give up.
⁹ Those who work with flax
  will be dismayed;
  those combing it and weaving linen
  will turn pale.ᶜ
¹⁰ Egypt's weaversᴰ will be dejected;
  all her wage earners
  will be demoralized.

¹¹ The princes of Zoan
  are complete fools;
  Pharaoh's wisest advisers
  give stupid advice!
  How can you say to Pharaoh,
  "I am oneᴱ of the wise,
  a student of easternᶠ kings"?
¹² Where then are your wise men?
  Let them tell you and reveal
  what the LORD of Armies has planned
  against Egypt.

18:2 Hb obscure **18:7** DSS, LXX, Vg; MT omits *from* ᶜ**19:9** DSS, Tg; MT reads *weavers of white cloth* ᴰ**19:10** Or *foundations* ᴱ**19:11** Lit *a son* ᶠ**19:11** Lit *a son of ancient*

spoke a **strange language** and were feared. The best understanding of this is that the command is addressed to Judean envoys to go to Cush since the description describes that nation, rather than as a command to the Ethiopian messengers to return home. The verse describes hectic diplomatic activity. **18:3** In spite of human diplomatic efforts, a decisive moment will occur in the future when an army gathers for battle. The **banner** marks the rallying point (5:26; 11:10,12; 13:2), and the **ram's horn** signals the start of war. **18:5–6** God's judgment is compared to pruning a grapevine before the grapes ripen. Those fallen in battle would be left to the **wild animals**.

18:7 The Ethiopians (Cushites), described as **tall and smooth-skinned** people (v. 2), are pictured as bringing tribute. This is a sign of their submission to God's temple on **Zion** after the judgment. **19:1** The **swift cloud**, a storm cloud, is God's war chariot. The image is found elsewhere in Scripture (Pss 18:10; 68:33; 104:3; Nah 1:3). Fear strikes the hearts of **Egypt's . . . idols** again, just as the plagues were described as a victory over Egypt's gods at the time of the exodus (Ex 12:12). **19:2** God will use Egyptian civil war to judge that nation. **19:4** Egypt's punishment is to be delivered into the control of **harsh masters**, a **strong king**.

19:5–7 The waters of the **Nile** River were the lifeblood of Egypt. God's judgment of Egypt is pictured as a drying up of the **water**. As a result, farmland will vanish. **19:8** The disappearance of the Nile waters will not only affect farmers but also those who make their living by fishing. **19:9–10** Another major industry associated with Egypt was the production of **flax**, a fiber from which clothes were made. The loss of this industry would lead to economic depression. **19:11 Zoan** was an important city (also known as Tanis), formerly a capital of Egypt. It is mentioned in this verse because it was the residence of Pharaoh's wisest advisers. This pronouncement mocks their wisdom.

¹³ The princes of Zoan have been fools;
the princes of Memphis are deceived.
Her tribal chieftains have led
Egypt astray.
¹⁴ The LORD has mixed within her a spirit
of confusion.
The leaders have made Egypt stagger
in all she does,
as a drunkard staggers in his vomit.
¹⁵ No head or tail, palm or reed,
will be able to do anything for Egypt.

Egypt Will Know the LORD

¹⁶ On that day Egypt will be like women and will tremble with fear because of the threatening hand of the LORD of Armies when he raises it against them. ¹⁷ The land of Judah will terrify Egypt; whenever Judah is mentioned, Egypt will tremble because of what the LORD of Armies has planned against it.

¹⁸ On that day five cities in the land of Egypt will speak the language of Canaan and swear loyalty to the LORD of Armies. One of the cities will be called the City of the Sun.^{A,B}

¹⁹ On that day there will be an altar to the LORD in the center of the land of Egypt and a pillar to the LORD near her border. ²⁰ It will be a sign and witness to the LORD of Armies in the land of Egypt. When they cry out to the LORD because of their oppressors, he will send them a savior and leader, and he will rescue them. ²¹ The LORD will make himself known to Egypt, and Egypt will know the LORD on that day. They will offer sacrifices and offerings; they will make vows to the LORD and fulfill them. ²² The LORD will strike Egypt, striking and healing. Then they will turn to the LORD, and he will be receptive to their prayers and heal them.

²³ On that day there will be a highway from Egypt to Assyria. Assyria will go to Egypt, Egypt to Assyria, and Egypt will worship with Assyria. ²⁴ On that day Israel will form a triple alliance with Egypt and Assyria — a blessing within the land. ²⁵ The LORD of Armies will bless them, saying, "Egypt my people, Assyria my handiwork, and Israel my inheritance are blessed."

No Help from Cush or Egypt

20 In the year that the chief commander, sent by King Sargon of Assyria, came to Ashdod and attacked and captured it — ² during that time the LORD had spoken through Isaiah son of Amoz, saying, "Go, take off your sackcloth from your waist and remove the sandals from your feet," and he did that, going stripped and barefoot — ³ the LORD said, "As my servant Isaiah has gone stripped and barefoot three years as a sign and omen against Egypt and Cush, ⁴ so the king of Assyria will lead the captives of Egypt and the exiles of Cush, young and old alike, stripped and barefoot, with bared buttocks — to Egypt's shame. ⁵ Those who made Cush their hope and Egypt their boast will be dismayed and ashamed. ⁶ And the inhabitants of this coastland will say on that day, 'Look, this is what has happened to those we relied on and fled to for help to rescue us from the king of Assyria! Now, how will we escape?'"

A Judgment on Babylon

21 A pronouncement concerning the desert by the sea:
Like storms that pass over the Negev,
it comes from the desert, from the land
of terror.

---

^A19:18 Some Hb mss, DSS, Sym, Tg, Vg, Arabic; other Hb mss read *of Destruction*; LXX reads *of Righteousness* ^B19:18 = the ancient Egyptian city Heliopolis

---

19:14 Egyptian **leaders** and wise men are pictured as drunk, in a state of heightened confusion.
19:15 The expression **head or tail, palm or reed** points to a totality (9:14).
19:16 **On that day** points to a future but unspecified time (vv. 18–19,23). It was an insult to say that Egypt's troops will be **like women** (Jr 50:37; 51:30).
19:18 **On that day**, see note at v. 16. The **five cities** cannot be identified and may be a symbolic number for "a few." But the **City of the Sun** is well known. It was Heliopolis, closely associated with the worship of the sun god. That the worship of the Lord would be taken up in this city is a sign of a radical transformation.
19:19 **On that day**, see note at v. 16. As a sign of an Egyptian conversion to the worship of the true God, there will be an **altar** set up in the center of the land and a memorial **pillar** at the border. The land will be dedicated to the worship of the true God.
19:20 The language of this verse is reminiscent of that of the book of Judges.
19:22 Egypt's conversion will be after that country experiences God's judgment; **healing** will follow **striking**.

19:23 **On that day**, see note at v. 16. **Assyria** and **Egypt** had been enemies for many years, but this amazing passage envisions a time when travel will be free and easy between them. They will be united in the worship of God.
19:24 Here **Israel** is added to Assyria and Egypt in an intimate relationship of love and worship of the Lord.
19:25 The description of God blessing Israel and the two most powerful Gentile nations of the time anticipates the fulfillment of the Abrahamic promise that God would **bless** not only Abraham's descendants but other nations as well (Gn 12:1–3).
20:1 The events narrated in this verse took place between 713 and 711 BC. Sargon II attacked the Philistine city of **Ashdod** after its king, Azuri, revolted. Azuri probably thought that Egypt under Shabaka would provide aid. The Assyrians deposed Azuri and placed his brother Ahimeti on the throne. But Ahimeti was deposed by a person named Yamani, so Sargon had to come back. Yamani fled to Egypt, but under the Assyrian threat, Egypt handed the rebel over. This should have served as a warning to others who

believed Egypt could provide help against their enemies.
20:2–4 God commanded Isaiah to perform a symbolic action that would support his spoken pronouncement. Isaiah had been wearing **sackcloth**, a symbol of mourning, but he was told to go about **stripped**. This would represent the coming humiliation and destitution of Egypt.
20:5 Those who trusted **Egypt** and **Cush** for help against their enemies would be sorely disappointed. God was the only proper object of the people's trust.
20:6 The pronouncement envisioned other nations coming to recognize that Egypt was an unreliable ally. The implicit message is that Judah should come to the same realization.
21:1–10 The pronouncement in these verses was against the **desert by the sea**. This designation is ambiguous when first stated, but the end of the passage (v. 9) makes it clear that Babylon was meant. The description of the fall of Babylon is mysterious. Debate surrounds whether it anticipates an Assyrian defeat of Babylon in the late eighth or early seventh century BC (three times: 710, 700, 689) or the ultimate defeat of Babylon

2 A troubling vision is declared to me:
"The treacherous one
     acts treacherously,
and the destroyer destroys.
Advance, Elam! Lay siege, you Medes!
I will put an end to all the groaning."

3 Therefore I am^A filled with anguish.
Pain grips me, like the pain of a woman
     in labor.
I am too perplexed to hear,
too dismayed to see.
4 My heart staggers;
horror terrifies me.
He has turned my last glimmer of hope^B
into sheer terror.
5 Prepare a table, and spread out a carpet!
Eat and drink!
Rise up, you princes, and oil the shields!

6 For the Lord has said to me,
"Go, post a lookout;
let him report what he sees.
7 When he sees riders —
pairs of horsemen,
riders on donkeys,
riders on camels —
he must pay close attention."
8 Then the lookout^C reported,
"Lord, I stand on the watchtower all day,
and I stay at my post all night.
9 Look, riders come —
horsemen in pairs."
And he answered, saying,
"Babylon has fallen, has fallen.
All the images of her gods
have been shattered on the ground."

10 My people who have been crushed
on the threshing floor,

I have declared to you
what I have heard from the Lord
of Armies,
the God of Israel.

A Pronouncement against Dumah

11 A pronouncement concerning Dumah:^D
One calls to me from Seir,
"Watchman, what is left of the night?
Watchman, what is left of the night?"
12 The watchman said,
"Morning has come, and also night.
If you want to ask, ask!
Come back again."

A Pronouncement against Arabia

13 A pronouncement concerning Arabia:
In the desert^E brush
you will camp for the night,
you caravans of Dedanites.
14 Bring water for the thirsty.
The inhabitants of the land of Tema
meet^F the refugees with food.
15 For they have fled from swords,
from the drawn sword,
from the bow that is strung,
and from the stress of battle.

16 For the Lord said this to me: "Within one year, as a hired worker counts years, all the glory of Kedar will be gone. 17 The remaining Kedarite archers will be few in number." For the Lord, the God of Israel, has spoken.

A Pronouncement against Jerusalem

22 A pronouncement concerning the Valley of Vision:
What's the matter with you?
Why have all of you gone up
to the rooftops?

^A 21:3 Lit *my waist is*, or *my insides are*   ^B 21:4 Lit *my twilight*   ^C 21:8 DSS, Syr; MT reads *Then a lion*   ^D 21:11 Some Hb mss, LXX read *Edom*   ^E 21:13 LXX, Syr, Tg, Vg read *desert at evening*   ^F 21:14 LXX, Syr, Tg, Vg read *meet* as a command

by Persia in 539 BC. A good argument can be made that both the earlier and the later defeats are alluded to in this prophecy. The intention of this prophecy at the time of Isaiah was to show that Babylon would not be an effective ally against Assyria as even King Hezekiah of Judah at one point had hoped (chap. 39).
21:1 The **desert** (lit "wilderness") **by the sea** in connection with Babylon could be taken as a reference to the area in the extreme south of Mesopotamia, the swampland next to what today is called the Persian Gulf. The **Negev** was to the extreme south of Jerusalem and was itself a wilderness area. The storms that pass through that area even today are particularly violent.
21:2 Elam and Media (**Medes**) were countries on the Iranian plateau east of Babylon. In this verse they are called to advance, but against whom? In the late eighth century BC, they were allies with Babylon and would have fought against Assyria. In 539 BC they were both parts of the Persian Empire that defeated Babylon. Perhaps the ambiguity

intends the reader at a later time to recognize allusions to both events.
21:3 Isaiah used the theme of a **woman in labor**. This was a graphic image of the pain and distress that would fall on the object of God's warring activity.
21:5 Attack would come in the midst of celebrative feasting, reminiscent of Dn 5 when Belshazzar ate and drank on the eve of Babylon's destruction. It is unclear whether such banqueting indicated a lack of preparedness for battle or whether it was a pre-battle rally (Est 1). The reference to the oiling of **shields** may indicate the latter since this was done before battle.
21:6 The **lookout** was posted at some point distant from the battle. He looked for signs of victory or defeat.
21:9 The attacking army returned intact with the announcement that **Babylon has fallen**. The focus is on the defeat of Babylon's gods.
21:10 The **crushed** people were the people of Israel.
21:11-12 Dumah was an oasis in Arabia that controlled trade routes. Besides designating

an oasis in north central Arabia, the Hebrew word *Dumah* means "silence," like the silence of death (Ps 94:17). Thus, the name sets the mood for the pronouncement. The Greek translation of the OT understood "Dumah" as a reference to Edom. **Seir** is a reference to an important part of Edom, but here Edom spoke to Dumah. The theme of the **watchman** continues from the preceding pronouncement. The question the watchman was asked is enigmatic, but it may be a way of asking how much longer the suffering (**night**) would last.
21:13-17 Dedan, Tema, and Kedar are references to geographical and/or political entities in northern **Arabia**. They were likely allies of Babylon during the eighth century BC. These tribes were defeated by Assyria between 691-689 BC.
22:1 From later in the pronouncement, it is clear that the **Valley of Vision** is a reference to Jerusalem. The significance of the **rooftops** is also difficult, but it probably refers to getting a better perspective on the withdrawal of a besieging army. Most think

2 The noisy city, the jubilant town,
is filled with celebration.
Your dead did not die by the sword;
they were not killed in battle.
3 All your rulers have fled together,
captured without a bow.
All your fugitives
were captured together;
they had fled far away.
4 Therefore I said,
"Look away from me!
Let me weep bitterly!
Do not try to comfort me
about the destruction
of my dearᴬ people."
5 For the Lord GOD of Armies
had a day of tumult, trampling,
and confusion
in the Valley of Vision —
people shoutingᴮ and crying
to the mountains;
6 Elam took up a quiver
with chariots and horsemen,ᶜ
and Kir uncovered the shield.
7 Your best valleys were full of chariots,
and horsemen were positioned
at the city gates.
8 He removed the defenses of Judah.

On that day you looked to the weapons in the House of the Forest. 9 You saw that there were many breaches in the walls of the city of David. You collected water from the lower pool. 10 You counted the houses of Jerusalem so that you could tear them down to fortify the wall. 11 You made a reservoir between the walls for the water of the ancient pool, but you did not look to the one who made it, or consider the one who created it long ago.

12 On that day the Lord GOD of Armies
called for weeping, for wailing,
for shaven heads,
and for the wearing of sackcloth.
13 But look: joy and gladness,
butchering of cattle,
slaughtering of sheep and goats,
eating of meat, and drinking of wine —
"Let's eat and drink, for tomorrow
we die!"
14 The LORD of Armies has
directly revealed to me:
"This iniquity will not be wiped out for
you people as long as you live."ᴰ
The Lord GOD of Armies has spoken.

A Pronouncement against Shebna

15 The Lord GOD of Armies said, "Go to Shebna, that steward who is in charge of the palace, and say to him: 16 What are you doing here? Who authorized you to carve out a tomb for yourself here, carving your tomb on the height and cutting a resting place for yourself out of rock? 17 Look, you strong man! The LORD is about to shake you violently. He will take hold of you, 18 wind you up into a ball, and sling you into a wide land.ᴱ There you will die, and there your glorious chariots will be — a disgrace to the house of your lord. 19 I will remove you from your office; you will be ousted from your position.

20 "On that day I will call for my servant, Eliakim son of Hilkiah. 21 I will clothe him with your robe and tie your sash around him. I will hand your authority over to him, and he will be like a father to the inhabitants of Jerusalem and to the house of Judah. 22 I will place the key of the house of David on his shoulder; what he opens, no one can close; what he closes, no one

ᴬ22:4 Lit of the daughter of my ᴮ22:5 Or Vision — a tearing down of a wall, or Vision — Kir raged; Hb obscure
ᶜ22:6 Lit chariots of man ᴰ22:14 Lit for you until you die ᴱ22:17–18 Hb obscure

the historical reference is to the withdrawal of the Assyrian army from Jerusalem in 701 BC (chaps. 36–37).
22:2 The inhabitants were **jubilant** because the attacking army had withdrawn from its siege. The reference to those who died apart from battle may be to those who starved or contracted disease during the siege.
22:3 The description of fleeing **rulers** does not accord with what we know about the siege of 701 BC, but some connect it with an Assyrian account of the battle that mentions the capture of some of Hezekiah's paid troops.
22:4–5 The prophet Isaiah (the first-person speaker) did not share the joy of the city.
22:6–7 Elam (located on the Iranian plateau east of Babylon) and **Kir** (of uncertain location) appear to have fought along with the Assyrians.
22:8 The **House of the Forest** is likely the same as the storehouse in the palace complex known as the House of the Forest of Lebanon (1Kg 7:1–12). **Weapons** were stored there.
22:9–11 Refortifying the wall with construction materials taken from demolished homes

and building an emergency reservoir within the city are taken again by the prophet as a sign of human self-reliance. The reference to collecting water from the lower **pool** may connect to the fact that Hezekiah built a tunnel to bring water inside the city walls (2Kg 20:20).
22:12 Shaving one's head and wearing **sackcloth** were rituals of mourning in ancient Israel.
22:13–14 God called for mourning (v. 12), but the people celebrated the lifting of the siege on the city. The fact that the **iniquity** of the people would never be removed boded poorly for the future of the city. Paul quotes v. 13 in 1Co 15:32.
22:15–25 The pronouncement against Jerusalem in these verses concludes with an evaluation of two stewards. Shebna abused his office and would be replaced by Eliakim. Eliakim was competent, and Isaiah praised him, but even Eliakim eventually failed. The message is that politicians cannot be relied on to solve problems that only God can solve.
22:15 The office of **steward** was an important role. **Shebna** is known elsewhere as a

high-ranking officer in the court of Hezekiah (36:3,11,22; 37:2; 2Kg 18:18; 19:2), though in these passages he is called a "secretary" which may indicate that he had been demoted.
22:16 Shebna was concerned more about himself and his own glory than with the well-being of the city. Rock-hewn tombs from antiquity may be seen today all around Jerusalem, but particularly east of the city.
22:18 Shebna not only exalted himself by the type of tomb he was building, but also by driving **glorious chariots**.
22:20 Shebna's replacement will be **Eliakim son of Hilkiah**, also known as a high official in King Hezekiah's court (36:3,11,22; 37:22; 2Kg 18:18,26,37). He will be God's **servant**, a title used elsewhere for Isaiah (20:3).
22:21 The **robe** and **sash** were symbols of the office of steward. As opposed to self-serving Shebna, Eliakim will function **like a father**, looking after the needs of his people.
22:22 The **key**, whether literal or metaphorical, indicates the control the steward had over the distribution of resources.

can open. ²³ I will drive him, like a peg, into a firm place. He will be a throne of honor for his father's family. ²⁴ They will hang on him all the glory of his father's family: the descendants and the offshoots — all the small vessels, from bowls to every kind of jar. ²⁵ On that day" — the declaration of the LORD of Armies — "the peg that was driven into a firm place will give way, be cut off, and fall, and the load on it will be destroyed." Indeed, the LORD has spoken.

A Pronouncement against Tyre

23 A pronouncement concerning Tyre:
Wail, ships of Tarshish,
for your haven has been destroyed.
Word has reached them from the land
of Cyprus.^A
² Mourn, inhabitants of the coastland,
you merchants of Sidon;
your agents have crossed the sea^B
³ over deep water.
Tyre's revenue was the grain
from Shihor —
the harvest of the Nile.
She was the merchant
among the nations.
⁴ Be ashamed, Sidon, the stronghold
of the sea,
for the sea has spoken:
"I have not been in labor or given birth.
I have not raised young men
or brought up young women."
⁵ When the news reaches Egypt,
they will be in anguish over the news
about Tyre.
⁶ Cross over to Tarshish;
wail, inhabitants of the coastland!
⁷ Is this your jubilant city,

whose origin was in ancient times,
whose feet have taken her
to reside far away?
⁸ Who planned this against Tyre,
the bestower of crowns,
whose traders are princes,
whose merchants are the honored ones
of the earth?
⁹ The LORD of Armies planned it,
to desecrate all its glorious beauty,
to disgrace all the honored ones
of the earth.
¹⁰ Overflow^C your land like the Nile,
daughter of Tarshish;
there is no longer anything
to restrain you.^D
¹¹ He stretched out his hand over the sea;
he made kingdoms tremble.
The LORD has commanded
that the Canaanite fortresses
be destroyed.
¹² He said,
"You will not celebrate anymore,
ravished young woman,
daughter of Sidon.
Get up and cross over to Cyprus —
even there you will have no rest!"
¹³ Look at the land of the Chaldeans —
a people who no longer exist.
Assyria destined it for desert creatures.
They set up their siege towers
and stripped its palaces.
They made it a ruin.
¹⁴ Wail, ships of Tarshish,
because your fortress is destroyed!

¹⁵ On that day Tyre will be forgotten for seventy years — the life span of one king. At the

---

^A23:1 Hb *Kittim*   ^B23:2 DSS; MT reads *Sidon, whom the seafarers have filled*   ^C23:10 DSS, LXX read *Work*   ^D23:10 Or *longer any harbor*

22:23 The metaphor probably refers to a **peg** driven into a plastered wall to hold up shelves.
22:24–25 Eliakim is compared to a shelf on which his family put a tremendous burden. The weight ultimately sheared off the **peg**, causing the shelf (Eliakim) to crash and its contents (his family's burdens) to break. The message of the pronouncement seems to be that the people could not trust even a competent, well-intentioned person to resolve Jerusalem's problems.
23:1 Tyre was the southernmost major city of Phoenicia. It was a wealthy city due to its development and control of sea trade. As an island city (with overflow population living on the mainland) its major port was easily protected. Tyre had established a trading colony on **Tarshish**, thought to be in what is modern Spain (Tartessus). The ships of Tarshish were particularly impressive, since they traveled so far between Tyre and Iberia. The destruction of Tyre prophetically described in this pronouncement is difficult to pin down from the description made here. The pronouncement may also look forward to Nebuchadnezzar's attack on Tyre (including a

thirteen-year siege) in the sixth century and perhaps even to the final destruction of Tyre by Alexander the Great in 332 BC. **Cyprus** was a large island about seventy-five miles west of Tyre and would have been the last port of call before reaching Tyre.
23:2 Sidon was another important Phoenician trade port north of Tyre. Its mention indicates that, though the pronouncement was specifically directed toward Tyre (the city closest to Jerusalem), the whole of Phoenicia was under judgment.
23:3 Shihor is a name for the Nile valley. Phoenicia carried on trade with Egypt during much of its history. Egypt was well known for its production and export of **grain**.
23:5 Egypt will be upset because it had lost an important trading partner.
23:6 Because of the destruction of the Phoenician **coastland**, its inhabitants will have to disperse, some perhaps going as far as the trading colony of **Tarshish** (see note at v. 1).
23:7 The **jubilant city** is Tyre, the ancient city that established Tarshish as a colony. After it is destroyed, its inhabitants will flee to Tarshish.
23:9 In answer to the question of v. 8, the pronouncement proclaims that the one

who planned the fall of the magnificent city of Tyre was none other than the **LORD of Armies**.
23:10 The Nile's waters **overflow** annually. Now **Tarshish** will overflow with all the refugees from the destroyed cities of the Phoenician coastland.
23:11 Phoenicia was considered a part of Canaan, and its fortresses may be referred to as **Canaanite fortresses**.
23:12 Sidon is compared to a rape victim, who must leave to seek refuge in **Cyprus**.
23:13–14 An analogy is drawn between the fall of the **Chaldeans** (the Aramaic-speaking tribe that produced the two rebels against Assyria—Merodach-baladan at the end of the eighth century and Nabopolassar at the end of the seventh century BC) and the fall of Tyre. Since the verse goes on to imply the fall of Babylon at the hands of the Assyrians, it probably refers to the first of these, not the second in which Babylon was victorious.
23:15–18 The pronouncement against Tyre ends with a note about its restoration. It also suggests that the city will turn to the Lord.

end of seventy years, what the song says about the prostitute will happen to Tyre:

¹⁶ Pick up your lyre,
stroll through the city,
you forgotten prostitute.
Play skillfully,
sing many a song
so that you will be remembered.

¹⁷ And at the end of the seventy years, the LORD will restore Tyre and she will go back into business, prostituting herself with all the kingdoms of the world throughout the earth. ¹⁸ But her profits and wages will be dedicated to the LORD. They will not be stored or saved, for her profit will go to those who live in the LORD's presence, to provide them with ample food and sacred clothing.

The Earth Judged

24 Look, the LORD is stripping
the earth bare
and making it desolate.
He will twist its surface and scatter
its inhabitants:
² people and priest alike,
servant and master,
female servant and mistress,
buyer and seller,
lender and borrower,
creditor and debtor.
³ The earth will be stripped
completely bare
and will be totally plundered,
for the LORD has spoken this message.

⁴ The earth mourns and withers;
the world wastes away and withers;
the exalted people of the earth
waste away.
⁵ The earth is polluted
by its inhabitants,
for they have transgressed teachings,
overstepped decrees,
and broken the permanent covenant.

⁶ Therefore a curse has consumed
the earth,
and its inhabitants have become guilty;
the earth's inhabitants
have been burned,
and only a few survive.
⁷ The new wine mourns;
the vine withers.
All the carousers now groan.
⁸ The joyful tambourines have ceased.
The noise of the jubilant has stopped.
The joyful lyre has ceased.
⁹ They no longer sing and drink wine;
beer is bitter to those who drink it.
¹⁰ The city of chaos is shattered;
every house is closed to entry.
¹¹ In the streets they cryᴬ for wine.
All joy grows dark;
earth's rejoicing goes into exile.
¹² Only desolation remains in the city;
its gate has collapsed in ruins.
¹³ For this is how it will be on earth
among the nations:
like a harvested olive tree,
like a gleaning after a grape harvest.

¹⁴ They raise their voices, they sing out;
they proclaim in the west
the majesty of the LORD.
¹⁵ Therefore, in the east honor the LORD!
In the coasts and islands of the west
honor the name of the LORD,
the God of Israel.
¹⁶ From the ends of the earth
we hear songs:
The Splendor of the Righteous One.

But I said, "I waste away! I waste away!ᴮ
Woe is me."
The treacherous act treacherously;
the treacherous deal very treacherously.

¹⁷ Panic, pit, and trap await you
who dwell on the earth.
¹⁸ Whoever flees at the sound of panic

ᴬ **24:11** Lit *streets she cries*   ᴮ **24:16** Hb obscure

23:16 This song speaks of an old **forgotten prostitute** who tried to attract attention by singing songs. The revived Tyre is like this prostitute.
23:18 Surprisingly, though, Tyre's restored trade will go to the work of the Lord, specifically to the priests.
24:1 While chaps. 13–23 focused on the judgment of particular nations, chaps. 24–27 speak of the whole **earth** (a word repeated twenty-three times) as the object of God's punishment.
24:2 This long list of pairs of opposites is a striking way of saying that all human inhabitants of the earth will be judged without regard for social standing.
24:3–4 For the LORD has spoken this message gives the reason Isaiah knew that God was going to act.

24:5 The reference to **permanent covenant** reminds the reader of the Noahic covenant between God and all the inhabitants of the earth (Gn 9:16).
24:7–9 God's judgment brings joyful singing and drinking alcoholic beverages to an end. Both of these involved celebration. **Wine** and **beer** were the two main types of alcoholic drinks in the ancient Near East.
24:10 The **city of chaos** is not a specific city. It represents evil men and women who are subject to God's judgment.
24:12 The **gate** in a walled city represented its defenses.
24:13 A harvested **olive tree** or a **grape** vine after **harvest** had only a few olives or grapes. So the cities of the nations will have just a few people left when God's judgment falls.

24:14–16a Those who **sing out** are not specifically identified. They could be Israel or the remnant from all the nations. The fact that they are in the **west**, the **east**, the **coasts and islands of the west**, and the **ends of the earth**, suggests that if it does refer to Israel, then it imagines a time when they will be scattered among the nations. In any case, these verses indicate that there were some people who celebrated the downfall of the wicked described in the previous verses.
24:16b Isaiah (the first-person speaker) does not join the chorus of celebration of vv. 14–16a.
24:17–18 The words **panic, pit, and trap** stand for the judgment that God has prepared for the sinful inhabitants of the earth. The open **floodgates** of the sky imply rain and suggest devastating flood. The shaking **foundations** would be experienced as earthquakes.

will fall into a pit,
and whoever escapes from the pit
will be caught in a trap.
For the floodgates on high are opened,
and the foundations of the earth
are shaken.
19 The earth is completely devastated;
the earth is split open;
the earth is violently shaken.
20 The earth staggers like a drunkard
and sways like a hut.
Earth's rebellion weighs it down,
and it falls, never to rise again.

21 On that day the LORD will punish
the army of the heights in the heights
and the kings of the ground on the
ground.
22 They will be gathered together
like prisoners in a pit.
They will be confined to a dungeon;
after many days they will be punished.
23 The moon will be put to shame
and the sun disgraced,
because the LORD of Armies will reign
as king
on Mount Zion in Jerusalem,
and he will display his glory
in the presence of his elders.

Salvation and Judgment on That Day

25 LORD, you are my God;
I will exalt you. I will praise
your name,
for you have accomplished wonders,
plans formed long ago,
with perfect faithfulness.
2 For you have turned the city into a pile
of rocks,
a fortified city, into ruins;
the fortress of barbarians is no longer
a city;
it will never be rebuilt.
3 Therefore, a strong people
will honor you.
The cities of violent nations will fear you.
4 For you have been a stronghold
for the poor person,

a stronghold for the needy
in his distress,
a refuge from storms and a shade
from heat.
When the breath of the violent
is like a storm against a wall,
5 like heat in a dry land,
you will subdue the uproar
of barbarians.
As the shade of a cloud cools the heat
of the day,
so he will silence the song of the violent.

6 On this mountain,[A]
the LORD of Armies will prepare for all
the peoples a feast of choice meat,
a feast with aged wine, prime cuts of
choice meat,[B] fine vintage wine.
7 On this mountain
he will swallow up the burial shroud,
the shroud over all the peoples,
the sheet covering all the nations.
8 When he has swallowed up death
once and for all,
the Lord GOD will wipe away the tears
from every face
and remove his people's disgrace
from the whole earth,
for the LORD has spoken.

9 On that day it will be said,
"Look, this is our God;
we have waited for him, and he has
saved us.
This is the LORD; we have waited
for him.
Let's rejoice and be glad in his salvation."
10 For the LORD's power will rest
on this mountain.

But Moab will be trampled in his place[C]
as straw is trampled in a dung pile.
11 He will spread out his arms
in the middle of it,
as a swimmer spreads out his arms
to swim.
His pride will be brought low,
along with the trickery of his hands.

[A]25:6 = Mount Zion   [B]25:6 Lit wine, fat full of marrow   [C]25:10 Or trampled under him

---

24:19 The verse is very emphatic (lit: "broken is broken the earth, split is split the earth, shaken is shaken the earth").
24:20 A **drunkard** cannot think or stand straight. A lightweight **hut** sways in the wind. Both ultimately will fall down. This judgment is connected to **rebellion** against God by virtually all people on earth.
24:21 The phrase **on that day** points to a future but unspecified time. God's judgment is extensive. It not only covers the earth but also the **army of the heights**, a phrase that either indicates the stars (perhaps also suggesting pagan deities) or fallen angels.

25:1 The prophet Isaiah is the first-person speaker (**I**) who praises God for his plan that includes judgment.
25:2 The **city** described in this and the following verses is the same as the "city of chaos" of 24:10. It is not a specific place but a city that represents human evil.
25:4–5 God is their protection, not city walls or weapons. God's protection of the humble poor is illustrated by the image of **a refuge from storms** and **a shade from heat**. Violent people are the rain and the heat from which God provides protection for the vulnerable.
25:6 The **mountain** refers to the mountain of God's presence—Zion.

25:7–8 God not only conquers the evil nations but also **death** and **tears** and **disgrace**. He will **swallow** them **up**. Paul quotes v. 8 in 1Co 15:54.
25:9 On that day, see note at 24:21. **Salvation** indicates rescue from powerful, evil enemies.
25:10 The **mountain** is where God will make his presence known—Zion. **Moab**, a small nation east of the Dead Sea, is a prime example of the sinful pride of the nations.
25:11 Continuing the image from the previous verse, Isaiah described Moab as swimming in dung.

¹² The high-walled fortress
　　will be brought down,
　　thrown to the ground, to the dust.

The Song of Judah

26 On that day this song will be sung in
　　the land of Judah:
We have a strong city.
Salvation is established as walls
　　and ramparts.
² Open the gates
　　so a righteous nation can come in —
　　one that remains faithful.
³ You will keep the mind that is
　　dependent on you
　　in perfect peace,
　　for it is trusting in you.
⁴ Trust in the LORD forever,
　　because in the LORD, the LORD himself, is
　　an everlasting rock!
⁵ For he has humbled those who live
　　in lofty places —
　　an inaccessible city.
He brings it down; he brings it down
　　to the ground;
he throws it to the dust.
⁶ Feet trample it,
the feet of the humble,
the steps of the poor.

God's People Vindicated

⁷ The path of the righteous is level;
　　you clear a straight path
　　for the righteous.
⁸ Yes, LORD, we wait for you
　　in the path of your judgments.
Our desire is for your name and renown.
⁹ I long for you in the night;
yes, my spirit within me
　　diligently seeks you,
for when your judgments are
　　in the land,
the inhabitants of the world
　　will learn righteousness.
¹⁰ But if the wicked man is shown favor,
he does not learn righteousness.
In a righteous land he acts unjustly
and does not see the majesty
　　of the LORD.

¹¹ LORD, your hand is lifted up
　　to take action,
but they do not see it.
Let them see your zeal for your people
and be put to shame.
Let fire consume your adversaries.
¹² LORD, you will establish peace for us,
for you have also done all our work
　　for us.
¹³ LORD our God, lords other than you
　　have owned^A us,
but we remember your name alone.

¹⁴ The dead do not live;
departed spirits do not rise up.
Indeed, you have punished
　　and destroyed them;
you have wiped out all memory
　　of them.
¹⁵ You have added to the nation, LORD.
You have added to the nation;
　　you are honored.
You have expanded all the borders
　　of the land.
¹⁶ LORD, they went to you in their distress;
they poured out whispered prayers
because your discipline fell on them.^B
¹⁷ As a pregnant woman
　　about to give birth
writhes and cries out in her pains,
so we were before you, LORD.
¹⁸ We became pregnant, we writhed
　　in pain;
we gave birth to wind.
We have won no victories on earth,
and the earth's inhabitants
　　have not fallen.

¹⁹ Your dead will live; their bodies^C
　　will rise.
Awake and sing, you who dwell
　　in the dust!
For you will be covered
　　with the morning dew,^D
and the earth will bring out
　　the departed spirits.

²⁰ Go, my people, enter your rooms
and close your doors behind you.

---

^A 26:13 Or *married*　　^B 26:16 Hb obscure　　^C 26:19 Lit *live; my body they*　　^D 26:19 Lit *For your dew is a dew of lights*

26:1 The **strong city** contrasts with the "city of chaos" (see note at 24:10). That city represents human evil and has walls that crumble, but this city's strength (its **walls and ramparts**) is defined by **salvation**.
26:3–4 Trust is the defining trait of those who depend on God. The image of the **everlasting rock** points to God's persistent protection of his people.
26:5 The **inaccessible city**, like the "city of chaos" (see note at 24:10), represents the proud who do not humble themselves before God. Though it is called "inaccessible," God is able to defeat this city in spite of its pretensions.

26:7 The image of the **path** is drawn from Wisdom literature (Pr 1–9) and stands for the course of a person's life.
26:8 In this verse Isaiah expressed longing for God's coming judgment on the wicked. But even in the context of passionate desire for God, he expressed confidence (**we wait**).
26:11 God's upraised **hand** is an image of the imminent judgment against the wicked.
26:14 A contrast exists between this statement and v. 19. In this verse, the wicked **dead** stay dead. God's judgment will not be reversed.

26:15 God blesses the righteous. In this verse his blessing takes the form of an expanded **land**.
26:16–18 God's people experienced suffering similar to the excruciating pain of a woman in labor. A pregnant woman goes through that pain and receives a positive result at the end—a baby. However, God's people went through the pain and simply passed gas (**gave birth to wind**). There was no deliverance, no victory over enemies.
26:19 In contrast to the wicked who die and stay dead (v. 14), God's people will **live** again.

Hide for a little while until the wrath
    has passed.
21 For look, the LORD is coming
    from his place
to punish the inhabitants of the earth
    for their iniquity.
The earth will reveal the blood shed
    on it
and will no longer conceal her slain.

Leviathan Slain

27 On that day the LORD with his relentless, large, strong sword will bring judgment on Leviathan, the fleeing serpent —Leviathan, the twisting serpent. He will slay the monster that is in the sea.

The LORD's Vineyard

2 On that day
    sing about a desirable vineyard:
3 I am the LORD, who watches over it
to water it regularly.
So that no one disturbs it,
    I watch over it night and day.
4 I am not angry.
If only there were thorns and briers
    for me to battle,
I would trample them
and burn them to the ground.
5 Or let it take hold of my strength;
let it make peace with me —
    make peace with me.
6 In days to come, Jacob will take root.
Israel will blossom and bloom
and fill the whole world with fruit.

7 Did the LORD strike Israel
as he struck the one
    who struck Israel?
Was Israel killed like those killed by the
    LORD?
8 You disputed with Israel
by banishing and driving her away.^A
He removed her with his severe storm
on the day of the east wind.

9 Therefore Jacob's iniquity
    will be atoned for in this way,
and the result of the removal of his sin
    will be this:
when he makes all the altar stones
    like crushed bits of chalk,
no Asherah poles or incense altars
    will remain standing.
10 For the fortified city will be desolate,
    pastures deserted and abandoned
    like a wilderness.
Calves will graze there,
and there they will spread out and strip
    its branches.
11 When its branches dry out, they will be
    broken off.
Women will come and make fires
    with them,
for they are not a people
    with understanding.
Therefore their Maker will not
    have compassion on them,
and their Creator will not be gracious
    to them.

12 On that day
    the LORD will thresh grain
    from the Euphrates River
as far as the Wadi of Egypt,
and you Israelites will be gathered
    one by one.
13 On that day
a great ram's horn will be blown,
and those lost in the land of Assyria
    will come,
as well as those dispersed in the land
    of Egypt;
and they will worship the LORD
at Jerusalem on the holy mountain.

Woe to Samaria

28 Woe to the majestic crown
    of Ephraim's drunkards,
and to the fading flower
    of its beautiful splendor,

---

^27:8 Hb obscure

The **morning dew** is an image of freshness and renewal.
27:1 On that day refers to a future but unspecified time. **Leviathan** was a sea monster, representing chaos and evil in this verse.
27:2–6 The **desirable vineyard** is a metaphor for God's people. The poem has many contrasts with the vineyard song of 5:1–7. There the vineyard image is used to emphasize God's judgment on sin; here the vineyard image describes the restoration of his people after judgment.
27:4–5 In these verses the **thorns and briers** seem to represent rebellion against God—the type of behavior that led to judgment in the first place. The thorns and briers have two possible courses of action: they can experience the devastating punishment of God or they can **make peace** with him.

27:6 The phrase **in days to come**, like "on that day" (see note at v. 1), refers to a future but unspecified time. The prophet Isaiah saw a prosperous future for God's people, one that would bring prosperity to the **whole world** (Gn 12:1–3).
27:8 Rather than annihilating his people, God will scatter them. The image of a windy storm (the **east wind** was a particularly hot, dangerous wind coming off the desert) evokes the picture of chaff being blown away.
27:9 God's punishment of his people will be a cleansing (**will be atoned for**), a renewing, not a complete destruction. In particular, their idolatrous practices will be removed. On **Asherah poles** see note at 17:7–8.
27:10–11 The **fortified city**, like the "city of chaos" (see note at 24:10) and the

"inaccessible city" (see note at 26:5), represents arrogant human evil. In the aftermath of God's judgment, this city will become grazing land.
27:12 On that day, see note at 24:21. The **Euphrates River** and the **Wadi of Egypt** were the far northern and southern boundaries of the promised land. The image of threshing **grain** represents refining judgment since the process separated the wheat from the chaff.
27:13 On that day, see note at 24:21. The Israelites will come back for the purpose of worship. The **holy mountain** refers to Zion, the location of the temple.
28:1 Woe marks the beginning of a pronouncement connected to a funeral procession (see note at 1:4). This is the first woe in chaps. 28–33 (29:1,15; 30:1; 31:1; 33:1). The effect of the pronouncement is to announce

which is on the summit above
  the rich valley.
Woe to those overcome with wine.
2 Look, the Lord has a strong
  and mighty one —
like a devastating hail storm,
like a storm with strong flooding water.
He will bring it across the land
  with his hand.
3 The majestic crown
  of Ephraim's drunkards
will be trampled underfoot.
4 The fading flower
  of his beautiful splendor,
which is on the summit
  above the rich valley,
will be like a ripe fig
  before the summer harvest.
Whoever sees it will swallow it
  while it is still in his hand.
5 On that day
the Lord of Armies will become a crown
  of beauty
and a diadem of splendor
to the remnant of his people,
6 a spirit of justice
to the one who sits in judgment,
and strength
to those who repel attacks at the city
  gate.

7 Even these stagger because of wine
and stumble under the influence
  of beer:
Priest and prophet stagger
  because of beer.
They are confused by wine.
They stumble because of beer.
They are muddled in their visions.
They stumble in their judgments.
8 Indeed, all their tables are covered
  with vomit;
there is no place without a stench.

9 Who is he trying to teach?
Who is he trying to instruct?
Infants[A] just weaned from milk?
Babies[A] removed from the breast?
10 "Law after law, law after law,
line after line, line after line,
a little here, a little there."[B]
11 For he will speak to this people
with stammering speech
and in a foreign language.
12 He had said to them,
"This is the place of rest;
let the weary rest;
this is the place of repose."
But they would not listen.

13 The word of the Lord will come
  to them:
"Law after law, law after law,
line after line, line after line,
a little here, a little there,"
so they go stumbling backward,
to be broken, trapped, and captured.

A Deal with Death

14 Therefore hear the word of the Lord,
  you scoffers
who rule this people in Jerusalem.
15 For you said, "We have made a covenant
  with Death,
and we have an agreement
  with Sheol;
when the overwhelming catastrophe[C]
  passes through,
it will not touch us,
because we have made falsehood
  our refuge
and have hidden behind treachery."
16 Therefore the Lord God said:
"Look, I have laid a stone in Zion,
a tested stone,
a precious cornerstone,
a sure foundation;

[A]28:9 Lit *Those*   [B]28:10 Hb obscure, also in v. 13   [C]28:15 Or *whip*; Hb obscure, also in v. 18

that the object of the pronouncement, in this case the northern kingdom of Israel (called by the name of its major tribe Ephraim), is as good as dead. The **majestic crown** of Ephraim may be a reference to its capital city Samaria, which sat atop a large hill overlooking the area. The reference to heavy drinking in the northern kingdom may be because of an abuse of alcohol in the region, particularly among its leaders, but this also fits with the prophetic theme of the cup of wrath (Jr 12). **28:2** God's judgment is compared to the devastating effects of a **hail storm** and a flood. **28:3–4** Appealing again to the images of **crown** and **flower** from v. 1, the prophet describes the devastating punishment coming on Ephraim. He adds the picture of the **ripe fig** ready to be plucked and devoured. **28:5–6 On that day**, see note at 24:21. While the majestic crown of Ephraim will be "trampled underfoot" (28:3), God himself

will become a **crown of beauty** for the **remnant**—for the righteous who survive the punishments to come and form the nucleus for a new people of God. Inspired by God, judges will again be just and soldiers will again have the strength to defend their city. **28:7–13** While vv. 1–6 criticize the nobility for their drunken behavior, this section focuses on the priests and prophets. **28:7–8** The priests and prophets were crucial to the spiritual leadership of the nation, but here they had clouded their thought with drink. They had drunk so much alcohol that they were covered with **vomit**. **28:9–10** These decadent leaders were acting as if they were teaching **babies** and not adults. The content of their teaching was mocked. **28:11–12** Since God's people had been so irresponsible and had refused to **rest** contentedly in God, he will speak to his people

with **stammering speech** and in a **foreign language**—Akkadian, the language of the Assyrians. Paul quotes these verses in 1Co 14:21 in the context of speaking in other languages. **28:14–22** The pronouncement now shifts its focus from the northern to the southern kingdom. **28:14 Scoffers** were those who did not fear God and who made fun of those who did (Pr 1:22; 9:7–8,12; 13:1). **28:15** The rulers of Judah had entered a dangerous agreement. The agreement is said to be with **Death** and **Sheol**. Sheol refers to the grave and in some contexts signifies the underworld. Isaiah probably referred to treaties with foreign nations to try to keep Assyria (**the overwhelming catastrophe**) from defeating them. **28:16** A precise identification of the **tested stone** is elusive. This verse is quoted in Rm 9:33; 10:11; 1Pt 2:6.

the one who believes
    will be unshakable.^A
17 And I will make justice the measuring line
    and righteousness the mason's level."
Hail will sweep away the false refuge,
    and water will flood your hiding place.
18 Your covenant with Death
    will be dissolved,
    and your agreement with Sheol
    will not last.
When the overwhelming catastrophe
    passes through,
    you will be trampled.
19 Every time it passes through,
    it will carry you away;
    it will pass through every morning —
    every day and every night.
Only terror will cause you
    to understand the message.^B
20 Indeed, the bed is too short
    to stretch out on,
and its cover too small to wrap up in.
21 For the LORD will rise up as he did
    at Mount Perazim.
He will rise in wrath, as at the Valley
    of Gibeon,
to do his work, his unexpected work,
    and to perform his task,
    his unfamiliar task.
22 So now, do not scoff,
    or your shackles will become stronger.
Indeed, I have heard from the Lord GOD
    of Armies
a decree of destruction
    for the whole land.

God's Wonderful Advice

23 Listen and hear my voice.
    Pay attention and hear what I say.
24 Does the plowman plow every day
    to plant seed?
Does he continuously break up
    and cultivate the soil?
25 When he has leveled its surface,
    does he not then scatter black cumin
    and sow cumin?

He plants wheat in rows and barley
    in plots,
    with spelt as their border.
26 His God teaches him order;
    he instructs him.
27 Certainly black cumin is not threshed
    with a threshing board,
    and a cart wheel is not rolled
    over the cumin.
But black cumin is beaten out
    with a stick,
    and cumin with a rod.
28 Bread grain is crushed,
    but is not threshed endlessly.
Though the wheel
    of the farmer's cart rumbles,
    his horses do not crush it.
29 This also comes from the LORD
    of Armies.
He gives wondrous advice;
    he gives great wisdom.

Woe to Jerusalem

29 Woe to Ariel,^C Ariel,
    the city where David camped!
Continue year after year;
    let the festivals recur.
2 I will oppress Ariel,
    and there will be mourning and crying,
    and she will be to me like an Ariel.
3 I will camp in a circle around you;
    I will besiege you with earth ramps,
    and I will set up my siege towers
    against you.
4 You will be brought down;
    you will speak from the ground,
    and your words will come from low
    in the dust.
Your voice will be like that of a spirit
    from the ground;
    your speech will whisper from the dust.
5 Your many foes^D will be like fine dust,
    and many of the ruthless,
    like blowing chaff.
Then suddenly, in an instant,

---

^A 28:16 Lit will not hurry ^B 28:19 Or The understanding of the message will cause sheer terror ^C 29:1 Or Altar Hearth, or Lion of God; Hb obscure, also in v. 2 ^D 29:5 Lit foreigners

28:18 On the dark pact with **Death**, see note at v. 15.
28:21 At **Perazim** (described in 2Sm 5:20 as a "bursting flood") God gave David a great victory over the Philistines. At the **Valley of Gibeon**, God used hailstones to allow Joshua to defeat the southern coalition of Canaanite city-states (Jos 10:11).
28:22 Though God's judgment against the mocking leaders of Judah is certain, their future behavior will determine whether it becomes even worse (**your shackles will become stronger**).
28:23-29 In this section Isaiah drew an analogy between a farmer's task and God's treatment of Judah. Good results come from

different actions and different methods applied at different times.
28:24-26 The farmer (**plowman**) does not just keep plowing; he also sows seed. He places the various seeds in their separate places. This **order** comes from God himself.
28:27 Each plant has its proper treatment. The analogy may point to the fact that God exercises his judgment against sinners in a way that is appropriate to their specific situation.
28:28-29 But the crushing and threshing, images of judgment, are not endless activities. It comes to an end.
29:1 **Ariel** stands for Jerusalem. What the word means is difficult to discern. It could

mean "lion of God," but more likely it refers to "altar hearth," its meaning in Ezk 43:15 in reference to the hearth of the sanctuary. This chapter is a pronouncement of **woe** (see note at 1:4) against Jerusalem. This is the second woe presented in chaps. 28-33 (28:1; 29:15; 30:1; 31:1; 33:1).
29:2 God will turn Jerusalem into an **Ariel**—an altar hearth. The meaning seems to be that he will destroy it by fire.
29:4 God speaks to Jerusalem in the second person (**you . . . your**).
29:5-8 **Suddenly** the pronouncement shifts from judgment against Jerusalem to the restoration of the city.

6 you will be punished by the LORD
    of Armies
with thunder, earthquake,
    and loud noise,
storm, tempest, and a flame
    of consuming fire.
7 All the many nations
going out to battle against Ariel —
all the attackers, the siege works
    against her,
and those who oppress her —
will then be like a dream, a vision
    in the night.
8 It will be like a hungry one who dreams
    he is eating,
then wakes and is still hungry;
and like a thirsty one who dreams
    he is drinking,
then wakes and is still thirsty,
    longing for water.
So it will be for all the many nations
who go to battle against Mount Zion.

9 Stop and be astonished;
blind yourselves and be blind!
They are drunk,^A but not with wine;
they stagger,^B but not with beer.
10 For the LORD has poured out on you
an overwhelming urge to^C sleep;
he has shut your eyes (the prophets)
and covered your heads (the seers).
11 For you the entire vision will be like the
words of a sealed document. If it is given to
one who can read and he is asked to read it,^D
he will say, "I can't read it, because it is sealed."
12 And if the document is given to one who cannot read and he is asked to read it,^E he will say,
"I can't read."
    13 The Lord said:
These people approach me
    with their speeches
to honor me with lip-service,^F
yet their hearts are far from me,
and human rules direct their worship
    of me.^G

14 Therefore, I will again confound
    these people
with wonder after wonder.
The wisdom of their wise will vanish,
and the perception of their perceptive
    will be hidden.

15 Woe to those who go to great lengths
to hide their plans from the LORD.
They do their works in the dark,
and say, "Who sees us? Who knows us?"
16 You have turned things around,
as if the potter were the same
    as the clay.
How can what is made say
    about its maker,
"He didn't make me"?
How can what is formed
say about the one who formed it,
"He doesn't understand
what he's doing"?

17 Isn't it true that in just a little while
Lebanon will become an orchard,
and the orchard will seem
    like a forest?
18 On that day the deaf will hear
the words of a document,
and out of a deep darkness
the eyes of the blind will see.
19 The humble will have joy
after joy in the LORD,
and the poor people will rejoice
in the Holy One of Israel.
20 For the ruthless one will vanish,
the scorner will disappear,
and all those who lie in wait
    with evil intent
    will be killed —
21 those who, with their speech,
accuse a person of wrongdoing,
who set a trap for the one mediating at
    the city gate
and without cause deprive
    the righteous of justice.

---

^A 29:9 LXX, Tg, Vg read *Be drunk*   ^B 29:9 Tg, Vg read *wine; stagger*   ^C 29:10 Lit *you a spirit of*   ^D 29:11 Lit *If one gives it to one who knows the document, saying, "Read this, please"*   ^E 29:12 Lit *who does not know the document, saying, "Read this, please"*   ^F 29:13 Lit *their mouth and honor me with its lips*   ^G 29:13 Lit *their fearing of me is a taught command of men*

29:6 When God comes as warrior, he often takes the form of **earthquake . . . storm**, and **fire**.
29:11–12 God has laid it all out for the people (**the entire vision**), but they were spiritually dull and could not make sense of it. In ancient Israel documents were written on papyrus or vellum scrolls. After being rolled into a tube, they were **sealed** with wax or clay, then stamped with an impression that identified the sender.
29:13 Jesus quotes these words in Mt 15:8–9 and Mk 7:6–7.
29:14 The **wisdom** offered by the **wise** would **vanish** because it is based on the past, and God was going to do new wonders, such as the fall of Jerusalem, the return from

captivity, and the sending of a Savior. Paul quotes this verse in 1Co 1:19.
29:15 A new **woe** oracle (see note at 1:4) begins with this verse and extends to the end of the chapter. This is the third woe presented in chaps. 28–33 (v. 1; 28:1; 30:1; 31:1; 33:1). Those who did evil thought they could **hide** their actions from God.
29:16 The metaphor of God as a **potter** is used in a few key places in prophetic literature (45:9; 64:8; Jr 18:1–12; see also Rm 9:21). The prophets pointed out how crazy it was for God's creatures, the pots made from clay, to challenge or question their Maker, the Potter.
29:17–24 As with the previous woe oracle, there is a shift in this pronouncement from judgment to hope (see note at vv. 5–8).

29:17 Lebanon was known for its cedar forests, but it will be transformed into an **orchard**—a place for fruit-bearing trees. The cedar is often used in the Bible as a symbol of power and arrogance, so perhaps the transformation has to do with a change from pride to humble service.
29:18 The coming transformation is also pictured as the **deaf** hearing and the **blind** seeing. The **document** probably is an allusion to vv. 11–12. In those verses the document could not be understood, but here it could.
29:21 The **city gate** was where public hearings and judicial proceedings were held. The mediator was the person who heard a case. His removal would lead to injustice.

²² Therefore, the LORD who redeemed Abraham says this about the house of Jacob:
Jacob will no longer be ashamed,
and his face will no longer be pale.
²³ For when he sees his children,
the work of my hands within his nation,
they will honor my name,
they will honor the Holy One of Jacob
and stand in awe of the God of Israel.
²⁴ Those who are confused
will gain understanding,
and those who grumble
will accept instruction.

Condemnation of the Egyptian Alliance

30 Woe to the rebellious children!
This is the LORD's declaration.
They carry out a plan, but not mine;
they make an alliance,
but against my will,
piling sin on top of sin.
² Without asking my advice
they set out to go down to Egypt
in order to seek shelter
under Pharaoh's protection
and take refuge in Egypt's shadow.
³ But Pharaoh's protection will become
your shame,
and refuge in Egypt's shadow
your humiliation.
⁴ For though his^A princes are at Zoan
and his messengers reach
as far as Hanes,
⁵ everyone will be ashamed
because of a people who can't help.
They are of no benefit, they are
no help;
they are good for nothing but shame
and disgrace.

⁶ A pronouncement concerning the animals of the Negev:^B
Through a land of trouble and distress,
of lioness and lion,
of viper and flying serpent,

they carry their wealth on the backs
of donkeys
and their treasures on the humps
of camels,
to a people who will not help them.
⁷ Egypt's help is completely worthless;
therefore, I call her:
Rahab Who Just Sits.

⁸ Go now, write it on a tablet
in their presence
and inscribe it on a scroll;
it will be for the future,
forever and ever.
⁹ They are a rebellious people,
deceptive children,
children who do not want to listen to
the LORD's instruction.
¹⁰ They say to the seers, "Do not see,"
and to the prophets,
"Do not prophesy the truth to us.
Tell us flattering things.
Prophesy illusions.
¹¹ Get out of the way!
Leave the pathway.
Rid us of the Holy One of Israel."
¹² Therefore the Holy One of Israel says:
"Because you have rejected
this message
and have trusted in oppression
and deceit,
and have depended on them,
¹³ this iniquity of yours will be
like a crumbling gap,
a bulge in a high wall
whose collapse will come in an instant
— suddenly!
¹⁴ Its collapse will be like the shattering
of a potter's jar, crushed to pieces,
so that not even a fragment of pottery
will be found among
its shattered remains —
no fragment large enough to take fire
from a hearth
or scoop water from a cistern."

^A 30:4 Or *Judah's*   ^B 30:6 Or *Southland*

30:1 On **woe**, see note at 1:4. This is the fourth woe in chaps. 28–33 (28:1; 29:1,15; 31:1; 33:1). The **rebellious children** were God's people who sought help from a foreign nation rather than from God himself.
30:2 The plan was to form an alliance with **Egypt** to counter the Assyrian threat. **Shelter . . . protection**, and **shadow** imply the relationship with Egypt would not be as equal partners; God's people would be the junior partner. This arrangement involved the payment of annual tribute as well as the forfeiture of an independent foreign policy.
30:3 The purpose of the foreign alliance was to protect Israel against an Assyrian invasion. It would lead to **shame** because Egypt was an unreliable ally.
30:4 Zoan (also known as Tanis) was an important city, formerly a capital of Egypt,

mentioned in this verse because it was the residence of Pharaoh's wisest advisers (see note at 19:11). This is the only mention of **Hanes** in the Bible. According to extrabiblical sources, it is identified with Heracleopolis Magna.
30:5 God's attitude toward Israel's alliance with Egypt reaches its climax here. **They are good for nothing but shame and disgrace.**
30:6 The **Negev** was the wilderness region south of the southern Israelite city of Beersheba. It was on the way to Egypt. Nomadic peoples and various animals such as those listed in the first part of this verse populated this area. The people who carried their **wealth on the backs of donkeys** describe those who took tribute to Egypt to buy protection against the Assyrian threat. Isaiah saw this as a waste of money.

30:7 In the book of Job, **Rahab** is a monster representing chaos, which is parallel to Leviathan (Jb 26:12–13), but the name is used here and elsewhere to refer to Egypt (Ps 87:4).
30:8 A record of the prophecy of destruction would demonstrate to future generations that what happened had been predicted.
30:9 On **rebellious people**, see note at v. 1.
30:10–11 The **Holy One of Israel** is one of Isaiah's favorite titles for God, appearing more than twenty-five times in his book. It emphasizes God's distaste for sin (see note at 1:4).
30:12–14 They thought that Egypt would be a **high wall** of protection against the Assyrians, but the wall had a huge crack. It would eventually be obliterated.

15 For the Lord GOD, the Holy One of Israel,
        has said:
    "You will be delivered by returning
        and resting;
    your strength will lie
        in quiet confidence.
    But you are not willing."
16 You say, "No!
    We will escape on horses" —
        therefore you will escape! —
    and, "We will ride on fast horses" —
    but those who pursue you will be faster.
17 One thousand will flee at the threat
        of one,
    at the threat of five you will flee,
    until you remain
    like a solitary pole on a mountaintop
    or a banner on a hill.

The LORD's Mercy to Israel

18 Therefore the LORD is waiting
        to show you mercy,
    and is rising up
        to show you compassion,
    for the LORD is a just God.
    All who wait patiently for him
        are happy.

19 For people will live on Zion in Jerusalem.
You will never weep again; he will show favor
to you at the sound of your outcry; as soon as
he hears, he will answer you. 20 The Lord will
give you meager bread and water during oppression, but your Teacher^A will not hide any
longer. Your eyes will see your Teacher, 21 and
whenever you turn to the right or to the left,
your ears will hear this command behind you:
"This is the way. Walk in it." 22 Then you will defile your silver-plated idols and your gold-plated images. You will throw them away like
menstrual cloths, and call them filth.
    23 Then he will send rain for your seed that
you have sown in the ground, and the food, the

produce of the ground, will be rich and plentiful. On that day your cattle will graze in open
pastures. 24 The oxen and donkeys that work
the ground will eat salted fodder scattered with
winnowing shovel and fork. 25 Streams flowing
with water will be on every high mountain and
every raised hill on the day of great slaughter
when the towers fall. 26 The moonlight will be
as bright as the sunlight, and the sunlight will
be seven times brighter — like the light of sev-
en days — on the day that the LORD bandages
his people's injuries and heals the wounds he
inflicted.

Annihilation of the Assyrians

27 Look! The name of the LORD is coming
        from far away,
    his anger burning and heavy
        with smoke.^B
    His lips are full of fury,
    and his tongue is like a consuming fire.
28 His breath is like an overflowing torrent
    that rises to the neck.
    He comes to sift the nations in a sieve
        of destruction
    and to put a bridle on the jaws
        of the peoples
    to lead them astray.
29 Your singing will be like that
    on the night of a holy festival,
    and your heart will rejoice
    like one who walks to the music of a flute,
    going up to the mountain of the LORD,
    to the Rock of Israel.
30 And the LORD will make the splendor
        of his voice heard
    and reveal his arm striking in
        angry wrath
    and a flame of consuming fire,
    in driving rain, a torrent, and hailstones.
31 Assyria will be shattered by the voice
        of the LORD.
    He will strike with a rod.

---

^A 30:20 Or *teachers*   ^B 30:27 Hb obscure

30:18 God was **waiting** for the people to repent before turning his judgment into **compassion** and restoration.
30:19 The **outcry** of the people refers to their repentance, an acknowledgment of their sin, and a turn to God for help. As a result, he would respond with his **favor**. They will live on **Zion in Jerusalem** near the presence of God. The beginning of the fulfillment of this promise occurred after the Jews began returning from Babylonian exile in 539 BC.
30:20 The word **oppression** refers to the future exile and political oppression by foreign nations (Assyria, followed by Babylon, followed by Persia) that happened because of their sin. The **Teacher** of the people of God is a reference to God himself who would show them the right way to behave.
30:21 Walking in the **way** is reminiscent of the language of Ps 1 and Proverbs.

30:22 Menstrual cloths were especially impure because a woman was considered unclean during her menstrual period (Lv 15:19–24).
30:23–24 Based on the lists of covenant blessings found in places like Dt 28, God will grant agricultural prosperity to his restored people. Even the **oxen and donkeys** would have plenty of good food.
30:25 Israel's prosperity was normally tenuous because of limited water supplies. Here the picture is of overflowing waters. The reference to the **great slaughter** and the fall of **towers** is probably a reference to the downfall of their oppressors.
30:27–33 The pronouncement in these verses describes God's appearance as a judging warrior. The object of his wrath is not revealed until v. 31 where Assyria, the oppressor of God's people, is named.
30:27–28 God's anger is described in human terms as if he had **lips** ... **tongue** ... **breath**,

and **neck**. He will take the wayward nations and **bridle** them as if they were a donkey or horse. Then he will guide them in the way he wants them to go.
30:29 The scene shifts to the people of God who will celebrate this act of God. The judgment of their enemies is a cause for rejoicing. They will praise God as if it were a **holy festival** like Passover or the Festival of Shelters. The **mountain of the LORD** refers to Zion where God (their **Rock**, a title that signifies shelter and protection) will make his presence known.
30:30 God often uses weather as his weapon against the objects of his anger (see 28:21).
30:31 Assyria, the region's superpower, will be punished.
30:32 The blows of weapons are compared to the beating of **tambourines**. Babylon was the **appointed staff** of God to bring down Assyria in the late seventh century BC.

³² And every stroke of the appointed^A staff
that the LORD brings down on him
will be to the sound of tambourines
and lyres;
he will fight against him
with brandished weapons.
³³ Indeed! Topheth has been ready
for the king for a long time.
Its funeral pyre is deep and wide,
with plenty of fire and wood.
The breath of the LORD, like a torrent
of burning sulfur,
kindles it.

The LORD, the Only Help

31 Woe to those who go down to Egypt
for help
and who depend on horses!
They trust in the abundance
of chariots
and in the large number of horsemen.
They do not look to the Holy One
of Israel,
and they do not seek the LORD.
² But he also is wise and brings disaster.
He does not go back on what he says;
he will rise up against the house
of the wicked
and against the allies of evildoers.
³ Egyptians are men, not God;
their horses are flesh, not spirit.
When the LORD raises his hand to strike,
the helper will stumble
and the one who is helped will fall;
both will perish together.

⁴ For this is what the LORD said to me:
As a lion or young lion growls
over its prey
when a band of shepherds is called out
against it,
and it is not terrified by their shouting
or subdued by their noise,
so the LORD of Armies will come down
to fight on Mount Zion
and on its hill.

⁵ Like hovering birds,
so the LORD of Armies
will protect Jerusalem;
by protecting it, he will rescue it;
by passing over it, he will deliver it.

⁶ Return to the one the Israelites have greatly rebelled against. ⁷ For on that day, every one of you will reject the worthless idols of silver and gold that your own hands have sinfully made.
⁸ Then Assyria will fall,
but not by human sword;
a sword will devour him,
but not one made by man.
He will flee from the sword;
his young men will be put
to forced labor.
⁹ His rock^B will pass away because of fear,
and his officers will be afraid because of
the signal flag.
This is the LORD's declaration — whose fire
is in Zion and whose furnace is in Jerusalem.

The Righteous Kingdom Announced

32 Indeed, a king will reign righteously,
and rulers will rule justly.
² Each will be like a shelter
from the wind,
a refuge from the rain,
like flowing streams in a dry land
and the shade of a massive rock
in an arid land.
³ Then the eyes of those who see will not
be closed,
and the ears of those who hear
will listen.
⁴ The reckless mind will gain knowledge,
and the stammering tongue
will speak clearly and fluently.
⁵ A fool will no longer be called a noble,
nor a scoundrel said to be important.
⁶ For a fool speaks foolishness
and his mind plots iniquity.
He lives in a godless way
and speaks falsely about the LORD.
He leaves the hungry empty

---

^A30:32 Some Hb mss read *punishing*   ^B31:9 Perhaps the Assyrian king

30:33 Topheth was located in the Valley of Ben Hinnom (Jr 7:30–34). This valley was immediately south and west of Jerusalem. At times it functioned as a garbage heap for the city. In Greek, this valley was known as "Gehenna," which became associated with hell. It had been a place where the foreign god Molech was worshiped. Jeremiah said it epitomized the sin and guilt of the people (Jr 7:30–32; 19:6–13). Here though it is being used for a good purpose—the burning of the body of the king of Assyria after his defeat. **31:1** On **woe**, see note at 1:4. This is the fifth woe in chaps. 28–33 (28:1; 29:1,15; 30:1; 33:1). The issue again is that God's people were trusting foreign nations (in this case Egypt) rather than God for help against their enemies (30:1–17).

31:2–3 Israel's attempt to get help from Egypt will backfire because God will cause both **helper** (Egypt) and **helped** (God's people) to be destroyed. **31:4–5** In these verses, Isaiah uses two images to describe God's protection. He is a fearless **lion** on behalf of Israel against the foreign armies (represented by the **shepherds** who try to fend him off). He is also **hovering** over his people like **birds** hover over their prey. **31:6–7** The restoration of God's people has two sides: returning to him, which implies repentance, and rejecting false gods in the form of **idols of silver and gold**. **31:8** God is the real reason **Assyria will fall**. He will use Babylon for this task.

31:9 Though the reference is unusual, the **rock** is probably a reference to the Assyrian king. The **signal flag** is a reference to a battle standard used to rally troops. Zion's **fire** and Jerusalem's **furnace** may point to the fire that will come out of Jerusalem to destroy the attacking enemy. **32:1** Scholars are divided over whether the **king** who will **reign righteously** is a direct reference to the Messiah or whether it describes a historical king like Hezekiah or Josiah. **32:6–7** The book of Proverbs makes it clear that a **fool** is someone who rejects God and has a detrimental effect on the community. Here Isaiah claims that folly among the leadership leads to hunger and thirst among the people.

and deprives the thirsty of drink.

7 The scoundrel's weapons
   are destructive;
he hatches plots to destroy the needy
   with lies,
even when the poor person says
   what is right.

8 But a noble person plans noble things;
   he stands up for noble causes.

9 Stand up, you complacent women;
   listen to me.
Pay attention to what I say,
   you overconfident daughters.

10 In a little more than a year
   you overconfident ones will shudder,
for the grapes will fail
   and the harvest will not come.

11 Shudder, you complacent ones;
   tremble, you overconfident ones!
Strip yourselves bare
   and put sackcloth around your waists.

12 Beat your breasts in mourning
   for the delightful fields
      and the fruitful vines,

13 for the ground of my people
   growing thorns and briers,
indeed, for every joyous house
   in the jubilant city.

14 For the palace will be deserted,
   the busy city abandoned.
The hill and the watchtower
   will become
barren places forever,
   the joy of wild donkeys,
   and a pasture for flocks,

15 until the Spirit[A] from on high
   is poured out on us.
Then the desert will become an orchard,
   and the orchard will seem like a forest.

16 Then justice will inhabit the wilderness,
   and righteousness will dwell
      in the orchard.

17 The result of righteousness
   will be peace;
the effect of righteousness
   will be quiet confidence forever.

18 Then my people will dwell
   in a peaceful place,
in safe and secure dwellings.

19 But hail will level the forest,[B]
   and the city will sink into the depths.

20 You will be happy as you sow seed
   beside abundant water,
and as you let oxen and donkeys
   range freely.

The LORD Rises Up

33 Woe, you destroyer never destroyed,
   you traitor never betrayed!
When you have finished destroying,
   you will be destroyed.
When you have finished betraying,
   they will betray you.

2 LORD, be gracious to us! We wait for you.
   Be our strength every morning
and our salvation in time of trouble.

3 The peoples flee
   at the thunderous noise;
the nations scatter when you rise
   in your majesty.

4 Your spoil will be gathered as locusts
   are gathered;
people will swarm over it
   like an infestation of locusts.

5 The LORD is exalted, for he dwells
   on high;
he has filled Zion with justice
   and righteousness.

6 There will be times of security
   for you —
a storehouse of salvation, wisdom,
   and knowledge.
The fear of the LORD is Zion's treasure.

7 Listen! Their warriors cry loudly
   in the streets;
the messengers of peace weep bitterly.

8 The highways are deserted;
   travel has ceased.
An agreement has been broken,
   cities[C] despised,
   and human life disregarded.

[A]32:15 Or *a wind*   [B]32:19 Hb obscure   [C]33:8 DSS read *witnesses*

32:8 Noble speaks of character.
32:9 The prophetic pronouncement now addresses the **women** in the community of the people of God. They also show pride in human resources rather than in the Lord. They are **complacent** and **overconfident**.
32:11–12 Tearing and removing one's clothes (**strip yourselves bare**) and replacing them with **sackcloth** along with beating one's breast were mourning customs.
32:13 The land will produce **thorns and briers**, useless plants, instead of grains and vines. The idea is similar to the curse against Adam in Gn 3:17–18.
32:14 Not only will the fields be desolate and unproductive, but so will the city of

Jerusalem. It will be turned into the haunt of wild animals.
32:15 However, because of God (**the Spirit from on high**) a miraculous transformation will take place in the future. What has been unproductive will produce fruit-bearing trees.
33:1 This is the sixth and final **woe** in chaps. 28–33 (28:1; 29:1,15; 30:1; 31:1). The woe pronounces the destruction of a betrayer. Many interpreters believe the reference is to Sennacherib, whom King Hezekiah of Judah paid to back off from the siege of Jerusalem (chaps. 36–37). But others believe it is a general reference to the deception of the nations. They will receive their due.

33:2 Since the nations have let them down, God's people have no recourse but to **wait** for God to save them.
33:3–4 Locusts are often symbols of a large destroying army (Jl 1; Nah 3:15–16).
33:6 Zion's **treasure** is not gold, silver, or weapons. Its treasure is the **fear of the LORD**.
33:7–13 This passage describes a future attack (perhaps Sennacherib's attack on Jerusalem in 701 BC; v. 1) as if it were happening in the present.
33:8 The **agreement** that was **broken** may be a direct reference to the agreement that Sennacherib made to withdraw from Jerusalem after being paid tribute—a promise he

9 The land mourns and withers;
    Lebanon is ashamed and wilted.
    Sharon is like a desert;
    Bashan and Carmel shake off
        their leaves.
10 "Now I will rise up," says the LORD.
    "Now I will lift myself up.
    Now I will be exalted.
11 You will conceive chaff;
    you will give birth to stubble.
    Your breath is fire that will
        consume you.
12 The peoples will be burned to ashes,
    like thorns cut down and burned in a fire.
13 You who are far off, hear what
        I have done;
    you who are near, know my strength."

14 The sinners in Zion are afraid;
    trembling seizes the ungodly:
    "Who among us can dwell
        with a consuming fire?
    Who among us can dwell
        with ever-burning flames?"
15 The one who lives righteously
    and speaks rightly,
    who refuses profit from extortion,
    whose hand never takes a bribe,
    who stops his ears from listening
        to murderous plots
    and shuts his eyes against
        evil schemes —
16 he will dwell on the heights;
    his refuge will be the rocky fortresses,
    his food provided, his water assured.

17 Your eyes will see the King in his beauty;
    you will see a vast land.
18 Your mind will meditate
        on the past terror:
    "Where is the accountant?ᴬ
    Where is the tribute collector?ᴮ
    Where is the one who spied out
        our defenses?"ᶜ

19 You will no longer see the barbarians,
    a people whose speech is difficult
        to comprehend —
    who stammer in a language that is
        not understood.
20 Look at Zion, the city
        of our festival times.
    Your eyes will see Jerusalem,
    a peaceful pasture, a tent
        that does not wander;
    its tent pegs will not be pulled up
    nor will any of its cords be loosened.
21 For the majestic one, our LORD,
        will be there,
    a place of rivers and broad streams
    where ships that are rowed
        will not go,
    and majestic vessels will not pass.
22 For the LORD is our Judge,
    the LORD is our Lawgiver,
    the LORD is our King.
    He will save us.
23 Your ropes are slack;
    they cannot hold the base of the mast
    or spread out the flag.
    Then abundant spoil will be divided,
    the lame will plunder it,
24 and none there will say, "I am sick."
    The people who dwell there
    will be forgiven their iniquity.

The Judgment of the Nations

34 You nations, come here and listen;
    you peoples, pay attention!
    Let the earth and all that fills it hear,
    the world and all that comes from it.
2 The LORD is angry with all the nations,
    furious with all their armies.
    He will set them apart for destruction,
    giving them over to slaughter.
3 Their slain will be thrown out,
    and the stench of their corpses will rise;
    the mountains will flowᴰ
        with their blood.

ᴬ33:18 Lit *counter*   ᴮ33:18 Lit *weigher*   ᶜ33:18 Lit *who counts towers*   ᴰ34:3 Or *melt*, or *dissolve*

did not honor. Since the army is on the brink of attack, all **travel has ceased**.
33:9 Lebanon was north of Israel. **Sharon**, the western foothills famous for its wild flowers, as well as **Bashan and Carmel** were known as lush regions. But because of conflict these areas are described as bare wilderness.
33:11–12 In spite of the efforts of the enemy army to win a victory, they will achieve nothing productive. They **conceive** and **give birth**, not to life but to death, here represented by dead vegetation that is good for nothing (**chaff** and **stubble**).
33:14 The anticipation of such a powerful, judging God frightens sinners and causes everyone to ask, **Who . . . can dwell** with such a God?
33:15 Righteousness is described in this verse in relational terms. God will dwell with those who refrain from acts that exploit other people. The righteous person will avoid **extortion**, bribery, and murder.
33:16 The righteous will be protected and sustained by God.
33:17 The picture of the **King in his beauty** looks to the future after the judgment and the destruction of the enemy when God's people will be restored.
33:19 The **barbarians** at the end of the eighth century were the Assyrians, who spoke a **language** (Akkadian) that the people of God could not understand. They destroyed the northern kingdom and subjected the south to vassalage and threatened their existence.
33:20–21 Describing Jerusalem as a **tent** may be a way of emphasizing the fragility of the city. A tent is easy to pull down or destroy. However, since God will be for them, this tent will not move. To describe **Zion** as a place of **rivers and broad streams** is to paint a picture of future blessing since Jerusalem had nothing of the kind. The prevention of shipping in these rivers may refer to war vessels.
33:22 God is **Judge . . . Lawgiver**, and **King**, offices that provide internal and external stability and security.
33:23 The pronouncement changes the addressee. **Your** must refer to the enemy who tries to capture the people of God.
33:24 The change from judgment to salvation for the people of God takes place for one reason: they will be **forgiven their iniquity**.
34:1 God is not just the God of Israel. He is the God of the whole **world**, so he calls on all the **nations** to **hear** him when he speaks.
34:2–3 God's anger is directed toward the armies of the **nations**.

4 All[A] the stars in the sky will dissolve.
The sky will roll up like a scroll,
and its stars will all wither
as leaves wither on the vine,
and foliage on the fig tree.

The Judgment of Edom

5 When my sword has drunk its fill[B]
in the heavens,
it will then come down on Edom
and on the people I have set apart
for destruction.
6 The LORD's sword is covered with blood.
It drips with fat,
with the blood of lambs and goats,
with the fat of the kidneys of rams.
For the LORD has a sacrifice in Bozrah,
a great slaughter in the land of Edom.
7 The wild oxen will be struck[C] down
with them,
and young bulls with the mighty bulls.
Their land will be soaked with[D] blood,
and their soil will be saturated with fat.

8 For the LORD has a day of vengeance,
a time of paying back Edom
for its hostility against Zion.
9 Edom's streams will be turned
into pitch,
her soil into sulfur;
her land will become burning pitch.
10 It will never go out — day or night.
Its smoke will go up forever.
It will be desolate, from generation
to generation;
no one will pass through it forever
and ever.
11 Eagle owls[E] and herons[F] will possess it,
and long-eared owls and ravens
will dwell there.
The LORD will stretch out
a measuring line
and a plumb line over her
for her destruction and chaos.
12 No nobles will be left to proclaim a king,

and all her princes will come
to nothing.
13 Her palaces will be overgrown
with thorns;
her fortified cities, with thistles
and briers.
She will become a dwelling for jackals,
an abode[G] for ostriches.
14 The desert creatures will meet hyenas,
and one wild goat will call to another.
Indeed, the night birds will stay there
and will find a resting place.
15 Sand partridges[H] will make
their nests there;
they will lay and hatch their eggs
and will gather their broods
under their shadows.
Indeed, the birds of prey
will gather there,
each with its mate.
16 Search and read the scroll of the LORD:
Not one of them will be missing,
none will be lacking its mate,
because he has ordered it
by my[I] mouth,
and he will gather them by his Spirit.
17 He has cast the lot for them;
his hand allotted their portion
with a measuring line.
They will possess it forever;
they will dwell in it from generation
to generation.

The Ransomed Return to Zion

35 The wilderness and the dry land
will be glad;
the desert will rejoice and blossom
like a wildflower.[J]
2 It will blossom abundantly
and will also rejoice with joy
and singing.
The glory of Lebanon will be given to it,
the splendor of Carmel and Sharon.
They will see the glory of the LORD,
the splendor of our God.

[A]34:4 DSS read *And the valleys will be split, and all* [B]34:5 DSS read *sword will appear* [C]34:7 Or *will go* [D]34:7 Or *will drink its fill of* [E]34:11 Or *Pelicans* [F]34:11 Or *hedgehogs* [G]34:13 DSS, LXX, Syr, Tg; MT reads *jackals, grass* [H]34:15 Or *Arrow snakes,* or *Owls* [I]34:16 Some Hb mss; other Hb mss, DSS, Syr, Tg read *his* [J]35:1 Or *meadow saffron;* traditionally *rose*

34:4 The nations thought of the **stars** as representing their gods. This language points to the fact that their gods, who are not gods at all, will suffer defeat at the hands of the true God.
34:5 Victory over heavenly forces (v. 4) is followed by a description of one representative nation, **Edom**. This nation was south of Moab in the region southeast of the Dead Sea. **Set apart for destruction** translates a single Hebrew verb (*cherem*) that is used frequently in Joshua to indicate that every man, woman, and child would be killed. It also describes the death of the enemy as a type of sacrifice to God.
34:6-7 Bozrah was the capital of ancient Edom.

34:8 Edom had a reputation for taking advantage of Israel whenever Israel was weak (Ps 137:7; Lm 4:22; Ezk 35:15; Ob 10–14).
34:9–10 God would punish Edom with the same type of punishment (**pitch . . . sulfur . . . burning pitch**) that he had brought against Sodom and Gomorrah (Gn 19:24–28).
34:11 This verse describes animals that lived in ruins and desolate places. **Owls** were considered unclean (Lv 11:15–16). For similar use of the word in contexts of judgment, see Is 34:13; Jr 50:38; Mc 1:8. While the **measuring line** and the **plumb line** were normally used in construction, God will use them to plan for the destruction of Edom.
34:12 Edom's kingship was ancient, preceding that of Israel (Gn 36:31–43), but God will

bring that institution to an end since he is bringing the nation itself to a close.
34:16–17 The meaning of the **scroll of the LORD** is unknown. It may be a reference to a heavenly scroll, but if so, it is difficult to know how the hearer could refer to this document. The appeal to the scroll could be a rhetorical device to emphasize the certainty of Edom's destruction and its transformation into a haunt for wild animals.
35:1–10 This chapter is a mirror image of chap. 34 where God announced that he would turn the nations into a wilderness. In chap. 35, he proclaimed that he would transform the people of God from a wilderness into a garden.
35:2 Lebanon . . . Carmel, and **Sharon** were regions especially lush in vegetation (33:9).

³ Strengthen the weak hands,
    steady the shaking knees!
⁴ Say to the cowardly:
    "Be strong; do not fear!
    Here is your God;
    vengeance is coming.
    God's retribution is coming; he will
        save you."
⁵ Then the eyes of the blind
        will be opened,
    and the ears of the deaf unstopped.
⁶ Then the lame will leap like a deer,
    and the tongue of the mute will sing
        for joy,
    for water will gush in the wilderness,
    and streams in the desert;
⁷ the parched ground will become a pool,
    and the thirsty land, springs.
    In the haunt of jackals, in their lairs,
    there will be grass, reeds,
        and papyrus.
⁸ A road will be there and a way;
    it will be called the Holy Way.
    The unclean will not travel on it,
    but it will be for the one who walks
        the path.
    Fools will not wander on it.
⁹ There will be no lion there,
    and no vicious beast will go up on it;
    they will not be found there.
    But the redeemed will walk on it,
¹⁰ and the ransomed of the Lord
        will return
    and come to Zion with singing,
    crowned with unending joy.
    Joy and gladness will overtake them,
    and sorrow and sighing will flee.

Sennacherib's Invasion

36 In the fourteenth year of King Hezekiah, King Sennacherib of Assyria attacked all the fortified cities of Judah and captured them. ² Then the king of Assyria sent his royal spokesman, along with a massive army, from Lachish to King Hezekiah at Jerusalem. The Assyrian stood near the conduit of the upper pool, by the road to Launderer's Field. ³ Eliakim son of Hilkiah, who was in charge of the palace, Shebna the court secretary, and Joah son of Asaph, the court historian, came out to him.

⁴ The royal spokesman said to them, "Tell Hezekiah:

The great king, the king of Assyria, says this: What are you relying on? ⁵ You^ think mere words are strategy and strength for war. Who are you now relying on that you have rebelled against me? ⁶ Look, you are relying on Egypt, that splintered reed of a staff that will pierce the hand of anyone who grabs it and leans on it. This is how Pharaoh king of Egypt is to all who rely on him. ⁷ Suppose you say to me, 'We rely on the Lord our God.' Isn't he the one whose high places and altars Hezekiah has removed, saying to Judah and Jerusalem, 'You are to worship at this altar'?

⁸ "Now make a deal with my master, the king of Assyria. I'll give you two thousand horses if you're able to supply riders for them! ⁹ How then can you drive back a single officer among the least of my master's servants? How can you rely on Egypt for chariots and horsemen? ¹⁰ Have I attacked

---

^36:5 Many Hb mss, DSS, 2Kg 18:20; MT reads I

35:3–4 God's retribution refers to the punishment due the wicked and the reward due the righteous.
35:5–7 God's work transforms those who are **blind ... deaf ... lame**, and **mute**. Elsewhere in Isaiah these physical disabilities are metaphors for spiritual shortcomings (29:18; 42:18–19; 43:8). They have been physically dead to godliness, but in the future they will come alive. Not only will the lame walk, but they will **leap like a deer**. Not only will the mute speak, but they will **sing for joy**. A similar transformation is described with the language of nature. The **parched ground** will flow with water. Land that was only suitable for wilderness animals like **jackals** will be verdant.
35:8 Israel, with its deep wadis and mountainous terrain, was a hard land to cross, but Isaiah foresaw a **road**. This road will be the **Holy Way**, a name indicating that it would provide access to God. While the **unclean** would not travel on it since it led to the presence of a holy God, even the **fools** would not get lost if they sought to walk this **path**.
35:9–10 The road described in v. 8 will be a safe road, and it will lead to **Zion**.
36:1 The year was 701 BC. The Assyrians had defeated the northern kingdom of Israel in

722 BC and put Judah in a position where they had to pay annual tribute to keep the Assyrians from attacking them. In 703 BC **Sennacherib** succeeded his father Sargon on the throne of Assyria. Many nations, including Judah, seized upon this succession in leadership as an opportunity to rebel against Assyria. After taking care of rebellions in other parts of his empire, Sennacherib turned his attention to Judah in 701 BC. He easily took many of the smaller **fortified cities** on the way to Jerusalem. For accounts of this confrontation, see 2Kg 18–19 and 2Ch 32.
36:2 Lachish was an important garrison city about thirty miles west of Jerusalem. Along with other cities, it guarded the road that led to Jerusalem. The king of Assyria, along with his armies, was still at Lachish when he sent **his royal spokesman** (perhaps a Hebrew representation of an Akkadian title "chief cupbearer"), to present an ultimatum to Jerusalem. The **spokesman** stood at the same place where Isaiah had confronted Ahaz at an earlier time (7:3).
36:4–5 The purpose of the spokesman's speech was to try to get **Hezekiah** to surrender. He first questioned whether the people of Judah were militarily prepared to counter the Assyrian threat.

36:6 The royal spokesman then undermined any confidence the nation of Judah might have in **Egypt** as an ally. He used the metaphor of a **splintered reed of a staff**. A staff was something a person leaned on for support. However, this staff was made out of a reed that could not support a person's weight.
36:7 Finally, the spokesman questioned whether God would provide protection to **Hezekiah**. His argument shows that he did not understand the religion of Judah. Indeed, the removal of all altars except the one on Mount Zion was in conformity with the law of centralization in Dt 12.
36:8–9 The spokesman then taunted Judah by offering them **two thousand horses**, suggesting that they could not find riders for them.
36:10 Here the spokesman's statement reflects ancient Near Eastern pagan theology. The Assyrians believed that the God of Israel was a real deity, though perhaps not a strong one. The spokesman claimed that Judah's God had ordered the nation's destruction. In this case the spokesman was wrong, as further developments of the confrontation between Assyria and Israel would indicate.

this land to destroy it without the LORD's approval? The LORD said to me, 'Attack this land and destroy it.'"

¹¹ Then Eliakim, Shebna, and Joah said to the royal spokesman, "Please speak to your servants in Aramaic, since we understand it. Don't speak to us in Hebrewᴬ within earshot of the people who are on the wall." ¹² But the royal spokesman replied, "Has my master sent me to speak these words to your master and to you, and not to the men who are sitting on the wall, who are destined with you to eat their own excrement and drink their own urine?" ¹³ Then the royal spokesman stood and called out loudly in Hebrew:

Listen to the words of the great king, the king of Assyria! ¹⁴ This is what the king says: "Don't let Hezekiah deceive you, for he cannot rescue you. ¹⁵ Don't let Hezekiah persuade you to rely on the LORD, saying, 'The LORD will certainly rescue us! This city will not be handed over to the king of Assyria.'"

¹⁶ Don't listen to Hezekiah, for this is what the king of Assyria says: "Make peaceᴮ with me and surrender to me. Then every one of you may eat from his own vine and his own fig tree and drink water from his own cistern ¹⁷ until I come and take you away to a land like your own land — a land of grain and new wine, a land of bread and vineyards. ¹⁸ Beware that Hezekiah does not mislead you by saying, 'The LORD will rescue us.' Has any one of the gods of the nations rescued his land from the power of the king of Assyria? ¹⁹ Where are the gods of Hamath and Arpad? Where are the gods of Sepharvaim? Have they rescued Samaria from my power? ²⁰ Who among all the gods of these lands ever rescued his

land from my power? So will the LORD rescue Jerusalem from my power?"

²¹ But they kept silent; they didn't say anything, for the king's command was, "Don't answer him." ²² Then Eliakim son of Hilkiah, who was in charge of the palace, Shebna the court secretary, and Joah son of Asaph, the court historian, came to Hezekiah with their clothes torn and reported to him the words of the royal spokesman.

Hezekiah Seeks Isaiah's Counsel

37 When King Hezekiah heard their report, he tore his clothes, covered himself with sackcloth, and went to the LORD's temple. ² He sent Eliakim, who was in charge of the palace, Shebna the court secretary, and the leading priests, who were covered with sackcloth, to the prophet Isaiah son of Amoz. ³ They said to him, "This is what Hezekiah says: 'Today is a day of distress, rebuke, and disgrace. It is as if children have come to the point of birth, and there is no strength to deliver them. ⁴ Perhaps the LORD your God will hear all the words of the royal spokesman, whom his master the king of Assyria sent to mock the living God, and will rebuke him for the words that the LORD your God has heard. Therefore offer a prayer for the surviving remnant.'"

⁵ So the servants of King Hezekiah went to Isaiah, ⁶ who said to them, "Tell your master, 'The LORD says this: Don't be afraid because of the words you have heard, with which the king of Assyria's attendants have blasphemed me. ⁷ I am about to put a spirit in him and he will hear a rumor and return to his own land, where I will cause him to fall by the sword.'"

Sennacherib's Letter

⁸ When the royal spokesman heard that the king of Assyria had pulled out of Lachish, he left and found him fighting against Libnah.

ᴬ36:11 Lit Judahite, also in v. 13   ᴮ36:16 Lit a blessing

36:11 The spokesman probably had been speaking Hebrew to the Judean delegation. The leaders of Judah did not want the people to be frightened by the spokesman's speech. Perhaps because they did not know how to speak Akkadian, they requested that the conversation take place in Aramaic. This language was closely related to Hebrew. It was known more broadly throughout the ancient Near East, but not by the people who were listening to this conversation. 36:12 However, it served the spokesman's propagandistic purpose to have the people hear and be frightened by the coming Assyrian army, so he refused this request. He reminded them of the consequences of a long siege. They would run out of water and have to drink their urine; they would run out of food and have to eat their excrement. 36:16–17 Assyria's imperialistic policy called for the deportation of a subjugated people. The spokesman presented his ultimatum for surrender. Such a policy was put into place in 722 BC when the Assyrians conquered the northern kingdom and deported the vast majority of the native population and then brought in foreigners to live there. This policy was intended to break the connection between a people and the god of their land. 36:18–20 The spokesman argued that the God of Judah, Yahweh, could not save Judah any more than the gods of other nations and cities that had been defeated by Assyria. He specifically mentioned the defeat of three cities whose gods were unable to rescue their inhabitants. Arpad and Hamath were cities in northern Syria known to have been defeated by Assyria at an earlier time. The exact identification of Sepharvaim is unknown. 36:21–22 Hezekiah did not give his officials authority to negotiate with Assyria. They simply reported the proceedings to the king. Their clothes that were torn were a customary sign of mourning, showing their deep distress. 37:1 The report from Hezekiah's officials (36:22) led the king to assume a posture of mourning, indicated by the customary tearing of his clothes and putting on sackcloth, a rough and uncomfortable material. He then went to the temple, demonstrating the proper response to such a crisis. 37:2–4 Hezekiah then sent two of his officials, Eliakim and Shebna, along with senior priests, to elicit prayers on behalf of the nation from the prophet Isaiah. 37:5–6 Isaiah assured King Hezekiah through his men that God would remedy the threat presented by the Assyrian army. 37:7 God would send a spirit of deception to the Assyrian king so he would hear and believe a falsehood that would cause him to retreat. 37:8 When the royal spokesman had traveled to Jerusalem, the Assyrian king and his army was at Lachish (36:2); but when the spokesman returned, the king was at Libnah,

⁹ The king had heard concerning King Tirhakah of Cush, "He has set out to fight against you." So when he heard this, he sent messengers to Hezekiah, saying, ¹⁰ "Say this to King Hezekiah of Judah: 'Don't let your God, on whom you rely, deceive you by promising that Jerusalem won't be handed over to the king of Assyria. ¹¹ Look, you have heard what the kings of Assyria have done to all the countries: they completely destroyed them. Will you be rescued? ¹² Did the gods of the nations that my predecessors destroyed rescue them — Gozan, Haran, Rezeph, and the Edenites in Telassar? ¹³ Where is the king of Hamath, the king of Arpad, the king of the city of ^A Sepharvaim, Hena, or Ivvah?' "

Hezekiah's Prayer

¹⁴ Hezekiah took the letter from the messengers' hands, read it, then went up to the LORD's temple and spread it out before the LORD. ¹⁵ Then Hezekiah prayed to the LORD:

¹⁶ LORD of Armies, God of Israel, enthroned between the cherubim, you are God — you alone — of all the kingdoms of the earth. You made the heavens and the earth. ¹⁷ Listen closely, LORD, and hear; open your eyes, LORD, and see. Hear all the words that Sennacherib has sent to mock the living God. ¹⁸ LORD, it is true that the kings of Assyria have devastated all these countries and their lands. ¹⁹ They have thrown their gods into the fire, for they were not gods but made from wood and stone by human hands. So they have destroyed them. ²⁰ Now, LORD our God, save us from his power so that all the kingdoms of the earth may know that you, LORD, are God^B — you alone.

God's Answer through Isaiah

²¹ Then Isaiah son of Amoz sent a message to Hezekiah: "The LORD, the God of Israel, says, 'Because you prayed to me about King Sennacherib of Assyria, ²² this is the word the LORD has spoken against him:

Virgin Daughter Zion
despises you and scorns you;
Daughter Jerusalem shakes her head
behind your back.
²³   Who is it you have mocked
        and blasphemed?
Against whom have you raised your voice
and lifted your eyes in pride?
Against the Holy One of Israel!
²⁴   You have mocked the Lord
        through your servants.
You have said, "With my many chariots
I have gone up to the heights
        of the mountains,
to the far recesses of Lebanon.
I cut down its tallest cedars,
its choice cypress trees.
I came to its distant heights,
its densest forest.
²⁵   I dug wells and drank water in foreign
        lands.^C
I dried up all the streams of Egypt
with the soles of my feet."

²⁶   Have you not heard?
I designed it long ago;
I planned it in days gone by.
I have now brought it to pass,
and you have crushed fortified cities
into piles of rubble.
²⁷   Their inhabitants have become powerless,
dismayed, and ashamed.
They are plants of the field,
tender grass,
grass on the rooftops,
blasted by the east wind.^D

²⁸   But I know your sitting down,
your going out and your coming in,
and your raging against me.

---

^A 37:13 Or *king of Lair*,   ^B 37:20 *are God* supplied for clarity; see v. 16   ^C 37:25 DSS, 2Kg 19:24; MT omits *in foreign lands*   ^D 37:27 DSS; MT reads *rooftops, field before standing grain*

---

a town about eight miles northeast of Lachish. Sennacherib had completed the capture of Lachish and had moved on to the next city on what seemed to be an unstoppable march toward Jerusalem.
37:9 King Tirhakah of Cush at this point in history (701 BC) may have been crown prince of Egypt. He became pharaoh of all Egypt in 690 BC and ruled until 664 BC.
37:10 The rumor of Tirhakah's advance on his rear flank caused Sennacherib to retreat from his advance on **Jerusalem**, but before he left he sent a message in the form of a "letter" (v. 14) to warn Hezekiah that his departure was only temporary.
37:11–13 Sennacherib again told Hezekiah (see the spokesman's speech in 36:18–20) that he should not trust the Lord. After all, the **gods** of other **nations** and cities conquered by Assyria in the past had been unable to help them. Most of the sites listed here were in what is today eastern Turkey

(**Haran**, the city where Abraham and his family stayed for a while before descending into the promised land; see Gn 11:31–32) or northern Syria (**Gozan . . . Rezeph** and Eden). One site, **Telassar**, has been associated with a location (Til-Ashshuri) in what is today Iraq near the Diyala River. On **Hamath . . . Arpad**, and **Sepharvaim**, see note at 36:18–20. The locations of **Hena** and **Ivvah** are unknown.
37:14–15 Hezekiah immediately goes to the Lord, his only hope. He does not suppose to inform God of the contents of the letter, but lays it out as an expression of faith.
37:16 Hezekiah addressed his prayer to God whom he described as **enthroned between the cherubim**. The cherubim were among the most powerful of God's heavenly creatures and are often represented at places close to the divine presence. In particular, this refers to the statues of two cherubim whose wings covered the ark of the covenant as it rested in the holy of holies in the tabernacle

and temple. Hezekiah appealed to God as the one who **made the heavens and the earth**—the one who is sovereign over all kingdoms, not just Judah—since Sennacherib had mocked God as a mere local deity.
37:18–20 Hezekiah appealed to God based on his glory.
37:21 God responded to **Hezekiah** through his divinely chosen spokesman, the prophet **Isaiah**. As Isaiah spoke, he spoke in the name of **God**.
37:22 Daughter Zion is a personification of Zion, the most holy location in Judah.
37:25 It was always the dream of Mesopotamian kings to defeat Egypt. Sennacherib had boasted that he was able to travel to Egypt.
37:26–27 Now God revealed to Sennacherib the true nature of things—his victories had come about only because God had willed it.
37:28 In language reminiscent of Ps 139, God asserted his extensive knowledge of the Assyrian king.

29 Because your raging against me
and your arrogance have reached
my ears,
I will put my hook in your nose
and my bit in your mouth;
I will make you go back
the way you came.

30 " 'This will be the sign for you: This year
you will eat what grows on its own, and in the
second year what grows from that. But in the
third year sow and reap, plant vineyards and
eat their fruit. **31** The surviving remnant of the
house of Judah will again take root downward
and bear fruit upward. **32** For a remnant will go
out from Jerusalem, and survivors from Mount
Zion. The zeal of the LORD of Armies will accomplish this.'

33 "Therefore, this is what the LORD says
about the king of Assyria:

He will not enter this city,
shoot an arrow here,
come before it with a shield,
or build up a siege ramp against it.
34 He will go back
the way he came,
and he will not enter this city.
This is the LORD's declaration.
35 I will defend this city and rescue it
for my sake
and for the sake of my servant David."

Defeat and Death of Sennacherib

36 Then the angel of the LORD went out and
struck down one hundred eighty-five thousand in the camp of the Assyrians. When the
people got up the next morning, there were all
the dead bodies! **37** So King Sennacherib of Assyria broke camp and left. He returned home
and lived in Nineveh.

38 One day, while he was worshiping in the
temple of his god Nisroch, his sons Adrammelech and Sharezer struck him down with the
sword and escaped to the land of Ararat. Then
his son Esar-haddon became king in his place.

Hezekiah's Illness and Recovery

38 In those days Hezekiah became terminally ill. The prophet Isaiah son of
Amoz came and said to him, "This is what the
LORD says: 'Set your house in order, for you are
about to die; you will not recover.' "ᴬ

2 Then Hezekiah turned his face to the wall
and prayed to the LORD. **3** He said, "Please, LORD,
remember how I have walked before you faithfully and wholeheartedly, and have done what
pleases you." And Hezekiah wept bitterly.

4 Then the word of the LORD came to Isaiah:
5 "Go and tell Hezekiah, 'This is what the LORD
God of your ancestor David says: I have heard
your prayer; I have seen your tears. Look, I am
going to add fifteen years to your life.ᴮ **6** And I
will rescue you and this city from the grasp of
the king of Assyria; I will defend this city. **7** This
is the sign to you from the LORD that he will do
what he has promised: **8** I am going to make the
sun's shadow that goes down on the stairway of
Ahaz go back by ten steps.'" So the sun's shad-
owᶜ went back the ten steps it had descended.

9 A poem by King Hezekiah of Judah after
he had been sick and had recovered from his
illness:

10 I said: In the primeᴰ of my life
I must go to the gates of Sheol;

ᴬ**38:1** Lit *live* ᴮ**38:5** Lit *days*, also in v. 10 ᶜ**38:8** Lit *And the sun* ᴰ**38:10** Lit *quiet*

37:29 It was Assyrian practice, as illustrated
in the bas-reliefs that adorned their palaces,
to put a **hook** in the nose or the mouth of
captives as they carried them into exile. God
told Sennacherib that he would be subjected
to this brutal and degrading treatment.
37:30-32 God directed these words to
Hezekiah, king of Judah, to show him that
the future would see a turn for the better
for God's people.
37:30 Because of the siege by Assyria, the
Judeans were penned up behind the walls
of Jerusalem and had not been able to plant
their crops. Thus, they would eat what grew
on its own, an unreliable volunteer crop.
After Assyria lifted the siege, they would
be able to plant, but not until the third year
would agriculture get back to normal.
37:31-32 Now the pronouncement speaks
of a metaphorical harvest—of the **surviving
remnant** of the people of God. The future
will see the remnant become productive.
37:33-35 God directed his attention back
to the **king of Assyria**. He announced that
Sennacherib would fail at his attempt to take
the city. He would not even begin the assault
but would return to Assyria.
37:36-37 God sent his **angel** to kill the **Assyrians** without a battle. No proximate cause

is given for the death of the enemy soldiers,
though it is likely that God used disease to
accomplish his goal.
37:38 Nisroch was an unknown Assyrian
god or, more likely, the name given by the
Hebrews to a god known by another name.
Ararat was a region located around Lake Van
north of Assyria. It was known in antiquity as
Urartu and was a long-standing foe of Assyria, thus a likely place for the murderous sons
of Sennacherib to escape. While **Adrammelech and Sharezer** are not known by name,
Esar-haddon is known to have succeeded
his father Sennacherib after the king's death
in 683 BC. Since these events happened in
683 BC, it appears that almost twenty years
passed from the time Sennacherib withdrew
from Jerusalem in 701 BC to the time when
he died at the hands of his sons.
38:1-3 In those days should not be taken to
mean that chap. 38 follows chap. 37 chronologically. Hezekiah's illness occurred before
God delivered Jerusalem, as v. 6 makes clear.
38:4-5 God **heard** the **prayer** of Hezekiah and increased his lifespan by **fifteen
years**. Interestingly, God is described as
the LORD God of your ancestor David.
Hezekiah may not have had an heir at
this time (his heir, Manasseh, was twelve

years old when Hezekiah died, 2Kg 21:1).
This meant that if he died prior to the fif-
teen-year extension, the Davidic dynasty
would come to an end.
38:6 The reference to the deliverance of the
city from the **king of Assyria** may indicate
that this episode took place during the Assyrian threat described in chaps. 36–37.
38:7 Hezekiah's **sign** brings to mind the
sign offered to his father Ahaz in chap. 7.
Hezekiah did not try to refuse the sign. Their
contrasting responses reveal the difference
between Ahaz, who trusted in other nations,
and Hezekiah, who trusted in God.
38:8 The return of the **sun's shadow** on
the stairway indicated a lengthening of
the day that would be comparable to God's
lengthening of the life of Hezekiah. The parallel account in 2Kg 20:9–11 indicates that
Hezekiah was allowed to choose whether
the shadow would go ahead or go back **ten
steps**. Hezekiah chose the latter since he
considered that the more difficult feat.
38:9 The introduction to Hezekiah's poem
states that it was written **after he had been
sick and had recovered**. In this respect,
the poem is like the thanksgiving songs in
Psalms. In the first part of this poem, Hezekiah spoke as if he were going to die, but from

I am deprived of the rest of my years.
¹¹ I said: I will never see the LORD,
the LORD in the land of the living;
I will not look on humanity
    any longer
with the inhabitants of what is
    passing away.ᴬ
¹² My dwelling is plucked up and removed
    from me
like a shepherd's tent.
I have rolled up my life like a weaver;
he cuts me off from the loom.
By nightfallᴮ you make an end of me.
¹³ I thought until the morning:
He will break all my bones like a lion.
By nightfall you make an end of me.
¹⁴ I chirp like a swallow or a crane;
I moan like a dove.
My eyes grow weak looking upward.
Lord, I am oppressed; support me.

¹⁵ What can I say?
He has spoken to me,
    and he himself has done it.
I walk along slowly all my years
because of the bitterness
    of my soul.
¹⁶ Lord, by such things people live,
and in every one of them my spirit
    finds life;
you have restored me to health
and let me live.
¹⁷ Indeed, it was for my own well-being
that I had such intense bitterness;
but your love has delivered me
from the Pit of destruction,
for you have thrown all my sins
    behind your back.
¹⁸ For Sheol cannot thank you;
Death cannot praise you.
Those who go down to the Pit
cannot hope for your faithfulness.
¹⁹ The living, only the living can thank you,
as I do today;

a father will make your faithfulness
    known to children.
²⁰ The LORD is ready to save me;
we will play stringed instruments
all the days of our lives
at the house of the LORD.

²¹ Now Isaiah had said, "Let them take a lump of pressed figs and apply it to his infected skin, so that he may recover." ²² And Hezekiah had asked, "What is the sign that I will go up to the LORD's temple?"

Hezekiah's Folly

39 At that time Merodach-baladan son of Baladan, king of Babylon, sent letters and a gift to Hezekiah since he heard that he had been sick and had recovered. ² Hezekiah was pleased with the letters, and he showed the envoys his treasure house — the silver, the gold, the spices, and the precious oil — and all his armory, and everything that was found in his treasuries. There was nothing in his palace and in all his realm that Hezekiah did not show them.

³ Then the prophet Isaiah came to King Hezekiah and asked him, "What did these men say, and where did they come to you from?"

Hezekiah replied, "They came to me from a distant country, from Babylon."

⁴ Isaiah asked, "What have they seen in your palace?"

Hezekiah answered, "They have seen everything in my palace. There isn't anything in my treasuries that I didn't show them."

⁵ Then Isaiah said to Hezekiah, "Hear the word of the LORD of Armies: ⁶ 'Look, the days are coming when everything in your palace and all that your predecessors have stored up until today will be carried off to Babylon; nothing will be left,' says the LORD. ⁷ 'Some of your descendants — who come from you, whom you father — will be taken away, and they will become eunuchs in the palace of the king of Babylon.'"

ᴬ 38:11 Some Hb mss, Tg read *of the world*   ᴮ 38:12 Lit *From day until night*, also in v. 13

---

the second half of the poem it is clear that it was written after he was healed.
38:10 Sheol refers to the grave and in some contexts signifies the ancient concept of an underworld.
38:11 The **land of the living** refers to this world.
38:12 Hezekiah used multiple metaphors to describe the fragility and brevity of life.
38:14 The groans of Hezekiah's lamentation sound like the chirping of a bird.
38:17 Hezekiah's **bitterness** (see also v. 15) refers to his mournful reaction to news of his impending death. This bitterness is what led him to seek God in prayer and ultimately to God's relenting from his death sentence. The king referred to the grave (and the afterlife) as a **Pit of destruction**. After all, in the grave the body rots and turns to dust.

38:18 Sheol (see note at v. 10) and **Death** are personified. The implication, as made clear by the phrase **those who go down to the Pit**, is that the dead can no longer praise God.
38:19 God benefits from keeping his saints alive. The living can praise God, and they can share that praise with the following generations.
38:21–22 These verses are an appendix that fills in some facts from earlier in the story.
39:1 Merodach-baladan was king of Babylon, at this time a province of the Assyrian Empire, during two different times—721–710 BC and 705–703 BC. In 703 BC Sennacherib, to whom Merodach-baladan had been a constant irritant looking for opportunities to revolt, removed him. Even after his removal from Babylon, Merodach-baladan went to Elam and continued to plot against Assyria until his death. The **letters and a gift** that he sent to Hezekiah

were part of a strategy to get Hezekiah to join with him in a rebellious alliance. This story in 39:1–8 finds its parallel in 2Kg 20:12–19.
39:2 Hezekiah responded positively to Merodach-baladan, showing him the wealth of his kingdom as well as the strength of his armaments.
39:5–7 The king's actions demonstrated that he was trusting foreign nations like **Babylon** for his protection rather than God. The Lord's punishment would take away the wealth that Hezekiah had been showing off to Merodach-baladan. Another part of the punishment was that some of the king's **descendants** would be taken away and would become **eunuchs** in Babylon.
39:8 The implication of the announced punishment was that it would happen in a future generation. Hezekiah's selfish relief does not speak well for him.

⁸ Then Hezekiah said to Isaiah, "The word of the LORD that you have spoken is good," for he thought: There will be peace and security during my lifetime.

God's People Comforted

40 "Comfort, comfort my people,"
says your God.
² "Speak tenderly toᴬ Jerusalem,
and announce to her
that her time of hard service is over,
her iniquity has been pardoned,
and she has received
from the LORD's hand
double for all her sins."

³ A voice of one crying out:
Prepare the way of the LORD
in the wilderness;
make a straight highway for our God
in the desert.
⁴ Every valley will be lifted up,
and every mountain and hill
will be leveled;
the uneven ground
will become smooth
and the rough places, a plain.
⁵ And the glory of the LORD will appear,
and all humanityᴮ together will see it,
for the mouth of the LORD has spoken.

⁶ A voice was saying, "Cry out!"
Another said,ᶜ "What should I cry out?"
"All humanity is grass,
and all its goodness is like the flower
of the field.
⁷ The grass withers, the flowers fade
when the breathᴰ of the LORD blows
on them;ᴱ
indeed, the people are grass.
⁸ The grass withers, the flowers fade,
but the word of our God
remains forever."

⁹ Zion, herald of good news,
go up on a high mountain.
Jerusalem, herald of good news,
raise your voice loudly.
Raise it, do not be afraid!
Say to the cities of Judah,
"Here is your God!"
¹⁰ See, the Lord GOD comes with strength,
and his power establishes his rule.
His wages are with him,
and his reward accompanies him.
¹¹ He protects his flock like a shepherd;
he gathers the lambs in his arms
and carries them in the fold
of his garment.
He gently leads those that are nursing.

¹² Who has measured the waters
in the hollow of his hand
or marked off the heavens with the span
of his hand?
Who has gathered the dust of the earth
in a measure
or weighed the mountains
on a balance
and the hills on the scales?
¹³ Who has directedᶠ the Spirit of the LORD,
or who gave him counsel?
¹⁴ Who did he consult?
Who gave him understanding
and taught him the paths of justice?
Who taught him knowledge
and showed him the way
of understanding?
¹⁵ Look, the nations are like a drop
in a bucket;
they are considered as a speck of dust
on the scales;
he lifts up the islands like fine dust.
¹⁶ Lebanon's cedars are not enough
for fuel,
or its animals enough
for a burnt offering.

ᴬ 40:2 Lit *Speak to the heart of*   ᴮ 40:5 Lit *flesh*   ᶜ 40:6 DSS, LXX, Vg read *I said*   ᴰ 40:7 Or *wind,* or *Spirit*   ᴱ 40:7 Lit *it*
ᶠ 40:13 Or *measured,* or *comprehended*

40:1 Though the hearer of God's words is not here specified, it is best to see these words as being directed to the prophet Isaiah, who was commanded to bring words of **comfort** rather than judgment to God's people. The words address the prophet as if he were living in the time of the future exile of Judah to Babylon.

40:2 The **time of hard service** refers to the future Babylonian exile (586–539 BC). That the people had received **double** punishment is a way of saying that their sentence was fully satisfied before God.

40:3–4 The wilderness was difficult to cross because it had deep wadis and high mountains, but in preparation for the return this rough terrain would become like **a plain**, easy to travel. The fulfillment most immediately in view is the return of Jewish people after the end of the exile, but the ultimate fulfillment of these verses is in the work of Jesus Christ as signaled by the quotation of v. 3 along with Mal 3:1 in Mk 1:2–3 and the identification of the voice as that of John the Baptist. Also see Mt 3:3; Mk 1:3; Lk 3:4–6; Jn 1:23.

40:6–8 Another herald compared humanity to **grass** and the **flower of the field**, both of which have short-lived and fragile beauty. The contrast is with the **word of God** that endures. Peter quotes these words in 1Pt 1:24–25.

40:9–10 **His power** is literally "his arm," which is found frequently in Isaiah (30:30; 33:2; 48:14; 50:2; 51:5,9; 52:10; 53:1).

40:11 In the Bible and throughout the ancient Near East, the **shepherd** was a familiar image for a ruler. The nation would once again have a strong and compassionate shepherd—God himself (Ps 23).

40:12–26 The series of rhetorical questions that appear in these verses have one intention—to demonstrate the uniqueness of the one true God.

40:13–14 Paul quotes these words in Rm 11:34 and 1Co 2:16.

#36 **99 Essential Christian Truths**

SIN AS MISSING THE MARK

One aspect of sin is missing the mark of God's standards set for humanity. This missing of the mark is not a simple mistake but a falling short of God's glory through conscious choosing of sin. We may refer to sin as a failure on the part of humans to live according to God's standards, but we must recognize that failure is intentional. We miss the mark when we deliberately choose to cast aside God's intention for us.

17 All the nations are as nothing
  before him;
they are considered by him
as empty nothingness.

18 With whom will you compare God?
What likeness will you set up for
  comparison with him?
19 An idol? — something that a smelter casts
and a metalworker plates with gold
and makes silver chains for?
20 A poor person contributes wood for
  a pedestal
that will not rot.^A
He looks for a skilled craftsman
to set up an idol that will not fall over.

21 Do you not know?
Have you not heard?
Has it not been declared to you
from the beginning?
Have you not considered
the foundations of the earth?
22 God is enthroned above the circle
  of the earth;
its inhabitants are like grasshoppers.
He stretches out the heavens
  like thin cloth
and spreads them out like a tent
  to live in.
23 He reduces princes to nothing
and makes judges of the earth like a
  wasteland.
24 They are barely planted, barely sown,
their stem hardly takes root
  in the ground
when he blows on them
  and they wither,
and a whirlwind carries them away
  like stubble.

25 "To whom will you compare me,
or who is my equal?" asks the Holy One.
26 Look up and see!
Who created these?
He brings out the stars by number;
he calls all of them by name.
Because of his great power
  and strength,
not one of them is missing.

27 Jacob, why do you say,
and Israel, why do you assert,

"My way is hidden from the LORD,
and my claim is ignored by my God"?
28 Do you not know?
Have you not heard?
The LORD is the everlasting God,
the Creator of the whole earth.
He never becomes faint or weary;
there is no limit to his understanding.
29 He gives strength to the faint
and strengthens the powerless.
30 Youths may become faint and weary,
and young men stumble and fall,
31 but those who trust in the LORD
will renew their strength;
they will soar on wings like eagles;
they will run and not become weary,
they will walk and not faint.

The LORD versus the Nations' Gods

41 "Be silent before me, coasts and
  islands!
And let peoples renew their strength.
Let them approach; let them testify;
let's come together for the trial.
2 Who has stirred up someone
  from the east?
In righteousness he calls him to serve.^B,C
The LORD hands nations over to him,
and he subdues kings.
He makes them like dust with his sword,
like wind-driven stubble with his bow.
3 He pursues them, going on safely,
hardly touching the path with his feet.
4 Who has performed and done this,
calling the generations
  from the beginning?
I am the LORD, the first
and with the last — I am he."

5 The coasts and islands see
  and are afraid,
the whole earth trembles.
They approach and arrive.
6 Each one helps the other,
and says to another, "Take courage!"
7 The craftsman encourages
  the metalworker;
the one who flattens with the hammer
encourages the one who strikes
  the anvil,
saying of the soldering, "It is good."
He fastens it with nails so that it will not
  fall over.

---

^A 40:20 Or *who is too poor for such an offering*, or *who chooses mulberry wood as a votive gift*; Hb obscure ^B 41:2 Or *Righteousness calls him to serve* ^C 41:2 Lit *to his foot*

40:25–26 The fact that God knew **the stars** by name indicates that they were his creation and they were protected (**not one of them is missing**) by his power. **40:29–31** The criterion for receiving God's strength was not youth but **trust**. Those who trusted God would have an unlimited source of strength.

41:1 The **coasts and islands** refer to far-off lands and thus represent all the nations of the world. The prophets often used the language of the courtroom. Here God will try the nations and their idols. The nations were to be quiet as God presented evidence in support of his case. **41:2** The one **from the east** who subdues kings is a reference to Cyrus, king of Persia

(45:1), whom God used to defeat Babylon in 539 BC. This brought the exile of Judah to an end. **41:5–7** On **coasts and islands**, see note at v. 1. The **craftsman** and the **metalworker** were those who created the idols in whom the nations trusted.

8 But you, Israel, my servant,
Jacob, whom I have chosen,
descendant of Abraham, my friend —
9 I brought^A you from the ends
of the earth
and called you from its farthest corners.
I said to you: You are my servant;
I have chosen you; I haven't
rejected you.
10 Do not fear, for I am with you;
do not be afraid, for I am your God.
I will strengthen you; I will help you;
I will hold on to you with my righteous
right hand.

11 Be sure that all who are enraged
against you
will be ashamed and disgraced;
those who contend with you
will become as nothing and will perish.
12 You will look for those who contend
with you,
but you will not find them.
Those who war against you
will become absolutely nothing.
13 For I am the LORD your God,
who holds your right hand,
who says to you, "Do not fear,
I will help you.
14 Do not fear, you worm Jacob,
you men^B of Israel.
I will help you" —
this is the LORD's declaration.
Your Redeemer is the Holy One of Israel.
15 See, I will make you
into a sharp threshing board,
new, with many teeth.
You will thresh mountains
and pulverize them
and make hills into chaff.
16 You will winnow them
and a wind will carry them away,
a whirlwind will scatter them.
But you will rejoice in the LORD;
you will boast in the Holy One of Israel.

17 The poor and the needy seek water,
but there is none;
their tongues are parched with thirst.

I will answer them.
I am the LORD, the God of Israel.
I will not abandon them.
18 I will open rivers on the barren heights,
and springs in the middle of the plains.
I will turn the desert into a pool
and dry land into springs.
19 I will plant cedar, acacia, myrtle,
and olive trees
in the wilderness.
I will put juniper, elm, and cypress trees
together
in the desert,
20 so that all may see and know,
consider and understand,
that the hand of the LORD has done this,
the Holy One of Israel has created it.

21 "Submit your case," says the LORD.
"Present your arguments,"
says Jacob's King.
22 "Let them come and tell us
what will happen.
Tell us the past events,
so that we may reflect on them
and know the outcome,
or tell us the future.
23 Tell us the coming events,
then we will know that you are gods.
Indeed, do something good or bad,
then we will be in awe^C when we see it.
24 Look, you are nothing
and your work is worthless.
Anyone who chooses you is detestable.

25 "I have stirred up one from the north,
and he has come,
one from the east who invokes my^D name.
He will march over rulers as if
they were mud,
like a potter who treads the clay.
26 Who told about this from the beginning,
so that we might know,
and from times past,
so that we might say, 'He is right'?
No one announced it,
no one told it,
no one heard your words.
27 I was the first to say to Zion,^E

^A41:9 Or seized   ^B41:14 LXX reads small number; DSS read dead ones   ^C41:23 DSS read we may hear   ^D41:25 DSS read his
^E41:27 Lit First to Zion

41:10 God's **right hand** is often associated with his military might, thus his ability to protect his people.
41:15 The **threshing board** was a heavy wooden sledge with many stone or iron teeth on its underside. It was dragged across sheaves to separate the grain from the chaff in the winnowing process. The metaphor emphasizes how thoroughly and violently Israel would defeat the nations.
41:16 Winnowing involved throwing grain in the air so the wind caught the chaff, or waste matter, and blew it away.

41:17–18 The phrase **the poor and the needy** here refers to God's own down-and-out people whom he has punished. But God will restore them, turning their dry land into a watery paradise.
41:19–20 The **wilderness** has become an orchard, an act that only God could perform—the word translated **created** (Hb *bara'*) is the same as in Gn 1:1.
41:21 Again (see note at v. 1) God used legal language as he challenged the nations and their idols. **Jacob's King** is none other than God himself.

41:25 King Cyrus of Persia is in mind here. He is said to be from the **east** (see note at v. 2) because his homeland was geographically east of Israel. On the other hand, he could at the same time be from the **north** because that was the direction from which he attacked Babylon.
41:26–27 The coming of Cyrus was **good news** to Jerusalem because his defeat of Babylon would mean that the exiles could come home.

'Look! Here they are!'
And I gave Jerusalem a herald
with good news.

28 When I look, there is no one;
there is no counselor among them;
when I ask them, they have
nothing to say.

29 Look, all of them are a delusion;[A]
their works are nonexistent;
their images are wind and emptiness.

The Servant's Mission

42 "This is my servant; I strengthen him,
this is my chosen one; I delight
in him.
I have put my Spirit on him;
he will bring justice[B] to the nations.

2 He will not cry out or shout
or make his voice heard in the streets.

3 He will not break a bruised reed,
and he will not put out
a smoldering wick;
he will faithfully bring justice.

4 He will not grow weak
or be discouraged
until he has established justice
on earth.
The coasts and islands will wait
for his instruction."

5 This is what God, the LORD, says —
who created the heavens and stretched
them out,
who spread out the earth
and what comes from it,
who gives breath to the people on it
and spirit to those who walk on it —

6 "I am the LORD. I have called you
for a righteous purpose,[C]
and I will hold you by your hand.
I will watch over you, and I will appoint
you
to be a covenant for the people

and a light to the nations,

7 in order to open blind eyes,
to bring out prisoners
from the dungeon,
and those sitting in darkness
from the prison house.

8 I am the LORD. That is my name,
and I will not give my glory to another
or my praise to idols.

9 The past events have indeed happened.
Now I declare new events;
I announce them to you
before they occur."

A Song of Praise

10 Sing a new song to the LORD;
sing his praise from the ends
of the earth,
you who go down to the sea with all
that fills it,
you coasts and islands
with your[D] inhabitants.

11 Let the desert and its cities shout,
the settlements where Kedar dwells
cry aloud.
Let the inhabitants of Sela sing for joy;
let them cry out from the mountaintops.

12 Let them give glory to the LORD
and declare his praise in the coasts
and islands.

13 The LORD advances like a warrior;
he stirs up his zeal like a soldier.
He shouts, he roars aloud,
he prevails over his enemies.

14 "I have kept silent from ages past;
I have been quiet and restrained myself.
But now, I will groan like a woman
in labor,
gasping breathlessly.

15 I will lay waste mountains and hills
and dry up all their vegetation.
I will turn rivers into islands

[A]41:29 DSS, Syr read *are nothing*   [B]42:1 DSS read *his justice*   [C]42:6 Or *you by my righteousness*; lit *you in righteousness*
[D]42:10 Lit *their*

42:1–9 A number of songs in the latter half of Isaiah focus on the servant of the Lord (49:1–6; 50:4–6; 52:13–53:12). The identity of the servant is much debated, and most modern commentaries give full lists of options. The context of these verses points in the first instance to Israel or Judah filling the role of the servant. After all, 41:8–9 addresses the nation as the servant. Christian readers recognize that the NT writers (Mt 12:15–21) applied the description of the servant, both here and in the three other songs, to Jesus Christ (CSB). **42:1** God will choose and anoint his servant with the **Spirit**. Such anointing in the OT granted the recipient the ability to perform a divinely given task, in this case to bring justice to the nations. God commissioned Israel with this task beginning with the promises to Abraham that included their being a blessing

to the **nations** (cp. Gn 12:1–3), but it is Jesus who will perform his Father's will perfectly in this regard. Jesus's work of justice included bringing judgment on sinners (Mt 12:15–21; Rv 19:11). **42:2** The servant will not be loud or obnoxious in carrying out his task. He will not cry out in pain. This assumes suffering as part of the servant's future (chap. 53). At Gethsemane Jesus went quietly when arrested (Mt 26:47). Later he quietly bore the crossbeam of his cross a portion of the way as he walked the streets toward his execution site: Golgotha (Jn 19:17). **42:3** The servant's work of bringing justice to the world is also characterized by compassion. The servant will not crush anyone, provided there is even a glimmer of hope in them (**a bruised reed . . . a smoldering wick**).

42:4 The **coasts and islands** refers to the distant nations, so it is a way of referring to all the nations. **42:10–17** This song celebrating God's making all things new through his judgment follows the first "servant song." **42:10** The expression **new song** occurs only in Isaiah, Psalms (Pss 33:3; 40:3; 98:1; 149:1), and Revelation (Rv 5:9; 14:3). With only minor exceptions, "new song" is associated, as here, with the image of God as a warrior. It is the warrior who causes all things to become new through his refining warfare. On **coasts and islands**, see note at 41:1. **42:11 Kedar** refers to a desert-dwelling Arabic tribe, while **Sela** was a major city in Edom, a mountainous region. The two sites thus represent isolated desert and mountain regions. **42:12** On **coasts and islands**, see note at 41:1.

and dry up marshes.
16 I will lead the blind by a way
they did not know;
I will guide them on paths
they have not known.
I will turn darkness to light in front
of them
and rough places into level ground.
This is what I will do for them,
and I will not abandon them.
17 They will be turned back
and utterly ashamed —
those who trust in an idol
and say to a cast image,
'You are our gods!'

Israel's Blindness and Deafness
18 "Listen, you deaf!
Look, you blind, so that you may see.
19 Who is blind but my servant,
or deaf like my messenger I am sending?
Who is blind like my dedicated one,^A
or blind like the servant of the LORD?
20 Though seeing many things,^B
you pay no attention.
Though his ears are open,
he does not listen."

21 Because of his righteousness, the LORD
was pleased
to magnify his instruction
and make it glorious.
22 But this is a people plundered
and looted,
all of them trapped in holes
or imprisoned in dungeons.
They have become plunder
with no one to rescue them
and loot, with no one saying,
"Give it back!"
23 Who among you will hear this?
Let him listen and obey in the future.
24 Who gave Jacob to the robber,^C
and Israel to the plunderers?
Was it not the LORD?
Have we not sinned against him?
They were not willing to walk
in his ways,

and they would not listen
to his instruction.
25 So he poured out his furious anger
and the power of war on Jacob.
It surrounded him with fire,
but he did not know it;
it burned him, but he didn't take it to
heart.

Restoration of Israel
43 Now this is what the LORD says —
the one who created you, Jacob,
and the one who formed you, Israel —
"Do not fear, for I have redeemed you;
I have called you by your name;
you are mine.
2 When you pass through the waters,
I will be with you,
and the rivers will not overwhelm you.
When you walk through the fire,
you will not be scorched,
and the flame will not burn you.
3 For I am the LORD your God,
the Holy One of Israel, and your Savior.
I have given Egypt as a ransom for you,
Cush and Seba in your place.
4 Because you are precious in my sight
and honored, and I love you,
I will give people in exchange for you
and nations instead of your life.
5 Do not fear, for I am with you;
I will bring your descendants
from the east,
and gather you from the west.
6 I will say to the north, 'Give them up!'
and to the south,
'Do not hold them back!'
Bring my sons from far away,
and my daughters from the ends
of the earth —
7 everyone who bears my name
and is created for my glory.
I have formed them;
indeed, I have made them."

8 Bring out a people who are blind,
yet have eyes,
and are deaf, yet have ears.

---

^A 42:19 Hb obscure ^B 42:20 Alt Hb tradition reads *You see many things;* ^C 42:24 Lit *to loot*

42:18–25 The chapter ends with a pronouncement that explains why God's people will experience judgment before they receive the deliverance described in the previous hymn (vv. 10–17).
42:18–20 God describes his **servant** Israel as **blind** and **deaf**. These physical disabilities represent spiritual disabilities; they don't perceive God's guidance.
42:22 The reference to **holes** is to makeshift prisons, similar to the cistern in which Jeremiah was held (Jr 38).
43:1 Calling a person by **name** indicates a high level of familiarity. The intention of this pronouncement is expressed clearly at

the start (**Do not fear**; see also 43:5). God informed his people about their coming deliverance to keep them from caving in to fear.
43:2 The **waters** can be naturally dangerous just like the **fire** mentioned in the second half of the verse. However, the waters in particular can stand for the forces of chaos and evil (Dn 7:1–9) or some kind of personal duress (Ps 69:1–3).
43:3–4 God's people are so **precious** that he is willing to save them at the price (**ransom**) of **Egypt** . . . **Cush**, and **Seba**. The land of Cush was south of Egypt, on the upper (southern) portion of the Nile River, roughly identical to modern Ethiopia. Seba's location

is unknown. Some scholars take this as a reference to the fact that while King Cyrus of Persia decreed the restoration of Judah, his successors went on to attack Egypt and Cush. Indeed, God is willing to give much more than these three countries in place of his people.
43:5–6 God will **gather** his people from all over the world, **east** and **west** . . . **north** and **south**. The reference is to the restoration from the exile. The returns under Sheshbazzar and Zerubbabel as well as the later returns under Ezra and Nehemiah show that the Lord kept his promise.

⁹ All the nations are gathered together,
    and the peoples are assembled.
Who among them can declare this,
    and tell us the former things?
Let them present their witnesses
    to vindicate themselves,
so that people may hear and say,
    "It is true."
¹⁰ "You are my witnesses" —
        this is the LORD's declaration —
    "and my servant whom I have chosen,
so that you may know and believe me
    and understand that I am he.
No god was formed before me,
    and there will be none after me.
¹¹ I — I am the LORD.
    Besides me, there is no Savior.
¹² I alone declared, saved,
        and proclaimed —
    and not some foreign godᴬ among you.
So you are my witnesses" —
        this is the LORD's declaration —
    "andᴮ I am God.
¹³ Also, from today on I am he alone,
    and none can rescue from my power.
I act, and who can reverse it?"

God's Deliverance of Rebellious Israel

¹⁴ This is what the LORD, your Redeemer, the
Holy One of Israel says:
    Because of you, I will send an armyᶜ
        to Babylon
    and bring all of them as fugitives,ᴰ
    even the Chaldeans in the ships
        in which they rejoice.ᴱ
¹⁵ I am the LORD, your Holy One,
    the Creator of Israel, your King.

¹⁶ This is what the LORD says —
    who makes a way in the sea,
    and a path through raging water,
¹⁷ who brings out the chariot and horse,
    the army and the mighty one together
    (they lie down, they do not rise again;
    they are extinguished, put out
        like a wick) —
¹⁸ "Do not remember the past events;
    pay no attention to things of old.
¹⁹ Look, I am about to do something new;
    even now it is coming. Do you not see it?

Indeed, I will make a way
        in the wilderness,
    riversᶠ in the desert.
²⁰ Wild animals —
    jackals and ostriches — will honor me,
    because I provide water
        in the wilderness,
    and rivers in the desert,
    to give drink to my chosen people.
²¹ The people I formed for myself
    will declare my praise.

²² "But, Jacob, you have not called on me,
    because, Israel, you have become weary
        of me.
²³ You have not brought me your sheep
        for burnt offerings
    or honored me with your sacrifices.
I have not burdened you with offerings
    or wearied you with incense.ᴳ
²⁴ You have not bought me aromatic cane
        with silver,
    or satisfied me with the fat
        of your sacrifices.
But you have burdened me
    with your sins;
you have wearied me
    with your iniquities.

²⁵ "I am the one, I sweep away
        your transgressions
    for my own sake
    and remember your sins no more.
²⁶ Remind me. Let's argue
        the case together.
Recount the facts, so that you may
    be vindicated.
²⁷ Your first father sinned,
    and your mediators have rebelled
        against me.
²⁸ So I defiled the officers of the sanctuary,
    and set Jacob apart for destruction
    and Israel for scorn.

Spiritual Blessing

4️⃣4️⃣ "And now listen, Jacob my servant,
        Israel whom I have chosen.
² This is the word of the LORD
    your Maker, the one who formed you
        from the womb:

ᴬ43:12 Lit *not a foreigner* ᴮ43:12 Or *that* ᶜ43:14 *an army* supplied for clarity ᴰ43:14 Or *will break down all their bars*
ᴱ43:14 Hb obscure ᶠ43:19 DSS read *paths* ᴳ43:23 I.e., with demands for offerings and incense

---

43:14 Chaldeans were an Aramaic-speaking tribe of Babylon that rose up in the seventh century BC to lead the charge against Assyria, thus establishing the Neo-Babylonian Empire. The Chaldean tribe's home base was at the point where the Tigris and Euphrates rivers emptied into what is today called the Persian Gulf. Thus shipping was very important to them.
43:18–19 The exodus poetically described in vv. 16–17 is described as **past events**, the **things of old**. But God turns the

hearers' attention to **something new**, a new exodus. This time God will create not "a way in the sea" (v. 16), but **a way in the wilderness**. This future deliverance is pictured as a reversal of nature, with **rivers in the desert**.
43:25 The people sinned, but God forgave. The idea of removal of sin is communicated by the action of sweeping as well as the mental act of forgetting. To remember something is to act on it, and to forget is to hold back from acting.

43:26–28 Once again a court setting is introduced. God challenged his people to **argue** their **case** against him. The reference to Israel's **first father** is likely Jacob, whose name was changed to Israel. Jacob was well known for his foolish and sinful ways (Hs 12:1–6).
44:2–3 The phrase **formed you from the womb** evokes the metaphor of God as the mother who gave birth to Israel. **Jeshurun** is used as a name for Israel (Dt 32:15; 33:5,26) in contexts that indicate it is a term of endearment. It is obscure in meaning but may

He will help you.
Do not fear, Jacob my servant,
Jeshurun^A whom I have chosen.
³ For I will pour water on the thirsty land
and streams on the dry ground;
I will pour out my Spirit
on your descendants
and my blessing on your offspring.
⁴ They will sprout among^B the grass
like poplars by flowing streams.
⁵ This one will say, 'I am the LORD's';
another will use the name of Jacob;
still another will write on his hand,
'The LORD's,'
and take on the name of Israel."

No God Other Than the LORD

⁶ This is what the LORD, the King of Israel and
its Redeemer, the LORD of Armies, says:
I am the first and I am the last.
There is no God but me.
⁷ Who, like me, can announce the future?
Let him say so and make a case
before me,
since I have established
an ancient people.
Let these gods declare^C
the coming things,
and what will take place.
⁸ Do not be startled or afraid.
Have I not told you and declared it
long ago?
You are my witnesses!
Is there any God but me?
There is no other Rock;
I do not know any.

⁹ All who make idols are nothing,
and what they treasure benefits no one.
Their witnesses do not see
or know anything,
so they will be put to shame.
¹⁰ Who makes a god or casts a metal image
that benefits no one?
¹¹ Look, all its worshipers will be
put to shame,
and the craftsmen are humans.
They all will assemble and stand;
they all will be startled
and put to shame.

¹² The ironworker labors over the coals,
shapes the idol with hammers,

and works it with his strong arm.
Also he grows hungry
and his strength fails;
he doesn't drink water and is faint.
¹³ The woodworker stretches out
a measuring line,
he outlines it with a stylus;
he shapes it with chisels
and outlines it with a compass.
He makes it according to a human form,
like a beautiful person,
to dwell in a temple.
¹⁴ He cuts down^D cedars for his use,
or he takes a cypress or an oak.
He lets it grow strong among the trees
of the forest.
He plants a laurel, and the rain
makes it grow.
¹⁵ A person can use it for fuel.
He takes some of it and warms himself;
also he kindles a fire and bakes bread;
he even makes it into a god
and worships it;
he makes an idol from it and bows down
to it.
¹⁶ He burns half of it in a fire,
and he roasts meat on that half.
He eats the roast and is satisfied.
He warms himself and says, "Ah!
I am warm, I see the blaze."
¹⁷ He makes a god or his idol with the rest
of it.
He bows down to it and worships;
he prays to it, "Save me, for you are
my god."
¹⁸ Such people^E do not comprehend
and cannot understand,
for he has shut their eyes^F
so they cannot see,
and their minds
so they cannot understand.
¹⁹ No one comes to his senses;^G
no one has the perception or insight
to say,
"I burned half of it in the fire,
I also baked bread on its coals,
I roasted meat and ate.
Should I make something detestable
with the rest of it?
Should I bow down to a block of wood?"
²⁰ He feeds on^H ashes.
His deceived mind has led him astray,
and he cannot rescue himself,

^A44:2 = Upright One   ^B44:4 Some Hb mss, DSS, LXX read *as among*   ^C44:7 Lit *declare them* —   ^D44:14 Lit *To cut down for himself*   ^E44:18 Lit *They*   ^F44:18 Or *for their eyes are shut*   ^G44:19 Lit *No one returns to his heart*   ^H44:20 Or *He shepherds*

be related to the Hebrew word *yashar,* which means "virtuous." The theme of turning dry land into fertile land is an image of physical and/or spiritual transformation. The results are growth, in this case among the **descendants** of the people of God.
44:5 Writing on one's **hand** signified intimacy, though some believe it refers to a slave

mark showing ownership. In either case, the idea is that people will want to identify and align themselves with the Lord.
44:6 A long argument against idols (vv. 6–23) begins with an assertion of the uniqueness of God. The words **I am the first and I am the last** are used of Christ in Rv 1:17; 2:8; 21:6; 22:13.

44:8 The invocation of **witnesses** places this passage in a courtroom setting. These witnesses will bear testimony to the fact that only the Lord is a **Rock**—a place of protection and stability—unlike the false gods of the nations.

or say, "Isn't there a lie
    in my right hand?"

21 Remember these things, Jacob,
    and Israel, for you are my servant;
    I formed you, you are my servant;
    Israel, you will never be forgotten
      by me.^A
22 I have swept away your transgressions
    like a cloud,
    and your sins like a mist.
    Return to me,
    for I have redeemed you.
23 Rejoice, heavens, for the LORD has acted;
    shout, depths of the earth.
    Break out into singing, mountains,
    forest, and every tree in it.
    For the LORD has redeemed Jacob,
    and glorifies himself through Israel.

Restoration of Israel through Cyrus

24 This is what the LORD, your Redeemer who
formed you from the womb, says:
    I am the LORD, who made everything;
    who stretched out the heavens
      by myself;
    who alone spread out the earth;
25 who destroys the omens
    of the false prophets
    and makes fools of diviners;
    who confounds the wise
    and makes their knowledge foolishness;
26 who confirms the message
    of his servant
    and fulfills the counsel
    of his messengers;
    who says to Jerusalem, "She will
      be inhabited,"
    and to the cities of Judah, "They will
      be rebuilt,"
    and I will restore her ruins;
27 who says to the depths of the sea,
    "Be dry,"
    and I will dry up your rivers;
28 who says to Cyrus, "My shepherd,
    he will fulfill all my pleasure"

and says to Jerusalem, "She will
    be rebuilt,"
and of the temple, "Its foundation
    will be laid."

45 The LORD says this to Cyrus,
    his anointed,
    whose right hand I have grasped
    to subdue nations before him
    and disarm^B kings,
    to open doors before him,
    and even city gates will not be shut:
2 "I will go before you
    and level the uneven places;^C
    I will shatter the bronze doors
    and cut the iron bars in two.
3 I will give you the treasures
    of darkness
    and riches from secret places,
    so that you may know that I am the
      LORD.
    I am the God of Israel, who calls you
      by your name.
4 I call you by your name,
    for the sake of my servant Jacob
    and Israel my chosen one.
    I give a name to you,
    though you do not know me.
5 I am the LORD, and there is no other;
    there is no God but me.
    I will strengthen^D you,
    though you do not know me,
6 so that all may know from the rising
    of the sun to its setting
    that there is no one but me.
    I am the LORD, and there is no other.
7 I form light and create darkness,
    I make success and create disaster;
    I am the LORD, who does all these things.

8 "Heavens, sprinkle from above,
    and let the skies shower righteousness.
    Let the earth open up
    so that salvation will sprout
    and righteousness will spring up with it.
    I, the LORD, have created it.

---

^A 44:21 DSS, LXX, Tg read *Israel, do not forget me* ^B 45:1 Lit *unloosen the waist of* ^C 45:2 DSS, LXX read *the mountains*
^D 45:5 Lit *gird*

44:24–28 In these verses God's sovereignty over his creation and the future is asserted. God affirmed his prophets over those prophets who deceived.
44:24 This description demonstrates God's control over the cosmos. He puts it up like a Bedouin erects a tent.
44:25 The type of **prophets** this verse has in mind were diviners, not those who received revelation from God. Diviners manipulated or observed such things as sheep livers, cloud formations, and the stars to determine the future.
44:28 God announced the agent of his rescue of exiled Judah—**Cyrus** the Great. Thus Isaiah, whose ministry spanned four kings whose reigns stretched from 742 to

686 BC, named a ruler who was not yet born. The prophetic reference is to Persia's defeat of Babylon under the leadership of Cyrus in 539 BC, an event that led to permission for the Jews to return to their homeland and rebuild Jerusalem. Cyrus is called a **shepherd**, a common metaphor for a royal figure. The rebuilding of Jerusalem is associated with the rebuilding of the **temple**, a hope that became reality in 515 BC.
45:1–8 In this section, written at least 140 years before it was fulfilled, God speaks to Cyrus and announces how he intends to use him as his agent. The passage divinely commissions Cyrus. There is no reason to believe that Cyrus was conscious of his role as God's

agent of redemption. Indeed, the final lines of vv. 4 and 5 state as much.
45:1 God called Cyrus his **anointed**. The Hebrew word can be rendered "Messiah" in English. In the ancient Near East, when a god **grasped** the **right hand** of someone, it indicated special favor, commissioning, guidance, and divine endowment with skill.
45:3 As Cyrus defeated nations (including Medes, Lydians, and Babylonians), their wealth would come into his possession. These **treasures** were hidden away from the world and thus are associated with **darkness** and considered **secret**.

⁹ "Woe to the one who argues
        with his Maker —
    one clay pot among many.^A
    Does clay say to the one forming it,
    'What are you making?'
    Or does your work say,
    'He has no hands'?^B
¹⁰ Woe to the one who says to his father,
    'What are you fathering?'
    or to his mother,^C
    'What are you giving birth to?'"
¹¹ This is what the LORD,
        the Holy One of Israel
        and its Maker, says:
    "Ask me what is to happen to^D my sons,
    and instruct me about the work
        of my hands.
¹² I made the earth,
        and created humans on it.
    It was my hands that stretched out
        the heavens,
    and I commanded everything in them.
¹³ I have stirred him up in righteousness,
    and will level all roads for him.
    He will rebuild my city,
    and set my exiles free,
    not for a price or a bribe,"
    says the LORD of Armies.

God Alone Is the Savior

¹⁴ This is what the LORD says:
    "The products of Egypt
        and the merchandise of Cush
    and the Sabeans, men of stature,
    will come over to you
    and will be yours;
    they will follow you,
    they will come over in chains
    and bow down to you.
    They will confess^E to you,
    'God is indeed with you, and there is
        no other;
    there is no other God.'"

¹⁵ Yes, you are a God who hides,
    God of Israel, Savior.
¹⁶ All of them are put to shame,
        even humiliated;
    the makers of idols
        go in humiliation together.
¹⁷ Israel will be saved by the LORD
    with an everlasting salvation;

    you will not be put to shame
        or humiliated
    for all eternity.

¹⁸ For this is what the LORD says —
        the Creator of the heavens,
    the God who formed the earth
        and made it,
    the one who established it
    (he did not create it to be a wasteland,
    but formed it to be inhabited) —
    he says, "I am the LORD,
        and there is no other.
¹⁹ I have not spoken in secret,
    somewhere in a land of darkness.
    I did not say to the descendants
        of Jacob:
    Seek me in a wasteland.
    I am the LORD, who speaks righteously,
    who declares what is right.

²⁰ "Come, gather together,
    and approach, you fugitives
        of the nations.
    Those who carry their wooden idols
    and pray to a god who cannot save
    have no knowledge.
²¹ Speak up and present your case^F —
    yes, let them consult each other.
    Who predicted this long ago?
    Who announced it
        from ancient times?
    Was it not I, the LORD?
    There is no other God but me,
    a righteous God and Savior;
    there is no one except me.
²² Turn to me and be saved,
    all the ends of the earth.
    For I am God,
        and there is no other.
²³ By myself I have sworn;
    truth has gone from my mouth,
    a word that will not be revoked:
    Every knee will bow to me,
    every tongue will swear allegiance.
²⁴ It will be said about me, 'Righteousness
        and strength
    are found only in the LORD.'"
    All who are enraged against him
    will come to him and be put to shame.
²⁵ All the descendants of Israel
    will be justified and boast in the LORD.

---

^A45:9 Lit *a clay pot with clay pots of the ground*   ^B45:9 Or *making? Your work has no hands.*   ^C45:10 Lit *to a woman*
^D45:11 Or *me the coming things about*   ^E45:14 Lit *pray*   ^F45:21 Lit *and approach*

45:9–13 The woe oracle in these verses responds to those who would argue with God for using a pagan king like Cyrus to accomplish his purposes.
45:9 On **woe** oracles, see notes at 1:4; 5:8–30. Humans are the **pot** and God is the potter. This image reminds humans of their proper place in relationship to God.

45:10 The second metaphor of God as parent (**father** and **mother**) and his human creation as the child also expresses an unbalanced power relationship. A baby does not question his birth any more than a pot questions its creation. So why should Israel question God's plan?
45:11 On **Holy One of Israel**, see note at 1:4.
45:13 The one **stirred ... up** is Cyrus.

45:14 Egypt and **Cush** (Ethiopia; see note at 18:1–7) were nations associated with the Nile Valley. The **Sabeans** were an Arabian tribe.
45:21 The challenge to **speak up and present your case** indicates that this passage has a legal background. The issue involves the gods' ability to reveal the future.
45:23 Paul quotes this verse in Rm 14:11.

There Is No One Like God

46

Bel crouches; Nebo cowers.
Idols depicting them are consigned
   to beasts and cattle.
The images you carry are loaded,
   as a burden for the weary animal.

2 The gods cower; they crouch together;
   they are not able to rescue the burden,
   but they themselves go into captivity.

3 "Listen to me, house of Jacob,
   all the remnant of the house of Israel,
   who have been sustained
      from the womb,
   carried along since birth.

4 I will be the same until your old age,
   and I will bear you up when you
      turn gray.
   I have made you, and I will carry you;
   I will bear and rescue you.

5 "To whom will you compare me
   or make me equal?
Who will you measure me with,
   so that we should be like each other?

6 Those who pour out their bags of gold
   and weigh out silver on scales —
   they hire a goldsmith and he makes it
      into a god.
Then they kneel and bow down to it.

7 They lift it to their shoulder
   and bear it along;
they set it in its place, and there
   it stands;
it does not budge from its place.
They cry out to it but it doesn't answer;
   it saves no one from his trouble.

8 "Remember this and be brave;^A
   take it to heart, you transgressors!

9 Remember what happened long ago,
   for I am God, and there is no other;
   I am God, and no one is like me.

10 I declare the end from the beginning,
   and from long ago what is not yet done,
   saying: my plan will take place,

and I will do all my will.

11 I call a bird of prey^B from the east,
   a man for my purpose
      from a far country.
Yes, I have spoken; so I will also
   bring it about.
I have planned it; I will also do it.

12 Listen to me, you hardhearted,
   far removed from justice:

13 I am bringing my justice near;
   it is not far away,
   and my salvation will not delay.
I will put salvation in Zion,
   my splendor in Israel.

The Fall of Babylon

47

"Go down and sit in the dust,
   Virgin Daughter Babylon.
Sit on the ground without a throne,
   Daughter Chaldea!
For you will no longer be called
   pampered and spoiled.

2 Take millstones and grind flour;
   remove your veil,
strip off your skirt, bare your thigh,
   wade through the streams.

3 Your nakedness will be uncovered,
   and your disgrace will be exposed.
I will take vengeance;
   I will spare no one."^A

4 The Holy One of Israel is our Redeemer;
   The Lord of Armies is his name.

5 "Daughter Chaldea,
   sit in silence and go into darkness.
For you will no longer be called mistress
   of kingdoms.

6 I was angry with my people;
   I profaned my possession,
   and I handed them over to you.
You showed them no mercy;
   you made your yoke very heavy
      on the elderly.

7 You said, 'I will be the queen forever.'
You did not take these things to heart
   or think about their outcome.

^A46:8; 47:3 Hb obscure   ^B46:11 = Cyrus

46:1 Bel means "lord" and is likely a reference to Marduk, the chief god of Babylon. **Nebo** is the Hebrew name for Nabu, Marduk's son and an important deity in his own right. Nabu was the god of wisdom, the god of the scribes. These gods, or more precisely the idols that represented them, had to be carried on carts to move from one place to another. They were a heavy burden for the draft animals that carried them.
46:2 When one ancient Near Eastern power defeated another, they would carry off the idols of the vanquished nation.
46:3–4 The **remnant** were those Israelites who would survive the coming judgment.
46:8–9 To **remember** means to draw strength by contemplating God's past acts of power.

46:10–11 Cyrus—the king of Persia (45:1), a country **east** of Israel—was the **bird of prey**. This is the theme of the prediction. The Lord demonstrates his sovereignty by declaring **the end from the beginning.**
46:12–13 The **hardhearted** here are the same as the "transgressors" in v. 8. They are Israelites who refuse to trust the Lord for deliverance.
47:1 To **sit in the dust**, just like sitting on the **ground**, was a sign of subservience and humiliation. Babylon, the mighty nation that achieved special status among the other nations of the world (**pampered and spoiled**), will be put in a position of shame. Up to this point in the book, God's people have been called **daughter** by the Lord (1:8; 3:16; 37:22). In this passage not

only is Babylon given this title of intimacy, but it is qualified by **virgin**, indicating purity as well as dependence on the father, or God. However, here "virgin" is sarcastic. **Chaldea** refers to the Aramaic-speaking tribe of the southern marsh region of Babylon that came to dominate the entire nation during the Neo-Babylonian period (626–586 BC).
47:2–3 Babylon, personified as a young woman, will do her lowly chores—in contrast to her former exalted status—and then will **strip** to cross a stream. As she does so, her **disgrace** (her promiscuity that contradicted her apparent virginity) will be exposed.
47:4 On **Holy One of Israel**, see notes at 1:4; 30:10–11.

8 "So now hear this, lover of luxury,
    who sits securely,
who says to herself,
    'I am, and there is no one else.
I will never be a widow
    or know the loss of children.'
9 These two things will happen to you
    suddenly, in one day:
    loss of children and widowhood.
They will happen to you
        in their entirety,
in spite of your many sorceries
    and the potency of your spells.
10 You were secure in your wickedness;
    you said, 'No one sees me.'
Your wisdom and knowledge
    led you astray.
You said to yourself,
    'I am, and there is no one else.'
11 But disaster will happen to you;
    you will not know how to avert it.
And it will fall on you,
    but you will be unable to ward it off.^
Devastation will happen to you suddenly
    and unexpectedly.
12 So take your stand with your spells
    and your many sorceries,
    which you have wearied yourself with
        from your youth.
Perhaps you will be able to succeed;
    perhaps you will inspire terror!
13 You are worn out
    with your many consultations.
So let the astrologers stand
    and save you —
    those who observe the stars,
    those who predict monthly
    what will happen to you.
14 Look, they are like stubble;
    fire burns them.
They cannot rescue themselves
    from the power of the flame.
This is not a coal
    for warming themselves,
    or a fire to sit beside!
15 This is what they are to you —
    those who have wearied you
    and have traded with you
        from your youth —
    each wanders on his own way;
    no one can save you.

Israel Must Leave Babylon

48 "Listen to this, house of Jacob —
    those who are called
    by the name Israel
    and have descended from^ Judah,
    who swear by the name of the Lord
    and declare the God of Israel,
    but not in truth or righteousness.
2 For they are named after the holy city,
    and lean on the God of Israel;
    his name is the Lord of Armies.
3 I declared the past events long ago;
    they came out of my mouth;
        I proclaimed them.
Suddenly I acted, and they occurred.
4 Because I know that you are stubborn,
    and your neck is iron^
    and your forehead bronze,
5 therefore I declared to you long ago.
I announced it to you
        before it occurred,
so you could not claim, 'My idol
        caused them;
    my carved image and cast idol
        control them.'
6 You have heard it. Observe it all.
    Will you not acknowledge it?
From now on I will announce
        new things to you,
    hidden things that you have not known.
7 They have been created now, and not
        long ago;
    you have not heard of them
        before today,
    so you could not claim, 'I already
        knew them!'
8 You have never heard; you have
        never known;
    for a long time your ears have not
        been open.
For I knew that you
        were very treacherous,
    and were known as a rebel
        from birth.
9 I will delay my anger for the sake
        of my name,
    and I will restrain myself
        for your benefit and for my praise,
    so that you will not be destroyed.
10 Look, I have refined you, but not
        as silver;

---

^47:11 Or to atone for it   ^48:1 Lit have come from the waters of   ^48:4 Lit is an iron sinew

---

47:8–9 Babylon is personified as a woman consistently in this chapter. Before she was the "Virgin Daughter," but in these verses she is a woman who is blessed with marriage and **children**. The future judgment of Babylon is compared to a woman who will lose husband and children in **one day**. A woman without husband and children had no value and no protection in ancient times. This disaster will befall Babylon even though she was a sorceress.

47:12–13 Babylonian culture was known for its infatuation with **sorceries** and **spells**, which represented a way to manipulate the gods. In particular, Babylon was known for attempts to determine the future by consulting the stars. Indeed, even after Babylon disappeared as an empire, the term "Chaldean" was used to designate **astrologers**.
48:4 Nothing can get through a **bronze** forehead. An **neck** of **iron** is stiff and cannot

turn around. This imagery shows the refusal of God's people to hear him or to repent.
48:6–7 Up to this point God has been announcing judgment, but now he will announce **new things**—a message of grace after the judgment. The new things include God's use of Cyrus to deliver his people (vv. 14–15).
48:8 "To hear" means more than just listening; it implies acting on what is heard.
48:10 Pure **silver** is made by subjecting ore to high temperatures and removing the

I have tested^A you in the furnace
   of affliction.
11 I will act for my own sake,
   indeed, my own,
for how can I^B be defiled?
I will not give my glory to another.

12 "Listen to me, Jacob,
   and Israel, the one called by me:
I am he; I am the first,
   I am also the last.
13 My own hand founded the earth,
   and my right hand spread out
    the heavens;
when I summoned them,
   they stood up together.
14 All of you, assemble and listen!
Who among the idols^C has declared
   these things?
The LORD loves him;^D
he will accomplish his will
   against Babylon,
and his arm will be against
   the Chaldeans.
15 I — I have spoken;
   yes, I have called him;
I have brought him,
and he will succeed in his mission.
16 Approach me and listen to this.
From the beginning I have not spoken
   in secret;
from the time anything existed,
   I was there."
And now the Lord GOD
   has sent me and his Spirit.

17 This is what the LORD, your Redeemer, the
Holy One of Israel says:
I am the LORD your God,
who teaches you for your benefit,
who leads you in the way
   you should go.
18 If only you had paid attention
   to my commands.
Then your peace would have been
   like a river,
and your righteousness like the waves
   of the sea.

19 Your descendants would have been
   as countless as the sand,
and the offspring of your body
   like its grains;
their name would not be cut off
   or eliminated from my presence.

20 Leave Babylon,
flee from the Chaldeans!
Declare with a shout of joy,
   proclaim this,
let it go out to the end of the earth;
announce,
   "The LORD has redeemed
    his servant Jacob!"
21 They did not thirst
when he led them through the deserts;
he made water flow from the rock
   for them;
he split the rock, and water gushed out.
22 "There is no peace for the wicked,"
   says the LORD.

The Servant Brings Salvation

49 Coasts and islands,^E listen to me;
   distant peoples, pay attention.
The LORD called me before I was born.
He named me while I was
   in my mother's womb.
2 He made my words like a sharp sword;
he hid me in the shadow of his hand.
He made me like a sharpened arrow;
he hid me in his quiver.
3 He said to me, "You are my servant,
Israel, in whom I will be glorified."
4 But I myself said: I have labored in vain,
I have spent my strength for nothing
   and futility;
yet my vindication is with the LORD,
and my reward is with my God.
5 And now, says the LORD,
who formed me from the womb to be
   his servant,
to bring Jacob back to him
so that Israel might be gathered to him;
for I am honored in the sight
   of the LORD,
and my God is my strength —

^A48:10 DSS; MT reads *chosen*   ^B48:11 DSS, Syr; MT reads *it*   ^C48:14 Lit *among them*   ^D48:14 = Cyrus   ^E49:1 Or *Islands*

impurities. The image of refining is often used in the Bible to refer to removing sin from a person or a community (1:22), in this case, through **affliction**.
48:14–15 The one whom the Lord **loves** is Cyrus (44:24–45:8)—the pagan king of Persia whom the Lord will use to deliver his people from the Babylonians. On **Chaldeans**, see note at 13:19.
48:17–18 On **Holy One of Israel**, see note at 1:4.
48:19 The allusion to **sand** goes back to the patriarchal promise that Abraham would have numerous descendants (Gn 22:17; 32:12; 41:49). It was Israel's sin that led to a reduction of the population.

48:20–22 The chapter ends with a divine directive to **leave Babylon**. The assumption is that the people should do this after the work of God's Messiah, in this case Cyrus (see note at 45:1).
48:20 On **Chaldeans**, see note at 13:19.
49:1 Coasts and islands (see note at 41:1) refers to the distant places of the earth. The servant began by recounting his calling that began even before he was born.
49:2 The servant was made to be a weapon in the arsenal of God the warrior to wage war against the chaos of the world.
49:3 The **servant** is identified as **Israel**. As in 42:1–9 (see note there, as well as note at

42:1), the more precise identification is the purified remnant within Israel (an alternative idea views the servant as Isaiah himself). However, as with all the servant songs, the NT authors recognized a second and deeper identification of the servant as they associated these texts with Jesus Christ (Mt 8:17; 12:17–21; Jn 12:38; Ac 8:30–35).
49:5 In v. 3 the **servant** identified himself as Israel; here the servant speaks as if he is the agent of Israel's restoration. This seeming inconsistency is resolved once it is realized that it is the remnant, and ultimately the remnant of one—Jesus—who functions in this way (see note at 42:1).

6 he says,
"It is not enough for you to be
my servant
raising up the tribes of Jacob
and restoring the protected ones
of Israel.
I will also make you a light
for the nations,
to be my salvation to the ends
of the earth."
7 This is what the LORD,
the Redeemer of Israel,
his Holy One, says
to one who is despised,
to one abhorred by people,[A]
to a servant of rulers:
"Kings will see, princes will stand up,
and they[B] will all bow down
because of the LORD, who is faithful,
the Holy One of Israel
— and he has chosen you."

8 This is what the LORD says:
I will answer you in a time of favor,
and I will help you in the day
of salvation.
I will keep you, and I will appoint you
to be a covenant for the people,
to restore the land,
to make them possess
the desolate inheritances,
9 saying to the prisoners, "Come out,"
and to those who are in darkness,
"Show yourselves."
They will feed along the pathways,
and their pastures will be on all
the barren heights.
10 They will not hunger or thirst,
the scorching heat or sun will not
strike them;
for their compassionate one
will guide them,
and lead them to springs.
11 I will make all my mountains
into a road,
and my highways will be raised up.
12 See, these will come
from far away,
from the north and from the west,[C]
and from the land of Sinim.[D,E]

13 Shout for joy, you heavens!
Earth, rejoice!
Mountains break into joyful shouts!
For the LORD has comforted his people,
and will have compassion
on his afflicted ones.

Zion Remembered

14 Zion says, "The LORD
has abandoned me;
the Lord has forgotten me!"
15 "Can a woman forget
her nursing child,
or lack compassion for the child
of her womb?
Even if these forget,
yet I will not forget you.
16 Look, I have inscribed you on the palms
of my hands;
your walls are continually before me.
17 Your builders[F] hurry;
those who destroy and devastate you
will leave you.
18 Look up, and look around.
They all gather together; they come
to you.
As I live" —
this is the LORD's declaration —
"you will wear all your children[G]
as jewelry,
and put them on as a bride does.
19 For your waste and desolate places
and your land marked by ruins
will now be indeed too small
for the inhabitants,
and those who swallowed you up will be
far away.
20 Yet as you listen, the children
that you have been deprived of will say,
'This place is too small for me;
make room for me so that I may settle.'
21 Then you will say within yourself,
'Who fathered these for me?
I was deprived of my children
and unable to conceive,
exiled and wandering —
but who brought them up?
See, I was left by myself —
but these, where did they
come from?'"[H]

[A]49:7 Or by the nation [B]49:7 Lit princes and they [C]49:12 Lit sea [D]49:12 DSS read of the Syenites [E]49:12 Perhaps modern Aswan in southern Egypt [F]49:17 DSS, Aq, Theod, Vg; MT, Syr, Sym read sons [G]49:18 Lit all of them [H]49:21 Lit where are they

---

49:6 The servant will do more than restore Israel to its former glory. He will serve as an agent of **salvation** to the **nations**, thus fulfilling the divine promise to Abraham that through his descendants God would be a blessing to "all the peoples on earth" (Gn 12:3). Paul and Barnabas quote these words in Ac 13:47. **49:8** Here the emphasis is on the promise of the **land**. God will restore his people to the land he gave them and which they forfeited. Paul quotes this verse in 2Co 6:2.

49:11–12 Sinim is typically associated with modern Aswan, postexilic Elephantine in Egypt. **49:13** Isaiah began with a pronouncement calling on **heavens** and **earth** to serve as witnesses to testify that God's people deserved their punishment (1:2); now they rejoice in their restoration. **49:16** To inscribe something on one's **hands** (tattooing perhaps) placed the writing on a bodily location that would be readily seen. In

particular the defensive **walls** of Jerusalem were a concern of the Lord. **49:17** Those who will build will hurry home to Judah. The word for **builders** is from the Dead Sea Scroll. The Masoretic text here reads "sons." **49:18** The picture of Zion wearing her children like wedding **jewelry** suggests that the passage understood God to be her husband. The returned **children** were a wedding gift.

²² This is what the Lord God says:
Look, I will lift up my hand
   to the nations,
and raise my banner to the peoples.
They will bring your sons in their arms,
and your daughters will be carried
   on their shoulders.

²³ Kings will be your guardians
and their queens^A your nursing mothers.
They will bow down to you
with their faces to the ground
and lick the dust at your feet.
Then you will know that I am the Lord;
those who put their hope in me
will not be put to shame.

²⁴ Can the prey be taken from
   a mighty man,
or the captives of a tyrant^B be delivered?

²⁵ For this is what the Lord says:
"Even the captives of a mighty man
   will be taken,
and the prey of a tyrant will be delivered;
I will contend with the one
   who contends with you,
and I will save your children.

²⁶ I will make your oppressors eat
   their own flesh,
and they will be drunk
   with their own blood
as with sweet wine.
Then all humanity will know
that I, the Lord, am your Savior,
and your Redeemer, the Mighty One
   of Jacob."

50

This is what the Lord says:
Where is your mother's
   divorce certificate
that I used to send her away?
Or to which of my creditors
   did I sell you?
Look, you were sold for your iniquities,
and your mother was sent away
because of your transgressions.

² Why was no one there when I came?
Why was there no one to answer
   when I called?
Is my arm too weak to redeem?
Or do I have no power to rescue?
Look, I dry up the sea by my rebuke;
I turn the rivers into a wilderness;

their fish rot because of lack of water
and die of thirst.

³ I dress the heavens in black
and make sackcloth their covering.

The Obedient Servant

⁴ The Lord God has given me
the tongue of those who are instructed
to know how to sustain the weary
   with a word.
He awakens me each morning;
he awakens my ear to listen like those
   being instructed.

⁵ The Lord God has opened my ear,
and I was not rebellious;
I did not turn back.

⁶ I gave my back to those who beat me,
and my cheeks to those who tore out
   my beard.
I did not hide my face from scorn
   and spitting.

⁷ The Lord God will help me;
therefore I have not been humiliated;
therefore I have set my face like flint,
and I know I will not be put to shame.

⁸ The one who vindicates me is near;
who will contend with me?
Let us confront each other.^C
Who has a case against me?^D
Let him come near me!

⁹ In truth, the Lord God will help me;
who will condemn me?
Indeed, all of them will wear out
   like a garment;
a moth will devour them.

¹⁰ Who among you fears the Lord
and listens to his servant?
Who among you walks in darkness,
and has no light?
Let him trust in the name of the Lord;
let him lean on his God.

¹¹ Look, all you who kindle a fire,
who encircle yourselves with^E torches;
walk in the light of your fire
and of the torches you have lit!
This is what you'll get from my hand:
you will lie down in a place of torment.

Salvation for Zion

51

Listen to me, you
   who pursue righteousness,
you who seek the Lord:

---

^A 49:23 Lit *princesses*   ^B 49:24 DSS, Syr, Vg; MT reads *a righteous man*   ^C 50:8 Lit *us stand*   ^D 50:8 Lit *Who is lord of my judgment*   ^E 50:11 Syr reads *who set ablaze*

49:22–23 The deportation that began the exile saw the people of God dragged off in chains by foreign armies. The picture of the return views the **nations** carrying them back to their land and showing subservience. **50:1** God put away Zion but did not divorce her (there is no **divorce certificate**; Dt 24:1– 4). God sold his children, but not to settle a

debt (so there are no **creditors**). Why did he do it? Because of their sins. **50:3 Sackcloth** was a rough material, irritating to the skin, worn as part of mourning rites. The **heavens** mourned because of God's acts of judgment. **50:4–5** The first-person speaker (**me**) is the servant (v. 10). The servant ultimately is identified with Christ, though the original

audience probably identified the servant as purified Israel (see note at 42:1–9). Alternatively, a number of scholars identify the servant in this poem as Isaiah. **50:6–7** Allusions to this verse are found in Mt 26:67; 27:30. **51:1–2** Abraham was the **rock** from which the people of God were cut and Sarah the **quarry** from which they were dug. From the

Look to the rock from which
you were cut,
and to the quarry from which
you were dug.

2 Look to Abraham your father,
and to Sarah who gave birth to you.
When I called him, he was only one;
I blessed him and made him many.

3 For the LORD will comfort Zion;
he will comfort all her waste places,
and he will make her wilderness
like Eden,
and her desert like the garden
of the LORD.
Joy and gladness will be found in her,
thanksgiving and melodious song.

4 Pay attention to me, my people,
and listen to me, my nation;
for instruction will come from me,
and my justice for a light
to the nations.
I will bring it about quickly.

5 My righteousness is near,
my salvation appears,
and my arms will bring justice
to the nations.
The coasts and islands will put
their hope in me,
and they will look to my strength.^A

6 Look up to the heavens,
and look at the earth beneath;
for the heavens will vanish like smoke,
the earth will wear out like a garment,
and its inhabitants will die like gnats.^B
But my salvation will last forever,
and my righteousness will never
be shattered.

7 Listen to me, you who
know righteousness,
the people in whose heart is
my instruction:
do not fear disgrace by men,
and do not be shattered by their taunts.

8 For moths will devour them
like a garment,
and worms will eat them like wool.
But my righteousness will last forever,
and my salvation for all generations.

9 Wake up, wake up!
Arm of the LORD, clothe yourself with
strength.
Wake up as in days past,
as in generations long ago.
Wasn't it you who hacked Rahab to pieces,
who pierced the sea monster?

10 Wasn't it you who dried up the sea,
the waters of the great deep,
who made the sea-bed into a road
for the redeemed to pass over?

11 And the ransomed of the LORD will return
and come to Zion with singing,
crowned with unending joy.
Joy and gladness will overtake them,
and sorrow and sighing will flee.

12 I — I am the one who comforts you.
Who are you that you should
fear humans who die,
or a son of man who is given up
like grass?

13 But you have forgotten the LORD,
your Maker,
who stretched out the heavens
and laid the foundations of the earth.
You are in constant dread all day long
because of the fury of the oppressor,
who has set himself to destroy.
But where is the fury of the oppressor?

14 The prisoner^C is soon to be set free;
he will not die and go to the Pit,
and his food will not be lacking.

15 For I am the LORD your God
who stirs up the sea so that
its waves roar —
his name is the LORD of Armies.

16 I have put my words in your mouth,
and covered you in the shadow
of my hand,
in order to plant^D the heavens,
to found the earth,
and to say to Zion, "You are my people."

17 Wake yourself, wake yourself up!
Stand up, Jerusalem,
you who have drunk the cup of his fury
from the LORD's hand;
you who have drunk the goblet
to the dregs —

^A 51:5 Lit *arm* ^B 51:6 Or *die in like manner* ^C 51:14 Hb obscure ^D 51:16 Syr reads *to stretch out*

one man came **many** descendants, according to the promise of the Abrahamic covenant (Gn 12:1–3).
51:4–5 The **coasts and islands** represent the distant nations (49:1). Invoking human imply that all the nations of the world will put their **hope** in the Lord.
51:6 From a human perspective the **heavens** and the **earth** look permanent. But God's **salvation** and **righteousness** make even the heavens and the earth appear temporary.
51:9–10 God is encouraged to **wake up** from slumber and go about his redemptive

work (Pss 44:23; 78:65). Past victories are then recounted in the form of the defeat of **Rahab**, a sea monster (see 30:7; Jb 26:12; Ps 89:10). Rahab in other texts clearly stands for Egypt. Here we have a poetic allusion to God's victory over the Egyptians at the time of the exodus. God, after all, dried up the **sea-bed** and made it a **road** at the Red Sea (Ex 14–15). God's past deliverance of his people from Egyptian bondage bodes well for their future deliverance from Babylonian captivity.
51:14 The word **prisoner** refers to those who were exiled by the Babylonians.

51:18 In the ancient Near East, it was the duty of the children to care for a drunk parent. Noah's son Ham acted in a reprehensible manner when his father was drunk (Gn 9:18–29). Here Jerusalem's children, God's people, did not take hold of her hand when she was drunk after drinking the cup of God's fury.
51:21–23 Once Jerusalem has experienced the full force of God's judgment, once they have drunk of the **cup** of his **fury**, he will take it away and give it to their **tormentors**. Among the latter, Babylon is particularly in mind.

the cup that causes people to stagger.

¹⁸ There is no one to guide her
among all the children she has raised;
there is no one to take hold of her hand
among all the offspring
she has brought up.

¹⁹ These two things have happened to you:
devastation and destruction,
famine and sword.
Who will grieve for you?
How can I^A comfort you?

²⁰ Your children have fainted;
they lie at the head of every street
like an antelope in a net.
They are full of the LORD's fury,
the rebuke of your God.

²¹ So listen to this, suffering
and drunken one — but not with wine.

²² This is what your Lord says —
the LORD, even your God,
who defends his people —
"Look, I have removed from your hand
the cup that causes staggering;
that goblet, the cup of my fury.
You will never drink it again.

²³ I will put it into the hands
of your tormentors,
who said to you,
'Lie down, so we can walk over you.'
You made your back like the ground,
and like a street for those who walk on it.

52 "Wake up, wake up;
put on your strength, Zion!
Put on your beautiful garments,
Jerusalem, the holy city!
For the uncircumcised and the unclean
will no longer enter you.

² Stand up, shake the dust off yourself!
Take your seat, Jerusalem.
Remove the bonds^B from your neck,
captive Daughter Zion."

³ For this is what the LORD says:
"You were sold for nothing,
and you will be redeemed without silver."

⁴ For this is what the Lord GOD says:
"At first my people went down to Egypt
to reside there,
then Assyria oppressed them
without cause.^C

⁵ So now what have I here" —
this is the LORD's declaration —
"that my people are taken away
for nothing?
Its rulers wail" —
this is the LORD's declaration —
"and my name is continually
blasphemed all day long.

⁶ Therefore my people will know my name;
therefore they will know on that day
that I am he who says,
'Here I am.'"

⁷ How beautiful on the mountains
are the feet of the herald,
who proclaims peace,
who brings news of good things,
who proclaims salvation,
who says to Zion, "Your God reigns!"

⁸ The voices of your watchmen —
they lift up their voices,
shouting for joy together;
for every eye will see
when the LORD returns to Zion.

⁹ Be joyful, rejoice together,
you ruins of Jerusalem!
For the LORD has comforted his people;
he has redeemed Jerusalem.

¹⁰ The LORD has displayed his holy arm
in the sight of all the nations;
all the ends of the earth will see
the salvation of our God.

¹¹ Leave, leave, go out from there!
Do not touch anything unclean;

^A51:19 DSS, LXX, Syr, Vg read *you? Who can* ^B52:2 Alt Hb tradition reads *The bonds are removed* ^C52:4 Or *them at last*, or *them for nothing*

52:1 For the third time in this section, the call to **wake up** occurs (51:9,17; see also 50:4). This time it is addressed to Zion, again personified as a woman (49:14–50:4). The description is of a renewed, refreshed, and restored Jerusalem. The city is no longer contaminated by the uncircumcised and the unclean.
52:3 God was so anxious to get rid of sinful Zion that he **sold** her for **nothing**. Since he sold her for nothing, he can now redeem her for nothing.
52:4 The prophecy speaks from a prophetic perspective as if Isaiah were living at the time of the Babylonian captivity. From that time in the future, he looks back on two previous traumatic periods in Israelite history—the exodus from Egypt in the second millennium BC and the Assyrian invasion of the northern kingdom during Isaiah's lifetime (722 BC). The Babylonian captivity dates to 586–539 BC.

52:5–6 God's **people** come to **know** him through this process of punishment and restoration. Paul quotes v. 5 in Rm 2:24.
52:7 In the ancient world, news was carried by a **herald**. In this verse the herald announces the end of hostilities and the fact that **God reigns** as King over his people. Paul quotes this verse in Rm 10:15.
52:8–9 Watchmen were posted on city walls to keep an eye out for attack, or in this case to be the first to witness the return of the Lord to his Holy City, Jerusalem. Their words are recorded in v. 9.
52:10 The **salvation** referred to here is the conspicuous restoration of Jerusalem after it had been reduced to ruins by the Babylonians.
52:11 The priests (**who carry the vessels of the LORD**) are now encouraged to leave, presumably from Babylonian captivity

(48:20–22). Ezekiel 1:5–11 recounts the return of the temple vessels under the leadership

#37 **99 Essential Christian Truths**

CHRIST AS SACRIFICE

There are several signs, symbols, and pointers in the Old Testament that foreshadowed Christ as being the sacrificial Lamb of God who would take away the sins of the world. However, unlike the sacrifices of the Old Testament sacrificial system, which were unable to take away sin, Christ's sacrifice on the cross was able to permanently, once for all, take away sins (Heb 10:1–14).

go out from her, purify yourselves,
you who carry the vessels of the LORD.
12 For you will not leave in a hurry,
and you will not have to take flight;
because the LORD is going before you,
and the God of Israel is your rear guard.

The Servant's Suffering and Exaltation

13 See, my servant[A] will be successful;[B]
he will be raised and lifted up
and greatly exalted.
14 Just as many were appalled at you[c] —
his appearance was so disfigured
that he did not look like a man,
and his form did not resemble
a human being —
15 so he will sprinkle many nations.[D]
Kings will shut their mouths
because of him,
for they will see
what had not been told them,
and they will understand
what they had not heard.

53 Who has believed
what we have heard?[E]
And to whom has the arm of the LORD
been revealed?
2 He grew up before him
like a young plant
and like a root out of dry ground.
He didn't have an impressive form
or majesty that we should look at him,
no appearance that we should
desire him.
3 He was despised and rejected by men,
a man of suffering who knew
what sickness was.
He was like someone
people turned away from;[F]

he was despised, and we didn't
value him.
4 Yet he himself bore our sicknesses,
and he carried our pains;
but we in turn regarded him stricken,
struck down by God, and afflicted.
5 But he was pierced because of
our rebellion,
crushed because of our iniquities;
punishment for our peace was on him,
and we are healed by his wounds.
6 We all went astray like sheep;
we all have turned to our own way;
and the LORD has punished him
for[G] the iniquity of us all.

7 He was oppressed and afflicted,
yet he did not open his mouth.
Like a lamb led to the slaughter
and like a sheep silent
before her shearers,
he did not open his mouth.
8 He was taken away because of
oppression and judgment,
and who considered his fate?[H]
For he was cut off from the land
of the living;
he was struck because of
my people's rebellion.
9 He was assigned a grave
with the wicked,
but he was with a rich man
at his death,
because he had done no violence
and had not spoken deceitfully.

10 Yet the LORD was pleased to crush him
severely.[I]
When[J] you make him a guilt offering,

[A]52:13 Tg adds *the Messiah* [B]52:13 Or *will act wisely* [c]52:14 Some Hb mss, Syr, Tg read *him* [D]52:15 LXX reads *so many nations will marvel at him* [E]53:1 Or *believed our report* [F]53:3 Lit *And like a hiding of faces from him* [G]53:6 Or *has placed on him*; lit *with* [H]53:8 Or *and as for his generation, who considered him?* [I]53:10 Or *him; he made him sick.* [J]53:10 Or *If*

of Sheshbazzar. This pronouncement exhorts the priests not to defile themselves ritually because they are going back to a Zion that is not stained by impurity (Is 52:1). Paul quotes this verse in 2Co 6:17.
52:12 Unlike in the first exodus (Ex 12:11) they will not go out in haste because there will be no one chasing them. The imagery of the **rear guard** is from Jos 6:9; 8:13.
52:13–53:12 See the note at 42:1–9 for the view that the servant in this passage represents the purified remnant of Israel and ultimately the Messiah. The NT authors recognized that the description of a suffering servant, who "bore the sin of many" (53:12), fits Jesus Christ, who died on the cross for the sins of his people. This chapter's description is the most individualistic of all the servant songs in the book of Isaiah, and thus most clearly points to application beyond Israel.
52:13 The poem begins with the end point—the exaltation of the servant (53:11–12). Glory will be the end result of his suffering.

52:15 Much debate surrounds the meaning of the servant sprinkling **many nations**. The main problem is that the verse does not specify what the servant will use to **sprinkle** them. The best guess is that it refers to a ritual act like the sprinkling of blood (Lv 4:6,17; 16:14–15,19; Nm 19:4) or oil (Lv 8:11). The effect of this sprinkling is either to purify or to dedicate to a holy status. Paul quotes this verse in Rm 15:21.
53:1 The **arm of the LORD** refers to his victorious power, ironically revealed through a suffering servant. This verse is quoted in Jn 12:38 and Rm 10:16.
53:2–3 A **young plant** growing up in **dry ground** would be withered, thus providing an appropriate image of the **man of suffering**. Just like a withered plant is uprooted and thrown away, so the suffering servant was **rejected by men**.
53:4–6 For the first time the reader learns that the servant suffered on behalf of others. Even so, people did not recognize it, and he was rejected as one **struck down by God**

for his own supposed sins. Verse 4 is quoted in Mt 8:17.
53:7 Though not suffering for his own sins, the servant suffered silently and willingly. Philip used this passage to tell the Ethiopian eunuch the good news about Jesus, who silently bore his crucifixion (Ac 8:31–35; 1Pt 2:22–23).
53:8 For the first time the passage reveals that the servant's suffering culminated in death.
53:9 The pairing of the wicked with the rich man implies that the wealthy man got his riches by deceit. Jesus was literally buried by a rich man when he was placed in the tomb of Joseph of Arimathea (Mt 27:57–60).
53:10–11 That God was **pleased to crush** the servant sounds mean-spirited, but his pleasure is explained by the fact that the servant's suffering **will justify many**. What seems harsh will turn out to be gracious. The servant's pain, suffering, and death will function like a restitution offering (Lv 5:14–6:7; 7:1–10)—a sacrifice offered when

he will see his seed, he will prolong
     his days,
and by his hand, the Lord's pleasure
     will be accomplished.
11 After his anguish,
he will see light^A^ and be satisfied.
By his knowledge,
my righteous servant will justify many,
and he will carry their iniquities.
12 Therefore I will give him^B^ the many
     as a portion,
and he will receive^C^ the mighty as spoil,
because he willingly submitted to death,
and was counted among the rebels;
yet he bore the sin of many
and interceded for the rebels.

Future Glory for Israel

54 "Rejoice, childless one, who did not
     give birth;
burst into song and shout,
you who have not been in labor!
For the children of the desolate one
     will be more
than the children
     of the married woman,"
says the Lord.
2 "Enlarge the site of your tent,
and let your tent curtains
     be stretched out;
do not hold back;
lengthen your ropes,
and drive your pegs deep.
3 For you will spread out to the right
     and to the left,
and your descendants
     will dispossess nations
and inhabit the desolate cities.

4 "Do not be afraid, for you will not
     be put to shame;
don't be humiliated, for you will not
     be disgraced.
For you will forget the shame
     of your youth,
and you will no longer remember
the disgrace of your widowhood.
5 Indeed, your husband is your Maker —
his name is the Lord of Armies —

and the Holy One of Israel is
     your Redeemer;
he is called the God of the whole earth.
6 For the Lord has called you,
like a wife deserted and wounded
     in spirit,
a wife of one's youth
     when she is rejected,"
says your God.
7 "I deserted you for a brief moment,
but I will take you back
     with abundant compassion.
8 In a surge of anger
I hid my face from you for a moment,
but I will have compassion on you
with everlasting love,"
says the Lord your Redeemer.
9 "For this is like the days^D^ of Noah to me:
when I swore that the water of Noah
would never flood the earth again,
so I have sworn that I will not be angry
     with you
or rebuke you.
10 Though the mountains move
and the hills shake,
my love will not be removed from you
and my covenant of peace will not
     be shaken,"
says your compassionate Lord.

11 "Poor Jerusalem, storm-tossed,
     and not comforted,
I will set your stones in black mortar,^E^
and lay your foundations in lapis lazuli.
12 I will make your fortifications^F^
     out of rubies,
your gates out of sparkling stones,
and all your walls out of precious stones.
13 Then all your children will be taught
     by the Lord,
their prosperity will be great,
14 and you will be established
on a foundation of righteousness.
You will be far from oppression,
you will certainly not be afraid;
you will be far from terror,
it will certainly not come near you.
15 If anyone attacks you,
it is not from me;

---

^A^53:11 DSS, LXX; MT omits *light*   ^B^53:12 Or *him with*   ^C^53:12 Or *receive with*   ^D^54:9 DSS, Cairo Geniza; MT, LXX read *waters*
^E^54:11 Lit *in antimony*   ^F^54:12 Lit *suns*; perhaps *shields*; Ps 84:11

---

there was a transgression against the sacred things of the Lord.
53:12 Returning to the theme at the beginning of the poem (52:13), the suffering of the servant will give way to his exaltation. Jesus's suffering culminated in the crucifixion but gave way to the resurrection. This verse is quoted in Lk 22:37.
54:1 A **childless** woman was often scorned in the ancient Near East. In this verse Jerusalem is a barren woman who will have a child (like Sarah, Rachel, or Hannah). Indeed she will have many **children**. Thus her sadness

will turn to joy (Ps 113:9). Paul quotes this verse in Gl 4:27.
54:4–5 A worse fate than childlessness was being a widow. The pronouncement tells the widow Israel not to be afraid because God has married her. She has gone from nothing to everything, as the list of divine names makes clear.
54:6–8 The metaphor changes in this verse. Israel is no longer a widow; she is a divorcee. God, her husband, has abandoned her; now he will take her back. He rejected Israel because of her sin (**in a surge of anger**),

but now he takes her back with **everlasting covenant love**.
54:9–10 The **covenant of peace** may be an allusion to the covenant with Noah, symbolized by the rainbow.
54:11–12 Jerusalem is now personified as a **storm-tossed** city that God will restore to unprecedented splendor, made of precious **stones** and metals, which anticipates new Jerusalem in Rv 21:15–21.
54:13 Jesus quotes this verse in Jn 6:45.
54:15 Those who attacked Jerusalem (the Assyrians in 701 BC and the Babylonians in 605,

whoever attacks you
will fall before you.
[16] Look, I have created the craftsman
who blows on the charcoal fire
and produces a weapon suitable
for its task;
and I have created the destroyer
to cause havoc.
[17] No weapon formed against you
will succeed,
and you will refute any accusation[A]
raised against you in court.
This is the heritage
of the Lord's servants,
and their vindication is from me."
This is the Lord's declaration.

Come to the Lord

55 "Come, everyone who is thirsty,
come to the water;
and you without silver,
come, buy, and eat!
Come, buy wine and milk
without silver and without cost!
[2] Why do you spend silver on what
is not food,
and your wages on what
does not satisfy?
Listen carefully to me, and eat
what is good,
and you will enjoy the choicest of foods.[B]
[3] Pay attention and come to me;
listen, so that you will live.
I will make a permanent covenant
with you
on the basis of the faithful kindnesses
of David.[C]
[4] Since I have made him a witness
to the peoples,
a leader and commander
for the peoples,
[5] so you will summon a nation
you do not know,
and nations who do not know you
will run to you.
For the Lord your God,
even the Holy One of Israel,
has glorified you."

[6] Seek the Lord while he may be found;
call to him while he is near.

[7] Let the wicked one abandon his way
and the sinful one his thoughts;
let him return to the Lord,
so he may have compassion on him,
and to our God, for he will freely forgive.

[8] "For my thoughts are not your thoughts,
and your ways are not my ways."
This is the Lord's declaration.
[9] "For as heaven is higher than earth,
so my ways are higher than your ways,
and my thoughts than your thoughts.
[10] For just as rain and snow fall from heaven
and do not return there
without saturating the earth
and making it germinate and sprout,
and providing seed to sow
and food to eat,
[11] so my word that comes from my mouth
will not return to me empty,
but it will accomplish what I please
and will prosper in what I send it to do."

[12] You will indeed go out with joy
and be peacefully guided;
the mountains and the hills will break
into singing before you,
and all the trees of the field will clap
their hands.
[13] Instead of the thornbush, a cypress
will come up,
and instead of the brier, a myrtle
will come up;
this will stand as a monument for the
Lord,
an everlasting sign that will not
be destroyed.

A House of Prayer for All

56 This is what the Lord says:
Preserve justice and do what is right,
for my salvation is coming soon,
and my righteousness will be revealed.
[2] Happy is the person who does this,
the son of man who holds it fast,
who keeps the Sabbath
without desecrating it,
and keeps his hand from doing any evil.

[3] No foreigner who has joined himself
to the Lord

[A]54:17 Lit refute every tongue   [B]55:2 Lit enjoy fatness   [C]55:3 Or with you, the faithful acts of kindness shown to David

---

597, and 586 BC) did so with God's permission, but after the restoration, their enemies will not be God-sent and will fall for that reason. **54:16–17** Using both military (**weapon**) and legal (**accusation**) metaphors, God proclaims that his people will withstand all attacks because of his protection. **55:1** God will not only freely give water, but also the more substantial drinks of **milk** and **wine**. These drinks represent spiritual as well as physical nourishment.

55:3 The **covenant with** David is found in 2Sm 7. David's dynasty would be established forever (2Sm 7:16). The NT understood the unconditional promise to be fulfilled in Jesus Christ, a descendant of David. Paul quotes this verse in Ac 13:34. **56:1 Salvation** here is equivalent to victory or rescue since it envisions release from Babylonian bondage. This verse does not call for obedience that earns salvation. Obedience is a response to the promise

of God's coming deliverance, not a way to earn his favor. **56:2** God pronounces **happy** (see Ps 1) those who are obedient and who avoid evil. The **Sabbath** commandment (Ex 20:8–11; Dt 5:12–15) is singled out because it was considered the epitome (the "sign") of the Mosaic covenant (Ex 31:13). **56:3** God reminds his people that foreigners who convert to the Lord are not excluded from worship.

A Biblical View of History

by Thomas S. Kidd

Christians believe the God of the Bible is the Lord of history. The history of everything—from an individual human life to the vast universe—is under God's sovereign control. By using the word *history*, I certainly mean the great stories of wars, kings, and political affairs, but I also mean the quieter narratives of forgotten people, those who do not appear in history books. Many are forgotten to human history, but they appear in God's view of it no matter how humble they are. Christ tells us that God does not even forget sparrows, and we are worth much more than they. Even the hairs of our heads are counted by him (Lk 12:6–7). God has never overlooked anything or anyone.

Nevertheless, God does not directly cause everything to happen in history. Most notably, he does not cause evil, for he is not the author of sin. On the other hand, nothing happens without his permission or consent, not even a sparrow's death (Mt 10:29). Critics have argued that this distinction between God's allowing evil to occur but not actually causing it is a hollow one. Christians, however, affirm that God is absolutely holy, that he directs history toward the ultimate triumph of good, and that he has permitted evil and suffering to enter the world by the agency of fallen people and the devil.

History and God's Purpose

As opposed to secular or materialistic philosophies that see no overarching point to history or human existence, Christians have a linear, purposeful view of the past, present, and future. Christians embrace three core convictions about history: "that God intervenes in it; that he guides it in a straight line; and that he will bring it to the conclusion that he has planned" (David Bebbington, *Patterns in History: A Christian Perspective* [Grand Rapids: Baker, 1990], 43). These ideas are central to the Christian belief in God's providence. God created the world with purpose—primarily to glorify himself—and since the fall of humanity in the garden of Eden, God has also been working out a plan of redemption, also for his own glory.

God even plays a sustaining role in what might, at first glance, seem to be the "natural" things of history and everyday life. Hebrews 1:2–3 tells us that God the Father made the universe through the Son, who sustains "all things by his powerful word." Through Christ "all things hold together" (Col 1:17). God is, in a sense, always intervening to sustain and preserve his creatures and all creation. He has not even relinquished control of forces such as gravity or time.

But God also intervenes in special ways and particular places and times to accomplish his purposes. One could cite any number of examples. For instance, God raised up King Cyrus of Persia in order to bring about the return of the Jewish exiles to Jerusalem. Ezra 1:1 and 2 Chronicles 36:22 speak of how God "roused the spirit of King Cyrus" to decree the return of the exiles, in spite of the fact that Cyrus probably worshiped pagan gods. In Isaiah 44:28 God calls Cyrus his "shepherd" who would fulfill all God's "pleasure" with regard to his chosen people, the Jews.

The fact of God's sovereignty over history is not just a dry philosophical proposition, but it lies at the heart of our personal trust in God's loving control over our lives. We all experience disappointments and sometimes tragedies, and in those times many are tempted to wonder where God is. What is he doing? Does he not care? Knowing that nothing takes God by surprise proves a great comfort; moreover, "all things work together for the good of those who love God, who are called according to his purpose" (Rm 8:28). We may not understand or like what is happening in the moment, but it is reassuring to know that God remains sovereign over everything—not only in our lives but throughout the entire universe.

History and Humility

A great challenge for Christians regarding history is our limited ability to discern God's purposes. Our limitations come from living in a time-bound state and having minds only partially redeemed from the effects of the fall of humankind. God, conversely, is not bound by time or space; he is infinitely powerful and holy. Humans simply do not share God's level of understanding, as he says in Isaiah 55:8: "My thoughts are not your thoughts, and your ways are not my ways." Joseph had no idea when he was sold into slavery in Genesis 37 that it would result in his elevation to authority in Pharaoh's court as well as in the deliverance of his family. Yet in Genesis 50:20 Joseph makes a statement to his brothers that reveals a humble and wonderful shift in perspective: "You planned evil against me; God planned it for good to bring about the present result."

Because of our limited understanding of God's specific purposes, we should be humble about asserting that we know exactly what God is doing in history except in matters such as those revealed in Scripture. In some cases we may safely assert that God was moving in a certain event or in a person's life, including our own. Seminal events in church history, such as the Reformation of the sixteenth century or the Great Awakening of the eighteenth century, have obvious marks of God's providence.

Understanding God's role in other historical episodes, such as the creation of the United States, requires more reflection and caution. Many American Christians eagerly assert that America's founding was a special work of God's providence. Indeed, a number of the founding fathers saw it that way as well. We must certainly agree that America's independence from Britain, just as with any similar political transformation, happened by God's sovereign permission. But we must also remember that God's primary purpose in history is the building of his kingdom, not the building of a nation (outside of biblical Israel).

Similarly, we must be cautious about asserting that we understand God's purposes in allowing natural disasters or the acts of sinful people. In the wake of events such as the September 11, 2001, terrorist attacks, or Hurricane Katrina's devastation of New Orleans in 2005, certain Christians said these events were products of God's wrath. But other Christians contended that we are not given such direct insight into the workings of God's providence, absent the divine knowledge reserved for the Bible's prophetic authors. If New Orleans, for instance, was subject to God's judgment, then why not other American cities? And what of the godly people and churches that were devastated by the storm and floods? Does every hurricane represent God's judgment? Or just particularly devastating ones? The more we think about such questions, the harder it is for us, with our restricted vision, to know just what to make of such events from the divine perspective.

Though God does not permit us to understand the purpose for everything that happens in history, Scripture does certainly give assurance that God controls it all. It also tells us about God's most important purposes in history, especially about the redemption of believers in Jesus Christ and the building of the kingdom of God to his glory.

should say,
"The LORD will exclude me
from his people,"
and the eunuch should not say,
"Look, I am a dried-up tree."
4 For the LORD says this:
"For the eunuchs who keep
my Sabbaths,
and choose what pleases me,
and hold firmly to my covenant,
5 I will give them, in my house and within
my walls,
a memorial and a name
better than sons and daughters.
I will give each of them
an everlasting name
that will never be cut off.
6 As for the foreigners who join
themselves to the LORD
to minister to him, to
love the name of the LORD,
and to become his servants —
all who keep the Sabbath
without desecrating it
and who hold firmly to my covenant —
7 I will bring them to my holy mountain
and let them rejoice in my house
of prayer.
Their burnt offerings and sacrifices
will be acceptable on my altar,
for my house will be called a house
of prayer
for all nations."
8 This is the declaration
of the Lord GOD,
who gathers the dispersed of Israel:
"I will gather to them still others
besides those already gathered."

Unrighteous Leaders Condemned

9 All you animals of the field and forest,
come and eat!
10 Israel's^A watchmen are blind,
all of them,
they know nothing;
all of them are mute dogs,

they cannot bark;
they dream, lie down,
and love to sleep.
11 These dogs have fierce appetites;
they never have enough.
And they are shepherds
who have no discernment;
all of them turn to their own way,
every last one for his own profit.
12 "Come, let me get some wine,
let's guzzle some beer;
and tomorrow will be like today,
only far better!"

57 The righteous person perishes,
and no one takes it to heart;
the faithful are taken away,
with no one realizing
that the righteous person is taken away
because of^B evil.
2 He will enter into peace —
they will rest on their beds^C —
everyone who lives uprightly.

Pagan Religion Denounced

3 But come here,
you witch's sons,
offspring of an adulterer
and a prostitute!^D
4 Who are you mocking?
Who are you opening your mouth
and sticking out your tongue at?
Isn't it you, you rebellious children,
you offspring of liars,
5 who burn with lust among the oaks,
under every green tree,
who slaughter children in the wadis
below the clefts of the rocks?
6 Your portion is
among the smooth stones
of the wadi;
indeed, they are your lot.
You have even poured out
a drink offering to them;
you have offered a grain offering;
should I be satisfied with these?

56:4 Eunuchs were typically excluded from worship according to Dt 23:1. However, this verse describes an obedient eunuch and thus one who had become a eunuch accidentally or who had converted to worship of God after becoming a eunuch. Such devout eunuchs were invited to join in the worship of God.
56:5 Eunuchs could not have children and thus lacked progeny who would perpetuate their names. God proclaims that he will provide a memorial for them.
56:6 This verse gives the positive word regarding foreigners, matching the negative in v. 3.
56:7 God's house, the temple, will be a place where everyone can come to pray. This verse is quoted in Mt 21:13; Mk 11:17; and Lk 19:46.

56:9–10 Watchmen were supposed to keep wild animals away from the crops, but these watchmen—Israel's leaders—were ineffective, silent (mute dogs), and asleep.
56:11 In v. 10 the watchmen were called "mute dogs." This verse picks up on that image to describe their voracious appetites.
57:1–2 Retribution does not always happen in this life. Even so, v. 2 hints at future resolution of this problem when it talks about death for the righteous as an entering into peace.
57:3–13 In this section God blasts those who practice idolatry and warns them of coming judgment. In the last half of the final verse of the section, he affirms the righteous.

57:5 In ancient Israel illegitimate worship took place under trees, perhaps suggesting a fertility religion and sexual rites (Dt 12:2; Jr 2:20; 3:6,13). At times during the OT period, gruesome acts like child sacrifice were also included among the false religious practices of Israel (2Kg 23:10).
57:6–10 These verses describe idolatrous rituals, many features of which are obscure (e.g., the smooth stones of the wadi). Even so, the sexual nature of these practices comes through clearly at points (see references to bed and genitals), suggesting a connection with the fertility religion of ancient Canaan from which the Israelites were supposed to separate themselves.

7 You have placed your bed
on a high and lofty mountain;
you also went up there to offer sacrifice.
8 You have set up your memorial
behind the door and doorpost.
For away from me, you stripped,
went up, and made your bed wide,
and you have made a bargain^A
for yourself with them.
You have loved their bed;
you have gazed on their genitals.^B,C
9 You went to the king with oil
and multiplied your perfumes;
you sent your envoys far away
and sent them down even to Sheol.
10 You became weary
on your many journeys,
but you did not say, "It's hopeless!"
You found a renewal of your strength;^D
therefore you did not grow weak.
11 Who was it you dreaded and feared,
so that you lied and didn't
remember me
or take it to heart?
I have kept silent for a long time,
haven't I?^E
So you do not fear me.
12 I will announce your righteousness,
and your works — they will not
profit you.
13 When you cry out,
let your collection of idols rescue you!
The wind will carry all of them off,
a breath will take them away.
But whoever takes refuge in me
will inherit the land
and possess my holy mountain.

Healing and Peace

14 He said,
"Build it up, build it up, prepare the way,
remove every obstacle
from my people's way."
15 For the High and Exalted One,
who lives forever, whose name is holy,
says this:
"I live in a high and holy place,
and with the oppressed and lowly
of spirit,
to revive the spirit of the lowly
and revive the heart of the oppressed.
16 For I will not accuse you forever,
and I will not always be angry;

for then the spirit would grow weak
before me,
even the breath, which I have made.
17 Because of his sinful greed I was angry,
so I struck him; I was angry and hid;
but he went on turning back
to the desires of his heart.
18 I have seen his ways, but I will heal him;
I will lead him and restore comfort
to him and his mourners,
19 creating words of praise."^F
The LORD says,
"Peace, peace to the one who is far
or near,
and I will heal him.
20 But the wicked are
like the storm-tossed sea,
for it cannot be still,
and its water churns up mire and muck.
21 There is no peace for the wicked,"
says my God.

True Fasting

58 "Cry out loudly, don't hold back!
Raise your voice like a ram's horn.
Tell my people their transgression
and the house of Jacob their sins.
2 They seek me day after day
and delight to know my ways,
like a nation that does what is right
and does not abandon the justice
of their God.
They ask me for righteous judgments;
they delight in the nearness of God."

3 "Why have we fasted,
but you have not seen?
We have denied ourselves,
but you haven't noticed!"^G

"Look, you do as you please on the day
of your fast,
and oppress all your workers.
4 You fast with contention and strife
to strike viciously with your fist.
You cannot fast as you do today,
hoping to make your voice heard
on high.
5 Will the fast I choose be like this:
A day for a person to deny himself,
to bow his head like a reed,
and to spread out sackcloth and ashes?
Will you call this a fast

---

^A 57:8 Lit you cut   ^B 57:8 Lit hand   ^C 57:8 In Hb, the word "hand" is probably a euphemism for genitals.   ^D 57:10 Lit found life of your hand   ^E 57:11 LXX reads And I, when I see you, I pass by   ^F 57:19 Lit creating fruit of the lips   ^G 58:3 These are Israel's words to God.

57:11–12 God would expose his people's **righteousness**, which was no righteousness at all.

57:14–21 Reversing the proportions of the previous pronouncement (vv. 3–13), this section has a long statement about God's good intentions toward the righteous, with a brief

statement about the fate of the wicked at the end (vv. 20–21).

58:2–3a God acknowledged that his people appeared pious on the surface. They had even **fasted**, expecting God to do something for them. The people of God complained about getting no divine response from

their self-initiated fast, while they failed to observe the Sabbath, one of the OT's most important commands (vv. 13–14).

58:3b–5 God responded to his people's challenge. Their fasting led to divisions in the community and exploitative behavior toward underlings, as well as self-absorption.

and a day acceptable to the LORD?

6 Isn't this the fast I choose:
To break the chains of wickedness,
to untie the ropes of the yoke,
to set the oppressed free,
and to tear off every yoke?

7 Is it not to share your bread
with the hungry,
to bring the poor and homeless
into your house,
to clothe the naked when you see him,
and not to ignore your own flesh
and blood?[A]

8 Then your light will appear
like the dawn,
and your recovery will come quickly.
Your righteousness will go before you,
and the LORD's glory will be
your rear guard.

9 At that time, when you call, the LORD
will answer;
when you cry out, he will say,
'Here I am.'
If you get rid of the yoke among you,
the finger-pointing
and malicious speaking,

10 and if you offer yourself[B] to the hungry,
and satisfy the afflicted one,
then your light will shine
in the darkness,
and your night will be like noonday.

11 The LORD will always lead you,
satisfy you in a parched land,
and strengthen your bones.
You will be like a watered garden
and like a spring whose water
never runs dry.

12 Some of you will rebuild
the ancient ruins;
you will restore the foundations laid
long ago;
you will be called the repairer
of broken walls,
the restorer of streets where people live.

13 "If you keep from desecrating
the Sabbath,
from doing whatever you want
on my holy day;

if you call the Sabbath a delight,
and the holy day of the LORD honorable;
if you honor it, not going
your own ways,
seeking your own pleasure,
or talking business;[C,D]

14 then you will delight in the LORD,
and I will make you ride
over the heights of the land,
and let you enjoy the heritage
of your father Jacob."
For the mouth of the LORD has spoken.

Sin and Redemption

59 Indeed, the LORD's arm is not
too weak to save,
and his ear is not too deaf to hear.

2 But your iniquities are separating you
from your God,
and your sins have hidden his face
from you
so that he does not listen.

3 For your hands are defiled with blood
and your fingers, with iniquity;
your lips have spoken lies,
and your tongues mutter injustice.

4 No one makes claims justly;
no one pleads honestly.
They trust in empty
and worthless words;
they conceive trouble and give birth
to iniquity.

5 They hatch viper's eggs
and weave spider's webs.
Whoever eats their eggs will die;
crack one open, and a viper is hatched.

6 Their webs cannot become clothing,
and they cannot cover themselves
with their works.
Their works are sinful works,
and violent acts are in their hands.

7 Their feet run after evil,
and they rush to shed innocent blood.
Their thoughts are sinful thoughts;
ruin and wretchedness are
in their paths.

8 They have not known the path of peace,
and there is no justice in their ways.
They have made their roads crooked;

[A]58:7 Lit *not hide yourself from your flesh*   [B]58:10 Some Hb mss, LXX, Syr read *offer your bread*   [C]58:13 Or *idly*   [D]58:13 Lit *or speak a word*

God's idea of fasting extended far beyond public expressions of mourning.
58:6 After condemning the people's idea of fasting, God defined what he understood to be legitimate and effective fasting. The emphasis is on social justice.
58:7 Proper fasting is also connected to care for those in need, including the **hungry** and those who needed shelter and clothing (cp. Mc 6:6–8). **Flesh and blood** is a reference to fellow Israelites.
58:11–12 The pronouncement looks forward to the restoration when God's people will

leave their captivity and return to the land, but the land and its cities, especially Jerusalem, will be in **ruins**.
58:13–14 While God's people kept fasts not commanded in the Bible, they flouted **Sabbath** observance, which was one of the central commands of the OT. It was the fourth commandment, considered the sign of the Mosaic covenant (see note at 56:2).
59:3–4 A selection of the sins that separated God from his people is listed. The list begins with acts of violence and moves on to deceit and **injustice**. They were guilty in thought

and action (**they conceive trouble and give birth to iniquity**).
59:5–6 These sinners produced **viper's eggs**. Eggs promise life, but these eggs produced death. Thus, the works of God's people may look promising, but they kill. In a similar vein, God's people produce **spider's webs**. They may look beautiful in their intricacy, but they have no practical value.
59:7 Again (v. 4), the pronouncement emphasizes that the people are sinful in thought and deed. They show their eagerness when they **run after evil**.

no one who walks on them
will know peace.

9 Therefore justice is far from us,
and righteousness does not reach us.
We hope for light, but there is darkness;
for brightness, but we live in the night.

10 We grope along a wall like the blind;
we grope like those without eyes.
We stumble at noon as though
it were twilight;
we are like the dead among those
who are healthy.

11 We all growl like bears
and moan like doves.
We hope for justice, but there is none;
for salvation, but it is far from us.

12 For our transgressions have multiplied
before you,
and our sins testify against us.
For our transgressions are with us,
and we know our iniquities:

13 transgression and deception
against the LORD,
turning away from following our God,
speaking oppression and revolt,
conceiving and uttering lying words
from the heart.

14 Justice is turned back,
and righteousness stands far off.
For truth has stumbled
in the public square,
and honesty cannot enter.

15 Truth is missing,
and whoever turns from evil
is plundered.

The LORD saw that there was
no justice,
and he was offended.

16 He saw that there was no man —
he was amazed that there was
no one interceding;
so his own arm brought salvation,

and his own righteousness
supported him.

17 He put on righteousness as body armor,
and a helmet of salvation on his head;
he put on garments of vengeance
for clothing,
and he wrapped himself in zeal
as in a cloak.

18 So he will repay according to
their deeds:
fury to his enemies,
retribution to his foes,
and he will repay the coasts and islands.

19 They will fear the name of the LORD
in the west
and his glory in the east;[A]
for he will come like a rushing stream
driven by the wind of the LORD.

20 "The Redeemer will come to Zion,
and to those in Jacob who turn
from transgression."
This is the LORD's declaration.

21 "As for me, this is my covenant with them,"
says the LORD: "My Spirit who is on you, and my
words that I have put in your mouth, will not
depart from your mouth, or from the mouths
of your children, or from the mouths of your
children's children, from now on and forever," says the LORD.

The LORD's Glory in Zion

60 Arise, shine, for your light has come,
and the glory of the LORD shines
over you.[B]

2 For look, darkness will cover the earth,
and total darkness the peoples;
but the LORD will shine over you,
and his glory will appear over you.

3 Nations will come to your light,
and kings to your shining brightness.

4 Raise your eyes and look around:
they all gather and come to you;
your sons will come from far away,

59:8 Isaiah used the words **path** and **roads** to refer to the course of a person's life. Paul quotes vv. 7–8 in Rm 3:15–17.

59:9 Note the transition from third person plural speech ("they" in previous verses) to first person (**we**) that begins in this verse and continues until v. 15a. The prophet included himself along with the people.

59:11 Bears growl out of anger, and **doves** make a sound like the groans of a suffering person. These metaphors suggest that God's people were angry and sad about their present state.

59:15b–21 The chapter concludes with a description of God's reaction to the sin and helplessness of his people. He will intercede and rescue his people in spite of their sin and helplessness.

59:15b–16 The section begins with a statement of God's recognition of human injustice

and the offense that he takes at it. It also goes on to describe his amazement that no human was interceding on behalf of the people. Perhaps the intercession of Moses (Ex 33) or the other prophets is what is in mind here. In any case, God proclaims that in the absence of such a human intercessor, he himself will step into the gap between his people and himself.

59:17 To save his people, God assumed the guise of a warrior. However, his armor and his weapons are not physical but spiritual. The description of God's armor and weapons remind believers of Paul's description of the spiritual weapons available to Christians as they wage battle against "evil, spiritual forces in the heavens" (Eph 6:12).

59:18–19 God's **enemies** do not get off without punishment. The mention of the **coasts and islands** indicates that the

far-flung nations, indeed the whole world (**west** and **east**), are in mind here. The whole world will **fear the name of the LORD** after his work of retribution.

59:20–21 The climax of this pronouncement announces the future arrival of God **the Redeemer** at **Zion**, God's holy mountain in Jerusalem. God's Spirit will be given to his people to cleanse their mouths, so they will proclaim the glory of God to future generations. Paul quotes these verses in Rm 11:26–27.

60:1–2 Now God announces the arrival of the **light**, whose source is the glory of God. **Darkness will cover the earth** (a reference to pervasive sin), but God's hovering glory will illuminate the way for his people.

60:3 Though the light comes to God's people, the **nations** will share in it by coming to the light.

and your daughters on the hips
of nursing mothers.
⁵ Then you will see and be radiant,
and your heart will tremble
and rejoice,^A
because the riches of the sea
will become yours
and the wealth of the nations will come
to you.
⁶ Caravans of camels will cover
your land^B —
young camels of Midian and Ephah —
all of them will come from Sheba.
They will carry gold and frankincense
and proclaim the praises of the Lord.
⁷ All the flocks of Kedar will be gathered
to you;
the rams of Nebaioth will serve you
and go up on my altar
as an acceptable sacrifice.
I will glorify my beautiful house.

⁸ Who are these who fly like a cloud,
like doves to their shelters?
⁹ Yes, the coasts and islands will wait
for me
with the ships of Tarshish in the lead,
to bring your children from far away,
their silver and gold with them,
for the honor of the Lord your God,
the Holy One of Israel,
who has glorified you.
¹⁰ Foreigners will rebuild your walls,
and their kings will serve you.
Although I struck you in my wrath,
yet I will show mercy to you
with my favor.
¹¹ Your city gates will always be open;
they will never be shut day or night
so that the wealth of the nations
may be brought into you,
with their kings being led
in procession.
¹² For the nation and the kingdom
that will not serve you will perish;
those nations will be annihilated.

¹³ The glory of Lebanon will come
to you —
its pine, elm, and cypress together —
to beautify the place of my sanctuary,
and I will glorify my dwelling place.^C
¹⁴ The sons of your oppressors
will come and bow down to you;
all who reviled you
will fall facedown at your feet.
They will call you the City of the Lord,
Zion of the Holy One of Israel.
¹⁵ Instead of your being deserted
and hated,
with no one passing through,
I will make you an object
of eternal pride,
a joy from age to age.
¹⁶ You will nurse on the milk of nations,
and nurse at the breast of kings;
you will know that I, the Lord,
am your Savior
and Redeemer, the Mighty One of Jacob.

¹⁷ I will bring gold instead of bronze;
I will bring silver instead of iron,
bronze instead of wood,
and iron instead of stones.
I will appoint peace as your government
and righteousness as your overseers.
¹⁸ Violence will never again be heard of
in your land;
devastation and destruction
will be gone from your borders.
You will call your walls Salvation
and your city gates Praise.
¹⁹ The sun will no longer be your light
by day,
and the brightness of the moon
will not shine on you.
The Lord will be your everlasting light,
and your God will be your splendor.
²⁰ Your sun will no longer set,
and your moon will not fade;
for the Lord will be
your everlasting light,
and the days of your sorrow will be over.

^A60:5 Lit expand ^B60:6 Lit cover you ^C60:13 Lit glorify the place of my feet

60:5–6 As they return to their homeland, the people will bring the **wealth of the nations. Camels** carried freight on the caravan trails of the ancient Near East. Here they are described as carrying precious items like **gold and frankincense.** The camels will come from **Midian,** a nomadic Arabic tribe. **Ephah** was associated with Midian by way of genealogy (Gn 25:4; 1Ch 1:33), but not much else is known about it. **Sheba** was also an Arabian kingdom. It was famous because of the queen of Sheba, whose wealth flowed to Israel because of her admiration for Solomon's wisdom (1Kg 10:1–10). **60:7** Sacrificial animals that will be offered at the temple (**my beautiful house**) are described. On **Kedar,** see note at 21:13–17.

Nebaioth is elsewhere in the Bible a personal name, the son of Kedar, showing a relationship between these two nomadic tribes (Gn 25:13; 36:3; 1Ch 1:29). **60:9** The **coasts and islands** refer to distant lands and thus represent all the nations of the world. The **ships of Tarshish,** thought to be what is today Spain (Tartessus), were particularly impressive since they traveled so far between Tyre and Iberia. **60:10** The future will see foreign nations serve God's people. One thinks of Nehemiah, who received the permission of the Persian king Artaxerxes to rebuild the **walls** of Jerusalem. **60:11** Open **gates** indicated that a city felt secure. But the gates will also be open

because the **wealth of the nations** is flowing into Jerusalem. **60:12** In the day of Israel's glory there will no longer be nations who do not worship the Lord. **60:13** The trees (**glory**) of Lebanon were renowned for their beauty and quality. The pronouncement envisions their use in the temple of the Lord. **60:17 Peace** and **righteousness** will abound, indicating a new quality of spirituality in the city. **60:19–20** The pronouncement returns to the theme with which it began: God's people will experience **light,** not darkness. This is a supernatural light provided by God, not the **sun.** God will be perpetually present with his people.

21 All your people will be righteous;
they will possess the land forever;
they are the branch I planted,
the work of my^A hands,
so that I may be glorified.
22 The least will become a thousand,
the smallest a mighty nation.
I am the LORD;
I will accomplish it quickly in its time.

Messiah's Jubilee

61 The Spirit of the Lord GOD is on me,
because the LORD has anointed me
to bring good news to the poor.
He has sent me to heal^B
the brokenhearted,
to proclaim liberty to the captives
and freedom to the prisoners;
2 to proclaim the year of the LORD's favor,
and the day of our God's vengeance;
to comfort all who mourn,
3 to provide for those who mourn in Zion;
to give them a crown of beauty
instead of ashes,
festive oil instead of mourning,
and splendid clothes instead of despair.^C
And they will be called righteous trees,
planted by the LORD
to glorify him.

4 They will rebuild the ancient ruins;
they will restore
the former devastations;
they will renew the ruined cities,
the devastations of many generations.
5 Strangers will stand and feed
your flocks,
and foreigners will be your plowmen
and vinedressers.
6 But you will be called the LORD's priests;
they will speak of you as ministers
of our God;
you will eat the wealth of the nations,

and you will boast in their riches.
7 In place of your shame, you will have
a double portion;
in place of disgrace, they will rejoice
over their share.
So they will possess double in their land,
and eternal joy will be theirs.

8 For I the LORD love justice;
I hate robbery and injustice;^D
I will faithfully reward my people
and make a permanent covenant
with them.
9 Their descendants will be known
among the nations,
and their posterity among the peoples.
All who see them will recognize
that they are a people the LORD
has blessed.

10 I rejoice greatly in the LORD,
I exult in my God;
for he has clothed me with the garments
of salvation
and wrapped me in a robe
of righteousness,
as a groom wears a turban
and as a bride adorns herself
with her jewels.
11 For as the earth produces its growth,
and as a garden enables what is sown
to spring up,
so the Lord GOD
will cause righteousness and praise
to spring up before all the nations.

Zion's Restoration

62 I will not keep silent because of Zion,
and I will not keep still
because of Jerusalem,
until her righteousness shines
like a bright light
and her salvation, like a flaming torch.

---

^A 60:21 LXX, DSS read his ^B 61:1 Lit bind up ^C 61:3 Lit a dim spirit ^D 61:8 Some Hb mss, DSS, LXX, Syr, Tg, Vg; other Hb mss read robbery with a burnt offering

---

61:1–3 Much debate surrounds the identity of the first-person speaker of the first three verses of this chapter. He identified himself as having the **Spirit**. This reference provides a connection to the servant on whom God had placed his Spirit (see note at 42:1–9). Isaiah 11:2 states of the Messiah that "the Spirit of the LORD will rest on him." It is significant that 61:1–3 uses the language of anointing from which the word *Messiah* ("anointed one") comes. Thus, it is best to consider the first-person speaker in this pronouncement to be none other than the Messiah-Servant. Jesus identified himself as the embodiment of this passage when he read these verses in a synagogue, to the amazement of all who heard him (Lk 4:16–30).
61:1 The description of this future day as one in which **prisoners** will be freed and the **poor** will receive **good news** associates

this time with the Jubilee, where slaves were freed and land reverted to the original owners (Lv 25).
61:2 The same act can be designated as displaying the **LORD's favor** as well as **God's vengeance**, depending on whether a person is on God's side or not.
61:3 This verse emphasizes the reversal of fortune (from suffering to restoration) expressed in chap. 60.
61:5–6 Like chap. 60, this pronouncement repeats the themes of **foreigners** serving rather than oppressing the people of God as well as **the wealth of the nations** flowing to Jerusalem. The idea that all of God's people will function as **priests** toward the nations points back to Ex 19:6 where God told Moses that the Israelites would be "my kingdom of priests and my holy nation."

61:7 Double portion seems to allude to the inheritance awarded to the firstborn (Gn 48:22; Dt 21:17).
61:10 Isaiah broke out in a hymn of praise in response to the pronouncement he had just delivered. He used the theme of clothing to describe his taking on God's salvation and righteousness. These were not just any clothes but the clothes of a bride. This image implies the metaphor of God as husband of his people.
62:1–12 The theme of the transformation of God's people continues in this chapter. From shame, they will rise up in glory—thanks to their God.
62:1 The first-person speaker here is either the Servant-Messiah of 61:1–3 or the prophet Isaiah. He will speak until Jerusalem's spiritual transformation is complete. **Light** is an important theme describing God's work

2 Nations will see your righteousness
and all kings, your glory.
You will be given a new name
that the LORD's mouth will announce.
3 You will be a glorious crown
in the LORD's hand,
and a royal diadem in the palm
of your God's hand.
4 You will no longer be called Deserted,
and your land will not
be called Desolate;
instead, you will be called My Delight
Is in Her,^A
and your land Married;^B
for the LORD delights in you,
and your land will be married.
5 For as a young man marries
a young woman,
so your sons will marry you;
and as a groom rejoices over his bride,
so your God will rejoice over you.

6 Jerusalem,
I have appointed watchmen
on your walls;
they will never be silent, day or night.
There is no rest for you,
who remind the LORD.
7 Do not give him rest
until he establishes
and makes Jerusalem
the praise of the earth.

8 The LORD has sworn
with his right hand
and his strong arm:
I will no longer give your grain
to your enemies for food,
and foreigners will not drink
the new wine
for which you have labored.
9 For those who gather grain will eat it
and praise the LORD,
and those who harvest the grapes
will drink the wine
in my holy courts.

10 Go out, go out through the city gates;
prepare a way for the people!
Build it up, build up the highway;
clear away the stones!
Raise a banner for the peoples.
11 Look, the LORD has proclaimed
to the ends of the earth,
"Say to Daughter Zion:
Look, your salvation is coming,
his wages are with him,
and his reward accompanies him."
12 And they will be called^C
the Holy People,
the LORD's Redeemed;
and you will be called Cared For,
A City Not Deserted.

The LORD's Day of Vengeance

63 Who is this coming from Edom
in crimson-stained garments
from Bozrah —
this one who is splendid
in his apparel,
striding in his formidable^D might?

It is I, proclaiming vindication,^E
powerful to save.

2 Why are your clothes red,
and your garments like one who treads
a winepress?

3 I trampled the winepress alone,
and no one from the nations was
with me.
I trampled them in my anger
and ground them underfoot
in my fury;
their blood spattered my garments,
and all my clothes were stained.
4 For I planned the day of vengeance,
and the year of my redemption^F came.
5 I looked, but there was no one to help,
and I was amazed that no one assisted;
so my arm accomplished victory for me,
and my wrath assisted me.

---

^A 62:4 Or *Hephzibah*   ^B 62:4 Or *Beulah*   ^C 62:12 Lit *will call them*   ^D 63:1 Syr, Vg read *apparel, striding forward in*   ^E 63:1 Or *righteousness*   ^F 63:4 Or *blood retribution*

---

among his people (58:10; 60:1–13). It is also connected with the Messiah (10:17; 42:6).
62:2 Names and their meaning often were connected with a person's character or reputation. Israel's **new** divinely given name indicates a change of condition for the people of God (vv. 4,12).
62:4–5 Israel's names are changed from ones that indicated her loneliness (**Deserted** and **Desolate**) to those that show intimate relationship (**My Delight Is in Her** and **Married**). The metaphor of God married to his people as a husband is to his bride communicates the intimacy and exclusivity of the relationship (see note at 61:10). As a bride can have only one husband, so Israel can have only one God.

62:6–7 The leaders of God's people are compared to watchmen whose responsibilities included the encouragement of the people's relationship with God. Isaiah urged them to keep after God to maintain his efforts at restoring Jerusalem until it was truly "the joy of the whole earth" (Ps 48:1).
62:10 A **highway** is a frequent image in Isaiah for the removal of barriers between God and his people (11:16; 19:23; 33:8; 35:8; 40:3; 49:11). A **banner** marked a gathering place for the regathered remnant (see note at 11:10) and a rallying point for an army (see note at 13:2).
62:11 The "triumphal entry" quotation in Mt 21:5 is a combination of Zch 9:9 and this verse.

63:1–6 This passage is similar to 59:15b–20. Both passages describe God as a warrior going to battle to defeat the forces of evil.
63:1 The verse opens with a question from the watchman, and God responds. The warrior God has waged war and is returning blood stained and victorious. Perhaps **Edom**, with its capital city of **Bozrah**, is representative of all the nations that had exploited God's people through the years (which may also explain its role in 34:5–17).
63:3 God responded to the watchman's second question by describing his work of anger against the foes (identified as "nations" in v. 6). He described his killing work as trampling the enemy underfoot like a winemaker tramples on grapes. This image is picked up by the book

6 I crushed nations in my anger;
I made them drunk with my wrath
and poured out their blood
on the ground.

Remembrance of Grace

7 I will make known
the LORD's faithful love
and the LORD's praiseworthy acts,
because of all the LORD has done
for us —
even the many good things
he has done for the house of Israel,
which he did for them based on
his compassion
and the abundance of his faithful love.
8 He said, "They are indeed my people,
children who will not be disloyal,"
and he became their Savior.
9 In all their suffering, he suffered,[A]
and the angel of his presence saved them.
He redeemed them
because of his love and compassion;
he lifted them up and carried them
all the days of the past.
10 But they rebelled
and grieved his Holy Spirit.
So he became their enemy
and fought against them.
11 Then he[B] remembered the days of the past,
the days of Moses and his people.
Where is he who brought them
out of the sea
with the shepherds[C] of his flock?
Where is he who put his Holy Spirit
among the flock?
12 He made his glorious strength
available at the right hand of Moses,
divided the water before them
to make an eternal name for himself,
13 and led them through the depths
like a horse in the wilderness,
so that they did not stumble.
14 Like cattle that go down into the valley,
the Spirit of the LORD gave them[D] rest.
You led your people this way
to make a glorious name for yourself.

Israel's Prayer

15 Look down from heaven and see
from your lofty home
— holy and beautiful.
Where is your zeal and your might?
Your yearning[E] and your compassion
are withheld from me.
16 Yet you are our Father,
even though Abraham does not
know us
and Israel doesn't recognize us.
You, LORD, are our Father;
your name is Our Redeemer
from Ancient Times.
17 Why, LORD, do you make us stray
from your ways?
You harden our hearts so we do not
fear[F] you.
Return, because of your servants,
the tribes of your heritage.
18 Your holy people had a possession[G]
for a little while,
but our enemies have trampled down
your sanctuary.
19 We have become like those
you never ruled,
like those who did not bear your name.

64 If only you would tear
the heavens open
and come down,
so that mountains would quake
at your presence —
2 just as fire kindles brushwood,
and fire boils water —
to make your name known
to your enemies,
so that nations would tremble
at your presence!
3 When you did awesome works
that we did not expect,
you came down,
and the mountains quaked
at your presence.
4 From ancient times no one has heard,
no one has listened to,
no eye has seen any God except you
who acts on behalf of the one who waits
for him.
5 You welcome the one who joyfully does
what is right;
they remember you in your ways.
But we have sinned, and you were angry.
How can we be saved if we remain in
our sins?[H]
6 All of us have become
like something unclean,

[A]63:9 Alt Hb tradition reads *did not suffer* [B]63:11 Or *they* [C]63:11 LXX, Tg, Syr read *shepherd* [D]63:14 Lit *him* [E]63:15 Lit *The agitation of your inward parts* [F]63:17 Lit *our heart from fearing* [G]63:18 Or *Your people possessed your holy place* [H]64:5 Lit *angry; in them continually and we will be saved*; Hb obscure

---

of Revelation to describe Jesus as warrior at the final battle in Rv 19:13.
63:6 Finally, the object of God's warring anger is explicitly identified as the **nations**. The description of the nations as **drunk** with God's wrath invokes the metaphor of the cup of God's anger.
63:10 Holy Spirit is literally "Spirit of his holiness."

63:15 Isaiah began a lament that continues to 64:12. It bemoaned the fact that God had not yet enacted his exodus mercies (63:11–14). God seemed to be up in his heavenly home, distant from his people.
64:1–2 God seemed to be up in heaven (see note at 63:15), and Isaiah asked that he **come down** to help them in their need. When God

appears as a warrior, **mountains . . . quake** (see Nah 1:5) and **nations . . . tremble**.
64:3–4 Verse 4 is the basis for Paul's quote in 1Co 2:9.
64:5–7 A polluted garment means clothes stained by menstrual blood and thus rendered ritually unclean (Lv 15:19–33).

and all our righteous acts are
  like a polluted^A garment;
all of us wither like a leaf,
and our iniquities carry us away
  like the wind.

⁷ No one calls on your name,
striving to take hold of you.
For you have hidden your face from us
and made us melt because of^{B,C}
  our iniquity.

⁸ Yet Lᴏʀᴅ, you are our Father;
we are the clay, and you are our potter;
we all are the work of your hands.
⁹ Lᴏʀᴅ, do not be terribly angry
or remember our iniquity forever.
Please look — all of us are your people!
¹⁰ Your holy cities have become
  a wilderness;
Zion has become a wilderness,
Jerusalem a desolation.
¹¹ Our holy and beautiful^D temple,
where our ancestors praised you,
has been burned down,
and all that was dear to us lies in ruins.
¹² Lᴏʀᴅ, after all this, will you
  restrain yourself?
Will you keep silent and afflict
  us severely?

The Lᴏʀᴅ's Response

65 "I was sought by those
  who did not ask;
I was found by those
  who did not seek me.
I said, 'Here I am, here I am,'
to a nation that did not call
  on^E my name.
² I spread out my hands all day long
to a rebellious people
who walk in the path that is not good,
following their own thoughts.
³ These people continually anger me

to my face,
sacrificing in gardens,
burning incense on bricks,
⁴ sitting among the graves,
spending nights in secret places,
eating the meat of pigs,
and putting polluted broth
  in their bowls.^F
⁵ They say, 'Keep to yourself,
don't come near me, for I am too holy
  for you!'
These practices are smoke
  in my nostrils,
a fire that burns all day long.
⁶ Look, it is written in front of me:
I will not keep silent, but I will repay;
I will repay them fully^G
⁷ for your iniquities and the iniquities
of your^H ancestors together,"
says the Lᴏʀᴅ.
"Because they burned incense
  on the mountains
and reproached me on the hills,
I will reward them fully^I
for their former deeds."

⁸ The Lᴏʀᴅ says this:
"As the new wine is found in a bunch
  of grapes,
and one says, 'Don't destroy it,
for there's some good^J in it,'
so I will act because of my servants
and not destroy them all.
⁹ I will produce descendants
  from Jacob,
and heirs to my mountains
  from Judah;
my chosen ones will possess it,
and my servants will dwell there.
¹⁰ Sharon will be a pasture for flocks,
and the Valley of Achor a place for herds
  to lie down,
for my people who have sought me.

^A**64:6** Lit *menstrual* ^B**64:7** LXX, Syr, Vg, Tg read *and delivered us into the hand of* ^C**64:7** Lit *melt by the hand of* ^D**64:11** Or *glorious*; Is 60:7 ^E**65:1** Or *that was not called by* ^F**65:3–4** These vv. describe pagan worship. ^G**65:6** Lit *repay into their lap* ^H**65:7** LXX, Syr read *for their iniquities and the iniquities of their* ^I**65:7** Lit *reward into their lap* ^J**65:8** Or *there's a blessing*

64:8 Isaiah appealed to God as their **Father**. The prophet also appealed to God as their Creator, using the image of the **potter** and his **clay**.

64:10–12 Isaiah foresaw the time when the Babylonians would destroy the city of Jerusalem and burn the temple in 586 BC. Isaiah appealed to God to turn things around and restore the city and its temple.

65:1–2 In these and the following verses, God responded to the people's prayer uttered by Isaiah. God first described his total openness and accessibility to the people. Even more, he sought them out, though they should be the ones who were seeking him out. God would **spread out** his hands in welcome to people who had passed him by. Paul quotes these verses in Rm 10:20–21.

65:3 The rebellion of the people is enumerated in terms of their false worship. False worship

modeled on the pattern of Canaanite religion was carried on in garden areas. Canaanite worship was part of fertility worship, often featuring sacred **gardens** and trees. Such false religion was condemned in Dt 12:2; Jr 3:9; and Hs 4:13. **Incense** offerings are often associated with the worship of a god like Baal or a goddess like Asherah (17:8; 27:9; Ezk 6:6; Hs 11:2).

65:4 God's description of false religion continues with a mention of those who sat **among the graves**. The worship of departed ancestors was a feature of Canaanite religion. Eating the meat of **pigs** was particularly sinful because pork was considered an unclean food (Lv 11:7).

65:5 Ironically, these sinful people claimed to be holy, which God considered extremely irritating.

65:6–7 God accused his people of reproaching him on the **mountains** and **hills**. False

worship on "high places" was condemned (Dt 12:2; 2Kg 17:10; Jr 2:20–21; Ezk 6:13; 20:28; Hs 4:13).

65:8–9 Using the analogy of a **bunch of grapes**, God announced that he would not destroy the good grapes out of the bunch but would use them to make **new wine**. The analogy presents the idea that God will preserve a faithful remnant of his people after the judgment.

65:10 Sharon was the name of the foothills west of Jerusalem, famous for wildflowers. In 33:9 Sharon was described as a desert as a result of God's judgment (35:2). The **Valley of Achor** (lit "Valley of Trouble") received its name in the early days of the conquest of Canaan (Jos 7:16–26) when Achan stole some of the plunder from the city of Jericho. Because of his theft, Israel was defeated at the city of Ai. In Isaiah's vision of a restored remnant,

11 But you who abandon the Lord,
   who forget my holy mountain,
   who prepare a table for Fortune
   and fill bowls of mixed wine
      for Destiny,^A
12 I will destine you for the sword,
   and all of you will kneel down
      to be slaughtered,
   because I called and you did not answer,
   I spoke and you did not hear;
   you did what was evil in my sight
   and chose what I did not delight in."

13 Therefore, this is what the Lord God says:
   "Look! My servants will eat,
   but you will be hungry.
   Look! My servants will drink,
   but you will be thirsty.
   Look! My servants will rejoice,
   but you will be put to shame.
14 Look! My servants will shout for joy
      from a glad heart,
   but you will cry out
      from an anguished heart,
   and you will lament out of a broken spirit.
15 You will leave your name behind
   as a curse for my chosen ones,
   and the Lord God will kill you;
   but he will give his servants another name.
16 Whoever asks for a blessing in the land
   will ask for a blessing by the God of truth,
   and whoever swears in the land
   will swear by the God of truth.
   For the former troubles
      will be forgotten
   and hidden from my sight.

A New Creation

17 "For I will create new heavens
      and a new earth;
   the past events will not be remembered
      or come to mind.

18 Then be glad and rejoice forever
   in what I am creating;
   for I will create Jerusalem to be a joy
   and its people to be a delight.
19 I will rejoice in Jerusalem
   and be glad in my people.
   The sound of weeping and crying
   will no longer be heard in her.
20 In her, a nursing infant will no longer live
   only a few days,^B
   or an old man not live out his days.
   Indeed, the one who dies at a hundred
      years old
   will be mourned as a young man,^C
   and the one who misses
      a hundred years
   will be considered cursed.
21 People will build houses and live
      in them;
   they will plant vineyards and eat
      their fruit.
22 They will not build and others live
      in them;
   they will not plant and others eat.
   For my people's lives will be
   like the lifetime of a tree.
   My chosen ones will fully enjoy
   the work of their hands.
23 They will not labor without success
   or bear children destined for disaster,
   for they will be a people blessed
      by the Lord
   along with their descendants.
24 Even before they call, I will answer;
   while they are still speaking, I will hear.
25 The wolf and the lamb
      will feed together,^D
   and the lion will eat straw like cattle,
   but the serpent's food will be dust!
   They will not do what is evil or destroy
   on my entire holy mountain,"
   says the Lord.

---

^A 65:11 Pagan gods   ^B 65:20 Lit her, no longer infant of days   ^C 65:20 Lit the youth of a hundred years will die   ^D 65:25 Lit as one

---

Achor was a peaceful and prosperous place. Since the Valley of Achor was located in the east (near Jericho) and Sharon was in the west, the two together signified that all of Israel would be prosperous. **65:11–12 Fortune** (Hb *gad*) and **Destiny** (Hb *meni*) are personified as objects of false worship. *Gad* is thought to be a minor Canaanite god, while *Meni* is more obscure but thought to be venerated by the Arabs. While God had good things in store for the faithful remnant, those among his people who continued to worship false deities would meet a horrible end. **65:13–16** In this section God continued the distinction between those who followed him and were his servants and those who rejected him. The former will enjoy life; the latter will suffer. **65:15** Because of their sin, the wicked have a bad reputation (**name**). What they do to create that reputation becomes a curse for God's people. On the other hand, God's

people will get a new name (see note at 62:2), a new start after the judgment. **65:16** Blessing, a pleasant and prosperous life, comes only through God, not through false gods like Fortune and Destiny (see note at vv. 11–12). **65:17** Just as God will give his people a "new name" after his judgment and restoration (see v. 15; 62:2), so he will create **new heavens and a new earth**. The **past events** are acts of sin by the people that resulted in God's judgment. **65:18–19** God's original intention for **Jerusalem** will be fulfilled (see Ps 48:1 where it is called "the joy of the whole earth"). Its sin and God's judgment had reduced it to the point where it was "a horror to all the earth's kingdoms" (Jr 34:17), but now it will be **a joy**. **65:20–22** The future blessing of Jerusalem includes long life for its inhabitants. Infant mortality rates will disappear and **old** people will survive even longer. If someone dies at age one hundred, it will be considered tragic

because he was just a **young man** compared to others. Further blessing will come in the form of shelter and agricultural abundance. **65:23** In the past the **labor** of God's people had been enjoyed by others as he allowed foreign nations to take them over. Their **children** had been born to disaster since the enemy would either kill them or deport them. But this will change in God's "new heavens" and "new earth" (see note at v. 17). The blessing of work and of childbearing was first troubled at the time of the fall into sin (Gn 3:16–19). The language of this verse suggests a reversal of these curses. **65:24** The relationship with the Lord will be so close that he will anticipate their needs, and they will pray in accordance with his will. **65:25** The pronouncement uses language that suggests a restoration of Eden-like conditions. Wolves would normally eat lambs, but they will eat peacefully together. The **lion**, another predator, will **eat straw** rather than other animals. The serpent will eat

Final Judgment and Joyous Restoration

66 This is what the LORD says:
Heaven is my throne,
and earth is my footstool.
Where could you possibly build a house
for me?
And where would my resting place be?
² My hand made all these things,
and so they all came into being.
This is the LORD's declaration.
I will look favorably on this kind
of person:
one who is humble,
submissive^A in spirit,
and trembles at my word.
³ One person slaughters an ox,
another kills a person;
one person sacrifices a lamb,
another breaks a dog's neck;
one person offers a grain offering,
another offers pig's blood;
one person offers incense,
another praises an idol —
all these have chosen their ways
and delight in their abhorrent practices.
⁴ So I will choose their punishment,
and I will bring on them
what they dread
because I called and no one answered;
I spoke and they did not listen;
they did what was evil in my sight
and chose what I did not delight in.

⁵ You who tremble at his word,
hear the word of the LORD:
"Your brothers who hate
and exclude you
for my name's sake have said,
'Let the LORD be glorified
so that we can see your joy!'
But they will be put to shame."

⁶ A sound of uproar from the city!
A voice from the temple —

the voice of the LORD,
paying back his enemies
what they deserve!

⁷ Before Zion was in labor,
she gave birth;
before she was in pain, she delivered
a boy.
⁸ Who has heard of such a thing?
Who has seen such things?
Can a land be born in one day
or a nation be delivered in an instant?
Yet as soon as Zion was in labor,
she gave birth to her sons.
⁹ "Will I bring a baby to the point of birth
and not deliver it?"
says the LORD;
"or will I who deliver, close the womb?"
says your God.
¹⁰ Be glad for Jerusalem and rejoice
over her,
all who love her.
Rejoice greatly with her,
all who mourn over her —
¹¹ so that you may nurse and be satisfied
from her comforting breast
and drink deeply and delight yourselves
from her glorious breasts.

¹² For this is what the LORD says:
I will make peace flow to her like a river,
and the wealth^B of nations like a flood;
you will nurse and be carried on her hip
and bounced on her lap.
¹³ As a mother comforts her son,
so I will comfort you,
and you will be comforted in Jerusalem.

¹⁴ You will see, you will rejoice,
and you^C will flourish like grass;
then the LORD's power will be revealed
to his servants,
but he will show his wrath
against his enemies.

---

^A**66:2** Lit *broken*   ^B**66:12** Or *glory*   ^C**66:14** Lit *your bones*

---

dust, reminiscent of the serpent's role in Gn 3. The similar language in Is 11:6–9 suggests a connection with the theme of the Messiah expressed in those verses.
66:1 One of the presumptions of the preexilic people of God was that the temple literally was the place where God lived (Jr 7:3–4). This attitude had no justification, especially in light of the speech King Solomon gave when he dedicated the temple (1Kg 8:27). Thus, God began the final pronouncement in the book of Isaiah by reminding his people that his presence fills heaven (**my throne**) and earth (**my footstool**). Stephen quotes vv. 1–2 in Ac 7:49–50 just before becoming the first Christian martyr.
66:2 God made everything. This means that people should honor and fear God, which will result in humility, submissiveness to him, and total obedience to his commands.

66:3 This verse links four legitimate ritual acts with four perverse acts. The people did both, rendering even the legitimate ritual acts **abhorrent practices**.
66:4 This verse repeats 65:12.
66:5–6 Trembling at God's word (v. 2) indicates the kind of submission to God that leads to obedience. The **brothers** (fellow Israelites) mocked the faithful by saying **Let the LORD be glorified** because they did not think that would happen. God will see that the mockers get **what they deserve**.
66:7–8 Zion or Jerusalem has been described as Israel's mother before (see 49:14; 50:1). Here the return to Judah after the exile is described as Zion giving **birth** painlessly (again reversing a punishment of the fall; see note at Gn 3:16) to many sons.
66:9 In previous passages (see note at 50:1) God is imagined to be the husband of Zion.

That idea might also be operative here, but he is definitely pictured as the doctor who delivered Zion's babies.
66:10–11 Zion, the mother of the returned exiles, will not only give them birth but will succor them and give them life.
66:12 Zion (Jerusalem) will be a place of abundant (**like a river**) peace and overflowing (**like a flood**) wealth (on **the wealth of nations**, see 60:1–61:11). Zion, the mother, will care for and play with her children, the returned inhabitants of Jerusalem.
66:13 God, who is typically featured as the Father, speaks in the first person as the **mother** (a role typically played by Zion).
66:14–16 God will save his people and punish those who disobey him. While God blesses and punishes in historical time, the ultimate expression of God's salvation and judgment will take place at the final

¹⁵ Look, the LORD will come with fire —
 his chariots are like the whirlwind —
to execute his anger with fury
 and his rebuke with flames of fire.
¹⁶ For the LORD will execute judgment
 on all humanity with his fiery sword,
 and many will be slain by the LORD.

¹⁷ "Those who dedicate and purify themselves to enter the groves following their leader,^A eating meat from pigs, vermin,^B and rats, will perish together."
This is the LORD's declaration.
¹⁸ "Knowing^C their works and their thoughts, I have come to gather all nations and languages; they will come and see my glory. ¹⁹ I will establish a sign among them, and I will send survivors from them to the nations — to Tarshish, Put,^D Lud (who are archers), Tubal, Javan, and the coasts and islands far away — who have not heard about me or seen my glory. And they will proclaim my glory among the nations. ²⁰ They will bring all your brothers from all the nations as a gift to the LORD on horses and chariots, in litters, and on mules and camels, to my holy mountain Jerusalem," says the LORD, "just as the Israelites bring an offering in a clean vessel to the house of the LORD. ²¹ I will also take some of them as priests and Levites," says the LORD.
²² "For just as the new heavens
 and the new earth,
 which I will make,
 will remain before me" —
 this is the LORD's declaration —
 "so your offspring and your name
 will remain.
²³ All humanity will come
 to worship me
from one New Moon to another
and from one Sabbath to another,"
 says the LORD.

²⁴ "As they leave, they will see the dead bodies of those who have rebelled against me; for their worm will never die, their fire will never go out, and they will be a horror to all humanity."

^66:17 Hb obscure   ᵇ66:17 Lit *abhorrent things*   ᶜ66:18 LXX, Syr; MT omits *Knowing*   ᴰ66:19 LXX; MT reads *Pul*

judgment (pictured most graphically in the book of Revelation).
66:17 The wicked who receive the punishment described in vv. 14–16 are those who entered illegitimate worship sites (**groves**). They ate the most unclean food, defiantly rejecting God's law for Israel.
66:18 God was never interested in Israel alone. His promise to Abraham extended to the **nations** (Gn 12:3). Isaiah looked forward to the day when the nations would recognize God's **glory**.
66:19 The survivors, the remnant of God's people who survive the judgment, will go out to **the nations** to speak of God's **glory**. Among the representative nations named are those at great distance. **Tarshish** is modern day Spain (likely Tartessus); **Put** (ancient Punt) is equivalent to modern Somaliland (though some think a part of Libya; Nah 3:9 lists Libya along with Put); **Tubal** is an area near the Black Sea; **Javan** is modern Greece. The **coasts and islands** refer to distant lands and thus represent all the nations of the world.
66:20 The missionaries of v. 19 will bring back the fruit of their labor, **all your brothers**, from the nations. This would be Gentile converts coming to Jerusalem.
66:21 The most natural antecedent to **them** is the nations. Thus, Isaiah presented a remarkable picture of the nations producing people set apart for service to the Lord like **priests and Levites**.
66:22 On **new heavens** and **new earth**, see note at 65:17.
66:23 In this future day, no one will neglect the regular worship of the Lord. The **New Moon** festival was a monthly sacred observance (1:13; Nm 29:6; 2Kg 4:23; Ezr 3:5; Ps 81:3).
66:24 Isaiah ended his book with one last description of the fate of the wicked. If his intention was to describe a departure from Jerusalem, then perhaps he referred to the Hinnom Valley—a place where garbage was burned and bodies were left to rot. The purpose of this graphic image was to move people toward God and redemption.

▼ Introduction to Jeremiah

Circumstances of Writing

Jeremiah was a priest from the town of Anathoth (1:1). At the Lord's command, he neither married nor had children because of the impending judgment that would come upon the next generation. His ministry as a prophet began in 626 BC and ended after 586 BC. He was a contemporary of Habakkuk and possibly Obadiah.

The book of Jeremiah discusses the last days of Judah. King Hezekiah reigned for forty-two years (729–686 BC) and began to reverse Judah's spiritual bankruptcy. But when Hezekiah's son, Manasseh, came to the throne, idolatrous and superstitious cultic practices and rites came back like a flood. Manasseh's son Amon ruled for only two years (642–640 BC). He also reinstated idol worship as the official religion of Judah (2Ch 33:22–23).

Amon's eight-year-old son, Josiah, succeeded him on the throne. This lad walked in the ways of the former King David. When he was eighteen years old (622 BC), he called for long-delayed repairs to be made to the temple. During this work, a copy of the law of Moses was found. On the basis of hearing this word, the young king and all his people renewed the covenant with the Lord. However, this reformation failed to overcome the effects of the wickedness Manasseh and Amon had instituted.

Contribution to the Bible

The best-known passage in Jeremiah is the new covenant text in 31:31–34. Not only is it the largest Old Testament text quoted in the New Testament (Heb 8:8–12; 10:16–17), but arguably better than any other passage it links God's ancient promises to Eve (Gn 3:15), Abraham (Gn 12:1–3), and David (2Sm 7:16–19) with New Testament assurances that God in Christ grants believers new hearts, salvation, and fellowship with him.

Structure

One date rings throughout the entire book of Jeremiah: "the fourth year of Jehoiakim son of Josiah, king of Judah." That year, 605 BC, brought major change to the political situation of the ancient Near East. Both Egypt and Assyria were defeated at the battle of Carchemish (Jr 46:2–12; 2Kg 24:7; 2Ch 35:20). Nebuchadnezzar ascended the throne of Babylon. In that same year God instructed Jeremiah to put his prophecies into writing as a final test of King Jehoiakim's responsiveness to the Word of God.

This significant dateline, "the fourth year of Jehoiakim," was placed at 25:1; 36:1; and 45:1, thereby dividing the prophet's book into three main sections: the prophet's faithfulness in carrying out God's commission (chaps. 2–24), the fierce opposition to his ministry (chaps. 25–35), and the collapse of Judah (chaps. 36–45).

The book of Jeremiah includes poetic sections (especially in chaps. 2–25) and prose accounts as well. Critical scholars generally say that the poetry is Jeremiah's and the prose is either the work of his friends or a person

---

Jeremiah Timeline

650–625 BC

Under Ashurbanipal, Assyrians capture and destroy Babylon. **649**

Birth of Jeremiah **640?**

Ashurbanipal (**668–629**) rules over a declining Assyrian Empire that experienced revolts (**642**) and contributes to the assassination of Amon of Judah (**641**) and the rise of Amon's son Josiah. (**641–609**).

Initial reforms of Josiah **631**

Jeremiah is called to be a prophet; he warns of an invasion from the north. **626**

625–605 BC

Second phase of Josiah's reforms when the book of the law is found in the temple **622**

Under Nabopolassar (**626–605**), Asshur and Nineveh fall, marking the end of the Assyrian Empire. **612**

Babylonians and Medes take Harran from what remained of Assyrian forces. **610**

Jeremiah's temple sermon **609**

Josiah killed by the Egyptians at Megiddo **609**

Josiah's son, Jehoahaz II, succeeds him and is deposed; he's replaced by his brother, Jehoiakim. **609**

who is labeled a Deuteronomic writer (so designated because the prose sections are said to reflect the book of Deuteronomy). But we may ask, could not Jeremiah have written in both poetic and prose form? There is no reason to suppose he was incapable of writing in both forms.

Key verse in Jeremiah

29:11 "For I know the plans I have for you" — this is the LORD's declaration — "plans for your well-being, not for disaster, to give you a future and a hope."

605–600 BC

Nebuchadnezzar attacks Jerusalem and leads citizens of Judah into exile. **605, 597, 586, 582**
Jehoiakim makes a decision to turn from his alliance with Egypt and submit to Nebuchadnezzar. **604**
Jehoiakim ignores Jeremiah's warning and turns back to Egypt for support after Egypt defeats Babylon at Migdol. **601**
A reinforced Babylonian army approaches Judah; Jehoiakim dies. **598**

600–575 BC

Jehoiachin succeeds his father, Jehoiakim, and reigns three months and ten days. **597**
Jehoiachin and Judah's queen mother are brought to Babylon by Nebuchadnezzar. **597**
Zedekiah succeeds Jehoiachin; reigns 597–586
Ezekiel is exiled in Babylon. **597**

1 The words of Jeremiah, the son of Hilkiah, one of the priests living in Anathoth in the territory of Benjamin. ² The word of the LORD came to him in the thirteenth year of the reign of Josiah son of Amon, king of Judah. ³ It also came throughout the days of Jehoiakim son of Josiah, king of Judah, until the fifth month of the eleventh year of Zedekiah son of Josiah, king of Judah, when the people of Jerusalem went into exile.

The Call of Jeremiah

⁴ The word of the LORD came to me:
⁵ I chose you before I formed you
 in the womb;
 I set you apart
 before you were born.
 I appointed you a prophet
 to the nations.

⁶ But I protested, "Oh no, Lord GOD! Look, I don't know how to speak since I am only a youth."
⁷ Then the LORD said to me:
 Do not say, "I am only a youth,"
 for you will go to everyone I send you to
 and speak whatever I tell you.
⁸ Do not be afraid of anyone,
 for I will be with you to rescue you.
 This is the LORD's declaration.

⁹ Then the LORD reached out his hand, touched my mouth, and told me:
 I have now filled your mouth
 with my words.
¹⁰ See, I have appointed you today
 over nations and kingdoms
 to uproot and tear down,
 to destroy and demolish,
 to build and plant.

1:1–4 Jeremiah was the instrument through whom God spoke, but it was the divine **word** that **came to him**. This was a favorite expression of Jeremiah, indicating that God's word took possession of him and exerted deep influence in his life. Verse 4 repeats this expression. God's word came to Jeremiah over many years, ending with the Babylonian exile. The revelations began during the reign of the Judean King **Josiah** (640–609 BC) and continued during the reigns of Jehoahaz (reigned for three months in 609 BC); **Jehoiakim** (609–597 BC); Jehoiachin (reigned for three months in 597 BC); and **Zedekiah** (597–586 BC). Jeremiah did not mention the brief reigns of Jehoahaz or Jehoiachin in his list (v. 3). The Hebrew expression for the "word" (*dabar*) means not only the spoken word, as it is frequently

and correctly rendered, but also "thing," "action," or "event." Accordingly, Jeremiah both preached and acted out some of his messages in symbolic performances in order to bring the word of God home more forcibly to his audience.

1:5 The prophet was told that God **chose** him **before** he **formed** him **in the womb**. The word for **chose** is the Hebrew verb *yada*, which also carries the connotation "knew." God had more than an intellectual knowledge of Jeremiah; he had a personal relationship with him. He was **set . . . apart** or separated (as in the root "to be holy," or "set apart" to the Lord) and **appointed** to be a **prophet to the nations**.

1:6 Youth can refer to an infant (Ex 2:6), a child (1Sm 1:22), a boy (1Sm 3:1), or even a young man (Gn 22:3; 34:19).

1:7–8 The word **rescue** also means to "deliver." This was the same strong assurance God had given to his people in the exodus from Egypt (Ex 3:8; 12:27) and when he rescued David from a lion (1Sm 17:37).

1:9 Here is an anthropomorphism (description of God in human terms) that promises that God will personally be the source of his message. Later Jeremiah will speak of having eaten God's word (Jr 15:16). These words became like fire in his mouth (5:14). The word of God in Jeremiah's mouth was "like a hammer that pulverizes rock" (Jr 23:29).

1:10 Six metaphors — **uproot** . . . **tear down** . . . **destroy** . . . **demolish** . . . **build**, and **plant**—will constitute Jeremiah's message to the nations; four negative and two positive.

Q & A: Is DNA evidence for the existence of God?

by Frank Turek

I once read an atheist who complained that there was not enough evidence to believe in God. When a Christian asked him what kind of evidence he would need to believe, he said he would believe if he looked up and saw written in the sky, "Hey, Roger! This is God. I certainly do exist!"

The immediacy and specificity of such a message would rule out a skywriter. Roger certainly couldn't explain it away as a chance collection of cloud material or an unusual cloud formation. Nor would he say that, given enough time, the clouds would form that way naturally due to some kind of cloud evolution. A message such as this would have to be the product of intelligence. Why? Because natural laws don't create specific, complex messages. In all our experience, the only forces we see creating specific complex messages are intelligent minds. Natural forces never do it.

That's why when you're walking down the beach and you see "John loves Mary" scribbled in the sand, you know a human being has been there. You don't assume that a crab wrote the message or that the lapping waves produced it. Only minds produce messages. This is why archaeologists know that inscriptions dug up from the ground were made by ancient humans, not natural forces.

Well, it turns out that all life forms contain messages that are far more specified and complex than the message the

atheist above said he'd like to see in the sky or any messages found scribbled on beaches or ancient tablets.

How much more?

The simplest independent life we know about (the amoeba) is a miniature machine of astonishing complexity. Even the ardent Darwinist, Richard Dawkins, admits that the amount of information in this one-celled life form has as much information in its DNA as one thousand complete sets of an encyclopedia—that's thirty volumes times one thousand in a cell that's much smaller than a grain of salt. Now, believing that thirty thousand books came into existence from non-living chemicals by natural law without any intelligent intervention is like believing that an entire library resulted from an explosion in a printing shop! I don't have enough faith to believe that.

This is not a God-of-the-gaps argument, which is a kind of argument that says God must be the explanation for things we don't know or understand. We don't simply lack a natural explanation for the complexity of DNA. Rather, evidence for the complexity of DNA is positive and empirically-detectable, and it points to the work of an intelligent Creator. There is no natural force that can create such a message, especially one that is thirty thousand books long. Messages only come from minds.

In summary, DNA points to a supreme intelligence. This is why Francis Collins, former head of the Human Genome Project, calls DNA the language of God. To paraphrase the seventeenth-century mathematician, physicist, and religious philosopher Blaise Pascal, God never performed a miracle to convince an atheist because his ordinary works provide sufficient evidence. DNA is one of those ordinary works.

Two Visions

¹¹ Then the word of the LORD came to me, asking, "What do you see, Jeremiah?"

I replied, "I see a branch of an almond tree."

¹² The LORD said to me, "You have seen correctly, for I watch over^A my word to accomplish it." ¹³ Again the word of the LORD came to me asking, "What do you see?"

And I replied, "I see a boiling pot, its lip tilted from the north to the south."

¹⁴ Then the LORD said to me, "Disaster will be poured out^B from the north on all who live in the land. ¹⁵ Indeed, I am about to summon all the clans and kingdoms of the north."

This is the LORD's declaration.

They will come, and each king
    will set up his throne
at the entrance to Jerusalem's gates.
They will attack
    all her surrounding walls
    and all the other cities of Judah.

¹⁶ "I will pronounce my judgments against them for all the evil they did when they abandoned me to burn incense to other gods and to worship the works of their own hands.

¹⁷ "Now, get ready. Stand up and tell them everything that I command you. Do not be intimidated by them or I will cause you to cower before them. ¹⁸ Today, I am the one who has made you a fortified city, an iron pillar, and bronze walls against the whole land — against the kings of Judah, its officials, its priests, and the population. ¹⁹ They will fight against you but never prevail over you, since I am with you to rescue you."

This is the LORD's declaration.

Israel Accused of Apostasy

2 The word of the LORD came to me: ² "Go and announce directly to Jerusalem that this is what the LORD says:

I remember the loyalty of your youth,
    your love as a bride —
how you followed me in the wilderness,
    in a land not sown.
³   Israel was holy to the LORD,
    the firstfruits of his harvest.
All who ate of it found
        themselves guilty;
disaster came on them."
    This is the LORD's declaration.

⁴   Hear the word of the LORD,
        house of Jacob
    and all families of the house of Israel.
⁵   This is what the LORD says:

What fault did your ancestors find
    in me
that they went so far from me,
followed worthless idols,
    and became worthless themselves?
⁶   They stopped asking, "Where is
        the LORD
who brought us from the land of Egypt,
who led us through the wilderness,
through a land of deserts and ravines,
through a land of drought
        and darkness,^C
a land no one traveled through
    and where no one lived?"
⁷   I brought you to a fertile land
        to eat its fruit and bounty,

---

^A 1:12 In Hb, the word for *almond tree* sounds like the word for *watch over*   ^B 1:14 LXX reads *will boil*   ^C 2:6 Or *shadow of death*

1:11–12 In the first of two visions, God showed the prophet a **branch** of an **almond tree**, one of the first trees to blossom in the spring. In 1:12 the Lord interpreted this imagery by saying, **I watch over my word**. The "almond" is *shaqed* in Hebrew, and the verb "to watch" is *shoqed*; thus, these verses involve a pun in the original language. Just as the almond tree blossoms early in Israel's springtime and signifies the coming of a fruitful season, God told Jeremiah that he would soon cause him to "blossom" with fruitful words from God.
1:13–15 Next the prophet saw **a boiling pot** or cauldron, tilted toward the south, spilling its contents of disaster from the north. This was the direction from which foreign armies would come against Israel and Judah. This enemy is identified in 25:9 as Babylon, but the threat collectively came from **all the clans and kingdoms of the north**. Each northern king would **set up his throne**, symbolizing his conquest and rule over defeated Judah.
1:16 The reason for such a severe judgment was Judah's burning **incense to other gods**. The Hebrew verb shows these were repeated acts still going on.
1:17–19 Jeremiah was given three commands: (1) **stand up**, (2) **tell them everything that**

I command you, and (3) **do not be intimidated by them**. The command to stand up is literally "gird your loins," or "brace yourself." It is used of getting ready for work, battle, debate, or for the tiring job of preaching to an unreceptive audience. The prophet was not to speak out of his own thoughts, but everything that God commanded him. The word for "to be intimidated" (also meaning "to be terrified," "to be confounded," or "to panic") plays on the word **to cower** (same Hb verb; "to ruin [you]" or "to make [you] a failure") **before them**. God would make Jeremiah **a fortified city, an iron pillar, and bronze walls against the whole land**. The prophet would be made strong, resistant, and as impregnable as these objects. There would be strong opposition to his message, but **kings . . . officials**, and **priests** would not prevail over God's prophet.
2:1–20 In this section God recalled the "honeymoon" he had enjoyed with Israel from the time of the exodus to the events at Mount Sinai (Ex 3–24). During that time the people believed the Lord and worshiped him (Ex 4:29–31; 12:22–28; 14:31; see also Hs 2:15; 9:10). However, Israel soon murmured, grumbled, and complained (Ex 14:11; 15:24; 16:2; 17:2). These early "gripe sessions" illustrated a lack of faith, but full-fledged rebellion and

apostasy were often the marks of Israel in the years following the establishment of the covenant at Mount Sinai (known as the Sinaitic covenant).
2:2 The **loyalty of your youth** uses the beautiful Hebrew word *chesed* for "loyalty." It occurs 248 times in the OT and speaks of the "loving-kindness" or "unfailing devotion" Israel (depicted as a bride) initially showed to her bridegroom, the Lord.
2:3 That Israel will be the **firstfruits of his harvest**, rather than the *only* fruits, anticipates other peoples and nations coming to the Lord. **Israel was holy to the LORD** in the same way that certain offerings were called "holy" or "hallowed." They were set aside from common or ordinary use to be reserved for the Lord (Nm 18:8–19,26–29).
2:5 The rhetorical **what fault did your ancestors find in me** uses the language of divorce proceedings (Dt 24:1), as if God had proven to be an unworthy marital partner. But God was not to blame for Israel's apostasy. God had remained faithful, but Israel departed from the covenant to follow **worthless idols**. The word for "worthless" is the same term used in Ecclesiastes for "vanity."
2:7 The words **fertile land** are literally "land of Carmel." Mount Carmel was renowned

but after you entered, you defiled
    my land;
you made my inheritance detestable.
8   The priests quit asking, "Where is
        the LORD?"
    The experts in the law no longer
        knew me,
    and the rulers rebelled against me.
    The prophets prophesied by^A Baal
    and followed useless idols.

9   Therefore, I will bring a case
        against you again.
    This is the LORD's declaration.
    I will bring a case
        against your children's children.
10 Cross over to the coasts of Cyprus^B
        and take a look.
    Send someone to Kedar
        and consider carefully;
    see if there has ever been
        anything like this:
11 Has a nation ever exchanged its gods?
    (But they were not gods!)
    Yet my people have exchanged
        their^C Glory
    for useless idols.
12 Be appalled at this, heavens;
    be shocked and utterly desolated!
    This is the LORD's declaration.

13 For my people have committed
        a double evil:
    They have abandoned me,
        the fountain of living water,
    and dug cisterns for themselves —
        cracked cisterns that cannot hold water.

Consequences of Apostasy

14 Is Israel a slave?
    Was he born into slavery?^D
    Why else has he become a prey?

15 The young lions have roared at him;
    they have roared loudly.
    They have laid waste his land.
    His cities are in ruins,
        without inhabitants.
16 The men of Memphis and Tahpanhes
    have also broken your skull.
17 Have you not brought this on yourself
    by abandoning the LORD your God
    while he was leading you along the way?
18 Now what will you gain
    by traveling along the way to Egypt
    to drink the water of the Nile?^E
    What will you gain
    by traveling along the way to Assyria
    to drink the water of the Euphrates?
19 Your own evil will discipline you;
    your own apostasies
        will reprimand you.
    Recognize^F how evil and bitter it is
    for you to abandon the LORD your God
    and to have no fear of me.
    This is the declaration
        of the Lord GOD of Armies.

20 For long ago I^G broke your yoke;
    I^G tore off your chains.
    You insisted, "I will not serve!"
    On every high hill
    and under every green tree
    you lay down like a prostitute.
21 I planted you, a choice vine
    from the very best seed.
    How then could you turn into
    a degenerate, foreign vine?

22 Even if you wash with lye
    and use a great amount of bleach,^H
    the stain of your iniquity is still
        in front of me.
    This is the Lord GOD's declaration.

---

^A 2:8 = in the name of   ^B 2:10 Lit to the islands of Kittim   ^C 2:11 Alt Hb tradition reads my   ^D 2:14 Lit born of a house
^E 2:18 Lit of Shihor   ^F 2:19 Lit Know and see   ^G 2:20 LXX reads you   ^H 2:22 Lit cleansing agent

---

for its luxurious vegetation and crops (Am 1:2; Mc 7:14).

2:8 Four types of leaders are charged for failing to carry out their responsibilities and for allowing apostasy and unfaithfulness to take over in Israel: **priests . . . experts in the law . . . rulers** (lit "the shepherds," used metaphorically of political leaders in the OT), and false **prophets** who **prophesied by Baal**.

2:9 Therefore introduces a prophetic announcement about coming judgment. God will take his nation to court, and he will act as both plaintiff and judge.

2:10–12 Here is God's courtroom accusation: Israel had behaved ludicrously. They **exchanged their Glory for useless idols**. Look from Cyprus to **Kedar** in the desert east of Transjordan, God says, and nowhere will you find another nation making such a foolish exchange.

2:13 As the **fountain of living water**, or a flowing spring, God is the source of

everlasting life (17:13; Is 55:1; Zch 13:1; Jn 4:10–14; 7:37–39). In defiance of God as the source of life, Judah had dug her own wells (metaphorically speaking) in the earth and plastered their sides to hold in stale rainwater, only to have the plaster crack, the **cisterns** fail, and the water escape. Such is the futility of false religion.

2:14–19 God asks six rhetorical questions. In contrast to the safety they enjoyed in their honeymoon days with the Lord, now the nations attack Israel at will. How did she become everyone else's prey? God says the **discipline** was a result of Israel's **own evil** (v. 19).

2:15 The **young lions** figuratively designate Israel's enemies, especially the Assyrians.

2:16 Memphis was the capital of Lower Egypt, approximately thirteen miles south of Cairo. **Tahpanhes** was a fortress close to the northeastern boundary of Egypt. The Egyptians would become allies in the destruction of Judah.

2:18 The Hebrew word translated **Nile** is shichor, meaning "blackness." Referring to the Nile River in this way denigrates its status as a god among the Egyptians. Hence, it was futile for Judah to trust Assyria or Egypt to rescue them from the coming threat.

2:20–28 Five images in this section describe Judah's breaking the covenant with God: (1) a beast that has broken loose from its yoke, (2) choice grapes that have gone wild, (3) a stain that will not wash off, (4) a young female camel that cannot walk straight, and (5) a wild donkey in heat, sniffing the wind for a male companion.

2:21 The Sorek vine (**a choice vine**) grew in the Wadi al-Sarar and yielded a muchprized red wine. Israel was once this vine, but turned **degenerate** and yielded inferior grapes.

2:22 Lye is probably a reference to niter, a mineral alkali deposited on the shores of some lakes in Egypt. **Bleach** was a vegetable

23 How can you protest, "I am not defiled;
I have not followed the Baals"?
Look at your behavior in the valley;
acknowledge what you have done.
You are a swift young camel
twisting and turning on her way,

24 a wild donkey at home[A]
in the wilderness.
She sniffs the wind in the heat
of her desire.
Who can control her passion?
All who look for her will not
become weary;
they will find her in her mating season.[B]

25 Keep your feet from going bare
and your throat from thirst.
But you say, "It's hopeless;
I love strangers,
and I will continue to follow them."

26 Like the shame of a thief
when he is caught,
so the house of Israel has been
put to shame.
They, their kings, their officials,
their priests, and their prophets

27 say to a tree, "You are my father,"
and to a stone, "You gave birth to me."
For they have turned their back to me
and not their face,
yet in their time of disaster they beg,
"Rise up and save us!"

28 But where are your gods you made
for yourself?
Let them rise up and save you
in your time of disaster if they can,
for your gods are as numerous
as your cities, Judah.

Judgment Deserved

29 Why do you bring a case against me?
All of you have rebelled against me.
This is the LORD's declaration.

30 I have struck down your children
in vain;
they would not accept discipline.
Your own sword has devoured
your prophets
like a ravaging lion.

31 Evil generation,
pay attention to the word of the LORD!
Have I been a wilderness to Israel
or a land of dense darkness?
Why do my people claim,
"We will go where we want;[C]
we will no longer come to you"?

32 Can a young woman forget her jewelry
or a bride her wedding sash?
Yet my people have forgotten me
for countless days.

33 How skillfully you pursue love;
you also teach evil women your ways.

34 Moreover, your skirts are stained
with the blood of the innocent poor.
You did not catch them breaking
and entering.
But in spite of all these things

35 you claim, "I am innocent.
His anger is sure to turn away
from me."
But I will certainly judge you
because you have said, "I have
not sinned."

36 How unstable you are,
constantly changing your ways!
You will be put to shame by Egypt
just as you were put to shame
by Assyria.

37 Moreover, you will be led out from here
with your hands on your head
since the LORD has rejected
those you trust;
you will not succeed even with
their help.[D]

Wages of Apostasy

3 If[E] a man divorces his wife
and she leaves him to marry another,
can he ever return to her?
Wouldn't such a land[F] become
totally defiled?
But you!
You have prostituted yourself
with many partners —
can you return to me?
This is the LORD's declaration.

A 2:24 Lit *donkey taught*   B 2:24 Lit *her month*   C 2:31 Or *"We have taken control,* or *"We can roam*   D 2:37 Lit *with them*
E 3:1 One Hb ms, LXX, Syr; other Hb mss read *Saying: If*   F 3:1 LXX reads *woman*

---

alkali, made by pouring water through wood ashes.
2:23 A **swift young camel** could cause a lot of damage if turned loose in a crowded place, for it would be reckless in its direction and unsteady in its gait.
2:24 This female **wild donkey** was frantic for a male in the time of her heat. She could not be diverted from her sexual goal. This image depicts Judah mindlessly lusting after foreign gods.
2:26–28 God satirically mocked his people's adoption of Canaanite worship by reversing the genders of the pagan gods. He depicts

Judah saying to **a tree** (representing the goddess Asherah in the form of a standing pole), **You are my father**, and **to a stone** (probably the stone pillars representing the male Canaanite deity), **You gave birth to me.**
2:31 We will go where we want signifies the rejection of divine guidance.
2:34–35 In the Mosaic law there was no guilt on someone who beat to death a thief caught breaking into his house (Ex 22:2).
2:36 Judah will **be put to shame** by Egypt, just as they had been by Assyria. Pharaoh Psammetich II (663–610 BC) had gained

Egypt's independence from Assyria while King Ashurbanipal of Assyria was fending off revolutionaries. Judah thought the time was right to form an alliance with Egypt against Assyria, but this was doomed to failure.
3:1 The phrase **Wouldn't such a land become totally defiled?** alludes to the divorce law in Dt 24:1–4, where a man is not allowed to remarry his ex-wife if she has married and been divorced by another man. In a similar way, God asks Judah, **can you return to me** after defiling the land by your infidelities with false gods?

² Look to the barren heights and see.
   Where have you not been immoral?
 You sat waiting for them
     beside the highways
 like a nomad in the desert.
 You have defiled the land
   with your prostitution and wickedness.
³ This is why the showers
     haven't come —
 why there has been no spring rain.
 You have the brazen look of a prostitute^A
   and refuse to be ashamed.
⁴ Haven't you recently called to me,
     "My Father!
 You were my friend in my youth.
⁵ Will he bear a grudge forever?
 Will he be endlessly infuriated?"
 This is what you have said,
 but you have done the evil things
   you are capable of.

Unfaithful Israel, Treacherous Judah

⁶ In the days of King Josiah the Lord asked me, "Have you seen what unfaithful Israel has done? She has ascended every high hill and gone under every green tree to prostitute herself there. ⁷ I thought, 'After she has done all these things, she will return to me.' But she didn't return, and her treacherous sister Judah saw it. ⁸ I^B observed that it was because unfaithful Israel had committed adultery that I had sent her away and had given her a certificate of divorce. Nevertheless, her treacherous sister Judah was not afraid but also went and prostituted herself. ⁹ Indifferent to^c her prostitution, she defiled the land and committed adultery with stones and trees. ¹⁰ Yet in spite of all this, her treacherous sister Judah didn't return to me with all her heart — only in pretense."

This is the Lord's declaration.

¹¹ The Lord announced to me, "Unfaithful Israel has shown herself more righteous than treacherous Judah. ¹² Go, proclaim these words to the north, and say,

 'Return, unfaithful Israel.
     This is the Lord's declaration.

 I will not look on you with anger,^D
   for I am unfailing in my love.
     This is the Lord's declaration.
 I will not be angry forever.
¹³ Only acknowledge your guilt —
   you have rebelled against the Lord
     your God.
 You have scattered your favors
     to strangers
 under every green tree
 and have not obeyed me.
     This is the Lord's declaration.

¹⁴ "'Return, you faithless children — this is the Lord's declaration — for I am your master,^E and I will take you, one from a city and two from a family, and I will bring you to Zion. ¹⁵ I will give you shepherds who are loyal to me,^F and they will shepherd you with knowledge and skill. ¹⁶ When you multiply and increase in the land, in those days — this is the Lord's declaration — no one will say again, "The ark of the Lord's covenant." It will never come to mind, and no one will remember or miss it. Another one will not be made.^G ¹⁷ At that time Jerusalem will be called The Lord's Throne, and all the nations will be gathered to it, to the name of the Lord in Jerusalem. They will cease to follow the stubbornness of their evil hearts. ¹⁸ In those days the house of Judah will join with the house of Israel, and they will come together from the land of the north to the land I have given your ancestors to inherit.'"

True Repentance

¹⁹ I thought, "How I long to make you
     my sons
 and give you a desirable land,
 the most beautiful inheritance of all
     the nations."
 I thought, "You will call me 'My Father'
 and never turn away from me."
²⁰ However, as a woman may betray
     her lover,^H
 so you have betrayed me,
     house of Israel.
     This is the Lord's declaration.

---

^A3:3 Lit *have a prostitute's forehead* ^B3:8 One Hb ms, Syr read *She* ^C3:9 Lit *From the lightness of* ^D3:12 Lit *not cause my face to fall on you* ^E3:14 Or *husband* ^F3:15 Lit *shepherds according to my heart* ^G3:16 Or *It will no longer be done* ^H3:20 Lit *friend*

3:2 Like a nomad compares lustful Judah to a Bedouin waiting in ambush to rob a caravan.

3:3 The false god Baal whom Judah worshiped was thought to be the god of **rain**, dew, thunder, and fertility. The true God withheld these things, demonstrating the futility of false religion.

3:6–7 Apostate northern Israel **ascended every high hill** to practice the fertility cult. **3:8** The **certificate of divorce** is referred to in Dt 24:1.

3:9 Judah regarded her sins lightly, in spite of what had happened to the ten tribes of northern Israel when the capital city, Samaria, fell to the Assyrians.

3:12 I am unfailing in my love refers to God's loyalty, mercy, and grace. On the Hebrew word *chesed*, or "unfailing love," see note at 2:2.

3:15 The **shepherds** mentioned here do not refer to political rulers but to the spiritual leaders (Jeremiah himself was counted as such in 17:16).

3:16 The future messianic era is signaled by the introductory phrase **in those days**. Israel and Judah will **multiply and increase in the land** in this messianic era. The ark of the covenant, the most central and precious symbol at the heart of Israel's worship, will not even be remembered then because something more significant will take its place.

3:17 At that time Jerusalem will be called the **Lord's Throne**, replacing the ark of the covenant as the symbol of his presence (Lv 16:2,13; Ps 80:1). The result will be that **all the nations will be gathered** to Jerusalem, and they will **cease to follow the stubbornness of their evil hearts**.

3:19 The land of promise is called **a desirable land**, or literally "pleasant land" (Ps 106:24; Zch 7:14). Having been rejected as Israel's husband, God was now rejected by the people of Judah as their Father.

3:20 The verb for betray can also mean "deal treacherously with." See Jr 5:11.

21 A sound is heard on the barren heights:
the children of Israel weeping
    and begging for mercy,
for they have perverted their way;
they have forgotten the Lord their God.
22 Return, you faithless children.
I will heal your unfaithfulness.
"Here we are, coming to you,
for you are the Lord our God.
23 Surely, falsehood comes from the hills,
commotion from the mountains,
but the salvation of Israel
is only in the Lord our God.
24 From the time of our youth
the shameful one[A] has consumed
what our ancestors have worked for —
their flocks and their herds,
their sons and their daughters.
25 Let us lie down in our shame;
let our disgrace cover us.
We have sinned against the Lord
    our God,
both we and our ancestors,
from the time of our youth
    even to this day.
We have not obeyed the Lord our God."

Blessing or Curse

4 If you return,[B] Israel —
    this is the Lord's declaration —
you will return to me,
if you remove your abhorrent idols
from my presence
and do not waver,
2 then you can swear, "As the Lord lives,"
in truth, justice, and righteousness,
and then the nations will be blessed[C]
    by him
and will boast in him.

3 For this is what the Lord says to the men
of Judah and Jerusalem:
Break up the unplowed ground;
do not sow among the thorns.
4 Circumcise yourselves to the Lord;
remove the foreskin of your hearts,
men of Judah and residents
    of Jerusalem.
Otherwise, my wrath will break out
    like fire

and burn with no one to extinguish it
because of your evil deeds.

Judgment from the North

5 Declare in Judah, proclaim in Jerusalem, and
say,
Blow the ram's horn
    throughout the land.
Cry out loudly and say,
"Assemble yourselves,
and let's flee to the fortified cities."
6 Lift up a signal flag toward Zion.
Run for cover! Don't stand still!
For I am bringing disaster
    from the north —
a crushing blow.
7 A lion has gone up from his thicket;
a destroyer of nations has set out.
He has left his lair
to make your land a waste.
Your cities will be reduced
    to uninhabited ruins.
8 Because of this, put on sackcloth;
mourn and wail,
for the Lord's burning anger
has not turned away from us.

9 "On that day" — this is the Lord's declaration — "the king and the officials will lose
their courage. The priests will tremble in fear,
and the prophets will be scared speechless."
10 I said, "Oh no, Lord God, you have certainly deceived this people and Jerusalem, by announcing, 'You will have peace,' while a sword
is at[D] our throats."
11 "At that time it will be said to this people
and to Jerusalem, 'A searing wind blows from
the barren heights in the wilderness on the
way to my dear[E] people. It comes not to winnow or to sift; 12 a wind too strong for this
comes at my call.[F] Now I will also pronounce
judgments against them.'"
13 Look, he advances like clouds;
his chariots are like a storm.
His horses are swifter than eagles.
Woe to us, for we are ruined!
14 Wash the evil from your heart, Jerusalem,
so that you will be delivered.
How long will you harbor
malicious thoughts?

[A]3:24 = Baal   [B]4:1 Or Repent   [C]4:2 Or will bless one another   [D]4:10 Lit sword touches   [E]4:11 Lit to the daughter of my
[F]4:12 Lit comes for me

3:24–25 Baal is designated by the derisive term often used for him: the shameful one. 4:3 Unplowed ground was soil long untended and abandoned to wild growth. Ground that had lain fallow too long needed to be broken up and cultivated again. Jeremiah and Hosea (Hs 10:12) used this image to picture the need for spiritual renewal. 4:4 A hard buildup around the hearts of the people had to be cut away (Dt 10:16; Rm 2:28–29).

4:5–31 In this section Jeremiah was so sure that God's judgment was imminent that he described it as already present. 4:7 Jeremiah used many animals, including the lion, to portray the furious warfare that would come from the north. Add to this the eagle (v. 13), wolf, and leopard (5:6), plus the images of the hot winds of the sirocco (4:11), or fire (v. 4), and the threatened disaster grows more frightening. 4:10 This is one of the most controversial verses in Jeremiah. Was Jeremiah accusing

God of deceiving the nation? James 1:13 says God does not do that. Scripture is often silent about secondary causes, and since God rules history even things he merely permits can be attributed to him. In the present case, God allowed false prophets to mislead the nation by saying peace was on the way. 4:11 The phrase my dear people (lit "the daughter of my people") occurs for the first time here. It occurs a total of eight times between here and 9:7 where it ends (to be picked up again five times in Lamentations).

15 For a voice announces from Dan,
  proclaiming malice
    from Mount Ephraim.
16 Warn the nations: Look!
  Proclaim to Jerusalem:
  Those who besiege are coming
    from a distant land;
  they raise their voices
    against the cities of Judah.
17 They have her surrounded
    like those who guard a field,
  because she has rebelled against me.
    This is the LORD's declaration.
18 Your way and your actions
    have brought this on you.
  This is your punishment. It is very bitter,
    because it has reached your heart!

Jeremiah's Lament

19 My anguish, my anguish!^A I writhe
    in agony!
  Oh, the pain in^B my heart!
  My heart pounds;
  I cannot be silent.
  For you, my soul,
    have heard the sound
      of the ram's horn —
    the shout of battle.
20 Disaster after disaster is reported
  because the whole land is destroyed.
  Suddenly my tents are destroyed,
    my tent curtains, in a moment.
21 How long must I see the signal flag
    and hear the sound of the ram's horn?

22 "For my people are fools;
    they do not know me.
  They are foolish children,
    without understanding.
  They are skilled in doing what is evil,
    but they do not know how to do
      what is good."

23 I looked at the earth,
    and it was formless and empty.
  I looked to the heavens,
    and their light was gone.
24 I looked at the mountains,
    and they were quaking;

25 all the hills shook.
  I looked, and there was no human being,
    and all the birds of the sky had fled.
26 I looked, and the fertile field was
    a wilderness.
  All its cities were torn down
    because of the LORD
      and his burning anger.

27 For this is what the LORD says:
  "The whole land will be a desolation,
    but I will not finish it off.
28 Because of this, the earth will mourn;
    the skies above will grow dark.
  I have spoken; I have planned,
    and I will not relent or turn back
      from it."

29 Every city flees
    at the sound of the horseman
      and the archer.
  They enter the thickets
    and climb among the rocks.
  Every city is abandoned;
    no inhabitant is left.
30 And you, devastated one, what are
    you doing
  that you dress yourself in scarlet,
    that you adorn yourself
      with gold jewelry,
  that you enhance your eyes
    with makeup?
  You beautify yourself for nothing.
  Your lovers reject you;
    they intend to take your life.
31 I hear a cry like a woman in labor,
    a cry of anguish like one bearing
      her first child.
  The cry of Daughter Zion
    gasping for breath,
  stretching out her hands:
  "Woe is me, for my life is weary
    because of the murderers!"

The Depravity of Jerusalem

5 Roam through the streets of Jerusalem.
  Investigate;^C
  search in her squares.
  If you find one person,

---

^A 4:19 Lit My inner parts, my inner parts ^B 4:19 Lit the walls of ^C 5:1 Lit See and know

---

Sometimes it is the Lord who uses it, and sometimes it is the prophet.

4:15–17 The advances of the enemy from the north can be heard from **Dan**, at the northern limit of Israel and at the headwaters of the Jordan River, on down to **Mount Ephraim**, the highlands stretching from Shechem to Bethel.

4:19–22 These verses contain the first of Jeremiah's "confessions" (see his other confessions at 11:18–23; 12:1–6; 15:10–11,15–21; 17:14–18; 18:18–23; 20:7–13,14–18; and possibly 5:3–5; 8:18–9:1). The confessions reflect the pain Jeremiah experienced about the calamity that awaited his people.

4:23–28 This is one of the most haunting passages in all the Prophets because of its vivid, realistic portrayal of God's coming wrath against sin. The judgment moves beyond the Babylonian conquest to the coming day of the Lord at the end of history.

4:23 Jeremiah borrowed the phrase **the earth . . . was formless and empty** from Gn 1:2. The imagery portrays the reversal of God's acts of creation. Such will be the devastation of the coming day of the Lord.

4:30 Jeremiah depicted Jerusalem in her death agony, still rejecting God as her husband. Instead of choosing repentance and

mourning, she dressed in **scarlet**, adorned herself with **gold jewelry**, and enhanced her eyes with **makeup**. This imagery plays off the fact that women of Bible times applied a silver-white metallic substance as a base for black kohl on the upper and lower eyelids. But Jerusalem prettied herself **for nothing**; her **lovers** would only take her life.

5:1–2 The phrase **find one person** is a hyperbole. Jeremiah and his scribe Baruch would certainly count as two righteous persons. This reminds us of the five cities of the plain, which would have been spared

any who acts justly,
who pursues faithfulness,
then I will forgive her.
2 When they say, "As the LORD lives,"
they are swearing falsely.
3 LORD, don't your eyes
look for faithfulness?
You have struck them, but they felt
no pain.
You finished them off,
but they refused to accept discipline.
They made their faces harder than rock,
and they refused to return.

4 Then I thought:
They are just the poor;
they have been foolish.
For they don't understand the way
of the LORD,
the justice of their God.
5 I will go to the powerful
and speak to them.
Surely they know the way of the LORD,
the justice of their God.
However, these also had broken
the yoke
and torn off the chains.
6 Therefore, a lion from the forest
will strike them down.
A wolf from arid plains
will ravage them.
A leopard stalks their cities.
Anyone who leaves them will be torn
to pieces
because their rebellious acts are many,
their unfaithful deeds numerous.

7 Why should I forgive you?
Your children have abandoned me
and sworn by those who are not gods.
I satisfied their needs, yet they
committed adultery;
they gashed themselves
at the^A prostitute's house.
8 They are well-fed,^B eager^C stallions,
each neighing after someone else's wife.
9 Should I not punish them
for these things?
This is the LORD's declaration.
Should I not avenge myself
on such a nation as this?

10 Go up among her vineyard terraces
and destroy them,
but do not finish them off.
Prune away her shoots,
for they do not belong to the LORD.
11 They, the house of Israel and the house
of Judah,
have dealt very treacherously with me.
This is the LORD's declaration.
12 They have contradicted the LORD
and insisted, "It won't happen.^D
Harm won't come to us;
we won't see sword or famine."
13 The prophets become only wind,
for the LORD's word is not in them.
This will in fact happen to them.

Coming Judgment

14 Therefore, this is what the Lord GOD of Armies says:
Because you have spoken this word,
I am going to make my words
become fire in your mouth.
These people are the wood,
and the fire will consume them.
15 I am about to bring a nation
from far away against you,
house of Israel.
This is the LORD's declaration.
It is an established nation,
an ancient nation,
a nation whose language
you do not know
and whose speech
you do not understand.
16 Their quiver is like an open grave;
they are all warriors.
17 They will consume your harvest
and your food.
They will consume your sons
and your daughters.
They will consume your flocks
and your herds.
They will consume your vines
and your fig trees.
With the sword they will destroy
your fortified cities in which you trust.

18 "But even in those days" — this is the
LORD's declaration — "I will not finish you off.
19 When people ask, 'For what offense has the

---

^A5:7 Or adultery and trooped to the, or adultery and lodged at the; Hb obscure   ^B5:8 Lit well-equipped; Hb obscure
^C5:8 Lit early-rising; Hb obscure   ^D5:12 Lit "He does not exist

---

had just ten righteous people lived there (Gn 18:22–32). To act **justly** is to act according to the norms of behavior that God has established.
5:4–5 Jeremiah probably was expressing irony because the prominent citizens of Judah were no more loyal to the covenant than were the poor people.
5:7 The phrase **I satisfied their needs** is literally "I fed them to the full." **They gashed**

themselves as in the Canaanite cultic practices (1Kg 18:28).
5:8–9 Jeremiah pictured the people of Judah as **well-fed, eager stallions** or "lusty stallions." Their sexual immorality at the brothels of pagan temples was like horses whinnying after a mate.
5:10–11 The branches will be pruned back, but the root and stock will remain, much as Paul argued in Rm 11:17–24.

5:12 This attitude, **it won't happen**, mistakenly presumed that God's promises to bless Israel precluded the possibility of judgment for sins.
5:14–17 In a solemn introduction, Jeremiah declared his message in the name of **the Lord GOD of Armies**. The description of the enemy nation as being **established ... ancient**, with an unintelligible **language**, and boasting **warriors** fits Babylon well.

LORD our God done all these things to us?' You will respond to them, 'Just as you abandoned me and served foreign gods in your land, so will you serve strangers in a land that is not yours.'

²⁰ "Declare this in the house of Jacob; proclaim it in Judah, saying:

²¹   Hear this,
      you foolish and senseless^A people.
   They have eyes, but they don't see.
   They have ears, but they don't hear.
²²   Do you not fear me?
      This is the LORD's declaration.
   Do you not tremble before me,
   the one who set the sand
      as the boundary of the sea,
   an enduring barrier that
      it cannot cross?
   The waves surge, but they
      cannot prevail.
   They roar but cannot pass over it.
²³   But these people have stubborn
      and rebellious hearts.
   They have turned aside
      and have gone away.
²⁴   They have not said to themselves,
   'Let's fear the LORD our God,
   who gives the seasonal rains,
      both autumn and spring,
   who guarantees to us the fixed weeks
      of the harvest.'
²⁵   Your guilty acts have diverted
      these things from you.
   Your sins have withheld my bounty
      from you,
²⁶   for wicked men live among my people.
   They watch like hunters^B
      lying in wait.^C
   They set a trap;
      they catch men.
²⁷   Like a cage full of birds,
   so their houses are full of deceit.
   Therefore they have grown powerful
      and rich.
²⁸   They have become fat and sleek.
   They have also excelled in evil matters.
   They have not taken up cases,

such as the case of the fatherless,
   so they might prosper,
and they have not defended the rights
   of the needy.
²⁹   Should I not punish them
      for these things?
   This is the LORD's declaration.
   Should I not avenge myself
   on such a nation as this?

³⁰   "An appalling, horrible thing
      has taken place in the land.
³¹   The prophets prophesy falsely,
      and the priests rule
      by their own authority.
   My people love it like this.
   But what will you do at the end of it?

Threatened Siege of Jerusalem

6   "Run for cover
      out of Jerusalem, Benjaminites.
   Sound the ram's horn in Tekoa;
   raise a smoke signal
      over Beth-haccherem,^D
   for disaster threatens from the north,
      even a crushing blow.
²   Though she is beautiful and delicate,
   I will destroy^E Daughter Zion.
³   Shepherds and their flocks will come
      against her;
   they will pitch their tents all around her.
   Each will pasture his own portion.
⁴   Set them apart for war against her;
   rise up, let's attack at noon.
   Woe to us, for the day is passing;
   the evening shadows grow long.
⁵   Rise up, let's attack by night.
   Let's destroy her fortresses."

⁶ For this is what the LORD of Armies says:
   Cut down the trees;
   raise a siege ramp against Jerusalem.
   This city must be punished.
   There is nothing but oppression
      within her.
⁷   As a well gushes out its water,
   so she pours out her evil.^F

---

^A 5:21 Lit *without heart*   ^B 5:26 Lit *hunters of birds*   ^C 5:26 Hb obscure   ^D 6:1 = House of the Vineyard   ^E 6:2 Or *silence*
^F 6:7 Or *well keeps its water fresh, so she keeps her evil fresh*

5:20–21 The word for **hear this** is the same Hebrew word (*shema*) that introduces the great Shema of Dt 6:4. It called Israel to covenantal accountability.
5:24 The **fixed weeks of the harvest** were the seven weeks from Passover to Pentecost in which the barley harvest was gathered first, followed by the wheat harvest.
5:25 As water can be **diverted** or dammed up, so Israel's sin and guilt have kept God's blessings from reaching them.
5:26–28 As fowlers set a net with several tame birds in the net to attract wild, unsuspecting birds, so too **wicked men** preyed upon innocent victims.

5:30 The word **horrible** is derived from a Hebrew stem meaning "filthiness" or "rottenness" (29:17; Hs 6:10). Here it describes the wickedness of the false prophets, priests, and people.
5:31 The phrase **priests rule by their own authority** is literally "rule by their hands," meaning either at the direction of the false prophets, or on the priests' own authority.
6:1 Tekoa, about five miles south of Bethlehem, was the hometown of the prophet Amos. **Beth-haccherem** was either 'Ain Karim, west of Jerusalem, or modern Ramat Rachel (ancient Khirbet Salih), located on the road from Jerusalem to Bethlehem. A **smoke**

signal was sent to warn about the approach of an enemy (Jdg 20:38,40).
6:3 The enemy and his troops are called **shepherds** and **their flocks**.
6:4–5 Attacking **at noon** or **by night** means that the battle can occur anytime.
6:6–7 Cut down the trees; raise a siege ramp refers to military actions that the Assyrians and Babylonians boasted about in their victory memorials. They carried dirt in baskets, pouring it against the city walls until the slope was halfway up the wall. Then they built towers from felled trees to hurl heavy stones and firebrands against the wall (2Sm 20:15; Ezk 29:18). Evil was erupting so

Violence and destruction resound
in her.
Sickness and wounds keep coming
to my attention.
⁸ Be warned, Jerusalem,
or I will turn away from you;
I will make you a desolation,
a land without inhabitants.

Wrath on Israel
⁹ This is what the LORD of Armies says:
Glean the remnant of Israel
as thoroughly as a vine.
Pass your hand once more
like a grape gatherer
over the branches.

¹⁰ Who can I speak to and give
such a warningᴬ
that they will listen?
Look, their ear is uncircumcised,ᴮ
so they cannot pay attention.
See, the word of the LORD
has become contemptible to them —
they find no pleasure in it.
¹¹ But I am full of the LORD's wrath;
I am tired of holding it back.
Pour it out on the children in the street,
on the gathering of young men as well.
For both husband and wife
will be captured,
the old with the very old.ᶜ
¹² Their houses will be turned over
to others,
their fields and wives as well,
for I will stretch out my hand
against the inhabitants of the land.
This is the LORD's declaration.

¹³ For from the least to the greatest
of them,
everyone is making profit dishonestly.
From prophet to priest,
everyone deals falsely.
¹⁴ They have treated
my people's brokenness superficially,
claiming, "Peace, peace,"
when there is no peace.
¹⁵ Were they ashamed when they acted
so detestably?
They weren't at all ashamed.
They can no longer feel humiliation.
Therefore, they will fall
among the fallen.

When I punish them, they will collapse,
says the LORD.

Disaster because of Disobedience
¹⁶ This is what the LORD says:
Stand by the roadways and look.
Ask about the ancient paths,
"Which is the way to what is good?"
Then take it
and find rest for yourselves.
But they protested, "We won't!"
¹⁷ I appointed watchmen over you
and said, "Listen for the sound
of the ram's horn."
But they protested, "We won't listen!"

¹⁸ Therefore listen, you nations
and you witnesses,
learn what the charge is against them.
¹⁹ Listen, earth!
I am about to bring disaster
on these people,
the fruit of their own plotting,
for they have paid no attention
to my words.
They have rejected my instruction.
²⁰ What use to me is frankincense
from Sheba
or sweet cane from a distant land?
Your burnt offerings are not acceptable;
your sacrifices do not please me.
²¹ Therefore, this is what the LORD says:
I am going to place stumbling blocks
before these people;
fathers and sons together will stumble
over them;
friends and neighbors will also perish.

A Cruel Nation from the North
²² This is what the LORD says:
Look, an army is coming
from a northern land;
a great nation will be stirred up
from the remote regions of the earth.
²³ They grasp bow and javelin.
They are cruel and show no mercy.
Their voice roars like the sea,
and they ride on horses,
lined up like men in battle formation
against you, Daughter Zion.

²⁴ We have heard about it,
and our hands have become weak.
Distress has seized us —

ᴬ6:10 Or *and bear witness* ᴮ6:10 They are unresponsive to God. ᶜ6:11 Lit *with fullness of days*

spontaneously in Judah by now that Jeremiah compared it to a gushing **well**.
6:10 An **uncircumcised** ear was closed, impervious to God's Spirit and word.
6:16 The ancient paths were the ones followed by Noah and the patriarchs, who believed God's promises and walked with God.

6:20 Frankincense came from southern Arabia. It was an aromatic resin from trees used in perfume and incense. **Sheba** was a country in southwestern Arabia, the center of incense and spices trade. Incense and **burnt offerings** were no substitute for obeying God (7:21–24; Is 1:11–15; Am 5:21; Mc 6:6–8).

6:21 The **stumbling blocks** in this verse are undefined.
6:22 This begins another oracle regarding a foe from the north.
6:23 The word **javelin** probably refers to a sword.

pain, like a woman in labor.
25 Don't go out to the fields;
don't walk on the road.
For the enemy has a sword;
terror is on every side.

26 My dear^A people, dress yourselves
in sackcloth
and roll in the dust.
Mourn as you would for an only son,
a bitter lament,
for suddenly the destroyer will come
on us.

Jeremiah Appointed as an Examiner

27 I have appointed you to be an assayer
among my people —
a refiner^B —
so you may know and assay their way
of life.
28 All are stubborn rebels
spreading slander.
They are bronze and iron;
all of them are corrupt.
29 The bellows blow,
blasting the lead with fire.
The refining is completely in vain;
the evil ones are not separated out.
30 They are called rejected silver,
for the LORD has rejected them.

False Trust in the Temple

7 This is the word that came to Jeremiah
from the LORD: 2 "Stand in the gate of the
house of the LORD and there call out this word:
'Hear the word of the LORD, all you people of
Judah who enter through these gates to worship the LORD.
3 " 'This is what the LORD of Armies, the God
of Israel, says: Correct your ways and your actions, and I will allow you to live in this place.
4 Do not trust deceitful words, chanting, "This is
the temple of the LORD, the temple of the LORD,
the temple of the LORD." 5 Instead, if you really correct your ways and your actions, if you

act justly toward one another,^C 6 if you no longer oppress the resident alien, the fatherless,
and the widow and no longer shed innocent
blood in this place or follow other gods, bringing harm on yourselves, 7 I will allow you to live
in this place, the land I gave to your ancestors
long ago and forever. 8 But look, you keep trusting in deceitful words that cannot help.
9 " 'Do you steal, murder, commit adultery,
swear falsely, burn incense to Baal, and follow
other gods that you have not known? 10 Then
do you come and stand before me in this house
that bears my name and say, "We are rescued,
so we can continue doing all these detestable
acts"? 11 Has this house, which bears my name,
become a den of robbers in your view? Yes, I
too have seen it.
This is the LORD's declaration.

Shiloh as a Warning

12 " 'But return to my place that was at Shiloh, where I made my name dwell at first. See
what I did to it because of the evil of my people Israel. 13 Now, because you have done all
these things — this is the LORD's declaration
— and because I have spoken to you time and
time again^D but you wouldn't listen, and I have
called to you, but you wouldn't answer, 14 what
I did to Shiloh I will do to the house that bears
my name, the house in which you trust, the
place that I gave you and your ancestors. 15 I
will banish you from my presence, just as I banished all of your brothers, all the descendants
of Ephraim.'

Do Not Pray for Judah

16 "As for you, do not pray for these people.
Do not offer a cry or a prayer on their behalf,
and do not beg me, for I will not listen to you.
17 Don't you see how they behave in the cities
of Judah and in the streets of Jerusalem? 18 The
sons gather wood, the fathers light the fire, and
the women knead dough to make cakes for
the queen of heaven,^E and they pour out drink
offerings to other gods so that they provoke

---

^A 6:26 Lit *Daughter of my*   ^B 6:27 Text emended; MT reads *fortress*   ^C 7:5 Lit *justly between a man and his neighbor*   ^D 7:13 Lit
you rising early and speaking   ^E 7:18 = a pagan goddess

6:25 The phrase **terror is on every side** is
a favorite saying of Jeremiah. The people
turned Jeremiah's saying around and used
it against him, saying that all he saw were
terrors coming from every direction.
6:26 The death of **an only son** meant that
hope for descendants was gone (Gn 22:2).
6:27 An assayer was a metallurgist who
tested the quality of ore (in this case, the
quality of the people).
6:28 The people are described as **stubborn
rebels** ("rebel of rebels," or "the most stubborn of rebels"), active in **spreading slander**.
6:29 To refine silver, **lead** and silver were
heated together so that the oxidized lead
would bind impurities (dross), leaving pure
silver (Ps 66:10). However, here the ore (the
people of Judah) was so impure that the

alloys remained. The refining process failed.
The **evil ones** were the dross that could not
be **separated** from the pure silver.
7:1 Jeremiah's temple gate sermon from this
chapter is repeated in chap. 26.
7:4 This refers not only to the temple itself,
but to the complex of buildings around the
temple. The people came to believe that the
temple was a talisman (good luck charm) that
would never be destroyed.
7:9 The sins of the people included violations
of the eighth, sixth, seventh, ninth, first, and
second of the Ten Commandments.
7:11 They were making God's house **a den of
robbers**, or literally "a cave" used by bandits
(cp. Mt 21:13).
7:12,14 Shiloh, eighteen miles north of Jerusalem, near modern Seilun, was where the

tabernacle and the ark of the covenant were
set up after the conquest of Canaan (Jos 18:1;
22:12; Jdg 21:19). This place was destroyed by
the Philistines in 1050 BC (Ps 78:60–64) after
the battle of Ebenezer (1Sm 4:1–11).
7:16–17 The Lord commanded the prophet,
do not pray for these people. The nation
had passed the point of no return (11:14;
14:11; 15:1). God would no longer listen to
intercessions on behalf of the people of
Judah.
7:18 The **queen of heaven** was the Assyr-
ian-Babylonian goddess Ishtar, parallel to the
Canaanite goddess Astarte. Both were astral
deities (perhaps Venus) linked with love, fertility, and warfare. The women made **cakes**,
perhaps in the shape of stars (44:15–19) as
part of her worship ritual. King Manasseh

me to anger. **19** But are they really provoking me? " This is the LORD's declaration. "Isn't it they themselves being provoked to disgrace? "

20 Therefore, this is what the Lord GOD says: "Look, my anger — my burning wrath — is about to be poured out on this place, on people and animals, on the tree of the field, and on the produce of the land. My wrath will burn and not be quenched."

Obedience over Sacrifice

21 This is what the LORD of Armies, the God of Israel, says: "Add your burnt offerings to your other sacrifices, and eat the meat yourselves, **22** for when I brought your ancestors out of the land of Egypt, I did not speak with them or command them concerning burnt offering and sacrifice. **23** However, I did give them this command: 'Obey me, and then I will be your God, and you will be my people. Follow every way I command you so that it may go well with you.' **24** Yet they didn't listen or pay attention but followed their own advice and their own stubborn, evil heart. They went backward and not forward. **25** Since the day your ancestors came out of the land of Egypt until today, I have sent all my servants the prophets to you time and time again.^ **26** However, my people wouldn't listen to me or pay attention but became obstinate; they did more evil than their ancestors.

A Lament for Disobedient Judah

27 "When you speak all these things to them, they will not listen to you. When you call to them, they will not answer you. **28** Therefore, declare to them, 'This is the nation that would not listen to the LORD their God and would not accept discipline. Truth° has perished — it has disappeared from their mouths. **29** Cut off the hair of your sacred vow° and throw it away. Raise up a dirge on the barren heights, for the LORD has rejected and abandoned the generation under his wrath.'

30 "For the Judeans have done what is evil in my sight." This is the LORD's declaration. "They have set up their abhorrent things in the house that bears my name in order to defile it. **31** They have built the high places of Topheth° in Ben Hinnom Valley° in order to burn their sons and daughters in the fire, a thing I did not command; I never entertained the thought.

32 "Therefore, look, the days are coming" — the LORD's declaration — "when this place will no longer be called Topheth and Ben Hinnom Valley, but Slaughter Valley. Topheth will become a cemetery,° because there will be no other burial place. **33** The corpses of these people will become food for the birds of the sky and for the wild animals of the land, with no one to scare them away. **34** I will remove from the cities of Judah and the streets of Jerusalem the sound of joy and gladness and the voices of the groom and the bride, for the land will become a desolate waste.

Death over Life

8 "At that time" — this is the LORD's declaration — "the bones of the kings of Judah, the bones of her officials, the bones of the priests, the bones of the prophets, and the bones of the residents of Jerusalem will be brought out of their graves. **2** They will be exposed to the sun, the moon, and all the stars in the sky, which they have loved, served, followed, consulted, and worshiped. Their bones will not be collected and buried but will become like manure on the soil's surface. **3** Death will be chosen over life by all the survivors of this evil family, those who remain wherever I have banished them." This is the declaration of the LORD of Armies.

4 "You are to say to them: This is what the LORD says:

Do people fall and not get up again?
If they turn away, do they not return?
5 Why have these people turned away?
Why is Jerusalem always turning away?
They take hold of deceit;
they refuse to return.
6 I have paid careful attention.
They do not speak what is right.
No one regrets his evil,

^7:25 Lit you, each day rising early and sending °7:28 Or Faithfulness °7:29 Lit off your consecration °7:31 Lit of the fireplace °7:31 A valley south of Jerusalem °7:32 Lit They will bury in Topheth

---

introduced this false worship (2Kg 21:1–9), and it revived after King Josiah's death.
7:21–23 The point is that God never commanded his people to perform empty rituals. Rather, their offerings and sacrifices were to be heartfelt and born of a desire for obedience.
7:27–28 The verb for **disappeared** (lit "severed"), is as if their tongues were cut out. The word for **truth** can also mean "integrity."
7:29 The undefiled Nazirites were required to cut and burn their hair when the term of their vow was fulfilled (Nm 6:13–18). Now Judah is told that she must **cut off the hair of your sacred vow and throw it away** not because she has completed her vow, but

rather because she has violated it. She is no longer consecrated to the Lord.
7:30 This would have been an act of Jehoiakim. See Ezk 5:11.
7:31 Topheth is an Aramaic word meaning "fire pit," "fireplace," or "hearth." This high place was located in **Ben Hinnom Valley**, south of Jerusalem. Kings Ahaz (2Kg 16:3) and Manasseh (2Kg 21:5–6) instituted pagan sacrifices here, including the offering of Judah's children to the god Baal or Molech. Child sacrifice was forbidden by Mosaic law (Lv 18:21; 20:2–5; Dt 18:10). This practice was abolished under King Josiah (2Kg 23:10). During Jeremiah's days the sacrifices appear to have been revived. Later generations dumped their garbage in the Ben Hinnom

Valley. Understandably, this place became a symbol for the place of future judgment called Gehenna (Mt 5:22).
7:32–34 So devastating will be the invasion of Judah that corpses will lie everywhere.
8:1 At that time links what follows with Jeremiah's temple gate sermon in chap. 7. The exhuming of **bones** (here of kings, officials, priests, prophets, and residents) **out of their graves** will be the ultimate insult to the defeated people.
8:2 In an ironic demonstration of the futility of false religion, "the bones" (v. 1) will be exposed. The astral deities Judah worshiped will look down, powerless to prevent this desecration.
8:4–5 Once again the emphasis is on the word "turn/return" or "repent" (Hb *shuv*).

asking, 'What have I done?'
Everyone has stayed his course
like a horse rushing into battle.
[7] Even storks in the sky
know their seasons.
Turtledoves, swallows, and cranes[A]
are aware of their migration,
but my people do not know
the requirements of the LORD.

Punishment for Judah's Leaders

[8] "How can you claim, 'We are wise;
the law of the LORD is with us'?
In fact, the lying pen of scribes
has produced falsehood.
[9] The wise will be put to shame;
they will be dismayed and snared.
They have rejected the word
of the LORD,
so what wisdom do they really have?
[10] Therefore, I will give their wives
to other men,
their fields to new occupants,
for from the least to the greatest,
everyone is making profit dishonestly.
From prophet to priest,
everyone deals falsely.
[11] They have treated the brokenness
of my dear[B] people superficially,
claiming, 'Peace, peace,'
when there is no peace.
[12] Were they ashamed when they acted
so detestably?
They weren't at all ashamed.
They can no longer feel humiliation.
Therefore, they will fall
among the fallen.
When I punish them, they will collapse,"
says the LORD.

[13] "I will gather them and bring them
to an end."[C]
This is the LORD's declaration.
"There will be no grapes on the vine,
no figs on the fig tree,
and even the leaf will wither.
Whatever I have given them will be lost
to them."

God's People Unrepentant

[14] Why are we just sitting here?
Gather together; let's enter
the fortified cities
and perish there,[D]
for the LORD our God has destroyed[E] us.
He has given us poisoned water
to drink,
because we have sinned
against the LORD.
[15] We hoped for peace, but there was
nothing good;
for a time of healing, but there was
only terror.

[16] From Dan, the snorting
of horses is heard.
At the sound of the neighing
of mighty steeds,
the whole land quakes.
They come to devour the land
and everything in it,
the city and all its residents.
[17] Indeed, I am about to send snakes
among you,
poisonous vipers that cannot
be charmed.
They will bite you.
This is the LORD's declaration.

Lament over Judah

[18] My joy has flown away;
grief has settled on me.
My heart is sick.
[19] Listen — the cry of my dear people
from a faraway land,
"Is the LORD no longer in Zion,
her King not within her?"
Why have they angered me
with their carved images,
with their worthless foreign idols?
[20] Harvest has passed, summer has ended,
but we have not been saved.
[21] I am broken by the brokenness
of my dear people.
I mourn; horror has taken hold of me.
[22] Is there no balm in Gilead?
Is there no physician there?

[A]8:7 Hb obscure [B]8:11 Lit of the daughter of my, also in vv. 19,21,22 [C]8:13 Lit Gathering I will end them [D]8:14 Or there be silenced [E]8:14 Or silenced

---

8:7 Storks . . . turtledoves, swallows, and cranes are migratory birds. They instinctively obey the laws of nature set by their Creator. This contrasts with God's rational and intelligent beings who saw the impending signs of disaster but decided to do nothing to correct their path.
8:8–9 In the hands of the scribes, God's law was twisted into a covering for corruption.
8:12 On **they weren't at all ashamed**, see note at 3:3.
8:13–9:23 This section spells out the doom of Judah and its inhabitants.

8:14–15 God will give Judah **poisoned water** to drink. This metaphor occurs again in 9:15 and 23:15 as a judgment on the people.
8:16 The city of **Dan**, to the far north and bordering on Phoenicia, marked the route that the enemy from the east would take. The desert to the east was virtually impassable.
8:17 The battle metaphors change from the speed of the horse to the creeping terror of the snake. God will send poisonous **snakes** among the people. The point is that there will be no escape.

8:18–21 Jeremiah speaks in vv. 18,19a, and 21. The people speak through Jeremiah in vv. 19b,20; and the Lord speaks in v. 19c—in the center.
8:20 The phrase **harvest has passed, summer has ended, but we have not been saved** is a proverbial saying meaning that all opportunities have passed and no hope of rescue exists.
8:22 Gilead was a territory in Transjordan, north of Moab, where its northern regions were heavily wooded. It was well known for its medicinal **balm**, a resin from the balsam

So why has the healing
   of my dear people
not come about?

9 If my head were a flowing spring,
   my eyes a fountain of tears,
I would weep day and night
   over the slain of my dear^A people.
² If only I had a traveler's lodging place
   in the wilderness,
I would abandon my people
   and depart from them,
for they are all adulterers,
   a solemn assembly
      of treacherous people.

³ They bent their tongues like their bows;
   lies and not faithfulness prevail
      in the land,
for they proceed from one evil
      to another,
and they do not take me into account.
   This is the LORD's declaration.

Imminent Ruin and Exile

⁴ Everyone has to be on guard
      against his friend.
Don't trust any brother,
   for every brother will certainly deceive,
and every friend spread slander.
⁵ Each one betrays his friend;
   no one tells the truth.
They have taught their tongues
      to speak lies;
they wear themselves out
      doing wrong.
⁶ You live in a world of deception.^B
   In their deception they refuse to know
      me.
   This is the LORD's declaration.

⁷ Therefore, this is what the LORD of Armies says:
   I am about to refine them and test them,
   for what else can I do
because of my dear^C people?^D
⁸ Their tongues are deadly arrows —
   they speak deception.
With his mouth
   one speaks peaceably with his friend,
but inwardly he sets up an ambush.

⁹ Should I not punish them
      for these things?
   This is the LORD's declaration.
Should I not avenge myself
   on such a nation as this?

¹⁰ I will raise weeping and a lament
      over the mountains,
a dirge over the wilderness
      grazing land,
for they have been so scorched
   that no one passes through.
The sound of cattle is no longer heard.
From the birds of the sky to the animals,
   everything has fled — they have
      gone away.
¹¹ I will make Jerusalem a heap of rubble,
   a jackals' den.
I will make the cities of Judah
      a desolation,
   an uninhabited place.

¹² Who is the person wise enough to understand this? Who has the LORD spoken to, that he may explain it? Why is the land destroyed and scorched like a wilderness, so no one can pass through? ¹³ The LORD said, "It is because they abandoned my instruction, which I set before them, and did not obey my voice or walk according to it. ¹⁴ Instead, they followed the stubbornness of their hearts and followed the Baals as their ancestors taught them." ¹⁵ Therefore, this is what the LORD of Armies, the God of Israel, says: "I am about to feed this people wormwood and give them poisonous water to drink. ¹⁶ I will scatter them among the nations that they and their ancestors have not known. I will send a sword after them until I have finished them off."

Mourning over Judah

¹⁷ This is what the LORD of Armies says:
   Consider, and summon the women
      who mourn;
   send for the skillful women.
¹⁸ Let them come quickly to raise a lament
      over us
so that our eyes may overflow
      with tears,
our eyelids be soaked with weeping.

^A 9:1 Lit *slain among the daughter of my* ^B 9:6 LXX reads *Oppression on oppression, deceit on deceit* ^C 9:7 Lit *of the daughter of my* ^D 9:7 LXX, Tg read *because of their evils*

tree that was applied to wounds. Neither healing nor healer could cure the hurt of the people.
9:1 From here and 13:17; 14:17 derives the designation of Jeremiah as "the weeping prophet." He is brokenhearted (8:21).
9:2 The prophet longed to take a break and get some rest from his ministry to the people.
9:3 The Lord speaks here. The word rendered **faithfulness** can also be rendered "integrity."

9:4 Every brother will certainly deceive, Jeremiah argued, punning on Jacob's name (Gn 27:36).
9:15 Wormwood belonged to the aster family. It had a bitter taste and the same effect as the **poisonous water**.
9:16 God's declaration **I will scatter them among the nations** is just what Moses had warned would happen if the people abandoned the Lord (Lv 26:33; Dt 28:36,64).

9:17–22 This section is a poem about death, the grim reaper. Death is personified as an intruder who sneaks in through the window at night.
9:17 The **women who mourn** were professional mourners whose dirges would start the mourning process for the conquered nation.

19 For a sound of lamentation is heard
from Zion:
How devastated we are.
We are greatly ashamed,
for we have abandoned the land;
our dwellings have been torn down.

20 Now hear the word of the LORD,
you women.
Pay attention to^A the words
from his mouth.
Teach your daughters a lament
and one another a dirge,
21 for Death has climbed
through our windows;
it has entered our fortresses,
cutting off children from the streets,
young men from the squares.

22 "Speak as follows: 'This is what the LORD declares: Human corpses will fall like manure on the surface of the field, like newly cut grain after the reaper with no one to gather it.

Boast in the LORD

23 "This is what the LORD says:
The wise person should not boast
in his wisdom;
the strong should not boast
in his strength;
the wealthy should not boast
in his wealth.
24 But the one who boasts should boast
in this:
that he understands and knows me —
that I am the LORD,
showing faithful love,
justice, and righteousness on the earth,
for I delight in these things.
This is the LORD's declaration.

25 "'Look, the days are coming — this is the LORD's declaration — when I will punish all the circumcised yet uncircumcised: 26 Egypt, Judah, Edom, the Ammonites, Moab, and all the inhabitants of the desert who clip the hair on their temples.^B All these nations are uncircumcised, and the whole house of Israel is uncircumcised in heart.'"

False Gods Contrasted with the Creator

10 Hear the word that the LORD has spoken to^C you, house of Israel. 2 This is what the LORD says:
Do not learn the way of the nations
or be terrified by signs in the heavens,
although the nations are terrified
by them,
3 for the customs of the peoples
are worthless.
Someone cuts down a tree
from the forest;
it is worked by the hands of a craftsman
with a chisel.
4 He decorates it with silver and gold.
It is fastened with hammer and nails,
so it won't totter.
5 Like scarecrows in a cucumber patch,
their idols cannot speak.
They must be carried because
they cannot walk.
Do not fear them for they can do
no harm —
and they cannot do any good.

6 LORD, there is no one like you.
You are great;
your name is great in power.
7 Who should not fear you,
King of the nations?
It is what you deserve.
For among all the wise people
of the nations
and among all their kingdoms,
there is no one like you.
8 They are both stupid and foolish,
instructed by worthless idols
made of wood!
9 Beaten silver is brought from Tarshish
and gold from Uphaz.^D
The work of a craftsman
and of a goldsmith's hands
is clothed in blue and purple,
all the work of skilled artisans.
10 But the LORD is the true God;
he is the living God and eternal King.
The earth quakes at his wrath,
and the nations cannot endure
his fury.

^A 9:20 Lit Your ears must receive ^B 9:26 Or who live in distant places ^C 10:1 Or against ^D 10:9 Or Ophir

9:23–24 Two contrasting ways are described in two triads of values. Wisdom … strength, and wealth are the values that the wise … the strong, and the wealthy aspire to. But the person who understands and knows the Lord sets his highest values on the fact that God alone is the LORD. He shows faithful love (Hb chesed; used 248 times in the OT, meaning "loyalty, steadfast love, grace"), justice, and righteousness. God's people should note what he delights in and order their priorities accordingly.
9:25 The circumcised yet uncircumcised lumps Judah in with four other nations

that practiced circumcision of the flesh but neglected circumcision of the heart (4:4; Gl 5:2–5). If circumcision alone were enough to please God, the pagan nations mentioned here would enjoy God's favor.
9:26 The phrase inhabitants … who clip the hair on their temples refers to Arabian tribes that cut hair from the corners of their temples to honor Bacchus, the pagan god of wine. Israel was forbidden to do this (Lv 19:27; Dt 14:1).
10:2–3 The way of the nations involved their religious practices and customs. Those ways were worthless ("fog, mist, or breath").

This word is used almost forty times in the book of Ecclesiastes and is usually rendered "vanity" or "worthless."
10:4 The idol makers used silver from Tarshish (often linked with Spain) and gold from Uphaz (perhaps the same city as Ophir, which may have been located in Africa or Arabia), to beautify and overlay the carved wooden form.
10:5 The idols are compared to scarecrows, though the word can be rendered "palm tree" (as in the KJV and ASV) or "pillar."
10:9 On Tarshish and Uphaz, see note at v. 4.

¹¹ You are to say this to them: "The gods that did not make the heavens and the earth will perish from the earth and from under these heavens."[A]

¹² He made the earth by his power,
    established the world by his wisdom,
    and spread out the heavens
        by his understanding.
¹³ When he thunders,[B]
    the waters in the heavens are in turmoil,
    and he causes the clouds to rise
    from the ends of the earth.
    He makes lightning for the rain
    and brings the wind
        from his storehouses.

¹⁴ Everyone is stupid and ignorant.
    Every goldsmith is put to shame
    by his carved image,
    for his cast images are a lie;
    there is no breath in them.
¹⁵ They are worthless, a work
        to be mocked.
    At the time of their punishment
    they will be destroyed.
¹⁶ Jacob's Portion[C] is not like these
    because he is the one who formed
        all things.
    Israel is the tribe of his inheritance;
    the LORD of Armies is his name.

Exile after the Siege

¹⁷ Gather up your belongings[D]
        from the ground,
    you who live under siege.

¹⁸ For this is what the LORD says:
    Look, I am flinging away
    the land's residents at this time
    and bringing them such distress
    that they will feel it.

Jeremiah Grieves

¹⁹ Woe to me because of my brokenness —
    I am severely wounded!
    I exclaimed, "This is
        my intense suffering,
    but I must bear it."

²⁰ My tent is destroyed;
    all my tent cords are snapped.
    My sons have departed from me and are
        no more.
    I have no one to pitch my tent again
    or to hang up my curtains.
²¹ For the shepherds are stupid:
    They don't seek the LORD.
    Therefore they have not prospered,
    and their whole flock is scattered.
²² Listen! A noise — it is coming —
    a great commotion from the land
        to the north.
    The cities of Judah will be
        made desolate,
    a jackals' den.

²³ I know, LORD,
    that a person's way of life is not
        his own;
    no one who walks determines
        his own steps.
²⁴ Discipline me, LORD, but with justice —
    not in your anger,
    or you will reduce me to nothing.
²⁵ Pour out your wrath on the nations
    that don't recognize you
    and on the families
    that don't call on your name,
    for they have consumed Jacob;
    they have consumed him and finished
        him off
    and made his homeland desolate.

Reminder of the Covenant

11 This is the word that came to Jeremiah from the LORD: ² "Listen to the words of this covenant and tell them to the men of Judah and the residents of Jerusalem. ³ Tell them, 'This is what the LORD, the God of Israel, says: "Let a curse be on the man who does not obey the words of this covenant, ⁴ which I commanded your ancestors when I brought them out of the land of Egypt, out of the iron furnace." I declared, "Obey me, and do everything that I command you, and you will be my people, and I will be your God," ⁵ in order to establish the oath I swore to your ancestors, to

---

^[A]10:11 This is the only Aramaic v. in Jr. ᴮ10:13 Lit *At his giving of the voice* ᶜ10:16 = the LORD ᴰ10:17 Lit *bundle*

10:11 This is the only verse in the book of Jeremiah that is in Aramaic, a language similar to Hebrew. These idol merchants probably could understand Aramaic well since their business dealings required that they know this language.
10:12–16 This section is repeated in 51:15–19.
10:16 Jacob's Portion refers to the Lord, because he had given himself as Israel's **inheritance**.
10:18–20 This is a description of the exile.
10:22 A **great commotion** would announce the arrival of the Babylonian army in 587 BC. The imagery of being **made desolate** and becoming **a jackals' den** is often used to

describe the total destruction of conquered cities (51:37; Zph 2:13–15).
10:23–25 This is a personal prayer by Jeremiah, but it applied to the entire nation of Judah.
10:24 Discipline me, LORD, is a verb used frequently in the Wisdom literature of the OT for educational or corrective punishment. Jeremiah, like the prophet Daniel (Dn 9:4–19), prayed in the first person, identifying himself with his people. But neither the prophet nor the nation wanted God to deal with them according to what they really deserved. Jeremiah may have reasoned that if God disciplined **with justice**, there would be

a chance that he would offer mercy. If he disciplined **in . . . anger**, however, he would certainly destroy them.
11:1–2 The phrase **listen** (pl.) **to the words of this covenant and tell** (pl.) **them** is difficult in Hebrew because Jeremiah is addressed personally, yet the verbs are plural. Perhaps the problem is solved by emphasizing the "words" or terms of the covenant.
11:3 At the heart of the covenant given by the Lord at Sinai were two terms: a **curse** and the call to **obey** the words of the covenant.
11:5 A **land flowing with milk and honey** was a figure of speech indicating the fruitfulness of Canaan (32:22; Ezk 20:6,15).

give them a land flowing with milk and honey, as it is today.'"

I answered, "Amen, LORD."

⁶ The LORD said to me, "Proclaim all these words in the cities of Judah and in the streets of Jerusalem: 'Obey the words of this covenant and carry them out.' ⁷ For I strongly warned your ancestors when I brought them out of the land of Egypt until today, warning them time and time again,^ 'Obey me.' ⁸ Yet they would not obey or pay attention; each one followed the stubbornness of his evil heart. So I brought on them all the curses of this covenant, because they had not done what I commanded them to do."

⁹ The LORD said to me, "A conspiracy has been discovered among the men of Judah and the residents of Jerusalem. ¹⁰ They have returned to the iniquities of their ancestors who refused to obey my words and have followed other gods to worship them. The house of Israel and the house of Judah broke my covenant I made with their ancestors.

¹¹ "Therefore, this is what the LORD says: I am about to bring on them disaster that they cannot escape. They will cry out to me, but I will not hear them. ¹² Then the cities of Judah and the residents of Jerusalem will go and cry out to the gods they have been burning incense to, but they certainly will not save them in their time of disaster. ¹³ Your gods are indeed as numerous as your cities, Judah, and the altars you have set up to Shame^B —altars to burn incense to Baal —as numerous as the streets of Jerusalem.

¹⁴ "As for you, do not pray for these people. Do not raise up a cry or a prayer on their behalf, for I will not be listening when they call out to me at the time of their disaster.

¹⁵ What right does my beloved have
to be in my house,
having carried out so many
evil schemes?
Can holy meat^C prevent your disaster^D
so you can celebrate?
¹⁶ The LORD named you
a flourishing olive tree,
beautiful with well-formed fruit.

He has set fire to it,
and its branches are consumed^E
with the sound of a mighty tumult.

¹⁷ "The LORD of Armies who planted you has decreed disaster against you, because of the disaster^F the house of Israel and the house of Judah brought on themselves when they angered me by burning incense to Baal."

¹⁸ The LORD informed me, so I knew.
Then you helped me to see their deeds,
¹⁹ for I was like a docile^G lamb led
to slaughter.
I didn't know that they had devised plots
against me:
"Let's destroy the tree with its fruit;^H
let's cut him off from the land
of the living
so that his name will no longer
be remembered."
²⁰ But, LORD of Armies,
who judges righteously,
who tests heart^I and mind,
let me see your vengeance on them,
for I have presented my case to you.

²¹ Therefore, here is what the LORD says concerning the people of Anathoth who intend to take your life. They warn, "Do not prophesy in the name of the LORD, or you will certainly die at our hand." ²² Therefore, this is what the LORD of Armies says: "I am about to punish them. The young men will die by the sword; their sons and daughters will die by famine. ²³ They will have no remnant, for I will bring disaster on the people of Anathoth in the year of their punishment."

Jeremiah's Complaint

12 You will be righteous, LORD,
even if I bring a case against you.
Yet, I wish to contend with you:
Why does the way of the wicked
prosper?
Why do all the treacherous live at ease?
² You planted them, and they
have taken root.
They have grown and produced fruit.

---

^11:7 Lit *today, rising early and warning* ^B11:13 = Baal ^C11:15 = sacrificial meat ^D11:15 LXX; MT reads *meat pass from you* ^E11:16 Vg; MT reads *broken* ^F11:17 Or *evil* ^G11:19 Or *pet* ^H11:19 Lit *bread* ^I11:20 Lit *kidneys*

Its plentiful grass was turned into milk by grazing livestock, and the nectar of flowering plants was changed into honey by bees. **11:6–7 Until today** shows that this warning had been issued year after year, even up to "today" (the time of Jeremiah), to no avail. **11:9–10** There appears to have been a general **conspiracy** and revolt against King Josiah's call for reform and revival in Judah. But it did not escalate into political action (e.g., a coup); instead, it was a revolt against God. **11:14** Again as in 7:16–17 (see note there), God did not permit Jeremiah to pray for the people. It was now too late (14:11–12; 15:1).

11:15 Judah had been the Lord's **beloved** (12:7; Pss 78:68–72; 82:2). God asked, **What right does my beloved have to be in my house?** Like a son or daughter expelled for bad behavior, Judah's sin caused her to lose her privileges. **11:18–23** This is another of Jeremiah's "confessions" (see note at 4:19–22). **11:18–19** Because Jeremiah had not suspected all the plots and schemes arrayed against him, he was like **a docile lamb led to slaughter**. His enemies planned to **destroy the tree with its fruit** (lit "its bread"), a proverbial expression indicating that they

would destroy both him and whatever he produced ("food" or "bread"). Jeremiah was not married, so this refers to the destruction of his life's work, not a wife or children. **11:21–23** Jeremiah's hometown of **Anathoth** plotted against him. **12:1–4** This is another of Jeremiah's "confessions" (see note at 4:19–22). **12:1** Even though God is **righteous** in all his actions and judgments, Jeremiah pressed the age-old question, **Why does the way of the wicked prosper?** Asaph wanted the same question answered (Ps 73), and so did David (Ps 37).

You are ever on their lips,[A]
but far from their conscience.[B]

3 As for you, Lord, you know me;
you see me.
You test whether my heart is with you.
Drag the wicked away like sheep
to slaughter
and set them apart for the day of killing.

4 How long will the land mourn
and the grass of every field wither?
Because of the evil of its residents,
animals and birds have been
swept away,
for the people have said,
"He cannot see what our end will be."[C]

The Lord's Response

5 If you have raced with runners
and they have worn you out,
how can you compete with horses?
If you stumble[D] in a peaceful land,
what will you do in the thickets
of the Jordan?

6 Even your brothers
— your own father's family —
even they were treacherous to you;
even they have cried out loudly
after you.
Do not have confidence in them,
though they speak well of you.

7 I have abandoned my house;
I have deserted my inheritance.
I have handed the love of my life
over to her enemies.

8 My inheritance has behaved toward me
like a lion in the forest.
She has roared against me.
Therefore, I hate her.

9 Is my inheritance like a hyena[E] to me?
Are birds of prey circling her?
Go, gather all the wild animals;
bring them to devour her.

10 Many shepherds have destroyed
my vineyard;
they have trampled my plot of land.

They have turned my desirable plot
into a desolate wasteland.

11 They have made it a desolation.
It mourns, desolate, before me.
All the land is desolate,
but no one takes it to heart.

12 Over all the barren heights
in the wilderness
the destroyers have come,
for the Lord has a sword that devours
from one end of the earth to the other.
No one has peace.

13 They have sown wheat
but harvested thorns.
They have exhausted themselves
but have no profit.
Be put to shame by your harvests
because of the Lord's burning anger.

14 This is what the Lord says: "Concerning all my evil neighbors who attack the inheritance that I bequeathed to my people, Israel, I am about to uproot them from their land, and I will uproot the house of Judah from them. **15** After I have uprooted them, I will once again have compassion on them and return each one to his inheritance and to his land. **16** If they will diligently learn the ways of my people — to swear by my name, 'As the Lord lives,' just as they taught my people to swear by Baal — they will be built up among my people. **17** However, if they will not obey, then I will uproot and destroy that nation." This is the Lord's declaration.

Linen Underwear

13 This is what the Lord said to me: "Go and buy yourself a linen undergarment and put it on.[F] But do not put it in water." **2** So I bought underwear as the Lord instructed me and put it on.

3 Then the word of the Lord came to me a second time: **4** "Take the underwear that you bought and are wearing,[G] and go at once to the Euphrates[H] and hide it in a rocky crevice." **5** So I went and hid it by the Euphrates, as the Lord commanded me.

[A]12:2 Lit are near in their mouth [B]12:2 Lit kidneys [C]12:4 LXX reads see our ways [D]12:5 Or you are secure [E]12:9 Hb obscure
[F]13:1 Lit around your waist [G]13:4 Lit wearing around your waist [H]13:4–7 Perhaps a place near Anathoth with the same spelling as the river

12:5–6 The Lord responded to Jeremiah's complaint (see vv. 1–4). If running refers to the false prophets who "ran" even though the Lord did not send them (23:21), how did Jeremiah hope to **compete with horses?** This may be an allusion to the Babylonian horses that would soon descend on Judah and the prophet. Or it may be that if Jeremiah thought his family and friends in Anathoth were hard to deal with, he would not know what to do when the wicked (riders on horses) were turned loose on him. **12:7** God still referred to the nation of Judah as **my house . . . my inheritance**, and the **love of my life**. But these descriptions he must now abandon and give Judah into the

hands of her **enemies**. The word *inheritance* or "heritage" occurs five times in this chapter, usually of God's gift of the land of Canaan to Israel (vv. 7,9,14–15), but in v. 8 it refers to the people. **12:8–9** The phrase **I hate her** is the language of rejection. God determined to treat his people as his enemy. **12:14–17** This section deals with Israel's **evil neighbors**, who will be **uprooted** (cp. 1:10) just as Judah will be. But like Judah, they will be built up by God (cp. Jr 10) if they will repent and turn to the Lord. **13:1–2** The Lord told Jeremiah to purchase a new **linen undergarment**. This item of clothing extended from the waist to the

thighs. It was made of valuable linen, material usually reserved for priests (Lv 16:4). **13:3–7** Jeremiah was then instructed to **take the underwear** he had **bought** and was **wearing** and **hide it in a rocky crevice** along the Euphrates River, which lay about 350 miles northeast of Anathoth—a round trip journey of 700 miles. The Hebrew word for the Euphrates is *perath*. Another site, using the same word, *perath*, was a spring at Wadi Farah, about four miles northeast of doomed Anathoth. Since the Hebrew names for both sites are the same, each suggests that destruction (symbolized by the ruined underwear, v. 7) would come from the region of the Euphrates River.

⁶ A long time later the LORD said to me, "Go at once to the Euphrates and get the underwear that I commanded you to hide there." ⁷ So I went to the Euphrates and dug up the underwear and got it from the place where I had hidden it, but it was ruined — of no use at all.

⁸ Then the word of the LORD came to me: ⁹ "This is what the LORD says: Just like this I will ruin the great pride of both Judah and Jerusalem. ¹⁰ These evil people, who refuse to listen to me, who follow the stubbornness of their own hearts, and who have followed other gods to serve and bow in worship — they will be like this underwear, of no use at all. ¹¹ Just as underwear clings to one's waist, so I fastened the whole house of Israel and of Judah to me" — this is the LORD's declaration — "so that they might be my people for my fame, praise, and glory, but they would not obey.

The Wine Jars

¹² "Say this to them: 'This is what the LORD, the God of Israel, says: Every jar should be filled with wine.' Then they will respond to you, 'Don't we know that every jar should be filled with wine?' ¹³ And you will say to them, 'This is what the LORD says: I am about to fill all who live in this land — the kings who reign for David on his throne, the priests, the prophets, and all the residents of Jerusalem — with drunkenness. ¹⁴ I will smash them against each other, fathers and sons alike — this is the LORD's declaration. I will allow no mercy, pity, or compassion to keep me from destroying them.' "

The LORD's Warning

¹⁵ Listen and pay attention.
     Do not be proud,
for the LORD has spoken.
¹⁶ Give glory to the LORD your God
before he brings darkness,
before your feet stumble
on the mountains at dusk.
You wait for light,
but he brings darkest gloom^A

and makes total darkness.
¹⁷ But if you will not listen,
my innermost being will weep in secret
because of your pride.
My eyes will overflow with tears,
for the LORD's flock has been
     taken captive.

¹⁸ Say to the king and the queen mother:
Take a humble seat,
for your glorious crowns
have fallen from your heads.
¹⁹ The cities of the Negev are under siege;
no one can help them.
All of Judah has been taken into exile,
taken completely into exile.
²⁰ Look up and see
those coming from the north.
Where is the flock entrusted to you,
the sheep that were your pride?

The Destiny of Jerusalem

²¹ What will you say when he appoints
close friends as leaders over you,
ones you yourself trained?
Won't labor pains seize you,
as they do a woman in labor?
²² And when you ask yourself,
"Why have these things happened
     to me?"
it is because of your great guilt
that your skirts have been stripped off,
your body exposed.^B
²³ Can the Cushite change his skin,
or a leopard his spots?
If so, you might be able to do
     what is good,
you who are instructed in evil.
²⁴ I will scatter you^C like drifting chaff
before the desert wind.
²⁵ This is your lot,
what I have decreed for you —
     this is the LORD's declaration —
because you have forgotten me
and trusted in lies.

---

^A 13:16 Or *brings a shadow of death*   ^B 13:22 Lit *your heels have suffered violence*   ^C 13:24 Lit *them*

13:8–10 God's interpretation of this symbolic action was: **Just like this I will ruin the great pride of both Judah and Jerusalem.** **13:12–14** God had Jeremiah announce a common proverb: **Every jar should be filled with wine.** The people's derisive reply was essentially, "Why of course, what do you think those jars are for anyway?" But the metaphor meant that the people themselves were the earthen jars that should be filled with wine. Everyone from the top of society to the bottom would be filled with **drunkenness,** or the wrath of God (25:15–16,27). God would **smash** these jars.
13:15–17 The word **pride** ties this section together with the two parables in vv. 1–11.
13:16 The nation of Judah is depicted as a weary traveler on a mountain caught in the dark, stumbling about, anxious for the dawn,

and accepting directions from no one—not even God. The command to **give glory to the LORD your God** can be a call to confess one's sins (Jos 7:19; Jn 9:24).
13:18 The Lord commanded Jeremiah to address the **king** (Jehoiachin) and his **queen mother,** Queen Nehushta, who were deported to Babylon by Nebuchadnezzar in 597 BC (2Kg 24:8–15). Jehoiachin was only eighteen years old when he ascended the throne for a short rule of three months. His mother probably exerted a lot of influence over him. Neither of them was receptive to God's call through the prophet.
13:19 Nebuchadnezzar of Babylon will strike the cities of south Judah, the **Negev** first. But eventually **all of Judah** will be **taken into exile.** The words "all" and "taken completely into exile" are hyperbolic. The

Babylonians did leave a remnant along with Jeremiah in the land (39:9–10).
13:22 Speaking euphemistically, God promised to expose Judah's secret parts (politely expressed as **your skirts have been stripped off,** i.e., they will be sexually attacked; see Lv 18:6–19; 20:17; Dt 22:30). **Your body exposed** is literally "your heels have suffered violence," another euphemism for sexual attack.
13:23–24 The question **Can the Cushite** (a Nubian or an Ethiopian) **change his skin,** or **a leopard his spots?** anticipates a negative answer. It was unlikely that Judah would change after centuries of acting in such an evil way.
13:25 Judah had **trusted in lies** or *the Lie,* a derisive term for the pagan gods, especially Baal.

26 I will pull your skirts up over your face
   so that your shame might be seen.
27 Your adulteries and
      your lustful neighing,
   your depraved prostitution
      on the hills, in the fields —
   I have seen your abhorrent acts.
   Woe to you, Jerusalem!
   You are unclean —
      for how long yet?

The Drought

14 This is the word of the LORD that came
   to Jeremiah concerning the drought:
2 Judah mourns;
   her city gates languish.
   Her people are on the ground
      in mourning;
   Jerusalem's cry rises up.
3 Their nobles send their servants[A]
      for water.
   They go to the cisterns;
   they find no water;
   their containers return empty.
   They are ashamed and humiliated;
   they cover their heads.
4 The ground is cracked
   since no rain has fallen on the land.
   The farmers are ashamed;
   they cover their heads.
5 Even the doe in the field
   gives birth and abandons her fawn
   since there is no grass.
6 Wild donkeys stand
      on the barren heights
   panting for air like jackals.
   Their eyes fail
   because there are no green plants.

7 Though our iniquities testify against us,
   LORD, act for your name's sake.
   Indeed, our rebellions are many;
   we have sinned against you.
8 Hope of Israel,
   its Savior in time of distress,
   why are you like a resident alien
      in the land,
   like a traveler stopping only
      for the night?

9 Why are you like a helpless man,
   like a warrior unable to save?
   Yet you are among us, LORD,
   and we bear your name.
   Don't leave us!

10 This is what the LORD says concerning
these people:
   Truly they love to wander;
   they never rest their feet.
   So the LORD does not accept them.
   Now he will remember their iniquity
   and punish their sins.

False Prophets to Be Punished

11 Then the LORD said to me, "Do not pray for
the well-being of these people. 12 If they fast, I
will not hear their cry of despair. If they offer
burnt offering and grain offering, I will not
accept them. Rather, I will finish them off by
sword, famine, and plague."
13 And I replied, "Oh no, Lord GOD! The prophets are telling them, 'You won't see sword or
suffer famine. I will certainly give you lasting
peace in this place.'"
14 But the LORD said to me, "These prophets are prophesying a lie in my name. I did not
send them, nor did I command them or speak
to them. They are prophesying to you a false
vision, worthless divination, the deceit of their
own minds.
15 "Therefore, this is what the LORD says
concerning the prophets who prophesy in
my name, though I did not send them, and
who say, 'There will never be sword or famine in this land.' By sword and famine these
prophets will meet their end. 16 The people
they are prophesying to will be thrown into
the streets of Jerusalem because of the famine and the sword. There will be no one to
bury them — they, their wives, their sons,
and their daughters. I will pour out their own
evil on them."

Jeremiah's Request

17 You are to speak this word to them:
   Let my eyes overflow with tears;
   day and night may they not stop,
   for my dearest people[B]

A **14:3** Lit *little ones*   B **14:17** Lit *for the virgin daughter of my people*

13:26 On **I will pull your skirts up over your face**, see note at v. 22.
13:27 This verse cites three sexual descriptions of Judah's wickedness: **adulteries . . . lustful neighing**, and **prostitution**. These refer to the people's practices out in the open as they went after sex with an animalistic passion in their worship of Canaanite gods.
14:1–17:27 The message in this long section was delivered during a severe drought that hit Judah.
14:2–6 This section is a lament with the devastation pictured as a crisis where there was **no water** . . . **no grass**, and **no green plants**.

14:2 Her city gates represents the cities of Judah.
14:7 Either Jeremiah, acting on behalf of the people, or the nation itself acknowledged that the drought had struck as a result of their sin.
14:8 The Lord is described in one of the prophet's favorite names for God: **Hope of Israel** (see 17:7,13; 50:7; Ps 71:5; Ac 28:20; Col 1:27; 1Tm 1:1). The complaint was that God seemed to show no more interest in Judah than a **resident alien** or a **traveler** who was just passing through the land.
14:9 Jeremiah knew God had the power to deliver his people if he wanted. Thus he

knew the issue was not a lack of power on God's part, but a decree to punish. **We bear your name** means "we belong to you, Lord."
14:11–12 Once again the prophet was forbidden to pray for the people of Judah (see notes at 7:16–17; 15:1).
14:14 This verse cites four methods the false prophets were using: (1) they were **prophesying a lie** in the Lord's name, (2) they were using **false** visions and (3) **worthless divination**, and (4) they were speaking **the deceit of their own minds**.

have been destroyed by a crushing blow,
an extremely severe wound.
¹⁸ If I go out to the field,
look — those slain by the sword!
If I enter the city,
look — those ill from famine!
For both prophet and priest
travel to a land they do not know.

¹⁹ Have you completely rejected Judah?
Do you detest Zion?
Why do you strike us
with no hope of healing for us?
We hoped for peace,
but there was nothing good;
for a time of healing,
but there was only terror.
²⁰ We acknowledge our wickedness, LORD,
the iniquity of our ancestors;
indeed, we have sinned against you.
²¹ For your name's sake, don't despise us.
Don't disdain your glorious throne.
Remember your covenant with us;
do not break it.
²² Can any of the worthless idols
of the nations bring rain?
Or can the skies alone give showers?
Are you not the LORD our God?
We therefore put our hope in you,
for you have done all these things.

The LORD's Negative Response

15 Then the LORD said to me, "Even if Moses and Samuel should stand before me,
my compassions would not reach out to these
people. Send them from my presence, and let
them go. ² If they ask you, 'Where will we go?'
tell them: This is what the LORD says:

Those destined for death, to death;
those destined for the sword,
to the sword.
Those destined for famine, to famine;
those destined for captivity, to captivity.

³ "I will ordain four kinds^ of judgment for
them" — this is the LORD's declaration — "the
sword to kill, the dogs to drag away, and the
birds of the sky and the wild animals of the
land to devour and destroy. ⁴ I will make them
a horror to all the kingdoms of the earth because of Manasseh son of Hezekiah, the king
of Judah, for what he did in Jerusalem.
⁵ Who will have pity on you, Jerusalem?
Who will show sympathy toward you?
Who will turn aside
to ask about your well-being?
⁶ You have left me."
This is the LORD's declaration.
"You have turned your back,
so I have stretched out my hand
against you
and destroyed you.
I am tired of showing compassion.
⁷ I scattered them
with a winnowing fork
at the city gates of the land.
I made them childless; I destroyed
my people.
They would not turn from their ways.
⁸ I made their widows more numerous
than the sand of the seas.
I brought a destroyer at noon
against the mother of young men.
I suddenly released on her
agitation and terrors.
⁹ The mother of seven grew faint;
she breathed her last breath.
Her sun set while it was still day;
she was ashamed and humiliated.
The rest of them I will give over
to the sword
in the presence of their enemies."
This is the LORD's declaration.

Jeremiah's Complaint

¹⁰ Woe is me, my mother,
that you gave birth to me,
a man who incites dispute
and conflict
in all the land.
I did not lend or borrow,
yet everyone curses me.

---

^15:3 Lit families

14:18 The word **travel** means "to go about" as a herdsman, or "to travel about" as a merchant or tradesperson. The false prophets and priests could practice their illegitimate trade in exile, Jeremiah declared.
14:19–22 In desperation they pleaded for God's help for three reasons: (1) **your name's sake**, (2) **your glorious throne**, and (3) **your covenant**. God's throne was Jerusalem, particularly the temple (2Kg 19:15; Ps 99:1).
15:1 **Even if** great prayer warriors such as **Moses** and **Samuel** came before him, they could not persuade God to change his decision. The people had gone so far in sin that no prayer would help them. Moses successfully interceded for Israel numerous times (Ex 32:7–14,30–32; Nm 14:13–19; Dt 9:13–29) as did

Samuel (1Sm 7:8–9; 12:17–25). But Judah was now beyond all hope.
15:3 The fourfold curses (death, sword, famine, captivity) appear frequently in Jeremiah and Ezekiel. The same afflictions appear with the four horseman of Revelation (Rv 6:1–8).
15:4 This verse contains the only reference to King **Manasseh** (696–642 BC) in the book of Jeremiah. He is listed here as the reason for the terrible state of affairs in Judah. So far-reaching was the evil Manasseh introduced that Judah was still bound for destruction, even after the revival introduced by his grandson, King Josiah, in 621 BC (2Kg 23:26).
15:5 The understood answer to these questions is "No one."

15:7 God will use a **winnowing fork** to toss the nation of Judah like grain into the wind so the chaff will be blown away. The metaphor suggests that the destruction would not be total. The phrase **city gates of the land** refers to the outlying towns of Judah.
15:8–9 The image of the **sand of the seas** is familiar from Gn 41:49 but here has just the opposite meaning. **The mother of seven** was the image of fruitfulness until she lost all seven.
15:10–12 This is another "confession" of Jeremiah (see note at 4:19–22). He wished he had never been born. He was tempted to reject his call and mission.
15:10 The prophet felt he had incited **dispute** and **conflict**—words for legal strife

The Lord's Response

11 The Lord said:

Haven't I set you loose for
your good?
Haven't I punished you
in a time of trouble,
in a time of distress with the enemy?[A]

12 Can anyone smash iron,
iron from the north, or bronze?

13 I will give up your wealth
and your treasures as plunder,
without cost, for all your sins
in all your borders.

14 Then I will make you serve
your enemies[B]
in a land you do not know,
for my anger will kindle a fire
that will burn against you.

Jeremiah's Prayer for Vengeance

15 You know, Lord;
remember me and take note of me.
Avenge me against my persecutors.
In your patience,[C] don't take me away.
Know that I suffer disgrace
for your honor.

16 Your words were found,
and I ate them.
Your words became a delight to me
and the joy of my heart,
for I bear your name,
Lord God of Armies.

17 I never sat with the band of revelers,
and I did not celebrate with them.
Because your hand was on me,
I sat alone,
for you filled me with indignation.

18 Why has my pain become unending,
my wound incurable,
refusing to be healed?
You truly have become like a mirage
to me —
water that is not reliable.

Jeremiah Told to Repent

19 Therefore, this is what the Lord says:

If you return, I will take you back;
you will stand in my presence.
And if you speak noble words,
rather than worthless ones,
you will be my spokesman.
It is they who must return to you;
you must not return to them.

20 Then I will make you a fortified wall
of bronze
to this people.
They will fight against you
but will not overcome you,
for I am with you
to save you and rescue you.
This is the Lord's declaration.

21 I will rescue you from the power
of evil people
and redeem you from the grasp
of the ruthless.

No Marriage for Jeremiah

16 The word of the Lord came to me: **2** "Do not marry or have sons or daughters in this place. **3** For this is what the Lord says concerning sons and daughters born in this place as well as concerning the mothers who bear them and the fathers who father them in this land: **4** They will die from deadly diseases. They will not be mourned or buried but will be like manure on the soil's surface. They will be finished off by sword and famine. Their corpses will become food for the birds of the sky and for the wild animals of the land.

5 "For this is what the Lord says: Don't enter a house where a mourning feast is taking place.[D] Don't go to lament or sympathize with them, for I have removed my peace from these people as well as my faithful love and compassion." This is the Lord's declaration. **6** "Both great and small will die in this land without burial. No lament will be made for

[A] 15:11 Hb obscure [B] 15:14 Some Hb mss, LXX, Syr, Tg; other Hb mss read *you pass through* [C] 15:15 Lit *In the slowness of your anger* [D] 16:5 Lit *house of mourning*

and contention—always taking his people to court.

15:12 Anyone may actually refer to the false prophet Hananiah. He had broken the wooden yoke around Jeremiah's neck, but he would not be able to break the yoke of iron (28:10–13). Neither would he be able to stop the **iron from the north**—Babylon.

15:13–14 This prophecy was given to Pashhur the priest in 20:5 and was fulfilled in 597 BC (2Kg 24:13).

15:15–18 This is another of Jeremiah's "confessions" (see note at 4:19–22). God's answer occurs in 15:19–21.

15:15 Jeremiah did not seek his own retribution but left it to God.

15:16 Both Jeremiah and Ezekiel (Ezk 2:8–3:3) initially found God's words delightful. In the expression **Your words were found**, there may be an allusion to the discovery of the

book of the law in the temple in King Josiah's time (2Kg 22:13; 23:2).

15:18 Jeremiah accused God of being **a mirage**, or "a deceitful brook"—a stream that went dry in the summer and could not be depended on to supply water. Contrast this image with 2:13, where the prophet described God as a "fountain of living water."

15:19 God startled the prophet by calling on him to **return** (Hb *shuv*, "turn, repent"). God wanted him to stop talking this way so he could **take** him **back** (Hb *shuv, hiphil*, "cause to turn") and make him **stand in** his **presence** once again. God called Jeremiah's words in vv. 15–18 **worthless**. The prophet must repent if he is to continue to serve as the Lord's **spokesman**.

15:20–21 These words amount to a recommissioning service for Jeremiah (1:18–19). God would make him a **fortified wall of**

bronze (see note at 1:17–19) in the presence of his people who had become his enemies. The three verbs of rescue, featured also in the exodus story, emphasize several sides of God's salvation/redemption: **save**, to bring out from bondage into a wide place; **rescue**, to snatch a person from a predator or a powerful oppressor; and **redeem**, to liberate a person by paying a ransom to set him free.

16:1–2 Jeremiah's call to celibacy was unusual for an Israelite. Already the prophet was isolated from his own citizens (15:10) and lonely (15:17); now he must face celibacy and restrictions against going to funeral feasts (16:5) or times of festivity (v. 8). He became a social outcast.

16:6 According to the pagan mourning customs of that time, people **cut** themselves or shaved their heads (cp. 41:5; 47:5; 48:37; Is 15:2–3; 22:12; Ezk 7:18; Am 8:10;

them, nor will anyone cut himself or shave his head for them.[A] [7] Food won't be provided for the mourner to comfort him because of the dead. A consoling drink won't be given him for the loss of his father or mother. [8] Do not enter the house where feasting is taking place to sit with them to eat and drink. [9] For this is what the LORD of Armies, the God of Israel, says: I am about to eliminate from this place, before your very eyes and in your time, the sound of joy and gladness, the voice of the groom and the bride.

Abandoning the LORD and His Law

[10] "When you tell these people all these things, they will say to you, 'Why has the LORD declared all this terrible disaster against us? What is our iniquity? What is our sin that we have committed against the LORD our God?' [11] Then you will answer them, 'Because your ancestors abandoned me — this is the LORD's declaration — and followed other gods, served them, and bowed in worship to them. Indeed, they abandoned me and did not keep my instruction. [12] You did more evil than your ancestors. Look, each one of you was following the stubbornness of his evil heart, not obeying me. [13] So I will hurl you from this land into a land that you and your ancestors have not known. There you will worship other gods both day and night, for I will not grant you grace.'[B]

[14] "However, look, the days are coming" — the LORD's declaration — "when it will no longer be said, 'As the LORD lives who brought the Israelites from the land of Egypt,' [15] but rather, 'As the LORD lives who brought the Israelites from the land of the north and from all the other lands where he had banished them.' For I will return them to their land that I gave to their ancestors.

Punishment of Exile

[16] "I am about to send for many fishermen" — this is the LORD's declaration — "and they will fish for them. Then I will send for many hunters, and they will hunt them down on every mountain and hill and out of the clefts of the rocks, [17] for my gaze takes in all their ways. They are not concealed from me, and their iniquity is not hidden from my sight. [18] I will first repay them double for their iniquity and sin because they have polluted my land. They have filled my inheritance with the carcasses of their abhorrent and detestable idols."

[19]   LORD, my strength and my stronghold,
         my refuge in a time of distress,
     the nations will come to you
         from the ends of the earth,
             and they will say,
     "Our ancestors inherited only lies,
         worthless idols of no benefit at all."
[20]   Can one make gods for himself?
         But they are not gods.
[21]   "Therefore, I am about to inform them,
         and this time I will make them know
     my power and my might;
         then they will know that my name
             is the LORD."

The Persistent Sin of Judah

17   The sin of Judah is inscribed
         with an iron stylus.
     With a diamond point
         it is engraved on the tablet
             of their hearts
     and on the horns of their[c] altars,
[2]   while their children remember
             their altars
     and their Asherah poles,
         by the green trees
     on the high hills —
[3]   my mountains in the countryside.
     I will give up your wealth
         and all your treasures as plunder
     because of the sin
         of your high places[D]
     in all your borders.
[4]   You will, on your own, relinquish
             your inheritance
     that I gave you.
     I will make you serve your enemies
         in a land you do not know,
     for you have set my anger on fire;
         it will burn forever.

[A]16:6 This custom demonstrated pagan mourning rituals.   [B]16:13 Or *compassion*   [c]17:1 Some Hb mss, Syr, Vg; other Hb mss read *your*   [D]17:3 Lit *plunder, your high places because of sin*

Mc 1:16). Since these were pagan customs, Israel was forbidden to practice them (Lv 21:5; Dt 14:1).
16:7 Neighbors apparently brought food and drink for the relatives of the deceased (**food and a consoling drink**).
16:13 The expression **day and night** means "all the time."
16:14–15 These verses sound a theme that will reverberate later—a new exodus from Babylon.
16:18 The Hebrew word *mishneh* usually means "twofold" or **double** (cp. Is 40:2), but tablets from Alalakh contain a similar

word meaning "equivalent." If "double" is the correct translation, it means "ample, full, or complete" punishment. If "equivalent" is the correct rendering, the sentence means God would repay them the equivalent of their sinful iniquity. In either case, the Israelites reaped what they sowed.
17:1–27 There is no central theme in this chapter. It is a collection of wise sayings on how life should be lived.
17:1 The **iron stylus** that had **a diamond point** (cp. Jb 19:24) was an iron engraver's tool that chiseled the sin of Judah onto their hard **hearts** and the **horns of their altars**.

These horns were the projections at the four stone corners on top of the altar (Ex 27:2; 29:12; 30:1–3,10; Lv 4:7).
17:2 Asherah poles were upright carved wooden objects representing the fertility mother goddess of the Canaanites (2Kg 13:6; 17:16; 18:4; 21:3; 23:6,15).
17:3 High places were elevated platforms on top of a mountain or hill. An altar to a pagan god and a carved pole for the fertility goddess Asherah were located on these sites (2Kg 21:3; 2Ch 14:3). They also featured a stone pillar symbolizing the male deity (2Kg 3:2).

Curse and Blessing

⁵ This is what the LORD says:

Cursed is the person who trusts
　in mankind.
He makes human flesh his strength,
　and his heart turns from the LORD.
⁶ He will be like a juniper in the Arabah;
he cannot see when good comes
but dwells in the parched places
　in the wilderness,
in a salt land where no one lives.
⁷ The person who trusts in the LORD,
whose confidence indeed is the LORD, is
　blessed.
⁸ He will be like a tree planted by water:
it sends its roots out toward a stream,
it doesn't fear when heat comes,
and its foliage remains green.
It will not worry in a year of drought
or cease producing fruit.

The Deceitful Heart

⁹ The heart is more deceitful
　than anything else,
and incurable
　— who can understand it?
¹⁰ I, the LORD, examine the mind,
I test the heartᴬ
to give to each according to his way,
according to what
　his actions deserve.
¹¹ He who makes a fortune unjustly
is like a partridge that hatches eggs
　it didn't lay.
In the middle of his life
his riches will abandon him,
so in the end he will be a fool.

¹² A glorious throne
on high from the beginning
is the place of our sanctuary.
¹³ LORD, the hope of Israel,
all who abandon you
will be put to shame.
All who turn away from me
will be written in the dirt,

for they have abandoned
　the LORD, the fountain of living water.

Jeremiah's Plea

¹⁴ Heal me, LORD, and I will be healed;
save me, and I will be saved,
for you are my praise.
¹⁵ Hear how they keep challenging me,
"Where is the word of the LORD?
Let it come!"
¹⁶ But I have not run away from being
　your shepherd,
and I have not longed for the fatal day.
You know my words were spoken
　in your presence.
¹⁷ Don't become a terror to me.
You are my refuge in the day of disaster.
¹⁸ Let my persecutors be put to shame,
but don't let me be put to shame.
Let them be terrified, but don't let me
　be terrified.
Bring on them the day of disaster;
shatter them with totalᴮ destruction.

Observing the Sabbath

¹⁹ This is what the LORD said to me, "Go and stand at the People's Gate, through which the kings of Judah enter and leave, as well as at all the gates of Jerusalem. ²⁰ Announce to them, 'Hear the word of the LORD, kings of Judah, all Judah, and all the residents of Jerusalem who enter through these gates. ²¹ This is what the LORD says: Watch yourselves; do not pick up a load and bring it in through Jerusalem's gates on the Sabbath day. ²² Do not carry a load out of your houses on the Sabbath day or do any work, but keep the Sabbath day holy, just as I commanded your ancestors. ²³ They wouldn't listen or pay attention but became obstinate, not listening or accepting discipline.

²⁴ " 'However, if you listen to me — this is the LORD's declaration — and do not bring loads through the gates of this city on the Sabbath day, but keep the Sabbath day holy and do no work on it, ²⁵ kings and princes will enter through the gates of this city. They will sit on

---

ᴬ17:10 Lit *kidneys*　ᴮ17:18 Lit *double*

17:5–13 The poem in these verses has close parallels with Ps 1 and the Wisdom literature of Job, Proverbs, and Ecclesiastes. It focuses on two ways of death and two ways of life. **17:5–6** In these verses there is a play on the words for **person** . . . **mankind** and **flesh**. In Hebrew, the first word is *gever*, meaning "strong one," man as male. The second is *'adam*, "man made of dust." The third is *basar*, "flesh." Put together, these indicate a poor substitute for trusting in the Lord. The people's misplaced trust is like **a juniper in the Arabah**, a bush that shriveled in the scorching heat. The Arabah, part of the Great Rift Valley that stretches from the south end of the Dead Sea to the Gulf of Aqabah, is desertlike.

17:9–11 These verses contain three wisdom sayings: (1) **The heart is more deceitful than anything** and is **incurable** (lit "perverse" or "beyond cure," 13:23). (2) **I, the LORD, examine the mind** (Hb, "heart"), **I test the heart** (lit "kidneys"). The "mind" and the "heart" are hidden elements of a human personality, but God sees them perfectly. (3) The **partridge** (perhaps a sand grouse) **hatches eggs it didn't lay**. Some people amass wealth via the sweat of others, but like these birds, they will discover that their wealth does not last forever (Pr 23:4–5). **17:12** The phrase **a glorious throne** refers to the temple where the Lord dwelled, and thus to his rule (Lm 5:19).

17:13 On **LORD, the hope of Israel**, see note at 14:8. Judah had turned her back on her hope and had **abandoned the LORD, the fountain of living water** (see note at 2:13). **17:14–18** This is another of Jeremiah's "confessions" (see note at 4:19–22). **17:18** This is an imprecation as is often found in the Psalms (e.g., Pss 69:22–28; 139:19–22). Jeremiah recognized his enemies as the enemies of God. **17:19** The **People's Gate** was not the gate of the temple. The gate Jeremiah referred to is unknown, but it was apparently a place where people commonly gathered. **17:20–27** The **Sabbath day** is mentioned several times in these verses.

the throne of David; they will ride in chariots and on horses with their officials, the men of Judah, and the residents of Jerusalem. This city will be inhabited forever. ²⁶ Then people will come from the cities of Judah and from the area around Jerusalem, from the land of Benjamin and from the Judean foothills, from the hill country and from the Negev bringing burnt offerings and sacrifices, grain offerings and frankincense, and thanksgiving sacrifices to the house of the LORD. ²⁷ But if you do not listen to me to keep the Sabbath day holy by not carrying a load while entering the gates of Jerusalem on the Sabbath day, I will set fire to its gates, and it will consume the citadels of Jerusalem and not be extinguished.'"

Parable of the Potter

18 This is the word that came to Jeremiah from the LORD: ² "Go down at once to the potter's house; there I will reveal my words to you." ³ So I went down to the potter's house, and there he was, working away at the wheel.^A ⁴ But the jar that he was making from the clay became flawed in the potter's hand, so he made it into another jar, as it seemed right for him to do.

⁵ The word of the LORD came to me: ⁶ "House of Israel, can I not treat you as this potter treats his clay?" — this is the LORD's declaration. "Just like clay in the potter's hand, so are you in my hand, house of Israel. ⁷ At one moment I might announce concerning a nation or a kingdom that I will uproot, tear down, and destroy it. ⁸ However, if that nation about which I have made the announcement turns from its evil, I will relent concerning the disaster I had planned to do to it. ⁹ At another time I might announce concerning a nation or a kingdom that I will build and plant it. ¹⁰ However, if it does what is evil in my sight by not listening to me, I will relent concerning the good I had said I would do to it. ¹¹ So now, say to the men of Judah and to the residents of

Jerusalem, 'This is what the LORD says: Look, I am about to bring harm to you and make plans against you. Turn now, each from your evil way, and correct your ways and your deeds.' ¹² But they will say, 'It's hopeless. We will continue to follow our plans, and each of us will continue to act according to the stubbornness of his evil heart.'"

Deluded Israel

¹³ Therefore, this is what the LORD says:

Ask among the nations,
who has heard things like these?
Virgin Israel has done
a most horrible thing.
¹⁴ Does the snow of Lebanon ever leave
the highland crags?
Or does cold water flowing
from a distance ever fail?
¹⁵ Yet my people have forgotten me.
They burn incense to worthless idols
that make them stumble in their ways
on the ancient roads,
and make them walk on new paths,
not the highway.
¹⁶ They have made their land a horror,
a perpetual object of scorn;^B
all who pass by it will be appalled
and shake their heads.
¹⁷ I will scatter them before the enemy
like the east wind.
I will show them^C my back and not
my face
on the day of their calamity.

Plot against Jeremiah

¹⁸ Then certain ones said, "Come, let's make plans against Jeremiah, for instruction will never be lost from the priest, or counsel from the wise, or a word from the prophet. Come, let's denounce him^D and pay no attention to all his words."
¹⁹ Pay attention to me, LORD.
Hear what my opponents are saying!

^A**18:3** Lit *pair of stones*   ^B**18:16** Lit *hissing*   ^C**18:17** LXX, Lat, Syr, Tg; MT reads *will look at them*   ^D**18:18** Lit *let's strike him with the tongue*

#38 **99 Essential Christian Truths**

GOD'S PROVIDENCE

Providence refers to God's continuing work and involvement in his creation. This includes, in various degrees, God's preservation of the created order, his governance, and his care for his people (Gn 8:21–22; Col 1:17; Heb 1:3). Christians believe the world, and even the cosmos itself, is contingent upon God, incapable of existing apart from him. Christians also believe in God's personal and direct intervention in the world— as opposed to a hands-off approach to creation—that affects not only the natural order but also the individuals and events within human history.

17:26 The **land of Benjamin** was north of Judah; the **Judean foothills** were the western lowlands, west and southwest of Judah; the **hill country** was the central part of the country; and the **Negev** was the dry, arid land south of Judah. **Frankincense** was not the incense offering, but the incense that was added *to* the offerings (Ex 30:7–9). **Thanksgiving sacrifices** were a type of peace or fellowship offering (Lv 7:11).
18:1–2 The trip to the **potter's house** provided Jeremiah with a symbolic action message. Potters commonly used a wheel, turned by foot, as they shaped a lump of clay with their hands. The vessel was then fired in a kiln to make it hard.
18:7–10 The lesson of the potter illustrates God's grace for all who will repent and turn back to him.
18:12 **It's hopeless** is also found in 2:25. The people's stubborn hearts are also mentioned in 3:17; 5:23; 7:24; 9:14; 11:8; 13:10; 16:12; 23:17.

18:16 Judah had become a land of **horror** and an **object of scorn**, or of "hissing" or "whistling." This was the ultimate expression in the Near Eastern "loss of face." People would make a hissing sound at a guilty person and shake their heads in scorn and disbelief.
18:17 The **east wind** was the hot wind or sirocco from the desert (4:11; 13:24; Hs 13:15), the same direction from which Babylon would come. The Lord has turned his back—a universal symbol of rejection (Hs 5:15).
18:19–23 This is another of Jeremiah's "confessions" (see note at 4:19–22). His accusers said, "Come, let's denounce him" (18:18), or literally, "Let us smite him with the tongue." Jeremiah charged his opponents with the following: (1) paying "no attention to all his words" (v. 18), (2) digging **a pit** for him (vv. 20,22), (3) hiding **snares** for his **feet** (v. 22), and (4) planning to kill him (v. 23).

²⁰ Should good be repaid with evil?
  Yet they have dug a pit for me.
  Remember how I stood before you
  to speak good on their behalf,
  to turn your anger from them.
²¹ Therefore, hand their children
  over to famine,
  and give them over to the power of the
  sword.
  Let their wives become childless
  and widowed,
  their husbands slain by deadly disease,^A
  their young men struck down
  by the sword in battle.
²² Let a cry be heard from their houses
  when you suddenly bring raiders
  against them,
  for they have dug a pit to capture me
  and have hidden snares for my feet.
²³ But you, Lord, know
  all their deadly plots against me.
  Do not wipe out their iniquity;
  do not blot out their sin before you.
  Let them be forced to stumble
  before you;
  deal with them in the time
  of your anger.

The Clay Jar

19 This is what the Lord says: "Go, buy a potter's clay jar. Take^B some of the elders of the people and some of the leading priests ² and go out to Ben Hinnom Valley near the entrance of the Potsherd Gate. Proclaim there the words I speak to you. ³ Say, 'Hear the word of the Lord, kings of Judah and residents of Jerusalem. This is what the Lord of Armies, the God of Israel, says: I am going to bring such a disaster on this place that everyone who hears about it will shudder^C ⁴ because they have abandoned me and made this a foreign place. They have burned incense in it to other gods that they, their ancestors, and the kings of Judah have never known. They have filled this place with the blood of the innocent. ⁵ They have built high places to Baal on which to burn their children in the fire as burnt offerings to Baal, something I have

never commanded or mentioned; I never entertained the thought.^D

⁶ "'Therefore, look, the days are coming — this is the Lord's declaration — when this place will no longer be called Topheth and Ben Hinnom Valley, but Slaughter Valley. ⁷ I will spoil the plans of Judah and Jerusalem in this place. I will make them fall by the sword before their enemies, by the hand of those who intend to take their life. I will provide their corpses as food for the birds of the sky and for the wild animals of the land. ⁸ I will make this city desolate, an object of scorn. Everyone who passes by it will be appalled and scoff because of all its wounds. ⁹ I will make them eat the flesh of their sons and their daughters, and they will eat each other's flesh in the distressing siege inflicted on them by their enemies who intend to take their life.'

¹⁰ "Then you are to shatter the jar in the presence of the people going with you, ¹¹ and you are to proclaim to them, 'This is what the Lord of Armies says: I will shatter these people and this city, like one shatters a potter's jar that can never again be mended. They will bury the dead in Topheth because there is no other place for burials. ¹² That is what I will do to this place — this is the declaration of the Lord — and to its residents, making this city like Topheth. ¹³ The houses of Jerusalem and the houses of the kings of Judah will become impure like that place Topheth — all the houses on whose rooftops they have burned incense to all the stars in the sky and poured out drink offerings to other gods.'"

¹⁴ Jeremiah returned from Topheth, where the Lord had sent him to prophesy, stood in the courtyard of the Lord's temple, and proclaimed to all the people, ¹⁵ "This is what the Lord of Armies, the God of Israel, says: 'I am about to bring on this city — and on all its cities — every disaster that I spoke against it, for they have become obstinate, not obeying my words.'"

Jeremiah Beaten by Pashhur

20 Pashhur the priest, the son of Immer and chief official in the temple of the Lord, heard Jeremiah prophesying these

---

^A18:21 Lit by death   ^B19:1 Syr, Tg; MT omits Take   ^C19:3 Lit about it, his ears will tingle; Hb obscure   ^D19:5 Lit mentioned, and it did not arise on my heart

---

19:1 The Lord told Jeremiah to buy a **potter's clay jar** as his next symbolic action. This was probably a narrow-necked water jar.
19:2 Along with some elders, Jeremiah was told to go to **Ben Hinnom Valley** (later Gehenna; see note at 7:31) **near the entrance of the Potsherd Gate**. This gate, south of the Jerusalem wall, was the gate through which broken pottery and other trash were transported to the city dump.
19:4 The **blood of the innocent** refers to the practice of offering children as burnt offerings to Baal or Molech (see note at 7:31).

19:5 Judah had **built high places to Baal** in the Ben Hinnom Valley.
19:6-7 Topheth (see note at 7:31) and **Ben Hinnom Valley** would then be called **Slaughter Valley** to reflect God's judgment. The corpses of Judah's dead would remain unburied, a sign of judgment as **birds of the sky** and **wild animals** fed on their remains (7:33; 16:4; 34:20; Dt 28:26).
19:9 So severe would be the conditions of the siege that Judah's survivors would **eat the flesh of their sons** and **daughters**. This cannibalism is attested in the siege of Samaria (2Kg 6:26-29) and in the Babylonian siege in

587 BC (Lm 2:20; 4:10). According to Josephus in *Wars of the Jews*, this also happened in AD 70 when Jerusalem fell to the Romans.
19:10-11 On **Topheth**, see note at 7:31.
19:14-15 Judgment will fall on **this city** (Jerusalem) and **its cities**, meaning the rest of Judah's cities.
20:1 Ironically, **Pashhur**, the **chief official** or "overseer" of **the temple of the Lord**, came against Jeremiah. This Pashhur is probably the same as the father of Gedaliah (38:1), but not the same as another official named Pashhur in 21:1; 38:1. Jeremiah predicted Pashhur would go into exile in Babylon (20:6).

things. [2] So Pashhur had the prophet Jeremiah beaten and put him in the stocks at the Upper Benjamin Gate in the LORD's temple. [3] The next day, when Pashhur released Jeremiah from the stocks, Jeremiah said to him, "The LORD does not call you Pashhur, but Terror Is on Every Side,[A] [4] for this is what the LORD says, 'I am about to make you a terror to both yourself and those you love. They will fall by the sword of their enemies before your very eyes. I will hand Judah over to the king of Babylon, and he will deport them to Babylon and put them to the sword. [5] I will give away all the wealth of this city, all its products and valuables. Indeed, I will hand all the treasures of the kings of Judah over to their enemies. They will plunder them, seize them, and carry them off to Babylon. [6] As for you, Pashhur, and all who live in your house, you will go into captivity. You will go to Babylon. There you will die, and there you will be buried, you and all your friends to whom you prophesied lies.'"

Jeremiah Compelled to Preach

[7] You deceived me, LORD,
    and I was deceived.
You seized me and prevailed.
I am a laughingstock all the time;
    everyone ridicules me.
[8] For whenever I speak, I cry out,
I proclaim, "Violence and destruction!"
    so the word of the LORD
    has become my
constant disgrace and derision.
[9] I say, "I won't mention him
    or speak any longer in his name."
But his message becomes a fire burning
    in my heart,
shut up in my bones.
I become tired of holding it in,
    and I cannot prevail.
[10] For I have heard the gossip
    of many people,
"Terror is on every side!
Report him; let's report him!"

Everyone I trusted[B] watches
    for my fall.
"Perhaps he will be deceived
so that we might prevail against him
and take our vengeance on him."
[11] But the LORD is with me
    like a violent warrior.
Therefore, my persecutors will stumble
    and not prevail.
Since they have not succeeded,
    they will be utterly shamed,
an everlasting humiliation that will
    never be forgotten.
[12] LORD of Armies, testing
    the righteous
and seeing the heart[C] and mind,
let me see your vengeance on them,
for I have presented my case to you.
[13] Sing to the LORD!
Praise the LORD,
for he rescues the life of the needy
    from evil people.

Jeremiah's Lament

[14] May the day I was born
    be cursed.
May the day my mother bore me
    never be blessed.
[15] May the man be cursed
    who brought the news
        to my father, saying,
"A male child is born to you,"
    bringing him great joy.
[16] Let that man be like the cities
    the LORD demolished
        without compassion.
Let him hear an outcry in the morning
    and a war cry at noontime
[17] because he didn't kill me in the womb
    so that my mother might have been
        my grave,
    her womb eternally pregnant.
[18] Why did I come out of the womb
    to see only struggle and sorrow,
        to end my life in shame?

[A] 20:3 = Magor-missabib   [B] 20:10 Lit Every man of my peace   [C] 20:12 Lit kidneys

---

20:2 Pashhur ordered that Jeremiah be **beaten**. This was the first act of violence against the prophet. The **Upper Benjamin Gate** (built by King Jotham; 2Kg 15:35) was the northern gate of the upper temple court and the most prominent gate in the city.
20:3 By God's commission, Jeremiah changed Pashhur's name to Magor-missabib, meaning **Terror Is on Every Side** This name appears five times in Jeremiah (v. 10; 6:25; 46:5; 49:29) and in Lm 2:22. Elsewhere the term is found only in Ps 31:13 and Is 31:9.
20:4 This is the first time the **king of Babylon** is mentioned in the book of Jeremiah. His inclusion here prompts some scholars to date this prophecy after the battle of Carchemish in 605 BC. This was roughly the halfway mark of Jeremiah's forty-year ministry.

20:5-6 Even though **Pashhur** was a priest, he had apparently prophesied falsely along with his **friends**. For this sin he would face captivity and death in a foreign land.
20:7-18 This is the last of Jeremiah's "confessions" (see note at 4:19–22). As his saddest and most bitter complaint, it is one of his most revealing self-disclosures.
20:7 Jeremiah cried, **You deceived me, LORD**. So bold, offensive, and verging on blasphemous were these words that many have tried to soften them by translating them as "enticed," or "persuaded." Jeremiah did not accuse God of lying. But the Hebrew verb *pathah* means "to seduce" as a virgin is seduced (Ex 22:16). Thus, he thought God had "twisted his arm" in calling him to prophetic ministry. Jeremiah's audiences made him a **laughingstock**.

20:9 Whenever Jeremiah decided to quit and no longer speak in God's name, the divine message became **a fire burning** in his **heart, shut up** in his **bones**. Thus he felt compelled to speak, no matter how unpopular his message.
20:10 A gossip campaign began to build against Jeremiah as they nicknamed him Mr. **Terror . . . on every side**.
20:12 This verse is virtually the same as 11:20, bracketing the first and last of the prophet's "confessions."
20:14-15 Whereas a messenger who brought **news** of a birth was usually rewarded in that culture, Jeremiah said the man who announced his birth should have been **cursed**.

Zedekiah's Request Denied

21 This is the word that came to Jeremiah from the LORD when King Zedekiah sent Pashhur son of Malchijah and the priest Zephaniah son of Maaseiah to Jeremiah, asking, ² "Inquire of the LORD on our behalf, since King Nebuchadnezzar^A of Babylon is making war against us. Perhaps the LORD will perform for us something like all his past wondrous works so that Nebuchadnezzar will withdraw from us."

³ But Jeremiah answered, "This is what you are to say to Zedekiah: ⁴ 'This is what the LORD, the God of Israel, says: I am about to repel the weapons of war in your hands, those you are using to fight the king of Babylon and the Chaldeans^B who are besieging you outside the wall, and I will bring them into the center of this city. ⁵ I myself will fight against you with an outstretched hand and a strong arm, with anger, fury, and intense wrath. ⁶ I will strike the residents of this city, both people and animals. They will die in a severe plague. ⁷ Afterward — this is the LORD's declaration — King Zedekiah of Judah, his officers, and the people — those in this city who survive the plague, the sword, and the famine — I will hand over to King Nebuchadnezzar of Babylon, to their enemies, yes, to those who intend to take their lives. He will put them to the sword; he won't spare them or show pity or compassion.'

A Warning for the People

⁸ "But tell this people, 'This is what the LORD says: Look, I am setting before you the way of life and the way of death. ⁹ Whoever stays in this city will die by the sword, famine, and plague, but whoever goes out and surrenders to the Chaldeans who are besieging you will live and will retain his life like the spoils of war. ¹⁰ For I have set my face against this city to bring disaster and not good — this is the LORD's declaration. It will be handed over to the king of Babylon, who will burn it.'

¹¹ "And to the house of the king of Judah say this: 'Hear the word of the LORD! ¹² House of David, this is what the LORD says:

Administer justice every morning,
and rescue the victim of robbery
from his oppressor,
or my anger will flare up like fire
and burn unquenchably
because of your evil deeds.
¹³ Beware! I am against you,
you who sit above the valley,
you atop the rocky plateau —
this is the LORD's declaration —
you who say, "Who can come down
against us?
Who can enter our hiding places?"
¹⁴ I will punish you according to
what you have done —
this is the LORD's declaration.
I will kindle a fire in your forest
that will consume everything
around it.' "

Judgment against Sinful Kings

22 This is what the LORD says: "Go down to the palace of the king of Judah and announce this word there. ² You are to say, 'Hear the word of the LORD, king of Judah, you who sit on the throne of David — you, your officers, and your people who enter these gates. ³ This is what the LORD says: Administer justice and righteousness. Rescue the victim of robbery from his oppressor. Don't exploit or brutalize the resident alien, the fatherless, or the widow. Don't shed innocent blood in this place. ⁴ For if you conscientiously carry out this word, then kings sitting on David's throne will enter through the gates of this palace riding on chariots and horses — they, their officers, and their people. ⁵ But if you do not obey these words, then I swear by myself — this is the LORD's declaration — that this house will become a ruin.' "

---

^A **21:2** Lit *Nebuchadrezzar*   ^B **21:4** = Babylonians

21:1–14 This chapter contains three messages that God revealed to Jeremiah: (1) a message to King Zedekiah of Judah, (2) a message to the people of Jerusalem, and (3) a message to **the house of the king of Judah**.
21:1 This **Pashhur** is not the same person as the Pashhur in 20:1. **Zephaniah** was the successor of Jehoiada the priest (29:25–26; 37:3; 52:24) and second in rank below the high priest.
21:2 King Zedekiah of Judah, who reigned 597–586 BC, depended on Pharaoh Hophra of Egypt to take care of Nebuchadnezzar, king of Babylon. Zedekiah sent Pashhur to Jeremiah to foretell what the outcome of his foolish rebellion against Babylon would be. He was hopeful that the Lord would perform **wondrous works** for Judah, just as he had done in the days of Hezekiah (2Kg 18–19) and Jehoshaphat (2Ch 20).
21:3–4 Chaldeans is the usual term for Babylonians. The tribal groups living in the

area between the Tigris and Euphrates rivers and between the city of Babylon and the Persian Gulf were called Chaldeans. A Chaldean dynasty was started under Nabopolassar, whose son was Nebuchadnezzar.
21:5 An **outstretched hand** and a **strong arm** are routine metaphors describing God's miraculous intervention in times past.
21:6–7 During military sieges, the possibility of an epidemic or **severe plague** is heightened. Such illness would further weaken the people's ability to defend against attackers. Then those who survived would be killed by the sword.
21:9 The prophet counseled defection for the citizens of Judah. The person who surrendered to Babylon would **retain his life like the spoils of war**. This is an idiomatic expression meaning literally "his soul will be to him for booty" (38:2; 39:18; 45:5).

21:11–14 House refers to the dynasty of the king.
21:13 The phrases **you who sit above the valley** and **you atop the rocky plateau** refer to the city of Jerusalem as well as the king. The city, with its palace complex, was surrounded by valleys. Complacently and proudly the people asked, **Who can come down against us?** The short answer: God himself.
21:14 The word **forest** is used here figuratively for the royal palace (1Kg 7:2; 10:21).
22:3 The sins mentioned here fit the reigns of all the Judean kings of this period, but they were especially fitting for Jehoiakim's time (2Kg 23:35).
22:5 To underline the solemnity of this message, the Lord declared, **I swear by myself**, giving the strongest possible authentication to Jeremiah's words.

⁶ For this is what the LORD says concerning the house of the king of Judah:

> "You are like Gilead to me,
> or the summit of Lebanon,
> but I will certainly turn you
> into a wilderness,
> uninhabited cities.
> ⁷ I will set apart destroyers against you,
> each with his weapons.
> They will cut down the choicest
> of your cedars
> and throw them into the fire.

⁸ "Many nations will pass by this city and ask one another, 'Why did the LORD do such a thing to this great city?' ⁹ They will answer, 'Because they abandoned the covenant of the LORD their God and bowed in worship to other gods and served them.'"

A Message concerning Shallum

> ¹⁰ Do not weep for the dead;
> do not mourn for him.
> Weep bitterly for the one
> who has gone away,
> for he will never return again
> and see his native land.

¹¹ For this is what the LORD says concerning Shallum son of Josiah, king of Judah, who became king in place of his father Josiah, and who has left this place: "He will never return here again, ¹² but he will die in the place where they deported him, never seeing this land again."

A Message concerning Jehoiakim

> ¹³ Woe for the one who builds his palace
> through unrighteousness,
> his upstairs rooms through injustice,
> who makes his neighbor serve
> without pay
> and will not give him his wages,
> ¹⁴ who says, "I will build myself
> a massive palace,
> with spacious upstairs rooms."
> He will cut windows^A in it,

> and it will be paneled with cedar
> and painted bright red.
> ¹⁵ Are you a king because you excel
> in cedar?
> Didn't your father eat and drink
> and administer justice
> and righteousness?
> Then it went well with him.
> ¹⁶ He took up the case of the poor
> and needy;
> then it went well.
> Is this not what it means to know me?
> This is the LORD's declaration.
> ¹⁷ But you have eyes and a heart
> for nothing
> except your own dishonest profit,
> shedding innocent blood
> and committing extortion
> and oppression.

¹⁸ Therefore, this is what the LORD says concerning Jehoiakim son of Josiah, king of Judah:

> They will not mourn for him, saying,
> "Woe, my brother!" or "Woe, my sister!"
> They will not mourn for him, saying,
> "Woe, lord! Woe, his majesty!"
> ¹⁹ He will be buried like a donkey,
> dragged off and thrown
> outside Jerusalem's gates.
> ²⁰ Go up to Lebanon and cry out;
> raise your voice in Bashan;
> cry out from Abarim,
> for all your lovers^B have been crushed.
> ²¹ I spoke to you when you were secure.
> You said, "I will not listen."
> This has been your way since youth;
> indeed, you have never listened to me.
> ²² The wind will take charge of^C all
> your shepherds,
> and your lovers will go into captivity.
> Then you will be ashamed
> and humiliated
> because of all your evil.
> ²³ You residents of Lebanon,
> nestled among the cedars,

---

^A 22:14 Lit my windows   ^B 22:20 Or friends, or allies, also in v. 22   ^C 22:22 Lit will shepherd

---

22:6-9 These verses refer not to the Davidic line, but to the royal palace. The regions of **Gilead** and **Lebanon** were noted for trees such as **cedars** (1Kg 5:6,8–10; 7:2–5; 10:27). However, the lofty and startling cedar columns of the palace would be burned up in the fall of Jerusalem.
22:9 The phrase **they abandoned the covenant of the LORD** occurs only here and at Dt 29:25. It refers to the Sinaitic covenant, not God's covenant with David (2Sm 7).
22:10-12 Instead of weeping for **the dead** King Josiah, who was killed at the battle of Megiddo in 609 BC (2Kg 23:29–35; 2Ch 35:24–25), Jeremiah told the people to reserve their tears for Josiah's son, King **Shallum**. This king was also known as Jehoahaz. After a short reign of three months, Jehoahaz would be

exiled to Egypt, where he would die (2Kg 23:34). In that sense, Josiah would be better off than his son. Jehoahaz would be the first Judean king to die in exile.
22:13-16 Jeremiah denounced King Jehoiakim, who reigned 609–598 BC, more severely than he denounced any other king. In a manic building campaign, Jehoiakim violated Mosaic law (Lv 19:13; Dt 24:14–15) by forcing Judean laborers to build and remodel his palace without paying them any wages.
22:17 Not only was Jehoiakim tyrannical, covetous, and oppressive; he was also guilty of shedding **innocent blood**. For example, because the prophet Uriah had prophesied against him, the king brought Uriah back from Egypt and had him executed (26:20–23).

22:18-19 A humiliating death awaited evil King Jehoiakim. That he would be buried like a **donkey, dragged off and thrown outside Jerusalem's gates** meant no burial at all, which was considered a curse (Dt 28:26).
22:20 The people are told to pick a mountain in the north, **Lebanon**, for example, or **Bashan** in northern Transjordan, or **Abarim**, the mountains of Moab, east of the Dead Sea. From these heights they could broadcast their lament over what was about to happen. The words **your lovers** refer to the faithful patriots in Judah, the leaders of the nation, or perhaps Egypt and those countries to whom King Jehoiakim had looked for help against Babylon.
22:21 The word rendered **secure** can also mean "complacent."

how you will groan[A] when pains
come on you,
agony like a woman in labor.

A Message concerning Coniah

[24] "As I live" — this is the LORD's declaration — "though you, Coniah[B] son of Jehoiakim, the king of Judah, were a signet ring on my right hand, I would tear you from it. [25] In fact, I will hand you over to those you dread, who intend to take your life, to Nebuchadnezzar king of Babylon and the Chaldeans. [26] I will hurl you and the mother who gave birth to you into another land, where neither of you were born, and there you will both die. [27] They will never return to the land they long to return to."

[28] Is this man Coniah
a despised, shattered pot,
a jar no one wants?
Why are he and his descendants
hurled out
and cast into a land
they have not known?
[29] Earth, earth, earth,
hear the word of the LORD!

[30] This is what the LORD says:
Record this man as childless,
a man who will not be successful
in his lifetime.
None of his descendants will succeed
in sitting on the throne of David
or ruling again in Judah.

The LORD and His Sheep

23 "Woe to the shepherds who destroy and scatter the sheep of my pasture!" This is the LORD's declaration. [2] "Therefore, this is what the LORD, the God of Israel, says about the shepherds who tend my people: You have scattered my flock, banished them, and have not attended to them. I am about to attend to you because of your evil acts" — this is the LORD's declaration. [3] "I will gather the remnant of my flock from all the lands where I have banished them, and I will return them to their grazing land. They will become fruitful and numerous. [4] I will raise up shepherds over them who will tend them. They will no longer be afraid or discouraged, nor will any be missing." This is the LORD's declaration.

The Righteous Branch of David

[5] "Look, the days are coming" — this is
the LORD's declaration —
"when I will raise up a Righteous
Branch for David.
He will reign wisely as king
and administer justice and
righteousness in the land.
[6] In his days Judah will be saved,
and Israel will dwell securely.
This is the name he will be called:
The LORD Is Our Righteousness.[C]

[7] "Look, the days are coming" — the LORD's declaration — "when it will no longer be said, 'As the LORD lives who brought the Israelites from the land of Egypt,' [8] but, 'As the LORD lives, who brought and led the descendants of the house of Israel from the land of the north and from all the other countries where I[D] had banished them.' They will dwell once more in their own land."

False Prophets Condemned

[9] Concerning the prophets:
My heart is broken within me,
and all my bones tremble.
I have become like a drunkard,
like a man overcome by wine,
because of the LORD,
because of his holy words.
[10] For the land is full of adulterers;
the land mourns because of the curse,
and the grazing lands in the wilderness
have dried up.
Their way of life[E] has become evil,
and their power is not rightly used
[11] because both prophet and priest
are ungodly,

---

^A22:23 LXX, Syr, Vg; MT reads *will be pitied* B22:24 = Jehoiachin C23:6 = *Yahweh-zidkenu* D23:8 LXX reads *he* E23:10 Lit *Their manner of running*

22:24–30 In these verses Jehoiachin (son of Jehoiakim) is condemned. He reigned for only three months. Jehoiachin was also called Coniah (vv. 24,28).
22:24 A **signet ring** contains the king's official seal, which he used to stamp official documents. Such documents bore the sign of royal authority (Hg 2:23). Because of Jehoiachin's sins, God says in figurative language that, were the king a signet ring on his right hand, he would rip that privilege away from him. Jehoiachin was exiled to Babylon in 597 BC (2Kg 24:8–17; 25:27–30).
22:26 Jehoiachin's **mother** was Nehushta (2Kg 24:8).
22:29 The repetition of **earth** gives a strong and solemn emphasis to the message God was about to deliver.

22:30 The words **record this man as childless** are startling since Jehoiachin had seven sons (1Ch 3:17). This is an allusion to the fact that **none of his descendants** would ascend to the throne. Jehoiachin's uncle, Zedekiah, reigned after him, but he died before Jehoiachin died in Babylon. Thus Jehoiachin was the last living Judean king in the line of David.
23:1–2 The **shepherds** were not only Zedekiah and the three godless Judean kings mentioned in chap. 22, but all leaders of Judah, including spiritual and civil leaders. The phrases **the sheep of my pasture . . . my people**, and **my flock** are used by Jeremiah more than forty times to designate the close relationship between God and the people of Judah.

23:3–4 The upcoming exile was a sure thing, but so too was the future regathering. The good **shepherds** that God would raise up were not only Zerubbabel, Ezra, and Nehemiah, but leaders far into the future.
23:5 The expression **the days are coming** points to messianic times. It is used fifteen times in the book of Jeremiah. **Branch for David** refers to the Messiah.
23:6 In contrast to the name *Zedekiah*, meaning "The LORD is righteousness" (a name given to Mattaniah by Nebuchadnezzar in 2Kg 24:17), the coming Messiah will be named **The LORD Is Our Righteousness**. Zedekiah was nothing like the Messiah in character or actions.
23:11–31 Both **prophet** and **priest** were accomplices in corrupting and misleading the

even in my house I have found their evil.
This is the LORD's declaration.

¹² Therefore, their way will seem
like slippery paths in the gloom.
They will be driven away
and fall down there,
for I will bring disaster on them,
the year of their punishment.
This is the LORD's declaration.

¹³ Among the prophets of Samaria
I saw something disgusting:
They prophesied by Baal
and led my people Israel astray.

¹⁴ Among the prophets of Jerusalem also
I saw a horrible thing:
They commit adultery and walk in lies.
They strengthen the hands of evildoers,
and none turns his back on evil.
They are all like Sodom to me;
Jerusalem's residents are
like Gomorrah.

¹⁵ Therefore, this is what the LORD of Armies
says concerning the prophets:
I am about to feed them wormwood
and give them poisoned water
to drink,
for from the prophets of Jerusalem
ungodliness^ has spread
throughout the land.

¹⁶ This is what the LORD of Armies says: "Do
not listen to the words of the prophets who
prophesy to you. They are deluding you. They
speak visions from their own minds, not from
the LORD's mouth. ¹⁷ They keep on saying to
those who despise me, 'The LORD has spoken:
You will have peace.' They have said to everyone who follows the stubbornness of his heart,
'No harm will come to you.' "

¹⁸ For who has stood in the council
of the LORD
to see and hear his word?
Who has paid attention to his word
and obeyed?

¹⁹ Look, a storm from the LORD!
Wrath has gone out,
a whirling storm.

It will whirl about the heads
of the wicked.

²⁰ The LORD's anger will not turn away
until he has completely fulfilled
the purposes of his heart.
In time to come you will
understand it clearly.

²¹ I did not send out these prophets,
yet they ran.
I did not speak to them,
yet they prophesied.

²² If they had really stood in my council,
they would have enabled my people
to hear my words
and would have turned them
from their evil ways
and their evil deeds.

²³ "Am I a God who is only near" — this is the
LORD's declaration — "and not a God who is
far away? ²⁴ Can a person hide in secret places
where I cannot see him?" — the LORD's declaration. "Do I not fill the heavens and the earth?"
— the LORD's declaration.

²⁵ "I have heard what the prophets who
prophesy a lie in my name have said: 'I had
a dream! I had a dream!' ²⁶ How long will
this continue in the minds of the prophets
prophesying lies, prophets of the deceit of
their own minds? ²⁷ Through their dreams
that they tell one another, they plan to cause
my people to forget my name as their ancestors forgot my name through Baal worship.
²⁸ The prophet who has only a dream should
recount the dream, but the one who has my
word should speak my word truthfully, for
what is straw compared to grain?" — this is
the LORD's declaration. ²⁹ "Is not my word like
fire" — this is the LORD's declaration — "and
like a hammer that pulverizes rock? ³⁰ Therefore, take note! I am against the prophets"
— the LORD's declaration — "who steal my
words from each other. ³¹ I am against the
prophets" — the LORD's declaration — "who
use their own tongues to make a declaration.
³² I am against those who prophesy false
dreams" — the LORD's declaration — "telling them and leading my people astray with

---

^23:15 Or pollution

---

people. Jeremiah had more to say against false
prophets than any other OT writer (vv. 9–40;
2:8; 5:30–31; 6:13–14; 8:10–11; 14:13–15; 18:18–23;
26:8,11,16; 27:1–28:16). His four charges against
them were: (1) low morals and character
(23:14), (2) they invented their own messages
(v. 16), (3) they did not have a call from God
(vv. 21–22), and (4) they were plagiarists (v. 30).
23:13 The **something disgusting** ("offensive thing") that Jeremiah saw was Israel
being **led . . . astray** as prophets prophesied
in Baal's name.
23:15 What the false prophets were about
to experience would be like eating **worm-**

wood—a shrub with a bitter taste—and
drinking **poisoned water** (9:15).
23:16–17 These **peace** prophets created
messages as figments of their **own minds**.
They deceived the people by promising
peace, prosperity, and success. The false
prophets were **deluding** the people.
23:18 Some understand the **council of the
LORD** to be a gathering of divine beings over
whom God presided or consulted. But the
biblical concept is different. The "council of
the LORD" referred to God's desire to share
his teaching with his prophets, as Amos declared (Am 3:7).

23:19–20 This announcement of judgment
is repeated almost identically in 30:23–24.
23:23–24 God is both immanent (**near**) and
transcendent (**far**).
23:25–29 The dreams to which the prophet
referred here were fabricated and preyed on
the gullible. The dreams of the false prophets
were like **straw**, not **grain**. God's word, by
contrast, was **like a hammer that pulverizes rock**.
23:30 Since they did not truly speak from
God, God said the false prophets could only
plagiarize **my words from each other** as
they made up false messages in God's name.

their reckless lies. It was not I who sent or commanded them, and they are of no benefit at all to these people" — this is the LORD's declaration.

The Burden of the LORD

³³ "Now when these people or a prophet or a priest asks you, 'What is the burden^A of the LORD?' you will respond to them, 'What is the burden? I will throw you away! This is the LORD's declaration.' ³⁴ As for the prophet, priest, or people who say, 'The burden of the LORD,' I will punish that man and his household. ³⁵ This is what each man is to say to his friend and to his brother: 'What has the LORD answered?' or 'What has the LORD spoken?' ³⁶ But no longer refer to^B the burden of the LORD, for each man's word becomes his burden and you pervert the words of the living God, the LORD of Armies, our God. ³⁷ Say to the prophet, 'What has the LORD answered you?' or 'What has the LORD spoken?' ³⁸ But if you say, 'The burden of the LORD,' then this is what the LORD says: Because you have said, 'The burden of the LORD,' and I specifically told you not to say, 'The burden of the LORD,' ³⁹ I will surely forget you.^C I will throw you away from my presence — both you and the city that I gave you and your ancestors. ⁴⁰ I will bring on you everlasting disgrace and humiliation that will never be forgotten."

The Good and the Bad Figs

24 After King Nebuchadnezzar of Babylon had deported Jeconiah^D son of Jehoiakim king of Judah, the officials of Judah, and the craftsmen and metalsmiths from Jerusalem and had brought them to Babylon, the LORD showed me two baskets of figs placed in front of the temple of the LORD. ² One basket contained very good figs, like early figs, but the other basket contained very bad figs, so

bad they were inedible. ³ The LORD said to me, "What do you see, Jeremiah?"

I said, "Figs! The good figs are very good, but the bad figs are extremely bad, so bad they are inedible."

⁴ The word of the LORD came to me: ⁵ "This is what the LORD, the God of Israel, says: Like these good figs, so I regard as good the exiles from Judah I sent away from this place to the land of the Chaldeans. ⁶ I will keep my eyes on them for their good and will return them to this land. I will build them up and not demolish them; I will plant them and not uproot them. ⁷ I will give them a heart to know me, that I am the LORD. They will be my people, and I will be their God because they will return to me with all their heart.

⁸ "But as for the bad figs, so bad they are inedible, this is what the LORD says: In this way I will deal with King Zedekiah of Judah, his officials, and the remnant of Jerusalem — those remaining in this land or living in the land of Egypt. ⁹ I will make them an object of horror and a disaster to all the kingdoms of the earth, an example for disgrace, scorn, ridicule, and cursing, wherever I have banished them. ¹⁰ I will send the sword, famine, and plague against them until they have perished from the land I gave to them and their ancestors."

The Seventy-Year Exile

25 This is the word that came to Jeremiah concerning all the people of Judah in the fourth year of Jehoiakim son of Josiah, king of Judah (which was the first year of King Nebuchadnezzar of Babylon). ² The prophet Jeremiah spoke concerning all the people of Judah and all the residents of Jerusalem as follows: ³ "From the thirteenth year of Josiah son of Amon, king of Judah, until this very day — twenty-three years — the word of the LORD has come to me, and I have spoken to you time

---

^A**23:33** The Hb word for *burden* (Ex 23:5; 2Sm 15:33) can also mean "oracle" (Is 13:1; Nah 1:10). ^B**23:36** Or *longer remember* ^C**23:39** Some Hb mss; other Hb mss, LXX, Syr, Vg read *surely lift you up* ^D**24:1** = Jehoiachin

---

23:33–38 The word **burden** comes from a Hebrew verbal root meaning "to lift up." All instances of the Hebrew noun imply a "burden," for all are judgment passages. So when the people or the false prophets asked, **What is the burden of the LORD?** (v. 33), the answer was the short retort given in the Latin Vulgate and the Greek Septuagint (LXX): "You are the burden." The pun of the two senses of "burden" (prophetic burden of judgment and the burden of trying to speak to stubborn people) recurs throughout this section. **24:1–10** In this vision Jeremiah saw **two baskets of figs**, one good and one bad. **24:1** The phrase **the LORD showed me** marks a supernatural revelation to the prophet, much like that in Am 7:1,4,7. This happened in a vision and not in reality because bad figs could not be offered to the Lord (Dt 26:2). **24:2** The **early figs**, which ripened in May–June, were very juicy and were considered a delicacy.

24:5 God regarded as **good the exiles from Judah** that he **sent away** to Babylon in 597 BC. They were the pride of the nation in skills, leadership, and craftsmanship. Some of the leaders in that deportation had intervened on Jeremiah's behalf on several occasions (chaps. 26; 36). There were ten thousand deported at that time, including King Jehoiachin (aka Jeconiah) and the prophet Ezekiel. **24:7** The new heart did not depend on the people returning to God, because he had already given them a heart to know him. **24:8–10** The **bad figs** were **inedible**. This describes those who were still living in the land or those who had fled to Egypt. **25:1–38** This chapter describes a critical year in the history of the Near East. In this year, 605 BC, Jeremiah dictated his prophecies to his scribe Baruch (36:1–6), the battle of Carchemish unfolded, and Nebuchadnezzar ascended the throne of Babylon (see notes at 36:1; 45:1–5).

25:1 That the **first year of King Nebuchadnezzar** paralleled the **fourth year** of King Jehoiakim of Judah is not in conflict with Dn 1:1, which says Nebuchadnezzar laid siege in Jehoiakim's "third year." The two countries used different methods of reckoning the initiation of a king's reign. Judah used the accession-year principle, where the portion of the calendar year that remained when the king came to power was called his first year of reign. Babylon used the non-accession-year principle, where the first year of reign was calculated only with the advent of the new calendar year (hence, a king who took the throne on January 2 would begin his first year of reign on January 1 of the next calendar year). **25:2–4** Jeremiah had ministered in Judah for **twenty-three years**, but he had to conclude that the people had **not obeyed**. Jeremiah was not the only prophet sent by God during this time (Uriah, Zephaniah, and Habakkuk).

and time again,^ but you have not obeyed. ⁴ The LORD sent all his servants the prophets to you time and time again, ᴮ but you have not obeyed or even paid attention.ᶜ ⁵ He announced, 'Turn, each of you, from your evil way of life and from your evil deeds. Live in the land the LORD gave to you and your ancestors long ago and forever. ⁶ Do not follow other gods to serve them and to bow in worship to them, and do not anger me by the work of your hands. Then I will do you no harm.

⁷ " 'But you have not obeyed me' — this is the LORD's declaration — 'with the result that you have angered me by the work of your hands and brought disaster on yourselves.'

⁸ "Therefore, this is what the LORD of Armies says: 'Because you have not obeyed my words, ⁹ I am going to send for all the families of the north' — this is the LORD's declaration — 'and send for my servant Nebuchadnezzar king of Babylon, and I will bring them against this land, against its residents, and against all these surrounding nations, and I will completely destroy them and make them an example of horror and scorn, and ruins forever. ¹⁰ I will eliminate the sound of joy and gladness from them — the voice of the groom and the bride, the sound of the millstones and the light of the lamp. ¹¹ This whole land will become a desolate ruin, and these nations will serve the king of Babylon for seventy years. ¹² When the seventy years are completed, I will punish the king of Babylon and that nation' — this is the LORD's declaration — 'the land of the Chaldeans, for their iniquity, and I will make it a ruin forever. ¹³ I will bring on that land all my words I have spoken against it, all that is written in this book that Jeremiah prophesied against all the nations. ¹⁴ For many nations and great kings will enslave them, and I will repay them according to their deeds and the work of their hands.' "

The Cup of God's Wrath

¹⁵ This is what the LORD, the God of Israel, said to me: "Take this cup of the wine of wrath from my hand and make all the nations to whom I am sending you drink from it. ¹⁶ They will drink, stagger,ᴰ and go out of their minds because of the sword I am sending among them."

¹⁷ So I took the cup from the LORD's hand and made all the nations to whom the LORD sent me drink from it.

¹⁸ Jerusalem and the other cities of Judah, its kings and its officials, to make them a desolate ruin, an example for scorn and cursing — as it is today;
¹⁹ Pharaoh king of Egypt, his officers, his leaders, all his people,
²⁰ and all the mixed peoples;
all the kings of the land of Uz;
all the kings of the land of the Philistines
— Ashkelon, Gaza, Ekron, and the remnant of Ashdod;
²¹ Edom, Moab, and the Ammonites;
²² all the kings of Tyre,
all the kings of Sidon,
and the kings of the coasts and islands;
²³ Dedan, Tema, Buz, and all those who clip the hair on their temples;ᴱ
²⁴ all the kings of Arabia,
and all the kings of the mixed peoples who have settled in the desert;
²⁵ all the kings of Zimri,
all the kings of Elam,
and all the kings of Media;
²⁶ all the kings of the north, both near and far from one another;
that is, all the kingdoms of the world throughout the earth.
Finally, the king of Sheshakᶠ will drink after them.

²⁷ "Then you are to say to them, 'This is what the LORD of Armies, the God of Israel, says: Drink, get drunk, and vomit. Fall down and never get up again, as a result of the sword I am sending among you.' ²⁸ Ifᴳ they refuse to accept the cup from your hand and drink, you are to say to them, 'This is what the LORD of Armies says: You must drink! ²⁹ For I am already bringing disaster on the city that bears my name, so

---

^25:3 Lit you; rising early and speaking   ᴮ25:4 Lit to you, rising early and sending   ᶜ25:4 Lit even inclined your ear to hear   ᴰ25:16 Or vomit   ᴱ25:23 Or who live in distant places   ᶠ25:26 = Babylon   ᴳ25:28 Or When

---

In spite of his efforts, four times in vv. 3–8 Judah's disobedience is emphasized. The **thirteenth year** of King Josiah was 626 BC. **25:8–9 All the families of the north** meant Babylon's allies or the many nations and tribes within the Babylonian Empire. **Nebuchadnezzar** is called **my servant** three times in Jeremiah (v. 9; 27:6; 43:10). He was called by God as an instrument of his plan to **completely destroy** Judah and the surrounding nations. "Completely destroy" is related to the Hebrew noun *cherem*, where the enemy was "put under the ban" and set apart for destruction. **25:11** The **seventy years** is often regarded as a round number, but here it is the literal

period of time between 606/605 BC when Daniel was taken captive, and 536 BC when Zerubbabel led the first group of resettlers back to Judah. **25:12–14** The LXX inserts Jeremiah's oracles against the nations (chaps. 46–51) after the words **in this book**. **25:15–16** The prophet did not physically take the **cup** to all the nations, but all nations would experience that cup in the tragedies of the future. **25:17–18** The Lord's wrath would begin with **Jerusalem and the other cities of Judah**. **25:19–22** All the nations listed in chaps. 46–51, except Damascus, are included in this section. The list runs from south to north.

25:20 The **land of Uz** is mentioned in Jb 1:1. It was probably east of Edom. The **remnant of Ashdod** is singled out because Pharaoh Psammetik I of Egypt (663–609 BC) took the city after a twenty-nine-year siege. **25:23–24 Dedan** and **Tema** are both in northwest Arabia, but **Buz** is unknown. For **all those who clip the hair on their temples**, see 9:26. **25:25** The location of **Zimri** is unknown, though the name appears in Nm 25:14 and elsewhere. **Elam** and **Media** were east of the Tigris River. **25:26 Sheshak** is probably a cipher code for Babylon, written in what the Hebrews called *atbash*, where letters of the Hebrew alphabet

how could you possibly go unpunished? You will not go unpunished, for I am summoning a sword against all the inhabitants of the earth. This is the declaration of the LORD of Armies.'

Judgment on the Whole World

³⁰ "As for you, you are to prophesy all these things to them, and say to them:

The LORD roars from on high;
he makes his voice heard
from his holy dwelling.
He roars loudly over his grazing land;
he calls out with a shout, like those
who tread grapes,
against all the inhabitants of the earth.
³¹ The tumult reaches to the ends
of the earth
because the LORD brings a case
against the nations.
He enters into judgment
with all humanity.
As for the wicked, he hands them over
to the sword —
this is the LORD's declaration.

³² "This is what the LORD of Armies says:
Pay attention! Disaster spreads
from nation to nation.
A huge storm is stirred up
from the ends of the earth."

³³ Those slain by the LORD on that day will be scattered from one end of the earth to the other. They will not be mourned, gathered, or buried. They will be like manure on the soil's surface.

³⁴ Wail, you shepherds, and cry out.
Roll in the dust, you leaders of the flock.
Because the days of your slaughter
have come,
you will fall and become shattered
like a precious vase.
³⁵ Flight will be impossible
for the shepherds,
and escape, for the leaders of the flock.
³⁶ Hear the sound of the shepherds' cry,
the wail of the leaders of the flock,
for the LORD is destroying their pasture.
³⁷ Peaceful grazing land
will become lifeless

because of the LORD's burning anger.
³⁸ He has left his den like a lion,
for their land has become a desolation
because of the sword^A of the oppressor,
because of his burning anger.

Jeremiah's Speech in the Temple

26 At the beginning of the reign of Jehoiakim son of Josiah, king of Judah, this word came from the LORD: ² "This is what the LORD says: Stand in the courtyard of the LORD's temple and speak all the words I have commanded you to speak to all Judah's cities that are coming to worship there. Do not hold back a word. ³ Perhaps they will listen and turn — each from his evil way of life — so that I might relent concerning the disaster that I plan to do to them because of the evil of their deeds. ⁴ You are to say to them, 'This is what the LORD says: If you do not listen to me by living according to my instruction that I set before you ⁵ and by listening to the words of my servants the prophets — whom I have been sending to you time and time again,^B though you did not listen — ⁶ I will make this temple like Shiloh. I will make this city an example for cursing for all the nations of the earth.'"

Jeremiah Seized

⁷ The priests, the prophets, and all the people heard Jeremiah speaking these words in the temple of the LORD. ⁸ When he finished the address the LORD had commanded him to deliver to all the people, immediately the priests, the prophets, and all the people took hold of him, yelling, "You must surely die! ⁹ How dare you prophesy in the name of the LORD, 'This temple will become like Shiloh and this city will become an uninhabited ruin'!" Then all the people crowded around Jeremiah at the LORD's temple.

¹⁰ When the officials of Judah heard about these things, they went from the king's palace to the LORD's temple and sat at the entrance of the New Gate of the LORD's temple.^C ¹¹ Then the priests and prophets said to the officials and all the people, "This man deserves the death sentence because he has prophesied against this city, as you have heard with your own ears."

^A 25:38 Some Hb mss, LXX, Tg; other Hb mss read *burning*   ^B 26:5 Lit *you, rising early and sending*   ^C 26:10 Many Hb mss, Syr, Tg, Vg; other Hb mss read *the New Gate of the LORD*

---

are substituted for their opposite (see note at 51:1). Here the letters *bet-bet-lamed* of Babylon are changed to *shin-shin-khet*. **25:30–33** The imagery changes from a cup of wine to a lion. It changes again to an image of the Lord treading out **grapes** in the winepress (Is 63:3; Rv 14:19–20; 19:15), and once more to the image of **a huge storm** as nation after nation succumbs to Babylon's advances. **25:34–38** Three times in these verses Jeremiah used the shepherd metaphor and

then switched over to describe the nations' impending disaster. **26:1–24** This chapter is connected with chap. 7, the prophet's famous temple gate sermon. **26:1** The date for this event is set as **the beginning of the reign of Jehoiakim** (609 BC). This is chronologically earlier than 25:1, Jehoiakim's "fourth year." King Josiah had died that year, and Jehoahaz had ruled only three months. **26:4–6** This is a summary of the more complete message in chap. 7 with three

emphases: (1) the call to obey God's law, (2) the alignment of Jeremiah's message with **my servants the prophets**, and (3) the seriousness of the impending threat against the city of Jerusalem and the temple. **26:6,9** On **Shiloh**, see note at 7:12,14. **26:10–11** The **New Gate** is thought to be the gate leading to the inner court of the temple (36:10). This was the place where trials were held. King Jotham built it (2Kg 15:35).

Jeremiah's Defense

¹² Then Jeremiah said to all the officials and all the people, "The LORD sent me to prophesy all the words that you have heard against this temple and city. ¹³ So now, correct your ways and deeds, and obey the LORD your God so that he might relent concerning the disaster he had pronounced against you. ¹⁴ As for me, here I am in your hands; do to me what you think is good and right. ¹⁵ But know for certain that if you put me to death, you will bring innocent blood on yourselves, on this city, and on its residents, for it is certain the LORD has sent me to speak all these things directly to you."

Jeremiah Released

¹⁶ Then the officials and all the people told the priests and prophets, "This man doesn't deserve the death sentence, for he has spoken to us in the name of the LORD our God!"

¹⁷ Some of the elders of the land stood up and said to all the assembled people, ¹⁸ "Micah the Moreshite prophesied in the days of King Hezekiah of Judah and said to all the people of Judah, 'This is what the LORD of Armies says:

Zion will be plowed like a field,
Jerusalem will become ruins,
and the temple's mountain will be
    a high thicket.'

¹⁹ Did King Hezekiah of Judah and all the people of Judah put him to death? Did not the king fear the LORD and plead for the LORD's favor,ᴬ and did not the LORD relent concerning the disaster he had pronounced against them? We are about to bring a terrible disaster on ourselves!"

The Prophet Uriah

²⁰ Another man was also prophesying in the name of the LORD — Uriah son of Shemaiah from Kiriath-jearim. He prophesied against this city and against this land in words like all those of Jeremiah. ²¹ King Jehoiakim, all his warriors, and all the officials heard his words, and the king tried to put him to death. When Uriah heard, he fled in fear and went to Egypt. ²² But King Jehoiakim sent men to Egypt: Elnathan son of Achbor and certain other men with him went to Egypt. ²³ They brought Uriah out of Egypt and took him to King Jehoiakim, who executed him with the sword and threw his corpse into the burial place of the common people.ᴮ

²⁴ But Ahikam son of Shaphan supported Jeremiah, so he was not handed over to the people to be put to death.

The Yoke of Babylon

27 At the beginning of the reign of Zedekiahᶜ son of Josiah, king of Judah, this word came to Jeremiah from the LORD:ᴰ ² This is what the LORD said to me: "Make chains and yoke bars for yourself and put them on your neck. ³ Send word to the king of Edom, the king of Moab, the king of the Ammonites, the king of Tyre, and the king of Sidon through messengers who are coming to King Zedekiah of Judah in Jerusalem. ⁴ Command them to go to their masters, saying, 'This is what the LORD of Armies, the God of Israel, says: Tell this to your masters: ⁵ "By my great strength and outstretched arm, I made the earth, and the people, and animals on the face of the earth. I give it to anyone I please.ᴱ ⁶ So now I have placed all these lands under the authority of my servant Nebuchadnezzar, king of Babylon. I have even given him the wild animals to serve him. ⁷ All nations will serve him, his son, and his grandson until the time for his own land comes, and then many nations and great kings will enslave him.

ᴬ26:19 Or and appease the LORD ᴮ26:23 Lit the sons of the people ᶜ27:1 Some Hb mss, Syr, Arabic; other Hb mss, DSS read Jehoiakim ᴰ27:1 LXX omits this v. ᴱ27:5 Lit to whomever is upright in my eyes

26:12–15 Jeremiah defended himself with great courage, unusual brevity, and straightforward accounting for his twenty years of ministry among them (cp. 25:3, three years earlier).

26:16 Jeremiah's defense convinced **the officials and all the people**.

26:17–18 **Micah the Moreshite** alludes to Mc 1:1. The quoted verse is almost identical to Mc 3:12. Moresheth was a village twenty-three miles southwest of Jerusalem. Micah's warnings were heeded, and the nation was delivered because the people responded with repentance. This argument from the past was effective, and Jeremiah was released.

26:19 The example of Micah and Hezekiah convince them that they dare not harm Jeremiah.

26:20–23 These verses show that **Uriah son of Shemaiah** did not fare as well as Micah did.

26:20 **Kiriath-jearim** was about eight miles northwest of Jerusalem where the ark of the covenant was kept after it was returned by the Philistines (1Sm 7:1–2).

26:22 **Elnathan son of Achbor** might have been one of the sons of Achbor son of Micaiah, an official of King Josiah (2Kg 22:12,14). Elnathan tried to stop King Jehoiakim from burning Jeremiah's scroll (Jr 36:25).

26:23 Uriah was **brought . . . out of Egypt** by King Jehoiakim of Judah.

26:24 **Ahikam son of Shaphan supported Jeremiah**. Shaphan was the scribe of King Josiah's reform (2Kg 22:3–14). Gemariah, another son of Shaphan, argued that King Jehoiakim should not burn Jeremiah's scroll (Jr 36:10,25). A third son of Shaphan, Gedaliah, was appointed governor of Judah after the fall of Jerusalem (39:14; 40:5–16).

27:1 The **beginning of the reign of Zedekiah** was in 594 BC (28:1). The LXX may preserve the more accurate reading: "in the fourth year of Zedekiah." Nebuchadnezzar of Babylon had just put down an uprising by some of his troops. News of this palace revolt may have stirred false hopes, especially in Judah.

27:2 Jeremiah was commanded by God to **make chains and yoke bars** for himself.

27:3 The phrase **send word** (Hb, "send them") implies that Jeremiah made a separate yoke for each king of the five nations mentioned here, apparently giving an appropriate message for each ambassador. The enumeration of the nations from the south to the north may indicate that they were prompted by Pharaoh Psammetik II of Egypt to revolt when it appeared Babylon was going through internal troubles.

27:6 Revolt was futile because God had already assigned Babylon to execute judgment over these nations on his behalf. Again, Nebuchadnezzar is called **my servant** (see note at 25:8–9).

27:7 Nebuchadnezzar, **his son, and his grandson** were given power over all the mentioned nations. Their dominance lasted for three generations, including the kings Nebuchadnezzar, Evil-Merodach (52:31; 2Kg 25:27), and Belshazzar (Dn 5:2).

⁸ " ' "As for the nation or kingdom that does not serve King Nebuchadnezzar of Babylon and does not place its neck under the yoke of the king of Babylon, that nation I will punish by sword, famine, and plague — this is the LORD's declaration — until through him I have destroyed it. ⁹ So you should not listen to your prophets, diviners, dreamers, fortune-tellers, or sorcerers who say to you, 'Don't serve the king of Babylon!' ' ¹⁰ They are prophesying a lie to you so that you will be removed from your land. I will banish you, and you will perish. ¹¹ But as for the nation that will put its neck under the yoke of the king of Babylon and serve him, I will leave it in its own land, and that nation will cultivateᴬ it and reside in it. This is the LORD's declaration." ' "

Warning to Zedekiah

¹² I spoke to King Zedekiah of Judah in the same way: "Put your necks under the yoke of the king of Babylon, serve him and his people, and live! ¹³ Why should you and your people die by the sword, famine, and plague as the LORD has threatened against any nation that does not serve the king of Babylon? ¹⁴ Do not listen to the words of the prophets who are telling you, 'Don't serve the king of Babylon,' for they are prophesying a lie to you. ¹⁵ 'I have not sent them' — this is the LORD's declaration — 'and they are prophesying falsely in my name; therefore, I will banish you, and you will perish — you and the prophets who are prophesying to you.' "

¹⁶ Then I spoke to the priests and all these people, saying, "This is what the LORD says: 'Do not listen to the words of your prophets. They are prophesying to you, claiming, "Look, very soon now the articles of the LORD's temple will be brought back from Babylon." They are prophesying a lie to you. ¹⁷ Do not listen to them. Serve the king of Babylon and live! Why should this city become a ruin? ¹⁸ If they are indeed prophets and if the word of the LORD is with them, let them intercede with the LORD of Armies not to let the articles that remain in

the LORD's temple, in the palace of the king of Judah, and in Jerusalem go to Babylon.' ¹⁹ For this is what the LORD of Armies says about the pillars, the basin,ᴮ the water carts, and the rest of the articles that still remain in this city, ²⁰ those King Nebuchadnezzar of Babylon did not take when he deported Jeconiahᶜ son of Jehoiakim, king of Judah, from Jerusalem to Babylon along with all the nobles of Judah and Jerusalem. ²¹ Yes, this is what the LORD of Armies, the God of Israel, says about the articles that remain in the temple of the LORD, in the palace of the king of Judah, and in Jerusalem: ²² 'They will be taken to Babylon and will remain there until I attend to them again.' This is the LORD's declaration. 'Then I will bring them up and restore them to this place.' "

Hananiah's False Prophecy

28 In that same year, at the beginning of the reign of King Zedekiah of Judah, in the fifth month of the fourth year, the prophet Hananiah son of Azzur from Gibeon said to me in the temple of the LORD in the presence of the priests and all the people, ² "This is what the LORD of Armies, the God of Israel, says: 'I have broken the yoke of the king of Babylon. ³ Within two years I will restore to this place all the articles of the LORD's temple that King Nebuchadnezzar of Babylon took from here and transported to Babylon. ⁴ And I will restore to this place Jeconiahᶜ son of Jehoiakim, king of Judah, and all the exiles from Judah who went to Babylon' — this is the LORD's declaration — 'for I will break the yoke of the king of Babylon.' "

Jeremiah's Response to Hananiah

⁵ The prophet Jeremiah replied to the prophet Hananiah in the presence of the priests and all the people who were standing in the temple of the LORD. ⁶ The prophet Jeremiah said, "Amen! May the LORD do that. May the LORD make the words you have prophesied come true and may he restore the articles of the LORD's temple and all the exiles from

---

ᴬ27:11 Lit work   ᴮ27:19 Lit sea   ᶜ27:20; 28:4 = Jehoiachin

27:9–11 Five different types of false foretellers are listed here: false **prophets, diviners** (prophesied from the way arrows fell), **dreamers, fortune-tellers** (or "enchanters" who interpreted various signs), and **sorcerers** (conjurers). All these were banned from Israel (Dt 18:9–13). Their message (**don't serve the king of Babylon!**) was nothing but falsehood. **27:13–15** What is said to the nations in vv. 8–11 is here applied to Judah. **27:16** The **articles** (not just "vessels," "utensils," or "furnishings") from the temple would not be coming back to Judah soon. Nothing was returned until the beginning of the reign of Cyrus of Persia in 536 BC. **27:17** The message of **Serve the king of Babylon and live** continued after 586 BC (see 40:9; 2Kg 25:24).

27:19 The **pillars**, made of bronze and placed in front of the temple, were called Jachin and Boaz (1Kg 7:15–22). These would be broken up because they were too big to be taken away intact. The **basin** was a massive cast bowl sitting on the backs of twelve cast oxen. The **water carts** were stands on wheels that supported the lavers (1Kg 7:27–37). The same three items are singled out in Jr 52:17. **28:1–17** The phrase **in that same year** places the incident in this chapter not long after the events in chap. 27. **28:1 Hananiah son of Azzur**, whom the LXX calls a "false prophet," was a native of **Gibeon**, a city of priests five miles northwest of Jerusalem (modern el-Jib). He publicly

contradicted Jeremiah's prophecy about the yoke (chap. 27). **28:2** Hananiah had the audacity to use the same introductory formula for a divine message that God had given Jeremiah, his genuine prophet. **28:3 Within two years**, Hananiah predicted, everything would be restored. Such specificity must have made him look credible, but when his prophecy failed, he deserved the penalty prescribed in Dt 18:21–22. **28:4 Jeconiah** is another name for King Jehoiachin of Judah (27:20). **28:5–6** Jeremiah responded to Hananiah's brazen prediction with an **Amen!** Perhaps he did so sarcastically.

Babylon to this place! ⁷ Only listen to this message I am speaking in your hearing and in the hearing of all the people. ⁸ The prophets who preceded you and me from ancient times prophesied war, disaster,^ and plague against many lands and great kingdoms. ⁹ As for the prophet who prophesies peace — only when the word of the prophet comes true will the prophet be recognized as one the LORD has truly sent."

Hananiah Breaks Jeremiah's Yoke

¹⁰ The prophet Hananiah then took the yoke bar from the neck of the prophet Jeremiah and broke it. ¹¹ In the presence of all the people Hananiah proclaimed, "This is what the LORD says: 'In this way, within two years I will break the yoke of King Nebuchadnezzar of Babylon from the neck of all the nations.'" The prophet Jeremiah then went on his way.

The LORD's Word against Hananiah

¹² After the prophet Hananiah had broken the yoke bar from the neck of the prophet Jeremiah, the word of the LORD came to Jeremiah: ¹³ "Go say to Hananiah, 'This is what the LORD says: You broke a wooden yoke bar, but in its place you will make an iron yoke bar. ¹⁴ For this is what the LORD of Armies, the God of Israel, says: I have put an iron yoke on the neck of all these nations that they might serve King Nebuchadnezzar of Babylon, and they will serve him. I have even put the wild animals under him.'" ¹⁵ The prophet Jeremiah said to the prophet Hananiah, "Listen, Hananiah! The LORD did not send you, but you have led these people to trust in a lie. ¹⁶ Therefore, this is what the LORD says: 'I am about to send you off the face of the earth. You will die this year because you have preached rebellion against the LORD.'" ¹⁷ And the prophet Hananiah died that year in the seventh month.

Jeremiah's Letter to the Exiles

29 This is the text of the letter that the prophet Jeremiah sent from Jerusalem to the remaining exiled elders, the priests, the prophets, and all the people Nebuchadnezzar had deported from Jerusalem to Babylon. ² This was after King Jeconiah,ᴮ the queen mother, the court officials, the officials of Judah and Jerusalem, the craftsmen, and the metalsmiths had left Jerusalem. ³ He sent the letter with Elasah son of Shaphan and Gemariah son of Hilkiah, whom Zedekiah king of Judah sent to Babylon to King Nebuchadnezzar of Babylon. The letter stated:

⁴ This is what the LORD of Armies, the God of Israel, says to all the exiles I deported from Jerusalem to Babylon: ⁵ "Build houses and live in them. Plant gardens and eat their produce. ⁶ Find wives for yourselves, and have sons and daughters. Find wives for your sons and give your daughters to men in marriage so that they may bear sons and daughters. Multiply there; do not decrease. ⁷ Pursue the well-beingᶜ of the city I have deported you to. Pray to the LORD on its behalf, for when it thrives, you will thrive."

⁸ For this is what the LORD of Armies, the God of Israel, says: "Don't let your prophets who are among you and your diviners deceive you, and don't listen to the dreams you elicit from them, ⁹ for they are prophesying falsely to you in my name. I have not sent them." This is the LORD's declaration.

¹⁰ For this is what the LORD says: "When seventy years for Babylon are complete, I will attend to you and will confirm my promise concerning you to restore you to this place. ¹¹ For I know the plans I have for you" — this is the LORD's declaration — "plans for your well-being, not for disaster, to give you a future and a hope. ¹² You will call to me and come and pray to me, and I will listen to you. ¹³ You will seek me and find me when you search for me with all your heart. ¹⁴ I will be found by you" — this is the LORD's declaration — "and I will restore your fortunesᴰ and gather you from all the nations and places where I banished you" — this is the LORD's declaration. "I will restore you to the place from which I deported you."

^28:8 Some Hb mss, Vg read famine ᴮ29:2 = Jehoiachin ᶜ29:7 Or peace ᴰ29:14 Or will end your captivity

28:12–14 The Lord told Jeremiah to **make an iron yoke bar** because Hananiah had made Jeremiah's word about God's judgment all the more certain and hardened.
28:15–17 In another wordplay the Lord declared that since he had not sent Hananiah to prophesy, he would **send** him **off the face of the earth**. Two months later Hananiah died. We are not told how this happened, but the reason for his death is that he had **preached rebellion against the LORD** (see Dt 13:5).
29:2 **King Jeconiah** is another name for King Jehoiachin (see note at 22:24–30).

29:3 Jeremiah sent his letter to the exiles in Babylon by two of King Zedekiah's emissaries to Nebuchadnezzar. The two men who carried the letter were **Elasah** son of Shaphan and **Gemariah** son of Hilkiah. Shaphan was a sort of secretary of state under King Josiah (2Kg 22:8–14), and Gemariah was the high priest under Josiah (2Ch 34–35). These men show that some people remained faithful to the Lord, even during the worst of times.
29:4–7 Jeremiah's letter must have arrived in Babylon shortly after the **exiles** did. It warned that this would not be a short exile.

29:7 Jeremiah urged them to **pray** for Babylon and its prosperity. By doing this, the exiles would **thrive** as well (1Tm 2:1–2).
29:10 The **seventy years for Babylon** are also noted in 25:11. The duration of the Babylonian kingdom is linked with the length of the exile (see note at 25:11). From Nebuchadnezzar's accession to the throne in 605 BC to the fall of Babylon in 539 BC was sixty-six years.
29:12–14 These verses are a renewal of God's promise in Dt 30:3–5.

¹⁵ You have said, "The LORD has raised up prophets for us in Babylon!" ¹⁶ But this is what the LORD says concerning the king sitting on David's throne and concerning all the people living in this city — that is, concerning your brothers who did not go with you into exile. ¹⁷ This is what the LORD of Armies says: "I am about to send sword, famine, and plague against them, and I will make them like rotten figs that are inedible because they are so bad. ¹⁸ I will pursue them with sword, famine, and plague. I will make them a horror to all the kingdoms of the earth — a curse and a desolation, an object of scorn and a disgrace among all the nations where I have banished them. ¹⁹ I will do this because they have not listened to my words" — this is the LORD's declaration — "the words that I sent to them with my servants the prophets time and time again.^A And you too have not listened." This is the LORD's declaration.

²⁰ Hear the word of the LORD, all you exiles I have sent from Jerusalem to Babylon. ²¹ This is what the LORD of Armies, the God of Israel, says about Ahab son of Kolaiah and concerning Zedekiah son of Maaseiah, the ones prophesying a lie to you in my name: "I am about to hand them over to King Nebuchadnezzar of Babylon, and he will kill them before your very eyes. ²² Based on what happens to them, all the exiles of Judah who are in Babylon will create a curse that says, 'May the LORD make you like Zedekiah and Ahab, whom the king of Babylon roasted in the fire!' ²³ because they have committed an outrage in Israel by committing adultery with their neighbors' wives and have spoken in my name a lie, which I did not command them. I am he who knows, and I am a witness." This is the LORD's declaration.

²⁴ To Shemaiah the Nehelamite you are to say, ²⁵ "This is what the LORD of Armies,

the God of Israel, says: You^B in your own name have sent out letters to all the people of Jerusalem, to the priest Zephaniah son of Maaseiah, and to all the priests, saying, ²⁶ 'The LORD has appointed you priest in place of the priest Jehoiada to be the chief officer in the temple of the LORD, responsible for every madman who acts like a prophet. You must confine him in the stocks and an iron collar. ²⁷ So now, why have you not rebuked Jeremiah of Anathoth who has been acting like a prophet among you? ²⁸ For he has sent word to us in Babylon, claiming, "The exile will be long. Build houses and settle down. Plant gardens and eat their produce."'" ²⁹ The priest Zephaniah read this letter in the hearing of the prophet Jeremiah.

A Message about Shemaiah

³⁰ Then the word of the LORD came to Jeremiah: ³¹ "Send a message to all the exiles, saying, 'This is what the LORD says concerning Shemaiah the Nehelamite. Because Shemaiah prophesied to you, though I did not send him, and made you trust a lie, ³² this is what the LORD says: I am about to punish Shemaiah the Nehelamite and his descendants. There will not be even one of his descendants living among these people, nor will any ever see the good that I will bring to my people — this is the LORD's declaration — for he has preached rebellion against the LORD.'"

Restoration from Captivity

30 This is the word that came to Jeremiah from the LORD. ² "This is what the LORD, the God of Israel, says: Write on a scroll all the words that I have spoken to you, ³ for look, the days are coming" — this is the LORD's declaration — "when I will restore the fortunes^C of my people Israel and Judah," says the LORD. "I will restore them to the land I gave to their ancestors and they will possess it."

⁴ These are the words the LORD spoke to Israel and Judah. ⁵ This is what the LORD says:

^A29:19 Lit prophets, rising up early and sending ^B29:25 Lit Because you ^C30:3 Or will end the captivity

29:15-19 Many interpreters think these verses are misplaced since Jeremiah was so critical of Zedekiah in a letter carried by his ambassadors. But vv. 4–23 may not be a single letter. Verses 15–19 could be a second letter not carried to Babylon by the king's officials. **29:17** The people left in Jerusalem who were not among the initial exiles will be made like **rotten figs**. This same imagery appears in chap. 24. **29:20-23** Ahab son of Kolaiah and Zedekiah son of Maaseiah were two prophets singled out for **committing adultery with their neighbors' wives** as well as prophesying lies. There is a wordplay here. The name Kolaiah is related to the Hebrew term *qelalah* ("curse") and *qalah* ("to burn"). Thus they would roast in the **fire**.

29:24-25 Shemaiah the Nehelamite was another false prophet. He had apparently ordered **the priest Zephaniah** to silence Jeremiah. Zephaniah was warden over police regulations in the temple (21:1; 37:3; 52:24). **29:26** Shemaiah charged Jeremiah with being a **madman**. **29:29-32 Zephaniah** the priest read Shemaiah's **letter** to Jeremiah, who responded with another letter from the Lord to the exiles. He exposed Shemaiah's hypocrisy and set his punishment—that he would have no **descendants** and he would not live to see the restoration God had predicted. **30:1-33:26** These chapters were written during the final days of the siege of Jerusalem (the last eighteen months of that siege; 32:1-2); yet they foretell a bright future.

Jeremiah was in prison and the city was in dire straits; nevertheless, he foresaw in the distant future the restoration of the nation to its land, the new covenant of redemption, the rule of a purified Davidic king over a purified Zion, and a large number of Gentiles coming to the Messiah. **30:3 The days are coming** announces eschatological times (3:16; 16:14; 23:5; 31:27,31). The phrase **I will restore the fortunes** (lit "turn the turnings" or "reverse the fortunes") appears often in these chapters. **Restore them to the land I gave to their ancestors** looks to a time beyond the future return from the exile. **30:4-8 On that day** must be the time when God will judge all nations. "That day" is used in Scripture to introduce the "Day of the LORD" (Am 5:18–20; Zph 1:14–18).

We have heard a cry of terror,
of dread — there is no peace.
⁶ Ask and see
whether a male can give birth.
Why then do I see every man
with his hands on his stomach
like a woman in labor
and every face turned pale?
⁷ How awful that day will be!
There will be no other like it!
It will be a time of trouble for Jacob,
but he will be saved out of it.

⁸ On that day —
this is the declaration of the LORD
of Armies —
I will break his yoke from your neck
and tear off your chains,
and strangers will never again enslave
him.
⁹ They will serve the LORD their God
and David their king,
whom I will raise up for them.

¹⁰ As for you, my servant Jacob,
do not be afraid —
this is the LORD's declaration —
and do not be discouraged, Israel,
for without fail I will save you out of a
distant place,
your descendants, from the land
of their captivity!
Jacob will return and have calm
and quiet
with no one to frighten him.
¹¹ For I will be with you —
this is the LORD's declaration —
to save you!
I will bring destruction
on all the nations
where I have scattered you;
however, I will not bring destruction
on you.
I will discipline you justly,
and I will by no means
leave you unpunished.

Healing Zion's Wounds

¹² For this is what the LORD says:
Your injury is incurable;

your wound most severe.
¹³ You have no defender for your case.
There is no remedy for your sores,
and no healing for you.ᴬ
¹⁴ All your lovers have forgotten you;
they no longer look for you,
for I have struck
you as an enemy would,
with the discipline of someone cruel,
because of your enormous guilt
and your innumerable sins.
¹⁵ Why do you cry out about your injury?
Your pain has no cure!
I have done these things to you
because of your enormous guilt
and your innumerable sins.
¹⁶ Nevertheless, all who devoured you
will be devoured,
and all your adversaries
— all of them —
will go off into exile.
Those who plunder you
will be plundered,
and all who raid you will be raided.
¹⁷ But I will bring you health
and will heal you of your wounds —
this is the LORD's declaration —
for they call you Outcast,
Zion whom no one cares about.

Restoration of the Land

¹⁸ This is what the LORD says:
I will certainly restore the fortunesᴮ
of Jacob's tents
and show compassion on his dwellings.
Every city will be rebuilt on its mound;
every citadel will stand
on its proper site.
¹⁹ Thanksgiving will come out of them,
a sound of rejoicing.
I will multiply them,
and they will not decrease;
I will honor them, and they will not
be insignificant.
²⁰ His children will be as in past days;
his congregation will be established
in my presence.
I will punish all his oppressors.
²¹ Jacob's leader will be one of them;
his ruler will issue from him.

ᴬ**30:13** Or *No one pleads that your sores should be healed. There is no remedy for you.*   ᴮ**30:18** Or *certainly end the captivity*

30:9 David their king, whom God **will raise up for them** refers to the future ideal king, a so-called "second David." This messianic person in the line of David is paired with **the LORD their God**.
30:12–17 Israel's wounds will be beyond human help, but the Lord will serve as their physician (**but I will bring you health,** see 3:22; 33:6). Israel's sad condition appears in three metaphors: no medicine, no physician, and no lovers.
30:15–16 Some argue that there is a radical change in God's attitude between these

two verses. But God remains the same. His judgment must fall to bring Israel to the point where he can restore them. Israel's enemies will experience the same things Israel went through. (1) The nations **who devoured you will be devoured.** (2) Those who sent Israel into captivity **will go off into exile.** (3) The plunderers **will be plundered.** (4) Those who raided Israel **will be raided.**
30:18–20 In these verses a whole new day, not just a restoration, is promised for Israel. Jerusalem will be rebuilt, repopulated, and

ruled by a new leader who is responsive to God.
30:18 Every city will be rebuilt on its mound denotes a mound that stands on the ruins of a destroyed or abandoned town.
30:21–22 This messianic prophecy emphasizes three functions. (1) The Messiah will be a native (**one of them**), not a foreigner. (2) He will carry the priestly prerogative, which allows him to **approach** the Lord like Melchizedek (Heb 5:5–6). (3) He will declare **You will be my people, and I will be your God.**

I will invite him to me, and he will
     approach me,
for who would otherwise risk his life
     to approach me?
This is the LORD's declaration.
22 You will be my people,
     and I will be your God.

The Wrath of God
23 Look, a storm from the LORD!
Wrath has gone out,
a churning storm.
It will whirl about the heads
     of the wicked.
24 The LORD's burning anger will not
     turn back
until he has completely fulfilled
     the purposes of his heart.
In time to come you will understand it.

God's Relationship with His People

31 "At that time" — this is the LORD's declaration — "I will be the God of all
the families of Israel, and they will be my
people."
2 This is what the LORD says:
The people who survived
     the sword
found favor in the wilderness.
When Israel went to find rest,
3 the LORD appeared to him^A
     from far away.
I have loved you
     with an everlasting love;
therefore, I have continued to extend
     faithful love to you.
4 Again I will build you so that you will
     be rebuilt,
Virgin Israel.
You will take up
     your tambourines again
and go out in joyful dancing.
5 You will plant vineyards again
on the mountains of Samaria;
the planters will plant and will enjoy
     the fruit.
6 For there will be a day when watchmen
     will call out
in the hill country of Ephraim,
"Come, let's go up to Zion,
     to the LORD our God!"

God's People Brought Home
7 For this is what the LORD says:
Sing with joy for Jacob;
shout for the foremost
     of the nations!
Proclaim, praise, and say,
"LORD, save your people,
     the remnant of Israel!"
8 Watch! I am going to bring them
     from the northern land.
I will gather them from remote regions
     of the earth —
the blind and the lame will be
     with them,
along with those who are pregnant
     and those about to give birth.
They will return here
     as a great assembly!
9 They will come weeping,
but I will bring them back
     with consolation.^B
I will lead them to wadis filled
     with water,
by a smooth way where
     they will not stumble,
for I am Israel's Father,
     and Ephraim is my firstborn.
10 Nations, hear the word of the LORD,
and tell it among the far off coasts and
     islands!
Say, "The one who scattered Israel
     will gather him.
He will watch over him as a shepherd
     guards his flock,
11 for the LORD has ransomed Jacob
and redeemed him from the power
     of one stronger than he."
12 They will come and shout for joy
     on the heights of Zion;
they will be radiant with joy
     because of the LORD's goodness,
because of the grain, the new wine,
     the fresh oil,
and because of the young of the flocks
     and herds.
Their life will be
     like an irrigated garden,
and they will no longer grow weak
     from hunger.
13 Then the young women will rejoice
     with dancing,

---

^A **31:3** LXX; MT reads *me*   ^B **31:9** LXX; MT reads *supplications*

31:1–6 In these verses God declared that he will reunify all Israel. His words of comfort are addressed to **all the families of Israel**. **31:2** The combining of **the wilderness** with those who **survived the sword** links the exodus and wilderness experience with the return from exile in Babylon. **31:4–5** With a threefold repetition of **again**, Israel's future will parallel her past. **31:6** The assumption is that the temple will be rebuilt in Jerusalem. **Ephraim**, standing for the ten northern tribes of Israel, will again **go up to Zion** to worship. **31:7** Five imperatives (**sing . . . shout . . . proclaim, praise . . . say**) are given to Israel to celebrate the great deliverance of God for the **remnant of Israel**. **31:8** God's future restoration will come not only from the **northern land** (Assyria and Babylon), but it will come from **remote regions of the earth**. This refers to a worldwide regathering in which no one will be excluded. **31:9** The phrase **Ephraim is my firstborn** means not first in chronology (Ephraim was Joseph's second son), but first in rank and priority. **31:11** The words **redeemed him** recall the practice of a family redeemer (Hb *ga'al*; cp. Lv 25:25,48; Nm 35:12,19; Ru 2:20; 3:9,8,14), a man who was expected to rescue a close relative from danger or hardship.

while young and old men
　　rejoice together.
I will turn their mourning into joy,
　　give them consolation,
　　and bring happiness out of grief.
14 I will refresh the priests
　　　with an abundance,^A
　　and my people will be satisfied
　　　with my goodness.
　　This is the LORD's declaration.

Lament Turned to Joy

15 This is what the LORD says:
　　A voice was heard in Ramah,
　　　a lament with bitter weeping—
　　Rachel weeping for her children,
　　refusing to be comforted
　　　for her children
　　because they are no more.

16 This is what the LORD says:
　　Keep your voice from weeping
　　　and your eyes from tears,
　　for the reward for your work will come—
　　　this is the LORD's declaration—
　　and your children will return
　　　from the enemy's land.
17 There is hope for your future—
　　　this is the LORD's declaration—
　　and your children will return
　　　to their own territory.
18 I have surely heard Ephraim moaning,
　　"You disciplined me,
　　　and I have been disciplined
　　like an untrained calf.
　　Take me back, so that I can return,
　　for you, LORD, are my God.
19 After my return, I felt regret;
　　After I was instructed, I struck my thigh
　　　in grief.

I was ashamed and humiliated
　　because I bore the disgrace
　　　of my youth."
20 Isn't Ephraim a precious son to me,
　　　a delightful child?
　　Whenever I speak against him,
　　I certainly still think about him.
　　Therefore, my inner being yearns
　　　for him;
　　I will truly have compassion on him.
　　This is the LORD's declaration.

Repentance and Restoration

21 Set up road markers for yourself;
　　　establish signposts!
　　Keep the highway in mind,
　　　the way you have traveled.
　　Return, Virgin Israel!
　　Return to these cities of yours.
22 How long will you turn here and there,
　　　faithless daughter?
　　For the LORD creates something new
　　　in the land^B—
　　a female^C will shelter^D a man.

23 This is what the LORD of Armies, the God
of Israel, says: "When I restore their fortunes,^E
they will once again speak this word in the land
of Judah and in its cities: 'May the LORD bless
you, righteous settlement, holy mountain.'
24 Judah and all its cities will live in it together—also farmers and those who move^F with
the flocks—25 for I satisfy the thirsty person
and feed all those who are weak."
26 At this I awoke and looked around. My
sleep had been most pleasant to me.
27 "Look, the days are coming"—this is the
LORD's declaration—"when I will sow the house
of Israel and the house of Judah with the seed
of people and the seed of animals. 28 Just as I

---

^A 31:14 Lit *fatness*　^B 31:22 Or *new on earth*　^C 31:22 Or *woman*　^D 31:22 Or *female surrounds*, or *female courts*; Hb obscure
^E 31:23 Or *I end their captivity*　^F 31:24 Tg, Vg, Aq, Sym; MT reads *and they will move*

31:15 **Rachel**, Joseph's mother, is pictured as **weeping** in **Ramah**, a town five miles north of Jerusalem. Ramah served as the staging grounds for the deportation to Babylon (40:1–4). Rachel was Jacob's favorite wife. She died giving birth to Benjamin (Gn 35:18). The citation in Mt 2:17–18 depicts Rachel as the embodiment of all Israel's mothers weeping for their slain children, a tragedy that Herod's atrocities called to mind once more. 31:16–17 Rachel is twice told to stop weeping, because **your children will return**. 31:16 The **reward for** Rachel's **work** is that her children will come back from exile from all over the world. 31:18–20 **Ephraim**, representing the ten northern tribes, finally saw how he had acted as **an untrained** [or "undisciplined"] **calf** (cp. Hs 10:11) and as a rebel against God. But now chastened and repentant, he **struck his thigh** . . . **ashamed and humiliated**. Ephraim will be forgiven and, like the prodigal, will return home. God's love will triumph over Israel's rebellion (Hs 11:1–11). 31:21 These **road markers** and **signposts** would lead Israel back home from Babylon and function as signposts.

31:22 The phrase **a female will shelter a man** is perhaps the most obscure phrase in all of Jeremiah. Some see this as a prophecy of the virgin birth of Christ. But the word "female" does not have a definite article with it, and such a general word for "woman" cannot be made to mean a virgin. Further, "to shelter" does not mean conceiving, nor does any of this fit the context. No one interpretation satisfies all difficulties since the intention of the verb "to shelter" is uncertain. **Something new** may mean that "woman" refers to Israel and "man" to the Lord, so a new relationship between Israel and her God will arise in the latter days. 31:23–25 **Holy mountain** refers to Zion. It occurs twenty-three times in the Prophets and Psalms. Even the lowest classes are promised security. 31:27–28 **Look, the days are coming** occurs fourteen times in Jeremiah, and seven times elsewhere in the OT. Here it echoes the use in 30:3 (see note there). Verse 28 recalls Jeremiah's commissioning in 1:10,12.

watched over them to uproot and to tear them down, to demolish and to destroy, and to cause disaster, so will I watch over them to build and to plant them" — this is the LORD's declaration. ²⁹ "In those days, it will never again be said,

'The fathers have eaten sour grapes,
and the children's teeth are set on edge.'

³⁰ Rather, each will die for his own iniquity. Anyone who eats sour grapes — his own teeth will be set on edge.

The New Covenant

³¹ "Look, the days are coming" — this is the LORD's declaration — "when I will make a new covenant with the house of Israel and with the house of Judah. ³² This one will not be like the covenant I made with their ancestors on the day I took them by the hand to lead them out of the land of Egypt — my covenant that they broke even though I am their master"ᴬ — the LORD's declaration. ³³ "Instead, this is the covenant I will make with the house of Israel after those days" — the LORD's declaration. "I will put my teaching within them and write it on their hearts. I will be their God, and they will be my people. ³⁴ No longer will one teach his neighbor or his brother, saying, 'Know the LORD,' for they will all know me, from the least to the greatest of them" — this is the LORD's declaration. "For I will forgive their iniquity and never again remember their sin.

³⁵ "This is what the LORD says:

The one who gives the sun for light
by day,
the fixed order of moon and stars
for light by night,
who stirs up the sea and makes
its waves roar —

the LORD of Armies is his name:
³⁶ If this fixed order departs
from before me —
this is the LORD's declaration —
only then will Israel's descendants
cease
to be a nation before me forever.

³⁷ "This is what the LORD says:
Only if the heavens above
can be measured
and the foundations
of the earth below explored,
will I reject all of Israel's descendants
because of all they have done —
this is the LORD's declaration.

³⁸ "Look, the days are coming" — the LORD's declaration — "when the cityᴮ from the Tower of Hananel to the Corner Gate will be rebuilt for the LORD. ³⁹ A measuring line will once again stretch out straight to the hill of Gareb and then turn toward Goah. ⁴⁰ The whole valley — the corpses, the ashes, and all the fields as far as the Kidron Valley to the corner of the Horse Gate to the east — will be holy to the LORD. It will never be uprooted or demolished again."

Jeremiah's Land Purchase

32 This is the word that came to Jeremiah from the LORD in the tenth year of King Zedekiah of Judah, which was the eighteenth year of Nebuchadnezzar. ² At that time, the army of the king of Babylon was besieging Jerusalem, and the prophet Jeremiah was imprisoned in the guard's courtyard in the palace of the king of Judah. ³ King Zedekiah of Judah

---

ᴬ31:32 Or husband ᴮ31:38 = Jerusalem

31:29–30 The proverb about the **fathers** eating **sour grapes, and the children's teeth** being **set on edge** reflects the widespread belief that they were being unfairly punished for the sins of the previous generation, but Moses taught that this was not true (Dt 24:16). Ezekiel also refuted this proverb (Ezk 18:2–4).
31:31–34 The NT frequently used this passage about the new covenant (Lk 22:20; 1Co 11:25; 2Co 3:5–14; and Heb 8:8–12, the longest quote from the OT in the NT). It is a classic text that has shaped much of Christian theological reflection.
31:31 The new covenant is set in eschatological times of the Messiah and the consummation of history (**the days are coming**). The name of this **new covenant** suggests a radical break from past covenants. But the word for "new" in Hebrew can also mean "renewed covenant," especially since three-fourths of the contents of this covenant recall the Abrahamic-Davidic covenants. The principal parties of the covenant are **the house of Israel** and **the house of Judah**. This new covenant also applies to the church because Gentiles were part of this continuing Abrahamic-Davidic

new covenant when God promised that in Abraham's seed all nations would be blessed.
31:32 The problem with the old covenant was not with its Maker or its contents, but with God's people who **broke** their marriage vows to him (cp. 11:10).
31:34 Teaching will also be a thing of the past. **From the least to the greatest of them** indicates all people no matter their social class ("great" to the "poor," cp. 5:4–5) or age ("youngest" to the "oldest," cp. 6:13). The phrase **I will forgive . . . and never again remember their sin** reflects the grace of God that forgives sin and the omniscience of God that chooses not to call it to mind or to hold it against us.
31:35–37 The permanence of God's promise to Israel is compared to the durability of the cosmos.
31:38 Once again in days connected to the consummation of history, Jerusalem will be rebuilt **from the Tower of Hananel to the Corner Gate**. The Tower of Hananel was in the northeast corner of Jerusalem (Neh 3:1; 12:39; Zch 14:10), and the Corner Gate was probably at the northwest corner of the city wall (2Kg 14:13; 2Ch 26:9).

31:39 The **hill of Gareb** and **Goah** are unknown to us today. Since the other places mentioned were on the north side of Jerusalem, it may be assumed that these unknown places were on the south.
31:40 The **valley**, presumably composed of **corpses** and **ashes**, must be the Ben Hinnom Valley (see note at 7:31), where Israel buried the dead. The **Horse Gate** apparently was on the eastern wall of the city at the northern end of the Kidron Valley (Neh 3:28).
32:1–2 The promise of a bright future was given during one of Judah's darkest moments in 588 BC when Jeremiah was **imprisoned in the guard's courtyard** (33:1), in the **tenth year of King Zedekiah of Judah** and the **eighteenth year of Nebuchadnezzar**. This dating is correct if Nebuchadnezzar's reign is based on his accession year in the fall of 605 BC (see note at 25:1). His first official full year as king was 604 BC (52:29). Otherwise, his eighteenth year by Jewish reckoning was his seventeenth by Babylonian reckoning.
32:3–5 The Babylonian siege, which began in King Zedekiah's ninth year (39:1), was temporarily lifted when news came that the Egyptian army was approaching (37:5). Jeremiah was arrested during this lull in the siege on

had imprisoned him, saying, "Why are you prophesying as you do? You say, 'This is what the LORD says: Look, I am about to hand this city over to Babylon's king, and he will capture it. ⁴ King Zedekiah of Judah will not escape from the Chaldeans; indeed, he will certainly be handed over to Babylon's king. They will speak face to face^A and meet eye to eye. ⁵ He will take Zedekiah to Babylon, where he will stay until I attend to him — this is the LORD's declaration. For you will fight the Chaldeans, but you will not succeed.' "

⁶ Jeremiah replied, "The word of the LORD came to me: ⁷ Watch! Hanamel, the son of your uncle Shallum, is coming to you to say, 'Buy my field in Anathoth for yourself, for you own the right of redemption to buy it.'

⁸ "Then, as the LORD had said, my cousin Hanamel came to the guard's courtyard and urged me, 'Please buy my field in Anathoth in the land of Benjamin, for you own the right of inheritance and redemption. Buy it for yourself.' Then I knew that this was the word of the LORD. ⁹ So I bought the field in Anathoth from my cousin Hanamel, and I weighed out the silver to him — seventeen shekels^B of silver. ¹⁰ I recorded it on a scroll, sealed it, called in witnesses, and weighed out the silver on the scales. ¹¹ I took the purchase agreement — the sealed copy with its terms and conditions and the open copy — ¹² and gave the purchase agreement to Baruch son of Neriah, son of Mahseiah. I did this in the sight of my cousin^C Hanamel, the witnesses who had signed the purchase agreement, and all the Judeans sitting in the guard's courtyard.

¹³ "I charged Baruch in their sight, ¹⁴ 'This is what the LORD of Armies, the God of Israel, says: Take these scrolls — this purchase agreement with the sealed copy and this open copy — and put them in an earthen storage jar so they will last a long time. ¹⁵ For this is what the

LORD of Armies, the God of Israel, says: Houses, fields, and vineyards will again be bought in this land.'

¹⁶ "After I had given the purchase agreement to Baruch, son of Neriah, I prayed to the LORD: ¹⁷ Oh, Lord GOD! You yourself made the heavens and earth by your great power and with your outstretched arm. Nothing is too difficult for you! ¹⁸ You show faithful love to thousands but lay the fathers' iniquity on their sons' laps after them, great and mighty God whose name is the LORD of Armies, ¹⁹ the one great in counsel and powerful in action. Your eyes are on all the ways of the children of men^D in order to reward each person according to his ways and as the result of his actions. ²⁰ You performed signs and wonders in the land of Egypt and still do today, both in Israel and among all mankind. You made a name for yourself, as is the case today. ²¹ You brought your people Israel out of Egypt with signs and wonders, with a strong hand and an outstretched arm, and with great terror. ²² You gave them this land you swore to give to their ancestors, a land flowing with milk and honey. ²³ They entered and possessed it, but they did not obey you or live according to your instructions. They failed to perform all you commanded them to do, and so you have brought all this disaster on them. ²⁴ Look! Siege ramps have come against the city to capture it, and the city, as a result of the sword, famine, and plague, has been handed over to the Chaldeans who are fighting against it. What you have spoken has happened. Look, you can see it! ²⁵ Yet you, Lord GOD, have said to me, 'Purchase the field and call in witnesses' — even though the city has been handed over to the Chaldeans!"

²⁶ The word of the LORD came to Jeremiah: ²⁷ "Look, I am the LORD, the God over every creature. Is anything too difficult for me? ²⁸ Therefore, this is what the LORD says: I am

---

^A 32:4 Lit *His mouth will speak with his mouth*   ^B 32:9 About seven ounces   ^C 32:12 Some Hb mss, LXX, Syr; other Hb mss read *uncle*   ^D 32:19 Or *Adam*

---

the grounds that he was trying to escape and because he was encouraging Judah to surrender to Babylon (37:11–14). Zedekiah would be left in Babylon until God attended to him. **Attend** in this context connotes a sense of threat.

32:6 After the parenthetical explanation in vv. 2–5, v. 6 picks up from v. 1 with a first-person description of what is about to take place.

32:7 Jeremiah was given symbolic evidence for the hope he had just preached about Israel's future. His cousin, **Hanamel**, would offer him **the right of redemption** for family property in his hometown of **Anathoth**. The legal precedent for this action is found in Lv 25:25–28.

32:9 The prophet purchased the land for **seventeen shekels of silver**. This refers to the weight of the silver. Coins were not used until the Persian period in the seventh century BC. Monetary values were set by weighing

ingots of precious metals. Silver was one of the chief forms of payment.

32:10–11 Four steps were involved in this real estate transaction: Jeremiah **recorded** the transaction **on a scroll, sealed it, called in witnesses**, and stored it in two copies, a **sealed copy** and an **open copy**. The sealed copy was rolled up with a seal placed on the outside as a backup copy to verify that no tampering had taken place. The open copy was a duplicate.

32:12 Baruch son of Neriah, son of Mahseiah, was Jeremiah's scribe.

32:13–14 The **earthen storage jar** that Jeremiah used was the kind in which the Dead Sea Scrolls were sealed.

32:15 Jeremiah's purchase of the field at Anathoth symbolized Israel's future restoration to the land.

32:16–17 Only twice in his book is Jeremiah recorded as praying—here and in 42:4. In this prayer the prophet declared, **Nothing**

is too difficult for you! His emphasis was not on the difficulty of what God does, but on the "wondrous" nature of the divine work in creation and history (Gn 18:14; Ex 3:20; 15:11).

32:18 The phrase **You show faithful love to thousands** occurs also in Ex 20:6; Dt 5:10 (cp. Ex 34:7; Dt 7:9). God's retribution is just and fair, not capricious. He only lays **the fathers' iniquity on their sons' laps** when they themselves repeat those sins.

32:19–20 Note the Lord watches not only his people but **all the ways of the children of men.**

32:23–25 Buying a field seems absurd in the light of current circumstances.

32:26–27 On **Is anything too difficult for me?** see note at vv. 16–17.

32:28–35 The first-person pronoun appears ten times in these verses. God's anger is real, but its expression is always contingent on Israel's repentance.

about to hand this city over to the Chaldeans, to Babylon's king Nebuchadnezzar, and he will capture it. ²⁹ The Chaldeans who are fighting against this city will come and set this city on fire. They will burn it, including the houses where incense has been burned to Baal on their rooftops and where drink offerings have been poured out to other gods to anger me. ³⁰ From their youth, the Israelites and Judeans have done nothing but what is evil in my sight! They have done nothing but anger me by the work of their hands" — this is the LORD's declaration — ³¹ "for this city has caused my wrath and fury from the day it was built until now. I will therefore remove it from my presence ³² because of all the evil the Israelites and Judeans have done to anger me — they, their kings, their officials, their priests, and their prophets, the men of Judah, and the residents of Jerusalem. ³³ They have turned their backs to me and not their faces. Though I taught them time and time again,^A they do not listen and receive discipline. ³⁴ They have placed their abhorrent things in the house that bears my name and have defiled it. ³⁵ They have built the high places of Baal in Ben Hinnom Valley to sacrifice their sons and daughters in the fire^B to Molech — something I had not commanded them. I had never entertained the thought^c that they do this detestable act causing Judah to sin! ³⁶ "Now therefore, this is what the LORD, the God of Israel, says to this city about which you said, 'It has been handed over to Babylon's king through sword, famine, and plague': ³⁷ I will certainly gather them from all the lands where I have banished them in my anger, fury, and intense wrath, and I will return them to this place and make them live in safety. ³⁸ They will be my people, and I will be their God. ³⁹ I will give them integrity of heart and action^D so that they will fear me always, for their good and for the good of their descendants after them. ⁴⁰ "I will make a permanent covenant with them: I will never turn away from doing good to them, and I will put fear of me in their hearts

so they will never again turn away from me. ⁴¹ I will take delight in them to do what is good for them, and with all my heart and mind I will faithfully plant them in this land.

⁴² "For this is what the LORD says: Just as I have brought all this terrible disaster on these people, so am I about to bring on them all the good I am promising them. ⁴³ Fields will be bought in this land about which you are saying, 'It's a desolation without people or animals'; it has been handed over to the Chaldeans!' ⁴⁴ Fields will be purchased, the transaction written on a scroll and sealed, and witnesses will be called on in the land of Benjamin, in the areas surrounding Jerusalem, and in Judah's cities — the cities of the hill country, the cities of the Judean foothills, and the cities of the Negev — because I will restore their fortunes."^E This is the LORD's declaration.

Israel's Restoration

33 While he was still confined in the guard's courtyard, the word of the LORD came to Jeremiah a second time: ² "The LORD who made the earth,^F the LORD who forms it to establish it, the LORD is his name, says this: ³ Call to me and I will answer you and tell you great and incomprehensible things you do not know. ⁴ For this is what the LORD, the God of Israel, says concerning the houses of this city and the palaces of Judah's kings, the ones torn down for defense against the assault ramps and the sword: ⁵ The people coming to fight the Chaldeans will fill the houses with the corpses of their own men that I strike down in my wrath and fury. I have hidden my face from this city because of all their evil. ⁶ Yet I will certainly bring health and healing to it and will indeed heal them. I will let them experience the abundance^G of true peace. ⁷ I will restore the fortunes^H of Judah and of Israel and will rebuild them as in former times. ⁸ I will purify them from all the iniquity they have committed against me, and I will forgive all the iniquities they have committed against me, rebelling

---

^A32:33 Lit *them, rising up early and teaching*   ^B32:35 Lit *to make their sons and daughters pass through the fire*   ^C32:35 Lit *them, and it did not arise on my heart*   ^D32:39 Lit *give them one heart and one way*   ^E32:44 Or *will end their captivity*   ^F33:2 LXX; MT reads *made it*   ^G33:6 Or *fragrance*; Hb obscure   ^H33:7 Or *will end the captivity, also in v. 11*

32:33 Once again, Israel had **turned their backs** to God and **not their faces** (see note at 18:17).

32:35 The idolatrous worship of **Baal** and **Molech**, in which Israel sacrificed **their sons and daughters in the fire** (see notes at 7:31; 19:4) is also banned in Lv 18:21 and 20:2–5.

32:36–44 In six remarkable promises in these verses, God declared that he will: (1) **gather** his people from all lands (23:3; 29:14; 30:10; 31:8–14; Is 11:12; Ezk 11:17; 36:24); (2) **make them live in safety**; (3) declare that **they will be my people, and I will be their God**; (4) **give them integrity of heart and action so that they will fear me always**; (5) **make a permanent covenant with them** (Is 55:3; 61:8; Ezk 16:60; 37:26);

and (6) **take delight in them** and faithfully **plant them in this land**.

32:41 God pledges to carry this out with all his **heart and mind**. This is the only place in the OT where this expression is used of God.

32:42–44 The last verses of this chapter return to Jeremiah's purchase of the field in Anathoth. This was a sure sign that fields in Judah would once again belong to Hebrews in the future. This will include all the geographical areas in Israel, from **Benjamin**, where Jeremiah's purchase was made, to **Jerusalem . . . Judah's cities** and all the way south to the **Negev**.

33:1 The phrase **a second time** links vv. 1–13 with the previous chapter.

33:2–3 The things that God will reveal are **incomprehensible**, or "inaccessible." The Hebrew word is used of "walled up" cities that were "fortified."

33:4–5 The sense of these verses seems to be that all efforts to rescue Jerusalem will fail. These actions include tearing down houses for stones to plug up holes in the city wall and to set up barricades. The **corpses** will be citizens of Judah, not Babylonian soldiers.

33:6 The word for **health** is literally "new flesh" (8:22); thus, the exile will have a healing effect on Judah. The word **abundance** occurs only here. Related to the Hebrew word for "crown" or "diadem," it means "treasures."

33:8 Three key Hebrew words for "sin" are used in this verse.

against me. ⁹ This city will bear on my behalf a name of joy, praise, and glory before all the nations of the earth, who will hear of all the prosperity I will give them. They will tremble with awe because of all the good and all the peace I will bring about for them.

¹⁰ "This is what the LORD says: In this place, which you say is a ruin, without people or animals — that is, in Judah's cities and Jerusalem's streets that are a desolation without people, without inhabitants, and without animals — there will be heard again ¹¹ a sound of joy and gladness, the voice of the groom and the bride, and the voice of those saying,

Give thanks to the LORD of Armies,
for the LORD is good;
his faithful love endures forever

as they bring thanksgiving sacrifices to the temple of the LORD. For I will restore the fortunes of the land as in former times, says the LORD.

¹² "This is what the LORD of Armies says: In this desolate place — without people or animals — and in all its cities there will once more be a grazing land where shepherds may rest flocks. ¹³ The flocks will again pass under the hands of the one who counts them in the cities of the hill country, the cities of the Judean foothills, the cities of the Negev, the land of Benjamin — the areas around Jerusalem and in Judah's cities, says the LORD.

God's Covenant with David

¹⁴　"Look, the days are coming" —
this is the LORD's declaration —
"when I will fulfill the good promise
that I have spoken
concerning the house of Israel
and the house of Judah.
¹⁵　In those days and at that time
I will cause a Righteous Branch
to sprout up for David,
and he will administer justice
and righteousness in the land.
¹⁶　In those days Judah will be saved,
and Jerusalem will dwell securely,
and this is what she will be named:
The LORD Is Our Righteousness.ᴬ

¹⁷ "For this is what the LORD says: David will never fail to have a man sitting on the throne of the house of Israel. ¹⁸ The Levitical priests will never fail to have a man always before me to offer burnt offerings, to burn grain offerings, and to make sacrifices."

¹⁹ The word of the LORD came to Jeremiah: ²⁰ "This is what the LORD says: If you can break my covenant with the day and my covenant with the night so that day and night cease to come at their regular time, ²¹ then also my covenant with my servant David may be broken. If that could happen, then he would not have a son reigning on his throne and the Levitical priests would not be my ministers. ²² Even as the stars of heaven cannot be counted, and the sand of the sea cannot be measured, so too I will make innumerable the descendants of my servant David and the Levites who minister to me."

²³ The word of the LORD came to Jeremiah: ²⁴ "Have you not noticed what these people have said? They say, 'The LORD has rejected the two families he had chosen.' My people are treated with contempt and no longer regarded as a nation among them. ²⁵ This is what the LORD says: If I do not keep my covenant with the day and with the night, and if I fail to establish the fixed order of heaven and earth, ²⁶ then I might also reject the descendants of Jacob and of my servant David. That is, I would not take rulers from his descendants to rule over the descendants of Abraham, Isaac, and Jacob. But in fact, I will restore their fortunesᴮ and have compassion on them."

Jeremiah's Word to King Zedekiah

34 This is the word that came to Jeremiah from the LORD when King Nebuchadnezzar of Babylon, his whole army, all the kingdoms of the lands under his control, and all other peoples were fighting against Jerusalem and all its surrounding cities: ² "This is what the LORD, the God of Israel, says: Go, speak to King Zedekiah of Judah, and tell him, 'This is what the LORD says: I am about to hand this city over to the king of Babylon, and he will burn it. ³ As for you, you will not escape from him but are

---

ᴬ33:16 = Yahweh-zidkenu　ᴮ33:26 Or I will end their captivity

33:13 The one who counts them refers to a person who counted sheep as they came into the sheepfold at night to make sure that none were missing.
33:14–26 These verses are not in the LXX.
33:15 On the **Righteous Branch**, see notes at 23:5; 23:6.
33:16 The name **The LORD Is Our Righteousness** was formerly a name applied to the Messiah. In this verse it is applied to Jerusalem (see note at 23:6).
33:17–18 These verses do not literally promise the constant presence of a Davidic king and a Levitical priesthood (history shows this did not happen). Rather, it means that there will be no

cessation of David's dynasty or of the office of the priesthood. Jesus fulfills the offices of King and Priest (Ps 110:4). Christ's priesthood does not follow Levi's line, but the line of Melchizedek, the priest of Salem (Gn 14:17–20).
33:19–22 God compared the irrevocability of his promises to David (2Sm 7) and Levi's lines (Nm 17) with his unbreakable covenant with **day and night**.
33:23–24 Some disbelieving Israelites were saying that **the LORD** had **rejected the two families he had chosen**. These families were not the royal and priestly families referred to in vv. 21–22, but the northern and southern kingdoms of Israel.

33:25–26 Count on the natural order collapsing and going out of existence before God's promises to David, Levi, and the nation evaporate.
34:1 The attack against Jerusalem and **all its surrounding cities** is spoken of in hyperbolic, global terms—**all the kingdoms of the lands** or of the earth. It was as if the whole world was lined up against Judah.
34:2–3 The fate of Jerusalem and of King Zedekiah is foretold. Zedekiah would meet the Babylonian king **eye to eye and speak face to face**. There his eyes would be put out after he was forced to watch the execution of his sons (39:5–7; 52:8–11).

---

certain to be captured and handed over to him. You will meet the king of Babylon eye to eye and speak face to face;[A] you will go to Babylon.

⁴ " 'Yet hear the LORD's word, King Zedekiah of Judah. This is what the LORD says concerning you: You will not die by the sword; ⁵ you will die peacefully. There will be a burning ceremony for you just like the burning ceremonies for your ancestors, the kings of old who came before you. "Oh, master!" will be the lament for you, for I have spoken this word. This is the LORD's declaration.' "

⁶ So the prophet Jeremiah related all these words to King Zedekiah of Judah in Jerusalem ⁷ while the king of Babylon's army was attacking Jerusalem and all of Judah's remaining cities — that is, Lachish and Azekah, for they were the only ones left of Judah's fortified cities.

The People and Their Slaves

⁸ This is the word that came to Jeremiah from the LORD after King Zedekiah made a covenant with all the people who were in Jerusalem to proclaim freedom to them. ⁹ As a result, each was to let his male and female Hebrew slaves go free, and no one was to enslave his fellow Judean. ¹⁰ All the officials and people who entered into covenant to let their male and female slaves go free — in order not to enslave them any longer — obeyed and let them go free. ¹¹ Afterward, however, they changed their minds and took back their male and female slaves they had let go free and forced them to become slaves again.

¹² Then the word of the LORD came to Jeremiah from the LORD: ¹³ "This is what the LORD, the God of Israel, says: I made a covenant with your ancestors when I brought them out of the land of Egypt, out of the place of slavery, saying, ¹⁴ 'At the end of seven years, each of you must let his fellow Hebrew who sold himself[B] to you go. He may serve you six years, but then you must let him go free from your service.' But

your ancestors did not obey me or pay any attention. ¹⁵ Today you repented and did what pleased me, each of you proclaiming freedom for his neighbor. You made a covenant before me at the house that bears my name. ¹⁶ But you have changed your minds and profaned my name. Each has taken back his male and female slaves who had been set free to go wherever they wanted, and you have again forced them to be your slaves.

¹⁷ "Therefore, this is what the LORD says: You have not obeyed me by proclaiming freedom, each for his fellow Hebrew and for his neighbor. I hereby proclaim freedom for you — this is the LORD's declaration — to the sword, to plague, and to famine! I will make you a horror to all the earth's kingdoms. ¹⁸ As for those who disobeyed my covenant, not keeping the terms of the covenant they made before me, I will treat them like the calf they cut in two in order to pass between its pieces. ¹⁹ The officials of Judah and Jerusalem, the court officials, the priests, and all the people of the land who passed between the pieces of the calf — ²⁰ all these I will hand over to their enemies, to those who intend to take their life. Their corpses will become food for the birds of the sky and for the wild animals of the land. ²¹ I will hand King Zedekiah of Judah and his officials over to their enemies, to those who intend to take their lives, to the king of Babylon's army that is withdrawing. ²² I am about to give the command — this is the LORD's declaration — and I will bring them back to this city. They will fight against it, capture it, and burn it. I will make Judah's cities a desolation, without inhabitant."

The Rechabites' Example

35 This is the word that came to Jeremiah from the LORD in the days of Jehoiakim son of Josiah, king of Judah: ² "Go to the house of the Rechabites, speak to them, and bring them to one of the chambers of the temple of the LORD to offer them a drink of wine."

[A]34:3 Lit *and his mouth will speak to your mouth*   [B]34:14 Or *who was sold*

34:4–5 Zedekiah would not be killed. He would die in Babylon and have **a burning ceremony** just like the "funeral fire" at other royal funerals (2Ch 16:14; 21:19). This ceremony involved burning spices on the coffins, but it did not necessarily involve cremation.
34:6–7 Only **Lachish and Azekah** remained of all of Judah's cities as the siege of Jerusalem continued. Lachish was a fortified city thirty miles southwest of Jerusalem. Azekah, likewise fortified, was northeast of Lachish.
34:8–10 The motivation for King Zedekiah issuing this **covenant**, or proclamation of emancipation, that all **male and female Hebrew slaves** should be set free is not given. It seems to have come just before the temporary lifting of Nebuchadnezzar's siege against Jerusalem in late spring or early summer of 588 BC due to a rumor about the approach of the Egyptian army.

34:11–16 When the siege was lifted, the people abandoned their panic-inspired piety, with the result that slave owners repudiated their solemn oath to God in violation of the provisions in Ex 21:2–6 and Dt 15:12–18, thus profaning God's **name**.
34:17 With a devastating play on words and an irony of ironies, God would take Judah's revoked proclamation of emancipation and make his own proclamation: Judah would experience **freedom** from his protection, thus falling to **sword, to plague, and to famine**.
34:18–20 In a covenant ceremony, a **calf** was **cut in two in order** that the parties to the covenant could **pass between its pieces**. Parties who passed between the pieces were in effect saying, "If I do not keep the terms of this covenant, may I die like this slaughtered animal." God would hand over to their enemies everyone who passed between the pieces.

34:21–22 Nebuchadnezzar's army had withdrawn briefly, but God would give the command to **bring them back to this city** (Jerusalem).
35:1–19 After devoting several chapters to King Zedekiah, Jeremiah returns to a decade earlier when Zedekiah's older brother Jehoiakim ruled Judah (609–598 BC).
35:2 The **house** [household] **of the Rechabites** is known largely from this chapter. Their founder was Jonadab or Jehonadab, son of Rechab, who lived under King Jehu of the northern kingdom. Jehonadab apparently supported the king's radical reform movements (2Kg 10:15–23), which included demolishing the Baal cult and other elements of Canaanite culture. The Rechabites also promised their ancestor that they would not build houses or plant vineyards, apparently so they would be able to remain

³ So I took Jaazaniah son of Jeremiah, son of Habazziniah, and his brothers and all his sons — the entire house of the Rechabites — ⁴ and I brought them into the temple of the LORD to a chamber occupied by the sons of Hanan son of Igdaliah, a man of God, who had a chamber near the officials' chamber, which was above the chamber of Maaseiah son of Shallum the doorkeeper. ⁵ I set jars filled with wine and some cups before the sons of the house of the Rechabites and said to them, "Drink wine!"

⁶ But they replied, "We do not drink wine, for Jonadab, son of our ancestor Rechab, commanded, 'You and your descendants must never drink wine. ⁷ You must not build a house or sow seed or plant a vineyard. Those things are not for you. Rather, you must live in tents your whole life, so you may live a long time on the soil where you stay as a resident alien.' ⁸ We have obeyed Jonadab, son of our ancestor Rechab, in all he commanded us. So we haven't drunk wine our whole life — we, our wives, our sons, and our daughters. ⁹ We also have not built houses to live in and do not have vineyard, field, or seed. ¹⁰ But we have lived in tents and have obeyed and done everything our ancestor Jonadab commanded us. ¹¹ However, when King Nebuchadnezzar of Babylon marched into the land, we said, 'Come, let's go into Jerusalem to get away from the Chaldean and Aramean armies.' So we have been living in Jerusalem."

¹² Then the word of the LORD came to Jeremiah: ¹³ "This is what the LORD of Armies, the God of Israel, says: Go, say to the men of Judah and the residents of Jerusalem, 'Will you not accept discipline by listening to my words? — this is the LORD's declaration. ¹⁴ The words of Jonadab, son of Rechab, have been carried out. He commanded his descendants not to drink wine, and they have not drunk to this day because they have obeyed their ancestor's command. But I have spoken to you time and time again,ᴬ and you have not obeyed me! ¹⁵ Time and time againᴮ I have sent you all my servants the prophets, proclaiming, "Turn, each one from his evil way, and correct your actions.

Stop following other gods to serve them. Live in the land that I gave you and your ancestors." But you did not pay attention or obey me. ¹⁶ Yes, the sons of Jonadab son of Rechab carried out their ancestor's command he gave them, but these people have not obeyed me. ¹⁷ Therefore, this is what the LORD, the God of Armies, the God of Israel, says: I will certainly bring on Judah and on all the residents of Jerusalem all the disaster I have pronounced against them because I have spoken to them, but they have not obeyed, and I have called to them, but they did not answer.'"

¹⁸ But to the house of the Rechabites Jeremiah said, "This is what the LORD of Armies, the God of Israel, says: 'Because you have obeyed the command of your ancestor Jonadab and have kept all his commands and have done everything he commanded you, ¹⁹ this is what the LORD of Armies, the God of Israel, says: Jonadab son of Rechab will never fail to have a man to stand before me always.'"

Jeremiah Dictates a Scroll

36 In the fourth year of Jehoiakim son of Josiah, king of Judah, this word came to Jeremiah from the LORD: ² "Take a scroll, and write on it all the words I have spoken to you concerning Israel, Judah, and all the nations from the time I first spoke to you during Josiah's reign until today. ³ Perhaps when the house of Judah hears about all the disaster I am planning to bring on them, each one of them will turn from his evil way. Then I will forgive their iniquity and their sin."

⁴ So Jeremiah summoned Baruch son of Neriah. At Jeremiah's dictation,ᶜ Baruch wrote on a scroll all the words the LORD had spoken to Jeremiah. ⁵ Then Jeremiah commanded Baruch, "I am restricted; I cannot enter the temple of the LORD, ⁶ so you must go and read from the scroll — which you wrote at my dictationᴰ — the words of the LORD in the hearing of the people at the temple of the LORD on a day of fasting. Read his words in the hearing of all the Judeans who are coming from their cities. ⁷ Perhaps their petition will come before

ᴬ35:14 Lit you, rising up early and speaking ᴮ35:15 Lit Rising up early and sending ᶜ36:4 Lit From Jeremiah's mouth ᴰ36:6 Lit wrote from my mouth

mobile. They were devout worshipers of the Lord. The Lord told Jeremiah to invite the Rechabites into the temple **to offer them a drink of wine**.
35:3–4 Jaazaniah and **Habazziniah** are not mentioned elsewhere. The father of Jaazaniah, identified here as Jeremiah, is not the unmarried prophet. Jaazaniah must have been the head of the Rechabites at this time.
35:4 Maaseiah son of Shallum the doorkeeper may have been the father of the priest Zephaniah (21:1; 29:25; 37:3).
35:5 The **jars filled with wine** were large drinking bowls with dipping **cups**.

35:6–11 The Rechabites were just the illustration Jeremiah needed to teach obedience to the Lord's commands.
35:12–16 Judah is being rebuked here. Three times in these verses Jeremiah contrasted the Rechabites' obedience to a human command with Judah's disobedience to the living God.
35:17–19 What happened to the Rechabites after 587 BC is unknown except for Malchijah son of Rechab. He repaired the Dung Gate in the days of Nehemiah (Neh 3:14).
36:1 This **fourth year of Jehoiakim** in 605–604 BC was a critical time (25:1; 45:1). Nebuchadnezzar of Babylon had defeated

the Assyrian forces at Carchemish on the Euphrates River and had begun his move south to Syria and Israel.
36:2–3 The prophet was instructed to **take a scroll**, which in Hebrew was called a *megillath sepher*, "a book-scroll," made of goat skins or papyrus. Jeremiah was to write on this scroll all the words God had spoken **concerning Israel, Judah, and all the nations**.
36:4 Baruch son of Neriah came from a well-known family (see note at 32:12). Baruch acted as Jeremiah's secretary.
36:6 A number of months passed between the writing of the scroll and its public reading, as seen from the dates in Jr 36:1,9,22.

the LORD, and each one will turn from his evil way, for the anger and fury that the LORD has pronounced against this people are intense." **8** So Baruch son of Neriah did everything the prophet Jeremiah had commanded him. At the LORD's temple he read the LORD's words from the scroll.

Baruch Reads the Scroll

9 In the fifth year of Jehoiakim son of Josiah, king of Judah, in the ninth month, all the people of Jerusalem and all those coming in from Judah's cities into Jerusalem proclaimed a fast before the LORD. **10** Then at the LORD's temple, in the chamber of Gemariah son of Shaphan the scribe, in the upper courtyard at the opening of the New Gate of the LORD's temple, in the hearing of all the people, Baruch read Jeremiah's words from the scroll.

11 When Micaiah son of Gemariah, son of Shaphan, heard all the words of the LORD from the scroll, **12** he went down to the scribe's chamber in the king's palace. All the officials were sitting there — Elishama the scribe, Delaiah son of Shemaiah, Elnathan son of Achbor, Gemariah son of Shaphan, Zedekiah son of Hananiah, and all the other officials. **13** Micaiah reported to them all the words he had heard when Baruch read from the scroll in the hearing of the people. **14** Then all the officials sent word to Baruch through Jehudi son of Nethaniah, son of Shelemiah, son of Cushi, saying, "Bring the scroll that you read in the hearing of the people, and come." So Baruch son of Neriah took the scroll and went to them. **15** They said to him, "Sit down and read it in our hearing." So Baruch read it in their hearing.

16 When they had heard all the words, they turned to each other in fear and said to Baruch, "We must surely tell the king all these things." **17** Then they asked Baruch, "Tell us, how did you write all these words? At his dictation?"^A **18** Baruch said to them, "At his dictation. He recited all these words to me while I was writing on the scroll in ink."

Jehoiakim Burns the Scroll

19 The officials said to Baruch, "You and Jeremiah must hide and tell no one where you are." **20** Then, after depositing the scroll in the chamber of Elishama the scribe, the officials came to the king at the courtyard and reported

everything in the hearing of the king. **21** The king sent Jehudi to get the scroll, and he took it from the chamber of Elishama the scribe. Jehudi then read it in the hearing of the king and all the officials who were standing by the king. **22** Since it was the ninth month, the king was sitting in his winter quarters with a fire burning in front of him. **23** As soon as Jehudi would read three or four columns, Jehoiakim would cut the scroll^B with a scribe's knife and throw the columns into the fire in the hearth until the entire scroll was consumed by the fire in the hearth. **24** As they heard all these words, the king and all his servants did not become terrified or tear their clothes. **25** Even though Elnathan, Delaiah, and Gemariah had urged the king not to burn the scroll, he did not listen to them. **26** Then the king commanded Jerahmeel the king's son, Seraiah son of Azriel, and Shelemiah son of Abdeel to seize the scribe Baruch and the prophet Jeremiah, but the LORD hid them.

Jeremiah Dictates Another Scroll

27 After the king had burned the scroll and the words Baruch had written at Jeremiah's dictation,^C the word of the LORD came to Jeremiah: **28** "Take another scroll, and once again write on it the original words that were on the original scroll that King Jehoiakim of Judah burned. **29** You are to proclaim concerning King Jehoiakim of Judah, 'This is what the LORD says: You have burned the scroll, asking, "Why have you written on it that the king of Babylon will certainly come and destroy this land and cause it to be without people or animals?" **30** Therefore, this is what the LORD says concerning King Jehoiakim of Judah: He will have no one to sit on David's throne, and his corpse will be thrown out to be exposed to the heat of day and the frost of night. **31** I will punish him, his descendants, and his officers for their iniquity. I will bring on them, on the residents of Jerusalem, and on the people of Judah all the disaster, which I warned them about but they did not listen.'" **32** Then Jeremiah took another scroll and gave it to Baruch son of Neriah, the scribe, and he wrote on it at Jeremiah's dictation^D all the words of the scroll that Jehoiakim, Judah's king, had burned in the fire. And many other words like them were added.

---

^A36:17 Lit *From his mouth*, also in v. 18   ^B36:23 Lit *columns, he would tear it*   ^C36:27 Lit *written from Jeremiah's mouth*
^D36:32 Lit *it from Jeremiah's mouth*

36:9–10 Shaphan was King Josiah's secretary of state (2Kg 22:3,8,12). **Gemariah** was the brother of Ahikam, one of Jeremiah's few friends (Jr 26:24), but he was not the Gemariah mentioned in 29:3. Gemariah allowed Baruch to use his room in the temple's inner court, which provided a setting in which the assembled people could hear Baruch's reading.

36:9 The **fifth year of Jehoiakim** was 604 BC, and the **ninth month** (December 604 BC) was when the Babylonians sacked the Philistine city of Ashkelon. This event may have forced Jehoiakim to switch his allegiance from Egypt to Babylon. **36:11–13** When **Micaiah son of Gemariah** and grandson of Shephan—a family supportive of Jeremiah—heard what Baruch

read, he repeated the words to all the king's officials (v. 12). **36:22–25** His **winter quarters** was a warm section of the palace apparently facing the winter sun (Am 3:15). **36:32** In creating the replacement scroll, Jeremiah dictated to Baruch the words that had been on the first scroll plus **many other words like them**. Presumably, these

Jerusalem's Last Days

37 Zedekiah son of Josiah reigned as king in the land of Judah in place of Coniah[A] son of Jehoiakim, for King Nebuchadnezzar of Babylon made him king. [2] He and his officers and the people of the land did not obey the words of the LORD that he spoke through the prophet Jeremiah.

[3] Nevertheless, King Zedekiah sent Jehucal son of Shelemiah and Zephaniah son of Maaseiah, the priest, to the prophet Jeremiah, requesting, "Please pray to the LORD our God on our behalf!" [4] Jeremiah was going about his daily tasks[B] among the people, for he had not yet been put into the prison. [5] Pharaoh's army had left Egypt, and when the Chaldeans, who were besieging Jerusalem, heard the report, they withdrew from Jerusalem.

[6] The word of the LORD came to the prophet Jeremiah: [7] "This is what the LORD, the God of Israel, says: This is what you will say to Judah's king, who is sending you to inquire of me: 'Watch: Pharaoh's army, which has come out to help you, is going to return to its own land of Egypt. [8] The Chaldeans will then return and fight against this city. They will capture it and burn it. [9] This is what the LORD says: Don't deceive yourselves by saying, "The Chaldeans will leave us for good," for they will not leave. [10] Indeed, if you were to strike down the entire Chaldean army that is fighting with you, and there remained among them only the badly wounded[C] men, each in his tent, they would get up and burn this city.'"

Jeremiah's Imprisonment

[11] When the Chaldean army withdrew from Jerusalem because of Pharaoh's army, [12] Jeremiah started to leave Jerusalem to go to the land of Benjamin to claim his portion there among the people. [13] But when he was at the Benjamin Gate, an officer of the guard was there, whose name was Irijah son of Shelemiah, son of Hananiah, and he apprehended the prophet Jeremiah, saying, "You are defecting to the Chaldeans."

[14] "That's a lie," Jeremiah replied. "I am not defecting to the Chaldeans!" Irijah would not listen to him but apprehended Jeremiah and took him to the officials. [15] The officials were angry at Jeremiah and beat him and placed him in jail in the house of Jonathan the scribe, for it had been made into a prison. [16] So Jeremiah went into a cell in the dungeon and stayed there many days.

Jeremiah Summoned by Zedekiah

[17] King Zedekiah later sent for him and received him, and in his house privately asked him, "Is there a word from the LORD?"

"There is," Jeremiah responded. He continued, "You will be handed over to the king of Babylon." [18] Then Jeremiah said to King Zedekiah, "How have I sinned against you or your servants or these people that you have put me in prison? [19] Where are your prophets who prophesied to you, claiming, 'The king of Babylon will not come against you and this land'? [20] So now please listen, my lord the king. May my petition come before you. Don't send me back to the house of Jonathan the scribe, or I will die there."

[21] So King Zedekiah gave orders, and Jeremiah was placed in the guard's courtyard. He was given a loaf of bread each day from the bakers' street until all the bread was gone from the city. So Jeremiah remained in the guard's courtyard.

Jeremiah Thrown into a Cistern

38 Now Shephatiah son of Mattan, Gedaliah son of Pashhur, Jucal[D] son of Shelemiah, and Pashhur son of Malchijah heard the words Jeremiah was speaking to all the people: [2] "This is what the LORD says: 'Whoever stays in this city will die by the sword, famine, and plague, but whoever surrenders to the Chaldeans will live. He will retain his life like

---

[A] 37:1 = Jehoiachin [B] 37:4 Lit was coming in and going out [C] 37:10 Lit the pierced [D] 38:1 = Jehucal in Jr 37:3

---

new words dealt with the fulfillment of his prophecies about Judah as events unfolded after the burning of the first scroll.
37:1–21 Eighteen years passed between the events of chaps. 36 and 37.
37:1 In fulfillment of Jeremiah's prophecy in 36:30, **Zedekiah** (a brother of Jehoiakim) was placed on the throne **in place of Coniah** [aka Jehoiachin] **son of Jehoiakim.** Nebuchadnezzar of Babylon **made** Zedekiah **king.**
37:3 For the second time (21:1–2), Zedekiah sent messengers to Jeremiah asking for intercessory prayer.
37:5 The phrase **Pharaoh's army had left Egypt** probably refers to Pharaoh Hophra (44:30), called "Apries" by Herodotus (2.161; 4.159). This caused Babylon to withdraw temporarily from the siege of Jerusalem in the summer of 588 BC. The Babylonians soon

defeated the Egyptians, and the siege of Jerusalem resumed.
37:11–12 Jeremiah was arrested as he set out to inspect and **claim his portion** of the property in his native town of Anathoth (1:1; 32:8). He had just purchased this property from his cousin Hanamel (chap. 32).
37:13–14 An **officer of the guard** presumed Jeremiah was defecting to the enemy. After all, the prophet had encouraged others to surrender to the Babylonians (see note at 21:9). But Jeremiah denied the charge.
37:16 Jeremiah was placed in **a cell in the dungeon** (lit "the house of a cistern-pit"). This was a vault adjoining an underground dungeon, where he could have been left to die (v. 20).
37:17 King Zedekiah called for Jeremiah a third time, but this time in secrecy. Perhaps he hoped this would encourage a good

word from the Lord. But the word from the prophet was not good. He, the king of Judah, would be **handed over to the king of Babylon.**
37:21 Zedekiah reversed his officials' decision and transferred Jeremiah to the **guard's courtyard.** Here he was given a **loaf of bread each day from the bakers' street.** Streets of Near Eastern cities were often named after those whose businesses were on that street, hence Bakers' Street—the only street name in ancient Jerusalem known to us.
38:1 Jucal and **Pashhur,** already mentioned in 21:1 and 37:3, were among the four persons who heard Jeremiah's messages from the guard's courtyard (37:21).
38:2 The **Chaldeans** derived their name from an ancient name Chaldai, which referred to a group of Aramean tribes that moved

the spoils of war and will live.' **3** This is what the LORD says: 'This city will most certainly be handed over to the king of Babylon's army, and he will capture it.'"

4 The officials then said to the king, "This man ought to die, because he is weakening the morale^A of the warriors who remain in this city and of all the people by speaking to them in this way. This man is not pursuing the welfare of this people, but their harm."

5 King Zedekiah said, "Here he is; he's in your hands since the king can't do anything against you." **6** So they took Jeremiah and dropped him into the cistern of Malchiah the king's son, which was in the guard's courtyard, lowering Jeremiah with ropes. There was no water in the cistern, only mud, and Jeremiah sank in the mud.

7 But Ebed-melech, a Cushite court official in the king's palace, heard Jeremiah had been put into the cistern. While the king was sitting at the Benjamin Gate, **8** Ebed-melech went from the king's palace and spoke to the king: **9** "My lord the king, these men have been evil in all they have done to the prophet Jeremiah. They have dropped him into the cistern where he will die from hunger, because there is no more bread in the city."

10 So the king commanded Ebed-melech, the Cushite, "Take from here thirty men under your authority^B and pull the prophet Jeremiah up from the cistern before he dies."

11 So Ebed-melech took the men under his authority^C and went to the king's palace to a place below the storehouse.^D From there he took old rags and worn-out clothes and lowered them by ropes to Jeremiah in the cistern. **12** Ebed-melech the Cushite called down to Jeremiah, "Place these old rags and clothes between your armpits and the ropes." Jeremiah did this. **13** They pulled him up with the ropes and lifted him out of the cistern, but he remained in the guard's courtyard.

Zedekiah's Final Meeting with Jeremiah

14 King Zedekiah sent for the prophet Jeremiah and received him at the third entrance of the LORD's temple. The king said to Jeremiah, "I am going to ask you something; don't hide anything from me."

15 Jeremiah replied to Zedekiah, "If I tell you, you will kill me, won't you? Besides, if I give you advice, you won't listen to me anyway."

16 King Zedekiah swore to Jeremiah in private, "As the LORD lives, who has given us this life, I will not kill you or hand you over to these men who intend to take your life."

17 Jeremiah therefore said to Zedekiah, "This is what the LORD, the God of Armies, the God of Israel, says: 'If indeed you surrender to the officials of the king of Babylon, then you will live, this city will not be burned, and you and your household will survive. **18** But if you do not surrender to the officials of the king of Babylon, then this city will be handed over to the Chaldeans. They will burn it, and you yourself will not escape from them.'"

19 But King Zedekiah said to Jeremiah, "I am worried about the Judeans who have defected to the Chaldeans. They may hand me over to the Judeans to abuse me."

20 "They will not hand you over," Jeremiah replied. "Obey the LORD in what I am telling you, so it may go well for you and you can live. **21** But if you refuse to surrender, this is the verdict^E that the LORD has shown me: **22** 'All the women^F who remain in the palace of Judah's king will be brought out to the officials of the king of Babylon and will say to you,^G

"Your trusted friends^H misled^I you
and overcame you.
Your feet sank into the mire,
and they deserted you."

23 All your wives and children will be brought out to the Chaldeans. You yourself will not escape from them, for you will be seized by the king of Babylon and this city will burn.'"

24 Then Zedekiah warned Jeremiah, "Don't let anyone know about this conversation^J or you will die. **25** The officials may hear that I have spoken with you and come and demand of you, 'Tell us what you said to the king; don't hide anything from us and we won't kill you.

^A38:4 Lit *hands* ^B38:10 Lit *men in your hand* ^C38:11 Lit *men in his hand* ^D38:11 Or *treasury* ^E38:21 Or *promise*; lit *word*
^F38:22 Or *wives* ^G38:22 *to you* supplied for clarity ^H38:22 Lit *"The men of your peace* ^I38:22 Or *incited* ^J38:24 Lit *about these words*

into lower Mesopotamia somewhere around 1000 to 900 BC. After they moved from their tribal settlements to urban settings, they acquired the name *Babylonians*, or more precisely, *Neo-Babylonians*; thus, "Chaldeans" and "Babylonians" are used interchangeably. **38:6** Malchiah the king's son was not one of Zedekiah's sons, but a royal prince (see 36:26 for a similar expression).
38:7–9 Ebed-melech, a Cushite court official, whose name means "servant of the king," was a royal official of Ethiopian descent. He told Zedekiah what the officials had done and how desperate Jeremiah's situation was. It took real courage for him to

oppose those who were determined to stop Jeremiah's proclamations.
38:10 Ebed-melech was authorized to take thirty men to pull Jeremiah up from the cistern before he dies. One Hebrew manuscript and the Greek Septuagint read "three" for "thirty," but this is not enough evidence to overrule the Hebrew text as it stands. Perhaps thirty were needed for the total task: some for protection and some for pulling the prophet out of the pit.
38:11–13 The old rags and worn-out clothes were needed to protect Jeremiah from the ropes, since he was mired down in mud (v. 6). The narrative in 37:17–21 does not

include all these details about Jeremiah's rescue, but both record the prophet's plea not to be sent back to this cistern (37:20; 38:26).
38:14 The third entrance, where this secret discussion between Jeremiah and the king took place, is otherwise unknown. Could it have been the king's private entrance to the temple?
38:22 Zedekiah feared the ridicule of Judah's defectors (v. 19), but he was even more frightened of the women (his own harem) who would remain in the palace of Judah's king. They might shower insult and ridicule on him for being so gullible that he trusted weak allies and false prophets. The

Also, what did the king say to you?' [26] If they do, tell them, 'I was bringing before the king my petition that he not return me to the house of Jonathan to die there.'" [27] All the officials did come to Jeremiah, and they questioned him. He reported the exact words to them the king had commanded, and they quit speaking with him because the conversation^A had not been overheard. [28] Jeremiah remained in the guard's courtyard until the day Jerusalem was captured, and he was there when it happened.^B

The Fall of Jerusalem to Babylon

39 In the ninth year of King Zedekiah of Judah, in the tenth month, King Nebuchadnezzar of Babylon advanced against Jerusalem with his entire army and laid siege to it. [2] In the fourth month of Zedekiah's eleventh year, on the ninth day of the month, the city was broken into. [3] All the officials of the king of Babylon entered and sat at the Middle Gate: Nergal-sharezer, Samgar, Nebusarsechim^c the chief of staff, Nergal-sharezer the chief soothsayer, and all the rest of the officials of Babylon's king.

[4] When King Zedekiah of Judah and all the fighting men saw them, they fled. They left the city at night by way of the king's garden through the city gate between the two walls. They left along the route to the Arabah. [5] However, the Chaldean army pursued them and overtook Zedekiah in the plains of Jericho. They arrested him and brought him up to Nebuchadnezzar, Babylon's king, at Riblah in the land of Hamath. The king passed sentence on him there.

[6] At Riblah the king of Babylon slaughtered Zedekiah's sons before his eyes, and he also slaughtered all Judah's nobles. [7] Then he blinded Zedekiah and put him in bronze chains to take him to Babylon. [8] The Chaldeans next burned down the king's palace and the people's houses and tore down the walls of Jerusalem. [9] Nebuzaradan, the captain of the guards, deported the rest of the people to Babylon — those who had remained in the city and those deserters who had defected to him along with the rest of the people who remained. [10] However, Nebuzaradan, the captain of the guards, left in the land of Judah some of the poor people who owned nothing, and he gave them vineyards and fields at that time.

Jeremiah Freed by Nebuchadnezzar

[11] Speaking through Nebuzaradan, captain of the guards, King Nebuchadnezzar of Babylon gave orders concerning Jeremiah: [12] "Take him and look after him. Don't do him any harm, but do for him whatever he says." [13] Nebuzaradan, captain of the guards, Nebushazban the chief of staff, Nergal-sharezer the chief soothsayer, and all the captains of Babylon's king [14] had Jeremiah brought from the guard's courtyard and turned him over to Gedaliah son of Ahikam, son of Shaphan, to take him home. So he settled among his own people.

[15] Now the word of the LORD had come to Jeremiah when he was confined in the guard's courtyard: [16] "Go tell Ebed-melech the Cushite, 'This is what the LORD of Armies, the God of Israel, says: I am about to fulfill my words for disaster and not for good against this city. They will take place before your eyes on that day. [17] But I will rescue you on that day — this is the LORD's declaration — and you will not be handed over to the men you dread. [18] Indeed, I will certainly deliver you so that you do not fall by the sword. Because you have trusted in me, you will retain your life like the spoils of war. This is the LORD's declaration.'"

---

^A 38:27 Lit word   ^B 38:28 Or captured. This is what happened when Jerusalem was captured: ^c 39:3 LXX; MT reads Samgar-nebu, Sarsechim

---

women would try to curry favor with their new Babylonian overlords.
39:1-2 The siege of Jerusalem began in January of 588 BC and lasted until July of 587 BC, except for a brief interlude in the summer of 588 BC (52:4–6).
39:3 The names and titles of the Babylonians are not entirely clear. **Nergal-sharezer** was the **Samgar**, which is either a Babylonian title or a district in Babylon named "Simmagir." **Nebusarsechim** may be the same as "Nebushazban" (v. 13). Both are called the **chief of staff**. A second person named **Nergal-sharezer** was a **chief soothsayer**, another obscure Babylonian title. This one was Nebuchadnezzar's son-in-law who later became king of Babylon (560–556 BC). One more name appears in vv. 9–10,13 as part of the Babylonian entourage—Nebuzaradan, the commander or captain of the guards. The **Middle Gate** at which the officials of the king of Babylon . . . sat was probably between the upper and lower portions of Jerusalem. This is where the Babylonian officials set up the occupational court and government.

39:4–5 The **king's garden** and the **gate between the two walls** are otherwise unknown. King Zedekiah fled to the **Arabah**, referring to the Jordan Valley, where **Jericho** was located about twenty miles east of Jerusalem. After he was captured he was taken to Nebuchadnezzar's headquarters at **Riblah in the land of Hamath**, about sixtyfive miles north of Damascus.
39:6–8 So important and tragic was the fall of Jerusalem that it is recorded in Scripture four times: chaps. 39; 52; 2Kg 25; and 2Ch 36. Zedekiah saw the slaughter of his sons and his nobles (Jr 39:6) just before his eyes were put out by Nebuchadnezzar. Then he was carted off to Babylon in **bronze chains**. His palace was burned, along with the houses of the people, and the **walls of Jerusalem** were torn down.
39:9–10 The Babylonians **deported** the people of Judah to Babylon. This was the final deportation, coming eleven years after king Jehoiachin was taken away in 598 BC. **The poor people who owned nothing** were given **vineyards and fields**. The

word for "fields" has an uncertain meaning and could be translated "wells" or "watering places."
39:11–14 Jeremiah was turned over to **Gedaliah son of Ahikam, son of Shaphan**, whom the Babylonians had just appointed governor of Judah. Ironically, the prophet received better treatment from the enemy than he had received from his own people. Some have declared there is a contradiction between the events described in vv. 11–14 and those in 40:1–6, but the two accounts supplement each other. Jeremiah was released from prison into Gedaliah's care (39:14). Jeremiah mingled with the captives as they were getting ready to be sent off to Babylon (v. 14). Unrecognized at first, Jeremiah was placed in chains and readied for deportation to Babylon (40:1). At Ramah, Jeremiah was recognized and released (40:4).
39:15–18 Ebed-melech is commended for his courageous act of rescuing Jeremiah from the muddy cistern (see notes at 38:7–9; 38:10).

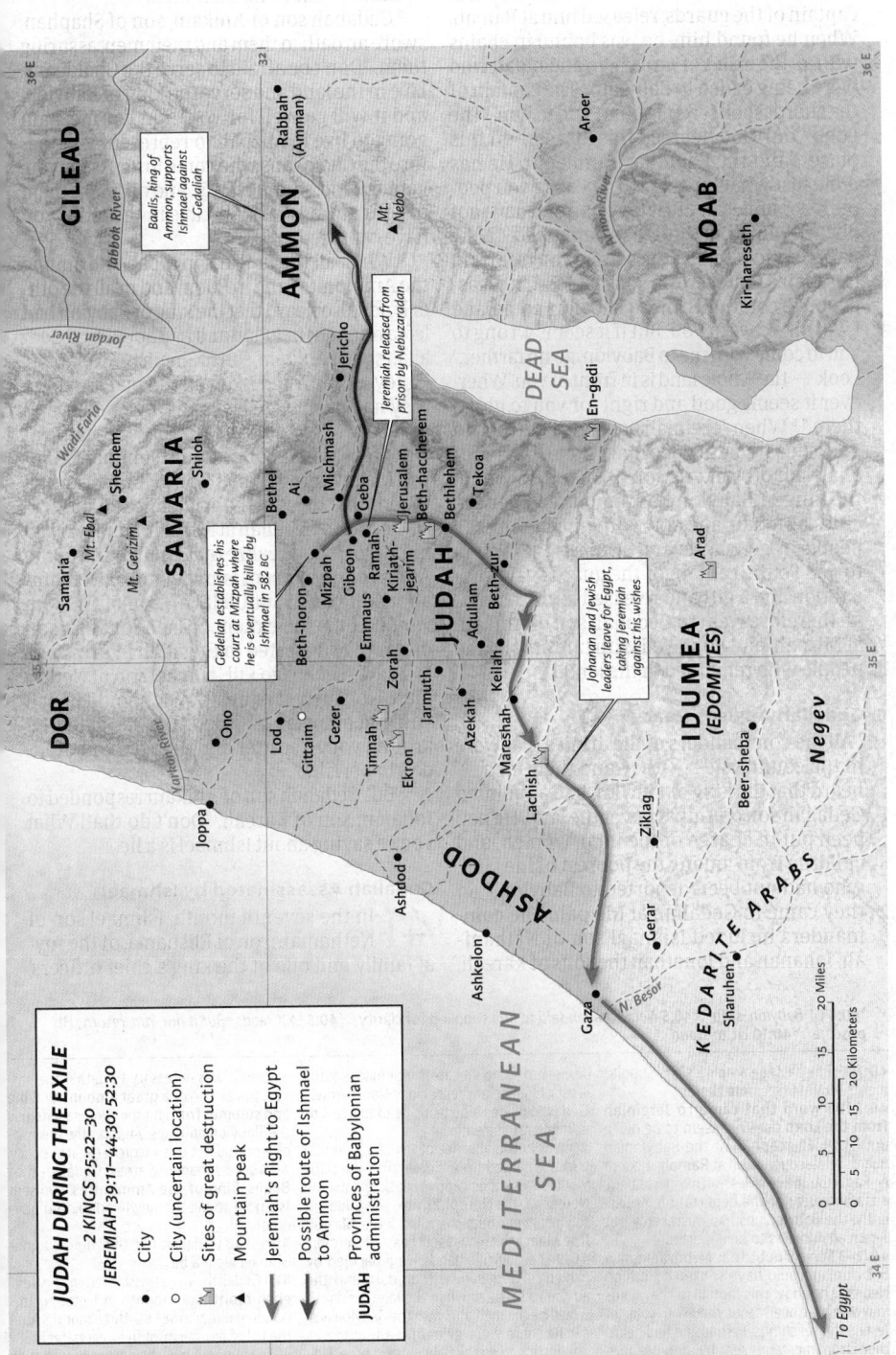

JUDAH DURING THE EXILE

2 KINGS 25:22–30
JEREMIAH 39:11–44:30; 52:30

- • City
- ○ City (uncertain location)
- Sites of great destruction
- ▲ Mountain peak
- Jeremiah's flight to Egypt
- Possible route of Ishmael to Ammon
- JUDAH Provinces of Babylonian administration

Baalis, king of Ammon, supports Ishmael against Gedaliah

Jeremiah released from prison by Nebuzaradan

Gedeliah establishes his court at Mizpah where he is eventually killed by Ishmael in 582 BC

Johanan and Jewish leaders leave for Egypt, taking Jeremiah against his wishes

GILEAD

SAMARIA

DOR

AMMON

JUDAH

IDUMEA (EDOMITES)

MOAB

DEAD SEA

MEDITERRANEAN SEA

Negev

ASHDOD

KEDARITE ARABS

Jordan River

Jabbok River

Wadi Farìa

Yarkon River

N. Besor

Arnon River

Rabbah (Amman)

Aroer

Mt. Nebo

Kir-hareseth

En-gedi

Jericho

Samaria

Mt. Ebal

Mt. Gerizim

Shechem

Shiloh

Bethel

Ai

Michmash

Geba

Beth-haccherem

Jerusalem

Bethlehem

Tekoa

Beth-horon

Mizpah

Gibeon

Ramah

Kiriath-jearim

Emmaus

Adullam

Beth-zur

Arad

Zorah

Jarmuth

Azekah

Keilah

Mareshah

Lachish

Ono

Lod

Gittaim

Gezer

Timnah

Ekron

Joppa

Ashdod

Ashkelon

Gaza

Ziklag

Gerar

Beer-sheba

Sharuhen

To Egypt

0   5   10   15   20 Miles

0   5   10   15   20 Kilometers

Jeremiah Stays in Judah

40 This is the word that came to Jeremiah from the LORD after Nebuzaradan, captain of the guards, released him at Ramah. When he found him, he was bound in chains with all the exiles of Jerusalem and Judah who were being exiled to Babylon. ² The captain of the guards took Jeremiah and said to him, "The LORD your God decreed this disaster on this place, ³ and the LORD has fulfilled it. He has done just what he decreed. Because you people have sinned against the LORD and have not obeyed him, this thing has happened. ⁴ Now pay attention: Today I am setting you free from the chains that were on your hands. If it pleases you to come with me to Babylon, come, and I will take care of you. But if it seems wrong to you to come with me to Babylon, go no farther.^A Look — the whole land is in front of you. Wherever it seems good and right for you to go, go there." ⁵ When Jeremiah had not yet turned to go, Nebuzaradan said to him,^B "Return^C to Gedaliah son of Ahikam, son of Shaphan, whom the king of Babylon has appointed over the cities of Judah, and stay with him among the people or go wherever it seems right for you to go." So the captain of the guards gave him a ration and a gift and released him. ⁶ Jeremiah therefore went to Gedaliah son of Ahikam at Mizpah, and he stayed with him among the people who remained in the land.

Gedaliah Advises Peace

⁷ All the commanders of the armies that were in the countryside — they and their men — heard that the king of Babylon had appointed Gedaliah son of Ahikam over the land. He had been put in charge of the men, women, and children from among the poorest of the land, who had not been deported to Babylon. ⁸ So they came to Gedaliah at Mizpah. The commanders included Ishmael son of Nethaniah, Johanan and Jonathan the sons of Kareah,

Seraiah son of Tanhumeth, the sons of Ephai the Netophathite, and Jezaniah son of the Maacathite — they and their men.

⁹ Gedaliah son of Ahikam, son of Shaphan, swore an oath to them and their men, assuring them, "Don't be afraid to serve the Chaldeans. Live in the land and serve the king of Babylon, and it will go well for you. ¹⁰ As for me, I am going to live in Mizpah to represent you^D before the Chaldeans who come to us. As for you, gather wine, summer fruit, and oil, place them in your storage jars, and live in the cities you have captured."

¹¹ When all the Judeans in Moab and among the Ammonites and in Edom and in all the other lands also heard that the king of Babylon had left a remnant in Judah and had appointed Gedaliah son of Ahikam, son of Shaphan, over them, ¹² they all returned from all the places where they had been banished and came to the land of Judah, to Gedaliah at Mizpah, and harvested a great amount of wine and summer fruit.

¹³ Meanwhile, Johanan son of Kareah and all the commanders of the armies in the countryside came to Gedaliah at Mizpah ¹⁴ and warned him, "Don't you realize that Baalis, king of the Ammonites, has sent Ishmael son of Nethaniah to kill you?" But Gedaliah son of Ahikam would not believe them. ¹⁵ Then Johanan son of Kareah suggested to Gedaliah in private at Mizpah, "Let me go kill Ishmael son of Nethaniah. No one will know it. Why should he kill you and allow all of Judah that has gathered around you to scatter and the remnant of Judah to perish?"

¹⁶ But Gedaliah son of Ahikam responded to Johanan son of Kareah, "Don't do that! What you're saying about Ishmael is a lie."

Gedaliah Assassinated by Ishmael

41 In the seventh month, Ishmael son of Nethaniah, son of Elishama, of the royal family and one of the king's chief officers,

---

^A 40:4 Lit Babylon, stop   ^B 40:5 Nebuzaradan said to him supplied for clarity   ^C 40:5 LXX reads "But if not, run, return"; Hb obscure   ^D 40:10 Lit to stand

---

40:1–6 This passage amplifies and supplements 39:11–14 (see note there).

40:1 The **word that came to Jeremiah from the LORD** does not seem to be given until 42:9. The captain of the Babylonian guards released Jeremiah at **Ramah**, modern er-Ram, about five miles north of Jerusalem, a staging area for the deportation. Apparently, the Babylonians had mistakenly put Jeremiah in chains to be deported.

40:2–3 Some doubt that Nebuzaradan, a Babylonian, could have spoken such high Hebrew theology. This captain of the guards may also have been acquainted with some of Jeremiah's teachings. Perhaps he had heard them from messages sent by ambassadors, from Jeremiah's letters to those in exile, and from defectors.

40:6 Mizpah was perhaps present-day Tell en-Nasbeh, about eight miles north of

Jerusalem. Others locate it four miles southwest of Ramah at present-day Nabi Samwil. Gedaliah made this site his headquarters or administrative center.

40:7–8 In the absence of leaders, guerrilla bands emerged from hiding after the Babylonians took their captives back to Babylon. Netophah (the **Netophathite**) was a Judean town between Bethlehem and Tekoa. Maacah (the **Maacathite**) was southeast of Hermon.

40:9 The guerrilla bands were pacified by Governor Gedaliah with an oath and advice to settle down in the land. Gedaliah would be the mediator with the Babylonians.

40:10 There were evidently a few towns not destroyed by the Babylonians, especially north of Jerusalem.

40:11–12 Refugee Jews started returning from all over **Moab**, Ammon, **Edom**, and **all the other lands**. Summer was coming to an

end, so it was necessary to gather the harvest (consisting of **a great amount of wine and summer fruit**) for the winter and to pay the Babylonian taxes. Apparently, the conquerors did not use a scorched-earth policy.

40:13–14 Johanan warned Gedaliah that **Baalis, king of the Ammonites**, had sent **Ishmael** to kill the newly appointed governor.

40:15–16 Gedaliah felt the rumors about Ishmael were **a lie**.

41:1 Gedaliah was assassinated in the **seventh month**, our month of October. This occurred either in 587 BC, three months after the fall of Jerusalem, or five years later in 582 BC in connection with another deportation of Jews mentioned in 52:30. The year cannot be fixed with certainty. **Ishmael son of Nethaniah . . . of the royal family**, was a member of the Davidic line and one of King

came with ten men to Gedaliah son of Ahikam at Mizpah. They ate a meal together there in Mizpah, ² but then Ishmael son of Nethaniah and the ten men who were with him got up and struck down Gedaliah son of Ahikam, son of Shaphan, with the sword; he killed the one the king of Babylon had appointed in the land. ³ Ishmael also struck down all the Judeans who were with Gedaliah at Mizpah, as well as the Chaldean soldiers who were there.

⁴ On the day after he had killed Gedaliah, when no one knew yet, ⁵ eighty men came from Shechem, Shiloh, and Samaria who had shaved their beards, torn their clothes, and gashed themselves, and who were carrying grain and incense offerings to bring to the temple of the LORD. ⁶ Ishmael son of Nethaniah came out of Mizpah to meet them, weeping as he came. When he encountered them, he said, "Come to Gedaliah son of Ahikam!" ⁷ But when they came into the city, Ishmael son of Nethaniah and the men with him slaughtered them and threw them into^A a cistern.

⁸ However, there were ten men among them who said to Ishmael, "Don't kill us, for we have hidden treasure in the field — wheat, barley, oil, and honey!" So he stopped and did not kill them along with their companions. ⁹ Now the cistern where Ishmael had thrown all the corpses of the men he had struck down was a large one^B that King Asa had made in the encounter with King Baasha of Israel. Ishmael son of Nethaniah filled it with the slain.

¹⁰ Then Ishmael took captive all the rest of the people of Mizpah including the daughters of the king — all those who remained in Mizpah over whom Nebuzaradan, captain of the guards, had appointed Gedaliah son of Ahikam. Ishmael son of Nethaniah took them captive and set off to cross over to the Ammonites.

The Captives Rescued by Johanan

¹¹ When Johanan son of Kareah and all the commanders of the armies with him heard of all the evil that Ishmael son of Nethaniah had done, ¹² they took all their men and went to fight with Ishmael son of Nethaniah. They found him by the great pool in Gibeon. ¹³ When all the people held by Ishmael saw Johanan son of Kareah and all the commanders of the army with him, they rejoiced. ¹⁴ All the people whom Ishmael had taken captive from Mizpah turned around and rejoined Johanan son of Kareah. ¹⁵ But Ishmael son of Nethaniah escaped from Johanan with eight men and went to the Ammonites. ¹⁶ Johanan son of Kareah and all the commanders of the armies with him then took from Mizpah all the remnant of the people whom he had recovered from Ishmael son of Nethaniah after Ishmael had killed Gedaliah son of Ahikam — men, soldiers, women, children, and court officials whom he brought back from Gibeon. ¹⁷ They left, stopping in Geruth Chimham, which is near Bethlehem, in order to make their way into Egypt, ¹⁸ away from the Chaldeans. For they feared them because Ishmael son of Nethaniah had struck down Gedaliah son of Ahikam, whom the king of Babylon had appointed over the land.

The People Seek Jeremiah's Counsel

42 Then all the commanders of the armies, along with Johanan son of Kareah, Jezaniah son of Hoshaiah, and all the people from the least to the greatest, approached ² the prophet Jeremiah and said, "May our petition come before you; pray to the LORD your God on our behalf, on behalf of this entire remnant (for few of us remain out of the many, as you can see with your own eyes), ³ that the LORD your God may tell us the way we should go and the thing we should do."

---

^A 41:7 Syr; MT reads *slaughtered them in*   ^B 41:9 LXX; MT reads *down by the hand of Gedaliah*

Zedekiah's chief officers. He did not agree with Jeremiah's advice to surrender to the Babylonians either before or after the fall of Jerusalem.

41:2–3 Ishmael came with his **ten men** and sat down for a meal with Gedaliah, who did not suspect treachery. In a breach of Eastern hospitality, they killed both **Judeans** and **Chaldean soldiers** on the spot.

41:4–5 Ishmael continued his slaughter by killing seventy of the **eighty men** who came from **Shechem, Shiloh, and Samaria**, carrying **grain and incense offerings . . . to the temple**. Though the temple was destroyed (note that these were bloodless sacrifices), the plot of ground it had occupied was still regarded as sacred. Even though these men lived in pagan northern Israel, they continued to worship God in Jerusalem.

41:5 Though the eighty pilgrims were genuine worshipers of the Lord, syncretism was evident in the fact that they **gashed themselves**, a cultic practice adopted from Baal

worship yet forbidden in the law of God (5:7; Dt 14:1; 1Kg 18:28).

41:8 Ishmael spared **ten men** among the eighty because they offered him **hidden treasure in the field**. Ishmael's greed and deceit showed his true character.

41:9 The **cistern** into which Ishmael stuffed the bodies of the slain was **a large one** from the time of **King Asa**. Three hundred years previously, Asa had built a fortress at Mizpah from the material he had dragged off from Baasha's construction of a fortress at Ramah (1Kg 15:22; 2Ch 16:6).

41:10 The phrase **daughters of the king** is puzzling. There are no references anywhere else to Zedekiah's daughters, so they may have been women of royal descent.

41:11–18 **Johanan**, who opposed Ishmael, apparently returned to Mizpah, where he learned about Ishmael's treachery. Johanan tracked Ishmael with all the captives he had taken from Mizpah to **the great pool in Gibeon**, about three miles away. This large

pit, hewn out of rock, is about eighty-two feet deep. Twelve of Joab's men fought twelve of Abner's men (2Sm 2:12–16) near this pool at what is today the city of el-Jib. Johanan rescued the captives, and Ishmael escaped with **eight men**. Johanan feared what the Babylonians might do as reprisals for Ishmael's killing spree, so he was determined to take the remnant of people left in Judah off to Egypt.

42:1–3 The commanders and all the people came to Jeremiah to pray for guidance on what to do. They wanted Jeremiah to plead to **the LORD your God** so he would direct them. The prophet agreed to do so. How Jeremiah reached this group—or whether he had been living in Mizpah when Ishmael's attack happened—is not revealed. This **Jezaniah** is not the same as the Jezaniah of 40:8, but he is the same as the Azariah of 43:2; the Greek Septuagint reads Azariah in both 42:1 and 43:2. Then as now, men were known by more than one name.

⁴ So the prophet Jeremiah said to them, "I have heard. I will now pray to the LORD your God according to your words, and I will tell you every word that the LORD answers you; I won't withhold a word from you."

⁵ And they said to Jeremiah, "May the LORD be a true and faithful witness against us if we don't act according to every word the LORD your God sends you to tell us. ⁶ Whether it is pleasant or unpleasant, we will obey the LORD our God to whom we are sending you so that it may go well with us. We will certainly obey the LORD our God!"

Jeremiah's Advice to Stay

⁷ At the end of ten days, the word of the LORD came to Jeremiah, ⁸ and he summoned Johanan son of Kareah, all the commanders of the armies who were with him, and all the people from the least to the greatest.

⁹ He said to them, "This is what the LORD says, the God of Israel to whom you sent me to bring your petition before him: ¹⁰ 'If you will indeed stay in this land, then I will rebuild and not demolish you, and I will plant and not uproot you, because I relent concerning the disaster that I have brought on you. ¹¹ Don't be afraid of the king of Babylon whom you now fear; don't be afraid of him' — this is the LORD's declaration — 'because I am with you to save you and rescue you from him. ¹² I will grant you compassion, and heᴬ will have compassion on you and allow you to return to your own soil.'

¹³ "But if you say, 'We will not stay in this land,' in order to disobey the LORD your God, ¹⁴ and if you say, 'No, instead we'll go to the land of Egypt where we will not see war or hear the sound of the ram's horn or hunger for food, and we'll live there,' ¹⁵ then hear the word of the LORD, remnant of Judah! This is what the LORD of Armies, the God of Israel, says: 'If you are firmly resolved to go to Egypt and stay there for a while, ¹⁶ then the sword you fear will overtake you there in the land of Egypt, and the famine you are worried about will follow on your heelsᴮ there to Egypt, and you will die there. ¹⁷ All who resolve to go to Egypt to stay there for a while will die by the sword, famine, and plague. They will have no survivor or fugitive from the disaster I will bring on them.'

¹⁸ "For this is what the LORD of Armies, the God of Israel, says: 'Just as my anger and fury were poured out on Jerusalem's residents, so will my fury pour out on you if you go to Egypt. You will become an example for cursing, scorn, execration, and disgrace, and you will never see this place again.' ¹⁹ The LORD has spoken concerning you, remnant of Judah: 'Don't go to Egypt.' Know for certain that I have warned you today! ²⁰ You have gone astray at the cost of your livesᶜ because you are the ones who sent me to the LORD your God, saying, 'Pray to the LORD our God on our behalf, and as for all that the LORD our God says, tell it to us, and we'll act accordingly.' ²¹ For I have told you today, but you have not obeyed the LORD your God in everything he has sent me to tell you. ²² Now therefore, know for certain that by the sword, famine, and plague you will die in the place where you desired to go to stay for a while."

Jeremiah's Counsel Rejected

43 When Jeremiah had finished speaking to all the people all the words of the LORD their God — all these words the LORD their God had sent him to give them — ² then Azariahᴰ son of Hoshaiah, Johanan son of Kareah, and all the other arrogant men responded to Jeremiah, "You are speaking a lie! The LORD our God has not sent you to say, 'You must not go to Egypt to stay there for a while!' ³ Rather, Baruch son of Neriah is inciting you against us to hand us over to the Chaldeans to put us to death or to deport us to Babylon!"

⁴ So Johanan son of Kareah, all the commanders of the armies, and all the people failed to obey the LORD's command to stay in the land of Judah. ⁵ Instead, Johanan son of Kareah and all the commanders of the armies led away the whole remnant of Judah, those who had returned to stay in the land of Judah from all the nations where they had been banished. ⁶ They led away the men, women, children, king's daughters, and everyone whom Nebuzaradan, captain of the guards, had allowed to remain with Gedaliah son of Ahikam son of Shaphan. They also led the prophet Jeremiah and Baruch son of Neriah away. ⁷ They went to the land of Egypt because they did not obey the LORD. They went as far as Tahpanhes.

ᴬ**42:12** LXX reads *I* ᴮ**42:16** Lit *will cling after you* ᶜ**42:20** Or *You have led your own selves astray* ᴰ**43:2** = Jezaniah

---

42:4-6 Three times the people affirmed that they would do whatever the Lord told Jeremiah. They would **certainly** (lit "yes, indeed") **obey the LORD.**

42:7-9 Jeremiah was unwilling to speak until he had the Lord's answer, so it took **ten days.** This must have caused more jitters about reprisals from the Babylonians.

42:8-12 Once again Jeremiah delivered an unpopular message. God said he would **not uproot** them if they stayed in the land. This message disappointed them, for they wished to flee to Egypt rather than remain.

42:13-17 If the remnant of Judah's citizens trusted in humans and not in God, terrifying consequences awaited them in Egypt—**sword . . . famine,** and death. Though Egypt was defeated at the battle of Carchemish in 605 BC, she had not experienced warfare in her own country; indeed, Egypt was the only country that had escaped this scourge. The **remnant of Judah** are those who remained after the city's fall in 587 BC.

42:18-22 The disobedient refugees would experience exactly what they were trying to avoid by going to Egypt. The trio of judgments is sounded once more: **sword, famine, and plague** (cp. vv. 16–17; 14:12).

43:1-3 The leaders accused Jeremiah of **speaking a lie.** They charged that Baruch (Jeremiah's secretary) was inciting him against them to **deport** them to **Babylon.**

43:4-7 These verses are bookended in a paragraph that has at its beginning and end the words "they **did not obey the LORD**" (see vv. 4,7). The rebellious group arrived in Egypt at **Tahpanhes,** a fortified city on the northern border of Lower Egypt where one of Pharaoh's palaces was situated. It was

God's Sign to the People in Egypt

8 Then the word of the LORD came to Jeremiah at Tahpanhes: **9** "Pick up some large stones and set them in the mortar of the brick pavement that is at the opening of Pharaoh's palace at Tahpanhes. Do this in the sight of the Judean men **10** and tell them, 'This is what the LORD of Armies, the God of Israel, says: I will send for my servant Nebuchadnezzar king of Babylon, and I will place his throne on these stones that I have embedded, and he will pitch his pavilion over them. **11** He will come and strike down the land of Egypt — those destined for death, to death; those destined for captivity, to captivity; and those destined for the sword, to the sword. **12** I* will kindle a fire in the temples of Egypt's gods, and he will burn them and take them captive. He will clean the land of Egypt as a shepherd picks lice off* his clothes, and he will leave there unscathed. **13** He will smash the sacred pillars of the sun temple** in the land of Egypt and burn the temples of the Egyptian gods.'"

God's Judgment against His People in Egypt

44 This is the word that came to Jeremiah for all the Jews living in the land of Egypt — at Migdol, Tahpanhes, Memphis, and in the land of Pathros: **2** "This is what the LORD of Armies, the God of Israel, says: You have seen all the disaster I brought against Jerusalem and all Judah's cities. Look, they are a ruin today without an inhabitant in them **3** because of the evil they committed to anger me, by going and burning incense to serve other gods that they, you, and your ancestors did not know. **4** So I sent you all my servants the prophets time and time again,* saying, 'Don't commit this detestable action that I hate.' **5** But they did not listen or pay attention; they did not turn from their evil or stop burning incense to other gods. **6** So my fierce wrath poured out

and burned in Judah's cities and Jerusalem's streets so that they became the desolate ruin they are today.

7 "So now, this is what the LORD, the God of Armies, the God of Israel, says: Why are you doing such terrible harm to yourselves? You are cutting off man and woman, infant and nursing baby from Judah, leaving yourselves without a remnant. **8** You are angering me by the work of your hands. You are burning incense to other gods in the land of Egypt where you have gone to stay for a while. As a result, you will be cut off and become an example for cursing and insult among all the nations of earth. **9** Have you forgotten the evils of your ancestors, the evils of Judah's kings, the evils of their wives, your own evils, and the evils of your wives that were committed in the land of Judah and in the streets of Jerusalem? **10** They have not become humble to this day, and they have not feared or followed my instruction or my statutes that I set before you and your ancestors.

11 "Therefore, this is what the LORD of Armies, the God of Israel, says: I am about to set my face against you to bring disaster, to cut off all Judah. **12** And I will take away the remnant of Judah, those who have set their face to go to the land of Egypt to stay there. All of them will meet their end in the land of Egypt. They will fall by the sword; they will meet their end by famine. From the least to the greatest, they will die by the sword and by famine. Then they will become an example for cursing, scorn, execration, and disgrace. **13** I will punish those living in the land of Egypt just as I punished Jerusalem by sword, famine, and plague. **14** Then the remnant of Judah — those going to live for a while there in the land of Egypt — will have no fugitive or survivor to return to the land of Judah where they are longing* to return to stay, for they will not return except for a few fugitives."

^43:12 LXX, Syr, Vg read *He*   ^43:12 Or *will wrap himself in the land of Egypt as a shepherd wraps himself in*   ^43:13 Or *Beth-shemesh*   ^43:13 = of Heliopolis   ^44:4 Lit *prophets, rising up early and sending*   ^44:14 Lit *lifting up their soul*

probably modern Tell el-Dafenneh. Ironically, the remnant of Jews fled back to the land they had escaped from about nine hundred years earlier.

43:8–11 The Lord told Jeremiah to pick up some large stones and set them in the mortar of the brick pavement **at the opening of Pharaoh's palace**. Then Jeremiah was to announce to the remnant of Judah that Nebuchadnezzar would **place his throne on these stones** (v. 10). Egypt would experience the same thing that Judah had been through. Nebuchadnezzar did invade Egypt in the twenty-seventh year of his reign (568–567 BC; cp. Ezk 29:17–20), as Jeremiah predicted. What happened to Jeremiah and Baruch remains a mystery.

43:13 The **sun temple** is a reference to Heliopolis (Hb *On*), known for its temple to the sun god Re. This city, five miles northeast of Cairo, was noted for its obelisks (**sacred**

pillars). Besides those that were smashed, these obelisks were later carted off to New York, Rome, London, Istanbul, and Alexandria, leaving only one at On. Originally two rows of pillars lined the approach to Re's temple.

44:1–30 This chapter contains Jeremiah's last recorded public words. It is not known where or when he died. One tradition says he was murdered in Egypt by his fellow citizens of Judah.

44:1 Migdol, meaning "Tower," was on Egypt's northeastern border. It is located in modern Tell el-Her and is mentioned in the time of the exodus (Ex 14:2; Nm 33:7) as well as in Ezekiel's time (Ezk 29:10; 30:6). On **Tahpanhes**, see note at 43:4–7. **Memphis**, or Noph, was located on the west bank of the Nile River about fifteen miles south of Cairo, approximately at the head of the Nile delta. **Pathros** (lit "the land of the south") was located in Upper (i.e., southern) Egypt,

approximately halfway between Cairo and the Aswan Dam, about three hundred miles south of Memphis.

44:2–14 This passage is divided into three sections, each beginning with **this is what the LORD of Armies, the God of Israel, says** (vv. 2,7,11). Verses 2–6 review Israel's history, vv. 7–10 indict the rebellious fugitives in Egypt, and vv. 11–14 announce judgment on the disobedient people.

44:7–9 In these verses God posed four questions. (1) Why are you **doing such terrible harm to yourselves**? (2) Why are you **angering me by the work of your hands**? (3) Why are you **burning incense to other gods in . . . Egypt**? (4) How can you have **forgotten** the long history of evil that has marked your lives?

44:11–14 This is an enlarged warning over what Jeremiah declared in 42:17–18.

The People's Stubborn Response

[15] However, all the men who knew that their wives were burning incense to other gods, all the women standing by — a great assembly — and all the people who were living in the land of Egypt at Pathros answered Jeremiah, [16] "As for the word you spoke to us in the name of the LORD, we are not going to listen to you! [17] Instead, we will do everything we promised:[A] we will burn incense to the queen of heaven[B] and offer drink offerings to her just as we, our ancestors, our kings, and our officials did in Judah's cities and in Jerusalem's streets. Then we had enough food, we were well off, and we saw no disaster, [18] but from the time we ceased to burn incense to the queen of heaven and to offer her drink offerings, we have lacked everything, and through sword and famine we have met our end."

[19] And the women said,[C] "When we burned incense to the queen of heaven and poured out drink offerings to her, was it apart from our husbands' knowledge that we made sacrificial cakes in her image and poured out drink offerings to her?"

[20] But Jeremiah responded to all the people — the men, women, and all the people who were answering him: [21] "As for the incense you burned in Judah's cities and in Jerusalem's streets — you, your ancestors, your kings, your officials, and the people of the land — did the LORD not remember them? He brought this to mind. [22] The LORD can no longer bear your evil deeds and the detestable acts you have committed, so your land has become a waste, a desolation, and an example for cursing, without inhabitant, as you see today. [23] Because you burned incense and sinned against the LORD and didn't obey the LORD and didn't follow his instruction, his statutes, and his testimonies, this disaster has come to you, as you see today."

[24] Then Jeremiah said to all the people, including all the women, "Hear the word of the LORD, all you people of Judah who are in the land of Egypt. [25] This is what the LORD of Armies, the God of Israel, says: 'As for you and your wives, you women have spoken with your mouths, and you men fulfilled it by your deeds, saying, "We will keep our vows that we have made to burn incense to the queen of heaven and to pour out drink offerings for her." Go ahead, confirm your vows! Keep your vows!'

[26] "Therefore, hear the word of the LORD, all you Judeans who live in the land of Egypt: 'I have sworn by my great name, says the LORD, that my name will never again be invoked by anyone of Judah in all the land of Egypt, saying, "As the Lord GOD lives." [27] I am watching over them for disaster and not for good, and everyone from Judah who is in the land of Egypt will meet his end by sword or famine until they are finished off. [28] Those who escape the sword will return from the land of Egypt to the land of Judah only few in number, and the whole remnant of Judah, the ones going to the land of Egypt to stay there for a while, will know whose word stands, mine or theirs! [29] This will be a sign to you' — this is the LORD's declaration — 'that I will punish you in this place, so you may know that my words of disaster concerning you will certainly come to pass. [30] This is what the LORD says: I am about to hand over Pharaoh Hophra, Egypt's king, to his enemies, to those who intend to take his life, just as I handed over Judah's King Zedekiah to Babylon's King Nebuchadnezzar, who was his enemy, the one who intended to take his life.'"

The LORD's Message to Baruch

45 This is the word that the prophet Jeremiah spoke to Baruch son of Neriah when he wrote these words on a scroll at Jeremiah's dictation[D] in the fourth year of Jehoiakim son of Josiah, king of Judah: [2] "This is what the LORD, the God of Israel, says to you, Baruch: [3] 'You have said, "Woe is me, because the LORD has added misery to my pain! I am worn out with[E] groaning and have found no rest."'

[4] "This is what you are to say to him: 'This is what the LORD says: "What I have built I am

---

[A] **44:17** Lit *do every word that came from our mouth*   [B] **44:17** = Ashtoreth, or Astarte   [C] **44:19** LXX, Syr; MT omits *And the women said*   [D] **45:1** Lit *scroll from Jeremiah's mouth*   [E] **45:3** Lit *I labored in my*

44:15–19 This is one of the most surprising passages in the Bible. In blatant defiance of God, **all the men** stated their preference for the **queen of heaven** (see note at 7:18), for by their logic their harsh fate was not a punishment from the God of Israel but was instead a result of ceasing sacrifices to her! **44:16–18** From the perspective of the renegade troupe of Judeans in Egypt, Judah's economy and overall health were good before the 621 BC revival under King Josiah, but since that revival, only hardships had come. **44:20–30** Chronologically speaking these verses contain the last messages of Jeremiah recorded in this book. The remaining chapters stem from an earlier time in his life.

44:24–25 Jeremiah took up a second point in the rebels' argument—that they must be faithful to their vows (cp. v. 17). His response was ironic, if not sarcastic: **Go ahead, confirm your vows! Keep your vows!** Jeremiah must have had in mind 42:4–6, where the people had vowed to do whatever the Lord commanded. How could they keep vows to a pagan idol when they could not even keep their vows to the living God? **44:30 Pharaoh Hophra** of Egypt (589–570 BC) was an ally of King Zedekiah of Judah. He had sent his troops to help besieged Jerusalem (37:5). But he would also die by the hands of his enemies, just as surely as King Zedekiah fell into Babylonian hands. Pharaoh Hophra was assassinated by Amasis, who

became Pharaoh in 570 BC, just before the Babylonians invaded Egypt (43:13–26; Ez 29:17–20; 30:20–26). **45:1–5** Once again, 605 BC seems to be a marker for the history of Israel and Judah and for the grand story of the Bible (see notes at 25:1; 36:1). **45:1 Baruch** ("Blessed") **son of Neriah** ("The Lord is my lamp") came from a notable family. He was the grandson of Mahseiah (32:12), governor of Jerusalem under King Josiah (2Ch 34:8, Maaseiah). The phrase **these words** is usually linked with the scroll that King Zedekiah burned in chap. 36. This could be the reason for Baruch's depression in this chapter. His brother had attained status in government, but his work of writing down

about to demolish, and what I have planted I am about to uproot — the whole land! ⁵ But as for you, do you pursue great things for yourself? Stop pursuing! For I am about to bring disaster on all humanity" — this is the LORD's declaration — "but I will grant you your life like the spoils of war wherever you go." ' "

PROPHECIES AGAINST THE NATIONS

46 This is the word of the LORD that came to the prophet Jeremiah about the nations:

Prophecies against Egypt

² About Egypt and the army of Pharaoh Neco, Egypt's king, which was defeated at Carchemish on the Euphrates River by King Nebuchadnezzar of Babylon in the fourth year of Judah's King Jehoiakim son of Josiah:

³   Deploy small shields and large;
     approach for battle!
⁴   Harness the horses;
     mount the steeds;^A
     take your positions
         with helmets on!
     Polish the lances;
     put on armor!
⁵   Why have I seen this?
     They are terrified,
     they are retreating,
     their warriors are crushed,
     they flee headlong,
     they never look back,
     terror is on every side!
         This is the LORD's declaration.
⁶   The swift cannot flee,
     and the warrior cannot escape!

     In the north by the bank
         of the Euphrates River,
     they stumble and fall.

⁷   Who is this, rising like the Nile,
     with waters that churn like rivers?
⁸   Egypt rises like the Nile,
     and its waters churn like rivers.
     He boasts, "I will go up, I will cover
         the earth;
     I will destroy cities with their residents."
⁹   Rise up, you cavalry!
     Race furiously, you chariots!
     Let the warriors march out —
     Cush and Put,
     who are able to handle shields,
     and the men of Lud,
     who are able to handle and string
         the bow.
¹⁰ That day belongs to the Lord, the GOD
         of Armies,
     a day of vengeance to avenge himself
         against his adversaries.
     The sword will devour and be satisfied;
     it will drink its fill of their blood,
     because it will be a sacrifice to the Lord,
         the GOD of Armies,
     in the northern land
         by the Euphrates River.

¹¹ Go up to Gilead and get balm,
     Virgin Daughter Egypt!
     You have multiplied remedies in vain;
     there is no healing for you.
¹² The nations have heard
         of your dishonor,
     and your cries fill the earth,

---

^A 46:4 Or *mount up, riders*

---

the dictated words from Jeremiah the prophet had gone up in smoke. He had nothing to show for his labors.
45:5 It is not clear what **great things** Baruch was pursuing for himself. He may have been guilty of self-serving ambition. On the other hand, he may have wanted to see the mighty deeds of God that were promised in Dt 10:21 (cp. Ps 71:19). The most God promised to Baruch was that he would **grant** him his **life like the spoils of war**. That was the same promise given to the Ethiopian eunuch who saved Jeremiah's life (39:18).
46:1–51:64 Even though the Greek Septuagint version of the OT (third century BC) placed these prophecies against the nations after 25:13, there is no reason to doubt that they came from Jeremiah the prophet. It was not unusual for prophets to include a word from God for the foreign nations. Often these messages were sent to foreign capitals by ambassadors living in Jerusalem. Rarely were they delivered personally by the prophet. The prophecies focus on ten nations—Egypt, Philistia, Moab, Ammon, Edom, Syria (Damascus), Kedar, Hazor, Elam, and Babylon. Possibly the messages were given at various times during Jeremiah's ministry, then collected under the common theme of judgment for failure to live up to God's standards.

46:1 This verse with its introduction serves as a superscription for the entire collection in chaps. 46 through 51. The same formula appears at 14:1; 47:1; and 49:34.
46:2 The phrase **the army of Pharaoh Neco, Egypt's king, which was defeated at Carchemish** refers to the Pharaoh who killed King Josiah at Megiddo in 609 BC. Neco placed Jehoahaz on the throne for three months and then removed him, imprisoned him at Riblah, and installed Jehoiakim in his place. In Jehoiakim's fourth year, Neco II went to aid the Assyrians against the rising Babylonian menace, but was defeated at the battle of Carchemish in 605 BC.
46:3–12 These verses contain one of the most vivid poems in the OT. It was written either just before or just after the Babylonians thrashed Egypt. The poem describes the Egyptian army preparing for its confrontation with Nebuchadnezzar. It bristles with sarcasm.
46:3 The Egyptians used **small shields** (small round bucklers used by lightly armed soldiers) and **large** (for protecting the whole body of the heavily armed soldier) in this battle.
46:4 The words **horses** and **steeds** show the charioteers were readied at the same time as the infantry.

46:5 No sooner had the battle begun than the Egyptians broke ranks and fled for their lives. **Terror is on every side!** shows that panic was widespread. This expression is a favorite of Jeremiah. He used it of the "foe from the north" (see 6:25), and for his detractor (20:3). It was also used as a taunt against Jeremiah himself (20:10).
46:7–8 Egypt's resurgence under Pharaoh Neco II is compared to the annual flood of the Nile River. Egypt fancied itself as one who **will cover the earth**, presumably like the Nile River. The same metaphor is used of Assyria (Is 8:7–8).
46:9 Apparently mercenary troops accompanied the Egyptian army from **Cush**, or Ethiopia, to the south of Egypt. **Put** may be the Punt of Egyptian literature. It bordered the east African coast. **Lud** is variously understood as Lydia in Asia Minor (cp. the Ludites of Ezk 30:5) or the land in North Africa (Gn 10:13).
46:10 A theological interpretation of Egypt's defeat is given here. Egypt's defeat is viewed as **a sacrifice to the Lord** (cp. Is 34:5–7; Ezk 39:17–20; Zph 1:7).
46:11 Gilead's plant that produced healing medicine cannot be identified with certainty, but the association of this healing balm with Gilead is strong (8:22; 51:8; Gn 37:25). **Virgin**

because warrior stumbles
against warrior
and together both of them have fallen.

¹³ This is the word the LORD spoke to the prophet Jeremiah about the coming of King Nebuchadnezzar of Babylon to defeat the land of Egypt:

¹⁴ Announce it in Egypt, and proclaim it
in Migdol!
Proclaim it in Memphis
and in Tahpanhes!
Say, "Take positions! Prepare yourself,
for the sword devours all around you."
¹⁵ Why have your strong ones
been swept away?
Each has not stood,
for the LORD has thrust him down.
¹⁶ He continues to stumble.
Indeed, each falls over the other.
They say, "Get up! Let's return to our people
and to our native land,
away from the oppressor's sword."
¹⁷ There they will cry out,
"Pharaoh king of Egypt was all noise;
he let the opportune moment pass."

¹⁸ As I live —
this is the King's declaration;
the LORD of Armies is his name —
the king of Babylon^A will come
like Tabor among the mountains
and like Carmel by the sea.
¹⁹ Get your bags ready for exile,
inhabitant of Daughter Egypt!
For Memphis will become a desolation,
uninhabited ruins.

²⁰ Egypt is a beautiful young cow,
but a horsefly from the north is coming
against her.^B

²¹ Even her mercenaries among her
are like stall-fed calves.
They too will turn back;
together they will flee;
they will not take their stand,
for the day of their calamity is coming
on them,
the time of their punishment.
²² Egypt will hiss like a slithering snake,^C
for the enemy will come with an army;
with axes they will come against her
like those who cut trees.
²³ They will cut down her forest —
this is the LORD's declaration —
though it is dense,
for they are more numerous
than locusts;
they cannot be counted.
²⁴ Daughter Egypt will be put to shame,
handed over to a northern people.

²⁵ The LORD of Armies, the God of Israel, says, "I am about to punish Amon, god of Thebes, along with Pharaoh, Egypt, her gods, and her kings — Pharaoh and those trusting in him. ²⁶ I will hand them over to those who intend to take their lives — to King Nebuchadnezzar of Babylon and his officers. But after this, Egypt^D will be inhabited again as in ancient times." This is the LORD's declaration.

Reassurance for Israel
²⁷ But you, my servant Jacob,
do not be afraid,
and do not be discouraged, Israel,
for without fail I will save you
from far away,
and your descendants from the land
of their captivity!
Jacob will return and have calm and quiet
with no one to frighten him.

---

^A 46:18 Lit *He*   ^B 46:20 Some Hb mss, LXX, Syr; other Hb mss read *is coming, coming goes*   ^C 46:22 Lit *Her sound is like a snake as it*   ^D 46:26 Lit *it*

Daughter Egypt is an unusual title for that nation, since it brings to mind "Virgin Israel" (18:13; 31:4,21).
46:13 With the defeat of the Egyptian force at Carchemish, Nebuchadnezzar advanced toward Egypt. In August of 605 BC Nabopolassar, the father of Nebuchadnezzar, died. His son rushed back to Babylon to secure his throne. But the advance on Egypt soon resumed. By the end of 604 BC the Babylonian army had captured and sacked Ashkelon (47:2–9). Then it pressed on toward Egypt.
46:14 Migdol was on the northeastern border of Egypt. Noph or **Memphis** was the ancient capital of Lower Egypt, situated twenty-five to thirty miles south of Cairo. Its kings were the pyramid builders. **Tahpanhes** or Daphne was a fortress southwest of the Pelusium near the northwest border of Egypt (see note at 2:16). Egypt was to **take positions** and prepare themselves. The battle with Babylon was about to begin.

46:16 **They say** introduces two sentences spoken by the foreign mercenaries supporting Egypt. They decided to **get up** and **return** home.
46:17 Pharaoh Hophra of Egypt had boasted of what he would do, but he was **all noise**. He **let the opportune moment pass**. This Pharaoh had promised to come to the aid of King Zedekiah during the final siege of Jerusalem (37:5–6), but it was only talk.
46:18 Tabor rises 1,800 feet in the Plain of Esdraelon while **Carmel by the sea** (Mediterranean Sea) rises 1,700 feet on its western face. Neither peak is especially tall, but because of their isolated positions and their steep slopes, they stand out against their surroundings. So victorious Babylon would tower over Egypt like these mountain peaks.
46:19 Jeremiah advised the Egyptians to pack their **bags** for **exile**. Memphis, capital of Lower Egypt, would become **uninhabited ruins**.

46:20 Egypt is pictured as a "beautiful heifer," but King Nebuchadnezzar is depicted as a **horsefly from the north** that would sting this young cow.
46:22–24 The **snake** figure for Egypt was appropriate. It was their insignia of royalty. Despite the snake's hiding in the **forest**, the woodcutters will chop down the forest. Egypt will be handed over to the Babylonians.
46:25–26 The **God of Israel** will punish **Amon, god of Thebes**. Amon was the chief god of the city of Thebes, the capital of Upper Egypt. Later the god Amon was merged with Re to become Amon-Re, the sun god and the god of the rulers of Egypt. However, after Thebes is punished, there is a promise of restoration, which is repeated for other nations as well (48:47; 49:6,39).
46:27–28 These verses are virtually the same as 30:10–11. If Egypt had the prospect of restoration, this was even truer for Israel and Judah.

²⁸ And you, my servant Jacob,
   do not be afraid —
     this is the LORD's declaration —
for I will be with you.
I will bring destruction
   on all the nations
where I have banished you,
but I will not bring destruction on you.
I will discipline you with justice,
and I will by no means
   leave you unpunished.

Prophecies against the Philistines

47 This is the word of the LORD that came to the prophet Jeremiah about the Philistines before Pharaoh defeated Gaza. ² This is what the LORD says:

Look, water is rising from the north
and becoming an overflowing wadi.
It will overflow the land and everything
   in it,
the cities and their inhabitants.
The people will cry out,
and every inhabitant of the land
   will wail.
³ At the sound of the stomping hooves
   of his stallions,
the rumbling of his chariots,
and the clatter of their wheels,
fathers will not turn back for their sons.
They will be utterly helpless^A
⁴ on account of the day that is coming
to destroy all the Philistines,
to cut off from Tyre and Sidon
every remaining ally.
Indeed, the LORD is about to destroy
   the Philistines,

the remnant of the coastland
   of Caphtor.^B
⁵ Baldness is coming to Gaza;
Ashkelon will become silent.
Remnant of their valley,
how long will you gash yourself?

⁶ Oh, sword of the LORD!
How long will you be restless?
Go back to your sheath;
be still; be silent!
⁷ How can it^C rest
when the LORD has given it a command?
He has assigned it
against Ashkelon and the shore
   of the sea.

Prophecies against Moab

48 About Moab, this is what the LORD of Armies, the God of Israel, says:

Woe to Nebo, because it is
   about to be destroyed;
Kiriathaim will be put to shame;
   it will be taken captive.
The fortress will be put to shame
   and dismayed!
² There is no longer praise for Moab;
they plan harm against her
   in Heshbon:
Come, let's cut her off
   from nationhood.
Also, Madmen, you will be silenced;
the sword will follow you.
³ A voice cries out from Horonaim,
"devastation and a crushing blow!"
⁴ Moab will be shattered;
her little ones will cry out.

---

^A47:3 Lit *Because of weakened hands*   ^B47:4 Probably Crete   ^C47:7 LXX, Vg; MT reads *you*

47:1 The phrase **before Pharaoh defeated Gaza** is part of the chronological notation, because the real invader will come out of the north and not from Egypt. But on what occasion did Pharaoh capture Gaza? Some link it with Neco's 609 BC defeat and slaying of King Josiah at Megiddo. This happened as Neco went to assist the Assyrians against the Babylonians. Others say Gaza was attacked in late 601 BC after Neco met Nebuchadnezzar and sent him home to Babylon to regroup his forces when Neco captured Gaza. The matter is not certain.
47:2 The reference to the **water . . . rising from the north** surely points to the Babylonians.
47:3 So deep will be the terror be that the Philistines will be powerless to fight, forsaking even their own children.
47:4 The Philistines and the Phoenicians are grouped together here; presumably there was an alliance between their cities. If so, then Nebuchadnezzar's actions against the Phoenician cities of **Tyre and Sidon** were merely preparatory for what was to come for the Philistine cities. Nebuchadnezzar besieged Tyre in 594 and 587 BC. The phrase **the Philistines, the remnant of the coastland of Caphtor** accords with Am 9:7 where Caphtor is described as the original home of

the Philistines. Caphtor is usually identified with the island of Crete and the Aegean Islands. The Philistines apparently belonged to a group known as the Sea Peoples.
47:5 There are three signs of mourning here: shaving one's head to **baldness**, being **silent**, and inflicting gashes on oneself (16:6; 41:5). Two alternate translations for a **remnant of their valley** should be noted. First, the Hebrew word *'emeq*, rendered "valley," may be the same as the Ugaritic/Canaanite word *'mq*, meaning "strength." In this light the phrase could be translated, "O you last of their strength." Second, the LXX reads "Anakim," which links the people of Gaza and Ashkelon with the giants that were in the land before the Israelites invaded it (Nm 13:22–23; Dt 1:28). Joshua 11:22 notes remnants of this people group still lived in Gaza, Gath, and Ashdod.
47:6-7 Attempts to quiet the **sword of the LORD** would prove futile. What had been decreed by the Lord **against Ashkelon and the shore of the sea** was finished when Nebuchadnezzar overran Ashkelon after a siege in 604–603 BC. The attack against Ashkelon prompted King Jehoiakim to proclaim a fast in Jerusalem (chap. 36). This fast gave Baruch the opportunity to read Jeremiah's scroll.

48:1–47 This chapter contains Jeremiah's prophecy against the Moabites. The Moabites were the descendants of Lot's incestuous relationship with his oldest daughter (Gn 19:30–38). Moab was located east of the Dead Sea, bounded on the south by the river Zered, on the north by the river Arnon, on the east by the desert, and on the west by the Dead Sea. A few towns mentioned in this chapter were north of the Arnon, since this small country extended north from time to time. The tribes of Reuben and Gad originally occupied this land (Nm 32:33–38). But in the time of Mesha, king of Moab (ninth century BC), Moab regained these areas. It was mostly a plateau with fertile lands.
48:1 **Nebo** was twelve miles east of the northern tip of the Dead Sea. **Kiriathaim** is possibly modern el-Qereiyat, about five miles northwest of Dibon.
48:2 **Heshbon** was the capital city of the Amorite king Sihon (Nm 21:25–30).
48:3–4 **Horonaim** is unknown. **Her little ones will cry out** is rendered in the LXX as "their cry can be heard clear to Zoar." Zoar, one of the five cities of the plain (Gn 13:10–11), was probably located at the end of the Dead Sea.

⁵ For on the Ascent to Luhith
they will be weeping continually,ᴬ
and on the descent to Horonaim
will be heard cries of distress
over the destruction:

⁶ Flee! Save your lives!
Be like a juniper bushᴮ
in the wilderness.

⁷ Because you trust in your works
and treasures,
you will be captured also.
Chemosh will go into exile
with his priests and officials.

⁸ The destroyer will move
against every town;
not one town will escape.
The valley will perish,
and the plain will be annihilated,
as the LORD has said.

⁹ Make Moab a salt marsh,ᶜ
for she will run away;ᴰ
her towns will become a desolation,
without inhabitant.

¹⁰ The one who does
the LORD's business deceitfullyᴱ
is cursed,
and the one who withholds
his sword from bloodshed is cursed.

¹¹ Moab has been left quiet
since his youth,
settled like wine on its dregs.
He hasn't been poured
from one container to another
or gone into exile.
So his taste has remained the same,
and his aroma hasn't changed.

¹² Therefore look, the days
are coming —
this is the LORD's declaration —
when I will send pourers to him,
who will pour him out.

They will empty his containers
and smash his jars.
¹³ Moab will be put to shame
because of Chemosh,
just as the house of Israel was
put to shame
because of Bethel
that they trusted in.

¹⁴ How can you say,
"We are warriors —
valiant men for battle"?

¹⁵ The destroyer of Moab and its towns
has come up,ᶠ
and the best of its young men
have gone down to slaughter.
This is the King's declaration;
the LORD of Armies is his name.

¹⁶ Moab's calamity is near at hand;
his disaster is rushing swiftly.

¹⁷ Mourn for him,
all you surrounding nations,
everyone who knows his name.
Say, "How the mighty scepter
is shattered,
the glorious staff!"

¹⁸ Come down from glory;
sit on parched ground,
resident of the daughter of Dibon,
for the destroyer of Moab has come
against you;
he has destroyed your fortresses.

¹⁹ Stand by the highway and watch,
resident of Aroer!
Ask him who is fleeing or her
who is escaping,
"What happened?"

²⁰ Moab is put to shame,
indeed dismayed.
Wail and cry out!
Declare by the Arnon
that Moab is destroyed.

ᴬ48:5 Lit *Luhith, weeping goes up with weeping*   ᴮ48:6 Or *like Aroer*; Is 17:2; Jr 48:19   ᶜ48:9 LXX reads *a sign*; Vg reads *a flower*; Syr, Tg read *a crown*   ᴰ48:9 Hb obscure   ᴱ48:10 Or *negligently*   ᶠ48:15 Or *Moab is destroyed; he has come up against its cities*

48:5 The **Ascent to Luhith** is otherwise unknown.

48:7 Chemosh, the national deity of Moab (Nm 21:29, 1Kg 11:7,33), is known on the Moabite Stone as Ashtar-Kemosh. Ashtar in Canaan was associated with the morning star, so it seems he was one of the astral deities. Solomon built a high place for Chemosh (1Kg 11:7) so the Moabite women in his harem could have a place of worship.

48:8 The valley probably refers to the Jordan Valley, which bordered Moab on the west. The **plain** signifies the plateau of the Transjordanian highland where most Moabite cities were located.

48:9 The phrase **make Moab a salt marsh** is the preferred reading following Ugaritic/Canaanite *sisuma*, "salt." Sowing an enemy's fields with salt was a way to destroy his land (Jdg 9:45). **She will run away** is obscure, but

it could also be rendered, "She shall surely be laid in ruins."

48:11 Complacency is implied by the phrase **settled like wine on its dregs**—an apt metaphor for Moab and her renowned vineyards. Moab **has been left quiet**. Even though she had been a tributary nation to Israel, she had never gone into exile. Since she was off the main trail, she had experienced few if any invasions.

48:12 God will send **pourers to him** [Moab], **who will pour him out** (lit "I will send tilters who will tilt him"). Tilters worked in wine cellars to decant the wine. In order for wine to age properly, it was not left to settle on its dregs in the vessel too long (Zph 1:12). After forty days or so it was poured into other vessels and separated from its dregs. If not handled properly, the wine would not achieve the quality the tilters sought. In the

same way Moab had rested on her laurels, but this time of complacency was over.

48:13 Moab will be put to shame because of Chemosh. In parallel to Chemosh, **the house of Israel** [would be] **put to shame because of Bethel**. This must be an allusion to the calf worship set up by King Jeroboam in Bethel (1Kg 12:26–33).

48:17 In about 580 BC Moab lost her independence forever.

48:18 The phrase **resident of the daughter of Dibon** addresses this city that stood on two hills. Dibon, modern Diban, was thirteen miles east of the Dead Sea and four miles north of the Arnon River. The Moabite Stone, which mentions Dibon, was discovered here in AD 1868.

48:19 Aroer was the northernmost city of Reuben on the north side of the Arnon River.

²¹ "Judgment has come to the land of the plateau — to Holon, Jahzah, Mephaath, ²² Dibon, Nebo, Beth-diblathaim, ²³ Kiriathaim, Beth-gamul, Beth-meon, ²⁴ Kerioth, Bozrah, and all the towns of the land of Moab, those far and near. ²⁵ Moab's horn is chopped off; his arm is shattered."

This is the LORD's declaration.

²⁶ "Make him drunk, because he has exalted himself against the LORD. Moab will wallow in his own vomit, and he will also become a laughingstock. ²⁷ Wasn't Israel a laughingstock to you? Was he ever found among thieves? For whenever you speak of him you shake your head."

²⁸   Abandon the towns! Live in the cliffs,
    residents of Moab!
  Be like a dove
    that nests inside the mouth of a cave.

²⁹   We have heard of Moab's pride,
    great pride, indeed —
  his insolence, arrogance, pride,
    and haughty heart.
³⁰   I know his outburst.
    This is the LORD's declaration.
  It is empty.
  His boast is empty.
³¹   Therefore, I will wail over Moab.
  I will cry out for Moab, all of it;
  he will moan for the men of Kir-heres.
³²   I will weep for you, vine of Sibmah,
  with more than the weeping
    for Jazer.
  Your tendrils have extended
    to the sea;
  they have reached to the sea
    and to Jazer.ᴬ
  The destroyer has fallen
    on your summer fruit
    and grape harvest.
³³   Gladness and celebration are taken
    from the fertile field
    and from the land of Moab.
  I have stopped the flow of wine
    from the winepresses;

no one will tread with shouts of joy.
The shouting is not a shout of joy.

³⁴ "There is a cry from Heshbon to Elealeh; they make their voices heard as far as Jahaz — from Zoar to Horonaim and Eglath-shelishiyah — because even the Waters of Nimrim have become desolate. ³⁵ In Moab, I will stop" — this is the LORD's declaration — "the one who offers sacrifices on the high place and burns incense to his gods. ³⁶ Therefore, my heart moans like flutes for Moab, and my heart moans like flutes for the people of Kir-heres. And therefore, the wealth he has gained has perished. ³⁷ Indeed, every head is bald and every beard is chopped short. On every hand is a gash and sackcloth around the waist. ³⁸ On all the rooftops of Moab and in her public squares, everyone is mourning because I have shattered Moab like a jar no one wants." This is the LORD's declaration. ³⁹ "How broken it is! They wail! How Moab has turned his back! He is ashamed. Moab will become a laughingstock and a shock to all those around him."

⁴⁰ For this is what the LORD says:
  Look! He will swoop down like an eagle
    and spread his wings against Moab.
⁴¹   The towns haveᴮ been captured,
    and the strongholds seized.
  In that day the heart
    of Moab's warriors
  will be like the heart of a woman
    with contractions.
⁴²   Moab will be destroyed as a people
  because he has exalted himself
    against the LORD.
⁴³   Panic, pit, and trap
  await you, resident of Moab.
    This is the LORD's declaration.
⁴⁴   He who flees from the panic will fall
    in the pit,
  and he who climbs from the pit
  will be captured in the trap,
  for I will bring against Moab
    the year of their punishment.
    This is the LORD's declaration.

ᴬ48:32 Some Hb mss read *reached as far as Jazer*   ᴮ48:41 Or *Kerioth has*

48:21–24 Eleven towns of Moab are mentioned in these verses.
48:21 The Moabite Stone mentions the towns of **Jahzah** . . . **Dibon** . . . **Beth-diblathaim, Kiriathaim** . . . **Beth-meon, Kerioth,** and **Bozrah,** even though the identification of some of these towns is uncertain. Likewise, the locations for **Holon** and **Mephaath** (a Levitical city in Jos 21:37) are unknown. **Beth-gamul** may be Khirbet el Jemeil, eight miles east of Dibon. Kerioth is referred to in Am 2:2. Bozrah may be Bezer (Dt 4:43; Jos 20:8; 21:36), but not the Edomite city by the same name in Jr 49:13,22.
48:25 The **horn** and **arm** are OT metaphors for strength and military might.
48:26 Drunkenness is an apt figure for the Moabite wine-producing industry. It is also

an apt allusion given the origin of Moab in Gn 19:30–38.
48:27 The translation of this verse is uncertain.
48:29–30 Jeremiah piled up several synonymous terms to depict Moab's pride: **insolence, arrogance,** and **haughty heart.**
48:31–36 In these verses four different Hebrew verbs are used for the Moabite weeping and wailing.
48:31 Kir-heres (lit "city of potsherds") is probably the Kir-hareseth of 2 Kg 3:25 and Is 16:7 (cp. Is 16:11). It may be identified with el-Kerak, about seventeen miles south of the Arnon River and eleven miles east of the Dead Sea.
48:32 God would **weep** more for the **vine of Sibmah** than **for Jazer.** Sibmah's branches

reached down to the Dead Sea with its famous vineyards and gardens, but her destruction would include all its renowned vegetation and grape vineyards.
48:33 The **shouts** heard are not those of the joyous grape treaders, but the shouting of warriors who have come to conquer Moab.
48:34 Another seven towns of Moab are mentioned in this verse along with the eleven Moabite towns in vv. 21–24. The mention of the cities here seems to move from north to south.
48:36 Flutes were used at funerals; they signified mourning.
48:37 On these four symbols of mourning, see note at 47:5.
48:38 The phrase **like a jar no one wants** was used of King Jehoiachin (22:28).

45 Those who flee will stand exhausted
   in Heshbon's shadow
because fire has come out from Heshbon
   and a flame from within Sihon.
It will devour Moab's forehead
   and the skull of the noisemakers.
46 Woe to you, Moab!
The people of Chemosh have perished
because your sons have been
   taken captive
and your daughters have gone
   into captivity.
47 Yet, I will restore the fortunes^A of Moab
   in the last days.
This is the LORD's declaration.
The judgment on Moab ends here.

Prophecies against Ammon

49 About the Ammonites, this is what the
LORD says:
Does Israel have no sons?
Is he without an heir?
Why then has Milcom^B,^C
   dispossessed Gad
and his people settled in their cities?
2 Therefore look, the days are coming —
   this is the LORD's declaration —
when I will make the shout of battle heard
against Rabbah of the Ammonites.
It will become a desolate mound,
and its surrounding villages will be set
   on fire.
Israel will dispossess
   their dispossessors,
says the LORD.

3 Wail, Heshbon, for Ai is devastated;
   cry out, daughters of Rabbah!
Clothe yourselves with sackcloth,
   and lament;
run back and forth within your walls,^D
because Milcom will go into exile
   together with his priests
   and officials.
4 Why do you boast about your valleys,
   your flowing valley,^E
you faithless daughter —
you who trust in your treasures
and say, "Who can attack me?"
5 Look, I am about to bring terror
   on you —
this is the declaration of the Lord GOD
   of Armies —
from all those around you.
You will be banished,
   each person headlong,
with no one to gather up the fugitives.
6 But after that, I will restore the fortunes^F
   of the Ammonites.
This is the LORD's declaration.

Prophecies against Edom

7 About Edom, this is what the LORD of Armies
says:
Is there no longer wisdom in Teman?
Has counsel perished from the prudent?
Has their wisdom rotted away?
8 Run! Turn back! Lie low,
   residents of Dedan,
for I will bring Esau's calamity on him
   at the time I punish him.

---

^A48:47 Or will end the captivity   ^B49:1 LXX, Syr, Vg; MT reads Malkam   ^C49:1 = Molech   ^D49:3 Or sheep pens   ^E49:4 Or about your strength, your ebbing strength   ^F49:6 Or will end the captivity, also in v. 39

48:45–46 Some believe these verses may be a free quotation from an old Hesbon song mentioned in Nm 21:28–29 and 24:17. If so, the words of Balaam the prophet seem poised to be fulfilled.
48:47 In spite of all the dire predictions against Moab, God will restore its fortunes in the future. The prophecies of restoration are not limited to Israel and Judah.
49:1–6 Ammon was a country east of the Jordan River and north of Moab. Its boundaries were not well fixed, and it often was in conflict with Israel. Its capital city was Rabbah, modern Amman, Jordan, situated in the valley of the Jabbok River. The Ammonites were descended from Ben-Ammi, son of Lot (Gn 19:38). During the reign of the Judean King Zedekiah, the Ammonites participated with Judah in a revolt against Babylon (Jr 27:3); they continued their revolt beyond the fall of Jerusalem in 587 BC. Nebuchadnezzar's army took the country around 582 BC.
49:1 This verse reflects the territorial dispute between the Ammonites and the tribe of Gad (cp. Jdg 11:23–24). The Lord asked through Jeremiah, should Ammon and its god have dispossessed Gad, who was still living there and who had been given that territory? (See Nm 21:21–31; 32:1–39.) Milcom, also known as Molech, was the national deity of Ammon. His name meant "the king," but

the Hebrews refused to pronounce it in a way that signified "king." They substituted the vowels of "o" and "e" from the Hebrew word bosheth, meaning "shame," thereby stigmatizing the name of Ammon's deity (see note at 7:31).
49:2 Rabbah was the capital city of the Ammonites. It is identified with modern Amman, Jordan. The archaeological term tell signifies the ruins of a city. It appears in the phrase a desolate mound.
49:3 Heshbon was referred to as a Moabite city (48:2), but it must have belonged to Ammon at this time. The Ai referred to here is not the same as the Ai in Israel, but is another town with the same name, meaning "ruin." The phrase run back and forth within your walls could also be rendered "rush to and fro in confusion among the sheep pens." The picture is one of people darting about in the open areas of the city in total confusion.
49:4 Ammon was bragging about their valleys, their flowing valley. An alternative translation would render "valleys" as "strength" (see note at 47:5). In either case ("valleys" or "strength") the Ammonites were complacent and needed rebuffing.
49:6 As God would do with Egypt (46:26), Moab (48:47), and Elam (49:39), he would one day restore the fortunes of Ammon as well.

49:7–22 Edom descended from Esau, brother of Jacob. The Edomites were the subject of more judgment prophecies than any other nation (Ps 137:7; Is 34:1–17; 63:1–6; Lm 4:21–22; Ezk 25:12–14; 35:1–15; Am 1:11–12; Obadiah; Mal 1:2–5). Jeremiah was surprisingly softer in his tone against them than he was in his prophecies against other nations. Edom stretched from the Gulf of Aqabah, east of the Sinai Peninsula about a hundred miles north, to the River Zered, which flowed into the southern end of the Dead Sea and marked the border between Moab and Edom. Edom was mostly mountainous. It was settled originally by the Horim ("cave people") whom Edom expelled (Dt 2:12,22). Edom's prosperity came from its iron and copper mines as well as its position on the King's Highway (Nm 20:17,19).
49:7 God began his prophecy against Edom with a set of rhetorical questions. The first was about wisdom in Teman. Teman was famous for wisdom (Ob 8 and possibly the book of Job), but it does not seem to have served them well. Teman was Esau's first grandson (Gn 36:11,15). Often the name stands for the whole country or as here for a city or province in Edom.
49:8 The residents of Dedan, a region not too far away in north Arabia, are told to steer their caravans away from Edom because of the destruction God will bring on the nation.

⁹ If grape harvesters came to you,
   wouldn't they leave a few grapes?
   Were thieves to come in the night,
   they would destroy only
      what they wanted.
¹⁰ But I will strip Esau bare;
   I will uncover his secret places.
   He will try to hide, but he will be unable.
   His descendants will be destroyed
   along with his relatives and neighbors.
   He will exist no longer.
¹¹ Abandon your fatherless;
      I will preserve them;
   let your widows trust in me.

¹² For this is what the LORD says: "If those
who do not deserve to drink the cup must
drink it, can you possibly remain unpunished?
You will not remain unpunished, for you must
drink it too. ¹³ For by myself I have sworn" —
this is the LORD's declaration — "Bozrahᴬ will
become a desolation, a disgrace, a ruin, and an
example for cursing, and all its surrounding
cities will become ruins forever."
¹⁴   I have heard an envoy from the LORD;
      a messenger has been sent
         among the nations:
      Assemble yourselves to come
         against her.
      Rise up for war!

¹⁵   I will certainly make you insignificant
         among the nations,
      despised among humanity.
¹⁶   As to the terror you cause,ᴮ
      your arrogant heart has deceived you.
      You who live in the clefts of the rock,ᶜ
      you who occupy the mountain summit,
         though you elevate your nest
      like the eagles,
      even from there I will bring you down.
      This is the LORD's declaration.

¹⁷ "Edom will become a desolation. Everyone
who passes by her will be appalled and scoff
because of all her wounds. ¹⁸ As when Sodom
and Gomorrah were overthrown along with

their neighbors," says the LORD, "no one will
live there; no human being will stay in it even
temporarily.
¹⁹ "Look, it will be like a lion coming from the
thicketsᴰ of the Jordan to the watered grazing
land. I will chase Edom away from her land in
a flash. I will appoint whoever is chosen for
her. For who is like me? Who will issue me a
summons? Who is the shepherd who can stand
against me?"
²⁰ Therefore, hear the plans that the LORD
has drawn up against Edom and the strategies he has devised against the people of Teman: The flock's little lambs will certainly be
dragged away, and their grazing land will be
made desolate because of them. ²¹ At the sound
of their fall the earth will quake; the sound of
her cry will be heard at the Red Sea. ²² Look!
It will be like an eagle soaring upward, then
swooping down and spreading its wings over
Bozrah. In that day the hearts of Edom's warriors will be like the heart of a woman with
contractions.

Prophecies against Damascus

²³ About Damascus:
      Hamath and Arpad are put to shame,
      for they have heard a bad report
         and are agitated,
      likeᴱ the anxious sea that cannot
         be calmed.
²⁴   Damascus has become weak;
      she has turned to run;
      panic has gripped her.
      Distress and labor pains
         have seized her
      like a woman in labor.
²⁵   How can the city of praise
         not be abandoned,
      the town that brings me joy?
²⁶   Therefore, her young men will fall
         in her public squares;
      all the warriors will perish in that day.
      This is the declaration of the LORD
         of Armies.
²⁷   I will set fire to the wall of Damascus;
      it will consume Ben-hadad's citadels.

ᴬ49:13 = Edom's capital ᴮ49:16 Lit *Your horror* ᶜ49:16 = Petra ᴰ49:19 Lit *pride* ᴱ49:23 Lit *in*

49:12 The image of drinking from **the cup** is a metaphor for the judgment God will bring to the nations (25:12–29; 48:26; cp. Is 34:5–6; Lm 4:21).
49:13 Bozrah was the capital and chief city of Edom in Jeremiah's time. It is identified with modern el-Buseira, about twenty miles southeast of the Dead Sea. It is not to be confused with the Moabite Bozrah (48:24).
49:16 Edom thought they were unconquer-able, because the people lived in the **clefts of the rock**. The rocks were later called Sela or Petra, which became the fortress and cap-ital of the Edomites.
49:19–22 God is compared to a **lion** and an **eagle**. He will drag away the **lambs** (the

Edomites, v. 20) and swoop down on them as his prey. Verses 19–21 are repeated in 50:44–46 and applied to Babylon.
49:23–27 Damascus was the capital city of Syria (Aram); therefore, this city stands for the entire nation. It appears that the Syrian/Aramaean armies joined Babylon in its attack on Jerusalem in 597 BC.
49:23–24 Hamath and **Arpad** were two smaller Aramaean/Syrian city-states. Ha-math, often called a Canaanite and then later a Hethite city (Gn 10:18), was 110 miles north of **Damascus** on the Orontes River. Arpad was ninety-five miles north of Ha-math. All three cities were conquered by the Assyrian king, Tiglath-pileser, in 738 BC

(Is 10:9; 36:19; 37:13). Sargon II crushed a rebellion in 720 BC in Damascus. This city was also captured by Nebuchadnezzar in 605 BC. Damascus was **agitated** and troubled like **the . . . sea**, even though it had no seacoast. Fear and anguish gripped this city like **a woman in labor**. Jeremiah used this figure of many nations, including Israel, Moab, Edom, and Babylon (v. 22; 6:24; 48:41; 50:43).
49:25 Damascus was a delight to God. He called it **the town that brings me joy**.
49:27 Ben-hadad was a royal name for Ar-amaean kings stretching from the ninth to the eighth centuries BC.

Prophecies against Kedar and Hazor

28 About Kedar and the kingdoms of Hazor, which King Nebuchadnezzar of Babylon defeated, this is what the LORD says:

Rise up, attack Kedar,
and destroy the people of the east!
29 They will take their tents
and their flocks
along with their tent curtains
and all their equipment.
They will take their camels
for themselves.
They will call out to them,
"Terror is on every side!"
30 Run! Escape quickly! Lie low,
residents of Hazor —
this is the LORD's declaration —
for King Nebuchadnezzar of Babylon
has drawn up a plan against you;
he has devised a strategy against you.

31 Rise up, attack a nation at ease,
one living in security.
This is the LORD's declaration.
They have no doors, not even a gate bar;
they live alone.
32 Their camels will become plunder,
and their massive herds of cattle will
become spoil.
I will scatter them to the wind
in every direction,
those who clip the hair on their temples;
I will bring calamity on them
across all their borders.
This is the LORD's declaration.
33 Hazor will become a jackals' den,
a desolation forever.
No one will live there;
no human being will stay in it even
temporarily.

Prophecies against Elam

34 This is the word of the LORD that came to the prophet Jeremiah about Elam[A] at the beginning of the reign of King Zedekiah of Judah. **35** This is what the LORD of Armies says:

I am about to shatter Elam's bow,
the source[B] of their might.
36 I will bring the four winds against Elam
from the four corners of the heavens,
and I will scatter them
to all these winds.
There will not be a nation
to which Elam's banished ones
will not go.
37 I will devastate Elam
before their enemies,
before those who intend to take
their lives.
I will bring disaster on them,
my burning anger.
This is the LORD's declaration.
I will send the sword after them
until I finish them off.
38 I will set my throne in Elam,
and I will destroy the king and officials
from there.
This is the LORD's declaration.

39 Yet, in the last days,
I will restore the fortunes of Elam.
This is the LORD's declaration.

Prophecies against Babylon

50 This is the word the LORD spoke about Babylon, the land of the Chaldeans, through the prophet Jeremiah:
2 Announce to the nations;
proclaim and raise up a signal flag;
proclaim, and hide nothing.
Say, "Babylon is captured;

A **49:34** = modern Iran   B **49:35** Lit *first*

49:28–33 Kedar was an Ishmaelite tribe in the Arabian desert (Gn 25:13) that is frequently referred to in the OT (Is 21:16,17; 42:11; 60:7; Ezk 27:21). They were known for their sheep-breeding (Is 60:7), their dwelling east of the Ammonites (Is 42:11), their trading with Tyre (Ezk 27:21), and their archery skills (Is 21:16–17).
49:28 This **Hazor** is not the city in northern Israel (Jos 11:1–13). It was apparently a now-unknown town in a desert region. The Lord gave a command for **Nebuchadnezzar** to **rise up** and **destroy the people of the east**. The "people/sons of the east" are identified with the Midianites and Amalekites in Jdg 6:3 and with other nomadic peoples who often raided Israelite territory (Gn 29:1; Jdg 7:12; 8:10; 1Kg 4:30; Jb 1:3; Is 11:14; Ezk 25:4).
49:29 The five items that will be taken (**tents . . . flocks . . . tent curtains . . . equipment**, and **camels**) are what we would expect nomads rather than city dwellers to own.
49:30 The exact date of the Babylonian campaign against the desert tribes is unknown, but Nebuchadnezzar did conduct a

raid against them in 599–598 BC, before his attack on Jerusalem.
49:33 Conventional expressions are used for the extent of the destruction on these tribes. They will become **a jackals' den** (9:11; 10:22; 51:37) and **a desolation forever** (v. 2; 4:27; 6:8; 9:11; 10:22; 12:10–11; 32:43; 44:6; 50:13). **No one will live there** (4:7,29; 9:11; 26:9; 33:10; 44:22; 46:19; 51:29,37).
49:34–39 Elam was the first of Shem's sons (Gn 10:22). It was an ancient kingdom (Gn 14:1) about two hundred miles east of Babylon in modern southwestern Iran. Its capital city was Shushan, also known as Susa (Neh 1:1; Est 1:2,5; Dn 8:2). Elam may be a general name for Persia. It was subdued by Assyria and later came under Babylonian and Persian rule.
49:34 This prophecy came at **the beginning of the reign of King Zedekiah of Judah** (ca 597 BC).
49:35 Elamites were known for their skill in archery (Is 22:6), but the Lord would take that away. When Elam was absorbed into the Persian Empire about 539 BC, landowners were required to furnish the Persian king

with a bowman or to pay a bow tenure—a sum of money to hire an archer in his place.
49:36–37 The expression **four winds** is used elsewhere to depict military might (Ezk 37:9; Dn 8:8; Zch 2:6; 6:5).
49:39 As with Israel (29:14), Moab (48:47), Ammon (49:6), and Egypt (46:26), God promised to restore the fortunes of Elam.
50:1–51:64 Jeremiah's final prophecy against the nations is reserved for Babylon. Almost as much space is devoted to Babylon as to all the other nations combined. This argues against those who felt Jeremiah was so pro-Babylonian that he could see no wrong with them.
50:1 The **land of the Chaldeans** reverts to the name of the seminomadic tribe that settled south of Ur (see note at 21:3–4). Nebuchadnezzar's father, Nabopolassar, was a native Chaldean who ascended the throne in 626 BC and gave birth to the Neo-Babylonian period that continued until the fall of Babylon in 539 BC.
50:2 Bel, meaning "lord," was the title of the storm god Enlil, chief god of Nippur. Later "Bel" became a name for Marduk. As the

Bel is put to shame;
Marduk is terrified."
Her idols are put to shame;
her false gods, devastated.
³ For a nation from the north will attack
her;
it will make her land desolate.
No one will be living in it —
both people and animals will escape.^A
⁴ In those days and at that time —
this is the Lord's declaration —
the Israelites and Judeans
will come together,
weeping as they come,
and will seek the Lord their God.
⁵ They will ask about Zion,
turning their faces to this road.
They will come and join themselves^B
to the Lord
in a permanent covenant that will never
be forgotten.

⁶ My people were lost sheep;
their shepherds led them astray,
guiding them the wrong way
in the mountains.
They wandered from mountain to hill;
they forgot their resting place.
⁷ Whoever found them devoured them.
Their adversaries said, "We're not guilty;
instead, they have sinned
against the Lord,
their righteous grazing land,
the hope of their ancestors, the Lord."

⁸ Escape from Babylon;
depart from the Chaldeans' land.
Be like the rams that lead the flock.
⁹ For I will soon stir up and bring
against Babylon
an assembly of great nations
from the north country.
They will line up in battle formation
against her;
from there she will be captured.
Their arrows will be like a skilled^c warrior
who does not return empty-handed.
¹⁰ The Chaldeans will become plunder;
all Babylon's plunderers will be
fully satisfied.
This is the Lord's declaration.

¹¹ Because you rejoice,
because you celebrate —
you who plundered my inheritance —
because you frolic like a young cow
treading grain
and neigh like stallions,
¹² your mother will be utterly humiliated;
she who bore you will be put to shame.
Look! She will lag behind
all^D the nations —
an arid wilderness, a desert.
¹³ Because of the Lord's wrath,
she will not be inhabited;
she will become a desolation, every bit
of her.
Everyone who passes
through Babylon
will be appalled
and scoff because of all her wounds.
¹⁴ Line up in battle formation
around Babylon,
all you archers!
Shoot at her! Do not spare an arrow,
for she has sinned against the Lord.
¹⁵ Raise a war cry against her
on every side!
She has thrown up her hands
in surrender;
her defense towers have fallen;
her walls are demolished.
Since this is the Lord's vengeance,
take your vengeance on her;
as she has done, do the same to her.
¹⁶ Cut off the sower from Babylon
as well as him who wields the sickle
at harvest time.
Because of the oppressor's sword,
each will turn to his own people,
each will flee to his own land.

The Return of God's People

¹⁷ Israel is a stray lamb, chased by lions.
The first who devoured him was
the king of Assyria;
the last who crushed his bones
was King Nebuchadnezzar of Babylon.

¹⁸ Therefore, this is what the Lord of Armies,
the God of Israel, says: I am about to punish the
king of Babylon and his land just as I punished
the king of Assyria.

---

^A **50:3** Lit *escape; they will walk*   ^B **50:5** LXX; MT reads *Come and join yourselves*   ^c **50:9** Some Hb mss, LXX, Syr; other Hb mss
read *bereaving*   ^D **50:12** Lit *Look! The last of*

50: major god of Babylon, Marduk was the Babylonian creator-god. The word for **false gods** in Hebrew is *gillulim* (lit "balls of excrement"). **50:3** The **nation from the north** is not immediately identified, but here the prophet seems to refer to Persia, since the attack will be against Babylon. **50:7** Babylon claimed they were not to blame for their treatment of Israel. They lay the blame on Israel's God for forsaking them.

50:8 With judgment so certain for Babylon, those who live there are told to **escape**. Just as male goats ("rams") rush out to lead the flock when the pen is opened, so should those left in Babylon scatter before the judgment begins. **50:11–12** Frolicked **like a young cow treading grain** is an image of a heifer frisking around the threshing floor, eating whatever she wanted to eat. Babylon's **mother** is the city of Babylon.

50:16 The **sower** and the one who **wields the sickle** depict the rural population that will feel the onslaught of warfare even before the city dwellers. **50:17–20 Assyria** crushed Israel in the eighth century BC, and the Babylonians did the same thing to Judah in the sixth.

19 I will return Israel to his grazing land,
  and he will feed on Carmel and Bashan;
  he will be satisfied
  in the hill country of Ephraim
  and of Gilead.
20 In those days and at that time —
  this is the LORD's declaration —
  one will search for Israel's iniquity,
  but there will be none,
  and for Judah's sins,
  but they will not be found,
  for I will forgive those I leave
  as a remnant.

The Invasion of Babylon

21 Attack the land of Merathaim,
  and those living in Pekod.
  Put them to the sword;
  completely destroy them —
  this is the LORD's declaration —
  do everything I have commanded you.
22 The sound of war is in the land —
  a crushing blow!
23 How the hammer of the whole earth
  is cut down and smashed!
  What a horror Babylon has become
  among the nations!
24 Babylon, I laid a trap for you, and you
  were caught,
  but you did not even know it.
  You were found and captured
  because you pitted yourself
  against the LORD.
25 The LORD opened his armory
  and brought out his weapons of wrath,
  because it is a task of the Lord GOD
  of Armies
  in the land of the Chaldeans.
26 Come against her
  from the most distant places.^
  Open her granaries;
  pile her up like mounds of grain
  and completely destroy her.
  Leave her no survivors.
27 Put all her young bulls to the sword;
  let them go down to the slaughter.
  Woe to them because their day has come,
  the time of their punishment.

The Humiliation of Babylon

28 There is a voice of fugitives
  and refugees
  from the land of Babylon.

The voice announces in Zion
  the vengeance of the LORD our God,
  the vengeance for his temple.
29 Summon the archers to Babylon,
  all who string the bow;
  camp all around her; let none escape.
  Repay her according to her deeds;
  just as she has done, do the same to her,
  for she has acted arrogantly
  against the LORD,
  against the Holy One of Israel.
30 Therefore, her young men will fall
  in her public squares;
  all the warriors will perish in that day.
  This is the LORD's declaration.
31 Look, I am against you,
  you arrogant one —
  this is the declaration of
  the Lord GOD of Armies —
  for your day has come,
  the time when I will punish you.
32 The arrogant will stumble and fall
  with no one to pick him up.
  I will set fire to his cities,
  and it will consume everything
  around him.

The Desolation of Babylon

33 This is what the LORD of Armies says:
  Israelites and Judeans alike
  have been oppressed.
  All their captors hold them fast;
  they refuse to release them.
34 Their Redeemer is strong;
  the LORD of Armies is his name.
  He will fervently champion their cause
  so that he might bring rest to the earth
  but turmoil to those who live
  in Babylon.
35 A sword is over the Chaldeans —
  this is the LORD's declaration —
  against those who live in Babylon,
  against her officials, and against
  her sages.
36 A sword is against the diviners,
  and they will act foolishly.
  A sword is against her heroic warriors,
  and they will be terrified.
37 A sword is against his horses
  and chariots
  and against all the foreigners
  among them,
  and they will be like women.

---

^**50:26** Lit *from the end*

50:21 Babylon's enemies are to attack **Merathaim** and **those living in Pekod**. Merathaim was probably the district of Marratim at the head of the Persian Gulf. Pekod was probably *puqudu*, a people of eastern Babylonia. The phrase **completely destroy them** translates the Hebrew word *cherem* ("to place under the ban" and "to render to God as an involuntary offering").

50:22–24 Babylon is called **the hammer of the whole earth**. Persia is referred to with similar imagery (51:20). **50:26–27 Survivors** is a term that also means "remnant" (see v. 20). **Young bulls** probably refers to warriors. **50:29–32** The **archers** are urged to press the attack against Babylon because of the nation's insolence, defiance, and arrogance against **the Holy One of Israel** (Is 1:4; 5:19,24).

50:35–38 Babylon's enemies are depicted as God's **sword** that hangs heavy over Babylon's **officials**...**her sages**...**her heroic warriors**, their **horses and chariots**, and **her treasuries**. The **terrifying things** (Hb *'emim*) is a contemptuous way of referring to Babylon's gods.

A sword is against her treasuries,
and they will be plundered.
38 A drought will come on her waters,
and they will be dried up.
For it is a land of carved images,
and they go mad because of
terrifying things.^A

39 Therefore, desert creatures^B will live
with hyenas,
and ostriches will also live in her.
It will never again be inhabited
or lived in through all generations.
40 Just as God demolished Sodom
and Gomorrah
and their neighboring towns —
this is the LORD's declaration —
so no one will live there;
no human being will stay in it even
temporarily
as a temporary resident.

The Conquest of Babylon
41 Look! A people comes from the north.
A great nation and many kings will be
stirred up
from the remote regions of the earth.
42 They grasp bow and javelin.
They are cruel and show no mercy.
Their voice roars like the sea,
and they ride on horses,
lined up like men in battle formation
against you, Daughter Babylon.
43 The king of Babylon has heard
about them;
his hands have become weak.
Distress has seized him —
pain, like a woman in labor.

44 "Look, it will be like a lion coming from
the thickets^C of the Jordan to the watered grazing land. I will chase Babylon^D away from her
land in a flash. I will appoint whoever is chosen for her. For who is like me? Who will issue
me a summons? Who is the shepherd who can
stand against me?"
45 Therefore, hear the plans that the LORD has
drawn up against Babylon and the strategies
he has devised against the land of the Chaldeans: Certainly the flock's little lambs will be

dragged away; certainly the grazing land will
be made desolate because of them. 46 At the
sound of Babylon's conquest the earth will
quake; a cry will be heard among the nations.

God's Judgment on Babylon
51 This is what the LORD says:
I am about to rouse the spirit of a
destroyer^E against Babylon
and against the population
of Leb-qamai.^F,G
2 I will send strangers to Babylon
who will scatter her and strip
her land bare,
for they will come against her
from every side in the day of disaster.
3 Don't let the archer string his bow;
don't let him put on^H his armor.
Don't spare her young men;
completely destroy her entire army!
4 Those who were slain will fall
in the land of the Chaldeans,
those who were pierced through,
in her streets.
5 For Israel and Judah are not
left widowed
by their God, the LORD of Armies,
though their land is full of guilt
against the Holy One of Israel.

6 Leave Babylon;
save your lives, each of you!
Don't perish because of her guilt.
For this is the time
of the LORD's vengeance —
he will pay her what she deserves.
7 Babylon was a gold cup
in the LORD's hand,
making the whole earth drunk.
The nations drank her wine;
therefore, the nations go mad.
8 Suddenly Babylon fell
and was shattered.
Wail for her;
get balm for her wound —
perhaps she can be healed.
9 We tried to heal Babylon,
but she could not be healed.
Abandon her!

---

^A 50:38 Or of dreaded gods ^B 50:39 Or desert demons ^C 50:44 Lit pride ^D 50:44 Lit them ^E 51:1 Or to stir up a destructive wind ^F 51:1 Lit heart of my adversaries ^G 51:1 = Chaldeans ^H 51:3 Hb obscure

---

50:40 Babylon's destruction will be as severe and as permanent as the destruction of **Sodom** and **Gomorrah** (49:18; Gn 19:24–25; Is 13:19). 50:41–43 These verses repeat 6:22–24 with only a few minor variations. Previously addressed to Judah, they are now directed to Babylon. 50:44–46 These verses repeat with some minor changes the condemnation of Edom (49:19–21). 51:1–64 The judgment message against Babylon continues in the longest chapter

in the book of Jeremiah, concluding with a special message to Babylon. 51:1 Leb-qamai (lit "the heart of those who rise against me") is a figure of speech called atbash, a Jewish device where letters are substituted for their opposites in the alphabet. In the English equivalent, the letter A would be changed to Z, B to Y, and so on. "Leb-qamai" is therefore a cipher for Kasdim or Chaldea (Babylonia). It is not clear why Jeremiah used atbash in these cases since elsewhere he clearly points to Babylon. The **spirit** or breath or

wind **of a destroyer** is known elsewhere in the OT as the east wind or sirocco. This wind is an apt figure for the winnowing (v. 2) that God will perform on Babylon. 51:3–4 Behind the translation of **completely destroy** is the Hebrew word cherem (see note at 50:21). 51:9 The phrase **her judgment extends to the sky and reaches as far as the clouds** is a proverbial expression indicating that Babylon's judgment will be severe (Nm 13:28; Dt 1:28).

Let each of us go to his own land,
for her judgment extends to the sky
and reaches as far as the clouds.

¹⁰ The LORD has brought about
our vindication;
come, let's tell in Zion
what the LORD our God
has accomplished.

¹¹ Sharpen the arrows!
Fill the quivers!ᴬ
The LORD has roused the spirit
of the kings of the Medes
because his plan is aimed at Babylon
to destroy her,
for it is the LORD's vengeance,
vengeance for his temple.

¹² Raise up a signal flag
against the walls of Babylon;
fortify the watch post;
set the watchmen in place;
prepare the ambush.
For the LORD has both planned
and accomplished
what he has threatened
against those who live in Babylon.

¹³ You who reside by abundant water,
rich in treasures,
your end has come,
your life thread is cut.

¹⁴ The LORD of Armies has sworn by himself:
I will fill you up with men
as with locusts,
and they will sing the victory song
over you.

¹⁵ He made the earth by his power,
established the world by his wisdom,
and spread out the heavens
by his understanding.

¹⁶ When he thunders,ᴮ
the waters in the heavens are tumultuous,
and he causes the clouds
to rise from the ends of the earth.
He makes lightning for the rain
and brings the wind
from his storehouses.

¹⁷ Everyone is stupid and ignorant.
Every goldsmith is put to shame
by his carved image,

for his cast images are a lie;
there is no breath in them.

¹⁸ They are worthless, a work
to be mocked.
At the time of their punishment
they will be destroyed.

¹⁹ Jacob's Portionᶜ is not like these
because he is the one who formed
all things.
Israel is the tribe of his inheritance;
the LORD of Armies is his name.

²⁰ You are my war club,
my weapons of war.
With you I will smash nations;
with you I will bring kingdoms to ruin.

²¹ With you I will smash the horse
and its rider;
with you I will smash the chariot
and its rider.

²² With you I will smash man and woman;
with you I will smash the old man
and the youth;
with you I will smash the young man
and the young woman.

²³ With you I will smash the shepherd
and his flock;
with you I will smash the farmer
and his ox-team.ᴰ
With you I will smash governors
and officials.

²⁴ "Before your very eyes, I will repay Babylon and all the residents of Chaldea for all their evil they have done in Zion."
This is the LORD's declaration.

²⁵ Look, I am against you,
devastating mountain.
This is the LORD's declaration.
You devastate the whole earth.
I will stretch out my hand against you,
roll you down from the cliffs,
and turn you into a charred mountain.

²⁶ No one will be able to retrieve
a cornerstone
or a foundation stone from you,
because you will become
desolate forever.
This is the LORD's declaration.

²⁷ Raise a signal flag in the land;
blow a ram's horn among the nations;
set apart the nations against her.

ᴬ51:11 Or Grasp the shields!   ᴮ51:16 Lit At his giving of the voice   ᶜ51:19 = The LORD   ᴰ51:23 Lit yoke

51:11–12 Babylon's enemies are identified for the first time in these verses as **the Medes**. Media was a country northeast of Babylon (in modern Iran) with its capital at Ecbatana. Media rose to prominence in the seventh century BC. In 549 BC it came under Persian rule and joined Cyrus in the defeat of the Babylonian Empire.

51:13–14 The one who resided **by abundant water** was Babylon. The Euphrates and Tigris rivers were symbolic of her strength.
51:15–19 God is **Jacob's Portion** (cp. 10:16).
51:20–23 The phrase **with you** ("you" being God's **war club**) falls ten times in these verses like the beat of a heavy battle drum. Many see King Cyrus of Persia (Is 41:2–4,25;

45:1–6) as the unnamed "war club." The verb **will smash** is repeated nine times, like the beat of a second battle drum.
51:25–26 The image is of a volcano that spews rock and hot coals, leaving a burned-out crater.
51:27–28 Three kingdoms of the Median Empire—**Ararat, Minni, and Ashkenaz**—

Summon kingdoms against her —
Ararat, Minni, and Ashkenaz.
Appoint a marshal against her;
bring up horses like a swarm[A] of locusts.
28 Set apart the nations for battle
against her —
the kings of Media,
her governors and all her officials,
and all the lands they rule.
29 The earth quakes and trembles
because the LORD's intentions
against Babylon stand:
to make the land of Babylon
a desolation, without inhabitant.
30 Babylon's warriors have
stopped fighting;
they sit in their strongholds.
Their might is exhausted;
they have become like women.
Babylon's homes have been set ablaze,
her gate bars are shattered.
31 Messenger races to meet messenger,
and herald to meet herald,
to announce to the king of Babylon
that his city has been captured
from end to end.
32 The fords have been seized,
the marshes set on fire,
and the fighting men are terrified.

33 For this is what the LORD of Armies, the
God of Israel, says:
Daughter Babylon is like a threshing floor
at the time it is trampled.
In just a little while her harvest time
will come.

34 "King Nebuchadnezzar of Babylon
has devoured me;
he has crushed me.
He has set me aside like an empty dish;
he has swallowed me like a sea monster;
he filled his belly with my delicacies;
he has vomited me out.[B]
35 Let the violence done to me
and my family be done to Babylon,"
says the inhabitant of Zion.
"Let my blood be on the inhabitants
of Chaldea,"
says Jerusalem.

36 Therefore, this is what the LORD says:
I am about to champion your cause
and take vengeance on your behalf;
I will dry up her sea
and make her fountain run dry.
37 Babylon will become a heap of rubble,
a jackals' den,
a desolation and an object of scorn,
without inhabitant.
38 They will roar together like young lions;
they will growl like lion cubs.
39 While they are flushed with heat,
I will serve them a feast,
and I will make them drunk so that
they celebrate.[C]
Then they will fall asleep forever
and never wake up.
This is the LORD's declaration.
40 I will bring them down like lambs
to the slaughter,
like rams together with male goats.

41 How Sheshak[D] has been captured,
the praise of the whole earth seized.
What a horror Babylon has become
among the nations!
42 The sea has risen over Babylon;
she is covered
with its tumultuous waves.
43 Her cities have become a desolation,
an arid desert,
a land where no one lives,
where no human being even
passes through.
44 I will punish Bel in Babylon.
I will make him vomit
what he swallowed.
The nations will no longer stream
to him;
even Babylon's wall will fall.

45 Come out from among her, my people!
Save your lives, each of you,
from the LORD's burning anger.
46 May you not become cowardly
and fearful
when the report is proclaimed
in the land,
for the report will come one year,
and then another the next year.

[A]51:27 Hb obscure   [B]51:34 Lit *has rinsed me off*   [C]51:39 LXX reads *pass out*   [D]51:41 = Babylon

are invited to join battle against Babylon. These kingdoms were northwest of Babylon in what is today generally called Armenia. Ararat occupied southeastern Turkey and the northern regions of Iraq and Iran, about the same area where the Kurdish people live today. Minni or Mannaya (aka the Maneans) lived south of Lake Urmia in the southwestern regions of modern Iran. Ashkenaz generally refers to Indo-European peoples whom Herodotus called Scythians.

51:29–32 Babylon was completely demoralized by this announcement and became **like women**. The reed-filled **marshes** that surrounded Babylon were set on fire, cutting off escape and flushing out fugitives. **51:41** On the cipher **Sheshak**, see note at 25:26. **51:44** God will destroy two things for which Babylon was famous—the idol **Bel** (see note at 50:2) and the **wall** around Babylon. The outer wall was twelve feet thick with a lane twenty-three feet wide between it and the

inner wall, which was twenty-one feet thick. The walls were so thick that several chariots could drive abreast atop them. Towers rose from the walls every sixty feet. Outside the walls, a moat-like ditch was bricked and filled with water from the Euphrates River. **51:46–48** Nebuchadnezzar's son, Amel-Marduk (Evil-Merodach) was assassinated in 560 BC by his brother-in-law Neriglissar (560–556 BC). Neriglissar's heir, Labashi-Marduk had a short reign of a few months and was replaced by Nabonidus (556–539 BC).

There will be violence in the land
with ruler against ruler.

47 Therefore, look, the days are coming
when I will punish
Babylon's carved images.
Her entire land will suffer shame,
and all her slain will lie fallen
within her.

48 Heaven and earth and everything
in them
will shout for joy over Babylon
because the destroyers from the north
will come against her.
This is the LORD's declaration.

49 Babylon must fall because of the slain
of Israel,
even as the slain of the
whole earth fell
because of Babylon.

50 You who have escaped the sword,
go and do not stand still!
Remember the LORD from far away,
and let Jerusalem come to your mind.

51 We are ashamed
because we have heard insults.
Humiliation covers our faces
because foreigners have entered
the holy places of the LORD's temple.

52 Therefore, look, the days are coming —
this is the LORD's declaration —
when I will punish
her carved images,
and the wounded will groan
throughout her land.

53 Even if Babylon should ascend
to the heavens
and fortify her tall fortresses,
destroyers will come against her
from me.
This is the LORD's declaration.

54 The sound of a cry from Babylon!
The sound of terrible destruction
from the land of the Chaldeans!

55 For the LORD is going
to devastate Babylon;
he will silence her mighty voice.
Their waves roar like a huge torrent;
the tumult of their voice resounds,

56 for a destroyer is coming against her,
against Babylon.

Her warriors will be captured,
their bows shattered,
for the LORD is a God of retribution;
he will certainly repay.

57 I will make her princes
and sages drunk,
along with her governors, officials,
and warriors.
Then they will fall asleep forever
and never wake up.
This is the King's declaration;
the LORD of Armies is his name.

58 This is what the LORD of Armies says:
Babylon's thick walls will be
totally demolished,
and her high gates set ablaze.
The peoples will have labored
for nothing;
the nations will weary themselves
only to feed the fire.

59 This is what the prophet Jeremiah commanded Seraiah son of Neriah son of Mahseiah, the quartermaster, when he went to Babylon with King Zedekiah of Judah in the fourth year of Zedekiah's reign. 60 Jeremiah wrote on one scroll about all the disaster that would come to Babylon; all these words were written against Babylon. 61 Jeremiah told Seraiah, "When you get to Babylon, see that you read all these words aloud. 62 Say, 'LORD, you have threatened to cut off this place so that no one will live in it — people or animals. Indeed, it will remain desolate forever.' 63 When you have finished reading this scroll, tie a stone to it and throw it into the middle of the Euphrates River. 64 Then say, 'In the same way, Babylon will sink and never rise again because of the disaster I am bringing on her. They will grow weary.'"

The words of Jeremiah end here.

The Fall of Jerusalem

52 Zedekiah was twenty-one years old when he became king, and he reigned eleven years in Jerusalem. His mother's name was Hamutal daughter of Jeremiah; she was from Libnah. 2 Zedekiah did what was evil in the LORD's sight just as Jehoiakim had done. 3 Because of the LORD's anger, it came to the point in Jerusalem and Judah that he finally banished them from his presence. Then Zedekiah rebelled against the king of Babylon.

51:50–58 The structure of this section is similar to vv. 45–49.
51:59–64 One final symbolic act has Jeremiah speaking with **Seraiah**, brother of Baruch. Seraiah was to accompany King Zedekiah during the fourth year of his reign on a trip to Babylon (594/593 BC). This was the year of the plot to rebel against Babylon (2Ch 27), a plot in which Zedekiah was implicated. He

would take a **scroll** on which the prophet had recorded his prophecies against Babylon. Seraiah was to read aloud these words, then pray that God would fulfill them, making Babylon an uninhabited place. Then he was to **tie a stone** to the scroll and throw it into the **Euphrates River** and declare, **In the same way, Babylon will sink and never rise again.**

The note that **the words of Jeremiah end here** are probably from the compiler, who wanted to separate chap. 51 from chap. 52. The final chapter parallels 2Kg 24:18–25:30, even though they differ in some respects.
52:1–34 A shortened form of this material is found in 39:1–10. A longer form is preserved in 2Kg 24:18–25:30, which in turn is condensed in 2Ch 36:11–21.

⁴ In the ninth year of Zedekiah's reign, on the tenth day of the tenth month, King Nebuchadnezzar of Babylon advanced against Jerusalem with his entire army. They laid siege to the city and built a siege wall against it all around. ⁵ The city was under siege until King Zedekiah's eleventh year.

⁶ By the ninth day of the fourth month the famine was so severe in the city that the common people had no food. ⁷ Then the city was broken into, and all the warriors fled. They left the city at night by way of the city gate between the two walls near the king's garden, though the Chaldeans surrounded the city. They made their way along the route to the Arabah. ⁸ The Chaldean army pursued the king and overtook Zedekiah in the plains of Jericho. Zedekiah's entire army left him and scattered. ⁹ The Chaldeans seized the king and brought him to the king of Babylon at Riblah in the land of Hamath, and he passed sentence on him.

¹⁰ At Riblah the king of Babylon slaughtered Zedekiah's sons before his eyes, and he also slaughtered the Judean commanders. ¹¹ Then he blinded Zedekiah and bound him with bronze chains. The king of Babylon brought Zedekiah to Babylon, where he kept him in custody^A until his dying day.

¹² On the tenth day of the fifth month — which was the nineteenth year of King Nebuchadnezzar, king of Babylon — Nebuzaradan, the captain of the guards, entered Jerusalem as the representative of^B the king of Babylon. ¹³ He burned the LORD's temple, the king's palace, all the houses of Jerusalem; he burned down all the great houses. ¹⁴ The whole Chaldean army with the captain of the guards tore down all the walls surrounding Jerusalem. ¹⁵ Nebuzaradan, the captain of the guards, deported some of the poorest of the people, as well as the rest of the people who remained in the city, the deserters who had defected to the king of Babylon, and the rest of the craftsmen. ¹⁶ But Nebuzaradan, the captain of the guards, left some of the poorest of the land to be vinedressers and farmers.

¹⁷ Now the Chaldeans broke into pieces the bronze pillars for the LORD's temple and the water carts and the bronze basin^C that were

in the LORD's temple, and they carried all the bronze to Babylon. ¹⁸ They also took the pots, shovels, wick trimmers, sprinkling basins, dishes, and all the bronze articles used in the temple service. ¹⁹ The captain of the guards took away the bowls, firepans, sprinkling basins, pots, lampstands, pans, and drink offering bowls — whatever was gold or silver.

²⁰ As for the two pillars, the one basin, with the twelve bronze oxen under it, and the water carts^D that King Solomon had made for the LORD's temple, the weight of the bronze of all these articles was beyond measure. ²¹ One pillar was 27 feet^E tall, had a circumference of 18 feet,^F was hollow — four fingers thick — ²² and had a bronze capital on top of it. One capital, encircled by bronze grating and pomegranates, stood 7½ feet^G high. The second pillar was the same, with pomegranates. ²³ Each capital had ninety-six pomegranates all around it. All the pomegranates around the grating numbered one hundred.

²⁴ The captain of the guards also took away Seraiah the chief priest, Zephaniah the priest of the second rank, and the three doorkeepers. ²⁵ From the city he took a court official^H who had been appointed over the warriors; seven trusted royal aides^I found in the city; the secretary of the commander of the army, who enlisted the people of the land for military duty; and sixty men from the common people^J who were found within the city. ²⁶ Nebuzaradan, the captain of the guards, took them and brought them to the king of Babylon at Riblah. ²⁷ The king of Babylon put them to death at Riblah in the land of Hamath. So Judah went into exile from its land.

²⁸ These are the people Nebuchadnezzar deported: in the seventh year, 3,023 Jews; ²⁹ in his eighteenth year,^K 832 people from Jerusalem; ³⁰ in Nebuchadnezzar's twenty-third year, Nebuzaradan, the captain of the guards, deported 745 Jews. Altogether, 4,600 people were deported.

Jehoiachin Pardoned

³¹ On the twenty-fifth day of the twelfth month of the thirty-seventh year of the exile of Judah's King Jehoiachin, King Evil-merodach

^A 52:11 Lit *in a house of guards* ^B 52:12 Lit *Jerusalem; he stood before* ^C 52:17 Lit *sea* ^D 52:20 LXX, Syr; MT reads *oxen under the water carts* ^E 52:21 Lit *18 cubits* ^F 52:21 Lit *12 cubits* ^G 52:22 Lit *five cubits* ^H 52:25 Or *a eunuch* ^I 52:25 Lit *seven men who look on the king's face* ^J 52:25 Lit *the people of the land* ^K 52:29 Some Hb mss, Syr add *he deported*

52:4–11 The siege of Jerusalem, with its horrible famine, began in **the ninth year of Zedekiah's reign** (January 588 BC); it persisted until July of 587 BC, **Zedekiah's eleventh year**. The king and his warriors attempted to escape by the **king's garden**, but they were overtaken by the Babylonian army in the plains of Jericho. At **Riblah** the Babylonian king had Zedekiah's sons **slaughtered** before his eyes just before Zedekiah was blinded. 52:12–23 One month after the fall of Jerusalem, the Babylonian army returned

under the command of **Nebuzaradan** to burn down the temple, the **king's palace**, the **houses** of the city, and to raze the city **walls**. The vessels of the temple are listed one by one, as if to prolong the agony of the report and to note that all the most cherished items of the temple were dismantled. 52:24–30 Seventy-four priestly, royal, and military leaders were executed. These included the chief priest **Seraiah** (not the same Seraiah as 40:8 and 51:59) and **Zephaniah**

the priest of the second rank. Most leaders were exiled to Babylon; why these specific leaders were executed is not known. This was the third and last deportation. The first deportation in 606 BC involved Daniel and other youths. The second deportation in 597 BC involved ten thousand persons, including Ezekiel (2Kg 24:14). 52:31–34 About twenty-six years after the destruction of Jerusalem, **King Jehoiachin** found favor in exile under the Babylonian king **Evil-merodach**. The former Judean

of Babylon, in the first year of his reign, pardoned King Jehoiachin of Judah and released him from prison. [32] He spoke kindly to him and set his throne above the thrones of the kings who were with him in Babylon. [33] So Jehoiachin changed his prison clothes, and he dined regularly in the presence of the king of Babylon for the rest of his life. [34] As for his allowance, a regular allowance was given to him by the king of Babylon, a portion for each day until the day of his death, for the rest of his life.

---

king was given a standing above all the other exiled kings in Babylon, was awarded a place at the royal table, and was provided with new robes and privileges. No reason is given for this special treatment. In another twenty years, King Cyrus of Persia would allow the exiles to return home (538 BC, Ezr 1:14).

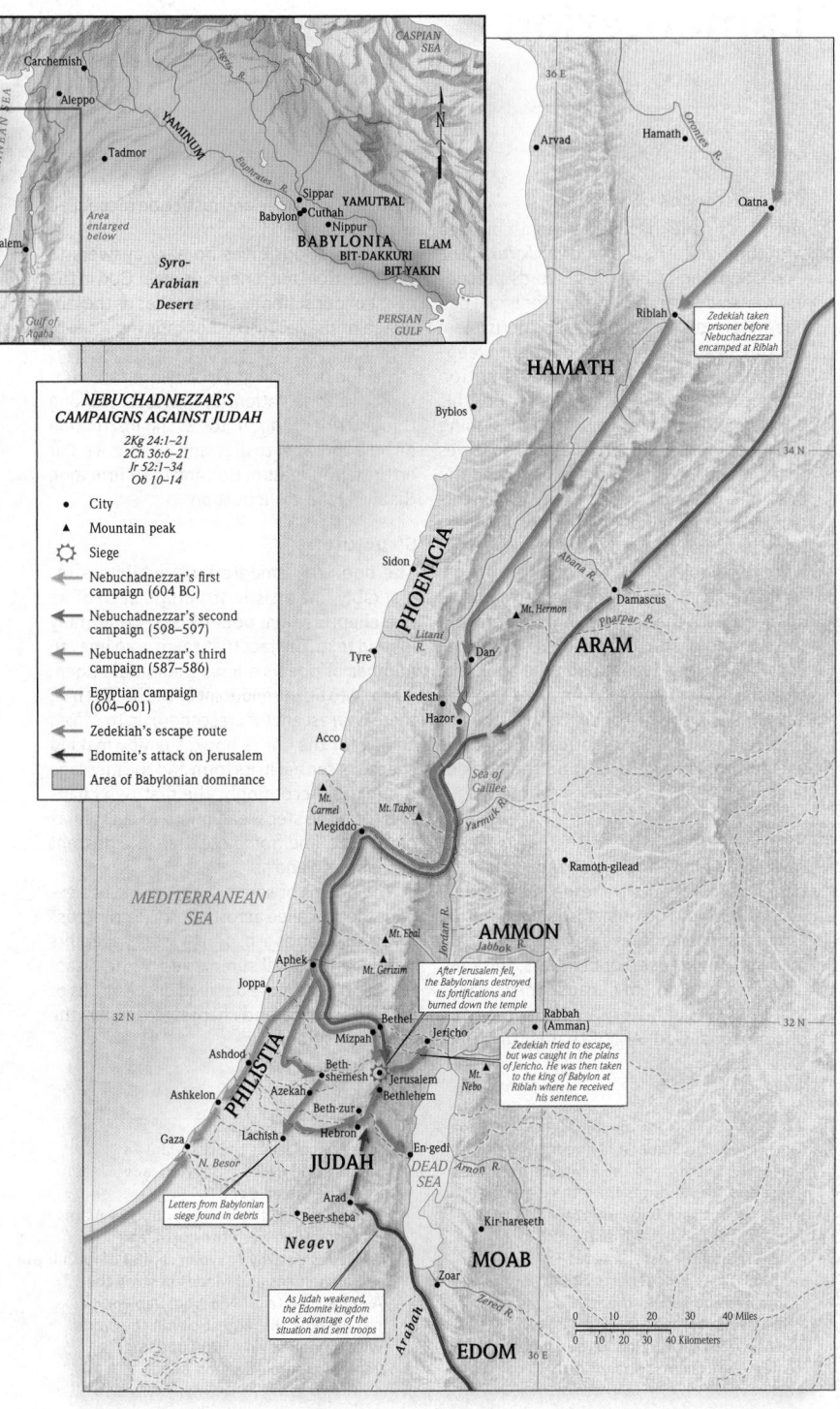

CASPIAN SEA

Carchemish
Aleppo
Tadmor
YAMINUM
Euphrates R.
Tigris R.
36 E

Jerusalem
Area enlarged below

MEDITERRANEAN SEA
Gulf of Aqaba

Sippar
Babylon
Cuthah
Nippur
YAMUTBAL
BABYLONIA
BIT-DAKKURI
BIT-YAKIN
ELAM

Syro-Arabian Desert

PERSIAN GULF

Arvad
Hamath
Orontes R.
Qatna

HAMATH
34 N

Byblos

Zedekiah taken prisoner before Nebuchadnezzar encamped at Riblah
Riblah

NEBUCHADNEZZAR'S CAMPAIGNS AGAINST JUDAH

2Kg 24:1–21
2Ch 36:6–21
Jr 52:1–34
Ob 10–14

- • City
- ▲ Mountain peak
- ☼ Siege
- ← Nebuchadnezzar's first campaign (604 BC)
- ← Nebuchadnezzar's second campaign (598–597)
- ← Nebuchadnezzar's third campaign (587–586)
- ← Egyptian campaign (604–601)
- ← Zedekiah's escape route
- ← Edomite's attack on Jerusalem
- ▨ Area of Babylonian dominance

Sidon
PHOENICIA
Mt. Hermon
Abana R.
Damascus
Pharpar R.
ARAM

Litani R.
Tyre
Dan
Kedesh
Hazor
Acco
Sea of Galilee

Mt. Carmel
Mt. Tabor
Megiddo
Yarmuk R.

Ramoth-gilead

MEDITERRANEAN SEA

Jordan R.
Mt. Ebal
Mt. Gerizim
AMMON
Jabbok R.

Aphek
Joppa
32 N

After Jerusalem fell, the Babylonians destroyed its fortifications and burned down the temple

Bethel
Mizpah
Jericho
Rabbah (Amman)
32 N

Ashdod
PHILISTIA
Beth-shemesh
Azekah
Ashkelon
Beth-zur
Gaza
Lachish
Hebron
Jerusalem
Bethlehem
Mt. Nebo

Zedekiah tried to escape, but was caught in the plains of Jericho. He was then taken to the king of Babylon at Riblah where he received his sentence.

En-gedi
JUDAH
DEAD SEA
Arnon R.

Letters from Babylonian siege found in debris
Arad
Beer-sheba
N. Besor
Negev

Kir-hareseth
MOAB

Zoar
Zered R.

As Judah weakened, the Edomite kingdom took advantage of the situation and sent troops

Arabah
EDOM
36 E

0 10 20 30 40 Miles
0 10 20 30 40 Kilometers

Introduction to Lamentations

Circumstances of Writing

Jeremiah's name has long been associated with this book. The Alexandrian form of the Greek Septuagint has these words preceding 1:1: "And it came to pass, after Israel had been carried away captive, and Jerusalem became desolate, that Jeremiah sat weeping, and lamented with this lamentation over Jerusalem." The Latin Vulgate adds this phrase: "and with a sorrowful mind, sighing and moaning, he said." The Talmud observes that "Jeremiah wrote his own book and the book of Kings and Lamentations." Given this rich tradition linking Jeremiah to Lamentations, it seems safe to conclude he did indeed write this book.

The sad background for these five poems of lament was the sacking of Jerusalem and the burning of the temple in 587 BC by the Babylonian army. Even though the book lists only one proper name ("Edom"; 4:21–22), the allusions and the historical connections to the events listed so dramatically in 2 Kings 25; 2 Chronicles 36:11–21; and the book of Jeremiah are unmistakable.

Contribution to the Bible

Few things contrast religious and humanistic traditions more than their respective responses to suffering. The humanist sees suffering as a bare, impersonal event without ultimate meaning or purpose. For believers, suffering is a personal problem because they believe that all events of history are under the hand of a personal God. And if that is true, then how can God's love and justice be reconciled with our pain?

Lamentations gives no easy answers to this question, but it helps us meet God in the midst of our suffering and teaches us the language of prayer. Instead of offering a set of techniques, easy answers, or inspiring slogans for facing pain and grief, Lamentations supplies: (1) an orientation, (2) a voice for working through grief from "A" to "Z," (3) instruction on how and what to pray, and (4) a focal point on the faithfulness of God and the affirmation that he alone is our portion.

Structure

The book of Lamentations exhibits a remarkably fine artistic structure. Each of its five chapters (five poems) is a structurally unified text. The fact that there is an uneven number of poems allows the middle poem (chap. 3) to be the midpoint of the book. Thus, there is an ascent (or crescendo) up to a fixed climax for the entire book, thereby making chapter 3 central in its form and the message it imparts. Accordingly, the first two chapters form the steps leading up to the climax of 3:22–24, and from here there is a descent in chapters 4 and 5.

The poems or songs of this book also exhibit the so-called acrostic form (a crisscross inversion such as a-b, b-a). As such, chapters 1 and 5 are overall summaries of the disaster, 2 and 4 are more detailed descriptions of what took place, and chapter 3 occupies the central position.

Lamentations Timeline

2000–700 BC

Lament for Ur, a Sumerian lament composed after the fall of Ur to the Elamites from the east and the Amorites from the west **2000**

The Assyrians sack Babylon. **1240**

Samaria, the capital of Israel, captured by the Assyrians **722**

Sargon II of Assyria deports 28,000 Israelites and settles them throughout the Assyrian Empire. **722**

The Assyrians capture numerous Judean cities—Jerusalem is spared. **701**

700–605 BC

Ashurbanipal leads the Assyrians to capture and destroy Babylon. **649**

Birth of Jeremiah **640?**

Jeremiah is called to be a prophet; he warns of an invasion from the north. **626**

The Medes destroy Assyrian capital of Asshur **614**

The Babylonians and Medes destroy the Assyrian capital of Nineveh. Babylon has become the largest city in the world with a population of 200,000. **612**

Jeremiah's temple sermon **609**

Lamentations also uses the form of the alphabetic acrostic with the twenty-two-letter Hebrew alphabet. In chapter 5, each of its twenty-two stanzas consists of a single line, but this is the only chapter that is not in an alphabetic acrostic. Chapter 3 is the most structured of the five poems.

Outline

605–600 BC

Babylonians defeat Pharaoh Neco of Egypt at Carchemish. The Babylonians hold the balance of power in the region. **605**

Babylonian force is exercised in the destruction of the Philistine cities of Ashkelon, Ashdod, and Ekron. **604**

Jehoiakim makes a decision to turn from his alliance with Egypt and submit to Nebuchadnezzar. **604**

Jehoiakim ignores Jeremiah's warning and turns back to Egypt for support after Egypt defeats Babylon at Migdol. **601**

A reinforced Babylonian army approaches Judah; Jehoiakim dies. **598**

600–585 BC

Nebuchadnezzar plunders the temple, takes Jehoiachin and the royal family into exile, and Zedekiah becomes king. **597**

Nebuchadnezzar destroys Jerusalem and the temple. **586**

Nebuchadnezzar appoints Gedaliah as governor of Judah. **585**

Judah's provincial capital is moved from Jerusalem to Mizpah. **585**

Gedaliah is assassinated after only two months by a group of fanatically zealous nationalists under the leadership of Ishmael. **585**

Lamentations **585**

Lament over Jerusalem

א Aleph

1 How[A] she sits alone,
the city once crowded with people!
She who was great among the nations
has become like a widow.
The princess among the provinces
has been put to forced labor.

ב Beth

2 She weeps bitterly during the night,
with tears on her cheeks.
There is no one to offer her comfort,
not one from all her lovers.[B]
All her friends have betrayed her;
they have become her enemies.

ג Gimel

3 Judah has gone into exile
following[C] affliction and harsh slavery;
she lives among the nations
but finds no place to rest.
All her pursuers have overtaken her
in narrow places.

ד Daleth

4 The roads to Zion mourn,
for no one comes
to the appointed festivals.
All her gates are deserted;
her priests groan,
her young women grieve,
and she herself is bitter.

ה He

5 Her adversaries have become
her masters;
her enemies are at ease,
for the LORD has made her suffer
because of her many transgressions.
Her children have gone away
as captives before the adversary.

ו Waw

6 All the splendor has vanished
from Daughter Zion.
Her leaders are like stags
that find no pasture;
they stumble away exhausted
before the hunter.

ז Zayin

7 During the days of her affliction
and homelessness
Jerusalem remembers all
her precious belongings
that were hers in days of old.
When her people fell
into the adversary's hand,
she had no one to help.
The adversaries looked at her,
laughing over her downfall.

ח Cheth

8 Jerusalem has sinned grievously;
therefore, she has become an object
of scorn.[D]
All who honored her now despise her,
for they have seen her nakedness.
She herself groans and turns away.

ט Teth

9 Her uncleanness stains her skirts.
She never considered her end.
Her downfall was astonishing;
there was no one to comfort her.
LORD, look on my affliction,
for the enemy boasts.

י Yod

10 The adversary has seized
all her precious belongings.
She has even seen the nations
enter her sanctuary —
those you had forbidden
to enter your assembly.

כ Kaph

11 All her people groan
while they search for bread.
They have traded
their precious belongings for food
in order to stay alive.
LORD, look and see
how I have become despised.

ל Lamed

12 Is this nothing to you, all you
who pass by?
Look and see!
Is there any pain like mine,

---

^1:1 The stanzas in Lm 1–4 form an acrostic.   ^1:2 = Jerusalem's political allies   ^1:3 Or *because of*   ^1:8 Or *become impure*

1:1–22 This chapter is an alphabetic acrostic where each verse begins with a successive letter of the twenty-two-letter Hebrew alphabet.
1:1–7 In this section the poet uses the third person as he speaks on behalf of Jerusalem. It is her loneliness that strikes the poet as the losses mount up: loss of abundance (v. 1), loss of allies (v. 2), loss of a resting place (v. 3), loss of happiness (v. 4), loss of prestige (v. 5), loss of courage (v. 6), and loss of worship (v. 7).

1:1 The poet begins with an exclamatory word **How**—a word used in biblical texts for laments and funerals. Three contrasts of status are listed. Jerusalem was once populous, **great among the nations**, the queen of the cities; now she is solitary, a **widow**, and a tributary slave.
1:7 This verse summarizes the whole section with the name of **Jerusalem** appearing for the first time.
1:8–11 This section explores some of the sources of Judah's grief. Notable are its

shame (v. 8), its defilement (v. 9), its desecration (v. 10), and famine (v. 11).
1:10 Judah lost the most outstanding of all her glorious possessions—the temple of God. The sanctuary was off limits to Gentiles previously, but now the nations tramped through it with disregard.
1:12–17 The second half of this first lament intensifies as the plan and purpose of God are unveiled.

which was dealt out to me,
which the LORD made me suffer
on the day of his burning anger?

מ Mem

¹³ He sent fire from on high
into my bones;
he made it descend.ᴬ
He spread a net for my feet
and turned me back.
He made me desolate,
sick all day long.

נ Nun

¹⁴ My transgressions have been formed
into a yoke,ᴮ,ᶜ
fastened together by his hand;
they have been placed on my neck,
and the Lord has broken my strength.
He has handed me over
to those I cannot withstand.

ס Samek

¹⁵ The Lord has rejected
all the mighty men within me.
He has summoned an armyᴰ against me
to crush my young warriors.
The Lord has trampled
Virgin Daughter Judah
like grapes in a winepress.

ע Ayin

¹⁶ I weep because of these things;
my eyes flowᴱ with tears.
For there is no one nearby
to comfort me,
no one to keep me alive.
My children are desolate
because the enemy has prevailed.

פ Pe

¹⁷ Zion stretches out her hands;
there is no one to comfort her.
The LORD has issued a decree
against Jacob
that his neighbors should be
his adversaries.
Jerusalem has become
something impure among them.

צ Tsade

¹⁸ The LORD is just,
for I have rebelled
against his command.
Listen, all you people;
look at my pain.
My young women and young men
have gone into captivity.

ק Qoph

¹⁹ I called to my lovers,
but they betrayed me.
My priests and elders
perished in the city
while searching for food
to keep themselves alive.

ר Resh

²⁰ LORD, see how I am in distress.
I am churning within;
my heart is broken,ᶠ
for I have been very rebellious.
Outside, the sword takes the children;
inside, there is death.

ש Shin

²¹ People have heard me groaning,
but there is no one to comfort me.
All my enemies have heard
of my misfortune;
they are glad that you have caused it.
Bring on the day you have announced,
so that they may become like me.

ת Taw

²² Let all their wickedness come
before you,
and deal with them
as you have dealt with me
because of all my transgressions.
For my groans are many,
and I am sick at heart.

Judgment on Jerusalem

א Aleph

2 How the Lord has overshadowed
Daughter Zion with his anger!
He has thrown down Israel's glory
from heaven to earth.

ᴬ**1:13** DSS, LXX; MT reads *bones, and it prevailed against them*   ᴮ**1:14** Some Hb mss, LXX read *He kept watch over my transgressions*   ᶜ**1:14** Or *The yoke of my transgressions is bound*; Hb obscure   ᴰ**1:15** Or *has announced an appointed time*   ᴱ**1:16** Lit *my eye, my eye flows*   ᶠ**1:20** Lit *is turned within me*

:13–15 Four strong metaphors depict the sufferings that Jerusalem endured: (1) **fire from on high**, (2) a hunter's **net** for her **feet**, (3) an animal **yoke** on her **neck**, and (4) being **trampled** and crushed like grapes in **a winepress**. Each figure depicted the "day of wrath" belonging to the Lord. The fire from on high was nothing less than fire from God (Gn 19:24; Ps 11:6). So was the net from God, because it came as a check on one's lifestyle (Ps 94:13; Jr 50:24; Ezk 12:13; 17:20; 2:3; Hs 7:12). The yoke recalled Jeremiah's

encounter with the false prophet Hananiah (Jr 28). Likewise, the winepress was a symbol of the final judgment (Is 63:1–4; Jr 6:9; Jl 3:13; Rv 14:18–20; 19:13–15).
1:17 Once again, for the fourth time in this chapter, the mournful words fall: **there is no one to comfort her**.
1:18–22 After structuring his first poem around the first seventeen letters of the Hebrew alphabet, describing all the while Israel's bitter response to her suffering, with the eighteenth letter Jeremiah begins a brief

interlude in which Judah confesses that the Lord is in the right and asks him to **deal with them** [Judah's enemies] **as you have dealt with me**.
1:20–21 Two requests are issued in these verses: (1) for the Lord to witness the enormous mental and emotional **distress** Judah was experiencing, and (2) for the Lord to pay back the jeering nations.
2:1–22 God's anger is mentioned elsewhere in Lamentations (1:12; 3:1,43,66; 4:11; 5:22), but the theme is especially common

He did not acknowledge his footstool
  in the day of his anger.

ב Beth
2 Without compassion the Lord
  has swallowed up
  all the dwellings of Jacob.
In his wrath he has demolished
  the fortified cities of Daughter Judah.
He brought them to the ground
  and defiled the kingdom
  and its leaders.

ג Gimel
3 He has cut off every horn of Israel
  in his burning anger
and withdrawn his right hand
  in the presence of the enemy.
He has blazed against Jacob
  like a flaming fire
  that consumes everything.

ד Daleth
4 He has strung his bow like an enemy;
his right hand is positioned
  like an adversary.
He has killed everyone who was the
  delight to the eye,
pouring out his wrath like fire
  on the tent of Daughter Zion.

ה He
5 The Lord is like an enemy;
  he has swallowed up Israel.
He swallowed up all its palaces
  and destroyed its fortified cities.
He has multiplied mourning
  and lamentation
  within Daughter Judah.

ו Waw
6 He has wrecked his temple[A]
  as if it were merely a shack in a field,[B]
  destroying his place of meeting.
The Lord has abolished
  appointed festivals and Sabbaths
  in Zion.
He has despised king and priest
  in his fierce anger.

ז Zayin
7 The Lord has rejected his altar,
  repudiated his sanctuary;

he has handed the walls
  of her palaces
  over to the enemy.
They have raised a shout in the house
  of the Lord
  as on the day of an appointed festival.

ח Cheth
8 The Lord determined to destroy
  the wall of Daughter Zion.
He stretched out a measuring line
  and did not restrain himself
  from destroying.
He made the ramparts
  and walls grieve;
  together they waste away.

ט Teth
9 Zion's gates have fallen to the ground;
  he has destroyed and shattered the bars
  on her gates.
Her king and her leaders live
  among the nations,
instruction[C] is no more,
  and even her prophets receive
  no vision from the Lord.

י Yod
10 The elders of Daughter Zion
  sit on the ground in silence.
They have thrown dust
  on their heads
  and put on sackcloth.
The young women of Jerusalem
  have bowed their heads to the ground.

כ Kaph
11 My eyes are worn out from weeping;
  I am churning within.
My heart is poured out in grief[D]
  because of the destruction
  of my dear people,
because infants and nursing
  babies faint
  in the streets of the city.

ל Lamed
12 They cry out to their mothers,
  "Where is the grain and wine?"
as they faint like the wounded
  in the streets of the city,
as their life pours out
  in the arms of their mothers.

[A]2:6 Lit *booth*   [B]2:6 Lit *it were a garden*   [C]2:9 Or *the law*   [D]2:11 Lit *My liver is poured out on the ground*

---

in this section. The first ten verses of chap. 2 contain forty descriptions of God's anger and judgment. This chapter is an alphabetic acrostic where each verse begins with a successive letter of the twenty-two-letter Hebrew alphabet.
2:1 The phrase **Israel's glory** must mean that the temple of God has been destroyed.

2:3 God's work is described both actively (**He has cut off every horn of Israel**, meaning all strength and power) and passively (he has **withdrawn his right hand**). The destruction of Jerusalem was as much a work of God as it was an accomplishment of Babylon.
2:7 God **rejected** and **repudiated** not only the temple with its altar and sanctuary, but also **the walls of her palaces**. The royal

palace, state buildings, the temple—God judged every aspect of Jerusalem. **The enemy**, not Hebrew worshipers, raised shouts **in the house of the Lord**.
2:8–9 The ruin of the **ramparts and walls** leaves Jerusalem defenseless.
2:10 Being clothed in **sackcloth** with **dust on their heads** were symbols of extreme distress and mourning.

מ Mem

13 What can I say on your behalf?
What can I compare you to,
    Daughter Jerusalem?
What can I liken you to,
so that I may console you,
    Virgin Daughter Zion?
For your ruin is as vast as the sea.
Who can heal you?

נ Nun

14 Your prophets saw visions for you
that were empty and deceptive;[A]
they did not reveal your iniquity
and so restore your fortunes.
They saw pronouncements for you
that were empty and misleading.

ס Samek

15 All who pass by
scornfully clap their hands at you.
They hiss and shake their heads
at Daughter Jerusalem:
Is this the city that was called
the perfection of beauty,
the joy of the whole earth?

פ Pe

16 All your enemies
open their mouths against you.
They hiss and gnash their teeth,
saying, "We have swallowed her up.
This is the day we have waited for!
We have lived to see it."

ע Ayin

17 The LORD has done what he planned;
he has accomplished his decree,
which he ordained in days of old.
He has demolished
    without compassion,
letting the enemy gloat over you
and exalting the horn
    of your adversaries.

צ Tsade

18 The hearts of the people cry out
to the Lord.

Wall of Daughter Zion,
let your tears run down like a river
day and night.
Give yourself no relief
and your[B] eyes no rest.

ק Qoph

19 Arise, cry out in the night
from the first watch of the night.
Pour out your heart like water
before the Lord's presence.
Lift up your hands to him
for the lives of your children
who are fainting from hunger
at the head of every street.

ר Resh

20 LORD, look and consider
to whom you have done this.
Should women eat their own children,
the infants they have nurtured?[C]
Should priests and prophets
be killed in the Lord's sanctuary?

ש Shin

21 Both young and old
are lying on the ground in the streets.
My young women and young men
have fallen by the sword.
You have killed them in the day
    of your anger,
slaughtering without compassion.

ת Taw

22 You summon those who terrorize me[D]
    on every side,
as if for an appointed festival day;
on the day of the LORD's anger
no one escaped or survived.
My enemy has destroyed
those I nurtured[E] and reared.

Hope through God's Mercy

א Aleph

3 I am the man who has seen affliction
under the rod of God's wrath.
2 He has driven me away and forced me
    to walk

[A]2:14 Or insipid [B]2:18 Lit and the daughter of your [C]2:20 Or infants in a healthy condition; Hb obscure [D]2:22 Or terrors
[E]2:22 Or I bore healthy; Hb obscure

2:13 Words fail Jeremiah as he struggles to make sense of what has happened. It is as catastrophic as a churning sea.
2:19 Judah is to call on the name of the Lord with her **heart** poured out **like water**, starting with **the first watch**—from sunset until 10:00 p.m.
2:20 **Should women eat their own children**? This is how desperate conditions became during the siege of Jerusalem. People fought over whose child should be eaten next (4:10; see Jr 19:9; Ezk 5:10).
2:22 The phrase **those who terrorize me on every side** may also be rendered "terrors on

every side." This jeer was hurled at Jeremiah repeatedly during his ministry (Jr 6:25; 20:3,10; 46:5; 49:29).
3:1–66 This is the central chapter of the lament. It is distinctive in form and content from all others in the book. Like chaps. 1; 2; 4, it is an alphabetic acrostic, but here there are three verses devoted to each of the successive letters of the twenty-two-letter Hebrew alphabet. The identity of **I am the man** (v. 1) strikes us immediately. Who is speaking here? It is an individual "I" (vv. 1–24) that changes to a "we" (vv. 22,40–47) and back to "I" again in vv. 48–66. Some

say it is a generalized "everyman," others suggest a historical personage such as King Jehoiachin. But it is probably Jeremiah speaking as a collective personage. He suffered as an "I" while carrying out his unpopular role as prophet, prayer warrior, and pleader for his people; and he also suffered as a "we" as his people and his city were destroyed.
3:1 The **rod of God's wrath** was Babylon.
3:2 **He has driven** is usually used of driving flocks to good places (Ex 3:1), but here it is the opposite.

in darkness instead of light.
³ Yes, he repeatedly turns his hand
against me all day long.

ᴊ Beth

⁴ He has worn away my flesh and skin;
he has broken my bones.
⁵ He has laid siege against me,
encircling me with bitterness
and hardship.
⁶ He has made me dwell in darkness
like those who have been dead for ages.

ᴊ Gimel

⁷ He has walled me in so I cannot get out;
he has weighed me down with chains.
⁸ Even when I cry out and plead for help,
he blocks out my prayer.
⁹ He has walled in my ways with blocks
of stone;
he has made my paths crooked.

ᴛ Daleth

¹⁰ He is^A a bear waiting in ambush,
a lion in hiding.
¹¹ He forced me off my way and tore me
to pieces;
he left me desolate.
¹² He strung his bow
and set me as the target for his arrow.

ᴊ He

¹³ He pierced my kidneys
with shafts from his quiver.
¹⁴ I am a laughingstock to all my people,^B

mocked by their songs all day long.
¹⁵ He filled me with bitterness,
satiated me with wormwood.

ᴊ Waw

¹⁶ He ground my teeth with gravel
and made me cower^C in the dust.
¹⁷ I have been deprived^D of peace;
I have forgotten what prosperity is.
¹⁸ Then I thought, "My future^E is lost,
as well as my hope from the Lᴏʀᴅ."

ᴊ Zayin

¹⁹ Remember^F my affliction
and my homelessness,
the wormwood and the poison.
²⁰ I continually remember them
and have become depressed.^G
²¹ Yet I call this to mind,
and therefore I have hope:

ᴊ Cheth

²² Because of the Lᴏʀᴅ's faithful love
we do not perish,^H
for his mercies never end.
²³ They are new every morning;
great is your faithfulness!
²⁴ I say, "The Lᴏʀᴅ is my portion,
therefore I will put my hope in him."

ᴊ Teth

²⁵ The Lᴏʀᴅ is good to those who wait
for him,
to the person who seeks him.
²⁶ It is good to wait quietly

---

^A3:10 Lit *is to me* ^B3:14 Some Hb mss, LXX, Vg; other Hb mss, Syr read *all peoples* ^C3:16 Or *and trampled me* ^D3:17 Syr, Vg; MT reads *You deprived my soul* ^E3:18 Or *splendor* ^F3:19 Or *I remember* ^G3:20 Alt Hb tradition reads *and you cause me to collapse* ^H3:22 One Hb mss, Syr, Tg read *The LORD's faithful love, indeed, does not perish*

3:4–6 The days of rebellion by the people against God had aged the poet and left him like a dead man. Like the nation, Jeremiah could sense life ebbing away.

3:6 Dwelling in **darkness** implies that death and adversity had wrapped themselves around Jeremiah (Jb 12:25; Am 5:18).

3:7–9 God had **walled . . . in** his representative Jeremiah and **weighed** him **down** so

that he felt he was walking in a maze—paths that led nowhere, full of dead ends.

3:10–11 In another bold figure of speech, God is compared to **a bear waiting in ambush** or **a lion in hiding** (see Hs 13:8; Am 5:19). There is a mixing of metaphors here; Jeremiah had already compared Israel's enemies to lions (Jr 5:6; 49:19; 50:44). Thus what God had permitted the nation's enemy to do (stalk

and destroy Judah) could also be attributed to God himself.

3:12 God is depicted as an archer (Jb 16:12–13) who shoots with deadly accuracy at his prey.

3:19 Four terms show the depth of Jeremiah's sorrow: **affliction . . . homelessness . . . wormwood**, and **poison**. Jeremiah's memory of the past was bitter to the utmost.

3:20–24 Just as quickly as the prophet was tempted by bitter thoughts, he adopted a better line of thought: instead of brooding over his anguish and sorrow, he will put his hope in the love of the Lord because **his mercies never end**. The fact that Jeremiah was still alive was proof that God's **faithful love** was constant. Here is the heart of this book: **Great is your faithfulness!** The Lord himself was the poet's **portion** (see Pss 16:5; 73:26; 119:57; 142:5).

3:25–39 The dominant thought of this section is that **the Lord is good**. All five triads in this section (vv. 25–27,28–30,31–33,34–36,37–39) begin not only with the same letter from the Hebrew alphabet, but with the same Hebrew word or related words in each line.

3:25–27 God's goodness is presented in three aspects. (1) God is good in his nature and being. (2) God is good to those who have learned to wait silently and endure his

for salvation from the LORD.
27 It is good for a man to bear the yoke
while he is still young.

י Yod
28 Let him sit alone and be silent,
for God has disciplined[A] him.
29 Let him put his mouth in the dust —
perhaps there is still hope.
30 Let him offer his cheek
to the one who would strike him;
let him be filled with disgrace.

כ Kaph
31 For the Lord
will not reject us forever.
32 Even if he causes suffering,
he will show compassion
according to the abundance of his
faithful love.
33 For he does not enjoy bringing affliction
or suffering on mankind.

ל Lamed
34 Crushing all the prisoners of the land[B]
beneath one's feet,
35 denying justice to a man
in the presence of the Most High,
36 or subverting a person in his lawsuit —
the Lord does not approve of these things.

מ Mem
37 Who is there who speaks
and it happens,
unless the Lord has ordained it?
38 Do not both adversity and good
come from the mouth of the Most High?
39 Why should any living person complain,
any man, because of the punishment
for his sins?

נ Nun
40 Let's examine and probe our ways,
and turn back to the LORD.

41 Let's lift up our hearts and our hands
to God in heaven:
42 "We have sinned and rebelled;
you have not forgiven.

ס Samek
43 "You have covered yourself in anger
and pursued us;
you have killed without compassion.
44 You have covered yourself with a cloud
so that no prayer can get through.
45 You have made us disgusting filth
among the peoples.

פ Pe
46 "All our enemies
open their mouths against us.
47 We have experienced panic and pitfall,
devastation and destruction."
48 My eyes flow with streams of tears
because of the destruction
of my dear people.

ע Ayin
49 My eyes overflow unceasingly,
without end,
50 until the LORD looks down
from heaven and sees.
51 My eyes bring me grief
because of the fate of all the women
in my city.

צ Tsade
52 For no reason, my enemies[C]
hunted me like a bird.
53 They smothered my life in[D] a pit
and threw stones on me.
54 Water flooded over my head,
and I thought, "I'm going to die!"

ק Qoph
55 I called on your name, LORD,
from the depths of the pit.
56 You heard my plea:

[A]**3:28** Lit *has laid a burden on* [B]**3:34** Or *earth* [C]**3:52** Or *Those who were my enemies for no reason* [D]**3:53** Or *They ended my life in*; Hb obscure

lessons through suffering. (3) God is good to those who submit agreeably to divine providence. **3:28–30** This triad teaches how a person is to suffer patiently. (1) **Sit alone and be silent**, which allows for reflection with God. (2) **Put your mouth in the dust**, which keeps you from speaking in anger. (3) **Offer** your **cheek** to the striker, an attitude of humility. Each tactic is increasingly difficult, and each raises the hope that God will deliver his people from trouble. **3:31–33** There are three reasons for hope. (1) The **Lord will not reject** his people **forever**. (2) God's **compassion** outweighs the sorrow he sends. (3) God **does not enjoy bringing affliction or suffering on mankind**. **3:40–47** Jeremiah shifted to the first-person plural pronoun (us and our) for the rest of this

chapter. In these verses his representative role is made plain. He will lead his people in a confession of their sins and exhort them to return to the Lord. **3:40** No phrase is more characteristic of the prophets—especially Jeremiah—than **turn back to the LORD** (see Jr 3:1). It is the OT word for repentance. It called for the people to **examine and probe** their **ways**, an act that implied their sin was hidden from the eyes and hearts of those who had been deceived (Jr 17:9). **3:41** Here is an appeal to prayer, as signified by the lifting of one's **hands** (2:19). **3:42** This verse states the content of the prayer. The contrast between **we** and the Lord (**you**) is emphatic and specific. **3:46–48** The third line of the triad of vv. 46–48 dramatically (as in v. 40) breaks

back into the first-person pronoun with its reference to **my eyes** (which continues in v. 49), so this is a lament against Israel's enemies. **3:52–54 Water flooded over my head** is a metaphor for all sorts of distress (Jb 27:20; Pss 42:7; 66:12; 88:7; 124:4; Is 43:2). **3:55–66** The final twelve verses of this chapter are a prayer for deliverance, which is how chapters 1 and 2 end. **3:55** Like the psalmist, Jeremiah called on God's name **from the depths of the pit** (see Ps 130:1). **3:56–57** God **heard** Jeremiah's **plea**. His words of assurance were, **Do not be afraid**.

Do not ignore my cry for relief.

57 You came near whenever I called you;
you said, "Do not be afraid."

ר Resh

58 You championed my cause, Lord;
you redeemed my life.

59 LORD, you saw the wrong done to me;
judge my case.

60 You saw all their vengefulness,
all their plots against me.

ש Sin/ ש Shin

61 LORD, you heard their insults,
all their plots against me.

62 The slander[A] and murmuring
of my opponents
attack me all day long.

63 When they sit and when they rise, look,
I am mocked by their songs.

ת Taw

64 You will pay them back
what they deserve, LORD,
according to the work of their hands.

65 You will give them a heart
filled with anguish.[B]
May your curse be on them!

66 You will pursue them in anger
and destroy them
under your heavens.[C]

Terrors of the Besieged City

א Aleph

4 How the gold has become tarnished,
the fine gold become dull!
The stones of the temple[D] lie scattered
at the head of every street.

ב Beth

2 Zion's precious children —
once worth their weight in pure gold —
how they are regarded as clay jars,
the work of a potter's hands!

ג Gimel

3 Even jackals offer their breasts
to nurse their young,
but my dear people have become cruel
like ostriches in the wilderness.

ד Daleth

4 The nursing baby's tongue
clings to the roof of his mouth
from thirst.
Infants beg for food,
but no one gives them any.

ה He

5 Those who used to eat delicacies
are destitute in the streets;
those who were reared
in purple garments
huddle in trash heaps.

ו Waw

6 The punishment of my dear people
is greater than that of Sodom,
which was overthrown in an instant
without a hand laid on it.

ז Zayin

7 Her dignitaries were brighter
than snow,
whiter than milk;
their bodies[E] were more ruddy
than coral,
their appearance like lapis lazuli.

ח Cheth

8 Now they appear darker than soot;
they are not recognized in the streets.
Their skin has shriveled on their bones;
it has become dry like wood.

ט Teth

9 Those slain by the sword are better off
than those slain by hunger,
who waste away, pierced with pain
because the fields lack produce.

י Yod

10 The hands of compassionate women
have cooked their own children;
they became their food
during the destruction
of my dear people.

כ Kaph

11 The LORD has exhausted his wrath,
poured out his burning anger;

[A]3:62 Lit lips   [B]3:65 Or them an obstinate heart; Hb obscure   [C]3:66 Lit under the LORD's heavens   [D]4:1 Or The sacred gems
[E]4:7 Lit bones

4:1–22 This chapter is an alphabetic acrostic where each verse begins with a successive letter of the twenty-two-letter Hebrew alphabet. **4:1–2** God's people were **worth their weight** in gold. The prophet used three terms for gold: the general term **gold, fine gold**, and **pure gold**. That is what the holy nation was before God; but now smeared with sin, they were regarded as **clay jars**, like pieces of broken pottery. **4:3–4** The **jackals** offer their **breasts to nurse their young**, but Israel's parents neglected their young during the crisis. They are like **ostriches**, which are known for their habit of laying eggs and then leaving them (Jb 39:13–18). **4:7–8** The phrase **her dignitaries** is often rendered as "her Nazirites," but Gn 49:26 and Dt 33:16 use it of a person who is "separated" by rank and task from his contemporaries. Hence, these dignitaries, once **ruddy** and glamorous, were now **darker than soot**. Their skin was **shriveled on their bones**. **4:9** A swift death by the **sword** was better than a slow death by starvation. **4:10** So horrific were the effects of the famine during the siege of Jerusalem that even **compassionate women**, who under normal circumstances would never think of such a thing, **cooked their own children** for **food** (see note at 2:20). **4:11 Exhausted his wrath** means his planned judgment was fulfilled, not that he became weary and thus relented.

he has ignited a fire in Zion,
and it has consumed her foundations.

ל Lamed

12 The kings of the earth
and all the world's inhabitants
did not believe
that an enemy or adversary
could enter Jerusalem's gates.

מ Mem

13 Yet it happened because of the sins
of her prophets
and the iniquities of her priests,
who shed the blood of the righteous
within her.

נ Nun

14 Blind, they stumbled in the streets,
defiled by this blood,
so that no one dared
to touch their garments.

ס Samek

15 "Stay away! Unclean!" people shouted
at them.
"Away, away! Don't touch us!"
So they wandered aimlessly.
It was said among the nations,
"They can stay here no longer."

פ Pe

16 The LORD himself
has scattered them;
he no longer watches over them.
The priests are not respected;
the elders find no favor.

ע Ayin

17 All the while our eyes were failing
as we looked in vain for help;
we watched from our towers
for a nation that would not save us.

צ Tsade

18 Our steps were closely followed
so that we could not walk in our streets.
Our end approached; our time ran out.
Our end had come!

ק Qoph

19 Those who chased us were swifter
than eagles in the sky;
they relentlessly pursued us
over the mountains
and ambushed us in the wilderness.

ר Resh

20 The LORD's anointed, the breath
of our life,ᴬ
was captured in their traps.
We had said about him,
"We will live under his protection
among the nations."

שׁ Sin

21 So rejoice and be glad, Daughter Edom,
you resident of the land of Uz!
Yet the cup will pass to you as well;
you will get drunk and expose yourself.

תּ Taw

22 Daughter Zion, your punishment
is complete;
he will not lengthen your exile.ᴮ
But he will punish your iniquity,
Daughter Edom,
and will expose your sins.

Prayer for Restoration

5 LORD, remember what has happened
to us.
Look, and see our disgrace!
2 Our inheritance has been turned over
to strangers,
our houses to foreigners.
3 We have become orphans, fatherless;
our mothers are widows.
4 We must pay for the water we drink;
our wood comes at a price.
5 We are closely pursued;
we are tired, and no one offers us rest.
6 We made a treaty withᶜ Egypt
and with Assyria, to get enough food.
7 Our ancestors sinned;
they no longer exist,
but we bear their punishment.
8 Slaves rule over us;
no one rescues us from them.

ᴬ4:20 Lit nostrils ᴮ4:22 Or not deport you again ᶜ5:6 Lit We gave the hand to

---

4:13–14 That no one dared to touch their garments means the prophets and the priests were the outcasts of society.
4:15–16 The survivors, who once cheered the false prophets and priests, now yelled at them: Unclean! . . . Away, away! Don't touch us! They were now homeless, aimless, and despised.
4:18–19 The imagery of closely followed is that of a hunter stalking his prey.
4:20 Likewise, their trust in the heir of the Davidic line (The LORD's anointed, the

breath of our life) proved futile. He was also captured in their traps. King Zedekiah was chained, blinded after watching his sons being massacred, and exiled to Babylon.
4:21–22 The nation of Edom might jeer for the moment, but the cup of God's wrath would fall on them also (Jr 25:15–29; Hab 2:15–16; Obadiah).
5:1–22 Chapter 5 has twenty-two verses, but it is not an alphabetic acrostic in Hebrew. It is as if things have gotten so bad that even poetry is chaotic.

5:1 To remember in Scripture is never just calling something to mind. It involves a corresponding action.
5:5 The people of God were without rest, implying spiritual and physical troubles (Heb 3:16–4:11).
5:8 A great reversal has occurred, signifying a bad situation. Slaves have been made masters (see Pr 30:21–23).

⁹ We secure our food at the risk
  of our lives
because of the sword
  in the wilderness.
¹⁰ Our skin is as hot^A as an oven
  from the ravages of hunger.
¹¹ Women have been raped in Zion,
  virgins in the cities of Judah.
¹² Princes have been hung up
  by their hands;
elders are shown no respect.
¹³ Young men labor at millstones;
  boys stumble under loads of wood.
¹⁴ The elders have left the city gate,
  the young men, their music.
¹⁵ Joy has left our hearts;
  our dancing has turned to mourning.

¹⁶ The crown has fallen from our head.
  Woe to us, for we have sinned.
¹⁷ Because of this, our heart is sick;
  because of these, our eyes grow dim:
¹⁸ because of Mount Zion,
  which lies desolate
and has jackals prowling in it.
¹⁹ You, LORD, are enthroned forever;
  your throne endures from generation
  to generation.
²⁰ Why do you continually forget us,
  abandon us for our entire lives?
²¹ LORD, bring us back to yourself, so we
  may return;
renew our days as in former times,
²² unless you have completely rejected us
  and are intensely angry with us.

^A5:10 Or *black*; Hb obscure

5:9 Even the scanty harvests were subject to predatory raids by desert tribes.
5:10 Figuratively speaking, the people's skin was as **hot as an oven** as they suffered from the fever of extreme **hunger**.
5:11–14 Hardly anyone in Jerusalem was left unscathed.

5:16 The fallen **crown** symbolized Israel's loss of honor and glory. The reason was clear: **we have sinned**.
5:17 **Because of this/these** refers to the situation and events of vv. 2–16. Elsewhere **eyes** growing **dim** refers to the loss of vitality as through aging.

5:22 Had God been so **intensely angry** with his people that he had **completely rejected** them? No. He would restore and renew them as he had done in the past.

Introduction to Ezekiel

Circumstances of Writing

There is sufficient reason for maintaining that the prophet Ezekiel composed the book of Ezekiel in Babylon. The work demonstrates such homogeneity and literary coherence that it is reasonable to conclude that all editorial work was done by the prophet himself.

The inclusion of historical dates at the beginning of many of the oracles and prophecies in Ezekiel is another important unifying factor. The book is one of the most chronologically ordered books of the Bible. Thirteen times a passage is introduced by an indication of time. The common point of orientation for the dates given in Ezekiel is the exile of King Jehoiachin of Judah in 598/597 BC. The occurrence of visions throughout the book (chaps. 1; 8–11; 40–48) is another strong argument in favor of its overall unity. Finally, stylistic features throughout the book strengthen the unity argument.

Ezekiel, son of Buzi, was among the approximately ten thousand citizens of Judah deported to Babylon when King Nebuchadnezzar invaded Jerusalem in 598/597 BC (2Kg 24:10–17). His prophetic call came to him five years later (the fifth year of King Jehoiachin's exile), in 593 BC. He received his call at the age of thirty (1:1), the year he should have begun his duties as a priest (Nm 4:3). The last dated oracle in the book occurs in the twenty-seventh year of King Jehoiachin (29:17), thus indicating that Ezekiel's ministry lasted twenty-two or twenty-three years. The prophet lived during the greatest crisis in Israel's history—the destruction of Jerusalem and its temple, plus the exile of Judah's leading citizens to Babylon.

Contribution to the Bible

There are few quotations of the book of Ezekiel in the New Testament, but there are some notable correlations. For instance, the structure of the book of Revelation, which begins with a vision of Christ, corresponds to the appearances of God in Ezekiel's visions. The end of the book of Revelation also reflects the end of Ezekiel, where the river flows from the presence of God (47:1–12; Rv 21:1–22:6). Finally, the depiction of the return of the exiles as resurrected from the dead is analogous to Paul's concept of regeneration (Eph 2:5).

Structure

The prophet Ezekiel displayed a distinct style throughout his prophetic work. The phrase "son of man" occurs ninety-three times as a title for Ezekiel, focusing on the prophet's human nature. The expression "the hand of the Lord was on me," which is said elsewhere only of Elijah (1Kg 18:46) and Elisha (2Kg 3:15), occurs in the various major sections of Ezekiel (1:3; 3:22; 33:22; 37:1). The so-called recognition formula, that "you [or they] may know that I am the Lord," a characteristic phrase of the exodus narrative (Ex 6:6–8; 7:5; 10:1–2; 14:4,18), occurs about sixty times in Ezekiel. The introductory oracle phrase "the word of the Lord came to me"

Ezekiel Timeline

625–590 BC

Year of Ezekiel's birth **623**
First siege of Jerusalem by the Babylonians and first wave of exiles, including Daniel, taken to Babylon **605**
Babylonians' second siege of Jerusalem; King Jehoiachin and 10,000 citizens of Judah, including Ezekiel, exiled to Babylon **597**
God calls Ezekiel, then thirty years old, to prophesy. **593**
Ezekiel prophesies against pagan practices at the temple in Jerusalem. **592**
Elders of Israel seek a word of the Lord from Ezekiel. **591**

590–585 BC

The Lord tells Ezekiel to let the captives know that the king of Babylon has once again laid siege to Jerusalem. **588**
Ezekiel prophesies Egypt's ruin and the destruction of Pharaoh and his army. **587**
Ezekiel prophesies the downfall of Tyre. **586**
After a two-year siege, the walls of Jerusalem and the temple are destroyed; a third wave of exiles is taken to Babylon. **586**
A messenger from Jerusalem comes to Ezekiel to announce the downfall of the city. **586/585**
Ezekiel's lament for Pharaoh **585**

occurs forty-six times in the book and alerts the reader to the beginning of a separate section. The phrase "I, the LORD, have spoken" also occurs frequently in Ezekiel. Another feature for which Ezekiel is well known is his performance of symbolic, dramatic actions. He also used the literary technique of allegory to communicate his prophecies. His allegories include Jerusalem as a vine (chap. 15) and majestic eagles (17:1–21),

the Davidic dynasty as a lioness (19:1–9) and a vineyard (19:10–14), a sword as judgment (21:1–17), and Oholah and Oholibah as corrupt sisters (23:1–35).

A final characteristic of the book is the citation of previously written Scripture in Ezekiel's prophecies. This is evident in the judgment oracles of chapters 4–5 that depend heavily on the curses listed in Leviticus 26.

Outline

575–550 BC

The Lord gives Ezekiel a vision of the new temple. **573**
The Lord shows Ezekiel that Egypt will be given over to the Babylonians. **571**
Nebuchadnezzar invades Egypt in fulfillment of both Jeremiah's and Ezekiel's prophecies. **569**
Evil-merodach, Nebuchadnezzar's son, succeeds him as king of Babylon. **562**
Evil-merodach releases Judean King Jehoiachin from prison. **561**
Nergal-sharezer becomes king of Babylon. **560**
Cyrus the Great founds the Persian Empire. **559**

550–500 BC

Cyrus captures Babylon without resistance. **539**
Cyrus issues decree allowing the Jews to return to Judah **538**
Work begins on rebuilding the temple in Jerusalem. **536**
Renewed work on the temple **520–518**
New temple dedicated **515**
The Greek thinker Hecataeus of Miletus draws the first recognizable map of the Mediterranean basin and writes the first known geography book. **500**

In the thirtieth year, in the fourth month, on the fifth day of the month, while I was among the exiles by the Chebar Canal, the heavens were opened and I saw visions of God. ² On the fifth day of the month — it was the fifth year of King Jehoiachin's exile — ³ the word of the LORD came directly to the priest Ezekiel son of Buzi, in the land of the Chaldeans by the Chebar Canal. The LORD's hand was on him there.

Vision of the LORD's Glory

⁴ I looked, and there was a whirlwind coming from the north, a huge cloud with fire flashing back and forth and brilliant light all around it. In the center of the fire, there was a gleam like amber. ⁵ The likeness of four living creatures came from it, and this was their appearance: They looked something like a human, ⁶ but each of them had four faces and four wings. ⁷ Their legs were straight, and the soles of their feet were like the hooves of a calf, sparkling like the gleam of polished bronze. ⁸ They had human hands under their wings on their four sides. All four of them had faces and wings. ⁹ Their wings were touching. The creatures did not turn as they moved; each one went straight ahead. ¹⁰ Their faces looked something like the face of a human, and each of the four had the face of a lion on the right, the face of an ox on the left, and the face of an eagle. ¹¹ That is what their faces were like. Their wings were spread upward; each had two wings touching that of another and two wings covering its body. ¹² Each creature went straight ahead. Wherever the Spirit^A

wanted to go, they went without turning as they moved.

¹³ The likeness of the living creatures was like the appearance of blazing coals of fire or like torches. Fire was moving back and forth between the living creatures; it was bright, with lightning coming out of it. ¹⁴ The creatures were darting back and forth like flashes of lightning.

¹⁵ When I looked at the living creatures, there was one wheel on the ground beside each of the four-faced creatures. ¹⁶ The appearance of the wheels and their craftsmanship was like the gleam of beryl, and all four had the same likeness. Their appearance and craftsmanship was like a wheel within a wheel. ¹⁷ When they moved, they went in any of the four directions, without turning as they moved. ¹⁸ Their four rims were tall and awe-inspiring, completely covered with eyes. ¹⁹ When the living creatures moved, the wheels moved beside them, and when the creatures rose from the earth, the wheels also rose. ²⁰ Wherever the Spirit wanted to go, the creatures went in the direction the Spirit was moving. The wheels rose alongside them, for the spirit of the living creatures was in the wheels. ²¹ When the creatures moved, the wheels moved; when the creatures stopped, the wheels stopped; and when the creatures rose from the earth, the wheels rose alongside them, for the spirit of the living creatures was in the wheels.

²² Over the heads of the living creatures the likeness of an expanse was spread out. It gleamed like awe-inspiring crystal, ²³ and under the expanse their wings extended one

---

^1:12 Or *spirit*, also in v. 20

1:1 The editorial explanation in verse 2 takes **the thirtieth year** as equivalent to "the fifth year of Jehoiachin's exile" (593 BC). Thirty was the age at which priests qualified for induction into their office (Nm 4:30).

Ezekiel was among the ten thousand soldiers and nobility who had been sent into exile along with the king (2Kg 24:14–16) in 597 BC. The **Chebar**, a river in Babylonia where the Jewish exiles settled, was the site of Ezekiel's visions (vv. 1,3; 3:15,23; 10:15,20,22; 43:3). The only other reference in the OT to the opening of **the heavens** occurs in Gn 7:11. In the NT, the heavens were opened at Christ's baptism (Mt 3:16). Stephen saw the heavens open and was given supernatural perception of heavenly realities (Ac 7:56). Similar cases of the heavens opening are found in Rv 4:1; 19:11.

1:2 Jehoiachin reigned only three months and ten days (2Kg 24:8; 2Ch 36:9). His removal and deportation to Babylon was April 22, 597 BC.

1:3 The name **Ezekiel** means "may God strengthen or toughen." In Ezekiel the name **Chaldeans** is interchanged with "Babylonians" (12:13; 23:15,23). God's **hand** is a manifestation of his power (Ex 9:3; Dt 2:15; 1Sm 5:9; Is 41:20). The power of the Spirit of God on the prophets enabled them to communicate divine truth.

1:4 God's approach is described as an atmospheric storm. Storms and clouds were often associated with appearances of God (Jb 38:1; Pss 18:7–15; 29:3–9; 104:3; Is 29:6). The phrase **fire flashing back and forth** occurs elsewhere only in Ex 9:24 in the account of the plague of hail. The pillar of fire and the pillar of cloud led the Hebrews in the wilderness (Ex 13:17–22). God's appearance on Mount Sinai was characterized by lightning, smoke, and fire (Ex 19:16–18). The storm arrives from the north, the same direction from which the Babylonian army will come to invade and destroy Judah.

1:5 From Ezk 10 we know that the **four . . . creatures** were cherubim (10:5,20). Cherubim were embroidered on the curtain of the tabernacle (Ex 26:31). They were placed on top of the ark of the covenant in the most holy place, where the tablets of covenant were kept (Ex 25:18–22). When Adam and Eve were thrown out of the garden of Eden, cherubim were appointed to prohibit their entry back into the garden (Gn 3:24). Elsewhere God is said to be he who "is enthroned between the cherubim" (1Sm 4:4; 2Sm 6:2; Ps 99:1).

1:7–8 The **straight** legs means they were unjointed.

1:9 The outspread **wings** of the cherubim in the most holy place "touched" one another (1Kg 6:27); the verb used here occurs in Ex

26:3 and elsewhere for the interlinking of cloth strips that made up the curtains of the desert tabernacle. Whatever direction the four living creatures wished to take was **straight ahead** for one of the four. Thus, all directions were "straight ahead."

1:10 The **lion** was considered the fiercest of beasts (Nm 23:24; 24:9; Jdg 14:18; 2Sm 1:23; 17:10), while the **eagle** was the most magnificent of birds (Dt 28:49; 2Sm 1:23; Jb 39:27; Jr 48:40; Lm 4:19). The **ox** was the most valued of domestic animals (Jb 21:10; Pr 14:4; cp. Ex 21:36).

1:11 Each creature had one pair of **wings** raised upward, touching the wing tips of the adjacent creature. This feature is identical to the cherubim over the ark of the covenant in the most holy place.

1:15–17 The **wheels** were built so that the chariot could travel in any direction.

1:16 The Septuagint took **beryl** to refer to a bright yellow precious stone, probably topaz.

1:18 The eyes in the **rims** symbolized divine omniscience and watchfulness (2Ch 16:9; Pr 15:3; Zch 3:9; 4:10; Rv 4:6).

1:19–21 Note the repetition in these verses indicating that the wheels appeared to the prophet to be alive.

1:22–25 The word for **expanse** is the same as in Gn 1:6. It may signify a kind of platform on which the throne rested. Below the expanse

toward another. They each also had two wings covering their bodies. ²⁴ When they moved, I heard the sound of their wings like the roar of a huge torrent, like the voice of the Almighty, and a sound of tumult like the noise of an army. When they stopped, they lowered their wings.

²⁵ A voice came from above the expanse over their heads; when they stopped, they lowered their wings. ²⁶ Something like a throne with the appearance of lapis lazuli was above the expanse over their heads. On the throne, high above, was someone who looked like a human. ²⁷ From what seemed to be his waist up, I saw a gleam like amber, with what looked like fire enclosing it all around. From what seemed to be

his waist down, I also saw what looked like fire. There was a brilliant light all around him. ²⁸ The appearance of the brilliant light all around was like that of a rainbow in a cloud on a rainy day. This was the appearance of the likeness of the LORD's glory. When I saw it, I fell facedown and heard a voice speaking.

Mission to Rebellious Israel

2 He said to me, "Son of man, stand up on your feet and I will speak with you." ² As he spoke to me, the Spirit entered me and set me on my feet, and I listened to the one who was speaking to me. ³ He said to me, "Son of man, I am sending you to the Israelites, to^ the

---

^2:3 Or *Israelites and to*

---

the sound of the creatures was like **the roar of a huge torrent**, and above the expanse came the voice of the Almighty himself.
1:26 The **lapis lazuli** was one of the most prized stones in the ancient world.
1:28 The **rainbow** in Ezekiel's vision recalls the ancient covenant God made with Noah and the human race (Gn 9). The **glory** of the Lord is a visible manifestation of God (Ex 16:7; 24:16–17; 40:34–35). The glory of the Lord also refers to the "pillar of fire" that accompanied the Israelites in their desert wanderings (Ex 13:21–22; Nm 14:14). Clouds, like fire, are frequently associated with the

appearance of God (Ex 19:16; Jdg 5:4). Ezekiel declared that he **fell facedown**. This is the posture a person assumed before a king in ancient times.
2:1 The expression **son of man** occurs about ninety times in the book of Ezekiel. It should be distinguished from the same phrase in Dn 7:13, where it reflects a messianic title. Unlike the usage in Dn 7:13, Ezekiel's usage of the phrase can mean simply a "member of humanity." It could also be translated, "descendants of Adam."
2:2 The same **Spirit** of God that activated the chariot wheels (1:12,19; 10:16–17) and the

living beings now **entered** Ezekiel. The Spirit would supply the strength to accomplish Ezekiel's prophetic ministry.
2:3 Normally in the OT the Israelites are referred to as a "people" and Gentiles as "nations." Here the designations are reversed. The traditional language of election has been turned on its head so that the Gentiles have become a people while Israel has become **pagans**. The people of God have become no different than the pagan people around them. The phrase **who have rebelled against me** is used of subjects who refused to be loyal to their king (17:15; 2Kg 18:7).

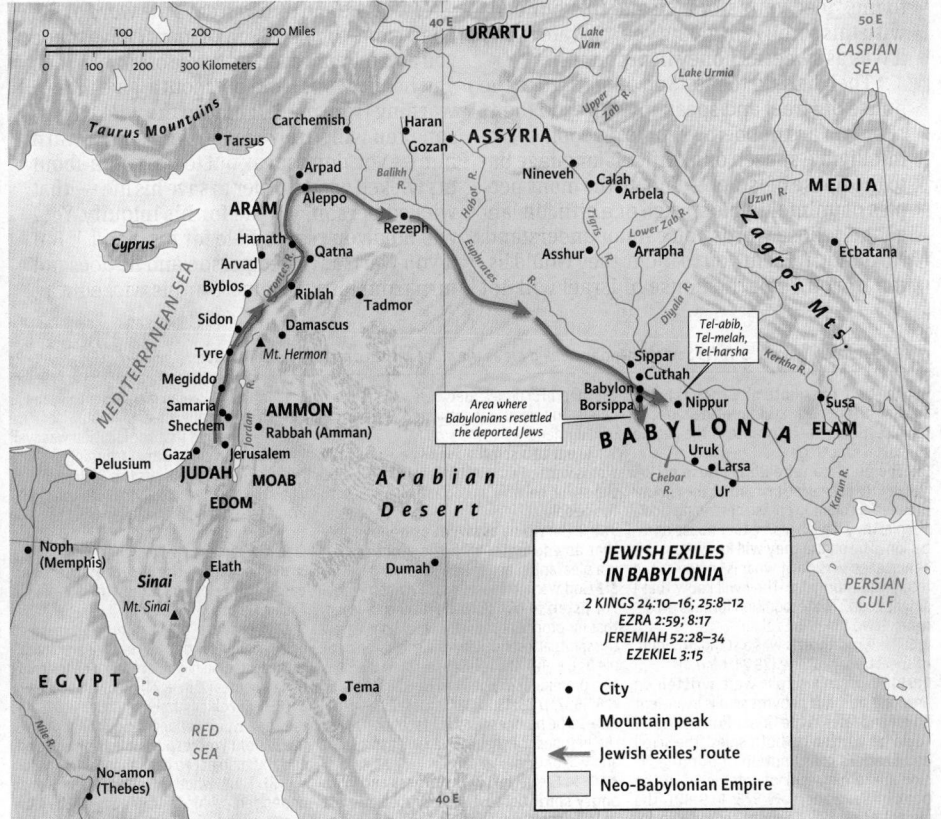

JEWISH EXILES IN BABYLONIA

2 KINGS 24:10–16; 25:8–12
EZRA 2:59; 8:17
JEREMIAH 52:28–34
EZEKIEL 3:15

• City
▲ Mountain peak
← Jewish exiles' route
Neo-Babylonian Empire

rebellious pagans who have rebelled against me. The Israelites and their ancestors have transgressed against me to this day. **⁴** The descendants are obstinate^A and hardhearted. I am sending you to them, and you must say to them, 'This is what the Lord GOD says.' **⁵** Whether they listen or refuse to listen — for they are a rebellious house — they will know that a prophet has been among them.

⁶ "But you, son of man, do not be afraid of them and do not be afraid of their words, even though briers and thorns are beside you and you live among scorpions. Don't be afraid of their words or discouraged by the look on their faces, for they are a rebellious house. **⁷** Speak my words to them whether they listen or refuse to listen, for they are rebellious.

⁸ "And you, son of man, listen to what I tell you: Do not be rebellious like that rebellious house. Open your mouth and eat what I am giving you." **⁹** So I looked and saw a hand reaching out to me, and there was a written scroll in it. **¹⁰** When he unrolled it before me, it was written on the front and back; words of lamentation, mourning, and woe were written on it.

3 He said to me, "Son of man, eat what you find here. Eat this scroll, then go and speak to the house of Israel." **²** So I opened my mouth, and he fed me the scroll. **³** "Son of man," he said to me, "feed your stomach and fill your belly with this scroll I am giving you." So I ate it, and it was as sweet as honey in my mouth.

⁴ Then he said to me, "Son of man, go to the house of Israel and speak my words to them. **⁵** For you are not being sent to a people of unintelligible speech or a difficult language but to the house of Israel — **⁶** not to the many peoples of unintelligible speech or a difficult language, whose words you cannot understand. No doubt, if I sent you to them, they would listen to you. **⁷** But the house of Israel will not

want to listen to you because they do not want to listen to me. For the whole house of Israel is hardheaded and hardhearted. **⁸** Look, I have made your face as hard as their faces and your forehead as hard as their foreheads. **⁹** I have made your forehead like a diamond, harder than flint. Don't be afraid of them or discouraged by the look on their faces, though they are a rebellious house."

¹⁰ Next he said to me, "Son of man, listen carefully to all my words that I speak to you and take them to heart. **¹¹** Go to your people, the exiles, and speak to them. Tell them, 'This is what the Lord GOD says,' whether they listen or refuse to listen."

¹² The Spirit then lifted me up, and I heard a loud rumbling sound behind me — bless the glory of the LORD in his place! — **¹³** with the^B sound of the living creatures' wings brushing against each other and the sound of the wheels beside them, a loud rumbling sound. **¹⁴** The Spirit lifted me up and took me away. I left in bitterness and in an angry spirit, and the LORD's hand was on me powerfully. **¹⁵** I came to the exiles at Tel-abib, who were living by the Chebar Canal, and I sat there among them stunned for seven days.

Ezekiel as a Watchman

¹⁶ Now at the end of seven days the word of the LORD came to me: **¹⁷** "Son of man, I have made you a watchman over the house of Israel. When you hear a word from my mouth, give them a warning from me. **¹⁸** If I say to the wicked person, 'You will surely die,' but you do not warn him — you don't speak out to warn him about his wicked way in order to save his life — that wicked person will die for his iniquity. Yet I will hold you responsible for his blood. **¹⁹** But if you warn a wicked person and he does not turn from his wickedness or his wicked way,

---

^A **2:4** Lit *hard of face*   ^B **3:12–13** Some emend to *behind me as the glory of the LORD rose from his place:* ^13*the*

2:4 The term **obstinate** often occurs in the phrase "stiff of neck, stubborn." It emphatically illustrates the resistance of the people to Ezekiel's message.
2:5 The phrase **a rebellious house** occurs frequently in Ezekiel; instead of the "house of Israel," a common phrase describing God's people, they have become the "house of rebellion." The phrase **they will know** contains a shortened version of what is known as the recognition formula: "They will know that I am the LORD." The recognition formula occurs ninety-two times in Ezekiel.
2:6 The word **thorns** was a standard figure of speech for hostility (28:24; Mc 7:4).
2:9–10 Normally scrolls were **written** on only one side, but papyrus scrolls in ancient Egypt and later in the Greco-Roman period could be written on both sides. The scroll and Ezekiel's consumption of it in the vision are reminiscent of references in the book of Revelation (Rv 5; 6; 10:9–10). The lament or dirge is thought to derive from

the mournful dirges that were wailed at funerals. The scroll was saturated with words of judgment.
3:1 To **eat this scroll** signifies devouring the words written on it. After Ezekiel consumed the scroll, he would proclaim the words to the people.
3:2–3 The words **as sweet as honey** show that an encounter with the Word of God is a pleasant experience (Pss 19:10; 119:103).
3:7 God warned Moses that Pharaoh would not **listen** to him (Ex 3:19). God told Isaiah that his prophetic ministry would only show the spiritual insensitivity of a corrupted people (Is 6:9–10). The refusal-to-listen theme is also prominent in Jeremiah (Jr 3:25; 7:13; 9:13; 11:8; 16:12; 17:23; 18:10; 19:15; 22:5; 25:3–4,7).
3:8–9 The hardness of their faces portrayed the hardness of their will against the word and will of God.
3:10–14 Ezekiel **left in bitterness and in an angry spirit** because of the rebelliousness of the people.

3:15 In the Akkadian language, the phrase **Tel-abib** literally means "mound of the flood," indicating that the location was well known as a ruined site. Mourning for the dead lasted **seven days** (Gn 50:10; Jb 2:13). The consecration ceremony for admission into the priesthood, which Ezekiel had anticipated for himself before the exile, also lasted seven days (Lv 8:33).
3:16 The phrase **the word of the LORD came to me** occurs almost fifty times in Ezekiel.
3:17 In order to give a timely warning of approaching danger, lookouts or watchmen were posted on high places such as the roofs of gatehouses (2Sm 18:24) or towers (2Kg 9:17).
3:18–19 Ezekiel's failure to deliver God's message would render him guilty of murder (**I will hold you responsible for his blood**) and thus subject to capital punishment (Gn 9:5–6). Thus, whether Ezekiel lived or died depended on his faithfulness to the holy commission he had received.

he will die for his iniquity, but you will have rescued yourself. ²⁰ Now if a righteous person turns from his righteousness and acts unjustly, and I put a stumbling block in front of him, he will die. If you did not warn him, he will die because of his sin, and the righteous acts he did will not be remembered. Yet I will hold you responsible for his blood. ²¹ But if you warn the righteous person that he should not sin, and he does not sin, he will indeed live because he listened to your warning, and you will have rescued yourself."

²² The hand of the LORD was on me there, and he said to me, "Get up, go out to the plain, and I will speak with you there." ²³ So I got up and went out to the plain. The LORD's glory was present there, like the glory I had seen by the Chebar Canal, and I fell facedown. ²⁴ The Spirit entered me and set me on my feet. He spoke with me and said, "Go, shut yourself inside your house. ²⁵ As for you, son of man, they will put ropes on you and bind you with them so you cannot go out among them. ²⁶ I will make your tongue stick to the roof of your mouth, and you will be mute and unable to be a mediator forᴬ them, for they are a rebellious house. ²⁷ But when I speak with you, I will open your mouth, and you will say to them, 'This is what the Lord GOD says.' Let the one who listens, listen, and let the one who refuses, refuse — for they are a rebellious house.

Jerusalem's Siege Dramatized

4 "Now you, son of man, take a brick, set it in front of you, and draw the city of Jerusalem on it. ² Then lay siege against it: Construct a siege wall, build a ramp, pitch military camps, and place battering rams against it on all sides. ³ Take an iron plate and set it up as an iron wall between yourself and the city. Face it so that it is under siege, and besiege it. This will be a sign for the house of Israel.

⁴ "Then lie down on your left side and place the iniquityᴮ of the house of Israel on it. You will bear their iniquity for the number of days you lie on your side. ⁵ For I have assigned you the years of their iniquity according to the number of days you lie down, 390 days; so you will bear the iniquity of the house of Israel. ⁶ When you have completed these days, lie down again, but on your right side, and bear the iniquity of the house of Judah. I have assigned you forty days, a day for each year. ⁷ Face the siege of Jerusalem with your arm bared, and prophesy against it. ⁸ Be aware that I will put cords on you so you cannot turn from side to side until you have finished the days of your siege.

⁹ "Also take wheat, barley, beans, lentils, millet, and spelt. Put them in a single container and make them into bread for yourself. You are to eat it during the number of days you lie on your side, 390 days. ¹⁰ The food you eat each day will weigh eight ounces;ᶜ you will eat it at set times.ᴰ ¹¹ You will also drink a ration of water, a sixth of a gallon,ᴱ which you will drink at set times. ¹² You will eat it as you would a barley cake and bake it over dried human excrement in their sight." ¹³ The LORD said, "This is how the Israelites will eat their bread — ceremonially unclean — among the nations where I will banish them."

¹⁴ But I said, "Oh, Lord GOD, I have never been defiled. From my youth until now I have not eaten anything that died naturally or was mauled by wild beasts. And impure meat has never entered my mouth."

¹⁵ He replied to me, "Look, I will let you use cow dung instead of human excrement, and you can make your bread over that." ¹⁶ He said to me, "Son of man, I am going to cut off the supply of bread in Jerusalem. They will anxiously eat food they have weighed out and in dread drink rationed water ¹⁷ for lack of bread and water. Everyone will be devastated and waste away because of their iniquity.

ᴬ3:26 Or to rebuke ᴮ4:4 Or punishment ᶜ4:10 Lit 20 shekels ᴰ4:10 Lit from time to time, also in v. 11 ᴱ4:11 Lit hin

3:20 To lay a **stumbling block** before a person was to expose him to danger (Jr 6:21). **3:21** Those who responded faithfully to the watchman's proclamation would **live**. This signified not just physical life but the fullness of fellowship with the Lord that flows from obedience. **3:22–23** Ezekiel had his second encounter with the Lord in **the plain**. **3:24–25** Being **shut** in the **house** illustrates the siege of Jerusalem. This does not mean that Ezekiel was literally never to leave his house (cp. 5:2; 12:3); instead, he was to refrain from open fellowship with others. Leaders often came to him at his house to receive God's word (8:1; 14:1; 20:1). General confinement to his home is reflected in all the locations of prophesying mentioned in the book (8:1; 14:1; 20:1; 33:30). **3:26** The expression **tongue stick to the roof of your mouth** is an idiomatic way of saying that a person cannot talk (Jb 29:10; Ps 137:6).

Ezekiel's speechlessness lasted seven years (Ezk 33:21–22). He remained silent, except when God instructed him to deliver a message. **4:1–2** Sketching a city plan on a clay **brick** was not an uncommon practice in the ancient world. Ezekiel was instructed to sketch the siege of **Jerusalem**. Nebuchadnezzar's construction of the siege wall around Jerusalem is described in 2Kg 25:1 and Jr 52:4. The purpose of a **siege** was to wear enemies down by halting their flow of food and supplies. Battering rams were pushed up siege ramps to attack the city walls. **4:3** The setting of God's **face** behind an **iron plate** indicated that he would no longer look favorably upon the people. **4:4–6** The 430-year period was chosen to represent the period of Israel's stay in Egypt. By depicting the total period of sin and judgment in terms of a renewed Egyptian bondage, the prophet invited the hope that the end of the appointed time of punishment

would result in a new exodus and a new entry into the promised land. **4:8** The **siege** that Ezekiel was predicting lasted two years (2Kg 25:1–8). **4:9** The food products mentioned in this verse, all native to Mesopotamia, constitute a siege diet. **4:10–13** Because Ezekiel was aware of the laws regarding the removal of **human excrement**, he reacted with disgust (Dt 23:11–13). **4:14–15** Eating flesh that had been **mauled by wild beasts** disqualified a priest from priestly service (44:31; Lv 22:8). **Impure meat** was sacrificial meat that had not been eaten by the third day after the animal was slaughtered (Lv 7:18; 19:7). **4:16** The expression **supply of bread** indicates the destruction of the whole food supply (Lv 26:26; Is 3:1). **4:17** To be defeated or **devastated** in war was to experience a covenant curse (Lv 26:17,37; Dt 28:25,49,52; 32:23–24,30,42).

Ezekiel Dramatizes Jerusalem's Fall

5 "Now you, son of man, take a sharp sword, use it as you would a barber's razor, and shave your head and beard. Then take a set of scales and divide the hair. ² You are to burn a third of it in the city when the days of the siege have ended; you are to take a third and slash it with the sword all around the city; and you are to scatter a third to the wind, for I will draw a sword to chase after them. ³ But you are to take a few strands from the hair and secure them in the folds of your robe. ⁴ Take some more of them, throw them into the fire, and burn them in it. A fire will spread from it to the whole house of Israel.

⁵ "This is what the Lord GOD says: I have set this Jerusalem in the center of the nations, with countries all around her. ⁶ She has rebelled against my ordinances with more wickedness than the nations, and against my statutes more than the countries that surround her. For her people have rejected my ordinances and have not walked in my statutes.

⁷ "Therefore, this is what the Lord GOD says: Because you have been more insubordinate than the nations around you — you have not walked in my statutes or kept my ordinances; you have not even kept the ordinances of the nations around you — ⁸ therefore, this is what the Lord GOD says: See, I myself am against you, Jerusalem, and I will execute judgments within you in the sight of the nations. ⁹ Because of all your detestable practices, I will do to you what I have never done before and what I will never do again. ¹⁰ As a result, fathers will eat their sons within Jerusalem,ᴬ and sons will eat their fathers. I will execute judgments against you and scatter all your survivors to every direction of the wind.

¹¹ "Therefore, as I live" — this is the declaration of the Lord GOD — "I will withdraw and show you no pity, because you have defiled my

sanctuary with all your abhorrent acts and detestable practices. Yes, I will not spare you. ¹² A third of your people will die by plague and be consumed by famine within you; a third will fall by the sword all around you; and I will scatter a third to every direction of the wind, and I will draw a sword to chase after them. ¹³ When my anger is spent and I have vented my wrath on them, I will be appeased. Then after I have spent my wrath on them, they will know that I, the LORD, have spoken in my jealousy.

¹⁴ "I will make you a ruin and a disgrace among the nations around you, in the sight of everyone who passes by. ¹⁵ So youᴮ will be a disgrace and a taunt, a warning and a horror, to the nations around you when I execute judgments against you in anger, wrath, and furious rebukes. I, the LORD, have spoken. ¹⁶ When I shoot deadly arrows of famine at them, arrows for destruction that I will send to destroy you, inhabitants of Jerusalem, I will intensify the famine against you and cut off your supply of bread. ¹⁷ I will send famine and dangerous animals against you. They will leave you childless. Plague and bloodshed will sweep through you, and I will bring a sword against you. I, the LORD, have spoken."

Prophecy against Israel's Idolatry

6 The word of the LORD came to me: ² "Son of man, face the mountains of Israel and prophesy against them. ³ You are to say: Mountains of Israel, hear the word of the Lord GOD! This is what the Lord GOD says to the mountains and the hills, to the ravines and the valleys: I am about to bring a sword against you, and I will destroy your high places. ⁴ Your altars will be desolated and your shrinesᶜ smashed. I will throw down your slain in front of your idols. ⁵ I will lay the corpses of the Israelites in front of their idols and scatter your bones around your altars. ⁶ Wherever you live the

ᴬ5:10 Lit *you* ᴮ5:15 DSS, LXX, Syr, Tg, Vg; MT reads *she* ᶜ6:4 Or *incense altars*, also in v. 6

5:1 Shaving one's **head** was often associated with mourning rites (7:18; 27:31; Jb 1:20; Is 7:20; 15:2–3; Jr 7:29; 48:37). Mourning for the dead in this way was prohibited for the Israelites (Dt 14:1). Weighing on **scales** was a symbol of evaluation for impending judgment (Pr 21:2; Dn 5:27).
5:2–4 Two-thirds of the population would be killed in the invasion, and one-third would be taken into exile. From the last third of **hair** that was consigned to dispersion, Ezekiel was to take and bind some in the **folds** of his **robe**. This portrayed survival of only a remnant of exiles. Hair scattered to the wind would be impossible to retrieve. By tucking the remnants of hair into his garment, Ezekiel indicated that the future of the people of God lay with the Babylonian exiles (Lv 26:36–39; Hg 2:12). Destruction would reach even some of those in exile.
5:10 Cannibalism was prohibited in the law of Moses (Lv 26:29; Dt 28:53–57) and was

denounced by the prophets (Is 9:19–21; Jr 19:9; Zch 11:9). Tragically, the Israelites resorted to cannibalism in Jerusalem during the siege and the subsequent fall to Babylon's forces in 588–586 BC (Lm 1:7–14; 2:20–22; 4:4–10).
5:11 The expression **show you no pity** was used to discourage leniency in criminal cases (Dt 7:16; 13:8; 19:13,21; 25:12). The defilement of the holy **sanctuary** is the sole issue in 8:1–18.
5:12 **Famine** and **plague** often accompanied the siege of a city. These were also numbered among the covenant curses of Lv 26:25–26.
5:14–15 The nation that was chosen for honor (Dt 26:19) now became the moral spectacle of the nations (**you will be a disgrace and a taunt**).
5:16–17 The phrase **when I shoot deadly arrows of famine at them** begins a list of judgments. These are identical to the standard types of covenant curses associated with disobedience of God's law (famine, Lv 26:26,29; wild animals, Lv 26:22; Dt 32:24; disease, Dt 28:21; bloodshed, Dt 32:42).

6:1–2 When God tells the prophet to **face the mountains of Israel**, it reflects the Lord's adverse attitude toward his people. The phrase "mountains of Israel" does not occur outside the book of Ezekiel. Mountains represent the whole land because the land of Israel was mountainous and hilly (Dt 11:11). Mountains were often centers of idolatrous worship; thus, reference to Israel as "mountainous" is a reference to Israel's apostasy (Ezk 6:13; 18:6,11; 22:9).
6:3 **High places** were elevated platforms where sacrifices were performed. They existed in the land of Canaan before the Israelite conquest and were supposed to have been destroyed (Nm 33:52).
6:4–5 For the Hebrews, burning corpses on **altars** defiled the altars (1Kg 13:2; 2Kg 23:16). Ezekiel's favorite word for idol is associated with round dung pellets. This graphically expressed Ezekiel's disposition toward useless idols.
6:6 The Hebrew verb rendered "to wipe out" is used in Gn 6:7; 7:4,23 to describe the

cities will be in ruins and the high places will be desolate, so that your altars will lie in ruins and be desecrated,ᴬ your idols smashed and obliterated, your shrines cut down, and what you have made wiped out. ⁷ The slain will fall among you, and you will know that I am the Lᴏʀᴅ.

⁸ "Yet I will leave a remnant when you are scattered among the nations, for throughout the countries there will be some of you who will escape the sword. ⁹ Then your survivors will remember me among the nations where they are taken captive, how I was crushed by their promiscuous hearts that turned away from me and by their eyes that lusted after their idols. They will loathe themselves because of the evil things they did, their detestable actions of every kind. ¹⁰ And they will know that I am the Lᴏʀᴅ; I did not threaten to bring this disaster on them without a reason.

Lament over the Fall of Jerusalem

¹¹ "This is what the Lord Gᴏᴅ says: Clap your hands, stamp your feet, and cry out over all the evil and detestable practices of the house of Israel, who will fall by the sword, famine, and plague. ¹² The one who is far off will die by plague; the one who is near will fall by the sword; and the one who remains and is sparedᴮ will die of famine. In this way I will exhaust my wrath on them. ¹³ You will all know that I am the Lᴏʀᴅ when their slain lie among their idols around their altars, on every high hill, on all the mountaintops, and under every green tree and every leafy oak — the places where they offered pleasing aromas to all their idols. ¹⁴ I will stretch out my hand against them, and wherever they live I will make the land a desolate waste, from the wilderness to Riblah.ᶜ Then they will know that I am the Lᴏʀᴅ."

Announcement of the End

7 The word of the Lᴏʀᴅ came to me: ² "Son of man, this is what the Lord Gᴏᴅ says to the land of Israel:

An end! The end has come
on the four corners of the earth.
³   The end is now upon you;

I will send my anger against you
and judge you according to your ways.
I will punish you for all
    your detestable practices.
⁴   I will not look on you with pity
    or spare you,
but I will punish you for your ways
and for your detestable practices
    within you.
Then you will know that I am
    the Lᴏʀᴅ."

⁵ This is what the Lord Gᴏᴅ says:
Look, one disaster after another
    is coming!
⁶   An end has come; the end has come!
It has awakened against you.
Look, it is coming!
⁷   Doomᴰ has come on you,
inhabitants of the land.
The time has come; the day is near.
There will be panic on the mountains
and not celebration.

⁸   I will pour out my wrath on you
very soon;
I will exhaust my anger against you
and judge you according to your ways.
I will punish you for all your
    detestable practices.
⁹   I will not look on you with pity
    or spare you.
I will punish you for your ways
and for your detestable practices
    within you.
Then you will know
that it is I, the Lᴏʀᴅ, who strikes.

¹⁰   Here is the day! Here it comes!
Doom is on its way.
The rod has blossomed;
arrogance has bloomed.
¹¹   Violence has grown into a rod
    of wickedness.
None of them will remain:
none of that crowd,
none of their wealth,
and none of the eminentᴱ among them.

ᴬ6:6 Hb obscure   ᴮ6:12 Or *besieged*   ᶜ6:14 Some Hb mss, some LXX mss; other Hb mss read *Diblah*; 2Kg 23:33; Jr 39:5
ᴰ7:7 Or *A leash*; Hb obscure, also in v. 10   ᴱ7:11 Some Hb mss, Syr, Vg read *and no rest*

---

decimation of the human race by the flood (2Kg 21:13).
6:7 The phrase **you will know that I am the Lᴏʀᴅ** is known as a recognition formula. It is used some sixty times in Ezekiel. It was frequently used in the context of the exodus from Egypt (Ex 7:5; 14:4).
6:8–9 Here is the first explicit reference in Ezekiel to leaving a **remnant**. See 12:16; 14:22; 39:28.
6:10 The expression **threaten to bring this disaster on them** occurs outside this passage only in the account of the golden calf (Ex 32:14).

6:11–12 Ezekiel was commanded to sing a number of taunt songs against Israel's enemies (e.g., chaps. 27–28; 31–32).
6:13 In the pagan belief system of the ancient Near East, people sought the assistance of gods and goddesses of nature to bless themselves and make themselves productive.
7:1–2 This particular Hebrew expression for the **land of Israel** occurs only in Ezekiel. In the use of the term here, the emphasis is on the ground or soil rather than the land or the nation. The expression **the end has come** refers not to the end of the latter days but to the end of great corruption, as in Gn 6:13.

7:3–6 Detestable practices is sometimes rendered "abominations" and typically carries the death penalty.
7:7 The **day** of the Lord refers to a time of God's intervention in history to deliver or to judge (Is 2:12–22; 13). But in some ways the day of the Lord focuses on an event rather than a definite extent of time. The nearness of the day of the Lord is a common theme in prophetic literature (Ezk 30:3; Jl 1:15; 2:1; Zph 1:7,14).
7:8–11 The **rod** that had **blossomed** refers to Aaron's rod that meant not only God's choice but also his judgment on the arrogant (Nm 17:8).

12 The time has come; the day has arrived.
  Let the buyer not rejoice
  and the seller not mourn,
  for wrath is on her whole crowd.
13 The seller will certainly not return
  to what was sold
  as long as he and the buyer
    remain alive.^A
  For the vision concerning
    her whole crowd
  will not be revoked,
  and because of the iniquity
    of each one,
  none will preserve his life.

14 They have blown the trumpet
  and prepared everything,
  but no one goes to war,
  for my wrath is on her whole crowd.
15 The sword is on the outside;
  plague and famine are on the inside.
  Whoever is in the field will die
    by the sword,
  and famine and plague will devour
  whoever is in the city.

16 The survivors among them will escape
  and live on the mountains.
  Like doves of the valley,
  all of them will moan,
  each over his own iniquity.
17 All their hands will become weak,
  and all their knees will run
    with urine.^B
18 They will put on sackcloth,
  and horror will overwhelm them.
  Shame will cover all their faces,
  and all their heads will be bald.

19 They will throw their silver
    into the streets,
  and their gold will seem like
    something filthy.
  Their silver and gold will be unable
    to save them
  in the day of the LORD's wrath.
  They will not satisfy their appetites
  or fill their stomachs,
  for these were the stumbling blocks
  that brought about their iniquity.

20 He appointed his beautiful ornaments
    for majesty,
  but^c they made their detestable images
    from them,
  their abhorrent things.
  Therefore, I have made these
  into something filthy to them.
21 I will hand these things over
  to foreigners as plunder
  and to the wicked of the earth as spoil,
  and they will profane them.
22 I will turn my face from them
  as they profane my treasured place.
  Violent men will enter it and profane it.

23 Forge the chain,
  for the land is filled with crimes
    of bloodshed,
  and the city is filled with violence.
24 So I will bring the most evil of nations
  to take possession of their houses.
  I will put an end to the pride
    of the strong,
  and their sacred places will be profaned.
25 Anguish is coming!
  They will look for peace,
    but there will be none.
26 Disaster after disaster will come,
  and there will be rumor after rumor.
  Then they will look for a vision
    from a prophet,
  but instruction will perish
    from the priests
  and counsel from the elders.
27 The king will mourn;
  the prince will be clothed in grief;
  and the hands of the people of the land
    will tremble.
  I will deal with them according to
    their own conduct,
  and I will judge them
    by their own standards.
  Then they will know that I am the LORD.

Visionary Journey to Jerusalem

8 In the sixth year, in the sixth month, on the fifth day of the month, I was sitting in my house and the elders of Judah were sitting in front of me, and there the hand of the Lord GOD came down on me. ² I looked, and there

---

^A**7:13** Lit sold, while still in life is their life   ^B**7:17** Lit knees will go water   ^c**7:20** Or They turned their beautiful ornaments into objects of pride, and

---

7:12 Land was sold only under dire circumstances, hence the mourning. But in times of judgment nothing else mattered.
7:13 After the seventh sabbatical year (forty-nine years) the Year of Jubilee took place, during which each person who had lost or sold his land received back his personal property (Lv 25:8–22).
7:19 The **filthy** thing was the technical term used for the ceremonial impurity that resulted from menstruation (Lv 15:19–33) and the

touching of a corpse (Nm 19:13–21). Wealth had become the people's stumbling block.
7:20 Beautiful ornaments is an allusion to the temple, as in v. 22 (cp. Dn 1:2; 5:3–4).
7:22 Many Israelites considered themselves invincible because the presence of God resided in Jerusalem (**my treasured place**)—they thought that God would never let his holy dwelling be destroyed (Jr 7:1–5)—but even the temple would not escape God's judgment (Mc 3:12).

7:23 The phrase **the city is filled with violence** clearly echoes Gn 6:11.
7:24–25 The **sacred places** refers to high places. See Lv 26:30.
8:1 The words **in the sixth year, in the sixth month, on the fifth day of the month** show that Ezekiel had reflected on his first vision for fourteen months.
8:2–5 The nearest analogy to Ezekiel's experience occurred with Elijah, who was carried about by the **Spirit** (1Kg 18:12; 2Kg

was someone who looked like a man.^A From what seemed to be his waist down was fire, and from his waist up was something that looked bright, like the gleam of amber. ³ He stretched out what appeared to be a hand and took me by the hair of my head. Then the Spirit lifted me up between earth and heaven and carried me in visions of God to Jerusalem, to the entrance of the inner gate that faces north, where the offensive statue that provokes jealousy was located. ⁴ I saw the glory of the God of Israel there, like the vision I had seen in the plain.

Pagan Practices in the Temple

⁵ The LORD said to me, "Son of man, look toward the north." I looked to the north, and there was this offensive statue north of the Altar Gate, at the entrance. ⁶ He said to me, "Son of man, do you see what they are doing here — more detestable acts that the house of Israel is committing — so that I must depart from my sanctuary? You will see even more detestable acts."

⁷ Then he brought me to the entrance of the court, and when I looked there was a hole in the wall. ⁸ He said to me, "Son of man, dig through the wall." So I dug through the wall and discovered a doorway. ⁹ He said to me, "Go in and see the detestable, wicked acts they are committing here."

¹⁰ I went in and looked, and there engraved all around the wall was every kind of abhorrent thing — crawling creatures and beasts — as well as all the idols of the house of Israel. ¹¹ Seventy elders from the house of Israel were standing before them, with Jaazaniah son of Shaphan standing among them. Each had a firepan in his hand, and a fragrant cloud of incense was rising up. ¹² He said to me, "Son of man, do you see what the elders of the house of Israel are doing in the darkness, each at the shrine of his idol? For they are saying, 'The LORD does not see us. The LORD has abandoned the land.' " ¹³ Again he said to me, "You

will see even more detestable acts that they are committing."

¹⁴ Then he brought me to the entrance of the north gate of the LORD's house, and I saw women sitting there weeping for Tammuz. ¹⁵ And he said to me, "Do you see this, son of man? You will see even more detestable acts than these."

¹⁶ So he brought me to the inner court of the LORD's house, and there were about twenty-five men at the entrance of the LORD's temple, between the portico and the altar, with their backs to the LORD's temple and their faces turned to the east. They were bowing to the east in worship of the sun. ¹⁷ And he said to me, "Do you see this, son of man? Is it not enough for the house of Judah to commit the detestable acts they are doing here, that they must also fill the land with violence and repeatedly anger me, even putting the branch to their nose?^B ¹⁸ Therefore I will respond with wrath. I will not show pity or spare them. Though they call loudly in my hearing, I will not listen to them."

Vision of Slaughter in Jerusalem

9 Then he called loudly in my hearing, "Come near, executioners of the city, each of you with a destructive weapon in his hand." ² And I saw six men coming from the direction of the Upper Gate, which faces north, each with a war club in his hand. There was another man among them, clothed in linen, carrying writing equipment. They came and stood beside the bronze altar.

³ Then the glory of the God of Israel rose from above the cherub where it had been, to the threshold of the temple. He called to the man clothed in linen and carrying writing equipment. ⁴ "Pass throughout the city of Jerusalem," the LORD said to him, "and put a mark on the foreheads of the men who sigh and groan over all the detestable practices committed in it."

⁵ He spoke to the others in my hearing: "Pass through the city after him and start killing; do

---

^A8:2 LXX; MT, Vg read *like fire*   ^B8:17 Alt Hb tradition reads *my nose*

2:1–12,16–18). The term translated **offensive statue** occurs elsewhere only in Dt 4:16 and 2Ch 33:7,15. This image may have been one of the Asherahs set up in the temple by Manasseh (2Kg 21:7; 2Ch 33:7,15). This conclusion is suggested by the use of the same word in reference to Manasseh's idol in 2Ch 33:7,15.

8:10 The phrase **every kind of abhorrent thing** is reminiscent of Rm 1:23.

8:11 The **seventy elders** were probably the leaders of the nation whose position was established by Moses's appointment of officials to assist him in governing God's people (Ex 24:1,9; Nm 11:16–25). The prophet echoed the critical moment in the Day of Atonement ceremonies when the **cloud of incense** screened the ark from the vision of the high priest (Lv 16:2,13).

8:12–13 They were in **darkness** to hide from God, who they claimed had abandoned Israel.

8:14–15 Weeping for Tammuz was a Babylonian ritual marking the death and descent into the underworld of the Sumerian god Dumuzi. The mythological course of death and return for Dumuzi (Tammuz) was thought to be parallel to the annual rhythm of nature.

8:16 The final and supreme act of idolatry took place within the **inner court** of the **temple** itself, where **twenty-five men** bowed toward the **east**, worshiping the **sun**. According to 2Kg 21:5, worship of the sun god appears to have gained sponsorship during the reign of Manasseh, who built altars for foreign gods in the courts of the temple. The area **between the portico and the altar** was probably for use by priests alone and was where they prayed to God on a fast day (Jl 2:17).

8:17–18 The phrase **putting the branch to their nose** may have referred to an idolatrous

practice, or possibly it is an idiomatic expression indicating contempt for God.

9:1–2 Linen was often worn by angelic messengers (Dn 10:5; Rv 15:6), but it was also the fabric for priestly garments (Ex 28:42); linen thus portrays purity and holiness. The **bronze altar**, originally built by Solomon (2Ch 4:1), was relocated during the reign of Ahaz to the northeast corner of the temple to make room for his own pagan altar (2Kg 16:14).

9:3–4 It is possible that those to be spared received the sign of the cross (**put a mark on the foreheads**), like those sealed for deliverance in Rv 7:3–4; 14:1.

9:5–6 This deliverance from judgment (**do not come near anyone who has the mark**) resembles the Passover story, where the household was spared if the blood of a sacrificial lamb was placed above the door (Ex 12:7,13).

not show pity or spare them! **6** Slaughter the old men, the young men and women, as well as the children and older women, but do not come near anyone who has the mark. Begin at my sanctuary." So they began with the elders who were in front of the temple. **7** Then he said to them, "Defile the temple and fill the courts with the slain. Go!" So they went out killing people in the city.

8 While they were killing, I was left alone. And I fell facedown and cried out, "Oh, Lord God! Are you going to destroy the entire remnant of Israel when you pour out your wrath on Jerusalem?"

9 He answered me, "The iniquity of the house of Israel and Judah is extremely great; the land is full of bloodshed, and the city full of perversity. For they say, 'The Lord has abandoned the land; he does not see.' **10** But as for me, I will not show pity or spare them. I will bring their conduct down on their own heads."

11 Then the man clothed in linen and carrying writing equipment reported back, "I have done all that you commanded me."

God's Glory Leaves the Temple

10 Then I looked, and there above the expanse over the heads of the cherubim was something like a throne with the appearance of lapis lazuli. **2** The Lord spoke to the man clothed in linen and said, "Go inside the wheelwork beneath the cherubim. Fill your hands with blazing coals from among the cherubim and scatter them over the city." So he went in as I watched.

3 Now the cherubim were standing to the south of the temple when the man went in, and the cloud filled the inner court. **4** Then the glory of the Lord rose from above the cherub to the threshold of the temple. The temple was filled with the cloud, and the court was filled with the brightness of the Lord's glory. **5** The sound of the cherubim's wings could be heard as far as the outer court; it was like the voice of God Almighty when he speaks.

6 After the Lord commanded the man clothed in linen, saying, "Take fire from inside the wheelwork, from among the cherubim," the man went in and stood beside a wheel.

7 Then the cherub reached out his hand to the fire that was among them. He took some and put it into the hands of the man clothed in linen, who took it and went out. **8** The cherubim appeared to have the form of human hands under their wings.

9 I looked, and there were four wheels beside the cherubim, one wheel beside each cherub. The luster of the wheels was like the gleam of beryl. **10** In appearance, all four looked alike, like a wheel within a wheel. **11** When they moved, they would go in any of the four directions, without pivoting as they moved. But wherever the head faced, they would go in that direction, without pivoting as they went. **12** Their entire bodies, including their backs, hands, wings, and the wheels that the four of them had, were full of eyes all around. **13** As I listened the wheels were called "the wheelwork." **14** Each one had four faces: one was the face of a cherub, the second the face of a human, the third the face of a lion, and the fourth the face of an eagle.

15 The cherubim ascended; these were the living creatures I had seen by the Chebar Canal. **16** When the cherubim moved, the wheels moved beside them, and when they lifted their wings to rise from the earth, even then the wheels did not veer away from them. **17** When the cherubim stopped, the wheels stood still, and when they ascended, the wheels ascended with them, for the spirit of the living creatures was in them.

18 Then the glory of the Lord moved away from the threshold of the temple and stopped above the cherubim. **19** The cherubim lifted their wings and ascended from the earth right before my eyes; the wheels were beside them as they went. The glory of the God of Israel was above them, and it stopped at the entrance to the eastern gate of the Lord's house.

20 These were the living creatures I had seen beneath the God of Israel by the Chebar Canal, and I recognized that they were cherubim. **21** Each had four faces and each had four wings, with what looked something like human hands under their wings. **22** Their faces looked like the same faces I had seen by the Chebar Canal. Each creature went straight ahead.

9:7 The historical fulfillment of this event (**fill the courts with the slain**) is depicted in 2Ch 36:17–19.

9:9–11 Verse 9 is an apparent echo of the flood (Gn 6:11). The saying of the lawless (**the Lord has abandoned the land; he does not see**) repeats in inverted form what the idolatrous elders had said in 8:12.

10:1 The inner curtains and the veil that closed off the most holy place in the tabernacle were adorned with **cherubim** (Ex 26:1,31; 36:8,35). Two golden cherubim with extended wings were part of the covering of the ark of the covenant within the most holy place of the tabernacle (Ex 25:18–22; 37:7–9). Cherubim were also carved in the walls of the Jerusalem temple and covered with gold (1Kg 6:29; 2Ch 3:7; Ezk 41:18–20). In both the tabernacle and the temple, the cherubim constituted a throne for God's invisible presence and glory (1Sm 4:4; 2Sm 6:2; 2Kg 19:15; Pss 18:10; 80:1; 99:1). The creatures in the vision in Ezk 1 were not named. Ezekiel recognized these creatures to be cherubim.

10:2 The image of a burned **city** came true for Jerusalem in 586 BC (2Kg 25:9).

10:3 All the time that the glory of the Lord dwelt in the temple, the **cloud** that accompanied it to reveal the glory of the Lord **filled** the **court** (see Ex 19:9; Lv 16:2).

10:4–5 Verse 4 repeats 9:3.

10:6–8 Fire in the Bible is often associated with God's judgment against wickedness and sin (Gn 19:24; Dt 32:22; Am 1–2).

10:9–13 This is a repetition from chap. 1. In 1:18 only the wheels were "full of eyes all around," whereas here the creatures in their entirety were **full of eyes**. The four creatures John saw around God's throne were also covered with eyes (Rv 4:8).

10:14–17 The faces in v. 14 are the same as in 1:10 except that the "ox" is replaced with the **cherub**. The **cherubim** and the Lord's glory slowly begin their movement from the temple.

10:19 The movement of God's glory to the **eastern gate** anticipated its ultimate

Vision of Israel's Corrupt Leaders

11 The Spirit then lifted me up and brought me to the eastern gate of the LORD's house, which faces east, and at the gate's entrance were twenty-five men. Among them I saw Jaazaniah son of Azzur, and Pelatiah son of Benaiah, leaders of the people. **2** The LORD^A said to me, "Son of man, these are the men who plot evil and give wicked advice in this city. **3** They are saying, 'Isn't the time near to build houses?^B The city is the pot, and we are the meat.' **4** Therefore, prophesy against them. Prophesy, son of man!"

5 Then the Spirit of the LORD came on me, and he told me, "You are to say, 'This is what the LORD says: That is what you are thinking, house of Israel; and I know the thoughts that arise in your mind. **6** You have multiplied your slain in this city, filling its streets with them.

7 "'Therefore, this is what the Lord GOD says: The slain you have put within it are the meat, and the city is the pot, but I^C will take you out of it. **8** You fear the sword, so I will bring the sword against you. This is the declaration of the Lord GOD. **9** I will take you out of the city and hand you over to foreigners; I will execute judgments against you. **10** You will fall by the sword, and I will judge you at the border of Israel. Then you will know that I am the LORD. **11** The city will not be a pot for you, and you will not be the meat within it. I will judge you at the border of Israel, **12** so you will know that I am the LORD, whose statutes you have not followed and whose ordinances you have not practiced. Instead, you have acted according to the ordinances of the nations around you.'"

13 Now while I was prophesying, Pelatiah son of Benaiah died. Then I fell facedown and cried out loudly, "Oh, Lord GOD! You are bringing the remnant of Israel to an end!"

Promise of Israel's Restoration

14 The word of the LORD came to me again: **15** "Son of man, your own relatives, those who have the right to redeem your property,^D,E along with the entire house of Israel — all of them — are those to whom the residents of Jerusalem have said, 'You are far from the LORD; this land has been given to us as a possession.'

16 "Therefore say, 'This is what the Lord GOD says: Though I sent them far away among the nations and scattered them among the countries, yet for a little while I have been a sanctuary for them in the countries where they have gone.'

17 "Therefore say, 'This is what the Lord GOD says: I will gather you from the peoples and assemble you from the countries where you have been scattered, and I will give you the land of Israel.'

18 "When they arrive there, they will remove all its abhorrent acts and detestable practices from it. **19** I will give them integrity of^F heart and put a new spirit within them; I will remove their heart of stone from their bodies^G and give them a heart of flesh, **20** so that they will follow my statutes, keep my ordinances, and practice them. They will be my people, and I will be their God. **21** But as for those whose hearts pursue their desire for abhorrent acts and detestable practices, I will bring their conduct down on their own heads." This is the declaration of the Lord GOD.

God's Glory Leaves Jerusalem

22 Then the cherubim, with the wheels beside them, lifted their wings, and the glory of

---

^A **11:2** Lit *He* ^B **11:3** Or *"The time is not near to build houses.* ^C **11:7** Some Hb mss, LXX, Syr, Tg, Vg; other Hb mss read *he*
^D **11:15** LXX, Syr read *your relatives, your fellow exiles* ^E **11:15** Or *own brothers, your relatives* ^F **11:19** Lit *give them one*
^G **11:19** Lit *flesh*

---

departure from the temple complex and Jerusalem (11:22–23). The east gate would also be the site of the final judgment for Jews (Zch 14:1–9).

MISSION OF THE CHURCH

The church is a sign and instrument of the kingdom of God, a people united by faith in the gospel announcement of the crucified and risen King Jesus. The mission of the church is to go into the world in the power of the Spirit and make disciples by proclaiming this gospel, calling people to respond in ongoing repentance and faith, and demonstrating the truth and power of the gospel by living under the lordship of Christ for the glory of God and the good of the world.

11:1 This verse mentions the same **twenty-five men** who had been described earlier (see note at 8:16).

11:2–4 In 24:3–5 Jerusalem is portrayed as a pot being filled with the choicest morsels. The people thought they could go ahead and build houses because they belonged in Jerusalem, whereas the exiles were like the entrails that were discarded as unfit for the cooking pot.

11:5 On **the Spirit of the LORD came on me**, see note at 2:2.

11:6 This accusation of the leaders of Judah is illustrated in 19:3,6, where kings are charged with devouring humans, and in 22:27, where Ezekiel portrays Israel's leaders as ravenous, violent animals.

11:7–8 Only the **slain** will be left in Jerusalem. The rest will be taken into exile.

11:11–12 This prophecy **I will judge you at the border of Israel** was literally fulfilled at Riblah (2Kg 25:18–21; Jr 52:24–27).

11:13 Ezekiel's lament is also found in 9:8.

11:16 The **sanctuary** was a symbol of the Lord's presence among the Israelites. Here the Lord

promised personally to be for the exiles what the temple had been for them in Jerusalem.

11:17 The regathering (**I will gather you from the peoples**) refers to the end of the Babylonian exile but also may refer to a future gathering of Israel at the beginning of the millennial kingdom (36:24–38; 37:11–28).

11:18 Some scholars believe the historical fulfillment of these actions occurred in Ezr 6–10.

11:19 The **heart of stone** is that of the unregenerate, those who refuse to submit to the will of God (Zch 7:12).

11:20–21 The restoration of Israel's relationship with God (**They will be my people, and I will be their God**) will fulfill the goal of the first exodus (Ex 6:7; cp. Gn 17:7–8; 2Co 6:16; Rv 21:3). But the promise did not apply to everyone.

11:22–23 The **glory** of God, leaving the city, took the direction of King David's flight from Absalom, **on the mountain** [Mount of Olives] **east of the city** (see 2Sm 15:23). Jesus Christ ascended to heaven from the Mount of Olives and promised to return to the same place (cp. Zch 14:4; Ac 1:9–12).

the God of Israel was above them. ²³ The glory of the LORD rose up from within the city and stopped on the mountain east of the city.^A ²⁴ The Spirit lifted me up and brought me to Chaldea and to the exiles in a vision from the Spirit of God. After the vision I had seen left me, ²⁵ I spoke to the exiles about all the things the LORD had shown me.

Ezekiel Dramatizes the Exile

12 The word of the LORD came to me: ² "Son of man, you are living among a rebellious house. They have eyes to see but do not see, and ears to hear but do not hear, for they are a rebellious house.

³ "Now you, son of man, get your bags ready for exile and go into exile in their sight during the day. You will go into exile from your place to another place while they watch; perhaps they will understand, though they are a rebellious house. ⁴ During the day, bring out your bags like an exile's bags while they look on. Then in the evening go out in their sight like those going into exile. ⁵ As they watch, dig through the wall and take the bags out through it. ⁶ And while they look on, lift the bags to your shoulder and take them out in the dark; cover your face so that you cannot see the land. For I have made you a sign to the house of Israel."

⁷ So I did just as I was commanded. In the daytime I brought out my bags like an exile's bags. In the evening I dug through the wall by hand; I took them out in the dark, carrying them on my shoulder in their sight.

⁸ In the morning the word of the LORD came to me: ⁹ "Son of man, hasn't the house of Israel, that rebellious house, asked you, 'What are you doing?' ¹⁰ Say to them, 'This is what the Lord GOD says: This pronouncement concerns the prince^B in Jerusalem and the whole house of Israel living there.'^C ¹¹ You are to say, 'I am a sign for you. Just as I have done, it will be done to them; they will go into exile, into captivity.' ¹² The prince who is among them will lift his bags to his shoulder in the dark and go out. They^D will dig through the wall to bring him out through it. He will cover his face so he cannot

see the land with his eyes. ¹³ But I will spread my net over him, and he will be caught in my snare. I will bring him to Babylon, the land of the Chaldeans, yet he will not see it, and he will die there. ¹⁴ I will also scatter all the attendants who surround him and all his troops to every direction of the wind, and I will draw a sword to chase after them. ¹⁵ They will know that I am the LORD when I disperse them among the nations and scatter them among the countries. ¹⁶ But I will spare a few of them from the sword, famine, and plague, so that among the nations where they go they can tell about all their detestable practices. Then they will know that I am the LORD."

Ezekiel Dramatizes Israel's Anxiety

¹⁷ The word of the LORD came to me: ¹⁸ "Son of man, eat your bread with trembling and drink your water with anxious shaking. ¹⁹ Then say to the people of the land, 'This is what the Lord GOD says about the residents of Jerusalem in the land of Israel: They will eat their bread with anxiety and drink their water in dread, for their^E,F land will be stripped of everything in it because of the violence of all who live there. ²⁰ The inhabited cities will be destroyed, and the land will become dreadful. Then you will know that I am the LORD.'"

A Deceptive Proverb Stopped

²¹ Again the word of the LORD came to me: ²² "Son of man, what is this proverb you people have about the land of Israel, which goes, 'The days keep passing by, and every vision fails'? ²³ Therefore say to them, 'This is what the Lord GOD says: I will put a stop to this proverb, and they will not use it again in Israel.' But say to them, 'The days have arrived, as well as the fulfillment of every vision. ²⁴ For there will no longer be any false vision or flattering divination within the house of Israel. ²⁵ But I, the LORD, will speak whatever message I will speak, and it will be done. It will no longer be delayed. For in your days, rebellious house, I will speak a message and bring it to pass. This is the declaration of the Lord GOD.'"

---

^A **11:23** = the Mount of Olives   ^B **12:10** = King Zedekiah   ^C **12:10** Lit *Israel among them*   ^D **12:12** LXX, Syr read *He*   ^E **12:19** Lit *its*   ^F **12:19** = Jerusalem's

---

12:1–2 Blindness (unseeing **eyes**) and deafness (unhearing **ears**) often indicate disobedience or disbelief (Dt 29:1–4; Is 6:9–10; 43:8; Jr 5:21; Mt 13:13–15; Mk 8:18; Jn 12:39–40; Ac 28:26–27). The phrase **rebellious house** occurs in the prophetic commissioning of Ezekiel (Ezk 2:5–8; 3:9), but it also occurs in 3:26–27. **12:3–6** Ezekiel's readers understood that breaking through a wall indicated exile, since the conquering armies would **dig through the wall** at strategic points in order to enter the city (Am 4:3). **12:7** The **exile's bags** symbolize the remnant that will be led out of the homeland as captives.

12:12 The covering of King Zedekiah's **face** was Ezekiel's symbolic prophecy of the blinding of the king of Judah by Nebuchadnezzar and his exile to Babylon (2Kg 25:7). **12:13** The phrase **I will spread my net over him** uses the image of a bird hunter (Hs 7:12) or animal hunter (Ezk 19:8). The words **yet he will not see it** refer to the ancient Near Eastern custom of gouging out the eyes of captives. **12:14–15** Some of the people would escape to other **countries**. **12:16** The statement **I will spare a few of them** refers to a remnant that will be preserved by the Lord. They will realize their

guilt and turn to the Lord in heathen lands (6:8–10). **12:17–20** The phrase **because of the violence** reflects the rationale for the judgment of the earth by the flood (Gn 6:11,13). **12:21–22** The expression **the days keep passing by, and every vision fails** reflects the test of true prophecy (Dt 18:20–22). If a prophecy did not come true, the person who made the prediction was a false prophet. **12:23–28** In Ezekiel's day **false** prophets opposed the claims of God's true messengers in Jerusalem (Jr 28:1–4) and Babylon (Jr 29:1,8–9).

26 The word of the LORD came to me: **27** "Son of man, notice that the house of Israel is saying, 'The vision that he sees concerns many years from now; he prophesies about distant times.' **28** Therefore say to them, 'This is what the Lord GOD says: None of my words will be delayed any longer. The message I speak will be fulfilled. This is the declaration of the Lord GOD.'"

Israel's False Prophets Condemned

13 The word of the LORD came to me: **2** "Son of man, prophesy against the prophets of Israel who are prophesying. Say to those who prophesy out of their own imagination, 'Hear the word of the LORD! **3** This is what the Lord GOD says: Woe to the foolish prophets who follow their own spirit and have seen nothing. **4** Your prophets, Israel, are like jackals among ruins. **5** You did not go up to the gaps or restore the wall around the house of Israel so that it might stand in battle on the day of the LORD. **6** They saw false visions and their divinations were a lie. They claimed, "This is the LORD's declaration," when the LORD did not send them, yet they wait for the fulfillment of their message. **7** Didn't you see a false vision and speak a lying divination when you proclaimed, "This is the LORD's declaration," even though I had not spoken?

8 "'Therefore, this is what the Lord GOD says: You have spoken falsely and had lying visions; that's why you discover that I am against you. This is the declaration of the Lord GOD. **9** My hand will be against the prophets who see false visions and speak lying divinations. They will not be present in the council of my people or be recorded in the register of the house of Israel, and they will not enter the land of Israel. Then you will know that I am the Lord GOD.

10 "'Since they have led my people astray by saying, "Peace," when there is no peace, and since when a flimsy wall is being built, they plaster it with whitewash, **11** therefore, tell those plastering it with whitewash that it will fall. Torrential rain will come, and I will send hailstones plunging^A down, and a whirlwind will be released. **12** When the wall has fallen, will you not be asked, "Where's the whitewash you plastered on it?"

13 "'So this is what the Lord GOD says: I will release a whirlwind in my wrath. Torrential rain will come in my anger, and hailstones will fall in destructive fury. **14** I will demolish the wall you plastered with whitewash and knock it to the ground so that its foundation is exposed. The city will fall, and you will be destroyed within it. Then you will know that I am the LORD. **15** After I exhaust my wrath against the wall and against those who plaster it with whitewash, I will say to you, "The wall is no more and neither are those who plastered it — **16** those prophets of Israel who prophesied to Jerusalem and saw a vision of peace for her when there was no peace." This is the declaration of the Lord GOD.'

17 "Now you, son of man, face^B the women among your people who prophesy out of their own imagination, and prophesy against them. **18** Say, 'This is what the Lord GOD says: Woe to the women who sew magic bands on the wrist of every hand and who make veils for the heads of people of every size in order to ensnare lives. Will you ensnare the lives of my people but preserve your own? **19** You profane me among my people for handfuls of barley and scraps of bread; you put those to death who should not die and spare those who should not live, when you lie to my people, who listen to lies.

20 "'Therefore, this is what the Lord GOD says: I am against your magic bands with which you ensnare people like birds, and I will tear them from your arms. I will free the people you have ensnared like birds. **21** I will also tear off your veils and rescue my people from your hands, so that they will no longer be prey in your hands. Then you will know that I am the LORD. **22** Because you have disheartened the righteous person with lies (when I intended no distress), and because you have supported^C the wicked person so that he does not turn from his evil way to save his life, **23** therefore you will no longer see false visions or practice divination. I will rescue my people from your hands. Then you will know that I am the LORD.'"

Idolatrous Elders Punished

14 Some of the elders of Israel came to me and sat down in front of me. **2** Then the word of the LORD came to me: **3** "Son of man,

---

^A **13:11** One Hb ms, LXX, Vg; other Hb mss read *and you, hailstones, will plunge*   ^B **13:17** Lit *set your face*   ^C **13:22** Lit *strengthened the hand of*

13:1–3 In no sense were these people prophets of God. The source of their message was **their own imagination** (i.e., their heart) and **their own spirit**. According to Dt 18:18, genuine prophets receive their messages directly from God and speak for him.
13:4 The sight of **jackals** scavenging in the **ruins** of the city pictures the despair of the people after the fall of Jerusalem (Lm 5:18).
13:5–7 The **gaps** in the wall are figurative. The prophets should have strengthened the people morally and spiritually.

13:8–9 The phrase **I am against you** is addressed to Israel one other time in Ezekiel (21:3). It was normally directed toward foreign nations.
13:10–16 The destructive **hailstones** recall the seventh plague on Egypt (Ex 9:13–35), Joshua's victory over the five Amorite kings (Jos 10:1–15), God's judgment on Samaria (Is 28:2,17), and the Lord's defeat of Assyria (Is 30:30; cp. Ps 148:8).
13:17–23 Women practiced magic in Jerusalem (Jr 7:18; 44:17,19) as well as in Babylon.

The Mosaic law condemned witches and necromancers (Lv 20:27; 1Sm 28:9; cp. Lv 19:31). There were a number of legitimate prophetesses in the OT, including Miriam (Ex 15:20), Deborah (Jdg 4:4), Huldah (2Kg 22:14), and Noadiah (Neh 6:14). Prophetesses are also mentioned in the NT (Lk 2:36–38; Ac 21:9; 1Co 11:5).
14:1–3 The phrase **set up idols in their hearts** literally reads, "raised idols in their heart," conveying the notion of commitment to the service of an idol. This word

these men have set up idols in their hearts and have put their sinful stumbling blocks in front of themselves. Should I actually let them inquire of me?

⁴ "Therefore, speak to them and tell them, 'This is what the Lord GOD says: When anyone from the house of Israel sets up idols in his heart and puts his sinful stumbling block in front of himself, and then comes to the prophet, I, the LORD, will answer him appropriately.^A I will answer him according to his many idols, ⁵ so that I may take hold of the house of Israel by their hearts. They are all estranged from me because of their idols.'

⁶ "Therefore, say to the house of Israel, 'This is what the Lord GOD says: Repent and turn away from your idols; turn your faces away from all your detestable things. ⁷ For when anyone from the house of Israel or from the aliens who reside in Israel separates himself from me, setting up idols in his heart and putting his sinful stumbling block in front of himself, and then comes to the prophet to inquire of me, I, the LORD, will answer him myself. ⁸ I will turn against that one and make him a sign and a proverb; I will cut him off from among my people. Then you will know that I am the LORD.

⁹ " 'But if the prophet is deceived and speaks a message, it was I, the LORD, who deceived that prophet. I will stretch out my hand against him and destroy him from among my people Israel. ¹⁰ They will bear their punishment — the punishment of the one who inquires will be the same as that of the prophet — ¹¹ in order that the house of Israel may no longer stray from following me and no longer defile themselves with all their transgressions. Then they will be my people and I will be their God. This is the declaration of the Lord GOD.' "

Four Devastating Judgments

¹² The word of the LORD came to me: ¹³ "Son of man, suppose a land sins against me by acting faithlessly, and I stretch out my hand against it to cut off its supply of bread, to send famine through it, and to wipe out both people and animals from it. ¹⁴ Even if these three men — Noah, Daniel, and Job — were in it, they would rescue only themselves by their righteousness." This is the declaration of the Lord GOD.

¹⁵ "Suppose I allow dangerous animals to pass through the land and depopulate it so that it becomes desolate, with no one passing through it for fear of the animals. ¹⁶ Even if these three men were in it, as I live" — the declaration of the Lord GOD — "they could not rescue their sons or daughters. They alone would be rescued, but the land would be desolate.

¹⁷ "Or suppose I bring a sword against that land and say, 'Let a sword pass through it,' so that I wipe out both people and animals from it. ¹⁸ Even if these three men were in it, as I live" — the declaration of the Lord GOD — "they could not rescue their sons or daughters, but they alone would be rescued.

¹⁹ "Or suppose I send a plague into that land and pour out my wrath on it with bloodshed to wipe out both people and animals from it. ²⁰ Even if Noah, Daniel, and Job were in it, as I live" — the declaration of the Lord GOD — "they could not rescue their son or daughter. They would rescue only themselves by their righteousness.

²¹ "For this is what the Lord GOD says: How much worse will it be when I send my four devastating judgments against Jerusalem — sword, famine, dangerous animals, and plague — in order to wipe out both people and animals from it! ²² Even so, there will be survivors left in it, sons and daughters who will be brought out. Indeed, they will come out to you, and you will observe their conduct and actions. Then you will be consoled about the devastation I have brought on Jerusalem, about all I have brought on it. ²³ They will bring you consolation when you see their conduct and actions, and you will know that it was not without cause that I have done what I did to it." This is the declaration of the Lord GOD.

---

^A **14:4** Alt Hb tradition reads *him who comes*

---

for idols was used in 6:4–6,13. It literally denotes "dung pellets," thus indicating what the prophet thought of idols. While the idolatry in Jerusalem was openly displayed (chap. 8), the idolatry practiced by Hebrew exiles in Babylon was more subtle, as revealed by the people's heart convictions.
14:4–5 God wanted to **take hold of the house of Israel by their hearts**.
14:7 The word **aliens** refers to non-Israelites who had relocated and identified themselves with the people of God and who sometimes became proselytes to the true faith.
14:8 To be **cut . . . off** refers to experiencing premature death, perhaps by means of the death penalty (Lv 20:2–5).
14:9 If the people continued to refuse to listen to prophets whom God sent to tell them the truth, the Lord would judge them by sending lying prophets to tell them what

they wanted to hear rather than what they needed to hear.
14:10 The expression **they will bear their punishment** is a legal phrase from Lv 20:17. In that passage as here, the concept of being "cut off" accompanies this statement of judgment.
14:11 The formula **then they will be my people and I will be their God** has its origin in Ex 6:7 in connection with the establishment of the covenant relationship between Yahweh and his people. It recurs in the description of the ultimate bliss in the covenantal blessings (Lv 26:12).
14:12–14 Some people of Judah must have wondered whether the impending judgment on Jerusalem might be diverted if some well-known righteous man or men (**Noah, Daniel, and Job**) could be found (Gn 18). Ezekiel's reference to these men affirmed

that moral responsibility is not transferable; it is individual.
14:21 Sword curses (predictions of punishment by war) occur in Lv 26:25,33; Dt 32:41–42. On **famine** curses, see Lv 26:26,29; Dt 28:53–56; 32:24. **Dangerous** animal curses appear in Lv 26:22; Dt 32:24. Pestilence or **plague** curses are found in Lv 26:16,25; Dt 28:21–22; 32:24. These four curses are also mentioned in Ezk 5.
14:22–23 When the exiles saw the wicked behavior of the survivors of the perilous judgments (**you will observe their conduct and actions**), they would be assured of God's justice—that he had acted righteously in his judgment. The exiles would regard the destruction of Judah's capital as well deserved.
15:1–8 The **vine** as an image of Israel goes back to Nm 13:23 where it appears as a

Parable of the Useless Vine

15 Then the word of the Lord came to me: ² "Son of man, how does the wood of the vine, that branch among the trees of the forest, compare to any other wood? ³ Can wood be taken from it to make something useful? Or can anyone make a peg from it to hang things on? ⁴ In fact, it is put into the fire as fuel. The fire devours both of its ends, and the middle is charred. Can it be useful for anything? ⁵ Even when it was whole it could not be made into a useful object. How much less can it ever be made into anything useful when the fire has devoured it and it is charred!"

⁶ Therefore, this is what the Lord God says, "Like the wood of the vine among the trees of the forest, which I have given to the fire as fuel, so I will give up the residents of Jerusalem. ⁷ I will turn against them. They may have escaped from the fire, but it will still consume them. And you will know that I am the Lord when I turn against them. ⁸ I will make the land desolate because they have acted unfaithfully." This is the declaration of the Lord God.

Parable of God's Adulterous Wife

16 The word of the Lord came to me again: ² "Son of man, confront Jerusalem with her detestable practices. ³ You are to say, 'This is what the Lord God says to Jerusalem: Your origin and your birth were in the land of the Canaanites. Your father was an Amorite and your mother a Hethite. ⁴ As for your birth, your umbilical cord wasn't cut on the day you were born, and you weren't washed clean^A with water. You were not rubbed with salt or wrapped in cloths. ⁵ No one cared enough about you to do even one of these things out of compassion for you. But you were thrown out into the open field because you were despised on the day you were born.

⁶ " 'I passed by you and saw you thrashing around in your blood, and I said to you as you lay in your blood, "Live!" Yes, I said to you as you lay in your blood, "Live!"^B ⁷ I made you thrive^C like plants of the field. You grew up and matured and became very beautiful.^D Your breasts were formed and your hair grew, but you were stark naked.

⁸ " 'Then I passed by you and saw you, and you were indeed at the age for love. So I spread the edge of my garment over you and covered your nakedness. I pledged myself to you, entered into a covenant with you — this is the declaration of the Lord God — and you became mine. ⁹ I washed you with water, rinsed off your blood, and anointed you with oil. ¹⁰ I clothed you in embroidered cloth and provided you with fine leather^A sandals. I also wrapped you in fine linen and covered you with silk. ¹¹ I adorned you with jewelry, putting bracelets on your wrists and a necklace around your neck. ¹² I put a ring in your nose, earrings on your ears, and a beautiful crown on your head. ¹³ So you were adorned with gold and silver, and your clothing was made of fine linen, silk, and embroidered cloth. You ate fine flour, honey, and oil. You became extremely beautiful and attained royalty. ¹⁴ Your fame spread among the nations because of your beauty, for it was perfect through my splendor, which I had bestowed on you. This is the declaration of the Lord God.

¹⁵ " 'But you trusted in your beauty and acted like a prostitute because of your fame. You lavished your sexual favors on everyone who passed by. Your beauty became his.^A ¹⁶ You took some of your clothing and made colorful high places for yourself, and you engaged

---

^A **16:4,10,15** Hb obscure   ^B **16:6** Some Hb mss, LXX, Syr omit *Yes, I said to you as you lay in your blood, "Live!"*
^C **16:7** LXX reads *Thrive; I made you*   ^D **16:7** Or *matured and developed the loveliest of ornaments*

---

symbol of the richness of Canaan, the land promised to Israel. The image of the vine portrays God's loving care for the nation as a vinedresser taking care of what he had planted (Ps 80:8–9; Is 5:1–7). It is clear from Mt 21:33–41 that God desires fruit (good works) from his vine. **Fire** is a frequent figure for destruction in Ezekiel (5:2,4; 10:2; 16:41; 23:47; 24:10–11). The burning of the **wood** accompanied the destruction of **Jerusalem**. In Babylonian invasions fire accompanied annihilation (2Kg 25:9; 2Ch 36:19).

16:1–63 This chapter is similar in purpose to 20:3–31, where a review of Israel's history set the context for its coming judgment.

16:1–3 Jerusalem had a centuries-old, pre-Israelite history (Gn 14:18), and the city resisted Israelite conquest in the days of Joshua (Jos 15:63). It became an Israelite city only after David's conquest (2Sm 5:6–9). In biblical ethnography **Canaanites**, Amorites, and Hethites were closely related. Moreover, these three were related to the Jebusites, the pre-Israelite inhabitants of Jerusalem (Gn 10:15–18; Jdg 19:11; 2Sm 5:6). The Amorites were pre-Israelite, Semitic inhabitants of Palestine (Gn 48:22; Jos 5:1; 10:5; Jdg 1:34–36). The Hethites were descendants of Heth, son of Canaan, who had flourished in the land of Canaan during the second millennium BC (Gn 10:15; 23:10–20; 26:34; Dt 7:1). By going back to the people's origin, Ezekiel emphasized that the people had always been characterized by rebellion and idol worship.

16:4–6 Exposure of unwanted babies, especially girls, was common in the ancient world. In this description the infant was abandoned, apparently still attached to the placenta, and left to die (**you were not rubbed with salt or wrapped in cloths**). The phrase **saw you thrashing around in your blood** emphasizes that Israel was abandoned by her mother.

16:7–8 The special word for **love** (Hb *dodim*) in v. 8 refers to the love that leads to sexual relations (23:17; Sg 1:2,4; 4:10; 5:1; 7:13). Spreading a **garment** over a person was a proposal of marriage (Ru 3:9). The portrayal is of Israel as the Lord's wife (**you became mine**). A wife's obligation to remain true to her husband offered a fitting parallel to Israel's obligations to God.

16:9 The expression **rinsed off your blood** may be associated with bleeding that occurs with the first experience of sexual intercourse (Dt 22:13–21). Or it may refer to menstrual blood, indicating sexual maturity.

16:10 Jerusalem is **clothed** in materials that are elsewhere used in decorating the tabernacle (**embroidered cloth**). This is a subtle suggestion that Jerusalem was the home of the temple (Pss 48:2; 50:2; Lm 2:15).

16:11–14 Jerusalem became beautiful because God's **splendor** resided there.

16:15–16 The accusation (**acted like a prostitute**) referred both to a spiritual turning away from the Lord and to physical involvement with the fertility rites of Canaanite paganism (Jr 3:1–5; Hs 4:13–14; 9:1; cp. Gn 38:14–16). Jerusalem played the harlot; she committed the sin of idolatry (Jms 4:4). Her pride led her astray (Dt 32:15; Jr 7:4; Mc 3:11).

in prostitution on them. These places should not have been built, and this should never have happened!^A ^17 You also took your beautiful jewelry made from the gold and silver I had given you, and you made male images so that you could engage in prostitution with them. ^18 Then you took your embroidered clothing to cover them and set my oil and incense before them. ^19 The food that I gave you — the fine flour, oil, and honey that I fed you — you set it before them as a pleasing aroma. That is what happened. This is the declaration of the Lord GOD.

^20 " 'You even took your sons and daughters you bore to me and sacrificed them to these images as food. Wasn't your prostitution enough? ^21 You slaughtered my children and gave them up when you passed them through the fire to the images. ^22 In all your detestable practices and acts of prostitution, you did not remember the days of your youth when you were stark naked and thrashing around in your blood.

^23 " 'Then after all your evil — Woe, woe to you! — the declaration of the Lord GOD — ^24 you built yourself a mound and made yourself an elevated place in every square. ^25 You built your elevated place at the head of every street and turned your beauty into a detestable thing. You spread your legs to everyone who passed by and increased your prostitution. ^26 You engaged in promiscuous acts with Egyptian men, your well-endowed neighbors, and increased your prostitution to anger me.

^27 " 'Therefore, I stretched out my hand against you and reduced your provisions. I gave you over to the desire of those who hate you, the Philistine women, who were embarrassed by your indecent conduct. ^28 Then you engaged in prostitution with the Assyrian men because you were not satisfied. Even though you did this with them, you were still not satisfied. ^29 So you extended your prostitution to Chaldea, the land of merchants, but you were not even satisfied with this!

^30 " 'How your heart was inflamed with lust^B — the declaration of the Lord GOD — when you did all these things, the acts of a brazen prostitute, ^31 building your mound at the head

of every street and making your elevated place in every square. But you were unlike a prostitute because you scorned payment. ^32 You adulterous wife, who receives strangers instead of her husband! ^33 Men give gifts to all prostitutes, but you gave gifts to all your lovers. You bribed them to come to you from all around for your sexual favors. ^34 So you were the opposite of other women in your acts of prostitution; no one solicited you. When you paid a fee instead of one being paid to you, you were the opposite.

^35 " 'Therefore, you prostitute, hear the word of the LORD! ^36 This is what the Lord GOD says: Because your lust was poured out and your nakedness exposed by your acts of prostitution with your lovers, and because of all your detestable idols and the blood of your children that you gave to them, ^37 I am therefore going to gather all the lovers you pleased — all those you loved as well as all those you hated. I will gather them against you from all around and expose your nakedness to them so they see you completely naked. ^38 I will judge you the way adulteresses and those who shed blood are judged. Then I will bring about the shedding of your blood in jealous wrath. ^39 I will hand you over to them, and they will demolish your mounds and tear down your elevated places. They will strip off your clothes, take your beautiful jewelry, and leave you stark naked. ^40 They will bring a mob against you to stone you and to cut you to pieces with their swords. ^41 They will burn your houses and execute judgments against you in the sight of many women. I will stop you from being a prostitute, and you will never again pay fees for lovers. ^42 So I will satisfy my wrath against you, and my jealousy will turn away from you. Then I will be calm and no longer angry. ^43 Because you did not remember the days of your youth but enraged me with all these things, I will also bring your conduct down on your own head. This is the declaration of the Lord GOD. Haven't you committed depravity in addition to all your detestable practices?

^44 " 'Look, everyone who uses proverbs will quote this proverb about you: "Like mother,

---

^A 16:16 Hb obscure   ^B 16:30 Or was sick

like daughter." ⁴⁵ You are the daughter of your mother, who despised her husband and children. You are the sister of your sisters, who despised their husbands and children. Your mother was a Hethite and your father an Amorite. ⁴⁶ Your older sister was Samaria, who lived with her daughters to the north of you, and your younger sister was Sodom, who lived with her daughters to the south of you. ⁴⁷ Didn't you walk in their ways and do their detestable practices? It was only a short time before all your ways were more corrupt than theirs.

⁴⁸ "As I live — the declaration of the Lord GOD — your sister Sodom and her daughters have not behaved as you and your daughters have. ⁴⁹ Now this was the iniquity of your sister Sodom: She and her daughters had pride, plenty of food, and comfortable security, but didn't supportᴬ the poor and needy. ⁵⁰ They were haughty and did detestable acts before me, so I removed them when I saw this.ᴮ ⁵¹ But Samaria did not commit even half your sins. You have multiplied your detestable practices beyond theirs and made your sisters appear righteous by all the detestable acts you have committed. ⁵² You must also bear your disgrace, since you have helped your sisters out.ᶜ For they appear more righteous than you because of your sins, which you committed more detestably than they did. So you also, be ashamed and bear your disgrace, since you have made your sisters appear righteous.

⁵³ "'I will restore their fortunes, the fortunes of Sodom and her daughters and those of Samaria and her daughters. I will also restoreᴰ your fortunes among them, ⁵⁴ so you will bear your disgrace and be ashamed of all you did when you comforted them. ⁵⁵ As for your sisters, Sodom and her daughters and Samaria and her daughters will return to their former state. You and your daughters will also return to your former state. ⁵⁶ Didn't you treat your sister Sodom as an object of scorn when you were proud, ⁵⁷ before your wickedness was exposed? It was like the time you were scorned by the daughters of Aramᴱ and all those around her, and by the daughters of the Philistines — those who treated you with contempt from every side. ⁵⁸ You yourself must bear the consequences of your depravity and detestable practices — this is the LORD's declaration.

⁵⁹ "'For this is what the Lord GOD says: I will deal with you according to what you have done, since you have despised the oath by breaking the covenant. ⁶⁰ But I will remember the covenant I made with you in the days of your youth, and I will establish a permanent covenant with you. ⁶¹ Then you will remember your ways and be ashamed when youᶠ receive your older and younger sisters. I will give them to you as daughters, but not because of your covenant. ⁶² I will establish my covenant with you, and you will know that I am the LORD, ⁶³ so that when I make atonement for all you have done, you will remember and be ashamed, and never open your mouth again because of your disgrace. This is the declaration of the Lord GOD.'"

Parable of the Eagles

17 The word of the LORD came to me: ² "Son of man, pose a riddle and speak a parable to the house of Israel. ³ You are to say, 'This is what the Lord GOD says: A huge eagle with powerful wings, long feathers, and full plumage of many colors came to Lebanon and took the top of the cedar. ⁴ He plucked off its topmost shoot, brought it to the land of merchants, and set it in a city of traders. ⁵ Then he took some of the land's seed and put it in a fertile field; he set it like a willow, a plant⁶ by abundant water. ⁶ It sprouted and became a spreading vine,

---

ᴬ16:49 Lit strengthen the hand of   ᴮ16:50 Or them as you have seen   ᶜ16:52 Lit you have been the advocate for your sisters   ᴰ16:53 LXX, Vg; MT reads Samaria and her daughters and the fortunes of   ᴱ16:57 Some Hb mss, Syr read Edom   ᶠ16:61 Some LXX mss, Syr read I   ⁶17:5 Hb obscure

---

corruption (Dt 32:32; Is 1:10; Jr 23:14). The Bible frequently compares cities or peoples to Sodom, which was taken to be the epitome of evil and degradation (Dt 29:23; 32:32; Is 1:9–10; 3:9; Lm 4:6; Mt 10:15; 11:23–24; Jd 7).
16:48–52 Samaria and Sodom were Judah's **sisters** in sin. If God had not punished Judah, whose sins were so much worse than Samaria's and Sodom's, he would have been unjust.
16:56 The phrase **when you were proud** refers to the golden days of Jerusalem during the reign of David and the beginning of Solomon's reign.
16:59 Jerusalem's contempt toward the oath and the **breaking** of **the covenant** would be answered by the suspension of God's own covenant obligations.
16:60–61 References to the Lord remembering his **covenant** occur only in relationship to the patriarchal covenants (Gn 9:15–16; Ex 2:24; 6:5; Lv 26:42,45; Ps 105:8). The mention of

God remembering his covenant is contrasted with Jerusalem's forgetting the terms of her relationship with God (Ezk 16:22,43). When this new relationship is established, the people will remember their ways and be ashamed. The **permanent covenant** is the new covenant spoken of in Is 59:21; 61:8; and Jr 31:31–34, but it should be viewed as closely related to the Abrahamic covenant. The features of the new covenant are actually the outworking of the basic elements of God's promises to Abraham (Is 55:3; Jr 32:40).
16:62 Prophetic passages that announce the restoration of Israel (**I will establish my covenant with you**) reflect the teaching of Dt 30:3.
17:1–2 A **riddle** is an obscure and mysterious saying. It hides the truth it imparts, while a **parable** elucidates the truth that underlies it by putting it in fresh light.
17:3 The **huge eagle** in this verse is Nebuchadnezzar of Babylon (v. 12). The fulfillment

of the riddle came in Nebuchadnezzar's campaign against Jerusalem in 597 BC and his deportation of Jehoiachin (and Ezekiel) as part of the second deportation to Babylon (2Kg 24:10–12). The historical background behind this passage may be found in 2Kg 24:8–20; 2Ch 36:9–13; Jr 37; 52:1–17. **Lebanon** refers to Jerusalem (Ezk 17:12). In ancient times the Lebanon mountain range was covered with cedars. The **cedar** refers to David's dynasty, his royal family. The top of the cedar removed by the king of Babylon was Jehoiachin, who was taken into exile in 597 BC (2Kg 24:8–16).
17:4 Here the phrase **land of merchants** refers to Babylon (16:29), the great center of commerce in all Asia.
17:5 The **land's seed** in this verse is King Zedekiah of Judah, son of Josiah (2Kg 23–34).
17:6 This image (**low in height with its branches turned toward him**) represents Zedekiah turning toward Nebuchadnezzar to whom he owed his power.

low in height with its branches turned toward him, yet its roots stayed under it. So it became a vine, produced branches, and sent out shoots. ⁷ " 'But there was another huge eagle with powerful wings and thick plumage. And this vine bent its roots toward him! It stretched out its branches to him from the plot where it was planted, so that he might water it. ⁸ It had been planted in a good field by abundant water in order to produce branches, bear fruit, and become a splendid vine.'

⁹ "You are to say, 'This is what the Lord God says: Will it flourish? Will he not tear out its roots and strip off its fruit so that it shrivels? All its fresh leaves will wither! Great strength and many people will not be needed to pull it from its roots. ¹⁰ Even though it is planted, will it flourish? Won't it wither completely when the east wind strikes it? It will wither on the plot where it sprouted.'"

¹¹ The word of the Lord came to me: ¹² "Now say to that rebellious house, 'Don't you know what these things mean?' Tell them, 'The king of Babylon came to Jerusalem, took its king and officials, and brought them back with him to Babylon. ¹³ He took one of the royal family and made a covenant with him, putting him under oath. Then he took away the leading men of the land, ¹⁴ so that the kingdom would be humble and not exalt itself but would keep his covenant in order to endure. ¹⁵ However, this king revolted against him by sending his ambassadors to Egypt so they might give him horses and a large army. Will he flourish? Will the one who does such things escape? Can he break a covenant and still escape?

¹⁶ " 'As I live — this is the declaration of the Lord God — he will die in Babylon, in the land of the king who put him on the throne, whose oath he despised and whose covenant he broke. ¹⁷ Pharaoh with his mighty army and vast company will not help him in battle, when ramps are built and siege walls constructed to destroy many lives. ¹⁸ He despised the oath by breaking the covenant. He did all these things even though he gave his hand in pledge. He will not escape!

¹⁹ " 'Therefore, this is what the Lord God says: As I live, I will bring down on his head my oath that he despised and my covenant that he broke. ²⁰ I will spread my net over him, and he will be caught in my snare. I will bring him to Babylon and execute judgment on him there for the treachery he committed against me. ²¹ All the fugitives^A among his troops will fall by the sword, and those who survive will be scattered to every direction of the wind. Then you will know that I, the Lord, have spoken.

²² " 'This is what the Lord God says:

I will take a sprig
from the lofty top of the cedar
and plant it.
I will pluck a tender sprig
from its topmost shoots,
and I will plant it
on a high towering mountain.
²³ I will plant it on Israel's high mountain
so that it may bear branches,
produce fruit,
and become a majestic cedar.
Birds of every kind will nest under it,
taking shelter in the shade of its branches.
²⁴ Then all the trees of the field will know
that I am the Lord.
I bring down the tall tree,
and make the low tree tall.
I cause the green tree to wither
and make the withered tree thrive.
I, the Lord, have spoken
and I will do it.' "

Personal Responsibility for Sin

18 The word of the Lord came to me: ² "What do you mean by using this proverb concerning the land of Israel:

'The fathers eat sour grapes,
and the children's teeth are set on edge'?
³ As I live" — this is the declaration of the Lord God — "you will no longer use this proverb in

---

^17:21 Some Hb mss, LXX, Syr, Tg read *choice men*

17:7–8 While the first eagle represents the king of Babylon, the second **huge eagle** is Egypt. This eagle is the Egyptian pharaoh, either Psammetichus II (595–589 BC) or Hophra (589–570 BC). King Zedekiah of Judah attempted to seek Egypt's aid in order to break free from the Babylonian yoke. For the details of these events, see 2Ch 36:13; Jr 35:5–7; 44:30; 52:11.
17:9 Taking up the **roots** signifies the abolition of national existence (Am 2:9). In this specific case, it refers to the deportation of Judah to Babylon.
17:10 The **east wind** is the hot, dry wind. It is an instrument of God's will.
17:11–15 See note on vv. 7–8.
17:13 The phrase **he took one of the royal family and made a covenant with him** describes Nebuchadnezzar's installation of his own puppet king, Mattaniah, whom he

renamed Zedekiah after Jehoiachin was removed from the throne. The people of the upper class of the land were carried away with Jehoiachin to Babylon (2Kg 24:15).
17:16–18 This prophecy (**he will die in Babylon**) was fulfilled in 2Kg 25:7.
17:19–21 Nebuchadnezzar had forced his vassal **covenant** on King Zedekiah of Judah (2Ch 36:13). The **oath** had been sworn to the God of Israel, so a violation of the agreement would bring the anger of the Lord.
17:22 In this context, a **sprig** serves as a forerunner of the messianic figure mentioned later. God would replant a king from the line of David on the **mountain** heights of Israel. The mountain on which the cedar will be planted is the symbol of a mighty kingdom (Is 2:2; Mc 4:1).
17:24 The concept of the Messiah as the **low tree** or "dry tree" awaiting glorification fits

with the view of the Messiah as Suffering Servant.
18:1–2 The Hebrew word for **set on edge** describes the effect on the **teeth** that results from eating tart **grapes** (Jr 31:29–30). In the Ten Commandments, God said he would visit sin on the third and fourth generations of those who rebel against him (Ex 20:5). The people in Ezekiel's day misconstrued this reality, as reflected in this proverb accusing God of unfairness. God does not punish the innocent for the sins of others. The proverb was current in Jerusalem as well (Jr 31:29–30); see Dt 24:16.
18:3–4 God demanded that the people not recite this false **proverb**. It not only misconstrued God's conduct and character, but those who recited it regarded themselves as completely innocent (Pr 26:9).

Israel. ⁴ Look, every life belongs to me. The life of the father is like the life of the son — both belong to me. The person who sins is the one who will die.

⁵ "Suppose a man is righteous and does what is just and right: ⁶ He does not eat at the mountain shrines^A or look to the idols of the house of Israel. He does not defile his neighbor's wife or approach a woman during her menstrual impurity. ⁷ He doesn't oppress anyone but returns his collateral to the debtor. He does not commit robbery, but gives his bread to the hungry and covers the naked with clothing. ⁸ He doesn't lend at interest or for profit but keeps his hand from injustice and carries out true justice between men. ⁹ He follows my statutes and keeps my ordinances, acting faithfully. Such a person is righteous; he will certainly live." This is the declaration of the Lord God.

¹⁰ "But suppose the man has a violent son, who sheds blood and does any of these things, ¹¹ though the father has done none of them. Indeed, when the son eats at the mountain shrines and defiles his neighbor's wife, ¹² and when he oppresses the poor and needy, commits robbery, and does not return collateral, and when he looks to the idols, commits detestable acts, ¹³ and lends at interest or for profit, will he live? He will not live! Since he has committed all these detestable acts, he will certainly die. His death will be his own fault.^B

¹⁴ "Now suppose he has a son who sees all the sins his father has committed, and though he sees them, he does not do likewise. ¹⁵ He does not eat at the mountain shrines or look to the idols of the house of Israel. He does not defile his neighbor's wife. ¹⁶ He doesn't oppress anyone, hold collateral, or commit robbery. He gives his bread to the hungry and covers the naked with clothing. ¹⁷ He keeps his hand from harming the poor, not taking interest or profit on a loan. He practices my ordinances and follows my statutes. Such a person will not die for his father's iniquity. He will certainly live. ¹⁸ "As for his father, he will die for his own iniquity because he practiced fraud, robbed his brother, and did among his people what was not good. ¹⁹ But you may ask, 'Why doesn't the son suffer punishment for the father's iniquity?' Since the son has done what is just and right, carefully observing all my statutes, he will certainly live. ²⁰ The person who sins is the one who will die. A son won't suffer punishment for the father's iniquity, and a father won't suffer punishment for the son's iniquity. The righteousness of the righteous person will be on him, and the wickedness of the wicked person will be on him.

²¹ "But if the wicked person turns from all the sins he has committed, keeps all my statutes, and does what is just and right, he will certainly live; he will not die. ²² None of the transgressions he has committed will be held against him. He will live because of the righteousness he has practiced. ²³ Do I take any pleasure in the death of the wicked?" This is the declaration of the Lord God. "Instead, don't I take pleasure when he turns from his ways and lives? ²⁴ But when a righteous person turns from his righteousness and acts unjustly, committing the same detestable acts that the wicked do, will he live? None of the righteous acts he did will be remembered. He will die because of the treachery he has engaged in and the sin he has committed.

²⁵ "But you say, 'The Lord's way isn't fair.' Now listen, house of Israel: Is it my way that is unfair? Instead, isn't it your ways that are unfair? ²⁶ When a righteous person turns from his righteousness and acts unjustly, he will die for this. He will die because of the injustice he has committed. ²⁷ But if a wicked person turns from the wickedness he has committed and does what is just and right, he will preserve his life. ²⁸ He will certainly live because he thought it over and turned from all the transgressions he had committed; he will not die. ²⁹ But the house of Israel says, 'The Lord's way isn't fair.' Is it my ways that are unfair, house of Israel? Instead, isn't it your ways that are unfair?

³⁰ "Therefore, house of Israel, I will judge each one of you according to his ways." This

---

^A 18:6 Lit the mountains, also in vv. 11,15   ^B 18:13 Lit His blood will be on him

---

18:6 To **approach a woman** is a euphemism for sexual intercourse (Lv 18:14; Dt 22:14; Is 8:3).

18:7 On **returns his collateral to the debtor**, see Ex 22:26; Dt 24:12–13. **Robbery** refers to the seizure of property, usually by the rich (Is 3:14; 10:2; Mc 2:2).

18:8 The law prohibited charging **interest** on loans made to fellow Israelites (Ex 22:25; Lv 25:35–37; Dt 23:19–20). Deuteronomy 23:20 allowed an Israelite to charge interest to a foreigner.

18:9 For the righteous person in the OT, to **live** refers to life in all its fullness. A meaningful life is one that enjoys the fullness of relationship with God and thus includes communion with God (Pss 63:3; 73:27–28).

18:10–11 The phrase **sheds blood** occurs often in Ezekiel (16:38; 22:3,27; 23:45; 33:25). Its frequency indicates that human life was not valued among the Israelites at the time of the exile.

18:12 The **poor** and **needy** are often mentioned together in the OT (Dt 24:14; Jr 22:16; Pss 35:10; 37:14).

18:13 The expression **his death will be his own fault** indicated that the one who performed a justified capital punishment (i.e., the executioner) was free of any guilt. The blame lay with the offender.

18:14–17 This is the case of a son who learns wisdom from his father's bad example.

18:22–23 There is no reason for a person to live under condemnation for past sins if he is truly repentant and has experienced the new birth (Rm 8:1–17).

18:24 On turning from **righteousness** to acting **unjustly**, see Heb 2:3 and 2Pt 2:20–22. These verses contain warnings against those who knowingly and willfully turn from God. Those who are right with God will persevere to the end (Mt 10:22; 22:13; Mk 4:1–20).

18:25–29 The people charge that God does not measure his actions but acts arbitrarily. God's response is that they are the ones who do not measure their actions.

18:30 Every person will face a final judgment in which obedience to God's commands will be fairly and justly evaluated.

is the declaration of the Lord GOD. "Repent and turn from all your rebellious acts, so they will not become a sinful stumbling block to you. ³¹ Throw off all the transgressions you have committed, and get yourselves a new heart and a new spirit. Why should you die, house of Israel? ³² For I take no pleasure in anyone's death." This is the declaration of the Lord GOD. "So repent and live!

A Lament for Israel's Princes

19 "As for you, take up a lament for the princes of Israel, ² and say:

What was your mother? A lioness!
She lay down among the lions;
she reared her cubs
   among the young lions.
³ She brought up one of her cubs,
and he became a young lion.
After he learned to tear prey,
he devoured people.
⁴ When the nations heard about him,
he was caught in their pit.
Then they led him away with hooks
to the land of Egypt.

⁵ When she saw that she waited in vain,
that her hope was lost,
she took another of her cubs
and made him a young lion.
⁶ He prowled among the lions,
and he became a young lion.
After he learned to tear prey,
he devoured people.
⁷ He devastated their strongholds^A
and destroyed their cities.
The land and everything in it shuddered
at the sound of his roaring.
⁸ Then the nations from
   the surrounding provinces

set out against him.
They spread their net over him;
he was caught in their pit.
⁹ They put a wooden yoke on him^B
   with hooks
and led him away to the king of Babylon.
They brought him into the fortresses
so his roar could no longer be heard
on the mountains of Israel.

¹⁰ Your mother was like a vine
   in your vineyard,^C
planted by the water;
it was fruitful and full of branches
because of abundant water.
¹¹ It had strong branches, fit for
   the scepters of rulers;
its height towered among the clouds.^D
So it was conspicuous for its height
as well as its many branches.
¹² But it was uprooted in fury,
thrown to the ground,
and the east wind dried up its fruit.
Its strong branches were torn off
   and dried up;
fire consumed them.
¹³ Now it is planted in the wilderness,
in a dry and thirsty land.
¹⁴ Fire has gone out from its main branch^E
and has devoured its fruit,
so that it no longer has a strong branch,
a scepter for ruling.

This is a lament and should be used as a lament."

Israel's Rebellion

20 In the seventh year, in the fifth month, on the tenth day of the month, some of Israel's elders came to inquire of the LORD, and they sat down in front of me. ² Then the word

^A**19:7** Tg, Aq; MT reads *knew their widows*   ^B**19:9** Or *put him in a cage*   ^C**19:10** Some Hb mss; other Hb mss read *blood*
^D**19:11** Or *thick foliage*   ^E**19:14** Lit *from the branch of its parts*

18:31 What had been promised earlier in the book (11:19) is viewed now as attainable but not inevitable. Later in the book of Ezekiel (36:26–27) the people of Israel are promised **a new heart and a new spirit.** In this verse the people are commanded to obtain these new qualities.
19:1 Sad songs of the type found in chap. 19 are known in Hebrew by the name *qinah,* which means "funeral dirge" or "funerary **lament**." They have a unique meter, and their content is similar to modern eulogies (2Sm 1:19–27). The switch of subjects from Ezk 18 seems to indicate that the emphasis on individual responsibility also applies to the monarchy of Judah.
19:2 The **mother** in this allegory is the nation of Israel, who had produced the kings of the nation.
19:3 Genesis 49:9 seems to be the background for Judah, the royal line, being compared to a **lion.** In the Balaam oracles, the nation itself is compared to a lion (Nm 23:24; 24:9). The first cub-king represents

Jehoahaz, son of Josiah. He was crowned by the people after Josiah's death but was almost immediately deposed by Pharaoh Neco. He was then taken to Egypt in fetters after reigning only three months (2Kg 23:30–34).
19:5–9 This **lion** displayed greater power than the first by tearing down strongholds and devastating towns. The nations trapped him also, leading him with hooks to the land of Babylon. This second lion appears to refer to Jehoiachin. After a reign of only three months and ten days (2Ch 36:9), Jehoiachin was imprisoned in Babylon for thirty-seven years until the Babylonian king Evil-merodach released him.
19:10–11 Ezekiel used the vine metaphor in 15:1–8 and 17:5–10 with reference to the decline and fall of Judah (Is 24:7; Jr 2:21; 6:9). Just this imagery of the **vine** typifies the nation of Israel as a whole (Pss 80:8–16; Is 5:1–7; 27:2–6).
19:12 The **east wind** represents Nebuchadnezzar of Babylon and his army. The image refers to the capture and death of King Zedekiah and the destruction of Jerusalem in the siege of 586 BC.

19:13 Zedekiah was captured in the desert (**wilderness**) near Jericho, blinded, bound in chains, and taken to Babylon (2Kg 25; Jr 52).
19:14 The Davidic dynasty and the Israelite monarchy appear to come to a sudden end in Zedekiah. **Fire** is alternatively a symbol for annihilation or ongoing punishment (Gn 19:24; Is 66:24; Jr 50:32; Am 1:4,7,10,12,14; 2:2,5; 7:4; Mt 25:41; Rv 20:14). The **scepter** will be temporarily removed from Judah as a punishment for sins. In the person of Christ, however, God's promise that the scepter will not depart from the line of Judah (Gn 49:10) will be ultimately fulfilled.
20:1 As in 8:1 and 14:1, a delegation of **elders** came to Ezekiel's home seeking an oracle from the Lord. It had been almost eleven months since the vision of the abominations of the temple in 8:1. The date indicated is 591 BC.
20:2–3 God refused to respond to their questions. Rather, he had his own message for them.

of the LORD came to me: ³ "Son of man, speak with the elders of Israel and tell them, 'This is what the Lord GOD says: Are you coming to inquire of me? As I live, I will not let you inquire of me. This is the declaration of the Lord GOD.'

⁴ "Will you pass judgment against them, will you pass judgment, son of man? Explain the detestable practices of their ancestors to them. ⁵ Say to them, 'This is what the Lord GOD says: On the day I chose Israel, I swore an oath[A] to the descendants of Jacob's house and made myself known to them in the land of Egypt. I swore to them, saying, "I am the LORD your God." ⁶ On that day I swore[B] to them that I would bring them out of the land of Egypt into a land I had searched out for them, a land flowing with milk and honey, the most beautiful of all lands. ⁷ I also said to them, "Throw away, each of you, the abhorrent things that you prize,[C] and do not defile yourselves with the idols of Egypt. I am the LORD your God."

⁸ "But they rebelled against me and were unwilling to listen to me. None of them threw away the abhorrent things that they prized,[D] and they did not abandon the idols of Egypt. So I considered pouring out my wrath on them, exhausting my anger against them within the land of Egypt. ⁹ But I acted for the sake of my name, so that it would not be profaned in the eyes of the nations they were living among, in whose sight I had made myself known to Israel by bringing them out of Egypt.

¹⁰ "So I brought them out of the land of Egypt and led them into the wilderness. ¹¹ Then I gave them my statutes and explained my ordinances to them — the person who does them will live by them. ¹² I also gave them my Sabbaths to serve as a sign between me and them, so that they would know that I am the LORD who consecrates them.

¹³ "But the house of Israel rebelled against me in the wilderness. They did not follow my statutes and they rejected my ordinances — the person who does them will live by them. They also completely profaned my Sabbaths. So I considered pouring out my wrath on them in the wilderness to put an end to them. ¹⁴ But I acted for the sake of my name, so that it would not be profaned in the eyes of the nations in whose sight I had brought them out. ¹⁵ However, I swore to them in the wilderness that I would not bring them into the land I had given them — the most beautiful of all lands, flowing with milk and honey — ¹⁶ because they rejected my ordinances, profaned my Sabbaths, and did not follow my statutes. For their hearts went after their idols. ¹⁷ Yet I spared them from destruction and did not bring them to an end in the wilderness.

¹⁸ "Then I said to their children in the wilderness, "Don't follow the statutes of your fathers, defile yourselves with their idols, or keep their ordinances. ¹⁹ I am the LORD your God. Follow my statutes, keep my ordinances, and practice them. ²⁰ Keep my Sabbaths holy, and they will be a sign between me and you, so you may know that I am the LORD your God."

²¹ "But the children rebelled against me. They did not follow my statutes or carefully keep my ordinances — the person who does them will live by them. They also profaned my Sabbaths. So I considered pouring out my wrath on them and exhausting my anger against them in the wilderness. ²² But I withheld my hand and acted for the sake of my name, so that it would not be profaned in the eyes of the nations in whose sight I brought them out. ²³ However, I swore to them in the wilderness that I would disperse them among the nations and scatter them among the countries. ²⁴ For they did not practice my ordinances but rejected my statutes and profaned my Sabbaths, and their eyes were fixed on their

---

[A]20:5 Lit *I lifted my hand*   [B]20:6 Lit *lifted my hand*, also in vv. 15,23,28,42   [C]20:7 Lit *things of your eyes*   [D]20:8 Lit *things of their eyes*

20:4 Like chaps. 16 and 23, chap. 20 presents a negative view of Israel's history; unlike them, it does not use allegory.
20:5 The phrase **I swore an oath** is literally "I raise my hand in oath." The uplifted hand (vv. 5,15,23,42) was apparently a gesture used when a person made an oath (36:7; 44:12; 47:14; Ex 6:8; Neh 9:15; Ps 106:26). The phrase **descendants of Jacob's house** is a reference to all Israel (i.e., Israel and Judah; see 37:25). The statement **made myself known to them in the land of Egypt** recalls the Lord's encounter with Moses in Ex 6:2–8, where Yahweh swore by oath and revealed his name.
20:7 Joshua 24:14 also mentions that the Israelites had worshiped foreign gods. On Israel's idolatry in Egypt, see Lv 17:7; 18:3; Ps 106:7; Ezk 23:3; Am 5:25–27.
20:9 Moses used this argument effectively in his intercession for Israel after the golden calf incident and in the wilderness (Ex 32:12; Nm 14:16).

20:11 The phrase **the person who does them will live by them** appears to come from Lv 18:5. Deuteronomy 30:15–19 states forcefully that to follow the commandments is to choose life and blessing; not to follow them is to choose death and cursing.
20:12 The Sabbath was a visible manifestation of the Mosaic covenant (Is 56:1–8). The Sabbath was a perpetual reminder of the Lord's covenant with his people.
20:13–14 The Sabbath was **profaned** if it was not observed (Jr 17:21–23) or was improperly observed (Am 8:5).
20:15 The phrase **I swore to them** is literally "I lifted up my hand." The upraised hand was used earlier in reference to God's oath to bring the chosen people into the promised land (v. 5). Now the expression is used to refer to the solemn oath that this generation would never enter that land (v. 15). Later, Ezekiel used the formula to describe God's

announcement that the people would go into exile (v. 23).
20:16–17 Israel failed to enter the land of Canaan because of unbelief (Nm 14) expressed in four specific violations: they **rejected my ordinances, profaned my Sabbaths . . . did not follow my statutes . . . went after their idols**.
20:18–20 The **statutes** and **ordinances** of their **fathers** were not literal but referred to their practices.
20:21 This refers to acts of apostasy following the incident of the spies during the wilderness wanderings—in particular, the events at Meribah (Nm 20) and Baal Peor (Nm 25).
20:22 See vv. 9,14.
20:23–24 This oath that God **swore** could refer to the Lord's words through Moses in Lv 26:14–46 and Dt 28; 32. It is also alluded to in Ps 106:27. God made this oath before his people had even entered the land.

fathers' idols. ²⁵ I also gave them statutes that were not good and ordinances they could not live by. ²⁶ When they sacrificed every firstborn in the fire,ᴬ I defiled them through their gifts in order to devastate them so they would know that I am the Lᴏʀᴅ.'

²⁷ "Therefore, son of man, speak to the house of Israel, and tell them, 'This is what the Lord Gᴏᴅ says: In this way also your ancestors blasphemed me by committing treachery against me: ²⁸ When I brought them into the land that I swore to give them and they saw any high hill or leafy tree, they offered their sacrifices and presented their offensive offerings there. They also sent up their pleasing aromas and poured out their drink offerings there. ²⁹ So I asked them, "What is this high place you are going to?" And it is still called Bamahᴮ today.'

³⁰ "Therefore say to the house of Israel, 'This is what the Lord Gᴏᴅ says: Are you defiling yourselves the way your ancestors did, and prostituting yourselves with their abhorrent things? ³¹ When you offer your gifts, sacrificing your children in the fire,ᶜ you still continue to defile yourselves with all your idols today. So should I let you inquire of me, house of Israel? As I live — this is the declaration of the Lord Gᴏᴅ — I will not let you inquire of me!

Israel's Restoration

³² " 'When you say, "Let's be like the nations, like the clans of other countries, serving wood and stone," what you have in mind will never happen. ³³ As I live — the declaration of the Lord Gᴏᴅ — I will reign over you with a strong hand, an outstretched arm, and outpoured wrath. ³⁴ I will bring you from the peoples and gather you from the countries where you were scattered, with a strong hand, an

outstretched arm, and outpoured wrath. ³⁵ I will lead you into the wilderness of the peoples and enter into judgment with you there face to face. ³⁶ Just as I entered into judgment with your ancestors in the wilderness of the land of Egypt, so I will enter into judgment with you. This is the declaration of the Lord Gᴏᴅ. ³⁷ I will make you pass under the rod and will bring you into the bond of the covenant. ³⁸ I will purge you of those who rebel and transgress against me. I will bring them out of the land where they live as foreign residents, but they will not enter the land of Israel. Then you will know that I am the Lᴏʀᴅ.

³⁹ " 'As for you, house of Israel, this is what the Lord Gᴏᴅ says: Go and serve your idols, each of you. But afterward you will surely listen to me, and you will no longer defile my holy name with your gifts and idols. ⁴⁰ For on my holy mountain, Israel's high mountain — the declaration of the Lord Gᴏᴅ — there the entire house of Israel, all of them, will serve me in the land. There I will accept them and will require your contributions and choicest gifts, all your holy offerings. ⁴¹ When I bring you from the peoples and gather you from the countries where you have been scattered, I will accept you as a pleasing aroma. And I will demonstrate my holiness through you in the sight of the nations. ⁴² When I lead you into the land of Israel, the land I swore to give your ancestors, you will know that I am the Lᴏʀᴅ. ⁴³ There you will remember your ways and all your deeds by which you have defiled yourself, and you will loathe yourselves for all the evil things you have done. ⁴⁴ You will know that I am the Lᴏʀᴅ, house of Israel, when I have dealt with you for the sake of my name rather than according to your evil ways and corrupt acts. This is the declaration of the Lord Gᴏᴅ.' "

ᴬ20:26 Lit *they made every firstborn pass through the fire*   ᴮ20:29 = High Place   ᶜ20:31 Lit *gifts, making your children pass through the fire*

20:25–27 One of the ways that God punishes sin is to abandon people to it so that they suffer its consequences. Thus the **statutes** and **ordinances** in this verse refer to the futile and blameworthy commandments of the pagan religions to which Israel had turned. These laws "required" the Israelites to sacrifice every firstborn (v. 26), a practice condemned by God (Lv 20:1–5). These statutes and ordinances devastated rather than blessed the people who obeyed them. The phrase **they sacrificed every firstborn in the fire** refers to the child sacrifices made by followers of the god Molech. According to pagan perception, sacrifices made to a god put that god in your debt, such that the god was bound to act favorably toward you. **20:32** The designation of the heathen gods as **wood and stone** should have been enough to signal that these heathen gods were mere fictions. The same expression occurs in Dt 4:28; 28:36. **20:33** A **strong hand** and **outstretched arm** call to mind God's strength in delivering

his people from Egypt (Dt 4:34; 5:15; 7:19; 11:2; 26:8; Ps 136:12). Ironically, now his hand and arm will bring wrath rather than deliverance for his people. **20:35–36** Israel's exile among the nations is compared to the **wilderness** tradition recorded in the book of Numbers. **20:37–38** The phrase **pass under the rod** appears to be an allusion to the Levitical law of counting animals for the tithe (Lv 27:32–33). While the selection in Leviticus was for dedication, here it is for destruction. God uses this metaphor to portray the purge of Israel that will take place when the temple is destroyed. **20:39** Desecrations of the **holy name** are recorded in Lv 18:21; 20:3; 21:6; 22:32. **20:40** The phrase **on my holy mountain** occurs only here in the book of Ezekiel. It refers to Jerusalem or Zion (Pss 2:6; 3:4; 15:1; Is 11:9; 56:7; 57:13; 65:11; Ob 16; Zph 3:11). The term "serve" is a technical word for priestly ministry; thus, this expression (**serve me in the land**) is in harmony with the goal established

at Mount Sinai—that the created nation would be a kingdom of priests (Ex 19:6). **20:41–42** The Lord will accept the people as a soothing or **pleasing aroma**, an expression used of God's response to an animal sacrifice. Only here in the OT is the expression used in reference to people as a soothing aroma. This paves the way for Paul's application of the expression to the church in 2Co 2:14–16. In Eph 5:2 the term refers to Christ. **20:43** Ezekiel's expression **you will loathe yourselves for all the evil things you have done** describes a thorough repentance (6:9; 16:63; 36:31; Lk 15:17–19). Perceiving God in his holiness and majesty causes one to abhor one's sinful ways (Jb 42:5–6; Is 6:5). **20:44** The first fulfillment of this promise (**when I have dealt with you for the sake of my name**) took place immediately after the exile. It also awaits a future fulfillment, according to Paul in Rm 11:25. When used in application to morality, the term **corrupt acts** occurs elsewhere only in Gn 6:11–12,

Fire in the South

45 The word of the LORD came to me: **46** "Son of man, face the south and preach against it. Prophesy against the forest land in the Negev, **47** and say to the forest there, 'Hear the word of the LORD! This is what the Lord GOD says: I am about to ignite a fire in you, and it will devour every green tree and every dry tree in you. The blazing flame will not be extinguished, and every face from the south to the north will be scorched by it. **48** Then all humanity will see that I, the LORD, have kindled it. It will not be extinguished.'"

49 Then I said, "Oh, Lord GOD, they are saying of me, 'Isn't he just composing parables?'"

God's Sword of Judgment

21 The word of the LORD came to me again: **2** "Son of man, face Jerusalem and preach against the sanctuaries. Prophesy against the land of Israel, **3** and say to it, 'This is what the LORD says: I am against you. I will draw my sword from its sheath and cut off from you both the righteous and the wicked. **4** Since I will cut off^A both the righteous and the wicked, my sword will therefore come out of its sheath against all humanity from the south to the north. **5** So all humanity will know that I, the LORD, have taken my sword from its sheath — it will not be sheathed again.'

6 "But you, son of man, groan! Groan bitterly with a broken heart^B right before their eyes. **7** And when they ask you, 'Why are you groaning?' then say, 'Because of the news that is coming. Every heart will melt, and every hand will become weak. Every spirit will be discouraged, and all knees will run with urine.^C Yes, it is coming and it will happen. This is the declaration of the Lord GOD.'"

8 The word of the LORD came to me: **9** "Son of man, prophesy, 'This is what the Lord says!' You are to proclaim,

'A sword! A sword is sharpened
and also polished.
10 It is sharpened for slaughter,
polished to flash like lightning!
Should we rejoice?
The scepter of my son,
the sword despises every tree.^D
11 The sword is given to be polished,
to be grasped in the hand.
It is sharpened, and it is polished,
to be put in the hand of the slayer.'

12 "Cry out and wail, son of man, for it is against my people. It is against all the princes of Israel! They are given over to the sword with my people. Therefore strike your thigh in grief. **13** Surely it will be a trial! And what if the sword despises even the scepter? The scepter will not continue."^D This is the declaration of the Lord GOD.

14 "So you, son of man, prophesy and clap your hands together:

Let the sword strike two times,
even three.
It is a sword for massacre,
a sword for great massacre —
it surrounds^E them!
15 I have appointed a sword for slaughter^D
at all their gates,
so that their hearts may melt
and many may stumble.
Yes! It is ready to flash like lightning;
it is drawn^D for slaughter.
16 Slash to the right;
turn to the left —
wherever your blade is directed.

17 I also will clap my hands together, and I will satisfy my wrath. I, the LORD, have spoken."

18 The word of the LORD came to me: **19** "Now you, son of man, mark out two roads that the sword of Babylon's king can take. Both of them should originate from the same land. And make a signpost at the fork in the road

---

^A**21:4** Lit *off from you*   ^B**21:6** Lit *insides*, or *waist*   ^C**21:7** Lit *knees will go water*   ^D**21:10,13,15** Hb obscure   ^E**21:14** Or *penetrates*

---

where it describes the corruption of the human race before the flood.
20:45–46 The orientation in the phrase **face the south and preach against it** would be from the north, the direction of a Babylonian invasion.
20:47–49 Fire is routinely a means of divine punishment in the Bible (Gn 19:23–28; Dt 28:24; 32:22; Rv 20:15). Ezekiel complained that he was not being taken seriously because he was speaking in **parables**, so in chap. 21 God will clearly interpret any previous symbolic language.
21:1–2 Every time God tells Ezekiel to **face** a city or a direction, it is in a judgment context.
21:3 God's opposition to his people is expressed by the image of the drawn **sword**, the common way of referring to warfare in the OT. History would prove that God's drawn sword was King Nebuchadnezzar of Babylon and his armies.

21:4 No one will survive the coming invasion, not even the **righteous**. The Bible advocates corporate responsibility. For Judah as a nation, it was too late to repent; destruction was decreed. Individuals could repent and have assurance of eternal life, but many righteous people were going to be swept up in the coming destruction.
21:5 God will not bring upon his people a partial defeat and exile this time, as was the case in 598 BC when Ezekiel was exiled. This time, God will finish the job through his agent, the Babylonians.
21:6–9 The coming **sword** is the reason for groaning.
21:10 The **scepter** symbolized the Lord's covenant promise to David that his house would have the eternal title to the throne of Jerusalem (2Sm 7). This promise was rooted in the blessing spoken by Jacob, which said that the scepter would never pass from Judah (Gn 49:10). This

interpretation is reinforced by the Hebrew expression *beni* (**my son**), an echo of Gn 49:9 and 2Sm 7:14. Judah's hope in the midst of judgment was that the ultimate "scepter of Judah," the Messiah, would never be extinguished.
21:11–13 The practice of striking one's thigh in grief is also found in Jr 31:19 and may have its origin in Gn 32:32.
21:14 In v. 17 the act of clapping the **hands together** is associated with God's wrath. It should also be viewed here as an expression of anger (6:11). The mention of **three** strikes of the **sword** may refer to the three attacks and deportations that the Babylonians launched against Jerusalem in 605, 597, and 588–586 BC.
21:18–20 Rabbah was the capital of Ammon (Jr 49:2). It is the location of modern Amman, the capital of Jordan. The combined conspiracy of Judah and Ammon against Babylonia in 589 BC undoubtedly precipitated this coming of the Babylonian army (Jr 27:3).

to each city. ²⁰ Mark out a road that the sword can take to Rabbah of the Ammonites and to Judah into fortified Jerusalem. ²¹ For the king of Babylon stands at the split in the road, at the fork of the two roads, to practice divination: he shakes the arrows, consults the idols, and observes the liver. ²² The answer marked^A Jerusalem appears in his right hand, indicating that he should set up battering rams, give the order to^B slaughter, raise a battle cry, set battering rams against the gates, build a ramp, and construct a siege wall. ²³ It will seem like false divination to those who have sworn an oath to the Babylonians,^C but it will draw attention to their guilt so that they will be captured.

²⁴ "Therefore, this is what the Lord God says: Because you have drawn attention to your guilt, exposing your transgressions, so that your sins are revealed in all your actions — since you have done this, you will be captured by them. ²⁵ And you, profane and wicked prince of Israel,^D the day has come for your punishment.^E

²⁶ "This is what the Lord God says:
Remove the turban, and take off
    the crown.
Things will not remain as they are;^F
exalt the lowly and bring down
    the exalted.
²⁷ A ruin, a ruin,
I will make it a ruin!
Yet this will not happen
until he comes;
I have given the judgment to him.^G

²⁸ "Now you, son of man, prophesy, and say, 'This is what the Lord God says concerning the Ammonites and their contempt.' You are to proclaim,

'A sword! A sword
is drawn for slaughter,
polished to consume, to flash
    like lightning.

²⁹ While they offer false visions
and lying divinations about you,
the time has come to put you
to the necks of the profane wicked ones;
the day has come
for final punishment.

³⁰ "'Return it to its sheath!

"'I will judge you^H
in the place where you were created,
in the land of your origin.
³¹ I will pour out my indignation on you;
I will blow the fire of my fury on you.
I will hand you over to brutal men,
skilled at destruction.
³² You will be fuel for the fire.
Your blood will be spilled
    within the land.
You will not be remembered,
for I, the Lord, have spoken.'"

Indictment of Sinful Jerusalem

22 The word of the Lord came to me: ² "As for you, son of man, will you pass judgment? Will you pass judgment against the city of blood? Then explain all her detestable practices to her. ³ You are to say, 'This is what the Lord God says: A city that sheds blood within her walls so that her time of judgment has come and who makes idols for herself so that she is defiled! ⁴ You are guilty of the blood you have shed, and you are defiled from the idols you have made. You have brought your judgment^I days near and have come to your years of punishment.^J Therefore, I have made you a disgrace to the nations and a mockery to all the lands. ⁵ Those who are near and those far away from you will mock you, you infamous one full of turmoil.

⁶ "'Look, every prince of Israel within you has used his strength to shed blood. ⁷ Father and mother are treated with contempt, and the

---

^A 21:22 Lit The divination for   ^B 21:22 Lit rams, open the mouth in   ^C 21:23 Lit them   ^D 21:25 = King Zedekiah   ^E 21:25 Lit come in the time of the punishment of the end, also in v. 29   ^F 21:26 Lit This not this   ^G 21:27 Or comes to whom it rightfully belongs, and I will give it to him   ^H 21:30 = the Ammonites   ^I 22:4 judgment supplied for clarity   ^J 22:4 punishment supplied for clarity

---

21:21–23 The practice of shaking marked **arrows** in a quiver, letting them fall to the ground or shooting them into the distance and then interpreting the pattern, was known as belomancy (2Kg 13:15–19). It was a form of casting lots. The **idols** (Hb teraphim) appear to have been miniature household gods that were consulted even by Israelites (Gn 31:30; Hs 3:4; Zch 10:2). The examination of the **liver** of a sacrificial animal—called hepatoscopy—is mentioned only here in the OT. Though God did not condone **divination** in any form (Dt 18:10; 2Kg 17:17), as sovereign over the earth he controls all things; thus, in some sense even pagan practices could, by God's choice, reveal his will (Jnh 1:7).
21:23 The phrase **sworn an oath to the Babylonians** probably refers to the treaty oaths made by Babylonia and Judah.

21:24–25 Wicked prince of Israel refers to King Zedekiah.
21:26 The removal of the priesthood and the kingship from Judah is symbolized by the removal of the high priest's **turban** (Ex 28:4,37,39; 29:6) and the king's **crown**.
21:27 The turban and the crown would not be worn again **until he comes**—a clear reference to Gn 49:10 and the king-priest Messiah (cp. Heb 5–7).
21:28–30 The **Ammonites**, who participated in the judgment of Jerusalem, would themselves be objects of wrath.
21:31–32 The **fire** of the Lord's **fury** reflects the covenant curses. Fire was a symbol of divine judgment (Dt 28:24; 32:22).
22:1–2 Seven times in this prophecy (vv. 1–16) the words **blood** or "bloodshed" occur, suggesting that the crimes against

God's covenant were routine as well as thoroughgoing in Jerusalem. Rabbinic tradition relates this oracle to Manasseh's shedding of innocent blood in Jerusalem (2Kg 21:6). As in Ezk 18, the catalog of crimes listed here derives especially from the Holiness Code in Lv 17–26. The **city** is personified as a person violating the Mosaic law.
22:3–4 These two sins (**sheds blood ... makes idols**) summarize the violation of the Ten Commandments, which legislated stipulations about a person's relationship to God as well as to his fellow man.
22:6 The indictment of vv. 6–12 contains a catalog of sins based on the regulations in Lv 18–20. The kings are specifically indicted because it was their responsibility to make sure justice was administered in the community,

resident alien is exploited within you. The fatherless and widow are oppressed in you. **8** You despise my holy things and profane my Sabbaths. **9** There are men within you who slander in order to shed blood. People who live in you eat at the mountain shrines;^A they commit depraved acts within you. **10** Men within you have sexual intercourse with their father's wife and violate women during their menstrual impurity. **11** One man within you commits a detestable act with his neighbor's wife; another defiles his daughter-in-law with depravity; and yet another violates his sister, his father's daughter. **12** People who live in you accept bribes in order to shed blood. You take interest and profit on a loan and brutally extort your neighbors. You have forgotten me. This is the declaration of the Lord GOD.

13 " 'Now look, I clap my hands together against the dishonest profit you have made and against the blood shed among you. **14** Will your courage endure or your hands be strong in the days when I deal with you? I, the LORD, have spoken, and I will act. **15** I will disperse you among the nations and scatter you among the countries; I will purge your uncleanness. **16** You^B will be profaned in the sight of the nations. Then you will know that I am the LORD.' "

Jerusalem as God's Furnace

17 The word of the LORD came to me: **18** "Son of man, the house of Israel has become merely dross to me. All of them are copper, tin, iron, and lead inside the furnace; they are just dross from silver. **19** Therefore, this is what the Lord GOD says: Because all of you have become dross, I am about to gather you into Jerusalem. **20** Just as one gathers silver, copper, iron, lead, and tin into the furnace to blow fire on them and melt them, so I will gather you in my anger and wrath, put you inside, and melt you. **21** Yes, I will gather you together and blow on you with the fire of my fury, and you will be melted within the city. **22** As silver is melted inside a furnace, so you will be melted inside the city. Then you will know that I, the LORD, have poured out my wrath on you."

Indictment of a Sinful Land

23 The word of the LORD came to me: **24** "Son of man, say to her, 'You are a land that has not been cleansed, that has not received rain in the day of indignation.' **25** The conspiracy of her prophets within her is^C like a roaring lion tearing its prey: they devour people, seize wealth and valuables, and multiply the widows within her. **26** Her priests do violence to my instruction and profane my holy things. They make no distinction between the holy and the common, and they do not explain the difference between the clean and the unclean. They close their eyes to my Sabbaths, and I am profaned among them. **27** "Her officials within her are like wolves tearing their prey, shedding blood, and destroying lives in order to make profit dishonestly. **28** Her prophets plaster for them with whitewash by seeing false visions and lying divinations, saying, 'This is what the Lord GOD says,' when the LORD has not spoken. **29** The people of the land have practiced extortion and committed robbery. They have oppressed the poor and needy and unlawfully exploited the resident alien. **30** I searched for a man among them who would repair the wall and stand in the gap before me on behalf of the land so that I might not destroy it, but I found no one. **31** So I have poured out my indignation on them and consumed them with the fire of my fury. I have brought their conduct down on their own heads." This is the declaration of the Lord GOD.

---

^A 22:9 Lit the mountains ^B 22:16 One Hb ms, LXX, Syr, Vg read I ^C 22:24–25 LXX reads indignation, ^25 whose princes within her are

---

especially by protecting the poor and weak (Ps 72:1–4).
22:7 The lack of concern for those in need (**fatherless and widow**) was a clear violation of the Mosaic covenant (Ex 22:21; 23:9,12; Dt 14:29; 16:11,14; 24:19–21; 26:12–19).
22:8 On profaning the Sabbath, see 20:12–13.
22:9 Leviticus 19:16 contains the only other occurrence of the legal word **slander** in the Bible. There it is also associated with bloodshed. Ezekiel's use of the Hebrew word for **depraved acts** to denote unchastity (vv. 9,11; 16:27,58; 23:21,27,35,44,48) followed the tradition in the Mosaic law (Lv 18:17–18; 19:29; 20:14).
22:10 The reference to **their father's wife** means stepmother rather than birth mother. Lewdness with one's stepmother is a violation of the law in Lv 20:11 (cp. 1Co 5:1; see Dt 22:30; Am 2:7).
22:11 All the sins mentioned in this verse were specifically forbidden in the law (Lv 18:7–20; 20:10–21; Dt 22:22–23,30; 27:22).
22:12 You have forgotten me is the explanation for all the listed violations. Forgetting

God is another way of saying that they have rejected his covenant (Dt 4:23; 8:19).
22:13–14 On hand clapping, see 21:15–17.
22:15–16 The residents of Jerusalem will be scattered all over the world (**among the countries**) if they continue to pursue disobedience. Moses had warned Israel that continual national disobedience would lead to dispersion (Lv 26:27–39; Dt 28:64–68).
22:17–20 Just as precious metals are melted to remove **dross**, Israel will be purified by **fire** to remove sins and impurities. The Babylonians would execute this fire of God's **wrath** when they burned and sacked Jerusalem.
22:21–22 The phrase **will be melted within the city** may refer to the misery of being besieged by foreign enemies, which in itself was a divine punishment (Dt 28:52–57).
22:23–24 Ezekiel's combination of **rain** and judgment goes back to the account of the biblical flood in Genesis (Gn 6–8). The withholding of rain was a covenant curse (Lv 26:19).

22:25 The Hebrew has **her prophets** (ne-vi'eyha) whereas the LXX has "her princes" (nesiy'eyha), read by NIV, NLT, NRSV.
22:26–27 Government **officials** were supposed to protect people. The denunciation of the leadership in Ezk 22:25–28 has close affinities to the denunciation of leaders in Zph 3:1–4. For instance, each passage contains a nearly identical list of leaders. Even more striking is the fact that both passages describe the officials as **wolves** (Zph 3:3) and the priests as those who **do violence to my instruction** (Zph 3:4). It is possible that Ezekiel knew this oracle from the prophet Zephaniah.
22:30–31 This proposal (**I searched for a man among them who would repair the wall**) is reminiscent of Gn 18:22–33, where God promised to spare Sodom and Gomorrah if only ten righteous persons were found there. Intercession (**stand in the gap**) is part of a prophet's task (1Sm 12:23; Jr 37:3; 42:2).

The Two Immoral Sisters

23 The word of the Lord came to me again: ² "Son of man, there were two women, daughters of the same mother, ³ who acted like prostitutes in Egypt, behaving promiscuously in their youth. Their breasts were fondled there, and their virgin nipples caressed. ⁴ The older one was named Oholah,^ and her sister was Oholibah.^ They became mine and gave birth to sons and daughters. As for their names, Oholah represents Samaria and Oholibah represents Jerusalem.

⁵ "Oholah acted like a prostitute even though she was mine. She lusted after her lovers, the Assyrians: warriors ⁶ dressed in blue, governors and prefects, all of them desirable young men, horsemen riding on steeds. ⁷ She offered her sexual favors to them; all of them were the elite of Assyria. She defiled herself with all those she lusted after and with all their idols. ⁸ She didn't give up her promiscuity that began in Egypt, when men slept with her in her youth, caressed her virgin nipples, and poured out their lust on her. ⁹ Therefore, I handed her over to her lovers, the Assyrians she lusted for. ¹⁰ They exposed her nakedness, seized her sons and daughters, and killed her with the sword. Since they executed judgment against her, she became notorious among women.

¹¹ "Now her sister Oholibah saw this, but she was even more depraved in her lust than Oholah, and made her promiscuous acts worse than those of her sister. ¹² She lusted after the Assyrians: governors and prefects, warriors splendidly dressed, horsemen riding on steeds, all of them desirable young men. ¹³ And I saw that she had defiled herself; both of them had taken the same path. ¹⁴ But she increased her promiscuity when she saw male figures carved on the wall, images of the Chaldeans, engraved in bright red, ¹⁵ wearing belts on their waists and flowing turbans on their heads; all of them looked like officers, a depiction of the Babylonians in Chaldea, their native land. ¹⁶ At the sight of them^c she lusted after them and sent messengers to them in Chaldea. ¹⁷ Then the Babylonians came to her, to the bed of love, and defiled her with their lust. But after she was defiled by them, she turned away from them in disgust. ¹⁸ When she flaunted her promiscuity and exposed her nakedness, I turned away from her in disgust just as I turned away from her sister. ¹⁹ Yet she multiplied her acts of promiscuity, remembering the days of her youth when she acted like a prostitute in the land of Egypt ²⁰ and lusted after their lovers, whose sexual members^D were like those of donkeys and whose emission was like that of stallions. ²¹ So you revisited the depravity of your youth, when the Egyptians caressed your nipples to enjoy your youthful breasts.

²² "Therefore, Oholibah, this is what the Lord God says: I am going to incite your lovers against you, those you turned away from in disgust. I will bring them against you from every side: ²³ the Babylonians and all the Chaldeans; Pekod, Shoa, and Koa; and all the Assyrians with them — desirable young men, all of them governors and prefects, officers and administrators, all of them riding on steeds. ²⁴ They will come against you with an assembly of peoples and with weapons, chariots, and^E wagons. They will set themselves against you on every side with large and small shields and helmets. I will delegate judgment to them, and they will judge you by their own standards. ²⁵ When I vent my jealous fury on you, they will deal with you in wrath. They will cut off your nose and ears, and

---

^23:4 = Her Tent   ^B23:4 = My Tent Is in Her   ^C23:16 Lit of her eyes   ^D23:20 Lit whose flesh   ^E23:24 LXX reads peoples, from the north, chariots and; Hb obscure

---

23:1–2 Since Israel was often portrayed as the wife of God (Jr 2–3; Hs 1–3), Ezekiel used the metaphor of harlotry (**two women**) to describe Samaria and Jerusalem. While chap. 16 focuses on Judah's idolatry, chap. 23 emphasizes Judah's illicit foreign alliances in addition to her idolatry. In chap. 16 the issue is Israel's trust in other gods; here she trusts in other nations.

23:3 Adultery and prostitution were both odious to God and punishable by death, according to numerous legal passages in Leviticus (Lv 19:29; 20:10; 21:9) and Deuteronomy (Dt 23:17). The adulterous cities will be destroyed.

23:4 Samaria, **the older one**, embraced idolatry and international alliances much earlier than Jerusalem. She would also precede Jerusalem in captivity. The phrase **they became mine** recalls marriage rituals described in 16:8–13. The two names **Oholah** and **Oholibah** relate to the Hebrew noun 'ohel, "tent," corresponding to the cities they represent. The names recall the period when Israel lived in tents in the desert, reinforcing the notion of long-standing harlotry since that was a

time in which Israel suffered punishment for its idolatries. The mention of the mother of the sisters emphasizes their common origin from the united nation of Israel that existed for a time. The cities were the capital cities of the northern and southern kingdoms, respectively.

23:5–9 Prostitution here represents political alliances with pagan powers—not idolatry as in chap. 16 (v. 15). The graphic language underscores God's disgust with Israel for playing the game of international politics rather than relying on him for security and support. Samaria's (**Oholah**) relations with the officers of Assyria presupposes the earlier alliance under Jehu's descendants, Menahem (2Kg 15:17–22) and Hoshea (2Kg 17:1–6).

23:10 The expression **they exposed her nakedness** refers to the fall of Samaria in 722 BC.

23:11–13 Rather than embracing her God-given mission to bring the message of salvation to the nations (Gn 12:1–3), as a prostitute Jerusalem used the nations for her own advantage. Judah allied with Assyria (2Kg 16:7–9) and then Babylon (Ezk

17:13; 2Kg 24:1,17; cp. Is 39:1–8). Ezekiel may also have had in mind the disastrous political move of King Ahaz, who willingly made Judah Assyria's vassal. Rather than trusting God for deliverance (as Isaiah urged him to do), Ahaz enlisted Assyria's aid. With that act Judah became a vassal of Assyria for the next century (2Kg 16:5–9; Is 7).

23:14–19 Like the idols of the house of Israel in 8:10, these **male** images were **carved** on a **wall**. Visual art in Bible times was often painted on walls.

23:20–21 The reference to relations with Egypt (**lusted after their lovers**) may recall Solomon's early alliance with Egypt (1Kg 3:1) and Jehoiakim's support from Pharaoh Neco before he turned to Babylonia (2Kg 23:31–24:7).

23:22–23 The word **Chaldeans**, often interchanged with **Babylonians**, initially referred to the people living north of the Persian Gulf. **Pekod, Shoa, and Koa** were Aramean tribes east of the Tigris River that were allied with Babylonia.

23:24–30 God would **delegate judgment** to the Babylonians and Assyrians. Israel and the rest of you^ will fall by the sword. They will seize your sons and daughters, and the rest of you will be consumed by fire. ²⁶ They will strip off your clothes and take your beautiful jewelry. ²⁷ So I will put an end to your depravity and sexual immorality, which began in the land of Egypt, and you will not look longingly at them or remember Egypt anymore.

²⁸ "For this is what the Lord GOD says: I am going to hand you over to those you hate, to those you turned away from in disgust. ²⁹ They will treat you with hatred, take all you have worked for, and leave you stark naked, so that the shame of your debauchery will be exposed, both your depravity and promiscuity. ³⁰ These things will be done to you because you acted like a prostitute with the nations, defiling yourself with their idols. ³¹ You have followed the path of your sister, so I will put her cup in your hand."

³² This is what the Lord GOD says:

"You will drink your sister's cup,
which is deep and wide.
You will be an object of⁸ ridicule and scorn,
for it holds so much.
³³   You will be filled with drunkenness
and grief,
with a cup of devastation
and desolation,
the cup of your sister Samaria.
³⁴   You will drink it and drain it;
then you will gnaw its broken pieces,
and tear your breasts.
For I have spoken."

This is the declaration of the Lord GOD.

³⁵ Therefore, this is what the Lord GOD says: "Because you have forgotten me and cast me behind your back, you must bear the consequences of your indecency and promiscuity."

³⁶ Then the LORD said to me, "Son of man, will you pass judgment against Oholah and Oholibah? Then declare their detestable practices to them. ³⁷ For they have committed adultery, and blood is on their hands; they have committed adultery with their idols. And the children

they bore to me they have sacrificed in the fire^c as food for the idols. ³⁸ They also did this to me: they defiled my sanctuary on that same day and profaned my Sabbaths. ³⁹ On the same day they slaughtered their children for their idols, they entered my sanctuary to profane it. Yes, that is what they did inside my house.

⁴⁰ "In addition, they sent for men who came from far away when a messenger was dispatched to them. And look how they came! You bathed, painted your eyes, and adorned yourself with jewelry for them. ⁴¹ You sat on a luxurious couch with a table spread before it, on which you had set my incense and oil. ⁴² The sound of a carefree crowd was there. Drunkards^D from the desert were brought in, along with common men. They put bracelets on the women's hands and beautiful tiaras on their heads. ⁴³ Then I said concerning this woman worn out by adultery: Will they^E now have illicit sex with her, even her? ⁴⁴ Yet they had sex with her as one does with a prostitute. This is how they had sex with Oholah and Oholibah, those depraved women. ⁴⁵ But righteous men will judge them the way adulteresses and those who shed blood are judged, for they are adulteresses and blood is on their hands.

⁴⁶ "This is what the Lord GOD says: Summon^F an assembly against them and consign them to terror and plunder. ⁴⁷ The assembly will stone them and cut them down with their swords. They will kill their sons and daughters and burn their houses. ⁴⁸ So I will put an end to depravity in the land, and all the women will be admonished not to imitate your depraved behavior. ⁴⁹ They will punish you for your depravity, and you will bear the consequences for your sins of idolatry. Then you will know that I am the Lord GOD."

Parable of the Boiling Pot

24 The word of the LORD came to me in the ninth year, in the tenth month, on the tenth day of the month: ² "Son of man, write down today's date, this very day. The king of Babylon has laid siege to Jerusalem this very day. ³ Now speak a parable to the rebellious

---

^23:25 Or *and your descendants*   ⁸23:32 Or *It will bring*   ^c23:37 Lit *have made pass through the fire*   ^D23:42 Or *Sabeans*
^E23:43 Or *They will*   ^F23:46 Or *I will summon*

Judah's sin is traced all the way back to Egypt, to their very beginning.
23:31–33 The **cup** in the Bible is a neutral metaphor. It was most frequently used, however, to refer to a toxic or intoxicating drink (Ps 75:8; Jr 25:15–16; Lm 4:21; Hab 2:15–16)—a cup of judgment or a cup of wrath (Is 51:17; Jr 51:7; Rv 17:3–4; 18:6).
23:34 Beating the breast was the customary response to a crisis (Is 32:12; Nah 2:7). The tearing of breasts intensified the image.
23:38–39 The defiling of God's **sanctuary** in Jerusalem was documented in chap. 8. Samaria, by its practice of worship at the illegal sanctuary of Bethel, defiled God's true sanctuary (1Kg 12:25–30).

23:40–41 **Incense** and **oil** not only belonged to the Lord, but they were products used in the offering of sacrifices.
23:42 The word **drunkards** may also be rendered as "men from Sheba." Sheba was located at the southwest corner of the Arabian Peninsula (modern Yemen) and was known for trading (27:22; 38:13; 1Kg 10:1–10; Jb 6:19).
23:46 **Terror** and **plunder** were standard types of covenant punishments (Lv 26:16–17; Dt 28:31,66–67; 32:25).
23:47 Stoning was the prescribed punishment for idolatry, child sacrifice, and adultery (Lv 20:2; Dt 13:10; 17:5; 22:21,24). These are the same judgments Ezekiel had pronounced earlier (16:40–41).

24:1–2 The date of this prophecy is significant. This was the day that Nebuchadnezzar's siege of Jerusalem began in January of 588 BC. Later in Israel's history the date became an appointed fast day and was observed as early as the time of the prophet Zechariah (Zch 8:19). This was the day Ezekiel had been pointing to for more than four years. The date was so significant that it was also mentioned by the writer of 1 and 2 Kings (2Kg 25:1) and by the prophet Jeremiah (Jr 39:1; 52:4).
24:3 This is the last occurrence of the phrase **the rebellious house**, which is unique to Ezekiel (2:5–6,8; 3:9,26–27; 12:2–3,9,25; 17:12). Those left in Jerusalem were like the choice

house. Tell them, 'This is what the Lord GOD says:

Put the pot on the fire —
    put it on,
    and then pour water into it!
4 Place the pieces of meat in it,
    every good piece —
    thigh and shoulder.
    Fill it with choice bones.
5 Take the choicest of the flock
    and also pile up the fuelᴬ under it.
    Bring it to a boil
    and cook the bones in it.

6 " 'Therefore, this is what the Lord GOD says:
Woe to the city of bloodshed,
    the pot that has corrosion inside it,
    and its corrosion has not come out of it!
    Empty it piece by piece;
    lots should not be cast for its contents.
7 For the blood she shedᴮ is still
        within her.
    She put it out on the bare rock;
    she didn't pour it on the ground
    to cover it with dust.
8 In order to stir up wrath
        and take vengeance,
    I have put her blood on the bare rock,
    so that it would not be covered.

9 " 'Therefore, this is what the Lord GOD says:
Woe to the city of bloodshed!
    I myself will make the pile
        of kindling large.
10 Pile on the logs and kindle the fire!
    Cook the meat well
    and mix in the spices!ᶜ,ᴰ
    Let the bones be burned!
11 Set the empty pot on its coals
    so that it becomes hot
        and its copper glows.
    Then its impurity will melt inside it;
    its corrosion will be consumed.
12 It has frustrated every effort;ᴱ
    its thick corrosion will not come off.
    Into the fire with its corrosion!

13 Because of the depravity
        of your uncleanness —
    since I tried to purify you,
    but you would not be purified
        from your uncleanness —
    you will not be pure again
    until I have satisfied my wrath on you.
14 I, the LORD, have spoken.
    It is coming, and I will do it!
    I will not refrain, I will not show pity,
        and I will not relent.
    Iᶠ will judge you
    according to your ways and deeds.
    This is the declaration
        of the Lord GOD.' "

The Death of Ezekiel's Wife: A Sign

15 Then the word of the LORD came to me: 16 "Son of man, I am about to take the delight of your eyes away from you with a fatal blow. But you must not lament or weep or let your tears flow. 17 Groan quietly; do not observe mourning rites for the dead. Put on your turban and strap your sandals on your feet; do not cover your mustache or eat the bread of mourners."ᴳ

18 I spoke to the people in the morning, and my wife died in the evening. The next morning I did just as I was commanded. 19 Then the people asked me, "Won't you tell us what these things you are doing mean for us?"

20 So I answered them, "The word of the LORD came to me: 21 Say to the house of Israel, 'This is what the Lord GOD says: I am about to desecrate my sanctuary, the pride of your power, the delight of your eyes, and the desire of your heart. Also, the sons and daughters you left behind will fall by the sword. 22 Then you will do just as I have done: You will not cover your mustache or eat the bread of mourners. 23 Your turbans will remain on your heads and your sandals on your feet. You will not lament or weep but will waste away because of your iniquities and will groan to one another. 24 Now Ezekiel will be a sign for you. You will do everything that he has done. When this happens, you will know that I am the Lord GOD.'

ᴬ24:5 Lit *bones*　ᴮ24:7 Lit *For her blood*　ᶜ24:10 Some Hb mss read *well; remove the broth* ; LXX reads *fire so that the meat may be cooked and the broth may be reduced*　ᴰ24:10 Or *and stir the broth*　ᴱ24:12 Hb obscure　ᶠ24:14 Some Hb mss, LXX, Syr, Tg, Vg; other Hb mss read *They*　ᴳ24:17 Lit *men*, also in v. 22

---

meat intended for the **pot**, as opposed to the discarded by-products that represented the people taken away into exile. Now Ezekiel will utter a parable based on the same sort of imagery, once again (11:11) condemning rather than reassuring Jerusalem.
24:4 The phrase **every good piece** refers to choice offerings (Nm 18:12), including the breast and thigh (Gn 32:32; Ex 29:26–28; Lv 7:28–36; 10:12–15; Nm 18:18).
24:5 The **flock** elsewhere in Ezekiel represents the people of Israel (chap. 34). Thus the pieces of meat (**choicest of the flock**) probably picture Jerusalem's inhabitants, who would be "boiled" in the judgment fire of Nebuchadnezzar's siege.

24:6 Jerusalem is called the **city of bloodshed**, just as the pagan city of Nineveh is Nah 3:1. **Corrosion** represents injustice and bloodguilt (22:6–12).
24:7–8 Uncovered **blood** evoked God's vengeance (Gn 4:10; Is 26:21).
24:9–14 Because of **bloodshed**, the fire under the **pot** will be made extremely hot to burn up the contents and even the rust.
24:15–16 The statement **take the delight of your eyes away from you** is reminiscent of God's command to Abraham (Gn 22) to offer his son as a sacrifice. A **blow** resulted in a sudden death either from combat (1Sm 4:17; 2Sm 18:7) or from plague or disease (Ex 9:14; Nm 14:37; 17:13; 25:8–9).

24:17 In this passage five of the typical gestures of ancient Israelite mourning are alluded to: groaning (Is 24:7; Mal 2:13), removing one's **turban** or **sandals** (2Sm 15:30), covering one's lips (Mc 3:7), and eating special mourning **bread** (Hs 9:4). In addition, dust was often thrown atop the head (Jos 7:6; 1Sm 4:12). These practices were never prescribed in the law, but they became standard responses to tragedy.
24:18–21 Ezekiel's behavior was so unusual that the people asked him to explain. The destruction of the **sanctuary** included the fall of the city. God's destruction of the people's sanctuary is one of the covenant punishments prescribed for national disobedience

²⁵ "As for you, son of man, know that on that day I will take from them their stronghold — their pride and joy, the delight of their eyes, and the longing of their hearts — as well as their sons and daughters. ²⁶ On that day a fugitive will come to you and report the news. ²⁷ On that day your mouth will be opened to talk with him; you will speak and no longer be mute. So you will be a sign for them, and they will know that I am the LORD."

PROPHECIES AGAINST THE NATIONS
Judgment against Ammon

25 Then the word of the LORD came to me: ² "Son of man, face the Ammonites and prophesy against them. ³ Say to the Ammonites, 'Hear the word of the Lord GOD: This is what the Lord GOD says: Because you said, "Aha!" about my sanctuary when it was desecrated, about the land of Israel when it was laid waste, and about the house of Judah when they went into exile, ⁴ therefore I am about to give you to the people of the east as a possession. They will set up their encampments and

pitch their tents among you. They will eat your fruit and drink your milk. ⁵ I will make Rabbah a pasture for camels and Ammon a resting place for sheep. Then you will know that I am the LORD.

⁶ " 'For this is what the Lord GOD says: Because you clapped your hands, stamped your feet, and rejoiced over the land of Israel with wholehearted contempt, ⁷ therefore I am about to stretch out my hand against you and give you as plunder to the nations. I will cut you off from the peoples and eliminate you from the countries. I will destroy you, and you will know that I am the LORD.

Judgment against Moab

⁸ " 'This is what the Lord GOD says: Because Moab and Seir said, "Look, the house of Judah is like all the other nations." ⁹ Therefore I am about to expose Moab's flank beginning with its^A frontier cities, the splendor of the land: Beth-jeshimoth, Baal-meon, and Kiriathaim. ¹⁰ I will give it along with Ammon to the people of the east as a possession, so that Ammon will not be remembered among the nations. ¹¹ So I

^A25:9 Lit with the cities, with its

---

n the Mosaic law (Lv 26:31). Jerusalem died as did Ezekiel's wife), and with it the temple and the prescribed methods of worship. This created a first-rate identity crisis for Hebrews who wished to remain faithful to God. **24:25–26** This prophecy, which says a **fugitive** arriving from fallen Jerusalem will mark the end of Ezekiel's silence, is fulfilled n 33:21–22. **24:27** Ezekiel's ability to **speak** again will signal that his six-year ministry of announcing judgment is over; a new ministry of consolation will begin. **25:1–32:32** This section of Ezekiel includes the book's message of doom and its message of hope. Doom for Israel's antagonists spells hope for Israel itself. The placement of these oracles at this point disrupts the

flow of the book and heightens the tension as the destruction of the temple is imminent. God's judgment on these nations is based on the Abrahamic covenant, which said that those who cursed Israel would be cursed by God (Gn 12:1–3). All the nations named in the oracle had either taken part in Jerusalem's destruction or had rejoiced over it. The audience for these oracles was Judean, and so they had cause for future hope. **25:1–7** Ammon, Moab, and Edom are mentioned in the order of their geographic location, from north to south. The **Ammonites** were descendants of Abraham's nephew, Lot (Gn 19:30–38). They were known for their idolatry (1Kg 11:7,33), cruelty (Am 1:13), pride (Zph 2:9–10), and opposition to God's people

(Dt 23:3–4; Jdg 3:13; 1Sm 11:1–3; 2Sm 10:1–14; 2Kg 24:2; Neh 4:3,7–8). With ironic justice, the nation that rejoiced over the destruction of Judah (v. 3) will suffer the same fate. They will be conquered and oppressed by their enemies. **25:8–11** Like the Ammonites, the people of **Moab** were descendants of Lot and one of his daughters (Gn 19:30–38). Shortly after the Israelites were released from Egyptian bondage, the Moabites caused a great setback for the young Israelite nation by introducing them to Baal worship (Nm 21:1–25; 31:16). During Ezekiel's time, Moabite troops joined forces with Nebuchadnezzar and attacked King Jehoiakim of Jerusalem (2Kg 24:2). When Judah was defeated, the Moabites responded with delight (Jr 48:29; Zph 2:8–9).

Q & A: Is religion the cause of evil in the world?

by Alison Thomas

Many people believe the world would be a better place without religion. They say religion leads to violence. After all, who caused the Crusades? Religious people. Who was in charge of the Spanish Inquisition? Religious people. The solution seems simple: get rid of religion, and we'll get rid of evil, right? Not so fast!

First, we have to admit that religion can be a cause of evil in the world, as when people use it to suppress others. As Christians, we should admit that evil things have been done in the name of Christianity. However, it is also important to remember that not everything done in the name of Christianity actually reflects genuine Christian teaching. Christianity is misused when used as justification for violence.

Second, what about all the violence done in the name of secularism? If religion is responsible for all the violence done in its name, what about atheism? Religion is not the only cause of evil in the world. In fact, more people have been killed by atheist regimes in the twentieth century

than in all the religious persecutions of Western history. Mao was responsible for over forty million deaths; Stalin for more than twenty million; Hitler's count is over ten million. And those are just the big three atheists—we haven't mentioned other tyrants like Pol Pot, Enver Hoxha, Nicolae Ceaușescu, Fidel Castro, and Kim Jong-il. In a single century, atheists have killed more than one hundred million people.

Secularist violence is the result of man playing God. It sees man, not God, as the measure of all things. Instead of seeing humankind as sinful and in need of redemption, secularism is convinced that humans can become perfect and create utopia here on earth. Secularist regimes do whatever it takes to achieve this, including taking control of society and murdering those who get in the way. Without God, anything goes. Without God, we cannot even distinguish between what is good and what is evil.

It is true that the pages of history are stained with the blood of religious violence. But those same pages are also stained by the blood of Jesus. On the cross, God the Son not only took evil on himself but gave us the hope and power to overcome it. Instead of blaming God for the world's evils, we must look to him for the solution.

will execute judgments against Moab, and they will know that I am the LORD.

Judgment against Edom

¹² " 'This is what the Lord GOD says: Because Edom acted vengefully against the house of Judah and incurred grievous guilt by taking revenge on them, ¹³ therefore this is what the Lord GOD says: I will stretch out my hand against Edom and cut off both people and animals from it. I will make it a wasteland; they will fall by the sword from Teman to Dedan. ¹⁴ I will take my vengeance on Edom through my people Israel, and they will deal with Edom according to my anger and wrath. So they will know my vengeance. This is the declaration of the Lord GOD.

Judgment against Philistia

¹⁵ " 'This is what the Lord GOD says: Because the Philistines acted in vengeance and took revenge with deep contempt, destroying because of their perpetual hatred, ¹⁶ therefore this is what the Lord GOD says: I am about to stretch out my hand against the Philistines, cutting off the Cherethites and wiping out what remains of the coastal peoples.^A ¹⁷ I will execute severe vengeance against them with furious rebukes. They will know that I am the LORD when I take my vengeance on them.' "

The Downfall of Tyre

26 In the eleventh year, on the first day of the month, the word of the LORD came to me: ² "Son of man, because Tyre said about Jerusalem, 'Aha! The gateway to the peoples is shattered. She has been turned over to me.^B I will be filled now that she lies in ruins,' ³ therefore this is what the Lord GOD says: See, I am

against you, Tyre! I will raise up many nations against you, just as the sea raises its waves. ⁴ They will destroy the walls of Tyre and demolish her towers. I will scrape the soil from her and turn her into a bare rock. ⁵ She will become a place in the sea to spread nets, for I have spoken." This is the declaration of the Lord GOD. "She will become plunder for the nations, ⁶ and her villages on the mainland will be slaughtered by the sword. Then they will know that I am the LORD."

⁷ For this is what the Lord GOD says: "See, I am about to bring King Nebuchadnezzar^C of Babylon, king of kings, against Tyre from the north with horses, chariots, cavalry, and a huge assembly of troops. ⁸ He will slaughter your villages on the mainland with the sword. He will set up siege works, build a ramp, and raise a wall of shields against you. ⁹ He will direct the blows of his battering rams against your walls and tear down your towers with his iron tools. ¹⁰ His horses will be so numerous that their dust will cover you. When he enters your gates as an army entering a breached city, your walls will shake from the noise of cavalry, wagons, and chariots. ¹¹ He will trample all your streets with the hooves of his horses. He will slaughter your people with the sword, and your mighty pillars will fall to the ground. ¹² They will take your wealth as spoil and plunder your merchandise. They will also demolish your walls and tear down your beautiful homes. Then they will throw your stones, timber, and soil into the water. ¹³ I will put an end to the noise of your songs, and the sound of your lyres will no longer be heard. ¹⁴ I will turn you into a bare rock. You will be a place to spread nets. You will never be rebuilt, for I, the LORD, have spoken." This is the declaration of the Lord GOD.

---

^A **25:16** Lit *the seacoast*   ^B **26:2** Or *It has swung open for me*   ^C **26:7** Lit *Nebuchadrezzar*

25:12–14 The struggle between **Edom** and **Judah** began when their respective patriarchs were born as twin brothers. Jacob, who went on to father the Israelites, grabbed the heel of Esau, who fathered the Edomites, as they struggled to emerge from Rebekah's womb (Gn 25:21–34). Centuries later, shortly after the Israelites emerged from bondage in Egypt, Edom refused to let them pass through their land en route to Canaan (Nm 20:14–21). This was the beginning of a long adversarial relationship between Israel and Edom. The most blatant example was Edom's role in the destruction of the Jerusalem temple (Ps 137:7; Lm 4:21–22; Ob 1–14). Like the Moabites and Ammonites, the Edomites were a warring (Gn 27:39–40), idolatrous (2Ch 25:14,20), cruel (Am 1:11–12), and vengeful (Ezk 25:12–14) people. This prophecy was fulfilled when Edom was defeated by the Maccabees and incorporated into the Jewish state. God's judgment on Edom is further expanded in 35:1–36:15.
25:15 The **Philistines** migrated to the coast of Palestine from the Greek coasts and islands of the Aegean Sea (Jr 47:4; Am 9:7; Zph

2:5). As early as the time of the judges they were constant adversaries of Israel (Jdg 3:31; 10:7; 13–16; 1Sm 4; 13; 31; 2Sm 5; 2Kg 18:8; 2Ch 21:16–17; 28:18). David was credited with the final subjugation of the Philistines during his reign (2Sm 5:17–25).
25:16–17 The **Cherethites** (possibly Cretans) were presumably an ethnic group of Aegean origin that settled along the southwestern coast of Canaan. By David's time they had such a positive relationship with Israel that David chose many Cherethites as his personal guardsmen (1Sm 30:14; 2Sm 8:18). They are frequently mentioned along with the Pelethite forces that together formed a mercenary unit during the time of David (2Sm 8:18; 20:23).
26:1–14 The Phoenicians represented the remnants of the original population that occupied Canaan before the Israelites arrived. As the most powerful city on the Phoenician coast, **Tyre** dominated not only other coastal cities but much of the Phoenician inland areas as well. Tyre's Hebrew name means "rock." Built atop an island off the Phoenician coast, Tyre was virtually impregnable by sea or land. Relations between Israel and Tyre

were often cordial (1Kg 5; 7). Tyre, the preeminent maritime power of the ancient world, joined Judah in revolt against the Babylonian Empire (Jr 27:3). After Nebuchadnezzar defeated Jerusalem, he besieged Tyre for thirteen years (585–572 BC) but was unsuccessful in his campaign to conquer the offshore rock fortress. In the fourth century BC, Alexander built a causeway of stone, timber, and rubble a half mile long and two hundred feet wide from the mainland to the island. By this means Tyre was finally conquered, thus fulfilling Ezekiel's prophecy (27:36).
This is the fifth date in Ezekiel (1:1; 8:1; 20:1; 24:1), but there is a textual problem: the month is missing in the MT. The **eleventh year** would fall between April 587 BC and April 586 BC. But since Jerusalem's fall did not occur until July 586 BC and the city was not burned until August 586 BC (2Kg 25:3,8), other possibilities have been proposed. One is that Ezekiel is prophesying that Tyre will celebrate Judah's downfall in the near future. Another proposal is that words have dropped out of the date formula, and it originally read, "In the eleventh month of the twelfth year."

¹⁵ This is what the Lord God says to Tyre: "Won't the coasts and islands quake at the sound of your downfall, when the wounded groan and slaughter occurs within you? ¹⁶ All the princes of the sea will descend from their thrones, remove their robes, and strip off their embroidered garments. They will clothe themselves with trembling; they will sit on the ground, tremble continually, and be appalled at you. ¹⁷ Then they will lament for you and say of you,

> 'How you have perished, city of renown,
> you who were populated from the seas!ᴬ
> She who was powerful on the sea,
> she and all of her inhabitants
> inflicted their terror.ᴮ

¹⁸ Now the coastlands tremble
on the day of your downfall;
the islands in the sea
are alarmed by your demise.' "

¹⁹ For this is what the Lord God says: "When I make you a ruined city like other deserted cities, when I raise up the deep against you so that the mighty waters cover you, ²⁰ then I will bring you down to be with those who descend to the Pit, to the people of antiquity. I will make you dwell in the underworldᶜ likeᴰ the ancient ruins, with those who descend to the Pit, so that you will no longer be inhabited or display your splendorᴱ in the land of the living. ²¹ I will make you an object of horror, and you will no longer exist. You will be sought but will never be found again." This is the declaration of the Lord God.

The Sinking of Tyre

27 The word of the Lord came to me: ² "Now, son of man, lament for Tyre. ³ Say to Tyre, who is situated at the entrance of the sea, merchant of the peoples to many coasts and islands, 'This is what the Lord God says:

> Tyre, you declared,
> "I am perfect in beauty."
⁴ Your realm was in the heart of the sea;
> your builders perfected your beauty.
⁵ They constructed all your planking
> with pine trees from Senir.
> They took a cedar from Lebanon
> to make a mast for you.

⁶ They made your oars of oaks
> from Bashan.
> They made your deck of cypress wood
> from the coasts of Cyprus,
> inlaid with ivory.
⁷ Your sail was made of
> fine embroidered linen from Egypt,
> and served as your banner.
> Your awning was of blue
> and purple fabric
> from the coasts of Elishah.
⁸ The inhabitants of Sidon and Arvad
> were your rowers.
> Your wise men were within you, Tyre;
> they were your captains.
⁹ The elders of Gebal and its wise men
> were within you, repairing your leaks.

> "'All the ships of the sea and their sailors
> came to you to barter for your goods.
¹⁰ Men of Persia, Lud, and Put
> were in your army, serving
> as your warriors.
> They hung shields and helmets in you;
> they gave you splendor.
¹¹ Men of Arvad and Helech
> were stationed on your walls all around,
> and Gammadites were in your towers.
> They hung their shieldsᶠ all around
> your walls;
> they perfected your beauty.

¹² "'Tarshish was your trading partner because of your abundant wealth of every kind. They exchanged silver, iron, tin, and lead for your merchandise. ¹³ Javan, Tubal, and Meshech were your merchants. They exchanged slavesᴳ and bronze utensils for your goods. ¹⁴ Those from Beth-togarmah exchanged horses, war horses, and mules for your merchandise. ¹⁵ Men of Dedanᴴ were also your merchants; many coasts and islands were your regular markets. They brought back ivory tusks and ebony as your payment. ¹⁶ Aramᴵ was your trading partner because of your numerous products. They exchanged turquoise,ᴶ purple and embroidered cloth, fine linen, coral,ᴶ and rubiesᴶ for your merchandise. ¹⁷ Judah and the land of Israel were your merchants. They exchanged

---

ᴬ **26:17** Some LXX mss read *How you were destroyed from the seas, city of renown!* ᴮ **26:17** Lit *and all her inhabitants who put their terror on all her inhabitants*; Hb obscure ᶜ **26:20** Lit *the lower parts of the earth* ᴰ **26:20** Some Hb mss, LXX; other Hb mss, Syr read *in* ᴱ **26:20** LXX reads *or appear* ᶠ **27:11** Or *quivers*; Hb obscure ᴳ **27:13** Lit *souls of men* ᴴ **27:15** LXX reads *Rhodes* ᴵ **27:16** Some Hb mss, Aq, Syr read *Edom* ᴶ **27:16** Hb obscure

---

26:15–18 The **princes of the sea** are the rulers of islands and coastal lands with which Tyre had traded.
26:19 The Lord threatened Tyre with a judgment reminiscent of the Genesis flood (Gn 6–8).
26:20–21 The phrase **the Pit** is a figurative way of expressing death. It is virtually synonymous with the grave (Pr 1:12; Is 14:15; 38:18).
27:1–11 Ezekiel portrayed Tyre as a well-built ship. This symbolizes the way Tyre achieved

wealth through maritime trade. **Cedar from Lebanon** was prized for its height and strength (1Kg 4:33; 5:6; 1Ch 17:1–6; Ezr 3:7; Is 2:13). The material was often imported into Israel from Lebanon for building projects. Egypt was known for its fine **linen** (Gn 41:42; Pr 7:16). Verses 8–11 point to the greatness of Tyre.
27:12–25 Some of these places that traded with Tyre still exist, but many have changed their names or no longer exist.

27:12 There is much debate about the exact location of **Tarshish**. It has often been linked with Tartessus—a Phoenician colony in western Spain. The nation of Spain was a source of metals in the ancient world.
27:16 Phoenicia was known for trade in **purple** dye derived from shellfish. Both names for the country, *Phoenicia* and *Canaan*, mean "purple."

wheat from Minnith, meal,^A honey, oil, and balm, for your goods. **18** Damascus was also your trading partner because of your numerous products and your abundant wealth of every kind, trading in wine from Helbon and white wool.^B **19** Vedan^C and Javan from Uzal^D dealt in your merchandise; wrought iron, cassia, and aromatic cane were exchanged for your goods. **20** Dedan was your merchant in saddlecloths for riding. **21** Arabia and all the princes of Kedar were your business partners, trading with you in lambs, rams, and goats. **22** The merchants of Sheba and Raamah traded with you. For your merchandise they exchanged the best of all spices and all kinds of precious stones as well as gold. **23** Haran, Canneh, Eden, the merchants of Sheba, Asshur, and Chilmad traded with you. **24** They were your merchants in choice garments, cloaks of blue and embroidered materials, and multicolored carpets,^D which were bound and secured with cords in your marketplace. **25** Ships of Tarshish were the carriers for your goods.

> " 'So you became full and heavily loaded^E
> in the heart of the sea.
> **26** Your rowers have brought you
> onto the high seas,
> but the east wind has wrecked you
> in the heart of the sea.
> **27** Your wealth, merchandise, and goods,
> your sailors and captains,
> those who repair your leaks,
> those who barter for your goods,
> and all the warriors on board,
> with all the other people within you,
> sink into the heart of the sea
> on the day of your downfall.
> **28** " 'The countryside shakes
> at the sound of your sailors' cries.
> **29** All the oarsmen
> disembark from their ships.
> The sailors and all the captains
> of the sea
> stand on the shore.
> **30** Because of you, they raise their voices
> and cry out bitterly.
> They throw dust on their heads;
> they roll in ashes.
> **31** They shave their heads because of you
> and wrap themselves in sackcloth.
> They weep over you
> with deep anguish
> and bitter mourning.
> **32** " 'In their wailing they lament for you,
> mourning over you:
> "Who was like Tyre,
> silenced^D in the middle of the sea?
> **33** When your merchandise was unloaded
> from the seas,
> you satisfied many peoples.
> You enriched the kings of the earth
> with your abundant wealth and goods.
> **34** Now you are wrecked by the sea
> in the depths of the waters;
> your goods and the people within you
> have gone down.
> **35** All the inhabitants of the coasts
> and islands
> are appalled at you.
> Their kings shudder with fear;
> their faces are contorted.
> **36** Those who trade among the peoples
> scoff^F at you;
> you have become an object of horror
> and will never exist again." ' "

The Fall of Tyre's Ruler

28 The word of the LORD came to me: **2** "Son of man, say to the ruler of Tyre, 'This is what the Lord GOD says: Your^G heart is proud, and you have said, "I am a god; I sit in the seat of gods in the heart of the sea." Yet you are a man and not a god, though you have regarded your heart as that of a god. **3** Yes, you are wiser than Daniel; no secret is hidden from you! **4** By your wisdom and understanding you have acquired wealth for yourself. You have acquired gold and silver for your treasuries. **5** By your great skill in trading you have increased your wealth, but your heart has become proud because of your wealth.

> **6** " 'Therefore, this is what the Lord GOD says:
> Because you regard your heart as that
> of a god,
> **7** I am about to bring strangers against you,
> ruthless men from the nations.
> They will draw their swords
> against your magnificent wisdom
> and will pierce your splendor.
> **8** They will bring you down to the Pit,
> and you will die a violent death
> in the heart of the sea.
> **9** Will you still say, "I am a god,"
> in the presence of those who slay^H you?
> Yet you will be only a man, not a god,
> in the hands of those who kill you.
> **10** You will die the death
> of the uncircumcised

---

^A **27:17** Or *resin*; Hb obscure   ^B **27:18** Or *and wool from Zahar*   ^C **27:19** Or *Dan*   ^D **27:19,24,32** Hb obscure   ^E **27:25** Or *and very glorious*   ^F **27:36** Lit *hiss*   ^G **28:2** Lit *Because your*   ^H **28:9** Some Hb mss, LXX, Syr, Vg; other Hb mss read *of the one who kills*

27:23 Eden was a district south of **Haran**. **27:26–36** Tyre's ruin came in the very element where she was most at home—the open **seas**. **28:1–2** This **ruler of Tyre** may be identified as Ithobaal II, whose name meant "Baal is

with him," or Ethbaal III. Possibly the language was kept vague so that the condemnation could aptly describe any Tyrian king. **28:3–5** The fame of the prophet **Daniel** had spread in the exile, even beyond the bounds

of his own people (14:14,20; Dn 1:20; 2:48; 4:18–27; 5:11–12; 6:3). **28:10** In his disgraceful **death**, the king of Tyre will join the ranks of the **uncircumcised**. Since Phoenicians as well as most

at the hands of strangers.
For I have spoken.
This is the declaration
of the Lord God.'"

A Lament for Tyre's King

¹¹ The word of the LORD came to me: ¹² "Son of man, lament for the king of Tyre and say to him, 'This is what the Lord GOD says:

You were the seal^A of perfection,^B
full of wisdom and perfect in beauty.
¹³ You were in Eden, the garden of God.
Every kind of precious stone
covered you:
carnelian, topaz, and diamond,^B
beryl, onyx, and jasper,
lapis lazuli, turquoise^C and emerald.^D
Your mountings and settings
were crafted in gold;
they were prepared on the day
you were created.
¹⁴ You were an anointed guardian cherub,
for^E I had appointed you.
You were on the holy mountain of God;
you walked among the fiery stones.
¹⁵ From the day you were created
you were blameless in your ways
until wickedness was found in you.
¹⁶ Through the abundance of your trade,
you were filled with violence,
and you sinned.
So I expelled you in disgrace
from the mountain of God,
and banished you, guardian cherub,^F
from among the fiery stones.
¹⁷ Your heart became proud because of
your beauty;
For the sake of your splendor
you corrupted your wisdom.
So I threw you down to the ground;^G
I made you a spectacle before kings.
¹⁸ You profaned your sanctuaries
by the magnitude of your iniquities
in your dishonest trade.
So I made fire come from within you,
and it consumed you.
I reduced you to ashes on the ground

in the sight of everyone watching you.
¹⁹ All those who know you
among the peoples
are appalled at you.
You have become an object of horror
and will never exist again.'"

A Prophecy against Sidon

²⁰ The word of the LORD came to me: ²¹ "Son of man, face Sidon and prophesy against it. ²² You are to say, 'This is what the Lord GOD says:

Look! I am against you, Sidon,
and I will display my glory within you.
They will know that I am the LORD
when I execute judgments against her
and demonstrate my holiness
through her.
²³ I will send a plague against her
and bloodshed in her streets;
the slain will fall within her,
while the sword is against her^H
on every side.
Then they will know that I am the LORD.

²⁴ "The house of Israel will no longer be hurt by^I prickly briers or painful thorns from all their neighbors who treat them with contempt. Then they will know that I am the Lord GOD.

²⁵ "This is what the Lord GOD says: When I gather the house of Israel from the peoples where they are scattered, I will demonstrate my holiness through them in the sight of the nations, and they will live in their own land, which I gave to my servant Jacob. ²⁶ They will live there securely, build houses, and plant vineyards. They will live securely when I execute judgments against all their neighbors who treat them with contempt. Then they will know that I am the LORD their God.'"

A Prophecy of Egypt's Ruin

29 In the tenth year, in the tenth month on the twelfth day of the month, the word of the LORD came to me: ² "Son of man, face Pharaoh king of Egypt and prophesy against him and against all of Egypt. ³ Speak to him and say, 'This is what the Lord GOD says:

---

^A 28:12 Or *sealer*   ^B 28:12,13 Hb obscure   ^C 28:13 Or *malachite,* or *garnet*   ^D 28:13 Or *beryl*   ^E 28:14 Or *With an anointed guardian cherub*   ^F 28:16 Or *and the guardian cherub banished you*   ^G 28:17 Or *earth*   ^H 28:23 Or *within her by the sword*   ^I 28:24 Lit *longer have*

---

other ancient Near Eastern males practiced circumcision, Ezekiel's use of the term must be figurative. The point is that the king will be assigned to the most undesirable compartment of the netherworld, along with other degraded and unclean persons (31:18; 32:17–32).
28:11–13 The prideful **king of Tyre** is compared either to a guardian angel at the "mountain of God" (v. 14) or to errant Adam in the **garden** of Eden. Nine of the twelve **precious** gemstones listed here were included on the high priest's breastpiece (Ex 28:15–20; 39:10–13).

28:14–17 Though the context is an oracle against the king of Tyre, many believe that this **anointed . . . cherub** should ultimately be identified as Satan himself. In that case the passage would have double reference.
28:18–19 These verses have the king clearly in view. Verse 19 repeats 27:36.
28:20–21 Sidon was another key Phoenician port city. It was located twenty-five miles north of Tyre. Sidon and Tyre often are mentioned together (Jr 27:3; 47:4; Jl 3:4). During times when Tyre was in decline, Sidon would increase in prominence. In the Persian period, Sidon stood at the head of the Phoenician cities.

28:24 The insults of the nations are compared to **prickly briers** and **painful thorns**. See Nm 33:55.
28:26 Once the nations that treated Israel with **contempt** are destroyed, the exiles will return to the land of Israel (Gn 12; 28; 35) and rebuild their community. Then they will exhibit God's holiness in the world.
29:1–2 Egypt was Israel's constant foe after keeping the nation in bondage for four hundred years during its early history. Ezekiel's first oracle against Egypt (there are seven) is dated to January 587 BC, when Hophra was Pharaoh.

Look, I am against you, Pharaoh
    king of Egypt,
the great monster[A] lying in the middle
    of his Nile,
who says, "My Nile is my own;
    I made it for myself."
4   I will put hooks in your jaws
    and make the fish of your streams
        cling to your scales.
    I will haul you up
    from the middle of your Nile,
    and all the fish of your streams
        will cling to your scales.
5   I will leave you in the desert,
    you and all the fish of your streams.
    You will fall on the open ground
    and will not be taken away
        or gathered for burial.
    I have given you
    to the wild creatures of the earth
    and the birds of the sky as food.

6   "'Then all the inhabitants of Egypt
    will know that I am the LORD,
    for they[B] have been a staff
        made of reed
    to the house of Israel.
7   When Israel grasped you by the hand,
    you splintered, tearing all
        their shoulders;
    when they leaned on you,
    you shattered and made all
        their hips unsteady.[C]

8 " 'Therefore, this is what the Lord GOD says:
I am going to bring a sword against you and cut
off both people and animals from you. 9 The
land of Egypt will be a desolate ruin. Then they
will know that I am the LORD. Because you[D]
said, "The Nile is my own; I made it," 10 therefore, I am against you and your Nile. I will turn
the land of Egypt into ruins, a desolate waste
from Migdol to Syene, as far as the border of
Cush. 11 No human foot will pass through it, and
no animal foot will pass through it. It will be
uninhabited for forty years. 12 I will make the
land of Egypt a desolation among[E] desolate

lands, and its cities will be a desolation among[F]
ruined cities for forty years. I will disperse the
Egyptians among the nations and scatter them
throughout the lands.

13 " 'For this is what the Lord GOD says: At the
end of forty years I will gather the Egyptians
from the peoples where they were dispersed.
14 I will restore the fortunes of Egypt and bring
them back to the land of Pathros, the land of
their origin. There they will be a lowly kingdom. 15 Egypt will be the lowliest of kingdoms
and will never again exalt itself over the nations. I will make them so small they cannot
rule over the nations. 16 It will never again be
an object of trust for the house of Israel, drawing attention to their iniquity of turning to the
Egyptians. Then they will know that I am the
Lord GOD.' "

Babylon Receives Egypt as Compensation

17 In the twenty-seventh year, in the first
month, on the first day of the month, the word
of the LORD came to me: 18 "Son of man, King
Nebuchadnezzar of Babylon made his army
labor strenuously against Tyre. Every head
was made bald and every shoulder chafed, but
he and his army received no compensation
from Tyre for the labor he expended against
it. 19 Therefore, this is what the Lord GOD says:
I am going to give the land of Egypt to King
Nebuchadnezzar of Babylon, and he will carry off its wealth, seizing its spoil and taking
its plunder. This will be his army's compensation. 20 I have given him the land of Egypt as
the pay he labored for, since they worked for
me." This is the declaration of the Lord GOD.
21 "In that day I will cause a horn to sprout for
the house of Israel, and I will enable you to
speak out among them. Then they will know
that I am the LORD."

Egypt's Doom

30 The word of the LORD came to me:
2 "Son of man, prophesy and say, 'This
is what the Lord GOD says:
    Wail, "Woe because of that day!"

[A]29:3 Or crocodile   [B]29:6 LXX, Syr, Vg read you   [C]29:7 LXX, Syr, Vg; MT reads and you caused their hips to stand   [D]29:9 LXX,
Syr, Vg; MT reads he   [E]29:12 Or Egypt the most desolate of   [F]29:12 Or be the most desolate of

---

29:3 In ancient Near Eastern literature,
the word **monster** (Hb *tannin*) refers to
the mythical sea monster, the chaos god,
known elsewhere as Rahab or Leviathan.
Ezekiel equates **Pharaoh** with *tannin*. Like
the ruler of Tyre in chap. 28, Pharaoh dared
to defy the Lord.
29:7 Egypt's guilt stemmed from its pact
to assist King Zedekiah of Judah in his defiance of Nebuchadnezzar, the agent of God's
wrath against Judah. By resisting Nebuchadnezzar, Pharaoh Hophra was hindering
the execution of God's plan. The phrase **you
splintered, tearing all their shoulders;
when they leaned on you** looks back to

Hophra's unsuccessful attempt to give military support during the siege of Jerusalem.
His attack against Nebuchadnezzar in the
spring of 588 BC failed to relieve Jerusalem
(Jr 37:5-10).
29:12 In the Bible **forty years** is a frequent
expression for a complete and lengthy period
of time (Nm 14:33; 1Kg 2:11). If Egypt fell to
the Babylonians in 568 BC, as most ancient
Near Eastern histories maintain, then this
forty-year "captivity" of Egypt ended when
the Persians came to power.
29:16 After the Babylonians were defeated
and the Persians seized control, Egypt was
never again a formidable world power.

29:17-20 Nebuchadnezzar labored over **Tyre**
but received no plunder. The Lord gave Egypt
to him as compensation for all his labor.
29:21 Horn was used as a metaphor for
strength or power (1Sm 2:1; 1Kg 22:11; Ps 92:10;
Jr 48:25). Here the reference is to the strength
of the Messiah and the future restoration
of the Davidic monarchy in the aftermath
of Egypt's collapse (Ps 132:17; Is 11:1-16). The
word *grow* or *sprout* is a specific messianic
image. The ultimate fulfillment of this verse
is found in Christ (Ezk 17:22-24).
30:1-2 The **day** of the Lord theme occurs
in many prophetic books (Is 2:6-21; 13-14; Jl
1-2; Am 5:18-20; Obadiah; Zph 1:2-18; 2:1-3).

³ For a day is near;
   a day belonging to the LORD is near.
It will be a day of clouds,
   a time of doom^A for the nations.
⁴ A sword will come against Egypt,
   and there will be anguish in Cush
when the slain fall in Egypt,
   and its wealth is taken away,
   and its foundations are demolished.
⁵ Cush, Put, and Lud,
   and all the various foreign troops,^B
plus Libya^C and the men
      of the covenant land
will fall by the sword along with them.
⁶ This is what the LORD says:
Those who support Egypt will fall,
   and its proud strength will collapse.
From Migdol to Syene
they will fall within it by the sword.
      This is the declaration
      of the Lord GOD.
⁷ They will be desolate
   among^D desolate lands,
and their cities will lie
   among ruined^E cities.
⁸ They will know that I am the LORD
   when I set fire to Egypt
   and all its allies are shattered.
⁹ On that day, messengers will go out from me
in ships to terrify confident Cush. Anguish will
come over them on the day of Egypt's doom.^F
For indeed it is coming.

¹⁰ " 'This is what the Lord GOD says:
I will put an end to the hordes^G of Egypt
   by the hand of King Nebuchadnezzar
   of Babylon.
¹¹   He along with his people,
   ruthless men from the nations,
will be brought in to destroy the land.
   They will draw their swords
      against Egypt
   and fill the land with the slain.
¹²   I will make the streams dry
   and sell the land to evil men.
I will bring desolation
   on the land and everything in it
   by the hands of foreigners.
I, the LORD, have spoken.

¹³ " 'This is what the Lord GOD says:
I will destroy the worthless idols

and put an end to the false gods
   in Memphis.
There will no longer be
   a prince from the land of Egypt.
And I will instill fear in that land.
¹⁴ I will make Pathros desolate,
   set fire to Zoan,
   and execute judgments on Thebes.
¹⁵ I will pour out my wrath on Pelusium,
   the stronghold of Egypt,
   and will wipe out the hordes of Thebes.
¹⁶ I will set fire to Egypt;
   Pelusium will writhe in anguish,
Thebes will be breached,
   and Memphis will face foes
      in broad daylight.^H
¹⁷ The young men of On^I and Pi-beseth
   will fall by the sword,
   and those cities^J will go into captivity.
¹⁸ The day will be dark^K in Tehaphnehes,
   when I break the yoke of Egypt there
and its proud strength
   comes to an end in the city.
A cloud will cover Tehaphnehes,^L
   and its surrounding villages will go
      into captivity.
¹⁹ So I will execute judgments
      against Egypt,
   and they will know that I am the LORD.' "

Pharaoh's Power Broken

²⁰ In the eleventh year, in the first month, on
the seventh day of the month, the word of the
LORD came to me: ²¹ "Son of man, I have broken the arm of Pharaoh king of Egypt. Look,
it has not been bandaged — no medicine has
been applied and no splint put on to bandage
it so that it can grow strong enough to handle a sword. ²² Therefore, this is what the Lord
GOD says: Look! I am against Pharaoh king of
Egypt. I will break his arms, both the strong
one and the one already broken, and will make
the sword fall from his hand. ²³ I will disperse
the Egyptians among the nations and scatter
them among the countries. ²⁴ I will strengthen
the arms of Babylon's king and place my sword
in his hand. But I will break the arms of Pharaoh, and he will groan before him as a mortally wounded man. ²⁵ I will strengthen the arms
of Babylon's king, but Pharaoh's arms will fall.
They will know that I am the LORD when I place
my sword in the hand of Babylon's king and

---

^A 30:3 *of doom* supplied for clarity   ^B 30:5 Or *all Arabia*   ^C 30:5 Lit *Cub*; Hb obscure   ^D 30:7 Or *be the most desolate of*
^E 30:7 Or *will be the most ruined of*   ^F 30:9 Lit *of Egypt*   ^G 30:10 Or *pomp, or wealth,* also in v. 15   ^H 30:16 Or *foes daily*
^I 30:17 LXX, Vg; MT reads *iniquity*   ^J 30:17 Or *and the women*; lit *and they*   ^K 30:18 Some Hb mss, LXX, Syr, Tg, Vg; other Hb
mss read *will withhold*   ^L 30:18 Or *Egypt*

30:3 Clouds often appear in texts that address the changes that take place in the end
times (v. 18; 32:7–8; 34:12; Jl 2:2; Zph 1:15).
30:5 The phrase **men of the covenant land**
is literally "sons of the land of the covenant."
It contains an implied reference to Jewish
mercenaries who fought with Pharaoh's forces.

30:6–12 Ruin would even come on Egypt's
allies, and Cush, its neighbor, would tremble
in fear. Foreigners would bring desolation
on Egypt.
30:14–19 Judgment would come on the
major cities of **Egypt**, centers of religious,
political, and military influence.

30:20 The date formula indicates that this
oracle was announced shortly before the
fall of Jerusalem. The date may allude to
Pharaoh Hophra's attempt to intervene to
deliver Judah from the crisis (Jr 37:5).
30:21–26 The figurative expression **I have
broken the arm of Pharaoh** refers to

he wields it against the land of Egypt. **26** When I disperse the Egyptians among the nations and scatter them among the countries, they will know that I am the LORD."

Downfall of Egypt and Assyria

31 In the eleventh year, in the third month, on the first day of the month, the word of the LORD came to me: **2** "Son of man, say to Pharaoh king of Egypt and to his hordes,

'Who are you like in your greatness?
3   Think of Assyria, a cedar in Lebanon,
      with beautiful branches and shady foliage
      and of lofty height.
      Its top was among the clouds.^A
4   The waters caused it to grow;
      the underground springs made it tall,
      directing their rivers all around
      the place where the tree was planted
      and sending their channels
      to all the trees of the field.
5   Therefore the cedar became greater
         in height
      than all the trees of the field.
      Its branches multiplied,
      and its boughs grew long
      as it spread them out
      because of the abundant water.
6   All the birds of the sky
      nested in its branches,
      and all the animals of the field
      gave birth beneath its boughs;
      all the great nations lived in its shade.
7   It was beautiful in its size,
      in the length of its limbs,
      for its roots extended
      to abundant water.
8   The cedars in God's garden could not
         eclipse it;
      the pine trees couldn't compare
         with its branches,
      nor could the plane trees match
         its boughs.
      No tree in the garden of God
      could compare with it in beauty.
9   I made it beautiful with its many limbs,
      and all the trees of Eden,
      which were in God's garden, envied it.

10 " 'Therefore, this is what the Lord GOD says: Since it^B towered high in stature and set its top among the clouds, and it^C grew proud on account of its height, **11** I determined to hand it over to a ruler of nations; he would surely deal with it. I banished it because of its wickedness. **12** Foreigners, ruthless men from the nations, cut it down and left it lying. Its limbs fell on the mountains and in every valley; its boughs lay broken in all the earth's ravines. All the peoples of the earth left its shade and abandoned it. **13** All the birds of the sky nested on its fallen trunk, and all the animals of the field were among its boughs. **14** This happened so that no trees planted beside water would become great in height and set their tops among the clouds, and so that no other well-watered trees would reach them in height. For they have all been consigned to death, to the underworld, among the people^D who descend to the Pit.

15 " 'This is what the Lord GOD says: I caused grieving on the day the cedar went down to Sheol. I closed off the underground deep because of it:^E I held back the rivers of the deep, and its abundant water was restrained. I made Lebanon mourn on account of it, and all the trees of the field fainted because of it. **16** I made the nations quake at the sound of its downfall, when I threw it down to Sheol to be with those who descend to the Pit. Then all the trees of Eden, the choice and best of Lebanon, all the well-watered trees, were comforted in the underworld. **17** They too descended with it to Sheol, to those slain by the sword. As its allies^F,G they had lived in its shade among the nations.

18 " 'Who then are you like in glory and greatness among Eden's trees? You also will be brought down to the underworld to be with the trees of Eden. You will lie among the uncircumcised with those slain by the sword. This is Pharaoh and all his hordes. This is the declaration of the Lord GOD.' "

A Lament for Pharaoh

32 In the twelfth year, in the twelfth month, on the first day of the month, the word of the LORD came to me: **2** "Son of man, lament for Pharaoh king of Egypt and say to him,

'You compare yourself to a lion
   of the nations,
but^H you are like a monster^I in the seas.
You thrash about in your rivers,
churn up the waters with your feet,
and muddy the^J rivers.

---

^A31:3 Or *thick foliage*, also in vv. 10,14   ^B31:10 Syr, Vg; MT, LXX read *you*   ^C31:10 Lit *its heart*   ^D31:14 Or *the descendants of Adam*   ^E31:15 Or *I covered it with the underground deep*   ^F31:17 LXX, Syr read *offspring*   ^G31:17 Lit *arm*   ^H32:2 Or *'Lion of the nations, you are destroyed;*   ^I32:2 Or *crocodile*   ^J32:2 Lit *their*

Nebuchadnezzar's defeat of Hophra, who attempted to relieve Jerusalem in 588 BC (2Kg 24:7; Jr 37:5).

31:1–3 The **cedar** was a renowned ancient Near Eastern symbol of royalty and majesty. In the Bible it is frequently mentioned in texts describing the production of palaces and temples. The fall of **Assyria** forms the precedent and paradigm for the fall of Egypt. This fifth oracle against Egypt is dated to June 587 BC.

31:10–14 Because the tree representing the Pharaoh had become prominent (**towered high in stature**), it would be cut down (Is 2:6–21; 10:5–34).

31:18 The **trees** would die disgracefully as **uncircumcised** foreigners without a decent burial. This reality would be particularly poignant for Egyptian royalty because they built pyramids in the hopes of making themselves comfortable in the afterlife.

32:1–2 This sixth oracle against Egypt is dated to March 585 BC.

3 " 'This is what the Lord GOD says:
    I will spread my net over you
    with an assembly of many peoples,
    and they[A] will haul you up in my net.
4   I will abandon you on the land
    and throw you onto the open field.
    I will cause all the birds of the sky
    to settle on you
    and let the wild creatures
        of the entire earth
    eat their fill of you.
5   I will put your flesh on the mountains
    and fill the valleys with your carcass.
6   I will drench the land
    with the flow of your blood,
    even to the mountains;
    the ravines will be filled with your gore.

7   " 'When I snuff you out,
    I will cover the heavens
    and darken their stars.
    I will cover the sun with a cloud,
    and the moon will not give its light.
8   I will darken all the shining lights
    in the heavens over you,
    and will bring darkness on your land.
    This is the declaration
        of the Lord GOD.

9   " 'I will trouble the hearts
        of many peoples,
    when I bring about your destruction
    among the nations,
    in countries you have not known.
10 I will cause many peoples to be appalled
    at you,
    and their kings will shudder with fear
        because of you
    when I brandish my sword
        in front of them.
    On the day of your downfall
    each of them will tremble
    every moment for his life.

11 " 'For this is what the Lord GOD says:
    The sword of Babylon's king
    will come against you!
12 I will make your hordes fall
    by the swords of warriors,
    all of them ruthless men
    from the nations.

They will ravage Egypt's pride,
    and all its hordes will be destroyed.
13 I will slaughter all its cattle
    that are beside many waters.
    No human foot will churn them again,
    and no cattle hooves will disturb them.
14 Then I will let their waters settle
    and will make their rivers flow like oil.
    This is the declaration
        of the Lord GOD.
15 When I make the land of Egypt
        a desolation,
    so that it is emptied of everything in it,
    when I strike down all who live there,
    then they will know that I am the LORD.

16 " 'The daughters of the nations will chant
that lament. They will chant it over Egypt and
all its hordes. This is the declaration of the Lord
GOD.' "

Egypt in Sheol

17 In the twelfth year,[B] on the fifteenth day of
the month, the word of the LORD came to me:
18 "Son of man, wail over the hordes of Egypt
and bring Egypt and the daughters of mighty
nations down to the underworld,[C] to be with
those who descend to the Pit:
19   Who do you surpass in loveliness?
        Go down and be laid to rest
            with the uncircumcised!
20   They will fall among those slain
            by the sword.
        A sword is appointed!
        They drag her and all her hordes away.
21   Warrior leaders will speak
        from the middle of Sheol
        about him[D] and his allies:
        'They have come down;
        the uncircumcised lie
        slain by the sword.'

22 "Assyria is there with
        her whole assembly;
    her graves are all around her.
    All of them are slain, fallen
        by the sword.
23 Her graves are set in the deepest regions
        of the Pit,
    and her assembly is all around
        her burial place.

A32:3 LXX, Vg read / B32:17 LXX reads *year, in the first month,* C32:18 Lit *the lower parts of the earth,* also in v. 24
D32:21 Either Pharaoh or Egypt

32:3–5 The Lord will cast his **net** over Pharaoh, a method by which hunters captured crocodiles and lions (19:8).
32:6 The image of flowing **blood** recalls the plague of blood, the first plague in the exodus account (Ex 7:19–24).
32:7–8 The darkness in this verse recalls the exodus plague of darkness against Egypt (Ex 10:21–29) as well as the darkness that will accompany the day of the

Lord. On the day of the Lord the heavens will be darkened, and the **sun**, **moon**, and **stars** will fail to give **light** (Jl 2:1–2; 3:15; Zph 1:15).
32:17–18 This oracle, the last of the seven against Egypt, is probably to be dated two weeks after the sixth oracle (compare 32:1,17). But the textual problem of the specific lack of the month places it between April 586 BC and April 585 BC.

32:19–21 The phrase **the uncircumcised** is used ten times in chap. 32 (vv. 19,21,24–30,32) to emphasize that the death of the pharaoh will be a death of shame and defeat. In this oracle, Egypt was the climactic seventh nation that occupied the underworld (v. 18).
32:22–30 Here is a macabre roll call of other uncircumcised peoples in the Pit, felled by the sword: **Assyria**, **Elam**, **Meshech and**

All of them are slain, fallen
     by the sword —
those who once spread terror
     in the land of the living.

²⁴ "Elam is there
with all her hordes around her grave.
All of them are slain, fallen
     by the sword —
those who went down
     to the underworld uncircumcised,
who once spread their terror
     in the land of the living.
They bear their disgrace
     with those who descend to the Pit.
²⁵ Among the slain
they prepare a bed for Elam
     with all her hordes.
Her graves are all around her.
All of them are uncircumcised,
     slain by the sword,
although their terror was once spread
     in the land of the living.
They bear their disgrace
     with those who descend to the Pit.
They are placed among the slain.

²⁶ "Meshech and Tubal^A are there,
     with all their hordes.
Their graves are all around them.
All of them are uncircumcised,
     slain by the sword,
although their terror was once spread
     in the land of the living.
²⁷ They do not lie down
with the fallen warriors
     of the uncircumcised,^B
who went down to Sheol
     with their weapons of war,
whose swords were placed
     under their heads^C
and their shields^D
     rested on their bones,
although the terror of these warriors
     was once in the land of the living.
²⁸ But you will be shattered
and will lie down
     among the uncircumcised,
with those slain by the sword.

²⁹ "Edom is there, her kings and all
     her princes,
who, despite their strength,
     have been placed
among those slain by the sword.
They lie down
     with the uncircumcised,
with those who descend to the Pit.
³⁰ All the leaders of the north
and all the Sidonians are there.
They went down in shame
     with the slain,
despite the terror
     their strength inspired.
They lie down uncircumcised
with those slain by the sword.
They bear their disgrace
with those who descend to the Pit.

³¹ "Pharaoh will see them
and be comforted over all his hordes —
Pharaoh and his whole army,
     slain by the sword."
     This is the declaration
         of the Lord God.
³² "For I will spread my^E terror
     in the land of the living,
so Pharaoh and all his hordes
will be laid to rest
     among the uncircumcised,
with those slain by the sword."
     This is the declaration
         of the Lord God.

Ezekiel as Israel's Watchman

33 The word of the Lord came to me: ² "Son of man, speak to your people and tell them, 'Suppose I bring the sword against a land, and the people of that land select a man from among them, appointing him as their watchman. ³ And suppose he sees the sword coming against the land and blows his ram's horn to warn the people. ⁴ Then, if anyone hears the sound of the ram's horn but ignores the warning, and the sword comes and takes him away, his death will be his own fault.^F ⁵ Since he heard the sound of the ram's horn but ignored the warning, his death is his own fault.^G If he had taken warning, he would have saved

---

^A32:26 Lit *Meshech-tubal*   ^B32:27 LXX reads *of antiquity*   ^C32:27 Or *Do they not . . . heads?*   ^D32:27 Emended; MT reads *iniquities*   ^E32:32 Alt Hb tradition, LXX, Syr read *his*   ^F33:4 Lit *his blood will be on his head*   ^G33:5 Lit *his blood will be on him*

Tubal, Edom, and **all the leaders of the north and all the Sidonians**.
32:26 Meshech and Tubal (see 27:13) were probably located on the northern border of modern Turkey. They are the allies of Gog in chaps. 38–39.
33:1–2 This announcement of a new oracle (**Son of man, speak to your people**) begins a transitional section in the book, bridging the oracles about the nations to prophecies of consolation that close the book.

33:2 In ancient times every major town had a **watchman** stationed at a high point, either at the city gate (2Sm 18:24) or on a lookout tower (2Kg 9:17). The watchman was not responsible for the fate of the people in the city if he warned them of pending danger. Conversely, he was responsible if he failed to raise the alarm. The watchman is used here as a prophetic agent calling for repentance. The metaphor of the lookout was first applied to Ezekiel in a private message at the start of his career. The prophet's role as sentinel

explains how the intention behind Ezekiel's doom prophecy was not death but life—a warning call to repentance.
33:3 The **ram's horn** was used to **warn the people** of approaching danger (Neh 4:18–20; Jr 4:19; Am 3:6; 1Co 14:8) as well as to announce the beginnings of religious celebrations (Day of Atonement, Lv 25:9; New Moon festival, Ps 81:3).
33:4–5 It is the responsibility of those who hear the **warning** to act.

his life. **⁶** However, suppose the watchman sees the sword coming but doesn't blow the ram's horn, so that the people aren't warned, and the sword comes and takes away their lives. Then they have been taken away because of their iniquity, but I will hold the watchman accountable for their blood.'

⁷ "As for you, son of man, I have made you a watchman for the house of Israel. When you hear a word from my mouth, give them a warning from me. **⁸** If I say to the wicked, 'Wicked one, you will surely die,' but you do not speak out to warn him about his way, that wicked person will die for his iniquity, yet I will hold you responsible for his blood. **⁹** But if you warn a wicked person to turn from his way and he doesn't turn from it, he will die for his iniquity, but you will have rescued yourself.

¹⁰ "Now as for you, son of man, say to the house of Israel, 'You have said this: "Our transgressions and our sins are heavy on us, and we are wasting away because of them! How then can we survive?" ' **¹¹** Tell them, 'As I live — this is the declaration of the Lord God — I take no pleasure in the death of the wicked, but rather that the wicked person should turn from his way and live. Repent, repent of your evil ways! Why will you die, house of Israel?'

¹² "Now, son of man, say to your people, 'The righteousness of the righteous person will not save him on the day of his transgression; neither will the wickedness of the wicked person cause him to stumble on the day he turns from his wickedness. The righteous person won't be able to survive by his righteousness on the day he sins. **¹³** When I tell the righteous person that he will surely live, but he trusts in his righteousness and acts unjustly, then none of his righteousness will be remembered, and he will die because of the injustice he has committed.

¹⁴ " 'So when I tell the wicked person, "You will surely die," but he repents of his sin and does what is just and right — **¹⁵** he returns collateral, makes restitution for what he has stolen, and walks in the statutes of life without committing injustice — he will certainly live;

he will not die. **¹⁶** None of the sins he committed will be held^A against him. He has done what is just and right; he will certainly live.

¹⁷ " 'But your people say, "The Lord's way isn't fair," even though it is their own way that isn't fair. **¹⁸** When a righteous person turns from his righteousness and commits injustice, he will die for it. **¹⁹** But if a wicked person turns from his wickedness and does what is just and right, he will live because of it. **²⁰** Yet you say, "The Lord's way isn't fair." I will judge each of you according to his ways, house of Israel.' "

The News of Jerusalem's Fall

²¹ In the twelfth year of our exile, in the tenth month, on the fifth day of the month, a fugitive from Jerusalem came to me and reported, "The city has been taken!" **²²** Now the hand of the Lord had been on me the evening before the fugitive arrived, and he opened my mouth before the man came to me in the morning. So my mouth was opened and I was no longer mute.

Israel's Continued Rebellion

²³ Then the word of the Lord came to me: **²⁴** "Son of man, those who live in the^B ruins in the land of Israel are saying, 'Abraham was only one person, yet he received possession of the land. But we are many; surely the land has been given to us as a possession.' **²⁵** Therefore say to them, 'This is what the Lord God says: You eat meat with blood in it, you look to your idols, and you shed blood. Should you then receive possession of the land? **²⁶** You have relied on your swords, you have committed detestable acts, and each of you has defiled his neighbor's wife. Should you then receive possession of the land?'

²⁷ "Tell them this: 'This is what the Lord God says: As surely as I live, those who are in the ruins will fall by the sword, those in the open field I have given to wild animals to be devoured, and those in the strongholds and caves will die by plague. **²⁸** I will make the land a desolate waste, and its proud strength will come to an end. The mountains of Israel will become

---

^A **33:16** Lit *remembered*   ^B **33:24** Lit *these*

33:6 Given its essential role in biological systems, **blood** is synonymous with life (see Gn 9:5; 42:22).
33:10–20 This section in many ways paraphrases sections of 18:21–32. This is the first time the exiles expressed a consciousness of their **sins**. Previously they had placed the blame for their predicaments on their fathers (18:2) and even God (18:19,25).
33:12 This section (vv. 12–20) addresses the same subject as 18:21–29. Each person, whether **righteous** or **wicked**, has a choice to live faithfully each day.
33:15 This description of the obedient life answers the question of v. 10: "How then can we survive?"
33:21–22 The six messages in 33:21–39:29 are dated in this verse. The date was January 8,

585 BC. The time it took for the bearer of the news to reach Ezekiel was five to six months. The siege of Jerusalem lasted two years and seven months (2Kg 25:8). Now that the prophet had been informed of Jerusalem's fall, he would address the restoration of Israel (Ezk 33:21–39:29) and the temple (chaps. 40–48). Many of the prophecies of restoration reverse the earlier images of devastation and ruin. The fall of Jerusalem was a watershed, fulfilling the prophetic judgments; now it was time for a message of hope and promise. This marks a turning point in the prophet's relation to his listeners. Verse 22 also fulfills the Lord's word to Ezekiel in 3:26–27 and 24:27. Ezekiel's enforced silence had lasted for over a decade, during which he had served as a "sign" to his people (24:27).

33:23–24 This saying (**Abraham was only one person**) is based on Gn 15, in which Abraham, still childless, was promised innumerable descendants and possession of the land. Those who remained behind were repeating their claim to the land.
33:25–26 The list of sins in these verses is similar to basic prohibitions for Gentile believers in Ac 15:29. The list is also similar to OT laws for strangers.
33:27–28 The dangers mentioned in these verses (**sword . . . wild animals . . . plague**) are also typical of Mosaic covenant punishment predictions (Lv 26:22; Dt 32:24; cp. 2Kg 17:25–26). Notice the threefold threat in Ezk 5:12; 7:15; 12:16 and the fourfold threat in 14:12–21. Ezekiel's strategy was deliberate. Those **who are in the ruins**

desolate, with no one passing through. ²⁹ They will know that I am the LORD when I make the land a desolate waste because of all the detestable acts they have committed.'

³⁰ "As for you, son of man, your people are talking about you near the city walls and in the doorways of their houses. One person speaks to another, each saying to his brother, 'Come and hear what the message is that comes from the LORD!' ³¹ So my people come to you in crowds,^A sit in front of you, and hear your words, but they don't obey them. Their mouths go on passionately, but their hearts pursue dishonest profit. ³² Yes, to them you are like a singer of passionate songs who has a beautiful voice and plays skillfully on an instrument. They hear your words, but they don't obey them. ³³ Yet when all this comes true — and it definitely will — then they will know that a prophet has been among them."

The Shepherds and God's Flock

34 The word of the LORD came to me: ² "Son of man, prophesy against the shepherds of Israel. Prophesy, and say to them, 'This is what the Lord GOD says to the shepherds: Woe to the shepherds of Israel, who have been feeding themselves! Shouldn't the shepherds feed their flock? ³ You eat the fat, wear the wool, and butcher the fattened animals, but you do not tend the flock. ⁴ You have not strengthened the weak, healed the sick, bandaged the injured, brought back the strays, or sought the lost. Instead, you have ruled them with violence and cruelty. ⁵ They were scattered for lack of a shepherd; they became food for all the wild animals when they were scattered. ⁶ My flock went astray on all the mountains and every high hill. My flock was scattered over the whole face of the earth, and there was no one searching or seeking for them.

⁷ " 'Therefore, you shepherds, hear the word of the LORD. ⁸ As I live — this is the declaration of the Lord GOD — because my flock, lacking a shepherd, has become prey and food for every wild animal, and because my shepherds do not search for my flock, and because the shepherds feed themselves rather than my flock, ⁹ therefore, you shepherds, hear the word of the LORD!

¹⁰ " 'This is what the Lord GOD says: Look, I am against the shepherds. I will demand my flock from them^B and prevent them from shepherding the flock. The shepherds will no longer feed themselves, for I will rescue my flock from their mouths so that they will not be food for them.

¹¹ " 'For this is what the Lord GOD says: See, I myself will search for my flock and look for them. ¹² As a shepherd looks for his sheep on the day he is among his scattered flock, so I will look for my flock. I will rescue them from all the places where they have been scattered on a day of clouds and total darkness. ¹³ I will bring them out from the peoples, gather them from the countries, and bring them to their own soil. I will shepherd them on the mountains of Israel, in the ravines, and in all the inhabited places of the land. ¹⁴ I will tend them in good pasture, and their grazing place will be on Israel's lofty mountains. There they will lie down in a good grazing place; they will feed in rich pasture on the mountains of Israel. ¹⁵ I will tend my flock and let them lie down. This is the declaration of the Lord GOD. ¹⁶ I will seek the lost, bring back the strays, bandage the injured, and strengthen the weak, but I will destroy^C the fat and the strong. I will shepherd them with justice.

¹⁷ " 'As for you, my flock, the Lord GOD says this: Look, I am going to judge between one sheep and another, between the rams and goats. ¹⁸ Isn't it enough for you to feed on the

---

^A 33:31 Lit you like the coming of a people   ^B 34:10 Lit their hand   ^C 34:16 Some Hb mss, LXX, Syr, Vg read watch over

---

33:29 Detestable acts denotes sexual violations of the Holiness Code, particularly Lv 18:26–30 (Ezk 5:17; 14:21). Because they disobeyed the Mosaic covenant stipulations, the Israelites failed to receive the Abrahamic covenant blessings, one of which was the blessing of occupying the promised land (Ex 20:4–5,13–14; Lv 17:10–14; 18:6; 19:26).

34:1 Ezekiel 34 is a self-contained literary unit. It begins with the introductory phrase **the word of the LORD came to me** and concludes with the recognition formula (vv. 30–31). The passage is similar to Jr 23:1–6.

34:2–3 The **shepherds of Israel** is a figurative expression referring to political leaders, perhaps primarily the kings. Kings and other leaders were commonly called "shepherds" (2Sm 7:7; Ps 78:70–72; Is 44:28; 63:11; Jr 10:21; 23:1–6; 25:34–38; Mc 5:4–5; Zch 11:4–17).

are very unlike faithful Abraham, who received God's promise of land but was also enjoined to walk before God and be blameless (Gn 17:1–8).

34:4 This characteristic feature of a shepherd (**sought the lost**) is mentioned in many biblical texts (Jr 50:6; Mt 18:12–14; Lk 15:4; 19:10). The word **cruelty** is the same word used to compare the oppression of the taskmasters who ruled brutally over the Israelites during their bondage in Egypt (Ex 1:13–14). This type of action was prohibited in the Mosaic law (Lv 25:43,46). A member of the community of Israel was not to be treated this way.

34:5 The verb **scattered** was often used by Ezekiel to describe Israel's exile and dispersion (11:16–17; 12:15; 20:23,34,41; 22:15; 28:25).

34:6 This dispersion may allude to the Assyrian and Babylonian captivities, which **scattered** Israel and Judah among the nations.

34:11 The verb **look for** is used in Leviticus to refer to the physical examination of a leper (Lv 13:36). In passages that address the offering of sacrifices, the verb describes the examination of a prospective sacrificial animal (Lv 27:33).

34:12 While most exiles were sent to Babylon, this was not the only foreign country that received displaced Israelites (Jr 43:1–7).

34:13–15 This promise of restoration (**I will bring them ... to their own soil**) is mentioned in 11:17 and repeated in 20:34,41–42; 28:25. The restoration of the nation is especially emphasized in Ezk 38–39 (see also 36:24; 37:21). These three phrases represent and reflect the exodus from Egypt. Hence, God's rescuing of Israel from Babylon and restoring her to Canaan follows the model of the formative saving event in the OT—the exodus from Egypt.

34:16 God is the good shepherd (Ps 23; Is 40:11; Jr 23:3; 31:10; Mc 2:12; 4:6–8) who will gather the dispersed flock. Concern for social **justice** was a common topic for Ezekiel and other prophets (Is 3:13–15; 5:8; Am 5:12; 6:1–7; Mc 2:1–5). God will execute judgment against **the fat and the strong**, greedy sheep who trample good pasture and muddy clear waters, gorging themselves while depriving the needy of life's essential resources.

good pasture? Must you also trample the rest of the pasture with your feet? Or isn't it enough that you drink the clear water? Must you also muddy the rest with your feet? **19** Yet my flock has to feed on what your feet have trampled, and drink what your feet have muddied.

20 " 'Therefore, this is what the Lord GOD says to them: See, I myself will judge between the fat sheep and the lean sheep. **21** Since you have pushed with flank and shoulder and butted all the weak ones with your horns until you scattered them all over, **22** I will save my flock. They will no longer be prey, and I will judge between one sheep and another. **23** I will establish over them one shepherd, my servant David, and he will shepherd them. He will tend them himself and will be their shepherd. **24** I, the LORD, will be their God, and my servant David will be a prince among them. I, the LORD, have spoken.

25 " 'I will make a covenant of peace with them and eliminate dangerous creatures from the land, so that they may live securely in the wilderness and sleep in the forest. **26** I will make them and the area around my hill a blessing: I will send down showers in their season; they will be showers of blessing. **27** The trees of the field will yield their fruit, and the land will yield its produce; my flock will be secure in their land. They will know that I am the LORD when I break the bars of their yoke and rescue them from the power of those who enslave them. **28** They will no longer be prey for the nations, and the wild creatures of the earth will not consume them. They will live securely, and no one will frighten them. **29** I will establish for them a place renowned for its agriculture,^A and they will no longer be victims of famine in the land. They will no longer endure the insults of the nations. **30** Then they will know that I, the

LORD their God, am with them, and that they, the house of Israel, are my people. This is the declaration of the Lord GOD. **31** You are my flock, the human flock of my pasture, and I am your God. This is the declaration of the Lord GOD.' "

A Prophecy against Edom

35 The word of the LORD came to me: **2** "Son of man, face Mount Seir and prophesy against it. **3** Say to it, 'This is what the Lord GOD says:

Look! I am against you, Mount Seir.
I will stretch out my hand against you
    and make you a desolate waste.
4 I will turn your cities into ruins,
    and you will become a desolation.
Then you will know that I am the LORD.

5 " 'Because you maintained a perpetual hatred and gave the Israelites over to the power of the sword in the time of their disaster, the time of final punishment, **6** therefore, as I live — this is the declaration of the Lord GOD — I will destine you for bloodshed, and it will pursue you. Since you did not hate bloodshed, it will pursue you. **7** I will make Mount Seir a desolate waste and will cut off from it those who come and go. **8** I will fill its mountains with the slain; those slain by the sword will fall on your hills, in your valleys, and in all your ravines. **9** I will make you a perpetual desolation; your cities will not be inhabited. Then you will know that I am the LORD.

10 " 'Because you said, "These two nations and two lands will be mine, and we will possess them" — though the LORD was there — **11** therefore, as I live — this is the declaration of the Lord GOD — I will treat you according to the anger and jealousy you showed in your

---

^A **34:29** LXX, Syr read a *plant of peace*

34:23–24 In addition to God becoming the **shepherd** for Israel, he also promised to appoint a ruler, the Messiah, from the line of **David** (see 2Sm 7:12–14a; Ps 89:4,20,29). Thus Yahweh would be Israel's God; the Messiah, called **my servant David**, would be Israel's ruler on earth after he restored Israel to her land. This covenant was ultimately fulfilled in the person of Jesus, the Messiah.
34:25 This covenant should be equated with the new covenant relationship, which will provide peace (Nm 25:12; Jos 9:15; 10:1; Pss 29:11; 85:8; Is 54:10). The **covenant of peace** looks forward to the blessings Israel will experience in the millennium.
34:26 In Israel, autumn rains signaled the beginning of the rainy season, and spring rains the end (Jr 5:24). **Blessing** is a term that occurs frequently in the creation account, and this depends on the work of the Creator.
34:27 Most occurrences of **yoke** in the Bible are figurative, as in Ezk 34:27, which represents foreign domination (Dt 28:48; Jr 27:8–12).
34:28 Ezekiel's idyllic picture of the Messianic Age as a time of universal peace, involving even the animal world, recalls Is 11:6–9 and

Hs 2:18–23. The doom prophecies of Ezk 1–24 drew on the curses of the covenant documents (particularly Lv 26), and now the restoration visions draw on the language of blessings for covenant obedience (especially those of Lv 26) and present them as unconditional prophecies of future bliss.
34:29 Agricultural bounty is a standard way of describing the benefits of the restoration age (Dt 30:9; Am 9:13).
35:1–3 Mount Seir was the central mountain of the Edomite nation and thus was synonymous with the country of Edom itself (Gn 32:3). In 126 BC Edom was subjugated by John Hyrcanus the Hasmonean. He compelled the Edomites to become Jews (1Macc 5:3,65). King Herod, who sought desperately to kill Jesus as a baby, was an Idumean, or Edomite. Mount Seir is used in this oracle as a foil for "the mountains of Israel" in Ezk 36. Most likely Edom was mentioned here to represent the judgment that God would inflict on all nations who opposed Israel. For Ezekiel's other oracle against Edom, see 25:12–14.
35:4 This curse (**I will turn your cities into ruins**) echoes the covenant curse against Israel for its continual disobedience (Lv 26:31).

35:5 The bitter relations between Israel and Edom began in the womb of Rebekah (Gn 25:22–23) and continued with Jacob's deception of Isaac for Esau's blessing (Gn 27). The phrase **perpetual hatred** occurs elsewhere in the Bible only in 25:15 in reference to the actions of the Philistines. "Hatred" here refers to the hostility between Jacob and Esau, as their personal rivalry (Gn 27:41) spilled over into a national conflict (Nm 20:14–21; 2Sm 8:13–14). When Nebuchadnezzar leveled Jerusalem, the Edomites stood by clapping their hands with joy at this **disaster** (Ps 137; Lm 4:21; Jl 3:19; Ob 1–14; Mal 1:2–5).
35:6 Twice it is stated in this verse that blood will **pursue** the Edomites. This is retribution in kind, as the punishment is commensurate with the crime (Ps 109:17; Mt 7:2; 26:52). "Disaster," "blood," and "Edom" sound similar in Hebrew and are thus interrelated in this passage.
35:7–9 Edom would not only be destroyed but would be a **perpetual desolation**.
35:10–13 I will treat you according to indicates that Edom's punishment would be commensurate with her crime.

hatred of them. I will make myself known among them[A] when I judge you. [12] Then you will know that I, the Lord, have heard all the blasphemies you uttered against the mountains of Israel, saying, "They are desolate. They have been given to us to devour!" [13] You boasted against me with your mouth, and spoke many words against me. I heard it myself!

[14] " 'This is what the Lord God says: While the whole world rejoices, I will make you a desolation. [15] Just as you rejoiced over the inheritance of the house of Israel because it became a desolation, I will deal the same way with you: you will become a desolation, Mount Seir, and so will all Edom in its entirety. Then they will know that I am the Lord.'

Restoration of Israel's Mountains

36 "Son of man, prophesy to the mountains of Israel and say, 'Mountains of Israel, hear the word of the Lord. [2] This is what the Lord God says: Because the enemy has said about you, "Aha! The ancient heights have become our possession,"' [3] therefore, prophesy and say, 'This is what the Lord God says: Because they have made you desolate and have trampled you from every side, so that you became a possession for the rest of the nations and an object of people's gossip and slander, [4] therefore, mountains of Israel, hear the word of the Lord God. This is what the Lord God says to the mountains and hills, to the ravines and valleys, to the desolate ruins and abandoned cities, which have become plunder and a mockery to the rest of the nations all around:

[5] " 'This is what the Lord God says: Certainly in my burning zeal I speak against the rest of the nations and all of Edom, who took[B] my land as their own possession with wholehearted rejoicing and utter contempt so that

its pastureland became[C] plunder. [6] Therefore, prophesy concerning Israel's land, and say to the mountains and hills, to the ravines and valleys: This is what the Lord God says: Look, I speak in my burning zeal because you have endured the insults of the nations. [7] Therefore, this is what the Lord God says: I swear[D] that the nations all around you will endure their own insults.

[8] " 'You, mountains of Israel, will produce your branches and bear your fruit for my people Israel, since their arrival is near. [9] Look! I am on your side; I will turn toward you, and you will be tilled and sown. [10] I will fill you with people, with the whole house of Israel in its entirety. The cities will be inhabited and the ruins rebuilt. [11] I will fill you with people and animals, and they will increase and be fruitful. I will make you inhabited as you once were and make you better off than you were before. Then you will know that I am the Lord. [12] I will cause people, my people Israel, to walk on you; they will possess you, and you will be their inheritance. You will no longer deprive them of their children.

[13] " 'This is what the Lord God says: Because some are saying to you, "You devour people and deprive your nation of children," [14] therefore, you will no longer devour people and deprive your nation of children.[E] This is the declaration of the Lord God. [15] I will no longer allow the insults of the nations to be heard against you, and you will not have to endure the reproach of the peoples anymore; you will no longer cause your nation to stumble.[F] This is the declaration of the Lord God.' "

Restoration of Israel's People

[16] The word of the Lord came to me: [17] "Son of man, while the house of Israel lived in their

---

[A]35:11 LXX reads *you*　[B]36:5 Lit *gave*　[C]36:5 Or *contempt, to empty it of*; Hb obscure　[D]36:7 Lit *lift up my hand*　[E]36:14 Alt Hb tradition reads *and cause your nation to stumble*　[F]36:15 Some Hb mss, Tg read *no longer bereave your nation of children*

35:14–15 As Edom **rejoiced** over Judah's fall (Ob 12), so the world would later rejoice over Edom's fall.

36:1 Chapter 36 is set in antithesis to chap. 35. When God intervenes on Israel's behalf, the "mountains" of Israel's enemies will be judged (35:1–3,8) but the **mountains of Israel** will be blessed. The terrain of Israel was an elevated region between the Jordan Valley and the Mediterranean Sea coast characterized by mountainous areas (Dt 11:11). Thus, this reference to the "mountains of Israel" should be understood as a reference to the entire nation.

36:2–3 That Israel would become the **object** of ridicule had been foretold in Dt 28:37 and reiterated in Jr 24:9.

36:4–5 The phrase **burning zeal** occurs elsewhere only in v. 6. Formerly God's passion was kindled by Israel's rebellion against him; now it flares against the arrogant Gentiles. **Edom** is once again pictured as representative of all nations that sought to harm Israel (Is 34; 63:1–6). God's personal identification

with the land of Israel is demonstrated by the phrase **my land** (see Lv 25:23).

36:6 The word translated "land" is not the normal term used in the expression **Israel's land**. This term could be rendered "soil" in this context. It would be appropriate in this prophecy of renewal of the land's fertility (Gn 4:2; Pr 12:11).

36:7 The phrase **I swear** means literally "with uplifted hand." This gesture accompanied the taking of an oath (20:5,15,23; 47:14).

36:8 In the OT, agricultural abundance was seen as a blessing from God (Dt 30:9) and a preview of the blessings of the coming Messianic Age. This oracle reverses the judgments on the **mountains of Israel** in Ezk 6.

36:9 The phrase **I will turn toward you** also occurs in Lv 26:9 in the context of the covenant blessings that would accompany obedience to the Mosaic law. Thus the renewed abundance of fruitfulness in the land would coincide with the blessings that accompanied obedience to the Mosaic law (Lv 26:1–13).

36:10 The phrase **whole house of Israel** refers to the twelve tribes that had originally made up the nation, not just Judah alone. As in 37:15–23, Ezekiel was speaking of the restoration of all Israel.

36:11 The references to increased fertility and population growth (**increase and be fruitful**) refer back to the creation account where God's blessing upon animals (Gn 1:22) and humans (Gn 1:28) resulted in them filling the earth (Gn 9:1,7).

36:12 Walking through land was a way to claim ownership (Gn 13:17; Jos 24:3; 1Kg 21:16). This promise reverses the desolation predicted in Ezk 6:14.

36:13–15 The threat of the land "devouring" (Hb *klt*) inhabitants not only recalls 5:13–17 but also echoes, for a second time, the statements of the faithless spies who reported about the land of Canaan.

36:16–17 Since under Jewish law a woman's monthly **menstrual** period rendered her unclean (Lv 15:19–30; 18:19), God categorized the conduct of Israel as uncleanness or

land, they defiled it with their conduct and actions. Their behavior before me was like menstrual impurity. ¹⁸ So I poured out my wrath on them because of the blood they had shed on the land, and because they had defiled it with their idols. ¹⁹ I dispersed them among the nations, and they were scattered among the countries. I judged them according to their conduct and actions. ²⁰ When they came to the nations where they went, they profaned my holy name, because it was said about them, 'These are the people of the LORD, yet they had to leave his land in exile.' ²¹ Then I had concern for my holy name, which the house of Israel profaned among the nations where they went.

²² "Therefore, say to the house of Israel, 'This is what the Lord GOD says: It is not for your sake that I will act, house of Israel, but for my holy name, which you profaned among the nations where you went. ²³ I will honor the holiness of my great name, which has been profaned among the nations — the name you have profaned among them. The nations will know that I am the LORD — this is the declaration of the Lord GOD — when I demonstrate my holiness through you in their sight.

²⁴ "'For I will take you from the nations and gather you from all the countries, and will bring you into your own land. ²⁵ I will also sprinkle clean water on you, and you will be clean. I will cleanse you from all your impurities and all your idols. ²⁶ I will give you a new heart and put a new spirit within you; I will remove your heart of stone^A and give you a heart of flesh. ²⁷ I will place my Spirit within you and

cause you to follow my statutes and carefully observe my ordinances. ²⁸ You will live in the land that I gave your ancestors; you will be my people, and I will be your God. ²⁹ I will save you from all your uncleanness. I will summon the grain and make it plentiful, and I will not bring famine on you. ³⁰ I will also make the fruit of the trees and the produce of the field plentiful, so that you will no longer experience reproach among the nations on account of famine.

³¹ "'You will remember your evil ways and your deeds that were not good, and you will loathe yourselves for your iniquities and detestable practices. ³² It is not for your sake that I will act — this is the declaration of the Lord GOD — let this be known to you. Be ashamed and humiliated because of your ways, house of Israel!

³³ "This is what the Lord GOD says: On the day I cleanse you from all your iniquities, I will cause the cities to be inhabited, and the ruins will be rebuilt. ³⁴ The desolate land will be cultivated instead of lying desolate in the sight of everyone who passes by. ³⁵ They will say, "This land that was desolate has become like the garden of Eden. The cities that were once ruined, desolate, and demolished are now fortified and inhabited." ³⁶ Then the nations that remain around you will know that I, the LORD, have rebuilt what was demolished and have replanted what was desolate. I, the LORD, have spoken and I will do it.

³⁷ "This is what the Lord GOD says: I will respond to the house of Israel and do this for them: I will multiply them in number like a

---

^A 36:26 Lit stone from your flesh

---

defilement. A woman in this condition was not eligible to take part in religious activities. Her **impurity** lasted seven days, after which she was considered clean and fit to return to the house of the Lord.
36:18 The dual offenses of **blood they had shed on the land** and idolatry summarize Israel's social injustices and idolatrous practices (22:3). The people have sinned against God and their fellow man—the two categories of sin outlined in the Ten Commandments.
36:19 To be faithful and loyal, God had no choice but to bring on his people the curses of the covenant they had broken—namely, scattering them **among the nations** (see Dt 29:22–28).
36:20–21 Though Yahweh expelled his people from the promised land for the purpose of chastening and eventually restoring them, their exile reflected unfavorably upon God among foreign nations. The ancients believed that if a people were forced from their land, it was a sign that their god was not strong enough to protect and care for them (2Kg 18:32–35; 19:10–12). Thus the Hebrew exile was taken as a sign that Israel's God was weaker than the gods of the nations that defeated Jerusalem. The nations **profaned** God's **holy name**, meaning they defamed his essence, character, and reputation.
36:22 In chap. 20 the expression **but for my holy name** states the reason for

the withholding of divine punishment (20:9,14,22). Here it is the reason for divine restoration.
36:23 The ultimate purpose of God's plans for Israel was that Israel and the whole world would **know** the true God.
36:24–25 This figurative language is based on water purification practices when the priest threw water on persons or objects to **cleanse** them of impurity (Nm 19:13,20). The first order of business for the Israelites when they return to their homeland will be to pay attention to their spiritual condition (Ps 119:9; Is 4:4; Zch 13:1; Heb 10:22). The Lord himself will **sprinkle** his people with **clean water**.
36:26 The statement **I will give you a new heart and put a new spirit within you** reflects the teaching of Dt 30:6–8—that the Lord will circumcise the hearts of his people so they may live in obedience. This radical new creation (Ezk 11:19; 18:31; Jr 31:31–34) was necessary to break the people's bondage to the cycle of sin and retribution emphasized in Ezk 20.
36:27 More than any other prophet, Ezekiel emphasizes the Holy Spirit's role in regeneration. When God places his **Spirit** in his people, they will be able to follow his decrees and keep his laws. Thus, the people will be transformed, never again to profane God's holy name.
36:28 This contains the covenant formula that first appears in Ex 6:7. (Also see Lv 26:12; Jr 7:23; 11:4; 30:22.)

36:29–30 What is described in this passage (**you will no longer experience reproach among the nations**) does not refer to the return to Canaan under Zerubbabel, Ezra, and Nehemiah. Rather, it looks to a final and complete restoration under the Messiah in the end times.
36:31–32 God's unmerited grace causes sinners to **loathe** their ways, leading to reflection and repentance.
36:33–36 In this prophecy for the land of Israel, God will restore the land to a "better than original" state. It will **become like the garden of Eden**, the ultimate symbol of fertility and fruitfulness (28:13; 31:9; cp. Is 51:3; Jl 2:3). The replenishing of the land so that it resembles the garden of Eden (Gn 2–3) will reveal God to the nations. The mention of this idyllic state suggests a future fulfillment beyond that which occurred in the return from Babylon under the leadership of Zerubbabel, Ezra, and Nehemiah. These conditions will not be realized until the Messianic Age. Supernatural fertility of the land is one of the characteristics of the messianic kingdom (Is 35:1–2; 55:13; Ezk 47:1–12; Zch 8:12).
36:37–38 The number of people is compared to the numerous **sheep** that passed through Jerusalem at the time of the appointed festivals (Lv 23). The phrase **a flock of people** conveys the idea of abundance (1Kg 8:63; 1Ch 29:21; 2Ch 35:7).

flock.[A] [38] So the ruined cities will be filled with a flock of people, just as Jerusalem is filled with a flock of sheep for sacrifice[B] during its appointed festivals. Then they will know that I am the LORD.'"

The Valley of Dry Bones

37 The hand of the LORD was on me, and he brought me out by his Spirit and set me down in the middle of the valley; it was full of bones. [2] He led me all around them. There were a great many of them on the surface of the valley, and they were very dry. [3] Then he said to me, "Son of man, can these bones live?" I replied, "Lord GOD, only you know." [4] He said to me, "Prophesy concerning these bones and say to them: Dry bones, hear the word of the LORD! [5] This is what the Lord GOD says to these bones: I will cause breath to enter you, and you will live. [6] I will put tendons on you, make flesh grow on you, and cover you with skin. I will put breath in you so that you come to life. Then you will know that I am the LORD."

[7] So I prophesied as I had been commanded. While I was prophesying, there was a noise, a rattling sound, and the bones came together, bone to bone. [8] As I looked, tendons appeared on them, flesh grew, and skin covered them, but there was no breath in them. [9] He said to me, "Prophesy to the breath,[C] prophesy, son of man. Say to it: This is what the Lord GOD says: Breath, come from the four winds and breathe into these slain so that they may live!" [10] So I prophesied as he commanded me; the breath entered them, and they came to life and stood on their feet, a vast army.

[11] Then he said to me, "Son of man, these bones are the whole house of Israel. Look how they say, 'Our bones are dried up, and our hope has perished; we are cut off.' [12] Therefore,

prophesy and say to them, 'This is what the Lord GOD says: I am going to open your graves and bring you up from them, my people, and lead you into the land of Israel. [13] You will know that I am the LORD, my people, when I open your graves and bring you up from them. [14] I will put my Spirit in you, and you will live, and I will settle you in your own land. Then you will know that I am the LORD. I have spoken, and I will do it. This is the declaration of the LORD.'"

The Reunification of Israel

[15] The word of the LORD came to me: [16] "Son of man, take a single stick and write on it: Belonging to Judah and the Israelites associated with him. Then take another stick and write on it: Belonging to Joseph — the stick of Ephraim — and all the house of Israel associated with him. [17] Then join them together into a single stick so that they become one in your hand. [18] When your people ask you, 'Won't you explain to us what you mean by these things?' — [19] tell them, 'This is what the Lord GOD says: I am going to take the stick of Joseph, which is in the hand of Ephraim, and the tribes of Israel associated with him, and put them together with the stick of Judah. I will make them into a single stick so that they become one in my hand.' [20] "When the sticks you have written on are in your hand and in full view of the people, [21] tell them, 'This is what the Lord GOD says: I am going to take the Israelites out of the nations where they have gone. I will gather them from all around and bring them into their own land. [22] I will make them one nation in the land, on the mountains of Israel, and one king will rule over all of them. They will no longer be two nations and will no longer be divided into two kingdoms. [23] They will not defile themselves anymore with their idols, their abhorrent things, and all their transgressions. I will save

---

[A]36:37 Lit *flock of people*   [B]36:38 Lit *as the consecrated flock, as the flock of Jerusalem*   [C]37:9 Or *wind*, or *spirit*, also in v. 10

37:1 The introductory phrase **the hand of the LORD was on me** indicates a new subject. The hand is often used metaphorically for power in Scripture. The arrival of the hand of the Lord upon the prophet speaks of the overwhelming force with which the prophet was seized by God. On the "hand of the LORD" coming upon Ezekiel to overpower him; see 1:3; 3:14; 8:1; 40:1. The work of the Spirit in transporting Ezekiel to a different location occurs in 3:14; 8:3; 11:1,24; 43:5, indicating the beginning of a visionary revelation. As an Israelite trained in the priesthood, Ezekiel knew the importance of treating a human corpse properly. This vast array of skeletons left unburied (**it was full of bones**) reminded Ezekiel of the execution of the judgment curses for disobedience (Dt 28:26).
37:2 Bones that were **very dry** indicated that death had taken place long ago. Hence, life was obviously beyond resuscitation (1Kg 17:17–24; 2Kg 4:18–37; but see 2Kg 13:21).
37:3 Ezekiel was aware that God had the power to raise people from the dead (1Kg

17:17–24; 2Kg 4:18–37; Is 26:19; Dn 12:1–2). But these bones were dry, meaning that the flesh had decayed. This seemed to make resuscitation impossible.
37:7–9 The **four winds** probably indicate the full power of the entering **breath** since the winds come from every direction.
37:11 **These bones** symbolize the restoration of the **whole house of Israel** to its own land.
37:12–13 Continuing his explanation of the vision, God added a new dimension to the resurrection of the dry bones. He declared that he would **open the graves** of his people and take them from their place of burial, demonstrating the reality of national rebirth.
37:14 I will settle you in your own land picks up the theme from the exodus and conquest. It also explains Paul's statement that the reincorporation of Israel into the community of faith was like "life from the dead" (Rm 11:15). The prophecy will be fulfilled when God gathers believing Israelites

to the land (Jr 31:33; 33:14–16) at the second coming of Christ (Mt 24:30–31).
37:15–16 The key word *one* (**single** in this verse) occurs ten times in vv. 15–28. On the use of a **stick** or staff to represent a tribe, see Nm 17.
37:17 By being placed end to end, the two sticks would appear to be a **single stick**. This is Ezekiel's prophetic vision of a reunited Israel (cp. Jr 3:12,14; 31:2–6; Ezk 4:4–8; 16:53). Fundamental to all prophecy concerning Israel is the presupposition of a united people, a healing of the breach in the commonwealth of God's people (Is 11:12–13). The prophets recognized the northern tribes as still in existence and knew of no lost tribes (Is 43:5–7; 49:5–6; Jr 3:12–15).
37:18–19 God will reunite the two kingdoms that had been separated since Solomon's death (1Kg 12).
37:20–23 Israel and Judah will become the kingdom of God, God's holy people. Note the covenant formula again in v. 23.

them from all their apostasies by which^A they sinned, and I will cleanse them. Then they will be my people, and I will be their God. ²⁴ My servant David will be king over them, and there will be one shepherd for all of them. They will follow my ordinances, and keep my statutes and obey them.

²⁵ "They will live in the land that I gave to my servant Jacob, where your ancestors lived. They will live in it forever with their children and grandchildren, and my servant David will be their prince forever. ²⁶ I will make a covenant of peace with them; it will be a permanent covenant with them. I will establish and multiply them and will set my sanctuary among them forever. ²⁷ My dwelling place will be with them; I will be their God, and they will be my people. ²⁸ When my sanctuary is among them forever, the nations will know that I, the LORD, sanctify Israel.'"

The Defeat of Gog

38 The word of the LORD came to me: ² "Son of man, face Gog, of the land of Magog, the chief prince of^B Meshech and Tubal. Prophesy against him ³ and say, 'This is what the Lord GOD says: Look, I am against you, Gog, chief prince of Meshech and Tubal. ⁴ I will turn you around, put hooks in your jaws, and bring you out with all your army, including horses and riders, who are all splendidly dressed, a huge assembly armed with large and small shields, all of them brandishing swords. ⁵ Persia, Cush, and Put are with them, all of them with shields and helmets; ⁶ Gomer with all its troops; and Beth-togarmah from the remotest parts of the north along with all its troops — many peoples are with you.

⁷ "'Be prepared and get yourself ready, you and your whole assembly that has been mobilized around you; you will be their guard. ⁸ After a long time you will be summoned. In the last years you will enter a land that has been restored from war^C and regathered from many peoples to the mountains of Israel, which had long been a ruin. They were brought out from the peoples, and all of them now live securely. ⁹ You, all of your troops, and many peoples with you will advance, coming like a thunderstorm; you will be like a cloud covering the land.

¹⁰ "'This is what the Lord GOD says: On that day, thoughts will arise in your mind, and you will devise an evil plan. ¹¹ You will say, "I will advance against a land of open villages; I will come against a tranquil people who are living securely, all of them living without walls and without bars or gates" — ¹² in order to seize spoil and carry off plunder, to turn your hand against ruins now inhabited and against a people gathered from the nations, who have been acquiring cattle and possessions and who live at the center of the world. ¹³ Sheba and Dedan and the merchants of Tarshish with all its rulers^D will ask you, "Have you come to seize spoil? Have you mobilized your assembly to carry off plunder, to make off with silver and gold, to take cattle and possessions, to seize plenty of spoil?"'

¹⁴ "Therefore prophesy, son of man, and say to Gog, 'This is what the Lord GOD says: On that day when my people Israel are dwelling securely, will you not know this ¹⁵ and come from your place in the remotest parts of the north — you and many peoples with you, who are all riding horses — a huge assembly, a powerful army? ¹⁶ You will advance against my people Israel like a cloud covering the land. It will happen in the last days, Gog, that I will bring you against my land so that the nations may know

---

^A**37:23** Some Hb mss, LXX, Sym; other Hb mss read *their settlements where*　　^B**38:2** Or *the prince of Rosh,*　　^C**38:8** Lit *from the sword*　　^D**38:13** Lit *young lions,* or *villages*

37:24 The "servant" language (cp. Is 49; 53) is characteristic of messianic prophecies. The Davidic heritage, represented by such terms as **king** and **my servant David** (cp. 2Sm 7:5,8; Ps 89:20) will establish national unity and keep at bay abuses that were prevalent in Judah's preexilic history. The reunification of the tribes is connected to the fostering of messianic hope (Ezk 37:25–28; cp. Rm 11:25–36).

37:25–28 The new covenant is here referred to as **a covenant of peace** and a **permanent covenant.**

38:1 The introductory phrase **the word of the LORD came to me** indicates a change of subject from the previous chapter. The message in chaps. 38–39 should be seen as the sixth and last in Ezekiel's series of messages delivered the night before the news about the fall of Jerusalem arrived. The chapters describe the final attempt by foreigners to possess the land of Israel.

38:2 Gog may most immediately refer to Gyges, king of Lydia, from the seventh century BC. Even so, the reference transcends this Gog's historical circumstances to refer to a leader who will oppose Israel in the far future. The only other occurrence of "Gog" is in Rv 20:8. Gog seems to transcend historical categories, serving as a symbol of the forces of the antichrist. In Ezk 25–32 the prophet addressed nations that Judah was familiar with. Now, we read about the plan of God for distant, unknown nations. This is parallel to the book of Revelation's depiction of the battle of Armageddon. Revelation 20:8 identifies Gog and Magog as a figure for all the pagan foes of Israel and the Messiah. On **Meshech** and **Tubal**, see 32:26.

38:6 Gomer is mentioned as early as Gn 10:2–3. In 1Ch 1:6 he is listed as one of the sons of Japheth. According to Gn 10:3, Togarmah was one of the children of Gomer.

38:7–9 After a long time (lit "in the end of years") is a prophetic phrase that is sometimes applied to the end times (Jr 32:14; Dn 8:26). It alludes to the nearly identical phrase "end of days", which designates the time of

the messianic kingdom (Gn 49:1; Is 2:2; Jr 23:20; 30:24; Hs 3:5; Mc 4:1). The attack will be so massive that the invading troops will appear to be **like a cloud covering the land.** The cloud and the storm are common images in biblical literature announcing prophetic threats (Jr 4:13).

38:10–11 The phrase **living securely** describes messianic security after Israel's restoration.

38:12 The phrase **center of the world** may be translated "navel of the earth." Since the Hebrew word for "land" can also mean "earth," it could be argued that theologically Jerusalem will be the center of both the land of Israel and indeed all the earth.

38:13 Sheba (27:22), **Dedan** (25:13; 27:20), and **Tarshish** (27:12) are mentioned in chap. 27 as engaged in trade with Tyre. Sheba, located in the southwestern corner of the Arabian Peninsula (modern Yemen), was known for its trading (Jb 6:19; see 1Kg 10:1–2; Ezk 27:22).

38:14–16 This invasion will take place in the end times, after the people of Israel have

me, when I demonstrate my holiness through you in their sight.

¹⁷ " 'This is what the Lord God says: Are you the one I spoke about in former times through my servants, the prophets of Israel, who for years prophesied in those times that I would bring you against them? ¹⁸ Now on that day, the day when Gog comes against the land of Israel — this is the declaration of the Lord God — my wrath will flare up.^ ¹⁹ I swear in my zeal and fiery wrath: On that day there will be a great earthquake in the land of Israel. ²⁰ The fish of the sea, the birds of the sky, the animals of the field, every creature that crawls on the ground, and every human being on the face of the earth will tremble before me. The mountains will be demolished, the cliffs will collapse, and every wall will fall to the ground. ²¹ I will call for a sword against him on all my mountains — this is the declaration of the Lord God — and every man's sword will be against his brother. ²² I will execute judgment on him with plague and bloodshed. I will pour out torrential rain, hailstones, fire, and burning sulfur on him, as well as his troops and the many peoples who are with him. ²³ I will display my greatness and holiness, and will reveal myself in the sight of many nations. Then they will know that I am the Lord.'

The Disposal of Gog

39 "As for you, son of man, prophesy against Gog and say, 'This is what the Lord God says: Look, I am against you, Gog, chief prince of^B Meshech and Tubal. ² I will turn you around, drive you on, and lead you up from the remotest parts of the north. I will bring you against the mountains of Israel. ³ Then I will knock your bow from your left hand and make your arrows drop from your right hand. ⁴ You, all your troops, and the peoples who are with you will fall on the mountains of Israel. I will give you as food to every kind of predatory bird

and to the wild animals. ⁵ You will fall on the open field, for I have spoken. This is the declaration of the Lord God.

⁶ " 'I will send fire against Magog and those who live securely on the coasts and islands. Then they will know that I am the Lord. ⁷ So I will make my holy name known among my people Israel and will no longer allow it to be profaned. Then the nations will know that I am the Lord, the Holy One in Israel. ⁸ Yes, it is coming, and it will happen. This is the declaration of the Lord God. This is the day I have spoken about.

⁹ " 'Then the inhabitants of Israel's cities will go out, kindle fires, and burn the weapons — the small and large shields, the bows and arrows, the clubs and spears. For seven years they will use them to make fires. ¹⁰ They will not gather wood from the countryside or cut it down from the forests, for they will use the weapons to make fires. They will take the loot from those who looted them and plunder those who plundered them. This is the declaration of the Lord God.

¹¹ " 'Now on that day I will give Gog a burial place there in Israel — the Travelers' Valley^C east of the Sea. It will block those who travel through, for Gog and all his hordes will be buried there. So it will be called Hordes of Gog^D Valley. ¹² The house of Israel will spend seven months burying them in order to cleanse the land. ¹³ All the people of the land will bury them and their fame will spread on the day I display my glory. This is the declaration of the Lord God.

¹⁴ " 'They will appoint men on a full-time basis to pass through the land and bury the invaders^E who remain on the surface of the ground, in order to cleanse it. They will make their search at the end of the seven months. ¹⁵ When they pass through the land and one of them sees a human bone, he will set up a marker next to it until the buriers have buried

---

^38:18 Lit *up in my anger*   ^39:1 Or *Gog, prince of Rosh*,   ^39:11 Hb obscure   ^39:11 = Hamon-gog, also in v. 15   ^39:14 Or *basis, some to pass through the land, and with them some to bury those*

---

been restored to the promised land and are living securely under the Messiah's rule and protection.
38:17–20 When Gog advances, a **great earthquake** will occur. Such listings of **animals** in v. 20 are used to allude to the entire created order in the creation story (Gn 1) and elsewhere (Gn 9:2; 1Kg 4:33; Jb 12:7–8).
38:21 God will bring such confusion on those who oppose his people that they will kill one another (Lv 26:37; Dt 28:29). For a similar event in the time of King Jehoshaphat, see 2Ch 20:22–23.
38:22–23 These judgments against Gog are consistent with the covenant curses of **plague** (Dt 32:24), **bloodshed** (Dt 32:42), flood (Gn 6), hail, **fire**, and **burning sulfur** (Jos 10:11). The defeat of Gog by the sword and natural elements highlights God's role as Creator and governor of nature. The

destruction is also reminiscent of the destruction of Sodom and Gomorrah (Gn 18–19).
39:1–3 These verses essentially repeat verses from chap. 38.
39:4–9 These verses are similar to Rv 19:17–18, perhaps referring to the same event.
39:6 The sending of **fire** (in this case, **against Magog**) is a common expression for divine judgment (Hs 8:14; Am 1:12).
39:7 As a result of his actions against Gog and the coalition, his **holy name** will never be **profaned** again (v. 25; 20:9; 36:20–23; 43:7–9).
39:9–10 Up to this point in the prophecy about the invasion of Gog, only God has defended his people against this enemy. Now for the first time Israel is called to act, but her role is to conduct a "mopping up" exercise. The carnage left in the aftermath of the defeat of Gog will be so massive that the

Israelites will fuel their fires for **seven years** with the weapons of their slain enemies.
39:11 This **burial** project will be so massive that it will block travel through the land. The name of the valley will be changed to **Hordes of Gog Valley**. The only major valley that ran in an east-west direction in Israel was the Jezreel Valley, a vital strategic link on the route from Egypt to Damascus in biblical times. This valley will be the location of the great battle of the tribulation period known as Armageddon (Rv 16:13–16).
39:12–16 Because corpses were considered unclean (Lv 11:11; 22:4; Nm 5:2; 6:6–12; 31:19), the Mosaic law required all humans to be given a proper burial (Dt 21:22–23). Numbers 19:11–22 explains not only the contaminating effects of a corpse but also the process by which a person so defiled could be ceremonially cleansed.

it in Hordes of Gog Valley. ¹⁶ There will even be a city named Hamonah⁴ there. So they will cleanse the land.'

¹⁷ "Son of man, this is what the Lord GOD says: Tell every kind of bird and all the wild animals, 'Assemble and come! Gather from all around to my sacrificial feast that I am slaughtering for you, a great feast on the mountains of Israel; you will eat flesh and drink blood. ¹⁸ You will eat the flesh of mighty men and drink the blood of the earth's princes: rams, lambs, male goats, and all the fattened bulls of Bashan. ¹⁹ You will eat fat until you are satisfied and drink blood until you are drunk, at my sacrificial feast that I have prepared for you. ²⁰ At my table you will eat your fill of horses and riders, of mighty men and all the warriors. This is the declaration of the Lord GOD.'

Israel's Restoration to God

²¹ "I will display my glory among the nations, and all the nations will see the judgment I have executed and the hand I have laid on them. ²² From that day forward the house of Israel will know that I am the LORD their God. ²³ And the nations will know that the house of Israel went into exile on account of their iniquity, because they dealt unfaithfully with me. Therefore, I hid my face from them and handed them over to their enemies, so that they all fell by the sword. ²⁴ I dealt with them according to their uncleanness and transgressions, and I hid my face from them.

²⁵ "So this is what the Lord GOD says: Now I will restore the fortunes of Jacob and have compassion on the whole house of Israel, and I will be jealous for my holy name. ²⁶ They will feel remorse for^B,C their disgrace and all the

unfaithfulness they committed against me, when they live securely in their land with no one to frighten them. ²⁷ When I bring them back from the peoples and gather them from the countries of their enemies, I will demonstrate my holiness through them in the sight of many nations. ²⁸ They will know that I am the LORD their God when I regather them to their own land after having exiled them among the nations. I will leave none of them behind.^D ²⁹ I will no longer hide my face from them, for I will pour out my Spirit on the house of Israel." This is the declaration of the Lord GOD.

The New Temple

40 In the twenty-fifth year of our exile, at the beginning of the year, on the tenth day of the month in the fourteenth year after Jerusalem had been captured, on that very day the LORD's hand was on me, and he brought me there. ² In visions of God he took me to the land of Israel and set me down on a very high mountain. On its southern slope was a structure resembling a city. ³ He brought me there, and I saw a man whose appearance was like bronze, with a linen cord and a measuring rod in his hand. He was standing by the city gate. ⁴ He spoke to me: "Son of man, look with your eyes, listen with your ears, and pay attention to everything I am going to show you, for you have been brought here so that I might show it to you. Report everything you see to the house of Israel."

The Wall and Outer Gates

⁵ Now there was a wall surrounding the outside of the temple. The measuring rod in the man's hand was six units of twenty-one inches;^E each

---

^A39:16 In Hb, *Hamonah* is related to the word "horde."　^B39:26 Some emend to *will forget*　^C39:26 Lit *will bear*　^D39:28 Lit *behind there any longer*　^E40:5 = a long cubit

---

39:17–20 The mention of the **fattened bulls of Bashan** in v. 18 is further confirmation that this is the Lord's sacrificial feast because fat and blood were normally reserved for him (44:15; Lv 3:17). Bashan, east and northeast of the Sea of Galilee, was famous for its fertile land and fat cows (Dt 32:14; Ps 22:12; Am 4:1). **39:17** This **sacrificial feast** (Is 34:6–8; Zph 1:7) will consist of the flesh and blood of the armies of Gog that had been killed. Birds and beasts will eat fat and drink blood, elements that were reserved exclusively for the Lord when the Hebrews made animal sacrifices (Lv 3:17). Mention of the fat and blood therefore may be a way of highlighting the Lord's participation in the annihilation of Israel's enemies. **39:21–24** The image of God hiding his **face** (v. 24), turning away from Israel and choosing not to help them, also appears in Dt 31:17–18; Ps 13:1–2. **39:27–29** Before the destruction of Jerusalem God had promised to "pour out" his wrath on Israel (7:8; 9:8; 20:13,21; 22:22; 36:18). Now in restoring his people he will **pour out** his **Spirit**. This reference to the Spirit of God connects the passage in its entirety to chaps. 36–37 with their focus on the Spirit.

40:1 This date (**in the twenty-fifth year of our exile**) is the thirteenth and final date formula in Ezekiel. This was April 573 BC. This was twelve years after the oracle in 32:1, fourteen years after the destruction of Jerusalem, and twenty years after Ezekiel's first vision of the temple (8:1). The tenth day of the first month marked the beginning of the Passover that was celebrated four days later. Moreover, the twenty-fifth year was the halfway point to the next Jubilee Year when freedom and release would be observed (Lv 25). Whereas the opening vision of the heavenly King on his throne had been dated from the exile of the earthly king—Jehoiachin—this vision of the heavenly city is dated from the destruction of the earthly city, Jerusalem. **40:2** This vision provides a literary and conceptual envelope for the entire book. It complements especially the visions of God's departure and the temple's destruction in chaps. 9–11. This vision is the longest vision in the Bible apart from the book of Revelation. As Ezekiel received legislation for the new age upon this **high mountain**, it is natural to compare the experience of Moses

receiving the law on Mount Sinai. Indeed, Ezekiel is the only person in the OT except Moses who transmitted legislation that he received directly from God. As Ezekiel's vision was a vision of the city of Jerusalem, it is likely that this "very high mountain" is a reference to Mount Zion, often cited in the OT for its great height (17:22; Is 2:2; Mc 4:1; see Zch 14:10). **40:3** The **measuring rod** was used for short measurements. It was about ten feet four inches in length. **40:4** This shows the importance of this final revelation of the book. **40:5–16** Ezekiel's angelic tour guide begins his tour outside the temple. **40:5** The dimensions of the **temple** and the city are dominated by multiples of five. The gate structure measured twenty-five by fifty cubits; the temple house with its adjoining structures, fifty by a hundred cubits; the inner court and the quadrangles of the temple area, a hundred by a hundred cubits; and the entire temple complex, five hundred by five hundred cubits. The number of steps (7 + 8 + 10) leading to the temple adds up to twenty-five. The length of the measuring unit was the standard length plus three inches.^ He measured the thickness of the wall structure; it was 10½ feet,[8] and its height was the same. [6] Then he came to the gate that faced east and climbed its steps. He measured the threshold of the gate; it was 10½ feet deep — one threshold was 10½ feet deep. [7] Each recess was 10½ feet long and 10½ feet deep, and there was a space of 8¾ feet[c] between the recesses. The inner threshold of the gate on the temple side next to the gate's portico was 10½ feet. [8] Next he measured the gate's portico; [9] it[D] was 14 feet,[E] and its jambs were 3½ feet.[F] The gate's portico was on the temple side.

[10] There were three recesses on each side of the east gate, each with the same measurements, and the jambs on either side also had the same measurements. [11] Then he measured the width of the gate's entrance; it was 17½ feet,[G] while the width[H] of the gate was 22¾ feet.[I] [12] There was a barrier of 21 inches[J] in front of the recesses on both sides, and the recesses on each side were 10½ feet[K] square. [13] Then he measured the gate from the roof of one recess to the roof of the opposite one; the distance was 43¾ feet.[L] The openings of the recesses faced each other. [14] Next, he measured the porch — 105 feet.[M,N] [15] The distance from the front of the gate at the entrance to the front of the gate's portico on the inside was 87½ feet.[O] [16] The recesses and their jambs had beveled windows all around the inside of the gate. The porticoes also had windows all around on the inside. Each jamb was decorated with palm trees.

[17] Then he brought me into the outer court, and there were chambers and a paved surface laid out all around the court. Thirty chambers faced the pavement, [18] which flanked the courtyard's gates and corresponded to the length of the gates; this was the lower pavement. [19] Then

he measured the distance from the front of the lower gate to the exterior front of the inner court; it was 175 feet.[P] This was the east; next the north is described.

[20] He measured the gate of the outer court facing north, both its length and width. [21] Its three recesses on each side, its jambs, and its portico had the same measurements as the first gate: 87½ feet long and 43¾ feet wide. [22] Its windows, portico, and palm trees had the same measurements as those of the gate that faced east. Seven steps led up to the gate, and its portico was ahead of them. [23] The inner court had a gate facing the north gate, like the one on the east. He measured the distance from gate to gate; it was 175 feet.

[24] He brought me to the south side, and there was also a gate on the south. He measured its jambs and portico; they had the same measurements as the others. [25] Both the gate and its portico had windows all around, like the other windows. It was 87½ feet long and 43¾ feet wide. [26] Its stairway had seven steps, and its portico was ahead of them. It had palm trees on its jambs, one on each side. [27] The inner court had a gate on the south. He measured from gate to gate on the south; it was 175 feet.

The Inner Gates

[28] Then he brought me to the inner court through the south gate. When he measured the south gate, it had the same measurements as the others. [29] Its recesses, jambs, and portico had the same measurements as the others. Both it and its portico had windows all around. It was 87½ feet long and 43¾ feet wide. [30] (There were porticoes all around, 43¾ feet long and 8¾ feet wide.[Q]) [31] Its portico faced the outer court, and its jambs were decorated with palm trees. Its stairway had eight steps.

^40:5 Lit *six cubits by the cubit and a handbreadth* [B]40:5 Lit *was one rod*, also in v. 7 [C]40:7 Lit *five cubits*, also in v. 30 [D]40:8–9 Some Hb mss, Syr, Vg; other Hb mss read *gate facing the temple side; it was one rod.* [E]Then he measured the gate's portico; it [F]40:9 Lit *eight cubits* [G]40:9 Lit *two cubits* [H]40:11 Lit *10 cubits* [I]40:11 Lit *length* [J]40:11 Lit *13 cubits* [K]40:12 Lit *one cubit*, also in v. 42 [L]40:12 Lit *six cubits* [M]40:13 Lit *25 cubits*, also in vv. 21,25,29,33,36 [N]40:14 MT adds *To the jamb of the court, the gate was all around*; Hb obscure [O]40:14 Lit *60 cubits* [P]40:15 Lit *50 cubits*, also in vv. 21,25,29,33, 36 [Q]40:19 Lit *100 cubits*, also in vv. 23,27,47 [R]40:30 Some Hb mss, LXX omit v. 30

rod (**six units of twenty-one inches**; lit "six cubits, with a cubit and a handbreadth") followed the later cubit length. The shorter cubit, eighteen inches, was used in former times (2Ch 3:3).
40:6–7 The alcoves, guardrooms, or **recesses** inside the temple gates were one rod long

and one rod wide (**10 ½ feet long and 10 ½ feet deep**; see also v. 10). The projecting walls between the alcoves were five cubits thick. Guardrooms were also a part of the Solomonic temple (2Ch 12:11).
40:16 Representations of the **palm** tree also decorated Solomon's temple (1Kg 6:29,32,35).

40:17–27 Ezekiel's tour proceeds to the outer court.
40:17–19 A **paved surface** functioned something like a border around the outside edges of the **outer court**. Along this pavement were thirty rooms used by the Levites (perhaps for meals) in other Israelite temples (Neh 13:4–14; Jr 35:2–4). The distance from the outer gate to the exterior of the inner court was a hundred cubits, or **175 feet**. The dimensions of the northern and southern gates as well as the space between these gates to the inner court were identical to the dimensions of the east gate (vv. 17–27).
40:28–41:26 Ezekiel's tour reaches the inner court, which is the focus of the tour.
40:28 There was no western gate for this temple because the temple occupied the western side of the compound.

#42 99 Essential Christian Truths

REGENERATION

Regeneration takes place at the beginning of the Christian life and is the miraculous transformation—the new birth—that takes place within an individual through the supernatural work of the Holy Spirit (Jn 3:3–8; Ti 3:5). It is the divine side of conversion (turning to Christ in repentance and faith), being the work of God within a person's life that causes him or her to be born again, a work that human effort is unable to produce.

³² Then he brought me to the inner court on the east side. When he measured the gate, it had the same measurements as the others. ³³ Its recesses, jambs, and portico had the same measurements as the others. Both it and its portico had windows all around. It was 87 ½ feet long and 43 ¾ feet wide. ³⁴ Its portico faced the outer court, and its jambs were decorated with palm trees on each side. Its stairway had eight steps.

³⁵ Then he brought me to the north gate. When he measured it, it had the same measurements as the others, ³⁶ as did its recesses, jambs, and portico. It also had windows all around. It was 87 ½ feet long and 43 ¾ feet wide. ³⁷ Its portico^A faced the outer court, and its jambs were decorated with palm trees on each side. Its stairway had eight steps.

Rooms for Preparing Sacrifices

³⁸ There was a chamber whose door opened into the gate's portico.^B The burnt offering was to be washed there. ³⁹ Inside the gate's portico there were two tables on each side, on which to slaughter the burnt offering, sin offering, and guilt offering. ⁴⁰ Outside, as one approaches the entrance of the north gate, there were two tables on one side and two more tables on the other side of the gate's portico. ⁴¹ So there were four tables inside the gate and four outside, eight tables in all on which the slaughtering was to be done. ⁴² There were also four tables of cut stone for the burnt offering, each 31 ½ inches^C long, 31 ½ inches wide, and 21 inches high. The utensils used to slaughter the burnt offerings and other sacrifices were placed on them. ⁴³ There were three-inch^D hooks^E fastened all around the inside of the room, and the flesh of the offering was to be laid on the tables.

Rooms for Singers and Priests

⁴⁴ Outside the inner gate, within the inner court, there were chambers for the singers:^F one^G beside the north gate, facing south, and another beside the south^H gate, facing north.

⁴⁵ Then the man said to me, "This chamber that faces south is for the priests who keep charge of the temple. ⁴⁶ The chamber that faces north is for the priests who keep charge of the altar. These are the sons of Zadok, the ones from the sons of Levi who may approach the Lord to serve him." ⁴⁷ Next he measured the court. It was square, 175 feet long and 175 feet wide. The altar was in front of the temple.

⁴⁸ Then he brought me to the portico of the temple and measured the jambs of the portico; they were 8 ¾ feet thick on each side. The width of the gate was 24 ½ feet,^I and the side walls of the gate were^J 5 ¼ feet^K wide on each side. ⁴⁹ The portico was 35 feet^L across and 21 feet^M feet^N deep, and 10 steps led^O up to it. There were pillars by the jambs, one on each side.

Inside the Temple

41 Next he brought me into the great hall and measured the jambs; on each side the width of the jamb was 10 ½ feet.^P,Q ² The width of the entrance was 17 ½ feet,^R and the side walls of the entrance were 8 ¾ feet^S wide on each side. He also measured the length of the great hall, 70 feet,^T and the width, 35 feet.^U ³ He went inside the next room and measured the jambs at the entrance; they were 3 ½ feet^V wide. The entrance was 10 ½ feet wide, and the width of the entrance's side walls on each side^W was 12 ¼ feet.^X ⁴ He then measured the length of the room adjacent to the great hall, 35 feet, and the width, 35 feet. And he said to me, "This is the most holy place."

Outside the Temple

⁵ Then he measured the wall of the temple; it was 10 ½ feet thick. The width of the side rooms all around the temple was 7 feet.^Y ⁶ The side rooms were arranged one above another in three stories of thirty rooms each.^Z There were ledges on the wall of the temple all around to serve as supports for the side rooms, so that the supports would not be in the temple wall

---

^A 40:37 LXX; MT reads *jambs*   ^B 40:38 Text emended; MT reads *door was by the jambs, at the gates*   ^C 40:42 Lit *one and a half cubits*   ^D 40:43 Lit *one handbreadth*   ^E 40:43 Or *ledges*   ^F 40:44 LXX reads *were two chambers*   ^G 40:44 LXX; MT reads *singers, which was*   ^H 40:44 LXX; MT reads *east*   ^I 40:48 Lit *14 cubits*   ^J 40:48 LXX; MT omits *24 ½ feet, and the side walls of the gate were*   ^K 40:48 Lit *three cubits*   ^L 40:49 Lit *20 cubits*   ^M 40:49 LXX; MT reads *19 ½*   ^N 40:49 Lit *12 cubits*   ^O 40:49 MT reads *and it was on steps that they would go*   ^P 41:1 LXX; MT reads *jambs; they were 10 ½ feet wide on each side — the width of the tabernacle*   ^Q 41:1 Lit *six cubits,* also in vv. 3,5   ^R 41:2 Lit *10 cubits*   ^S 41:2 Lit *five cubits,* also in vv. 9,11,12   ^T 41:2 Lit *40 cubits*   ^U 41:2 Lit *20 cubits,* also in vv. 4,10   ^V 41:3 Lit *two cubits,* also in v. 22   ^W 41:3 LXX; MT reads *width of the entrance*   ^X 41:3 Lit *seven cubits*   ^Y 41:5 Lit *four cubits*   ^Z 41:6 Lit *another three and thirty times*

40:39 The **burnt offering** may be considered the most important sacrifice since it was the most prominent sacrifice in the festivals (Nm 28–29). It was distinctive insomuch as the entire offering (apart from the skin) was offered, leaving none for the priest to eat.

For inadvertent sins, some were to be purified for the **sin offering** (Lv 4:1–5:13) while others required a **guilt offering** (Lv 5:14–6:7). In distinction to the sin offering, the guilt or restitution offering was required for offenses that created a debt between humans and God.

40:46 According to the book of Ezekiel, the Zadokites will be distinguished from the Levites in the coming age. The Zadokites were **sons of Zadok**, who traced his Levitical lineage to Aaron through Aaron's son Eleazar (1Ch 6:50–53). Zadok served as a priest under David, along with Abiathar (2Sm 8:17; 15:24–29; 20:25). Zadok was appointed chief priest during Solomon's reign because he supported Solomon as king (1Kg 1:32–35; 2:26–27,35). The Zadokites were elevated and the Levites demoted out of concern for ritual purity, a dominant subject in Ezk 40–46.

40:47 In Ezekiel's temple, **square** shapes (**175 feet long and 175 feet wide**) are often associated with holy places. The most holy place was a perfect cube (41:4).

41:3–4 While the angel previously brought Ezekiel with him into the great hall (v. 1), only the angel went into the **next room** and the **most holy place**. This corresponds to the restrictions given in the law (Lv 16; Heb 9:7).

41:6 There were three tiers or **stories** of **thirty rooms** per tier on the sides of the temple (1Kg 6:5–10), yielding a total of ninety **side rooms**. The rooms widened as one went

itself. ⁷ The side rooms surrounding the temple widened at each successive story, for the structure surrounding the temple went up by stages. This was the reason for the temple's broadness as it rose. And so, one would go up from the lowest story to the highest by means of the middle one.ᴬ

⁸ I saw that the temple had a raised platform surrounding it; this foundation for the side rooms was 10 ½ feet high.ᴮ ⁹ The thickness of the outer wall of the side rooms was 8 ¾ feet. The free space between the side rooms of the temple ¹⁰ and the outer chambers was 35 feet wide all around the temple. ¹¹ The side rooms opened into the free space, one entrance toward the north and another to the south. The area of free space was 8 ¾ feet wide all around.

¹² Now the building that faced the temple yard toward the west was 122 ½ feetᶜ wide. The wall of the building was 8 ¾ feet thick on all sides, and the building's length was 157 ½ feet.ᴰ

¹³ Then the man measured the temple; it was 175 feetᴱ long. In addition, the temple yard and the building, including its walls, were 175 feet long. ¹⁴ The width of the front of the temple along with the temple yard to the east was 175 feet. ¹⁵ Next he measured the length of the building facing the temple yard to the west, with its galleriesᶠ on each side; it was 175 feet.

Interior Wooden Structures

The interior of the great hall and the porticoes of the court — ¹⁶ the thresholds, the beveled windows, and the balconies all around with their three levels opposite the threshold — were overlaid with wood on all sides. They were paneled from the ground to the windows (but the windows were covered), ¹⁷ reaching to the top of the entrance, and as far as the inner temple and on the outside. On every wall all around, on the inside and outside, was a pattern ¹⁸ carved with cherubim and palm trees. There was a palm tree between each pair of cherubim. Each cherub had two faces: ¹⁹ a human face turned toward the palm tree on one side, and a lion's face turned toward it on the other. They were carved throughout the temple on all sides. ²⁰ Cherubim and palm trees were carved from the ground to the top of the entrance and on the wall of the great hall.

²¹ The doorposts of the great hall were square, and the front of the sanctuary had the same appearance. ²² The altar wasᴳ made of wood, 5 ¼ feetᴴ high and 3 ½ feet long.ᴵ It had corners, and its lengthᴶ and sides were of wood. The man told me, "This is the table that stands before the LORD."

²³ The great hall and the sanctuary each had a double door, ²⁴ and each of the doors had two swinging panels. There were two panels for one door and two for the other. ²⁵ Cherubim and palm trees were carved on the doors of the great hall like those carved on the walls. There was a wooden canopyᴬ outside, in front of the portico. ²⁶ There were beveled windows and palm trees on both sides, on the side walls of the portico, the side rooms of the temple, and the canopies.ᴬ

The Priests' Chambers

42 Then the man led me out by way of the north gate into the outer court. He brought me to the group of chambers opposite the temple yard and opposite the building to the north. ² Along the length of the chambers, which was 175 feet,ᴷ there was an entrance on the north; the width was 87 ½ feet.ᴸ ³ Opposite the 35 foot spaceᴹ belonging to the inner court and opposite the paved surface belonging to the outer court, the structure rose gallery by gallery in three tiers. ⁴ In front of the chambers was a walkway toward the inside, 17 ½ feetᴺ wide and 175 feet long,ᴼ and their entrances were on the north. ⁵ The upper chambers were narrower because the galleries took away more space from them than from the lower and middle stories of the building. ⁶ For they were arranged in three stories and had no pillars like the pillars of the courts; therefore the upper chambers were set back from the ground more than the lower and middle stories. ⁷ A wall on the outside ran in front of the chambers, parallel to them, toward the outer court; it was 87 ½ feet long. ⁸ For the chambers on the outer court were 87 ½ feet long, while those facing the great hall were 175 feet long. ⁹ At the base of these chambers there was an entryway on the east side as one enters them from the outer court.

ᴬ**41:7,25,26** Hb obscure ᴮ**41:8** Lit a full rod of six cubits of a joint; Hb obscure ᶜ**41:12** Lit 70 cubits ᴰ**41:12** Lit 90 cubits ᴱ**41:13** Lit 100 cubits ᶠ**41:15** Or ledges ᴳ**41:21–22** Or and in front of the sanctuary was something that looked like ²²an altar ᴴ**41:22** Lit three cubits ᴵ**41:22** LXX reads long and 3½ feet wide ᴶ**41:22** LXX reads base ᴷ**42:2** Lit 100 cubits, also in vv. 4,8 ᴸ**42:2** Lit 50 cubits, also in v. 7 ᴹ**42:3** Lit 20 cubits ᴺ**42:4** Lit 10 cubits ᴼ**42:4** LXX, Syr; MT reads wide, a way of one cubit

upward because the walls of the lower stories were thicker for structural reasons. They may have been designated for the storage of temple equipment and temple treasures (1Kg 6:5–10; 14:26; 2Kg 14:14).

41:18–19 Cherubim and palm trees were carved on the wall of the outer sanctuary and into the structure of Solomon's temple (1Kg 6:29–30). Cherubim were associated with the appearance of God in the visions of Ezk 1:4–28 and chap. 10. Unlike the cherubim in the earlier visions, the cherubim in the temple had only two faces—a human face and a lion's face—instead of four faces. In the Genesis narrative, the cherubim served as guards of the garden (Gn 3:24). Here in the temple as well as in Ezekiel's earlier visions, the cherubim likewise served as guards over God's dwelling place.

41:22 This **altar** stood outside the most holy place. This table was probably for the Bread of the Presence (Ex 25:30; Lv 24:5–9; 1Kg 7:48).

42:1–14 Ezekiel's tour goes back through the outer court.

[10] In the thickness of the wall of the court toward the south,[A] there were chambers facing the temple yard and the western building, [11] with a passageway in front of them, just like the chambers that faced north. Their length and width, as well as all their exits, measurements, and entrances, were identical. [12] The entrance at the beginning of the passageway, the way in front of the corresponding[B] wall as one enters on the east side, was similar to the entrances of the chambers that were on the south side.

[13] Then the man said to me, "The northern and southern chambers that face the courtyard are the holy chambers where the priests who approach the LORD will eat the most holy offerings. There they will deposit the most holy offerings — the grain offerings, sin offerings, and guilt offerings — for the place is holy. [14] Once the priests have entered, they are not to go out from the holy area to the outer court until they have removed the clothes they minister in, for these are holy. They are to put on other clothes before they approach the public area."

Outside Dimensions of the Temple Complex

[15] When he finished measuring inside the temple complex, he led me out by way of the gate that faced east and measured all around the complex.

[16] He measured the east side with a measuring rod;
it was 875 feet[C] by the measuring rod.[D]
[17] He[E] measured the north side;
it was 875 feet by the measuring rod.
[18] He[F] measured the south side;
it was 875 feet by the measuring rod.
[19] Then he turned to the west side and measured 875 feet by the measuring rod.
[20] He measured the temple complex on all four sides. It had a wall all around it, 875 feet long and 875 feet wide, to separate the holy from the common.

Return of the LORD's Glory

43 He led me to the gate, the one that faces east, [2] and I saw the glory of the God of Israel coming from the east. His voice sounded like the roar of a huge torrent, and the earth shone with his glory. [3] The vision I saw was like the one I had seen when he[G] came to destroy the city, and like the ones I had seen by the Chebar Canal. I fell facedown. [4] The glory of the LORD entered the temple by way of the gate that faced east. [5] Then the Spirit lifted me up and brought me to the inner court, and the glory of the LORD filled the temple.

[6] While the man was standing beside me, I heard someone speaking to me from the temple. [7] He said to me, "Son of man, this is the place of my throne and the place for the soles of my feet, where I will dwell among the Israelites forever. The house of Israel and their kings will no longer defile my holy name by their religious prostitution and by the corpses[H] of their kings at their high places.[I] [8] Whenever they placed their threshold next to my threshold and their doorposts beside my doorposts, with only a wall between me and them, they were defiling my holy name by the detestable acts they committed. So I destroyed them in my anger. [9] Now let them remove their prostitution and the corpses of their kings far from me, and I will dwell among them forever.

[10] "As for you, son of man, describe the temple to the house of Israel, so that they may be ashamed of their iniquities. Let them measure its pattern, [11] and they will be ashamed of all that they have done. Reveal[J] the design of the temple to them — its layout with its exits and entrances — its complete design along with all its statutes, design specifications, and laws. Write it down in their sight so that they may observe its complete design and all its statutes

[A]42:10 LXX; MT reads east   [B]42:12 Or protective; Hb obscure   [C]42:16 Lit 500 in rods, also in vv. 17,18,19   [D]42:16 Lit rod all around, also in vv. 17,18,19   [E]42:17 LXX reads Then he turned to the north and   [F]42:18 LXX reads Then he turned to the south and   [G]43:3 Some Hb mss, Theod, Vg; other Hb mss, LXX, Syr read I   [H]43:7 Or monuments, also in v. 9   [I]43:7 Some Hb mss, Theod, Tg read their death   [J]43:10–11 LXX, Vg; MT reads pattern. [11]And if they are ashamed . . . done, reveal

42:13 It was customary for Israelite **priests** to eat a portion of the **most holy offerings** that the Israelites offered to the Lord (Lv 2:3; 5:13; 6:16,26,29; 7:6,10). **Grain offerings** were usually offered with a burnt offering and often with the fellowship offering as well. The grain offering was a gift to the Lord that honored him as the source of life and the land's fertility. 42:15–20 After the guide had finished measuring what was inside the temple area, Ezekiel was brought outside to survey the temple from the outside. 42:20 The **temple complex** had a **wall all around it, 875 feet long and 875 feet wide,** a complete square. In the tabernacle only the most holy place was square. 43:1–2 In chap. 43 the return of God's **glory** to the temple indicates a reversal of the tragedy

described in chaps. 10–11. God's glory is always described as radiant or very bright (10:4; Lk 2:9; Rv 21:11,23). The glory of the Lord returned through the **east** gate, the gate from which it had earlier departed (10:18–19; 11:23). The **roar of a huge torrent** often accompanies a vision of God (1:24; Rv 1:15; 14:2; 19:6). 43:3 This verse interrupts the narrative of the vision with Ezekiel's reaction. For the former visions see chaps. 8–11. Ezekiel's fall-ing **facedown** recalls his reaction to his first vision of God (1:28). 43:4–5 Chapters 40–42 focused on structures and spaces during temple construction. Now the focus is on filling those spaces. The climax to Israel's restoration as a nation now took place as God's **glory** reentered the new temple in Jerusalem.

43:6–9 The filling of the temple with God's glory will begin with the most holy place (vv. 1–9) and end at the corners of the outer court, with the description of the activities in the kitchens (46:24). The **place for the soles of my feet** is another way to describe the "footstool," the place for a king's feet when seated on a **throne** (1Ch 28:2; Pss 99:5; 132:7; Lm 2:1). The phrase **I will dwell among the Israelites forever** indicates God's reason for entering the temple. This renews the promise of 37:26–28 (cp. 43:9; 1Kg 6:13; Zch 2:11). The **corpses of their kings** refers to the burial of kings near the temple. The proximity of these graves to the temple defiled the temple (1Kg 2:10; 11:43; 2Kg 21:18,26).

and may carry them out. ¹² This is the law of the temple: All its surrounding territory on top of the mountain will be especially holy. Yes, this is the law of the temple.

The Altar

¹³ "These are the measurements of the altar in units of length (each unit being the standard length plus three inches):^A The gutter is 21 inches^B deep and 21 inches wide, with a rim of nine inches^C around its edge. This is the base^D of the altar. ¹⁴ The distance from the gutter on the ground to the lower ledge is 3½ feet,^E and the width of the ledge is 21 inches. There are 7 feet^F from the small ledge to the large ledge, whose width is also 21 inches. ¹⁵ The altar hearth^G is 7 feet high, and four horns project upward from the hearth. ¹⁶ The hearth is square, 21 feet^H long by 21 feet wide. ¹⁷ The ledge is 24½ feet^I long by 24½ feet wide, with four equal sides. The rim all around it is 10½ inches,^J and its gutter is 21 inches all around it. The altar's steps face east."

¹⁸ Then he said to me, "Son of man, this is what the Lord GOD says: These are the statutes for the altar on the day it is constructed, so that burnt offerings may be sacrificed on it and blood may be splattered on it: ¹⁹ You are to give a bull from the herd as a sin offering to the Levitical priests who are from the offspring of Zadok, who approach me in order to serve me." This is the declaration of the Lord GOD. ²⁰ "You are to take some of its blood and apply it to the four horns of the altar, the four corners of the ledge, and all around the rim. In this way you will purify the altar and make atonement for it. ²¹ Then you are to take away the bull for the sin offering, and it must be burned outside the sanctuary in the place appointed for the temple.

²² "On the second day you are to present an unblemished male goat as a sin offering. They will purify the altar just as they did with the bull. ²³ When you have finished the purification, you are to present a young, unblemished bull and an unblemished ram from the flock.

²⁴ You are to present them before the LORD; the priests will throw salt on them and sacrifice them as a burnt offering to the LORD. ²⁵ You will offer a goat for a sin offering each day for seven days. A young bull and a ram from the flock, both unblemished, are also to be offered. ²⁶ For seven days the priests are to make atonement for the altar and cleanse it. In this way they will consecrate it^K ²⁷ and complete the days of purification. Then on the eighth day and afterward, the priests will offer your burnt offerings and fellowship offerings on the altar, and I will accept you." This is the declaration of the Lord GOD.

The Prince's Privilege

44 The man then brought me back toward the sanctuary's outer gate that faced east, and it was closed. ² The LORD said to me, "This gate will remain closed. It will not be opened, and no one will enter through it, because the LORD, the God of Israel, has entered through it. Therefore it will remain closed. ³ The prince himself will sit in the gate to eat a meal before the LORD. He is to enter by way of the portico of the gate and go out the same way."

⁴ Then the man brought me by way of the north gate to the front of the temple. I looked, and the glory of the LORD filled his temple. And I fell facedown. ⁵ The LORD said to me, "Son of man, pay attention; look with your eyes and listen with your ears to everything I tell you about all the statutes and laws of the LORD's temple. Take careful note of the entrance of the temple along with all the exits of the sanctuary.

The Levites' Duties and Privileges

⁶ "Say to the rebellious people, the house of Israel, 'This is what the Lord GOD says: I have had enough of all your detestable practices, house of Israel. ⁷ When you brought in foreigners, uncircumcised in both heart and flesh, to occupy my sanctuary, you defiled my temple while you offered my food — the fat and the blood.

---

^A 43:13 Lit in cubits (a cubit being a cubit plus a handbreadth) ^B 43:13 Lit one cubit, also in vv. 14,17 ^C 43:13 Lit one span
^D 43:13 LXX reads height ^E 43:14 Lit two cubits ^F 43:14 Lit four cubits, also in v. 15 ^G 43:15 Hb obscure ^H 43:16 Lit 12 cubits
^I 43:17 Lit 14 cubits ^J 43:17 Lit one-half cubit ^K 43:26 Lit will fill its hands

---

43:13–17 After the return of the glory of the Lord to the temple, the first issue to be addressed is the **altar**, the place of sacrifice. The altar was mentioned in 40:47 but now becomes the focus of temple activities. Because of the altar's size and height, it was necessary that steps led up to it on the east side (Ex 20:26).
43:18–20 On **blood . . . splattered on it**, see Ex 29:16; Lv 4:6; 5:9.
43:21 Some sacrificial animals were taken **outside the sanctuary** (Ex 29:14; Lv 4:12,21; 8:17; 9:11; 16:27). This action foreshadows one aspect of Christ's sacrifice (Heb 13:11–13).
43:22–26 The consecration of the **altar** for **seven days** was performed at the Festival of Shelters (1Kg 8:65–66; Ezr 3:1–7). It resembled the ordination of **priests** (Ex 29:1–37; Lv 8).

43:27 The **fellowship** offering was prescribed on three specific occasions: the Festival of Weeks (Lv 23:19–20), the completion of the Nazirite vow (Nm 6:17–20), and the installation of the priests (Lv 9:18,22). This offering appears to have been closely associated with the burnt offering, which it followed. What was distinctive about the fellowship offering was that the offerer could share in the sacrifice. As such it expressed the joy of fellowship around a shared meal.
44:1–2 After the ceremony for the consecration of the altar had ended, the guide brought Ezekiel back to the **outer gate** of the sanctuary, the one that **faced east**. Then the Lord informed the prophet that the gate

was to **remain closed** because the God of Israel had entered through, giving it a special degree of holiness.
44:3 The reader is introduced to a new character, **the prince**, who is the topic of 45:21–46:12.
44:4 Compare 43:3 and 1:28.
44:5 After the entrance of God into the temple (as when God descended on Mount Sinai), God revealed **statutes and laws** to his prophet.
44:6 A **rebellious . . . house** is a common phrase in the book of Ezekiel (2:5–6,8; 3:9,26–27; 12:3,9,25; 17:12; 24:3).
44:7–9 This description of the defilement of God's **sanctuary** may refer to the practice of using **foreigners** as guards in the temple

You^ broke my covenant by all your detestable practices. **8** You have not kept charge of my holy things but have appointed others to keep charge of my sanctuary for you.'

9 "This is what the Lord GOD says: No foreigner, uncircumcised in heart and flesh, may enter my sanctuary, not even a foreigner who is among the Israelites. **10** Surely the Levites who wandered away from me when Israel went astray, and who strayed from me after their idols, will bear the consequences of their iniquity. **11** Yet they will occupy my sanctuary, serving as guards at the temple gates and ministering at the temple. They will slaughter the burnt offerings and other sacrifices for the people and will stand before them to serve them. **12** Because they ministered to the house of Israel before their idols and became a sinful stumbling block to them, therefore I swore an oath^B against them" — this is the declaration of the Lord GOD — "that they would bear the consequences of their iniquity. **13** They must not approach me to serve me as priests or come near any of my holy things or the most holy things. They will bear their disgrace and the consequences of the detestable acts they committed. **14** Yet I will make them responsible for the duties of the temple — for all its work and everything done in it.

The Priests' Duties and Privileges

15 "But the Levitical priests descended from Zadok, who kept charge of my sanctuary when the Israelites went astray from me, will approach me to serve me. They will stand before me to offer me fat and blood." This is the declaration of the Lord GOD. **16** "They are the ones who may enter my sanctuary and approach my table to serve me. They will keep my mandate. **17** When they enter the gates of the inner court they are to wear linen garments; they must not have on them anything made of wool when they minister at the gates of the inner court and within it. **18** They are to wear linen turbans on their heads and linen undergarments around their waists. They are not to put

on anything that makes them sweat. **19** Before they go out to the outer court,^c to the people, they must take off the clothes they have been ministering in, leave them in the holy chambers, and dress in other clothes so that they do not transmit holiness to the people through their clothes.

20 "They may not shave their heads or let their hair grow long, but are to carefully trim their hair. **21** No priest may drink wine before he enters the inner court. **22** He is not to marry a widow or a divorced woman, but may marry only a virgin from the offspring of the house of Israel, or a widow who is the widow of a priest. **23** They are to teach my people the difference between the holy and the common, and explain to them the difference between the clean and the unclean.

24 "In a dispute, they will officiate as judges and decide the case according to my ordinances. They are to observe my laws and statutes regarding all my appointed festivals, and keep my Sabbaths holy. **25** A priest may not come near a dead person so that he becomes defiled. However, he may defile himself for a father, a mother, a son, a daughter, a brother, or an unmarried sister. **26** After he is cleansed, he is to count off seven days for himself. **27** On the day he goes into the sanctuary, into the inner court to minister in the sanctuary, he is to present his sin offering." This is the declaration of the Lord GOD.

28 "This will be their inheritance: I am their inheritance. You are to give them no possession in Israel: I am their possession. **29** They will eat the grain offering, the sin offering, and the guilt offering. Everything in Israel that is permanently dedicated to the LORD will belong to them. **30** The best of all the firstfruits of every kind and contribution of every kind from all your gifts will belong to the priests. You are to give your first batch of dough to the priest so that a blessing may rest on your homes. **31** The priests may not eat any bird or animal that died naturally or was mauled by wild beasts.

---

^44:7 LXX, Syr, Vg; MT reads *They*   ^44:12 Lit *I lifted my hand*   ^44:19 Some Hb mss, LXX, Syr, Vg; other Hb mss read *court, to the outer court*

(2Kg 11:14–15; see Jos 9:23,27). Nehemiah carried out this statute when he dismissed Tobiah (Neh 13:8), an Ammonite (Neh 2:10; cp. Dt 23:3).
44:10 This event (**Levites who wandered away from me when Israel went astray**) may refer to the rebellion of the Israelites during Israel's wilderness wanderings (Nm 16–18).
44:11 This restriction regarding **sacrifices** goes beyond the earlier stipulations that allowed laymen to present and sacrifice their offerings (Lv 1:1–5,11).
44:12–14 The specific violation described in these verses (**ministered to the house of Israel before their idols**) is not clear.

44:15–16 The priest **Zadok** traced his Levitical lineage to Aaron through Aaron's son Eleazar (1Ch 6:50–53). He served as priest under David, along with Abiathar (2Sm 8:17; 15:24–29; 20:25). Zadok supported Solomon and thus secured for himself and his descendants the privilege of serving in the Jerusalem temple (1Kg 1:32–35; 2:26–27,35).
44:17–22 When the Zadokites entered the sanctuary, they had to be appropriately dressed for service to God. Clothes **made of wool** were forbidden because this material caused the wearer to perspire. Sweat, like other bodily excretions, was considered defiling (Dt 23:11–13). Other rules also would govern their behavior.

44:23 On **teach...the difference between the holy and the common**, see a similar purpose for priests in Lv 10:10–11.
44:24 Priests functioned as **judges** early in Israel's history (1Sm 4:18; see also 2Ch 19:8–11).
44:25–27 The same requirements for priests (**may not come near a dead person**) are found in the Mosaic law (Lv 21:1–3).
44:28–30 The statement that priests were not to own land (**I am their inheritance**) is identical to the Mosaic legislation (Nm 18:20,23–24; Dt 10:9; Jos 13:14,33; 18:7).
44:31 The **priests** were not allowed to **eat** anything that had been torn by a wild animal or was found dead (Lv 22:8; Dt 14:21).

The Sacred Portion of the Land

45 "When you divide the land by lot as an inheritance, set aside a donation to the LORD, a holy portion of the land, 8 ⅓ miles^A long and 6 ⅔ miles^B wide. This entire region will be holy. ² In this area there will be a square section^C for the sanctuary, 875 by 875 feet,^D with 87 ½ feet^E of open space all around it. ³ From this holy portion,^F you will measure off an area 8 ⅓ miles long and 3 ⅓ miles^G wide, in which the sanctuary, the most holy place, will stand.^H ⁴ It will be a holy area of the land to be used by the priests who minister in the sanctuary, who approach to serve the LORD. It will be a place for their houses, as well as a holy area for the sanctuary. ⁵ There will be another area 8 ⅓ miles long and 3 ⅓ miles wide for the Levites who minister in the temple; it will be their possession for towns to live in.^I

⁶ "As the property of the city, set aside an area 1 ⅔ miles^J wide and 8 ⅓ miles long, adjacent to the holy donation of land. It will be for the whole house of Israel. ⁷ And the prince will have the area on each side of the holy donation of land and the city's property, adjacent to the holy donation and the city's property, stretching to the west on the west side and to the east on the east side. Its length will correspond to one of the tribal portions from the western boundary to the eastern boundary. ⁸ This will be his land as a possession in Israel. My princes will no longer oppress my people but give the rest of the land to the house of Israel according to their tribes.

⁹ "This is what the Lord GOD says: You have gone too far,^K princes of Israel! Put away violence and oppression and do what is just and right. Put an end to your evictions of my people." This is the declaration of the Lord GOD. ¹⁰ "You are to have honest scales, an honest dry measure,^L and an honest liquid measure.^M ¹¹ The dry measure^N and the liquid measure^O will be uniform, with the liquid measure containing 5 ½ gallons^P and the dry measure holding half a bushel.^P Their measurement will be a tenth of the standard larger capacity measure.^Q ¹² The

shekel^R will weigh twenty gerahs. Your mina will equal sixty shekels.

The People's Contribution to the Sacrifices

¹³ "This is the contribution you are to offer: Three quarts^S from six bushels^T of wheat and^U three quarts from six bushels of barley. ¹⁴ The quota of oil in liquid measures^V will be one percent of every^W cor. The cor equals ten liquid measures or one standard larger capacity measure,^X since ten liquid measures equal one standard larger capacity measure. ¹⁵ And the quota from the flock is one animal out of every two hundred from the well-watered pastures of Israel. These are for the grain offerings, burnt offerings, and fellowship offerings, to make atonement for the people." This is the declaration of the Lord GOD. ¹⁶ "All the people of the land must take part in this contribution for the prince in Israel. ¹⁷ Then the burnt offerings, grain offerings, and drink offerings for the festivals, New Moons, and Sabbaths — for all the appointed times of the house of Israel — will be the prince's responsibility. He will provide the sin offerings, grain offerings, burnt offerings, and fellowship offerings to make atonement on behalf of the house of Israel.

¹⁸ "This is what the Lord GOD says: In the first month, on the first day of the month, you are to take a young, unblemished bull and purify the sanctuary. ¹⁹ The priest is to take some of the blood from the sin offering and apply it to the temple doorposts, the four corners of the altar's ledge, and the doorposts of the gate of the inner court. ²⁰ You are to do the same thing on the seventh day of the month for everyone who sins unintentionally or through ignorance. In this way you will make atonement for the temple.

²¹ "In the first month, on the fourteenth day of the month, you are to celebrate the Passover, a festival of seven days during which unleavened bread will be eaten. ²² On that day the prince will provide a bull as a sin offering on behalf of himself and all the people of the land.

---

^A 45:1 Lit 25,000 cubits, also in vv. 3,5,6   ^B 45:1 LXX reads 20,000 cubits; MT reads 10,000 cubits   ^C 45:2 Lit square all around   ^D 45:2 Lit 500 by 500 cubits   ^E 45:2 Lit 50 cubits   ^F 45:3 Lit this measured portion   ^G 45:3 Lit 10,000 cubits, also in v. 5   ^H 45:3 Lit be   ^I 45:5 LXX; MT, Syr, Tg, Vg read possession — 20 chambers   ^J 45:6 Lit 5,000 cubits   ^K 45:9 Lit Enough of you   ^L 45:10 Lit an honest ephah   ^M 45:10 Lit and an honest bath   ^N 45:11 Lit The ephah   ^O 45:11 Lit the bath   ^P 45:11 Lit one-tenth of a homer   ^Q 45:11 Lit be based on the homer   ^R 45:12 A shekel is about two-fifths of an ounce of silver   ^S 45:13 Lit One-sixth of an ephah   ^T 45:13 Lit a homer   ^U 45:13 LXX, Vg; MT reads and you are to give   ^V 45:14 Lit oil, the bath, the oil   ^W 45:14 Lit be a tenth of the bath from the   ^X 45:14 Lit 10 baths, a homer

---

45:1–4 In Ezekiel the allotments of the land were aligned with the east-west orientation of the temple. This differed from the divisions after the conquest in Joshua's time. The allotment of the land is outlined in greater detail in 47:13–48:35.
45:5 The designation of the Levite settlements as towns or cities recalls the Levitical cities prescribed in Nm 35:1–8. The centralization of the priests in this new arrangement contrasts with the rest of OT history when

priests and Levites were scattered throughout the land.
45:6–8 On either side of the central district, the prince would have land. He would oversee the division of land to the tribes.
45:9 Israel's political leaders had disregarded the rights of others throughout their history (19:1–9; 22:6,25; 34:1–10).
45:10–12 The law warned against cheating people with false weights and measures (Lv 19:35–36; Dt 25:13–16; Mc 6:10–12). Holiness

in the temple required just, standardized, honest measures as well (Pr 11:1; 20:10; Am 8:5).
45:13–17 The people were responsible to make regular contributions to the prince for the operation of the sacrificial system.
45:18–20 The first day of the first month was to be a time of purification of the temple.
45:21–22 The fact that the prince will make a sin offering for himself shows that he was not the promised Messiah.

²³ During the seven days of the festival, he will provide seven bulls and seven rams without blemish as a burnt offering to the LORD on each of the seven days, along with a male goat each day for a sin offering. ²⁴ He will also provide a grain offering of half a bushel^A per bull and half a bushel per ram, along with a gallon^B of oil for every half bushel. ²⁵ At the festival that begins on the fifteenth day of the seventh month,^C he will provide the same things for seven days — the same sin offerings, burnt offerings, grain offerings, and oil.

Sacrifices at Appointed Times

46 "This is what the Lord GOD says: The gate of the inner court that faces east is to be closed during the six days of work, but it will be opened on the Sabbath day and opened on the day of the New Moon. ² The prince should enter from the outside by way of the gate's portico and stand at the gate's doorpost while the priests sacrifice his burnt offerings and fellowship offerings. He will bow in worship at the gate's threshold and then depart, but the gate is not to be closed until evening. ³ The people of the land will also bow in worship before the LORD at the entrance of that gate on the Sabbaths and New Moons.

⁴ "The burnt offering that the prince presents to the LORD on the Sabbath day is to be six unblemished lambs and an unblemished ram. ⁵ The grain offering will be half a bushel^D with the ram, and the grain offering with the lambs will be whatever he wants to give, as well as a gallon^E of oil for every half bushel. ⁶ On the day of the New Moon, the burnt offering is to be a young, unblemished bull, as well as six lambs and a ram without blemish. ⁷ He will provide a grain offering of half a bushel with the bull, half a bushel with the ram, and whatever he can afford with the lambs, together with a gallon of oil for every half bushel. ⁸ When the prince enters, he is to go in by way of the gate's portico and go out the same way.

⁹ "When the people of the land come before the LORD at the appointed times,^F whoever enters by way of the north gate to worship is to go out by way of the south gate, and whoever enters by way of the south gate is to go out by way of the north gate. No one may return through the gate by which he entered, but is to go out by the opposite gate. ¹⁰ When the people enter, the prince will enter with them, and when they leave, he will leave. ¹¹ At the festivals and appointed times, the grain offering will be half a bushel with the bull, half a bushel with the ram, and whatever he wants to give with the lambs, along with a gallon of oil for every half bushel.

¹² "When the prince makes a freewill offering, whether a burnt offering or a fellowship offering as a freewill offering to the LORD, the gate that faces east is to be opened for him. He is to offer his burnt offering or fellowship offering just as he does on the Sabbath day. Then he will go out, and the gate is to be closed after he leaves.

¹³ "You are to offer an unblemished year-old male lamb as a daily burnt offering to the LORD; you will offer it every morning. ¹⁴ You are also to prepare a grain offering every morning along with it: three quarts,^G with one-third of a gallon^H of oil to moisten the fine flour — a grain offering to the LORD. This is a permanent statute to be observed regularly. ¹⁵ They will offer the lamb, the grain offering, and the oil every morning as a regular burnt offering.

Transfer of Royal Lands

¹⁶ "This is what the Lord GOD says: If the prince gives a gift to each of his sons as their inheritance, it will belong to his sons. It will become their property by inheritance. ¹⁷ But if he gives a gift from his inheritance to one of his servants, it will belong to that servant until the year of freedom, when it will revert to the prince. His inheritance belongs only to his sons; it is theirs. ¹⁸ The prince must not take any of the people's inheritance, evicting them from their property. He is to provide an inheritance for his sons from his own property, so that none of my people will be displaced from his own property."

---

^A 45:24 Lit *an ephah* ^B 45:24 Lit *a hin* ^C 45:25 = the Festival of Shelters ^D 46:5 Lit *an ephah*, also in vv. 7,11 ^E 46:5 Lit *a hin*, also in vv. 7,11 ^F 46:9 Or *the festivals* ^G 46:14 Lit *one-sixth of an ephah* ^H 46:14 Lit *one-third of a hin*

46:1 While the east gate of the outer court was permanently closed (44:2), the east **gate of the inner court** could be opened during special days like the **Sabbath** and the **New Moon** festival.
46:2 On the Sabbath and the New Moon festival, the **prince** was to enter from the outside through the portico of the temple, and the **priests** were to sacrifice his **burnt offerings** and his **fellowship offerings**.
46:3 People of the land in this part of Ezekiel (vv. 3,9; 45:16,22) refers to the whole community that worshiped Yahweh in this manner.

46:4–8 These are the burnt offerings and grain offerings required of the prince on the Sabbath and New Moon.
46:4 The Mosaic law called for two **lambs** and no **ram** for the offering on the Sabbath (Nm 28:9).
46:9–11 These are regulations for the worship offered by the **people of the land**.
46:12–15 These are regulations for the **freewill** offerings of the prince and the regular daily offerings.
46:16 The fact that the **prince** had **sons** argues against identifying him with the Messiah.

46:17 Unlike the time when Israel was ruled by a king, the land that belonged to the prince was to be carefully regulated. The sons of the prince could inherit lands from him, but if the prince made a gift from his inheritance to one of his **servants**, the servant was to return the property in the Year of Jubilee, or **year of freedom** (see Lv 25:8–15).
46:18 Because the prince's land will remain in his family, he was prohibited from seizing the property of his fellow Israelites. Adherence to this law would prevent some of the abuses of previous times (34:3–4; 1Kg 21:1–16; Mc 2:1–2).

The Temple Kitchens

19 Then he brought me through the entrance that was at the side of the gate, into the priests' holy chambers, which faced north. I saw a place there at the far western end. **20** He said to me, "This is the place where the priests will boil the guilt offering and the sin offering, and where they will bake the grain offering, so that they do not bring them into the outer court and transmit holiness to the people." **21** Next he brought me into the outer court and led me past its four corners. There was a separate court in each of its corners. **22** In the four corners of the outer court there were enclosed^A courts, 70 feet^B long by 52 ½ feet^C wide. All four corner areas had the same dimensions. **23** There was a stone wall^D around the inside of them, around the four of them, with ovens built at the base of the walls on all sides. **24** He said to me, "These are the kitchens where those who minister at the temple will cook the people's sacrifices."

The Life-Giving River

47 Then he brought me back to the entrance of the temple and there was water flowing from under the threshold of the temple toward the east, for the temple faced east. The water was coming down from under the south side of the threshold of the temple, south of the altar. **2** Next he brought me out by way of the north gate and led me around the outside to the outer gate that faced east; there the water was trickling from the south side. **3** As the man went out east with a measuring line in his hand, he measured off a third of a mile^E and led me through the water. It came up to my ankles. **4** Then he measured off a third of a mile and led me through the water. It came up to my knees. He measured off another third of a mile and led me through the water. It came up to my waist. **5** Again he measured off a third of a mile, and it was a river that I could not cross

on foot. For the water had risen; it was deep enough to swim in, a river that could not be crossed on foot.

6 He asked me, "Do you see this, son of man?" Then he led me back to the bank of the river. **7** When I had returned, I saw a very large number of trees along both sides of the riverbank. **8** He said to me, "This water flows out to the eastern region and goes down to the Arabah. When it enters the sea, the sea of foul water,^F,G the water of the sea becomes fresh. **9** Every kind of living creature that swarms will live wherever the river flows,^H and there will be a huge number of fish because this water goes there. Since the water will become fresh, there will be life everywhere the river goes. **10** Fishermen will stand beside it from En-gedi to En-eglaim.^I These will become places where nets are spread out to dry. Their fish will consist of many different kinds, like the fish of the Mediterranean Sea. **11** Yet its swamps and marshes will not be healed; they will be left for salt. **12** All kinds of trees providing food will grow along both banks of the river. Their leaves will not wither, and their fruit will not fail. Each month they will bear fresh fruit because the water comes from the sanctuary. Their fruit will be used for eating and their leaves for healing."

The Borders of the Land

13 This is what the Lord GOD says: "This is^J the border you will use to divide the land as an inheritance for the twelve tribes of Israel. Joseph will receive two shares. **14** You will inherit it in equal portions, since I swore^K to give it to your ancestors. So this land will fall to you as an inheritance.

15 This is to be the border of the land:

On the north side it will extend from the Mediterranean Sea by way of Hethlon and Lebo-hamath to Zedad,^L **16** Berothah, and Sibraim (which is between the border of Damascus and the border of Hamath), as

---

^A**46:22** Hb obscure ^B**46:22** Lit 40 cubits ^C**46:22** Lit 30 cubits ^D**46:23** Or a row ^E**47:3** Lit 1,000 cubits, also in vv. 4,5 ^F**47:8** Or enters the sea, being brought out to the sea ; Hb obscure ^G**47:8** = the Dead Sea ^H**47:9** LXX, Vg; MT reads the two rivers flow ^I**47:10** Two springs near the Dead Sea ^J**47:13** Tg, Vg; Syr reads The valley of ^K**47:14** Lit lifted my hand ^L**47:15** LXX; MT reads and Lebo to Zedad, Hamath ; Ezk 48:1

46:19–24 This section describes the holy chambers and the four **kitchens** used by the priests to cook the sacrifices that have been brought in by the people.

47:1–5 By its correlation with the book of Revelation, Ezk 47–48 addresses the consummation of all human history. This is perhaps best seen in this river of life **flowing** from God's **temple** to bring healing to the land (vv. 1–12).

47:6–7 The abundance of **trees** in this vision correlates to the fruitfulness of the garden of Eden, suggesting that Ezekiel was shown a new creation for the coming age (Gn 2:9). Here as in the garden account, the surplus is possible because a marvelous stream, the river of life, flows in its midst (Gn 2:10–14). Since the river now comes from the temple

and not the garden, the temple is the new center of creation (Ps 46:4).

47:8 The **sea of foul water** is another way of referring to the Dead Sea. The future blessing on this region is the subject of other prophetic passages (Is 35:1–2,6–7; Jl 3:18). The Dead Sea is approximately six times saltier than the ocean.

47:9–11 This scene is reminiscent of Gn 1:20–21. The Dead Sea will be full of life.

47:12 Like the trees in the garden (Gn 2:15–17), these **trees** will remain perpetually green and provide an endless supply of food for nourishment. The fruit trees will **bear** . . . **fruit** every **month** (Ezk 34:27; 36:30) because they draw nourishment from the water that comes from **the sanctuary**. The **fruit** of these trees will be **for eating**, but their **leaves** will be **for healing** (Zch 13:1; Rv 22:1–2).

47:13 Ezekiel's promised new exodus and settlement (Ezk 20:33–38) will result in a new allotment of **the land** with boundaries similar to those of the Davidic Empire and that of Jeroboam II (2Sm 8:5–12; 2Kg 14:25; cp. Nm 34). The land will be divided equally among the tribes, fulfilling the promise given to the Israelite forefathers (Ezk 20:6; 36:28; Gn 12:1–3; 15:9–21; 17:8). Strikingly absent from the land is the territory of Transjordan (Nm 34).

47:14 A sworn promise made under oath (20:5,15,42; 36:7–8; Neh 9:15) was accompanied by the gesture of an uplifted hand.

47:15–20 The borders of the land are listed here.

47:15 Lebo-hamath was the northernmost location in the previous land divisions of Israel (Nm 13:21; 1Kg 8:65).

far as Hazer-hatticon, which is on the border of Hauran. ¹⁷ So the border will run from the sea to Hazar-enon at the border of Damascus, with the territory of Hamath to the north. This will be the northern side.

¹⁸ On the east side it will run between Hauran and Damascus, along the Jordan between Gilead and the land of Israel; you will measure from the northern border to the eastern sea.ᴬ This will be the eastern side.

¹⁹ On the south side it will run from Tamar to the Waters of Meribath-kadesh,ᴮ and on to the Brook of Egypt as far as the Mediterranean Sea. This will be the southern side.

²⁰ On the west side the Mediterranean Sea will be the border, from the southern border up to a point opposite Lebo-hamath. This will be the western side.

²¹ "You are to divide this land among yourselves according to the tribes of Israel. ²² You will allot it as an inheritance for yourselves and for the aliens residing among you, who have fathered children among you. You will treat themᶜ like native-born Israelites; along with you, they will be allotted an inheritance among the tribes of Israel. ²³ In whatever tribe the alien resides, you will assign his inheritance there." This is the declaration of the Lord GOD.

The Tribal Allotments

48 "Now these are the names of the tribes:
From the northern end, along the road of Hethlon, to Lebo-hamath as far as Hazar-enon, at the northern border of Damascus, alongside Hamath and extending from the eastern side to the sea, will be Dan — one portion.
² Next to the territory of Dan, from the east side to the west, will be Asher — one portion.
³ Next to the territory of Asher, from the east side to the west, will be Naphtali — one portion.

⁴ Next to the territory of Naphtali, from the east side to the west, will be Manasseh — one portion.
⁵ Next to the territory of Manasseh, from the east side to the west, will be Ephraim — one portion.
⁶ Next to the territory of Ephraim, from the east side to the west, will be Reuben — one portion.
⁷ Next to the territory of Reuben, from the east side to the west, will be Judah — one portion.

⁸ "Next to the territory of Judah, from the east side to the west, will be the portion you donate to the LORD, 8⅓ milesᴰ wide, and as long as one of the tribal portions from the east side to the west. The sanctuary will be in the middle of it.
⁹ "The special portion you donate to the LORD will be 8⅓ miles long and 3⅓ milesᴱ wide. ¹⁰ This holy donation will be set apart for the priests alone. It will be 8⅓ miles long on the northern side, 3⅓ miles wide on the western side, 3⅓ miles wide on the eastern side, and 8⅓ miles long on the southern side. The LORD's sanctuary will be in the middle of it. ¹¹ It is for the consecrated priests, the sons of Zadok, who kept my charge and did not go astray as the Levites did when the Israelites went astray. ¹² It will be a special donation for them out of the holy donation of the land, a most holy place adjacent to the territory of the Levites.
¹³ "Next to the territory of the priests, the Levites will have an area 8⅓ miles long and 3⅓ miles wide. The total length will be 8⅓ miles and the width 3⅓ miles. ¹⁴ They must not sell or exchange any of it, and they must not transfer this choice part of the land, for it is holy to the LORD.
¹⁵ "The remaining area, 1⅔ milesᶠ wide and 8⅓ miles long, will be for common use by the city, for both residential and open space. The city will be in the middle of it. ¹⁶ These are the city's measurements:
1½ milesᴳ on the north side;
1½ miles on the south side;
1½ miles on the east side;
and 1½ miles on the west side.

ᴬ47:18 = the Dead Sea ᴮ47:19 = Kadesh-barnea ᶜ47:22 Lit *They will be to you* ᴰ48:8 Lit *25,000 cubits*, also in vv. 9,10,13, 15,20,21 ᴱ48:9 Lit *10,000 cubits*, also in vv. 10,13,18 ᶠ48:15 Lit *5,000 cubits* ᴳ48:16 Lit *4,500 cubits*, also in vv. 30,32,33,34

47:19 The **Brook of Egypt**, Wadi el-Arish, marked the southernmost extremity of Solomon's kingdom (1Kg 8:65).

47:20 The western boundary of the land would be the Great Sea, also known as the **Mediterranean Sea**. In the eternal state there will be no sea (Rv 21:1).

47:21–23 Aliens will be allotted **an inheritance** among the tribes of Israel. The distinctions between resident aliens and Israelites will be eliminated.

48:1–29 The tribal allotments of Israel in the coming age will begin at the northern frontier with **Dan**. Since the tribe of Levi was not to receive land (v. 28), Joseph's two sons Manasseh and Ephraim would inherit land just as they had done throughout Israel's history (Gn 48:8–22). The order of the tribes listed here has no conformity to any other such list in Israel's history. The tribes that originated through the handmaids of Jacob's wives will be placed on the outer extremities. The tribes that originated from Jacob's wives Rachel and Leah will be given land in the center of the nation (cp. Gn 35:23–26). Judah and Benjamin will occupy the privileged positions next to the land's special sacred portion. Ezekiel 48:8–22 enlarges and expands on 45:1–8.

48:15 The site of Jerusalem, with the surrounding **open** land, was exactly fifty times that of the temple (42:20).

¹⁷ The city's open space will extend:
425 feet^A to the north,
425 feet to the south,
425 feet to the east,
and 425 feet to the west.

¹⁸ "The remainder of the length alongside the holy donation will be 3 ⅓ miles to the east and 3 ⅓ miles to the west. It will run alongside the holy donation. Its produce will be food for the workers of the city. ¹⁹ The city's workers from all the tribes of Israel will cultivate it. ²⁰ The entire donation will be 8 ⅓ miles by 8 ⅓ miles; you are to set apart the holy donation along with the city property as a square area.

²¹ "The remaining area on both sides of the holy donation and the city property will belong to the prince. He will own the land adjacent to the tribal portions, next to the 8 ⅓ miles of the donation as far as the eastern border and^B next to the 8 ⅓ miles of the donation as far as the western border. The holy donation and the sanctuary of the temple will be in the middle of it. ²² Except for the Levitical property and the city property in the middle of the area belonging to the prince, the area between the territory of Judah and that of Benjamin will belong to the prince.

²³ "As for the rest of the tribes:
From the east side to the west, will be Benjamin — one portion.
²⁴ Next to the territory of Benjamin, from the east side to the west, will be Simeon — one portion.
²⁵ Next to the territory of Simeon, from the east side to the west, will be Issachar — one portion.

²⁶ Next to the territory of Issachar, from the east side to the west, will be Zebulun — one portion.
²⁷ Next to the territory of Zebulun, from the east side to the west, will be Gad — one portion.
²⁸ Next to the territory of Gad toward the south side, the border will run from Tamar to the Waters of Meribath-kadesh, to the Brook of Egypt, and out to the Mediterranean Sea. ²⁹ This is the land you are to allot as an inheritance to Israel's tribes, and these will be their portions." This is the declaration of the Lord GOD.

The New City

³⁰ "These are the exits of the city:
On the north side, which measures 1 ½ miles, ³¹ there will be three gates facing north, the gates of the city being named for the tribes of Israel: one, the gate of Reuben; one, the gate of Judah; and one, the gate of Levi.
³² On the east side, which is 1 ½ miles, there will be three gates: one, the gate of Joseph; one, the gate of Benjamin; and one, the gate of Dan.
³³ On the south side, which measures 1 ½ miles, there will be three gates: one, the gate of Simeon; one, the gate of Issachar; and one, the gate of Zebulun.
³⁴ On the west side, which is 1 ½ miles, there will be three gates: one, the gate of Gad; one, the gate of Asher; and one, the gate of Naphtali.
³⁵ The perimeter of the city will be six miles,^C and the name of the city from that day on will be The LORD Is There."

---

^A 48:17 Lit *250 cubits* ^B 48:21 Lit *border, and to the west,* ^C 48:35 Lit *18,000 cubits*

48:21 What will belong to the **prince** includes twenty-five thousand cubits from both the eastern and western borders. This area will lie between the borders of Judah and Benjamin. The prince will have a higher rank than the average Israelite, yet his role will be below that of priests and Levites.

48:30–34 The names of the city gates adhere more to Israel's conventional genealogical traditions.

48:35 The city was square, as is the city in Revelation (specifically, it is a cube; Rv 21:16). They appear to be identical. In many ways the presence of God is the object of the final vision, and perhaps of the book of Ezekiel

as a whole. It is the emphatic resolution to the tragic event of God leaving his people in Ezk 8–11 (esp. 10:18–19; see Is 60:14; Jr 23:6). It also fulfills the prophetic promises about the reality of God's presence among his people in Zion (Is 1:26; 62:2; Zch 8:3). The name **The LORD Is There** reverses Ezk 10:18–19.

▼ Introduction to Daniel

Circumstances of Writing

The critical view of the book of Daniel suggests it was written by a second-century-BC Jewish author, not the historical Daniel. This view is largely based on a naturalistic perspective that denies the possibility of the authentic foretelling found in Daniel. On the other hand, the traditional view maintains that Daniel the prophet did indeed write this book sometime shortly after the end of the Babylonian captivity (sixth century BC). Internal testimony supports this claim. In the text itself, Daniel claimed to have written down visions given by God (8:2; 9:2,20; 12:5). Passages which contain third-person references to Daniel do not disprove his authorship. The prophet Ezekiel referred to Daniel several times (Ezk 14:14,20; 28:3), a prominence that would befit the writing prophet. Finally, Jesus Christ attributed the book of Daniel to Daniel himself (Mt 24:15; Mk 13:14).

The historical setting of the book of Daniel is the Babylonian captivity. The book opens after King Nebuchadnezzar's first siege of Judah (605 BC) when he brought Daniel and his friends to Babylon along with other captives among the Judean nobility. Nebuchadnezzar assaulted Judah again in 597 and brought ten thousand captives back to Babylon. In 586, he once again besieged Jerusalem, this time destroying the city, the holy temple, and exiling the people of Judah to Babylon. Daniel's ministry began in 605 when he arrived at Babylon with the first Jewish captives, extended throughout the Babylonian captivity (which ended in 539), and concluded sometime after the third year of Cyrus the Great, the Medo-Persian king who overthrew Babylonia (see Dn 1:21; 10:1).

When was the book written? While the critical view maintains a date of 165 BC in the Maccabean period primarily because of the precise prophecies related to that time, the traditional view asserts that it was written just after the end of the Babylonian captivity in the late sixth century BC. The book contains a factual recounting of events from the life of Daniel, supernatural prediction of events that took place during the intertestamental period, and prophecies that are yet to be fulfilled.

Manuscript evidence supports the early date. Fragments from Daniel were found among the Dead Sea Scrolls, a collection that included other books of the Bible that were written well before the second century. Historical evidence also supports the early date. For example, Daniel accurately described Belshazzar as coregent with another king (Nabonidus), a fact that was not known elsewhere until modern times. In summary, the late-date view is driven by a presuppositional rejection of supernatural prophecy and not objective evidence.

Contribution to the Bible

Daniel's book establishes the validity of predictive prophecy and lays the foundation for understanding end-times prophecy, especially the book of Revelation in the New Testament. Most important, it emphasizes that the Lord has dominion over all the kingdoms

Daniel Timeline

650–620 BC

Under Ashurbanipal, Assyrians capture and destroy Babylon. **649**
Birth of Jeremiah **640?**
Jeremiah's call to be a prophet; warns of invasion from the north **626**
Birth of Ezekiel **623**
Birth of Daniel **620**

620–605 BC

Under Nabopolassar **(626–605)** Asshur and Nineveh fall, marking the end of the Assyrian Empire. **612**
Babylonians and Medes take Harran from what remained of Assyrian forces. **610**
Jeremiah's temple sermon **609**
Josiah killed by the Egyptians at Megiddo **609**
Babylonians defeat Pharaoh Neco of Egypt at Carchemish. The Babylonians hold the balance of power in the region. **605**

of the earth, even in evil days when wicked empires reign. Two key words in the book are king (used more than 150 times) and kingdom (used more than 50 times). Above all, Daniel teaches that the God of Israel is the Sovereign of the universe, "for his dominion is an everlasting dominion, and his kingdom is from generation to generation" (4:34).

Structure

The genre of the book of Daniel is narrative, recounting historical events for the purpose of present and future instruction. The narrative contains history, prophecy, and apocalyptic visions. Apocalyptic literature refers to revelation by God given through visions and symbols with a message of eschatological (end-time) triumph.

Noting that the book of Daniel contains both history (chaps. 1–6) and prophecy (chaps. 7–12), some divide the book into two sections. A better way to view the book's structure is based on the two languages it uses: 1:1–2:3 (Hebrew); 2:4–7:28 (Aramaic); and 8:1–12:13 (Hebrew). The Hebrew sections pertain primarily to the people of Israel, which is fitting since Hebrew was Israel's national language. Aramaic was the international language of that time. The Aramaic section of Daniel demonstrates God's dominion over the international Gentile nations.

605–560 BC

The Babylonians besiege Jerusalem; some of the royal family and nobles, including Daniel, are taken to Babylon. **605**

Daniel and his Hebrew companions are trained to serve Nebuchadnezzar. **604–603**

Nebuchadnezzar's dream of the colossal statue and Daniel's interpretation **602**

Jerusalem falls to the third Babylonian siege and the temple is destroyed. **586**

Nebuchadnezzar's seven years of insanity **573–566**

Evil-merodach, Nebuchadnezzar's son, succeeds him as king of Babylon. **562**

560–525 BC

Daniel interprets the handwriting on the wall for Belshazzar. Cyrus captures Babylon without resistance. **539**

Gabriel visits Daniel with the message of 70 weeks. **539**

Cyrus issues a decree allowing the Jews to return to Judah. **538**

Daniel, now 84 years old, is thrown into the lions' den. **536**

Daniel receives vision of future events **535**

Daniel's Captivity in Babylon

1 In the third year of the reign of King Jehoiakim of Judah, King Nebuchadnezzar^A of Babylon came to Jerusalem and laid siege to it. ² The Lord handed King Jehoiakim of Judah over to him, along with some of the vessels from the house of God. Nebuchadnezzar carried them to the land of Babylon,^B to the house of his god,^C and put the vessels in the treasury of his god.

³ The king ordered Ashpenaz, his chief eunuch, to bring some of the Israelites from the royal family and from the nobility — ⁴ young men without any physical defect, good-looking, suitable for instruction in all wisdom, knowledgeable, perceptive, and capable of serving in the king's palace. He was to teach them the Chaldean language and literature. ⁵ The king assigned them daily provisions from the royal food and from the wine that he drank. They were to be trained for three years, and at the end of that time they were to attend the king.^D ⁶ Among them, from the Judahites, were Daniel, Hananiah, Mishael, and Azariah. ⁷ The chief eunuch gave them names; he gave the name Belteshazzar to Daniel, Shadrach to Hananiah, Meshach to Mishael, and Abednego to Azariah.

Faithfulness in Babylon

⁸ Daniel determined that he would not defile himself with the king's food or with the wine he drank. So he asked permission from the chief eunuch not to defile himself. ⁹ God had granted Daniel kindness and compassion from the chief eunuch, ¹⁰ yet he said to Daniel, "I fear my lord the king, who assigned your food and drink. What if he sees your faces looking thinner than the other young men your age? You would endanger my life^E with the king."

¹¹ So Daniel said to the guard whom the chief eunuch had assigned to Daniel, Hananiah, Mishael, and Azariah, ¹² "Please test your servants for ten days. Let us be given vegetables to eat and water to drink. ¹³ Then examine our appearance and the appearance of the young men who are eating the king's food, and deal with your servants based on what you see."

---

^A 1:1 Or *Nebuchadrezzar* ^B 1:2 Lit *Shinar* ^C 1:2 Or *gods* ^D 1:5 Lit *to stand before the king* ^E 1:10 Lit *would make my head guilty*

1:1 Although Daniel recorded these events as taking place **in the third year of . . . Jehoiakim**, Jeremiah wrote that it was in the fourth year (Jr 25:1,9; 46:1). Daniel probably used the Babylonian system which did not count a king's year of accession, while Jeremiah used the Israelite system of counting, which did include the accession year. The events took place during the accession year of **King Nebuchadnezzar of Babylon**, probably when he was still coregent with his father and just after the battle of Carchemish (605 BC).

1:2 Nebuchadnezzar took **vessels from the house of God**, in fulfillment of Isaiah's prediction when Hezekiah showed them to the Babylonian king a century beforehand (Is 39:2,6). **1:3** **His chief eunuch** could also be translated "his chief official." **1:4** The Hebrew word for **young men** here literally means "children" or "boys" and probably refers to teenagers, a good estimate being around age fifteen. **Chaldean language and literature** refers to an ancient university-style education in Sumerian, Akkadian, and Aramaic.

1:6–7 Daniel and his friends, whose original names honored the God of Israel, were given other **names** intended to honor the false gods of Babylon. **Daniel** ("God Is My Judge") became **Belteshazzar** ("Bel Protect Him"); **Hananiah** ("God Has Been Gracious") became **Shadrach** ("The Command of Akku"); **Mishael** ("Who Is What God Is?") became **Meshach** ("Who Is What Aku Is?"); **Azariah** ("The Lord Has Helped") became **Abednego** ("Servant of Nebo"). **1:8** The word **determined** means literally "set upon his heart," referring to inner resolve.

Character profile:
Daniel

From a historical perspective, it seems that Daniel came of age at exactly the wrong time in Israel. He was born just in time to see his once-great nation fall to the Babylonians. As punishment for their centuries of unfaithfulness and disobedience, God allowed his people to be defeated by their enemies. Daniel—like many other young, strong, and capable people in Israel—was carried away into captivity in Babylon.

From a spiritual perspective, however, it's apparent that Daniel came of age at exactly the right time. During his years as a captive in Babylon, Daniel made a lasting impression on key figures in the Babylonian and (later) Persian governments. He revealed God's power and protectiveness in ways no one would forget.

Under God's guiding hand, Daniel made a name for himself as a wise and trusted adviser to King Nebuchadnezzar. His later quick rise to prominence in Darius's government made him a marked man among that king's other advisers.

Daniel could not follow the royal edict that commanded the king's subjects to pray to no one but the king for thirty days under penalty of being cast into a den of lions. This decree, which was dreamed up by a faction of rogue advisers, was nothing more than a shrewd political maneuver—a way for Daniel's enemies to create a fatal trap. But the king didn't know that when he put it into writing, making it an inviolable law that even he couldn't revoke.

Daniel certainly recognized the decree for what it was. He knew his opponents had found a way to use his devotion to God against him. He understood that the next time he prayed could be his last. But for Daniel there was no debate. As soon as the new law was announced, he went straight to his room, dropped to his knees, and prayed to the Lord—in full view of his enemies, who were carefully watching.

King Darius, much to his dismay, was forced to throw Daniel into a pit of hungry lions and then seal the pit with a stone. At the first light of dawn, Darius rushed back to the pit. To his shock, Daniel was alive, preserved by his God.

Daniel's willingness to die for his faith and God's willingness to save his faithful servant made a powerful impact on the king. His first order of business was to sentence to death the men who had brought the charges against Daniel. His second order of business? To issue a decree that all the people in his royal dominion would "tremble in fear before the God of Daniel," the "living God," whose "dominion has no end," who "rescues and delivers" and "performs signs and wonders in the heavens and on the earth" (Dn 6:26–27).

Taking a bold stand for God always pays dividends. That's not to suggest that a miraculous outcome like Daniel's awaits everyone who stands firm in the face of overwhelming opposition. Millions of Christian martyrs could testify to that fact.

Yet one person's stand has the power to bring glory to God, to inspire others, to change hearts, and to produce results far beyond immediate circumstances. The better prepared you are to take a stand for your faith when circumstances dictate, the bigger the impact you can have.

¹⁴ He agreed with them about this and tested them for ten days. ¹⁵ At the end of ten days they looked better and healthier^A than all the young men who were eating the king's food. ¹⁶ So the guard continued to remove their food and the wine they were to drink and gave them vegetables.

Faithfulness Rewarded

¹⁷ God gave these four young men knowledge and understanding in every kind of literature and wisdom. Daniel also understood visions and dreams of every kind. ¹⁸ At the end of the time that the king had said to present them, the chief eunuch presented them to Nebuchadnezzar. ¹⁹ The king interviewed them, and among all of them, no one was found equal to Daniel, Hananiah, Mishael, and Azariah. So they began to attend the king. ²⁰ In every matter of wisdom and understanding that the king consulted them about, he found them ten times^B better than all the magicians and mediums in his entire kingdom. ²¹ Daniel remained there until the first year of King Cyrus.

Nebuchadnezzar's Dream

2 In the second year of his reign, Nebuchadnezzar had dreams that troubled him, and sleep deserted him. ² So the king gave orders to summon the magicians, mediums, sorcerers, and Chaldeans^c to tell the king his dreams. When they came and stood before the king, ³ he said to them, "I have had a dream and am anxious to understand it."

⁴ The Chaldeans spoke to the king (Aramaic^D begins here): "May the king live forever. Tell your servants the dream, and we will give the interpretation."

⁵ The king replied to the Chaldeans, "My word is final: If you don't tell me the dream and its interpretation, you will be torn limb from limb,^E and your houses will be made a garbage dump. ⁶ But if you make the dream and its interpretation known to me, you'll receive gifts, a reward, and great honor from me. So make the dream and its interpretation known to me."

⁷ They answered a second time, "May the king tell the dream to his servants, and we will make known the interpretation."

⁸ The king replied, "I know for certain you are trying to gain some time, because you see that my word is final. ⁹ If you don't tell me the dream, there is one decree for you. You have conspired to tell me something false or fraudulent until the situation changes. So tell me the dream and I will know you can give me its interpretation."

¹⁰ The Chaldeans answered the king, "No one on earth can make known what the king requests. Consequently, no king, however great and powerful, has ever asked anything like this of any magician, medium, or Chaldean. ¹¹ What the king is asking is so difficult that no one can make it known to him except the gods, whose dwelling is not with mortals." ¹² Because of this, the king became violently angry and gave orders to destroy all the wise men of Babylon. ¹³ The decree was issued that the wise men were to be executed, and they searched for Daniel and his friends, to execute them.

¹⁴ Then Daniel responded with tact and discretion to Arioch, the captain of the king's guard,^F who had gone out to execute the wise men of Babylon. ¹⁵ He asked Arioch, the king's officer, "Why is the decree from the king so harsh?"^G Then Arioch explained the situation to Daniel. ¹⁶ So Daniel went and asked the king to give him some time, so that he could give the king the interpretation.

¹⁷ Then Daniel went to his house and told his friends Hananiah, Mishael, and Azariah about the matter, ¹⁸ urging them to ask the God of the heavens for mercy concerning this mystery, so Daniel and his friends would not be destroyed with the rest of Babylon's wise men. ¹⁹ The mystery was then revealed to Daniel in a vision at night, and Daniel praised the God of the heavens ²⁰ and declared:

> May the name of God
> be praised forever and ever,
> for wisdom and power belong to him.
> ²¹ He changes the times and seasons;
> he removes kings and establishes kings.
> He gives wisdom to the wise
> and knowledge to those
> who have understanding.
> ²² He reveals the deep and hidden things;
> he knows what is in the darkness,
> and light dwells with him.
> ²³ I offer thanks and praise to you,
> God of my ancestors,
> because you have given me
> wisdom and power.
> And now you have let me know

---

^A1:15 Lit *fatter of flesh*   ^B1:20 Lit *hands*   ^C2:2 In this chap. Chaldeans are influential Babylonian wise men.
^D2:4 Dn 2:4–7:28 is written in Aramaic.   ^E2:5 Lit *be made into limbs*   ^F2:14 Or *executioners*   ^G2:15 Or *urgent*

1:21 The first year of King Cyrus was 539 BC.
2:1 Nebuchadnezzar's dreams took place **in the second year of his reign**, which was in 602 BC.
2:2–3 Chaldeans, as used here, is a specific term for priests who served as astrologers, soothsayers, and wise men in the king's government.

2:4–7:28 The narrative switches from Hebrew to **Aramaic** in v. 4 and continues in Aramaic until 7:28. Chapters 2–7 pertain to God's revelations about the Gentile nations.
2:5–9 Some versions translate the phrase **my word is final** as "the dream is forgotten." It is better to translate it as referring to the certainty and finality of the king's demand. Nebuchadnezzar withheld the facts of the

dream not because he could not remember them but because he wanted to test his wise men.
2:17–19 The mystery refers to a secret that can only be known by divine revelation.
2:20–23 Daniel's song of praise includes the two key ideas of the chapter: God is sovereign over the political affairs of humanity and God alone can give revelation.

1. Head of Gold

2. Chest & Arms of Silver

3. Stomach & Thighs of Bronze

4. Legs of Iron

5. Feet of Iron & Fired Clay

Abe Goolsby

Nebuchadnezzar's Dream / Daniel 2

what we asked of you,
for you have let us know
the king's mystery.^A

²⁴ Therefore Daniel went to Arioch, whom the king had assigned to destroy the wise men of Babylon. He came and said to him, "Don't destroy the wise men of Babylon! Bring me before the king, and I will give him the interpretation." ²⁵ Then Arioch quickly brought Daniel before the king and said to him, "I have found a man among the Judean exiles who can let the king know the interpretation." ²⁶ The king said in reply to Daniel, whose name was Belteshazzar, "Are you able to tell me the dream I had and its interpretation?" ²⁷ Daniel answered the king, "No wise man, medium, magician, or diviner is able to make known to the king the mystery he asked about. ²⁸ But there is a God in heaven who reveals mysteries, and he has let King Nebuchadnezzar know what will happen in the last days. Your dream and the visions that came into your mind as you lay in bed were these: ²⁹ Your Majesty, while you were in your bed, thoughts came to your mind about what will happen in the future.^B The revealer of mysteries has let you know what will happen. ³⁰ As for me, this mystery has been revealed to me, not because I have more wisdom than anyone living, but in order that the interpretation might be made known to the king, and that you may understand the thoughts of your mind.

The Dream's Interpretation

³¹ "Your Majesty, as you were watching, suddenly a colossal statue appeared. That statue, tall and dazzling, was standing in front of you, and its appearance was terrifying. ³² The head of the statue was pure gold, its chest and arms were silver, its stomach and thighs were bronze, ³³ its legs were iron, and its feet were partly iron and partly fired clay. ³⁴ As you were watching, a stone broke off without a hand touching it,^C struck the statue on its feet of iron and fired clay, and crushed them. ³⁵ Then the iron, the fired clay, the bronze, the silver, and the gold were shattered and became like chaff from the summer threshing floors. The wind carried them away, and not a trace of them could be found. But the stone that struck the statue became a great mountain and filled the whole earth.

³⁶ "This was the dream; now we will tell the king its interpretation. ³⁷ Your Majesty, you are king of kings. The God of the heavens has given you sovereignty, power, strength, and glory. ³⁸ Wherever people live — or wild animals, or birds of the sky — he has handed them over to you and made you ruler over them all. You are the head of gold.

³⁹ "After you, there will arise another kingdom, inferior to yours, and then another, a third kingdom, of bronze, which will rule the whole earth. ⁴⁰ A fourth kingdom will be as strong as iron; for iron crushes and shatters everything, and like iron that smashes, it will crush and smash all the others.^D ⁴¹ You saw the feet and toes, partly of a potter's fired clay and partly of iron — it will be a divided kingdom, though some of the strength of iron will be in it. You saw the iron mixed with clay, ⁴² and that the toes of the feet were partly iron and partly fired clay — part of the kingdom will be strong, and part will be brittle. ⁴³ You saw the iron mixed with clay — the peoples will mix with one another^E but will not hold together, just as iron does not mix with fired clay.

⁴⁴ "In the days of those kings, the God of the heavens will set up a kingdom that will never be destroyed, and this kingdom will not be left to another people. It will crush all these kingdoms and bring them to an end, but will itself endure forever. ⁴⁵ You saw a stone break off from the mountain without a hand touching it,^F and it crushed the iron, bronze, fired clay, silver, and gold. The great God has told the king what will happen in the future. The dream is certain, and its interpretation reliable."

Nebuchadnezzar's Response

⁴⁶ Then King Nebuchadnezzar fell facedown, worshiped Daniel, and gave orders to present an offering and incense to him. ⁴⁷ The king said to Daniel, "Your God is indeed God of gods, Lord of kings, and a revealer of mysteries, since you were able to reveal this mystery." ⁴⁸ Then the king promoted Daniel and gave him many generous gifts. He made him ruler over the entire province of Babylon and chief governor over all the wise men of Babylon. ⁴⁹ At Daniel's request, the king appointed Shadrach, Meshach, and Abednego to manage the province of Babylon. But Daniel remained at the king's court.

---

^A 2:23 Lit matter ^B 2:29 Lit happen after this, also in v. 45 ^C 2:34 Lit off not by hands ^D 2:40 Lit all these ^E 2:43 Lit another in the seed of men ^F 2:45 Lit mountain, not by hands

---

2:27 **Diviner** refers to a person who is able to determine another's fate.
2:28 **In the last days** indicates that the king's dream would find its complete fulfillment only in the end times.
2:31–45 Daniel interpreted the parts of the colossal statue to represent four empires in historical succession. The **head** represented the kingdom of Babylon (605–539 BC).

The **chest and arms** symbolized the Medo-Persian Empire (539–331 BC). The **stomach and thighs** stood for the Greek Empire (331–146 BC). The **legs** referred to the Roman Empire (146 BC–AD 1476 in the West and AD 1453 in the East). The feet were mixed of **iron** and **clay** and represented a future continuation or revival of Rome. The material of each section of the statue

decreased in value but increased in strength (except for the feet; see vv. 42–43). Daniel also described a **stone** that would shatter the final kingdom and grow into a mountain that **filled the whole earth**. This "stone" is the kingdom of God.
2:37 In Ezk 26:7 God himself calls Nebuchadnezzar **king of kings**. King Artaxerxes claims the title for himself in Ezr 7:12. But the title

Nebuchadnezzar's Gold Statue

3 King Nebuchadnezzar made a gold statue, ninety feet high and nine feet wide.^A He set it up on the plain of Dura in the province of Babylon. ² King Nebuchadnezzar sent word to assemble the satraps, prefects, governors, advisers, treasurers, judges, magistrates, and all the rulers of the provinces to attend the dedication of the statue King Nebuchadnezzar had set up. ³ So the satraps, prefects, governors, advisers, treasurers, judges, magistrates, and all the rulers of the provinces assembled for the dedication of the statue the king had set up. Then they stood before the statue Nebuchadnezzar had set up.

⁴ A herald loudly proclaimed, "People of every nation and language, you are commanded: ⁵ When you hear the sound of the horn, flute, zither,^B lyre,^C harp, drum,^D and every kind of music, you are to fall facedown and worship the gold statue that King Nebuchadnezzar has set up. ⁶ But whoever does not fall down and worship will immediately be thrown into a furnace of blazing fire."

⁷ Therefore, when all the people heard the sound of the horn, flute, zither, lyre, harp, and every kind of music, people of every nation and language fell down and worshiped the gold statue that King Nebuchadnezzar had set up.

The Furnace of Blazing Fire

⁸ Some Chaldeans took this occasion to come forward and maliciously accuse^E the Jews. ⁹ They said to King Nebuchadnezzar, "May the king live forever. ¹⁰ You as king have issued a decree that everyone who hears the sound of the horn, flute, zither, lyre, harp, drum, and every kind of music must fall down and worship the gold statue. ¹¹ Whoever does not fall down and worship will be thrown into a furnace of blazing fire. ¹² There are some Jews you have appointed to manage the province of Babylon: Shadrach, Meshach, and Abednego. These men have ignored you, the king; they do not serve your gods or worship the gold statue you have set up."

¹³ Then in a furious rage Nebuchadnezzar gave orders to bring in Shadrach, Meshach, and Abednego. So these men were brought before the king. ¹⁴ Nebuchadnezzar asked them, "Shadrach, Meshach, and Abednego, is it true that you don't serve my gods or worship the gold statue I have set up? ¹⁵ Now if you're ready, when you hear the sound of the horn, flute, zither, lyre, harp, drum, and every kind of music, fall down and worship the statue I made. But if you don't worship it, you will immediately be thrown into a furnace of blazing fire — and who is the god who can rescue you from my power?"

¹⁶ Shadrach, Meshach, and Abednego replied to the king, "Nebuchadnezzar, we don't need to give you an answer to this question. ¹⁷ If the God we serve exists, then he can rescue us from the furnace of blazing fire, and he can^F rescue us from the power of you, the king. ¹⁸ But even if he does not rescue us,^G we want you as king to know that we will not serve your gods or worship the gold statue you set up."

¹⁹ Then Nebuchadnezzar was filled with rage, and the expression on his face changed toward Shadrach, Meshach, and Abednego. He gave orders to heat the furnace seven times more than was customary, ²⁰ and he commanded some of the best soldiers in his army to tie up Shadrach, Meshach, and Abednego and throw them into the furnace of blazing fire. ²¹ So these men, in their trousers, robes, head coverings,^H and other clothes, were tied up and thrown into the furnace of blazing fire. ²² Since the king's command was so urgent^I and the furnace extremely hot, the raging flames^J killed those men who carried up Shadrach, Meshach, and Abednego. ²³ And these three men, Shadrach, Meshach, and Abednego fell, bound, into the furnace of blazing fire.

Delivered from the Fire

²⁴ Then King Nebuchadnezzar jumped up in alarm. He said to his advisers, "Didn't we throw three men, bound, into the fire?"

"Yes, of course, Your Majesty," they replied to the king.

²⁵ He exclaimed, "Look! I see four men, not tied, walking around in the fire unharmed; and the fourth looks like a son of the gods."^K

---

^A 3:1 Lit statue, its height sixty cubits, its width six cubits   ^B 3:5 Or lyre   ^C 3:5 Or sambuke   ^D 3:5 Or pipe   ^E 3:8 Lit and eat the pieces of   ^F 3:17 Or If the God whom we serve is willing to save us from the furnace of blazing fire, then he will   ^G 3:18 Lit But if not   ^H 3:21 The identity of these articles of clothing is uncertain.   ^I 3:22 Or harsh   ^J 3:22 Lit the flame of the fire   ^K 3:25 Or of a divine being

---

belongs truly only to Jesus Christ (1Tm 6:15; Rv 17:14; 19:16).
3:1 The events of Dn 3 probably took place shortly after Daniel explained the king's dream (cp. Dn 2), although some estimate that it could have been ten or even twenty years later. The **gold statue** was not likely solid gold but was instead overlaid with it. The location of **the plain of Dura** has not been conclusively identified. Daniel was not involved in the events here since he remained in the capital city "at the king's court" (2:49). **3:4–5** Three of the instruments mentioned — **zither . . . harp,** and **drum** — are the only

Greek loanwords in Daniel. Although some conjecture that the **gold statue** was of Nebuchadnezzar himself, this is unlikely because the Babylonians did not believe their king was divine. More likely, the image was of a Babylonian god, perhaps Nebuchadnezzar's patron Nabu or the chief Babylonian god Marduk.
3:6 Incineration in **a furnace of blazing fire** — a punishment that Nebuchadnezzar had also used on two Judean false prophets, Zedekiah and Ahab (Jr 29:22) — was a normal Babylonian penalty, as seen in the Code of Hammurabi.

3:8 On **Chaldeans,** see 2:2–3.
3:19 Seven times more than was customary is an idiom for "as hot as possible."
3:23 The furnace was built on a small hill or mound with openings at the top and side. So the three men **fell . . . into the furnace** from the top, and the king was able to see four men in the furnace (v. 25) as he looked in through the side opening.
3:24–25 A **fourth** figure who looked **like a son of the gods** may have been an angel or even a preincarnate appearance of God the Son.

²⁶ Nebuchadnezzar then approached the door of the furnace of blazing fire and called, "Shadrach, Meshach, and Abednego, you servants of the Most High God — come out!" So Shadrach, Meshach, and Abednego came out of the fire. ²⁷ When the satraps, prefects, governors, and the king's advisers gathered around, they saw that the fire had no effect onᴬ the bodies of these men: not a hair of their heads was singed, their robes were unaffected, and there was no smell of fire on them. ²⁸ Nebuchadnezzar exclaimed, "Praise to the God of Shadrach, Meshach, and Abednego! He sent his angelᴮ and rescued his servants who trusted in him. They violated the king's command and risked their lives rather than serve or worship any god except their own God. ²⁹ Therefore I issue a decree that anyone of any people, nation, or language who says anything offensive against the God of Shadrach, Meshach, and Abednego will be torn limb from limb and his house made a garbage dump. For there is no other god who is able to deliver like this." ³⁰ Then the king rewarded Shadrach, Meshach, and Abednego in the province of Babylon.

Nebuchadnezzar's Proclamation

4 King Nebuchadnezzar,

To those of every people, nation, and language, who live on the whole earth:

May your prosperity increase. ² I am pleased to tell you about the miracles and wonders the Most High God has done for me.

³   How great are his miracles,
        and how mighty his wonders!
      His kingdom is an eternal kingdom,
        and his dominion is from generation
           to generation.

The Dream

⁴ I, Nebuchadnezzar, was at ease in my house and flourishing in my palace. ⁵ I had a dream, and it frightened me; while in my bed, the images and visions in my mind alarmed me. ⁶ So I issued a decree to bring all the wise men of Babylon to me in order that they might make the dream's interpretation known to me. ⁷ When the magicians, mediums, Chaldeans, and diviners came in, I told them the dream, but they could not make its interpretation known to me.

⁸ Finally Daniel, named Belteshazzar after the name of my god — and a spirit of the holy gods is in him — came before me. I told him the dream: ⁹ "Belteshazzar, head of the magicians, because I know that you have the spirit of the holy gods and that no mystery puzzles you, explain to me the visions of my dream that I saw, and its interpretation. ¹⁰ In the visions of my mind as I was lying in bed, I saw this:

      There was a tree in the middle
          of the earth,
        and it was very tall.
¹¹   The tree grew large and strong;
        its top reached to the sky,
      and it was visible to the ends
          of theᶜ earth.
¹²   Its leaves were beautiful, its fruit
          was abundant,
      and on it was food for all.
      Wild animals found shelter under it,
      the birds of the sky lived in its branches,
      and every creature was fed from it.

¹³ "As I was lying in my bed, I also saw in the visions of my mind a watcher, a holy one,ᴰ coming down from heaven. ¹⁴ He called out loudly:

      Cut down the tree and chop off
          its branches;
      strip off its leaves and scatter its fruit.
      Let the animals flee from under it,
        and the birds from its branches.
¹⁵   But leave the stump with its roots
          in the ground
      and with a band of iron and bronze
          around it
      in the tender grass of the field.
      Let him be drenched with dew
          from the sky
      and share the plants of the earth
          with the animals.
¹⁶   Let his mind be changed from that
          of a human,
      and let him be given the mind
          of an animal

ᴬ3:27 Lit fire had not overcome   ᴮ3:28 Or messenger   ᶜ4:11 Lit of all the   ᴰ4:13 = an angel

---

3:26–27 Hebrews 11:34 cites this miracle of faith, referring to those who "quenched the raging of fire."
4:1–3 These verses come at the end of chap. 3 in Aramaic rather than at the beginning of chap. 4. As an introduction to chap. 4, the miracles and wonders include the dream in chap. 4 and its aftermath.
4:4–36 The text does not indicate when King Nebuchadnezzar had his **dream**, but it was likely some ten years before the end of his forty-three-year reign. Then God in

his grace allowed him one year to repent followed by seven years of madness. Once he came to his senses, Nebuchadnezzar lived another two or three years before dying in 562 BC.
4:7 Unlike the dream of Dn 2, the king **told them the dream**. But similarly **they could not make its interpretation known** to him.
4:8 Beginning in this verse and throughout the chapter, Daniel is most frequently called by his Babylonian name **Belteshazzar**, seemingly because this section is written from

the perspective of the Babylonian king, not a Hebrew exile.
4:13 The **watcher, a holy one**, was an angel.
4:14–17 The fact that **the stump with its roots** would remain **in the ground** indicated the continuation of life. The **band of iron and bronze** pointed to the protection of the stump. The tree plainly represents a man (the king) because the angel declared that **his mind** would **be changed from that of a human** to **an animal for seven periods of time** or for seven years.

for seven periods of time."^,B

17 This word is by decree of the watchers,
and the decision is by command
from the holy ones.
This is so that the living will know
that the Most High is ruler
over human kingdoms.
He gives them to anyone he wants
and sets the lowliest of people
over them.

18 This is the dream that I, King Nebuchadnezzar, had. Now, Belteshazzar, tell me the interpretation, because none of the wise men of my kingdom can make the interpretation known to me. But you can, because you have a spirit of the holy gods."

The Dream Interpreted

19 Then Daniel, whose name is Belteshazzar, was stunned for a moment, and his thoughts alarmed him. The king said, "Belteshazzar, don't let the dream or its interpretation alarm you."

Belteshazzar answered, "My lord, may the dream apply to those who hate you, and its interpretation to your enemies! 20 The tree you saw, which grew large and strong, whose top reached to the sky and was visible to the whole earth, 21 and whose leaves were beautiful and its fruit abundant — and on it was food for all, under it the wild animals lived, and in its branches the birds of the sky lived — 22 that tree is you, Your Majesty. For you have become great and strong: your greatness has grown and even reaches the sky, and your dominion extends to the ends of the earth.

23 "The king saw a watcher, a holy one, coming down from heaven and saying, 'Cut down the tree and destroy it, but leave the stump with its roots in the ground and with a band of iron and bronze around it in the tender grass of the field. Let him be drenched with dew from the sky and share food with the wild animals for seven periods of time.' 24 This is the interpretation, Your Majesty, and this is the decree of the Most High that has been issued against my lord the king: 25 You will be driven away from people to live with the wild animals. You will feed on grass like cattle and be drenched with dew from the sky for seven periods of time, until you acknowledge that the Most High is ruler over human kingdoms, and he gives them to anyone he wants. 26 As for the command to leave the tree's stump with its roots, your kingdom will be restored^c to you as soon as you acknowledge that Heaven^D rules. 27 Therefore, may my advice seem good to you my king. Separate yourself from your sins by doing what is right, and from your injustices by showing mercy to the needy. Perhaps there will be an extension of your prosperity."

The Sentence Executed

28 All this happened to King Nebuchadnezzar. 29 At the end of twelve months, as he was walking on the roof of the royal palace in Babylon, 30 the king exclaimed, "Is this not Babylon the Great that I have built to be a royal residence by my vast power and for my majestic glory?" 31 While the words were still in the king's mouth, a voice came from heaven: "King Nebuchadnezzar, to you it is declared that the kingdom has departed from you. 32 You will be driven away from people to live with the wild animals, and you will feed on grass like cattle for seven periods of time, until you acknowledge that the Most High is ruler over human kingdoms, and he gives them to anyone he wants."

33 At that moment the message against Nebuchadnezzar was fulfilled. He was driven away from people. He ate grass like cattle, and his body was drenched with dew from the sky, until his hair grew like eagles' feathers and his nails like birds' claws.

Nebuchadnezzar's Praise

34 But at the end of those days, I, Nebuchadnezzar, looked up to heaven, and my sanity returned to me. Then I praised the Most High and honored and glorified him who lives forever:

For his dominion is
an everlasting dominion,
and his kingdom is from generation
to generation.
35 All the inhabitants of the earth
are counted as nothing,
and he does what he wants
with the army of heaven
and the inhabitants of the earth.
There is no one who can block his hand
or say to him, "What have you done?"

36 At that time my sanity returned to me, and my majesty and splendor returned to me for the glory of my kingdom. My advisers and my nobles sought me out, I was reestablished over

---

^A4:16 Lit *animal as seven times pass over him* ^B4:16 Perhaps seven years ^C4:26 Lit *enduring* ^D4:26 = God

---

4:26 This is the only place in the OT where **Heaven** is used as a euphemism for God. **4:29–30** Nebuchadnezzar had no less than three palaces in the city of Babylon. He was **walking on the roof** of one of them when he was overcome with the glory of the city and was consumed with pride. In his exclamation **Is this not Babylon the Great that I** (lit "I, myself") **have built** ...

by my vast power and for my majestic glory?, Nebuchadnezzar proclaimed himself the source of majesty. He failed to give God the credit and glory as the ultimate giver of all good gifts. **4:33** Nebuchadnezzar may have suffered from boanthropy, a rare mental illness in which people believe they are actually cattle.

4:34 Boanthropy does not render its victims entirely unable to reason or understand what has happened to them, so it was possible for the king to realize that his own pride had caused his insanity. Realizing the cause of his state, **Nebuchadnezzar** repented of his pride and acknowledged the Most High God. His **sanity returned** to him instantly, a signal that God had lifted his sentence.

my kingdom, and even more greatness came to me. [37] Now I, Nebuchadnezzar, praise, exalt, and glorify the King of the heavens, because all his works are true and his ways are just. He is able to humble those who walk in pride.

Belshazzar's Feast

5 King Belshazzar held a great feast for a thousand of his nobles and drank wine in their presence. [2] Under the influence of[A] the wine, Belshazzar gave orders to bring in the gold and silver vessels that his predecessor[B] Nebuchadnezzar had taken from the temple in Jerusalem, so that the king and his nobles, wives, and concubines could drink from them. [3] So they brought in the gold[C] vessels that had been taken from the temple, the house of God in Jerusalem, and the king and his nobles, wives, and concubines drank from them. [4] They drank the wine and praised their gods made of gold and silver, bronze, iron, wood, and stone.

The Handwriting on the Wall

[5] At that moment the fingers of a man's hand appeared and began writing on the plaster of the king's palace wall next to the lampstand. As the king watched the hand[D] that was writing, [6] his face turned pale,[E] and his thoughts so terrified him that he soiled himself[F] and his knees knocked together. [7] The king shouted to bring in the mediums, Chaldeans, and diviners. He said to these wise men of Babylon, "Whoever reads this inscription and gives me its interpretation will be clothed in purple, have a gold chain around his neck, and have the third highest position in the kingdom." [8] So all the king's wise men came in, but none could read the inscription or make its interpretation known to him. [9] Then King Belshazzar became even more terrified, his face turned pale,[G] and his nobles were bewildered.

[10] Because of the outcry of the king and his nobles, the queen[H] came to the banquet hall. "May the king live forever," she said. "Don't let your thoughts terrify you or your face be pale.[I] [11] There is a man in your kingdom who has a spirit of the holy gods in him. In the days of your predecessor he was found to have insight, intelligence, and wisdom like the wisdom of the gods. Your predecessor, King Nebuchadnezzar, appointed him chief of the magicians, mediums, Chaldeans, and diviners. Your own predecessor, the king, [12] did this because Daniel, the one the king named Belteshazzar, was found to have an extraordinary spirit, knowledge and intelligence, and the ability to interpret dreams, explain riddles, and solve problems.[J] Therefore, summon Daniel, and he will give the interpretation."

Daniel before the King

[13] Then Daniel was brought before the king. The king said to him, "Are you Daniel, one of the Judean exiles that my predecessor the king brought from Judah? [14] I've heard that you have a spirit of the gods in you, and that insight, intelligence, and extraordinary wisdom are found in you. [15] Now the wise men and mediums were brought before me to read this inscription and make its interpretation known to me, but they could not give its interpretation. [16] However, I have heard about you that you can give interpretations and solve problems. Therefore, if you can read this inscription and give me its interpretation, you will be clothed in purple, have a gold chain around your neck, and have the third highest position in the kingdom."

[17] Then Daniel answered the king, "You may keep your gifts and give your rewards to someone else; however, I will read the inscription for the king and make the interpretation known to

---

[A]5:2 Or *When he tasted* [B]5:2 Or *father*, or *grandfather* [C]5:3 Theod, Vg add *and silver* [D]5:5 Lit *part of the hand*
[E]5:5–6 Lit *writing*, [F]*the king's brightness changed* [F]5:6 Or *that the joints of his hips gave way*; lit *that the knots of his loins
were untied* [G]5:9 Lit *his brightness changed on him* [H]5:10 Perhaps the queen mother [I]5:10 Lit *your brightness change*
[J]5:12 Lit *and untie knots*; also in v. 16

4:37 The last sentence of the chapter summarizes the message of the story—that God is **able to humble those who walk in pride. 5:1** The developments in Dn 5 occurred about twenty-three years after the events in the previous chapter. Nebuchadnezzar had died in 562 BC, shortly after his time of madness and subsequent repentance. After his death, a series of intrigues and assassinations resulted in several obscure kings ruling Babylon until Nabonidus took the throne (556–539 BC). **King Belshazzar held a great feast for a thousand of his nobles**, probably to bolster morale after Nabonidus had experienced a crushing defeat at the hands of the Persians. The Greek historians Herodotus and Xenophon confirm that Babylon fell while a great feast was in progress (v. 30). **5:2–4** By drinking libations to Babylonian gods with the **vessels . . . taken from the temple** devoted to the true God of Israel,

Belshazzar was acting in an unusually aggressive and blasphemous way. **Nebuchadnezzar** is called Belshazzar's **predecessor** (lit "his father"). Most likely, Belshazzar's father, Nabonidus, married Nebuchadnezzar's daughter to establish his own claim to the throne of Babylon, making Nebuchadnezzar the grandfather of Belshazzar.
5:5 The appearance of **a man's hand** beginning to write was not a vision seen by Belshazzar alone, but a miracle seen by everyone present.
5:7 The **third highest position in the kingdom** was after Nabonidus and Belshazzar.
5:10 The **queen** who **came to the banquet hall** was the queen mother, not the wife of King Belshazzar since all his wives were already present (cp. v. 3).
5:11–12 Daniel was approximately eighty years old at this point and was either retired or forgotten. The queen mother,

being the daughter of Nebuchadnezzar, remembered Daniel's **extraordinary spirit** and **ability to interpret dreams** during her father's reign.

#43 99 Essential Christian Truths

GOD IS HOLY

God's holiness refers to his uniqueness in being separate from all he has created. The Hebrew word for *holy* means "separate" or "set apart." God's holiness also refers to his absolute purity. God is unstained by the evil of the world. His goodness is perfect, and the moral code we find in the Scriptures is a reflection of his holy nature. As people made in God's image, we are called to holiness.

him. **18** Your Majesty, the Most High God gave sovereignty, greatness, glory, and majesty to your predecessor Nebuchadnezzar. **19** Because of the greatness he gave him, all peoples, nations, and languages were terrified and fearful of him. He killed anyone he wanted and kept alive anyone he wanted; he exalted anyone he wanted and humbled anyone he wanted. **20** But when his heart was exalted and his spirit became arrogant, he was deposed from his royal throne and his glory was taken from him. **21** He was driven away from people, his mind was like an animal's, he lived with the wild donkeys, he was fed grass like cattle, and his body was drenched with dew from the sky until he acknowledged that the Most High God is ruler over human kingdoms and sets anyone he wants over them.

22 "But you his successor, Belshazzar, have not humbled your heart, even though you knew all this. **23** Instead, you have exalted yourself against the Lord of the heavens. The vessels from his house were brought to you, and as you and your nobles, wives, and concubines drank wine from them, you praised the gods made of silver and gold, bronze, iron, wood, and stone, which do not see or hear or understand. But you have not glorified the God who holds your life-breath in his hand and who controls the whole course of your life.^A **24** Therefore, he sent the hand, and this writing was inscribed.

The Inscription's Interpretation

25 "This is the writing that was inscribed: MENE, MENE, TEKEL, and PARSIN. **26** This is the interpretation of the message:

'Mene'^B means that God has numbered^C
the days of your kingdom and brought it
to an end.

27 'Tekel'^D means that you have been weighed^E on the balance and found deficient.

28 'Peres'^F,^G means that your kingdom has been divided and given to the Medes and Persians."^H

29 Then Belshazzar gave an order, and they clothed Daniel in purple, placed a gold chain around his neck, and issued a proclamation concerning him that he should be the third ruler in the kingdom.

30 That very night Belshazzar the king of the Chaldeans was killed, **31** and Darius the Mede received the kingdom at the age of sixty-two.

The Plot against Daniel

6 Darius decided^I to appoint 120 satraps over the kingdom, stationed throughout the realm, **2** and over them three administrators, including Daniel. These satraps would be accountable to them so that the king would not be defrauded. **3** Daniel^J distinguished himself above the administrators and satraps because he had an extraordinary spirit, so the king planned to set him over the whole realm. **4** The administrators and satraps, therefore, kept trying to find a charge against Daniel regarding the kingdom. But they could find no charge or corruption, for he was trustworthy, and no negligence or corruption was found in him. **5** Then these men said, "We will never find any charge against this Daniel unless we find something against him concerning the law of his God."

6 So the administrators and satraps went together to the king and said to him, "May King Darius live forever. **7** All the administrators of the kingdom — the prefects, satraps, advisers, and governors — have agreed that the king

---

^A **5:23** Lit *and all your ways belong to him*   ^B **5:26** Or *a mina*   ^C **5:26** The Aramaic word for *numbered* sounds like *mene.*
^D **5:27** Or *a shekel*   ^E **5:27** The Aramaic word for *weighed* sounds like *tekel.*   ^F **5:28** Or *half a shekel*   ^G **5:28** In Aramaic, the word *peres* is the sg form of "parsin" in v. 25.   ^H **5:28** The Aramaic word for *divided* and *Persians* sounds like *peres.*
^I **6:1** Lit *It was pleasing before Darius*   ^J **6:3** Lit *Now this Daniel*

5:18–24 According to ancient Babylonian texts, Belshazzar had served in the government of King Neriglissar in 560 BC. This indicates that he had been old enough to be aware of the events at the end of Nebuchadnezzar's life. The specific sins Daniel cited were pride, blasphemy, idolatry, and failure to glorify the true God.
5:28 Although the third word was written in the plural form (PARSIN), Daniel explained its meaning by using the singular form (**Peres**). The prediction that Belshazzar's **kingdom has been divided** does not indicate that the Babylonian Empire would be divided equally by two kingdoms (**Medes** and **Persians**) but rather that Babylon would be destroyed or dissolved and taken over by the Medo-Persian Empire. The third word on the wall (PARSIN) has the same letters as the Aramaic word for "Persian." It was a play on words, indicating that the kingdom would fall to the Persian army.
5:30 The Babylonians had twenty years of provisions, and the city was a seemingly

impregnable fortress. Nevertheless, Darius diverted the waters of the Euphrates River so his forces could enter through the channel, passing below the water gates. He took the city **that very night** without a battle and killed Belshazzar, who was engaged in a drunken feast.
5:31 The identity of **Darius the Mede**, who **received the kingdom at the age of sixty-two**, is uncertain. Some believe he was Gubaru, the governor of Babylon, called Darius, an honorific title meaning "royal one." Others maintain that "Darius the Mede" was an alternate title for the Persian emperor, Cyrus the Great, also viewing the word "Darius" as a royal title.
6:1 In one of the best-known stories in the book, Daniel was cast into the lions' den for his faith. Since Daniel was about fifteen years old in 605 BC when the Babylonians brought him as a captive to Babylon, and since the events in Dn 6 most likely took place in the second or third year after the Medo-Persian

conquest of Babylon in 539 BC, Daniel would have been approximately eighty-two years old when he was thrown to the lions. Darius began organizing the newly conquered Babylonian Empire and immediately **decided to appoint 120 satraps over the kingdom**. These 120 satraps were lower tier officials who helped rule the entire empire or just over the part of the empire that was formerly under Babylonian control.
6:2 The king appointed **three administrators** over the 120 satraps to assure that taxes would be properly collected without any embezzlement or corruption by the 120 government officials. He chose **Daniel** as one of these officials.
6:3 Daniel proved to be a superlative administrator, therefore, **the king planned to set him over the whole realm** as prime minister.
6:6–7 By agreeing to the edict, Darius's goal was to unite the Babylonian realm under the new Persian Empire.

should establish an ordinance and enforce an edict that, for thirty days, anyone who petitions any god or man except you, the king, will be thrown into the lions' den. [8] Therefore, Your Majesty, establish the edict and sign the document so that, as a law of the Medes and Persians, it is irrevocable and cannot be changed." [9] So King Darius signed the written edict.

Daniel in the Lions' Den

[10] When Daniel learned that the document had been signed, he went into his house. The windows in its upstairs room opened toward Jerusalem, and three times a day he got down on his knees, prayed, and gave thanks to his God, just as he had done before. [11] Then these men went as a group and found Daniel petitioning and imploring his God. [12] So they approached the king and asked about his edict: "Didn't you sign an edict that for thirty days any person who petitions any god or man except you, the king, will be thrown into the lions' den?"

The king answered, "As a law of the Medes and Persians, the order stands[A] and is irrevocable."

[13] Then they replied to the king, "Daniel, one of the Judean exiles, has ignored you, the king, and the edict you signed, for he prays three times a day." [14] As soon as the king heard this, he was very displeased; he set his mind on rescuing Daniel and made every effort until sundown to deliver him.

[15] Then these men went together to the king and said to him, "You know, Your Majesty, that it is a law of the Medes and Persians that no edict or ordinance the king establishes can be changed."

[16] So the king gave the order, and they brought Daniel and threw him into the lions' den. The king said to Daniel, "May your God, whom you continually serve, rescue you!" [17] A stone was brought and placed over the mouth of the den. The king sealed it with his own signet ring and with the signet rings of his nobles, so that nothing in regard to Daniel could be changed. [18] Then the king went to his palace and spent the night fasting. No diversions[B] were brought to him, and he could not sleep.

Daniel Released

[19] At the first light of dawn the king got up and hurried to the lions' den. [20] When he reached the den, he cried out in anguish to Daniel. "Daniel, servant of the living God," the king said,[C] "has your God, whom you continually serve, been able to rescue you from the lions?"

[21] Then Daniel spoke with the king: "May the king live forever. [22] My God sent his angel and shut the lions' mouths; and they haven't harmed me, for I was found innocent before him. And also before you, Your Majesty, I have not done harm."

[23] The king was overjoyed and gave orders to take Daniel out of the den. When Daniel was brought up from the den, he was found to be unharmed, for he trusted in his God. [24] The king then gave the command, and those men who had maliciously accused Daniel[D] were brought and thrown into the lions' den — they, their children, and their wives. They had not reached the bottom of the den before the lions overpowered them and crushed all their bones.

Darius Honors God

[25] Then King Darius wrote to those of every people, nation, and language who live on the whole earth: "May your prosperity abound. [26] I issue a decree that in all my royal dominion, people must tremble in fear before the God of Daniel:

For he is the living God,
and he endures forever;
his kingdom will never be destroyed,
and his dominion has no end.
[27] He rescues and delivers;
he performs signs and wonders
in the heavens and on the earth,
for he has rescued Daniel
from the power of the lions."

[28] So Daniel prospered during the reign of Darius and[E] the reign of Cyrus the Persian.

[A] 6:12 Lit the word is certain [B] 6:18 Aramaic obscure [C] 6:20 Lit said to Daniel [D] 6:24 Lit had eaten his pieces [E] 6:28 Or Darius, even

---

6:8–9 The irrevocability of **a law of the Medes and Persians** is confirmed elsewhere in Scripture (Est 1:19; 8:8) and secular literature (Diodorus of Sicily, XVII:30).
6:10 Jewish people in exile always pray **toward Jerusalem**, just as Solomon had instructed in his prayer of dedication for the temple (1Kg 8:44–49).
6:14–15 The king was **very displeased** not because Daniel had defied him but because he came to understand that the true purpose of the law was to trap Daniel, whom he respected.
6:16 The Persians used mutilation by lions as one of several brutal forms of execution. It was Daniel's continual service to God that

caused him to be cast into the lions' den; now the king hoped that this devotion would cause God to deliver Daniel. The word for **den** can also be translated as "pit."
6:17–18 Daniel was cast into a pit over which **a stone** was placed and sealed with the **signet rings** of the king and his nobles. King Darius then spent the night **fasting** and presumably praying for Daniel.
6:21–23 This may have been an angel or even the angel of the Lord (i.e., a preincarnate appearance of the Messiah). Daniel was not claiming perfection in declaring that he was **found innocent** before God. Rather, Daniel claimed that his allegiance to God made him guiltless in this matter.

6:24 Although executing family members is exceptionally cruel, this was a common Persian practice according to Herodotus (Histories, 3.119).
6:25–27 Just as King Nebuchadnezzar before him, King Darius issued a decree to **every people, nation, and language** (cp. 4:2), declaring praise to the God of Daniel. It is unlikely that Darius came to a saving faith here. He instead accepted the God of Israel as just one of many gods.
6:28 Some maintain that this verse draws a distinction between **Darius** and **Cyrus**, such that Darius could only be identified with Gubaru and not with Cyrus the Persian (see note at 5:31). But it is also possible to

No Matter the Cost

BIBLICAL CHARACTER(S)	THE THREAT
Shadrach, Meshach, and Abednego	Worship the king's statue or be thrown into the fiery furnace *(Dn 3:13–15)*
Daniel	For a thirty-day period, pray only to the king or be thrown into the lions' den *(Dn 6:6–9)*
Esther	Approaches the king without being summoned in order to rescue her people from destruction, but doing so risked the death penalty *(Est 4:8–11)*
Zerubbabel, Jeshua, Haggai, and Zechariah	The names of the leaders rebuilding the temple were taken and sent to the king for a decision regarding this matter *(Ezr 4:24–5:17)*.
Ezra	Potential harm from enemies on the journey from Babylon to Jerusalem *(Ezr 8:21–22)*
Nehemiah	Unknown potential consequences for sadness of heart in the king's presence, causing overwhelming fear *(Neh 2:1–2)*
Jesus	The shame and death of a cross *(Heb 12:2)*

DEATH-DEFYING FAITH	THE RESULT
God can rescue us, but even if he doesn't, we won't worship your statue (Dn 3:16–18).	Thrown into the furnace, but God rescued them from the fire (Dn 3:19–29; see Heb 11:34)
Prayed to God as he had always done (Dn 6:10)	Thrown into the lions' den, but God rescued him from the lions' mouths (Dn 6:16–23; see Heb 11:33)
Believing she might be in her position "for such a time as this," she fasted and prayed for three days and then approached the king (Est 4:14–17).	She won the approval of the king and was able to thwart the destruction of her people (Est 5–9).
Continued the reconstruction of the temple and named themselves the servants of the God of heaven and earth (Ezr 5:11–16)	The king protected the rebuilding of the temple and even supported it from his taxes so that it was completed (Ezr 6:1–15).
Refused to ask the king for protection, having said God would help them; prayed and fasted for God's protection (Ezr 8:21–23)	God strengthened and protected his people from the power of the enemy and from ambush along the way (Ezr 8:31).
Explained his sadness, prayed silently to the God of heaven, and then requested to leave the king's service and go and rebuild his city; also asked for supplies to do so (Neh 2:3–8)	The king granted his requests, for he was graciously strengthened by God; returned to Jerusalem and rebuilt the wall (Neh 2:8–6:16)
Endured the cross and despised the shame for the joy that lay before him (Heb 12:2)	Now seated at the right hand of the throne of God (Heb 12:2)

Daniel's Vision of the Four Beasts

7 In the first year of King Belshazzar of Babylon, Daniel had a dream with visions in his mind as he was lying in his bed. He wrote down the dream, and here is the summary[A] of his account. ² Daniel said, "In my vision at night I was watching, and suddenly the four winds of heaven stirred up the great sea. ³ Four huge beasts came up from the sea, each different from the other.

⁴ "The first was like a lion but had eagle's wings. I continued watching until its wings were torn off. It was lifted up from the ground, set on its feet like a man, and given a human mind.

⁵ "Suddenly, another beast appeared, a second one, that looked like a bear. It was raised up on one side, with three ribs in its mouth between its teeth. It was told, 'Get up! Gorge yourself on flesh.'

⁶ "After this, while I was watching, suddenly another beast appeared. It was like a leopard with four wings of a bird on its back. It had four heads, and it was given dominion.

⁷ "After this, while I was watching in the night visions, suddenly a fourth beast appeared, frightening and dreadful, and incredibly strong, with large iron teeth. It devoured and crushed, and it trampled with its feet whatever was left. It was different from all the beasts before it, and it had ten horns.

⁸ "While I was considering the horns, suddenly another horn, a little one, came up among them, and three of the first horns were uprooted before it. And suddenly in this horn there were eyes like the eyes of a human and a mouth that was speaking arrogantly.

The Ancient of Days and the Son of Man

⁹ "As I kept watching,
thrones were set in place,
and the Ancient of Days took his seat.

His clothing was white like snow,
and the hair of his head
like whitest wool.
His throne was flaming fire;
its wheels were blazing fire.
¹⁰ A river of fire was flowing,
coming out from his presence.
Thousands upon thousands served him;
ten thousand times ten thousand
stood before him.
The court was convened,
and the books were opened.

¹¹ "I watched, then, because of the sound of the arrogant words the horn was speaking. As I continued watching, the beast was killed and its body destroyed and given over to the burning fire. ¹² As for the rest of the beasts, their dominion was removed, but an extension of life was granted to them for a certain period of time. ¹³ I continued watching in the night visions,

and suddenly one like a son of man
was coming with the clouds of heaven.
He approached the Ancient of Days
and was escorted before him.
¹⁴ He was given dominion
and glory and a kingdom,
so that those of every people,
nation, and language
should serve him.
His dominion is
an everlasting dominion
that will not pass away,
and his kingdom is one
that will not be destroyed.

Interpretation of the Vision

¹⁵ "As for me, Daniel, my spirit was deeply distressed within me,[B] and the visions in my mind

---

[A]7:1 Lit beginning   [B]7:15 Lit was distressed in the middle of its sheath

---

translate this verse as "during the reign of Darius, *even* Cyrus the Persian."

7:1–28 This chapter of Daniel is one of the most important in the entire OT, an essential guide to biblical prophecy. Moreover, the vision of the Son of Man is the centerpiece of OT revelation concerning the Messiah.

7:1 Belshazzar became coregent with Nabonidus in 553 BC. Assuming Daniel was about fifteen when he was exiled to Babylon, he would have received this vision when he was approximately sixty-seven years old. The events described in this chapter precede those of Dn 5.

7:2 The **four winds** stirring up **the great sea** refers to the convulsions of the Gentile nations in the times of the Gentiles.

7:3 The **four huge beasts** represent the four nations previously identified in the vision of the colossus in Dn 2 (see note at 2:31–45). These four beasts are increasingly violent, perhaps indicating the growing moral degeneracy of the respective kingdoms they represent.

7:4 The **lion** with **eagle's wings** represents the Babylonian Empire. The winged lion was

a fitting symbol because some biblical passages represent Nebuchadnezzar as a lion (Jr 4:7; 49:19; 50:17,44) and others as an eagle (Jr 49:22; Lm 4:19; Ezk 17:3; Hab 1:8). The Babylonian Empire used lions to represent itself, and statues with winged lions were common there. Perhaps the **wings** being **torn off** represents Nebuchadnezzar's madness, and the lion's being **set on its feet like a man** indicates his restoration.

7:5 The **bear . . . with three ribs in its mouth** represents the Medo-Persian Empire and its three main conquests: Babylon (539 BC), Lydia (546 BC), and Egypt (525 BC). Its lopsided nature expresses the Persian dominance in this joint empire.

7:6 The **leopard** represents the Greek Empire. Its **four wings** refer to the great speed of Alexander's conquests, and its **four heads** represent the four principle sections of the empire: Greece and Macedonia, Thrace and Asia Minor, Syria and Babylonia, and Egypt and Israel.

7:7 The terrifying **fourth beast** represents the Roman Empire. It was **different** from the previous three because it was more

powerful and had longer dominion. **Horns** commonly represent kings or kingdoms in Scripture (Ps 132:17; Zch 1:18; Rv 13:1; 17:12), as the angel's later interpretation plainly indicates (Dn 7:24).

7:8 A **little . . . horn** represents a king who starts small in power but becomes dominant. The little horn's **eyes like the eyes of a human** indicates its shrewdness and its **mouth that was speaking arrogantly** points to its boasting blasphemously against God (cp. v. 25). This little horn is a future world ruler whom Scripture also calls "the coming ruler" (9:26); the king who "will do whatever he wants" (11:36); "the man of lawlessness," "the man doomed to destruction" (2Th 2:3); "the beast" (Rv 13:1–10); and the "antichrist" (1Jn 2:18).

7:9–10 The phrase **the Ancient of Days** refers to God's eternal nature.

7:13–14 The **son of man** is none other than the divine Messiah himself, who will fulfill the destiny of humanity (Ps 8; Heb 2:5–18). Jesus understood it to be a messianic title (Mk 14:61–62), and he used it to speak of himself.

terrified me. [16] I approached one of those who were standing by and asked him to clarify all this. So he let me know the interpretation of these things: [17] 'These huge beasts, four in number, are four kings who will rise from the earth. [18] But the holy ones of the Most High will receive the kingdom and possess it forever, yes, forever and ever.'

[19] "Then I wanted to be clear about the fourth beast, the one different from all the others, extremely terrifying, with iron teeth and bronze claws, devouring, crushing, and trampling with its feet whatever was left. [20] I also wanted to know about the ten horns on its head and about the other horn that came up, before which three fell — the horn that had eyes, and a mouth that spoke arrogantly, and that looked bigger than the others. [21] As I was watching, this horn waged war against the holy ones and was prevailing over them [22] until the Ancient of Days arrived and a judgment was given in favor of the holy ones of the Most High, for the time had come, and the holy ones took possession of the kingdom.

[23] "This is what he said: 'The fourth beast will be a fourth kingdom on the earth, different from all the other kingdoms. It will devour the whole earth, trample it down, and crush it. [24] The ten horns are ten kings who will rise from this kingdom. Another king, different from the previous ones, will rise after them and subdue three kings. [25] He will speak words against the Most High and oppress[A] the holy ones of the Most High. He will intend to change religious festivals[B] and laws, and the holy ones will be handed over to him for a time, times, and half a time.[C] [26] But the court will convene, and his dominion will be taken away, to be completely destroyed forever. [27] The kingdom, dominion, and greatness of the kingdoms under all of heaven will be given to the people, the holy ones of the Most High. His kingdom will be an everlasting kingdom, and all rulers will serve and obey him.'

[28] "This is the end of the account. As for me, Daniel, my thoughts terrified me greatly, and my face turned pale,[D] but I kept the matter to myself."

The Vision of a Ram and a Goat

8 In the third year of King Belshazzar's reign, a vision appeared to me, Daniel, after the one that had appeared to me earlier. [2] I saw the vision, and as I watched, I was in the fortress city of Susa, in the province of Elam. I saw in the vision that I was beside the Ulai Canal. [3] I looked up,[E] and there was a ram standing beside the canal. He had two horns. The two horns were long, but one was longer than the other, and the longer one came up last. [4] I saw the ram charging to the west, the north, and the south. No animal could stand against him, and there was no rescue from his power. He did whatever he wanted and became great.

[5] As I was observing, a male goat appeared, coming from the west across the surface of the entire earth without touching the ground. The goat had a conspicuous horn[F] between his eyes. [6] He came toward the two-horned ram I had seen standing beside the canal and rushed at him with savage fury. [7] I saw him approaching the ram, and infuriated with him, he struck the ram, breaking his two horns, and the ram was not strong enough to stand against him. The goat threw him to the ground and trampled him, and there was no one to rescue the ram from his power. [8] Then the male goat acted

---

[A]**7:25** Lit *wear out*   [B]**7:25** Lit *change times*   [C]**7:25** Or *for three and a half years*   [D]**7:28** Lit *my brightness changed on me*
[E]**8:3** Lit *I lifted my eyes and looked*   [F]**8:5** Lit *a horn of a vision*

7:18 The **holy ones of the Most High** is most likely a reference to Israel when the nation turns in faith to their Messiah Jesus (Zch 12:10; Rm 11:26). The literal covenant people will **receive the kingdom**, emphasizing that Messiah's final kingdom will be a literal kingdom on earth.

7:19–24a After a summary of the vision's meaning (vv. 19–22), the angel explains that the fourth kingdom, in its future state, will **devour the whole earth**, indicating world domination. The **ten kings** could be a metaphor for completeness. More likely, it refers to an empire with a literal confederation of ten kings (cp. Rv 17:12–13).

7:24b–26 Another king, the antichrist (cp. vv. 7–8), described in the vision as the little horn, will arise and take control of this last human empire by subduing **three kings**. He will be characterized by blasphemy (**words against the Most High**), anti-Semitism (he will **oppress the holy ones of the Most High**), and religious corruption (he will **intend to change religious festivals and laws**). He will oppress the Jewish people for **time, times, and half a time**, meaning three and one-half years, or the second half of the future tribulation (cp. Rv 7:14). This oppression is yet future. When the heavenly **court will convene**, the antichrist will **be completely destroyed forever**.

7:27 The Son of Man will take his throne and rule over his **everlasting kingdom**. Then the **people**—the believing remnant of Israel, also called **holy ones**—will receive this kingdom under the authority of their Messiah, the Son of Man.

8:1–27 Daniel 8:1–12:13 was written in Hebrew, focusing on God's people during the times of the Gentiles. The vision in Dn 8 predicted events that involved the second and third world empires within a time frame from the sixth to second centuries BC.

8:1 Belshazzar became coregent with Nabonidus in 553 BC. Assuming Daniel was about fifteen when he was exiled to Babylon, he would have received this vision in 550 BC when he was about seventy years old. The events in this chapter precede those described in Dn 5.

8:2 Daniel was probably in Babylon when he received this vision. He was only in Susa in a visionary sense.

8:3 As in the previous chapter, Daniel saw a vision of animals that stood for world empires. First, he saw a **ram**, representing the Medo-Persian Empire (v. 20). It had **two horns**, representing the two nations in this confederated empire. **One was longer than the other, and the longer one came up last**, signifying the dominant status of Persia in the empire, even though it originally was the weaker kingdom.

8:4 Most of the conquests of the Medo-Persian Empire were to the west, north, and south.

8:5 Daniel also saw **a male goat**, representing the Greek Empire. The goat's **conspicuous horn** represents Alexander the Great (v. 21). The goat crossed **the surface of the entire earth** so rapidly that it did not touch **the ground**. This refers to Alexander the Great's speedy conquest of the entire Near East in only three years.

8:6–7 The goat **struck the ram** and shattered **his two horns**, indicating the Greek Empire's crushing defeat of Medo-Persia (331 BC).

8:8 At the height of his power **the large horn was broken**. This refers to Alexander's

even more arrogantly, but when he became powerful, the large horn was broken. Four conspicuous horns came up in its place, pointing toward the four winds of heaven.

The Little Horn

⁹ From one of them a little horn emerged and grew extensively toward the south and the east and toward the beautiful land.ᴬ ¹⁰ It grew as high as the heavenly army, made some of the army and some of the starsᴮ fall to the earth, and trampled them. ¹¹ It acted arrogantly even against the Prince of the heavenly army; it revoked his regular sacrifice and overthrew the place of his sanctuary. ¹² In the rebellion, the army was given up, together with the regular sacrifice. The horn threw truth to the ground and was successful in what it did.

¹³ Then I heard a holy one speaking, and another holy one said to the speaker, "How long will the events of this vision last — the regular sacrifice, the rebellion that makes desolate, and the giving over of the sanctuary and of the army to be trampled?"

¹⁴ He said to me,ᶜ "For 2,300 evenings and mornings; then the sanctuary will be restored."

Interpretation of the Vision

¹⁵ While I, Daniel, was watching the vision and trying to understand it, there stood before me someone who appeared to be a man. ¹⁶ I heard a human voice calling from the middle of the Ulai: "Gabriel, explain the vision to this man."

¹⁷ So he approached where I was standing; when he came near, I was terrified and fell facedown. "Son of man," he said to me, "understand that the vision refers to the time of the end." ¹⁸ While he was speaking to me, I fell

into a deep sleep, with my face to the ground. Then he touched me, made me stand up, ¹⁹ and said, "I am here to tell you what will happen at the conclusion of the time of wrath, because it refers to the appointed time of the end. ²⁰ The two-horned ram that you saw represents the kings of Media and Persia. ²¹ The shaggy goat represents the king of Greece, and the large horn between his eyes represents the first king.ᴰ ²² The four horns that took the place of the broken horn represent four kingdoms. They will rise from that nation, but without its power.

²³ Near the end of their kingdoms,
  when the rebels have reached
  the full measure of their sin,ᴱ
  a ruthlessᶠ king, skilled in intrigue,ᴳ
  will come to the throne.

²⁴ His power will be great,
  but it will not be his own.
  He will cause outrageous destruction
  and succeed in whatever he does.
  He will destroy the powerful
  along with the holy people.

²⁵ He will cause deceit to prosper
  through his cunning
  and by his influence,
  and in his own mind he will
  exalt himself.
  He will destroy many in a time of peace;
  he will even stand against the Prince
  of princes.
  Yet he will be broken — not by
  human hands.

²⁶ The vision of the evenings
  and the mornings
  that has been told is true.
  Now you are to seal up the vision
  because it refers to many days
  in the future."

ᴬ8:9 = Israel   ᴮ8:10 Or *some of the army, that is, some of the stars*   ᶜ8:14 LXX, Theod, Syr, Vg read *him*   ᴰ8:21 = Alexander the Great   ᴱ8:23 Lit *have become complete*   ᶠ8:23 Lit *strong of face*   ᴳ8:23 Lit *king, and understanding riddles*

---

sudden death at the peak of his greatness (323 BC). His kingdom was divided by four of his generals (Cassander over Macedon and Greece, Lysimachus over Thrace and Asia Minor, Seleucus over Syria and Babylon, Ptolemy over Egypt), described in the vision as **four conspicuous horns** that replaced him.

8:9–12 As opposed to the little horn that will come from the fourth kingdom (Rome) described in 7:8, a different **little horn** emerged out of one of the four kingdoms that divided the Greek Empire. This one was Antiochus IV (175–163 BC), ruler of the Seleucid dynasty, who conquered surrounding areas to **the south** and to **the east** but especially dominated **the beautiful land** of Israel. He brutally **trampled** and persecuted the Jewish people from 170–164 BC. Antiochus blasphemously presented himself as **the Prince of the heavenly army**, God himself (called the "Prince of princes" in 8:25), stopping **regular sacrifice** and defiling the holy temple (**his sanctuary**) in Jerusalem (167 BC). He **was successful**, but only temporarily.

8:13–14 An angel announced that Antiochus's defilement of Israel would last only **2,300 evenings and mornings**, until the temple was rededicated by Judas Maccabeus in 164 BC. This event is still celebrated by Jewish people today during the festival of *Chanukah* (Eng "Dedication," see Jn 10:22–23).

8:15–16 Daniel received the interpretation of the vision from the angel **Gabriel**, only one of two angels (along with Michael) who are named in Scripture. Gabriel would also give the message of Daniel's seventy weeks (9:24–27) and announce the birth of John the Baptist to Zechariah (Lk 1:19) and the birth of the Messiah Jesus to Mary (Lk 1:26).

8:17 Gabriel addressed Daniel as **son of man**, but he did not use the Hebrew equivalent of the Aramaic title given to the Messiah, which points to Messiah's divinity (7:13). The phrase used here emphasizes the human weakness and mortality of Daniel. Gabriel also indicated that the vision referred **to the time of the end**. Antiochus as the little horn of chap. 8 typifies the coming end-time antichrist. So, although this chapter does directly

refer to Antiochus, it also pertains to the end times. Thus there is a double-fulfillment of this vision.

8:18–22 Here begins the interpretation of the ram and the goat.

8:23–25 After his summary explanation of Daniel's vision, Gabriel expanded his description of Antiochus. He would take the throne through deceit against the rightful heir, his nephew Demetrius. His great power would **not be his own** but would have a satanic source. He would **succeed** at first, defeating **powerful** rulers and generals and destroying many of God's **holy people** Israel and deceive himself, thinking himself great enough to oppose God. Nevertheless, he would ultimately and suddenly be **broken**, not through assassination or battle but through some ailment sent by God.

8:26 Gabriel instructed Daniel to **seal up the vision** not for the purpose of hiding its meaning from faithful readers of Scripture but rather to secure the document for safe-keeping into the distant future, meaning the time of Antiochus (some four hundred

²⁷ I, Daniel, was overcome and lay sick for days. Then I got up and went about the king's business. I was greatly disturbed by the vision and could not understand it.

Daniel's Prayer

9 In the first year of Darius, the son of Ahasuerus, a Mede by birth, who was made king over the Chaldean kingdom — ² in the first year of his reign, I, Daniel, understood from the books according to the word of the LORD to the prophet Jeremiah that the number of years for the desolation of Jerusalem would be seventy. ³ So I turned my attention to the Lord God to seek him by prayer and petitions, with fasting, sackcloth, and ashes.

⁴ I prayed to the LORD my God and confessed: Ah, Lord — the great and awe-inspiring God who keeps his gracious covenant with those who love him and keep his commands — ⁵ we have sinned, done wrong, acted wickedly, rebelled, and turned away from your commands and ordinances. ⁶ We have not listened to your servants the prophets, who spoke in your name to our kings, leaders, ancestors, and all the people of the land.

⁷ Lord, righteousness belongs to you, but this day public shame belongs to us: the men of Judah, the residents of Jerusalem, and all Israel — those who are near and those who are far, in all the countries where you have banished them because of the disloyalty they have shown toward you. ⁸ LORD, public shame belongs to us, our kings, our leaders, and our ancestors, because we have sinned against you. ⁹ Compassion and forgiveness belong to the Lord our God, though we have rebelled against him ¹⁰ and have not obeyed the LORD our God by following his instructions that he set before us through his servants the prophets.

¹¹ All Israel has broken your law and turned away, refusing to obey you. The promised curse^A written in the law of Moses, the servant of God, has been poured out on us because we have sinned against him. ¹² He has carried out his words that he spoke against us and against our rulers^B by bringing on us a disaster that is so great that nothing like what has been done to Jerusalem has ever been done under all of heaven. ¹³ Just as it is written in the law of Moses, all this disaster has come on us, yet we have not sought the favor of the LORD our God by turning from our iniquities and paying attention to your truth. ¹⁴ So the LORD kept the disaster in mind and brought it on us, for the LORD our God is righteous in all he has done. But we have not obeyed him.

¹⁵ Now, Lord our God — who brought your people out of the land of Egypt with a strong hand and made your name renowned as it is this day — we have sinned, we have acted wickedly. ¹⁶ Lord, in keeping with all your righteous acts, may your anger and wrath turn away from your city Jerusalem, your holy mountain; for because of our sins and the iniquities of our ancestors, Jerusalem and your people have become an object of ridicule to all those around us.

¹⁷ Therefore, our God, hear the prayer and the petitions of your servant. Make your face shine on your desolate sanctuary for the Lord's sake. ¹⁸ Listen closely,^C my God, and hear. Open your eyes and see our desolations and the city that bears your name. For we are not presenting our petitions before you based on our righteous acts, but based on your abundant compassion. ¹⁹ Lord, hear! Lord, forgive! Lord, listen and act! My God, for your own sake, do not delay, because your city and your people bear your name.

The Seventy Weeks of Years

²⁰ While I was speaking, praying, confessing my sin and the sin of my people Israel, and presenting my petition before the LORD my God concerning the holy mountain of my God — ²¹ while I was praying, Gabriel, the man I had seen in the first vision, reached me in my extreme weariness, about the time of the evening

---

^A 9:11 Lit *The curse and the oath*   ^B 9:12 Lit *against rulers who ruled us*   ^C 9:18 Lit *Stretch out your ear*

---

years after the vision was given) and the time of the antichrist which is yet future and is typified by Antiochus.
8:27 Daniel did not understand the timing of the events, their full implications, or the identity of the evil king who would oppress the Jews.
9:1 If Daniel was approximately fifteen when he went into captivity, he would have been about eighty-one years old at the time of this vision. The name **Ahasuerus** was probably a Persian royal title rather than a

personal name. It refers to an ancestor of Cyrus the Great or Governor Gubaru (see note at 5:31), not Ahasuerus (485–465 BC), the king mentioned in the book of Esther (Est 1:1).
9:2 Although the book of **Jeremiah** was completed only a generation before the events described in Dn 9, Daniel already recognized it as Scripture. Jeremiah predicted that **the desolation of Jerusalem** would endure for seventy years (Jr 25:11–13; 29:10). Daniel calculated that since the first

captives had been taken to Babylon in 605 BC, the seventy years were nearly complete.
9:3 Daniel's prayer was with **fasting, sackcloth, and ashes**, three customary ways to express sorrow and contrition (Ezr 8:23; Neh 9:1; Est 4:1,3,16; Jb 2:12; Jnh 3:5–6).
9:21 The angel **Gabriel** appears for a second time in Daniel (8:16), here called a **man** because he appeared in human form. Had the temple still stood, the **time of the evening offering** would have been between 3:00 and 4:00 p.m.

offering. [22] He gave me this explanation: "Daniel, I've come now to give you understanding. [23] At the beginning of your petitions an answer went out, and I have come to give it, for you are treasured by God.[A] So consider the message and understand the vision:

[24] Seventy weeks are decreed
about your people and your holy city —
to bring the rebellion to an end,
to put a stop to sin,
to atone for iniquity,
to bring in everlasting righteousness,
to seal up vision and prophecy,
and to anoint the most holy place.

[25] Know and understand this:
From the issuing of the decree
to restore and rebuild Jerusalem
until an Anointed One, the ruler,[B]
will be seven weeks
and sixty-two weeks.
It will be rebuilt with a plaza and a moat,
but in difficult times.

[26] After those sixty-two weeks
the Anointed One will be cut off
and will have nothing.
The people of the coming ruler
will destroy the city and the sanctuary.[C]
The[D] end will come with a flood,
and until the end there will be[E] war;
desolations are decreed.

[27] He will make a firm covenant[F]
with many for one week,
but in the middle of the week
he will put a stop to sacrifice
and offering.
And the abomination
of desolation
will be on a wing of the temple[G,H]
until the decreed destruction
is poured out on the desolator."

Vision of a Glorious One

10 In the third year of King Cyrus of Persia, a message was revealed to Daniel, who was named Belteshazzar. The message was true and was about a great conflict. He understood the message and had understanding of the vision.

[2] In those days I, Daniel, was mourning for three full weeks. [3] I didn't eat any rich food, no meat or wine entered my mouth, and I didn't put any oil on my body until the three weeks were over. [4] On the twenty-fourth day of the first month,[I] as I was standing on the bank of the great river, the Tigris, [5] I looked up, and there was a man dressed in linen, with a belt of gold from Uphaz[J] around his waist. [6] His body was like beryl,[K] his face like the brilliance of lightning, his eyes like flaming torches, his arms and feet like the gleam of polished

---

[A]9:23 by God added for clarity   [B]9:25 Or until an anointed one, a prince   [C]9:26 MT; Theod, some mss read The city and the sanctuary will be destroyed when the ruler comes.   [D]9:26 Lit Its, or His   [E]9:26 Or end of a   [F]9:27 Or will enforce a covenant   [G]9:27 LXX; MT reads of abominations   [H]9:27 Or And the desolator will be on the wing of abominations, or And the desolator will come on the wings of monsters (or of horror); Hb obscure   [I]10:4 = Nisan (March–April)   [J]10:5 Some Hb mss read Ophir   [K]10:6 The identity of this stone is uncertain.

9:22–24 Seventy weeks probably refers to seventy periods of seven years, or 490 years, during which six objectives would be accomplished. The first three pertain to bringing **rebellion . . . sin**, and **iniquity** to an end. The final three relate to consummating prophetic events by bringing in a kingdom of **everlasting righteousness**, fulfilling **vision and prophecy**, and setting apart **the most holy place** (lit "the holy of holies"), referring to a yet future, literal, millennial temple (cp. Ezk 40–48).
9:25 It is likely that the decree that is the beginning point is Artaxerxes's second decree in 444 BC, authorizing Nehemiah to rebuild the walls of Jerusalem (Neh 2:1–8). There will be a period of **seven weeks** of years (forty-nine years) followed by **sixty-two weeks** of years (434 years), making a total of sixty-nine weeks of years or 483 years from the decree until the coming of **an Anointed One, the ruler**. The starting point of the prophecy would have begun on Nisan 1 (March 5), 444 BC, followed by sixty-nine weeks of 360-day biblical/prophetic years or 173,880 days, and culminated on Nisan 10 (March 30), AD 33, the date of Jesus the Messiah's triumphal entry into Jerusalem (Lk 19:28–40).
9:26 Several events are said to follow the seven weeks and the **sixty-two weeks** (or the sixty-nine weeks). First, **the Anointed One** would **be cut off**, a prediction of the death of the Messiah Jesus. Thus, the book of Daniel, written in the sixth century BC,

predicted not only the precise date of the Messiah's coming (v. 25) but also that the Messiah would be put to death some time before the destruction of Jerusalem in AD 70. This was fulfilled when Jesus was crucified in AD 33 (AD 30 according to some interpreters). Second, **the people of the coming ruler** would **destroy the city** of Jerusalem and the second temple. The "coming ruler" probably is a reference to the future ruler described as the little horn in Dn 7, also known as the beast or the antichrist. He is not said to be the one to destroy Jerusalem and the temple; rather, it is *his people* who will do it. Since Dn 7 clearly viewed this ruler as coming from the fourth major world power, or Rome, this prophecy predicts that the Romans would destroy Jerusalem, as they did in AD 70. Third, there appears to be a significant time gap from the end of the sixty-ninth week to the beginning of the seventieth week.
9:27 The final seven-year period, or the seventieth week, will begin when **he** (the coming prince) **will make a firm covenant** of peace **with many** in the leadership of Israel. The antichrist will desecrate the future temple and put a stop to worship there. This covenant is yet future and will mark the beginning of a time of oppression of the Jewish people called "a time of trouble for Jacob" (Jr 30:7) or the tribulation period (Mt 24:29; Mk 13:24). **In the middle of the week**, or after the first three and one-half years, the antichrist will break his

covenant with Israel, leading to a time of unprecedented persecution of the Jewish people (Mt 24:21; Mk 13:19) and followers of Jesus (Rv 7:14) that will last for another three and one-half years (Dn 7:25; Rv 11:2–3; 12:14; 13:5). When the antichrist breaks his covenant, he will also **put a stop to sacrifice** in the rebuilt temple (7:25) and will commit **the abomination of desolation** (Mt 24:15), desecrating the temple and declaring himself to be God (2Th 2:4; Rv 13:5–7). The antichrist's oppression and abominations will continue until God's **decreed destruction is poured out on the desolator** (11:45; Rv 19:20).
10:1 Daniel received this vision in 536 BC. Assuming Daniel was about fifteen when taken captive, he was approximately eighty-four years old at the time. The vision was about **a great conflict** in the future, recounted in 11:2–12:3. The last three chapters of Daniel are about the same vision.
10:2 The Hebrew text contains the words "weeks of days" in describing Daniel's mourning period to distinguish it from the weeks of years in the previous chapter (Dn 9:24–27).
10:4 The **Tigris** River was some twenty miles from Babylon.
10:5–6 Despite his similarity to Christ's appearance as described in Rv 1:12–16, the angel in the form of **a man dressed in linen** cannot have been the preincarnate Messiah because Christ would not need help from the angel Michael.

bronze, and the sound of his words like the sound of a multitude.

[7] Only I, Daniel, saw the vision. The men who were with me did not see it, but a great terror fell on them, and they ran and hid. [8] I was left alone, looking at this great vision. No strength was left in me; my face grew deathly pale,[A] and I was powerless. [9] I heard the words he said, and when I heard them I fell into a deep sleep,[B] with my face to the ground.

Angelic Conflict

[10] Suddenly, a hand touched me and set me shaking on my hands and knees. [11] He said to me, "Daniel, you are a man treasured by God.[C] Understand the words that I'm saying to you. Stand on your feet, for I have now been sent to you." After he said this to me, I stood trembling. [12] "Don't be afraid, Daniel," he said to me, "for from the first day that you purposed to understand and to humble yourself before your God, your prayers were heard. I have come because of your prayers. [13] But the prince of the kingdom of Persia opposed me for twenty-one days. Then Michael, one of the chief princes, came to help me after I had been left there with the kings of Persia. [14] Now I have come to help you understand what will happen to your people in the last days, for the vision refers to those days."

[15] While he was saying these words to me, I turned my face toward the ground and was speechless. [16] Suddenly one with human likeness touched my lips. I opened my mouth and said to the one standing in front of me, "My lord, because of the vision, anguish overwhelms me and I am powerless. [17] How can someone like me, your servant,[D] speak with someone like you, my lord? Now I have no strength, and there is no breath in me."

[18] Then the one with a human appearance touched me again and strengthened me. [19] He said, "Don't be afraid, you who are[E] treasured by God. Peace to you; be very strong!"

As he spoke to me, I was strengthened and said, "Let my lord speak, for you have strengthened me."

[20] He said, "Do you know why I've come to you? I must return at once to fight against the prince of Persia, and when I leave, the prince of Greece will come. [21] However, I will tell you what is recorded in the book of truth. (No one has the courage to support me against those

11
princes except Michael, your prince. [1] In the first year of Darius the Mede, I stood up to strengthen and protect him.) [2] Now I will tell you the truth.

Prophecies about Persia and Greece

"Three more kings will arise in Persia, and the fourth will be far richer than the others. By the power he gains through his riches, he will stir up everyone against the kingdom of Greece. [3] Then a warrior king will arise; he will rule a vast realm and do whatever he wants. [4] But as soon as he is established, his kingdom will be broken up and divided to the four winds of heaven, but not to his descendants; it will not be the same kingdom that he ruled, because his kingdom will be uprooted and will go to others besides them.

Kings of the South and the North

[5] "The king of the South will grow powerful, but one of his commanders will grow more powerful and will rule a kingdom greater than his. [6] After some years they will form an alliance, and the daughter of the king of the South will go to the king of the North to seal the agreement. She will not retain power, and his

---

[A] 10:8 Lit *my splendor was turned on me to ruin* [B] 10:9 Lit *a sleep on my face* [C] 10:11 *by God* added for clarity, also in v. 19
[D] 10:17 Lit *Can I, a servant of my lord* [E] 10:19 Lit *afraid, man*

10:7 The Hebrew for **only I, Daniel, saw the vision** is emphatic: "I saw, I, Daniel, I alone." His companions sensed a powerful and terrifying presence but saw nothing, so **they ran and hid** (cp. Ac 9:7).
10:8–11 In v. 11 the phrase **treasured by God** is used; that also occurs in 9:23.
10:12–13 The Persian **prince** had to be supernatural to oppose this angel, and he had to be evil to oppose God's purposes. Therefore, we conclude that he was a demonic spirit seeking to influence the political affairs of Persia and oppose God's purposes. The unnamed angel was able to prevail over the demon associated with Persia only because the angel **Michael . . . came to help** him. Michael (whose name means "who is like God") is the guardian angel of Israel (cp. v. 21; 12:1; Rv 12:7), and he is designated an archangel in the NT (Jd 9).
10:14 The angel revealed that the first purpose of the vision was to reveal what would happen to Israel **in the last days**.
10:15–19 The angel came not only to reveal the future but also to strengthen Daniel, first

by his touch (v. 18) and secondly with his words of encouragement (v. 19).
10:20–21 The **prince of Greece** is an allusion to the prediction that Greece would follow Persia as the next major world power (8:4–8,20–22). The angel's final purpose was to reveal **what is recorded in the book of truth** (lit "the writings of truth"), a reference not to a particular earthly book but to God's heavenly decrees about the future of all nations.
11:1–45 This chapter contains some of the most precise predictions in the entire Bible.
11:1 Although the angel visited Daniel "In the third year of King Cyrus of Persia" (10:1), he revealed to Daniel that he had **stood up to strengthen and protect** Darius since the first year of his reign (539 BC). God is active in the political affairs of the world.
11:2 The **three . . . kings** in Persia were Cambyses (530–522 BC), Pseudo-Smerdis (522 BC), and Darius I Hystaspes (522–486 BC). Ahasuerus was **the fourth** king who would be **far richer than the others**.

11:3–4 The **warrior king** predicted here was Alexander the Great (336–323 BC). As prophesied, his kingdom was **divided to the four winds of heaven**, referring to the division of his empire among his four generals rather than **his descendants** (see note at 8:8).
11:5 The **king of the South** is Ptolemy I Soter of Egypt (323–285 BC), who was outstripped by **one of his commanders**, Seleucus I Nicator (311–280 BC), who had abandoned Ptolemy I to become ruler of Babylonia, Media, and Syria, and establish the Seleucid kingdom that grew to be **greater than** that of Ptolemy's Egypt.
11:6 The **king of the South**, Ptolemy II Philadelphus (285–246 BC), would make **an alliance** with the **king of the North**, Antiochus II Theos (261–246 BC), sealing the agreement by giving his daughter, the Ptolemaic princess Berenice, to marry Antiochus. Yet Berenice would not **retain power**, as Antiochus's former wife Laodice would murder Antiochus, Berenice, and their child.

strength will not endure. She will be given up, together with her entourage, her father,^A and the one who supported her during those times. ⁷ In the place of the king of the South, one from her family^B will rise up, come against the army, and enter the fortress of the king of the North. He will take action against them and triumph. ⁸ He will take even their gods captive to Egypt, with their metal images and their precious articles of silver and gold. For some years he will stay away from the king of the North, ⁹ who will enter the kingdom of the king of the South and then return to his own land.

¹⁰ "His sons will mobilize for war and assemble a large number of armed forces. They will advance, sweeping through like a flood,^C and will again wage war as far as his fortress. ¹¹ Infuriated, the king of the South will march out to fight with the king of the North, who will raise a large army, but they will be handed over to his enemy. ¹² When the army is carried off, he will become arrogant and cause tens of thousands to fall, but he will not triumph. ¹³ The king of the North will again raise a multitude larger than the first. After some years^D he will advance with a great army and many supplies.

¹⁴ "In those times many will rise up against the king of the South. Violent ones among your own people will assert themselves to fulfill a vision, but they will fail. ¹⁵ Then the king of the North will come, build up a siege ramp, and capture a well-fortified city. The forces of the South will not stand; even their select troops will not be able to resist. ¹⁶ The king of the North who

comes against him will do whatever he wants, and no one can oppose him. He will establish himself in the beautiful land^E with total destruction in his hand. ¹⁷ He will resolve to come with the force of his whole kingdom and will reach an agreement with him.^F He will give him a daughter in marriage^G to destroy it,^H but she will not stand with him or support him. ¹⁸ Then he will turn his attention to the coasts and islands^I and capture many. But a commander will put an end to his taunting; instead, he will turn his taunts against him. ¹⁹ He will turn his attention back to the fortresses of his own land, but he will stumble, fall, and be no more.

²⁰ "In his place one will arise who will send out a tax collector for the glory of the kingdom; but within a few days he will be broken, though not in anger^J or in battle.

²¹ "In his place a despised person will arise; royal honors will not be given to him, but he will come during a time of peace^K and seize the kingdom by intrigue. ²² A flood of forces will be swept away before him; they will be broken, as well as the covenant prince. ²³ After an alliance is made with him, he will act deceitfully. He will rise to power with a small nation.^L ²⁴ During a time of peace,^M he will come into the richest parts of the province and do what his fathers and predecessors never did. He will lavish plunder, loot, and wealth on his followers, and he will make plans against fortified cities, but only for a time.

²⁵ "With a large army he will stir up his power and his courage against the king of the

---

11:7–9 One from Berenice's **family**, her brother Ptolemy III Euergetes (246–221 BC), would avenge her murder by storming Antioch, **the fortress** of **the king of the North**, Seleucus II Callinicus (246–226 BC), and killing Laodice. Ptolemy III would even seize Seleucid **gods** and valuables, bringing them back to **Egypt.**

11:10 The sons of Seleucus II—Seleucus III Ceraunus (226–223 BC) and Antiochus III (223–187 BC)—would **wage war** as far as the Ptolemaic **fortress** Raphia in southern Israel.

11:11–12 The king of the South, Ptolemy IV Philopator (221–203 BC) of Egypt, would counterattack **the king of the North,** Antiochus III (219–218 BC). Although both would command large armies, the result would be a great victory for the Ptolemies. As a result of his success, Ptolemy IV would **become arrogant** and slaughter **tens of thousands** of Seleucid troops, yet he would not be able to maintain his dominance over the Seleucid kingdom.

11:13–15 Fifteen years later, **the king of the North,** Antiochus III, would raise an even greater army and attack the Ptolemies in Phoenicia and Israel. Antiochus III would receive support against **the king of the South,** Ptolemy V Epiphanes (203–181 BC), and the Ptolemies. This support would come from Jewish rebels, here called **violent ones among**

your own people. Antiochus III's forces would win a resounding victory, even capturing the **well-fortified city** of Sidon (199–198 BC).

11:16–17 The **king of the North,** Antiochus III, would make **the beautiful land** of Israel a possession of the Seleucid kingdom in 198 BC and force a peace agreement on the Ptolemies. Antiochus III would **give** his **daughter** Cleopatra to Ptolemy V as a wife, hoping to control the Ptolemaic kingdom through her. This failed because Cleopatra helped her Ptolemaic husband and did **not stand with . . . or support** her father Antiochus III.

11:18–19 Antiochus III would then **turn his attention** to the lands around the Mediterranean Sea but would be defeated by the Roman **commander** Lucius Cornelius Scipio at Thermopylae (191 BC) and then Magnesia (190 BC). This would force Antiochus to focus on his own country where he would **stumble, fall, and be no more,** being killed by a mob defending the temple of Zeus in Elymais as Antiochus tried to pillage it.

11:20 The king who would arise **in his place** was Seleucus IV Philopator (187–175 BC), who would send his **tax collector,** Heliodorus, to collect money with which to pay the heavy indemnity he owed to Rome. After his short reign, Seleucus IV was killed **not in anger or in battle** but by poison from his tax collector.

11:21–35 Antiochus IV Epiphanes (175–163 BC), the little horn in 8:9–12,23–25 (cp. notes there), is emphasized in this section because he would have a terrible and oppressive effect on the Jewish people in the near term, and his reign is a picture of the future world ruler (the antichrist) who will also oppress the Jewish people.

11:21 Antiochus IV was not of the **royal** line, but took control by **intrigue** while the rightful heir, Demetrius, was held in Rome. The prediction called him **a despised person** because of his hatred of the Jewish people, his attempt to destroy Judaism, his desecration of the temple, and his megalomania displayed in calling himself Epiphanes ("Manifest One, Illustrious One"). People of that time also called him Epimanes ("madman").

11:22 Despite Ptolemy VI Philometor (181–146 BC) attacking with **a flood of forces,** Antiochus IV would be able to defeat them and depose **the covenant prince,** the Jewish high priest Onias III.

11:23–24 Antiochus IV would increase in **power** by sharing the wealth of his conquests, lavishing **plunder, loot, and wealth on his followers.**

11:25–26 These verses refer back to the war with Ptolemy VI (v. 22), predicting that not only would the power of Antiochus IV defeat

South. The king of the South will prepare for battle with an extremely large and powerful army, but he will not succeed, because plots will be made against him. ²⁶ Those who eat his provisions will destroy him; his army will be swept away, and many will fall slain. ²⁷ The two kings, whose hearts are bent on evil, will speak lies at the same table but to no avail, for still the end will come at the appointed time. ²⁸ The king of the North will return to his land with great wealth, but his heart will be set against the holy covenant;^ he will take action, then return to his own land.

²⁹ "At the appointed time he will come again to the South, but this time⁸ will not be like the first. ³⁰ Ships of Kittim^C will come against him, and being intimidated, he will withdraw. Then he will rage against the holy covenant and take action. On his return, he will favor those who abandon the holy covenant. ³¹ His forces will rise up and desecrate the temple fortress. They will abolish the regular sacrifice and set up the abomination of desolation. ³² With flattery he will corrupt those who act wickedly toward the covenant, but the people who know their God will be strong and take action. ³³ Those who have insight among the people will give understanding to many, yet they will fall by the sword and flame, and they will be captured and plundered for a time. ³⁴ When they fall, they will be helped by some, but many others will join them insincerely. ³⁵ Some of those who have insight will fall so that they may be refined, purified, and cleansed until the time of the end, for it will still come at the appointed time.

³⁶ "Then the king will do whatever he wants. He will exalt and magnify himself above every god, and he will say outrageous things against

the God of gods. He will be successful until the time of wrath is completed, because what has been decreed will be accomplished. ³⁷ He will not show regard for the gods^D of his ancestors, the god desired by women, or for any other god, because he will magnify himself above all. ³⁸ Instead, he will honor a god of fortresses — a god his ancestors did not know — with gold, silver, precious stones, and riches. ³⁹ He will deal with the strongest fortresses with the help of a foreign god. He will greatly honor those who acknowledge him,^E making them rulers over many and distributing land as a reward.

⁴⁰ "At the time of the end, the king of the South will engage him in battle, but the king of the North will storm against him with chariots, horsemen, and many ships. He will invade countries and sweep through them like a flood. ⁴¹ He will also invade the beautiful land, and many will fall. But these will escape from his power: Edom, Moab, and the prominent people^F of the Ammonites. ⁴² He will extend his power against the countries, and not even the land of Egypt will escape. ⁴³ He will get control over the hidden treasures of gold and silver and over all the riches of Egypt. The Libyans and Cushites will also be in submission.^G ⁴⁴ But reports from the east and the north will terrify him, and he will go out with great fury to annihilate and completely destroy many. ⁴⁵ He will pitch his royal tents between the sea and^H the beautiful holy mountain, but he will meet his end with no one to help him.

12 At that time
Michael, the great prince
who stands watch over your people,
will rise up.
There will be a time of distress

^11:28 Or the Jewish people and religion   ⁸11:29 Lit but the last   ^C11:30 = the Romans   ^D11:37 Or God   ^E11:39 Or those he acknowledges   ^F11:41 Lit the first   ^G11:43 Lit Cushites at his steps   ^H11:45 Or the seas at

Ptolemy VI but also that **plots . . . against him** would cause **his army to be swept away**.
11:27-28 After the defeat of Ptolemy VI, Ptolemy VII took control of Egypt. Then the other **two kings**, Antiochus IV and Ptolemy VI, would meet, speaking **lies at the same table**, to plot Ptolemy VI's restoration to the throne. After initial limited success, they would eventually fail. Then Antiochus IV (**the king of the North**), having plundered Egypt, would return to his land, with his **heart . . . set against the holy covenant**. On the way home, he would attack Israel, kill eighty thousand Jewish men, women, and children, and plunder the holy temple (169 BC).
11:29-30 Antiochus IV would launch another attack against Egypt, but this time **ships of Kittim** (cp. Nm 24:24)—the Roman fleet led by Gaius Popilius Laenas—would force him to **withdraw** in humiliation.
11:31-32 Antiochus IV would once again attack Israel (167 BC) while returning to Syria, this time desecrating **the temple** in Jerusalem. Antiochus would prefigure the future antichrist's actions (9:27; 12:11) by

abolishing the **regular sacrifice** and committing **the abomination of desolation**. In response, **the people who know their God will . . . take action**, as expressed in the Maccabean revolt (see note at 8:13-14).
11:33-35 The Maccabees would experience suffering in their battle with Antiochus. In **the end**, the Maccabees would defeat Antiochus, rededicate the holy temple in Jerusalem, and establish the festival of *Chanukah* (Eng "Dedication") which the Lord Jesus celebrated (Jn 10:22) and which Jewish people still observe today.
11:36-45 At this point, the predictions shift away from Antiochus IV and focus on the end of days. **The king** mentioned in this section is the future antichrist, already identified as the "little" horn (7:8,20,24-25) and "the coming ruler" (9:26).
11:36-39 These verses provide a clear description of the future antichrist. **The god desired by women** (lit "the desire of women") may be a reference to the longing of Jewish women to give birth to the Messiah.
11:40-44 During the great tribulation, the antichrist will be attacked in a pincer movement from both the north and the south.

Yet he will be successful, sweeping through **like a flood**. He will also invade Israel, **the beautiful land**, ignoring some nations that are in alliance with him but conquering others, including **Egypt**, Libya, and Sudan (the **Cushites**). Reports of nations from **the east and the north** coming to attack will both **terrify** and infuriate him, leading him to pursue a course of genocidal warfare against his enemies, killing especially many of the Jewish people (cp. Zch 13:8-9).
11:45 The antichrist will establish his military capital in Israel, pitching **his royal tents** between the Mediterranean Sea and the city of Jerusalem, situated on **the beautiful holy mountain**. There the nations of the earth will gather (Zch 14:2) at Mount Megiddo to begin the campaign of Armageddon (Rv 16:13-16). At that time, when the nation of Israel calls on the Messiah Jesus, he will return (Mt 23:37-39) to deliver them, and the antichrist **will meet his end with no one to help him**.
12:1 At that time refers to the events predicted in the previous paragraph (11:36-45), which details the antichrist's furious attempt to destroy and annihilate the Jewish people

such as never has occurred
since nations came into being
    until that time.
But at that time all your people
who are found written in the book
    will escape.
² Many who sleep in the dust
of the earth will awake,
some to eternal life,
and some to disgrace
    and eternal contempt.
³ Those who have insight will shine
like the bright expanse of the heavens,
and those who lead many
    to righteousness,
like the stars forever and ever.

⁴ "But you, Daniel, keep these words secret
and seal the book until the time of the end.
Many will roam about, and knowledge will
increase."ᴬ

⁵ Then I, Daniel, looked, and two others
were standing there, one on this bank of the
river and one on the other. ⁶ One of them said
to the man dressed in linen, who was above

the water of the river, "How long until the end
of these wondrous things?" ⁷ Then I heard the
man dressed in linen, who was above the water of the river. He raised both his handsᴮ toward heaven and swore by him who lives
eternally that it would be for a time, times,
and half a time. When the power of the holy
people is shattered, all these things will be
completed.

⁸ I heard but did not understand. So I asked,
"My lord, what will be the outcome of these
things?"

⁹ He said, "Go on your way, Daniel, for the
words are secret and sealed until the time of
the end. ¹⁰ Many will be purified, cleansed, and
refined, but the wicked will act wickedly; none
of the wicked will understand, but those who
have insight will understand. ¹¹ From the time
the daily sacrifice is abolished and the abomination of desolation is set up, there will be
1,290 days. ¹² Happy is the one who waits for
and reaches 1,335 days. ¹³ But as for you, go on
your way to the end;ᶜ you will rest, and then
you will riseᴰ to receive your allotted inheritance at the end of the days."

ᴬ**12:4** LXX reads *and the earth will be filled with unrighteousness*   ᴮ**12:7** Lit *raised his right and his left*   ᶜ**12:13** LXX omits *to the end*   ᴰ**12:13** Or *stand*

(11:44). Then the archangel **Michael ... who stands watch** over the Jewish people will rise to their defense to preserve them (see note at 10:12–13; cp. Rv 12:7). This will be necessary because the great tribulation (the second half of Daniel's seventieth week; Dn 9:27) will be a time of unprecedented **distress**. Despite the horrific nature of the persecution of Israel, the result will be that the surviving remnant of the Jewish nation will turn in faith to their Messiah Jesus (Zch 12:10; Rm 11:25–27) and he will deliver them. **The book** refers to the heavenly book of life in which the names of the elect are listed (Ps 69:28; Php 4:3; Rv 13:8; 17:8; 20:15).
12:2 Following the deliverance of Israel, there will be a resurrection of those **who sleep in the dust**. The word *sleep* is used as a metaphor to emphasize the temporary state of bodily death before being physically raised at the resurrection (cp. Jn 11:11–15). Although telescoped together here (as is common in prophecy), the resurrection of the faithful and the unfaithful are two distinct events separated by the one-thousand-year messianic kingdom (Rv 20:4–6). Dn 12:2 contains the clearest statement of resurrection in the OT.
12:3 The phrase **those who have insight** refers to those with the wisdom to turn in faith to the Messiah Jesus. As a result, they will **lead many** others to faith and **righteousness**.
12:4 Although it is possible that Daniel was told to keep these words of the vision **secret**,

an alternative rendering of the Hebrew is to "close up the words" **and seal the book**, a reference to preservation of the text of Daniel **until the time of the end**. Preserving Daniel's prophecy was necessary because in the end of days, **many will roam about** seeking answers that will be found in the book of Daniel. Moreover, in that day, **knowledge will increase**, possibly referring to the understanding of Daniel's prophecies as informed observers recognize the fulfillment of his predictions.
12:5–7 Daniel saw **two others**, meaning angels, who served as witnesses for the oath of the linen-dressed angel (10:5). Two was the minimum number of witnesses necessary for an oath (Dt 19:15). One of the witnessing angels asked **how long until the end** of the predicted time of distress. The angel dressed in linen answered that the time of the great tribulation (the second half of Daniel's seventieth week) would be for **a time, times, and half a time**, or three and one-half years (7:25; Rv 12:7). By the end of the great tribulation, **the power of the holy people** Israel will be **shattered**, causing them to turn in faith to their long-rejected Messiah Jesus (Zch 12:10). At that time, he will return and deliver them (Zch 14:1–21) and **all these things will be completed**.
12:8–10 Daniel's statement that he **heard but did not understand** means that he did not understand precisely how these events would happen. Daniel was told to go on his way, because **the words are**

secret (or "closed") **and sealed until the time of the end**, meaning they would not be fully recognized until their fulfillment at the end of days. At that time, the wicked will fail to comprehend their situation **but those who have insight will understand** the fulfillment of Daniel's words and turn in faith to the God of Israel and his Messiah Jesus.
12:11–12 Two periods of time were revealed to Daniel. First, from the middle of the tribulation when the antichrist stops **daily sacrifice** and commits **the abomination of desolation** until the end, **there will be 1,290 days**. The great tribulation is said to be three and one-half years (v. 7) or 1,260 days (Rv 12:6; 13:5). Here it is thirty days longer, probably to include time for the judgment of the nations (Mt 25:31–46). Second, a blessing awaits **the one who ... reaches 1,335 days**, a period that includes not only the thirty days for judging the nations but an additional forty-five days, perhaps to establish the government of the messianic kingdom. Those who enter that kingdom are said to be **happy** because they will be part of the most glorious world, governed by its greatest King, the Lord Jesus himself.
12:13 The angel told Daniel that he was to continue **to the end** of his life, at which point he would **rest**, a euphemism for death. Yet he was given the promise that he too would **rise** from the dead, **at the end of** time (v. 2).

▼ Introduction to Hosea

Circumstances of Writing

According to the first verse, Hosea's prophetic career spanned at least forty years. It began sometime during the reign of Jeroboam II, who ruled Israel, the northern kingdom, as coregent with his father Jehoash from 793 to 782 BC, then independently until 753 BC. Hosea's ministry ended sometime during the reign of Hezekiah, who ruled Judah from 716 to 686 BC.

Although the southern kingdom of Judah was not neglected in Hosea's prophecy (e.g., 1:7,11; 6:11; 12:2), his messages were directed primarily to the northern kingdom of Israel, often referred to as "Ephraim" (5:3,12–14; 6:4; 7:1) and represented by the royal city Samaria (7:1; 8:5–6; 10:5,7; 13:16). Hosea apparently lived and worked in or around Samaria, probably moving to Jerusalem at least by the time Samaria fell to the Assyrians in 722 BC.

The reign of Jeroboam II, the northern kingdom's greatest ruler by worldly standards, was a time of general affluence, military might, and national stability. The economy was strong, the future looked bright, and the mood of the country was optimistic—at least for the upper class (Hs 12:8; Am 3:15; 6:4–6). Syria was a constant problem to Israel, but Adad-nirari III of Assyria had brought Israel relief with an expedition against Damascus, the Syrian capital, in 805 BC.

After Adad-nirari's death in 783 BC, Israel and Judah expanded during a time of Assyrian weakness (the time of Jonah). But after Jeroboam's death in 753 BC, Israel sank into near anarchy, going through six kings in about thirty years, four of whom were assassinated (Zechariah, Shallum, Pekahiah, and Pekah). Since Assyria also regained power during this time, Israel was doomed. Of course the real reason Israel crumbled was God's determination to judge the people for their sins, as Hosea and Amos made clear. Most of Hosea's messages were probably delivered during these last thirty years of Israel's nationhood.

Contribution to the Bible

Hosea compared the relationship between God and his people to that of a husband and his wife, drawing a parallel between spiritual and marital unfaithfulness. "The Bible is very clear in its moral code that the sexual act can only legitimately take place within the context of the marriage relationship. Thus the image of marriage and sex, a relationship that is purely exclusive and allows no rivals, is an ideal image of the relationship between God and his people." Yet nothing can quench God's love for his covenant people. Like a marriage partner, God is deeply involved in our lives and is pained when we go our own way. God demands love and loyalty from his own. Often God's people have failed to demonstrate whole-hearted love for him, but he stands ready to forgive and restore those who turn to him in repentance. In buying Gomer's freedom, Hosea pointed ahead to God's love perfectly expressed in Christ, who bought the freedom of his bride, the church, with his own life.

* *Dictionary of Biblical Imagery* (Downers Grove, IL: InterVarsity, 1988), 778.

Hosea Timeline

850–775 BC

Jehu, king of northern kingdom **841–814**
Jehoahaz, king of northern kingdom **814–798**
Jehoash, king of northern kingdom **798–782**
Jeroboam II, king of northern kingdom **793–753**
Uzziah, king of southern kingdom **792–740**
Amos is called to prophetic ministry. **783**

775–740 BC

Zechariah, king of northern kingdom **753–752**, assassinated by Shallum
Shallum, king of northern kingdom **752**, assassinated by Menahem
Menahem, king of northern kingdom **752–742**
Pekah, king of northern kingdom **752–732**, assassinated by Hoshea
Micah is called to be a prophet. **750**
Jotham, king of southern kingdom **750–732**
Hosea's prophetic ministry **750–710?**
Pekahiah, king of northern kingdom **742–740**, assassinated by Pekah

Structure

The first three chapters of the book establish a parallel between the Lord and Hosea. Both were loving husbands of unfaithful wives. Hosea's three children, whose names served as messages to Israel, represent an overture to the second main division of the book, which presents its accusations and the calls to repentance in groups of three. Just as chapter 1—a third-person account of Hosea's family—is balanced by chapter 3—a first-person account—so the final main division of the book alternates between first-person announcements of God's message and third-person reports from the prophet.

Outline

I. The Pain and Persistence of Divine Love (1:1–3:5)
   A. God's message to Israel through Hosea's family (1:1–2:23)
   B. Hosea's testimony to his restored marriage (3:1–5)

II. Threefold Accusation and Call to Repent (4:1–7:16)
   A. Indictment and warning (4:1–5:15)
   B. Call to repent and God's grief at Israel's refusal (6:1–7:16)

III. Alternating Lament of the Lord and Hosea (8:1–14:9)
   A. Failure of false hopes (8:1–10:15)
   B. Israel's punishment for rebellion (11:1–13:16)
   C. Final call to repent (14:1–9)

740–730 BC

Isaiah is called to be a prophet. **740**
Ahaz, king of southern kingdom **735–716**
Damascus and Israel attack Jerusalem
  hoping to replace Ahaz with a king
  favorable to their alliance. **735**
Tiglath-pileser's continued expansion takes
  territory along the Mediterranean coast,
  destroys Damascus, and captures most
  of the northern kingdom. **733–732**

730–675 BC

Hoshea, last king of northern kingdom **732–722**
Tiglath-pileser III's successor, Shalmaneser V
  besieges Samaria. **725–722**
Samaria falls to the hands of Shalmaneser's
  successor, Sargon II. **722**
Sargon's inscriptions say that nearly 28,000
  captives were deported from Israel. **722**
Hezekiah, king of southern kingdom **716–686**

1 The word of the Lord that came to Hosea son of Beeri during the reigns of Uzziah, Jotham, Ahaz, and Hezekiah, kings of Judah, and of Jeroboam son of Jehoash, king of Israel.

Hosea's Marriage and Children

² When the Lord first spoke to Hosea, he said this to him:

Go and marry a woman of promiscuity,
and have children of promiscuity,
for the land is committing
blatant acts of promiscuity
by abandoning the Lord.

³ So he went and married Gomer daughter of Diblaim, and she conceived and bore him a son. ⁴ Then the Lord said to him:

Name him Jezreel,ᴬ for in a little while
I will bring the bloodshed of Jezreel
on the house of Jehu
and put an end to the kingdom
of the house of Israel.
⁵ On that day I will break the bow of Israel
in Jezreel Valley.

⁶ She conceived again and gave birth to a daughter, and the Lord said to him:

Name her Lo-ruhamah,ᴮ
for I will no longer have compassion
on the house of Israel.
I will certainly take them away.
⁷ But I will have compassion on the house
of Judah,
and I will deliver them by
the Lord their God.
I will not deliver them by bow, sword,
or war,
or by horses and cavalry.

⁸ After Gomer had weaned Lo-ruhamah, she conceived and gave birth to a son. ⁹ Then the Lord said:

Name him Lo-ammi,ᶜ
for you are not my people,
and I will not be your God.ᴰ
¹⁰ Yet the number of the Israelites
will be like the sand of the sea,
which cannot be measured or counted.
And in the place where they were told:
You are not my people,
they will be called: Sons of the living God.
¹¹ And the Judeans and the Israelites
will be gathered together.
They will appoint for themselves
a single ruler
and go up fromᴱ the land.
For the day of Jezreel will be great.

2 Callᶠ your brothers: My People
and your sisters: Compassion.

Israel's Adultery Rebuked

² Rebuke your mother; rebuke her.
For she is not my wife and I am not
her husband.
Let her remove the promiscuous look
from her face
and her adultery
from between her breasts.
³ Otherwise, I will strip her naked
and expose her as she was on the day
of her birth.
I will make her like a desert
and like a parched land,
and I will let her die of thirst.
⁴ I will have no compassion
on her children
because they are the children
of promiscuity.
⁵ Yes, their mother is promiscuous;
she conceived them
and acted shamefully.
For she thought, "I will follow my lovers,
the men who give me my food
and water,

ᴬ1:4 = God Sows   ᴮ1:6 = No Compassion   ᶜ1:9 = Not My People   ᴰ1:9 Lit *not be yours*   ᴱ1:11 Or *and flourish in*; Hb obscure
ᶠ2:1 Lit *Say to*

1:1 See the Introduction on authorship, Hosea, and the kings listed here.
1:2-3 Hosea's initial call to the prophetic ministry began with perplexing instructions to find a wife among the promiscuous women of Israel (of which there were apparently many; 4:11). This was no mere parable or vision but an actual command to enter a literal marriage that would vividly portray God's perspective on Israel. **A woman of promiscuity** describes her behavior and character when Hosea married her. Hosea, like the Lord, had a wayward wife and a broken heart. **Children of promiscuity** indicates that the paternity of Gomer's children would be questioned.
1:4-5 Jehu had carried out God's judgment (2Kg 9:7) by putting the last of Omri's dynasty to the sword at the city of Jezreel (2Kg 9:24–10:11). Hosea named his first child **Jezreel**, symbolizing that Jehu's dynasty would likewise suffer annihilation at Jezreel.

Zechariah, Jehu's last royal descendant, was assassinated by Shallum in 752 BC, probably at Ibleam in Jezreel (2Kg 15:10).
1:6-7 Hosea's second child, a **daughter**, was given the pathetic Hebrew name **Lo-ruhamah**, meaning "No Compassion," symbolic of the fact that by her continual unfaithfulness Israel had forfeited God's love.
1:8-9 The Hebrew name of Hosea's third child, **Lo-ammi**, meaning "Not My People," was a symbolic proclamation that Israel had broken covenant with God (Ex 6:7; Lv 26:12). **I will not be your God** amounted to a decree of divorce.
1:10-11 Allusion to the Abrahamic covenant in the phrase **like the sand of the sea** (cp. Gn 22:17) indicates that God's "divorce" of Israel was not final but applied only to that generation. The division between Israel and Judah was temporary, a theme to be repeated later (Ezk 37:18–25; Hs 3:5).
2:1-23 These verses elaborate on the "Not My People" oracle in 1:9–11. They open with

the divorce formula in v. 2 that begins the rebuke in vv. 1–13: "**She is not my wife and I am not her husband.**" The forgiveness section in vv. 14–23 announces the restoration of Israel. The Lord again becomes **my husband** (v. 16), and Israel becomes **my wife** (v. 19); "No Compassion" also receives compassion, and "Not My People" becomes **my people** (v. 23).
2:2 Here is the first command to repent in the book (4:15; 6:1; 10:12; 12:6; 14:1–2,9), followed by alternating verses of judgment (2:3–4,6–7,9–11) and indictment (vv. 5,8,12–13). The children, representing the common people of Israel, are urged to **rebuke** their mother, representing Israel's leadership.
2:3 Captured exiles are often depicted in antiquity as being led away **naked** (cp. Is 20:1–6).
2:5 The nation's **lovers** were other gods (idols), which she **thought** could meet her needs.

my wool and flax, my oil and drink."

⁶ Therefore, this is what I will do:
I will block her^A way with thorns;
I will enclose her with a wall,
so that she cannot find her paths.

⁷ She will pursue her lovers
but not catch them;
she will look for them
but not find them.
Then she will think,
"I will go back to my former husband,
for then it was better for me than now."

⁸ She does not recognize
that it is I who gave her the grain,
the new wine, and the fresh oil.
I lavished silver and gold on her,
which they used for Baal.

⁹ Therefore, I will take back my grain
in its time
and my new wine in its season;
I will take away my wool and linen,
which were to cover her nakedness.

¹⁰ Now I will expose her shame
in the sight of her lovers,
and no one will rescue her
from my power.

¹¹ I will put an end to all her celebrations:
her feasts, New Moons, and Sabbaths —
all her festivals.

¹² I will devastate her vines and fig trees.
She thinks that these are her wages
that her lovers have given her.
I will turn them into a thicket,
and the wild animals will eat them.

¹³ And I will punish her for the days
of the Baals,
to which she burned incense.
She put on her rings and her jewelry
and followed her lovers,
but she forgot me.
This is the LORD's declaration.

Israel's Adultery Forgiven

¹⁴ Therefore, I am going
to persuade her,
lead her to the wilderness,
and speak tenderly to her.^B

¹⁵ There I will give her vineyards
back to her
and make the Valley of Achor^C
into a gateway of hope.
There she will respond as she did
in the days of her youth,
as in the day she came out of the land
of Egypt.

¹⁶ In that day —
this is the LORD's declaration —
you will call me "my husband"
and no longer call me "my Baal."^D

¹⁷ For I will remove the names
of the Baals
from her mouth;
they will no longer be remembered
by their names.

¹⁸ On that day I will make a covenant
for them
with the wild animals, the birds
of the sky,
and the creatures that crawl
on the ground.
I will shatter bow, sword,
and weapons of war in the land^E
and will enable the people
to rest securely.

¹⁹ I will take you to be my wife forever.
I will take you to be my wife
in righteousness,
justice, love, and compassion.

²⁰ I will take you to be my wife
in faithfulness,
and you will know the LORD.

²¹ On that day I will respond —
this is the LORD's declaration.
I will respond to the sky,
and it will respond to the earth.

²² The earth will respond to the grain,
the new wine, and the fresh oil,
and they will respond to Jezreel.

²³ I will sow her^F in the land for myself,
and I will have compassion
on Lo-ruhamah;
I will say to Lo-ammi:
You are my people,
and he will say, "You are my God."

---

^A2:6 LXX, Syr; MT reads *your*   ^B2:14 Lit *speak to her heart*   ^C2:15 = Trouble   ^D2:16 Or *my master*   ^E2:18 Or *war on the earth*   ^F2:23 = Israel

---

2:8 The name **Baal** occurs seven times in Hosea, all but one for the Canaanite god.
2:9 The word for **I will take back** is essentially the same Hebrew word as "I will go back" in v. 7. If Israel did not return to her husband, the Lord, he would take back his blessings.
2:10 The noun translated **shame** refers literally to a woman's private parts. Israel's punishment would include the disgrace of having her sins exposed for everyone to see.
2:13 The words of rebuke (vv. 1–13) conclude with the common prophetic refrain **This is the LORD's declaration**. God's promised

eventual redemption and restoration in vv. 14–23 follow.
2:14–15 The word **therefore** begins an announcement of salvation. The place of judgment, the **wilderness**, will also be the place of salvation. The Lord would carry Israel back to the wilderness where he would renew and restore her faith as it had been in **her youth** (cp. Hs 13:5). **Speak tenderly** is literally "speak to her heart." It occurs elsewhere for Joseph's comforting assurance of favor and forgiveness to his brothers, who had done evil to him (Gn 50:21; cp. Gn 34:3; Jdg 19:3; Is 40:2). **Achor** means "trouble" and alludes to the trouble

that Achan caused Israel (Jos 7:24–26; see Is 65:10).
2:16–17 The phrase **the LORD's declaration** is repeated in vv. 16,21 to echo its use in v. 13 and highlight Israel's radical change from Baal's mistress to Yahweh's restored wife. The Hebrew noun *ba'al* could mean "husband" as well as the name of the Canaanite deity.
2:18 The **covenant** refers figuratively to the peace God will bring between man and beast (Jb 5:23; Is 11:6–9; Ezk 34:25).
2:21–23 These verses are parallel to 1:3–2:1 in that they refer back to Hosea's three children. God will **respond** to Israel's cries for help and the earth's need for rain. **Jezreel** generally

Waiting for Restoration

3 Then the LORD said to me, "Go again; show love to a woman who is loved by another man and is an adulteress, just as the LORD loves the Israelites though they turn to other gods and love raisin cakes."

² So I bought her for fifteen shekels of silver and nine bushels of barley,^A,B ³ I said to her, "You are to live with me many days. You must not be promiscuous or belong to any man, and I will act the same way toward you."

⁴ For the Israelites must live many days without king or prince, without sacrifice or sacred pillar, and without ephod or household idols. ⁵ Afterward, the people of Israel will return and seek the LORD their God and David their king. They will come with awe to the LORD and to his goodness in the last days.

God's Case against Israel

4 Hear the word of the LORD,
    people of Israel,
  for the LORD has a case
    against the inhabitants of the land:
  There is no truth, no faithful love,
  and no knowledge of God in the land!
² Cursing, lying, murder, stealing,
    and adultery are rampant;
  one act of bloodshed follows another.
³ For this reason the land mourns,
  and everyone who lives in it languishes,
    along with the wild animals
    and the birds of the sky;
  even the fish of the sea disappear.
⁴ But let no one dispute; let no one argue,
  for my case is against you priests.^C,D
⁵ You will stumble by day;
  the prophet will also stumble with you
    by night.
  And I will destroy your mother.

⁶ My people are destroyed for lack
    of knowledge.
  Because you have rejected knowledge,
  I will reject you from serving
    as my priest.
  Since you have forgotten the law
    of your God,
  I will also forget your sons.

⁷ The more they multiplied,
  the more they sinned against me.
  I^E will change their^F honor into disgrace.
⁸ They feed on the sin^G of my people;
  they have an appetite for their iniquity.
⁹ The same judgment will happen
    to both people and priests.
  I will punish them for their ways
  and repay them for their deeds.
¹⁰ They will eat but not be satisfied;
  they will be promiscuous
    but not multiply.
  For they have abandoned their devotion
    to the LORD.
¹¹ Promiscuity, wine, and new wine
  take away one's understanding.

¹² My people consult their wooden idols,
  and their divining rods inform them.
  For a spirit of promiscuity
    leads them astray;
  they act promiscuously
    in disobedience to^H their God.
¹³ They sacrifice on the mountaintops,
  and they burn offerings on the hills,
  and under oaks, poplars, and terebinths,
    because their shade is pleasant.
  And so your daughters
    act promiscuously
  and your daughters-in-law
    commit adultery.

---

^A3:2 LXX reads *barley and a measure of wine* ^B3:2 Lit *silver, a homer of barley, and a lethek of barley* ^C4:4 Text emended; MT reads *argue, and your people are like those contending with a priest* ^D4:4 Hb obscure ^E4:7 Alt Hb tradition, Syr, Tg read *They* ^F4:7 Alt Hb tradition reads *my* ^G4:8 Or *sin offerings* ^H4:12 Lit *promiscuously from under*

---

meant bloodshed, but here it means "God plants" (cp. 1:10) and refers to Israel.
3:1 Even though Gomer, like Israel, had joined herself to **another man** (lit "a neighbor"; cp. Dt 5:21; Jr 3:1,20) and so committed adultery, Hosea was told to take her back. She is called **a woman** rather than "your wife" because she had broken the covenant and had no claim on him. Like Hosea, God would show love to Israel even though she had forfeited her right to his love. **Raisin cakes** were apparently used in Canaanite religious rites, possibly as an aphrodisiac. With its four uses of the word *love*, this verse graphically depicts the foolishness of Israel's attitude toward God.
3:2-3 Why Hosea had to buy Gomer is not stated. Hosea's instructions to Gomer probably mean they would refrain from conjugal relations for a time after she returned to him. Verses 4-5 compare this to Israel's coming time of exile when they would be without ruler or worship. During this time the Lord would be expecting Israel to seek him (5:15). The time

would end "in the last days" when Israel would seek their messianic king (descended from David, 3:5) in repentance and faith (Is 11:1-10; Jr 23:5-6; 33:15-16; Mt 1:1; 21:9; Rm 11:23).
3:4-5 This prophesies the exile and restoration and even the last days when Israel is led by their Messiah.
4:1-5:15 This section is centered on the commands in 4:15. Three repetitions of indictment plus judgment both precede and follow these commands.
4:1-3 The prophetic call to **hear the word of the LORD** is found twenty-nine times in the OT, but only twice in the Minor Prophets—here and in Am 7:16. This central indictment section begins with a summary of the Lord's charges and a call to the true **people** (lit "sons") **of Israel** to recognize the moral and spiritual corruption of the rest of their countrymen who have abandoned their God and forfeited their right to be called his people. These adulterous **inhabitants** have abandoned: (1) **truth** or integrity, the quality of

being reliable and genuine; (2) **faithful love** or kindness and mercy to friends and associates; and (3) the **knowledge of God**. They had ceased to care about knowing him or the truth about him (Rm 1:18-32). As a result they were violating the Ten Commandments (Hs 4:2) and suffering the consequences (v. 3).
4:4-7 Especially guilty were the priests who were responsible for teaching the people.
4:8 The term for **sin** can also mean "sin offering," which the priests were to eat (Lv 6:25-26). The priests were using Israel's sin and the sacrificial system for their own advantage.
4:9-10 The fertility religion that had infected apostate Israel, even the priesthood, was about prosperity, but the Lord would see to it that the opposite results occurred. They would **not multiply**. More references to promiscuity occur in vv. 10-15,18 than anywhere else in the book (10 of the 22 times in Hosea).
4:11 This proverb concludes the section.

14 I will not punish your daughters
　　when they act promiscuously
　　or your daughters-in-law
　　when they commit adultery,
　　for the men themselves go off
　　　　with prostitutes
　　and make sacrifices
　　　　with cult prostitutes.
　　People without discernment
　　　　are doomed.

Warnings for Israel and Judah

15 Israel, if you act promiscuously,
　　don't let Judah become guilty!
　　Do not go to Gilgal
　　or make a pilgrimage to Beth-aven,ᴬ
　　and do not swear an oath:
　　　　As the Lᴏʀᴅ lives!

16 For Israel is as obstinate
　　　　as a stubborn cow.
　　Can the Lᴏʀᴅ now shepherd them
　　　　like a lamb in an open meadow?
17 Ephraim is attached to idols;
　　leave him alone!
18 When their drinking is over,
　　they turn to promiscuity.
　　Israel's leadersᴮ fervently
　　　　love disgrace.ᶜ
19 A wind with its wings will
　　　　carry them off,ᴰ
　　and they will be ashamed
　　　　of their sacrifices.

5 Hear this, priests!
　　Pay attention, house of Israel!
　　Listen, royal house!

ᴬ**4:15** = House of Wickedness　　ᴮ**4:18** Lit *Her shields*; Ps 47:9; 89:18　　ᶜ**4:18** Hb obscure　　ᴰ**4:19** Lit *wind will bind it in its wings*

4:14 God's statement that he would **not punish your daughters** must be understood as a rhetorical way of saying that God placed heavier blame on the men who supported the vile practice of cult prostitution. All would suffer when God brought judgment against Israel.
4:15 This verse contains the first of three exhortations (cp. 5:1,8) that divide this section into three warnings. Although the warnings are mainly directed against Israel, Judah was also in danger of following Israel in apostasy and punishment (5:5,10,12–14). Hosea used **Beth-aven** as a derogatory term for Bethel, which meant "house of

God." Beth-aven meant "house of disaster, wickedness, nothingness, or idolatry." **Gilgal** and Bethel had become centers of Israelite apostate religion (Am 5:5). The name of God continued to be used, but its attachment to idolatry made its utterance not only hypocritical but blasphemous. The Hebrew verb *'asham* ("be guilty") occurs here for the first of five times in the book (Hs 5:15; 10:2; 13:1,16), more than in any other book except Leviticus (11 times). "Guilty" is the legal condition of unpunished lawbreakers.
4:17 This verse has the first of thirty-seven references to **Ephraim** in Hosea, more than in any other book. The name was given to

Joseph's second son, then to the tribe he fathered, then to the northern hill country where they lived.
4:19 Because of Israel's adulterous idolatry, arrogance, and stubbornness, they were warned that God would blow them away as with a whirlwind, the first of three metaphors used in this section to make vivid the coming judgment. He would also eat away at them like rot or a moth (5:12) and tear them to pieces like a lion (5:14).
5:1–2 Verses 1–7 contain a second exhortation directed against the corrupt leaders. **House of Israel** probably refers to unofficial leaders of society (Jr 2:26). **Mizpah** and

---

▼ Seeing Jesus in the Prophets

▼ Old Testament

Hosea: Pursued His Adulterous Wife; Bought Her Back from Slavery for Purity *(Hs 3)*

Jonah: In the Belly of a Great Fish Three Days and Nights *(Jnh 1:17)*

Joel: Prophesied God's Spirit Poured Out on Those Who Call on the Lord *(Jl 2:28–32)*

Jeremiah: Prophesied a New Covenant for the Forgiveness of Sin *(Jr 31:31–34)*

Ezekiel: Prophesied a Resurrection for God's People, a Restoration to the Land *(Ezk 37)*

▼ New Testament

Jesus: Gave Himself for His Church to Make Her Holy and Blameless *(Eph 5:25–27)*

Jesus, the Better Jonah: In the Heart of the Earth Three Days and Nights *(Mt 12:39–41)*

Jesus: Pours Out His Spirit on All Who Call on Him to Be Saved *(Ac 2; Rm 10)*

Jesus: Shed His Blood to Establish the Covenant for the Forgiveness of Sin *(Mt 26:28)*

Jesus: The Resurrection and the Life for All Who Believe in Him *(Jn 11:25–26)*

For the judgment applies to you
because you have been a snare
at Mizpah
and a net spread out on Tabor.

² Rebels are deeply involved in slaughter;
I will be a punishment for all of them.ᴬ

³ I know Ephraim,
and Israel is not hidden from me.
For now, Ephraim,
you have acted promiscuously;
Israel is defiled.

⁴ Their actions do not allow them
to return to their God,
for a spirit of promiscuity
is among them,
and they do not know the LORD.

⁵ Israel's arrogance testifies
against them.ᴮ
Both Israel and Ephraim stumble
because of their iniquity;
even Judah will stumble with them.

⁶ They go with their flocks and herds
to seek the LORD
but do not find him;
he has withdrawn from them.

⁷ They betrayed the LORD;
indeed, they gave birth
to illegitimate children.
Now the New Moon will devour them
along with their fields.

⁸ Blow the ram's horn in Gibeah,
the trumpet in Ramah;
raise the war cry in Beth-aven:
Look behind you,ᶜ Benjamin!

⁹ Ephraim will become a desolation
on the day of punishment;
I announce what is certain
among the tribes of Israel.

¹⁰ The princes of Judah are like those
who move boundary markers;
I will pour out my fury on them
like water.

¹¹ Ephraim is oppressed,
crushed in judgment,
for he is determined to follow
what is worthless.ᴰ

¹² So I am like rot to Ephraim

and like decay to the house of Judah.

¹³ When Ephraim saw his sickness
and Judah his wound,
Ephraim went to Assyria
and sent a delegation to the great king.ᴱ
But he cannot cure you or heal
your wound.

¹⁴ For I am like a lion to Ephraim
and like a young lion to the house
of Judah.
Yes, I will tear them to pieces
and depart.
I will carry them off,
and no one can rescue them.

¹⁵ I will depart and return to my place
until they recognize their guilt and seek
my face;
they will search for me in their distress.

A Call to Repentance

6 Come, let's return to the LORD.
For he has torn us,
and he will heal us;
he has wounded us,
and he will bind up our wounds.

² He will revive us after two days,
and on the third day he will raise us up
so we can live in his presence.

³ Let's strive to know the LORD.
His appearance is as sure as the dawn.
He will come to us like the rain,
like the spring showers that water
the land.

The LORD's First Lament

⁴ What am I going to do
with you, Ephraim?
What am I going to do
with you, Judah?
Your love is like the morning mist
and like the early dew that vanishes.

⁵ This is why I have used the prophets
to cut them down;ᶠ
I have killed them with the words
from my mouth.
My judgment strikes like lightning.ᴳ

⁶ For I desire faithful love
and not sacrifice,

ᴬ5:2 Hb obscure ᴮ5:5 Lit *against his face* ᶜ5:8 Or *We will follow you* ᴰ5:11 Or *follow a command*; Hb obscure ᴱ5:13 Or *to King Yareb* ᶠ6:5 Or *have cut down the prophets* ᴳ6:5 LXX, Syr, Tg; MT reads *Your judgments go out as light*

Mount **Tabor** are described as **a snare** and **a net** respectively because of the unauthorized sanctuary at Mizpah (Jr 41:4–6) and a high place on Mount Tabor, where false religion was practiced.
5:3–4 Although God knew all about **Ephraim**, they did not **know** him.
5:7 Israel's leaders had produced a generation of **illegitimate children** who did not know God and were therefore "not my people." The **New Moon** refers to the monthly festival held when the moon first appeared. It was accompanied by trumpets and special offerings of animals, grain, and wine (Nm

28:11–15; Ps 81:3). The sense may be that with every "new moon" God would send another wave of judgments.
5:8–9 These cities were in Benjamin between Ephraim (the northern kingdom of Israel) and Judah. The battle alarm would be sounded because a battle would be fought there. The outcome would be desolation for Israel (v. 9) and divine fury for Judah (v. 10).
5:11 Crushed in judgment could be rendered "justice is crushed," and **what is worthless** could be rendered "command" or "policy."
5:12–13 Rot and **decay** are striking similes for God to use of himself. The term for "rot"

can also mean "maggot" or "pus." It pictures a man whose festering wounds were divinely inflicted. Israel's efforts to heal these wounds through human means would be futile. This is the first of nine references to **Assyria** in Hosea.
5:14 The Lord's power to destroy is contrasted with Assyria's so-called power to deliver.
6:1–3 After a short time in exile, Israel would be resurrected.
6:5 This verse answers the question of v. 4.
6:6 Quoted by Jesus in Mt 9:13 and 12:7, this verse does not reject **sacrifice** but rather ritualism and worship that is not accompanied

the knowledge of God rather than
    burnt offerings.

7 But they, like Adam,^ have violated
    the covenant;
there they have betrayed me.
8 Gilead is a city of evildoers,
    tracked with bloody footprints.
9 Like raiders who wait in ambush
    for someone,
a band of priests murders on the road
    to Shechem.
They commit atrocities.
10 I have seen something horrible
    in the house of Israel:
Ephraim's promiscuity is there;
    Israel is defiled.
11 A harvest is also appointed
    for you, Judah.

When I restore the fortunes of
    my people,

7 1 when I heal Israel,
the iniquity of Ephraim and the crimes
    of Samaria
will be exposed.
For they practice fraud;
a thief breaks in;
a raiding party pillages outside.
2 But they never consider
    that I remember all their evil.
Now their actions are all around them;
they are right in front of my face.

Israel's Corruption

3 They please the king with their evil,
    the princes with their lies.
4 All of them commit adultery;
they are like an oven heated by a baker
who stops stirring the fire
from the kneading of the dough
    until it is leavened.
5 On the day of our king,
    the princes are sick with the heat
    of wine —
there is a conspiracy with traitors.^B
6 For they — their hearts like an oven —

draw him into their oven.
Their anger smolders all night;
in the morning it blazes
    like a flaming fire.
7 All of them are as hot as an oven,
and they consume their rulers.
All their kings fall;
not one of them calls on me.^C

8 Ephraim has allowed himself
    to get mixed up with the nations.
Ephraim is unturned bread
    baked on a griddle.
9 Foreigners consume his strength,
    but he does not notice.
Even his hair is streaked with gray,
    but he does not notice.
10 Israel's arrogance testifies
    against them,^D
yet they do not return to the LORD
    their God,
and for all this, they do not seek him.

11 So Ephraim has become like a silly,
    senseless dove;
they call to Egypt, and they go to Assyria.
12 As they are going, I will spread my net
    over them;
I will bring them down like birds
    of the sky.
I will discipline them in accordance
with the news that reaches^E
    their assembly.

The LORD's Second Lament

13 Woe to them, for they fled from me;
destruction to them, for they rebelled
    against me!
Though I want to redeem them,
    they speak lies against me.
14 They do not cry to me from their hearts;
rather, they wail on their beds.
They slash themselves^F for grain
    and new wine;
they turn away from me.
15 I trained and strengthened their arms,
but they plot evil against me.

---

^6:7 Or they, as at Adam, or they, like men,   ^7:5 Lit wine — he stretches out his hand to scorners; Hb obscure   ^7:3–7 These vv. may refer to a king's assassination; Hb obscure.   ^7:10 Lit against his face   ^7:12 Lit news to   ^7:14 Some Hb mss, LXX; other Hb mss read They stay

---

by faithfulness and love and is not based on the **knowledge of God** (4:1).
6:7 The relation between God and the first man, **Adam**, is often described as covenantal.
6:8–11a Judgment approaching **Judah** is here described as a coming **harvest** because the people were growing ripe with wickedness (Jr 51:33; Jl 3:13; Rv 14:14–16).
7:3–7 The king cared nothing for God but loved to hear of evil, deceptive schemes, for which reason he would **fall. All of them** in the government burned with passions like a baker's **oven**. The king's conspiratorial counselors lured him into drunkenness, passion,

and death. The **baker** may be an image of the king whose debauchery allowed evil to flourish.
7:8–10 Ephraim's leaders were negligent in allowing the people to become like the other nations. They were like careless cooks who failed to turn the **bread**, allowing it to burn on one side. Yet they did not even **notice** what was happening.
7:11–12 Israel was like a bird that had forgotten its way home. The **news that reaches their assembly** was probably news that their efforts to find security in foreign governments had failed.

7:13 Woe to them is a declaration of coming judgment (9:12; Is 3:9; Jr 50:27; Jl 11). The term for **fled** is often used of birds (Is 16:2; Jr 4:25) and can also refer to restless wandering (Pr 27:8). Israel could flee from God in rebellion, but they could not escape **destruction**. The phrase **I want to redeem** can also be translated "I redeemed," referring to the exodus (Dt 7:8; 9:26; Mc 6:4). God's deliverance should cause his people to declare the truth about him.
7:14 Israel's wailing and slashing probably involved pagan rituals (1Kg 18:28; Ezk 8:14).
7:15 Here is the second of two contrasts between "I" and "they" in the passage (cp. v. 13).

16 They turn, but not to what is above;[A]
  they are like a faulty bow.
  Their leaders will fall by the sword
  because of their insolent tongue.
  They will be ridiculed for this in the land
      of Egypt.

Israel's False Hopes

8 Put the ram's horn to your mouth!
  One like an eagle comes
  against the house of the LORD,
  because they transgress my covenant
  and rebel against my law.
2 Israel cries out to me,
  "My God, we know you!"
3 Israel has rejected what is good;
  an enemy will pursue him.

4 They have installed kings,
  but not through me.
  They have appointed leaders,
  but without my approval.
  They make their silver and gold
  into idols for themselves
  for their own destruction.[B]
5 Your calf-idol[C] is rejected, Samaria.
  My anger burns against them.
  How long will they be incapable
    of innocence?
6 For this thing is from Israel—
  a craftsman made it, and it is not God.
  The calf of Samaria will be smashed
    to bits!

7 Indeed, they sow the wind
  and reap the whirlwind.
  There is no standing grain;
  what sprouts fails to yield flour.
  Even if they did,
  foreigners would swallow it up.
8 Israel is swallowed up!
  Now they are among the nations
  like discarded pottery.

9 For they have gone up to Assyria
  like a wild donkey going off on its own.
  Ephraim has paid for love.
10 Even though they hire lovers
    among the nations,
  I will now round them up,
  and they will begin to decrease
    in number
  under the burden of the king
    and leaders.

11 When Ephraim multiplied his altars
    for sin,
  they became his altars for sinning.
12 Though I were to write out for him
  ten thousand points of my instruction,
  they would be[D] regarded
    as something strange.
13 Though they offer sacrificial gifts[E]
  and eat the flesh,
  the LORD does not accept them.
  Now he will remember their guilt
  and punish their sins;
  they will return to Egypt.
14 Israel has forgotten his Maker
    and built palaces;
  Judah has also multiplied
    fortified cities.
  I will send fire on their cities,
  and it will consume their citadels.

The Coming Exile

9 Israel, do not rejoice jubilantly
    as the nations do,
  for you have acted promiscuously,
    leaving your God.
  You love the wages of a prostitute
  on every grain-threshing floor.
2 Threshing floor and wine vat will not
    sustain them,
  and the new wine will fail them.
3 They will not stay in the land
    of the LORD.

[A]7:16 Some emend to *turn to what is useless*   [B]8:4 Lit *themselves that it might be cut off*   [C]8:5 Lit *calf*   [D]8:12 Or *Though I wrote out … instruction, they are*   [E]8:13 Hb obscure

---

God had **trained** Israel to be a mighty nation, but they had turned their might **against** him. **7:16** Israel's **leaders** were as helpful as a faulty bow that could not send arrows to hit the mark (Ps 78:57). Israel's **insolent tongue** may refer to their bitter words against God or the prophets (2Ch 36:16). The consequent ridicule may be what they would experience when they sought help from Egypt (Hs 7:11) or when they were destroyed (v. 13). **8:1–3** God speaks in vv. 1–14. An alarm was to sound because God was sending an army to swoop down on Israel like an **eagle** on its prey (Dt 28:49; Lm 4:19; Hab 1:8). Israel was treating their covenant with God (**we know you**) as if it were a blank check for sin. **House of the LORD** may refer to Israel (9:8) rather than the temple. **8:4–6 Samaria**, Israel's capital, refers to the entire northern kingdom (Is 10:10–11). Israel had arrogantly sought success and

security through idolatry, military might, and political power. All their efforts would produce just the opposite of what they desired. **8:7** Idols were worshiped because they were thought to grant fertility. But the "planting" of idolatry would be like planting **wind**, and the harvest would be nothing but a **whirlwind**—a storm representing divine judgment (Pr 1:27; 10:25; Is 17:13; 29:6; 66:15; Nah 1:3). Whatever sprouted would be blown away. Foreigners would take everything the people produced. **8:8–10** These verses use three images to make the point that Israel's search for help from the nations has been in vain. Israel has ended up like discarded pottery, like a wandering donkey, and like someone who wasted all his money on prostitutes. **8:11–12** Israel built altars to cleanse them from **sin** (Lv 4:35), but the altars only increased Israel's sinning, perhaps by giving them a false

sense of security. Their hypocritical sacrifices only added to their sin (Is 1:14; Jr 7:11; Am 5:21 Mk 11:17). Having God's written **instruction** likewise did them no good because they disregarded it as **something strange** and adopted Baal worship as their native religion. **8:13 Return to Egypt** is probably not literal but indicates the people would have to start over in foreign slavery (9:3). The northern kingdom fell to Assyria in 722 BC (2Kg 18:9–12), but Hosea did not neglect Judah, which was to suffer invasion by the Assyrians in 701 BC (2Kg 18:13). **9:1–3** Hosea speaks in vv. 1–9. Israel was seeking prosperity by serving pagan fertility gods as the **nations** did, just as a woman would seek **the wages of a prostitute**. They could not **rejoice jubilantly** at the "LORD's feast" (v. 5), however, because the Lord withheld the harvest, causing deprivation that would increase during Israel's exile (v. 3)

Instead, Ephraim will return to Egypt,
and they will eat unclean food
  in Assyria.

4 They will not pour out
their wine offerings to the LORD,
and their sacrifices will not please him.
Their food will be like the bread
  of mourners;
all who eat it become defiled.
For their bread will be
  for their appetites alone;
it will not enter the house of the LORD.

5 What will you do on a festival day,
on the day of the LORD's feast?

6 For even if they flee from devastation,
Egypt will gather them, and Memphis
  will bury them.
Thistles will take possession
  of their precious silver;
thorns will invade their tents.

7 The days of punishment have come;
the days of retribution have come.
Let Israel recognize it!
The prophet is a fool,
and the inspired man is insane,
because of the magnitude
  of your iniquity and hostility.

8 Ephraim's watchman is with my God.
Yet the prophet encounters a bird trap
  on all his pathways.
Hostility is in the house of his God!

9 They have deeply corrupted themselves
as in the days of Gibeah.
He will remember their iniquity;
he will punish their sins.

Ephraim Bereaved of Offspring

10 I discovered Israel
like grapes in the wilderness.
I saw your ancestors
like the first fruit of the fig tree
  in its first season.

But they went to Baal-peor,
consecrated themselves to Shame,^A
and became abhorrent,
  like the thing they loved.

11 Ephraim's glory will fly away
  like a bird:
no birth, no pregnancy, no conception.

12 Even if they raise children,
I will bereave them of each one.
Yes, woe to them when I depart
  from them!

13 I have seen Ephraim like Tyre,
planted in a meadow,
so Ephraim will bring out his children
to the executioner.

14 Give them, LORD —
What should you give?
Give them a womb that miscarries
and breasts that are dry!

15 All their evil appears at Gilgal,
for there I began to hate them.
I will drive them from my house
because of their evil, wicked actions.
I will no longer love them;
all their leaders are rebellious.

16 Ephraim is struck down;
their roots are withered;
they cannot bear fruit.
Even if they bear children,
I will kill the precious offspring
  of their wombs.

17 My God will reject them
because they have not listened to him;
they will become wanderers
  among the nations.

The Vine and the Calf

10 Israel is a lush^B vine;
it yields fruit for itself.
The more his fruit increased,
the more he increased the altars.
The better his land produced,
the better they made the sacred pillars.

---

^A 9:10 = Baal   ^B 10:1 Or ravaged

9:4–6 Israel's failed harvest would leave the people with barely enough to eat, with nothing for **offerings** and **sacrifices**. The **bread of mourners** was food defiled by association with death. It could not be offered to God. Israel would seek refuge from **devastation** in Egypt, but they would die there outside their land.
9:7–9 God had sent prophets to warn the people, but their **iniquity** and **hostility** were such that they considered God's **inspired** messengers to be **insane** fools. Nevertheless, God was with them. **Watchman** is a common biblical image for prophets (Jr 6:17; Ezk 3:17; 33:2). The **bird trap** may be what the prophet was to the **pathways** of foolish Israel (Is 8:14; 2Co 2:16). On **the days of Gibeah**, see note at 10:9.
9:10 God speaks in vv. 10–17. Israel initially brought God as much pleasure as **grapes**

found in the **wilderness** or **the first fruit of the fig tree**, but that changed with the incident of pagan sexuality at **Baal-peor** (Nm 25:1–9; Ps 106:28–30) where the people tried to ensure fertility by worshiping Baal, here referred to as **Shame**. The point is that Israel was now repeating its foolish behavior.
9:11–12 **Ephraim's glory** was the Lord, whose departure would end their fertility and cause them **woe**.
9:13 God had placed both Ephraim and Tyre in surroundings in which they should have flourished (**meadow** is figurative; Ezk 17:5–8), but both had turned to Baal worship and practiced child sacrifice. Both Tyre and Samaria were besieged by the Assyrian king Shalmaneser V. Both cities fell to Sargon II of Assyria in 722 BC.
9:14 The prophet asks the Lord to give Israel what they deserve: the opposite of Jacob's

blessing in Gn 49:25: "blessings of the breasts and the womb."
9:15–17 Just as vv. 10–14 begin with an allusion to Baal-peor, these verses begin with an allusion to **Gilgal** (cp. 4:15; 12:11), a town so full of evil that God had rejected them (**hate** in v. 15 = **reject** in v. 17).
10:1–4 Hosea speaks in vv. 1–8. Although once a **lush vine** (cp. Is 5; Jn 15), Israel only yielded **fruit for itself**. They had turned the Lord's blessings into gifts for the calf idols of Baal. The word rendered "lush" more often means "ravaging" (Nah 2:2), which it may mean here. Rather than producing fruit for harvest, they were **devious** and acted like **poisonous weeds** (cp. Dt 32:32; 2Kg 4:39; Jr 2:21). They recognized no external authority (**no king**), but pretended to worship the Lord with **false oaths**. **Lawsuits** can also be rendered "justice," the fruit God was looking for.

2 Their hearts are devious;[A]
now they must bear their guilt.
The LORD will break down their altars
and demolish their sacred pillars.
3 In fact, they are now saying,
"We have no king!
For we do not fear the LORD.
What can a king do for us?"
4 They speak mere words,
taking false oaths
while making covenants.
So lawsuits break out
like poisonous weeds in the furrows
of a field.

5 The residents of Samaria will have anxiety
over the calf of Beth-aven.
Indeed, its idolatrous priests rejoiced
over it;
the people will mourn over it,
over its glory.
It will certainly go into exile.
6 The calf itself will be taken to Assyria
as an offering to the great king.[B]
Ephraim will experience shame;
Israel will be ashamed of its counsel.
7 Samaria's king will disappear[C]
like foam[D] on the surface of the water.
8 The high places of Aven, the sin of Israel,
will be destroyed;
thorns and thistles will grow
over their altars.
They will say to the mountains,
"Cover us!"
and to the hills, "Fall on us!"

Israel's Defeat because of Sin

9 Israel, you have sinned
since the days of Gibeah;
they have taken their stand there.
Will not war against the unjust
overtake them in Gibeah?

10 I will discipline them at my discretion;
nations will be gathered against them
to put them in bondage[E]
for their double iniquity.

11 Ephraim is a well-trained calf
that loves to thresh,
but I will place a yoke on[F] her fine neck.
I will harness Ephraim;
Judah will plow;
Jacob will do the final plowing.
12 Sow righteousness for yourselves
and reap faithful love;
break up your unplowed ground.
It is time to seek the LORD
until he comes and sends righteousness
on you like the rain.

13 You have plowed wickedness
and reaped injustice;
you have eaten the fruit of lies.
Because you have trusted
in your own way[G]
and in your large number of soldiers,
14 the roar of battle will rise
against your people,
and all your fortifications
will be demolished
in a day of war,
like Shalman's destruction of Beth-arbel.
Mothers will be dashed to pieces
along with their children.
15 So it will be done to you, Bethel,
because of your extreme evil.
At dawn the king of Israel will be
totally destroyed.

The LORD's Love for Israel

11 When Israel was a child, I loved him,
and out of Egypt I called my son.
2 Israel called to the Egyptians
even as Israel was leaving them.[H]

[A]10:2 Or divided　[B]10:6 Or to King Yareb　[C]10:7 Or will be cut off　[D]10:7 Or a stick　[E]10:10 LXX, Syr, Vg read against them when they are disciplined　[F]10:11 Lit will pass over　[G]10:13 LXX reads your chariots　[H]11:2 Lit They called to them; thus they went from before them

---

10:5 Will have anxiety indicates that the **residents of Samaria** feared **the calf of Beth-aven.** This refers to the calf god worshiped at Bethel (see note at 4:15). **Go into exile** is explained by v. 6.
10:6 For an account of Israel's troubles with **Assyria,** see 2Kg 15:19–20,29; 17:3–6.
10:8 When the **high places** were destroyed, the people would cry out to be buried by the very places of their idolatry (Dt 12:2; Lk 23:30).
10:9 God speaks in vv. 9–15. Allusions to **Gibeah** in 9:9 and 10:9 (see also 5:8) recall the civil war occasioned by a Levite's concubine being raped, murdered, and cut into pieces (Jdg 19–21). Like Samaria, Gibeah was a hill with a fortress; it served as Saul's capital during his kingship but was later deserted. So it represents both depravity and militarism and may have figuratively referred to Samaria.
10:11 Calves were sometimes allowed to walk atop fresh grain stalks that had been laid out

on the ground in order to separate the husks from the kernels (Mc 4:13). Little effort was involved, and the calves could eat some of the grain (Dt 25:4; 1Co 9:9; 1Tm 5:18). Israel would cease to be like the calf and would have to plow with the yoke of discipline.
10:12–13 The exhortations to **sow . . . reap,** and **seek** are essentially identical in meaning. Israel was to seek **righteousness . . . faithful love,** and **the LORD.** This is the summary of a life that pleases God (2:19; Pss 33:5; 36:10; 89:14; 103:17; Pr 21:21; Jr 9:24). But Israel had sought **wickedness . . . injustice,** and **the fruit of lies.** The latter is probably the "false fruit" of idolatry and military power.
10:14–15 The identities of Shalman and **Beth-arbel** are uncertain, but Shalman may refer to the Assyrian king Shalmaneser. Hosea's hearers were apparently familiar with the incident. This battle, like the one prophesied, started at **dawn.**

11:1–4 In these verses the Lord alternates between "I did this" and "but Israel did that."
11:1 I loved him speaks of Yahweh drawing Israel into his affectionate heart and of his faithfulness to his covenant with the patriarchs in redeeming Israel and choosing them for a covenant relationship (Dt 7:7–8). As a loving Father (Ex 4:22; Mal 2:10) God had brought (where "brought" is a strong use of the word "call"; cp. Ex 2:7; Is 41:4; Am 5:8) Israel to himself and to a destiny. But now he grieved as a father abandoned by his son (Hs 6:4). Like 6:2, 11:1 is understood in the NT to have messianic significance in that Jesus, God's Son like Israel, was also brought out of Egypt in the context of hatred (Mt 2:15; cp. Ex 4:22).
11:2–3 Israel's not knowing their own God, not recognizing him at work in their lives, and not praising his faithfulness but instead attributing the effects of his grace to other causes, is a major theme in Hosea.

They kept sacrificing to the Baals
and burning offerings to idols.
³ It was I who taught Ephraim to walk,
taking them^A by the hand,^B
but they never knew that I healed them.
⁴ I led them with human cords,
with ropes of love.
To them I was like one
who eases the yoke from their jaws;
I bent down to give them food.
⁵ Israel will not return to the land
of Egypt
and Assyria will be his king,
because they refused to repent.
⁶ A sword will whirl through his cities;
it will destroy and devour the bars
of his gates,^C
because of their schemes.
⁷ My people are bent on turning from me.
Though they call to him on high,
he will not exalt them at all.

⁸ How can I give you up, Ephraim?
How can I surrender you, Israel?
How can I make you like Admah?
How can I treat you like Zeboiim?
I have had a change of heart;
my compassion is stirred!
⁹ I will not vent the full fury of my anger;
I will not turn back to destroy Ephraim.
For I am God and not man,
the Holy One among you;
I will not come in rage.^D
¹⁰ They will follow the LORD;
he will roar like a lion.
When he roars,
his children will come trembling
from the west.
¹¹ They will be roused like birds
from Egypt
and like doves from the land
of Assyria.

Then I will settle them in their homes.
This is the LORD's declaration.
¹² Ephraim surrounds me with lies,
the house of Israel, with deceit.
Judah still wanders with God
and is faithful to the holy ones.^E

God's Case against Jacob's Heirs

12 Ephraim chases^F the wind
and pursues the east wind.
He continually multiplies lies
and violence.
He makes a covenant with Assyria,
and olive oil is carried to Egypt.

² The LORD also has a dispute
with Judah.
He is about to punish Jacob
according to his conduct;
he will repay him based on his actions.
³ In the womb he grasped
his brother's heel,
and as an adult he wrestled with God.
⁴ Jacob struggled with the angel
and prevailed;
he wept and sought his favor.
He found him at Bethel,
and there he spoke with him.^G
⁵ The LORD is the God of Armies;
the LORD is his name.
⁶ But you must return to your God.
Maintain love and justice,
and always put your hope in God.

⁷ A merchant loves to extort
with dishonest scales in his hands.
⁸ But Ephraim thinks,
"How rich I have become;
I made it all myself.
In all my earnings,
no one can find any iniquity in me
that I can be punished for!"^H

---

^A11:3 LXX, Syr, Vg; MT reads him　^B11:3 Lit them on his arms　^C11:6 Or devour his empty talkers, or devour his limbs; Hb obscure　^D11:9 Or come into any city; Hb obscure　^E11:12 Hb obscure　^F12:1 Or grazes on, or tends　^G12:4 LXX, Syr; MT reads us　^H12:8 Lit iniquity which is sin

---

#44 99 Essential Christian Truths

GOD'S GLORY

The glory of God is his manifest work, the way he represents his perfect character through his activity. It also refers to his excellent reputation and is given as one of the reasons we are to praise his name. Another sense of the word is the inherent beauty of God, the unbearable brightness and beauty of his being as he radiates his own attributes and characteristics for all to witness. The Scriptures speak of humanity as having fallen short of God's glory (Rm 3:23) because we have rejected the purpose for which God created us—to glorify him.

11:5–7 In these verses the Lord announces the penalty for Israel's ingratitude. Israel would be delivered to Assyria, who would oppress them as Egypt had done (7:16; 10:6). **11:8–11** The Lord refused to annihilate Israel but promised a new exodus for a believing remnant.
11:8–9 The point of God's manner of speaking here is that nothing stands in the way of the deserved abandonment and destruction of Israel but God's gracious compassion.
11:10 Whereas the Lord is like a **lion** as Israel's fierce predator in 5:14 and 13:7, here the comparison is a positive one as the divine lion is Israel's champion restoring them to the land. The **trembling** signifies submissive excitement at hearing the Lord's voice (Jb 37:1–4).
11:11 The phrase **this is the LORD's declaration** concludes the promise of restoration in vv. 8–11 and echoes its use in a similar blessing passage in 2:16,21.

11:12 The section ends by declaring that both **Ephraim** or Israel and **Judah** were grieving the Lord. The last two lines of this verse are difficult. The Hebrew term for God is not the usual *Elohim* but *El*, which can refer to God but also to the Canaanite god of that name. The term for **wanders** is rare but suggests rebellion (Gn 27:40; Jr 2:31). **Holy ones** elsewhere refers to godly people or to angels (Pss 16:3; 89:5; Dn 7:18; 8:13), but it could refer in this context to Canaanite deities or cult prostitutes.
12:3–5 Hosea rebuked Israel by pointing out that although their namesake **Jacob** (whose name God changed to Israel) had once been a faithless, self-centered conniver, he met God first at Bethel and was later changed in the encounter at the Jabbok River. The people of Israel, on the other hand, met Baal at Bethel (Beth-aven) and, in effect, died (13:1).
12:6 Again Hosea exhorted a threefold repentance (cp. 6:1; 10:12; 14:2–3).

Judgment on Apostate Israel

9 I have been the LORD your God
  ever since[A] the land of Egypt.
  I will make you live in tents again,
    as in the festival days.
10 I will speak through the prophets
  and grant many visions;
  I will give parables
    through the prophets.
11 Since Gilead is full of evil,
  they will certainly come to nothing.
  They sacrifice bulls in Gilgal;
  even their altars will be like piles of
    rocks
  on the furrows of a field.

Further Indictment of Jacob's Heirs

12 Jacob fled to the territory of Aram.
  Israel worked to earn a wife;
  he tended flocks for a wife.
13 The LORD brought Israel from Egypt
    by a prophet,
  and Israel was tended by a prophet.

14 Ephraim has provoked bitter anger,
  so his Lord will leave his bloodguilt
    on him
  and repay him for his contempt.

13 When Ephraim spoke,
    there was trembling;
  he was exalted in Israel.
  But he incurred guilt through Baal
    and died.

2 Now they continue to sin
  and make themselves a cast image,
  idols skillfully made
    from their silver,
  all of them the work of craftsmen.
  People say about them,
  "Let the men who sacrifice[B] kiss
    the calves."
3 Therefore, they will be
    like the morning mist,
  like the early dew that vanishes,
  like chaff blown from a threshing floor,
  or like smoke from a window.

Death and Resurrection

4 I have been the LORD your God
  ever since[C] the land of Egypt;
  you know no God but me,
  and no Savior exists besides me.
5 I knew[D] you in the wilderness,
  in the land of drought.
6 When they had pasture,
  they became satisfied;
  they were satisfied,
  and their hearts became proud.
  Therefore they forgot me.
7 So I will be like a lion to them;
  I will lurk like a leopard on the path.
8 I will attack them
  like a bear robbed of her cubs
  and tear open the rib cage
    over their hearts.
  I will devour them there like a lioness,
  like a wild beast that would rip
    them open.
9 I will destroy you, Israel;
  you have no help but me.[E]
10 Where now is your king,[F]
  that he may save you in all your cities,
  and the[G] rulers[H] you demanded, saying,
  "Give me a king and leaders"?
11 I give you a king in my anger
  and take away a king in my wrath.
12 Ephraim's guilt is preserved;
  his sin is stored up.
13 Labor pains come on him.
  He is not a wise son;
  when the time comes,
  he will not be born.[I]

14 I will ransom them from the power
    of Sheol.
  I will redeem[J] them from death.
  Death, where are your barbs?
  Sheol, where is your sting?
  Compassion is hidden from my eyes.

The Coming Judgment

15 Although he flourishes
    among his brothers,[K]
  an east wind will come,

---

^12:9 LXX reads God who brought you out of ^13:2 Or "Those who make human sacrifices ^13:4 DSS, LXX read God who brought you out of ^13:5 LXX, Syr read fed ^13:9 LXX reads At your destruction, Israel, who will help you? ^13:10 LXX, Syr, Vg; MT reads I will be your king ^13:10 Lit your ^13:10 Or judges ^13:13 Lit he will not present himself at the opening of the womb for sons ^13:14 Or Should I ransom . . . ? Should I redeem . . . ? ^13:15 Or among reeds

---

12:9 The Lord was going to cause Israel to live in the wilderness again, in tents, as during the Feast of Shelters.
12:10–11 The second line of v. 10 can be rendered "and I am the one who caused visions to abound." But Israel disposed of God's revelation and pursued pagan sacrifices at Gilead and Gilgal, for which they would receive nothing but piles of rocks.
12:12–13 The prophet took up here where he left off in v. 4 and compared Israel's experience in Egypt to that of Jacob in

Aram. Both man and nation went seeking for refuge in a foreign land but ended up being enslaved instead. But whereas Jacob came out shepherding flocks (Gn 31:17–18), the nation was led like a flock by a shepherd (Moses, see Ex 13).
13:7–9 Those who are lulled into believing God is indulgent of our sins are shocked into reality by this picture of God being like a lion (cp. 11:10), a leopard, or a bear, tearing, ripping, and devouring. Israel had no help but God, and God himself had come to destroy.

13:10–13 Verses 10–11 allude to 1Sm 8:4–5 where Israel demands a king "as all the other nations have." Verse 12 means that Ephraim's guilt must be contained and taken away. Verse 13 compares Ephraim to a woman in labor whose child is breech, so that both woman and child will probably die. Both the institutions of Israel (the mother) and her child (the people) are doomed.
13:14 As in 6:1–2, although Israel was doomed, the Lord is able to bring life out of death.

a wind from the LORD rising up
   from the desert.
His water source will fail,
and his spring will run dry.
The wind[A] will plunder the treasury
of every precious item.

16 Samaria will bear her guilt
    because she has rebelled
       against her God.
    They will fall by the sword;
    their children will be dashed to pieces,
    and their pregnant women
       ripped open.

A Plea to Repent

14 Israel, return to the LORD your God,
    for you have stumbled
       in your iniquity.
2   Take words of repentance with you
    and return to the LORD.
    Say to him, "Forgive all our iniquity
    and accept what is good,
    so that we may repay you
    with praise[B] from our[C] lips.
3   Assyria will not save us,
    we will not ride on horses,
    and we will no longer proclaim,
       'Our gods!'
    to the work of our hands.
    For the fatherless receives compassion
       in you."

A Promise of Restoration

4   I will heal their apostasy;
    I will freely love them,
    for my anger will have turned from him.
5   I will be like the dew to Israel;
    he will blossom like the lily
    and take root like the cedars of Lebanon.
6   His new branches will spread,
    and his splendor will be
       like the olive tree,
    his fragrance, like the forest of Lebanon.
7   The people will return and live
       beneath his shade.
    They will grow grain
    and blossom like the vine.
    His renown will be like the wine
       of Lebanon.

8   Ephraim, why should I[D] have
       anything more
    to do with idols?
    It is I who answer and watch over him.
    I am like a flourishing pine tree;
    your fruit comes from me.

9   Let whoever is wise understand
       these things,
    and whoever is insightful
       recognize them.
    For the ways of the LORD are right,
    and the righteous walk in them,
    but the rebellious stumble in them.

[A]13:15 Probably the Assyrian king   [B]14:2 LXX reads *with the fruit*   [C]14:2 Lit *repay the bulls of our*   [D]14:8 LXX reads *he*

14:1–3 This final invitation to repent (6:1–3) even gives a "sinner's prayer."
14:4 A believing remnant will experience restoration and blessing. God promised to **heal their apostasy**.
14:5–7 God promised to restore life and beauty to Israel as to a dead, abandoned garden. Israel would again be a blessing to the nations as it was originally intended to be (Gn 12:1–3; Is 2:2–4), signified by

the fragrant **olive tree** furnishing not only food, fuel, and medicine but also **shade** (Lk 13:18–19). **His renown** is literally "his memory," probably referring to God's remembrance of Israel that will prompt him to restore them by his grace (Gn 8:21). **Lebanon** is referred to three times in vv. 5–7 but nowhere else in the book. The reason may be that flourishing Lebanon had been the origin of Israel's Baal cult (1Kg 16:31–33).

14:8 By **idols** God means the "topic" of idols. **Him** refers to the nation of Israel. The reference to the **flourishing pine tree** means that the Lord is the source of all they had been looking for in fertility gods.
14:9 Hosea concluded by exhorting readers to persevere in the study of his prophecy, so as to **understand** and **recognize** the things he had communicated.

◥ Introduction to Joel

Circumstances of Writing

Joel ("Yahweh is God") is identified as the son of Pethuel. He is not easily identified with the other Joels of Scripture (1Sm 8:2; 1Ch 4:35; 6:33; 11:38; 15:7; Ezr 10:43; Neh 11:9), leaving us only his book to know him, his calling from God, and his work. The book itself gives no biographical information other than his father's name.

Dating the book of Joel has always been difficult and mainly conjecture, with suggestions ranging as widely as premonarchial Israel to the postexilic period, sometimes well into the Hellenistic period.

Contribution to the Bible

The book of Joel shows us the Creator and Redeemer God of all the universe in complete control of nature. Joel made it clear that the God of judgment also is a God of mercy who stands ready to redeem and restore when his people come before him in repentance. Joel points to a time when the spirit of God would be present upon all people. On the day of Pentecost, Peter proclaimed that the new day of Spirit–filled discipleship, foretold by Joel, had arrived (Ac 2:17–21).

Structure

Joel's use of repetition gives the book the appearance of a series of folding doors, in some cases doors within doors. The overall structure balances the section on God's judgment through the locust plague (1:1–20) with a section on the land's physical restoration (2:21–27). The prophecy of an invading army (2:1–11) is balanced by a prophecy on the destruction of this army (2:20). In the center is the highly prominent call to repent and the promise of renewal (2:12–19). But this balanced structure overlaps with another. The prophecy of the destruction of the invading army (2:20) is also balanced with the final prophecy of the Lord's vengeance against all the nations (3:1–21). Finally, the assurance of the land's physical restoration through rain (2:21–27) is balanced by the promise of the people's spiritual restoration through the outpouring of God's Spirit (2:28–32).

Outline

600–450 BC

Second temple construction begins under
  Zerubbabel's and Joshua's leadership. **536**
Haggai and Zechariah encourage the people
  to finish rebuilding the temple. **520–518**
Second temple is dedicated. **515**
Events in Esther **486–465**
Greek victory over Persians in Battle of
  Salamis, **480**, and Plain of Plataea, **479**,
  thwarted Persian expansion into Europe
  and were keys to Greek hegemony in
  the Mediterranean Basin and Europe.
Ezra goes to Jerusalem. **458**

450–400 BC

Joel's prophecy occurred sometime after **445**
  when Jerusalem's walls had been rebuilt.
  (See events under **725** for a different
  view of when Joel prophesied.)
Events in Nehemiah **445–430**
Nehemiah's ministry **445–420?**
Nehemiah in Jerusalem **445–432**
Jerusalem's walls rebuilt **445**
The Peloponnesian War between
  Sparta and Athens **431–404**

1 The word of the LORD that came to Joel son of Pethuel:

A Plague of Locusts

2 Hear this, you elders;
   listen, all you inhabitants of the land.
   Has anything like this ever happened
      in your days
   or in the days of your ancestors?
3 Tell your children about it,
   and let your children tell their children,
   and their children the next generation.
4 What the devouring locust has left,
   the swarming locust has eaten;
   what the swarming locust has left,
   the young locust has eaten;
   and what the young locust has left,
   the destroying locust has eaten.

5 Wake up, you drunkards, and weep;
   wail, all you wine drinkers,
   because of the sweet wine,
   for it has been taken from your mouth.
6 For a nation has invaded my land,
   powerful and without number;
   its teeth are the teeth of a lion,
   and it has the fangs of a lioness.
7 It has devastated my grapevine
   and splintered my fig tree.
   It has stripped off its bark
      and thrown it away;
   its branches have turned white.
8 Grieve like a young woman dressed
      in sackcloth,
   mourning for the husband of her youth.
9 Grain and drink offerings have been
      cut off
   from the house of the LORD;
   the priests, who are ministers
      of the LORD, mourn.
10 The fields are destroyed;
   the land grieves;
   indeed, the grain is destroyed;
   the new wine is dried up;
   and the fresh oil fails.
11 Be ashamed, you farmers,

wail, you vinedressers,^A
   over the wheat and the barley,
   because the harvest of the field
      has perished.
12 The grapevine is dried up,
   and the fig tree is withered;
   the pomegranate, the date palm,
      and the apple —
   all the trees of the orchard
      — have withered.
   Indeed, human joy has dried up.

13 Dress in sackcloth and lament,
      you priests;
   wail, you ministers of the altar.
   Come and spend the night in sackcloth,
   you ministers of my God,
   because grain and drink offerings
   are withheld from the house
      of your God.
14 Announce a sacred fast;
   proclaim a solemn assembly!
   Gather the elders
   and all the residents of the land
   at the house of the LORD your God,
   and cry out to the LORD.

The Day of the LORD
15 Woe because of that day!
   For the day of the LORD is near
   and will come as devastation
      from the Almighty.
16 Hasn't the food been cut off
   before our eyes,
   joy and gladness
   from the house of our God?
17 The seeds lie shriveled in their casings.^B
   The storehouses are in ruin,
   and the granaries are broken down,
   because the grain has withered away.
18 How the animals groan!
   The herds of cattle wander
      in confusion
   since they have no pasture.
   Even the flocks of sheep and goats
      suffer punishment.

---

^A 1:11 Or *The farmers are dismayed, the vinedressers wail*   ^B 1:17 Or *clods*; Hb obscure

---

1:1 Nothing more is known of this man **Joel**.
1:2–3 Joel addressed both the **elders** and the **inhabitants of the land** with a question designed to arrest their attention. A unique locust plague served as a warning of two future events: a coming war and the day of the Lord.
1:4 The use of four different Hebrew words for "locusts" in this verse emphasizes the totality of their destruction.
1:5 Joel addressed a third group—the **drunkards**. Their wine-induced stupor kept them from realizing what was happening around them. Now out of wine, they sobered up and faced the devastation.
1:6–7 Grapevines and figs were two of the principle crops of the land. They were

damaged during wars or plague, impacting the food supply and the economy.
1:8 The proper response to this catastrophe was grief, symbolized by donning **sackcloth**, a rough, uncomfortable fabric that chafed and irritated the skin.
1:9 The **priests** lamented the fact that **offerings** were **cut off** not just because the temple would lack its sacrifices, but also because they would lack the food portion they took from these offerings. Empty altars also meant empty stomachs.
1:10–12 The farm workers were to mourn and wail because the agricultural economy had been ruined. Starvation was imminent.
1:13–14 The **priests** were to take the lead in mourning rituals by dressing in **sackcloth**

and spending the night at the temple. The whole assembly was to gather together and **cry out to the LORD**, an expression of their corporate guilt before God.
1:15–20 The people gathered at the temple for a communal lament. These verses give the content of their prayer. The major theme of the book is the **day of the LORD**, and the people were terrified as they considered that coming day. It would be a time when the Lord punished sin and judged the nations. They were out of food and could not offer fellowship offerings to commune with God. The **storehouses** for grain were empty. The plague appears to be compounded with a drought and perhaps with a **fire**, so the **pastures** were ruined. Even **sheep**

19 I call to you, LORD,
for fire has consumed
the pastures of the wilderness,
and flames have devoured
all the trees of the orchard.

20 Even the wild animals cry out to[A] you,
for the river beds are dried up,
and fire has consumed
the pastures of the wilderness.

2 Blow the ram's horn in Zion;
sound the alarm on my holy mountain!
Let all the residents of the land tremble,
for the day of the LORD is coming;
in fact, it is near —

2 a day of darkness and gloom,
a day of clouds and total darkness,
like the dawn spreading
over the mountains;
a great and strong people appears,
such as never existed in ages past
and never will again
in all the generations to come.

3 A fire devours in front of them,
and behind them a flame blazes.
The land in front of them
is like the garden of Eden,
but behind them,
it is like a desert wasteland;
there is no escape from them.

4 Their appearance is like that of horses,
and they gallop like war horses.

5 They bound on the tops of the mountains.
Their sound is like the sound of chariots,
like the sound of fiery flames
consuming stubble,
like a mighty army deployed for war.

6 Nations writhe in horror before them;
all faces turn pale.

7 They attack as warriors attack;
they scale walls as men of war do.
Each goes on his own path,
and they do not change their course.

8 They do not push each other;
each proceeds on his own path.
They dodge the arrows,
never stopping.

9 They storm the city;
they run on the wall;
they climb into the houses;
they enter through the windows
like thieves.

10 The earth quakes before them;
the sky shakes.
The sun and moon grow dark,
and the stars cease their shining.

11 The LORD makes his voice heard
in the presence of his army.
His camp is very large;
those who carry out his command
are powerful.
Indeed, the day of the LORD is terrible
and dreadful —
who can endure it?

God's Call for Repentance

12 Even now —
this is the LORD's declaration —
turn to me with all your heart,
with fasting, weeping, and mourning.

13 Tear your hearts,
not just your clothes,
and return to the LORD your God.
For he is gracious and compassionate,
slow to anger,
abounding in faithful love,
and he relents from sending disaster.

14 Who knows? He may turn and relent
and leave a blessing behind him,

^1:20 Or *animals pant for*; Hb obscure

and goats that could survive in barren lands were suffering. The speaker in v. 19 expressed the community's complaint and petition for mercy. The **animals**, domestic and wild, also joined in crying out to the Lord. Without water, death would soon come to man and beast.
2:1 Commentators are divided over the identity of the invading northern army (see note at v. 20) described in chap. 2. (1) Some see it as a figurative description of the locust invasion of chap. 1. (2) Some see literal enemy troops coming from the north, described as invading locusts. (3) Revelation 9:3–11 compares demonic forces to locusts. Whether this army was man or insect, it represented the judgment force of the Lord. The prophet was called to **sound the alarm** to the nation from Jerusalem, from the place where the temple stood.
2:2 The people of God have often longed for the coming of the Lord. But Joel insisted that this day would be a day of

darkness . . . **gloom**, blackness, and destruction (Zph 1:14–17).
2:7–8 In many biblical passages (e.g., Jdg 6:5; Is 33:4; Jr 51:14) armies are compared to locusts and sometimes locusts are compared to armies (Pr 30:27).
2:9–11 Joel continued the interplay of soldiers with the imagery and actions of a locust plague. The swarming locusts ate everything in the fields and then came into the **city** and finally into the **houses**. So also invading armies breached the city walls and then plundered the houses. Joel used end-time language and moved beyond what happens in normal locust or military invasions. The very heavens were now engaged; Yahweh and his heavenly armies were ready to wreak havoc. Judgment day had come.
2:12–13 The tone of the prophet changes from this verse to the end of his message. The phrase **even now**—**this is the LORD's declaration** announces a wonderful possibility. Yahweh is a God of mercy and compassion to repentant sinners. "The LORD's

declaration" is a solemn promise. This is the only place where this phrase appears in Joel.
2:14 The question **Who knows?** expresses hope based on the fact that God is free to choose pardon or punishment (2Sm 12:22).

#45 99 Essential Christian Truths

GOD IS LOVE

To say that God is love is to say that God is the essence of love, or that perfect love both resides and resonates within God himself—one God in three persons. The imperfect love that human beings share between one another is a dim reflection, a sign that points to the perfect love that resides within God. The greatest act of love by God toward humans isn't the giving of earthly goods but the giving of himself in Christ so that we might become reconciled to him.

so you can offer a grain offering and
a drink offering
to the LORD your God.

15 Blow the ram's horn in Zion!
Announce a sacred fast;
proclaim a solemn assembly.
16 Gather the people;
sanctify the congregation;
assemble the aged;^A
gather the infants,
even babies nursing at the breast.
Let the groom leave his bedroom,
and the bride
her honeymoon chamber.
17 Let the priests, the LORD's ministers,
weep between the portico and the altar.
Let them say,
"Have pity on your people, LORD,
and do not make your inheritance
a disgrace,
an object of scorn among the nations.
Why should it be said
among the peoples,
'Where is their God?'"

God's Response to His People

18 Then the LORD became jealous for his land
and spared his people. 19 The LORD answered
his people:

Look, I am about to send you
grain, new wine, and fresh oil.
You will be satiated with them,
and I will no longer make you
a disgrace among the nations.

20 I will drive the northerner
far from you
and banish him to a dry
and desolate land,
his front ranks into the Dead Sea,
and his rear guard
into the Mediterranean Sea.
His stench will rise;
yes, his rotten smell will rise,
for he has done astonishing things.

21 Don't be afraid, land;
rejoice and be glad,
for the LORD has done
astonishing things.
22 Don't be afraid, wild animals,
for the wilderness pastures
have turned green,
the trees bear their fruit,
and the fig tree and grapevine yield
their riches.
23 Children of Zion, rejoice and be glad
in the LORD your God,
because he gives you the autumn rain^B
for your vindication.^C
He sends showers for you,
both autumn and spring rain as before.
24 The threshing floors will be full of grain,
and the vats will overflow
with new wine and fresh oil.

25 I will repay you for the years
that the swarming locust ate,
the young locust, the destroying locust,
and the devouring locust —
my great army that I sent against you.
26 You will have plenty to eat
and be satisfied.
You will praise the name of the
LORD your God,
who has dealt wondrously with you.
My people will never again be put
to shame.
27 You will know that I am present
in Israel
and that I am the LORD your God,
and there is no other.
My people will never again be put
to shame.

God's Promise of His Spirit

28 After this
I will pour out my Spirit on all humanity;
then your sons and your daughters
will prophesy,
your old men will have dreams,
and your young men will see visions.

---

^A 2:16 Or *elders*   ^B 2:23 Or *the teacher of righteousness*   ^C 2:23 Or *righteousness*

2:15–17 The trumpet call summoned the people to **a solemn assembly** for worship and petition. This contrasts with the **ram's horn** call of v. 1, which heralded war. This time everyone was to come, even those who normally were exempt from such gatherings. The **priests** were given special instructions because they were to lead the expression of the national lament and petition.
2:18–19 Starting in v. 19 the Lord speaks directly to the people. His covenant blessings will be restored, and the people will be protected from their enemies.
2:20 Who was this northern army? Some interpreters say it was an army of locusts. Almost every military invasion of Israel came from the north, so it would be difficult to identify a specific army. The best approach is to interpret

the enemy from the north as a reference to the end-time attack of the nations against God's people (Is 34:1–7; Ezk 38; Dn 11:36–45).
2:21–22 The destruction caused by the locust invasion (or the invading army) is now reversed. Both **land** and **animals** will participate in the salvation of God's people (Rm 8:19–23; Rv 21).
2:23–24 Israel was dependent on **autumn** and **spring** rains for the prosperity of the land. The phrase **autumn rain for your vindication** can also be translated as "teacher of (or for) righteousness." This could be a veiled allusion to a coming Davidic leader-teacher who would bring righteousness to the believing remnant (Dt 18:15; Jr 33:14–17).
2:25–27 The locusts served as symbols of all the invading armies that had attacked Israel

and decimated the land. That God would say **my great army** of a pagan military force reminded Israel that Yahweh is the sovereign Lord of history. He is in control of all nations and they ultimately serve his purposes no matter their intentions (Is 45:1–7).
2:28–29 The giving of his **Spirit** would take place at the time of the forgiveness of their sins. Peter on the day of Pentecost announced the gift of the Spirit and the forgiveness of sins by calling on God's name (Ac 2:21,38–40). The Lord's promise of the Spirit in Joel was not reserved for a few but for anyone who from **all humanity** would believe. Peter saw that this gift was not limited to Israel, but was for "all who are far off, as many as the Lord our God will call" (Ac 2:39).

Seeing Jesus
in the Divided Kingdom

▼ **Old Testament**

▼ **New Testament**

THE LORD: High and Lifted Up; His Glory Fills the Whole Earth *(Is 6)*

JESUS: Isaiah Saw Jesus's Glory and Spoke of Him *(Jn 12:37–41)*

Elijah the Prophet: Encountered God in a Still, Small Voice on Mount Horeb *(1Kg 19)*

God's Son: Revealed His Glory with Elijah and Moses at the Transfiguration *(Mt 17:1–5)*

Naaman the Syrian: Healed of Leprosy; Praised the God in Israel *(2Kg 5:14–15)*

Jesus the Savior: Healed Leprosy by His Touch; He Is God in Israel *(Lk 5:12–15)*

The Suffering Servant: Rejected by Men; Wounded for Our Healing *(Is 52:13–53:12)*

The Suffering Christ: Reviled by Men; Bore Our Sins on the Tree *(1Pt 2:21–25)*

Hezekiah: Prayed for God's Glory in the Saving of His People from Assyria *(2Kg 19)*

Jesus: Prayed for God's Glory in the Saving of People from Their Sin *(Jn 17)*

Hosea: Pursued His Adulterous Wife; Bought Her Back from Slavery for Purity *(Hs 3)*

Jesus: Gave Himself for His Church to Make Her Holy and Blameless *(Eph 5:25–27)*

Jonah: In the Belly of a Great Fish Three Days and Nights *(Jnh 1:17)*

Jesus, the Better Jonah: In the Heart of the Earth Three Days and Nights *(Mt 12:39–41)*

Joel: Prophesied God's Spirit Poured Out on Those Who Call on the Lord *(Jl 2:28–32)*

Jesus: Pours Out His Spirit on All Who Call on Him to Be Saved *(Ac 2; Rm 10)*

Jeremiah: Prophesied a New Covenant for the Forgiveness of Sin *(Jr 31:31–34)*

Jesus: Shed His Blood to Establish the Covenant for the Forgiveness of Sin *(Mt 26:28)*

The Kings of Judah: Sinned, Calling the Davidic Covenant into Question *(2Kg 24:19–20)*

The Son of David: God Remained Faithful to His Covenant with David *(Mt 1:1–17)*

Ezekiel: Prophesied a Resurrection for God's People, a Restoration to the Land *(Ezk 37)*

Jesus: The Resurrection and the Life for All Who Believe in Him *(Jn 11:25–26)*

²⁹ I will even pour out my Spirit
    on the male and female slaves
       in those days.
³⁰ I will display wonders
    in the heavens and on the earth:
    blood, fire, and columns of smoke.
³¹ The sun will be turned to darkness
    and the moon to blood
    before the great and terrible day
       of the LORD comes.
³² Then everyone who calls
    on the name of the LORD will be saved,
    for there will be an escape
    for those on Mount Zion
       and in Jerusalem,
    as the LORD promised,
    among the survivors the LORD calls.

Judgment of the Nations

3 Yes, in those days and at that time,
    when I restore the fortunes of Judah
       and Jerusalem,
² I will gather all the nations
    and take them to the Valley
       of Jehoshaphat.^A
    I will enter into judgment
    with them there
    because of my people,
       my inheritance Israel.
    The nations have scattered the Israelites
    in foreign countries
    and divided up my land.
³ They cast lots for my people;
    they bartered a boy for a prostitute
    and sold a girl for wine to drink.

⁴ And also: Tyre, Sidon, and all the territories of Philistia — what are you to me? Are you paying me back or trying to get even with me? I will quickly bring retribution on your heads. ⁵ For you took my silver and gold and carried my finest treasures to your temples. ⁶ You sold the people of Judah and Jerusalem to the Greeks to remove them far from their own territory. ⁷ Look, I am about to rouse them up from the place where you sold them; I will

bring retribution on your heads. ⁸ I will sell your sons and daughters to the people of Judah, and they will sell them to the Sabeans,^B to a distant nation, for the LORD has spoken.
⁹ Proclaim this among the nations:
    Prepare for holy war;
    rouse the warriors;
    let all the men of war advance and attack!
¹⁰ Beat your plows into swords
    and your pruning knives into spears.
    Let even the weakling say, "I am
       a warrior."
¹¹ Come quickly,^C all
    you surrounding nations;
    gather yourselves.
    Bring down your warriors there, LORD.

¹² Let the nations be roused
    and come to the Valley of Jehoshaphat,
    for there I will sit down
    to judge all the surrounding nations.
¹³ Swing the sickle
    because the harvest is ripe.
    Come and trample the grapes
    because the winepress is full;
    the wine vats overflow
    because the wickedness of the nations
       is extreme.

¹⁴ Multitudes, multitudes
    in the valley of decision!
    For the day of the LORD is near
    in the valley of decision.
¹⁵ The sun and moon will grow dark,
    and the stars will cease their shining.
¹⁶ The LORD will roar from Zion
    and make his voice heard
       from Jerusalem;
    heaven and earth will shake.
    But the LORD will be a refuge
       for his people,
    a stronghold for the Israelites.

Israel Blessed

¹⁷ Then you will know
    that I am the LORD your God,

---

^A3:2 = The LORD Will Judge   ^B3:8 Probably the south Arabian kingdom of Sheba (modern Yemen)   ^C3:11 LXX, Syr, Tg read *Gather yourselves and come*; Hb obscure

---

2:30–31 The cosmic signs that are part of the **day of the LORD** inspire awe for believers and terror for unbelievers. This day is one of salvation as well as judgment (Rv 6:12–17). **2:32** This verse shows the human obligation (**calls on the name of the LORD**) and the divine role in salvation (**among the survivors the LORD calls**). Both "calls" are necessary for salvation. God does not save those who do not call on him, and none call whom he has not called. **3:1–2** Sometime after Judah is restored the Lord will judge the nations, who will gather at Jerusalem (Is 66:18; Zph 3:8; Zch 12:3; 14:2–3; Rv 16:14–16; 19:11–16). The **Valley of Jehoshaphat** is literally "the valley where

Yahweh judged," but the name is probably symbolic. Some identify it with the valley of Jezreel near Megiddo and cite Rv 16:16, but that would be too far from Jerusalem. Others identify it with the Kidron Valley. **3:3–4** When Israel lost wars, their children would be sold by their enemies as slaves. **Tyre** and **Sidon** were trading hubs for slaves. **3:5–6** The crimes of these enemies were not only against Israel but against the Lord. It was God's **silver and gold** that they took. The slaves were sent as far away as Greece. **3:7–8** The Jews were sent in exile to the northwest, and so those who exiled them would be sent to the southeast. The **Sabeans** dominated the trade routes to the south.

3:9–12 The nations are summoned to battle. **3:13** The Lord will trample his enemies like **grapes** in a **winepress** (Is 63:1–6; Rv 14:14–20). **3:14–17 Multitudes, multitudes** are hordes of people in the valley of judgment. The **decision** is the verdict that the Lord is pronouncing on an unbelieving world, not a decision that people are making to follow God. It is too late because it is judgment day for Israel's enemies but salvation day for the people of Yahweh—**a refuge . . . a stronghold**. This will be a time of revelation to Israel and the nations because the Lord will be known as he is.

who dwells in Zion, my holy mountain.
Jerusalem will be holy,
and foreigners will never
   overrun it again.
18 In that day
the mountains will drip
   with sweet wine,
and the hills will flow with milk.
All the streams of Judah will flow
   with water,
and a spring will issue
   from the LORD's house,

watering the Valley of Acacias.^A
19 Egypt will become desolate,
and Edom a desert wasteland,
because of the violence done
   to the people of Judah
in whose land they shed innocent blood.
20 But Judah will be inhabited forever,
and Jerusalem from generation
   to generation.
21 I will pardon their bloodguilt,^B
which I have not pardoned,
for the LORD dwells in Zion.

---

^A **3:18** Or *Shittim* ^B **3:21** LXX, Syr read *I will avenge their blood*

3:18–21 Joel summarized the result of the day of the Lord. The land of Israel will have miraculous fertility and fruitfulness. Traditional enemies will be punished. The Lord will dwell with his people, and they will receive pardon for their sins.

◥ Introduction to Amos

Circumstances of Writing

Amos was a shepherd from Tekoa, a village about ten miles south of Jerusalem. He received a call from God to go north and prophesy against Samaria and the kingdom of Israel around 760 BC. We do not know how long he actually was in the north; it appears to have been a fairly short time. He provoked a great deal of opposition and anger, as illustrated by his encounter with Amaziah, the priest of Bethel (7:10–17). He wrote his book, a summary of his prophecies, after his return to Judah. He probably wrote it with the aid of a scribe.

Amos prophesied during the reigns of Uzziah of Judah (792–740 BC) and Jeroboam II of Israel (793–753 BC). This was a time of great prosperity and military success for both nations, as all their traditional enemies were in a weakened condition. Samaria, the capital city of Israel, enjoyed enormous wealth, and luxuries flowed into the city.

At the same time, decades of struggle with Damascus had left the population exhausted. Many farmers were reduced to poverty. Their more affluent neighbors, and especially the aristocracy, swooped in with loans that the poor could not repay and then reduced the debtors to slavery and seized their lands. The leaders of society believed they had no reason to fear for the future. Their city had high walls and fortified citadels, and their army was everywhere victorious. They were the chosen people of God, and they considered themselves immune from judgment.

Contribution to the Bible

Amos reminds us of the sovereignty of God in his involvement with his people. God will bring his judgment, a reality that certainly came to pass. Amos's emphasis on "the day of the LORD" had implications for his contemporaries, but it also reminds the modern reader of a coming day referred to repeatedly in the New Testament—the day of Christ's return.

Structure

After the superscription (1:1), the book of Amos is divided into seven parts. The first part, the introduction, is a single verse (1:2). This is followed by six major divisions: 1:3–2:16; 3:1–15; 4:1–13; 5:1–6:14; 7:1–8:3; 8:4–9:15. Remarkably, formulas of divine speech (statements such as "the LORD says," "the LORD has spoken," and "the LORD's declaration") are evenly distributed in these sections. Amos 1:3–2:16 has fourteen such formulas, and each of the following sections have seven each, for a total of forty-nine. The basic structure and content of each section is described in the notes.

Amos Timeline

800–760 BC

Adad-nirari III led his Assyrian army to victory over Syria and the destruction of Damascus. **802**
For half a century after the fall of Damascus, Assyrian expansion was thwarted by internal problems. **802–745**
Jeroboam II, king of northern kingdom, enjoyed an era of peace, expansion, increased trade, and affluence. **793–753**
Uzziah, king of southern kingdom **792–740**
Eclipse of the sun visible in Judah/Israel **JUNE 15, 763**
Earthquake at Hazor between **765** and **755**

760–750 BC

Amos is called to travel from Judah to Israel to prophesy in Samaria. **760**
Zechariah, king of northern kingdom **753–752**, assassinated by Shallum
Shallum, king of northern kingdom **752**, assassinated by Menahem
Menahem, king of northern kingdom **752–742**
Hosea's prophetic ministry **750–722?**
Micah called to be a prophet **750**

Outline

750–740 BC

Assyrian aggression was thwarted by internal problems until **745** when Tiglath-pileser III came to power.

Pekahiah, king of northern kingdom **742–740**, assassinated by Pekah

Death of King Uzziah of Judah **740**

Isaiah's call to be a prophet **740**

Other states in the region pay tribute to the growing power of Assyria. **740**

740–700 BC

Tiglath-pileser III's invasions of Israel **734–732**

Pekah of Israel and Rezin of Damascus form a mutual defense alliance against Assyria and invite Ahaz of Judah to join them. **734**

Ahaz refuses Isaiah's counsel and seeks protection from Assyria by paying tribute to them, creating a heavy financial burden on Judah for years to come. **734**

Alliance between Syria and Israel collapses with the fall of Damascus **(732)** and the fall of Samaria **(722)**

Pekah, king of northern kingdom **752–732**, assassinated by Hoshea, last king of northern kingdom **732–722**

The words of Amos, who was one of the sheep breeders^A from Tekoa — what he saw regarding Israel in the days of King Uzziah of Judah and Jeroboam son of Jehoash, king of Israel, two years before the earthquake.

² He said:

The LORD roars from Zion
and makes his voice heard
from Jerusalem;
the pastures of the shepherds mourn,^B
and the summit of Carmel withers.

Judgment on Israel's Neighbors

³ The LORD says:

I will not relent
from punishing Damascus
for three crimes, even four,
because they threshed Gilead
with iron sledges.
⁴ Therefore, I will send fire
against Hazael's palace,
and it will consume
Ben-hadad's citadels.
⁵ I will break down the gates^C
of Damascus.
I will cut off the ruler
from the Valley of Aven,
and the one who wields the scepter
from Beth-eden.
The people of Aram will be exiled to Kir.
The LORD has spoken.

⁶ The LORD says:

I will not relent from punishing Gaza
for three crimes, even four,
because they exiled a whole community,
handing them over to Edom.
⁷ Therefore, I will send fire
against the walls of Gaza,
and it will consume its citadels.
⁸ I will cut off the ruler from Ashdod,
and the one who wields the scepter
from Ashkelon.

I will also turn my hand against Ekron,
and the remainder of the Philistines
will perish.
The Lord GOD has spoken.

⁹ The LORD says:

I will not relent from punishing Tyre
for three crimes, even four,
because they handed over
a whole community of exiles to Edom
and broke^D a treaty of brotherhood.
¹⁰ Therefore, I will send fire
against the walls of Tyre,
and it will consume its citadels.

¹¹ The LORD says:

I will not relent from punishing Edom
for three crimes, even four,
because he pursued his brother
with the sword.
He stifled his compassion,
his anger tore at him continually,
and he harbored his rage incessantly.
¹² Therefore, I will send fire
against Teman,
and it will consume the citadels
of Bozrah.

¹³ The LORD says:

I will not relent from punishing
the Ammonites
for three crimes, even four,
because they ripped open
the pregnant women of Gilead
in order to enlarge their territory.
¹⁴ Therefore, I will set fire to the walls
of Rabbah,
and it will consume its citadels.
There will be shouting on the day
of battle
and a violent wind on the day
of the storm.
¹⁵ Their king and his princes

---

^A 1:1 Or *the shepherds*   ^B 1:2 Or *dry up*   ^C 1:5 Lit *gate bars*   ^D 1:9 Lit *and did not remember*

1:1 Some believe that Amos was a very poor man, being no more than a day laborer who tended livestock and worked in orchards (7:14), but **sheep breeders** may imply Amos owned sheep and cattle and that he was in the middle or upper-middle class. Although Amos was from Judah, his message was primarily designated for **Israel**, the northern kingdom. The **earthquake** was evidently of such severity that other events were dated relative to it. The fact that the book is precisely dated to **two years** before the earthquake suggests that Amos's preaching career was fairly short.
1:2 This verse sets the theme of the book: God is like a roaring lion. This symbolically portrays his giving a message to his prophets and his readiness to pounce and attack (3:4–8).
1:3–2:16 The first section of Amos is a series of oracles against the nations. The order of the nations slowly tightens around Israel. First is Damascus, to the northeast; then

Gaza, to the southwest; then Tyre, to the northwest; then Edom, to the southeast; and next come Ammon and Moab, across the Jordan River to the east; and finally before Israel comes Judah, located immediately south of Israel. The focus is on Israel, which is last and is given by far the longest oracle.
1:3 The significance of the expression **for three crimes, even four** is debated. But it could be translated as "for three crimes, and for [another] four," implying that the number of offenses had reached seven and was therefore complete, requiring judgment. **Damascus** regularly struggled with Israel for control of **Gilead**, east of the Sea of Galilee. It used brutal military tactics there, symbolically described as going over the countryside with **iron sledges**.
1:4 *Hazael* and *Ben-hadad* were throne names used by all the kings of Damascus.
1:5 Judgment will fall on the main areas of population. **Kir** is the region from which the

Arameans came (Am 9:7). The Assyrians exiled the Arameans there (2 Kg 16:9).
1:6 The Philistines captured villages in order to sell the entire populace into slavery.
1:7–8 All the major cities of the Philistines (**Gaza . . . Ashdod . . . Ashkelon**, and **Ekron**) are mentioned except Gath, which by the time of Amos had already been substantially wiped out.
1:9 **Tyre** also raided towns to sell the people into slavery, and it did so in violation of treaty obligations.
1:11 **Edom** committed border raids (probably against Judah) in which they exterminated entire populations.
1:13 The **Ammonites** sought to exterminate the population of **Gilead** by slaughtering the **pregnant women**.
1:14–15 Verse 14 begins with the standard punishment oracle (vv. 4,10,12). The leaders will receive special attention.

will go into exile together.
The LORD has spoken.

2 The LORD says:
I will not relent from punishing Moab
for three crimes, even four,
because he burned the bones
of the king of Edom to lime.
² Therefore, I will send fire against Moab,
and it will consume the citadels
of Kerioth.
Moab will die with a tumult,
with shouting and the sound
of the ram's horn.
³ I will cut off the judge from the land
and kill all its officials with him.
The LORD has spoken.

Judgment on Judah

⁴ The LORD says:
I will not relent from punishing Judah
for three crimes, even four,
because they have rejected
the instruction of the LORD
and have not kept his statutes.
The lies that their ancestors followed
have led them astray.
⁵ Therefore, I will send fire against Judah,
and it will consume the citadels
of Jerusalem.

Judgment on Israel

⁶ The LORD says:
I will not relent from punishing Israel
for three crimes, even four,
because they sell a righteous person
for silver
and a needy person for a pair of sandals.

⁷ They trample the heads of the poor
on the dust of the ground
and obstruct the path of the needy.
A man and his father
have sexual relations
with the same girl,
profaning my holy name.
⁸ They stretch out beside every altar
on garments taken as collateral,
and in the house of their God
they drink wine obtained through fines.

⁹ Yet I destroyed the Amorite
as Israel advanced;
his height was like the cedars,
and he was as sturdy as the oaks;
I destroyed his fruit above
and his roots beneath.
¹⁰ And I brought you from the land of Egypt
and led you forty years
in the wilderness
in order to possess the land
of the Amorite.
¹¹ I raised up some of your sons
as prophets
and some of your young men
as Nazirites.
Is this not the case, Israelites?
This is the LORD's declaration.
¹² But you made the Nazirites drink wine
and commanded the prophets,
"Do not prophesy."
¹³ Look, I am about to crush^A you
in your place
as a wagon crushes when full of grain.
¹⁴ Escape will fail the swift,
the strong one will not
maintain his strength,

---

^**2:13** Or *hinder*; Hb obscure

2:1–3 Interpreters puzzle over the charge that Moab **burned the bones of the king of Edom to lime.** Some say the act displayed simple disrespect for a human body, and others that it was motivated by a belief that burning the bones would prevent the victim

#46 99 Essential Christian Truths

EDIFICATION

Edification refers to the progressive growth and maturity of the church, both individually and collectively. The Bible talks about different ways that edification, or maturity, may happen, such as through the fellowship Christians share with one another (1Co 12:26; Gl 6:2). In addition, edification takes place through the church's preaching and teaching of Scripture (Eph 4:11–12), helping people understand and internalize the whole counsel of God. Ultimately, edification is building up the body of Christ, equipping people to live on mission for the kingdom of God.

from participating in the resurrection. Lime was used for plastering walls.
2:4–5 All the Gentile nations are accused of crimes against humanity, but **Judah** is charged with unfaithfulness to its covenant with Yahweh as described in the law. The **lies** mentioned here are idols.
2:6 Selling a **needy person for a pair of sandals** probably refers to selling a debtor into slavery over a trifling sum of money.
2:7–8 This text describes outrages committed at the religious shrines. Men had sexual relations with shrine prostitutes, even going to the point of **a man and his father** sharing the same woman; they did this while lying on **garments** that they had taken from poor people as **collateral** for loans; they did this at pagan altars all over the countryside; and they combined this with drinking bouts at the shrines, using **wine** they had taken from powerless people.
2:9–12 In this section God gives a historical retrospective, comparing his favors toward Israel with Israel's impudent rejection of him.
2:9–10 Disregarding historical sequence, the conquest of Canaan (v. 9) is mentioned before the exodus and wilderness wandering (v. 10).

2:11–12 The **prophets**, as exponents of God's will, and the **Nazirites**, as examples of great devotion to God, came to the Israelites as representatives sent by God to turn the people to righteousness. The Israelite rejection of both groups represents their rejection of God himself.
2:13 The Hebrew of this verse is difficult. An alternative translation is, "Behold I am weighed down beneath you, just as a cart that is filled with sheaves is weighed down." If this is correct, it expresses God's frustration with Israel's stubborn attitude.
2:14–16 The Israelite army will be routed in battle. In v. 14, **swift** refers to any soldier who runs quickly and therefore would normally escape defeat, and **strong** refers to anyone who would normally prevail in battle. At the end of v. 14 and in v. 15, we have four military specializations: the **warrior** (referring to the heavy infantry in the main line of battle), the **archer**, the **swift of foot** (light infantry), and the **one riding a horse** (the cavalry). Finally, in v. 16, **the most courageous of the warriors** (who would be expected to stand fast in the face of an onslaught) will **flee naked** (cast away their armor, shields, and weapons).

and the warrior will not save his life.
15 The archer will not stand his ground,
   the one who is swift of foot
   will not save himself,
   and the one riding a horse will not save
     his life.
16 Even the most courageous
     of the warriors
   will flee naked on that day —
     this is the LORD's declaration.

God's Reasons for Punishing Israel

3 Listen to this message that the LORD has
   spoken against you, Israelites, against
the entire clan that I brought from the land
of Egypt:
2 I have known only you
     out of all the clans of the earth;
   therefore, I will punish you for all
     your iniquities.
3 Can two walk together
   without agreeing to meet?
4 Does a lion roar in the forest
   when it has no prey?
   Does a young lion growl from its lair
   unless it has captured something?
5 Does a bird land in a trap on the ground
   if there is no bait for it?
   Does a trap spring from the ground
   when it has caught nothing?
6 If a ram's horn is blown in a city,
   aren't people afraid?
   If a disaster occurs in a city,
   hasn't the LORD done it?
7 Indeed, the Lord GOD does nothing
   without revealing his counsel
   to his servants the prophets.
8 A lion has roared;
   who will not fear?
   The Lord GOD has spoken;
   who will not prophesy?

9 Proclaim on the citadels in Ashdod
   and on the citadels in the land of Egypt:

Assemble on the mountains of Samaria,
   and see the great turmoil in the city
   and the acts of oppression within it.
10 The people are incapable
     of doing right —
   this is the LORD's declaration —
   those who store up violence
     and destruction
   in their citadels.

11 Therefore, the Lord GOD says:
   An enemy will surround the land;
   he will destroy your strongholds
   and plunder your citadels.

12 The LORD says:
   As the shepherd snatches two legs
   or a piece of an ear
   from the lion's mouth,
   so the Israelites who live in Samaria
   will be rescued
   with only the corner of a bed
   or the^A cushion^B of a couch.^C

13 Listen and testify against the house
     of Jacob —
   this is the declaration
     of the Lord GOD,
     the God of Armies.
14 I will punish the altars of Bethel
   on the day I punish Israel for its crimes;
   the horns of the altar will be cut off
   and fall to the ground.
15 I will demolish the winter house
   and the summer house;
   the houses inlaid with ivory
     will be destroyed,
   and the great houses will come
     to an end.
   This is the LORD's declaration.

Social and Spiritual Corruption

4 Listen to this message, you cows
     of Bashan
   who are on the hill of Samaria,

---

^A 3:12 Or Israelites will be rescued, those who sit in Samaria on a corner of a bed or a   ^B 3:12 Hb obscure   ^C 3:12 LXX, Aq, Sym,
Theod, Syr, Tg, Vg read or in Damascus

3:1–15 In this chapter, Amos answered those who claimed that he had no right to prophesy against Israel because they were the chosen people of God. Against this charge, Amos made three claims. (1) Their election guaranteed that they will be judged rather than escape judgment (vv. 1–3). (2) God has spoken, and therefore his prophet must speak (vv. 4–8). (3) Israel was so wicked that even pagan nations could sit in judgment against them (vv. 9–11). This passage concludes with a portrait of Israel's destruction (vv. 12–15).
3:3 The phrase without agreeing to meet means "without coming to terms."
3:4–8 These verses include a short epigram, a series of poetic verses that teach some kind of lesson and may contain a riddle (vv. 4–6). After this there is a short commentary on

the epigram (vv. 7–8). The epigram makes the point that when one thing is true (for example, that a lion roars), it is reasonable that something else is also true (he has prey). The commentary in vv. 7–8 tells us that because God has roared, disaster must come and his prophets must prophesy. Notice that all the examples in the epigram are violent in nature.
3:9–10 Ashdod (the Philistines) and Egypt were two traditional oppressors of Israel, but even they did not oppress the Israelites as cruelly as the Israelites oppressed themselves through their rebellion against God. Thus these pagans could sit in judgment on Israel.
3:11–15 Israel's punishment is described in this section.
3:12 Behind this verse one can detect a common viewpoint among the people of Israel:

that if an enemy should attack, the Israelites would be rescued by God. Amos responded sarcastically by saying that they would be "rescued" like a piece of an ear from the lion's mouth. When only pieces of an ear or legs are snatched from a lion's mouth, obviously the lamb is dead. The main point is that Israel will be completely destroyed.
3:14–15 The phrase altars of Bethel refers to Israel's religious sins, and the winter house and the summer house refer to the destruction of the oppressive upper classes.
4:1–13 This chapter has two major parts, and each is an accusation followed by a religious statement used in an ironic and threatening manner. The first part (vv. 1–5) includes an accusation against the aristocratic women of Samaria (vv. 1–3) followed by an ironic benediction (actually a malediction) upon

women who oppress the poor
and crush the needy,
who say to their husbands,
"Bring us something to drink."

² The Lord God has sworn by his holiness:
Look, the days are coming^A
when you will be taken away
with hooks,
every last one of you with fishhooks.
³ You will go through breaches
in the wall,
each woman straight ahead,
and you will be driven along
toward Harmon.
This is the Lord's declaration.

⁴ Come to Bethel and rebel;
rebel even more at Gilgal!
Bring your sacrifices every morning,
your tenths every three days.
⁵ Offer leavened bread as
a thanksgiving sacrifice,
and loudly proclaim
your freewill offerings,
for that is what you Israelites love to do!
This is the declaration
of the Lord God.

God's Discipline and Israel's Apostasy

⁶ I gave you absolutely nothing to eat^B
in all your cities,
a shortage of food in all
your communities,
yet you did not return to me.
This is the Lord's declaration.

⁷ I also withheld the rain from you
while there were still three months
until harvest.
I sent rain on one city
but no rain on another.
One field received rain
while a field with no rain withered.
⁸ Two or three cities staggered
to another city to drink water
but were not satisfied,

yet you did not return to me.
This is the Lord's declaration.

⁹ I struck you with blight and mildew;
the locust devoured
your many gardens and vineyards,
your fig trees and olive trees,
yet you did not return to me.
This is the Lord's declaration.

¹⁰ I sent plagues like those of Egypt;
I killed your young men
with the sword,
along with your captured horses.
I caused the stench of your camp
to fill your nostrils,
yet you did not return to me.
This is the Lord's declaration.

¹¹ I overthrew some of you
as I^C overthrew Sodom and Gomorrah,
and you were like a burning stick
snatched from a fire,
yet you did not return to me —
This is the Lord's declaration.

¹² Therefore, Israel, that is what I will do
to you,
and since I will do that to you,
Israel, prepare to meet your God!
¹³ He is here:
the one who forms the mountains,
creates the wind,
and reveals his thoughts to man,
the one who makes the dawn
out of darkness
and strides on the heights of the earth.
The Lord, the God of Armies,
is his name.

Lamentation for Israel

5 Listen to this message that I am singing for
you, a lament, house of Israel:
² She has fallen;
Virgin Israel will never rise again.
She lies abandoned on her land
with no one to raise her up.

---

^A 4:2 Lit *coming on you*   ^B 4:6 Lit *you cleanness of teeth*   ^C 4:11 Lit *God*

---

the pilgrims going to the religious shrines (vv. 4–5). The second part (vv. 6–13) accuses Israel of having disregarded all preliminary judgments sent against them, and it asserts that they must be ready for final judgment (vv. 6–12). After this, Amos gives a doxology that is threatening rather than encouraging (v. 13).
4:1 The expression **cows of Bashan** derisively refers to the upper-class women of Samaria. Bashan, located east of the Sea of Galilee, was famous for its lush pasture and fine livestock (Dt 32:14; Ezk 39:18). Like the cattle of that region, these aristocratic women were well fed and pampered. The women spoken of by Amos were cruel and

unfeeling, as shown by their indifference to the suffering of the poor. Their arrogance was apparent in how they treated even their husbands as household slaves.
4:2–3 The Hebrew of this verse is difficult. The word translated as **taken away** literally means to "lift up," and the words translated as **hooks** and **fishhooks** are obscure and may not refer to hooks at all. But if "hooks" is correct, the metaphor may describe the bodies of the "cows" being hoisted on meat hooks. Also, the location of **Harmon** is unknown. Still, the main point is clear: many people will be slaughtered, and those who survive will file out of the ruined walls of the city into exile.

4:4–5 Amos asserted sarcastically that when the Israelites went to their shrines, it only increased their guilt.
4:13 This is a fitting conclusion to the previous passage. Amos had told the Israelites to be ready to meet their God, and this is the kind of God they will meet.
5:1–6:14 This lengthy and complex passage presents the core of the accusation against Israel. The passage begins with the lament in 5:2 that there was no one to **raise . . . up** fallen **Israel**, and it ends in 6:14 with God **raising up** an enemy against Israel. The idea of lamentation dominates the passage. The main accusations are given in 5:4–6:7 in two sets of verses (5:4–15 and

◤ The Gospel and Social Ministry

by Mary Anne Poe

Social ministry is generally defined by its aim to provide assistance to those with physical or social needs, whether in the form of food, shelter, emotional or mental health care, family life support, or advocacy for social justice. The Scriptures and church tradition point to the centrality of social ministry as evidence of the power of the gospel at work in human lives. While the church throughout its history has debated about and vacillated between an emphasis on social ministry or an emphasis on preaching and evangelism, Jesus's teaching and his works of service suggest that both preaching and social ministries are central to the gospel. What Jesus taught, what Jesus did, and the tradition of the church attest to what has become known as the integral mission of the church.

Jesus and Social Ministry

Jesus announced his mission at the inauguration of his public ministry in the synagogue through a reading from the prophet Isaiah: "The Spirit of the Lord is on me, because he has anointed me to preach good news to the poor. He has sent me to proclaim release to the captives and recovery of sight to the blind, to set free the oppressed, to proclaim the year of the Lord's favor" (Lk 4:18–19).

By using this text, Jesus asserted that God's purpose through Christ is wholeness and healing in body, soul, and spirit through the coming kingdom of God. Jesus announced that because of his coming the poor will be blessed, the blind will see, the lame will walk, and relationships will be restored. The worldwide impact of Jesus's coming was not only the promise of a future spiritual kingdom but an effect on the present realities of the broken human condition.

At the conclusion of his earthly ministry and prior to his ascent into heaven, Jesus instructed the disciples about what their mission, and the mission of all future disciples, was to be: "Go, therefore, and make disciples of all nations, baptizing them in the name of the Father and of the Son and of the Holy Spirit, teaching them to observe everything I have commanded you" (Mt 28:19–20).

Being a follower of Christ means we should do what Jesus did, commit to his purpose, and invite others to join us in observing what he taught. Following Jesus is costly and strenuous. His teaching was unambiguous as he drew a distinction between true discipleship and simple assent to a religious teaching. The gospel Jesus proclaimed from beginning to end addressed the concrete realities of the present world as well as the spiritual hope for all eternity.

Jesus teaches us to pay careful attention to all aspects of our social relationships. The Sermon on the Mount speaks to a wide range of social issues: forgiveness, anger, broken relationships, divorce, truthfulness, responses to evil, love for friends and enemies, almsgiving, use of wealth, anxiety, and social justice. All of these issues can be addressed through social ministries offered through the church or other faith-based organizations.

Jesus described his kingdom as a place where justice and righteousness prevail: good seed bears fruit; lost sheep, coins, and sons are restored; faithful stewardship is compensated; issues of wealth and poverty are explored; labor practices are examined; and helping the downtrodden is rewarded. The examples Jesus gave of what the kingdom would be like are not mere abstractions but concrete ways he is calling us to live. Social ministries help the church to address the concerns of human relationships in practical and tangible ways.

The example of Jesus's life and ministry reinforces his teachings and demonstrates the significance of social ministry as a central aspect of the gospel. What Jesus did with his time and energy emphasized engagement with people, especially those who lived on the margins of society. Jesus experienced the hardships of homelessness, alienation, hunger, betrayal, and physical pain. This allowed him to be a sympathetic Savior (Hb 4:15).

The first-century world was amazed by what Jesus did. His public ministry focused on healing the sick, feeding the hungry, reconciling outcasts to the community, loving the poor, challenging the wealthy, touching the leprous, condemning religious hypocrites, eating with prostitutes and tax collectors, confronting the powerful, and restoring mental health. He defied societal and cultural structures and belief systems that created oppressive conditions. Simple conversations with people, such as the Samaritan woman, tax collectors, those with leprosy, and children violated cultural norms and aroused the antipathy of those who would keep oppressive systems in place.

Clearly, Jesus's expectations for his followers included acts of kindness, advocacy for social justice, and demolition of social barriers that marginalized groups of people. His invitation to the disciples was to do what he did, to follow him, in demonstrating the love and mercy of God—especially to people who might not otherwise experience a compassionate and hospitable world. His miraculous works served to show the consistency with his character and message, confirming his teachings by meeting concrete human needs as well as bearing witness to his deity. Jesus taught that those who will be invited to inherit the kingdom are those who have demonstrated the same character and message by engaging in social ministries like feeding the hungry, visiting the prisoners, and offering hospitality to strangers (Mt 25:31–46).

The Early Church and Social Ministry
The church was notable from its inception for the radical nature of her social relationships and ministry. In Acts 2 and 4 Luke highlights the nature of the church as a place of continual fellowship, teaching, and prayer. Participants were inspired to sell property and possessions and share with all so no one had need of anything. The resurrection of Jesus and the coming of the Holy Spirit on the church allowed the work and ministry of Jesus to continue through the lives of those who believed. The social ministry of the church in the early centuries drew attention to the transformative power of the gospel to shape relationships among people. Rather than an entirely spiritualized, otherworldly religion, the Christian faith promised eternal life that changed how people lived in the present.

The church in its earliest history became known for its array of social ministries to care for the poor, the ill, and outcasts. Hospitals and other refuges provided care for those who suffered while simultaneously offering the presence and power of God for all eternity through their teaching and preaching. In the centuries following, Christians have been noted for establishing orphanages, schools, hospitals, and refuges as well as advocating for social justice for those who are oppressed.

In the twentieth century Dietrich Bonhoeffer asserted that one cannot understand and preach the gospel concretely enough. He gave his life in the battle against the oppression of the Nazi regime much like other Christians in other times and places have done to advance the cause of the gospel in the face of social injustice. Present-day followers of Christ continue to provide leadership in all kinds of social ministry as churches and faith-based organizations around the world fight poverty and injustice in myriad ways as part of the compelling mission and message of the gospel.

³ For the Lord GOD says:
  The city that marches out
    a thousand strong
  will have only a hundred left,
  and the one that marches out
    a hundred strong
  will have only ten left in the house
    of Israel.

Seek God and Live

⁴ For the LORD says to the house of Israel:
  Seek me and live!
⁵   Do not seek Bethel
  or go to Gilgal
  or journey to Beer-sheba,
  for Gilgal will certainly go into exile,
  and Bethel will come to nothing.
⁶   Seek the LORD and live,
  or he will spread like fire
  throughout the house of Joseph;
  it will consume everything
  with no one at Bethel to extinguish it.
⁷   Those who turn justice into wormwood
  also throw righteousness to the ground.

⁸   The one who made the Pleiades
    and Orion,
  who turns darkness ᴬ into dawn
  and darkens day into night,
  who summons the water of the sea
  and pours it out over the surface
    of the earth —
  the LORD is his name.
⁹   He brings destruction ᴮ on the strong, ᶜ
  and it falls on the fortress.

¹⁰   They hate the one who convicts
    the guilty
  at the city gate,
  and they despise the one who speaks
    with integrity.
¹¹   Therefore, because you trample on
    the poor
  and exact a grain tax from him,
  you will never live in the houses
    of cut stone
  you have built;
  you will never drink the wine
  from the lush vineyards
  you have planted.

¹²   For I know your crimes are many
  and your sins innumerable.
  They oppress the righteous, take a bribe,
  and deprive the poor of justice
    at the city gates.
¹³   Therefore, those who have insight
    will keep silent ᴰ
  at such a time,
  for the days are evil.

¹⁴   Pursue good and not evil
  so that you may live,
  and the LORD, the God of Armies,
  will be with you
  as you have claimed.
¹⁵   Hate evil and love good;
  establish justice at the city gate.
  Perhaps the LORD, the God of Armies,
    will be gracious
  to the remnant of Joseph.

¹⁶ Therefore the LORD, the God of Armies, the
Lord, says:
  There will be wailing in all
    the public squares;
  they will cry out in anguish ᴱ in all
    the streets.
  The farmer will be called on to mourn,
  and professional mourners ᶠ to wail.
¹⁷   There will be wailing in all
    the vineyards,
  for I will pass among you.
  The LORD has spoken.

The Day of the LORD

¹⁸   Woe to you who long for the day
    of the LORD!
  What will the day of the LORD
    be for you?
  It will be darkness and not light.
¹⁹   It will be like a man who flees
    from a lion
  only to have a bear confront him.
  He goes home and rests his hand
    against the wall
  only to have a snake bite him.
²⁰   Won't the day of the LORD
  be darkness rather than light,
  even gloom without any brightness
    in it?

ᴬ **5:8** Or *turns the shadow of death* ᴮ **5:9** Hb obscure ᶜ **5:9** Or *stronghold* ᴰ **5:13** Or *who are prudent will perish* ᴱ **5:16** Lit *will say, "Alas! Alas!"* ᶠ **5:16** Lit *and those skilled in lamentation*

5:18–6:7), and these two sets are similar. In the first set, Israel presumptuously assumed that its pilgrimages satisfied God (5:4–7), even while they were oppressing the poor (5:10–15). In the second set, Israel again assumed its worship and festivals satisfied God, presumptuously certain that the day of the Lord would bring them no trouble (5:18–24) even while they lived in arrogant luxury in Samaria (6:1–7). In both sets, therefore, their religious arrogance is placed alongside their arrogant indifference toward the poor. Also, in the first set, God is praised as Maker of the heavens (5:8–9), while in the second set, ironically, Israel worships the sky gods (5:25–27). Amos 6:8–11 pictures the judgment that is coming to Israel. Finally, 6:12–14 summarizes the whole with a proverb (v. 12), an accusation (v. 13), and a judgment (v. 14).
5:4–5 Bethel . . . Gilgal, and **Beer-sheba** were three pilgrimage shrines. Bethel was where Jacob had his vision of the stairway into heaven (Gn 28:12–19), but it was also one of the places where King Jeroboam I of Israel set up calf idols (1Kg 12:28–29). Gilgal was the embarkation point for the crossing of the Jordan River and the invasion of Canaan, and Joshua set up a memorial there (Jos 4:19–20). Beer-sheba, far to the south, is closely associated with the sojourns of Abraham (Gn 21:14), and we know from archaeology that there was a shrine there.

²¹ I hate, I despise, your feasts!
I can't stand the stench
of your solemn assemblies.
²² Even if you offer me
your burnt offerings
and grain offerings,
I will not accept them;
I will have no regard
for your fellowship offerings
of fattened cattle.
²³ Take away from me the noise
of your songs!
I will not listen to the music
of your harps.
²⁴ But let justice flow like water,
and righteousness,
like an unfailing stream.

²⁵ "House of Israel, was it sacrifices and grain offerings that you presented to me during the forty years in the wilderness? ²⁶ But you have taken up^A Sakkuth your king and Kaiwan your star god,^B images you have made for yourselves. ²⁷ So I will send you into exile beyond Damascus." The LORD, the God of Armies, is his name. He has spoken.

Woe to the Complacent

6 Woe to those who are at ease in Zion
and to those who feel secure on the hill
of Samaria —
the notable people in this first
of the nations,
those the house of Israel comes to.
² Cross over to Calneh and see;
go from there to great Hamath;
then go down to Gath of the Philistines.
Are you better than these kingdoms?
Is their territory larger than yours?
³ You dismiss any thought of the evil day
and bring in a reign of violence.

⁴ They lie on beds inlaid with ivory,
sprawled out on their couches,
and dine on lambs from the flock
and calves from the stall.

⁵ They improvise songs^C to the sound
of the harp
and invent^D their own
musical instruments like David.
⁶ They drink wine by the bowlful
and anoint themselves
with the finest oils
but do not grieve over the ruin
of Joseph.
⁷ Therefore, they will now go into exile
as the first of the captives,
and the feasting of those
who sprawl out
will come to an end.

Israel's Pride Judged

⁸ The Lord GOD has sworn by himself — this is the declaration of the LORD, the God of Armies:
I loathe Jacob's pride
and hate his citadels,
so I will hand over the city
and everything in it.

⁹ And if there are ten men left in one house, they will die. ¹⁰ A close relative^E and burner^F will remove his corpse^G from the house. He will call to someone in the inner recesses of the house, "Any more with you?"
That person will reply, "None."
Then he will say, "Silence, because the LORD's name must not be invoked."
¹¹ For the LORD commands:
The large house will be smashed
to pieces,
and the small house to rubble.

¹² Do horses gallop on the cliffs?
Does anyone plow there with oxen?^H
Yet you have turned justice
into poison
and the fruit of righteousness
into wormwood —
¹³ you who rejoice over Lo-debar
and say, "Didn't we
capture Karnaim
for ourselves by our own strength?"

^A5:26 Or *you will lift up* ^B5:26 LXX reads *taken up the tent of Molech and the star of your god Rephan*; Ac 7:43 ^C6:5 Hb obscure ^D6:5 Or *compose on* ^E6:10 Lit *His uncle* ^F6:10 A burner of incense, a memorial fire, or a body; Hb obscure ^G6:10 Lit *remove bones* ^H6:12 Some emend to *plow the sea*

5:25–26 This text is the source of great confusion because it appears to teach that the Israelites made no **sacrifices** during the **wilderness** period, contrary to what is recorded in the Pentateuch (Ex 24:5). Probably Am 5:25 should be joined to v. 26, as follows: "Did you offer sacrifices and grain offerings to me forty years in the wilderness, House of Israel, while you were taking up Sakkuth your king?" Read this way, Israel did make sacrifices to God in the wilderness, but the people also carried images of the **Sakkuth** and other gods. During Amos's time, however, they were more brazenly combining the worship of the Lord with the worship of these pagan gods. "Sakkuth" and **Kaiwan** were names of the sky deity of the planet Saturn.

6:2 Calneh (Calno, Is 10:9) was in Syria. It had been destroyed by the Assyrians in the mid-ninth century. **Hamath**, another Syrian city, was conquered by Jeroboam II, king of Israel during the ministry of Amos (2Kg 14:28; it may be that Calneh also was subdued by Jeroboam II). **Gath**, a Philistine city, was destroyed by another contemporary of Amos, King Uzziah of Judah (2Ch 26:6). These fallen cities served as warnings to the people of Samaria, who assumed their city was indestructible.

6:9–10 The LORD's name must not be invoked indicates that instead of giving the normal funeral dirges and laments—which may have included invocations of Israel's God (Lm 1:20)—Yahweh's name will not be mentioned at all (probably because God's name should not be mentioned in the midst of so much carnage, and also because the dead were evidently under God's curse).

6:12–13 Verse 12 is a proverb concerning absurd, irrational behavior. The point is that the boasting of v. 13 is equally absurd. **Lo-debar** was a city east of the Sea of Galilee that the Israelites boasted about capturing, but the name "Lo-debar" sounds like the Hebrew for the word *nothing*. **Karnaim**, another town in Transjordan, means "two horns." In other words, the people boasted

¹⁴ But look, I am raising up a nation
against you, house of Israel —
    this is the declaration of the Lord,
    the GOD of Armies —
and they will oppress you
from the entrance of Hamath^A
to the Brook of the Arabah. ^B

First Vision: Locusts

7 The Lord GOD showed me this: He was forming a swarm of locusts at the time the spring crop first began to sprout — after the cutting of the king's hay. ² When the locusts finished eating the vegetation of the land, I said, "Lord GOD, please forgive! How will Jacob survive since he is so small?" ³ The LORD relented concerning this. "It will not happen," he said.

Second Vision: Fire

⁴ The Lord GOD showed me this: The Lord GOD was calling for a judgment by fire. It consumed the great deep and devoured the land. ⁵ Then I said, "Lord GOD, please stop! How will Jacob survive since he is so small?" ⁶ The LORD relented concerning this. "This will not happen either," said the Lord GOD.

Third Vision: A Plumb Line

⁷ He showed me this: The Lord was standing there by a vertical wall with a plumb line in his hand. ⁸ The LORD asked me, "What do you see, Amos?"
I replied, "A plumb line."
Then the Lord said, "I am setting a plumb line among my people Israel; I will no longer spare them:
⁹   Isaac's high places will be deserted,
    and Israel's sanctuaries will be in ruins;

I will rise up
    against the house of Jeroboam
    with a sword."

Amaziah's Opposition

¹⁰ Amaziah the priest of Bethel sent word to King Jeroboam of Israel, saying, "Amos has conspired against you right here in the house of Israel. The land cannot endure all his words, ¹¹ for Amos has said this: 'Jeroboam will die by the sword, and Israel will certainly go into exile from its homeland.' "

¹² Then Amaziah said to Amos, "Go away, you seer! Flee to the land of Judah. Earn your living^C and give your prophecies there, ¹³ but don't ever prophesy at Bethel again, for it is the king's sanctuary and a royal temple."

¹⁴ So Amos answered Amaziah, "I was^D not a prophet or the son of a prophet;^E rather, I was^D a herdsman, and I took care of sycamore figs. ¹⁵ But the LORD took me from following the flock and said to me, 'Go, prophesy to my people Israel.' "

¹⁶ Now hear the word of the LORD. You say:
Do not prophesy against Israel;
    do not preach against the house
        of Isaac.

¹⁷ Therefore, this is what the LORD says:
Your wife will be a prostitute
    in the city,
your sons and daughters will fall
    by the sword,
and your land will be divided up
    with a measuring line.
You yourself will die on pagan^F soil,
    and Israel will certainly go
        into exile
    from its homeland.

---

^A6:14 Or from Lebo-hamath   ^B6:14 Probably the Valley of Zared at the southeast end of the Dead Sea   ^C7:12 Lit Eat bread
^D7:14 Or am   ^E7:14 = a prophet's disciple or a member of a prophetic guild   ^F7:17 Lit unclean

---

of having conquered "nothing" and "two horns."

6:14 The **entrance of Hamath** (also called Lebo-hamath) was the northern limit of Israel's domain. The **Brook of the Arabah** is only mentioned here, but it may be the same as the Brook of Egypt, the traditional southern border of Israel (Jos 15:4). The point is that the Israelites will be driven from all the lands that had been allotted to them by the Lord.

7:1–8:3 This section contains four visions (locusts, 7:1–3; fire, 7:4–6; plumb line, 7:7–9; basket of summer fruit, 8:1–3). Between the third and fourth visions is a biographical unit describing a confrontation between Amos and Amaziah, the chief priest of the Bethel shrine.

7:1–3 In the Bible **locusts** are a common image of God's wrath. In this case, however, Israel was not actually struck with a locust plague; Amos merely saw it in a vision and, in response to his pleas, God relented and no locust plague came.

7:3 The phrase, **the LORD relented**, here and in v. 6 seems to imply that God changed his mind. The same expression is used in Ex 32:14. Readers wonder how an omniscient God could change his mind. The "change" of God's mind would of course be something he foreknew he would do in response to Amos's intercession.

7:4–6 The vision of **fire** is probably symbolic of a ferocious, all-consuming drought. But in response to Amos's intercession, it did not happen.

7:7–8 The Hebrew text does not contain a word meaning **vertical**, and the word translated as **plumb line** is an enigma; no one really knows what this Hebrew word means.

If the CSB is correct, God is about to bring a plumb line to show that the people of **Israel** are crooked. This may be a reference to the function of the law in bringing sin to light (Rm 7:7). A wall that was not plumb would be torn down.

7:9 The **high places** referred to are probably the **sanctuaries** at Bethel, Gilgal, Beersheba, Samaria, and Dan. The term *Isaac* being used to refer to the northern kingdom is unique here and in v. 16. Perhaps it is because Isaac worshiped at Beersheba. The **house of Jeroboam** II ended with the assassination of his son Zechariah in 753 BC.

7:10–17 The account of Amos's confrontation with Amaziah in this section interrupts the sequence of visions. Amaziah represented the Israelite hierarchy, who considered Amos to be either a charlatan or a conspirator against King Jeroboam.

7:14 The Hebrew for **I was not a prophet** is ambiguous; it could be past tense, as here in the CSB, or it could be present tense, "I am not a prophet." That is, Amos *is* not a prophet in the sense that Amaziah meant it: a hireling who peddles his messages for gain (v. 12). A **son of a prophet** refers not to a prophet's biological son but to a member of a prophetic guild.

Sycamore **figs** had to be scraped or split in order to ripen properly. Apparently one part of Amos's occupation was cutting such figs, but we do not know if he did it as a day laborer and was therefore poor or if he actually owned a grove of fig trees.

Fourth Vision: A Basket of Summer Fruit

8 The Lord God showed me this: a basket of summer fruit. ² He asked me, "What do you see, Amos?"

I replied, "A basket of summer fruit."^A

The Lord said to me, "The end has come for my people Israel; I will no longer spare them. ³ In that day the temple⁸ songs will become wailing" — this is the Lord God's declaration. "Many dead bodies, thrown everywhere! Silence!"

4   Hear this, you who trample
on the needy
and do away with the poor of the land,
5   asking, "When will the New Moon
be over
so we may sell grain,
and the Sabbath,
so we may market wheat?
We can reduce the measure
while increasing the price^C
and cheat with dishonest scales.
6   We can buy the poor with silver
and the needy for a pair of sandals
and even sell the chaff!"

7 The Lord has sworn by the Pride of Jacob:^D
I will never forget all their deeds.
8   Because of this, won't the land quake
and all who dwell in it mourn?
All of it will rise like the Nile;
it will surge and then subside
like the Nile in Egypt.

9   And in that day —
this is the declaration of the Lord
God —
I will make the sun go down at noon;
I will darken the land in the daytime.
10   I will turn your feasts into mourning
and all your songs into lamentation;

I will cause everyone^E to wear sackcloth
and every head to be shaved.
I will make that grief
like mourning for an only son
and its outcome like a bitter day.

11   Look, the days are coming —
this is the declaration of the Lord
God —
when I will send a famine
through the land:
not a famine of bread or a thirst
for water,
but of hearing the words of the Lord.
12   People will stagger from sea to sea
and roam from north to east
seeking the word of the Lord,
but they will not find it.
13   In that day the beautiful young women,
the young men also, will faint
from thirst.
14   Those who swear by the guilt
of Samaria
and say, "As your god lives, Dan,"
or, "As the way^F,G of Beer-sheba lives" —
they will fall, never to rise again.

Fifth Vision: The Lord beside the Altar

9 I saw the Lord standing beside the altar, and he said:
Strike the capitals of the pillars
so that the thresholds shake;
knock them down on the heads of all
the people.
Then I will kill the rest of them
with the sword.
None of those who flee will get away;
none of the fugitives will escape.
2   If they dig down to Sheol,
from there my hand will take them;
if they climb up to heaven,

---

^A 8:2 In Hb the word for *summer fruit* sounds like the word for *end.*   ^B 8:3 Or *palace*   ^C 8:5 Lit *reduce the ephah and make the shekel great*   ^D 8:7 = the Lord or the promised land   ^E 8:10 Lit *every waist*   ^F 8:14 LXX reads *god*   ^G 8:14 Or *power*

8:1–3 The Hebrew word for **summer fruit** sounds almost identical to the word translated as **end** in v. 2. Just as the fruit in the basket had ripened, so also Israel was ripe for judgment.

8:4–9:15 This, the last major segment of Amos, is in four sections. First, God accused the merchants and the wealthy class of cheating people in the sale of grain and of enslaving people for the sake of trifling debts (8:4–6). Next, there is a judgment in which God swears an oath, the land heaves like the Nile River, people mourn, and there is a famine for the word of God (8:7–14). For the third section, another judgment passage follows: God stands by the altar (in effect swearing another oath), the Israelites are hunted down, and the land again heaves like the Nile River (9:1–6). In the final section, Israel is compared to the nations to which it must go in exile, but abruptly the judgment is reversed, and Israel becomes predominant among all the nations and very prosperous (9:7–15).

8:5–6 Three accusations are combined here: contempt for the **Sabbath**, cheating customers when selling them food, and enslaving people who could not pay even the smallest of debts.

8:7 It is odd that God swears in this verse by the **Pride of Jacob**. In 6:8, he said that he hated "Jacob's pride," and in that case the pride of Jacob was the citadels and wealth of Israel. It is not likely that God would swear by something he hated. In 4:2 God swore by his "holiness," and in 6:8 he swore by "himself." In this verse, therefore, the "Pride of Jacob" is probably again Yahweh himself.

8:9 The darkening of the **sun** implies the coming of the day of the Lord.

8:11–12 The **famine** for **hearing the words of the Lord** suggests the time of Israel's exile and Diaspora, when Jewish people would wander through the nations, alienated from their God and Messiah.

8:13 The thirst here is probably figurative as in v. 11. If **beautiful** (vigorous) **young**

women and **men** faint, how much more would the rest of the population.

8:14 The **guilt of Samaria** is the shrines the people made throughout the land, but especially at Dan and Bethel. The **way of Beer-sheba** probably refers to the pilgrimage devotees made to Beer-sheba and by extension to the pagan god they worshiped there.

9:1 The phrase **knock them down on the heads of all the people** could be translated as "sever them at the head—all of them!" The shrines, fortresses, and palaces will come down. Also, the leaders of the people are described here metaphorically as the **pillars** that will be cut down. The common people are called **the rest of them**. The point is that no one, whether of high or low status, will escape God's judgment.

9:2–4 None of the Israelites will be able to **hide** from God (v. 3). The language here is hyperbole (exaggeration for rhetorical effect). Obviously no one can literally climb into **heaven** or hide at the bottom of the **sea**.

from there I will bring them down.
³ If they hide
on the top of Carmel,
from there I will track them down
and seize them;
if they conceal themselves
from my sight on the sea floor,
from there I will command
the sea serpent to bite them.
⁴ And if they are driven
by their enemies into captivity,
from there I will command
the sword to kill them.
I will keep my eye on them
for harm and not for good.

⁵ The Lord, the GOD of Armies —
he touches the earth;
it melts, and all who dwell
in it mourn;
all of it rises like the Nile
and subsides like the Nile of Egypt.
⁶ He builds his upper chambers
in the heavens
and lays the foundation of his vault
on the earth.
He summons the water of the sea
and pours it out over the surface
of the earth.
The LORD is his name.

Announcement of Judgment

⁷ Israelites, are you not like the Cushites
to me?
This is the LORD's declaration.
Didn't I bring Israel from the land
of Egypt,
the Philistines from Caphtor,ᴬ
and the Arameans from Kir?
⁸ Look, the eyes of the Lord GOD
are on the sinful kingdom,
and I will obliterate it
from the face of the earth.
However, I will not totally destroy

the house of Jacob —
this is the LORD's declaration —
⁹ for I am about to give the command,
and I will shake the house of Israel
among all the nations,
as one shakes a sieve,
but not a pebble will fall to the ground.
¹⁰ All the sinners among my people
who say, "Disaster will never overtakeᴮ
or confront us,"
will die by the sword.

Announcement of Restoration

¹¹ In that day
I will restore the fallen shelter of David:
I will repair its gaps,
restore its ruins,
and rebuild it as in the days of old,
¹² so that they may possess
the remnant of Edom
and all the nations
that bear my nameᶜ —
this is the declaration of the LORD;
he will do this.

¹³ Look, the days are coming —
this is the LORD's declaration —
when the plowman will overtake
the reaper
and the one who treads grapes,
the sower of seed.
The mountains will drip
with sweet wine,
and all the hills will flow with it.
¹⁴ I will restore the fortunes
of my people Israel.ᴰ
They will rebuild and occupy
ruined cities,
plant vineyards and drink their wine,
make gardens and eat their produce.
¹⁵ I will plant them on their land,
and they will never again be uprooted
from the land I have given them.
The LORD your God has spoken.

ᴬ9:7 Probably Crete   ᴮ9:10 Or "You will not let disaster come near   ᶜ9:12 LXX reads so that the remnant of man and all the nations . . . may seek me; Ac 15:17   ᴰ9:14 Or restore my people Israel from captivity

9:7 The **Cushites** were people from Nubia, directly south of Egypt. **Caphtor** was either Crete or Cyprus, and it represented the Aegean Sea area from which the Philistines came. **Kir** was probably east of Mesopotamia, in the area of Elam. The point is that God had moved many nations, not just Israel, to their homelands.
9:11–12 The **fallen shelter of David** refers to the dynasty and empire of David (normally called the "house" of David but here a "shelter," symbolic of the pathetic condition of this once-mighty line of kings). **Edom** is representative of the Gentiles that hated and persecuted Israel. Many will **bear my name**, implies that Gentiles will belong to Yahweh. James cited this passage as being fulfilled in the mission to the Gentiles (Ac 15:14–18). James's citation of Am 9:12 in Ac 15:17 differs somewhat from the Hebrew because he seems to be loosely quoting from the Greek Septuagint translation of Amos. Also, the Hebrew word for "Edom" is similar to the word for "humanity" (adam), which explains why Amos has "Edom" but James has "humanity."
9:13–15 Just as God had promised to bring famine to Israel and nearly to exterminate the nation, he promises in these verses to give them abundant crops and a large population. The statement that **the plowman will overtake the reaper** is hyperbole for fruitfulness and served to assure the people that they would enjoy eternal well-being.

◤ Introduction to Obadiah

Circumstances of Writing

Presumably Obadiah (v. 1) was the author of this book, but nothing else is known about him. His common Hebrew name, denoting "servant of the Lord," is shared by at least a dozen men in the Old Testament.

The time of writing of Obadiah is disputed, with a wide variety of proposed dates from the tenth to the fifth centuries BC, depending on when the invasion and plunder of Jerusalem (vv. 11–14) occurred. The two most popular views are during the reign of King Jehoram of Judah (ca 848–841 BC) and shortly after the final destruction of Jerusalem by the Babylonians (587/586 BC).

The former date (ca 845 BC) was when the Philistines and Arabs plundered Judah (2Ch 21:16–17) and the Edomites revolted (2Kg 8:20), presumably then becoming allies of the invaders. Since the text does not explicitly indicate the cooperation of the Edomites with the Philistines and Arabs, the latter date (mid-sixth or even fifth century BC) fits the biblical data better, including Obadiah 20 (the dispersed exiles of the Israelites and of Jerusalem to be restored), as opposed to dates before the dispersion of Israel (by 722 BC) or of Judah (605–586 BC). This postexilic view is also supported by the mention of Edomite involvement in Jerusalem's downfall (vv. 10–14, gloating over the fall of Jerusalem, as in other sixth-century-BC texts—Lm 4:21; Ezk 35:15; see Lm 2:15–17—and participating in the plunder), which would result in the Lord's promised justice ("As you have done, it will be done to you"; Ob 15) on their heads.

Contribution to the Bible

Like the book of Revelation, which proclaims the downfall of the persecuting Roman Empire, the book of Obadiah sustains faith in God's moral government and hope in the eventual triumph of his just will. It brings a pastoral message to aching hearts that God is on his throne and he cares for his own.

Structure

The text declares the book of Obadiah is a prophetic "vision" from the Lord (v. 1) that also appears to be a war oracle (v. 1) communicating the Lord's imminent judgment upon Edom (vv. 2–9). As a subtype of the prophetic "oracle against foreign nations" (Is 13–23; Jr 46–51; Ezk 25–32; Am 1–2; Zph 2:4–15), it is typical in announcing judgment on a foreign power (specifically Edom; see also Lm 4:21–22) to bring deliverance for Judah (Ob 17–20; see Jr 46:25–28; Nah 1:1–15; Zph 3:14–20). Yet it, like Nahum and Jonah, is atypical in focusing solely on judgment for a foreign nation, rather than specifying judgment for Israel as well.

This shortest Old Testament book consists of several parts. A war oracle from the Lord announces certain judgment on Edom for their arrogant presumption and self-deception (Ob 3) that they were immune from divine intervention (vv. 1–9). Next is an explanation of the further cause for coming

Obadiah Timeline

1900–1000 BC

Edomites are descendants of Esau and seen as "brothers of Israel." **1900**
The Edomites refused the Israelites' passage through their land as Israel journeyed from Egypt to Canaan. **1406**
Egyptian texts from about **1300–1100** refer to Shasu, apparently semi-nomadic tribes, from Seir and Edom.
Saul delivers Israel from the hands of neighbors on almost all sides, including Edom. **1020**

1000–900 BC

David resisted Edom's encroachment on Israel by striking down 18,000 Edomites in the region of the Dead Sea. To further secure Israel's southeastern flank, David builds garrisons throughout Edom, which are then subject to David. **982**
Hadad, a member of Edom's royal family, flees to Egypt during the time David subjected Edom. When Solomon was king, God brought Hadad back as an enemy of Solomon, a disciplinary measure for Solomon's turning away from God. **940**

judgment on Edom (vv. 10–14), a lack of brotherly commitment (vv. 10–11) in gloating over the day of disaster for God's people Judah (vv. 12–13) and cooperating with Judah's enemies in her destruction (vv. 10–11,13–14). Then the text focuses on the day of the Lord (vv. 15–21), in which imminent judgment falls on the historical nation of Edom (vv. 15–16), followed by ultimate judgment on "Edom" as representative of Israel's end-time enemies (v. 16) that would result in the deliverance of both Judah and Israel (vv. 17–21).

900–800 BC

During Jehoram's reign as king of the southern kingdom, Edom begins to rebel against domination by Judah and becomes an independent state with its own king. **848–841**
Some interpreters place Obadiah's prophecy in the ninth century when Edom rebelled against Judah. **848–841**

600–500 BC

Edom puts aside its hostilities toward Judah during the reign of Zedekiah. **594**
Edom becomes Judah's ally in resisting the Babylonians. **594**
Edom soon commits an act of hostility against Judah that brings impassioned denunciation of Edom from Jeremiah, a psalmist (Ps 137), and Ezekiel. **586**
The more likely setting of Obadiah's prophecy is in this era surrounding the Babylonian devastation of Jerusalem and the temple. **586**

T he vision of Obadiah.

Edom's Certain Judgment

This is what the Lord GOD has said about Edom:
We have heard a message
 from the LORD;
an envoy has been sent
 among the nations:
"Rise up, and let's go to war
 against her."^A
2 Look, I will make you insignificant
 among the nations;
you will be deeply despised.
3 Your arrogant heart has deceived you,
you who live in clefts of the rock^B,C
in your home on the heights,
who say to yourself,
"Who can bring me down
 to the ground?"
4 Though you seem to soar^D like an eagle
and make your nest among the stars,
even from there I will bring you down.
 This is the LORD's declaration.

5 If thieves came to you,
if marauders by night —
how ravaged you would be! —
wouldn't they steal only
 what they wanted?
If grape harvesters came to you,
wouldn't they leave a few grapes?
6 How Esau will be pillaged,
his hidden treasures searched out!
7 Everyone who has a treaty with you
will drive you to the border;
everyone at peace with you
will deceive and conquer you.
Those who eat your bread
will set^E a trap for you.

He will be unaware of it.
8 In that day —
 this is the LORD's declaration —
will I not eliminate the wise ones
 of Edom
and those who understand
 from the hill country of Esau?
9 Teman,^F your warriors will be terrified
so that everyone
 from the hill country of Esau
will be destroyed by slaughter.

Edom's Sins against Judah

10 You will be covered with shame
 and destroyed forever
because of violence done
 to your brother Jacob.
11 On the day you stood aloof,
on the day strangers captured
 his wealth,^G
while foreigners entered his city gate
and cast lots for Jerusalem,
you were just like one of them.
12 Do not^H gloat over your brother
in the day of his calamity;
do not rejoice over the people of Judah
 in the day of their destruction;
do not boastfully mock^I
 in the day of distress.
13 Do not enter my people's city gate
in the day of their disaster.
Yes, you — do not gloat
 over their misery
in the day of their disaster,
and do not appropriate
 their possessions
in the day of their disaster.
14 Do not stand at the crossroads^J
 to cut off their fugitives,

^A1 = Edom   ^B3 Or in Sela ; probably = Petra   ^C3 Probably Petra   ^D4 Or to build high   ^E7 Some LXX mss, Sym, Tg, Vg; MT reads They will set your bread as   ^F9 = a region or city in Edom   ^G11 Or forces   ^H12–14 Or You should not throughout vv. 12–14   ^I12 Lit not make your mouth big   ^J14 Hb obscure

1 The parallel passage in Jr 49:14 more clearly indicates that God is calling the nations together to **go to war against** Edom.
2 **Insignificant** can also mean "small, unimportant, inferior."
3 **Clefts of the rock** may also be translated as "clefts of Sela" (or Petra). The Nabateans, who built the famed rock-hewn temples at

Petra, drove out the Edomites, who settled in southern Judah (Idumea in NT times). The Edomites may have been completely destroyed by about AD 70 (with "no survivor," v. 18), possibly suffering the same fate as many Jews when Jerusalem fell to the Romans.
4 The Edomites thought they were unconquerable. But even eagles **among the stars** cannot get away from God. See Jb 39:27.
5 **Thieves** . . . **grape harvesters** is a twofold illustration of the thoroughness of the impending judgment (Jr 49:9). Even more completely than thieves pillaging from their victims' houses (cp. Ob 11, Edomites' ravaging of Israel's wealth) or farmers harvesting crops, this destruction would leave no remnant behind (v. 5; Jr 49:10). The mention of **grapes** (lit "gleanings of grapes or olives") alludes to the practice of leaving leftovers from the harvest in the corners of the field for widows, orphans, and aliens to gather (Lv 23:22; Ru 2). Whereas gleaning in the OT often entails a remnant (Is 17:6; Jr 6:9), Obadiah left no room for hope. No remnant would be left for Edom (cp. Ob 18).

6 **Esau**, the brother of Jacob (vv. 10,12), was the father of the Edomites. Thus his descendants the Edomites would be **pillaged** and destroyed like stubble (v. 18). In vv. 9,21, everyone from the hill country of Esau would be destroyed so that it would become the possession of Jacob's descendants (vv. 17–18).
7 Near the end of the sixth century BC the Edomites were driven from Edom by the Arabs, who may have had a **treaty** with them.
8–9 Edom was known for its wisdom (Job's companion Eliphaz was from Teman, Jb 2:11; Jr 49:7); but God would take away their wisdom and understanding. **Teman**, the area east of Petra, is use d to refer to Edom.
10 To harmonize the phrase **destroyed forever** with the seemingly contradictory statement in Am 9:12, see note at Ob 18.
11 Conquering soldiers who **cast lots** (Jl 3:2–3; Nah 3:10) probably did so by shaking a container of marked pebbles until one fell out. He whose stone fell out first picked the choice portions of **Jerusalem**.
12–14 The repetition of the **day** of their disaster emphasizes the calamity and suffering

#47 99 Essential Christian Truths

SIN AS TRANSGRESSION

The word *transgression* means "to cross over" or "to pass by" and is often used in reference to transgressing God's explicit commands. When God gives a specific command, as he did with Adam and Eve in the garden of Eden, and when that command is disobeyed, transgression has taken place (Rm 5:14; 1Tm 2:14). In this sense, sin is law-breaking.

and do not hand over their survivors
in the day of distress.

Judgment of the Nations

15 For the day of the LORD is near,
against all the nations.
As you have done, it will be done to you;
what you deserve will return
on your own head.
16 As you have drunk
on my holy mountain,
so all the nations will
drink continually.
They will drink and gulp down
and be as though they had never been.
17 But there will be a deliverance
on Mount Zion,
and it will be holy;
the house of Jacob will dispossess
those who dispossessed them.^A
18 Then the house of Jacob will be
a blazing fire,
and the house of Joseph,
a burning flame,
but the house of Esau will be stubble;

Jacob^B will set them on fire
and consume Edom.^C
Therefore no survivor will remain
of the house of Esau,
for the LORD has spoken.

Future Blessing for Israel

19 People from the Negev will possess
the hill country of Esau;
those from the Judean foothills
will possess
the land of the Philistines.
They^D will possess
the territories of Ephraim and Samaria,
while Benjamin will possess Gilead.
20 The exiles of the Israelites who are
in Halah^E
and who are among the Canaanites
as far as Zarephath
as well as the exiles of Jerusalem
who are in Sepharad
will possess the cities of the Negev.
21 Saviors^F will ascend Mount Zion
to rule over the hill country of Esau,
and the kingdom will be the LORD's.

^A17 DSS, LXX, Syr, Vg, Tg; MT reads *Jacob will possess its inheritance*   ^B18 Lit *they*   ^C18 Lit *them*   ^D19 = The house of Jacob
^E20 Or *of this host of the Israelites*; Hb obscure   ^F21 Or *Those who have been delivered*

of Judah at the time of Edom's mistreatment. Ironically this preoccupation with distress and disaster prepared the way for the "day of the LORD" (v. 15), when God would pay back Edom accordingly (cp. v. 8, "in that day"). **15** The **day of the LORD** was a time of retribution for the Edomites because of their cooperation with the conquering Babylonians in the day of Judah's distress (see note at vv. 12–14). **What you deserve** is literally "your payback or retribution." Retribution would come upon Babylon the ally of Edom (Ps 137:8) and all who had insulted Judah (Lm 3:61–64). The promise of "retribution on your heads" to all Israel's enemies will be fulfilled in the last days (Jl 3:4,7). **16** The initial occasion for the drinking bout (**as you have drunk on my holy mountain**) may have been the Edomite celebration over

the recent demise of Judah (ca 586 BC). However, the reference to future drinking (**so all the nations will drink continually**) does not picture celebration but rather judgment against Edom (see notes at Ps 75:8; Is 19:14). Drunken, they would stagger and "fall down and never get up again" as the sword swept through the land (Jr 25:27–29). "Edom" represents not just the Edomites, but ultimately all the nations who oppose Israel in the end times. They will all fall under God's judgment. **17** This **deliverance** (lit "escape; escaped ones") for God's people in the last days is also prophesied in Jl 2:32 and Is 4:2–4. The surviving righteous remnant of Jerusalem will be **holy**. **18** God's burning anger will consume his enemies like grass or chaff. He will use Israel as

a blazing fire consumes grass to destroy their enemies (Zch 12:6). The phrase **no survivor** (cp. Ob 10, "destroyed forever") is in tension with Am 9:12, which states that Israel will possess "the remnant of Edom." Will there or won't there be a remnant? The most likely solution is that "remnant of Edom" in Am 9:12 broadly represents Israel's remaining enemies in the end times, not the Edomites specifically (see note at Ob 16). **19–21** The land of Edom will be given to the Israelites living in the **Negev**, or the southern section of the land. God's people, who were once **exiles**, will once again possess the land that they had taken originally from the **Canaanites**. **Saviors**, or deliverers, will rule the **hill country of Esau**, and Yahweh will rule over the entire **kingdom**.

▼ Introduction to Jonah

Circumstances of Writing

Jonah appears in 2 Kings 14:25 as a prophet from Gath-hepher in the territory of Zebulun in northern Israel. He was active around the first half of the eighth century BC. Jonah predicted the restoration of the northern kingdom's boundaries. This occurred during the reign of Jeroboam II (ca 793–753 BC). This book about Jonah could have been composed at any time from the eighth century to the end of the Old Testament period.

Jonah preached to the city of Nineveh. Nineveh was a major city of the Assyrians, a cruel and warlike people who were longtime enemies of Israel. Assyrian artwork emphasizes war, including scenes of execution, impalement, flaying the skin off prisoners, and beheadings. This explains Jonah's reluctance to preach to the infamous city of Nineveh.

The key debate about the book of Jonah is the question of its genre. Is Jonah history or parable? The parable view argues that Jonah is a fictional story or fable made up to convey a theological point about God's attitude toward Gentiles. Proponents of the parable view argue that the ironic and fantastic events described by the book (e.g., Jonah living and praying in the stomach of a fish) is the author's way of tipping the reader off that this is not literal history. There are also historical difficulties that the fictional view would resolve: the exaggerated size of Nineveh (3:3) and the lack of extrabiblical, Assyrian evidence to confirm that the city ever repented.

Five considerations suggest taking the book of Jonah as genuine history. First, Jonah was a real historical figure, said to be a prophet in 2 Kings 14:25. The book of Jonah portrays Jonah as a flawed character. Were the book of Jonah a piece of fiction, it would be guilty of slander, saying something derogatory and untrue about a real person who is elsewhere presented positively.

Second, Jonah is part of the collection of twelve Minor Prophets. All the other books of this collection convey prophecies by genuine, historical prophets.

Third, the miracles in Jonah are not impossible for the God of the Bible. Presuming otherwise, some interpreters allow their anti-supernaturalism to drive them to the parable view of Jonah.

Fourth, Jesus in Matthew 12:39–41 and Luke 11:29–32 spoke of Jonah being in the fish and preaching in Nineveh as if these were real events. In particular, Jesus's statement that "the men of Nineveh will stand up at the judgment with this generation and condemn it, because they repented at Jonah's preaching" (Mt 12:41; Lk 11:32) makes little sense if the people of Nineveh never actually repented due to Jonah's preaching. Unless one is willing to affirm that Jesus was wrong, it is best to say that the book of Jonah is historical.

Contribution to the Bible

The book of Jonah shows God's gracious concern for the whole world, his power over nature, and the futility of running from him. In addition, it foreshadows Jesus's burial and resurrection. Matthew 12:38–45 and Luke 11:24–32 compare

---

Jonah Timeline

5000–1000 BC

Earliest settlement of Nineveh **5000**

Three major Assyrian cities, Nineveh, Asshur, and Calah, engage in vigorous trading as far as Cappadocia. **1900**

An expanding Assyria wars with Babylon's King Hammurabi shortly before breaking up into smaller city-states. **1700**

Adad-nirari establishes the first Assyrian Empire. **1307**

Tiglath-pileser I is monarch of the second Assyrian Empire. **1115–1077**

At Tiglath-pileser's death the empire falls into a 166-year decline. **1077–911**

1000–850 BC

Neo-Assyrian Empire established by Ashur-dan II, lays the foundation for a unified rule in the ancient Near East from Egypt to the Caspian Sea **934**

Adad-nirari II **(911–891)** and his grandson, Ashurnasirpal II **(883–859)**, lead a resurgent Assyria.

Ashurnasirpal's son, Shalmaneser III **(859–824)**, fights a coalition of twelve kings including Ben-hadad of Aram-Damascus and Ahab of Israel at Qarqar in north Syria. **853**

the ministry of Jesus with that of Jonah, Jesus being the greater. Both texts see Jonah's great fish as a foreshadowing of Jesus's burial in the tomb, making Jonah a "type" of Christ.

Structure

The book of Jonah exhibits a high degree of Hebrew literary excellence. Its style is rich and varied. It is considered by many as a masterpiece of rhetoric. There is symmetry and balance in the book, and it can be divided into two sections of two chapters each. The peak of the first discourse is marked by its poetic form, which has a higher prominence in narrative than prose. The peak in the second discourse is marked by the dialogue between Jonah and God. The Lord and Jonah are indicated as the two main characters of the story by being the only ones who are named; the other characters are anonymous.

Phenomena of nature also serve in each half as props: wind, storm, sea, dry land, and fish in the first half; herd and flock, plant, worm, sun, and wind in the second half. When placed side by side, chapters 1 and 3 and chapters 2 and 4 can be seen as parallel. Finally, both chapters 1 and 3 begin with Jonah receiving a word from the Lord consisting of a call to go to Nineveh.

Outline

I. Jonah's Flight from God (1:1–17)
    A. The Lord calls; Jonah rebels (1:1–3)
    B. The Lord sends a storm (1:4–6)
    C. The sailors intervene (1:7–16)
    D. The Lord sends a big fish (1:17)
II. Jonah's Prayer of Thanksgiving from the Fish (2:1–10)
    A. Jonah prays (2:1–9)
    B. The Lord delivers Jonah (2:10)
III. Jonah's Preaching in Nineveh (3:1–10)
    A. Jonah obeys the call (3:1–4)
    B. King and Ninevites repent (3:5–9)
    C. The Lord withholds judgment (3:10)
IV. Jonah's Anger at God's Mercy (4:1–11)
    A. The Lord displeases Jonah (4:1–5)
    B. Jonah displeases the Lord (4:6–10)
    C. The Lord shows great pity (4:11)

850–750 BC

Shalmaneser defeats Hazael of Damascus and receives tribute from Israel's King Jehu (**841**). This scene is carved in relief on the Black Obelisk of Shalmaneser, unearthed at Nimrud, Iraq, in AD 1846. With the death of Shalmaneser III, Assyrian expansion is held in check. **824–745**

Jonah prophesies that the Lord will restore the border of Israel from Lebo-hamath as far as the Sea of the Arabah. Jeroboam II strengthens Israel. **793–753**

God calls Jonah to go to Nineveh and preach repentance. During its time of weakness, Assyria experiences two severe plagues (**765** and **759**) and a total eclipse (**763**).

750–700 BC

Tiglath-pileser III checks the aggression of the Kingdom of Urartu on Assyria's north and leads an expansion of Assyria, conquering Babylon and greatly reducing Israel's territory. **745–727**

Assyria's Shalmaneser V besieges Samaria. **725–722**

Samaria falls to Assyria's Sargon II; nearly 28,000 Israelites are sent into exile, and Gentiles from Assyrian-controlled territories are resettled into what was the northern kingdom. **722**

Jonah's Flight

1 The word of the LORD came to Jonah son of Amittai: [2] "Get up! Go to the great city of Nineveh and preach against it because their evil has come up before me." [3] Jonah got up to flee to Tarshish from the LORD's presence. He went down to Joppa and found a ship going to Tarshish. He paid the fare and went down into it to go with them to Tarshish from the LORD's presence.

[4] But the LORD threw a great wind onto the sea, and such a great storm arose on the sea that the ship threatened to break apart. [5] The sailors were afraid, and each cried out to his god. They threw the ship's cargo into the sea to lighten the load. Meanwhile, Jonah had gone down to the lowest part of the vessel and had stretched out and fallen into a deep sleep.

[6] The captain approached him and said, "What are you doing sound asleep? Get up! Call to your god.[A] Maybe this god will consider us, and we won't perish."

[7] "Come on!" the sailors said to each other. "Let's cast lots. Then we'll know who is to blame for this trouble we're in." So they cast lots, and the lot singled out Jonah. [8] Then they said to him, "Tell us who is to blame for this trouble we're in. What is your business, and where are you from? What is your country, and what people are you from?"

[9] He answered them, "I'm a Hebrew. I worship[B] the LORD, the God of the heavens, who made the sea and the dry land."

[10] Then the men were seized by a great fear and said to him, "What have you done?" The men knew he was fleeing from the LORD's

^A 1:6 Or *God* ^B 1:9 Or *fear*

1:1 Jonah in Hebrew means "dove." His father's name **Amittai** means "faithful [is Yahweh]."
1:2 Nineveh on the east bank of the Tigris River became the Assyrian capital after 705 BC, well after Jonah's day. Its ruins are found in the northern part of modern Iraq, opposite the city of Mosul 220 miles northwest of Baghdad. For Jonah, Nineveh was an arduous journey of more than 500 miles to the northeast of Samaria. His probable route—first traveling north and then east—would have made the trip closer to 600 miles. God showed himself judge of the world by holding these distant pagans accountable for **their evil**, though he also showed his mercy by commanding his prophet to warn them.
1:3 To flee . . . from before the LORD's presence is to attempt the impossible

since God is everywhere. **Joppa** on the Mediterranean coast just south of modern Tel Aviv was one of Israel's few natural seaports. **Tarshish** has sometimes been identified with Paul's home of Tarsus in Cilicia or the city of Tharros on the island of Sardinia west of Italy. But the most probable identification of Tarshish is the Phoenician colony of Tartessus, located on the Guadalquivir River on the southwestern coast of Spain about 2,000 miles west of Palestine. This is about as far in the opposite direction from Nineveh as Jonah could have gone.
1:5–6 Jonah's spiritual decline is depicted in parallel with the descriptions of his response to God's call. He was told to "get up" (v. 2) to go to Nineveh, but instead he "went down to Joppa" (v. 3), "went down"

to the ship (v. 3), and finally went **down to the lowest part of the vessel.** Eventually he will be swallowed by a fish and sink down "to the foundations of the mountains" at the bottom of the sea (2:6). His **deep sleep** in the midst of a storm also symbolizes his spiritual condition.
1:9 Worship is literally "fear." Fear of God in the OT is the respect that a person has for God, causing him to turn from evil and obey God's commandments (Gn 22:12; Jb 1:8; 28:28; Pr 8:13). Ironically, God's prophet Jonah showed no such fear by his disobedience. The title **the LORD** renders "Yahweh," God's personal name in the OT.
1:10–11 Perhaps what frightened the sailors was that Jonah's God had created the sea. They hoped that some kind of sacrifice might calm the **sea.**

Character profile:
Jonah

J onah stands alone among the prophets of the Old Testament. Certainly, he was the only one to spend three days in the belly of a fish. In the bigger picture, though, he was the only one to flatly refuse an assignment from God.

The Lord instructed Jonah to go to Nineveh to preach against the wickedness of the people. Instead, Jonah booked passage on a boat heading to Tarshish—that is, away from Nineveh. Some part of him must have believed—or at least desperately hoped—that he could escape his prophetic assignment.

The reason Jonah didn't want to go to Nineveh is because he feared that, in response to his preaching, they would actually turn to God in repentance. If that happened, Jonah feared that they would receive God's mercy instead of his judgment. The bad guys would be pardoned.

Nineveh was the capital city of Assyria, Israel's bitter enemy. The Assyrians had plagued the Israelites for centuries. The prospect of an entire Assyrian city being destroyed by God's judgment must have been tantalizing to an Israelite like Jonah. Likewise, the prospect of the entire city being spared by God, if Jonah preached to them (and the Ninevites repented), must have seemed absolutely intolerable to him. That's why he ran.

Nevertheless, he didn't get far. The boat to Tarshish encountered foul weather as soon as it hit the open sea. The boat's crewmen recognized that what they were facing was no ordinary storm. They sensed a divine judgment in the squall that threatened to sink their vessel. They cast lots (similar to rolling dice) to determine which of their

passengers was the focus of wrath. The results pointed to Jonah.

Jonah resigned himself to his fate. He advised the crew to throw him overboard to stop the storm. The sailors resisted at first, but they finally had no choice. When Jonah plunged into the sea, the waters immediately grew calm and Jonah was swallowed by a giant fish—in which he spent three days. That's a lot of time for a man to assess his life and rethink some of his choices.

Jonah prayed to God from his rancid surroundings. If the Lord wanted him to go to Nineveh, that's where he would go. The fish vomited Jonah back on shore, and Jonah headed for Nineveh, where he watched his worst-case scenario unfold before his eyes.

Jonah delivered God's warning according to his instructions. As a result, the Ninevites rightly responded with extreme humility and repentance. The king of Nineveh urged his people to call on God to withhold his judgment and to spare them.

Much to Jonah's displeasure, God honored their prayers and relented from the disaster with which he had threatened them. The people of Nineveh lived to see another day, thanks to God's great forgiveness and mercy.

God's plan for your life will take you outside your comfort zone, perhaps frequently. God will put you in situations that force you to resist your natural instincts. If you're not prepared to sacrifice your own desires for the greater good, you may struggle, as Jonah did. If you insist on clinging to your own agenda, you will miss out on the blessings God has in store for you.

If, on the other hand, you're willing to cede control to him, you'll find that God will work in and through you to accomplish some extraordinary things.

presence because he had told them. ¹¹ So they said to him, "What should we do to you so that the sea will calm down for us?" For the sea was getting worse and worse.

¹² He answered them, "Pick me up and throw me into the sea so that it will calm down for you, for I know that I'm to blame for this great storm that is against you." ¹³ Nevertheless, the men rowed hard to get back to dry land, but they couldn't because the sea was raging against them more and more.

¹⁴ So they called out to the Lord, "Please, Lord, don't let us perish because of this man's life, and don't charge us with innocent blood! For you, Lord, have done just as you pleased." ¹⁵ Then they picked up Jonah and threw him into the sea, and the sea stopped its raging. ¹⁶ The men were seized by great fear of the Lord, and they offered a sacrifice to the Lord and made vows.

¹⁷ The Lord appointed a great fish to swallow Jonah, and Jonah was in the belly of the fish three days and three nights.

Jonah's Prayer

2 Jonah prayed to the Lord his God from the belly of the fish:

² I called to the Lord in my distress,
and he answered me.
I cried out for help
from deep inside[A] Sheol;
you heard my voice.

³ When you threw me into the depths,
into the heart of the seas,
the current[B] overcame me.
All your breakers and your billows
swept over me.

⁴ And I said, "I have been banished
from your sight,
yet I will look[C] once more

toward your holy temple."

⁵ The water engulfed me up to the neck;[D]
the watery depths overcame me;
seaweed was wrapped around my head.

⁶ I sank to the foundations
of the mountains,
the earth's gates shut
behind me forever!
Then you raised my life from the Pit,
Lord my God!

⁷ As my life was fading away,
I remembered the Lord,
and my prayer came to you,
to your holy temple.

⁸ Those who cherish worthless idols
abandon their faithful love,

⁹ but as for me, I will sacrifice to you
with a voice of thanksgiving.
I will fulfill what I have vowed.
Salvation[E] belongs to the Lord.

¹⁰ Then the Lord commanded the fish, and it vomited Jonah onto dry land.

Jonah's Preaching

3 The word of the Lord came to Jonah a second time: ² "Get up! Go to the great city of Nineveh and preach the message that I tell you." ³ Jonah got up and went to Nineveh according to the Lord's command.

Now Nineveh was an extremely great city,[F] a three-day walk. ⁴ Jonah set out on the first day of his walk in the city and proclaimed, "In forty days Nineveh will be demolished!" ⁵ Then the people of Nineveh believed God. They proclaimed a fast and dressed in sackcloth — from the greatest of them to the least.

⁶ When word reached the king of Nineveh, he got up from his throne, took off his royal

---

[A] 2:2 Lit from the stomach of   [B] 2:3 Lit river   [C] 2:4 LXX reads sight. Will I look . . . ?   [D] 2:5 Or me, threatening my life   [E] 2:9 Or Deliverance   [F] 3:3 Or was a great city to God

---

1:12–15 Despite Jonah's confession of guilt, these pagan Gentiles had moral scruples about sending a man to his death and tried to row ashore instead. Only after they saw no other option and had prayed that the Lord would not hold them accountable for taking a human life did they throw Jonah into the sea.
1:16 When the sea calmed, these Gentile sailors **were seized by great fear of the Lord.** They were so overpowered by the experience that they could do nothing but worship the Lord (see note at 1:9).
1:17 The **great fish** that swallowed Jonah was not necessarily a whale. **Three days and three nights** parallels Christ's resurrection on the third day (Mt 12:40).
2:1–2 Sheol is the realm of the dead, often the grave. The fish's stomach is metaphorically like a tomb. But God was present in Sheol (**you heard my voice**) to receive Jonah's prayer.
2:3–5 Verses 3 and 5 depict Jonah's dire circumstances. He sees both the **breakers** and

the **billows** as judgment tools of God. But v. 4 sounds a note of faith and hope. Though he had been **banished** from God's sight, he expected to **look once more** toward his **holy temple,** which means he expected he would live to pray again and perhaps even worship in the Jerusalem temple. **Neck** (Hb nephesh) in v. 5 can also be rendered "life," but originally it meant "throat." The image of water up to the prophet's throat fits this context well.
2:8–9 What I have vowed refers to a promised gift to God if he should answer prayer (Nm 21:2; 1Sm 1:11). Jonah promised praise and animal sacrifice. A fellowship offering was used to worship God at the completion of a vow (Nm 6:21; 2Sm 15:7–8; Pr 7:14).
2:10 Vomited, an ignoble means of exiting the fish.
3:1–3 Jonah went to Nineveh as God had commanded. **Extremely great city** (lit "a great city to God"; see textual footnote) may have a double meaning: great in size (where "God," Hb elohim, is used as a superlative for

"extremely") and a city "important to God" even though inhabited by Gentiles. **Three-day walk** could refer to greater Nineveh that included the region around Nineveh proper. More likely it refers to how long it would take for Jonah to preach thoroughly throughout Nineveh itself, street corner by street corner.
3:4 Forty often refers to a period of testing or judgment in the Bible (Lk 4:2; Heb 3:9), serving here to give Nineveh time to repent. Jonah preached only on **the first day** of his three-day task (see note at 3:1–3), showing his half-hearted obedience. **Demolished** has a secondary meaning of "changed" which is not the sense Jonah meant, but ironically that is how the word of prophecy was actually fulfilled. Nineveh was not destroyed, but was instead changed.
3:5–8 After recounting that Nineveh **believed God.** The text then explains that this overwhelming response was a result of a royal decree. The king led by example. **Sackcloth** was worn during times

robe, covered himself with sackcloth, and sat in ashes. **⁷** Then he issued a decree in Nineveh: By order of the king and his nobles: No person or animal, herd or flock, is to taste anything at all. They must not eat or drink water. **⁸** Furthermore, both people and animals must be covered with sackcloth, and everyone must call out earnestly to God. Each must turn from his evil ways and from his wrongdoing.^A **⁹** Who knows? God may turn and relent; he may turn from his burning anger so that we will not perish.

¹⁰ God saw their actions — that they had turned from their evil ways — so God relented from the disaster he had threatened them with. And he did not do it.

Jonah's Anger

4 Jonah was greatly displeased and became furious. **²** He prayed to the LORD, "Please, LORD, isn't this what I said while I was still in my own country? That's why I fled toward Tarshish in the first place. I knew that you are a gracious and compassionate God, slow to anger, abounding in faithful love, and one who relents from sending disaster. **³** And now, LORD, take my life from me, for it is better for me to die than to live."

⁴ The LORD asked, "Is it right for you to be angry?"

⁵ Jonah left the city and found a place east of it. He made himself a shelter there and sat in its shade to see what would happen to the city. **⁶** Then the LORD God appointed a plant, and it grew over Jonah to provide shade for his head to rescue him from his trouble.^B Jonah was greatly pleased with the plant. **⁷** When dawn came the next day, God appointed a worm that attacked the plant, and it withered.

⁸ As the sun was rising, God appointed a scorching east wind. The sun beat down on Jonah's head so much that he almost fainted, and he wanted to die. He said, "It's better for me to die than to live."

⁹ Then God asked Jonah, "Is it right for you to be angry about the plant?"

"Yes, it's right!" he replied. "I'm angry enough to die!"

¹⁰ And the LORD said, "You cared about the plant, which you did not labor over and did not grow. It appeared in a night and perished in a night. **¹¹** So may I not care about the great city of Nineveh, which has more than a hundred twenty thousand people who cannot distinguish between their right and their left, as well as many animals?"

---

^A 3:8 Or *injustice*, or *violence*   ^B 4:6 Or *disaster*, or *evil*

#48 99 Essential Christian Truths

THE GOSPEL

The Bible teaches that the gospel is both an event and a story. First, it is an event that took place at a specific point in history: the life, death, and resurrection of Jesus Christ for the redemption of sinners (1Co 15; 2Co 5:21). Second, the gospel is also the story of redemption that God has planned since "before the foundation of the world" (Eph 1:4), which runs through Scripture, and which culminates in a restored and redeemed creation—a new heaven and new earth where sin, death, and suffering will never again plague humanity and where God's people will live with him forever (Is 25:8; 2Pt 3:13; Rv 21). The event and story do not exist apart from or in conflict with one another, but together inspire us to a life of devotion and mission.

of mourning and repentance, usually while sitting atop ashes (Gn 37:34; 1Kg 21:27; Mt 11:21). **Person or animal** means even the animals fasted, bellowing miserably to heaven along with the people.

3:9 Who knows? indicates that Jonah had not explicitly stated that judgment against the city could be averted by repentance. The king of Nineveh took a shot in the dark.

3:10 Prophecies of doom are often conditional warnings that can be averted through repentance (Jr 18:8–10).

4:1–2 The unexpected and overwhelming success of Jonah's preaching resulted in Nineveh's escape from calamity. However, this brought emotional calamity to the angry and self-pitying prophet, who wished he were dead. Jonah had initially fled from preaching to Nineveh because he feared that God, being excessively **gracious and compassionate** (see Ex 34:6–7), would forgive these pagan, warlike Gentiles.

4:3–4 Take my life echoes the words of the prophet Elijah (1Kg 19:4), who despaired over the failure of his mission, just as Jonah despaired over the success of his.

4:5–8 Another factor behind Jonah's death wish was the blisteringly hot weather and the dry **east wind**, making him extremely uncomfortable as he sat watching to see what God would do to Nineveh. He was also upset over the withering of a **plant**, perhaps a castor-oil plant or a climbing gourd that had sprung up to give him temporary relief from the sun.

4:9–11 God used Jonah's emotional reaction to the death of the plant as an object lesson to rebuke him for being more concerned about a plant than the destruction of **a hundred twenty thousand people** who could not **distinguish between their right and their left**. This probably does not refer to small children in Nineveh, but that the people themselves were immature and uninformed morally and spiritually. **As well as many animals** was a final rebuke. If Jonah could not feel compassion for Gentile people, he should at least feel sorry for the hungry livestock that were bellowing their misery (see 3:7–8). The book ends without telling us whether Jonah responded positively to the Lord's closing reprimand.

◥ Introduction to Micah

Circumstances of Writing

Micah's hometown of Moresheth-gath (1:1,14) in the lowlands of Judah was about twenty-five miles southwest of Jerusalem. The fact that his hometown is mentioned probably means that Micah ministered elsewhere, including Jerusalem, and since no genealogy is given we can probably assume that his family was not prominent. Micah was a skilled orator, a master of metaphors with a genius for wordplay and blunt, vivid imagery. Few prophets saw the future more clearly. Micah prophesied the fall of Samaria (1:5–9), Jerusalem's destruction (1:1–16; 3:12), the Babylonian captivity and return from exile (4:6–10), as well as the birth of God's future Davidic ruler in Bethlehem (5:2).

Micah's ministry probably began late in Jotham's reign and ended early in Hezekiah's, dating between 730 and 690 BC. His reference to the future judgment of Samaria (1:6) shows that his ministry began sometime before 722 BC. As such, Micah's ministry overlapped Isaiah's. The elders in Jeremiah's day remembered Micah's prophecy as having spurred Hezekiah's religious reform (Jr 26:17–19).

Both Israel and Judah experienced affluence and material prosperity in the late eighth century BC. In the south, King Uzziah's military victories brought wealth for some. A wealthy merchant class developed, and many poorer farmers found themselves at the mercy of government-supported businessmen. As business dealings became more corrupt, God's prophets spoke to the nation, confronting the ill-gotten wealth and accompanying godlessness. Amos and Hosea prophesied in the northern kingdom of Israel, and Isaiah and Micah prophesied in Judah to the south.

Judah's commercial and secular culture replaced God's covenant ideal. The rich became wealthy at the expense of the poor. The growing affluence in Micah's day led to increasing callousness toward the weak (Mc 2:1–2) and a blatant disregard for God's foundational laws (6:10–12). Judges and lawmakers became involved in conspiracy, bribery, and other corruption (3:1–3,9–11; 7:3). Religious leaders were concerned more about making money than teaching God's Word (3:11). The wealthy learned to separate their worship from everyday practice.

At this time, the ancient Near East experienced an international power shift. Assyria was ascending, becoming one of the most evil, bloodthirsty, manipulative, and arrogant empires of the ancient world. Four Assyrian kings made military inroads into Palestine during Micah's ministry, taking Samaria in 722 BC and making Israel an Assyrian province. In 701 BC, Sennacherib took forty-six Judean towns and villages and besieged Jerusalem. King Hezekiah had allied with Egypt and Babylon against Assyria, for which both Micah and Isaiah urged him to repent. God miraculously spared Jerusalem (2Kg 19:35–36; 2Ch 32:22–23; Is 37:36–37); according to Micah, the Jerusalem siege was both an act of God's judgment and an occasion for God's deliverance.

---

750 BC

Jotham, king of Judah **750–732**
Micah begins his prophetic ministry. **750**
Tiglath-pileser III comes to power as king of Assyria and begins a program of expansion and domination of the region. **745**
Death of King Uzziah of Judah **740**
Isaiah's call to be a prophet **740**
Ahaz, king of Judah **735–716**

735 BC

Tiglath-pileser III's invasions of Israel **734–732**
Pekah of Israel and Rezin of Damascus form a mutual defense alliance against Assyria and invite Ahaz of Judah to join them. **734**
Ahaz refuses Isaiah's counsel and seeks protection from Assyria by paying tribute to them, creating a heavy financial burden on Judah for years to come. **734**
Micah prophesies the fall of Samaria.
Alliance between Syria and Israel collapses with the fall of Damascus. **732**

Judah never learned its lesson. The people wavered between faith and apostasy and suffered many crises. As the rulers proved increasingly unfaithful, Micah prophesied Judah's destruction and exile by the Babylonians (586 BC). Beyond that, however, he saw a future restoration for a remnant of the people (539 BC).

Contribution to the Bible

Micah's holy and just God demands holiness and justice from all people. This is the "good" he requires (6:8). The people had grown content with going through the religious motions while practicing very little genuine spiritual devotion. Even the religious leaders chose to speak popular messages in order to support their standard of living. Micah preached that true religion comes from a heart tuned to God, resulting in godly living. As such, religion and ethics are inseparable. People who refuse to repent will face his judgment, but the faithful will find his salvation and be led by God's King, who would usher in his peace and prosperity.

Structure

Structured thematically as a balanced chiasm, the book highlights the central and final sections. Each matching section reflects on the other. This literary structure emphasizes Micah's main themes of Judah's social sins, the moral failure of its leadership, and the establishment of God's kingship over the land.

Outline

I. Coming Defeat and Destruction (1:1–16)
II. Corruption of the People (2:1–13)
III. Corruption of the Leaders (3:1–12)
IV. Hope for a Glorious Future Restoration (4:1–5:15)
V. Corruption of the City and Its Leaders (6:1–16)
VI. Corruption of the People (7:1–7)
VII. Future Reversal of Defeat and Destruction (7:8–20)

Key verse in Micah

6:8   Mankind, he has told each of you what is good and what it is the LORD requires of you: to act justly, to love faithfulness, and to walk humbly with your God.

725–600 BC

Assyria's Shalmaneser V besieges Samaria **(725–722)**, which falls to Sargon II. **722**
Hezekiah, king of Judah **716–687**
Micah prophesies Jerusalem's destruction, the Babylonian captivity, the return from exile, and the birth of God's future Davidic ruler in Bethlehem.
Hezekiah's reforms **715**
Assyria's King Sennacherib conquers forty-six Judean towns and villages and besieges Jerusalem. **701**
Micah's prophetic work ends about the time of Hezekiah's death. **686**
Josiah's reforms **622**

600–5 BC

Nebuchadnezzar attacks Jerusalem and leads citizens of Judah into exile. The temple is destroyed. **605, 597, 586**
Cyrus issues decree allowing the Jews to return to Judah **538**
Events in Ezra **538–457**
Second temple construction under Zerubbabel's and Joshua's leadership. **536–515**
Second temple dedicated **515**
Jesus of Nazareth, son of David, is born in Bethlehem. **5**

1 The word of the LORD that came to Micah the Moreshite — what he saw regarding Samaria and Jerusalem in the days of Jotham, Ahaz, and Hezekiah, kings of Judah.

Coming Judgment on Israel

2 Listen, all you peoples;
pay attention, earth^A and everyone in it!
The Lord GOD will be a witness against you,
the Lord, from his holy temple.
3 Look, the LORD is leaving his place
and coming down to trample
the heights^B of the earth.
4 The mountains will melt beneath him,
and the valleys will split apart,
like wax near a fire,
like water cascading down
a mountainside.
5 All this will happen because of
Jacob's rebellion
and the sins of the house of Israel.
What is the rebellion of Jacob?
Isn't it Samaria?
And what is the high place of Judah?
Isn't it Jerusalem?
6 Therefore, I will make Samaria
a heap of ruins in the countryside,
a planting area for a vineyard.
I will roll her stones into the valley
and expose her foundations.
7 All her carved images will be smashed
to pieces;
all her wages will be burned in the fire,
and I will destroy all her idols.
Since she collected the wages
of a prostitute,
they will be used again for a prostitute.

Micah's Lament

8 Because of this I will lament and wail;
I will walk barefoot and naked.
I will howl like the jackals
and mourn like ostriches.^C
9 For her wound is incurable
and has reached even Judah;
it has approached my people's
city gate,
as far as Jerusalem.

10 Don't announce it in Gath,
don't weep at all.
Roll in the dust in Beth-leaphrah.
11 Depart in shameful nakedness,
you residents of Shaphir;
the residents of Zaanan will not
come out.
Beth-ezel is lamenting;
its support^D is taken from you.
12 Though the residents of Maroth
anxiously wait for something good,
disaster has come from the LORD
to the gate of Jerusalem.
13 Harness the horses to the chariot,
you residents of Lachish.
This was the beginning of sin
for Daughter Zion
because Israel's acts of rebellion
can be traced to you.
14 Therefore, send farewell gifts
to Moresheth-gath;
the houses of Achzib are a deception
to the kings of Israel.
15 I will again bring a conqueror
against you who live in Mareshah.
The nobility^E of Israel will come
to Adullam.
16 Shave yourselves bald and cut off
your hair
in sorrow for your precious children;
make yourselves as bald as an eagle,
for they have been taken from you
into exile.

---

^A 1:2 Or *land*   ^B 1:3 Or *high places*   ^C 1:8 Or *eagle owls*; lit *daughters of the desert*   ^D 1:11 Lit *its standing place*; Hb obscure
^E 1:15 Lit *glory*

1:1 Samaria and Jerusalem, the capitals of the northern and southern kingdoms, are representative of the entire nations of Israel and Judah respectively. The three kings of Judah's dates of rule were: **Jotham** (750–735 BC), **Ahaz** (735–715 BC), and **Hezekiah** (715–687 BC).
1:2–5 Rebellion or "revolt" denotes a willful, criminal breaking of a covenant (1Kg 12:19; Jr 2:29). **Sins** are literally deviations from a target (Jdg 20:16; Pr 19:2), God's holiness in this case. Samaria's idolatry and immorality were so deep that God marked her for destruction (Mc 1:6–7). Micah compared worship in **Jerusalem** with pagan worship in the north. Hezekiah repented through Micah's preaching (Jr 26:19) and removed every **high place**, stone altar, and pagan Asherah pole (2Kg 18:1–6).
1:6–7 Assyria captured **Samaria** in 722 BC (2Kg 17:3–6). Israel's apostasy included participating in pagan cultic prostitution, which involved paying **wages** to prostitutes;

Assyrian troops would pillage Samaria, steal these wages, and use the money yet again on prostitutes.
1:8–16 This section declares that sinful Judah will also face God's wrath. Micah grieved over the towns of Judah facing destruction, even his hometown (v. 14). Sennacherib of Assyria marched through Judah to Jerusalem in 701 BC (Is 10:28–32). He captured at least forty-six Judean towns in this campaign but failed to take Jerusalem.
1:10–15 David lamented, **Don't announce it in Gath** when Saul and Jonathan died in battle; for otherwise he knew the Philistines would gloat (2Sm 1:20). In the same spirit, Micah did not want the Assyrians to gloat in their success. **Beth-leaphrah** (lit "house of dust") would **roll in the dust** as a sign of humiliating defeat (Gn 3:14; Ps 44:25). Those living in **Shaphir** (lit "pleasant") would have the unpleasant experience of being stripped naked and led into exile. Neighboring **Zaanan** would not go out to help,

and **Beth-ezel** (lit "house of taking away") would remove its support.
Maroth (sounds like "bitter") wanted something sweet but would instead face the Lord's **disaster**. This trouble would approach **the gate of Jerusalem** but would not enter it. **Lachish**, a major fortification and military garrison (2Ch 11:9), would need riding steeds to power chariots in a fast getaway. Reliance on military might was **the beginning of sin** leading to **acts of rebellion** among God's people (Is 30:15–17). Like a father giving away his betrothed daughter, Judah would have to give away **Moresheth-gath** (sounds like "betrothed") to Assyria. Though it promised help, **Achzib** (lit "deception") would not come through. **Mareshah** (sounds like "the conqueror") would be conquered. Israel's leaders would flee to **Adullam** to hide like David had done (1Sm 22:1; 2Sm 23:13).
1:16 On baldness as a sign of grief and mourning see Jb 1:20; Jr 16:6; Ezk 27:31.

Oppressors Judged

2 Woe to those who dream up wickedness
and prepare evil plans on their beds!
At morning light they accomplish it
because the power is in their hands.

² They covet fields and seize them;
they also take houses.
They deprive a man of his home,
a person of his inheritance.

³ Therefore, the LORD says:
I am now planning a disaster
against this nation;
you cannot free your necks from it.
Then you will not walk so proudly
because it will be an evil time.

⁴ In that day one will take up a taunt
against you
and lament mournfully, saying,
"We are totally ruined!
He measures out the allotted land
of my people.
How he removes it from me!
He allots our fields to traitors."

⁵ Therefore, there will be no one
in the assembly of the LORD
to divide the land by casting lots.ᴬ

God's Word Rejected

⁶ "Quit your preaching," theyᴮ preach.
"They should not preach these things;
shame will not overtake us."ᶜ

⁷ House of Jacob, should it be asked,
"Is the Spirit of the LORD impatient?
Are these the things he does?"
Don't my words bring good
to the one who walks uprightly?

⁸ But recently my people have risen up
like an enemy:
You strip off the splendid robe
from those who are
passing through confidently,
like those returning from war.

⁹ You force the women of my people
out of their comfortable homes,
and you take my blessingᴰ
from their children forever.

¹⁰ Get up and leave,
for this is not your place of rest

because defilement
brings destruction —
a grievous destruction!

¹¹ If a man comes
and utters empty lies —
"I will preach to you about wine
and beer" —
he would be just the preacher
for this people!

The Remnant Regathered

¹² I will indeed gather all of you, Jacob;
I will collect the remnant of Israel.
I will bring them together like sheep
in a pen,
like a flock in the middle
of its pasture.
It will be noisy with people.

¹³ One who breaks open the way
will advance before them;
they will break out, pass
through the city gate,
and leave by it.
Their King will pass through
before them,
the LORD as their leader.

Unjust Leaders Judged

3 Then I said, "Now listen,
leaders of Jacob,
you rulers of the house of Israel.
Aren't you supposed to know
what is just?

² You hate good and love evil.
You tear off people's skin
and strip their flesh
from their bones.

³ You eat the flesh of my people
after you strip their skin from them
and break their bones.
You chop them up
like flesh for the cooking pot,
like meat in a cauldron."

⁴ Then they will cry out to the LORD,
but he will not answer them.
He will hide his face from them
at that time
because of the crimes
they have committed.

ᴬ2:5 Lit LORD stretching the measuring line by lot   ᴮ2:6 = the prophets   ᶜ2:6 Text emended; MT reads *things. Shame will not depart*   ᴰ2:9 Perhaps *the land*

2:1–5 Micah pronounced a "woe oracle" against wealthy men who devised wicked schemes to seize houses and lands from the weak. God's law prohibited such acts, even in cases where it was deemed legal (Lv 19:13). Thus the Lord was **planning a disaster** against this corrupt nation. Their own lands would be seized by the Assyrians. No one would be left **to divide the land by casting lots**, as in the time of Joshua (Jos 14:2; 18:8,10).
2:6–7 Popular false prophets rejected Micah's message of God's judgment. They

told him to **quit your preaching**, because **shame will not overtake us**. Focusing only on God's love and patience, they lost sight of God's holiness and judgment (Ex 34:6–7).
2:8–11 Greedy oppressors were **an enemy** of the people, attacking innocent passers-by, evicting **women** from their **homes**, and taking from them God's material **blessing**. God ordered these oppressors to **get up and leave**, a reference to the exile. With intense sarcasm Micah said the people deserved the false prophecy they received.

2:12–13 Micah promised salvation beyond the judgment for a righteous remnant.
3:1–12 In this chapter Micah declared that corrupt rulers, prophets, and priests plagued God's people. Political and judicial leaders perverted justice, and the spiritual leaders perverted God's word.
3:1–4 Leaders should be **just**. Instead, Micah saw rulers who hated **good** and loved **evil**. He described their sin in cannibalistic terms (**you eat the flesh of my people**), for such is the impact of false teaching about God. Because they offered no justice to others,

False Prophets Judged

5 This is what the LORD says
concerning the prophets
who lead my people astray,
who proclaim peace
when they have food to sink
their teeth into
but declare war against the one
who puts nothing in their mouths.

6 Therefore, it will be night for you —
without visions;
it will grow dark for you —
without divination.
The sun will set on these prophets,
and the daylight will turn black
over them.

7 Then the seers will be ashamed
and the diviners disappointed.
They will all cover their mouths[A]
because there will be no answer
from God.

8 As for me, however, I am filled
with power
by the Spirit of the LORD,
with justice and courage,
to proclaim to Jacob his rebellion
and to Israel his sin.

Zion's Destruction

9 Listen to this, leaders of the house
of Jacob,
you rulers of the house of Israel,
who abhor justice
and pervert everything that is right,

10 who build Zion with bloodshed
and Jerusalem with injustice.

11 Her leaders issue rulings for a bribe,
her priests teach for payment,
and her prophets practice divination
for silver.
Yet they lean on the LORD, saying,
"Isn't the LORD among us?
No disaster will overtake us."

12 Therefore, because of you,
Zion will be plowed like a field,

Jerusalem will become ruins,
and the temple's mountain
will be a high thicket.

The LORD's Rule from Restored Zion

4 In the last days
the mountain of the LORD's house
will be established
at the top of the mountains
and will be raised above the hills.
Peoples will stream to it,

2 and many nations will come and say,
"Come, let's go up to the mountain
of the LORD,
to the house of the God of Jacob.
He will teach us about his ways
so we may walk in his paths."
For instruction will go out of Zion
and the word of the LORD
from Jerusalem.

3 He will settle disputes
among many peoples
and provide arbitration for strong nations
that are far away.
They will beat their swords into plows
and their spears into pruning knives.
Nation will not take up the sword
against nation,
and they will never again train for war.

4 But each person will sit
under his grapevine
and under his fig tree
with no one to frighten him.
For the mouth of the LORD of Armies
has spoken.

5 Though all the peoples walk
in the name of their own gods,
we will walk in the name of the
LORD our God
forever and ever.

6 On that day —
this is the LORD's declaration —
I will assemble the lame
and gather the scattered,
those I have injured.

[A] 3:7 Lit mustache

---

they would find no solace in the Lord, who would **hide his face from them** (see Dt 31:17).
3:8 But God had left a faithful witness distinctly different from the false prophets. Empowered by **the Spirit of the LORD**, Micah had a powerful voice of **justice** (see Is 58:1–2). He preached about **rebellion** and **sin** (cp. Mc 1:5,13), dealing with issues that would not be resolved until God's people confessed and abandoned their sin.
3:9–11 The corrupt leaders were known to **abhor justice** and **pervert everything that is right**. They were guilty of **bloodshed** and **injustice**, influenced by **a bribe** . . . **payment**, and **silver**.
3:12 Micah's sermon spurred King Hezekiah's reform (Jr 26:17–19; cp. 2Kg 18:1–6; 2Ch

29:1–31:21) and helped save Jeremiah's life a century later (Jr 26:7–19).
4:1–5:15 This central section portrays Yahweh establishing himself as the true ruler over his people and all nations. He would replace Israel's wicked rulers with his own ruler, who would bring God's reign and peace to the world (5:4–5a).
4:1–4 This oracle (also in Is 2:1–4) refers to **the last days** when God's kingdom will be established. The temple mount, representing God's dwelling on earth, though previously destroyed (3:12), would **be established at the top of the mountains**, and God would exalt himself among the nations (Ps 46:10). Many peoples will be drawn to him saying, **Come, let's go up to the mountain of the LORD.** They will want to learn **his**

ways, and they will be changed by the truth of his **instruction** (Hb *torah*). God himself will bring peace between **peoples** and **nations**, causing bloodshed to end (3:10) and instruments of death to be remade into implements promoting life. Nations will **never again train for war**. Peace and security are certain because **the mouth of the LORD of Armies has spoken**.
4:5 Though outnumbered by unbelievers, faithful worshipers promised to **walk in the name of the LORD our God forever**. Looking in hope, they would always follow his leadership, trusting him to work out his plan in history.
4:6–8 Though they had been **injured** by God's judgment, God would also **gather** his **lame** and **scattered** people once more. From

⁷ I will make the lame into a remnant,
   those far removed into a strong nation.
   Then the LORD will reign over them
      in Mount Zion
   from this time on and forever.
⁸ And you, watchtower for the flock,
   fortified hillᴬ of Daughter Zion,
   the former rule will come to you;
   sovereignty will come
      to Daughter Jerusalem.

From Exile to Victory

⁹ Now, why are you shouting loudly?
   Is there no king with you?
   Has your counselor perished
   so that anguish grips you like a woman
      in labor?
¹⁰ Writhe and cry out,ᴮ Daughter Zion,
   like a woman in labor,
   for now you will leave the city
   and camp in the open fields.
   You will go to Babylon;
   there you will be rescued;
   there the LORD will redeem you
   from the grasp of your enemies!
¹¹ Many nations have now assembled
      against you;
   they say, "Let her be defiled,
   and let us feast our eyes on Zion."
¹² But they do not know
      the LORD's intentions
   or understand his plan,
   that he has gathered them
   like sheaves to the threshing floor.
¹³ Rise and thresh, Daughter Zion,
   for I will make your horns iron
   and your hooves bronze

so you can crush many peoples.
   Then youᶜ will set apart their plunder
      for the LORD,
   their wealth for the Lord of the
      whole earth.

From Defeated Ruler to Conquering King

5 Now, daughter who is under attack,
   you slash yourself in grief;
   a siege is set against us!
   They are striking the judge of Israel
   on the cheek with a rod.
² Bethlehem Ephrathah,
   you are small among the clans of Judah;
   one will come from you
   to be ruler over Israel for me.
   His originᴰ is from antiquity,
   from ancient times.
³ Therefore, Israel will be abandoned
      until the time
   when she who is in labor
      has given birth;
   then the rest of the ruler's brothers
      will return
   to the people of Israel.
⁴ He will stand and shepherd them
   in the strength of the LORD,
   in the majestic name of the LORD
      his God.
   They will live securely,
   for then his greatness will extend
   to the ends of the earth.
⁵ He will be their peace.
   When Assyria invades our land,
   when it marches against our fortresses,
   we will raise against it seven shepherds,
   even eight leaders of men.

ᴬ4:8 Or *flock, Ophel* ᴮ4:10 Hb obscure ᶜ4:13 LXX, Syr, Tg; MT reads *I* ᴰ5:2 Lit *His going out*

---

this godly **remnant** he would build **a strong nation**. Thus God's people could expect to suffer before being redeemed. He **will reign over them . . . forever**. The greatness of the Davidic Empire in the past would return once more to *Migdal-eder* (**watchtower for the flock**), a location near Bethlehem (Gn 35:19–21).

4:9–10 But first (**now**) the people must face God's judgment. Zion's inhabitants were **shouting loudly** and in **anguish** much like **a woman in labor** before their enemies. They had forgotten the Lord, their **king** and **counselor** who would not abandon his people in their time of need. They would leave the city of Jerusalem, **camp in the open fields** on their way to exile, and go to **Babylon**. But God would not forget them, for they would be rescued and the Lord's power would **redeem** them.

4:11–5:1 Judah's oppressors did not **know** God's ultimate wisdom or **understand** the purpose of **his plan**. Yahweh had actually **gathered** these oppressors to be threshed like **sheaves** of grain. His sovereign power will make his weak and frail people into a mighty army who will **rise and thresh** God's enemies and glorify **the Lord of the whole earth**. But until that glorious day of

deliverance, Jerusalem would suffer **attack** and **siege** and her ruler would be utterly humiliated.

5:2–5a God would raise up another **ruler** from David's hometown of **Bethlehem Ephrathah** (Ru 4:11) who would be his servant (**for me**; cp. 1Sm 16:1). This "ruler" will extend God's kingdom **to the ends of the earth** (see Pss 2:8; 72:8) and bring God's "wholeness" or **peace** (Hb *shalom*) with his righteous reign (Is 9:6). His people will **live securely** in his kingdom. His **origin** (lit "goings out") will be **from antiquity**, and **from ancient times** (lit "from days long ago"). Both terms can refer just to a very long time ago, perhaps the beginnings of messianic prophecy (Gn 3:15; 12:3; 49:10, etc.), or to eternity (Ps 74:12; Pr 8:23; Hab 1:12, etc.). God had not forgotten his promise of granting an eternal kingship to David (2Sm 7:4–17). This coming Davidic ruler would appear **when she who is in labor has given birth**. Varying interpretations of this woman include: (1) the mother of Messiah (i.e., Mary); (2) Bethlehem, the birthplace of Messiah; (3) a righteous remnant bringing forth salvation; and (4) a historical reference to the upcoming exile (4:10). The exiles would go forth as from the womb into captivity

and **return** once more (v. 3). See Matthew's application of these verses (and 2Sm 5:2) to Jesus in Mt 2:6.

5:5b–9 People confident in their own strength believed that they could **raise** up

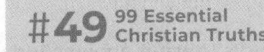

#49 99 Essential Christian Truths

CHRIST AS SUBSTITUTE

At the heart of the atonement is Jesus Christ substituting himself for sinners as he died on the cross. This truth is seen against the backdrop of the Old Testament sacrificial system, which provided a picture of humanity's need for sin to be covered and guilt to be removed by an innocent sacrifice. Jesus perfectly revealed and did the will of God, taking upon himself human nature with its demands and necessities and identifying himself completely with humankind yet without sin. He honored the divine law by his personal obedience, and in his substitutionary death on the cross, he made provision for the redemption of humanity from sin.

6 They will shepherd the land of Assyria
    with the sword,
    the land of Nimrod with a drawn blade.[A]
So he will rescue us from Assyria
    when it invades our land,
    when it marches against our territory.

The Glorious and Purified Remnant

7 Then the remnant of Jacob
    will be among many peoples
    like dew from the Lord,
    like showers on the grass,
    which do not wait for anyone
    or linger for mankind.

8 Then the remnant of Jacob
    will be among the nations,
      among many peoples,
    like a lion among animals of the forest,
    like a young lion among flocks of sheep,
    which tramples and tears
      as it passes through,
    and there is no one to rescue them.

9 Your hand will be lifted up
    against your adversaries,
    and all your enemies will be destroyed.

10 In that day —
    this is the Lord's declaration —
I will remove your horses from you
    and wreck your chariots.

11 I will remove the cities of your land
    and tear down all your fortresses.

12 I will remove sorceries from your hands,
    and you will not have
      any more fortune-tellers.

13 I will remove your carved images
    and sacred pillars from you
so that you will no longer worship
    the work of your hands.

14 I will pull up the Asherah poles
    from among you
and demolish your cities.[B]

15 I will take vengeance in anger and wrath
    against the nations that have not
      obeyed me.

God's Lawsuit against Judah

6 Now listen to what the Lord is saying:
    Rise, plead your case
      before the mountains,
    and let the hills hear
      your complaint.[C]

2 Listen to the Lord's lawsuit,
    you mountains
      and enduring foundations
      of the earth,
because the Lord has a case
    against his people,
and he will argue it against Israel.

3 My people, what have I done to you,
    or how have I wearied you?
Testify against me!

4 Indeed, I brought you up from the land
    of Egypt
and redeemed you from that place
    of slavery.
I sent Moses, Aaron, and Miriam
    ahead of you.

5 My people,
    remember what King
      Balak of Moab proposed,
what Balaam son of Beor
      answered him,
and what happened from
      the Acacia Grove[D] to Gilgal
so that you may acknowledge
    the Lord's righteous acts.

6 What should I bring
      before the Lord
when I come to bow before God
    on high?
Should I come before him
      with burnt offerings,
with year-old calves?

7 Would the Lord be pleased
    with thousands of rams
or with ten thousand streams of oil?
Should I give my firstborn
    for my transgression,
the offspring of my body
    for my own sin?

8 Mankind, he has told each of you
    what is good
and what it is the Lord requires
    of you:
to act justly,
to love faithfulness,
and to walk humbly with your God.

[A]5:6 Aq, Vg; MT, Sym read *Nimrod at its gateways*   [B]5:14 Or *shrines*   [C]6:1 Lit *voice*   [D]6:5 Or *from Shittim*

---

for themselves numerous **leaders** against their enemies, even ruling over **Assyria** and **Nimrod**, or Babylon. Micah asserted that only **he** [God's ruler] **will rescue us from Assyria**, not any human leaders. God would make the faithful **remnant . . . like dew** and rain **showers**, which are God-caused phenomena that humans cannot control (Jdg 6:36–40; Jb 38:28). People must not rely on human strength and initiative for their future but must instead trust in God's power and wait for him to act. He can make a feeble remnant become **like a**

young lion to execute judgment on their **enemies**.
5:10–15 God revealed how he would bring about eschatological peace. He would purge his people of anything that hindered their relationship with him—such as reliance on military might (vv. 10–11), divination (v. 12), and idolatry (vv. 13–14)—judging any nation that refused to submit to his rule (v. 15).
6:1–16 In this chapter Micah sealed God's indictment with a covenant lawsuit. He announced the case (vv. 1–2), defended God's benevolent actions (vv. 3–5), heard

a response from the people (vv. 6–7), reported the basis for God's judgment (v. 8), brought specific accusations (vv. 9–12), and pronounced God's verdict and punishment (vv. 13–16).
6:1–5 On v. 5, see Nm 24–25. Between **the Acacia Grove** (Nm 25:1) and **Gilgal** (Jos 4:19) was the beginning of the conquest.
6:8 The people already knew the **good** things that God required (see Pss 14:1,3; 37:3). They were to **act justly** under God's standards. They were to **love faithfulness**, treating one another with love and mercy. They were to

Verdict of Judgment

9 The voice of the Lord calls out
   to the city[A]
   (and it is wise to fear your name):
   "Pay attention to the rod
   and the one who ordained it.[B]

10 Are there still[C] the treasures
   of wickedness
   and the accursed short measure
   in the house of the wicked?

11 Can I excuse wicked scales
   or bags of deceptive weights?

12 For the wealthy of the city are full
   of violence,
   and its residents speak lies;
   the tongues in their mouths
   are deceitful.

13 "As a result, I have begun to strike
   you severely,[D]
   bringing desolation because of
   your sins.

14 You will eat but not be satisfied,
   for there will be hunger within you.
   What you acquire, you cannot save,
   and what you do save,
   I will give to the sword.[C]

15 You will sow but not reap;
   you will press olives
   but not anoint yourself with oil;
   and you will tread grapes
   but not drink the wine.

16 The statutes of Omri
   and all the practices of Ahab's house
   have been observed;
   you have followed their policies.
   Therefore, I will make you
   a desolate place
   and the city's[E] residents an object
   of contempt;[F]
   you will bear the scorn of my people."[G]

Israel's Moral Decline

7 How sad for me!
   For I am like one who —
   when the summer fruit
   has been gathered
   after the gleaning
   of the grape harvest —
   finds no grape cluster to eat,
   no early fig, which I crave.

2 Faithful people have vanished
   from the land;
   there is no one upright
   among the people.
   All of them wait in ambush
   to shed blood;
   they hunt each other with a net.

3 Both hands are good
   at accomplishing evil:
   the official and the judge demand
   a bribe;
   when the powerful man communicates
   his evil desire,
   they plot it together.

4 The best of them is like a brier;
   the most upright is worse than a hedge
   of thorns.
   The day of your watchmen,
   the day of your punishment, is coming;
   at this time their panic is here.

5 Do not rely on a friend;
   don't trust in a close companion.
   Seal your mouth
   from the woman who lies
   in your arms.

6 Surely a son considers his father a fool,
   a daughter opposes her mother,
   and a daughter-in-law is
   against her mother-in-law;
   a man's enemies are the men
   of his own household.

7 But I will look to the Lord;
   I will wait for the God of my salvation.
   My God will hear me.

Zion's Vindication

8 Do not rejoice over me, my enemy!
   Though I have fallen, I will stand up;
   though I sit in darkness,
   the Lord will be my light.

9 Because I have sinned against him,
   I must endure the Lord's fury
   until he champions my cause
   and establishes justice for me.
   He will bring me into the light;
   I will see his salvation.[H]

10 Then my enemy will see,
   and she will be covered with shame,
   the one who said to me,
   "Where is the Lord your God?"
   My eyes will look at her in triumph;

[A]6:9 = Jerusalem [B]6:9 Or attention, you tribe. Who has ordained it?; Hb obscure [C]6:10,14 Hb obscure [D]6:13 LXX, Aq,
Theod, Syr, Vg; MT reads I have made you sick by striking you down [E]6:16 Lit and its [F]6:16 Lit residents a hissing
[G]6:16 LXX reads of the peoples [H]7:9 Or righteousness

---

walk humbly with God as their constant
companion, conforming their lives to his will.
6:13–16 God's verdict of judgment for sins
is certain because they had followed the
example of the wicked and idolatrous kings
Omri and Ahab (see 1Kg 16:25–33).
7:1–6 As Micah's society disintegrated, he
found that no faithful or upright people
were left in the land, and the moral fabric

of society was decayed. Homes and family
relationships had disintegrated to the point
that no man could trust a friend or even his
wife. Children dishonored and rebelled against
their parents, making family members their
enemies. Jesus quoted Mc 7:6 in Mt 10:35–36
to describe the ramifications of his ministry.
7:8–20 In these verses, Micah's message looked past the coming defeat and

destruction (1:1–16) to the future day when the
Lord would reverse that judgment. Repentant
people would be raised again (7:8–9). Enemies
would be defeated and Israel would be rebuilt
(vv. 10–11). The exiles would be gathered (v.
12), and a new exodus would take place (v. 15).
Because of his promise to Abraham (v. 20), God
would forgive sinners who deserved no mercy
(vv. 18–19). God always keeps his promises.

at that time she will be trampled
like mud in the streets.

11 A day will come for rebuilding
    your walls;
  on that day your boundary
    will be extended.
12 On that day people will come to you
  from Assyria and the cities of Egypt,
  even from Egypt to the Euphrates River
  and from sea to sea
  and mountain to mountain.
13 Then the earth will become a wasteland
  because of its inhabitants
  and as a result of their actions.

Micah's Prayer Answered
14 Shepherd your people with your staff,
  the flock that is your possession.
  They live alone in a woodland
  surrounded by pastures.
  Let them graze in Bashan and Gilead
  as in ancient times.

15 I will perform miracles for them^A
  as in the days of your exodus
  from the land of Egypt.

16 Nations will see and be ashamed
  of^B all their power.
  They will put their hands
    over their mouths,
  and their ears will become deaf.
17 They will lick the dust like a snake;
  they will come trembling out of
    their hiding places
  like reptiles slithering on the ground.
  They will tremble in the presence of the
    LORD our God;
  they will stand in awe of you.

18 Who is a God like you,
  forgiving iniquity and passing
    over rebellion
  for the remnant of his inheritance?
  He does not hold on to his anger forever
  because he delights in faithful love.
19 He will again have compassion on us;
  he will vanquish our iniquities.
  You will cast all our^C sins
  into the depths of the sea.
20 You will show loyalty to Jacob
  and faithful love to Abraham,
  as you swore to our ancestors
  from days long ago.

^A 7:15 = Israel   ^B 7:16 Or ashamed in spite of   ^C 7:19 Some Hb mss, LXX, Syr, Vg; other Hb mss read their

7:18-20 Micah described God's forgiveness as **forgiving iniquity** from his sight and **passing over rebellion** as no longer relevant. God would **vanquish** their **iniquities** like a conqueror, and cast their **sins** into the **depths of the sea**. God will deal with people's sins completely.

◥ Introduction to Nahum

Circumstances of Writing

The presumed author, Nahum (1:1), is the only person with that name in the Old Testament. Like Jonah in the previous century, Nahum prophesied judgment upon Nineveh. The Ninevites in Jonah's time had repented (Jnh 3). But now that Nineveh's leaders had resumed their wicked actions, the Lord called Nahum to reaffirm his coming judgment. Ironically Nahum's Hebrew name means "comfort"— comfort for Judah (Nah 1:12–15) because its cruel overlord Assyria would be punished without any comforters (3:7). Except for the name of his hometown Elkosh (1:1), nothing certain is known about Nahum.

Two events circumscribe the earliest and latest possible dates for the composition of the book of Nahum: the capture and downfall of Thebes in about 663 BC and the announcements of Nineveh's certain destruction (1:1; 2:8; 3:7) which would happen in 612 BC. The book's emphasis on the fall of Thebes, seemingly a recent event, would favor a date shortly after 663 BC, during the reign of the notoriously wicked King Manasseh (ca 686–642 BC) and/or his evil son Amon (642–640 BC). Certainly Nahum 1:12 (Assyria was still "strong [at full strength] and numerous") suggests a time before the decline of that empire. This fits the reign of cruel Ashurbanipal (ca 668–627 BC) when Assyria was at the pinnacle of its power.

Contribution to the Bible

The book of Nahum provides a great view of a powerful, just God who maintains his absolute moral standards and offers hope to those who are despised and downtrodden. Nahum teaches us to trust God. Even when we despair of any help, we can know that God will stand with those who belong to him.

Structure

Nahum interweaved typical prophetic strands such as judgment songs against God's enemies (1:9–11,14; cp. 2:13; 3:5–7), a woe oracle or mock lament (3:1–7), salvation oracles for his people Judah (1:12–15), a victory hymn to Yahweh the divine warrior (1:2–8; see Ex 15; Ps 98), and a sarcastic "word vision" of imminent enemy invasion (Nah 2:1–10; see 3:2–3). He colored this literary tapestry with satirical "taunt songs" mocking Nineveh's soon-coming role reversal (2:11–12; 3:8–19; see 2:1–2; 3:4–5). He ridiculed Nineveh's practice of scattering of peoples to other nations by announcing that God's "scatterer" (2:1–2; 3:18–19) would pay her back in like manner. He taunted that her lion's lair of military booty would soon be looted (2:11–13). He also mocked her as a witch-prostitute condemned to appropriate punishment: nakedness exposed with shame (3:4–7).

Using psychological warfare (as the Assyrians had used against Judah), Nahum taunted Nineveh's dependence on allies and other supposed defenses (3:8–10; see Is 36:4–20). Esar-haddon, father of Ashurbanipal, had threatened King Manasseh of Judah in 672 BC with treaty curses from the gods if they rebelled. The Lord converted borrowed treaty terminology to reverse this curse on Judah. It would not be Judah but Assyria's military men

Nahum Timeline

800–705 BC

At a time the Assyrian Empire is in decline, God calls Jonah to go to Nineveh and preach repentance. This was likely during the reigns of Uzziah of Judah (**792–740**) and Jeroboam II of Israel (**793–753**). During its time of weakness, Assyria experiences two severe plagues (**765** and **759**) and a total eclipse (**763**). Nineveh repents in response to Jonah's preaching and is spared God's judgment. Assyria's Shalmaneser V besieges Samaria. **725–722** Samaria falls to Assyria's Sargon II; nearly 28,000 Israelites are sent into exile. **722**

705–675 BC

Sennacherib establishes Nineveh as the capital of the Assyrian Empire. **705–681** Sennacherib captures and devastates Judah, besieging but not capturing Jerusalem. **701** When Babylon rebels against Sennacherib, he destroys the city. **689** Sennacherib is murdered by his two sons, one of whom, Esar-haddon (**681–669**), succeeds him as king. **681** Esar-haddon immediately begins the rebuilding of Babylon, an act that wins the allegiance of the local populace.

who would become defenseless like women (Nah 3:13). The Assyrians' ravaging of the land like a swarming army of locusts (see Jl 1:4–12; 2:4–9) was evoked and modified to mock Nineveh's merchants and military personnel, comparing them to harmless locusts on a wall, easily frightened and scattered (Nah 3:15–18). The incurable disease threatened from their gods would boomerang and inflict Assyria instead (3:19).

Yahweh as the caring warrior who would bring vengeance on his enemies, especially Nineveh, to save Judah, forms the backbone of Nahum's purpose statement and also of the book's literary structure.

Outline

I. Prelude (1:1–10)
II. Nineveh's Destruction as Part of God's Plan (1:11–15)
   A. Deliverance of Judah (1:12–13,15)
   B. Judgment against Assyria (1:11,14)
III. Nineveh's Destruction to Be Complete (2:1–13)
   A. Successful siege (2:1–9)
   B. Despair of the people (2:10–13)
IV. Nineveh's Destruction the Result of Sin (3:1–18)
   A. Inevitability of judgment (3:1–4)
   B. National annihilation (3:5–18)
V. Postlude (3:19)

Key verse in Nahum

1:7   The LORD is good, a stronghold in a day of distress;
     he cares for those who take refuge in him.

675–610 BC

Nahum **(675–612)** prophesies that just as Assyria destroyed Thebes, Nineveh (Assyria's capital) will be destroyed.
Esar-haddon invades Egypt. **671**
Egypt rebels **(669)** and Esar-haddon's son, Ashurbanipal **(668–627)**, sets out to reconquer Egypt. **667**
Egypt rebels again, so Ashurbanipal destroys Thebes. **665**
Calah is destroyed and the combined armies of the Babylonians and the Medes lay siege to Nineveh. After two months, the city falls. **612**

610–600 BC

An Assyrian general claims the throne and rallies what is left of the Assyrian army in Haran. An alliance with Egypt brings a few troops to Assyria's aid, but as the Babylonians approach, Haran is abandoned. **610**
The last remnants of the battered Assyrian Empire, along with their recent Egyptian allies, are defeated at the battle of Carchemish, bringing the Assyrian Empire to an end. **605**

1 The pronouncement concerning Nineveh. The book of the vision of Nahum the Elkoshite.

God's Vengeance

² The LORD is a jealous and avenging God;
the LORD takes vengeance
and is fierce in^A wrath.
The LORD takes vengeance
against his foes;
he is furious with his enemies.
³ The LORD is slow to anger but great
in power;
the LORD will never leave
the guilty unpunished.
His path is in the whirlwind and storm,
and clouds are the dust beneath his feet.
⁴ He rebukes the sea and dries it up,
and he makes all the rivers run dry.
Bashan and Carmel wither;
even the flower of Lebanon withers.
⁵ The mountains quake before him,
and the hills melt;
the earth trembles^B,C at his presence —
the world and all who live in it.
⁶ Who can withstand his indignation?
Who can endure his burning anger?
His wrath is poured out like fire;
even rocks are shattered before him.

Destruction of Nineveh

⁷ The LORD is good,
a stronghold in a day of distress;
he cares for those who take refuge
in him.
⁸ But he will completely destroy Nineveh^D
with an overwhelming flood,

and he will chase his enemies
into darkness.
⁹ Whatever you^E plot against the LORD,
he will bring it to complete destruction;
oppression will not rise up
a second time.
¹⁰ For they will be consumed
like entangled thorns,
like the drink of a drunkard
and like straw that is fully dry.^F
¹¹ One has gone out from you,^G
who plots evil against the LORD,
and is a wicked counselor.

Promise of Judah's Deliverance

¹² This is what the LORD says:
Though they are strong^H
and numerous,
they will still be mowed down,
and he^I will pass away.
Though I have punished you,^J
I will punish you no longer.
¹³ For I will now break off his yoke
from you
and tear off your shackles.

The Assyrian King's Demise

¹⁴ The LORD has issued an order concerning you:
There will be no offspring
to carry on your name.^K
I will eliminate the carved idol
and cast image
from the house of your gods;
I will prepare your grave,
for you are contemptible.

---

^A 1:2 Lit *is a master of* ^B 1:5 Some emend to *earth is laid waste* ^C 1:5 Lit *lifts* ^D 1:8 Lit *her place* ^E 1:9 = Nineveh ^F 1:10 Hb obscure ^G 1:11 Possibly Nineveh ^H 1:12 Lit *intact* ^I 1:12 Either the king of Assyria or his army ^J 1:12 = Judah ^K 1:14 Lit *It will not be sown from your name any longer*

1:2–8 This is a victory hymn to the Lord.
1:2 Like a **jealous** (or zealous) husband, the Lord would tolerate no rivals for Israel's affection, whether other so-called gods (Ex 34:14–16) or foreign nations and their kings.
1:3 That God was **slow to anger but great in power** indicates his wrath was not that of a hot-tempered tyrant.

1:4 Bashan and Carmel **wither** (and even the **flower of Lebanon**) because of a severe drought, parching the most fertile lands in Palestine (Is 33:9)—from the east, Bashan in Transjordan, to the northwest borders of the storm god Baal's home territory near Mount Carmel and the Lebanon mountains. Bashan was famous for its lush pasturelands (Jr 50:19), fine cattle (Dt 32:14), and rich forests (Is 2:13; Ezk 27:6), and Carmel (lit "garden-land") was known for its verdant vegetation (Jr 50:19; Am 1:2).
1:5 Verse 5 compares the terrifying power of the Lord's anger to the experience of earthquakes and volcanoes that shake the earth.
1:6 Verse 6 provides a "so then" to the whole. If the Lord is a God of vengeance against his enemies, and if he is greater even than his creation, then **Who can withstand his indignation? Who can endure his burning anger?** The obvious answer is "No one." His wrath is like fire that is poured out and is so hot that it shatters the rocks.
1:7 Verse 7 is the first clue to the primary message the prophet has for Judah. By somewhat indirect means, Nahum is telling Judah to **take refuge** in their God. "Take

refuge" is one of the many expressions the OT has for faith.
1:9 The verse is spoken against the Assyrians.
1:11 The one who **plots evil against the Lord, and is a wicked counselor** may be any Assyrian ruler. Sennacherib had plotted evil, but his objective to destroy Jerusalem (ca 701 BC) was thwarted (2Kg 19:20–28,32–34).
1:12 **Strong** and **numerous** mean that a formidable army is in view. **You** in the last two lines refers to Judah.
1:13 The imagery of the **yoke** and **shackles** is a divine promise of release from Babylonian subjugation.
1:14 Whereas "you" and "your" in v. 13 are feminine singular referring to Judah, **you** and **your** in v. 14 are consistently masculine singular referring to Nineveh or its king. The first judgment is that the king's dynasty would end, and his reputation would be lost after his death (cp. Is 56:5; 66:22). The second judgment is that his idols and images would be removed from the temple (Zch 13:2), so that the Assyrian gods would no longer be worshiped and would be angry with him in the afterlife. The third judgment

¹⁵ Look to the mountains —
the feet of the herald,
who proclaims peace.
Celebrate your festivals, Judah;
fulfill your vows.
For the wicked one will never again
march through you;
he will be entirely wiped out.

Attack against Nineveh

2 One who scatters is coming up
against you.
Man the fortifications!
Watch the road!
BraceᴬΩΩ yourself!
Summon all your strength!

² For the Lᴏʀᴅ will restore the majesty
of Jacob,
yes,ᴮ the majesty of Israel,
though ravagers have ravaged them
and ruined their vine branches.

³ The shields of hisᶜ warriors
are dyed red;
the valiant men are dressed in scarlet.
The fittings of the chariot flash
like fire
on the day of its battle preparations,
and the spears are brandished.

⁴ The chariots dash madly
through the streets;
they rush around in the plazas.
They look like torches;
they dart back and forth like lightning.

⁵ He gives orders to his officers;
they stumble as they advance.
They race to its wall;
the protective shield is set in place.

⁶ The river gates are opened,
and the palace erodes away.

⁷ Beautyᴰ is stripped;ᴱ
she is carried away;
her ladies-in-waiting moan
like the sound of doves
and beat their breasts.

⁸ Nineveh has been like a pool of water
from her first days,ᴱ
but they are fleeing.

"Stop! Stop!" they cry,
but no one turns back.

⁹ "Plunder the silver! Plunder the gold!"
There is no end to the treasure,
an abundance
of every precious thing.

¹⁰ Desolation, decimation, devastation!
Hearts melt,
knees tremble,
insides churn,
every face grows pale!

¹¹ Where is the lions' lair,
or the feeding ground
of the young lions,
where the lion and lioness prowled,
and the lion's cub,
with nothing to frighten them away?

¹² The lion mauled whatever
its cubs needed
and strangled prey for its lionesses.
It filled up its dens with the kill,
and its lairs with mauled prey.

¹³ Beware, I am against you.
This is the declaration of the Lᴏʀᴅ
of Armies.
I will make your chariots go up
in smoke,ᶠ
and the sword will devour
your young lions.
I will cut off your prey from the earth,
and the sound of your messengers
will never be heard again.

Nineveh's Downfall

3 Woe to the city of blood,
totally deceitful,
full of plunder,
never without prey.

² The crack of the whip
and rumble of the wheel,
galloping horse
and jolting chariot!

³ Charging horseman,
flashing sword,
shining spear;
heaps of slain,
mounds of corpses,
dead bodies without end —
they stumble over their dead.

ᴬ2:1 Lit *Strengthen*   ᴮ2:2 Or *like*   ᶜ2:3 = the army commander attacking Nineveh   ᴰ2:7 Text emended; MT reads *Huzzab*
ᴱ2:7,8 Hb obscure   ᶠ2:13 Lit *will burn her chariots in smoke*

---

may involve not only the king's death but also the desecration of his **grave**.
2:1 Nahum the "Watchman" mockingly begins to cheer the Assyrians on as they prepared for siege warfare (3:14).
2:2 This verse gives the reason Nineveh is being attacked. It is because the Lord is restoring the majesty of Jacob/Israel, which requires Nineveh's destruction.
2:3–10 To heighten the suspense and surprise, **shields of his warriors . . . dyed red** and **valiant men . . . dressed in scarlet**

initiate an intentionally ambiguous description of the battle's outcome. Were these uniforms dyed red or were they spattered with blood? Not until v. 8 is it clear that **Nineveh** is the defeated party, whose **hearts** would **melt** with fear.
2:11–13 The **lions' lair** with **lion** and **lioness** plays on two lion motifs commonly employed by Assyrian kings. The kings described themselves as "lions" crushing their enemies. Ashurbanipal often portrayed himself killing literal lions single-handedly, with a weapon

or even bare-handed. Ironically reversing this imagery, the Lord mocked Nineveh, the once-mighty lion who preyed on its enemies. Now Nineveh was being hunted and made prey. Its **young lions** (warriors) would be killed in battle.
3:1–3 Again, the author is initially vague (cp. note at 2:3–10) about the identity of the bloody city with its **mounds of corpses**, but the attentive reader knows that it is Nineveh, the once-formidable city, which God will now devastate.

4 Because of the continual prostitution
     of the prostitute,
  the attractive mistress of sorcery,
  who treats nations
     and clans like merchandise
  by her prostitution and sorcery,
5 I am against you.
     This is the declaration of the LORD
     of Armies.
  I will lift your skirts over your face
  and display your nakedness to nations,
     your shame to kingdoms.
6 I will throw filth on you
  and treat you with contempt;
  I will make a spectacle of you.
7 Then all who see you will recoil
     from you, saying,
  "Nineveh is devastated;
  who will show sympathy to her?"
  Where can I find anyone
     to comfort you?

8 Are you better than Thebes[A]
  that sat along the Nile
  with water surrounding her,
  whose rampart was the sea,
  the river[B,C] her wall?
9 Cush and Egypt were her endless source
     of strength;
  Put and Libya were among her[D] allies.
10 Yet she became an exile;
  she went into captivity.
  Her children were also dashed to pieces
  at the head of every street.
  They cast lots for her dignitaries,
  and all her nobles were bound in chains.
11 You[E] also will become drunk;
  you will hide.[F]
  You also will seek refuge
     from the enemy.

12 All your fortresses are fig trees
  with figs that ripened first;

  when shaken, they fall—
  right into the mouth of the eater!

13 Look, your troops are like women
     among you;
  your land's city gates
  are wide open to your enemies.
  Fire will devour the bars of your gates.
14 Draw water for the siege;
  strengthen your fortresses.
  Step into the clay and tread the mortar;
  take hold of the brick-mold!
15 The fire will devour you there;
  the sword will cut you down.
  It will devour you like the young locust.
  Multiply yourselves
     like the young locust;
  multiply like the swarming locust!
16 You have made your merchants
  more numerous than the stars
     of the sky.
  The young locust strips[G] the land
  and flies away.
17 Your court officials are
     like the swarming locust,
  and your scribes like clouds of locusts,
  which settle on the walls on a cold day;
  when the sun rises, they take off,
  and no one knows where they are.

18 King of Assyria,
     your shepherds slumber;
  your officers sleep.
  Your people are scattered
     across the mountains
  with no one to gather them together.
19 There is no remedy for your injury;
  your wound is severe.
  All who hear the news about you
  will clap their hands because of you,
  for who has not experienced
  your constant cruelty?

A 3:8 Hb No-amon   B 3:8 LXX, Syr, Vg read water   C 3:8 Lit sea from sea   D 3:9 Lit your   E 3:11 = Nineveh   F 3:11 Or will be overcome   G 3:16 Or sheds its skin

---

3:4–6 On a prostitute's punishment, compare Jr 13:26.
3:7 Their motive to **recoil** is now clearly not fright but rather horror and amazement.
3:8–9 Thebes, located about 400 miles south of the Mediterranean at modern Karnak and Luxor, spanned both sides of the Nile River. It became a prominent city during the Sixth Dynasty, about 2200 BC. By the Twelfth Dynasty (ca 1990–1776 BC) its temple to Amon-Re was one of the most important temples in Egypt, and its god was called "King of the Gods, and who is over the Two Lands." During the New Kingdom era (1550–1076 BC) Thebes reached even greater heights of influence and was noted as the burial city of kings, in the Valley of the Kings. Many temples were built there to Egyptian gods. It continued to be a major city until it was sacked by Ashurbanipal and the Assyrians in 663 BC.

3:10 The Egyptian **children** were **dashed to pieces** by the Assyrians, just as Assyria had recently done to Israel in fulfillment of Hs 13:16 (cp. Ps 137:9; Hs 10:14–15). The atrocities included ripping pregnant women open. Such cruelty was not unique to the Assyrians (see note at vv. 18–19); other invading armies did similar things (see 2Kg 8:12; Is 13:16).
3:11–12 Drunkenness is found several times referring to judgment on God's enemies. The message of v. 12 is that regardless how secure and invincible Nineveh felt itself to be, before the Lord's forces they were as exposed and vulnerable as figs on a ripe fig tree.
3:13 Assyria's troops, known for their ruthless efficiency and skill, are called **women**. This is a common curse in the ancient Near East. See Is 19:16.
3:14 This verse contains ironic or rhetorical exhortations to prepare for the coming siege.

3:15–17 Under Ashurbanipal western Asia was dominated by a single political rule. Locusts are known for appearing and then leaving as quickly as they arrive. Nahum alludes to this characteristic in v. 17. And this is what God is going to cause to happen to the Assyrians.
3:18–19 These final verses are addressed to Nineveh's king regarding his impending death, which will bring celebration. As attested in the Babylonian Chronicle, between 615 and 612 BC the major cities of Assyria were annihilated: Kalah, Assur, Dur-Sharrukin, and Nineveh. Ashurballit II (612–609 BC) set himself up as king and regrouped his forces at Haran. But the Babylonians under Nebuchadnezzar crushed them at the battle of Carchemish in 605 BC.

◤ Introduction to Habakkuk

Circumstances of Writing

Habakkuk is not mentioned anywhere else in the Bible. His name is thought to derive from the Hebrew word *chabaq*, "to embrace," but its form appears non-Hebraic. More likely, the name is related to *habbaququ*, a word found in the related Semitic language of Akkadian. It denotes a species of garden plant or fruit tree.

Habakkuk predicted the invasion of Judah by the Chaldeans (1:6). The term *Chaldean* (Hb *kasdim*; Akk *kaldu*) was originally used of an ethnic group that appeared in southern Babylonia in the ninth century BC. In the eighth century BC, Chaldeans began to rise to power in Babylon. By the time of Habakkuk, *Chaldean* had come to be a synonym for "Babylonian."

These world events came to affect Judah. Pharaoh Neco of Egypt passed through Palestine in an attempt to support the remnant of the Assyrians in northern Syria against Babylon. The godly King Josiah confronted him at Megiddo but was killed by Neco in 609 BC. Judah then fell into the hands of Egypt from 609 to 605 BC.

Judah's fortunes changed again when Nebuchadnezzar II defeated Neco at the battle of Carchemish (May/June 605 BC) and succeeded his father on the throne of Babylon in September of that year. The Babylonian army pursued Neco back to Egypt. This led to Judah falling under control of the Babylonians by 604 BC.

Habakkuk predicted the Chaldean devastation of Judah (1:5–11), but that does not seem to have been fulfilled by the relatively bloodless Babylonian occupation in 604 BC. But when Jehoiakim, whom Neco had placed on Judah's throne in 609 BC, rebelled against Babylon in roughly 600 BC, Nebuchadnezzar eventually invaded the land and besieged Jerusalem from 598 to 597 BC. This led to Jehoiakim being deposed and killed in 598 and his son Jehoiachin going into Babylonian exile in 597. The last king of Judah, Zedekiah, brought even more devastation upon Judah by rebelling against Babylon in 588 BC. When Judah fell to the Babylonians in August of 587 or 586 BC, Nebuchadnezzar devastated Jerusalem and destroyed the temple. And yet as Habakkuk predicted (2:6–20), Babylon had its own day of reckoning in 539 BC when Cyrus of Persia conquered it.

These historical events help us to attach a date to the book of Habakkuk. Habakkuk probably wrote his prophecy during the time of trouble after the death of King Josiah of Judah in 609 BC but before the devastations of Judah in 598/597 BC and 587/586 BC by the Chaldeans. That places the prophecy during the reign of Jehoiakim (ca 609–599 BC), probably in the period of Egyptian domination before Babylon invaded Judah (609–605 BC).

Contribution to the Bible

The book of Habakkuk looks at an issue that often confronts people: trying to discern God's purposes in the midst of this world. There is a realization of the will of God for this world. This truth is seen throughout the Scripture: God's promises to Abraham; God's desire for us to have life abundantly; and God's will for a human community of joy, security, and righteousness. We ultimately triumph in the world and live abundantly only through faith. Habakkuk's message that the righteous will live by faith prepared the way for the greater understanding of this truth in the New Testament, which emphasizes salvation through faith in Christ (Rm 1:17; Gl 3:11; Heb 10:38–39).

Structure

The first two chapters consist of a dialogue between the prophet and God. Habakkuk first complained of injustice in Judah (1:2–4). God responded by announcing that he was sending the Chaldeans to punish Judah (1:5–11). Habakkuk then complained about God's answer, arguing that it seemed unfair for God to use the more wicked Babylonians to punish the less wicked Judeans (1:12–2:1). God responded that the Babylonians were indeed arrogant and would ultimately be punished; nonetheless, God would use the Babylonians just as he had determined (2:2–20). The final chapter consists of a psalm in which Habakkuk reflected on this dialogue with God.

Outline

I. Dialogue Between God and Habakkuk (1:1–2:20)
- A. Habakkuk's first complaint: injustice (1:1–4)
- B. God's first response: Chaldeans will invade (1:5–11)
- C. Habakkuk's second complaint: God seems unfair (1:12–2:1)
- D. God's second response: have faith, justice will prevail (2:2–20)

II. Habakkuk's Psalm (3:1–19)
- A. Habakkuk's fear (3:1)
- B. God's theophany (3:2–15)
- C. Habakkuk's faith (3:16–19)

1 The pronouncement that the prophet Habakkuk saw.

Habakkuk's First Prayer

2 How long, LORD, must I call for help
    and you do not listen
    or cry out to you about violence
    and you do not save?
3 Why do you force me to look
    at injustice?
Why do you tolerate^A wrongdoing?
Oppression and violence are right
    in front of me.
Strife is ongoing, and conflict escalates.
4 This is why the law is ineffective
    and justice never emerges.
For the wicked restrict the righteous;
    therefore, justice comes out perverted.

God's First Answer

5 Look at the nations^B and observe —
    be utterly astounded!
For I am doing something in your days
    that you will not believe
    when you hear about it.
6 Look! I am raising up the Chaldeans,^C

that bitter, impetuous nation
    that marches across
    the earth's open spaces
    to seize territories not its own.
7 They are fierce and terrifying;
    their views of justice and sovereignty
    stem from themselves.
8 Their horses are swifter than leopards
    and more fierce^D than wolves
    of the night.
Their horsemen charge ahead;
    their horsemen come
    from distant lands.
They fly like eagles,
    swooping to devour.
9 All of them come to do violence;
    their faces are set in determination.^E
They gather prisoners like sand.
10 They mock kings,
    and rulers are a joke to them.
They laugh at every fortress
    and build siege ramps to capture it.
11 Then they sweep by like the wind
    and pass through.
They are guilty;^F their strength
    is their god.

^A1:3 Lit observe, also in v. 13   ^B1:5 DSS, LXX, Syr read Look, you treacherous people   ^C1:6 = the Babylonians   ^D1:8 Or and quicker   ^E1:9 Hb obscure   ^F1:11 Or wind, and transgress and incur guilt

1:1 **Pronouncement** is a prophetic proclamation, literally a "lifting up [of voice]." "Burden" (KJV) is another meaning, though it does not fit the present context well.
1:2–4 Habakkuk lamented to God (**how long**?) about overt **violence . . . injustice**, and **oppression** during Jehoiakim's reign.

1:5–6 God responded that he would punish the sins of Judah through an invasion by the **Chaldeans** (the Babylonians).
1:8 Comparisons with predatory animals (**leopards . . . wolves**, and **eagles**) illustrate the speed, brutality, and efficiency of the Babylonian military machine.

1:9 **Violence** here and in v. 2 refers to violation of the rights of others. It could also be rendered "injustice," "oppression," or simply "lawlessness."
1:10–11 The mighty Babylonian army scoffed at all opposition. The phrase **their strength is their god** suggests they worshiped their

Q & A: Are There Contradictions in the Bible?

by Lenny Esposito

Skeptics say the Bible contains contradictions. If true, this would suggest it is not inspired by God since God is all knowing. However, close examination reveals that the Bible doesn't contain actual contradictions.

A writer is guilty of contradiction when two facts are affirmed that can't both possibly be true at the same time and in the same manner. But it is not always easy to establish that a writer is guilty of this. For example, it would seemingly be a contradiction to say, "The apple is red, and the apple is not red." But what if the author was referring to two different apples? Or perhaps he was referring to the skin first and then the pulp. Or maybe he described the apple over a span of time, from when it was ripe and red to when it was rotted and brown.

We need sufficient information before we can conclude that an actual contradiction is present, and writers sometimes don't supply more than bare details. We should presume innocence until guilt is proven. Those who claim the Bible contains contradictions must prove the statements in question could not be resolved by additional information. Here's a list of common Bible phenomena that are *not* contradictions or errors:

Different individuals reported at a location: Matthew reports only *one* angel at Jesus's tomb (Mt 28:2-7), while Luke reports two (Lk 24:4). But this is no more a contradiction than telling one friend, "I saw a movie last night," giving the impression that you went alone, while telling another, "My family and I went to the movies together," which indicates that you were not alone.

- *Applying modern definitions to ancient texts:* Critics highlight apparent mistakes in science in Scripture as a way of showing that the Bible contains errors (e.g., rabbits chewing cud, Dt 14:7), but it is only natural that ancient writers used terms and descriptions that were accepted in their era.

- *Misunderstanding popular idioms:* Idioms shouldn't be taken literally. For example, Jesus foretold that he'd be in the tomb three days (Mk 8:31). Technically, Friday at sundown to Sunday morning is not three whole days, but Jesus did not mean three days in the literal sense. Rather, he used a Hebrew idiom that counts any part of a day as the whole.

- *Differences in perspective:* The creation accounts in Genesis 1 and 2 are markedly different. Rather than indicating a contradiction, scholars note that Genesis 1 gives a broad overview of creation, while Genesis 2 focuses on the creation of humans during the sixth day.

- *Copying mistakes by a scribe:* In 2 Chronicles 9:25 we read that Solomon had four thousand horses, while 1 Kings 4:26 reports forty thousand. This is merely a copyist's error, not an original contradiction.

- *Different vantage points or details of the same event:* The accounts of Jesus's resurrection vary in theme and detail. Far from counting as contradictions that undermine confidence in Scripture, the differences indicate that the accounts are drawn from eyewitnesses who recounted the events they experienced.

Habakkuk's Second Prayer

12 Are you not from eternity,
     LORD my God?
   My Holy One, you^A will not die.
   LORD, you appointed them
     to execute judgment;
   my Rock, you destined them
     to punish us.
13 Your eyes are too pure to look on evil,
   and you cannot tolerate wrongdoing.
   So why do you tolerate those
     who are treacherous?
   Why are you silent
   while one^B who is wicked swallows up
   one^C who is more righteous
     than himself?
14 You have made mankind
   like the fish of the sea,
   like marine creatures that have no ruler.
15 The Chaldeans pull them all up
     with a hook,
   catch them in their dragnet,
   and gather them in their fishing net;
   that is why they are glad and rejoice.
16 That is why they sacrifice
     to their dragnet
   and burn incense to their fishing net,
   for by these things their portion is rich
   and their food plentiful.
17 Will they therefore empty their net
   and continually slaughter nations
     without mercy?

Habakkuk Waits for God's Response

2 I will stand at my guard post
   and station myself on the lookout tower.
   I will watch to see what he will say to me
   and what I should^D reply
     about my complaint.

God's Second Answer

2 The LORD answered me:
   Write down this vision;
   clearly inscribe it on tablets
   so one may easily read it.^E
3 For the vision is yet
   for the appointed time;

it testifies about the end and will not lie.
Though it delays, wait for it,
since it will certainly come and not
     be late.
4 Look, his ego is inflated;^F
   he is without integrity.
   But the righteous one will live
     by his faith.^G
5 Moreover, wine^H betrays;
   an arrogant man is never at rest.^I
   He enlarges his appetite like Sheol,
   and like Death he is never satisfied.
   He gathers all the nations to himself;
   he collects all the peoples for himself.

The Five Woe Oracles

6 Won't all of these take up a taunt
     against him,
   with mockery and riddles about him?
   They will say,
   "Woe to him who amasses
     what is not his —
   how much longer? —
   and loads himself with goods
     taken in pledge."
7 Won't your creditors suddenly arise,
   and those who disturb you wake up?
   Then you will become spoil for them.
8 Since you have plundered
     many nations,
   all the peoples who remain
     will plunder you —
   because of human bloodshed
   and violence against lands, cities,
   and all who live in them.

9 Woe to him who dishonestly makes
   wealth for his house^J
   to place his nest on high,
   to escape the grasp of disaster!
10 You have planned shame for your house
   by wiping out many peoples
   and sinning against your own self.
11 For the stones will cry out
     from the wall,
   and the rafters will answer them
   from the woodwork.

own military power (v. 16), though the verse
possibly means that they attributed their
strength to their national god Marduk (see
note at 2:18–20).
1:12 All manuscripts literally read "we will
not die" (see textual footnote) rather than
you will not die, but CSB follows a Jewish
tradition that says "you" was original.
1:13 Habakkuk complained that rewarding
the more wicked in order to punish the less
wicked seemed inconsistent with God's **pure**
goodness. As bad as the Jews were (see note
at vv. 2–4), they were **more righteous** than
the **wicked** Babylonian invaders.

1:14–16 Like fishermen who pull in a huge
catch of **fish** from **the sea** and as a result
begin worshiping their **net,** so Babylon captured hordes of people and thus worshiped
its own military strength (cp. v. 11).
2:1 Habakkuk braced himself for God's response. The Syriac translation (see textual
footnote) preserves another text for 2:1b:
"What he will reply about my reproof [of
him]."
2:4–5 The **arrogant** Babylonians were just
as wicked as Habakkuk supposed. Yet v. 4b
says **righteous** people such as Habakkuk
must exercise **faith** in God's goodness

despite his use of evil Babylon. Verse 4 conveys the central message of the book. The NT
cites it to show how the Christian life from
beginning to end is based on faith (Rm 1:17;
Gl 3:11; Heb 10:38).
2:6–8 Even though God used Babylon to
punish Judah, Babylon would not go unpunished. Five woes in conjunction with
taunt (or "proverb") are pronounced upon
them. Babylon's plunder from the **nations**
is like a debt from **creditors** that they must
eventually repay.
2:9–14 Babylon built its **house** (empire, v.
9) with stolen **stones** and its **rafters** from

¹² Woe to him who builds a city
    with bloodshed
    and founds a town with injustice!
¹³ Is it not from the LORD of Armies
    that the peoples labor only to fuel
      the fire
    and countries exhaust themselves
      for nothing?
¹⁴ For the earth will be filled
    with the knowledge of the LORD's glory,
    as the water covers the sea.

¹⁵ Woe to him who gives
    his neighbors drink,
    pouring out your wrathᴬ
    and even making them drunk,
    in order to look at their nakedness!
¹⁶ You will be filled with disgrace
    instead of glory.
    You also — drink,
    and expose your uncircumcision!ᴮ
    The cup in the LORD's right hand
    will come around to you,
    and utter disgrace will cover your glory.
¹⁷ For your violence against Lebanon
    will overwhelm you;
    the destruction of animals
      will terrify youᶜ
    because of your human bloodshed
      and violence
    against lands, cities, and all who live
      in them.

¹⁸ What use is a carved idol
    after its craftsman carves it?
    It is only a cast image, a teacher of lies.
    For the one who crafts its shape
      trusts in it
    and makes worthless idols
    that cannot speak.
¹⁹ Woe to him who says to wood: Wake up!
    or to mute stone: Come alive!

Can it teach?
    Look! It may be plated with gold
      and silver,
    yet there is no breath in it at all.

²⁰ But the LORD is in his holy temple;
    let the whole earth
    be silent in his presence.

Habakkuk's Third Prayer

3 A prayer of the prophet Habakkuk. According to *Shigionoth.*ᴰ
² LORD, I have heard the report
    about you;
    LORD, I stand in awe of your deeds.
    Revive your work in these years;
    make it known in these years.
    In your wrath remember mercy!

³ God comes from Teman,
    the Holy One from Mount Paran.   *Selah*
    His splendor covers the heavens,
    and the earth is full of his praise.
⁴ His brilliance is like light;
    rays are flashing from his hand.
    This is where his power is hidden.
⁵ Plague goes before him,
    and pestilence follows in his steps.
⁶ He stands and shakesᴱ the earth;
    he looks and startles the nations.
    The age-old mountains break apart;
    the ancient hills sink down.
    His pathways are ancient.
⁷ I see the tents of Cushanᶠ in distress;
    the tent curtains of the land
      of Midian tremble.
⁸ Are you angry at the rivers, LORD?
    Is your wrath against the rivers?
    Or is your fury against the sea
    when you ride on your horses,
    your victorious chariot?
⁹ You took the sheath from your bow;

ᴬ2:15 Or *venom*   ᴮ2:16 DSS, LXX, Aq, Syr, Vg read *and stagger*   ᶜ2:17 DSS, LXX, Aq, Syr, Tg, Vg; MT reads *them*   ᴰ3:1 Perhaps a passionate song with rapid changes of rhythm, or a dirge   ᴱ3:6 Or *surveys*   ᶠ3:7 = Midian

---

stolen lumber. This involved the **bloodshed** and **injustice** of slave labor. God in his **glory** would make it all **fuel** for the **fire** when Persia toppled Babylon in 539 BC.
2:15–17 Babylon's shameless perversity foisted upon its **neighbors** such as **Lebanon** (whose famous forests provided much of the stolen lumber of v. 11) would come back in

the form of **violence** against itself. By degrading and humiliating conquered peoples, the invaders sought to break their will and render them incapable of further resistance.
2:18–20 Though the Babylonians attributed their strength to their god Marduk (see note at 1:10–11), their god was only a lifeless **idol**, a piece of **wood** or **stone**, but the Lord lives and will have the last word. There is an allusion here (**Wake up! . . . Come alive!**) to Egyptian and Mesopotamian rituals that were used to consecrate new idols. Called the "opening of the mouth," these rituals were supposed to prepare the idol for habitation by the god.
3:1 The **prayer** of Hab 3 is a psalm to be sung to musical instruments and presented to a music director (v. 19). This psalm represents the prophet's response to God's message to him. The Hebrew word *shigionoth* refers to a type of song. Its precise meaning is unknown. "Dirge" is an educated guess.

3:2 The **report about you** (or "what you have reported") perhaps alludes to the revelation that God was punishing Judah through Babylon (1:5–11). God's coming **deeds** made Habakkuk **stand in awe** (lit "fear") and beg for **mercy**.
3:3–7 This vision portrays God marching north in power and wrath from the direction of Mount Sinai (**Teman** was in Edom to the south; **Paran** was in the wilderness of Sinai; Dt 33:2). God was casting lightning bolts (Hab 3:4) and was accompanied front and back by personified **plague** and **pestilence**. Earthquakes associated with God's presence terrorized bedouin peoples such as the **Cushan** and **Midian**.
3:8–15 The purpose of God's march was to subdue his people's enemies, who were symbolized by elements of nature. He will punish the **wicked** Babylonians and **save** his **people** and their **anointed** Davidic lineage.

#51 **99 Essential Christian Truths**

CHRIST AS PROPHET

As one of his offices, Jesus fulfills the role of prophet: He alone is the ultimate teacher and has the words of eternal life (Jn 6:68). Jesus is also God's ultimate revelation of himself, the very Word of God (Jn 1:1).

the arrows are ready^A to be used
with an oath.^B   *Selah*
You split the earth with rivers.
10 The mountains see you and shudder;
a downpour of water sweeps by.
The deep roars with its voice
and lifts its waves^c high.
11 Sun and moon stand still
in their lofty residence,
at the flash of your flying arrows,
at the brightness of your shining spear.
12 You march across the earth
with indignation;
you trample down the nations
in wrath.
13 You come out to save your people,
to save your anointed.^D
You crush the leader of the house
of the wicked
and strip him from foot^E to neck.   *Selah*
14 You pierce his head
with his own spears;
his warriors storm out to scatter us,
gloating as if ready to secretly devour
the weak.
15 You tread the sea with your horses,
stirring up the vast water.

Habakkuk's Confidence in God Expressed

16 I heard, and I trembled within;
my lips quivered at the sound.
Rottenness entered my bones;
I trembled where I stood.
Now I must quietly wait for the day
of distress
to come against the people
invading us.
17 Though the fig tree does not bud
and there is no fruit on the vines,
though the olive crop fails
and the fields produce no food,
though the flocks disappear
from the pen
and there are no herds in the stalls,
18 yet I will celebrate in the LORD;
I will rejoice in the God
of my salvation!
19 The LORD my Lord is my strength;
he makes my feet like those
of a deer
and enables me to walk
on mountain heights!
For the choir director: on^F stringed instruments.

^A3:9 Or *set* ^B3:9 Hb obscure ^c3:10 Lit *hands* ^D3:13 The Davidic king or the nation of Israel ^E3:13 Lit *foundation*
^F3:19 Lit *on my*

3:16 The Hebrew of v. 16b is ambiguous. Did the prophet await **the day of distress to come against the people invading us** (CSB) or "for the day of distress, for a people to come and attack us" (NJPS)? With the first rendering the prophet awaited a double distress: invasion of Judah and judgment on Babylon (vv. 13–15; 2:6–20). With the second rendering the focus is on the predicted Babylonian invasion (1:5–11). In either case, Habakkuk's feeling of dread (**my lips quivered . . . I trembled**) best relates to the invasion of Judah that must come first. **3:17–19** But come what may, the prophet will trust in God, finding his **strength** and sure footing through faith. The prophet applied to his own life the message of 2:4.

◥ Introduction to Zephaniah

Circumstances of Writing

Zephaniah's lengthy genealogy (1:1, four generations back to Hezekiah) suggests he was of royal lineage. Why list four generations (other prophets, at most, listed two generations; see Zch 1:1) unless this final name was significant? Perhaps because his father's name was Cushi, people tended to suspect that Zephaniah was of mixed ancestry, including Cushite bloodlines. In fact, Zephaniah twice mentions the Cushites/Cush (Ethiopians) in his short prophecy (2:12; 3:10), possibly suggesting his Cushite roots.

Internal evidence indicates the book of Zephaniah was written sometime between 640 and 612 BC. Zephaniah 1:1 refers to King Josiah's reign (ca 640–609 BC), and 2:13–15 prophesies Nineveh's fall. Since Nineveh fell in 612 BC, Zephaniah's prophecy would have been given prior to that time. Furthermore, existing idolatrous practices in Judah (1:4–6) imply Zephaniah's ministry began before Josiah's reforms in roughly 621 BC (2Kg 23).

King Josiah's father, King Amon (Zph 1:1), was a wicked man, as was his father before him, King Manasseh (2Kg 21:1–7,11,16,20–22). This heritage of wickedness helps explain the rampant idolatry in the land when Josiah inherited the throne in 640 BC. Josiah struggled to squelch idolatry in Judah (Zph 1:4–9). Together pagan and "orthodox priests" led worship of the Lord while also bowing before Baal, Molech, and other pagan gods (1:4–6). The public reading of the book of the law (ca 621 BC) helped spawn the reforms of Josiah as people repented and tore down the numerous altars (cp. Jr 11:13) and other idolatrous paraphernalia of Baal and Molech (2Kg 23:1–14; see Zph 1:3–4). This included abolishing the false priests (2Kg 23:5).

Contribution to the Bible

The promise of a remnant illustrates God's amazing grace counterbalancing his jealous wrath and blazing fury against the wicked (Nah 1:2–8). He would judge the proud nations (Zph 2:8–11,13–15) and purge the haughty braggarts from his people (3:11) to preserve the humble. Thus Zephaniah invited everyone who humbly obeyed the Lord to seek him for possible deliverance (2:2–3). The New Testament highlights the wonderful truth that all of us can find salvation through faith in Christ. Paul underscored the idea of the Jewish remnant and reminded us that the remnant is "chosen by grace," not by works (Rm 11:5–6).

Structure

"The word of the Lord [Yahweh]" (Zph 1:1a) and "the Lord [Yahweh] has spoken" (3:20b) frame the whole book of Zephaniah to emphasize crucial complementary messages: imminent, universal judgment (1:1–3:8) but

---

Zephaniah Timeline

800–725 BC

Amos is called to travel from Judah to Israel to prophesy in Samaria. **783**

Jonah is called to go to Nineveh and preach repentance.

Hosea's prophetic ministry **750–722?**

Micah begins his prophetic ministry. **750**

Assyria emerges from years of decline as Tiglath-pileser III invades Israel and other territories in the region. **745–727**

Isaiah is called to be a prophet. **740**

725–640 BC

Assyria's Shalmaneser V besieges Samaria. **725–722**

Samaria falls to Assyria's Sargon II, nearly 28,000 Israelites are sent into exile, and Gentiles from Assyrian-controlled territories are resettled into what was the northern kingdom. **722**

Third temple reform under Hezekiah **715**

Years of prophetic silence **(698–626)** in Judah coincide with some of Judah's darkest years under the rule of Manasseh **(697–642)** and Amon **(642–640)**.

eventual blessing for the remnant (3:9–20). The chiastic first section, interlaced by the reinforcing refrain "this is the LORD's declaration" (see 1:2–3,10a; 2:9a; 3:8a; cp. 2:5, "word of the LORD"), highlights an all-inclusive judgment.

Zephaniah 3:8 is a transitional exhortation that looks both backward ("therefore"; v. 8a) and forward (wait patiently for God to consummate judgment which will yield salvation for the remnant; vv. 9–13, introduced by Hb *ki*, "for/because" in vv. 9,11). To offer hope during judgment in 3:8–13 may synthesize two exhortations: 1:7 (hush/wait for the day of the Lord's "cutting off" the wicked) and 2:1–3 (pivotal invitation to seek him for possible salvation).

640–615 BC

Josiah is placed on Judah's throne at the age of eight when his father, Amon, is assassinated. **640**
Initial reforms of Josiah **631**
Zephaniah's years of prophecy range between **626** and **612**.
Jeremiah called to be a prophet; warns of invasion from the north **626**
The book of the law is found and read publicly, spurring additional reform under Josiah. **621**
Zephaniah and Nahum both prophesy the fall of Nineveh that occurred in **621**.

615–580 BC

With the fall of Nineveh, the Babylonian Empire succeeds the Assyrian Empire as the dominant force in the ancient Near East. **612**
Josiah killed in battle by Pharaoh Neco **609**
Habakkuk prophesies shortly before or after the battle at Carchemish (**605**) to point out what the growing Babylonian strength means for Judah.
Nebuchadnezzar attacks Jerusalem and leads citizens of Judah into exile. **605, 597, 586, 582**

1 The word of the LORD that came to Zephaniah son of Cushi, son of Gedaliah, son of Amariah, son of Hezekiah, in the days of Josiah son of Amon, king of Judah.

The Great Day of the LORD

2 I will completely
    sweep away everything
from the face of the earth —
    this is the LORD's declaration.
3 I will sweep away people and animals;
I will sweep away the birds of the sky
    and the fish of the sea,
and the ruins[A] along with the wicked.
I will cut off mankind
    from the face of the earth.
    This is the LORD's declaration.

4 I will stretch out my hand against Judah
and against all the residents of Jerusalem.
I will cut off every vestige of Baal
    from this place,
the names of the pagan priests
    along with the priests;
5 those who bow in worship
    on the rooftops
to the stars in the sky;
those who bow and pledge loyalty
    to the LORD
but also pledge loyalty to Milcom;[B]
6 and those who turn back
    from following the LORD,
who do not seek the LORD or inquire
    of him.

7 Be silent in the presence of the Lord GOD,
for the day of the LORD is near.
Indeed, the LORD has prepared
    a sacrifice;
he has consecrated his guests.

8 On the day of the LORD's sacrifice
I will punish the officials,
    the king's sons,

and all who are dressed
    in foreign clothing.
9 On that day I will punish
all who skip over the threshold,[C]
who fill their master's house
    with violence and deceit.

10 On that day —
    this is the LORD's declaration —
there will be an outcry
    from the Fish Gate,
a wailing from the Second District,
and a loud crashing from the hills.
11 Wail, you residents of the Hollow,[D]
for all the merchants[E] will be silenced;
all those loaded with silver will be
    cut off.

12 And at that time I will search Jerusalem
    with lamps
and punish
    those who settle down comfortably,[F]
who say to themselves:
The LORD will do nothing
    — good or bad.
13 Their wealth will become plunder
and their houses a ruin.
They will build houses but never live
    in them,
plant vineyards but never drink
    their wine.

14 The great day of the LORD is near,
near and rapidly approaching.
Listen, the day of the LORD —
    then the warrior's cry is bitter.
15 That day is a day of wrath,
a day of trouble and distress,
a day of destruction and desolation,
a day of darkness and gloom,
a day of clouds and total darkness,
16 a day of ram's horn and battle cry
against the fortified cities,

---

^1:3 Perhaps objects connected with idolatry   ^B1:5 Some LXX mss, Syr, Vg; MT, other LXX mss read *their king*
^C1:9 Hb obscure   ^D1:11 Or *the market district*   ^E1:11 Or *Canaanites*   ^F1:12 Lit *who thicken on their dregs*

1:2 The prophetic **declaration**, God **will completely sweep away everything** on **earth**, is hyperbole.
1:3 The judgment language is more comprehensive than Noah's flood (Gn 6:7, no fish mentioned). Here the creatures are listed in reverse order from Gn 1:20–28 (sea creatures, birds, beasts, and man). **The ruins along with the wicked** were apparently idol paraphernalia.
1:4 The Hebrew phrase meaning literally "stretch out the hand" occurs thirteen times in the Exodus narrative, all but one (Ex 7:5) with Moses or Aaron as the subject. Clearly this is not a call to repentance, but to an intervention of God that is comparable to the judgments on Egypt.
1:5 To **pledge loyalty to Milcom** involved religious syncretism, combining pseudo-worship of the Lord with worship of a false god.

Milcom was the Ammonite god (Jr 49:1–3), interchangeable with "Molech" (1Kg 11:7; Jr 32:35). Worship of this god apparently included child sacrifice. This worship continued Manasseh's pagan practices which Josiah would disrupt (2Kg 23:10–13).
1:6 To follow the Lord is to keep the statutes of the covenant, so to **turn back** is to desert the Lord and violate the covenant.
1:7–8 Verse 7 announces the coming of **the day of the LORD**. The proper response is reverential silence in his presence. The **sacrifice** the Lord has **prepared** refers to a slaughter, and the consecrated guests are the scavenger birds and wild animals, as in Ezk 39:17–18. The birds and animals represent the powers that will execute the judgment. The phrase **king's sons** is not likely to be taken literally since Josiah became king at age eight. It is probably a title for the king's council of

advisers. **Foreign clothing** may have referred to the vestments of Baal worship.
1:9 To **skip over the threshold** probably reflected a foreign, fearful superstition.
1:10–11 Verse 10 lists three sounds of destruction that will be heard in various parts of Jerusalem. **The Hollow** in v. 11 was apparently another district of the city, where the merchants did business. It was probably in what was later called the Tyropoeon Valley.
1:12–13 Verse 12 speaks of the Lord's meticulous search to punish men **who settle down comfortably**. The end of v. 13 quotes Dt 28:30b, which is one of the curses for refusing to follow the Lord's "commands and statutes" (Dt 28:15).
1:14 The **day of the LORD** was imminent (**near**, v. 7; cp. Is 13:6; Ezk 30:3; Jl 2:1; 3:14; Ob 15) and **rapidly approaching**. On this day God would judge Judah for its rampant

and against the high corner towers.
17 I will bring distress on mankind,
and they will walk like the blind
because they have sinned
against the LORD.
Their blood will be poured out like dust
and their flesh like dung.
18 Their silver and their gold
will be unable to rescue them
on the day of the LORD's wrath.
The whole earth will be consumed
by the fire of his jealousy,
for he will make a complete,
yes, a horrifying end
of all the inhabitants of the earth.

A Call to Repentance

2 Gather yourselves together;
gather together, undesirable[A] nation,
2 before the decree takes effect
and the day passes like chaff,
before the burning of the LORD's anger
overtakes you,
before the day of the LORD's anger
overtakes you.
3 Seek the LORD, all you humble
of the earth,
who carry out what he commands.
Seek righteousness, seek humility;
perhaps you will be concealed
on the day of the LORD's anger.

Judgment against the Nations

4 For Gaza will be abandoned,
and Ashkelon will become a ruin.
Ashdod will be driven out at noon,
and Ekron will be uprooted.

5 Woe, inhabitants of the seacoast,
nation of the Cherethites![B]
The word of the LORD is against you,
Canaan, land of the Philistines:
I will destroy you until there is
no one left.
6 The seacoast will become pasturelands
with caves for shepherds and pens
for sheep.
7 The coastland will belong
to the remnant of the house of Judah;
they will find pasture there.
They will lie down in the evening
among the houses of Ashkelon,
for the LORD their God will return
to them
and restore their fortunes.

8 I have heard the taunting of Moab
and the insults of the Ammonites,
who have taunted my people
and threatened their territory.
9 Therefore, as I live —
this is the declaration of the LORD
of Armies,
the God of Israel —
Moab will be like Sodom
and the Ammonites like Gomorrah:
a place overgrown with weeds,
a salt pit, and a perpetual wasteland.
The remnant of my people
will plunder them;
the remainder of my nation
will dispossess them.
10 This is what they get for their pride,
because they have taunted
and acted arrogantly

^A 2:1 Or shameless   ^B 2:5 = Sea Peoples

---

idolatry (vv. 4–7). The Lord's destruction of Judah by the Babylonians in 586 BC (Lm 2:1–3,22; 4:11) partially fulfilled this day of his burning anger (Zph 1:18; 2:2–3) as he punished them for abominable idolatries (1:4–11; cp. Ezk 7:8–11,14–21; 8:5–18). Ultimately all earthly inhabitants would be judged (Jl 3:1–2,12–16; Zph 1:2–3) and consumed by his fiery anger (vv. 17–18; 3:8; cp. 2Pt 3:10–12).
1:17 The judgment **walk like the blind** is based on Dt 28:28–29. Blindness represents ignorance of God, helplessness, and hopelessness.
1:18 When King Asa of Judah was threatened by Israel, he sent silver and gold to Aram to purchase deliverance (2Ch 16:1–3). When Ahaz king of Judah was threatened by the kings of Aram and Israel, he sent silver and gold to the king of Assyria to purchase deliverance (2Kg 16:7–9). King Jehoiakim of Judah gave silver and gold to Pharaoh Neco for deliverance (2Kg 23:35). But all the silver and gold in the earth will not be able to deliver anyone on the day of the Lord. Ezekiel 7:19 quotes Zephaniah.
2:1–2 The term for **gather** is related to the word for "straw, stubble." Judah has become an **undesirable nation**.
2:3 The triple occurrence of **seek** prescribes an antidote for idolatry and self-sufficiency—

humbly **seek the LORD** and **righteousness** (1:6b; cp. Am 5:14–15), while waiting on him to respond (Zph 3:8).
2:4 In the Hebrew of this verse, similar sounding words (**Gaza** and **abandoned**) and puns (**Ekron** and **uprooted**) eloquently expressed judgment upon four of the five Philistine cities (Am 1:6–9; cp. Zph 2:5).
2:5–6 The relationship between the Cherethites and the Philistines is unknown, but here the **nation** and **land** seem to be identical. See also Ezk 25:16.
2:7 Restore their fortunes is an OT technical formula (lit "restore the captivity") for total restoration, whether physical (cp. Jr 33:10–13) or spiritual (Ps 85:1–4; Jr 32:44; cp. Zph 3:20).
2:8–11 Unlike the previous prophecy of judgment against the Philistines, this prophecy gives reasons for the judgment. The prophecy against Moab and Ammon is in two parts. In vv. 8–9 the Lord speaks, and in v. 10–11 the prophet speaks. Each speech consists of an indictment (vv. 8,10) and what the Lord will do as a result (vv. 9,11). In v. 8 the Lord himself testifies to their **taunting** and their **insults** because he himself has **heard** them.
2:9 God's universal judgment (1:2–3,17–18) allowed for godly survivors—the **remnant of my people** or **my nation** (cp. Am 5:14–15;

9:8b). This remnant was primarily of Judah (Zph 2:7) and ultimately of all Israel (3:12–13). Remarkably, the two primary characteristics of this human remnant that was allowed to **plunder** enemies were meekness and humility (3:12). The Lord would give the godly remnant the territory of other nations (2:7,9), reversing the curse of Dt 28:62–66. He also promised to bless the eschatological remnant (Zph 3:14–17), including the lame and other outcasts (3:18–19; cp. Mc 4:6–7).

#52 **99 Essential Christian Truths**

LIFE AFTER DEATH

The Bible teaches that when a Christian dies, he or she immediately is with the Lord (Lk 23:43; 2Co 5:8). This is what some people call an intermediate state, given that the final state for believers takes place at the future resurrection (Rv 6:10–11). For those who are not in Christ, life after death results in being separated from Christ in a state of suffering, even though future judgment remains (Lk 16:19–31).

against the people of the Lord
of Armies.
11 The Lord will be terrifying to them
when he starves all the gods
of the earth.
Then all the distant coasts and islands
of the nations
will bow in worship to him,
each in its own place.

12 You Cushites will also be slain
by my sword.

13 He will also stretch out his hand
against the north
and destroy Assyria;
he will make Nineveh a desolate ruin,
dry as the desert.
14 Herds will lie down in the middle of it,
every kind of wild animal.^A
Both eagle owls^B and herons^C
will roost in the capitals of its pillars.
Their calls will sound^D from the window,
but devastation^E will be
on the threshold,
for he will expose the cedar work.^F
15 This is the jubilant city
that lives in security,
that says to herself:
I exist, and there is no one else.
What a desolation she has become,
a place for wild animals to lie down!
Everyone who passes by her
scoffs^G and shakes his fist.

Woe to Oppressive Jerusalem

3 Woe to the city that is rebellious^H
and defiled,
the oppressive city!
2 She has not obeyed;
she has not accepted discipline.
She has not trusted in the Lord;
she has not drawn near to her God.
3 The^I princes within her are
roaring lions;
her judges are wolves of the night,
which leave nothing for^J the morning.

4 Her prophets are reckless —
treacherous men.
Her priests profane the sanctuary;
they do violence to instruction.
5 The righteous Lord is in her;
he does no wrong.
He applies his justice morning
by morning;
he does not fail at dawn,
yet the one who does wrong
knows no shame.

6 I have cut off nations;
their corner towers are destroyed.
I have laid waste their streets,
with no one to pass through.
Their cities lie devastated,
without a person,
without an inhabitant.
7 I said: You will certainly fear me
and accept correction.
Then her dwelling place^K
would not be cut off
based on all that I had allocated
to her.
However, they became more corrupt
in all their actions.
8 Therefore, wait for me —
this is the Lord's declaration —
until the day I rise up for plunder.^L
For my decision is to gather nations,
to assemble kingdoms,
in order to pour out my indignation
on them,
all my burning anger;
for the whole earth will be consumed
by the fire of my jealousy.

Final Restoration Promised

9 For I will then restore
pure speech to the peoples
so that all of them may call
on the name of the Lord
and serve him with a single purpose.^M
10 From beyond the rivers of Cush
my supplicants, my dispersed people,
will bring an offering to me.

---

^A 2:14 Lit every wild animal of a nation ^B 2:14 Or the pelicans ^C 2:14 Or the hedgehogs ^D 2:14 Lit sing ^E 2:14 LXX, Vg read ravens ^F 2:14 Hb obscure ^G 2:15 Or hisses ^H 3:1 Or filthy ^I 3:3 Lit Her ^J 3:3 Or that had nothing to gnaw in ^K 3:7 LXX, Syr read her eyes ^L 3:8 LXX, Syr read for a witness; Vg reads up forever ^M 3:9 Lit with one shoulder

---

2:11 The phrase **starves all the gods** may indicate that the Lord will literally cut off sacrifices (food and drink) to the "gods" (cult statues) by destroying (cp. 1:4; Jr 50:2–3; 51:43–44,52–53) or converting their worshipers (Zph 3:9).
2:12–15 God's judgment will reach the south (v. 12) and the north (vv. 13–15).
2:13 The word **also** may indicate a connection with 1:4 where the Lord stretched out **his hand against** Judah and Jerusalem.
2:15 God will judge each **jubilant city** (Assyria, v. 15; Babylon, Is 47:8–10) that makes God-like claims such as **I exist, and there is no one else** (cp. Is 45:5–6,19,21).

3:1–2 Verses 1–8 repeatedly refer to **the city**, which is nowhere specified. That Jerusalem is the referent is clear from v. 5 that says "the righteous Lord is in her."
3:5 On **in her** (or "in her midst") cp. vv. 15,17.
3:6–7 **You will certainly fear me and accept correction** follows up v. 2, where Jerusalem neither "accepted discipline" nor "trusted in the Lord" (Pr 1:7; 3:5,7). It also follows logically after v. 6. What God did to **nations** was supposed to teach his people a lesson. But it did not.
3:8 The **fire of my jealousy** may incorporate two OT themes: (1) the Lord's fierce, jealous

judgment of Israel by covenant curses (Dt 29:20–21) because they ignored warnings against idol worship (Dt 29:16–18); and (2) his zeal or jealousy for his people (cp. Zch 8:2), resulting in fire upon his enemies (Is 26:11) during earth's universal judgment (Is 24) to bring salvation to the remnant (Zch 8:6–8).
3:9–10 The phrase **restore pure speech to the peoples** may reflect a reversal of the Babel motif (cp. Is 2:2–4; 19:18–25) or international worship without language barriers. But its meaning apparently also involves genuine worship of the Lord without deceit (Zph

11 On that day you^ will not be put
   to shame
because of everything you have done
in rebelling against me.
For then I will remove
from among you your jubilant,
   arrogant people,
and you will never again be haughty
on my holy mountain.

12 I will leave
a meek and humble people among you,
and they will take refuge in the name
   of the LORD.

13 The remnant of Israel will no longer
do wrong or tell lies;
a deceitful tongue will not be found
in their mouths.
They will pasture and lie down,
with nothing to make them afraid.

14 Sing for joy, Daughter Zion;
shout loudly, Israel!
Be glad and celebrate with all
   your heart,
Daughter Jerusalem!

15 The LORD has removed
   your punishment;
he has turned back your enemy.
The King of Israel, the LORD,
is among you;

you need no longer fear harm.

16 On that day it will be said to Jerusalem:
"Do not fear;
Zion, do not let your hands grow weak.

17 The LORD your God is among you,
a warrior who saves.
He will rejoice over you with gladness.
He will be quiet^B in his love.
He will delight in you with singing."

18 I will gather those
   who have been driven
from the appointed festivals;
they will be a tribute from you^C
and a reproach on her.^D

19 Yes, at that time
I will deal with all who oppress you.
I will save the lame and gather
   the outcasts;
I will make those
   who were disgraced
throughout the earth
receive praise and fame.

20 At that time I will bring you^E back,
yes, at the time I will gather you.
I will give you fame and praise
among all the peoples of the earth,
when I restore your fortunes
   before your eyes.
The LORD has spoken.

^3:11 = Israel   ^B 3:17 LXX, Syr read *He will renew you*   ^C 3:18 = Jerusalem   ^D 3:18 Hb obscure   ^E 3:20 = people of Israel

---

3:13–14; cp. Rv 14:5). Zephaniah 3:10 describes dispersed Israelites joining the nations in worship.
3:11 In v. 5 they had no shame because they had no conscience and no repentance. Here they have no shame because they are forgiven and purged of sin.

3:12–13 Pride had been at the base of Israel's sinfulness. Humility, then, is the preeminent characteristic of the righteous remnant, who are finally ready to seek **refuge** in the Lord's **name**. The key behavioral characteristic of the remnant is their truthfulness, and their reward is peace.

3:14–15 Verse 14 is a hymnic call to praise.
3:19–20 These verses describe seven things the Lord promises to do for his redeemed people.

▼ Introduction to Haggai

Circumstances of Writing

There is no statement that strictly identifies who wrote this book, but the words recorded are repeatedly connected to what God spoke to the prophet Haggai (1:1,3,13; 2:1,10,14,20).

In 587 BC, Nebuchadnezzar came to Jerusalem for the third time, this time destroying the walls, the temple, and the city (2Kg 25:8–21; Jr 39–40). Most of the people were taken into Babylonian captivity for seventy years (Jr 25:11–12; 29:10), although Jeremiah and a few survivors stayed in Jerusalem (Jr 41–43). God predicted through Isaiah that the strong king named Cyrus (Is 44:24–45:2) would defeat Babylon and her gods (Is 46–47). After the Persian King Cyrus defeated Babylon, he issued a decree in 538 BC that allowed the exiled nations in Babylon to return to their homelands (Ezr 1:1–4; Cyrus Cylinder). Sheshbazzar (Ezr 1:8–11) led about forty-three thousand Jewish pilgrims back to the state of Yehud (Judah) to rebuild the temple in Jerusalem (Ezr 2:64–65). In the seventh month, the governor Zerubbabel and the high priest Joshua led the people in building an altar to worship God (Ezr 3:1–7); in their second year, the people laid the foundation of the new temple (Ezr 3:8–10). But this effort was stopped for the next sixteen years because the Samaritan people who lived north of Jerusalem frustrated these rebuilding efforts, plus they hired lawyers to cause the Persian authorities to stop supporting the work on this temple (Ezr 4:1–5). This led to a period of great discouragement. Apathy set in because many of the hopes of the Jewish people were unfulfilled. The walls of the city were not repaired, the temple was not rebuilt, there was a famine in the land (Hg 2:9–11), and the people were still under Persian control. They could do nothing without the approval of Tattenai, the governor of the "region west of the Euphrates River," and his officials (Ezr 5:3–5). There seemed to be no way to move forward and rebuild the temple.

After the death of Cyrus, his son Cambyses became king (530–522 BC). He marched through Judah and conquered most of Egypt, but on his way home he died (possibly an assassination). A high army official named Darius took control of the Persian army, marched back to Babylon, defeated a rebel force led by Gaumata, and became king in 522 BC. Darius put down several revolts and then reformed the satrapy administrative system, with the result that by 520 BC the Persian Empire was at peace.

In the second year of Darius (520 BC; Hg 1:1; Ezr 4:24–5:2) when the conflict over political control of the empire was over, God directed Haggai to encourage the leaders in Jerusalem to rebuild the temple. When governor Tattenai heard about this rebuilding, he questioned the plan's legitimacy and wrote to Darius to find out whether the government was sanctioning this project (Ezr 5:3–17). Darius approved the rebuilding campaign and even supported it through the royal treasury, as was confirmed by the discovery of Cyrus's original decree in a palace at Ecbatana (Ezr 6:1–12). Consequently, the temple rebuilding was completed in four years (Ezr 6:15).

Haggai Timeline

605–540 BC

Babylonian campaign against Jerusalem begins; Daniel and others of Israelite nobility taken to Babylon **605**

A second deportation to Babylon includes the prophet Ezekiel. **597**

Nebuchadnezzar's siege of Jerusalem begins. **JANUARY, 588**

Jerusalem and the temple are destroyed by the Babylonians; a third wave of exiles taken to Babylon **586**

Cyrus, who ruled the Persian Empire from **559** to **530**, takes Babylon with little resistance. **539**

540–525 BC

Cyrus issues a decree allowing the Jews to return to Judah and rebuild the temple. **538**

Events in Ezra **538–457**

Second temple construction begins under Zerubbabel's and Joshua's leadership. **536**

Cyrus dies in battle and his son Cambyses succeeds him and rules from **530** to **522**.

Discouragement reinforced by opposition from transplanted people brings work on the temple to a halt. **526**

Darius succeeds Cambyses and rules from **522** to **486**.

Contribution to the Bible

Throughout the Bible, there is a call and a reminder to place God first. The period following the return from exile was no exception. Haggai's challenge was to call the postexilic community of Jews living in Jerusalem not simply to focus on their own creature comforts but to honor God. This commitment would be reflected in their work on the temple. Haggai's call was later reflected in the words of Jesus: "Seek first the kingdom of God and his righteousness, and all these things will be provided for you" (Mt 6:33).

Haggai's call for the people to get their priorities in order and place God first by rebuilding his temple was of great importance. For the people to return to this task was a sign of their priorities. It also showed that God was with the remnant and that his promises of restoration had begun to be fulfilled. Their obedience in this matter declared God's glory and thus brought him pleasure. It served to vindicate the Lord since the temple's destruction had disgraced the Lord's name. Finally, their obedience to Haggai's words served as a pledge of the new covenant and the messianic age. The restoration of the temple was a sign that God had not revoked his covenant with Levi or his covenant with David. He would provide cleansing and restoration through a glorious temple and a messianic ruler.

Structure

The book of Haggai contains four short confrontational speeches in chronological order that identify ways the leaders and people in Jerusalem should change their theological thinking and behavior. There is a logical progression in the structure. People must glorify God (1:1–15), stay committed to God's plans (2:1–9), please God by living holy lives (2:10–19), and serve him faithfully (2:20–23).

Outline

I. Reprimand and Call to Rebuild the House of God (1:1–15)
II. Reminder of the Lord's Presence and Future Glory of the Temple (2:1–9)
III. Religious Principles about Holiness and Uncleanness (2:10–19)
IV. Restoration of Davidic Line Promised (2:20–23)

525–520 BC

Haggai and Zechariah encourage the people to resume construction of the temple. **520–518**
Haggai's first message **AUGUST 29, 520**
Temple building resumes **SEPTEMBER 21, 520**
Haggai's second message **OCTOBER 17, 520**

520–515 BC

Haggai's third and fourth messages **DECEMBER 18, 520**
Zechariah's night visions **FEBRUARY 15, 519**
Temple completed **MARCH 12, 515**

Command to Rebuild the Temple

1 In the second year of King Darius,^ on the first day of the sixth month, the word of the LORD came through the prophet Haggai to Zerubbabel son of Shealtiel, the governor of Judah, and to Joshua son of Jehozadak, the high priest: ² "The LORD of Armies says this: These people say: The time has not come for the house of the LORD to be rebuilt." ³ The word of the LORD came through the prophet Haggai: ⁴ "Is it a time for you yourselves to live in your paneled houses, while this house^B lies in ruins?" ⁵ Now, the LORD of Armies says this: "Think carefully about^C your ways:
⁶ You have planted much
but harvested little.
You eat
but never have enough to be satisfied.
You drink
but never have enough to be happy.
You put on clothes
but never have enough to get warm.
The wage earner puts his wages
into a bag with a hole in it."

⁷ The LORD of Armies says this: "Think carefully about your ways. ⁸ Go up into the hills, bring down lumber, and build the house; and I will be pleased with it and be glorified," says the LORD. ⁹ "You expected much, but then it amounted to little. When you brought the harvest to your house, I ruined^D it. Why?" This is the declaration of the LORD of Armies. "Because my house still lies in ruins, while each of you is busy with his own house.

¹⁰ So on your account,^E
the skies have withheld the dew
and the land its crops.
¹¹ I have summoned a drought
on the fields and the hills,
on the grain, new wine, fresh oil,
and whatever the ground yields,
on people and animals,
and on all that your hands produce."

The People's Response

¹² Then Zerubbabel son of Shealtiel, the high priest Joshua son of Jehozadak, and the entire remnant of the people obeyed the LORD their God and the words of the prophet Haggai, because the LORD their God had sent him. So the people feared the LORD. ¹³ Then Haggai, the LORD's messenger, delivered the LORD's message to the people: "I am with you — this is the LORD's declaration." ¹⁴ The LORD roused the spirit of Zerubbabel son of Shealtiel, governor of Judah, the spirit of the high priest Joshua son of Jehozadak, and the spirit of all the remnant of the people. They began work on the house of the LORD of Armies, their God, ¹⁵ on the twenty-fourth day of the sixth month, in the second year of King Darius.

Encouragement and Promise

2 On the twenty-first day of the seventh month, the word of the LORD came through the prophet Haggai: ² "Speak to Zerubbabel son of Shealtiel, governor of Judah, to the high priest Joshua son of Jehozadak, and to

---

^1:1 King of Persia reigned 522–486 BC   ^1:4 = the temple   ^1:5 Lit *Place your heart on*, also in v. 7   ^1:9 Lit *blew on*
^1:10 Or *So above you*

1:1 The king named **Darius** is Darius I (522–486 BC), not the earlier Darius the Mede (Dn 5:31; 6:1,6,9) or the later Darius II Nothus (Neh 12:12). **Zerubbabel** is listed as the **governor** because under Persian control Judah had no Hebrew king. His father **Shealtiel** was the son of King Jehoiachin (1Ch 3:17). As leaders, Zerubbabel and **Joshua** ... **the high priest** (1Ch 6:14–15; Ezr 3:2) carried the responsibility of guiding the people, so **the word of the**

LORD was directed specifically to them. The date was August 29, 520 BC.
1:2 A common name for God in Haggai is **the LORD of Armies** (used 14 times). This title views God as the Divine Warrior in charge of the armies of heaven. The people were saying to each other **the time has not come** to finish the work of building God's temple.
1:3–4 Your paneled houses refers to the upper-income homes of Zerubbabel and Joshua. Their homes had expensive wood interior paneling to cover the ugly and uneven stones.
1:5 Think carefully about your ways (lit "set your heart on your ways") is a call for serious thinking on the decisions the people were making and what these choices say about their priorities.
1:6 You have planted much but harvested little indicates that God was not blessing the work of their hands.
1:7 A repetition of the expression in v. 5. Note it occurs again in 2:18.
1:8 God's desire was that the people **build the house** and give priority to worshiping God. Whatever one does, God should always **be pleased with it and be glorified** by it.
1:9 I ruined it (lit "I blew on it") explains why the people never had enough in v. 6.
1:10 The covenant curses in Dt 28:38–39 indicate that when God's covenant people

do not love and serve him, he will neither bless their crops nor send rain (Dt 28:23–24). Thus these problems were **on your account.**
1:12 When the leaders **obeyed** God, the people followed their example.
1:13 I am with you is a foundational promise that God gives to his people (cp. 2:4). Things may be tough at times, but God is always there to care for the people he loves.
1:15 In the second year of King Darius is sometimes connected with the date in 2:1 (the dating system in 1:1 and 2:10 includes the month and year). On the other hand, since 2:1 and 2:20 do not give the year, a shortened formula is an acceptable way of identifying a date. The people began the work on the temple twenty-three days after Haggai's first prophecy—September 21, 520 BC.
2:1 The twenty-first day of the seventh month was the last day of the Feast of Shelters in which the people celebrated the blessings of a good harvest and commemorated the time when their ancestors lived in tents during their wilderness wanderings (Lv 23:33–43; Nm 29:12–40; Dt 16:13–17). There was a large crowd gathered for this feast, so it was a good time to address many people. This was October 17, 520 BC.
2:2–3 Many had a negative attitude, saying this temple would be greatly inferior to Solomon's gold-covered temple (1Kg 6:2–35).

#53   99 Essential Christian Truths

INERRANCY OF SCRIPTURE

Inerrancy refers to the belief that Scripture is completely truthful, without any mixture of error, in all its teachings, no matter what subject it addresses. Believing Scripture to be inerrant does not preclude the biblical authors' inclusion of observations from a human observer, the use of round numbers, unusual grammatical constructions, or varying perspectives on a particular event. It does mean, however, that Scripture is an infallible guide to salvation and that it is truthful in all that it affirms (Mt 5:18; Jn 10:35; Ti 1:2; Heb 6:18).

the remnant of the people:³ 'Who is left among you who saw this house in its former glory? How does it look to you now? Doesn't it seem to you like nothing by comparison? ⁴ Even so, be strong, Zerubbabel — this is the LORD's declaration. Be strong, Joshua son of Jehozadak, high priest. Be strong, all you people of the land — this is the LORD's declaration. Work! For I am with you — the declaration of the LORD of Armies. ⁵ This is the promise I made to you when you came out of Egypt, and my Spirit is present among you; don't be afraid.' "

⁶ For the LORD of Armies says this: "Once more, in a little while, I am going to shake the heavens and the earth, the sea and the dry land. ⁷ I will shake all the nations so that the treasures of all the nations will come, and I will fill this house with glory," says the LORD of Armies. ⁸ "The silver and gold belong to me" — this is the declaration of the LORD of Armies. ⁹ "The final glory of this house^A will be greater than the first," says the LORD of Armies. "I will provide peace in this place" — this is the declaration of the LORD of Armies.

From Deprivation to Blessing

¹⁰ On the twenty-fourth day of the ninth month, in the second year of Darius, the word of the LORD came to the prophet Haggai: ¹¹ "This is what the LORD of Armies says: Ask the priests for a ruling. ¹² If a man is carrying consecrated meat in the fold of his garment, and it touches bread, stew, wine, oil, or any other food, does it become holy?"

The priests answered, "No."
¹³ Then Haggai asked, "If someone defiled by contact with a corpse touches any of these, does it become defiled?"

The priests answered, "It becomes defiled."
¹⁴ Then Haggai replied, "So is this people, and so is this nation before me — this is the LORD's declaration. And so is every work of their hands; even what they offer there is defiled.

¹⁵ "Now from this day on, think carefully: Before one stone was placed on another in the LORD's temple, ¹⁶ what state were you in?^B When someone came to a grain heap of twenty measures, it only amounted to ten; when one came to the winepress to dip fifty measures from the vat, it only amounted to twenty. ¹⁷ I struck you — all the work of your hands — with blight, mildew, and hail, but you didn't turn to me — this is the LORD's declaration. ¹⁸ From this day on, think carefully; from the twenty-fourth day of the ninth month, from the day the foundation of the LORD's temple was laid; think carefully. ¹⁹ Is there still seed left in the granary? The vine, the fig, the pomegranate, and the olive tree have not yet produced. But from this day on I will bless you."

Promise to Zerubbabel

²⁰ The word of the LORD came to Haggai a second time on the twenty-fourth day of the month: ²¹ "Speak to Zerubbabel, governor of Judah: I am going to shake the heavens and the earth. ²² I will overturn royal thrones and destroy the power of the Gentile kingdoms. I will overturn chariots and their riders. Horses and their riders will fall, each by his brother's sword. ²³ On that day" — this is the declaration of the LORD of Armies — "I will take you, Zerubbabel son of Shealtiel, my servant" — this is the LORD's declaration — "and make you like my signet ring, for I have chosen you." This is the declaration of the LORD of Armies.

---

^2:9 Or *The glory of this latter house*   ^B 2:16 Hb obscure

2:4 Be strong (mentioned 3 times) is an encouragement for the leaders Zerubbabel and Joshua, as well as the rest of the people, to be bold and firmly committed. They should not question the worthiness of building a temple to glorify God.
2:5 My Spirit is present among you promises that the power that enabled the people to escape Egypt (cp. Ex 33:14–17) was still actively present to help in this crisis situation.
2:6 This verse is quoted in Heb 12:26.
2:7 The treasures of all the nations will come is not a messianic hope, but a promise that God will provide all the gold and silver that is needed (v. 8 says they "belong to me") to make the unimpressive temple glorious. Ezra 6:8 marks the fulfillment of this prophecy, for the Persians paid the full cost of reconstruction.
2:9 The final glory of this house will be greater may be an eschatological promise (cp. Is 60:1–9; Ezk 40:1–44:8).

2:10–12 This prophecy is dated December 18, 520 BC, three months after work began on the temple. This would have been planting season. **Does it become holy?** asks if touching something holy can transfer holiness. The answer is no.
2:13 Does it become defiled? inquires about the transfer of uncleanness. The answer is yes (cp. Nm 19:11).
2:14 So is this people indicates that these people in Jerusalem will not become holy simply by touching the holy temple while rebuilding it.
2:15–16 From this day on, cp. v. 18. Grain production was down 50 percent and wine production 60 percent.
2:17 I struck you . . . but you didn't turn to me describes past failures to repent and God's past discipline of them when he gave them poor crops (cp. 1:6,9–11; Am 4:9).
2:18–19 From this day on, think carefully . . . I will bless you implies acts of

confession and spiritual revival took place at this time. The date was mid-December 520 BC.
2:20–22 Although Zerubbabel was discouraged with little power and few military resources, God promised to work on his behalf to determine who would win the wars at that time.
2:23 My servant identifies Zerubbabel not as an insignificant governor, but as a key obedient person who followed God's directions. **Make you like my signet ring** indicates that Zerubbabel will carry the authority to act as God's legitimate Davidic ruler, a right that God removed from the evil King Jehoiachin (Coniah) in Jr 22:24. This no doubt gave some hope about a future Davidic ruler who would someday rule on David's throne (Is 9:6–7; Jr 23:5–6).

◥ Introduction to Zechariah

Circumstances of Writing

Zechariah returned to Judah with the former exiles and was apparently a priest (Neh 12:16). He was a contemporary of Haggai. Though nothing is known of cooperation between the two prophets, they had similar missions and are credited with the successful reconstruction of the temple (Ezr 5:1–2; 6:14). Zechariah gave dates for two periods of his prophetic ministry (520 and 518 BC; Zch 1:1,7; 7:1). Whether he was the author of the entire book is debated. Many scholars, impressed with the differences between chapters 1–8 and 9–14, conclude that Zechariah did not write the last six chapters. The concept of authorship at the time of the Bible, however, was different from modern standards. In the Old Testament, there is evidence of portions of books under a single author's name that were not written by that author (Nm 12:3; Dt 34:5–12; Jr 51:64c).

A key moment in the history of the Israelites came after King Cyrus of Persia granted the captives permission to return to Palestine (538 BC). The chosen people had just come through one of the worst experiences possible in the ancient world. Their homeland was devastated by invading armies, their capital city and temple were plundered and flattened, many of their people and leaders were killed, and most of the rest were carried off into pagan lands. The returnees who made the long trek back to Judah were faced with the challenge of reestablishing Jerusalem and the temple. Based on the account in the book of Ezra, work began immediately. But after the altar was rebuilt and the foundation stones were laid, problems arose and the work stopped (Ezr 3:1–4:24). Though sacrifices were offered on the altar, the temple continued to lie in ruins for almost two more decades.

Contribution to the Bible

The book of Zechariah is full of the language of judgment, but it is also full of God's promises. The Lord challenged his people to undertake an overwhelmingly difficult task, and he assured them of their success through his power. But the nature of these promises extended beyond rebuilding the temple. From beginning to end, the Bible tells the story of God's redemptive plan, culminating in God's triumph over evil and salvation for sinners. Zechariah's prophecies anticipate this grand culmination of history, describing a coming glorious king, a God who triumphs over all, and a world with all wrongs corrected. These promises set the stage for God's future kingdom, as evidenced by the quotes and allusions to Zechariah in the New Testament.

Structure

The book of Zechariah is complex, sometimes with seemingly disjointed units, like a series of snapshots that need to be put in order. The apparent lack of organization may reflect the oral origin of the book, a collection of sermons that were patched together in written form. But it may also have been intentional. With the goal of shocking the hearers and bringing them to their senses, rapid-fire movement from one thought to another may

---

Zechariah Timeline

625–525 BC

Jeremiah prophesies that the Babylonian exile will last seventy years. **605**
Nebuchadnezzar's three invasions of Judah **605, 597, 586**
Jerusalem and the temple are destroyed. **586**
Fall of Babylon and rise of Persia **539**
Cyrus's decree allows return of Jews from exile; 42,360 return initially. **538**
Second temple construction begins under Zerubbabel's and Joshua's leadership. **536**
Discouragement reinforced by opposition from transplanted peoples brought work on the temple to a halt. **526**

525–520 BC

Aeschylus (**525–456**), Greek tragedian, many of whose plays dealt with the Persian invasion of Greece; he participated in the Greek victories at Marathon and Salamis.
Haggai and Zechariah encourage the people to resume construction of the temple. **520–518**
Haggai's first message **AUGUST 29, 520**
Temple building resumes **SEPTEMBER 21, 520**
Haggai's second message **OCTOBER 17, 520**
Zechariah's first prophetic message **OCTOBER/NOVEMBER 520**

have been part of Zechariah's technique. Chapters 1–8 contain carefully dated visions and sermons, while chapters 9–14 consist of undated poetic oracles and narrative descriptions of judgment and blessing.

Zechariah used a mix of genres. His sermons, poetry, and oracles of judgment and salvation were typical of the prophetic genre. But his visions had similarities with apocalyptic literature, best represented in the Old Testament by the book of Daniel. The content of some of his oracles, describing divine intervention and a radically different world, are also typical of apocalyptic literature. Thus Zechariah may represent a stage of development between a prophetic form and an apocalyptic form.

Outline

I. Call to Conversion (1:1–6)
II. Visionary Disclosure of God's Purposes (1:7–6:15)
III. A Prophetic Message to the People (7:1–8:23)
    A. Empty worship and judgment (7:1–14)
    B. Incredible blessings (8:1–23)
IV. The Emerging Kingdom (9:1–14:21)
    A. The King and his kingdom (9:1–11:3)
    B. Two shepherds (11:4–17)
    C. Jerusalem attacked and delivered (12:1–9)
    D. Inward blessings promised (12:10–14)
    E. Threefold purification (13:1–6)
    F. Death of the shepherd (13:7–9)
    G. The day of the Lord (14:1–21)

A Plea for Repentance

1 In the eighth month, in the second year of Darius, the word of the LORD came to the prophet Zechariah son of Berechiah, son of Iddo: ² "The LORD was extremely angry with your ancestors. ³ So tell the people, 'This is what the LORD of Armies says: Return to me — this is the declaration of the LORD of Armies — and I will return to you, says the LORD of Armies. ⁴ Do not be like your ancestors; the earlier prophets proclaimed to them: This is what the LORD of Armies says: Turn from your evil ways and your evil deeds. But they did not listen or pay attention to me — this is the LORD's declaration. ⁵ Where are your ancestors now? And do the prophets live forever? ⁶ But didn't my words and my statutes that I commanded my servants the prophets overtake your ancestors?'"

So the people repented and said, "As the LORD of Armies decided to deal with us for our ways and our deeds, so he has dealt with us."

THE NIGHT VISIONS

⁷ On the twenty-fourth day of the eleventh month, which is the month of Shebat, in the second year of Darius, the word of the LORD came to the prophet Zechariah son of Berechiah, son of Iddo:

First Vision: Horsemen

⁸ I looked out in the night and saw a man riding on a chestnut^A horse. He was standing among the myrtle trees in the valley.^B Behind him were chestnut, brown, and white horses. ⁹ I asked, "What are these, my lord?"

The angel who was talking to me replied, "I will show you what they are."

¹⁰ Then the man standing among the myrtle trees explained, "They are the ones the LORD has sent to patrol the earth."

¹¹ They reported to the angel of the LORD standing among the myrtle trees, "We have patrolled the earth, and right now the whole earth is calm and quiet."

¹² Then the angel of the LORD responded, "How long, LORD of Armies, will you withhold mercy from Jerusalem and the cities of Judah that you have been angry with these seventy years?" ¹³ The LORD replied with kind and comforting words to the angel who was speaking with me.

¹⁴ So the angel who was speaking with me said, "Proclaim: The LORD of Armies says: I am extremely jealous for Jerusalem and Zion. ¹⁵ I am fiercely angry with the nations that are at ease, for I was a little angry, but they made the destruction worse.^C ¹⁶ Therefore, this is what the LORD says: In mercy, I have returned to Jerusalem; my house will be rebuilt within it — this is the declaration of the LORD of Armies — and a measuring line will be stretched out over Jerusalem.

¹⁷ "Proclaim further: This is what the LORD of Armies says: My cities will again overflow with prosperity; the LORD will once more comfort Zion and again choose Jerusalem."

Second Vision: Four Horns and Craftsmen

¹⁸ Then I looked up and saw four horns. ¹⁹ So I asked the angel who was speaking with me, "What are these?"

And he said to me, "These are the horns that scattered Judah, Israel, and Jerusalem."

²⁰ Then the LORD showed me four craftsmen. ²¹ I asked, "What are they coming to do?"

He replied, "These are the horns that scattered Judah so no one could raise his head. These craftsmen have come to terrify them, to cut off^D the horns of the nations that raised a horn against the land of Judah to scatter it."

Third Vision: Surveyor

2 I looked up and saw a man with a measuring line in his hand. ² I asked, "Where are you going?"

---

^A 1:8 Lit red ^B 1:8 Lit depths ^C 1:15 Lit they helped for evil ^D 1:21 Lit throw down

1:1 Zechariah and Haggai began their ministries only two months apart (Hg 1:1) in the fall of 520 BC, nineteen years after Cyrus, king of Persia, issued an edict giving the Israelites permission to return from exile to their homeland. Both prophets were instrumental in the temple being rebuilt; completed in 516/515 BC (Ezr 5:1–2; 6:14). 1:3 Return (or "turn, repent," Hb shuv) is a key motif throughout Zechariah. It applied to the Israelites in two senses: a return from captivity (a spatial return) and a return to the Lord (a spiritual return). It applied to God in two senses: "return" referred to showing favor again and God's "turn" could also denote the change from judging the people to blessing them. God's offer to return was contingent on the people returning to him. 1:4 They did not listen or pay attention to me are some of the saddest words in the Bible.

1:7 The string of visions that came to the prophet Zechariah brought to life the answer for people on the brink of despair: God is in control and is on your side. 1:8–11 I looked out in the night apparently introduces all eight of the prophet's visions. They offer a mix of the ordinary and the surreal—a world somewhere between heaven and earth. The scene unfolds gradually, with clues appearing along the way and with the angel (or "messenger") interpreting certain details. The man riding on a chestnut horse is the one standing among the myrtle trees, and he is the angel of the LORD. Hearing that the whole earth is calm and quiet underscores the contrast with the turbulence that the people of Israel faced. 1:12–13 The angel's question of how long the mercy of the Lord would be withheld was one that God's people were eager to have answered.

1:14–17 The declaration that my house will be rebuilt suggests that the function of this vision and the ones to follow was to energize the people to unite in rebuilding God's temple. On a measuring line, see note at 2:1–5. 1:18–21 The imagery of four horns that scattered the people so that no one could raise his head suggests the terrifying power and merciless ruin enacted by Israel's enemies. The craftsmen designate skilled artisans (blacksmiths, if the horns were iron) could cut off or carve up horns for various purposes. With the horns in the vision removed, the chosen people could return to the promised land. 2:1–5 The third vision revisits the promise of Jerusalem being rebuilt but enlarges the scope dramatically. With measuring line (1:16)—a common tool of the building trade but in regard to sacred sites signifying divine commissioning—in hand, a surveyor set

He answered me, "To measure Jerusalem to determine its width and length." **3** Then the angel who was speaking with me went out, and another angel went out to meet him. **4** He said to him, "Run and tell this young man: Jerusalem will be inhabited without walls because of the number of people and animals in it." **5** The declaration of the LORD: "I myself will be a wall of fire around it, and I will be the glory within it."

6 "Listen! Listen! Flee from the land of the north" — this is the LORD's declaration — "for I have scattered you like the four winds of heaven" — this is the LORD's declaration. **7** "Listen, Zion! Escape, you who are living with Daughter Babylon." **8** For the LORD of Armies says this: "In pursuit of his glory, he sent me against the nations plundering you, for whoever touches you touches the pupil^A of my^B eye. **9** For look, I am raising my hand against them, and they will become plunder for their own servants. Then you will know that the LORD of Armies has sent me.

10 "Daughter Zion, shout for joy and be glad, for I am coming to dwell among you" — this is the LORD's declaration. **11** "Many nations will join themselves to the LORD on that day and become my^C people. I will dwell among you, and you will know that the LORD of Armies has sent me to you. **12** The LORD will take possession of Judah as his portion in the Holy Land, and he will once again choose Jerusalem. **13** Let all humanity be silent before the LORD, for from his holy dwelling he has roused himself."

Fourth Vision: High Priest and Branch

3 Then he showed me the high priest Joshua standing before the angel of the LORD, with Satan^D standing at his right side to accuse him. **2** The LORD^E said to Satan, "The LORD rebuke you, Satan! May the LORD who has chosen Jerusalem rebuke you! Isn't this man a burning stick snatched from the fire?"

3 Now Joshua was dressed with filthy^F clothes as he stood before the angel. **4** So the angel of the LORD^G spoke to those^H standing before him, "Take off his filthy clothes!" Then he said to him, "See, I have removed your iniquity from you, and I will clothe you with festive robes."

5 Then I said, "Let them put a clean turban on his head." So a clean turban was placed on his head, and they clothed him in garments while the angel of the LORD was standing nearby.

6 Then the angel of the LORD charged Joshua, **7** "This is what the LORD of Armies says: If you walk in my ways and keep my mandates, you will both rule my house and take care of my courts; I will also grant you access among these who are standing here.

8 "Listen, High Priest Joshua, you and your colleagues sitting before you; indeed, these men are a sign that I am about to bring my servant, the Branch. **9** Notice the stone I have set before Joshua; on that one stone are seven eyes. I will engrave an inscription on it" — this is the declaration of the LORD of Armies — "and I will take away the iniquity of this land in a single day. **10** On that day, each of you will invite his neighbor to sit under his vine and

---

^A 2:8 Or *apple*   ^B 2:8 Alt Hb tradition; MT reads *his*   ^C 2:11 LXX, Syr read *his*   ^D 3:1 Or *the accuser*   ^E 3:2 Syr reads *The Angel of the LORD*   ^F 3:3 Probably stained with human excrement   ^G 3:4 Lit *he*   ^H 3:4 = the angels

---

to determine its **width and length**, apparently intending to measure from wall to wall (probably an allusion to Ezk 40:3–42:20). But an angelic messenger spoke with urgency: **Tell this young man** that the city could not be measured because there were no walls. A wall-less city symbolized three ideas. (1) The city would be so vast that walls could not contain it, **because of the number of people and animals**. (2) The city would be at peace, and the only protection needed would be provided by God himself. (3) **A wall of fire around it**, makes clear that a physical wall would be unnecessary. His **glory within it** need not be an eschatological reference, but is more likely a reference to God's glory returning to the tabernacle or temple (Ex 40:34–35; Lv 9:23–24).

2:6–13 The extent of the divine declarations in these verses suggests that they are not a continuation of the vision in vv. 1–5 but are a pause in the action.

2:6 God appealed to exiles to return from **the land of the north**. The initial return in 537 BC preceded Zechariah's prophecies (Ezr 2:64–67; Neh 7:66–69). At least two more groups made the long journey (458 BC and 445 BC), while many remained behind in the dispersion.

2:7 Daughter Babylon may be a hint of tenderness toward this pagan nation, even with

judgment impending (vv. 8–9). It anticipates "Daughter Zion" (v. 10) and suggests that God's love for the nation of Israel, though special, does not mean he does not love the other nations.

2:8 Pupil of my eye refers to the most valuable yet vulnerable part of the body and more accurately translates "gate of the eye" rather than the traditional "apple of the eye." The metaphor functions to express God's deepest feelings for his chosen people (cp. Dt 32:10; Ps 17:8; Pr 7:2).

2:11 Many nations will . . . become my people underscores a paradox of unexpected double reversal. The nations that God had used to enact judgment—which in an act of reversal came under his judgment—have now come into his blessing, yet another act of reversal.

3:1–10 The fourth vision signaled even more encouragement for the returnees to rebuild the temple. The priesthood, which did not operate during the exile, would be restored, and God would grant the chosen people the blessings of forgiveness, service, and peace. The high priest is representative of the nation of Israel.

3:1–2 Joshua was the first high priest after the exile. He is mentioned numerous times in Ezra, Nehemiah, and Haggai. As in Jb

1:6–12; 2:1–6, **Satan** (or "the adversary") had access to God's courtroom and functioned as prosecutor. **A burning stick snatched from the fire** is the first clue that Joshua is symbolic for the chosen people, based on the prophet Amos using this same image for Israel (Am 4:11).

3:3–5 The forgiveness of sin is vividly portrayed by a change of apparel. The **filthy clothes** (lit "defiled by excrement") underscores the gruesome guilt of the people, which had resulted in the severity of God's judgment. In an unexpected reversal, which could only happen by divine decree, Joshua is given clean clothes.

3:6–7 Lest the people become presumptuous on God's gift of forgiveness, **the angel of the LORD charged** (or "admonished solemnly") **Joshua** that obedience was a prerequisite if he were to enjoy God's favor and perform his duties as high priest, including having access to God's presence.

3:8–10 Not only was the priesthood restored and forgiveness granted, but a descendant of David would become their ruler, as indicated by **my servant, the Branch**, probably a reference to Zerubbabel (Hg 2:23; see notes at Zch 4:11–14; 6:12–13; cp. Jr 33:15). The same is true for the **stone** of Zch 3:9 (see Is 8:14; 28:16).

fig tree." This is the declaration of the Lord of Armies.

Fifth Vision: Gold Lampstand

4 The angel who was speaking with me then returned and roused me as one awakened out of sleep. [2] He asked me, "What do you see?"

I replied, "I see a solid gold lampstand with a bowl at the top. The lampstand also has seven lamps at the top with seven spouts for each of[A] the lamps. [3] There are also two olive trees beside it, one on the right of the bowl and the other on its left."

[4] Then I asked the angel who was speaking with me, "What are these, my lord?"

[5] "Don't you know what they are?" replied the angel who was speaking with me.

I said, "No, my lord."

[6] So he answered me, "This is the word of the Lord to Zerubbabel: 'Not by strength or by might, but by my Spirit,' says the Lord of Armies. [7] 'What are you, great mountain? Before Zerubbabel you will become a plain. And he will bring out the capstone accompanied by shouts of: Grace, grace to it!'"

[8] Then the word of the Lord came to me: [9] "Zerubbabel's hands have laid the foundation of this house, and his hands will complete it. Then you will know that the Lord of Armies has sent me to you. [10] For who despises the day of small things? These seven eyes of the Lord, which scan throughout the whole earth, will rejoice when they see the ceremonial stone[B] in Zerubbabel's hand."

[11] I asked him, "What are the two olive trees on the right and left of the lampstand?" [12] And I questioned him further, "What are the two streams[C] of the olive trees, from which the golden oil is pouring through the two golden conduits?"

[13] Then he inquired of me, "Don't you know what these are?"

"No, my lord," I replied.

[14] "These are the two anointed ones,"[D] he said, "who stand by the Lord of the whole earth."

Sixth Vision: Flying Scroll

5 I looked up again and saw a flying scroll. [2] "What do you see?" he asked me.

"I see a flying scroll," I replied, "thirty feet[E] long and fifteen feet[F] wide."

[3] Then he said to me, "This is the curse that is going out over the whole land, for everyone who is a thief, contrary to what is written on one side, has gone unpunished, [G] and everyone who swears falsely, contrary to what is written on the other side, has gone unpunished. [4] I will send it out," — this is the declaration of the Lord of Armies — "and it will enter the house of the thief and the house of the one who swears falsely by my name. It will stay inside his house and destroy it along with its timbers and stones."

Seventh Vision: Woman in the Basket

[5] Then the angel who was speaking with me came forward and told me, "Look up and see what this is that is approaching."

[6] So I asked, "What is it?"

He responded, "It's a measuring basket[H] that is approaching." And he continued, "This is their iniquity[I] in all the land." [7] Then a lead cover was lifted, and there was a woman sitting inside the basket. [8] "This is Wickedness," he said. He shoved her down into the basket and pushed the lead weight over its opening. [9] Then I looked up and saw two women approaching with the wind in their wings. Their wings were like those of a stork, and they lifted up the basket between earth and sky.

[10] So I asked the angel who was speaking with me, "Where are they taking the basket?"

[11] "To build a shrine for it in the land of Shinar," he told me. "When that is ready, the basket will be placed there on its pedestal."

[A]4:2 Or seven lips to   [B]4:10 Lit the tin stone   [C]4:12 Or branches   [D]4:14 = Joshua and Zerubbabel   [E]5:2 Lit 20 cubits   [F]5:2 Lit 10 cubits   [G]5:3 Or side, will be removed   [H]5:6 Lit It's an ephah   [I]5:6 One Hb ms, LXX, Syr; other Hb mss read eye

---

4:1–10 Faced with rebuilding their temple and city, the chosen people felt small, powerless, and overwhelmed. Opposition came from within and without. But Zechariah saw things differently. God would empower the people and their leader Zerubbabel. The vision was particularly evocative: **For who despises the day of small things?** (4:10). **4:2–3** The **lampstand** described here is surrealistic, with an inexplicable arrangement of containers of oil—**a bowl** . . . **seven lamps** . . . **seven spouts**, and **two olive trees**—perhaps signifying an abundance of oil. On the lampstand in the tabernacle, see Ex 25:31–37. **4:4–6** The angel's question **Don't you know what they are?** heightens the anticipation of what the answer will be and underscores the necessity of supernatural insight. What the angel said to Zerubbabel about the

Spirit provides insight into the interpretation of the lampstand. Oil was symbolic of God's Spirit (1Sm 16:13). Thus, while Zerubbabel would be instrumental in accomplishing God's purposes, it could only happen through the plentiful supply of God's Spirit. **4:6–7** While **Zerubbabel** was a legitimate heir to David's throne, his role was apparently limited to governor, even though he is spoken of in elevated terms (Hg 2:21–23). In hyperbolic language, he would be able to move mountains. But since God deserved all the credit, shouts of **grace, grace** to the temple were very appropriate. **4:10** It is often suggested that multiple eyes may signify wisdom or knowledge. **4:11–14** Given the placement of this vision next to the preceding one, it is likely that **the two anointed ones** (Hb, "two men of oil," v. 14) are Joshua and Zerubbabel.

5:1–4 The sixth vision focuses on the Torah (the five books of the Law), disclosing what God expects his people to do. **5:2** The dimensions of the **scroll** are unusual, though the proportions suggest a partly unrolled scroll, as if it were waiting to be read. **5:3** The **curse** for disobedience is not unexpected (Dt 27:15–26; 28:15–68). The selection of two commandments (Ex 20:7,15) is probably representative of all ten (for different selections, see Zch 7:4–14). **5:5–8** The seventh vision with **Wickedness** being transported in a basket back to Babylon signifies that idolatry belonged there, not in the promised land. **5:7–8** The Hebrew word for "Wickedness" is feminine in gender and may be connected with the Canaanite goddess Asherah. **5:11 Shinar** is an older name for Babylon (Gn 11:1–2). If the chosen people were going

Eighth Vision: Four Chariots

6 Then I looked up again and saw four chariots coming from between two mountains.
The mountains were made of bronze. ² The first
chariot had chestnut^A horses, the second chariot black horses, ³ the third chariot white horses, and the fourth chariot dappled horses — all
strong horses. ⁴ So I inquired of the angel who
was speaking with me, "What are these, my
lord?"
⁵ The angel told me, "These are the four spir-
its^B of heaven going out after presenting themselves to the Lord of the whole earth. ⁶ The one
with the black horses is going to the land of the
north, the white horses are going after them,
but the dappled horses are going to the land of
the south." ⁷ As the strong horses went out, they
wanted to go patrol the earth, and the LORD
said, "Go, patrol the earth." So they patrolled
the earth. ⁸ Then he summoned me saying, "See,
those going to the land of the north have pacified my Spirit in the northern land."

Crowning of the Branch

⁹ The word of the LORD came to me: ¹⁰ "Take an
offering from the exiles, from Heldai, Tobijah,
and Jedaiah, who have arrived from Babylon,
and go that same day to the house of Josiah
son of Zephaniah. ¹¹ Take silver and gold, make
a crown,^C and place it on the head of Joshua
son of Jehozadak, the high priest. ¹² You are to
tell him: This is what the LORD of Armies says:
Here is a man whose name is Branch; he will
branch out from his place and build the LORD's
temple. ¹³ Yes, he will build the LORD's temple;

he will bear royal splendor and will sit on his
throne and rule. There will be a priest on his
throne, and there will be peaceful counsel between the two of them. ¹⁴ The crown will reside
in the LORD's temple as a memorial to Heldai,
Tobijah, Jedaiah, and Hen^D son of Zephaniah.
¹⁵ People who are far off will come and build
the LORD's temple, and you will know that the
LORD of Armies has sent me to you. This will
happen when you fully obey the LORD your
God."

Disobedience and Fasting

7 In the fourth year of King Darius, the word
of the LORD came to Zechariah on the
fourth day of the ninth month, which is Chislev. ² Now the people of Bethel had sent Sharezer, Regem-melech, and their men to plead
for the LORD's favor ³ by asking the priests who
were at the house of the LORD of Armies as well
as the prophets, "Should we mourn and fast in
the fifth month as we have done these many
years?"
⁴ Then the word of the LORD of Armies came
to me: ⁵ "Ask all the people of the land and the
priests: When you fasted and lamented in the
fifth and in the seventh months for these seventy years, did you really fast for me? ⁶ When
you eat and drink, don't you eat and drink simply for yourselves? ⁷ Aren't these the words
that the LORD proclaimed through the earlier
prophets when Jerusalem was inhabited and
secure,^E along with its surrounding cities, and
when the southern region and the Judean foothills were inhabited?"

---

^A 6:2 Lit red   ^B 6:5 Or winds   ^C 6:11 Lit crowns   ^D 6:14 Probably Josiah   ^E 7:7 Or prosperous

---

to be idolatrous, they might as well do it
in style back in Babylon, with a shrine in
their honor.
6:1–8 The first and eighth visions functioned
as bookends for the intervening visions and
convey the same message: God is sovereign
and is in control of the whole earth. However,
there is a change of outcome between the
two visions. While both picture four horses
patrolling the earth, when the report came
in the first vision that there was peace on
earth, the angel asked a troubling question
about the lack of peace in Jerusalem. Visions
two through seven address this question.
This eighth vision (vv. 1–8) provides the final
resolution. God's Spirit is pacified. Here as in
1:12, the angel is the angel of the Lord—often
construed as a theophany.
6:1–3 The **mountains . . . made of bronze**
may represent heaven or its gates since the
chariots seem to originate there (v. 5).
6:5 The chariots are identified as **the four
spirits of heaven**. The point is that God's
Spirit is present over the whole earth.
6:6–7 The horses going **to the land of
the north** designate the nations that had
destroyed Israel. The other direction in and
out of Palestine was to the south. Thus the
whole earth was **patrolled**.
6:9–15 This passage concludes the first
section of Zechariah, presenting three prerequisites for rebuilding the temple. (1) There

will need to be harmony between the civil
and priestly leadership. (2) Israelites who
have not returned from captivity should lend
their support. (3) Everyone will need to be
obedient to God's law.
6:10–11 The naming of specific individuals
suggests that these are envoys representing
Israelites still in exile in Babylon. Dedicating
a memorial to them (v. 14) functioned as encouragement to those who had not returned.
6:12–13 On Zerubbabel as the **Branch**, see
the fourth vision (see note at 3:8–10; cp. Hg
2:23). Joshua the high priest and Zerubbabel
were previously identified as the key leaders
in the building of the temple (see note at Zch
4:11–14; cp. Hg 2:2). Some see a reference to
a messianic figure in this passage (see note
at Zch 3:8–10).
6:15 People who are far off refers to exiles
who had not returned but should have done
so. Strengthening the call to return, God's
authority will be validated if they come
back. **When you fully obey the LORD
your God** is nearly an exact quote from
Dt 28:1, which emphasizes contingency in
the covenant.
7:1–14 This second section of Zechariah begins in similar fashion to the first, looking
back on the disobedient ancestors, their
stubbornness, and the display of God's anger
(cp. 1:4–6). The question still begged for an
answer: Had the returnees learned the lesson

of exile? Another issue under consideration
was whether the temple in Jerusalem had
regained its religious authority.
7:1 The second section of Zechariah is marked
by a date two years later than when the
word of the Lord first came to Zechariah (cp.
1:1,7). Chislev compares to our November–
December thus December 7, 518 BC. In contrast to the first section of the book, which
consists primarily of visions, this section is
a sermon that develops themes introduced
in the visions.
7:2–3 Bethel had been a center of worship for the northern ten tribes (1Kg 12:29).
Some Israelites who remained in the land
during the exile worshiped there, but they
were willing to defer to the authority of
the religious leaders in Jerusalem as long
as they found evidence of God's blessing
being restored.
7:4–7 The answer to the question posed in
v. 3 involved a series of convicting questions
from the "LORD of Armies" (v. 9), designed to
accomplish three purposes: (1) to validate
Zechariah as a true prophet of the Lord,
for God was speaking through him as he
did through the **earlier prophets**; (2) to
demonstrate that God was endowing the
returned community with the same authority it had before the exile; and (3) to
underscore what God required in order to
have his blessing.

⁸ The word of the LORD came to Zechariah: ⁹ "The LORD of Armies says this: 'Make fair decisions. Show faithful love and compassion to one another. ¹⁰ Do not oppress the widow or the fatherless, the resident alien or the poor, and do not plot evil in your hearts against one another.' ¹¹ But they refused to pay attention and turned a stubborn shoulder; they closed their ears so they could not hear. ¹² They made their hearts like a rock so as not to obey the law or the words that the LORD of Armies had sent by his Spirit through the earlier prophets. Therefore intense anger came from the LORD of Armies. ¹³ Just as he had called, and they would not listen, so when they called, I would not listen, says the LORD of Armies. ¹⁴ I scattered them with a windstorm over all the nations that had not known them, and the land was left desolate behind them, with no one coming or going. They turned a pleasant land into a desolation."

Obedience and Feasting

8 The word of the LORD of Armies came: ² The LORD of Armies says this: "I am extremely jealous for Zion; I am jealous for her with great wrath." ³ The LORD says this: "I will return to Zion and live in Jerusalem. Then Jerusalem will be called the Faithful City; the mountain of the LORD of Armies will be called the Holy Mountain." ⁴ The LORD of Armies says this: "Old men and women will again sit along the streets of Jerusalem, each with a staff in hand because of advanced age. ⁵ The streets of the city will be filled with boys and girls playing in them." ⁶ The LORD of Armies says this: "Though it may seem impossible to the remnant of this people in those days, should it also seem impossible to me?" — this is the declaration of the LORD of Armies. ⁷ The LORD of Armies says this: "I will save my people from the land of the east and the land of the west.^8 I will bring them back to live in Jerusalem. They will be my people, and I will be their faithful and righteous God."

⁹ The LORD of Armies says this: "Let your hands be strong, you who now hear these words that the prophets spoke when the foundations were laid for the rebuilding of the temple, the house of the LORD of Armies. ¹⁰ For prior to those days neither people nor animals had wages. There was no safety from the enemy for anyone who came or went, for I turned everyone against his neighbor. ¹¹ But now, I will not treat the remnant of this people as in the former days" — this is the declaration of the LORD of Armies. ¹² "For they will sow in peace: the vine will yield its fruit, the land will yield its produce, and the skies will yield their dew. I will give the remnant of this people all these things as an inheritance. ¹³ As you have been a curse among the nations, house of Judah and house of Israel, so I will save you, and you will be a blessing. Don't be afraid; let your hands be strong." ¹⁴ For the LORD of Armies says this: "As I resolved to treat you badly when your ancestors provoked me to anger, and I did not relent," says the LORD of Armies, ¹⁵ "so I have resolved again in these days to do what is good to Jerusalem and the house of Judah. Don't be afraid. ¹⁶ These are the things you must do: Speak truth to one another; make true and sound decisions within your city gates. ¹⁷ Do not plot evil in your hearts against your neighbor, and do not love perjury, for I hate all this" — this is the LORD's declaration.

¹⁸ Then the word of the LORD of Armies came to me: ¹⁹ The LORD of Armies says this: "The fast of the fourth month, the fast of the fifth, the

^8:7 Lit *sunset*

7:8–10 Social injustice is the focus here. Taking advantage of the poor earned the most severe punishment (Jr 5:28–29; Am 5:11–17).
7:11–12 **Stubborn shoulder . . . closed . . . ears**, and **hearts like a rock** are billboard-like metaphors for the insensitivity of the chosen people. They repeatedly refused to make the Lord their God.
7:13–14 With the parade of sinfulness summarized in vv. 4–12, God was justified in stirring up a **windstorm** that **scattered** the participants in all directions. Typical of prophetic language, judgment is expressed in hyperbole.
8:1–8 The sermon now turns dramatically from judgment to blessing, from complete dispersion to total restoration. Spectacular blessings from God had already been proclaimed in the visions (1:16–17; 2:4–5,11–12; 3:9–10). But with the returnees barely existing in the land, Zechariah sought to energize them with the potential of becoming something magnificent.
8:2 The connection between a **jealous** God and a God of **wrath** suggests that his deep desire for relationship was matched by decisive judgment against anything that

would interfere—whether from within or without (Zch 1:18–21; 2:9; 5:4; 7:12–14; cp. Heb 12:4–11).
8:3 In a remarkable reversal, God announced restoration instead of the dispersion. Whether announcing judgment or blessing, the object was the same—to enforce the covenant and encourage obedience. Calling Jerusalem the **Faithful City** was another reversal; it had previously been referred to as a harlot (Is 1:21; Jr 3:1–2; Lm 1:8–9).
8:6 The reference to the **remnant** identifies the returnees as the true community of restoration, as promised in the Prophets (Is 10:21–22; 11:11,16; Jr 23:3).
8:7–8 **They will be my people, and I will be their . . . God** indicates full restoration of the covenant relationship.
8:9 Zechariah's sermon was presented approximately halfway between laying the foundation and the completion of the temple. **Let your hands be strong** (cp. v. 13; Hg 2:4) suggests that the sermon included encouragement for persistence in the work of rebuilding.
8:10–11 **Prior to those days** means before laying the foundation of the temple.

8:12 Everything the returnees could have hoped for was addressed in this sermon, which was rich with blessings (cp. Ezk 34:25–29). The **peace . . . fruit . . . produce**, and **dew** were the opposite of their experience in the land during the previous two decades (Hg 1:6–11; 2:15–19).
8:13–15 By referring to them as **house of Judah and house of Israel** Zechariah taught that the postexilic community represented the whole covenant people. The exhortation **let your hands be strong** (v. 13) also begins v. 9. They could be encouraged because God's resolve to do them good was as certain as was his resolve to do them harm previously.
8:16–17 **These are the things you must do** reveals that the function of the sermon was more than simply rebuilding the walls (v. 9). In order for the returnees to enjoy the incredible blessings that God offered, they would need to obey the covenant's standard of social justice (7:8–10). In Eph 4:25 Paul quotes Zch 8:16 as an exhortation to NT believers.
8:18–19 In response to the question that initiated the sermon—whether it was necessary to continue fasting and mourning the

fast of the seventh, and the fast of the tenth will become times of joy, gladness, and cheerful festivals for the house of Judah. Therefore, love truth and peace." [20] The LORD of Armies says this: "Peoples will yet come, the residents of many cities; [21] the residents of one city will go to another, saying: Let's go at once to plead for the LORD's favor and to seek the LORD of Armies. I am also going. [22] Many peoples and strong nations will come to seek the LORD of Armies in Jerusalem and to plead for the LORD's favor." [23] The LORD of Armies says this: "In those days, ten men from nations of every language will grab the robe of a Jewish man tightly, urging: Let us go with you, for we have heard that God is with you."

Judgment of Zion's Enemies

9 A pronouncement:
The word of the LORD
is against the land of Hadrach,
and Damascus is its resting place —
for the eyes of humanity
and all the tribes of Israel
are on the LORD[A] —
[2] and also against Hamath,
which borders it,
as well as Tyre and Sidon,
though they are very shrewd.
[3] Tyre has built herself a fortress;
she has heaped up silver like dust
and gold like the dirt of the streets.
[4] Listen! The Lord will impoverish her
and cast her wealth into the sea;
she herself will be consumed by fire.

[5] Ashkelon will see it and be afraid;
Gaza too, and will writhe in great pain,
as will Ekron, for her hope will fail.
There will cease to be a king in Gaza,
and Ashkelon will become uninhabited.
[6] A mongrel people will live in Ashdod,
and I will destroy the pride
of the Philistines.
[7] I will remove the blood
from their mouths
and the abhorrent things
from between their teeth.
Then they too will become a remnant
for our God;
they will become like a clan in Judah
and Ekron like the Jebusites.
[8] I will encamp at my house as a guard,
against those who march
back and forth,
and no oppressor will march
against them again,
for now I have seen with my own eyes.

The Coming of Zion's King

[9] Rejoice greatly, Daughter Zion!
Shout in triumph, Daughter Jerusalem!
Look, your King is coming to you;
he is righteous and victorious,[B]
humble and riding on a donkey,
on a colt, the foal of a donkey.
[10] I will cut off the chariot from Ephraim
and the horse from Jerusalem.
The bow of war will be removed,
and he will proclaim peace
to the nations.

[A]9:1 Or eyes of the LORD are on mankind — [B]9:9 Or and has salvation

---

destruction of Jerusalem (7:3,5)—the Lord announced a reversal. Fasts of lamentation were to be transformed into **times of joy, gladness, and cheerful festivals.**
8:20–22 Such an ingathering was a sign of greatness, both of Jerusalem and of God's presence. The image was a fitting conclusion to Zechariah's sermon. The seemingly insignificant city of Jerusalem was now seen as the most important city in the world.
8:23 Grabbing the hem of a garment was an act of submission and supplication. Since the Israelites spent years under foreign domination, to have Gentiles show submission to them would be an astonishing reversal (Gn 27:29).
9:1–17 The third section of Zechariah is an extended poem, beginning with a description of God as victorious Conqueror and King. Since poetry is often characterized by multiplying images to emphasize a point, it is not surprising to find God's overpowering strength expressed in numerous ways and against many different enemies. The poet included obscure cities and regions not mentioned elsewhere in the Bible (Zch 9:1–2). The intent was to underscore the contrast between the enemies who would be consumed by God's power and the new king ruling from Jerusalem.
9:1 Pronouncement denotes a message from God, often language of judgment, here

marking the beginning of a new section. For **the eyes of humanity and all the tribes of Israel** to be on the Lord suggests the reuniting of the twelve tribes (Judah and Israel, cp. 8:13) and the inclusion of Gentiles.
9:3–4 Tyre was well known as a naval and commercial power with an impregnable fortified island one-half mile off the Mediterranean coast. Alexander the Great and his army spent seven months dismantling the city on the mainland and building a causeway to the island.
9:5–7 The cities of Philistia represented the archenemy of the Israelites in the days of the monarchy. Removing **blood from their mouths** suggests judgment that was also an act of cleansing, bringing the people into conformity with God's law (Lv 17:11–12). Announcing that **they too will become a remnant** is an extraordinary measure of divine compassion granted to enemies (cp. 2:11; 8:20–23).
9:8 The preceding verses denote the conqueror's movement through Palestine, from north to south, eventually arriving in Jerusalem—the path followed by Alexander the Great (332 BC). It is better to understand the statement that **no oppressor will march against them again** as poetic language for God's general protection (Is 45:17; Jr 17:25).
9:9 The chosen people had longed for a king of similar stature to David or Solomon, but

none had come forth until the announcement of this **King** who is **righteous**. Instead of riding a mule, which was common for kings, he would ride a **donkey**—signifying unexpected humility. This prophecy applied to Jesus's triumphal entry into Jerusalem (Mt 21:5; Jn 12:15).
9:10–15 In this passage God's actions are typical of a victorious conqueror, cutting down **chariot . . . horse**, and **bow**, extending the kingdom's **dominion**, releasing **prisoners**, and taking on distant enemies (**Greece**).

His dominion will extend from sea
  to sea,
from the Euphrates River
  to the ends of the earth.
11 As for you,
because of the blood of your covenant,
I will release your prisoners
  from the waterless cistern.
12 Return to a stronghold,
  you prisoners who have hope;
today I declare that I will restore double
  to you.
13 For I will bend Judah as my bow;
I will fill that bow with Ephraim.
I will rouse your sons, Zion,
  against your sons, Greece.^A
I will make you like a warrior's sword.
14 Then the LORD will appear over them,
and his arrow will fly like lightning.
The Lord GOD will sound the ram's horn
and advance with the southern storms.
15 The LORD of Armies will defend them.
They will consume and conquer
  with slingstones;
they will drink and be rowdy as if
  with wine.
They will be as full as
  the sprinkling basin,
like those at the corners of the altar.
16 The LORD their God will save them
  on that day
as the flock of his people;
for they are like jewels in a crown,
sparkling over his land.
17 How lovely and beautiful!
Grain will make the young men flourish,
and new wine, the young women.

The LORD Restores His People

10 Ask the LORD for rain
  in the season of spring rain.
The LORD makes the rain clouds,
and he will give them showers of rain
and crops in the field for everyone.
2 For the idols speak falsehood,
and the diviners see illusions;
they relate empty dreams
and offer empty comfort.
Therefore the people wander like sheep;

they suffer affliction because there is
  no shepherd.
3 My anger burns against the shepherds,
so I will punish the leaders.^B
For the LORD of Armies has tended
  his flock,
the house of Judah;
he will make them
  like his majestic steed in battle.
4 The cornerstone, the tent peg,
  the battle bow, and every ruler —
all will go out from him together.
5 They will be like warriors in battle
trampling down the mud of the streets.
They will fight because the LORD is
  with them,
and they will put horsemen to shame.
6 I will strengthen the house of Judah
and deliver the house of Joseph.^C
I will restore^D them
because I have compassion on them,
and they will be
  as though I had never rejected them.
For I am the LORD their God,
and I will answer them.
7 Ephraim will be like a warrior,
and their hearts will be glad as if
  with wine.
Their children will see it and be glad;
their hearts will rejoice in the LORD.
8 I will whistle and gather them
because I have redeemed them;
they will be as numerous as
  they once were.
9 Though I sow them among the nations,
they will remember me
  in the distant lands;
they and their children will live
  and return.
10 I will bring them back from the land
  of Egypt
and gather them from Assyria.
I will bring them to the land of Gilead
  and to Lebanon,
but it will not be enough for them.
11 The LORD^E will pass through the sea
  of distress
and strike the waves of the sea;

---

^9:13 Lit *Javan* ^10:3 Lit *male goats* ^10:6 = the northern kingdom ^10:6 Other Hb mss, LXX read *settle* ^10:11 Lit *He*

10:1–2 With a lack of leadership (referred to as shepherds), the Israelites had been turning to false sources of blessings. Zechariah rebuked them, instructing them to **ask the LORD for rain** (see Jr 14:22; Jl 2:23) instead of appealing to household deities (**idols**) and false prophets (**diviners**), which was forbidden in the law (Dt 18:9–14).
10:3–5 The phrase **my anger burns against the shepherds** reflects a common concern of the prophets about inept and misguided leadership (Ezk 34:1–10; Mc 3:1–4). Conversely, when God **tended his flock**, they became like a **majestic steed**, a **cornerstone**, a **tent**

peg, a **battle bow**, or as "jewels in a crown, sparkling over his land" (9:16). They will even **put horsemen to shame**. **Cornerstone** can be a metaphor for leader (Is 19:13). It is used as a metaphor for Jesus in the NT (Ac 4:11; 1Pt 2:6–8).
10:6–9 Judah designates the southern two tribes, while the northern ten tribes can be referred to by **Joseph**, his son **Ephraim**, or Israel. When the chosen people were marched hundreds of miles into exile (Israel into Assyria and Judah into Babylonia), it seemed impossible that they could ever return. Once some exiles from Judah had

returned, the lingering question concerned Israel. After almost two hundred years in Assyria, was restoration to their land even possible? The answer was yes. God would **whistle and gather them** and reverse his rejection of them (Ezk 37:15–28; Hs 1:10–11). There is no biblical evidence that this has been fulfilled yet. Interpreters are divided on how the ultimate fulfillment will come about and what it will look like.
10:10–12 Egypt and **Assyria** were representative of various nations where the chosen people went into captivity. Even though the promised land is expanded to include outlying

all the depths of the Nile will dry up.
The pride of Assyria will be
    brought down,
and the scepter of Egypt will come
    to an end.
¹² I will strengthen them in the Lord,
and they will march in his name —
    this is the Lord's declaration.

Israel's Shepherds: Good and Bad

11 Open your gates, Lebanon,
    and fire will consume your cedars.
² Wail, cypress, for the cedar has fallen;
    the glorious trees are destroyed!
Wail, oaks of Bashan,
    for the stately forest has fallen!
³ Listen to the wail of the shepherds,
    for their glory is destroyed.
Listen to the roar of young lions,
    for the thickets of the Jordan
    areᴬ destroyed.

⁴ The Lord my God says this: "Shepherd the flock intended for slaughter. ⁵ Those who buy them slaughter them but are not punished. Those who sell them say, 'Blessed be the Lord because I have become rich!' Even their own shepherds have no compassion for them. ⁶ Indeed, I will no longer have compassion on the inhabitants of the land" — this is the Lord's declaration. "Instead, I will turn everyone over to his neighbor and his king. They will devastate the land, and I will not rescue it from their hand."

⁷ So I shepherded the flock intended for slaughter, the oppressed of the flock.ᴮ I took two staffs, calling one Favor and the other Union, and I shepherded the flock. ⁸ In one month I got rid of three shepherds. I became impatient with them, and they also detested me. ⁹ Then I said, "I will no longer shepherd you. Let what is dying die, and let what is perishing

perish; let the rest devour each other's flesh." ¹⁰ Next I took my staff called Favor and cut it in two, annulling the covenant I had made with all the peoples. ¹¹ It was annulled on that day, and so the oppressed of the flockᶜ who were watching me knew that it was the word of the Lord. ¹² Then I said to them, "If it seems right to you, give me my wages; but if not, keep them." So they weighed my wages, thirty pieces of silver. ¹³ "Throw it to the potter,"ᴰ the Lord said to me — this magnificent price I was valued by them. So I took the thirty pieces of silver and threw it into the house of the Lord, to the potter.ᴱ ¹⁴ Then I cut in two my second staff, Union, annulling the brotherhood between Judah and Israel.

¹⁵ The Lord also said to me, "Take the equipment of a foolish shepherd. ¹⁶ I am about to raise up a shepherd in the land who will not care for those who are perishing, and he will not seek the lostᶠ or heal the broken. He will not sustain the healthy,ᴳ but he will devour the flesh of the fat sheep and tear off their hooves.
¹⁷   Woe to the worthless shepherd
    who deserts the flock!
May a sword strikeᴴ his arm
    and his right eye!
May his arm wither away
    and his right eye go completely blind!"

Judah's Security

12 A pronouncement:
    The word of the Lord
    concerning Israel.
A declaration of the Lord,
who stretched out the heavens,
laid the foundation of the earth,
and formed the spirit of man
    within him.

² "Look, I will make Jerusalem a cup that causes staggering for the peoples who surround the city. The siege against Jerusalem will

---

ᴬ11:3 Lit for the majesty of the Jordan is   ᴮ11:7 LXX reads slaughter that belonged to the sheep merchants   ᶜ11:11 LXX reads and the sheep merchants   ᴰ11:13 Syr reads treasury   ᴱ11:13 One Hb ms, Syr read treasury   ᶠ11:16 Or young   ᴳ11:16 Or exhausted   ᴴ11:17 Lit be against

regions (**Gilead** and **Lebanon**), that **will not be enough** for the number of returnees. **11:1–11** The rich symbolism in this scene recalls the visions in the first section of the book, though here the form is more like a parable. Given the failure of the shepherds to lead the people in the right paths (see note at 10:3–5), God appointed the prophet as a figurative shepherd. When the people failed to follow him, the Lord canceled his relationship with them and turned them over to worthless leaders. **11:1–3 Open your gates, Lebanon** may be a symbolic reference to the temple and its gates (timbers from Lebanon were used in the building of the temple), which suggests that the leadership in view is that of the religious authorities. **11:4–6** The temple precinct was full of sheep **intended for slaughter**, which was their proper purpose in the sacrificial system. But

they had become objects for personal gain, and with **their own shepherds** having **no compassion for them**, God withdrew and turned neighboring kingdoms loose on the chosen people and their land. **11:7–9** The shepherd named one of his staffs **Favor** (or Grace) and the other **Union** (or Unity), the former symbolizing the covenant (v. 10) and the latter representing reunited Israel (v. 14). But the failure of the shepherds to be good leaders resulted in letting the people self-destruct. The phrase **three shepherds** probably does not refer to anyone in particular. **11:10–11** Most interpreters do not consider **the covenant** mentioned here to be one of the biblical covenants but a general covenant of protection between Judah and her neighboring nations. **11:12–13** The **thirty pieces of silver** may be an allusion to the value of a slave (Ex 21:32). Throwing the **magnificent price** (probably

sarcastic) to the **potter** in the temple was an act of desecration. Matthew used some of this wording in reference to Judas (Mt 27:9–10), though stating that it was Jeremiah's prophecy that was fulfilled (Jr 32:6–9). **11:14** The hoped-for reunification of Israel and Judah was canceled (see note at 10:6–9). **11:15–16** If the people were not going to follow a good shepherd, they might as well follow a bad one, so God responded in satire and appointed the prophet as a **foolish shepherd**. **12:1 Pronouncement** marks the beginning of the fourth section of Zechariah (see note at 9:1), which recapitulates themes treated earlier in the book. God's great power—highlighted by reference to creation—is now focused on Jerusalem, which God promised to protect and exalt so it would be bigger and more significant than all other nations. **12:2–9** A **cup that causes staggering** recalls other prophets' descriptions of the

also involve Judah. ³ On that day I will make Jerusalem a heavy stone for all the peoples; all who try to lift it will injure themselves severely when all the nations of the earth gather against her. ⁴ On that day" — this is the LORD's declaration — "I will strike every horse with panic and its rider with madness. I will keep a watchful eye on the house of Judah but strike all the horses of the nations with blindness. ⁵ Then each of the leaders of Judah will think to himself: The residents of Jerusalem are my strength through the LORD of Armies, their God. ⁶ On that day I will make the leaders of Judah like a firepot in a woodpile, like a flaming torch among sheaves; they will consume all the peoples around them on the right and the left, while Jerusalem continues to be inhabited on its site, in Jerusalem. ⁷ The LORD will save the tents of Judah first, so that the glory of David's house and the glory of Jerusalem's residents may not be greater than that of Judah. ⁸ On that day the LORD will defend the inhabitants of Jerusalem, so that on that day the one who is weakest among them will be like David on that day, and the house of David will be like God, like the angel of the LORD, before them. ⁹ On that day I will set out to destroy all the nations that come against Jerusalem.

Mourning for the Pierced One

¹⁰ "Then I will pour out a spiritᴬ of grace and prayer on the house of David and the residents of Jerusalem, and they will look atᴮ me whom they pierced. They will mourn for him as one mourns for an only child and weep bitterly for him as one weeps for a firstborn. ¹¹ On that day the mourning in Jerusalem will be as great as the mourning of Hadad-rimmon in the plain of Megiddo. ¹² The land will mourn, every family by itself: the family of David's house by itself and their women by themselves; the family of Nathan'sᶜ house by itself and their women by themselves; ¹³ the family of Levi's house by itself and their women by themselves; the family of Shimeiᴰ by itself and their women by themselves; ¹⁴ all the remaining families, every family by itself, and their women by themselves.

God's People Cleansed

13 "On that day a fountain will be opened for the house of David and for the residents of Jerusalem, to wash away sin and impurity. ² On that day" — this is the declaration of the LORD of Armies — "I will remove the names of the idols from the land, and they will no longer be remembered. I will banish the prophetsᴱ and the unclean spirit from the land. ³ If a man still prophesies, his father and his mother who bore him will say to him, 'You cannot remain alive because you have spoken a lie in the name of the LORD.' When he prophesies, his father and his mother who bore him will pierce him through. ⁴ On that day every prophet will be ashamed of his vision when he prophesies; they will not put on a hairy cloak in order to deceive. ⁵ He will say, 'I am not a prophet; I work the land, for a man purchasedᶠ me as a servant since my youth.' ⁶ If someone asks him, 'What are these wounds on your chest?'ᴳ — then he will answer, 'I received the wounds in the house of my friends.'

⁷   Sword, awake against my shepherd,
     against the man who is my associate —
       this is the declaration of the LORD
       of Armies.
     Strike the shepherd, and the sheep
       will be scattered;
     I will turn my hand
       against the little ones.
⁸   In the whole land —
       this is the LORD's declaration —
     two-thirdsᴴ will be cut off and die,
     but a third will be left in it.
⁹   I will put this third through the fire;
     I will refine them as silver is refined

ᴬ12:10 Or *out the Spirit*   ᴮ12:10 Or *to*   ᶜ12:12 = a son of David   ᴰ12:13 = a descendant of Levi   ᴱ13:2 = false prophets
ᶠ13:5 Or *sold*   ᴳ13:6 Lit *wounds between your hands*   ᴴ13:8 Lit *two-thirds in it*

cup of God's wrath (Jr 25:15–17,27–29; cp. Is 51:17; Ezk 23:32–34). What may taste good at first—when the nations attack Jerusalem—will leave them staggering around helplessly. Jerusalem's destruction would involve moving **heavy** stones, but in this case the stones would be too large, resulting in severe injury to anyone who attempted it. Placing a **firepot in a woodpile** or a **flaming torch among sheaves** would result in a quick conflagration, signaling the ease with which Jerusalem's enemies would be defeated. An especially vivid picture is seeing **the one who is weakest** transformed into a superior fighter **like David**. To declare that Jerusalem would become the **house of David** and that it would be **like God** is the highest exaltation possible—an amazing reversal from God forsaking his people (11:9–10).
12:3 On that day may be translated "in the future." **When all the nations of the earth**

gather against her may be a hyperbolic statement and not necessarily a reference to a final epic battle. However, some commentators think this language refers to a specific battle in the end times (Armageddon). In either case, Zechariah's intent was to energize the current inhabitants of Jerusalem by looking ahead to God's blessings.
12:10–14 The announcement of God's blessing on Jerusalem shifts to spiritual reconciliation, which is dependent on divine grace and human contrition. The interpretive crux is the identity of **me whom they pierced**, especially when the prophet declared, **they will mourn for him**. The best explanation is that God's true followers will recognize that by their disobedience and rejection of the divine Shepherd, they in effect pierced God's soul. Verse 10 also anticipates Jesus's crucifixion, as indicated by the quotation in Jn 19:37.

13:1–6 The oracle turns to two of the most heinous sins that needed to be washed away—worshiping other gods and prophesying falsely in God's name. False prophecy is so detestable that a counterfeit prophet's own parents would kill him.
13:4–6 A **hairy cloak** is an allusion to Elijah's clothes (2Kg 1:8), not necessarily an indication that all prophets dressed this way. The attempt of false prophets to hide their identity involved displaying **wounds** that were probably self-inflicted (1Kg 18:28). Claiming that the "wounds" were routine from a scuffle with **friends** would lead to more suspicion because the Hebrew word translated "friends" may denote illicit lovers.
13:7–9 Though the identity of the **shepherd** is ambiguous, the overall point of the passage is clear: to purge and refine, separating the true from the false. God desires followers worthy of the affirmation that **they are my**

and test them as gold is tested.
They will call on my name,
and I will answer them.
I will say, 'They are my people,'
and they will say, 'The Lord is our God.' "

The Lord's Triumph and Reign

14 Look, a day belonging to the Lord is coming when the plunder taken from you will be divided in your presence. ² I will gather all the nations against Jerusalem for battle. The city will be captured, the houses looted, and the women raped. Half the city will go into exile, but the rest of the people will not be removed from the city.

³ Then the Lord will go out to fight against those nations as he fights on a day of battle. ⁴ On that day his feet will stand on the Mount of Olives, which faces Jerusalem on the east. The Mount of Olives will be split in half from east to west, forming a huge valley, so that half the mountain will move to the north and half to the south. ⁵ You will flee by my mountain valley,^ for the valley of the mountains will extend to Azal. You will flee as you fled⁸ from the earthquake in the days of King Uzziah of Judah. Then the Lord my God will come and all the holy ones with him.^

⁶ On that day there will be no light; the sunlight and moonlight will diminish.^D,E ⁷ It will be a unique day known only to the Lord, without day or night, but there will be light at evening.

⁸ On that day living water will flow out from Jerusalem, half of it toward the eastern sea^F and the other half toward the western sea,^G in summer and winter alike. ⁹ On that day the Lord will become King over the whole earth — the Lord alone, and his name alone. ¹⁰ All the land from Geba to Rimmon south of Jerusalem will be changed into a plain. But Jerusalem will be raised up and will remain^H on its site from the Benjamin Gate to the place of the First

Gate,^I to the Corner Gate, and from the Tower of Hananel to the royal winepresses. ¹¹ People will live there, and never again will there be a curse of complete destruction. So Jerusalem will dwell in security.

¹² This will be the plague with which the Lord strikes all the people who have warred against Jerusalem: their flesh will rot while they stand on their feet, their eyes will rot in their sockets, and their tongues will rot in their mouths. ¹³ On that day a great panic from the Lord will be among them, so that each will seize the hand of another, and the hand of one will rise against the other. ¹⁴ Judah will also fight at Jerusalem, and the wealth of all the surrounding nations will be collected: gold, silver, and clothing in great abundance. ¹⁵ The same plague as the previous one will strike^J the horses, mules, camels, donkeys, and all the animals that are in those camps.

¹⁶ Then all the survivors from the nations that came against Jerusalem will go up year after year to worship the King, the Lord of Armies, and to celebrate the Festival of Shelters. ¹⁷ Should any of the families of the earth not go up to Jerusalem to worship the King, the Lord of Armies, rain will not fall on them. ¹⁸ And if the people^K of Egypt will not go up and enter, then rain will not fall on them; this will be the plague the Lord inflicts on the nations who do not go up to celebrate the Festival of Shelters. ¹⁹ This will be the punishment of Egypt and all the nations that do not go up to celebrate the Festival of Shelters.

²⁰ On that day, the words Holy to the Lord will be on the bells of the horses. The pots in the house of the Lord will be like the sprinkling basins before the altar. ²¹ Every pot in Jerusalem and in Judah will be holy to the Lord of Armies. All who sacrifice will come and use the pots to cook in. And on that day there will no longer be a Canaanite^L in the house of the Lord of Armies.

---

^A 14:5 Some Hb mss, LXX, Sym, Tg read *The valley of my mountains will be blocked*　^B 14:5 LXX reads *It will be blocked as it was blocked*　^C 14:5 Some Hb mss, LXX, Vg, Tg, Syr; other Hb mss read *you*　^D 14:6 LXX, Sym, Syr, Tg, Vg read *no light or cold or ice*　^E 14:6 Lit *no light; the precious ones will congeal*　^F 14:8 = the Dead Sea　^G 14:8 = the Mediterranean Sea　^H 14:10 Or *will be inhabited*　^I 14:10 Or *the former gate*　^J 14:15 Lit *be on*　^K 14:18 Lit *family*　^L 14:21 Or *merchant*

---

people (see note at 8:7–8). God scattered them and cut off two-thirds in order to gain a remnant that would sincerely say, the Lord is our God. Possibilities for the meaning of "my shepherd" being struck include a flashback to striking the arm of the worthless shepherd (11:17). Alternatively, Jesus's quote of the lines with regard to his death and his disciples falling away (Mt 26:31) suggests that "shepherd" may have anticipated the messianic King.

14:1–21 The book of Zechariah ends in classic prophetic fashion. The nations attack Jerusalem, God intervenes and blesses Jerusalem miraculously, God announces curses for Jerusalem's enemies, and the peoples of the world go up to Jerusalem to worship. Everything from cooking pots to horses' bells is set apart as Holy to the Lord, a privilege previously extended only to the temple and priests (Ex 28:36–38).

14:2–5 The venue for God's great triumph is the city of Jerusalem under severe duress, not only being plundered but with the enemy dividing up belongings in the presence of the inhabitants (vv. 1–2). Yet the victory involved a huge valley providing a miraculous way of escape. On God as Divine Warrior, see note at 9:10–15. Holy ones refers to angelic forces from heaven (Ps 89:5,7; Jd 14). 14:8 Since water was a premium in Palestine, and Jerusalem was not near a river, the picture of a year-round source of living water flowing from the city with sufficient quantity to reach the Dead Sea and the Mediterranean Sea was inspiring. It would require supernatural redesign of the geography of the region. "Living water" refers to fresh spring water as opposed to water stored in cisterns.

14:10 Isaiah envisioned Jerusalem to be on the highest mountain of the world, with

people streaming to it from all over the earth (Is 2:2–3; cp. Mc 4:1–2). Here the picture is of people coming to Jerusalem for the Festival of Shelters (Tabernacles, cp. v. 16; see Dt 16:13–15). 14:12–13 The judgment of these verses recalls that inflicted on the army of Sennacherib during the reign of Hezekiah (2Kg 19:35). 14:14–15 These verses are a reversal of vv. 1–2 (cp. Hg 2:7–8). 14:16–19 Rain will not fall on them is standard language of judgment. 14:20–21 The holiness once residing in the temple will be transferred to the entire city of Jerusalem. Canaanite is a pejorative term since the Israelites considered the Canaanites vile and morally reprehensible. But the Israelites had become "Canaanites" by their disobedience. The announcement that there would be no Canaanite in the temple signified the purity of God's chosen people.

Introduction to Malachi

Circumstances of Writing

Nothing is known about the author except his name. The book emphasizes the message rather than the messenger; God is the speaker in about forty-seven of the fifty-five verses. The one prophesied in 3:1 to "clear the way" for God to come to his temple is identified as *malakiy,* "my messenger," a Hebrew word identical to the name of the book's author.

Although the book is not dated by a reference to a ruler or a specific event, internal evidence, as well as its position in the canon, favors a postexilic date. Reference to a governor in 1:8 favors the Persian period when Judah was a province or subprovince of the Persian satrapy Abar Nahara, which included Palestine, Syria, Phoenicia, Cyprus, and, until 485 BC, Babylon. The temple had been rebuilt (515 BC) and worship reestablished there (1:6–11; 2:1–3; 3:1,10). But the excitement and enthusiasm for which the prophets Haggai and Zechariah were the catalysts had waned. The social and religious problems that Malachi addressed reflect the situation portrayed in Ezra 9 and 10 and Nehemiah 5 and 13, suggesting dates not long before Ezra's return to Judah (ca 460 BC) or Nehemiah's second term as governor of Judah (Neh 13:6–7; ca 435 BC). Linguistic data favors the earlier date.

Contribution to the Bible

Malachi was the last prophetic message from God before the close of the Old Testament period. This book is a fitting conclusion to the Old Testament and a transition for understanding the kingdom proclamation in the New Testament. Malachi spoke to the hearts of a troubled people whose circumstances of financial insecurity, religious skepticism, and personal disappointments were similar to those often experienced by God's people today. The book contains a message that must not be overlooked by those who wish to encounter God and his kingdom and to lead others to a similar encounter. We have a great, loving, and holy God, who has unchanging and glorious purposes for his people. Our God calls us to genuine worship, fidelity to himself and to one another, and to expectant faith in what he is doing and says he will do in this world and for his people.

God's love is paramount. It is expressed in Malachi in terms of God's election and protection of Israel above all the nations of the world. Since God had served the interests of Judah out of his unchanging love, he required Judah to live up to its obligations by obedience, loyalty, and sincere worship. This love relationship between God and Judah is the model for how people were expected to treat other members of the redeemed community. They were required to be faithful in all their dealings with one another.

As a community devoted to God, his people enjoy his protection and provision. But failure to live right before God and one another will bring God's judgment. Thus God's people could not expect the joy of his blessings if they continued to fail in their duties to him and to one another. Before God would hold Judah in the balance of judgment, he would

Malachi Timeline

625–525 BC

The Assyrian Empire comes to an end when the Babylonians and Medes destroy Nineveh. **612**

The Babylonians level Jerusalem and the temple. **586**

Cyrus, founding ruler of the Medo-Persian Empire, captures Babylon with little resistance. **539**

Cyrus's decree allows return of Jews from exile; 42,360 return initially. **538**

Second temple construction begins under Zerubbabel's and Joshua's leadership. **536**

Cambyses, son of Cyrus, rules Persian Empire. **530–522**

525–480 BC

Discouragement reinforced by opposition from transplanted people brings work on the temple to a halt. **526**

Darius I (Darius the Great) succeeds Cambyses. **521–486**

Haggai and Zechariah encourage the people to resume construction of the temple. **520–518**

Temple completed **MARCH 12, 515**

Xerxes (Ahasuerus) ascends the throne of Persia upon the death of his father, Darius I. **486**

grant one last call for repentance. A forerunner would precede the fearsome day of the Lord and herald the coming of God's kingdom on earth.

Structure

Malachi's message is communicated in three interrelated addresses. Each address contains five sections arranged in a mirrorlike repetitive structure surrounding a central section (a-b-c-b-a).

The first two addresses begin with positive motivation or hope (1:2–5; 2:10a) and end with negative motivation or judgment (2:1–9; 3:1–6). In between is God's indictment (1:6–9,11–14; 2:10b–15a,17) surrounding his commands (1:10; 2:15b–16). The final climactic address begins and ends with commands to repent (3:7–10a; 4:4–6). In between are sections of motivation (3:10b–12; 3:16–4:3) surrounding the indictment (3:13–15).

Key verse in Malachi

3:10 "Bring the full tenth into the storehouse so that there may be food in my house. Test me in this way," says the LORD of Armies. "See if I will not open the floodgates of heaven and pour out a blessing for you without measure."

480–460 BC

Greek victories over Persians in battles of Salamis **(480)** and Plain of Plataea **(479)** thwart Persian expansion into Europe and are keys to Greek hegemony in the Mediterranean Basin and Europe.
Esther becomes queen of Persia. **479**
Esther intercedes with Xerxes for her people. **474**
First celebration of Purim **473**
Xerxes I (Ahasuerus), husband of Esther, assassinated **465**
Artaxerxes I succeeds his father. **465–423**

460–425 BC

Malachi's prophecy **460**
Ezra leads second group of Jewish exiles to Jerusalem. **458**
Events in Nehemiah **445–430**
Jerusalem's walls rebuilt under Nehemiah's leadership **445**
Nehemiah returns to Persia. **432**
The second of the Peloponnesian Wars between Athens and other Greek city-states **431–404**
Nehemiah returns to Jerusalem. **425**

The LORD's Love for Israel

1 A pronouncement:
The word of the LORD to Israel through Malachi.[A]

[2] "I have loved you," says the LORD.

Yet you ask, "How have you loved us?"

"Wasn't Esau Jacob's brother?" This is the LORD's declaration. "Even so, I loved Jacob, [3] but I hated Esau. I turned his mountains into a wasteland, and gave his inheritance to the desert jackals."

[4] Though Edom says, "We have been devastated, but we will rebuild[B] the ruins," the LORD of Armies says this: "They may build, but I will demolish. They will be called a wicked country and the people the LORD has cursed[C] forever. [5] Your own eyes will see this, and you yourselves will say, 'The LORD is great, even beyond[D] the borders of Israel.'

Disobedience of the Priests

[6] "A son honors his father, and a servant his master. But if I am a father, where is my honor? And if I am a master, where is your fear of me? says the LORD of Armies to you priests, who despise my name."

Yet you ask, "How have we despised your name?"

[7] "By presenting defiled food on my altar."

"How have we defiled you?" you ask.

When you say, "The LORD's table is contemptible."

[8] "When you present a blind animal for sacrifice, is it not wrong? And when you present a lame or sick animal, is it not wrong? Bring it to your governor! Would he be pleased with you or show you favor?" asks the LORD of Armies.

[9] "And now plead for God's favor. Will he be gracious to us? Since this has come from your hands, will he show any of you favor?" asks the LORD of Armies. [10] "I wish one of you would shut the temple doors, so that you would no longer kindle a useless fire on my altar! I am not pleased with you," says the LORD of Armies, "and I will accept no offering from your hands.

[11] "My name will be great among the nations, from the rising of the sun to its setting. Incense[E] and pure offerings will be presented in my name in every place because my name will be great among the nations,"[F] says the LORD of Armies.

[12] "But you are profaning it when you say, 'The Lord's table is defiled, and its product, its food, is contemptible.' [13] You also say, 'Look, what a nuisance!' And you scorn[G] it,"[H] says the LORD of Armies. "You bring stolen,[I] lame, or sick animals. You bring this as an offering! Am I to accept that from your hands?" asks the LORD.

[14] "The deceiver is cursed who has an acceptable male in his flock and makes a vow but sacrifices a defective animal to the Lord. For I am a great King," says the LORD of Armies, "and my name will be feared among the nations.

Warning to the Priests

2 "Therefore, this decree is for you priests: [2] If you don't listen, and if you don't take it to heart to honor my name," says the LORD of Armies, "I will send a curse among you, and I will curse your blessings. In fact, I have already begun to curse them because you are not taking it to heart.

[3] "Look, I am going to rebuke your descendants, and I will spread animal waste[J] over

---

[A] 1:1 = My Messenger [B] 1:4 Or *will return and build* [C] 1:4 Or *LORD is angry with* [D] 1:5 Or *great over* [E] 1:11 Or *Burnt offerings* [F] 1:11 Or *is great . . . are presented . . . is great* [G] 1:13 Lit *blow at* [H] 1:13 Alt Hb tradition reads *me* [I] 1:13 Or *injured* [J] 2:3 Dung or entrails

---

1:2 The Lord reminded the people in 1:2–5 of his faithful love throughout their history (Jr 31:3). But Judah disputed God's love, showing they had allowed life's trials to blind them to his faithfulness and loving presence. Such spiritual depletion was at the root of not only

Israel's insulting religious rites (Mal 1:6–14) but also the moral decay and spiritual indifference that Malachi described. **1:3–5** God's love had been abundantly demonstrated in recent history, in contrast to his dealings with the nation of **Edom** (descended from Jacob's twin brother, Gn 25). **I loved Jacob** refers to God's choosing him over Esau as recipient and instrument of his blessing (Gn 25:23; Rm 9:10–13) as well as to God's enduring love for Jacob's descendants. God **hated Esau** insomuch as he did not choose to make a covenant of blessing with him and his descendants (the Edomites) but instead destroyed them for their rebellion. **1:6** The only appropriate response to God's holiness is **fear**, which is essential to wisdom (Pr 1:7; Mc 6:9) and true faith (Is 33:6; 50:10), as well as wholehearted devotion and obedience. **1:7** The temple **altar** is compared to a divinely hosted dinner **table**, a symbol of hospitality and relationship (Ezk 44:16). Their casual attitude toward the altar showed how little the people valued their relationship with God.

1:8–9 They were bringing to their God what they wouldn't dare offer their **governor**. Besides, these offerings were in violation of the Mosaic law (Lv 22:18–25; Dt 15:21). **Plead for God's favor** in v. 9 is ironic and is understood as a kind of condition. Both the questions here are assumed to have a negative reply. **1:10** King Ahaz in earlier years had **shut the temple doors** to pursue the worship of idols (2Ch 28:24). **1:11–14** A time is coming when even Gentiles everywhere will recognize the Lord's greatness and worship him (Is 59:19; Ezk 36:20–36; 39:7; Mt 8:11–12; Rm 11:11–12). But God's own children, his kingdom of priests who were to mediate his grace to the nations, were **profaning** his **name**. God's "name" is his nature, character, and worth as he reveals it in his words and acts (Gn 16:13; 17:5; 22:14; Ex 33:19; 1Kg 8:43). **2:1–3** God decreed that if the priests' attitude and behavior did not change, he would treat them with contempt (as they had treated him). The **waste** consisted of the dung and unclean sacrificial remains after a temple festival that were disposed of "outside the camp" (Ex 29:14; Lv 16:27–28).

#55 99 Essential Christian Truths

SIN'S EFFECTS IN THE WORLD

Sin not only affects our relationship with God but is also the root of our broken relationships with the people around us. Human sinfulness is the reason the creation groans in anticipation for redemption and deliverance from its bondage to evil powers (Rm 8:20–22). Sin has infected and redirected the social structures of society, leading to injustice and oppression. The distorting effects of sin are visible all around us, but the good news of the gospel is that the battle against these powers will be won through the work of Christ.

your faces, the waste from your festival sacrifices, and you will be taken away with it. **4** Then you will know that I sent you this decree, so that my covenant with Levi may continue," says the LORD of Armies. **5** "My covenant with him was one of life and peace, and I gave these to him; it called for reverence, and he revered me and stood in awe of my name. **6** True instruction was in his mouth, and nothing wrong was found on his lips. He walked with me in peace and integrity and turned many from iniquity. **7** For the lips of a priest should guard knowledge, and people should desire instruction from his mouth, because he is the messenger of the LORD of Armies.

8 "You, on the other hand, have turned from the way. You have caused many to stumble by your instruction. You have violated^A the covenant of Levi," says the LORD of Armies. **9** "So I in turn have made you despised and humiliated before all the people because you are not keeping my ways but are showing partiality in your instruction."

Judah's Marital Unfaithfulness

10 Don't all of us have one Father? Didn't one God create us? Why then do we act treacherously against one another, profaning the covenant of our ancestors? **11** Judah has acted treacherously, and a detestable act has been done in Israel and in Jerusalem. For Judah has profaned the LORD's sanctuary,^B which he loves, and has married the daughter of a foreign god.^C **12** May the LORD cut off from the tents of Jacob the man who does this, whoever he may be,^D even if he presents an offering to the LORD of Armies.

13 This is another thing you do. You are covering the LORD's altar with tears, with weeping and groaning, because he no longer respects your offerings or receives them gladly from your hands. **14** And you ask, "Why?" Because even though the LORD has been a witness between you and the wife of your youth, you have acted treacherously against her. She was your marriage partner and your wife by covenant. **15** Didn't God make them one and give them a portion of spirit? What is the one seeking?^D Godly offspring. So watch yourselves carefully,^E so that no one acts treacherously against the wife of his^F youth. **16** "If he hates and divorces his wife," says the LORD God of Israel, "he^G covers his garment with injustice," says the LORD of Armies. Therefore, watch yourselves carefully,^H and do not act treacherously.

Judgment at the LORD's Coming

17 You have wearied the LORD with your words. Yet you ask, "How have we wearied him?"

When you say, "Everyone who does what is evil is good in the LORD's sight, and he is delighted with them, or else where is the God of justice?"

3 "See, I am going to send my messenger, and he will clear the way before me. Then the Lord you seek will suddenly come

---

^A**2:8** Lit *corrupted*   ^B**2:11** Or *profaned what is holy to the LORD*   ^C**2:11** = a woman who worshiped a foreign god
^D**2:12,15** Hb obscure   ^E**2:15** Lit *So guard yourselves in your spirit*   ^F**2:15** Lit *your*   ^G**2:16** Or *The LORD God of Israel says
that he hates divorce and the one who*   ^H**2:16** Lit *Therefore, guard yourselves in your spirit*

2:4–9 The **covenant with** or of **Levi** in vv. 4,8 refers not to a covenant with the son of Jacob but to the "covenant of peace" that God made with the Levite Phinehas, Aaron's grandson. God promised Phinehas and his descendants a "perpetual priesthood" in return for his zeal in protecting Israel from the corruption of idolatry (Nm 25:1–13). The tribe's function was to teach the law to Israel and in that sense to be God's **messenger** and to officiate at the altar (Lv 10:8–11; Dt 33:8–11). The priests had **violated** the covenant. **2:10** The words **act treacherously** that occur in vv. 10–11,14–16 designate failure to fulfill one's promised obligations—i.e., to betray another. The **covenant of our ancestors** is the Mosaic covenant (Jdg 2:20; 1Kg 8:21). To "profane" it meant to treat it with contempt (Mal 1:12; 2:11) by violating it. **2:11–12** The most obvious way Judah was violating the covenant was by intermarriage with women who worshiped foreign gods, thus introducing a spiritually destructive element into the covenant community (Ex 34:11–16; Dt 7:3–4; Ezr 9:1–2; Neh 13:26; 2Co 6:14–17). A **detestable act** was one that caused such serious defilement that destruction or death was required (Lv 18:29; Dt 7:25; 13:15; Jr 44:22–23). Anyone who did this was cursed (Mal 2:12). The last clause (lit "and presenting an offering to Yahweh of hosts")

probably explains more precisely why their sin profaned the sanctuary: They were continuing to sacrifice to God despite their sin. **2:13–14** To marry pagan women, some men were divorcing their Jewish wives to whom they had sworn faithfulness before God. An **other thing you do** is not the *weeping* of v. 13, but introduces the issue of divorce in v. 14. Divorce, after intermarriage, was the second detestable act of treachery that was profaning the sanctuary (v. 11). Divorce profaned the sanctuary because the people continued to offer their sacrifices (v. 13) despite their marital betrayals. God's refusal to respond favorably to their offerings (hence their tears; see Gn 4:4–5; Ps 6:6–9) was probably linked to their continuing economic and social troubles (Neh 9:32–37; Hg 1:6,9–11; 2:16–19). Persistent sin renders worship meaningless. **Marriage partner** renders a word for someone with whom one is bound by covenant. **2:15** Verse 15a seems to indicate that the marriage bond is not only earthly and easily dissolved but also the product of God's Spirit, whose purpose is to produce **godly offspring.** **2:16** This verse ends by repeating v. 15b with one significant change. After speaking to "you" in vv. 13–15a, v. 15b switches back to third person "he" as in vv. 11–12, ending literally, "and with the wife of your youth let him

not act treacherously." Verse 16 opens with a verb that clearly means "he hates," although most translations change it to "I hate." But the subject apparently is the one who "acts treacherously," and who also **covers his garment with injustice.** The one speaking is **the LORD God of Israel,** and contrary to KJV, NKJV, etc., there is no indication of indirect discourse ("says that"), so God cannot be the subject of "he hates." This verse specifies how wives were being betrayed. Their husbands were "hating" so as to "divorce" them for no legitimate reason (Dt 24:3), which was a heinous injustice. Such a cold-blooded and unscrupulous traitor to his marital responsibilities, who would deny his wife the very things he had pledged to provide—devotion, care, companionship, protection, intimacy, peace, justice (Gn 2:24; Ex 21:10; Dt 22:13–19; Pr 5:15–20)—stood condemned by God, and he wore the stain of his crime like a garment for all to see (Ps 73:6). **2:17** They accused God of injustice for not coming to their aid and punishing people they considered "evil" (1:2; 3:15). God's ironic reply was to announce in 3:1–6 a coming messenger of "judgment" (3:5; the same Hb word as **justice**) who would purge and purify God's people, including the priests. **3:1–5** God's **messenger** here is the "voice . . . in the wilderness" of Is 40:3, which the NT interprets as the "Elijah" of Mal 4:5,

◥ A Biblical Basis for Science

by John A. Bloom

A popular myth in our culture says that science and theology have always been at war with each other. It may come as a surprise to learn that most historians of science believe this idea to be untrue. In fact, the Bible provided some of the key intellectual foundations for the development of the sciences in the West.

God as Master of the Universe

The first foundation is the expectation of regularity in nature, which stems from the Bible's monotheistic view of God. Polytheistic and pantheistic religions see the universe as run by committee, with unpredictable events arising from conflicts among the many supernatural personalities involved. As a result, nature is seen as capricious, without any expectation of regularity.

By contrast, the Bible presents God as the sole master of the universe (Ps 89:11–13; Is 48:12–13), which he spoke into existence (Pss 33:6–9; 148:5) and over which he rules (Is 40:26). Since one God is in control of nature and has said that he does not change (Nm 23:19; Mal 3:6), we can expect his universe to run in a regular way. This is more than an inference: God explicitly says that he established the heavens and earth to follow regular laws (Gn 8:22; Jr 33:20,25).

Science as a Worthy Pursuit

Another foundation is the Bible's teaching that the study of nature is a worthy pursuit in gaining wisdom and glorifying God. God's creation is good, and even though it is corrupted by sin, we are encouraged to learn from it (Ps 19:1; Pr 6:6). Job 38–39 and Psalm 104 praise God's wisdom, sovereignty, and control over creation. Scientists such as Isaac Newton and Johannes Kepler often stated that they sought to glorify God by studying his creation. By contrast, many world religions view nature in a dualistic manner, regarding the spiritual world as good and the material world as evil.

The Complexity of God's World

A third biblical foundation for science is that God's creation is not simple to understand. God informs us, "My thoughts are not your thoughts, and your ways are not my ways" (Is 55:8; see also Pr 25:2). Yet "the LORD founded the earth by wisdom and established the heavens by understanding" (3:19). This suggests that, through difficult study, we may be able to glimpse some of God's wisdom. When doing science, as Kepler quipped, we are "thinking God's thoughts after Him."

God's Contingency

The last foundation to mention here is God's contingency: God created the world as he wanted it to be; he was not bound by outside constraints like human logic or philosophical principles. God "does whatever he pleases in heaven and on earth, in the seas and all the depths" (Ps 135:6; see also 115:3). Therefore, we cannot predict how God created; we must study God's handiwork itself to see what he has done. Thus, good science is based on direct observations and experiments while theories are held tentatively until proven beyond doubt.

Tensions between Science and Theology

While the Bible is not a scientific textbook, we find that it provides the correct perspectives for viewing nature and the proper motivations for studying it. Science is arguably one of the tasks mankind is commissioned to do: Adam was to "name" the animals in the garden of Eden (Gn 2:19), and he was given stewardship over the earth (1:28), a task that required study and wisdom to do it well. Although the Bible has higher priorities than explaining how the heavens work, biblical descriptions of nature are profoundly true while simply stated. Examples are the creation event in Genesis 1:1 (see also Is 44:24; Heb 11:3) and the heavens and the earth's wearing out over time (Ps 102:25–26), an echo of the second law of thermodynamics.

If the study of nature was historically grounded in biblical insights, how did the modern tensions between science and theology arise? The drift started in the late 1600s when the philosophers of the Enlightenment freed themselves from the shackles of Aristotle and other ancient authorities by attempting to rely only on reason and experience to establish truth claims. Newton's discovery of the laws of motion and gravity led philosophers and theologians away from a theistic view (where God is actively involved in nature) to a deistic view (where God created the universe but now allows it to operate via laws he established). In the 1800s T. H. Huxley and others desired to ground all knowledge on physical cause and effect, removing religious authority from society and replacing it with the authority of science. This narrowed the practice of science, limiting it to purely naturalistic explanations of the world.

Thus, the issues between the sciences and theology today hinge on the religious differences between naturalism and theism. In other words, should we view the universe as purely a machine which God cannot touch, or as a musical instrument which God plays for his glory? The difference is profound with respect to the explanations we can accept for natural phenomena. For example, if naturalism is assumed, something like Darwinism must be the "scientific" explanation for how life developed because God's guidance or intervention in nature is ruled out. Any naturalistic explanation must be preferred, no matter how implausible it is, because others would not be naturalistic. Unfortunately, by ignoring some possible answers, science today may be missing the truth. This is perhaps most evident in the fields of biology, psychology, and the social sciences where the abandonment of man's special place in creation in favor of explaining him as a machine or an animal has led to the devaluing of human life and personhood.

Strikingly, this philosophical shift in the foundation of science from theism to naturalism leaves people with little justification to pursue science. Better technology can earn one fame and fortune, a military advantage, or more comfortable living, but naturalistically minded scientists have no reason to expect mathematics to explain and predict how the universe behaves, no reason to expect the world to operate in a regular manner, and no explanation for what put the "material" in materialism in the first place. The ad hoc nature of the naturalistic presupposition has become more glaring with the recognition that our universe is not eternal but had a beginning and that the physical laws and constants themselves appear to be fine-tuned to allow for the possibility of complex, intelligent life. Naturalists sometimes suggest that our universe is just one among countless universes in a so-called multiverse and that with so many universes the chances were good that at least one would turn out to be fine-tuned for life. But importantly, there is no evidence indicating that other universes exist.

Christians and Science

Is it possible for the sciences to return to a biblical basis? For Christians it certainly is. We should look beyond the naturalistic, materialistic, and mechanistic blinders that limit the perspective of our culture. Christians who marvel at the wisdom, power, and creativity demonstrated in God's handiwork, as the biblical writers and early scientists did, have a strong motive to pursue the sciences even if their colleagues espouse a narrower viewpoint.

The fine-tuning of our universe and the fact that it had a beginning strongly imply that someone is behind it. So too does the dizzying complexity of life, which is becoming more evident as biochemistry unravels the secrets of life. If, through continued discoveries like these, the naturalistic straitjacket on valid scientific explanations comes to be seen for what it is, perhaps science will soon shed naturalism. Perhaps then it will return to its theistic roots—the most fruitful perspective for viewing nature.

to his temple, the Messenger of the covenant you delight in — see, he is coming," says the Lord of Armies. ² But who can endure the day of his coming? And who will be able to stand when he appears? For he will be like a refiner's fire and like launderer's bleach.ᴬ ³ He will be like a refiner and purifier of silver; he will purify the sons of Levi and refine them like gold and silver. Then they will present offerings to the Lord in righteousness. ⁴ And the offerings of Judah and Jerusalem will please the Lord as in days of old and years gone by.

⁵ "I will come to you in judgment, and I will be ready to witness against sorcerers and adulterers; against those who swear falsely; against those who oppress the hired worker, the widow, and the fatherless; and against those who deny justice to the resident alien. They do not fear me," says the Lord of Armies. ⁶ "Because I, the Lord, have not changed, you descendants of Jacob have not been destroyed.ᴮ

Robbing God

⁷ "Since the days of your ancestors, you have turned from my statutes; you have not kept them. Return to me, and I will return to you," says the Lord of Armies.

Yet you ask, "How can we return?"

⁸ "Will a man rob God? Yet you are robbing me!"

"How do we rob you?" you ask.

"By not making the payments of the tenth and the contributions. ⁹ You are suffering under a curse, yetᶜ you — the whole nation — are still robbing me. ¹⁰ Bring the full tenth into the storehouse so that there may be food in my house. Test me in this way," says the Lord of Armies. "See if I will not open the floodgates of heaven and pour out a blessing for you without

measure. ¹¹ I will rebuke the devourerᴰ for you, so that it will not ruin the produce of your land and your vine in your field will not fail to produce fruit," says the Lord of Armies. ¹² "Then all the nations will consider you fortunate, for you will be a delightful land," says the Lord of Armies.

The Righteous and the Wicked

¹³ "Your words against me are harsh," says the Lord.

Yet you ask, "What have we spoken against you?"

¹⁴ You have said, "It is useless to serve God. What have we gained by keeping his requirements and walking mournfully before the Lord of Armies? ¹⁵ So now we consider the arrogant to be fortunate. Not only do those who commit wickedness prosper, they even test God and escape."

¹⁶ At that time those who feared the Lord spoke to one another. The Lord took notice and listened. So a book of remembrance was written before him for those who feared the Lord and had high regard for his name. ¹⁷ "They will be mine," says the Lord of Armies, "my own possession on the day I am preparing. I will have compassion on them as a man has compassion on his son who serves him. ¹⁸ So you will again see the difference between the righteous and the wicked, between one who serves God and one who does not serve him.

The Day of the Lord

4 "For look, the day is coming, burning like a furnace, when all the arrogant and everyone who commits wickedness will become stubble. The coming day will consume them," says the Lord of Armies, "not leaving them root or branches. ² But for you who fear my name,

---

ᴬ3:2 Lit *cleansing agent*　　ᴮ3:6 Or *Because I, the Lord, do not change, you descendants of Jacob are not destroyed*　　ᶜ3:9 Or *because*　　ᴰ3:11 Perhaps locusts

---

fulfilled (conditionally) by John the Baptist (Mt 3:3; 11:14; 17:10–13). His goal would be to exhort the people to repent and prepare for God's other **Messenger** (see Jn 1:14–17). This "Messenger" is distinguished from God by referring to him as **he**, and yet also identified with God by calling him **the Lord** in v. 1 and **I** in v. 5. Verse 1 is quoted in Mt 11:10; Mk 1:2; Lk 7:27.

3:6 In reply to charges that he had been unfaithful, God declared that if he were not the immutable God whose purposes and promises were irrevocable, Israel's rebellion would have destroyed them long ago. **3:7–10a** The final, climactic address begins with a command to **return** (Jr 3:22–4:4; 24:7; Hs 14:1–2; Zch 1:3) to the Lord, and it ends with a command to "remember" his instructions (Mal 4:4). Evidence of the people's return to God would be to resume bringing tithes and other **contributions** to support the priests, Levites, and landless poor (Lv 27:30–33; Nm 18:8–32; Dt 12:5–19; 14:22–29; 26:12–15; Neh 10:38; 13:10). Such offerings

would demonstrate a proper attitude toward their possessions as God's gifts (Dt 6:10–12; 8:17–18). **3:10b–12** Although testing God with complaining, rebellion, and unbelief is wrong (v. 15; Ex 17:2–7; Ps 95:8–9), testing his faithfulness with our obedience is not. The phrase rendered **without measure** may also mean "only what you need" (Pr 25:16). The Mosaic covenant promised material blessings or curses (Dt 28) to the nation as a whole, not necessarily to the individual. **3:13–15** On the **harsh** words, see Jdg 14–15. Judah's current difficulties had led them to conclude there was no advantage in serving God (Is 5:20; Mal 2:17). The word for **gained** refers to dishonest gain (see Is 56:11). **3:16–18** The **book of remembrance** was the royal archives where the most significant events of a king's reign were recorded (Ezr 4:15; 5:17). As Mordecai was rewarded on the basis of the royal archives (Est 2:23; 6:1–3), so it will be for all who fear God and treasure his name. God has already determined the

day when he will come with compassion to retrieve his **own possession** (see Ex 19:5; Dt 7:6; 14:1–2; 26:18; Ps 135:4), all who serve him in faith (Ezk 34:11–31; Gl 1:4; Eph 1:14). **4:1** The fiery element of the coming day echoes similar images in eschatological passages such as Jl 2:3–5 (see Ps 21:9; Is 31:9). The wicked may seem powerful, but they will be removed, both **root** and **branches**, from the earth like dry **stubble** thrown into a **furnace**. **4:2–3** Darkness in the Bible often symbolizes earthly life full of evil, ignorance, pain, and death (Gn 1:4; 1Sm 2:9; Is 8:22–9:2). God promises to invade this world with **righteousness** as the **sun** invades the night, driving the darkness away (Dt 33:2; 2Sm 23:3–4; Is 60:1–3,19–21). This image represents the Messiah, whose coming will be celebrated like the dawn (Lk 1:76–79). As a bird's **wings** offer protection (Dt 32:11), God's "wings" will bring healing to his children (Ps 91:4; Is 53:5; 57:18–19), who will never again fear **the wicked**.

Seeing Jesus
in the Exile and Return

▼ Old Testament	▼ New Testament
THE LORD: Will Send His Messenger to Prepare His Way *(Mal 3:1)*	**JESUS, THE LORD:** His Ways Are Prepared by John the Baptist *(Lk 1:76–77)*
Daniel: Determined Not to Defile Himself with the King's Food or Wine *(Dn 1:8)*	**Jesus:** Came to Take Away Sins, and There Is No Sin in Him *(1Jn 3:5)*
The Fourth Man: One "like a son of the gods" in the Furnace with the Exiles *(Dn 3:25)*	**The Son of God:** The One Who Endured the Fire of God's Wrath for Us *(Rm 3:25)*
Daniel: A Man of Wisdom, Said to Have "the spirit of the holy gods" in Him *(Dn 5:11–14)*	**Christ Jesus:** The Man of Wisdom, God-Given Wisdom for Our Salvation *(1Co 1:30)*
One Like a Son of Man: Coming on the Clouds to Rule *(Dn 7:13–14)*	**The Son of Man:** Jesus Coming on the Clouds with Power and Glory *(Mt 24:30)*
Cyrus the Persian: Anointed by God to Rule and Rebuild the Temple *(Is 44:24–45:7)*	**Jesus the Messiah:** Anointed by God to Rule—He Is the Temple *(Jn 1:41; 2:21)*
Zerubbabel: A Descendant of Jehoiachin; Returned from the Exile *(1Ch 3:19)*	**Jesus Christ:** A Descendant of Zerubbabel; the End the Exile *(Mt 1:12–17)*
Esther: Chosen as Queen "for such a time as this" to Save Her People *(Est 4:14)*	**Jesus:** Born in the Fullness of Time to Redeem Those Under the Law *(Gl 4:4–5)*
Ezra: Devoted Himself to Studying, Obeying, and Teaching the Law of the Lord *(Ezr 7:10)*	**Jesus:** The Scriptures, Including the Law of the Lord, Testify About Him *(Jn 5:39,46)*
Nehemiah: A Man of Prayer *(Neh 1:5–11; 2:4; 4:9; 5:19; 6:9,14; 13:14,22,29,31)*	**Jesus:** A Man of Prayer *(Mt 26:36–44; Lk 11:1–13; Jn 17; Rm 8:34; Heb 7:25)*
The Sun of Righteousness: Will Rise with Healing in Its Wings *(Mal 4:2)*	**The Dawn:** Jesus Will Visit Us and Guide Us into the Way of Peace *(Lk 1:78–79)*

the sun of righteousness will rise with healing in its wings, and you will go out and playfully jump like calves from the stall.[A] [3] You will trample the wicked, for they will be ashes under the soles of your feet on the day I am preparing," says the Lord of Armies.

A Final Warning

[4] "Remember the instruction of Moses my servant, the statutes and ordinances I commanded

him at Horeb for all Israel. [5] Look, I am going to send you the prophet Elijah before the great and terrible day of the Lord comes. [6] And he will turn the hearts of fathers to their children and the hearts of children to their fathers. Otherwise, I will come and strike the land[B] with a curse."

[A] 4:2 Or *like stall-fed calves*   [B] 4:6 Or *earth*

4:4–6 Malachi called the people of Israel to **remember** God's **instruction** through **Moses** (see Ps 119:16). On the **great and terrible day of the Lord**, see Jl 2:31 (the only other place where this phrase occurs). This will be a day of blessing for God's people as well as a time of judgment on his enemies. **Elijah**, mentioned twenty-eight times in the NT, was viewed as the preeminent prophet of repentance. Both Moses and Elijah were connected with **Horeb**, God's mountain (Ex 3:1; 1Kg 19:8). Although this prophecy was provisionally fulfilled by John the Baptist (Mal 3:1–5), it will be further fulfilled at Jesus's return (Mt 11:14; 17:11; Rv 11:3) and it will be accompanied by a great revival of faith in Israel (Dt 30:1–2). Mal 4:6, quoted in Lk 1:16–17, describes a time of reconciliation when "the disobedient" will accept the wisdom of "the righteous" and when **fathers** and their **children** will no longer live self-serving lives but will regard one another with compassion and respect (2:15; Ezk 5:10; Rm 1:30).

◤ The
New Testament

Introduction to the Gospels and Acts

by Andreas J. Köstenberger

The Fourfold Gospel

The Gospels (in the plural) are more accurately described as the "Fourfold Gospel" (in the singular) according to Matthew, Mark, Luke, and John. This is the way in which the canonical Gospels were viewed by the early church, as is reflected in their ancient titles "The Gospel according to Matthew," "The Gospel according to Mark," "The Gospel according to Luke," and "The Gospel according to John." This understanding attests to the Gospels' unity and complementary witness to the one gospel of the life, crucifixion, burial, and resurrection of the Lord Jesus Christ.

The fact that Luke and Acts are separated in the New Testament canon by the Gospel of John shows that genre considerations overrode keeping Luke–Acts together as a two-volume work. Just as the opening genealogy in Matthew provides a fitting introduction not only to Matthew but to all four Gospels, John's conclusion furnishes a suitable ending to the entire fourfold Gospel. Matthew's genealogy presents Jesus as the virgin-born son of Abraham and son of David (Mt 1:1–18); John's conclusion references the selectivity involved in the task of writing a Gospel (Jn 21:24–25; cp. 20:30–31).

In between these two Gospels, both of which were most likely aimed originally at a predominantly Jewish audience, are two Gospels that are addressed to a predominantly Gentile readership. Mark, most likely writing for a Roman audience, presents Jesus as the "Son of God," attested by a Roman centurion at the climax of his Gospel (Mk 15:39). Luke—a highly educated Gentile—drew on eyewitness accounts to highlight the fulfillment of messianic expectations in Jesus and to defend Christianity against charges of political subversiveness.

The Inclusion of the Gospels into the Canon

The fourfold Gospel canon has strong early support. The earliest canonical list, the Muratorian Canon (which most likely dates to ca AD 180), includes Matthew, Mark, Luke, and John—and only these four Gospels. The church father Irenaeus, likewise, attests to the fourfold Gospel. Other early canonical lists and church writers also reference these four Gospels, citing only these as Scripture. Conversely, there is no mention of the Gospel of Thomas (dated to the second century AD) or other early "Gospels" in any canonical lists alongside Matthew, Mark, Luke, and John.

It is therefore not accurate to say, as some scholars have done, that the four Gospels were selected for inclusion in the canon only in the fourth century AD. While it is true that the canon was formalized and finalized at that time, a "canon consciousness" was present in the church at least by the second century, as canonical lists and patristic citations attest. In fact, of the handful of possible rivals to the Gospels included in the New Testament, none comes even close in terms of date (first century), connection to apostolic eyewitness testimony, and other characteristics. The Gospel of Thomas, for example, is not only late but also constitutes a mere collection of some of Jesus's alleged sayings, completely lacking any narrative structure. Thus, to call Thomas a "Gospel" is really a misnomer.

Interpreting the Gospels and Acts

The Gospels are properly interpreted as coherent narratives centering on Jesus's messianic mission culminating in his crucifixion and resurrection. Along these lines, each Gospel exhibits a distinctive structure and literary plan as well as particular theological emphases. This unity in diversity results in a fourfold portrait of Jesus that highlights certain aspects of his messianic identity and mission that together provide a rich, full-orbed testimony to this most remarkable individual who came to secure salvation for those who place their trust in him.

Matthew's Gospel presents Jesus as the son of Abraham and son of David, showing how Jesus fulfilled God's promises to both Abraham and David. Matthew structures his Gospel around five major discourses of Jesus, beginning with the Sermon on the Mount (Mt 5–7) and continuing with Jesus's commissioning discourse (Mt 10), instructions in (kingdom) parables (Mt 13; 18), and teaching on the end times (Mt 24–25). These discourse sections alternate with narrative portions, showing Jesus to be the Messiah in both word and deed.

Mark's Gospel presents Jesus as the "Son of God" (Mk 1:1) who wields unparalleled authority over nature, sickness, death, and even the evil supernatural (demons). The plot pivots on Peter's confession of Jesus as Messiah halfway through the Gospel (Mk 8:29) and climaxes in the Roman centurion's confession of Jesus as the "Son of God" (Mk 15:39). Otherwise, mostly demons confess Jesus as the "Son of God" (e.g., Mk 3:11; 5:7), while Jesus's true identity remains largely veiled even for his closest followers.

Luke conceived of his Gospel and the book of Acts, both addressed to Theophilus (see Lk 1:1–4; Ac 1:1–3), as a coherent two-part narrative, viewing Acts as the sequel to his Gospel that picked up where it left off. Luke's Gospel traces Jesus's ministry from the early beginnings in Galilee to his later ministry in Judea. The latter spans ten chapters and builds drama and suspense as Jesus moves inexorably to Jerusalem, the eventual site of his confrontation with the Jewish authorities culminating in his crucifixion (Lk 9:51–19:27). Like Matthew and Mark, Luke tells the story of Jesus's demise in an extended passion narrative, featuring several distinctive resurrection appearances of the risen Jesus.

John structures his Gospel in four parts. The account is framed by a prologue (Jn 1:1-18) and epilogue (chap. 21). In between, the first half tells the story of Jesus's mission to the Jews (Jn 1:19–12:50), featuring seven messianic signs of Jesus. Once rejected by his own people (Jn 12:36–50), Jesus turns to the Twelve, the new messianic community (chaps. 13–17). Like the other Gospels, John includes a passion narrative, though focusing on the Roman rather than Jewish phase of Jesus's trial. The second half of the Gospel (chaps. 13–20) culminates in a commissioning scene and purpose statement.

In the book of Acts, Luke narrates the fulfillment of Jesus's vision that the believing community "will receive power when the Holy Spirit has come on you, and you will be my witnesses . . . to the end of the earth" (Ac 1:8). In this way, Jesus's mission is shown to be extended through the church's global, Spirit-empowered mission. Attention in Acts is divided between Peter (Ac 1–12) and Paul (Ac 13–28; though see chap. 9). Luke may have conceived of his narrative in Acts as a sort of biography of the Holy Spirit, the ultimate agent standing behind the apostles.

The Gospels and Acts lay an indispensable foundation for the New Testament canon as a whole. In narrating the life of the earthly Jesus and the continued activity of the exalted Jesus through the Holy Spirit, they build on the Old Testament foundation. At the same time, the Gospels and Acts themselves lay the foundation for the remainder of the New Testament and occupy a central location at the heart of the church's message of forgiveness and salvation in Jesus Christ.

◤ Introduction to Matthew

Circumstances of Writing

The author did not identify himself in the text. However, the title that ascribes this Gospel to Matthew appears in the earliest manuscripts and is possibly original. Titles became necessary to distinguish one Gospel from another when the four Gospels began to circulate as a single collection. Many early church fathers (Papias, Irenaeus, Pantaenus, and Origen) acknowledged Matthew as the author. Papias also contended that Matthew first wrote in Hebrew, implying that this Gospel was later translated into Greek.

Many modern scholars dispute these traditional claims. They argue that if the early church, following Papias's opinion, was wrong about the original language, they were likely incorrect about the author as well. However, even if Papias was wrong about the Gospel's original language, this does not imply that he and other early church leaders were wrong to identify Matthew as the author of this Gospel. In fact, the early church unanimously affirmed that the apostle Matthew authored the Gospel of Matthew. It would require impressive evidence to overturn this early consensus.

Determining the date of composition of Matthew's Gospel depends largely on the relationship of the Gospels to one another. Most scholars believe that Matthew used Mark's Gospel in writing his own Gospel. If this is correct, Matthew's Gospel must postdate Mark's.

The date of composition for Mark is best inferred from the date of Luke and Acts. The abrupt ending of Acts, which left Paul under house arrest in Rome, implies that Acts was written before Paul's release. Since one of the major themes of Acts is the legality of Christianity in the Roman Empire, one would have expected Luke to mention Paul's release by the emperor if it had already occurred. This evidence dates Acts to the early 60s. Luke and Acts were two volumes of a single work, as the prologues to these books demonstrate. Luke was written before Acts. Given the amount of research that Luke invested in the book and the travel that eyewitness interviews probably required, a date in the late 50s is reasonable. If Luke used Mark in writing his own Gospel, as seems likely, by implication Mark was written some time before the late 50s, perhaps the early to mid-50s. Thus, despite Matthew's dependence on Mark, Matthew may have been written any time beginning in the mid-50s once Mark was completed.

Contribution to the Bible

As the first book in the New Testament, the Gospel of Matthew serves as a gateway between the two testaments. Of the New Testament books, and certainly of the four Gospels, Matthew has the strongest connections to the Old Testament. Matthew gave us God's entire plan from Genesis to Revelation. Matthew looked back and referred to Hebrew prophecies some sixty times ("was fulfilled" and "so that what was spoken . . . might be fulfilled"). He also looked forward by dealing not only with Messiah's coming and his ministry, but also his future plan for his church and kingdom.

Matthew Timeline

2200–1800 BC	1526–1000 BC	1000–586 BC
ABRAHAM 2166–1991	MOSES 1526–1406	DAVID 1050?–970
ISAAC 2066–1886	Exodus **1446**	SOLOMON 990?–931
JACOB 2006–1859	JOSHUA 1490?–1380?	REHOBOAM 971?–913
JOSEPH 1915–1805	Destruction of Jericho **1406**	JEROBOAM 971–909
	Judges **1380?–1060?**	Fall of the northern kingdom **722**
	RUTH 1175?–1125?	Fall of the southern kingdom **586**
	SAMUEL 1105?–1025?	
	SAUL 1080?–1010	

Structure

Matthew divided his Gospel into three major sections. He introduced new major sections with "from then on Jesus began to" (4:17; 16:21). These transitional statements divide the Gospel into the introduction (1:1–4:16), body (4:17–16:20), and conclusion (16:21–28:20). Matthew also divided his Gospel into five major blocks of teaching, each of which concludes with a summary statement (8:1; 11:1; 13:53; 19:1; 26:1). Some scholars believe these five major discourses were meant to correspond to the five books of Moses and to confirm Jesus's identity as the new Moses.

Outline

I. Birth and Infancy of Jesus (1:1–2:23)
II. Beginning of Jesus's Ministry in Galilee (3:1–4:25)
III. Discourse One: The Sermon on the Mount (5:1–7:29)
IV. Jesus's First Miracles (8:1–9:38)
V. Discourse Two: Ministry of Jesus's Disciples (10:1–42)
VI. Responses to Jesus's Ministry (11:1–12:50)
VII. Discourse Three: Parables about the Kingdom (13:1–58)
VIII. Close of Jesus's Ministry in Galilee (14:1–17:27)
IX. Discourse Four: Character of Jesus's Disciples (18:1–35)
X. Jesus's Ministry on the Way to Jerusalem (19:1–20:34)
XI. Jesus's Ministry in Jerusalem (21:1–23:39)
XII. Discourse Five: Olivet Discourse (24:1–25:46)
XIII. Betrayal, Crucifixion, and Burial (26:1–27:66)
XIV. Resurrection and Commission (28:1–20)

Key verses in Matthew

1:21 She will give birth to a son, and you are to name him Jesus, because he will save his people from their sins.

4:10 Then Jesus told him, "Go away, Satan! For it is written: Worship the Lord your God, and serve only him."

5:16 In the same way, let your light shine before others, so that they may see your good works and give glory to your Father in heaven.

5:44 But I tell you, love your enemies and pray for those who persecute you.

21:22 And if you believe, you will receive whatever you ask for in prayer.

28:19–20 Go, therefore, and make disciples of all nations, baptizing them in the name of the Father and of the Son and of the Holy Spirit, teaching them to observe everything I have commanded you. And remember, I am with you always, to the end of the age.

586–63 BC

Babylonian exile **586–538**
Temple completed **515**
Greeks thwart Persian expansion into Europe with victories at Plataea and Mycale. **479**
Jerusalem's walls completed **445**
Alexander the Great invades Persia. **334**
Greek control of Palestine **323–167**
Years of Jewish independence **167–63**
Roman dominance begins. **63**

5 BC–AD 33

Jesus's birth **WINTER 5 BC**
Herod the Great's death **4 BC**
John the Baptist's ministry begins. **AD 29**
Jesus's ministry begins. **AD 29**
Jesus's final week **MARCH 28–APRIL 3, AD 33**
Jesus's resurrection **APRIL 5, AD 33**
Jesus's ascension **MAY 14, AD 33**
Feast of Pentecost **MAY 24, AD 33**

The Genealogy of Jesus Christ

1 An account of the genealogy of Jesus Christ, the Son of David, the Son of Abraham:

From Abraham to David

2 Abraham fathered^A Isaac,
Isaac fathered Jacob,
Jacob fathered Judah and his brothers,
3 Judah fathered Perez and Zerah
by Tamar,
Perez fathered Hezron,
Hezron fathered Aram,
4 Aram fathered Amminadab,
Amminadab fathered Nahshon,
Nahshon fathered Salmon,
5 Salmon fathered Boaz by Rahab,
Boaz fathered Obed by Ruth,
Obed fathered Jesse,
6 and Jesse fathered King David.

From David to the Babylonian Exile

David fathered Solomon^B
by Uriah's wife,
7 Solomon fathered Rehoboam,
Rehoboam fathered Abijah,
Abijah fathered Asa,^C
8 Asa^C fathered Jehoshaphat,
Jehoshaphat fathered Joram,^D
Joram fathered Uzziah,
9 Uzziah fathered Jotham,
Jotham fathered Ahaz,
Ahaz fathered Hezekiah,
10 Hezekiah fathered Manasseh,
Manasseh fathered Amon,^E

Amon fathered Josiah,
11 and Josiah fathered Jeconiah
and his brothers
at the time of the exile to Babylon.

From the Exile to the Messiah

12 After the exile to Babylon
Jeconiah fathered Shealtiel,
Shealtiel fathered Zerubbabel,
13 Zerubbabel fathered Abiud,
Abiud fathered Eliakim,
Eliakim fathered Azor,
14 Azor fathered Zadok,
Zadok fathered Achim,
Achim fathered Eliud,
15 Eliud fathered Eleazar,
Eleazar fathered Matthan,
Matthan fathered Jacob,
16 and Jacob fathered Joseph the husband
of Mary,
who gave birth to Jesus who is called
the Messiah.

17 So all the generations from Abraham to David were fourteen generations; and from David until the exile to Babylon, fourteen generations; and from the exile to Babylon until the Messiah, fourteen generations.

The Nativity of the Messiah

18 The birth of Jesus Christ came about this way: After his mother Mary had been engaged^F to Joseph, it was discovered before they came together that she was pregnant from the Holy

^A1:2 In vv. 2–16 either a son, as here, or a later descendant, as in v. 8   ^B1:6 Other mss add *King*   ^C1:7,8 Other mss read *Asaph*
^D1:8 = Jehoram   ^E1:10 Other mss read *Amos*   ^F1:18 Or *betrothed*

1:1 The title of this genealogy introduces several important themes in Matthew. Jesus is identified as the **Christ**, Messiah, the King anointed by God to rule over his people. This is reiterated by identifying Jesus as **Son of David** (v. 20; 2:2; 9:27; 12:3,23; 15:22; 20:30–31; 21:9,15). OT prophecies like 2Sm 7:16 and Is 9:2–7 foretold that Messiah (the "anointed one") would be a descendant of King David. Jesus's Davidic lineage shows that he meets this qualification. Though the genealogy is otherwise arranged in chronological order, Matthew shifted "Son of David" ahead of **Son of Abraham** to lay emphasis on the royal title.
The title "Son of Abraham" implies that just as Abraham was the father of national Israel, Jesus will be the founder of a new spiritual Israel. The phrase **an account of the genealogy of Jesus** is unusual. OT genealogies are consistently named after the earliest ancestor in the lineage because the Jews considered that person to be most significant since everyone else derived from them. That Matthew names his genealogy after Jesus, the final descendant in the lineage, implies that Jesus is more important than anyone who preceded him.
1:2–6 Matthew mentioned four women in his genealogy, all of them Gentiles. **Tamar** was a Canaanite. **Rahab** was from Jericho. **Ruth** was a Moabitess. **Uriah's wife** Bathsheba was probably a Hethite. The mention

of these women signals God's intention to include Gentiles and women in his redemptive plan. Several kings are named also, but only David is explicitly given the title **King**. This highlights that the Son of David (Jesus) will likewise be a kingly figure.
1:7–16 Matthew's genealogy agrees with the genealogies of 1Ch 1–3 and Lk 3:23–38 from the generation of Abraham down to David. After David, Matthew's genealogy agrees with that of 1 Chronicles except for a few intentional gaps, but departs significantly from Luke's. Some interpreters argue from this that one or both of the NT genealogies is inaccurate. However, Jews in David's line carefully preserved their genealogies because they knew from the OT prophecies that one of their descendants would be the Messiah. David's descendants also had the privilege of providing firewood for the altar in Jerusalem (*m. Ta'an.* 4:5). Naturally, they kept careful records to demonstrate their Davidic descent and preserve their privileges. Evidence in Josephus (*Life* 1) and rabbinic texts suggests that genealogical archives were kept in public registers.
Scholars suggest several ways in which the genealogies of Matthew and Luke may be harmonized. First, one may preserve the genealogy of Jesus through Mary and Luke other through Joseph. Second, the custom of levirate marriage resulted in a child having different biological and legal fathers. Perhaps one genealogy follows the biological line

while the other follows the legal. Third, one genealogy may trace David's legal descendants who would have reigned if the Davidic kingdom had continued, while the other lists descendants in Joseph's specific line. A combination of these approaches is also possible.
In English, it is difficult to identify the antecedent of the first occurrence of the pronoun **who** in v. 16. However, in Matthew's Greek, the pronoun is feminine. Thus, although the rest of the genealogy focuses on fathers and only rarely mentions mothers, Matthew identified a human mother but not a human father of Jesus, thus implying Jesus's virginal conception.
1:17 Matthew's arrangement of Jesus's genealogy into three sets of **fourteen generations** is probably an example of gematria, a system that assigns numerical value to letters of the alphabet (e.g., A = 1, B = 2, etc.) in order to communicate a subtle message. In Hebrew, the numerical value of the letters composing the name *David* is fourteen. Thus Matthew's artistic arrangement probably highlights Jesus's Davidic lineage. If Matthew did intentionally use gematria, this supports the view that he originally wrote his Gospel in Hebrew, for the gematria functions in the Hebrew version of the genealogy but not the Greek.
1:18 The words **of Jesus Christ** are in an emphatic position in the Greek text, implying that the circumstances of Jesus's birth differed from those of everyone else in the

Spirit. ¹⁹ So her husband, Joseph, being a righteous man, and not wanting to disgrace her publicly, decided to divorce her secretly. ²⁰ But after he had considered these things, an angel of the Lord appeared to him in a dream, saying, "Joseph, son of David, don't be afraid to take Mary as your wife, because what has been conceived in her is from the Holy Spirit. ²¹ She will give birth to a son, and you are to name him Jesus, because he will save his people from their sins."

²² Now all this took place to fulfill what was spoken by the Lord through the prophet:

²³   See, the virgin will become pregnant
        and give birth to a son,
        and they will name him Immanuel,^A

which is translated "God is with us."

²⁴ When Joseph woke up, he did as the Lord's angel had commanded him. He married her ²⁵ but did not have sexual relations with her until she gave birth to a son.^B And he named him Jesus.

Wise Men Visit the King

2 After Jesus was born in Bethlehem of Judea in the days of King Herod, wise men from the east arrived in Jerusalem, ² saying,

A1:23 Is 7:14 B1:25 Other mss read *to her firstborn son*

---

genealogy. Although several of those people were conceived by miracles, they all had a human father. Only Jesus was born of a virgin. **Mary had been engaged to Joseph.** However, ancient Jewish engagement was as legally binding as marriage. The couple did not live together or engage in sexual intercourse. But the engagement could only be ended by divorce (thus, Joseph's decision in 1:19). **Before they came together** means that Joseph and Mary had not yet had intercourse. Joseph thus assumed that Mary had been unfaithful. **Pregnant from the Holy Spirit** means that Mary's pregnancy was a miracle performed by the Spirit, not that God assumed material form and physically impregnated her. This makes Jesus's conception dramatically different from Greek myths that speak of children born to gods who lay with women.
1:19 Joseph did not want to humiliate Mary publicly because he was a **righteous man.** His peers most likely expected him to expose her apparent sin, but true righteousness is characterized by compassion and mercy, an important theme for Matthew (5:6–7,21–26,38–48).
1:20 God spoke to Joseph through dreams, just as he did to his OT namesake (Gn 37:1–11). The title **son of David** reminded Joseph of his royal lineage and prepared him for the

announcement of Messiah's birth. On **conceived . . . from the Holy Spirit,** see note at v. 18.
1:21 Jesus is the Greek form of the Hebrew name *Joshua* which means "Yahweh saves." The angel explained that Jesus's name revealed his purpose: He would rescue sinners from the punishment they deserve. This salvation would be experienced by **his people,** identified as those who follow Jesus.
1:22 Spoken by the Lord through the prophet implies that God was the ultimate author of the messages spoken and written by the prophets. The grammar that Matthew uses to introduce the quote from Is 7:14 (see Mt 1:23) suggests that the angel quoted this verse to Joseph during his announcement. Some interpreters argue that Matthew mishandled Is 7:14, but he seems to have handled it just as the angel did, which means his usage is backed by angelic authority.
1:23 The name **Immanuel** (God with us) implies Jesus's deity. Mary's virgin-born Son would be God himself living among his people. The Immanuel of Is 7:14 is to be identified with the person described in Is 9:2–7 and 11:1–9.
1:24–25 These verses emphasize Joseph's absolute obedience to the angel's instructions, a prevalent theme in these early chapters (2:13–15,19–21). Joseph is a model of the

obedience that should characterize Jesus's disciples (5:19–20). **Did not have sexual relations with her** confirms again that Jesus was the product of a virginal conception.
2:1 The **wise men** were magi. Eastern magi mixed Zoroastrianism with astrology and black magic. They are described in Dn 2:2,4–5,10, where they are associated with diviner-priests, mediums, and sorcerers. The Greek word for *magus* (sg. of *magi*) appears only once in the NT. It describes the sorcerer whom Paul portrayed as "full of all kinds of deceit and trickery" and a "son of the devil and enemy of all that is right" (Ac 13:6–10). The magus of whom Paul spoke would have held beliefs that were similar to those of the wise men. Thus, the summons of the magi to visit Jesus demonstrates God's intention to save Gentiles from their futile religions. As an adult, Jesus cast out demons and broke Satan's grip on beleaguered people. Here we see that even in his infancy, Christ plundered Satan's kingdom and set captives free. The **east** may refer to Babylonia or Persia. **King Herod** was actually a client king ruling under Roman authority. Though he was Idumean and not a Jew, the Roman Senate named him king of Judea in 40 BC. He was an able ruler but brutal and suspicious.
2:2 The question posed by the wise men was an unintentional challenge to Herod's reign.

Character profile:
Joseph, the Husband of Mary

Though Joseph's name doesn't appear often in the New Testament, the fact remains that God chose him for a reason. Jesus's heavenly Father selected Joseph to serve as Jesus's earthly father. As such, Joseph played a pivotal role in Jesus's life.

Mary wasn't the only one who received a visit from an angel prior to Jesus's birth. God sent a heavenly messenger to assure Joseph that Mary's pregnancy was not only legitimate but also a world-changing event. So Joseph stood with Mary, despite the inevitable gossip and attacks on his character that surely came with his decision. He risked his reputation and his standing in the community for the sake of God's plan.

When Joseph and Mary traveled to Bethlehem to register for taxation in accordance with Caesar Augustus's decree, Joseph found a safe place for his expectant wife in a town overrun with crowds. Joseph's plan was to return to Nazareth with Mary and the newborn Jesus after their brief stay in Bethlehem. However, he learned from an angel in a dream that Herod was intent on killing all baby boys to prevent the rise of the "King of the Jews" (Mt 2:2).

Following the angel's instructions, Joseph immediately relocated his family to Egypt and stayed there until the threat ended. Joseph went to great lengths to protect the wife and son that God had entrusted to him.

It seems Joseph was a hands-on father to Jesus. The two likely spent hours together every day in Joseph's carpentry shop. Joseph almost certainly taught Jesus the skills he needed to make a living as a carpenter.

Joseph also gave Jesus an identity of sorts. When Jesus returned to Nazareth during his public ministry, the people there still remembered him—even if they were suspicious of his new spiritual authority. They asked one another, "Isn't this the carpenter's son?" (Mt 13:55). In their minds, Jesus's identity was still linked to Joseph's.

Bible scholars believe Joseph died before Jesus started his public ministry. If that is true, he didn't get a chance to see the fruition of what he helped nurture through the early days of Jesus's life.

Yet traces of Joseph's legacy can be seen. As Jesus hung on the cross, enduring unimaginable physical and spiritual agony, he summoned the strength to make one last heartfelt request of his disciple John, who stood nearby.

As the eldest son of his earthly family, Jesus instructed John to take care of his mother, Mary, after his death. He concerned himself with the well-being of those in his care, just as Joseph had done before him.

There is no such thing as an insignificant role in God's plan. No act of mercy, no use of a spiritual gift, and no personal sacrifice ever goes unnoticed by God. If you wonder about your significance in God's plan, ask the Lord to show you the difference you're making and the example you're setting for others.

"Where is he who has been born king of the Jews? For we saw his star at its rising and have come to worship him."ᴬ

³ When King Herod heard this, he was deeply disturbed, and all Jerusalem with him. ⁴ So he assembled all the chief priests and scribes of the people and asked them where the Messiah would be born.

⁵ "In Bethlehem of Judea," they told him, "because this is what was written by the prophet:

⁶ And you, Bethlehem, in the land
of Judah,
are by no means least
among the rulers of Judah:
Because out of you will come a ruler
who will shepherd my people
Israel."ᴮ

⁷ Then Herod secretly summoned the wise men and asked them the exact time the star appeared. ⁸ He sent them to Bethlehem and said, "Go and search carefully for the child. When you find him, report back to me so that I too can go and worship him."ᶜ

⁹ After hearing the king, they went on their way. And there it was — the star they had seen at its rising. It led them until it came and stopped above the place where the child was.

¹⁰ When they saw the star, they were overwhelmed with joy. ¹¹ Entering the house, they saw the child with Mary his mother, and falling to their knees, they worshiped him.ᴰ Then they opened their treasures and presented him with gifts: gold, frankincense, and myrrh. ¹² And being warned in a dream not to go back to Herod, they returned to their own country by another route.

The Flight into Egypt

¹³ After they were gone, an angel of the Lord appeared to Joseph in a dream, saying, "Get up! Take the child and his mother, flee to Egypt, and stay there until I tell you. For Herod is about to search for the child to kill him." ¹⁴ So he got up, took the child and his mother during the night, and escaped to Egypt. ¹⁵ He stayed there until Herod's death, so that what was spoken by the Lord through the prophet might be fulfilled: Out of Egypt I called my Son.ᴱ

The Massacre of the Innocents

¹⁶ Then Herod, when he realized that he had been outwitted by the wise men, flew into a rage. He gave orders to massacre all the boys in and around Bethlehem who were two years old and under, in keeping with the time he had

---

ᴬ 2:2 Or to pay him homage ᴮ 2:6 Mc 5:2 ᶜ 2:8 Or and pay him homage ᴰ 2:11 Or they paid him homage ᴱ 2:15 Hs 11:1

Jesus was **born king** in the sense that he was from David's line and thus king by birthright. Herod, however, was neither a full Jew nor a descendant of David and thus was not genuinely qualified to reign as king. The word translated **star** can indicate many different astronomical phenomena, including comets, meteors, or planetary conjunctions. Matthew later (v.9) described the star as moving through the sky in order to point the magi to Jesus's precise location. This indicates that it was no ordinary star. **At its rising** indicates that the star mysteriously appeared in the eastern sky to signal Messiah's birth. The interest of the magi in astrology, a practice condemned in the Bible (Is 47:13–15), probably first directed their attention to the star. In another profound display of grace, God condescended to use the magi's pagan superstitions to draw them to Jesus.
2:3 Herod was **disturbed** by reports of the birth of a legitimate claimant to his throne. The people of **Jerusalem** were equally disturbed because they feared Herod's paranoid and delusional rages. In the past he had killed even his favorite wife and sons in order to protect his rule.
2:4 Herod summoned expert scribes to learn where the OT said **the Messiah** would be born. To this point the star had guided the wise men near to Jesus, but now the witness of the Scriptures was necessary before God caused the star to reappear and pinpoint the exact location. Thus the value of biblical revelation was upheld even as new revelations unfolded.
2:5–6 The "chief priests and scribes" (v. 4) knew Scripture well enough to identify **Bethlehem** as Christ's birthplace (Mc 5:2; Jn 7:42), but nevertheless they later opposed his teachings. Knowledge of Scripture does

not guarantee that your heart is right with God. The priestly opposition to Jesus is foreshadowed here by the fact that they made no effort to go visit him even as the magi undertook the last leg of a long journey to do so. Micah 5:2 foretold that Bethlehem would be the birthplace of a king, a ruler who would **shepherd** . . . **Israel**. Although Micah said that the promised prince would "rule" over Israel, Matthew's translation says that Messiah will "shepherd" Israel. Matthew likely chose this word to reflect Micah's use in 5:4 and thus show that the entirety of the Mc 5 applies to Jesus. This indicates that Jesus is eternal since Micah says, "His origin is from antiquity, from ancient times" (v. 2). Micah's prophecy also said that the shepherd's "greatness will extend to the ends of the earth" (v. 4).
2:7–8 Herod questioned the magi about the **exact time** of the star's appearance under the assumption that the star first appeared at the time of the child's birth. On the basis of this date, he ordered the execution of all male children in Bethlehem two years of age and under (v. 16). This implies that the magi's journey was lengthy and involved great sacrifice. Herod's pretended desire to worship Messiah highlights his deceitfulness.
2:9–12 In contrast to the stable in which Jesus was born (Lk 2), Jesus's family now lived in a **house**. This shows that the magi visited Jesus after the visit of the shepherds described by Luke. The magi worshiped Jesus openly, as did many other people during his lifetime (8:2; 9:18; 14:33; 15:25; 20:20; 28:9,17). Jesus's reception of worship reinforces his identity as Immanuel, "God is with us" (1:23). **Gold, frankincense, and myrrh** were costly gifts. The latter two are aromatic resins. Frankincense was used in making incense and

perfume (see Ex 30:34–35). Myrrh was used as an ingredient in anointing oil (30:23–25), as a perfume (Ps 45:8), and in burial preparations (Jn 19:39).
2:13–14 Again **an angel** visited Joseph **in a dream** warning him of Herod's intent. Herod was a cruel and paranoid ruler. See note at 2:3. So it is not surprising that he would commit treachery against children due to a perceived threat (v. 16). Joseph promptly obeyed when he was told to **flee to Egypt**. See note at 1:24–25.
2:15 That **what was spoken** had to be fulfilled indicates that the Bible is inspired by God and authoritative over history. In its original context, the calling of the son **out of Egypt** in Hs 11 is a reference to Israel's exodus from slavery to Egypt, not young Messiah's trip back home. Matthew understood this, but under the Spirit's direction he recognized Jesus as the new Moses who will lead a new and climactic exodus. Just as Moses delivered his people from slavery to Pharaoh, Jesus will deliver people from slavery to Satan. Thus Matthew rightly regarded Hs 11:1 and other portions of the OT as foreshadows of Jesus and events in his life.
2:16 Skeptics deny that Herod ever slaughtered the boys of Bethlehem since no extra-biblical source documents this horrific event. However, the murders are consistent with his documented dealings, such as his murdering his own family. The Jewish historian Josephus reported that Herod arranged for many Jewish nobles to be murdered upon his death in order to ensure that the land mourned his passing (*Ant.* 17.167–69). Herod's behavior is reminiscent of Pharaoh's around the time of Moses's birth (Ex 1:15–22). This and other striking similarities to Moses's birth narrative strengthen Matthew's presentation of Jesus

learned from the wise men. ¹⁷ Then what was spoken through Jeremiah the prophet was fulfilled:

¹⁸ A voice was heard in Ramah,
  weeping,ᴬ and great mourning,
  Rachel weeping for her children;
  and she refused to be consoled,
  because they are no more.ᴮ

The Return to Nazareth

¹⁹ After Herod died, an angel of the Lord appeared in a dream to Joseph in Egypt, ²⁰ saying, "Get up, take the child and his mother, and go to the land of Israel, because those who intended to kill the child are dead." ²¹ So he got up, took the child and his mother, and entered the land of Israel. ²² But when he heard that Archelaus was ruling over Judea in place of his father Herod, he was afraid to go there. And being warned in a dream, he withdrew to the region of Galilee. ²³ Then he went and settled in a town called Nazareth to fulfill what was spoken through the prophets, that he would be called a Nazarene.

The Herald of the Messiah

3 In those days John the Baptist came, preaching in the wilderness of Judea ² and saying, "Repent, because the kingdom of heaven has come near!" ³ For he is the one spoken of through the prophet Isaiah, who said:

A voice of one crying out
  in the wilderness:
Prepare the way for the Lord;
  make his paths straight!ᶜ

⁴ Now John had a camel-hair garment with a leather belt around his waist, and his food was locusts and wild honey. ⁵ Then people from Jerusalem, all Judea, and all the vicinity of the Jordan were going out to him, ⁶ and they were baptized by him in the Jordan River, confessing their sins. ⁷ When he saw many of the Pharisees and Sadducees coming to his baptism, he said to

---

ᴬ2:18 Other mss read *Ramah, lamentation, and weeping,*   ᴮ2:18 Jr 31:15   ᶜ3:3 Is 40:3

---

as the new Moses whom God promised in Dt 18:15–19. Ancient Jews thought of Moses as a deliverer (Ac 7:25,35). By highlighting parallels between Moses and Jesus, Matthew shows that Jesus was the promised deliverer who would save his people from their sins (see notes at Mt 1:7–16 and 2:20–21). Herod killed all boys **two years old and under** in and around Bethlehem because the star had appeared to the magi two years previously, presumably at the moment of Jesus's birth. **2:17–18** Once again Matthew introduces a quotation in a way that implies that the OT author (Jeremiah in this case) was used by God to proclaim his message. This was the unquestioned view among religious Jews from the day of the prophets down to Jesus's day. In v. 18 Matthew quotes Jr 31:15, which originally expressed the lament of mothers who grieved over sons who were sent into exile. Matthew's application here implies that Israel was again in exile, estranged from God, and in need of redemption. Since Jr 31 includes the weeping and then climaxes with the joyous promise that God would establish a new covenant with his people, one in which he would forgive their sins and write his law on their hearts, Matthew likely intends to call this to mind and apply it to the Bethlehem massacre and the coming of Jesus. Just as the weeping of mothers preceded the promise of the new covenant in Jr 31, so now the **weeping** of mothers preceded the establishment of the new covenant through Jesus (see note at 26:27–28). **2:19** Since **Herod died** in 4 BC and since Jesus was born roughly two years before Herod ordered the massacre of the Bethlehem boys, it seems that Jesus was born in 5 or 6 BC. It also seems likely that the shameless Bethlehem massacre was one of Herod's final acts. **2:20–21** The angel's words are almost identical to the words the Lord spoke to Moses from the burning bush (Ex 4:19, LXX). This allusion to the Moses narrative again identifies Jesus as the new Moses (see notes at 2:15 and 2:16). Jesus, now perhaps three years old, returns from Egypt with his family.

2:22–23 Archelaus, son of Herod the Great, inherited his father's violent traits. His rule over Judea signaled that the holy family should settle elsewhere, and so Joseph led his family to resettle in the obscure Galilean village of **Nazareth,** where Joseph and Mary had previously lived (Lk 1:26). Matthew states that the decision was a fulfillment of an OT prophecy that Messiah **would be called a Nazarene.** Rather than a specific OT text, Matthew was probably referring to an OT theme, the prophecies that describe the Messiah as a "branch." The term used for "branch" in Is 11:1 (*netser*) may be transliterated with the first three consonants (nzr) that compose the nouns "Nazareth" and "Nazarene." This messianic prophecy is closely connected to others (Is 4:2; Jr 23:5; 33:15) that told of a righteous descendant of David whose wise and just rule would be empowered by the Spirit and who would bring salvation to Judah. **3:1 In those days** means "during the time of Jesus's residence in Nazareth" rather than "during the reign of Archelaus." After all, Archelaus reigned from 4 BC to AD 6, too early for **John the Baptist** to have begun his ministry since he would have been under age twelve. In OT usage, "in those days" often refers to a time of prophetic fulfillment (Is 10:20; Am 9:11; Zph 1:15; Zch 12:3–4). Matthew probably used the phrase in conjunction with his references to fulfilled prophecy to emphasize that God's promises were being fulfilled through Jesus and John the Baptist, herald and predecessor of Messiah. The location of John's ministry (**wilderness of Judea**) is reminiscent of the ministry of the prophet Elijah (1Kg 17:3; 19:3–18; 2Kg 2:1–12), whom many Jews believed would appear again to prepare the way for Messiah (Mt 17:10–13). Josephus described John's ministry in a way that closely matches the Gospel accounts (*Ant.* 18.114–119). **3:2** John's message focused on repentance and the coming **kingdom of heaven**. Jesus emphasized the same thing from the outset of his ministry (see note at 4:17). The kingdom is defined as the rule that God exercises

through the person, work, and teachings of Jesus. The call to **repent** means we must abandon sinful lifestyles and express sorrow for sins. **3:3** Matthew's application of Is 40:3 to John the Baptist tells us as much about Jesus as it does about John. After all, in its original context the prophecy spoke of one who prepared the way for the coming of the Lord, God himself. By using a text about the coming of the Lord to describe the coming of Jesus, Matthew proclaims that Jesus is divine. **3:4** John's **garment** was similar to Elijah's (2Kg 1:8) and his ministry and lifestyle paralleled Elijah's also, including his residence in the Judean wilderness, his austere diet, his call for Israel to repent, and his confrontation with an evil king and his wife. Jesus explained the significance of these parallels in Mt 11:14; 17:12–13. **3:5–6** Although Jews required Gentiles to immerse themselves in water in order to convert from paganism to Judaism, John demanded that repentant Jews be **baptized** as well. This bold move implied that Jews did not belong to God merely by virtue of their descent from Abraham (see note at vv. 7–9). Like anyone else, ethnic Jews needed to repent in order to enter the coming kingdom. Unlike the repetitive ritual washings of other religious groups, John's baptism appears to have been a one-time event associated with a permanent repentance and a transformed life. **3:7–9** In Mt 2:4 the chief priests and scribes identified the place of Christ's birth but made no effort to visit him. Their attention was on worldly power instead. That negative portrayal is now followed by John's charge that the leading priests of the Jews were a **brood of vipers** (see 12:34; 23:33) fleeing from God's **coming wrath**. The **Pharisees** were the largest and most important Jewish religious group. They controlled the synagogues and exercised great control over the population. The **Sadducees** were an aristocratic party of high priestly families. They had charge of the temple and accepted only

them, "Brood of vipers! Who warned you to flee from the coming wrath? **8** Therefore produce fruit consistent with[A] repentance. **9** And don't presume to say to yourselves, 'We have Abraham as our father.' For I tell you that God is able to raise up children for Abraham from these stones. **10** The ax is already at the root of the trees. Therefore, every tree that doesn't produce good fruit will be cut down and thrown into the fire.

11 "I baptize you with[B] water for repentance, but the one who is coming after me is more powerful than I. I am not worthy to remove[C] his sandals. He himself will baptize you with the Holy Spirit and fire. **12** His winnowing shovel is in his hand, and he will clear his threshing floor and gather his wheat into the barn. But the chaff he will burn with fire that never goes out."

The Baptism of Jesus

13 Then Jesus came from Galilee to John at the Jordan, to be baptized by him. **14** But John tried to stop him, saying, "I need to be baptized by you, and yet you come to me?"

15 Jesus answered him, "Allow it for now, because this is the way for us to fulfill all righteousness." Then John allowed him to be baptized.

16 When Jesus was baptized, he went up immediately from the water. The heavens suddenly opened for him,[D] and he saw the Spirit of God descending like a dove and coming down on him. **17** And a voice from heaven said, "This is my beloved Son, with whom I am well-pleased."

The Temptation of Jesus

4 Then Jesus was led up by the Spirit into the wilderness to be tempted by the devil. **2** After he had fasted forty days and forty nights,

---

A3:8 Lit *fruit worthy of* **B3:11** Or *in* **C3:11** Or *to carry* **D3:16** Other mss omit *for him*

---

the Pentateuch (first five books of the OT) as authoritative. John stressed that the coming kingdom would be accompanied by blessing for God's people and by punishment for the unrepentant. John knew that the Pharisees and Sadducees had no intention of confessing their sins because they presumed that descent from Abraham guaranteed that they would escape God's wrath. This belief was reflected in the Mishnah, which stated: "All Israel will have a share in the world to come." John's statement about raising up **children for Abraham from these stones** involves a wordplay in Aramaic. The word "child" (*ben*) sounds similar to the word "stone" (*eben*). A stone has no intrinsic value, yet Almighty God can transform worthless rock into a person and include him in his covenant people if he so chooses (Is 51:1–2). Consequently, descent from Abraham gave the Jews no grounds for boasting. John's warning foreshadows the incorporation of believing Gentiles into the people of God, an important theme in Matthew's Gospel. **3:10** Just as the owner of an orchard laid the **ax** to barren trees, so too God will punish those who fail to produce "fruit consistent with repentance" (v. 8). In the teachings of John and Jesus, **fruit** represents good works that result from a miraculous inner transformation (7:15–20; 12:33; 13:23). Later, the cursing of the fig tree and the parable of the wicked tenants illustrated the consequences of failing to produce good fruits (21:18–22,33–43). **3:11** Removing the master's **sandals** was a task so menial that Hebrew slave owners could not require it of Hebrew slaves. John, however, saw himself as unworthy to perform for Jesus the very task that slaves were spared from performing. John expressed this deep humility because Jesus was **more powerful** than he, and this greater power expressed itself through a new baptism that was vastly superior to John's. John's baptism was a public expression of **repentance**, but his baptism could not change a person's heart. Jesus, however, baptized the repentant **with the Holy Spirit**, making them holy through inner transformation. Matthew's quotation from Jr 31:15 in Mt 2:18 was probably intended to remind his readers of the

promise of the new covenant (Jr 31:31–34). The reference to baptism with the Spirit recalls the related promise in Ezk 36:27 in which God declared, "I will place my Spirit within you and cause you to follow my statutes and carefully observe my ordinances." This work of the Spirit was highlighted again at Jesus's baptism (3:16). Jesus would have the power to transform human character in a way that John could not. Jesus would also baptize people with **fire**, a reference to divine judgment against unrepentant sinners. **3:12** A **winnowing shovel** was used to toss grain into the air. The wind would blow the useless husks (called **chaff**) aside, while the heavier grain kernels fell to the threshing floor. The chaff would then be gathered up and burned. John's parable thus described a coming divine judgment in which all people are sifted, with the result that Christ's followers will be preserved by God, while the unrepentant are gathered for punishment. Though chaff is highly flammable and burns away quickly, possibly giving the impression that divine judgment is only temporary, John made clear that the fire that awaits the unrepentant will never go out. God's punishment against unrepentant sinners is eternal. **3:13** Apparently Jesus and his family still lived in Nazareth (in **Galilee**) at this time. **3:14** John **tried to stop him** because he recognized Jesus's superiority. By his protest John further identified Jesus as the one who would come after him (v. 11). John knew that he needed Jesus's baptism, the baptism of the Spirit, but he also understood that sinless Jesus did not seek water baptism as an expression of repentance. **3:15** Jesus explained that baptism was essential to his perfection. Jesus wished to please his Father by obeying the commands of the prophets (John was the greatest of the prophets, 11:9–13) and by identifying with God's righteous cause among the people. If he had refused to participate in John's baptism, Jesus would have seemed like a rebel rather than one who came to **fulfill all righteousness**. **3:16** The opening of the **heavens** demonstrates that both the voice and the descending **Spirit** came from heaven and were divine. First-century Jews associated the

dove with the Spirit since Gn 1:2 describes the Spirit as hovering over the primeval waters. The Hebrew verb translated "hover" is the same word used to describe a bird rapidly fluttering its wings. Consequently, both the Qumran Scrolls and the Talmud associated God's Spirit in Gn 1:2 with the dove. The descent of the Spirit thus alludes to Gn 1 and identifies Jesus not only as one empowered by the Spirit but also as one who brings new creation (2Co 5:17; Gl 6:15). **3:17** The Father speaks directly only twice in Matthew—here at Jesus's baptism and later at the transfiguration. On both occasions he identified Jesus as his **Son** and expressed approval of him (see 17:5). The Father's words at Jesus's baptism blend together two important OT texts: Ps 2:7 and Is 42:1. Psalm 2 was a song sung at the crowning of Israel's kings. The Father's application of this text to Jesus identified him as a divinely appointed King who would rule with divine authority and whose kingdom would extend to the ends of the earth (Ps 2:1–12). The allusion to Is 42 identified Jesus as the Servant, the messianic figure whom Is 53:5 promised would be "pierced because of our rebellion, crushed because of our iniquities." Matthew 12:18–21 explicitly applies Is 42 to Jesus, and Mt 8:17 explicitly applies Is 53 to Jesus. With this OT background in mind, we see that the Father's words identify Jesus as King and Savior. **4:1–2** The temptation of Christ highlights numerous parallels between Jesus and OT Israel. Deuteronomy 8:2–3 says that the Lord led Israel into the wilderness to be tested for forty years. Similarly, **Jesus was led up by the Spirit into the wilderness** to be tested for **forty days**. The three temptations Jesus faced parallel the tests Israel faced in the wilderness, and every Scripture that Jesus quoted in response to his temptations were drawn from God's message to the Israelites about their wilderness test (Dt 6–8). Israel failed its tests, but Jesus passed his and in doing so "fulfilled all righteousness" (see Mt 3:15). Thus he is qualified to create a new spiritual Israel. Several features of Matthew confirm Jesus's intention to gather a new people for God. He chose twelve disciples to parallel Israel's twelve tribes. This was a conscious effort to identify his followers

The Work of the Spirit

OLD TESTAMENT	JESUS CHRIST	NEW TESTAMENT
God's Spirit **hovered** over the waters to carry out God's word (Gn 1:2–3; Ps 33:6).	The Holy Spirit **overshadowed** Mary so that the child she miraculously conceived would be called the Son of God (Lk 1:30–35).	The Holy Spirit **dwells in** believers as the firstfruits of the coming new creation (Rm 8:22–25).
The Spirit of the Lord **anointed** people for leadership and service to God's people (Ex 35:30–35; 1Sm 16:13).	God's Spirit descended upon Jesus at his baptism in the form of a dove, **anointing** him as God's Son and empowering his ministry as Messiah (Mt 3:16–17; Lk 4:14–21).	The Holy Spirit testifies to God's children and **gives gifts** to them so they can lead and serve the body of Christ (Rm 8:14–17; 1Co 12).
The Lord **led** the Israelites in the wilderness for forty years to humble them and test them (Dt 8:2).	The Spirit **led** Jesus into the wilderness to be tempted by the devil after forty days and nights of fasting (Mt 4:1–2).	The Holy Spirit **leads** Jesus's followers in carrying out the Great Commission (Mt 10:16–20; Ac 1:8).
The Spirit was promised to indwell God's people, to **transform** them and cause them to obey God's law (Ezk 36:25–27).	Jesus baptized with the Holy Spirit, **transforming** his disciples (Mt 3:11).	The Spirit brings about the **new birth** so people can enter the kingdom of God (Jn 3:3–8,34; Ti 3:4–7).

he was hungry. ³ Then the tempter approached him and said, "If you are the Son of God, tell these stones to become bread."

⁴ He answered, "It is written: Man must not live on bread alone but on every word that comes from the mouth of God."ᴬ

⁵ Then the devil took him to the holy city, had him stand on the pinnacle of the temple, ⁶ and said to him, "If you are the Son of God, throw yourself down. For it is written:

He will give his angels orders
concerning you,
and they will support you
with their hands
so that you will not strike
your foot against a stone."ᴮ

⁷ Jesus told him, "It is also written: Do not test the Lord your God."ᶜ

⁸ Again, the devil took him to a very high mountain and showed him all the kingdoms of the world and their splendor. ⁹ And he said to him, "I will give you all these things if you will fall down and worship me."ᴰ

¹⁰ Then Jesus told him, "Go away,ᴱ Satan! For it is written: Worship the Lord your God, and serve only him."ᶠ

¹¹ Then the devil left him, and angels came and began to serve him.

Ministry in Galilee

¹² When he heard that John had been arrested, he withdrew into Galilee. ¹³ He left Nazareth and went to live in Capernaum by the sea, in the region of Zebulun and Naphtali. ¹⁴ This was to fulfill what was spoken through the prophet Isaiah:

¹⁵   Land of Zebulun and land
of Naphtali,
along the road by the sea,
beyond the Jordan,
Galilee of the Gentiles.
¹⁶   The people who live
in darkness
have seen a great light,
and for those living in the land of the
shadow of death,
a light has dawned.ᴳ,ᴴ

ᴬ**4:4** Dt 8:3   ᴮ**4:6** Ps 91:11–12   ᶜ**4:7** Dt 6:16   ᴰ**4:9** Or *and pay me homage*   ᴱ**4:10** Other mss read *"Get behind me*
ᶠ**4:10** Dt 6:13   ᴳ**4:16** Lit *dawned on them*   ᴴ**4:15–16** Is 9:1–2

---

as the new Israel. The fact that Jesus **was hungry** shows that he was truly human as well as divine.

4:3 The **stones** that littered the wilderness floor resembled small round loaves of **bread** in shape, size, and color. Interpreters disagree as to why it would have been wrong for Jesus to transform and eat the stones. Most suggest that he was tempted to exercise supernatural power rather than depend on God's provision. Clues in the text suggest that the Spirit, who led Jesus into the wilderness, commanded this fast. Thus, breaking the fast prematurely would have been an act of disobedience, preventing Jesus from fulfilling every act of righteousness (3:15). Jesus aimed to end his fast when the test was over and no sooner. God would signal the end by providing food. Matthew 4:11 shows that at fast's end, angels came and "began to serve" Jesus. The verb *serve* means "to serve as a table-waiter" and implies that the angels fed Jesus. During their wilderness wanderings, Israel failed to trust God to provide food and water. Jesus, the embodiment of the new Israel, had unwavering trust in God's care. On **Son of God**, see note at 3:17.

4:4 Jesus quoted Dt 8:3. His reference to **every word that comes from the mouth of God** recalls the OT theme that God's words are not idle but are to be received as commands. Deuteronomy 8:1,6 emphasize the need to obey God's commands, and Dt 8:1 teaches that man lives by following God's commandments just as 8:3 says that man lives by what comes from God's mouth (Dt 6:24). Thus the OT text that Jesus quoted teaches that obeying God is more important than being well-fed. Israel struggled to learn this truth (Ex 16:3; Nm 11:4–5). In contrast, Jesus hungered for righteousness more than bread and thirsted for obedience more than water. He urged his disciples to have the same priority (Mt 5:6).

4:5–7 Satan quoted Ps 91:11–12 out of context, trying to convince Jesus that the Father

would supernaturally protect him even if he gambled with his life. Jesus responded by quoting Dt 6:16 which refers to the time when Israel, angry and thirsty, questioned God's presence until he miraculously produced a stream of water from a rock: "They tested the Lᴏʀᴅ, saying, 'Is the Lᴏʀᴅ among us or not?'" (Ex 17:7). Had Jesus succumbed to Satan's temptation, it would indicate that his faith was frail and depended on God's miraculous action. Jumping from the **pinnacle of the temple** would test God by attempting to force him to perform a miracle.

Satan implied that God is trustworthy only when he rescues us from suffering and danger. Jesus knew better. God is trustworthy even when he allows us or even causes us to suffer. True faith recognizes this and perseveres through hard times. When Jesus suffered on the cross (27:41–44), those who tormented him used arguments similar to that of the devil: "If you are the Son of God, come down from the cross." They even quoted Ps 22:8 to argue that Jesus would be rescued if God really loved him, much as Satan quoted Ps 91:11–12 to argue that God would rescue Jesus from a deadly fall if he were really God's Son. Again, Jesus knew better. He trusted God even through a brutal scourging, even when nails were driven through his limbs, and even when God let him suffer a horrible death.

4:8–9 Although Satan exercises some authority over the world (Lk 4:6; Jn 12:31), the **kingdoms of the world** belong to God, and he promised to give them to his Son (Ps 2:8).

4:10–11 Jesus responded to Satan by quoting from Dt 6:14 and 10:20. If Jesus had worshiped Satan in order to gain worldly power, it would have indicated that he valued creation more than the Creator and the kingdoms of the earth more than the kingdom of God. Jesus insisted that **only** God is worthy of **worship**. After citing Dt 6:13, Jesus's reception of worship later in this Gospel (8:2; 9:18; 14:33; 15:25; 20:20; 28:9,17)

without rebuking the worshiper (cp. Ac 10:25–26; 14:11–15) strongly implies his deity. That the **angels came** to **serve** Jesus further implies his superior status.

4:12 John the Baptist **had been arrested** because he dared to say that Herod Antipas's marriage to his brother's wife was immoral. As tetrarch of Galilee and Perea (Lk 3:1), Herod did not have jurisdiction over Judea, the locale of Jesus's baptism and wilderness temptation. Thus Jesus fearlessly marched into the heart of Herod's territory when he heard of John's arrest. In Lk 13:31–33, the Pharisees urged Jesus to leave Galilee in order to escape arrest by Herod. Jesus replied by calling Herod "that fox" and insisted that he would travel to Jerusalem only because it was necessary for him to die there, not to flee Herod. Jesus caused kings to tremble (2:3; 14:1–2), but he himself feared no man.

4:13 At this point Jesus made an important strategic move by shifting his headquarters from **Nazareth** to **Capernaum**. Nazareth was an obscure village, but Capernaum was a much larger fishing center on the shores of Lake Galilee. It boasted a tax collection station and a Roman garrison of at least a hundred soldiers. **By the sea** alludes to Isaiah's prophecies, which describe the area as "the way of the sea," an ancient trade route stretching from Damascus down to Caesarea Maritima on the coast of the Mediterranean Sea. By the time of Christ, the Romans had built a stone road along the route, allowing caravans to travel from Syria and pass through Capernaum on the way to Caesarea. Since Capernaum was on the coast of the Sea of Galilee, it also provided easy access to every other city along the Galilean coast. Thus by choosing high-traffic Capernaum as his headquarters, Jesus was able to reach many Jews and Gentiles.

4:14–16 Matthew's quotation of Is 9:1–2 highlights the international focus of Jesus's ministry by describing Galilee as **Galilee of the Gentiles**. Second Kings 15:29 and

¹⁷ From then on Jesus began to preach, "Repent, because the kingdom of heaven has come near."

The First Disciples

¹⁸ As he was walking along the Sea of Galilee, he saw two brothers, Simon (who is called Peter), and his brother Andrew. They were casting a net into the sea — for they were fishermen. **¹⁹** "Follow me," he told them, "and I will make you fish for[A] people." **²⁰** Immediately they left their nets and followed him.

²¹ Going on from there, he saw two other brothers, James the son of Zebedee, and his brother John. They were in a boat with Zebedee their father, preparing their nets, and he called them. **²²** Immediately they left the boat and their father and followed him.

Teaching, Preaching, and Healing

²³ Now Jesus began to go all over Galilee, teaching in their synagogues, preaching the good news of the kingdom, and healing every[B] disease and sickness[C] among the people. **²⁴** Then the news about him spread throughout Syria. So they brought to him all those who were afflicted, those suffering from various diseases and intense pains, the demon-possessed, the epileptics, and the paralytics. And he healed them. **²⁵** Large crowds followed him from Galilee, the Decapolis, Jerusalem, Judea, and beyond the Jordan.

THE SERMON ON THE MOUNT

5 When he saw the crowds, he went up on the mountain, and after he sat down, his disciples came to him. **²** Then[D] he began to teach them, saying:

The Beatitudes

³   "Blessed are the poor in spirit,
     for the kingdom of heaven
     is theirs.

[A]4:19 Or *you fishers of*   [B]4:23 Or *every kind of*   [C]4:23 Or *physical ailment*   [D]5:2 Lit *Then opening his mouth*

17:24–27 show that after the Jews were deported from the northern kingdom of Israel, foreigners flooded into Galilee. For instance, reports from the geographer Strabo and first-century Jewish historian Josephus show that Egyptians, Arabians, Phoenicians, and Greeks lived in Galilee. The Apocrypha (1 Macc 5) says Galilee's population was largely Gentile and heathen. Jesus's move to Galilee and the strategically located city of Capernaum shows his intention to save Gentiles as well as Jews. Matthew's application of Is 9:3 shows that Jesus was the great King called "Mighty God" who would reign from David's throne over a universal and eternal kingdom, liberate God's people from spiritual slavery, and bring peace and joy to the world (Is 9:3–7).

4:17 The words from *then on Jesus began to* introduce the main body of Matthew's Gospel (cp. 16:21). Jesus's message was identical to the message proclaimed by John the Baptist before his arrest. This identifies Jesus as the one who came after John (3:11) whom John had identified as the Lord God himself (Is 40:3; see note at Mt 3:3).

4:18–22 Jesus's command, **Follow me**, urged the disciples not just to accompany him on his travels but to follow his example and emulate his character. Following Jesus involved significant sacrifice for **Simon . . . Andrew . . . James, and John.** They abandoned their careers as fishermen. The words **they left . . . their father** indicate that following Jesus also required the disciples to place commitment to Jesus above commitment to their own families (10:37; 19:29).

4:23 Jesus's ministry in the **synagogues** shows that he initially focused his ministry on the Jewish population of Galilee, but this focus then widened to include Gentiles from there and beyond. The **good news of the kingdom,** the primary topic of Jesus's preaching, was that the long-awaited Christ, the human ruler through whom God would establish his reign on earth, had come at last. This was the message proclaimed by John the Baptist (3:2), preached by Jesus (4:17), and emphasized by Matthew through his mention of Jesus's Davidic lineage, the account

of his miraculous birth, and his record of the visit of the magi. Jesus healed **every disease and sickness among the people.** The adjective "every" shows that no type of ailment was beyond Jesus's power to heal. In the Greek text, the adjective "every" is repeated, placing emphasis on Jesus's unlimited power to heal (9:35).

4:24 Syria was located just north of Galilee. Not surprisingly, word of Jesus's healings quickly **spread** to that region, crossing geographical and language barriers. Soon Syrians began bringing their sick for Jesus to heal. By consenting to this, Jesus distinguished himself from some later Jewish interpreters who urged Jews to give no aid to a drowning Gentile or a Gentile woman giving birth (Maimonides). Matthew says Jesus healed **demon-possessed** people, but some scholars argue that these people were just epileptics. However, this verse distinguishes epilepsy from demon possession, which proves that the ancients differentiated between the two conditions.

4:25 Jesus's earliest followers hailed from Jewish and Gentile regions. **Jerusalem** and **Judea** were Jewish regions, **Galilee** had a mixture of Jews and Gentiles, and **the Decapolis** was a group of predominantly Gentile cities. These geographical references and the diverse peoples entailed by them demonstrate Jesus's desire to serve, heal, teach, and save all the nations of the earth (28:18–20). He came as the world's Messiah.

5:1–2 Jesus ascended a mountain **when he saw the crowds** because he deemed the mountainside to be a better setting for teaching a large group. As the new Moses, his delivery of God's message from a mountaintop provides yet another parallel with the ancient Moses. The Greek words translated **he went up on the mountain** are used three times in the Greek OT (Ex 19:3; 24:18; 34:42), and all three fall in the section describing Moses's ascent of Mount Sinai. This fits with Matthew's repeated theme of drawing out parallels between Moses and Jesus. For instance, Jesus's birth paralleled several events surrounding Moses's birth. Herod attempted to kill the infant Christ

by ordering the slaughter of Bethlehem's boys (Mt 2:16–18) much as Pharaoh ordered the execution of newborn male Israelites (Ex 1:15–18,22). Furthermore, the angel's pronouncement that danger had passed ("those who intended to kill the child are dead," Mt 2:20) is a clear echo of Ex 4:19, "All the men who wanted to kill you are dead" (see note at Mt 2:15).

5:3 Since Matthew introduces the Sermon on the Mount by highlighting the connection between Jesus and Moses, the Beatitudes (Mt 5:3–12) should probably be read against the backdrop of Moses's teachings. The only time the Septuagint (ancient Greek translation of the OT) used the adjective "Blessed" (Gk *makarios*) to translate Moses's words was in his blessing on Israel (Dt 33:29): "How happy [or "blessed"] you are, Israel! Who is like you, a people saved by the LORD? He is the shield that protects you, the sword you boast in. Your enemies will cringe before you, and you will tread on their backs." Israel's blessing had both a historical and future focus. "Saved by the LORD" referred to Israel's exodus from Egypt. The remainder of the blessing assured the Israelites of success in their conquest of the promised land. Against this backdrop, the blessings of the new Moses identify Jesus's disciples as the new Israel who will enjoy a new exodus and conquest. The new Moses is a spiritual deliverer rather than a political one, and his promises must be understood in that light. In the Beatitudes, the new Moses pronounces spiritual salvation (exodus from slavery to sin) and promises spiritual victory (conquest and inheritance of a new promised land) to the new Israel. This background is confirmed by the allusion to Israel's exodus and conquest in the promise that the meek will "inherit the earth" (5:5).

In the OT, the **poor** were those who cried out for God's help, depended entirely on him for their needs, had a humble and contrite spirit, experienced his deliverance, and enjoyed his undeserved favor (Ps 86:1–5). In light of this background, Jesus was describing his disciples as unworthy sinners who depend on God's grace for salvation. Although the promises in Mt 5:4–9 are expressed in the

4 Blessed are those who mourn,
  for they will be comforted.
5 Blessed are the humble,
  for they will inherit the earth.
6 Blessed are those who hunger and thirst
  for righteousness,
  for they will be filled.
7 Blessed are the merciful,
  for they will be shown mercy.
8 Blessed are the pure in heart,
  for they will see God.
9 Blessed are the peacemakers,
  for they will be called sons of God.
10 Blessed are those who are persecuted
   because of righteousness,
   for the kingdom of heaven is theirs.

11 "You are blessed when they insult you and
persecute you and falsely say every kind of evil
against you because of me. 12 Be glad and rejoice, because your reward is great in heaven.
For that is how they persecuted the prophets
who were before you.

Believers Are Salt and Light

13 "You are the salt of the earth. But if the salt
should lose its taste, how can it be made salty?^A
It's no longer good for anything but to be
thrown out and trampled under people's feet.
14 "You are the light of the world. A city situated on a hill cannot be hidden. 15 No one lights
a lamp and puts it under a basket, but rather
on a lampstand, and it gives light for all who

^5:13 Or *how can the earth be salted?*

---

future tense, the affirmation **the kingdom of heaven is theirs** is in the present tense (5:3,10). This suggests that the kingdom had already arrived through the coming of Jesus but that the fulfillment of many kingdom promises will occur only in the future. This future fulfillment awaits Christ's second coming. The statement "the kingdom of heaven is theirs" appears at the beginning and end of the main body of the Beatitudes (5:3,10). This bracketing device suggests that the Beatitudes constitute promises only to those who belong to the kingdom. Isaiah 61:1 promised that Messiah would bring good news to the poor. This beatitude serves as a fulfillment of that prophecy (Lk 4:16–21).
5:4 This beatitude is also dependent on Is 61: "He has sent me to heal the brokenhearted . . . to comfort all who mourn, to provide for those who mourn in Zion; to give them a crown of beauty instead of ashes, festive oil instead of mourning, and splendid clothes instead of despair" (vv. 1–3). The context of Is 61 portrays mourning as expressive of Israel's sorrow over the exile that their sins had caused. In this light, Mt 5:4 expresses the grief of those suffering the consequences of sin. Theirs is an attitude of repentance.
5:5 Like the preceding Beatitudes, this one parallels Is 61. Isaiah 61:7 (LXX) uses the words "they will inherit the earth," an exact parallel to Mt 5:5b. The first three Beatitudes thus confirm Jesus's identity as the Servant of Is 61. This identification is important for understanding the sacrificial nature of Jesus's death since Is 52:14–53:12 describes the Servant as suffering the punishment that sinners deserved (see Mt 8:17 and 12:17–21 which appeal to Is 53:4 and 42:1–4). This beatitude also echoes Ps 37:11 in which the **humble** are those who trust God and surrender to his authority even when they cannot make sense of their circumstances. **Inherit the earth** (land) in the OT refers to inheriting the promised land of Canaan. Thus most of Jesus's hearers recognized that his disciples were a new Israel that would inherit the land promised to Abraham. In the context of the Sermon on the Mount and the Gospel of Matthew as a whole, "inheriting the earth" involves more than the promise of living in Palestine. It refers to living in a recreated earth over which Christ rules eternally. Matthew 19:28 anticipates the renewal of earth and assures Jesus's disciples that they will enjoy great reward in the eternal kingdom.
5:6 Hunger and **thirst** are metaphors for a disciple's fervent desire for **righteousness**.

The words **they will be filled** are in the passive voice, indicating that righteousness is not something disciples can achieve by their own efforts. The verb here, like those in the promises of vv. 4,6–7 (and possibly v. 9), is a "divine passive" that describes an act of God. He alone imparts the righteousness for which disciples hunger and thirst. This is crucial to understanding the theology of the Sermon on the Mount, where Jesus required his disciples to keep the least of the commandments (v. 19), surpass the righteousness of the scribes and Pharisees (v. 20), and to "be perfect . . . as your heavenly Father is perfect" (v. 48). Such demands can be twisted into a false theology in which righteousness is achieved by works, but the righteousness Jesus demands of us is actually a divine gift given to his followers.
5:7 The **merciful** are those who relate to others with a forgiving and compassionate spirit (6:2–4; 18:21–35). God will show mercy to the merciful.
5:8 The words **pure in heart** refer to someone who is authentically righteous in the inner person. Righteousness can be faked, as was the case with the Pharisees (23:25–28). Jesus said true purity is attained when God grants it to the person who hungers and thirsts for it. Complete fulfillment of this divine promise will occur at Jesus's return, but the identification of his disciples as those who are pure shows that dramatic transformation occurs even in this lifetime. The promise that Jesus's disciples **will see God** looks forward to the time when they will literally behold God in all his glory. The words are not to be interpreted figuratively as if they refer merely to special insight into God's nature or to a visionary experience. The new Moses promises his followers access to God that not even the ancient Moses was allowed to experience (Ex 33:12–23).
5:9 The ministry of peacemaking involves resolving conflict by making prompt apologies and acts of restitution, refusing to seek revenge, and humbly serving and loving one's enemies (vv. 21–26,38–41,43–48). The promise that **peacemakers . . . will be called sons of God** probably means that Jesus's authentic disciples emulate God by undertaking the ministry of reconciliation. Thus at the final judgment they shall be accepted as the sons (and daughters) of God.
5:10 The purest form of **righteousness** is pursued by disciples who know that their good deeds will demand great sacrifice and will result in pain rather than immediate

reward. This is the epitome of the kingdom righteousness demanded by the Sermon on the Mount. Jesus pronounced that the kingdom of heaven belongs to those who suffer for righteousness. In the Greek text, **theirs** is shifted from its normal position at the end of the clause to the beginning instead. This gives the pronoun a special emphasis indicating that the kingdom belongs to righteous sufferers and to them alone. Those who always endeavor to evade persecution are not true disciples and will not have a share in the kingdom because true disciples follow Jesus even at the cost of their lives (16:24–27). The **kingdom of heaven** is the reign of God in the person of Jesus Christ. Righteous sufferers are subjects of God's rule through their submission to Jesus's authority. Jesus inaugurated this kingdom during his ministry, but it will be consummated in the end time.
5:11–12 Jesus's words show that persecution is typically either verbal or violent. Verbal forms include insult and slander. The word *persecute* includes acts of physical violence like the slap of Mt 5:39. Jesus promised that the cost of discipleship will be offset by the enormity of the **reward** the disciple enjoys **in heaven**. Jewish leaders rejected and vehemently **persecuted** the OT **prophets**, and Jesus repeatedly denounced this persecution (21:34–36; 23:29–37). By treating Jesus's followers in the same way they had treated the prophets, Jewish persecutors unwittingly bestowed on them a prophet's honor.
5:13 Salt has many uses, but in the OT it is most often a purifying agent (Ex 30:35; Lv 2:13; 2Kg 2:21; Ezk 16:4). As **the salt of the earth**, Jesus's disciples are to purify a corrupt world through their example of righteous living and their proclamation of the gospel. However, contaminated salt does not promote purity. The verb translated **lose its taste** indicates foolish and immoral behavior. It refers to a professing disciple whose unrighteous lifestyle promotes destruction rather than purification. Such salt is only good for spreading over ground where you want to kill vegetation. Such is the fatal effect of an unrighteous disciple's lifestyle. Nothing grows where they go. The verb **thrown out** describes the disposal of something worthless, and the verb **trampled** alludes to the treatment an immoral disciple receives from the world.
5:14–16 You are the light of the world is an allusion to Is 9:1–2; 42:6; 49:6—texts that describe the ministry of Messiah, Servant of

are in the house. **¹⁶** In the same way, let your light shine before others, so that they may see your good works and give glory to your Father in heaven.

Christ Fulfills the Law

¹⁷ "Don't think that I came to abolish the Law or the Prophets. I did not come to abolish but to fulfill. **¹⁸** For truly I tell you, until heaven and earth pass away, not the smallest letter^A or one stroke of a letter will pass away from the law until all things are accomplished. **¹⁹** Therefore, whoever breaks one of the least of these commands and teaches others to do the same will be called least in the kingdom of heaven. But whoever does and teaches these commands will be called great in the kingdom of heaven. **²⁰** For I tell you, unless your righteousness surpasses that of the scribes and Pharisees, you will never get into the kingdom of heaven.

Murder Begins in the Heart

²¹ "You have heard that it was said to our ancestors, **Do not murder,**^B and whoever murders will be subject to judgment. **²²** But I tell you, everyone who is angry with his brother or sister^C will be subject to judgment. Whoever insults^D his brother or sister, will

be subject to the court.^E Whoever says, 'You fool!' will be subject to hellfire.^F **²³** So if you are offering your gift on the altar, and there you remember that your brother or sister has something against you, **²⁴** leave your gift there in front of the altar. First go and be reconciled with your brother or sister, and then come and offer your gift. **²⁵** Reach a settlement quickly with your adversary while you're on the way with him to the court, or your adversary will hand you over to the judge, and the judge to^G the officer, and you will be thrown into prison. **²⁶** Truly I tell you, you will never get out of there until you have paid the last penny.^H

Adultery Begins in the Heart

²⁷ "You have heard that it was said, **Do not commit adultery.**^I **²⁸** But I tell you, everyone who looks at a woman lustfully has already committed adultery with her in his heart. **²⁹** If your right eye causes you to sin, gouge it out and throw it away. For it is better that you lose one of the parts of your body than for your whole body to be thrown into hell. **³⁰** And if your right hand causes you to sin, cut it off and throw it away. For it is better that you lose one of the parts of your body than for your whole body to go into hell.

---

^A**5:18** Or *not one iota*; *iota* is the smallest letter of the Gk alphabet.   ^B**5:21** Ex 20:13; Dt 5:17   ^C**5:22** Other mss add *without a cause*   ^D**5:22** Lit *Whoever says 'Raca'*; an Aramaic term of abuse that puts someone down, insulting one's intelligence   ^E**5:22** Lit *Sanhedrin*   ^F**5:22** Lit *the gehenna of fire*   ^G**5:25** Other mss read *judge will hand you over to*   ^H**5:26** Lit *quadrans*, the smallest and least valuable Roman coin, worth 1/₆₄ of a daily wage   ^I**5:27** Ex 20:14; Dt 5:18

---

the Lord. This indicates that Jesus's disciples are to be extensions of his ministry, carrying salvation to the ends of the earth. Such ministry is intrinsic to true discipleship. A disciple should no more conceal his righteousness or the gospel message than a glowing **city** should douse its light at night. The reference to giving light **for all** combines with the reference to "the world" to show that Christ's ministry is intended for all people. This anticipates the Great Commission of Mt 28:18–20.

Jesus's words make clear that the disciple is not the ultimate author of his good works. If the disciple were the author of his good works, he would justly receive praise. However, Jesus taught that only the **Father in heaven** is to be praised for a disciple's good works, for he is the true source of such works (see note at v. 6). This must not be overlooked. The righteousness demanded by the Sermon on the Mount is a divine gift that God imparts to Jesus's followers.

5:17–20 Jesus defended himself against charges that he defied the law (9:3,11,14; 12:2,10; 15:1–2; 17:24; 19:3; 22:34–36) by insisting that he came to **fulfill** both the **Law** and the **Prophets**, which together amount to the entire OT. The word *fulfill* may refer to fulfillment of OT prophecies (1:22; 2:15,17,23; 4:14; 8:17; 12:17; 13:35; 21:4; 26:54,56; 27:9). This is suggested by the words **all things are accomplished**. However, it can also refer to obedience to God's commands (3:15). This additional meaning is implied by the reference to practicing **these commands**. Consequently, Jesus's words imply that he

would fulfill all of the OT promises and obey all its commandments. The **smallest letter** of the Hebrew alphabet is the *yod*, which resembles an English apostrophe. The **stroke of a letter** is a slight pen stroke that distinguishes similar letters. Jesus's statement shows that he regarded the OT as accurate and reliable down to the smallest detail. In keeping with this conviction, Jesus taught that fidelity to the OT witness determines a disciple's stature in his kingdom. True fidelity to God's commands is made possible by God's miraculous work in a disciple's heart (see note at v. 6).

5:21–22 Matthew 5:21 begins a section of the Sermon on the Mount generally known as the "six antitheses." The title may seem to imply that Jesus opposed the OT in some way, but in reality he always upheld its authority. Rather than contradicting or overturning OT teachings, Jesus opposed the misguided interpretations of the scribes and Pharisees. These men were concerned only with superficial matters, but Jesus went deeper. He argued that the law prohibits not just actual **murder** but murderous attitudes as well. Similarly, violent temperaments are condemned just as surely as violent deeds.

5:23–24 Disciples must attempt at their earliest opportunity to reconcile with a **brother or sister** who **has something against** them, even if doing so interrupts important business. Speaking to the context of his day, Jesus said disciples should seek reconciliation even if it meant halting in the middle of offering sacrifices at the Jerusalem temple.

This interruption was significant since Jesus's original audience (located away from Jerusalem) would have to abandon their **gift** at the **altar**, travel for days to reach Galilee and seek reconciliation, and then return to Judea to complete the sacrifice. Such is the priority of reconciliation.

5:25–26 A person can typically pay a smaller penalty for their offense by seeking an out-of-court settlement rather than waiting for the issue to be settled in court. This illustrates that reconciliation is urgent because the longer it is postponed, the more severe the consequences.

5:27–28 Jesus said that gazing on a member of the opposite sex for the purpose of arousing illicit sexual desire is **adultery** of the **heart**. This does not mean lustful thoughts are equally as sinful as the act of adultery. Rather it means the law prohibits adulterous desires as well as adulterous actions. Sin begins in the mind before it is committed outwardly. True righteousness therefore seeks to avoid not only adulterous acts but also adulterous thoughts.

5:29–30 Self-mutilation and amputation are not effective ways to overcome sin. After all, sin arises from a corrupt heart rather than flesh and bone (15:19). Jesus here uses hyperbole (intentional exaggeration for the sake of making a point) and allegory (in which the **eye** represents a lustful perspective and the **hand** represents an immoral deed) in order to convey a vital requirement of discipleship. Disciples should put a stop to thoughts and behaviors that contribute to immorality.

Divorce Practices Censured

31 "It was also said, **Whoever divorces his wife must give her a written notice of divorce.**^A **32** But I tell you, everyone who divorces his wife, except in a case of sexual immorality, causes her to commit adultery. And whoever marries a divorced woman commits adultery.

Tell the Truth

33 "Again, you have heard that it was said to our ancestors, **You must not break your oath, but you must keep your oaths to the Lord.**^B **34** But I tell you, don't take an oath at all: either by heaven, because it is God's throne; **35** or by the earth, because it is his footstool; or by Jerusalem, because it is the city of the great King. **36** Do not swear by your head, because you cannot make a single hair white or black. **37** But let your 'yes' mean 'yes,' and your 'no' mean 'no.' Anything more than this is from the evil one.

Go the Second Mile

38 "You have heard that it was said, **An eye for an eye** and **a tooth for a tooth.**^C **39** But I tell you, don't resist^D an evildoer. On the contrary, if anyone slaps you on your right cheek, turn the other to him also. **40** As for the one who wants to sue you and take away your shirt, let him have your coat as well. **41** And if anyone forces you to go one mile, go with him two. **42** Give to the one who asks you, and don't turn away from the one who wants to borrow from you.

Love Your Enemies

43 "You have heard that it was said, **Love your neighbor**^E and hate your enemy. **44** But I tell you, love your enemies^F and pray for those who^G persecute you, **45** so that you may be^H children of your Father in heaven. For he causes his sun to rise on the evil and the good, and sends rain on the righteous and the unrighteous. **46** For if you love those who love you, what reward will you have? Don't even the tax collectors do the same? **47** And if you greet only your brothers and sisters, what are you doing out of the ordinary?^I Don't even the Gentiles^J do the same? **48** Be perfect, therefore, as your heavenly Father is perfect.

^A**5:31** Dt 24:1 ^B**5:33** Lv 19:12; Nm 30:2; Dt 23:21 ^C**5:38** Ex 21:24; Lv 24:20; Dt 19:21 ^D**5:39** Or *don't set yourself against*, or *don't retaliate against* ^E**5:43** Lv 19:18 ^F**5:44** Other mss add *bless those who curse you, do good to those who hate you,* ^G**5:44** Other mss add *mistreat you and* ^H**5:45** Or *may become*, or *may show yourselves to be* ^I**5:47** Or *doing that is superior*; lit *doing more* ^J**5:47** Other mss read *tax collectors*

5:31–32 Jesus challenged a loose rabbinic paraphrase of Dt 24:1 that distorted the original meaning of the text. In the hands of the rabbis, Dt 24:1 greatly multiplied the number of offenses that could justify **divorce**. For instance, rabbinic commentaries on Dt 24 cited minor complaints such as a wife's fading beauty or her tendency to burn food as legitimate grounds for divorce. However, Jesus kept true to Dt 24:1 and insisted that **sexual immorality** is legitimate grounds for divorce. People who divorce for frivolous reasons and remarry are guilty of adultery since their original marriage covenant has not been genuinely dissolved.

5:33–37 Oaths to the Lord (i.e., "I swear to God") were considered binding, but since Jews avoided use of God's personal name and instead used reverent substitutions, clever liars could take an oath that seemed to appeal to God without technically doing so (23:16–22). Jesus taught that swearing oaths is wrong since oaths call for the destruction of an object or person if the oath is broken. Thus, swearing by **heaven** . . . **earth** . . . **Jerusalem**, or even one's own **head** is inappropriate because it implies that we have the authority to destroy things over which God alone has authority. Swearing against God or his belongings aligns us with the **evil one** who attempted to assume God's position as ruler of the universe.

5:38–39 Jesus explained that **eye for an eye** (Ex 21:24; Lv 24:20; Dt 19:21) was given not as a mandate for personal vengeance but as a principle to guide courts in determining appropriate punishments. The slap on **your right cheek** was a back-handed slap that was both insulting and injurious. For this act Jewish law imposed a fine that was double the one for an open-palmed blow on the left cheek. Thus we see that Jesus urged his disciples not to seek vengeance even against the most offensive kind of blow. The words

don't resist an evildoer do not indicate, however, that we should not seek justice or defend ourselves when threatened with serious bodily harm.

5:40 Frivolous lawsuits were rare in first-century Israel, and so the suit described here was probably a legitimate one that the plaintiff was likely to win. Ordinarily, defendants are upset if the judgment goes against them, but Jesus commanded his disciples to seek reconciliation with their opponents by going above and beyond the legal requirements in order to make amends. Jewish law permitted an opponent to sue for possession of an offender's inner garment, the **shirt**. Typically it was a sleeved tunic that extended to the ankles and was made of wool or linen. These could be valuable and were frequently used for bartering or making payments. The **coat** was an outer robe or wrap. It was the more essential piece of clothing since it provided warmth and could double as a blanket for the poor. Based on OT texts such as Ex 22:26–27 and Dt 24:12–13, Jewish law insisted that the coat was exempt from seizure by the courts (*m. B. Qam.* 8:6). Taking the coat was too severe a punishment. Jesus thus commanded his disciples to do even more than the courts allowed when seeking reconciliation with an opponent.

5:41 Jesus likely had in mind the much-resented practice of compulsion, in which Roman officials could force their subjects to perform menial tasks such as hauling a load on their backs (27:32). It is often said that soldiers could legally compel a subject to carry a load for only one mile before letting him go, but no surviving text establishes this as law. Most likely compulsion was usually limited to a mile simply out of common sense: people are tired after hauling a load for a mile, and soldiers who pressed for more than this risked fostering dangerous resentment among subjugated peoples. In contrast

to this, Jesus said his disciples should carry their oppressor's pack out of obligation for the first mile, but then exceed all expectations by going a second mile as an act of love and service.

5:42 Since this entire paragraph is devoted to Jesus's teaching against retaliation, this verse probably prohibits disciples from seeking vengeance against opponents by refusing to help them in a time of need. By giving the necessities of life to an enemy, disciples may restore broken relationships (Rm 12:19–21).

5:43 The words **love your neighbor** appear in Lv 19:18. However, the command **hate your enemy** does not appear anywhere in the OT. Evidently some of Jesus's contemporaries argued that the command to love your neighbor also implied the opposite—that a person was to hate everyone who was not his neighbor.

5:44–45 Loving **enemies** and praying for one's persecutors does not make a person God's child. Only rebirth does that. However, the sort of forgiving love Jesus mentions displays your family resemblance to the heavenly Father, and thus serves as a sign to your true identity. God blesses both the **evil and the good** with **sun** and **rain**.

5:46–47 Tax collectors were despised because they often collected more than the legal tax and served Rome at the expense of their downtrodden fellow Jews. Jesus taught that selfish behavior and loving only **those who love you** resembles the behavior of tax collectors and pagan **Gentiles**, not the character of the heavenly Father.

5:48 Much as a child resembles his biological parents, spiritual children bear close resemblance to their **heavenly Father**. Consequently, Jesus's disciples are commanded to exhibit moral perfection. The close connection between this verse and Jesus's teaching about love (vv. 43–47) suggests that unconditional love is the most crucial

How to Give

6 "Be careful not to practice your righteousness^ in front of others to be seen by them. Otherwise, you have no reward with your Father in heaven. [2] So whenever you give to the poor, don't sound a trumpet before you, as the hypocrites do in the synagogues and on the streets, to be applauded by people. Truly I tell you, they have their reward. [3] But when you give to the poor, don't let your left hand know what your right hand is doing, [4] so that your giving may be in secret. And your Father who sees in secret will reward you.[B]

How to Pray

[5] "Whenever you pray, you must not be like the hypocrites, because they love to pray standing in the synagogues and on the street corners to be seen by people. Truly I tell you, they have their reward. [6] But when you pray, go into your private room, shut your door, and pray to your Father who is in secret. And your Father who sees in secret will reward you.[C] [7] When you pray, don't babble like the Gentiles, since they imagine they'll be heard for their many words. [8] Don't be like them, because your Father knows the things you need before you ask him.

The Lord's Prayer

[9] "Therefore, you should pray like this:

Our Father in heaven,
    your name be honored as holy.
[10]   Your kingdom come.
    Your will be done
    on earth as it is in heaven.
[11]   Give us today our daily bread.[D]
[12]   And forgive us our debts,
    as we also have forgiven our debtors.
[13]   And do not bring us
        into[E] temptation,
    but deliver us from the evil one.[F]

[14] "For if you forgive others their offenses, your heavenly Father will forgive you as well. [15] But if you don't forgive others,[G] your Father will not forgive your offenses.

How to Fast

[16] "Whenever you fast, don't be gloomy like the hypocrites. For they disfigure their faces so that their fasting is obvious to people. Truly I tell you, they have their reward. [17] But when you fast, put oil on your head and wash your face, [18] so that your fasting isn't obvious to others but to your Father who is in secret.

---

^6:1 Other mss read *charitable giving*   ^6:4 Other mss read *will himself reward you openly*   ^C 6:6 Other mss add *openly*
^D 6:11 Or *our necessary bread*, or *our bread for tomorrow*   ^E 6:13 Or *do not cause us to come into*   ^F 6:13 Or *from evil*; some later mss add *For yours is the kingdom and the power and the glory forever. Amen.*   ^G 6:15 Other mss add *their wrongdoing*

---

expression of God's character in the life of his followers.
6:1 Jesus did not prohibit public acts of righteousness (see note at 5:14–16), but he warned that the motivation for such acts is more important than the bare fact of performing them. All such deeds must be done for God's glory, not human reputation. Those who seek human acclaim when performing good works will receive no heavenly reward. In Mt 6:2–18, Jesus supplies general principles for performing righteous acts.
6:2–4 The words **whenever you give** assume that disciples will regularly assist needy people. The prohibition **don't sound a trumpet** stems from the fact that the offering chests in the temple (shofar chests or trumpet chests) were trumpet-shaped with a wide opening where coins were deposited and a winding, ever-narrower funnel that, at its narrowest point, exits into the chest. This arrangement prevented thieves from sticking their hands into the chest (*Sheqal.* 2:1; 6:1,5). Thus, "sounding the trumpet" is likely a reference to tossing coins noisily into the trumpet-shaped coffer and thereby calling attention to one's generosity. Jesus described such conduct as hypocritical. The word **hypocrites** (Gk *hupocrites*) originally referred to actors who performed in Greek or Roman theaters. The hypocrites to whom Jesus referred are spiritual actors who pretend to have piety in order to win human approval. The instructions about the **left hand** and the **right hand** prohibit a person from celebrating personal acts of righteousness. Give liberally, but never dwell on the fact that you do so.
6:5 Standing in the synagogues (gathering places for Jewish worship) or **on the street corners** when praying ensured that

many people saw the hypocrites praying, but Jesus taught that God has no regard for such actions.
6:6 A **private room** (Gk *tameion*) was a room that did not have doors or windows to the building's exterior. Closing the **door** granted total privacy. Since the true disciple prays for a heavenly rather than a human audience, privacy is ideal for genuine prayer. Jesus described the Father as the one **who is in secret**. God is ever-present. The disciple can encounter him in the most obscure locations. Jesus's words do not prohibit public prayers—which are encouraged in the church (see 1Co 14:26).
6:7 The babbling of **Gentiles** may refer to the meaningless gibberish that appears in Greek magical papyri. Like the familiar "abracadabra," these formulas were nonsensical combinations of sounds that were believed to have special power. Ancient texts show that Jews sometimes embraced these practices.
6:8 Genuine and effective prayers don't need to be long prayers.
6:9 By commanding his disciples to **pray like this** rather than simply "pray this," Jesus demonstrated that this prayer was offered as a model rather than a mantra to be recited. The first person plural pronoun **Our** implies that Jesus intended this prayer to be a model for corporate prayer, i.e., a prayer for when disciples gather as a group. This confirms that Mt 6:5 was not intended to prohibit disciples from praying together publicly in the synagogue or other gatherings but instead prohibited prayers that were motivated by religious showmanship. **Your name be honored as holy** suggests that Jesus expected his disciples to live righteous lives that honor

rather than profane God's name (5:16; Lv 22:31–32). This is an important precondition for successful prayer.
6:10 In light of parallels with contemporary Jewish prayers and Jesus's teaching that the kingdom of God is a present reality but also awaits a fuller future consummation, the petition **your kingdom come** has a present and a future focus. The petition asks that disciples submit more fully to God's **will** as subjects of his reign through Jesus. We should daily pray for the future consummation of God's rule in which he will reign fully and completely over the world.
6:11 Daily bread was the amount of bread necessary to survive for a day. The request is reminiscent of Pr 30:8–9. Jesus wanted his disciples to live in a state of constant dependence on God and his provision.
6:12 The Greek grammar indicates that the disciple prays for forgiveness from God only after having first expressed forgiveness to others.
6:13 Do not bring us into temptation. As James makes clear, God does not tempt anyone (Jms 1:13). Moreover, God certainly permits his people to undergo temptation. The idea is "do not let us fall to temptation" or "do not abandon us to temptation." According to Paul, though believers experience temptation, they do not have to yield to it. For God provides "a way out" (1Co 10:13).
6:14–15 God forgives those who are truly repentant. True repentance results in a willingness to **forgive others**.
6:16–18 They disfigure their faces refers to the Jewish practice of smearing ashes on the face and wearing grim expressions during times of fasting. Although these acts originally expressed true repentance, hypocrites adopted them as a mask of false piety.

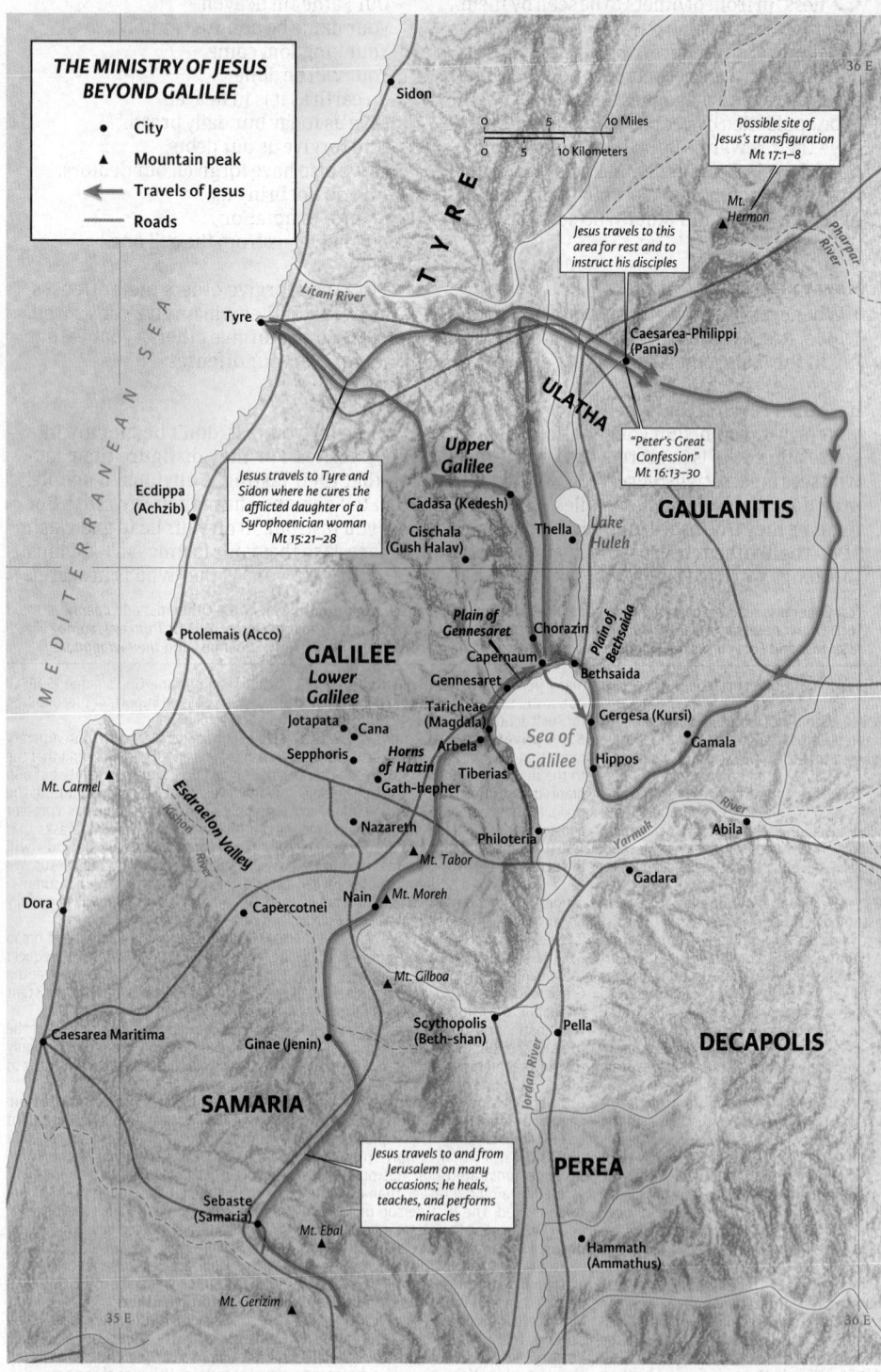

THE MINISTRY OF JESUS BEYOND GALILEE

- • City
- ▲ Mountain peak
- ← Travels of Jesus
- Roads

Sidon

0 5 10 Miles
0 5 10 Kilometers

Possible site of Jesus's transfiguration Mt 17:1–8

Mt. Hermon

Jesus travels to this area for rest and to instruct his disciples

Litani River

Tyre

Caesarea-Philippi (Panias)

ULATHA

Upper Galilee

"Peter's Great Confession" Mt 16:13–30

GAULANITIS

Ecdippa (Achzib)

Jesus travels to Tyre and Sidon where he cures the afflicted daughter of a Syrophoenician woman Mt 15:21–28

Cadasa (Kedesh)

Gischala (Gush Halav)

Thella

Lake Huleh

Ptolemais (Acco)

GALILEE
Lower Galilee

Plain of Gennesaret

Chorazin

Plain of Bethsaida

Capernaum

Bethsaida

Gennesaret

Taricheae (Magdala)

Gergesa (Kursi)

Jotapata

Cana

Sepphoris

Horns of Hattin

Arbela

Tiberias

Gamala

Hippos

Sea of Galilee

Gath-hepher

Mt. Carmel

Esdraelon Valley

Kishon River

Nazareth

Philoteria

Abila

Mt. Tabor

Yarmuk River

Dora

Capercotnei

Nain

Mt. Moreh

Gadara

Mt. Gilboa

Scythopolis (Beth-shan)

Pella

DECAPOLIS

Caesarea Maritima

Ginae (Jenin)

Jordan River

SAMARIA

PEREA

Jesus travels to and from Jerusalem on many occasions; he heals, teaches, and performs miracles

Sebaste (Samaria)

Mt. Ebal

Hammath (Ammathus)

Mt. Gerizim

35 E

36 E

MEDITERRANEAN SEA

TYRE

And your Father who sees in secret will reward you.^A

God and Possessions

^19 "Don't store up for yourselves treasures^B on earth, where moth and rust destroy and where thieves break in and steal. ^20 But store up for yourselves treasures in heaven, where neither moth nor rust destroys, and where thieves don't break in and steal. ^21 For where your treasure is, there your heart will be also.

^22 "The eye is the lamp of the body. If your eye is healthy, your whole body will be full of light. ^23 But if your eye is bad, your whole body will be full of darkness. So if the light within you is darkness, how deep is that darkness!

^24 "No one can serve two masters, since either he will hate one and love the other, or he will be devoted to one and despise the other. You cannot serve both God and money.

The Cure for Anxiety

^25 "Therefore I tell you: Don't worry about your life, what you will eat or what you will drink; or about your body, what you will wear. Isn't life more than food and the body more than clothing? ^26 Consider the birds of the sky: They don't sow or reap or gather into barns, yet your heavenly Father feeds them. Aren't you worth more than they? ^27 Can any of you add one moment to his life span^C by worrying? ^28 And why do you worry about clothes? Observe how the wildflowers of the field grow: They don't labor or spin thread. ^29 Yet I tell you that not even Solomon in all his splendor was adorned like one

of these. ^30 If that's how God clothes the grass of the field, which is here today and thrown into the furnace tomorrow, won't he do much more for you — you of little faith? ^31 So don't worry, saying, 'What will we eat?' or 'What will we drink?' or 'What will we wear?' ^32 For the Gentiles eagerly seek all these things, and your heavenly Father knows that you need them. ^33 But seek first the kingdom of God^D and his righteousness, and all these things will be provided for you. ^34 Therefore don't worry about tomorrow, because tomorrow will worry about itself. Each day has enough trouble of its own.

Do Not Judge

7 "Do not judge, so that you won't be judged. ^2 For you will be judged by the same standard with which you judge others, and you will be measured by the same measure you use. ^3 Why do you look at the splinter in your brother's eye but don't notice the beam of wood in your own eye? ^4 Or how can you say to your brother, 'Let me take the splinter out of your eye,' and look, there's a beam of wood in your own eye? ^5 Hypocrite! First take the beam of wood out of your eye, and then you will see clearly to take the splinter out of your brother's eye. ^6 Don't give what is holy to dogs or toss your pearls before pigs, or they will trample them under their feet, turn, and tear you to pieces.

Ask, Search, Knock

^7 "Ask, and it will be given to you. Seek, and you will find. Knock, and the door^E will be opened to you. ^8 For everyone who asks receives, and the

---

^A6:18 Other mss add *openly*   ^B6:19 Or *valuables*   ^C6:27 Or *add a single cubit to his height*   ^D6:33 Other mss omit *of God*   ^E7:7 Lit *and it*

6:19–20 Jesus emphasized the fleeting value of worldly wealth. The larvae of the **moth** could quickly destroy valuable fabrics that were treasured by the ancients. The word **rust** is literally "eating." It can refer to the pitting of metal coins or to vermin that ruin valuable food stores.
6:21 Jesus taught that one's **heart** truly belongs to what it most treasures. Since a disciple is to love God with all one's heart (22:37; Dt 6:4), love for material possessions and riches is a subtle form of idolatry (Col 3:5).
6:22–23 In Jewish writings, a good **eye** represented a generous attitude and a bad eye a stingy, miserly attitude. The bad eye (an improper perspective on wealth) results in a deep internal **darkness**, a moral blindness that diminishes the ability to see and pursue what is good.
6:24 People have a sinful tendency to make an idol of **money**, which then competes with God for their allegiance.
6:25 Isn't life more than food is a rabbinic style of argument. It reasons that if God does a greater thing for us, he will also do lesser things. Specifically, if God created you (the greater accomplishment), he is certainly capable of feeding you (a lesser accomplishment).
6:26 Jesus here reversed his previous argument and reasoned that if God bothers to do a lesser

thing (feed **the birds**), he will assuredly accomplish the greater thing of feeding humans.
6:27 Add one moment to his life span refers to longevity. Worry is futile and cannot prolong your life.
6:28–30 Jesus revealed that the real cause of anxiety is when disciples have **little faith**, meaning doubt about God's power and disbelief in his desire to provide for his children.
6:31–32 Obsession with material possessions displays the warped priorities of **Gentiles**.
6:33 Disciples who value the reign of God over their lives and who diligently pursue righteous living can trust God to satisfy their needs.
6:34 Jesus did not prohibit planning for the future, but he did prohibit worrying about it. He urged his disciples instead to focus on the challenges of the present.
7:1 Jesus did not intend to prohibit all acts of judgment. Elsewhere he commanded believers to discern the actions of others (v. 15; 18:15–20). What Jesus condemned is hypocritical judgment that focuses on the faults of others while excusing one's own sins.
7:2 Jesus warned that those who use a harsh standard of judgment when evaluating others can expect God to use the same harsh standard when they face his judgment.
7:3–5 The **splinter** represents a small fault. The **beam of wood** represents a major moral

fault. Those who correct the minor faults of others without attending to their own more serious faults are hypocrites. Believers do have a responsibility to help one another repent of sins but only after first dealing with their own serious sins.
7:6 What is holy probably refers to sacrificial meat. **Dogs** would devour it insensibly without appreciating its sacredness. In Jesus's allegory, this sacrificial meat symbolizes his own sacred teachings. The dogs symbolize the wicked who disregard the value of his teachings. First-century teachers referred to **pearls** symbolically to speak of insightful and valuable teaching. Consequently, the pearls here symbolize Jesus's teachings given by the disciples. **Pigs** were ritually unclean animals. They symbolize the wicked and unclean. Pigs eat spoiled food but have no appreciation for pearls, just as the wicked consume wicked pleasures but disregard the gospel. This contempt for the gospel is pictured by the pig trampling the pearls underfoot. That pigs may turn against the one offering the pearls shows that contempt for the gospel message can become contempt for the gospel messenger, as has often happened in history.
7:7–8 While some people interpret these verses as a promise that God will give disciples whatever they pray for, linguistic connections

one who seeks finds, and to the one who knocks, the door will be opened. ⁹ Who among you, if his son asks him for bread, will give him a stone? ¹⁰ Or if he asks for a fish, will give him a snake? ¹¹ If you then, who are evil, know how to give good gifts to your children, how much more will your Father in heaven give good things to those who ask him. ¹² Therefore, whatever you want others to do for you, do also the same for them, for this is the Law and the Prophets.

Entering the Kingdom

¹³ "Enter through the narrow gate. For the gate is wide and the road broad that leads to destruction, and there are many who go through it. ¹⁴ How narrow is the gate and difficult the road that leads to life, and few find it.

¹⁵ "Be on your guard against false prophets who come to you in sheep's clothing but inwardly are ravaging wolves. ¹⁶ You'll recognize them by their fruit. Are grapes gathered from thornbushes or figs from thistles? ¹⁷ In the same way, every good tree produces good fruit, but a bad tree produces bad fruit. ¹⁸ A good tree can't produce bad fruit; neither can a bad tree produce good fruit. ¹⁹ Every tree that doesn't produce good fruit is cut down and thrown into the fire. ²⁰ So you'll recognize them by their fruit.

²¹ "Not everyone who says to me, 'Lord, Lord,' will enter the kingdom of heaven, but only the one who does the will of my Father in heaven. ²² On that day many will say to me, 'Lord, Lord, didn't we prophesy in your name, drive out demons in your name, and do many miracles in your name?' ²³ Then I will announce to them, 'I never knew you. **Depart from me, you lawbreakers!** ' ^A,B

The Two Foundations

²⁴ "Therefore, everyone who hears these words of mine and acts on them will be like a wise man who built his house on the rock. ²⁵ The rain fell, the rivers rose, and the winds blew and pounded that house. Yet it didn't collapse, because its foundation was on the rock. ²⁶ But everyone who hears these words of mine and doesn't act on them will be like a foolish man who built his house on the sand. ²⁷ The rain fell, the rivers rose, the winds blew and pounded that house, and it collapsed. It collapsed with a great crash."

²⁸ **When Jesus had finished saying these things, the crowds were astonished at his teaching, ²⁹ because he was teaching them like one who had authority, and not like their scribes.**

A Man Cleansed

8 When he came down from the mountain, large crowds followed him. ² Right away a man with leprosy^c came up and knelt before

---

^A 7:23 Lit *you who work lawlessness*   ^B 7:23 Ps 6:8   ^C 8:2 Gk *lepros*; a term for various skin diseases, also in v. 3; see Lv 13–14

---

between these verses and other portions of the Sermon on the Mount suggest that Jesus promised that those who ask, search, and knock will be invited to enter his kingdom. The command to **ask** is tied to the promise of "good things" to those who ask in v. 11. In the Lukan parallel, these good things are interpreted as the Holy Spirit who transforms the disciple and makes him fit for the kingdom. **Seek** uses the same Greek verb as 6:33, "Seek first the kingdom of God and his righteousness." Since the word **door** is not in the Greek text of v. 7, and because ancient people knocked on gates as well as doors to request entrance (Ac 12:13), **knock** likely refers to knocking on the gate of the kingdom (mentioned in Mt 7:13–14).
7:9–10 Round loaves of bread resemble smooth, brown stones. Certain **fish** in the Sea of Galilee resemble snakes.
7:11 Jesus's description of humans as **you . . . who are evil** disproves the modern concept that people are basically good. Although Jesus acknowledged that humans may perform gracious acts like providing for their children, he insisted that they do so contrary to their sinful nature. God's gracious acts, on the other hand, express our heavenly Father's perfect nature.
7:12 The word **therefore** suggests that the "Golden Rule" of this verse draws an application from the preceding section. Since the preceding verse describes God's gracious and loving provision for others, the conjunction probably implies that following the Golden Rule shows the disciple's resemblance to the heavenly Father (see notes at 5:44–45; 5:48).
7:13–14 The **narrow gate** symbolizes the exclusive nature of Christ's kingdom. Entrance

requires the disciple to do the will of the Father in heaven (v. 21). The **gate** that is **wide** indicates that hell grants unrestricted entrance and that many will enter through its gates. The **difficult** (lit "narrow") . . . **road** may symbolize the life of hardship and persecution that the disciple must face. However, since Jewish literature often used the symbol of the road to represent a moral path (Jdg 2:22; Is 30:21; Jr 6:16; 2Jn 6) and because the law was portrayed as a narrow road from which a person was not to deviate (Dt 5:32; 17:20; 28:14; Jos 1:7; 2Kg 22:2), the narrow road probably represents Jesus's morally restrictive teaching. The wide road permits travelers to meander and pursue worldly desires, but the narrow path requires travelers to stick to God's will (Mt 7:21).
7:15–20 False prophets don sheep's clothing to disguise the fact that they are **ravaging wolves** masquerading as true disciples. However, a prophet's character and behavior (his **fruit**) indicates whether he is true or false. Other NT texts insist that a teacher's doctrine must also be examined (1Jn 4:2–3). True disciples bear the fruit of good works, and this confirms their identity as Jesus's disciples (Mt 7:21–23). The image of cutting down and burning a bad **tree** portrays the judgment and eternal punishment of false disciples. The test Jesus gives is not quick and easy but one that proves itself over time.
7:21–23 By referring to himself as **Lord** and depicting himself as the ultimate judge of humanity, Jesus implied his deity. True disciples affirm Jesus's lordship, submit to his authority, and obey his commands. Jesus insisted that a person is confirmed as a

true disciple not by prophecy, exorcism, or working miracles but by living a transformed life made possible by God. The disobedient lifestyles of **lawbreakers** are inconsistent with genuine discipleship. Jesus's words, **I never knew you**, show that these were never truly disciples.
7:24–27 The adjectives **wise** and **foolish** describe a person's spiritual and moral state, not his intellect. Whether one is considered wise or foolish is determined by his response to Jesus's teaching. Since OT writers described God's wrath using the image of a great storm (Is 28:16–17; Ezk 13:10–13), the storm that destroys the **house on the sand** is a picture of divine judgment. Hence, the person who **hears** and **acts** on Jesus's teaching is prepared for judgment. The one who **hears** but **doesn't act** on Jesus's **words** will be destroyed in the storm of judgment.
7:28–29 Jesus amazed the crowds with an **authority** that surpassed that of other teachers. First-century Jewish teachers appealed to the authority of their rabbinic predecessors. However, Jesus introduced his teachings with the contrast, "You have heard that it was said . . . but I tell you" (5:21,27,31,33,38,43). By this Jesus made clear that he had the authority to interpret the law independent from and even contrary to the Jewish oral tradition and the most esteemed rabbis. The words **when Jesus had finished** mark the end of the first of five major blocks of teaching in Matthew's Gospel (cp. 11:1; 13:53; 19:1; 26:1).
8:1–2 Regarding **leprosy**, the Greek term can refer to several conditions, ranging from fungal infections to Hansen's Disease. The OT law

him, saying, "Lord, if you are willing, you can make me clean."
³ Reaching out his hand, Jesus touched him, saying, "I am willing; be made clean." Immediately his leprosy was cleansed. ⁴ Then Jesus told him, "See that you don't tell anyone; but go, show yourself to the priest, and offer the gift that Moses commanded, as a testimony to them."

A Centurion's Faith

⁵ When he entered Capernaum, a centurion came to him, pleading with him, ⁶ "Lord, my servant is lying at home paralyzed, in terrible agony."
⁷ He said to him, "Am I to come and heal him?"ᴬ
⁸ "Lord," the centurion replied, "I am not worthy to have you come under my roof. But just say the word, and my servant will be healed. ⁹ For I too am a man under authority, having soldiers under my command.ᴮ I say to this one, 'Go,' and he goes; and to another, 'Come,' and he comes; and to my servant, 'Do this!' and he does it."
¹⁰ Hearing this, Jesus was amazed and said to those following him, "Truly I tell you, I have not found anyone in Israel with so great a faith. ¹¹ I tell you that many will come from east and west to share the banquetᶜ with Abraham, Isaac, and Jacob in the kingdom of heaven. ¹² But the sons of the kingdom will be thrown

into the outer darkness where there will be weeping and gnashing of teeth." ¹³ Then Jesus told the centurion, "Go. As you have believed, let it be done for you." And his servant was healed that very moment.ᴰ

Healings at Capernaum

¹⁴ Jesus went into Peter's house and saw his mother-in-law lying in bed with a fever. ¹⁵ So he touched her hand, and the fever left her. Then she got up and began to serve him. ¹⁶ When evening came, they brought to him many who were demon-possessed. He drove out the spirits with a word and healed all who were sick, ¹⁷ so that what was spoken through the prophet Isaiah might be fulfilled:

He himself took our weaknesses
and carried our diseases.ᴱ

The Cost of Following Jesus

¹⁸ When Jesus saw a large crowdᶠ around him, he gave the order to go to the other side of the sea. ¹⁹ A scribe approached him and said, "Teacher, I will follow you wherever you go."
²⁰ Jesus told him, "Foxes have dens, and birds of the sky have nests, but the Son of Man has no place to lay his head."
²¹ "Lord," another of his disciples said, "first let me go bury my father."
²² But Jesus told him, "Follow me, and let the dead bury their own dead."

ᴬ8:7 Or "I will come and heal him." ᴮ8:9 Lit under me ᶜ8:11 Lit recline at the table ᴰ8:13 Or that hour; lit very hour
ᴱ8:17 Is 53:4 ᶠ8:18 Other mss read saw large crowds

---

required lepers to be isolated from society (Lv 13:45–46). By kneeling before Jesus and addressing him as Lord (Gk *kurios*, the Greek translation of the Hebrew name *Yahweh*), the man recognized Jesus as far more than just a man. His confidence in Jesus's ability to heal his condition hints that his act of worship involved full recognition of Jesus's deity. After all, only God was capable of healing lepers in the OT (Ex 4:6–7; Nm 12:10–16; 2Kg 5:1–15, esp. v. 7). The man's qualification, **if you are willing**, may indicate that other so-called healers had mistreated or failed him.
8:3 Although Jesus frequently healed by touch (v. 15; 9:20,25), he could heal by command and even at great distance from the sufferer (8:5–13; 9:6). Touching a leper was an expression of boldness and deep compassion since doing so was prohibited by OT law (Lv 5:3).
8:4 By being inspected and declared clean by the priest, the healed man could authenticate the miracle that Jesus performed.
8:5–6 A **centurion** was an officer of the Roman army who commanded about one hundred soldiers.
8:7–10 Jesus's willingness to enter the home of a Gentile shocked the centurion, for Jewish law banned Jews from doing this (Ac 10:28). God's grace to Gentiles and his intention to include them in his redemptive plan is a prominent theme in Matthew. The centurion was confident that Jesus had the authority to heal his servant even though the servant was in another location.

8:11 The **kingdom of heaven** is open to anyone who places their faith in Jesus. Believing Gentiles will be equal even to the great Jewish patriarchs **Abraham, Isaac, and Jacob**.
8:12 The **sons of the kingdom** refers to Jews to whom the kingdom was originally promised but who will be excluded because they rejected Jesus. **Outer darkness** is a metaphor for damnation in ancient Jewish texts. **Weeping and gnashing of teeth** denotes anguish expressed by those who suffer eternal torment.
8:13 The centurion's faith in Jesus was wisely placed.
8:14 Mention of Peter's **mother-in-law** confirms that Peter was married. His marriage was foundational to Paul's argument that apostles had the right to marry and to have their wives accompany them in their missionary labors (1Co 9:5).
8:15 The woman's ability to get up immediately and serve a meal indicates that her healing was instant and complete.
8:16 Jesus's ability to drive out **spirits** by command stands in contrast to the drastic measures used by Jewish exorcists. These included using offensive odors to drive demons away or nose rings to hook them (Tob 6:7–8,16–17; Josephus, *Ant.* 8.45–49). That Jesus could heal **all who were sick** indicates that no disease could thwart his healing powers.
8:17 In one sense Jesus was able to heal physical illnesses because his impending sacrificial death purchased spiritual atonement from

sin. All sickness is ultimately a consequence of Adam's sinful choice. Jesus could remove these consequences because he would bear the full penalty for sin on the cross. Matthew's application of Is 53:4 shows that he understood Jesus's death as an act of substitution, an atonement in which Jesus was "pierced because of our rebellion" and bore punishment "for the iniquity of us all" (Is 53:5–6).
8:18–20 Following Jesus can involve sacrificing the comforts of home. Jesus is more than worthy of such sacrifice because he is the **Son of Man**. This title was drawn from Dn 7:13–14 where it described a ruler of heavenly origin who would reign over a universal and eternal kingdom. This was Jesus's favorite self-designation. It is used twenty-eight times in Matthew.
8:21–22 Jesus's demand seems harsh to modern readers, for today funerals would only briefly delay a commitment to follow him. However, ancient Jewish burials stretched over an entire year. A year after the initial interment, the eldest son was obligated to gather the skeletal remains and place them in an ossuary for second burial. Many Jews regarded the commandment to honor father and mother as the supreme commandment, and they also viewed giving parents an honorable burial as its most important implication. Jesus insisted that following him was to be an even higher priority. Since obligation to God supersedes obligation to parents (Dt 13:5–6), Jesus assumed a divine prerogative in this teaching.

Wind and Waves Obey Jesus

23 As he got into the boat, his disciples followed him. **24** Suddenly, a violent storm arose on the sea, so that the boat was being swamped by the waves — but Jesus kept sleeping. **25** So the disciples came and woke him up, saying, "Lord, save us! We're going to die!"

26 He said to them, "Why are you afraid, you of little faith?" Then he got up and rebuked the winds and the sea, and there was a great calm. **27** The men were amazed and asked, "What kind of man is this? Even the winds and the sea obey him!"

Demons Driven Out by Jesus

28 When he had come to the other side, to the region of the Gadarenes,^ two demon-possessed men met him as they came out of the tombs. They were so violent that no one could pass that way. **29** Suddenly they shouted, "What do you have to do with us,^B Son of God? Have you come here to torment us before the time?"

30 A long way off from them, a large herd of pigs was feeding. **31** "If you drive us out," the demons begged him, "send us into the herd of pigs."

32 "Go!" he told them. So when they had come out, they entered the pigs, and the whole herd rushed down the steep bank into the sea and perished in the water. **33** Then the men who tended them fled. They went into the city and reported everything, especially what had happened to those who were demon-possessed.

34 At that, the whole town went out to meet Jesus. When they saw him, they begged him to leave their region.

The Son of Man Forgives and Heals

9 So he got into a boat, crossed over, and came to his own town. **2** Just then some men^C brought to him a paralytic lying on a stretcher. Seeing their faith, Jesus told the paralytic, "Have courage, son, your sins are forgiven."

3 At this, some of the scribes said to themselves, "He's blaspheming!"

4 Perceiving their thoughts, Jesus said, "Why are you thinking evil things in your hearts?^D **5** For which is easier: to say, 'Your sins are forgiven,' or to say, 'Get up and walk'? **6** But so that you may know that the Son of Man has authority on earth to forgive sins" — then he told the paralytic, "Get up, take your stretcher, and go home." **7** So he got up and went home. **8** When the crowds saw this, they were awestruck^E,F and gave glory to God, who had given such authority to men.

The Call of Matthew

9 As Jesus went on from there, he saw a man named Matthew sitting at the tax office, and he said to him, "Follow me," and he got up and followed him.

10 While he was reclining at the table in the house, many tax collectors and sinners came to eat with Jesus and his disciples. **11** When the

---

^8:28 Other mss read *Gergesenes* ^B8:29 Other mss add *Jesus* ^C9:2 Lit *then they* ^D9:4 Or *minds* ^E9:8 Other mss read *amazed* ^F9:8 Lit *afraid*

8:23–27 Jesus's authority over **winds** and **sea** identified him as the creator and ruler of nature.
8:28 Early manuscripts of Matthew describe this event as occurring in **the region of the Gadarenes**. In contrast, early manuscripts of Mark and Luke describe it as occurring in "the region of the Gerasenes" (Mk 5:1; Lk 8:26). Gadara and Gerasa were located in the same province. The different readings mean very little in this light, and they likely arose due to transcription errors rather than disagreement between the original texts of the Gospels. These regions were Gentile lands, as confirmed by the large herd of pigs nearby. The **tombs** were burial caves in which fugitives sometimes hid. The presence of the **demon-possessed** among the tombs indicates their obsession with things profane and unclean.
8:29 Although Jesus's disciples were slow to recognize his divine Sonship, the demons were not. Jesus was first identified as God's Son by the Father during his baptism (3:17). Later, Satan acknowledged Jesus's divine Sonship (4:3,6). Now demons reiterated Jesus's identity. **Son of God** was a messianic title drawn from Ps 2:7,12 (see note at Mt 3:17). The demons also recognized Jesus as the one who would judge and punish them.
8:30–32 No longer able to continue their destructive and violent work in the lives of the two men, the demons begged for permission to enter the **herd of pigs** where the demons'

deceptive and murderous nature was clearly displayed in the senseless destruction of the entire herd. Here is a picture of Satan's ultimate aim for the world.
8:33–34 Gentiles from the nearby town may have thought that Jesus personally destroyed the herd as a statement against Gentile idolatry and uncleanness, and they naturally feared destruction of other valuable herds (see note at v. 28).
9:1 Crossed over refers to the Sea of Galilee. Jesus's **own town** was Capernaum, the headquarters of his ministry (see note at 4:13).
9:2 Jesus elsewhere insisted that illness is not necessarily a direct consequence of a person's sin (Jn 9:1–3). **Seeing their faith** implies that personal faith ("their" included the paralytic and his friends) was necessary to receive Jesus's healing and forgiveness. On the association of personal faith with Jesus's miracles, see vv. 22,28–29; 8:13. In chap. 9, Jesus healed people who were lame (vv. 1–8), blind (vv. 27–31), and unable to speak (vv. 32–34). A Jewish audience who knew OT prophecies would recognize these miracles as the fulfillment of Is 35:5–6.
9:3 Scribes were a guild of scholars skilled in copying and interpreting the OT. They viewed themselves as guardians of Jewish traditions. The scribes considered Jesus's pronouncement of forgiveness to be blasphemous since only God can forgive sins. By asserting this divine right, Jesus put himself in God's place (Mk 2:7).

9:4 Jesus's ability to know the scribes' secret **thoughts** implies supernatural knowledge.
9:5 Jesus proved his authority to forgive sins by removing the physical consequences of sin.
9:6 Jesus associated his **authority** to forgive sins with his identity as the **Son of Man** (see note at 8:18–20). Although first-century Jews did not associate forgiveness of sin with Messiah, Is 53 showed that Messiah would offer the sacrifice that accomplished atonement for sin. Matthew alludes to this in Mt 8:17 (see also 20:28).
9:7–8 Although other individuals do not share Jesus's authority to forgive sins, Jesus did impart to his disciples the authority to heal sickness and disease (10:1). The amazement of the **crowds** shows that the scribes were incapable of performing such miracles even though they claimed to be God's authoritative spokespersons.
9:9 Parallel texts (Mk 2:14; Lk 5:27) identify this tax collector as Levi. Most Jews had two or three names. **Matthew** means "gift of Yahweh," and it may have been a nickname given to Levi by Jesus (cp. Mt 16:17–18) to remind him that his conversion and call were gifts from God. Many interpreters believe this verse identifies Matthew as the author of this Gospel.
9:10–11 Tax collectors were detested by many first-century Jews because they served the oppressive Roman government and often abused their authority for their own financial gain.

◀ Are Miracles and Science Compatible?

by Douglas Groothuis

One of the secular claims against Christianity is that the modern world's increasing knowledge of the natural world through science has made belief in miracles unjustified at best and positively irrational at worst. Recently, biologist and atheist Richard Dawkins has led this charge, especially in his best-selling book *The God Delusion* (2007). Before responding to this challenge, we need to define our two basic terms: *miracle* and *science*.

Biblically understood, a miracle is God's supernatural intervention in creation, which produces an effect otherwise not possible given the operation of natural laws. Since God as Creator and Sustainer of the universe is the one who has established so-called natural laws, he is also free to act outside such laws. After all, natural laws simply reflect God's design for the way things normally occur. If he decides to act outside this normal design, he is not breaking the laws of nature since they are not "laws" for God; they are simply patterns that reflect his own will.

So why, then, do secularists think science is incompatible with belief in miracles? There are three main reasons.

First, if one believes there is no God, then there is no divine agent (or conscience actor) to produce a miracle. In other words, if you begin with the presupposition that God does not exist, then you cannot believe in miracles.

Nevertheless, there are ample reasons drawn from science and philosophy to believe that a personal Creator and Designer does exist. Cosmology indicates that the universe began from nothing a finite time ago with a big bang. Such an event requires a cause outside the universe. The best explanation is that God caused this event. From one point of view, the creation of the universe from nothing is God's first supernatural action, since natural laws do not allow something to be made from nothing. Physics also reveals that the laws and proportions of the universe are finely tuned for the support of human life. Chance and mindless natural law do not explain this adequately. God's purpose and design provide the best explanation.

Science, in and of itself, does not preclude the work of God within nature. But if scientists presuppose that God does not exist, then such explanations are dismissed. Consequently, many secularists define science in such a way as to exclude miracles. Science is seen as offering only natural explanations for natural events.

Second, scientific endeavor is regarded as the only legitimate source for knowledge about the natural world. No supernatural explanations are allowed in principle. So, even if the universe began from nothing, science cannot even suggest a Creator's involvement in it. Neither can science speak to the existence of a Designer to explain the fine-tuning of the universe. Inevitably, the result is that no one can be intellectually justified in believing in miracles.

But this claim for science is neither grounded in the history of science (many leaders of the scientific revolution were theists) nor is it philosophically credible. Science becomes a knowledge blocker if, in fact, God has left recognizable signs of his existence in the cosmos. Whether or not we can find evidence for God in the natural world should be a question open to rigorous investigation.

Furthermore, when science is regarded as the *only* source of rational knowledge, it logically refutes itself. This approach, known as scientism, claims that (1) science is limited to giving natural explanations for natural events based on logical reasoning; and that (2) science is the sole conduit for knowledge (or credible, true beliefs). These two statements rightly receive the following rebuttals: First, the claim that science is the only source of knowledge is not justified by any natural event or logical reasoning. Scientism is, rather, a philosophical claim. And therefore, second, since this materialistic view of science is not supported by its own understanding of science, scientism must be false. This destroys the argument for science as the one source of knowledge about reality. It cannot be the only means of acquiring genuine knowledge.

Third, some affirm that the development of technology, especially in the twentieth century, is incompatible with belief in

Pharisees saw this, they asked his disciples, "Why does your teacher eat with tax collectors and sinners?"

¹² Now when he heard this, he said, "It is not those who are well who need a doctor, but those who are sick. ¹³ Go and learn what this means: **I desire mercy and not sacrifice.**ᴬ For I didn't come to call the righteous, but sinners."ᴮ

A Question about Fasting

¹⁴ Then John's disciples came to him, saying, "Why do we and the Pharisees fast often, but your disciples do not fast?"

¹⁵ Jesus said to them, "Can the wedding guestsᶜ be sad while the groom is with them? The timeᴰ will come when the groom will be taken away from them, and then they will fast. ¹⁶ No one patches an old garment with unshrunk cloth, because the patch pulls away from the garment and makes the tear worse. ¹⁷ And no one putsᴱ new wine into old wineskins. Otherwise, the skins burst, the wine spills out, and the skins are ruined. No, they put new wine into fresh wineskins, and both are preserved."

A Girl Restored and a Woman Healed

¹⁸ As he was telling them these things, suddenly one of the leaders came and knelt down before him, saying, "My daughter just died,ᶠ but come and lay your hand on her, and she will live." ¹⁹ So Jesus and his disciples got up and followed him.

²⁰ Just then, a woman who had suffered from bleeding for twelve years approached from behind and touched the end of his robe, ²¹ for she

---

ᴬ**9:13** Hs 6:6   ᴮ**9:13** Other mss add *to repentance*   ᶜ**9:15** Lit *the sons of the bridal chamber*   ᴰ**9:15** Lit *days*   ᴱ**9:17** Lit *And they do not put*   ᶠ**9:18** Lit *daughter has now come to the end*

9:12–13 Hosea 6:6 is an important text in Matthew, since it is quoted twice (see 12:7). In its original context, the verse meant that sacrifice would not secure atonement for anyone who sought God's mercy but did not extend it to others. Jesus often insisted that those who seek forgiveness from God must also offer it to others (5:23–24; 6:14–15; 18:21–35). The two Hs 6:6 citations are the only times that Matthew uses the term **sacrifice**. Elsewhere when he refers to sacrifice, he uses the term *gift* (Gk *doron*). This is likely because Jesus's death was the one true sacrifice that secured atonement for sins (8:17; 20:28). Matthew wanted Jewish Christians who continued to practice temple rituals to view their sacrifices as gifts expressing gratitude for forgiveness already received through Jesus rather than acts that accomplish atonement.
9:14–15 This conversation with **John's disciples** occurred while John was in prison (Mt 4:12). The presence of Messiah gave the disciples an irrepressible joy that was inconsistent with fasting.
9:16–17 The images of a shrinking **patch** tearing the **garment** that it was intended to repair and brittle **wineskins** rupturing from the gases released by fermenting wine picture the incompatibility of traditional Jewish teaching and Jesus's teaching.
9:18–19 The man was a leader of the synagogue.
9:20–22 This woman's condition left her perpetually unclean (Lv 25:15–31; Is 64:6). The penalty for entering the temple while

---

miracles. A twentieth-century biblical scholar, not a scientist, put this starkly: Rudolph Bultmann said that no one who uses a transistor radio can believe in the miraculous world presented in the NT. But the development of technology is not incompatible with miracles since these technologies depend on scientific discoveries and methods that themselves do not refute miracles, as argued above.

Detecting a miracle in human experience is a matter of historical inquiry—not hard science such as chemistry, biology, or physics. That is, we cannot know through the methods of science that Caesar crossed the Rubicon. But this does not mean we have no knowledge of historical matters, such as social change within cultures, the rise and fall of empires, or biography. One's method of acquiring knowledge must fit the subject of study. History consults written and unwritten items from the past to discern what happened. While many historians simply dismiss God and the supernatural from knowable history, ignoring the Bible's claims to record such, there is no good reason to do so. If it is possible that God exists, then miracles are possible. If they are possible, we may investigate miraculous claims to see if there are any actual miracles.

While many religions claim miracles, none are as well substantiated as New Testament miracles. This is especially true of Jesus's miracles and his resurrection in particular. In fact, Christianity is the only religion that attributes miracles to its founder in its earliest and foundational documents—the books comprising the New Testament. For example, the resurrection of Jesus from the dead is affirmed in all four Gospels. It is also directly or indirectly affirmed throughout the rest of the New Testament. These documents were written by eyewitnesses (Jn 19:35) or by those who consulted eyewitnesses (Lk 1:1–4).

Christians need not fear that the advancement of science somehow undermines the rationality of their belief in miracles. Miracles are not incompatible with science. Only an unhelpful understanding of science, miracles, or both generates this false impression. Both science and history corroborate the biblical teaching that God is a wonder-working God of space-time history and eternity.

said to herself, "If I can just touch his robe, I'll be made well."[A]
[22] Jesus turned and saw her. "Have courage, daughter," he said. "Your faith has saved you."[B] And the woman was made well from that moment.[C]
[23] When Jesus came to the leader's house, he saw the flute players and a crowd lamenting loudly. [24] "Leave," he said, "because the girl is not dead but asleep." And they laughed at him. [25] After the crowd had been put outside, he went in and took her by the hand, and the girl got up. [26] Then news of this spread throughout that whole area.

Healing the Blind

[27] As Jesus went on from there, two blind men followed him, calling out, "Have mercy on us, Son of David!"
[28] When he entered the house, the blind men approached him, and Jesus said to them, "Do you believe that I can do this?"
They said to him, "Yes, Lord."
[29] Then he touched their eyes, saying, "Let it be done for you according to your faith." [30] And their eyes were opened. Then Jesus warned them sternly, "Be sure that no one finds out." [31] But they went out and spread the news about him throughout that whole area.

Driving Out a Demon

[32] Just as they were going out, a demon-possessed man who was unable to speak was brought to him. [33] When the demon had been driven out, the man who had been mute spoke, and the crowds were amazed, saying, "Nothing like this has ever been seen in Israel!"
[34] But the Pharisees said, "He drives out demons by the ruler of the demons."

The Lord of the Harvest

[35] Jesus continued going around to all the towns and villages, teaching in their synagogues, preaching the good news of the kingdom, and healing every[D] disease and every sickness.[E,F] [36] When he saw the crowds, he felt compassion for them, because they were distressed and dejected, like sheep without a shepherd. [37] Then he said to his disciples, "The harvest is abundant, but the workers are few. [38] Therefore, pray to the Lord of the harvest to send out workers into his harvest."

Commissioning the Twelve

10 Summoning his twelve disciples, he gave them authority over unclean spirits, to drive them out and to heal every[D] disease and sickness.[F] [2] These are the names of the twelve apostles: First, Simon, who is called Peter, and Andrew his brother; James the son of Zebedee, and John his brother; [3] Philip and Bartholomew; Thomas and Matthew the tax collector; James the son of Alphaeus, and Thaddaeus;[G] [4] Simon the Zealot,[H] and Judas Iscariot, who also betrayed him.
[5] Jesus sent out these twelve after giving them instructions: "Don't take the road that leads to the Gentiles, and don't enter any Samaritan town. [6] Instead, go to the lost sheep of the house of Israel. [7] As you go, proclaim, 'The kingdom of heaven has come near.' [8] Heal the sick, raise the dead, cleanse those with leprosy,[I] drive out demons. Freely you received, freely give. [9] Don't acquire gold, silver, or copper for your money-belts. [10] Don't take a traveling bag for the road, or an extra shirt, sandals, or a staff, for the worker is worthy of his food. [11] When you enter any town or village, find out who is worthy,

---

[A] **9:21** Or *be saved* [B] **9:22** Or *has made you well* [C] **9:22** Lit *hour* [D] **9:35; 10:1** Or *every kind of* [E] **9:35** Other mss add *among the people* [F] **9:35; 10:1** Or *physical ailment* [G] **10:3** Other mss read *and Lebbaeus, whose surname was Thaddaeus* [H] **10:4** Lit *the Cananaean* [I] **10:8** Gk *lepros*; a term for various skin diseases; see Lv 13–14

---

unclean ranged from forty lashes to death by stoning (*m. Ker.* 1:1).
9:23–26 The presence of mourners and **flute players** indicate that the girl had been dead for a while and that her funeral had begun (*m. Ketub.* 4:4). The word **asleep** implies that death is a state from which believers will be awakened at the resurrection (1Th 4:13–14).
9:27 On the meaning of **Son of David**, see note at 1:1. The healing of the **blind** recalls Is 35:5–6 and confirms Jesus's identity as Messiah.
9:28–31 On the relationship between **faith** and Jesus's healing miracles, see note at v. 2.
9:32–33 The healing of a man who was **unable to speak** recalls Is 35:5–6 and confirms Jesus's identity as Messiah (see notes at vv. 2 and 27).
9:34 Because they were unable to deny Jesus's repeated exorcisms, the Pharisees attempted to dismiss them as evidence of his alliance with Satan. Jesus later showed how unreasonable this accusation was (12:25–32).
9:35 On Jesus's ministry in the region of Galilee, see note at 4:23. These two very

similar verses bracket Mt 4:23–9:34 as a single literary unit.
9:36 The words **like sheep without a shepherd** recall Ezk 34. They imply that Israel's spiritual condition reflected the failures of its spiritual shepherds. By showing **compassion** for the abused and neglected sheep of God's flock, Jesus identified himself as the Shepherd of God's people, Lord and Servant of David (Ezk 34:11–16,20–24). See also Mt 25:32; 26:31.
9:37–38 By sending out the Twelve in Mt 10:5, Jesus identified himself as **Lord of the harvest**. Since OT texts and rabbinic parables presented the Lord as master of the harvest in portrayals of eschatological judgment (Is 18:4–5; 27:12; Hs 6:11; Jl 3:13), this identification strongly implies Jesus's deity (3:11–12; 13:39,41).
10:1 The emphasis on Jesus's selection of **twelve disciples** (cp. 11:1) reminds readers of the twelve tribes of Israel (Mt 19:28) and identifies Jesus's followers (the church) as the new and true Israel, the beneficiaries of God's promises to Abraham (Gn 12:1–3; 15:6; see note at Mt 1:1).

10:2–4 Only here in Matthew are the Twelve called "apostles." This is one of four lists of the apostles in the NT. See Mk 3:16–19; Lk 6:14–16; Ac 1:13.
10:5–6 Jesus prioritized the mission to Israel. Although he had already served Gentiles (8:5–13) and would do so again (15:21–28), Jews were the main focus of the earliest Christian missions (see Acts 13:14,15,43; 14:1; 17:1–17; 18:1–8).
10:7–8 They are to declare and demonstrate that the kingdom of heaven is breaking in.
10:9–10 Jesus prohibited his disciples from carrying the provisions normally taken on lengthy trips. This invited utter dependence on God. The disciples trusted that God would provide for them just as he had for OT Israel (Dt 8:3–4). Some suggest that the prohibition against a **staff** here contradicts permission to carry one in Mk 6:8. However, the texts can be harmonized by several explanations. For example, Matthew may prohibit acquiring a staff while Mark allows those who already own one to take it along.
10:11–14 Those who were **worthy** would welcome the disciples and their message

and stay there until you leave. ¹² Greet a household when you enter it, ¹³ and if the household is worthy, let your peace be on it; but if it is unworthy, let your peace return to you. ¹⁴ If anyone does not welcome you or listen to your words, shake the dust off your feet when you leave that house or town. ¹⁵ Truly I tell you, it will be more tolerable on the day of judgment for the land of Sodom and Gomorrah than for that town.

Persecutions Predicted

¹⁶ "Look, I'm sending you out like sheep among wolves. Therefore be as shrewd as serpents and as innocent as doves. ¹⁷ Beware of them, because they will hand you over to local courts^A and flog you in their synagogues. ¹⁸ You will even be brought before governors and kings because of me, to bear witness to them and to the Gentiles. ¹⁹ But when they hand you over, don't worry about how or what you are to speak. For you will be given what to say at that hour, ²⁰ because it isn't you speaking, but the Spirit of your Father is speaking through you. ²¹ "Brother will betray brother to death, and a father his child. Children will rise up against parents and have them put to death. ²² You will be hated by everyone because of my name. But the one who endures to the end will be saved. ²³ When they persecute you in one town, flee to another. For truly I tell you, you will not have gone through the towns of Israel before the Son of Man comes. ²⁴ A disciple^B is not above his teacher, or a slave above his master. ²⁵ It is enough for a disciple to become like his teacher and a slave like his master. If they called the head of the house 'Beelzebul,' how much more the members of his household!

Fear God

²⁶ "Therefore, don't be afraid of them, since there is nothing covered that won't be uncovered and nothing hidden that won't be made known. ²⁷ What I tell you in the dark, speak in the light. What you hear in a whisper,^C proclaim on the housetops. ²⁸ Don't fear those who kill the body but are not able to kill the soul; rather, fear him who is able to destroy both soul and body in hell. ²⁹ Aren't two sparrows sold for a penny?^D Yet not one of them falls to the ground without your Father's consent.^E ³⁰ But even the hairs of your head have all been counted. ³¹ So don't be afraid; you are worth more than many sparrows.

Acknowledging Christ

³² "Therefore, everyone who will acknowledge me before others, I will also acknowledge him before my Father in heaven. ³³ But whoever denies me before others, I will also deny him before my Father in heaven. ³⁴ Don't assume that I came to bring peace on the earth. I did not come to bring peace, but a sword. ³⁵ For I came to turn

a man against his father,
a daughter against her mother,
a daughter-in-law against
    her mother-in-law;
³⁶ and a man's enemies will be
    the members of his household.^F

³⁷ The one who loves a father or mother more than me is not worthy of me; the one who loves a son or daughter more than me is not worthy of me. ³⁸ And whoever doesn't take up his cross and follow me is not worthy of me. ³⁹ Anyone who finds his life will lose it, and anyone who loses his life because of me will find it.

---

^A10:17 Or *sanhedrins* ^B10:24 Or *student* ^C10:27 Lit *in the ear* ^D10:29 Gk *assarion*, a small copper coin ^E10:29 Lit *ground apart from your Father* ^F10:35–36 Mc 7:6

(see note at 7:6). Those who were unworthy would neither welcome them nor listen. The typical Jewish greeting *Shalom* ("Peace be unto you") pronounced a blessing, but those who rejected the gospel were unworthy of such a greeting. Jews shook the **dust off** their **feet** when they returned to Israel from pagan lands. By doing this when rejected, Jesus's disciples marked those who rejected the gospel as pagans who did not truly belong to Israel. Paul and Barnabas practiced this at Antioch of Pisidia (Ac 13:51).
10:15 God destroyed **Sodom and Gomorrah** because of their wickedness (Gn 19:24–29). Jesus declared in Mt 11:23–24 that even these notorious cities would have repented if they had heard the message the disciples announced and had witnessed the miracles they performed.
10:16 Just as **wolves** stalk and destroy **sheep**, persecutors will attempt to hunt and destroy Jesus's disciples. **Serpents** are **shrewd** because they flee from danger (see note at 3:7–9). Similarly, Jesus's disciples must be prepared to take strategic action when persecution threatens (10:23). However, like **doves**, they should be **innocent** and not use violent means to answer persecution.

10:17–20 The reference to **synagogues** show that Jews sponsored the first anti-Christian persecution. Jewish persecutors appealed to **governors** and **kings** because only Roman officials had the authority to order executions. However, persecution by the highest levels of government gave the disciples opportunity to **bear witness . . . to the Gentiles.**
10:21–22 Followers of Christ must be prepared for even their families to turn against them. **Everyone** means all kinds of people.
10:23 The phrase **you will not have gone through the towns of Israel before the Son of Man comes** may mean that Christian disciples will not complete their mission in the Jewish people before the second coming of Christ. The towns of Israel likely include the far-flung cities of the world where Jews settled down after several dispersions from Israel. However, Jesus's promise is closely linked to the first half of the verse by the conjunction **for** and by the repetition of the word **town**. Thus "will not have gone through the towns" primarily means that the disciples will not have run out of Jewish towns to which to escape before Messiah comes. The mission to the nations in Mt

28:19–20 augments rather than replaces the mission to Israel.
10:24–25 On the meaning of **Beelzebul**, see note at 12:24.
10:26–28 Most may not see the truth of the gospel now, but they will. And "the worst [the persecutors] can do does not match the worst God can do" (D. A. Carson).
10:29–31 If God must consent to the fall of **sparrows**, no disciple can suffer persecution without his consent. The God who has numbered **even the hairs of your head** has also numbered the days of your life. His plan for his disciples cannot be cut short by persecution.
10:32–34 Jesus's words do not imply that his disciples should take up the **sword** in violent reprisal against persecutors. The sword is merely a symbol for conflict and division (Lk 12:51).
10:35–37 This is an even more emphatic statement of 10:21–22.
10:38 Taking up a **cross** does not refer to evangelism. Instead, Jesus refers here to the death march that leads to crucifixion. The point is that disciples must be prepared to die (literally and figuratively) as martyrs for Christ.
10:39 Worldly "life" and true **life** in the world to come are incompatible.

A Cup of Cold Water

[40] "The one who welcomes you welcomes me, and the one who welcomes me welcomes him who sent me. [41] Anyone who welcomes a prophet because he is a prophet[A] will receive a prophet's reward. And anyone who welcomes a righteous person because he's righteous[B] will receive a righteous person's reward. [42] And whoever gives even a cup of cold water to one of these little ones because he is a disciple,[C] truly I tell you, he will never lose his reward."

John the Baptist Doubts

11 When Jesus had finished giving instructions to his twelve disciples, he moved on from there to teach and preach in their towns. [2] Now when John heard in prison what the Christ was doing, he sent a message through his disciples [3] and asked him, "Are you the one who is to come, or should we expect someone else?"

[4] Jesus replied to them, "Go and report to John what you hear and see: [5] The blind receive their sight, the lame walk, those with leprosy[D] are cleansed, the deaf hear, the dead are raised, and the poor are told the good news, [6] and blessed is the one who isn't offended by me."

[7] As these men were leaving, Jesus began to speak to the crowds about John: "What did you go out into the wilderness to see? A reed swaying in the wind? [8] What then did you go out to see? A man dressed in soft clothes? See, those who wear soft clothes are in royal palaces. [9] What then did you go out to see? A prophet? Yes, I tell you, and more than a prophet. [10] This is the one about whom it is written:

> See, I am sending my messenger
> ahead of you;
>
> he will prepare your way before you.[E]

[11] "Truly I tell you, among those born of women no one greater than John the Baptist has appeared,[F] but the least in the kingdom of heaven is greater than he. [12] From the days of John the Baptist until now, the kingdom of heaven has been suffering violence,[G] and the violent have been seizing it by force. [13] For all the prophets and the law prophesied until John. [14] And if you're willing to accept it, he is the Elijah who is to come. [15] Let anyone who has ears[H] listen.

An Unresponsive Generation

[16] "To what should I compare this generation? It's like children sitting in the marketplaces who call out to other children:

> [17] We played the flute for you,
> but you didn't dance;
> we sang a lament,
> but you didn't mourn!'

[18] For John came neither eating nor drinking, and they say, 'He has a demon!' [19] The Son of Man came eating and drinking, and they say, 'Look, a glutton and a drunkard, a friend of tax collectors and sinners!' Yet wisdom is vindicated[I] by her deeds."[K]

[A]**10:41** Lit *prophet in the name of a prophet*   [B]**10:41** Lit *person in the name of a righteous person*   [C]**10:42** Lit *little ones in the name of a disciple*   [D]**11:5** Gk *lepros*; a term for various skin diseases; see Lv 13–14   [E]**11:10** Mal 3:1   [F]**11:11** Lit *arisen*   [G]**11:12** Or *has been forcefully advancing*   [H]**11:15** Other mss add *to hear*   [I]**11:17** Or *beat your chests in grief*   [J]**11:19** Or *declared right*   [K]**11:19** Other mss read *children*

10:40–42 The person who welcomes a persecuted disciple **welcomes** Jesus and the one who sent him. He can expect to receive a heavenly **reward**, just as the person who welcomes a prophet or righteous person receives the reward that a prophet or **righteous person** deserves.

11:1 The words **when Jesus had finished** mark the end of the second of five major blocks of teaching in Matthew's Gospel (cp. 7:28; 13:53; 19:1; 26:1).

11:2–3 John the Baptist previously expressed faith in Jesus as **the Christ** (3:14; Jn 2:29–37; 3:22–30). John's doubts here were likely the result of his prolonged imprisonment and his disappointment that a "baptism of fire" had not yet occurred (Mt 3:11–12). Jesus identified himself as the one anointed by the Spirit in Is 61:1–3. However, Is 61:1 promised that the anointed one would "proclaim liberty to the captives, and freedom to the prisoners." John probably interpreted the prophecy literally and thus mistakenly expected a miraculous release from prison.

11:4–5 Jesus confirmed his identity as the Christ by appealing to his miraculous and gracious works (Is 29:18–19; 35:5–6; 61:1).

11:6 Jesus pronounced blessing on those who were willing to suffer without being **offended** at him. John thus serves as a model for those who persevere in faith despite suffering.

11:7 A **reed swaying in the wind** is a metaphor for someone who lacks conviction and is easily swayed by public opinion (1Kg 14:15; 2Kg 18:21).

11:8–9 Unlike false prophets, John did not allow himself to be bought off by a king who wished to purchase favorable prophecies (see 1Kg 22:13–28).

11:10 John the Baptist's ministry was foretold in Scripture. See note at 3:3.

11:11 John was imprisoned and executed before Jesus's reign was established through his death and resurrection (Ac 2:32–36; Rm 1:4). Thus disciples who enjoy the present reign of Christ enjoy blessings that John yearned for but did not experience (Mt 13:17). The description of the OT prophets in 1Pt 1:10–12 accurately portrays the experience of John. These men did not live to see the messianic sufferings and the glories that followed.

11:12 The arrest, imprisonment, and eventual execution of John and the Jewish leaders' violent opposition to Jesus were attempts to seize and control the unfolding **kingdom of heaven**. The words **until now** hint that the kingdom will someday break free from the grip of those who seek to restrain it (see note at vv. 13–15).

11:13–15 Malachi 4:5 promised that the day of the Lord, a time of divine judgment for the wicked but healing and joy for God's people, would be preceded by the sending of **Elijah**. Jesus explained that John the Baptist fulfilled this role and that his ministry signaled the dawn of the day of the Lord. Malachi 4:3 promised that the day of the Lord would be a time when God's people "will trample the wicked, for they will be ashes under the soles of your feet." This signals that violent suppression of the kingdom will soon end (see note at Mt 11:12).

11:16–19 Jesus portrayed his unbelieving contemporaries as spoiled children who whined when they did not get their way. In an ancient version of the game "Simon says," if a designated child **played** a pretend **flute**, the other children were supposed to **dance**. If he **sang a lament**, they were supposed to **mourn**. However, like unresponsive children, Israel did not pay heed to the ministries of Jesus and John the Baptist. The reference to wisdom's **deeds** parallels the reference to Messiah's deeds (v. 2) and implies that Jesus's claims were vindicated by the acts described in vv. 4–6. Between the time of the OT and the NT, Jewish interpreters elaborated on Pr 8:32–36 and taught that **wisdom** was an eternal being who served as God's agent in the creation of the world. By identifying himself with personified Wisdom, Jesus hinted that he is the eternal one through whom the Father created everything (Jn 1:3).

²⁰ Then he proceeded to denounce the towns where most of his miracles were done, because they did not repent: ²¹ "Woe to you, Chorazin! Woe to you, Bethsaida! For if the miracles that were done in you had been done in Tyre and Sidon, they would have repented in sackcloth and ashes long ago. ²² But I tell you, it will be more tolerable for Tyre and Sidon on the day of judgment than for you. ²³ And you, Capernaum, will you be exalted to heaven? No, you will go down to Hades. For if the miracles that were done in you had been done in Sodom, it would have remained until today. ²⁴ But I tell you, it will be more tolerable for the land of Sodom on the day of judgment than for you."

The Son Gives Knowledge and Rest

²⁵ At that time Jesus said, "I praise you, Father, Lord of heaven and earth, because you have hidden these things from the wise and intelligent and revealed them to infants. ²⁶ Yes, Father, because this was your good pleasure.ᴬ ²⁷ All things have been entrusted to me by my Father. No one knows the Son except the Father, and no one knows the Father except the Son and anyone to whom the Son desiresᴮ to reveal him.

²⁸ "Come to me, all of you who are weary and burdened, and I will give you rest. ²⁹ Take up my yoke and learn from me, because I am lowly and humble in heart, and you will find rest for your souls. ³⁰ For my yoke is easy and my burden is light."

Lord of the Sabbath

12 At that time Jesus passed through the grainfields on the Sabbath. His disciples were hungry and began to pick and eat some heads of grain. ² When the Pharisees saw this, they said to him, "See, your disciples are doing what is not lawful to do on the Sabbath."

³ He said to them, "Haven't you read what David did when he and those who were with him were hungry: ⁴ how he entered the house of God, and they ateᶜ the bread of the Presence — which is not lawful for him or for those with him to eat, but only for the priests? ⁵ Or haven't you read in the law that on Sabbath days the priests in the temple violate the Sabbath and are innocent? ⁶ I tell you that something greater than the temple is here. ⁷ If you had known what this means, **I desire mercy and not sacrifice**,ᴰ you would not have condemned the innocent. ⁸ For the Son of Man is Lord of the Sabbath."

The Man with the Shriveled Hand

⁹ Moving on from there, he entered their synagogue. ¹⁰ There he saw a man who had a shriveled hand, and in order to accuse him they asked him, "Is it lawful to heal on the Sabbath?"

¹¹ He replied to them, "Who among you, if he had a sheep that fell into a pit on the Sabbath, wouldn't take hold of it and lift it out? ¹² A person is worth far more than a sheep; so it is lawful to do what is good on the Sabbath."

¹³ Then he told the man, "Stretch out your hand." So he stretched it out, and it was restored, as good as the other. ¹⁴ But the Pharisees went out and plotted against him, how they might kill him.

The Servant of the Lord

¹⁵ Jesus was aware of this and withdrew. Large crowdsᴱ followed him, and he healed them all.

ᴬ**11:26** Lit *was well-pleasing in your sight*   ᴮ**11:27** Or *wills*, or *chooses*   ᶜ**12:4** Other mss read *he ate*   ᴰ**12:7** Hs 6:6
ᴱ**12:15** Other mss read *Many*

11:20–24 These verses remind us that the Gospels are not exhaustive accounts of Jesus's life. Jesus performed most of his **miracles** in **Chorazin** . . . **Bethsaida**, and **Capernaum**, and yet the Gospels do not describe his miracles at Chorazin and mention only two that were performed at Bethsaida (Mk 6:45; 8:22; Lk 9:10). God's judgment against sin is **more tolerable** for people to whom little revelation is given. On the other hand, those who have received much revelation bear greater responsibility and thus incur greater judgment for their unbelief. On **Tyre and Sidon**, see note on 15:21. On **Sodom**, see Gn 19:1–29.

11:25–26 God hides the truth from those who will not believe but are enamored with their own learning.

11:27 Jesus's statement resembles those attributed to him in John's Gospel (Jn 7:29; 10:14–15; 17:25). This shows how substantially John and the Synoptic Gospels agree on the portrait of Jesus.

11:28–30 Jesus's words recall a statement made by personified Wisdom in a Jewish document dating to several hundred years before Christ (Sir 6:18–31; 51:23–27). When combined with Mt 11:19, this suggests that

Jesus portrayed himself as personified Wisdom, the one who exists eternally and acted on the Lord's behalf to create the world (1Co 1:24; see note at Mt 11:16–19). Jesus's teaching provided an easy **yoke** in contrast to the heavy, suppressive yoke of rabbinic teaching (23:4; Ac 15:10).

12:1–2 Work was prohibited on the **Sabbath**. First-century rabbis divided work into thirty-nine categories, each having many subcategories. Three prohibited categories were picking, threshing, and winnowing. The disciples picked **grain** and rubbed it between their hands to remove the husks and thus broke the highly restrictive rabbinic law on three different counts. Handpicking grain from a neighbor's field was not considered stealing (Dt 23:25).

12:3–7 Jesus taught that **Sabbath** law was overridden by priorities such as (1) genuine human need (1Sm 21:1–6); (2) worship (Nm 28:9–10); and (3) acts of kindness (Hs 6:6).

12:8 Son of Man was Jesus's favorite self-designation. **Lord of the Sabbath** refers to God since he instituted the Sabbath (Gn 2:1–3), commanded the Sabbath (Ex 20:10), and was the Lord for whom the Sabbath was observed (Lv 23:3). By calling himself "Lord of

the Sabbath," Jesus clearly meant to identify himself as God Almighty.

12:9–10 Many rabbis permitted healing on the Sabbath only when a life was at risk (*m. Yoma* 8:6). Otherwise, it was illegal to tie a bandage, set a broken bone, or administer medicine. Some rabbis even banned prayer for the sick on the Sabbath.

12:11–12 With the exception of the Essenes (CD 11:13–14), most Jews believed it was permissible to rescue a beast of burden (e.g., a donkey) on the Sabbath. It was inconsistent to refuse the same privilege to humans since God values people more than animals. The Sabbath was to be kept holy (Ex 20:8–11), but a ban on good deeds is unholy and dishonors God.

12:13 The man's paralyzed **hand** had wasted away from disuse. Jesus **restored** the hand's function and also renewed the wasted muscle. Thus this miracle was an act of creation. Since the Creator God had instituted the Sabbath (Gn 2:1–3), the miracle confirmed Jesus's self-confessed identity as Lord of the Sabbath.

12:14 The plotting continued. See Mt 26:4; 27:1.

12:15–21 Matthew recognized Jesus as the fulfillment of Is 42:1–4. This implies: (1)

16 He warned them not to make him known, **17** so that what was spoken through the prophet Isaiah might be fulfilled:

18   Here is my servant
      whom I have chosen,
   my beloved in whom I delight;
   I will put my Spirit on him,
   and he will proclaim justice
      to the nations.
19   He will not argue or shout,
   and no one will hear his voice
      in the streets.
20   He will not break a bruised reed,
   and he will not put out
      a smoldering wick,
   until he has led justice to victory.^A
21   The nations will put their hope
      in his name.^B

A House Divided

22 Then a demon-possessed man who was blind and unable to speak was brought to him. He healed him, so that the man^c could both speak and see. **23** All the crowds were astounded and said, "Could this be the Son of David?" **24** When the Pharisees heard this, they said, "This man drives out demons only by Beelzebul, the ruler of the demons."

25 Knowing their thoughts, he told them, "Every kingdom divided against itself is headed for destruction, and no city or house divided against itself will stand. **26** If Satan drives out Satan, he is divided against himself. How then will his kingdom stand? **27** And if I drive out demons by Beelzebul, by whom do your sons drive them out? For this reason they will be your judges. **28** If I drive out demons by the Spirit of God, then the kingdom of God has come upon you. **29** How can someone enter a strong man's house and steal his possessions unless he first ties up the strong man? Then he can plunder his house. **30** Anyone who is not with me is against me, and anyone who does not gather with me scatters. **31** Therefore, I tell you, people will be forgiven every sin and blasphemy, but the blasphemy against^D the Spirit will not be forgiven.^E **32** Whoever speaks a word against the Son of Man, it will be forgiven him; but whoever speaks against the Holy Spirit, it will not be forgiven him, either in this age or in the one to come.

A Tree and Its Fruit

33 "Either make the tree good and its fruit will be good, or make the tree bad^F and its fruit will be bad; for a tree is known by its fruit. **34** Brood of vipers! How can you speak good things when you are evil? For the mouth speaks from the overflow of the heart. **35** A good person produces good things from his storeroom of good, and an evil person produces evil things from his storeroom of evil. **36** I tell you that on the day of judgment people will have to account for every careless^G word they speak."^H **37** For by your words you will be acquitted, and by your words you will be condemned."

The Sign of Jonah

38 Then some of the scribes and Pharisees said to him, "Teacher, we want to see a sign from you."

39 He answered them, "An evil and adulterous generation demands a sign, but no sign will be given to it except the sign of the prophet Jonah. **40** For as Jonah was in the belly of the huge fish^I three days and three nights, so the Son of Man will be in the heart of the earth three days

---

^A **12:20** Or *until he has successfully put forth justice* ^B **12:18–21** Is 42:1–4 ^c **12:22** Lit *mute* ^D **12:31** Or *of* ^E **12:31** Other mss add *people* ^F **12:33** Or *decayed*; lit *rotten* ^G **12:36** Lit *worthless* ^H **12:36** Lit *will speak* ^I **12:40** Or *sea creature*; Jnh 1:17

---

he is God's Son/**servant**; (2) he is **chosen** and loved by God; (3) he pleases God with his obedience; (4) he bears God's **Spirit** (5) he will rule over a universal kingdom that includes all **nations**; (6) he is humble and nonviolent; and (7) he will include Gentiles in his redemptive plan. Matthew's identification of Jesus as "servant" is closely connected to his interpretation of Is 53 (see note at 8:17).

12:22–23 On **Son of David**, see note at 1:1.
12:24 **Beelzebul** was probably an ancient name for Baal, a Canaanite storm/fertility god. Worship of Baal competed with worship of the Lord in the OT. Although gods were nonexistent, demonic spirits were at work in the pagan religions (Ps 106:28,36–39; 1Co 10:19–20). Satan himself was deemed to be the spirit at work in Baal worship. Consequently, Beelzebul became an alternate name for Satan.
12:25–27 Jesus argued that Satan is too smart to undermine his own kingdom. Also, the objection of the Pharisees (v. 24) indicted their own disciples, for they too claimed to cast out demons.

12:28–29 Jesus's power to cast out **demons** proved that the **kingdom of God** was overthrowing Satan's kingdom. Jesus was tying up the **strong man** (Satan) so he could **plunder his house**, or claim Satan's captives as citizens of his own kingdom.
12:30 See Lk 11:23. The demands of Jesus and the world are so opposite that one cannot be neutral.
12:31–32 Jesus claimed to cast out demons "by the Spirit of God" (v. 28). By refuting this and attributing his exorcisms to Satan's power instead, Jesus's opponents were guilty of **blasphemy against the Spirit** in whose power Jesus worked the miracles. Their attempt to dismiss Jesus's supernatural power would not **be forgiven** because it expressed a resolute, permanent rejection of Jesus.
12:33–37 The evil words spoken by the Pharisees divulged the true nature of their hearts.
12:38 The Jewish leaders had already witnessed several of Jesus's miracles (vv. 9–14; 9:1–8).
12:39–40 The word **adulterous** refers to the scribes' and Pharisees' spiritual adultery exhibited by their rejection of Jesus.

#56 **99 Essential Christian Truths**

UNITY OF THE CHURCH

Christ's desire for the church is that we are united as one in him by the gospel (Php 2:1–2), reflecting the oneness of our trinitarian God (Jn 17:20–23). As such, we are to allow for no divisions to separate us (1Co 1:10), such as ethnicity, socio-economics, nationality, language, politics, or secondary doctrinal beliefs. Our objective is not simply to work around or look past these differences within the body of Christ but to celebrate the diversity of God's people made one in Christ (1Cor 12:12–13; Eph 4:4–6,11–13), demonstrating humility (Rm 12:3,16; Php 2:5–11) and freely loving and forgiving one another (Col 3:13–14) to reflect the power of Christ who reconciles all things to himself (Ps 133:1; Eph 1:10; 2:14).

and three nights. **41** The men of Nineveh will stand up at the judgment with this generation and condemn it, because they repented at Jonah's preaching; and look — something greater than Jonah is here. **42** The queen of the south will rise up at the judgment with this generation and condemn it, because she came from the ends of the earth to hear the wisdom of Solomon; and look — something greater than Solomon is here.

An Unclean Spirit's Return

43 "When an unclean spirit comes out of a person, it roams through waterless places looking for rest but doesn't find any. **44** Then it says, 'I'll go back to my house that I came from.' Returning, it finds the house vacant, swept, and put in order. **45** Then it goes and brings with it seven other spirits more evil than itself, and they enter and settle down there. As a result, that person's last condition is worse than the first. That's how it will also be with this evil generation."

True Relationships

46 While he was still speaking with the crowds, his mother and brothers were standing outside wanting to speak to him. **47** Someone told him, "Look, your mother and your brothers are standing outside, wanting to speak to you."**A** **48** He replied to the one who was speaking to him, "Who is my mother and who are my brothers?" **49** Stretching out his hand toward his disciples, he said, "Here are my mother and my brothers! **50** For whoever does the will of my Father in heaven is my brother and sister and mother."

The Parable of the Sower

13 On that day Jesus went out of the house and was sitting by the sea. **2** Such large crowds gathered around him that he got into a boat and sat down, while the whole crowd stood on the shore.

3 Then he told them many things in parables, saying, "Consider the sower who went out to sow. **4** As he sowed, some seed fell along the path, and the birds came and devoured them. **5** Other seed fell on rocky ground where it didn't have much soil, and it grew up quickly since the soil wasn't deep. **6** But when the sun came up, it was scorched, and since it had no root, it withered away. **7** Other seed fell among thorns, and the thorns came up and choked it. **8** Still other seed fell on good ground and produced fruit: some a hundred, some sixty, and some thirty times what was sown. **9** Let anyone who has ears**B** listen."

Why Jesus Used Parables

10 Then the disciples came up and asked him, "Why are you speaking to them in parables?"

11 He answered, "Because the secrets of the kingdom of heaven have been given for you to know, but it has not been given to them. **12** For whoever has, more will be given to him, and he will have more than enough; but whoever does not have, even what he has will be taken away from him. **13** That is why I speak to them in parables, because looking they do not see, and hearing they do not listen or understand. **14** Isaiah's prophecy is fulfilled in them, which says:

You will listen and listen,
　but never understand;
you will look and look,
　but never perceive.
15　For this people's heart
　　has grown callous;
　their ears are hard of hearing,
　and they have shut their eyes;
　otherwise they might see
　　with their eyes,
　and hear with their ears, and
　understand with their hearts,

A12:47 Other mss omit this v.　**B**13:9 Other mss add *to hear*

Mention of the **sign of . . . Jonah** is Jesus's first reference to his death in Matthew. Jonah was as good as dead for **three days and three nights** (Jnh 1:17). His prayer compared his experience to being in the grave. Thus Jonah's experience was analogous to Jesus's experience of being interred for three days. Since Jesus's resurrection occurred on Sunday, some have argued that the reference to three days and three nights requires a Thursday or Wednesday crucifixion. However, 1Sm 30:12–13 suggests that "three days and three nights" could be idiomatic for a span of time that covered all of one day and parts of two others. Thus Jesus's interment late on Friday and his resurrection early Sunday counts as three days. **12:41–42** Ninevites and the queen of Sheba (**queen of the south**) were pagan Gentiles who repented and sought the truth. Jesus is greater than **Jonah** and **Solomon**, whom these pagans heard and obeyed.

12:43–45 The words **that's how it will also be with this evil generation** show that this discussion functioned like a parable. Jesus cast evil spirits out of afflicted people, but the Jewish leaders discouraged them from accepting God's help and rule through the person of Jesus. This left them empty and vulnerable to even greater evil. **12:46–50** On the response of Jesus's family members to him, see notes on Mk 3:20–21, 31–35 and Jn 7:3–5. Jesus valued his spiritual relationship with his disciples above his physical relationship with his family. Later, once faith had dawned in their hearts, his family members understood and adopted this value system (Jms 1:1; Jd 1). His brothers are named in 13:55. **13:1** The word **parables** can refer to a wide variety of figurative speech. Although many interpreters insist that Jesus's parables were simple metaphors that teach only one main truth, Jesus's interpretation of his own parables may suggest that many of them

were allegories that carried multiple points of symbolism, teaching several related truths (Jesus explained this parable in vv. 18–23). **13:10–13** Jesus's parables had two distinct purposes: (1) to reveal truth to those who were willing to hear and believe, and (2) to conceal truth from those who willingly rejected truth because of their calloused hearts (v. 15). The hiddenness component of Jesus's teaching may seem harsh, but since greater exposure to truth increases one's accountability to God in judgment (11:20–24), the concealment may represent God's graciousness toward those whom he knew would be unresponsive. **13:14–16** Matthew frequently explains how Jesus's ministry fulfilled prophecy. Here Jesus himself described the fulfillment of Is 6:9–10. The application of this text to Jesus's contemporaries probably implies that Israel's hardened rejection of Jesus was not permanent, since Is 6:11–13 showed that the hearts of the people would someday be softened

and turn back —
and I would heal them.^A
¹⁶ "Blessed are your eyes because they do see, and your ears because they do hear. ¹⁷ For truly I tell you, many prophets and righteous people longed to see the things you see but didn't see them, to hear the things you hear but didn't hear them.

The Parable of the Sower Explained

¹⁸ "So listen to the parable of the sower: ¹⁹ When anyone hears the word about the kingdom and doesn't understand it, the evil one comes and snatches away what was sown in his heart. This is the one sown along the path. ²⁰ And the one sown on rocky ground — this is one who hears the word and immediately receives it with joy. ²¹ But he has no root and is short-lived. When distress or persecution comes because of the word, immediately he falls away. ²² Now the one sown among the thorns — this is one who hears the word, but the worries of this age and the deceitfulness^B of wealth choke the word, and it becomes unfruitful. ²³ But the one sown on the good ground — this is one who hears and understands the word, who does produce fruit and yields: some a hundred, some sixty, some thirty times what was sown."

The Parable of the Wheat and the Weeds

²⁴ He presented another parable to them: "The kingdom of heaven may be compared to a man who sowed good seed in his field. ²⁵ But while people were sleeping, his enemy came, sowed weeds among the wheat, and left. ²⁶ When the plants sprouted and produced grain, then the weeds also appeared. ²⁷ The landowner's servants came to him and said, 'Master, didn't you sow good seed in your field? Then where did the weeds come from?'

²⁸ "'An enemy did this,' he told them.

" 'So, do you want us to go and pull them up?' the servants asked him.

²⁹ " 'No,' he said. 'When you pull up the weeds, you might also uproot the wheat with them. ³⁰ Let both grow together until the harvest. At harvest time I'll tell the reapers: Gather the weeds first and tie them in bundles to burn them, but collect the wheat in my barn.' "

The Parables of the Mustard Seed and of the Leaven

³¹ He presented another parable to them: "The kingdom of heaven is like a mustard seed that a man took and sowed in his field. ³² It's the smallest of all the seeds, but when grown, it's taller than the garden plants and becomes a tree, so that the birds of the sky come and nest in its branches."

³³ He told them another parable: "The kingdom of heaven is like leaven^C that a woman took and mixed into fifty pounds^D of flour until all of it was leavened."

Using Parables Fulfills Prophecy

³⁴ Jesus told the crowds all these things in parables, and he did not tell them anything without a parable, ³⁵ so that what was spoken through the prophet might be fulfilled:

I will open my mouth in parables;
I will declare things kept secret
from the foundation of the world.^E,F

Jesus Interprets the Parable of the Wheat and the Weeds

³⁶ Then he left the crowds and went into the house. His disciples approached him and said, "Explain to us the parable of the weeds in the field."

³⁷ He replied, "The one who sows the good seed is the Son of Man; ³⁸ the field is the world; and the good seed — these are the children of the kingdom. The weeds are the children of the

---

^A 13:14–15 Is 6:9–10   ^B 13:22 Or *pleasure*   ^C 13:33 Or *yeast*   ^D 13:33 Lit *three sata*; about forty liters   ^E 13:35 Some mss omit *of the world*   ^F 13:35 Ps 78:2

---

and that God would preserve a righteous remnant in Israel. Thus the picture is of stony resistance, not permanent resistance.
13:17 The OT **prophets** and saints had eagerly awaited Messiah's coming (see 1Pt 1:10–12).
13:18–23 The four types of soil represent types of people and their differing responses to Jesus. The first three types represent those who reject Jesus outright (7:26–27) and those who falsely claim to be his disciples (7:15–23; 10:35–39). These are all **unfruitful**. Only the last type **does produce fruit**. Since producing the fruit of good deeds is an essential expression of discipleship (3:8,10; 7:16–20; 12:33; 21:18–19,33–41), only the last type is a true disciple. A harvest of ten to twenty times **what was sown** was considered a bumper crop, given the primitive agricultural technology of the period. The amazing harvest described by Jesus's parable (**a hundred . . . sixty . . . thirty**) shows that true disciples produce fruit in a miraculous quantity.

13:24–30 The **weeds** were probably darnel. This plant is related to wheat and resembles it during the early stages of growth, but darnel is actually a poisonous weed. Roman law prohibited sowing darnel in another's field, which suggests Jesus's story was realistic. The root systems of wheat and darnel become intertwined as the crop matures and makes it difficult to uproot the weeds without damaging the **wheat**. For the interpretation of this parable, see note at vv. 36–43.
13:31–32 Like the **mustard seed**, the **kingdom of heaven** began as something small and seemingly insignificant but later grew to be large. The mustard seed was **the smallest of all the seeds** commonly planted in Palestine at that time.
13:33 The image of a pinch of **leaven** permeating **fifty pounds** of dough parallels the great impact the kingdom would have despite its small beginnings.

13:34–35 Like Asaph in Ps 78, Jesus taught in **parables** and revealed to his disciples truths that had not previously been understood.
13:36–43 This parable is frequently interpreted as if the wheat represents true disciples and the weeds false disciples. But Jesus's interpretation shows that the subject is not the mixture of true and false disciples in the church but rather the presence of both good and evil people in the broader world. Many Jews expected Messiah to immediately destroy evildoers and vindicate the righteous. Thus they were puzzled as to why Jesus didn't do this if he truly were the **Son of Man** (see Dn 7:13–14). In this parable Jesus demonstrated (1) that he is not the source of evil (13:27–28,36–39); (2) the entire world belongs to the Son of Man, and the devil had no right to bring evil into it; and (3) the Son of Man would assert his kingship over the world by punishing the wicked and blessing the righteous at an appropriate future time.

evil one, [39] and the enemy who sowed them is the devil. The harvest is the end of the age, and the harvesters are angels. [40] Therefore, just as the weeds are gathered and burned in the fire, so it will be at the end of the age. [41] The Son of Man will send out his angels, and they will gather from his kingdom all who cause sin[A] and those guilty of lawlessness. [B] [42] They will throw them into the blazing furnace where there will be weeping and gnashing of teeth. [43] Then the righteous will shine like the sun in their Father's kingdom. Let anyone who has ears[C] listen.

The Parables of the Hidden Treasure and of the Priceless Pearl

[44] "The kingdom of heaven is like treasure, buried in a field, that a man found and reburied. Then in his joy he goes and sells everything he has and buys that field.

[45] "Again, the kingdom of heaven is like a merchant in search of fine pearls. [46] When he found one priceless[D] pearl, he went and sold everything he had and bought it.

The Parable of the Net

[47] "Again, the kingdom of heaven is like a large net thrown into the sea. It collected every kind of fish, [48] and when it was full, they dragged it ashore, sat down, and gathered the good fish into containers, but threw out the worthless ones. [49] So it will be at the end of the age. The angels will go out, separate the evil people from the righteous, [50] and throw them into the blazing furnace, where there will be weeping and gnashing of teeth.

The Storehouse of Truth

[51] "Have you understood all these things?"[E]

They answered him, "Yes."

[52] "Therefore," he said to them, "every teacher of the law[F] who has become a disciple in the kingdom of heaven is like the owner of a house who brings out of his storeroom treasures new and old."

Rejection at Nazareth

[53] When Jesus had finished these parables, he left there. [54] He went to his hometown and began to teach them in their synagogue, so that they were astonished and said, "Where did this man get this wisdom and these miraculous powers? [55] Isn't this the carpenter's son? Isn't his mother called Mary, and his brothers James, Joseph,[G] Simon, and Judas? [56] And his sisters, aren't they all with us? So where does he get all these things?" [57] And they were offended by him.

Jesus said to them, "A prophet is not without honor except in his hometown and in his household." [58] And he did not do many miracles there because of their unbelief.

John the Baptist Beheaded

14 At that time Herod the tetrarch heard the report about Jesus. [2] "This is John the Baptist," he told his servants. "He has been raised from the dead, and that's why miraculous powers are at work in him."

[3] For Herod had arrested John, chained[H] him, and put him in prison on account of Herodias, his brother Philip's wife, [4] since John had been telling him, "It's not lawful for you to have her." [5] Though Herod wanted to kill John, he feared the crowd since they regarded John as a prophet.

[6] When Herod's birthday celebration came, Herodias's daughter danced before them[I] and pleased Herod. [7] So he promised with an oath to give her whatever she asked. [8] Prompted by her mother, she answered, "Give me John the Baptist's head here on a platter." [9] Although the king regretted it, he commanded that it be granted because of his oaths and his guests. [10] So he sent orders and had John beheaded in the prison. [11] His head was brought on

---

A 13:41 Or *stumbling*   B 13:41 Or *those who do lawlessness*   C 13:43 Other mss add *to hear*   D 13:46 Or *very precious*
E 13:51 Other mss add *Jesus asked them*   F 13:52 Or *every scribe*   G 13:55 Other mss read *Joses*; Mk 6:3   H 14:3 Or *bound*
I 14:6 Lit *danced in the middle*

13:44–46 These parables teach that the **kingdom of heaven** is so valuable that the wise are willing to sacrifice anything in order to gain it (19:21–26).

13:47–50 The parable of the net closely parallels the parable of the wheat and weeds (vv. 24–30,38–43). It describes the final judgment in which the righteous (Jesus's disciples) are separated from those who reject him and his rule and are sentenced to everlasting punishment.

13:51–52 Because of their exposure to Jesus's teaching, which disclosed what had previously been hidden (vv. 34–35), Jesus's disciples were better qualified than the scribes and Pharisees to serve as teachers of the law. In their storeroom of instruction, they had **old** treasures (the OT) and **new** treasures (the teachings of Jesus).

13:53 The words **when Jesus had finished** mark the end of the third of five major blocks of teaching in Matthew's Gospel (cp. 7:28; 11:1; 19:1; 26:1).

13:55 This verse and its parallels (Mk 6:3; Lk 4:22) are the only references to Joseph's and Jesus's trade in the NT. Jewish tradition dictated that fathers teach their trade to their sons. The word *carpenter* (Gk *tektōn*) was occasionally used to describe stone masons, but normally referred to woodworkers. One early tradition says that Jesus primarily made yokes and plows. Both **James** and **Judas** later became followers of Jesus and authored NT books.

13:56–57 Jesus identified himself as a prophet, but also more than a prophet (12:41). Prophets were typically rejected (23:37).

14:1 Herod Antipas was the son of Herod the Great and ruled as **tetrarch** of Galilee and Perea from about 4 BC until he was banished for seeking the kingship in AD 39 (Josephus, *Ant.* 18.252–54). In general, a tetrarch was one step below an ethnarch, which was in turn a step below king.

14:2–5 The explanatory conjunction **for** (Gk *gar*) shows that Herod's belief that **John** had been resurrected and possessed supernatural powers was a product of paranoia fed by his guilty conscience. John was arrested because he criticized Herod's illicit marriage to his brother's wife.

14:6–12 Herodias's daughter Salome danced erotically for her uncle Herod. This seems to have enticed a drunken Herod to make an oath he would later regret. Herodias preferred beheading as the means of execution so she could display John's head as a trophy. The Gospel accounts of this event

a platter and given to the girl, who carried it to her mother. ¹² Then his disciples came, removed the corpse,ᴬ buried it, and went and reported to Jesus.

Feeding of the Five Thousand

¹³ When Jesus heard about it, he withdrew from there by boat to a remote place to be alone. When the crowds heard this, they followed him on foot from the towns. ¹⁴ When he went ashore,ᴮ he saw a large crowd, had compassion on them, and healed their sick.

¹⁵ When evening came, the disciples approached him and said, "This place is deserted, and it is already late.ᶜ Send the crowds away so that they can go into the villages and buy food for themselves."

¹⁶ "They don't need to go away," Jesus told them. "You give them something to eat."

¹⁷ "But we only have five loaves and two fish here," they said to him.

¹⁸ "Bring them here to me," he said. ¹⁹ Then he commanded the crowds to sit down on the grass. He took the five loaves and the two fish, and looking up to heaven, he blessed them. He broke the loaves and gave them to the disciples, and the disciples gave them to the crowds. ²⁰ Everyone ate and was satisfied. They picked up twelve baskets full of leftover pieces. ²¹ Now those who ate were about five thousand men, besides women and children.

Walking on the Water

²² Immediately heᴰ made the disciples get into the boat and go ahead of him to the other side, while he dismissed the crowds. ²³ After dismissing the crowds, he went up on the mountain by himself to pray. Well into the night, he was there alone. ²⁴ Meanwhile, the boat was already some distanceᴱ from land,ᶠ battered by the waves, because the wind was against them. ²⁵ Jesus came toward them walking on the sea very early in the morning.ᴳ ²⁶ When the disciples saw him walking on the sea, they were terrified. "It's a ghost!" they said, and they cried out in fear.

²⁷ Immediately Jesus spoke to them. "Have courage! It is I. Don't be afraid."

²⁸ "Lord, if it's you," Peter answered him, "command me to come to you on the water."

²⁹ He said, "Come."

And climbing out of the boat, Peter started walking on the water and came toward Jesus. ³⁰ But when he saw the strength of the wind,ᴴ he was afraid, and beginning to sink he cried out, "Lord, save me!"

³¹ Immediately Jesus reached out his hand, caught hold of him, and said to him, "You of little faith, why did you doubt?"

³² When they got into the boat, the wind ceased. ³³ Then those in the boat worshiped him and said, "Truly you are the Son of God."

Miraculous Healings

³⁴ When they had crossed over, they came to shore at Gennesaret. ³⁵ When the men of that place recognized him, they alerted the whole vicinity and brought to him all who were sick. ³⁶ They begged him that they might only touch the end of his robe, and as many as touched it were healed.

ᴬ14:12 Other mss read body　ᴮ14:14 Lit Coming out (of the boat)　ᶜ14:15 Lit and the time (for the evening meal) has already passed　ᴰ14:22 Other mss read Jesus　ᴱ14:24 Lit already many stadia; one stadion = 600 feet　ᶠ14:24 Other mss read already in the middle of the sea　ᴳ14:25 Lit fourth watch of the night = 3 to 6 a.m.　ᴴ14:30 Other mss read saw the wind

were probably dependent on an informant in Herod's court, possibly Joanna or Manaen (Lk 8:3; 24:10; Ac 13:1).
14:13–14 On Jesus's **compassion** for the **crowd**, see note at 9:36.
14:15–17 Loaves of bread and small **fish** were staple foods in Galilee. The loaves were the size of dinner rolls. John's description of the fish (Gk opsarion) indicates that they were either dried or pickled (Jn 6:9). He also identified the loaves as made of barley, food of the poor. He implied that the loaves and fish were small since they were sufficient for only one boy's lunch.
14:18–21 This is the only miracle of Jesus recorded by all four Gospels. A true miracle is clearly expressed by the words **everyone ate and was satisfied**. Normally, a few small loaves and fish divided among so many people would provide each person with only a very tiny crumb. However, everyone ate to satisfaction and the disciples collected in leftovers more food than was originally available. Collecting these **baskets full of leftover pieces** served as a powerful reminder of Jesus's ability to provide abundance for his disciples (6:11,25–33). John's Gospel shows that many bystanders compared Jesus's miracles to God's provision of manna in the wilderness (Jn 6:22–33). The

miracle also closely resembles a miracle of Elisha (2Kg 4:42–44). Although the miracle is referred to as the "Feeding of the Five Thousand," the **five thousand men, besides women and children** might equal a total of fifteen thousand people. Thus Jesus's miracle was far greater than that performed by Elisha.
14:22–24 The boat was already some distance from land. The Greek is literally "many stadia"—a stadia equaling about six hundred feet (see Jn 6:19). The Sea of Galilee is about eight miles wide at its widest point.
14:25 Very early in the morning is literally "during the fourth watch of the night." The Romans divided the period from 6:00 p.m. to 6:00 a.m. into four watches of three hours each. Thus the fourth watch lasted from 3:00 a.m. to 6:00 a.m.
14:26 The word **ghost** (Gk phantasma) was used in Greek literature to describe dream visions or spirit apparitions. In the NT a closely related term referred to a dream or vision in which one saw something that was not real (Is 28:7; Jb 20:8 [LXX]). Matthew's usage may imply that the disciples thought their eyes were deceiving them. The language of the text does not imply that the Bible supports the belief that spirits of the dead roam the earth.

14:27 The words **it is I** are literally "I am." The statement is Jesus's purposeful echo of OT texts like Ex 3:14 and identifies him as Yahweh.
14:28–33 Truly you are the Son of God. Their awe of Jesus reached a new level as he exercised mastery over the created order—something God alone could do (Jb 9:8; Ps 77:19). The disciples' confession of Jesus as Son of God is not surprising in light of close connections between this miracle and important OT parallels. The title "Son of God" often serves as a messianic title in the NT (see note at 3:17), but here it also implies Jesus's deity. The disciples likely interpreted the miracle in light of Jb 9:8 (LXX) which states that the Lord walked on the sea as if it were dry land. Their worship of Jesus also confirmed their growing recognition of his divine nature (see note at Mt 4:10–11).
14:34 Gennesaret was located on the northwestern shore of the Sea of Galilee about five miles south of Capernaum.
14:35–36 The people of Gennesaret appeared to be aware of the healing of the woman in Mt 9:20. This miracle occurred in nearby Capernaum and set a precedent for healing by touching **the end of his robe**.

The Tradition of the Elders

15 Then Jesus was approached by Pharisees and scribes from Jerusalem, who asked, [2] "Why do your disciples break the tradition of the elders? For they don't wash their hands when they eat."[A]

[3] He answered them, "Why do you break God's commandment because of your tradition? [4] For God said:[B] Honor your father and your mother;[C] and, Whoever speaks evil of father or mother must be put to death.[D] [5] But you say, 'Whoever tells his father or mother, "Whatever benefit you might have received from me is a gift committed to the temple," [6] he does not have to honor his father.'[E] In this way, you have nullified the word of God[F] because of your tradition. [7] Hypocrites! Isaiah prophesied correctly about you when he said:

[8]   This people[G] honors me with their lips,
       but their heart is far from me.
[9]   They worship me in vain,
       teaching as doctrines
       human commands."[H]

Defilement Is from Within

[10] Summoning the crowd, he told them, "Listen and understand: [11] It's not what goes into the mouth that defiles a person, but what comes out of the mouth — this defiles a person."

[12] Then the disciples came up and told him, "Do you know that the Pharisees took offense when they heard what you said?"

[13] He replied, "Every plant that my heavenly Father didn't plant will be uprooted. [14] Leave them alone! They are blind guides.[I] And if the blind guide the blind, both will fall into a pit."

[15] Then Peter said, "Explain this parable to us."

[16] "Do you still lack understanding?" he[J] asked. [17] "Don't you realize[K] that whatever goes into the mouth passes into the stomach and is eliminated?[L] [18] But what comes out of the mouth comes from the heart, and this defiles a person. [19] For from the heart come evil thoughts, murders, adulteries, sexual immoralities, thefts, false testimonies, slander. [20] These are the things that defile a person; but eating with unwashed hands does not defile a person."

A Gentile Mother's Faith

[21] When Jesus left there, he withdrew to the area of Tyre and Sidon. [22] Just then a Canaanite woman from that region came and kept crying out,[M] "Have mercy on me, Lord, Son of David! My daughter is severely tormented by a demon."

[23] Jesus did not say a word to her. His disciples approached him and urged him, "Send her away because she's crying out after us."

[24] He replied, "I was sent only to the lost sheep of the house of Israel."

[A]15:2 Lit eat bread = eat a meal   [B]15:4 Other mss read commanded, saying   [C]15:4 Ex 20:12; Dt 5:16   [D]15:4 Ex 21:17; Lv 20:9   [E]15:6 Other mss read then he does not have to honor his father or mother   [F]15:6 Other mss read commandment   [G]15:8 Other mss add draw near to me with their mouths, and   [H]15:8–9 Is 29:13 LXX   [I]15:14 Other mss add for the blind   [J]15:16 Other mss read Jesus   [K]15:17 Other mss add yet   [L]15:17 Lit and goes out into the toilet   [M]15:22 Other mss read and cried out to him

---

15:1–2 The Mishnah devotes an entire tractate of Jewish law to a discussion on how the hands should be washed. Good Jews were expected to perform ritual hand washing before, during, and after each meal. A person would first pour water over his hands with the fingers pointing up and with the water reaching the wrist, then he would point the fingers down and pour the water again, this time allowing the water to drip off the fingers. If one mixed up this order or poured the water both times with the hands pointed down or up, the hands were still ritually unclean. Each hand had to be rubbed with the other, but this could not be done until the other hand was clean. To neglect the first or third washing was considered a serious sin, possibly a deadly one. Such washing was not prescribed by OT law, but was a tradition passed down to first-century Jews by their elders. Many teachers gave these human traditions an authority equal to that of OT commandments.

15:3–4 Jesus taught that the authority of the Scriptures trumps all human tradition, and he condemned the Pharisees and scribes for valuing human tradition above Scripture. For the Scripture quote see Ex 20:12; 21:17; Lv 20:9; Dt 5:16.

15:5–6 Jewish law required sons to care for their aging parents. However, corrupt priests allowed sons who were tired of caring for their parents to take a vow of corban. This

vow dedicated to God and the Jerusalem temple the resources they would otherwise have used to support their parents. Since one's obligation to God truly outweighs all other obligations, the priests taught that such a maneuver was righteous. Jesus strongly condemned it, however.

15:7–9 For the Scripture see Is 29:13 (LXX).

15:10–12 The laws regarding purification of the hands were concerned with ritual purity, not sanitation. After all, Jewish law permitted the water to be drawn from vessels made of cow manure. Further, it permitted the water to be so filthy that cattle refused to drink it (m. Ta'an. 1). Jesus argued that food consumed with unpurified hands does not spiritually defile a person. The words that proceed from the mouth defile a person because they show the sinful condition of the heart (v. 18). That the Pharisees took offense at Jesus's teaching suggests that they understood that he was referring to their hypocritical speech, which honored God even as their hearts refused to worship him (vv. 8–9).

15:13 Based on texts like Is 60:21 and 61:3, first-century Jews described themselves as the "plant of the Lord." Every plant that my heavenly Father didn't plant represents national Jews who neither understood nor practiced true righteousness. Like the weeds in the parable of Mt 13:24–30, these imposters would be uprooted and destroyed.

15:14 Jewish teachers like the Pharisees and scribes prided themselves on being guides for the blind (Rm 2:19). In ironic reversal, Jesus claimed the guides themselves were blind.

15:15–20 Jesus taught that the human heart is innately corrupt, but he also described his followers as "pure in heart" (5:8). From this we conclude that following Jesus results in a transformation of the heart that greatly diminishes our love of sin.

15:21 Tyre and Sidon were port cities on the coast of the Mediterranean Sea north of Galilee. Because these cities were denounced in Is 23 and Ezk 28, first-century Jews viewed them as notoriously wicked and deserving of divine wrath (11:21).

15:22 By labeling the woman a Canaanite (cp. Mk 7:26), Matthew associates her with the most notorious pagan enemy of Israel. Like the magi of Mt 2, her role shows that Gentiles may follow Christ and be blessed by him (see note at 2:1). Her use of the title Son of David indicates that she recognized Jesus as the Jewish Messiah (see note at 1:1).

15:23 The disciples' request to send her away could imply either that he would help her or he would not. The former was probably their intention because of Jesus's reply in v. 24.

15:24 Matthew emphasized Jesus's intention to include Gentiles in his kingdom, but he also stressed that Jesus focused his earthly

25 But she came, knelt before him, and said, "Lord, help me!"
26 He answered, "It isn't right to take the children's bread and throw it to the dogs."
27 "Yes, Lord," she said, "yet even the dogs eat the crumbs that fall from their masters' table."
28 Then Jesus replied to her, "Woman, your faith is great. Let it be done for you as you want." And from that moment^A her daughter was healed.

Healing Many People

29 Moving on from there, Jesus passed along the Sea of Galilee. He went up on a mountain and sat there, **30** and large crowds came to him, including the lame, the blind, the crippled, those unable to speak, and many others. They put them at his feet, and he healed them. **31** So the crowd was amazed when they saw those unable to speak talking, the crippled restored, the lame walking, and the blind seeing, and they gave glory to the God of Israel.

Feeding of the Four Thousand

32 Jesus called his disciples and said, "I have compassion on the crowd, because they've already stayed with me three days and have nothing to eat. I don't want to send them away hungry, otherwise they might collapse on the way."
33 The disciples said to him, "Where could we get enough bread in this desolate place to feed such a crowd?"
34 "How many loaves do you have?" Jesus asked them.
"Seven," they said, "and a few small fish."

35 After commanding the crowd to sit down on the ground, **36** he took the seven loaves and the fish, gave thanks, broke them, and gave them to the disciples, and the disciples gave them to the crowds. **37** They all ate and were satisfied. They collected the leftover pieces — seven large baskets full. **38** Now there were four thousand men who had eaten, besides women and children. **39** After dismissing the crowds, he got into the boat and went to the region of Magadan.^B

The Leaven of the Pharisees and the Sadducees

16 The Pharisees and Sadducees approached, and tested him, asking him to show them a sign from heaven. **2** He replied, "When evening comes you say, 'It will be good weather because the sky is red.' **3** And in the morning, 'Today will be stormy because the sky is red and threatening.' You^C know how to read the appearance of the sky, but you can't read the signs of the times.^D **4** An evil and adulterous generation demands a sign, but no sign will be given to it except the sign of^E Jonah." Then he left them and went away.

5 The disciples reached the other shore,^F and they had forgotten to take bread. **6** Then Jesus told them, "Watch out and beware of the leaven^G of the Pharisees and Sadducees."
7 They were discussing among themselves, "We didn't bring any bread."
8 Aware of this, Jesus said, "You of little faith, why are you discussing among yourselves that you do not have bread? **9** Don't you understand yet? Don't you remember the five loaves for

---

^A**15:28** Lit *hour*   ^B**15:39** Other mss read *Magdala*   ^C**16:3** Other mss read *Hypocrites! You*   ^D**16:2–3** Other mss omit *When (v. 2) through end of v. 3*   ^E**16:4** Other mss add *the prophet*   ^F**16:5** Lit *disciples went to the other side*   ^G**16:6** Or *yeast*, also in vv. 11,12

---

ministry on Israelites who had been abused by their spiritual leaders (10:5–6).
15:25–27 Comparison of the Canaanite woman to a dog sounds like a racial slur to modern readers, but the word **dogs** (Gk *kunarion*) was a diminutive used as a term of endearment. It typically referred to house dogs that slept in the master's lap. Jesus's metaphorical statement merely implies that he had a higher obligation to serve his fellow Jews, not that he despised Gentiles. The woman replied that Jesus need not neglect Jews by meeting Gentile needs any more than children go hungry because **crumbs** that fall from their **table** are eaten by their pets.
15:28 The faith that Jesus most highly commended in Matthew was expressed by Gentiles (see notes at 8:7–10,11). The faith of the Canaanite woman even compared favorably to that of the twelve disciples (14:31).
15:29–31 The location is apparently the northern shores of the **Sea of Galilee**, still in Gentile territory. The list of ailments that Jesus cured is reminiscent of Is 35:5–6 and identifies Jesus as Messiah (Mt 11:1–6). The people's praise to **the God of Israel** shows that Jesus's ministry pointed Gentiles to the one true God.

15:32–38 This miracle is similar to the previous feeding (Mt 14:13–21). In both cases Jesus was moved with **compassion**, used **loaves** and **fish**, and satisfied the people so completely that **leftover pieces** were collected. One notable difference is the audience. The first miracle was performed for Israelites, the second for Gentiles.
15:39 The **Magadan** mentioned here was probably ancient Magdala on the northwestern shore of the Sea of Galilee.
16:1 The Pharisees and Sadducees disagreed on major theological and political views. They united only because of their joint opposition to John the Baptist and Jesus (3:7).
16:2–3 Jesus's opponents could skillfully read signs for the coming weather, but they missed the more obvious signs (Jesus's miracles) about the coming kingdom of God (see note at v. 4).
16:4 Jesus's description of Israel's religious leaders is reminiscent of Dt 32:5, where Moses rebuked Israel for rejecting the Lord. Jesus thus compared Israel's rejection of God with its rejection of himself. By doing this, he equated himself with God. The context of Dt 32:5 uses meteorological terms like *heavens, rain, dew,* and *showers* (Dt 32:1–2) and

Moses elsewhere calls "heaven and earth as witnesses" against rebellious Israel (Dt 4:26; 30:19). Jesus used a meteorological illustration in order to tie in the OT text. On the **sign of Jonah**, see note at 12:39–40.
16:5–7 The disciples should have collected leftovers from Jesus's feeding miracle in order to sustain themselves on their next journey. Their failure to do so may have been an act of carelessness, but it may also indicate that they expected Jesus to perform signs and wonders at every turn, as did the sect leaders (vv. 1–4). The verb **had forgotten** (Gk *epilanthanomai*) often implies willful neglect (Ezk 23:35, LXX). **Leaven** was used as a metaphor for something seemingly insignificant that could have enormous influence (see note at 13:33). It could be used to indicate positive influence, but here it is used negatively. **The Pharisees and Sadducees** disagreed about many doctrines, so reference to their common teaching likely meant their joint skepticism regarding Jesus's messiahship.
16:8–12 The disciples' memory of Jesus's feeding miracles should have been enough to sustain their faith. Their constant desire for miracles paralleled the Pharisees' and

the five thousand and how many baskets you collected? ¹⁰ Or the seven loaves for the four thousand and how many large baskets you collected? ¹¹ Why is it you don't understand that when I told you, 'Beware of the leaven of the Pharisees and Sadducees,' it wasn't about bread?" ¹² Then they understood that he had not told them to beware of the leaven in bread, but of the teaching of the Pharisees and Sadducees.

Peter's Confession of the Messiah

¹³ When Jesus came to the region of Caesarea Philippi,ᴬ he asked his disciples, "Who do people say that the Son of Man is?"ᴮ

¹⁴ They replied, "Some say John the Baptist; others, Elijah; still others, Jeremiah or one of the prophets."

¹⁵ "But you," he asked them, "who do you say that I am?"

¹⁶ Simon Peter answered, "You are the Messiah, the Son of the living God."

¹⁷ Jesus responded, "Blessed are you, Simon son of Jonah,ᶜ because flesh and blood did not reveal this to you, but my Father in heaven. ¹⁸ And I also say to you that you are Peter, and on this rock I will build my church, and the gates of Hades will not overpower it. ¹⁹ I will give you the keys of the kingdom of heaven, and whatever you bind on earth will have been boundᴰ in heaven, and whatever you loose on earth will have been loosedᴱ in heaven." ²⁰ Then he gave the disciples orders to tell no one that he wasᶠ the Messiah.

His Death and Resurrection Predicted

²¹ From then on Jesus began to point out to his disciples that it was necessary for him to go to Jerusalem and suffer many things from the elders, chief priests, and scribes, be killed, and be raised the third day. ²² Peter took him aside and began to rebuke him, "Oh no,ᴳ Lord! This will never happen to you!"

²³ Jesus turned and told Peter, "Get behind me, Satan! You are a hindrance to me because you're not thinking about God's concernsᴴ but human concerns."

Take Up Your Cross

²⁴ Then Jesus said to his disciples, "If anyone wants to follow after me, let him deny himself, take up his cross, and follow me. ²⁵ For whoever wants to save his life will lose it, but whoever loses his life because of me will find it. ²⁶ For what will it benefit someone if he gains the whole world yet loses his life? Or what will anyone give in exchange for his life? ²⁷ For the Son of Man is going to come with his angels in the glory of his Father, and then he will reward each according to what he has done. ²⁸ Truly I tell you, there are some standing here who will not taste death until they see the Son of Man coming in his kingdom."

The Transfiguration

17 After six days Jesus took Peter, James, and his brother John and led them up on a high mountain by themselves. ² He was transfigured in front of them, and his face shone

---

ᴬ**16:13** A town north of Galilee at the base of Mount Hermon   ᴮ**16:13** Other mss read *that I, the Son of Man, am*   ᶜ**16:17** Or *son of John*   ᴰ**16:19** Or *earth will be bound*   ᴱ**16:19** Or *earth will be loosed*   ᶠ**16:20** Other mss add *Jesus*   ᴳ**16:22** Lit *"Mercy to you = "May God have mercy on you*   ᴴ**16:23** Lit *about the things of God*

Sadducees' demand for a "sign from heaven" (v. 1) and demonstrated that they were people **of little faith**.

16:13 Two cities in ancient Israel were named Caesarea. Caesarea Maritima was located on the Mediterranean coast. **Caesarea Philippi** was an inland city located approximately twenty-five miles north of the Sea of Galilee. This was the site of worship for a nature god known as Pan and the home of a temple dedicated to Augustus Caesar. That Jesus's identity as Messiah was announced here demonstrates that Jesus's kingdom is superior to Caesar's and that he is likewise superior to all idols and mythical gods. On the meaning of **Son of Man**, see note at 8:18–20.

16:14 Many of Jesus's contemporaries recognized his prophetic role. Herod suspected he was **John the Baptist** resurrected (14:2). Some of Jesus's miracles were similar to those of **Elijah** (cp. 1Kg 17:9–16 and Mt 14:13–21; 1Kg 17:17–24 and Mt 9:18–19,23–26), leading people to believe he was the fulfillment of Elijah's promised return (Mal 4:5). Like **Jeremiah**, Jesus was a much-rejected preacher of judgment.

16:15–16 On the titles **Messiah** and **Son of the living God**, see notes at 1:1 and 3:17. Although Matthew called Jesus Messiah earlier (1:1,16), this is the first time the disciples called him this. Peter used the title "living

God" to contrast the Lord with lifeless pagan deities, such as the false god Pan who was represented in a nearby pagan temple.

16:17–18 Simon understood Jesus's identity due to divine revelation (11:25–27), which is why Jesus nicknamed him **Peter**. Although Matthew previously referred to Simon as Peter, this is the first time in the Gospel that Jesus did so. Jesus identified Peter (Gk *petros*) as the **rock** (Gk *petra*) on which his church would be founded. Peter and the other apostles' proclamation of Jesus's messiahship laid the foundation for the church (Eph 2:19–20; Rv 21:14). **I will build** demonstrates that Jesus is ultimately responsible for the growth and expansion of the church. The word **church** was the word used in the OT to describe sacred Jewish assemblies. Jesus's use of the word implies that his followers constitute the new Israel, the true people of God who submit to his kingly reign.

16:19 The **keys** are a symbol of authority. The rabbis used the words **bind** and **loose** to denote decisions about what was or was not permitted. Note that Peter will permit or prohibit only what had already been permitted or prohibited in heaven. Peter was an agent of divine revelation.

16:20 Jesus's contemporaries, even his **disciples**, were slow to understand the nature of his messiahship.

16:21–22 The words **from then on Jesus began to** introduce the conclusion of Matthew's Gospel (cp. 4:17). Jesus referred to his death and resurrection earlier (12:40), but this is the first of three major predictions from this point on (see 17:22; 20:17–19). **Peter** could not accept the warning because his messianic expectations did not include a suffering, executed Messiah.

16:23 The cross was central to Jesus's purposes on earth. Because Peter's statement essentially tempted Jesus to evade the cross, he unwittingly became a spokesman for **Satan**.

16:24–26 Take up his cross refers to the death march of the Christian disciple, who is figuratively sentenced to crucifixion over his decision to follow Christ. The Christian must be prepared to give his life for Jesus. **Follow me** requires the disciple to follow the example of his Master, emulating Jesus's character and behavior.

16:27 Jesus applied to himself Ps 62:12 and Zch 14:5, statements which referred to the Lord. On the title **Son of Man**, see note at 8:18–20.

16:28 This promise refers to Jesus's transfiguration, which foreshadowed his resurrection and glorification (2Pt 1:16–18).

17:1–8 The reference to **six days** indicates the rapidity of the fulfillment of Jesus's promise in Mt 16:28, but it also may draw

like the sun; his clothes became as white as the light. ³ Suddenly, Moses and Elijah appeared to them, talking with him. ⁴ Then Peter said to Jesus, "Lord, it's good for us to be here. If you want, I will set up^A three shelters here: one for you, one for Moses, and one for Elijah."

⁵ While he was still speaking, suddenly a bright cloud covered^B them, and a voice from the cloud said, "This is my beloved Son, with whom I am well-pleased. Listen to him!" ⁶ When the disciples heard this, they fell facedown and were terrified.

⁷ Jesus came up, touched them, and said, "Get up; don't be afraid." ⁸ When they looked up they saw no one except Jesus alone.

⁹ As they were coming down the mountain, Jesus commanded them, "Don't tell anyone about the vision until the Son of Man is raised^C from the dead."

¹⁰ So the disciples asked him, "Why then do the scribes say that Elijah must come first?"

¹¹ "Elijah is coming^D and will restore everything," he replied.^E ¹² "But I tell you: Elijah has already come, and they didn't recognize him. On the contrary, they did whatever they pleased to him. In the same way the Son of Man is going to suffer at their hands." ¹³ Then the disciples understood that he had spoken to them about John the Baptist.

The Power of Jesus over a Demon

¹⁴ When they reached the crowd, a man approached and knelt down before him. ¹⁵ "Lord," he said, "have mercy on my son, because he has seizures^F and suffers terribly. He often falls into the fire and often into the water. ¹⁶ I brought him to your disciples, but they couldn't heal him."

¹⁷ Jesus replied, "You unbelieving and perverse generation, how long will I be with you? How long must I put up with you? Bring him here to me." ¹⁸ Then Jesus rebuked the demon,^G and it^H came out of him, and from that moment^I the boy was healed.

¹⁹ Then the disciples approached Jesus privately and said, "Why couldn't we drive it out?"

²⁰ "Because of your little faith," he^J told them. "For truly I tell you, if you have faith the size of^K a mustard seed, you will tell this mountain, 'Move from here to there,' and it will move. Nothing will be impossible for you."^L

The Second Prediction of His Death

²² As they were gathering together^M in Galilee, Jesus told them, "The Son of Man is about to be betrayed into the hands of men. ²³ They will kill him, and on the third day he will be raised up." And they were deeply distressed.

Paying the Temple Tax

²⁴ When they came to Capernaum, those who collected the temple tax approached Peter and said, "Doesn't your teacher pay the temple tax?"

²⁵ "Yes," he said.

When he went into the house, Jesus spoke to him first,^N "What do you think, Simon? From whom do earthly kings collect tariffs or taxes? From their sons or from strangers?"^O

a parallel between Jesus's transfiguration and God's revelation of himself to **Moses** in Ex 24:13–18. Other parallels include the reference to a **cloud**, a brilliant **light**, a **mountain**, and the separation of a small number of men from the larger group. Moses's face shone brilliantly after he met with God (Ex 34:29–35), so Jesus's transfiguration serves to identify him as the new Moses. This seems confirmed by the words **listen to him** which echo Dt 18:15, a text from the prophet-like-Moses prophecy (Dt 18:15–19). On the new Moses theme, see notes at Mt 2:15 and 2:16. However, the description of Jesus transcends that of Moses. In the transfiguration of the glorified Moses. In Ex 34:29–35, only Moses's face was radiant and this radiance was concealed by his veil. Jesus's face had radiance too glorious to conceal and **his clothes became as white as the light**. The description of Jesus parallels the description of the Ancient of Days in Dn 7:9–10 and shows that Jesus possessed the glory of his Father (Mt 16:27).

The presence of Moses and Elijah indicates that the necessary conditions for Messiah's coming had been fulfilled (v. 10; Dt 18:15–19; Mal 4:5). Peter's request to build **shelters** unjustly suggested equal treatment for Jesus and his guests. The Father's voice from

heaven showed Jesus's superiority to Moses and Elijah. Jesus is God's **beloved Son** and the focus of true disciples. God spoke from heaven only twice in Matthew, both times to express his love for Jesus and his delight in his works (v. 5; 3:17). On the meaning of "Son," see note at 3:17. The disciples' reaction is understandable, for the OT shows that direct encounters with God inspire fright (e.g., Is 6:1–5).

17:9 The disciples could report the transfiguration only after the resurrection when the nature of Jesus's messianic reign became clear.

17:10–13 The view of the **scribes** was prompted by Mal 4:5. John the Baptist was the fulfillment of the Elijah prophecy since his ministry had many similarities to Elijah's. See notes at Mt 3:1,4 and 11:13–15.

17:14–16 Like the magi (2:11), the leper (8:2), the father of the deceased daughter (9:18), and Jesus's disciples (14:33), this father worshiped Jesus (cp. 4:10). The **seizures** were probably the result of epilepsy. Epilepsy is distinguished from demon possession in Mt 4:24. However, Jesus recognized in this rare instance that the seizures were the result of demonic activity. The apparent suicidal tendencies described in v. 15 show the destructive influence of demons.

17:17–18 Jesus's description of his own disciples as an **unbelieving and perverse generation** is similar to his description of the Jewish leaders who rejected him (11:16; 12:39,45).

17:19–21 Moving a **mountain** was a metaphor for accomplishing an impossible task (1Co 13:2). Nothing that Christ authorizes his followers to do will be **impossible**.

17:22–23 This is Jesus's second major prediction of his death since Peter's confession in 16:13–20 (see 16:21). Each prediction adds additional details. This prophecy adds that Jesus will be thrust **into the hands of men** by an act of betrayal.

17:24 On **Capernaum**, see note at 4:13. The **temple tax** was collected from every Jewish male over the age of twenty and used for the upkeep of the Jerusalem temple (Ex 30:13; 38:25–26; Josephus, Ant. 18.9.1; War 7.6.6). This episode is recorded only in Matthew and provides evidence for the pre-AD 70 date of Matthew.

17:25–26 Because Jesus's disciples were children of the true King, they were exempt from the obligation to support the temple. This had enormous implications for Jewish Christians. If temple taxes were no longer obligatory, sacrifices and other offerings were also now optional.

26 "From strangers," he said.[A] "Then the sons are free," Jesus told him. **27** "But, so we won't offend them, go to the sea, cast in a fishhook, and take the first fish that you catch. When you open its mouth you'll find a coin.[B] Take it and give it to them for me and you."

Who Is the Greatest?

18 At that time[C] the disciples came to Jesus and asked, "So who is greatest in the kingdom of heaven?" **2** He called a small child and had him stand among them. **3** "Truly I tell you," he said, "unless you turn and become like little children, you will never enter the kingdom of heaven. **4** Therefore, whoever humbles himself like this child — this one is the greatest in the kingdom of heaven. **5** And whoever welcomes[D] one child like this in my name welcomes me.

6 "But whoever causes one of these little ones who believe in me to fall away — it would be better for him if a heavy millstone were hung around his neck and he were drowned in the depths of the sea. **7** Woe to the world because of offenses. For offenses will inevitably come, but woe to that person by whom the offense comes. **8** If your hand or your foot causes you to fall away, cut it off and throw it away. It is better for you to enter life maimed or lame than to have two hands or two feet and be thrown into the eternal fire. **9** And if your eye causes you to fall away, gouge it out and throw it away. It is better for you to enter life with one eye than to have two eyes and be thrown into hellfire.[E]

The Parable of the Lost Sheep

10 "See to it that you don't despise one of these little ones, because I tell you that in heaven their angels continually view the face of my Father in heaven.[F] **12** What do you think? If someone has a hundred sheep, and one of them goes astray, won't he leave the ninety-nine on the hillside and go and search for the stray? **13** And if he finds it, truly I tell you, he rejoices over that sheep[G] more than over the ninety-nine that did not go astray. **14** In the same way, it is not the will of your Father in heaven that one of these little ones perish.

Restoring a Brother

15 "If your brother sins against you,[H] go tell him his fault, between you and him alone. If he listens to you, you have won your brother. **16** But if he won't listen, take one or two others with you, so that **by the testimony[I] of two or three witnesses every fact may be established.**[J] **17** If he doesn't pay attention to them, tell the church.[K] If he doesn't pay attention even to the church, let him be like a Gentile and a tax collector to you. **18** Truly I tell you, whatever you bind on earth will have been bound[L] in heaven, and whatever you loose on earth will have been loosed[M] in heaven. **19** Again, truly I tell you, if two of you on earth agree about any matter that you[N] pray for, it will be done for you[O] by my Father in heaven. **20** For where two or three

---

[A]17:26 Other mss read *Peter said to him* [B]17:27 Gk *stater*, worth 2 double-drachmas [C]18:1 Lit *hour* [D]18:5 Or *receives* [E]18:9 Lit *gehenna of fire* [F]18:10 Some mss include v. 11: *For the Son of Man has come to save the lost.* [G]18:13 Lit *over it* [H]18:15 Other mss omit *against you* [I]18:16 Lit *mouth* [J]18:16 Dt 19:15 [K]18:17 Or *congregation* [L]18:18 Or *earth will be bound* [M]18:18 Or *earth will be loosed* [N]18:19 Lit *they* [O]18:19 Lit *for them*

17:27 Though Jesus insisted that the temple tax was not obligatory for his disciples, he gladly paid it to avoid offending his fellow Jews. His action provided an important model for believers who dealt with issues of ritual later in the early church (Rm 14:13–23). Several ancient texts refer to fishermen discovering valuable items inside fish. Through supernatural knowledge, Jesus knew that a nearby **fish** had swallowed an amount of money that was sufficient to pay the tax. He also exercised authority over nature, ensuring that the fish would take the bait Peter offered.
18:1–5 These verses are commonly said to promote childlike innocence or naïveté, but Jesus's statement actually urged disciples to adopt childlike humility. The desire to be the **greatest in the kingdom** displayed a pride that was inconsistent with genuine discipleship. Humility is the path to true greatness. Jesus urged kind and gracious treatment of children by teaching that anyone welcoming a **small child** in his **name** would be rewarded as if having received Messiah himself.
18:6–7 Jesus shifted the topic from literal children to spiritual **little ones who believe in** him, meaning his disciples. The **heavy millstone** was a large round stone turned by a donkey rather than the much smaller stone

used to pound grain by hand. Drowning was a particularly horrifying way to die in the mindset of first-century Jews, for Israel was not a seafaring nation.
18:8–9 Those who cause Jesus's disciples to sin will face severe punishment. Nevertheless, disciples are responsible for their own actions and must commit to purity (see note at 5:29–30).
18:10 Daniel 10:10–14 teaches that **angels** are assigned to represent and protect the nations. In similar fashion, Jesus appears to teach that angels are assigned to represent believers to God. Jesus said that these angels **continually view the face of my Father,** meaning they have access to the heavenly throne and constantly present the needs of believers to God.
18:12–14 Sinful believers who are restored to church fellowship should not be received begrudgingly or hesitantly but with the jubilation of a shepherd who finds a **sheep** that **goes astray.** The heavenly Shepherd cannot accept the loss of even a single believer. Like the shepherd of this parable, he will rescue his stray sheep.
18:15–17 These verses outline the process by which disciples demonstrate the Great Shepherd's concern for stray sheep. The words **against you** do not appear in the earliest

and best manuscripts of v. 15. Thus the process is not intended merely for dealing with personal grievances but rather for any sinful conduct on the part of a Christian **brother** (or sister) that indicates they are straying from Christ. The purpose of the process is not to punish, but to restore the sinful disciple (**you have won your brother**). If, at the final step of the process, the professing disciple refuses to heed the church's call to repentance, the **church** must assume that they are not a true believer and must exclude them from fellowship (see 1Co 5:1–13).
18:18 On binding and loosing, see note at 16:19. The decisions made by the church about what behavior is permissible or unacceptable reflect decisions already made by God in heaven.
18:19–20 A common but mistaken interpretation holds that these verses promise that God will do whatever two or more believers ask. This violates the context. There is a clear connection with the immediately preceding discussion about restoring a sinning disciple. Verses 18–19 relate the restoration/disciplinary actions of Jesus's disciples **on earth** to the decisions of the Father **in heaven.** The word **again** at the beginning of v. 19 suggests that this verse restates the principle of v. 18. The **two or three** mentioned in v. 20

Church Discipline

by Mark E. Dever

Jesus Christ founded and purchased the church with his blood (Ac 20:28), and he builds it upon acknowledgment and faith in him as Messiah (Mt 16:18). This means the church belongs to Jesus and represents him to the nations. In this light, the purity of the church is vital. Rightly practiced, church discipline helps ensure that purity.

Two Categories of Church Discipline

Two categories of church discipline describe ways a church may teach its members right living and right beliefs.

Formative Discipline: Formative discipline is a preventative measure. It includes the positive, direct teaching of biblical truth through sermons and Bible teaching. It also includes modeling godliness and mentoring new believers.

Corrective Discipline: Corrective discipline is used when trouble arises. It can include contradicting, challenging, rebuking, and excommunicating a member for unrepentance or erroneous teachings. Corrective discipline may seem controversial, but Jesus clearly taught that if a believer continues to sin despite the call to repentance, the church should treat him as if he were "a Gentile and a tax collector" (Mt 18:17). This exclusion from church membership is generically called "church discipline." It is also called "excommunication" because those under discipline are not permitted to participate in Communion (the Lord's Supper).

Correcting Misconceptions about Church Discipline

Excommunication is the final stage of church discipline. It is undertaken only if other corrective measures fail to bring the sinner to repentance. Though painful and traumatic, excommunication is not an unloving act. One of the obligations of love is to not leave someone in their sin. "Better an open reprimand than concealed love. The wounds of a friend are trustworthy, but the kisses of an enemy are excessive" (Pr 27:5–6).

Excommunication does not mean that the person should stop attending church. Except in rare cases, the congregation desires the disciplined sinner to continue attending and sitting under the preaching of God's Word. By this the sinner is confronted by Scripture and his life is observed by the faith community that has disciplined him.

Church discipline need not be permanent. One goal is the repentance of the sinner. Paul rebuked the Corinthian church for not readmitting into membership repentant members whom they had disciplined (2Co 2:6–7). Finally, church discipline is not an infallible assessment of the eternal state of the person disciplined. It is instead a fallible but serious warning about an evident lack of spiritual regeneration.

Why Church Discipline Is Important

Church discipline presents to the world and believers a clarifying picture of what it means to follow Christ. It is important to make sinners aware of their sin (e.g., 1Co 5). By confronting persistent sin, the church may reveal hypocrites—both to themselves so that they might repent, and to the church so that the church might distinguish sheep from wolves (see Mt 7).

The practice of church discipline is also an important part of glorifying God, for the church is to reflect God's holy character in a fallen world (1Pt 1:14–16). God is both merciful and holy. To neglect either aspect of his character is to distort his image and lie about him.

are gathered together in my name, I am there among them."

The Parable of the Unforgiving Servant

²¹ Then Peter approached him and asked, "Lord, how many times must I forgive my brother or sister who sins against me? As many as seven times?"

²² "I tell you, not as many as seven," Jesus replied, "but seventy times seven.^A

²³ "For this reason, the kingdom of heaven can be compared to a king who wanted to settle accounts with his servants. ²⁴ When he began to settle accounts, one who owed ten thousand talents^B was brought before him. ²⁵ Since he did not have the money to pay it back, his master commanded that he, his wife, his children, and everything he had be sold to pay the debt.

²⁶ "At this, the servant fell facedown before him and said, 'Be patient with me, and I will pay you everything.' ²⁷ Then the master of that servant had compassion, released him, and forgave him the loan.

²⁸ "That servant went out and found one of his fellow servants who owed him a hundred denarii.^C He grabbed him, started choking him, and said, 'Pay what you owe!'

²⁹ "At this, his fellow servant fell down^D and began begging him, 'Be patient with me, and I will pay you back.' ³⁰ But he wasn't willing. Instead, he went and threw him into prison until he could pay what was owed. ³¹ When the other servants saw what had taken place, they were deeply distressed and went and reported to their master everything that had happened. ³² Then, after he had summoned him,

his master said to him, 'You wicked servant! I forgave you all that debt because you begged me. ³³ Shouldn't you also have had mercy on your fellow servant, as I had mercy on you?' ³⁴ And because he was angry, his master handed him over to the jailers to be tortured until he could pay everything that was owed. ³⁵ So also my heavenly Father will do to you unless every one of you forgives his brother or sister^E from your^F heart."

The Question of Divorce

19 When Jesus had finished saying these things, he departed from Galilee and went to the region of Judea across the Jordan. ² Large crowds followed him, and he healed them there. ³ Some Pharisees approached him to test him. They asked, "Is it lawful for a man to divorce his wife on any grounds?"

⁴ "Haven't you read," he replied, "that he who created^G them in the beginning **made them male and female,**" ⁵ and he also said, '**For this reason a man will leave his father and mother and be joined to his wife, and the two will become one flesh'?**^I ⁶ So they are no longer two, but one flesh. Therefore, what God has joined together, let no one separate."

⁷ "Why then," they asked him, "did Moses command us to give divorce papers and to send her away?"

⁸ He told them, "Moses permitted you to divorce your wives because of the hardness of your hearts, but it was not like that from the beginning. ⁹ I tell you, whoever divorces his wife, except for sexual immorality, and marries another commits adultery."^J

---

^A 18:22 Or *but seventy-seven times* ^B 18:24 A talent is worth about 6,000 denarii, or twenty years' wages for a laborer ^C 18:28 A denarius = one day's wage ^D 18:29 Other mss add *at his feet* ^E 18:35 Other mss add *their trespasses* ^F 18:35 Lit *his* ^G 19:4 Other mss read *made* ^H 19:4 Gn 1:27; 5:2 ^I 19:5 Gn 2:24 ^J 19:9 Other mss add *Also whoever marries a divorced woman commits adultery*; Mt 5:32

---

are thus the two or three witnesses that were first mentioned in v. 16. Christ is present with his disciples when they gather and seek his leadership about troubling behavior among disciples. He will answer their prayer for the sinning believer's restoration.

18:21–22 Although forgiving someone only **seven times** seems stingy, this standard was generous considering the fact that some rabbis required their students to forgive offenders only three times. Interpreters dispute whether Jesus demanded forgiving one's **brother or sister** seventy-seven times or 490 times (seventy times seven), but Jesus's point was that forgiveness should be unlimited when true repentance is present. **18:23–27** In Jewish parables, a king symbolizes God and to **settle accounts** symbolizes divine judgment. The **ten thousand talents** was equivalent to a billion days' worth of peasant wages. This was more money than was circulating in all of Palestine. The talent was the largest unit of currency (equivalent to approximately six thousand days' worth of wages), and ten thousand is the highest single number that can be expressed in Greek. Thus we see that in this allegory the

sum represents the sinner's hopeless debt to God. Selling the debtor, his family, and possessions would hardly begin to recoup this debt. Forgiving such a loan is an astounding act of grace.

18:28–31 A hundred denarii (about a hundred day's wages) was negligible compared to the first servant's debt to the king. The contrast shows that the sins of others against us are trivial in comparison to the enormity of our own sins against God. The **fellow servant** begged the servant to **be patient** just as the servant had begged before the king, but the fellow servant was more honest in his pleas and promises since his debt was actually manageable. **18:32–35** The parable's point is now revealed. Since God has shown believers such great mercy by pardoning their sins, they should in turn forgive the sins of others from their heart. The word **jailers** literally means "torturers." The debtor's torture would continue until the debt was paid in full. Since the debt could not possibly be repaid, the torture symbolizes eternal punishment. **19:1** The words **when Jesus had finished** mark the end of the fourth of five major

blocks of teaching in Matthew's Gospel (cp. 7:28; 11:1; 13:53; 26:1). **19:2–3** First-century Pharisees who associated themselves with Hillel's school were liberal toward **divorce**. They permitted it for virtually any reason, including such ridiculous grounds as the wife burning her husband's supper or having physical defects like bushy eyebrows. **19:4–6** God ordained marriage both by creation and command. He created two complementary genders, **male and female**, and commanded one man and one woman to unite in marriage. Since God ordained marriage, human efforts to dissolve it constitute an attack on God's own work. **19:7–9** Although the Pharisees described divorce as something **Moses** commanded, Jesus described it as something Moses merely **permitted**. No provision for divorce was given at **the beginning**. Only after human **hearts** became hardened by sin was divorce permitted. The hearts of Jesus's disciples are transformed (5:8), enabling them to be faithful to their marital covenant. Jesus permitted divorce and remarriage for marital unfaithfulness because

10 His disciples said to him, "If the relationship of a man with his wife is like this, it's better not to marry."

11 He responded, "Not everyone can accept this saying, but only those to whom it has been given. **12** For there are eunuchs who were born that way from their mother's womb, there are eunuchs who were made by men, and there are eunuchs who have made themselves that way because of the kingdom of heaven. The one who is able to accept it should accept it."

Blessing the Children

13 Then little children were brought to Jesus for him to place his hands on them and pray, but the disciples rebuked them. **14** Jesus said, "Leave the little children alone, and don't try to keep them from coming to me, because the kingdom of heaven belongs to such as these."[A] **15** After placing his hands on them, he went on from there.

The Rich Young Ruler

16 Just then someone came up and asked him, "Teacher, what good must I do to have eternal life?"

17 "Why do you ask me about what is good?"[B] he said to him. "There is only one who is good.[C] If you want to enter into life, keep the commandments."

18 "Which ones?" he asked him.

Jesus answered: Do not murder; do not commit adultery; do not steal; do not bear false witness; **19** honor your father and mother; and love your neighbor as yourself.[D]

20 "I have kept all these,"[E] the young man told him. "What do I still lack?"

21 "If you want to be perfect,"[F] Jesus said to him, "go, sell your belongings and give to the poor, and you will have treasure in heaven. Then come, follow me."

22 When the young man heard that, he went away grieving, because he had many possessions.

Possessions and the Kingdom

23 Jesus said to his disciples, "Truly I tell you, it will be hard for a rich person to enter the kingdom of heaven. **24** Again I tell you, it is easier for a camel to go through the eye of a needle than for a rich person to enter the kingdom of God."

25 When the disciples heard this, they were utterly astonished and asked, "Then who can be saved?"

26 Jesus looked at them and said, "With man this is impossible, but with God all things are possible."

27 Then Peter responded to him, "See, we have left everything and followed you. So what will there be for us?"

28 Jesus said to them, "Truly I tell you, in the renewal of all things, when the Son of Man sits on his glorious throne, you who have followed me will also sit on twelve thrones, judging the twelve tribes of Israel. **29** And everyone who has left houses or brothers or sisters or father or mother[G] or children or fields because of my name will receive a hundred times more and will inherit eternal life. **30** But many who are first will be last, and the last first.

The Parable of the Vineyard Workers

20 "For the kingdom of heaven is like a landowner who went out early in the morning to hire workers for his vineyard. **2** After agreeing with the workers on one denarius,[H] he sent them into his vineyard for the day. **3** When he went out about nine in the morning,[I] he saw others standing in the marketplace doing nothing. **4** He said to them, 'You also go into my vineyard, and I'll give you whatever is right.' So off they went. **5** About noon and about three,[J] he went out again and did the same thing. **6** Then about five[K] he went and found others standing around[L] and said to them, 'Why have you been standing here all day doing nothing?'

7 "'Because no one hired us,' they said to him.

[A]**19:14** Lit *heaven is of such ones*   [B]**19:17** Other mss read *"Why do you call me good?"*   [C]**19:17** Other mss read *"No one is good but one — God*   [D]**19:18–19** Ex 20:12–16; Lv 19:18; Dt 5:16–20   [E]**19:20** Other mss add *from my youth*   [F]**19:21** Or *complete*   [G]**19:29** Other mss add *or wife*   [H]**20:2** A denarius = one day's wage, also in vv. 9,10,13   [I]**20:3** Lit *about the third hour*   [J]**20:5** Lit *about the sixth hour and the ninth hour*   [K]**20:6** Lit *about the eleventh hour*, also in v. 9   [L]**20:6** Other mss add *doing nothing*

sexual infidelity effectively destroys the one-flesh union of marriage.
19:10–12 The disciples rashly concluded that if marriage covenants are permanent, lifelong celibacy is the wisest option. Jesus upheld the value of marriage, but in this case he affirms those who chose celibacy in order to devote themselves wholly to God. **Eunuchs who have made themselves that way** are those who voluntarily abstain from marriage. Jesus did not condone self-emasculation.
19:13–15 On Jesus's blessing of children, see note at 18:1–5.
19:16–17 This story is related by Mark and Luke. Matthew identifies the man as "young" (v. 22). Luke notes he was a "ruler" and "very rich" (Lk 18:18,23). Thus the story is often labeled "The Rich Young Ruler." This man's question wrongly assumed that **eternal**

life can be earned through good deeds. The statement **there is only one who is good** was intended to shatter the man's deluded notion of attaining a personal goodness that merited salvation.
19:18–22 Jesus's command to **sell your belongings . . . Then come, follow me** was designed to show the young man that (1) his covetousness defied the spirit of the tenth commandment, (2) his neglect of the poor defied the commandment to love his neighbor, and possibly (3) his love for his possessions surpassed his love for God, thus breaking the commandment against idolatry.
19:23–26 The image of the largest animal in Palestine, a **camel**, passing through a small opening was an oft-used metaphor for impossible events. The salvation of **rich** people (tempted as they are to trust themselves

and their possessions) is possible only by divine miracle.
19:27–30 The renewal of all things will take place **when the Son of Man sits on his glorious throne**, reigning over the new heaven and new earth. The reign of the twelve disciples over Israel demonstrates that Jesus's disciples constitute the new Israel, the chosen people of God who will benefit from his covenant with Abraham. In a great divine reversal in which the first become last and the last become first, those who made personal sacrifices for Christ will enjoy enormous blessings, and those like the rich young ruler, who loved wealth more than Christ, will be punished.
20:1–7 In Jewish parables, authority figures like a wealthy **landowner** typically represent God. A **denarius** was the wage for a day's work in the first century.

" 'You also go into my vineyard,' he told them.[A] [8] When evening came, the owner of the vineyard told his foreman, 'Call the workers and give them their pay, starting with the last and ending with the first.'

[9] "When those who were hired about five came, they each received one denarius. [10] So when the first ones came, they assumed they would get more, but they also received a denarius each. [11] When they received it, they began to complain to the landowner: [12] 'These last men put in one hour, and you made them equal to us who bore the burden of the day's work and the burning heat.'

[13] "He replied to one of them, 'Friend, I'm doing you no wrong. Didn't you agree with me on a denarius? [14] Take what's yours and go. I want to give this last man the same as I gave you. [15] Don't I have the right to do what I want with what is mine? Are you jealous[B] because I'm generous?'[C]

[16] "So the last will be first, and the first last."[D]

The Third Prediction of His Death

[17] While going up to Jerusalem, Jesus took the twelve disciples aside privately and said to them on the way, [18] "See, we are going up to Jerusalem. The Son of Man will be handed over to the chief priests and scribes, and they will condemn him to death. [19] They will hand him over to the Gentiles to be mocked, flogged,[E] and crucified, and on the third day he will be raised."[F]

Suffering and Service

[20] Then the mother of Zebedee's sons approached him with her sons. She knelt down to ask him for something. [21] "What do you want?" he asked her.

"Promise,"[G] she said to him, "that these two sons of mine may sit, one on your right and the other on your left, in your kingdom."

[22] Jesus answered, "You don't know what you're asking. Are you able to drink the cup that I am about to drink?"[H]

"We are able," they said to him.

[23] He told them, "You will indeed drink my cup,[I] but to sit at my right and left is not mine to give; instead, it is for those for whom it has been prepared by my Father."

[24] When the ten disciples heard this, they became indignant with the two brothers. [25] Jesus called them over and said, "You know that the rulers of the Gentiles lord it over them, and those in high positions act as tyrants over them. [26] It must not be like that among you. On the contrary, whoever wants to become great among you must be your servant, [27] and whoever wants to be first among you must be your slave; [28] just as the Son of Man did not come to be served, but to serve, and to give his life as a ransom for many."

Two Blind Men Healed

[29] As they were leaving Jericho, a large crowd followed him. [30] There were two blind men sitting by the road. When they heard that Jesus was passing by, they cried out, "Lord, have mercy on us, Son of David!" [31] The crowd demanded that they keep quiet, but they cried out all the more, "Lord, have mercy on us, Son of David!" [32] Jesus stopped, called them, and said, "What do you want me to do for you?"

[33] "Lord," they said to him, "open our eyes."

[34] Moved with compassion, Jesus touched their eyes. Immediately they could see, and they followed him.

[A]20:7 Other mss add *and you'll get whatever is right.*   [B]20:15 Lit *Is your eye evil;* an idiom for jealousy or stinginess   [C]20:15 Lit *good*   [D]20:16 Other mss add *"For many are called, but few are chosen."*   [E]20:19 Or *scourged*   [F]20:19 Other mss read *will rise again*   [G]20:21 Lit *Say*   [H]20:22 Other mss add *and (or) to be baptized with the baptism which I am baptized?"*   [I]20:23 Other mss add *and be baptized with the baptism with which I am baptized.*

20:8 The words **starting with the last and ending with the first** recall 19:30 and show that this parable is an illustration of the principle taught there.
20:9–12 Since those who worked only **one hour** received a **denarius**, a full day's wage, other workers expected to be paid proportionately—one denarius an hour.
20:13–15 The workers had no right to protest their pay since their wage was the normally accepted sum and since they had agreed to work for this wage in the first place (v. 2). Just as the landowner was free to dispense his wealth as he saw fit, God is free to dispense his grace as he determines. The first workers hired represent people who consider themselves to be of greater importance to God, like the self-righteous man in 19:16–26. The last workers hired represent people like the twelve disciples, who live sacrificially but will be rewarded far more generously than they expect or deserve.
20:16 This repeats 19:30. Since this is repeated immediately before and after the parable of the vineyard workers, it is the key

to interpreting the parable. The conjunction at the beginning of 19:30 links this discussion with the one about the unexpected reward of Jesus's disciples.
20:17–19 This is Jesus's third major prediction of his death since Peter's confession (see 16:21; 17:22–23). Each prediction adds additional details. This time he added that he would be **mocked, flogged, and crucified** at the hands of **Gentiles**.
20:20 Zebedee's sons were James and John (see note at 4:18–22).
20:21 Jesus had promised that his disciples would sit on twelve thrones ruling over Israel in the renewal of all things (19:28–29). Now James and John sought, through their mother, to gain prominence over their fellows. Along with Peter, they were members of Jesus's inner circle. Because Jesus rebuked Peter in 16:23, they may have aspired to usurp Peter's position of prominence as well.
20:22–23 The **cup** was a metaphor for suffering (26:39). Jesus's question probed the disciples' willingness to suffer for him like he would suffer for them. **You will indeed**

drink my cup foretells the sufferings of James (Ac 12:1–2) and John. The parable in Mt 20:1–16 demonstrated that the Father distributes reward as he chooses, not according to merit. Jesus confirmed again the principle of the Father's freedom to determine who will enjoy heaven's greatest blessings.
20:24–28 The competition between the disciples exposed their pride. Jesus called his disciples to the same humble servitude that he modeled. The ultimate expression of his humility was his own sacrificial death that served as a **ransom** for believers. Jesus's words echo the themes of Is 53, which Matthew applied to Jesus in Mt 8:17.
20:29–34 The parallel passage in Mk 10:46–52 refers to only one blind man, not **two blind men.** However, since Mark gives the name of the blind man he mentions, he was probably known to Mark's original readers. Mark did not mention the other blind man because he wished to focus attention only on the man with whom his readers were familiar. On **Son of David,** see note at 1:1.

The Triumphal Entry

21 When they approached Jerusalem and came to Bethphage at the Mount of Olives, Jesus then sent two disciples, **2** telling them, "Go into the village ahead of you. At once you will find a donkey tied there with her colt. Untie them and bring them to me. **3** If anyone says anything to you, say that the Lord needs them, and he will send them at once."

4 This took place so that what was spoken through the prophet might be fulfilled:

5   Tell Daughter Zion,
     "See, your King is coming to you,
     gentle, and mounted on a donkey,
     and on a colt,
     the foal of a donkey."^A

6 The disciples went and did just as Jesus directed them. **7** They brought the donkey and the colt; then they laid their clothes on them, and he sat on them. **8** A very large crowd spread their clothes on the road; others were cutting branches from the trees and spreading them on the road. **9** Then the crowds who went ahead of him and those who followed shouted:

    Hosanna to the Son of David!
    Blessed is he who comes in the name of the Lord!^B
    Hosanna in the highest heaven!

10 When he entered Jerusalem, the whole city was in an uproar, saying, "Who is this?" **11** The crowds were saying, "This is the prophet Jesus from Nazareth in Galilee."

Cleansing the Temple

12 Jesus went into the temple^C and threw out all those buying and selling. He overturned the tables of the money changers and the chairs of those selling doves. **13** He said to them, "It is written, **my house will be called a house of prayer,**^D but you are making it **a den of thieves!**"^E

Children Praise Jesus

14 The blind and the lame came to him in the temple, and he healed them. **15** When the chief priests and the scribes saw the wonders that he did and the children shouting in the temple, "*Hosanna* to the Son of David!" they were indignant **16** and said to him, "Do you hear what these children are saying?"

Jesus replied, "Yes, have you never read:
    You have prepared^F praise
     from the mouths of infants
     and nursing babies?"^G

17 Then he left them, went out of the city to Bethany, and spent the night there.

The Barren Fig Tree

18 Early in the morning, as he was returning to the city, he was hungry. **19** Seeing a lone fig tree by the road, he went up to it and found nothing on it except leaves. And he said to it, "May no fruit ever come from you again!" At once the fig tree withered.

20 When the disciples saw it, they were amazed and said, "How did the fig tree wither so quickly?"

21 Jesus answered them, "Truly I tell you, if you have faith and do not doubt, you will not only do what was done to the fig tree, but even if you tell this mountain, 'Be lifted up and thrown into the sea,' it will be done. **22** And if you believe, you will receive whatever you ask for in prayer."

^A **21:5** Is 62:11; Zch 9:9   ^B **21:9** Ps 118:25–26   ^C **21:12** Other mss add *of God*   ^D **21:13** Is 56:7   ^E **21:13** Jr 7:11   ^F **21:16** Or *restored*   ^G **21:16** Ps 8:2

21:1 The **Mount of Olives** was a large hill on the eastern side of Jerusalem. It was mentioned in Zch 14:4, and ancient rabbis interpreted the text as referring to Messiah (Mt 24:3). **Bethphage** was a small village on the slopes of the hill.
21:2–3 Jesus may have made previous arrangements to use the animals mentioned here, but since Matthew often refers to Jesus's supernatural knowledge (17:27; 20:17–19), it is also possible that Jesus used supernatural knowledge here, in which case he has commandeered the animals in a show of messianic authority.
21:4–5 The formula that Matthew used to introduce the OT quotation affirms that God spoke through the OT prophets. The quotation is a combination of one line from Is 62:11 and excerpts from Zch 9:9. The first text refers to the coming of the Lord, while the second refers to the approach of the divine King. Both texts imply Jesus's deity and messiahship.
21:6–7 The mother **donkey** was led alongside her untamed **colt** in order to calm it. The **clothes** of bystanders were draped across the backs of both animals, serving as makeshift decorative saddles. The words **he sat**

on them refer to Jesus sitting atop the robes, not to his riding both animals simultaneously.
21:8 The scattering of **clothes** and **branches** in Jesus's path recalls the way in which kings entered their royal cities (2Kg 9:13).
21:9 These words of celebration echo Ps 118:25–26. The people pleaded for salvation from God and blessed God for sending a deliverer who came in the **name of the Lord**.
21:10–11 All Jerusalem was also stirred when Jesus was born. See Mt 2:3. They asked the right question, but they got an incomplete answer.
21:12 Since Roman currency had idolatrous images stamped on it, the temple accepted only idol-free Tyrian currency. **Money changers** exchanged pagan coins for acceptable currency for a fee. Merchants sold sacrificial animals to those who had traveled long distances. **Doves** were sacrificed by poor pilgrims who could not afford lambs (Lv 5:7). Although the merchants and money changers normally performed their services outside the temple precincts, they occasionally set up shop in the court of the Gentiles.
21:13 Jesus's quote is from Is 56:7 and Jr 7:11. The commotion in the court made the temple unsuitable as a **house of prayer**. Zechariah

6:12–13 foretold that Messiah would purify the temple. See also Zch 14:21.
21:14 Evidence suggests that first-century Jews extended the demands of Lv 21:16–20 to exclude handicapped persons from entering the temple (2Sm 5:8, LXX). By healing the **blind** and **lame**, Jesus identified himself as Messiah (Is 35:5–6). By doing so in the **temple**, he demonstrated that the handicapped were welcomed by a gracious God.
21:15–16 Both the wonders performed by Jesus and the words spoken by the **children** identified Jesus as the Son of David and Messiah (see notes at v. 14 and 1:1). Jesus argued from Ps 8:2 that the children's celebration was appropriate and divinely inspired. After all, God had **prepared praise from the mouths of infants**.
21:17–19 On his way from **Bethany** to Jerusalem, Jesus passed again through Bethphage (v. 1), meaning, "the house of unripe figs." In light of Mc 5:7, the fruitless **fig tree** symbolized Israel's moral barrenness. The cursing of the tree forewarned of God's coming judgment against Jerusalem and its temple.
21:20–22 Jesus's disciples apparently overlooked the symbolic significance of Jesus's

The Authority of Jesus Challenged

²³ When he entered the temple, the chief priests and the elders of the people came to him as he was teaching and said, "By what authority are you doing these things? Who gave you this authority?"

²⁴ Jesus answered them, "I will also ask you one question, and if you answer it for me, then I will tell you by what authority I do these things. ²⁵ Did John's baptism come from heaven, or was it of human origin?"

They discussed it among themselves, "If we say, 'From heaven,' he will say to us, 'Then why didn't you believe him?' ²⁶ But if we say, 'Of human origin,' we're afraid of the crowd, because everyone considers John to be a prophet." ²⁷ So they answered Jesus, "We don't know."

And he said to them, "Neither will I tell you by what authority I do these things.

The Parable of the Two Sons

²⁸ "What do you think? A man had two sons. He went to the first and said, 'My son, go work in the vineyard today.'

²⁹ "He answered, 'I don't want to,' but later he changed his mind and went. ³⁰ Then the man went to the other and said the same thing. 'I will, sir,' he answered, but he didn't go. ³¹ Which of the two did his father's will?"

They said, "The first."

Jesus said to them, "Truly I tell you, tax collectors and prostitutes are entering the kingdom of God before you. ³² For John came to you in the way of righteousness, and you didn't believe him. Tax collectors and prostitutes did believe him; but you, when you saw it, didn't even change your minds then and believe him.

The Parable of the Vineyard Owner

³³ "Listen to another parable: There was a landowner, who planted a vineyard, put a fence around it, dug a winepress in it, and built a watchtower. He leased it to tenant farmers and went away. ³⁴ When the time came to harvest fruit, he sent his servants to the farmers to collect his fruit. ³⁵ The farmers took his servants, beat one, killed another, and stoned a third. ³⁶ Again, he sent other servants, more than the first group, and they did the same to them. ³⁷ Finally, he sent his son to them. 'They will respect my son,' he said.

³⁸ "But when the tenant farmers saw the son, they said to each other, 'This is the heir. Come, let's kill him and take his inheritance.' ³⁹ So they seized him, threw him out of the vineyard, and killed him. ⁴⁰ Therefore, when the owner of the vineyard comes, what will he do to those farmers?"

⁴¹ "He will completely destroy those terrible men," they told him, "and lease his vineyard to other farmers who will give him his fruit at the harvest."

⁴² Jesus said to them, "Have you never read in the Scriptures:

The stone that the builders rejected
has become the cornerstone.ᴬ
This is what the Lord has done
and it is wonderful in our eyes?ᴮ

⁴³ Therefore I tell you, the kingdom of God will be taken away from you and given to a people producing its fruit. ⁴⁴ Whoever falls on this stone will be broken to pieces; but on whomever it falls, it will shatter him."ᶜ

⁴⁵ When the chief priests and the Pharisees heard his parables, they knew he was speaking about them. ⁴⁶ Although they were looking

---

ᴬ**21:42** Lit *the head of the corner*　ᴮ**21:42** Ps 118:22–23　ᶜ**21:44** Some mss omit this verse

---

miracle and simply focused on the power of his command. Although **this mountain** could be a reference to the Mount of Olives (Zch 14:4) or the temple mount, it probably referred to God's power to do humanly impossible things in response to prayer (1Co 13:2).

21:23–27 John the Baptist said that Christ would pour out the transforming Spirit on his disciples and punish the unrepentant with fiery judgment (see note at 3:11). John also identified Jesus as the promised Christ (see note at 3:14). Admission that John was a prophet would require the Jewish leaders to acknowledge Jesus's authority also.

21:28–32 The father here symbolizes God. The **first** son symbolizes notorious sinners like **tax collectors** and **prostitutes** who initially rebel against the Father's will but later repent and obey. The other son represents the chief priests and elders who promised obedience to God but never fulfilled their commitment.

21:33–41 The **landowner** represents God; the **vineyard** stands first for Israel (Is 5:1–7), then Jerusalem, then the kingdom; the **tenant farmers** represent the Jewish leaders; the **servants**, the OT prophets; the **son**, Jesus. Because the Jewish leaders refused to give God the fruits of righteousness that he demanded and because they rejected and murdered his Son, God would destroy them, take his kingdom away from them, and entrust it to Jesus's disciples.

21:42–44 Jesus quoted Ps 118:22–23, the same psalm from which the people in Mt 21:9 drew their expressions of praise. The image of a **stone** that was **rejected** as worthless by builders but later used as the **cornerstone**—the most important part of the structure—foreshadowed the fact that though Jesus was rejected by the Jewish leaders, he would be vindicated by God and would become the focal point of God's kingdom. Verse 43 interprets and applies the parable of the vineyard owner: God would take his **kingdom** away from the Jewish leaders and entrust it to Jesus's disciples. Verse 44 alludes to Is 8:14–15 and Dn 2:34,44–45. In Isaiah, the stone is the Lord over whom the people of Israel stumble, fall, and are broken. By identifying himself as the stone, Jesus strongly implied his deity. In Daniel, the stone symbolized a powerful kingdom that would destroy all others and endure forever. The OT allusion thus describes Jesus's deity and kingship and the destruction of all who reject him.

21:45–46 The background for these verses is 21:10–11.

#57　99 Essential Christian Truths

GOD IS TRUTHFUL

The Scriptures are clear that in God there is no falsehood (Ti 1:2; Heb 6:18). God represents things as they really are. Everything he says can be trusted because God guarantees the truth of everything he tells us. The call for humans to be honest and not to bear false witness is rooted in the utter truthfulness of our Creator. Telling the truth is one way we bear the image of God, whose Son is "the way, the truth, and the life" (Jn 14:6).

for a way to arrest him, they feared the crowds, because the people regarded him as a prophet.

The Parable of the Wedding Banquet

22 Once more Jesus spoke to them in parables: ² "The kingdom of heaven is like a king who gave a wedding banquet for his son. ³ He sent his servants to summon those invited to the banquet, but they didn't want to come. ⁴ Again, he sent out other servants and said, 'Tell those who are invited: See, I've prepared my dinner; my oxen and fattened cattle have been slaughtered, and everything is ready. Come to the wedding banquet.'

⁵ "But they paid no attention and went away, one to his own farm, another to his business, ⁶ while the rest seized his servants, mistreated them, and killed them. ⁷ The king^A was enraged, and he sent out his troops, killed those murderers, and burned down their city.

⁸ "Then he told his servants, 'The banquet is ready, but those who were invited were not worthy. ⁹ Go then to where the roads exit the city and invite everyone you find to the banquet.' ¹⁰ So those servants went out on the roads and gathered everyone they found, both evil and good. The wedding banquet was filled with guests.^B ¹¹ When the king came in to see the guests, he saw a man there who was not dressed for a wedding. ¹² So he said to him, 'Friend, how did you get in here without wedding clothes?' The man was speechless.

¹³ "Then the king told the attendants, 'Tie him up hand and foot,^C and throw him into the outer darkness, where there will be weeping and gnashing of teeth.'

¹⁴ "For many are invited, but few are chosen."

God and Caesar

¹⁵ Then the Pharisees went and plotted how to trap him by what he said.^D ¹⁶ So they sent their disciples to him, along with the Herodians. "Teacher," they said, "we know that you are truthful and teach truthfully the way of God. You don't care what anyone thinks nor do you show partiality.^E ¹⁷ Tell us, then, what you think. Is it lawful to pay taxes to Caesar or not?"

¹⁸ Perceiving their malicious intent, Jesus said, "Why are you testing me, hypocrites? ¹⁹ Show me the coin used for the tax." They brought him a denarius.^F ²⁰ "Whose image and inscription is this?" he asked them.

²¹ "Caesar's," they said to him.

Then he said to them, "Give, then, to Caesar the things that are Caesar's, and to God the things that are God's." ²² When they heard this, they were amazed. So they left him and went away.

The Sadducees and the Resurrection

²³ That same day some Sadducees, who say there is no resurrection, came up to him and questioned him: ²⁴ "Teacher, Moses said, **if a man dies, having no children, his brother is to marry his wife and raise up offspring for his brother.**^G ²⁵ Now there were seven brothers among us. The first got married and died. Having no offspring, he left his wife to his brother. ²⁶ The same thing happened to the second also, and the third, and so on to all seven. ²⁷ Last of all, the woman died. ²⁸ In the resurrection, then, whose wife will she be of the seven? For they all had married her."^H

²⁹ Jesus answered them, "You are mistaken, because you don't know the Scriptures or the

---

^A 22:7 Other mss read *But when the (that) king heard about it he* ^B 22:10 Lit *those reclining* (to eat) ^C 22:13 Other mss add *take him away* ^D 22:15 Lit *trap him in a word* ^E 22:16 Lit *don't look on the face of men* ^F 22:19 A denarius = one day's wage ^G 22:24 Dt 25:5 ^H 22:28 Lit *all had her*

22:1–7 This parable is an allegory of Israel's history. The **king** represents God; the **son**, Jesus; the **servants**, the prophets and possibly Jesus's disciples; and the **wedding banquet** symbolizes the great messianic feast that Jews expected to share with Messiah at the beginning of his rule. Those who rejected, persecuted, and murdered the servants represent OT Israel and their rejection of the prophets. The destruction of the **city** represents God's judgment on those who refuse to honor his Son. This destruction, like the penalty described in v. 13, portrays eternal punishment but may also hint at the destruction of Jerusalem in AD 70.

22:8–12 The **guests** represent Jesus's disciples who are invited into the kingdom despite their unworthiness. The improperly dressed guest represents a false disciple (7:15–23). His presence seems initially to honor the Son, but his refusal to wear festive garments dishonors him. Similarly, many false disciples appear to honor by calling him "Lord," but their lack of true faith and repentance offends him.

22:13–14 On the guest's punishment, see note at 8:12. Many people are **invited** to

God's kingdom, but only those who repent and honor the Son are **chosen** to enter.

22:15–17 The question was a trap. By expressing approval, Jesus would have seemed to be supporting the Roman occupation. On the other hand, by disapproving, he would have been seen as treasonous against Rome. Matthew mentioned the **Herodians** only here. Little is known about them. They were probably Jews who preferred the rule of the Herodian dynasty over the rule of Roman procurators.

22:18 On **hypocrites**, see note at 6:2–4.

22:19 The parallel texts in Mark and Luke refer to the coin as a **denarius** (see notes at vv. 20–22 and 20:1–7), but Matthew also uses the more precise term for "state coin" (Gk *nomisma*). This may reflect his background as a tax collector.

22:20–22 The denarius was a Roman silver coin that bore a portrait of Emperor Tiberius, a Latin superscription that said "Tiberius Caesar, son of the Divine Augustus," an image of a goddess, and superscripted titles of the Roman high priest. Thus the coins were loaded with propaganda for the worship of emperors and pagan gods, and the

Jews considered them to be idolatrous. Jesus approved the payment of taxes to Rome. However, he said that coins ultimately belong to the one whose **image** it bears, which implied that all a person is and has belongs to God since we bear God's image and likeness (Gn 1:26–27).

22:23 The **Sadducees** believed that humans cease to exist at the moment of physical death (Ac 23:6–8; Josephus, *Ant.* 18.16; *War* 2.164–65).

22:24–28 The Sadducees appealed to the law of levirate marriage (Dt 25:5) in an attempt to disprove the doctrine of resurrection. Although many first-century Jews practiced polygamy, they generally rejected polyandry (a woman having multiple husbands). The Sadducees tried to force Jesus either to reject the doctrine of resurrection or admit the legitimacy of polyandry.

22:29–33 Like **angels**, resurrected people will not marry because they are eternal and have no need to procreate. This shows that the dilemma described by the Sadducees is false. The Sadducees accepted only the Pentateuch (Genesis–Deuteronomy) as Scripture, and so they dismissed resurrection texts like

power of God. ³⁰ For in the resurrection they neither marry nor are given in marriage but are like^ angels in heaven. ³¹ Now concerning the resurrection of the dead, haven't you read what was spoken to you by God: ³² I am the God of Abraham and the God of Isaac and the God of Jacob?ᴮ Heᶜ is not the God of the dead, but of the living."

³³ And when the crowds heard this, they were astonished at his teaching.

The Primary Commands

³⁴ When the Pharisees heard that he had silenced the Sadducees, they came together. ³⁵ And one of them, an expert in the law, asked a question to test him: ³⁶ "Teacher, which command in the law is the greatest?"

³⁷ He said to him, "Love the Lord your God with all your heart, with all your soul, and with all your mind.ᴰ ³⁸ This is the greatest and most important ᴱ command. ³⁹ The second is like it: Love your neighbor as yourself.ᶠ ⁴⁰ All the Law and the Prophets depend ᴳ on these two commands."

The Question about the Messiah

⁴¹ While the Pharisees were together, Jesus questioned them, ⁴² "What do you think about the Messiah? Whose son is he?"

They replied, "David's."

⁴³ He asked them, "How is it then that David, inspired by the Spirit,ᴴ calls him 'Lord':

⁴⁴ The Lord declared to my Lord,
'Sit at my right hand
until I put your enemies
under your feet'?ᴵᴶ

⁴⁵ "If David calls him 'Lord,' how, then, can he be his son?" ⁴⁶ No one was able to answer him at all,ᴷ and from that day no one dared to question him anymore.

Religious Hypocrites Denounced

23 Then Jesus spoke to the crowds and to his disciples: ² "The scribes and the Pharisees are seated in the chair of Moses. ³ Therefore do whatever they tell you, and observe it. But don't do what they do, because they don't practice what they teach. ⁴ They tie up heavy loads that are hard to carryᴸ and put them on people's shoulders, but they themselves aren't willing to lift a finger to move them. ⁵ They do everythingᴹ to be seen by others: They enlarge their phylacteries and lengthen their tassels.ᴺ ⁶ They love the place of honor at banquets, the front seats in the synagogues, ⁷ greetings in the marketplaces, and to be called 'Rabbi' by people.

⁸ "But you are not to be called 'Rabbi,' because you have one Teacher,ᴼ and you are all brothers and sisters. ⁹ Do not call anyone on earth your father, because you have one Father, who is in heaven. ¹⁰ You are not to be called instructors either, because you have one Instructor, the Messiah. ¹¹ The greatest among you will be your servant. ¹² Whoever exalts himself will be humbled, and whoever humbles himself will be exalted.

¹³ "Woe to you, scribes and Pharisees, hypocrites! You shut the door of the kingdom of heaven in people's faces. For you don't go in, and you don't allow those entering to go in.ᴾ

¹⁵ "Woe to you, scribes and Pharisees, hypocrites! You travel over land and sea to make one convert, and when he becomes one, you make him twice as much a child of hell as you are!

¹⁶ "Woe to you, blind guides, who say, 'Whoever takes an oath by the temple, it means nothing. But whoever takes an oath by the gold

^22:30 Other mss add God's   ᴮ22:32 Ex 3:6,15–16   ᶜ22:32 Other mss read God   ᴰ22:37 Dt 6:5   ᴱ22:38 Lit and first   ᶠ22:39 Lv 19:18   ᴳ22:40 Or hang   ᴴ22:43 Lit David in Spirit   ᴵ22:44 Other mss read until I make your enemies your footstool'   ᴶ22:44 Ps 110:1   ᴷ22:46 Lit answer him a word   ᴸ23:4 Other mss omit that are hard to carry   ᴹ23:5 Lit do all their works   ᴺ23:5 Other mss add on their robes   ᴼ23:8 Other mss add the Christ   ᴾ23:13 Some mss include v. 14: "Woe to you, scribes and Pharisees, hypocrites! You devour widows' houses and make long prayers just for show. This is why you will receive a harsher punishment."

Is 26:19 and Dn 12:2. In order to convince them of the resurrection, Jesus needed to appeal to the books they revered. Thus he cited Ex 3:6,15–16, where God spoke to Moses from the burning bush, and he referred to the dead patriarchs in a manner that implied that they still existed, i.e., **I am the God of Abraham** rather than "I was the God of Abraham."
22:34–39 Deuteronomy 6:4–5, known as the *Shema*, was recited several times daily by faithful Jews.
22:40 Deuteronomy 6:4 and Lv 19:18 summarized the essence of God's demands in Scripture by calling individuals to love God and their fellow man (Mt 5:43–47).
22:41–42 After having been questioned by his opponents repeatedly (vv. 17,23–28,34–36), Jesus entrapped them with a question of his own. *Son* was used in ancient Greek and Hebrew to describe any male descendant. Due to several OT prophecies, the Christ was expected to be **David's** descendant (see note at 1:1).

22:43–46 Psalm 110:1 describes Yahweh's command to David's **Lord** (Gk *kurios*; Hb *adon*). "Lord" was a title of authority and/ or deity that portrayed the Christ as David's divine superior, not just his descendant. Psalm 110:1–4 is quoted more often in the NT than any other OT passage.
23:1–2 Chair of Moses may figuratively identify the **scribes** and **Pharisees** as representatives of Moses as they taught the OT. Several centuries after Jesus, seats reserved for teachers in synagogues were regularly called "Moses' seat."
23:3 Jesus did not intend to impose all the teachings of the Pharisees on his disciples. After all, he criticized many of their beliefs. His command meant "obey the Pharisees' teachings whenever they accurately interpret the Scriptures."
23:4 The Pharisees sought to "build a fence around the law," i.e., establish rules so strict that people would not even come close to breaking God's law (Ac 15:10).

23:5–7 Phylacteries were small boxes containing tiny scrolls of Ex 13:2–16 and Dt 6:4–9; 11:13–21. They were worn by faithful Jewish men on one arm and on the forehead (Dt 6:8; 11:18). **Tassels** made of blue or white threads were worn at the four corners of the outer garment (Nm 15:38–39; Dt 22:12). The Pharisees enlarged the phylacteries and lengthened the tassels in a bid to appear more pious.
23:8–12 Jesus prohibited the use of honorific titles for spiritual leaders that might encourage a sense of superiority in them or detract from the reverence that is properly due the **Father** and **Messiah**.
23:13–15 Woe was a term used by OT prophets to express condemnation (Is 5:8–23; Hab 2:6–9). Pharisees prevented people from entering the **kingdom of heaven** by discouraging them from following Jesus.
23:16–22 First-century laws declared some oaths to be valid and others invalid. The system was corrupt insomuch as it allowed

of the temple is bound by his oath.'ᴬ ¹⁷ Blind fools! For which is greater, the gold or the temple that sanctified the gold? ¹⁸ Also, 'Whoever takes an oath by the altar, it means nothing; but whoever takes an oath by the gift that is on it is bound by his oath.' ¹⁹ Blind people!ᴮ For which is greater, the gift or the altar that sanctifies the gift? ²⁰ Therefore, the one who takes an oath by the altar takes an oath by it and by everything on it. ²¹ The one who takes an oath by the temple takes an oath by it and by him who dwells in it. ²² And the one who takes an oath by heaven takes an oath by God's throne and by him who sits on it.

²³ "Woe to you, scribes and Pharisees, hypocrites! You pay a tenth ofᶜ mint, dill, and cumin, and yet you have neglected the more important matters of the law — justice, mercy, and faithfulness.ᴰ These things should have been done without neglecting the others. ²⁴ Blind guides! You strain out a gnat, but gulp down a camel!

²⁵ "Woe to you, scribes and Pharisees, hypocrites! You clean the outside of the cup and dish, but inside they are full of greedᴱ and self-indulgence. ²⁶ Blind Pharisee! First clean the inside of the cup,ᶠ so that the outside of itᴳ may also become clean.

²⁷ "Woe to you, scribes and Pharisees, hypocrites! You are like whitewashed tombs, which appear beautiful on the outside, but inside are full of the bones of the dead and every kind of impurity. ²⁸ In the same way, on the outside you seem righteous to people, but inside you are full of hypocrisy and lawlessness.

²⁹ "Woe to you, scribes and Pharisees, hypocrites! You build the tombs of the prophets and decorate the graves of the righteous,

³⁰ and you say, 'If we had lived in the days of our ancestors, we wouldn't have taken part with them in shedding the prophets' blood.' ³¹ So you testify against yourselves that you are descendants of those who murdered the prophets. ³² Fill up, then, the measure of your ancestors' sins!

³³ "Snakes! Brood of vipers! How can you escape being condemned to hell?ᴴ ³⁴ This is why I am sending you prophets, sages, and scribes. Some of them you will kill and crucify, and some of them you will flog in your synagogues and pursue from town to town. ³⁵ So all the righteous blood shed on the earth will be charged to you,ᴵ from the blood of righteous Abel to the blood of Zechariah, son of Berechiah, whom you murdered between the sanctuary and the altar. ³⁶ Truly I tell you, all these things will come on this generation.

Jesus's Lamenting over Jerusalem

³⁷ "Jerusalem, Jerusalem, who kills the prophets and stones those who are sent to her. How often I wanted to gather your children together, as a hen gathers her chicksᴶ under her wings, but you were not willing! ³⁸ See, your house is left to you desolate. ³⁹ For I tell you, you will not see me again until you say, '**Blessed is he who comes in the name of the Lord'!** "ᴷ

Destruction of the Temple Predicted

24 As Jesus left and was going out of the temple, his disciples came up and called his attention to its buildings. ² He replied to them, "Do you see all these things? Truly I tell you, not one stone will be left here on another that will not be thrown down."

ᴬ**23:16** Lit *is obligated*, also in v. 18   ᴮ**23:19** Other mss read *Fools and blind*   ᶜ**23:23** Or *You tithe*   ᴰ**23:23** Or *faith*   ᴱ**23:25** Or *full of violence*   ᶠ**23:26** Other mss add *and dish*   ᴳ**23:26** Other mss read *of them*   ᴴ**23:33** Lit *escape from the judgment of gehenna*   ᴵ**23:35** Lit *will come on you*   ᴶ**23:37** Or *as a mother bird gathers her young*   ᴷ**23:39** Ps 118:26

---

loopholes that justified lies and manipulated naïve or credulous people. See note at 5:33–37.

23:23–24 In accordance with Lv 27:30; Nm 18:21–32; and Dt 14:22, the scribes and Pharisees meticulously tithed a **tenth** of everything, including their tiny garden herbs. Jesus did not discourage this since **these things should have been done.** However, he rebuked the Jewish leaders for obsessing with ritual matters while overlooking the true essence of religion as described in Mc 5:24. Like those who strain a **gnat** out of their drink but leave a **camel** floating in it, they were obsessed with tiny matters but overlooked important ones.

23:25–26 Some first-century rabbis debated whether cleansing the **outside** or **inside** of vessels was more important. Jesus cited this to illustrate their obsession with ritual purity and their neglect of inner spiritual purity.

23:27–28 First-century Jews **whitewashed** the **tombs** in Jerusalem to alert people to their location so they would not unintentionally draw too near and thus defile themselves. The whitewash also beautified the tombs. Despite this outer beauty, Jewish purity laws regarded the inside of tombs as

defiled. Jesus said this resembled individuals whose outer piety (the whitewash) masks an inner corruption (spiritual defilement).

23:29–32 By persecuting God's representatives (John the Baptist, Jesus, the disciples), the scribes and Pharisees continued the rebellion of their ancestors and probed the limits of God's patience.

23:33 On **snakes** and **brood of vipers**, see note at 3:7–9.

23:34 This echoes Lk 11:49 but identifies Jesus as "the wisdom of God."

23:35–36 Jesus, in an apparent allusion to the coming destruction of the temple in AD 70, warned that his generation would suffer God's wrath for its abuse of the **righteous** Abel's murder is recorded in Gn 4, while Zechariah's is recorded in 2Ch 24:20–21. Second Chronicles was the final book of the OT in the typical order of the Hebrew Bible, so the martyrdoms of **Abel** and **Zechariah** were recorded in the first and last books of the Hebrew OT. Thus Jesus apparently meant to cite the whole span of martyrdom in the OT. Some interpreters argue that he confused the Zechariah of 2 Chronicles (identified as the son of Jehoiada) with the prophet Zechariah (described as the son of Berechiah in Zch

1:1). However, the Hebrew phrase **son of** was used to identify sons, grandsons, and even remote descendants. Consequently, Jesus probably identified the Zechariah of 2 Chronicles by an earlier or later ancestor. It is not unreasonable to suggest that both Zechariahs had ancestors named **Berechiah.**

23:37 In Ps 17:8; 91:4; and Is 31:5, the image of a **hen** sheltering her **chicks** portrayed the Lord's protection of Israel. By rejecting Jesus, **Jerusalem** rejected God's protection. The image implies Jesus's identity as the Lord.

23:38–39 The word **desolate** means "abandoned." It denotes God's abandonment of his **house**, the temple. This occurred when Jesus departed from the temple with the words **you will not see me again . . . 'Blessed is he who comes in the name of the Lord!'** echoes Ps 118:26 and was the jubilant greeting that welcomed Jesus into Jerusalem in Mt 21:9. Before the week was out, many of these same voices would be calling for Jesus's death.

24:1–2 This remarkable prophecy must have stunned the disciples. Josephus (*Ant.* 15.392) stated that the temple was constructed of blocks of white limestone that measured thirty-seven and a half feet long, twelve feet

◥ Christ as King

A King: Appointed by God as a shepherd for his people, administering justice, and leading in the way of righteousness; devotes himself to and delights himself in the law of the Lord and bears witness to the truth for the blessing of God to pour out over his people and into the world *(Dt 17:15–20; Pss 1–2; Jn 18:36–37)*.

WHO WAS AN OLD TESTAMENT KING?

DOs

- Appointed as king according to the Lord's choice *(Dt 17:15)*
- Appointed from among the Israelites *(Dt 17:15)*

The King . . .
- Must write a copy of the law for himself on a scroll in the presence of the priests *(Dt 17:18)*
- Must read from his copy of the law every day of his life so he may learn to fear the Lord and obey him *(Dt 17:19)*

DON'Ts

- Don't appoint a foreigner as king *(Dt 17:15)*
- Don't appoint a non-Israelite as king *(Dt 17:15)*

The King . . .
- Must not acquire many horses *(Dt 17:16)*
- Must not acquire many wives *(Dt 17:17)*
- Must not acquire large amounts of silver and gold *(Dt 17:17)*
- Must not exalt himself above his countrymen *(Dt 17:20)*
- Must not turn away from the Lord *(Dt 17:20)*

WHAT RESPONSIBILITIES DID THE KING HAVE?

- Lead the people to worship and obey the Lord *(Jdg 21:25)*
- Judge the people, go out before them, and fight their battles *(1Sm 8:20)*

FROM WHOM DID THE LORD APPOINT HIS KINGS OVER HIS PEOPLE?

- Kings would come from Abraham through Sarah *(Gn 17:6,16)*.
- Kings would come from Jacob *(Gn 35:11)*.
- Kings would come from Judah *(Gn 49:10)*.
- Kings would come from David *(2Sm 7:11–16)*.

THE DAVIDIC COVENANT

- The Lord would make a house, a dynasty, for David and raise up his descendant to sit on his throne *(2Sm 7:11–12)*.

- David's descendant would build a house (temple) for the Lord's name *(2Sm 7:13)*.

- The Lord would be a father to David's descendant, and he would be a son to the Lord *(2Sm 7:14)*.

- The Lord would discipline David's descendant but never remove his faithful love from him *(2Sm 7:14–15)*.

- David's house and kingdom would endure forever and his throne would be established forever *(2Sm 7:16)*.

SOLOMON, SON OF DAVID

- Solomon rode on David's mule to be anointed as king, and then he sat down on David's throne *(1Kg 1:32–40)*.

- Solomon built the temple for the Lord's name, and the glory of the Lord filled the temple *(1Kg 5–8)*.

- The Lord chose Solomon to be his son, and he would be his Father *(1Ch 28:6)*.

- Solomon's many wives turned his heart away to follow other gods, so the Lord took away the peace of the kingdom and sent enemies against Solomon; he also took the kingdom away from Solomon's son, leaving only one tribe to him for the sake of David *(1Kg 11)*.

- Solomon failed to persevere in keeping the Lord's commands, so his kingdom was not established forever *(1Ch 28:7)*.

HOW WAS JESUS A KING?

HE WAS A DESCENDANT OF...

 **Abraham**
Matthew 1:1–2,17; Luke 3:34

 **Jacob**
Matthew 1:2
Luke 3:34

 Judah
Matthew 1:2–3;
Luke 3:33

 **David**
Matthew 1:1,
6,17; Luke 3:31

DOs

The King . . .

- Must write a copy of the law for himself on a scroll in the presence of the priests (Dt 17:18)

- Must read from the law every day so he may learn to fear and obey the Lord (Dt 17:19)

Jesus . . .

- Taught with authority, giving the full meaning of the law and fulfilling the Law and the Prophets (Mt 5–7)

- Had the law in his heart, quoting from it to fight temptation from the devil (Mt 4:1–11)

DON'Ts

The King . . .

- Must not acquire many horses (Dt 17:16)

- Must not acquire many wives (Dt 17:17)

- Must not acquire large amounts of silver and gold (Dt 17:17)

- Must not exalt himself above his countrymen (Dt 17:20)

- Must not turn away from the Lord (Dt 17:20)

Jesus . . .

- Borrowed a donkey for his entry into Jerusalem (Mt 21:1–11)

- Has one bride—the church (Rv 21)

- Had no place to lay his head (Mt 8:20)

- Washed his disciples' feet as a servant (Jn 13:1–17)

- Was tempted in every way as we are, yet without sin (Heb 4:15)

HOW IS JESUS THE KING?

THE DAVIDIC COVENANT

- The Lord would make David a house (dynasty), and place a descendant on his throne (2Sm 7:11–12).

- David's descendant would build a house (temple) for the Lord's name (2Sm 7:13).

- The Lord would be a father to David's descendant (2Sm 7:14).

- The Lord would discipline David's descendant but never remove his faithful love from him (2Sm 7:14–15).

- David's throne will be established forever (2Sm 7:16).

JESUS, THE SON OF DAVID

- Jesus is the promised Son of David (Mt 1:1–17).

- Jesus declared himself to be the temple of God, raised up in three days (Jn 2:13–22).

- Jesus is the Son of God (Mt 3:16–17; 17:5; Lk 1:30–33; Heb 1:5).

- Jesus is the good shepherd who laid down his life for his sheep, so they will never lose God's faithful love (Mt 26:26–29; Jn 10:11–18, 27–30).

- Jesus received all authority in heaven and on earth, and he will be with his disciples forever (Mt 28:18–20; Lk 1:32–33)

God expected his image-bearers to rule over the creation. But sin brought exile from the garden kingdom and separation from the King, resulting in suffering and injustice. As God promised, a holy and righteous King—**Jesus**—would come to set everything right. The Son of God's perfect obedience and sacrificial death were vindicated in his resurrection, and he has received all authority in heaven and on earth. From his throne at the Father's right hand, he pours out the Holy Spirit on his ambassadors to proclaim the gospel of the kingdom until his enemies are made his footstool (Ps 110:1). He has won victory over sin and death. At his second coming, his peace will rest over all creation.

Signs of the End of the Age

³ While he was sitting on the Mount of Olives, the disciples approached him privately and said, "Tell us, when will these things happen? And what is the sign of your coming and of the end of the age?"

⁴ Jesus replied to them, "Watch out that no one deceives you. ⁵ For many will come in my name, saying, 'I am the Messiah,' and they will deceive many. ⁶ You are going to hear of wars and rumors of wars. See that you are not alarmed, because these things must take place, but the end is not yet. ⁷ For nation will rise up against nation, and kingdom against kingdom. There will be famines ᴬ and earthquakes in various places. ⁸ All these events are the beginning of labor pains.

Persecutions Predicted

⁹ "Then they will hand you over to be persecuted, and they will kill you. You will be hated by all nations because of my name. ¹⁰ Then many will fall away, betray one another, and hate one another. ¹¹ Many false prophets will rise up and deceive many. ¹² Because lawlessness will multiply, the love of many will grow cold. ¹³ But the one who endures to the end will be saved. ¹⁴ This good news of the kingdom will be proclaimed in all the world ᴮ as a testimony to all nations, and then the end will come.

The Great Tribulation

¹⁵ "So when you see the abomination of desolation,ᶜ spoken of by the prophet Daniel, standing in the holy place" (let the reader understand), ¹⁶ "then those in Judea must flee to the mountains. ¹⁷ A man on the housetopᴰ must not come down to get things out of his house, ¹⁸ and a man in the field must not go back to get his coat. ¹⁹ Woe to pregnant women and nursing mothers in those days! ²⁰ Pray that your escape may not be in winter or on a Sabbath. ²¹ For at that time there will be great distress,ᴱ the kind that hasn't taken place from the beginning of the world until now and never will again. ²² Unless those days were cut short, no one wouldᶠ be saved. But those days will be cut short because of the elect.

²³ "If anyone tells you then, 'See, here is the Messiah!' or, 'Over here!' do not believe it. ²⁴ For false messiahs and false prophets will arise and perform great signs and wonders to lead astray, if possible, even the elect. ²⁵ Take note: I have told you in advance. ²⁶ So if they tell you, 'See, he's in the wilderness!' don't go out; or, 'See, he's in the storerooms!' do not believe it. ²⁷ For as the lightning comes from the east and flashes as far as the west, so will be the coming of the Son of Man. ²⁸ Wherever the carcass is, there the vultures ᴳ will gather.

The Coming of the Son of Man

²⁹ "Immediately after the distress of those days, the sun will be darkened, and the moon will not shed its light; the stars will fall from the sky, and the powers of the heavens will be shaken. ³⁰ Then the sign of the Son of Man will appear in the sky, and then all the peoples of the earth ᴴ will mourn;ᴵ and they will see the Son of Man coming on the clouds of heaven with power and great glory. ³¹ He will send out his angels with a loud trumpet, and they will gather his elect from the four winds, from one end of the sky to the other.

ᴬ 24:7 Other mss add *epidemics*   ᴮ 24:14 Or *in all the inhabited earth*   ᶜ 24:15 Dn 9:27   ᴰ 24:17 Or *roof*   ᴱ 24:21 Or *tribulation,* also in v. 29   ᶠ 24:22 Lit *short, all flesh would not*   ᴳ 24:28 Or *eagles*   ᴴ 24:30 Or *all the tribes of the land*   ᴵ 24:30 Lit *will beat; that is, beat their chests*

The Parable of the Fig Tree

32 "Learn this lesson from the fig tree: As soon as its branch becomes tender and sprouts leaves, you know that summer is near. **33** In the same way, when you see all these things, recognize^A that he^B is near — at the door. **34** Truly I tell you, this generation will certainly not pass away until all these things take place. **35** Heaven and earth will pass away, but my words will never pass away.

No One Knows the Day or Hour

36 "Now concerning that day and hour no one knows — neither the angels of heaven nor the Son^C — except the Father alone. **37** As the days of Noah were, so the coming of the Son of Man will be. **38** For in those days before the flood they were eating and drinking, marrying and giving in marriage, until the day Noah boarded the ark. **39** They didn't know until the flood came and swept them all away. This is the way the coming of the Son of Man will be. **40** Then two men will be in the field; one will be taken and one left. **41** Two women will be grinding grain with a hand mill; one will be taken and one left. **42** Therefore be alert, since you don't know what day^D your Lord is coming. **43** But know this: If the homeowner had known what time^E the thief was coming, he would have stayed alert and not let his house be broken into. **44** This is why you are also to be ready, because the Son of Man is coming at an hour you do not expect.

Faithful Service to Christ

45 "Who then is a faithful and wise servant, whom his master has put in charge of his household, to give them food at the proper time? **46** Blessed is that servant whom the master finds doing his job when he comes. **47** Truly I tell you, he will put him in charge of all his possessions. **48** But if that wicked servant says in his heart,

'My master is delayed,' **49** and starts to beat his fellow servants, and eats and drinks with drunkards, **50** that servant's master will come on a day he does not expect him and at an hour he does not know. **51** He will cut him to pieces and assign him a place with the hypocrites, where there will be weeping and gnashing of teeth.

The Parable of the Ten Virgins

25 "At that time the kingdom of heaven will be like ten virgins^F who took their lamps^G and went out to meet the groom. **2** Five of them were foolish and five were wise. **3** When the foolish took their lamps, they didn't take oil with them; **4** but the wise ones took oil in their flasks with their lamps. **5** When the groom was delayed, they all became drowsy and fell asleep.

6 "In the middle of the night there was a shout: 'Here's the groom! Come out to meet him.'

7 "Then all the virgins got up and trimmed their lamps. **8** The foolish ones said to the wise ones, 'Give us some of your oil, because our lamps are going out.'

9 "The wise ones answered, 'No, there won't be enough for us and for you. Go instead to those who sell oil, and buy some for yourselves.'

10 "When they had gone to buy some, the groom arrived, and those who were ready went in with him to the wedding banquet, and the door was shut. **11** Later the rest of the virgins also came and said, 'Master, master, open up for us!'

12 "He replied, 'Truly I tell you, I don't know you!'

13 "Therefore be alert, because you don't know either the day or the hour."^H

The Parable of the Talents

14 "For it is just like a man about to go on a journey. He called his own servants and entrusted

---

^A**24:33** Or *things, you know*   ^B**24:33** Or *it*; that is, summer   ^C**24:36** Other mss omit *nor the Son*   ^D**24:42** Other mss read *hour*; = time   ^E**24:43** Lit *watch*; a division of the night in ancient times   ^F**25:1** Or *bridesmaids*   ^G**25:1** Or *torches*, also in vv. 3,4,7,8   ^H**25:13** Other mss add *in which the Son of Man is coming.*

---

the elect, his followers both living and dead, from heaven and earth. The angels are **his angels** because he has absolute authority over them (see note at 4:10–11).
24:32–34 All these things refers to the distress that will precede Jesus's return, not the second coming itself. **He is near** means that Christ is prepared to return at any moment, not that he must return immediately after these events unfold. All of these events occurred within Jesus's **generation**, particularly in the circumstances surrounding the fall of Jerusalem in AD 70. Thus Christ's followers must always be ready for his return. Others interpret "this generation" to refer to those alive during the final period of distress before the end.
24:35 Jesus's words have the same reliability and enduring quality as the OT itself (5:18).
24:36–44 Close observation of world events will not enable us to predict the time of

Christ's return. Rather, Jesus's followers should live in a state of constant preparation. Some interpret the words **one will be taken and one left** to mean that some will be gathered by Christ at his return while others will be left behind. Others understand this to mean that some are **taken** in judgment while others are **left** with Christ. On **Son of Man**, see note at 8:18–20.
24:45–51 We must not take advantage of the delay in Christ's return by pursuing sinful pleasures. Rather, we must live each day as if it were the day of his return.
25:1–5 Whereas the previous parable warned against postponing preparation for Christ's coming, this one warns against making preparations that are inadequate for the lengthy delay that precedes his second coming.
25:6–9 The **virgins** least expected the groom to arrive in the **middle of the night**.

This signifies the suddenness of Jesus's return (24:36,42). The **shout** announcing the groom's arrival parallels the trumpet blast in 24:31.
25:10–13 The foolish **virgins** represent those who fail to persevere by waiting for Jesus's return with constant vigilance. **Master, master** (Gk *kurie, kurie*) is identical to the cry of the false disciples in 7:21. **I don't know you** echoes 7:23 and expresses exclusion from Christ's kingdom. The parable does not describe a true disciple who loses his salvation, but a false one whose commitment to Jesus was deficient from the start. By portraying himself as a spiritual bridegroom, Jesus implied his deity. God was often portrayed as a bridegroom in the OT (Is 54:4–6; Ezk 16:7–34; Hs 2:19).
25:14–30 The **man** on the long **journey** symbolizes Jesus and the lengthy delay that will precede his second coming. The **talents**

his possessions to them. ¹⁵ To one he gave five talents,^ to another two talents, and to another one talent, depending on each one's ability. Then he went on a journey. Immediately ¹⁶ the man who had received five talents went, put them to work, and earned five more. ¹⁷ In the same way the man with two earned two more. ¹⁸ But the man who had received one talent went off, dug a hole in the ground, and hid his master's money.

¹⁹ "After a long time the master of those servants came and settled accounts with them. ²⁰ The man who had received five talents approached, presented five more talents, and said, 'Master, you gave me five talents. See, I've earned five more talents.'

²¹ "His master said to him, 'Well done, good and faithful servant! You were faithful over a few things; I will put you in charge of many things. Share your master's joy.'

²² "The man with two talents also approached. He said, 'Master, you gave me two talents. See, I've earned two more talents.'

²³ "His master said to him, 'Well done, good and faithful servant! You were faithful over a few things; I will put you in charge of many things. Share your master's joy.'

²⁴ "The man who had received one talent also approached and said, 'Master, I know you. You're a harsh man, reaping where you haven't sown and gathering where you haven't scattered seed. ²⁵ So I was afraid and went off and hid your talent in the ground. See, you have what is yours.'

²⁶ "His master replied to him, 'You evil, lazy servant! If you knew that I reap where I haven't sown and gather where I haven't scattered, ²⁷ then^B you should have deposited my money with the bankers, and I would have received my money^C back with interest when I returned. ²⁸ "'So take the talent from him and give it to the one who has ten talents. ²⁹ For to everyone who has, more will be given, and he will have more than enough. But from the one who does not have, even what he has will be taken away from him. ³⁰ And throw this good-for-nothing

servant into the outer darkness, where there will be weeping and gnashing of teeth.'

The Sheep and the Goats

³¹ "When the Son of Man comes in his glory, and all the angels^D with him, then he will sit on his glorious throne. ³² All the nations^E will be gathered before him, and he will separate them one from another, just as a shepherd separates the sheep from the goats. ³³ He will put the sheep on his right and the goats on the left. ³⁴ Then the King will say to those on his right, 'Come, you who are blessed by my Father; inherit the kingdom prepared for you from the foundation of the world.

³⁵ "'For I was hungry and you gave me something to eat; I was thirsty and you gave me something to drink; I was a stranger and you took me in; ³⁶ I was naked and you clothed me; I was sick and you took care of me; I was in prison and you visited me.'

³⁷ "Then the righteous will answer him, 'Lord, when did we see you hungry and feed you, or thirsty and give you something to drink? ³⁸ When did we see you a stranger and take you in, or without clothes and clothe you? ³⁹ When did we see you sick, or in prison, and visit you?'

⁴⁰ "And the King will answer them, 'Truly I tell you, whatever you did for one of the least of these brothers and sisters of mine, you did for me.'

⁴¹ "Then he will also say to those on the left, 'Depart from me, you who are cursed, into the eternal fire prepared for the devil and his angels! ⁴² For I was hungry and you gave me nothing to eat; I was thirsty and you gave me nothing to drink; ⁴³ I was a stranger and you didn't take me in; I was naked and you didn't clothe me, sick and in prison and you didn't take care of me.'

⁴⁴ "Then they too will answer, 'Lord, when did we see you hungry, or thirsty, or a stranger, or without clothes, or sick, or in prison, and not help you?'

⁴⁵ "Then he will answer them, 'Truly I tell you, whatever you did not do for one of the least of these, you did not do for me.'

---

^25:15 A talent is worth about 6,000 denarii, or twenty years' wages for a laborer   ^25:26–27 Or *So you knew ... scattered? Then* (as a question)   ^25:27 Lit *received what is mine*   ^25:31 Other mss read *holy angels*   ^25:32 Or *the Gentiles*

#58 99 Essential Christian Truths

ELECTION

Election is the gracious purpose of God, according to which he regenerates, justifies, sanctifies, and glorifies sinners. It is consistent with the free agency of man and comprehends all the means in connection with the end. It is the glorious display of God's sovereign goodness, and is infinitely wise, holy, and unchangeable. It excludes boasting and promotes humility.

(whose value equaled six thousand days of wages) represent the financial resources, gifts, privileges, and opportunities that Jesus entrusts to his disciples. The **faithful** servants (true disciples) used their gifts and resources responsibly and were generously rewarded. The **evil, lazy servant** (a false disciple) failed to use the resources and was severely punished. He attempted to excuse his failure by assaulting the character of his **master** (v. 24). However, the master's treatment of the other servants demonstrates that the wicked servant's slander was unfair.

25:31–46 This passage uses figurative language (**shepherd ... sheep ... goats**) drawn from Ezk 34:17–19 in Mt 25:32–33, but the rest

is too literal to be classified as a parable. The passage is therefore best taken as a literal description of the final judgment. Verses 33 and 34 define the title **Son of Man** as **King** (see note at 8:18–20). The King, Jesus, will judge people based on their reception and treatment of **the least of** his **brothers and sisters**. In light of 12:50, the words refer to Jesus's followers who seek to do God's will. Humble and compassionate treatment of Jesus's followers necessarily accompanies acceptance of the gospel that they proclaim (10:40–42). Those who show no compassion to Jesus's followers betray their lack of devotion to him. As in 7:21–23, Jesus identifies himself as the final Judge, a role that Jews expected the Lord to fulfill.

⁴⁶ "And they will go away into eternal punishment, but the righteous into eternal life."

The Plot to Kill Jesus

26 When Jesus had finished saying all these things, he told his disciples, ² "You know^A that the Passover takes place after two days, and the Son of Man will be handed over to be crucified."

³ Then the chief priests^B and the elders of the people assembled in the courtyard of the high priest, who was named Caiaphas, ⁴ and they conspired to arrest Jesus in a treacherous way and kill him. ⁵ "Not during the festival," they said, "so there won't be rioting among the people."

The Anointing at Bethany

⁶ While Jesus was in Bethany at the house of Simon the leper,^C ⁷ a woman approached him with an alabaster jar of very expensive perfume. She poured it on his head as he was reclining at the table. ⁸ When the disciples saw it, they were indignant. "Why this waste?" they asked. ⁹ "This might have been sold for a great deal and given to the poor."

¹⁰ Aware of this, Jesus said to them, "Why are you bothering this woman? She has done a noble thing for me. ¹¹ You always have the poor with you, but you do not always have me. ¹² By pouring this perfume on my body, she has prepared me for burial. ¹³ Truly I tell you, wherever this gospel is proclaimed in the whole world, what she has done will also be told in memory of her."

¹⁴ Then one of the Twelve, the man called Judas Iscariot, went to the chief priests ¹⁵ and said, "What are you willing to give me if I hand him over to you?" So they weighed out thirty pieces of silver for him. ¹⁶ And from that time he started looking for a good opportunity to betray him.

Betrayal at the Passover

¹⁷ On the first day of Unleavened Bread the disciples came to Jesus and asked, "Where do you want us to make preparations for you to eat the Passover?"

¹⁸ "Go into the city to a certain man," he said, "and tell him, 'The Teacher says: My time is near; I am celebrating the Passover at your place^D with my disciples.'" ¹⁹ So the disciples did as Jesus had directed them and prepared the Passover. ²⁰ When evening came, he was reclining at the table with the Twelve. ²¹ While they were eating, he said, "Truly I tell you, one of you will betray me."

²² Deeply distressed, each one began to say to him, "Surely not I, Lord?" ²³ He replied, "The one who dipped his hand with me in the bowl — he will betray me. ²⁴ The Son of Man will go just as it is written about him, but woe to that man by whom the Son of Man is betrayed! It would have been better for him if he had not been born."

²⁵ Judas, his betrayer, replied, "Surely not I, Rabbi?"

"You have said it," he told him.

The First Lord's Supper

²⁶ As they were eating, Jesus took bread, blessed and broke it, gave it to the disciples, and said, "Take and eat it; this is my body." ²⁷ Then he took a cup, and after giving thanks, he gave

---

^A 26:2 Or "Know (as a command)   ^B 26:3 Other mss add and the scribes   ^C 26:6 Gk lepros; a term for various skin diseases; see Lv 13–14   ^D 26:18 Lit Passover with you

---

26:1–2 Passover was a celebration that commemorated the Israelites' flight from Egypt in the days of Moses (Ex 12). The timing of Jesus's death (at Passover) confirms his identity as the new Moses who will lead his disciples on a new spiritual exodus. On **Son of Man**, see note at 8:18–20. The temporal reference that Passover **takes place after two days** means that Jesus's prophecy was given on Tuesday.

26:3 Joseph **Caiaphas** served as high priest from AD 18 to 36, after he replaced his father-in-law, Annas. His burial cave was discovered in 1990 south of Abu Tor.

26:4–5 The fear of **rioting** during Passover was well-founded since riots had previously occurred (Josephus, War 1.88). A riot would cause the Romans to strengthen their grip on Jerusalem and the Jewish leadership.

26:6 Jesus had apparently healed **Simon** of leprosy at a previous date since he now lived in a house (rather than a leper colony) and entertained Jewish guests before the Passover.

26:7 The unnamed **woman** was Mary (Jn 12:3). Her **perfume** was **very expensive**, worth a year's wages. Since Jesus was the Christ (a title meaning "anointed one"), anointing his head was especially

meaningful. It recalled the anointing of OT kings (1Sm 10:1; 2Kg 9:3,6).

26:8–11 According to Jn 12:4, Judas was the primary critic of the woman. Here the different evaluations of the woman's act—a **waste** or **a noble thing**—shows how little the disciples understood of Jesus. His remarks echo Dt 15:11.

26:12 Corpses were perfumed in first-century Palestine to mask the odor of putrefaction. Jesus interpreted Mary's act as preparation for his **burial**. Messiah was beginning his reign but, to the surprise of his disciples, his throne would be a cross and his diadem a crown of thorns.

26:13 Jesus is predicting the preaching of the "good news of the kingdom" (Mt 24:14) in all the world.

26:14–16 If the **thirty pieces of silver** are thirty shekels, the amount was equal to 120 days' wages. Thus by his traitorous act **Judas** earned an amount of money that equaled only one-third of the value of Mary's lavish gift (see note at v. 7). On the significance of this amount, see note at 27:9–10.

26:17 The feast of **Unleavened Bread** was a seven or eight-day feast associated with the one-day **Passover**. During this feast, the Jews refused to eat anything containing yeast in

order to commemorate the speed with which God delivered them from Egypt (Ex 13:7–8; Dt 16:3–4). The feast began on the day before Passover, Thursday of Passion Week.

26:18–19 Mark's account of this event more clearly implies that Jesus's instructions to his disciples indicate that he had used supernatural knowledge (Mk 14:13–16).

26:20–24 Just as it is written indicates that Jesus's sufferings were foretold in the OT. Jesus probably had in mind texts such as Is 53 and Ps 22.

26:25 Judas's words betray his flagrantly deceptive and hypocritical heart.

26:26 The Passover meal was rich with symbolic meaning. Jews ate lamb to commemorate the lamb whose blood protected firstborn Israelites from the death plague before the exodus. Bitter herbs were reminiscent of their enslavement. Unleavened bread symbolized the haste of their departure from Egypt (Ex 12). Jesus invested the meal with new symbolism: the unleavened **bread** symbolized his own **body**, which would be torn by scourging and crucifixion. His sacrifice would begin a new exodus in which people were liberated from slavery to sin.

26:27–28 The making of a **covenant** was normally accompanied by an act of sacrifice.

it to them and said, "Drink from it, all of you. ²⁸ For this is my blood of the covenant,^A which is poured out for many for the forgiveness of sins. ²⁹ But I tell you, I will not drink from this fruit of the vine from now on until that day when I drink it new with you in my Father's kingdom." ³⁰ After singing a hymn, they went out to the Mount of Olives.

Peter's Denial Predicted

³¹ Then Jesus said to them, "Tonight all of you will fall away because of me, for it is written:

I will strike the shepherd,
and the sheep of the flock
will be scattered.^B

³² But after I have risen, I will go ahead of you to Galilee."

³³ Peter told him, "Even if everyone falls away because of you, I will never fall away."

³⁴ "Truly I tell you," Jesus said to him, "tonight, before the rooster crows, you will deny me three times."

³⁵ "Even if I have to die with you," Peter told him, "I will never deny you," and all the disciples said the same thing.

The Prayer in the Garden

³⁶ Then Jesus came with them to a place called Gethsemane, and he told the disciples, "Sit here while I go over there and pray." ³⁷ Taking along Peter and the two sons of Zebedee, he began to be sorrowful and troubled. ³⁸ He said to them, "I am deeply grieved^c to the point of death. Remain here and stay awake with me." ³⁹ Going a little farther,^D he fell facedown and prayed, "My Father, if it is possible, let this cup pass from me. Yet not as I will, but as you will."

⁴⁰ Then he came to the disciples and found them sleeping. He asked Peter, "So, couldn't you stay awake with me one hour? ⁴¹ Stay awake and pray, so that you won't enter into temptation. The spirit is willing, but the flesh is weak."

⁴² Again, a second time, he went away and prayed, "My Father, if this^E cannot pass^F unless I drink it, your will be done." ⁴³ And he came again and found them sleeping, because they could not keep their eyes open.

⁴⁴ After leaving them, he went away again and prayed a third time, saying the same thing once more. ⁴⁵ Then he came to the disciples and said to them, "Are you still sleeping and resting? See, the time is near. The Son of Man is betrayed into the hands of sinners. ⁴⁶ Get up; let's go. See, my betrayer is near."

Judas's Betrayal of Jesus

⁴⁷ While he was still speaking, Judas, one of the Twelve, suddenly arrived. A large mob with swords and clubs was with him from the chief priests and elders of the people. ⁴⁸ His betrayer had given them a sign: "The one I kiss, he's the one; arrest him." ⁴⁹ So immediately he went up to Jesus and said, "Greetings, Rabbi!" and kissed him.

⁵⁰ "Friend," Jesus asked him, "why have you come?"^G

Then they came up, took hold of Jesus, and arrested him. ⁵¹ At that moment one of those with Jesus reached out his hand and drew his sword. He struck the high priest's servant and cut off his ear.

⁵² Then Jesus told him, "Put your sword back in its place because all who take up the sword will perish by the sword. ⁵³ Or do you think that I cannot call on my Father, and he will provide

The slaughter of the animal signified the consequences that would befall anyone who broke the covenant. The old covenant was sealed by such a sacrifice (Ex 24:8). Now, Jesus's sacrifice enacted the new covenant that had been promised in the OT (Jr 31:31–34). In this covenant God vowed to forgive and forget his people's sins. He also promised to write his law on the hearts of his people so that they will fulfill his righteous demands. **26:29** Many Jews expected Messiah to begin his reign by sharing a great banquet with his subjects. The final cup of the meal anticipated that great messianic feast and encouraged Jesus's disciples to eagerly wait "until he comes" (1Co 11:26). **26:30** Jews typically sang portions of OT psalms like Pss 113–118 during the Passover meal. **26:31** Many Jews regarded Zch 13:7, which Jesus quoted here, as a prophecy about the Messiah. Jesus's quote implied that the Father himself would **strike** him. Although his crucifixion involved the conspiracy of religious leaders, Roman officials, and the betrayal of a friend, Jesus viewed his death

ultimately as the fulfillment of God's righteous plan (see also Ac 4:27–28). **26:32** Jesus's reference to his resurrection goes right over the disciples' heads. **26:33–35** For the fulfillment of Jesus's prophecy, see vv. 69–75. **26:36–38** Jesus's sorrow resulted from his anticipation of his physical, emotional, and spiritual suffering, especially his alienation from his Father as he bore the sins of the world on the cross. **26:39** In the OT, the "cup" is often an image of divine wrath and judgment (Ps 75:7–8; Is 51:17). The cup that Jesus faced was God's wrath against sin. With the words **if it is possible, let this cup pass**, Jesus asked his Father to provide forgiveness by some means other than his sacrificial death. Jesus knew that God's power made it possible for him to evade the power of Jewish and Roman executioners (see note at vv. 52–53), but he did not want to reject the Father's plan to provide salvation to his people. **26:40–41** Luke 22:45 explains that the disciples were "exhausted from their grief." Peter's boast in v. 35 is quickly proving empty.

26:42–46 Jesus's second and third petitions in Gethsemane assumed that his sacrificial death was necessary. Matthew 26:54 shows that God had predicted Jesus's death in the OT. The Scriptures, being God's Word, had to be fulfilled. This second petition closely parallels Jesus's model prayer in 6:9–13. Both prayers address God as **Father** and contain the petition **your will be done**. **26:47–50** Jewish men did not **kiss** one another publicly except on formal occasions. Such a kiss expressed respect and affection. Thus Judas's kiss was an act of shameful hypocrisy. Jesus's question may also be read as a command ("Do what you came for") or a statement ("I know why you are here"). **26:51** The servant was named Malchus (Jn 18:10). Jesus restored his severed **ear** (Lk 22:51). **26:52–53** A Roman legion consisted of six thousand soldiers. A roughly equal number of auxiliary troops supported each legion. Thus **twelve legions of angels** would be equivalent to 72,000 or even 144,000 angels, more than enough to defend Jesus against arrest and crucifixion.

me here and now with more than twelve legions of angels? [54] How, then, would the Scriptures be fulfilled that say it must happen this way?"

[55] At that time Jesus said to the crowds, "Have you come out with swords and clubs, as if I were a criminal,[A] to capture me? Every day I used to sit, teaching in the temple, and you didn't arrest me. [56] But all this has happened so that the writings of the prophets would be fulfilled." Then all the disciples deserted him and ran away.

Jesus Faces the Sanhedrin

[57] Those who had arrested Jesus led him away to Caiaphas the high priest, where the scribes and the elders had convened. [58] Peter was following him at a distance right to the high priest's courtyard. He went in and was sitting with the servants to see the outcome.

[59] The chief priests and the whole Sanhedrin were looking for false testimony against Jesus so that they could put him to death, [60] but they could not find any, even though many false witnesses came forward.[B] Finally, two[c] who came forward [61] stated, "This man said, 'I can destroy the temple of God and rebuild it in three days.'"

[62] The high priest stood up and said to him, "Don't you have an answer to what these men are testifying against you?" [63] But Jesus kept silent. The high priest said to him, "I charge you under oath by the living God: Tell us if you are the Messiah, the Son of God."

[64] "You have said it," Jesus told him. "But I tell you, in the future[D] you will see the Son of Man seated at the right hand of Power and coming on the clouds of heaven."[E]

[65] Then the high priest tore his robes and said, "He has blasphemed! Why do we still need witnesses? See, now you've heard the blasphemy. [66] What is your decision?"

They answered, "He deserves death!" [67] Then they spat in his face and beat him; others slapped him [68] and said, "Prophesy to us, Messiah! Who was it that hit you?"

Peter Denies His Lord

[69] Now Peter was sitting outside in the courtyard. A servant girl approached him and said, "You were with Jesus the Galilean too."

[70] But he denied it in front of everyone: "I don't know what you're talking about."

[71] When he had gone out to the gateway, another woman saw him and told those who were there, "This man was with Jesus the Nazarene!"

[72] And again he denied it with an oath: "I don't know the man!"

[73] After a little while those standing there approached and said to Peter, "You really are one of them, since even your accent[F] gives you away."

[74] Then he started to curse and to swear with an oath, "I don't know the man!" Immediately a rooster crowed, [75] and Peter remembered the words Jesus had spoken, "Before the rooster crows, you will deny me three times." And he went outside and wept bitterly.

Jesus Handed Over to Pilate

27 When daybreak came, all the chief priests and the elders of the people plotted against Jesus to put him to death. [2] After tying him up, they led him away and handed him over to Pilate,[G] the governor.

[A]26:55 Lit as against a criminal [B]26:60 Other mss add they found none [c]26:60 Other mss add false witnesses [D]26:64 Lit you, from now [E]26:64 Ps 110:1; Dn 7:13 [F]26:73 Or speech [G]27:2 Other mss read Pontius Pilate

---

26:54–56 Jesus expressed the same view of the **Scriptures** that he taught in the Sermon on the Mount (5:17–20). **The writings of the prophets** that were being **fulfilled** would include such OT texts as those quoted in v. 31 and 21:42, as well as Is 52:13–53:12 which describes the Lord's Suffering Servant (see notes at 8:17; 12:15–21).
26:57–58 John 18:13 adds that they first visited Annas.
26:59–60 The **Sanhedrin** was obligated to interview witnesses separately and then compare their testimonies to determine if they were consistent (Mk 14:55–59). Inconsistent testimonies were considered invalid.
26:61–63 The testimony was based on a confused understanding of Jesus's statement in Jn 2:19. Since both 2Sm 7:13–14 and Zch 6:12 portrayed Messiah as one who would build a temple for God, the high priest regarded the statement about building the temple in **three days** as a claim to messiahship. The **high priest** appears to use the titles **Messiah** and **Son of God** interchangeably, suggesting that many Jews saw the title "Son of God" as messianic in light of Ps 2.
26:64 Jesus's confession acknowledged that he is Messiah and the Son of God. However,

he countered confused interpretations of his messianic role by describing himself as the **Son of Man**. Both "Son of Man" and the phrase **coming on the clouds** of heaven were drawn from Dn 7:13. Jesus's words confirmed that he intended this title to express not just his humanity but his identity as a King who would reign over an eternal kingdom. The words **seated at the right hand** echo Ps 110:1 (see note at Mt 22:43–46). Jesus's application of Ps 110:1 to himself gave the impression that he was claiming to be God's equal. The unbelieving Jewish leaders regarded this as blasphemy, a crime worthy of death (Lv 24:10–23).
26:65 Tearing one's **robes** was a common expression of deep grief and was the customary Jewish response to blasphemy. However, because the robes of the high priest were sacred, Lv 21:10 prohibited "the priest who is highest among his brothers" from tearing his garments. Thus the high priest's anger at Jesus's statement prompted him to commit an act of sacrilege.
26:66 Execution by stoning was the prescribed OT penalty for blasphemy (Lv 24:10–23).
26:67–68 Mark 14:65 shows that the men covered Jesus's face before they beat him.

Thus Jesus was expected to identify his abusers by name without seeing their faces or hearing their voices. This mock test of messiahship was probably based on a misinterpretation of Is 11:3 which said that Messiah "will not judge by what he sees with his eyes . . . [or] by what he hears with his ears." A century later Bar Kochba was executed after his claims to be Messiah were disproved by his inability to judge by smell.
26:69–71 The emphasis on Jesus's identity as a **Galilean** and a **Nazarene** may imply that one of the arguments used to refute his messianic claims was that he did not come from Bethlehem, the city of David. This city is identified as the birthplace of Messiah in Mc 5:2. Thus, this argument against Jesus's messiahship confused his hometown with his birthplace (Mt 2:4–11).
26:72–73 Galileans spoke with an **accent** that distinguished them from the inhabitants of Judah.
26:74–75 This event fulfilled Jesus's prophecy in v. 34.
27:1–2 This early morning meeting of the Sanhedrin was convened to compensate for the illegal procedures of the previous night. According to Jewish law, judges had

Judas Hangs Himself

[3] Then Judas, his betrayer, seeing that Jesus had been condemned, was full of remorse and returned the thirty pieces of silver to the chief priests and elders. [4] "I have sinned by betraying innocent blood," he said.

"What's that to us?" they said. "See to it yourself!" [5] So he threw the silver into the temple and departed. Then he went and hanged himself.

[6] The chief priests took the silver and said, "It's not permitted to put it into the temple treasury, since it is blood money." [7] They conferred together and bought the potter's field with it as a burial place for foreigners. [8] Therefore that field has been called "Field of Blood" to this day. [9] Then what was spoken through the prophet Jeremiah was fulfilled: **They took**[A] **the thirty pieces of silver, the price of him whose price was set by the Israelites,** [10] **and they gave**[B] **them for the potter's field, as the Lord directed me.**[C]

Jesus Faces the Governor

[11] Now Jesus stood before the governor. "Are you the king of the Jews?" the governor asked him.

Jesus answered, "You say so." [12] While he was being accused by the chief priests and elders, he didn't answer.

[13] Then Pilate said to him, "Don't you hear how much they are testifying against you?" [14] But he didn't answer him on even one charge, so that the governor was quite amazed.

Jesus or Barabbas

[15] At the festival the governor's custom was to release to the crowd a prisoner they wanted.

[16] At that time they had a notorious prisoner called Barabbas.[D] [17] So when they had gathered together, Pilate said to them, "Who is it you want me to release for you — Barabbas, or Jesus who is called Christ?" [18] For he knew it was because of envy that they had handed him over.

[19] While he was sitting on the judge's bench, his wife sent word to him, "Have nothing to do with that righteous man, for today I've suffered terribly in a dream because of him."

[20] The chief priests and the elders, however, persuaded the crowds to ask for Barabbas and to execute Jesus. [21] The governor asked them, "Which of the two do you want me to release for you?"

"Barabbas!" they answered.

[22] Pilate asked them, "What should I do then with Jesus, who is called Christ?"

They all answered, "Crucify him!"

[23] Then he said, "Why? What has he done wrong?"

But they kept shouting all the more, "Crucify him!"

[24] When Pilate saw that he was getting nowhere, but that a riot was starting instead, he took some water, washed his hands in front of the crowd, and said, "I am innocent of this man's blood.[E] See to it yourselves!"

[25] All the people answered, "His blood be on us and on our children!" [26] Then he released Barabbas to them and, after having Jesus flogged, handed him over to be crucified.

Mocked by the Military

[27] Then the governor's soldiers took Jesus into the governor's residence and gathered

---

^A **27:9** Or *I took* ^B **27:10** Some mss read *I gave* ^C **27:9–10** Jr 32:6–9; Zch 11:12–13 ^D **27:16** Other mss read *Jesus Barabbas*, also in v. 17 ^E **27:24** Other mss read *this righteous man's blood*

---

to conduct and conclude capital trials during daylight hours (*m. Sanh.* 4:1). The law also prohibited conducting trials on the eve of the Sabbath. The Jewish leaders also needed to plot and secure Roman approval for the intended execution of Jesus. Pontius **Pilate** was the Roman prefect of Judea during AD 26–36. The title **governor** (Gk *hegemon*) was an acceptable Greek translation of the Latin title "prefect" and was also used of Pilate by Josephus (*Ant.* 18.55).
27:3–4 Betraying innocent blood is a heinous offense that results in a divine curse (Dt 27:25). The reaction of the chief priests and elders shows that they realized that Jesus was innocent.
27:5 Some Jews believed that criminals received atonement from God through their execution (*m. Sanh.* 6:3). Once he realized the horror of his crime, guilt-stricken Judas ended his life, perhaps hoping to earn atonement. But only one death brings atonement: that of Jesus Christ.
27:6–8 Verse 8 hints that Matthew wrote his Gospel before the destruction of Jerusalem in AD 70. That such a burial field could be located and recognized by name decades after the utter destruction of Jerusalem is unlikely.

27:9–10 Matthew's appeal to the OT blends themes from Zch 11:12–13 and Jr 32:6–9. The first text describes Israel's rejection of its spiritual Shepherd, the low estimation they had of him (worth **thirty pieces of silver**, the price of a slave; Ex 21:32), and destruction of Jerusalem by the Romans. The second text assures that Israel will be restored after its devastation by the Babylonians. The two prophecies do more than just foretell the events surrounding Judas's actions. By merging these texts, Matthew shows that Jerusalem's rejection of Messiah would result in its destruction, but that God would restore the city in due time.
27:11–14 According to Roman law, the refusal to offer a defense counted as an admission of guilt. Jesus's silence before his accusers recalls Is 53:7.
27:15 The custom of releasing a **prisoner** for Passover seems to be attested in one Jewish text (*m. Pes.* 8:6: "they may slaughter a Passover lamb for one . . . whom they have promised to bring out of prison").
27:16–18 Mark 15:7 describes **Barabbas** as a murderous rebel. Some ancient manuscripts of Matthew and some important figures in the early church mention that Barabbas's

full name was Jesus Bar Abbas, which might indicate that he was the son of a renowned teacher ("son of Rabba"). Thus Pilate apparently offered the Jews a choice between a Jesus who was the son of a teacher and a Jesus who was the Son of God.
27:19 Greeks and Romans believed the gods spoke to them in dreams.
27:20–25 Both Judas (vv.. 3–5) and **Pilate** (v. 24) feared being accountable for Jesus's death, but the people gladly accepted responsibility. Many later Christians speculated that the destruction of Jerusalem was the penalty for this self-confessed guilt. Pilate's actions could not absolve him of the guilt of crucifying an innocent Jesus (see Ac 4:27).
27:26 Roman flogging utilized an instrument of torture called the (Gk) *flagellum*, a leather whip that had thongs laced with sharp pieces of iron or bone. Although beatings in the Jewish synagogue were limited to thirty-nine blows, no limit was imposed on Roman flogging. Ancient writers described victims being disemboweled or having their bones laid bare by the *flagellum*.
27:27–31 With their mock royal **robe** . . . **crown**, and scepter, the soldiers ridiculed Jesus's messianic claims.

the whole company^A around him. **28** They stripped him and dressed him in a scarlet robe. **29** They twisted together a crown of thorns, put it on his head, and placed a staff in his right hand. And they knelt down before him and mocked him: "Hail, king of the Jews!" **30** Then they spat on him, took the staff, and kept hitting him on the head. **31** After they had mocked him, they stripped him of the robe, put his own clothes on him, and led him away to crucify him.

Crucified Between Two Criminals

32 As they were going out, they found a Cyrenian man named Simon. They forced him to carry his cross. **33** When they came to a place called *Golgotha* (which means Place of the Skull), **34** they gave him wine^B mixed with gall to drink. But when he tasted it, he refused to drink it. **35** After crucifying him, they divided his clothes by casting lots.^C **36** Then they sat down and were guarding him there. **37** Above his head they put up the charge against him in writing: THIS IS JESUS, THE KING OF THE JEWS.

38 Then two criminals^D were crucified with him, one on the right and one on the left. **39** Those who passed by were yelling insults at^E him, shaking their heads **40** and saying, "You who would destroy the temple and rebuild it in three days, save yourself! If you are the Son of God, come down from the cross!" **41** In the same way the chief priests, with the scribes and elders,^F mocked him and said, **42** "He saved others, but he cannot save himself! He

is the King of Israel! Let him^G come down now from the cross, and we will believe in him. **43** He trusts in God; let God rescue him now — if he takes pleasure in him!^H For he said, 'I am the Son of God.'" **44** In the same way even the criminals who were crucified with him taunted him.

The Death of Jesus

45 From noon until three in the afternoon,^I darkness came over the whole land.^J **46** About three in the afternoon Jesus cried out with a loud voice, *"Elí, Elí, lemá^K sabachtháni?"* that is, "My God, my God, why have you abandoned me?"^L

47 When some of those standing there heard this, they said, "He's calling for Elijah." **48** Immediately one of them ran and got a sponge, filled it with sour wine, put it on a stick, and offered him a drink. **49** But the rest said, "Let's see if Elijah comes to save him."

50 But Jesus cried out again with a loud voice and gave up his spirit. **51** Suddenly, the curtain of the sanctuary was torn in two from top to bottom, the earth quaked, and the rocks were split. **52** The tombs were also opened and many bodies of the saints who had fallen asleep were raised. **53** And they came out of the tombs after his resurrection, entered the holy city, and appeared to many.

54 When the centurion and those with him, who were keeping watch over Jesus, saw the earthquake and the things that had happened, they were terrified and said, "Truly this man was the Son of God!"

---

^27:27 Lit *cohort* ^B27:34 Other mss read *sour wine* ^C27:35 Other mss add *that what was spoken by the prophet might be fulfilled: "They divided my clothes among them, and for my clothing they cast lots."* ^D27:38 Or *revolutionaries* ^E27:39 Lit *passed by, or were blaspheming* ^F27:41 Other mss add *and Pharisees* ^G27:42 Other mss read *If he . . . Israel, let him* ^H27:43 Or *if he wants him* ^I27:45 Lit *From the sixth hour to the ninth hour* ^J27:45 Or *whole earth* ^K27:46 Some mss read *lama*; other mss read *lima* ^L27:46 Ps 22:1

27:32 Crucifixion victims normally carried the cross's (Gk) *patibulum* (crossbeam) to the execution site. Having lost much blood, Jesus was too weak to carry it beyond the city walls. The soldiers impressed (see note at 5:41) **Simon**, a **Cyrenian**, to carry the rest of the way. Simon's sons were later known in the early church (Mk 15:21). This suggests that Simon became a disciple of Jesus. Cyrene was situated near the Mediterranean coast in northern Africa. Simon was probably an ethnic Jew visiting Jerusalem for the Passover (Ac 6:9).

27:33–34 This **wine** was probably intended to dull the pain of crucifixion or hasten death. Jesus's refusal **to drink** it expressed his determination to suffer the full agony of the cross.

27:35–36 Crucifixion was a horrifying and torturous means of execution. Naked victims were tied or nailed (Jn 20:25) to a cross. The victim might remain alive for days, and after death they were often consumed by dogs, carrion birds, or insects. Josephus described crucifixion as "the most wretched of all ways of dying" (*War* 7.5.4). Cicero (106–43 BC) said that crucifixion so frightened Roman citizens that they refused to speak the word *cross*.

27:37 A wooden placard called a *titulus* was often tied around the criminal's neck as he marched to death. This sign announced the reason for his crucifixion. When Jesus arrived at Golgotha, the placard was nailed over his head. Although Roman crosses were sometimes shaped like X or T, the placement of the *titulus* on Jesus's cross shows that it was shaped like a lowercase letter "t."

27:38–44 Jesus's final temptation was to abandon the cross. But "although he was the Son, he learned obedience from what he suffered" and thereby was "perfected" so that "he became the source of eternal salvation for all who obey him" (Heb 5:8–9). "It was the power of love, not nails, that kept him there" (Robert H. Mounce).

27:45 The bystanders naturally interpreted the **darkness** as God's judgment (Am 8:9). While they likely thought the judgment was against Jesus (as if he were a heretic), in light of his later resurrection they came to see the darkness as judgment against the sin that Jesus became on our behalf (2Co 5:21).

27:46–49 Jesus's lament quotes Ps 22:1. The psalm reads as if it were written by someone standing near the cross (see esp. Ps 22:7–8,14–18). Jesus's cry expressed the alienation from

God that he endured as he bore the Father's wrath against sin. Although Jesus elsewhere addressed God as "Father," he addressed him merely as **my God** in this verse.

27:50–51 Jesus's death at 3:00 p.m. coincided with the afternoon sacrifice. Thus the priests were present in the temple to observe the rending of the curtain. The **curtain of the sanctuary** separated the holy of holies from the rest of the temple. According to the Mishnah, it was sixty feet long, thirty feet wide, and as thick as a man's palm. It was so heavy that it took three hundred men to lift it when it was wet (*m. Shek.* 8:5). That it was **torn in two from top to bottom** shows that it was torn by God. This signified that Jesus's death granted sinners new access to God (Heb 6:19–20; 10:19–20).

27:52–53 Although the **tombs** were ruptured at the time of Jesus's death, the **saints** did not depart from them until after Jesus's resurrection. This demonstrated that Jesus's victory over death guaranteed that God would also raise his people (1Co 15:20).

27:54 Gentiles again recognized and confessed Jesus's true identity. This hints at God's worldwide plan for salvation (see note at 28:19).

[55] Many women who had followed Jesus from Galilee and looked after him were there, watching from a distance. [56] Among them were Mary Magdalene, Mary the mother of James and Joseph, and the mother of Zebedee's sons.

The Burial of Jesus

[57] When it was evening, a rich man from Arimathea named Joseph came, who himself had also become a disciple of Jesus. [58] He approached Pilate and asked for Jesus's body. Then Pilate ordered that it[A] be released. [59] So Joseph took the body, wrapped it in clean, fine linen, [60] and placed it in his new tomb, which he had cut into the rock. He left after rolling a great stone against the entrance of the tomb. [61] Mary Magdalene and the other Mary were seated there, facing the tomb.

The Closely Guarded Tomb

[62] The next day, which followed the preparation day, the chief priests and the Pharisees gathered before Pilate [63] and said, "Sir, we remember that while this deceiver was still alive he said, 'After three days I will rise again.' [64] So give orders that the tomb be made secure until the third day. Otherwise, his disciples may come, steal him, and tell the people, 'He has been raised from the dead,' and the last deception will be worse than the first."

[65] "Take[B] guards," Pilate told them. "Go and make it as secure as you know how." [66] They went and secured the tomb by setting a seal on the stone and placing the guards.

Resurrection Morning

28 After the Sabbath, as the first day of the week was dawning, Mary Magdalene and the other Mary went to view the tomb. [2] There was a violent earthquake, because an angel of the Lord descended from heaven and approached the tomb. He rolled back the stone and was sitting on it. [3] His appearance was like lightning, and his clothing was as white as snow. [4] The guards were so shaken by fear of him that they became like dead men.

[5] The angel told the women, "Don't be afraid, because I know you are looking for Jesus who was crucified. [6] He is not here. For he has risen, just as he said. Come and see the place where he lay. [7] Then go quickly and tell his disciples, 'He has risen from the dead and indeed he is going ahead of you to Galilee; you will see him there.' Listen, I have told you."

[8] So, departing quickly from the tomb with fear and great joy, they ran to tell his disciples the news. [9] Just then[C] Jesus met them and said, "Greetings!" They came up, took hold of his feet, and worshiped him. [10] Then Jesus told them, "Do not be afraid. Go and tell my brothers to leave for Galilee, and they will see me there."

The Soldiers Bribed to Lie

[11] As they were on their way, some of the guards came into the city and reported to the chief priests everything that had happened. [12] After the priests[D] had assembled with the elders and agreed on a plan, they gave the soldiers a large sum of money [13] and told them, "Say this, 'His disciples came during the night and stole him while we were sleeping.' [14] If this reaches the governor's ears, we will deal with[E] him and keep you out of trouble." [15] They took the money and did as they were instructed, and this story has been spread among Jewish people to this day.

The Great Commission

[16] The eleven disciples traveled to Galilee, to the mountain where Jesus had directed them.

---

^A 27:58 Other mss read *that the body*   ^B 27:65 Or *"You have*   ^C 28:9 Other mss add *as they were on their way to tell the news to his disciples*   ^D 28:12 Lit *After they*   ^E 28:14 Lit *will persuade*

27:55–56 Mary **the mother of James and Joseph** was probably the mother of two of Jesus's lesser-known disciples (Mk 15:40).
27:57–61 Joseph, a member of the Sanhedrin (Mk 15:43), had opposed their condemnation of Jesus (Lk 23:50–51). Though Jesus taught that rich people cannot enter God's kingdom by their own efforts, Joseph is proof that God can save anyone by his grace (Mt 19:24–26). The bodies of crucified victims were normally allowed to rot on the cross, but Pilate respected Jewish scruples and allowed the dead to be buried.
27:62–64 The Jewish leaders may have been remembering Jesus's resurrection prediction in Mt 12:38–40. They misjudged the disciples, whose grief was such that they had no notion of Jesus rising from the grave.
27:65 Pilate sent a detachment of **guards** to protect the tomb from disciples who might attempt to stage a fake resurrection. The Greek term for the detachment does not specify the number of soldiers in the unit.

27:66 The seal consisted of wax bearing the imprint of an official Roman seal. This ensured that no one could tamper with the tomb without being detected. Any unauthorized persons who broke the seal defied the authority of Rome and could be punished by death.
28:1 These events occurred early Sunday morning. For the identity of **the other Mary**, see note at 27:55–56. Mark indicates Salome went with them (Mk 16:1). Since the ancients did not view women as trustworthy, a writer who made up an account designed to convince readers of Jesus's resurrection would not have made women the first witnesses of the resurrection. That Matthew included the women confirms that he was faithful to record actual events, even if they would be seen as discreditable by society.
28:2–3 The angel's **appearance** identified him as a heavenly being (see Dn 7:9; 10:6).
28:4 The soldiers lost consciousness and fell to the ground.
28:5–7 The words **just as he said** recall Jesus's prophecies about his resurrection

(12:40; 16:21; 17:23; 20:19). Jesus taught that the OT prophecies had to be fulfilled since they came from God (5:18; 26:54,56).
28:8–10 During his wilderness temptation (4:10), Jesus quoted Dt 6:13, "Worship the Lord your God, and serve only him" (Mt 4:10). By accepting worship here, Jesus identified himself as "the Lord your God."
28:11–15 Wide circulation of this story probably led to the emperor's edict in the Nazareth Inscription (likely dated ca AD 41–54) that threatened death to anyone who removed an entombed body. Several aspects of the soldiers' story make no sense. If the soldiers were all asleep, they could not have known that it was Jesus's disciples who removed his body. Furthermore, it is extremely unlikely that all of the soldiers would have slept at the same time. Finally, soldiers were severely punished or even executed for sleeping on duty.
28:16–17 On the significance of the disciples' worship, see note at 28:8–10. The lingering confusion among them about Jesus's

¹⁷ When they saw him, they worshiped,^A but some doubted. ¹⁸ Jesus came near and said to them, "All authority has been given to me in heaven and on earth. ¹⁹ Go, therefore, and make disciples of⁸ all nations, baptizing them in the name of the Father and of the Son and of the Holy Spirit, ²⁰ teaching them to observe everything I have commanded you. And remember,ᶜ I am with you always,ᴰ to the end of the age."

^A 28:17 Other mss add *him*   ⁸ 28:19 Or *and disciple*   ᶜ 28:20 Lit *see*   ᴰ 28:20 Lit *all the days*

resurrection undermines the skeptical theory that the disciples shared a hallucination of Jesus's resurrection because they all expected him to arise.

28:18 Before the resurrection, Jesus had authority (7:29; 9:6,8; 11:27; 21:23). However, through the resurrection, the Father granted him **all authority** over **heaven and . . . earth**, an authority far greater than that which Satan had vainly promised him (see note at 4:8–9).

28:19 The command to extend their mission worldwide brings to a climax Matthew's repeated theme of Gentile participation in God's salvation. The inclusion of four Gentile women in Jesus's genealogy and the summons of the magi to worship the infant Christ foreshadowed the disciples' mission of making **disciples of all nations**. Baptism marked a person's entrance into the faith community. **In the name of the Father and of the Son and of the**

Holy Spirit is a reference to the Trinity. Matthew's language shows that a clear understanding of Jesus's nature and identity as God was required before baptism.

28:20 The Great Commission (vv. 19–20) is preceded by a reference to Jesus's authority and followed by the promise of Jesus's spiritual presence among us. Both are necessary if we are to fulfill our God-given mission.

◥ The Holy Trinity

by Timothy George

The word *trinity* is not mentioned in the Bible, but the doctrine of the Trinity is thoroughly biblical. The Christian church confesses with the people of Israel, "The LORD our God, the LORD is one" (Dt 6:4), an affirmation also quoted by Jesus himself (see Mk 12:29–39). Jesus believed and taught the oneness of God as foundational to his own messianic vocation. And in the New Testament the one, eternal, and living God of the Bible, the only real God, is further revealed as three personal agents: the Father, the Son, and the Holy Spirit. Together these agents plan, provide, and perform the salvation of sinners.

In Scripture, self-differentiation in God is presented with unmistakable clarity through the incarnation. Nowhere is this more clearly shown than in the baptism of Jesus. There the voice of the Father from heaven identified the one being baptized by John as his beloved Son, while the Spirit of God descended like a dove, attesting to the unique Sonship of Christ and inaugurating his public ministry (Mt 3:13–17). Subsequently, Jesus commanded his disciples to be baptized in the one name of the Father, the Son, and the Holy Spirit (Mt 28:19–20).

The mature doctrine of the Trinity that came to full expression in the classic creeds of the fourth century was a necessary implication of Christian conversion in the first century. Just as the Father sent his Son into the world, so too he has sent into our hearts his Spirit—who is the Spirit of the Son no less than the Spirit of the Father (Gl 4:4–6). It is the Spirit who places the believer in Christ, and it is the Spirit who cries out to the Father, "Abba" (Rm 8:15–17). In other words, through believing in Jesus, being baptized in God's triune name, and communing with the risen Christ in the Lord's Supper, the early Christians came to know and love increasingly the one eternal God—the Father who had sent his Spirit-conceived Son to die on the cross for their sins. This is the same Father who also sent the Spirit of his risen Son into their hearts, giving them a new life fit for eternity.

The doctrine of the Trinity is the necessary theological framework for understanding the story of Jesus as the story of God.

The church's teaching about the Trinity bears witness to both the Old Testament affirmation, "God is one," and the New Testament confession, "Jesus is Lord."

It is not surprising, however, given the complex nature of the doctrine of the three-in-one God, that both God's oneness and his triune-ness have been doubted, denied, and debated throughout the history of the church. *Modalism* teaches that Father, Son, and Holy Spirit are simply names or roles taken by one person at different moments in time, as if our Maker is an actor who plays three parts in a multi-act drama. *Tritheism* goes to another extreme, positing three deities working together in a cluster. Neither view is faithful to the Bible's teaching about God.

The doctrine of the Trinity was forged on the anvil of the church's encounters with heresy. In the second century, a false teacher named Marcion proposed that the entire Old Testament be expunged from the Bible as the antiquated revelation of a Jewish deity made irrelevant by the coming of Jesus. The church of that time responded wisely, claiming the Old Testament as Christian Scripture and declaring that the Father of Jesus was none other than the God of Israel. In doing so, the church affirmed a fundamental connection between creation and redemption.

Several centuries later, a man named Arius denied both the lordship and deity of Jesus Christ. In AD 325 the church responded at the Council of Nicaea that the one Christians adored and loved in their worship—Jesus the Redeemer—was of the same essence as the Father.

Later, there arose others known as the Pneumatomachi, "the Spirit-fighters," who understood the Holy Spirit as a force, an energy, a power—but not God. Against them, the church declared that God is one in essence and three in persons. The Holy Spirit is a person in eternal relationship with the Father and the Son—one God forever and ever.

In the biblical view, relationship is constitutive for God himself: the Father gives, the Son obediently receives, and the Holy Spirit proceeds from both of them. In the eternal and blessed intercommunion of the Father, the Son, and the Holy Spirit, the one true God is united without confusion and divided without separation. The doctrine of the Trinity is crucial for understanding the biblical God of holiness and love.

The Holy Trinity is not a puzzle to be solved; it is a mystery to be adored. The doctrine of the Trinity, though infinitely complex, is not a matter for philosophical speculation but rather an essential teaching of the faith that evokes wonder, love, and praise. The doctrine should be not only believed but also taught, preached, and made central in every act of public worship.

We can never fully fathom or comprehend completely the reality of the God who is one-in-three and three-in-one; nevertheless, we can confess our Trinitarian faith joyfully, reverently, and with a sense of humility. To sing, pray, and worship the one triune God of holiness and love is to bridge heaven and earth. The white-robed throng of saints and martyrs gathered around the throne of God join their voices with other heavenly beings to sing, day and night: "Holy, holy, holy, Lord God, the Almighty, who was, who is, and who is to come" (Rv 4:8; see also 7:9–17). Those of us still in this world are invited to join their chorus and to add our voices to theirs.

▼ Introduction to Mark

Circumstances of Writing

The Gospel of Mark is anonymous. Eusebius, the early church historian, writing in AD 326, preserved the words of Papias, an early church father. Papias quoted "the elder," probably John, as saying that Mark recorded Peter's preaching about the things Jesus said and did, but not in order. Thus Mark was considered the author of this Gospel even in the first century.

The Mark who wrote this Gospel was John Mark, the son of a widow named Mary, in whose house the church in Jerusalem sometimes gathered (Ac 12:12–17) and where Jesus possibly ate the Last Supper with his disciples. Mark was the cousin of Barnabas (Col 4:10), and he accompanied Barnabas and Paul back to Antioch after their famine relief mission to Jerusalem (Ac 12:25). Mark next went with Barnabas and Paul on part of the first missionary journey as an assistant (Ac 13:5), but at Perga, Mark turned back (Ac 13:13).

When the apostle Peter wrote to the churches in Asia Minor shortly before his martyrdom, he sent greetings from Mark, whom he called "my son" (1Pt 5:13). Then shortly before his execution, Paul asked Timothy to "bring Mark with you, for he is useful to me in the ministry" (2Tm 4:11). After Paul's execution, Mark is said to have moved to Egypt, established churches, and served them in Alexandria (Eusebius, *Ecclesiastical History* 2:16). Some have suggested the young man in Mark 14:51–52 was Mark himself.

Background

According to the early church fathers, Mark wrote his Gospel in Rome just before or just after Peter's martyrdom. Further confirmation of the Roman origin of Mark's Gospel is found in Mark 15:21 where Mark noted that Simon, a Cyrenian who carried Jesus's cross, was the father of Alexander and Rufus, men apparently known to the believers in Rome.

Because Mark wrote primarily for Roman Gentiles, he explained Jewish customs, translated Aramaic words and phrases into Greek, used Latin terms rather than their Greek equivalents, and rarely quoted from the Old Testament. Most Bible scholars are convinced that Mark was the earliest Gospel and served as one of the sources for Matthew and Luke.

Contribution to the Bible

Many concepts of the Messiah existed in Jesus's day, and several individuals laid claim to the title. What Mark contributes is a clarification of the concept of Messiah and a redefining of the term. Peter's insightful confession at Caesarea Philippi in 8:29 became the turning point at which Jesus began to explain that the divine conception of the Messiah involved rejection, suffering, death, and then resurrection (8:31). Mark also shows us the human side of Jesus. In fact, more than the other Gospel writers, Mark emphasizes Jesus's human side and his emotions. Thus Mark gives us a strong picture of both the humanity and the divinity of Jesus.

Mark Timeline

75–50 BC

Spartacus, the Roman gladiator, leads a slave revolt based near Mount Vesuvius. **73**

Pompey conquers Jerusalem. **63**

Rome's Gallic wars begin after Julius Caesar becomes Roman governor of Gaul. **58–51**

Pompey builds first stone amphitheater in Rome. **55**

Julius Caesar invades Britain. **55–54**

50 BC–AD 9

Circus Maximus is built in Rome. **50**

Mark Antony controls Rome; Julius Caesar is assassinated. **44**

Parthians conquer Jerusalem. **40–37**

Herod becomes "king of the Jews." **37**

Qumran is abandoned as a result of an earthquake in the vicinity of Jericho. **31**

Octavian becomes Augustus Caesar. **27**

Structure

Mark's Gospel begins with a prologue (1:1–13), which is then followed by three major sections. The first (1:14–8:21) tells of Jesus's Galilean ministry. There Jesus healed and cast out demons and worked miracles. The second section (8:22–10:52) is transitional. Jesus began his journey that would take him to Jerusalem.

The final section (11:1–16:8) involves a week in Jerusalem. From the time Jesus entered the city, he was at odds with the religious leaders, who quickly brought about his execution. A brief appendix (16:9–20) recording some of Jesus's appearances, his commissioning of his disciples, and his ascension is attached to the Gospel.

Outline

  I. Prologue to the Gospel (1:1–13)
  II. Jesus's Ministry in Galilee (1:14–8:21)
  III. On the Way to Jerusalem (8:22–10:52)
  IV. A Week in Jerusalem (11:1–16:8)
  V. Appendix: Jesus's Appearances (16:9–20)

Key verse in Mark

13:31 Heaven and earth will pass away, but my words will never pass away.

AD 9–30

Jesus visits the temple at the age of twelve. **9**
Tiberius, Rome's second emperor **14–37**
Caiaphas, Jewish high priest **18–36**
Jesus is baptized and begins calling disciples. **29**
Jesus's early ministry in Judea **AUTUMN**
  29 TO SPRING 30 (Jn 2–4)

AD 30–33

Jesus's Galilean ministry **SUMMER 30 TO SPRING 32**
  (all four Gospels)
Jesus travels with disciples and engages in
  intensive training. **SUMMER AND EARLY**
  AUTUMN 32 (Matthew, Mark, and Luke)
Jesus's later ministry in Judea **LATE AUTUMN**
  AND EARLY WINTER 32 (Luke and John)
Jesus's Perean ministry **LATE WINTER AND**
  EARLY SPRING 33 (Luke and John)
Jesus's crucifixion, resurrection,
  exaltation **33** (all four Gospels)

The Messiah's Herald

1 The beginning of the gospel of Jesus Christ, the Son of God.[A] [2] As it is written in Isaiah the prophet:[B]

See, I am sending my messenger
ahead of you;
he will prepare your way.[C,D]
[3] A voice of one crying out
in the wilderness:
Prepare the way for the Lord;
make his paths straight![E]

[4] John came baptizing[F] in the wilderness and proclaiming a baptism of repentance for the forgiveness of sins. [5] The whole Judean countryside and all the people of Jerusalem were going out to him, and they were baptized by him in the Jordan River, confessing their sins. [6] John wore a camel-hair garment with a leather belt around his waist and ate locusts and wild honey.

[7] He proclaimed, "One who is more powerful than I am is coming after me. I am not worthy to stoop down and untie the strap of his sandals. [8] I baptize you with[G] water, but he will baptize you with the Holy Spirit."

The Baptism of Jesus

[9] In those days Jesus came from Nazareth in Galilee and was baptized in the Jordan by John.

[10] As soon as he came up out of the water, he saw the heavens being torn open and the Spirit descending on him like a dove. [11] And a voice came from heaven: "You are my beloved Son; with you I am well-pleased."

The Temptation of Jesus

[12] Immediately the Spirit drove him into the wilderness. [13] He was in the wilderness forty days, being tempted by Satan. He was with the wild animals, and the angels were serving him.

Ministry in Galilee

[14] After John was arrested, Jesus went to Galilee, proclaiming the good news[H,I] of God: [15] "The time is fulfilled, and the kingdom of God has come near. Repent and believe the good news!"

The First Disciples

[16] As he passed alongside the Sea of Galilee, he saw Simon and Andrew, Simon's brother, casting a net into the sea — for they were fishermen. [17] "Follow me," Jesus told them, "and I will make you fish for[J] people." [18] Immediately they left their nets and followed him. [19] Going on a little farther, he saw James

---

[A]1:1 Some mss omit *the Son of God* [B]1:2 Other mss read *in the prophets* [C]1:2 Other mss add *before you* [D]1:2 Mal 3:1
[E]1:3 Is 40:3 [F]1:4 Or *John the Baptist came* [G]1:8 Or *in* [H]1:14 Other mss add *of the kingdom* [I]1:14 Or *gospel* [J]1:17 Or *you to become fishers of*

1:1 Mark's Gospel starts at **the beginning of the gospel** (Gk *euangelion*, meaning "good news"). The name **Jesus** is the Greek equivalent of the Hebrew name *Joshua*, meaning "Yahweh is salvation." Jesus is identified as **Christ** (or Messiah) and **Son of God**. Jesus is often identified as God's Son in Mark: at his baptism (v. 11), by demons (3:11; 5:7), at the transfiguration (9:7), at his trial (14:61), and by the centurion's confession (15:39).
1:2–3 As it is written is a formulaic expression indicating the authoritative character of the OT (7:6; 9:13; 11:17; 14:21,27). The phrase **in Isaiah the prophet** introduces a mixed quotation from Ex 23:20; Is 40:3; and Mal 3:1. Hence some manuscripts read "in the prophets." In its original context, **Lord** refers to God. The **messenger** announces the coming of God himself. The Gospel writers applied the words to Jesus, who is God in flesh (Jn 1:14).
1:4 Mark introduces John as **baptizing in the wilderness**, a place that recalled Israel's disobedience (Jos 5:6) and God's redemption. John called for **a baptism of repentance for the forgiveness of sins.** "Repentance" means "to change one's mind." It involves a deliberate turn from sins.
1:5 That John attracted **the whole Judean countryside and all the people of Jerusalem** indicates his appeal among both country folk and urbanites.
1:6 John's dress was like Elijah's (2Kg 1:8) and other prophets (Zch 13:4). Mark's description suggests that John was the Elijah who was expected to return and call the nation to repent before the day of the Lord (Mal 4:5–6).
1:7–8 John announced that the coming one was **more powerful** and that he was **not**

worthy to stoop down and untie the strap of his sandals—a task for Gentile slaves. The coming one was also superior in his work: **he will baptize you with the Holy Spirit** (Ac 11:16; see note at Ac 1:8). John's baptism was symbolic; Jesus's baptism would introduce the reality.
1:9–11 Nazareth is mentioned only here in Mark (cp. 6:1). Three things occurred **as soon as** Jesus **came up out of the water.** The **heavens** were **torn open . . . the Spirit** descended, and God's **voice** came **from heaven. My beloved Son** indicates the Son's uniqueness and recalls Abraham's love for Isaac (Gn 22:2,12,16). Only Israel (Ex 4:23) and Israel's king (Ps 2:7) were called God's son in the OT. The divine declaration in Mk 1:11 announced Jesus's eternal relationship to God. All three persons of the Trinity are represented at Jesus's baptism.
1:12–13 The **same Spirit** who descended on Jesus at his baptism now **drove him into the wilderness.** "Drove" is a strong term used for the driving out of demons (vv. 34,39; 3:15,22–23; 6:13; 7:26; 9:18,28,38) and other forced expulsions (5:40; 9:47; 12:8). **In the wilderness forty days** recalls Israel's testing for forty years as well as Moses's (Dt 9:18) and Elijah's (1Kg 19:8) forty-day wilderness fasts. **The angels were serving him** may indicate that they ministered to Jesus in unstated ways throughout his temptation, though he was not fed until the end (Mt 4:11). Angels also ministered to Elijah during his forty-day wilderness fast (1Kg 19:1–8).
1:14–15 The words **after John was arrested** indicate an interval between vv. 13 and 14, possibly as long as a year if this parallels Jn 4:3,43. Mark did not include Jesus's early

Judean ministry (Jn 3:22–36). Further details about John's arrest and execution appear in Mk 6:17–29. **The time is fulfilled** points to the fulfillment of the OT promises. In the person of Jesus, the **kingdom of God** was so near that announcement of its arrival demanded immediate response—**repent and believe.**
1:16–20 Mark included two accounts of Jesus calling fishermen, two pairs of brothers, to become his disciples. These four formed the core of the group (v. 29; 3:16–18; 13:3; see notes at 5:37; 9:2; 14:33). Mark emphasized Jesus's authority to call people to leave all and follow him. According to Lk 5:7–10, the two pairs of brothers were partners in the fishing business.
1:16–18 The **Sea of Galilee** was a freshwater lake about twelve miles long and seven miles wide that lay seven hundred feet below sea level. Also known as the Sea of Gennesaret (Lk 5:1) and the Sea of Tiberias (Jn 21:1), it hosted a thriving fishing industry. Brothers **Simon** and **Andrew** hailed from Bethsaida, across the northern end of the lake (Jn 1:44), but they now lived in Capernaum (Mk 1:29). **Follow me** is the heart of NT discipleship. It involves adopting Jesus's values and lifestyle. **I will make you fish for people** expands on their former profession. The words also point to a second aspect of discipleship—the call to serve the Lord and people through ministry.
1:19–20 The phrase **going on a little farther** links the call of the second pair of brothers—**James** and **John**—in time and place to the first pair. The fact that **hired men** were present implies their fishing business was prosperous. Leaving this to follow Jesus meant leaving a nice living. Like the first pair

Differences in the Gospels

by Robert H. Stein

Serious readers of the Gospels notice various differences between them. One difference involves geographical arrangement. In the Synoptic Gospels (Matthew, Mark, and Luke), Jesus visits Jerusalem only once during his entire ministry. For instance, all of the events in Mark 1:1–11:10 take place either in Galilee (1:1–8:21) or on the way to Jerusalem (8:22–11:10). Only from 11:11 forward is Jesus recorded as entering Jerusalem.

The Gospel of John takes a different approach. John records Jesus visiting Jerusalem several times throughout his ministry (2:13–4:45; 5:1–47; 7:1–10:40; and 12:12–20:31), including an early temple cleansing (John 2:13–22). The Synoptics say nothing about an early temple cleansing, and John in turn says nothing about the later cleansing that the Synoptics recount (Mt 21:12–13; Mk 11:15–18; Lk 19:45–48).

It seems the authors chose different ways of using geography as a tool for arranging their accounts of Jesus's life. Mark, whose Gospel likely predated and influenced Matthew and Luke, chose not to discuss any of Jesus's doings in Jerusalem until the climactic events beginning in 11:11. This literary approach builds a steady tension that finally explodes with Jesus's crucifixion in the sacred city. John, writing years after the Synoptics, took a different approach, sprinkling Jerusalem throughout his account.

Another literary consideration that helps account for differences among the Gospels is how the authors chose to group Jesus's teachings. Matthew is organized around alternating blocks of stories (S) of Jesus and teachings (T) of Jesus. Here is the arrangement: chapters 1–4 (S); 5–7 (T); 8–9 (S); 10 (T); 11–12 (S); 13 (T); 14–17 (S); 18 (T); 19–22 (S); 23–25 (T); 26–28 (S). Luke, on the other hand, places the teachings of Jesus in two large sections: 6:20–8:3 and 9:51–18:14. Different approaches such as this explain why the Gospel authors often place sayings of Jesus in different contexts, as for instance when Matthew records the Lord's Prayer early in Jesus's ministry (6:9-13) while Luke places it later (11:1-4). The Gospel writers arranged much of their material on topical and logical grounds rather than chronological.

The earliest reference to any Gospel was made by Papias, a church father who in the first decade of the second century stated that Mark wrote accurately but *not in chronological order* the traditions he learned from Peter. Thus, early readers noticed the differences between the Gospels, understood some of the basic causes of the differences, and did not regard them as problematic.

Another reason for differences involves the literary style of the individual Gospel writers. In Matthew 8:5–13 and Luke 7:1–10 we have two accounts of Jesus healing a centurion's servant. In Luke the conversation takes place between Jesus and Jewish elders who speak on behalf of the centurion. In Matthew the conversation is directly between Jesus and the centurion. There is no conflict in these accounts when we realize that Matthew has abbreviated the story (103 words compared to 186 words in Luke). Matthew omitted unessential material, and the elders (serving as go-betweens) are the least important element in the story. Thus, just as modern-day journalists report on meetings between heads of state without mentioning the go-betweens, Matthew makes no mention of the elders.

Furthermore, the Gospel authors understood themselves to be inspired interpreters, not mere stenographers of Jesus's acts and teachings. They felt free to clarify and add explanatory comments to the traditions they were recording. For example, whereas Matthew in 7:11 records Jesus as saying God the Father gives "good things" to those who ask, Luke has Jesus saying God gives "the Holy Spirit." In this case, Luke has done some interpretive extension: of all the good things God gives, the Holy Spirit is the best of them. Other examples of inspired editorial work include:

The Baptism of Jesus
- In Matthew 3:17 the voice from heaven states, "This is my beloved Son."
- In Mark 1:11 and Luke 3:22 the voice states, "You are my beloved Son."

Explanation: In Mark and Luke, God's voice addresses Jesus. Matthew shifts the audience to the bystanders in order to make clear to his readers that God would have them know

the son of Zebedee and his brother John in a boat putting their nets in order. **20** Immediately he called them, and they left their father Zebedee in the boat with the hired men and followed him.

Driving Out an Unclean Spirit

21 They went into Capernaum, and right away he entered the synagogue on the Sabbath and began to teach. **22** They were astonished at his teaching because he was teaching them as one who had authority, and not like the scribes. **23** Just then a man with an unclean spirit was in their synagogue. He cried out, **24** "What do you have to do with us, Jesus of Nazareth? Have you come to destroy us? I know who you are — the Holy One of God!"

25 Jesus rebuked him saying, "Be silent, and come out of him!" **26** And the unclean spirit threw him into convulsions, shouted with a loud voice, and came out of him. **27** They were all amazed, and so they began to ask each other, "What is this? A new teaching with authority!^ He commands even the unclean spirits, and they obey him." **28** At once the news about him spread throughout the entire vicinity of Galilee.

Healings at Capernaum

29 As soon as they left the synagogue, they went into Simon and Andrew's house with James and John. **30** Simon's mother-in-law was lying in bed with a fever, and they told him about her at once. **31** So he went to her, took her by the

^**1:27** Other mss read *"What is this? What is this new teaching? For with authority"*

of brothers in v. 18, these **followed** Jesus. Mark's words in the Greek directly link their response in v. 20 to Jesus's command in v. 17. **1:21–22 Capernaum,** on the northwestern shore of the Sea of Galilee, became Jesus's home (2:1) and headquarters (Mt 4:13). Mark did not record what Jesus **began to teach** in the **synagogue,** but he did say that the people were **astonished**. This was a regular reaction to Jesus's teachings (6:2; 7:37; 10:26; 11:18). What impressed listeners was the **authority** with which Jesus taught. His authority contrasted with that of **the scribes** who mastered the Torah and treasured traditional interpretations (oral traditions). In Mark the scribes were Jesus's fiercest opponents (2:6,16; 11:27) and were among the main instigators leading to his death (8:31; 10:33; 11:18; 14:1,43,53; 15:1,31).

1:23–24 Just then links this event to vv. 21–22. Mark used **unclean spirit** to denote a demonic spirit. "Unclean spirit" contrasts with the demons' identification of Jesus as **the Holy One of God. Have you come to destroy us?** Clearly the demons recognized and acknowledged the person and work of Jesus before humans did. **1:25–26** On the basis of the authority of his word, Jesus **rebuked** and expelled the spirit, commanding it to **be silent,** [lit "be muzzled"] **and come out of him**. The spirit **threw him into convulsions** (see note at 9:26–27), and **shouted** its desperate but futile resistance to Jesus. **1:27–28** The people were **amazed** to see an exorcism, especially given the authoritative manner in which Jesus accomplished it. Their statement that **the unclean spirits . . . obey**

him indicates their belief that what he did to one spirit, he could do to all. **At once** indicates how quickly the story of these events traveled **throughout . . . Galilee**. **1:29–31 As soon as they left the synagogue** connects vv. 29–34 to the same Sabbath day as vv. 21–28. **Simon and Andrew's house** was large enough to host Jesus and his followers. Archaeologists have identified such a house near the synagogue in Capernaum. **Simon's mother-in-law** indicates that Peter was married. First Co 9:5 suggests Peter's wife was supportive of his ministry. Jesus did not speak any words to heal Peter's mother-in-law; he simply **took her by the hand**. The phrase **raised her up** is a common expression for Jesus's healings in Mark (2:9,11; 3:3; 5:41; 9:27; 10:49).

that Jesus is his Son. The overall meaning is unchanged.

The Beatitudes
· In Matthew 5:3 the first beatitude reads, "Blessed are the poor in spirit . . ."
· Luke 6:20 has, "Blessed are you who are poor . . ."

Explanation: Matthew gives a "thought for thought" rather than "word for word" translation of the original. He adds "in spirit" to help his readers understand that in this context "poor" refers to spiritual humility. A similar usage of "poor" occurs in Psalm 86:1, where King David (who was financially wealthy) speaks of being "poor and needy."

Peter's Denial of Christ
· Mark tells his readers of Peter's denial in Mark 14:53–54 and 14:66–72. Wedged between this two-part account is the story of Jesus's trial.

· Luke completes the entire account of Peter's denial before telling of Jesus's trial.

Explanation: Rather than a chronological discrepancy, these are two different ways of telling two separate stories. Mark follows one of his favored stylistic techniques and "sandwiches" Jesus's trial between the two halves of the story of Peter's denial. Luke chooses to treat them separately.

We have avoided terms such as "discrepancy" and "contradiction" when discussing differences among the Gospels. When we seek to understand what the Gospel writers are doing as interpreters of Jesus's life, we often find that their different approaches help clarify and draw out implications from Jesus's acts and teachings. This often entails sharing the stories of Jesus's life in a topical or logical order, not chronological. In this light, alleged "discrepancies" and "contradictions" are seen as mere "differences."

hand, and raised her up. The fever left her,^A and she began to serve them.

³² When evening came, after the sun had set, they brought to him all those who were sick and demon-possessed. ³³ The whole town was assembled at the door, ³⁴ and he healed many who were sick with various diseases and drove out many demons. And he would not permit the demons to speak, because they knew him.

Preaching in Galilee

³⁵ Very early in the morning, while it was still dark, he got up, went out, and made his way to a deserted place; and there he was praying. ³⁶ Simon and his companions searched for him, ³⁷ and when they found him they said, "Everyone is looking for you."

³⁸ And he said to them, "Let's go on to the neighboring villages so that I may preach there too. This is why I have come."

A Man Cleansed

³⁹ He went into all of Galilee, preaching in their synagogues and driving out demons. ⁴⁰ Then a man with leprosy⁸ came to him and, on his knees,ᶜ begged him, "If you are willing, you can make me clean." ⁴¹ Moved with compassion,ᴰ Jesus reached out his hand and touched him. "I am willing," he told him. "Be made clean." ⁴² Immediately the leprosy left him, and he was made clean. ⁴³ Then he sternly warned him and sent him away at once, ⁴⁴ telling him, "See that you say nothing to anyone; but go and show yourself to the priest, and offer what Moses commanded for your cleansing, as a testimony to them."ᴱ ⁴⁵ Yet he went out and began to proclaim it widely and to spread the news, with the result that Jesus could no longer enter a town openly. But he was out in deserted places, and they came to him from everywhere.

The Son of Man Forgives and Heals

2 When he entered Capernaum again after some days, it was reported that he was at home. ² So many people gathered together that there was no more room, not even in the doorway, and he was speaking the word to them. ³ They came to him bringing a paralytic, carried by four of them. ⁴ Since they were not able to bring him toᶠ Jesus because of the crowd, they removed the roof above him, and after digging through it, they lowered the mat on which the paralytic was lying. ⁵ Seeing their faith, Jesus told the paralytic, "Son, your sins are forgiven."

⁶ But some of the scribes were sitting there, questioning in their hearts: ⁷ "Why does he speak like this? He's blaspheming! Who can forgive sins but God alone?"

⁸ Right away Jesus perceived in his spirit that they were thinking like this within themselves and said to them, "Why are you thinking these things in your hearts? ⁹ Which is easier: to say to the paralytic, 'Your sins are forgiven,' or to say, 'Get up, take your mat, and walk'? ¹⁰ But so that you may know that the Son of Man has authority on earth to forgive sins" — he told the paralytic — ¹¹ "I tell you: get up, take your mat, and go home."

---

^1:31 Other mss add *at once* ᴮ1:40 Gk *lepros*; a term for various skin diseases, also in v. 42; see Lv 13–14 ᶜ1:40 Other mss omit *on his knees* ᴰ1:41 Other mss *Moved with indignation* ᴱ1:44 Or *against them* ᶠ2:4 Other mss read *able to get near*

1:32–34 The expressions **when evening came** and **after the sun had set** emphasize that the Sabbath prohibitions against work were over since the Sabbath ended at sunset. **Those who were sick and demon-possessed** recalls the two types of healings Jesus performed earlier that day (vv. 23–26 and 30–31). That there is a difference between disease and demon possession is affirmed by Mark's description of Jesus's actions: He **healed** the **sick** but **drove out** the **demons** (3:10–11; 6:13). That Jesus healed **various diseases** points to the comprehensive nature of his healing powers.

1:35–39 Very early in the morning and **while it was still dark** together indicate that Jesus did not rest much after the previous evening's activity. The early hour explains how he got out of town undetected. The motion verbs **got up, went out, and made his way** describe Jesus's search for **a deserted place**, the same word used for the wilderness where John preached (v. 4) and where Jesus was tempted (v. 12). **Simon and his companions** refer to the four disciples Jesus called. This is the first time Mark depicted Peter as the leading disciple. Apparently everyone expected more miracles, but Jesus intended to **preach**, thus returning the focus to the start of his ministry (vv. 14–15).

1:40–45 Legislation related to **leprosy** appears in Lv 13–14. **Came to him** shows the sick man initiated the action and that

he broke protocol in doing so. His words **if you are willing, you can make me clean** affirmed Jesus's ability while submitting to his willingness. That Jesus was **moved with compassion** is a detail only Mark recorded (see parallels in Mt 8:1–4; Lk 5:12–16). To touch someone with leprosy violated OT law and rendered a person unclean. Nevertheless, **Jesus reached out his hand and touched him**, healing the man immediately. Jesus told him to follow the requirements of Lv 13:47–54 **as a testimony** to the priests of his cure. We do not know whether he completed the prescribed rites, but he disobeyed Jesus's command to **say nothing to anyone** about his healing.

2:1–3:6 This section contains five conflict stories relating to Jesus's authority. In each, Jesus was accused of blasphemy, challenged about his association with sinners, rebuked for neglecting religious customs, and accused of breaking Sabbath laws.

2:1 He was at home probably refers to Peter's house (see note at 1:29–31).

2:2 The word (Gk *logos*, see also 4:33; 8:32) was later used to refer to Christian missionary preaching (Ac 6:4; 8:4; 17:11; Gl 6:6; Col 4:3). Here, it refers to the good news (Mk 1:14–15).

2:3 This is the only time Mark mentioned **a paralytic** (cp. Mt 8:6).

2:4 Removed the roof. Most houses in Palestine were single-story, flat-roofed structures with an outside staircase. The roof

was used for work, drying laundry, sleeping, or prayer. Over the crossbeams small poles or branches were placed and covered with thatch and mud. A **mat** (vv. 4,9,11–12) was a poor person's pallet (6:55; Jn 5:8–11; Ac 5:15).

2:5 Their faith refers to those who carried the paralyzed man as well as the paralytic himself. Rather than a word of healing, Jesus spoke forgiveness over the paralytic after addressing him as **son**. **Your sins** is plural and possibly specific. Only here did Jesus link sin and infirmity. Possibly there was a direct relationship between this man's sins and his paralysis.

2:6–7 The scribes supposed Jesus was **blaspheming** when they heard him declare the man's sins forgiven. Death by stoning was the prescribed penalty for blasphemy (Lv 24:16; Jn 10:33), and it was the charge on which Jesus was eventually executed (Mk 14:64).

2:8–11 The answer to Jesus's question **which is easier** is of course the unverifiable claim to have forgiven the paralytic's sins. After all, forgiveness of sins is a quality that cannot be checked against visible evidence, and so anyone can claim to forgive sins. Actually having the authority to do it is another thing altogether. To prove his right to forgive sins, Jesus undertook the more verifiable (yet still remarkable) task of healing the man. **Son of Man** was Jesus's favorite self-designation. It derives from Dn 7:13–14, where the messianic

¹² Immediately he got up, took the mat, and went out in front of everyone. As a result, they were all astounded and gave glory to God, saying, "We have never seen anything like this!"

The Call of Levi

¹³ Jesus went out again beside the sea. The whole crowd was coming to him, and he was teaching them. ¹⁴ Then, passing by, he saw Levi the son of Alphaeus sitting at the tax office, and he said to him, "Follow me," and he got up and followed him.

¹⁵ While he was reclining at the table in Levi's house, many tax collectors and sinners were eating ᴬ with Jesus and his disciples, for there were many who were following him. ¹⁶ When the scribes who were Pharisees ᴮ saw that he was eating with sinners and tax collectors, they asked his disciples, "Why does he eat ᶜ with tax collectors and sinners?"

¹⁷ When Jesus heard this, he told them, "It is not those who are well who need a doctor, but those who are sick. I didn't come to call the righteous, but sinners."

A Question about Fasting

¹⁸ Now John's disciples and the Pharisees ᴰ were fasting. People came and asked him, "Why do John's disciples and the Pharisees' disciples fast, but your disciples do not fast?"

¹⁹ Jesus said to them, "The wedding guests cannot fast while the groom is with them, can they? As long as they have the groom with them, they cannot fast. ²⁰ But the time ᴱ will come when the groom will be taken away from them, and then they will fast on that day. ²¹ No one sews a patch of unshrunk cloth on an old garment. Otherwise, the new patch pulls away from the old cloth, and a worse tear is made. ²² And no one puts new wine into old wineskins. Otherwise, the wine will burst the skins, and the wine is lost as well as the skins. No, new wine is put into fresh wineskins."

Lord of the Sabbath

²³ On the Sabbath he was going through the grainfields, and his disciples began to make their way, picking some heads of grain. ²⁴ The Pharisees said to him, "Look, why are they doing what is not lawful on the Sabbath?"

²⁵ He said to them, "Have you never read what David and those who were with him did when he was in need and hungry — ²⁶ how he entered the house of God in the time of Abiathar the high priest and ate the bread of the Presence — which is not lawful for anyone to eat except the priests — and also gave some to his companions?" ²⁷ Then he told them, "The Sabbath was made for ᶠ man and not man for the Sabbath. ²⁸ So then, the Son of Man is Lord even of the Sabbath."

ᴬ 2:15 Lit *reclining together*   ᴮ 2:16 Other mss read *scribes and Pharisees*   ᶜ 2:16 Other mss add *and drink*   ᴰ 2:18 Other mss read *The disciples of John and of the Pharisees*   ᴱ 2:20 Or *the days*   ᶠ 2:27 Or *because of*

Son of Man is given **authority** (see note at 1:21–22).

2:12 This proved that Jesus could forgive sins. **They were all astounded** recalls 1:27. The scribes accused Jesus of usurping God's prerogatives (2:7), but the crowd **gave glory to God** because of Jesus.

2:13–14 Sea refers to the Sea of Galilee. Only Mark identified the tax collector as **Levi the son of Alphaeus** (cp. Mt 9:9; Lk 5:27, from which we learn that "Levi" was another name for Matthew; Mt 10:3). The **tax office** was probably a local customs booth. Tax collectors were regarded as no better than thieves or Gentiles. **Follow me** recalls 1:17–18. This is the standard term in the Gospels for discipleship. **He got up and followed him** shows Levi's response to Jesus's call was immediate.

2:15–17 Reclining at the floor-level **table** on an elbow with the feet extended across the floor was the traditional dining posture. Levi invited Jesus and his disciples to a banquet that included notorious figures—**sinners and tax collectors** (cp. Lk 5:29). "Sinners" refers to those who deliberately violate God's laws. By dining with such people, Jesus in some sense identified with them. Far from condoning their sins, Jesus dwelt among them because he had come to save sinners. On **scribes**, see note at 1:21–22. Most scribes were **Pharisees**. Pharisees ("separated ones") strictly observed the written and oral law, believed in angels and resurrection, opposed Greek influence, and were esteemed by the people. They were constantly in conflict with Jesus. The **righteous** whom Jesus says he

didn't come to call is an ironical reference to the self-righteous Pharisees.

2:18 The question about **fasting** arose because the behavior of Jesus's disciples contrasted with that of disciples who belonged to John the Baptist and the Pharisees. Fasting was only required on the Day of Atonement (Lv 16:29–30, but see Est 9:31 and Zch 8:19 for fasts originating in the postexilic period). In NT times, the Pharisees fasted on Mondays and Thursdays (Lk 18:12). It was considered an act of piety (Mt 6:16–18).

2:19–20 A **wedding** typically lasted seven days. **Guests** (lit "sons of the bridal chamber") may refer to wedding guests or the groom's attendants. **The groom** recalls John the Baptist's designation of Jesus (Jn 3:29). **Will be taken away** suggests forcible removal and shifts the focus to Jesus's coming death. Jesus stated that after he had been violently "taken away" as John the Baptist had been (1:14), his disciples would fast as John's disciples were doing now.

2:21–22 These are Jesus's first parables in Mark. **Wineskins** were made from soft, pliable goatskins. Old wineskins that already had been used to ferment wine lost their elasticity, became brittle, and would burst if used again, resulting in the loss of the containers and the new wine. Both sayings indicate the impossibility of integrating Jesus's teachings (the **new**) with the religious structures and practices of traditional Judaism (the **old**).

2:23–24 What is not lawful does not specify what regulations were broken. The

controversy was that they did this **on the Sabbath**, a day of rest on which no work was permitted (Ex 20:8–11; Dt 5:12–15). Harvesting and threshing grain on the Sabbath was specifically forbidden (Ex 34:21). The ripened grain places this narrative in late spring or early summer. On **the Pharisees**, see note at vv. 15–17.

2:25–26 Jesus defended his disciples by appealing to David's flight from King Saul (1Sm 21:1–6). **In the time of Abiathar the high priest** is peculiar to Mark (cp. Mt 12:3; Lk 6:3) and is debated because the event actually happened when Abiathar's father Ahimelech was high priest. However, Abiathar was the only high priest to escape Saul's slaughter of the priests (1Sm 22:19–20), and he was well-known throughout David's era. Thus Mark's reference is a fitting approximation. The **bread of the Presence** refers to twelve loaves of unleavened bread placed in the temple's holy place to represent Israel's twelve tribes. These were replaced every Sabbath, and only priests could eat them (Lv 24:5–9). **Which is not lawful** is a repetition of the Pharisees' phrase in v. 24, allowing Jesus to declare that while David's actions were technically a violation of OT law they were not condemned.

2:27–28 Mark alone recorded Jesus's declaration about God's priorities regarding the Sabbath and humans. On **Son of Man**, see note at vv. 8–11. **Lord even of the Sabbath** turned the issue to Jesus's authority and affirmed his status.

3 Jesus entered the synagogue again, and a man was there who had a shriveled hand. ² In order to accuse him, they were watching him closely to see whether he would heal him on the Sabbath. ³ He told the man with the shriveled hand, "Stand before us." ⁴ Then he said to them, "Is it lawful to do good on the Sabbath or to do evil, to save life or to kill?" But they were silent. ⁵ After looking around at them with anger, he was grieved at the hardness of their hearts and told the man, "Stretch out your hand." So he stretched it out, and his hand was restored. ⁶ Immediately the Pharisees went out and started plotting with the Herodians against him, how they might kill him.

Ministering to the Multitude

⁷ Jesus departed with his disciples to the sea, and a large crowd followed from Galilee, and a large crowd followed from Judea, ⁸ Jerusalem, Idumea, beyond the Jordan, and around Tyre and Sidon. The large crowd came to him because they heard about everything he was doing. ⁹ Then he told his disciples to have a small boat ready for him, so that the crowd wouldn't crush him. ¹⁰ Since he had healed many, all who had diseases were pressing toward him to touch him. ¹¹ Whenever the unclean spirits saw him, they fell down before him and cried out, "You are the Son of God!" ¹² And he would strongly warn them not to make him known.

The Twelve Apostles

¹³ Jesus went up the mountain and summoned those he wanted, and they came to him. ¹⁴ He appointed twelve, whom he also named apostles,ᴬ to be with him, to send them out to preach, ¹⁵ and to have authority toᴮ drive out demons. ¹⁶ He appointed the Twelve:ᶜ To Simon, he gave the name Peter; ¹⁷ and to James the son of Zebedee, and to his brother John, he gave the name "Boanerges" (that is, "Sons of Thunder"); ¹⁸ Andrew; Philip and Bartholomew; Matthew and Thomas; James the son of Alphaeus, and Thaddaeus; Simon the Zealot, ¹⁹ and Judas Iscariot, who also betrayed him.

A House Divided

²⁰ Jesus entered a house, and the crowd gathered again so that they were not even able to eat.ᴰ ²¹ When his family heard this, they set out to restrain him, because they said, "He's out of his mind." ²² The scribes who had come down from Jerusalem said, "He is possessed by Beelzebul,"

ᴬ3:14 Other mss omit *he also named them apostles* ᴮ3:15 Other mss add *heal diseases, and to* ᶜ3:16 Other mss omit *He appointed the Twelve* ᴰ3:20 Or *eat a meal*; lit *eat bread*

3:1–2 The **synagogue** that Jesus **entered** . . . **again** was probably the one in Capernaum. **To accuse** is a legal term for bringing a charge against someone (cp. 15:3–4). The Pharisees are almost certainly the ones who were **watching him closely** (v. 6). **To see whether he would heal** indicates they did not question Jesus's ability to heal. They only wanted to know whether he would dare to do so **on the Sabbath**. Only life-saving medical treatment and preventive medical measures were regarded as legal on the Sabbath. **3:3–4 Stand before us** indicates that Jesus was about to heal the man (1:31; 2:9,11–12; 5:41; 10:49). **Is it lawful** recalls the previous exchange (2:24,26). **3:5** The reason for Jesus's emotion was **the hardness of their hearts**, an expression describing willful rejection of God's truth. Mark used this phrase twice of the disciples (6:52; 8:17). **3:6** Only Mark mentions **the Herodians** here (cp. Mt 12:14; Lk 6:11). They are also mentioned in Mk 12:13 and Mt 22:16, and possibly alluded to in Mk 8:15. The Herodians were Jewish supporters of Herod the Great and his family, here specifically Herod Antipas of Galilee. The Herodians are allied with the Pharisees in the NT, which is ironic because the Herodians supported Hellenism (Greek influence), while the Pharisees opposed it. The linking of these groups indicates that opposition to Jesus involved the unlikely unification of diverse political and religious factions. **3:7–8** Galilee and Judea, including **Jerusalem**, were Jewish areas. **Idumea** was the OT Edomite area south of Judea in the Negev. Its population was mixed Jewish-Gentile. **Beyond the Jordan** refers to the Jewish area of Perea, east of the Jordan River. **Tyre**

and **Sidon** were in the old Phoenician area north of Galilee and were largely Gentile, but they included a Jewish presence. The phrase **large crowd** emphasizes the large area over which Jesus's fame had spread. **3:9–10** Jesus **had healed many**. Therefore, those who were afflicted with **diseases** sought to **touch him**. Mark describes one such encounter in 5:24–34. **3:11–12** On **you are the Son of God**, compare 1:1,11,24. To this point in Mark, only the Father and the unclean spirits fully understood Jesus's identity. **Not to make him known** recalls 1:25,34,44. **3:13–15** The **mountain** here is not identified. Jesus spent the night praying (Lk 6:12). **Summoned those he wanted** seems to indicate more than just the twelve disciples (cp. Lk 6:13). The number **twelve** recalls the twelve tribes of Israel (cp. Mt 19:28; Lk 22:30). The purpose clauses identify the apostles' functions: They were **to be with him** and learn his message, **to preach**, and **to have authority to drive out demons**. **3:16–17** Verses 16–19 identify **the Twelve** men whom Jesus appointed as apostles. The NT contains three other such lists (Mt 10:2–4; Lk 6:14–16; Ac 1:13), and these contain variations in names and order. Only Mark says that Jesus nicknamed **James** and **John** the **Sons of Thunder**, possibly because of their temperament (Lk 9:54). Peter, James, and John made up Jesus's inner circle (Mk 5:37; 9:2; 14:33). **3:18–19** On **Andrew**, Peter's brother, see note at 1:16–18. **Philip** is not mentioned again in Mark. **Bartholomew** may be Nathaniel (Jn 1:45–46) otherwise he is not mentioned in the Gospels again. **Matthew** is mentioned only here in Mark, but he is the same person

as Levi the tax collector (2:14; Mt 9:9; 10:3). **Thomas** appears in Jn 11:16; 20:24. **James the son of Alphaeus** is not mentioned again. He is distinguished from James who was the son of Zebedee. **Thaddaeus** is not mentioned again in the NT and is not in Luke's lists (Lk 6:14–16; Ac 1:13). Possibly he is the same as "Judas the son of James" (Lk 6:16; Ac 1:13). **Simon the Zealot** (cp. Lk 6:15) is literally "Simon the Cananean," an Aramean rendering of "zealous" and not an indication that he was a Canaanite. The term was used of religious and political zealots but here likely refers to Simon's piety (cp. Ac 21:20; 22:3; Gl 1:14) and distinguishes him from Simon Peter. Nothing more is said about him in the NT. **Judas Iscariot** appears last in each list. "Judas" is the Greek form of "Judah." "Iscariot" probably indicates that he hailed from Kerioth and thus may identify him as the only Judean among the group. **3:20–21** To this point Mark has not mentioned Jesus's **family**, and after this extended section they are mentioned only in 6:3. After introducing them in 3:21, Mark picks them up again in vv. 31–35. **To restrain him** is the same verb used for "arrest" in 6:17; 12:12; 14:1,44. Mark hinted that Jesus's family tried to do what the Jewish authorities sought to do. Neither Matthew nor Luke mention that Jesus's family thought he was **out of his mind** (cp. Ps 69:8). **3:22** Between the introduction of Jesus's family (v. 21) and discussing their actions (vv. 31–35), Mark places an incident with the scribes (v. 22) and two parabolic sayings (vv. 23–26,27–30). The description of **the scribes** as those **who had come down from Jerusalem** indicates they were an official delegation (cp. 7:1). They were saying

and, "He drives out demons by the ruler of the demons."

²³ So he summoned them and spoke to them in parables: "How can Satan drive out Satan? ²⁴ If a kingdom is divided against itself, that kingdom cannot stand. ²⁵ If a house is divided against itself, that house cannot stand. ²⁶ And if Satan opposes himself and is divided, he cannot stand but is finished. ²⁷ But no one can enter a strong man's house and plunder his possessions unless he first ties up the strong man. Then he can plunder his house.

²⁸ "Truly I tell you, people will be forgiven for all sins and whatever blasphemies they utter. ²⁹ But whoever blasphemes against the Holy Spirit never has forgiveness, but is guilty of an eternal sin"^ — ³⁰ because they were saying, "He has an unclean spirit."

True Relationships

³¹ His mother and his brothers came, and standing outside, they sent word to him and called him. ³² A crowd was sitting around him and told him, "Look, your mother, your brothers, and your sisters⁸ are outside asking for you."

³³ He replied to them, "Who are my mother and my brothers?" ³⁴ Looking at those sitting in a circle around him, he said, "Here are my mother and my brothers! ³⁵ Whoever does the will of God is my brother and sister and mother."

The Parable of the Sower

4 Again he began to teach by the sea, and a very large crowd gathered around him. So he got into a boat on the sea and sat down, while the whole crowd was by the sea on the shore. ² He taught them many things in parables, and in his teaching he said to them, ³ "Listen! Consider the sower who went out to sow. ⁴ As he sowed, some seed fell along the path, and the birds came and devoured it. ⁵ Other seed fell on rocky ground where it didn't have much soil, and it grew up quickly, since the soil wasn't deep. ⁶ When the sun came up, it was scorched, and since it had no root, it withered away. ⁷ Other seed fell among thorns, and the thorns came up and choked it, and it didn't produce fruit. ⁸ Still other seed fell on good ground and it grew up, producing fruit that increased thirty, sixty, and a hundred times." ⁹ Then he said, "Let anyone who has ears to hear listen."

Why Jesus Used Parables

¹⁰ When he was alone, those around him with the Twelve asked him about the parables. ¹¹ He answered them, "The secret of the kingdom of God has been given to you, but to those outside, everything comes in parables ¹² so that

they may indeed look,
and yet not perceive;
they may indeed listen,
and yet not understand;

---

^3:29 Other mss read *is subject to eternal judgment*   ⁸3:32 Other mss omit *and your sisters*

---

that he was **possessed by Beelzebul** (see notes at Mt 12:24; Lk 11:14–16) and **drives out demons by the ruler of the demons** (see note at Mt 9:34). The scribes and Pharisees did not deny Jesus's power; instead, they attributed his power to Satan (Mk 1:13; cp. Mt 10:25; 12:24,27; Lk 11:15,18–19).

3:23–27 This is the first mention of **parables** in Mark, though Jesus had already used them (2:17,21–22). A parable is an analogy or comparison that includes proverbial sayings, allegories, or narrative. Jesus used parables to reject the scribes' logic of 3:22. Neither a **kingdom** nor a **house** is strengthened by internal divisions. Attacks on Satan's kingdom came not from within but from God's kingdom. In Jesus's reference to external attack on **a strong man's house** and tying him up, Satan was the strong man (v. 27; cp. Is 49:24–26; Rv 20:1–3).

3:28–30 Truly I tell you is a declaration of Jesus's authority to declare truth. This is the first time it appears in Mark (8:12; 9:1,41; 10:15,29; 11:23; 13:30; 14:25,30). **All sins** that people commit, including blasphemies (see note at 2:6–7), can be **forgiven**—except whoever blasphemes against the Holy **Spirit**. This person **never has forgiveness**, and **is guilty of an eternal sin** (a sin with eternal consequences). Blasphemy against the Holy Spirit is attributing Jesus's works to Satan, claiming that Jesus was empowered by evil.

3:31–35 This completes the account begun in vv. 20–21. Mark did not name Jesus's **mother**, his **brothers**, or his **sisters** (cp. 6:3). Possibly

Joseph was dead by this time. The phrases **standing outside** and **sent word** indicate there was no direct contact between Jesus and his family, only messages exchanged. **Whoever** signifies that being part of Jesus's most significant family, his spiritual family, is a possibility for all people.

4:1–20 Between the parable (vv. 3–9) and its interpretation (vv. 13–20), Mark places Jesus's explanation for why he spoke in parables (vv. 10–12). For Mark, the parable of the seeds and soils is the key to understanding the rest of Jesus's parables (v. 13).

4:1 Again recalls 2:13 and 3:1. **The sea** refers to the Sea of Galilee (see note at 1:16–18). **He got into a boat** to use it as a floating platform from which to **teach**.

4:2–3 The imperative **listen** calls for obedience to what is taught, not mere comprehension. **The sower** represents Jesus.

4:4–7 Three failures based on soil type and circumstances are pictured. The seed that **fell along the path** did not have time to germinate (profess faith) before **birds** (Satan) **devoured it**. The seed that **fell on rocky ground** . . . **grew up quickly**, meaning there was early evidence of faith, but it rapidly **withered away** when the **sun** (pressure, persecution) came. The seed that **fell among thorns** (worries) was **choked** and **didn't produce fruit**.

4:8 The seed that **fell on good ground** . . . produced **fruit that increased**. Jesus pointed to the productive nature of the good soil versus the unproductive or transitory yield of the others. He reinforced this by specifying

a bountiful increase (cp. Gn 26:12) of **thirty, sixty, and a hundred times**.

4:9 Let anyone who has ears to hear listen recalls his initial admonition ("Listen!") in v. 3 and prepares his listeners for the important information in vv. 10–12 (cp. v. 23; 7:14; 8:18).

4:10–12 These verses, among the most difficult in the NT, give Jesus's rationale for teaching in **parables**. Interpreters are divided as to their meaning. It may be that one of Jesus's purposes in using parables was to deliver judgment against hard-hearted listeners.

4:10 Verses 10–12 were not part of Jesus's lakeside teaching but were spoken **when he was alone**. This is the first mention of **the Twelve** since they were chosen in 3:14.

4:11 Jesus distinguished two audiences: **you** (pl) to whom revelation **has been given** (by God) and **those outside**. Outsiders only heard **parables**; insiders learned the **secret**. "Secret" is literally "mystery" (Gk *mustērion*). In the NT, *mustērion* refers not to esoteric knowledge or secret rites that are discoverable by human effort, but to truth that is hidden and can be known only if God reveals it (Dn 2:18–19,27–30,47). The secret relates to **the kingdom of God**, which is what Jesus came to announce (1:15) and what he will begin to explain in 4:26–32.

4:12 So that (Gk *hina*) can indicate purpose or result. Thus Jesus's quotation of Is 6:9–10 either offers the reason for his teaching in parables or describes the result. Matthew 13:13 reads "because" (Gk *hoti*),

otherwise, they might turn back and be forgiven."[A,B]

The Parable of the Sower Explained

[13] Then he said to them, "Don't you understand this parable? How then will you understand all of the parables? [14] The sower sows the word. [15] Some are like the word sown on the path. When they hear, immediately Satan comes and takes away the word sown in them.[C] [16] And others are like seed sown on rocky ground. When they hear the word, immediately they receive it with joy. [17] But they have no root; they are short-lived. When distress or persecution comes because of the word, they immediately fall away. [18] Others are like seed sown among thorns; these are the ones who hear the word, [19] but the worries of this age, the deceitfulness[D] of wealth, and the desires for other things enter in and choke the word, and it becomes unfruitful. [20] And those like seed sown on good ground hear the word, welcome it, and produce fruit thirty, sixty, and a hundred times what was sown."

Using Your Light

[21] He also said to them, "Is a lamp brought in to be put under a basket or under a bed? Isn't it to be put on a lampstand? [22] For there is nothing hidden that will not be revealed, and nothing concealed that will not be brought to light. [23] If anyone has ears to hear, let him listen." [24] And he said to them, "Pay attention to what you hear. By the measure you use, it will be measured to you — and more will be added to you.

[25] For whoever has, more will be given to him, and whoever does not have, even what he has will be taken away from him."

The Parable of the Growing Seed

[26] "The kingdom of God is like this," he said. "A man scatters seed on the ground. [27] He sleeps and rises night and day; the seed sprouts and grows, although he doesn't know how. [28] The soil produces a crop by itself — first the blade, then the head, and then the full grain on the head. [29] As soon as the crop is ready, he sends for the sickle, because the harvest has come."

The Parable of the Mustard Seed

[30] And he said, "With what can we compare the kingdom of God, or what parable can we use to describe it? [31] It's like a mustard seed that, when sown upon the soil, is the smallest of all the seeds on the ground. [32] And when sown, it comes up and grows taller than all the garden plants, and produces large branches, so that the birds of the sky can nest in its shade."

Using Parables

[33] He was speaking the word to them with many parables like these, as they were able to understand. [34] He did not speak to them without a parable. Privately, however, he explained everything to his own disciples.

Wind and Waves Obey Jesus

[35] On that day, when evening had come, he told them, "Let's cross over to the other side of the sea." [36] So they left the crowd and took him

---

[A]4:12 Other mss read *and their sins forgiven them*　[B]4:12 Is 6:9–10　[C]4:15 Other mss read *in their hearts*　[D]4:19 Or *seduction*

---

states the result of the hearers' unwillingness, not its cause. Mark's abbreviated quotation of Is 6:9–10 reverses the first two clauses, drops the first half of v. 10, and changes "and be healed" to **and be forgiven. Turn back** expresses repentance. "Be forgiven" is a divine passive, meaning "be forgiven by God."
4:13–20 Jesus responded to the question of v. 10 and interpreted his own parable.
4:13 For Mark this verse is key: Whoever does not **understand this parable** will not understand all of the parables of Jesus.
4:14–20 In Jesus's explanation, the seed sown (cp. 1Co 3:5–9) is **the word** (cp. 2:2); the birds become **Satan**; the sun and its scorching become **distress or persecution** (i.e., religious persecution); withered becomes **fall away**; the choking from the thorns is specified as **the worries of this age, the deceitfulness of wealth, and the desires for other things** (i.e., from misplaced priorities, see Mt 6:24–34); and the good ground is identified as those who **hear the word, welcome it, and produce fruit.** Clearly Jesus's emphasis was on "the word" (Gk *logos*)—used eight times in these verses—and on "hear," used four times. Those who hear the word, welcome it, and produce a crop are true disciples, even though they produce varying results (Mt 25:14–30).

4:21–34 Mark concludes his section on Jesus teaching in parables with four epigrams (vv. 21–25), two parables about the kingdom of God (vv. 26–29,30–32), and a brief explanation of Jesus's parabolic teaching method (vv. 33–34).
4:21–23 Lamp refers to a small clay lamp that was placed on a **lampstand** to maximize illumination. The lamp represents Jesus. A **basket** refers to a grain container that would hold about two gallons. The rhetorical questions assume that light should not be hidden. The sayings in v. 22 are an example of synonymous parallelism that emphasizes that Jesus is only temporarily to be concealed.
4:24–25 Pay attention to what you hear reinforces vv. 9 and 23 and the emphasis on hearing in vv. 13–20. Jesus's words to his disciples are almost the opposite of those given to outsiders in v. 12. Hearing is vital (Rm 10:17), and God will grant more revelation and understanding to those who listen to and respond. Some will neither hear nor benefit from revelation (Mk 4:25).
4:26–29 Mark includes two parables related to **the kingdom of God** (vv. 26–29,30–32; cp. 1:15). Like **seed**, God's kingdom contains within itself the power to grow. The only human role is planting. Once planted, seeds grow and become a **harvest.** The **sickle** is

a symbol of the final judgment (Jl 3:13; Rv 14:15).
4:30–32 Mark's second kingdom parable (cp. Mt 13:31–32 and Lk 13:18–19) contrasts a small beginning with disproportionate growth. Technically **a mustard seed** is not **the smallest of all the seeds,** but it was apparently the smallest seed used in Jesus's time and thus was metaphorical for very small things (Mt 17:20; Lk 17:6). The mustard seed produces a bush up to six feet tall with **large branches** on which **the birds of the sky can nest.** The OT used this image for Gentiles finding a place among God's people (Ps 104:12; Ezk 17:22–23; 31:6; Dn 4:9–21).
4:33–34 Mark concludes his section on Jesus's parabolic teaching with a final explanation. **With many parables like these** indicates Mark (and the other Gospel writers) included only a selection of Jesus's parables (cp. v. 2). **He did not speak to them without a parable** indicates that parables were Jesus's regular method of public teaching, but in private **he explained everything to his own disciples.**
4:35–36 On that day refers to the same day that Jesus delivered his teaching in vv. 1–34. **When evening had come** is typical of Mark's dual references in which the second time marker is more specific than the first. In this case the words indicate that Jesus had

along since he was in the boat. And other boats were with him. **37** A great windstorm arose, and the waves were breaking over the boat, so that the boat was already being swamped. **38** He was in the stern, sleeping on the cushion. So they woke him up and said to him, "Teacher! Don't you care that we're going to die?"

39 He got up, rebuked the wind, and said to the sea, "Silence! Be still!" The wind ceased, and there was a great calm. **40** Then he said to them, "Why are you afraid? Do you still have no faith?"

41 And they were terrified^A and asked one another, "Who then is this? Even the wind and the sea obey him!"

Demons Driven Out by Jesus

5 They came to the other side of the sea, to the region of the Gerasenes.^B **2** As soon as he got out of the boat, a man with an unclean spirit came out of the tombs and met him. **3** He lived in the tombs, and no one was able to restrain him anymore — not even with a chain — **4** because he often had been bound with shackles and chains, but had torn the chains apart and smashed the shackles. No one was strong enough to subdue him. **5** Night and day among the tombs and on the mountains, he was always crying out and cutting himself with stones.

6 When he saw Jesus from a distance, he ran and knelt down before him. **7** And he cried out with a loud voice, "What do you have to do with me, Jesus, Son of the Most High God? I beg you before God, don't torment me!" **8** For he had told him, "Come out of the man, you unclean spirit!"

9 "What is your name?" he asked him.

"My name is Legion," he answered him, "because we are many." **10** And he begged him earnestly not to send them out of the region. **11** A large herd of pigs was there, feeding on the hillside. **12** The demons^C begged him, "Send us to the pigs, so that we may enter them." **13** So he gave them permission, and the unclean spirits came out and entered the pigs. The herd of about two thousand rushed down the steep bank into the sea and drowned there.

14 The men who tended them ran off and reported it in the town and the countryside, and people went to see what had happened. **15** They came to Jesus and saw the man who had been demon-possessed, sitting there, dressed and in his right mind; and they were afraid. **16** Those who had seen it described to them what had happened to the demon-possessed man and

^A **4:41** Or *were filled with awe* ^B **5:1** Some mss read *Gadarenes*; other mss read *Gergesenes* ^C **5:12** Other mss read *All the demons*

been teaching all day, and they help build suspense for what follows since a storm on the water at night is more frightening. **The other side of the sea** refers to the eastern side, which was Gentile territory.

4:37 The Sea of Galilee lies almost seven hundred feet below sea level. It is surrounded by highlands. To the northeast is Mount Hermon, which rises over nine thousand feet above sea level. When the cold air from Mount Hermon meets the rising warm air from the sea, it often results in a storm that sweeps down onto the lake from the heights. Because fishing boats of the day had low sides, **the boat was already being swamped.**

4:38 The **stern** (rear) of the boat had a raised deck on which fishermen could sit or lay. **The cushion** was for the helmsman. For the only time recorded in the Gospels, Jesus was **sleeping.** Exhausted from teaching, he entrusted himself to God (cp. v. 27; Pss 3:5; 4:8). **Don't you care that we're going to die** was softened in Mt 8:25 and Lk 8:24. The words recall Jnh 1:14.

4:39 The phrase **Silence! Be still!** recalls the exorcism of 1:25 in which Jesus rebuked and silenced the demon. The use of the perfect tense means "be still, and stay still." Nature responded immediately. The **great calm** of v. 39 contrasts with the great storm of v. 37. This transformation was accomplished by just a word from Jesus.

4:40 Jesus's rebuke of his disciples was not as harsh in Mt 8:26 and Lk 8:25. **Afraid** refers to timidity and lack of confidence in God. **Faith** is trust in God. Lack of faith thus made them fearful in the crisis.

4:41 **They were terrified** is literally "they feared a great fear." The great storm that Jesus

turned into great calm now led to great fear. Their terror is understandable in light of the teaching that only God can make **the wind and the sea obey him** (cp. Pss 65:7; 89:8–9).

5:1–20 The healing of the demoniac is recorded in Mt 8:28–34 in shortened form and in Lk 8:26–39. Jesus brought calm to a raging man just as he brought calm to the raging sea.

5:1 The region where Jesus and his disciples landed is unclear.

5:2 A man is reported as "two demon-possessed men" in Mt 8:28. On **unclean spirit,** see note at 1:23–24.

5:3–5 Mark's description is the most detailed in the Gospels. Three times he mentioned **the tombs** where the demoniac lived. They were cut from rock or were natural mountain caves. Tombs, burial places, and items associated with the dead were unclean for Jews. Though **shackles and chains** were repeatedly used, **no one was able to restrain** or **subdue him.** "Subdue" can refer to taming a wild animal (Jms 3:7). The man's supernatural strength is indicated by the fact that he **had torn the chains apart and smashed the shackles.** The man was **always crying out,** his shrieks echoing **among the tombs and on the mountains.** He was a danger to himself and others.

5:6 From a distance does not indicate discrepancy between vv. 2 and 6. Verse 6 resumes the story from v. 2 after Mark's description of the demon-possessed man.

5:7–8 What do you have to do with me virtually repeats the unclean spirit's words from 1:24. The demoniac's identification of **Jesus** as **Son of the Most High God** answered the disciples' question from 4:41 and underscored that the spirits knew who Jesus

was. Ironically the spirits asked Jesus not to **torment** them as they had tormented the possessed man.

5:9 My name is Legion indicated the strength of the demons. A Roman military legion consisted of about six thousand soldiers (cp. the number of pigs in v. 13). The name "Legion" thus serves to indicate a large number (**because we are many**), explains the supernatural strength of the man, and magnifies the fact that Jesus was the "more powerful" one (1:7) who could "enter a strong man's house" and tie him up (3:27).

5:10 Out of the region may refer to the false idea that demons were territorial.

5:11 Pigs were unclean to Jews. Herding them was forbidden (Lv 11:7; Dt 14:8). The **large herd** reminds us that this event took place in a Gentile area.

5:12 In v. 10 the unclean spirits begged Jesus not to send them out of the region. In this verse they **begged** to be sent into unclean animals.

5:13 Drowned refers to the **pigs,** not the spirits (cp. Mt 12:43–44). None of the Gospel authors comment on the loss of animal life or its economic impact. The action of the demon-possessed pigs reemphasizes the self-destructive impulse caused by demon possession (Mk 5:5).

5:14–15 Sitting . . . dressed . . . in his right mind proved the man's healing. **They were afraid** echoes the reaction of the disciples in 4:41. Ironically, the people were more afraid of the one who cast out demons than they were of the demoniac.

5:16–18 The spirits begged Jesus (vv. 10,12), the people of the region begged Jesus (v. 17), and now the healed man **begged** to stay with Jesus.

told about the pigs. ¹⁷ Then they began to beg him to leave their region.

¹⁸ As he was getting into the boat, the man who had been demon-possessed begged him earnestly that he might remain with him. ¹⁹ Jesus did not let him but told him, "Go home to your own people, and report to them how much the Lord has done for you and how he has had mercy on you." ²⁰ So he went out and began to proclaim in the Decapolis how much Jesus had done for him, and they were all amazed.

A Girl Restored and a Woman Healed

²¹ When Jesus had crossed over again by boat^A to the other side, a large crowd gathered around him while he was by the sea. ²² One of the synagogue leaders, named Jairus, came, and when he saw Jesus, he fell at his feet ²³ and begged him earnestly, "My little daughter is dying. Come and lay your hands on her so that she can get well^B and live." ²⁴ So Jesus went with him, and a large crowd was following and pressing against him.

²⁵ Now a woman suffering from bleeding for twelve years ²⁶ had endured much under many doctors. She had spent everything she had and was not helped at all. On the contrary, she became worse. ²⁷ Having heard about Jesus, she came up behind him in the crowd and touched his clothing. ²⁸ For she said, "If I just touch his clothes, I'll be made well." ²⁹ Instantly her flow of blood ceased, and she sensed in her body that she was healed of her affliction.

³⁰ Immediately Jesus realized that power had gone out from him. He turned around in the crowd and said, "Who touched my clothes?"

³¹ His disciples said to him, "You see the crowd pressing against you, and yet you say, 'Who touched me?'"

³² But he was looking around to see who had done this. ³³ The woman, with fear and trembling, knowing what had happened to her, came and fell down before him, and told him the whole truth. ³⁴ "Daughter," he said to her, "your faith has saved you. Go in peace and be healed from your affliction."

³⁵ While he was still speaking, people came from the synagogue leader's house and said, "Your daughter is dead. Why bother the teacher anymore?"

³⁶ When Jesus overheard^C what was said, he told the synagogue leader, "Don't be afraid. Only believe." ³⁷ He did not let anyone accompany him except Peter, James, and John, James's brother. ³⁸ They came to the leader's house, and he saw a commotion — people weeping and wailing loudly. ³⁹ He went in and said to them, "Why are you making a commotion and weeping? The child is not dead but asleep." ⁴⁰ They laughed at him, but he put them all outside. He took the child's father, mother, and those who were with him, and entered the place where the child was. ⁴¹ Then he took the child by the hand and said to her, "*Talitha koum*"^D (which is translated, "Little girl, I say to you, get up"). ⁴² Immediately the girl got up and began to walk. (She was twelve years old.) At this they

---

^A5:21 Other mss omit *by boat*   ^B5:23 Or *she might be saved*   ^C5:36 Or *ignored*   ^D5:41 An Aramaic expression

---

5:19–20 Jesus told the man to tell his **own people . . . how much the Lord** had done for him. People changed by Jesus must tell the world about his miraculous works. **The Decapolis** (lit "ten cities") refers to a league of ten Greek cities spread throughout Syria, Jordan, and Palestine. They were predominantly Gentile and were largely independent from Rome.
5:21–43 The intertwined miracles involving Jairus's daughter and the bleeding woman occur in all three Synoptic Gospels (cp. Mt 9:18–26; Lk 8:40–56). Both miracles involved uncleanness.
5:21 The other side refers to the western side of the Sea of Galilee. Mark has already recorded key ministry events **by the sea** (1:16–20; 2:13–15; 4:1–34). Mark's description of Jesus's return is virtually identical to that given in 4:1 before he crossed the lake.
5:22–23 Synagogue leaders such as Jairus were respected laymen responsible for synagogue oversight and activities. **Fell at his feet and begged him earnestly** shows Jairus's desperate concern for his **little daughter**. Luke recorded that she was his only daughter (Lk 8:42). The ruler's request **lay your hands on her** shows awareness of Jesus's method in other healings (1:31,41; 6:5; 7:32; 8:23,25). Jairus's word for **get well** also means "be saved." The same word was used of the woman in v. 28 and in Jesus's proclamation in v. 34.

5:24–26 The implication is that the **woman suffering from bleeding** was beset with vaginal bleeding, making her unclean according to OT law (Lv 15:19–33). That this had gone on for twelve years (cp. v. 42) and she had been treated by **many doctors** but **not helped at all** indicates an illness that was beyond the help of current medicine. Furthermore, she was financially depleted—**she had spent everything she had**.
5:27–29 The climax that has been building since v. 25 is finally reached with **touched**. The woman fulfilled her intent to reach out and touch Jesus. **His clothing** is clarified in Mt 9:20 as "the end of his robe." Many Jews wore tassels on the corners of their outer garments (Nm 15:38–39; Dt 22:12). On **instantly**, see note at 1:9–11.
5:30–31 Immediately is the same word as "instantly" (v. 29). As soon as the woman was healed, Jesus knew that **power** (Gk *dunamis*) **had gone out from him**. This reaction is not reported in his other healings.
5:32–33 Fell down before him recalls the actions of Jairus (v. 22) and the demoniac (v. 6).
5:34 Only here did Jesus address someone as **daughter**. It reassured the trembling woman. **Your faith has saved you** recalls the healing of the paralytic in 2:5 and anticipates 10:52. **Go in peace** was the usual Hebrew blessing at dismissal (Ex 4:18; Jdg 18:6; 1Sm 1:17; 25:35; 2Sm 15:9; 2Kg 5:19; Lk 7:50; Ac 16:36;

Jms 2:16). Jesus used the word **affliction** (v. 29) to assure the woman that her cure was permanent.
5:35 This resumes Jairus's story (vv. 21–24) after the interruption. Precious time had been lost, with the result that the girl had died.
5:36 Jesus's words to Jairus (**only believe**) are a present tense imperative, "Keep believing."
5:37 On other important occasions (9:2; 14:33), **Peter, James, and John** accompanied Jesus while the other disciples waited behind (see note at 1:16–20).
5:38–39 The **commotion** and **people weeping and wailing** were typical of Middle Eastern funerals. Flute players were also present (Mt 9:23). The mourners could have been friends or hired professionals. Before even seeing the girl, Jesus declared she was **not dead but asleep**. This earned him much derision. He meant that her sleep was not the sleep of final death.
5:40 The laughing indicates skepticism and mockery. **Those who were with him** refers to Peter, James, and John (v. 37).
5:41 Taking the girl's body **by the hand** technically made Jesus unclean. **Talitha koum** (lit "little lamb, arise!") is Aramaic. Her spirit returned at this command (Lk 8:55).
5:42–43 That Jesus arranged for the girl to get **something to eat** proves his practical concern for her.

were utterly astounded. **43** Then he gave them strict orders that no one should know about this and told them to give her something to eat.

Rejection at Nazareth

6 He left there and came to his hometown, and his disciples followed him. **2** When the Sabbath came, he began to teach in the synagogue, and many who heard him were astonished. "Where did this man get these things?" they said. "What is this wisdom that has been given to him, and how are these miracles performed by his hands? **3** Isn't this the carpenter, the son of Mary, and the brother of James, Joses, Judas, and Simon? And aren't his sisters here with us?" So they were offended by him.

4 Jesus said to them, "A prophet is not without honor except in his hometown, among his relatives, and in his household." **5** He was not able to do a miracle there, except that he laid his hands on a few sick people and healed them. **6** And he was amazed at their unbelief. He was going around the villages teaching.

Commissioning the Twelve

7 He summoned the Twelve and began to send them out in pairs and gave them authority over unclean spirits. **8** He instructed them to take nothing for the road except a staff — no bread, no traveling bag, no money in their belts, **9** but to wear sandals and not put on an extra

---

6:1 Jesus's **hometown** was Nazareth (see note at 1:9–11).
6:2 The words **he began to teach** assume Jesus was invited to do so. Unlike Luke (Lk 4:16–21), Mark did not focus on the content of Jesus's teaching. In Galilee Jesus regularly taught (Mk 1:21–22,39) or performed miracles (1:23–28,39; 3:1–6) in the synagogues. After his rejection at Nazareth, there is no record of Jesus entering a synagogue again. Synagogues are mentioned again only in Mark as places of hypocrisy and persecution (12:39; 13:9). As was true in Capernaum (1:22), people in Nazareth **were astonished** by Jesus's teaching.
6:3 Isn't this the carpenter? The parallel in Mt 13:55 reads, "Isn't this the carpenter's son?" Luke 4:22 has, "Isn't this Joseph's son?" A carpenter (Gk *tektōn*) was a craftsman in wood and stone. **Son of Mary** may hint at Jesus's supposed illegitimacy or indicate that Joseph had died (no mention is made of him in v. 4 or elsewhere in Mark, but see Jn 6:42). This is the only time Jesus's mother is

mentioned by name in Mark. Jesus's brother **James** later became leader of the Jerusalem church and was killed on orders from the high priest in AD 62 (Josephus, *Ant.*, 20.9.1). He authored the book of James. **Judas** probably was the author of the book of Jude. **Joses** ("Joseph") and **Simon** are not named again in the NT (but see Jn 2:12; 7:5; Ac 1:14; 1Co 9:5). Jesus's **sisters** are not named, but the plural indicates he had more than one.
6:4 Jesus used this self-applied proverb elsewhere (Jn 4:44). In Mark's version (cp. parallels in Mt 13:57; Lk 4:24) Jesus named three settings where **a prophet** is dishonored—**in his hometown, among his relatives** (referring to 3:20–21,31–35)**, and in his household**.
6:5–6a Matthew treats **he was not able** not as a statement about limitations of power but as a statement of fact ("he did not do," Mt 13:58). The reason was the people's **unbelief**. Previously they were astonished at Jesus (v. 2). In an ironic twist, Mark alone ended the narrative (cp. Lk 4:25–30) with

Jesus being **amazed** at *them*. What amazed him was their lack of faith. The people of Nazareth did not refer to Jesus by name but only as "this man," a sign of contempt.
6:6b This is the third time Jesus went on a preaching circuit in Galilee (1:14,39).
6:7 He summoned the Twelve recalls 3:13. **To send them out** recalls 3:14. **Authority over unclean spirits** recalls 3:15. **In pairs** reflects common-sense wisdom (Ec 4:9–10) and was Jesus's usual practice (Mk 11:1; 14:13; Lk 10:1), which was followed in the early church (Ac 8:14; 9:38; 11:30; 12:25; 13:2; 15:39–40). The practice ensured companionship and mutual support, and it fulfilled the OT requirement of two witnesses (Dt 17:6; 19:15; 2Co 13:1). "The Twelve" are called "apostles" after they returned (Mk 6:30).
6:8–9 According to Mark, the disciples were to take **a staff** ... **belts** ... **sandals** ... **shirt**. These were the same items God told the Israelites to take on their departure from Egypt (Ex 12:11). Matthew's and Luke's accounts prohibit the walking stick (Mt 10:10; Lk 9:3)

Character profile:
John the Baptist

T he circumstances of John the Baptist's birth are memorable. His mother, Elizabeth, was a relative of Jesus's mother, Mary. His father, Zechariah, served as a priest in the temple. One day the angel Gabriel appeared to Zechariah to announce that he and his wife would have a son. When Zechariah asked how that could be possible, since he and Elizabeth were well past childbearing years, Gabriel told him that, because of his unbelief, he would be mute until his son was born (see Lk 1:5–20).

Zechariah and Elizabeth named their son John in accordance with the angel's instructions. In time, he would become known as John the Baptist.

From a distance, John the Baptist may seem like an inscrutable eccentric—a cross between a slightly deranged street-corner preacher and a hardcore wilderness survivalist. The man lived in the desert outskirts of civilization, and he ate locusts and wild honey.

A closer look at John, however, reveals a person whose passion and struggles are quite relatable—and whose example deserves careful consideration. John understood from an early age that he was set apart by God for a purpose. It seems his whole life was geared to fulfilling that purpose.

John was among the first to know that the long-awaited Messiah had finally come (see Jn 1:29). However, John also was one of the few people who understood that the Jewish people weren't ready for what was about to happen.

His God-given mandate was to prepare the people of Israel, to serve as the Messiah's forerunner—and he took the

responsibility seriously. He challenged them to turn away from their sin and publicly demonstrate their repentance by being baptized. Hundreds responded to his message.

One day Jesus showed up at John's ministry site and asked John to baptize him. With humility, John admitted that he was unworthy to baptize Jesus. But when Jesus explained that his baptism was part of God's plan, John fulfilled his responsibility (see Mt 3:13–17).

With the advent of Jesus's public ministry, John challenged Herod, the king of Judea, to repent of his sins—specifically, his illegal marriage to the ex-wife of his brother. John paid a steep price for his boldness: Herod threw him into prison. At his lowest point he sent his disciples to Jesus to get assurance that Jesus was indeed the Messiah.

But that momentary display of weakness makes John's boldness throughout the rest of his life all the more remarkable. He refused to back down, even though he was angering the most powerful people in Israel. He spoke the words God had given him and left the consequences in God's hands.

Eventually John paid the ultimate price for his radical boldness and obedience. Although Herod was inclined to keep John alive, Herod's illegitimate wife had other ideas. She devised a scheme that resulted in John's execution (Mk 6:17–29).

Yet death could do little to diminish his legacy. Jesus himself said of John, "I tell you, among those born of women no one is greater than John" (Lk 7:28).

Living your Christian faith with a spirit of boldness and courage can make a lasting impression on the people you encounter. As John demonstrated, when you represent God you have no reason to be fearful or timid. Ultimately, no opposition can stand against you.

shirt. **10** He said to them, "Whenever you enter a house, stay there until you leave that place. **11** If any place does not welcome you or listen to you, when you leave there, shake the dust off your feet as a testimony against them."^A **12** So they went out and preached that people should repent. **13** They drove out many demons, anointed many sick people with oil and healed them.

John the Baptist Beheaded

14 King Herod heard about it, because Jesus's name had become well known. Some^B said, "John the Baptist has been raised from the dead, and that's why miraculous powers are at work in him." **15** But others said, "He's Elijah." Still others said, "He's a prophet, like one of the prophets from long ago." **16** When Herod heard of it, he said, "John, the one I beheaded, has been raised!"

17 For Herod himself had given orders to arrest John and to chain him in prison on account of Herodias, his brother Philip's wife, because he had married her. **18** John had been telling Herod, "It is not lawful for you to have your brother's wife." **19** So Herodias held a grudge against him and wanted to kill him. But she could not, **20** because Herod feared John and protected him, knowing he was a righteous and holy man. When Herod heard him he would be very perplexed,^C and yet he liked to listen to him.

21 An opportune time came on his birthday, when Herod gave a banquet for his nobles, military commanders, and the leading men of Galilee. **22** When Herodias's own daughter^D came in and danced, she pleased Herod and his guests. The king said to the girl, "Ask me whatever you want, and I'll give it to you." **23** He promised her with an oath: "Whatever you ask me I will give you, up to half my kingdom."

24 She went out and said to her mother, "What should I ask for?"

"John the Baptist's head," she said.

25 At once she hurried to the king and said, "I want you to give me John the Baptist's head on a platter immediately." **26** Although the king was deeply distressed, because of his oaths and the guests^E he did not want to refuse her. **27** The king immediately sent for an executioner and commanded him to bring John's head. So he went and beheaded him in prison, **28** brought his head on a platter, and gave it to the girl. Then the girl gave it to her mother. **29** When John's disciples heard about it, they came and removed his corpse and placed it in a tomb.

Feeding of the Five Thousand

30 The apostles gathered around Jesus and reported to him all that they had done and taught. **31** He said to them, "Come away by yourselves to a remote place and rest for a while." For many people were coming and going, and they did not even have time to eat. **32** So they went away in the boat by themselves to a remote place, **33** but many saw them leaving and recognized them, and they ran on

---

^A **6:11** Other mss add *Truly I tell you, it will be more tolerable for Sodom or Gomorrah on judgment day than for that town.* ^B **6:14** Other mss read *He* ^C **6:20** Other mss read *When he heard him, he did many things* ^D **6:22** Other mss read *When his daughter Herodias* ^E **6:26** Lit *and those reclining at the table*

---

and Matthew forbids sandals (Mt 10:10; cp. Lk 10:4). According to Mark, they were not to take **bread,** a **traveling bag . . . money,** or **an extra** shirt.
6:10–11 The disciples were to **stay** in one home until they left a given town and did look for better lodging. If they were not welcomed, they were to **shake the dust off** their **feet.** Jesus elaborated more on this when he sent out the seventy-two (Lk 10:10–11), and it was the practice of the earliest missionaries (Ac 13:51; cp. Ac 18:6). **As a testimony against them** can be rendered "as a witness to them," signifying a call to repentance (cp. 1:44; 13:9).
6:12–13 That people should repent was the content of their preaching, modeling the messages of John the Baptist (1:4) and Jesus (1:15). The ministry of the Twelve is summarized as preaching and teaching (6:30), exorcism, and healing. Anointing **sick people with oil** is mentioned here, in a parable in Lk 10:34, and in Jms 5:14.
6:14–15 The story of Herod Antipas, Herodias, and John is similar to that of Ahab, Jezebel, and Elijah in 1Kg 21. In fact, Elijah's name is closely tied to this story (Mk 6:15). **King Herod** was Herod Antipas (born 20 BC), a son of Herod the Great. He ruled Galilee and Perea from 4 BC to AD 39. Jesus **had become well known** because of his circuit preaching and the mission of the Twelve. The three opinions about Jesus's identity (that he

was **John the Baptist . . . Elijah,** or **a prophet**) are given again in 8:28 as reflections of popular opinion.
6:16–17 Herod's belief that Jesus was John the Baptist resurrected prompted him to reflect fearfully on **the one** he had **beheaded** (see Josephus, *Ant.*, 18.5.2). John was imprisoned (1:14) **on account of Herodias.** Herodias was formerly married to Herod's half-**brother,** Herod Philip, and had a daughter with him named Salome. Herod Antipas convinced Herodias to leave Philip and marry him instead. To clear the way, Herod Antipas had to divorce his own wife.
6:18 John the Baptist repeatedly condemned this marriage as **not lawful** (Lv 18:16; 20:21).
6:19–20 These verses contrast Herodias's and Herod Antipas's conflicting opinions about John the Baptist. Herodias **held a grudge . . . wanted to kill him,** and asked for a way to do so. Antipas, on the other hand, **feared John and protected him,** and considered him **a righteous and holy man.**
6:21 It is ironic that wicked Herod's **birthday** became the death day for righteous John.
6:22 Mark does not name Salome, but the Jewish historian Josephus does (Josephus, *Ant.*, 18.5.4). **Girl** (vv. 22,28) is the same word Jesus used of the twelve-year-old in 5:41. **Danced** and **pleased** do not necessarily carry a nuance of sensuousness, though it is possible.

6:23 Herod's **oath** recalls King Ahasuerus's words to Esther (Est 5:3,6; 7:2). Since Antipas was only a deputy of Rome, the promise was a hyperbolic figure of speech, not a literal promise (cp. 1Kg 13:8).
6:24–25 From this point the story moves quickly to conclusion. Note the double reference to **immediately** (vv. 25,27) and the words **hurried** and **at once** in v. 25. Salome was a pawn in her mother's hands.
6:26–28 Herod was **deeply distressed.** The only other time Mark uses this word concerns Jesus in the garden of Gethsemane (14:33).
6:30–31 Mark refers to the Twelve as **the apostles** only here and in 3:14 when they were appointed. **Reported to him all that they had done and taught** refers to the mission of vv. 7–13. **A remote place** recalls 1:3–5,12–13,35,45 and provides the ideal setting for the miracle that echoes the provision of bread in the wilderness. **They did not even have time to eat** recalls 3:20 and prepares the way for the story that follows.
6:32 Mark does not name the **remote place** (cp. Lk 9:10). In Mark this was Jesus's third journey by **boat** (4:35–5:1,21–22).
6:33–34 The word for **compassion** refers to intestinal organs, which were thought to be the seat of the emotions. The word is only used of Jesus in the NT (see note at 1:40–45). Jesus saw the people as leaderless and needy (**like sheep without a shepherd**). In fulfillment of Is 40:11, Jesus cared for his flock.

foot from all the towns and arrived ahead of them.[A]

[34] When he went ashore, he saw a large crowd and had compassion on them, because they were like sheep without a shepherd. Then he began to teach them many things.

[35] When it grew late, his disciples approached him and said, "This place is deserted, and it is already late. [36] Send them away so that they can go into the surrounding countryside and villages to buy themselves something to eat."

[37] "You give them something to eat," he responded.

They said to him, "Should we go and buy two hundred denarii[B] worth of bread and give them something to eat?"

[38] He asked them, "How many loaves do you have? Go and see."

When they found out they said, "Five, and two fish." [39] Then he instructed them to have all the people sit down in groups on the green grass. [40] So they sat down in groups of hundreds and fifties. [41] He took the five loaves and the two fish, and looking up to heaven, he blessed and broke the loaves. He kept giving them to his disciples to set before the people. He also divided the two fish among them all. [42] Everyone ate and was satisfied. [43] They picked up twelve baskets full of pieces of bread and fish. [44] Now those who had eaten the loaves were five thousand men.

Walking on the Water

[45] Immediately he made his disciples get into the boat and go ahead of him to the other side, to Bethsaida, while he dismissed the crowd. [46] After he said good-bye to them, he went away to the mountain to pray. [47] Well into the night, the boat was in the middle of the sea, and he was alone on the land. [48] He saw them straining at the oars,[C] because the wind was against them. Very early in the morning[D] he came toward them walking on the sea and wanted to pass by them. [49] When they saw him walking on the sea, they thought it was a ghost and cried out, [50] because they all saw him and were terrified. Immediately he spoke with them and said, "Have courage! It is I. Don't be afraid." [51] Then he got into the boat with them, and the wind ceased. They were completely astounded, [52] because they had not understood about the loaves. Instead, their hearts were hardened.

Miraculous Healings

[53] When they had crossed over, they came to shore at Gennesaret and anchored there. [54] As they got out of the boat, people immediately recognized him. [55] They hurried throughout that region and began to carry the sick on mats to wherever they heard he was. [56] Wherever he went, into villages, towns, or the country, they laid the sick in the marketplaces and begged him that they might touch just the end

[A]6:33 Other mss add *and gathered around him* [B]6:37 A denarius = one day's wage [C]6:48 Or *them being battered as they rowed* [D]6:48 Lit *Around the fourth watch of the night* = 3 to 6 a.m.

6:35–44 The feeding of the five thousand is the only miracle recorded in all four Gospels (Mt 14:13–21; Lk 9:10–17; Jn 6:1–15).

6:35–36 The words **this place is deserted** mark the third mention of the remoteness of the place (vv. 31–32,35). After pointing out it was **late**, the disciples commanded Jesus to **send them away**.

6:37 Jesus responded with a command of his own. **You** is emphatic. Obviously the disciples did not have **two hundred denarii** (a denarius was a day's wage). In fact they had just returned from a mission on which they had taken no bread or money (v. 8). Feeding this many people was a big challenge. (Cp. Moses's wilderness situation in Ex 16:1–35; Nm 11:13,22; and Elijah's in 2Kg 4:42–44.)

6:38 The disciples focused on what they lacked, but Jesus focused on what they had—**five** ... **loaves** and **two fish**. The loaves were probably small, round, flat barley biscuits; the fish were probably dried.

6:39–40 Matthew (14:19) and John (6:10) mention the **grass** on which the people sat, but only Mark says it was **green**, indicating springtime.

6:41 Looking **up to heaven** was a position of prayer (cp. 7:34). The Gospel writers did not record Jesus's prayer, but the traditional Jewish blessing over bread would have been appropriate: "Blessed art Thou, Lord our God, King of the world, who bringeth forth bread from the earth."

6:42 The verb **was satisfied** is used of fattening animals. Thus Jesus provided abundance, not just sustenance.

6:43 The **twelve baskets** matches the number of apostles and tribes of Israel. The word for "baskets" denotes large, heavy containers.

6:44 A total of **five thousand men** were fed. Mark's word (Gk) *andres* ("males") is gender specific. Matthew adds "besides women and children" (Mt 14:21), which means that considerably more than five thousand people were fed.

6:45 The word **immediately** is characteristic. **Made** is a strong verb that carries the sense of "compelled." Mark did not say why Jesus rushed his disciples away, but Jn 6:14–15 indicates that the people wanted to make him king.

6:46 After he said good-bye to them refers to the disciples. For the second time in Mark, Jesus went off by himself **to pray**.

6:47 Well into the night apparently refers to a time quite late since v. 48 refers to "very early in the morning."

6:48 The phrases **straining at the oars** and **the wind was against them** do not picture the same situation as 4:35–41 when Jesus calmed wind and sea. **Very early in the morning** (lit "around the fourth watch of the night") reflects the Roman method of dividing the night into four watches. The fourth was from 3:00 a.m. to 6:00 a.m. **Walking on the sea** is meant literally and is verbally parallel to "on the land" (v. 47).

6:49 The disciples thought Jesus was a **ghost** (Gk *phantasma*), which expresses the idea of illusion.

6:50 Jesus reassured the disciples with two commands: **Have courage** and **don't be afraid**. The words **it is I** are literally "I am" (Gk *egō eimi*), the divine name of God in Ex 3:14 (cp. Is 41:4; 43:10–11; 48:12). Jesus did what God alone could do and used God's name to identify himself.

6:51 In 4:35–41 **the wind ceased** when Jesus commanded it to stop; here it stopped when **he got into the boat.** ... **Astounded** was the usual reaction to Jesus's power (cp. 1:22,27; 2:12; 5:15,20,42).

6:52 Mark diagnosed a twofold problem: the disciples **had not understood** and **their hearts were hardened.** Hard hearts (spiritual insensitivity) characterized the Pharisees at the synagogue in Capernaum (3:5).

6:53–56 This is Mark's third summary of Jesus's ministry (cp. 1:35–39; 3:7–12).

6:53 Gennesaret was a fertile plain on the western shore of the Sea of Galilee between Capernaum and Tiberias.

6:54 The **people immediately recognized** Jesus. This contrasts with the disciples, who had failed to recognize him (v. 49).

6:55 The **mats** on which **the sick** were carried were the same type used by the paralytic (2:2–12).

6:56 Villages, towns, and **country** sum up the entire region of Galilee. **Marketplaces** (Gk *agora*) were the busiest centers of local life. The statement that **the sick** ... **begged**

of his robe. And everyone who touched it was healed.

The Traditions of the Elders

7 The Pharisees and some of the scribes who had come from Jerusalem gathered around him. [2] They observed that some of his disciples were eating bread with unclean — that is, unwashed — hands. [3] (For the Pharisees and all the Jews do not eat unless they give their hands a ceremonial washing, keeping the tradition of the elders. [4] When they come from the marketplace, they do not eat unless they have washed. And there are many other customs they have received and keep, like the washing of cups, pitchers, kettles, and dining couches.[A]) [5] So the Pharisees and the scribes asked him, "Why don't your disciples live[B] according to the tradition of the elders, instead of eating bread with ceremonially unclean[C] hands?"

[6] He answered them, "Isaiah prophesied correctly about you hypocrites, as it is written:

This people honors me with their lips,
but their heart is far from me.
[7] They worship me in vain,
teaching as doctrines
human commands.[D]

[8] Abandoning the command of God, you hold on to human tradition."[E] [9] He also said to them, "You have a fine way of invalidating God's command in order to set up[F] your tradition! [10] For Moses said: Honor your father and your mother;[G] and Whoever speaks evil of father

or mother must be put to death.[H] [11] But you say, 'If anyone tells his father or mother: Whatever benefit you might have received from me is *corban*' " (that is, an offering devoted to God), [12] "you no longer let him do anything for his father or mother. [13] You nullify the word of God by your tradition that you have handed down. And you do many other similar things."

[14] Summoning the crowd again, he told them, "Listen to me, all of you, and understand: [15] Nothing that goes into a person from outside can defile him but the things that come out of a person are what defile him."[I]

[17] When he went into the house away from the crowd, his disciples asked him about the parable. [18] He said to them, "Are you also as lacking in understanding? Don't you realize that nothing going into a person from the outside can defile him? [19] For it doesn't go into his heart but into the stomach and is eliminated" (thus he declared all foods clean). [20] And he said, "What comes out of a person is what defiles him. [21] For from within, out of people's hearts, come evil thoughts, sexual immoralities, thefts, murders, [22] adulteries, greed, evil actions, deceit, self-indulgence, envy,[J] slander, pride, and foolishness. [23] All these evil things come from within and defile a person."

A Gentile Mother's Faith

[24] He got up and departed from there to the region of Tyre.[K] He entered a house and did not want anyone to know it, but he could not escape notice. [25] Instead, immediately after

---

Jesus to heal them recalls the man with skin disease (1:40), the demoniac (5:10,12,17–18), and the synagogue ruler (5:23) where the same word is used. Their desire to **touch just the end of his robe** recalls the desire of the bleeding woman (5:28).

7:1–23 This is Jesus's longest conflict speech in the Gospel of Mark.

7:1 On the **Pharisees** and **scribes**, see notes at 1:21–22; 2:15–17; and 3:22.

7:2 As in 2:18,24, the dispute occurred over the actions of Jesus's disciples. **Unclean** . . . **hands** refers to ritual cleansing, not hygiene.

7:3–4 These verses are an explanatory parenthesis. This is Mark's only reference to **the Jews** as a group. **The tradition of the elders** (cp. vv. 5,8–9,13) refers to oral traditions that had grown up around the written law. Such traditions became the heart of rabbinic Judaism. Apparently when the Pharisees returned from the **marketplace** they did more than just ritually wash their hands; they thoroughly purified themselves.

7:5 Jesus replied in v. 8 that the **tradition of the elders** is merely "human tradition."

7:6–7 The word for **hypocrites** refers to an actor who hid behind a mask. Thus the word means "pretender." Jesus's quotation from Is 29:13 clearly defined what a hypocrite was and focused on God's condemnation of those who taught **as doctrines human commands**.

7:8–9 Jesus accused the scribes and Pharisees of **abandoning the command of God** while keeping **human tradition**. They made their oral traditions more important than God's law.

7:10 By quoting the fifth commandment (Ex 20:12; Dt 5:16) and Ex 21:17 (Lv 20:9), Jesus introduced a specific example of what he charged in Mk 7:8–9.

7:11–13 **You say** is emphatic and pits the rabbis' teaching against **the word of God**. The rabbinic custom of **corban** (modified from Lv 27:28; Nm 18:14) allowed a person to devote all his material goods to the Lord. The rabbis shamefully allowed corban to excuse sons from meeting the material needs of their aging parents. **You do many other similar things** emphasized that the corban practice was representative of other hypocritical Pharisaic practices.

7:14–15 Jesus broadened his audience to the **crowd** and expanded his topic to true defilement. Verse 15 is the heart of his teaching. A person is defiled by what comes out, not what goes in.

7:17–18 The disciples asked Jesus privately about **the parable** of v. 15. Jesus repeated what he had said and rebuked them for their lack of **understanding**.

7:19 What goes into a person's stomach doesn't defile because it is digested and

eliminated. Recall that Mark was written under Peter's influence and that Peter learned in Ac 10:15 that all foods are clean. Thus the parenthetical statement of Mk 7:19 indicates that Mark, Peter, and others looked back afresh on Jesus's saying and realized that he had pronounced all foods clean. They failed fully to grasp this when Jesus originally uttered it.

7:20–23 Jesus listed thirteen moral problems to illustrate his point about internal defilement. The first seven are plural and indicate repeated acts. **Sexual immoralities** (Gk *porneia*) includes all illicit sexual practices outside marriage. **Evil actions** is a term for maliciousness. The last six evils are all singular, indicating attitudes. **Envy** refers to jealousy, covetousness, and a grudging attitude. The word for **pride** refers to exalting oneself above others. **Foolishness** is lack of moral judgment.

7:24–8:10 These verses describe Jesus's ministry in the Gentile areas of Tyre, Sidon, and the Decapolis.

7:24 Tyre was on the Mediterranean coast northwest of Galilee. Jesus went to **the region of Tyre**, which refers to the administrative district around Tyre and not to the city itself.

7:25–26 This woman was **a Gentile** who lived according to Greek culture. **A Syrophoenician** (a Phoenician from Syria)

hearing about him, a woman whose little daughter had an unclean spirit came and fell at his feet. [26] The woman was a Gentile,[A] a Syrophoenician by birth, and she was asking him to cast the demon out of her daughter. [27] He said to her, "Let the children be fed first, because it isn't right to take the children's bread and throw it to the dogs."

[28] But she replied to him, "Lord, even the dogs under the table eat the children's crumbs."

[29] Then he told her, "Because of this reply, you may go. The demon has left your daughter." [30] When she went back to her home, she found her child lying on the bed, and the demon was gone.

Jesus Does Everything Well

[31] Again, leaving the region of Tyre, he went by way of Sidon to the Sea of Galilee, through[B] the region of the Decapolis. [32] They brought to him a deaf man who had difficulty speaking and begged Jesus to lay his hand on him. [33] So he took him away from the crowd in private. After putting his fingers in the man's ears and spitting, he touched his tongue. [34] Looking up to heaven, he sighed deeply and said to him, "*Ephphatha!*"[C] (that is, "Be opened!"). [35] Immediately his ears were opened, his tongue loosened, and he began to speak clearly. [36] He ordered them to tell no one, but the more he ordered them, the more they proclaimed it. [37] They were extremely astonished and said, "He has done everything well. He even makes the deaf hear and the mute speak."

Feeding Four Thousand

8 In those days there was again a large crowd, and they had nothing to eat. He called the disciples and said to them, [2] "I have compassion on the crowd, because they've already stayed with me three days and have nothing to eat. [3] If I send them home hungry, they will collapse on the way, and some of them have come a long distance."

[4] His disciples answered him, "Where can anyone get enough bread here in this desolate place to feed these people?"

[5] "How many loaves do you have?" he asked them.

"Seven," they said. [6] He commanded the crowd to sit down on the ground. Taking the seven loaves, he gave thanks, broke them, and gave them to his disciples to set before the people. So they served them to the crowd. [7] They also had a few small fish, and after he had blessed them, he said these were to be served as well. [8] They ate and were satisfied. Then they collected seven large baskets of leftover pieces. [9] About four thousand were there. He dismissed them. [10] And he immediately got into the boat with his disciples and went to the district of Dalmanutha.

The Leaven of the Pharisees and Herod

[11] The Pharisees came and began to argue with him, demanding of him a sign from heaven to test him. [12] Sighing deeply in his spirit, he said, "Why does this generation demand a sign? Truly I tell you, no sign will be given to

---

[A]**7:26** Or *a Greek (speaker)* [B]**7:31** Or *into* [C]**7:34** An Aramaic expression

---

reflects Mark's use of double expression, with the second term being more specific. **Fell at his feet** recalls the actions of Jairus (5:23) and the Gerasene demoniac (5:6).
7:27 In Jesus's curt statement, **the children** refers to the Jews (cp. Mt 15:24). Jews typically referred to Gentiles as **dogs**. Since Jews considered dogs unclean (Ex 22:31; 1Kg 21:23; 22:38; 2Kg 9:36; Pr 26:11; Mt 7:6; 2Pt 2:22), calling someone a dog was an insult (1Sm 17:43; 24:14; 2Sm 16:9; Is 56:10–11).
7:28 Lord can be a divine title or just a polite address. The woman asserted that even though dogs did not eat with the children at the table, they did eat the **crumbs** that fell to the floor (cp. Lk 16:21). She accepted the priority of Jesus's mission to the Jews but pointed out that Israel's privileges did not exclude Gentiles from enjoying the overflow.
7:29–30 The narrative returns to the exorcism, which was the occasion for the woman's coming to Jesus. His words **because of this reply** in Matthew's account focus on the greatness of the woman's faith (Mt 15:28).
7:31–37 This account is likely part of a larger healing ministry in the Decapolis that Matthew summarized (Mt 15:29–31). Jesus's reception this time contrasts with that of his first visit (cp. Mk 5:17) and possibly hints at the success of the Gerasene demoniac's proclamation (5:20).
7:31 By way of Sidon . . . the Decapolis indicates Jesus traveled more than twenty

miles farther north before turning southeast. The entire journey was more than 120 miles. On the Decapolis, see note at 5:19–20.
7:32 Difficulty speaking is also used in the Greek version of Is 35:5–6, a passage that Jesus fulfilled with this miracle.
7:33–34 Only here and in 8:22–26 did Jesus take the person he healed aside **in private**. **Spitting** (cp. 8:23) probably means Jesus spit into his hand and applied saliva to the man's tongue (Jn 9:6). **Looking up to heaven** is a sign of prayer (see note at 6:41). **Sighed deeply** indicates Jesus's deep emotional involvement. Mark translates the Aramaic word **Ephphatha** parenthetically (cp. 5:41).
7:35 He began to speak clearly indicates that, like many deaf people, he was previously able to make sounds but not form coherent words.
7:36 Proclaimed is the word Mark used for telling others about Jesus (Gk *kērussō*). The people of the Decapolis now responded as the Gerasene demoniac had done (5:20).
7:37 While Jesus's other healing miracles brought astonishment and amazement (1:22,27; 2:12; 5:20,42; 6:2,6,51), this is the only time that **extremely** or "beyond all measure" appears. **He has done everything well** echoes the Septuagint wording of Gn 1:31. Once again, Jesus had done what only God could do (Ex 4:11).
8:1–10 The feeding of the four thousand fulfilled the request of the Syrophoenician

woman in 7:28 for the Gentiles to eat the children's crumbs.
8:1 In those days refers to the time Jesus spent in the Decapolis (7:31).
8:7 The phrase **a few small fish** can refer to sardines or fish scraps.
8:8 Seven large baskets corresponds to the number of loaves (v. 5). The Greek word for *baskets* differs from the Jewish term in 6:43. This term refers to a hamper large enough to hold a person (Ac 9:25).
8:9 The number **four thousand** is not gender specific as in 6:44. It implies men, women, and children (as Mt 15:38 makes clear).
8:10 The **district of Dalmanutha** is mentioned only here in the NT and in ancient literature. Matthew identifies the place as Magadan, which was on the western shore of the Sea of Galilee.
8:11 Back on the western side of the lake, Jesus was again accosted by the Pharisees. On **Pharisees**, see note at 2:15–17. A **sign from heaven** could refer to "a sign from God" or to "a cosmic phenomenon." The Pharisees demanded further divine confirmation to **test** Jesus. They were trying to discredit him and his authority.
8:12 The word for **sighing deeply** points to despair rather than anger. **In his spirit** (cp. 2:8) refers to Jesus's inner being and the depth of his dismay. On **truly I tell you**, see note at 3:28–30.

this generation." [13] Then he left them, got back into the boat, and went to the other side.

[14] The disciples had forgotten to take bread and had only one loaf with them in the boat. [15] Then he gave them strict orders: "Watch out! Beware of the leaven[A] of the Pharisees and the leaven of Herod." [16] They were discussing among themselves that they did not have any bread. [17] Aware of this, he said to them, "Why are you discussing the fact you have no bread? Don't you understand or comprehend? Do you have hardened hearts? [18] Do you have eyes and not see; do you have ears and not hear?[B] And do you not remember? [19] When I broke the five loaves for the five thousand, how many baskets full of leftovers did you collect?"

"Twelve," they told him.

[20] "When I broke the seven loaves for the four thousand, how many baskets full of pieces did you collect?"

"Seven," they said.

[21] And he said to them, "Don't you understand yet?"

Healing a Blind Man

[22] They came to Bethsaida. They brought a blind man to him and begged him to touch him. [23] He took the blind man by the hand and brought him out of the village. Spitting on his eyes and laying his hands on him, he asked him, "Do you see anything?"

[24] He looked up and said, "I see people — they look like trees walking."

[25] Again Jesus placed his hands on the man's eyes. The man looked intently and his sight was restored and he saw everything clearly. [26] Then he sent him home, saying, "Don't even go into the village."[C]

Peter's Confession of the Messiah

[27] Jesus went out with his disciples to the villages of Caesarea Philippi. And on the road he asked his disciples, "Who do people say that I am?"

[28] They answered him, "John the Baptist; others, Elijah; still others, one of the prophets."

[29] "But you," he asked them, "who do you say that I am?"

Peter answered him, "You are the Messiah."
[30] And he strictly warned them to tell no one about him.

His Death and Resurrection Predicted

[31] Then he began to teach them that it was necessary for the Son of Man to suffer many things and be rejected by the elders, chief priests, and scribes, be killed, and rise after three days. [32] He spoke openly about this. Peter

[A] 8:15 Or yeast   [B] 8:18 Jr 5:21; Ezk 12:2   [C] 8:26 Other mss add *or tell anyone in the village*

8:13 He left them marks Jesus's break with the Pharisees. After v. 15 they are mentioned only in 10:2 and 12:13. **The other side** where Jesus went was Bethsaida on the northeastern shore of the Sea of Galilee (see note at v. 22).

8:14 One loaf of bread was not enough to feed those in the boat.

8:15 Jesus's double warning indicates strong admonition. **Leaven** permeates, spreads, and grows. It is a symbol for evil or corruption (1Co 5:6–8; Gl 5:9). In Matthew the leaven is identified as the teaching of the Pharisees (Mt 16:12), while in Luke it is their hypocrisy (Lk 12:1). After this, nothing more is said about leaven or Pharisees.

8:16–20 Jesus used the disciples' discussion about bread to rebuke them. His reference to deafness recalled his healing of a man who

was deaf (7:32–37); his reference to blindness anticipated his next miracle (8:22–26). He was disappointed that his disciples lacked spiritual perception.

8:21 This repeats the question of v. 17. The disciples still did not get it. This is Jesus's most severe rebuke of the disciples in the Gospel of Mark, but there was a bright spot. They didn't understand **yet** what Jesus was about.

8:22–10:52 In this section, Jesus completed his ministry in Galilee and began his journey to Jerusalem. It was time to leave the crowds, limit his miracles, and teach the disciples about his impending death.

8:22 Bethsaida, on the northeastern shore of the Sea of Galilee, was the hometown of Philip, Andrew, and Peter (Jn 1:44; 12:21). Mark does not record Jesus's previous visit to Bethsaida, but Luke associates it with the feeding of the five thousand (Lk 9:10). **They brought** presumably refers to the blind man's friends (cp. 2:3–5; 7:32). This is Mark's first account about the healing of **a blind man** (cp. 10:46–52).

8:23 Jesus's taking the blind man **out of the village** and then **spitting** on him recalls 7:33 (cp. Jn 9:6–7). **Laying his hands on him** recalls 5:23; 6:2,5.

8:24–25 After Jesus's first action, the man's vision was only partially restored. This is the only miracle of Jesus in which healing did not occur immediately and completely.

8:26 No reason is given for Jesus's command to avoid **the village**.

8:27–30 Peter's confession near Caesarea Philippi is the watershed of Mark's Gospel.

8:27–28 Caesarea Philippi was twenty-five miles north of Bethsaida in the foothills of Mount Hermon. Caesar Augustus gave the

city to Herod the Great. Herod's son Philip rebuilt, enlarged, and renamed it in honor of Caesar Augustus. **The villages** refers to surrounding settlements. Jesus's question and the disciples' response recall the opinions voiced to Antipas in 6:14–15.

8:29 The words **but you** are emphatic and call for a deeper answer. Jesus asked his disciples to state their own belief. **Peter** responded, **you are the Messiah**. This is the first time in Mark's Gospel that a person made this identification. To this point, only God (1:11) and demons (1:24,34; 3:11; 5:7) had testified to Jesus's true identity. The word "Messiah" (Christ) means "anointed one" and refers to God's appointed deliverer and King.

8:30 Strictly warned is the same Greek verb Jesus used (1:25; 3:12) to silence unclean spirits. His command to **tell no one** was a response to the popular misunderstanding that the Messiah would be a military conqueror. Jesus had to teach his disciples that the Messiah would actually suffer and die.

8:31 This is the first of three times in Mark that Jesus predicted his death (see notes at 9:31; 10:33–34). On **Son of Man**, see note at 2:8–11. Jesus will now use this title often, including in his death predictions. **It was necessary** points to the fact that his suffering and death were essential to God's purposes. The **elders**, the **chief priests**, and the **scribes** were the three power groups of the Sanhedrin, the ruling Jewish body. Jesus would **be killed**, not by a lawless mob but by Israel's religious leaders. Each of his predictions also ends with his resurrection as the final part of the divine necessity.

8:32 Peter could not accept a suffering Messiah. He took Jesus **aside** in a bid to convince him to stop speaking of his death.

#59   99 Essential Christian Truths

WORK OF THE HOLY SPIRIT IN LIFE OF THE CHRISTIAN

The Spirit's work in the life of a Christian begins in the work of salvation in bringing a person to faith in Christ and is continued through the work of sanctification in helping the Christian to become progressively more like Christ throughout the course of his or her life. The Spirit also empowers and indwells believers, intercedes on their behalf, and equips them with special gifts for the service of God's kingdom. He is the Comforter to the believer and aids us in properly interpreting the Bible.

took him aside and began to rebuke him. ³³ But turning around and looking at his disciples, he rebuked Peter and said, "Get behind me, Satan! You are not thinking about God's concerns^A but human concerns."

Take Up Your Cross

³⁴ Calling the crowd along with his disciples, he said to them, "If anyone wants to follow after me, let him deny himself, take up his cross, and follow me. ³⁵ For whoever wants to save his life will lose it, but whoever loses his life because of me and the gospel will save it. ³⁶ For what does it benefit someone to gain the whole world and yet lose his life? ³⁷ What can anyone give in exchange for his life? ³⁸ For whoever is ashamed of me and my words in this adulterous and sinful generation, the Son of Man will also be ashamed of him when he comes in the glory of his Father with the holy angels."

9 Then he said to them, "Truly I tell you, there are some standing here who will not taste death until they see the kingdom of God come in power."

The Transfiguration

² After six days Jesus took Peter, James, and John and led them up a high mountain by themselves to be alone. He was transfigured in front of them, ³ and his clothes became dazzling — extremely white as no launderer on earth could whiten them. ⁴ Elijah appeared to them with Moses, and they were talking with Jesus. ⁵ Peter said to Jesus, "Rabbi, it's good for us to be here. Let's set up three shelters: one for you, one for Moses, and one for Elijah" — ⁶ because he did not know what to say, since they were terrified.

⁷ A cloud appeared, overshadowing them, and a voice came from the cloud: "This is my beloved Son; listen to him!"

⁸ Suddenly, looking around, they no longer saw anyone with them except Jesus.

⁹ As they were coming down the mountain, he ordered them to tell no one what they had seen until the Son of Man had risen from the dead. ¹⁰ They kept this word to themselves, questioning what "rising from the dead" meant.

¹¹ Then they asked him, "Why do the scribes say that Elijah must come first?"

¹² "Elijah does come first and restores all things," he replied. "Why then is it written that the Son of Man must suffer many things and be treated with contempt? ¹³ But I tell you that Elijah has come, and they did whatever they pleased to him, just as it is written about him."

The Power of Faith over a Demon

¹⁴ When they came to the disciples, they saw a large crowd around them and scribes

---

^A**8:33** Or *about the things of God*

8:33 Get behind me, Satan are the same words Jesus spoke to the devil during the wilderness temptation (Mt 4:10).
8:34 The kind of Messiah Jesus was had implications for **anyone** who wanted to be his follower. An incorrect understanding of Jesus's messiahship leads to an incorrect understanding of discipleship. **Deny himself** is found only here and in the parallels (Mt 16:24; Lk 9:23). It refers to a denial of self-centered interests. To **take up** a **cross** refers to the fact that crucifixion victims were made to carry the crossbeam to the site of their execution.
8:35–37 The words **save** and **lose** show that Jesus was speaking not merely of physical life but of the essence of humanity: the soul. The sure way to save the soul is to lose it (entrust it to Jesus). There is no exchange rate high enough for the soul; money cannot buy it. Jesus's words echo Ps 49:7–9.
8:38 The phrase **my words** refers to the gospel. **This adulterous and sinful generation** is used only here in the NT (cp. Mt 12:39; 16:4) and is based on the language of OT prophets (Is 1:4; 57:3–13; Ezk 16:32–41; Hs 2:2–6). Jesus's present rejection is contrasted with his future **glory**. His coming **with the holy angels** is spelled out in 13:26–27.
9:1 Jesus previously used this solemn introductory formula (**Truly I tell you**) in 3:28 and 8:12. **Some standing here** is clarified by v. 2. **Until they see the kingdom of God come in power** is clarified by Jesus's transfiguration in vv. 2–13. This saying precedes the transfiguration in all three Synoptic Gospels (Mt 16:28; Lk 9:27).
9:2 Six days appears to refer to the time between Peter's confession and Jesus's transfiguration. It may also tie Jesus's experience to Moses's (Ex 24:15–17). On **Peter, James, and John** as Jesus's inner circle, see note at 1:16–20. The **high mountain** is often identified as Mount Tabor, but Mount Hermon or Mount Meron may be better candidates. As he was **transfigured**, Jesus's nature was not changed but unveiled.
9:3 Dazzling connotes extreme whiteness that is beyond natural explanation (Mt 17:2 describes them as "white as the light"). Matthew (17:2; cp. Lk 9:29) adds that Jesus's face glowed like the sun (cp. Ex 34:35).
9:4 Mark probably intended to indicate Moses as the greater OT figure by saying **Elijah** appeared **with Moses**.
9:5 The **three shelters** Peter mentioned relate to the Jewish custom of building booth-like shelters during the Festival of Shelters (Lv 23:39–43). Perhaps Peter wished to prolong this experience, but his words wrongly implied equality among the three persons.
9:6 Peter proves that when you don't know what to say, it's best to keep quiet. But he was not alone in his uncertainty; all the disciples were **terrified**.
9:7 A **cloud** is often a symbol of God's presence in the OT (Ex 40:34–38). The **voice** from within echoes Ex 24:15–18. **Them** probably refers to all six persons on the mountain. The divine announcement recalls the divine words at Jesus's baptism (see note at 1:9–11). This time Jesus's Sonship is confirmed to others, not just to Jesus, and the hearers are told to **listen to him** (cp. Dt 18:15). God's words affirmed Jesus's teaching in Mk 8:31–38 about his suffering and the requirements for discipleship.
9:8 Not even Moses or Elijah can compare with Jesus. The spotlight was on him and him alone.
9:9 Nine times in Mark's Gospel Jesus enjoined people to be quiet about his messiahship. This is the only time when he put a time limit on the injunction. Jesus's prohibition indicated that his glory and mission could not be understood fully until after his death and resurrection.
9:10 This verse indicates continued lack of understanding among Jesus's inner circle (cp. 8:31).
9:11 On **the scribes**, see note at 1:21–22. The question here was based on Mal 4:5–6.
9:12–13 Jesus affirmed the scribal teaching about Elijah and his role, but Elijah's coming did not change the fact that **the Son of Man must suffer many things** (cp. 8:31). Jesus then made two startling statements: **Elijah** had **come** already, and he suffered because the people **did whatever they pleased to him**. Jesus was identifying Elijah with John the Baptist. The treatment John received (6:16–29) foreshadowed the way Jesus would be treated.
9:14–29 These verses reveal what the other disciples were doing while Jesus and his inner circle were on the Mount of Transfiguration. Mark's account is twice as long as the parallels (Mt 17:14–20; Lk 9:37–43).
9:14 The **scribes**, again showing hostility toward the disciples (cp. 2:6,16; 3:22; 7:1), have no further role in Mark's account.

disputing with them. **15** When the whole crowd saw him, they were amazed and ran to greet him. **16** He asked them, "What are you arguing with them about?"

17 Someone from the crowd answered him, "Teacher, I brought my son to you. He has a spirit that makes him unable to speak. **18** Whenever it seizes him, it throws him down, and he foams at the mouth, grinds his teeth, and becomes rigid. I asked your disciples to drive it out, but they couldn't."

19 He replied to them, "You unbelieving generation, how long will I be with you? How long must I put up with you? Bring him to me." **20** So they brought the boy to him. When the spirit saw him, it immediately threw the boy into convulsions. He fell to the ground and rolled around, foaming at the mouth. **21** "How long has this been happening to him?" Jesus asked his father.

"From childhood," he said. **22** "And many times it has thrown him into fire or water to destroy him. But if you can do anything, have compassion on us and help us."

23 Jesus said to him, "'If you can'?^A Everything is possible for the one who believes."

24 Immediately the father of the boy cried out, "I do believe; help my unbelief!"

25 When Jesus saw that a crowd was quickly gathering, he rebuked the unclean spirit, saying to it, "You mute and deaf spirit, I command you: Come out of him and never enter him again."

26 Then it came out, shrieking and throwing him into terrible convulsions. The boy became like a corpse, so that many said, "He's dead." **27** But Jesus, taking him by the hand, raised him, and he stood up.

28 After he had gone into the house, his disciples asked him privately, "Why couldn't we drive it out?"

29 And he told them, "This kind can come out by nothing but prayer."^B

The Second Prediction of His Death

30 Then they left that place and made their way through Galilee, but he did not want anyone to know it. **31** For he was teaching his disciples and telling them, "The Son of Man is going to be betrayed^C into the hands of men. They will kill him, and after he is killed, he will rise three days later." **32** But they did not understand this statement, and they were afraid to ask him.

Who Is the Greatest?

33 They came to Capernaum. When he was in the house, he asked them, "What were you arguing about on the way?" **34** But they were silent, because on the way they had been arguing with one another about who was the greatest. **35** Sitting down, he called the Twelve and said to them, "If anyone wants to be first, he must be last and servant of all." **36** He took a child, had him stand among them, and taking him in his arms, he said to them, **37** "Whoever welcomes^D one little child such as this in my name welcomes me. And whoever welcomes me does not welcome me, but him who sent me."

In His Name

38 John said to him, "Teacher, we saw someone^E driving out demons in your name, and we tried to stop him because he wasn't following us."

39 "Don't stop him," said Jesus, "because there is no one who will perform a miracle in

---

^A **9:23** Other mss add *believe*   ^B **9:29** Other mss add *and fasting*   ^C **9:31** Or *handed over*   ^D **9:37** Or *"Whoever receives*
^E **9:38** Other mss add *who didn't go along with us*

9:15 Only Mark in the entire NT used the verb for **were amazed** (cp. 14:33; 16:5–6). It refers to intense emotion.
9:16–18 That the disciples couldn't **drive . . . out** this demon is surprising because Jesus had commissioned them to do this (3:15; 6:7) and they had previously succeeded in doing so (6:13). The symptoms were similar to epilepsy, but Mark says they were the result of unclean spirits (9:17,20,25).
9:19 Jesus's words **you unbelieving generation** recalls 8:38.
9:20 The reaction of **the spirit** when it *saw* Jesus was similar to that of other demonic spirits (see notes at 1:25–26 and 5:7–8).
9:21 The duration of the condition made Jesus's healing all the more impressive.
9:22 To destroy him shows the evil intention of demons. The father asked for **help** based on Jesus's **compassion** (see notes at 1:40–45 and 6:33–34). **If you can** was an appropriate qualifier, considering the disciples' failure to cast out the demon.
9:23 At issue was not Jesus's ability but the father's faith—**everything is possible for the one who believes** (cp. 5:36; 10:27).

9:24 Both faith and unbelief resided in the father's heart. Mark previously used **unbelief** when describing the people of Nazareth (see note at 6:5–6a).
9:25 The demonic spirit was **mute and deaf**, rendering the boy mute (v. 17). When Jesus issued the **command** to **come out of him**, he used a word that emphasized his authority. The demon was able to resist the disciples, but not the Lord. Jesus's command to **never enter him again** is unique in all the exorcisms in the Gospels.
9:26–27 The unclean spirit responded like one that Jesus had cast out earlier (see note at 1:25–26).
9:28–29 To the disciples' question **why**, Jesus told them **this kind** (apparently a very resistant and powerful evil being) required spiritual preparation on the part of the exorcist, specifically **prayer**.
9:30 This is the last reference in Mark to **Galilee** until after Jesus's resurrection (see 14:28; 16:7 and notes there).
9:31 Jesus's second death prediction is the briefest of the three (see notes at 8:31; 10:33–34), and has much in common with the others. The new element in this prediction is that he would be **betrayed**.

9:32 Luke explains why the disciples **did not understand**: "It was concealed from them so that they could not grasp it" (Lk 9:45).
9:33 This is the last time Jesus returned to **Capernaum**. The **house** may have been Peter's (see note at 1:29–31).
9:34 **They were silent** also described the people in the Capernaum synagogue (3:4).
9:35 **Sitting down** was the posture assumed by a teacher (4:1–2; Mt 5:1). Jesus's teaching reversed human thinking. In his value system, being **first** did not come through aggressiveness and privilege but through humility (Mt 18:4) and by being **servant of all**.
9:36–37 Jesus used **a child** as an object lesson. He did not command his disciples to become like children but to **welcome** those who are like a **little child**. A child is an example of a person with no status and no rights.
9:38 It is ironic that the disciples told this man to stop **driving out demons** when they had failed at the same task (vv. 14–29). Apparently they thought they were the only ones authorized to do this (3:14–15; 6:7,13). The episode recalls Nm 11:26–29.
9:39–41 Jesus gave three reasons not to stop the man. First, anyone who performed

my name who can soon afterward speak evil of me. **40** For whoever is not against us is for us. **41** And whoever gives you a cup of water to drink in my name, because you belong to Christ — truly I tell you, he will never lose his reward.

Warnings from Jesus

42 "But whoever causes one of these little ones who believe in me to fall away — it would be better for him if a heavy millstone were hung around his neck and he were thrown into the sea. **43** "And if your hand causes you to fall away, cut it off. It is better for you to enter life maimed than to have two hands and go to hell, the unquenchable fire.^ **45** And if your foot causes you to fall away, cut it off. It is better for you to enter life lame than to have two feet and be thrown into hell.^B **47** And if your eye causes you to fall away, gouge it out. It is better for you to enter the kingdom of God with one eye than to have two eyes and be thrown into hell, **48** where **their worm does not die, and the fire is not quenched.**^C **49** For everyone will be salted with fire.^D,E **50** Salt is good, but if the salt should lose its flavor, how can you season it? Have salt among yourselves, and be at peace with one another."

The Question of Divorce

10 He set out from there and went to the region of Judea and across the Jordan. Then crowds converged on him again, and as was his custom he taught them again.

2 Some Pharisees came to test him, asking, "Is it lawful for a man to divorce his wife?" **3** He replied to them, "What did Moses command you?" **4** They said, "Moses permitted us to write divorce papers and send her away." **5** But Jesus told them, "He wrote this command for you because of the hardness of your hearts. **6** But from the beginning of creation God^F made them male and female.^G **7** For this reason a man will leave his father and mother^H **8** and the two will become one flesh.^I So they are no longer two, but one flesh. **9** Therefore what God has joined together, let no one separate."

10 When they were in the house again, the disciples questioned him about this matter. **11** He said to them, "Whoever divorces his wife and marries another commits adultery against her. **12** Also, if she divorces her husband and marries another, she commits adultery."

Blessing the Children

13 People were bringing little children to him in order that he might touch them, but the disciples rebuked them. **14** When Jesus saw it, he was indignant and said to them, "Let the little children come to me. Don't stop them, because the kingdom of God belongs to such as these. **15** Truly I tell you, whoever does not receive^I the kingdom of God like a little child will never enter it." **16** After taking them in his

---

^**9:43** Some mss include v. 44: *Where their worm does not die, and the fire is not quenched.*   ^**9:45** Some mss include v. 46: *Where their worm does not die, and the fire is not quenched.*   ^**9:48** Is 66:24   ^**9:49** Other mss add *and every sacrifice will be salted with salt*   ^**9:49** Lv 2:13; Ezk 43:24   ^**10:6** Other mss omit *God*   ^**10:6** Gn 1:27; 5:2   ^**10:7** Some mss add *and be joined to his wife*   ^**10:15** Or *not welcome*

---

a miracle in Jesus's **name** wouldn't turn and **speak evil** of him. Second, there is no middle ground. A person is either **against** or **for** Jesus. Third, anyone who extends a kind gesture (giving **a cup of water** was a basic Eastern courtesy) **in my name . . . will never lose his reward.**
9:42 To cause someone to **fall away** refers to hindering discipleship or causing someone to sin. **Little ones** refers to immature disciples. A **heavy millstone** was the one donkeys turned to grind wheat. As terrible as drowning was, Jesus said it would be **better** than suffering the punishments of vv. 43–48.
9:43–48 The body parts and admonitions are figures of speech that warn disciples to guard their sight and actions against participation in evil, for recklessness here can lead to spiritual downfall (cp. Jb 31:1,5,7). This is the only place where Mark used the word for **hell** (Gk *gehenna*). The imagery for hell developed from the Hinnom Valley southwest of Jerusalem. This valley was used for pagan human sacrifice (2Kg 16:3; 21:6; Jr 7:31), hence the association with **unquenchable fire** and perpetual rot (**their worm does not die**).
9:49–50 Jesus's puzzling statement in v. 49 probably drew on the association of fire and salt in the sacrificial context of Lv 2:13. The first salt saying of Mk 9:50 occurs elsewhere (Mt 5:13; Lk 14:34) and focuses on the **good** uses of salt, which disciples must reflect on (Mt 5:13). Salt from deposits around the Dead

Sea could **lose its flavor** since it was not pure sodium chloride. Disciples who lose their saltiness are no longer effective witnesses. The second "salt saying" of v. 50 draws on the OT custom of using salt in making covenants of peace (Lv 2:13; Nm 18:19; 2Ch 13:5; cp. Col 4:6).
10:1 The words **from there** probably refer to Capernaum (9:33). **Judea** was south; **across the Jordan** refers to Perea or Transjordan. This latter area was under the jurisdiction of Antipas and may explain the reason for the question in v. 2.
10:2 Two major schools of thought differed on the justifications for divorce (Mt 19:3). Shammai's school was strict; Hillel's liberal. The Pharisees' motive was to **test** Jesus (8:11; 12:15). Perhaps if this encounter occurred in Antipas's territory, they hoped Jesus would answer as John the Baptist had done and suffer the same fate (see note at 6:16–17).
10:3–4 Jesus asked, **What did Moses command you?** They responded based on Dt 24:1–4, but this passage did not command divorce. It only acknowledged it, protected the woman's rights, and prohibited a husband from remarrying his original wife if he married another woman in between. Once again the Pharisees were misusing Scripture.
10:5 The phrase **hardness of your hearts** refers to closing one's heart to God's truths. Moses allowed divorce as a concession to spiritual hardness.
10:6–8 Through the use of two quotations from Genesis, Jesus moved from the later

concession to God's original intention **from the beginning of creation.** By quoting Gn 1:27 Jesus established that marriage is between a **male and female.**
10:9 Jesus emphasized that marriage is a divinely established institution. His final statement, **let no one separate**, refers to the husband, not a judicial court (cp. v. 11). Thus Jesus answered the question of v. 2 and ruled out divorce.
10:10 Jesus's disciples were stunned by his teaching and asked what he meant.
10:11–12 Though Jesus appeared to associate remarriage with **adultery**, he did not rule out all remarriage but emphasized that if a divorce is not grounded in biblically valid reasons, subsequent marriage is adulterous. Mark did not include the exception clauses of Mt 5:32 and 19:9. This is a reminder that this passage does not contain all of Jesus's teaching on divorce and remarriage.
10:13 People probably refers to parents. **Little children** was clarified by Luke as "infants" (Lk 18:15). **Touch them** is clarified in v. 16 as "blessed them."
10:14 This is the only place in the Gospels where Jesus was **indignant** (cp. 3:5). The word indicates strong anger. Jesus allowed the children to come to him, but the real point related to **such as these.** This saying pertains to the kind of people to whom God's kingdom **belongs.**
10:15 Jesus's second saying relates to how a person welcomes and enters **the kingdom**

arms, he laid his hands on them and blessed them.

The Rich Young Ruler

¹⁷ As he was setting out on a journey, a man ran up, knelt down before him, and asked him, "Good teacher, what must I do to inherit eternal life?"

¹⁸ "Why do you call me good?" Jesus asked him. "No one is good except God alone. ¹⁹ You know the commandments: Do not murder; do not commit adultery; do not steal; do not bear false witness; do not defraud; honor your father and mother."ᴬ

²⁰ He said to him, "Teacher, I have kept all these from my youth."

²¹ Looking at him, Jesus loved him and said to him, "You lack one thing: Go, sell all you have and give to the poor, and you will have treasure in heaven. Then come,ᴮ follow me."

²² But he was dismayed by this demand, and he went away grieving, because he had many possessions.

Possessions and the Kingdom

²³ Jesus looked around and said to his disciples, "How hard it is for those who have wealth to enter the kingdom of God!"

²⁴ The disciples were astonished at his words. Again Jesus said to them, "Children, how hard it isᶜ to enter the kingdom of God! ²⁵ It is easier for a camel to go through the eye of a needle than for a rich person to enter the kingdom of God."

²⁶ They were even more astonished, saying to one another, "Then who can be saved?"

²⁷ Looking at them, Jesus said, "With man it is impossible, but not with God, because all things are possible with God."

²⁸ Peter began to tell him, "Look, we have left everything and followed you."

²⁹ "Truly I tell you," Jesus said, "there is no one who has left house or brothers or sisters or mother or fatherᴰ or children or fields for my sake and for the sake of the gospel, ³⁰ who will not receive a hundred times more, now at this time — houses, brothers and sisters, mothers and children, and fields, with persecutions — and eternal life in the age to come. ³¹ But many who are first will be last, and the last first."

The Third Prediction of His Death

³² They were on the road, going up to Jerusalem, and Jesus was walking ahead of them. The disciples were astonished, but those who followed him were afraid. Taking the Twelve aside again, he began to tell them the things that would happen to him. ³³ "See, we are going up to Jerusalem. The Son of Man will be handed over to the chief priests and the scribes, and they will condemn him to death. Then they will hand him over to the Gentiles, ³⁴ and they will mock him, spit on him, flogᴱ him, and kill him, and he will rise after three days."

ᴬ**10:19** Ex 20:12–16; Dt 5:16–20 ᴮ**10:21** Other mss add *taking up the cross, and* ᶜ**10:24** Other mss add *for those trusting in wealth* ᴰ**10:29** Other mss add *or wife* ᴱ**10:34** Or *scourge*

---

of God. A little child accepts what is given as a gift without asserting his rights or claims (cp. Mt 18:3). To **enter** God's kingdom a person must accept it as a gracious gift.

10:16 The phrase **taking them in his arms** is one word in Greek. Jesus not only received the children but also **blessed** them. The word for "blessed" is intensified, conveying Jesus's sincerity.

10:17 The **journey** language continues, reminding readers that Jesus was on his final sweep toward Jerusalem (v. 1; 8:27; 9:2,30,33). Matthew (Mt 19:22) states that this man who approached Jesus was "young," and Luke (Lk 18:18) that he was "a ruler." Mark indicates that he was wealthy (Mk 10:22). Hence the man is referred to as "The Rich Young Ruler." His actions—**ran up, knelt down**—suggest earnestness and respect. He knew he was not entitled to life after death. Verse 23 shows that **eternal life** and "the kingdom of God" are synonymous.

10:18 Jesus's rebuff directed the man to **God**. In asserting that only God is **good**, Jesus did not deny his own deity. He only indicated that human judgment cannot serve as ultimate judge of good and bad.

10:19 The **commandments** were from the second tablet of the law, those that focused on behavior and relationships (Ex 20:12–16; Dt 5:16–20).

10:20 The young man again addressed Jesus as **teacher**, but this time he did not add "good" (v. 18).

10:21 Looking at him is an intensified form of the verb, indicating close scrutiny. Only Mark states that **Jesus loved him**. The phrase **you lack one thing** shows that perfect obedience to the law does not merit eternal life. The "one thing" involved divesting himself of his possessions and becoming a disciple (1:17; 2:14). In exchange for earthly possessions, he would **have treasure in heaven**.

10:22 He was dismayed is a descriptive verb used only here in Mark. It means "shocked" or "appalled." The effect of Jesus's **demand** must have been visible on the young man's face. Rather than following Jesus (v. 21), he **went away**, choosing his **many possessions** over Jesus. He is an example of 4:19 (see note at 4:14–20).

10:23 How hard it is refers to extreme difficulty. Rather than an advantage, possessions are a hindrance to entering God's kingdom.

10:24 On **were astonished**, see note at 1:21–22. Perhaps the disciples understood wealth as a sign of God's blessing (Dt 28:1–14).

10:25 Jesus used a proverb for impossibility. The **camel** was the largest animal in Palestine, and one certainly could not squeeze through **the eye of a needle**.

10:26 The astonishment of Jesus's disciples increased from "astonished" in v. 24 to **even more astonished** in v. 26. **Be saved** (Gk *sōzō*) is equivalent to "enter the kingdom of God" (vv. 23–25), "eternal life" (vv. 17,30), "heaven" (v. 21), and "the age to come" (v. 30).

10:27 The phrase **looking at** connotes great intensity. It recalls how Jesus looked at the young man (v. 21).

10:28 As usual, **Peter** served as spokesman for the disciples (8:29,32; 9:5; 11:21). In his judgment, he and the disciples had done what Jesus commanded the rich man to do (10:21).

10:29 Truly I tell you was Jesus's solemn oath formula. He placed equal importance on himself and **the gospel**.

10:30 The promised compensation (**a hundred times more**) covered **this time** (see 3:34–35) and **the age to come**. Following Jesus provides no protection against suffering, but the reward includes **eternal life**. The rich ruler sought this (v. 17) but walked away from it (v. 22).

10:31 Jesus emphasized the reversal of values that is so prominent in Christian discipleship (cp. Mt 19:30; 20:16; Lk 13:30).

10:32 The road trip continues (vv. 1,17; 8:27; 9:2,30,33–34). The eastern approach to Jerusalem goes **up** because of the city's elevation. Jesus was **walking ahead of them**, showing he was not afraid of what awaited him.

10:33–34 This is Jesus's third and most detailed prediction of his passion and resurrection. Jesus's use of **we** must have frightened the disciples even further. In this final prediction, Jesus declared that the **chief priests** and the **scribes** would **condemn him to death** (see notes at 14:53 and 14:64)

Suffering and Service

35 James and John, the sons of Zebedee, approached him and said, "Teacher, we want you to do whatever we ask you."
36 "What do you want me to do for you?" he asked them.
37 They answered him, "Allow us to sit at your right and at your left in your glory."
38 Jesus said to them, "You don't know what you're asking. Are you able to drink the cup I drink or to be baptized with the baptism I am baptized with?"
39 "We are able," they told him.
Jesus said to them, "You will drink the cup I drink, and you will be baptized with the baptism I am baptized with. **40** But to sit at my right or left is not mine to give; instead, it is for those for whom it has been prepared."
41 When the ten disciples heard this, they began to be indignant with James and John. **42** Jesus called them over and said to them, "You know that those who are regarded as rulers of the Gentiles lord it over them, and those in high positions act as tyrants over them. **43** But it is not so among you. On the contrary, whoever wants to become great among you will be your servant, **44** and whoever wants to be first among you will be a slave to all. **45** For even the Son of Man did not come to be served, but to serve, and to give his life as a ransom for many."ᴬ

A Blind Man Healed

46 They came to Jericho. And as he was leaving Jericho with his disciples and a large crowd, Bartimaeus (the son of Timaeus), a blind beggar, was sitting by the road. **47** When he heard that it was Jesus of Nazareth, he began to cry out, "Jesus, Son of David, have mercy on me!" **48** Many warned him to keep quiet, but he was crying out all the more, "Have mercy on me, Son of David!"
49 Jesus stopped and said, "Call him."
So they called the blind man and said to him, "Have courage! Get up; he's calling for you." **50** He threw off his coat, jumped up, and came to Jesus.
51 Then Jesus answered him, "What do you want me to do for you?"
"*Rabboni*,"ᴮ the blind man said to him, "I want to see."
52 Jesus said to him, "Go, your faith has saved you." Immediately he could see and began to follow Jesus on the road.

The Triumphal Entry

11 When they approached Jerusalem, at Bethphage and Bethany near the Mount of Olives, he sent two of his disciples **2** and told them, "Go into the village ahead of you. As soon as you enter it, you will find a colt tied there, on which no one has ever sat. Untie it and bring it. **3** If anyone says to you, 'Why are you doing this?' say, 'The Lord needs it and will send it back here right away.'"
4 So they went and found a colt outside in the street, tied by a door. They untied it, **5** and some of those standing there said to them, "What are you doing, untying the colt?" **6** They answered them just as Jesus had said; so they let them go. **7** They brought the colt to Jesus and threw their clothes on it, and he sat on it. **8** Many people spread their clothes on the road, and others

---

ᴬ**10:45** Or *in the place of many*; Is 53:10–12　　ᴮ**10:51** Hb word for *my lord*

---

and **hand him over to the Gentiles** since they lacked authority to carry out the sentence (15:1–2).
10:35–45 James and John failed to realize the implications of Jesus's suffering and death.
10:35–36 This is the only time in Mark that James and John acted on their own apart from the other disciples, and they did so selfishly. Most likely they asked Jesus to grant their request even before they spelled it out because they knew they were being selfish.
10:37 The **right** side was the highest position of honor, the **left** the second. James and John caught a glimpse of Jesus's **glory** in the transfiguration (9:2–13); now they wanted more. It was their mother who suggested they make this request (Mt 20:20–21).
10:38 The cup and **baptism** refer to Jesus's suffering and death (14:36).
10:39–40 You will may predict James's martyrdom (Ac 12:2) and John's exile (Rv 1:9). **It is for those for whom it has been prepared** is a divine passive, indicating that God would decide who would receive places of honor.
10:41 The other disciples became **indignant**, the same verb used of Jesus in v. 14.
10:42 That Jesus instructed all his apostles in this lesson shows that all of them struggled with the same greed that led James and John to seek places of honor.

10:43–44 Becoming **great** in Christian leadership means becoming a **servant**—that is, doing your Master's will and humbly working for the good of others.
10:45 The greatest example of servant leadership is **the Son of Man**. Giving is the essence of servanthood, and Jesus gave **his life as a ransom for many** (cp. Is 53:10–12). "Ransom" refers to the price paid to release a slave. The words of v. 45 are crucial to Jesus's self-understanding of his death.
10:46–52 Mark concludes the "on the road" section just as he began it—with the story of a blind man (8:22–26). This account contrasted what the blind man could see with what the disciples could not (10:35–45).
10:46 The city of **Jericho** lay seventeen miles northeast and 3,500 feet below Jerusalem. The **large crowd** was made up of Passover pilgrims.
10:47–48 This is the second time Mark identifies him as **Jesus of Nazareth** (1:24), and the only time in Mark that someone addressed Jesus as **Son of David**, a messianic designation based on 2Sm 7:11–14 (cp. Mk 11:10; 12:35–37).
10:52 In contrast to his healing of the blind man in 8:22–25, Jesus simply announced **your faith has saved you**, and Bartimaeus **could see**.
11:1–11 Mark 11–16 covers "Holy Week." The material Mark devotes to these last seven

days of Jesus's life comprises one-third of Mark's entire Gospel. Thus Jesus's final days in Jerusalem are crucial to a proper understanding of Jesus and his mission. Jesus's royal procession into Jerusalem took place on what is now called "Palm Sunday." His entry into Jerusalem is recorded in all four Gospels.
11:1 This is Jesus's first recorded visit to **Jerusalem** in Mark. (Lk 2:41–52 records Jesus's visit as a boy and John's Gospel indicates several visits.) **Bethphage** (lit "house of unripe figs") was located on the slope of the **Mount of Olives**, a large hill east of Jerusalem. **Bethany** was two miles east of Jerusalem.
11:2 The village ahead of you was probably Bethphage.
11:3 Commentator R.T. France supposes that these words were a "prearranged password."
11:4 Outside in the street indicates the **colt** was in plain sight.
11:5 Someone did ask as Jesus predicted in v. 5.
11:6 This verse may indicate that Jesus arranged in advance to borrow the colt.
11:7 The two unnamed disciples **threw their clothes** on the donkey to create a makeshift saddle. Even though Mark did not quote Zch 9:9 in this account (as did Mt 21:5; Jn 12:15), the messianic symbolism of Jesus's action is clear.
11:8 Clothes and **leafy branches** were traditionally draped across the road to receive a king (cp. 2Kg 9:13).

ca AD 50 (ALL VIEWS SHOWN ARE LOOKING WEST)

Interior View

INTERIOR VIEW
1. Lampstand
2. Altar of Incense
3. Table of the Bread of the Presence
4. Veil (separating Holy Place from Most Holy Place)

EXTERIOR VIEWS
1. Temple
2. Altar of Burnt Offering
3. Golden Vine (mentioned by Josephus)
4. Lamp of Queen Helena of Adiabene
5. Veil at Entrance to Holy Place (mentioned by Josephus)
6. Council Chambers and Priests' Quarters
7. Nicanor Gate
8. Court of the Women
9. Chamber of the Lepers
10. Chamber of the Nazirites
11. Soreg (partition wall separating Court of the Gentiles from temple area)
12. Court of the Gentiles
13. Royal Stoa
14. Solomon's Porch
15. Beautiful Gate (Shushan Gate)
16. Muster Gate
17. Fortress of Antonia

Exterior View

spread leafy branches cut from the fields.^A ^9 Those who went ahead and those who followed shouted:

> Hosanna!
> Blessed is he who comes
> in the name of the Lord!^B
> ^10 Blessed is the coming kingdom
> of our father David!
> Hosanna in the highest heaven!

^11 He went into Jerusalem and into the temple. After looking around at everything, since it was already late, he went out to Bethany with the Twelve.

The Barren Fig Tree Is Cursed

^12 The next day when they went out from Bethany, he was hungry. ^13 Seeing in the distance a fig tree with leaves, he went to find out if there was anything on it. When he came to it, he found nothing but leaves; for it was not the season for figs. ^14 He said to it, "May no one ever eat fruit from you again!" And his disciples heard it.

Cleansing the Temple

^15 They came to Jerusalem, and he went into the temple and began to throw out those buying and selling. He overturned the tables of the money changers and the chairs of those selling doves, ^16 and would not permit anyone to carry goods through the temple. ^17 He was teaching them: "Is it not written, My house will be called a house of prayer for all nations?^C But you have made it a den of thieves!"^D

^18 The chief priests and the scribes heard it and started looking for a way to kill him. For they were afraid of him, because the whole crowd was astonished by his teaching. ^19 Whenever evening came, they would go out of the city.

The Barren Fig Tree Is Withered

^20 Early in the morning, as they were passing by, they saw the fig tree withered from the roots up. ^21 Then Peter remembered and said to him, "Rabbi, look! The fig tree that you cursed has withered."

^22 Jesus replied to them, "Have faith in God. ^23 Truly I tell you, if anyone says to this mountain, 'Be lifted up and thrown into the sea,' and does not doubt in his heart, but believes that what he says will happen, it will be done for him. ^24 Therefore I tell you, everything you pray and ask for — believe that you have received^E it and it will be yours. ^25 And whenever you stand praying, if you have anything against anyone, forgive him, so that your Father in heaven will also forgive you your wrongdoing."^F

---

^A 11:8 Other mss read *others were cutting leafy branches from the trees and spreading them on the road* ^B 11:9 Ps 118:26 ^C 11:17 Is 56:7 ^D 11:17 Jr 7:11 ^E 11:24 Some mss read *you receive*; other mss read *you will receive* ^F 11:25 Some mss include v. 26: *"But if you don't forgive, neither will your Father in heaven forgive your wrongdoing."*

11:9 The two groups (**those who went ahead . . . those who followed**) may refer to fellow pilgrims traveling with Jesus (10:46) and those who came out of Jerusalem to meet them (Jn 12:9; cp. Mt 21:10–11). The crowd's shouts were recitations from Ps 118:25–26, the last of the Hallel psalms sung at Passover. *Hosanna* is Hebrew for "save us."

11:10 Only Mark recorded this shout from the crowd. The words echo Bartimaeus's cry (10:47–48).

11:11 Herod's **temple** was being reconstructed, a project that had been going on for more than forty-five years (13:1; Jn 2:20). **Bethany**, two miles east of Jerusalem, was where Jesus apparently lodged during Passover.

11:12–26 Matthew recorded the temple clearing (Mt 21:12–17) and the cursing of the fig tree (21:18–20) as distinct events. Mark divided the cursing of the fig tree (Mk 11:12–14) from its withering (vv. 20–21) and placed the clearing of the temple in between (vv. 15–19). Thus he meant for readers to see the connection between the barren fig tree (symbolic for Israel) and the barren temple. Jesus's cursing of the fig tree was an acted-out parable of God's judgment on Jerusalem and the temple.

11:12 The **next day** was Monday of Holy Week.

11:13 Jesus spotted a **fig tree** that bore **nothing but leaves**. Even though **it was not the season for figs**, the leafy tree should have been covered with edible buds (Gk *paggim*).

11:14 Jesus's words express a curse (v. 21). This is the last of Jesus's miracles recorded in Mark and the only miracle of destruction in the Gospels. In the OT, the fig tree was a symbol of Israel (Jr 24:1–10; Hs 9:10; cp. Lk 13:6–9). The episode recalls Jr 8:13; Hs 2:12; and Mc 7:1.

11:15–18 Scripture prophesied that the Messiah would purify the temple (Ezk 37:26–28; Mal 3:1–4). Jesus's temple cleansing is clearly messianic. John recorded a cleansing at the beginning of his Gospel (Jn 2:13–17).

11:15 Having noted all that went on in the **temple** the day before, Jesus now returned, probably to the Court of the Gentiles, where most **buying and selling** occurred. People who traveled from afar needed to purchase pure, unblemished animals once they arrived for Passover. **Money changers** exchanged idol-engraved Greek and Roman coinage for imageless Tyrian or Jewish temple coins that could be used to buy sacrificial items or pay the temple tax (Ex 30:11–16). **Doves** were offered by women after childbirth (Lv 12:6–8; Lk 2:22–24), by cleansed lepers (Lv 14:22), by those healed of bodily discharges (15:14,29), and by those who could not afford more expensive sacrifices (5:7,11). Sheep and cattle were sold also (Jn 2:14). The Court of the Gentiles had become a virtual stockyard.

11:16 Only Mark adds the information in this verse, indicating further inappropriate use of the temple as a thoroughfare or shortcut.

11:17 The **written** text Jesus quoted was Is 56:7. Only Mark added **for all nations**.

The **den of thieves** quotation is from Jr 7:11, part of Jeremiah's sermon in which he condemned temple goers for their attitudes and behaviors and predicted the temple's destruction (7:12–15).

11:18 Jesus's last word in v. 17, "thieves" (Gk *lēstēs*), involved foreshadowing since within three days he would be arrested as if he were a thief ("criminal," 14:48) and within four days would be crucified between two thieves ("criminals," 15:27). The words **a way to kill him** recall the plot in 3:6 by the Pharisees and Herodians.

11:19–20 The destruction of the fig tree echoes Hs 9:10,16.

11:21 This is the second time Mark records Peter addressing Jesus as **Rabbi** (9:5). Peter served as spokesman for the disciples (8:29,32; 9:5; 10:28).

11:22 The proper object of **faith** is **God**, not the temple.

11:23–24 Jesus's saying on faith and impossibilities (cp. 1Co 13:2) began with his solemn formula, **Truly I tell you** (cp. 3:28; 8:12; 9:1,41; 10:15,29). He gave a negative condition (**does not doubt in his heart**) and a positive condition (**but believes**) for fulfillment of this promise (cp. Jms 1:6).

11:25 A second condition to petitions being granted is to **forgive** others. Standing while **praying** was the usual Jewish posture for public prayers (cp. Lk 18:9–14). **If you have anything against anyone** recalls Mt 5:23–24 (cp. Mt 18:21–35).

The Authority of Jesus Challenged

²⁷ They came again to Jerusalem. As he was walking in the temple, the chief priests, the scribes, and the elders came ²⁸ and asked him, "By what authority are you doing these things? Who gave you this authority to do these things?"

²⁹ Jesus said to them, "I will ask you one question; then answer me, and I will tell you by what authority I do these things. ³⁰ Was John's baptism from heaven or of human origin? Answer me."

³¹ They discussed it among themselves: "If we say, 'From heaven,' he will say, 'Then why didn't you believe him?' ³² But if we say, 'Of human origin'" — they were afraid of the crowd, because everyone thought that John was truly a prophet. ³³ So they answered Jesus, "We don't know."

And Jesus said to them, "Neither will I tell you by what authority I do these things."

The Parable of the Vineyard Owner

12 He began to speak to them in parables: "A man planted a vineyard, put a fence around it, dug out a pit for a winepress, and built a watchtower. Then he leased it to tenant farmers and went away. ² At harvest time he sent a servant to the farmers to collect some of the fruit of the vineyard from them. ³ But they took him, beat him, and sent him away empty-handed. ⁴ Again he sent another servant to them, and theyᴬ hit him on the head and treated him shamefully.ᴮ ⁵ Then he sent another, and they killed that one. He also sent many others; some they beat, and others they killed. ⁶ He still had one to send, a beloved son. Finally he sent him to them, saying, 'They will respect my son.' ⁷ But those tenant farmers said to one another, 'This is the heir. Come, let's kill him, and the inheritance will be ours.' ⁸ So they seized him, killed him, and threw him out of the vineyard. ⁹ What then will the ownerᶜ of the vineyard do? He will come and kill the farmers and give the vineyard to others. ¹⁰ Haven't you read this Scripture:

The stone that the builders rejected
has become the cornerstone.
¹¹   This came about from the Lord
and is wonderful in our eyes?"ᴰ

¹² They were looking for a way to arrest him but feared the crowd because they knew he had spoken this parable against them. So they left him and went away.

God and Caesar

¹³ Then they sent some of the Pharisees and the Herodians to Jesus to trap him in his words. ¹⁴ When they came, they said to him, "Teacher, we know you are truthful and don't care what anyone thinks, nor do you show partiality but teach the way of God truthfully. Is it lawful to pay taxes to Caesar or not? Should we pay or shouldn't we?"

¹⁵ But knowing their hypocrisy, he said to them, "Why are you testing me? Bring me a denariusᴱ to look at." ¹⁶ They brought a coin. "Whose image and inscription is this?" he asked them.

"Caesar's," they replied.

¹⁷ Jesus told them, "Give to Caesar the things that are Caesar's, and to God the things that are God's." And they were utterly amazed at him.

ᴬ12:4 Other mss add *threw stones and*   ᴮ12:4 Other mss add *and sent him off*   ᶜ12:9 Or *lord*   ᴰ12:10–11 Ps 118:22–23
ᴱ12:15 A denarius = one day's wage

11:27–12:44 In this section Mark recorded a series of conflict stories with the religious leaders.

11:27 The **chief priests**, the **scribes**, and the **elders** made up the Sanhedrin, the seventy-member governing body of the Jews. These were representatives, not the whole body. In his first death prediction, Jesus named these groups as those who would put him to death (see note at 8:31).

11:28 The questions focused on the nature (**by what**) of Jesus's **authority** (Gk *exousia*) and on **who gave** it to him. Jesus's authority had been at issue since the beginning (1:22,27; 2:10). **These things** probably refers to his temple clearing and his royal entry into the city.

11:29–30 John's baptism encapsulates John the Baptist's entire ministry. **From heaven** means "from God." Jesus's question turned the tables on the Pharisees. If they admitted that John was sent by God, they would have to admit the same about Jesus.

11:31–33 A genuine **prophet** has authority from heaven. If John was a prophet from God, Jesus was even more so. Unwilling to admit this, the authorities refused to answer Jesus.

12:1 The phrase **a man planted a vineyard** points to the song of Is 5:1–7 in which Israel is symbolized by a vineyard. **Tenant farmers** and absentee landlords stand for Israel's leaders.

12:2–5 Harvest time for a vineyard might be as late as the fifth year after the vines are planted (Lv 19:23–25). The mistreated servants stand for the prophets.

12:6 The **beloved son** in this parable is Jesus. The adjective "beloved" is used two other times in Mark—both spoken by the Father in reference to Jesus (1:11; 9:7).

12:7 Come, let's kill him were the words spoken by Joseph's brothers (Gn 37:20).

12:8 Matthew (Mt 21:39) and Luke (Lk 20:15) report that the son was cast out before being killed. Mark's order (**seized him, killed him, and threw him out**) indicates they did not give the son a proper burial.

12:9 The man who planted the vineyard (v. 1) and sent his servants and son is identified as **the owner**. . . . **Give the vineyard to others** alludes to the upcoming gospel mission to the Gentiles.

12:10–11 Jesus concluded by quoting Ps 118:22–23, the first verse of which is also quoted elsewhere (Lk 20:17; Ac 4:11; Rm 9:33; 1Pt 2:6–8). Only Mark and Matthew (Mt 21:42) includes Ps 118:23, which adds a strong providential element. **Cornerstone**

may refer to a foundation cornerstone, the capstone on a column, or the keystone in an arch.

12:12 Fear of **the crowd** is also mentioned in 11:32; 14:1–2.

12:13 The fact that **the Pharisees** (see note at 2:15–17) and **the Herodians** (see note at 3:6) were **sent** indicates an approved delegation. The same groups are united in 3:6 in the plot against Jesus in Galilee. They hoped to **trap** Jesus with a trick question.

12:14 The specific tax the Pharisees and Herodians had in mind was the Roman poll tax imposed when Judea became a Roman province in AD 6. This tax was particularly offensive to Jews as it represented their subjugation to Rome.

12:15 If Jesus answered "yes," he would be seen as pro-Roman and would alienate the crowds. If he said "no," the Pharisees and Herodians would denounce him as a revolutionary (Lk 20:20). Jesus was not fooled. He saw their **hypocrisy** and realized they were **testing** him. A **denarius** was the equivalent of a day's wages (Mt 20:9–10).

12:16–17 The denarius bore an **image** of Tiberius Caesar (reigned AD 14–37) with an **inscription** professing his divinity. Since Jesus was asked about giving (vv. 14–15), he

The Sadducees and the Resurrection

18 Sadducees, who say there is no resurrection, came to him and questioned him: **19** "Teacher, Moses wrote for us that **if a man's brother dies**, leaving a wife behind but **no child, that man should take the wife and raise up off-spring for his brother.**^A **20** There were seven brothers. The first married a woman, and dying, left no offspring. **21** The second also took her, and he died, leaving no offspring. And the third likewise. **22** None of the seven^B left off-spring. Last of all, the woman died too. **23** In the resurrection, when they rise,^C whose wife will she be, since the seven had married her?"

24 Jesus spoke to them, "Isn't this the reason why you're mistaken: you don't know the Scriptures or the power of God? **25** For when they rise from the dead, they neither marry nor are given in marriage but are like angels in heaven. **26** And as for the dead being raised — haven't you read in the book of Moses, in the passage about the burning bush, how God said to him: **I am the God of Abraham and the God of Isaac and the God of Jacob?**^D **27** He is not the God of the dead but of the living. You are badly mistaken."

The Primary Commands

28 One of the scribes approached. When he heard them debating and saw that Jesus answered them well, he asked him, "Which command is the most important of all?"

29 Jesus answered, "The most important^E is Listen, Israel! The Lord our God, the Lord is one.^F **30** Love the Lord your God with all your heart, with all your soul, with all your mind, and with all your strength.^G,H **31** The second is, Love your neighbor as yourself.^I There is no other command greater than these."

32 Then the scribe said to him, "You are right, teacher. You have correctly said that he is one, and there is no one else except him. **33** And to love him with all your heart, with all your understanding,^J and with all your strength, and to love your neighbor as yourself, is far more important than all the burnt offerings and sacrifices."

34 When Jesus saw that he answered wisely, he said to him, "You are not far from the kingdom of God." And no one dared to question him any longer.

The Question about the Messiah

35 While Jesus was teaching in the temple, he asked, "How can the scribes say that the Messiah is the son of David? **36** David himself says by the Holy Spirit:

The Lord declared to my Lord,
'Sit at my right hand
until I put your enemies
under your feet.'^K

37 David himself calls him 'Lord.' How, then, can he be his son?" And the large crowd was listening to him with delight.

---

^A **12:19** Gn 38:8; Dt 25:5   ^B **12:22** Other mss add *had taken her and*   ^C **12:23** Other mss omit *when they rise*   ^D **12:26** Ex 3:6,15–16   ^E **12:29** Other mss add *of all the commands*   ^F **12:29** Or *the Lord our God is Lord alone.*   ^G **12:30** Other mss add *This is the first commandment.*   ^H **12:30** Dt 6:4–5; Jos 22:5   ^I **12:31** Lv 19:18   ^J **12:33** Other mss add *with all your soul*   ^K **12:36** Ps 110:1

---

replied with a lesson about ownership. The coin had Caesar's image, so it belonged to Caesar. Jesus supported the legitimacy of human government, but he raised the issue of **things that are God's**, but since humans bear God's image (Gn 1:27), we have an obligation to give to God that which bears his image—ourselves.
12:18 The **Sadducees** arose in the second century BC during the Maccabean revolt. They were closely associated with aristocratic and priestly classes; accepted only the books of Moses (the Pentateuch) as Scripture; denied bodily resurrection, future judgment, the existence of angels, demons, and spirits; and affirmed human free will (v. 18; Ac 23:6–8; Josephus, *Ant.*, 18.1.4).
12:19–23 The Sadducees approached Jesus with a situation based on the books of **Moses**. Specifically, the case involved the levirate (or brother-in-law) marriage law (Dt 25:5–6). This law obligated a male sibling to marry his deceased brother's widow in order to preserve the family name and inheritance. Based on this, the Sadducees presented a scenario designed to make the doctrine of resurrection look absurd. Their question assumed that the future life will be like the temporal life.
12:24–27 Jesus declared that the afterlife will be different from life on earth. In heaven people will not **marry** or be **given in marriage**. By going to **the book of Moses**,

specifically Ex 3 and the passage about **the burning bush**, Jesus used the part of the OT that the Sadducees recognized as Scripture. The point of the OT quotation is that **Abraham . . . Isaac**, and **Jacob** were long dead by the time God spoke to Moses, but God declared he was their God. Since God **is not the God of the dead but of the living**, they must still be alive.
12:28–40 This section describes three encounters with the scribes. The scribes were allies of the chief priests and elders (see note at 11:27).
12:28 The phrase **one of the scribes** may indicate that others were standing by ready to challenge Jesus (cp. Mt 22:34–35). This is the first time in the temple that an individual **approached** Jesus rather than a group. He wanted to know which **command** was the **most important**. The rabbis had counted 613 commandments in the books of Moses. They classified 365 as prohibitions and 248 as commands. They further divided the commandments into weightier and lesser ("least" in Mt 5:19).
12:29–30 Jesus quoted the Shema (Dt 6:4–5), a Scripture passage that pious Jews recited every morning and evening. The words affirmed monotheistic orthodoxy (**the Lord is one**), identified the primary affection with which people were to relate to God (**love**), and emphasized the necessity to do so with one's total being: **heart** (affections); **soul** (spirit); **mind** (intelligence); and **strength** (the will).

12:31 The scribe asked Jesus for one commandment, but Jesus gave him two. Love for neighbors is rooted in love for God, the first commandment. No one before Jesus had combined these commandments (Lv 19:18; Dt 6:5), but it became standard for his followers (Rm 13:8–10; Gl 5:14; Jms 2:8–11; 1Jn 4:11,19–20).
12:32–33 Only Mark records the scribe's response and Jesus's praise. The scribe saw that the love Jesus spoke of was far more **important** than all the **burnt offerings and sacrifices**.
12:34 **Jesus** told the scribe that he had **answered wisely**. Ironically the scene ended with Jesus judging the scribe rather than vice versa. Having foiled all questioners, Jesus now posed his own question (v. 35).
12:35 Jesus's question related to **the scribes** and their understanding of **Messiah** (1:1; 8:29) as **son of David** (see note at 10:47–48). This identification, based on God's promise in 2Sm 7:12–16, was commonplace in Jesus's time.
12:36–37 Jesus quoted Ps 110:1, the OT text quoted and alluded to most frequently in the NT (thirty-three times). Jesus affirmed the psalm's Davidic authorship and inspiration by **the Holy Spirit** (cp. 2Sm 23:2; Ac 1:16). The scribes identified Messiah as David's **son** (vv. 35–36), but David identified Messiah as his **Lord**. Therefore, Messiah was not just a descendant of David. He was David's Lord.

Warning against the Scribes

38 He also said in his teaching, "Beware of the scribes, who want to go around in long robes and who want greetings in the marketplaces, **39** the best seats in the synagogues, and the places of honor at banquets. **40** They devour widows' houses and say long prayers just for show. These will receive harsher judgment."

The Widow's Gift

41 Sitting across from the temple treasury, he watched how the crowd dropped money into the treasury. Many rich people were putting in large sums. **42** Then a poor widow came and dropped in two tiny coins worth very little. **43** Summoning his disciples, he said to them, "Truly I tell you, this poor widow has put more into the treasury than all the others. **44** For they all gave out of their surplus, but she out of her poverty has put in everything she had — all she had to live on."

Destruction of the Temple Predicted

13 As he was going out of the temple, one of his disciples said to him, "Teacher, look! What massive stones! What impressive buildings!"

2 Jesus said to him, "Do you see these great buildings? Not one stone will be left upon another — all will be thrown down."

Signs of the End of the Age

3 While he was sitting on the Mount of Olives across from the temple, Peter, James, John, and Andrew asked him privately, **4** "Tell us, when will these things happen? And what will be the sign when all these things are about to be accomplished?" **5** Jesus told them, "Watch out that no one deceives you. **6** Many will come in my name, saying, 'I am he,' and they will deceive many. **7** When you hear of wars and rumors of wars, don't be alarmed; these things must take place, but it is not yet the end. **8** For nation will rise up against nation, and kingdom against kingdom. There will be earthquakes in various places, and famines.[A] These are the beginning of birth pains.

Persecutions Predicted

9 "But you, be on your guard! They will hand you over to local courts,[B] and you will be flogged in the synagogues. You will stand before governors and kings because of me, as a witness to them. **10** And it is necessary that the

---

[A] 13:8 Other mss add *and disturbances*   [B] 13:9 Or *sanhedrins*

12:38–39 The phrase **he also said** indicates that Mark's summary in vv. 38–40 is only a brief part of the extensive condemnations of the scribes and Pharisees (cp. Mt 23; Lk 11:37–54). Naming four examples of what the scribes took pleasure in, Jesus first condemned them for showmanship. Their **long robes** were festive garments that were unreasonable for everyday wear. **Greetings in the marketplaces** refers to the fact that people were expected to rise in the presence of scribes. The **best seats** faced the congregation, identifying those seated as teachers and distinguished persons. For **places of honor at banquets**, see Jesus's comments in Lk 14:7–11.

12:40 Jesus condemned the scribes for dishonesty and hypocrisy. **Widows** were among the most vulnerable people. To defraud them was despicable (Is 1:17,23; 10:2; Jr 7:6; Ezk 22:7; Zch 7:10), whether by embezzlement or other fraudulent means, Jesus identified these greedy scribes as thieves. The phrase **these will receive harsher judgment** refers to God's eschatological judgment (cp. 9:42–48).

12:41 Previously Jesus was in the Court of the Gentiles. The **temple treasury** was in the Court of the Women, so named not because only women were allowed there but because that was as close as women could come to the sanctuary. The treasury consisted of thirteen trumpet-shaped chests into which worshipers deposited their freewill offerings. Apparently the trumpet shape of the collection boxes amplified the sound of coins when they were dropped in, making it obvious when **rich people** deposited **large sums**.

12:42–44 The **two tiny coins** are identified as *lepta*—copper coins of little value. The widow's gift meant more than the larger

gifts of rich people because she gave in spite of her poverty. The phrase **all she had to live on** meant she would not have enough for her next meal.

13:1–37 This chapter is often called Jesus's Olivet Discourse (cp. Mt 24–25; Lk 21). The themes of the destruction of Jerusalem and the temple by the Romans in AD 70 seem to be interwoven with the final tribulation and Jesus's return. Some interpreters assign all of Mk 13 to the destruction of Jerusalem and the temple. Most believe Jesus used the earlier destruction to foreshadow the end times. Some who hold this latter view assign vv. 1–13 to the first-century events and vv. 14–37 to earth's last days. Others assign vv. 1–31 to the first century and vv. 32–37 to the end times. Still others find an A1–B1–A2–B2 pattern and assign vv. 1–13 and 28–31 to first century and vv. 14–27 and 32–37 to end times.

13:1 The **massive stones** and **buildings** of the temple complex were truly impressive. Herod's temple had been under construction for almost fifty years, and the Jewish historian Josephus said some of the stones were sixty feet long. Archaeologists have found stones forty-two feet long, eleven feet high, and fourteen feet deep, weighing more than a million pounds.

13:2 Jesus prophesied (announced, not merely predicted) the destruction of the **great buildings**. Symbolically in the withering of the fig tree (11:12–14,20–21) Jesus had already prophesied their end. Some question the accuracy of **not one stone will be left upon another** because some stones remain today in the Western Wall, but this was not part of the temple itself but the foundation that supported the platform on which the temple stood.

13:3 The **Mount of Olives** rose three hundred feet above Jerusalem, across the Kidron Valley. It provided a panoramic view of the **temple** and Jerusalem.

13:4 These things and all these things refer to Jesus's comment in v. 2 and the temple's destruction. According to Mark and Luke (Lk 21:7), the disciples asked a double question. Their first question was about **when** the destruction would occur; their second asked what **sign** would precede it.

13:5–13 Jesus began his discourse by warning that his followers would experience persecution **because of** him. (v. 13).

13:5 Watch out (cp. vv. 9,23,33) lays on the disciples the responsibility to avoid being deceived. Jesus had accused the Sadducees of being deceived (12:24,27).

13:6 False claimants and false teachers can be popular. The phrase **in my name** may mean these imposters would claim to teach in Jesus's name or that they would claim to be Messiah (cp. Mt 24:5).

13:7 Wars and **rumors of wars** are not signs of **the end** but characterize the entire age. Jesus said **these things must take place,** meaning they are part of God's plan.

13:8 Natural disasters are not signs of the end, only **the beginning of birth pains.** Though troubling, these pains are harbingers of hope and new life.

13:9 Hand you over refers to betrayal. On being **flogged,** see 2Co 11:24–25. **Governors and kings** referred to Roman political authorities. Thus Jesus's disciples could expect to experience persecution from Jewish and Gentile powers, from religious and secular authorities.

13:10 Persecution is the context in which universal proclamation of the **gospel** will take place.

gospel be preached to all nations. ¹¹ So when they arrest you and hand you over, don't worry beforehand what you will say, but say whatever is given to you at that time, for it isn't you speaking, but the Holy Spirit. ¹² "Brother will betray brother to death, and a father his child. Children will rise up against parents and have them put to death. ¹³ You will be hated by everyone because of my name, but the one who endures to the end will be saved.

The Great Tribulation

¹⁴ "When you see the abomination of desolation^A standing where it should not be" (let the reader understand), "then those in Judea must flee to the mountains. ¹⁵ A man on the housetop must not come down or go in to get anything out of his house, ¹⁶ and a man in the field must not go back to get his coat. ¹⁷ Woe to pregnant women and nursing mothers in those days! ¹⁸ "Pray it^B won't happen in winter. ¹⁹ For those will be days of tribulation, the kind that hasn't been from the beginning of creation until now and never will be again. ²⁰ If the Lord had not cut those days short, no one would be saved. But he cut those days short for the sake of the elect, whom he chose.

²¹ "Then if anyone tells you, 'See, here is the Messiah! See, there!' do not believe it. ²² For false messiahs and false prophets will arise and will perform signs and wonders to lead astray, if possible, the elect. ²³ And you must watch! I have told you everything in advance.

The Coming of the Son of Man

²⁴ "But in those days, after that tribulation: The sun will be darkened, and the moon will not shed its light; ²⁵ the stars will be falling from the sky, and the powers in the heavens will be shaken. ²⁶ Then they will see the Son of Man coming in clouds with great power and glory. ²⁷ He will send out the angels and gather his elect from the four winds, from the ends of the earth to the ends of heaven.

The Parable of the Fig Tree

²⁸ "Learn this lesson from the fig tree: As soon as its branch becomes tender and sprouts leaves, you know that summer is near. ²⁹ In the same way, when you see these things happening, recognize^C that he^D is near — at the door. ³⁰ "Truly I tell you, this generation will certainly not pass away until all these things take

---

^A13:14 Dn 9:27　^B13:18 Other mss read *"Pray that your escape*　^C13:29 Or *you know*　^D13:29 Or *it*

13:11 Jesus admonished his disciples against anxiety that would distract them from their witness. God would give the appropriate response through his **Holy Spirit**. This is the last reference to the Spirit in Mark (1:8,10,12; 3:29; 12:36) and the only one that pictures his role with believers. On the Holy Spirit as Counselor, see Jn 14:16,26; 15:26; 16:7.
13:12 Some Christians will experience betrayal by family members, even to the point of **death** (cp. Mt 10:34–36).
13:13 You will be hated indicates the animosity unbelievers often feel toward Christians because of the **name** of Jesus (cp. 1Pt 4:16). Jesus did not warn his followers so they could seek safety but so they would endure faithfully.
13:14 The abomination of desolation is drawn from Dn 9:27; 11:31; 12:11 (cp. Mt 24:15) and was used to describe the desecration of the temple by Antiochus Epiphanes in 167 BC (see the apocryphal book 1Macc 1:54). Jesus's reference may be to some event prior

to AD 70 or to the "man of lawlessness" (2Th 2:3–10; cp. Rv 13:1–10,14–15). Mark did not identify the location for **standing where it should not be**, but Matthew (Mt 24:15) said "in the holy place," meaning the temple's sanctuary (cp. 2Th 2:4).
13:15–16 On **housetop**, see note at 2:4. Laborers who worked in the fields often laid aside their outer garments as they worked.
13:17 Woe is not a condemnation as in Mt 23:13–32 but a cry of pity for **pregnant women** and **nursing mothers** unable to move quickly.
13:18 Winter weather along with swollen streams that could not be crossed would add to the difficulty of their flight (cp. Mt 24:20).
13:19 This verse is drawn from Dn 12:1. The intensity of these **days of tribulation** (cp. Rv 7:14) will exceed what was experienced in the destruction of Jerusalem in AD 70.
13:20 The Lord will curtail the tribulation for the sake of **the elect**, emphasizing God's sovereign choice.
13:21–22 False prophets were a problem in both the OT (Dt 13:1–5; 18:20–22) and the NT (Mt 7:15; 24:11; Lk 6:26; Ac 13:6; 2Pt 2:1; 1Jn 4:1). **Signs and wonders** is a standard expression for miracles in the OT and NT. The false messiahs and false prophets will have no trouble performing signs—but their purpose will be to **lead astray**. These words foreshadow Paul's in 2Th 2:9–12.
13:23 Jesus had also told them to **watch** in v. 5.
13:24–25 Just as Jesus warned of earthly signs occurring before the tribulation, he also spoke of cosmic signs occurring **after** the tribulation. He declared that **the powers in the heavens will be shaken** as if with a heavenly earthquake (cp. Heb 12:26–29). His language is drawn from Is 13:9–10; Jl 2:10–11,30–31; 3:14–16.

13:26 Jesus drew the wording for this verse from Dn 7:13. **They will see** refers to those living when these events occur. The **clouds** are a reference to God's presence (9:7; 14:62; Ex 19:9; 1Kg 8:10–11; Ps 97:2; Dn 7:13). The phrase **with great power and glory** contrasts with the Son of Man's first coming in weakness and humility.
13:27 The **angels** are regularly pictured as accompanying Christ on his return (8:38; Mt 13:39–41; 16:27; 25:31). The two phrases **from the four winds** and **from the ends of the earth to the ends of heaven** stand in apposition to each other. The language is based on Dt 13:7; 30:4; and Zch 2:6. The former refers to the cardinal points—north, south, east, and west. The latter refers to extremities of earth and heaven. There is no place in all creation where the elect are that will be overlooked (cp. Ps 107:1–3; Is 45:5–7; 49:12; Mt 8:11; Lk 13:29).
13:28 For Jesus's previous use of a **fig tree**, see notes at 11:13 and 11:19–20. When the fig tree **sprouts**, usually in March or April around Passover, **summer is near.**
13:29 Just as Jesus's followers knew how to read the signs of the coming summer, so also when they saw **these things happening** they were to know that a cataclysmic event was near. It is unclear whether Jesus was referring to Jerusalem's fall or his return in the end time.
13:30 Truly I tell you was Jesus's standard indication of a solemn pronouncement. The **generation** that will **not pass away** until **all these things take place** is either Jesus's contemporary generation that would live to see the destruction of Jerusalem and the temple (cp. 8:12,38; 9:19) or the eschatological generation that will be alive when the end begins.

#60　**99 Essential Christian Truths**

JUSTIFICATION BY FAITH

Justification refers to the moment when a person is objectively declared righteous before God based on the righteousness of Christ's atoning death (Rm 8:33–34). This act of declaration takes place through faith in Christ and not as a result of human works or effort (Eph 2:8–9). Through justification, a person is made to be in right standing before God, changing what was once an estranged and hostile relationship to one of adoption into the family of God.

place. **³¹** Heaven and earth will pass away, but my words will never pass away.

No One Knows the Day or Hour

³² "Now concerning that day or hour no one knows — neither the angels in heaven nor the Son — but only the Father. **³³** "Watch! Be alert!^ For you don't know when the time is coming. **³⁴** "It is like a man on a journey, who left his house, gave authority to his servants, gave each one his work, and commanded the doorkeeper to be alert. **³⁵** Therefore be alert, since you don't know when the master of the house is coming — whether in the evening or at midnight or at the crowing of the rooster or early in the morning. **³⁶** Otherwise, when he comes suddenly he might find you sleeping. **³⁷** And what I say to you, I say to everyone: Be alert!"

The Plot to Kill Jesus

14 It was two days before the Passover and the Festival of Unleavened Bread. The chief priests and the scribes were looking for a cunning way to arrest Jesus and kill him. **²** "Not during the festival," they said, "so that there won't be a riot among the people."

The Anointing at Bethany

³ While he was in Bethany at the house of Simon the leper,ᴮ as he was reclining at the table, a woman came with an alabaster jar of very expensive perfume of pure nard. She broke the jar and poured it on his head. **⁴** But some were expressing indignation to one another: "Why has this perfume been wasted? **⁵** For this perfume might have been sold for more than three hundred denariiᶜ and given to the poor." And they began to scold her.

⁶ Jesus replied, "Leave her alone. Why are you bothering her? She has done a noble thing for me. **⁷** You always have the poor with you, and you can do what is good for them whenever you want, but you do not always have me. **⁸** She has done what she could; she has anointed my body in advance for burial. **⁹** Truly I tell you, wherever the gospel is proclaimed in the whole world, what she has done will also be told in memory of her."

¹⁰ Then Judas Iscariot, one of the Twelve, went to the chief priests to betray Jesus to them. **¹¹** And when they heard this, they were glad and promised to give him money. So he started looking for a good opportunity to betray him.

Preparation for Passover

¹² On the first day of Unleavened Bread, when they sacrifice the Passover lamb, his disciples asked him, "Where do you want us to go and prepare the Passover so that you may eat it?"

¹³ So he sent two of his disciples and told them, "Go into the city, and a man carrying a jar of water will meet you. Follow him. **¹⁴** Wherever he enters, tell the owner of the house, 'The Teacher says, "Where is my guest room where

---

^**13:33** Other mss add *and pray*　ᴮ**14:3** Gk *lepros*; a term for various skin diseases; see Lv 13–14　ᶜ**14:5** A denarius = one day's wage

---

13:31 Heaven and earth will pass away because they are temporal by nature. Jesus's **words**, however, will **never pass away**. Only God can make this claim (Is 40:8; 51:6). Jesus's words are as sure and permanent as God's Word (Mt 5:18; Lk 16:17).

13:32 That day or hour indicates Jesus was speaking of the eschatological future. When the end will come is unknown to **angels** or even **the Son**. Only the **Father** knows (Ac 1:7).

13:33 Be alert expresses the idea of staying awake and watchful. Even though Jesus's disciples **don't know when the time is coming**, they are to be ready and faithful.

13:34–37 Jesus's followers are to be like the **doorkeeper**, always on the alert for the master's **coming. Evening . . . midnight . . . the crowing of the rooster**, and **early in the morning** are the four watches of the night based on the Roman identification of them. **Suddenly** indicates not the speed but the unexpectedness of the master's return.

14:1 The temporal clause—**it was two days before**—points to the start of the Jewish **Passover** and the **Festival of Unleavened Bread**. This means the Sanhedrin plotted **to kill** Jesus sometime between sunset on Tuesday and sunset on Wednesday.

14:2 The Sanhedrin hesitated to act because of Jesus's popularity **among the people** who had flooded into town for Passover.

14:3 On **Bethany**, see notes at 11:1 and 11:11. An **alabaster jar** was a long-necked perfume vase that was considered a luxury item. A woman (Mary of Bethany, according to Jn 12:2–3) poured **expensive perfume of pure nard** on Jesus's head.

14:4–5 Some people expressed **indignation** at the waste of expensive **perfume**, which was the equivalent of **three hundred denarii**.

14:6 Jesus rebuked the critics of this woman. What they considered wasteful was actually **a noble thing** (lit "a good work"). Her act was noble because she did it for the Son of God, who is worthy of great sacrifices.

14:7 Christ's followers could **always** minister to the poor, but they would **not always** have the chance to serve Jesus in person. On concern for the poor, see Dt 15:1–11.

14:8 The phrase **she has done what she could** is almost identical to what Jesus said about the poor widow's donation (see note at 12:42–44). The widow gave almost nothing of monetary value; this woman gave a wealthy gift, but Jesus commended both equally. Jesus interpreted the perfume as a makeshift anointing oil for his coming **burial**.

14:9 Jesus anticipated that **the gospel** would be **proclaimed** in the **whole world** (cp. 13:10). When this happened, this woman's act would be told **in memory of her** (cp. Mt 26:13). Your reading of this verse fulfills this promise.

14:10 Mark mentions **Judas Iscariot** here, in the account of Jesus's arrest (vv. 43–45), and in the listing of the Twelve (3:19). The phrase **went to** places the initiative for Jesus's betrayal clearly on Judas; he wasn't recruited by the authorities. **Betray** is used of John the Baptist (1:14), of Jesus (9:31; 10:33; 14:10–11,18,21,41–42,44; 15:1,10,15), and of Jesus's disciples after him (13:9,11–12). Judas's actions stand in strong contrast to those of Mary in 14:3–9.

14:11 Only Matthew (Mt 26:15) indicates how much **money** Judas was given. The phrase **a good opportunity** recalls the Sanhedrin's hope to arrest Jesus "when the crowd was not present" (Lk 22:6) so they would not cause a riot (Mk 14:1–2).

14:12 Jesus decided where they would observe the Passover, but his disciples were responsible to **prepare** it. Preparations included obtaining and preparing a lamb, bitter herbs, unleavened bread, wine, crushed fruit, etc.

14:13–14 Luke (Lk 22:8) identifies the **two . . . disciples** as Peter and John. **Go into the city** indicates they were outside Jerusalem, probably at Bethany. **A man carrying a jar of water** was unusual. Normally women carried water in earthenware pitchers whereas men used animal skins. **Meet** could mean either "encounter" or that the man was looking for them. **The owner of the house** was apparently acquainted with Jesus since they identified him only as **the Teacher**.

I may eat the Passover with my disciples?"' ¹⁵ He will show you a large room upstairs, furnished and ready. Make the preparations for us there." ¹⁶ So the disciples went out, entered the city, and found it just as he had told them, and they prepared the Passover.

Betrayal at the Passover

¹⁷ When evening came, he arrived with the Twelve. ¹⁸ While they were reclining and eating, Jesus said, "Truly I tell you, one of you will betray me — one who is eating with me."

¹⁹ They began to be distressed and to say to him one by one, "Surely not I?"

²⁰ He said to them, "It is one of the Twelve — the one who is dipping bread in the bowl with me. ²¹ For the Son of Man will go just as it is written about him, but woe to that man by whom the Son of Man is betrayed! It would have been better for him if he had not been born."

The First Lord's Supper

²² As they were eating, he took bread, blessed and broke it, gave it to them, and said, "Take it; this is my body." ²³ Then he took a cup, and after giving thanks, he gave it to them, and they all drank from it. ²⁴ He said to them, "This is my blood of the covenant,ᴬ which is poured out for many. ²⁵ Truly I tell you, I will no longer drink of the fruit of the vine until that day when I drink it newᴮ in the kingdom of God."

²⁶ After singing a hymn, they went out to the Mount of Olives.

Peter's Denial Predicted

²⁷ Then Jesus said to them, "All of you will fall away,ᶜ because it is written:

I will strike the shepherd,
and the sheep will be scattered.ᴰ

²⁸ But after I have risen, I will go ahead of you to Galilee."

²⁹ Peter told him, "Even if everyone falls away, I will not."

³⁰ "Truly I tell you," Jesus said to him, "today, this very night, before the rooster crows twice, you will deny me three times."

³¹ But he kept insisting, "If I have to die with you, I will never deny you." And they all said the same thing.

The Prayer in the Garden

³² Then they came to a place named Gethsemane, and he told his disciples, "Sit here while I pray." ³³ He took Peter, James, and John with him, and he began to be deeply distressed and troubled. ³⁴ He said to them, "I am deeply grievedᴱ to the point of death. Remain here and stay awake." ³⁵ He went a little farther, fell to the ground, and prayed that if it were possible, the hour might pass from him. ³⁶ And he said, "Abba,ᶠ Father! All things are possible for you. Take this cup away from me. Nevertheless,

---

ᴬ 14:24 Other mss read *the new covenant*   ᴮ 14:25 Or *drink new wine*; lit *drink it new*   ᶜ 14:27 Other mss add *because of me this night*   ᴰ 14:27 Zch 13:7   ᴱ 14:34 Or *"My soul is swallowed up in sorrow"*   ᶠ 14:36 Aramaic for *father*

14:15–16 The "guest room" (v. 14) was **a large room upstairs**, probably the spacious roof chamber of a wealthy man. The room was **ready** to accommodate a large group. **Found it just as he had told them** stresses the exact fulfillment of Jesus's words.

14:17 When evening came marked the start of a new day by Jewish reckoning. According to Ex 12:8, the Passover meal had to be eaten at night and be finished by midnight.

14:18 Jesus had said earlier that he would be betrayed (9:31; 10:33). Now he added that the betrayer would be one of his disciples. The words **one who is eating with me** did not immediately identify the betrayer since all of the disciples were dining together. Rather, the words point to Ps 41:9 and add to the magnitude of the treachery since eating together in the ancient Orient involved a certain intimacy and demanded one restrain from hostile actions.

14:19 No one attempted to refute Jesus or make accusations. Apparently Judas was above all suspicion at this point. The disciples' statement **surely not I** expected both a negative response and a word of reassurance from Jesus.

14:20 That the betrayer was **dipping bread** with Jesus meant he was seated nearby (Mt 26:25; Jn 13:23–30).

14:21 On **Son of Man**, see note at 2:8–11. Previously Jesus had stated his betrayal was predicted by Scripture (9:12). This verse unites God's prophesied plan (**just as it is written**) with human actions and responsibility.

14:22 The institution of the Last Supper is recorded in all three Synoptic Gospels (vv. 22–26; Mt 26:26–29; Lk 22:19–20) and by Paul (1Co 11:23–25). Mark did not specify at what point in the traditional course of the Passover meal Jesus instituted the Last Supper. **This is my body** is metaphorical.

14:23 They **all drank from** one cup. "Eucharist" derives from the Greek word for **giving thanks**.

14:24 The phrase **blood of the covenant** recalls the institution of the Mosaic covenant at Sinai when the Israelites were sprinkled with blood (Ex 24:1–8; cp. Heb 9:19–20; 10:28–30). Jesus's blood established a new covenant. **Poured out for many** recalls Jesus's words in 10:45 and Isaiah's words (Is 53:11–12) about Messiah dying on behalf of others.

14:25 Jesus's solemn formula **Truly I tell you** focused the group's attention on the eschatological future. Even though Jesus had explained his death and its meaning, it would not be the end for him. The day (cp. 13:17,19–20,24,32) would come when he would **drink** with them in the **kingdom of God** (cp. 15:43–46).

14:26 The Passover meal traditionally ended with **singing** the Hallel psalms (Pss 115–118).

14:27 Jesus told his disciples, **All of you will fall away.** . . . **It is written** grounds Jesus's prediction in OT Scripture, specifically Zch 13:7. Jesus's prediction of the disciples' desertion and of Peter's denial is recorded in all four Gospels (Mt 26:31–35; Mk 14:27–31; Lk 22:31–34; Jn 13:36–38).

14:28 Jesus referred to his resurrection and added that he would gather his disciples again in **Galilee** for a new mission (cp. 16:7).

14:29–31 Quick-tongued Peter declared his steadfastness, but Jesus infallibly foreknew that Peter would cower in the face of opposition. Not only would he desert like the others, but he would also **deny** Jesus **three times.**

14:32 Gethsemane means "olive press." Located across the Kidron Valley on the western slope of the Mount of Olives, it was Jesus's regular meeting place with his disciples (Jn 18:2).

14:33 Peter, James, and John were the inner circle of Jesus's disciples (5:37; 9:2; 13:3). Each had pledged his willingness to die with Jesus (10:38–39; 14:29,31). Mark uses two rare words to describe Jesus's emotions. **Deeply distressed** occurs only in Mark (v. 33; 9:15; 16:5–6) and has the nuance of "greatly alarmed." The word for **troubled** expresses extreme anxiety, and it occurs elsewhere in Mt 26:37 and Php 2:26.

14:34 The phrase **to the point of death** indicates the depth of Jesus's distress. Lk 22:44 adds, "His sweat became like drops of blood falling to the ground."

14:35 Fell to the ground pictures Jesus collapsing under his burden (Mt 26:39; cp. Lk 22:41). **The hour** refers to Jesus's divinely appointed death (Jn 7:30; 8:20; 12:23,27; 13:1; 17:1). **If it were possible** was a request for God to change his divine plan.

14:36 Abba is Aramaic for "father" and is a term of intimacy. Jesus's words **all things**

not what I will, but what you will." **37** Then he came and found them sleeping. He said to Peter, "Simon, are you sleeping? Couldn't you stay awake one hour? **38** Stay awake and pray so that you won't enter into temptation.^A The spirit is willing, but the flesh is weak." **39** Once again he went away and prayed, saying the same thing. **40** And again he came and found them sleeping, because they could not keep their eyes open. They did not know what to say to him. **41** Then he came a third time and said to them, "Are you still sleeping and resting? Enough! The time has come. See, the Son of Man is betrayed into the hands of sinners. **42** Get up; let's go. See, my betrayer is near."

Judas's Betrayal of Jesus

43 While he was still speaking, Judas, one of the Twelve, suddenly arrived. With him was a mob, with swords and clubs, from the chief priests, the scribes, and the elders. **44** His betrayer had given them a signal. "The one I kiss," he said, "he's the one; arrest him and take him away under guard." **45** So when he came, immediately he went up to Jesus and said, "Rabbi!" and kissed him. **46** They took hold of him and arrested him. **47** One of those who stood by drew his sword, struck the high priest's servant, and cut off his ear.

48 Jesus said to them, "Have you come out with swords and clubs, as if I were a criminal,^B

to capture me? **49** Every day I was among you, teaching in the temple, and you didn't arrest me. But the Scriptures must be fulfilled." **50** Then they all deserted him and ran away. **51** Now a certain young man, wearing nothing but a linen cloth, was following him. They caught hold of him, **52** but he left the linen cloth behind and ran away naked.

Jesus Faces the Sanhedrin

53 They led Jesus away to the high priest, and all the chief priests, the elders, and the scribes assembled. **54** Peter followed him at a distance, right into the high priest's courtyard. He was sitting with the servants,^C warming himself by the fire.

55 The chief priests and the whole Sanhedrin were looking for testimony against Jesus to put him to death, but they could not find any. **56** For many were giving false testimony against him, and the testimonies did not agree. **57** Some stood up and gave false testimony against him, stating, **58** "We heard him say, 'I will destroy this temple made with human hands, and in three days I will build another not made by hands.'" **59** Yet their testimony did not agree even on this.

60 Then the high priest stood up before them all and questioned Jesus, "Don't you have an answer to what these men are testifying against you?" **61** But he kept silent and did not answer.

---

^A**14:38** Or *won't be put to the test*   ^B**14:48** Or *insurrectionist*   ^C**14:54** Or *temple police*, or *officers*, also in v. 65

---

are possible for you affirmed God's power and recalled his teaching (10:27). **This cup** refers to personal suffering and death (cp. 10:38–39) but also to God's judgment on sin (14:24; cp. Jr 25:15–16; 2Co 5:21; 1Pt 2:24). **Not what I will, but what you will** recalls Jesus's model prayer (Mt 6:10). Not his personal desire but the Father's will defined Jesus's life (Jn 5:30; 6:38).
14:37 Peter was singled out for his failure to stay awake because of his bold claims earlier in the evening (vv. 29–31). **One hour** may be idiomatic rather than literal.
14:38 Though Jesus addressed Peter in v. 37, his warning in v. 38 is addressed to the others as well since the verbs are plural in Greek. The warning to **pray so that you won't enter into temptation** recalls the petition from Jesus's model prayer (Mt 6:13). Jesus's acknowledgment that the **flesh** is weak may have applied to himself also that night, given his suffering. Natural human weaknesses (hunger, fatigue, etc.) can pose great spiritual danger.
14:39–40 The stupefied disciples **did not know what to say to him**. This recalls Peter's experience on the Mount of Transfiguration (9:6) and the disciples' silence in 9:34.
14:41–42 **Enough** was a cry of exasperation and served to awaken the sleepers. Jesus had prayed "that if it were possible, the hour might pass from him" (v. 35), but God did not grant that request. **Get up; let's go** was a call to meet the mob head on, not an encouragement to flee (cp. Jn 14:31). **See** indicates they could see the torches of the approaching throng.

14:43 In fulfillment of Jesus's prediction in 8:31, the **mob** hailed from the **chief priests**, the **scribes**, and the **elders**—the three parties of the Sanhedrin. This was an officially sanctioned arrest party.
14:44 **Signal** refers to a sign agreed on in advance. The specific signal was a **kiss** (probably on the cheek). While a kiss was a common greeting (Lk 7:45; Ac 20:37; Rm 16:16), this is the only time a disciple is recorded as greeting Jesus this way (cp. 2Sm 20:9–10).
14:45 **Rabbi** means "my great one." It was an address of honor to one's teacher.
14:46–47 The attack on **the high priest's servant** is recorded in all four Gospels (Mt 26:51–52; Lk 22:49–51; Jn 18:10–11). John identifies the attacker as Peter and the servant as Malchus (Jn 18:10). Apparently Jesus's disciples asked if they should defend him with swords (Lk 22:49), but Peter didn't wait for a reply. On Jesus's disciples carrying swords, see note at Lk 22:35–38. Jesus restored Malchus's ear (Lk 22:51).
14:48–50 The **Scriptures** that **must be fulfilled** are not identified, but v. 50 points to Zch 13:7 (quoted in v. 27) as one of them. **They all deserted him** refers to the fleeing disciples.
14:51–52 The **young man** is unidentified. Some have suggested he was John Mark, the author of this Gospel.
14:53–65 No single Gospel comprehensively records Jesus's trials, and each emphasizes different perspectives and events. It is clear, however, that both Roman political authorities and Jewish religious leaders

were involved in handing down Jesus's death sentence.
14:53 **They** refers to those who arrested Jesus (vv. 43,46). Matthew said **the high priest** was Caiaphas, who served from AD 18–36 (Mt 26:57). That all three parties **assembled** indicates this was a meeting of the Sanhedrin (vv. 43,55).
14:54 Peter followed the arrest party and ended up **warming himself** (cp. Jn 18:18) in **the high priest's courtyard.**
14:55–56 The entire Sanhedrin, especially **the chief priests**, had already decided to put Jesus to death, so they went looking for evidence to justify their plan. Many witnesses gave **false testimony** that **did not agree** under cross-examination. The OT required the agreement of two witnesses in a capital case (Nm 35:30; Dt 17:6; 19:15).
14:57–58 Some who gave **false testimony** claimed firsthand experience. **Made with human hands** indicates human agency; **not made by hands** indicates divine agency (cp. Ac 7:48; 17:24; Heb 9:11,24).
14:59 Only Mark notes that the accusers **did not agree even on this** (cp. Mt 26:60). The Jews took threats against the temple seriously (cp. Jr 26:7–24). This charge was issued against Jesus again while he hung on the cross (Mk 15:29).
14:60 Frustrated with the ineptitude of the proceedings, Caiaphas **stood up** and questioned Jesus himself.
14:61–62 **Kept silent** points to the prophesied Suffering Servant's response in Is 53:7 (cp. Ac 8:32; 1Pt 2:21,23). Throughout Mark's Gospel, Jesus had shied away from

Again the high priest questioned him, "Are you the Messiah, the Son of the Blessed One?"

62 "I am," said Jesus, "and you will see the Son of Man seated at the right hand of Power and coming with the clouds of heaven."[A]

63 Then the high priest tore his robes and said, "Why do we still need witnesses? **64** You have heard the blasphemy. What is your decision?" They all condemned him as deserving death.

65 Then some began to spit on him, to blindfold him, and to beat him, saying, "Prophesy!" The temple servants also took him and slapped him.

Peter Denies His Lord

66 While Peter was in the courtyard below, one of the high priest's maidservants came. **67** When she saw Peter warming himself, she looked at him and said, "You also were with Jesus, the man from Nazareth."

68 But he denied it: "I don't know or understand what you're talking about." Then he went out to the entryway,[B] and a rooster crowed.[C]

69 When the maidservant saw him again, she began to tell those standing nearby, "This man is one of them."

70 But again he denied it. After a little while those standing there said to Peter again, "You certainly are one of them, since you're also a Galilean."[D]

71 Then he started to curse and swear, "I don't know this man you're talking about!"

72 Immediately a rooster crowed a second time, and Peter remembered when Jesus had spoken the word to him, "Before the rooster crows twice, you will deny me three times." And he broke down and wept.

Jesus Faces Pilate

15 As soon as it was morning, having held a meeting with the elders, scribes, and the whole Sanhedrin, the chief priests tied Jesus up, led him away, and handed him over to Pilate. **2** So Pilate asked him, "Are you the king of the Jews?"

He answered him, "You say so."

3 And the chief priests accused him of many things. **4** Pilate questioned him again, "Aren't you going to answer? Look how many things they are accusing you of!" **5** But Jesus still did not answer, and so Pilate was amazed.

Jesus or Barabbas

6 At the festival Pilate used to release for the people a prisoner whom they requested. **7** There was one named Barabbas, who was in prison with rebels who had committed murder during the rebellion. **8** The crowd came up and began to ask Pilate to do for them as was his custom. **9** Pilate answered them, "Do you want me to release the king of the Jews for you?" **10** For he knew it

---

A14:62 Ps 110:1; Dn 7:13　**B14:68** Or *forecourt*　**C14:68** Other mss omit *and a rooster crowed*　**D14:70** Other mss add *and your speech shows it*

---

the title *Messiah* to avoid misunderstanding, but here he embraced it. **I am** (cp. Mt 26:64; Lk 22:67) echoes the divine name (Ex 3:14). Jesus then switched to his favorite self-designation **Son of Man** and quoted from Ps 110:2 and Dn 7:13. To be **seated at the right hand** was an honor (cp. 10:37,40). **Coming with the clouds of heaven** is often understood as a reference to the second coming, but **you will see** leads some interpreters to understand that Jesus was referring to his post-ascension enthronement in heaven.
14:63 Tearing one's clothes symbolized grief (Gn 37:34; Jos 7:6; 2Sm 1:11–12; 2Kg 2:12) or horror at blasphemy (2Kg 18:37; 19:1). **Witnesses** were no longer needed since Jesus had incriminated himself by claiming he was the Messiah.
14:64 Deserving death indicates death by stoning for blasphemy (Lv 24:10–16).
14:65 To **spit** in a person's face (Mt 26:67) was the ultimate insult (Nm 12:14; Dt 25:9; Jb 30:9–10). Jesus predicted this would happen (Mk 10:34; cp. 15:19). Isaiah described this as one of the sufferings of the Servant of the Lord (Is 50:6).
14:66 This picks up from v. 54. The phrase **the courtyard below** indicates Jesus's hearing was held in the hall above the entry level to the high priest's house.
14:67 As Peter stood in the courtyard of the high priest's house (see note at v. 54), a servant said she had seen him with **the man from Nazareth** (a contemptuous usage, as is "the Galilean," Mt 26:69).

14:68 Only Mark records Jesus as predicting a rooster would crow twice (vv. 29–31). This is a logical place for the first crowing, even though it apparently escaped Peter's notice.
14:69 This time **those standing nearby** were made aware of Peter's identity.
14:70 Peter's accent identified him as a **Galilean** (Mt 26:73).
14:71 Peter's denials escalated. **To curse** means to call down God's curse on oneself (cp. Ac 23:12,14,21). To **swear** refers to taking an oath in God's name. Peter's cursing and swearing backed his strongest denial—**I don't know this man**.
14:72 Immediately links Peter's third denial to the fulfillment of Jesus's prophecy (vv. 26–31). Jesus turned and looked at Peter (Lk 22:61) and then he **remembered** Jesus's prediction and his own vow of steadfastness. The last sentence of the verse indicates Peter's total remorse.
15:1 This verse is often seen as a third Jewish trial in which **the whole Sanhedrin** legalized their verdict in the **morning** (cp. Lk 22:66–71). Decisions reached at night were not binding. Being **handed . . . over** is repeatedly emphasized in this chapter (vv. 1,10,15) and throughout Mark. **Pilate** was a Roman official among the Jews during AD 26–36. Pilate resided at Caesarea Maritima but found it expedient to stay in Jerusalem during Passover and other major Jewish festivals because of the large number of pilgrims flooding the city and the potential for unrest.
15:2 Pilate focused on whether Jesus claimed to be **king of the Jews**. Clearly the

Sanhedrin's condemnation based on blasphemy (14:64) had turned into charges of sedition and treason. This is the first use of this title in Mark's Gospel, but Pilate repeatedly used it (15:2,9,12,26; cp. v. 32). The words recall the quest of the wise men at Jesus's birth (Mt 2:2). Jesus's reply, **you say so,** can be understood as either noncommittal or as an acknowledgement, but not as a denial.
15:3–5 Pilate's question involves a double negative. It is matched by Mark's double negative that Jesus **did not answer**. Pilate was amazed at Jesus's silence because he could free him if his answers were satisfactory.
15:6 Mark is silent about Pilate's attempt to extricate himself from the situation by sending Jesus to Herod Antipas (cp. Lk 23:5–12), the same Herod as in Mk 6:14–29. Here, in 15:6–15, Pilate tried another maneuver involving a custom **to release for the people a prisoner**. This custom is not documented outside the NT and was apparently done only at the Passover **festival** (Jn 18:39).
15:7 The **rebels** who were **in prison** with Barabbas probably included the two criminals who were crucified with Jesus. Mark gave no other details about **the rebellion,** which may indicate that his readers were familiar with it and thus did not need him to spell it out.
15:8–9 **The crowd**, coached by Jesus's enemies, asked Pilate to follow **his custom** of releasing a prisoner. Pilate instinctively offered them **the king of the Jews** (vv. 2,9,12,26). Thus Pilate unknowingly confessed Jesus's true status.

was because of envy that the chief priests had handed him over. ¹¹ But the chief priests stirred up the crowd so that he would release Barabbas to them instead. ¹² Pilate asked them again, "Then what do you want me to do with the one you call the king of the Jews?"

¹³ Again they shouted, "Crucify him!"

¹⁴ Pilate said to them, "Why? What has he done wrong?"

But they shouted all the more, "Crucify him!"

¹⁵ Wanting to satisfy the crowd, Pilate released Barabbas to them; and after having Jesus flogged, he handed him over to be crucified.

Mocked by the Military

¹⁶ The soldiers led him away into the palace (that is, the governor's residence) and called the whole company together. ¹⁷ They dressed him in a purple robe, twisted together a crown of thorns, and put it on him. ¹⁸ And they began to salute him, "Hail, king of the Jews!" ¹⁹ They were hitting him on the head with a stick and spitting on him. Getting down on their knees, they were paying him homage. ²⁰ After they had mocked him, they stripped him of the purple robe and put his clothes on him.

Crucified between Two Criminals

They led him out to crucify him. ²¹ They forced a man coming in from the country, who was passing by, to carry Jesus's cross. He was Simon of Cyrene, the father of Alexander and Rufus. ²² They brought Jesus to the place called *Golgotha* (which means Place of the Skull). ²³ They tried to give him wine mixed with myrrh, but he did not take it.

²⁴ Then they crucified him and divided his clothes, casting lots for them to decide what each would get. ²⁵ Now it was nine in the morning^A^ when they crucified him. ²⁶ The inscription of the charge written against him was: THE KING OF THE JEWS. ²⁷ They crucified two criminals^B^ with him, one on his right and one on his left.^C^

²⁹ Those who passed by were yelling insults at^D^ him, shaking their heads, and saying, "Ha! The one who would destroy the temple and rebuild it in three days, ³⁰ save yourself by coming down from the cross!" ³¹ In the same way, the chief priests with the scribes were mocking him among themselves and saying, "He saved others, but he cannot save himself! ³² Let the Messiah, the King of Israel, come down now from the cross, so that we may see and believe." Even those who were crucified with him taunted him.

The Death of Jesus

³³ When it was noon,^E^ darkness came over the whole land until three in the afternoon.^F^

---

^A^15:25 Lit *was the third hour* ^B^15:27 Or *revolutionaries* ^C^15:27 Some mss include v. 28: *So the Scripture was fulfilled that says: And he was counted among criminals.* ^D^15:29 Or *passed by blasphemed* ^E^15:33 Lit *the sixth hour* ^F^15:33 Lit *the ninth hour*, also in v. 34

15:10 Pilate recognized that **envy** was why the **chief priests** wanted Jesus dead.

15:11–12 Again **the chief priests** (vv. 1,3,10) manipulated the course of events. **Stirred up** suggests they incited the crowd to riot. Ironically, the crowd chose **Barabbas** ("son of the father") over Jesus, the true Son of the Father.

15:13–14 This is Mark's first reference to crucifixion. None of Jesus's death predictions specifically mentioned crucifixion, though he had hinted at it (8:34). R.T. France points out that it was the usual provincial penalty for political rebellion.

15:15 Wanting to satisfy the crowd at the cost of justice, Pilate **handed** Jesus **over**. Being **flogged** means Jesus was whipped with leather cords that had pieces of bone or metal tied in them that would rip the flesh off one's back. Being **crucified** was a punishment for slaves and rebels.

15:16 Company reflects the Greek equivalent of the Latin "cohors/cohort," which totaled six hundred soldiers. Mark does not use "company" in its technical sense, but he indicates that a large group of soldiers mocked Jesus.

15:17 The soldiers used makeshift substitutes for the **robe** . . . **crown**, and scepter of a king. **Purple** was a royal color.

15:18 Hail, king of the Jews was a mocking corruption of the greeting, "Hail, Caesar."

15:19 They beat the King of the Jews **on the head with a stick.**

15:20 The phrase **led him out to crucify him** refers to the centurion and the company of soldiers.

15:21 Condemned prisoners customarily carried the crossbeam, or *patibulum*, to the site of their execution, where it was attached to the vertical beam. The Greek biographer Plutarch wrote: "Every criminal condemned to death bears his cross on his back" (*Moralia*, 554 A/B). Apparently Jesus was too weak from being flogged and beaten to carry it all the way. Roman soldiers had the right to press citizens of subject nations into compulsory service (Mt 5:41), so they forced Simon to **carry** Jesus's **cross**. **Simon** was a Jewish Cyrenian from the north coast of Africa. He was **the father of Alexander and Rufus**, indicating that readers in Rome probably knew these men (Rm 16:13). Simon apparently became a Christian due to this experience.

15:22 Golgotha is Aramaic for **Place of the Skull**. The traditional site of the crucifixion is the Church of the Holy Sepulcher, located outside the city walls (Lv 24:14; Nm 15:35–36; Heb 13:12).

15:23 Wine mixed with myrrh was a primitive narcotic. The offer fulfilled Ps 69:21.

15:24 They crucified him is all Mark writes about the main event of the gospel. The crucifixion took place on Friday, now known as Good Friday. That the four soldiers of the execution squad **divided his clothes** and cast lots for them fulfilled Ps 22:18 (cp. Jn 19:23–24).

15:25 Nine in the morning is literally "the third hour." Jews reckoned the time of day from sunrise.

15:26 The **charge** on which a person was condemned was often **written** on a placard

and hung around his neck. In Jesus's case, it was nailed to his cross (Jn 19:19). All four Gospels record the words differently (cp. Mt 27:37; Lk 23:38; Jn 19:19), possibly because the **inscription** was trilingual (Jn 19:20). **THE KING OF THE JEWS** ironically proclaimed the truth about Jesus.

15:27 Criminals is the word used to describe Barabbas in Jn 18:40 (cp. Mk 14:48). Jesus's crucifixion between criminals was meant as a parody of his kingship (as if he had attendants on either side) but by God's design the whole event really was his royal enthronement. The phrase **one on his right and one on his left** recalls the request of James and John (10:37,40).

15:29–30 Insults means "blasphemies." **Those who passed by** were thus guilty of the very thing for which the Sanhedrin had condemned Jesus (14:64). The bystanders' insults and **shaking** of their **heads** fulfilled Ps 22:7 and Lm 2:15.

15:31 Once again the **chief priests** led the mockery of Jesus. Their derision along with that of **the scribes** went to the heart of Jesus's mission: To save others, Jesus refused to **save himself** (10:45).

15:32 On **Messiah**, see note at 8:29. The religious leaders' mockery recalls the second charge Jesus faced before the Sanhedrin (14:61). Mark reported that the two **crucified** with Jesus also taunted him. One of them repented (Lk 23:39–43).

15:33 Noon was literally "the sixth hour," and **three in the afternoon** was "the ninth hour." The **darkness** was supernatural and

34 And at three Jesus cried out with a loud voice, *"Eloi, Eloi, lemá sabachtháni?"* which is translated, "My God, my God, why have you abandoned me?"[A] **35** When some of those standing there heard this, they said, "See, he's calling for Elijah." **36** Someone ran and filled a sponge with sour wine, fixed it on a stick, offered him a drink, and said, "Let's see if Elijah comes to take him down." **37** Jesus let out a loud cry and breathed his last. **38** Then the curtain of the temple was torn in two from top to bottom. **39** When the centurion, who was standing opposite him, saw the way he[B] breathed his last, he said, "Truly this man was the Son of God!"[C]

40 There were also women watching from a distance. Among them were Mary Magdalene, Mary the mother of James the younger and of Joses, and Salome. **41** In Galilee these women followed him and took care of him. Many other women had come up with him to Jerusalem.

The Burial of Jesus

42 When it was already evening, because it was the day of preparation (that is, the day before the Sabbath), **43** Joseph of Arimathea, a prominent member of the Sanhedrin who was himself looking forward to the kingdom of God, came and boldly went to Pilate and asked for Jesus's body. **44** Pilate was surprised that he was already dead. Summoning the centurion, he asked him whether he had already died. **45** When he found out from the centurion, he gave the corpse to Joseph. **46** After he bought some linen cloth, Joseph took him down and wrapped him in the linen. Then he laid him in a tomb cut out of the rock and rolled a stone against the entrance to the tomb. **47** Mary Magdalene and Mary the mother of Joses were watching where he was laid.

Resurrection Morning

16 When the Sabbath was over, Mary Magdalene, Mary the mother of James, and Salome bought spices, so that they could go and anoint him. **2** Very early in the morning, on the first day of the week, they went to the tomb at sunrise. **3** They were saying to one another, "Who will roll away the stone from the entrance to the tomb for us?" **4** Looking up, they noticed that the stone — which was very large — had been rolled away.

5 When they entered the tomb, they saw a young man dressed in a white robe

---

[A]**15:34** Ps 22:1   [B]**15:39** Other mss read *saw that he cried out like this and*   [C]**15:39** Or *a son of God*

---

represented God's judgment (Ex 10:21–23; Am 8:9–10).
15:34 At 3:00 p.m. Jesus **cried out with a loud voice** the Aramaic phrase, *Eloi, Eloi, lemá sabachtháni.* As usual, Mark provided a translation. Even when Jesus felt most **abandoned** by God, he affirmed his relationship with his Father—**my God, my God,** quoting the opening words of Ps 22:1. Jesus endured God's wrath as the sin-bearer.
15:35–36 Perhaps bystanders mistook *Eloi* for **Elijah** (Aramaic *Eli*) since there was a tradition in Judaism that Elijah would return (9:11–13; Mal 4:5). **Sour wine,** made with vinegar and water, was a drink of the soldiers, not the wine of v. 23. This action fulfilled Ps 69:21 (see note at Jn 19:28–29).
15:37 The content of Jesus's **loud cry** (reported by all three Synoptic Gospels) is specified in Jn 19:30—"It is finished." Luke records Jesus's final words (Lk 23:46).
15:38 The **curtain of the temple** hung before the most holy place in the temple. Its tearing symbolizes unhindered access to God, made possible because of Jesus's atonement for sin on the cross (Heb 6:19–20; 9:3; 10:19–22). The only other use of the Greek word for **torn** in Mark is in 1:10 when God tore open the heavens at Jesus's baptism.
15:39 The Gentile **centurion** who presided over the execution was the first in Mark's Gospel to confess Jesus as **the Son of God** (cp. 1:11,24; 3:11; 5:9; 9:7). His confession matched Mark's opening statement (1:1).
15:40 This is the first reference to **Mary Magdalene** in Mark. Jesus expelled seven demons from her (16:9; Lk 8:2). She came from Magdala on the western side of the Sea of Galilee. **Mary the mother of James the younger and of Joses** is called "the other Mary" in Mt 27:61. Possibly she was

the mother of James the son of Alphaeus (Mk 3:18). **Salome** is named only in Mark (v. 40; 16:1). She was the mother of James and John, the sons of Zebedee (Mt 20:20; 27:56).
15:41 In Mark, only women (v. 41; 1:31) and angels (1:13) serve or help Jesus. The **many other women** who made the pilgrimage **to Jerusalem** did so for Passover.
15:42–47 Jesus's burial, an important element in early Christian proclamation (1Co 15:3–4), is recorded also in Mt 27:57–61; Lk 23:50–56; and Jn 19:38–42.
15:42 Jesus's burial was hastily performed because it was **already evening** on Friday. The Sabbath was soon to begin, a time when burial labors were not permitted. **The day of preparation** (the day before the Sabbath) was when pious Jews prepared whatever they needed for the Sabbath.
15:43 Joseph of Arimathea was a secret follower of Jesus (Mt 27:57; Jn 19:38). That he was **a prominent member of the Sanhedrin** and opposed their verdict (Lk 23:51) shows that this group was not unanimous in its decision to seek Jesus's execution (cp. Mk 14:55,64; 15:1). Joseph went **boldly** to Pilate to ask for Jesus's body. This contrasts with his formerly secret discipleship (Jn 19:38). The Romans often let criminals rot on their crosses, but the Jews objected to leaving the dead hanging overnight (Dt 21:22–23).
15:44 Crucifixion victims often survived for days before dying. Jesus died in about six hours. Thus he **surprised** Pilate a second time (v. 5).
15:45 Pilate **gave** Joseph Jesus's body without demanding the bribe that families sometimes had to pay to retrieve the bodies of their loved ones.
15:46 Only Mark mentions that Joseph **bought some linen cloth** in which Jesus was **wrapped.** Matthew (Mt 27:60) informs

readers that the **tomb** was Joseph's own. Luke (Lk 23:53) and John (Jn 19:41) add that it had never been used. Readers should understand the tomb as a family tomb, not an individual burial crypt. To seal the tomb and prevent looting, they **rolled a stone against the entrance.** The large, circular, flat stone rolled in a track cut into the rock at the tomb entrance.
15:47 The women who witnessed Jesus's death also witnessed his burial.
16:1–8 Women were the first to know that Jesus was risen (Mt 28:1–8; Lk 24:1–8; Jn 20:1–2). Mary Magdalene's name heads the list in all four Gospels. The role of women in this account is astonishing since Judaism did not accept the testimony of women as legally valid.
16:1 The **Sabbath was over** at about 6:00 p.m. on Saturday. This allowed the women to buy more **spices** that evening. All three women had witnessed Jesus's crucifixion (15:40), and two of them had witnessed his burial (15:47). They would also be the first witnesses to his resurrection. On **Mary the mother of James,** see note at 15:40. The Jews anointed bodies to cover the stench of decay.
16:2 The **first day of the week** was Sunday. **Very early in the morning** probably indicates when the women left for the tomb, whereas **at sunrise** indicates when they arrived.
16:3 That the women wondered who would **roll away the stone** reveals that they did not know that the tomb was sealed or guarded (Mt 27:62–66).
16:4 According to Matthew (Mt 28:2–4) an angel had rolled away **the stone.**
16:5 The stone was not moved to let Jesus out but to let witnesses enter. That the women **entered the tomb** confirms it was a large

sitting on the right side; they were alarmed. **6** "Don't be alarmed," he told them. "You are looking for Jesus of Nazareth, who was crucified. He has risen! He is not here. See the place where they put him. **7** But go, tell his disciples and Peter, 'He is going ahead of you to Galilee; you will see him there just as he told you.' "

8 They went out and ran from the tomb, because trembling and astonishment overwhelmed them. And they said nothing to anyone, since they were afraid.

[Some of the earliest mss conclude with 16:8.]^A

The Longer Ending of Mark: Appearances of the Risen Lord

[**9** Early on the first day of the week, after he had risen, he appeared first to Mary Magdalene, out of whom he had driven seven demons. **10** She went and reported to those who had been with him, as they were mourning and weeping. **11** Yet, when they heard that he was alive and had been seen by her, they did not believe it.

12 After this, he appeared in a different form to two of them walking on their way into the country. **13** And they went and reported it to the rest, who did not believe them either.

The Great Commission

14 Later he appeared to the Eleven themselves as they were reclining at the table. He rebuked their unbelief and hardness of heart, because they did not believe those who saw him after he had risen. **15** Then he said to them, "Go into all the world and preach the gospel to all creation. **16** Whoever believes and is baptized will be saved, but whoever does not believe will be

^A **16:8** Other mss include vv. 9–20 as a longer ending. The following shorter ending is found in some mss between v. 8 and v. 9 and in one ms after v. 8 (each of which omits vv. 9–20): *And all that had been commanded to them they quickly reported to those around Peter. After these things, Jesus himself sent out through them from east to west, the holy and imperishable proclamation of eternal salvation. Amen.*

---

family tomb. The **young man dressed in a white robe** (Mt 28:3; Ac 1:10; 10:30) was an angel (Mt 28:5; Lk 24:4). Luke mentions two angels (Lk 24:3–4); Mark focuses on the spokesman.

16:6 The words of reassurance (**don't be alarmed**) are a standard feature in angelic manifestations (Dn 10:12,19; Mt 28:5; Lk 1:13,30; 2:10; Ac 27:24). On three previous occasions in Mark, he was designated **Jesus of Nazareth** (1:23; 10:47; 14:67). Here the word serves to connect the historical Jesus **who**

was crucified to the one who **has risen**. . . . **See the place where they put him** recalls 15:47 (cp. Jn 20:6–7) and indicates the shelf inside the tomb on which Jesus's body was placed.

16:7 Go, tell are the two things that all followers of Jesus are to do. **Peter** is given special mention only in Mark as an encouragement following his denials of Jesus (14:66–72). The message for the disciples to meet Jesus in **Galilee** recalls Jesus's prophecy in 14:28.

16:8 Trembling and **astonishment overwhelmed** the women, whether from fear or excitement (cp. Mt 28:8). Most likely it was both. The phrase **they said nothing to anyone**, stated only by Mark, is a strong double negative. It does not imply that they forever kept silent but that they initially refused to speak about their bewildering experience (Mt 28:8; Lk 24:9–10).

16:9–20 These verses do not appear in some of the earliest manuscripts of Mark's Gospel.

Character profile:
Mary Magdalene

Mary Magdalene was from Magdala, a small town in Galilee in northern Israel. At some point early in his Galilee ministry, Jesus encountered her and cast seven demons out of her. We don't know exactly how the seven evil spirits afflicted Mary. But from the grim descriptions of demon-possessed individuals elsewhere in the New Testament, it's safe to assume Mary endured a miserable existence.

That is, until Jesus set her free. Immediately this transformed woman became one of Jesus's most committed disciples. She latched on to Christ like a drowning person grabs a life ring.

She became part of his traveling entourage (with a group of other devoted women; see Lk 8:1–3). They gave their time, energy, material resources—in short, their entire lives—to Jesus. Over the course of Christ's three-year ministry, many of his followers or would-be disciples turned away (see Mk 10:17–23; Jn 6:66)—but not Mary Magdalene.

She was there at the foot of the cross on the day of his death (even when most of his disciples had gone into hiding; see Mk 15:40; Jn 19:25). She was present at his burial (see Mk 15:47) and returned to his tomb following the Sabbath to properly anoint his body (see Mk 16:1). Mary also enjoyed the privilege of being one of the first witnesses of the empty tomb (see Mt 28:1–7; Mk 16:1–7; Lk 24:1–8).

In their shock and confusion, the women rushed to tell the apostles, who were skeptical and insisted upon seeing these things for themselves. In the chaos and commotion of that mind-boggling morning, many of Christ's disciples investigated the empty tomb. Eventually, however, they all left.

All except for Mary. She stood outside the tomb crying. Then she stooped to look inside. John tells us what happened next (Jn 20:12–17). Mary noticed two angels there. One asked, "Woman, why are you crying?" She told them her Lord had been taken away, and she didn't know where they'd put his body.

That's when another voice asked the same question: "Woman, why are you crying?" Only this time, it was the risen Lord Jesus himself. Yet, Mary was oblivious and thought he was the gardener! She pleaded with him to tell her where the body had been placed.

Then, Jesus called her by name. And immediately she recognized him. All her sorrow turned to joy. He told her, "Don't cling to me since I have not yet ascended to the Father. But go to my brothers and tell them that I am ascending to my Father and your Father, to my God and your God."

How fitting that in this happiest and most amazing of moments, Mary Magdalene instinctively desired to do what she'd been doing ever since she met Jesus: cling to him.

There are those who scoff at faith in Christ, saying, "That stuff is for the weak. It's a crutch for spiritual and emotional cripples." It's not far-fetched to think that Mary would respond, "Of course! That's why I cling to him—and that's why everyone should."

Jesus said, "It is not those who are well who need a doctor, but those who are sick" (Mt 9:12).

condemned. ¹⁷ And these signs will accompany those who believe: In my name they will drive out demons; they will speak in new tongues;^A ¹⁸ they will pick up snakes;^B if they should drink anything deadly, it will not harm them; they will lay hands on the sick, and they will get well."

^A16:17 = languages   ^B16:18 Other mss add *with their hands*

The Ascension

¹⁹ So the Lord Jesus, after speaking to them, was taken up into heaven and sat down at the right hand of God. ²⁰ And they went out and preached everywhere, while the Lord worked with them and confirmed the word by the accompanying signs.]

▼ Introduction to Luke

Circumstances of Writing

The author of the Third Gospel is not named. Considerable evidence points to Luke as its author. Much of that proof is found in the book of Acts, which identifies itself as a sequel to Luke (Ac 1:1–3). A major line of evidence has to do with the so-called "we" sections of the book (Ac 16:10–17; 20:5–15; 21:1–18; 27:1–37; 28:1–16). Most of Acts is narrated in third-person plural ("they," "them"), but some later sections having to do with the ministry of the apostle Paul unexpectedly shift to first-person plural ("we," "us"). This indicates that the author had joined the apostle Paul for the events recorded in those passages. Since there are no "we" passages in the Gospel of Luke, that fits with the author stating that he used eyewitness testimony to the life of Jesus (1:2), indicating he was not such an eyewitness himself.

Since Luke is not named among the workers who were "of the circumcised" (i.e., a Jew; Col 4:11), he was almost certainly a Gentile. That explains the healthy emphasis on Gentiles in Luke (6:17; 7:1–10). Luke also reflects an interest in medical matters (e.g., 4:38; 14:2).

Traditionally, the Gospel of Luke is believed to have been written after both Matthew and Mark. Those who date Matthew and Mark in the AD 60s or 70s have tended to push the dating of Luke back to the AD 70s or 80s.

Since Luke wrote both the Third Gospel and the book of Acts (Ac 1:1–3), it is relevant to consider the dating of both books together. The events at the end of Acts occurred around AD 62–63, the earliest point at which Acts could have been written. If Acts was written in the early AD 60s from Rome, where Paul was imprisoned for two years (Ac 28:30), the Third Gospel could date from an earlier stage of that period of imprisonment.

Contribution to the Bible

Nearly 60 percent of the material in the Gospel of Luke is unique. The following are notable among the larger distinctive portions: (1) much of the material in Luke 1–2 about the births of John the Baptist and Jesus, (2) the only biblical material on Jesus's childhood and preministry adult life (2:40–52), (3) a genealogy for Jesus (3:23–38) that is significantly different from the one in Matthew 1:1–17, (4) most of the "travelogue" section about Jesus's journey to Jerusalem (Lk 9:51–19:44), (5) a considerably different slant on the destruction of the temple (21:5–38) from the Olivet Discourse in Matthew 24–25 and Mark 13, and (6) quite a bit of fresh material in the post resurrection appearances, including the Emmaus Road, a distinctive statement of the Great Commission, and the only description in the Gospels of Jesus's ascension into heaven (Lk 24:13–53).

Structure

Luke's distinctive "narrative about the events" (1:1) of the life of Jesus is written in "orderly sequence" (1:3), though not strict chronological sequence in many cases. Generally, after the key events leading up to the beginning of Christ's public ministry (1:5–4:13), the flow of the book is from his early ministry in and around Galilee (4:14–9:50), through an extended description of ministry related to his journey to Jerusalem (9:51–19:44), climaxing in the events of Passion Week and post resurrection appearances (19:45–24:53).

Luke Timeline

50–5 BC

Augustus Caesar's reign begins. **MARCH 15, 44 BC**
Roman Senate declares Herod king of the Jews. **39 BC**
Herod assumes possession of the domain to which he had been named earlier. **37 BC**
Herod begins thorough expansion of the temple in Jerusalem in **20 BC**. The inner sanctuary was completed in one and a half years and the rest of the temple was finished in **AD 63**, only seven years before it was destroyed.
Imperial census in territory governed by Herod **6 TO 4 BC**

5 BC–AD 9

Jesus's birth **5 BC**
Eclipse of the moon just prior to Herod's death **MARCH 12/13, 4 BC**
Passover celebrated just after Herod's death **APRIL 11, 4 BC**
Herod's sons, Herod Phillip, Herod Antipas, and Archelaus divide Palestine and rule three territories under the aegis of Rome. **4 BC**
Jesus travels with his parents from Nazareth to Jerusalem for the Passover Festival. **AD 9**

Outline

I. Preparation for the Ministry of Jesus (1:1–4:13)
- A. Formal prologue (1:1–4)
- B. Births of John the Baptist and Jesus (1:5–2:20)
- C. Childhood and early adulthood of Jesus (2:21–52)
- D. Ministry of John the Baptist (3:1–22)
- E. Genealogy of Jesus (3:23–38)
- F. Testing of Jesus by the devil (4:1–13)

II. Jesus's Ministry in Galilee (4:14–9:50)
- A. Early preaching (4:14–44)
- B. Calling of disciples, then apostles (5:1–6:16)
- C. The Sermon on the Plain (6:17–49)
- D. Faith issues; the sending out of the Twelve (7:1–9:17)
- E. Peter's confession and the transfiguration (9:18–50)

III. Jesus's Ministry in Judea and Perea (9:51–19:44)
- A. Setting out toward Jerusalem (9:51–13:21)
- B. Continuing toward Jerusalem (13:22–18:30)
- C. Final approach to Jerusalem (18:31–19:44)

IV. Climax of Jesus's Ministry in Jerusalem (19:45–24:53)
- A. Controversies and teaching (19:45–21:4)
- B. Prediction of the temple's destruction (21:5–38)
- C. Events of Jesus's final Passover (22:1–46)
- D. Betrayal, arrest, and trials (22:47–23:25)
- E. Crucifixion and burial (23:26–56)

Key verses in Luke

1:37 For nothing will be impossible with God.

2:11 Today in the city of David a Savior was born for you, who is the Messiah, the Lord.

2:52 And Jesus increased in wisdom and stature, and in favor with God and with people.

6:31 Just as you want others to do for you, do the same for them.

6:37 Do not judge, and you will not be judged. Do not condemn, and you will not be condemned. Forgive, and you will be forgiven.

11:9 So I say to you, ask, and it will be given to you. Seek, and you will find. Knock, and the door will be opened to you.

19:10 For the Son of Man has come to seek and to save the lost.

24:34 The Lord has truly been raised and has appeared to Simon!

AD 10–30

Caiaphas is high priest. **18–36**
Pontius Pilate is prefect of Judea. **26–36**
John the Baptist's ministry begins. **29**
Jesus's baptism **29**
Jesus's wilderness temptations **29**
Jesus's call of his first disciples **29**
The first Passover of Jesus's ministry, an occasion on which it was said that the temple (inner sanctuary) had stood for 46 years **30**
Jesus goes from Judea to Galilee when he learns of John the Baptist's death. **30**

AD 31–33

In the second Passover of Jesus's ministry, he comes under increasing scrutiny for plucking grain on the Sabbath. **31**
Jesus feeds the 5,000 around the time of his third Passover. **32**
Between Passover of **32** and **33** Jesus withdraws from public ministry and focuses on preparing his disciples. During this time period is Peter's confession at Caesarea Philippi and Jesus's transfiguration.
Jesus's trials, death, and resurrection
NISAN 14–16 or **APRIL 3–5, 33**

The Dedication to Theophilus

1 Many have undertaken to compile a narrative about the events that have been fulfilled[A] among us, [2] just as the original eyewitnesses and servants of the word handed them down to us. [3] So it also seemed good to me, since I have carefully investigated everything from the very first, to write to you in an orderly sequence, most honorable Theophilus, [4] so that you may know the certainty of the things about which you have been instructed.[B]

Gabriel Predicts John's Birth

[5] In the days of King Herod of Judea, there was a priest of Abijah's division named Zechariah. His wife was from the daughters of Aaron, and her name was Elizabeth. [6] Both were righteous in God's sight, living without blame according to all the commands and requirements of the Lord. [7] But they had no children because Elizabeth could not conceive, and both of them were well along in years.

[8] When his division was on duty and he was serving as priest before God, [9] it happened that he was chosen by lot, according to the custom of the priesthood, to enter the sanctuary of the Lord and burn incense. [10] At the hour of incense the whole assembly of the people was praying outside. [11] An angel of the Lord appeared to him, standing to the right of the altar of incense. [12] When Zechariah saw him, he was terrified and overcome with fear. [13] But the angel said to him, "Do not be afraid, Zechariah, because your prayer has been heard. Your wife Elizabeth will bear you a son, and you will name him John. [14] There will be joy and delight for you, and many will rejoice at his birth. [15] For he will be great in the sight of the Lord and will never drink wine or beer. He will be filled with the Holy Spirit while still in his mother's womb. [16] He will turn many of the children of Israel to the Lord their God. [17] And he will go before him in the spirit and power of Elijah, to turn the hearts of fathers to their children, and the disobedient to the understanding of the righteous, to make ready for the Lord a prepared people."

[18] "How can I know this?" Zechariah asked the angel. "For I am an old man, and my wife is well along in years."

[19] The angel answered him, "I am Gabriel, who stands in the presence of God, and I was sent to speak to you and tell you this good news. [20] Now listen. You will become silent

---

[A] 1:1 Or *events that have been accomplished,* or *events most surely believed*   [B] 1:4 Or *informed*

1:1–4 Using elegant Greek, Luke begins his narrative about the events of Jesus's life and ministry with a formal preface. This was a common practice in historical works of Luke's era. His prologue (1) acknowledges previous treatments of the subject, (2) states his methodology, (3) identifies the recipient, and (4) articulates his purpose in writing. **1:1 Many have undertaken to compile a narrative** means that a number of others had previously written about the life and works of Jesus. This may include the Gospels of Mark and Matthew since they preceded Luke's writing. **Events . . . fulfilled among us** speaks of how Jesus fulfilled many OT prophecies (see note at 24:44–45). **1:2 Original eyewitnesses** included Mary, the mother of Jesus, about whom Luke wrote more than any other NT author. Mary may have still been alive when Luke wrote his Gospel. **Servants of the word** refers to the apostles of Jesus but may also include his brothers, James and Jude. Tradition says both brothers wrote NT books. **1:3 It also seemed good to me** does not mean that Luke found the previous narratives (v. 1) to be erroneous or inadequate. Rather, he wrote his Gospel to complement what was already written. **Carefully investigated everything from the very first** means Luke studied the life and ministry of Jesus in meticulous detail ("carefully") and with comprehensive scope ("everything"), including many aspects related to the births of John the Baptist and Jesus ("from the very first") that are not found in the other Gospels. **Orderly sequence** does not mean strict chronological sequence, but in an orderly manner, whether chronological (generally) or topical. On **most honorable Theophilus**, see Introduction. **1:4** Luke's stated purpose in writing his Gospel was to provide historical **certainty** and theological clarity for Theophilus in regard

to what he had been taught (**instructed** about Jesus. **1:5 King Herod** the Great was an Idumean appointed by the Roman emperor who ruled from 37–4 BC. His realm covered not only **Judea** but also Samaria, Galilee, and parts of Perea and Syria. **In the days of** indicates that the events that immediately follow probably occurred in 7–6 BC. The priesthood of Israel was made up of twenty-four divisions, including the house of Abijah (1Ch 24:10). **Daughters of Aaron** reveals that **Elizabeth** and her husband **Zechariah** were from priestly families. It is also the first instance of Luke's regular emphasis on the vital role that women played throughout Jesus's life. **1:6–7** The words **righteous . . . living without blame** refers to consistent obedience to God's **commands and requirements**, but more foundationally to living by faith. This is how Abraham was justified **in God's sight** (Gn 15:6; Gl 3:6–7,9). Like Abraham and Sarah, despite their godliness, Zechariah and Elizabeth **had no children** and were **well along in years** (past the age of child-bearing). It was considered a curse from God for a woman to be unable to bear children (see note at vv. 24–25). **1:8–9** Twice a year the priestly **division** of Abijah (see note at v. 5) was **on duty** at Jerusalem temple for a week. Out of hundreds of priests in that division, Zechariah was **chosen** by the casting of a **lot** (see notes at Pr 16:33; Ac 1:24–26) to **burn incense** on the altar in front of the most holy place (**the sanctuary**), a privileged duty that a priest could perform only once in his life. In fact, many never enjoyed this privilege because the lot never fell to them. **1:10** The **hour of incense** occurred at 9:00 a.m. and 3:00 p.m. daily. The presence of a sizable **assembly of the people** makes it more likely that this incident took place in the afternoon.

1:11–12 On **an angel of the Lord**, see note at v. 19. To be **overcome with fear** upon seeing an angel is common in Luke (v. 29; 2:9) and elsewhere in Scripture (Jdg 6:22–23; Dn 8:16–17). **1:13 Your prayer** may refer to Zechariah and Elizabeth praying to have a child (**your wife . . . will bear you a son**), or it could have been the prayer a priest was to offer at the altar for the redemption of Israel. **John** means "the Lord is gracious." **1:14–15 Joy** is the prevailing mood of the first two chapters of Luke's Gospel (vv. 44,47,58; 2:10). As **great in the sight of the Lord** as John would be, he was still only the forerunner for the coming Messiah. **Never drink wine or beer** indicates that John the Baptist was under a lifelong Nazirite vow (Nm 6:1–21). On **filled with the Holy Spirit . . . in his mother's womb**, see note at v. 41–45. On the meaning of being filled with the Holy Spirit, see Eph 5:18. **1:16–17 Turn . . . to the Lord their God** speaks of conversion, the result of repentance, which John the Baptist preached forcefully (3:3). **Go before him . . . to make ready for the Lord a prepared people** echoes the essence of the prophecy in Is 40:3–5 (see Lk 3:4–6). Malachi 4:5–6 prophesied that an Elijah-like figure would come and **turn the hearts of fathers to their children**. That new "Elijah" would be John the Baptist. **1:18** Like Abraham (Gn 15:8) and Sarah (Gn 18:10–15), Zechariah had a difficult time believing God would fulfill his promise in his **old** age. **1:19 Gabriel** means "(mighty) man of God." He is one of only two angels named in Scripture. The other is Michael (Dn 12:1; Rv 12:7). **1:20** As punishment for doubting the angel's pronouncement, Zechariah was rendered mute (**silent and unable to speak**).

and unable to speak until the day these things take place, because you did not believe my words, which will be fulfilled in their proper time."

²¹ Meanwhile, the people were waiting for Zechariah, amazed that he stayed so long in the sanctuary. ²² When he did come out, he could not speak to them. Then they realized that he had seen a vision in the sanctuary. He was making signs to them and remained speechless. ²³ When the days of his ministry were completed, he went back home.

²⁴ After these days his wife Elizabeth conceived and kept herself in seclusion for five months. She said, ²⁵ "The Lord has done this for me. He has looked with favor in these days to take away my disgrace among the people."

Gabriel Predicts Jesus's Birth

²⁶ In the sixth month, the angel Gabriel was sent by God to a town in Galilee called Nazareth, ²⁷ to a virgin engaged^A to a man named Joseph, of the house of David. The virgin's name was Mary. ²⁸ And the angel came to her and said, "Greetings, favored woman! The Lord is with you."^B ²⁹ But she was deeply troubled by this statement, wondering what kind of greeting this could be. ³⁰ Then the angel told her, "Do not be afraid, Mary, for you have found favor with God. ³¹ Now listen: You will conceive and give birth to a son, and you will name him Jesus. ³² He will be great and will be called the Son of the Most High, and the Lord God will give him the throne of his father David. ³³ He will reign over the house of Jacob forever, and his kingdom will have no end."

^A 1:27 Lit betrothed   ^B 1:28 Other mss add Blessed are you among women.

and possibly deaf as well (v. 62). **The day these things take place** was the time that began at John's birth and culminated at his circumcision (vv. 57–64).

1:21–22 The **people . . . waiting** for Zechariah to come out of the **sanctuary** were surprised because he did not emerge when expected. Since Gabriel had rendered him **speechless** (v. 20), Zechariah was unable to pronounce the traditional Aaronic blessing (Nm 6:24–26) upon the crowd. They realized **he had seen a vision**, likely because they noted his facial expressions and the excited **signs** he made with his hands.

1:23 Since each priest was on duty only for a week at a time, Zechariah would have been able to go **home** soon after his encounter with Gabriel (vv. 10–20). His home was in the Judean hill country, not far from Jerusalem (v. 39).

1:24–25 Elizabeth withdrew and **kept herself in seclusion for five months** after she miraculously **conceived**. Why did she do this? Some speculate that she feared miscarrying during the early months of pregnancy. More likely she recognized that her unusual

pregnancy would draw unwelcome attention if it became widely known. Better to have a restful start to a pregnancy that came so late in life.

1:26–38 Here the announcement of Jesus's coming birth is told from Mary's perspective. Matthew gives it from Joseph's vantage point (Mt 1:18–23).

1:26 In the **sixth month** of Elizabeth's pregnancy, **Gabriel**, the same angel who had appeared to Zechariah previously (v. 19), was dispatched by God to **Nazareth**. This was a small village in **Galilee**, a region north of Judea and Samaria.

1:27 Virgin (Gk parthenos) may echo the prophecy of the virgin birth in Is 7:14 (Mt 1:18–25). According to Jewish law, being **engaged** was just as legally binding as being married (Mt 1:18–19). The **house of David** was a clan in the tribe of Judah, from which prophecies said the Messiah would come (Gn 49:9–10).

1:28–30 Mary was **favored** because **the Lord** set his undeserved grace upon her, not because she had earned good standing. Understandably, she was **deeply troubled**

by Gabriel's visit and greeting, **wondering** how she had come to receive such an honor. Gabriel's admonishment that Mary **not be afraid** was the same thing he said to Zechariah (v. 13).

1:31–33 The miracle that would cause Mary to **conceive and give birth to a son** would be a far greater miracle than the one that caused Elizabeth to conceive in old age (vv. 13,18) because, unlike Elizabeth, Mary was still a virgin (v. 34). The name **Jesus** (Gk Iesous) is equivalent to the Hebrew Yeshoshua (Joshua), meaning "the Lord is salvation." Being **the Son of the Most High** means Jesus was the Son of God himself (v. 35) because God created the life in Mary's womb without the aid of a human father (see note at vv. 34–35). Humanly speaking, though, Jesus's lineage would be traced legitimately through the royal family of **David** (see note at 3:23–38) because Joseph, Jesus's adoptive father, was a descendant of David. This made Jesus heir to David's **throne** according to God's eternal covenant (**forever . . . his kingdom will have no end**, v. 33; see 2Sm 7:13,16).

Character profile:
Mary, the Mother of Jesus

M ary had a front-row seat for an unbelievable life full of amazing stories: the angel Gabriel showing up out of the blue to tell her that she, a virgin, was pregnant (see Lk 1:26–38)—and not just expecting, but expecting the Messiah; the baby's birth in a manger far from home (see Lk 2:1–7); the odd parade of well-wishers saying beautiful and occasionally frightening things (see Mt 2:1–12; Lk 2:8–38); the mad dash to Egypt to escape Herod's wrath (see Mt 2:13–14).

After Herod's death, Mary and her husband, Joseph, eventually returned to the land of promise and settled again in Nazareth (see Mt 2:19–23). They had other children (see Mt 13:55). But her oldest son was different.

When he was twelve, she watched him dumbfound the religious experts at the temple in Jerusalem (see Lk 2:41–50). She was there for his first miracle—providing wine for a wedding reception in Cana of Galilee (see Jn 2:1–11). She heard the stories of his skyrocketing popularity. She heard the reports of his heated verbal confrontations with the Pharisees, the scribes, and the Sadducees. Eventually, the Sanhedrin got involved. Mary was there when the Roman authorities (with the full approval of the Jewish leaders) nailed her naked son to a cross

and lifted him before a mocking crowd. Helpless to do anything, she watched as her firstborn, in his final moments of life, selflessly arranged for one of his trusted disciples to care for her (see Jn 19:25–27).

The Bible isn't clear if Mary was there for all the joyous confusion surrounding Jesus's resurrection, but she is mentioned a few weeks later as being with the group of disciples who were waiting in Jerusalem for the outpouring of God's Spirit (see Ac 1:12–14).

It's worth noting that the last recorded words we have of Mary are found in John 2:5: "Do whatever he tells you." And maybe at the end of it all, that's how she would most want to be remembered—less as Jesus's loving mother and more as his obedient follower.

Some Christian traditions incorrectly revere Mary. Others don't honor her nearly enough. She wasn't divine, but she is most definitely worth studying—and emulating. When called as an unmarried virgin to become the mother of the Messiah (with all the difficult social implications that came with it), she responded in profound submission to her God: "I am the Lord's servant. . . . May it happen to me as you have said" (Lk 1:38).

We marvel at that kind of surrender, but Mary's reply sounds an awful lot like the attitude displayed by her son when he faced his own excruciating calling. He told his Father in heaven, "Not my will, but yours, be done" (Lk 22:42).

³⁴ Mary asked the angel, "How can this be, since I have not had sexual relations with a man?"ᴬ

³⁵ The angel replied to her, "The Holy Spirit will come upon you, and the power of the Most High will overshadow you. Therefore, the holy one to be born will be called the Son of God. ³⁶ And consider your relative Elizabeth — even she has conceived a son in her old age, and this is the sixth month for her who was called childless. ³⁷ For nothing will be impossible with God."

³⁸ "See, I am the Lord's servant," said Mary. "May it happen to me as you have said." Then the angel left her.

Mary's Visit to Elizabeth

³⁹ In those days Mary set out and hurried to a town in the hill country of Judah ⁴⁰ where she entered Zechariah's house and greeted Elizabeth. ⁴¹ When Elizabeth heard Mary's greeting, the baby leaped inside her, and Elizabeth was filled with the Holy Spirit. ⁴² Then she exclaimed with a loud cry, "Blessed are you among women, and your child is blessed!ᴮ ⁴³ How could this happen to me, that the mother of my Lord should come to me? ⁴⁴ For you see, when the sound of your greeting reached my ears, the baby leaped for joy inside me. ⁴⁵ Blessed is she who has believed that the Lord would fulfill what he has spoken to her!"

Mary's Praise

⁴⁶ And Mary said:

My soul magnifies the Lord,
⁴⁷   and my spirit rejoices in God my Savior,
⁴⁸   because he has looked with favor
    on the humble condition of his servant.

ᴬ1:34 Lit *since I do not know a man*   ᴮ1:42 Lit *and the fruit of your abdomen* (or *womb*) *is blessed*

1:34–35 The difference between Mary's response (**how can this be**) and Zechariah's (v. 18) is that Mary asked her question not from unbelief but from puzzlement (v. 38; see note at v. 20). Mary's question about how she could get pregnant without having **sexual relations with a man** is that the **Holy Spirit** would **overshadow** her and cause her to conceive (see note at vv. 31–33). Because the Holy Spirit was the agent of conception, the child (**the holy One**; 2Co 5:21; Heb 4:15) would be **the Son of God**. **1:36–37** There is no way of knowing whether **your relative Elizabeth** means Elizabeth was Mary's aunt or cousin. On **she has conceived . . . the sixth month**, see note at vv. 24–25. If ever Mary was tempted to doubt

God's promise to her, she could recall Gabriel's words that **nothing will be impossible with God**, as had been shown in the lives of Abraham and Sarah (Gn 18:14). **1:38** Mary's response is a classic model of humble commitment (**I am the Lord's servant**) and willing obedience (**may it happen to me as you have said**). **1:39–40** Shortly after Gabriel left, Mary traveled to **Judah** to check on her relative, **Elizabeth**, whom she had just learned (from the angel) was pregnant (see note at vv. 36–37). **1:41–45** The baby (John) being "filled with the Holy Spirit" (v. 15) fulfilled Gabriel's prediction to Zechariah. But **Elizabeth** was **filled with the Holy Spirit** also (v. 41), and

the Spirit's revelations to her were apparently the source of her knowledge about the blessed roles and identities of Mary and her unborn child. When baby John **leaped** inside Elizabeth, she understood that he had experienced great **joy** at Mary's presence. **1:46–55** Mary's hymn of praise is known as the "Magnificat," so named for the Latin term rendered as **magnifies**. It is similar in tone to the song of Hannah (1Sm 2:1–10). **1:46–49** There is a beautiful balance in Mary's hymn of praise. She expressed **humble** recognition of the **great** and **holy** nature of God and his grace (**favor**) on his voluntary servant, but also an awareness that God's unique calling on her life would result in all future generations calling her

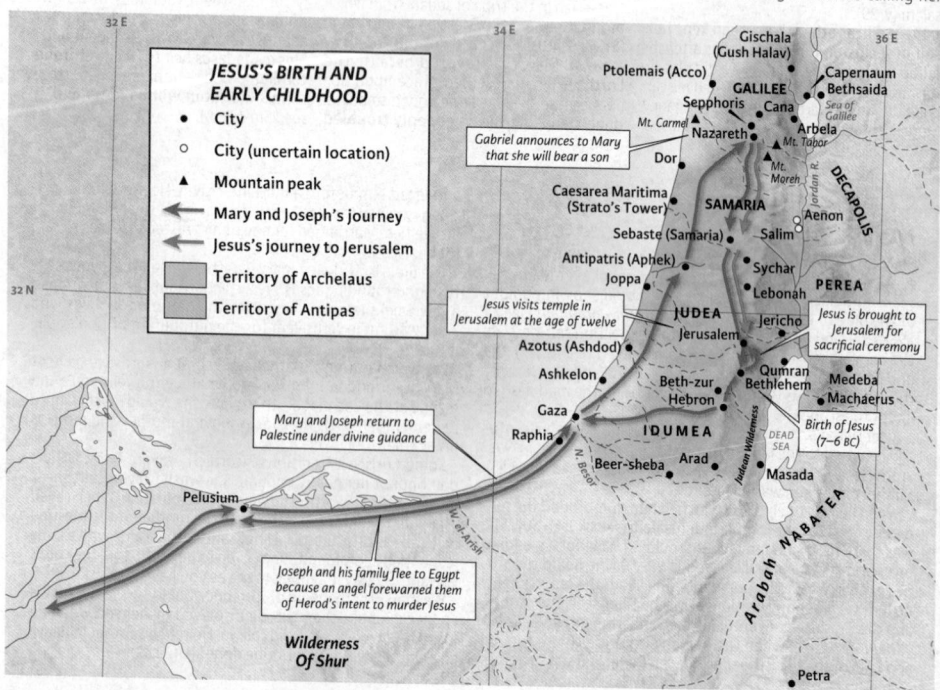

Surely, from now on all generations
will call me blessed,
49 because the Mighty One
has done great things for me,
and his name is holy.
50 His mercy is from generation
to generation
on those who fear him.
51 He has done a mighty deed
with his arm;
he has scattered the proud
because of the thoughts of their hearts;
52 he has toppled the mighty
from their thrones
and exalted the lowly.
53 He has satisfied the hungry
with good things
and sent the rich away empty.
54 He has helped his servant Israel,
remembering his mercy
55 to Abraham and his
descendants^A forever,
just as he spoke to our ancestors.

56 And Mary stayed with her about three months; then she returned to her home.

The Birth and Naming of John
57 Now the time had come for Elizabeth to give birth, and she had a son. 58 Then her neighbors and relatives heard that the Lord had shown her his great mercy, and they rejoiced with her. 59 When they came to circumcise the child on the eighth day, they were going to name him Zechariah, after his father. 60 But his mother responded, "No. He will be called John."

61 Then they said to her, "None of your relatives has that name." 62 So they motioned to his father to find out what he wanted him to be called. 63 He asked for a writing tablet and wrote, "His name is John." And they were all amazed. 64 Immediately his mouth was opened and his tongue set free, and he began to speak, praising God. 65 Fear came on all those who lived around them, and all these things were being talked about throughout the hill country of Judea. 66 All who heard about him took it to heart, saying, "What then will this child become?" For, indeed, the Lord's hand was with him.

Zechariah's Prophecy
67 Then his father Zechariah was filled with the Holy Spirit and prophesied:
68 Blessed is the Lord, the God of Israel,
because he has visited
and provided redemption for his people.
69 He has raised up a horn of salvation
for us
in the house of his servant David,
70 just as he spoke by the mouth
of his holy prophets in ancient times;
71 salvation from our enemies
and from the hand of those who hate us.
72 He has dealt mercifully
with our ancestors
and remembered his holy covenant—
73 the oath that he swore to our father
Abraham,
to grant that we,
74 having been rescued
from the hand of our enemies,

^A1:55 Or *offspring*; lit *seed*

blessed. She viewed herself as both humbled and exalted.
1:50–53 These verses recall the descriptions of God's justice found throughout the Psalms (e.g., Pss 100:5; 103:11). Those who fear him is an OT expression that is equivalent to the NT idea of faith. Fear of God is faith in God. His arm is figurative for God's power. God is a Spirit being (Jn 4:24) and does not have a physical body, but bodily metaphors are effective in communicating some of God's attributes and actions. God is against the proud . . . the mighty, and the rich, who imagine themselves self-sufficient. By contrast, he champions the cause of the lowly and the hungry, for they acknowledge their need for him.
1:54–55 In sending Jesus to be born to Mary, God mercifully helped . . . Israel, in keeping with promises he had made centuries earlier to Abraham and his descendants (see Gn 12:1–3; 22:15–18).
1:56–57 Mary visited Elizabeth shortly after hearing she was "in the sixth month" of her pregnancy (vv. 36,39–40) and Mary may have returned to Nazareth either shortly before or after the birth of Elizabeth's son, John. Given their spiritual bond and the great roles their sons would play in God's plan, it seems likely that Mary stayed for John's birth.
1:58 Since Elizabeth remained secluded for the early months of her pregnancy (see note at vv. 24–25), it is possible that many of her neighbors and relatives first learned of God's great mercy toward her at or near the time of John's birth. The birth of a son was seen as favor from God.
1:59–63 In the OT, a child's name was more often given at birth. Perhaps Zechariah's inability to speak at John's birth caused the delay. Because Luke was writing for a Gentile audience that was unfamiliar with Jewish rites, he explained that Mosaic law (Lv 12:3) required parents to circumcise a male child (i.e., cut off the foreskin of his sex organ) on the eighth day. It was customary to name a boy baby after his father, in this case Zechariah, or his grandfather. Elizabeth had apparently already learned from Zechariah in writing that God wished for them to name the baby John. That neighbors and relatives motioned to Zechariah (rather than spoke) may imply that he was temporarily deaf as well as mute (vv. 20,22). A writing tablet was a small wooden board covered with wax. A wooden stylus was used to etch words into the wax.
1:64 That Zechariah was again able to speak fulfilled Gabriel's prediction (see note at v. 20).
1:65–66 The overall outcome of the preceding episode is that it was clear that the
Lord's hand was with the newborn John in a remarkable way and that everyone living in the region continued to ponder (took . . . to heart) the question, What . . . will this child become?
1:67 On the meaning of filled with the Holy Spirit, see Eph 5:18. It is ironic that Zechariah, being a priest (v. 5) and having prophesied, set the stage for the ministry of his son, John the Baptist. Though John hailed from a priestly family, he was called to serve as a prophet of the Most High (v. 76).
1:68–79 Zechariah's prophecy is traditionally called the "Benedictus," from the first word (blessed) of v. 68 in the Latin Vulgate Bible.
1:68–70 The births of John the Baptist, the forerunner (v. 17; Is 40:1–5; Mal 4:5–6), and Jesus, the Messiah, marked the initiation of the final stages of God's plan of salvation for his people. This salvation would require a payment of redemption on the cross by Jesus. An animal's horn symbolized strength or power (Dt 33:17). Jesus was from the house of . . . David (see v. 27; 3:30).
1:71–75 The ministries of John the Baptist and Jesus fulfilled God's covenant with David (v. 69; 2Sm 7:12–16) and the oath that he swore to . . . Abraham (see Gn 12:1–3). As a result, in the Messiah's future reign, Israel would have full salvation from their enemies and would serve God in holiness and righteousness.

would serve him without fear
75 in holiness and righteousness
in his presence all our days.
76 And you, child, will be called
a prophet of the Most High,
for you will go before the Lord
to prepare his ways,
77 to give his people knowledge
of salvation
through the forgiveness of their sins.
78 Because of our God's merciful
compassion,
the dawn from on high will visit us
79 to shine on those who live in darkness
and the shadow of death,
to guide our feet into the way of peace.

80 The child grew up and became strong in spirit,^A and he was in the wilderness until the day of his public appearance to Israel.

The Birth of Jesus

2 In those days a decree went out from Caesar Augustus that the whole empire^B should be registered. ² This first registration took place while^C Quirinius was governing Syria. ³ So everyone went to be registered, each to his own town.

⁴ Joseph also went up from the town of Nazareth in Galilee, to Judea, to the city of David,

which is called Bethlehem, because he was of the house and family line of David, ⁵ to be registered along with Mary, who was engaged to him^D and was pregnant. ⁶ While they were there, the time came for her to give birth. ⁷ Then she gave birth to her firstborn son, and she wrapped him tightly in cloth and laid him in a manger,^E because there was no guest room available for them.

The Shepherds and the Angels

⁸ In the same region, shepherds were staying out in the fields and keeping watch at night over their flock. ⁹ Then an angel of the Lord stood before them, and the glory of the Lord shone around them, and they were terrified.^F ¹⁰ But the angel said to them, "Don't be afraid, for look, I proclaim to you good news of great joy that will be for all the people:^G ¹¹ Today in the city of David a Savior was born for you, who is the Messiah, the Lord. ¹² This will be the sign for you: You will find a baby wrapped tightly in cloth and lying in a manger."

¹³ Suddenly there was a multitude of the heavenly host^H with the angel, praising God and saying:

14   Glory to God in the highest heaven,
and peace on earth to people
he favors!^I,J

---

^1:80 Or *strong in the Spirit*   ^B2:1 Or *the whole inhabited world*   ^C2:2 Or *This registration was the first while*, or *This registration was before*   ^D2:5 Lit *betrothed*   ^E2:7 Or *feeding trough*, also in vv. 12,16   ^F2:9 Lit *they feared a great fear*   ^G2:10 Or *the whole nation*   ^H2:13 Lit *heavenly army*   ^I2:14 Other mss read *earth good will to people*   ^J2:14 Or *earth to men of good will*

1:76 John was to be the **prophet of the Most High** who would go before Jesus, "the Son of the Most High" (see note at vv. 31–33) to **prepare his ways** (see Is 40:3; Mal 3:1).
1:77 To give **knowledge of salvation** through the forgiveness of sins was the emphasis of John the Baptist's preaching (see note at 3:2–3).
1:78–79 Dawn from on high speaks of the coming Messiah (Mal 4:2). The Lord's visitation began with John's birth. The next part of that **visit** would be Jesus's birth (2:1–20). The phrase **those who live in darkness and the shadow of death** probably echoes Is 9:1–2, which is cited in Mt 4:16. The **way of peace** with God is through faith in Christ (Rm 5:1).
1:80 This verse about John's upbringing is parallel to 2:51–52, which is about Jesus's upbringing. Because Zechariah and Elizabeth were already quite old when John was born (see note at 1:6–7), they probably died while he was fairly young, which may explain why he **grew up . . . in the wilderness** of Judea, between Jerusalem and the Dead Sea. **The day of his public appearance** is recounted in 3:1–3. Since ministry for a Levite (which John was) began at thirty years old (Nm 4:46–47), this is probably when he launched his ministry, as did Jesus (Lk 3:23).
2:1 Augustus (meaning "Exalted," a title approved by the Roman Senate in 27 BC) was the Roman **Caesar** from 31 BC to AD 14. This **decree . . . that the whole empire should be registered** was a census for the purposes of taxation and military service.

2:2 It is thought that **Quirinius** served two terms as Roman governor of **Syria**: from 6 to 4 BC, and then AD 6 to 9. Jesus was born during the period of the **first registration**. There was also a census registration in Quirinius's second term (Ac 5:37).
2:3–4 His own town refers not to where Joseph presently lived (**Nazareth in Galilee**) but to the town of his ancestral roots (**Bethlehem** in **Judea**), which was called **the city of David** because King David grew up there (1Sm 16:1). Joseph was descended from David (Lk 1:27). The trip from Nazareth to Bethlehem would have taken three days and covered roughly ninety miles.
2:5–6 As months before in 1:27, **Mary** at this time was still only **engaged** to Joseph because they had not yet consummated their marriage via intercourse. Nevertheless, she was **pregnant** (see note at 1:31–33) and ready to **give birth**.
2:7 The words **her firstborn son** naturally implies that Mary later had other children (Mt 13:55–56). That baby Jesus was **laid . . . in a manger** indicates that the family was forced to stay in a stable, or perhaps a cave that served as a stable, because there was no other room available in Bethlehem.
2:8 The sheep used for temple sacrifices in Jerusalem were kept in fields outside Bethlehem. The work of **shepherds** was more important **at night** because of the threats from thieves and predators. Though the social position of shepherds was lowly, the role is often viewed positively in the Bible. God is pictured as a shepherd (Gn 49:24; Ps

23:1). King David was the shepherd of God's people (2Sm 5:2). Jesus called himself "the good shepherd" (Jn 10:11).
2:9–10 The **glory of the Lord** was a bright light (in the midst of the darkness of night), indicating God's glorious presence. It is only natural to be **terrified** at the sight of an angel (see note at 1:11–12), not to mention a sudden, overwhelming light from the sky. The angel spoke to calm the shepherds and refocus their attention on the proclamation of the gospel (**good news**). **All the people** could refer to Israel, but given Luke's emphasis on the gospel spreading to the Gentiles, it probably means "all nations."
2:11–12 Savior means "deliverer, redeemer." **Messiah** (Gk *christos*, equivalent to the Hb *meshiach*) means "anointed one," especially focusing on being anointed as king. **Lord** (Gk *kurios*) was used of secular rulers, but it is also the standard translation of the primary name of God in Hebrew, *Yahweh*. The shepherds would have been shocked to hear that a divine messianic ruler had been born, but to be told he was **lying in a manger** and born to a man and woman of humble means would have seemed preposterous.
2:13–14 The praise of **the heavenly host** is well-known today as the "Gloria in Excelsis Deo," from the first words of v. 14 in the Latin Vulgate (**Glory to God in the highest**). To give "glory to God" does not give him something he otherwise lacks. Rather, it is a confession of the wondrous glory he forever possesses. The **peace** to be found **on earth** was not the *Pax Romana* (the "universal

15 When the angels had left them and returned to heaven, the shepherds said to one another, "Let's go straight to Bethlehem and see what has happened, which the Lord has made known to us." **16** They hurried off and found both Mary and Joseph, and the baby who was lying in the manger. **17** After seeing them, they reported the message they were told about this child, **18** and all who heard it were amazed at what the shepherds said to them. **19** But Mary was treasuring up all these things in her heart and meditating on them. **20** The shepherds returned, glorifying and praising God for all the things they had seen and heard, which were just as they had been told.

The Circumcision and Presentation of Jesus

21 When the eight days were completed for his circumcision, he was named Jesus — the name given by the angel before he was conceived. **22** And when the days of their purification according to the law of Moses were finished, they brought him up to Jerusalem to present him to the Lord **23** (just as it is written in the law of the Lord, **Every firstborn male will be dedicated**[A] **to the Lord**[B]) **24** and to offer a sacrifice (according to what is stated in the law of the Lord, **a pair of turtledoves or two young pigeons**[C]).

Simeon's Prophetic Praise

25 There was a man in Jerusalem whose name was Simeon. This man was righteous and devout, looking forward to Israel's consolation, and the Holy Spirit was on him. **26** It had been revealed to him by the Holy Spirit that he would not see death before he saw the Lord's Messiah. **27** Guided by the Spirit, he entered the temple. When the parents brought in the child Jesus to perform for him what was customary under the law, **28** Simeon took him up in his arms, praised God, and said,

29   Now, Master,
     you can dismiss your servant in peace,
     as you promised.
30   For my eyes have seen your salvation.
31   You have prepared it
     in the presence of all peoples —
32   a light for revelation to the Gentiles[D]
     and glory to your people Israel.

33 His father and mother[E] were amazed at what was being said about him. **34** Then Simeon blessed them and told his mother Mary, "Indeed, this child is destined to cause the fall and rise of many in Israel and to be a sign that will be opposed[F] — **35** and a sword will pierce your own soul — that the thoughts[G] of many hearts may be revealed."

Anna's Testimony

36 There was also a prophetess, Anna, a daughter of Phanuel, of the tribe of Asher. She was well along in years, having lived with her husband seven years after her marriage,[H] **37** and was a widow for eighty-four years.[I] She did not leave the temple, serving God night and day with fasting and prayers. **38** At

---

[A]**2:23** Lit *be called holy*   [B]**2:23** Ex 13:2,12   [C]**2:24** Lv 5:11; 12:8   [D]**2:32** Or *the nations*   [E]**2:33** Other mss read *But Joseph and his mother*   [F]**2:34** Or *spoken against*   [G]**2:35** Or *schemes*   [H]**2:36** Lit *years from her virginity*   [I]**2:37** Or *she was a widow until the age of eighty-four*

---

peace" of the Roman Empire) but peace with God through faith in Jesus Christ (Rm 5:1; see note at Lk 1:78–79). The people whom God favors are those who have found God's undeserved favor, or grace, through Christ.
2:15 What has happened refers to the birth of the Savior, who is Christ and Lord (see note at vv. 11–12).
2:16 On **lying in the manger**, see note at v. 7.
2:17 On **the message they were told about this child**, see note at vv. 9–10.
2:18 All who heard it included anyone in or around Bethlehem with whom the shepherds had the opportunity to share their story (vv. 8–14).
2:19 It is possible that Luke gained much of his knowledge about what happened in chaps. 1 and 2 from talking to **Mary**, who recalled the things she had "treasured" in her heart.
2:20 The **shepherds returned** to the fields outside Bethlehem to tend their flocks. They were **glorifying and praising God** because everything they found in Bethlehem was just as the angel said it would be (vv. 10–12).
2:21 On **eight days** and **circumcision**, see note at 1:59–63. On the name **Jesus**, see note at 1:31–33.
2:22–24 The **days of their purification** lasted another thirty-three days after the

child's circumcision (Lv 12:2–8). **To present him to the Lord** was what was done with **every firstborn male** in Israel (Ex 13:2,12). On the sacrifice of **turtledoves** or **pigeons**, see Lv 12:8 and note there.
2:25–26 Like Zechariah and Elizabeth (see note at 1:6–7), **Simeon** was a **righteous** person. **Israel's consolation** spoke of the comfort and hope the people had in regard to God's plan for his people, but, more specifically, it referred to Messiah's role in that plan. In the OT, the **Holy Spirit** came on a few selected people (Nm 24:2; 1Sm 10:10; 16:13). After the day of Pentecost, the Spirit has indwelt all believers (Jn 14:16–17; 1Co 3:16). The Holy Spirit filled Zechariah so he could prophesy about John (Lk 1:67–79). In this case, the Spirit assured Simeon that he would live long enough to see the Messiah, so that he could prophesy about Jesus (2:29–32).
2:27 The Holy Spirit **guided** Simeon to the right place (**the temple**) at the right time (when **the child Jesus** was brought to **perform** . . . **what was customary under the law**). See notes at vv. 21,22–24.
2:28–32 Simeon's words here are traditionally called the "Nunc Dimittis," from wording in the Latin Vulgate translation. Simeon's Divine **Master** had kept his promise that he would live to see Christ (i.e., **your salvation**), so he

could now die (**dismiss your servant**). God's salvation in Christ (v. 30) is for **all peoples** (**the Gentiles** and Israel). The worldwide scope of the gospel is Luke's ongoing theme in both of his writings (his Gospel and the book of Acts).
2:33–35 Legally, Joseph was Jesus's **father** (see note at 3:23–38) even though it was the Holy Spirit who caused Mary to conceive (see note at 1:34–35). Jesus was a spiritual divider of society (**a sign** . . . **opposed**). In considering the gospel about Christ, **many in Israel** "fell" eternally due to unbelief and others rose by faith to eternal life. Mary would suffer great pain in watching Jesus rejected and executed. How people respond to Jesus is the difference between pardon and condemnation, eternity in heaven or hell.
2:36–38 The immediate shift of focus from Simeon, a male who prophesied, to **Anna**, the **prophetess**, fits with Luke's emphasis on women. The other prophetesses mentioned in the NT are Philip's daughters (Ac 21:8–9). If Anna had been married for **seven years** and **a widow for eighty-four years**, she was well over a hundred years old. The Greek text can also be read to mean that she was a widow until age eighty-four, but that reading does not fit the circumstances well. Besides being a prophetess, Anna's other ministry

that very moment,[A] she came up and began to thank God and to speak about him to all who were looking forward to the redemption of Jerusalem.[B]

The Family's Return to Nazareth

39 When they had completed everything according to the law of the Lord, they returned to Galilee, to their own town of Nazareth. **40** The boy grew up and became strong, filled with wisdom, and God's grace was on him.

In His Father's House

41 Every year his parents traveled to Jerusalem for the Passover Festival. **42** When he was twelve years old, they went up according to the custom of the festival. **43** After those days were over, as they were returning, the boy Jesus stayed behind in Jerusalem, but his parents[C] did not know it. **44** Assuming he was in the traveling party, they went a day's journey. Then they began looking for him among their relatives and friends. **45** When they did not find him, they returned to Jerusalem to search for him. **46** After three days, they found him in the temple sitting among the teachers, listening to them and asking them questions. **47** And all those who heard him were astounded at his understanding and his answers. **48** When his parents saw him, they were astonished, and his mother said to him, "Son, why have you treated us like

this? Your father and I have been anxiously searching for you."

49 "Why were you searching for me?" he asked them. "Didn't you know that it was necessary for me to be in my Father's house?"[D] **50** But they did not understand what he said to them.

In Favor with God and with People

51 Then he went down with them and came to Nazareth and was obedient to them. His mother kept all these things in her heart. **52** And Jesus increased in wisdom and stature, and in favor with God and with people.

The Messiah's Herald

3 In the fifteenth year of the reign of Tiberius Caesar, while Pontius Pilate was governor of Judea, Herod was tetrarch[E] of Galilee, his brother Philip tetrarch of the region of Iturea and Trachonitis, and Lysanias tetrarch of Abilene, **2** during the high priesthood of Annas and Caiaphas, God's word came to John the son of Zechariah in the wilderness. **3** He went into all the vicinity of the Jordan, proclaiming a baptism of repentance for the forgiveness of sins, **4** as it is written in the book of the words of the prophet Isaiah:

A voice of one crying out
  in the wilderness:
Prepare the way for the Lord;
  make his paths straight!

[A]2:38 Lit *very hour*   [B]2:38 Other mss read *in Jerusalem*   [C]2:43 Other mss read *but Joseph and his mother*   [D]2:49 Or *be involved in my Father's interests* (or *things*), or *be among my Father's people*   [E]3:1 Or *ruler*

included devotion to prayer. Since Jerusalem was the Jewish capital, **the redemption of Jerusalem** means the redemption of all the people of Israel.
2:39 Luke did not include several of the well-known incidents that appear in the Gospel of Matthew, including the visit of the magi and the trip to Egypt to avoid an attempt by Herod the Great to kill the infant Messiah (Mt 2:1–23).
2:40 This description of Jesus as a young boy is similar to that of John the Baptist in 1:80. The additional elements emphasized that Jesus was **filled with wisdom, and God's grace was on him** (see the similar description of Stephen in Ac 6:8,10).
2:41–42 This is the only incident Scripture reports about Jesus's life between the time he was a small child and his baptism by John (3:21–22). Adult Jewish males and their families were expected to make a pilgrimage to **Jerusalem** for the annual festivals of **Passover**, Pentecost, and Shelters. The *Bar Mitzvah* (Hb, "son of the commandment") ceremony at age thirteen marked the time when a Jewish male was recognized as a man. Since Jesus was now **twelve years old**, this was his last Passover before adulthood.
2:43–45 Joseph and Mary **went a day's journey** before worrying about Jesus because they assumed he was with the traveling party. It was completely out of character (see v. 51) for him not to obey them in every respect.

2:46–47 Three days included one day traveling from Jerusalem, one coming back, and the third searching for Jesus in the city. The **teachers** were rabbis who were scholars of the Mosaic law. It was highly unusual for a boy to be welcomed by a group of rabbis, much less amaze them with brilliant scriptural **understanding**.
2:48–50 Joseph and Mary **did not understand** that Jesus was referring to his heavenly Father (**my Father's house**; i.e., the temple), whom he also had to obey even when such obedience entailed giving his parents' concerns less priority.
2:51 The phrase **kept all these things in her heart**, like v. 19, implies that Mary herself was Luke's source for much of the unique material in chaps. 1 and 2.
2:52 During the years in which Jesus lived in obedience to Joseph and Mary, he continually increased in **wisdom** (intellect and practical holiness), **stature** (growing to adult size), **favor with God** (spiritual closeness to the Father), and favor with **people** (social respect). Jesus's wisdom was already noteworthy as a young boy (see note at v. 40), and the rabbis marveled at his understanding at age twelve. His advancement would have been astounding by the time he began his ministry.
3:1 The **fifteenth year of** . . . **Tiberius Caesar** could be as early as AD 26 or as late as AD 29 because Tiberius had been delegated some of the authority of his stepfather, Augustus (see note at 2:1), several years before

he died. **Pontius Pilate was governor of Judea**, Samaria, and Idumea (south of Judea, west of the Dead Sea), AD 26–36. He was responsible for regional administration and tax collection. At the death of Herod the Great (4 BC), his son, **Herod** Antipas, became **tetrarch** (a secondary prince) of **Galilee** and Perea (east of the Jordan River), while another son, Herod **Philip**, was **tetrarch** . . . **of Iturea and Trachonitis** (east and northeast of the Sea of Galilee), AD 4–34. Nothing else is known about **Lysanias tetrarch of Abilene** (the area near Damascus).
3:2–3 Technically, the **high priesthood of** Annas ended by AD 18. However, he continued to use the title and exercise considerable influence while his son-in-law **Caiaphas** was high priest during most of the period until AD 37. **John** the Baptist lived in **the wilderness** of Judea for a number of years before this (see note at 1:80), then moved a few miles northeast to **the vicinity of the Jordan** River, probably not far north of the Dead Sea. John preached **repentance** (a change of mind and heart about one's personal sins) **for the forgiveness of sins**, with water **baptism** being the outer sign of inner cleansing.
3:4–6 The quotation from Is 40:3–5 shows that John was the forerunner of the Messiah (**prepare the way for the Lord**; see Mal 3:1; 4:5). The apocalyptic language figuratively depicts the earth becoming level (**every mountain** . . . **made low**) and all **paths straight** before the coming Christ.

⁵ Every valley will be filled,
and every mountain and hill will be
made low;ᴬ
the crooked will become straight,
the rough ways smooth,
⁶ and everyone will see the salvation
of God.ᴮ

⁷ He then said to the crowds who came out to be baptized by him, "Brood of vipers! Who warned you to flee from the coming wrath? ⁸ Therefore produce fruit consistent with repentance. And don't start saying to yourselves, 'We have Abraham as our father,' for I tell you that God is able to raise up children for Abraham from these stones. ⁹ The ax is already at the root of the trees. Therefore, every tree that doesn't produce good fruit will be cut down and thrown into the fire."

¹⁰ "What then should we do?" the crowds were asking him.

¹¹ He replied to them, "The one who has two shirts must share with someone who has none, and the one who has food must do the same."

¹² Tax collectors also came to be baptized, and they asked him, "Teacher, what should we do?"

¹³ He told them, "Don't collect any more than what you have been authorized."

¹⁴ Some soldiers also questioned him, "What should we do?"

He said to them, "Don't take money from anyone by force or false accusation, and be satisfied with your wages."

¹⁵ Now the people were waiting expectantly, and all of them were questioning in their hearts whether John might be the Messiah. ¹⁶ John answered them all, "I baptize you with water, but one who is more powerful than I am is coming. I am not worthy to untie the strap of his sandals. He will baptize you withᶜ the Holy Spirit and fire. ¹⁷ His winnowing shovel is in his hand to clear his threshing floor and gather the wheat into his barn, but the chaff he will burn with fire that never goes out." ¹⁸ Then, along with many other exhortations, he proclaimed good news to the people. ¹⁹ But when John rebuked Herod the tetrarch because of Herodias, his brother's wife, and all the evil things he had done, ²⁰ Herod added this to everything else — he locked up John in prison.

The Baptism of Jesus

²¹ When all the people were baptized, Jesus also was baptized. As he was praying, heaven opened, ²² and the Holy Spirit descended on him in a physical appearance like a dove. And a voice came from heaven: "You are my beloved Son; with you I am well-pleased."

The Genealogy of Jesus Christ

²³ As he began his ministry, Jesus was about thirty years old and was thought to be the son of Joseph, son of Heli,
²⁴   son of Matthat, son of Levi,
son of Melchi, son of Jannai,

ᴬ 3:5 Lit be humbled   ᴮ 3:4–6 Is 40:3–5   ᶜ 3:16 Or in

Everyone (lit "all flesh") indicates that both Gentiles and Jews would see God's salvation. **3:7** Some among **the crowds** who flocked to hear John preach (see note at vv. 2–3) and **be baptized** were not sincere. John called them poisonous snakes and warned them to change their attitudes and **flee . . . the coming wrath** (judgment based on God's righteous anger). Jesus rescues believers from "the coming wrath" (1Th 1:10). **3:8–9** The **fruit** (behavioral impact) of **repentance** (see note at vv. 10–14), or the lack of it, proves whether or not a person has truly repented. At the time of judgment (**the ax is already at the root of the trees**), the claim of Jewish lineage (**Abraham as our father**) will mean nothing unless a person's faith is genuine, like Abraham's (see Gn 15:6; Gl 3:6–7). **3:10–14** The question **the crowds** asked John (**What then should we do?**) is the same as the one addressed to Peter on the day of Pentecost (Ac 2:37). To the general population, John answered: be compassionate (**share with someone who has none**); to the **tax collectors** (who were allowed to raise taxes to cover "expenses"): **don't collect any more** than is owed; to the **soldiers**: don't abuse military power but instead **be satisfied with your wages**. **3:15–17** John knew that the throngs of **people** wondered if he was the long-awaited **Messiah**. He answered that there was no comparison between him baptizing with **water** and Messiah baptizing with the

Holy Spirit (see Ac 1:5; 2:4; 1Co 12:13) and **fire** of judgment. On **winnowing**, see Ru 3:1–3. **Chaff** (symbolizing unbelievers) is the worthless husk that covers **wheat** (standing for believers); it is separated at harvest and burned. A **fire that never goes out** refers, ultimately, to the eternal lake of fire (Rv 20:10,14–15). **3:18** As well as preaching related to repentance (v. 3), John also **proclaimed good news** consistent with the message Messiah was prophesied to deliver (see note at 4:18). **3:19** On **Herod** Antipas, **the tetrarch**, see note at v. 1. Antipas divorced his wife, the daughter of King Aretas IV of Arabia, so he could marry the wife of his brother Philip (Mt 14:3; see note at Lk 3:1). Such a marriage was forbidden by Mosaic law (Lv 18:16; 20:21). **3:20** The events here are not given in chronological sequence, since **John** could not have baptized Jesus (see note at vv. 21–22) while he was **in prison**. Luke wrapped up his discussion of John's ministry before moving on to the beginning of Jesus's ministry. John was arrested at some point after Jesus began his public ministry (Jn 3:22–24). Josephus, the Jewish historian, stated John was held in the Machaerus prison, east of the Dead Sea. **3:21–22** Jesus was not **baptized** for the forgiveness of sins, as were all the other people whom John baptized. Rather, Jesus was baptized to identify himself and his ministry with the ministry and message of his forerunner (see notes at vv. 4–6,15–17). Prayer, especially Jesus's **praying**, is a strong

emphasis of Luke's Gospel. This is the first of three times in the Gospels when a voice from heaven spoke about Jesus. The other two were at the transfiguration (see note at 9:34–35) and in the temple during Passion Week (Jn 12:28). This is a relatively rare scriptural passage in which all three persons of the Godhead are mentioned: (1) the Father who said, **you are my beloved Son**, (2) Jesus the Divine Son, who was being baptized, and (3) **the Holy Spirit** who was in **physical appearance like a dove**. The words "you are my beloved Son" echo Ps 2:7, while **with you I am well-pleased** looks back to a key prophecy of the messianic servant in Is 42:1. **3:23–38** The family tree of Jesus in the Gospel of Luke is considerably different from the one in Mt 1:1–17. Luke's genealogy traces Jesus's lineage all the way back to Adam, emphasizing Jesus's relation to all humankind, while Matthew's version starts with Abraham and moves forward to Jesus, emphasizing Jesus's relation to Israel (i.e., that he was the Son of Abraham, fulfiller of the Abrahamic promises, and the messianic Son of David). In Luke, the family tree moves through Nathan, a younger son of David (Lk 3:30), while in Matthew it goes through Solomon (Mt 1:6–7), inheritor of Israel's throne after David. Since Lk 1–2 narrates events from Mary's point of view, 3:23–38 follows Jesus's *physical* line through Mary since v. 23 says Jesus was only "thought to be the son of Joseph." By contrast, Mt 1:1–17, in the midst of a section from Joseph's point

son of Joseph, ²⁵ son of Mattathias,
son of Amos, son of Nahum,
son of Esli, son of Naggai,
²⁶ son of Maath, son of Mattathias,
son of Semein, son of Josech,
son of Joda, ²⁷ son of Joanan,
son of Rhesa, son of Zerubbabel,
son of Shealtiel, son of Neri,
²⁸ son of Melchi, son of Addi,
son of Cosam, son of Elmadam,
son of Er, ²⁹ son of Joshua,
son of Eliezer, son of Jorim,
son of Matthat, son of Levi,
³⁰ son of Simeon, son of Judah,
son of Joseph, son of Jonam,
son of Eliakim, ³¹ son of Melea,
son of Menna, son of Mattatha,
son of Nathan, son of David,
³² son of Jesse, son of Obed,
son of Boaz, son of Salmon,ᴬ
son of Nahshon,
³³ son of Amminadab,
son of Ram,ᴮ son of Hezron,
son of Perez, son of Judah,
³⁴ son of Jacob, son of Isaac,
son of Abraham, son of Terah,
son of Nahor, ³⁵ son of Serug,
son of Reu, son of Peleg,
son of Eber, son of Shelah,
³⁶ son of Cainan,ᶜ son of Arphaxad,
son of Shem, son of Noah,
son of Lamech, ³⁷ son of Methuselah,
son of Enoch, son of Jared,
son of Mahalalel, son of Cainan,
³⁸ son of Enos, son of Seth,
son of Adam, son of God.

The Temptation of Jesus

4 Then Jesus left the Jordan, full of the Holy Spirit, and was led by the Spirit in the wilderness ² for forty days to be tempted by the devil. He ate nothing during those days, and when they were over, he was hungry. ³ The devil said to him, "If you are the Son of God, tell this stone to become bread."

⁴ But Jesus answered him, "It is written: Man must not live on bread alone."ᴰ,ᴱ

⁵ So he took him upᶠ and showed him all the kingdoms of the world in a moment of time. ⁶ The devil said to him, "I will give you their splendor and all this authority, because it has been given over to me, and I can give it to anyone I want. ⁷ If you, then, will worship me,ᴳ all will be yours."

⁸ And Jesus answered him,ᴴ "It is written: Worship the Lord your God, and serve him only."ᴵ

⁹ So he took him to Jerusalem, had him stand on the pinnacle of the temple, and said to him, "If you are the Son of God, throw yourself down from here. ¹⁰ For it is written:

He will give his angels orders
concerning you,
to protect you,'ᴶ ¹¹ and
they will support you
with their hands,
so that you will not strike
your foot against a stone."ᴷ

¹² And Jesus answered him, "It is said: Do not test the Lord your God."ᴸ

¹³ After the devil had finished every temptation, he departed from him for a time.

ᴬ3:32 Other mss read *Sala*   ᴮ3:33 Other mss read *Amminadab, son of Aram, son of Joram*; other mss read *Amminadab, son of Admin, son of Arni*   ᶜ3:36 Some mss omit *son of Cainan*   ᴰ4:4 Other mss add *but on every word of God*   ᴱ4:4 Dt 8:3   ᶠ4:5 Other mss read *So the devil took him up on a high mountain*   ᴳ4:7 Lit *will fall down before me*   ᴴ4:8 Other mss add "Get behind me, Satan!   ᴵ4:8 Dt 6:13   ᴶ4:10 Ps 91:11   ᴷ4:11 Ps 91:12   ᴸ4:12 Dt 6:16

of view (Mt 1–2), tracks Jesus's *legal* lineage. This demonstrates his right to the throne of David through his adoptive father, Joseph. **3:23** Jesus **began his ministry at about thirty years old**—the age when a Levite began priestly service (Nm 4:46–47; see note at Lk 1:80). **Thought to be the son of Joseph** affirms the prophecy of the virgin birth of Jesus (see notes at 1:31–33,34–35). Jesus was not Joseph's *physical* son, as everyone around them mistakenly assumed (see note at 4:22). **3:38** Adam is called **son of God** in this genealogy because he was directly created by God (see Gn 2:7). **4:1–2** When Jesus returned from being baptized by John (see note at 3:21–22), he was full of the **Holy Spirit** and was led by the Spirit to his encounter with **the devil in the wilderness**. The role of the Holy Spirit here is significant for at least three reasons: (1) the Spirit's role in driving Jesus to the wilderness shows Jesus's face-off with the devil was ordained by God; (2) the Spirit's activity is a repeated emphasis in Luke's Gospel; (3) the Spirit's involvement in Jesus's life highlights Jesus's genuine humanity. The filling (Eph 5:18) and leading of the Spirit (Gl 5:18) are key aspects of empowerment for the Christian

life. The wilderness is where Israel failed its test of faith before God (Nm 14). Jesus would pass the wilderness test that Israel could not. Also, Jesus was being tested as "the last Adam" (1Co 15:45), the one who would succeed where the first Adam failed. **4:3–4** Satan tested Jesus at the point of his physical weakness—hunger ("tell this stone to become bread," v. 3). The phrase **if you are the Son of God** expresses no doubt that Jesus is God and is best understood as, "*Since* you are the Son of God." The devil tried to bait Jesus into satisfying his extreme hunger by exercising his divine powers. Jesus's duty, however, was to suffer and patiently endure hardship as a perfectly obedient human who waited for God's deliverance and empowerment (v. 1). Jesus answered by citing the written Word of God (Dt 8:3). The context of this citation deals with Israel's needs being met in the wilderness for forty years, physically through the manna and spiritually by the presence and Word of God. **4:5–12** The order of the second and third tests is reversed in chap. 4 from Mt 4. The obvious reason would be that the wider structure of the Gospel of Luke depicted Jesus moving toward Jerusalem, with the

final test in Luke taking place on the pinnacle of the temple in Jerusalem. **4:5–8** As Messiah, Jesus will rule over **all the kingdoms of the world** at the end of the age (see Rv 11:15). The devil tried to entice Jesus with a shortcut to that kind of worldwide authority. Even though Satan is called "the ruler of this world" (Jn 12:31), his claim that the world was **given over** to him and that he can **give it to anyone** he wants is untrue. The devil is a usurper of God's realm. It is no surprise that he did not tell the truth here, for he is "a liar and the father of lies" (Jn 8:44). Jesus quoted Dt 6:13 to make clear that only God is worthy of **worship**, a point that echoes the first of the Ten Commandments (Ex 20:3). **4:9–12** After two failed tests (vv. 3–8), the devil attempted to catch Jesus off balance by quoting Scripture. In challenging Jesus to **throw** himself from **the pinnacle of the temple** (from which the fall may have been over one hundred feet), the devil referred to Ps 9:11–12, claiming that **angels** would rush to the rescue if Jesus jumped. Jesus did not deny the truth of the Scripture the devil quoted, just the application he gave it. In clear contrast, he cited Dt 6:16, which recalls

Ministry in Galilee

14 Then Jesus returned to Galilee in the power of the Spirit, and news about him spread throughout the entire vicinity. **15** He was teaching in their synagogues, being praised^A^ by everyone.

Rejection at Nazareth

16 He came to Nazareth, where he had been brought up. As usual, he entered the synagogue on the Sabbath day and stood up to read. **17** The scroll of the prophet Isaiah was given to him, and unrolling the scroll, he found the place where it was written:

18 The Spirit of the Lord is on me,
   because he has anointed me
   to preach good news to the poor.
 He has sent me^B^
   to proclaim release^C^ to the captives
   and recovery of sight to the blind,
   to set free the oppressed,
19 to proclaim the year
   of the Lord's favor.^D^

20 He then rolled up the scroll, gave it back to the attendant, and sat down. And the eyes of everyone in the synagogue were fixed on him. **21** He began by saying to them, "Today as you listen, this Scripture has been fulfilled."

22 They were all speaking well of him^E^ and were amazed by the gracious words that came from his mouth; yet they said, "Isn't this Joseph's son?"

23 Then he said to them, "No doubt you will quote this proverb^F^ to me: 'Doctor, heal yourself. What we've heard that took place in Capernaum, do here in your hometown also.'"

24 He also said, "Truly I tell you, no prophet is accepted in his hometown. **25** But I say to you, there were certainly many widows in Israel in Elijah's days, when the sky was shut up for three years and six months while a great famine came over all the land. **26** Yet Elijah was not sent to any of them except a widow at Zarephath in Sidon. **27** And in the prophet Elisha's time, there were many in Israel who had leprosy,^G^ and yet not one of them was cleansed except Naaman the Syrian."

28 When they heard this, everyone in the synagogue was enraged. **29** They got up, drove him out of town, and brought him to the edge of the hill that their town was built on, intending to hurl him over the cliff. **30** But he passed right through the crowd and went on his way.

Driving Out an Unclean Spirit

31 Then he went down to Capernaum, a town in Galilee, and was teaching them on the Sabbath. **32** They were astonished at his teaching because his message had authority. **33** In the synagogue there was a man with an unclean

---

^A^**4:15** Or *glorified*   ^B^**4:18** Other mss add *to heal the brokenhearted,*   ^C^**4:18** Or *freedom,* or *forgiveness*   ^D^**4:18–19** Is 61:1–2   ^E^**4:22** Or *They were testifying against him*   ^F^**4:23** Or *parable*   ^G^**4:27** Gk *lepros*; a term for various skin diseases; see Lv 13–14

---

the tragedy of Israel's complaining and testing God at Meribah and Massah (Ex 17:1–7). **4:13** Only three tests are recorded in Mt 4 and Lk 4, but the wording **every temptation** may imply that there were more. The devil was thwarted this time, but he **departed** from Jesus only to wait for the right **time** (Gk *kairos*, "time"—as an occasion or opportunity) to try again. **4:14–15** The same **power** of the Holy **Spirit** (see note at vv. 1–2) by which Jesus countered every test thrown at him by the devil was present in his **teaching** in the **synagogues**, bringing initial acceptance by virtually **everyone**. **4:16–17** Jesus lived (was **brought up**) in **Nazareth** in Galilee from the time he was a small boy (2:39,51) until he began his public ministry, when he was "about thirty years old" (see note at 3:23). When Jesus lived at his family home in Nazareth, he always worshiped in this **synagogue** on the **Sabbath**. From what is known about synagogue services of that era, the reading from the Mosaic law (Hb *torah*) was usually prescribed, while the person chosen to read from the books of the Prophets (Hb *nebi'im*) had the latitude to choose any passage he wished. When Jesus was given the **Isaiah** scroll, he unrolled it and began reading from Is 61:1. **4:18** Jesus's ministry throughout Galilee demonstrated that **the Spirit of the Lord** was on him (v. 14). As Messiah, he was **anointed** as the rightful king of Israel. But here the anointing was as a prophet (**to preach good news**). Even though the message Jesus preached was first to those

who were captivated by sin, the mention of **the poor . . . the captives . . . the blind,** and **the oppressed** is in keeping with Luke's emphasis on the poor and downtrodden. **4:19–21** Jesus stopped reading from Is 61 in the middle of v. 2 and **sat down** (the normal posture for reading Scripture was standing; teaching was done while sitting). He ended the reading precisely at the phrase **to proclaim the year of the Lord's favor** because this is exactly what his preaching proclaimed: the season of God's grace had come in Messiah's ministry. The very next phrase in Is 61:2, which Jesus did not read, is "and the day of our God's vengeance." This refers to the second coming of Christ and his judgment of the world (Rv 19:11–21). Thus Jesus read in the synagogue the part of Is 61:1–2 that was being **fulfilled** at that time but held off on reading the portion that would not be fulfilled until the time of judgment. **4:22** The immediate response to Jesus's message in the synagogue was mostly positive, as it had been elsewhere in Galilee (see note at vv. 14–15). But knowing Is 61 was a messianic prophecy, it greatly troubled the people that the young preacher whom they thought of merely as **Joseph's son** (see note at 3:23–38) was claiming to be the long-awaited Messiah. **4:23–24** The people in Jesus's **hometown** of Nazareth, motivated by curiosity rather than genuine spiritual interest, expected to see him **heal,** as they had heard about him doing in nearby **Capernaum**. Instead of satisfying them, Jesus illustrated a principle that often

proved true in OT times: A **prophet** (see 4:18; Is 61:1) is not **accepted in his hometown**. **4:25–27** Jesus's first example of a prophet being rejected by his own people was **Elijah**, who was so unpopular in Israel during the **three years and six months** of a drought that he had to seek refuge in the home of a widow in the Gentile town of **Zarephath** in Phoenicia, on the Mediterranean coast, northwest of Galilee (1Kg 17:1–24). The second example was the prophet Elisha, who skipped over all the lepers of Israel in his time and only **cleansed . . . Naaman the Syrian**, a Gentile general (2Kg 7:1–19). **4:28–30** The crowd in the synagogue **was enraged** because Jesus's examples implied God's acceptance of Gentiles and his rejection of Israel. Jesus foiled their attempt at mob violence by walking **right through the crowd**, an odd circumstance that may imply a miracle. Alternatively, it may only indicate that Jesus's presence was so forceful that the people, though angry, willingly stepped aside and let him through. **4:31–32** Luke does not elaborate on the exact nature of the **authority** that Jesus demonstrated through his **teaching** in Capernaum on the **Sabbath**. Most likely the authority derived from the fact that Jesus's message was directly from God, not merely from the religious authorities of earlier generations whom Jewish teachers typically cited. **4:33–36** This is an example of the far-reaching authority Jesus displayed in Capernaum. He cast out **an unclean demonic spirit** that had possessed a man in the synagogue. Jesus

demonic spirit who cried out with a loud voice, [34] "Leave us alone! What do you have to do with us, Jesus of Nazareth? Have you come to destroy us? I know who you are — the Holy One of God!"

[35] But Jesus rebuked him and said, "Be silent and come out of him!" And throwing him down before them, the demon came out of him without hurting him at all.

[36] Amazement came over them all, and they were saying to one another, "What is this message? For he commands the unclean spirits with authority and power, and they come out!" [37] And news about him began to go out to every place in the vicinity.

Healings at Capernaum

[38] After he left the synagogue, he entered Simon's house. Simon's mother-in-law was suffering from a high fever, and they asked him about her. [39] So he stood over her and rebuked the fever, and it left her. She got up immediately and began to serve them.

[40] When the sun was setting, all those who had anyone sick with various diseases brought them to him. As he laid his hands on each one of them, he healed them. [41] Also, demons were coming out of many, shouting and saying, "You are the Son of God!" But he rebuked them and would not allow them to speak, because they knew he was the Messiah.

[42] When it was day, he went out and made his way to a deserted place. But the crowds were searching for him. They came to him and tried to keep him from leaving them. [43] But he said to them, "It is necessary for me to proclaim the good news about the kingdom of God to the other towns also, because I was sent for this purpose." [44] And he was preaching in the synagogues of Judea. [A]

The First Disciples

5 As the crowd was pressing in on Jesus to hear God's word, he was standing by Lake Gennesaret. [B] [2] He saw two boats at the edge of the lake; the fishermen had left them and were washing their nets. [3] He got into one of the boats, which belonged to Simon, and asked him to put out a little from the land. Then he sat down and was teaching the crowds from the boat.

[4] When he had finished speaking, he said to Simon, "Put out into deep water and let down your nets for a catch."

[5] "Master," Simon replied, "we've worked hard all night long and caught nothing. But if you say so, I'll let down the nets." [C]

[6] When they did this, they caught a great number of fish, and their nets [c] began to tear. [7] So they signaled to their partners in the other boat to come and help them; they came and filled both boats so full that they began to sink.

[8] When Simon Peter saw this, he fell at Jesus's knees and said, "Go away from me, because I'm a sinful man, Lord!" [9] For he and all those with him were amazed at the catch of fish they had taken, [10] and so were James and John, Zebedee's sons, who were Simon's partners.

"Don't be afraid," Jesus told Simon. "From now on you will be catching people." [11] Then they brought the boats to land, left everything, and followed him.

A Man Cleansed

[12] While he was in one of the towns, a man was there who had leprosy [D] all over him. He saw Jesus, fell facedown, and begged him, "Lord, if you are willing, you can make me clean."

[13] Reaching out his hand, Jesus touched him, saying, "I am willing; be made clean," and immediately the leprosy left him. [14] Then he

---

[A] 4:44 Other mss read *Galilee* [B] 5:1 Another name for the Sea of Galilee [C] 5:5,6 Other mss read *net* (Gk sg) [D] 5:12 Gk *lepros*; a term for various skin diseases, also in v. 13; see Lv 13–14

---

did this simply by the rebuke, **Be silent and come out of him**. The crowds wondered about Jesus, his message, and his power over the demonic realm, but the demon knew exactly who Jesus was—**the Holy One of God**—a title that Simon Peter also used of Jesus (Jn 6:69).

4:38–40 Jesus's authority also extended to physical illness. As he had done with the demon, Jesus **rebuked the fever**, and Simon Peter's **mother-in-law** was immediately healed. As a result, word of Jesus's authority over sickness spread through Capernaum. He **laid his hands** on many people with **various diseases**, healing all of them.

4:41 As he healed the physical diseases of many people in Capernaum, Jesus also cast out more **demons**. This leaves the strong impression that demons were able to cause some diseases. As with the demon in the man in the synagogue (vv. 33–36), the demons identified Jesus as divine. Jesus **rebuked** the demons for revealing that he was **the Messiah** because they were attempting to

assert control over him by revealing who he was before the appropriate time.

4:42–44 This is the first of more than thirty times that **the kingdom of God** is mentioned in Luke's Gospel. A full-blown concept of the kingdom includes: (1) the King (ruler), (2) the rule itself (sovereignty to rule), (3) the realm being ruled (this world), and (4) those ruled (individuals who believe the **good news** of Jesus Christ). In addition, some passages in the Gospels present the kingdom of God as already present in at least some senses (Mt 12:28) while others speak of it as being still future (Mt 6:10).

5:1–3 Lake Gennesaret was an alternate name for the Sea of Galilee, which is also called the Sea of Tiberias (Jn 6:1; 21:1). The boat Jesus chose belonged to **Simon** Peter, whose mother-in-law he had recently healed (4:38–39). Jesus **sat down** in the boat; this was the normal posture for a teacher (see note at 4:19–21).

5:4–7 In spite of the fact that his night labors had been fruitless, at Jesus's command Peter

responded in faith (**if you say so, I'll let down the nets**). His faith was rewarded with a catch so big that their nets tore and the boats almost sank.

5:8–11 Peter's realization of Jesus's divine power and holiness through **the catch of fish** was essentially the same as that of Job (Jb 42:6) and Isaiah (Is 6:5). **James and John**, along with Simon Peter, formed Jesus's inner circle (9:28; Mt 26:37). Jesus used the huge catch of fish to illustrate the kind of evangelistic impact Simon would have (**catching people**; see Ac 2:41; 4:4). Peter and the other fishermen **left everything** and followed Jesus. This thoroughgoing commitment is the essence of true discipleship (14:26).

5:12–14 Jesus responded to the faith of a man with **leprosy** and immediately healed him. However, he did not want word about the miracle to spread. He ordered the man to act according to the law of **Moses** (Lv 14:1–32) for **cleansing** and let the visual proof of his healing take the place of verbal **testimony** before a Jewish **priest**.

ordered him to tell no one: "But go and show yourself to the priest, and offer what Moses commanded for your cleansing as a testimony to them."

¹⁵ But the news^A about him spread even more, and large crowds would come together to hear him and to be healed of their sicknesses. ¹⁶ Yet he often withdrew to deserted places and prayed.

The Son of Man Forgives and Heals

¹⁷ On one of those days while he was teaching, Pharisees and teachers of the law were sitting there who had come from every village of Galilee and Judea, and also from Jerusalem. And the Lord's power to heal was in him. ¹⁸ Just then some men came, carrying on a stretcher a man who was paralyzed. They tried to bring him in and set him down before him. ¹⁹ Since they could not find a way to bring him in because of the crowd, they went up on the roof and lowered him on the stretcher through the roof tiles into the middle of the crowd before Jesus. ²⁰ Seeing their faith he said, "Friend,^B your sins are forgiven."

²¹ Then the scribes and the Pharisees began to think to themselves, "Who is this man who speaks blasphemies? Who can forgive sins but God alone?"

²² But perceiving their thoughts, Jesus replied to them, "Why are you thinking this in your hearts?^C ²³ Which is easier: to say, 'Your sins are forgiven,' or to say, 'Get up and walk'? ²⁴ But so that you may know that the Son of Man has authority on earth to forgive sins" — he told the paralyzed man, "I tell you: Get up, take your stretcher, and go home."

²⁵ Immediately he got up before them, picked up what he had been lying on, and went home glorifying God. ²⁶ Then everyone was astounded, and they were giving glory to God. And they were filled with awe and said, "We have seen incredible things today."

The Call of Levi

²⁷ After this, Jesus went out and saw a tax collector named Levi sitting at the tax office, and he said to him, "Follow me." ²⁸ So, leaving everything behind, he got up and began to follow him.

²⁹ Then Levi hosted a grand banquet for him at his house. Now there was a large crowd of tax collectors and others who were reclining at the table with them. ³⁰ But the Pharisees and their scribes were complaining to his disciples,

---

^A 5:15 Lit *the word*   ^B 5:20 Lit *"Man*   ^C 5:22 Or *minds*

5:15–16 These verses reflect the difference between the public and private life of Jesus during his early ministry. On the one hand, **large crowds** heard him preach and were **healed of their sicknesses**. On the other hand, Jesus often sought out remote places where he could pray without interruption.
5:17–20 The **Pharisees** were the legalistic Jewish religious party. The **teachers of the law** of Moses were also known as "the scribes." They functioned essentially as lawyers who worked closely with the Pharisees. These leaders had heard about Jesus's preaching and **power to heal**, and they decided that he needed to be observed carefully. The persistence of the paralyzed man's friends to get him into the presence of Jesus reflects strong **faith**. But Jesus focused on the man's greatest need—forgiveness of sins through faith in God's Son.
5:21–25 The scribes and Pharisees understood that Jesus was acting as if he were God when he claimed to forgive the **sins** of the paralyzed man. Not only did they not believe he was God, but they also viewed his claims as **blasphemies**. Jesus was **perceiving their thoughts** because he knew what is in man (Jn 2:25). In Lk 5:23 Jesus expressed the heart of their doubt. It was much easier to just say **your sins are forgiven** than to heal a paralytic since there could be no visible proof of whether sins had been forgiven. To demonstrate that he had power to do the invisible miracle of forgiving sins, Jesus performed the visible miracle of healing the paralytic: **I tell you: Get up . . . and go home**. The man got up immediately and went home **glorifying God**.
5:26 The Pharisees and scribes together with everyone else in the crowd were **astounded** at Jesus's miracle. The "they" of **they were**

giving glory to God apparently included unbelieving scribes and Pharisees. There was simply no denying the wonder of what Jesus had done, but submitting to Jesus and the far-reaching implications of his claims was another thing altogether.
5:27–28 A **tax collector** would sit in a toll booth (**tax office**) and collect customs or duties, in this case likely on the international highway that ran through Galilee. **Levi** is another name for Matthew (Mt 9:9; 10:3). He demonstrated the discipleship commitment that Simon, James, and John had shown

earlier (**leaving everything behind . . . to follow him**; see note at vv. 8–11).
5:29–30 Levi's becoming a disciple was very open. He hosted a **grand banquet** in honor of Jesus, to which he invited his fellow **tax collectors**. The Pharisees and scribes (see note at vv. 17–20) were incensed because tax collectors were considered ritually unclean. Tax collectors and **sinners** (others who were ritually unclean) were socially off-limits to devout Jews. Although Levi was a fellow Jew, he was despised because he worked for the Roman government.

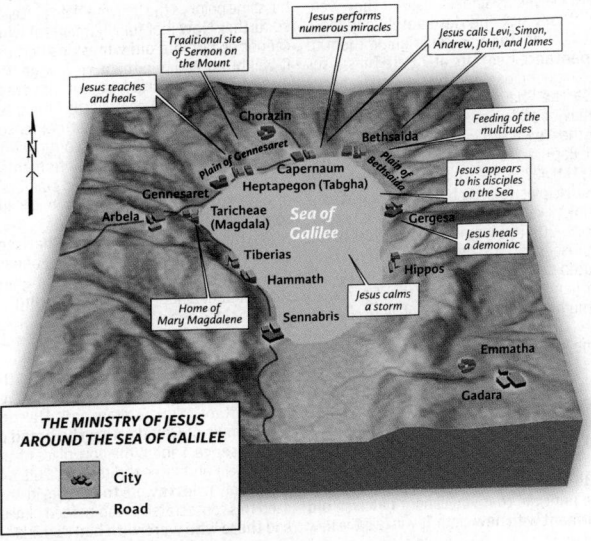

THE MINISTRY OF JESUS AROUND THE SEA OF GALILEE

City
Road

"Why do you eat and drink with tax collectors and sinners?"

31 Jesus replied to them, "It is not those who are healthy who need a doctor, but those who are sick. **32** I have not come to call the righteous, but sinners to repentance."

A Question about Fasting

33 Then they said to him, "John's disciples fast often and say prayers, and those of the Pharisees do the same, but yours eat and drink."

34 Jesus said to them, "You can't make the wedding guests fast while the groom is with them, can you? **35** But the time^A will come when the groom will be taken away from them — then they will fast in those days."

36 He also told them a parable: "No one tears a patch from a new garment and puts it on an old garment. Otherwise, not only will he tear the new, but also the piece from the new garment will not match the old. **37** And no one puts new wine into old wineskins. Otherwise, the new wine will burst the skins, it will spill, and the skins will be ruined. **38** No, new wine is put into fresh wineskins.^B **39** And no one, after drinking old wine, wants new, because he says, 'The old is better.' "^C

Lord of the Sabbath

6 On a Sabbath, he passed through the grainfields. His disciples were picking heads of grain, rubbing them in their hands, and eating them. **2** But some of the Pharisees said, "Why are you doing what is not lawful on the Sabbath?"

3 Jesus answered them, "Haven't you read what David and those who were with him did when he was hungry — **4** how he entered the house of God and took and ate the bread of the Presence, which is not lawful for any but the priests to eat? He even gave some to those who were with him." **5** Then he told them, "The Son of Man is Lord of the Sabbath."

6 On another Sabbath he entered the synagogue and was teaching. A man was there whose right hand was shriveled. **7** The scribes and Pharisees were watching him closely, to see if he would heal on the Sabbath, so that they could find a charge against him. **8** But he knew their thoughts and told the man with the shriveled hand, "Get up and stand here."^D So he got up and stood there. **9** Then Jesus said to them, "I ask you: Is it lawful to do good on the Sabbath or to do evil, to save life or to destroy it?" **10** After looking around at them all, he told him, "Stretch out your hand." He did, and his hand was restored.^E **11** They, however, were filled with rage and started discussing with one another what they might do to Jesus.

The Twelve Apostles

12 During those days he went out to the mountain to pray and spent all night in prayer to God. **13** When daylight came, he summoned his

---

^A **5:35** Lit *days*   ^B **5:38** Other mss add *And so both are preserved.*   ^C **5:39** Or *good*   ^D **6:8** Lit *stand in the middle*   ^E **6:10** Other mss add *as sound as the other*

5:31–32 Jesus referred to the Pharisees and their allies as the **healthy** and **righteous**. In contrast, he labeled tax collectors and their associates as the **sick** and **sinners**. He did not mean that the Pharisees were actually righteous but only that they saw themselves that way. By contrast, those whom the Pharisees viewed as sinners realized they were spiritually sick and desperately needed a spiritual **doctor** who could guide them to **repentance** (see note at 3:2–3). Thus Jesus had higher regard for the sick and sinners.
5:33 The Pharisees were offended at the behavior of Jesus's **disciples** as compared to their own disciples and those of John the Baptist. Jesus was not opposed to fasting (Mt 4:2; 6:16–18), but he also allowed his disciples to attend banquets (**eat and drink**), like that given by Levi (see note at vv. 29–30). This was in stark contrast to the Pharisees' rigid schedule of fasting. They fasted twice weekly (18:12), on the Day of Atonement (Lv 16:29), four times a year to remember the destruction of Jerusalem by the Babylonians (Zch 8:19), plus any other time it was deemed appropriate.
5:34–35 Jesus applied the issue of fasting to a **wedding**, as if he were the **groom**. It was not appropriate to fast during the joy of a wedding or before the divine groom was **taken away** (i.e., before the cross, resurrection, and ascension).
5:36 The first of Jesus's two parables applied the principle that you cannot patch an **old** garment with **new** cloth. It will tear the new

cloth and it won't match the old garment. On the heels of the controversy about fasting, Jesus illustrated the point that his message was radical (the new) and could not serve as a patch for the existing form of Judaism (the old garment).
5:37–39 Jesus's second parable initially made the same point as the first, but then proceeded further. **New** (not fully fermented) **wine** cannot be put into **old wineskins** because it will **burst** and ruin them. New wine (the message of Jesus) must be put into **fresh wineskins** (the church of Jesus Christ; see Mt 16:18). But there was a natural reason why many of Jesus's hearers continued to cling to Judaism: old (properly fermented and aged) wine (the established traditions of Judaism) tastes **better** (more familiar and comfortable).
6:1–2 The controversy with the **Pharisees** shifts to the issue of keeping the Sabbath day. Deuteronomy 23:25 permitted going through a neighbor's field and **picking . . . grain**, as long as a person did not use a sickle. The issue here was the permissibility of such behavior on the **Sabbath**.
6:3–5 Jesus's argument in answering the Pharisees was that there are exceptions even to important religious standards. He cited the example of **David** eating the **bread of the Presence**, kept in the holy place of the tabernacle and later the temple; 2Ch 2:4), which only **priests** were **to eat**. David once used this consecrated bread to feed himself and **those who were with him** (1Sm 21:1–6)

in a time of need. **Son of Man** is a messianic title (see Dn 7:13) that Jesus often used of himself (Lk 5:24; 19:10). As Messiah, Jesus was the same **Lord** who instituted the **Sabbath** regulations. Thus he had full authority to make an exception to the observance of this special day.
6:6–7 The second **Sabbath** controversy occurred in a **synagogue** while Jesus was teaching and a man whose hand **was shriveled** (cp. 5:17–25) was present. The **scribes and Pharisees** began watching his every move. They saw this as an opportunity to have Jesus charged and arrested.
6:8–10 On **he knew their thoughts**, see note at 5:21–25. When Jesus had the man with the **shriveled hand** get up and stand near him, he thrust the man's situation into the spotlight and confronted the Pharisees and scribes head-on. The answer to Jesus's rhetorical question was obvious. Everyone should agree that it was **lawful to do good** or **save life** on the Sabbath. Because healing was doing good, it would be wrong not to heal this man, even on the Sabbath. By stretching out his hand in obedience to Jesus's command, the man's hand was **restored**.
6:11 The Pharisees and scribes were **filled with rage** that Jesus had outwitted them again. The parallel passages in Mt 12:14 and Mk 3:6 state that they wanted to kill Jesus.
6:12–13 Although this is another example of Luke's emphasis on prayer, it is the only time it is said that Jesus **spent all night**

disciples, and he chose twelve of them, whom he also named apostles: [14] Simon, whom he also named Peter, and Andrew his brother; James and John; Philip and Bartholomew; [15] Matthew and Thomas; James the son of Alphaeus, and Simon called the Zealot; [16] Judas the son of James, and Judas Iscariot, who became a traitor.

Teaching and Healing

[17] After coming down with them, he stood on a level place with a large crowd of his disciples and a great number of people from all Judea and Jerusalem and from the seacoast of Tyre and Sidon. [18] They came to hear him and to be healed of their diseases; and those tormented by unclean spirits were made well. [19] The whole crowd was trying to touch him, because power was coming out from him and healing them all.

The Beatitudes

[20] Then looking up at his disciples, he said:
Blessed are you who are poor,
because the kingdom of God is yours.
[21] Blessed are you who are hungry now,
because you will be filled.
Blessed are you who weep now,
because you will laugh.
[22] Blessed are you when people hate you,
when they exclude you, insult you,
and slander your name as evil
because of the Son of Man.
[23] "Rejoice in that day and leap for joy. Take note — your reward is great in heaven, for this is the way their ancestors used to treat the prophets.

Woe to the Self-Satisfied

[24] But woe to you who are rich,
for you have received your comfort.
[25] Woe to you who are now full,
for you will be hungry.
Woe to you[A] who are now laughing,
for you will mourn and weep.
[26] Woe to you[A]
when all people speak well of you,
for this is the way their ancestors
used to treat the false prophets.

Love Your Enemies

[27] "But I say to you who listen: Love your enemies, do what is good to those who hate you, [28] bless those who curse you, pray for those who mistreat you. [29] If anyone hits you on the cheek, offer the other also. And if anyone takes away your coat, don't hold back your shirt either. [30] Give to everyone who asks you, and from someone who takes your things, don't ask for them back. [31] Just as you want others to do for you, do the same for them. [32] If you love those who love you, what credit is that to you? Even sinners love those who love them. [33] If you do what is good to those who are good to you, what credit is that to you? Even sinners do that. [34] And if you lend to those from whom you expect to receive, what credit is that to you? Even sinners lend to sinners to be repaid in full. [35] But love your enemies, do what is good, and lend, expecting nothing in return. Then your reward will be great, and you will be children of the Most High. For he is gracious to the

[A] 6:25,26 Other mss omit to you

in prayer. That Jesus prayed all night indicates the importance of the choice of the twelve ... apostles from the wider group of his disciples. It is not stated why he chose twelve apostles, though the fact that Israel had twelve tribes was likely the reason.
6:14–16 Other lists of the apostles appear in Mt 10:2–4; Mk 3:16–19; and Ac 1:13. Although certain details vary among the lists, Simon ... Peter is always listed first and Judas Iscariot ... the traitor, is listed last. "Iscariot" (Gk iskarioth) may be derived from Judas's hometown of Kerioth or an Aramaic word meaning "assassin." Bartholomew is probably another name for Nathanael (Jn 1:45). Matthew is an alternate name for Levi (5:27,29). Judas the son of James seems to be the same as Thaddaeus (Mt 10:3).
6:17–49 This section of Luke's Gospel is often referred to as the Sermon on the Plain. It has many similarities to the Sermon on the Mount in Mt 5–7, but it is much shorter. The two best explanations for the similarities and differences are: (1) after becoming acquainted with the material found in Matthew, Luke selected and shaped the content to fit his purposes in writing (see notes at Lk 1:1,2,3,4 in regard to Luke's editorial approach), or (2) since Jesus undoubtedly preached the same material in various locations, it is possible that the Sermon on the Mount and the Sermon on the Plain were presented on different occasions.

6:17 If this is the same event as the Sermon on the Mount (Mt 5–7), the level place would be a plateau on the side of a mountain where Jesus went up to pray in v. 12. In Matthew, the message is directed only to the disciples of Jesus (Mt 5:1), while Luke added two other groups: (1) a great number of people from all Judea and Jerusalem (i.e., where Jesus would minister later), and (2) many people from the seacoast of Tyre and Sidon (these were probably Gentile regions).
6:18–19 The crowd did not gather just to hear Jesus preach. Many came to be healed of physical diseases or spiritual oppression by unclean spirits (demons). Since power (Gk dunamis) was coming out from him, all who touched Jesus were healed.
6:20–26 Verses 24–26 in this section are the exact counterpart to vv. 20–23 (blessed vs. woe; poor vs. rich; hungry vs. full; when people hate you vs. when all people speak well of you). In Matthew, it is "the poor in spirit" and "those who hunger ... for righteousness" who are blessed. The same is true here, because the reward for the blessed ones is in heaven. Jesus noted that rejection was the way those in earlier generations used to treat the prophets, while speaking well was the way they treated the false prophets. The implication is that Jesus's growing rejection by the religious leaders is proof that he was a true prophet.
6:27–49 The remainder of the Sermon on the Plain in this section deals with the attitudes

and actions of those who are followers of Jesus.
6:27–30 Christ's disciples are to be characterized by actions of love (loving enemies, doing good to those who hate you, blessing those who curse you, praying for those who mistreat you, not retaliating against violence) and generosity (lit "giving the shirt off your back," lending and not expecting repayment).
6:31 This verse is usually referred to as the Golden Rule. This is apparently a restatement of the second greatest commandment: "Love your neighbor as yourself" (Lv 19:18).
6:32–34 Jesus discussed the logic of selfless love. It is not the kind of love his disciples display if they just return the love someone has shown them, or do ... good to someone as a sort of repayment, or lend when they are certain to be repaid. There is no spiritual credit in God's eyes for such behavior since even many unsaved sinners behave this way. Christians are to practice a deeper, selfless love.
6:35–36 The reward for obeying Jesus's command to love your enemies, do ... good and lend without expecting repayment will be great, though much of it will not be in this life. But your selfless love will reflect that you are children of the Most High. He is gracious and merciful to all people, and disciples of Jesus are to follow his example.

ungrateful and evil. **36** Be merciful, just as your Father also is merciful.

Do Not Judge

37 "Do not judge, and you will not be judged. Do not condemn, and you will not be condemned. Forgive, and you will be forgiven. **38** Give, and it will be given to you; a good measure — pressed down, shaken together, and running over — will be poured into your lap. For with the measure you use, it will be measured back to you."

39 He also told them a parable: "Can the blind guide the blind? Won't they both fall into a pit? **40** A disciple is not above his teacher, but everyone who is fully trained will be like his teacher. **41** "Why do you look at the splinter in your brother's eye, but don't notice the beam of wood in your own eye? **42** Or how can you say to your brother, 'Brother, let me take out the splinter that is in your eye,' when you yourself don't see the beam of wood in your own eye? Hypocrite! First take the beam of wood out of your eye, and then you will see clearly to take out the splinter in your brother's eye.

A Tree and Its Fruit

43 "A good tree doesn't produce bad fruit; on the other hand, a bad tree doesn't produce good fruit.^A **44** For each tree is known by its own fruit. Figs aren't gathered from thornbushes, or grapes picked from a bramble bush. **45** A good person produces good out of the good stored up in his heart. An evil person produces evil out of the evil stored up in his heart, for his mouth speaks from the overflow of the heart.

The Two Foundations

46 "Why do you call me 'Lord, Lord,' and don't do the things I say? **47** I will show you what someone is like who comes to me, hears my words, and acts on them: **48** He is like a man building a house, who dug deep and laid the foundation on the rock. When the flood came, the river crashed against that house and couldn't shake it, because it was well built. **49** But the one who hears and does not act is like a man who built a house on the ground without a foundation. The river crashed against it, and immediately it collapsed. And the destruction of that house was great."

A Centurion's Faith

7 When he had concluded saying all this to the people who were listening, he entered Capernaum. **2** A centurion's servant, who was highly valued by him, was sick and about to die. **3** When the centurion heard about Jesus, he sent some Jewish elders to him, requesting him to come and save the life of his servant. **4** When they reached Jesus, they pleaded with him earnestly, saying, "He is worthy for you to grant this, **5** because he loves our nation and has built us a synagogue."

6 Jesus went with them, and when he was not far from the house, the centurion sent friends to tell him, "Lord, don't trouble yourself, since I am not worthy to have you come under my roof. **7** That is why I didn't even consider myself worthy to come to you. But say the word, and my servant will be healed.^B **8** For I too am a man placed under authority, having soldiers under my command. I say to this one, 'Go,' and he goes; and to another, 'Come,' and he comes; and to my servant, 'Do this,' and he does it."

9 Jesus heard this and was amazed at him, and turning to the crowd following him, he said, "I tell you, I have not found so great a faith even in Israel." **10** When those who had been sent returned to the house, they found the servant in good health.

A Widow's Son Raised to Life

11 Afterward he was on his way to a town called Nain. His disciples and a large crowd

---

^A **6:43** Lit *on the other hand, again, a bad tree doesn't produce good fruit*   ^B **7:7** Other mss read *and let my servant be healed*

6:37 The problems here are hypocritical judgment, short-sighted condemnation, and an unforgiving spirit. These warnings do not mean that Jesus's followers should not practice careful discernment (judgment). **6:38** "Measure" involves weighing and judging. Be fair to others, because **the measure you use** will return to you. If you are generous, generosity will be returned to you in full measure. If you are stingy and uncharitable, such will be the standards by which you are judged. **6:39–40** This **parable** is a warning about following the wrong person. Spiritually blind leaders mislead disciples. **6:41–42** A person is a **hypocrite** (Gk *hupokrites*, "one who pretends to be someone else") if one harshly criticizes a small weakness (a **splinter**) in another person's life while overlooking a large fault (**beam of wood**) in one's own. We are in no position to criticize another person until we have dealt with our own shortcomings.

6:43–45 The type of **fruit** produced is determined by the type of **tree** that produces it. A person's actions and words come from the heart, whether good or evil. **6:46–49** The illustration of **building** on a solid **foundation** versus building **without a foundation** points out the necessity for a disciple's behavior to be consistent with his stated commitment. The difference between a life that can withstand storms and one that cannot depends not just on whether one comes to Christ and hears his words but also whether one **acts** on his teachings. **7:1 Capernaum** was Jesus's headquarters for his ministry in Galilee (4:14–9:50). **7:2–3** A **centurion** was a commander of a hundred men in the Roman army. This centurion was apparently a compassionate man, deeply concerned about the illness of his servant. He reached out to Jesus through some local **Jewish elders** (either recognized leaders in the community or respected older men). In the parallel passage

in Mt 8:5–10, the centurion approached Jesus directly. **7:4–8** The Jewish elders were willing to intervene with Jesus because they considered the centurion a truly **worthy** man. Though he was a Gentile, he loved Israel and had spent time and money constructing **a synagogue** in Capernaum. The centurion did not consider himself worthy of being in Jesus's presence, but he had faith that Jesus could heal his **servant**, even at a distance. He understood the spiritual authority Jesus commanded because he understood military authority (**I . . . am . . . under authority, having soldiers under my command**). **7:9–10** Jesus was **amazed** that the **faith** of the Gentile centurion was greater than the faith of any he had found in Israel. The centurion's faith was rewarded; his servant was restored to **good health** by Jesus. **7:11–12 Nain** was about six miles south of Nazareth, where Jesus grew up. Jesus's arrival coincided with a funeral procession for the

were traveling with him. ¹² Just as he neared the gate of the town, a dead man was being carried out. He was his mother's only son, and she was a widow. A large crowd from the town was also with her. ¹³ When the Lord saw her, he had compassion on her and said, "Don't weep." ¹⁴ Then he came up and touched the open coffin, and the pallbearers stopped. And he said, "Young man, I tell you, get up!"

¹⁵ The dead man sat up and began to speak, and Jesus gave him to his mother. ¹⁶ Then fear^A came over everyone, and they glorified God, saying, "A great prophet has risen among us," and "God has visited^B his people." ¹⁷ This report about him went throughout Judea and all the vicinity.

In Praise of John the Baptist

¹⁸ Then John's disciples told him about all these things. So John summoned two of his disciples ¹⁹ and sent them to the Lord, asking, "Are you the one who is to come, or should we expect someone else?"

²⁰ When the men reached him, they said, "John the Baptist sent us to ask you, 'Are you the one who is to come, or should we expect someone else?'"

²¹ At that time Jesus healed many people of diseases, afflictions, and evil spirits, and he granted sight to many blind people. ²² He replied to them, "Go and report to John what you have seen and heard: The blind receive their sight, the lame walk, those with leprosy^C are cleansed, the deaf hear, the dead are raised, and the poor are told the good news, ²³ and blessed is the one who isn't offended by me."

²⁴ After John's messengers left, he began to speak to the crowds about John: "What did you go out into the wilderness to see? A reed swaying in the wind? ²⁵ What then did you go out to see? A man dressed in soft clothes? See, those who are splendidly dressed and live in luxury are in royal palaces. ²⁶ What then did you go out to see? A prophet? Yes, I tell you, and more than a prophet. ²⁷ This is the one about whom it is written:

> See, I am sending my messenger
> ahead of you;
> he will prepare your way before you.^D

²⁸ I tell you, among those born of women no one is greater than John,^E but the least in the kingdom of God is greater than he."

²⁹ (And when all the people, including the tax collectors, heard this, they acknowledged God's way of righteousness, because they had been baptized with John's baptism. ³⁰ But since the Pharisees and experts in the law had not been baptized by him, they rejected the plan of God for themselves.)

An Unresponsive Generation

³¹ "To what then should I compare the people of this generation, and what are they like? ³² They are like children sitting in the marketplace and calling to each other:

> We played the flute for you,
> but you didn't dance;
> we sang a lament,
> but you didn't weep!

³³ For John the Baptist did not come eating bread or drinking wine, and you say, 'He has a demon!' ³⁴ The Son of Man has come eating and drinking, and you say, 'Look, a glutton and a drunkard, a friend of tax collectors and sinners!' ³⁵ Yet wisdom is vindicated by all her children."

^A7:16 Or awe ^B7:16 Or come to help ^C7:22 Gk lepros; a term for various skin diseases; see Lv 13–14 ^D7:27 Mal 3:1 ^E7:28 Other mss read women is not a greater prophet than John the Baptist

son of a widow, who was left childless and without a means of financial support. 7:13–15 Jesus acted out of compassion for the widow in bringing her son back from the dead. By custom Jewish funerals included an open coffin, but anyone who touched the corpse became ceremonially unclean (Nm 19:11). This is the first of several times that Jesus raised a person from the dead (Lk 8:40–56; Jn 11:38–44). 7:16–17 The phrase a great prophet has risen probably refers to Elijah (1Kg 17:17–24) and Elisha (2Kg 4:18–37) raising people from the dead. God has visited his people does not necessarily mean that the people at this early date believed that God had become a man in the person of Jesus (Jn 1:14). It can mean simply that the power of God had been experienced among his people. The fact that the report about this miracle reached Judea looks ahead to Jesus's journey to Jerusalem (9:51–19:44). 7:18–20 John the Baptist had to be told all these things because he was in prison (see note at 3:20). John's question grew out of confusion more than doubt. On the one hand, Jesus certainly did the works of the Messiah.

On the other hand, he had not acted to overturn Roman rule or free righteous prisoners, as the Jews expected the Messiah to do. So John decided to send two of his disciples to clear up the confusion by asking Jesus, Are you the one? 7:21–23 Verse 21 is a summary of the miracles Jesus was doing in his ministry, serving as a lead-in to his response to the question from John the Baptist's disciples. The things Jesus told John's disciples to report that they had seen and heard went beyond the prophecy of the Messiah in Is 61:1–2 (e.g., the dead are raised). Blessed looks back to 6:22. 7:24–28 The crowds were apparently asking Jesus why John the Baptist's messengers had come to him. So Jesus explained the significance of John and his ministry. He was not one who fit in with current thought or comfortable surroundings, and he had nothing to do with royalty and its excesses. Instead, he was a prophet and, beyond that, the forerunner for Messiah (my messenger ahead of you; see Mal 3:1). No mere human to that point was greater than John the Baptist. However, even the least Christian of the new covenant era

(the coming form of the kingdom of God), beginning with the day of Pentecost (Ac 2), would have greater spiritual resources than John due to the permanent indwelling of the Holy Spirit. 7:29–30 All of those who had repented and been baptized (see note at 3:2–3) by John acknowledged God's way of righteousness (John's message as forerunner to Jesus). But the Pharisees and experts in the law, who would not repent and humble themselves to be baptized by John, rejected the plan of God regarding salvation. 7:31–35 Jesus declared that it was impossible to please the people of his generation. They would not respond to the playing of a flute (a happy sound) or the singing of a lament (a sad sound). John the Baptist led a very strict lifestyle, but he was accused of having a demon. By contrast, Jesus was accused of living loosely and eating with sinners and thus was called a glutton and a drunkard. 7:35 The phrase wisdom is vindicated by all her children means that the teachings of John the Baptist and Jesus will be shown correct by all those who live (and live well) by following their teachings.

Much Forgiveness, Much Love

[36] Then one of the Pharisees invited him to eat with him. He entered the Pharisee's house and reclined at the table. [37] And a woman in the town who was a sinner found out that Jesus was reclining at the table in the Pharisee's house. She brought an alabaster jar of perfume [38] and stood behind him at his feet, weeping, and began to wash his feet with her tears. She wiped his feet with her hair, kissing them and anointing them with the perfume.

[39] When the Pharisee who had invited him saw this, he said to himself, "This man, if he were a prophet, would know who and what kind of woman this is who is touching him — she's a sinner!"

[40] Jesus replied to him, "Simon, I have something to say to you."

He said, "Say it, teacher."

[41] "A creditor had two debtors. One owed five hundred denarii,[A] and the other fifty. [42] Since they could not pay it back, he graciously forgave them both. So, which of them will love him more?"

[43] Simon answered, "I suppose the one he forgave more."

"You have judged correctly," he told him. [44] Turning to the woman, he said to Simon, "Do you see this woman? I entered your house; you gave me no water for my feet, but she, with her tears, has washed my feet and wiped them with her hair. [45] You gave me no kiss, but she hasn't stopped kissing my feet since I came in. [46] You didn't anoint my head with olive oil, but she has anointed my feet with perfume. [47] Therefore I tell you, her many sins have been forgiven; that's why she loved much. But the one who is forgiven little, loves little." [48] Then he said to her, "Your sins are forgiven."

[49] Those who were at the table with him began to say among themselves, "Who is this man who even forgives sins?"

[50] And he said to the woman, "Your faith has saved you. Go in peace."

Many Women Support Christ's Work

8 Afterward he was traveling from one town and village to another, preaching and telling the good news of the kingdom of God. The Twelve were with him, [2] and also some women who had been healed of evil spirits and sicknesses: Mary, called Magdalene (seven demons had come out of her); [3] Joanna the wife of Chuza, Herod's steward; Susanna; and many others who were supporting them from their possessions.

The Parable of the Sower

[4] As a large crowd was gathering, and people were coming to Jesus from every town, he said in a parable, [5] "A sower went out to sow his seed. As he sowed, some seed fell along the path; it was trampled on, and the birds of the sky devoured it. [6] Other seed fell on the rock; when it grew up, it withered away, since it lacked moisture. [7] Other seed fell among thorns; the thorns grew up with it and choked it. [8] Still other seed fell on good ground; when it grew up, it produced fruit: a hundred times what was sown." As he said this, he called out, "Let anyone who has ears to hear listen."

Why Jesus Used Parables

[9] Then his disciples asked him, "What does this parable mean?" [10] So he said, "The secrets of the kingdom of God have been given for you to know, but to the rest it is in parables, so that

A **7:41** A denarius = one day's wage

7:36–38 It is not clear whether the Pharisee who **invited** Jesus into his home wanted to learn from him, as did Nicodemus (Jn 3:1–2), or was seeking to trap him. The unnamed **woman** was probably a prostitute (**sinner**) who heard Jesus preach and repented. **Reclining** meant resting on your side, with your feet facing away from the **table**. Though she said nothing, her **tears** and her willingness to give the expensive **perfume** to anoint Jesus's feet were an eloquent testimony of her gratitude to Jesus.

7:39 The Pharisee who had invited Jesus into his home could not conceive that a true **prophet** would associate with this kind of woman—a known sinner. Being a **Pharisee** required him to be separated from sin and sinners like her.

7:40–43 A denarius (plural **denarii**) was the wage for a day's work in the first century. Jesus showed that he knew what **Simon**, the Pharisee, was thinking. The point of Jesus's story was simple: a person who is forgiven **more** appreciates it more.

7:44–47 Jesus drew a contrast between the Pharisee and the woman. Simon had failed to provide **water** to wash his **feet**, had given him **no kiss** of hospitality, and did not **anoint** his **head** with oil—all things she had done. Jesus did not mean that the Pharisee had little sin to be forgiven but that he did not think of himself as a sinner while the woman was profoundly aware of her sinfulness.

7:48–50 Based on her actions, which reflected true repentance of sins, Jesus forgave the woman who anointed his feet. He made it clear that her **faith** had **saved** her (see Eph 2:8–9). Once again, his authority to forgive **sins** was questioned (see note at 5:21–25).

8:1–3 As Jesus was **traveling** and **preaching** in Galilee, he was accompanied by **the Twelve** (see note at 6:14–16) and several well-to-do **women** who, out of gratitude for being healed by Jesus, financially supported him and the apostles. **Mary . . . Magdalene** (i.e., of the town of Magdala), who became a well-known follower (Mt 27:61), is introduced here. **Joanna**, who is also mentioned in 24:10, was married to a man who held a responsible position under Herod Antipas, the tetrarch of Galilee (see note at 3:1). Nothing else is known about **Susanna**.

8:4–8 From this point forward, Jesus used the parable approach much more, the purpose of which is explained in vv. 9–10. In an agricultural society, everyone would have understood what happened when a **sower** went out into a field to **sow his seed**. At least one **path** ran through most fields, and much of the terrain in Israel was rocky under a thin layer of topsoil. Dropping seeds along such paths was futile. Many fields had thorn bushes along the perimeters. Seeds falling there had no chance to grow and survive until harvest time. Others, however, did fall on fertile soil and produced a bumper crop (**a hundred times what was sown**). **Anyone who has ears to hear** should **listen** is a challenge to carefully consider the story and its hidden meaning and practical implications (Rv 2:7).

8:9–10 Jesus's disciples could not understand the point of the story, so they asked him its meaning. Quoting from Is 6:9, Jesus explained that he used parables as a way to reveal the truths of **the kingdom of God** to believers but that the story by itself actually concealed the meaning from unbelievers.

Looking they may not see,
and hearing they may not understand.ᴬ

The Parable of the Sower Explained

¹¹ "This is the meaning of the parable: The seed is the word of God. ¹² The seed along the path are those who have heard and then the devil comes and takes away the word from their hearts, so that they may not believe and be saved. ¹³ And the seed on the rock are those who, when they hear, receive the word with joy. Having no root, these believe for a while and fall away in a time of testing. ¹⁴ As for the seed that fell among thorns, these are the ones who, when they have heard, go on their way and are choked with worries, riches, and pleasures of life, and produce no mature fruit. ¹⁵ But the seed in the good ground — these are the ones who, having heard the word with an honest and good heart, hold on to it and by enduring, produce fruit.

Using Your Light

¹⁶ "No one, after lighting a lamp, covers it with a basket or puts it under a bed, but puts it on a lampstand so that those who come in may see its light. ¹⁷ For nothing is concealed that won't be revealed, and nothing hidden that won't be made known and brought to light. ¹⁸ Therefore take care how you listen. For whoever has, more will be given to him; and whoever does not have, even what he thinks he has will be taken away from him."

True Relationships

¹⁹ Then his mother and brothers came to him, but they could not meet with him because of the crowd. ²⁰ He was told, "Your mother and your brothers are standing outside, wanting to see you."

²¹ But he replied to them, "My mother and my brothers are those who hear and do the word of God."

Wind and Waves Obey Jesus

²² One day he and his disciples got into a boat, and he told them, "Let's cross over to the other side of the lake." So they set out, ²³ and as they were sailing he fell asleep. Then a fierce

ᴬ8:10 Is 6:9

8:11–12 The key to the parable is that the **seed** being sown stands for the preaching of **the word of God**. The seeds that fell on the hard dirt **along the path** did not penetrate the **hearts** of those who heard God's Word because the **devil** stole the seed away. So they remained unsaved.

8:13–14 The seeds on the rocky soil seemed to flourish at first, but they could not put down roots, so they soon withered and died. **The seed . . . among thorns** that **produce no mature fruit** may be: (1) those whose

unbelief is revealed by their response to **worries, riches,** and the **pleasures of life,** or (2) believers who are not fruitful (1Co 3:10–15).

8:15 The **seed in the good ground** represents fruitful believers (Jn 15:2) who receive God's **word** with an open heart and persevere in the faith.

8:16–18 How a person responds to God's revelation determines whether he will receive more **light** or lose what he has. In the end, God will bring everything to light.

8:19–21 Jesus's **brothers** (named in Mt 13:55) were later children of Joseph and Mary. Human relationships built upon mutual faith in Christ, spiritual openness to one another, and shared obedience to **the word of God** are more important than relationships with physical family members, especially if the family members are unbelievers.

8:22–25 When a boat trip across the Sea of Galilee ran into **a fierce windstorm,** Jesus slept in the boat while his disciples came up against the storm and feared they would die.

Character profile:

Joanna

Joanna is mentioned by name only twice in the New Testament, both occurrences in the Gospel of Luke. In Luke 8 we learn that she was the wife of Chuza, a prominent man employed by the notorious Herod Antipas—one of the sons of Herod the Great (the ruler who tried to murder Jesus shortly after his birth).

Antipas inherited one-fourth of his father's kingdom. During his life, Israel remained under the domination of Rome, meaning Herod Antipas's rule was limited in scope. Even so, he wielded great political power across his realm.

To rise to the position of steward, Chuza enjoyed Herod's full trust. Typically, a steward functioned like a personal assistant / business manager / right-hand man. Stewards oversaw a wealthy person's property and holdings. In some cases they even acted as a guardian or tutor of any children. Serving Herod Antipas in this capacity, Chuza would likely have enjoyed high compensation.

Because of Chuza's position, Joanna enjoyed more advantages, luxuries, and connections than most women. But as we know, wealth and power are not enough to ward off the troubles of life. So it was with Joanna. Luke lists her among a group of women "who had been healed of evil spirits and sicknesses" (Lk 8:2–3).

Luke doesn't tell us into which category Joanna fell. The only thing we know for sure is that she was grateful enough to support his ministry with her possessions. Did this cause tension at home or for her husband in his job? We don't know.

Luke tells us that for an unspecified period of time, Joanna and several other women with experiences like her own became part of Christ's entourage. They traveled with Christ and the disciples "from one town and village to another" (Lk 8:1). Perhaps they shared their own personal testimonies of how Jesus had changed their lives. Surely this caused eyebrows to rise and tongues to wag.

The only other mention of Joanna comes at the end of Luke's Gospel. She was one of the women who went to the tomb of Christ early on Sunday to anoint his body with spices. Upon arrival, they found the tomb open and the body gone. That's when they encountered "two men . . . in dazzling clothes" (Lk 24:4) who announced Christ's resurrection.

After this Joanna fades from view. Where did she go? What did she do? No one knows. But it's safe to assume this grateful woman spent the rest of her days telling others of God's gracious gift of his Son, Jesus Christ—the risen Lord who offers forgiveness and eternal life to all who will come to him.

One of the frequent charges leveled at Christianity is that it demeans women or at least denies them opportunities to use their strengths. This surely wasn't Joanna's experience with Christ. After experiencing his grace, she became one of his most devoted followers and generously shared her time, energy, and resources.

Joanna was an influential force in the spreading of the gospel. Regardless of your own circumstances, you too can have an impact for Christ's kingdom. Look for occasions to share your story. Look for opportunities to meet the needs of others through your local church.

windstorm came down on the lake; they were being swamped and were in danger. **²⁴** They came and woke him up, saying, "Master, Master, we're going to die!"

Then he got up and rebuked the wind and the raging waves. So they ceased, and there was a calm. **²⁵** He said to them, "Where is your faith?"

They were fearful and amazed, asking one another, "Who then is this? He commands even the winds and the waves, and they obey him!"

Demons Driven Out by Jesus

²⁶ Then they sailed to the region of the Gerasenes,ᴬ which is opposite Galilee. **²⁷** When he got out on land, a demon-possessed man from the town met him. For a long time he had worn no clothes and did not stay in a house but in the tombs. **²⁸** When he saw Jesus, he cried out, fell down before him, and said in a loud voice, "What do you have to do with me, Jesus, Son of the Most High God? I beg you, don't torment me!" **²⁹** For he had commanded the unclean spirit to come out of the man. Many times it had seized him, and though he was guarded, bound by chains and shackles, he would snap the restraints and be driven by the demon into deserted places.

³⁰ "What is your name?" Jesus asked him.

"Legion," he said, because many demons had entered him. **³¹** And they begged him not to banish them to the abyss.

³² A large herd of pigs was there, feeding on the hillside. The demons begged him to permit them to enter the pigs, and he gave them permission. **³³** The demons came out of the man and entered the pigs, and the herd rushed down the steep bank into the lake and drowned.

³⁴ When the men who tended them saw what had happened, they ran off and reported it in the town and in the countryside. **³⁵** Then people went out to see what had happened. They came to Jesus and found the man the demons had departed from, sitting at Jesus's feet, dressed and in his right mind. And they were afraid. **³⁶** Meanwhile, the eyewitnesses reported to them how the demon-possessed man was delivered. **³⁷** Then all the people of the Gerasene regionᴬ asked him to leave them, because they were gripped by great fear. So getting into the boat, he returned.

³⁸ The man from whom the demons had departed begged him earnestly to be with him. But he sent him away and said, **³⁹** "Go back to your home, and tell all that God has done for you." And off he went, proclaiming throughout the town how much Jesus had done for him.

A Girl Restored and a Woman Healed

⁴⁰ When Jesus returned, the crowd welcomed him, for they were all expecting him. **⁴¹** Just then, a man named Jairus came. He was a leader of the synagogue. He fell down at Jesus's feet and pleaded with him to come to his house, **⁴²** because he had an only daughter about twelve years old, and she was dying.

While he was going, the crowds were nearly crushing him. **⁴³** A woman suffering from bleeding for twelve years, who had spent all she had on doctorsᴮ and yet could not be healed by any, **⁴⁴** approached from behind and touched the end of his robe. Instantly her bleeding stopped.

⁴⁵ "Who touched me?" Jesus asked.

When they all denied it, Peterᶜ said, "Master, the crowds are hemming you in and pressing against you."ᴰ

ᴬ**8:26,37** Other mss read *the Gadarenes* ᴮ**8:43** Other mss omit *who had spent all she had on doctors* ᶜ**8:45** Other mss add *and those with him* ᴰ**8:45** Other mss add *and you say, 'Who touched me?'*

When Jesus was awakened, he demonstrated full authority over **wind** and **waves** by calming the storm. He also chided his disciples for their lack of **faith**. Had they genuinely trusted Jesus, they would not have feared even the fiercest winds and waves.

8:26 The **region of the Gerasenes** was probably around the town of Gergesa (or Khersa), on the eastern coast of the Sea of Galilee. The name for this predominantly Gentile region came from the city of Gerasa, located about thirty-five miles to the southeast.

8:27 In the parallel account in Mt 8:28, *two* **demon-possessed** men are mentioned. Apparently, Luke chose to focus on the one who did the talking. The phrase **did not stay in a house but in the tombs** may refer to an outdoor burial ground, but since the man was naked, it is more likely this refers to a cave, several of which have been found in that area.

8:28–31 The demon who spoke identified Jesus, just as the demons did in 4:34 and Ac 16:17. **Son of the Most High** was the wording

used by the angel in speaking to Mary (see note at 1:31–33). **Don't torment me** probably refers to sending the demon to the abyss, a place where some of the demons are currently confined (Rv 9:1–2,11). Demons enabled people whom they possessed to perform feats of great strength (**he would snap the restraints**). It is not clear whether Jesus was asking the name of the man or the demon, but the demon answered. A **legion** of Roman soldiers was a force of six thousand. Thus many demons possessed this man.

8:32–33 The presence of **a large herd of pigs** indicates that the region of the Gerasenes was heavily Gentile because Jews considered pigs to be unclean animals (Lv 11:7–8) and would never herd them. The cruel destructiveness of demons is seen in that, as soon as Jesus permitted them to enter the pigs, they caused them to drown in **the lake** (the Sea of Galilee).

8:34–37 Sitting at Jesus's feet is the position of a disciple (i.e., the pupil; see 10:38–42). The people were **afraid** when the demon-possessed man returned to normal,

for Jesus had exercised a power that revealed his supernatural identity.

8:38–39 Because he had been asked to leave, Jesus told the healed man to stay in that region and testify to what **God** had **done** for him. The man obeyed by proclaiming **how much Jesus had done for him**.

8:40–42 Jesus **returned** to Galilee. He likely had met this **Jairus** before. He had spoken in most of the synagogues in Galilee, and Jairus was a **leader** (Gk *archon*, "ruler"; probably the chief elder who conducted the services) in the local **synagogue**.

8:43–46 The account of the **woman suffering from bleeding for twelve years** interrupts the narrative to show that delay during a critical hour of the girl's illness could not keep Jesus from healing her. As for the woman, her bleeding was probably menstrual hemorrhaging, which had made her ceremonially unclean for all this time (Lv 15:25–31). As a doctor, Luke was especially sensitive to the fact that this woman had **spent** all her resources on **doctors and yet could not be healed**. Even with the crowd

46 "Someone did touch me," said Jesus. "I know that power has gone out from me." **47** When the woman saw that she was discovered, she came trembling and fell down before him. In the presence of all the people, she declared the reason she had touched him and how she was instantly healed. **48** "Daughter," he said to her, "your faith has saved you.^A Go in peace."

49 While he was still speaking, someone came from the synagogue leader's house and said, "Your daughter is dead. Don't bother the teacher anymore."

50 When Jesus heard it, he answered him, "Don't be afraid. Only believe, and she will be saved."^B **51** After he came to the house, he let no one enter with him except Peter, John, James, and the child's father and mother. **52** Everyone was crying and mourning for her. But he said, "Stop crying, because she is not dead but asleep."

53 They laughed at him, because they knew she was dead. **54** So he^C took her by the hand and called out, "Child, get up!" **55** Her spirit returned, and she got up at once. Then he gave orders that she be given something to eat. **56** Her parents were astounded, but he instructed them to tell no one what had happened.

Commissioning the Twelve

9 Summoning the Twelve, he gave them power and authority over all the demons and to heal diseases. **2** Then he sent them to proclaim the kingdom of God and to heal the sick.

3 "Take nothing for the road," he told them, "no staff, no traveling bag, no bread, no money; and don't take an extra shirt. **4** Whatever house you enter, stay there and leave from there. **5** If they do not welcome you, when you leave that town, shake off the dust from your feet as a testimony against them." **6** So they went out and traveled from village to village, proclaiming the good news and healing everywhere.

Herod's Desire to See Jesus

7 Herod the tetrarch heard about everything that was going on. He was perplexed, because some said that John had been raised from the dead, **8** some that Elijah had appeared, and others that one of the ancient prophets had risen. **9** "I beheaded John," Herod said, "but who is this I hear such things about?" And he wanted to see him.

Feeding of the Five Thousand

10 When the apostles returned, they reported to Jesus all that they had done. He took them along and withdrew privately to a^D town called Bethsaida. **11** When the crowds found out, they followed him. He welcomed them, spoke to them about the kingdom of God, and healed those who needed healing.

12 Late in the day, the Twelve approached and said to him, "Send the crowd away, so that they can go into the surrounding villages and countryside to find food and lodging, because we are in a deserted place here."

13 "You give them something to eat," he told them.

^A 8:48 Or has made you well ^B 8:50 Or she will be made well ^C 8:54 Other mss add having put them all outside ^D 9:10 Other mss add deserted place near a

---

pressing against Jesus from all sides, he was immediately aware of the touch of the woman who was instantly healed of her bleeding. No explanation is given for how he knew that healing **power** had gone out from him. **8:47–48** The woman was **instantly healed**, but she was understandably fearful when Jesus singled her out. After hearing her explanation, Jesus stated that her **faith** in him had **saved** her. **8:49–50** During the delay caused by Jesus's interaction with the bleeding woman, the **daughter** of the synagogue leader died. The natural conclusion was that she was now beyond the help of Jesus. However, he stated that the same kind of faith that had brought about the healing of the bleeding woman would bring the dead girl back to life. **8:51–53** In this passage **Peter, John**, and **James** are set apart by Jesus as the inner circle of the apostles (9:28; Mt 26:37). The sense of finality by the child's parents and, apparently, even the apostles was so profound that the people in the house **laughed** at Jesus when he seemingly denied that the girl was dead (**she is not dead but asleep**). **8:54–56** When Jesus commanded, **Child, get up,** her spirit returned to her body. Then **she got up** and had **something to eat**. It is not known why Jesus insisted that her parents not tell about him raising their

daughter from the dead. The crowd outside knew that the girl had genuinely died. Now she was alive just after Jesus went in to see her. There could be no hiding the fact that Jesus raised her. **9:1–2** After **the Twelve** had observed Jesus's ministry for several months, he delegated **power and authority** over **demons** and **diseases** to them (see note at 6:12–13). Their other mission was to **proclaim the kingdom of God**. In the parallel passage in Mt 10, the apostles were specifically instructed to avoid the Samaritans and Gentiles and to go only to "the lost sheep of the house of Israel" (Mt 10:6), but Luke did not include this restriction. **9:3–5** The apostles were to be dependent on hospitable hosts (**take nothing**) and were to move on if a family or town did not **welcome** them. **Shake off the dust from your feet** was a gesture of judgment against those who rejected the apostles and their message about Jesus. Paul and Barnabas practiced this at Antioch of Pisidia (Ac 13:51). **9:6 Proclaiming the good news** is paralleled here with "proclaim the kingdom of God" in v. 2. The message of the gospel of Jesus Christ is the means of entry into the kingdom of God. **9:7–9 Herod** Antipas (see note at 3:1) was at a loss (**perplexed**) to decide whether Jesus was John the Baptist raised from the dead.

The parallel passages (Mt 14:2; Mk 6:16) indicate he decided that Jesus was indeed the risen John. Others around Antipas, however, thought Jesus was the prophet **Elijah** (see Mal 4:5). John himself had partially fulfilled this prophecy (Mt 11:14). Still others believed that some other OT prophet had come back. Herod Antipas eventually would get to meet and interview Jesus (23:6–12)—but Jesus would not speak to him. **9:10–11** After the apostles returned from their mission, they **reported** their deeds, and Jesus again took the lead over the ministry of preaching and healing. **Bethsaida** was a town on the northeastern coast of the Sea of Galilee that had recently been rebuilt by Herod Philip (see note at 3:1). The attempt to find a private place outside Bethsaida where the apostles could rest and confer with Jesus was foiled by the following **crowds**. **9:12–17** Other than his resurrection from the dead, the feeding of the five thousand is the only miracle of Jesus that appears in all four Gospels (Mt 14:13–21; Mk 6:30–44; Jn 6:5–14). **9:12–14** According to John's Gospel, Jesus, already knowing what he was going to do, was the one who expressed concern initially over where the crowd would find **food and lodging** so late in the day (Jn 6:5–6). Here in Luke, Jesus responded to the question by the Twelve by challenging them to **give**

"We have no more than five loaves and two fish," they said, "unless we go and buy food for all these people." **14** (For about five thousand men were there.)

Then he told his disciples, "Have them sit down[A] in groups of about fifty each." **15** They did what he said, and had them all sit down. **16** Then he took the five loaves and the two fish, and looking up to heaven, he blessed and broke them. He kept giving them to the disciples to set before the crowd. **17** Everyone ate and was filled. They picked up twelve baskets of leftover pieces.

Peter's Confession of the Messiah

18 While he was praying in private and his disciples were with him, he asked them, "Who do the crowds say that I am?"

19 They answered, "John the Baptist; others, Elijah; still others, that one of the ancient prophets has come back."[B]

20 "But you," he asked them, "who do you say that I am?"

Peter answered, "God's Messiah."

His Death and Resurrection Predicted

21 But he strictly warned and instructed them to tell this to no one, **22** saying, "It is necessary that the Son of Man suffer many things and be rejected by the elders, chief priests, and scribes, be killed, and be raised the third day."

Take Up Your Cross

23 Then he said to them all, "If anyone wants to follow after[C] me, let him deny himself, take up his cross daily,[D] and follow me. **24** For whoever wants to save his life will lose it, but whoever loses his life because of me will save it. **25** For what does it benefit someone if he gains the whole world, and yet loses or forfeits himself? **26** For whoever is ashamed of me and my words, the Son of Man will be ashamed of him when he comes in his glory and that of the Father and the holy angels. **27** Truly I tell you, there are some standing here who will not taste death until they see the kingdom of God."

The Transfiguration

28 About eight days after this conversation, he took along Peter, John, and James and went up on the mountain to pray. **29** As he was praying, the appearance of his face changed, and his clothes became dazzling white. **30** Suddenly, two men were talking with him — Moses and Elijah. **31** They appeared in glory and were speaking of his departure, which he was about to accomplish in Jerusalem.

32 Peter and those with him were in a deep sleep,[E] and when they became fully awake, they saw his glory and the two men who were standing with him. **33** As the two men were departing from him, Peter said to Jesus, "Master,

---

[A]**9:14** Lit *them recline* [B]**9:19** Lit *has risen* [C]**9:23** Lit *come after* [D]**9:23** Other mss omit *daily* [E]**9:32** Lit *were weighed down with sleep*

---

them something to eat. The apostles had already surveyed the crowd and found only **five loaves** of bread and **two fish** to feed about five thousand men (who, with women and children, could easily have totaled fifteen thousand or more). To better manage distribution, Jesus had the apostles organize the huge crowd into **groups of about fifty** people.

9:16–17 It is likely that when Jesus looked **up to heaven** and **blessed and broke** the loaves, he uttered the traditional Jewish mealtime prayer: "Blessed are you, Lord our God, King of the universe, who brings out bread from the earth." The miracle of the multiplying of the loaves and fish took place in the hands of Jesus as he broke the food and **kept giving** it to the disciples to distribute. At the end, it appears that each of the twelve apostles picked up a full basket of **leftover pieces**, even after feeding thousands of people. The Jews were required to pick up scraps of food that fell during any meal.

9:18–20 These verses are another example of Luke's emphasis on prayer. The answers the disciples gave to Jesus's question about his identity prove that Herod Antipas was not the only person who was perplexed on this point (see note at vv. 7–9). When Jesus asked the disciples their personal opinion, **Peter** answered as spokesman for the group. His answer, that Jesus is **God's Messiah**, is the conclusion to which everything in Luke's Gospel points.

9:21–22 Jesus was not ready to present himself openly as the Messiah. In popular Jewish views of that time, Messiah was expected to overthrow Roman rule and, in a wave of popularity, take over as king of Israel. Contrary to this, Jesus's mission was to **suffer** and be **rejected** by the Jewish leadership before being **killed** and **raised** from the dead. This was the first of several predictions by Jesus of his death and/or resurrection (v. 44; 12:50; 17:25; 18:31–33).

9:23 To be a true disciple of Jesus requires self-denial. The **cross** was the most painful and humiliating form of execution in the Roman era. Thus to **take up** one's cross **daily** is to expect painful situations every day because of allegiance to Christ.

9:24 The principle that one must lose one's **life** to **save it** as opposed to living only for this world is Jesus's most common refrain in the Gospels (14:26–27; 17:33; Mt 10:38–39; 16:24–25; Mk 8:34–35; Jn 12:25). To follow him, we must lay down our devotions to this world and live for Christ and his mission.

9:25 No matter how wealthy a person is in this life (**gains the whole world**), he will be bankrupt eternally (**forfeits himself**) if he dies without Christ.

9:26 To be **ashamed** of Christ and his **words** indicates unbelief, which will bring eternal judgment (12:9; 2Tm 2:12) at his second coming. It is also possible for believers to temporarily cower in fear around unbelieving peers and act "ashamed" of Jesus, as Peter did in his denials of Christ. In such cases a believer may suffer loss of heavenly reward (1Co 3:10–15; 2Co 5:10) but not suffer eternal punishment.

9:27 This cryptic statement refers to the next event in the book—the transfiguration of Jesus (vv. 28–35). **Some standing here** indicates Peter, James, and John, who were with Jesus at his transfiguration (v. 28). **See the kingdom of God** apparently means that the glorious appearance of Jesus (vv. 29,32) was a preview of the coming kingdom.

9:28–29 On **Peter, John, and James**, see note at 8:51–53. The traditional candidate for **the mountain** in these verses is Mount Tabor, six miles east of Nazareth and about 1,900 feet in elevation. However, it is more likely that it was Mount Hermon, located between Caesarea Philippi and Damascus, which rises 9,000 feet above sea level. We are not told in what sense the **appearance** of Jesus's face **changed**. His clothes are described as **dazzling white** (gleaming, like a bolt of lightning). There may be an intended similarity here to Moses after he was with God on Mount Sinai (Ex 34:29–35) or to the vision of the Son of Man in Rv 1:13–16.

9:30–31 Jewish tradition expected **Moses** and **Elijah** (see Mal 4:5–6) to return before the arrival of the kingdom of God. Like Jesus, their appearances were almost blinding in this special appearance. The word translated **departure** (Gk *exodos*) can also refer to the OT exodus from Egypt. The choice of this word may be an association with the presence of Moses. **In Jerusalem** makes it clear that the "exodus" would be Jesus's death on the cross.

9:32–33 It is not clear whether Peter, James, and John were in a **deep sleep** because it was in the middle of the night or if they were caused to fall asleep as Daniel was when

it's good for us to be here. Let's set up three shelters: one for you, one for Moses, and one for Elijah" — not knowing what he was saying. **34** While he was saying this, a cloud appeared and overshadowed them. They became afraid as they entered the cloud. **35** Then a voice came from the cloud, saying, "This is my Son, the Chosen One;[A] listen to him!" **36** After the voice had spoken, Jesus was found alone. They kept silent, and at that time told no one what they had seen.

The Power of Jesus over a Demon

37 The next day, when they came down from the mountain, a large crowd met him. **38** Just then a man from the crowd cried out, "Teacher, I beg you to look at my son, because he's my only child. **39** A spirit seizes him; suddenly he shrieks, and it throws him into convulsions until he foams at the mouth; severely bruising him, it scarcely ever leaves him. **40** I begged your disciples to drive it out, but they couldn't." **41** Jesus replied, "You unbelieving and perverse[B] generation, how long will I be with you and put up with you? Bring your son here." **42** As the boy was still approaching, the demon knocked him down and threw him into severe convulsions. But Jesus rebuked the unclean spirit, healed the boy, and gave him back to his father. **43** And they were all astonished at the greatness of God.

The Second Prediction of His Death

While everyone was amazed at all the things he was doing, he told his disciples, **44** "Let these words sink in:[C] The Son of Man is about to be betrayed into the hands of men."

45 But they did not understand this statement; it was concealed from them so that they could not grasp it, and they were afraid to ask him about it.

Who Is the Greatest?

46 An argument started among them about who was the greatest of them. **47** But Jesus, knowing their inner thoughts,[D] took a little child and had him stand next to him. **48** He told them, "Whoever welcomes[E] this little child in my name welcomes me. And whoever welcomes me welcomes him who sent me. For whoever is least among you — this one is great."

In His Name

49 John responded, "Master, we saw someone driving out demons in your name, and we tried to stop him because he does not follow us." **50** "Don't stop him," Jesus told him, "because whoever is not against you is for you."[F]

The Journey to Jerusalem

51 When the days were coming to a close for him to be taken up, he determined[G] to journey to Jerusalem. **52** He sent messengers ahead of himself, and on the way they entered a village of the Samaritans to make preparations for him. **53** But they did not welcome him, because he determined to journey to Jerusalem. **54** When the disciples James and John saw this, they said, "Lord, do you want us to call down fire from heaven to consume them?"[H] **55** But he turned and rebuked them,[I] **56** and they went to another village.

---

^9:35 Other mss read *the Beloved* ^9:41 Or *corrupt*, or *perverted*, or *twisted*; Dt 32:5 ^9:44 Lit *"Put these words in your ears* ^9:47 Lit *the thoughts of their hearts* ^9:48 Or *receives*, throughout the verse ^9:50 Other mss read *against us is for us* ^9:51 Lit *he stiffened his face to go*; Is 50:7 ^9:54 Other mss add *as Elijah also did* ^9:55–56 Other mss add *and said, "You don't know what kind of spirit you belong to.* ^56*For the Son of Man did not come to destroy people's lives but to save them,"*

---

angels came (Dn 8:18; 10:9). Peter spoke as Moses and Elijah **were departing** in an attempt to prolong the glorious scene. But his idea was shortsighted for two reasons: (1) to make **three** equal **shelters** (temporary structures for housing) was to place Moses and Elijah on a level with Jesus and not to worship him exclusively (Rv 19:10; 22:8–9) and (2) Jesus's discussion of his coming "exodus" in Jerusalem (see note at Lk 9:30–31) meant there was no room for delay in God's plan of redemption.
9:34–35 The **cloud** that **overshadowed** the scene recalls the cloud that came over the tabernacle in the wilderness (Ex 40:34–35). The **voice . . . from the cloud** combines an echo of 3:22, at Jesus's baptism, and an allusion to Dt 18:15, where Israel was told to **listen** to the prophet like Moses who would come (the Messiah).
9:36 Luke does not state why the three apostles were **silent** about what they had experienced, though Mt 17:9 states that Jesus commanded them to tell no one until after his resurrection. In 2Pt 1:16–18, Peter recalls his experience at the transfiguration.

9:37–43a It is not known whether the **disciples** who could not heal the boy afflicted with seizures by a demon were the nine apostles who did not see Jesus's transfiguration or some of the wider group of disciples. It is not explained whether it was just the onlookers, or also the disciples, who were **unbelieving**. The boy was immediately **healed** when Jesus **rebuked** the demon.
9:43b–45 In the aftermath of the healing of the demon-possessed boy (vv. 38–43), Jesus shifted gears and announced that he would soon be **betrayed** and captured. The disciples were confused by Jesus's words. Luke states that it was **concealed from them** until after Jesus's death and resurrection. Meanwhile, their fear of Jesus's talk about betrayal and death kept them from asking him what he meant.
9:46–48 The question about **who was the greatest** among the apostles came up more than once (22:24). Jesus knew the competitive pride that fostered the argument and was quick to point out that, spiritually, **whoever** was **least** (truly humble as a disciple of Christ) was **great**.

9:49–50 Apparently the man casting out **demons** in Jesus's **name** was a true disciple, even though he did not **follow** Jesus from town to town. The spiritual principle here is to be careful about judging, because certain people who are **not against you** may be on your side. The opposite point is made in 11:23.
9:51 The phrase **the days . . . for him to be taken up** refers to Jesus's ascension to heaven and the events leading up to it. **Determined** means literally "to fix your face," a Hebrew expression for firmness of purpose in spite of danger. The mention of traveling to **Jerusalem** begins the third major section of Luke's Gospel (9:51–19:44).
9:52–56 The **Samaritans** would **not welcome** Jesus because he was headed to **Jerusalem** to worship in the temple and not to Mount Gerizim, their preferred site of worship (see Jn 4:20–21). In Mk 3:17, the apostles **James and John** were nicknamed by Jesus *Boanerges*, meaning "sons of thunder," likely indicating that they had fiery tempers. **Call down fire from heaven** recalls Elijah's action in 2Kg 1:9–16.

Following Jesus

57 As they were traveling on the road someone said to him, "I will follow you wherever you go." **58** Jesus told him, "Foxes have dens, and birds of the sky have nests, but the Son of Man has no place to lay his head." **59** Then he said to another, "Follow me."

"Lord," he said, "first let me go bury my father."

60 But he told him, "Let the dead bury their own dead, but you go and spread the news of the kingdom of God."

61 Another said, "I will follow you, Lord, but first let me go and say good-bye to those at my house."

62 But Jesus said to him, "No one who puts his hand to the plow and looks back is fit for the kingdom of God."

Sending Out the Seventy-Two

10 After this, the Lord appointed seventy-two^A others, and he sent them ahead of him in pairs to every town and place where he himself was about to go. **2** He told them, "The harvest is abundant, but the workers are few. Therefore, pray to the Lord of the harvest to send out workers into his harvest. **3** Now go; I'm sending you out like lambs among wolves. **4** Don't carry a money-bag, traveling bag, or sandals; don't greet anyone along the road. **5** Whatever house you enter, first say, 'Peace to this household.' **6** If a person of peace is there, your peace will rest on him; but if not, it will return to you. **7** Remain in the same house, eating and drinking what they offer, for the worker is worthy of his wages. Don't move from house to house. **8** When you enter any town, and they welcome you, eat the things set before you. **9** Heal the sick who are there, and tell them, 'The kingdom of God has come near you.' **10** When you enter any town, and they don't welcome you, go out into its streets and say, **11** 'We are wiping off even the dust of your town that clings to our feet as a witness against you. Know this for certain: The kingdom of God has come near.' **12** I tell you, on that day it will be more tolerable for Sodom than for that town.

Unrepentant Towns

13 "Woe to you, Chorazin! Woe to you, Bethsaida! For if the miracles that were done in you had been done in Tyre and Sidon, they would have repented long ago, sitting in sackcloth and ashes. **14** But it will be more tolerable for Tyre and Sidon at the judgment than for you. **15** And you, Capernaum, will you be exalted to heaven? No, you will go down to Hades. **16** Whoever listens to you listens to me. Whoever rejects you rejects me. And whoever rejects me rejects the one who sent me."

The Return of the Seventy-Two

17 The seventy-two^B returned with joy, saying, "Lord, even the demons submit to us in your name."

18 He said to them, "I watched Satan fall from heaven like lightning. **19** Look, I have given you the authority to trample on snakes and

---

^A10:1 Other mss read *seventy*   ^B10:17 Other mss read *The seventy*

9:57–58 Jesus warned this would-be disciple to count the cost before committing to follow him. After all, even Christ himself had **no place** to call home. To follow Christ is to loosen your grip on the things that normally provide physical and emotional security.

9:59–60 It is doubtful that this man's **father** had already died. If he had, the man would have been involved in burial rites instead of talking to Jesus. Thus the man's words were an excuse to delay, possibly for years, his responsibility to follow Jesus and **spread the news of the kingdom of God**.

9:61–62 In 14:26, Jesus made it clear that he must be the top priority in a disciple's life, even above one's family. **Puts his hand to the plow and looks back** means looking over your shoulder while plowing, making it impossible to plow a straight furrow. Christians cannot follow Christ by looking back. We must focus on serving him as we move ahead at his command.

10:1 Though not mentioned in 9:1–6, Jesus had apparently sent out the apostles previously **in pairs** (see Mk 6:7). In this verse he sent out seventy-two other followers to cover Judea with the message of good news in advance of his coming.

10:2 Christ seems to be saying that, as **abundant** as the spiritual **harvest** was, the seventy-two whom he sent out to preach were not enough. There was need for many more

to take the message, and prayers must be offered to meet this need.

10:3 Lambs among wolves was a common metaphor in Judaism for being in a dangerous situation.

10:4 On items for the journey, see note at 9:3–5.

10:5–6 Peace (Hb *shalom*) was a traditional Jewish greeting. But the word actually speaks of wholeness or well-being. "Person of" is a Jewish expression meaning "one characterized by" (Ac 4:36). In this context, **person of peace** and **your peace** appear to relate to the seventy-two who were offering the message of peace with God through faith in Jesus Christ (Rm 5:1).

10:7 On **remain in the same house**, see note at 9:3–5. **The worker is worthy of his wages** is a basic principle of fairness. This was quoted by the apostle Paul in making his case for ministers of God's Word being paid for their work (1Tm 5:17–18).

10:8–9 If the seventy-two disciples were made **welcome** in a **town**, it indicated that the hearts of the people were open to the gospel message. In some sense, the present tense aspects of **the kingdom of God** were present in the preaching of the gospel and the healing ministry delegated by Jesus to the seventy-two.

10:10–11 On wiping dust off the feet, see note at 9:3–5. On **the kingdom of God has come near**, see note at vv. 8–9.

10:12 That day is the day of judgment. **Sodom** was destroyed by the Lord because of its sin (Gn 19:23).

10:13–14 Chorazin and **Bethsaida** were towns in Galilee near Capernaum. **Tyre** and **Sidon** were Gentile cities in Phoenicia on the Mediterranean coast northwest of Galilee. **Sackcloth and ashes** were worn by those in mourning, sometimes as an expression of repentance from sin (Neh 9:1; Jnh 3:5).

10:15 Jesus spent more time in ministry in **Capernaum** than anywhere else in Galilee. Yet, in their arrogance (**exalted to heaven**), the people of this city rejected Jesus and, as a result of their unbelief, would be sent to **Hades** (death, the realm of death or punishment beyond the grave).

10:16 The principle here is that rejection of the disciples is ultimately rejection of God the Father (**the one who sent me**), for the Father sent the Son and the Son in turn sent out the seventy-two disciples to preach and heal (vv. 1,9). Since they were commissioned by Christ, to listen to the seventy-two was like listening to Jesus himself. Likewise, to reject the seventy-two was to reject Jesus. Finally, to reject Jesus was to reject God the Father.

10:17–20 Part of the healing that the seventy-two disciples performed (v. 9) included casting out demons. Some interpreters view the phrase **Satan fall from heaven** as an echo of Is 14:12. Though in context Isaiah

scorpions and over all the power of the enemy; nothing at all will harm you. ²⁰ However, don't rejoice that^ the spirits submit to you, but rejoice that your names are written in heaven."

The Son Reveals the Father

²¹ At that time he⁸ rejoiced in the Holy˂ Spirit and said, "I praise⁰ you, Father, Lord of heaven and earth, because you have hidden these things from the wise and intelligent and revealed them to infants. Yes, Father, because this was your good pleasure.ᴱ ²² All things haveᶠ been entrusted to me by my Father. No one knows who the Son is except the Father, and who the Father is except the Son, and anyone to whom the Son desiresᴳ to reveal him."

²³ Then turning to his disciples he said privately, "Blessed are the eyes that see the things you see! ²⁴ For I tell you that many prophets and kings wanted to see the things you see but didn't see them; to hear the things you hear but didn't hear them."

The Parable of the Good Samaritan

²⁵ Then an expert in the law stood up to test him, saying, "Teacher, what must I do to inherit eternal life?"
²⁶ "What is written in the law?" he asked him. "How do you read it?"
²⁷ He answered, "Love the Lord your God with all your heart, with all your soul, with all your strength, and with all your mind," and "your neighbor as yourself."ᴴ
²⁸ "You've answered correctly," he told him. "Do this and you will live."

²⁹ But wanting to justify himself, he asked Jesus, "And who is my neighbor?"

³⁰ Jesus took up the question and said, "A man was going down from Jerusalem to Jericho and fell into the hands of robbers. They stripped him, beat him up, and fled, leaving him half dead. ³¹ A priest happened to be going down that road. When he saw him, he passed by on the other side. ³² In the same way, a Levite, when he arrived at the place and saw him, passed by on the other side. ³³ But a Samaritan on his journey came up to him, and when he saw the man, he had compassion. ³⁴ He went over to him and bandaged his wounds, pouring on olive oil and wine. Then he put him on his own animal, brought him to an inn, and took care of him. ³⁵ The next day ' he took out two denarii,ᴶ gave them to the innkeeper, and said, 'Take care of him. When I come back I'll reimburse you for whatever extra you spend.'

³⁶ "Which of these three do you think proved to be a neighbor to the man who fell into the hands of the robbers?"

³⁷ "The one who showed mercy to him," he said.

Then Jesus told him, "Go and do the same."

---

^10:20 Lit *don't rejoice in this, that*   ᴮ10:21 Other mss read *Jesus*   ˂10:21 Other mss omit *Holy*   ᴰ10:21 Or *thank,* or *confess*   ᴱ10:21 Lit *was well-pleasing in your sight*   ᶠ10:22 Other mss read *And turning to the disciples, he said, "Everything has*   ᴳ10:22 Or *wills,* or *chooses*   ᴴ10:27 Lv 19:18; Dt 6:5   ᴵ10:35 Other mss add *as he was leaving*   ᴶ10:35 A denarius = one day's wage.

---

is pronouncing judgment upon Babylon, many have understood it as a description of Satan's original fall that the prophet has applied to Babylon. Thus the passage in Luke would be using the language of Satan's fall to speak of his further defeat through the disciples' ministry. Others do not interpret Is 14:12 as a reference to Satan but rather understand Jesus to be speaking metaphorically of the disciples' victory over Satan's power. Regardless, Jesus warns them that, as great as the power to cast out demons was, it was more significant that their names were written in the Lamb's book of life in heaven (Rv 13:8).
10:21–22 The mention of the **Holy Spirit** here is part of Luke's emphasis on the Spirit. The **wise** and **intelligent** people of the area had rejected the ministry of the seventy-two disciples, but the insignificant and children (**infants**) had accepted their message. This was part of the plan of God. In his **good pleasure** (see Eph 1:3–11), these things were hidden from some and revealed to others. It is impossible for spiritually dead humans to know God the **Father** or his **Son** unless the Son reveals both.
10:23–24 It was a truly **blessed** circumstance to see the ministry of Christ and even his delegated authority in healing and casting out demons. Peter stated that, beyond OT **prophets and kings**, even angels wanted to **see** and **hear** the things that Jesus was doing (see 1Pt 1:12).

10:25 Expert in the law refers to a scribe (11:45–46,52–53), many of whom were also Pharisees. The question asked was a standard one in Judaism and was intended to **test** Jesus. To **inherit eternal life** shows that many Jews thought their eternal destiny was based on their Jewish bloodline and their good deeds.
10:26–28 Jesus turned the tables on the scribe by asking him to answer his own question, then complimented the man on correctly citing Lv 19:18 and Dt 6:5. Jesus did not say that it is possible to earn eternal life by loving **God** and **your neighbor**. No human other than Jesus has been able to love perfectly in every situation. Since **heart . . . soul**, and **mind** are sometimes used interchangeably in Scripture, the terms here are not intended to speak of separate aspects of human existence. Rather, they describe the total person.
10:29 Having correctly answered the first question, this man asked for an important clarification. Certain kinds of neighbors are of course easy to love, while others, being argumentative or of different religious and moral persuasions, can be very hard to love. It seems that the man hoped Jesus would justify his bias against certain kinds of neighbors.
10:30–32 The road **from Jerusalem to Jericho**, a distance of seventeen miles with a descent of more than three thousand feet in elevation, was a dangerous route through

desert country. It had many places where **robbers** could lie in wait. It is possible that the **priest** and the **Levite . . . passed by on the other side** of the road because they thought the wounded man was dead and they would become ritually unclean by touching him, but it is more likely that they were afraid of being attacked by the same robbers or simply did not want to be bothered with the inconvenience of helping the man.
10:33–35 The Jews considered the Samaritans to be physical half-breeds who had intermarried with foreigners and who were guilty of false worship. For such a sworn enemy of the Jews to show **compassion** on an injured Jew and pay the expenses of his recuperation, while two Jewish religious officials did not, would deeply humiliate a Jew.
10:36–37 Now Jesus got back to the question with which this story began: Who is my neighbor? (see note at v. 29). His point was that the Samaritan **proved** he was a good **neighbor** by his gracious actions toward the man who had been attacked by robbers. It was impossible for the scribe to avoid acknowledging that it was the Samaritan who **showed mercy**. Jesus's reply to **go and do the same** emphasized that Jews should love their Samaritan neighbors even as the good Samaritan in the story had acted in love toward a Jew.

Martha and Mary

38 While they were traveling, he entered a village, and a woman named Martha welcomed him into her home.^A **39** She had a sister named Mary, who also sat at the Lord's^B feet and was listening to what he said.^C **40** But Martha was distracted by her many tasks, and she came up and asked, "Lord, don't you care that my sister has left me to serve alone? So tell her to give me a hand."^D

41 The Lord^E answered her, "Martha, Martha, you are worried and upset about many things, **42** but one thing is necessary.^F Mary has made the right choice,^G and it will not be taken away from her."

The Lord's Prayer

11 He was praying in a certain place, and when he finished, one of his disciples said to him, "Lord, teach us to pray, just as John also taught his disciples."

2 He said to them, "Whenever you pray, say,

Father,^H

your name be honored as holy.
Your kingdom come.'
3   Give us each day our daily bread.'
4   And forgive us our sins,
    for we ourselves also forgive everyone
    in debt to us.^K
    And do not bring us into temptation."^L

Ask, Search, Knock

5 He also said to them, "Suppose one of you^M has a friend and goes to him at midnight and says to him, 'Friend, lend me three loaves of bread, **6** because a friend of mine on a journey has come to me, and I don't have anything to offer him.' **7** Then he will answer from inside and say, 'Don't bother me! The door is already locked, and my children and I have gone to bed. I can't get up to give you anything.' **8** I tell you, even though he won't get up and give him anything because he is his friend, yet because of his friend's shameless boldness,^N he will get up and give him as much as he needs.

9 "So I say to you, ask, and it will be given to you. Seek, and you will find. Knock, and the door will be opened to you. **10** For everyone who asks receives, and the one who seeks finds, and to the one who knocks, the door will be opened. **11** What father among you, if his son^O asks for a fish, will give him a snake instead of a fish? **12** Or if he asks for an egg, will give him a scorpion? **13** If you then, who are evil, know how to give good gifts to your children, how much more will the heavenly Father give the Holy Spirit to those who ask him?"

A House Divided

14 Now he was driving out a demon that was mute. When the demon came out, the man who had been mute spoke, and the crowds were amazed. **15** But some of them said, "He drives out demons by Beelzebul, the ruler of the demons." **16** And others, as a test, were demanding of him a sign from heaven.

17 Knowing their thoughts, he told them, "Every kingdom divided against itself is headed

---

^A **10:38** Other mss omit *into her home*   ^B **10:39** Other mss read *at Jesus's*   ^C **10:39** Lit *to his word* or *message*   ^D **10:40** Or *tell her to help me*   ^E **10:41** Other mss read *Jesus*   ^F **10:42** Some mss read *few things are necessary*, or *only one*   ^G **10:42** Lit *has chosen the good part*, or *has chosen the better portion* ; = the right meal   ^H **11:2** Other mss read *Our Father in heaven*   ^I **11:2** Other mss add *Your will be done on earth as it is in heaven*   ^J **11:3** Or *our bread for tomorrow*   ^K **11:4** Or *everyone who wrongs us*   ^L **11:4** Other mss add *But deliver us from the evil one*   ^M **11:5** Lit *Who of you*   ^N **11:8** Or *persistence*   ^O **11:11** Other mss read *son asks for bread, would give him a stone? Or if he*

10:38–39 The **village** in v. 38 was Bethany, just over the Mount of Olives and two miles east of Jerusalem. **Martha** and **Mary** were the sisters of Lazarus, whom Jesus raised from the dead (Jn 11:1–44). **Sat at the Lord's feet** . . . **listening** was the posture of a committed disciple.
10:40–42 Martha was **distracted** from what should have been her highest priority—learning from Jesus. She was **worried and upset** about all the household chores that needed to be done and irritated with her sister Mary because it was the role of women to serve men in such a setting. Jesus indicated that Martha's exclusive focus should be the same as her sister's—discipleship, an eternally commendable choice (**it will not be taken away from her**).
11:1–4 This model prayer for Jesus's disciples is similar to the one in the Sermon on the Mount (Mt 6:9–13), but much shorter. Apparently, the **disciples** were motivated to learn to **pray** by both Jesus's example and that of John the Baptist and his disciples. It was unusual for Jews to refer to God as **Father**. Such an address would seem too personal and familiar. Even though Luke emphasized the offer of the kingdom of God (4:43) and

the nearness of the kingdom in Jesus's ministry (10:9,11), some aspects of the kingdom are still future (**your kingdom come**). All people are dependent on the Lord to meet their daily needs, as in **give us . . . our daily bread**. **In debt** refers to what is "owed" to us spiritually (i.e., having been sinned against). The phrase **do not bring us into temptation** is in contrast with Christ himself, who was led by the Holy Spirit to be tested by Satan (see note at 4:1–2). See also note on Mt 6:13.
11:5–8 The point of this story is that **shameless boldness** pays off. But, as with the story of the widow and the judge in 18:1–8, it must not be understood that God is like the hesitant homeowner in the story. If bold persistence is rewarded even by someone who is disposed against granting our request, how much more so will God, who cares about his children, delight in responding generously to our persistent prayers.
11:9–10 **Ask** . . . **seek** . . . **knock** refer to prayer and reflect the persistence theme emphasized in the story of vv. 5–8. The assurance that **everyone who asks receives** does not mean that every prayer is answered as we want it to be. Rather, it means that if we

persist in prayer, our prayers will eventually be answered according to God's best for us.
11:11–12 No human **father** who really loved his child would be so uncaring as to give him a **snake** in place of a **fish** or a **scorpion** in place of an **egg**.
11:13 The parallel passage in Mt 7:11 reads, "Give good things to those who ask him." If those good things are related to the **Holy Spirit**, the wording may be speaking of spiritual gifts (Rm 12; 1Co 12). This verse reflects Luke's emphasis on the Holy Spirit. Leading up to the day of Pentecost, the apostles and other believers waited in prayer (Ac 1:14) for the baptism of the Spirit to come. In that instance, **the heavenly Father** gave the Holy Spirit to those who asked him. See also note on Mt 7:11 regarding **you . . . who are evil**.
11:14–16 Instead of praising God for Jesus's healing of the **mute** demon-possessed man, some in the crowd accused him of casting out demons by the power of Satan. **Beelzebul**, the god worshiped by Philistines in Ekron, had become a nickname for Satan. Others were trying to trap Jesus by asking him to perform a miraculous **sign**.
11:17–20 A **kingdom** or **house** divided against itself is self-destructive. Jesus made

for destruction, and a house divided against itself falls. [18] If Satan also is divided against himself, how will his kingdom stand? For you say I drive out demons by Beelzebul. [19] And if I drive out demons by Beelzebul, by whom do your sons drive them out? For this reason they will be your judges. [20] If I drive out demons by the finger of God, then the kingdom of God has come upon you. [21] When a strong man, fully armed, guards his estate, his possessions are secure. [22] But when one stronger than he attacks and overpowers him, he takes from him all his weapons[A] he trusted in, and divides up his plunder. [23] Anyone who is not with me is against me, and anyone who does not gather with me scatters.

An Unclean Spirit's Return

[24] "When an unclean spirit comes out of a person, it roams through waterless places looking for rest, and not finding rest, it then[B] says, 'I'll go back to my house that I came from.' [25] Returning, it finds the house swept and put in order. [26] Then it goes and brings seven other spirits more evil than itself, and they enter and settle down there. As a result, that person's last condition is worse than the first."

True Blessedness

[27] As he was saying these things, a woman from the crowd raised her voice and said to him, "Blessed is the womb that bore you and the one who nursed you!"

[28] He said, "Rather, blessed are those who hear the word of God and keep it."

The Sign of Jonah

[29] As the crowds were increasing, he began saying, "This generation is an evil generation. It demands a sign, but no sign will be given to it except the sign of Jonah.[C] [30] For just as Jonah became a sign to the people of Nineveh, so also the Son of Man will be to this generation. [31] The queen of the south will rise up at the judgment with the men of this generation and condemn them, because she came from the ends of the earth to hear the wisdom of Solomon, and look — something greater than Solomon is here. [32] The men of Nineveh will stand up at the judgment with this generation and condemn it, because they repented at Jonah's preaching, and look — something greater than Jonah is here.

The Lamp of the Body

[33] "No one lights a lamp and puts it in the cellar or under a basket,[D] but on a lampstand, so that those who come in may see its light. [34] Your eye is the lamp of the body. When your eye is healthy, your whole body is also full of light. But when it is bad, your body is also full of darkness. [35] Take care, then, that the light in you is not darkness. [36] If, therefore, your whole body is full of light, with no part of it in darkness, it will be entirely illuminated, as when a lamp shines its light on you."

Religious Hypocrisy Denounced

[37] As he was speaking, a Pharisee asked him to dine with him. So he went in and reclined at the table. [38] When the Pharisee saw this, he was amazed that he did not first perform the ritual washing[E] before dinner. [39] But the Lord said

---

[A]11:22 Gk panoplia, the armor and weapons of a foot soldier; Eph 6:11,13   [B]11:24 Other mss omit then   [C]11:29 Other mss add the prophet   [D]11:33 Other mss omit or under a basket   [E]11:38 Lit he did not first wash

---

two key points in his defense: (1) It is nonsense to think that Satan would divide his own "house" by casting out his own **demons**, and (2) it is unlikely that Jewish exorcists were drawing on a different source of power than Jesus. Thus the best explanation of what happened was that Jesus drove out **demons by the finger of God** (God's power active in the world).
11:21–22 The **stronger** man can usually overpower the weaker man and disarm him. The implication is that Jesus, being stronger than Satan, was in the process of disarming him. **Divides up his plunder** may refer to the same thing as the giving of gifts related to Christ's victory in Eph 4:8.
11:23 This is the opposite principle from what is stated in 9:50. Since the context has to do with demonic activity and power, anyone who did not believe that Jesus cast out demons by the power of God was **against** Christ. **Anyone who does not gather with me scatters** is a reference to a shepherd gathering or scattering a flock of sheep. This could refer to either Israel or the church as a flock since Luke wrote his Gospel after the church's beginning.
11:24–26 These verses warn that the exorcism of a demon is incomplete unless Christ

enters by faith and indwells the person who is healed. Otherwise, there is nothing to prevent the demon and **seven other spirits** from reentering and possessing the person. In that case, this person's **last condition** is even **worse** than it was initially.
11:27–28 Jesus did not deny that his mother, Mary, was greatly **blessed**. Instead, he stated that a person who hears God's word and acts upon it in faith is even more blessed than anyone who has mere family ties to him (Rv 1:3).
11:29–32 There are two possible meanings of **the sign of Jonah.** (1) Since Jonah's preaching prompted repentance by **the people of Nineveh** (Jnh 3), such preaching was the only sign Israel would receive from Jesus, or (2) Jonah's three days and nights in the large fish (Jnh 1:17) was a foreshadowing of Jesus's death and resurrection, which was the sign that would be given to that **evil generation.** The queen of Sheba (**queen of the south**) responded to the wisdom of **Solomon**, which was not equal to the wisdom and salvation offered by Jesus, **the Son of Man.** If Nineveh repented at **Jonah's preaching,** how much more should the crowds repent at Jesus's preaching.
11:33–36 Jesus held forth the **light** of the gospel for all to see. Those who rejected

him and his message had **bad** spiritual eyes, which turned the light of Christ into **darkness.** But those who received Christ by faith were filled with light.
11:37–38 The **ritual washing** that took place before a meal was an ancient Jewish tradition, but it was not commanded in the Mosaic law (Mk 7:3).
11:39–41 Jesus declared that the problem of uncleanness on our **inside** is not taken care

#61 99 Essential Christian Truths

JESUS'S HUMANITY

In addition to being fully divine, Jesus is fully human. Not only does the Old Testament affirm that the promised one (Messiah) would be a man (Is 7:14; 9:6; Mc 5:3), but the New Testament also affirms that Jesus's earthly life bore all the marks of being a human. He experienced the circumstances common to living as a human being, such as hunger (Mt 4:2), thirst (Jn 19:28), weariness (Mt 8:24), sorrow (Jn 11:35), and pain (the crucifixion).

to him, "Now you Pharisees clean the outside of the cup and dish, but inside you are full of greed and evil. **40** Fools! Didn't he who made the outside make the inside too? **41** But give from what is within to the poor,^A and then everything is clean for you.

42 "But woe to you Pharisees! You give a tenth^B of mint, rue, and every kind of herb, and you bypass^C justice and love for God.^D These things you should have done without neglecting the others.

43 "Woe to you Pharisees! You love the front seat in the synagogues and greetings in the marketplaces.

44 "Woe to you!^E You are like unmarked graves; the people who walk over them don't know it."

45 One of the experts in the law answered him, "Teacher, when you say these things you insult us too."

46 Then he said, "Woe also to you experts in the law! You load people with burdens that are hard to carry, and yet you yourselves don't touch these burdens with one of your fingers.

47 "Woe to you! You build tombs^F for the prophets, and your fathers killed them. **48** Therefore, you are witnesses that you approve^G the deeds of your fathers, for they killed them, and you build their monuments."^H **49** Because of this, the wisdom of God said, 'I will send them prophets and apostles, and some of them they will kill and persecute,' **50** so that this generation may be held responsible for the blood of all the prophets shed since the foundation of the world^I— **51** from the blood of Abel to the blood of Zechariah, who perished between the altar and the sanctuary. "Yes, I tell you, this generation will be held responsible.^J

52 "Woe to you experts in the law! You have taken away the key to knowledge. You didn't go in yourselves, and you hindered those who were trying to go in."

53 When he left there,^K the scribes and the Pharisees began to oppose him fiercely and to cross-examine him about many things; **54** they were lying in wait for him to trap him in something he said.^L

Beware of Religious Hypocrisy

12 Meanwhile, a crowd of many thousands came together, so that they were trampling on one another. He began to say to his disciples first, "Be on your guard against the leaven^M of the Pharisees, which is hypocrisy. **2** There is nothing covered that won't be uncovered, nothing hidden that won't be made known. **3** Therefore, whatever you have said in the dark will be heard in the light, and what you have whispered in an ear in private rooms will be proclaimed on the housetops.

Fear God

4 "I say to you, my friends, don't fear those who kill the body, and after that can do nothing more. **5** But I will show you the one to fear: Fear him who has authority to throw people into hell after death. Yes, I say to you, this is the one to fear! **6** Aren't five sparrows sold for two pennies?^N Yet not one of them is forgotten in God's sight. **7** Indeed, the hairs of your head

---

^A **11:41** Or *But donate from the heart as charity* ^B **11:42** Or *a tithe* ^C **11:42** Or *neglect* ^D **11:42** Lit *the justice and the love of God* ^E **11:44** Other mss add *scribes and Pharisees, hypocrites!* ^F **11:47** Or *graves* ^G **11:48** Lit *witnesses and approve* ^H **11:48** Other mss omit *their monuments* ^I **11:50** Lit *so that the blood of all … world may be required of this generation* ^J **11:51** Lit *you, it will be required of this generation* ^K **11:53** Other mss read *And as he was saying these things to them* ^L **11:54** Other mss add *so that they might bring charges against him* ^M **12:1** Or *yeast* ^N **12:6** Lit *two assaria*; a small copper coin

---

of by cleansing our **outside** (hands, feet, etc.). The way to make sure everything is **clean** in God's eyes is to give freely from a heart devoted to God.

11:42–44 The first **woe** pronounced by Jesus on the **Pharisees** was not because they tithed everything but because they did not practice **justice and love**. The second woe was because they loved the spotlight, not the Lord. Regarding the third woe, if Jews walked over **unmarked graves**, they became defiled. Ironically, Jesus said that following the teachings of the Pharisees was like walking over an unmarked grave; you would become defiled without even knowing it. The teachings of the Pharisees seemed genuine and true, but in reality they were corrupted and misleading.

11:45–46 The scribe (expert **in the law**) standing by realized that the three woes Jesus had just pronounced against the Pharisees also reflected negatively on the scribes. So Jesus leveled an additional **woe** on the scribes. They burdened the average Jew with a **load** that they themselves did not carry. This could mean that the scribes were hypocritical in their keeping of the law or that

they had no compassion for the people who tried to live by their burdensome regulations. **11:47–48** Jesus's point in these verses is that the scribes and Pharisees were pleased to honor the **prophets** with **tombs**, now that the prophets were dead and silenced. The scribes and Pharisees were like their **fathers**, who **killed** God's prophets.

11:49–51 The Lord was not surprised when some of his **prophets and apostles** were persecuted or killed. Because of the presence of Jesus—who was far greater than prophets or apostles—that **generation** of Israel was held responsible (see the similar statement about Babylon the Great in Rv 18:20). The judgment for that responsibility was apparently the destruction of Jerusalem in AD 70. **Abel** was the victim of the first murder in Scripture (Gn 4:8), while Zechariah's murder is recorded in 2Ch 24:20–25. Since 2 Chronicles was the last book in the Hebrew Bible, that would make it the last murder in the Bible of Jesus's day.

11:52 In Mt 23:13, Jesus accused the scribes (**experts in the law**) of locking up "the kingdom of heaven." Here in Luke, **the key to knowledge** is the Scriptures, which the

scribes and Pharisees mishandled. Thus the people were locked out from understanding the things of God.

11:53–54 The **Pharisees** and **scribes** reacted with accusations and hostile questions. Their intent was to **trap** Jesus by some statement for which he could be arrested.

12:1–3 In the NT, **leaven** is normally a symbol of corruption or evil (Mt 16:6,11; 1Co 5:6–8; Gl 5:9). Here the symbol is defined as the evil of **hypocrisy**. Hypocritical behavior fools many people, but it will eventually be **uncovered** and **made known** by God, who is never fooled. Everything said in **private** will become public knowledge.

12:4–5 There are many people who can **kill** you physically, but that is the limit of the harm they can do. As natural as it is to **fear** such people, it makes more sense to fear God, for he presides over not just life and death but eternity. Those who remain opposed to him by their unbelief and unrepentant sins will be punished in **hell**.

12:6–7 If God does not overlook even the most insignificant birds (**sparrows**), he is aware of all the details of life (**the hairs of your head**) of every human being.

are all counted. Don't be afraid; you are worth more than many sparrows.

Acknowledging Christ

8 "And I say to you, anyone who acknowledges me before others, the Son of Man will also acknowledge him before the angels of God, 9 but whoever denies me before others will be denied before the angels of God. 10 Anyone who speaks a word against the Son of Man will be forgiven, but the one who blasphemes against the Holy Spirit will not be forgiven. 11 Whenever they bring you before synagogues and rulers and authorities, don't worry about how you should defend yourselves or what you should say. 12 For the Holy Spirit will teach you at that very hour what must be said."

The Parable of the Rich Fool

13 Someone from the crowd said to him, "Teacher, tell my brother to divide the inheritance with me."

14 "Friend," ^ he said to him, "who appointed me a judge or arbitrator over you? " 15 He then told them, "Watch out and be on guard against all greed, because one's life is not in the abundance of his possessions."

16 Then he told them a parable: "A rich man's land was very productive. 17 He thought to himself, 'What should I do, since I don't have anywhere to store my crops? 18 I will do this,' he said. 'I'll tear down my barns and build bigger ones and store all my grain and my goods there. 19 Then I'll say to myself, "You have many goods stored up for many years. Take it easy; eat, drink, and enjoy yourself." '

20 "But God said to him, 'You fool! This very night your life is demanded of you. And the things you have prepared—whose will they be?'

21 "That's how it is with the one who stores up treasure for himself and is not rich toward God."

The Cure for Anxiety

22 Then he said to his disciples, "Therefore I tell you, don't worry about your life, what you will eat; or about the body, what you will wear. 23 For life is more than food and the body more than clothing. 24 Consider the ravens: They don't sow or reap; they don't have a storeroom or a barn; yet God feeds them. Aren't you worth much more than the birds? 25 Can any of you add one moment to his life span B by worrying? 26 If then you're not able to do even a little thing, why worry about the rest?

27 "Consider how the wildflowers grow: They don't labor or spin thread. Yet I tell you, not even Solomon in all his splendor was adorned like one of these. 28 If that's how God clothes the grass, which is in the field today and is thrown into the furnace tomorrow, how much more will he do for you — you of little faith? 29 Don't strive for what you should eat and what you should drink, and don't be anxious. 30 For the Gentile world eagerly seeks all these things, and your Father knows that you need them. 31 "But seek his kingdom, and these things will be provided for you. 32 Don't be afraid, little flock, because your Father delights to give you the kingdom. 33 Sell your possessions and give to the poor. Make money-bags for yourselves that won't grow old, an inexhaustible treasure in heaven, where no thief comes near and no moth destroys. 34 For where your treasure is, there your heart will be also.

Ready for the Master's Return

35 "Be ready for service c and have your lamps lit. 36 You are to be like people waiting for their

---

^12:14 Lit Man   B 12:25 Or add a cubit to his height   c 12:35 Lit "Let your loins be girded; an idiom for tying up loose outer clothing in preparation for action; Ex 12:11

12:8–9 These verses add a positive element to Jesus's statement in 9:26. There, if a person is "ashamed" of Jesus (here it is **denies me before others**), he will face shame when Christ comes in judgment. Here, it is also stated that if a person **acknowledges** Christ, he will do likewise in heaven (in the presence of **the angels of God**).

12:10 Apparently, speaking against Jesus could be forgiven because of his human appearance (one aspect of the meaning of **Son of Man**). According to the parallel passage in Mk 3:28–30, blasphemy **against the Holy Spirit** is to attribute to Satan the works of the Spirit. That is the unforgivable sin.

12:11–12 These verses speak of the persecution the apostles would face at the hands of **rulers and authorities**. Classic examples where the **Holy Spirit** did teach them **what must be said** are in Ac 4:8–12; 5:29–32.

12:13–15 Disputes over family **inheritance** were normally handled by rabbis (teachers) in Jewish society, and Jesus was recognized as such. The person who approached Jesus was probably a younger brother who was upset because his older brother received twice the

inheritance, the Jewish tradition. Jesus refused to be drawn into the matter, realizing that the man's motivation was **greed**.

12:16–20 This parable is about the danger of greed, measured by the abundance of possessions (v. 15). The rich man was infatuated with hoarding his **goods**. In his self-centered perspective (there are at least ten self-references in vv. 17–19), he thought this was an effective strategy for a long life of leisure and pleasure. But God views such an outlook as foolish and shortsighted. When a person dies—which could be at any time—"you can't take it with you."

12:21 **Rich toward God** is what v. 33 and Mt 6:20 refer to as "treasures in heaven." Being "rich toward God" means living to glorify God and investing our earthly assets to make an eternal difference.

12:22–26 Jesus's advice to his disciples was not to be overcome with anxiety over the basic needs of life. Worrying won't change **even a little thing**. Since God feeds **the ravens**, who have no storeroom, will he not care for humans, his most valuable and beloved creatures?

12:27–32 If God "dresses" (**clothes**) nature so beautifully, he will certainly meet a disciple's basic needs. Unbelievers (the unsaved **Gentile world**) pursue provision and wealth as if life were all about these things and as if God is unconcerned about their needs, but this is not to be the focus of the Christian. In the parallel passage in Mt 6:33, Jesus declared, "Seek first the kingdom of God and his righteousness." Thus at least a key part of seeking God's **kingdom** for the believer is to strive to live by his standards. In regard to other benefits of the kingdom, believers can rest assured that the Father will give them to his children with joy.

12:33–34 When disciples are living for God's glory and his kingdom (v. 31), they will choose priorities in this life that are designed to reap **inexhaustible** heavenly dividends. These become the **treasure** of one's **heart**. Wealth on this earth can be stolen or destroyed, but heavenly treasures are eternally secure.

12:35–40 The point of this story is that we must practice constant readiness. **Waiting** for the **master to return** means waiting for master to return from the wedding banquet so that when he comes and knocks, they can open the door for him at once. **37** Blessed will be those servants the master finds alert when he comes. Truly I tell you, he will get ready,^ have them recline at the table, then come and serve them. **38** If he comes in the middle of the night, or even near dawn,^ and finds them alert, blessed are those servants. **39** But know this: If the homeowner had known at what hour the thief was coming, he would not have let his house be broken into. **40** You also be ready, because the Son of Man is coming at an hour you do not expect."

Rewards and Punishment

41 "Lord," Peter asked, "are you telling this parable to us or to everyone?"

42 The Lord said, "Who then is the faithful and sensible manager his master will put in charge of his household servants to give them their allotted food at the proper time? **43** Blessed is that servant whom the master finds doing his job when he comes. **44** Truly I tell you, he will put him in charge of all his possessions. **45** But if that servant says in his heart, 'My master is delaying his coming,' and starts to beat the male and female servants, and to eat and drink and get drunk, **46** that servant's master will come on a day he does not expect him and at an hour he does not know. He will cut him to pieces^ and assign him a place with the unfaithful.^ **47** And that servant who knew his master's will and didn't prepare himself or do it^ will be severely beaten. **48** But the one who did not know and did what deserved punishment will receive a light beating. From everyone who has been given much, much will be required; and from the one who has been entrusted with much, even more will be expected.^

Not Peace but Division

49 "I came to bring fire on the earth, and how I wish it were already set ablaze! **50** But I have a baptism to undergo, and how it consumes me until it is finished! **51** Do you think that I came here to bring peace on the earth? No, I tell you, but rather division. **52** From now on, five in one household will be divided: three against two, and two against three.

53 They will be divided, father
  against son,
son against father,
mother against daughter,
daughter against mother,
mother-in-law against
  her daughter-in-law,
and daughter-in-law
  against mother-in-law."^

Interpreting the Time

54 He also said to the crowds, "When you see a cloud rising in the west, right away you say, 'A storm is coming,' and so it does. **55** And when the south wind is blowing, you say, 'It's going to be hot,' and it is. **56** Hypocrites! You know how to interpret the appearance of the earth and the sky, but why don't you know how to interpret this present time?

Settling Accounts

57 "Why don't you judge for yourselves what is right? **58** As you are going with your adversary to the ruler, make an effort to settle with him on the way. Then he won't drag you before the judge, the judge hand you over to the bailiff, and the bailiff throw you into prison. **59** I tell you, you will never get out of there until you have paid the last penny."^

Repent or Perish

13 At that time, some people came and reported to him about the Galileans whose blood Pilate had mixed with their sacrifices. **2** And he^ responded to them, "Do you think that these Galileans were more sinful than all the other Galileans because they suffered these things? **3** No, I tell you; but unless you repent, you will all perish as well. **4** Or those eighteen

^**12:37** Lit *will gird himself* ^**12:38** Lit *even in the second or third watch* ^**12:46** Lit *him in two* ^**12:46** Or *unbelievers* ^**12:47** Lit *or do toward his will*, ^**12:48** Or *much* ^**12:53** Mc 7:6 ^**12:59** Gk *lepton*, the smallest and least valuable copper coin in use ^**13:2** Other mss read *Jesus*

Christ's second coming. It is not known when the return will take place, so it is necessary to be constantly vigilant. If a **thief** can come unexpectedly, how much more can the coming of Christ catch his servants by surprise? **12:41–44** Jesus previously told his disciples that his parables held secrets that were only for his followers (see note at 8:9–10). Jesus did not answer Peter's question directly. Instead, he told another story about a **master** and his **manager**. The story in vv. 35–40 emphasized that the master's servant should be watching, but this story made it clear that the servant must also be working. Disciples who persevere in faithfulness will be rewarded by the master. **12:45–48** If a **servant** of the **master** does not faithfully watch and work, there will be severe consequences when the master

comes. The reason for the difference in punishments is the principle of accountable stewardship. More is expected of those who have been **given much**. **12:49–50** Fire in these verses symbolizes judgment on **the earth** at the second coming of Christ. **A baptism to undergo** refers to the suffering of Christ, specifically his agony on the cross (Mk 10:38). **Consumes** expresses how focused Jesus was on completing his mission. **It is finished** are the words Jesus used on the cross to signal that redemption was accomplished (Jn 19:30). **12:51–53** Jesus Christ made **peace** with God possible for anyone who will choose to follow as his disciple (Rm 5:1). Unbelievers, however, remain at odds with God and his requirements for holiness. There will be such division over the gospel of Christ that some

families will be split down the middle. The spiritual family of God is more important than family bloodlines. **12:54–56** Storms in Palestine usually blow in from the **west**, off the Mediterranean Sea, or from the deserts to the south. A **cloud** coming from the west usually brought rain or a **storm**, while a **south wind** was dry and hot. In this context, **interpret** means "to discern." **Time** refers to "the opportune moment," in this case the presence of Messiah in their midst. **12:57–59** The need to **settle** accounts before undergoing judicial punishment pictures the need to be reconciled to God (Rm 5:10) before facing his judgment. At that point, it will be too late to seek reconciliation. **13:1–5** It is not known why Pontius **Pilate** (see note at 3:1) killed the **Galileans**

that the tower in Siloam fell on and killed — do you think they were more sinful than all the other people who live in Jerusalem? **⁵** No, I tell you; but unless you repent, you will all perish as well."

The Parable of the Barren Fig Tree

⁶ And he told this parable: "A man had a fig tree that was planted in his vineyard. He came looking for fruit on it and found none. **⁷** He told the vineyard worker, 'Listen, for three years I have come looking for fruit on this fig tree and haven't found any. Cut it down! Why should it even waste the soil?'

⁸ "But he replied to him, 'Sir,^ leave it this year also, until I dig around it and fertilize it. **⁹** Perhaps it will produce fruit next year, but if not, you can cut it down.'"

Healing a Daughter of Abraham

¹⁰ As he was teaching in one of the synagogues on the Sabbath, **¹¹** a woman was there who had been disabled by a spirit⁸ for over eighteen years. She was bent over and could not straighten up at all.^ **¹²** When Jesus saw her, he called out to her,^ "Woman, you are free of your disability." **¹³** Then he laid his hands on her, and instantly she was restored and began to glorify God.

¹⁴ But the leader of the synagogue, indignant because Jesus had healed on the Sabbath, responded by telling the crowd, "There are six days when work should be done; therefore come on those days and be healed and not on the Sabbath day."

¹⁵ But the Lord answered him and said, "Hypocrites! Doesn't each one of you untie his ox or donkey from the feeding trough on the Sabbath and lead it to water? **¹⁶** Satan has bound this woman, a daughter of Abraham, for eighteen years — shouldn't she be untied from this bondage^ on the Sabbath day?"

¹⁷ When he had said these things, all his adversaries were humiliated, but the whole crowd was rejoicing over all the glorious things he was doing.

The Parables of the Mustard Seed and of the Leaven

¹⁸ He said, therefore, "What is the kingdom of God like, and what can I compare it to? **¹⁹** It's like a mustard seed that a man took and sowed in his garden. It grew and became a tree, and the birds of the sky nested in its branches."

²⁰ Again he said, "What can I compare the kingdom of God to? **²¹** It's like leaven^ that a woman took and mixed into fifty pounds^ of flour until all of it was leavened."

The Narrow Way

²² He went through one town and village after another, teaching and making his way to Jerusalem. **²³** "Lord," someone asked him, "are only a few people going to be saved?"

He said to them, **²⁴** "Make every effort to enter through the narrow door, because I tell you, many will try to enter and won't be able **²⁵** once the homeowner gets up and shuts the door. Then you will stand outside and knock on the

^13:8 Or *Lord*   ^13:11 Lit *had a spirit of disability*   ^13:11 Or *straighten up completely*   ^13:12 Or *he summoned her*   ^13:16 Or *isn't it necessary that she be untied from this bondage*   ^13:21 Or *yeast*   ^13:21 Lit *three sata*; about forty liters

mentioned here. The mention of **their sacrifices** specifies that their deaths took place in the temple area, probably in relation to a major religious festival, when all Jewish men were required to make a pilgrimage to Jerusalem. Nor is anything else known about the **eighteen people** killed by the collapse of the **tower in Siloam** in the southeastern part of Jerusalem. Jesus's questions about the sinfulness of the Galileans and those killed by the tower was apparently inspired by widespread opinion that such things happen only as punishment for specific sins. Jesus countered this notion but nevertheless emphasized that every person must **repent** (see note at 3:2–3) or else perish spiritually for eternity.
13:6–9 The **fig tree** is often used as a symbol for the nation of Israel (Mt 24:32–33; Mk 11:12–14). Though young fig trees are slow to begin bearing fruit, three years was a sufficient length of time for trees to become mature and thus fruitful. The extra **year** requested by the vineyard worker represented one final chance for the trees to become fruitful. Otherwise they would be **cut . . . down**. This parable thus referred to Israel's last chance before judgment. If they rejected Jesus's message and miracles, the time for patience would be ended. But a future hope for Israel remains (Rm 11).
13:10–13 The mention of the **Sabbath** as the time of this healing calls to mind the

earlier controversy between Jesus and the religious leaders (6:1–11). The woman he healed had severe curvature of the spine, caused somehow by a demon (an evil **spirit**). The healing involved two acts: (1) the casting out of the demon, and (2) the straightening of the spine. This verse does not imply that deformities or illnesses are commonly caused by demons. This was apparently a very rare case, reflective of the heightened spiritual warfare during the time of Christ's earthly stay.
13:14–16 The **leader of the synagogue** rejected the healing as it was **work** done in violation of **the Sabbath day** (see note at Ex 20:8–11). Jesus's use of the plural **hypocrites** shows that he knew the leader spoke for many others who shared his view. He revealed their hypocrisy by showing that it was necessary for everyone to do some work on the Sabbath, notably related to the tending of farm animals. Should not a Jewish woman (**daughter of Abraham**) under bondage to Satan for such a long time also be **untied** on the Sabbath?
13:17 Those who had sided with the leader of the synagogue were **humiliated** because it made them look as if they had more compassion for animals than for a demonized, disfigured woman.
13:18–21 Both of these parables allude to the astonishing advancement of **the kingdom**

of God (God's rule in this world) that Jesus initiated. The first story focused on the kingdom's small beginning (**like a mustard seed**, which was proverbially considered the smallest seed in the ancient world) and dramatic spread (**a tree . . . its branches**) through Jesus's ministry. The second parable reinforced the first, with the implication that the kingdom of God would eventually permeate the entire earth much like leaven can spread through even **fifty pounds of flour**. While it is true that **leaven** often symbolizes evil in the Bible (1Co 5:6), this passage is a clear exception. Here leaven is used positively and calls to mind the potency of Jesus's message and works on behalf of humanity.
13:22–23 Luke structures his Gospel in a way that emphasizes that Jesus was **making his way to Jerusalem** in order to die on the cross. The question **are only a few people going to be saved?** may reflect two important realities about Jesus's ministry: (1) Many of his teachings insisted that true discipleship comes with many difficult challenges, and (2) though large crowds came to hear Jesus in every **town and village**, there were relatively few who authentically followed him as disciples.
13:24–27 Jesus's story here answered the question in v. 23 about why so few people were being saved. It is because they were not entering by **the narrow door** (faith in Jesus)

door, saying, 'Lord, open up for us!' He will answer you, 'I don't know you or where you're from.' [26] Then you will say, 'We ate and drank in your presence, and you taught in our streets.' [27] But he will say, 'I tell you, I don't know you or where you're from. Get away from me, all you evildoers!' [28] There will be weeping and gnashing of teeth in that place, when you see Abraham, Isaac, Jacob, and all the prophets in the kingdom of God, but yourselves thrown out. [29] They will come from east and west, from north and south, to share the banquet[A] in the kingdom of God. [30] Note this: Some who are last will be first, and some who are first will be last."

Jesus and Herod Antipas

[31] At that time some Pharisees came and told him, "Go, get out of here. Herod wants to kill you."

[32] He said to them, "Go tell that fox, 'Look, I'm driving out demons and performing healings today and tomorrow, and on the third day I will complete my work.'[B] [33] Yet it is necessary that I travel today, tomorrow, and the next day, because it is not possible for a prophet to perish outside of Jerusalem.

Jesus's Lamentation over Jerusalem

[34] "Jerusalem, Jerusalem, who kills the prophets and stones those who are sent to her. How often I wanted to gather your children together, as a hen gathers her chicks under her wings, but you were not willing! [35] See, your house is abandoned to you. I tell you, you will not see me until the time comes when[C] you say, 'Blessed is he who comes in the name of the Lord'! "[D]

A Sabbath Controversy

14 One Sabbath, when he went in to eat[E] at the house of one of the leading Pharisees, they were watching him closely. [2] There in front of him was a man whose body was swollen with fluid. [3] In response, Jesus asked the law experts and the Pharisees, "Is it lawful to heal on the Sabbath or not?" [4] But they kept silent. He took the man, healed him, and sent him away. [5] And to them, he said, "Which of you whose son or ox falls into a well, will not immediately pull him out on the Sabbath day?" [6] They could find no answer to these things.

Teachings on Humility

[7] He told a parable to those who were invited, when he noticed how they would choose the best places for themselves: [8] "When you are invited by someone to a wedding banquet, don't sit in the place of honor, because a more distinguished person than you may have been invited by your host. [9] The one who invited both of you may come and say to you, 'Give your place to this man,' and then in humiliation, you will proceed to take the lowest place.

[10] "But when you are invited, go and sit in the lowest place, so that when the one who invited you comes, he will say to you, 'Friend, move up higher.' You will then be honored in the presence of all the other guests. [11] For everyone who exalts himself will be humbled, and the one who humbles himself will be exalted."

[A]13:29 Lit *recline at the table*   [B]13:32 Lit *I will be finished*   [C]13:35 Other mss omit *the time comes when*   [D]13:35 Ps 118:26   [E]14:1 Lit *eat bread*

---

while the Lord gave them opportunity (in this case, while Jesus was present, preaching the gospel). Unbelievers may appeal that they knew Jesus in his social life (**we ate and drank**) and public ministry (**you taught in our streets**), but they don't know the Lord personally as Savior (**I don't know you or where you're from**). Because they had not been justified (declared righteous) through faith in Christ (Rm 5:1), they were ultimately **evildoers**.
13:28–29 An irony of eternal life in the **kingdom of God** is that many Jews, though they were the original people of God's covenant, will be excluded due to their unbelief, while many believing Gentiles will **share the banquet** in full fellowship because they have accepted God's offer of reconciliation in Jesus. There will be much anguish (**weeping and gnashing of teeth**) among excluded Jews.
13:30 The kingdom of God reverses many of the world's values. In the present context, the inversion apparently refers to the fact that believing Gentiles, though they were historically not part of God's covenant people Israel, became the first to receive the Messiah *en masse*. By contrast, the Jews were chronologically **first** in God's plan, but they became spiritually **last** since the bulk of their numbers rejected Christ. Jews

will receive Jesus widely near the end of the age (Rm 11:25–27).
13:31–34 Jesus seemed to take the warning of these **Pharisees** at face value, though it is doubtful that they really wished to protect Jesus from **Herod** Antipas (see note at 3:1). Most likely they simply wanted him to leave their region. Though v. 32 makes it seem that Jesus stayed put for three days more, the subsequent mention of **travel** to **Jerusalem** in order to die there makes it likely that this verse was a veiled reference to his coming resurrection. The mention of Jerusalem and his coming death as a prophet allowed Jesus to review the city's history of killing the **prophets** whom God **sent to her**. Jerusalem had repeatedly rejected God's compassionate outreach (pictured as a mother **hen** gathering her **chicks**). The city would soon do the same thing again by rejecting Jesus, God's Son.
13:35 Your house is abandoned reveals that God's blessing and protection would be removed, leading ultimately to judgment in the destruction of Jerusalem by the Romans in AD 70. **Blessed is he who comes in the name of the Lord** is from Ps 118:26 and was later cited in regard to Jesus's "triumphal entry" (see note at Lk 19:37–38). However, here it looks beyond that to the second coming of Christ (see Zch 12:10; Rv 1:7).

14:1–4 These verses continue the theme (see 6:1–11) of the Pharisees seeking to trap Jesus. **Swollen with fluid** describes a condition known as "dropsy," the major symptom of which was swollen limbs. Jesus performed five miracles on the Sabbath in Luke (vv. 1–4; 4:31,38; 6:6; 13:10,14). The probable reason the scribes (**law experts**) and Pharisees refused to answer Jesus's question about whether it was **lawful to heal on the Sabbath** was that others had been humiliated previously when they tried to debate Jesus on this topic (see note at 13:17).
14:5–6 The commandment not to work on **the Sabbath day** (Dt 5:12–14) should not have been taken to mean that rescue efforts (for people or animals) were forbidden on the Sabbath.
14:7–10 The **place of honor** at a dinner was next to the host. Jesus's parable made the point that the danger of arrogantly taking the best place at a banquet was that the person who invited you—here representing God—could ask you to move to the **lowest place** at the banquet table, causing humiliation rather than honor. It was wiser to sit in the seat of the humble and then be asked to **move up** to a seat of higher honor.
14:11 The principle that arrogance leads to humiliation appears repeatedly in the OT Wisdom Literature, especially Proverbs. That

¹² He also said to the one who had invited him, "When you give a lunch or a dinner, don't invite your friends, your brothers or sisters, your relatives, or your rich neighbors, because they might invite you back, and you would be repaid. ¹³ On the contrary, when you host a banquet, invite those who are poor, maimed, lame, or blind. ¹⁴ And you will be blessed, because they cannot repay you; for you will be repaid at the resurrection of the righteous."

The Parable of the Large Banquet

¹⁵ When one of those who reclined at the table with him heard these things, he said to him, "Blessed is the one who will eat bread in the kingdom of God!"

¹⁶ Then he told him, "A man was giving a large banquet and invited many. ¹⁷ At the time of the banquet, he sent his servant to tell those who were invited, 'Come, because everything is now ready.'

¹⁸ "But without exception^A they all began to make excuses. The first one said to him, 'I have bought a field, and I must go out and see it. I ask you to excuse me.'

¹⁹ "Another said, 'I have bought five yoke of oxen, and I'm going to try them out. I ask you to excuse me.'

²⁰ "And another said, 'I just got married, and therefore I'm unable to come.'

²¹ "So the servant came back and reported these things to his master. Then in anger, the master of the house told his servant, 'Go out quickly into the streets and alleys of the city, and bring in here the poor, maimed, blind, and lame.'

²² " 'Master,' the servant said, 'what you ordered has been done, and there's still room.'

²³ "Then the master told the servant, 'Go out into the highways and hedges and make them come in, so that my house may be filled. ²⁴ For I tell you, not one of those people who were invited will enjoy my banquet.' "

The Cost of Following Jesus

²⁵ Now great crowds were traveling with him. So he turned and said to them, ²⁶ "If anyone comes to me and does not hate his own father and mother, wife and children, brothers and sisters — yes, and even his own life — he cannot be my disciple. ²⁷ Whoever does not bear his own cross and come after me cannot be my disciple. ²⁸ "For which of you, wanting to build a tower, doesn't first sit down and calculate the cost to see if he has enough to complete it? ²⁹ Otherwise, after he has laid the foundation and cannot finish it, all the onlookers will begin to ridicule him, ³⁰ saying, 'This man started to build and wasn't able to finish.'

³¹ "Or what king, going to war against another king, will not first sit down and decide if he is able with ten thousand to oppose the one who comes against him with twenty thousand? ³² If not, while the other is still far off, he sends a delegation and asks for terms of peace. ³³ In the same way, therefore, every one of you who does not renounce^B all his possessions cannot be my disciple.

³⁴ "Now, salt is good, but if salt should lose its taste, how will it be made salty? ³⁵ It isn't fit for the soil or for the manure pile; they throw it out. Let anyone who has ears to hear listen."

The Parable of the Lost Sheep

15 All the tax collectors and sinners were approaching to listen to him. ² And the Pharisees and scribes were complaining, "This man welcomes sinners and eats with them."

³ So he told them this parable: ⁴ "What man among you, who has a hundred sheep and loses one of them, does not leave the ninety-nine in

---

^A14:18 Lit "And from one (voice)   ^B14:33 Or leave

humility can lead to exaltation is a common theme in the NT (18:14; Jms 4:10; 1Pt 5:6).
14:12–14 True hospitality (hosting a dinner or a banquet) will be **blessed** by the Lord if you invite those who cannot return the favor. The **resurrection of the righteous** is the positive side of the resurrection mentioned in Dn 12:2 and Jn 5:28–29. It is probably the same thing as "the first resurrection" mentioned in Rv 20:5–6.
14:15 The statement about being blessed to **eat bread** in the coming **kingdom of God** is true. However, the person who said this probably assumed (wrongly) that many at the table in the Pharisee's home (v. 1) would experience this blessing. The story Jesus told next (vv. 16–24) reflected a different reality.
14:16–20 This story symbolizes being **invited** to the messianic **banquet** in the future kingdom of God (v. 15). Those who were initially invited (the religious leaders of the Jewish people) all made excuses about why they could not attend.

14:21–24 After being rejected by those who symbolized the religious leaders, the unfortunate ones to whom Jesus came to minister (Is 61:1) were invited. However, there was **still room** for others. So a wider group (those from **the highways and hedges**) was also invited. These stand for Gentiles. Non-Jewish participation in the gospel is a common theme in Luke's Gospel.
14:25–26 Hate his own here hyperbolically expresses the same principle found in Mt 10:37, where Jesus says, "The one who loves a father or mother more than me is not worthy of me." Both Luke and Matthew convey the same point. Disciples must love Jesus more than they love their own family members.
14:27 On bearing a **cross**, see note at 9:23.
14:28–32 It is necessary to **calculate the cost** to be a disciple of Christ. Like a person who does not foresee the full cost of building **a tower** and suffers ridicule for starting something he cannot finish, a disciple must understand what it will take to complete the Christian life before he makes

the commitment. Similarly, a **king** must soberly consider the odds before deciding between war and peace.
14:33 The essence of being a disciple of Christ is unreserved commitment to him. This involves holding loosely the material things of this world.
14:34–35 Most **salt** of the ancient world was impure and lost its **taste** easily, making it unfit to use even as fertilizer or as a catalyst for burning **manure**. The danger for a person who lets his witness become "unsalty" is that he may be discarded from the Lord's service. On **ears to hear**, see note at 8:4–8.
15:1–2 On **tax collectors** and **sinners**, see note at 5:29–30. Then and now, to share a meal with someone typically indicates that you accept them.
15:3–7 Though it might be considered reckless to leave a flock of **ninety-nine** sheep to search for **the lost one**, Jesus's story emphasizes how much God cares for every lost **sinner** and how **joyfully** he responds when each one is found.

the open field^ and go after the lost one until he finds it? ⁵ When he has found it, he joyfully puts it on his shoulders, ⁶ and coming home, he calls his friends and neighbors together, saying to them, 'Rejoice with me, because I have found my lost sheep!' ⁷ I tell you, in the same way, there will be more joy in heaven over one sinner who repents than over ninety-nine righteous people who don't need repentance.

The Parable of the Lost Coin

⁸ "Or what woman who has ten silver coins, ᴮ·ᶜ if she loses one coin, does not light a lamp, sweep the house, and search carefully until she finds it? ⁹ When she finds it, she calls her friends and neighbors together, saying, 'Rejoice with me, because I have found the silver coin I lost!' ¹⁰ I tell you, in the same way, there is joy in the presence of God's angels over one sinner who repents."

The Parable of the Lost Son

¹¹ He also said, "A man had two sons. ¹² The younger of them said to his father, 'Father, give me the share of the estate I have coming to me.' So he distributed the assetsᴰ to them. ¹³ Not many days later, the younger son gathered together all he had and traveled to a distant country, where he squandered his estate in foolish living. ¹⁴ After he had spent everything, a severe famine struck that country, and he had nothing.ᴱ ¹⁵ Then he went to work for one of the citizens of that country, who sent him into his fields to feed pigs. ¹⁶ He longed to eat his fill fromᶠ the pods that the pigs were eating, but no one would give him anything. ¹⁷ When he came to his senses,ᴳ he said, 'How many of my

father's hired workers have more than enough food, and here I am dying of hunger!ᴴ ¹⁸ I'll get up, go to my father, and say to him, "Father, I have sinned against heaven and in your sight. ¹⁹ I'm no longer worthy to be called your son. Make me like one of your hired workers."' ²⁰ So he got up and went to his father. But while the son was still a long way off, his father saw him and was filled with compassion. He ran, threw his arms around his neck, and kissed him. ²¹ The son said to him, 'Father, I have sinned against heaven and in your sight. I'm no longer worthy to be called your son.'

²² "But the father told his servants, 'Quick! Bring out the best robe and put it on him; put a ring on his finger and sandals on his feet. ²³ Then bring the fattened calf and slaughter it, and let's celebrate with a feast, ²⁴ because this son of mine was dead and is alive again; he was lost and is found!' So they began to celebrate.

²⁵ "Now his older son was in the field; as he came near the house, he heard music and dancing. ²⁶ So he summoned one of the servants, questioning what these things meant. ²⁷ 'Your brother is here,' he told him, 'and your father has slaughtered the fattened calf because he has him back safe and sound.'

²⁸ "Then he became angry and didn't want to go in. So his father came out and pleaded with him. ²⁹ But he replied to his father, 'Look, I have been slaving many years for you, and I have never disobeyed your orders, yet you never gave me a goat so that I could celebrate with my friends. ³⁰ But when this son of yours came, who has devoured your assetsᴶ with prostitutes, you slaughtered the fattened calf for him.'

^15:4 Or *the wilderness* ᴮ15:8 Gk *ten drachmas* ᶜ15:8 A Gk drachma was equivalent to a Roman denarius = one day's wage ᴰ15:12 Or *life*, or *livelihood*, also in v. 30 ᴱ15:14 Lit *and he began to be in need* ᶠ15:16 Other mss read *to fill his stomach with* ᴳ15:17 Lit *to himself* ᴴ15:17 Or *dying in the famine*; v. 14 ᴶ15:27 Lit *him back healthy* ᴶ15:30 Or *life*, or *livelihood*

15:8–10 To search for a lost **coin** (Gk *drachma*; worth about a day's wage for the average worker) indoors required lighting **a lamp** since very few homes had windows. This search also required sweeping **the house** because the floor was earthen. **Joy in the presence of God's angels** speaks of God's joy over a repentant sinner.
15:11–12 Although this well-known parable (vv. 11–32) is usually called the parable of the

prodigal son, the other son and the father are also important characters. It was unusual, but not unheard of, for a father to settle his **estate** before his death. Since the older son got a double portion of his father's estate, the younger son's share (**share . . . I have coming to me**) would have been one-third of the estate.
15:13–16 The younger son had no intention of returning to his family. It is impossible to know whether his **foolish living** included prostitutes (v. 30) or if that was just an angry accusation made by the older brother. The irony of the penniless younger son's new job was that **pigs** were unclean animals to Jews (Lv 11:7). **Pods** were seed casings of a tree used as food for cattle, pigs, and sometimes the poor. He was at rock bottom in his new life.
15:17–19 It took extreme poverty and **hunger** to prompt the younger son to come to his senses and realize that, in spite of all he had done, the correct course of action was to return and become one of his father's **hired workers**. To do so, however, it would be necessary to confess that he had sinned greatly and was not **worthy** to be called his son. This is a vivid picture of a person

"hitting bottom" and finally realizing the magnitude of his sin.
15:20–23 That the father saw his son coming from **a long way off** indicates that he habitually looked for his return. Perhaps the normal parental reaction to the younger son's return would be anger or at least deep disappointment, but this father's response displayed: (1) **compassion**, (2) love (**threw his arms around his neck, and kissed him**), (3) celebration (a **feast**), and (4) joyful restoration of status for his son (a **robe** of distinction, signet **ring** of family authority, **sandals** worn by a son, in contrast to barefoot slaves).
15:24 This is the point at which the parable ties in to the two previous stories about God's joy in saving the **lost**. The father's celebratory attitude depicts the way in which God the Father receives repentant sinners. This contrasts with the contempt the Pharisees and scribes displayed for sinners who came to Jesus (v. 2).
15:25–30 Instead of the story ending on a note of joy and celebration, as might be expected, the spotlight shifts to the older brother. Unlike the father's positive attitude, the older brother (1) was surprised at the

---

#62 **99 Essential Christian Truths**

SINLESSNESS OF JESUS

While the Bible affirms the full humanity of Jesus, it also affirms that Jesus was completely sinless throughout his earthly life (2Co 5:21; Heb 7:26; 1Pt 2:22). Nevertheless, because Jesus was fully human, he experienced real temptation, as seen during his trials in the wilderness (Mt 4). Yet even though his trials and temptations were real and similar to the rest of humanity's, Hebrews 4:15 confirms that Jesus did not sin.

³¹ " 'Son,'ᴬ he said to him, 'you are always with me, and everything I have is yours. ³² But we had to celebrate and rejoice, because this brother of yours was dead and is alive again; he was lost and is found.' "

The Parable of the Dishonest Manager

16 Now he said to the disciples, "There was a rich man who received an accusation that his manager was squandering his possessions. ² So he called the manager in and asked, 'What is this I hear about you? Give an account of your management, because you can no longer be my manager.'

³ "Then the manager said to himself, 'What will I do since my master is taking the management away from me? I'm not strong enough to dig; I'm ashamed to beg. ⁴ I know what I'll do so that when I'm removed from management, people will welcome me into their homes.'

⁵ "So he summoned each one of his master's debtors. 'How much do you owe my master?' he asked the first one.

⁶ " 'A hundred measures of olive oil,' he said.

" 'Take your invoice,' he told him, 'sit down quickly, and write fifty.'

⁷ "Next he asked another, 'How much do you owe?'

" 'A hundred measures of wheat,' he said.

" 'Take your invoice,' he told him, 'and write eighty.'

⁸ "The master praised the unrighteous manager because he had acted shrewdly. For the children of this age are more shrewd than the children of light in dealing with their own people.ᴮ ⁹ And I tell you, make friends for yourselves by means of worldly wealthᶜ so that when it fails, they may welcome you into eternal dwellings. ¹⁰ Whoever is faithful in very little is also faithful in much, and whoever is unrighteous in very little is also unrighteous in much. ¹¹ So if you have not been faithful with worldly wealth, who will trust you with what is genuine? ¹² And if you have not been faithful with what belongs to someone else, who will give you what is your own? ¹³ No servant can serve two masters, since either he will hate one and love the other, or he will be devoted to one and despise the other. You cannot serve both God and money."

Kingdom Values

¹⁴ The Pharisees, who were lovers of money, were listening to all these things and scoffing at him. ¹⁵ And he told them, "You are the ones who justify yourselves in the sight of others, but God knows your hearts. For what is highly admired by people is revolting in God's sight.

¹⁶ "The Law and the Prophets were until John; since then, the good news of the kingdom of God has been proclaimed, and everyone is urgently invited to enter it.ᴰ ¹⁷ But it is

---

ᴬ15:31 Lit Child   ᴮ16:8 Lit own generation   ᶜ16:9 Lit unrighteous money, also in v. 11   ᴰ16:16 Or everyone is forcing his way into it

---

return of his sinning brother, (2) was offended and jealous at the father's celebration, (3) became angry at the father's forgiving love, (4) declared his own self-righteousness, and (5) focused on his brother's sinfulness rather than his newfound repentance. Jesus's representation of the religious leaders in the character of the older brother was a scathing rebuke of their self-righteousness. **15:31–32** The rebuke of the religious leaders continues. They did not understand (1) the opportunity for a close relationship with God, (2) the generosity of his grace, (3) his joy at the salvation of sinners, or (4) the profound transformation of conversion. Perhaps most crucial of all, however, is the reminder of kinship to the sinners intended in the phrase **this brother of yours**. Like the older brother in this story, the religious leaders refused to accept their Jewish brethren, the "sinners." **16:1–2** A **rich man** would often employ a **manager** (Gk oikonomos, "steward, administrator") who handled all the business affairs of his estate. The charge that this manager had squandered the rich man's **possessions**, indicating either neglectful management or criminal misconduct, must have been true. After all, the manager offered no defense when questioned. The landowner demanded a careful accounting of his assets, possibly so the next manager would have accurate data from the outset. **16:3–4** Realizing that he was being fired, the manager had to find a way to support

himself. Since he was not in condition to do physical labor and too proud to **beg**, he focused on a way to make his former clients willing to offer him hospitality. **16:5–7** Four explanations are offered for the manager's tactics in lowering these debts: (1) He dropped the price enough to ingratiate himself with the debtors, (2) he removed the interest charges on the debt, (3) he removed his commission on the transactions, or (4) he reduced the debt back to what it should have been in the first place, after having overcharged them previously in a bid to cover his mismanagement. All four tactics are possible, but it should be remembered that the manager was required to present a full accounting to the landowner. Therefore, his tactics here must have been legitimate. **16:8–9** Because the Greek word translated **master** is kurios ("lord"), some have thought that it was God who **praised the unrighteous manager**. However, it is much more likely that the story ends in the middle of v. 8. Thus it was the landowner rather than God who offered praise; and he did so only because the manager **acted shrewdly** in response to his errors. In the last half of v. 8 and all of v. 9, Jesus shares an implication of the story: the **children of this age** (unbelievers) typically deal shrewdly with each other and win friends by this means, whereas the **children of light** (believers) often fail to use their financial resources to win people to faith, who thus become friends forever

(**welcome you into eternal dwellings**). Thus Jesus encouraged his followers to use their money shrewdly (but innocently) in order to advance God's kingdom. **16:10–12** A second lesson that this story teaches is the need to be **faithful** before the Lord. Spiritually, every believer is a steward of the gifts God has given. If you are faithful with small amounts of money, the Lord may trust you with **much** more, including things of priceless eternal value. If you cannot be trusted with only a **little**, you would also be a poor steward if more were entrusted to you. **16:13** On **serve two masters**, see Mt 6:24. **16:14–15** The Pharisees, because they were **lovers of money**, were **scoffing** at Jesus, for they believed it was possible to serve both God and money (v. 13). In response, Jesus told the Pharisees that their desire to be **admired by people** was an abomination in **God's sight**, for he does not approve of the world's values. **16:16–17** **The Law and the Prophets** is a way of referring to the entire OT (v. 29; 24:27,44). The ministry of John the Baptist marked the end of the old covenant era. The ministry of Jesus began the offer of the gospel (**good news**), the new covenant era, and embodied the nearness of the **kingdom of God**. In this context, **everyone is urgently invited** probably refers to the urgency expressed by the evangelistic preaching efforts of John the Baptist, Jesus, and his apostles. On **one stroke of a letter**, see Mt 5:17–20.

easier for heaven and earth to pass away than for one stroke of a letter in the law to drop out. ¹⁸ "Everyone who divorces his wife and marries another woman commits adultery, and everyone who marries a woman divorced from her husband commits adultery.

The Rich Man and Lazarus

¹⁹ "There was a rich man who would dress in purple and fine linen, feasting lavishly every day. ²⁰ But a poor man named Lazarus, covered with sores, was lying at his gate. ²¹ He longed to be filled with what fell from the rich man's table, but instead the dogs would come and lick his sores. ²² One day the poor man died and was carried away by the angels to Abraham's side.^ The rich man also died and was buried. ²³ And being in torment in Hades, he looked up and saw Abraham a long way off, with Lazarus at his side. ²⁴ 'Father Abraham!' he called out, 'Have mercy on me and send Lazarus to dip the tip of his finger in water and cool my tongue, because I am in agony in this flame!'

²⁵ " 'Son,'ᴮ Abraham said, 'remember that during your life you received your good things, just as Lazarus received bad things, but now he is comforted here, while you are in agony. ²⁶ Besides all this, a great chasm has been fixed between us and you, so that those who want to pass over from here to you cannot; neither can those from there cross over to us.'

²⁷ " 'Father,' he said, 'then I beg you to send him to my father's house — ²⁸ because I have five brothers — to warn them, so that they won't also come to this place of torment.'

²⁹ "But Abraham said, 'They have Moses and the prophets; they should listen to them.'

³⁰ " 'No, father Abraham,' he said. 'But if someone from the dead goes to them, they will repent.'

³¹ "But he told him, 'If they don't listen to Moses and the prophets, they will not be persuaded if someone rises from the dead.' "

Warnings from Jesus

17 He said to his disciples, "Offenses will certainly come,ᶜ but woe to the one through whom they come! ² It would be better for him if a millstone were hung around his neck and he were thrown into the sea than for him to cause one of these little ones to stumble. ³ Be on your guard. If your brother sins,ᴰ rebuke him, and if he repents, forgive him. ⁴ And if he sins against you seven times in a day, and comes back to you seven times, saying, 'I repent,' you must forgive him."

Faith and Duty

⁵ The apostles said to the Lord, "Increase our faith."

⁶ "If you have faith the size ofᴱ a mustard seed," the Lord said, "you can say to this mulberry tree, 'Be uprooted and planted in the sea,' and it will obey you.

⁷ "Which one of you having a servant tending sheep or plowing will say to him when he comes in from the field, 'Come at once and sit down to eat'? ⁸ Instead, will he not tell him, 'Prepare something for me to eat, get ready, and serve me while I eat and drink; later you can eat and drink'? ⁹ Does he thank that servant because he did what was commanded?ᶠ ¹⁰ In the same way, when you have done all that you were commanded, you should say,

---

^16:22 Or *to Abraham's bosom*; lit *to the fold of Abraham's robe*; Jn 13:23   ᴮ16:25 Lit *Child*   ᶜ17:1 Lit *"It is impossible for offenses not to come*   ᴰ17:3 Other mss add *against you*   ᴱ17:6 Lit *faith like*   ᶠ17:9 Other mss add *I don't think so*

16:18 Remarriage after divorce constitutes **adultery** if the former marriage was dissolved for illegitimate reasons or motivations; hence the strict terms of this verse. The parallel passages in Mt 5:31–32 and 19:9 are more detailed. They indicate that remarriage is legitimate in cases where the former marriage was dissolved due to sexual immorality.
16:19–21 The **rich man** (called *Dives*, Latin for "rich man") clearly did not use his wealth to make friends in the "eternal dwellings" (see note at vv. 8–9). **Sores** is a medical term used only here in the NT, perhaps reflecting Luke's background as a physician (Col 4:14). It is ironic that the suffering **poor man** named **Lazarus** since a man by that name would later rise from the dead (Jn 11:1–44). On **dress in purple**, see Ac 16:14.
16:22–24 The circumstances were reversed after both men **died**. The Jewish Talmud refers to both paradise (23:43; 2Co 12:4) and **Abraham's side** (or "bosom") as names for the place of blessedness beyond the grave. **Hades**, the Greek equivalent of the Hebrew *Sheol*, is, generally, "the place of the dead." In this case, however, because of the mention of **being in torment**, Hades must be viewed as hell, the place of the unrighteous dead.

In this flame refers to the eternal lake of fire (Mt 25:41).
16:25 This verse is an application of the principle in 13:30. The rich man had been "first" in this life, having enjoyed many **good things**, but was now "last," referring to his **agony** in the afterlife. By contrast, Lazarus had been "last" during his earthly existence (vv. 20–21) but now was "first" (eternally **comforted**).
16:26 In the afterlife, there is a separation between believers and unbelievers that cannot be spanned. It is not possible to pass **over** from heaven to hell or hell to heaven.
16:27–29 Not being able to improve his own lot, the rich man finally showed concern for the eternal destiny of his **five brothers**. The phrase **Moses and the prophets** is another way of referring to the entire OT (see v. 16).
16:30–31 The irony here is that Luke, writing from a time after Jesus's resurrection, knew that very few people would be persuaded to **repent** even through witnessing the miracle of someone rising **from the dead** (Lazarus or Jesus). They must listen with "ears to hear" the message of salvation in the Scriptures. On **Moses and the prophets**, see notes at vv. 16–17,27–29.
17:1–2 Offenses (Gk *skandalon*, "that which causes sin") are unavoidable in life.

However, divine judgment awaits the person who causes a disciple of Christ (**one of these little ones**) to sin. A **millstone** was a large round stone used to grind grain. A large stone around the neck would cause a person thrown into the sea to sink and drown.
17:3–4 The purpose of rebuking a sinner is to get him to repent of his sin. If there is true repentance, there should be full forgiveness. **Seven** is the biblical number of completeness. To forgive "seven times" means to keep forgiving, no matter what (see Mt 18:21–22).
17:5–6 Genuine faith is powerful even in small quantities. The **mustard seed** was thought by farmers in Palestine to be the smallest of seeds. A **mulberry tree** has such an extensive and deep root system that it might live for several hundred years. It took a very powerful force to uproot such a tree.
17:7–10 A **servant** who only did his job, or what was **commanded**, got no special commendation since all he had done was to fulfill his responsibilities. Similarly, a disciple of Christ (v. 1) should not expect special commendation for doing what is required. We serve the Lord because this is what it means to follow him as disciples. It is our **duty**.

'We are unworthy servants; we've only done our duty.'"

Ten Men Healed

¹¹ While traveling to Jerusalem, he passed between^A Samaria and Galilee. ¹² As he entered a village, ten men with leprosy⁸ met him. They stood at a distance ¹³ and raised their voices, saying, "Jesus, Master, have mercy on us!" ¹⁴ When he saw them, he told them, "Go and show yourselves to the priests." And while they were going, they were cleansed.

¹⁵ But one of them, seeing that he was healed, returned and, with a loud voice, gave glory to God. ¹⁶ He fell facedown at his feet, thanking him. And he was a Samaritan. ¹⁷ Then Jesus said, "Were not ten cleansed? Where are the nine? ¹⁸ Didn't any return to give glory to God except this foreigner?" ¹⁹ And he told him, "Get up and go on your way. Your faith has saved you."ᶜ

The Coming of the Kingdom

²⁰ When he was asked by the Pharisees when the kingdom of God would come, he answered them, "The kingdom of God is not coming with something observable; ²¹ no one will say,ᴰ 'See here!' or 'There!' For you see, the kingdom of God is in your midst."ᴱ

²² Then he told the disciples, "The days are coming when you will long to see one of the days of the Son of Man, but you won't see it. ²³ They will say to you, 'See there!' or 'See here!' Don't follow or run after them. ²⁴ For as the lightning flashes from horizon to horizon and lights up the sky, so the Son of Man will be in his day. ²⁵ But first it is necessary that

he suffer many things and be rejected by this generation.

²⁶ "Just as it was in the days of Noah, so it will be in the days of the Son of Man: ²⁷ People went on eating, drinking, marrying and being given in marriage until the day Noah boarded the ark, and the flood came and destroyed them all. ²⁸ It will be the same as it was in the days of Lot: People went on eating, drinking, buying, selling, planting, building. ²⁹ But on the day Lot left Sodom, fire and sulfur rained from heaven and destroyed them all. ³⁰ It will be like that on the day the Son of Man is revealed. ³¹ On that day, a man on the housetop, whose belongings are in the house, must not come down to get them. Likewise the man who is in the field must not turn back. ³² Remember Lot's wife! ³³ Whoever tries to make his life secureᶠ,ᴳ will lose it, and whoever loses his life will preserve it. ³⁴ I tell you, on that night two will be in one bed; one will be taken and the other will be left. ³⁵ Two women will be grinding grain together; one will be taken and the other left."ᴴ

³⁷ "Where, Lord?" they asked him.

He said to them, "Where the corpse is, there also the vultures will be gathered."

The Parable of the Persistent Widow

18 Now he told them a parable on the need for them to pray always and not give up. ² "There was a judge in a certain town who didn't fear God or respect people. ³ And a widow in that town kept coming to him, saying, 'Give me justice against my adversary.'

⁴ "For a while he was unwilling, but later he said to himself, 'Even though I don't fear God or respect people, ⁵ yet because this widow keeps pestering me,' I will give her justice,

---

^17:11 Or *through the middle of*   ⁸17:12 Gk *lepros*; a term for various skin diseases; see Lv 13–14   ᶜ17:19 Or *faith has made you well*   ᴰ17:21 Lit *they will not say*   ᴱ17:21 Or *within you*   ᶠ17:33 Other mss read *to save his life*   ᴳ17:33 Or *tries to retain his life*   ᴴ17:35 Some mss include v. 36: "*Two will be in a field: One will be taken, and the other will be left.*"   ¹18:5 Lit *widow causes me trouble*

17:11 Jesus apparently walked along the border **between Samaria and Galilee**, then crossed the Jordan River at the nearest point, proceeding down the eastern bank of the Jordan toward the crossing point opposite Jericho (see note at 19:1–2), which is the next location mentioned in the narrative (18:35).

17:12–14 On **show yourselves to the priests** after being healed from **leprosy**, see note at 5:12–14.

17:15–19 It is striking that the only one of the ten men healed who **returned** and thanked Jesus was **a Samaritan . . . a foreigner**. This is in keeping with Luke's theme of the universal outreach of the gospel. Jesus's statement **your faith has saved you** implies that the Samaritan was healed physically and spiritually.

17:20–21 The Jews were looking for a **kingdom of God** that would come with signs in the sky and miracles (Jl 2:28–32), but that was yet in the future. The aspect of God's kingdom that Jesus emphasized in his ministry was not **observable** in that sense. The presence of the King (Jesus) and

his offer of the kingdom through the gospel meant that the kingdom was already "in their midst."

17:22–24 Jesus's disciples must not be led astray by false predictions of his coming. Instead, when he comes, it will be as obvious as **the lightning** flashing across the sky.

17:25 This is one of numerous predictions Jesus made about his suffering and rejection in Luke's Gospel (5:35; 9:22,43–44; 13:32–33; 18:32; 24:7).

17:26–29 Before Christ comes back, there will be no clear-cut warning signs that signal the end. Rather, it will be like (1) **the days of Noah**, when business as usual was carried on until the unexpected destruction of his flood, and (2) **the days of Lot**, when the status quo continued until, suddenly, fire and sulfur rained down on Sodom.

17:30–33 When Jesus returns, those on earth must not be attached to their possessions and earthly comforts, as was **Lot's wife** (see Gn 19:26). Commitment to Christ involves attachment only to spiritual and eternal realities. These provide the greatest security available.

17:34–36 The three aspects of life mentioned here cover the normal routine in an agricultural society: sleeping, **grinding grain**, and working in a field. It is not certain whether the one who is **taken** will be a believer taken by the Lord (see 1Th 4:15–17) or an unbeliever taken in judgment (Mt 13:40–42).

17:37 Jesus answered the disciples' question about where his coming would take place with a proverbial saying. It is easy to find a **corpse** by noting where the **vultures** are circling. Similarly, there will be no hiding Christ's second coming. It will be obvious to the entire world.

18:1 This parable speaks to the common tendency to **give up** and stop praying before receiving an answer from God.

18:2–3 This **judge** was not a religious or compassionate man. A **widow** in that culture was almost helpless. Her only hope was that her persistent plea for **justice** would be granted.

18:4–5 Though the judge was unprincipled and **unwilling** to grant the widow's request (perhaps he was waiting for the widow to offer a bribe), he eventually caved in and

so that she doesn't wear me out[A] by her persistent coming.'"

⁶ Then the Lord said, "Listen to what the unjust judge says. ⁷ Will not God grant justice to his elect who cry out to him day and night? Will he delay helping them?[B] ⁸ I tell you that he will swiftly grant them justice. Nevertheless, when the Son of Man comes, will he find faith on earth?"

The Parable of the Pharisee and the Tax Collector

⁹ He also told this parable to some who trusted in themselves that they were righteous and looked down on everyone else: ¹⁰ "Two men went up to the temple to pray, one a Pharisee and the other a tax collector. ¹¹ The Pharisee was standing and praying like this about himself:[C] 'God, I thank you that I'm not like other people — greedy, unrighteous, adulterers, or even like this tax collector. ¹² I fast twice a week; I give a tenth[D] of everything I get.'

¹³ "But the tax collector, standing far off, would not even raise his eyes to heaven but kept striking his chest and saying, 'God, have mercy on me,[E] a sinner!' ¹⁴ I tell you, this one went down to his house justified rather than the other, because everyone who exalts himself will be humbled, but the one who humbles himself will be exalted."

Blessing the Children

¹⁵ People were bringing infants to him so that he might touch them, but when the disciples saw it, they rebuked them. ¹⁶ Jesus, however, invited them: "Let the little children come to me,

and don't stop them, because the kingdom of God belongs to such as these. ¹⁷ Truly I tell you, whoever does not receive the kingdom of God like a little child will never enter it."

The Rich Young Ruler

¹⁸ A ruler asked him, "Good teacher, what must I do to inherit eternal life?"

¹⁹ "Why do you call me good?" Jesus asked him. "No one is good except God alone. ²⁰ You know the commandments: Do not commit adultery; do not murder; do not steal; do not bear false witness; honor your father and mother."[F]

²¹ "I have kept all these from my youth," he said.

²² When Jesus heard this, he told him, "You still lack one thing: Sell all you have and distribute it to the poor, and you will have treasure in heaven. Then come, follow me."

²³ After he heard this, he became extremely sad, because he was very rich.

Possessions and the Kingdom

²⁴ Seeing that he became sad,[G] Jesus said, "How hard it is for those who have wealth to enter the kingdom of God! ²⁵ For it is easier for a camel to go through the eye of a needle than for a rich person to enter the kingdom of God."

²⁶ Those who heard this asked, "Then who can be saved?"

²⁷ He replied, "What is impossible with man is possible with God."

²⁸ Then Peter said, "Look, we have left what we had and followed you."

²⁹ So he said to them, "Truly I tell you, there is no one who has left a house, wife or brothers

---

[A] 18:5 Or doesn't ruin my reputation   [B] 18:7 Or Will he put up with them?   [C] 18:11 Or by himself   [D] 18:12 Or give tithes   [E] 18:13 Or God, turn your wrath from me   [F] 18:20 Ex 20:12–16; Dt 5:16–20   [G] 18:24 Other mss omit he became sad

---

granted her **justice** because she was **persistent** and he knew she would soon wear him out.

18:6–8 Jesus intends to make a contrast between the **unjust judge** and **God**. Unlike the unjust judge, God will not only grant **justice** to his children who are praying consistently but will act **swiftly** in doing so. The last part of v. 8 refers to the fact that at the time just before Christ's second coming, genuine faith will be rare on earth (Mt 24:12–13).

18:9 The following parable focuses on a Pharisee (vv. 10–11). The phrase **some who trusted in themselves** describes the self-righteous outlook of the average Pharisee (vv. 11–12,14).

18:10–14 There were times around the morning and evening sacrifices at **the temple** when people could **pray**, although private prayer at other times was allowed. The Pharisee apparently kept the requirements of the Mosaic law and beyond (giving a **tenth** of earnings was all that was required). He was proud of his actions and his religious superiority to people such as the **tax collector**. By contrast, the tax collector knew that, as a **sinner**, he deserved only God's wrath. Jesus emphasized that God's justification is available to the humble, while the self-exalting will be brought low.

18:15–17 Jesus's disciples apparently thought his time was too precious to be taken up with infants. Jesus responded that **little children** coming to him demonstrate the kind of childlike faith that is necessary to **enter** the **kingdom of God**.

18:18–23 The ruler was under the impression that **eternal life** could be earned by works (**what must I do**). Jesus shifted the focus by asserting that goodness only comes

from God. Either the ruler had kept all the commandments listed in v. 20 or Jesus preferred not to argue about that. The latter is most likely, especially since Jesus's follow-up command revealed that the man was more interested in wealth on earth than **treasure in heaven** (where he would have eternal life). His unwillingness to distribute his wealth to **the poor** kept him from becoming Jesus's disciple.

18:24–27 Jesus contradicted the conventional wisdom that those with **wealth** would be blessed by God and would certainly be in his kingdom. A **camel** trying to go through the **eye of a needle** was apparently a proverbial saying for what was **impossible**; this explains the question from Jesus's hearers. His response was that people cannot be **saved** by their own efforts but only by salvation that comes by God's grace.

18:28–30 After hearing the earlier discussions, Peter—as spokesman for the apostles—indicated that they had done precisely what Jesus had instructed the rich ruler to do in v. 22. They had left everything and followed him. Jesus replied that not only would they have **eternal life in the age to come**, but they would also be greatly blessed in this life. To leave **wife** and **children** means

or sisters, parents or children because of the kingdom of God, ³⁰ who will not receive many times more at this time, and eternal life in the age to come."

The Third Prediction of His Death

³¹ Then he took the Twelve aside and told them, "See, we are going up to Jerusalem. Everything that is written through the prophets about the Son of Man will be accomplished. ³² For he will be handed over to the Gentiles, and he will be mocked, insulted, spit on; ³³ and after they flog him, they will kill him, and he will rise on the third day."

³⁴ They understood none of these things. The meaning of the saying^A was hidden from them, and they did not grasp what was said.

A Blind Man Receives His Sight

³⁵ As he approached Jericho, a blind man was sitting by the road begging. ³⁶ Hearing a crowd passing by, he inquired what was happening. ³⁷ "Jesus of Nazareth is passing by," they told him.

³⁸ So he called out, "Jesus, Son of David, have mercy on me!" ³⁹ Then those in front told him to keep quiet,^B but he kept crying out all the more, "Son of David, have mercy on me!"

⁴⁰ Jesus stopped and commanded that he be brought to him. When he came closer, he asked him, ⁴¹ "What do you want me to do for you?"

"Lord," he said, "I want to see."

⁴² "Receive your sight," Jesus told him. "Your faith has saved you." ⁴³ Instantly he could see, and he began to follow him, glorifying God.

All the people, when they saw it, gave praise to God.

Jesus Visits Zacchaeus

19 He entered Jericho and was passing through. ² There was a man named Zacchaeus who was a chief tax collector, and he was rich. ³ He was trying to see who Jesus was, but he was not able because of the crowd, since he was a short man. ⁴ So running ahead, he climbed up a sycamore tree to see Jesus, since he was about to pass that way. ⁵ When Jesus came to the place, he looked up and said to him, "Zacchaeus, hurry and come down because today it is necessary for me to stay at your house."

⁶ So he quickly came down and welcomed him joyfully. ⁷ All who saw it began to complain, "He's gone to stay with a sinful man."

⁸ But Zacchaeus stood there and said to the Lord, "Look, I'll give half of my possessions to the poor, Lord. And if I have extorted anything from anyone, I'll pay back four times as much."

⁹ "Today salvation has come to this house," Jesus told him, "because he too is a son of Abraham. ¹⁰ For the Son of Man has come to seek and to save the lost."

The Parable of the Ten Minas

¹¹ As they were listening to this, he went on to tell a parable because he was near Jerusalem, and they thought the kingdom of God was going to appear right away.

¹² Therefore he said, "A nobleman traveled to a far country to receive for himself authority to be king^C and then to return. ¹³ He called ten

---

^A 18:34 Lit This saying　^B 18:39 Or those in front rebuked him　^C 19:12 Lit to receive for himself a kingdom, or sovereignty, also in v. 15

---

itinerant ministry, not divorce or abandonment of domestic responsibilities.
18:31–34 This is the third major prediction of Jesus's death. The first is 9:21–22; the second is 9:43b–44. This is the most detailed of the three. As with the second prediction, the disciples did not understand. As is true through the entire middle portion of Luke's Gospel, the movement of the narrative is toward Jerusalem. The only passage in the OT **prophets** that deals with the **Son of Man** is found in Dn 7:13 and its context. However, there are several major prophecies about the sufferings of the Messiah, notably Ps 22 and Is 53. **Handed over** and **rise on the third day** give a preview of Luke's narrative in 22:63 to 24:12. The disciples did not understand what Jesus meant about these things until after his resurrection (24:25–27,44–46).
18:35–43 In Lk 17:11, Jesus apparently crossed the Jordan River to the east near the border between Galilee and Samaria. Now he crossed back to the west opposite **Jericho**. When the **blind man** inquired about the crowd, he was told only that **Jesus of Nazareth** (a Galilean village of little significance), was near. There is nothing messianic about such an identification. However, when he cried out that Jesus was the **Son of David** (see Mt 1:1), he was confessing Jesus as

Messiah. His faith became the basis for his healing. His cry, **have mercy on me**, prompted Jesus to restore his sight. It is ironic that the formerly blind man, who now became a disciple of Jesus, could **see** immediately, while the twelve apostles had no insight into where Jesus and his ministry were headed (see note at vv. 31–34).
19:1–2 Jericho is one of the oldest walled cities in the world. Today its ruins date back more than ten thousand years. It was located about five miles west of the Jordan River, ten miles northwest of the Dead Sea, and about seventeen miles by winding road from Jerusalem. **Chief tax collector** refers to a supervisor of other tax collectors in a certain tax district. **Zacchaeus** was rich because he had taken advantage of his position by extorting money (see note at vv. 5–9).
19:3–4 A **sycamore tree** might grow to be thirty to forty feet tall. However, it had low, spreading branches that even **a short man** could climb and that would support his weight.
19:5–9 It is necessary implies divine necessity in Jesus's statement about staying at Zacchaeus's **house**. The Jews greatly resented tax collectors because they worked for the Roman government that had invaded Israel, turning her into a subject nation. Thus

Jesus's decision to stay overnight with such a **sinful man** as Zacchaeus, who had sold out and mistreated his own people, seemed outrageous. But Zacchaeus's words and actions were those of a transformed man. It was considered extremely generous to give one-fifth of your possessions to the poor, but Zacchaeus stated he would give **half**. Also, while repayment for extortion was 20 percent over what had been extorted (Lv 6:5), Zacchaeus promised to repay **four times as much**. Zacchaeus had become a **son of Abraham** and gained **salvation** through faith in Jesus Christ (Gl 3:7).
19:10 Son of Man was both a messianic title for Jesus and a reflection of his full humanity. His mission was to **seek and to save** those who were **lost**.
19:11 In keeping with the messianic expectation of that day, Jesus's disciples believed that as soon as he arrived in **Jerusalem**, he would be declared ruler and overturn the Romans. Then the **kingdom of God** would appear in its glory.
19:12–13 This parable is similar to the one in Mt 25:14–30 in some respects but different enough that it was almost certainly told at a time distinct from the Matthew account. Jesus told the story to emphasize that he must go away in order to receive

of his servants, gave them ten minas,^ and told them, 'Engage in business until I come back.' ¹⁴ "But his subjects hated him and sent a delegation after him, saying, 'We don't want this man to rule over us.' ¹⁵ "At his return, having received the authority to be king, he summoned those servants he had given the money to, so that he could find out how much they had made in business. ¹⁶ The first came forward and said, 'Master, your mina has earned ten more minas.' ¹⁷ " 'Well done, good⁸ servant!' he told him. 'Because you have been faithful in a very small matter, have authority over ten towns.' ¹⁸ "The second came and said, 'Master, your mina has made five minas.' ¹⁹ "So he said to him, 'You will be over five towns.' ²⁰ "And another came and said, 'Master, here is your mina. I have kept it safe in a cloth ²¹ because I was afraid of you since you're a harsh man: you collect what you didn't deposit and reap what you didn't sow.' ²² "He told him, 'I will condemn you by what you have said, you evil servant! If you knew I was a harsh man, collecting what I didn't deposit and reaping what I didn't sow, ²³ why, then, didn't you put my money in the bank? And when I returned, I would have collected it with interest.' ²⁴ So he said to those standing there, 'Take the mina away from him and give it to the one who has ten minas.' ²⁵ "But they said to him, 'Master, he has ten minas.'

²⁶ " 'I tell you, that to everyone who has, more will be given; and from the one who does not have, even what he does have will be taken away. ²⁷ But bring here these enemies of mine, who did not want me to rule over them, and slaughterᶜ them in my presence.' "

The Triumphal Entry

²⁸ When he had said these things, he went on ahead, going up to Jerusalem. ²⁹ As he approached Bethphage and Bethany, at the place called the Mount of Olives, he sent two of the disciples ³⁰ and said, "Go into the village ahead of you. As you enter it, you will find a colt tied there, on which no one has ever sat. Untie it and bring it. ³¹ If anyone asks you, 'Why are you untying it?' say this: 'The Lord needs it.' " ³² So those who were sent left and found it just as he had told them. ³³ As they were untying the colt, its owners said to them, "Why are you untying the colt? " ³⁴ "The Lord needs it," they said. ³⁵ Then they brought it to Jesus, and after throwing their clothes on the colt, they helped Jesus get on it. ³⁶ As he was going along, they were spreading their clothes on the road. ³⁷ Now he came near the path down the Mount of Olives, and the whole crowd of the disciples began to praise God joyfully with a loud voice for all the miracles they had seen:

³⁸   Blessed is the King who comes
        in the name of the Lord.ᴰ
     Peace in heaven
     and glory in the highest heaven!

^19:13 = Gk coin worth a hundred drachmas or about a hundred days' wages   ⁸19:17 Or *capable*   ᶜ19:27 Or *execute*   ᴰ19:38 Ps 118:26

full **authority** (see Mt 28:18). Only after this would he **return** in the fullness of his glory and kingdom. A mina was equivalent to a hundred drachmas. A drachma was essentially a day's wages for an ordinary worker. So each mina would be worth about a hundred days' pay, roughly four months' wages. The command (**engage in business until I come back**) describes an undefined duration of absence by the nobleman (Jesus). This fits with the time between Jesus's ascension to heaven (24:50–53; Ac 1:9) and his eventual return (Ac 1:11).
19:14 Jesus warned about the dire consequences of the Jews rejecting his **rule** as Messiah.
19:15–19 Ten **servants** had been entrusted with one mina each, but only three were questioned about how much they had earned while the new king was gone. The first earned **ten more minas**, and his faithfulness resulted in his being given authority over **ten towns** in the kingdom. The second earned **five minas** and was also granted wider authority. Both servants are examples of the principle of v. 26: "To everyone who has, more will be given."
19:20–25 The third servant hid his mina because he feared his Master. It is also possible that he hoped the king would not return. In that case the money would become his. The **Master** did not accept his excuses, saying that even the small **interest** earned in a bank

account would have been more useful. That the **evil servant** had to hand over his mina to the servant who had ten minas demonstrates the principle of v. 26: "From the one who does not have, even what he does have will be taken away."
19:26–27 There is great reward for faithfulness to the Lord. Conversely, poor stewardship is punished by great loss. Those who do not want the Lord to **rule** their lives will be severely punished. It is likely that **slaughter them** refers to the destruction of Jerusalem in AD 70.
19:28–44 These verses describe Jesus's "triumphal entry" into Jerusalem (recorded in all four Gospels). Though he was not accepted as Messiah by most Jews, his entry was nevertheless triumphant insomuch as (1) the palm branches (Jn 12:13) that were waved and placed on the ground symbolized royalty and victory, and (2) his entry into Jerusalem represented the fulfillment of OT prophecy (Zch 9:9) and the triumph of God's plan of redemption.
19:28 Over the course of the seventeen miles from Jericho (see note at vv. 1–2) to **Jerusalem**, the elevation rises about 3,300 feet. Thus to travel that road was **going up** at the average rate of almost 200 feet per mile.
19:29 Bethphage and **Bethany** are small villages near the road from Jericho to Jerusalem. Bethany, the hometown of Lazarus, Mary, and Martha (Jn 11:1) was only

two miles east of Jerusalem, just over **the Mount of Olives**, a ridge across the Kidron Valley from the temple in Jerusalem. The **two . . . disciples** are not named in any of the Gospels.
19:30–34 Religious or political leaders in that time often borrowed property (**a colt**) for a short time, as here. Matthew 21:7 says that the mother donkey was also commandeered. This action fulfilled the prophecy of Zch 9:9: "Daughter Jerusalem . . . your King is coming to you . . . humble and riding on a donkey, on a colt, the foal of a donkey."
19:35–36 The **clothes** (outer garments) were cast down by the two disciples and by the crowd. **Spreading their clothes on the road** was a way to honor special dignitaries, as was done for Jehu when he was acclaimed king of Israel (2Kg 9:13).
19:37–38 As Jesus passed over the **Mount of Olives** (see note at v. 29) and began his descent into Jerusalem, the crowd of disciples praised God for **all the miracles they had seen**. The Gospel of John reports that the raising of Lazarus from the dead had recently occurred in Bethany, near the beginning point of the triumphal entry (Jn 11:1–44). The crowd was shouting Ps 118:26, which is messianic. In addition, they added the word **King** to their recitation of the OT Scripture, showing that they believed Jesus was the Messiah.

39 Some of the Pharisees from the crowd told him, "Teacher, rebuke your disciples." **40** He answered, "I tell you, if they were to keep silent, the stones would cry out."

Jesus's Love for Jerusalem

41 As he approached and saw the city, he wept for it, **42** saying, "If you knew this day what would bring peace — but now it is hidden from your eyes. **43** For the days will come on you when your enemies will build a barricade around you, surround you, and hem you in on every side. **44** They will crush you and your children among you to the ground, and they will not leave one stone on another in your midst, because you did not recognize the time when God visited you."

Cleansing the Temple

45 He went into the temple and began to throw out those who were selling,^A **46** and he said, "It is written, **my house will be a house of prayer,** but you have made it a **den of thieves!**"^B **47** Every day he was teaching in the temple. The chief priests, the scribes, and the leaders of the people were looking for a way to kill him, **48** but they could not find a way to do it, because all the people were captivated by what they heard.

The Authority of Jesus Challenged

20 One day as he was teaching the people in the temple and proclaiming the good news, the chief priests and the scribes, with the elders, came **2** and said to him, "Tell us, by what authority are you doing these things? Who is it who gave you this authority?"

3 He answered them, "I will also ask you a question. Tell me, **4** was the baptism of John from heaven or of human origin?" **5** They discussed it among themselves: "If we say, 'From heaven,' he will say, 'Why didn't you believe him?' **6** But if we say, 'Of human origin,' all the people will stone us, because they are convinced that John was a prophet." **7** So they answered that they did not know its origin. **8** And Jesus said to them, "Neither will I tell you by what authority I do these things."

The Parable of the Vineyard Owner

9 Now he began to tell the people this parable: "A man planted a vineyard, leased it to tenant farmers, and went away for a long time. **10** At harvest time he sent a servant to the farmers so that they might give him some fruit from the vineyard. But the farmers beat him and sent him away empty-handed. **11** He sent yet another servant, but they beat that one too, treated him shamefully, and sent him away empty-handed. **12** And he sent yet a third, but they wounded this one too and threw him out.

13 "Then the owner of the vineyard said, 'What should I do? I will send my beloved son. Perhaps^C they will respect him.' **14** "But when the tenant farmers saw him, they discussed it among themselves and said, 'This is the heir. Let's kill him, so that the inheritance will be ours.' **15** So they threw him out of the vineyard and killed him.

"What then will the owner of the vineyard do to them? **16** He will come and kill those farmers and give the vineyard to others."

But when they heard this they said, "That must never happen!"

^A**19:45** Other mss add *and buying in it* ^B**19:46** Is 56:7; Jr 7:11 ^C**20:13** Other mss add *when they see him*

19:39–40 The **Pharisees** asked Jesus to **rebuke** his disciples because they understood that the repetition of Ps 118:26 was a confession that Jesus was both Messiah and rightful king of Israel. Jesus replied that even if his disciples were to **keep silent,** God would make the truth known some other way (**the stones would cry out**), even if it took a miracle.

19:41–44 Jesus wept before Lazarus's tomb (Jn 11:35), and here he wept at the thought of his rejection by the city of Jerusalem. True, lasting peace with God comes through faith in Jesus Christ (Rm 5:1). The Jews enjoyed a temporal though imperfect peace under Roman rule, but such a peace cannot be secured forever, as the destructive events of AD 70 proved. Due to their unbelief, many Jews did not open their eyes to see Christ as Messiah (2Co 4:4) or recognize his coming as the time (Gk *kairos,* "opportune time") of God's visitation and offer of salvation.

19:45–46 The court of the Gentiles in the **temple** was where sacrificial animals were sold for outrageously high prices. According to Is 56:7, the temple (**my house**) was to be **a house of prayer.** The other quote (**a den of thieves**) is from Jr 7:11, which reflects a time when the corruption of the nation and its religious system was about to be judged

by God in the Babylonian captivity. Now, as Jesus beheld the corruption of the temple and the opposition arrayed against him, the nation faced an even greater season of judgment.

19:47–48 The religious **leaders** of Israel were increasingly desperate to get rid of Jesus, but they were hesitant to act because Jesus had gained considerable popularity among the masses.

20:1–2 Luke did not specify which day of the Passion Week is in view here, but the parallel account in Mk 11:19–20,27–33 indicates it was Tuesday. **Chief priests . . . scribes,** and **elders** were part of the Jewish ruling council, the Sanhedrin (see note at 22:66). The Jewish religious leaders questioned Jesus's **authority** for throwing the merchants out of the temple complex (19:45) because such an act was a direct attack on the heart of Jewish religion. To their mind, none but a blasphemer would dare do such a thing. Thus they sought to discredit Jesus in the eyes of the people gathered for Passover (see note at 19:47–48).

20:3–8 As he often did, Jesus turned the attention back on his questioners by asking them about the authority of John the Baptist's **baptism.** Finding themselves in a "no-win" situation, the religious leaders

stated that **they did not know** the basis of John's authority. Having caught his opponents in a trap, Jesus also refused to answer their question.

20:9–12 The **vineyard** was a symbol of Israel (Is 5:7), and its owner was God. The **tenant farmers** stood for the people of Israel, notably its religious leaders. The successive servants who suffered mistreatment from the tenants stood for the OT prophets who were sent from God but were rejected and even killed by Israel.

20:13–18 My beloved son stands for Jesus (see note at 3:21–22). The Jewish religious leaders did not want to kill Jesus to claim his inheritance but rather to forcefully and finally reject him as Messiah and heir to David's throne. The destruction of the **farmers** (Israel) by the **owner of the vineyard** (God) looks ahead to Gentiles being added to God's plan for his new covenant people, the church. This is one of Luke's major focuses in his next book, the Acts of the Apostles. The people in the temple area who were listening to Jesus (vv. 1,9) could not imagine God doing such a thing. In this quote from Ps 118:22, Jesus is **the stone** and **cornerstone** (see Ac 4:11; Eph 2:20; 1Pt 2:7). The **builders** are not identified, but they were undoubtedly Israel's religious leaders (vv. 1,19).

▼ Parables of the Kingdom

THE PARABLE	REFERENCE(S)	SOME DETAILS
The Sower and the Soils	*Matthew 13:1–9,18–23; Mark 4:1–9,13–20; Luke 8:4–8,11–15*	• Explanation given in Scripture • Specific allegorical interpretation
The Wheat and the Weeds	*Matthew 13:24–30, 36–43*	• Explanation given in Scripture • Specific allegorical interpretation
The Mustard Seed/the Leaven	*Matthew 13:31–33; Luke 13:18–21 (see also Mark 4:30–32)*	• Two parables with similar meanings
The Hidden Treasure and the Priceless Pearl	*Matthew 13:44–46*	• Two parables with similar meanings
The Unforgiving Servant	*Matthew 18:21–35*	• An extended story • Told in response to Peter's question about forgiving others
The Vineyard Owner	*Matthew 21:33–46; Mark 12:1–12; Luke 20:9–19*	• Specific allegorical interpretation • Pharisees recognized this parable was spoken against them
The Good Samaritan	*Luke 10:25–37*	• An extended story • Told in response to an expert in the law's question about eternal life and "Who is my neighbor?"
The Lost and Found Parables	*Luke 15*	• Three parables with similar meanings • Told in response to complaints from the Pharisees and teachers of the law that Jesus would welcome and eat with sinners
• The Lost Sheep/ the Lost Coin	*Luke 15:1–10*	• Two short parables about something of value being lost and then found
• The Lost Son(s)	*Luke 15:11–32*	• An extended story • Some allegorical interpretation • Just as much significance in the older brother who stayed as in the prodigal younger brother who returned
The Pharisee and the Tax Collector	*Luke 18:9–14*	• A short parable • Told in response to some who trusted in their own righteousness and looked down on others

KINGDOM SIGNIFICANCE

The word about the kingdom—the gospel—is **fruitful** only in a heart that hears and understands the good news, yet the message must still be shared like the indiscriminate casting of seed on the ground.

The Father's kingdom will come in its fullness at the end of the age when the unrighteous "children of the evil one" will be judged and condemned to hell and the **righteous** "children of the kingdom" will be glorified and blessed in the kingdom.

The kingdom will start small but will have a very large impact upon the world, permeating it in its entirety.

The kingdom is of such value that it is worth **sacrificing** everything we have in order to be a part of it.

The kingdom is comprised of people who **forgive** others from their heart because they recognize the infinite extent to which God has forgiven them.

The kingdom is comprised of people who produce its **fruit**; failure to produce fruit for God, exemplified in the rejection of his Son Jesus, is to reject participation in the kingdom of God.

The kingdom is comprised of those who see themselves as **neighbors** without boundaries and who show **mercy** to others.

The kingdom of heaven rejoices over even one sinner who **repents**.

The kingdom of heaven rejoices over a sinner who **repents**; refusal to **rejoice over a sinner's repentance** is to find oneself on the outside of the kingdom.

The kingdom is comprised of those who **humble** themselves before God and rely solely upon God's mercy for their salvation; these will be exalted, but those who exalt themselves will be humbled.

[17] But he looked at them and said, "Then what is the meaning of this Scripture:[A]

The stone that the builders rejected
has become the cornerstone?[B]

[18] Everyone who falls on that stone will be broken to pieces, but on whomever it falls, it will shatter him."

[19] Then the scribes and the chief priests looked for a way to get their hands on him that very hour, because they knew he had told this parable against them, but they feared the people.

God and Caesar

[20] They watched closely and sent spies who pretended to be righteous,[C] so that they could catch him in what he said, to hand him over to the governor's rule and authority. [21] They questioned him, "Teacher, we know that you speak and teach correctly, and you don't show partiality[D] but teach truthfully the way of God. [22] Is it lawful for us to pay taxes to Caesar or not?"

[23] But detecting their craftiness, he said to them,[E] [24] "Show me a denarius.[F] Whose image and inscription does it have?"

"Caesar's," they said.

[25] "Well then," he told them, "give to Caesar the things that are Caesar's, and to God the things that are God's."

[26] They were not able to catch him in what he said in public, and being amazed at his answer, they became silent.

The Sadducees and the Resurrection

[27] Some of the Sadducees, who say there is no resurrection, came up and questioned him: [28] "Teacher, Moses wrote for us that if a man's brother has a wife, and dies childless, his brother should take the wife and produce offspring for his brother.[G] [29] Now there were seven brothers. The first took a wife and died without children. [30] Also the second[H] [31] and the third took her. In the same way, all seven died and left no children. [32] Finally, the woman died too. [33] In the resurrection, therefore, whose wife will the woman be? For all seven had married her."

[34] Jesus told them, "The children of this age marry and are given in marriage. [35] But those who are counted worthy to take part in that age and in the resurrection from the dead neither marry nor are given in marriage. [36] For they can no longer die, because they are like angels and are children of God, since they are children of the resurrection. [37] Moses even indicated in the passage about the burning bush that the dead are raised, where he calls the Lord **the God of Abraham and the God of Isaac and the God of Jacob.**[I] [38] He is not the God of the dead but of the living, because all are living to[J] him."

[39] Some of the scribes answered, "Teacher, you have spoken well." [40] And they no longer dared to ask him anything.

The Question about the Messiah

[41] Then he said to them, "How can they say that the Messiah is the son of David? [42] For David himself says in the Book of Psalms:

The Lord declared to my Lord,
'Sit at my right hand
[43]   until I make your enemies
    your footstool.'[K]

[44] David calls him 'Lord.' How, then, can he be his son?"

[A]20:17 Lit *"What then is this that is written* [B]20:17 Ps 118:22 [C]20:20 Or *upright* [D]20:21 Lit *you don't receive a face* [E]20:23 Other mss add *"Why are you testing me?"* [F]20:24 A denarius = one day's wage [G]20:28 Dt 25:5 [H]20:30 Other mss add *took her as wife, and he died without children* [I]20:37 Ex 3:6,15 [J]20:38 Or *with* [K]20:42–43 Ps 110:1

20:19–21 The religious leaders (**scribes . . . chief priests**) understood that Jesus's preceding **parable** referred to them, and so they wanted to get rid of him immediately. But in order not to anger the people, they sought to trap him through a question that would allow them to turn him over to the Roman authorities. So, while attempting to sound pious and respectful, they asked for Jesus's view on one of the most divisive issues of the day—the Roman poll tax. **20:22–26** The religious leaders thought they had found the perfect way to trap Jesus, no matter how he answered. If he said it was **lawful** to pay the poll tax to Caesar, it would turn the Jewish people against him. If he said it was not lawful, it would provide grounds for the Romans to arrest him for treason. But Jesus did not fall into their trap. By asking for a **denarius**, the specific coin used to pay the poll tax, Jesus demonstrated that the religious leaders themselves found it necessary to cooperate with the ruling Roman government. **Give to Caesar the things that are Caesar's** was a proper recognition of the legitimate role of human government in God's plan (Rm 13:1–7). **To God the things that are God's** does not divide life into secular and sacred, which would imply that God is indifferent about some aspects of human existence. Rather, Jesus's statement demonstrates that all facets of life have reference to God, including the need to submit to governmental rule. This answer amazed the scribes and chief priests (v. 26), thwarting their efforts to catch Jesus in a self-condemning statement. **20:27–33** Another group among the religious leaders attempted to trap Jesus. The **Sadducees** did not believe in the **resurrection** from the dead because it was not taught in the Torah (Genesis–Deuteronomy). They asked Jesus a question that was designed to discredit the idea of resurrection by reducing it to absurdity. **If a man's brother . . . dies childless** refers to the law of levirate marriage in Dt 25:5. The Sadducees mistakenly assumed that life after **the resurrection** would include the same basic structures as earthly life. **20:34–36** Jesus answered that **marriage** is confined to **this age**. Those who are counted **worthy** are those who place faith in Christ because faith in Messiah is the only means by which anyone can be accepted by God (Rm 5:1; Gl 2:16). In heaven we will be **like angels**, who enjoy many meaningful relationships but do not marry or reproduce. After the resurrection, the human life cycle (birth, marriage, reproduction, death) is forever changed. **20:37–40** Jesus quoted Ex 3:1–6 to draw in the Sadducees, who revered the books of Moses. Jesus's logic is as follows: God could identify himself to Moses as the **God of Abraham . . . Isaac,** and **Jacob** only if they were still living in Moses's day. Since these men had died many years previously, there must be an afterlife. The religious leaders **no longer dared** to bait Jesus after this because he had **spoken well** and made them look foolish. **20:41–44** Jesus then asked his own difficult theological question based on Ps 110:1: how could the **Messiah** be both **the son of David** and the divine **Lord** of David? Though not given here, the answer is that Jesus, Messiah, was both fully God (Lord) and fully human (son of David).

Warning against the Scribes

45 While all the people were listening, he said to his disciples, **46** "Beware of the scribes, who want to go around in long robes and who love greetings in the marketplaces, the best seats in the synagogues, and the places of honor at banquets. **47** They devour widows' houses and say long prayers just for show. These will receive harsher judgment."

The Widow's Gift

21 He looked up and saw the rich dropping their offerings into the temple treasury. **2** He also saw a poor widow dropping in two tiny coins.^A3 "Truly I tell you," he said, "this poor widow has put in more than all of them. **4** For all these people have put in gifts out of their surplus, but she out of her poverty has put in all she had to live on."

Destruction of the Temple Predicted

5 As some were talking about the temple, how it was adorned with beautiful stones and gifts dedicated to God, he said, **6** "These things that you see — the days will come when not one stone will be left on another that will not be thrown down."

Signs of the End of the Age

7 "Teacher," they asked him, "so when will these things happen? And what will be the sign when these things are about to take place?"

8 Then he said, "Watch out that you are not deceived. For many will come in my name, saying, 'I am he,' and, 'The time is near.' Don't follow them. **9** When you hear of wars and rebellions,^B don't be alarmed. Indeed, it is necessary that these things take place first, but the end won't come right away."

10 Then he told them, "Nation will be raised up against nation, and kingdom against kingdom. **11** There will be violent earthquakes, and famines and plagues in various places, and there will be terrifying sights and great signs from heaven. **12** But before all these things, they will lay their hands on you and persecute you. They will hand you over to the synagogues and prisons, and you will be brought before kings and governors because of my name. **13** This will give you an opportunity to bear witness. **14** Therefore make up your minds^C not to prepare your defense ahead of time, **15** for I will give you such words and a wisdom that none of your adversaries will be able to resist or contradict. **16** You will even be betrayed by parents, brothers, relatives, and friends. They will kill some of you. **17** You will be hated by everyone because of my name, **18** but not a hair of your head will be lost. **19** By your endurance, gain^D your lives.

The Destruction of Jerusalem

20 "When you see Jerusalem surrounded by armies, then recognize that its desolation has come near. **21** Then those in Judea must flee to the mountains. Those inside the city must leave it, and those who are in the country must not enter it, **22** because these are days of vengeance to fulfill all the things that are written. **23** Woe to pregnant women and nursing mothers in

---

^A**21:2** Lit *two lepta*; the *lepton* was the smallest and least valuable Gk coin in use.   ^B**21:9** Or *insurrections*, or *revolutions*, or *chaos*   ^C**21:14** Lit *Therefore place* (determine) *in your hearts*   ^D**21:19** Other mss read *endurance, you will gain*

20:45–47 The **long robes** of **the scribes** were of white linen and had a decorative fringe. The **best seats** were where a person could be seen by everyone in attendance at the synagogue. **Devour widows' houses** probably means that some scribes defrauded helpless widows of their homes and their limited resources. Matthew 23:1–36 is an extended parallel passage describing the sins for which the scribes and Pharisees would be judged by God.

21:1–4 There were thirteen coffers shaped like inverted trumpets in the court of women in the temple and a **treasury** room nearby where supplicants could deposit their **offerings**. The **poor widow** did not have much to give, unlike the **rich** who made a great show of their offerings. **Tiny** copper **coins** traditionally called mites (Gk *lepta*) were the smallest Jewish currency at that time. Jesus commended the widow for giving sacrificially.

21:5 Herod the Great began renovating **the temple** in 20 BC. The work was completed in AD 63, some thirty years after Jesus's crucifixion. Some of the stones used for the foundation were forty feet long. Others were overlaid with gold.

21:6 Jesus declared that **not one stone will be left on another**. In AD 70, the Roman armies fulfilled this prophecy by leveling the temple and the city of Jerusalem. Many of the huge stones of the temple were toppled into lower areas surrounding the complex.

21:7 The parallel passages in Mt 24 and Mk 13 focus primarily on the end of the age, while Luke is concerned mostly about the near-term destruction of the temple (**these things**). But vv. 25–28 do speak of the second coming of Christ. The events leading to the destruction of the temple in AD 70 foreshadow the later time that leads up to Jesus's return.

21:8–10 The appearance of false messiahs and date-setting schemes (**the time is near**), as well as widespread **wars**, will continue throughout the present age. However, these things must occur and are part of an expected delay before the **end** of the age.

21:11 Earthquakes . . . famines, and **plagues** of varied intensity will occur through history all the way to the end of the age. **Great signs from heaven** probably refer to such cosmic phenomena as that prophesied in both Jl 2:28–32 and in Rv 6:13–14.

21:12–15 These verses return to discussion of the immediate circumstances of the apostles and their co-laborers in the gospel. Persecution by Jews (**the synagogues**) and Gentiles (**kings and governors**) will lead to opportunities to **witness** for Christ (Ac 4; 7; 22–24;

26). **I will give you such words** basically repeats Jesus's earlier promise in 12:11–12.

21:16–19 When troubles came upon them after Jesus's death, the disciples would draw comfort from their recollection of Jesus's forewarning that they would be **hated** and even **betrayed** by those closest to them. **Not a hair of your head** refers to spiritual security. **Endurance** is required of every true believer in Jesus Christ. Ultimately the strength to endure is supplied by God.

21:20–22 The words **Jerusalem** and **its desolation** indicate that this is the point where the questions in v. 7 are answered. **Surrounded by armies** is the "sign" that the temple and the city are about to be destroyed. Matthew 24:15 refers to "the abomination of desolation" spoken of by Daniel (Dn 9:27; 11:31; 21:11) that will be set up in the holy place in the temple. Luke spoke only of the desolation of Jerusalem. When the city was surrounded, it was imperative that its inhabitants and those in the surrounding areas (**Judea**) flee for their lives because the siege of the city was part of God's planned **vengeance** against Jerusalem.

21:23–24 Wrath is God's anger against sin expressed as righteous judgment. The survivors of the destruction of Jerusalem in AD 70 were spread all over the known world, even more extensively than the Diaspora

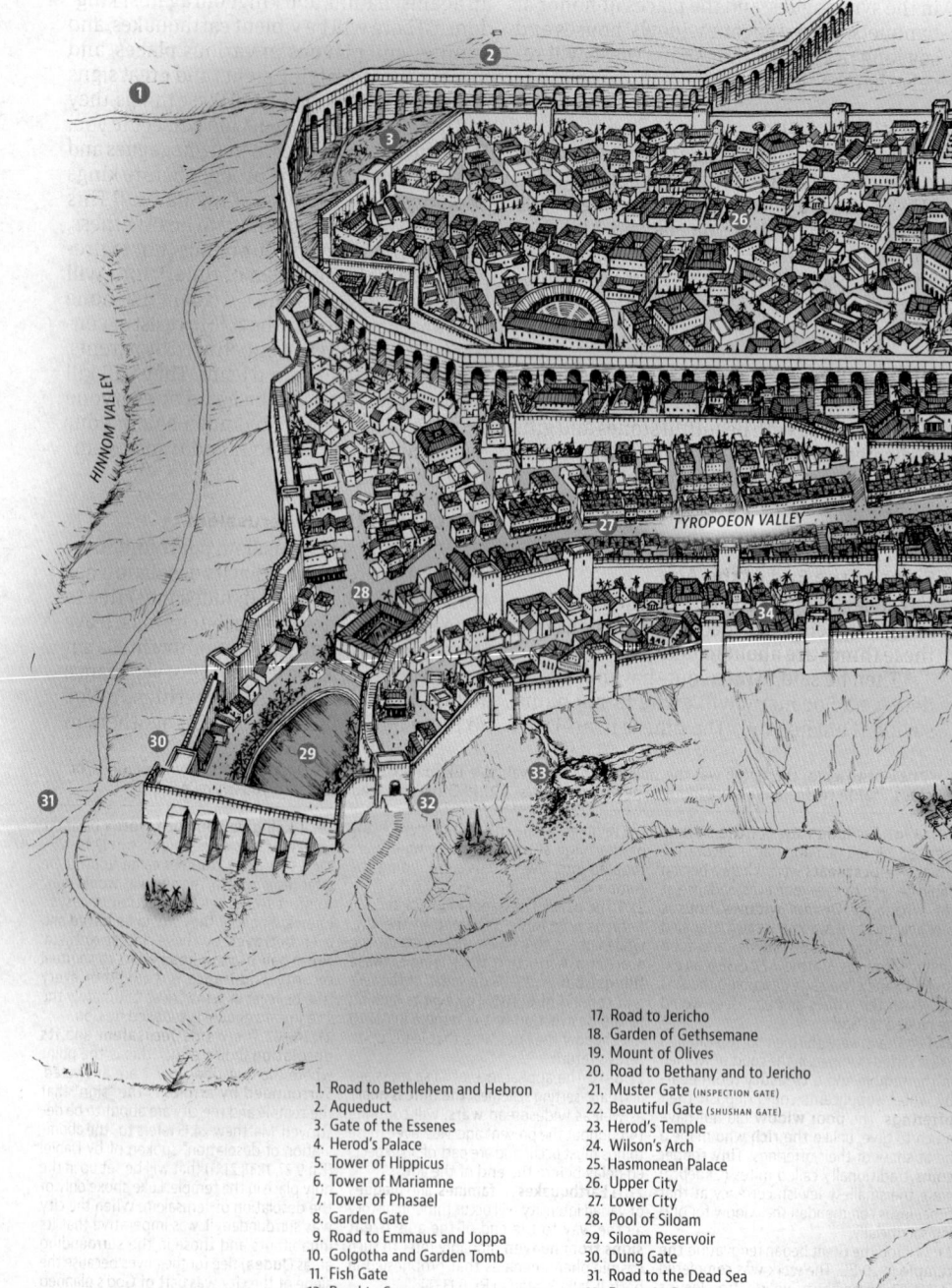

New Testament Jerusalem

ca AD 30 (VIEW IS LOOKING WESTWARD,
FROM A VANTAGE POINT ABOVE THE MOUNT OF OLIVES)

HINNOM VALLEY

TYROPOEON VALLEY

1. Road to Bethlehem and Hebron
2. Aqueduct
3. Gate of the Essenes
4. Herod's Palace
5. Tower of Hippicus
6. Tower of Mariamne
7. Tower of Phasael
8. Garden Gate
9. Road to Emmaus and Joppa
10. Golgotha and Garden Tomb
11. Fish Gate
12. Road to Caesarea
13. Pool of Bethesda
14. Fortress of Antonia
15. Sheep Gate
16. Pool of Israel
17. Road to Jericho
18. Garden of Gethsemane
19. Mount of Olives
20. Road to Bethany and to Jericho
21. Muster Gate (INSPECTION GATE)
22. Beautiful Gate (SHUSHAN GATE)
23. Herod's Temple
24. Wilson's Arch
25. Hasmonean Palace
26. Upper City
27. Lower City
28. Pool of Siloam
29. Siloam Reservoir
30. Dung Gate
31. Road to the Dead Sea
32. Fountain Gate
33. Tower of Siloam (RUINS)
34. Old City
35. Robinson's Arch
36. Temple Steps and Mikveh

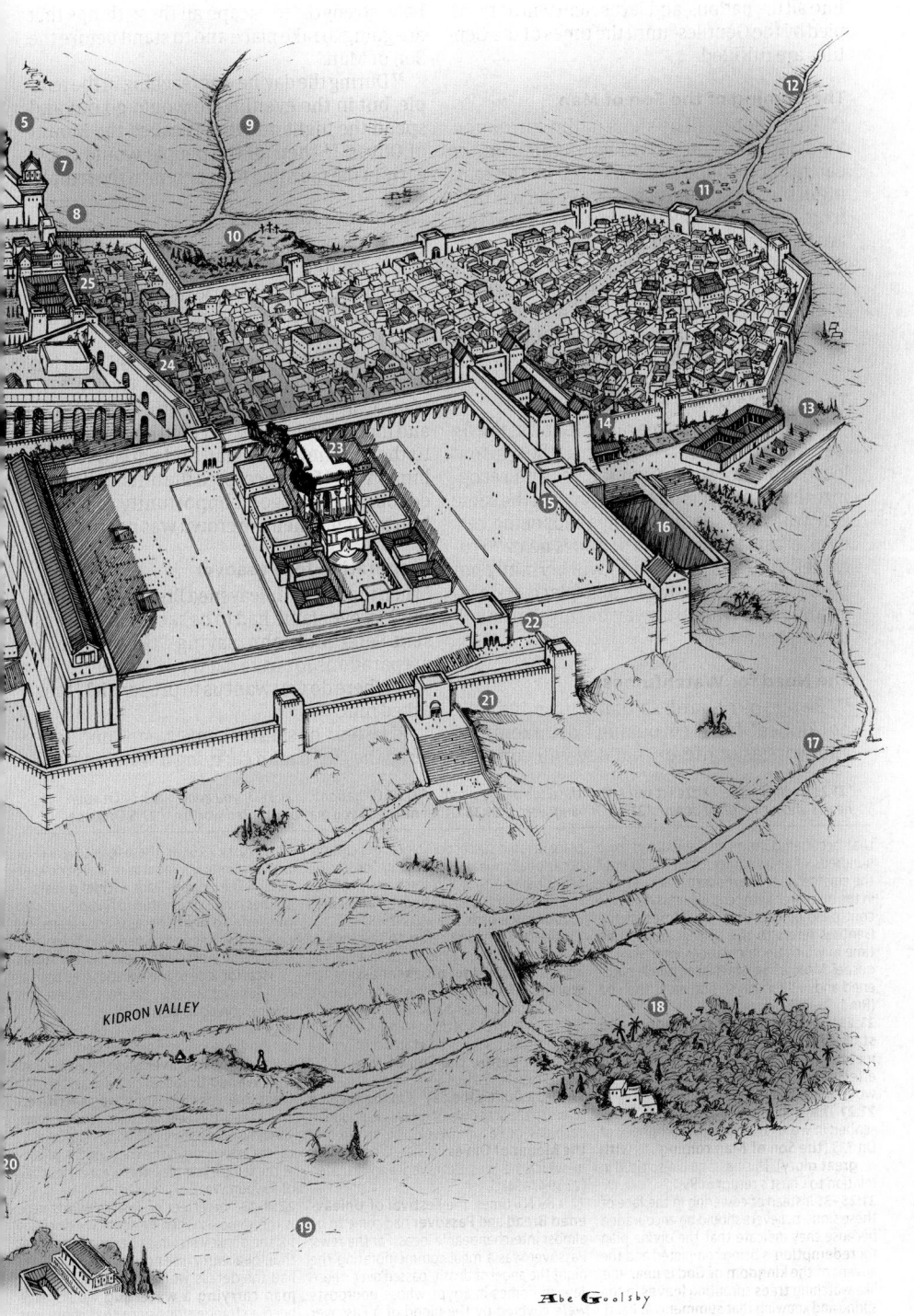

KIDRON VALLEY

Abe Goolsby

those days, for there will be great distress in the land[A] and wrath against this people. [24] They will be killed by the sword[B] and be led captive into all the nations, and Jerusalem will be trampled by the Gentiles[C] until the times of the Gentiles are fulfilled.

The Coming of the Son of Man

[25] "Then there will be signs in the sun, moon, and stars; and there will be anguish on the earth among nations bewildered by the roaring of the sea and the waves. [26] People will faint from fear and expectation of the things that are coming on the world, because the powers of the heavens will be shaken. [27] Then they will see the Son of Man coming in a cloud with power and great glory. [28] But when these things begin to take place, stand up and lift your heads, because your redemption is near."

The Parable of the Fig Tree

[29] Then he told them a parable: "Look at the fig tree, and all the trees. [30] As soon as they put out leaves you can see for yourselves and recognize that summer is already near. [31] In the same way, when you see these things happening, recognize[D] that the kingdom of God is near. [32] Truly I tell you, this generation will certainly not pass away until all things take place. [33] Heaven and earth will pass away, but my words will never pass away.

The Need for Watchfulness

[34] "Be on your guard, so that your minds are not dulled[E] from carousing,[F] drunkenness, and worries of life, or that day will come on

you unexpectedly [35] like a trap. For it will come on all who live on the face of the whole earth. [36] But be alert at all times, praying that you may have strength[G] to escape all these things that are going to take place and to stand before the Son of Man."

[37] During the day, he was teaching in the temple, but in the evening he would go out and spend the night on what is called the Mount of Olives. [38] Then all the people would come early in the morning to hear him in the temple.

The Plot to Kill Jesus

22 The Festival of Unleavened Bread, which is called Passover, was approaching. [2] The chief priests and the scribes were looking for a way to put him to death, because they were afraid of the people.

[3] Then Satan entered Judas, called Iscariot, who was numbered among the Twelve. [4] He went away and discussed with the chief priests and temple police how he could hand him over to them. [5] They were glad and agreed to give him silver.[H] [6] So he accepted the offer and started looking for a good opportunity to betray him to them when the crowd was not present.

Preparation for Passover

[7] Then the Day of Unleavened Bread came when the Passover lamb had to be sacrificed. [8] Jesus sent Peter and John, saying, "Go and make preparations for us to eat the Passover."

[9] "Where do you want us to prepare it?" they asked him.

[10] "Listen," he said to them, "when you've entered the city, a man carrying a water jug will

[A]21:23 Or *the earth*   [B]21:24 Lit *will fall by the edge of the sword*   [C]21:24 Or *nations*   [D]21:31 Or *you know*   [E]21:34 Lit *your hearts are not weighed down*   [F]21:34 Or *hangovers*   [G]21:36 Other mss read *you may be counted worthy*   [H]22:5 Or *money*

that occurred during the Babylonian exile hundreds of years earlier. From AD 70 until the emergence of the modern State of Israel in the mid-twentieth century, Jerusalem was controlled by **Gentiles**. The **times** of the Gentiles refers to the current opportune time in which Gentile nations embrace the gospel. Meanwhile, Israel is spiritually hardened and will remain so until near the end (Rm 11:25–26).
21:25–26 Signs in the sun, moon, and stars, probably referring to Jl 2:28,31, were mentioned earlier (Lk 21:11). These cosmic effects will cause great anxiety among the world population.
21:27 The second coming of Christ is described in words that echo the prophecy of Dn 7:13 (**the Son of Man coming** . . . **with** . . . **great glory**). This passage is also cited in relation to Christ's return in Rv 1:7.
21:28–31 Instead of cowering in the face of these signs, believers should be encouraged because they indicate that the divine plan for **redemption** is being completed and the advent of **the kingdom of God is near**. It is like watching **trees** sprouting **leaves** in the spring and knowing that **summer** is at hand.
21:32–33 This generation probably refers to those who will be alive when the various phenomena described by Jesus begin to take

place in rapid succession. Since "generation" occasionally means "family" or "posterity," some believe that it refers specifically to the people of Israel. On **heaven and earth** . . . **but my words**, see Mt 5:17–18.
21:34–36 That day refers to the time of Christ's return. Those caught up in a worldly lifestyle (**carousing, drunkenness**) or the **worries of life** will be caught off guard when Christ comes back. The proper outlook is prayerful alertness (18:8), which will prepare the believer to **stand** and not be ashamed **before the Son of Man** at his return (see 1Jn 2:28).
21:37–38 During the day . . . **in the evening** refers to the schedule that Jesus kept during each day of Passion Week. The mention of **the Mount of Olives** previews the incident in which he was betrayed and arrested (22:39,47–54).
22:1 By NT times, the **Festival of Unleavened Bread** and **Passover** had come to be almost interchangeable ideas. For the Jews, Passover was a meal commemorating the night the angel of death "passed over" those Jewish homes in Egypt whose doorposts were covered by the blood of a Passover lamb (Ex 12:1–14; Lv 23:5). Unleavened Bread was a weeklong feast immediately following Passover that commemorated the exodus (Ex

12:14–20; Lv 23:6–8). These feasts were celebrated during our months of March or April.
22:2–6 The religious leaders (**chief priests** . . . **scribes**) were committed to finding a way to **put** Jesus **to death** because they feared his popularity among the people. The perfect opportunity presented itself when **Judas** . . . **Iscariot**, one of the apostles (see note at 6:14–16), motivated by Satanic influence and money, agreed to **betray** Jesus.
22:7 All leaven, or yeast, was excluded from Jewish households from the beginning of the week of **Passover** and the Festival of **Unleavened Bread**. In that sense, the day when the Passover lamb was **sacrificed** was called the Day of Unleavened Bread. The lambs were sacrificed from midafternoon to late afternoon in the court of the priests at the temple complex. This was on Thursday of Passion Week.
22:8–13 The effect of Jesus's words here is the same as when he sent two disciples for the donkey on which he rode during the triumphal entry (see note at 19:30–34). God had the details worked out in advance. **A man carrying a water jug** would have been a strange sight since that chore was typically performed by women. Many homes in Jerusalem had an upstairs **guest room** with an outside entrance which could be

meet you. Follow him into the house he enters. [11] Tell the owner of the house, 'The Teacher asks you, "Where is the guest room where I can eat the Passover with my disciples?" ' [12] Then he will show you a large, furnished room upstairs. Make the preparations there."

[13] So they went and found it just as he had told them, and they prepared the Passover.

The First Lord's Supper

[14] When the hour came, he reclined at the table, and the apostles with him. [15] Then he said to them, "I have fervently desired to eat this Passover with you before I suffer. [16] For I tell you, I will not eat it again[A] until it is fulfilled in the kingdom of God." [17] Then he took a cup, and after giving thanks, he said, "Take this and share it among yourselves. [18] For I tell you, from now on I will not drink of the fruit of the vine until the kingdom of God comes."

[19] And he took bread, gave thanks, broke it, gave it to them, and said, "This is my body, which is given for you. Do this in remembrance of me." [20] In the same way he also took the cup after supper and said, "This cup is the new covenant in my blood, which is poured out for you.[B] [21] But look, the hand of the one betraying me is at the table with me. [22] For the Son of Man will go away as it has been determined, but woe to that man by whom he is betrayed!"

[23] So they began to argue among themselves which of them it could be who was going to do it.

The Dispute over Greatness

[24] Then a dispute also arose among them about who should be considered the greatest. [25] But he said to them, "The kings of the Gentiles lord it over them, and those who have authority over them have themselves called[C] 'Benefactors.' [26] It is not to be like that among you. On the contrary, whoever is greatest among you should become like the youngest, and whoever leads, like the one serving. [27] For who is greater, the one at the table or the one serving? Isn't it the one at the table? But I am among you as the one who serves. [28] You are those who stood by me in my trials. [29] I bestow on you a kingdom, just as my Father bestowed one on me, [30] so that you may eat and drink at my table in my kingdom. And you will sit on thrones judging the twelve tribes of Israel.

Peter's Denial Predicted

[31] "Simon, Simon,[D] look out. Satan has asked to sift you[E] like wheat. [32] But I have prayed for you[F] that your faith may not fail. And you, when you have turned back, strengthen your brothers."

[33] "Lord," he told him, "I'm ready to go with you both to prison and to death."

[34] "I tell you, Peter," he said, "the rooster will not crow today until[G] you deny three times that you know me."

Be Ready for Trouble

[35] He also said to them, "When I sent you out without money-bag, traveling bag, or sandals, did you lack anything?"

"Not a thing," they said.

[36] Then he said to them, "But now, whoever has a money-bag should take it, and also a traveling bag. And whoever doesn't have a sword should sell his robe and buy one. [37] For I tell you, what is written must be fulfilled in me:[H] And he

---

[A]22:16 Other mss omit *again* [B]22:19-20 Other mss omit *which is given for you* (v. 19) through the end of v. 20 [C]22:25 Or *them call themselves* [D]22:31 Other mss read *Then the Lord said, "Simon, Simon* [E]22:31 *you* is plural in Gk [F]22:32 *you* is singular in Gk [G]22:34 Other mss read *before* [H]22:37 Or *it is necessary that what is written be fulfilled in me*

---

rented to pilgrims observing a feast in the city. The wording suggests that the owner of this room knew Jesus or was even a disciple. **22:14** The Passover meal began at sundown. Participants **reclined** on their sides on low couches, leaning over the low **table** to eat. **22:15-18** By saying that he **fervently desired to eat this Passover** with his disciples before suffering (going to the cross), Jesus encouraged them to interpret the following events in light of Passover imagery. The **cup** here could have been the first or second cup of the traditional Jewish Passover ritual. **22:19** To institute a new memorial meal (the Lord's Supper), Jesus chose the unleavened **bread** of the Passover meal to represent his physical **body**, which would be broken on the cross much as bread was broken during the meal. His death would be offered (**given for you**) as a substitute for sinners, all of whom deserve to die for their sins. **22:20** The new memorial meal also lent fresh meaning to **the cup after supper** (probably the third of four cups in the Passover ritual). The cup was reinterpreted to refer to the **blood** of Christ, **poured out** as a payment for sins by Jesus, the ultimate

Lamb of God (Jn 1:29). The mention of the **new covenant** related to Christ's shed blood means that the prophesied new covenant (Jr 31:31-34) would be ratified by Jesus's death on the cross. **22:21-22** Judas was guilty as **the one betraying** Jesus (vv. 3-6), yet it remains the case that his actions were **determined** (planned, ordained) by God as part of the plan that would culminate in Jesus's crucifixion (Ac 2:23). **22:23-24** This argument recalls the earlier similar one on the way to Jerusalem (9:46-48). Luke is tenacious and honest about the immaturity of the disciples. After so great a spiritual experience as the Passover meal, conducted by the Lord himself, they argued over who was **greatest** among them. Had they misunderstood everything? **22:25-27** The wording in these verses is significantly different than that in Mt 20:25-28, suggesting that the apostles argued about greatness more than once. Greatness in the world is based on power and public recognition, but Christ taught that spiritual greatness requires humility and self-sacrifice. Jesus is our example because he came among us as **the one who serves**.

22:28-30 Because the apostles **stood by** Jesus in his **trials** (i.e., his troubles generally, not the trials he would soon face before Roman and Jewish authorities), they would be rewarded by the rights and privileges of leadership in the coming **kingdom**, including close fellowship with the King and rulership over eschatological Israel (Mt 19:28). **22:31-34** In these verses Jesus addressed **Simon** Peter as the leader of the apostles and their spokesman. The plural **you** indicates **Satan** wanted to sift all the apostles like wheat, a rough action that symbolizes tempting them to spiritual ruin. Peter protested that nothing would cause him to deny Jesus, but Jesus knew better. **When you have turned back** demonstrates that Jesus also knew that Peter's denial would be temporary and that he would play a significant role in church history. **22:35-38** On **when I sent you out without**, see notes at 9:1-2,3-5. Because of the rejection they would face, Jesus emphasized that the apostles must prepare to take care of their own needs (**money-bag, traveling bag**) and protect themselves physically (**a sword**). By arming themselves, Jesus's apostles unintentionally paved the way for

was counted among the lawless.ᵃ Yes, what is written about me is coming to its fulfillment." ³⁸ "Lord," they said, "look, here are two swords."

"That is enough!" he told them.

The Prayer in the Garden

³⁹ He went out and made his way as usual to the Mount of Olives, and the disciples followed him. ⁴⁰ When he reached the place, he told them, "Pray that you may not fall into temptation." ⁴¹ Then he withdrew from them about a stone's throw, knelt down, and began to pray, ⁴² "Father, if you are willing, take this cup away from me — nevertheless, not my will, but yours, be done."

⁴³ Then an angel from heaven appeared to him, strengthening him. ⁴⁴ Being in anguish, he prayed more fervently, and his sweat became like drops of blood falling to the ground.ᵇ ⁴⁵ When he got up from prayer and came to the disciples, he found them sleeping, exhausted from their grief. ⁴⁶ "Why are you sleeping?" he asked them. "Get up and pray, so that you won't fall into temptation."

Judas's Betrayal of Jesus

⁴⁷ While he was still speaking, suddenly a mob came, and one of the Twelve named Judas was leading them. He came near Jesus to kiss him, ⁴⁸ but Jesus said to him, "Judas, are you betraying the Son of Man with a kiss?"

⁴⁹ When those around him saw what was going to happen, they asked, "Lord, should we strike with the sword?" ⁵⁰ Then one of them struck the high priest's servant and cut off his right ear.

⁵¹ But Jesus responded, "No more of this!" And touching his ear, he healed him. ⁵² Then Jesus said to the chief priests, temple police, and the elders who had come for him, "Have you come out with swords and clubs as if I were a criminal?ᶜ ⁵³ Every day while I was with you in the temple, you never laid a hand on me. But this is your hour — and the dominion of darkness."

Peter Denies His Lord

⁵⁴ They seized him, led him away, and brought him into the high priest's house. Meanwhile Peter was following at a distance. ⁵⁵ They lit a fire in the middle of the courtyard and sat down together, and Peter sat among them. ⁵⁶ When a servant saw him sitting in the light, and looked closely at him, she said, "This man was with him too."

⁵⁷ But he denied it: "Woman, I don't know him." ⁵⁸ After a little while, someone else saw him and said, "You're one of them too."

"Man, I am not!" Peter said.

⁵⁹ About an hour later, another kept insisting, "This man was certainly with him, since he's also a Galilean."

⁶⁰ But Peter said, "Man, I don't know what you're talking about!" Immediately, while he was still speaking, a rooster crowed. ⁶¹ Then the Lord turned and looked at Peter. So Peter remembered the word of the Lord, how he had said to him, "Before the rooster crows today, you will deny me three times." ⁶² And he went outside and wept bitterly.

Jesus Mocked and Beaten

⁶³ The men who were holding Jesus started mocking and beating him. ⁶⁴ After blindfolding

---

ᵃ22:37 Is 53:12   ᵇ22:43–44 Other mss omit vv. 43–44   ᶜ22:52 Lit as against a thief, or a bandit

---

Jesus to fulfill the rebels' prophecy of Is 53:12. Jesus's call for a sword was likely only figurative, but the apostles responded that they had **two swords** among them.
22:39–41 Throughout Passion Week, Jesus and the apostles spent the nights on **the Mount of Olives** (21:37). John 18:1 says the location of this incident was a garden, and Mt 26:36 calls the place Gethsemane. On this occasion, Jesus instructed the apostles to linger in prayer so they would not be tempted by the devil and so their faith would not fail (Lk 22:32). Jesus then met the Father in prayer in order to seek strength in a time of deep suffering.
22:42 This cup refers to Jesus's upcoming judicial trials and execution on the cross (Mt 20:22–23). Jesus addressed God as **Father**, just as he had instructed his disciples to do (see note at 11:1–4). **If you are willing, take this cup** shows that Jesus, fully aware of the suffering that awaited him, struggled with going to the cross. He resolved his struggle in favor of doing God's **will**, which was always his focus (Jn 6:38).
22:43–44 Though God the Father would not allow Jesus to bypass the upcoming suffering (v. 42), he did send **an angel** to minister to him. However, this did not eliminate Jesus's **anguish**. As he prayed, Jesus's **sweat** poured

off his body as if he were bleeding. Some believe Luke is describing a condition called hematidrosis, in which sweat and blood mingle in extreme cases of anxiety, but most likely his language is figurative.
22:45–46 Human physical weakness (hunger, fatigue, etc.) can lead to spiritual weakness and **temptation** (see note at vv. 39–41).
22:47–48 Knowing exactly where Jesus would be spending the night (see note at 21:37–38), **Judas** Iscariot led a group of Jesus's enemies to arrest him. They are described as a **mob** because they carried swords and clubs. A **kiss** on the cheek was a common greeting between friends and family. Thus Judas used his intimacy with Jesus and his disciples as a platform for betraying the **Son of Man**.
22:49–51 The apostles' earlier misunderstanding about wielding the **sword** (see note at vv. 35–38) now came to a climax. Luke did not name the apostle who cut off the **ear** of the high priest's servant, but Jn 18:10 discloses that it was Peter. Jesus immediately **healed** the man's ear, averting certain disaster if the mob had attacked Peter.
22:52–53 That Jesus was viewed as a **criminal** fulfilled Is 53:12 (see note at Lk 22:35–38). Jesus's prior awareness of the time (**this is your hour**) and place (not in **the temple**)

of his arrest indicates that everything was according to God's design even though the **chief priests** and **elders** were in league with **the dominion of darkness** (Satan and the demons) in carrying out the arrest.
22:54 John 18:13 says that Jesus was first taken to the **house** of Annas, a former high priest who was the father-in-law of Caiaphas, the current high priest (see note at 3:2–3). Most of the apostles fled from Gethsemane, though **Peter** circled back and tracked down the arresting group, all the while careful to keep a safe **distance** in the darkness. John 18:15 indicates that "another disciple" (probably the apostle John) also followed.
22:55–62 In a period of only slightly over an **hour**, Peter disowned three years of discipleship. Jesus had predicted this only a few hours earlier (see note at vv. 31–34), and when **a rooster crowed** after Peter's denials, Jesus **turned and looked** at him. Immediately **Peter remembered** Jesus's prophecy and **wept** tears of shame and regret. Since Jesus was inside the high priest's house (v. 54), there must have been an open window or door through which he could look into **the courtyard** and catch Peter's eye.
22:63–65 Jesus's horrific treatment is also described in Mt 26:67 and Mk 14:65.

him, they kept^A asking, "Prophesy! Who was it that hit you?" ⁶⁵ And they were saying many other blasphemous things to him.

Jesus Faces the Sanhedrin

⁶⁶ When daylight came, the elders^B of the people, both the chief priests and the scribes, convened and brought him before their Sanhedrin. ⁶⁷ They said, "If you are the Messiah, tell us."

But he said to them, "If I do tell you, you will not believe. ⁶⁸ And if I ask you, you will not answer. ⁶⁹ But from now on, the Son of Man will be seated at the right hand of the power of God."

⁷⁰ They all asked, "Are you, then, the Son of God?"

And he said to them, "You say that I am."

⁷¹ "Why do we need any more testimony," they said, "since we've heard it ourselves from his mouth?"

Jesus Faces Pilate

23 Then their whole assembly rose up and brought him before Pilate. ² They began to accuse him, saying, "We found this man misleading our nation, opposing payment of taxes to Caesar, and saying that he himself is the Messiah, a king."

³ So Pilate asked him, "Are you the king of the Jews?"

He answered him, "You say so."^C

⁴ Pilate then told the chief priests and the crowds, "I find no grounds for charging this man."

⁵ But they kept insisting, "He stirs up the people, teaching throughout all Judea, from Galilee where he started even to here."

Jesus Faces Herod Antipas

⁶ When Pilate heard this,^D he asked if the man was a Galilean. ⁷ Finding that he was under Herod's jurisdiction, he sent him to Herod, who was also in Jerusalem during those days. ⁸ Herod was very glad to see Jesus; for a long time he had wanted to see him because he had heard about him and was hoping to see some miracle^E performed by him. ⁹ So he kept asking him questions, but Jesus did not answer him. ¹⁰ The chief priests and the scribes stood by, vehemently accusing him. ¹¹ Then Herod, with his soldiers, treated him with contempt, mocked him, dressed him in bright clothing, and sent him back to Pilate. ¹² That very day Herod and Pilate became friends.^F Previously, they had been enemies.

Jesus or Barabbas

¹³ Pilate called together the chief priests, the leaders, and the people, ¹⁴ and said to them, "You have brought me this man as one who misleads the people. But in fact, after examining him in your presence, I have found no grounds to charge this man with those things you accuse him of. ¹⁵ Neither has Herod, because he sent him back to us. Clearly, he has done nothing to deserve death. ¹⁶ Therefore, I will have him whipped^G and then release him."^H

¹⁸ Then they all cried out together, "Take this man away! Release Barabbas to us!"

---

^A22:64 Other mss add *striking him on the face and*   ^B22:66 Or *council of elders*   ^C23:3 Or *"That is true."*   ^D23:6 Other mss read *heard "Galilee"*   ^E23:8 Or *sign*   ^F23:12 Lit *friends with one another*   ^G23:16 Gk *paideuo*; to discipline or *"teach a lesson"*   ^H23:16 Some mss include v. 17: *For according to the festival he had to release someone to them.*

22:66 By rule it had to be **daylight** outside for the Sanhedrin (ruling council of the Jews) to hold a trial in which they decided on the death penalty (which could only be carried out by the Roman government). This explains why they waited for daylight. However, in several other respects the trial was illegal: (1) No trial could be held on the morning of a feast day (i.e., Passover), (2) there was no formal defense offered for Jesus, and (3) the verdict was reached in one day, not the two days required for capital offenses.

22:67–69 In a tactical move that may have been designed to keep Rome from thinking Jesus intended to ascend Israel's vacant throne, Jesus did not give a direct answer to the question of whether he was **the Messiah**. Since he knew he could not expect fair treatment from the members of the Sanhedrin, Jesus identified himself as **the Son of Man** who would sit as judge over them in a much higher court in heaven (**at the right hand**).

22:70–71 The Sanhedrin understood Jesus's previous claim to be Messiah, but they wanted to catch him in what they thought was a more clear-cut blasphemy: the claim that he was **the Son of God**. Jesus's response seems vague to modern readers, but those present understood it as a clear confession. Having

this in hand, they concluded there was no need for **any more testimony**.

23:1 On Pontius **Pilate**, see note at 3:1. Pilate's normal residence was in Caesarea Maritima, but he came to Jerusalem during the Jewish festivals to keep an eye on things. Since Jesus was crucified along with two criminals (vv. 32–33), a punishment that only the Romans could render, it seems that a couple of executions were already scheduled even before Jesus's sentencing. Thus Pilate came to town planning to execute criminals, but he left town having executed an innocent man.

23:2–4 The three charges the Jews brought against Jesus in Pilate's presence were fabrications. It was true that huge crowds had flocked to hear Jesus speak, but his teachings were not aimed at **misleading** Israel. The claim that he was **opposing payment of taxes to Caesar** was an outright lie (see note at 20:22–26). Jesus was **the Messiah**, but he carefully avoided giving the impression that he meant to topple Rome or ascend the throne as **king** of Israel. Pilate had undoubtedly heard about Jesus, and he saw right through the Sanhedrin's rush to judgment.

23:5–7 When Pilate heard that Jesus was from **Galilee**, he saw a convenient way to excuse himself from the Sanhedrin's headhunt.

He turned Jesus over to the proper **jurisdiction**, that of **Herod** Antipas, the ruler over Galilee (see note at 3:1). Like Pilate, Herod was in Jerusalem for the festivals of Passover and Unleavened Bread.

23:8–11 At an earlier **time**, Herod Antipas had been anxious to meet Jesus (9:7–9), and the Pharisees had claimed that Herod wanted to kill Jesus (13:31). Jesus's silence before Herod may have been designed to fulfill the prophecy in Is 53:7–8. In spite of the serious accusations of the Sanhedrin, Herod Antipas simply made sport of Jesus and **sent him back to Pilate** for final legal disposition. He dressed Jesus in **bright clothing** in order to ridicule him as a fake king and irritate the Sanhedrin since they charged him with claiming to be king (see note at vv. 2–4).

23:12–15 Herod Antipas and Pontius **Pilate** became friends because they both made the same assessment (**no grounds to charge this man**) of Jesus (vv. 14–15). Apparently they also shared the same low opinion of the Jewish Sanhedrin for pursuing a **death** sentence against Jesus.

23:16–19 In order to placate the Sanhedrin, Pilate was willing to have Jesus severely **whipped** and set free. It was his custom to release a prisoner in honor of Passover (Jn 18:39). However, the crowd demanded that

19 (He had been thrown into prison for a rebellion that had taken place in the city, and for murder.)

20 Wanting to release Jesus, Pilate addressed them again, **21** but they kept shouting, "Crucify! Crucify him!"

22 A third time he said to them, "Why? What has this man done wrong? I have found in him no grounds for the death penalty. Therefore, I will have him whipped and then release him."

23 But they kept up the pressure, demanding with loud voices that he be crucified, and their voices^ won out. **24** So Pilate decided to grant their demand **25** and released the one they were asking for, who had been thrown into prison for rebellion and murder. But he handed Jesus over to their will.

The Way to the Cross

26 As they led him away, they seized Simon, a Cyrenian, who was coming in from the country, and laid the cross on him to carry behind Jesus. **27** A large crowd of people followed him, including women who were mourning and lamenting him. **28** But turning to them, Jesus said, "Daughters of Jerusalem, do not weep for me, but weep for yourselves and your children. **29** Look, the days are coming when they will say, 'Blessed are the women without children, the wombs that never bore, and the breasts that never nursed!' **30** Then they will begin to say to the mountains, 'Fall on us!' and to the hills, 'Cover us!'^B **31** For if they do these things when the wood is green, what will happen when it is dry?"

Crucified between Two Criminals

32 Two others — criminals — were also led away to be executed with him. **33** When they arrived at the place called The Skull, they crucified him there, along with the criminals, one on the right and one on the left. **34** Then Jesus said, "Father, forgive them, because they do not know what they are doing."^C And they divided his clothes and cast lots.

35 The people stood watching, and even the leaders were scoffing: "He saved others; let him save himself if this is God's Messiah, the Chosen One!" **36** The soldiers also mocked him. They came offering him sour wine **37** and said, "If you are the king of the Jews, save yourself!"

38 An inscription was above him:^D THIS IS THE KING OF THE JEWS.

39 Then one of the criminals hanging there began to yell insults at^E him: "Aren't you the Messiah? Save yourself and us!"

40 But the other answered, rebuking him: "Don't you even fear God, since you are undergoing the same punishment? **41** We are punished justly, because we're getting back what we deserve for the things we did, but this man has done nothing wrong." **42** Then he said, "Jesus, remember me^F when you come into your kingdom."

43 And he said to him, "Truly I tell you, today you will be with me in paradise."

The Death of Jesus

44 It was now about noon,^G and darkness came over the whole land^H until three,^I **45** because the sun's light failed.^J The curtain of the sanctuary was split down the middle. **46** And Jesus

---

^**23:23** Other mss add *and those of the chief priests* ^B **23:30** Hs 10:8 ^C **23:34** Other mss omit *Then Jesus said, "Father, forgive them, because they do not know what they are doing."* ^D **23:38** Other mss add *written in Greek, Latin, and Hebrew letters* ^E **23:39** Or *began to blaspheme* ^F **23:42** Other mss add *Lord* ^G **23:44** Lit *about the sixth hour* ^H **23:44** Or *whole earth* ^I **23:44** Lit *the ninth hour* ^J **23:45** Other mss read *three, and the sun was darkened*

---

a criminal named **Barabbas**, who had committed **murder** and **rebellion** in Jerusalem, be released instead.
23:20–25 Pilate tried two more times to release Jesus, finding no valid basis for the **death penalty**. But he was repeatedly shouted down by a chorus of **Crucify him!** Finally, Pilate caved in to the crowd's demand, releasing Barabbas and handing Jesus over to be executed.
23:26 Condemned prisoners customarily carried the crossbeam or *patibulum* to the site of their execution, where it was attached to the vertical beam. Jesus was unable to carry the cross any farther after his earlier beating (22:63), so it was placed on the back of **Simon** of Cyrene. Simon was staying outside Jerusalem and **coming in from the country** to worship each day during the Festival of Unleavened Bread. Simon may have been part of the synagogue of the Cyrenians mentioned in Ac 6:9. Mk 15:21 mentions the names of Simon's sons (Rm 16:13 may refer to one of those sons).
23:27–31 Jesus told the crowds who were **mourning** his unjust crucifixion that they should weep for their own families because of the future destruction of Jerusalem. It

would be preferable not to have children in such awful times. Jesus then cited Hs 10:8, where it is said that people will request landslides to hide them from the military onslaught. The proverbial statement in Lk 23:31 implies that if things are this bad for an innocent man in a time of peace (**when the wood is green**), they will be much worse for those who deserve judgment during a time of war (**when it is dry**).
23:32–33 Being **executed** between **two** . . . **criminals** fulfilled the prophecy of Is 53:12, as well as Jesus's words in Lk 22:37. The place where Jesus was crucified was called **The Skull**. In Aramaic, the name is *Golgotha*. The Latin equivalent is *Calvary*.
23:34 Jesus forgave his executioners because they acted in ignorance of who he really was. Some early manuscripts do not include the first part of this verse. The phrase **they divided his clothes and cast lots** fulfilled Ps 22:18.
23:35–39 Four different groups (the **people** in general, the **leaders**, the **soldiers**, and **one of the criminals** being crucified) scoffed at Jesus and challenged him to save himself. None of them believed that Jesus was **the king of the Jews** . . . **the Messiah**,

even though the official inscription above his head on the cross charged him with posing as "the King of the Jews."
23:40–43 In the midst of this display of unbelief and mockery, the other criminal came to understand the difference between his own guilt and Jesus's innocence (**this man has done nothing wrong**). He also realized that Jesus was the Messiah and asked to take part in his coming **kingdom**. Jesus assured him that, after death, he would immediately be reunited with him in **paradise** (eternal life beyond the grave; see 2Co 12:4).
23:44–45 The three hours of darkness at midday (from **noon** . . . **until three**) was a sign of divine judgment against sin (which Jesus became on the cross) and the sinners who unjustly executed the Son of God. Matthew 27:51 explains that the splitting of **the curtain of the sanctuary** (between the holy place and the holy of holies in the temple) was caused by a great earthquake. The torn curtain symbolized open access to God, made possible by the death of Christ (see note at 22:20).
23:46 While expressing faith in God by reciting Ps 31:5, Jesus **breathed his last**. Jesus was placed on the cross at about 9:00 a.m.

called out with a loud voice, "Father, into your hands I entrust my spirit."[A] Saying this, he breathed his last.

47 When the centurion saw what happened, he began to glorify God, saying, "This man really was righteous!"[B] **48** All the crowds that had gathered for this spectacle, when they saw what had taken place, went home, striking their chests. **49** But all who knew him, including the women who had followed him from Galilee, stood at a distance, watching these things.

The Burial of Jesus

50 There was a good and righteous man named Joseph, a member of the Sanhedrin, **51** who had not agreed with their plan and action. He was from Arimathea, a Judean town, and was looking forward to the kingdom of God. **52** He approached Pilate and asked for Jesus's body. **53** Taking it down, he wrapped it in fine linen and placed it in a tomb cut into the rock, where no one had ever been placed.[C] **54** It was the preparation day, and the Sabbath was about to begin.[D] **55** The women who had come with him from Galilee followed along and observed the tomb and how his body was placed. **56** Then they returned and prepared spices and perfumes. And they rested on the Sabbath according to the commandment.

Resurrection Morning

24 On the first day of the week, very early in the morning, they[E] came to the tomb, bringing the spices they had prepared. **2** They found the stone rolled away from the tomb. **3** They went in but did not find the body of the Lord Jesus. **4** While they were perplexed about this, suddenly two men stood by them in dazzling clothes. **5** So the women were terrified and bowed down to the ground.

"Why are you looking for the living among the dead?" asked the men. **6** "He is not here, but he has risen! Remember how he spoke to you when he was still in Galilee, **7** saying, 'It is necessary that the Son of Man be betrayed into the hands of sinful men, be crucified, and rise on the third day'?" **8** And they remembered his words.

9 Returning from the tomb, they reported all these things to the Eleven and to all the rest. **10** Mary Magdalene, Joanna, Mary the mother of James, and the other women with them were telling the apostles these things. **11** But these words seemed like nonsense to them, and they did not believe the women. **12** Peter, however, got up and ran to the tomb. When he stooped to look in, he saw only the linen cloths.[F] So he went away, amazed at what had happened.

The Emmaus Disciples

13 Now that same day two of them were on their way to a village called Emmaus, which was about seven miles[G] from Jerusalem. **14** Together they were discussing everything that had taken place. **15** And while they were discussing and arguing, Jesus himself came near and began to walk along with them. **16** But they[H] were prevented from recognizing him.

---

^23:46 Ps 31:5   ^23:47 Or *innocent*   ^23:53 Or *interred,* or *laid*   ^23:54 Lit *was dawning*   ^24:1 Other mss add *and other women with them*   ^24:12 Other mss add *lying there*   ^24:13 Lit *about sixty stadia*; one *stadion* = 600 feet   ^24:16 Lit *their eyes*

(Mk 15:25) and died after only six hours—an unusually short time. Crucifixion victims sometimes lingered for two or three days before death occurred.

23:47 Compared to the parallel accounts, Luke muted the centurion's confession. Here the centurion merely observed that Jesus was truly **righteous** (not a criminal in any respect), whereas in Mt 27:54 and Mk 15:39 he is reported as acknowledging that Jesus is the Son of God.

23:48–49 Striking their chests could be a sign of grief, though in Lk 18:13 it appears to reflect contrition before the Lord. Significantly, the **women** from **Galilee**, who had generously supported Jesus's ministry financially (see note at 8:1–3), were spotlighted among those who were **watching** Jesus die on the cross. They stuck with him even after the male disciples abandoned him. The women are named in Mt 27:56 and Mk 15:40.

23:50–53 Even though **Joseph** of Arimathea was a **member of the Sanhedrin**, he had disagreed with their decision to execute Jesus (22:71–23:1). He was **a good and righteous man**, but he was also a secret disciple of Jesus (Jn 19:38). Jesus was laid in the **tomb** of the wealthy Joseph instead of the shallow common grave reserved for criminals. This fulfilled the prophecy of Is 53:9. Matthew (27:65–66) stated that soldiers were assigned to guard Jesus's tomb and that the stone

rolled in front of the tomb was stamped with the Roman seal of authority.

23:54–56 Preparation day (from Thursday sundown to Friday sundown) was the last day before the **Sabbath** when preparations for the Sabbath were completed. Joseph of Arimathea and Nicodemus did much to prepare Jesus's body for burial (Jn 19:39–40), but the women disciples from Galilee planned to finish the task (**prepared spices and perfumes**). They had to wait for the Sabbath to pass before they could carry out their plan.

24:1 The **first day of the week** was Sunday. It was so **early** in the morning that it was still dark (Jn 20:1) when the women arrived at Jesus's tomb to anoint his body.

24:2 On their way to the **tomb**, the women pondered the difficulty the sealing stone would present. Who would move it for them (Mk 16:3)? However, when they arrived, they found the **stone rolled away** from the entrance. The stone had been moved by "a violent earthquake" (Mt 28:2).

24:3–8 Jesus's **body** was nowhere to be found, and the women had no answer for why it was missing. The **two men** who suddenly appeared and terrified them were angels (v. 23; Jn 20:12). Matthew 28:2–3 and Mk 16:5 mention only one angel. The angels announced the resurrection of Jesus to the women and reminded them that he had predicted this would happen. As soon

as they were reminded of Jesus's assertion that he would **rise on the third day**, they **remembered his words.** Now they were better prepared to understand and believe the radical things Jesus had said.

24:9–10 In Jesus's day women were not considered to be credible witnesses. This is why **the Eleven** (the apostles who remained after Judas's act of betrayal) **did not believe** the women's report about what had happened at Jesus's tomb, viewing it as **nonsense**. However, Peter was curious enough to run to the tomb and look for himself. When he saw **only the linen cloths** in which Jesus had been wrapped (23:53), he was **amazed** but still skeptical.

24:13–14 Of the two disciples traveling **from Jerusalem** to **Emmaus** that Sunday, one was named Cleopas (v. 18). He was possibly the husband of one of the female disciples who watched Jesus die on the cross (Jn 19:25). They had heard about the women's report and Peter's experience at the empty tomb (Lk 24:19–24) before leaving Jerusalem.

24:15–16 That the two were **arguing** about what had happened indicates that there was no agreement among Jesus's disciples about what had occurred and why. Like Peter at the tomb, they were amazed and yet unconvinced. It is not known how God **prevented** the two disciples from **recognizing** Jesus at this point, but he eventually "opened their eyes" to recognize him (v. 31).

Christ in the Old Testament

by Craig A. Blaising

In Luke 24 Jesus showed himself alive to his disciples and explained that the cross and resurrection, and indeed much else in his life, were predicted in Scripture. Luke 24:27 states, "Then beginning with Moses and all the Prophets, he interpreted for them the things concerning himself in all the Scriptures." Then in 24:44 he told them that "everything written about me in the Law of Moses, the Prophets, and the Psalms must be fulfilled."

The New Testament applies many Old Testament texts to Jesus. This practice likely reflects Jesus's own teachings about how the Old Testament relates to him. Furthermore, because themes are repeated and developed in Scripture, the application of a particular text to Jesus is suggestive of other texts that relate to or repeat that theme. In this way we can see a rich portrait of Old Testament patterns, types, allusions, and predictions that present to us the person and work of Christ.

From beginning to end the Old Testament exudes an expectation that someone is coming. Genesis 3:15 speaks of the "offspring" of the woman who comes to crush the tempter's head. God promised Abraham that through his "offspring" blessing or curse would come to all nations (Gn 12:1-3; 22:15-18).

Among the descendants of Abraham many patterns and types pointed to a *coming one*. Isaac, born of promise (Gn 15:3–6; 17:19), was offered to God as a sacrifice but was redeemed by a substitute (Gn 22:1–14). Joseph, raised up to bless all peoples, was first rejected by his brothers but later was sought by them for forgiveness (Gn 37; 41–48; 50:15–21). Judah offered himself in place of his brother and received a promise of a scepter and the obedience of all peoples (Gn 49:1, 9–12). Moses failed to enter the promised land despite all his works, but it was said that a prophet like him would arise in the future (Dt 18:15–19). David, of the tribe of Judah, was raised up by God to deliver and shepherd Israel. God made a covenant to raise up David's son and seat him on his throne, establishing his kingdom forever (2Sm 7:8–17; 1Ch 17:7–15). God would be his Father, and he would be his son (2Sm 7:14).

The covenant with David is the key to messianic prophecy. It incorporates all former prophecies of a coming king, such as Balaam's prophecy that a star would arise from Jacob and exercise dominion (Nm 24:15–19; cp. 23:24; 24:7–9), plus it serves as the basis for later prophecies of a son who establishes the throne of David forever with peace, justice, and righteousness (Is 9:6–7); of a "shoot . . . from the stump of Jesse" upon whom the Spirit rests and who destroys the wicked, brings peace, righteousness, and extends the knowledge of God to the entire earth (Is 11:1–10); of a righteous "Branch" of David who will reign with justice and wisdom (Jr 23:5; 33:15); of a humble, righteous king bringing salvation, speaking peace to the nations, and ruling from sea to sea (Zch 9:9–10).

David's experiences of suffering, deliverance, and exaltation become types and patterns replayed and brought to a higher level of fulfillment in the experiences of his later son (descendant), Jesus. These include the rejected stone that becomes the cornerstone (Ps 118); the suffering that becomes a literal depiction of the cross (Ps 22); and the soul not abandoned to Sheol, the flesh that does not see decay (Ps 16).

Key among the prophecies of Isaiah are predictions of a coming servant who will bring Israel to God and be a light for the nations (Is 49), who will bear our sorrows, our griefs, be wounded for our iniquities, be bruised for our transgressions, and by whose wounds we will be healed. He would be like a lamb led to slaughter, and yet resurrected (Is 53:3–12). Through this prophecy, we are able to see types and images of Christ in the sacrificial system, especially the Passover and the Day of Atonement.

But we see more. In the line of David, one became incarnate whom we know across the pages of the Old Testament: one who forgives sins and heals diseases (Ps 103:3), feeds bread to a multitude in the wilderness (Ex 16), stills the sea (Jb 26:12), and is coming to reign as King (Zch 14). That son of David, son of Abraham, offspring of Eve, is none other than the eternal Son of God.

17 Then he asked them, "What is this dispute that you're having^A with each other as you are walking?" And they stopped walking and looked discouraged. **18** The one named Cleopas answered him, "Are you the only visitor in Jerusalem who doesn't know the things that happened there in these days?" **19** "What things?" he asked them.

So they said to him, "The things concerning Jesus of Nazareth, who was a prophet powerful in action and speech before God and all the people, **20** and how our chief priests and leaders handed him over to be sentenced to death, and they crucified him. **21** But we were hoping that he was the one who was about to redeem Israel. Besides all this, it's the third day since these things happened. **22** Moreover, some women from our group astounded us. They arrived early at the tomb, **23** and when they didn't find his body, they came and reported that they had seen a vision of angels who said he was alive. **24** Some of those who were with us went to the tomb and found it just as the women had said, but they didn't see him."

25 He said to them, "How foolish you are, and how slow^B to believe all that the prophets have spoken! **26** Wasn't it necessary for the Messiah to suffer these things and enter into his glory?" **27** Then beginning with Moses and all the Prophets, he interpreted for them the things concerning himself in all the Scriptures.

28 They came near the village where they were going, and he gave the impression that he was going farther. **29** But they urged him, "Stay with us, because it's almost evening, and now the day is almost over." So he went in to stay with them.

30 It was as he reclined at the table with them that he took the bread, blessed and broke it, and gave it to them. **31** Then their eyes were opened, and they recognized him, but he disappeared from their sight. **32** They said to each other, "Weren't our hearts burning within us while he was talking with us on the road and explaining the Scriptures to us?" **33** That very hour they got up and returned to Jerusalem. They found the Eleven and those with them gathered together, **34** who said, "The Lord has truly been raised and has appeared to Simon!" **35** Then they began to describe what had happened on the road and how he was made known to them in the breaking of the bread.

The Reality of the Risen Jesus

36 As they were saying these things, he himself stood in their midst. He said to them, "Peace to you!" **37** But they were startled and terrified and thought they were seeing a ghost. **38** "Why are you troubled?" he asked them. "And why do doubts arise in your hearts? **39** Look at my hands and my feet, that it is I myself! Touch me and see, because a ghost does not have flesh and bones as you can see I have." **40** Having said this, he showed them his hands and feet. **41** But while they still were amazed and in disbelief because of their joy, he asked them, "Do you have anything here to eat?" **42** So they gave him a piece of a broiled fish,^C **43** and he took it and ate in their presence.

44 He told them, "These are my words that I spoke to you while I was still with you — that

---

^A **24:17** Lit *"What are these words that you are exchanging*   ^B **24:25** Lit *slow of heart*   ^C **24:42** Other mss add *and some honeycomb*

24:17–18 The disciples were **discouraged** (Gk *skuthropos*, "sad, sullen") and shocked that the stranger (Jesus) seemed to know nothing about what had happened the past few days, though it was the talk of all Jerusalem.

24:19–20 The description of Jesus by the two disciples is short on both insight and faith. Jesus is referred to in relation to his hometown (**Nazareth**) and as a **prophet** and miracle worker, but not as the Son of God. In addition, nothing is said about the unjust nature of Jesus's betrayal, trials, and crucifixion—just that the **chief priests and leaders** got him **sentenced to death** and **crucified**. These disciples had not fully grasped Jesus's identity, nor had they understood the divine necessity of his death.

24:21–24 Jesus's death had dashed these disciples' hopes that he was the Messiah (**the one . . . to redeem Israel**), but the reports from the tomb that morning **astounded** them and made them wonder what was going on. The reports said: (1) the women disciples didn't find Jesus's body at the tomb, (2) the women had seen **a vision of angels** proclaiming his resurrection, and (3) some male disciples had verified that the tomb was indeed empty.

24:25–29 The stranger (Jesus) rebuked the two disciples for not believing the OT prophecies about **the Messiah**, particularly about his suffering and following **glory**. Then, during the remainder of the walk to Emmaus, Jesus worked his way through all the major messianic prophecies in the Hebrew Bible (**Moses and all the Prophets** refers to the entire OT), carefully interpreting their meaning to his hearers. Then, when Jesus **gave the impression** that he was not going to stop in Emmaus, they invited him to spend the night with them, probably so they could hear more.

24:30–33 During the evening meal, Jesus **blessed** and **broke** the **bread**. At that point, the two disciples were allowed to recognize Jesus, but he immediately **disappeared** from sight. Their first thought was to recall the things he had taught them as they walked along the road to Emmaus. With **hearts burning**, they ventured to Jerusalem through the darkness of night to meet with the apostles and tell them about their experience.

24:34–35 Unknown to the two disciples, the risen Christ had **appeared** to **Simon** Peter (an appearance mentioned elsewhere only in 1Co 15:5) sometime earlier in the day. This was a decisive event for Peter and the church because he led the apostles and the early church in the years to come. Now, in a room full of eager listeners, these disciples

told about their experiences on the road to Emmaus and the meal that followed. It had been a day of many wonders, but an even greater wonder would soon visit them all.

24:36–37 It is ironic that the group of disciples was **startled and terrified and thought they were seeing a ghost** when the risen Christ suddenly appeared in their midst. After all, they had been rejoicing about his resurrection (v. 34) and swapping stories about his several appearances that day. But their fear is understandable since Jesus appeared suddenly in the middle of a crowd in what was surely a locked room. **Peace to you** was a traditional Jewish greeting.

24:38–40 Jesus calmed the fears and doubts of his disciples with evidence of his resurrection body. In his **hands** and **feet** the nail scars were clearly visible. The crowd of disciples could touch him and verify that he had a human body and that he was not a **ghost**.

24:41–43 It is understandable that some were slow to believe. This was a highly unusual and unexpected event. Realizing their doubts, Jesus offered an additional piece of evidence. He showed them that he could eat food (**a piece of a broiled fish**), something no ghost could do.

24:44–45 The Law of Moses, the Prophets, and **the Psalms** represent the three

everything written about me in the Law of Moses, the Prophets, and the Psalms must be fulfilled." **⁴⁵** Then he opened their minds to understand the Scriptures. **⁴⁶** He also said to them, "This is what is written:ᴬ The Messiah will suffer and rise from the dead the third day, **⁴⁷** and repentance forᴮ forgiveness of sins will be proclaimed in his name to all the nations, beginning at Jerusalem. **⁴⁸** You are witnesses of these things. **⁴⁹** And look, I am sending youᶜ what my Father promised. As for you, stay in the cityᴰ until you are empoweredᴱ from on high."

The Ascension of Jesus

⁵⁰ Then he led them out to the vicinity of Bethany, and lifting up his hands he blessed them. **⁵¹** And while he was blessing them, he left them and was carried up into heaven. **⁵²** After worshiping him, they returned to Jerusalem with great joy. **⁵³** And they were continually in the temple praising God.ᶠ

ᴬ**24:46** Other mss add *and thus it was necessary that*   ᴮ**24:47** Many mss read *repentance and*   ᶜ**24:49** Lit *upon you*
ᴰ**24:49** Other mss add *of Jerusalem*   ᴱ**24:49** Lit *clothed with power*   ᶠ**24:53** Other mss read *praising and blessing God. Amen.*

---

major divisions of the Hebrew Bible. Jesus now did for the wider group of disciples essentially what he had already done for the two on the road to Emmaus. He explained the Scriptures (see note at vv. 25–29). **24:46–49** OT passages that clearly prophesy the suffering of **the Messiah** are Ps 22 and Is 53. A key OT passage for Messiah's resurrection, cited several times in the NT, is Ps 16:10. Significant OT passages that Jesus may have had in mind about **repentance . . . proclaimed . . . to all the nations, beginning at Jerusalem** are Is 2:1–4 and 49:6. Luke 24:47 is Luke's version of the Great Commission (Mt 28:19–20; Mk 16:15; Jn 20:21–22; Ac 1:8). These verses echo Ac 1:4–8. Since Luke wrote both

this Gospel and the book of Acts, he skillfully intertwined the conclusion of his first volume with the beginning of his second volume. **The city** refers to Jerusalem. **Empowered from on high** refers to the descent of the Spirit on Pentecost (Ac 2:1–13). **24:50–51 Bethany** was located just over the Mount of Olives, about two miles from Jerusalem. Acts 1:12 specifies that the ascension of Christ occurred at the Mount of Olives. **24:52–53** As Jesus had requested (v. 49), the disciples returned to Jerusalem and stayed there until the events of the day of Pentecost (Ac 2). Luke mentions the **great joy** of the apostles—a theme he has stressed from beginning to end (see 1:14; 2:10; 10:20;

13:17; 15:5,32; 19:37; 24:41,52). Although at least some disciples were **continually in the temple praising God** during that time and later (Ac 2:46; 3:1), it should not be assumed that all of them were always there. Acts 1:13–14 also speaks of the apostles, some of the women disciples, and Jesus's brothers (the sons of Joseph and Mary) being "continually united in prayer" in an upper room in Jerusalem. Such devotion to prayer was a fitting prelude and precondition to the wonderful things God would do through Christ's earliest messengers. Christ's church was set to explode onto the scene as a beacon of light and hope in a spiritually dark world.

◥ Introduction to John

Circumstances of Writing

A close reading of the Gospel of John suggests that the author was an apostle (1:14; cp. 2:11; 19:35), one of the Twelve ("the disciple Jesus loved"; 13:23; 19:26; 20:2; 21:20; cp. 21:24–25), and, still more specifically, John, the son of Zebedee. The church fathers, too, attested to this identification (e.g., Irenaeus). Because the apostolic office was foundational in the history of the church (Ac 2:42; Eph 2:20), the apostolic authorship of John's Gospel invests it with special authority as a firsthand eyewitness (Jn 15:27; 1Jn 1:1–4).

The most plausible date of writing is the period between AD 70 (the date of the destruction of the temple) and 100 (the end of John's lifetime), with a date in the 80s most likely. A date after 70 is suggested by the references to the Sea of Tiberias in 6:1 and 21:1 (a name widely used for the Sea of Galilee only toward the end of the first century); Thomas's confession of Jesus as "my Lord and my God" in 20:28 (possibly a statement against emperor worship in the time of Domitian); the reference to Peter's martyrdom, which occurred in 65 or 66 (21:19); the lack of reference to the Sadducees, who ceased to be a Jewish religious party after 70; and the comparative ease with which John equated Jesus with God (1:1,14,18; 10:30; 20:28).

The testimony of the early church also favors a date after AD 70. Clement of Alexandria stated, "Last of all, John, perceiving that the external facts had been made plain [in the other canonical Gospels] . . . composed a spiritual gospel" (Eusebius, *Ecclesiastical History* 6.14.7). The most likely place of writing is Ephesus (Irenaeus, *Against Heresies* 3.1.2; see Eusebius, *Ecclesiastical History* 3.1.1), one of the most important urban centers of the Roman Empire at the time, though the envisioned readership of John's Gospel transcends any one historical setting.

John's original audience was probably composed of people in the larger Greco-Roman world in Ephesus and beyond toward the close of the first century AD. Hence John frequently explained Jewish customs and Palestinian geography and translated Aramaic terms into Greek.

Contribution to the Bible

Of all the Gospels and any of the New Testament books, the Gospel of John most clearly teaches the deity and preexistence of Christ (1:1–2,18; 8:58; 17:5,24; 20:28). Together with the Gospel of Matthew, it provides the most striking proofs of Jesus's messiahship. It does so by narrating seven messianic signs, by seven "I am" statements of Jesus, by specific fulfillment quotations, especially at Jesus's passion, and by showing how Jesus fulfilled the symbolism inherent in a variety of Jewish festivals and institutions. Jesus's messianic mission is shown to originate with God the Father, "the one who sent" Jesus (7:16,18,28,33; 8:26,29; 15:21), and to culminate in his commissioning of his new messianic community in the power of his Spirit (20:21–22). John's Trinitarian teaching is among the most overt presentations of the tri-unity of the Godhead—Father, Son, and Spirit—in the entire New Testament and has provided much of the material for early Trinitarian and Christological formulations in the history of the church.

Structure

John is divided into two main parts. In the first section (chaps. 2–11) the focus is on both Jesus's ministry to "the world" and the signs he performed. Jesus performs seven signs that

AD 18–29

Caiaphas is high priest. **18–36**
Pontius Pilate is prefect of Judea. **26–36**
John the Baptist's ministry begins. **29**
Jesus's baptism **29**
Jesus's wilderness temptations **29**
Jesus's call of his first
   disciples **29**

AD 30–33

Jesus cleanses the temple at Passover. **30**
Jesus's ministry in Galilee **AUTUMN 30** to **SPRING 32**
Jesus's feeding of the 5,000 during Passover **32**
Jesus's teachings at the Festival
   of Shelters **AUTUMN 32**
Growing opposition to Jesus at the
   Festival of Dedication **WINTER 32/33**

meet with varying responses. The second major section (chaps. 12–21) reveals Jesus's teaching to his disciples and the triumphant "hour" of his passion. John's record of the passion focuses on Jesus's control of the events. He had to instruct his adversaries on how to arrest him (18:4–8). Pilate struggled with his decision, but Jesus knew what would happen. Jesus died as the Lamb and was sacrificed at the very time lambs were being sacrificed for Passover (19:14).

Outline

I. Prologue: Christ as the Eternal Word (1:1–18)
   A. The Word (1:1)
   B. The Word and creation (1:2–5)
   C. The Word and the world (1:6–18)
II. Presentation of Christ as the Son of God (1:19–12:50)
   A. By John the Baptist (1:19–34)
   B. To his disciples (1:35–51)
   C. Through miraculous signs (2:1–12:50)
III. Instruction of the Twelve by the Son of God (13:1–17:26)
   A. The Last Supper (13:1–38)
   B. The way to the Father (14:1–31)
   C. The true vine (15:1–27)
   D. The gift of the Spirit (16:1–33)
   E. Jesus's high-priestly prayer (17:1–26)
IV. Suffering of Christ as the Son of God (18:1–20:31)
   A. His arrest, trial, and death (18:1–19:42)
   B. His triumph over death (20:1–31)
V. Epilogue: The Continuing Work of the Son of God (21:1–25)
   A. Appearances to his disciples (21:1–14)
   B. Assignment to his disciples (21:15–25)

Key verses in John

3:16   For God loved the world in this way: He gave his one and only Son, so that everyone who believes in him will not perish but have eternal life.

4:24   God is spirit, and those who worship him must worship in Spirit and in truth.

8:32   You will know the truth, and the truth will set you free.

13:35 By this everyone will know that you are my disciples, if you love one another.

15:12-13 This is my command: Love one another as I have loved you. No one has greater love than this: to lay down his life for his friends.

AD 33

Jesus raises Lazarus from death. **WINTER 33**
Jesus's last journey to Jerusalem by way of Samaria and Galilee **LATE WINTER 33**
Jesus's triumphal entry into Jerusalem **SUNDAY, NISAN 9, 33**
Jesus's second cleansing of the temple **MONDAY, NISAN 10, 33**
Jesus teaches in the temple and prophesies the destruction of Jerusalem. **TUESDAY, NISAN 11, 33**

AD 33

Judas bargains with the Jewish leaders to betray Jesus. **TUESDAY EVENING, NISAN 11, 33**
Jesus celebrates Passover with his disciples. **THURSDAY EVENING, NISAN 13, 33**
Jesus's trials and crucifixion **FRIDAY, NISAN 14, 33**
Jesus's resurrection **SUNDAY, NISAN 16, 33**
Jesus's ascension; forty days after his resurrection **33**
Day of Pentecost; seven weeks following Jesus's resurrection **MAY 24, 33**

Prologue

1 In the beginning was the Word, and the Word was with God, and the Word was God. [2] He was with God in the beginning. [3] All things were created through him, and apart from him not one thing was created that has been created. [4] In him was life,[A] and that life was the light of men. [5] That light shines in the darkness, and yet the darkness did not overcome[B] it.

[6] There was a man sent from God whose name was John. [7] He came as a witness to testify about the light, so that all might believe through him.[C] [8] He was not the light, but he came to testify about the light. [9] The true light that gives light to everyone was coming into the world.[D]

[10] He was in the world, and the world was created through him, and yet the world did not recognize him. [11] He came to his own, and his own people did not receive him. [12] But to all who did receive him, he gave them the right to be[E] children of God, to those who believe in his name, [13] who were born, not of natural descent,[F] or of the will of the flesh, or of the will of man,[G] but of God.

[14] The Word became flesh and dwelt[H] among us. We observed his glory, the glory as the one and only Son[I] from the Father, full of grace and truth. [15] (John testified concerning him and exclaimed, "This was the one of whom I said, 'The one coming after me ranks ahead of me, because he existed before me.'") [16] Indeed, we have all received grace upon[J] grace from his fullness, [17] for the law was given through Moses; grace and truth came through Jesus Christ. [18] No one has ever seen God. The one and only Son, who is himself God and is at the Father's side[K] —he has revealed him.

John the Baptist's Testimony

[19] This was John's testimony when the Jews from Jerusalem sent priests and Levites to ask him, "Who are you?"

[A]1:3–4 Other punctuation is possible: . . . not one thing was created. What was created in him was life   [B]1:5 Or grasp, or comprehend, or overtake; Jn 12:35   [C]1:7 Or it (the light)   [D]1:9 Or The true light who comes into the world gives light to everyone, or The true light enlightens everyone coming into the world.   [E]1:12 Or become   [F]1:13 Lit blood   [G]1:13 Or not of human lineage, or of human capacity, or of human volition   [H]1:14 Or and dwelt in a tent; lit and tabernacled   [I]1:14 Son is implied from the reference to the Father and from Gk usage.   [J]1:16 Or in place of   [K]1:18 Other mss read The one and only Son, who is at the Father's side

1:1–18 John's prologue presents Jesus as the eternal, preexistent Word-become-flesh (vv. 1,14) and as the one-of-a-kind Son of the Father who is himself God (vv. 1,18). Jesus brought God's plan of salvation to a culmination. Previous to Jesus this plan included God giving the law through Moses (v. 17), his dwelling among his people in the tabernacle (v. 14), and the sending of John the Baptist (vv. 6–8,15). The prologue introduces several themes that are emphasized later in the Gospel, including Jesus as life, light, and truth, believers as God's children, and the world's rejection of Jesus.

1:1 In the beginning was the Word echoes Gn 1:1, "In the beginning God created the heavens and the earth." John located Jesus's existence in eternity past with God. **The Word was God**: Not only did Jesus exist before creation, but he is also the same God who created the heavens and the earth. "The Word" (Gk Logos) conveys the notion of divine self-expression or speech (Ps 19:1–4). God's Word is effective. He speaks, and things come into being (Gn 1:3,9; Is 55:11–12).

1:2–3 Everything that exists owes its existence to Jesus.

1:4–5 The references to **life . . . light**, and **darkness** continue to draw on Genesis themes (cp. Gn 1:3–5,14–18,20–31; 2:7; 3:20). Light symbolism is also found in later OT messianic passages (Is 9:2; 42:6–7; 49:6; 60:1–5; Mal 4:2; cp. Lk 1:78–79).

1:6 Unlike Jesus, John the Baptist was merely a **man**, but like Jesus he had a particular mission to perform.

1:7–8 On John as a **witness** to Jesus, see note at 5:31–47.

1:9 As the rest of John's Gospel makes clear, all did not in fact receive the light, though the light was available to all.

1:10–11 His **own people did not receive him** refers to the Jewish people, the recipients of God's covenants, the law, and promises of a Messiah (Rm 9:4). Messiah's rejection by the Jews despite convincing proofs of his messiahship (esp. the "signs")

is a major subject in the first half of John's Gospel (cp. 12:37).

1:12–13 Reference to **children of God** on the OT characterization of Israel as God's children (Dt 14:1; cp. Ex 4:22). **Born, not of natural descent . . . but of God** makes clear that true children of God come into being through faith in Messiah, not physical birth or ethnic descent (8:41–47; cp. 3:16). This opens the way for Gentiles to become God's children (11:51–52; cp. 10:16).

1:14 The Word continues the theme of 1:1. **Became flesh** does not mean the Word stopped being God; rather, the Word was made flesh. **Dwelt among us** literally means "pitched his tent" (Gk skenoō), an allusion to God's dwelling among the Israelites in the tabernacle (Ex 25:8–9; 33:7). In the past God demonstrated his presence to his people in the tabernacle and the temple. Now God has taken up residence among his people in the Word-made-flesh, Jesus Christ (Jn 1:17). The references to God's **glory** hark back to OT passages that describe the manifestation of God's presence and glory in theophanies (appearances of God), the tabernacle, or the temple (Ex 33:22; Nm 14:10; Dt 5:22). The Greek word monogenēs underlying **one and only Son from the Father** means "only child" (Jdg 11:34; Jr 6:26; Am 8:10; Zch 12:10). "Only" may mean "one of a kind," as in the case of Isaac, who is called Abraham's "one of a kind" son in Gn 22:2,12,16 (in contrast to Ishmael, cp. Heb 11:17). In the OT, Israel and the Son of David are called God's "firstborn" son (see Ps 89:27). The reference to God's "giving" of his "one and only Son" in Jn 3:16,18 may allude to Abraham's willingness to sacrifice Isaac (Gn 22). **Full of grace and truth** recalls "faithful love (Hb chesed) and truth (Hb emet)" in Ex 34:6 (cp. Ex 33:18–19), where the expression refers to God's covenant faithfulness to his people Israel. According to John, God's covenant faithfulness found ultimate expression in his sending of his "one and only Son," Jesus (see textual note at 1:14).

1:15 John the Baptist was six months older than Jesus (Lk 1:24,26), and he started his ministry earlier than Jesus (Lk 3:1–20). Usually, priority in time (such as being the firstborn) implied preeminence, but Jesus's preexistence overrode John's temporal precedence.

1:16 This verse resumes the thought of 1:14. **We** refers to the same group as "we" and "us" in v. 14, that is, the apostolic circle or the whole believing community.

1:17 The contrast between the **law** and **grace and truth** is not that the law was bad and Jesus was good; rather, both the giving of the law and the coming of Jesus Christ mark stages in God's reaching out to humanity. Jesus, however, marks the final, definitive revelation of God's grace and truth. He is superior to Abraham (8:53), Jacob (4:12), and Moses (5:46–47; cp. 9:28).

1:18 No one has ever seen God—not even Moses (Ex 33:18–23). God is spirit (4:24), and humans are sinful, preferring darkness to light (3:19). Thus humans are unable to see God in his fullness. But Jesus Christ, **the one and only Son, who is himself God** (1:1), has **revealed** God the Father in a way that Moses and the law (1:17) never could. As Jesus says later in John's Gospel, "The one who has seen me has seen the Father" (14:9).

1:19–2:11 This introductory unit presents the first week of Jesus's ministry: day 1, John's witness about Jesus (1:19–28); day 2, John's encounter with Jesus (1:29–34); day 3, John's referral of two of his disciples to Jesus (1:35–39); day 4, Andrew's introduction of his brother Peter to Jesus (1:40–42); day 5, the recruitment of Philip and Nathanael (1:43–51); and day 7, the wedding at Cana (2:1–11). During this early stage Jesus was hailed by John the Baptist as the "Lamb of God" (1:29,36), gathered his first disciples, and performed his first "sign"—turning water into wine (2:11).

1:19–21 John denied being the **Messiah** (cp. vv. 8,15; 3:28), **Elijah**, or **the Prophet**. "The Messiah" refers to the coming greater Son

Jesus is God

Preexistent

- In the beginning, the Word was with God, and the Word was God; all of creation was made through him—the Word became flesh *(Jn 1:1–3,14)*.

- John the Baptist testified that the one who came after him—Jesus—existed before him *(Jn 1:14–15)*.

The Son of God

- Conceived in Mary by the Holy Spirit, therefore called the Son of God *(Mt 1:18,20; Lk 1:35)*

- The fulfillment of the name "Immanuel," which means "God is with us" *(Mt 1:22–23)*

- The voice from heaven proclaimed about Jesus at his baptism: "This is my beloved Son" *(Mt 3:17)*.

- Inspired by the Father in heaven, Peter proclaimed Jesus is "the Messiah, the Son of the living God" *(Mt 16:15–17)*.

Worthy of Worship
Quoting the Old Testament, Jesus himself said worship should only be given to the Lord God *(Mt 4:10)*.

- The wise men worshiped Jesus at his home in Bethlehem and gave him gifts *(Mt 2:9–11)*.

- Jesus's disciples worshiped him after he walked on the water and came to them in their boat *(Mt 14:33)*.

- The women at Jesus's tomb worshiped him after seeing his resurrection *(Mt 28:9)*.

- Jesus's disciples worshiped him on the mountain before his ascension *(Mt 28:17)*.

Yahweh (the LORD) of the Old Testament

- John the Baptist's mission was to "prepare the way for the Lord," who is Jesus *(Mt 3:1–3; Is 40:3–5)*.

- John the Baptist was God's messenger to prepare his way in the person of Jesus *(Mal 3:1; Mt 11:10)*.

²⁰ He didn't deny it but confessed, "I am not the Messiah."

²¹ "What then?" they asked him. "Are you Elijah?"

"I am not," he said.

"Are you the Prophet?"

"No," he answered.

²² "Who are you, then?" they asked. "We need to give an answer to those who sent us. What can you tell us about yourself?"

²³ He said, "I am a voice of one crying out in the wilderness: Make straight the way of the Lordᴬ — just as Isaiah the prophet said."

²⁴ Now they had been sent from the Pharisees. ²⁵ So they asked him, "Why then do you baptize if you aren't the Messiah, or Elijah, or the Prophet?"

²⁶ "I baptize withᴮ water," John answered them. "Someone stands among you, but you don't know him. ²⁷ He is the one coming after me,ᶜ whose sandal strap I'm not worthy to untie." ²⁸ All this happened in Bethanyᴰ across the Jordan, where John was baptizing.

The Lamb of God

²⁹ The next day John saw Jesus coming toward him and said, "Look, the Lamb of God, who takes away the sin of the world! ³⁰ This is the one I told you about: 'After me comes a man who ranks ahead of me, because he existed before me.' ³¹ I didn't know him, but I came baptizing with water so that he might be revealed to Israel." ³² And John testified, "I saw the Spirit descending from heaven like a dove, and he

rested on him. ³³ I didn't know him, but he who sent me to baptize with water told me, 'The one you see the Spirit descending and resting on — he is the one who baptizes with the Holy Spirit.' ³⁴ I have seen and testified that this is the Son of God."ᴱ

³⁵ The next day, John was standing with two of his disciples. ³⁶ When he saw Jesus passing by, he said, "Look, the Lamb of God!"

³⁷ The two disciples heard him say this and followed Jesus. ³⁸ When Jesus turned and noticed them following him, he asked them, "What are you looking for?"

They said to him, "Rabbi" (which means "Teacher"), "where are you staying?"

³⁹ "Come and you'll see," he replied. So they went and saw where he was staying, and they stayed with him that day. It was about four in the afternoon.ᶠ

⁴⁰ Andrew, Simon Peter's brother, was one of the two who heard John and followed him. ⁴¹ He first found his own brother Simon and told him, "We have found the Messiah"ᴳ (which is translated "the Christ"), ⁴² and he brought Simon to Jesus.

When Jesus saw him, he said, "You are Simon, son of John.ᴴ You will be called Cephas" (which is translated "Peter")."

Philip and Nathanael

⁴³ The next day Jesus' decided to leave for Galilee. He found Philip and told him, "Follow me."

⁴⁴ Now Philip was from Bethsaida, the hometown of Andrew and Peter. ⁴⁵ Philip found

---

ᴬ1:23 Is 40:3   ᴮ1:26 Or in, also in vv. 31,33   ᶜ1:27 Other mss add who came before me   ᴰ1:28 Other mss read in Bethabara
ᴱ1:34 Other mss read is the Chosen One of God   ᶠ1:39 Lit about the tenth hour   ᴳ1:41 Both Hb Messiah and Gk Christos mean
"anointed one"   ᴴ1:42 Other mss read "Simon, son of Jonah   ᴵ1:42 Both Aramaic Cephas and Gk Petros mean "rock"
ᴶ1:43 Lit he

---

of David, predicted in the OT (2Sm 7:11–16; Hs 3:5). Elijah, who never died (2Kg 2:11), was expected to return in the end time (Mal 4:5) to "restore everything" (Mt 17:11; cp. Lk 1:17). John the Baptist resembled Elijah in his rugged lifestyle (Mt 3:4; cp. 2Kg 1:8) but denied being Elijah. Moses predicted the coming of "a prophet" in Dt 18:15,18 (cp. Ac 3:22; 7:37), who was expected in Jesus's time (Jn 6:14; 7:40); John denied being this prophet as well (though he was a prophet; see 10:40–41; Mt 11:11–14). **1:22–23** John was **a voice . . . crying out in the wilderness: Make straight the way of the Lord** in keeping with Isaiah's words (Is 40:3; cp. Mt 3:3; Mk 1:3; Lk 3:4). This messenger of God was to prepare the way for the Lord's coming by preaching repentance and divine judgment. Isaiah's vision in Is 40–55 drew heavily on exodus typology and envisioned a new exodus of God's people in which God's glory would be revealed and his people delivered. This would be accomplished by the coming of the Servant of the Lord (see esp. Is 52:13–53:12). **1:24–27** To **untie** and remove another's **sandal** was the task of a slave. John the Baptist does not fully answer their question until the next day, in 1:32–34. The purpose of his baptism was to prepare people for the Messiah.

1:28 John was baptizing at the Jordan River. Luke 3:1 places this event in the fifteenth year of the reign of Tiberius (AD 14–37), or AD 29. John would have been about thirty-three years old. The **Bethany across the Jordan** (cp. 10:40) was probably not the village near Jerusalem where Lazarus was raised (cp. 11:1,18) but the region of Batanea in the northeast (called Bashan in the OT). **1:29** On **the next day**, see note at 2:1–2. John the Baptist's references to Jesus as **the Lamb of God** may echo the lamb led to the slaughter mentioned in Is 53:7. John may also have proclaimed Jesus as the apocalyptic warrior lamb who would bring judgment (Rv 5:6,12; 7:17; cp. Mt 3:7–12; Lk 3:7–17). **Takes away the sin of the world** refers to Jesus's sacrificial, substitutionary death, which appeased God's wrath against sin and sinners (1Jn 2:2; 4:10). **1:30** Again the fact of Jesus's preexistence is declared. **1:31** By **I didn't know him**, John probably meant that he did not know Jesus was the Messiah until he saw the sign from God mentioned in vv. 32–33. **1:32–34** The **Spirit** did not just descend on Jesus, he **rested** on him (cp. 3:34)—a sign of Jesus's divine anointing. In the OT, the Spirit came upon people to enable them to accomplish specific tasks. Isaiah predicted that Messiah would be full of the Spirit at

all times (Is 11:2; 61:1; cp. Lk 4:18; see note at 5:31–47). **1:35** In 1:35–4:42 John narrated events that fell between Jesus's baptism and the start of his Galilean ministry. On **the next day**, see note at 2:1–2. **1:36–37** John the Baptist shows great humility here as he recommends Jesus as the greater teacher. What exactly the disciples understood by the **Lamb of God** is unclear, but they did not understand it fully. **1:38 "Rabbi" (which means "Teacher")** is one of six instances where John translated an Aramaic term for his readers. The others are *Messiah* (Christ, v. 41; 4:25); *Cephas* (Peter, 1:42); *Siloam* (Sent, 9:7); *Thomas* (Didymus, "Twin," 11:16; 20:24; 21:2); and "Place of the Skull" (*Golgotha*, 19:17). **1:39** Giving the time of day shows that this account was based on eyewitness testimony. **1:40 Andrew** was **one of the two**; the other disciple is not named. He was probably John, the son of Zebedee. **1:41** On **Messiah . . . the Christ**, see note at v. 38. **1:42 Cephas** is an Aramaic word meaning "rock" (cp. Mt 16:16–18; see note at Jn 1:38). In OT times, God frequently changed people's names to indicate their special calling. **1:43** On **the next day**, see note at 2:1–2. Jesus's calling of his disciples (**follow me**)

Nathanael and told him, "We have found the one Moses wrote about in the law (and so did the prophets): Jesus the son of Joseph, from Nazareth."

⁴⁶ "Can anything good come out of Nazareth?" Nathanael asked him.

"Come and see," Philip answered.

⁴⁷ Then Jesus saw Nathanael coming toward him and said about him, "Here truly is an Israelite in whom there is no deceit."

⁴⁸ "How do you know me?" Nathanael asked.

"Before Philip called you, when you were under the fig tree, I saw you," Jesus answered.

⁴⁹ "Rabbi," Nathanael replied, "You are the Son of God; you are the King of Israel!"

⁵⁰ Jesus responded to him, "Do you believe because I told you I saw you under the fig tree? You will see greater things than this." ⁵¹ Then he said, "Truly I tell you, you will see heaven opened and the angels of God ascending and descending on the Son of Man."

The First Sign: Turning Water into Wine

2 On the third day a wedding took place in Cana of Galilee. Jesus's mother was there, ² and Jesus and his disciples were invited to the wedding as well. ³ When the wine ran out, Jesus's mother told him, "They don't have any wine."

⁴ "What has this concern of yours to do with me,^A woman?" Jesus asked. "My hour has not yet come."

⁵ "Do whatever he tells you," his mother told the servants.

⁶ Now six stone water jars had been set there for Jewish purification. Each contained twenty or thirty gallons.^B

⁷ "Fill the jars with water," Jesus told them. So they filled them to the brim. ⁸ Then he said to them, "Now draw some out and take it to the headwaiter."^C And they did.

⁹ When the headwaiter tasted the water (after it had become wine), he did not know where it came from — though the servants who had drawn the water knew. He called the groom ¹⁰ and told him, "Everyone sets out the fine wine first, then, after people are drunk, the inferior. But you have kept the fine wine until now."

¹¹ Jesus did this, the first of his signs, in Cana of Galilee. He revealed his glory, and his disciples believed in him.

^A2:4 Or *"What does that have to do with you and me*; lit *"What to me and to you*; Mt 8:29; Mk 1:24; 5:7; Lk 8:28 ^B2:6 Lit *two or three measures* ^C2:8 Lit *ruler of the table*

---

differed from customary practice. Usually it was a disciple who took the initiative to follow a rabbi (15:16).
1:44 Most likely, **Andrew** and **Peter** grew up in **Bethsaida** and later moved to Capernaum (Mk 1:29; cp. Jn 1:21), located only a few miles west. Similarly, Jesus was born in Bethlehem, grew up in Nazareth (Jn 1:45), and later moved to Capernaum (Mt 4:13).
1:45 Nathanael is also mentioned in 21:2. Nathanael may be the personal name of Bartholomew (*Bar-Tholomaios* = son of Tholomaios), who is linked with **Philip** in all three Synoptic lists (Mt 10:3; Mk 3:18; Lk 6:14). Philip's reference to **the one Moses wrote about in the law** may allude to predictions of a coming prophet in Dt 18:15,18 (see note at Jn 1:19–21). The expression "the Law and the Prophets" commonly referred to the OT in its entirety (Mt 5:17; 7:12).
1:46 Nathanael, who hailed from the small village of Cana in Galilee (21:2; cp. 2:1–11), used something of a double standard when he displayed prejudice toward insignificant **Nazareth**. Nazareth was a small town of no more than two thousand people.
1:47 Here truly is an Israelite in whom there is no deceit. Note that Jacob/Israel was characterized by deceit.
1:48 Jesus displayed supernatural knowledge (**I saw you**), identifying himself as Messiah.
1:49 Son of God and **King of Israel** are both messianic titles. "Son of God" identifies Jesus as the prophesied Messiah (2Sm 7:14; Ps 2:7); "King of Israel" likewise is a common OT designation for Messiah (Zph 3:15). The two terms also appear in Mt 27:42; Mk 15:32.
1:50 Though Nathaniel had come to know who Jesus was, he had a great deal more to learn.
1:51 Truly I tell you translates Hebrew *amen, amen*, a solemn affirmation emphasizing the authoritative nature of Jesus's

pronouncement. The phrase appears twenty-five times in John's Gospel. **Heaven opened and the angels of God ascending and descending** recalls the story of Jacob in Gn 28:12–15. The greatness of the Son of Man will far surpass the vision of Jacob the patriarch (Jn 4:5–6,11–12). Jesus is the "new Bethel" where God is revealed, and the "new Israel." The expression **Son of Man** harks back to the mysterious figure of "one like a son of man" in Dn 7:13–14. The Son of Man would be "lifted up" by crucifixion (see note at Jn 3:14–15), provide divine revelation (6:27,53), and act with end-time authority (5:27; 9:39).
2:1–2 Third day is probably counted from Jesus's encounter with Nathanael. **Cana of Galilee** was later the site of Jesus's third sign ("the second sign" performed in Cana, 4:54). Jewish weddings were community events, a time of special focus not just on bride and groom but also on their extended families. **Jesus's mother** may have been a friend of the family, helping behind the scenes. Jesus's **disciples** probably included the five mentioned in 1:35–51.
2:3 The wedding party's running out of **wine** ironically calls to mind the spiritual barrenness of first-century Judaism.
2:4 Jesus's use of **woman** to address his mother established a polite but firm distance between them, as did his question: **What has this concern of yours to do with me?** On Jesus's **hour has not yet come**, cp. 7:6,8,30; 8:20. Because of misconceptions about the coming Messiah, Jesus chose not to reveal himself openly to Israel (though he did perform numerous messianic "signs"; see note at 2:11). John portrays Jesus as the "elusive Christ" via Jesus's pattern of occasional withdrawal (7:6–9; 10:40–41; 11:56–57), his realism about people's true motives (2:23–25), and his ability to elude his opponents when charged with blasphemy (7:44; 8:59; 10:39).

Jesus remained elusive until his time finally arrived (12:23,27; 13:1; 16:32; 17:1).
2:5 Mary's instruction, **Do whatever he tells you**, recalls Pharaoh's instructions in Gn 41:55.
2:6 The number of jars (**six**) may indicate incompleteness since seven represented fullness. Since **each contained twenty or thirty gallons**, this added up to as much as one hundred eighty gallons. The **Jewish purification** ritual may have involved the washing of the guests' hands and certain utensils used at the wedding.
2:7 Filled them to the brim points to the abundance of Jesus's messianic provision (3:34).
2:8–9 The **headwaiter** was in charge of catering. He supervised the serving of food and drink, and employed several servants.
2:10 John shows Jesus not only miraculously making wine but making high-quality wine.
2:11 The fact that Jesus's turning of water into wine at the wedding is called **the first of his signs, in Cana of Galilee**, leads the reader to expect more signs to follow. The corresponding reference in 4:54 is to Jesus's healing of the royal official's son again while at Cana, "the second sign Jesus performed after he came from Judea to Galilee." Beyond this, Jesus's signs include the nonmiraculous but prophetic temple clearing (2:13–22, one of Jesus's Judean signs; cp. v. 23; 3:2); his healing of a lame man (5:1–15); the feeding of the crowds (6:1–15); the healing of the man born blind (chap. 9); and the raising of Lazarus (chap. 11).
In each case, the emphasis is on the way the "sign" revealed Jesus's messianic nature (12:37–40; 20:30–31) and on the striking nature of the feat. These signs pointed unmistakably to Jesus as Messiah—whether it be the large quantity and high quality of wine (2:6,10); the short span required for Jesus to "rebuild" the temple (vv. 19–20); the

❧ Incarnation and Christology

by Stephen J. Wellum

The word *incarnation* derives from a Latin word that literally means "in the flesh." In Christian theology the term refers to the supernatural act of God, effected by the Holy Spirit, whereby the eternal Son of God, the Second Person of the Triune Godhead, took into union with himself a complete human nature apart from sin. As a result of that action, the Son of God became the God-man forever, the Word made flesh (Jn 1:1,14; Rm 1:3–4; 8:3; Gl 4:4; Php 2:6–11; 1Tm 3:16; Heb 2:5–18; 1Jn 4:2).

The means whereby the incarnation came about is the virgin conception, commonly known as the virgin birth—the miraculous action of the Holy Spirit in the womb of Mary—so that what was conceived was fully God and fully man in one person forever (Mt 1:18–25; Lk 1:26–38). He did this in order to become the Redeemer of the church, our Prophet, Priest, and King, and thus to save his people from their sins (Mt 1:21). By becoming one with us, the Lord of glory not only shares our sorrows and burdens but is also able to secure our redemption by bearing our sin on the cross as our substitute and being raised for our justification (see Rm 4:25; Heb 2:17–18; 4:14–16; 1Pt 3:18).

The Humanity and Deity of Jesus in Scripture

Biblical evidence for the full deity and humanity of Christ is abundant. In regard to his humanity, Jesus is presented as a Jewish man who was born, underwent the normal process of growth and development (Lk 2:52), and experienced a full range of human experiences (e.g., Mt 8:10,24; 9:36; Lk 22:44; Jn 19:28), including growth in knowledge (Mk 13:32) and death (Jn 19:30). Apart from his sinlessness, which Scripture unequivocally affirms (Jn 8:46; 2Co 5:21; Heb 4:15; 1Pt 1:19), he is one with us in every way.

Scripture also affirms that the *man* Christ Jesus is also the eternal Son of God and, thus, God—equal with the Father and Spirit. From the opening pages of the New Testament, Jesus is identified as the Lord: the one who establishes the divine rule and inaugurates the new covenant era in fulfillment of Old Testament expectation—something only

God can do (e.g., Is 9:6–7; 11:1–10; Jr 31:31–34; Ezk 34). That is why Jesus's miracles are not merely human acts empowered by the Spirit of God; rather, they are demonstrations of Jesus's own divine authority over nature (e.g., Mt 8:23–27; 14:22–23), Satan and his hosts (Mt 12:27–28), and all things (Eph 1:9–10,19–23). Because he is God the Son, Jesus has the authority to forgive sin (Mk 2:3–12), call himself the fulfillment of Scripture (Mt 5:17–19; 11:13), view his relationship with the Father as one of equality and reciprocity (Mt 11:25–27; Jn 5:16–30; 10:14–30), and do the very works of God in creation, providence, and redemption (Jn 1:1–18; Php 2:6–11; Col 1:15-20; Heb 1:1–3).

Theological Expression of Jesus's Natures

Later church reflection, especially at the Council of Chalcedon (AD 451), affirmed that we cannot do justice to Scripture without confessing that Jesus of Nazareth was fully God and fully man. God the Son, who gave personal identity to the human nature he had assumed and did so without putting aside or compromising his divine nature, must be confessed as one person who now exists in two natures. Additionally, Chalcedon affirmed that we must not think that the incarnation involved a change in the properties of each nature so that some kind of blending resulted which was neither divine nor human (as the Eutychians wrongly affirmed). Rather, we must affirm that the properties of each nature (human and divine) were preserved so that Jesus is all that God is in all of his perfections and all that we humans are except in terms of sin.

This affirmation entails at least two important points. First, *the man* Jesus from the moment of conception was personal by virtue of the union of the human nature in the person of the divine Son. At no point were there two persons or two centers of self-consciousness (as the Nestorians wrongly affirmed). That is why in our Lord Jesus Christ we come face-to-face with God. We meet him, not subsumed under human flesh, not merely associated with it, but in undiminished moral splendor. The deity and humanity coincide, not because the human has grown

¹² After this, he went down to Capernaum, together with his mother, his brothers, and his disciples, and they stayed there only a few days.

Cleansing the Temple

¹³ The Jewish Passover was near, and so Jesus went up to Jerusalem. ¹⁴ In the temple he found people selling oxen, sheep, and doves, and he also found the money changers sitting there. ¹⁵ After making a whip out of cords, he drove everyone out of the temple with their sheep and oxen. He also poured out the money changers' coins and overturned the tables. ¹⁶ He told those who were selling doves, "Get these things out of here! Stop turning my Father's house into a marketplace!"ᴬ

¹⁷ And his disciples remembered that it is written: Zeal for your house will consume me.ᴮ ¹⁸ So the Jews replied to him, "What sign will you show us for doing these things?" ¹⁹ Jesus answered, "Destroy this temple,ᶜ and I will raise it up in three days." ²⁰ Therefore the Jews said, "This temple took forty-six years to build,ᴰ and will you raise it up in three days?" ²¹ But he was speaking about the temple of his body. ²² So when he was raised from the dead, his disciples remembered that he had said this, and they believed the Scripture and the statement Jesus had made.

²³ While he was in Jerusalem during the Passover Festival, many believed in his name

---

ᴬ **2:16** Lit *a house of business*   ᴮ **2:17** Ps 69:9   ᶜ **2:19** Or *sanctuary*, also in vv. 20,21   ᴰ **2:20** Or *was built forty-six years ago*

---

ong-distance healing of the royal official's son (4:47,49–50); the lame man's thirty-eight years as an invalid (5:5); the abundance of food Jesus produced (6:13); the man's congenital blindness (9:1–2); or Lazarus's four days in the tomb (11:17,39). The phrases **he revealed his glory, and his disciples believed in him** hark back to 1:14.

2:12 Jesus **went down** from Cana (in the hill country) to **Capernaum** (situated by the Sea of Galilee). Capernaum was about fifteen miles northeast of Cana and could be reached in a day's journey. Capernaum served as Jesus's headquarters after John the Baptist's imprisonment (Mt 4:12–13; Lk 4:28–31; cp. Mt 9:1).

2:13–22 Jesus's first major confrontation with Jewish leaders in John's Gospel took place when he cleared the Jerusalem temple at Passover. The Synoptic Gospels record a later clearing, just before the crucifixion (Mk 11:15–19). By clearing the temple, Jesus displayed zeal for God's house (Jn 2:17; cp. Ps 69:9) and performed a sign of judgment on the Jewish leaders who had allowed worship to deteriorate into commerce. His action also prophetically foreshadowed his crucifixion and resurrection, which would establish him

as the new center of worship, replacing the old temple.

2:13 This is the first reference to a Jewish festival in John's Gospel and the first reference to **Passover**. Later, John referred to two more Passovers at 6:4 (Jesus in Galilee) and 11:55; 12:1 (Jesus's final Passover in Jerusalem). Beyond this, Mt 12:1 may refer to another Passover not recorded in John. If so, Jesus's ministry included four Passovers and extended over about three and one-half years, spanning from AD 29 to 33 (see note at Jn 1:28). Apart from these Passover references, John also mentioned Jesus's activities at an unnamed Jewish festival in 5:1 (possibly Shelters); at the Festival of Tabernacles (or Shelters in 7:2); and at the Festival of Dedication (or Hanukkah) in 10:22. People are described as traveling **up** to Jerusalem because it was located at a higher elevation than Galilee.

2:14 Merchants (**selling oxen, sheep, and doves**) and **money changers** (exchanging idol-free coins for those tainted with pagan engravings) eased the logistical burden on pilgrims traveling to Jerusalem from afar by providing them with appropriate animals and coins for sacrifices and offerings. By

conducting their business within the **temple**, however, they disrupted worship (esp. for Gentiles) and obstructed the temple's purpose.

2:17 Jesus's clearing of the temple reminded his disciples of the righteous sufferer in Ps 69:9. First-century Jews expected Messiah to purge and reconstitute the temple. Jesus was passionately concerned for the holiness and purity of God's **house**.

2:20 This temple took forty-six years to build seems to indicate that the reconstruction of the second temple had taken forty-six years. Alternatively, it can be read: "This sanctuary was completed forty-six years ago [and has stood since that time]." The Jews were amazed that Jesus claimed he could **raise it up in three days**, an impossibly short time. The misunderstanding is cleared up in v. 21.

2:22 The Scripture may be Ps 69:9 (cited in Jn 2:17). **The statement Jesus had made** refers to v. 19.

2:23–25 Believed . . . would not entrust himself is a wordplay in the original Greek. Jesus's knowledge of people's hearts was displayed in his encounters with Nicodemus and the Samaritan woman; see note at v. 4.

---

into the divine but because the divine Son has taken to himself a human nature for our salvation. He is the divine Son who subsists in two natures, who has lived his life for us as our representative head, died our death as our substitute, and been raised for our eternal salvation. This is why the Lord Jesus is utterly unique and without parallel and thus the only Lord and Savior.

Second, since in the incarnation the eternal Son took to himself a human nature, he can now live a fully human life. Yet he was not totally confined to that human nature as if for a period of time the divine nature was divested of its attributes or function. That is why Scripture affirms that even as the incarnate one, the divine Son continued to

uphold and sustain the universe (Col 1:15–17; Heb 1:1–3) even while he lived out his life on earth as a man dependent upon the Father and empowered by the Spirit (Jn 5:19–27; Ac 10:38).

Our affirmation of the biblical Jesus is beyond our full comprehension, but it is only in such a Jesus that we have one who can meet our every need. Apart from him as God the Son incarnate, we do not have a Redeemer who can stand on our behalf as a man, let alone satisfy God's own righteous demand upon us due to our sin. After all, it is only God who can save us. By becoming one with us, our Lord not only becomes our sympathetic Savior, he also accomplishes a work that saves us fully, completely, and finally.

when they saw the signs he was doing. ²⁴ Jesus, however, would not entrust himself to them, since he knew them all ²⁵ and because he did not need anyone to testify about man; for he himself knew what was in man.

Jesus and Nicodemus

3 There was a man from the Pharisees named Nicodemus, a ruler of the Jews. ² This man came to him at night and said, "Rabbi, we know that you are a teacher who has come from God, for no one could perform these signs you do unless God were with him." ³ Jesus replied, "Truly I tell you, unless someone is born again,ᴬ he cannot see the kingdom of God."

⁴ "How can anyone be born when he is old?" Nicodemus asked him. "Can he enter his mother's womb a second time and be born?" ⁵ Jesus answered, "Truly I tell you, unless someone is born of water and the Spirit, he cannot enter the kingdom of God. ⁶ Whatever is born of the flesh is flesh, and whatever is born of the Spirit is spirit. ⁷ Do not be amazed that I told you that you must be born again. ⁸ The wind blows where it pleases, and you hear its sound, but you don't know where it comes from or where it is going. So it is with everyone born of the Spirit."

⁹ "How can these things be?" asked Nicodemus. ¹⁰ "Are you a teacherᴮ of Israel and don't know these things?" Jesus replied. ¹¹ "Truly I tell you,

we speak what we know and we testify to what we have seen, but you do not accept our testimony. ¹² If I have told you about earthly things and you don't believe, how will you believe if I tell you about heavenly things? ¹³ No one has ascended into heaven except the one who descended from heaven — the Son of Man.ᶜ

¹⁴ "Just as Moses lifted up the snake in the wilderness, so the Son of Man must be lifted up, ¹⁵ so that everyone who believes in him mayᴰ have eternal life. ¹⁶ For God loved the world in this way:ᴱ He gaveᶠ his one and only Son, so that everyone who believes in him will not perish but have eternal life. ¹⁷ For God did not send his Son into the world to condemn the world, but to save the world through him. ¹⁸ Anyone who believes in him is not condemned, but anyone who does not believe is already condemned, because he has not believed in the name of the one and only Son of God. ¹⁹ This is the judgment: The light has come into the world, and people loved darkness rather than the light because their deeds were evil. ²⁰ For everyone who does evil hates the light and avoids it,ᴳ so that his deeds may not be exposed. ²¹ But anyone who lives byᴴ the truth comes to the light, so that his works may be shown to be accomplished by God."

Jesus and John the Baptist

²² After this, Jesus and his disciples went to the Judean countryside, where he spent time with them and baptized.

ᴬ 3:3 Or *from above*, also in v. 7 ᴮ 3:10 Or *the teacher* ᶜ 3:13 Other mss add *who is in heaven* ᴰ 3:15 Other mss add *not perish, but* ᴱ 3:16 Or *this much* ᶠ 3:16 Or *For in this way God loved the world, and so he gave*, or *For God so loved the world that he gave* ᴳ 3:20 Lit *and does not come to the light* ᴴ 3:21 Lit *who does*

3:1–4:42 The bulk of chaps. 3 and 4 is devoted to Jesus's encounters with Nicodemus, a representative of the Jewish religious establishment, and an unnamed woman representing Samaritan religion. Interspersed are explanatory sections (3:16–21,31–36) and a vignette on John the Baptist (3:22–30). The encounters with Nicodemus and the Samaritan woman are a study in contrasts. Nicodemus's status as a Sanhedrin member differs sharply from the lowly Samaritan woman who had a sinful past and present. Yet in both cases Jesus discerned deep spiritual need. He confronted Nicodemus about his need for regeneration and the woman about her sin. **3:1 Nicodemus** was a common name in first-century Palestine. **Ruler of the Jews** refers to the Jewish governing body known as the Sanhedrin. **3:2** Nicodemus's coming to Jesus **at night** may have negative overtones ("night" is probably negative in 13:30 but not in 21:3; see also the reference to the present event without apparent negative connotation in 19:39). Coming from a "teacher of Israel" (3:10), the address **rabbi** denoted respect, especially since it was known that Jesus did not have formal rabbinic training (7:15). The **signs** mentioned in John's Gospel presumably included those performed in Jerusalem (2:23), possibly the temple clearing (cp. 2:18; see note at 2:11). **3:3–8** The discussion of the need for spiritual rebirth develops the reference to the

"children of God" who are "born . . . of God" in the prologue (1:12–13). On "children of God," see 8:39–58 and 11:51–52. The phrase **born of water and the Spirit** probably refers to spiritual birth that cleanses from sin and brings spiritual transformation (Ezk 36:25–27). The **kingdom of God**, a major topic in the other Gospels, is mentioned by John only in vv. 3,5 (see the reference to Jesus's kingdom in 18:36). **3:7 You** is plural, probably indicating Nicodemus and other Sanhedrin members (cp. vv. 1,11). **3:8** Jesus illustrated his pronouncement of vv. 3–5 with an analogy between wind and a person born of the Spirit. **Wind** and **Spirit** translate the same Greek and Hebrew words (Gk *pneuma*; Hb *ruach*). While the wind's origin is invisible, its effects can be observed; it is the same with those born of the Spirit. **3:9–10** Jesus may here be "returning the compliment" (see note at v. 2), though he chastised Nicodemus for his lack of understanding. **3:11–12** Jesus's knowledge is firsthand rather than speculative or based on hearsay. The **earthly things** probably refers to the teaching on spiritual regeneration. **3:13** Jesus's statement may allude to Pr 30:4. Only Jesus **descended from heaven** and returned there (Lk 24:51; Ac 1:9). **3:14–15** The reference to the **Son of Man** being **lifted up** is the first of three "lifted up" sayings in John (8:28; 12:32). All three

speak of the future "lifting up" of the Son of Man in double meaning (possibly inspired by the language of Is 52:13). The reference in this verse invokes **Moses**'s lifting up of a serpent in the **wilderness** so that everyone who had been bitten by a poisonous snake and looked at the serpent in faith was healed (Nm 21:8–9). The third and final "lifted up" saying (Jn 12:32) emphasizes that the lifting up of the Son of Man refers to Jesus's crucifixion (cp. 12:33 and the similar reference to Peter's martyrdom in 21:19). **3:16–18** God, out of love, **gave his one and only Son** (cp. 1:14,18), so that everyone who believes in him will **have eternal life** (see notes at 5:26; 14:4–6). John's favorite designation for Jesus is the Son sent by the Father (3:34–36; 5:19–26; 6:40; 8:35–36; 14:13; 17:1), imagery taken from the Jewish concept of the *shaliach* (messenger), according to which the sent one is like the sender himself and faithfully pursues the sender's interests (13:16,20). Jesus is that "sent one" par excellence (9:7), and he in turn sends his disciples (see note at 20:21–22). Being sent implies that the commission, charge, and message are issued by the sender rather than originating with the ones sent. The messengers' role is to fulfill their commission according to their sender's will. **3:19–21** On Jesus as the **light**, see note at 8:12. **3:22** Jesus left the vicinity of Jerusalem and headed to the **Judean countryside**. In 4:3,

²³ John also was baptizing in Aenon near Salim, because there was plenty of water there. People were coming and being baptized, ²⁴ since John had not yet been thrown into prison. ²⁵ Then a dispute arose between John's disciples and a Jew^ about purification. ²⁶ So they came to John and told him, "Rabbi, the one you testified about, and who was with you across the Jordan, is baptizing — and everyone is going to him."

²⁷ John responded, "No one can receive anything unless it has been given to him from heaven. ²⁸ You yourselves can testify that I said, 'I am not the Messiah, but I've been sent ahead of him.' ²⁹ He who has the bride is the groom. But the groom's friend, who stands by and listens for him, rejoices greatly⁸ at the groom's voice. So this joy of mine is complete. ³⁰ He must increase, but I must decrease."

The One from Heaven

³¹ The one who comes from above is above all. The one who is from the earth is earthly and speaks in earthly terms.ᶜ The one who comes from heaven is above all. ³² He testifies to what he has seen and heard, and yet no one accepts his testimony. ³³ The one who has accepted his testimony has affirmed that God is true. ³⁴ For the one whom God sent speaks God's words, since heᴰ gives the Spirit without measure.

³⁵ The Father loves the Son and has given all things into his hands. ³⁶ The one who believes in the Son has eternal life, but the one who rejects the Sonᴱ will not see life; instead, the wrath of God remains on him.

Jesus and the Samaritan Woman

4 When Jesusᶠ learned that the Pharisees had heard he was making and baptizing more disciples than John ² (though Jesus himself was not baptizing, but his disciples were), ³ he left Judea and went again to Galilee. ⁴ He had to travel through Samaria; ⁵ so he came to a town of Samaria called Sychar near the propertyᴳ that Jacob had given his son Joseph. ⁶ Jacob's well was there, and Jesus, worn out from his journey, sat down at the well. It was about noon.ᴴ

⁷ A woman of Samaria came to draw water. "Give me a drink," Jesus said to her, ⁸ because his disciples had gone into town to buy food.

⁹ "How is it that you, a Jew, ask for a drink from me, a Samaritan woman?" she asked him. For Jews do not associate withᴵ Samaritans.ᴶ

¹⁰ Jesus answered, "If you knew the gift of God, and who is saying to you, 'Give me a drink,' you would ask him, and he would give you living water."

¹¹ "Sir," said the woman, "you don't even have a bucket, and the well is deep. So where do you get this 'living water'? ¹² You aren't greater than our father Jacob, are you? He gave us the well

---

^3:25 Other mss read *and the Jews*   ᴮ3:29 Lit *with joy rejoices*   ᶜ3:31 Or *of earthly things*   ᴰ3:34 Other mss read *since God*   ᴱ3:36 Or *refuses to believe in the Son*, or *disobeys the Son*   ᶠ4:1 Other mss read *the Lord*   ᴳ4:5 Lit *piece of land*   ᴴ4:6 Lit *about the sixth hour*   ᴵ4:9 Or *do not share vessels with*   ᴶ4:9 Other mss omit *For Jews do not associate with Samaritans.*

Jesus left Judea altogether, returning to Galilee (2:12) by way of Samaria.
3:23–25 The ministries of Jesus and John overlapped and led to a dispute between their respective disciples.
3:26 On John the Baptist as a witness to Jesus, see note at 5:31–47.
3:27 John points out that Jesus would not be having such success unless God was in it.
3:28 John's assertion that he had been sent ahead of the Messiah may allude to Mal 3:1 (cp. Mt 11:10; Mk 1:2; Lk 7:27).
3:29 John's reference to Jesus as the groom (cp. Mt 9:15) identified Jesus as Israel's long-awaited King and Messiah. In the OT, Israel is frequently depicted as God's "bride" (Is 62:4–5; Jr 2:2; Hs 2:16–20). John's role was that of **the groom's friend**, who selflessly rejoiced with the groom (1:6–9,15,19–36).
3:30 John the Baptist downplayed his disciples' concerns expressed in v. 26. Now that the light had come (1:6–9), the "lamp" had done its work (see note at 5:35).
3:31–32 The one who comes from above is Jesus. The **earthly** one is John the Baptist, but it speaks not of sin but of finiteness.
3:33 Has affirmed (Gk *sphragizo*) means literally "to seal" in the sense of confirming or authenticating something as true (see note at 6:27–29).
3:34 On Jesus as the recipient of God's Spirit, see note at 1:32–34 (see also Rv 3:1; 5:6).
3:35 The Father has given the Son authority over all things because of his love.

3:36 Has eternal life indicates that eternal life is not just a future expectation but is already a present experience. **The wrath of God remains on him** makes clear that unless a person believes in Jesus the Messiah, he remains under God's judgment (vv. 19–21).
4:1–42 Jesus's encounter with the Samaritan woman took place by divine necessity (v. 4). Unlike Nicodemus, the woman progressed in her understanding. She viewed him first as a Jew (v. 9), then as someone who could make her life easier (v. 15), then as a prophet (v. 19), and then possibly as Messiah (v. 29). The woman's fellow townspeople concluded that Jesus was the Savior of the world (v. 42).
4:1 The Pharisees had investigated John the Baptist's credentials (1:19,24); now they were looking into those of Jesus.
4:2 John the Evangelist, author of this Gospel, here clarified the earlier statement in 3:26.
4:3 On Jesus going from **Judea** to **Galilee**, see note at 3:22.
4:4 Had to travel may indicate that Jesus's itinerary was set by the sovereign plan of God (9:4; 10:16; 12:34; 20:9). **Through Samaria** was the most direct route from Judea to Galilee, but strict Jews, wishing to avoid defilement, bypassed Samaria by taking a longer, less direct route. This involved crossing the Jordan River and traveling across from Samaria on the eastern side of the river.
4:5 Sychar was located just east of Mount Gerizim and Mount Ebal. The reference to **the property that Jacob had given his**

son Joseph reflects the customary inference from Gn 48:21–22 and Jos 24:32 that Jacob gave his son Joseph the land at Shechem that he had bought from the sons of Hamor (Gn 33:18–19) and that later served as Joseph's burial place (Ex 13:19; Jos 24:32).
4:6 Jesus was **worn out from his journey**. This underscores his genuine, full humanity.
4:7 The first sentence would have raised the question: What will Jesus do? Those who knew the Samaritans would have been shocked by Jesus's request.
4:8 Jesus and his disciples usually carried little or nothing to eat on their journeys. Rather, they brought money to buy provisions along the way (12:6; 13:29). Purchasing food was a common assignment given to disciples. Jesus did not fear being defiled by **food** bought in a Samaritan village.
4:9 The author's aside that **Jews do not associate with Samaritans** explained to his Diaspora readership that rabbis considered Samaritans to be in a continual state of uncleanness.
4:10–15 The references to Jesus as the giver of **living water** involve double meaning (see notes at 3:3–8,14–15). Literally, the phrase refers to fresh spring water (Gn 26:19; Lv 14:6). God was known as the source of life (Gn 1:11–12,20–31; 2:7) and "the fountain of living water" (Jr 2:13; see Is 12:3). In Nm 20:8–11, water gushed out of the rock, a much-needed provision for the Israelites.
4:11 Jacob's **well** may have been the deepest well in Palestine. It is more than a hundred

and drank from it himself, as did his sons and livestock." **¹³** Jesus said, "Everyone who drinks from this water will get thirsty again. **¹⁴** But whoever drinks from the water that I will give him will never get thirsty again. In fact, the water I will give him will become a well^ of water springing up in him for eternal life."

¹⁵ "Sir," the woman said to him, "give me this water so that I won't get thirsty and come here to draw water."

¹⁶ "Go call your husband," he told her, "and come back here."

¹⁷ "I don't have a husband," she answered.

"You have correctly said, 'I don't have a husband,'" Jesus said. **¹⁸** "For you've had five husbands, and the man you now have is not your husband. What you have said is true."

¹⁹ "Sir," the woman replied, "I see that you are a prophet. **²⁰** Our ancestors worshiped on this mountain, but you Jews say that the place to worship is in Jerusalem."

²¹ Jesus told her, "Believe me, woman, an hour is coming when you will worship the Father neither on this mountain nor in Jerusalem. **²²** You Samaritans worship what you do not know. We worship what we do know, because salvation is from the Jews. **²³** But an hour is coming, and is now here, when the true worshipers will worship the Father in Spirit and in truth.^B Yes, the Father wants such people to worship him. **²⁴** God is spirit, and those who worship him must worship in Spirit and in truth."

²⁵ The woman said to him, "I know that the Messiah is coming" (who is called Christ). "When he comes, he will explain everything to us."

²⁶ Jesus told her, "I, the one speaking to you, am he."

The Ripened Harvest

²⁷ Just then his disciples arrived, and they were amazed that he was talking with a woman. Yet

---

^4:14 Or *spring*   ^B 4:23 Or *in spirit and truth*, also in v. 24

---

feet **deep** today and was probably deeper in Jesus's day.

4:12 The woman's account of **Jacob** giving the Samaritans the **well** and drinking from it **himself** was based on tradition, not Scripture. The book of Genesis does not record Jacob digging a well, drinking from it, and giving it to his sons.

4:14 The phrase **will become a well of water springing up in him** is reminiscent of Is 12:3 (cp. Is 44:3; 55:1–3).

4:16 Jesus's instructions gave the woman the opportunity to admit that she was living with a man who was not her husband.

4:17 While technically truthful, the woman's statement was potentially misleading because it could be taken to imply that she was unattached. Jesus knew the full truth.

4:18 The woman had had **five husbands**—or five "men" (the Gk *aner* can mean "husband" or "man")—having engaged in a series of illicit relationships, and she was not married to her current lover. Sexual relations outside of marriage are forbidden in both Testaments.

4:19 The woman recognized that Jesus knew her life circumstances without apparently having been told by anyone—hence he must be **a prophet** (cp. Lk 7:39).

4:20–21 The **ancestors** who worshiped on **this mountain**—a reference to Mount Gerizim (Dt 11:29; 27:12), the OT setting for the pronouncement of blessings for keeping the covenant, and the mountain on which Moses commanded an altar to be built (Dt 27:4–6)—included Abraham (Gn 12:7) and Jacob (Gn 33:20), who built altars in this region.

4:22 True worship must be based on true knowledge of God, and the Samaritans limited themselves to just the Pentateuch. **Salvation is from the Jews** means that in salvation history the Jews are the conduit through which salvation comes to the world.

4:23–24 Because **God is spirit**, the Israelites were not to make idols "in the shape of anything" as the surrounding nations did (Ex 20:4). Jesus's point was that since God is spirit, proper worship of him is also a matter of spirit rather than physical location.

4:25–26 On **Christ** as a title of Jesus, see note at 1:38.

4:27 The disciples' amazement that Jesus was **talking with a woman** stemmed from the common Jewish teaching that talking too much to a woman, even one's wife, was a

---

Character profile:
The Samaritan Woman

I sn't it amazing how an entire life can change in a moment? That's the way it happened for the unnamed woman we meet in John 4. One day in the Samaritan village of Sychar she went out to the well to fill her water jar.

Sitting alone near the well was a Jewish man. When he asked her for a drink, she almost dropped her container. Gathering herself, she asked, "How is it that you, a Jew, ask for a drink from me, a Samaritan woman?" (4:9). The intriguing stranger sidestepped the question. Then he explained that, if she knew who he was, she would ask him for "living water" (4:10). *A wise guy*, she thought. "You don't even have a bucket," she observed (4:11). Before she knew it, she was in a deep conversation. He kept talking about thirst. And when he looked at her, it was like he was seeing straight into her heart.

The clincher came when this kind but direct stranger gave her an accurate summary of her long and checkered marital past. She felt uncomfortable, unmasked. She tried to reroute the conversation toward theoretical chitchat about obtuse religious matters. When that didn't exactly work, she tried to end the discussion by concluding, "I know that the Messiah is coming. . . . When he comes, he will explain everything to us" (4:25). In response, the man said simply, "I, the one speaking to you, am he" (4:26). Pierced to the heart by this unanticipated

encounter, this unnamed woman set her water jar on the ground. Turning, she rushed back to the village where everyone knew all her secrets.

Then the woman with the sordid past told about her encounter, and "many Samaritans from that town believed in him because of what the woman said when she testified, 'He told me everything I ever did'" (4:39).

Why was it such a big deal that Jesus would have a discussion at a local watering hole with a Samaritan woman? There was a huge racial and cultural barrier. Jesus was a Jew; this anonymous woman was a citizen of Samaria. The Samaritans were the product of the Assyrian invasion and subjugation of the northern kingdom of Israel in 722 BC.

Intermarriage with foreign peoples who had been resettled in the promised land resulted in a race of people with mixed ancestry and diluted devotion to the Lord. "Pure-blooded" Jews viewed Samaritans with contempt; the Samaritans responded with equal hostility. John's statement that "Jews do not associate with Samaritans" (4:9) was putting it mildly.

In addition, there were issues of moral propriety. Jesus was a respected rabbi, a "holy man." This woman was regarded in her culture as a "sinner" and thus a social outcast. In every way Jesus's interaction with this woman was shocking.

This woman's encounter with Jesus reminds us of God's relentless love. It also screams the truth that life can change in a moment. Are you paying attention?

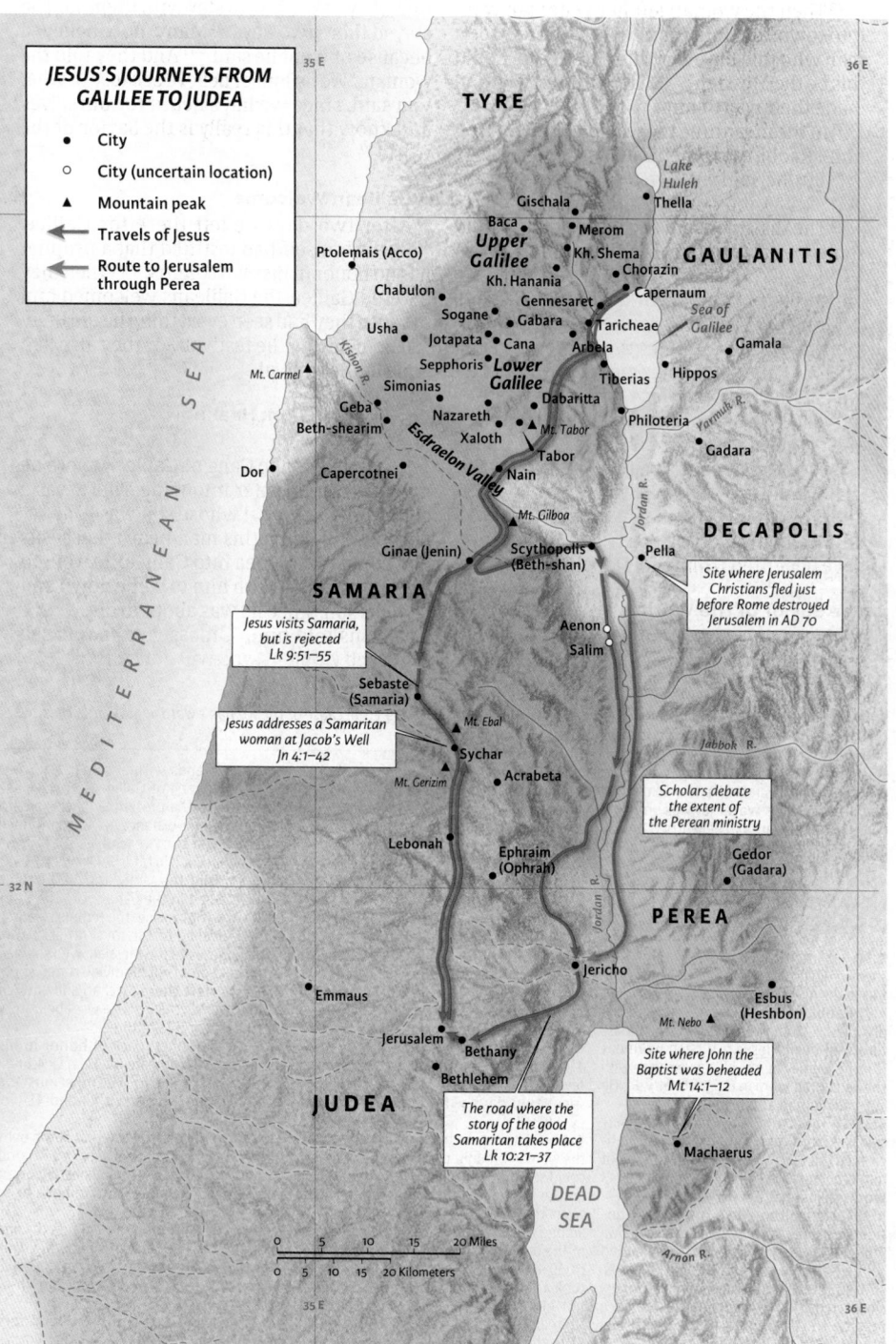

JESUS'S JOURNEYS FROM GALILEE TO JUDEA

- • City
- ○ City (uncertain location)
- ▲ Mountain peak
- ← Travels of Jesus
- ← Route to Jerusalem through Perea

35 E

36 E

MEDITERRANEAN SEA

TYRE

Lake Huleh

Gischala
Thella

Baca
Merom

GAULANITIS

Ptolemais (Acco)
Upper Galilee
Kh. Shema

Chabulon
Kh. Hanania
Chorazin
Capernaum

Sogane
Gabara
Gennesaret

Usha
Jotapata
Cana
Taricheae
Sea of Galilee

Sepphoris
Lower Galilee
Arbela
Gamala

Mt. Carmel ▲
Simonias
Tiberias
Hippos

Geba
Nazareth
Dabaritta

Beth-shearim
Xaloth
▲ Mt. Tabor
Philoteria
Yarmuk R.

Dor
Capercotnei
Tabor
Gadara

Esdraelon Valley
Nain

▲ Mt. Gilboa

Ginae (Jenin)
Scythopolis (Beth-shan)
Pella

DECAPOLIS

SAMARIA

Jesus visits Samaria, but is rejected
Lk 9:51–55

Aenon
Salim

Site where Jerusalem Christians fled just before Rome destroyed Jerusalem in AD 70

Sebaste (Samaria)

Jesus addresses a Samaritan woman at Jacob's Well
Jn 4:1–42

Mt. Ebal
Sychar

Mt. Gerizim ▲
Acrabeta

Jabbok R.

Scholars debate the extent of the Perean ministry

Lebonah
Ephraim (Ophrah)

Gedor (Gadara)

32 N

Jordan R.

PEREA

Jericho

Emmaus

Esbus (Heshbon)

Mt. Nebo ▲

Jerusalem
Bethany

Site where John the Baptist was beheaded
Mt 14:1–12

Bethlehem

JUDEA

The road where the story of the good Samaritan takes place
Lk 10:21–37

Machaerus

DEAD SEA

Arnon R.

0   5   10   15   20 Miles

0   5   10   15   20 Kilometers

35 E

36 E

Kishon R.

no one said, "What do you want?" or "Why are you talking with her?"

²⁸ Then the woman left her water jar, went into town, and told the people, ²⁹ "Come, see a man who told me everything I ever did. Could this be the Messiah?" ³⁰ They left the town and made their way to him.

³¹ In the meantime the disciples kept urging him, "Rabbi, eat something."

³² But he said, "I have food to eat that you don't know about."

³³ The disciples said to one another, "Could someone have brought him something to eat?" ³⁴ "My food is to do the will of him who sent me and to finish his work," Jesus told them. ³⁵ "Don't you say, 'There are still four more months, and then comes the harvest'? Listen to what I'm telling you: Open^A your eyes and look at the fields, because they are ready^B for harvest. ³⁶ The reaper is already receiving pay and gathering fruit for eternal life, so that the sower and reaper can rejoice together. ³⁷ For in this case the saying is true: 'One sows and another reaps.' ³⁸ I sent you to reap what you didn't labor for; others have labored, and you have benefited from^C their labor."

The Savior of the World

³⁹ Now many Samaritans from that town believed in him because of what the woman said^D

when she testified, "He told me everything I ever did." ⁴⁰ So when the Samaritans came to him, they asked him to stay with them, and he stayed there two days. ⁴¹ Many more believed because of what he said.^E ⁴² And they told the woman, "We no longer believe because of what you said, since we have heard for ourselves and know that this really is the Savior of the world."^F

A Galilean Welcome

⁴³ After two days he left there for Galilee. ⁴⁴ (Jesus himself had testified that a prophet has no honor in his own country.) ⁴⁵ When they entered Galilee, the Galileans welcomed him because they had seen everything he did in Jerusalem during the festival. For they also had gone to the festival.

The Second Sign: Healing an Official's Son

⁴⁶ He went again to Cana of Galilee, where he had turned the water into wine. There was a certain royal official whose son was ill at Capernaum. ⁴⁷ When this man heard that Jesus had come from Judea into Galilee, he went to him and pleaded with him to come down and heal his son, since he was about to die.

⁴⁸ Jesus told him, "Unless you people see signs and wonders, you will not believe."

---

^A **4:35** Lit *Raise* ^B **4:35** Lit *white* ^C **4:38** Lit *you have entered into* ^D **4:39** Lit *because of the woman's word* ^E **4:41** Lit *because of his word* ^F **4:42** Other mss add, *the Messiah*

---

waste of time, diverting one's attention from the study of Scripture and reflection on God.
4:28 The woman's **water jar** was probably a large earthenware pitcher carried on the shoulder or hip. She abandoned her original purpose for coming to the well in order to tell her townspeople about Jesus.
4:29 Who told me everything I ever did was an exaggeration—but understandable in light of her excitement. See note at v. 39.
4:30 It is interesting that the woman had such credibility that people left their work to see the man she spoke of.
4:31 Rabbi, eat something reflected the disciples' customary concern for their Master's well-being. Jesus had been worn out from his journey before his conversation with the Samaritan woman (see note at v. 6). He still had not had anything to eat.
4:32–34 The accomplishment of Jesus's mission was more important to him than physical food (Mt 6:25; Mk 3:20–21). His statement may echo Dt 8:3 (cp. Mt 4:4; Lk 4:4). On Jesus's **work**, see note at 17:4.
4:35 In agriculture there is always a considerable separation in time between sowing and harvesting. The disciples needed to realize that with the coming of Jesus, sowing (preaching) and reaping (conversions) coincided. The immediate reference may be to the approaching Samaritans (vv. 39–42).
4:36 This saying is reminiscent of Am 9:13, which depicted the prosperity of the new age. Hence Jesus claimed that he was ushering in the messianic age, a time of swift, abundant harvest.

4:37–38 This saying may allude to Mc 6:15, "You will sow but not reap." Yet Jesus's adaptation left judgment unmentioned. The others who had labored were Jesus and his predecessors, most recently John the Baptist, the final prophet associated with the OT era. Jesus's followers were the beneficiaries of their work and would bring in the harvest.
4:39 That town refers to Sychar (see note at v. 5). Though people would naturally be skeptical about religious pronouncements made by an immoral woman such as this Samaritan, her sincerity (and perhaps a noticeable change in her morality) convinced her townspeople to take her seriously as she spoke about Jesus.
4:40 Jesus obviously did not share in the Jewish bias against Samaritans since he spent **two days** with them (see notes at vv. 4,9).
4:41–42 As others had done (1:40–41,45), the woman brought people to Jesus so they could see for themselves. Ultimately, it was on the basis of a personal encounter with Jesus that they believed. His large harvest among the Samaritans marked the first sign of the universal scope of his saving mission (10:16; 11:51–52). The early church also undertook a Samaritan mission (Ac 8:4–25; cp. Ac 1:8). In fact, the pattern of Jesus's mission from Judea (Nicodemus, Jn 3), to Samaria (Jn 4), to the Gentiles (vv. 46–54; cp. 12:20–33), anticipated the post-Pentecost mission of the early church (Ac 1:8).
4:43–54 The healing of the royal official's son completes the "Cana cycle" in John's Gospel, which spans from 2:1 to 4:54 and

begins and ends with a "sign" performed by Jesus in Cana of Galilee (2:11; 4:54; see note at 2:11). The present sign is a rare instance of a long-distance healing performed by Jesus. The story resembles that of the Gentile centurion in Mt 8:5–13 and Lk 7:2–10, but this is not the same incident. All three signs featured in the Cana cycle (the turning of water into wine, the temple clearing, and the healing of the royal official's son) set forth Jesus as the Messiah, who showed convincing proofs of his divine commission.
4:43 Jesus **left there** (Sychar) and entered **Galilee**. From Sychar to Cana was about forty miles, a trip of two or three days.
4:44 On a prophet's lack of **honor in his own country**, compare Mt 13:57; Lk 4:24.
4:45 Jesus's Galilean welcome must be understood in light of vv. 44 and 48 (cp. 2:23–25).
4:46 The **royal official** was probably a Gentile centurion, possibly in service to Herod Antipas (Mk 6:14). His son's illness involved fever (Jn 4:52) and appears to have been terminal (vv. 47,49).
4:47 The distance from Capernaum to Cana was about fifteen miles. The journey was mostly uphill (see note at 2:12). Conversely, from Cana Jesus would **come down** to Capernaum.
4:48 The expression **signs and wonders** probably harks back to the series of miracles performed by Moses at the exodus. Jesus rebuked people for their dependence on the miraculous; for John, miracles were "signs" pointing to Jesus's messianic identity (see note at 2:11).

49 "Sir," the official said to him, "come down before my boy dies."

50 "Go," Jesus told him, "your son will live." The man believed what^A Jesus said to him and departed.

51 While he was still going down, his servants met him saying that his boy was alive. **52** He asked them at what time he got better. "Yesterday at one in the afternoon^B the fever left him," they answered. **53** The father realized this was the very hour at which Jesus had told him, "Your son will live." So he himself believed, along with his whole household.

54 Now this was also the second sign Jesus performed after he came from Judea to Galilee.

The Third Sign: Healing the Sick

5 After this, a Jewish festival took place, and Jesus went up to Jerusalem. **2** By the Sheep Gate in Jerusalem there is a pool, called Bethesda^C in Aramaic, which has five colonnades. **3** Within these lay a large number of the disabled — blind, lame, and paralyzed.^D **5** One man was there who had been disabled for thirty-eight years. **6** When Jesus saw him lying there and realized he had already been there a long time, he said to him, "Do you want to get well?"

7 "Sir," the disabled man answered, "I have no one to put me into the pool when the water is stirred up, but while I'm coming, someone goes down ahead of me."

8 "Get up," Jesus told him, "pick up your mat and walk." **9** Instantly the man got well, picked up his mat, and started to walk.

Now that day was the Sabbath, **10** and so the Jews said to the man who had been healed, "This is the Sabbath. The law prohibits you from picking up your mat."

11 He replied, "The man who made me well told me, 'Pick up your mat and walk.'"

12 "Who is this man who told you, 'Pick up your mat and walk'?" they asked. **13** But the man who was healed did not know who it was, because Jesus had slipped away into the crowd that was there.^E

14 After this, Jesus found him in the temple and said to him, "See, you are well. Do not sin anymore, so that something worse doesn't happen to you." **15** The man went and reported to the Jews that it was Jesus who had made him well. **16** Therefore, the Jews began persecuting Jesus^F because he was doing these things on the Sabbath.

Honoring the Father and the Son

17 Jesus responded to them, "My Father is still working, and I am working also." **18** This is why the Jews began trying all the more to kill him: Not only was he breaking the Sabbath, but he

---

^A**4:50** Lit *the word*   ^B**4:52** Lit *at the seventh hour*   ^C**5:2** Some mss read *Bethzatha*; other mss read *Bethsaida*   ^D**5:3** Some mss include vv. 3b-4: *— waiting for the moving of the water,* ⁴*because an angel would go down into the pool from time to time and stir up the water. Then the first one who got in after the water was stirred up recovered from whatever ailment he had.*   ^E**5:13** Lit *slipped away, there being a crowd in that place*   ^F**5:16** Other mss add *and trying to kill him*

4:49–50 This is a rare instance of a long-distance miracle. A similar incident is described in Mt 8:5–13 and Lk 7:2–10. The words **your son will live** may recall Elijah's statement in 1Kg 17:23. If so, Jesus's messianic activity is compared with the healing ministry of Elijah (Lk 4:23–27). **4:54** The **second sign** refers to signs done in Cana (see note at 2:11); in the interim, Jesus had performed signs in Jerusalem (2:23; 3:2; 4:45). Thus John closed the cycle of Jesus's first ministry circuit, starting and ending in Cana of Galilee (see note at vv. 43–54). **5:1–47** The "festival cycle" in John's Gospel spans from 5:1 to 10:42 and is characterized by escalating conflict between Jesus and the Jewish authorities. This cycle begins with yet another sign—Jesus's healing of a lame man at a feast in Jerusalem (see note at 2:11). The fact that the healing took place on a Sabbath provoked a major controversy. Jesus was accused of breaking the law by telling the man to pick up his mat (5:8–10). The controversy escalated to the point where the Jewish leaders charged Jesus with blasphemy for claiming to continue the work of God (v. 18). This provided an occasion for Jesus to defend his ministry and enumerate evidences for his identity. **5:1 After this** marks the passing of an indefinite period of time. Up to a year and a half may have passed after the last recorded festival, the Passover, when Jesus cleared

the temple and met with Nicodemus. The unnamed **Jewish festival** may have been the Festival of Shelters. On **Jesus went up to Jerusalem**, see note at 2:13. **5:2 Bethesda** may mean "house of mercy," a fitting term given the desperate state of the people who lay there hoping for a miraculous cure; see note at 1:38. **5:5** We do not know the invalid's age or how long he had been lying there, but he had been crippled for **thirty-eight years**, which is longer than many people in antiquity lived and roughly as long as Israel's wilderness wanderings (Dt 2:14). On John's penchant for selecting "difficult" and striking miracles, see note at 2:11. For a similar healing, see Mt 9:1–8. **5:6 Realized** probably indicates supernatural knowledge (see notes at 1:48; 4:19). Jesus's conversation with the man may have been occasioned by his request for alms (Ac 3:1–5). **5:7** Superstition attributed the stirring of the **water** to the actions of an angel (see the addition of v. 4 in some later mss). **5:8–9** A **mat** (Gk *krabattos*; as distinguished from "bed," Gk *klinarion*, e.g., Ac 5:15) was the poor man's bedding. Made of straw, it could be rolled up and carried. We are not told this day was the **Sabbath** until the miracle was performed. This sets the context for the tensions with the unbelieving Jews (cp. 9:14). **5:10** In a petty display of religious legalism, the Jewish leaders objected to the man's picking up his **mat** on the **Sabbath**. While

not actually breaking any biblical Sabbath regulations, the man was violating a rabbinical code that prohibited the carrying of an object "from one domain into another" (*m. Sabb.* 7:2). Hence Jesus was accused of enticing the man to sin. **5:11–13** It is interesting that Jesus did not make himself known to the man when he **healed** him. **5:14** Jesus met the man again in **the temple**, a short distance from the site of his healing. Jesus's words may imply that the man's suffering was due to sin but do not suggest that all suffering is caused by personal sin (see note at 9:2). **Something worse** may refer to eternal judgment for sin (vv. 22–30). **5:15–16** The man never thanked Jesus. He only **reported** him to the authorities. **5:17** While Gn 2:2–3 teaches that God rested (Hb *shabath*) on the seventh day of creation, Jewish rabbis agreed that God continually upheld the universe, yet without breaking the Sabbath. If God was above Sabbath regulations, so was Jesus (Mt 12:1–14). What is more, even the Jews made exceptions to the rule prohibiting work on the Sabbath, most notably in cases where circumcision occurred on a Sabbath (Jn 7:23). **5:18 Making himself equal to God** seemed to violate the OT teaching that there is only one God (Dt 6:4). Thus the Jewish leaders accused Jesus of blasphemy, which became the primary charge leveled against Jesus before Pilate (Jn 19:7).

was even calling God his own Father, making himself equal to God.

¹⁹ Jesus replied, "Truly I tell you, the Son is not able to do anything on his own, but only what he sees the Father doing. For whatever the Father[A] does, the Son likewise does these things. ²⁰ For the Father loves the Son and shows him everything he is doing, and he will show him greater works than these so that you will be amazed. ²¹ And just as the Father raises the dead and gives them life, so the Son also gives life to whom he wants. ²² The Father, in fact, judges no one but has given all judgment to the Son, ²³ so that all people may honor the Son just as they honor the Father. Anyone who does not honor the Son does not honor the Father who sent him.

Life and Judgment

²⁴ "Truly I tell you, anyone who hears my word and believes him who sent me has eternal life and will not come under judgment but has passed from death to life.

²⁵ "Truly I tell you, an hour is coming, and is now here, when the dead will hear the voice of the Son of God, and those who hear will live. ²⁶ For just as the Father has life in himself, so also he has granted to the Son to have life in himself. ²⁷ And he has granted him the right to pass judgment, because he is the Son of Man. ²⁸ Do not be amazed at this, because a time is coming when all who are in the graves will hear his voice ²⁹ and come out — those who have done good things, to the resurrection of life, but those who have done wicked things, to the resurrection of condemnation.

³⁰ "I can do nothing on my own. I judge only as I hear, and my judgment is just, because I do not seek my own will, but the will of him who sent me.

Witnesses to Jesus

³¹ "If I testify about myself, my testimony is not true. ³² There is another who testifies about me, and I know that the testimony he gives about me is true. ³³ You sent messengers to John, and he testified to the truth. ³⁴ I don't receive human testimony, but I say these things so that you may be saved. ³⁵ John[B] was a burning and shining lamp, and you were willing to rejoice for a while in his light.

³⁶ "But I have a greater testimony than John's because of the works that the Father has given me to accomplish. These very works I am doing testify about me that the Father has sent me. ³⁷ The Father who sent me has himself testified about me. You have not heard his voice at any time, and you haven't seen his form. ³⁸ You don't have his word residing in you, because you don't believe the one he sent. ³⁹ You pore over the Scriptures because you think you have eternal life in them, and yet they testify about me. ⁴⁰ But you are not willing to come to me so that you may have life.

⁴¹ "I do not accept glory from people, ⁴² but I know you — that you have no love for God within you. ⁴³ I have come in my Father's name, and yet you don't accept me. If someone else

---

[A]5:19 Lit whatever that one [B]5:35 Lit That man

5:19–26 On Jesus's relationship to the **Father** in these verses, see note at 3:16–18.
5:19 Jesus's claim that **the Son is not able to do anything on his own** echoes Moses's affirmation "that the LORD sent me to do all these things and that it was not of my own will" (Nm 16:28).
5:21 Jesus's statement that **the Son also gives life to whom he wants** is significant since raising the dead and giving life are the prerogatives of God alone (Dt 32:39; 1Sm 2:6; 2Kg 5:7).
5:22 Like life (v. 21), judgment is the exclusive prerogative of God (Gn 18:25; Jdg 11:27), and the Father **has given all judgment to the Son**.
5:23 Jesus characterized himself as God's authorized messenger. This is similar to Moses and the prophets, who served as God's agents and spokesmen. Of designated messengers (Hb *shaliach*), Jews held that "a man's agent is like the man himself" (*m. Ber.* 5:5). The statement **so that all people may honor the Son just as they honor the Father** in effect established Jesus's right to be worshiped and amounted to a claim of deity.
5:25 Jesus's words are reminiscent of Ezekiel's vision of the valley of dry bones (Ezk 37).
5:26 The claim that Jesus had **life in himself** echoes the affirmation in the prologue of John's Gospel that "in him [Jesus] was life" (1:4; see note at 14:4–6). It is further supported by Jesus's statement, "I am the

resurrection and the life" (11:25). Because he is "the life" and has life in himself, Jesus is able to give life (abundant life now; eternal life in the future) to all who place their trust in him (3:16; 10:10).
5:27 Because he is the Son of Man echoes Dn 7:13.
5:28–29 Compare these verses with Dn 12:2.
5:30 On **I can do nothing on my own**, see notes at vv. 19,23.
5:31–47 Jesus spoke of several witnesses who bore testimony about him: John the Baptist (vv. 32–36; cp. 1:7–8,15,19,32–34; 3:26); his own works (5:36; cp. 10:25,32,37–38; 15:24); God the Father (5:37–38; 8:18); and the Scriptures (5:39), particularly those written by Moses (vv. 45–47). Elsewhere in this Gospel, reference is made to the witness of Jesus himself (3:11,32; 8:14,18; 18:37), the Spirit (chaps. 14–16, esp. 15:26), the disciples (15:27), and the Fourth Evangelist (19:35; 21:24). The "witness" theme in John's Gospel is part of a larger "trial motif." This reverses the world's perspective of Jesus being put on trial. It becomes clear that it is really the world, not Jesus, that is on trial, with a multitude of witnesses bearing testimony to his true identity as Messiah. This section also emphasizes the world's guilt for rejecting Jesus.
5:31 Jesus did not deny his reliability. He was alluding to the importance of having multiple witnesses (Dt 17:6; 19:15; cp. Nm 35:30).
5:32 Jesus was speaking of God the Father (v. 37) when he said, **There is another who**

testifies about me. Avoiding God's name was a common way of showing reverence.
5:33 On Jesus as the **truth**, see note at 14:4–6 and the echo of this passage before Pilate (18:37). Compare 3Jn 3,12.
5:35 Jesus's characterization of John the Baptist as **a burning and shining lamp** seems to echo Ps 132:17 where God "prepared a lamp" for his Anointed One. John was a "lamp" but not "the light" (Jn 1:7–9); his witness was comparatively small and temporary. The past tense may imply that John was now dead or imprisoned. See notes at 3:29,30.
5:37 The Father . . . has himself testified may refer to the voice at Jesus's baptism (Mt 3:17), a passage not explicitly mentioned in John, though the primary reference may be to God's witness in Scripture (Jn 5:45–47; cp. Lk 24:27,44; Ac 13:27; 1Jn 5:9). Jesus's affirmation that his hearers had not **heard** God's **voice** or **seen his form** (cp. 1:18) seems to allude to wilderness Israel, which received the law at Mount Sinai without hearing God's voice or seeing his form.
5:38 Have his word residing in you recalls the depiction of a God-fearing person who has the word of God living in his heart (Jos 1:8–9; Ps 119:11).
5:39 Scripture itself does not impart life, but it witnesses to the one who does—Jesus (cp. vv. 46–47).
5:43 Jesus predicted the proliferation of false christs as a sign of the end times (Mt 24:5). The first-century Jewish historian Josephus

comes in his own name, you will accept him. **44** How can you believe, since you accept glory from one another but don't seek the glory that comes from the only God? **45** Do not think that I will accuse you to the Father. Your accuser is Moses, on whom you have set your hope. **46** For if you believed Moses, you would believe me, because he wrote about me. **47** But if you don't believe what he wrote, how will you believe my words?"

The Fourth Sign: Feeding of the Five Thousand

6 After this, Jesus crossed the Sea of Galilee (or Tiberias). **2** A huge crowd was following him because they saw the signs that he was performing by healing the sick. **3** Jesus went up a mountain and sat down there with his disciples.

4 Now the Passover, a Jewish festival, was near. **5** So when Jesus looked up and noticed a huge crowd coming toward him, he asked Philip, "Where will we buy bread so that these people can eat?" **6** He asked this to test him, for he himself knew what he was going to do.

7 Philip answered him, "Two hundred denarii^ worth of bread wouldn't be enough for each of them to have a little."

8 One of his disciples, Andrew, Simon Peter's brother, said to him, **9** "There's a boy here who has five barley loaves and two fish — but what are they for so many?"

10 Jesus said, "Have the people sit down." There was plenty of grass in that place; so they sat down. The men numbered about five thousand. **11** Then Jesus took the loaves, and after giving thanks he distributed them to those who were seated — so also with the fish, as much as they wanted.

12 When they were full, he told his disciples, "Collect the leftovers so that nothing is wasted." **13** So they collected them and filled twelve baskets with the pieces from the five barley loaves that were left over by those who had eaten.

14 When the people saw the sign^b he had done, they said, "This truly is the Prophet who is to come into the world."

15 Therefore, when Jesus realized that they were about to come and take him by force to make him king, he withdrew again to the mountain by himself.

The Fifth Sign: Walking on Water

16 When evening came, his disciples went down to the sea, **17** got into a boat, and started across the sea to Capernaum. Darkness had already set in, but Jesus had not yet come to them. **18** A high wind arose, and the sea began to churn. **19** After they had rowed about three or four

^6:7 A denarius = one day's wage   ^6:14 Other mss read *signs*

---

reported a string of messianic pretenders in the years before AD 70.
5:45–47 Jesus's appeal to **Moses** prepares the way for chap. 6, where Jesus is presented as the new Moses providing the new "bread from heaven." The reference to Moses as a witness or **accuser** against the Jews may allude to Dt 31:26–27 where the law was invoked as a witness against the Israelites. The reference to Moses writing about Jesus in Jn 5:46 may allude to the Pentateuch (attributed to Moses) or to the prediction of a "prophet like" Moses in Dt 18:15.
6:1–71 The feeding of the crowds (cp. Mt 14:13–23; Mk 6:30–44; Lk 9:10–17) is yet another of Jesus's messianic "signs" (see note at Jn 2:11), aligning Jesus with God's provision of manna to wilderness, Israel through Moses (6:30–31). In response to the people's demand that he perform a sign greater than Moses's signs at the exodus, Jesus claimed to be the "bread of life" that provides spiritual nourishment for all who believe in him (eat and drink of him). This controversial statement proved to be a watershed moment in Jesus's ministry, because many of his followers abandoned him at this point (vv. 60–66). But the Twelve, through Peter their spokesman, reaffirmed their allegiance (vv. 68–69).
6:1 After this again indicates the passing of an indefinite period of time (5:1). Half a year may have passed since the previous event. Sea of **Tiberias** (cp. 21:1) was an alternate name for the Sea of Galilee. Herod Antipas founded Tiberias, the largest city on the Sea of Galilee, in honor of his patron, the Roman emperor Tiberius (AD 14–37). The name gained currency toward the end of the first century.

6:2 Generally, John portrays the crowds as following primarily on account of his miracles, and as mired in confusion and ignorance.
6:3 Mountain may not refer to a specific mountain. It could designate the hill country east of the lake, known today as the Golan Heights (Mt 14:23; Mk 6:46). Like other rabbis, Jesus **sat down** to teach (Mt 5:1; Mk 4:1; 9:35; Lk 4:20), although teaching is not mentioned here.
6:4 This is the second of three Passovers mentioned by John, and the only one Jesus spent in Galilee (see note at 2:13).
6:5–6 The **huge crowd** apparently walked several miles around the north side of the lake and caught up with Jesus and the disciples. **Philip** would be the natural choice for Jesus's question since he, like Andrew (v. 8) and Peter, was a native of nearby Bethsaida (see note at 1:44). Jesus's question echoes Moses's query in the wilderness: "Where can I get meat to give all these people?" (Nm 11:13). Other parallels between Jn 6 and Nm 11 are the people's grumbling (Nm 11:1; Jn 6:41,43); the description of the manna (Nm 11:7–9; Jn 6:31); the reference to the eating of meat/Jesus's "flesh" (Nm 11:13; Jn 6:51); and the overabundance of the provision (Nm 11:22; Jn 6:7–9).
6:7 Two hundred denarii was roughly eight months' wages, since one denarius was about one day's pay for a common laborer (12:5; Mt 20:2).
6:8–9 Boy may refer to a child, a teenager, or even someone in his early twenties. The same word is used in the Septuagint (an ancient Gk translation of the OT, abbreviated LXX) to refer to young Joseph in Gn 37:30 and Daniel and his friends in Dn 1. **Barley** was

common food for the poor (the well-to-do preferred wheat bread); the **fish** were probably dried or preserved, perhaps pickled. In a similar account, Elisha fed one hundred men with twenty barley loaves (2Kg 4:42–44).
6:10 The men numbered **about five thousand**, plus women and children (Mt 14:21), totaling perhaps as many as fifteen thousand people. **Plenty of grass** may allude to the messianic age (10:9–10; Ps 23:2). Mark (Mk 6:39–40) mentioned that the grass was green, which points to springtime.
6:11 A common Jewish thanksgiving prayer was, "Blessed are you, O Lord our God, King of the universe, who brings forth bread from the earth."
6:12 Jesus's words echo Ru 2:14: "She ate and was satisfied and had some left over." Jesus took the same care in providing for those whom the Father gave him (Jn 10:28–29; 17:11–12,15).
6:13 The number of **baskets** may allude to Jesus's symbolic restoration of the twelve tribes of Israel.
6:14 The reference to **the Prophet who is to come into the world** alludes to Dt 18:15,18 (see notes at Jn 1:19–21; 7:40–41).
6:15 On Jesus's withdrawal to the **mountain**, see note at v. 3.
6:16–24 Jesus's walking across the Sea of Galilee may recall Job 9:8 (LXX) where God is said to walk on the water.
6:16–17 The disciples were on the eastern side of the lake, and they ventured to row the six or seven miles back **across the sea to Capernaum** on the western side.
6:19 They had rowed about **three or four miles**. If the feeding of the crowd occurred on the eastern shore, the shortest distance

miles,^ they saw Jesus walking on the sea. He was coming near the boat, and they were afraid. ²⁰ But he said to them, "It is I.ᴮ Don't be afraid." ²¹ Then they were willing to take him on board, and at once the boat was at the shore where they were heading.

The Bread of Life

²² The next day, the crowd that had stayed on the other side of the sea saw there had been only one boat.ᶜ They also saw that Jesus had not boarded the boat with his disciples, but that his disciples had gone off alone. ²³ Some boats from Tiberias came near the place where they had eaten the bread after the Lord had given thanks. ²⁴ When the crowd saw that neither Jesus nor his disciples were there, they got into the boats and went to Capernaum looking for Jesus. ²⁵ When they found him on the other side of the sea, they said to him, "Rabbi, when did you get here?"

²⁶ Jesus answered, "Truly I tell you, you are looking for me, not because you sawᴰ the signs, but because you ate the loaves and were filled. ²⁷ Don't work for the food that perishes but for the food that lasts for eternal life, which the Son of Man will give you, because God the Father has set his seal of approval on him."

²⁸ "What can we do to perform the works of God?" they asked.

²⁹ Jesus replied, "This is the work of God — that you believe in the one he has sent."

³⁰ "What sign, then, are you going to do so that we may see and believe you?" they asked. "What are you going to perform? ³¹ Our ancestors ate the manna in the wilderness, just as it is written: **He gave them bread from heaven to eat.**ᴱ

³² Jesus said to them, "Truly I tell you, Moses didn't give you the bread from heaven, but my Father gives you the true bread from heaven. ³³ For the bread of God is the one who comes down from heaven and gives life to the world."

³⁴ Then they said, "Sir, give us this bread always."

³⁵ "I am the bread of life," Jesus told them. "No one who comes to me will ever be hungry, and no one who believes in me will ever be thirsty again. ³⁶ But as I told you, you've seen me,ᶠ and yet you do not believe. ³⁷ Everyone the Father gives me will come to me, and the one who comes to me I will never cast out. ³⁸ For I have come down from heaven, not to do my own will, but the will of him who sent me. ³⁹ This is the will of him who sent me: that I should lose none of those he has given me but should raise them up on the last day. ⁴⁰ For this is the will of my Father: that everyone who sees the Son and believes in him will have eternal life, and I will raise him up on the last day."

⁴¹ Therefore the Jews started grumbling about him because he said, "I am the bread that came down from heaven." ⁴² They were saying, "Isn't this Jesus the son of Joseph, whose father and mother we know? How can he now say, 'I have come down from heaven'?"

⁴³ Jesus answered them, "Stop grumbling among yourselves. ⁴⁴ No one can come to me unless the Father who sent me drawsᴳ him, and I will raise him up on the last day. ⁴⁵ It is written in the Prophets: **And they will all be taught by God.**ᴴ Everyone who has listened

---

ᴬ **6:19** Lit *twenty-five or thirty stadia*; one *stadion* = 600 feet   ᴮ **6:20** Lit *"I am*   ᶜ **6:22** Other mss add *into which his disciples had entered*   ᴰ **6:26** Or *perceived*   ᴱ **6:31** Ex 16:4; Ps 78:24   ᶠ **6:36** Other mss omit *me*   ᴳ **6:44** Or *brings*, or *leads*   ᴴ **6:45** Is 54:13

---

to Capernaum would have been five to six miles.

6:20 It is I may have overtones of epiphany (cp. Ex 3:14; see note at Jn 6:35,48). The statement may allude to Ps 77:16,19, describing God's manifestation to Israel during the exodus.

6:21 The reference to the boat reaching the shore **at once** may allude to Ps 107:23–32 (esp. vv. 29–30).

6:23–24 Tiberias was and is the chief city on the western side of the lake (see note at v. 1). Whereas **Capernaum** was located on the northwestern edge of the lake, Tiberias is several miles to the south.

6:25 On the other side of the sea refers to the area in or around Capernaum (see note at vv. 23–24; cp. v. 59).

6:26 Jesus charged them with caring only about having full stomachs rather than about the significance of the **signs**.

6:27–29 People misunderstood Jesus's statement and asked about the **works** God required. Jesus said the only "work" required by God is faith in Messiah. On **seal of approval**, see note at 3:33.

6:30 Again, the people misunderstood. They demanded a **sign** as evidence of Jesus's claims (cp. 1Co 1:22). Jesus pointed to the significance

of the "sign" he had just performed—the feeding of the crowd (cp. 2:18). This revealed people's stubbornness, which led many of Jesus's disciples to leave (6:60–66) and prompted John to indict the Jews near the close of Jesus's public ministry (12:37–40).

6:31 This verse links exodus and Passover motifs with Jesus as the prophet like Moses and the expectation that God would again provide manna in the messianic age. The OT reference seems to involve several passages, with Ps 78:23–24 being most prominent (Ex 16:4,15; Neh 9:15; Ps 105:40).

6:32–34 The manna in the wilderness was pointing to **the true bread from heaven**, which is Jesus.

6:35,48 I am the bread of life is the first of Jesus's seven "I am" sayings in John. Subsequently he said he is "the light of the world" (8:12; 9:5); "the gate" of the sheep (10:7,9); the "good shepherd" (10:11,14); "the resurrection and the life" (11:25); "the way, the truth, and the life" (14:6); and "the true vine" (15:1). Apart from these sayings, there are statements where Jesus referred to himself as "I am" (6:20 textual note; 8:24,28,58; 18:5), a clear allusion to God's identification as "I AM" (Ex 3:14).

6:36 The earthly thinking of Jesus's audience resulted from their unbelief.

6:37,44 Jesus affirmed the twin themes of election and perseverance of the saints, prominent topics in John's Gospel. Those predestined by God will come to Jesus, and Jesus will preserve his own. No one can come to Jesus apart from the Father's drawing him. These themes continue in the good shepherd discourse (10:28–29) and Jesus's final prayer (17:6,9,11–12).

6:38–39 The believer's security is founded on the Son's faithfulness in doing the Father's will.

6:40 On Jesus's promise of **eternal life**, see note at 3:16–18.

6:41,43 The references to the **grumbling** of the **Jews** highlights the parallel between Jews of Jesus's day and wilderness Israel (cp. Ex 16:2,8–9; Nm 11:4–23; see note at Jn 6:5–6). The Israelites complained about the first giver of bread, Moses. Now they griped against the second giver, Jesus.

6:42 People showed no awareness of Jesus's virginal conception (Mt 1:18–25). They objected to Jesus's claim of descent from **heaven** since he was clearly human and was, they believed, conceived in the standard way (4:44).

6:44 On the "raising up" ministry of Jesus, see note at 12:32.

6:45 Citing Is 54:13, Jesus affirmed that, while his ministry fulfilled the prophetic

to and learned from the Father comes to me — [46] not that anyone has seen the Father except the one who is from God. He has seen the Father. [47] "Truly I tell you, anyone who believes[A] has eternal life. [48] I am the bread of life. [49] Your ancestors ate the manna in the wilderness, and they died. [50] This is the bread that comes down from heaven so that anyone may eat of it and not die. [51] I am the living bread that came down from heaven. If anyone eats of this bread he will live forever. The bread that I will give for the life of the world is my flesh."

[52] At that, the Jews argued among themselves, "How can this man give us his flesh to eat?"

[53] So Jesus said to them, "Truly I tell you, unless you eat the flesh of the Son of Man and drink his blood, you do not have life in yourselves. [54] The one who eats my flesh and drinks my blood has eternal life, and I will raise him up on the last day, [55] because my flesh is true food and my blood is true drink. [56] The one who eats my flesh and drinks my blood remains in me, and I in him. [57] Just as the living Father sent me and I live because of the Father, so the one who feeds on me will live because of me. [58] This is the bread that came down from heaven; it is not like the manna[B] your ancestors ate — and they died. The one who eats this bread will live forever."

[59] He said these things while teaching in the synagogue in Capernaum.

Many Disciples Desert Jesus

[60] Therefore, when many of his disciples heard this, they said, "This teaching is hard. Who can accept[C] it?"

[61] Jesus, knowing in himself that his disciples were grumbling about this, asked them, "Does this offend you? [62] Then what if you were to observe the Son of Man ascending to where he was before? [63] The Spirit is the one who gives life. The flesh doesn't help at all. The words that I have spoken to you are spirit and are life. [64] But there are some among you who don't believe." (For Jesus knew from the beginning those who did not[D] believe and the one who would betray him.) [65] He said, "This is why I told you that no one can come to me unless it is granted to him by the Father."

[66] From that moment[E] many of his disciples turned back and no longer accompanied him. [67] So Jesus said to the Twelve, "You don't want to go away too, do you?"

[68] Simon Peter answered, "Lord, to whom will we go? You have the words of eternal life. [69] We have come to believe and know that you are the Holy One of God."[F]

[70] Jesus replied to them, "Didn't I choose you, the Twelve? Yet one of you is a devil." [71] He was referring to Judas, Simon Iscariot's son,[G] one of the Twelve, because he was going to betray him.

The Unbelief of Jesus's Brothers

7 After this, Jesus traveled in Galilee, since he did not want to travel in Judea because the Jews were trying to kill him. [2] The Jewish Festival of Shelters[H] was near. [3] So his brothers said to him, "Leave here and go to Judea so that your disciples can see your works that you are doing. [4] For no one does anything in secret while he's seeking public recognition. If you do these things, show yourself to the world." [5] (For not even his brothers believed in him.)

[A]6:47 Other mss add in me　[B]6:58 Gk text lacks the manna　[C]6:60 Lit hear　[D]6:64 Other mss omit not　[E]6:66 Or Because of this　[F]6:69 Other mss read you are the Messiah, the Son of the Living God　[G]6:71 Or Judas Iscariot, Simon's son　[H]7:2 Or Tabernacles, or Booths

---

vision that one day all people would be taught by God, this applied only to those who were drawn by the Father and who came to believe in Jesus as Messiah.
6:46 Learning from the Father and seeing him are different. Only Jesus has seen the Father—not even Moses has seen him, which makes Jesus's revelation greater than Moses's.
6:47–52 Jesus contrasted the **manna in the wilderness** and the bread from **heaven**. Only the latter can provide **eternal life**. Jesus's **flesh** refers to his body on the cross, given for sin. Such talk raised questions from his audience.
6:53–59 Jesus meant for his words to be taken neither in a literal nor in a sacramental sense. The Hebrew idiom "flesh and blood" refers to the total person. Nowhere is Jesus's teaching more shocking than here. **Eternal life** comes from eating his **flesh** and drinking his **blood**—that is, from believing in him.
6:60–63 Even Jesus's disciples were offended by such talk. But Jesus explained that he was talking spiritually. Unaided by the **Spirit**, human reason cannot discern spiritual

truth. The Jews wrongly believed study of Scripture (see note at 5:39) and doing "works of God" (see note at 6:27–29) were sufficient for spiritual understanding.
6:64–66 Many of Jesus's disciples turned from him at this point, which is a watershed in John's Gospel. But Jesus was not surprised by the defection.
6:67–68 To whom will we go? may refer to transferring allegiance to another rabbi (cp. 1:35–37).
6:69 Peter's confession of Jesus as **the Holy One of God** anticipates later references to Jesus being set apart for God (10:36; 17:19). In the OT, God was called the "Holy One of Israel" (Ps 71:22; Is 43:3; 54:5). See similar confessions of Jesus in Mt 16:16; Mk 8:29; Lk 9:20.
6:70 This is the first reference to **the Twelve** in John's Gospel. Their existence and appointment are assumed from the testimony in the Synoptic Gospels. See notes at 1:43; 15:16.
6:71 Judas, Simon Iscariot's son, likely was the only non-Galilean among the Twelve.
7:1–8:59 On the heels of the unbelief of many disciples (6:60–66), chap. 7 opens with the unbelief of Jesus's brothers and

closes with the unbelief of the Jewish leaders (7:45–52). Chaps. 7 and 8 convey Jesus's teaching at the Festival of Shelters in Jerusalem. Jesus's teaching is given in two cycles (7:10–24,37–39; 8:12–30), climaxing in his invitation to all who are thirsty to come to him and drink. Once the Spirit was given, believers conveyed "streams of living water" (7:37–38). The second cycle begins with Jesus's startling affirmation that he is the "light of the world" (8:12).
7:1 Galilee (under the jurisdiction of Herod Antipas) was safer than **Judea** (under the Roman prefect) for Jesus since **the Jews were trying to kill him.**
7:2 The **Jewish Festival of Shelters** was celebrated in September or October, two months before the Festival of Dedication (see note at 10:22). People temporarily lived in shelters to remember God's faithfulness during Israel's wilderness wanderings (Lv 23:42–43; cp. Mt 17:4). See note at 2:13.
7:3–5 Jesus's **brothers** were naturally born sons of Mary. Their names were James, Joseph, Judas, and Simon (Mt 13:55 and Mk 6:3). Their poor advice stemmed from unbelief

⁶ Jesus told them, "My time has not yet arrived, but your time is always at hand. ⁷ The world cannot hate you, but it does hate me because I testify about it — that its works are evil. ⁸ Go up to the festival yourselves. I'm not going up to this festival,^ because my time has not yet fully come." ⁹ After he had said these things, he stayed in Galilee.

Jesus at the Festival of Shelters

¹⁰ After his brothers had gone up to the festival, then he also went up, not openly but secretly. ¹¹ The Jews were looking for him at the festival and saying, "Where is he?" ¹² And there was a lot of murmuring about him among the crowds. Some were saying, "He's a good man." Others were saying, "No, on the contrary, he's deceiving the people." ¹³ Still, nobody was talking publicly about him for fear of the Jews.

¹⁴ When the festival was already half over, Jesus went up into the temple and began to teach. ¹⁵ Then the Jews were amazed and said, "How is this man so learned, since he hasn't been trained?"

¹⁶ Jesus answered them, "My teaching isn't mine but is from the one who sent me. ¹⁷ If anyone wants to do his will, he will know whether the teaching is from God or whether I am speaking on my own. ¹⁸ The one who speaks on his own seeks his own glory; but he who seeks the glory of the one who sent him is true, and there is no unrighteousness in him. ¹⁹ Didn't Moses give you the law? Yet none of you keeps the law. Why are you trying to kill me?"

²⁰ "You have a demon!" the crowd responded. "Who is trying to kill you?"

²¹ "I performed one work, and you are all amazed," Jesus answered. ²² "This is why Moses has given you circumcision — not that it comes from Moses but from the fathers — and you circumcise a man on the Sabbath. ²³ If a man receives circumcision on the Sabbath so that the law of Moses won't be broken, are you angry at me because I made a man entirely well on the Sabbath? ²⁴ Stop judging according to outward appearances; rather judge according to righteous judgment."

The Identity of the Messiah

²⁵ Some of the people of Jerusalem were saying, "Isn't this the man they are trying to kill? ²⁶ Yet, look, he's speaking publicly and they're saying nothing to him. Can it be true that the authorities know he is the Messiah? ²⁷ But we know where this man is from. When the Messiah comes, nobody will know where he is from."

²⁸ As he was teaching in the temple, Jesus cried out, "You know me and you know where I am from. Yet I have not come on my own, but the one who sent me is true. You don't know him; ²⁹ I know him because I am from him, and he sent me."

---

^7:8 Other mss add *yet*

(Jn 7:5) and revealed a fundamental misunderstanding of Jesus's messianic identity (Mt 4:5–7).
7:6–10 On **my time has not yet arrived**, see note at 2:4. In 7:8, Jesus stated, **I'm not going up to this festival**. In v. 10, we learn that **he also went up, not openly but secretly** (see note at v. 1). It surprises many readers to realize that Jesus used craft and subterfuge to combat opposition and false expectations.
7:11 Particularly those who hadn't seen Jesus were eager to find him at the **festival**.
7:12 The charge that Jesus was **deceiving the people** may hark back to Dt 13:1–11 (cp.

Mt 27:63; Lk 23:2). Later Jewish literature called Jesus a deceiver.
7:13 The phrase **for fear of the Jews** (cp. 9:22; 19:38; 20:19) refers to Jerusalem authorities represented by the Sanhedrin (see note at 3:1).
7:14–15 **The Jews** may include Judean crowds and Jewish authorities. Jesus lacked formal rabbinic training (as did his disciples; Ac 4:13), but his teaching and authority came from God (Jn 7:16; 8:28; cp. Mt 5:21–26; 7:28–29).
7:16 Unlike other rabbis, Jesus claimed direct knowledge from God (8:28).
7:17 Only true believers, who are committed to following God's will, could rightly discern Jesus's teaching.
7:18–19 Jesus as an authoritative source contrasted himself with vain, false prophets (Dt 18:9–22). The Jews were proud of the fact that **Moses** had given them **the law** (cp. 9:28; Rm 2:17; 9:4).
7:20 This is one of several instances where Jesus was charged with **demon** possession (8:48; 10:20; Mt 12:24); the same charge was leveled against John the Baptist (Mt 11:18). Other charges against Jesus included breaking the Sabbath (Jn 5:16,18; 9:16), blasphemy (5:18; 8:58–59; 10:31,33,39; 19:7), deceiving the people (7:12,47), being a Samaritan (i.e., apostate; 8:48), madness (10:20), and criminal activity (18:30).
7:21 The **one work** Jesus referred to was probably the healing in 5:1–15.
7:22–23 **Circumcision** was given by **the fathers** (i.e., Abraham; Gn 17:9–14) and **Moses** (Ex 12:44,48–49; Lv 12:3). Jesus's argument was

"from the lesser to the greater." The Jews were to **circumcise** their males on the eighth day even if that day fell on the **Sabbath** (the "lesser" issue). If "perfecting" one part of a human body on the Sabbath was legitimate, how much more the healing of an entire person?
7:24 Jesus's statement about judging may allude to Lv 19:15 (cp. Dt 16:18–19; Is 11:3–4; Zch 7:9).
7:25–44 The next three scenes (vv. 25–31,32–36,37–44) center on the question, "Is Jesus the Christ?" Representative queries (in some cases involving misunderstanding) from the crowd serve as foils for dealing with this issue (vv. 27,31,42), in turn focusing on the supposedly unknown origins of Messiah, his performance of signs, and Bethlehem as Messiah's birthplace.
7:26 The authorities probably refers to the Sanhedrin (v. 48; 12:42; see notes at 3:1; 7:13).
7:27 Some rabbis taught that **Messiah** would be wholly unknown until he set out to procure salvation for Israel. Others felt his birthplace was foreknown (v. 42; cp. 2:1–6).
7:28–29 Telling the Jews that they didn't know God got a strong reaction.
7:30 On Jesus's ability to elude his enemies, see note at 2:4.
7:31 Since **Messiah** would be a prophet like Moses (Dt 18:15,18) and Moses performed many miraculous signs at the exodus (Ex 7–11), Messiah was expected to perform miracles as well (see notes at Jn 6:30,31). It would have been natural for people to wonder, after witnessing Jesus's miracles, if he was the Messiah.

#64 99 Essential Christian Truths

BAPTISM

Christian baptism is the immersion of a believer in water in the name of the Father, the Son, and the Holy Spirit. It is an act of obedience symbolizing the believer's faith in a crucified, buried, and risen Savior; the believer's death to sin; the burial of the old life; and the resurrection to walk in newness of life in Christ Jesus. It is a testimony to the believer's faith in the final resurrection of the dead. Being a church ordinance, it is prerequisite to the privileges of church membership and to the Lord's Supper.

30 Then they tried to seize him. Yet no one laid a hand on him because his hour had not yet come. **31** However, many from the crowd believed in him and said, "When the Messiah comes, he won't perform more signs than this man has done, will he?" **32** The Pharisees heard the crowd murmuring these things about him, and so the chief priests and the Pharisees sent servants^A to arrest him.

33 Then Jesus said, "I am only with you for a short time. Then I'm going to the one who sent me. **34** You will look for me, but you will not find me; and where I am, you cannot come."

35 Then the Jews said to one another, "Where does he intend to go that we won't find him? He doesn't intend to go to the Jewish people dispersed^B among the Greeks and teach the Greeks, does he? **36** What is this remark he made: 'You will look for me, and you will not find me; and where I am, you cannot come'?"

The Promise of the Spirit

37 On the last and most important day of the festival, Jesus stood up and cried out, "If anyone is thirsty, let him come to me^C and drink. **38** The one who believes in me, as the Scripture has said, will have streams of living water flow from deep within him." **39** He said this about the Spirit. Those who believed in Jesus were going to receive the Spirit, for the Spirit^D had not yet been given^E because Jesus had not yet been glorified.

The People Are Divided over Jesus

40 When some from the crowd heard these words, they said, "This truly is the Prophet." **41** Others said, "This is the Messiah." But some said, "Surely the Messiah doesn't come from Galilee, does he? **42** Doesn't the Scripture say that the Messiah comes from David's offspring^F and from the town of Bethlehem, where David lived?" **43** So the crowd was divided because of him. **44** Some of them wanted to seize him, but no one laid hands on him.

Debate over Jesus's Claims

45 Then the servants came to the chief priests and Pharisees, who asked them, "Why didn't you bring him?"

46 The servants answered, "No man ever spoke like this!"^G

47 Then the Pharisees responded to them, "Are you fooled too? **48** Have any of the rulers or Pharisees believed in him? **49** But this crowd, which doesn't know the law, is accursed."

50 Nicodemus — the one who came to him previously and who was one of them — said to them, **51** "Our law doesn't judge a man before it hears from him and knows what he's doing, does it?"

52 "You aren't from Galilee too, are you?" they replied. "Investigate and you will see that no prophet arises from Galilee."

[The earliest mss do not include 7:53–8:11.]^H

8 ^[53] Then each one went to his house. **1** But Jesus went to the Mount of Olives.

An Adulteress Forgiven

2 At dawn he went to the temple again, and all the people were coming to him. He sat down and began to teach them.

---

^A **7:32** Or *temple police*, or *officers*, also in vv. 45,46   ^B **7:35** Gk *diaspora*; Jewish people scattered throughout Gentile lands   ^C **7:37** Other mss omit *to me*   ^D **7:39** Other mss read *Holy Spirit*   ^E **7:39** Lit *the Spirit was not yet*   ^F **7:42** Lit *seed*   ^G **7:46** Other mss read *like this man*   ^H **7:53–8:11** Other mss include all or some of the passage after Jn 7:36,44,52; 21:25; or Lk 21:38.

7:32 The **chief priests and the Pharisees**, representing the Sanhedrin, deployed **servants** to **arrest** Jesus. His arrest implied that he was a criminal (but see note at vv. 45–52). The leaders hoped this would discourage people from following him.

7:33–34 Six months after Jesus issued this prediction, he was crucified.

7:35–36 People misunderstood Jesus's statement in v. 34. Ever since the exile, many Jews had not returned to Palestine but continued to live **dispersed among the Greeks** (synonymous with "Gentiles").

7:37 While v. 14 referred to the festival being "already half over," this was now the last and greatest day of the Festival of Shelters. Jesus's invitation harks back to OT prophetic passages such as Is 55:1 (cp. Is 12:3).

7:38–39 **Streams of living water** flowing from **deep within** Jesus's followers fulfill the end-time blessings predicted in the OT. John noted in v. 39 that these streams are emblematic of the **Spirit**, who would be given after Jesus's exaltation with the Father (20:22).

7:40–41 The Prophet is the figure referred to in Dt 18:15–18 (see note at Jn 1:19–21; cp.

6:14). This "Prophet" and the **Messiah** were thought to be different persons by some first-century Jews, but Jesus turned out to be both.

7:42 Bethlehem, south of Jerusalem in the heart of Judea, was foretold as Messiah's birthplace in Mc 5:2 (cp. Mt 2:5–6; see note at Jn 7:27). As David's city (1Sm 16:1,4; 20:6), Bethlehem had important messianic implications. In this verse the irony is apparent. Some people, knowing that Jesus hailed from Galilee, objected that **Messiah** was to be born in Bethlehem, not realizing that Bethlehem was in fact Jesus's birthplace.

7:43–44 On the right time for Jesus's death and resurrection, see note at 2:4.

7:45–52 The Sanhedrin's meeting highlighted the increasing threat that Jesus's popularity represented for the Jewish leadership. But Nicodemus's plea for fairness shows that the Sanhedrin was not yet united in opposition against Jesus.

7:45 On the attempt to arrest Jesus, see note at v. 32.

7:46 The **servants** (see v. 32) heard many people teach in the temple courts, but they

recognized Jesus's teaching as unique (Mt 7:28–29; see note at Jn 7:14–15).

7:48 Rulers probably refers to members of the Sanhedrin (see note at 3:1).

7:49 The disparaging reference to **this crowd, which doesn't know the law** reveals the arrogant contempt many rabbis had for the unschooled masses.

7:50 Jesus's previous encounter with Nicodemus is described in 3:1–15.

7:51 Old Testament law charged judges to investigate accusations fairly (Dt 1:16) and thoroughly (Jn 17:4; 19:18). Nicodemus's plea for fairness was later duplicated by the rabbi Gamaliel (Ac 5:34–39).

7:52 Contrary to the Pharisees' implication, prophets occasionally did arise from **Galilee**. These included Jonah (2Kg 14:25), possibly Elijah (1Kg 17:1), and Nahum (Nah 1:1).

7:53–8:11 The story of Jesus and the adulteress may be authentic, but it is doubtful that the account is part of John's original Gospel. Reasons include: (1) the account is absent from all the oldest copies of John; (2) where it does occur in later manuscripts, it is found at various places (after Jn 7:36,44,52; at the end of John's

3 Then the scribes and the Pharisees brought a woman caught in adultery, making her stand in the center. **4** "Teacher," they said to him, "this woman was caught in the act of committing adultery. **5** In the law Moses commanded us to stone such women. So what do you say?" **6** They asked this to trap him, in order that they might have evidence to accuse him.

Jesus stooped down and started writing on the ground with his finger. **7** When they persisted in questioning him, he stood up and said to them, "The one without sin among you should be the first to throw a stone at her." **8** Then he stooped down again and continued writing on the ground. **9** When they heard this, they left one by one, starting with the older men. Only he was left, with the woman in the center. **10** When Jesus stood up, he said to her, "Woman, where are they? Has no one condemned you?" **11** "No one, Lord,"^A she answered.

"Neither do I condemn you," said Jesus. "Go, and from now on do not sin anymore."]

The Light of the World

12 Jesus spoke to them again: "I am the light of the world. Anyone who follows me will never walk in the darkness but will have the light of life."

13 So the Pharisees said to him, "You are testifying about yourself. Your testimony is not valid."

14 "Even if I testify about myself," Jesus replied, "My testimony is true, because I know where I came from and where I'm going. But you don't know where I come from or where I'm going. **15** You judge by human standards.^B I judge no one. **16** And if I do judge, my judgment is true, because it is not I alone who judge, but I and the Father who sent me. **17** Even in your law it is written that the testimony of two witnesses is true. **18** I am the one who testifies about myself, and the Father who sent me testifies about me."

19 Then they asked him, "Where is your Father?"

"You know neither me nor my Father," Jesus answered. "If you knew me, you would also know my Father." **20** He spoke these words by the treasury, while teaching in the temple. But no one seized him, because his hour had not yet come.

Jesus Predicts His Departure

21 Then he said to them again, "I'm going away; you will look for me, and you will die in your sin. Where I'm going, you cannot come."

22 So the Jews said again, "He won't kill himself, will he, since he says, 'Where I'm going, you cannot come'?"

23 "You are from below," he told them, "I am from above. You are of this world; I am not of this world. **24** Therefore I told you that you will die in your sins. For if you do not believe that I am he, you will die in your sins."

25 "Who are you?" they questioned.

"Exactly what I've been telling you from the very beginning," Jesus told them. **26** "I have many things to say and to judge about you, but the one who sent me is true, and what I have heard from him — these things I tell the world."

27 They did not know he was speaking to them about the Father. **28** So Jesus said to them, "When you lift up the Son of Man, then you will know that I am he, and that I do nothing on my own. But just as the Father taught me, I say these things. **29** The one who sent me is with me. He has not left me alone, because I always do what pleases him."

Truth and Freedom

30 As he was saying these things, many believed in him. **31** Then Jesus said to the Jews who had believed him, "If you continue in my word,^C you really are my disciples. **32** You will know the truth, and the truth will set you free."

---

^8:11 Or *Sir*; Jn 4:15,49; 5:7; 6:34; 9:36   ^8:15 Lit *You judge according to the flesh*   ^8:31 Or *my teaching*, or *my message*, also in v. 37

Gospel; or after Lk 21:38); (3) virtually every verse from 8:1–11 (except for v. 5) features words not elsewhere found in John's Gospel, and standard vocabulary used in John is conspicuously absent; (4) the account appears to interrupt the narrative flow from 7:52 to 8:12, breaking the literary unit 7:1–8:59; and (5) the account was virtually unknown by early church fathers before the fourth century.
8:12 Jesus as **the light of the world** (see note at 6:35,48) develops further the affirmation in the prologue that Jesus was "the light of men" and that "that light shines in the darkness" (1:4–5). On this basis, Jesus exhorted his hearers to put their trust in the light while they had him with them, so they might become "children of light" (12:35–36). Jesus's concluding testimony is that he came into the world as light so that no one who

believes in him should remain in darkness (12:46). Yet, according to the Evangelist, the verdict is this: Light has come into the world, but people loved darkness rather than light because their deeds were evil (3:19–21).
8:13–14 The Pharisees' challenge and Jesus's response continue the acrimony of 5:31–47. Again, Mosaic stipulations were in view (Dt 17:6; 19:15).
8:14,18 On Jesus's testimony about himself, see note at 5:31–47.
8:15–16 Jesus's statement may echo 1Sm 16:7. People rejected Jesus because he did not come with regal fanfare, but appearances can be deceiving (Is 53:2–3).
8:17–18 On **the testimony of two witnesses**, see notes at Dt 17:6–7; 19:15.
8:19 Their question shows that they neither know who Jesus is nor do they know God.

8:20 On the timing of Jesus's **hour**, see note at 2:4.
8:21–23 You will look for me may mean that the Jews would continue looking for the Messiah after Jesus's death and ascension (D. A. Carson).
8:24,28 These statements hint at Jesus's deity (see notes at 6:35,48).
8:25–27 The question, **Who are you?** was not a request for information but a challenge, as in, Who do you think you are?
8:28 On the lifting up of Jesus, see note at 3:14–15.
8:29 This speaks of Jesus's sinlessness.
8:30–32 A disciple proves his genuineness by continuing to follow Jesus. Therefore, there is such a thing as a false disciple. To **know the truth** is to know Christ.

33 "We are descendants^A of Abraham," they answered him, "and we have never been enslaved to anyone. How can you say, 'You will become free'?"

34 Jesus responded, "Truly I tell you, everyone who commits sin is a slave of sin. **35** A slave does not remain in the household forever, but a son does remain forever. **36** So if the Son sets you free, you really will be free. **37** I know you are descendants of Abraham, but you are trying to kill me because my word has no place among you. **38** I speak what I have seen in the presence of the Father;^B so then, you do what you have heard from your father."

39 "Our father is Abraham," they replied.

"If you were Abraham's children," Jesus told them, "you would do what Abraham did. **40** But now you are trying to kill me, a man who has told you the truth that I heard from God. Abraham did not do this. **41** You're doing what your father does."

"We weren't born of sexual immorality," they said. "We have one Father — God."

42 Jesus said to them, "If God were your Father, you would love me, because I came from God and I am here. For I didn't come on my own, but he sent me. **43** Why don't you understand what I say? Because you cannot listen to^C my word. **44** You are of your father the devil, and you want to carry out your father's desires. He was a murderer from the beginning and does not stand in the truth, because there is no truth in him. When he tells a lie, he speaks from his own nature,^D because he is a liar and the father of lies. **45** Yet because I tell the truth, you do not believe me. **46** Who among you can convict me of sin? If I am telling the truth, why don't you believe me? **47** The one who is from God listens to God's words. This is why you don't listen, because you are not from God."

Jesus and Abraham

48 The Jews responded to him, "Aren't we right in saying that you're a Samaritan and have a demon?"

49 "I do not have a demon," Jesus answered. "On the contrary, I honor my Father and you dishonor me. **50** I do not seek my own glory; there is one who seeks it and judges. **51** Truly I tell you, if anyone keeps my word, he will never see death."

52 Then the Jews said, "Now we know you have a demon. Abraham died and so did the prophets. You say, 'If anyone keeps my word, he will never taste death.' **53** Are you greater than our father Abraham who died? And the prophets died. Who do you claim to be?"

54 "If I glorify myself," Jesus answered, "my glory is nothing. My Father — about whom you say, 'He is our God' — he is the one who glorifies me. **55** You do not know him, but I know him. If I were to say I don't know him, I would be a liar like you. But I do know him, and I keep his word. **56** Your father Abraham rejoiced to see my day; he saw it and was glad."

57 The Jews replied, "You aren't fifty years old yet, and you've seen Abraham?"^E

58 Jesus said to them, "Truly I tell you, before Abraham was, I am."

59 So they picked up stones to throw at him. But Jesus was hidden^F and went out of the temple.^G

The Sixth Sign: Healing a Man Born Blind

9 As he was passing by, he saw a man blind from birth. **2** His disciples asked him, "Rabbi, who sinned, this man or his parents, that he was born blind?"

---

^A**8:33** Or offspring; lit seed, also in v. 37; Jn 7:42   ^B**8:38** Other mss read of my Father   ^C**8:43** Or cannot hear   ^D**8:44** Lit from his own things   ^E**8:57** Other mss read and Abraham has seen you?   ^F**8:59** Or Jesus hid himself   ^G**8:59** Other mss add and having gone through their midst, he passed by

---

8:33 The OT extols the blessings of being descendants of Abraham (Ps 105:6; Is 41:8).
8:34–35 The contrast between **son** and **slave** may allude to Abraham's sons through Sarah and Hagar (Gn 21:1–21; see Ex 21:2).
8:36 On Jesus as the life-giving **Son**, see note at 3:16–18.
8:37–38 Even in the OT, physical descent from **Abraham** was insufficient to establish one's lineage (Jr 9:25–26; cp. Rm 2:28–29; 9:7; Gl 4:21–31).
8:39–58 On children of God, see note at 3:3–8.
8:40 Jesus had surreptitiously called them children of the devil, to which they replied that they were children of Abraham. Here Jesus argues that that cannot be the case.
8:41 Though the OT calls the Israelites God's children (Ex 4:22; Dt 14:1–2; 32:6; Is 63:16; 64:8; Jr 31:9; Mal 2:10), John said only those born of God (through faith) are God's children (Jn 1:12–13; 3:3–8).
8:42–43 The Jews had further declared that they were children of God; Jesus proceeded to prove that they were not.

8:44 The devil is **a murderer from the beginning**. He incited Cain to kill Abel (1Jn 3:15). He **does not stand in the truth** is a possible reference to Satan's fall (Is 14:12). At the fall of Adam and Eve, he blatantly contradicted God's word (Gn 3:3–4; cp. Gn 2:17).
8:45–46 Jesus always did what pleases God (v. 29; Is 53:9).
8:47 Jesus spoke boldly and plainly to the Jews, telling them, **you are not from God**.
8:48,52 On the accusation that Jesus had a demon, see note at 7:20.
8:49–53 Jesus countered the charge that he was demon-possessed by declaring that he honored his Father. Then he boldly said that keeping his word is the way to avoid death. This sounded insane to the Jews because all the great men of the faith had died. They responded, **Who do you claim to be?**
8:54–55 Jesus replied that he didn't have to glorify himself because God was doing it.
8:56 Jesus's statement refers to Abraham's joyful anticipation of the coming of the Messiah. See the later affirmation in 12:41 that Isaiah saw Jesus's glory.

8:57–58 On Jesus's **I am** statements, see note at 6:35,48.
8:59 Stoning was the prescribed punishment for blasphemy (Lv 24:16; cp. Dt 13:6–11; Jn 10:31–33; 11:8). However, this was never to be enacted by mob violence (Dt 17:2–7). In the OT, righteous men like Moses (Ex 17:4), Joshua and Caleb (Nm 14:10), and David (1Sm 30:6) were nearly stoned. As on previous occasions, Jesus evaded arrest (Jn 7:30,44; 8:20; see note at 2:4). His withdrawal from the Jews strikes a note of judgment similar to the removal of God's favor from King Saul (1Sm 15:23).
9:1–41 Jesus's identity as "the light of the world" was illustrated in his sixth and penultimate "sign" recorded in John's Gospel—the healing of a man born blind (see note at 2:11). As in chap. 5, Jesus healed on the Sabbath and thus suffered persecution from the Jewish leaders. But in contrast to the lame man of chap. 5, who showed no faith and reported Jesus to the authorities, the formerly blind man showed a progression of faith and ended up worshiping Jesus (9:38). Jesus

³ "Neither this man nor his parents sinned," Jesus answered. "This came about so that God's works might be displayed in him. ⁴ We^A must do the works of him who sent me^B while it is day. Night is coming when no one can work. ⁵ As long as I am in the world, I am the light of the world."

⁶ After he said these things he spit on the ground, made some mud from the saliva, and spread the mud on his eyes. ⁷ "Go," he told him, "wash in the pool of Siloam" (which means "Sent"). So he left, washed, and came back seeing.

⁸ His neighbors and those who had seen him before as a beggar said, "Isn't this the one who used to sit begging?" ⁹ Some said, "He's the one." Others were saying, "No, but he looks like him."

He kept saying, "I'm the one."

¹⁰ So they asked him, "Then how were your eyes opened?"

¹¹ He answered, "The man called Jesus made mud, spread it on my eyes, and told me, 'Go to Siloam and wash.' So when I went and washed I received my sight."

¹² "Where is he?" they asked.

"I don't know," he said.

The Healed Man's Testimony

¹³ They brought the man who used to be blind to the Pharisees. ¹⁴ The day that Jesus made the mud and opened his eyes was a Sabbath. ¹⁵ Then the Pharisees asked him again how he received his sight.

"He put mud on my eyes," he told them. "I washed and I can see."

¹⁶ Some of the Pharisees said, "This man is not from God, because he doesn't keep the Sabbath." But others were saying, "How can a sinful man perform such signs?" And there was a division among them.

¹⁷ Again they asked the blind man, "What do you say about him, since he opened your eyes?"

"He's a prophet," he said.

¹⁸ The Jews did not believe this about him — that he was blind and received sight — until they summoned the parents of the one who had received his sight. ¹⁹ They asked them, "Is this your son, the one you say was born blind? How then does he now see?"

²⁰ "We know this is our son and that he was born blind," his parents answered. ²¹ "But we don't know how he now sees, and we don't know who opened his eyes. Ask him; he's of age. He will speak for himself." ²² His parents said these things because they were afraid of the Jews, since the Jews had already agreed that if anyone confessed him as the Messiah, he would be banned from the synagogue. ²³ This is why his parents said, "He's of age; ask him."

²⁴ So a second time they summoned the man who had been blind and told him, "Give glory to God. We know that this man is a sinner."

²⁵ He answered, "Whether or not he's a sinner, I don't know. One thing I do know: I was blind, and now I can see!"

²⁶ Then they asked him, "What did he do to you? How did he open your eyes?"

²⁷ "I already told you," he said, "and you didn't listen. Why do you want to hear it again? You don't want to become his disciples too, do you?"

²⁸ They ridiculed him: "You're that man's disciple, but we're Moses's disciples. ²⁹ We know that God has spoken to Moses. But this man — we don't know where he's from."

---

^9:4 Other mss read I   ^B9:4 Other mss read *us*

---

condemned the Pharisees for their spiritual blindness (vv. 40–41).
9:2 The disciples' question reflected the assumption, customary in ancient Judaism, that suffering could be traced to specific sins (cp. Jb 4:7). The underlying concern of this assumption is to clear God of wrongdoing against innocent people (Ex 20:5; Nm 14:18; Dt 5:9). Yet the NT makes clear that suffering is not always a direct result of a person's sin (Lk 13:2–3; 2Co 12:7; Gl 4:13). We should not speculate about the cause of a person's suffering but realize that even evil can contribute to the greater glory of God (esp. the crucifixion; cp. Jn 12:28,37–41; 17:1,5).
9:3 Jesus did not explain why the man was born blind; he only announced what would be the result: God's glory.
9:4 That Jesus included the disciples in his ministry by saying **We must do the works** is remarkable. Jesus realized that his time on earth was limited.
9:5 On Jesus as **the light of the world**, see notes at 6:35,48; 8:12.
9:6–7 Jesus's sending the man to **wash in the pool of Siloam** is reminiscent of Elisha's

sending Naaman to wash in the Jordan River (2Kg 5:10–13). The words **which means "Sent"** may echo the messianic reference in Gn 49:10 (cp. Is 8:6, see notes at Jn 1:38; 3:16–18). After 9:7, Jesus is not heard from again until v. 35.
9:8–13 The man gave a clear testimony to all that he knew.
9:14 The mention of the **Sabbath** here (cp. 5:9) resumes the earlier Sabbath controversy in chap. 5. Jesus had moistened clay with his saliva and then kneaded it to make mud. Kneading dough, and by analogy kneading clay, was included among the thirty-nine classes of work forbidden on the Sabbath by Jewish rabbinic tradition (*m. Shabb.* 7:2).
9:15 Again the man gave his testimony, this time to the Pharisees.
9:16 The **division** among the Pharisees follows the differing ways of reasoning observed by the schools of Shammai and Hillel. The former argued from foundational principles ("anyone who breaks the law is a sinner"), the latter from the established facts of a case ("Jesus has performed a good work").

9:18–22 The parents were evasive, pleading ignorance because **they were afraid** of the Jewish authorities who had decided to expel from the **synagogue** anyone who **confessed** Jesus **as the Messiah**.
9:22–23 On **the Jews** and their power, see note at 7:13.
9:24 The Pharisees' exhortation to the healed man, **Give glory to God**, was a solemn warning for him to tell the truth (Jos 7:19; 2Ch 30:8; Jr 13:16).
9:25–27 The man spoke boldly.
9:28 The Pharisees' claim of being **Moses's disciples** was undermined by their failure to listen to the one of whom Moses wrote (see note at 5:45–47).
9:29 The Pharisees' assertion, **We know that God has spoken to Moses**, harks back to God's giving Moses the law at Mount Sinai (Ex 33:11; Nm 12:2–8; cp. Jn 1:17).
9:30–33 The healed man's major premise, that **God doesn't listen to sinners**, is borne out by the OT (Pss 34:15; 66:20; 109:7; 145:19). His minor premise, that there was no precedent for **opening the eyes of a person born blind**, is also confirmed by

30 "This is an amazing thing!" the man told them. "You don't know where he is from, and yet he opened my eyes. **31** We know that God doesn't listen to sinners, but if anyone is God-fearing and does his will, he listens to him. **32** Throughout history^A no one has ever heard of someone opening the eyes of a person born blind. **33** If this man were not from God, he wouldn't be able to do anything."

34 "You were born entirely in sin," they replied, "and are you trying to teach us?" Then they threw him out.

Spiritual Blindness

35 Jesus heard that they had thrown the man out, and when he found him, he asked, "Do you believe in the Son of Man?"^B

36 "Who is he, Sir, that I may believe in him?" he asked.

37 Jesus answered, "You have seen him; in fact, he is the one speaking with you."

38 "I believe, Lord!" he said, and he worshiped him.

39 Jesus said, "I came into this world for judgment, in order that those who do not see will see and those who do see will become blind."

40 Some of the Pharisees who were with him heard these things and asked him, "We aren't blind too, are we?"

41 "If you were blind," Jesus told them, "you wouldn't have sin. But now that you say, 'We see,' your sin remains.

The Good Shepherd

10 "Truly I tell you, anyone who doesn't enter the sheep pen by the gate but climbs in some other way is a thief and a robber. **2** The one who enters by the gate is the shepherd of the sheep. **3** The gatekeeper opens it for him, and the sheep hear his voice. He calls his own sheep by name and leads them out. **4** When he has brought all his own outside, he goes ahead of them. The sheep follow him because they know his voice. **5** They will never follow a stranger; instead they will run away from him, because they don't know the voice of strangers." **6** Jesus gave them this figure of speech, but they did not understand what he was telling them.

7 Jesus said again, "Truly I tell you, I am the gate for the sheep. **8** All who came before me^C are thieves and robbers, but the sheep didn't listen to them. **9** I am the gate. If anyone enters by me, he will be saved and will come in and go out and find pasture. **10** A thief comes only to steal and kill and destroy. I have come so that they may have life and have it in abundance. **11** "I am the good shepherd. The good shepherd lays down his life for the sheep. **12** The hired hand, since he is not the shepherd and doesn't own the sheep, leaves them^D and runs away when he sees a wolf coming. The wolf then snatches and scatters them. **13** This happens because he is a hired hand and doesn't care about the sheep.

---

^A**9:32** Lit *From the age*   ^B**9:35** Other mss read *the Son of God*   ^C**10:8** Other mss omit *before me*   ^D**10:12** Lit *leaves the sheep*

---

the absence of such instances cited in OT or extrabiblical sources. The man's conclusion, **If this man were not from God, he wouldn't be able to do anything** (cp. 3:2), fit with the common Jewish view that miracles were performed in answer to prayer.
9:34 The Pharisees' charge against the healed man may allude to Ps 51:5. **Threw him out** refers to expulsion from the synagogue (see v. 22). The way this was done suggests an impulsive action rather than excommunication based on a formal procedure.
9:35–38 Jesus the good shepherd sought out the man he had healed and led him to faith. The blind man progressed from identifying Jesus as "a prophet" (v. 17) to confessing him as **Lord** (v. 38).
9:39–41 Giving sight to the righteous blind (Ps 146:8; Is 29:18; 35:5; 42:7,18) and blinding unrighteous persons who can see (Is 6:10; 42:19; Jr 5:21; cp. Mt 13:13–15; Jn 12:40) are common OT themes. Elsewhere, Jesus called the Pharisees "blind guides" (Mt 23:16; cp. 15:14; 23:26).
10:1–42 In this discourse, Jesus criticized the Jewish leaders for failing to give Israel proper spiritual guidance. By contrast, Jesus is the good shepherd who lays down his life for the sheep. Chapter 10 provides a commentary on the previous chapter that revealed the Jewish leadership's legal pettiness, rigidity, and hardness toward God. Not only is Jesus the good shepherd, but he is also the door through which believers find abundant, eternal life (vv. 9–10). The following interchange, culminating in another attempt to

stone Jesus for blasphemy, took place at the Festival of Dedication (vv. 22–39). It is followed by a final reference to John the Baptist, which closes out the "festival cycle" of chaps. 5–10 and the entire section (1:19–10:42), which began with the ministry of John the Baptist and his witness to Jesus.
10:1 The **sheep pen** may have been a courtyard (18:15) near a house surrounded by a stone wall where several families kept their sheep. The **gate** would have been guarded by a hired gatekeeper (10:3). **Thief** may focus on the covert nature of entrance to the pen, and **robber** on violence (Lk 10:30,36).
10:2 The **shepherd** was the authorized caretaker of the flock.
10:3–4 On **gatekeeper**, see note at v. 1. The reference to the shepherd calling his **own sheep by name** and leading them out may allude to passages such as Nm 27:16–18 (esp. v. 17), possibly a messianic passage, or Ezk 34:13. Israel's exodus from Egypt is sometimes portrayed as a flock following its shepherd (Ps 77:20; Is 63:11,14; cp. Ps 78:52). Old Testament prophetic literature envisioned a similar end-time deliverance for God's people (Mc 2:12–13).
10:5–6 The **strangers** in the **figure of speech** are the Jewish leaders.
10:7,9 Jesus's reference to himself as **the gate** may hark back to messianic readings of passages such as Ps 118:20 (see notes at Jn 6:35,48 and 10:1).
10:8 All who came before me may hint at messianic pretenders who promised their followers freedom but led them into armed

conflict and doom instead (Ac 5:36–37; 21:38). The reference to **thieves and robbers** is reminiscent of the reference to Israel's shepherds "who have been feeding themselves" but not the flock (Ezk 34:2–4; see note at Jn 10:1).
10:9 Jesus is **the gate** to salvation (cp. 14:6). The NT elsewhere speaks of "entering" God's kingdom as through a door (see Mt 7:7,13; 25:10; Ac 14:22). **Will come in and go out** echoes covenant terminology, especially blessings for obedience (Dt 28:6; cp. Ps 121:8). It is also reminiscent of Moses's description of Joshua, who led Israel into the promised land (Nm 27:16–17). **Find pasture** depicts the assurance of God's provision (1Ch 4:40; Ps 23:2; Is 49:9–10; Ezk 34:12–15).
10:10 Jesus's promise of abundant life in the here and now brings to mind OT prophetic passages such as Ezk 34:12–15,25–31. See note at Jn 5:26.
10:11 Jesus is **the good shepherd** (see note at 6:35,48). In the OT, God as the true shepherd is contrasted with unfaithful shepherds whom God will judge (Jr 23:1–4; Ezk 34; Zch 11:4–17). David (or the Davidic Messiah) was also depicted as a good shepherd (2Sm 5:2; Ps 78:70–72; Ezk 37:24; Mc 5:4), as was Moses (Is 63:11; cp. Ps 77:20). The reference to the good shepherd who **lays down his life for the sheep** calls to mind young David (1Sm 17:34–37).
10:12–13 The **hired hand** does not care for the sheep and abandons them in times of danger. The hired hands of Israel (Ezk 22:27) are contrasted with God and his Messiah,

¹⁴ "I am the good shepherd. I know my own, and my own know me, ¹⁵ just as the Father knows me, and I know the Father. I lay down my life for the sheep. ¹⁶ But I have other sheep that are not from this sheep pen; I must bring them also, and they will listen to my voice. Then there will be one flock, one shepherd. ¹⁷ This is why the Father loves me, because I lay down my life so that I may take it up again. ¹⁸ No one takes it from me, but I lay it down on my own. I have the right to lay it down, and I have the right to take it up again. I have received this command from my Father."

¹⁹ Again the Jews were divided because of these words. ²⁰ Many of them were saying, "He has a demon and he's crazy. Why do you listen to him?" ²¹ Others were saying, "These aren't the words of someone who is demon-possessed. Can a demon open the eyes of the blind?"

Jesus at the Festival of Dedication

²² Then the Festival of Dedication took place in Jerusalem, and it was winter. ²³ Jesus was walking in the temple in Solomon's Colonnade. ²⁴ The Jews surrounded him and asked, "How long are you going to keep us in suspense?ᴬ If you are the Messiah, tell us plainly."ᴮ

²⁵ "I did tell you and you don't believe," Jesus answered them. "The works that I do in my Father's name testify about me. ²⁶ But you don't believe because you are not of my sheep.ᶜ ²⁷ My sheep hear my voice, I know them, and they follow me. ²⁸ I give them eternal life, and they will never perish. No one will snatch them out of my hand. ²⁹ My Father, who has given them to me, is greater than all. No one is able to snatch them out of the Father's hand. ³⁰ I and the Father are one."

Renewed Efforts to Stone Jesus

³¹ Again the Jews picked up rocks to stone him.

³² Jesus replied, "I have shown you many good works from the Father. For which of these works are you stoning me?"

³³ "We aren't stoning you for a good work," the Jews answered, "but for blasphemy, because you — being a man — make yourself God."

³⁴ Jesus answered them, "Isn't it written in your law,ᴰ I said, you are gods?ᴱ ³⁵ If he called those to whom the word of God came 'gods' — and the Scripture cannot be broken — ³⁶ do you say, 'You are blaspheming' to the one the Father set apart and sent into the world, because I said: I am the Son of God? ³⁷ If I am not doing my Father's works, don't believe me. ³⁸ But if I am doing them and you don't believe me, believe the works. This way you will know and understandᶠ that the Father is in me and I

ᴬ10:24 Lit *How long are you taking away our life?* ᴮ10:24 Or *openly*, or *publicly* ᶜ10:26 Other mss add *just as I told you*
ᴰ10:34 Other mss read *in the scripture* ᴱ10:34 Ps 82:6 ᶠ10:38 Other mss read *know and believe*

---

whose role is patterned after God's "good shepherd" par excellence, King David (1Sm 17:34–36).
10:14 On Jesus as **the good shepherd**, see note at v. 11.
10:15 "Whoever knows Jesus also knows the Father, and the Father loves those who love Jesus and believe in him" (Herman Ridderbos).
10:16 The **other sheep . . . not from this sheep pen** refers to Gentiles (Is 56:8). Jesus envisioned a future Gentile mission following his death on the cross. **One flock, one shepherd** alludes to Ezk 34:23; 37:24. Believing Jews and Gentiles will be united into one messianic community.
10:17 Jesus did not gain the Father's approval by sacrificing his life. Instead, his sacrifice was in obedience to the Father.

#65 99 Essential Christian Truths

GOD IS ONE IN THREE PERSONS

While the Bible affirms that God is one (Mk 12:29; 1Co 8:4–6), it also affirms that God exists in three persons: Father, Son, and Holy Spirit. Each person of the Trinity is fully divine—the Father is God (Jn 6:27); the Son is God (Php 2); the Spirit is God (Ac 5:3–4). And each person is distinct from the others (Mt 11:27; Jn 10:30; 14:16). This perfect unity within the three persons of the Trinity is a first-order doctrine; departing from it is to abandon orthodox Christianity.

10:18 Received this command is covenantal language, relating Jesus's relationship with the Father to the OT depiction of God's relationship with Israel. These words also remind readers that Jesus's death was not the result of events that got out of hand. This was the reason he came (see 12:27).
10:19–21 In ancient times insanity and demon possession were frequently linked. The reference to opening the **eyes of the blind** links the good shepherd discourse with the healing of the blind man in chap. 9. The charges of demon possession (which hark back to similar charges from earlier; see note at 7:20) and insanity were contradicted by OT teaching that it is the Lord who gives sight to the blind (Ps 146:8; cp. Ex 4:11).
10:22 The eight-day **Festival of Dedication** (also called Hanukkah and the Festival of Lights) celebrated the rededication of the Jewish temple in December of 164 BC after its desecration by the Seleucid ruler Antiochus Epiphanes in 167 BC (1Macc 1:59). **It was winter** refers to December. See note at 2:13.
10:23 Probably because of the cold winter weather, Jesus taught not out in the open but in the area called **Solomon's Colonnade**. The structure was commonly (though erroneously) thought to date back to Solomon's time. Later it became the gathering place for the early church (Ac 3:11; 5:12).
10:24–25 The demand, **If you are the Messiah, tell us plainly**, seems like double talk (Lk 22:67). If they had not understood Jesus's claim to be the Messiah, why did they repeatedly try to kill him? (Jn 5:18; 7:25; 8:59). Indeed, Jesus responded that he did make

this claim. On Jesus's **works** testifying about him, see note at 5:31–47.
10:26–29 Snatch (vv. 28–29) denotes the use of force (see note at v. 1). The comment contrasts with the figure of the hired man in vv. 12–13 who abandoned the flock in times of danger, and recalls OT statements that no one can rob from God's hand (Is 43:13).
10:30 Jesus's claim that he and the Father **are one** (cp. vv. 33–38; 5:17–18) echoes the Shema, the basic confession of Judaism (Dt 6:4) and amounts to a claim to deity. Jesus's unity with the Father is later said to be the basis on which Jesus's followers are to be unified (Jn 17:22).
10:31 On the attempt to stone Jesus for blasphemy, see notes at 5:18; 8:59.
10:32 On Jesus's **works** as a testimony to him, see note at 5:31–47.
10:33 The charge against Jesus appears to be grounded in Lv 24:16 (cp. Nm 15:30–31; Mk 14:61–64; see note at Jn 8:59).
10:34 Jesus's point in quoting Ps 82:6 was that if human judges can in some sense be called "god" in the Scriptures, this designation is even more appropriate for himself.
10:35 Jesus's statement that **the Scripture cannot be broken** is evidence for his belief in the inviolability of God's written Word (in this case, the Hebrew Scriptures; cp. Mt 5:18). Jesus and many of his opponents upheld the authority of God's Word.
10:36 The reference to Jesus being **set apart** for his mission echoes language used of appointed men such as Moses the lawgiver, Jeremiah the prophet, and the Aaronic priests.
10:37–38 On Jesus's **works** testifying about him, see note at 5:31–47.

in the Father." **39** Then they were trying again to seize him, but he escaped their grasp.

Many beyond the Jordan Believe in Jesus

40 So he departed again across the Jordan to the place where John had been baptizing earlier, and he remained there. **41** Many came to him and said, "John never did a sign, but everything John said about this man was true." **42** And many believed in him there.

Lazarus Dies at Bethany

11 Now a man was sick, Lazarus from Bethany, the village of Mary and her sister Martha. **2** Mary was the one who anointed the Lord with perfume and wiped his feet with her hair, and it was her brother Lazarus who was sick. **3** So the sisters sent a message to him: "Lord, the one you love is sick."

4 When Jesus heard it, he said, "This sickness will not end in death but is for the glory of God, so that the Son of God may be glorified through it." **5** Now Jesus loved Martha, her sister, and Lazarus. **6** So when he heard that he was sick, he stayed two more days in the place where he was. **7** Then after that, he said to the disciples, "Let's go to Judea again."

8 "Rabbi," the disciples told him, "just now the Jews tried to stone you, and you're going there again?"

9 "Aren't there twelve hours in a day?" Jesus answered. "If anyone walks during the day, he doesn't stumble, because he sees the light of this world. **10** But if anyone walks during the night, he does stumble, because the light is not in him."

11 He said this, and then he told them, "Our friend Lazarus has fallen asleep, but I'm on my way to wake him up."

12 Then the disciples said to him, "Lord, if he has fallen asleep, he will get well."

13 Jesus, however, was speaking about his death, but they thought he was speaking about natural sleep. **14** So Jesus then told them plainly, "Lazarus has died. **15** I'm glad for you that I wasn't there so that you may believe. But let's go to him."

16 Then Thomas (called "Twin"^A) said to his fellow disciples, "Let's go too so that we may die with him."

The Resurrection and the Life

17 When Jesus arrived, he found that Lazarus had already been in the tomb four days. **18** Bethany was near Jerusalem (less than two miles^B away). **19** Many of the Jews had come to Martha and Mary to comfort them about their brother.

20 As soon as Martha heard that Jesus was coming, she went to meet him, but Mary remained seated in the house. **21** Then Martha said to Jesus, "Lord, if you had been here, my brother wouldn't have died. **22** Yet even now I know that whatever you ask from God, God will give you."

23 "Your brother will rise again," Jesus told her.

24 Martha said to him, "I know that he will rise again in the resurrection at the last day."

25 Jesus said to her, "I am the resurrection and the life. The one who believes in me, even if he dies, will live. **26** Everyone who lives and believes in me will never die. Do you believe this?"

27 "Yes, Lord," she told him, "I believe you are the Messiah, the Son of God, who comes into the world."

---

^A**11:16** Gk *Didymus*   ^B**11:18** Lit *fifteen stadia*; one *stadion* = 600 feet

---

10:39 This was not the first attempt to arrest Jesus. See 7:30.
10:40–41 On the place where **John** was baptizing, see note at 1:28.
11:1–57 The raising of Lazarus is Jesus's seventh and climactic messianic sign in John's Gospel (see note at 2:11). This miracle (recorded only by John) anticipated Jesus's own resurrection and revealed him as "the resurrection and the life" (11:25). Resurrections are rare in the OT (1Kg 17:17–24; 2Kg 4:32–37; 13:21) and in the Gospels (Jesus's raising of Jairus's daughter, Mk 5:22–24,38–42; Jesus's raising of the widow's son at Nain, Lk 7:11–15). The raising of Lazarus served as the final event that triggered the Jewish leaders' resolve to arrest Jesus and try him for blasphemy (Jn 11:45–57).
11:1 The introduction of **Lazarus** is similar to 5:5. Lazarus (which means "whom God helps") was a common name. **Bethany**, called a **village** (Gk *kome*) as is Bethlehem (7:42), was not the Bethany mentioned in 1:28 and alluded to in 10:40–42. Bethany, where Lazarus lived, was located east of the Mount of Olives less than two miles from Jerusalem (11:18; cp. Mt 21:17; 26:6). The words **of Mary and her sister Martha** and the reference to Mary's anointing of Jesus anticipate chap. 12 and seems to

presuppose that readers knew these women, perhaps from Luke's Gospel (Lk 10:38–42).
11:2–5 The narrator makes sure the reader knows how much Lazarus meant to Jesus.
11:6 Jesus **stayed two more days . . . where he was.** Puzzling as this delay seems, it served to reveal God's glory (v. 4) since it enabled Jesus to perform an even "harder" miracle (v. 17).
11:7–8 Jesus's disciples assumed that Jesus would desire to stay alive.
11:9–10 Most people worked as long as there was daylight; once it was dark, work was over.
11:11 Fallen asleep means "died," as the following interchange makes clear (vv. 12–14). The OT equivalent is "slept with his fathers."
11:12–15 In view of Jesus's relationship with Lazarus and his family, the statement that **I'm glad . . . that I wasn't there** shows how important the faith of the disciples was.
11:16 On Thomas's designation as **Twin**, see note at 1:38.
11:17 By comforting Martha and Mary after Lazarus's death, Jesus fulfilled one of the most essential obligations in the Jewish

culture of his day—mourning with those who mourn. Burial usually followed shortly after death, so Lazarus had been dead **four days.**
11:18 On **Bethany**, see note at v. 1.
11:19 If the many Jews who **had come to Martha and Mary to comfort them** were from Jerusalem, this would indicate that their family had considerable social standing.
11:20 Seated in the house was the customary posture for those mourning a deceased loved one (Jb 2:8,13; Ezk 8:14).
11:21–22 Martha's statement, **whatever you ask from God**, could be taken to mean she was suggesting Jesus raise Lazarus from the dead. But her other statements indicate this was not the case.
11:23–24 Martha's belief in end-time **resurrection** agreed with Pharisaic beliefs (Ac 23:8), popular Jewish opinion, and Jesus's teaching (Jn 5:21,25–29; 6:39–44,54).
11:25 On **I am the resurrection and the life**, see notes at 5:26; 6:35,48.
11:26 Eternal life begins the moment that a person puts faith in Jesus (see note at 3:36).
11:27 Martha's reference to the one who **comes into the world** took up the messianic expression derived from Ps 118:26 (cp. Jn 12:13).

▼ Jesus's Signs

	MIRACLE	LOCATION	METHOD
First Sign	Turning Water into Wine (Jn 2:1–12)	Cana of Galilee	Jesus asked for six stone jars to be filled with water, and then the water became wine.
Second Sign	Healing an Official's Son (Jn 4:46–54)	Cana of Galilee/ Capernaum	Jesus, in Cana, told the official his son, in Capernaum, would live, and he recovered at that very hour.
Third Sign	Healing a Man Disabled for Thirty-eight Years (Jn 5:1–18)	Jerusalem, at the Pool of Bethesda	Jesus told the disabled man to get up, pick up his mat, and walk, which he did instantly.
Fourth Sign	Feeding of Five Thousand (Jn 6:1–15; see also Mt 14:13–21; Mk 6:30–44; Lk 9:10–17)	Near the Sea of Galilee	Jesus gave thanks for five barley loaves and two fish from a boy and distributed them to the people through the disciples.
Fifth Sign	Walking on Water (Jn 6:16–21; see also Mt 14:22–33; Mk 6:45–52)	On the Sea of Galilee	Jesus walked on the water to the disciples in a boat in a storm.
Sixth Sign	Healing a Man Born Blind (Jn 9)	Jerusalem	Jesus spit on the ground, made some mud, spread the mud on the man's eyes, and told him to wash in the pool of Siloam.
Seventh Sign	Raising Lazarus from the Dead (Jn 11)	Bethany, near Jerusalem	Jesus prayed and shouted, "Lazarus, come out!"

WITNESSES	PURPOSE	RESULT
Jesus's disciples and the servants at the wedding	Revealed Jesus's glory as the Son of God (Jn 2:11)	Jesus's disciples believed in Him (Jn 2:11).
The royal official and his whole household		The royal official and his household believed in Jesus (Jn 4:53).
The man who was healed, and later some of the Jews who objected to him carrying his mat on the Sabbath	Demonstrated Jesus's unity with the Father and authority over the Sabbath (Jn 5:17–18)	The Jews began persecuting Jesus because he healed and encouraged "work" on the Sabbath and made himself equal to God (Jn 5:16,18).
The disciples and the crowd of five thousand men	Demonstrated Jesus was greater than Moses, and he is the bread of life (Jn 6:32–35)	The crowd believed Jesus was the Prophet and wanted to make him king by force, but he withdrew from them (Jn 6:15)
The disciples	Demonstrated Jesus's identity as I am (Jn 6:20)	
The disciples, the formerly blind man, his parents, his neighbors, those who had seen him begging, and the Pharisees	Displayed God's works in the man's healing (Jn 9:3)	The man believed in Jesus and worshiped him (Jn 9:38).
Mary, Martha, the Jews who had come to comfort them, the disciples, and Lazarus	Displayed God's glory and glorified the Son of God (Jn 11:4)	Many believed in Jesus, but the Sanhedrin plotted to kill him (Jn 11:45–53).

John's Gospel was written with a singular purpose—so that his readers would believe Jesus is the Messiah, the Son of God, and by believing have eternal life in his name (Jn 20:30–31). While making references to many signs that Jesus performed, John highlighted seven specific signs through the first part of his Gospel to support this purpose.

Jesus Shares the Sorrow of Death

²⁸ Having said this, she went back and called her sister Mary, saying in private, "The Teacher is here and is calling for you."

²⁹ As soon as Mary heard this, she got up quickly and went to him. ³⁰ Jesus had not yet come into the village but was still in the place where Martha had met him. ³¹ The Jews who were with her in the house consoling her saw that Mary got up quickly and went out. They followed her, supposing that she was going to the tomb to cry there.

³² As soon as Mary came to where Jesus was and saw him, she fell at his feet and told him, "Lord, if you had been here, my brother wouldn't have died!"

³³ When Jesus saw her crying, and the Jews who had come with her crying, he was deeply moved^ in his spirit and troubled. ³⁴ "Where have you put him?" he asked.

"Lord," they told him, "come and see."

³⁵ Jesus wept.

³⁶ So the Jews said, "See how he loved him!" ³⁷ But some of them said, "Couldn't he who opened the blind man's eyes also have kept this man from dying?"

The Seventh Sign: Raising Lazarus from the Dead

³⁸ Then Jesus, deeply moved again, came to the tomb. It was a cave, and a stone was lying against it. ³⁹ "Remove the stone," Jesus said.

Martha, the dead man's sister, told him, "Lord, there is already a stench because he has been dead four days."

⁴⁰ Jesus said to her, "Didn't I tell you that if you believed you would see the glory of God?" ⁴¹ So they removed the stone. Then Jesus raised his eyes and said, "Father, I thank you that you heard me. ⁴² I know that you always hear me, but because of the crowd standing here I said

this, so that they may believe you sent me." ⁴³ After he said this, he shouted with a loud voice, "Lazarus, come out!" ⁴⁴ The dead man came out bound hand and foot with linen strips and with his face wrapped in a cloth. Jesus said to them, "Unwrap him and let him go."

The Plot to Kill Jesus

⁴⁵ Therefore, many of the Jews who came to Mary and saw what he did believed in him. ⁴⁶ But some of them went to the Pharisees and told them what Jesus had done.

⁴⁷ So the chief priests and the Pharisees convened the Sanhedrin and were saying, "What are we going to do since this man is doing many signs? ⁴⁸ If we let him go on like this, everyone will believe in him, and the Romans will come and take away both our place and our nation."

⁴⁹ One of them, Caiaphas, who was high priest that year, said to them, "You know nothing at all! ⁵⁰ You're not considering that it is to your^B advantage that one man should die for the people rather than the whole nation perish." ⁵¹ He did not say this on his own, but being high priest that year he prophesied that Jesus was going to die for the nation, ⁵² and not for the nation only, but also to unite the scattered children of God. ⁵³ So from that day on they plotted to kill him.

⁵⁴ Jesus therefore no longer walked openly among the Jews but departed from there to the countryside near the wilderness, to a town called Ephraim, and he stayed there with the disciples.

⁵⁵ Now the Jewish Passover was near, and many went up to Jerusalem from the country to purify themselves before the Passover. ⁵⁶ They were looking for Jesus and asking one another as they stood in the temple, "What do you think? He won't come to the festival,

---

^11:33 Or *angry*, also in v. 38   ^B 11:50 Other mss read *to our*

11:28 The Teacher was a natural way for a disciple to refer to Jesus before his resurrection (v. 8; 1:38,49; 3:2; 4:31; 6:25; 9:2; 20:16).
11:29–32 Although Mary says less than Martha had, her faith in Jesus was no less strong.
11:33 Jesus was **deeply moved in his spirit and troubled** in the face of human suffering and death (12:27; 13:21).
11:34–35 Jesus wept, or perhaps even better, "burst into tears," as the term is regularly translated in extrabiblical sources.
11:36–37 In this sacred scene were still skeptics who would soon have their world shocked.
11:38–39 While the Jews used spices at burials, this did not prevent decomposition of the body, as Martha pointed out.
11:40–42 Jesus's prayer finds an OT antecedent in Elijah's prayer (1Kg 18:37). Compare Jn 6:11.
11:43 Jesus raised Lazarus not by magic, incantations, or spells, but by the power of his word.
11:44 John did not record Lazarus's reaction or any of the aftermath of his raising.

Instead, he immediately moved (v. 45) to focus on the plot against Jesus.
11:45–46 Surprisingly, not all who were there at the raising of Lazarus put their faith in Jesus (see Lk 16:30–31).
11:47 On the **Sanhedrin**, see notes at 3:1; 7:45–52.
11:48 Our place almost certainly refers to the temple. Similar concerns resurface in Ac 6:13–14 and 21:28, where the temple is referred to as "this holy place" or "this place." **Take away . . . our nation** may refer to the feared removal of the Jews' semi-autonomous status by the Romans. Ironically, what the Sanhedrin sought to prevent by killing Jesus still came to pass when the Romans razed the temple and sacked Jerusalem in AD 70 (see note at 2:13–22).
11:49 That year need not imply that the high priestly office rotated annually. It simply indicates that Caiaphas happened to serve in this role the year Jesus was tried and crucified. In fact, Caiaphas was high priest for

eighteen years (AD 18–36), longer than any other first-century high priest.
11:50–51 Die for the people invokes memory of the Maccabean martyrs (2Macc 7:37–38). In the typical double meaning used in John's Gospel, Caiaphas's pronouncement anticipated the substitutionary atonement Jesus was to render. As the Jewish high priest, Caiaphas **prophesied**, speaking better than he knew.
11:52 The **scattered children of God** refers to the Gentiles (see note at 3:3–8).
11:53–54 From now on, "Jesus is not to be arrested in order to be tried; he is to be tried because he has already been found guilty (as Mk 14:1–2 presupposes)" (D. A. Carson).
11:55 This is the third and final **Passover** mentioned by John. See note at 2:13. People went **up to Jerusalem** early to **purify themselves** from any ceremonial uncleanness that would prevent them from celebrating Passover (Nm 9:4–14; 19:11–12).
11:56–57 On the timing of Jesus's arrest, see note at 2:4.

will he?"⁵⁷ The chief priests and the Pharisees had given orders that if anyone knew where he was, he should report it so that they could arrest him.

The Anointing at Bethany

12 Six days before the Passover, Jesus came to Bethany where Lazarus^ was, the one Jesus had raised from the dead. ² So they gave a dinner for him there; Martha was serving them, and Lazarus was one of those reclining at the table with him. ³ Then Mary took a pound of perfume, pure and expensive nard, anointed Jesus's feet, and wiped his feet with her hair. So the house was filled with the fragrance of the perfume. ⁴ Then one of his disciples, Judas Iscariot (who was about to betray him), said, ⁵ "Why wasn't this perfume sold for three hundred denarii⁸ and given to the poor?" ⁶ He didn't say this because he cared about the poor but because he was a thief. He was in charge of the money-bag and would steal part of what was put in it.

⁷ Jesus answered, "Leave her alone; she has kept it for the day of my burial. ⁸ For you always have the poor with you, but you do not always have me."

The Decision to Kill Lazarus

⁹ Then a large crowd of the Jews learned he was there. They came not only because of Jesus but also to see Lazarus, the one he had raised from the dead. ¹⁰ But the chief priests had decided to kill Lazarus also, ¹¹ because he was the reason many of the Jews were deserting them^c and believing in Jesus.

The Triumphal Entry

¹² The next day, when the large crowd that had come to the festival heard that Jesus was coming to Jerusalem, ¹³ they took palm branches and went out to meet him. They kept shouting:

"Hosanna!
Blessed is he who comes in the name of the Lordᴰ — the King of Israel!"

¹⁴ Jesus found a young donkey and sat on it, just as it is written:

¹⁵ **Do not be afraid,**
Daughter Zion. Look, your King is coming,
sitting on a donkey's colt.ᴱ

¹⁶ His disciples did not understand these things at first. However, when Jesus was glorified, then they remembered that these things had been written about him and that they had done these things to him.

¹⁷ Meanwhile, the crowd, which had been with him when he called Lazarus out of the tomb and raised him from the dead, continued to testify.ᶠ ¹⁸ This is also why the crowd met him, because they heard he had done this sign. ¹⁹ Then the Pharisees said to one another, "You see? You've accomplished nothing. Look, the world has gone after him!"

Jesus Predicts His Crucifixion

²⁰ Now some Greeks were among those who went up to worship at the festival. ²¹ So they

^12:1 Other mss read *Lazarus who died* ᴮ12:5 A denarius = one day's wage ᶜ12:11 Lit *going away* ᴰ12:13 Ps 118:25–26 ᴱ12:15 Zch 9:9 ᶠ12:17 Other mss read *Meanwhile the crowd, which had been with him, continued to testify that he had called Lazarus out of the tomb and raised him from the dead.*

12:1–11 The anointing by Mary of Bethany foreshadowed Jesus's imminent arrest, trial, condemnation, crucifixion, and burial (vv. 7–8). The account is closely linked with the raising of Lazarus, whose presence served as proof of Jesus's miracle-working power and thus fueled the Jewish leaders' hostility toward Jesus. What is more, the anointing also revealed Judas's antagonism toward Jesus (vv. 4–8). While only v. 3 is devoted to Mary's act of devotion, five verses speak of Judas's objection and Jesus's rebuke of Judas (vv. 4–8). **12:1** On this Passover, see notes at 2:13; 11:55. **Six days before the Passover** most likely refers to Saturday, which began Friday evening at sundown. **12:2 Dinner** (Gk *deipnon*) refers to the main meal of the day, which was usually held toward evening (Lk 14:12). The term may also refer to a festive banquet (Mt 23:6; Mk 6:21). It is used later of the Last Supper (Jn 13:2,4; 21:20). **Reclining at the table** may imply a banquet rather than a regular meal (13:2–5,23). **12:3** A **pound** or half a liter was a large amount of **perfume** (11:2). **Pure and expensive nard** was imported from northern India and used by the Romans for anointing the head. The Synoptic Gospels indicate that the perfume was kept in an alabaster jar (Mt

26:7; Mk 14:3). Attending to the **feet** of a guest was the work of servants (1:27; 13:5), so Mary's actions showed humility and devotion. Her wiping of Jesus's feet with her **hair** is remarkable since Jewish women rarely unbound their hair in public. **12:4–5 Three hundred denarii** was a lot of money for a jar of perfume and a lot of money to "waste" by breaking the jar, as **Judas Iscariot** observed. **12:6** Judas's motivation was impure. Before he betrayed Jesus, he was already a **thief**. **12:8** Jesus's response may have been an allusion to Dt 15:11. **12:9–11** The Synoptic Gospels tell us that the religious leaders demanded a sign from Jesus (e.g., Mt 12:38). John tells us the leaders admitted he had performed "many signs" (11:47), including raising Lazarus from the dead. But rather than believe in Jesus, they "plotted to kill him" (11:53) and **had decided to kill Lazarus also**. **12:12–19** Jesus's triumphal entry, with people waving palm branches to greet him, is celebrated in Christian tradition as Palm Sunday. Jesus's riding into Jerusalem on a donkey fulfilled OT Scripture (Zch 9:9; see Ps 118:25–26). The waving of palm branches, a symbolic act celebrating victory over one's enemy and/or reception of a king, may indicate that the people thought Jesus would take

Israel's vacant throne and deliver the nation from Roman occupation and suppression. Yet Jesus's popular acclaim would not last; some people who now hailed him as victor called for his crucifixion only a few days later. **12:12 The next day** probably refers to Sunday of Passion Week, now known as Palm Sunday. The **festival** was the Passover celebration. **12:13 Palm branches** were a Jewish national symbol. The people hailed Jesus as the Davidic king of Ps 118:26 (cp. Mt 21:4–9). Psalm 118 was part of the Hallel (Pss 113–118), sung by the temple choir at major Jewish festivals. **12:15** Jesus is depicted as the humble Shepherd-King of Zch 9:9 who came to the Holy City to take his rightful place. An early messianic prophecy spoke of a ruler from Judah who would command the obedience of nations and would ride on a donkey (Gn 49:10–11). **Do not be afraid** may be taken from Is 40:9, which refers to one who brings good tidings to Zion (Is 44:2). **12:19 The world** was an obvious exaggeration, highlighting the Pharisees' frustration (Ac 17:6). **12:20–50** This section concludes the first major unit of John's Gospel, which narrates Jesus's mission to the Jews. The approach of some Greeks signaled that Jesus's mission was approaching the climax in which he would die

came to Philip, who was from Bethsaida in Galilee, and requested of him, "Sir, we want to see Jesus." ²² Philip went and told Andrew; then Andrew and Philip went and told Jesus.

²³ Jesus replied to them, "The hour has come for the Son of Man to be glorified. ²⁴ Truly I tell you, unless a grain of wheat falls to the ground and dies, it remains by itself. But if it dies, it produces much fruit. ²⁵ The one who loves his life will lose it, and the one who hates his life in this world will keep it for eternal life. ²⁶ If anyone serves me, he must follow me. Where I am, there my servant also will be. If anyone serves me, the Father will honor him.

²⁷ "Now my soul is troubled. What should I say — Father, save me from this hour? But that is why I came to this hour. ²⁸ Father, glorify your name." ᴬ

Then a voice came from heaven: "I have glorified it, and I will glorify it again."

²⁹ The crowd standing there heard it and said it was thunder. Others said, "An angel has spoken to him."

³⁰ Jesus responded, "This voice came, not for me, but for you. ³¹ Now is the judgment of this world. Now the ruler of this world will be cast out. ³² As for me, if I am lifted up ᴮ from the earth I will draw all people to myself." ³³ He said this to indicate what kind of death he was about to die.

³⁴ Then the crowd replied to him, "We have heard from the law that the Messiah will remain forever. So how can you say, 'The Son of Man must be lifted up'? Who is this Son of Man?"

³⁵ Jesus answered, "The light will be with you only a little longer. Walk while you have the light so that darkness doesn't overtake you.

ᴬ12:28 Other mss read *your Son*   ᴮ12:32 Or *exalted*, also in v. 34

and thus reach all nations. His "hour" was now at hand (vv. 23–26; see note at 2:4); the Son of Man would shortly be "lifted up" (crucified) by men and highly exalted by God the Father (12:32; see note at 3:14–15). Jesus would then be able to draw people (Jews and non-Jews) to himself (12:32). Further, the Jewish nation would suffer judgment for rejecting Messiah, who had performed so many signs among them (vv. 37–40).
12:20 Greeks likely refers to Gentiles, not necessarily Grecians (see note at 7:35–36). They were "God-fearers" who came to Jerusalem to worship at the Passover festival.
12:21–22 On **Andrew** and **Philip**, see notes at 1:44; 6:5–6. The Greeks may have singled out Philip (who in turn went to get Andrew) because he and Andrew were the only two members of the Twelve with Greek names.
12:23,27 On Jesus's **hour**, see note at 2:4.
12:24 The principle of life through death is illustrated by an agricultural example.

12:25 Following Christ involves self-sacrifice, shown supremely at the cross.
12:26 This truth extends beyond a disciple's earthly life to his eternal destiny (7:34,36; 14:3; 17:24).
12:27 Jesus's expression of anguish may invoke Davidic psalms such as Ps 6:3 or 42:5,11.
12:28 This is one of only three times during Jesus's earthly ministry when a heavenly **voice** attested to his identity (cp. his baptism and his transfiguration, Mt 3:13–17; 17:1–13 and parallels).
12:29 God's revelation through **thunder** and angels is well documented in the OT. Thunder was part of God's appearance at Mount Sinai (Ex 19:16,19). Angels (or the angel of God) spoke to Hagar (Gn 21:17), Abraham (Gn 22:11), Moses (Ac 7:38), Elijah (2Kg 1:15), and Daniel (see Dn 10:4–11).
12:30–31 The **ruler of this world** in its fallen, sinful state is Satan (14:30; 16:11; 1Jn 5:19). **Now**, at the cross, the devil would be

cast out, or decisively defeated (Lk 10:18; Col 2:14–15).
12:32 This most explicit **lifted up** saying completes the earlier references in 3:14–15 (see note there) and 8:28. Very likely, the terminology echoes Is 52:13. **All people**, in the present context, means "all kinds of people"—both Jews and Gentiles (10:16; 11:52; cp. 12:20–21).
12:33 On the **kind of death** Jesus was about to die, see note at 21:19.
12:34 This is the final of several messianic misunderstandings featured in John's Gospel (cp. 7:27,31,41–42; see note at 7:25–44). This reference may find its basis in passages such as Ps 89:4,36–37 (which in turn is grounded in 2Sm 7:12–16); Ps 110:1; Is 9:7; and Dn 7:14.
12:35–36 Jesus's answer was indirect (see v. 46). In light of the fact that the light would be with people **only a little longer**, his crucifixion was near (7:33; 16:16–19). He urged

Character profile:
Mary, the Sister of Martha

T he New Testament is full of women named *Mary*, so it can be easy to get confused. The Mary we're considering was a resident of Bethany, near Jerusalem. She was the sister of Martha and Lazarus. We meet her in three separate stories in the New Testament.

In the first story, Mary seems *upset with Jesus* (see Jn 11:20, 28–33). Her brother, Lazarus, had fallen deathly ill. She and Martha sent word for Jesus to come *quickly to heal him*. Yet he took so long that he missed the funeral. When he showed up four days after Lazarus's burial, Mary refused at first to go greet him.

In the other two incidents, Mary is *praised by Jesus*. Once when Jesus showed up at dinnertime (see Lk 10:38–42), Martha frantically scrambled to get a meal on the table while Mary sat listening to Jesus. When Martha insisted that Mary lend a hand, Jesus gently chided her and commended Mary for her proper priorities.

The other event happened near the end of Jesus's life (see Mt 26:6–13; Mk 14:3–9; and Jn 12:1–8). Mary anointed him with expensive perfume during a feast thrown by Simon and Martha. Consider how Mary must have felt. Reclining at the dinner table was Lazarus—the brother she loved deeply and thought for sure she'd lost. There's Simon, the one who struggled for so long with the disfiguring disease of leprosy. The disciples

were there with all their amazing tales. Everyone in attendance had a story.

And there in the midst of them all was the guest of honor: Jesus of Nazareth, the one who brought her brother back from the grave, who made Simon well, whose words are truth and life itself. The Messiah was in *her* house.

Then she remembered it—her most precious possession. That alabaster jar of expensive fragrant oil, worth a small fortune (at least a year's salary).

With joy she retrieved it and broke it open. As the fragrance filled the room, she poured the precious substance on Christ's head. When it dripped down on his feet, she knelt and mopped up the excess.

All conversation ceased. The room went still. Finally Judas, one of the disciples, spoke. He criticized her about the "waste," insisting that the oil could have been sold and the money donated to the poor. Other disciples joined in the rebuke.

But Jesus wouldn't stand for it. "Leave her alone. Why are you bothering her? She has done a noble thing for me. . . . She has done what she could; she has anointed my body in advance for burial" (Mk 14:6,8). Jesus promised that Mary's actions would be forever told in memory of her.

If we had to guess, Mary wasn't trying to be noble when she anointed Christ. It was awe and gratitude that propelled her to be so generous. Mary's actions remind us that no act of genuine love is ever wasted. Are you a lavish person? When you feel grateful, are you generous with your words, your time, and your possessions?

The one who walks in darkness doesn't know where he's going. ³⁶ While you have the light, believe in the light so that you may become children of light." Jesus said this, then went away and hid from them.

Isaiah's Prophecies Fulfilled

³⁷ Even though he had performed so many signs in their presence, they did not believe in him. ³⁸ This was to fulfill the word of Isaiah the prophet, who said:ᴬ

Lord, who has believed our message?
And to whom has the arm of the Lord
been revealed?ᴮ

³⁹ This is why they were unable to believe, because Isaiah also said:
⁴⁰   He has blinded their eyes
and hardened their hearts,
so that they would not see
with their eyes
or understand with their hearts,
and turn,
and I would heal them.ᶜ
⁴¹ Isaiah said these things becauseᴰ he saw his glory and spoke about him.
⁴² Nevertheless, many did believe in him even among the rulers, but because of the Pharisees they did not confess him, so that they would not be banned from the synagogue. ⁴³ For they loved human praise more than praise from God.

A Summary of Jesus's Mission

⁴⁴ Jesus cried out, "The one who believes in me believes not in me, but in him who sent me.

⁴⁵ And the one who sees me sees him who sent me. ⁴⁶ I have come as light into the world, so that everyone who believes in me would not remain in darkness. ⁴⁷ If anyone hears my words and doesn't keep them, I do not judge him; for I did not come to judge the world but to save the world. ⁴⁸ The one who rejects me and doesn't receive my sayings has this as his judge:ᴱ The word I have spoken will judge him on the last day. ⁴⁹ For I have not spoken on my own, but the Father himself who sent me has given me a command to say everything I have said. ⁵⁰ I know that his command is eternal life. So the things that I speak, I speak just as the Father has told me."

Jesus Washes His Disciples' Feet

13 Before the Passover Festival, Jesus knew that his hour had come to depart from this world to the Father. Having loved his own who were in the world, he loved them to the end.

² Now when it was time for supper, the devil had already put it into the heart of Judas, Simon Iscariot's son,ᶠ to betray him. ³ Jesus knew that the Father had given everything into his hands, that he had come from God, and that he was going back to God. ⁴ So he got up from supper, laid aside his outer clothing, took a towel, and tied it around himself. ⁵ Next, he poured water into a basin and began to wash his disciples' feet and to dry them with the towel tied around him.

⁶ He came to Simon Peter, who asked him, "Lord, are you going to wash my feet?"

ᴬ12:38 Lit which he said ᴮ12:38 Is 53:1 ᶜ12:40 Is 6:10 ᴰ12:41 Other mss read when ᴱ12:48 Lit has the one judging him ᶠ13:2 Or Judas Iscariot, Simon's son

---

that they **believe in the light** (9:4; 11:10; see note at 8:12) while there was still time.
12:36 When Jesus **hid from them**, he illustrated God's imminent judgment and completed his revelatory work to the people of Israel (1:18).
12:37–50 This indictment identified Israel's wilderness generation with the unbelieving Jews in Jesus's day. Just as the ancient Jews saw God's power (performed through Moses) at the exodus (Dt 29:2–4) and turned away, so the Jews in Jesus's day watched miraculous signs (performed by Jesus) and responded with grumbling (Jn 6:41,61; cp. Ex 17:3; Nm 11:1) and unbelief (Jn 12:39).
12:38–40 John cited Is 53:1 and 6:10 to indicate that the Jewish rejection of Jesus was predicted by Scripture and thus served to confirm rather than thwart God's plan. Is 53:1 referred to the Servant of the Lord who was rejected by the people but exalted by God. Is 6:10 attributed people's hardening ultimately to God himself (similar to Pharaoh's). These verses are the first in a series of fulfillment quotations in the second half of John's Gospel.
12:41 A reference to Isaiah seeing **his** (Jesus's) **glory** may indicate that Isaiah foresaw that God would be pleased with a Suffering Servant who would be "raised and lifted up and greatly exalted" (Is 52:13).

Like Abraham, Isaiah saw "Jesus's day" (cp. Jn 8:58).
12:42–43 Among **the rulers** who believed in Jesus were Joseph of Arimathea and Nicodemus (see 7:50–57; 19:38–42). On fear of the Pharisees and the Sanhedrin, see note at 7:13.
12:44–50 This section summarizes Jesus's message and conveys his final appeal, bringing closure to the first major section of John's Gospel. **Sent me** presupposes the Jewish idea of representation, according to which a messenger's identity is inseparable from that of the one who sent him. Verses 48–50 echo Deuteronomy (Dt 18:19; 31:19,26).
13:1–17:26 In the second major unit of John's Gospel, Jesus prepared his messianic community (represented by the Twelve, minus Judas) for the time following his exaltation to the Father. The community was first cleansed literally (foot washing, 13:1–17), then figuratively through the removal of the betrayer (13:18–30). Jesus's farewell discourse (13:31–16:33) conveys instructions to his followers, particularly about the coming "Helping Presence" (Gk *paraklētos*), the Holy Spirit, and the disciples' need to remain in Jesus spiritually after his physical departure from earth. The discourse (unique to John's Gospel) concludes with Jesus's final prayer (chap. 17).
13:1–17 With his crucifixion imminent, Jesus washed his disciples' feet as a final proof

of his love and to give them an example of humility and service. In a striking demonstration of love for his enemies, Jesus washed all of his disciples' feet, including Judas's. Jesus's act is all the more remarkable because washing people's feet was considered a task so low it could be performed only by non-Jewish slaves. In a culture where people walked long distances on dusty roads in sandals, it was customary for the host to provide water for foot-washing. This was usually done upon arrival, not during the meal. The disciples probably felt guilty that none of them had thought to do this.
13:1 References to Jewish religious festivals and the coming of Jesus's **hour** (see note at 2:4) now converge. Jesus's **own** refers to the Twelve, the representatives of his new messianic community (1:11).
13:2–3 These verses show that Judas already was under Satan's influence and that Jesus had full knowledge of this before he washed the disciples' feet.
13:4–5 The practice of foot washing had a long OT tradition (Gn 18:4; 19:2; 24:32; 43:24; Jdg 19:21; 1Sm 25:41). Jesus's performance of this menial task exemplified his humility (Php 2:6–8).
13:6–11 What Peter failed to realize was the humiliating nature of Jesus's mission to be our Savior.

7 Jesus answered him, "What I'm doing you don't realize now, but afterward you will understand."

8 "You will never wash my feet," Peter said. Jesus replied, "If I don't wash you, you have no part with me."

9 Simon Peter said to him, "Lord, not only my feet, but also my hands and my head."

10 "One who has bathed," Jesus told him, "doesn't need to wash anything except his feet, but he is completely clean. You are clean, but not all of you." **11** For he knew who would betray him. This is why he said, "Not all of you are clean."

The Meaning of Foot Washing

12 When Jesus had washed their feet and put on his outer clothing, he reclined again and said to them, "Do you know what I have done for you? **13** You call me Teacher and Lord — and you are speaking rightly, since that is what I am. **14** So if I, your Lord and Teacher, have washed your feet, you also ought to wash one another's feet. **15** For I have given you an example, that you also should do just as I have done for you.

16 "Truly I tell you, a servant is not greater than his master,^A and a messenger is not greater than the one who sent him. **17** If you know these things, you are blessed if you do them. **18** I'm not speaking about all of you; I know those I have chosen. But the Scripture must be fulfilled: The one who eats my bread^B has raised his heel against me.^C **19** I am telling you now before it happens, so that when it does happen you will believe that I am he. **20** Truly I tell you, whoever receives anyone I send

receives me, and the one who receives me receives him who sent me."

Judas's Betrayal Predicted

21 When Jesus had said this, he was troubled in his spirit and testified, "Truly I tell you, one of you will betray me."

22 The disciples started looking at one another — uncertain which one he was speaking about. **23** One of his disciples, the one Jesus loved, was reclining close beside Jesus.^D **24** Simon Peter motioned to him to find out who it was he was talking about. **25** So he leaned back against Jesus and asked him, "Lord, who is it?"

26 Jesus replied, "He's the one I give the piece of bread to after I have dipped it." When he had dipped the bread, he gave it to Judas, Simon Iscariot's son.^E **27** After Judas ate the piece of bread, Satan entered him. So Jesus told him, "What you're doing, do quickly."

28 None of those reclining at the table knew why he said this to him. **29** Since Judas kept the money-bag, some thought that Jesus was telling him, "Buy what we need for the festival," or that he should give something to the poor. **30** After receiving the piece of bread, he immediately left. And it was night.

The New Command

31 When he had left, Jesus said, "Now the Son of Man is glorified, and God is glorified in him. **32** If God is glorified in him,^F God will also glorify him in himself and will glorify him at once. **33** Little children, I am with you a little while longer. You will look for me, and just as I told the Jews, so now I tell you, 'Where I am going, you cannot come.'

^A**13:16** Or *lord*   ^B**13:18** Other mss read *eats bread with me*   ^C**13:18** Ps 41:9   ^D**13:23** Lit *reclining at Jesus's breast*; that is, on his right; Jn 1:18   ^E**13:26** Or *Judas Iscariot, Simon's son*   ^F**13:32** Other mss omit *If God is glorified in him*

13:12–15 The phrase in 1Tm 5:10, "washed the saints' feet," shows that the disciples got Jesus's message.
13:16–17 On Jesus as the one **sent** as well as the sender, see note at 3:16–18.
13:18–30 Judas's betrayal of Jesus comes as no surprise to the alert reader. John repeatedly anticipated this treacherous act (vv. 10–11; 6:70–71; 12:4). It is shocking that one whom Jesus had chosen as an apostle would betray him. But far from indicating that Jesus made a mistake, the betrayal actually fulfilled Scripture (13:18, citing Ps 41:9; see note at Jn 17:12). God's plan was right on track. This section also contains the first mention of "the one Jesus loved" (13:23). He is frequently featured side by side with Peter in the second half of John's Gospel.
13:18 Judas's treachery fulfilled OT typology. Jesus cited Ps 41:9, which dealt with Absalom's rebellion against King David. Judas's betrayal came as no surprise to Jesus (Jn 13:19). Eating someone's **bread** indicated close fellowship, and yet Judas **raised his heel** against Jesus, an idiom that describes betrayal. Not only did Jesus's public foes plot against him; even his own disciples could not be trusted.
13:19–20 Jesus's statement is one of several references to his omniscience in this section

(14:29; 16:1,4,32,33). **I am he**, as in 6:35,48 (see note there), very likely had overtones of deity.
13:21–22 Jesus's being **troubled in his spirit** (cp. 11:33; 12:27) parallels the emotions of David, who expressed anguish over the betrayal of a close friend (Ps 55:2–14; cp. Pss 31:9–10; 38:10).
13:23 The reference to one of his disciples, **the one Jesus loved . . . reclining close beside Jesus** (Gk *kolpos*), echoes the description of Jesus as the one who is "at the Father's side" (Gk *kolpos*) in 1:18. This disciple is mentioned again in 21:20. Clearly he was an integral member of Jesus's group. Tradition identifies him as John, author of this Gospel.
13:24–28 See note at 13:18. On a human level, Jesus's action of giving bread to Judas constituted an indication of friendship as well as a final appeal that Judas rejected.
13:29 The supposition that Jesus may have sent Judas to **give something to the poor** harks back to 12:5, where Judas presented himself as a champion of charity. Almsgiving was an important part of Jewish piety (Mt 6:2–4).
13:30 The phrase **it was night** strikes an ominous note. Compare Lk 22:53: "But this is your hour—and the dominion of darkness"; see Mt 26:20; Mk 14:17; 1Co 11:23.

13:31 This verse echoes Isaiah (Is 49:3; see note at Jn 2:4).
13:31–16:33 Jesus's farewell discourse in John's Gospel is patterned after Moses's farewell discourse in Dt 31–33. Such discourses typically include predictions of a person's death and departure; predictions of future challenges for his followers after his death; arrangements for succession; exhortations to moral behavior; a final commission; an affirmation and renewal of God's covenant promises; and a closing doxology. While Jesus's farewell discourse is generally true to this pattern, there are differences as well. Jesus's farewell was only temporary (his followers will see him again after "a little while," Jn 14:19), so his final words focused on the future rather than the past. Also, the vine allegory in Jn 15 is distinct from OT or second-temple farewell discourses. Overall, Jesus made provision for the Holy Spirit to continue his mission through the disciples. Jesus himself would continue to direct their mission from his exalted position with the Father.
13:31–32 Looking through the eyes of faith, Jesus's glorification refers to his death.
13:33 Jesus's words repeated to the Jews and the disciples mean different things. The Jews would not be able to find him, but Jesus would prepare a place for his disciples.

³⁴ "I give you a new command: Love one another. Just as I have loved you, you are also to love one another. ³⁵ By this everyone will know that you are my disciples, if you love one another."

Peter's Denials Predicted

³⁶ "Lord," Simon Peter said to him, "where are you going?"

Jesus answered, "Where I am going you cannot follow me now, but you will follow later."

³⁷ "Lord," Peter asked, "why can't I follow you now? I will lay down my life for you."

³⁸ Jesus replied, "Will you lay down your life for me? Truly I tell you, a rooster will not crow until you have denied me three times.

The Way to the Father

14 "Don't let your heart be troubled. Believe^A in God; believe also in me. ² In my Father's house are many rooms. If it were not so, would I have told you that I am going to prepare a place for you? ³ If I go away and prepare a place for you, I will come again and take you to myself, so that where I am you may be also. ⁴ You know the way to where I am going."^B

⁵ "Lord," Thomas said, "we don't know where you're going. How can we know the way?"

⁶ Jesus told him, "I am the way, the truth, and the life. No one comes to the Father except through me. ⁷ If you know me, you will also know^C my Father. From now on you do know him and have seen him."

Jesus Reveals the Father

⁸ "Lord," said Philip, "show us the Father, and that's enough for us."

⁹ Jesus said to him, "Have I been among you all this time and you do not know me, Philip? The one who has seen me has seen the Father. How can you say, 'Show us the Father'? ¹⁰ Don't you believe that I am in the Father and the Father is in me? The words I speak to you I do not speak on my own. The Father who lives in me

^14:1 Or *You believe* ^B 14:4 Other mss read this verse: *And you know where I am going, and you know the way* ^C 14:7 Other mss read *If you had known me, you would have known*

13:34–35 Love must be the distinguishing mark of Jesus's disciples. Jesus's **new command** closely resembled the Mosaic commands to love the Lord (Dt 6:5) and one's neighbor as oneself (Lv 19:18; cp. Mk 12:28–33). Elsewhere Jesus said we must love even our enemies (Mt 5:43–48). While the command to love God and one's neighbor was thus not new, Jesus's example (**as I have loved you**) was unparalleled, as was his insistence that we should love our enemies. **13:36–38** Peter would indeed deny Jesus **three times** (see 18:15–18,25–27). After his resurrection, Jesus would ask Peter three times, "Do you love me?" (21:15–17). **14:1** Jesus's words echo similar admonitions in the OT (Dt 1:21,29; 20:1,3; Jos 1:9; cp. Jn 11:33; 12:27; 13:21). **Believe** denotes personal, relational trust in keeping with OT usage (Is 28:16).

14:2–3 Jesus elsewhere said his followers would be welcomed into "eternal dwellings" (Lk 16:9). The disciples' homecoming will be comparable to a son's return to his father's house (Lk 15:11–32). The words **I will come again and take you to myself, so that where I am you may be also** echoes the terminology in Sg 8:2. Jesus, the messianic bridegroom (Jn 3:29), said he would **prepare a place** for his followers in his **Father's house** and then come to take them home to be with him. **14:4–6** Jesus is **the way, the truth, and the life** (see note at 6:35,48), and **no one comes to the Father** except through him. Jesus alone is able to provide access to God because he alone paid the penalty for our sins (Is 53:5; Heb 1:3). He is the truth (Jn 1:14,17; 5:33; 18:37; cp. 8:40,45–46) and all

contrary claims are false. He alone is the life (1:4), having life in himself (5:26). He is thus able to confer eternal life on all those who believe in him (3:16). Jesus is truth and life, and he is the one and only way of salvation. **14:7** The emphasis on truly knowing Jesus and God the Father harks back to OT covenant language (Jr 24:7; 31:34; Hs 13:4). **14:8** Philip apparently wanted some sort of revelation of God. In the OT, Moses asked and was given a limited vision of God's glory (Ex 33:18; cp. Ex 24:10); Isaiah received a similar vision (Is 6:1; see note at Jn 12:41). In keeping with OT teaching, however, Jesus denied the possibility of a direct vision of God (1:18; 5:37; 6:46). **14:9–11** Jesus spoke of his unity with the Father, who made himself known in Jesus.

Q & A: Is Jesus the only way?

by Brett Kunkle

That Jesus is the only way to God may be the most controversial claim of Christianity. Is there good reason for this claim?

What does Jesus say? We don't want to claim something about Jesus that he wouldn't claim of himself. If the Gospels are historically reliable (and we have overwhelming evidence that they are), then we have Jesus's own words, and by examining them we discover that he claimed to be the only way to God.

In John 14:6, Jesus said, "I am the way, the truth, and the life. No one comes to the Father except through me." This doesn't leave much room for debate. Indeed, Jesus said whoever rejects him rejects God, for God sent him (Lk 10:16). So according to Jesus, there's no other path to God. If you wish to follow Jesus, you must accept the claims he made about himself.

Is Jesus special? Those who claim that all religions are basically the same haven't studied them closely, for religions often contradict one another. Hinduism says God is an impersonal force, while Christianity says God is a personal being. Both cannot be true. Also, Jesus is unique among religious figures. His disciples said he is God (Jn 1:1; Php 2:5–7) because Jesus himself said so (Mk 14:61–64; Jn 10:30–34). No other founder of a major world religion claimed to be God.

Jesus was either right or wrong to make his claim, and he provided a standard to verify it. He said his resurrection from the dead would be confirmation (Mt 12:38–42; Mk 14:28). Siddhartha, the founder of Buddhism, is still in his grave. Muhammad, the founder of Islam, is still dead. But not Jesus. He conquered death and thus provided the ultimate evidence for the truth of his unique claims.

Why is Jesus the only way? We are conditioned by our culture to think of religion as a personal preference. We are told, "You've got your religion, and I've got mine." To claim Jesus is the only way to God seems like claiming chocolate ice cream is the one true flavor. However, religious truth does not come down merely to differences in preference.

Instead, we should think of religion the same way we think of medicine. Each religion recognizes the world is sick and offers a diagnosis. In addition, each religion offers a means of being cured. Just like when our doctors must choose the right medicine to cure us, we must choose the religion that offers the genuine cure to our sickness.

In John 8:24, Jesus says "if you do not believe that I am he, you will die in your sins." Jesus offers both diagnosis and cure. Sin is the disease we're all infected with and Jesus is the one true cure. So, why is Jesus the only way? Because Jesus is the only medicine that can cure the spiritual disease—sin—that is killing us.

does his works. [11] Believe me that I am in the Father and the Father is in me. Otherwise, believe[A] because of the works themselves.

Praying in Jesus's Name

[12] "Truly I tell you, the one who believes in me will also do the works that I do. And he will do even greater works than these, because I am going to the Father. [13] Whatever you ask in my name, I will do it so that the Father may be glorified in the Son. [14] If you ask me[B] anything in my name, I will do it.[C]

Another Counselor Promised

[15] "If you love me, you will keep[D] my commands. [16] And I will ask the Father, and he will give you another Counselor[E] to be with you forever. [17] He is the Spirit of truth. The world is unable to receive him because it doesn't see him or know him. But you do know him, because he remains with you and will be[F] in you.

The Father, the Son, and the Holy Spirit

[18] "I will not leave you as orphans; I am coming to you. [19] In a little while the world will no longer see me, but you will see me. Because I live, you will live too. [20] On that day you will know that I am in my Father, you are in me, and I am in you. [21] The one who has my commands and keeps them is the one who loves me. And the one who loves me will be loved by my Father. I also will love him and will reveal myself to him."

[22] Judas (not Iscariot) said to him, "Lord, how is it you're going to reveal yourself to us and not to the world?"

[23] Jesus answered, "If anyone loves me, he will keep my word. My Father will love him, and we will come to him and make our home with him. [24] The one who doesn't love me will not keep my words. The word that you hear is not mine but is from the Father who sent me. [25] "I have spoken these things to you while I remain with you. [26] But the Counselor, the Holy Spirit, whom the Father will send in my name, will teach you all things and remind you of everything I have told you.

Jesus's Gift of Peace

[27] "Peace I leave with you. My peace I give to you. I do not give to you as the world gives. Don't let your heart be troubled or fearful. [28] You have heard me tell you, 'I am going away and I am coming to you.' If you loved me, you would rejoice that I am going to the Father, because the Father is greater than I. [29] I have told you now before it happens so that when it does happen you may believe. [30] I will not talk with you much longer, because the ruler of the world is coming. He has no power over me.[G] [31] On the contrary, so that the world may know that I love the Father, I do as the Father commanded me.

"Get up; let's leave this place.

The Vine and the Branches

15 "I am the true vine, and my Father is the gardener. [2] Every branch in me that does not produce fruit he removes, and he prunes every branch that produces fruit so that it will produce more fruit. [3] You are already clean

---

[A]14:11 Other mss read *believe me*   [B]14:14 Other mss omit *me*   [C]14:14 Other mss omit all of v. 14   [D]14:15 Other mss read *"If you love me, keep* (as a command)   [E]14:16 Or *advocate*, or *comforter*, also in v. 26   [F]14:17 Other mss read *and is*   [G]14:30 Lit *He has nothing in me*

14:12 The disciples' **greater works** are made possible because Jesus was **going to the Father** after his work on the cross (12:24; 15:13; 19:30). The works are greater because they are based on the totality of Jesus's work and will bear lasting fruit (Mt 11:11; Jn 15:8,16).
14:13–14 Praying in Jesus's **name** expresses alignment of one's desires and purposes with God (1Jn 5:14–15). See note at Jn 3:16–18.
14:15 Jesus's words echo the demands of the Deuteronomic covenant (Dt 5:10; 6:5–6; 7:9; 10:12–13; 11:13,22).
14:16–17 Another Counselor or the **Spirit of truth** is the Holy Spirit (v. 26), who guides disciples into all truth (16:13). The Spirit replaces Jesus's physical presence by permanently indwelling his followers. Divine presence for Jesus's followers includes the Spirit (14:15–17), Jesus (vv. 18–21), and the Father (vv. 22–24).
14:18 The Spirit's presence within disciples essentially amounts to Jesus's own presence, because the Spirit testifies about Jesus (15:26) and helps disciples understand the significance of what Jesus has done (16:14). Jesus's assurance, **I will not leave you as orphans**, echoes Moses's parting words to Israel (Dt 31:6; cp. Jos 1:5). By saying this, Jesus likely had in mind both his resurrection and the coming of the Spirit at Pentecost.

14:19–20 On that day probably refers to Jesus coming on his disciples in the Spirit at Pentecost.
14:21 The references to **the one who has my commands and keeps them** and the phrase **reveal myself** hark back to the giving of the law at Mount Sinai and to other OT appearances of God (Ex 33:13).
14:22 This **Judas (not Iscariot)** is probably "Judas the son of James," also known as Thaddaeus (see note at Mk 3:18–19), mentioned in Lk 6:16 and Ac 1:13, not Jude, the half-brother of Jesus (Mt 13:55; Mk 6:3).
14:23–24 Make our home with him recalls God's dwelling among his people in the tabernacle (Ex 25:8; 29:45; Lv 26:11–12) and the temple (1Kg 8:10–11; cp. Ac 7:46–47), and points forward to the time when the Spirit would come at Pentecost (Ac 2).
14:25–26 The **Holy Spirit** (1:33; 20:22) is mentioned infrequently in the OT (Ps 51:11; Is 63:9–10). Jesus's focus here was on the Spirit's future teaching ministry (1Jn 2:20,27).
14:27 The expression **peace** (Hb *shalom*) could serve as a greeting or announce blessing upon those who enjoyed a right relationship with God (Nm 6:24–26; cp. Ps 29:11; Hg 2:9). The OT prophesied a period of peace following Messiah's coming, for he is the "Prince of Peace" (Is 9:6), who would

"proclaim peace to the nations" (Zch 9:10; cp. 9:9). There would be tidings of peace and salvation (Is 52:7; cp. 54:13; 57:19), and God would establish an ever-lasting "covenant of peace" with his people (Ezk 37:26). Jesus's parting encouragement for his followers not to be **troubled or fearful** (cp. 14:1) echoes Moses's parting counsel (Dt 31:6,8).
14:28–29 After Jesus's exaltation, his disciples would be able to call on the exalted Jesus and the indwelling Spirit. **The Father is greater than I** refers not to ontology (Jesus and the Father are one), but to Jesus's subordination as eternal Son.
14:30 On **the ruler of the world**, see note at 12:30–31. Satan has no legal claim or hold on Jesus.
14:31 Some scholars view the transition from 14:31 to 15:1 as a literary seam, which would indicate that John's Gospel was pieced together from different sources (one ending at 14:31; another beginning at 15:1). More likely, John is simply describing Jesus's transition (**Get up; let's leave this place**) from the upper room to the garden of Gethsemane, where he arrived in 18:1.
15:1–17 This allegory is at the heart of Jesus's farewell discourse to the disciples. The OT used the vineyard or vine as a symbol for Israel, God's covenant people, especially in

because of the word I have spoken to you. ⁴ Remain in me, and I in you. Just as a branch is unable to produce fruit by itself unless it remains on the vine, neither can you unless you remain in me. ⁵ I am the vine; you are the branches. The one who remains in me and I in him produces much fruit, because you can do nothing without me. ⁶ If anyone does not remain in me, he is thrown aside like a branch and he withers. They gather them, throw them into the fire, and they are burned. ⁷ If you remain in me and my words remain in you, ask whatever you want and it will be done for you. ⁸ My Father is glorified by this: that you produce much fruit and prove to be^ my disciples.

Christlike Love

⁹ "As the Father has loved me, I have also loved you. Remain in my love. ¹⁰ If you keep my commands you will remain in my love, just as I have kept my Father's commands and remain in his love.
¹¹ "I have told you these things so that my joy may be in you and your joy may be complete. ¹² "This is my command: Love one another as I have loved you. ¹³ No one has greater love than this: to lay down his life for his friends. ¹⁴ You are my friends if you do what I command you. ¹⁵ I do not call you servants anymore, because a servant doesn't know what his master⁸ is doing. I have called you friends, because I have made known to you everything I have heard from my Father. ¹⁶ You did not choose me, but I chose you. I appointed you to go and produce fruit and that your fruit should remain, so that

whatever you ask the Father in my name, he will give you.
¹⁷ "This is what I command you: Love one another.

Persecutions Predicted

¹⁸ "If the world hates you, understand that it hated me before it hated you. ¹⁹ If you were of the world, the world would love you as its own. However, because you are not of the world, but I have chosen you out of it, the world hates you. ²⁰ Remember the word I spoke to you: 'A servant is not greater than his master.' If they persecuted me, they will also persecute you. If they kept my word, they will also keep yours. ²¹ But they will do all these things to you on account of my name, because they don't know the one who sent me. ²² If I had not come and spoken to them, they would not be guilty of sin. Now they have no excuse for their sin. ²³ The one who hates me also hates my Father. ²⁴ If I had not done the works among them that no one else has done, they would not be guilty of sin. Now they have seen and hated both me and my Father. ²⁵ But this happened so that the statement written in their law might be fulfilled: **They hated me for no reason.**ᶜ

The Counselor's Ministry

²⁶ "When the Counselor comes, the one I will send to you from the Father — the Spirit of truth who proceeds from the Father — he will testify about me. ²⁷ You also will testify, because you have been with me from the beginning.

^**15:8** Or *and become*   ⁸**15:15** Or *lord*   ᶜ**15:25** Ps 69:4

two "vineyard songs" (Is 5:1–7; 27:2–6). However, Israel's failure to produce fruit resulted in divine judgment. Jesus, by contrast, is the true vine, and his followers are to remain in him and produce much fruit for God.
15:1 I am the true vine is the last of Jesus's seven "I am" sayings in John's Gospel (see note at 6:35,48). "True" contrasts Jesus with OT Israel (see note at 15:1–17). Joseph was called a "fruitful vine" in Gn 49:22. The reference to the Father as **the gardener** harks back to Isaiah's first vineyard song, where God is depicted as tending his vineyard, only to be rewarded with worthless grapes (Is 5:1–7; cp. Ps 80:8–9).
15:2 To ensure maximal fruit production, the divine vineyard keeper **removes** dead branches and **prunes** all the others (Heb 6:7–8). In John's Gospel, Judas the betrayer is an example of the former scenario (Jn 13:10–11). Peter, who denied Jesus three times, is an example of the latter (18:15–18,25–27; 21:15–19).
15:3 On **you are already clean**, see 13:10–11.
15:4 The "**in**" terminology harks back to OT covenant theology, including prophetic texts about a future new covenant (Ex 25:8; 29:45; Lv 26:11–12; Ezk 37:27–28; 43:9).
15:4,5,8 The repeated reference to **fruit** underscores that fruitfulness is God's primary creative (Gn 1:11–12,22,28) and redemptive purpose (Jn 15:8,16). The OT prophets

envisioned a time when God's people would "blossom and bloom and fill the whole world with fruit" (Is 27:6; cp. Hs 14:4–8).
15:6 This verse echoes Ezk 15:1–8, where a barren vine is said to be fit only for burning. **Fire** is a common symbol for divine judgment (Is 30:27; 66:24; Mt 3:12; 5:22; 18:8; 25:41; see note at Jn 15:2).
15:7 See note at 14:13–14.
15:9–11 Obedience is not all gloom and doom; rather, it's a source of **joy**. The OT prophets envisioned a period of great end-time rejoicing (Is 25:9; 35:10; 51:3; 61:10; 66:10; Zch 9:9).
15:12–17 On Jesus's "love commandment," see note at 13:34–35.
15:13–14 In the OT, only Abraham (2Ch 20:7; Is 41:8) and, by implication, Moses (Ex 33:11) are called "friends of God." Jesus extended this privilege to all obedient believers.
15:16 In first-century Palestine, disciples typically took the initiative in attaching themselves to a particular rabbi, not vice versa. As a well-known dictum declared, "Provide yourself with a teacher." Jesus broke with this custom and called his own disciples. **Appointed** recalls the OT description of God's appointment of Abraham (Gn 17:5; cp. Rm 4:17), the ordination of Levites (Nm 8:10), and Moses's commissioning of Joshua (Nm 27:18).
15:18–16:33 This final major unit in Jesus's farewell discourse deals with the world's

hostility toward him and his followers and with the future ministry of the Holy Spirit.
15:18 Jesus's followers are to be known by their love (see 13:34–35 and note there).
15:19–23 Jesus's disciples have no control over how their message is received. People's responses will be determined by their attitude toward Jesus. The words in v. 23 belie those who claim to love God but will not accept Jesus. **They would not** be guilty of **sin** does not mean the world would be perfect. Rather it stresses the world's guilt since Jesus has come.
15:24 On Jesus's **works** as a witness to him, see note at 5:31–47.
15:25 Jesus declared that the Jews' hatred of him fulfilled OT Scripture, specifically Ps 69:4 (cp. Ps 35:19). This Davidic psalm depicts a righteous sufferer who is zealous for God but is persecuted by God's enemies **for no reason**. Thus Jesus saw David's experiences as a prefiguration of the hatred and rejection he suffered.
15:26 On Jesus's promise of the Holy Spirit, see notes at 14:16–17,25–26.
15:27 The call for Jesus's followers to serve as his witnesses recalls OT prophetic literature, where God's end-time people are called his "witnesses" to the nation (Is 43:10–12; 44:8). In the NT, believers are promised the Spirit's help in times of persecution (Mt 10:20; Mk 13:11; Lk 12:12), and the Spirit played a vital

16

"I have told you these things to keep you from stumbling. ² They will ban you from the synagogue. In fact, a time is coming when anyone who kills you will think he is offering service to God. ³ They will do these things because they haven't known the Father or me. ⁴ But I have told you these things so that when their time^A comes you will remember I told them to you. I didn't tell you these things from the beginning, because I was with you. ⁵ But now I am going away to him who sent me, and not one of you asks me, 'Where are you going?' ⁶ Yet, because I have spoken these things to you, sorrow has filled your heart. ⁷ Nevertheless, I am telling you the truth. It is for your benefit that I go away, because if I don't go away the Counselor will not come to you. If I go, I will send him to you. ⁸ When he comes, he will convict the world about sin, righteousness, and judgment: ⁹ About sin, because they do not believe in me; ¹⁰ about righteousness, because I am going to the Father and you will no longer see me; ¹¹ and about judgment, because the ruler of this world has been judged.

¹² "I still have many things to tell you, but you can't bear them now. ¹³ When the Spirit of truth comes, he will guide you into all the truth. For he will not speak on his own, but he will speak whatever he hears. He will also declare to you what is to come. ¹⁴ He will glorify me, because he will take from what is mine and declare it to you. ¹⁵ Everything the Father has is mine. This is why I told you that he takes from what is mine and will declare it to you.

Sorrow Turned to Joy

¹⁶ "In a little while, you will no longer see me; again in a little while, you will see me."^B

¹⁷ Then some of his disciples said to one another, "What is this he's telling us: 'In a little while, you will not see me; again in a little while, you will see me,' and, 'Because I am going to the Father'?" ¹⁸ They said, "What is this he is saying,^C 'In a little while'? We don't know what he's talking about."

¹⁹ Jesus knew they wanted to ask him, and so he said to them, "Are you asking one another about what I said, 'In a little while, you will not see me; again in a little while, you will see me'? ²⁰ Truly I tell you, you will weep and mourn, but the world will rejoice. You will become sorrowful, but your sorrow will turn to joy. ²¹ When a woman is in labor, she has pain because her time has come. But when she has given birth to a child, she no longer remembers the suffering because of the joy that a person has been born into the world. ²² So you also have sorrow^D now. But I will see you again. Your hearts will rejoice, and no one will take away your joy from you.

²³ "In that day you will not ask me anything. Truly I tell you, anything you ask the Father in my name, he will give you. ²⁴ Until now you have asked for nothing in my name. Ask and you will receive, so that your joy may be complete.

Jesus the Victor

²⁵ "I have spoken these things to you in figures of speech. A time is coming when I will no longer speak to you in figures, but I will tell you plainly about the Father. ²⁶ On that day you will ask in my name, and I am not telling you that I will ask the Father on your behalf. ²⁷ For the Father himself loves you, because you have loved me and have believed that I came from God.^E ²⁸ I came from the Father and have come into

---

^A **16:4** Other mss read *when the time*   ^B **16:16** Other mss add *because I am going to the Father*   ^C **16:18** Other mss omit *he is saying*   ^D **16:22** Other mss read *will have sorrow*   ^E **16:27** Other mss read *from the Father*

---

part in the church's mission (Ac 1:8; cp. Lk 24:48; Ac 5:32; 6:10).
16:1 These things refers to Jesus's warning about persecution in 15:18–27. **Stumbling** refers to apostasy.
16:2 The phrase **a time is coming** is reminiscent of prophetic or apocalyptic expressions such as "the days are coming" (Jr 7:32; 9:25; 16:14; 31:31,38; Am 9:13; cp. Zch 14:1). On expulsion from the synagogue, see note at Jn 9:34. **When anyone who kills you will think he is offering service to God** most likely refers to Jewish rather than Roman persecution. Some rabbis believed that killing heretics was an act of divine worship. Note Paul's comments in Ac 26:9–11 and Php 3:6.
16:3–4 Though the persecutors think they are serving God, they do not know God.
16:5–6 Jesus's disciples were so self-absorbed that they could not think of the positive implications of his departure.
16:7 Reference to **the Counselor** (see notes at 14:16–17,25–26) harks back to the anticipated coming of the Spirit and the inauguration of the age of the kingdom in OT prophetic literature (Is 11:1–10; 32:14–18; 42:1–4; 44:1–5;

Jr 31:31–34; Ezk 11:17–20; 36:24–27; 37:1–14; Jl 2:28–32).
16:8–11 The Holy Spirit will judge the world's **sin** of unbelief on the basis of his **righteousness**. On **the ruler of this world**, see note at 12:30–31.
16:12–13 On the **Spirit of truth**, see note at 14:16–17. The Spirit's ministry of guiding Jesus's followers into **all the truth** will fulfill the psalmists' longing for divine guidance (Pss 25:4–5; 43:3; 86:11; 143:10). Isaiah recounted how God led his people in the wilderness by the Holy Spirit (Is 63:14) and predicted God's renewed guidance in the future (Is 43:19). The word **declare** (Gk *anangello*) occurs more than forty times in the book of Isaiah, where declaring things to come is said to be the exclusive domain of God (Is 48:14) and where God challenges pretenders to declare the things to come (Is 42:9; 44:7; 46:10; cp. Is 41:21–29, esp. vv. 22–23; 45:19).
16:14–15 The Spirit would glorify Jesus by declaring all his words and actions.
16:16–19 In **a little while** harks back to previous instances of this expression in John's Gospel (7:33; 12:35; 13:33; 14:19). Similar terms

were used by OT prophets for announcing God's judgment (Is 10:25; Jr 51:33; Hs 1:4; Hg 2:6) and salvation (Is 29:17). In this situation the reference is to the brief period between Jesus's crucifixion and resurrection.
16:20 Jesus's prediction that his disciples' **sorrow will turn to joy** echoes the experiences of God's people in OT times (Est 9:22) and marks the fulfillment of OT prophecies (Is 61:2–3; Jr 31:13).
16:21 Jesus's illustration of a woman in childbirth resonates with human experience. While the **labor** preceding **birth** is intense, all anguish is forgotten the moment the new **child** is born. Jesus elsewhere spoke of the end times as "the beginning of labor pains" and times of "great distress" (Mt 24:8,21,29).
16:22–24 In that day here refers to the time of Jesus's resurrection.
16:25–27 These things in v. 25 refers to the entire farewell discourse. **A time is coming** occurs also in 16:2,32.
16:28 The depiction of Jesus as having come **from the Father . . . into the world** and as **leaving the world and going to the Father** is patterned after the portrayal of the Word of God which is sent, accomplishes

the world. Again, I am leaving the world and going to the Father."

29 His disciples said, "Look, now you're speaking plainly and not using any figurative language. **30** Now we know that you know everything and don't need anyone to question you. By this we believe that you came from God."

31 Jesus responded to them, "Do you now believe? **32** Indeed, an hour is coming, and has come, when each of you will be scattered to his own home, and you will leave me alone. Yet I am not alone, because the Father is with me. **33** I have told you these things so that in me you may have peace. You will have suffering in this world. Be courageous! I have conquered the world."

Jesus Prays for Himself

17 Jesus spoke these things, looked up to heaven, and said, "Father, the hour has come. Glorify your Son so that the Son may glorify you, **2** since you gave him authority over all people,^A so that he may give eternal life to everyone you have given him. **3** This is eternal life: that they may know you, the only true God, and the one you have sent — Jesus Christ. **4** I have glorified you on the earth by completing the work you gave me to do. **5** Now, Father, glorify me in your presence with that glory I had with you before the world existed.

Jesus Prays for His Disciples

6 "I have revealed your name to the people you gave me from the world. They were yours, you gave them to me, and they have kept your word. **7** Now they know that everything you have given en me is from you, **8** because I have given them the words you gave me. They have received them and have known for certain that I came from you. They have believed that you sent me. **9** "I pray^B for them. I am not praying for the world but for those you have given me, because they are yours. **10** Everything I have is yours, and everything you have is mine, and I am glorified in them. **11** I am no longer in the world, but they are in the world, and I am coming to you. Holy Father, protect^C them by your name that you have given me, so that they may be one as we are one. **12** While I was with them, I was protecting them by your name that you have given me. I guarded them and not one of them is lost, except the son of destruction,^D so that the Scripture may be fulfilled. **13** Now I am coming to you, and I speak these things in the world so that they may have my joy completed in them. **14** I have given them your word. The world hated them because they are not of the world, just as I am not of the world. **15** I am not praying that you take them out of the world but that you protect them from the evil one. **16** They are not of the world, just as I am not of

---

^17:2 Or *flesh*   ^17:9 Lit *ask* (throughout this passage)   ^17:11 Lit *keep* (throughout this passage)   ^17:12 The one destined for destruction, loss, or perdition

---

its purpose, and returns to the one who sent it (Is 55:11–12; see note at Jn 1:1).

16:29–31 Despite their confident confession, the disciples are no closer to understanding than before. Jesus's question (**Do you now believe?**) expresses skepticism and mild rebuke.

16:32 Jesus's prediction of a coming **hour** at which his followers will be **scattered** (cp. 19:27) may allude to Zch 13:7 (quoted in Mt 26:31; cp. Mt 26:56; 1Kg 22:17). The sheep would desert the Shepherd and return home, and yet Jesus would not be **alone** due to the constant presence of his Father.

16:33 Jesus's farewell discourse ends on a note of triumph (1Jn 2:13–14; 4:4; 5:4–5).

17:1–26 In his final prayer in this chapter, Jesus gave an account of his earthly mission to the Father who sent him. He prayed first for himself (vv. 1–5), then for his disciples (vv. 6–19), and finally for all future believers (vv. 20–26). In his prayer, Jesus adopted the stance of one who has completed his mission (v. 4; cp. 4:34), having been sent by the Father and now preparing to return (13:1; 16:28). His prayer was fulfilled when he cried out from the cross, saying of the mission of redemption and revelation he had come to accomplish, "It is finished" (19:30).

17:1–5 The first unit in Jesus's prayer is his intercession for himself.

17:1 Jesus **looked up to heaven**, striking a customary posture in prayer (Ps 123:1; Mk 7:34; Lk 18:13). On **the hour has come**, see note at 2:4. The opening petition, **Glorify your Son so that the Son may glorify you,**

is a claim to deity since the OT affirms that God will not give his glory to another (Is 42:8; 48:11). On Jesus as the sent Son, see note at Jn 3:16–18.

17:2 God's granting of **authority** to Jesus (5:27) marks the beginning of a new era (Is 9:6–7; Dn 7:13–14; see Mt 11:27; 28:18).

17:2–3 Eternal life comes from knowing God and the sent Son (1:4; 5:26; 20:31). Knowing God is not confined to intellectual knowledge; it involves living in fellowship with him. That God is **the only true God** is affirmed in the Shema (Dt 6:4; cp. Jn 5:44; 1Jn 5:20). Jesus, in turn, is the one and only sent by the Father (Jn 1:14,18; 3:16,18) and the only way to him (14:6). In the Gospel of John, the full name **Jesus Christ** is found only here and in 1:17, forming a literary *inclusio*. Note that in these verses Jesus referred to himself in the third person.

17:4 The reference to Jesus's **work** in the singular harks back to 4:34, another *inclusio*.

17:5 Again, Jesus claimed preexistence (v. 24; 1:1,14; 3:13; 6:62; 8:58; 16:28).

17:6–19 The second unit of Jesus's prayer contains his intercession for his disciples, beginning with a review of his ministry to them (vv. 6–8). Jesus's prayer for his followers in vv. 9–19 includes petitions for their protection (vv. 11–16) and for their consecration for service in the truth (vv. 17–19).

17:6 Jesus's revelation of God's **name** included making known the Father's works and words (1:18; 8:19,27; 10:38; 12:45; 14:9–11).

17:7–8 The portrayal of Jesus here is reminiscent of the description of the "prophet like" Moses in Dt 18:18.

17:9–11 Here begins Jesus's actual prayer for his disciples. His primary prayer is for protection from the evil one, which will be realized as they are unified and made holy in the truth, God's word.

17:12 Even Judas's betrayal happened in fulfillment of Scripture. The antecedent passage is probably Ps 41:9. This text is applied to Jesus in Jn 13:18. Other Scriptures fulfilled through Judas are Pss 69:25 and 109:8 (cited in Ac 1:20).

17:13–17 These things probably refers to the entire farewell discourse. In the midst of the world's hostility, Jesus's desire is that his followers have joy. The end of being made holy **by the truth** is being equipped for God's service.

the world. **17** Sanctify them by the truth; your word is truth. **18** As you sent me into the world, I also have sent them into the world. **19** I sanctify myself for them, so that they also may be sanctified by the truth.

Jesus Prays for All Believers

20 "I pray not only for these, but also for those who believe in me through their word. **21** May they all be one, as you, Father, are in me and I am in you. May they also be^ in us, so that the world may believe you sent me. **22** I have given them the glory you have given me, so that they may be one as we are one. **23** I am in them and you are in me, so that they may be made completely one, that the world may know you have sent me and have loved them as you have loved me.

24 "Father, I want those you have given me to be with me where I am, so that they will see my glory, which you have given me because you loved me before the world's foundation. **25** Righteous Father, the world has not known you. However, I have known you, and they have known that you sent me. **26** I made your name known to them and will continue to make it known, so that the love you have loved me with may be in them and I may be in them."

Jesus Betrayed

18 After Jesus had said these things, he went out with his disciples across the Kidron Valley, where there was a garden, and he and his disciples went into it. **2** Judas, who betrayed him, also knew the place, because Jesus often met there with his disciples. **3** So Judas took a company of soldiers and some officials^ from the chief priests and the Pharisees and came there with lanterns, torches, and weapons.

4 Then Jesus, knowing everything that was about to happen to him, went out and said to them, "Who is it that you're seeking?"

5 "Jesus of Nazareth," they answered.

"I am he," Jesus told them.

Judas, who betrayed him, was also standing with them. **6** When Jesus told them, "I am he," they stepped back and fell to the ground. **7** Then he asked them again, "Who is it that you're seeking?"

"Jesus of Nazareth," they said.

8 "I told you I am he," Jesus replied. "So if you're looking for me, let these men go." **9** This was to fulfill the words he had said: "I have not lost one of those you have given me."

10 Then Simon Peter, who had a sword, drew it, struck the high priest's servant, and cut off his right ear. (The servant's name was Malchus.) **11** At that, Jesus said to Peter, "Put your sword away! Am I not to drink the cup the Father has given me?"

Jesus Arrested and Taken to Annas

12 Then the company of soldiers, the commander, and the Jewish officials arrested Jesus and tied him up. **13** First they led him to Annas, since he was the father-in-law of Caiaphas, who was high priest that year. **14** Caiaphas was the one who had advised the Jews that it would be better for one man to die for the people.

Peter Denies Jesus

15 Simon Peter was following Jesus, as was another disciple. That disciple was an acquaintance of the high priest; so he went with Jesus

---

^**17:21** Other mss add *one*　　^**18:3** Or *temple police*, or *officers*, also in vv. 12,18,22

17:18–19 This verse looks forward to the commission that Jesus assigned his disciples after his resurrection (20:21).

17:20–26 Jesus did not stop at praying for himself (vv. 1–5) and his disciples (vv. 6–19); his vision transcended the present (Dt 29:14–15). Jesus was concerned for his followers' unity (Jn 17:21–23) and love (v. 26). The vision of a unified people of God was previously expressed in 10:16 and 11:52. Unity among believers results from the indivisible unity of God (10:38; 14:10–11,20,23; 15:4–5). Once unified, believers are able to bear witness to the true identity of Jesus as the one sent by God.

17:25 Jesus addressed God as **Righteous Father**. The OT teaches that God is righteous and just (Pss 116:5; 119:137; Jr 12:1). Though his betrayal, torture, and death were looming, Jesus affirmed the righteousness of God his Father.

17:26 The phrase **I may be in them** is filled with covenantal overtones (v. 23; 14:20). After the giving of the law at Sinai, God came to dwell in the midst of Israel in the tabernacle (Ex 40:34). As they moved toward the promised land, God frequently assured his people that he was in their midst (Ex 29:45–46; Dt 7:21; 23:14).

18:1–19:42 John's Passion Narrative appears in these chapters. The familiar sequence of events includes Jesus's betrayal by Judas (18:1–11), his informal hearing before Annas (18:12–14,19–24), Peter's denials (18:15–18,25–27), Jesus's Roman trial before Pilate (18:28–19:16a), and his crucifixion and burial (19:16b–42). Only John among all the Gospels featured Jesus's appearance before Annas, and his Roman trial is covered in more detail in John. On the other hand, John did not provide an account of Jesus's formal Jewish trial before Caiaphas and the Sanhedrin.

18:1–2 The **Kidron Valley** is mentioned frequently in the OT (2Sm 15:23; 1Kg 2:37; 15:13; 2Kg 23:4,6,12). The **garden** is called "Gethsemane" in the Synoptic Gospels (Mt 26:36; Mk 14:32). **Went into it** may suggest that it was a walled garden.

18:3 The **company of soldiers** was dispatched to prevent rioting. The **officials from the chief priests and the Pharisees** were the primary arresting officers. **Lanterns** and **torches** were needed to track down a suspect hiding in the dark garden. The presence of **weapons** shows that the arrest party anticipated resistance.

18:4 Jesus's supernatural knowledge is mentioned several times in the Gospel (e.g., 1:47–48; 2:24–25; 4:17–18).

18:5 I am he connotes deity (see note at 6:35,48). This is shown by the soldiers' reaction in the following verse.

18:6 Falling to the **ground** was a common reaction to divine revelation (Ezk 1:28; 44:4; Dn 2:46; 8:18; 10:9; Ac 9:4; 22:7; 26:14; Rv 1:17; 19:10; 22:8).

18:7 Jesus drew attention on himself and away from the disciples.

18:8–9 Jesus's statement summarized 17:12, which harks back to 6:39 and 10:28. Jesus is portrayed as the good shepherd who chose death to save his sheep (10:11,15,17–18,28).

18:10 Peter's **sword** was short and could be hidden under his robe (Lk 22:38). The name **Malchus** (stated only in John) indicates a **servant** of Arabic origin.

18:11 Drink the cup is a metaphor for death.

18:12 Tied him up is a customary expression in conjunction with arrest or imprisonment (Ac 9:2,14,21).

18:13 Annas, apart from being **the father-in-law of Caiaphas, who was high priest that year**, also had been high priest during AD 6–15. He continued to wield considerable influence.

18:14 On this description of Caiaphas, see notes at 11:49,50–51.

18:15–16 Another disciple was probably "the one Jesus loved" (20:2; see note at 13:23).

into the high priest's courtyard. ¹⁶ But Peter remained standing outside by the door. So the other disciple, the one known to the high priest, went out and spoke to the girl who was the doorkeeper and brought Peter in. ¹⁷ Then the servant girl who was the doorkeeper said to Peter, "You aren't one of this man's disciples too, are you?"

"I am not," he said. ¹⁸ Now the servants and the officials had made a charcoal fire, because it was cold. They were standing there warming themselves, and Peter was standing with them, warming himself.

Jesus before Annas

¹⁹ The high priest questioned Jesus about his disciples and about his teaching.

²⁰ "I have spoken openly to the world," Jesus answered him. "I have always taught in the synagogue and in the temple, where all the Jews gather, and I haven't spoken anything in secret. ²¹ Why do you question me? Question those who heard what I told them. Look, they know what I said."

²² When he had said these things, one of the officials standing by slapped Jesus, saying, "Is this the way you answer the high priest?"

²³ "If I have spoken wrongly," Jesus answered him, "give evidence^ about the wrong; but if rightly, why do you hit me?" ²⁴ Then Annas sent him bound to Caiaphas the high priest.

Peter Denies Jesus Twice More

²⁵ Now Simon Peter was standing and warming himself. They said to him, "You aren't one of his disciples too, are you?"

He denied it and said, "I am not."

²⁶ One of the high priest's servants, a relative of the man whose ear Peter had cut off, said, "Didn't I see you with him in the garden?" ²⁷ Peter denied it again. Immediately a rooster crowed.

Jesus before Pilate

²⁸ Then they led Jesus from Caiaphas to the governor's headquarters. It was early morning. They did not enter the headquarters themselves; otherwise they would be defiled and unable to eat the Passover. ²⁹ So Pilate came out to them and said, "What charge do you bring against this man?"

³⁰ They answered him, "If this man weren't a criminal,⁸ we wouldn't have handed him over to you."

³¹ Pilate told them, "You take him and judge him according to your law."

"It's not legal for us to put anyone to death," the Jews declared. ³² They said this so that Jesus's words might be fulfilled indicating what kind of death he was going to die.

³³ Then Pilate went back into the headquarters, summoned Jesus, and said to him, "Are you the king of the Jews?"

³⁴ Jesus answered, "Are you asking this on your own, or have others told you about me?"

³⁵ "I'm not a Jew, am I?" Pilate replied. "Your own nation and the chief priests handed you over to me. What have you done?"

³⁶ "My kingdom is not of this world," said Jesus. "If my kingdom were of this world, my servants would fight, so that I wouldn't be

---

^18:23 Or him, "testify ⁸18:30 Lit an evil doer

18:16–17 The **girl who was the doorkeeper** was probably one of the high priest's servants.
18:18 The Roman soldiers had returned to their barracks, entrusting the task of guarding Jesus to the **officials** (see note at v. 3). Another **charcoal fire** was lit at Peter's restoration in 21:9.
18:19 High priest refers to Annas (see note at v. 13). Questioning Jesus about **his disciples** and **his teaching** suggests that the primary concern was theological. Political charges were later added (19:7,12).
18:20 Jesus's words **I haven't spoken anything in secret** echo the book of Isaiah (Is 45:19; 48:16). Jesus did not mean that he never spoke in private with his disciples but that his message was the same in private as in public; he was not leading a conspiracy. John recorded instances of Jesus teaching both **in the synagogue** (cp. 6:59) and **in the temple.**
18:21 Jesus's response is understandable, especially if the questioning of prisoners was considered improper in his day. Note also the legal principle that a person's own testimony about himself was inadmissible (see note at 5:31).
18:22 One of the officials standing by was probably one of those who helped arrest Jesus (vv. 3,12). The slapping was likely a sharp blow with the flat of one's hand (Is 50:6, LXX;

cp. Mt 26:67; Ac 23:1–5). The question, **Is this the way you answer the high priest?** may refer to Ex 22:28: "You must not blaspheme God or curse a leader among your people" (quoted by Paul in Ac 23:5).
18:23 When challenged about his response to the high priest, Jesus alluded to the law of Ex 22:28 and denied having violated it.
18:24 Before Jesus could be brought to the Roman governor, charges had to be confirmed by the official high priest, Caiaphas, in his function as chairman of the Sanhedrin (see note at 3:1).
18:25 Now (Gk de) could also be rendered "meanwhile." **Warming himself,** repeated from v. 18, picks up the story from there.
18:26 On **one of the high priest's servants,** see note at 18:10.
18:27 On the crowing of a **rooster,** compare 13:38.
18:28 The **governor's headquarters** may refer to Herod's palace on the western wall of the temple or the Fortress of Antonia northwest of the temple grounds. **Early morning** probably means shortly after sunrise, when the Sanhedrin met in formal session and pronounced its verdict (Mt 27:1–2). The reference to Passover may mean the entire Festival of Unleavened Bread, which lasted seven days (cp. Lk 22:1: "the Festival of Unleavened Bread, which is called Passover"). **Eat the Passover**

probably means "observe the Festival" (see 2Ch 30:21).
18:29 Pilate was appointed by Emperor Tiberius, and he served as governor of Judea from AD 26 until 36/37. The famous "Pilate inscription," discovered in Caesarea in 1961, identified Pilate as prefect of Judea.
18:30 The Jews were evasive because of the weakness of their case against Jesus.
18:31 Like Gallio after him (Ac 18:14–15), Pilate was not interested in judging internal Jewish disputes. The Sanhedrin did not have the power of capital punishment.
18:32 Crucifixion horrified Jewish sensibilities. It was considered to be similar to hanging (Ac 5:30; 10:39), for which Mosaic law enunciated the principle, "Anyone hung on a tree is under God's curse" (Dt 21:23; cp. Gl 3:13). If Jesus had been put to death by the Sanhedrin, he would have been stoned, the method of execution for blasphemy (Lv 24:16; cp. Jn 10:33; Ac 7:57–58).
18:33 On **the headquarters,** see note at v. 28. **King of the Jews** had political overtones. Pilate's question aimed at determining whether Jesus was a threat to Rome's imperial power.
18:34–35 Pilate was exasperated because he didn't want to get involved in Jewish affairs.
18:36 Jesus's description of his kingdom echoes passages in Daniel (Dn 2:44; 7:14,27; cp. Jn 6:15).

handed over to the Jews. But as it is,^ my kingdom is not from here."

37 "You are a king then?" Pilate asked.

"You say that I'm a king," Jesus replied. "I was born for this, and I have come into the world for this: to testify to the truth. Everyone who is of the truth listens to my voice."

38 "What is truth?" said Pilate.

Jesus or Barabbas

After he had said this, he went out to the Jews again and told them, "I find no grounds for charging him. **39** You have a custom that I release one prisoner to you at the Passover. So, do you want me to release to you the king of the Jews?"

40 They shouted back, "Not this man, but Barabbas!" Now Barabbas was a revolutionary.^

Jesus Flogged and Mocked

19 Then Pilate took Jesus and had him flogged. **2** The soldiers also twisted together a crown of thorns, put it on his head, and clothed him in a purple robe. **3** And they kept coming up to him and saying, "Hail, king of the Jews!" and were slapping his face.

4 Pilate went outside again and said to them, "Look, I'm bringing him out to you to let you know I find no grounds for charging him." **5** Then Jesus came out wearing the crown of thorns and the purple robe. Pilate said to them, "Here is the man!"

Pilate Sentences Jesus to Death

6 When the chief priests and the temple servants^c saw him, they shouted, "Crucify! Crucify!"

Pilate responded, "Take him and crucify him yourselves, since I find no grounds for charging him."

7 "We have a law," the Jews replied to him, "and according to that law he ought to die, because he made himself the Son of God."

8 When Pilate heard this statement, he was more afraid than ever. **9** He went back into the headquarters and asked Jesus, "Where are you from?" But Jesus did not give him an answer. **10** So Pilate said to him, "Do you refuse to speak to me? Don't you know that I have the authority to release you and the authority to crucify you?"

11 "You would have no authority over me at all," Jesus answered him, "if it hadn't been given you from above. This is why the one who handed me over to you has the greater sin."

12 From that moment Pilate kept trying^D to release him. But the Jews shouted, "If you release this man, you are not Caesar's friend. Anyone who makes himself a king opposes Caesar!"

13 When Pilate heard these words, he brought Jesus outside. He sat down on the judge's seat in a place called the Stone Pavement (but in Aramaic,^E *Gabbatha*). **14** It was the preparation day for the Passover, and it was about noon.^F Then he told the Jews, "Here is your king!"

15 They shouted, "Take him away! Take him away! Crucify him!"

Pilate said to them, "Should I crucify your king?"

---

^18:36 Or *But now*   ^18:40 Or *robber*; see Jn 10:1,8 for the same Gk word used here   ^19:6 Or *temple police*, or *officers*   ^19:12 Lit *Pilate was trying*   ^19:13 Or *Hebrew*, also in vv. 17,20   ^19:14 Lit *about the sixth hour*

18:37 On **testify** and **truth**, see notes at 5:31–47; 14:4–6.
18:38 Ironically, the man charged with determining truth in the matter glibly dismissed the relevance of truth in the presence of the one who *is* truth incarnate (see note at 14:4–6). Pilate's comment may reflect disillusionment, if not bitterness, and a pragmatic viewpoint. On **he went out to the Jews again**, see vv. 28–29. Pilate exonerated Jesus three times (cp. 19:4,6), but Jewish pressures convinced him to press the prosecution (19:12–16).
18:39 At the Passover refers to the entire festival (see note at v. 28).
18:40 Barabbas means "son of the father" (Gk *barabbas*). Ironically, people wanted Barabbas released rather than the true Son of the Father—Jesus. **Revolutionary** refers to an insurrectionist or domestic terrorist, perhaps engaged in Zealot-style political extremism (Mk 15:7; Lk 23:19).
19:1 After the Jewish phase of the trial, Jesus's interrogation by Pilate, the sentencing stage of his trial began. On **Pilate**, see note at 18:29. The flogging weakened Jesus so much that he could not carry his crossbeam very far.
19:2 The **crown of thorns** represented a mock crown ridiculing Jesus's messiahship. The thorns would sink into his skull,

bloodying and distorting his face. The **purple robe** (cp. Mt 27:28; Mk 15:17) represented a mock royal robe. Purple was the imperial color (1Macc 8:14).
19:3 Hail, King of the Jews mimicked the "Ave Caesar" ("Hail, Caesar!") extended to the Roman emperor. Roman soldiers customarily played "mock king" games during the Saturnalia festival.
19:4 Usually Pilate's decision would be final, but the Jews would not let the matter drop.
19:5 Here is the man (Lat *ecce homo*) conveys a sense of, "Look at the poor fellow!" In his mock regal clothes, Jesus made a heartrending sight. In the context of John's Gospel, the statement may also highlight Jesus's humanity and invoke messianic passages such as Zch 6:12.
19:6 Pilate used sarcasm, being fully aware that the Jews did not have the authority to impose the death penalty (see note at 18:31).
19:7 The Jews' comment may refer to Lv 24:16: "Whoever blasphemes the name of the LORD must be put to death" (see note at Jn 5:18; cp. 8:59; 10:31,33).
19:8 Pilate was **more afraid than ever**. Earlier that morning his wife's dream had disturbed him (Mt 27:19).
19:9 Jesus's origin was frequently an issue with his opponents (7:27–28; 8:14; 9:29–30). For John, there were clear spiritual overtones

to Pilate's question, **Where are you from?** (cp. 18:36–37). Jesus's silence before Pilate is reminiscent of Is 53:7 (cp. Mk 14:61; 15:5; 1Pt 2:22–23).
19:10–11 In typical Jewish fashion, Jesus used **from above** to refer to God.
19:12 Unconvinced of Jesus's guilt, Pilate sentenced him to die only after intense Jewish pressure (vv. 13–16). **Caesar**, originally the surname of Gaius Julius Caesar (d. 44 BC), became the title of subsequent Roman emperors (cp. v. 15; Mt 22:17,21). **Caesar's friend** was a semiformal status indicating a person favored by the emperor. Pilate feared losing this status.
19:13 The **judge's seat** served as the platform for the judge's formal verdict (Ac 25:6,17). The kind of **Stone Pavement** mentioned here has been excavated on the lower level of the Fortress of Antonia, one of the two possible sites for the governor's residence (see note at 18:28).
19:14 The **preparation day for the Passover** may refer to the day before the Sabbath of Passover week (Mt 26:62; Mk 15:42; Lk 23:54; see note at Jn 18:28). If so, all four Gospels concur that Jesus's Last Supper was a Passover meal eaten on Thursday evening (which, by Jewish reckoning, was the beginning of Friday).
19:15 By professing to acknowledge Caesar alone as their king, the Jewish leaders

"We have no king but Caesar!" the chief priests answered. ¹⁶ Then he handed him over to be crucified.

The Crucifixion

Then they took Jesus away.^ ¹⁷ Carrying the cross by himself, he went out to what is called Place of the Skull, which in Aramaic is called *Golgotha*. ¹⁸ There they crucified him and two others with him, one on either side, with Jesus in the middle. ¹⁹ Pilate also had a sign made and put on the cross. It said: JESUS OF NAZARETH, THE KING OF THE JEWS. ²⁰ Many of the Jews read this sign, because the place where Jesus was crucified was near the city, and it was written in Aramaic, Latin, and Greek. ²¹ So the chief priests of the Jews said to Pilate, "Don't write, 'The king of the Jews,' but that he said, 'I am the king of the Jews.'"

²² Pilate replied, "What I have written, I have written."

²³ When the soldiers crucified Jesus, they took his clothes and divided them into four parts, a part for each soldier. They also took the tunic, which was seamless, woven in one piece from the top. ²⁴ So they said to one another, "Let's not tear it, but cast lots for it, to see who gets it." This happened that the Scripture might be fulfilled that says: **They divided my clothes among themselves, and they cast lots for my clothing.**ᴮ This is what the soldiers did.

Jesus's Provision for His Mother

²⁵ Standing by the cross of Jesus were his mother, his mother's sister, Mary the wife of Clopas, and Mary Magdalene. ²⁶ When Jesus saw his mother and the disciple he loved standing there, he said to his mother, "Woman, here is your son." ²⁷ Then he said to the disciple, "Here is your mother." And from that hour the disciple took her into his home.

The Finished Work of Jesus

²⁸ After this, when Jesus knew that everything was now finished that the Scripture might be fulfilled, he said, "I'm thirsty." ²⁹ A jar full of sour wine was sitting there; so they fixed a sponge full of sour wine on a hyssop branch and held it up to his mouth.

³⁰ When Jesus had received the sour wine, he said, "It is finished." Then bowing his head, he gave up his spirit.

Jesus's Side Pierced

³¹ Since it was the preparation day, the Jews did not want the bodies to remain on the cross on the Sabbath (for that Sabbath was a special ͨ day). They requested that Pilate have the men's legs broken and that their bodies be taken away. ³² So the soldiers came and broke the legs of the first man and of the other one who had been crucified with him. ³³ When they came to Jesus, they did not break his legs since they saw that he was already dead. ³⁴ But one of

---

^19:16 Other mss add *and led him out*   ᴮ19:24 Ps 22:18   ͨ19:31 Lit *great*

---

betrayed their national heritage and denied their own messianic expectations based on the promises of Scripture.
19:16a Upon pronouncement of the sentence, the person was scourged and then executed.
19:16b–42 The final unit in John's passion narrative describes Jesus's crucifixion and burial.
19:17 Jesus set out **carrying the cross by himself** until he collapsed. Simon of Cyrene was then pressed into service, and he carried it to the execution site (Mt 27:32). **He went out** means "out of the city," where Jewish custom prescribed that executions should take place (Lv 24:14,23; Nm 15:35–36; Dt 17:5; 21:19–21; 22:24; cp. Heb 13:12). **Place of the Skull** translates Aramaic **Golgotha**; the Latin equivalent used in the Vulgate is "Calvary" (see note at 1:38).
19:18 On crucifixion, see note at 18:32. Jesus's crucifixion between two criminals is reminiscent of Ps 22:16: "A gang of evildoers has closed in on me." The passage also echoes Is 53:12: "counted among the rebels."
19:19 The inscription on Jesus's cross specified the crime for which he was executed, probably to discourage others from committing similar acts.
19:20 On **the place . . . was near the city**, see note at v. 17. **Aramaic** was the language most widely understood by the Jewish population of Palestine; **Latin** was the official language of the Roman occupying force; and **Greek** was the "international language" of the empire, understood by most Diaspora Jews as well as Gentiles. The trilingual inscription ensured

that virtually anyone could read the crimes with which Jesus was charged.
19:21–22 Pilate was unwilling to give in to further Jewish pressures. For John, the inscription unintentionally confirmed Jesus's true kingship.
19:23 The **seamless** tunic may recall Joseph's robe (Gn 37:3,23). Similar to several later events at the crucifixion (Jn 19:28–37), the soldiers' division of Jesus's clothes and their casting of lots fulfilled Scripture (Ps 22:18). On other fulfillment quotations, see note at Jn 12:38–40.
19:24 The quotation is from Ps 22, a lament psalm ascribed to David. This is the first of several references to Jesus as the righteous sufferer in keeping with the experience of the psalmist (Jn 19:28,36–37). The soldiers did not want to tear Jesus's tunic because it was woven of one cloth. John may have purposefully shaped his account of Jesus's crucifixion in a way that highlighted the parallels and fulfillments between the experiences of David and Jesus. For instance, Ps 22:15–18 mentions the sufferer's thirst (v. 15), his pierced hands and feet (v. 16), and the preservation of all his bones (v. 17).
19:25 On Jesus's **mother**, see 2:1–5 and note at 19:26–27. **His mother's sister** may be Salome, the mother of the sons of Zebedee mentioned in Matthew and Mark. On **Mary Magdalene**, see 20:1–18 (cp. Lk 8:2–3).
19:26–27 In keeping with biblical injunctions to honor one's parents (Ex 20:12; Dt 5:16), Jesus made provision for his mother, who

was almost certainly widowed and probably in her early fifties, with little or no personal income. On the word **woman**, see note at 2:4. On **the disciple he loved**, see the notes at 13:23; 20:1–21:25; 21:7–8; 21:24.
19:28–29 The reference to Scripture being fulfilled builds on v. 24 (see note there), most likely in allusion to Ps 69:21: "They gave me vinegar to drink" (cp. Mt 27:34,48; see Ps 22:15). Soldiers and laborers used **sour wine** to quench their thirst (Mk 15:36). It is different from the "wine mixed with myrrh" Jesus refused on the way to the cross (Mk 15:23). **Hyssop** was a plant classified in 1Kg 4:33 as a humble shrub. It was used for the sprinkling of blood on the doorpost at the original Passover (Ex 12:22).
19:30 Gave up may echo "willingly submitted to death," which was prophesied of the Suffering Servant (Is 53:12).
19:31 On **preparation day**, see note at v. 14. That **Sabbath was . . . special** because it was the Sabbath of Passover week. For the Jews, bodies of hanged criminals were not to defile the land by remaining on a tree overnight (Dt 21:22–23; cp. Jos 8:29).
19:31–33 The **legs** of crucifixion victims were **broken** to hasten death. This prevented them from pushing themselves up with their legs to open the chest cavity and thus breathe better. Since the victims would now have to pull themselves up by the arms instead, suffocation occurred once their arm strength failed. See note at v. 36.
19:34 The flow of **blood and water** proved that Jesus was dead (1Jn 5:6–8). The passage

the soldiers pierced his side with a spear, and at once blood and water came out. ³⁵ He who saw this has testified so that you also may believe. His testimony is true, and he knows he is telling the truth. ³⁶ For these things happened so that the Scripture would be fulfilled: **Not one of his bones will be broken.**ᴬ ³⁷ Also, another Scripture says: **They will look at the one they pierced.**ᴮ

Jesus's Burial

³⁸ After this, Joseph of Arimathea, who was a disciple of Jesus — but secretly because of his fear of the Jews — asked Pilate that he might remove Jesus's body. Pilate gave him permission; so he came and took his body away. ³⁹ Nicodemus (who had previously come to him at night) also came, bringing a mixture of about seventy-five poundsᶜ of myrrh and aloes. ⁴⁰ They took Jesus's body and wrapped it in linen cloths with the fragrant spices, according to the burial custom of the Jews. ⁴¹ There was a garden in the place where he was crucified. A new tomb was in the garden; no one had yet been placed in it. ⁴² They placed Jesus there because of the Jewish day of preparation and since the tomb was nearby.

The Empty Tomb

20 On the first day of the week Mary Magdalene came to the tomb early, while it was still dark. She saw that the stone had been removed from the tomb. ² So she went running to Simon Peter and to the other disciple, the one Jesus loved, and said to them, "They've taken the Lord out of the tomb, and we don't know where they've put him!"

³ At that, Peter and the other disciple went out, heading for the tomb. ⁴ The two were running together, but the other disciple outran Peter and got to the tomb first. ⁵ Stooping down, he saw the linen cloths lying there, but he did not go in. ⁶ Then, following him, Simon Peter also came. He entered the tomb and saw the linen cloths lying there. ⁷ The wrapping that had been on his head was not lying with the linen cloths but was folded up in a separate place by itself. ⁸ The other disciple, who had reached the tomb first, then also went in, saw, and believed. ⁹ For they did not yet understand the Scripture that he must rise from the dead. ¹⁰ Then the disciples returned to the place where they were staying.

Mary Magdalene Sees the Risen Lord

¹¹ But Mary stood outside the tomb, crying. As she was crying, she stooped to look into the

---

ᴬ19:36 Ex 12:46; Nm 9:12; Ps 34:20   ᴮ19:37 Zch 12:10   ᶜ19:39 Lit *a hundred litrai*; a Roman *litrai* = 12 ounces

---

may also allude to Ex 17:6: "Hit the rock, water will come out of it and the people will drink" (cp. Nm 20:11). The **spear** was about three and one-half feet long and consisted of an iron spearhead joined to a shaft of wood.

19:35 On John's witness about Jesus, see notes at 5:31–47; 13:23; 21:24.

19:36 After vv. 24 and 28–29 (see notes there), this is the third scriptural proof that shows that Jesus's death fulfilled Scripture (Ex 12:46; Ps 34:20). Jesus escaped having his legs broken since he died so quickly, and the spear did not damage any of his bones.

19:37 The Roman soldiers again fulfilled prophecy without knowing it: "They will look at me whom they pierced" (Zch 12:10; also cited in Rv 1:7).

19:38 Joseph of Arimathea, a wealthy member of the Jewish ruling council (Mt 27:57), asked Pilate for Jesus's body. Thus Jesus was killed alongside criminals and was buried in a rich man's tomb. This fulfilled another Scripture: "He was assigned a grave with the wicked, but he was with a rich man at his death" (Is 53:9).

19:39–40 The amount of aromatic spices brought by Joseph and Nicodemus—about **seventy-five pounds of myrrh and aloes**—was considerable (2Ch 16:14). Myrrh was a fragrant resin used by Egyptians in embalming; aloes were a powder of aromatic sandalwood; the mixture cloaked the smell of decay.

19:41 On **the place where he was crucified**, see notes at vv. 17,20. The **garden** was apparently somewhat elaborate; note the mention of a gardener in 20:15. Garden burials are recorded in the OT (Manasseh in 2Kg 21:18; Amon in 2Kg 21:26).

19:42 On the **Jewish day of preparation**, see note at v. 14. Sabbath was rapidly

approaching, when all work ceased, including that of carrying spices or transporting a corpse. Thus we may see it as an instance of divine providence that the tomb was **nearby** (see note at 20:1).

20:1–21:25 The final two chapters of John's Gospel cover the aftermath of Jesus's crucifixion and burial, specifically the empty tomb, the risen Jesus's encounter with Mary Magdalene, three resurrection appearances to his disciples (20:14), the commissioning of the disciples (20:21), a special commissioning of Peter (21:15–23), conclusions to the Gospel proper (20:30–31), and the epilogue (21:24–25). The concluding statement in 20:30–31 reviews some of the major themes of the Gospel, particularly Jesus's identity as Messiah and Son of God, his messianic "signs," the importance of believing in Jesus, and the gift of eternal life. The conclusion to the epilogue identifies the "disciple Jesus loved" (who was one of the Twelve; cp. 21:20; 13:23) as the writer of John's Gospel (21:24; cp. 19:35) and affirms the truth of his testimony about Jesus (21:24).

20:1 The **first day of the week** was Sunday. **Mary Magdalene** (and several other women) decided to attend to some matters that had been left undone because of the beginning of the Sabbath (see note at 19:42). The need to complete the care for the dead may have overridden the customary seven-day mourning period (see note at 11:20). On **while it was still dark**, compare the slightly different time frame depicted in Mt 28:1 (cp. Mk 16:2; and Lk 24:1).

20:2 At this point Mary had no thought of Jesus's resurrection. The Jewish charge that his disciples stole his body (Mt 27:62–66; 28:11–15) shows that grave robbery was not uncommon. The plural **we** suggests the

presence of other women besides Mary. On **the other disciple**, see note at 18:15–16.

20:3–4 Went out translates a singular verb, suggesting perhaps the priority of Peter.

20:5–6 Apparently by now there was enough daylight to see inside the burial chamber through the small, low opening in the cave tomb. The other disciple **did not go in**, presumably in deference to Simon Peter, a leader among the Twelve.

20:7 Jesus's resurrection body apparently passed through the linen wrappings similar to the way in which he later appeared to his disciples in a locked room (vv. 19,26). This reference to the head wrapping being **folded up in a separate place by itself** counters the notion of grave robbers, who in their haste would not have taken the time to fold up this cloth.

20:8–9 The presence of two witnesses rendered the evidence admissible under Jewish law (Dt 17:6; 19:15). The **other disciple** believed based on what he **saw**, not on an understanding from Scripture that Jesus **must rise from the dead**. This lack of expectation of a resurrection shows that the disciples did not fabricate the resurrection story to fit their preconceived expectations. Rather, the resurrection shocked them and did not fit with what they understood from Scripture. Only later, aided by the Spirit's teaching (see notes at 14:25–26; 16:12–13), did they come to see that Jesus's resurrection was foretold in the OT.

20:10 When **the disciples returned to the place where they were staying**, "the other disciple Jesus loved" in all likelihood told the Lord's mother, whom he had taken "into his home" (19:27), that he was risen.

20:11 Mary was **crying**, not because Jesus had died, but because his body had vanished.

◄ The Missional Church

by Ed Stetzer

Most believers readily grasp the idea of Jesus being sent to the world. While speaking to his disciples at the well of Samaria, Jesus said, "My food is to do the will of him who *sent* me" (Jn 4:34; emphasis added). In John 4–8 Jesus spoke of being sent by his Father on fourteen separate occasions, such as saying, "I have come down from heaven, not to do my own will, but the will of him who *sent* me" (6:38; emphasis added) and "I am the one who testifies about myself, and the Father who *sent* me testifies about me" (8:18; emphasis added). Paul wrote of the same truth in Rm 8:3 (emphasis added) referring to God's "*sending* his own Son in the likeness of sinful flesh." When Jesus said, "the Father has sent me," it is not a surprise. The fact that Jesus was the "sent one" is one of the most fundamental identifications of Jesus. The incarnation of Christ is the definitive occurrence of being sent on mission—and a model for us to represent Christ in the world.

Believers know that they are sent on mission into the world. The word *sent* is replete through Paul's epistles as he mentions those such as Timothy and Titus who have been entrusted with a message and a mission. In the book of Acts, sending is a common occurrence as well. Ananias is sent to pray for Paul and open his eyes. Paul and Barnabas are sent out from the church in Antioch as missionaries with the gospel. "As they were worshiping the Lord and fasting, the Holy Spirit said, 'Set apart for me Barnabas and Saul for the work to which I have called them.' Then after they had fasted, prayed, and laid hands on them, they sent them off" (Ac 13:2–3). Most know that God sent *some*, but they often do not consider the breadth and depth of that sending (cp. Gn 12:1–3; Ex 19:5–6; Is 6:8; Mt 24:14; 28:18–20; Lk 24:46–48; Ac 1:8; 1Pt 2:9–10).

All of God's people are sent on mission, the only questions are "where?" and "among whom?" So, God has a kingdom mission and he entrusts that mission to the church—in other words, the church does not have a mission, but the mission has a church. Some are sent cross-culturally as missionaries (we call that missions), but all are sent (we call that being missional).

To understand the depth of this *sentness*, consider that the source of our missional identity is located in the nature of God. Further consider that this sending is as central to God's nature as his love, forgiveness, righteousness, and holiness. It must be since we are given example after example of it in his Word. Without God's sending nature we would know little else of his other attributes. Without his sending nature, we would not see the "bridegroom coming from his home" in creation (Ps 19:5), culminating in Jesus "present[ing] the church to himself in splendor" in the gospel (Eph 5:27).

God's sending is as tangible as any other attribute of the Godhead. And sending does belong to the Godhead: The Father sent his Son and the Holy Spirit. The Father, Son, and Spirit in indivisible unity send the church. We are to be missional, we are to live *sent*. Our sent-and-sending identity is connected ontologically with the very existence of the church. That is, just as it is the nature of God, it is in the nature of the church. When Jesus proclaimed, "As the Father has sent me, I also send you" (Jn 20:21), his mandate was a commissioning act for the disciples of that day. His command then develops into the missional task described by Peter in his first letter. "But you are a chosen race, a royal priesthood, a holy nation, a people for his possession, so that you may proclaim the praises of the one who called you out of darkness into his marvelous light" (1Pt 2:9).

The concept of a missional church is recognition that God is a sending God and we, the church and individual believers, are to live *sent*. The missional church is shaped by the idea that every believer is to live on mission. Being *sent* means that we move outside the walls of our church buildings and our Christian homes in order to engage all people with the gospel. The missional nature of the church calls for us to engage in and support the work of international missionaries to take the gospel across the world and the local mission-shaped believers to take the gospel and show the love of Christ across the street. There is a *sentness* inherent to being a follower of Jesus. It is the way of Jesus in us.

tomb. [12] She saw two angels in white sitting where Jesus's body had been lying, one at the head and the other at the feet. [13] They said to her, "Woman, why are you crying?"

"Because they've taken away my Lord," she told them, "and I don't know where they've put him."

[14] Having said this, she turned around and saw Jesus standing there, but she did not know it was Jesus. [15] "Woman," Jesus said to her, "why are you crying? Who is it that you're seeking?"

Supposing he was the gardener, she replied, "Sir, if you've carried him away, tell me where you've put him, and I will take him away."

[16] Jesus said to her, "Mary."

Turning around, she said to him in Aramaic,[A] "Rabboni!" — which means "Teacher."

[17] "Don't cling to me," Jesus told her, "since I have not yet ascended to the Father. But go to my brothers and tell them that I am ascending to my Father and your Father, to my God and your God."

[18] Mary Magdalene went and announced to the disciples, "I have seen the Lord!" And she told them what[B] he had said to her.

The Disciples Commissioned

[19] When it was evening on that first day of the week, the disciples were gathered together with the doors locked because they feared the Jews. Jesus came, stood among them, and said to them, "Peace be with you."

[20] Having said this, he showed them his hands and his side. So the disciples rejoiced when they saw the Lord.

[21] Jesus said to them again, "Peace be with you. As the Father has sent me, I also send you." [22] After saying this, he breathed on them and

[A] 20:16 Or Hebrew   [B] 20:18 Lit these things

20:12 She saw two angels in white. Angels often appeared in pairs (Ac 1:10) and are often depicted as dressed in white (Ezk 9:2; Dn 10:5–6; Rv 15:6). The angels were sitting . . . one at the head and the other at the feet of the burial shelf.
20:13–14 The resurrected Jesus is often not recognized immediately. His appearance since Mary saw him last must have changed dramatically. See 1Co 15:35–38.
20:15 Mary mistook Jesus for the gardener, which suggests that Jesus was indistinguishable from an ordinary person. Gardeners often tend to their grounds in the early morning.

20:16 Jesus had already spoken to her. It was when she heard her own name from his lips that she knew who it was.
20:17 My Father and your Father maintains a distinction between how Jesus and the disciples relate to God. Even so, Jesus called believers his brothers.
20:18 In view of the disregard for women in the culture, it is remarkable that Jesus appeared first to a woman and gave her the job of reporting his presence.
20:19,21,26 The common Jewish greeting Peace be with you (v. 21; representing Hb Shalom alekem) is still used today. Peace was Jesus's gift to his followers by virtue of his

sacrificial death on the cross. On feared the Jews (v. 19), see note at 7:13.
20:20 Jesus's scars proved that he was the very one who was crucified and prophesied his resurrection. Thus the disciples rejoiced.
20:21–22 These verses contain the Gospel of John's version of the Great Commission, which culminates in the presentation of Jesus as the one sent from the Father (see note at 3:16–18). Now the sent one (Jesus) had turned Sender, commissioning his followers to serve as his messengers and representatives (17:18). All three persons of the Godhead are involved in this commissioning. As Jesus was sent by God the Father, so he, the Son,

We are not sent on mission alone. God's people join him on his mission. We are commanded and empowered to participate with him. We know this because Jesus promised, "I am with you always, to the end of the age" (Mt 28:20). We are sent on a mission with the sender. As believers, we don't decide if we are on mission. It is our calling—because of God's nature. The only question is whether or not we are living up to the calling we have been given. Is our identity (sent on mission) aligning with our life (living on mission)?

Missional churches engage the people with the redemptive message of the gospel. To do so, the church emulates Christ in the engagement of the mission. He came announcing that he would serve the hurting (Lk 4) and save the lost (Lk 19:10). We are called to join him on that mission and show and share the good news of Jesus to a world Jesus loves. The missional church contends for the truth.

The missional church engages and inhabits the culture while seeking to remain separate from its sin and sinful structures. Jesus

Christ was a thoroughly Jewish, first-century man who engaged believers, doubters, scoffers, friends, and foes, yet never sinned. He was truly in the world without being of the world. We can engage the greedy without becoming greedy, the hateful without becoming hateful, and the proud without becoming prideful. The existence of temptation should not hinder us from missional living. Instead, we are to be a culturally relevant, counter-culture community for the kingdom.

Last, being sent by Jesus as the Father sent him means that the seed of the gospel will take root. The seed of the gospel must be sown in the soil of the culture, which necessitates Christians being engaged there. Scripture calls us salt and light and that requires presence and proclamation. The sending nature of the Father, the commission by Christ, and the empowerment of the Spirit creates a missional church. As believers, we should revel in the invitation by Christ to join his missional people.

said,[A] "Receive the Holy Spirit. [23] If you forgive the sins of any, they are forgiven them; if you retain the sins of any, they are retained."

Thomas Sees and Believes

[24] But Thomas (called "Twin"[B]), one of the Twelve, was not with them when Jesus came. [25] So the other disciples were telling him, "We've seen the Lord!"

But he said to them, "If I don't see the mark of the nails in his hands, put my finger into the mark of the nails, and put my hand into his side, I will never believe."

[26] A week later his disciples were indoors again, and Thomas was with them. Even though the doors were locked, Jesus came and stood among them and said, "Peace be with you." [27] Then he said to Thomas, "Put your finger here and look at my hands. Reach out your hand and put it into my side. Don't be faithless, but believe."

[28] Thomas responded to him, "My Lord and my God!"

[29] Jesus said, "Because you have seen me, you have believed.[C] Blessed are those who have not seen and yet believe."

The Purpose of This Gospel

[30] Jesus performed many other signs in the presence of his disciples that are not written in this book. [31] But these are written so that you may believe that Jesus is the Messiah, the Son of God,[D] and that by believing you may have life in his name.

Jesus's Third Appearance to the Disciples

21 After this, Jesus revealed himself again to his disciples by the Sea of Tiberias.[E] He revealed himself in this way:

[2] Simon Peter, Thomas (called "Twin"[B]), Nathanael from Cana of Galilee, Zebedee's sons, and two others of his disciples were together. [3] "I'm going fishing," Simon Peter said to them.

"We're coming with you," they told him. They went out and got into the boat, but that night they caught nothing.

[4] When daybreak came, Jesus stood on the shore, but the disciples did not know it was Jesus. [5] "Friends,"[F] Jesus called to them, "you don't have any fish, do you?"

"No," they answered.

[6] "Cast the net on the right side of the boat," he told them, "and you'll find some." So they did,[G] and they were unable to haul it in because of the large number of fish. [7] The disciple, the one Jesus loved, said to Peter, "It is the Lord!"

When Simon Peter heard that it was the Lord, he tied his outer clothing around him (for he had taken it off) and plunged into the sea. [8] Since they were not far from land (about a hundred yards[H] away), the other disciples came in the boat, dragging the net full of fish.

[9] When they got out on land, they saw a charcoal fire there, with fish lying on it, and bread. [10] "Bring some of the fish you've just caught," Jesus told them. [11] So Simon Peter climbed up and hauled the net ashore, full of large fish — 153 of them. Even though there were so many, the net was not torn.

[12] "Come and have breakfast," Jesus told them. None of the disciples dared ask him, "Who are you?" because they knew it was the Lord. [13] Jesus came, took the bread, and gave it to them. He did the same with the

---

[A] 20:22 Lit *he breathed and said to them*　[B] 20:24; 21:2 Gk *Didymus*　[C] 20:29 Or *have you believed?*　[D] 20:31 Or *that the Messiah, the Son of God, is Jesus*　[E] 21:1 Another name for the Sea of Galilee　[F] 21:5 Lit *"Children"*　[G] 21:6 Lit *they cast*　[H] 21:8 Lit *about two hundred cubits*

---

was sending out his disciples (20:21), equipping them with *the Holy Spirit* (v. 22). John thus demonstrated that each member of the Godhead is involved in the redemption plan and the mission of spreading the gospel to the world. **The Holy Spirit** was given dramatically and permanently a short time later (Acts 2).
20:23 The reference to forgiveness or lack thereof may echo the reference to "the key of the House of David" in Is 22:22 (cp. Rv 3:7). Jesus bestowed on his followers authority to announce access or disbarment from God's kingdom based on reception or denial of the gospel message. For those who reject Jesus, his messengers are commissioned to say that they do not have forgiveness of sins.
20:24 On Thomas as **Twin**, see note at 1:38.
20:25 Apparently Thomas thought the disciples had seen a ghost (Mt 14:26). Yet John was careful to affirm that Jesus's resurrection body was not that of a phantom or spirit apparition but a genuine (although glorified) human body (Jn 20:27).
20:26 A week later refers to the following Sunday, one week after Easter (v. 19).

20:27–28 Jesus condescended to allow Thomas's test of his identity. But when Thomas saw and heard Jesus, no such examination was necessary. He recognized that in some sense Jesus was God incarnate. The words **Lord** and **God** occur together in the OT more than one thousand times. The emperor Domitian also wished to be addressed as "our Lord and God."
20:29 Though they **have not seen** the risen Christ, readers of the Gospel of John may **yet believe** because John, by aid of the Holy Spirit, has written the truth about God's Son.
20:30–31 On Jesus's **signs** in John's Gospel, see note at 2:11. These verses summarize John's purpose for writing his Gospel.
21:1–25 This epilogue narrates Jesus's third and final resurrection appearance recorded in this Gospel and contrasts the callings of Peter and "the disciple Jesus loved."
21:1 With the weeklong Festival of Unleavened Bread now past, the disciples left Jerusalem and returned to Galilee (see note at 20:26; cp. Lk 2:43). On the **Sea of Tiberias**, see note at 6:1.

21:2 The names of **Zebedee's sons** are given in the Synoptic Gospels as James and John (Mt 4:21). Luke mentions that they were "Simon's partners" (Lk 5:10) in the fishing business before they were called to follow Jesus as disciples (see note at Jn 1:40).
21:3 Night was the preferred time for **fishing** in ancient times (Lk 5:5). This schedule allowed fish caught at night to be sold fresh in the morning market.
21:4–6 The disciples' failure to recognize Jesus may have been supernatural (Lk 24:16,37).
21:7–8 the **disciple . . . Jesus loved** must be one of the seven mentioned in v. 2, which included Zebedee's sons, and was almost certainly John the son of Zebedee, author of this Gospel (see note at v. 24).
21:9 On the **charcoal fire**, see note at 18:18.
21:10–11 Various attempts have been made to interpret the number **153** symbolically, but most likely it simply represents the actual number of fish. Large numbers elsewhere in John are meant literally as well (2:6; 12:3).
21:12–13 By taking the **bread** and **fish** and giving them to his disciples, Jesus acted as

fish. [14] This was now the third time Jesus appeared[A] to the disciples after he was raised from the dead.

Jesus's Threefold Restoration of Peter

[15] When they had eaten breakfast, Jesus asked Simon Peter, "Simon, son of John,[B] do you love me more than these?"

"Yes, Lord," he said to him, "you know that I love you."

"Feed my lambs," he told him. [16] A second time he asked him, "Simon, son of John, do you love me?"

"Yes, Lord," he said to him, "you know that I love you."

"Shepherd my sheep," he told him. [17] He asked him the third time, "Simon, son of John, do you love me?"

Peter was grieved that he asked him the third time, "Do you love me?" He said, "Lord, you know everything; you know that I love you."

"Feed my sheep," Jesus said. [18] "Truly I tell you, when you were younger, you would tie your belt and walk wherever you wanted. But when you grow old, you will stretch out your hands and someone else will tie you and carry you where you don't want to go." [19] He said this to indicate by what kind of death Peter would glorify God. After saying this, he told him, "Follow me."

Correcting a False Report

[20] So Peter turned around and saw the disciple Jesus loved following them, the one who had leaned back against Jesus at the supper and asked, "Lord, who is the one that's going to betray you?" [21] When Peter saw him, he said to Jesus, "Lord, what about him?"

[22] "If I want him to remain until I come," Jesus answered, "what is that to you? As for you, follow me."

[23] So this rumor[C] spread to the brothers and sisters that this disciple would not die. Yet Jesus did not tell him that he would not die, but, "If I want him to remain until I come, what is that to you?"

Epilogue

[24] This is the disciple who testifies to these things and who wrote them down. We know that his testimony is true.

[25] And there are also many other things that Jesus did, which, if every one of them were written down, I suppose not even the world itself could contain the books[D] that would be written.

---

^[A]21:14 Lit was revealed (v. 1)   [B]21:15–17 Other mss read "Simon, son of Jonah; Mt 16:17; Jn 1:42   [C]21:23 Lit this word   [D]21:25 Lit scroll

---

a Jewish host pronouncing the blessing at a meal (6:11,23).

21:14 This verse forms an *inclusio* with 21:1 and marks off 21:1–14 as a unit.

21:15 On **Simon, son of John**, see note at 1:42. Jesus's question **do you love me more than these?** probably meant, "Do you love me more than these disciples do?" rather than, "Do you love me more than these fish [i.e., his profession]?" or "Do you love me more than you love these men?" though each of the three meanings is possible.

21:15–17 Peter had denied Jesus three times (18:15–18,25–27); now Jesus asked him three times to reaffirm his love for him before recommissioning him for gospel service.

21:18 Stretch out your hands refers to crucifixion, where a person's hands and arms are spread out and nailed to the crossbeam. Tradition says Peter chose to be crucified upside down because he felt himself unworthy of dying in the same exact manner as Jesus.

21:19 The reference **to indicate by what kind of death Peter would glorify God** echoes the reference "to indicate what kind of death he [Jesus] was about to die" in 12:33. This verse therefore establishes a connection between the deaths of Jesus and Peter. As God's Lamb, Jesus died for the sins of the world (1:29,36); Peter died a martyr's death, giving his life as a witness to his faith in Jesus.

21:20 On **the disciple Jesus loved**, see note at 13:23.

21:21–23 Like the final chapter of Matthew, the closing verses of John's Gospel dispel a **rumor**. Matthew denied that Jesus's disciples stole his body (Mt 28:11–15; cp. Mt 27:62–66) while John sought to lay to rest the rumor that Christ had promised to return during John's lifetime.

21:24 This is the disciple in a third-person authorial self-reference. Again, this is "the disciple Jesus loved" (cp. v. 7; see note at 13:23), one of the Twelve (cp. 21:20), John the son of Zebedee, the apostle John, who referred to himself by the epithet "the beloved disciple." **We know** represents an instance of the authorial "we," by which the author included himself along with his audience.

21:25 John acknowledges that he had to be selective, choosing from a vast amount of material about Jesus (specifically, the "signs"; cp. 20:30–31).

◥ Introduction to Acts

Circumstances of Writing

The book of Acts is formally anonymous. The traditional view is that the author was the same person who wrote the Gospel of Luke— Luke the physician and traveling companion of Paul (Col 4:14; 2 Tm 4:11; Phm 24). As early as the second century AD, church leaders such as Irenaeus wrote that Luke was the author of Acts. Irenaeus based his view on the "we" passages in Acts, five sections where the author changed from the third person ("he/she," "they") to first-person plural ("we") as he narrated the action (16:10–17; 20:5–15; 21:1–18; 27:1–29; 28:1–16). Irenaeus and many scholars since his time have interpreted these passages to mean that the author of Acts was one of the eyewitness companions of Paul. Luke fits this description better than any other candidate, especially given the similar themes between the Gospel of Luke and the book of Acts.

The date of composition of the book of Acts is to a large extent directly tied to the issue of authorship. A number of scholars have argued that Acts should be dated to the early 60s (at the time of Paul's imprisonment). Acts closes with Paul still in prison in Rome (28:30–31). Although it is possible that Luke wrote at a later date, a time when Paul had been released, it is more plausible to think that he completed this book while Paul was still in prison. Otherwise he would have ended the book by telling about Paul's release.

Contribution to the Bible

The book of Acts ties together the other books of the New Testament. It does so by first providing "the rest of the story" to the Gospels. The gospel and the message of the kingdom of God did not end with Jesus's ascension to heaven forty days after his resurrection but continued on in the lives of his followers. Acts shows us how the words and promises of Jesus were carried out by the apostles and other believers through the power of the Holy Spirit. Second, the book of Acts gives us the context for much of the rest of the New Testament, especially the letters Paul wrote to the churches he had helped establish during his missionary journeys.

Structure

So far as literary form is concerned, the book of Acts is an ancient biography that focuses on several central characters, especially Peter and Paul. Ancient biography was not concerned simply with narrating events but with displaying the character of the people involved, especially their ethical behavior. Other features included genealogies and rhetorical elements such as speeches. Ancient biographies also commonly drew from both written and oral sources for information.

Acts 1:8 provides the introduction and outline for the book. Once empowered by the Holy Spirit, the disciples proclaimed the gospel boldly in Jerusalem. As the book progresses, the gospel spread farther into Judea and Samaria and then finally into the outer reaches of the known world through the missionary work of Paul.

Acts Timeline

AD 33–37

Tiberius Caesar **14–37**
Jesus's trials, death, resurrection, and
  ascension **NISAN 14-16** or **APRIL 3-5, 33**
Lunar eclipse; moon turns blood
  red **NISAN 15** or **APRIL 4, 33**
Pentecost **33**
Saul's conversion on the Damascus
  Road **OCTOBER 34**
Paul's years in Arabia **34–37**
Paul's first visit to Jerusalem
  following his conversion **37?**

AD 37–41

Paul returns to his native Tarsus. **SUMMER 37–40**
Caligula, Emperor of Rome **37–41**
Emperor Caligula removes Herod Antipas as
  Tetrarch of Galilee and replaces him with
  his nephew, Herod Agrippa, who had been
  a childhood companion of Caligula. **39**
Barnabas travels from Antioch of
  Syria to find Paul. **SUMMER 40**
Conversion of Cornelius and his family **40**
Barnabas and Saul serve together in Antioch. **41**

Outline

Key verses in Acts

1:8   But you will receive power when the Holy Spirit has come on you, and you will be my witnesses in Jerusalem, in all Judea and Samaria, and to the ends of the earth.

4:12   There is salvation in no one else, for there is no other name under heaven given to people by which we must be saved.

10:34   Peter began to speak: "Now I truly understand that God doesn't show favoritism."

16:31   They said, "Believe in the Lord Jesus, and you will be saved — you and your household."

AD 41–49

Claudius, Emperor of Rome **41–54**
Believers respond to famine
  prophesied by Agabus. **44–47**
Martyrdom of James, son of Zebedee **44**
Death of Herod Agrippa **44**
Paul, Barnabas, and John Mark make
  first missionary journey. **47–49**

AD 49–68

Paul and Silas take second
  missionary journey. **49–52**
Paul's third missionary journey **53–57**
Paul's arrest in Jerusalem (**57**) and
  imprisonment at Caesarea **58–59**
Paul's journey to Rome **LATE 59**
Paul's house arrest in Rome **60–62**
Martyrdom of James, half brother of Jesus **62**
Martyrdom of Peter and Paul in Rome **67** or **68**

Prologue

1 I wrote the first narrative, Theophilus, about all that Jesus began to do and teach [2] until the day he was taken up, after he had given instructions through the Holy Spirit to the apostles he had chosen. [3] After he had suffered, he also presented himself alive to them by many convincing proofs, appearing to them over a period of forty days and speaking about the kingdom of God.

The Holy Spirit Promised

[4] While he was [A] with them, he commanded them not to leave Jerusalem, but to wait for the Father's promise. "Which," he said, "you have heard me speak about; [5] for John baptized with water, but you will be baptized with the Holy Spirit in a few days."

[6] So when they had come together, they asked him, "Lord, are you restoring the kingdom to Israel at this time?"

[7] He said to them, "It is not for you to know times or periods that the Father has set by his own authority. [8] But you will receive power when the Holy Spirit has come on you, and you will be my witnesses in Jerusalem, in all Judea and Samaria, and to the ends of the earth."

The Ascension

[9] After he had said this, he was taken up as they were watching, and a cloud took him out of their sight. [10] While he was going, they were gazing into heaven, and suddenly two men in white clothes stood by them. [11] They said, "Men of Galilee, why do you stand looking up into heaven? This same Jesus, who has been taken from you into heaven, will come in the same way that you have seen him going into heaven."

United in Prayer

[12] Then they returned to Jerusalem from the Mount of Olives, which is near Jerusalem — a Sabbath day's journey away. [13] When they arrived, they went to the room upstairs where they were staying: Peter, John, James, Andrew, Philip, Thomas, Bartholomew, Matthew, James the son of Alphaeus, Simon the Zealot, and Judas the son of James. [14] They all were continually united in prayer, [B] along with the women, including Mary the mother of Jesus, and his brothers.

Matthias Chosen

[15] In those days Peter stood up among the brothers and sisters [C] — the number of people who were together was about a hundred twenty — and said, [16] "Brothers and sisters, it was necessary that the Scripture be fulfilled that the Holy Spirit through the mouth of David foretold about Judas, who became a guide to those who arrested Jesus. [17] For he was one of our number and shared in this ministry." [18] Now this man acquired a field with his unrighteous wages. He fell headfirst, his body burst open and his intestines spilled out. [19] This became known to all the residents of Jerusalem, so that in their own language that field is called *Hakeldama* (that is, "Field of Blood"). [20] "For it is written in the Book of Psalms:

Let his dwelling become desolate;
let no one live in it; [D] and

Let someone else take his position. [E]

[A] 1:4 Or *he was eating*, or *he was lodging*　[B] 1:14 Other mss add *and petition*　[C] 1:15 Other mss read *disciples*　[D] 1:20 Ps 69:25　[E] 1:20 Ps 109:8

1:1–3 The preface links the book of Acts explicitly with the **first narrative**, the Gospel of Luke (Lk 1:1–4). Like the first volume, the second is addressed to a person named **Theophilus**. Some speculate that Theophilus (Gk, "lover of God") was a literary figure representing Christians generally, but more likely he was an actual historical person. Some think that Theophilus was a seeker after God and Luke aimed to explain Christianity to him. Others think Theophilus was a recent convert who required instruction in his newfound faith. Still others suggest he was an early church leader for whom Luke provided a summary of events surrounding the rise of Christianity. Jesus presented himself by **many convincing proofs**, including appearing to the disciples during the **forty days** between his resurrection and ascension.

1:4 The **Father's promise** refers to the gift of the Holy Spirit, which would soon come (chap. 2).

1:6–7 Restoration of the **kingdom** of **Israel** was something for which all first-century Jews longed. It was commonly believed that Messiah, son of David and heir to his throne, would accomplish this restoration.

1:8 The major focus of the book of Acts is stated in this verse. Jesus said believers would **receive power** when the **Holy Spirit** came upon them, empowering them to be his **witnesses in Jerusalem** first and then spreading to **the ends of the earth**. Note three things about how this unfolds. First, the empowering presence is to be the Holy Spirit, not Jesus himself. Second, the growth of the church would come about through the witness of the disciples. Third, the result of this witness will be measurable, geographical growth. "The ends of the earth" may refer to the known world of that time, likely coextensive with the reach of the Roman Empire.

1:9–11 A cloud took him out recalls the presence of God depicted as a cloud elsewhere (e.g., Ex 13:21–22). Jesus's ascension to heaven provides overlap and transition between Luke's Gospel and the book of Acts. Jesus's return will be in the **same way** as he departed—bodily and visibly.

1:12–13 Lk 6:14–16 provides the same list of disciples. **Simon the Zealot** of Luke-Acts is probably Simon the Cananaean, and **Judas the son of James** in Luke-Acts may be Thaddaeus.

1:14 Jesus had six half-brothers according to Mk 6:3.

1:15–17 Peter began to assume his role as leader and spokesman for the apostles. The Scripture Peter referred to was Ps 69:25, quoted in v. 20.

1:18–19 The differences between the two NT accounts of Judas's death (here and Mt 27:3–8) should not be overemphasized. Both agree that he died a shameful death and that a field was named after his traitorous deed. Mt 27:5 says Judas hanged himself, while the present passage says he fell **headfirst** and **burst open**. Possibly after he hanged himself, Judas's body decayed and fell from the rope, bursting open.

1:20 See note on vv. 15–17.

#67 99 Essential Christian Truths

SIN AS REBELLION

Because the Bible portrays people as responsible beings, called to respond in faith and obedience to God's revelation, the Bible often portrays sin in terms of defiance and rebellion toward God the King. Isaiah 1:2 is one of many passages that describes sin in terms of rebellion against God: "I have raised children and brought them up, but they have rebelled against me." Seen in this light, sin is personal and willful disobedience, the raising of a clinched fist toward the one who made us.

21 "Therefore, from among the men who have accompanied us during the whole time the Lord Jesus went in and out among us — **22** beginning from the baptism of John until the day he was taken up from us — from among these, it is necessary that one become a witness with us of his resurrection." **23** So they proposed two: Joseph, called Barsabbas, who was also known as Justus, and Matthias. **24** Then they prayed, "You, Lord, know everyone's hearts; show which of these two you have chosen **25** to take the place^A in this apostolic ministry that Judas left to go where he belongs." **26** Then they cast lots for them, and the lot fell to Matthias and he was added to the eleven apostles.

Pentecost

2 When the day of Pentecost had arrived, they were all together in one place. **2** Suddenly a sound like that of a violent rushing wind came from heaven, and it filled the whole house where they were staying. **3** They saw tongues like flames of fire that separated and rested on each one of them. **4** Then they were all filled with the Holy Spirit and began to speak in different tongues,^B as the Spirit enabled them.

5 Now there were Jews staying in Jerusalem, devout people from every nation under heaven. **6** When this sound occurred, a crowd came together and was confused because each one heard them speaking in his own language. **7** They were astounded and amazed, saying,^C "Look, aren't all these who are speaking Galileans? **8** How is it that each of us can hear them in our own native language? **9** Parthians, Medes, Elamites; those who live in Mesopotamia, in Judea and Cappadocia, Pontus and Asia, **10** Phrygia and Pamphylia, Egypt and the parts of Libya near Cyrene; visitors from Rome (both Jews and converts), **11** Cretans and Arabs — we hear them declaring the magnificent acts of God in our own tongues." **12** They were all astounded and perplexed, saying to one another, "What

does this mean?"^13 But some sneered and said, "They're drunk on new wine."

Peter's Sermon

14 Peter stood up with the Eleven, raised his voice, and proclaimed to them, "Fellow Jews and all you residents of Jerusalem, let this be known to you, and pay attention to my words. **15** For these people are not drunk, as you suppose, since it's only nine in the morning.^D **16** On the contrary, this is what was spoken through the prophet Joel:

17   And it will be in the last days, says God,
        that I will pour out my Spirit
        on all people;
        then your sons and your daughters
        will prophesy,
        your young men will see visions,
        and your old men will dream dreams.
18   I will even pour out my Spirit
        on my servants in those days, both
        men and women
        and they will prophesy.
19   I will display wonders
        in the heaven above
        and signs on the earth below:
        blood and fire and a cloud of smoke.
20   The sun will be turned to darkness
        and the moon to blood
        before the great and glorious day of
        the Lord comes.
21   Then everyone who calls
        on the name of the Lord will be saved.^E

22 "Fellow Israelites, listen to these words: This Jesus of Nazareth was a man attested to you by God with miracles, wonders, and signs that God did among you through him, just as you yourselves know. **23** Though he was delivered up according to God's determined plan and foreknowledge, you used^F lawless people to nail him to a cross and kill him. **24** God raised him up, ending the pains of death, because it was not possible for him to be held by death. **25** For David says of him:

---

^A1:25 Other mss read *to share*   ^B2:4 languages, also in v. 11   ^C2:7 Other mss add *to one another*   ^D2:15 Lit *it's the third hour of the day*   ^E2:17–21 Jl 2:28–32   ^F2:23 Other mss read *you have taken*

1:24–26 The casting of **lots** was an acceptable method for making decisions in the era before the Holy Spirit was given. The sovereign Lord superintended the event, ensuring that the lot fell in such a way as to identify his chosen man.

2:1–12 Pentecost (also called the Festival of Weeks, Lv 23:15–16) commemorated the giving of the law on Mount Sinai and occurred fifty days after Passover and the Festival of Unleavened Bread. Jews either made pilgrimage to Jerusalem for Pentecost or remained there after Passover. The events of Pentecost, which mark the formal and public beginning of the church, involved a number of supernatural phenomena. These included the rush of violent wind from heaven, tongues like flames of fire, the infilling with the Holy

Spirit, and speaking in languages as the Spirit gave believers the ability to do so.

2:4 These **tongues** have been interpreted as (1) supernatural languages given specifically for the purpose of communicating with the people gathered from all over the Roman Empire, (2) human languages that were recognized by individuals from various lands, or (3) the Greek language that was common to all the people gathered from throughout the Roman world. The second option seems to best fit the context.

2:8–11 All the regions listed in vv. 9–10 are known to have had Jewish populations.

2:16–21 In his reply to the jeering crowd (v. 13), Peter cited three OT passages to demonstrate the biblical basis for the events of Pentecost. The first passage he cited was from

Jl 2:28–32. Peter identified Joel's prophecy with **the last days** and said those days had now arrived with the coming of the Spirit.

2:23 Peter's declaration articulates a major paradox of the Christian life: Jesus's death occurred as a result of the plan and foreknowledge of God, but it was the free (and sinful) acts of human beings that executed that plan.

2:24 Peter made several important statements about the resurrection in this verse. First, it was **God** who **raised** Jesus from the dead. Second, Jesus was literally dead before the resurrection, not simply injured. Third, death's power was overcome by the resurrection, which means that believers should no longer fear it.

2:25–28 The second OT passage Peter cited is Ps 16:8–11. Jesus was the one about whom

I saw the Lord ever before me;
because he is at my right hand,
I will not be shaken.
²⁶ Therefore my heart is glad
and my tongue rejoices.
Moreover, my flesh will rest in hope,
²⁷ because you will not abandon me in
Hades
or allow your holy one to see decay.
²⁸ You have revealed the paths of life
to me;
you will fill me with gladness
in your presence.ᴬ

²⁹ "Brothers and sisters, I can confidently speak to you about the patriarch David: He is both dead and buried, and his tomb is with us to this day. ³⁰ Since he was a prophet, he knew that God had sworn an oath to him to seat one of his descendantsᴮ on his throne. ³¹ Seeing what was to come, he spoke concerning the resurrection of the Messiah: Heᶜ was not abandoned in Hades, and his flesh did not experience decay.ᴰ ³² "God has raised this Jesus; we are all witnesses of this. ³³ Therefore, since he has been exalted to the right hand of God and has received from the Father the promised Holy Spirit, he has poured out what you both see and hear. ³⁴ For it was not David who ascended into the heavens, but he himself says:

The Lord declared to my Lord,
'Sit at my right hand
³⁵ until I make your enemies
your footstool.'ᴱ

³⁶ "Therefore let all the house of Israel know with certainty that God has made this Jesus, whom you crucified, both Lord and Messiah."

Call to Repentance

³⁷ When they heard this, they were pierced to the heart and said to Peter and the rest of the apostles, "Brothers, what should we do?"

³⁸ Peter replied, "Repent and be baptized, each of you, in the name of Jesus Christ for the forgiveness of your sins, and you will receive the gift of the Holy Spirit. ³⁹ For the promise is for you and for your children, and for all who are far off, as many as the Lord our God will call." ⁴⁰ With many other words he testified and strongly urged them, saying, "Be saved from this corruptᶠ generation!" ⁴¹ So those who accepted his message were baptized, and that day about three thousand people were added to them.

A Generous and Growing Church

⁴² They devoted themselves to the apostles' teaching, to the fellowship, to the breaking of bread, and to prayer. ⁴³ Everyone was filled with awe, and many wonders and signs were being performed through the apostles. ⁴⁴ Now all the believers were together and held all things in common. ⁴⁵ They sold their possessions and property and distributed the proceeds to all, as any had need. ⁴⁶ Every day they devoted themselves to meeting together in the temple, and broke bread from house to house. They ate their food with joyful and sincere hearts, ⁴⁷ praising God and enjoying the favor of all the people. Every day the Lord added to their numberᴳ those who were being saved.

Healing of a Lame Man

3 Now Peter and John were going up to the temple for the time of prayer at three in the afternoon.ᴴ ² A man who was lame from birth was being carried there. He was placed each day at the temple gate called Beautiful, so that he could beg from those entering the temple. ³ When he saw Peter and John about to enter the temple, he asked for money. ⁴ Peter, along with John, looked straight at him and said, "Look at us." ⁵ So he turned to them, expecting to get something from them. ⁶ But Peter said, "I don't have silver or gold, but what I

ᴬ2:25–28 Ps 16:8–11   ᴮ2:30 Other mss add *according to the flesh to raise up the Messiah*   ᶜ2:31 Other mss read *His soul*   ᴰ2:31 Ps 16:10   ᴱ2:34–35 Ps 110:1   ᶠ2:40 Or *crooked*, or *twisted*   ᴳ2:47 Other mss read *to the church*   ᴴ3:1 Lit *at the ninth hour*

David had prophesied, the one who would not see the **decay** of death (also in v. 31).
2:29–30 Peter identified **David** as a prophet because he had prophesied through his psalm about the Messiah.
2:31 The citation is from Ps 16:10, in which the meaning of the words describe more than just David's experience.
2:34–35 The third and final OT passage cited by Peter is Ps 110:1.
2:36 By calling Jesus **Lord and Messiah**, Peter was staking the biggest possible claims. "Lord" is reserved in the Greek translation of the OT (the Septuagint or LXX) for God (Yahweh). Thus Peter says Jesus is God. Peter further noted that Jesus was the Messiah (anointed one), Israel's hope for salvation.

2:38 Peter's answer to the question in v. 37 indicates three major components in conversion. One must **repent**, which means turning from sin. To **be baptized . . . in the name of Jesus** publicly declares our repentance and faith, plus it symbolically identifies us with the death, burial, and resurrection of Christ. The **Holy Spirit** is given as a gift and seal of conversion, empowering the believer for the life of faith.
2:39 The Gentiles were **far off** in two senses: they were geographically far removed from Israel, but even more significantly they were "far off" from knowledge of the one true God.
2:40 On **this corrupt generation**, see Ps 78:8.
2:41 Note the close link between coming to faith and being **baptized**. There was

apparently no delay between profession of faith and baptism. The large number of converts was made possible by the huge crowds who had traveled to Jerusalem from all over the Mediterranean region for the Passover celebration.
2:42 These four practices—**teaching** . . . **fellowship**, the **breaking of bread**, and **prayer**—provide insight into the priorities of early Christianity. The breaking of bread probably included fellowship meals and participation in the Lord's Supper (1Co 11:17–34).
2:46 Early Christian gatherings took place in two places: **the temple** and the homes of individual believers.
2:47 The early church was an evangelizing church.
3:2 This is the first healing miracle in Acts.

do have, I give you: In the name of Jesus Christ of Nazareth, get up and walk!" [7] Then, taking him by the right hand he raised him up, and at once his feet and ankles became strong. [8] So he jumped up and started to walk, and he entered the temple with them — walking, leaping, and praising God. [9] All the people saw him walking and praising God, [10] and they recognized that he was the one who used to sit and beg at the Beautiful Gate of the temple. So they were filled with awe and astonishment at what had happened to him.

Preaching in Solomon's Colonnade

[11] While he[A] was holding on to Peter and John, all the people, utterly astonished, ran toward them in what is called Solomon's Colonnade. [12] When Peter saw this, he addressed the people: "Fellow Israelites, why are you amazed at this? Why do you stare at us, as though we had made him walk by our own power or godliness? [13] The God of Abraham, Isaac, and Jacob, the God of our ancestors, has glorified his servant Jesus, whom you handed over and denied before Pilate, though he had decided to release him. [14] You denied the Holy and Righteous One and asked to have a murderer released to you. [15] You killed the source[B] of life, whom God raised from the dead; we are witnesses of this. [16] By faith in his name, his name has made this man strong, whom you see and know. So the faith that comes through Jesus has given him this perfect health in front of all of you.

[17] "And now, brothers and sisters, I know that you acted in ignorance, just as your leaders also did. [18] In this way God fulfilled what he had predicted through all the prophets — that his Messiah would suffer. [19] Therefore repent and turn back, so that your sins may be wiped out, [20] that seasons of refreshing may come from the presence of the Lord, and that he may send Jesus, who has been appointed for you as the Messiah. [21] Heaven must receive him until the time of the restoration of all things, which God spoke about through his holy prophets from

the beginning. [22] Moses said:[C] The Lord your God will raise up for you a prophet like me from among your brothers. You must listen to everything he tells you. [23] And everyone who does not listen to that prophet will be completely cut off from the people.[D]

[24] "In addition, all the prophets who have spoken, from Samuel and those after him, have also foretold these days. [25] You are the sons[E] of the prophets and of the covenant that God made with your ancestors, saying to Abraham, And all the families of the earth will be blessed through your offspring.[F] [26] God raised up his servant[G] and sent him first to you to bless you by turning each of you from your evil ways."

Peter and John Arrested

4 While they were speaking to the people, the priests, the captain of the temple police, and the Sadducees confronted them, [2] because they were annoyed that they were teaching the people and proclaiming in Jesus the resurrection of the dead. [3] So they seized them and took them into custody until the next day since it was already evening. [4] But many of those who heard the message believed, and the number of the men[H] came to about five thousand.

Peter and John Face the Jewish Leadership

[5] The next day, their rulers, elders, and scribes assembled in Jerusalem [6] with Annas the high priest, Caiaphas, John, Alexander, and all the members of the high-priestly family. [7] After they had Peter and John stand before them, they began to question them: "By what power or in what name have you done this?"

[8] Then Peter was filled with the Holy Spirit and said to them, "Rulers of the people and elders:[I] [9] If we are being examined today about a good deed done to a disabled man, by what means he was healed, [10] let it be known to all of you and to all the people of Israel, that by

---

^3:11 Other mss read *the lame man who was healed*　^B^3:15 Or *the Prince*, or *the Ruler*　^C^3:22 Other mss add *to the fathers*
^D^3:22–23 Dt 18:15–19　^E^3:25 = heirs　^F^3:25 Gn 12:3; 18:18; 22:18; 26:4　^G^3:26 Other mss add *Jesus*　^H^4:4 Or *people*
^I^4:8 Other mss add *of Israel*

3:12 Recognizing that the onlookers were **amazed**, Peter seized the chance to testify about Jesus Christ.
3:13–15 Peter emphasized the heinous nature of their deed by calling Jesus the **Holy and Righteous One** and by noting that they had asked Pilate to release a **murderer** in place of Jesus. Thus they killed the **source of life** instead of one who had taken life.
3:17 Ignorance here is not an excuse but is culpable, making repentance necessary.
3:18 The prophecy that the **Messiah** would suffer is an apparent reference to the Suffering Servant of Is 52:13–53:12. The suffering of the servant for sins (Is 53:10) had been fulfilled through Jesus.

3:20–21 God had foretold the time of **restoration** through the prophets, starting as far back as Moses (v. 22; see also Rm 8:18–25).
3:22–24 Peter appealed to Dt 18:15–19, where Moses foretold Israel that **God will raise up for you a prophet like me**. Over time this came to be recognized as a Messianic prophecy.
3:25–26 The Jews listening to Peter were **sons of the prophets** and inheritors of the covenant God made with Abraham. Thus they had a personal stake in the words of the prophets and the Pentateuch.
4:1–3 The religious authorities **confronted** and ultimately arrested Peter and John for **proclaiming in Jesus the resurrection of the dead**. The Sadducees in particular

were provoked by this, for they did not believe in resurrection because they did not think it was taught in the Pentateuch, the only portion of the Hebrew Bible they acknowledged as authoritative (Mt 22:23). The apostles were held in **custody** overnight because Sanhedrin trials were not conducted at night. Rome had granted the Sanhedrin legal authority over the temple area since disputes arising there were religious in nature rather than civic.
4:4 With the healing of the lame man, Peter's sermon, and the arrest of the apostles, the church grew **to about five thousand.**
4:5–7 The parties listed in vv. 5–6 represent all the most powerful players in the Jewish religious establishment. They made **Peter**

the name of Jesus Christ of Nazareth, whom you crucified and whom God raised from the dead — by him this man is standing here before you healthy. [11] This Jesus is

the stone rejected by you builders, which has become the cornerstone.[A]

[12] There is salvation in no one else, for there is no other name under heaven given to people by which we must be saved."

The Boldness of the Disciples

[13] When they observed the boldness of Peter and John and realized that they were uneducated and untrained men, they were amazed and recognized that they had been with Jesus. [14] And since they saw the man who had been healed standing with them, they had nothing to say in opposition. [15] After they ordered them to leave the Sanhedrin, they conferred among themselves, [16] saying, "What should we do with these men? For an obvious sign has been done through them, clear to everyone living in Jerusalem, and we cannot deny it. [17] But so that this does not spread any further among the people, let's threaten them against speaking to anyone in this name again." [18] So they called for them and ordered them not to speak or teach at all in the name of Jesus.

[19] Peter and John answered them, "Whether it's right in the sight of God for us to listen to you rather than to God, you decide; [20] for we are unable to stop speaking about what we have seen and heard."

[21] After threatening them further, they released them. They found no way to punish them because the people were all giving glory to God over what had been done. [22] For this sign of healing had been performed on a man over forty years old.

Prayer for Boldness

[23] After they were released, they went to their own people and reported everything the chief priests and the elders had said to them. [24] When they heard this, they raised their voices together to God and said, "Master, you are the one who made the heaven, the earth, and the sea, and everything in them. [25] You said through the Holy Spirit, by the mouth of our father David your servant:[B]

Why do the Gentiles rage
and the peoples plot futile things?
[26] The kings of the earth
take their stand
and the rulers assemble together
against the Lord and
against his Messiah.[C]

[27] "For, in fact, in this city both Herod and Pontius Pilate, with the Gentiles and the people of Israel, assembled together against your holy servant Jesus, whom you anointed, [28] to do whatever your hand and your will had predestined to take place. [29] And now, Lord, consider their threats, and grant that your servants may speak your word with all boldness, [30] while you stretch out your hand for healing, and signs and wonders are performed through the name of your holy servant Jesus." [31] When they had prayed, the place where they were assembled was shaken, and they were all filled with the Holy Spirit and began to speak the word of God boldly.

All Things in Common

[32] Now the entire group of those who believed were of one heart and mind, and no one claimed that any of his possessions was his own, but instead they held everything in common. [33] With great power the apostles were giving testimony to the resurrection of the Lord Jesus, and great grace was on all of them. [34] For there was not a needy person among them because all those who owned lands or houses sold them, brought the proceeds of what was sold, [35] and laid them at the apostles' feet. This was then distributed to each person as any had need.

[36] Joseph, a Levite from Cyprus by birth, the one the apostles called Barnabas (which is translated Son of Encouragement), [37] sold a field he owned, brought the money, and laid it at the apostles' feet.

Lying to the Holy Spirit

5 But a man named Ananias, with his wife Sapphira, sold a piece of property. [2] However, he kept back part of the proceeds with his wife's knowledge, and brought a portion of it and laid it at the apostles' feet.

[A]4:11 Ps 118:22 [B]4:25 Other mss read *through the mouth of David your servant* [C]4:25–26 Ps 2:1–2

---

and **John stand before them,** two men against all the powers of Israel. On **Annas** and **Caiaphas,** see the notes on Mt 26:3; Lk 3:2–3; Jn 18:13.
4:11 Peter again identified Jesus with OT testimony by citing Ps 118:22. Though Jesus was a **stone rejected** by the Jewish leaders, God made him **the cornerstone** (foundation) of the church.
4:12 Peter concluded by making clear the uncompromising claim of Christianity: There is **salvation in no one else** besides Jesus. This message rings throughout the NT. Jesus

himself said, "No one comes to the Father except through me" (Jn 14:6).
4:13–15 The word for **boldness** also refers to freedom of speech and could relate to articulateness.
4:24–28 When Peter and John told the members of their fellowship what had happened, they all recognized this persecution as fulfillment of Ps 2:1–2. **Gentiles and the people of Israel** had united in opposition to God's **holy servant Jesus** and his followers.
4:30 Besides boldness in testifying, the early Christians expected to receive power from

God to perform **healing, and signs and wonders** through the **name of . . . Jesus.**
4:31 Their prayer was answered immediately.
4:32–35 As long as there was complete unanimity of purpose and intention among them, the early Christians shared their **possessions** freely, such that **there was not a needy person among them.**
4:36–37 Joseph (aka **Barnabas**) led by example, selling his **field** and donating all the proceeds to the church. Such charitable acts inspired others to do good but also incited some to seek acclaim.

▼ Spirit-led Giving

ACTS OF GIVING	THE RESULTS	CHARACTERISTICS OF SPIRIT-LED GIVING
The believers held everything in common, so they sold possessions and property and distributed the proceeds to those among them in need (Ac 2:44–45; 4:32).	There was not a needy person among them; each person's basic needs were met (Ac 4:34–35).	**In love**, Jesus laid down his life for us, so we should lay down our lives for our brothers and sisters in Christ and take care of their needs (1Jn 3:16–17).
Peter and John did not have silver or gold to give but gave to a lame man what they did have and healed him in the name of Jesus Christ (Ac 3:1–7).	The lame man jumped up and entered the temple—walking, leaping, and praising God—giving Peter an opportunity to preach Christ to the gathering crowd (Ac 3:8–26).	Whatever you do, in word or in deed, **do everything in the name of the Lord Jesus**, giving thanks to God the Father through him (Col 3:17).
Joseph, also called Barnabas, sold a field he owned and brought the money and laid it at the apostles' feet (Ac 4:36–37).	Barnabas set an example of Spirit-led giving for the early church and all readers of the book of Acts.	Each person should do as he has decided in his heart, not out of reluctance or necessity, for God loves a **cheerful** giver (2Co 9:7).
Ananias and Sapphira sold a piece of property and laid the proceeds at the apostles' feet as if it were all of it, but secretly they kept back part of the money for themselves. (Acts 5:1–2)	They lied to God in testing the Holy Spirit and dropped dead for their deceit; great fear came on the whole church and on all who heard about these things (Ac 5:3–11).	We must not love only in word or speech but in **action** and **truth** (1Jn 3:18).
Simon the Samaritan saw Peter and John lay hands on the Samaritan believers and their receiving the Holy Spirit, so he offered money in order to obtain this power for himself (Ac 8:18–19).	Peter rebuked Simon, saying one cannot obtain the gift of God with money; he commanded Simon to repent of his wickedness and to pray to the Lord for forgiveness (Ac 8:20–24).	Salvation and the Holy Spirit are gifts from God that cannot be bought and sold—**freely you have received; freely give** (Mt 10:8; 1Co 2:12).
A prophesied famine throughout the Roman world prompted the Jewish and Gentile Christians in Antioch to send relief to the brothers and sisters in Judea, each giving according to his ability (Ac 11:27–29).	Barnabas and Saul (Paul) were sent from Antioch with the gift to the elders of the Jerusalem church, highlighting the unity of the church across geographical and ethnic lines (Ac 11:30).	Our giving should **testify to our faith in Christ** so that God will be glorified and the church will be unified (2Co 9:12–14).
After Lydia and the Philippian jailer each believed in the Lord, they welcomed Paul and Silas into their homes to care and provide for them (Ac 16:13–15, 25–34).	Lydia's house appears to have become a meeting place for the church in Philippi (Ac 16:40).	**Share with the saints in their needs** and pursue hospitality (Rm 12:13).
Paul was a tentmaker by trade, which provided for his own needs and the needs of his missionary partners and prevented him from becoming a burden to others as he shared the gospel (Ac 18:1–4; 20:33–34).	Paul demonstrated the necessity of helping the weak by the work of one's hands and illustrated the truth of Jesus's words: "It is more blessed to give than to receive" (Ac 20:35).	**Work with your own hands** so you are not dependent upon anyone and have something to share with those in need; in this way you will be **a godly example in the presence of unbelievers** (Eph 4:28; 1Th 4:11–12).

3 "Ananias," Peter asked, "why has Satan filled your heart to lie to the Holy Spirit and keep back part of the proceeds of the land? **4** Wasn't it yours while you possessed it? And after it was sold, wasn't it at your disposal? Why is it that you planned this thing in your heart? You have not lied to people but to God." **5** When he heard these words, Ananias dropped dead, and a great fear came on all who heard. **6** The young men got up, wrapped his body, carried him out, and buried him.

7 About three hours later, his wife came in, not knowing what had happened. **8** "Tell me," Peter asked her, "did you sell the land for this price?"

"Yes," she said, "for that price."

9 Then Peter said to her, "Why did you agree to test the Spirit of the Lord? Look, the feet of those who have buried your husband are at the door, and they will carry you out." **10** Instantly she dropped dead at his feet. When the young men came in, they found her dead, carried her out, and buried her beside her husband. **11** Then great fear came on the whole church and on all who heard these things.

Apostolic Signs and Wonders

12 Many signs and wonders were being done among the people through the hands of the apostles. They were all together in Solomon's Colonnade. **13** No one else dared to join them, but the people spoke well of them. **14** Believers were added to the Lord in increasing numbers — multitudes of both men and women. **15** As a result, they would carry the sick out into the streets and lay them on cots and mats so that when Peter came by, at least his shadow might fall on some of them. **16** In addition, a multitude came together from the towns surrounding Jerusalem, bringing the sick and those who were tormented by unclean spirits, and they were all healed.

In and out of Prison

17 Then the high priest rose up. He and all who were with him, who belonged to the party of the Sadducees, were filled with jealousy. **18** So they arrested the apostles and put them in the public jail. **19** But an angel of the Lord opened the doors of the jail during the night, brought them out, and said, **20** "Go and stand in the temple, and tell the people all about this life." **21** Hearing this, they entered the temple at daybreak and began to teach.

The Apostles on Trial Again

When the high priest and those who were with him arrived, they convened the Sanhedrin — the full council of the Israelites — and sent orders to the jail to have them brought. **22** But when the servants^A got there, they did not find them in the jail; so they returned and reported, **23** "We found the jail securely locked, with the guards standing in front of the doors, but when we opened them, we found no one inside." **24** As^B the captain of the temple police and the chief priests heard these things, they were baffled about them, wondering what would come of this.

25 Someone came and reported to them, "Look! The men you put in jail are standing in the temple and teaching the people." **26** Then the commander went with the servants and brought them in without force, because they were afraid the people might stone them. **27** After they brought them in, they had them stand before the Sanhedrin, and the high priest asked, **28** "Didn't we strictly order you not to teach in this name? Look, you have filled Jerusalem with your teaching and are determined to make us guilty of this man's blood."

29 Peter and the apostles replied, "We must obey God rather than people. **30** The God of our ancestors raised up Jesus, whom you had murdered by hanging him on a tree. **31** God exalted

---

^5:22 Or *temple police,* or *officers,* also in v. 26   ^5:24 Other mss add *the high priest and*

#68 99 Essential Christian Truths

DISCIPLESHIP

Discipleship is a process that takes place both formally and informally to effect spiritual maturity as people follow Jesus. Informal discipleship, as passages like Deuteronomy 6:4–9 suggest, happens everywhere, in every arena of life. Growing in our faith and deepening our walk with Christ is something that requires our whole life, not just the mind. Formal discipleship refers to periods of instruction. We make disciples through our words and actions, providing verbal instruction from God's Word and non-verbal examples through our lives (Ac 20:17–24).

5:3–4 Ananias and Sapphira assumed they were merely lying to men (the apostles), but in reality they had lied to the **Holy Spirit** who is ever-present in the church. Peter's wording indicates that the Holy Spirit is God. Peter's question (**wasn't it at your disposal?**) implies that Ananias and Sapphira would have been justified to sell the land and give only a portion to the church. Their sin lay in their deception and their desire to win praise.
5:11 On **fear** as a response to the workings of God, see v. 5; 2:43; 9:31; 19:17.
5:13–14 There is an apparent contradiction between these two verses. It seems that prior to the incident with Ananias and Sapphira many nonbelievers had been attracted to the Christian group because of the signs and wonders. That was now no longer the case. Nevertheless, many genuine believers were still joining them.

5:15–16 The people came to believe that there was something magical about **Peter** and that even his **shadow** would be enough to heal them.
5:19–20 Having been arrested again for their ministry in Jesus's name (v. 18), the apostles were set free by **an angel of the Lord** in such a way that aroused no attention. See 12:6–10 and note there for a similar episode.
5:21b–24 The Sanhedrin convened in the morning, intent on taking decisive action to halt the growth of the Christian faith. That the **servants** found **the jail securely locked** and the **guards** standing duty proves that the jailbreak was both miraculous and secretive.
5:29 Christians should obey the law of the land, but when human law conflicts with God's law, we must **obey God rather than people.**

this man to his right hand as ruler and Savior, to give repentance to Israel and forgiveness of sins. [32] We are witnesses of these things, and so is the Holy Spirit whom God has given to those who obey him."

Gamaliel's Advice

[33] When they heard this, they were enraged and wanted to kill them. [34] But a Pharisee named Gamaliel, a teacher of the law who was respected by all the people, stood up in the Sanhedrin and ordered the men[A] to be taken outside for a little while. [35] He said to them, "Men of Israel, be careful about what you're about to do to these men. [36] Some time ago Theudas rose up, claiming to be somebody, and a group of about four hundred men rallied to him. He was killed, and all his followers were dispersed and came to nothing. [37] After this man, Judas the Galilean rose up in the days of the census and attracted a following. He also perished, and all his followers were scattered. [38] So in the present case, I tell you, stay away from these men and leave them alone. For if this plan or this work is of human origin, it will fail; [39] but if it is of God, you will not be able to overthrow them. You may even be found fighting against God." They were persuaded by him. [40] After they called in the apostles and had them flogged, they ordered them not to speak in the name of Jesus and released them. [41] Then they went out from the presence of the Sanhedrin, rejoicing that they were counted worthy to be treated shamefully on behalf of the Name.[B] [42] Every day in the temple, and in various homes, they continued teaching and proclaiming the good news that Jesus is the Messiah.

Seven Chosen to Serve

6 In those days, as the disciples were increasing in number, there arose a complaint by the Hellenistic Jews against the Hebraic Jews that their widows were being overlooked in the daily distribution. [2] The Twelve summoned the whole company of the disciples and said, "It would not be right for us to give up preaching the word of God to wait on tables. [3] Brothers and sisters, select from among you seven men of good reputation, full of the Spirit and wisdom, whom we can appoint to this duty. [4] But we will devote ourselves to prayer and to the ministry of the word." [5] This proposal pleased the whole company. So they chose Stephen, a man full of faith and the Holy Spirit, and Philip, Prochorus, Nicanor, Timon, Parmenas, and Nicolaus, a convert from Antioch. [6] They had them stand before the apostles, who prayed and laid their hands on them.

[7] So the word of God spread, the disciples in Jerusalem increased greatly in number, and a large group of priests became obedient to the faith.

Stephen Accused of Blasphemy

[8] Now Stephen, full of grace and power, was performing great wonders and signs among the people. [9] Opposition arose, however, from some members of the Freedmen's Synagogue, composed of both Cyrenians and Alexandrians, and some from Cilicia and Asia, and they began to argue with Stephen. [10] But they were unable to stand up against his wisdom and the Spirit by whom he was speaking. [11] Then they secretly persuaded some men to say, "We heard him speaking blasphemous words against Moses and God." [12] They stirred

---

A [5:34] Other mss read apostles   B [5:41] Other mss add of Jesus, or of Christ

---

5:33–34 If the Jewish leaders had been willing to kill Jesus, much more were they prepared to **kill** the apostles, whose stubborn testimony was serving to prolong the Jesus controversy. But **Gamaliel** wisely cooled their rage. This was Gamaliel I, the teacher of Paul the apostle (22:3). It is uncertain whether he was the successor to the great rabbinic teacher Hillel or whether he founded his own school. In either case, he became a major rabbinic teacher. His conciliatory stance toward the apostles is consistent with what is known of his temperate attitude elsewhere. **5:35–36** Josephus, the Jewish historian, reported that many revolts against Roman rule occurred during the time of Jesus—some of them even having messianic overtones. **5:37 Judas the Galilean**, or Judas of Gamala, rebelled against the census that Quirinius took in AD 6. He was mentioned by Josephus as teaching that the Israelites were not to give tribute to pagan rulers. His revolt ended in defeat. **6:1** The distinction between **Hellenistic** and **Hebraic Jews** probably refers to their respective languages. Many Jews whose primary language was Greek were converted

to Christianity (e.g., Paul, Ac 9; see note at 22:3). Needy Hellenistic believers felt they had been neglected in the early church's charity **distribution**. The existing church structure proved unable to meet the growing demands. It was time for change. **6:2–4** The distinction between those responsible for **preaching** and those responsible for distribution of food marks the beginning of functional distinction of roles and responsibilities in the early church. The apostles (**the Twelve**) believed **prayer** and preaching were their primary duties. It is not that other roles were unimportant. In fact, the high requirements (**good reputation, full of the Spirit and wisdom**) that had to be met by the **seven men** who would take over the **duty** of food distribution signals the importance of all roles in Christian service. **6:5–6 Stephen** and six others (their Greek names probably identify them as Hellenistic believers) were selected. They were set apart for service by prayer and the laying on of **hands** by the apostles. The laying on of hands occurs in several contexts in Acts (8:17; 13:3; 19:6). Here, as in 13:3, it indicated the church's recognition that God had called these people

to a particular ministry. The ministry of **Philip** is highlighted in 8:4–13,26–40. **6:7** Luke did not specify who the **priests** were, but they were probably those who performed duties in connection with worship at the temple. This put them in a good position to hear the apostles preach on a regular basis. **6:8** A mark of the authenticity of Stephen's work is that it was distinguished by **great wonders and signs**. God often affirmed the apostolic message in this way (5:12). **6:9–10** Though Jews from several different backgrounds **began to argue with Stephen**, he swept them aside by use of his human intellectual gifts (**wisdom**) and divine empowerment (**the Spirit**). **6:11** Stephen's supposedly **blasphemous words** on this occasion were probably similar to his speech in Ac 7, which emphasized Israel's disobedience and the fulfillment of the OT in the ministry of Jesus, including his replacing the temple and the law. **6:12** Like the apostles before him, especially Peter and John, Stephen was taken before the **Sanhedrin** after those from the synagogues were unable to stand against him.

up the people, the elders, and the scribes; so they came, seized him, and took him to the Sanhedrin. [13] They also presented false witnesses who said, "This man never stops speaking against this holy place and the law. [14] For we heard him say that this Jesus of Nazareth will destroy this place and change the customs that Moses handed down to us." [15] And all who were sitting in the Sanhedrin looked intently at him and saw that his face was like the face of an angel.

Stephen's Sermon

7 "Are these things true?" the high priest asked.

[2] "Brothers and fathers," he replied, "listen: The God of glory appeared to our father Abraham when he was in Mesopotamia, before he settled in Haran, [3] and said to him: **Leave your country and relatives, and come to the land that I will show you.**[A]

[4] "Then he left the land of the Chaldeans and settled in Haran. From there, after his father died, God had him move to this land in which you are now living. [5] He didn't give him an inheritance in it — not even a foot of ground — but he promised to give it to him as a possession, and to his descendants after him, even though he was childless. [6] God spoke in this way: His **descendants** would **be strangers in a foreign country, and they** would **enslave and oppress them for four hundred years.** [7] I will judge the nation that they will serve as slaves, God said. After this, they will come out and worship me in this place.**[B]** [8] And so he gave Abraham the covenant of circumcision. After this, he fathered Isaac and circumcised him on the eighth day. Isaac became the father of Jacob, and Jacob became the father of the twelve patriarchs.

The Patriarchs in Egypt

[9] "The patriarchs became jealous of Joseph and sold him into Egypt, but God was with him [10] and rescued him out of all his troubles. He gave him favor and wisdom in the sight of Pharaoh, king of Egypt, who appointed him ruler over Egypt and over his whole

household. [11] Now a famine and great suffering came over all of Egypt and Canaan, and our ancestors could find no food. [12] When Jacob heard there was grain in Egypt, he sent our ancestors there the first time. [13] The second time, Joseph revealed himself to his brothers, and Joseph's family became known to Pharaoh. [14] Joseph invited his father Jacob and all his relatives, seventy-five people in all, [15] and Jacob went down to Egypt. He and our ancestors died there, [16] were carried back to Shechem, and were placed in the tomb that Abraham had bought for a sum of silver from the sons of Hamor in Shechem.

Moses, a Rejected Savior

[17] "As the time was approaching to fulfill the promise that God had made to Abraham, the people flourished and multiplied in Egypt [18] until a different king who did not know Joseph ruled over Egypt.[C] [19] He dealt deceitfully with our race and oppressed our ancestors by making them abandon their infants outside so that they wouldn't survive. [20] At this time Moses was born, and he was beautiful in God's sight. He was cared for in his father's home for three months. [21] When he was put outside, Pharaoh's daughter adopted and raised him as her own son. [22] So Moses was educated in all the wisdom of the Egyptians and was powerful in his speech and actions.

[23] "When he was forty years old, he decided to visit his own people, the Israelites. [24] When he saw one of them being mistreated, he came to his rescue and avenged the oppressed man by striking down the Egyptian. [25] He assumed his people would understand that God would give them deliverance through him, but they did not understand. [26] The next day he showed up while they were fighting and tried to reconcile them peacefully, saying, 'Men, you are brothers. Why are you mistreating each other?'

[27] "But the one who was mistreating his neighbor pushed Moses aside, saying: **Who appointed you a ruler and a judge over us?** [28] **Do you want to kill me, the same way you killed the Egyptian yesterday?**[D]

---

^7:3 Gn 12:1   ^7:6–7 Gn 15:13–14   ^7:18 Other mss omit *over Egypt*   ^7:27–28 Ex 2:14

6:13 The fact that Stephen had not actually spoken against the **holy place and the law** is confirmed by the fact that **false witnesses** were produced to sustain the charges against him.
7:2 Although the context of Gn 12:1 is **Haran** rather than Ur, Gn 15:7 implies that God called Abram out of Ur.
7:3–4 Stephen cited Gn 12:1, in which God directed Abraham to leave his home in Haran and go to the **land** that God would give him.
7:5 Although Abraham had no children at the time, God promised to give his **descendants** land **as a possession**. Thus it was

fundamentally on an act of trust (faith) that the nation of Israel had its beginning.
7:6–7 Stephen recalled Gn 15:13–14, where God foretold Abraham that his descendants would be enslaved **in a foreign country** (Egypt) before they would **come out and worship** in the promised land. Thus God's promise of blessing came with an equally sure promise of suffering.
7:8 The term **patriarchs** does not occur in Greek literature. This may be its first use.
7:9–16 Stephen explains how Israel came to be in Egypt.
7:17–19 Without the oppression, Israel might have remained in Egypt.

7:20–22 Moses, though born to Jewish parents, was reared by Pharaoh's daughter and **educated in all the wisdom** of the Egyptians, becoming powerful in **his speech and actions**. When God called Moses (Ex 3:1–4:17), it was as if a non-Hebrew became a follower of the Hebrew God.
7:23,30 Moses's life is divided into three periods of **forty years** each—forty in Egypt, forty in Midian, and forty in the wilderness.
7:24–28 The Israelites initially questioned Moses as their **ruler** (Ex 2:14). They had been wrong about Moses. Might they have been wrong about Jesus too?

29 "When he heard this, Moses fled and became an exile in the land of Midian, where he became the father of two sons. **30** After forty years had passed, an angel[A] appeared to him in the wilderness of Mount Sinai, in the flame of a burning bush. **31** When Moses saw it, he was amazed at the sight. As he was approaching to look at it, the voice of the Lord came: **32** I am the God of your ancestors — the God of Abraham, of Isaac, and of Jacob.[B] Moses began to tremble and did not dare to look.

33 "The Lord said to him: Take off the sandals from your feet, because the place where you are standing is holy ground. **34** I have certainly seen the oppression of my people in Egypt; I have heard their groaning and have come down to set them free. And now, come, I will send you to Egypt.[C]

35 "This Moses, whom they rejected when they said, Who appointed you a ruler and a judge?[D] — this one God sent as a ruler and a deliverer through the angel who appeared to him in the bush. **36** This man led them out and performed wonders and signs in the land of Egypt, at the Red Sea, and in the wilderness for forty years.

Israel's Rebellion against God

37 "This is the Moses who said to the Israelites: God[E] will raise up for you a prophet like me from among your brothers.[F] **38** He is the one who was in the assembly in the wilderness, with the angel who spoke to him on Mount Sinai, and with our ancestors. He received living oracles to give to us. **39** Our ancestors were unwilling to obey him. Instead, they pushed him aside, and in their hearts turned back to Egypt. **40** They told Aaron: Make us gods who will go before us. As for this Moses who brought us out of the land of Egypt, we don't know what's happened to him.[G] **41** They even made a calf in those days, offered sacrifice to the idol, and were celebrating what their hands had made. **42** God turned away and gave them up to worship the stars of heaven, as it is written in the book of the prophets:

House of Israel, did you bring me
    offerings and sacrifices
for forty years in the wilderness?
43 You took up the tent of Moloch
    and the star of your god Rephan,
    the images that you made to worship.
So I will send you into exile
    beyond Babylon.[H]

God's Real Tabernacle

44 "Our ancestors had the tabernacle of the testimony in the wilderness, just as he who spoke to Moses commanded him to make it according to the pattern he had seen. **45** Our ancestors in turn received it and with Joshua brought it in when they dispossessed the nations that God drove out before them, until the days of David. **46** He found favor in God's sight and asked that he might provide a dwelling place for the God[I] of Jacob. **47** It was Solomon, rather, who built him a house, **48** but the Most High does not dwell in sanctuaries made with hands, as the prophet says:

49 Heaven is my throne,
    and the earth my footstool.
What sort of house will you build
    for me?
says the Lord,
    or what will be my resting place?
50 Did not my hand make all
    these things?[J]

Resisting the Holy Spirit

51 "You stiff-necked people with uncircumcised hearts and ears! You are always resisting the Holy Spirit. As your ancestors did, you do also. **52** Which of the prophets did your ancestors not persecute? They even killed those who foretold the coming of the Righteous One, whose betrayers and murderers you have now become. **53** You received the law under the direction of angels and yet have not kept it."

The First Christian Martyr

54 When they heard these things, they were enraged[K] and gnashed their teeth at him. **55** Stephen, full of the Holy Spirit, gazed into heaven.

[A]7:30 Other mss add *of the Lord* [B]7:32 Ex 3:6,15 [C]7:33–34 Ex 3:5,7–8,10 [D]7:35 Ex 2:14 [E]7:37 Other mss read *The Lord your God* [F]7:37 Dt 18:15 [G]7:40 Ex 32:1,23 [H]7:42–43 Am 5:25–27 [I]7:46 Other mss read *house* [J]7:49–50 Is 66:1–2 [K]7:54 Or *were cut to the quick*

7:35–36 On **the angel**, see note on v. 53. **7:37–38** The **living oracles** to which Stephen referred were the Ten Commandments given by God to Moses for his people. **7:39–40** Though God accompanied the Hebrews in highly visible, powerful ways during their journey out from Egypt, they defied him and asked Aaron to **make . . . gods** for them (Ex 32:1). **7:41–43** Stephen's citation of Am 5:25–27 was perhaps intended to convey that just as the Hebrews rejected God in the desert, suffering exile and spiritual estrangement as a consequence, so too contemporary Israel was inviting similar consequences by rejecting Jesus.

7:51 The descriptors Stephen used to condemn Israel for unbelief and disobedience (**stiff-necked people with uncircumcised hearts and ears**) were commonly used by OT prophets (Lv 26:41; Jr 4:4; 6:10; 9:26; Ezk 44:7,9). This language was also adopted by Paul (Rm 2; Gl 5). Possibly Paul was influenced by Stephen's speech since he was present (Ac 7:58; 8:1), but the OT was the more obvious influence. **7:52** Stephen's words would either raise the ire of his audience or break their hearts, leading to repentance. The OT prophets had delivered messages similar to his own, and **your ancestors**, Stephen said, persecuted and killed them. Worse, his audience had

made themselves the **betrayers and murderers** of the **Righteous One** whom God promised through the prophets. **7:53** Even though the OT does not explicitly state that the **law** was given by **angels**, Stephen, Paul (Gl 3:19), and the author of Hebrews (Heb 2:2) stated that angels were involved in the process of lawgiving. This likely implied that the law was especially important since God entrusted its deliverance to angels. **7:54** Stephen's audience expressed displeasure both inwardly (**enraged**) and outwardly (**gnashed their teeth at him**). **7:55** Stephen was a stark contrast to his audience. They were fuming with rage, but he

◄ Christ as Prophet

A Prophet: Called by God, led by the Spirit of Christ, to deliver the word of the Lord to the people through words and sometimes deeds (Dt 18:15–19; Lk 24:19; 1Pt 1:10–12).

WHO WAS AN OLD TESTAMENT PROPHET?

WORDS

- Proclaimed the word of the Lord
- Recorded the word of the Lord
- Condemned sin
- Warned people of judgment
- Called people to repentance
- Proclaimed good news
- Interpreted present events
- Foretold future events

DEEDS

- Performed miracles (healings; even raised the dead)
- Acted out a prophetic message

WHO WERE SOME OF THE PROPHETS?

- **Abraham** (Gn 20:7)
- **Moses** (Dt 18:15–19; 34:10; Ac 7:37)
- **Samuel** (1Sm; Ac 13:20)
- **David** (Pss; Ac 2:29–30)
- **Nathan** (2Sm 7; 11–12; 1Kg 1)
- **Elijah** (1Kg 18:1; Lk 4:25–26)
- **Elisha** (2Kg 2:13–15; Lk 4:27)
- **Jonah** (2Kg 14:25; Jnh 1:1; Mt 12:39)
- **Isaiah** (2Kg 19:20; Is 1:1; Mt 3:3)
- **Jeremiah** (2Ch 36; Jr 1:1–2; Mt 2:17)
- **Ezekiel** (Ezk 1:1–3)
- **Zechariah** (Ezr 6:14; Zch 1:1; Mt 21:4)
- **Haggai** (Ezr 6:14; Hg 1:1)
- **Daniel** (Dn 1:17; Mt 24:15)
- **Hosea** (Hs 1:1; Mt 2:15)
- **Joel** (Jl 1:1; Ac 2:16)
- **Amos** (Am 1:1–3; Ac 7:42)
- **Obadiah** (Ob 1)
- **Micah** (Mc 1:1; Mt 2:5)
- **Nahum** (Nah 1:1)
- **Habakkuk** (Hab 1:1; Ac 13:40)
- **Zephaniah** (Zph 1:1)
- **Malachi** (Mal 1:1; Mt 11:10)

HOW WERE THE LORD'S PROPHETS CONFIRMED?

- Their message in the name of the Lord came true.
- They did not lead the people to worship other gods.

HOW WERE THE PROPHETS TREATED?

- Some enjoyed places of prominence and honor.
  - Moses was mourned at his death.
  - Nathan was an established prophet in David's kingdom.
  - Daniel was elevated in the Babylonian and Medo-Persian Empires.
- All were persecuted in one way or another.
  - Moses was routinely blamed for the people's wandering.
  - Elijah was threatened with death.
  - Jeremiah was imprisoned.
  - Zechariah was stoned to death.

HOW WAS JESUS A PROPHET?

WORDS

- His message: "Repent, because the kingdom of heaven has come near" *(Mt 4:17).*
- He preached the good news *(Mt 4:23)*
- He taught with authority: "But I tell you . . ." *(Mt 5:22,28; 7:29).*

DEEDS

- He healed disease and sickness *(Mt 4:23–24).*
- He raised the dead *(Lk 7:16; Jn 11:1–44).*
- He told the truth of the Samaritan woman's marital history *(Jn 4:16–19).*
- He fed the five thousand from five loaves of bread and two fish *(Jn 6:11–14).*
- He healed the blind *(Jn 9:17).*

WHAT PROPHECIES DID JESUS MAKE?

- His suffering, crucifixion, and resurrection *(Mk 8:31; 9:31; 10:33–34; Jn 2:18–22)*
- His raising Lazarus from the dead *(Jn 11:1–4)*

- The destruction of the temple in Jerusalem *(Mt 24:1–2)*
- Peter's denials of Jesus *(Mk 14:30)*
- His second coming *(Jn 14:1–3)*

HOW WAS JESUS TREATED?

- Some viewed him positively as a prophet of God.
  - Some thought he was one of the prophets *(Mt 16:13–14).*
  - Because of his teaching, some thought he was the Prophet *(Jn 7:40).*
  - The crowds at Jerusalem called him a prophet at his triumphal entry *(Mt 21:11).*
  - The Pharisees were afraid to arrest Jesus because the crowds believed him to be a prophet *(Mt 21:45–46).*
  - The disciples on the road to Emmaus described him as a prophet powerful in word and deed *(Lk 24:19).*

- Others persecuted him as a prophet of God.
  - His hometown was offended by him and refused to honor him *(Mt 13:53–58).*
  - The world hated him because he revealed the Father by his works *(Jn 15:18–25).*
  - The Pharisees denied he was a prophet *(Jn 7:52).*
  - The Sanhedrin took false testimony against him *(Mt 26:59–61).*
  - The Jews beat him and mocked him as a prophet *(Lk 22:63–65).*
  - His enemies crucified him *(Jn 19:17–30).*

HOW IS JESUS THE PROPHET?

- Jesus is the Word who was with God, was God, and became flesh *(Jn 1:1–14).*
- The law was given through Moses; grace and truth through Jesus Christ *(Jn 1:17).*
- "You have heard that it was said" in the law through Moses; "But I tell you" as Jesus gave the spirit of the law *(Mt 5).*
- God spoke through the prophets in the past, but in the last days he has spoken to us by his Son, who reveals God to us *(Heb 1:1–3).*

- "Moses and all the Prophets" testify to Jesus's coming, suffering, crucifixion, and resurrection *(Lk 24:26–27,44–45).*
- Moses wrote about Jesus *(Jn 5:45–47).*
- Moses had a fading glory reflecting God's presence; Jesus is God's glory *(2Co 3).*
- Jesus is the Prophet about whom Moses prophesied *(Ac 3:22).*

Long ago, inspired by the Holy Spirit, Moses prophesied of a Prophet to come, one like him to whom God's people should listen. This Prophet would speak God's words and perfectly obey him. The Lord would hold accountable those who did not listen to his Prophet *(Dt 18:15–19).* **Jesus** alone is the ultimate teacher and has the words of eternal life *(Jn 6:68).* He is also God's ultimate revelation of himself *(Heb 1:3).* He obeys God's Word; he speaks God's Word; he is God's Word. Jesus is God's Prophet calling us to repentance and faith so that we can be saved from our sins and live in peace with Almighty God.

He saw the glory of God, and Jesus standing at the right hand of God. [56] He said, "Look, I see the heavens opened and the Son of Man standing at the right hand of God!"

[57] They yelled at the top of their voices, covered their ears, and together rushed against him. [58] They dragged him out of the city and began to stone him. And the witnesses laid their garments at the feet of a young man named Saul. [59] While they were stoning Stephen, he called out, "Lord Jesus, receive my spirit!" [60] He knelt down and cried out with a loud voice, "Lord, do not hold this sin against them!" And after saying this, he fell asleep.

Saul the Persecutor

8 Saul agreed with putting him to death. On that day a severe persecution broke out against the church in Jerusalem, and all except the apostles were scattered throughout the land of Judea and Samaria. [2] Devout men buried Stephen and mourned deeply over him. [3] Saul, however, was ravaging the church. He would enter house after house, drag off men and women, and put them in prison.

Philip in Samaria

[4] So those who were scattered went on their way preaching the word. [5] Philip went down to a[a] city in Samaria and proclaimed the Messiah to them. [6] The crowds were all paying attention to what Philip said, as they listened and saw the signs he was performing. [7] For unclean spirits, crying out with a loud voice, came out of many who were possessed, and many who were paralyzed and lame were healed. [8] So there was great joy in that city.

The Response of Simon

[9] A man named Simon had previously practiced sorcery in that city and amazed the Samaritan people, while claiming to be somebody great. [10] They all paid attention to him, from the least of them to the greatest, and they said, "This man is called the Great Power of God."[b] [11] They were attentive to him because he had amazed them with his sorceries for a long time. [12] But when they believed Philip, as he proclaimed the good news about the kingdom of God and the name of Jesus Christ, both men and women were baptized. [13] Even Simon himself believed. And after he was baptized, he followed Philip everywhere and was amazed as he observed the signs and great miracles that were being performed.

Simon's Sin

[14] When the apostles who were at Jerusalem heard that Samaria had received the word of God, they sent Peter and John to them. [15] After they went down there, they prayed for them so that the Samaritans might receive the Holy Spirit because he had not yet come down on any of them. [16] (They had only been baptized in the name of the Lord Jesus.) [17] Then Peter and John laid their hands on them, and they received the Holy Spirit.

[18] When Simon saw that the Spirit[c] was given through the laying on of the apostles' hands, he offered them money, [19] saying, "Give me this power also so that anyone I lay hands on may receive the Holy Spirit."

[20] But Peter told him, "May your silver be destroyed with you, because you thought you could obtain the gift of God with money! [21] You have no part or share in this matter, because

---

[a]8:5 Other mss read the   [b]8:10 Or "This is the power of God called Great   [c]8:18 Other mss add Holy

---

was filled with the **Holy Spirit** and **gazed** peacefully into **heaven** even as he knew death was coming.
7:56–57 Son of Man was Jesus's favorite self-designation. Each use of this expression in the NT came from the lips of Jesus, except where others quoted his words back to him (Jn 12:34) and in this verse. Stephen's claim that Jesus was at God's right hand enraged the members of the Sanhedrin.
7:58 The Romans allowed the Jewish leaders to maintain the sanctity of the temple area but not to carry out the death penalty. In this instance, however, Stephen was killed illegally by an enraged mob. This is the first reference in Scripture to **Saul** (later called Paul). He "agreed" with the decision to stone Stephen (8:1).
7:59–60 Both of Stephen's requests are remarkable. His first, **Lord Jesus, receive my spirit,** proclaims that Jesus is Judge and Savior. Stephen's second request, that God **not hold this sin against** his executioners, illustrates the nonvindictive spirit of one who understands that his own sins have been forgiven by grace.
8:1 Events surrounding Stephen's testimony and murder led to **severe persecution** of

the church in Jerusalem. All believers **except the apostles** were **scattered** to nearby regions. Hence the persecution helped spread the gospel to surrounding areas such as **Judea** and **Samaria**. The facts that the apostles were not the focus of the persecution and that it came about after Stephen's death suggest that the persecution focused primarily on Hellenistic Jewish Christians, although the entire church was affected.
8:3 Paul, or **Saul,** seems to have become lead persecutor. His reputation as a destructive force in Jerusalem (**ravaging the church**), and possibly elsewhere, seems to have preceded him to Damascus (9:13).
8:4–5 Among those who scattered with the heightened persecution was **Philip,** who went to a **city in Samaria.** This territory near Judea was made up of those who had not left under the Assyrian exile and had intermarried with non-Jews. Jews generally looked down on Samaria; ministry here was a significant step for the church, for it indicated that old biases had no place in Christianity. For bias against the Samaritans among Jesus's own disciples, see Lk 9:51–55. For the antagonism between Jews and Samaritans, see Lk 10:29–37; Jn 4:9.

8:6–8 The **signs** that accompanied Philip's message about Jesus, including the casting out of **unclean spirits** and the healing of **many who were paralyzed and lame,** ensured that **the crowds were all paying attention.** God was vouching for Philip's preaching.
8:10–11 The term **Great Power of God** reflects pagan language.
8:12–13 The authenticity of Simon's belief is doubtful. He seems to have been fixated on the **signs** and **miracles** that accompanied Philip's preaching, not the person of Jesus Christ.
8:14–16 Some suggest that God withheld the Holy Spirit from **the Samaritans** so the apostles could come and witness that even the Samaritans were included in the Christian community.
8:18–19 Here we see Simon's true heart. He was used to impressing the crowds with magic; now he wanted to impress them with his ability to impart the **Holy Spirit.**
8:20–24 By saying that Simon had **no part or share in this matter,** Peter confirmed that Simon had not truly converted to Christianity. His heart (meaning his will, affections, allegiance) was still **not right before God.**

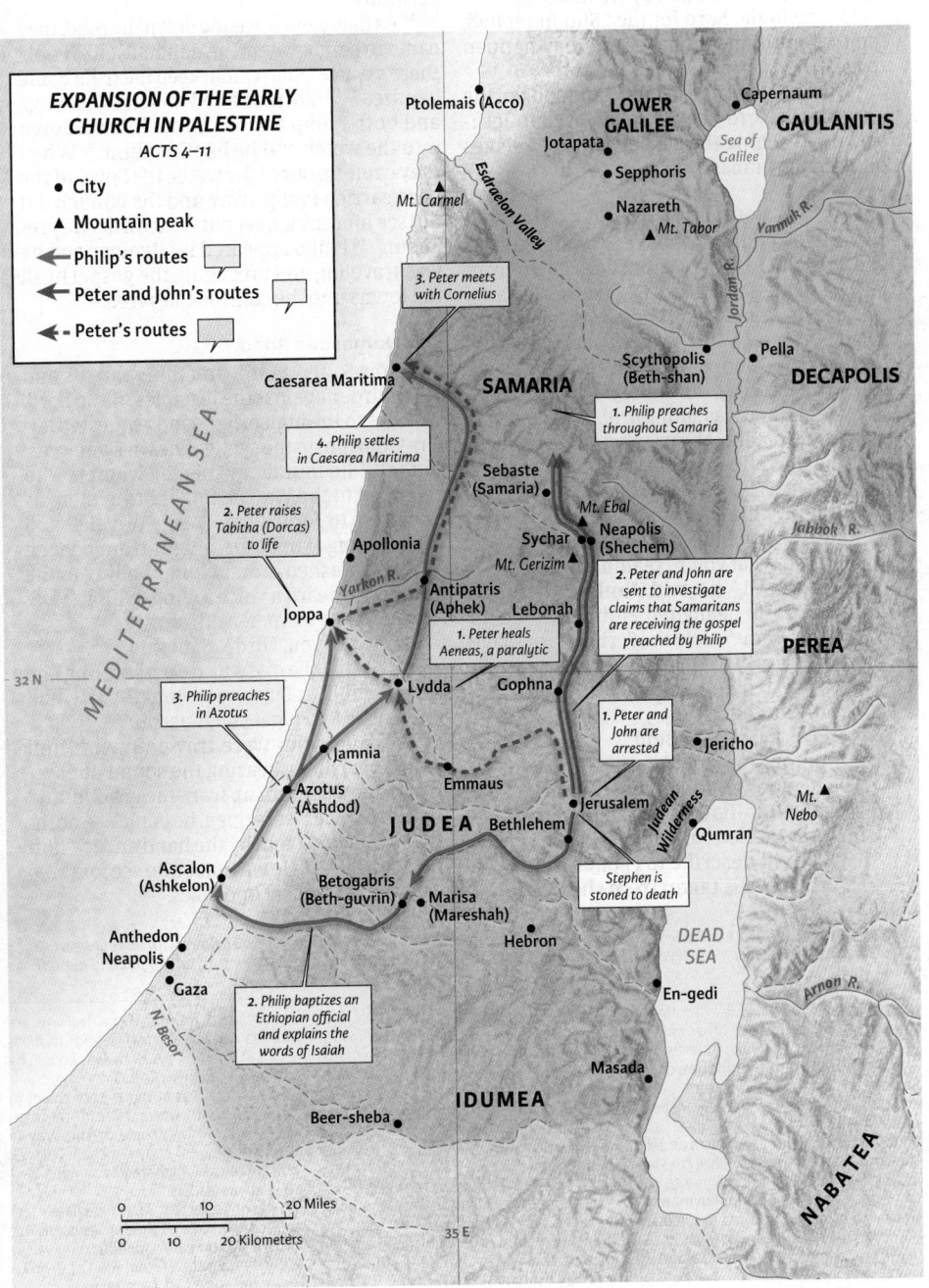

EXPANSION OF THE EARLY
CHURCH IN PALESTINE
ACTS 4–11

- ● City
- ▲ Mountain peak
- ← Philip's routes
- ← Peter and John's routes
- ←- Peter's routes

Ptolemais (Acco)

LOWER GALILEE

Capernaum

GAULANITIS

Jotapata

Sea of Galilee

● Sepphoris

Mt. Carmel

● Nazareth
▲ Mt. Tabor

Esdraelon Valley

Yarmuk R.

Jordan R.

3. Peter meets with Cornelius

Scythopolis (Beth-shan)

● Pella

DECAPOLIS

Caesarea Maritima

SAMARIA

1. Philip preaches throughout Samaria

4. Philip settles in Caesarea Maritima

Sebaste (Samaria) ●

Mt. Ebal

Neapolis (Shechem)

Jabbok R.

2. Peter raises Tabitha (Dorcas) to life

Apollonia

Sychar ●
Mt. Gerizim ▲

2. Peter and John are sent to investigate claims that Samaritans are receiving the gospel preached by Philip

PEREA

MEDITERRANEAN SEA

Yarkon R.

Antipatris (Aphek)

Lebonah

Joppa

1. Peter heals Aeneas, a paralytic

32 N

3. Philip preaches in Azotus

● Lydda

Gophna

1. Peter and John are arrested

● Jericho

Mt. ▲ Nebo

Jamnia

Emmaus

Jerusalem ●

Qumran

Judean Wilderness

Azotus (Ashdod)

JUDEA

Bethlehem

Stephen is stoned to death

DEAD SEA

Ascalon (Ashkelon) ●

Betogabris (Beth-guvrin) ●

● Marisa (Mareshah)

● Hebron

Anthedon
Neapolis ●

● Gaza

2. Philip baptizes an Ethiopian official and explains the words of Isaiah

● En-gedi

Arnon R.

N. Besor

● Masada

IDUMEA

NABATEA

Beer-sheba ●

0   10   20 Miles
0   10   20 Kilometers

35 E

your heart is not right before God. ²² Therefore repent of this wickedness of yours, and pray to the Lord that, if possible, your heart's intent may be forgiven. ²³ For I see you are poisoned by bitterness and bound by wickedness."

²⁴ "Pray to the Lord for me," Simon replied, "so that nothing you have said may happen to me."

²⁵ So, after they had testified and spoken the word of the Lord, they traveled back to Jerusalem, preaching the gospel in many villages of the Samaritans.

The Conversion of the Ethiopian Official

²⁶ An angel of the Lord spoke to Philip: "Get up and go south to the road that goes down from Jerusalem to Gaza." (This is the desert road.ᴬ) ²⁷ So he got up and went. There was an Ethiopian man, a eunuch and high official of Candace, queen of the Ethiopians, who was in charge of her entire treasury. He had come to worship in Jerusalem ²⁸ and was sitting in his chariot on his way home, reading the prophet Isaiah aloud. ²⁹ The Spirit told Philip, "Go and join that chariot."

³⁰ When Philip ran up to it, he heard him reading the prophet Isaiah, and said, "Do you understand what you're reading?"

³¹ "How can I," he said, "unless someone guides me?" So he invited Philip to come up and sit with him. ³² Now the Scripture passage he was reading was this:

> He was led like a sheep
>   to the slaughter,
> and as a lamb is silent
>   before its shearer,
> so he does not open his mouth.
> ³³   In his humiliation justice
>   was denied him.
> Who will describe his generation?
> For his life is taken from the earth.ᴮ

³⁴ The eunuch said to Philip, "I ask you, who is the prophet saying this about — himself or someone else?" ³⁵ Philip proceeded to tell him the good news about Jesus, beginning with that Scripture.

³⁶ As they were traveling down the road, they came to some water. The eunuch said, "Look, there's water. What would keep me from being baptized?"ᶜ ³⁸ So he ordered the chariot to stop, and both Philip and the eunuch went down into the water, and he baptized him. ³⁹ When they came up out of the water, the Spirit of the Lord carried Philip away, and the eunuch did not see him any longer but went on his way rejoicing. ⁴⁰ Philip appeared inᴰ Azotus,ᴱ and he was traveling and preaching the gospel in all the towns until he came to Caesarea.

The Damascus Road

9 Now Saul was still breathing threats and murder against the disciples of the Lord. He went to the high priest ² and requested letters from him to the synagogues in Damascus, so that if he found any men or women who belonged to the Way, he might bring them as prisoners to Jerusalem. ³ As he traveled and was nearing Damascus, a light from heaven suddenly flashed around him. ⁴ Falling to the ground, he heard a voice saying to him, "Saul, Saul, why are you persecuting me?"

⁵ "Who are you, Lord?" Saul said.

"I am Jesus, the one you are persecuting," he replied. ⁶ "But get up and go into the city, and you will be told what you must do."

⁷ The men who were traveling with him stood speechless, hearing the sound but seeing no one. ⁸ Saul got up from the ground, and though his eyes were open, he could see nothing. So they took him by the hand and led him into Damascus. ⁹ He was unable to see for three days and did not eat or drink.

ᴬ8:26 Or *is a desert place* ᴮ8:32–33 Is 53:7–8 ᶜ8:36 Some mss include v. 37: *Philip said, "If you believe with all your heart you may." And he replied, "I believe that Jesus Christ is the Son of God."* ᴰ8:40 Or *Philip was found at*, or *Philip found himself in* ᴱ8:40 Or *Ashdod*

8:25 After several episodes in Samaria, Peter, John, Philip, and any other apostles traveling with them returned to **Jerusalem**. They evangelized **many villages of the Samaritans** along the way, tearing down ethnic barriers with the global gospel of Jesus Christ.

8:26–29 Through the agency of **an angel of the Lord**, God arranged for Philip to stand in a place that would bring him into contact with an important **Ethiopian man** who would listen, believe, and in turn spread the gospel to other lands. **Candace** was not the queen's name but a title. Reading **aloud** was common, especially if the scroll was not in his native language. The **eunuch** was a Gentile God-fearer who **had come to worship in Jerusalem**. The Ethiopia of that time was not the modern country of Ethiopia but the ancient kingdom of Meroe, which covered what is now northern Sudan south of Aswan to Khartoum.

8:30–31 Philip's question and the Ethiopian's response imply that the OT passage the eunuch was reading (Is 53:7–8) required interpretation in light of what God had done in Jesus of Nazareth.

8:35 The phrase, **beginning with that Scripture**, may indicate that Philip went on to explain other relevant OT passages besides those in Isaiah.

8:38–40 The Ethiopian requested and was granted baptism just as soon as he believed (see note at 10:47–48). That they went **into the water** and then came **up out of the water** apparently indicates baptism by immersion. The Holy Spirit miraculously **carried Philip away** to his next appointment, a place called **Azotus**, the OT Philistine city of Ashdod, about thirty-five miles from Gaza.

9:1 The narrative returns to **Saul** (see 8:3), or Paul. His anger with Jesus's followers continued unabated, to the point that he was

threatening to **murder** them. Paul later acknowledged his zeal in persecuting Christians (Php 3:6), and this is how he was known by others (e.g., Ananias, Ac 9:13).

9:2 That Saul was authorized to travel to **Damascus** with warrants from the high priest to imprison people of **the Way** (a common name for early Christians; 19:9,23; 22:4) indicates his high standing among Jewish religious leaders.

9:5 It is doubtful that Saul immediately recognized the voice as that of Jesus. His use of **Lord** was probably honorific (equivalent to "sir") rather than recognition of divinity. Hence the voice said, **I am Jesus**.

9:7 This is the first of three accounts of Saul's conversion that appear in the book of Acts (22:6–11; 26:12–18). Here it appears that Saul's traveling companions heard a noise but did not recognize the words that were spoken. The comments, it seems, were intended only for Saul.

Saul's Baptism

¹⁰ There was a disciple in Damascus named Ananias, and the Lord said to him in a vision, "Ananias."

"Here I am, Lord," he replied.

¹¹ "Get up and go to the street called Straight," the Lord said to him, "to the house of Judas, and ask for a man from Tarsus named Saul, since he is praying there. ¹² In a vision[A] he has seen a man named Ananias coming in and placing his hands on him so that he may regain his sight."

¹³ "Lord," Ananias answered, "I have heard from many people about this man, how much harm he has done to your saints in Jerusalem. ¹⁴ And he has authority here from the chief priests to arrest all who call on your name."

¹⁵ But the Lord said to him, "Go, for this man is my chosen instrument to take my name to Gentiles, kings, and Israelites. ¹⁶ I will show him how much he must suffer for my name."

¹⁷ Ananias went and entered the house. He placed his hands on him and said, "Brother Saul, the Lord Jesus, who appeared to you on the road you were traveling, has sent me so that you may regain your sight and be filled with the Holy Spirit."

¹⁸ At once something like scales fell from his eyes, and he regained his sight. Then he got up and was baptized. ¹⁹ And after taking some food, he regained his strength.

Saul Proclaiming the Messiah

Saul was with the disciples in Damascus for some time. ²⁰ Immediately he began proclaiming Jesus in the synagogues: "He is the Son of God."

²¹ All who heard him were astounded and said, "Isn't this the man in Jerusalem who was causing havoc for those who called on this name and came here for the purpose of taking them as prisoners to the chief priests?"

²² But Saul grew stronger and kept confounding the Jews who lived in Damascus by proving that Jesus is the Messiah.

²³ After many days had passed, the Jews conspired to kill him, ²⁴ but Saul learned of their plot. So they were watching the gates day and night intending to kill him, ²⁵ but his disciples took him by night and lowered him in a large basket through an opening in the wall.

Saul in Jerusalem

²⁶ When he arrived in Jerusalem, he tried to join the disciples, but they were all afraid of him, since they did not believe he was a disciple. ²⁷ Barnabas, however, took him and brought him to the apostles and explained to them how Saul had seen the Lord on the road and that the Lord had talked to him, and how in Damascus he had spoken boldly in the name of Jesus. ²⁸ Saul was coming and going with them in Jerusalem, speaking boldly in the name of the Lord. ²⁹ He conversed and debated with the Hellenistic Jews, but they tried to kill him. ³⁰ When the brothers found out, they took him down to Caesarea and sent him off to Tarsus.

The Church's Growth

³¹ So the church throughout all Judea, Galilee, and Samaria had peace and was strengthened. Living in the fear of the Lord and encouraged by the Holy Spirit, it increased in numbers.

The Healing of Aeneas

³² As Peter was traveling from place to place, he also came down to the saints who lived in Lydda. ³³ There he found a man named Aeneas, who was paralyzed and had been bedridden for eight years. ³⁴ Peter said to him, "Aeneas, Jesus Christ heals you. Get up and make your bed,"[B] and immediately he got up. ³⁵ So all who lived in Lydda and Sharon saw him and turned to the Lord.

Dorcas Restored to Life

³⁶ In Joppa there was a disciple named Tabitha (which is translated Dorcas). She was always doing good works and acts of charity. ³⁷ About that time she became sick and died.

ᴬ 9:12 Other mss omit *In a vision*   ᴮ 9:34 Or *and get ready to eat*

9:11–14 Ananias's fear of Saul was such that he dared to question God's judgment. Saul's reputation as an enemy of the church was well earned, built as it was on the testimony of **many people**.

9:19–20 Saul stayed **in Damascus for some time**, likely becoming oriented to basic Christianity even as **he began proclaiming Jesus in the synagogues**.

9:21–22 Understandably, the initial response to Saul was skeptical amazement, but as he **grew stronger** he was able to confound unbelieving Jews, **proving that Jesus is the Messiah**. Apparently, he was able to explain the messianic connections between the OT and Jesus so clearly that the Jews in Damascus could not refute him.

9:23–25 After many days pictures Saul dutifully preaching Jesus as Messiah for long enough to become the uppermost enemy

of unbelieving Jews in Damascus. He had come to help their struggle against the growing Christian movement, but now he had become the chief cause of its growth. Thus they **conspired to kill him**. Unable to leave via the city gates, Saul escaped in a most undignified but effective manner: he was placed in a **large basket** and shoved **through an opening in the wall**.

9:26 Among believers in **Jerusalem**, Saul's reputation as a persecutor of the church was unchanged.

9:27 Barnabas was convinced of the genuineness of Saul's conversion.

9:28–30 Saul . . . conversed and debated with the Hellenistic Jews, some of whom may have been involved with him in Stephen's stoning (7:57–60). A Hellenistic Jew himself, Paul had been born in **Tarsus** and spoke Greek as his primary language. Seeing

one of their own, a former persecutor of the church no less, argue on behalf of Christianity was more than they could bear. They **tried to kill** Saul, with the result that he was whisked away to his hometown.

9:32 The saints at **Lydda** may have been there since Pentecost and the time of persecution that had scattered believers throughout Judea (8:1). It is also possible that they traced their origins to Philip's ministry (8:40).

9:33–35 Again we see that the apostles never hesitated to give all credit for healing miracles to **Jesus Christ** (3:6).

9:37–38 So powerfully had God worked wonders through Peter and the other apostles that even when Dorcas **died** and had been ceremonially washed and **placed . . . in a room upstairs** for viewing, Christians in **Joppa** did not give up hope but instead sent for **Peter**.

After washing her, they placed her in a room upstairs. [38] Since Lydda was near Joppa, the disciples heard that Peter was there and sent two men to him who urged him, "Don't delay in coming with us." [39] Peter got up and went with them. When he arrived, they led him to the room upstairs. And all the widows approached him, weeping and showing him the robes and clothes that Dorcas had made while she was with them. [40] Peter sent them all out of the room. He knelt down, prayed, and turning toward the body said, "Tabitha, get up." She opened her eyes, saw Peter, and sat up. [41] He gave her his hand and helped her stand up. He called the saints and widows and presented her alive. [42] This became known throughout Joppa, and many believed in the Lord. [43] Peter stayed for some time in Joppa with Simon, a leather tanner.

Cornelius's Vision

10 There was a man in Caesarea named Cornelius, a centurion of what was called the Italian Regiment. [2] He was a devout man and feared God along with his whole household. He did many charitable deeds for the Jewish people and always prayed to God. [3] About three in the afternoon^A he distinctly saw in a vision an angel of God who came in and said to him, "Cornelius."

[4] Staring at him in awe, he said, "What is it, Lord?"

The angel told him, "Your prayers and your acts of charity have ascended as a memorial offering before God. [5] Now send men to Joppa and call for Simon, who is also named Peter. [6] He is lodging with Simon, a tanner, whose house is by the sea."

[7] When the angel who spoke to him had gone, he called two of his household servants and a devout soldier, who was one of those who attended him. [8] After explaining everything to them, he sent them to Joppa.

Peter's Vision

[9] The next day, as they were traveling and nearing the city, Peter went up to pray on the roof about noon.^B [10] He became hungry and wanted to eat, but while they were preparing something, he fell into a trance. [11] He saw heaven opened and an object that resembled a large sheet coming down, being lowered by its four corners to the earth. [12] In it were all the four-footed animals and reptiles of the earth, and the birds of the sky. [13] A voice said to him, "Get up, Peter; kill and eat."

[14] "No, Lord!" Peter said. "For I have never eaten anything impure and ritually unclean."

[15] Again, a second time, the voice said to him, "What God has made clean, do not call impure." [16] This happened three times, and suddenly the object was taken up into heaven.

Peter Visits Cornelius

[17] While Peter was deeply perplexed about what the vision he had seen might mean, right away the men who had been sent by Cornelius, having asked directions to Simon's house, stood at the gate. [18] They called out, asking if Simon, who was also named Peter, was lodging there.

[19] While Peter was thinking about the vision, the Spirit told him, "Three men are here looking for you. [20] Get up, go downstairs, and go with them with no doubts at all, because I have sent them."

[21] Then Peter went down to the men and said, "Here I am, the one you're looking for. What is the reason you're here?"

[22] They said, "Cornelius, a centurion, an upright and God-fearing man, who has a good reputation with the whole Jewish nation, was divinely directed by a holy angel to call you to his house and to hear a message from you." [23] Peter then invited them in and gave them lodging.

The next day he got up and set out with them, and some of the brothers from Joppa went with him. [24] The following day he entered Caesarea. Now Cornelius was expecting them and had called together his relatives and close friends. [25] When Peter entered, Cornelius met him, fell at his feet, and worshiped him.

[26] But Peter lifted him up and said, "Stand up. I myself am also a man." [27] While talking with him, he went in and found a large gathering of people. [28] Peter said to them, "You know it's forbidden for a Jewish man to associate with or visit a foreigner, but God has shown

---

^A **10:3** Lit *About the ninth hour*   ^B **10:9** Lit *about the sixth hour*

me that I must not call any person impure or unclean. **29** That's why I came without any objection when I was sent for. So may I ask why you sent for me?"

30 Cornelius replied, "Four days ago at this hour, at three in the afternoon,^A I was^B praying in my house. Just then a man in dazzling clothing stood before me **31** and said, 'Cornelius, your prayer has been heard, and your acts of charity have been remembered in God's sight. **32** Therefore send someone to Joppa and invite Simon here, who is also named Peter. He is lodging in Simon the tanner's house by the sea.'^C **33** So I immediately sent for you, and it was good of you to come. So now we are all in the presence of God to hear everything you have been commanded by the Lord."

Good News for Gentiles

34 Peter began to speak: "Now I truly understand that God doesn't show favoritism, **35** but in every nation the person who fears him and does what is right is acceptable to him. **36** He sent the message to the Israelites, proclaiming the good news of peace through Jesus Christ — he is Lord of all. **37** You know the events that took place throughout all Judea, beginning from Galilee after the baptism that John preached: **38** how God anointed Jesus of Nazareth with the Holy Spirit and with power, and how he went about doing good and healing all who were under the tyranny of the devil, because God was with him. **39** We ourselves are witnesses of everything he did in both the Judean country and in Jerusalem, and yet they killed him by hanging him on a tree. **40** God raised up this man on the third day and caused him to be seen, **41** not by all the people, but by us whom God appointed as witnesses, who ate and drank with him after he rose from the dead. **42** He commanded us to preach to the people and to testify that he is the one appointed by God to be the judge of the living and the dead. **43** All the prophets testify about him that through his name everyone who believes in him receives forgiveness of sins."

Gentile Conversion and Baptism

44 While Peter was still speaking these words, the Holy Spirit came down on all those who heard the message. **45** The circumcised believers who had come with Peter were amazed because the gift of the Holy Spirit had been poured out even on the Gentiles. **46** For they heard them speaking in tongues^D and declaring the greatness of God.

Then Peter responded, **47** "Can anyone withhold water and prevent these people from being baptized, who have received the Holy Spirit just as we have?" **48** He commanded them to be baptized in the name of Jesus Christ. Then they asked him to stay for a few days.

Gentile Salvation Defended

11 The apostles and the brothers and sisters who were throughout Judea heard that the Gentiles had also received the word of God. **2** When Peter went up to Jerusalem, the circumcision party criticized him, **3** saying, "You went to uncircumcised men and ate with them."

4 Peter began to explain to them step by step, **5** "I was in the town of Joppa praying, and I saw, in a trance, an object that resembled a large sheet coming down, being lowered by its four corners from heaven, and it came to me. **6** When I looked closely and considered it, I saw the four-footed animals of the earth, the wild beasts, the reptiles, and the birds of the sky. **7** I also heard a voice telling me, 'Get up, Peter; kill and eat.'

8 "'No, Lord!' I said. 'For nothing impure or ritually unclean has ever entered my mouth.'

9 But a voice answered from heaven a second time, 'What God has made clean, you must not call impure.'

10 "Now this happened three times, and everything was drawn up again into heaven. **11** At that very moment, three men who had been sent to me from Caesarea arrived at the house where we were. **12** The Spirit told me to accompany them with no doubts at all. These six brothers also accompanied me, and we went into the man's house. **13** He reported to us how he had seen the angel standing in his house and saying, 'Send to Joppa, and call for Simon, who is also named Peter. **14** He will speak a message to you by which you and all your household will be saved.'

15 "As I began to speak, the Holy Spirit came down on them, just as on us at the beginning.

---

^A**10:30** Lit *at the ninth hour*   ^B**10:30** Other mss add *fasting and*   ^C**10:32** Other mss add *When he arrives, he will speak to you.*
^D**10:46** Or *other languages*

---

[16] I remembered the word of the Lord, how he said, 'John baptized with water, but you will be baptized with the Holy Spirit.' [17] If, then, God gave them the same gift that he also gave to us when we believed in the Lord Jesus Christ, how could I possibly hinder God?"

[18] When they heard this they became silent. And they glorified God, saying, "So then, God has given repentance resulting in life even to the Gentiles."

The Church in Antioch

[19] Now those who had been scattered as a result of the persecution that started because of Stephen made their way as far as Phoenicia, Cyprus, and Antioch, speaking the word to no one except Jews. [20] But there were some of them, men from Cyprus and Cyrene, who came to Antioch and began speaking to the Greeks[A] also, proclaiming the good news about the Lord Jesus. [21] The Lord's hand was with them, and a large number who believed turned to the Lord. [22] News about them reached[B] the church in Jerusalem, and they sent out Barnabas to travel[C] as far as Antioch. [23] When he arrived and saw the grace of God, he was glad and encouraged all of them to remain true to the Lord with devoted hearts, [24] for he was a good man, full of the Holy Spirit and of faith. And large numbers of people were added to the Lord.

[25] Then he went to Tarsus to search for Saul, [26] and when he found him he brought him to Antioch. For a whole year they met with the church and taught large numbers. The disciples were first called Christians at Antioch.

Famine Relief

[27] In those days some prophets came down from Jerusalem to Antioch. [28] One of them, named Agabus, stood up and predicted by the Spirit that there would be a severe famine throughout the Roman world.[D] This took place during the reign of Claudius. [29] Each of the disciples, according to his ability, determined to send relief to the brothers and sisters who lived in Judea. [30] They did this, sending it to the elders by means of Barnabas and Saul.

James Martyred and Peter Jailed

12 About that time King Herod violently attacked some who belonged to the church, [2] and he executed James, John's brother, with the sword. [3] When he saw that it pleased the Jews, he proceeded to arrest Peter too, during the Festival of Unleavened Bread. [4] After the arrest, he put him in prison and assigned four squads of four soldiers each to guard him, intending to bring him out to the people after the Passover. [5] So Peter was kept in prison, but the church was praying fervently to God for him.

Peter Rescued

[6] When Herod was about to bring him out for trial, that very night Peter, bound with two chains, was sleeping between two soldiers, while the sentries in front of the door guarded the prison. [7] Suddenly an angel of the Lord appeared, and a light shone in the cell. Striking Peter on the side, he woke him up and said, "Quick, get up!" And the chains fell off his wrists. [8] "Get dressed," the angel told him, "and put on your sandals." And he did. "Wrap your cloak around you," he told him, "and follow me." [9] So he went out and followed, and he did not know that what the angel did was really happening, but he thought he was seeing a vision. [10] After they passed the first and second guards, they came to the iron gate that leads into the city, which opened to them by itself. They went outside and passed one street, and suddenly the angel left him.

[11] When Peter came to himself, he said, "Now I know for certain that the Lord has sent his angel and rescued me from Herod's grasp and from all that the Jewish people expected." [12] As

---

[A]11:20 Lit *Hellenists* [B]11:22 Lit *reached the ears of* [C]11:22 Other mss omit *to travel* [D]11:28 Or *the whole world*

11:18 They became silent indicates these Jewish believers were having to process the same shocking revelation that had come to Peter at Joppa and then Caesarea (10:9–16,44–48). Eventually, however, **they glorified God** for what he had done.

11:19 The Christian mission continued to spread much farther afield, including areas well beyond Judea (**Phoenicia, Cyprus, and Antioch**).

11:20–21 The evangelization of **Antioch** was carried out by believers **from Cyprus and Cyrene**. As a result, Antioch became the center of the Gentile mission and the church that sent Paul out as a missionary (see chaps. 13 and following).

11:22–24 The spiritual qualities of **Barnabas** were obvious to the Jerusalem church (4:36–37; 9:27). No wonder they sent him to **Antioch**. He was probably sent to determine the genuineness of the conversions taking place there and encourage them to **remain true to the Lord**.

11:25 Saul (soon to be Paul, 13:9) had faded from the picture, while the evangelization of Antioch moved forward. Once again Barnabas played a central role in involving Paul in ministry (see note at 9:27). On **Tarsus**, see note at 9:28–30.

11:26 The term **Christians** probably came from Romans who labeled Jesus's followers in **Antioch** "little Christs." Though it was likely intended as an offense, the label is actually an honor insomuch as it indicates disciples are living Christlike lives.

11:27–28 Agabus was a prophet from Jerusalem who reappears in 21:10. The reign of **Claudius** (AD 41–54) was marked with numerous famines in various parts of the Roman Empire. The famine referred to here may have occurred around AD 46–47, with the effects of the famine lasting for a number of years after that.

11:29 The church at Antioch determined to provide relief for the believers in **Judea**. In

so doing, they gave back to the churches and believers who had brought the gospel to Antioch and abroad in the first place.

12:1 This **King Herod** was Herod Agrippa I, who ruled in Palestine from AD 37 to 44. He was the grandson of Herod the Great (see Mt 2). His attack apparently focused on the apostles in Jerusalem.

12:2 The **James** whom Herod **executed** was one of the sons of Zebedee, **John's brother**.

12:3–5 Peter would have been guarded by four soldiers at a time, who worked three-hour shifts.

12:6–10 Peter was again rescued from prison by an **angel of the Lord** (see note at 5:19–20), though this time he initially thought he was only seeing a vision.

12:12–16 The suggestion that it was Peter's **angel** reflected the common Jewish belief in guardian angels. It was believed that one's guardian angel would sometimes appear shortly after the person's death. It seems

soon as he realized this, he went to the house of Mary, the mother of John who was called Mark, where many had assembled and were praying. ¹³ He knocked at the door of the outer gate, and a servant named Rhoda came to answer. ¹⁴ She recognized Peter's voice, and because of her joy, she did not open the gate but ran in and announced that Peter was standing at the outer gate.

¹⁵ "You're out of your mind!" they told her. But she kept insisting that it was true, and they said, "It's his angel." ¹⁶ Peter, however, kept on knocking, and when they opened the door and saw him, they were amazed.

¹⁷ Motioning to them with his hand to be silent, he described to them how the Lord had brought him out of the prison. "Tell these things to James and the brothers," he said, and he left and went to another place.

¹⁸ At daylight, there was a great commotion among the soldiers as to what had become of Peter. ¹⁹ After Herod had searched and did not find him, he interrogated the guards and ordered their execution. Then Herod went down from Judea to Caesarea and stayed there.

Herod's Death

²⁰ Herod had been very angry with the people of Tyre and Sidon. Together they presented themselves before him. After winning over Blastus, who was in charge of the king's bedroom, they asked for peace, because their country was supplied with food from the king's country. ²¹ On an appointed day, dressed in royal robes and seated on the throne, Herod delivered a speech to them. ²² The assembled people began to shout, "It's the voice of a god and not of a man!" ²³ At once an angel of the Lord struck him because he did not give the glory to God, and he was eaten by worms and died.

²⁴ But the word of God spread and multiplied. ²⁵ After they had completed their relief mission, Barnabas and Saul returned to ^Jerusalem, taking along John who was called Mark.

Preparing for the Mission Field

13 Now in the church at Antioch there were prophets and teachers: Barnabas, Simeon who was called Niger, Lucius of Cyrene, Manaen, a close friend of Herod the tetrarch, and Saul.

² As they were worshiping ᴮ the Lord and fasting, the Holy Spirit said, "Set apart for me Barnabas and Saul for the work to which I have called them." ³ Then after they had fasted, prayed, and laid hands on them, they sent them off.

The Mission to Cyprus

⁴ So being sent out by the Holy Spirit, they went down to Seleucia, and from there they sailed to Cyprus. ⁵ Arriving in Salamis, they proclaimed the word of God in the Jewish synagogues. They also had John as their assistant. ⁶ When they had traveled the whole island as far as Paphos, they came across a sorcerer, a Jewish false prophet named Bar-Jesus. ⁷ He was with the proconsul, Sergius Paulus, an intelligent man. This man summoned Barnabas and Saul and wanted to hear the word of God. ⁸ But Elymas the sorcerer (that is the meaning of his name) opposed them and tried to turn the proconsul away from the faith.

⁹ But Saul — also called Paul — filled with the Holy Spirit, stared straight at Elymas ¹⁰ and said, "You are full of all kinds of deceit and trickery, you son of the devil and enemy of all that is right. Won't you ever stop perverting the straight paths of the Lord? ¹¹ Now, look, the Lord's hand is against you. You are going to

---

^12:25 Other mss read *from*   ᴮ13:2 Or *were ministering to*

---

the believers were better prepared to believe Peter had been executed than that he had been released!

12:17 Peter **went to another place** most likely in an attempt to throw Herod and the Jewish authorities off his trail. Peter instructed those present to tell **James**, Jesus's brother, mentioned here for the first time in Acts. James, apparently not a follower of Jesus until after the resurrection (1Co 15:7), emerged as a leader in the Jerusalem church (Ac 15:13–21; Gl 1:19).

12:18–19 According to the Roman code of Justinian, soldiers who allowed a captive to escape would suffer the same penalty their charge was to suffer. Thus we see Peter was to be executed.

12:23 Herod **died** because he claimed for himself the honor and **glory** that belong only to God. There have been various speculations about the immediate cause of Herod's death, including appendicitis, poisoning, and intestinal blockage.

12:25 Barnabas and Saul returned to Jerusalem after their relief mission. Here again we see the vital role Barnabas played

in assimilating Saul into leadership of the early church.

13:1 The **teachers** continued the apostolic function of transmitting Jesus's message (see note at 6:2–4), while **prophets** conveyed divine revelation via interpreting the OT or giving new insights (11:27). This is the only reference in Acts to teachers. The group of prophets and teachers was diverse, including people from Africa and Cyrene, and at least one person (**Manaen**) who was connected to Herod's household.

13:2–3 The routine of the prophets and teachers included **worshiping the Lord and fasting**. This helps to account for their openness to the Holy Spirit, who directed them to set aside **Barnabas and Saul** for a work to which the Spirit had called them. Barnabas and Saul were confirmed in their calling after a process of fasting, praying, and laying on of hands. This commissioning marks an important turning point in the history of the church, as Saul and Barnabas were selected to extend the gospel message beyond Judea and surrounding regions.

13:4 This verse describes the beginning of the first of Paul's three missionary journeys. This journey included the island of **Cyprus** and a part of Asia Minor.

13:5 Paul began his preaching efforts at local **synagogues**, continuing his early pattern (see 9:19–20). **John** ("John . . . Mark," 12:25) was with them for now (but see 13:13 and note).

13:6 Just as Peter had a confrontation with a magician (Simon), so Paul confronted a **sorcerer** on Cyprus.

13:7 A **proconsul** governed a Roman province.

13:8 The **sorcerer** Bar-Jesus (v. 6) is here called **Elymas**. Possibly *Elymas* is a Semitic word, as is *Bar-Jesus*, and "sorcerer" is its translation. In any case, true to his demonic influence, Elymas tried to keep Sergius Paulus from embracing the gospel.

13:9 From this point on in the book of Acts, Saul is referred to as **Paul** (except when he recounted his conversion experience in chaps. 22 and 26). Paul was the Roman version of Saul's name.

be blind, and will not see the sun for a time." Immediately a mist and darkness fell on him, and he went around seeking someone to lead him by the hand.

¹² Then, when he saw what happened, the proconsul believed, because he was astonished at the teaching of the Lord.

Paul's Sermon in Antioch of Pisidia

¹³ Paul and his companions set sail from Paphos and came to Perga in Pamphylia, but John left them and went back to Jerusalem.

¹⁴ They continued their journey from Perga and reached Pisidian Antioch. On the Sabbath day they went into the synagogue and sat down. ¹⁵ After the reading of the Law and the Prophets, the leaders of the synagogue sent word to them, saying, "Brothers, if you have any word of encouragement for the people, you can speak."

¹⁶ Paul stood up and motioned with his hand and said, "Fellow Israelites, and you who fear God, listen! ¹⁷ The God of this people Israel chose our ancestors, made the people prosper during their stay in the land of Egypt, and

---

13:12 The signs normally associated with conversion in Acts (baptism, reception of the Spirit) do not appear in this account of Sergius Paulus's conversion. Possibly Luke just abbreviated his account, but it is also possible that Paulus's belief amounted to nothing more than his being **astonished**

at the teaching and the blindness that befell Elymas.
13:13 John Mark (son of Mary, 12:12) **left them** at **Perga** and went back to **Jerusalem**. No reason is given for his leaving, but it must have seemed unwarranted to Paul, for on the second missionary journey Barnabas

suggested that they take John along, but Paul refused, pointing out that John had previously abandoned them (15:37–38).
13:16–41 This is Paul's first public speech and his first missionary speech in the book of Acts. It is the longest speech by him in a Jewish synagogue, and it probably represents

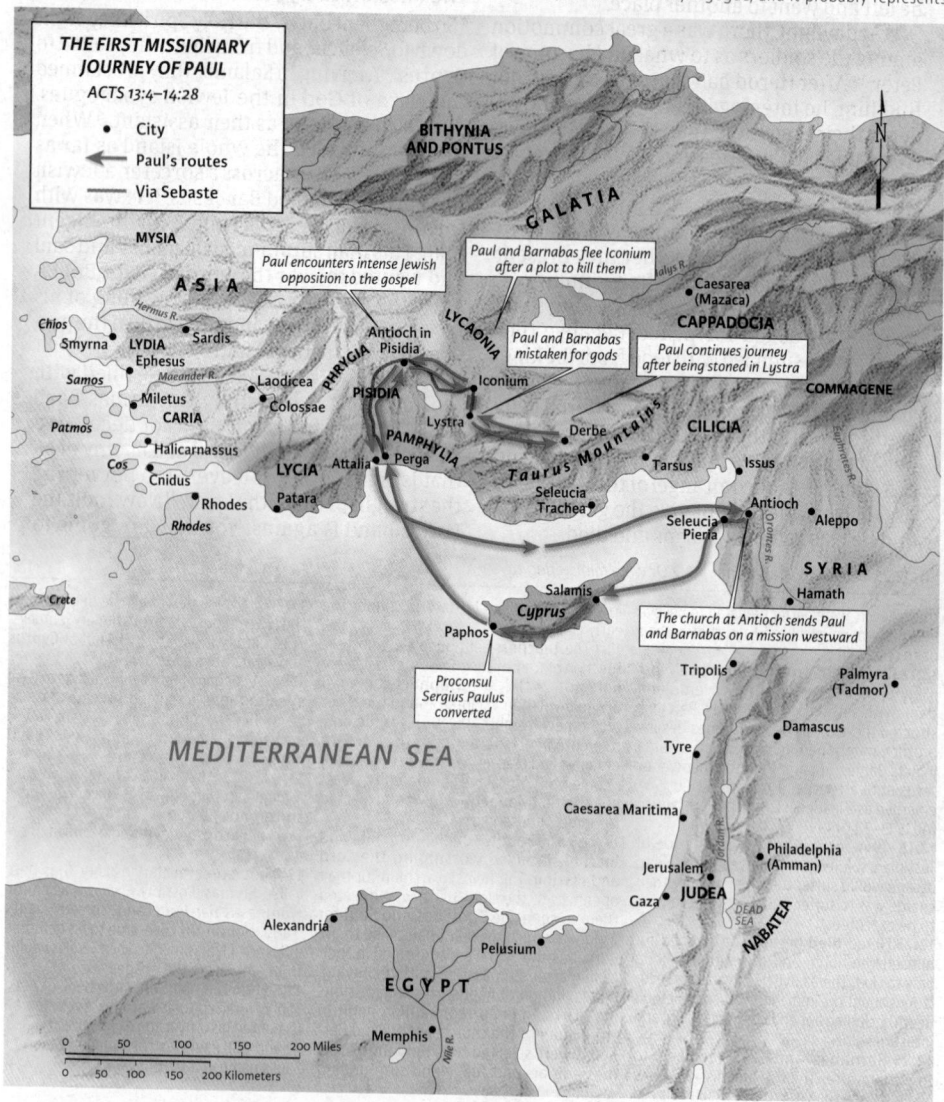

THE FIRST MISSIONARY JOURNEY OF PAUL
ACTS 13:4–14:28

• City

← Paul's routes

— Via Sebaste

Paul encounters intense Jewish opposition to the gospel

Paul and Barnabas flee Iconium after a plot to kill them

Paul and Barnabas mistaken for gods

Paul continues journey after being stoned in Lystra

The church at Antioch sends Paul and Barnabas on a mission westward

Proconsul Sergius Paulus converted

MEDITERRANEAN SEA

BITHYNIA AND PONTUS

GALATIA

MYSIA

ASIA

LYCAONIA

Caesarea (Mazaca)

CAPPADOCIA

COMMAGENE

Chios
Smyrna   LYDIA   Sardis
Ephesus
Samos   Laodicea
Miletus   Colossae
CARIA
Patmos
Halicarnassus
Cos
Cnidus
Rhodes
Rhodes   Patara

Antioch in Pisidia
PHRYGIA
PISIDIA
Iconium
Lystra
Derbe
CILICIA
Tarsus   Issus
Seleucia Trachea
Seleucia Pieria
Antioch   Aleppo
SYRIA
Hamath

LYCIA   Attalia   Perga
PAMPHYLIA

Taurus Mountains

Salamis
Cyprus
Paphos

Crete

Tripolis

Palmyra (Tadmor)

Damascus

Tyre

Caesarea Maritima

Jerusalem
Gaza   JUDEA
DEAD SEA
NABATEA

Philadelphia (Amman)

Alexandria

Pelusium

EGYPT

Memphis

0   50   100   150   200 Miles
0   50   100   150   200 Kilometers

led them out of it with a mighty^A arm. ¹⁸ And for about forty years he put up with them⁸ in the wilderness; ¹⁹ and after destroying seven nations in the land of Canaan, he gave them their land as an inheritance. ²⁰ This all took about 450 years. After this, he gave them judges until Samuel the prophet. ²¹ Then they asked for a king, and God gave them Saul the son of Kish, a man of the tribe of Benjamin, for forty years. ²² After removing him, he raised up David as their king and testified about him, 'I have found David the son of Jesse to be a man after my own heart,^c who will carry out all my will.'

²³ "From this man's descendants, as he promised, God brought to Israel the Savior, Jesus.^D ²⁴ Before his coming to public attention, John had previously proclaimed a baptism of repentance to all the people of Israel. ²⁵ Now as John was completing his mission, he said, 'Who do you think I am? I am not the one. But one is coming after me, and I am not worthy to untie the sandals on his feet.'

²⁶ "Brothers and sisters, children of Abraham's race, and those among you who fear God, it is to us that the word of this salvation has been sent. ²⁷ Since the residents of Jerusalem and their rulers did not recognize him or the sayings of the prophets that are read every Sabbath, they have fulfilled their words by condemning him. ²⁸ Though they found no grounds for the death sentence, they asked Pilate to have him killed. ²⁹ When they had carried out all that had been written about him, they took him down from the tree and put him in a tomb. ³⁰ But God raised him from the dead, ³¹ and he appeared for many days to those who came up with him from Galilee to Jerusalem, who are now his witnesses to the people. ³² And we ourselves proclaim to you the good news of the promise that was made to our ancestors. ³³ God has fulfilled this for us, their children, by raising up Jesus, as it is written in the second Psalm:

You are my Son;
today I have become your Father.^E,F

³⁴ As to his raising him from the dead, never to return to decay, he has spoken in this way,

I will give you the holy and sure promises of David.^G ³⁵ Therefore he also says in another passage, You will not let your Holy One see decay.^H ³⁶ For David, after serving God's purpose in his own generation, fell asleep, was buried with his fathers, and decayed, ³⁷ but the one God raised up did not decay. ³⁸ Therefore, let it be known to you, brothers and sisters, that through this man forgiveness of sins is being proclaimed to you. ³⁹ Everyone who believes is justified^I through him from everything that you could not be justified from through the law of Moses. ⁴⁰ So beware that what is said in the prophets does not happen to you:

⁴¹   Look, you scoffers,
        marvel and vanish away,
        because I am doing a work in your days,
        a work that you will never believe,
        even if someone were to explain it
        to you."^J

Paul and Barnabas in Antioch

⁴² As they were leaving, the people^K urged them to speak about these matters the following Sabbath. ⁴³ After the synagogue had been dismissed, many of the Jews and devout converts to Judaism followed Paul and Barnabas, who were speaking with them and urging them to continue in the grace of God.

⁴⁴ The following Sabbath almost the whole town assembled to hear the word of the Lord.^L ⁴⁵ But when the Jews saw the crowds, they were filled with jealousy and began to contradict what Paul was saying, insulting him.

⁴⁶ Paul and Barnabas boldly replied, "It was necessary that the word of God be spoken to you first. Since you reject it and judge yourselves unworthy of eternal life, we are turning to the Gentiles. ⁴⁷ For this is what the Lord has commanded us:

I have made you
a light for the Gentiles
to bring salvation
to the ends of the earth."^M

⁴⁸ When the Gentiles heard this, they rejoiced and honored the word of the Lord,

---

^A13:17 Lit with an uplifted   ⁸13:18 Other mss read he cared for them   ^c13:22 1Sm 13:14; Ps 89:20   ^D13:23 Other mss read brought salvation   ^E13:33 Or I have begotten you   ^F13:33 Ps 2:7   ^G13:34 Is 55:3   ^H13:35 Ps 16:10   ^I13:39 Or freed, also later in this verse   ^J13:41 Hab 1:5   ^K13:42 Other mss read they were leaving the synagogue of the Jews, the Gentiles   ^L13:44 Other mss read of God   ^M13:47 Is 49:6

---

a style of speech he used on many such occasions. Paul recounted the history of Israel to place the coming of Jesus Christ in historical perspective. He made it clear that the coming of Jesus was the fulfillment of God's promise (v. 23), as his resurrection confirmed (v. 33).
13:22–23 As he promised refers to 2Sm 7:12–16, where God promised through the prophet Nathan that he would raise up from David a descendant whose throne would be established "forever."
13:24–26 Verse 25 may point to Mal 3:1 and its promise of a forerunner to the Messiah.

13:36–37 Paul relied on the same verse, Ps 16:10, that Peter did in his Pentecost sermon (Ac 2:31) to prove the resurrection of Christ.
13:40–41 Paul cited Hab 1:5 as a fitting conclusion to his speech. This passage from the prophet referred to the work that God was doing and recognized that some people would scoff and refuse to believe what God was doing, even if it was explained to them.
13:42–43 Whether due to the speech's novelty or their genuine spiritual hunger, the people wanted to hear more. It was probably

in the "downtime" outside the synagogues, in small groups or individual meetings, that Paul and Barnabas accomplished their most effective teaching.
13:46–47 The NT consistently says the gospel message came first to the Jews (e.g., Mk 7:27), though the Gentiles were anticipated as eventual recipients.
13:48 This verse expresses one of the great enigmatic truths of Scripture: **all who had been appointed to eternal life believed**. This touches both on God's election ("appointed") and the human responsibility to choose ("believed").

and all who had been appointed to eternal life believed. **49** The word of the Lord spread through the whole region. **50** But the Jews incited the prominent God-fearing women and the leading men of the city. They stirred up persecution against Paul and Barnabas and expelled them from their district. **51** But Paul and Barnabas shook the dust off their feet against them and went to Iconium. **52** And the disciples were filled with joy and the Holy Spirit.

Growth and Persecution in Iconium

14 In Iconium they entered the Jewish synagogue, as usual, and spoke in such a way that a great number of both Jews and Greeks believed. **2** But the unbelieving Jews stirred up the Gentiles and poisoned their minds against the brothers. **3** So they stayed there a long time and spoke boldly for the Lord, who testified to the message of his grace by enabling them to do signs and wonders. **4** But the people of the city were divided, some siding with the Jews and others with the apostles. **5** When an attempt was made by both the Gentiles and Jews, with their rulers, to mistreat and stone them, **6** they found out about it and fled to the Lycaonian towns of Lystra and Derbe and to the surrounding countryside. **7** There they continued preaching the gospel.

Mistaken for Gods in Lystra

8 In Lystra a man was sitting who was without strength in his feet, had never walked, and had been lame from birth. **9** He listened as Paul spoke. After looking directly at him and seeing that he had faith to be healed, **10** Paul said in a loud voice, "Stand up on your feet!" And he jumped up and began to walk around.

11 When the crowds saw what Paul had done, they shouted, saying in the Lycaonian language, "The gods have come down to us in human form!" **12** Barnabas they called Zeus, and Paul, Hermes, because he was the chief speaker. **13** The priest of Zeus, whose temple was just outside the town, brought bulls and wreaths to the gates because he intended, with the crowds, to offer sacrifice.

14 The apostles Barnabas and Paul tore their robes when they heard this and rushed into the crowd, shouting, **15** "People! Why are you doing these things? We are people also, just like you, and we are proclaiming good news to you, that you turn from these worthless things to the living God, **who made the heaven, the earth, the sea, and everything in them.**^ **16** In past generations he allowed all the nations to go their own way, **17** although he did not leave himself without a witness, since he did what is good by giving you rain from heaven and fruitful seasons and filling you with food and your hearts with joy." **18** Even though they said these things, they barely stopped the crowds from sacrificing to them.

19 Some Jews came from Antioch and Iconium, and when they won over the crowds, they stoned Paul and dragged him out of the city, thinking he was dead. **20** After the disciples gathered around him, he got up and went into the town. The next day he left with Barnabas for Derbe.

Church Planting

21 After they had preached the gospel in that town and made many disciples, they returned to Lystra, to Iconium, and to Antioch, **22** strengthening the^b disciples by encouraging them to continue in the faith and by telling

---

^**14:15** Ex 20:11; Ps 146:6   ^b**14:22** Lit *the souls of the*

13:49 The whole region was predominantly Gentile, thus those who were historically "outside" God's people.

13:51 They shook the dust off their feet, obeying Jesus's command to his disciples (Lk 10:11).

14:1 The familiar pattern of evangelization took place in **Iconium**: Barnabas and Paul began in the **synagogue**. The **Greeks** were likely God-fearers (10:2).

14:2–7 Paul and Barnabas ministered **boldly** until they discovered that **both the Gentiles and Jews** had formed a plot to **stone them**. They left Iconium more from prudence than fear of risk.

14:8–13 Lystra apparently shared in the region's mythological tradition that said the Greek gods **Zeus** and **Hermes** (their Roman counterparts were Jupiter and Mercury) had once visited earth. The city had ongoing devotion to these gods.

14:14 That the apostles **tore their robes** indicates not just refusal to be worshiped as gods, but abject horror at the idea.

14:15–18 This speech, delivered by both Barnabas and Paul to a pagan audience (rather than Jews or God-fearers), is Paul's second missionary speech in Acts. It drew upon natural theology, which is knowledge of God that can be derived from creation. This approach was appropriate for a group of pagans who thought of their gods as part of nature.

14:15 Paul and Barnabas cited Ex 20:11 and Ps 146:6 about God creating **heaven, the earth, the sea, and everything in them.** This placed the natural order within the realm of God's creative power.

14:19 Agitators traveled from **Antioch** (about one hundred miles away) and **Iconium** to catalyze the about-face at Lystra. So seriously did unbelieving Jews take the threat from Christian growth that they followed Paul from town to town, seeking to thwart his missions work (see note at 17:13). In this case, they **stoned Paul** to death. Or so they believed.

14:20 Did Paul literally rise from the dead? Probably not, since Luke does not explicitly say so. The mob apparently jumped to conclusions once Paul fell under the hail of stones (v. 19). Paul recovered and reentered Lystra, presumably without being spotted. He left the next day but returned to Lystra soon afterward (v. 21). This was likely made possible by the Jews from Antioch and Iconium returning home.

14:21–22 After evangelizing Derbe (v. 20), Paul and Barnabas began their return journey to their home base of Antioch of Syria, stopping by each of the towns they had visited along the way (**Lystra** . . . **Iconium**, and **Antioch** of Pisidia). Their purpose was to strengthen the hearts of **the disciples** and be sure that they understood that **many hardships** come to those who seek **the kingdom of God**. Most of the churches Paul and Barnabas founded on this first missionary journey were in the Roman province of Galatia. These were probably the churches to which Paul addressed his letter to the Galatians.

them, "It is necessary to go through many hardships to enter the kingdom of God." ²³ When they had appointed elders for them in every church and prayed with fasting, they committed them to the Lord in whom they had believed.

²⁴ They passed through Pisidia and came to Pamphylia. ²⁵ After they had spoken the word in Perga, they went down to Attalia. ²⁶ From there they sailed back to Antioch where they had been commended to the grace of God for the work they had now completed. ²⁷ After they arrived and gathered the church together, they reported everything God had done with them and that he had opened the door of faith to the Gentiles. ²⁸ And they spent a considerable time with the disciples.

Dispute in Antioch

15 Some men came down from Judea and began to teach the brothers, "Unless you are circumcised according to the custom prescribed by Moses, you cannot be saved." ² After Paul and Barnabas had engaged them in serious argument and debate, Paul and Barnabas and some others were appointed to go up to the apostles and elders in Jerusalem about this issue. ³ When they had been sent on their way by the church, they passed through both Phoenicia and Samaria, describing in detail the conversion of the Gentiles, and they brought great joy to all the brothers and sisters.

⁴ When they arrived at Jerusalem, they were welcomed by the church, the apostles, and the elders, and they reported all that God had done with them. ⁵ But some of the believers who belonged to the party of the Pharisees stood up and said, "It is necessary to circumcise them and to command them to keep the law of Moses."

The Jerusalem Council

⁶ The apostles and the elders gathered to consider this matter. ⁷ After there had been much debate, Peter stood up and said to them, "Brothers, you are aware that in the early days God made a choice among you,ᴬ that by my mouth the Gentiles would hear the gospel message and believe. ⁸ And God, who knows the heart, bore witness to them by giving them the Holy Spirit, just as he also did to us. ⁹ He made no distinction between us and them, cleansing their hearts by faith. ¹⁰ Now then, why are you testing God by putting a yoke on the disciples' necks that neither our ancestors nor we have been able to bear? ¹¹ On the contrary, we believe that we are saved through the grace of the Lord Jesus in the same way they are."

¹² The whole assembly became silent and listened to Barnabas and Paul describe all the signs and wonders God had done through them among the Gentiles. ¹³ After they stopped speaking, James responded, "Brothers, listen to me. ¹⁴ Simeonᴮ has reported how God first intervened to take from the Gentiles a people for his name. ¹⁵ And the words of the prophets agree with this, as it is written:

¹⁶   **After these things I will return**
     and rebuild David's fallen tent.
     I will rebuild its ruins
     and set it up again,
¹⁷   **so that the rest of humanity**
     may seek the Lord —
     even all the Gentiles
     who are called by my name —
     declares the Lord
     who makes these things ¹⁸ known
       from long ago.ᶜ,ᴰ

¹⁹ Therefore, in my judgment, we should not cause difficulties for those among the Gentiles who turn to God, ²⁰ but instead we should write to them to abstain from things polluted

---

ᴬ15:7 Other mss read *us*   ᴮ15:14 Simon (Peter)   ᶜ15:17–18 Other mss read *says the Lord who does all these things. Known to God from long ago are all his works.*   ᴰ15:16–18 Am 9:11–12; Is 45:21

14:23 Elders in these early Pauline churches were apparently **appointed** by Paul and Barnabas to establish the first stages of church leadership.

14:24–28 They also visited some additional towns (Attalia, Perga). This ends the first missionary journey.

15:1 After arriving back in Antioch, Paul and Barnabas reported on what God had done in Asia on the first missionary journey, especially the evangelizing of the Gentiles (14:27). **Some men came down from Judea** and attempted to modify Paul's approach to non-Jews. By insisting that Gentiles be circumcised, they made observance of Jewish ritual a requirement for salvation.

15:2 Unable to reach an agreement, Paul and Barnabas were sent to the **elders in Jerusalem**, a sign that the Jerusalem church, with its **apostles** and elders, was still the center of the Christian movement.

15:3 On the way to Jerusalem, Paul and Barnabas shared details about **the conversion of the Gentiles** with believers in **Phoenicia and Samaria**, creating **great joy** among **the brothers and sisters**.

15:4–5 Though the **Pharisees** (including Paul) had opposed Jesus bitterly, some had become **believers** (6:7). In this case a group of them failed to understand the freedoms Christ had won for believers.

15:6 The central issue of the Jerusalem Council was whether Gentile Christians had to be circumcised and keep the law of Moses.

15:7–9 Peter reminded his hearers of four things: (1) God had chosen him to proclaim the gospel to the Gentiles (10:1–43). (2) The Gentiles believed Peter's message. (3) When the Gentiles believed, they received the Holy Spirit (10:44–46). (4) The pattern of Gentile conversion was the same as for Jewish believers. God was making no ethnic distinctions in building the church.

15:10 In light of the above points (see note at vv. 7–9), the believers from the "party of the Pharisees" (v. 5) were **testing God** and putting on Gentile converts a burden that neither Jewish **ancestors** nor contemporary Jews were **able to bear.**

15:13–14 As leader of the Jerusalem church, James, the brother of Jesus, assessed the claims and counterclaims. He began his address by recalling how **Simeon** (Peter) had reported God's plan to **take from the Gentiles a people for his name**, which had occasioned controversy of its own (11:2–18).

15:15–18 James cited the prophets Amos (Am 9:11–12) and Isaiah (Is 45:21) to show that God had long ago foretold that Gentiles would be called by his name.

15:20 Despite the common basis of salvation for Jews and Gentiles, a number of restrictions were required (v. 29; 21:25). It is more likely that these were designed to elevate the moral standards of the Gentiles by

◥ Suffering for Jesus

ACTS OF MINISTRY	THE RESPONSE OF ENEMIES
Peter, along with John, healed a lame man and then preached in Jesus's name to the gathering crowd (Ac 3:1–26).	The Jewish leaders were annoyed because they taught the people and proclaimed in Jesus the resurrection of the dead (Ac 4:1–2).
Through the apostles, the sick and those with unclean spirits were being healed (Ac 5:12–16).	The high priest and the Sadducees were filled with jealousy (Ac 5:17).
Stephen performed great wonders and signs among the people and spoke with wisdom from the Holy Spirit (Ac 6:8–10; 7:1–53).	Some Jews from the Freedmen's Synagogue opposed Stephen and argued with him (Ac 6:9).

Saul's persecution of the church was persecution of Jesus Christ, the head of the church; Jesus called Saul to himself as his chosen instrument to take his name to Gentiles, to kings, and to the Israelites, and Saul would now suffer for the name of Jesus (Ac 9:1–19).

ACTS OF MINISTRY	THE RESPONSE OF ENEMIES
—	—
Paul and Barnabas preached the gospel to both Jews and Gentiles in Pisidian Antioch (Ac 13:13–44).	The Jews were filled with jealousy at the gospel preached to Gentiles and rejected it (Ac 13:45–47).
Paul, along with Barnabas, healed a lame man and preached the gospel in Lystra (Ac 14:8–10).	Some Jews from Pisidian Antioch and Iconium came and won over the crowds against Paul and Barnabas (Ac 14:19).
Paul, along with Silas, freed a slave girl from demonic possession in the name of Jesus (Ac 16:16–18).	The slave girl's owners realized their hope for profit from her predictions of the future was gone (Ac 16:19).

THE FORM OF PERSECUTION	THE RESULTS
Peter and John were arrested by the Sanhedrin and threatened if they spoke in Jesus's name again *(Ac 4:3–22)*.	They reported the events to the church and then all prayed to the Lord for boldness in the face of opposition, which the Lord granted through his Holy Spirit *(Ac 4:23–31)*.
The apostles were arrested and tried by the Sanhedrin, flogged and ordered not to speak in Jesus's name *(Ac 5:18–41)*.	The apostles rejoiced that they were counted worthy to suffer for Jesus's name and continued proclaiming the good news about Jesus *(Ac 5:41–42)*.
• Stephen was falsely accused of blasphemy against the temple *(Ac 6:11–14; cp. Mt 26:59–61)*. • He was taken outside the city and stoned to death *(Ac 7:57–60; cp. Lk 23:32–33)*.	• Stephen prayed for Jesus to receive his spirit *(Ac 7:59; cp. Lk 23:46)*. • He prayed for forgiveness for those stoning him *(Ac 7:60; cp. Lk 23:34)*. • Persecution broke out against the church and scattered believers throughout the world preaching the word about Jesus *(Ac 8:1,4; 11:19–20)*.

Herod violently attacked some of the church: executed James, John's brother, with the sword and arrested Peter to try and execute him *(Ac 12:1–5)*.	Peter rescued from prison by an angel *(Ac 12:6–19)*
The Jews stirred up persecution against Paul and Barnabas and had them expelled from the district *(Ac 13:50)*.	Paul and Barnabas shook the dust off their feet against the Jews and moved on to preach elsewhere; the disciples left behind were filled with joy and the Holy Spirit *(Ac 13:51–52)*.
Paul was stoned and dragged out of the city by the mob, thinking he was dead *(Ac 14:19)*.	Paul miraculously recovered and went back into the city, and the next day left for Derbe *(Ac 14:20)*.
Paul and Silas were arrested, severely flogged, and imprisoned with their feet in the stocks *(Ac 16:19–24)*.	In prison they prayed and sang hymns to God before an earthquake freed them; then they shared the gospel with the jailer, who believed along with his entire household *(Ac 16:25–34)*.

Paul strengthened the disciples on his first missionary journey by telling them, "It is necessary to go through many hardships to enter the kingdom of God" *(Ac 14:22)*. In this he echoed Jesus's words to his disciples: "You will have suffering in this world. Be courageous! I have conquered the world" *(Jn 16:33)*.

by idols, from sexual immorality, from eating anything that has been strangled, and from blood. ²¹ For since ancient times, Moses has had those who proclaim him in every city, and every Sabbath day he is read aloud in the synagogues."

The Letter to the Gentile Believers

²² Then the apostles and the elders, with the whole church, decided to select men who were among them and to send them to Antioch with Paul and Barnabas: Judas, called Barsabbas, and Silas, both leading men among the brothers. ²³ They wrote:

"From the apostles and the elders, your brothers,

To the brothers and sisters among the Gentiles in Antioch, Syria, and Cilicia:

Greetings.

²⁴ Since we have heard that some without our authorization went out from us and troubled you with their words and unsettled your hearts,ᴬ ²⁵ we have unanimously decided to select men and send them to you along with our dearly loved Barnabas and Paul, ²⁶ who have risked their lives for the name of our Lord Jesus Christ. ²⁷ Therefore we have sent Judas and Silas, who will personally report the same things by word of mouth. ²⁸ For it was the Holy Spirit's decision — and ours — not to place further burdens on you beyond these requirements: ²⁹ that you abstain from food offered to idols, from blood, from eating anything that has been strangled, and from sexual immorality. You will do well if you keep yourselves from these things. Farewell."

The Outcome of the Jerusalem Letter

³⁰ So they were sent off and went down to Antioch, and after gathering the assembly, they delivered the letter. ³¹ When they read it, they rejoiced because of its encouragement. ³² Both Judas and Silas, who were also prophets themselves, encouraged the brothers and sisters and strengthened them with a long message. ³³ After spending some time there, they were sent back in peace by the brothers and sisters to those who had sent them.ᴮ,ᶜ ³⁵ But Paul and Barnabas, along with many others, remained in Antioch, teaching and proclaiming the word of the Lord.

Paul and Barnabas Part Company

³⁶ After some time had passed, Paul said to Barnabas, "Let's go back and visit the brothers and sisters in every town where we have preached the word of the Lord and see how they're doing." ³⁷ Barnabas wanted to take along John who was called Mark. ³⁸ But Paul insisted that they should not take along this man who had deserted them in Pamphylia and had not gone on with them to the work. ³⁹ They had such a sharp disagreement that they parted company, and Barnabas took Mark with him and sailed off to Cyprus. ⁴⁰ But Paul chose Silas and departed, after being commended by the brothers and sisters to the grace of the Lord. ⁴¹ He traveled through Syria and Cilicia, strengthening the churches.

Paul Selects Timothy

16 Paul went on to Derbe and Lystra, where there was a disciple named Timothy, the son of a believing Jewish woman, but his father was a Greek. ² The brothers and sisters

---

ᴬ15:24 Other mss add by saying, 'Be circumcised and keep the law,' ᴮ15:33 Other mss read the brothers to the apostles ᶜ15:33 Other mss add v. 34: But Silas decided to stay there.

prohibiting them from engaging in a number of the practices that were associated with pagan temple rites such as animal sacrifice, **sexual immorality,** and idolatry.
15:21 James's reason for invoking **Moses** and the widespread proclamation of the law is not entirely clear. He may have meant that Jewish people who spread throughout the world via the Diaspora had made Moses's law known among Gentiles through their public reading of Scripture. Alternatively, he may have been saying that the standards he demanded of Gentiles in v. 20 reflected universal moral laws that were enshrined in the law of Moses.
15:22–23a Judas and **Silas,** both **leading men among the brothers** in Jerusalem, accompanied Paul and Barnabas back to **Antioch** in order to vouch (personally and via hand-delivered letter) for the results of the Jerusalem Council.
15:23b–27 The letter not only conveyed the findings of the council but also commended the ministry of **Barnabas and Paul.**
15:28 James names both the Holy Spirit and human initiative (**ours**) as factors in the Council's decision. Throughout the NT,

there is interplay between divine guidance and human actions that accomplish God's purpose (e.g., Php 2:12–13).
15:29 The four things to avoid are repeated from v. 20 but in a different order.
15:30–31 The letter was an **encouragement** to the church at Antioch because it endorsed the strategy of Paul and Barnabas in evangelizing Gentiles and did not impose unnecessary burdens on new converts.
15:32–35 Judas and **Silas,** who were **prophets** in addition to being leading figures from the Jerusalem church, **encouraged** and **strengthened** the believers in Antioch with a **long message** that Scripture nowhere records. We are reminded yet again that many great speeches and vital events went unreported by the Bible's authors.
15:36 This verse marks the beginning of Paul's second missionary journey. Out of a sense of responsibility, Paul wanted to **visit** the converts in **every town** they had evangelized to see how they were progressing in the faith.
15:37–40 That Paul and Barnabas **parted company** over **John who was called Mark** shows that even within the apostolic

fellowship, perfect unity was not always obtainable. Sometimes God's workers have to agree to go separate ways. Paul took with him **Silas,** one of the men who had carried the Jerusalem letter to Antioch (vv. 23–34). Barnabas is not mentioned in the book of Acts after this incident.
15:41 Rather than going to Cyprus to strengthen the believers there, Paul and Silas went to **Syria** and the region of **Cilicia,** entering the province of Asia Minor.
16:1–3 Paul and Silas continued to retrace the first missionary journey by reentering Galatia. At Lystra, Paul invited a young **disciple named Timothy**—son of a Jewish woman and Greek man—to join him. Paul **circumcised** Timothy not because he was caving in to pressure from "believers who belonged to the party of the Pharisees" (15:5), but rather to show respect for Jewish law and identity given the fact that Timothy was half-Jewish. If Timothy had remained uncircumcised, it would seem to many Jews that he had rejected not just the Mosaic law but also his Jewish ethnicity. Paul's continuing mentorship of Timothy throughout his ministry resulted

at Lystra and Iconium spoke highly of him. ³ Paul wanted Timothy to go with him; so he took him and circumcised him because of the Jews who were in those places, since they all knew that his father was a Greek. ⁴ As they traveled through the towns, they delivered the decisions reached by the apostles and elders at Jerusalem for the people to observe. ⁵ So the churches were strengthened in the faith and grew daily in numbers.

Evangelization of Europe

⁶ They went through the region of Phrygia and Galatia; they had been forbidden by the Holy Spirit to speak the word in Asia. ⁷ When they came to Mysia, they tried to go into

Bithynia, but the Spirit of Jesus did not allow them. ⁸ Passing by Mysia they went down to Troas. ⁹ During the night Paul had a vision in which a Macedonian man was standing and pleading with him, "Cross over to Macedonia and help us!" ¹⁰ After he had seen the vision, we immediately made efforts to set out for Macedonia, concluding that God had called us to preach the gospel to them.

Lydia's Conversion

¹¹ From Troas we put out to sea and sailed straight for Samothrace, the next day to Neapolis, ¹² and from there to Philippi, a Roman colony and a leading city of the district of Macedonia. We stayed in that city for several days.

in, among other things, the writing of the letters 1 Timothy and 2 Timothy.
16:4 Besides evangelizing, Paul and his ministry partners conveyed the **decisions** of the **apostles and elders** in Jerusalem about circumcision and Gentile converts. Paul wanted to make clear that Gentiles could believe in Jesus without adhering to Jewish rites.
16:6–8 Paul and his companions passed through the region of **Galatia** (probably visiting Iconium and Antioch), and were **forbidden by the Holy Spirit to speak the word in Asia**. They were also prevented

by **the Spirit of Jesus** (i.e., Holy Spirit) from turning north **into Bithynia**. So they passed through **Mysia** and arrived at the coastal city of **Troas** in Asia. Luke did not indicate why the Spirit constrained Paul's plans or by what method he made known the restrictions.
16:9 In a **vision** Paul saw a **Macedonian man** plead with him to cross over the Aegean Sea to Europe and **help** them. Thus it seems Paul was restricted from preaching in other places because God planned for him to "preach the gospel" (v. 10) in Macedonia.

16:10 This is the beginning of the first "we" section in the book of Acts. It extends until v. 17. The "we" passages are vv. 10–17; 20:5–15; 21:1–18; 27:1–37; 28:1–16. The **we** likely indicates that Luke joined Paul's journey at these points. When connected together, the "we" passages form a continuous geographically joined narrative.
16:11–12 Philippi was a leading city of **Macedonia** but not the capital (Thessalonica). It was a **Roman colony** where a number of military veterans lived after completing their service. As a result, Roman law was in effect in Philippi.

THE SECOND MISSIONARY
JOURNEY OF PAUL

ACTS 15:36–18:22

• City
▲ Mountain peak
— Via Egnatia
⤫ Pass
← Route of Paul and Silas

[13] On the Sabbath day we went outside the city gate by the river, where we expected to find a place of prayer. We sat down and spoke to the women gathered there. [14] A God-fearing woman named Lydia, a dealer in purple cloth from the city of Thyatira, was listening. The Lord opened her heart to respond to what Paul was saying. [15] After she and her household were baptized, she urged us, "If you consider me a believer in the Lord, come and stay at my house." And she persuaded us.

Paul and Silas in Prison

[16] Once, as we were on our way to prayer, a slave girl met us who had a spirit by which she predicted the future. She made a large profit for her owners by fortune-telling. [17] As she followed Paul and us she cried out, "These men, who are proclaiming to you[a] a way of salvation, are the servants of the Most High God." [18] She did this for many days.

Paul was greatly annoyed. Turning to the spirit, he said, "I command you in the name of Jesus Christ to come out of her!" And it came out right away.

[19] When her owners realized that their hope of profit was gone, they seized Paul and Silas and dragged them into the marketplace to the authorities. [20] Bringing them before the chief magistrates, they said, "These men are seriously disturbing our city. They are Jews [21] and are promoting customs that are not legal for us as Romans to adopt or practice." [22] The crowd joined in the attack against them, and the chief magistrates stripped off their clothes and ordered them to be beaten with rods. [23] After they had severely flogged them, they threw them in jail, ordering the jailer to guard them carefully. [24] Receiving such an order, he put them into the inner prison and secured their feet in the stocks.

[a]16:17 Other mss read us

A Midnight Deliverance

[25] About midnight Paul and Silas were praying and singing hymns to God, and the prisoners were listening to them. [26] Suddenly there was such a violent earthquake that the foundations of the jail were shaken, and immediately all the doors were opened, and everyone's chains came loose. [27] When the jailer woke up and saw the doors of the prison standing open, he drew his sword and was going to kill himself, since he thought the prisoners had escaped. [28] But Paul called out in a loud voice, "Don't harm yourself, because we're all here!"

[29] The jailer called for lights, rushed in, and fell down trembling before Paul and Silas. [30] He escorted them out and said, "Sirs, what must I do to be saved?"

[31] They said, "Believe in the Lord Jesus, and you will be saved — you and your household." [32] And they spoke the word of the Lord to him along with everyone in his house. [33] He took them the same hour of the night and washed their wounds. Right away he and all his family were baptized. [34] He brought them into his house, set a meal before them, and rejoiced because he had come to believe in God with his entire household.

An Official Apology

[35] When daylight came, the chief magistrates sent the police to say, "Release those men."

[36] The jailer reported these words to Paul: "The magistrates have sent orders for you to be released. So come out now and go in peace."

[37] But Paul said to them, "They beat us in public without a trial, although we are Roman citizens, and threw us in jail. And now are they going to send us away secretly? Certainly not! On the contrary, let them come themselves and escort us out."

16:13 The **place of prayer** refers to the place where Jews of the city gathered. Philippi apparently did not have a synagogue, since only **women** and no men are mentioned. The establishment of a synagogue required the participation of at least ten Jewish men.

16:14 The name **Lydia** may have been a personal name, or it could merely indicate that this woman was from the city of Lydia. She is the only woman named in this passage (vv. 11–14). She was likely a prominent woman since Luke singled her out for her responsiveness to Paul's message. The **purple cloth** she sold had important uses in the Roman Empire. Luke combined both human and divine initiative in the description of Lydia's response. The Lord **opened her heart**, and she responded to what Paul said.

16:15 Household baptism is mentioned several times in the book of Acts (vv. 31–34; 18:8; cp. 11:14). It is never stated who exactly was involved in such baptisms. Lydia's response (16:14) and her question to Paul after her baptism suggest that only those of the household who were mature enough to make

their own positive response to the gospel would have been baptized.

16:16 That the **slave girl** had a **spirit by which she predicted the future** implies demonic possession.

16:17–18 Paul **was greatly annoyed**. Luke does not say why, but presumably Paul was irritated at the wild and distracting manner in which the girl carried on.

16:20–21 Paul and Silas were accused of causing civil disorder and **promoting customs** that were **not legal** among **Romans**. The practice of variant religion was not illegal in the Roman Empire, but any activity (religious or otherwise) that risked sparking civil unrest was frowned upon.

16:22–24 The **chief magistrates** acted rashly under the influence of **the crowd**. Paul and Silas were **stripped . . . beaten**, and thrown into **jail** before the charges against them were investigated.

16:27 If prisoners escaped, their Roman guards or jailers were forced to serve their sentences. Believing his **prisoners had escaped**, the Philippian jailer preferred a quick death over imprisonment or execution.

16:29–30 The jailer asked the most important question in the book of Acts: **What must I do to be saved?**

16:31 Paul and Silas had a direct answer for his straightforward question: **Believe in the Lord Jesus, and you will be saved—you and your household**. On household baptism, see note at v. 15.

16:32 Paul's initial response to the jailer was succinct and to the point. That Paul then **spoke the word of the Lord** may indicate that he followed his initial answer, which was aimed at bringing the jailer to saving faith, with a more detailed explanation aimed at building the new disciple's understanding of God and the Christian life.

16:33 Baptism for the jailer and **all his family** followed almost immediately upon their profession of faith in the Lord. On household baptism, see note at v. 15.

16:37 Paul knew the laws regulating punishment of Roman citizens. Having been illegally beaten and denied **trial**, he refused to be released and pretend nothing had happened. Paul's Roman citizenship is mentioned here for the first time in Acts (see 22:25–29; 23:27;

38 The police reported these words to the magistrates. They were afraid when they heard that Paul and Silas were Roman citizens. **39** So they came to appease them, and escorting them from prison, they urged them to leave town. **40** After leaving the jail, they came to Lydia's house, where they saw and encouraged the brothers and sisters, and departed.

A Short Ministry in Thessalonica

17 After they passed through Amphipolis and Apollonia, they came to Thessalonica, where there was a Jewish synagogue. **2** As usual, Paul went into the synagogue, and on three Sabbath days reasoned with them from the Scriptures, **3** explaining and proving that it was necessary for the Messiah to suffer and rise from the dead: "This Jesus I am proclaiming to you is the Messiah." **4** Some of them were persuaded and joined Paul and Silas, including a large number of God-fearing Greeks, as well as a number of the leading women.

Riot in the City

5 But the Jews became jealous, and they brought together some wicked men from the marketplace, formed a mob, and started a riot in the city. Attacking Jason's house, they searched for them to bring them out to the public assembly. **6** When they did not find them, they dragged Jason and some of the brothers before the city officials, shouting, "These men who have turned the world upside down have come here too, **7** and Jason has welcomed them. They are all acting contrary to Caesar's decrees, saying that there is another king — Jesus." **8** The crowd and city officials who heard

these things were upset. **9** After taking a security bond from Jason and the others, they released them.

The Bereans Search the Scriptures

10 As soon as it was night, the brothers and sisters sent Paul and Silas away to Berea. Upon arrival, they went into the synagogue of the Jews. **11** The people here were of more noble character than those in Thessalonica, since they received the word with eagerness and examined^A the Scriptures daily to see if these things were so. **12** Consequently, many of them believed, including a number of the prominent Greek women as well as men. **13** But when the Jews from Thessalonica found out that the word of God had been proclaimed by Paul at Berea, they came there too, agitating and upsetting^B the crowds. **14** Then the brothers and sisters immediately sent Paul away to go to the coast, but Silas and Timothy stayed on there. **15** Those who escorted Paul brought him as far as Athens, and after receiving instructions for Silas and Timothy to come to him as quickly as possible, they departed.

Paul in Athens

16 While Paul was waiting for them in Athens, he was deeply distressed when he saw that the city was full of idols. **17** So he reasoned in the synagogue with the Jews and with those who worshiped God, as well as in the marketplace every day with those who happened to be there. **18** Some of the Epicurean and Stoic philosophers also debated with him. Some said, "What is this ignorant show-off^C trying to say?"

---

^A 17:11 Or *asked about*   ^B 17:13 Other mss omit *and upsetting*   ^C 17:18 Lit *this seed picker*

25:11). Roman citizens were exempt from certain kinds of punishment (e.g., crucifixion) and were entitled to due process prior to punishment.

16:38 The fear of the magistrates is understandable. Philippi was a Roman colony that followed Roman law. Many people in the town would have known about the rights of a Roman citizen.

17:1 The next major stop on this second missionary journey was **Thessalonica**, where once again Paul began by visiting the local **synagogue**. He did this for three weeks (v. 2).
17:2–3 These verses give us insight into what Paul did when he visited synagogues. He **reasoned . . . from the Scriptures**, identifying Jesus as **Messiah** and explaining the necessity of his death and resurrection. Among Jews, who revered the OT as God's Word, Paul used the Scriptures as the basis for his argumentation.
17:4–5 The conversion of **a large number of God-fearing Greeks** and **leading women** prompted jealousy among unbelieving **Jews**. Paul had encountered resistance before, but this was an orchestrated movement involving the roundup of **wicked men from the marketplace**. Jason was apparently one of the Thessalonians who had become a

believer. He had welcomed Paul into his home (v. 7), so the **mob** attacked his house.
17:6 The phrase **these men who have turned the world upside down** may indicate that the Christians were mistaken for Jewish nationalists who had caused riots throughout the Roman Empire, but more likely it is an exaggerated reference to the unrest caused from town to town by Jews who opposed the Christian message.
17:7 Declaring that there was another king besides Caesar was a serious crime in the Roman Empire. This same false charge was used to condemn Jesus before Pilate (Lk 23:2).
17:8–9 The **security bond** from Jason probably promised he would send Paul and Silas away in order to guarantee the peace (cp. 1Th 2:14–18).
17:11 The Bereans exemplify the ideal stance of disciples: They were **of more noble character** and open to biblical instruction. They **examined the Scriptures daily** to see if the teachings were true.
17:13 Agitators from **Thessalonica** were unwilling to let faith flourish in **Berea**, and so **they came there too**, intent on thwarting the missionaries.
17:14 Paul set sail for Athens, while **Silas** and **Timothy** stayed behind and braved the

opposition in Berea. This seems to indicate that Paul had become the focal point of Jewish opposition to the Christian message.
17:15 Athens was 195 miles from Berea.
17:16 While waiting for Silas and Timothy to arrive from Berea, Paul observed **Athens** closely. He saw that it was **full of idols**. The city was also a center of intellectual, philosophical, and religious discussion. All of this **deeply distressed** Paul as a person who knew the one true God and his Son Jesus Christ.
17:17 Paul followed his custom and **reasoned in the synagogue**, but also expanded his audience even before the onset of trouble from the **Jews**, by taking the gospel to **the marketplace** and engaging whoever was there, likely including philosophers, rhetoricians, and teachers.
17:18 Epicurean and Stoic philosophers comprised two of the best-known philosophical schools of thought. Epicureans taught that one ought to lead a tranquil and contemplative life, free of passions and destructive emotions. They didn't deny the existence of gods but believed they were indifferent to humanity. Stoics were pantheists and believed the divine principle was found everywhere. Humans ought to live by

◥ The Bible and Civil Rights

by Kevin Smith

The Bible was central to the thought, rhetoric, and development of the civil rights movement. This was influenced by the essential role of Black churches and preachers in the organization of the movement. Not only was the movement characterized by meetings in churches and the singing of Negro spirituals, but it was also marked by biblical themes and language. Although many non-Christians participated in and supported the aims of the civil rights movement, the underlying truth claims about the nature of all humanity, regardless of ethnicity, were grounded in the Scriptures.

The central intellectual stream behind the movement focused on the issue of the equality of all humans, since they were created in the image of God (Gn 1:27), no matter the color of their skin. Throughout the Black freedom struggle in American history, the biblical teachings on creation and human dignity were foundational to the arguments being put forth both by scholars and by everyday people. Even those who were illiterate knew from the rhetoric of the movement that God had created all people from one man (Ac 17:26). This distinguishes the civil rights movement from other revolutions that may have been rooted in political, economic, philosophical, or other ideas. This unique biblical foundation provided a basis for the invocation of the God revealed in the Bible to be a participant in the movement—just as he had empowered the exodus.

In his famous "Letter from Birmingham Jail" written April 16, 1963, Dr. Martin Luther King Jr. used biblical examples as a defense when he was accused of being an interloper and an extremist for participating in demonstrations, sit-ins, and boycotts. When justifying his presence in Birmingham, Dr. King noted that he was invited by local organizers and that the Old Testament prophets left their villages to proclaim "thus saith the Lord" wherever God would send them. Additionally, he applauded the apostle Paul's travels in response to the call for help from the believers in Macedonia.

Grounding the movement morally in the Bible, King said, "A just law is a manmade code that squares with the moral law or the law of God." Therefore, the movement was able to attack laws that supported segregation and discrimination as laws that were ungodly, unjust, and against the clear teaching of Scripture. Certainly, America's founding documents—the Declaration of Independence and the U.S. Constitution—were an important part of the discourse, but the moral motivation and spiritual energy of the movement were grounded in the Bible. King even identified segregation as "sin" and called its proponents "sinful." He grounded his understanding of civil disobedience in the biblical example of Shadrach, Meshach, and Abednego, who refused to bow to the laws of Nebuchadnezzar because of their loyalty to a higher law—God's law. This was a vital part of his argument against passive or indifferent clergy, who sometimes grounded their opposition to King's actions in the rhetoric of "law and order." Many of the preachers involved in the movement would cite Old Testament prophets, especially Hosea and Amos, when "prophesying" against corrupt officials—especially sheriffs and other law enforcement officers who would attack protestors and demonstrators.

In a provocative section of his letter, King responds to charges that his activities will bring about negative consequences—conflict, possibly violent, between demonstrators and local law enforcement. The Baptist preacher chastised his critics by likening them to those who would say the teachings, actions, and devotions of Jesus the Christ "precipitated the evil act of crucifixion." This thinking was flawed and unethical in King's mind. In contrast to the violence that was brought to bear on protestors, King noted that the nonviolent approach of the civil rights movement was grounded in "the Negro church" and its biblical understanding of loving one's neighbor and praying for one's enemies.

Some of the clergy who refused to support King's efforts suggested the church should not get involved in "secular" affairs. Additionally, they retorted that the church's business was the saving of souls, not political concerns. The letter responds that such a neglect of social concerns is not logical, ethical, or biblical. In fact, King finds it a strange understanding of Christian ethics, saying, "I have watched many churches commit themselves to a completely otherworldly religion which makes a

Others replied, "He seems to be a preacher of foreign deities" — because he was telling the good news about Jesus and the resurrection. [19] They took him and brought him to the Areopagus,[A] and said, "May we learn about this new teaching you are presenting? [20] Because what you say sounds strange to us, and we want to know what these things mean." [21] Now all the Athenians and the foreigners residing there spent their time on nothing else but telling or hearing something new.

The Areopagus Address

[22] Paul stood in the middle of the Areopagus and said, "People of Athens! I see that you are extremely religious in every respect. [23] For as I was passing through and observing the objects of your worship, I even found an altar on which was inscribed, 'To an Unknown God.' Therefore, what you worship in ignorance, this I proclaim to you. [24] The God who made the world and everything in it — he is Lord of heaven and earth — does not live in shrines made by hands. [25] Neither is he served by human hands, as though he needed anything, since he himself gives everyone life and breath and all things. [26] From one man[B] he has made every nationality to live over the whole earth and has determined their appointed times and the boundaries of where they live. [27] He did this so that they might seek God, and perhaps they might reach out and find him, though he is not far from each one of us. [28] For in him we live and move and have our being, as even some of your own poets have said, 'For we are also his offspring.' [29] Since, then, we are God's offspring, we shouldn't think that the divine nature is like gold or silver or stone, an image fashioned by human art and imagination.

[A] 17:19 Or Mars Hill   [B] 17:26 Other mss read blood

---

reason, the divine principle within them, so as to achieve a virtuous life. An **ignorant** **show-off** was actually a slang term that meant "seed-picker."

17:19–21 The *Areopagus* was a rocky hill in Athens overlooking the marketplace. The word **Areopagus** was also used to refer to the council that originally met on the hill. During Hellenistic times, the council probably met in the *agora*—or marketplace. The Greek text here is ambiguous. So it could be that Paul gave an address on the hilltop or

that he appeared before this Athenian council elsewhere. The term *Areopagus* means "hill of Ares." Ares, the Greek god of war, was equivalent to the Roman god, Mars. So the hilltop was also known as Mars Hill. **17:22–31** This is Paul's third and final missionary speech in the book of Acts. He appealed to the Athenians' religious inclinations, drew upon observable data from nature to discuss the attributes of **God**, marshaled insights from pagan poets, and identified God and the need for humans to **repent** in

preparation for the **day** in which God will **judge the world in righteousness** through Jesus Christ, whom God vindicated **by raising him from the dead**. **17:22–23** As an example of Athenian superstition, Paul noted the altar erected **To an Unknown God**. Doubtless it was erected to ensure that no gods were overlooked (and thus angered) in the people's devotion. **17:28** Paul quoted (**For we are also his offspring**) someone whom these philosophers would have recognized—a Greek

---

strange, un-Biblical distinction between body and soul, between the sacred and the secular."

Finally, the Bible and its sweeping story are on display in an extended passage where King cites biblical leaders and figures from church history in defense against the assertion that he was an extremist.

Though I was initially disappointed at being categorized as an extremist, as I continued to think about the matter I gradually gained a measure of satisfaction from the label. Was not Jesus an extremist for love: "Love your enemies, bless them that curse you, do good to them that hate you, and pray for them which despitefully use you, and persecute you." Was not Amos an extremist for justice: "Let justice roll down like waters and righteousness like an everflowing stream." Was not Paul an extremist for the Christian gospel: "I bear in my body the marks of the Lord Jesus." Was not Martin Luther an extremist: "Here I stand; I cannot do otherwise, so help me God." And John Bunyan: "I will stay in jail until the end of my days before I make a butchery of my conscience." And Abraham

Lincoln: "This nation cannot survive half slave and half free." And Thomas Jefferson: "We hold these truths to be selfevident, that all men are created equal . . ." So the question is not whether we will be extremists, but what kind of extremists we will be. Will we be extremists for hate or for love? Will we be extremists for the preservation of injustice or for the extension of justice? In that dramatic scene on Calvary's hill three men were crucified. We must never forget that all three were crucified for the same crime— the crime of extremism. Two were extremists for immorality, and thus fell below their environment. The other, Jesus Christ, was an extremist for love, truth, and goodness, and thereby rose above his environment. Perhaps the South, the nation, and the world are in dire need of creative extremists.

Martin Luther King Jr. served many roles in the civil rights movement: he was its face, an ethicist, a theologian, an organizer, and a public relations agent. In all of these roles, his thinking and rhetoric were shaped and influenced by the Bible. Thus, so was the larger movement.

[30] "Therefore, having overlooked the times of ignorance, God now commands all people everywhere to repent, [31] because he has set a day when he is going to judge the world in righteousness by the man he has appointed. He has provided proof of this to everyone by raising him from the dead."

[32] When they heard about the resurrection of the dead, some began to ridicule him, but others said, "We'd like to hear from you again about this." [33] So Paul left their presence. [34] However, some people joined him and believed, including Dionysius the Areopagite, a woman named Damaris, and others with them.

Founding the Corinthian Church

18 After this, he[A] left Athens and went to Corinth, [2] where he found a Jew named Aquila, a native of Pontus, who had recently come from Italy with his wife Priscilla because Claudius had ordered all the Jews to leave Rome. Paul came to them, [3] and since they were of the same occupation, tentmakers by trade, he stayed with them and worked. [4] He reasoned in the synagogue every Sabbath and tried to persuade both Jews and Greeks.

[5] When Silas and Timothy arrived from Macedonia, Paul devoted himself to preaching the word[B] and testified to the Jews that Jesus is the Messiah. [6] When they resisted and blasphemed, he shook out his clothes and told them, "Your blood is on your own heads! I am innocent.[C] From now on I will go to the Gentiles." [7] So he left there and went to the house of a man named Titius Justus, a worshiper of God,

whose house was next door to the synagogue. [8] Crispus, the leader of the synagogue, believed in the Lord, along with his whole household. Many of the Corinthians, when they heard, believed and were baptized.

[9] The Lord said to Paul in a night vision, "Don't be afraid, but keep on speaking and don't be silent. [10] For I am with you, and no one will lay a hand on you to hurt you, because I have many people in this city." [11] He stayed there a year and a half, teaching the word of God among them.

[12] While Gallio was proconsul of Achaia, the Jews made a united attack against Paul and brought him to the tribunal. [13] "This man," they said, "is persuading people to worship God in ways contrary to the law."

[14] As Paul was about to open his mouth, Gallio said to the Jews, "If it were a matter of wrongdoing or of a serious crime, it would be reasonable for me to put up with you Jews. [15] But if these are questions about words, names, and your own law, see to it yourselves. I refuse to be a judge of such things." [16] So he drove them from the tribunal. [17] And they all[D] seized Sosthenes, the leader of the synagogue, and beat him in front of the tribunal, but none of these things mattered to Gallio.

The Return Trip to Antioch

[18] After staying for some time, Paul said farewell to the brothers and sisters and sailed away to Syria, accompanied by Priscilla and Aquila. He shaved his head at Cenchreae because of a vow he had taken. [19] When they reached Ephesus he left them there, but he himself

---

[A] 18:1 Other mss read Paul   [B] 18:5 Other mss read was urged by the Spirit   [C] 18:6 Lit clean   [D] 18:17 Other mss read Then all the Greeks

---

poet named Aratus who lived about 315–240 BC.

17:32–33 Neither Stoics nor Epicureans believed in the possibility of bodily **resurrection**, though the Stoics did believe the human spirit continued to exist after bodily death. In any event, Paul's talk about bodily resurrection earned him **ridicule** but also a measure of curiosity.

17:34 Paul's missionary efforts in Athens were not as successful as they were elsewhere since he founded no church there. But there were a number of converts. These included a member of the Areopagus, **Dionysius**, a man of distinction because of this prestigious membership. **Damaris** may also have been a woman of distinction since Luke bothered to name her (vv. 4–5).

18:1 Corinth was another leading city of Greece (Achaia). Its two harbors made it a center of trade for the Mediterranean area.

18:2 It appears that in AD 41 Emperor Claudius prohibited Jews from gathering together in Rome. Then in AD 49 he expelled them altogether, probably because the earlier measures did not work. Presumably **Aquila** and **Priscilla** were expelled at this time. That they had **recently** arrived from **Italy** suggests that Paul arrived in Corinth in about AD 50.

18:3 Tentmakers refers to people who worked in leather, possibly related to

working in the goat hair cloth that was made in Cilicia, Paul's home region.

18:4 The **Greeks** were likely God-fearers Paul encountered at the synagogue, but possibly outside as well.

18:5 When **Silas** and **Timothy** finally caught up with Paul in Corinth, he was engaged in what he did best—**preaching the word** and bearing witness to the Jews that Jesus was the **Messiah**.

18:6 Shook out his clothes symbolized that Paul was finished giving priority to Jewish evangelism, as if he were shaking the dust from the folds of his garment. He would concentrate on the more fruitful harvest among the **Gentiles**. Similarly, in 13:46 Paul and Barnabas responded to persistent Jewish rejection of the gospel by saying they were "turning to the Gentiles."

18:7–8 Paul's vow in v. 6 did not mean no one from the synagogue had accepted his message, as the conversion of **Crispus** and **his whole household** indicates. Also, since **Titius Justus** (a Gentile) was said to be a **worshiper of God**, he almost certainly had been a member of **the synagogue** that was right **next door** to his home.

18:9–11 Paul had experienced trouble in previous towns, including Philippi, Thessalonica, and Berea. But the Lord assured him that he would have a productive ministry in

Corinth, which explains why he stayed for **a year and a half**.

18:12 The time when **Gallio was proconsul of Achaia**, of which Corinth was the capital, is a relatively firm date in NT chronology. An inscription found at Delphi says Gallio was installed as proconsul in early AD 51. Paul appeared before him later that year.

18:13 For another instance in which Paul was accused of persuading people **to worship God in ways contrary to the law**, see 16:20–21 and the note there.

18:14–17 Gallio seemed both perceptive (**I refuse to be a judge of such things**) and negligent (the beating of **Sosthenes** did not concern him).

18:18 It is not clear that **Paul** was the one who **shaved his head at Cenchreae**. It may have been **Aquila**. The Greek syntax seems to indicate the latter, but it is uncertain. The vow may have been a Nazirite vow. If Paul was the person who made the vow, his going up to Jerusalem to visit "the church" (v. 22) may have included a stop at the temple to complete the vow and make an offering of his hair. Such activity was unusual for Paul, especially outside of Judea (cp. 21:26), but would have been consistent with his Jewish identity.

18:19–20 Paul's stop at **Ephesus** must have been very short since he apparently did not

entered the synagogue and debated with the Jews. **²⁰** When they asked him to stay for a longer time, he declined, **²¹** but he said farewell and added,^A "I'll come back to you again, if God wills." Then he set sail from Ephesus.

²² On landing at Caesarea, he went up to Jerusalem and greeted the church, then went down to Antioch.

²³ After spending some time there, he set out, traveling through one place after another in the region of Galatia and Phrygia, strengthening all the disciples.

The Eloquent Apollos

²⁴ Now a Jew named Apollos, a native Alexandrian, an eloquent man who was competent in the use of the Scriptures, arrived in Ephesus. **²⁵** He had been instructed in the way of the Lord; and being fervent in spirit,^B he was speaking and teaching accurately about Jesus, although he knew only John's baptism. **²⁶** He began to speak boldly in the synagogue. After Priscilla and Aquila heard him, they took him aside^C and explained the way of God to him more accurately. **²⁷** When he wanted to cross over to Achaia, the brothers and sisters wrote to the disciples to welcome him. After he arrived, he was a great help to those who by grace had believed. **²⁸** For he vigorously refuted the Jews in public, demonstrating through the Scriptures that Jesus is the Messiah.

---

^A **18:21** Other mss add *"By all means it is necessary to keep the coming festival in Jerusalem. But* ^B **18:25** Or *in the Spirit*
^C **18:26** Lit *they received him*

---

encounter Apollos (vv. 24–28) or the misguided teaching that he countered in his later, extended visit to Ephesus (chap. 19). **18:21** Paul promised to come back to Ephesus **if God wills**, as indeed he did (19:1). **18:22** Paul's return to **Antioch** marks the completion of his second missionary journey. **18:23** This marks the beginning of Paul's third missionary journey. Like the first two, this one began from Antioch and retraced his steps through Asia Minor, particularly the Phrygian region of the province of Galatia.

18:24–25 Apollos was from Alexandria, Egypt, the most learned city in the Greco-Roman world. Since Apollos had been **instructed in the way of the Lord**, we know that Christianity had reached Egypt by this time. However, his knowledge of Christianity was deficient since he **knew only the baptism** of John the Baptist. Nonetheless, some take **fervent in spirit** to mean that Apollos was already filled with the Holy Spirit. However, it is more likely that Apollos was serious about his dawning faith in

Christ but had not yet received the baptism of the Holy Spirit. **18:26** We see here that speaking **boldly** about Jesus is not enough. One must also **accurately** understand the faith. **Priscilla and Aquila** served both Apollos and the kingdom by taking time to instruct him. **18:27–28** Once Apollos's rhetorical skills were coupled with accurate understanding of the Christian faith, he left Ephesus and went to **Achaia** (Corinth, 19:1). He **vigorously refuted the Jews** using apologetic

THE THIRD MISSIONARY JOURNEY OF PAUL
ACTS 18:23–21:17

- City
- Site of the Seven Churches of Asia
- Mountain peak
- Roads
- Pass
- Paul's routes

Twelve Disciples of John the Baptist

19 While Apollos was in Corinth, Paul traveled through the interior regions and came to Ephesus. He found some disciples [2] and asked them, "Did you receive the Holy Spirit when you believed?"

"No," they told him, "we haven't even heard that there is a Holy Spirit."

[3] "Into what then were you baptized?" he asked them.

"Into John's baptism," they replied.

[4] Paul said, "John baptized with a baptism of repentance, telling the people that they should believe in the one who would come after him, that is, in Jesus."

[5] When they heard this, they were baptized into the name of the Lord Jesus. [6] And when Paul had laid his hands on them, the Holy Spirit came on them, and they began to speak in tongues[A] and to prophesy. [7] Now there were about twelve men in all.

In the Lecture Hall of Tyrannus

[8] Paul entered the synagogue and spoke boldly over a period of three months, arguing and persuading them about the kingdom of God. [9] But when some became hardened and would not believe, slandering the Way in front of the crowd, he withdrew from them, taking the disciples, and conducted discussions every day in the lecture hall of Tyrannus. [10] This went on for two years, so that all the residents of Asia, both Jews and Greeks, heard the word of the Lord.

Demonism Defeated at Ephesus

[11] God was performing extraordinary miracles by Paul's hands, [12] so that even facecloths or aprons[B] that had touched his skin were brought to the sick, and the diseases left them, and the evil spirits came out of them. [13] Now some of the itinerant Jewish exorcists also attempted to pronounce the name of the Lord Jesus over those who had evil spirits, saying, "I command you by the Jesus that Paul preaches!" [14] Seven sons of Sceva, a Jewish high priest, were doing this. [15] The evil spirit answered them, "I know Jesus, and I recognize Paul — but who are you?" [16] Then the man who had the evil spirit jumped on them, overpowered them all, and prevailed against them, so that they ran out of that house naked and wounded. [17] When this became known to everyone who lived in Ephesus, both Jews and Greeks, they became afraid, and the name of the Lord Jesus was held in high esteem.

[18] And many who had become believers came confessing and disclosing their practices, [19] while many of those who had practiced magic collected their books and burned them in front of everyone. So they calculated their value and found it to be fifty thousand pieces of silver. [20] In this way the word of the Lord spread and prevailed.

The Riot in Ephesus

[21] After these events, Paul resolved by the Spirit[C] to pass through Macedonia and Achaia and go to Jerusalem. "After I've been there," he said, "It is necessary for me to see Rome as well." [22] After sending to Macedonia two of those who assisted him, Timothy and Erastus, he himself stayed in Asia for a while.

[23] About that time there was a major disturbance about the Way. [24] For a person named Demetrius, a silversmith who made silver shrines of Artemis, provided a great deal of business for the craftsmen. [25] When he had assembled them, as well as the workers engaged in this type of business, he said, "Men, you know that our prosperity is derived from this business. [26] You see and hear that not only in Ephesus, but in almost all of Asia, this man Paul has persuaded and misled a considerable number of people by saying that gods made by hand are not gods. [27] Not only do we run a risk that our business may be discredited, but also that the temple of the great goddess Artemis may be despised and her magnificence come to the

and instructional techniques similar to Paul's.

19:1–6 This is one of the most difficult NT passages to interpret. The basic question is whether these disciples were genuine Christians when Paul first met them. Some argue that they were not since they had neither received the Holy Spirit nor been baptized into Christ. Others insist that they were genuine Christians who had not yet received full knowledge of the faith.

19:5–7 The order of conversion here follows the typical pattern in Acts except for the laying on of **hands**, the mention of **tongues**, and the ability to prophesy as immediate results of the Spirit's coming.

19:8 Paul's discussion there marks only the second time that Paul mentioned **the kingdom of God** in his preaching as recorded in Acts (14:22).

19:9 Tyrannus either owned the **lecture hall** or taught there regularly.

19:10 After three months of speaking in the synagogue (v. 8), Paul spent another **two years** teaching in Ephesus, making a significant impact on the province of **Asia**.

19:11–12 That **Paul's** personal items (**facecloths or aprons**) were involved demonstrates his identity as an apostle.

19:15–16 The **evil spirit** knew that the exorcists did not share in Christ's authority through faith. The consequences of frivolously invoking Jesus's name were severe. That the men fled **naked** was especially humiliating since Jews shunned nudity.

19:19–20 Books were expensive in ancient times. The **fifty thousand pieces of silver** could be the Greek drachma or the Roman denarius. Either way it would have been a large sum of money.

19:21 Paul intended to return to the places he had evangelized earlier on his second missionary trip and then go to **Jerusalem**. After taking the collection to Jerusalem, he planned to proceed to Rome.

19:22 Some believe the **Erastus** mentioned here is the same as in Rm 16:23, while others dispute this.

19:23–25 The cult of **Artemis** at Ephesus was part of a larger Greek cult of Artemis, the "Great Mother." As with many ancient cults, artisans like **Demetrius** made their living by fashioning cultic items such as idols. Paul's preaching jeopardized this vocation (vv. 25–26).

19:26–27 The Ephesian **temple** of Artemis, whose foundations went back to the eighth century BC, was one of the seven wonders of the ancient world. The ruins of the temple were discovered in the nineteenth century, and the altar was uncovered in 1965.

verge of ruin — the very one all of Asia and the world worship."

²⁸ When they had heard this, they were filled with rage and began to cry out, "Great is Artemis of the Ephesians!" ²⁹ So the city was filled with confusion, and they rushed all together into the amphitheater, dragging along Gaius and Aristarchus, Macedonians who were Paul's traveling companions. ³⁰ Although Paul wanted to go in before the people, the disciples did not let him. ³¹ Even some of the provincial officials of Asia, who were his friends, sent word to him, pleading with him not to venture^A into the amphitheater. ³² Some were shouting one thing and some another, because the assembly was in confusion, and most of them did not know why they had come together. ³³ Some Jews in the crowd gave instructions to Alexander^B after they pushed him to the front. Motioning with his hand, Alexander wanted to make his defense to the people. ³⁴ But when they recognized that he was a Jew, they all shouted in unison for about two hours, "Great is Artemis of the Ephesians!"

³⁵ When the city clerk had calmed the crowd down, he said, "People of Ephesus! What person is there who doesn't know that the city of the Ephesians is the temple guardian of the great^C Artemis, and of the image that fell from heaven? ³⁶ Therefore, since these things are undeniable, you must keep calm and not do anything rash. ³⁷ For you have brought these men here who are not temple robbers or blasphemers of our^D goddess. ³⁸ So if Demetrius and the craftsmen who are with him have a case against anyone, the courts are in session, and there are proconsuls. Let them bring charges against one another. ³⁹ But if you seek anything further, it must be decided in a legal assembly. ⁴⁰ In fact, we run a risk of being charged with

rioting for what happened today, since there is no justification that we can give as a reason for this disturbance." ⁴¹ After saying this, he dismissed the assembly.

Paul in Macedonia

20 After the uproar was over, Paul sent for the disciples, encouraged them, and after saying farewell, departed to go to Macedonia. ² And when he had passed through those areas and offered them many words of encouragement, he came to Greece ³ and stayed three months. The Jews plotted against him when he was about to set sail for Syria, and so he decided to go back through Macedonia. ⁴ He was accompanied^E by Sopater son of Pyrrhus^F from Berea, Aristarchus and Secundus from Thessalonica, Gaius from Derbe, Timothy, and Tychicus and Trophimus from the province of Asia. ⁵ These men went on ahead and waited for us in Troas, ⁶ but we sailed away from Philippi after the Festival of Unleavened Bread. In five days we reached them at Troas, where we spent seven days.

Eutychus Revived at Troas

⁷ On the first day of the week, we assembled to break bread. Paul spoke to them, and since he was about to depart the next day, he kept on talking until midnight. ⁸ There were many lamps in the room upstairs where we were assembled, ⁹ and a young man named Eutychus was sitting on a window sill and sank into a deep sleep as Paul kept on talking. When he was overcome by sleep, he fell down from the third story and was picked up dead. ¹⁰ But Paul went down, bent over him, embraced him, and said, "Don't be alarmed, because he's alive." ¹¹ After going upstairs, breaking the bread, and eating, Paul talked a long time until dawn. Then

^A 19:31 Lit *not to give himself*   ^B 19:33 Or *thought it was about Alexander*   ^C 19:35 Other mss add *goddess*   ^D 19:37 Other mss read *your*   ^E 20:4 Other mss add *to Asia*   ^F 20:4 Other mss omit *son of Pyrrhus*

19:29–31 The Ephesian **amphitheater** seated twenty-four thousand people and was thoroughly remodeled in the first century. **The disciples** wisely kept **Paul** from joining his **traveling companions**. It would have been a senseless self-sacrifice to enter into the clutches of such a hostile mob. That some of the **provincial officials** also pleaded with Paul to stay away shows that he had come to be well regarded by some leaders in the province.
19:32 True to mob mentality, **most of them** had no idea why they had gathered in the amphitheater.
19:33–34 The Jews of the city understandably wanted to distance themselves from the controversy caused by Paul and his followers. They shoved forward one of their own, **Alexander**, a Hellenistic Jew (as indicated by his name), to offer an apology on their behalf. Ironically, the Jews would have had the same view of the Artemis cult as Paul and his followers, but in this case they did not want to be lumped in with them. As for

the Ephesian mob, they disallowed such a distinction. They knew that anyone whose religious roots were Jewish represented opposition to Artemis.
19:35 The **image that fell from heaven** may indicate that the Artemis cult was inspired by a meteorite that fell to earth. Alternatively, this could be a way of saying that the cult was thought to originate with the gods.
19:36–39 In this case, the city clerk made it clear that the actions of Demetrius were against the law and did not follow due process.
19:40–41 Fear of Roman reprisal was a common motivator for clearing up civil unrest. There is no mention of further legal action taken. This shows that Paul and his followers had broken no laws. They were simply upsetting those who profited from the Artemis cult.
20:1 Paul took one last occasion to gather the believers in Ephesus before going to **Macedonia**.

20:2–3 Paul probably went to Philippi and Thessalonica in Macedonia before going to **Greece** (Achaia), where he stayed for **three months**, possibly in Athens and Corinth. Paul's Jewish opponents **plotted against him**, which caused him to change his travel plans. He decided to travel overland from Greece to Macedonia, where he caught a ship at Philippi.
20:4 A number of Paul's companions hailed from cities he had visited during his missionary journeys.
20:5 The "we" narrative resumes and continues through v. 15 (see note at 16:10).
20:7 On the first day of the week, Paul gathered with other believers to **break bread**, a tradition that apparently began soon after the resurrection and ascension of Christ. Because he was leaving the next day (this event occurred at the end of his week in Troas), Paul spoke **until midnight**.
20:9–10 It is not clear whether **Eutychus** was actually dead or just unconscious. Paul's statement that **he's alive** (lit "his life is in

he left. [12] They brought the boy home alive and were greatly comforted.

From Troas to Miletus

[13] We went on ahead to the ship and sailed for Assos, where we were going to take Paul on board, because these were his instructions, since he himself was going by land. [14] When he met us at Assos, we took him on board and went on to Mitylene. [15] Sailing from there, the next day we arrived off Chios. The following day we crossed over to Samos, and[A] the day after, we came to Miletus. [16] For Paul had decided to sail past Ephesus to avoid spending time in the province of Asia, because he was hurrying to be in Jerusalem, if possible, for the day of Pentecost.

Farewell Address to the Ephesian Elders

[17] Now from Miletus, he sent to Ephesus and summoned the elders of the church. [18] When they came to him, he said to them, "You know, from the first day I set foot in Asia, how I was with you the whole time, [19] serving the Lord with all humility, with tears, and during the trials that came to me through the plots of the Jews. [20] You know that I did not avoid proclaiming to you anything that was profitable or from teaching you publicly and from house to house. [21] I testified to both Jews and Greeks about repentance toward God and faith in our Lord Jesus.

[22] "And now I am on my way to Jerusalem, compelled by the Spirit,[B] not knowing what I will encounter there, [23] except that in every town the Holy Spirit warns me that chains and afflictions are waiting for me. [24] But I consider my life of no value to myself; my purpose is to finish my course[C] and the ministry I received from the Lord Jesus, to testify to the gospel of God's grace.

[25] "And now I know that none of you, among whom I went about preaching the kingdom, will ever see me again. [26] Therefore I declare to you this day that I am innocent[D] of the blood of all of you, [27] because I did not avoid declaring to you the whole plan of God. [28] Be on guard for yourselves and for all the flock of which the Holy Spirit has appointed you as overseers, to shepherd the church of God,[E] which he purchased with his own blood. [29] I know that after my departure savage wolves will come in among you, not sparing the flock. [30] Men will rise up even from your own number and distort the truth to lure the disciples into following them. [31] Therefore be on the alert, remembering that night and day for three years I never stopped warning each one of you with tears.

[32] "And now I commit you to God and to the word of his grace, which is able to build you up and to give you an inheritance among all who are sanctified. [33] I have not coveted anyone's silver or gold or clothing. [34] You yourselves know that I worked with my own hands to support myself and those who are with me. [35] In every way I've shown you that it is necessary to help the weak by laboring like this and to remember the words of the Lord Jesus, because he said, 'It is more blessed to give than to receive.'"

[36] After he said this, he knelt down and prayed with all of them. [37] There were many tears shed by everyone. They embraced Paul and kissed him, [38] grieving most of all over his statement that they would never see his face again. And they accompanied him to the ship.

Warnings on the Journey to Jerusalem

21 After we tore ourselves away from them, we set sail straight for Cos, the next day to Rhodes, and from there to Patara. [2] Finding a ship crossing over to Phoenicia, we boarded and set sail. [3] After we sighted Cyprus, passing to the south of it,[F] we sailed on to Syria and arrived at Tyre, since the ship was to unload

---

[A]20:15 Other mss add *after staying at Trogyllium*   [B]20:22 Or *in my spirit*   [C]20:24 Other mss add *with joy*   [D]20:26 Lit *clean*   [E]20:28 Some mss read *church of the Lord*; other mss read *church of the Lord and God*   [F]21:3 Lit *leaving it on the left*

him") suggests Eutychus was unconscious. If so, **picked up dead** would mean he appeared to be dead.
20:13–14 The narrative follows the events of those in the "we" group (see note at 16:10), who sailed from Troas to Assos, where they met Paul, who had traveled by **land**.
20:15 The group met in Assos, where Paul joined the ship, stopping at several ports before its arrival in **Miletus**. This verse ends the **we** section (see note at 16:10).
20:16 Paul appears to have consciously decided to **sail past Ephesus** in his hurry to get to Jerusalem for Pentecost. He may have wanted to avoid Ephesus because of the possibility that his presence would cause unrest (cp. 19:23–41). Also, he had close ties with the Ephesian church, and it might have been difficult to take leave of them if he had stopped in the city.

20:17 The port at **Miletus** was about thirty miles south of **Ephesus**. In this verse the leaders of the church in Ephesus are called **elders**, but they are referred to as "overseers" in v. 28. These terms designate a functional and formal title of church leadership.
20:18–35 This speech differs from Paul's others in Acts. It is the only one delivered to a group of believers.
20:21 Paul's message to both **Jews and Greeks** called for **repentance** toward God for one's sins and **faith** in the **Lord Jesus**. This is an excellent summary of the mission of the church.
20:25 Paul's intention after visiting Jerusalem was to head to Rome and beyond. This is why he declared to the Ephesian elders that he would not see any of them again (cp. v. 38).
20:28 The leaders of the Ephesian church are here called **overseers** rather than elders (see

note at v. 17), appointed by the **Holy Spirit** for their task. Reference here to redemption through the **blood** of Jesus is unique in Acts, but the language reflects Paul's statements elsewhere (Rm 3:25; 5:9; Eph 2:13).
20:33–35 Paul was more motivated by money. Jesus' saying, **It is more blessed to give than to receive**, is found only here. It resembles some of Jesus' sayings elsewhere (Lk 6:38). Jesus obviously said much more than is recorded in the Gospels (Jn 20:30–31; 21:25).
21:1 The shipboard journey continued from Ephesus by way of **Cos** to **Rhodes** and **Patara**. This is the third "we" section in Acts (see note at 16:10). It extends through 21:18.
21:2 They left the smaller ship at Patara and took a larger one able to travel the four hundred miles to Phoenicia.
21:3 The most common vessels sailing the Mediterranean were grain ships from Egypt,

its cargo there. [4] We sought out the disciples and stayed there seven days. Through the Spirit they told Paul not to go to Jerusalem. [5] When our time had come to an end, we left to continue our journey, while all of them, with their wives and children, accompanied us out of the city. After kneeling down on the beach to pray, [6] we said farewell to one another and boarded the ship, and they returned home.

[7] When we completed our voyage[A] from Tyre, we reached Ptolemais, where we greeted the brothers and sisters and stayed with them for a day. [8] The next day we left and came to Caesarea, where we entered the house of Philip the evangelist, who was one of the Seven, and stayed with him. [9] This man had four virgin daughters who prophesied.

[10] After we had been there for several days, a prophet named Agabus came down from Judea. [11] He came to us, took Paul's belt, tied his own feet and hands, and said, "This is what the Holy Spirit says: 'In this way the Jews in Jerusalem will bind the man who owns this belt and deliver him over to the Gentiles.'" [12] When we heard this, both we and the local people pleaded with him not to go up to Jerusalem.

[13] Then Paul replied, "What are you doing, weeping and breaking my heart? For I am ready not only to be bound but also to die in Jerusalem for the name of the Lord Jesus."

[14] Since he would not be persuaded, we said no more except, "The Lord's will be done."

Conflict over the Gentile Mission

[15] After this we got ready and went up to Jerusalem. [16] Some of the disciples from Caesarea also went with us and brought us to Mnason of Cyprus, an early disciple, with whom we were to stay.

[17] When we reached Jerusalem, the brothers and sisters welcomed us warmly. [18] The following day Paul went in with us to James, and all the elders were present. [19] After greeting them, he reported in detail what God had done among the Gentiles through his ministry.

[20] When they heard it, they glorified God and said, "You see, brother, how many thousands of Jews there are who have believed, and they are all zealous for the law. [21] But they have been informed about you — that you are teaching all the Jews who are among the Gentiles to abandon Moses, telling them not to circumcise their children or to live according to our customs. [22] So what is to be done?[B] They will certainly hear that you've come. [23] Therefore do what we tell you: We have four men who have made a vow. [24] Take these men, purify yourself along with them, and pay for them to get their heads shaved. Then everyone will know that what they were told about you amounts to nothing, but that you yourself are also careful about observing the law. [25] With regard to the Gentiles who have believed, we have written a letter containing our decision that[C] they should keep themselves from food sacrificed to idols, from blood, from what is strangled, and from sexual immorality."

The Riot in the Temple

[26] So the next day, Paul took the men, having purified himself along with them, and entered the temple, announcing the completion of the

---

[A] 21:7 Or *As we continued our voyage*   [B] 21:22 Other mss add *A multitude has to come together, since*   [C] 21:25 Other mss add *they should observe no such thing, except that*

---

heading to the rest of the Roman Empire (but especially Rome).

21:5–6 The departure from the Christians at Tyre resembled the departure from Miletus and the Ephesian elders (20:37–38). They knew Paul was heading for his deepest trouble yet.

21:7 Ptolemais is also known as Acco (Jdg 1:31).

21:8 Philip the evangelist was probably so called to distinguish him from other Philips. He was one of those selected to serve in the church in Jerusalem (see note at 6:5–6). Philip eventually settled with his daughters in **Caesarea**. He is identified as **one of the Seven** (6:3).

21:9 The word **virgin** means Philip's daughters were young and unmarried.

21:10–11 Agabus (see note at 11:27–28) explicitly stated that Paul would fall into hostile hands in Jerusalem. As it turned out (21:30–36), Paul was delivered by Gentiles out of Jewish hands, but then remained in Gentile hands throughout the rest of the book of Acts.

21:12 With such an explicit prophecy, it is not surprising that Paul's traveling companions and the locals **pleaded with him** not to go on to **Jerusalem**.

21:15–16 Mnason of Cyprus was a believer who had probably been saved during the

first missionary journey. "Mnason" may be a Hellenized form of a Jewish name, or he may have been a Gentile.

21:18 James, Jesus's half-brother, is singled out as the leader of the church in Jerusalem, along with a group of **elders**. This verse marks the end of this "we" section.

21:19 As Paul did in his previous major meeting in Jerusalem (15:4), he told James and the church elders what God had been doing **among the Gentiles** through his ministry. This was an appropriate follow-up to the original Jerusalem Council (see note at 15:2).

21:20 Having listened to Paul's report about what God had done "among the Gentiles" (v. 19), the Jerusalem leadership rejoiced but also answered back with something like one-upmanship. Mention of **many thousands of Jews** converting in Jerusalem was perhaps exaggeration, for the city had a population between twenty-five thousand and fifty thousand. At issue in the back-and-forth between Jerusalem leaders and Paul (minister to the Gentiles) is the role of the law in Christian faith; thus the emphasis on Jewish believers being **zealous for the law**. Perhaps this response also represented an attempt by believers in Jerusalem to strengthen their position as they saw the center of the church shift to Gentile Christians.

21:21 Rumor said Paul was teaching Jews who were dispersed among Gentiles to disregard Mosaic law and traditional Jewish rituals such as circumcision. To dismiss these fears, the brothers proposed a solution that would absolve Paul of the charges (vv. 23–24).

21:22–24 The elders worked out a solution through which Paul could demonstrate his respect for the law and his Jewish identity and put to rest rumors that he was against the law. Paul was not opposed to circumcising Timothy (16:3) or to taking Jewish vows (18:18). What he opposed was any claim that such observances of Jewish law merit salvation (Gl 2:15–16).

21:25 On the Jerusalem Council, see notes at 15:21,22–23a. The issue of the **letter** had been solved much earlier, and what Paul had or had not encouraged Jews living among Gentiles to do would not be clarified by the proposal of vv. 23–24. James was apparently succumbing to pressures from the Jewish believers in Jerusalem. Ultimately his proposal backfired (v. 27).

21:26 It is somewhat surprising that Paul agreed to perform the ritual of **purification**. Perhaps he sensed this was part of God's overall plan, to which he was partially privy (vv. 10–11; 20:22–23).

purification days when the offering would be made for each of them. [27] When the seven days were nearly over, some Jews from the province of Asia saw him in the temple, stirred up the whole crowd, and seized him, [28] shouting, "Fellow Israelites, help! This is the man who teaches everyone everywhere against our people, our law, and this place. What's more, he also brought Greeks into the temple and has defiled this holy place." [29] For they had previously seen Trophimus the Ephesian in the city with him, and they supposed that Paul had brought him into the temple.

[30] The whole city was stirred up, and the people rushed together. They seized Paul, dragged him out of the temple, and at once the gates were shut.

[31] As they were trying to kill him, word went up to the commander of the regiment that all Jerusalem was in chaos. [32] Taking along soldiers and centurions, he immediately ran down to them. Seeing the commander and the soldiers, they stopped beating Paul. [33] Then the commander approached, took him into custody, and ordered him to be bound with two chains. He asked who he was and what he had done. [34] Some in the crowd were shouting one thing and some another. Since he was not able to get reliable information because of the uproar, he ordered him to be taken into the barracks. [35] When Paul got to the steps, he had to be carried by the soldiers because of the violence of the crowd, [36] for the mass of people followed, yelling, "Get rid of him!"

Paul's Defense before the Jerusalem Mob

[37] As he was about to be brought into the barracks, Paul said to the commander, "Am I allowed to say something to you?"

He replied, "You know how to speak Greek? [38] Aren't you the Egyptian who started a revolt some time ago and led four thousand men of the Assassins into the wilderness?"

[39] Paul said, "I am a Jewish man from Tarsus of Cilicia, a citizen of an important city. Now I ask you, let me speak to the people."

[40] After he had given permission, Paul stood on the steps and motioned with his hand to the people. When there was a great hush, he addressed them in Aramaic:[A1] "Brothers and fathers, listen now to my defense before you." [2] When they heard that he was addressing them in Aramaic,[A] they became even quieter. [3] He continued, "I am a Jew, born in Tarsus of Cilicia but brought up in this city, educated at the feet of Gamaliel according to the strictness of our ancestral law. I was zealous for God, just as all of you are today. [4] I persecuted this Way to the death, arresting and putting both men and women in jail, [5] as both the high priest and the whole council of elders can testify about me. After I received letters from them to the brothers, I traveled to Damascus to arrest those who were there and bring them to Jerusalem to be punished.

Paul's Testimony

[6] "As I was traveling and approaching Damascus, about noon an intense light from heaven suddenly flashed around me. [7] I fell to the ground and heard a voice saying to me, 'Saul, Saul, why are you persecuting me?'

[8] "I answered, 'Who are you, Lord?'

"He said to me, 'I am Jesus of Nazareth, the one you are persecuting.' [9] Now those who were with me saw the light,[B] but they did not hear the voice of the one who was speaking to me.

[A]21:40; 22:2 Or *Hebrew*   [B]22:9 Other mss add *and were afraid*

21:27 There is no indication that the **Jews** from **Asia** were Christians.
21:28–29 Trophimus, an Ephesian, accompanied Paul to Jerusalem (20:4). It is unlikely that Paul ever brought Trophimus into the temple. After all, Paul was in the process of fulfilling the Jewish law, not ignoring or flaunting it. Even if the accusation was true, it would be Trophimus, not Paul, who would

have been guilty according to the law as stated in temple inscriptions.
21:31–32 Roman soldiers were stationed in the Antonia Fortress on the northwest side of the temple mount. One of their chief jobs was to put down disturbances such as this.
21:33 The **two chains** were perhaps attached to soldiers on either side.
21:34–36 Even with the soldiers protecting him, Paul **had to be carried** as the mob pressed in for the kill. Fortunately the **barracks** were nearby.
21:37–38 Paul asked permission to speak. His use of **Greek** surprised the Roman **commander** ("Claudius Lysias," 23:26). Lysias mistook Paul for an **Egyptian** rebel.
21:39 That **Paul** was a citizen of **Tarsus**, a city of importance in the Greco-Roman world, accounted for his knowledge of Greek.
21:40 Paul spoke **Aramaic** to the crowd in order to communicate clearly with them. In Paul's day Hebrew was used only by the religious elite.
22:1–2 Paul labeled his address a **defense** or an apology. This is his first apologetic speech in Acts.

22:3 Paul offered a number of important facts about himself. It appears that Paul spent his youth up to the age of thirteen or so in Tarsus where he was probably educated in the first stage of Jewish schooling. Then he went to Jerusalem (**this city**) and finished his education under **Gamaliel**. Elsewhere in Acts Paul indicated that much of his youth was spent in Jerusalem (26:4), and that he had relatives there (23:16).
22:4 Paul's admission that he **persecuted this Way to the death** indicates that he was more than a passive participant in events such as the stoning death of Stephen (7:58).
22:5–21 This is the second account of Paul's conversion in the book of Acts (9:7; 26:12–18).
22:9 According to 9:7, Paul's traveling companions heard the voice that spoke to him on the road to Damascus, but they did not see anyone. In this verse Paul himself said that they **did not hear the voice** of the one who was speaking to him. The grammar here supports the idea that Paul's traveling companions may have heard the voice but they did not understand it, or at least they did not understand it as the voice of the Lord.

#69 **99 Essential Christian Truths**

VIRGIN BIRTH

The Bible affirms that Jesus was conceived by the Holy Spirit and born of a virgin (Mt 1:18–25; Lk 1:26–38). The virgin birth affirms the historicity of the incarnation, in which the eternal Son of God took on human flesh. The virgin birth is significant in that it serves as a reminder of Old Testament prophecies (Is 7) while also affirming both the deity and humanity of Christ.

¹⁰ "I said, 'What should I do, Lord?'
"The Lord told me, 'Get up and go into Damascus, and there you will be told everything that you have been assigned to do.'
¹¹ "Since I couldn't see because of the brightness of the light,^A I was led by the hand by those who were with me, and went into Damascus.
¹² Someone named Ananias, a devout man according to the law, who had a good reputation with all the Jews living there, ¹³ came and stood by me and said, 'Brother Saul, regain your sight.' And in that very hour I looked up and saw him. ¹⁴ And he said, 'The God of our ancestors has appointed you to know his will, to see the Righteous One, and to hear the words from his mouth, ¹⁵ since you will be a witness for him to all people of what you have seen and heard. ¹⁶ And now, why are you delaying? Get up and be baptized, and wash away your sins, calling on his name.'

¹⁷ "After I returned to Jerusalem and was praying in the temple, I fell into a trance ¹⁸ and saw him telling me, 'Hurry and get out of Jerusalem quickly, because they will not accept your testimony about me.'

¹⁹ "But I said, 'Lord, they know that in synagogue after synagogue I had those who believed in you imprisoned and beaten. ²⁰ And when the blood of your witness Stephen was being shed, I stood there giving approval⁸ and guarding the clothes of those who killed him.'

²¹ "He said to me, 'Go, because I will send you far away to the Gentiles.'"

Paul's Roman Protection

²² They listened to him up to this point. Then they raised their voices, shouting, "Wipe this man off the face of the earth! He should not be allowed to live!"

²³ As they were yelling and flinging aside their garments and throwing dust into the air, ²⁴ the commander ordered him to be brought into the barracks, directing that he be interrogated with the scourge to discover the reason they were shouting against him like this. ²⁵ As they stretched him out for the lash, Paul said to the centurion standing by, "Is it legal for you to scourge a man who is a Roman citizen and is uncondemned?"

²⁶ When the centurion heard this, he went and reported to the commander, saying, "What are you going to do? For this man is a Roman citizen."

²⁷ The commander came and said to him, "Tell me, are you a Roman citizen?"
"Yes," he said.

²⁸ The commander replied, "I bought this citizenship for a large amount of money."
"But I was born a citizen," Paul said.

²⁹ So those who were about to examine him withdrew from him immediately. The commander too was alarmed when he realized Paul was a Roman citizen and he had bound him.

Paul before the Sanhedrin

³⁰ The next day, since he wanted to find out exactly why Paul was being accused by the Jews, he released him^C and instructed the chief priests and all the Sanhedrin to convene. He brought Paul down and placed him before them. ¹ Paul looked straight at the Sanhedrin and said, "Brothers, I have lived my life before God in all good conscience to this day." ² The high priest Ananias ordered those who were standing next to him to strike him on the mouth. ³ Then Paul said to him, "God is going to strike you, you whitewashed wall! You are sitting there judging me according to the law, and yet in violation of the law are you ordering me to be struck?"

⁴ Those standing nearby said, "Do you dare revile God's high priest?"

⁵ "I did not know, brothers, that he was the high priest," replied Paul. "For it is written, **You must not speak evil of a ruler of your people.**"ᴰ ⁶ When Paul realized that one part

23

---

^A 22:11 Lit the glory of that light　⁸ 22:20 Other mss add of his murder　ᶜ 22:30 Other mss add from his chains
ᴰ 23:5 Ex 22:28

22:10 This is the only account of Paul's conversion that has him asking two questions rather than one.
22:11 Note that Paul was the only one in his party who was blinded by the light.
22:14 The **Righteous One** was apparently a messianic designation.
22:17–21 Only this account of Paul's conversion mentions the **temple** vision. In his answer to the Lord (**But I said**), newly converted Paul seemed to expect his dramatic reversal from persecutor to advocate for Christianity would make his testimony powerful among Christian Jews in Jerusalem, but the Lord knew at this point they would **not accept** him. On early skepticism about Paul's conversion, see 9:26. On the execution of **Stephen**, see notes at v. 4; 7:58.
22:24 The Roman **commander** knew that Paul spoke Greek, but he also knew that he

was a Jew. Thus he assumed it was legal to scourge him as the first step in the interrogation.
22:25 Paul knew it was illegal to **scourge** an uncondemned **Roman citizen**; see note at 16:37.
22:26–28 Sometimes citizenship was granted to individuals who performed meritorious service for the empire. One of Paul's ancestors may have performed noteworthy service to Rome, including serving in the army or providing supplies for the army, such as making tents. Whatever the origin, Paul had inherited his Roman citizenship.
22:29 The significance of Roman citizenship is made clear, just as it was in Philippi (16:37). Stiff penalties could be handed down for mistreating a **Roman citizen** in this way.
22:30 Paul was either **released** from his chains or released from Roman imprisonment

while the **Sanhedrin** convened to try him on charges related to the Jewish law. During this time he remained under the protection of the Roman soldiers.
23:1–3 The high priest ordered Paul struck on the mouth because he thought Paul was lying about having a **good conscience** before God. Paul's accusation that the priest was a **whitewashed wall** meant the priest practiced outward piety but was inwardly corrupt.
23:4–5 Paul claimed not to have recognized the **high priest**, but most likely he was only being ironical. In this way he highlighted the high priest's inappropriate behavior.
23:6–9 Paul deflected the attention of the Sanhedrin by dividing his accusers over the doctrine of **resurrection**. The **Pharisees**, like Paul, believed in resurrection, while the **Sadducees**, of which the high priest Ananias

of them were Sadducees and the other part were Pharisees, he cried out in the Sanhedrin, "Brothers, I am a Pharisee, a son of Pharisees. I am being judged because of the hope of the resurrection of the dead!" [7] When he said this, a dispute broke out between the Pharisees and the Sadducees, and the assembly was divided. [8] For the Sadducees say there is no resurrection, and neither angel nor spirit, but the Pharisees affirm them all.

[9] The shouting grew loud, and some of the scribes of the Pharisees' party got up and argued vehemently, "We find nothing evil in this man. What if a spirit or an angel has spoken to him?" [A] [10] When the dispute became violent, the commander feared that Paul might be torn apart by them and ordered the troops to go down, take him away from them, and bring him into the barracks. [11] The following night, the Lord stood by him and said, "Have courage! For as you have testified about me in Jerusalem, so it is necessary for you to testify in Rome."

The Plot against Paul

[12] When it was morning, the Jews formed a conspiracy and bound themselves under a curse not to eat or drink until they had killed Paul. [13] There were more than forty who had formed this plot. [14] These men went to the chief priests and elders and said, "We have bound ourselves under a solemn curse that we won't eat anything until we have killed Paul. [15] So now you, along with the Sanhedrin, make a request to the commander that he bring him down to you [B] as if you were going to investigate his case more thoroughly. But, before he gets near, we are ready to kill him."

[16] But the son of Paul's sister, hearing about their ambush, came and entered the barracks and reported it to Paul. [17] Paul called one of the centurions and said, "Take this young man to the commander, because he has something to report to him."

[18] So he took him, brought him to the commander, and said, "The prisoner Paul called me

and asked me to bring this young man to you, because he has something to tell you."

[19] The commander took him by the hand, led him aside, and inquired privately, "What is it you have to report to me?"

[20] "The Jews," he said, "have agreed to ask you to bring Paul down to the Sanhedrin tomorrow, as though they are going to hold a somewhat more careful inquiry about him. [21] Don't let them persuade you, because there are more than forty of them lying in ambush — men who have bound themselves under a curse not to eat or drink until they have killed him. Now they are ready, waiting for your consent."

[22] So the commander dismissed the young man and instructed him, "Don't tell anyone that you have informed me about this."

To Caesarea by Night

[23] He summoned two of his centurions and said, "Get two hundred soldiers ready with seventy cavalry and two hundred spearmen to go to Caesarea at nine tonight. [C] [24] Also provide mounts to ride so that Paul may be brought safely to Felix the governor."

[25] He wrote the following letter: [D]

[26] Claudius Lysias,

To the most excellent governor Felix:

Greetings.

[27] When this man had been seized by the Jews and was about to be killed by them, I arrived with my troops and rescued him because I learned that he is a Roman citizen. [28] Wanting to know the charge they were accusing him of, I brought him down before their Sanhedrin. [29] I found out that the accusations were concerning questions of their law, and that there was no charge that merited death or imprisonment. [30] When I was informed that there was a plot against the man, [E] I sent him to you right away. I also ordered his accusers to state their case against him in your presence. [F]

[31] So the soldiers took Paul during the night and brought him to Antipatris as they were ordered.

^23:9 Other mss add *Let us not fight God.* ^B23:15 Other mss add *tomorrow* ^C23:23 Lit *at the third hour tonight* ^D23:25 Or *He wrote a letter to this effect:* ^E23:30 Other mss add *by the Jews* ^F23:30 Other mss add *Farewell*

was a member, did not. The ensuing debate led some of the scribes, who were associated with the Pharisees, to find no basis for charging Paul (v. 9).
23:10 Once again Roman intervention saved Paul's life; see 21:34–36 and note.
23:11 Again we see God's sovereign guidance of Paul's mission; see 22:17–21 and note.
23:12–15 Paradoxically, the very people who accused Paul of violating the law of Moses contemplated murdering him.
23:16 **Paul's** nephew reported the murder plot (vv. 12–15). It is unclear how many of Paul's family members were in Jerusalem (see vv. 17,22). Most likely Paul's sister lived in

Jerusalem, perhaps indicating that his entire family had moved there after Paul's childhood in Tarsus. The Greek of this verse suggests Paul's nephew was in his late teens. It is not stated how he came to know of the plot, but certainly the air was ripe for such a plot.
23:23 The commander acted decisively to get Paul out of harm's way. **Caesarea** Maritima was the headquarters for the province. Here Paul would be under the protection of the procurator, Felix.
23:24 Originally a slave, **Felix** became procurator of Judea in AD 52. He was removed from office around AD 59 for mishandling conflicts between Jews and Gentiles in Caesarea.

23:25–30 The letter from **Claudius Lysias**, the commander, followed the standard letter form of the time, with a greeting, the body of the letter, and a closing.
23:29–30 Lysias interpreted the conflict as a dispute over Jewish law, which meant the charge against Paul did not merit **death** or **imprisonment** under Roman law. His sending Paul to Felix might seem to imply otherwise, but this move was aimed at protecting Paul and allowing the Jewish authorities a chance to formally present their **case** before the Roman governor.
23:31–33 The distance from Jerusalem to **Antipatris** was approximately thirty-five

[32] The next day, they returned to the barracks, allowing the cavalry to go on with him. [33] When these men entered Caesarea and delivered the letter to the governor, they also presented Paul to him. [34] After he^ read it, he asked what province he was from. When he learned he was from Cilicia, [35] he said, "I will give you a hearing whenever your accusers also get here." He ordered that he be kept under guard in Herod's palace.^B

The Accusation against Paul

24 Five days later Ananias the high priest came down with some elders and a lawyer named Tertullus. These men presented their case against Paul to the governor. [2] When Paul was called in, Tertullus began to accuse him and said, "We enjoy great peace because of you, and reforms are taking place for the benefit of this nation because of your foresight. [3] We acknowledge this in every way and everywhere, most excellent Felix, with utmost gratitude. [4] But, so that I will not burden you any further, I request that you would be kind enough to give us a brief hearing. [5] For we have found this man to be a plague, an agitator among all the Jews throughout the Roman world, and a ringleader of the sect of the Nazarenes. [6] He even tried to desecrate the temple, and so we apprehended him.^C By examining him yourself you will be able to discern the truth about these charges we are bringing against him." [9] The Jews also joined in the attack, alleging that these things were true.

Paul's Defense before Felix

[10] When the governor motioned for him to speak, Paul replied, "Because I know you have

been a judge of this nation for many years, I am glad to offer my defense in what concerns me. [11] You can verify for yourself that it is no more than twelve days since I went up to worship in Jerusalem. [12] They didn't find me arguing with anyone or causing a disturbance among the crowd, either in the temple or in the synagogues or anywhere in the city. [13] Neither can they prove the charges they are now making against me. [14] But I admit this to you: I worship the God of my ancestors according to the Way, which they call a sect, believing everything that is in accordance with the law and written in the prophets. [15] I have a hope in God, which these men themselves also accept, that there will be a resurrection,^D both of the righteous and the unrighteous. [16] I always strive to have a clear conscience toward God and men. [17] After many years, I came to bring charitable gifts and offerings to my people. [18] While I was doing this, some Jews from Asia found me ritually purified in the temple, without a crowd and without any uproar. [19] It is they who ought to be here before you to bring charges, if they have anything against me. [20] Or let these men here state what wrongdoing they found in me when I stood before the Sanhedrin, [21] other than this one statement I shouted while standing among them, 'Today I am on trial before you concerning the resurrection of the dead.'"

The Verdict Postponed

[22] Since Felix was well informed about the Way, he adjourned the hearing, saying, "When Lysias the commander comes down, I will decide your case." [23] He ordered that the centurion keep Paul under guard, though he could have

---

^A23:34 Other mss read the governor ^B23:35 Or headquarters ^C24:6 Some mss include vv. 6b-8a: and wanted to judge him according to our law. ^7But Lysias the commander came and took him from our hands with great force, ^8commanding his accusers to come to you. ^D24:15 Other mss add of the dead

---

miles along the Roman road. The trip from Antipatris to **Caesarea** was along the coast and did not require such a large guard to ensure Paul's safety.
23:34–35 Felix could have sent Paul to the governor of Syria but decided to try the case himself, perhaps because he realized how flimsy the evidence against Paul was and wished to settle the case as quickly as possible. Paul was kept in custody in the procurator's **palace**, originally built by Herod the Great.
24:1 Luke's reporting of the case against Paul reflects standard Roman legal procedure, including the prosecution brought by a *rhetor* (lawyer). **Tertullus** was a common Roman name, but he may have been a Jew (v. 6), although he refers to the Jews objectively in v. 5.
24:2–4 Tertullus began with a *captatio benevolentiae*, the standard opening of a Greco-Roman speech designed to curry the favor of the listener, **Felix**.
24:5–6 Paul was accused by Tertullus of far more than just bringing a Gentile into the temple (**desecrate the temple**). Although the charge of desecrating the temple would

perhaps make Felix suspicious of Paul, the charges of being an **agitator** and **ringleader** would have genuinely alarmed him since it implied Paul was a threat to Roman rule.
24:8–9 Tertullus finished with another compliment toward Felix, this time expressing confidence in his abilities to rightly judge the case against Paul.
24:10 When Felix asked Paul to **speak**, Paul offered a less flattering *captatio benevolentiae* (see note at vv. 2–4). Instead of offering hyperbole, he recognized that Felix was an experienced governor of **many years** before whom he would gladly offer his **defense**. This is Paul's second apologetic or defensive speech in Acts; see 22:1–2 and note for the first.
24:11–13 The **twelve days** that Paul referred to did not include the time he had spent in Caesarea, but only time spent in **Jerusalem**. This was a sufficient amount of time for Paul's enemies to gather evidence that he was a troublemaker, and yet they were unable to **prove the charges**.
24:14 The phrase **the Way** is used throughout Acts as a self-designation by Christians (v. 22; 9:2; 19:9,23).

24:15 Paul's belief in the **resurrection**—of the **righteous** to their reward, the **unrighteous** to their punishment—aligned him with the Pharisees and against the Sadducees (23:6–9).
24:17 This collection is mentioned in Paul's letters (Rm 15:25–26; 1Co 16:3; 2Co 8:1–9:15; cp. Gl 2:10), but is not emphasized in Acts.
24:20–21 Paul justly demanded that the **Sanhedrin** representatives charge him with things they had personally witnessed or heard from him (including talk about **resurrection of the dead**).
24:22 Felix was familiar with **the Way**. Some have speculated that he learned of Christianity through his wife, Drusilla, the daughter of Herod Agrippa (v. 24). As procurator for more than five years, he would have had numerous chances to learn this new movement. Felix seemed to acknowledge that Tertullus had not been a faithful conveyor of the facts surrounding Paul's arrest when he stated that he would wait for the arrival of Claudius **Lysias** before deciding the case.
24:23 The circumstances of Paul's imprisonment in Caesarea allowed visits by **friends**

some freedom, and that he should not prevent any of his friends from meeting[A] his needs.

²⁴ Several days later, when Felix came with his wife Drusilla, who was Jewish, he sent for Paul and listened to him on the subject of faith in Christ Jesus. ²⁵ Now as he spoke about righteousness, self-control, and the judgment to come, Felix became afraid and replied, "Leave for now, but when I have an opportunity I'll call for you." ²⁶ At the same time he was also hoping that Paul would offer him money.[B] So he sent for him quite often and conversed with him.

²⁷ After two years had passed, Porcius Festus succeeded Felix, and because Felix wanted to do the Jews a favor, he left Paul in prison.

Appeal to Caesar

25 Three days after Festus arrived in the province, he went up to Jerusalem from Caesarea. ² The chief priests and the leaders of the Jews presented their case against Paul to him; and they appealed, ³ asking for a favor against Paul, that Festus summon him to Jerusalem. They were, in fact, preparing an ambush along the road to kill him. ⁴ Festus, however, answered that Paul should be kept at Caesarea, and that he himself was about to go there shortly. ⁵ "Therefore," he said, "let those of you who have authority go down with me and accuse him, if he has done anything wrong."

⁶ When he had spent not more than eight or ten days among them, he went down to Caesarea. The next day, seated at the tribunal, he commanded Paul to be brought in. ⁷ When he arrived, the Jews who had come down from Jerusalem stood around him and brought many serious charges that they were not able to prove. ⁸ Then Paul made his defense: "Neither against the Jewish law, nor against the temple, nor against Caesar have I sinned in any way."

⁹ But Festus, wanting to do the Jews a favor, replied to Paul, "Are you willing to go up to Jerusalem to be tried before me there on these charges?"

¹⁰ Paul replied, "I am standing at Caesar's tribunal, where I ought to be tried. I have done no wrong to the Jews, as even you yourself know very well. ¹¹ If then I did anything wrong and am deserving of death, I am not trying to escape death; but if there is nothing to what these men accuse me of, no one can give me up to them. I appeal to Caesar!"

¹² Then after Festus conferred with his council, he replied, "You have appealed to Caesar; to Caesar you will go."

King Agrippa and Bernice Visit Festus

¹³ Several days later, King Agrippa and Bernice arrived in Caesarea and paid a courtesy call on Festus. ¹⁴ Since they were staying there several days, Festus presented Paul's case to the king, saying, "There's a man who was left as a prisoner by Felix. ¹⁵ When I was in Jerusalem, the chief priests and the elders of the Jews presented their case and asked that he be condemned. ¹⁶ I answered them that it is not the Roman custom to give someone up[C] before the accused faces the accusers and has an opportunity for a defense against the charges. ¹⁷ So when they had assembled here, I did not delay. The next day I took my seat at the tribunal and ordered the man to be brought in. ¹⁸ The accusers stood up but brought no charge against him of the evils I was expecting. ¹⁹ Instead they had some disagreements with him about their own religion and about a certain Jesus, a dead man Paul claimed to be alive. ²⁰ Since I was at a loss in a dispute over such things, I asked him if he wanted to go to Jerusalem and be tried there regarding these matters. ²¹ But when Paul appealed to be held for trial by the Emperor,[D] I ordered him to be kept in custody until I could send him to Caesar."

ᴬ24:23 Other mss add *or visiting*   ᴮ24:26 Other mss add *so that he might release him*   ᶜ25:16 Other mss add *to destruction*
ᴰ25:21 Lit *his majesty*, also in v. 25

---

and colleagues. This privilege was likely made possible by his Roman citizenship.
24:24 Felix was interested enough in Christianity that he brought his wife, **Drusilla, who was Jewish,** to hear Paul.
24:25 Paul may have tailored his comments specifically for Felix, whose morals were publicly questioned. For instance, he took Drusilla from her first husband Azizus. Feeling the threat of divine judgment, **Felix became afraid** and sent Paul away.
24:26 Whatever hope Paul may have held for Felix's conversion, Felix's hidden motive for their ongoing discussions was base, illegal, and indicative of spiritual destitution.
24:27 Felix's immorality is on further display in the fact that he kept Paul imprisoned for **two years**, even though he did not find that Paul had committed any punishable offense, and then left him in this state when **Festus** became the new proconsul (ca AD 59).

25:1–3 The new governor, **Festus**, went up from his palace in **Caesarea** to **Jerusalem**, probably to get a sense of the most important Jewish city in the realm. Hoping to seize on his unfamiliarity with the case, the Jewish leaders tried to coax him into sending Paul to Jerusalem, giving them a chance to renew their plans for **ambush**.
25:4–5 Festus was known to be much more honest and able than his predecessor Felix or his successor Albinus.
25:9–11 Likely aware of the ongoing plan to murder him, Paul avoided **Jerusalem** by invoking his right as a Roman citizen to **appeal** directly to **Caesar**. Not all such appeals were granted by local governors, but Festus was glad to shift this case to another jurisdiction and free himself of the pressure to appease the Jews (see note at 26:32).
25:12 The council was only a local advisory body but would have probably included an expert in Roman law. Scholars disagree about

whether Festus was obligated to grant Paul's request.
25:13 Herod **Agrippa** II visited Caesarea with his sister **Bernice**, who had a checkered sexual and marital history. Herod was the last of the Herodian rulers. Festus was sly to bring Herod into the controversy over Paul, for Herod had responsibility for the temple and appointing the Jewish high priest. Thus he had an interest in the charges that Paul had violated the temple.
25:14–19 Festus portrayed himself in the best possible light. He had expected a more serious charge, like fomenting insurrection and revolution. He came to understand that the major issue was whether Jesus, who had died, was now **alive**.
25:20 Realizing that the theological debate was beyond him, Festus attempted to put a good spin on the push for Paul to **go to Jerusalem** for trial.
25:21–22 Perhaps Herod had heard of Jesus and was curious what Paul would say about him.

²² Agrippa said to Festus, "I would like to hear the man myself."

"Tomorrow you will hear him," he replied.

Paul before Agrippa

²³ So the next day, Agrippa and Bernice came with great pomp and entered the auditorium with the military commanders and prominent men of the city. When Festus gave the command, Paul was brought in. ²⁴ Then Festus said, "King Agrippa and all men present with us, you see this man. The whole Jewish community has appealed to me concerning him, both in Jerusalem and here, shouting that he should not live any longer. ²⁵ I found that he had not done anything deserving of death, but when he himself appealed to the Emperor, I decided to send him. ²⁶ I have nothing definite to write to my lord about him. Therefore, I have brought him before all of you, and especially before you, King Agrippa, so that after this examination is over, I may have something to write. ²⁷ For it seems unreasonable to me to send a prisoner without indicating the charges against him."

Paul's Defense before Agrippa

26 Agrippa said to Paul, "You have permission to speak for yourself."

Then Paul stretched out his hand and began his defense: ² "I consider myself fortunate that it is before you, King Agrippa, I am to make my defense today against all the accusations of the Jews, ³ especially since you are very knowledgeable about all the Jewish customs and controversies. Therefore I beg you to listen to me patiently.

⁴ "All the Jews know my way of life from my youth, which was spent from the beginning among my own people and in Jerusalem. ⁵ They have known me for a long time, if they are willing to testify, that according to the strictest sect of our religion I lived as a Pharisee. ⁶ And now I stand on trial because of the hope in what God promised to our ancestors, ⁷ the promise our twelve tribes hope to reach as they earnestly serve him night and day. King Agrippa, I am being accused by the Jews because of this hope. ⁸ Why do any of you consider it incredible that God raises the dead? ⁹ In fact, I myself was convinced that it was necessary to do many things in opposition to the name of Jesus of Nazareth. ¹⁰ I actually did this in Jerusalem, and I locked up many of the saints in prison, since I had received authority for that from the chief priests. When they were put to death, I was in agreement against them. ¹¹ In all the synagogues I often punished them and tried to make them blaspheme. Since I was terribly enraged at them, I pursued them even to foreign cities.

Paul's Account of His Conversion and Commission

¹² "I was traveling to Damascus under these circumstances with authority and a commission from the chief priests. ¹³ King Agrippa, while on the road at midday, I saw a light from heaven brighter than the sun, shining around me and those traveling with me. ¹⁴ We all fell to the ground, and I heard a voice speaking to me in Aramaic,^ 'Saul, Saul, why are you persecuting me? It is hard for you to kick against the goads.'

¹⁵ "I asked, 'Who are you, Lord?'

"And the Lord replied, 'I am Jesus, the one you are persecuting. ¹⁶ But get up and stand on your feet. For I have appeared to you for this purpose, to appoint you as a servant and a witness of what you have seen and will see of me. ¹⁷ I will rescue you from your people and from the Gentiles. I am sending you to them ¹⁸ to open their eyes so that they may turn⁸ from darkness to light and from the power of Satan to God, that they may receive forgiveness of sins and a share among those who are sanctified by faith in me.'

¹⁹ "So then, King Agrippa, I was not disobedient to the heavenly vision. ²⁰ Instead, I preached to those in Damascus first, and to

---

^26:14 Or *Hebrew* ⁸26:18 Or *to turn them*

25:23 The entrance of **Agrippa and Bernice** must have been quite an occasion, with the honored guests and other people forming an elaborate entourage.
25:25 Festus had not previously made it known publicly that he thought Paul was innocent. Since Paul had made his appeal to Caesar, Festus was now free to admit, without repercussion, that he believed the charges were groundless.
25:26–27 Festus found the case not only groundless but perplexing. He hoped **Agrippa** would be able to help him think of a way to specify to the emperor the **charges** laid against Paul.
26:1 This is Paul's third apologetic or defensive speech in Acts; see 22:1; 24:10.
26:2–3 Paul began his *captatio benevolentiae* (see notes at 24:2–4,10) by flattering Agrippa about how **fortunate** he was to be making his **defense** before an expert in **Jewish customs** and laws.

26:4–5 **My youth** indicates that Paul had lived in Jerusalem since his teens. All this time his **way of life** had been known and seen by others, and he lived **according to the strictest sect** of Jewish religion, the Pharisees. In this way Paul painted a portrait of his character for Agrippa.
26:6–8 Paul distilled the entire controversy down to **the hope in what God promised**— that is, the resurrection of the dead.
26:9–11 The reason for such a long narration is to show that Paul was a faithful Jew who also was a witness for Christ.
26:12–18 This is the third and final account of Paul's conversion in the book of Acts (9:1–7; 22:6–11).
26:14 Only in this account of his conversion did Paul say the voice from heaven spoke to him in **Aramaic**, the common tongue of the first-century Jew (see note at 21:40). **It is hard for you to kick against the goads**

probably meant that Paul should not resist the divine force that was moving him in a new direction.
26:16–18 These three verses are not included in the accounts of Paul's conversion in chaps. 9 or 22, even though the mention of Paul's ministry to the **Gentiles** was a message given to Ananias in Damascus (9:15; 22:15). Many scholars believe the essence of Paul's mission to the Gentiles was revealed to him at the time of his conversion. Certainly these three verses summarize Paul's ministry to both Jews and Gentiles.
26:19 **I was not disobedient** is a spectacular understatement in light of Paul's faithfulness to God's calling, even through remarkable hardships.
26:20–21 Paul's faithfulness to "the heavenly vision" (v. 19) was the very reason **the Jews seized** him and wanted him dead.

those in Jerusalem and in all the region of Judea, and to the Gentiles, that they should repent and turn to God, and do works worthy of repentance. [21] For this reason the Jews seized me in the temple and were trying to kill me. [22] To this very day, I have had help from God, and I stand and testify to both small and great, saying nothing other than what the prophets and Moses said would take place — [23] that the Messiah would suffer, and that, as the first to rise from the dead, he would proclaim light to our people and to the Gentiles."

Agrippa Not Quite Persuaded

[24] As he was saying these things in his defense, Festus exclaimed in a loud voice, "You're out of your mind, Paul! Too much study is driving you mad."

[25] But Paul replied, "I'm not out of my mind, most excellent Festus. On the contrary, I'm speaking words of truth and good judgment. [26] For the king knows about these matters, and I can speak boldly to him. For I am convinced that none of these things has escaped his notice, since this was not done in a corner. [27] King Agrippa, do you believe the prophets? I know you believe."

[28] Agrippa said to Paul, "Are you going to persuade me to become a Christian so easily?"[A]

[29] "I wish before God," replied Paul, "that whether easily or with difficulty,[B] not only you but all who listen to me today might become as I am — except for these chains."

[30] The king, the governor, Bernice, and those sitting with them got up, [31] and when they had left they talked with each other and said, "This man is not doing anything to deserve death or imprisonment."

[32] Agrippa said to Festus, "This man could have been released if he had not appealed to Caesar."

Sailing for Rome

27 When it was decided that we were to sail to Italy, they handed over Paul and some other prisoners to a centurion named Julius, of the Imperial Regiment.[C] [2] When we had boarded a ship of Adramyttium, we put to sea, intending to sail to ports along the coast of Asia. Aristarchus, a Macedonian of Thessalonica, was with us. [3] The next day we put in at Sidon, and Julius treated Paul kindly and allowed him to go to his friends to receive their care. [4] When we had put out to sea from there, we sailed along the northern coast[D] of Cyprus because the winds were against us. [5] After sailing through the open sea off Cilicia and Pamphylia, we reached Myra in Lycia. [6] There the centurion found an Alexandrian ship sailing for Italy and put us on board. [7] Sailing slowly for many days, with difficulty we arrived off Cnidus. Since the wind did not allow us to approach it, we sailed along the south side of Crete off Salmone. [8] With still more difficulty we sailed along the coast and came to a place called Fair Havens near the city of Lasea.

Paul's Advice Ignored

[9] By now much time had passed, and the voyage was already dangerous. Since the Day of Atonement[E] was already over, Paul gave his advice [10] and told them, "Men, I can see that this voyage is headed toward disaster and heavy loss, not only of the cargo and the ship but also of our lives." [11] But the centurion paid attention to the captain and the owner of the ship rather than to what Paul said. [12] Since the harbor was unsuitable to winter in, the majority decided to set sail from there, hoping somehow to reach Phoenix, a harbor on Crete facing the southwest and northwest, and to winter there.

Storm-Tossed Ship

[13] When a gentle south wind sprang up, they thought they had achieved their purpose. They

---

[A]26:28 Or *so quickly* [B]26:29 Or *whether a short time or long* [C]27:1 Or *Augustan Cohort* [D]27:4 Lit *sailed under the lee*, also in v. 7 [E]27:9 Lit *the Fast*

26:24 **Festus** took Paul to be **mad** because of talk about resurrection and Messiah, Jewish beliefs that seemed foolish to the Gentile world.
26:27 Paul played to the king's Jewishness. If **Agrippa** was a good Jew, he should have accepted the **prophets** and their message about Jesus.
26:28 Scholars disagree over whether Agrippa's response was sarcastic anger, a jest, or a sign that Paul's logic was close to persuading him.
26:32 The charges against Paul were found to be groundless before both Roman and Jewish authorities. Nevertheless, Paul's appeal to Rome put his case in a special category that must be discharged by Caesar himself.
27:1 This is the fourth **we** section in Acts (see note at 16:10), and it extends to v. 37. The most natural conclusion is that the author of the "we" source was along for the journey. There were a number of people besides Paul

and the other prisoners on the ship (e.g., Aristarchus, v. 2).
27:2 **Adramyttium** was in western Asia near the island of Lesbos. Like many ships sailing the Mediterranean Sea, the ship appears to have been a small grain vessel that would have worked its way from Caesarea along the **coast** until it reached Adramyttium.
27:3 There apparently were Christians in **Sidon**, although Acts does not record when the city was evangelized. Paul seemed to have **friends** there who provided for him, possibly friends made during an unrecorded visit as he traveled between Jerusalem and Antioch.
27:4 The route of travel reflects the need to sail close to land and to tack against the **winds**.
27:5–6 The ship from Adramyttium would have taken them out of their way since it was going to follow the coast of the province of

Asia. As a result, at **Myra**, on the southern coast of Asia Minor, the centurion found a ship from Alexandria that was going to Rome. The **Alexandrian ship** would have been part of the grain supply trade from Egypt to Rome (see note at v. 38).
27:7–9 The journey was being undertaken at the end of the sailing season, so the ship ran into difficulty. Sailing was dangerous from mid-September to mid-November, and waterways closed for travel from then until February (see note at 28:11). It appears that Paul's journey occurred in roughly mid-October. **Fair Havens** was not a suitable place to spend the winter because the harbor was exposed to the open sea (v. 12).
27:13–16 The crew thought the **gentle south wind** would push them to their destination, but the seasonal "**northeaster**" blew the ship away from Phoenix and into open sea.

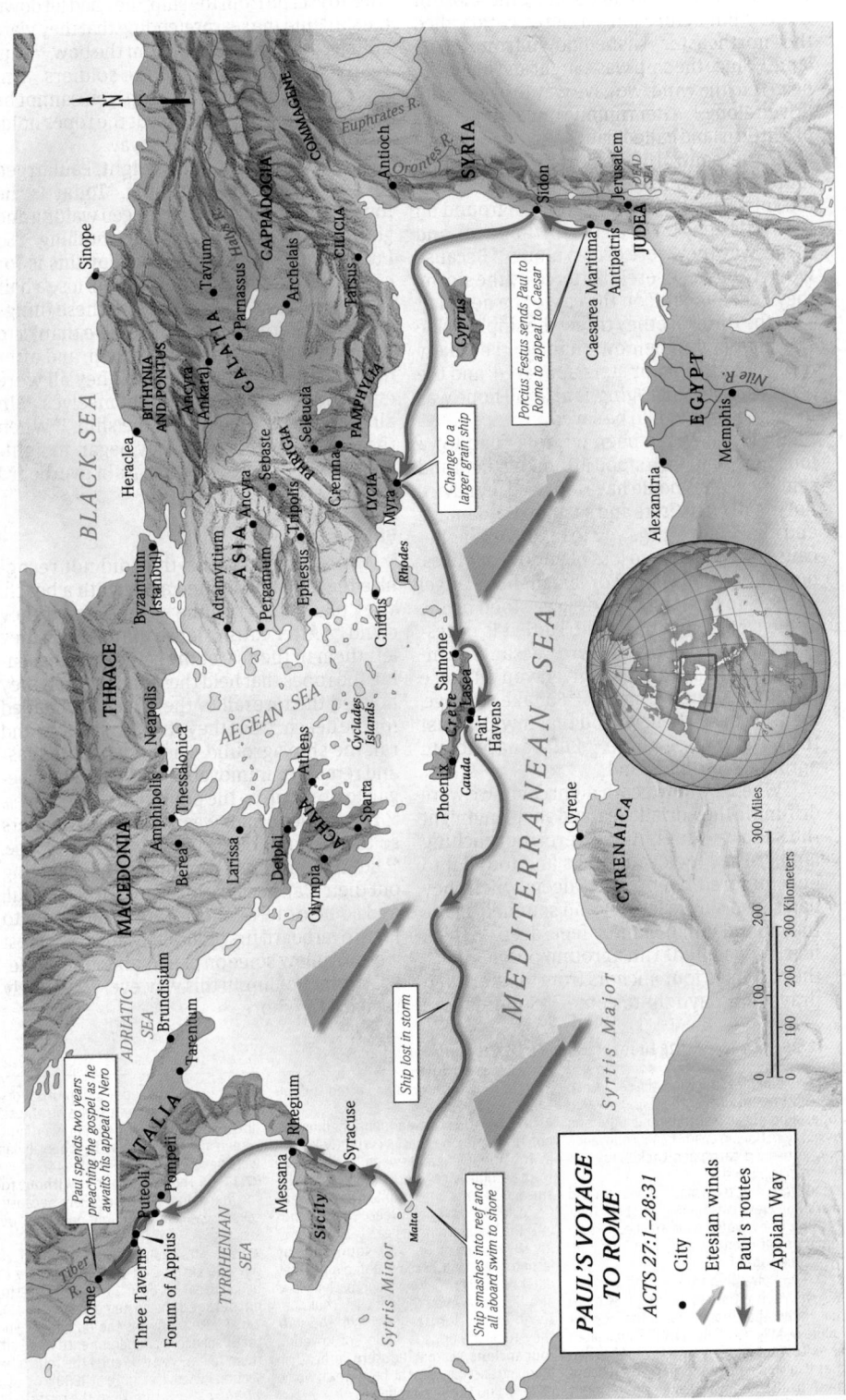

PAUL'S VOYAGE TO ROME

ACTS 27:1–28:31

- • City
- Etesian winds
- Paul's routes
- Appian Way

Change to a larger grain ship

Porcius Festus sends Paul to Rome to appeal to Caesar

Ship lost in storm

Ship smashes into reef and all aboard swim to shore

Paul spends two years preaching the gospel as he awaits his appeal to Nero

BLACK SEA

Sinope

Heraclea

BITHYNIA AND PONTUS

Byzantium (Istanbul)

THRACE

Neapolis

Amphipolis

MACEDONIA

Thessalonica

Berea

Larissa

Delphi

Olympia

ACHAIA

Athens

Sparta

AEGEAN SEA

Cyclades Islands

Adramyttium

Pergamum

Ephesus

ASIA

Ancyra

Tripolis

PHRYGIA

Seleucia

Cnidus

Rhodes

GALATIA

Ancyra (Ankara)

Sebaste

Tavium

Parnassus Halys

CAPPADOCIA

Archelais

CILICIA

Tarsus

COMMAGENE

Euphrates R.

Antioch

Orontes R.

SYRIA

Sidon

Jerusalem

JUDEA

DEAD SEA

Antipatris

Caesarea Maritima

Cyprus

PAMPHYLIA

PISIDIA

Cremna

LYCIA

Myra

Salmone

Crete

Lasea

Fair Havens

Phoenix

Cauda

MEDITERRANEAN SEA

Cyrene

CYRENAICA

Syrtis Major

Syrtis Minor

EGYPT

Nile R.

Memphis

Alexandria

Malta

Syracuse

Messana

Sicily

Rhegium

TYRRHENIAN SEA

Pompeii

Puteoli

Three Taverns

Forum of Appius

Rome

Tiber R.

ITALIA

Brundisium

Tarentum

ADRIATIC SEA

300 Miles

300 Kilometers

0   100   200

0   100   200

weighed anchor and sailed along the shore of Crete. [14] But before long, a fierce wind called the "northeaster" rushed down from the island. [15] Since the ship was caught and unable to head into the wind, we gave way to it and were driven along. [16] After running under the shelter of a little island called Cauda,[A] we were barely able to get control of the skiff. [17] After hoisting it up, they used ropes and tackle and girded the ship. Fearing they would run aground on the Syrtis, they lowered the drift-anchor, and in this way they were driven along. [18] Because we were being severely battered by the storm, they began to jettison the cargo the next day. [19] On the third day, they threw the ship's tackle overboard with their own hands. [20] For many days neither sun nor stars appeared, and the severe storm kept raging. Finally all hope was fading that we would be saved.

[21] Since they had been without food for a long time, Paul then stood up among them and said, "You men should have followed my advice not to sail from Crete and sustain this damage and loss. [22] Now I urge you to take courage, because there will be no loss of any of your lives, but only of the ship. [23] For last night an angel of the God I belong to and serve stood by me [24] and said, 'Don't be afraid, Paul. It is necessary for you to appear before Caesar. And indeed, God has graciously given you all those who are sailing with you.' [25] So take courage, men, because I believe God that it will be just the way it was told to me. [26] But we have to run aground on some island."

[27] When the fourteenth night came, we were drifting in the Adriatic Sea, and about midnight the sailors thought they were approaching land. [28] They took soundings and found it to be a hundred twenty feet[B] deep; when they had sailed a little farther and sounded again, they found it to be ninety feet[C] deep. [29] Then, fearing we might run aground on the rocks, they dropped four anchors from the stern and prayed for daylight to come. [30] Some sailors tried to escape from the ship; they had let down the skiff into the sea, pretending that they were going to put out anchors from the bow. [31] Paul said to the centurion and the soldiers, "Unless these men stay in the ship, you cannot be saved." [32] Then the soldiers cut the ropes holding the skiff and let it drop away.

[33] When it was about daylight, Paul urged them all to take food, saying, "Today is the fourteenth day that you have been waiting and going without food, having eaten nothing. [34] So I urge you to take some food. For this is for your survival, since none of you will lose a hair from your head." [35] After he said these things and had taken some bread, he gave thanks to God in the presence of all of them, and after he broke it, he began to eat. [36] They all were encouraged and took food themselves. [37] In all there were 276 of us on the ship. [38] When they had eaten enough, they began to lighten the ship by throwing the grain overboard into the sea.

Shipwreck

[39] When daylight came, they did not recognize the land but sighted a bay with a beach. They planned to run the ship ashore if they could. [40] After cutting loose the anchors, they left them in the sea, at the same time loosening the ropes that held the rudders. Then they hoisted the foresail to the wind and headed for the beach. [41] But they struck a sandbar and ran the ship aground. The bow jammed fast and remained immovable, while the stern began to break up by the pounding of the waves. [42] The soldiers' plan was to kill the prisoners so that no one could swim away and escape. [43] But the centurion kept them from carrying out their plan because he wanted to save Paul, and so he ordered those who could swim to jump overboard first and get to land. [44] The rest were to follow, some on planks and some on debris from the ship. In this way, everyone safely reached the shore.

[A]27:16 Or *Clauda*   [B]27:28 Lit *twenty fathoms*   [C]27:28 Lit *fifteen fathoms*

27:17–19 Caught in the wind, the sailors had virtually no control over the ship. They tied **ropes** around the hull to bind it tight and keep it from ripping apart. To gain buoyancy, they jettisoned **cargo** and **tackle**, but not the grain (cp. v. 38).

27:20 Since the storm blacked out **sun** and **stars**, the crew was unable to chart their location. They would have tracked the alternation between day and night by noting the vague light of day.

27:21–26 Refraining from eating was apparently due either to seasickness or to fear. Rather than reprimanding the crew for failure to take his advice (v. 21), Paul related his encounter with an **angel** who revealed that Paul had a greater destiny than death by shipwreck. He was destined to **appear before Caesar**, the world's premier power. The divine plan would not be thwarted,

especially by those who had acted so foolishly.

27:27 The **Adriatic Sea** mentioned here is not the same one that is currently known as the Adriatic Sea between Italy and the former Yugoslavia. It apparently refers instead to the modern day Ionian Sea between Crete, Malta, Italy, and Greece that extends into the Mediterranean Sea.

27:28–29 The sailors took **soundings** by letting down lengths of weighted rope. They determined that they were approaching land at a fast pace, even though they could not see it. In an effort to slow down the ship, they took the unusual action of lowering **four anchors**, all from the **stern**, rather than dropping anchors from the bow, which would have swung the ship around.

27:30–32 The prospect of imminent landfall after being adrift on the stormy sea for two

weeks (v. 27) enticed a group of sailors to attempt, selfishly, an escape on the **skiff** (lifeboat). Paul's wisdom in preventing this is seen in the next episode, when all hands were needed (vv. 37–38,40,43–44).

27:33–34 The men had gone **without food** for fourteen days, most likely because of severe seasickness brought on by the rough sea.

27:36 Paul's example of steady faith ("he gave thanks to God") and practicality ("he began to eat," v. 35) in the midst of the storm **encouraged** the battered sailors.

27:37 Luke mentions the number to show that Paul had managed to encourage all of them to eat. Verse 37 ends the fourth "we" section in Acts (see note at 16:10).

27:38 The crew threw out the **grain**, which had been acting as ballast for the ship, so they could run it aground (v. 39).

Malta's Hospitality

28 Once safely ashore, we then learned that the island was called Malta. [2] The local people showed us extraordinary kindness. They lit a fire and took us all in, since it was raining and cold. [3] As Paul gathered a bundle of brushwood and put it on the fire, a viper came out because of the heat and fastened itself on his hand. [4] When the local people saw the snake hanging from his hand, they said to one another, "This man, no doubt, is a murderer. Even though he has escaped the sea, Justice has not allowed him to live." [5] But he shook the snake off into the fire and suffered no harm. [6] They expected that he would begin to swell up or suddenly drop dead. After they waited a long time and saw nothing unusual happen to him, they changed their minds and said he was a god.

Ministry in Malta

[7] Now in the area around that place was an estate belonging to the leading man of the island, named Publius, who welcomed us and entertained us hospitably for three days. [8] Publius's father was in bed suffering from fever and dysentery. Paul went to him, and praying and laying his hands on him, he healed him. [9] After this, the rest of those on the island who had diseases also came and were healed. [10] So they heaped many honors on us, and when we sailed, they gave us what we needed.

Rome at Last

[11] After three months we set sail in an Alexandrian ship that had wintered at the island, with the Twin Gods[A] as its figurehead. [12] Putting in at Syracuse, we stayed three days. [13] From there, after making a circuit along the coast,[B] we reached Rhegium. After one day a south wind sprang up, and the second day we came to Puteoli. [14] There we found brothers and sisters and were invited to stay a week with them. And so we came to Rome. [15] Now the brothers and sisters from there had heard the news about us and had come to meet us as far as the Forum of Appius and the Three Taverns. When Paul saw them, he thanked God and took courage. [16] When we entered Rome,[C] Paul was allowed to live by himself with the soldier who guarded him.

Paul's First Interview with Roman Jews

[17] After three days he called together the leaders of the Jews. When they had gathered he said to them, "Brothers, although I have done nothing against our people or the customs of our ancestors, I was delivered as a prisoner from Jerusalem into the hands of the Romans. [18] After they examined me, they wanted to release me, since there was no reason for the death penalty in my case. [19] Because the Jews objected, I was compelled to appeal to Caesar; even though I had no charge to bring against my people. [20] For this reason I've asked to see you and speak to you. In fact, it is for the hope of Israel that I'm wearing this chain." [21] Then they said to him, "We haven't received any letters about you from Judea. None of the brothers has come and reported or spoken anything evil about you. [22] But we want to hear what your views are, since we know that people everywhere are speaking against this sect."

The Response to Paul's Message

[23] After arranging a day with him, many came to him at his lodging. From dawn to dusk he expounded and testified about the kingdom of God. He tried to persuade them about Jesus

---

[A] **28:11** Gk *Dioscuri*, twin sons of Zeus, Castor and Pollux [B] **28:13** Other mss read *From there, casting off,* [C] **28:16** Other mss add *the centurion turned the prisoners over to the military commander; but*

28:1 This is the fifth **we** section in Acts (see note at 16:10), and it extends through v. 16. The shipwreck happened on **Malta**, a small island south of Sicily.
28:2–4 The residents of Malta apparently thought **Justice**, a Greek goddess, had singled Paul out because he deserved death (cp. v. 6).
28:5–6 The superstitious natives of Malta quickly decided Paul was **a god** rather than a "murderer" (v. 4). Paul shrugged off this false praise just as easily as he had shaken off the snake.
28:7 **Leading man** or "first man" of Malta is a title reflected in inscriptional evidence from the island. **Publius** may have been a leading citizen or political leader.
28:8 Publius's **father** may have suffered from "Malta fever," which is caused by drinking impure goats' milk.
28:9–10 The **honors** that Paul received may have been monetary rewards or payment. The same word is used elsewhere in Acts to indicate money (5:2–3; 7:16; 19:19).

28:11 The journey aboard the other **Alexandrian ship** probably began in February or shortly thereafter. The **Twin Gods** were Castor and Pollux (Gemini), sons of Zeus. Sailors regarded them as gods and patrons of seafarers.
28:12 **Syracuse** was a port on the eastern side of Sicily.
28:13 **Rhegium** was a port city on the southern end of Italy, seventy miles from Syracuse. **Puteoli**, an important shipping harbor for transporting grain from Egypt to Rome, was about 130 miles southeast of Rome.
28:14 It is not known how the **brothers and sisters** came to be in Puteoli.
28:15 Believers from Rome came down the Appian Way to two small towns (**Forum of Appius** and **Three Taverns**) to greet and encourage Paul before his arrival in Rome.
28:16 While in Roman custody, Paul appears to have stayed on his own and at his own expense (cp. vv. 23,30), guarded only by one **soldier**. We know nothing more about his contact with the Roman government or the

disposition of his case. This verse is the end of the last **we** section in the book of Acts (see note at 16:10).
28:17 This is the final time in Acts in which Paul began his ministry in a new city. As usual, he started by contacting **the Jews**. Since he was in custody, he invited the Jewish leaders to visit him rather than going to their synagogue.
28:21–22 The Jews in Rome had heard about the **sect** of Christianity (24:14), but they had not received any official word about Paul from Jerusalem. This lack of communication between Jerusalem and Rome may have been caused by winter weather, or it may indicate that the Jewish leaders in Jerusalem had lost interest in Paul's case since he was now out of their sight, beyond their jurisdiction, and unlikely to cause them any more trouble. In any event, the Christians of Rome knew more about Paul's situation than did the unbelieving Jews (see 28:15 and note).
28:23 Like the risen Christ on the road to Emmaus (Lk 24:13–35), Paul showed how

from both the Law of Moses and the Prophets. [24] Some were persuaded by what he said, but others did not believe.

[25] Disagreeing among themselves, they began to leave after Paul made one statement:[A] "The Holy Spirit was right in saying to your[B] ancestors through the prophet Isaiah [26] when he said,

Go to these people and say:
You will always be listening,
    but never understanding;
and you will always
    be looking,
    but never perceiving.
[27] For the hearts of these people
    have grown callous,
their ears are hard of hearing,

and they have shut their eyes;
    otherwise they might see
    with their eyes
and hear with their ears,
    understand with their heart
and turn,
    and I would heal them.[C]
[28] Therefore, let it be known to you that this salvation of God has been sent to the Gentiles; they will listen."[D]

Paul's Ministry Unhindered

[30] Paul stayed two whole years in his own rented house. And he welcomed all who visited him, [31] proclaiming the kingdom of God and teaching about the Lord Jesus Christ with all boldness and without hindrance.

[A]28:25 Or *after they began to leave, Paul made one statement* [B]28:25 Other mss read *our* [C]28:26–27 Is 6:9–10
[D]28:28 Some mss include v. 29: *After he said these things, the Jews departed, while engaging in a vigorous debate among themselves.*

---

both the Law of Moses and the Prophets pointed to Jesus as God's Messiah.
28:24 Elsewhere in Acts the verb **were persuaded** refers to genuine conversion.
28:25–27 Luke identifies the turning point in the discussion as Paul's provocative **statement** that the Holy Spirit **was right** about Israel's spiritual stubbornness through Isaiah the prophet (Is 6:9–10).
28:28 On God's **salvation** being **sent to the Gentiles**, see notes at 13:46–47; 18:6.

28:30–31 The book of Acts ends in an unexpectedly open-ended fashion. Paul remained a prisoner **two whole years**. During this time he lived at his own expense and was allowed to have visitors to whom he proclaimed his message boldly and **without hindrance**. Church tradition has long held that Paul was beheaded during the persecution instigated by the Roman emperor Nero (AD 64 or 65). It is possible that Paul was executed in Rome after the "two whole years," though

church historian Eusebius believed Paul was released from Roman imprisonment, only to be rearrested at a later date, sent to Rome, and executed. The fact that Luke does not write of Paul's execution leads some scholars to conclude that Luke wrote the book of Acts previous to Paul's execution, though it is possible that Luke chose not to discuss the details of Paul's death because his aim was to show that God had fulfilled his purpose in Paul: taking the gospel to the Gentiles.

Introduction to the New Testament Letters

by Charles L. Quarles

Twenty-one of the twenty-seven books of the New Testament are letters. The books of Acts and Revelation also include letters within them (see Ac 15:23–29; 23:25–30; Rv 2:1–3:22). Since understanding these documents is key to understanding the New Testament message, we will briefly consider the practice of ancient letter writing, concerns about questions of authorship, and some basic principles of interpreting the New Testament letters.

Ancient Letter Writing

While we might imagine the New Testament authors penning the entirety of documents with their own hands, instead most ancient letters were handwritten by skilled scribes who were normally compensated for their work. Sometimes the author dictated the letter word for word to the scribe. The scribe initially used an ancient form of shorthand to preserve the precise content of the letter and later wrote out the letter in full. In other situations, the scribe had more input by suggesting specific expressions that might make a thought clearer or proposing a particular structure for the argument of the letter. Even when the scribe had greater influence on the content of the letter, the author had the opportunity to make corrections during a final reading to ensure that the letter still communicated exactly what he wished to say.

Understanding the approaches to letter writing helps explain some of the differences in style, vocabulary, and grammar that appear in different letters by the same NT author. Sometimes scholars point to differences between Romans and 2 Thessalonians, for example, to argue that the same author could not have produced both. However, several explanations can be given for these differences. Differences in vocabulary may be influenced by the specific needs of the audience, the nature of the author's relationship with them, and his own circumstances at the moment. Some of these differences may imply only that the letters were penned for Paul by different scribes. We know that the scribe Tertius, for example, penned the letter to the Romans for Paul (Rm 16:22). Second Thessalonians lists both Silas and Timothy as co-senders of the letter (2Th 1:1–2), and one of these men may have served as the scribe. These different influences may account for some of the subtle differences in expression between these two letters of Paul.

Modern letters have standard forms and style. Business letters place different elements in a distinct order and use formalities like "Dear Sir/Madam:" and "Sincerely," in the greeting and closing. Ancient letters had standard forms and styles too. The letters normally had three distinct sections: the opening, the body, and the closing. Each section normally contained several specific features. Ancient letters opened with a prescript that identified the sender and the recipient and expressed a greeting. The prescript was followed by a thanksgiving formula that expressed gratitude to the gods and offered prayer for the good health or safe travel of the recipient.

The New Testament letters use these conventions but modify them for theological purposes. For example, although the normal "greetings" formula is used by James (see also Ac 15:23; 23:26), Paul consistently changes the formula from "Greetings to you" (Gk *chairein*) to "Grace to you" (Gk *charis*).

New Testament letters also expand and modify the thanksgiving formula. In particular, the focus of thanksgiving and prayer is for the spiritual health rather than the physical health of the recipients. Philippians is a perfect example of this. Paul gave thanks for the Philippians' partnership in the gospel and for God's continued work among them. He prayed for the growth of their love and for their purity (Php 1:3–11).

The closing of ancient letters often contained greetings to individuals and an autograph. The autograph was used when a secretary penned the letter for the author. By writing a portion of the closing with his own hand, the author verified his identity.

The clearest examples of these features appear in Paul's letters. For example, the longest list of greetings to individuals in the New Testament appears in the closing of Romans 16:3–16. Paul has clear examples of the autograph as well. He closed Galatians with the statement: "Look at what large letters I use as I write to you in my own handwriting" (Gl 6:11). He closed 2 Thessalonians with the words: "I, Paul, am writing this greeting with my own hand, which is an authenticating mark in every letter; this is how I write" (2Th 3:17).

The simple shift from one handwriting sample to another made the autograph clear. Unfortunately, that shift is apparent in the original letter but not in copies or translations. Nevertheless, Paul's statement that the autograph was a sign "in every letter" indicates that he consistently used the autograph even when it is not conspicuous in our modern translations.

Authorship

Some scholars claim that a few of the New Testament letters are *pseudonymous*—that is, written under the name of an important figure who was not truly the author. These scholars claim that, although several letters claim to be written by Paul (such as Ephesians, 1–2 Timothy, and Titus), they are actually pseudonymous—written by someone else, perhaps a later disciple of Paul. This theory should be rejected, however, for several reasons.

First, few, if any, examples of ancient pseudonymous *letters* from among the Jews exist. Second, the New Testament clearly shows that the apostles objected to pseudonymous letters (see 2Th 2:2–3). Third, the early church also rejected pseudonymous letters. In the second century, someone wrote a letter that claimed to be the missing letter Paul wrote to the Laodiceans (see Col 4:16). Even though the letter did not contain dangerous doctrines, the early church rejected it simply because it was pseudonymous.

Interpreting the New Testament Letters

Read the letters as historical documents. Rather than reading the New Testament Letters as written by God directly to the modern reader, we should first study them as correspondence written to ancient churches that were facing specific challenges. These letters certainly communicate God's revelation for modern readers. But before we can understand what God intends to say *to us*, we must first determine what the letter was intended to communicate *to the original readers*. Therefore, we should seek to understand the original historical context of the letters as fully as possible. Good study Bibles and Bible commentaries will help readers to do this.

Read the letters as one would ordinarily read a letter. Modern readers often read the New Testament Letters very differently than they would read other letters. Few people receive a letter and read only a paragraph at a time. They recognize that if they are going to understand the letter, they must read it in a single sitting, so that they can properly appreciate the flow and progression of the author's thoughts. Yet many read New Testament Letters haphazardly and, as a result, miss the development of thought in the letter.

Read the letters being conscious of the important differences between then and now. Sometimes statements in the New Testament letters are culturally conditioned. They were written assuming the conditions of first-century Jewish or Gentile culture in various parts of the world. They may not apply to readers in a different culture or era *in precisely the same way* that they applied to the original readers. In order to interpret and apply the NT Letters, readers must appreciate the differences between then and now, there and here. The differences are sometimes significant and influence interpretation and application greatly. Prudent application of biblical texts involves an attempt to discover the moral or theological principles that apply in all situations and which lie behind directives addressed to a situation different from today.

The following questions will help: What instruction does the letter give to the original reader? What particular situation was the instruction addressing? How is my situation like that original situation? How is my situation different? If our situation is very similar to that of the original reader, the instruction may directly apply. However, if our situation is very different from that of the original reader, the instruction will still apply, but less directly.

◄ Introduction to Romans

Circumstances of Writing

Paul the apostle is the stated and indisputable author of the book of Romans. From the book of Acts and statements in Romans, we learn that Paul wrote this letter while he was in Corinth and on his way to Jerusalem in the spring of AD 57, to deliver an offering from the Gentile churches to poor Jewish Christians (Ac 20:3; Rm 15:25–29).

All of Paul's writings grew out of his missionary/pastoral work and were about the problems and needs of local churches. The book of Romans is also of this genre, but it is the least "local" in the sense that Paul had not yet been to Rome. This letter was his opportunity to expound the good news message (the gospel). He could discuss the essence of sin, the salvation accomplished on the cross, the union of the believer with Christ, how the Spirit works in the Christian to promote holiness, the place of the Jewish people in God's plan, future things, and Christian living or ethics. Though Paul did not write Romans as a systematic theology, his somewhat orderly exposition has been the fountain for the development of that discipline.

The origin of the Roman house churches is unknown. The founding of the Roman church likely goes back to the "visitors from Rome, (both Jews and converts)" who came to Jerusalem at Pentecost (Ac 2:10). Many of these visitors converted to Christianity (Ac 2:41), some of whom very likely hailed from Rome. In Acts 18:2, Luke mentioned Aquila and Priscilla, who left Rome because Emperor Claudius had ordered all Jews to leave the city (AD 49). This exodus was caused by strife among Jews over "Chrestus" (Christ). The remaining Christians in Rome would be from a Gentile background. The Jewish-Gentile tensions in Rome had a long history. These tensions are somewhat reflected throughout the letter, most specifically in chapters 2, 11, and 14–15.

Rome was the primary destination of this letter. Yet some manuscripts lack the phrase "in Rome" (1:7), giving some support to the conclusion that Paul intended a wider audience for the book of Romans and sent copies to other churches.

Contribution to the Bible

What is the gospel? The word *gospel* means "good news." The good news is about Jesus and what he did for us. Most Bible students would say that the gospel is outlined in 1 Corinthians 15:3–5. Romans fills in that outline and clarifies the gospel in relation to the Old Testament promises and the Mosaic law, the role of good works, and the gift of God's righteousness. Paul emphasized righteousness and justification in this letter to a depth and detail not found elsewhere in the Bible. Sin is traced to its core in our union with Adam and the imputation of original sin. Paul also mapped out the spread of human sin and its results in both believers and nonbelievers.

There are three passages in the New Testament (each one long sentence in the Greek text) that contain the most important theology of the New Testament: John 1:14 on the incarnation; Ephesians 1:3–14 about the triune purpose and glory of God; and Romans 3:21–26 on

Romans Timeline

800–450 BC

Mythical founding of Rome by Romulus and Remus **753**
Rome ruled by seven kings **753–509**
King Tarquin the Proud ousted and the Roman Republic founded **509**
Plebeian struggle with patricians results in greater voice in the governance of Rome **494**
Lucius Quinctius Cincinnatus, farmer, general, and consul of Rome from **460–438**
A *Decemviri*, committee of ten men, is commissioned to draw up Rome's first code of law, *The Twelve Tables*, binding on both patricians and plebeians. **451**

450–250 BC

The Via Appia, first of an unparalleled system of roads in the ancient world, is begun by Appius Claudius Caecus running in a southwesterly direction out of Rome. **312**
Rome gains control of the entire Italian peninsula as a prelude to far greater expansion and a series of wars with other peoples. **275–272**
The Romans begin minting coins. **269**
The first recorded gladiatorial games in Rome during the funeral of Junius Brutus. Three pairs of gladiators fought to the death. **264**

justification, redemption, and propitiation. If a Christian understands these three sentences, he has a solid foundation for faith.

Paul, in Romans 6–8, gave the most comprehensive development of our union with Christ and the Spirit's work in us. Romans 9–11 (on the role of Israel in God's plan) has been called the key to understanding the Bible. Romans 13 is the classic New Testament passage on the Christian's relation to and duties to the state. Romans 14–15 covers how Christians can relate to one another yet have different opinions and convictions on nonessential religious matters.

Structure

Paul wrote thirteen of the twenty-one letters (or "epistles") contained in the New Testament. The four Gospels, the book of Acts, and the book of Revelation are not classified as letters. Romans is the longest of Paul's letters, and it contains the elements found in a standard letter at that time: salutation (1:1–7); thanksgiving (1:8–17); the main body (1:18–16:18); and a farewell (16:19–24). Some scholars refer to Romans as a tractate (a formal treatise). But it bears all the marks of a real letter, although it is a finely tuned literary composition.

Outline

I. Introduction (1:1–15)
II. The Universal Need of Righteousness (1:16–3:20)
III. Justification: The Imputation of Righteousness (3:21–5:21)
IV. The New Life in Christ (6:1–8:39)
V. The Mystery of Israel (9:1–11:36)
VI. Exhortations about the Christian Life (12:1–15:13)
VII. Epilogue: Greetings and Travel Plans (15:14–16:27)

Key verses in Romans

8:28 We know that all things work together for the good of those who love God, who are called according to his purpose.

10:9 If you confess with your mouth, "Jesus is Lord," and believe in your heart that God raised him from the dead, you will be saved.

12:1 Therefore, brothers and sisters, in view of the mercies of God, I urge you to present your bodies as a living sacrifice, holy and pleasing to God; this is your true worship.

12:10 Love one another deeply as brothers and sisters. Take the lead in honoring one another.

14:12 So then, each of us will give an account of himself to God.

---

100 BC–AD 33

Romans develop the hypocaust, a central heating system, used in large villas and public baths. **85 BC**
Julius Caesar is assassinated on **MARCH 15, 44 BC**.
Octavian (Augustus), Rome's first emperor **27 BC–AD 14**
The birth of Jesus of Nazareth **5 BC**
The reign of Tiberius Caesar **AD 14–37**

AD 33–80

Agrippina, Emperor Claudius's third wife, brings Seneca out of an eight-year exile on Corsica to be the tutor of her son Nero. **41**
Agrippina poisons her husband Claudius; her son Nero becomes emperor of Rome. **54**
Jesus's trials, crucifixion, resurrection, and ascension **33**
Saul's conversion on the Damascus Road **OCTOBER 34**
Paul's letter to the church at Rome written in Corinth **57**
Nero blames Christians for the great fire in Rome. **64**
Roman Colosseum under construction **70–80**

The Gospel of God for Rome

1 Paul, a servant of Christ Jesus, called as an apostle[A] and set apart for the gospel of God — [2] which he promised beforehand through his prophets in the Holy Scriptures — [3] concerning his Son, Jesus Christ our Lord, who was a descendant of David[B] according to the flesh [4] and was appointed to be the powerful Son of God according to the Spirit of holiness[C] by the resurrection of the dead. [5] Through him we have received grace and apostleship to bring about[D] the obedience of faith for the sake of his name among all the Gentiles, [E] [6] including you who are also called by Jesus Christ.

[7] To all who are in Rome, loved by God, called as saints.

Grace to you and peace from God our Father and the Lord Jesus Christ.

Paul's Desire to Visit Rome

[8] First, I thank my God through Jesus Christ for all of you because the news of your faith[F] is being reported in all the world. [9] God is my witness, whom I serve with my spirit in telling the good news about his Son — that I constantly mention you, [10] always asking in my prayers that if it is somehow in God's will, I may now at last succeed in coming to you. [11] For I want very much to see you, so that I may impart to you some spiritual gift to strengthen you, [12] that

is, to be mutually encouraged by each other's faith, both yours and mine.

[13] Now I don't want you to be unaware, brothers and sisters, that I often planned to come to you (but was prevented until now) in order that I might have a fruitful ministry[G] among you, just as I have had among the rest of the Gentiles. [14] I am obligated both to Greeks and barbarians,[H] both to the wise and the foolish. [15] So I am eager to preach the gospel to you also who are in Rome.

The Righteous Will Live by Faith

[16] For I am not ashamed of the gospel,[I] because it is the power of God for salvation to everyone who believes, first to the Jew, and also to the Greek. [17] For in it the righteousness of God is revealed from faith to faith,[J] just as it is written: **The righteous will live by faith.**[K,L]

The Guilt of the Gentile World

[18] For God's wrath is revealed from heaven against all godlessness and unrighteousness of people who by their unrighteousness suppress the truth, [19] since what can be known[M] about God is evident among them, because God has shown it to them. [20] For his invisible attributes, that is, his eternal power and divine nature, have been clearly seen since the creation of the world, being understood through what

---

[A]1:1 Or *Jesus, a called apostle* [B]1:3 Lit *was of the seed of David* [C]1:4 Or *the spirit of holiness,* or the *Holy Spirit* [D]1:5 Or *him for; lit him into* [E]1:5 Or *nations,* also in v. 13 [F]1:8 Or *because your faith* [G]1:13 Lit *have some fruit* [H]1:14 Or *non-Greeks* [I]1:16 Other mss add *of Christ* [J]1:17 Or *revealed out of faith into faith* [K]1:17 Or *The one who is righteous by faith will live* [L]1:17 Hab 2:4 [M]1:19 Or *what is known*

1:1–2 In God's summons of Paul from his previous way of life, he commissioned him as an apostle (Ac 9). The good news is the fulfillment of the OT prophecies.
1:3 Jesus is God's **Son** in a different sense than are Christians. Jesus is God's Son first by being the eternal Son and Second Person of the Trinity (Is 9:6; Gl 4:4), and second by being the virgin-born incarnate Son, conceived as the Spirit came to Mary (Lk 1:35). Jesus was also the messianic Son who came in the family line of David (2Sm 7:12–16; Pss 2:6–7; 89:26–29,36). **Flesh** here means the real human nature of Jesus.
1:4 The **Spirit of holiness** (another title for the Holy Spirit) raised Jesus from the **dead**. This event testified that he was as God's unique Son exalted over death and Satan, and invested with all power (Mt 28:18).
1:5 The **obedience of faith** (cp. 10:16; 15:18) is best understood as the faith that issues in obedience.
1:6 Christians are **called by Jesus.** This calling is not a mere invitation. It is a sovereign summons that results in salvation as people respond in faith. God took the initiative in saving believers.
1:7 Called as saints does not mean called "to be" saints, as if this is something Christians might become in the future. Neither does it signify an unusually holy person. Rather, all Christians are saints by the sovereign call of God. They have been set apart just as the nation of Israel was set apart (Lv 11:44; 19:2).

1:8 Paul was thankful for the spread of the **faith.**
1:9–10 Paul continually prayed for the Roman Christians in his **spirit.** Paul had wanted to come to Rome, but God was in control of all his circumstances.
1:11–12 Paul was sure he would bring certain benefits or blessings as he taught among the house churches of Rome. The **spiritual gift** mentioned here was not the special gift(s) in 1Co 12–14 which were given by God (1Co 12:11) but gifts that Christians gave to one another. Paul was certain that the Roman Christians would minister to him since every part of the body of Christ has useful functions in relation to other parts (1Co 12:12–27).
1:14 Paul's conversion placed a special commission and obligation on him (Ac 9:15; 13:47; 1Co 9:16; Gl 2:8–9). His training and Roman citizenship equipped him to reach all varieties of pagans, including the educated and the **barbarians.** These barbarians included people from Spain and Asia Minor (Ac 14:11–18).
1:16 Why might someone be **ashamed of the gospel?** On the surface, the gospel seems like a very strange message. A crucified Messiah seemed to be a contradiction in terms to the Jews. A crucified **Jew** like foolishness to the Romans, who despised Jews in general. People are saved by faith, but faith is not the cause of **salvation.** The cause of salvation is the grace of God, the will of God, and the **power of God** working through the message.

1:17 The **righteousness of God** was the core of Paul's message. God's righteousness can be understood in several ways. First, God always does what is right and can be said to have righteousness as one of his attributes (Dt 32:4; Ps 119:142). Second, since God always does what is right, his actions or activities are sometimes identified as his righteousness (Is 45:8; 46:13; 51:5–6,8; 56:1). Third, God's righteousness is as a gift from him to us, justifying us in his sight. "Justification" is a courtroom term signifying that a judge declares a person to be "right" or "just." In the gospel, God reveals his righteousness (his nature, his activity, and his gift of right status) by faith. **From faith to faith** emphasizes that the entire process of being declared righteous comes to us from start to finish by faith.
1:18 All people need the gospel because they are under **God's wrath,** which stems from his holy revulsion to sin. Since the garden of Eden, people have been unrighteous, and they have suppressed **the truth.**
1:19 God as Creator has disclosed himself in creation (Ps 19:1; cp. Ac 14:15–17). God is at work to show himself in the world, yet the world is in rebellion against him.
1:20 Humanity's problem is not that they don't know the truth. The history of the human race discloses a determined effort to oppose the will of God. People are **without excuse** for their idolatry and practical atheism.

he has made. As a result, people are without excuse. ²¹ For though they knew God, they did not glorify him as God or show gratitude. Instead, their thinking became worthless, and their senseless hearts were darkened. ²² Claiming to be wise, they became fools ²³ and exchanged the glory of the immortal God for images resembling mortal man, birds, four-footed animals, and reptiles.

²⁴ Therefore God delivered them over in the desires of their hearts to sexual impurity, so that their bodies were degraded among themselves. ²⁵ They exchanged the truth of God for a lie, and worshiped and served what has been created instead of the Creator, who is praised forever. Amen.

From Idolatry to Depravity

²⁶ For this reason God delivered them over to disgraceful passions. Their womenᴬ exchanged natural sexual relationsᴮ for unnatural ones. ²⁷ The menᶜ in the same way also left natural relations with women and were inflamed in their lust for one another. Men committed shameless acts with men and received in their own personsᴰ the appropriate penalty of their error.

²⁸ And because they did not think it worthwhile to acknowledge God, God delivered them over to a corrupt mind so that they do what is not right. ²⁹ They are filled with all unrighteousness,ᴱ evil, greed, and wickedness. They are full of envy, murder, quarrels, deceit, and malice. They are gossips, ³⁰ slanderers, God-haters, arrogant, proud, boastful, inventors of evil,

disobedient to parents, ³¹ senseless, untrustworthy, unloving,ᶠ and unmerciful. ³² Although they know God's just sentence — that those who practice such things deserve to dieᴳ — they not only do them, but even applaudᴴ others who practice them.

God's Righteous Judgment

2 Therefore, every one of youᴵ who judges is without excuse. For when you judge another, you condemn yourself, since you, the judge, do the same things. ² Now we know that God's judgment on those who do such things is based on the truth. ³ Do you think — anyone of you who judges those who do such things yet do the same — that you will escape God's judgment? ⁴ Or do you despise the riches of his kindness, restraint, and patience, not recognizingᴶ that God's kindness is intended to lead you to repentance? ⁵ Because of your hardened and unrepentant heart you are storing up wrath for yourself in the day of wrath, when God's righteous judgment is revealed. ⁶ **He will repay each one according to his works:**ᴷ ⁷ eternal life to those who by persistence in doing good seek glory, honor, and immortality; ⁸ but wrath and anger to those who are self-seeking and disobey the truth while obeying unrighteousness. ⁹ There will be affliction and distress for every human being who does evil, first to the Jew, and also to the Greek; ¹⁰ but glory, honor, and peace for everyone who does what is good, first to the Jew, and also to the Greek. ¹¹ For there is no favoritism with God.

ᴬ**1:26** Lit *females*, also in v. 27   ᴮ**1:26** Lit *natural use*, also in v. 27   ᶜ**1:27** Lit *males*, also later in v.   ᴰ**1:27** Or *in themselves*
ᴱ**1:29** Other mss add *sexual immorality*   ᶠ**1:31** Other mss add *unforgiving*   ᴳ**1:32** Lit *things are worthy of death*   ᴴ**1:32** Lit *even take pleasure in*   ᴵ**2:1** Lit *Therefore, O man, every one*   ᴶ**2:4** Or *patience, because you do not recognize*   ᴷ**2:6** Ps 62:12; Pr 24:12

1:21 Because of human willfulness, people's knowledge of God became clouded and their thinking became **darkened**. Part of the wrath of God is revealed in humanity's loss of intelligent **thinking**.

1:23 Many people think that the history of religion developed along an evolutionary model. Instead of starting in polytheism, the Bible says humanity started with knowledge of the one true God and then declined into polytheism as humans were separated from God and fractured from one another.

1:24 Because they rejected the truths of God revealed in creation, God punished the Greco-Roman world by delivering them to the **desires of their hearts**.

1:25 The loss of the knowledge of God in the mind and heart leads to an exchange of **the truth** for **a lie**. Something created is served and worshiped rather than the Creator, and judgment is the result (Ps 81:12; Ac 7:42).

1:26–27 Lesbians and homosexuals often argue that this verse only prohibits sexual abuse of children, or else they say that **natural sexual relations** are not violated when men and women who are born with a tendency for homosexual desires (as they claim) practice homosexuality. But Paul clearly says

sexual relations between members of the same sex are **unnatural**, and the Bible elsewhere strictly prohibits all homosexuality (e.g., Lv 18:22). Such **disgraceful passions** result in **appropriate penalty**.

1:28–32 In v. 24 God is described as delivering society to impurity, in v. 26 to degrading the passions, and in v. 28 to a **corrupt mind**. The mind becomes (Gk) *adokimos* (disqualified), an untrustworthy guide in moral choices because people have rejected knowledge of God. Verses 29–31 contain a list of vices. Lesbian and homosexual practices may seem particularly objectionable, but any of the twenty-one sins listed (cp. Gl 5:19–21) cut people off from the life of God and bring spiritual death. When society applauds **others who practice** these sins, it has lost its moral compass.

2:1 Some interpreters think Paul is speaking about Gentile moralists in vv. 1–16, and then Jews beginning at v. 17. The majority of scholars, however, see the Jew as the subject throughout chap. 2. Judgment and condemnation follow sin as night follows day. Not all people commit the same sins, but all show by their judging and criticism that they do not live up to the moral law they know. No one is **without excuse**.

2:2 The coming **judgment** will be based on God's **truth**, which no amount of human opinion or protest can alter.

2:3 There will be no **escape** from God's coming **judgment**.

2:4 God's grace should lead people to repent of their sin (2Pt 3:7–13).

2:5 Like water pooling up behind a dam, people accumulate a debt of **wrath** as they continue to reject God's grace. One day the dam will break, and the flood of divine wrath will sweep up individuals and entire societies.

2:6–10 This is a controversial passage. The most likely interpretation is that **works** are the outcome of a person's faith. Christians are declared righteous by faith. At the moment of that declaration, the person is joined to Christ and regenerated by the Holy Spirit, becoming a new creation (2Co 5:17) created for good works (Eph 2:10). Thus the person of faith who seeks glory, honor, and immortality and continues to do good demonstrates that he is truly regenerate and thus is assured of eternal life. To the person who obeys **unrighteousness** and disobeys **truth**, however, **wrath** is his destiny.

2:11 No one should think that God's judgment is tainted with **favoritism**. He is a just Judge of both Jews and Gentiles.

¹² For all who sin without the law will also perish without the law, and all who sin under^A the law will be judged by the law. ¹³ For the hearers of the law are not righteous before God, but the doers of the law will be justified.^B ¹⁴ So, when Gentiles, who do not by nature have the law, do^C what the law demands, they are a law to themselves even though they do not have the law. ¹⁵ They show that the work of the law^D is written on their hearts. Their consciences confirm this. Their competing thoughts either accuse or even excuse them^E ¹⁶ on the day when God judges what people have kept secret, according to my gospel through Christ Jesus.

Jewish Violation of the Law

¹⁷ Now if^F you call yourself a Jew, and rely on the law, and boast in God, ¹⁸ and know his will, and approve the things that are superior, being instructed from the law, ¹⁹ and if you are convinced that you are a guide for the blind, a light to those in darkness, ²⁰ an instructor of the ignorant, a teacher of the immature, having the embodiment of knowledge and truth in the law — ²¹ you then, who teach another, don't you teach yourself? You who preach, "You must not steal" — do you steal? ²² You who say, "You must not commit adultery" — do you commit adultery? You who detest idols, do you rob temples? ²³ You who boast in the law, do you dishonor God by breaking the law?^G ²⁴ For, as it is written: **The name of God is blasphemed among the Gentiles because of you.**^H

Circumcision of the Heart

²⁵ Circumcision benefits you if you observe the law, but if you are a lawbreaker, your circumcision has become uncircumcision. ²⁶ So if an uncircumcised man keeps the law's requirements, will not his uncircumcision be counted as circumcision? ²⁷ A man who is physically uncircumcised, but who keeps the law, will judge you who are a lawbreaker in spite of having the letter of the law and circumcision. ²⁸ For a person is not a Jew who is one outwardly, and true circumcision is not something visible in the flesh. ²⁹ On the contrary, a person is a Jew who is one inwardly, and circumcision is of the heart — by the Spirit, not the letter.^I That person's praise is not from people but from God.

Paul Answers an Objection

3 So what advantage does the Jew have? Or what is the benefit of circumcision? ² Considerable in every way. First, they were entrusted with the very words of God. ³ What then? If some were unfaithful, will their unfaithfulness nullify God's faithfulness? ⁴ Absolutely not! Let God be true, even though everyone is a liar, as it is written:

> **That you may be justified in your words and triumph when you judge.**^J

⁵ But if our unrighteousness highlights^K God's righteousness, what are we to say? I am using a human argument:^L Is God unrighteous to inflict wrath? ⁶ Absolutely not! Otherwise, how will God judge the world? ⁷ But if by my lie God's truth abounds to his glory, why am I

---

^A 2:12 Lit *in* ^B 2:13 Or *acquitted* ^C 2:14 Or *who do not have the law, instinctively do* ^D 2:15 The code of conduct required by the law ^E 2:15 Internal debate, either in a person or among the pagan moralists ^F 2:17 Other mss read *Look —* ^G 2:23 Or *you dishonor God by breaking the law.* ^H 2:24 Is 52:5 ^I 2:29 Or *heart — spiritually, not literally* ^J 3:4 Ps 51:4 ^K 3:5 Or *shows,* or *demonstrates* ^L 3:5 Lit *I speak as a man*

2:12 This verse introduces the Mosaic **law** into the discussion of the coming judgment. Paul teaches that the law does not save a person but only reveals sin as people fall short of the law's requirements. Thus in the judgment, the possession of the law will be a basis of condemnation.
2:13 No one will be **justified** by obeying the law, for no one obeys the law perfectly (Rm 3:20,23; Gl 2:16; Jms 2:8–11).
2:14–15 The **Gentiles** do not have the Mosaic law as a moral guide, but they do have an inner **law** that informs their conscience. All humans have this as a component of their being created in God's image (Gn 1:26). This moral law will **accuse or even excuse** daily moral choices, but ultimately demonstrates that all people fall short of God's holiness.
2:16 God knows every **secret**, and Jesus will be the final Judge (Jn 5:22–30; Ac 17:31). The coming judgment will be according to truth, proportional to the rejection of revelation received, according to deeds done, without partiality, and in response to the **gospel**.
2:17–20 Paul listed eight grounds on which Jews rested their sense of moral superiority over the Gentiles; three times he cited the law as a grounds. However, mere possession of the law does not win divine favor.

2:21–23 Paul exposed Jewish hypocrisy. He did so with a series of five rhetorical questions that indicted his people for lacking essential righteousness. Paul did not mean that every Jew committed all these sins but that all transgress the law and lack the righteousness to enter God's presence.
2:24 Paul cited Is 52:5 from the Greek OT (the Septuagint, or LXX) as support that Jewish sin resulted in God's name being dishonored among the pagan nations when the Jews were defeated and exiled. To pagan perception, the Lord seemed powerless since he did not protect his people.
2:25–29 Circumcision was a sign and seal of a covenant that God made with Israel (Ex 12:44–49). The rite went back to Abraham and the covenant God made with him (Gn 17:9–14). Circumcision became a badge of Jewish identity and, it was thought, a guarantee of salvation. By implication, the way you lived made no difference. But Paul declared that circumcision without obedience is empty. Furthermore, Abraham was a man of faith who was accepted by God long before he was circumcised (Gn 15:1–20). The true Jew is one who has a spiritual **circumcision . . . of the heart**.
3:1–2 It might seem from chap. 2 that being a Jew and being circumcised conferred no

advantage, but Paul listed many Jewish advantages in 9:4–5. It is a great privilege to be Jewish — **considerable in every way**. They heard God speak the "ten words" or Ten Commandments (Ex 20:1–20) directly to them. Then through a long series of prophets, God's words came to them. No other people on earth had this privilege.
3:3 Even if some of the Jewish people **were unfaithful**, God will be faithful to his covenant and will bring his promises to fulfillment. Paul referred particularly to the promises centered in the Messiah, Jesus Christ.
3:4 After he was confronted by the prophet Nathan for his sins surrounding the Bathsheba incident, David confessed in Ps 51:4 that God is **justified** in his judgments. **Let God be true**, for it would be against his infinitely perfect nature to be otherwise.
3:5–8 Paul addresses several implications to which critics mistakenly thought his teachings would lead. For example, if God is shown to be in the right by man's sin and error, then God is honored by our shortcomings. How then can God punish us when we have helped display his righteousness? But Paul answered that as a matter of principle God's judgment of sin is always righteous. People who think otherwise deserve **condemnation**, for their true focus is not on

The Cross and the Gospel

by Bruce A. Ware

The cross of Christ and the gospel of Christ are inextricably linked. Indeed, the gospel is the good news of what took place when Christ died on the cross. To understand what Jesus accomplished on the cross, then, is to understand the gospel. To believe personally that what Christ did on the cross he did for you is to believe the gospel of Jesus Christ.

What Happened on the Cross?

What took place in Christ's death on the cross? The short answer is this: "Christ died for our sins" (1Co 15:3). Christ's death for our sin must be understood in two broad ways: First, when Jesus was nailed to the cross, the Father charged to him all of our sin (2Co 5:21) and judged the full penalty of our sin in Jesus as he died (Col 2:14). Second, Jesus conquered the power of Satan, darkness, and death as he died for our sin (Col 2:15; Heb 2:14), thus establishing his supreme authority and power over everything in creation (Eph 1:20–23). To summarize, in his death on the cross Jesus fully paid the penalty for our sin, and he totally defeated the power of sin.

Jesus's subsequent resurrection from the dead was not just a nice ending to the story but rather necessary evidence that his death for sin really worked (1Co 15:17). The penalty of sin is death, and the greatest power that sin has over us is death. But since the penalty of sin is death, and since Christ paid the penalty of sin fully by his death on the cross, his resurrection from the dead demonstrated that the penalty had been paid in full. And since the greatest power of sin is death, and since Christ conquered all of sin's power in his death on the cross, his resurrection also demonstrated that the complete power of sin had been defeated as he arose victorious from the grave.

Erasing the Certificate of Debt

It is only because Christ paid sin's penalty that he was able also to liberate us from sin's power. That is, his payment of sin's penalty is the basis for his conquering of sin's power. Consider one sample passage that shows this to be true. Colossians 2:13–14 teaches that believers are forgiven of all their trespasses through the death of Christ on the cross. The thrust here is on expiation: the liability we owed before a holy God to suffer the penalty for our violation of his law is removed because Christ took upon himself our record of debt. Jesus "erased the certificate of debt, with its obligations, that was against us and opposed to us, and has taken it away by nailing it to the cross" (2:14).

The substitutionary death Christ died, in which he cancelled out the debt of sinners, then, is the backdrop for the next glorious truth found in Colossians 2:15: Jesus "disarmed the rulers and authorities and disgraced them publicly," putting them to shame and triumphing over them. The death by which Satan is disarmed and put to shame, then, is a death that cancels our sin. The disarming of Satan and the death that cancels our sin are theologically linked in this way: the basis of Satan's power over sinners is sin itself; the only way to overthrow this power was for sin to be paid for and forgiven. Christ's forgiveness through his payment of sin's penalty ("penal substitution"), therefore, is the means by which we are freed from Satan's power.

An Analogy of Our Freedom

An analogy may assist in clarifying Scripture's teaching about the pardon Christ earned for believers on the cross. Under a just system of laws, a prisoner is jailed because he has been convicted of some crime whose penalty involves his incarceration. Notice, then, that his guilt forms the basis for his bondage. Only because he has been proven guilty of breaking the law does the state have the right to imprison him. Furthermore, if a prisoner can prove his actual innocence, such that the charge of guilt can be removed—e.g., if some forensic or DNA evidence available after his incarceration demonstrates his innocence—then the state is obligated to release him from prison. It is clear, then, that the power of the state to put criminals in bondage comes from the guilt they have incurred and the accompanying penalty directed at them as a result. Remove the guilt and its penalty, and you remove the just basis for the state's power to enforce bondage.

Similarly, Satan's power over sinners is tied specifically and exclusively to the sinner's

also still being judged as a sinner? **⁸ And why not say, just as some people slanderously claim we say, "Let us do what is evil so that good may come"? Their condemnation is deserved!**

The Whole World Guilty before God

⁹ What then? Are we any better off?ᴬ Not at all! For we have already charged that both Jews and Greeks are all under sin,ᴮ ¹⁰ as it is written:

> There is no one righteous,
>   not even one.
> ¹¹ There is no one who understands;
>   there is no one who seeks God.
> ¹² All have turned away;
>   all alike have become worthless.
> There is no one who does
>   what is good,
>   not even one.ᶜ
> ¹³ Their throat is an open grave;
>   they deceive with their tongues.ᴰ
> Vipers' venom is under their lips.ᴱ
> ¹⁴ Their mouth is full of cursing
>   and bitterness.ᶠ
> ¹⁵ Their feet are swift to shed blood;
> ¹⁶ ruin and wretchedness are
>   in their paths,

> ¹⁷ and the path of peace
>   they have not known.ᴳ
> ¹⁸ There is no fear of God
>   before their eyes.ᴴ

¹⁹ Now we know that whatever the law says, it speaks to those who are subject to the law,ᴵ so that every mouth may be shut and the whole world may become subject to God's judgment.ᴶ ²⁰ For no one will be justifiedᴷ in his sight by the works of the law, because the knowledge of sin comes through the law.

The Righteousness of God through Faith

²¹ But now, apart from the law, the righteousness of God has been revealed, attested by the Law and the Prophets.ᴸ ²² The righteousness of God is through faith in Jesus Christᴹ to all who believe, since there is no distinction. ²³ For all have sinned and fall short of theᴺ glory of God; ²⁴ they are justified freely by his grace through the redemption that is in Christ Jesus. ²⁵ God presented him as the mercy seatᴼ by his blood, through faith, to demonstrate his righteousness, because in his restraint God passed over the sins previously committed. ²⁶ God

---

ᴬ **3:9** Are we Jews any better than the Gentiles? ᴮ **3:9** Under sin's power or dominion ᶜ **3:10–12** Ps 14:1–3; 53:1–3; Ec 7:20 ᴰ **3:13** Ps 5:9 ᴱ **3:13** Ps 140:3 ᶠ **3:14** Ps 10:7 ᴳ **3:15–17** Is 59:7–8 ᴴ **3:18** Ps 36:1 ᴵ **3:19** Lit *those in the law* ᴶ **3:19** Or *become guilty before God*, or *may be accountable to God* ᴷ **3:20** Or *will be declared righteous*, or *will be acquitted* ᴸ **3:21** When capitalized, *the Law and the Prophets* = OT ᴹ **3:22** Or *through the faithfulness of Jesus Christ* ᴺ **3:23** Or *and lack the* ᴼ **3:25** Or *propitiation*, or *place of atonement*

---

glorifying God but on giving free rein to their sinful desires.

3:10–18 In these verses Paul linked seven OT passages to demonstrate that all of humanity is under sin's dominion. No one is righteous; no one **understands** (Jn 8:43–44; 1Co 2:14), and **no one . . . seeks God**. Paul cited Bible passages that show the extent of corruption.

3:19 Someone may argue that the seven passages Paul cited are addressed not to Jews but to pagan nations. But everything in the Hebrew Bible is first addressed to the Jews for their instruction so they can learn about sin's power. All people from every nation and ethnicity are sinners, and God will judge **the whole world**. In God's court, everyone is speechless.

3:20 No one can earn justification by obedience to the law's requirements. The law was never intended to be a means of salvation. A primary purpose of the law was to reveal sin in its full scope, thus pointing to humanity's need for the gift of righteousness.

3:21–26 The phrase **but now** marks a decisive shift in Paul's argument. This paragraph (one long sentence in the original Greek) is a wonderful compression of theology. The **righteousness of God** was manifested and given through the cross of Christ. Sinners gain pardon not through their adherence to the law, but through faith in the one who fulfilled all righteousness on their behalf. **The Law and the Prophets** refers to the OT, and the entire OT is correctly understood as a witness to Jesus and his work.

3:23 All have missed the mark that God intended for the human race and have lost the **glory** of the original creation (Ps 8:5).

3:24 Justified means that Christians are declared to be righteous (5:1,9; 8:30; 1Co 1:30; 6:11) because of Jesus's work on the cross. **Freely** means that God grants justification not due to any merit in Christians but solely by **his grace**, the undeserved love and mercy of God. **Redemption** is a commercial term that refers to purchasing freedom for slaves. All people are slaves to sin by their fallen nature. The purchase price for our freedom was the blood of **Christ Jesus** (see Mk 10:45; 1Pt 1:18–19).

3:25 Mercy seat translates the Greek word *hilastērion*, a term borrowed from the sacrificial system and the temple. God **presented**

---

guilt through sin. His hold on them is owing to their sinful rebellion against God. But remove the guilt through Christ's payment for their sin and you remove the basis for Satan's hold on them! So by his death Christ took upon himself the sin of others and paid the full penalty for their sin. As a consequence, the hold that Satan had upon sinners is necessarily broken since the basis for this bondage is removed. Remove the guilt and you remove the bondage.

The Cross Is Good News

The gospel is the good news that in the cross of Christ, the penalty of our sin was paid fully by Christ. By this, sin's powerful hold on our lives, which leads ultimately to death, has been completely defeated. If we will trust fully Christ's accomplishment for us—that he paid sin's penalty and conquered sin's power—and not look to our own works or accomplishments as if they could commend us to God, we will be saved (Eph 2:8–9).

presented him to demonstrate his righteousness at the present time, so that he would be just and justify the one who has faith in Jesus.

Boasting Excluded

27 Where, then, is boasting? It is excluded. By what kind of law?^A By one of works? No, on the contrary, by a law^B of faith. **28** For we conclude that a person is justified by faith apart from the works of the law. **29** Or is God the God of Jews only? Is he not the God of Gentiles too? Yes, of Gentiles too, **30** since there is one God who will justify the circumcised by faith and the uncircumcised through faith. **31** Do we then nullify the law through faith? Absolutely not! On the contrary, we uphold the law.

Abraham Justified by Faith

4 What then will we say that Abraham, our forefather according to the flesh, has found?^C **2** If Abraham was justified^D by works, he has something to boast about — but not before God. **3** For what does the Scripture say? **Abraham believed God, and it was credited to him for righteousness.**^E **4** Now to the one who works, pay is not credited as a gift, but as something owed. **5** But to the one who does not work, but believes on him who justifies the ungodly, his faith is credited for righteousness.

David Celebrating the Same Truth

6 Likewise, David also speaks of the blessing of the person to whom God credits righteousness apart from works:
7   **Blessed are those whose lawless acts are forgiven**
   and whose sins are covered.

8   **Blessed is the person**
   the Lord will never charge with sin.^F

Abraham Justified before Circumcision

9 Is this blessing only for the circumcised, then? Or is it also for the uncircumcised? For we say, **Faith was credited to Abraham for righteousness.**^E **10** In what way, then, was it credited — while he was circumcised, or uncircumcised? It was not while he was circumcised, but uncircumcised. **11** And he received the sign of circumcision as a seal of the righteousness that he had by faith^G while still uncircumcised. This was to make him the father of all who believe but are not circumcised, so that righteousness may be credited to them also. **12** And he became the father of the circumcised, who are not only circumcised but who also follow in the footsteps of the faith our father Abraham had while he was still uncircumcised.

The Promise Granted through Faith

13 For the promise to Abraham or to his descendants that he would inherit the world was not through the law, but through the righteousness that comes by faith. **14** If those who are of the law are heirs, faith is made empty and the promise nullified, **15** because the law produces wrath. And where there is no law, there is no transgression.

16 This is why the promise is by faith, so that it may be according to grace, to guarantee it to all the descendants — not only to the one who is of the law^H but also to the one who is of Abraham's faith. He is the father of us all. **17** As it is written: **I have made you the father**

^A**3:27** Or *what principle?* ^B**3:27** Or *a principle* ^C**4:1** Or *What then shall we say? Have we found Abraham to be our forefather according to the flesh?* or *What, then, shall we say that Abraham our forefather found according to the flesh?* ^D**4:2** Or *was declared righteous,* or *was acquitted* ^E**4:3,9** Gn 15:6 ^F**4:7–8** Ps 32:1–2 ^G**4:11** Lit *righteousness of faith,* also in v. 13 ^H**4:16** Or *not to the one who is of the law only*

---

his Son as the mercy seat. By means of Jesus's **blood**—his sacrificial death—God's holy wrath against sin was appeased, and the sins of those who place their **faith** in Christ are taken away. **3:26** The **present time** of the cross and preaching of the good news vindicated God, showing that he is **just** and justifies the **one who has faith in Jesus**. **3:27–28** No one can boast in one's **works**. No one can boast even in one's **faith**. Faith is not the *cause* of justification but the *means* of justification. The cause of salvation is grace and mercy. **3:29–30** There is only one God and only one way to be justified by him, no matter your ethnic and national identity: **by faith**. **3:31** Does the gospel destroy the **law**? To answer this question, Paul considered the case of Abraham (Rm 4). **4:1–25** Abraham was the father of the He- brew nation (Gn 12:1–3). Jews commonly believed that Abraham kept the whole law before it was given on Mount Sinai (Gn 26:5), so he had something to brag about. Paul refutes this, showing that Abraham was jus- tified by faith and had no grounds to boast.

4:3 Genesis 15:6 is the text that Paul cited. **4:4–5 Pay** and **gift** are as different as works and faith. **To the one who does not work, but believes on him who justifies the un- godly . . . for righteousness** is a shocking expression. The Reformation focused on this passage. God saves the ungodly, sinners, and his enemies (5:5,8,10). Though Jews took Abra- ham to be a paragon of virtue, Paul declared that he was just a sinner saved by grace. **4:6–8** David, Israel's greatest king, sang about the **blessing** that God gave him in the forgiveness of his deliberate **sins**. David understood that, in God's accounting ledger, his sins were wiped out and righteousness was inscribed in their place. Paul's quotation of Ps 32:1–2 clarifies and explains Gn 15:6. Paul links justification and the forgiveness of sin. **4:9–10** Paul returned to his key text in Gn 15:6 and showed that the crediting of righ- teousness to Abraham took place when he was **uncircumcised**, so God's blessing is also for Gentiles who believe. **4:11** Circumcision was a **sign** and a **seal**. It marked out a man as part of the nation of Israel. It was also to be a seal of the **righ- teousness** a man had received **by faith**. The

timing of Abraham's circumcision enabled him to be the spiritual **father** and model for justification by faith to both circumcised Jews and uncircumcised Gentiles. **4:12** Abraham was the physical **father** of the Hebrew nation, but his greatest legacy was his example of **faith**. **4:13** The **law** demanded obedience and per- formance. If the law was violated, wrath re- sulted. God's **promise** was one of grace. The promise to Abraham and his seed (Gl 3:16–18) was not through the law but through the **righteousness that comes by faith**. **4:14–15** If the inheritance of the **promise** came by legal obedience, then the way of **faith** is empty. Furthermore, no one would inherit the promise since no one could keep the law. **4:16–18** God's **promise is by faith** so that it may be guaranteed to both Jews and Gentiles who believe. If it were by law, no such guarantee would be possible. **Abraham** was also promised to be the **father** of many nations. It seemed humanly impossible for Abraham to become the **father of many nations** when he was old, but he placed his **hope** in God's promise.

of many nations — ^ in the presence of the God in whom he believed, the one who gives life to the dead and calls things into existence that do not exist. [18] He believed, hoping against hope, so that he became **the father of many nations**^ according to what had been spoken: **So will your descendants be.**[8] [19] He did not weaken in faith when he considered^ his own body to be already dead (since he was about a hundred years old) and also the deadness of Sarah's womb. [20] He did not waver in unbelief at God's promise but was strengthened in his faith and gave glory to God, [21] because he was fully convinced that what God had promised, he was also able to do. [22] Therefore, **it was credited to him for righteousness.**[D] [23] Now **it was credited to him**[D] was not written for Abraham alone, [24] but also for us. It will be credited to us who believe in him who raised Jesus our Lord from the dead. [25] He was delivered up for[E] our trespasses and raised for our justification.

Faith Triumphs

5 Therefore, since we have been justified by faith, we have peace[F] with God through our Lord Jesus Christ. [2] We have also obtained access through him by faith[G] into this grace in which we stand, and we boast[H] in the hope of the glory of God. [3] And not only that, but we also boast in our afflictions, because we know that affliction produces endurance, [4] endurance produces proven character, and proven character produces hope. [5] This hope will not disappoint us, because God's love has been poured out in our hearts through the Holy Spirit who was given to us.

The Justified Are Reconciled

[6] For while we were still helpless, at the right time, Christ died for the ungodly. [7] For rarely will someone die for a just person — though for a good person perhaps someone might even dare to die. [8] But God proves his own love for us in that while we were still sinners, Christ died for us. [9] How much more then, since we have now been justified by his blood, will we be saved through him from wrath. [10] For if, while we were enemies, we were reconciled to God through the death of his Son, then how much more, having been reconciled, will we be saved by his life. [11] And not only that, but we also boast in God through our Lord Jesus Christ, through whom we have now received this reconciliation.

Death through Adam and Life through Christ

[12] Therefore, just as sin entered the world through one man, and death through sin, in this way death spread to all people, because all sinned.[I] [13] In fact, sin was in the world before the law, but sin is not charged to a person's account when there is no law. [14] Nevertheless, death reigned from Adam to Moses, even over those who did not sin in the likeness of Adam's transgression. He is a type of the Coming One.

[15] But the gift is not like the trespass. For if by the one man's trespass the many died, how

---

^**4:17,18** Gn 17:5   ^**4:18** Gn 15:5   ^**4:19** Other mss read *He did not consider*   ^**4:22,23** Gn 15:6   ^**4:25** Or *because of*   ^**5:1** Other mss read *faith, let us have peace*, which can also be translated *faith, let us grasp the fact that we have peace*   ^**5:2** Other mss omit *by faith*   ^**5:2** Or *rejoice*, also in vv. 3,11   ^**5:12** Or *have sinned*

4:19–22 Abraham had a realistic evaluation of his prospects for fatherhood. He was about **a hundred years old**, and Sarah was childless and long past child-bearing years. Yet Abraham did not doubt **God's promise**, and God strengthened his **faith**. This is the kind of faith that receives **righteousness**.
4:23–24 Everything in Scripture is for our benefit. The experiences of **Abraham** are as relevant to us as they were to him. We are **credited** as righteous before God in the same manner as Abraham: by faith.
4:25 Jesus was **delivered up for our trespasses** as promised in Is 52:13–53:12. Who delivered up Jesus? Was it Judas? Pilate? The Jewish Sanhedrin? Satan? Certainly all these were causal agents in the crucifixion of Christ, but ultimately it was the sovereign God who brought it to pass in order to fulfill his plan of redemption (Ac 4:27–28). The Father delivered up Jesus for our trespasses, and raised him so that his righteous servant would justify many people (Is 53:11).
5:1 We have peace in some manuscripts can be read as "let us grasp the fact that we have peace." This peace is an objective, settled fact because Jesus has accomplished it once and for all.
5:2 Access to God's grace is the privilege of all believers. We have the freedom to enter his presence at all times.

5:3–4 Believers can **boast in** tough circumstances and **afflictions** because we know that through such things the Father is disciplining us for greater holiness (Heb 12:10).
5:5 The Christian's hope is certain because **God's love** is assured to us by the Holy Spirit's ministry within the core of our being (**our hearts**).
5:6–8 We can be sure of God's love since he did so much for us when we were **helpless**. We were **ungodly**, we were still **sinners**, and we were his enemies (v. 10). Jesus died for that kind of person. The word translated "for" is the Greek preposition *huper* used in substitution contexts. Jesus **died** in our place.
5:10–11 If by the death of Christ **we were reconciled to God**, how much surer must the good news of salvation be now that he has risen and lives forevermore!
5:12–21 In this section, Paul brings his major discussion of justification by faith to a close. He shows that grace in justification reaches and affects us in Christ much more than sin and death have affected us in Adam.
5:12 Therefore gives this verse a loose connection with the previous section. **Sin** and **death** are almost personified here (cp. v. 21, "sin reigned in death"). **Just as** introduces a long and difficult Greek sentence. The main comparisons are clear, but some of the details lead interpreters to different opinions. Paul

was thinking of how both the first Adam (Gn 1–3) and the last Adam (Jesus Christ) have a universal significance for humanity. Interpreters are divided over the phrase **because all sinned**. The two major interpretations are (1) all people commit sin and therefore die, and (2) somehow all humans sinned "in Adam." The second view is more likely and entails either that Adam was the federal head of the race and acted on behalf of us all, or that Adam was the seminal head of the race and we were somehow "in him."
5:13–14 These verses support the second interpretive option for v. 12 (see note there). Sin "reigned" (v. 21) over humanity before the giving of the law even though none had sinned in the way Adam sinned. Adam's sin was a personal, deliberate act that plunged the human race into physical and spiritual death. All humans are under death's domain. All people now are born spiritually dead (Eph 2:1–3). Adam's sin had this broad effect because he was a **type** (Gk *tupos*) or prefiguration of Jesus, the **Coming One**, and represented all of humanity just as Jesus would do on the cross.
5:15–16 The works of Adam and Jesus have similar scope but drastically different effect. One **sin** plunged humanity into ruin, but God gave the gift that issued in justification in spite of our many **trespasses**. What was

much more have the grace of God and the gift which comes through the grace of the one man Jesus Christ overflowed to the many. ¹⁶ And the gift is not like the one man's sin, because from one sin came the judgment, resulting in condemnation, but from many trespasses came the gift, resulting in justification.^ ¹⁷ If by the one man's trespass, death reigned through that one man, how much more will those who receive the overflow of grace and the gift of righteousness reign in life through the one man, Jesus Christ.

¹⁸ So then, as through one trespass there is condemnation for everyone, so also through one righteous act there is justification leading to life for everyone. ¹⁹ For just as through one man's disobedience the many were made sinners, so also through the one man's obedience the many will be made righteous. ²⁰ The law came along to multiply the trespass. But where sin multiplied, grace multiplied even more ²¹ so that, just as sin reigned in death, so also grace will reign through righteousness, resulting in eternal life through Jesus Christ our Lord.

The New Life in Christ

6 What should we say then? Should we continue in sin so that grace may multiply? ² Absolutely not! How can we who died to sin still live in it? ³ Or are you unaware that all of us who were baptized into Christ Jesus were baptized into his death? ⁴ Therefore we were buried with him by baptism into death, in order

that, just as Christ was raised from the dead by the glory of the Father, so we too may walk in newness⁸ of life. ⁵ For if we have been united with him in the likeness of his death, we will certainly also beᶜ in the likeness of his resurrection. ⁶ For we know that our old selfᴰ was crucified with him so that the body ruled by sinᴱ might be rendered powerless so that we may no longer be enslaved to sin, ⁷ since a person who has died is freedᶠ from sin. ⁸ Now if we died with Christ, we believe that we will also live with him, ⁹ because we know that Christ, having been raised from the dead, will not die again. Death no longer rules over him. ¹⁰ For the death he died, he died to sin once for all time; but the life he lives, he lives to God. ¹¹ So, you too consider yourselves dead to sin and alive to God in Christ Jesus.ᴳ

¹² Therefore do not let sin reign in your mortal body, so that you obeyᴴ its desires. ¹³ And do not offer any partsᴵ of it to sin as weapons for unrighteousness. But as those who are alive from the dead, offer yourselves to God, and all the parts of yourselves to God as weapons for righteousness. ¹⁴ For sin will not rule over you, because you are not under the law but under grace.

From Slaves of Sin to Slaves of God

¹⁵ What then? Should we sin because we are not under the law but under grace? Absolutely not! ¹⁶ Don't you know that if you offer yourselves to someoneᴶ as obedient slaves, you are slaves of that one you obey — either of sin leading

^5:16 Or *acquittal*   ᴮ6:4 Or *a new way*   ᶜ6:5 Be joined with him   ᴰ6:6 Lit *man*   ᴱ6:6 Lit *that the body of sin*   ᶠ6:7 Or *justified*; lit *acquitted*   ᴳ6:11 Other mss add *our Lord*   ᴴ6:12 Other mss add *sin* (lit *it*) *in*   ᴵ6:13 Or *members*, also in v. 19   ᴶ6:16 Lit *that to whom you offer yourselves*

gained through Jesus is far greater than that which was lost through Adam.
5:17 Death took the entire human race into its kingdom. Believers, who with the rest of humanity were once slaves in the kingdom of darkness (Col 1:13), were brought into Christ's kingdom as sons to **reign** with him.
5:18 Adam's sin resulted in **condemnation for everyone**, whereas Christ's substitutionary death made possible **justification leading to life for everyone**.

#70 99 Essential Christian Truths

PERSONHOOD OF THE HOLY SPIRIT

The Bible affirms not only the full divinity of the Holy Spirit but also his personhood. Many people have mistakenly believed that the Spirit is a force or power, not a person. However, Scripture affirms his personhood by acknowledging that he is treated as a person (Ac 5:3; 7:51; Heb 10:29), acts like a person (Jn 14:26, 15:26; Rm 8:14), has attributes of a person (1Co 2:10–11; Eph 4:30), and acts in personal ways (Is 63:10; Ac 13:2). In addition, the Bible affirms that Christians relate to him personally (Ac 5:3–4; 7:51).

5:19 The expression **will be made** does not refer to the last judgment, as if our salvation were pending until that time. Rather, it pictures the fact that believers are made **righteous** when they come to faith. Since Paul knew many people were yet to come to faith when he wrote, it was fitting to use future tense.
5:20–21 The **law** was never an end unto itself. Rather, its function was to **multiply the trespass** by bringing the knowledge of **sin**. By this the need for **grace** is highlighted, allowing God to bestow it **even more**.
6:1–2 Can a justified person live the same way as he did before justification? Paul rejected the invalid inference (v. 1) with the strong expression **absolutely not**. Paul argues that believers have **died to sin**. Having experienced such a transfer, dare we go on living in sin?
6:3 In defense of his claim that believers have died to sin, Paul points out that through baptism we were **baptized into Christ Jesus** and his **death**.
6:4 Believers are symbolically **buried** with Christ through baptism and **raised** with him **from the dead** in order that we may **walk in newness of life**. This makes clear the absurdity of the idea that we can "continue in sin so that grace may multiply" (v. 1).
6:6 Our old self (Gk *palaios anthropos*; lit "old man") is everything that we were before

we became Christians. By contrast, the new self is what we are once we become Christians (Eph 4:22–24; Col 3:9–10). We cannot live as we once did because the "old self" **was crucified with him** (Christ). In Christ the believer is a "new creation" (2Co 5:17).
6:7 Sin (personified) has no claim over a dead person and can claim no loyalty from him.
6:8–9 It was because of our sin that death fixed its grip on Jesus, but he arose to live forever. **Death no longer rules** the believer, for we **died with Christ**, who no longer dies.
6:10–11 Jesus went through an irreversible transformation in his death and resurrection. Believers also undergo an irreversible transformation. Like Jesus, the believer **lives to God**.
6:12–13 The believer, as a member of the new kingdom, must not offer any help to the old king (Satan, sin, death) and his kingdom. We must give ourselves as **weapons** to be used in this warfare on the side of the rightful King. Sin is no longer the believer's ruler. Sin gained its power by using the **law**, but the Christian is under the rule of **grace** rather than law.
6:16 Paul used the figure of **slaves**. Whoever you **obey**, you come under his power. Obedience to **sin** brings **death**. Obedience to God brings **righteousness** and the gift of eternal life.

to death or of obedience leading to righteousness? [17] But thank God that, although you used to be slaves of sin, you obeyed from the heart that pattern of teaching to which you were handed[A] over, [18] and having been set free from sin, you became enslaved to righteousness. [19] I am using a human analogy because of the weakness of your flesh. [B] For just as you offered the parts of yourselves as slaves to impurity, and to greater and greater lawlessness, so now offer them as slaves to righteousness, which results in sanctification. [20] For when you were slaves of sin, you were free with regard to righteousness.[C] [21] So what fruit was produced[D] then from the things you are now ashamed of? The outcome of those things is death. [22] But now, since you have been set free from sin and have become enslaved to God, you have your fruit, which results in sanctification — and the outcome is eternal life! [23] For the wages of sin is death, but the gift of God is eternal life in Christ Jesus our Lord.

An Illustration from Marriage

7 Since I am speaking to those who know the law, brothers and sisters, don't you know that the law rules over someone as long as he lives? [2] For example, a married woman is legally bound to her husband while he lives. But if her husband dies, she is released from the law regarding the husband. [3] So then, if she is married to another man while her husband is living, she will be called an adulteress. But if her husband dies, she is free from that law. Then, if she is married to another man, she is not an adulteress.

[4] Therefore, my brothers and sisters, you also were put to death in relation to the law through the body of Christ so that you may belong to another. You belong to him who was raised from the dead in order that we may bear fruit for God. [5] For when we were in the flesh, the sinful passions aroused through the law were working in us[E] to bear fruit for death. [6] But now we have been released from the law, since we have died to what held us, so that we may serve in the newness of the Spirit and not in the old letter of the law.

Sin's Use of the Law

[7] What should we say then? Is the law sin? Absolutely not! But I would not have known sin if it were not for the law. For example, I would not have known what it is to covet if the law had not said, **Do not covet.**[F] [8] And sin, seizing an opportunity through the commandment, produced in me coveting of every kind. For apart from the law sin is dead. [9] Once I was alive apart from the law, but when the commandment came, sin sprang to life again [10] and I died. The commandment that was meant for life resulted in death for me. [11] For sin, seizing an opportunity through the commandment, deceived me, and through it killed me. [12] So then, the law is holy, and the commandment is holy and just and good. [13] Therefore, did what is good become death to me? Absolutely not! But sin, in order to be recognized as sin, was producing death in me through what is good, so that through the commandment, sin might become sinful beyond measure.

[A]6:17 Or *entrusted* [B]6:19 Or *your human nature* [C]6:20 Lit *free to righteousness* [D]6:21 Lit *what fruit do you have* [E]7:5 Lit *in our members* [F]7:7 Ex 20:17

6:18–19 Slavery and redemption are common biblical metaphors for spiritual death and salvation.
6:20–23 As **slaves** of God, believers produce **fruit**. This is the work of **sanctification** or holiness in their lives, and the final product is eternal life. Lest the figure be misunderstood as a payment for merits earned, **eternal life** is a **gift of God** through Christ.
7:1 Roman Christians knew about Roman civil law, and many of them (especially those of a Jewish or proselyte background) knew the Mosaic law. Of course neither **law** could hold sway over a dead person.
7:2–3 A **married woman**, bound by law to her **husband** so long as he lived, was legally free to marry another man if her husband died.
7:4–5 Believers have died to the "old self" (6:2–6) and are free to marry another and **bear fruit for God**. The death of Messiah is the means by which we died to the Mosaic law (Gl 3:13–14; Col 2:14).
7:6 As new creations, believers serve in **newness** with a new power from the Spirit, not as old men (6:6) laboring vainly under the **letter of the law**.
7:7–8 The law itself is not evil or sinful, but one of its functions is to reveal **sin**. In fact Paul speaks as if sin is an unknown entity

apart from the law when he says, **I would not have known sin if it were not for the law.** Sin, **seizing an opportunity**, uses the law to motivate the flesh (fallen nature) to action. Once again Paul personified sin.
7:9–10 The phrase **once I was alive** has been variously interpreted as a reference to: (1) Paul before he came to know the law as a young Jewish boy, (2) Paul before his conversion and the conviction brought by the Holy Spirit, (3) Paul speaking as Adam in the garden of Eden before the command came, or (4) any Hebrew before the giving of the Mosaic law at Mount Sinai. The basic point is that God's intent in the law was **life**, but sin deceived man by the law and brought **death**.
7:11–12 Though **the law** makes sin known and is in fact used by sin to produce death, it is nevertheless **holy and just and good**, reflecting God's perfect and eternal holiness.
7:13 Did the **good** law cause **death**? The correct understanding is that sin used something good to bring human death. God used the law to accomplish his purpose to fully expose sin and point the sinner to God's only remedy for sin.
7:14–25 This section is probably the most difficult and controversial passage in the letter to the Romans. For the most part the

Eastern Church has interpreted it as referring to an unregenerate person (e.g., Paul before his conversion). The Western Church has followed Augustine, Martin Luther, and John Calvin in thinking it refers to a regenerate person (Paul after his conversion). Some suggest a mediating position. One such view interprets the subject as an OT believer who loves the law (Pss 1; 119) but struggles to perform it. Living before Christ and Pentecost, this person does not have the permanent and empowering gift of the Holy Spirit, as do new covenant believers. Another view holds that the subject is almost converted to Christ and is now under conviction of sin by the law.
The view that the subject of vv. 14–25 is a regenerate person is sometimes modified in the following ways. (1) The subject is saved but has not had "baptism" in the Pentecostal sense or a second work of grace (as held in some types of Wesleyan theology). (2) The subject is an immature believer, not yet equipped for warfare with his fleshly desires. (3) The subject is a believer trying to become sanctified by legalism.
The view outlined here takes the position that the subject is a regenerated believer, most obviously Paul himself but generically every believer. Paul describes the new self in relation to the law of God and is looking

The Problem of Sin in Us

14 For we know that the law is spiritual, but I am of the flesh,^A sold as a slave under sin. **15** For I do not understand what I am doing, because I do not practice what I want to do, but I do what I hate. **16** Now if I do what I do not want to do, I agree with the law that it is good. **17** So now I am no longer the one doing it, but it is sin living in me. **18** For I know that nothing good lives in me, that is, in my flesh. For the desire to do what is good is with me, but there is no ability to do it. **19** For I do not do the good that I want to do, but I practice the evil that I do not want to do. **20** Now if I do what I do not want, I am no longer the one that does it, but it is the sin that lives in me. **21** So I discover this law:^B When I want to do what is good,^C evil is present with me. **22** For in my inner self^D I delight in God's law, **23** but I see a different law in the parts of my body,^E waging war against the law of my mind and taking me prisoner to the law of sin in the parts of my body. **24** What a wretched man I am! Who will rescue me from this body of death? **25** Thanks be to God through Jesus Christ our Lord! So then, with my mind I myself am serving the law of God, but with my flesh, the law of sin.

The Life-Giving Spirit

8 Therefore, there is now no condemnation for those in Christ Jesus,^F **2** because the law^B of the Spirit of life in Christ Jesus has set you^G free from the law^B of sin and death. **3** For what the law could not do since it was weakened by the flesh, God did. He condemned sin in the flesh by sending his own Son in the likeness of sinful flesh as a sin offering,^H **4** in order that the law's requirement would be fulfilled in us who do not walk according to the flesh but according to the Spirit. **5** For those who live according to the flesh have their minds set on the things of the flesh, but those who live according to the Spirit have their minds set on the things of the Spirit. **6** Now the mindset of the flesh is death, but the mindset of the Spirit is life and peace. **7** The mindset of the flesh is hostile to God because it does not submit to God's law. Indeed, it is unable to do so. **8** Those who are in the flesh cannot please God. **9** You, however, are not in the flesh, but in the Spirit, if indeed the Spirit of God lives in you. If anyone does not have the Spirit of Christ, he does not belong to him. **10** Now if Christ is in you, the body is dead because of sin, but the Spirit^I gives life^J because of righteousness. **11** And if the Spirit of him who raised Jesus from the dead lives in you, then he who raised Christ from the dead will also bring your mortal bodies to life through^K his Spirit who lives in you.

The Holy Spirit's Ministries

12 So then, brothers and sisters, we are not obligated to the flesh to live according to the flesh, **13** because if you live according to the flesh, you are going to die. But if by the Spirit you put to death the deeds of the body, you will live. **14** For all those led by God's Spirit are God's sons. **15** For you did not receive a spirit of slavery to fall back into fear. Instead, you received the Spirit of adoption, by whom we cry out, "*Abba,*^L Father!" **16** The Spirit himself

---

^A**7:14** Or *unspiritual*   ^B**7:21; 8:2** Or *principle*   ^C**7:21** Or *I find with respect to the law that when I want to do good*   ^D**7:22** Lit *inner man*   ^E**7:23** Lit *my members*   ^F**8:1** Other mss add *who do not walk according to the flesh but according to the Spirit*   ^G**8:2** Other mss read *me*   ^H**8:3** Or *for sin*   ^I**8:10** Or *spirit*   ^J**8:10** Or *your spirit is alive*   ^K**8:11** Other mss read *because of*   ^L**8:15** Aramaic for *father*

---

at only one aspect of the person. The main reason for the position offered here is a consideration of what this person's problem really is. In v. 14 he is said to be **of the flesh** (Gk *sarkinos*, not *sarkikos*). Many translations confuse these two Greek words. The first word emphasizes composition while the second emphasizes tendency ("fleshy" vs. "fleshly"). In v. 18 **in my flesh** means the whole fallen nature that needs the resurrection body (Php 3:21). In v. 24 the **wretched man** cries out to be rescued ("out," Gk *ek*) **from this body of death**. As a believer in Christ, Paul longed to be delivered from the fallen human body which still has indwelling sin.

7:14–15 The law is from God and is therefore **spiritual**, but Paul is **of the flesh** (a metaphorical reference to spiritual fallenness) and thus finds himself conflicted with the heavenly law of God.

7:16–17 Paul agreed with the law and its goodness, but sin is an alien power that has residence within him and causes him to do things he hates.

7:18–19 Even after conversion, there is no part of a person that is sinless, no place without sin's presence, and the believer is unable to keep the whole law.

7:20–23 In the **inner self** (Gk *eso anthropos*), in one's deepest recesses, the believer delights in God's law, but he finds this alien power living within, waging war with him and taking him **prisoner to the law of sin**.

7:24–25 In v. 24 the subject cries out for deliverance from the fallen human condition. A cry of thanksgiving is then offered to God because the subject knows that Jesus will deliver him from his body. The believer recognizes that in his mind he wants to serve God's law since it is holy, just, good, and spiritual, but at the same time his fallen nature is in the service of this alien power—sin.

8:1–39 Romans 8 has been called the most wonderful chapter in the Bible. It begins with "no condemnation" (v. 1) and ends with no separation from God (v. 39). Whereas 7:14–25 describes the new self in relation to the law, chap. 8 describes the new self in relation to the Holy Spirit and his work in and through the new man.

8:1 There is **no condemnation** for believers because they are not under the law (6:14), and they have been released from the law (7:6).

8:2–4 The believer's freedom comes from Jesus's incarnation and his work as the **sin**

offering and by the Holy Spirit's operation in providing life.

8:5–11 Paul described the two kinds of people: two different kinds of existence or two "mindsets." The outcomes of the two ways of thinking are explained: **death** versus **life and peace**. Unregenerate people (Gk *en sarki*; lit "in the flesh") are **hostile to God** and **unable** to **submit to God's law** because they lack God's Spirit, which makes submission possible. Christians are in a new realm, for the **Spirit** indwells them. The Spirit's presence is the mark of Christ's ownership. The pledge and promise of the Spirit is that he will raise us as he did Jesus. Now the Spirit provides **life** and **righteousness**.

8:12–13 Freedom brings an obligation. If a person lives to the fallen nature, **death** is his destiny. The Christian is empowered by the Holy **Spirit** to stop doing the sinful deeds of the body. He can mortify the flesh and its activities, and he lives.

8:14 The leading of **God's Spirit** is his providential sanctification (Ps 23:3). It is common to all believers, it is constant, and it will bring the believer to glory (Rm 8:17). The leading of the Spirit is not mystical direction or ecstasy. It is the Spirit's empowerment for mortification of fleshly desires (v. 13).

▼ The Bible and Creation Care

by Glenn R. Kreider

The biblical story begins with God and his creative work. God spoke the universe into existence. He separated light from darkness, day from night, water under the expanse from water above it, and water from land. Then he caused vegetation to grow on the dry ground. He filled the waters with fish, the sky with flying creatures, and the earth with a variety of living things, each created according to its kind. He blessed the creatures he had made and commanded them to fill their domain (Gn 1:22). Then, as the pinnacle of his creative work, he made humanity (male and female) in his image and likeness and commanded them to fill the earth and rule over all the creatures he had made and blessed (Gn 1:26–28). Rather than caring for it himself, God entrusted the care of his creation to humans. He placed the man and woman "in the garden of Eden to work it and watch over it" (Gn 2:15). It was a world of order, harmony, and blessing for all created things.

But then order was turned to chaos, harmony to turmoil, blessing to curse, and life to death. Creation's caretakers chose to believe the serpent, a creature, rather than God (Gn 3:1–6). God cursed the ground as his judgment on these rebels. He removed them from the garden and promised them that death would be their end. Nevertheless, he did not rescind the command to rule over the earth and to care for the creation. Instead, he said that their creation care would be more difficult; their work would now be characterized as "painful labor" (Gn 3:17–19).

As humanity multiplied on the earth, they became more corrupt and filled with wickedness (Gn 3:1–5). God was "deeply grieved" (Gn 6:6). He sent judgment on the earth in the form of a flood in order to "wipe mankind, whom [he] created, off the face of the earth, together with the animals, creatures that crawl, and birds of the sky" (Gn 6:7). But God delivered Noah and his family and representatives of every kind of living creature. When the flood waters receded and the inhabitants of the ark returned to the dry ground, God reiterated his purpose for humanity when he said to Noah and his family, "Be fruitful and multiply and fill the earth" (Gn 9:1). God made a covenant with all living creatures and the earth itself, in which he promised never again to destroy all life on the planet (Gn 9:11). This covenant had a sign, a rainbow, which God established as a reminder of the everlasting covenant between him and "all the living creatures on earth" (Gn 9:16). The everlasting covenant presupposes an everlasting earth, cared for by those created in God's image and likeness.

In the incarnation, in Jesus of Nazareth, the eternal Son of God entered creation. The Creator took on flesh and resided in the world he had made (Jn 1:14). In so doing, he revealed God to the world and became its Savior (Jn 1:14–18,29). Christ's work of redemption is not merely good news for humans. The salvific plan of God is cosmic in scope.

The apostle Paul explains that creation has been longing for its redemption since the day it was cursed. Human creation care cannot remove the curse. That can only be done by the Creator, and he has promised to do so in the restoration of all things, in the redemption of all creation: "Creation eagerly waits with anticipation . . . in the hope that the creation itself will also be set free from the bondage to decay into the glorious freedom of God's children" (Rm 8:19–21). Creation's redemption is tied to humanity's redemption. Creation groans as it looks forward to its liberation. God's love for the world means that the world will be redeemed by the work of the Savior (Jn 3:16).

In his letter to the Colossians, Paul asserts that Jesus Christ is "the image of the invisible God" (Col 1:15), the one who created "everything" (Col 1:16), and the one who came "to have first place in everything" through his resurrection from the dead (Col 1:18). Paul concludes, "For God was pleased to have all his fullness dwell in him, and through him to reconcile everything to himself, whether things on earth or things in heaven, by making peace through his blood, shed on the cross" (Col 1:19–20). In the God-man, the Creator entered creation in order to redeem creation. As the head of his body, the church, Christ cares for his creation through his followers (Col 1:18).

The biblical story concludes with the promise of a new creation. In his vision of the completion of the work of redemption, John sees a new heaven and a new earth coming

testifies together with our spirit that we are God's children, ¹⁷ and if children, also heirs — heirs of God and coheirs with Christ — if indeed we suffer with him so that we may also be glorified with him.

From Groans to Glory

¹⁸ For I consider that the sufferings of this present time are not worth comparing with the glory that is going to be revealed to us. ¹⁹ For the creation eagerly waits with anticipation for God's sons to be revealed. ²⁰ For the creation was subjected to futility — not willingly, but because of him who subjected it — in the hope ²¹ that the creation itself will also be set free from the bondage to decay into the glorious freedom of God's children. ²² For we know that

the whole creation has been groaning together with labor pains until now. ²³ Not only that, but we ourselves who have the Spirit as the firstfruits — we also groan within ourselves, eagerly waiting for adoption, the redemption of our bodies. ²⁴ Now in this hope we were saved, but hope that is seen is not hope, because who hopes for what he sees? ²⁵ Now if we hope for what we do not see, we eagerly wait for it with patience.

²⁶ In the same way the Spirit also helps us in our weakness, because we do not know what to pray for as we should, but the Spirit himself intercedes for us^A with inexpressible groanings. ²⁷ And he who searches our hearts knows the mind of the Spirit, because he intercedes for the saints according to the will of God.

^A 8:26 Some mss omit *for us*

8:15–16 The Holy **Spirit** is the means of our **adoption** into God's family. By the Spirit we have a consciousness that God is our **Father**. The Spirit also gives us assurance of our status and therefore of our salvation. **Abba** is an Aramaic word meaning "father." Jesus used it in prayer to God the Father (Mk 14:36).
8:17 All God's **children** are his **heirs** and coheirs with Christ. We are joined to him in suffering but also in our future destiny.

8:19–21 The created order of this earth was cursed at the fall (Gn 3:17–19), and it will be restored in the regeneration. **8:22–23** Paul describes the **groaning** of cre-**ation**, the groaning of believers, and the groaning of the Holy Spirit (v. 26). **8:24–25** Our salvation is secure, but it is as yet unseen and thus a matter of **hope**. We wait in faith and patience. **8:26–27** In our **weakness** we have the help of the **Spirit**. Jesus is our intercessor

in heaven (Heb 7:25), and the Spirit is our intercessor on earth within our hearts. We are limited and ignorant, but the Spirit uses **inexpressible groanings** to communicate our needs. This is not "speaking in tongues or languages" (Gk *glossolalia*). It is instead wordless. The Spirit's requests are always **according to the will of God** and are always answered.

down to the earth from heaven. He also hears a voice from the throne of God:

Look, God's dwelling is with humanity, and he will live with them. They will be his peoples, and God himself will be with them and will be their God. He will wipe away every tear from their eyes. Death will be no more; grief, crying, and pain will be no more, because the previous things have passed away (Rv 21:3–4).

When redemption is completed, the curse and all its effects will be removed, the earth will be made new, and the Creator will make the creation his home forever (cp. Is 65:17–25). Then, forever, humans will serve God by caring for the world he made.

Humanity has been given the responsibility to serve God by caring for his creation, the place in which God will make his home eternally. Creation care is a stewardship given to us. It is a biblical mandate that predates the fall and has never been repealed. The fall makes our care more difficult, but it does not remove our responsibility.

One indication of the seriousness of this responsibility is seen in the declaration of the Judge that those who destroy the earth will

be judged. In Revelation 11:18, according to the song of the twenty-four elders, in the day of God's wrath, "the time has come for the dead to be judged and to give the reward to your servants the prophets, to the saints, and to those who fear your name, both small and great, and the time has come to destroy those who destroy the earth." Destruction of the planet is not merely accomplished by active and willful rebellion. Passivity, too, is failure to care for the earth and is tantamount to destroying it.

Several practical implications follow. (1) Creation care is a gospel concern, for it is a life issue. Healthy human and animal life depends on a good environment that includes clean air and water and one in which disease and decay are controlled. (2) In James 1:27 the apostle describes "pure and undefiled religion" as looking "after orphans and widows in their distress" and keeping "oneself unstained from the world." Later, he characterizes a faith that does not provide clothes and daily food for the needy as "dead" faith (Jms 2:15–17). Surely, providing clean air and water is as important as providing food and clothes. (3) Since no one knows when the end will come (Mt 24:36–44), caring for the creation benefits all inhabitants of the planet. Extending lifetimes and improving life's quality is good stewardship.

²⁸ We know that all things work together^A for the good^B of those who love God, who are called according to his purpose. ²⁹ For those he foreknew he also predestined to be conformed to the image of his Son, so that he would be the firstborn among many brothers and sisters. ³⁰ And those he predestined, he also called; and those he called, he also justified; and those he justified, he also glorified.

The Believer's Triumph

³¹ What, then, are we to say about these things? If God is for us, who is against us? ³² He did not even spare his own Son but gave him up for us all. How will he not also with him grant us everything? ³³ Who can bring an accusation against God's elect? God is the one who justifies. ³⁴ Who is the one who condemns? Christ Jesus is the one who died, but even more, has been raised; he also is at the right hand of God and intercedes for us. ³⁵ Who can separate us from the love of Christ? Can affliction or distress or persecution or famine or nakedness or danger or sword? ³⁶ As it is written:

> Because of you
> we are being put to death
> all day long;
> we are counted as sheep
> to be slaughtered.^C

³⁷ No, in all these things we are more than conquerors through him who loved us. ³⁸ For I am persuaded that neither death nor life, nor angels nor rulers, nor things present nor things to come, nor powers, ³⁹ nor height nor depth, nor any other created thing will be able to separate us from the love of God that is in Christ Jesus our Lord.

Israel's Rejection of Christ

9 I speak the truth in Christ — I am not lying; my conscience testifies to me through the Holy Spirit^D — ² that I have great sorrow and unceasing anguish in my heart. ³ For I could wish that I myself were cursed and cut off^E from Christ for the benefit of my brothers and sisters, my own flesh and blood. ⁴ They are Israelites, and to them belong the adoption, the glory, the covenants, the giving of the law, the temple service, and the promises. ⁵ The ancestors are theirs, and from them, by physical descent,^F came the Christ, who is God over all, praised forever.^G Amen.

God's Gracious Election of Israel

⁶ Now it is not as though the word of God has failed, because not all who are descended from Israel are Israel. ⁷ Neither is it the case that all of Abraham's children are his descendants.^H On the contrary, **your offspring will be traced**^I **through Isaac.**^J ⁸ That is, it is not the children by physical descent^K who are God's children, but the children of the promise are considered to be the offspring. ⁹ For this is the statement of the promise: **At this time I will come, and Sarah will have a son.**^L ¹⁰ And not only that, but Rebekah conceived children through one man, our father Isaac. ¹¹ For though her sons had not been born yet or done anything good or bad, so that God's purpose according to election

---

^8:28 Other mss read *that God works together in all things*   ^B8:28 The ultimate good   ^C8:36 Ps 44:22   ^D9:1 Or *testifying with me by the Holy Spirit*   ^E9:3 Lit *to be anathema*   ^F9:5 Lit *them, according to the flesh*   ^G9:5 Or *the Messiah, the one who is over all, the God who is blessed forever*, or *Messiah. God, who is over all, be blessed forever*   ^H9:7 Lit *seed*   ^I9:7 Lit *called*   ^J9:7 Gn 21:12   ^K9:8 Lit *children of the flesh*   ^L9:9 Gn 18:10,14

8:28 The **called** are all Christians (vv. 29–30). The promise of this verse is that God orders everything for believers so that all of life's experiences **work together** for our ultimate **good**. Not everything is good in and of itself, but God uses everything for our good (vv. 35–37).

8:29–30 God has a plan that spans from eternity past to eternity future. **Those he foreknew** refers to those whom God set his electing love upon in eternity past. **Predestined** means that God planned from eternity that "those [whom] he foreknew" would become like Christ through spiritual rebirth. **Called** is the "effectual" call in which God opens our heart so we can hear his voice (cp. Ac 16:14). **Justified** is God's act of declaration that we are "right" in his sight because Jesus paid our penalty and we received his righteousness (2Co 5:21). **Glorified** is the final stage of our salvation. Our future glorification is so certain that it is spoken of in the past tense.

8:31 If **God is for us** expresses not a hypothetical scenario, but a sure reality.

8:32 In contrast to Abraham who was permitted to spare Isaac (Gn 22:11–18), God did not **spare** his Son. If God did the greater (gave his Son), will he not do the lesser

and give us all that is necessary for life and godliness?

8:33 Our accusers are numerous, but God the Judge has already pronounced the final verdict.

8:34 The understood answer to the opening question of this verse is "no one." We can be sure that no one will be able to condemn us on the last day because of three facts listed here in increasing significance. First, Christ **died** for us. Second, and **even more** important, he was **raised**. And finally, he now **intercedes** for us.

8:37 We are **more than conquerors** not by our ability but because God **loved us**.

8:38–39 Paul's "grand persuasion" (Gk *pepeismai*) is in the perfect tense, which indicates a past action that has ongoing impact. Having been **persuaded** (by God), he stood firm in the belief that nothing could separate him from the **love of God**.

9:1–11:36 If Jesus really was the Messiah and yet God had not delivered Israel, how could anyone trust him to keep his gospel promises? And so the trustworthiness of God seemed to be on the line. Paul overturned these doubts by answering from three perspectives: (1) from the viewpoint of divine sovereignty (chap. 9), (2) from human

responsibility (chap. 10), and (3) from God's final purpose (chap. 11).

9:1–3 Paul insisted that he felt **great sorrow and unceasing anguish** over Jewish national unbelief and would willingly forsake his own salvation if it could save his **brothers and sisters**, his **own flesh and blood**.

9:4–5 Paul began in 3:1–2 to list Jewish national benefits. Now he returns to list their privileges, the greatest of which is the incarnation of God in Jewish flesh.

9:6 It is a basic misunderstanding of the OT promises to think that all who were in the nation of Israel were guaranteed to receive God's spiritual blessings. Paul provides examples in the following verses.

9:7 Abraham had children by Hagar and Keturah, but the promised line was through Sarah's son **Isaac**.

9:8–9 Ishmael was a physical son of Abraham, but Isaac was the **physical** son with the spiritual promises.

9:10–11 The case is clearer with **Rebekah** because she had twins. God's choice of the younger twin before their birth showed his gracious **election** and indicated again that God's blessings are his to hand out and that they were not an automatic birthright of all ethnic Jews; see note at v. 6.

might stand — [12] not from works but from the one who calls — she was told, **The older will serve the younger.**[A] [13] As it is written: **I have loved Jacob, but I have hated Esau.**[B]

God's Selection Is Just

[14] What should we say then? Is there injustice with God? Absolutely not! [15] For he tells Moses, **I will show mercy to whom I will show mercy, and I will have compassion on whom I will have compassion.**[C] [16] So then, it does not depend on human will or effort but on God who shows mercy. [17] For the Scripture tells Pharaoh, **I raised you up for this reason so that I may display my power in you and that my name may be proclaimed in the whole earth.**[D] [18] So then, he has mercy on whom he wants to have mercy and he hardens whom he wants to harden.

[19] You will say to me, therefore, "Why then does he still find fault? For who resists his will?" [20] On the contrary, who are you, a human being, to talk back to God? Will what is formed say to the one who formed it, "Why did you make me like this?" [21] Or has the potter no right over the clay, to make from the same lump one piece of pottery for honor and another for dishonor? [22] And what if God, wanting to display his wrath and to make his power known, endured with much patience objects of wrath prepared for destruction? [23] And what if he did this to make known the riches of his glory on objects of mercy that he prepared beforehand for glory — [24] on us, the ones he also called, not only from the Jews but also from the Gentiles? [25] As it[E] also says in Hosea,

**I will call Not My People, My People,
and she who is Unloved, Beloved.**[F]
[26] **And it will be in the place where
they were told,
you are not my people,**

**there they will be called sons
of the living God.**[G]
[27] But Isaiah cries out concerning Israel,

**Though the number of Israelites
is like the sand of the sea,
only the remnant will be saved;**
[28] **since the Lord will execute
his sentence
completely and decisively
on the earth.**[H,I]
[29] And just as Isaiah predicted:

**If the Lord of Armies had not left
us offspring,
we would have become like Sodom,
and we would have been made
like Gomorrah.**[J]

Israel's Present State

[30] What should we say then? Gentiles, who did not pursue righteousness, have obtained righteousness — namely the righteousness that comes from faith. [31] But Israel, pursuing the law of righteousness, has not achieved the righteousness of the law.[K] [32] Why is that? Because they did not pursue it by faith, but as if it were by works.[L] They stumbled over the stumbling stone. [33] As it is written,

**Look, I am putting a stone in Zion
to stumble over
and a rock to trip over,
and the one who believes on him
will not be put to shame.**[M]

Righteousness by Faith Alone

10 Brothers and sisters, my heart's desire and prayer to God concerning them[N] is for their salvation. [2] I can testify about them that they have zeal for God, but not according to knowledge. [3] Since they are ignorant of the righteousness of God and attempted to establish their own righteousness, they have not submitted to God's righteousness. [4] For

---

[A]9:12 Gn 25:23 [B]9:13 Mal 1:2–3 [C]9:15 Ex 33:19 [D]9:17 Ex 9:16 [E]9:25 Or *he* [F]9:25 Hs 2:23 [G]9:26 Hs 1:10 [H]9:28 Or *land* [I]9:27–28 Is 10:22–23; 28:22; Hs 1:10 [J]9:29 Is 1:9 [K]9:31 Other mss read *the law for righteousness* [L]9:32 Other mss add *of the law* [M]9:33 Is 8:14; 28:16 [N]10:1 Other mss read *God for Israel*

9:12–13 The divine purpose was revealed from the beginning of the Hebrew nation when God chose one twin over the other. **I have loved Jacob** means God chose or elected his descendants (the nation of Israel), whereas **I have hated Esau** means that God rejected the nation that stemmed from him (Edom). **9:14–15 Is there injustice with God?** is a rhetorical question. God does not need to treat all sinners the same in order to be just. A just God is perfectly free to make such choices. God does not owe **mercy** to anyone. Paul quoted Ex 33:19 to this effect. **9:16** Salvation does not depend on **human will or effort**. Salvation is based on God's **mercy**. The situation is not that people want to be saved but cannot be (2Tm 2:25–26), or that they are running after God but cannot find him. Apart from God's drawing them, none is seeking the one true God—not a single one (Rm 3:11–12).

9:19–22 Paul declared that the Judge of the earth is always just. Humans cannot judge God. The image of the village **potter** is common in the OT (Is 41:25; 45:9; Jr 18:1–12). Here the clay represents fallen humanity. Much as a potter, God works this material into shapes that fulfill his desires (Is 64:6–9). Some pots the Messiah and did not believe in him he chooses to be for **honor**; others he patiently endures until he displays his justified **wrath** against sin. **9:23–24** God desires to display his grace on **objects of mercy**, the ones on whom he has set his redeeming love. These come from both Jewish and Gentile backgrounds. **9:25–26** Drawing from Hosea's marriage, Paul compares Gentile salvation to mercy bestowed on an undeserving adulterous wife. **9:27–29** Paul also cited the words of **Isaiah** to show that God will save a remnant of Israel that he "calls."

9:30–33 Gentiles, who were not seeking **righteousness**, were granted it by grace through **faith**. They did not work for it or earn it. But **Israel** missed it by seeking righteousness through the **law** and by their **works**. They stumbled over the Messiah and did not believe in him (Is 8:14; 28:16). **10:1** Paul saw no contradiction between election and prayer. Only a sovereign God, who has rights to move unilaterally in the affairs of humanity, can answer **prayer**. Paul therefore prayed for Jewish **salvation**. **10:2–3** Both **zeal** and true **knowledge** are necessary if one is truly to know God and serve him. Unbelieving Jews, in spiritual blindness, not only missed God's way of **righteousness**, but they opposed it. **10:4** Christ is the **end of the law** in being both its fulfillment and its termination.

Christ is the end[A] of the law for righteousness to everyone who believes, [5] since Moses writes about the righteousness that is from the law: **The one who does these things will live by them.**[B] [6] But the righteousness that comes from faith speaks like this: **Do not say in your heart, "Who will go up to heaven?"**[C] that is, to bring Christ down [7] or, **"Who will go down into the abyss?"**[D] that is, to bring Christ up from the dead. [8] On the contrary, what does it say? **The message is near you, in your mouth and in your heart.**[E] This is the message of faith that we proclaim: [9] If you confess with your mouth, "Jesus is Lord," and believe in your heart that God raised him from the dead, you will be saved. [10] One believes with the heart, resulting in righteousness, and one confesses with the mouth, resulting in salvation. [11] For the Scripture says, **Everyone who believes on him will not be put to shame,**[F] [12] since there is no distinction between Jew and Greek, because the same Lord of all richly blesses all who call on him. [13] For **everyone who calls on the name of the Lord will be saved.**[G]

Israel's Rejection of the Message

[14] How, then, can they call on him they have not believed in? And how can they believe without hearing about him? And how can they hear without a preacher? [15] And how can they preach unless they are sent? As it is written: **How beautiful**[H] **are the feet of those who bring good news.**[I] [16] But not all obeyed the gospel. For Isaiah says, **Lord, who has believed our message?**[J] [17] So faith comes from what is heard, and what is heard comes through the message about Christ.[K] [18] But I ask, "Did they not hear?" Yes, they did:

Their voice has gone out to
 the whole earth,
and their words to the ends
 of the world.[L]

[19] But I ask, "Did Israel not understand?" First, Moses said,

I will make you jealous
 of those who are not a nation;
I will make you angry by a nation
 that lacks understanding.[M]

[20] And Isaiah says boldly,

I was found
 by those who were not looking
 for me;
I revealed myself
 to those who were not asking
 for me.[N]

[21] But to Israel he says, **All day long I have held out my hands to a disobedient and defiant people.**[O]

Israel's Rejection Not Total

11 I ask, then, has God rejected his people? Absolutely not! For I too am an Israelite, a descendant of Abraham, from the tribe of Benjamin. [2] God has not rejected his people whom he foreknew. Or don't you know what the Scripture says in the passage about Elijah — how he pleads with God against Israel? [3] **Lord, they have killed your prophets and torn down your altars. I am the only one left, and they are trying to take my life!**[P] [4] But what was God's answer to him? **I have left seven thousand for myself who have not bowed down to Baal.**[Q] [5] In the same way, then, there is also at the present time a remnant chosen by grace. [6] Now if by grace, then it is not by works; otherwise grace ceases to be grace.[R]

[7] What then? Israel did not find what it was looking for, but the elect did find it. The rest were hardened, [8] as it is written,

God gave them a spirit of stupor,
 eyes that cannot see
and ears that cannot hear,
 to this day.[S]

[A]10:4 Or *goal* [B]10:5 Lv 18:5 [C]10:6 Dt 9:4; 30:12 [D]10:7 Dt 30:13 [E]10:8 Dt 30:14 [F]10:11 Is 28:16 [G]10:13 Jl 2:32
[H]10:15 Or *welcome*, or *timely* [I]10:15 Is 52:7; Nah 1:15 [J]10:16 Is 53:1 [K]10:17 Other mss read *God* [L]10:18 Ps 19:4
[M]10:19 Dt 32:21 [N]10:20 Is 65:1 [O]10:21 Is 65:2 [P]11:3 1Kg 19:10,14 [Q]11:4 1Kg 19:18 [R]11:6 Other mss add *But if of works*
it is no longer grace; otherwise work is no longer work. [S]11:8 Dt 29:4; Is 29:10

10:5–7 Paul quoted **Moses** on both sides of the issue. In Lv 18:5 (cp. Gl 3:12) obedience to the law brings life, but no one can keep the law and gain righteousness (as implied by Paul's citation of Moses in v. 6). Faith-based righteousness is from **Christ**. Moses pointed out that God's revelation was accessible, and Paul quoted his words to show that Christ is accessible.

10:9–10 Jesus is Lord is a confession of faith. "Lord" is the translation of the Greek word *kurios*. This is the regular way of translating the Hebrew name for God (Yahweh) in the Greek OT (the LXX). Not only do we believe that the man Jesus was **raised** . . . **from the dead**, but we also believe that he shares the same nature with God.

10:11–13 Paul cited biblical support for the universal offer of salvation. Salvation is for both **Jew** and **Greek** (i.e., Gentiles) since the

same **Lord** (Gk *kurios*, v. 12) **richly blesses all who call on him.** The promise is for all who call on **the name of the Lord** (*kurios*, v. 13). As the prophet Joel said (Jl 2:32).

10:14–15 What must occur for someone to call on the name of the Lord? Someone must first be sent to proclaim the gospel message, and then listeners must pay attention and believe. In the absence of any one of these factors, no one can call on the name of the Lord.

10:16–21 Paul quoted several OT passages to show that the conditions described in vv. 14–15 had been met for Israel. The gospel message was proclaimed throughout the Roman Empire. The Jews listened and simply did not believe. The Gentiles heard too, and many embraced it. Paul's citations show that Gentile conversion was predicted in the OT. Ultimately, all peoples are **a disobedient and**

defiant people. Israel was singled out in this way due to their consistent rejection of God's message and messengers (see Ac 7:51–60).

11:1–4 Paul continued explaining that the unbelief of Israel is no argument against the gospel. Israel's blindness is not total, and God is still working with the nation. Paul himself was evidence that God was saving some Jews. God's election of the nation (**whom he foreknew**, v. 2; cp. 8:29) is immutable. Even in times of national apostasy, God saves a remnant.

11:5–6 Grace is by definition unmerited favor. Grace would cease **to be grace** if works played a role in election.

11:7–10 The Jewish nation missed salvation because they sought for it by works. Paul's portion was given mercy, but the majority was hardened in unbelief; OT citations are given to show that God has judged his people.

⁹ And David says,

> Let their table become a snare
>   and a trap,
>   a pitfall and a retribution to them.
> ¹⁰ Let their eyes be darkened
>   so that they cannot see,
>   and their backs be bent continually.ᴬ

Israel's Rejection Not Final

¹¹ I ask, then, have they stumbled so as to fall? Absolutely not! On the contrary, by their transgression, salvation has come to the Gentiles to make Israel jealous. ¹² Now if their transgression brings riches for the world, and their failure riches for the Gentiles, how much more will their fullness bring!

¹³ Now I am speaking to you Gentiles. Insofar as I am an apostle to the Gentiles, I magnify my ministry, ¹⁴ if I might somehow make my own peopleᴮ jealous and save some of them. ¹⁵ For if their rejection brings reconciliation to the world, what will their acceptance mean but life from the dead? ¹⁶ Now if the firstfruits are holy, so is the whole batch. And if the root is holy, so are the branches.

¹⁷ Now if some of the branches were broken off, and you, though a wild olive branch, were grafted in among them and have come to share in the rich rootᶜ of the cultivated olive tree, ¹⁸ do not boast that you are better than those branches. But if you do boast — you do not sustain the root, but the root sustains you. ¹⁹ Then you will say, "Branches were broken off so that I might be grafted in." ²⁰ True enough; they were broken off because of unbelief, but you stand by faith. Do not be arrogant, but beware,ᴰ ²¹ because if God did not spare the natural branches, he will not spare you either. ²² Therefore, consider God's kindness and severity: severity toward those who have fallen but God's kindness toward you — if you remain in his kindness. Otherwise you too will be cut off. ²³ And even they, if they do not remain in unbelief, will be grafted in, because God has the power to graft them in again. ²⁴ For if you were cut off from your native wild olive tree and against nature were grafted into a cultivated olive tree, how much more will these — the natural branches — be grafted into their own olive tree?

²⁵ I don't want you to be ignorant of this mystery, brothers and sisters, so that you will not be conceited: A partial hardening has come upon Israel until the fullness of the Gentiles has come in. ²⁶ And in this way allᴱ Israel will be saved, as it is written,

> The Deliverer will come from Zion;
>   he will turn godlessness away
>   from Jacob.
> ²⁷ And this will be my covenant
>   with themᶠ
>   when I take away their sins.ᴳ

²⁸ Regarding the gospel, they are enemies for your advantage, but regarding election, they are loved because of the patriarchs, ²⁹ since God's gracious gifts and calling are irrevocable.ᴴ ³⁰ As you once disobeyed God but now have received mercy through their disobedience, ³¹ so they too have now disobeyed, resulting in mercy to you, so that they also may nowᴵ receive mercy. ³² For God has imprisoned all in disobedience so that he may have mercy on all.

A Hymn of Praise

> ³³ Oh, the depth of the riches
>   and the wisdom and the knowledge
>   of God!
> How unsearchable his judgments
>   and untraceable his ways!
> ³⁴ For who has known the mind
>   of the Lord?
> Or who has been his counselor?
> ³⁵ And who has ever given to God,
>   that he should be repaid?ᴶ
> ³⁶ For from him and through him
>   and to him are all things.
> To him be the glory forever. Amen.

ᴬ11:9–10 Ps 69:22–23   ᴮ11:14 Lit flesh   ᶜ11:17 Other mss read the root and the richness   ᴰ11:20 Lit fear   ᴱ11:26 Or And then all   ᶠ11:26–27 Is 59:20–21   ᴳ11:27 Jr 31:31–34   ᴴ11:29 Or are not taken back   ᴵ11:31 Other mss omit now   ᴶ11:34–35 Jb 41:11; Is 40:13; Jr 23:18

11:11 Like a runner in a race, the Jewish nation had **stumbled**, but they had not totally fallen. Their stumbling had a purpose—to bring **salvation** to the **Gentiles**. Salvation for the Gentiles will eventually provoke the Jews to envy (Ac 13:45–51).

11:12,15–16 The future reception of Jews by God will result in **world** blessing. If their unbelief brought riches to the Gentiles, their future faith in Jesus as Messiah will enrich the world (cp. Is 2:2–4).

11:13–14 Paul magnified his **ministry** by working with all his strength to accomplish it. His purpose was to save as many Jews as possible, who would become **jealous**.

11:16–24 The **olive tree** was a symbol of the nation of Israel. It was used in this section by Paul as an illustration or allegory of God's dealings with Jews and Gentiles. The patriarchs are represented by the **root** of the tree. The Gentiles are a **wild** graft. Pruned off **branches** are the unbelieving Jews. Salvation is by faith, and the Gentiles need to be humble about their position. God is able to restore the Jewish people to the place of faith.

11:25–27 A **mystery** has been revealed by God: (1) A **partial hardening** has come to Israel; (2) this will continue **until the fullness of the Gentiles has come in;** and (3) then **all Israel will be saved.** "Israel" is the name for the Jewish people. Here in v. 26, "all Israel" means there will be a conversion of the Hebrew nation. It does not mean that every single Jew living will be saved. Salvation is defined in vv. 26–27 as the new **covenant** that the Messiah will inaugurate.

11:28–32 Israel's vocation and gifts are **irrevocable**, so their future salvation is certain. God in his mercy gives grace to the disobedient: both to Gentiles and Jews. Both were so **imprisoned** in their **disobedience** that there was no way to escape except by God's **mercy**.

11:33–36 In these verses Paul concludes his line of reasoning about Israel's current unbelief is no argument against the truth of the gospel. He is moved to exclamations of wonder at God's wisdom, power, and plan. Who could have foreseen what God was working out? Paul cites various OT texts to express God's incomprehensible purposes.

A Living Sacrifice

12 Therefore, brothers and sisters, in view of the mercies of God, I urge you to present your bodies as a living sacrifice, holy and pleasing to God; this is your true worship.[A] [2] Do not be conformed to this age, but be transformed by the renewing of your mind, so that you may discern what is the good, pleasing, and perfect will of God.

Many Gifts but One Body

[3] For by the grace given to me, I tell everyone among you not to think of himself more highly than he should think. Instead, think sensibly, as God has distributed a measure of faith to each one. [4] Now as we have many parts in one body, and all the parts do not have the same function, [5] in the same way we who are many are one body in Christ and individually members of one another. [6] According to the grace given to us, we have different gifts: If prophecy, use it according to the proportion of one's[B] faith; [7] if service, use it in service; if teaching, in teaching; [8] if exhorting, in exhortation; giving, with generosity; leading, with diligence; showing mercy, with cheerfulness.

Christian Ethics

[9] Let love be without hypocrisy. Detest evil; cling to what is good. [10] Love one another deeply as brothers and sisters. Take the lead in honoring one another. [11] Do not lack diligence in zeal; be fervent in the Spirit;[C] serve the Lord. [12] Rejoice in hope; be patient in affliction; be persistent in prayer. [13] Share with the saints in their needs; pursue hospitality. [14] Bless those who persecute you; bless and do not curse. [15] Rejoice with those who rejoice; weep with those who weep. [16] Live in harmony with one another. Do not be proud; instead, associate with the humble. Do not be wise in your own estimation. [17] Do not repay anyone evil for evil. Give careful thought to do what is honorable in everyone's eyes. [18] If possible, as far as it depends on you, live at peace with everyone. [19] Friends, do not avenge yourselves; instead, leave room for God's wrath, because it is written, **Vengeance belongs to me; I will repay,**[D] says the Lord. [20] But

If your enemy is hungry, feed him.
If he is thirsty, give him something
to drink.
For in so doing
you will be heaping fiery coals
on his head.[E]

[21] Do not be conquered by evil, but conquer evil with good.

A Christian's Duties to the State

13 Let everyone submit to the governing authorities, since there is no authority except from God, and the authorities that exist are instituted by God. [2] So then, the one who resists the authority is opposing God's command, and those who oppose it will bring judgment on themselves. [3] For rulers are not a terror to good conduct, but to bad. Do you want to be unafraid of the one in authority? Do what

^12:1 Or *your reasonable service*   ^12:6 Or *the*, also in v. 19   ^12:11 Or *in spirit*   ^12:19 Dt 32:35   ^12:20 Pr 25:21–22

12:1–2 Therefore … I urge you shows that the order of presentation is doctrine first and then duty. Our **true worship** entails offering our **bodies as a living sacrifice**, which means dedication of the total person to living for God's honor. We should experience a progressive transformation of life by **the renewing of** our **mind**. The mind is changed by prayer, by reading and reflection on God's Word, by worship, and by meditation on God's acts as the Holy Spirit works in us.

12:3–8 As part of a renewed mind, the Christian is to **think** wisely about himself and what his function is to be in the body of Christ (the church; see 1Co 12:12–28). **Measure of faith** may mean a person should measure himself by the gospel. Others see it as different apportionments of faith. Either way, Paul exhorts Christians to use what

 # 71 99 Essential Christian Truths

LORD'S SUPPER

The Lord's Supper is a symbolic act of obedience whereby members of the church, through partaking of the bread and the fruit of the vine, memorialize the death of Jesus Christ and anticipate his second coming (1Co 11:26).

God has given for the good of the body. Based on Rm 12:3; 1Co 12:8–10; Eph 4:11; 1Pt 4:10, Christians are given **gifts** to use for the good of others.

Only some of the gifts are explained in this present passage. **Prophecy** in the NT churches was direct revelation from God before the canon was completed. This gift was to be used and measured in concert with the objective body of Christian truths. **Service** (Gk *diakonia*) describes a gift of ministry. **Teaching** is an essential gift. Parents teach children, older believers teach younger believers, vocational pastor-teachers are the primary instructors in a church, and elders should be able to teach also. All believers can teach to some level, but those who have a special facility for teaching are responsible to develop and use it. **Exhortation** is the gift of motivating and encouraging. This gift is similar to the Holy Spirit's function. **Giving** is to be done with generosity. All can give, but capacities differ. **Leading** is a gift of vision and direction that is effective but should not be overbearing. **Mercy** is helping the sick, the poor, and the sorrowful. This gift is to be exercised with cheerfulness.

12:9–16 Transformed thinking is explained in a series of short exhortations. Christians are one family, and they should honor one another and **love one another deeply as brothers and sisters**. They should be **fervent in the Spirit** or let the Spirit kindle

and motivate their service. They should also **rejoice** in the hope of Jesus's return, **share** what they have, and share the joys and sorrows of the church family. Keep praying—in the afflictions and persecutions of life, members of the body are to support one another. Pride is a great sin and humility is a great virtue.

12:17–21 Christians often suffer hatred and persecution from society (1Pt 1:6; 2:11–12; 3:14–17; 4:12–16; 5:9). The normal response is to retaliate, but Christians are called to serve and minister God's grace to a lost and hostile world. As much as possible, we are to **live at peace with everyone**. God is the judge and the administrator of wrath. Our role is to display God's grace and love in our lives. God in Jesus conquered evil on the cross. We are not to let **evil** conquer us but to **conquer evil with good**.

13:1–7 Paul in these few short verses does not address some of the questions that we might ask him, but clearly he wanted Roman Christians to be good citizens. However, the same government put our Lord to death (Jn 19:10–11) and killed both Peter and Paul.

13:1 That **no authority** exists **except from God** indicates God's sovereignty over human affairs. It also shows why unwarranted rebellion against government is de facto rebellion against God (v. 2).

13:2–4 The Jewish nation rebelled against Rome in two costly wars, bringing **judgment**

is good, and you will have its approval. [4] For it is God's servant for your good. But if you do wrong, be afraid, because it does not carry the sword for no reason. For it is God's servant, an avenger that brings wrath on the one who does wrong. [5] Therefore, you must submit, not only because of wrath but also because of your conscience. [6] And for this reason you pay taxes, since the authorities are God's servants, continually attending to these tasks.^A [7] Pay your obligations to everyone: taxes to those you owe taxes, tolls to those you owe tolls, respect to those you owe respect, and honor to those you owe honor.

Love, Our Primary Duty

[8] Do not owe anyone anything, except to love one another, for the one who loves another has fulfilled the law. [9] The commandments, **Do not commit adultery; do not murder; do not steal;**^B **do not covet;**^C and any other commandment, are summed up by this commandment: **Love your neighbor as yourself.**^D [10] Love does no wrong to a neighbor. Love, therefore, is the fulfillment of the law.

Put On Christ

[11] Besides this, since you know the time, it is already the hour for you^E to wake up from sleep, because now our salvation is nearer than when we first believed. [12] The night is nearly over, and the day is near; so let us discard the deeds of darkness and put on the armor of light. [13] Let us walk with decency, as in the daytime: not in carousing and drunkenness; not in sexual impurity and promiscuity; not in quarreling and jealousy. [14] But put on the Lord Jesus Christ, and make no provision for the flesh to gratify its desires.

The Law of Liberty

14 Welcome anyone who is weak in faith, but don't argue about disputed matters. [2] One person believes he may eat anything, while one who is weak eats only vegetables. [3] One who eats must not look down on one who does not eat, and one who does not eat must not judge one who does, because God has accepted him. [4] Who are you to judge another's household servant? Before his own Lord he stands or falls. And he will stand, because the Lord is able^F to make him stand.

[5] One person judges one day to be more important than another day. Someone else judges every day to be the same. Let each one be fully convinced in his own mind. [6] Whoever observes the day, observes it for the honor of the Lord.^G Whoever eats, eats for the Lord, since he gives thanks to God; and whoever does not eat, it is for the Lord that he does not eat it, and he gives thanks to God. [7] For none of us lives for himself, and no one dies for himself. [8] If we live, we live for the Lord; and if we die, we die for the Lord. Therefore, whether we live or die, we belong to the Lord. [9] Christ died and returned to life for this: that he might be Lord over both the dead and the living. [10] But you, why do you judge your brother or sister? Or you, why do you despise your brother or sister? For we will all stand before the judgment seat of God.^H [11] For it is written,

As I live, says the Lord,
every knee will bow to me,
and every tongue will give praise
to God.^I

[12] So then, each of us will give an account of himself to God.

^A14:6 Lit *to this very thing*   ^B13:9 Other mss add *do not bear false witness*   ^C13:9 Ex 20:13–17; Dt 5:17–21   ^D13:9 Lv 19:18   ^E13:11 Other mss read *for us*   ^F14:4 Other mss read *For God has the power*   ^G14:6 Other mss add *but whoever does not observe the day, it is to the Lord that he does not observe it*   ^H14:10 Other mss read *of Christ*   ^I14:11 Is 45:23; 49:18

---

upon themselves at a cost of more than one million lives. Government is ordained by God to reward **good** and punish evil, providing peace and order for those whom it serves. **The sword** alludes to capital punishment. A government that rewards evil and punishes good will not long survive, for evil is innately destructive.
13:5–7 Since the civil government is ordained by God and gives us certain benefits, we are to **submit** to it. We are to **pay taxes** to support it, **honor** and **respect** it (see 1Tm 2:1–2).
13:8–10 The Christian is to pay all his obligations, but there is one debt we can never repay. This is the debt of **love**. Some have misinterpreted this verse as prohibiting all monetary debt, including having a mortgage on a house or buying a car on an installment plan. This verse has little to do with modern methods of finance. It is about fulfilling obligations of all kinds. We can never stop loving as long as we live.
13:11–14 Christians live between the ages. The old age is passing, and the new is dawning. We long for the new age to fully come,

and we recognize that our **salvation** will soon be completed. We need to wake up from spiritual lethargy. Paul used the image of taking off the old clothes of sinful behavior and putting on the **Lord Jesus Christ** as our way of life. This passage is famous for bringing Augustine of Hippo to salvation (*Confessions*, 8:12.22).
14:1–15:13 The exact historical background of the problem described in this section is unknown. Christians in Rome had different opinions on certain practices since they came from various backgrounds. Theologians have called these issues **disputed matters** (Gk *adiaphora*) since differences of opinion are allowed, but it is easy to see how some believers feel otherwise. The church must strive for tolerance and understanding on such matters, emphasizing the unity of believers, the expression of love for others, and the purity of the gospel message.
14:1 The believer **who is weak in faith** is overly conscientious about matters not regulated by Christian revelation. Paul commanded believers to **welcome** weak

Christians but not to get into arguments about **disputed matters**.
14:2 Jews were not normally vegetarians, but some were (e.g., Daniel; see Dn 1:8–12).
14:3–4 Mutual toleration is a Christian virtue. God accepts each believer, along with issues stemming from their background and maturity level, and is able to sanctify them.
14:6 Our religious practices are to be done out of conviction before God. How we live and die must come from the conviction that we belong to the Lord.
14:7–9 We are not our own. **We belong to the Lord**.
14:10–12 The **judgment seat of God** (Gk *bema*) is elsewhere called the "judgment seat of Christ" (2Co 5:10). Many interpreters distinguish this from the great white throne judgment in Rv 20:11–15. The "judgment seat of Christ" is where believers will be rewarded or suffer loss of rewards (1Co 3:13) based on their deeds and their stewardship of God-given responsibilities. In distinction to this, the great white throne judgment is the place where unbelievers will be raised for

The Law of Love

[13] Therefore, let us no longer judge one another. Instead decide never to put a stumbling block or pitfall in the way of your brother or sister. [14] I know and am persuaded in the Lord Jesus that nothing is unclean in itself. Still, to someone who considers a thing to be unclean, to that one it is unclean. [15] For if your brother or sister is hurt by what you eat, you are no longer walking according to love. Do not destroy, by what you eat, someone for whom Christ died. [16] Therefore, do not let your good be slandered, [17] for the kingdom of God is not eating and drinking, but righteousness, peace, and joy in the Holy Spirit. [18] Whoever serves Christ in this way is acceptable to God and receives human approval.

[19] So then, let us pursue what promotes peace and what builds up one another. [20] Do not tear down God's work because of food. Everything is clean, but it is wrong to make someone fall by what he eats. [21] It is a good thing not to eat meat, or drink wine, or do anything that makes your brother or sister stumble.[A] [22] Whatever you believe about these things, keep between yourself and God. Blessed is the one who does not condemn himself by what he approves. [23] But whoever doubts stands condemned if he eats, because his eating is not from faith,[B] and everything that is not from faith is sin.

Pleasing Others, Not Ourselves

15 Now we who are strong have an obligation to bear the weaknesses of those without strength, and not to please ourselves. [2] Each one of us is to please his neighbor for his good, to build him up. [3] For even Christ did not please himself. On the contrary, as it is written, The insults of those who insult you have fallen on me.[C] [4] For whatever was written in the past was written for our instruction, so that we may have hope through endurance and through the encouragement from the Scriptures. [5] Now may the God who gives[D] endurance and encouragement grant you to live in harmony with one another, according to Christ Jesus, [6] so that you may glorify the God and Father of our Lord Jesus Christ with one mind and one voice.

Glorifying God Together

[7] Therefore welcome one another, just as[E] Christ also welcomed you, to the glory of God. [8] For I say that Christ became a servant of the circumcised[F] on behalf of God's truth, to confirm the promises to the fathers, [9] and so that Gentiles may glorify God for his mercy. As it is written,

Therefore I will praise you
among the Gentiles,
and I will sing praise to your name.[G]

[10] Again it says, Rejoice, you Gentiles, with his people![H] [11] And again,

Praise the Lord, all you Gentiles;
let all the peoples praise him![I]

[12] And again, Isaiah says,

The root of Jesse will appear,
the one who rises to rule the Gentiles;
the Gentiles will hope in him.[J]

[13] Now may the God of hope fill you with all joy and peace as you believe so that you may overflow with hope by the power of the Holy Spirit.

From Jerusalem to Illyricum

[14] My brothers and sisters, I myself am convinced about you that you also are full of goodness, filled with all knowledge, and able to instruct one another. [15] Nevertheless, I have written to remind you more boldly on some

---

[A]14:21 Other mss add or offended or weakened   [B]14:23 Or conviction   [C]15:3 Ps 69:9   [D]15:5 Lit God of   [E]15:7 Or because   [F]15:8 The Jews   [G]15:9 2Sm 22:50; Ps 18:49   [H]15:10 Dt 32:43   [I]15:11 Ps 117:1   [J]15:12 Is 11:10

---

judgment. All people will bow before God and give **an account** of their lives.
14:13 Our goal must be to help all believers grow into spiritual maturity and not to hinder their progress.
14:14 This is one of Paul's most amazing statements. His background as a Pharisee trained him to emphasize the distinction between clean and **unclean**, but Jesus persuaded him that this distinction was no longer valid. But Paul also recognized that some believers, especially those from a Jewish background, had not made this transition. Mature believers should not recklessly push "weak" believers (v. 1) into such a transition.
14:15 A strong Christian must live in love and not violate the conscience of a weak believer. The conscience is the moral faculty of the mind. It can be educated by God through the Holy Spirit, but we must never teach others to go against their conscience. **Do not destroy** means that we can cause a person's spiritual ruin by teaching them to ignore or violate their conscience.

14:16–19 Christian liberty will get a bad name if love does not govern it. We are to promote **righteousness, peace, and joy** in the churches. Our actions should serve Christ and help other Christians grow and flourish.
14:20–21 Objectively, **everything is clean** (see 1Tm 4:4). Yet some immature believers might stumble over **meat** or **drink** (1Co 8:7–11).
14:22–23 A Christian's sense of freedom in these matters should not translate into public behavior if another believer finds the freedom scandalous.
15:1 Why should the **strong** "give in" to the conscience of the weak? The way of love demands it. The strong believer does not forsake his conscience by abstaining from certain of his freedoms, but the weaker believer would have to violate his in order to accommodate the liberties of the strong. Thus the strong should choose in accordance with the weak.
15:2–3 The strong Christian is to follow the example of one's Lord, who **did not please himself**.

15:4 Far from being irrelevant to Christian faith, the OT writings are for our **instruction** (2Tm 3:16).
15:5–6 Paul's prayer is that God will bring these house churches of Rome to the place of harmony, love, and unity that will enable them to best honor God.
15:7–8 These verses show that people from Jewish and Gentile backgrounds struggled with accepting one another.
15:9–12 A series of citations from the OT demonstrates God's plans. Quotes from the Law, History, Psalms, and Prophets refer to Gentile reception and praise of God.
15:13 Paul gave a second benediction for the churches with emphasis on hope in God produced by the Holy Spirit's work among them.
15:14–16 Paul was **convinced** that the Roman Christians were gifted by God for effective service and healthy church life. Yet Paul also knew that God had uniquely called and equipped him as an apostle to the Gentiles. So what he wrote was sure to be useful in helping the Roman house churches grow to maturity.

points^A because of the grace given me by God ^16 to be a minister of Christ Jesus to the Gentiles, serving as a priest of the gospel of God. God's purpose is that the Gentiles may be an acceptable offering, sanctified by the Holy Spirit. ^17 Therefore I have reason to boast in Christ Jesus regarding what pertains to God. ^18 For I would not dare say anything except what Christ has accomplished through me by word and deed for the obedience of the Gentiles, ^19 by the power of miraculous signs and wonders, and by the power of God's Spirit. As a result, I have fully proclaimed the gospel of Christ from Jerusalem all the way around to Illyricum.^B ^20 My aim is to preach the gospel where Christ has not been named, so that I will not build on someone else's foundation, ^21 but, as it is written,

Those who were not told about him
    will see,
and those who have not heard
    will understand.^C

Paul's Travel Plans

^22 That is why I have been prevented many times from coming to you. ^23 But now I no longer have any work to do in these regions,^D and I have strongly desired for many years to come to you ^24 whenever I travel to Spain.^E For I hope to see you when I pass through and to be assisted by you for my journey there, once I have first enjoyed your company for a while. ^25 Right now I am traveling to Jerusalem to serve the saints, ^26 because Macedonia and Achaia were pleased to make a contribution for the poor among the saints in Jerusalem. ^27 Yes, they were pleased, and indeed are indebted to them. For if the Gentiles have shared in their spiritual benefits, then they are obligated to minister to them in material needs. ^28 So when I have finished this and safely delivered the funds^F to them,^G I will visit you on the way to Spain. ^29 I know that when I come to you, I will come in the fullness of the blessing^H of Christ.

^30 Now I appeal to you, brothers and sisters, through our Lord Jesus Christ and through the love of the Spirit, to strive together with me in prayers to God on my behalf. ^31 Pray that I may be rescued from the unbelievers in Judea, that my ministry to^I Jerusalem may be acceptable to the saints, ^32 and that, by God's will, I may come to you with joy and be refreshed together with you.

^33 May the God of peace be with all of you. Amen.

Paul's Commendation of Phoebe

16 I commend to you our sister Phoebe, who is a servant^J of the church in Cenchreae. ^2 So you should welcome her in the Lord in a manner worthy of the saints and assist her in whatever matter she may require your help. For indeed she has been a benefactor of many — and of me also.

Greeting to Roman Christians

^3 Give my greetings to Prisca^K and Aquila, my coworkers in Christ Jesus, ^4 who risked their own necks for my life. Not only do I thank them, but so do all the Gentile churches. ^5 Greet also the church that meets in their home. Greet my dear friend Epaenetus, who is the first convert^L to Christ from Asia.^M ^6 Greet Mary,^N who has worked very hard for you.^O ^7 Greet Andronicus and Junia, my fellow Jews^P and fellow prisoners. They are noteworthy in the eyes of the apostles,^Q and they were also in Christ before me. ^8 Greet Ampliatus, my dear friend in the

^A15:15 Other mss add brothers ^B15:19 A Roman province northwest of Greece on the eastern shore of the Adriatic Sea ^C15:21 Is 52:15 ^D15:23 Lit now, having no longer a place in these parts ^E15:24 Other mss add I will come to you. ^F15:28 Lit delivered this fruit ^G15:28 Or and placed my seal of approval on this fruit for them ^H15:29 Other mss add of the gospel ^I15:31 Lit that my service for ^J16:1 Others interpret this term in a technical sense: deacon, or deaconess, or minister, or courier ^K16:3 Traditionally, Priscilla, as in Ac 18:2,18,26 ^L16:5 Lit the firstfruits ^M16:5 Other mss read Achaia ^N16:6 Or Maria ^O16:6 Other mss read us ^P16:7 Or family members ^Q16:7 Or They are noteworthy among the apostles

15:17-19 Paul wanted to **boast in Christ Jesus** to the Roman believers about how God had used him to spread the good news all the way from **Jerusalem** to the Roman province of **Illyricum** (modern Albania). God had approved of his ministry by authenticating **signs** and **wonders** and many conversions. The Roman believers would have been comforted by this testimony, for it illustrated the secure basis on which they had rested their hopes for salvation.
15:20-21 In ten years, God had used Paul as a pioneer church planter in the eastern section of the Roman Empire. Paul felt his ministry was in keeping with OT messianic prophecy (Is 52:15). He was the planter; others would come water the soil, and God would give growth (1Co 3:3-9).
15:22-24 God's **work** for Paul in the eastern half of the Roman Empire had kept him from going to Rome sooner, but now the work was

completed and he planned to **pass through** Rome on a mission trip to the western part of the Roman Empire (**Spain**). Scholars are divided on whether Paul ever made it to Spain. The Bible does not record a Spanish mission for Paul.
15:25-29 Paul was on his way to **Jerusalem** to bring a gift from the Gentile churches for the poor of the Jewish church in that city. He planned to come to Rome next. Little did he know he would be taken to Rome in custody (Ac 25:11-28:14,30-31).
15:30-33 Paul made three specific prayer requests: (1) for deliverance from unbelieving Jews in Judea, (2) that the gift from Gentile Christians would be welcomed by Jewish Christians, and (3) that he might come to Rome. All three were answered; see Ac 23:10; 21:17-20a; 25:11-12, respectively.
16:1-2 Phoebe was the probable carrier of this letter to Rome. Paul commended her for her service.

16:3-4 Prisca and Aquila (Ac 18:1-3,18,26; 2Tm 4:19) were Paul's **coworkers**. They had churches in their homes, they instructed Apollos, and they **risked their own necks** to save Paul.
16:5 Epaenetus means "beloved." He was Asia's first convert to Christ. **Asia** refers to the Roman province of that name in Asia Minor (present-day Turkey).
16:6 Several women are the recipients of Paul's greeting: Prisca, **Mary**, Junia, Tryphaena, Tryphosa, Persis, Rufus's mother, and Julia.
16:7 The phrase **noteworthy in the eyes of the apostles** is variously translated as "well-known to the apostles" or as "outstanding among the apostles." The word "apostle" can be used in a nontechnical sense, referring to a messenger rather than a commissioned apostle such as Paul.
16:8 Paul listed several as **my dear friend**: Epaenetus, **Ampliatus**, Stachys, and Persis.

Lord. ⁹ Greet Urbanus, our coworker in Christ, and my dear friend Stachys. ¹⁰ Greet Apelles, who is approved in Christ. Greet those who belong to the household of Aristobulus. ¹¹ Greet Herodion, my fellow Jew.ᴬ Greet those who belong to the household of Narcissus who are in the Lord. ¹² Greet Tryphaena and Tryphosa, who have worked hard in the Lord. Greet my dear friend Persis, who has worked very hard in the Lord. ¹³ Greet Rufus, chosen in the Lord; also his mother — and mine. ¹⁴ Greet Asyncritus, Phlegon, Hermes, Patrobas, Hermas, and the brothers and sisters who are with them. ¹⁵ Greet Philologus and Julia, Nereus and his sister, and Olympas, and all the saints who are with them. ¹⁶ Greet one another with a holy kiss. All the churches of Christ send you greetings.

Warning against Divisive People

¹⁷ Now I urge you, brothers and sisters, to watch out for those who create divisions and obstacles contrary to the teaching that you learned. Avoid them, ¹⁸ because such people do not serve our Lord Christ but their own appetites.ᴮ They deceive the hearts of the unsuspecting with smooth talk and flattering words.

Paul's Gracious Conclusion

¹⁹ The report of your obedience has reached everyone. Therefore I rejoice over you, but I want you to be wise about what is good, and yet innocent about what is evil. ²⁰ The God of peace will soon crush Satan under your feet. The grace of our Lord Jesus be with you.

²¹ Timothy, my coworker, and Lucius, Jason, and Sosipater, my fellow countrymen, greet you.

²² I, Tertius, who wrote this letter, greet you in the Lord.ᶜ

²³ Gaius, who is host to me and to the whole church, greets you. Erastus, the city treasurer, and our brother Quartus greet you.ᴰ

Glory to God

²⁵ Now to him who is able to strengthen you according to my gospel and the proclamation about Jesus Christ, according to the

ᴬ16:11 Or *family member* ᴮ16:18 Lit *belly* ᶜ16:22 Or *letter in the Lord, greet you* ᴰ16:23 Some mss include v. 24: *The grace of our Lord Jesus Christ be with you all.*

16:9 Listed as coworkers are Prisca and Aquila, and **Urbanus.**
16:10 Only **Apelles** is described as **approved in Christ**.
16:11 Herodion is called **my fellow Jew**, as were Andronicus and Junia in v. 7.
16:12 Several are described with **worked** (very) **hard (in the Lord)**: Mary (v. 6), Tryphaena, Tryphosa, and Persis.
16:13 Rufus was possibly the same Rufus whose father ("Simon of Cyrene") helped carry Jesus's cross to Golgotha (Mk 15:21–22). Only he is described as **chosen in the Lord**.

16:16 This encouragement to **greet one another with a holy kiss** is also found in 1Co 16:20; 2Co 13:12; 1Th 5:26.
16:17–20 Satan and false teachers will always assail the church (Ac 20:28–29; 2Co 11:13–15; Gl 5:10–12; Php 3:2,18–20; Col 2:16–19). Paul warned believers at Rome to be alert and **avoid** false teachers. Illustrating the familiar both/and relation between divine sovereignty and human responsibility to choose, we must be diligent in the battle against darkness, but ultimate victory is assured (**The God of peace will soon crush Satan**).

16:21 Timothy was Paul's close friend and **coworker** since the second missionary journey. **Lucius** is unknown. **Jason** is probably the one who gave Paul hospitality in Thessalonica (Ac 17:5–9). **Sosipater** is probably the Sopater from Berea who accompanied Paul for a while (Ac 20:4).
16:22–23 Tertius was Paul's scribe. **Erastus,** who had a responsible position as **city treasurer,** may be the same as that in Ac 19:22 and 2Tm 4:20.
16:25–27 By **my gospel,** Paul did not mean his preaching did not reflect God's

Character profile:

Phoebe

In Paul's letter to the Romans, he began with eleven deeply theological chapters, essentially answering the question, "What does the gospel really mean?" Then he wrote four practical chapters, answering the question, "What differences does the gospel make in a believer's everyday life?"

Yet, chapter 15 isn't the end of the book. Paul tacked on one more chapter—which is beautifully personal. In Romans 16 Paul included thirty-five individuals by name. It's a tiny but fascinating window into the life of the early church.

The first person we see there is a woman named Phoebe. Paul didn't write much about her, but he managed to paint a vivid picture of a competent and compassionate woman of tremendous impact.

First, Paul wrote, "I commend to you our sister Phoebe" (Rm 16:1). This almost surely means this little-known woman was the courier who hand delivered Paul's letter to its recipients in Rome. We owe a measure of gratitude to Phoebe. What a privilege and responsibility to be the bearer of such news.

Second, Paul called her "a servant of the church in Cenchreae" (16:1). Phoebe was a woman known for both her godly reputation and her tireless service in Cenchreae (a suburb of Corinth, Greece, where Paul wrote his letter to the Romans).

Finally, Paul urged the Roman Christians to "welcome her in the Lord in a manner worthy of the saints and assist her in whatever matter she may require your help. For indeed she has been a benefactor of many—and of me also" (16:2). Paul instructed them to show hospitality to this sister in the faith because Phoebe had been a "benefactor" to many, including Paul himself.

The word benefactor broadly means "helper." More specifically in this context it means "supporter" or "patroness." The strong indication is that Phoebe gave generously to the work of God. We don't know where she got her means or how she derived her income. But she apparently used her material resources to help fund the spread of the gospel.

Add such financial generosity to the other ways she served and supported the Lord's work. She spent her time tending to the spiritual needs of those in her local congregation. She spent great effort traveling more than six hundred miles from southern Greece to central Italy in order to deliver his world-changing letter. This was an era when travel was far more dangerous and much less convenient.

In just a few words, Paul paints the picture of a caring, capable, courageous woman. Who wouldn't want to be described in those terms? Paul's quick glimpse into Phoebe's life and character is inspiring.

How did she become such a respected individual? Phoebe's commendable life was built just like anyone else's—by one faithful act of service, one generous gift, one kind gesture at a time.

Do that long enough and you'll have a great reputation. More importantly, you'll have an eternal impact. Most importantly, you'll honor God.

revelation of the mystery kept silent for long ages **26** but now revealed and made known through the prophetic Scriptures, according to the command of the eternal God to advance the obedience of faith among all the Gentiles — **27** to the only wise God, through Jesus Christ — to him be the glory forever!^ Amen.

^**16:25–27** Other mss have these vv. at the end of chap. 14 or 15.

direct revelation (see Gl 1:11–12). He meant the gospel as he had faithfully preached it: a gospel of grace for all. In ages past this gospel was a **mystery kept silent**. In Christ the "mystery" is revealed to the world. In mentioning **the obedience of** **faith**, Paul concludes his letter where he began (1:5).

▼ Introduction to 1 Corinthians

Circumstances of Writing

First Corinthians ascribes Paul as its author (1:1; 16:21). Biblical scholars are almost unanimous that Paul wrote the letter. He wrote it during the last year of his three-year ministry at Ephesus, probably a few weeks before Pentecost in the spring of AD 56 (15:32; 16:8; see Ac 20:31).

During Paul's second missionary journey, he had a vision at Troas; he heard a man call to him, "Cross over to Macedonia and help us!" (Ac 16:9). That change in plans led Paul to Philippi, Thessalonica, Athens, and ultimately to Corinth (Ac 18:5). Paul ministered in Corinth for at least eighteen months (Ac 18:1–18). He left Corinth accompanied by Aquila and Priscilla (Ac 18:18), leaving them at Ephesus where they met and instructed "an eloquent man" named Apollos (Ac 18:24–26). Apollos then went to Corinth and had a powerful ministry there (Ac 18:27–19:1).

First Corinthians is the second letter that Paul wrote to the Corinthian church. He had written them an earlier letter that included an admonition not to mix with the sexually immoral (1Co 5:9). The writing of this second letter (1 Corinthians) was prompted by oral reports from Chloe's household about factional strife within the church (1:11). Paul had also received reports about an incestuous relationship among the membership (5:1), factions that arose during observance of the Lord's Supper (11:18), and confusion over the resurrection of the dead (15:12). As a result, Paul addressed these issues in 1 Corinthians.

Apparently, as he was writing the letter, he received a letter from the Corinthians asking his opinion on various issues (7:1,25; 8:1; 12:1; 16:1). Therefore, he included his replies within this letter to the Corinthian believers.

Contribution to the Bible

First Corinthians contributes greatly to our understanding of the Christian life, ministry, and relationships by showing us how the members of the church—Christ's body—are to function together. Problems can arise in any church because the church is composed of sinful people (redeemed certainly, but still prone to follow the tug of sin). Paul gave specific solutions to specific problems, but the underlying answer to all these problems is for the church and its members to live Christ-centered lives. It all comes down to living under the lordship and authority of Christ, the head of his body (the church).

Structure

Paul's writing is in the form of a letter, using the standard four parts of a first-century letter: salutation (1:1–3), thanksgiving (1:4–9), the main body (1:10–16:18), and a farewell (16:19–21). It is a pastoral letter, driven by the occasion and the present needs of the recipients.

Perhaps the most noteworthy feature of the way Paul structured his letter was his use of the word *about* to introduce a subject. It is apparent that "about" signals that Paul was responding to items on a list of questions that he had received—perhaps by way of a committee of men (16:17). These questions dealt with males and females in marriage (7:1); virgins (7:25); food offered to idols (8:1); spiritual gifts (12:1); the collection for the saints in Jerusalem (16:1); and Apollos (16:12).

Outline

I. Greetings and Thanksgiving (1:1–9)
II. Problems in the Church (1:10–6:20)
III. Replies to Questions from the Corinthians (7:1–14:40)
IV. The Resurrection of the Body (15:1–58)
V. Conclusion (16:1–24)

Key verses in 1 Corinthians

3:9   For we are God's coworkers. You are God's field, God's building.
3:16   Don't you yourselves know that you are God's temple and that the Spirit of God lives in you?
4:2   In this regard, it is required that managers be found faithful.
10:31   So, whether you eat or drink, or whatever you do, do everything for the glory of God.
14:40   But everything is to be done decently and in order.

---

50 BC–AD 50

Julius Caesar rebuilds Corinth as a colony of Rome naming it *Colonia Laus Julia Corinthiensis*. **44 BC**
Augustus Caesar makes Corinth the capital of Achaia. **27 BC**
Jesus's trials, death, resurrection, and ascension **NISAN 14–16** or **APRIL 3–5, AD 33**
Pentecost **AD 33**
Saul's conversion on the Damascus Road **OCTOBER AD 34**

AD 50–100

Paul arrives in Corinth and spends eighteen months planting the church. **50–51**
Paul's hearing before Corinth's proconsul, Gallio, brother of the Roman philosopher Seneca **51**
Paul writes 1 Corinthians from Ephesus. **56**
Paul writes 2 Corinthians from Ephesus. **56**
Paul spends the winter in Corinth, from where he writes Romans. **57**
Clement of Rome, the earliest of the apostolic fathers, sends a letter from Rome to the church at Corinth. This is thought to be the earliest Christian document outside the books of the New Testament. **96**

Greeting

1 Paul, called as an apostle of Christ Jesus by God's will, and Sosthenes our brother: ² To the church of God at Corinth, to those sanctified in Christ Jesus, called as saints, with all those in every place who call on the name of Jesus Christ our Lord — both their Lord and ours.

³ Grace to you and peace from God our Father and the Lord Jesus Christ.

Thanksgiving

⁴ I always thank my God for you because of the grace of God given to you in Christ Jesus, ⁵ that you were enriched in him in every way, in all speech and all knowledge. ⁶ In this way, the testimony about Christ was confirmed among you, ⁷ so that you do not lack any spiritual gift as you eagerly wait for the revelation of our Lord Jesus Christ. ⁸ He will also strengthen you to the end, so that you will be blameless in the day of our Lord Jesus Christ. ⁹ God is faithful; you were called by him into fellowship with his Son, Jesus Christ our Lord.

Divisions at Corinth

¹⁰ Now I urge you, brothers and sisters, in the name of our Lord Jesus Christ, that all of you agree in what you say, that there be no divisions among you, and that you be united with the same understanding and the same conviction. ¹¹ For it has been reported to me about you, my brothers and sisters, by members of Chloe's people, that there is rivalry among you. ¹² What I am saying is this: One of you says, "I belong to Paul," or "I belong to Apollos," or "I belong to Cephas," or "I belong to Christ." ¹³ Is Christ divided? Was Paul crucified for you? Or were you baptized in Paul's name? ¹⁴ I thank God^(A,B) that I baptized none of you except Crispus and Gaius, ¹⁵ so that no one can say you were baptized in my name. ¹⁶ I did, in fact, baptize the household of Stephanas; beyond that, I don't recall if I baptized anyone else. ¹⁷ For Christ did not send me to baptize, but to preach the gospel — not with eloquent wisdom, so that the cross of Christ will not be emptied of its effect.

Christ the Power and Wisdom of God

¹⁸ For the word of the cross is foolishness to those who are perishing, but it is the power of God to us who are being saved. ¹⁹ For it is written,

I will destroy the wisdom of the wise,
and I will set aside the intelligence
of the intelligent.^C

²⁰ Where is the one who is wise? Where is the teacher of the law?^D Where is the debater of this age? Hasn't God made the world's wisdom foolish? ²¹ For since, in God's wisdom, the world did not know God through wisdom, God was pleased to save those who believe through the foolishness of what is preached. ²² For the Jews ask for signs and the Greeks seek wisdom, ²³ but we preach Christ crucified, a stumbling block to the Jews and foolishness to the Gentiles,^E ²⁴ Yet to those who are called, both Jews and Greeks, Christ is the power of God and the wisdom of God, ²⁵ because God's foolishness is wiser than human wisdom, and God's weakness is stronger than human strength.

Boasting Only in the Lord

²⁶ Brothers and sisters, consider your calling: Not many were wise from a human perspective,^F not many powerful, not many of noble birth. ²⁷ Instead, God has chosen what is foolish in the world to shame the wise, and God has chosen what is weak in the world to shame the strong. ²⁸ God has chosen what is insignificant

---

^A 1:14 Other mss omit *God*　^B 1:14 Or *I am thankful*　^C 1:19 Is 29:14　^D 1:20 Or *scholar*　^E 1:23 Other mss read *Greeks*　^F 1:26 Lit *wise according to the flesh*

1:1 Paul generally used the designation **as an apostle . . . by God's will** when his apostolic authority was being challenged or when he was writing to correct his readers.
1:2 Paul attached two epithets that identified the church at Corinth: those who were **sanctified in Christ Jesus** and those who were **called as saints**.
1:3 Paul's standard greeting after the salutation identified two persons of the Trinity, **God** the Father and **the Lord** Jesus **Christ**.
1:4 Paul's chief reason for gratitude toward the Corinthian believers was the gift of grace **God** had given to them.
1:5–8 Their spiritual giftedness confirmed their reception of the **testimony** of the gospel.
1:9 In the introduction to 1 Corinthians, the word **Lord** occurs more than in any other letter introduction of Paul (vv. 2,3,7,8,9).
1:10–6:20 The letter includes Paul's responses to two reports. The first was regarding major divisions within the church (1:10–4:21).

The second regarded gross sexual immorality (5:1–6:20).
1:10 The phrase **the same conviction** refers to the shared conviction about the centrality and importance of the gospel message—Christ crucified (v. 17; 1:18–3:4). In Paul's mind, this central conviction was the key to church unity.
1:11–12 Paul disclosed the report from Chloe's household about the quarrelsome, divisive spirit in the church at Corinth. **Apollos** was a popular teacher at Corinth (Ac 18:24–19:1). **Cephas** is the Aramaic name of Peter.
1:13–16 Paul answered the rhetorical question **is Christ divided?** by illustrating from his own life and ministry two crucial issues related to who he was and what devotion others owed him. In rapid-fire fashion, he asked: **Was Paul crucified for you? Or were you baptized in Paul's name?** The answer to both questions was clearly no.
1:17 Not with eloquent wisdom emphasizes what the world sees as the gospel's

foolishness, that being the message of "Christ crucified" (vv. 18,23; 2:2).
1:18–19 The **cross** divides the human race. The division is between **those who are perishing**, to whom the cross is **foolishness**, and those **who are being saved**, to whom the cross is wisdom and power. Paul supported this truth by quoting Is 29:14.
1:20–21 The last question of the series (**Hasn't God made the world's wisdom foolish?**) shows the futility of unbelieving human wisdom. God determined to save people on the basis of their trust in **what is preached**—Christ crucified.
1:25 The term translated **foolishness** refers to the foolish content of the message preached—the offensive message of Christ crucified.
1:26–28 Because the Lord's people embrace the "nothing" message, the world views them as **nothing**. But in the next age God will **shame** the **wise** and the **strong** and bring to nothing the things that in this age are viewed as **something** (2:6; 3:18–20).

and despised in the world — what is viewed as nothing — to bring to nothing what is viewed as something, [29] so that no one^A may boast in his presence. [30] It is from him that you are in Christ Jesus, who became wisdom from God for us — our righteousness, sanctification, and redemption — [31] in order that, as it is written: **Let the one who boasts, boast in the Lord.**^B

Paul's Proclamation

2 When I came to you, brothers and sisters, announcing the mystery^C of God to you, I did not come with brilliance of speech or wisdom. [2] I decided to know nothing among you except Jesus Christ and him crucified. [3] I came to you in weakness, in fear, and in much trembling. [4] My speech and my preaching were not with persuasive words of wisdom^D but with a demonstration of the Spirit's power, [5] so that your faith might not be based on human wisdom but on God's power.

Spiritual Wisdom

[6] We do, however, speak a wisdom among the mature, but not a wisdom of this age, or of the rulers of this age, who are coming to nothing. [7] On the contrary, we speak God's hidden wisdom in a mystery, a wisdom God predestined before the ages for our glory. [8] None of the rulers of this age knew this wisdom, because if they had known it, they would not have crucified the Lord of glory. [9] But as it is written,

What no eye has seen, no ear
    has heard,
and no human heart has conceived —
    God has prepared these things
    for those who love him.^E

[10] Now God has revealed these things to us by the Spirit, since the Spirit searches everything, even the depths of God. [11] For who knows a person's thoughts^F except his spirit within him? In the same way, no one knows the thoughts of God except the Spirit of God. [12] Now we have not received the spirit of the world, but the Spirit who comes from God, so that we may understand what has been freely given to us by God. [13] We also speak these things, not in words taught by human wisdom, but in those taught by the Spirit, explaining spiritual things to spiritual people.^G [14] But the person without the Spirit^H does not receive what comes from God's Spirit, because it is foolishness to him; he is not able to understand it since it is evaluated^I spiritually. [15] The spiritual person, however, can evaluate^J everything, and yet he himself cannot be evaluated by anyone. [16] For

who has known the Lord's mind,
    that he may instruct him?^K
But we have the mind of Christ.

The Problem of Immaturity

3 For my part, brothers and sisters, I was not able to speak to you as spiritual people but as people of the flesh, as babies in Christ. [2] I gave you milk to drink, not solid food, since you were not yet ready for it. In fact, you are still not ready, [3] because you are still worldly. For since there is envy and strife^L among you, are you not worldly and behaving like mere humans? [4] For whenever someone says, "I belong to Paul," and another, "I belong to Apollos," are you not acting like mere humans?

---

^A1:29 Lit that not all flesh ^B1:31 Jr 9:24 ^C2:1 Other mss read testimony ^D2:4 Other mss read human wisdom ^E2:9 Is 52:15; 64:4 ^F2:11 Or things ^G2:13 Or things with spiritual words ^H2:14 Lit natural person ^I2:14 Or judged, or discerned, also in v. 15 ^J2:15 Or judge, or discern ^K2:16 Is 40:13 ^L3:3 Other mss add and divisions

---

1:30–31 By the Father's doing, believers have an identification **in Christ** (shorthand for "in Christ crucified," cp. vv. 23–24, 30; 2:2). Because of this they possess the wisdom of God—Christ crucified. Through this wisdom,

believers have justification at God's court, sanctification that allows their entrance into his presence, and ultimate redemption. **2:3–5** Paul's preaching was not with **persuasive words of wisdom**, but with **power** as demonstrated by the saving power of the Holy Spirit. **2:6–7** The phrase **hidden wisdom in a mystery** refers to a secret openly revealed by God—the secret being the glory of God—that the Lord of glory is truly the Christ crucified. **2:9** Paul validated this revelation of the "hidden wisdom" by quoting two OT texts (Is 52:15; 64:4). **2:10 Depths of God** refers to the deepest wisdom that God's Spirit reveals to believers. **2:11** Paul used an analogy of the lesser to the greater. Just as the human **spirit** (Gk pneuma) within a person knows what the person is thinking, so also **the Spirit** (Gk pneuma) **of God** knows the **thoughts** of God. **2:12** Paul declared that with the reception of **the Spirit … from God**, a person understands that "Christ and him crucified" (v. 2) is actually the highest wisdom.

2:13 Spiritual reception is brought about by the Spirit's revelation to **spiritual people** (Gk pneumatikoi; lit "spiritual ones"). **2:14** Throughout chaps. 1–2, **foolishness** is always a reference to "Christ and him crucified," or the gospel, the wisdom of God. **2:15–16** That the spiritual person … **cannot be evaluated by anyone** means he does not need to be concerned about negative human evaluations of the gospel because such a person has the right perspective—**the mind of Christ**. Paul validated his statement in v. 15 by appealing to Is 40:13. **3:1–3b** Many of the Corinthians were immature in the Lord. They were not able to receive **solid food** (advanced teaching) because they were full of **envy and strife** (rivalries), which marked them as **babies in Christ** who needed **milk** (fundamental Christian instruction) rather than adult fare. **3:3c–4** In a second analogy, this one borrowed from slavery, Paul observed that the Corinthian believers were **behaving like mere humans** (lit "walking according to man"), following human masters in a slavish,

---

#72 99 Essential Christian Truths

JESUS'S DEITY

Within the person of Jesus Christ, there are two natures—divine and human. Scripture teaches he is fully divine and fully human. His divinity is on display in passages that describe him as equal with God (Jn 1:1–18; Php 2:5–11; Col 1:15–20; Heb 1:1–3). The New Testament also points to the deity of Christ by showing how he possesses attributes that God alone possesses (Mc 5:2; Jn 1:4), performs works that only God performs (Mk 2:5–12; Jn 10:28; 17:2), and claims to be the Son of God (Mt 26:63–64; Jn 8:58; 10:30; 17:5).

The Role of God's Servants

⁵ What then is Apollos? What is Paul? They are servants through whom you believed, and each has the role the Lord has given. ⁶ I planted, Apollos watered, but God gave the growth. ⁷ So, then, neither the one who plants nor the one who waters is anything, but only God who gives the growth. ⁸ Now he who plants and he who waters are one,ᴬ and each will receive his own reward according to his own labor. ⁹ For we are God's coworkers.ᴮ You are God's field, God's building.

¹⁰ According to God's grace that was given to me, I have laid a foundation as a skilled master builder,ᶜ and another builds on it. But each one is to be careful how he builds on it. ¹¹ For no one can lay any foundation other than what has been laid down. That foundation is Jesus Christ. ¹² If anyone builds on the foundation with gold, silver, costly stones, wood, hay, or straw, ¹³ each one's work will become obvious. For the day will disclose it, because it will be revealed by fire; the fire will test the quality of each one's work. ¹⁴ If anyone's work that he has built survives, he will receive a reward. ¹⁵ If anyone's work is burned up, he will experienceᴰ loss, but he himself will be saved — but only as through fire.

¹⁶ Don't you yourselves know that you are God's temple and that the Spirit of God lives in you? ¹⁷ If anyone destroys God's temple, God will destroy him; for God's temple is holy, and that is what you are.

The Folly of Human Wisdom

¹⁸ Let no one deceive himself. If anyone among you thinks he is wise in this age, let him become a fool so that he can become wise. ¹⁹ For the wisdom of this world is foolishness with God, since it is written, **He catches the wise in their craftiness;**ᴱ ²⁰ and again, **The Lord knows the reasonings of the wise are futile.**ᶠ ²¹ So let no one boast in human leaders, for everything is yours — ²² whether Paul or Apollos or Cephas or the world or life or death or things present or things to come

— everything is yours, ²³ and you belong to Christ, and Christ belongs to God.

The Faithful Manager

4 A person should think of us in this way: as servants of Christ and managers of the mysteries of God. ² In this regard, it is required that managers be found faithful. ³ It is of little importance to me that I should be judged by you or by any human court.ᴳ In fact, I don't even judge myself. ⁴ For I am not conscious of anything against myself, but I am not justified by this. It is the Lord who judges me. ⁵ So don't judge anything prematurely, before the Lord comes, who will both bring to light what is hidden in darkness and reveal the intentions of the hearts. And then praise will come to each one from God.

The Apostles' Example of Humility

⁶ Now, brothers and sisters, I have applied these things to myself and Apollos for your benefit, so that you may learn from us the meaning of the saying: "Nothing beyond what is written." The purpose is that none of you will be arrogant, favoring one person over another. ⁷ For who makes you so superior? What do you have that you didn't receive? If, in fact, you did receive it, why do you boast as if you hadn't received it? ⁸ You are already full! You are already rich! You have begun to reign as kings without us — and I wish you did reign, so that we could also reign with you! ⁹ For I think God has displayed us, the apostles, in last place, like men condemned to die: We have become a spectacle to the world, both to angels and to people. ¹⁰ We are fools for Christ, but you are wise in Christ! We are weak, but you are strong! You are distinguished, but we are dishonored! ¹¹ Up to the present hour we are both hungry and thirsty; we are poorly clothed, roughly treated, homeless; ¹² we labor, working with our own hands. When we are reviled, we bless; when we are persecuted, we endure it; ¹³ when we are slandered, we respond graciously. Even now, we are like the scum of the earth, like everyone's garbage.

ᴬ**3:8** Or *of equal status,* or *united in purpose*　ᴮ**3:9** Or *are coworkers belonging to God*　ᶜ**3:10** Or *wise master builder*
ᴰ**3:15** Or *suffer*　ᴱ**3:19** Jb 5:13　ᶠ**3:20** Ps 94:11　ᴳ**4:3** Lit *a human day*

---

partisan manner. The phrase was often an idiom for living like a slave.
3:5–6 Paul made the Corinthian believers aware that both he and Apollos, the founding evangelists of the Corinthian church, were dispatched **servants** (Gk *diakonoi*) through whom they **believed** the message of the gospel. Most scholars understand **planted** to be a reference to Paul's founding of the church and **watered** to refer to Apollos's later ministry after Paul left Corinth.
3:7 The Lord was to receive all the credit for the growth; therefore, the servants were nothing.
3:9b–17 The word translated **building** usually designates a structure still under

construction. This fitting metaphor designates the church as a work both accomplished and ongoing: its foundation of Jesus Christ is secure and permanent (v. 11), but various builders continue the work of adding stones (believers) to the structure.
3:10a–c As a **skilled master builder**, Paul laid a foundation—the message of Christ crucified (v. 11; 2:2). The key word in this context is "skilled," referring to his expertise and wisdom as a builder to construct with "Jesus Christ and him crucified." The phrase **another builds on it** refers to later builders who would have a role in building the body of Christ at Corinth (v. 5). These builders included Apollos and others who followed Paul.

3:10d–12 As a "skilled master builder" (v. 10), Paul issued a warning (as found in construction contracts) to any builder-leader who should follow him to be **careful how he builds**, choosing to use only quality materials, which is symbolic of faithfulness to his God-given duties as builder of God's church. The urgent reason for this diligence is revealed in vv. 13–17.
3:13 When Paul wrote **the day will disclose it**, he was speaking of the eschatological inspection day when God will examine how builders have built the building of God, the body of Christ, on the foundation of the "foolish message" (1:18,23; 2:2,5).

Paul's Fatherly Care

14 I'm not writing this to shame you, but to warn you as my dear children. **15** For you may have countless instructors in Christ, but you don't have many fathers. For I became your father in Christ Jesus through the gospel. **16** Therefore I urge you to imitate me. **17** This is why I have sent Timothy to you. He is my dearly loved and faithful child in the Lord. He will remind you about my ways in Christ Jesus, just as I teach everywhere in every church.

18 Now some are arrogant, as though I were not coming to you. **19** But I will come to you soon, if the Lord wills, and I will find out not the talk, but the power of those who are arrogant. **20** For the kingdom of God is not a matter of talk but of power. **21** What do you want? Should I come to you with a rod, or in love and a spirit of gentleness?

Immoral Church Members

5 It is actually reported that there is sexual immorality among you, and the kind of sexual immorality that is not even tolerated[A]

among the Gentiles — a man is sleeping with his father's wife. **2** And you are arrogant! Shouldn't you be filled with grief and remove from your congregation the one who did this? **3** Even though I am absent in the body, I am present in spirit. As one who is present with you in this way, I have already pronounced judgment on the one who has been doing such a thing. **4** When you are assembled in the name of our Lord Jesus, and I am with you in spirit, with the power of our Lord Jesus, **5** hand that one over to Satan for the destruction of the flesh, so that his spirit may be saved in the day of the Lord.

6 Your boasting is not good. Don't you know that a little leaven[B] leavens the whole batch of dough? **7** Clean out the old leaven so that you may be a new unleavened batch, as indeed you are. For Christ our Passover lamb has been sacrificed.[C] **8** Therefore, let us observe the feast, not with old leaven or with the leaven of malice and evil, but with the unleavened bread of sincerity and truth.

[A]5:1 Other mss read *named*   [B]5:6 Or *yeast*, also in vv. 7,8   [C]5:7 Other mss add *for us*

3:14–17 In this section Paul gives three different scenarios describing three different types of subcontractors who were constructing the building of God. He begins each scenario with the expression **if anyone's work** ... **if anyone** (vv. 14–15,17; cp. v. 12).
3:14 In the ancient world, a **reward** (Gk *misthos*) was granted to those who constructed the building on time, within budget, and according to specifications.
3:15 Paul warned those who built carelessly that they would suffer loss.
3:17 Paul gave stern notice to those who corrupted the church (chap. 15; 2Co 11). In a wordplay on the verb **destroy**, Paul warned that anyone who "destroys" (Gk *phtheiro*, "ruin," "corrupt," "defraud," "destroy") God's **temple** will, as recompense, be destroyed by God. The word *destroy* was used in construction contracts to describe building a structure with the intent to defraud. Thus the image here is of a church leader (builder, v. 12) who is willfully negligent.
3:19–20 These verses are filled with courtroom terminology from OT Wisdom literature (e.g., Jb 5:12–13). Paul affirmed from these witnesses that any disputations (**reasonings**) made before God's bench would be foolish if based on human wisdom.
3:21–23 The remedy for divisions in the church is the recognition that all gospel servants — even prominent figures such as **Paul** ... **Apollos**, or **Cephas** — are not their own, but **belong to Christ**, who in turn belongs **to God**. In this light, servants must never become a distraction to the church, and believers must never mistake them for the Master.
4:3–5 Paul was aware that the examination of his stewardship with respect to "the mysteries of God" (v. 1) came from the Lord, not humans nor even himself. Paul cautions against passing judgment on a person's ministry. All will be revealed only in the final judgment.
4:6 Paul did not disclose the identity of these misguided, arrogant leaders; he used

himself and Apollos as a foil. Paul and Apollos had illustrated dramatically in their foolish message that they did **nothing beyond** what was **written**.
4:7 Paul offered a rhetorical response to those claiming superiority in the Corinthian church.
4:8 With a strong dose of irony, Paul says the boastful disposition of the Corinthian believers made them **full** and **rich**, as if their glorification was complete and they were already reigning **as kings** in eternity.
4:9 Paul's mention of a **spectacle** (Gk *theatron*, "theatrical display") refers to the arena where victims (usually criminals) were led in procession before the last public show of the day, and then executed before the eager spectators. But rather than pagan or unbelieving Jewish authorities, Paul knew that ultimately it was **God** himself who had chosen to display **the apostles** in a humiliating manner.
4:10 Paul presents an alarming contrast, likely intended as a warning to the Corinthian church. While the apostles were made out to be **fools** as they faithfully dispatched the gospel, the spiritually immature Corinthians were **wise** (Gk *phronimos*) in their escape from ostracism, hardship, and persecution.
4:11–13 Paul describes the lifestyle and character of apostolic ministry. The world with its human wisdom labeled them as **scum** and **garbage** (cp. 2Co 2:16), which is the refuse (Gk *perikatharma*) of chamber pots and the off scouring (Gk *peripsēma*) in waste vats and cesspools respectively. The Romans used these terms to describe the dregs of society. Yet Paul says they **bless** ... **endure**, and **respond graciously** as Christ had taught them (Lk 6:27–36).
4:15 Paul reminded the Corinthian believers that he was their father **through the gospel**. In contrast to their present **instructors**, he had founded the church in Corinth (Ac 18).
4:17 Timothy probably had been dispatched from Ephesus before the letter was sent (16:10–11).

4:18–20 Paul would come to examine their teaching from the standpoint of **power**, the standard for all those who were truly teaching the foolishness of Christ crucified — the only wisdom that has the power to save (1:18,22–24).
4:21 Rod pictures a father who is faithful to correct his disobedient children.
5:1–6:20 Paul shifts to discuss specific immoralities that had been reported to him. The three issues in this section involve incest (5:1–13), lawsuits (6:1–11), and prostitution (6:12–20).
5:1 The phrase **not even tolerated among the Gentiles** refers to Roman law. A son committing incest with his stepmother was a capital crime in a Roman colony, calling for death or banishment. It was also prohibited in the Mosaic law (Lv 18:8; Dt 22:30).
5:2 They should have removed the offender from their fellowship. The purpose of this measure is revealed in v. 5.
5:3 Taking up the language of a secular legal trial, Paul used at least ten legal idioms in these verses.
5:4–5 The assembled corporate body had the authority to remove him (2:2) from their midst for the **destruction of the flesh**. This may refer to physical judgments such as sickness or even death (11:30). If the person were a true believer, banishment to Satan's domain would cause misery and possibly repentance. Paul expressed hope for the guilty person's ultimate restoration with the legal phrase, **so that his spirit may be saved** on the appointed **day of the Lord** (Rm 2:6,9).
5:7–8 With a wordplay on the expression **Christ our Passover lamb**, Paul offered a threefold solution to this corporate arrogance: (1) their recognition of what Christ as their Passover lamb did to deliver them from death; (2) their acknowledgment that Christ as their Passover lamb rendered them clean (**unleavened**) before the Lord; and (3) their remembrance that as they observed Christ as the Passover lamb, they were to purge their

Church Discipline

⁹ I wrote to you in a letter not to associate with sexually immoral people. ¹⁰ I did not mean the immoral people of this world or the greedy and swindlers or idolaters; otherwise you would have to leave the world. ¹¹ But actually, I wrote^A you not to associate with anyone who claims to be a brother or sister and is sexually immoral or greedy, an idolater or verbally abusive, a drunkard or a swindler. Do not even eat with such a person. ¹² For what business is it of mine to judge outsiders? Don't you judge those who are inside? ¹³ God judges outsiders. **Remove the evil person from among you.**^B

Lawsuits among Believers

6 If any of you has a dispute against another, how dare you take it to court before the unrighteous,^C and not before the saints? ² Or don't you know that the saints will judge the world? And if the world is judged by you, are you unworthy to judge the trivial cases? ³ Don't you know that we will judge angels — how much more matters of this life? ⁴ So if you have such matters, do you appoint as your judges those who have no standing in the church? ⁵ I say this to your shame! Can it be that there is not one wise person among you who is able to arbitrate between fellow believers? ⁶ Instead, brother goes to court against brother, and that before unbelievers!

⁷ As it is, to have legal disputes against one another is already a defeat for you. Why not rather be wronged? Why not rather be cheated? ⁸ Instead, you yourselves do wrong and cheat — and you do this to brothers and sisters! ⁹ Don't you know that the unrighteous will not inherit God's kingdom? Do not be deceived: No sexually immoral people, idolaters,

adulterers, or males who have sex with males,^D ¹⁰ no thieves, greedy people, drunkards, verbally abusive people, or swindlers will inherit God's kingdom. ¹¹ And some of you used to be like this. But you were washed, you were sanctified, you were justified in the name of the Lord Jesus Christ and by the Spirit of our God.

Glorifying God in Body and Spirit

¹² "Everything is permissible for me," but not everything is beneficial. "Everything is permissible for me," but I will not be mastered by anything. ¹³ "Food is for the stomach and the stomach for food," and God will do away with both of them. However, the body is not for sexual immorality but for the Lord, and the Lord for the body. ¹⁴ God raised up the Lord and will also raise us up by his power. ¹⁵ Don't you know that your bodies are a part of Christ's body? So should I take a part of Christ's body and make it part of a prostitute? Absolutely not! ¹⁶ Don't you know that anyone joined to a prostitute is one body with her? For Scripture says, **The two will become one flesh.**^E ¹⁷ But anyone joined to the Lord is one spirit with him.

¹⁸ Flee sexual immorality! Every other sin^F a person commits is outside the body, but the person who is sexually immoral sins against his own body. ¹⁹ Don't you know that your body is a temple of the Holy Spirit who is in you, whom you have from God? You are not your own, ²⁰ for you were bought at a price. So glorify God with your body.^G

Principles of Marriage

7 Now in response to the matters you wrote^H about: "It is good for a man not to have sexual relations with a woman." ² But because sexual

^A 5:11 Or *But now I am writing*   ^B 5:13 Dt 17:7   ^C 6:1 Unbelievers; v. 6   ^D 6:9 Both passive and active participants in homosexual acts   ^E 6:16 Gn 2:24   ^F 6:18 Lit *Every sin*   ^G 6:20 Other mss add *and in your spirit, which belong to God.*   ^H 7:1 Other mss add *to me*   ^I 7:1 Or *"It is good for a man not to use a woman for sex"*; lit *"It is good for a man not to touch a woman."*

household of **malice and evil** to celebrate with **sincerity and truth**.
5:9 Paul's previous **letter** is long since lost.
5:10 Paul corrected a mistaken perception that his admonition in the letter (v. 9) had prohibited them from mixing socially with nonbelievers (**the immoral people of this world**). He actually had meant not to mix with believers who live like unbelievers (3:3).
5:11 To **eat** with such people could be taken as a sign of condoning their worldly lifestyle.
5:12–13 Paul concludes by quoting God's repeated exhortation in Dt (13:5; 17:7,12; 19:19; 21:21; 22:21,24; 24:7) to show that the church, just as Israel, must remove from their midst those who live in flagrant rebellion against God's law.
6:1 The phrase **how dare you take it to court before the unrighteous** refers to bringing a legal complaint against fellow members before unbelieving Roman judges at Corinth.
6:2–3 Paul called the church to an awareness of their own authority as a judicial body.

He argued their competency to judge cases by drawing from two greater-to-lesser analogies: (1) being qualified to judge **the world** (i.e., nonbelievers) at the end of the age qualified them to judge church members in this age, and (2) being qualified to judge **angels** at the end of the age qualified them to judge **matters of this life**.
6:5–6 The question in v. 5 is intentional irony, since the Corinthians were claiming to be wise.
6:9–11 Believers should **not be deceived** into thinking that unbelieving judges (**the unrighteous**) and their slap-on-the-wrist verdicts about serious sin can render justice in the church. These people have no inheritance in **God's kingdom**. Only believers, who are **washed . . . sanctified**, and **justified**, can rightly judge sins (v. 1). Paul reminds the believers that many of them were involved in such sins before their conversion, but they had experienced transformation so they could now live in conformity to their profession and status.

6:12–20 Paul quotes a slogan apparently put forth by the immature Corinthians (**Everything is permissible for me**) to introduce a series of admonitions emphasizing a dominant theme in this letter: a believer's freedom is to be limited to that which is profitable to the Lord.
6:12–14 Paul's reply to the slogan (v. 12) is that the Corinthian Christians are not their own; they are "bodies" belonging to the Lord (vv. 13,19–20; 1:2; 7:22–23; 10:26).
6:15–17 The words **one flesh** in this context refer to becoming one body through sexual relations with a **prostitute**. "One flesh" recalls Gn 24 and contrasts the proper marriage relationship with an illicit sexual relationship.
6:18–20 Sexual immorality is unique among sins insomuch as it is sin against the **body**. The point is that the believer's body is a sacred vessel, **bought at a price** by the Son of God. Believers thus have no business doing anything with the Lord's body that does not **glorify** God.
7:1 Paul responded to several **matters** about which the Corinthians had written to him

Christian Worldview and Same-Sex Marriage

by Andrew T. Walker

Same-sex marriage presents a significant cultural challenge to the Christian worldview. As it becomes increasingly normalized throughout Western culture, Christians will face a great temptation to grow indifferent toward biblical teaching on marriage, to fear culture's disapproval of Christian teaching about it, or to reluctantly accept same-sex marriage as a reality of civil life. But because the Bible's teaching on marriage is connected to the gospel and to God's vision for human flourishing, believers committed to the authority of the Bible must reject these temptations and remain committed to the Christian teaching that defines marriage as a union of two opposite-sexed persons.

Marriage and Gender in the Bible

Marriage is a gendered institution in the Bible. The early chapters of Genesis offer a blueprint for God's design for marriage. Being made male and female, Adam and Eve are sexually differentiated but made for each other. Because God has knit their distinction down to the deepest levels of their being, a male husband and a female wife are designed for each other emotionally, physically, and even anatomically. The complementarity of Adam and Eve is what makes their marriage union achievable and procreation possible (Gn 1:27–28; 2:24). Genesis paints a picture of marriage that is complementary (that is, relating between the two sexes), exclusive between two opposite-sexed persons, and meant to be permanent for the duration of their lives.

The most basic element of marriage, however, is the physical difference that exists between men and women, which manifests itself in sexual union. Together man and woman possess a design oriented toward procreation, but each requires the other in order to realize or fulfill reproduction. Marriage is a comprehensive union: "Marriage is ordered to family life because the act by which spouses make love also makes new life; one and the same act both seals a marriage and brings forth children. That is why marriage alone is the loving union of mind and body fulfilled by the procreation—and rearing—of whole new humans" (Robert P. George, Ryan T. Anderson, and Sherif Girgis, *What Is Marriage? Man and Woman: A Defense* [New York: Encounter, 2011], 33).

This pattern set forth in Genesis is a pattern Jesus Christ reaffirms as authoritative in the New Testament (Mt 19:4–6). The Bible always bundles these aspects of marriage together. Without complementarity and all that follows from it, it is difficult to explain why an institution like marriage would exist at all and why marriage ought to be both permanent and exclusive between only two persons. Marriage is what the Bible says it is, or else marriage does not exist. Christians have disagreed on many things throughout history, but they have always been united around basic truths that the Bible makes clear, and the biblical definition of marriage as between one man and one woman is one matter on which Christians have spoken clearly and uniformly.

The Impossibility of Same-Sex Marriage

The biblical picture of marriage presented above is why same-sex marriage is not only a violation of God's moral law governing sexual relations between men and women (Rm 1:18–32; 1 Co 6:9–11) but also why same-sex marriage cannot ever truly exist. Governments may create a legal entity that two persons of the same sex consider a marriage, but government does not have the authority to redefine God's moral law. According to the Bible, marriage can never exist between two persons of the same sex because marriage is designed exclusively for two persons of the opposite sex. This is an unpopular teaching in the eyes of the world, but faithfulness to Scripture demands our obedience on all matters—even those that are controversial.

The Implications of Revisionist Definitions of Marriage

Same-sex marriage is a bad path for society. It puts into principle troubling patterns that can hinder human flourishing. First, children need moms and dads. Same-sex marriage denies this truth altogether by insisting that there is no difference between mothers and fathers. Our consciences know this is false. Each of us recognizes that a mother's love and a father's love are different and yet necessary and vital for children. In reality, there is no such thing as "parenting"; there is only mothering and fathering. Therefore, it is in the best interest of government and society to promote the ideal place for children to be raised: in a married household with a mom and dad.

Redefining marriage hands immense power to the state, essentially allowing it to redefine the family. By cutting off biological connection to the definition of marriage and family life, natural foundations and natural rights that follow from family life are called into question. This is a dangerous precedent.

Redefining marriage does not simply expand who can marry; it fundamentally alters what marriage is and what the foundation of a stable social order consists of. Marriage is not something the state creates; rather, the state recognizes marriage as something that exists prior to the state, and thus the state acknowledges it has no control over it.

Same-sex marriage is based on incoherent premises that lead to the further erosion of marriage. By denying the truth that marriage is based on the physical differences of men and women, same-sex marriage is based on the premise that what makes marriage achievable is the emotional union and physical attraction that exists between two persons, regardless of sexual difference. But this is not a solid foundation. Indeed, same-sex marriage is a historical anomaly not found anywhere throughout human history. Why is this? Because all societies have understood that the basis of society hinges on the union of man and woman joined together in marriage. Were it not for the procreative potential between men and women, the institution of marriage would have little reason to exist in the first place. Society has no need for an institution like marriage if marriage is simply about licensing physical attraction between two persons who exchange legal benefits.

A Christian Response to Same-Sex Marriage

So, what is marriage? Marriage is the union of a man and a woman who come together as husband and wife to be father and mother to any children their union produces. Notice that the progression of roles in this definition relies centrally on the truth that men and women are distinct. Marriage is based on the anthropological truth that men and women are different, the biological fact that reproduction requires one man and one woman, and the sociological reality that children need moms and dads. Based on the definition above, same-sex marriage fundamentally rejects and thwarts these central truths about marriage.

The most consequential concern surrounding same-sex marriage is the message we who hold a Christian worldview send to our neighbors. The Bible condemns sexual relations between persons of the same sex. While some revisionists depict the Bible as condemning only certain forms of homosexual practice seen in ancient times, these flawed arguments overlook the Bible's broad and sweeping condemnation of homosexuality. Homosexuality violates the physical boundaries God placed between men and women. The New Testament lists homosexuality as an offense that provokes God's wrath and denies entry into the kingdom of God to those who choose indulging in it over submission to Christ (1Co 6:9–11). Therefore, if Christians are to love their neighbors, they can never support an institution based on sexual activities and disordered desires prohibited in Scripture. As Paul declares, "Love finds no joy in unrighteousness but rejoices in the truth" (13:6). We must tell the truth about marriage to our neighbors, work to uphold it in our laws, and seek to share it with all of society. Christians can never accommodate or accept same-sex marriage.

It is common to hear proponents of the issue saying something like this to those of us holding biblical convictions: "Same-sex marriage doesn't harm you, so why should you care?" This is demonstrably false. Same-sex marriage harms society by casting uncertainty onto marriage's role as the basic unit of society. It harms children by denying them their right to a mom and dad, and it evokes great challenges for religious liberty. Moreover, it harms individuals by putting them on a path that rejects God's design for marriage and sexual morality. While these truths are understandably challenging to uphold in a time like ours, God has given his people a wonderful opportunity to learn afresh his vision for marriage. Marriage is, ultimately, a picture of the gospel itself (Eph 5:22–33; Rv 19:6–9).

immorality is so common,^A each man should have sexual relations with his own wife, and each woman should have sexual relations with her own husband. ³ A husband should fulfill his marital duty to his wife, and likewise a wife to her husband. ⁴ A wife does not have the right over her own body, but her husband does. In the same way, a husband does not have the right over his own body, but his wife does. ⁵ Do not deprive one another — except when you agree for a time, to devote yourselves to⁸ prayer. Then come together again; otherwise, Satan may tempt you because of your lack of self-control. ⁶ I say this as a concession, not as a command. ⁷ I wish that all people were as I am. But each has his own gift from God, one person has this gift, another has that.

A Word to the Unmarried

⁸ I say to the unmarried^c and to widows: It is good for them if they remain as I am. ⁹ But if they do not have self-control, they should marry, since it is better to marry than to burn with desire.

About Married People

¹⁰ To the married I give this command — not I, but the Lord — a wife is not to leave^D her husband. ¹¹ But if she does leave, she must remain unmarried or be reconciled to her husband — and a husband is not to divorce his wife. ¹² But I (not the Lord) say to the rest: If any brother has an unbelieving wife and she is willing to live with him, he must not divorce her. ¹³ Also, if any woman has an unbelieving husband and he is willing to live with her, she must not divorce her husband.

¹⁴ For the unbelieving husband is made holy by the wife, and the unbelieving wife is made holy by the husband.^E Otherwise your children would be unclean, but as it is they are holy. ¹⁵ But if the unbeliever leaves, let him leave. A brother or a sister is not bound in such cases. God has called you^F to live in peace. ¹⁶ Wife, for all you know, you might save your husband. Husband, for all you know, you might save your wife.^G

Various Situations of Life

¹⁷ Let each one live his life in the situation the Lord assigned when God called him.^H This is what I command in all the churches. ¹⁸ Was anyone already circumcised when he was called? He should not undo his circumcision. Was anyone called while uncircumcised? He should not get circumcised. ¹⁹ Circumcision does not matter and uncircumcision does not matter. Keeping God's commands is what matters. ²⁰ Let each of you remain in the situation^I in which he was called. ²¹ Were you called while a slave? Don't let it concern you. But if you can become free, by all means take the opportunity.^J ²² For he who is called by the Lord as a slave is the Lord's freedman. Likewise he who is called as a free man is Christ's slave. ²³ You were bought at a price; do not become slaves of people. ²⁴ Brothers and sisters, each person is to remain with God in the situation in which he was called.

About the Unmarried and Widows

²⁵ Now about virgins:^K I have no command from the Lord, but I do give an opinion as one who

---

^A 7:2 Lit *because of immoralities*   ^B 7:5 Other mss add *fasting and to*   ^C 7:8 Or *widowers*   ^D 7:10 Or *separate from*, or *divorce*
^E 7:14 Lit *the brother*   ^F 7:15 Other mss read *us*   ^G 7:16 Or *Wife, how do you know that you will save your husband? Husband,
how do you know that you will save your wife?*   ^H 7:17 Lit *called each*   ^I 7:20 Lit *in the calling*   ^J 7:21 Or *But even though you
can become free, make the most of your position as a slave*   ^K 7:25 Or *betrothed*, or *those not yet married*

(see also 7:25; 8:1; 12:1; 16:1,12), in addition to what he had heard (1:10–11). The first matter Paul addressed was articulated by the Corinthians as, **"It is good for a man not to have sexual relations with a woman."** What a divide in the Corinthian church! Based on this quotation, it's apparent that some advocated marital celibacy. In contrast to this, others were engaged in gross immorality (see 5:9–13; 6:12–20).

7:2–4 Sexual desires, which can readily lead to **sexual immorality**, commend frequent sexual union between husband and wife. The phrase **have the right** in this context refers to sexual relations. Neither has exclusive right over his or her body, but each has a responsibility to meet the sexual needs of the other.

7:5 Paul issues an apostolic ruling: husbands and wives must **not deprive one another** in marriage, **except** when mutually agreed upon for the sake of devotion **to prayer.** But they must **come together again** to avoid temptation due to **lack of self-control.**

7:6–7 Paul did think it was good if the Corinthians stayed single as he was—but only if they had the **gift** to do so.

7:8–9 Paul speaks here to people in his situation—not currently married—but who do not have his gift. Paul gives another apostolic

ruling: unmarried persons who lack self-control should get married.

7:10 Paul reiterates the Lord's ruling to **the married,** giving an injunction to wives that they must remain in their marriage (Mt 19:1–9; Mk 10:1–12).

7:11 The wife who has separated from her husband has two options: remain apart from him, though celibate, or be **reconciled** to her **husband.** Completing his reiteration of the Lord's instructions for marriage, Paul insisted that the **husband is not to divorce his wife.**

7:12–13 The phrase **to the rest** is a reference to mixed marriages—a believer married to an unbeliever. Christians were only to marry "in the Lord" (cp. v. 39). The situation Paul addresses here assumes that both spouses were unbelievers when they married but that one of them thereafter converted to Christianity. Since Jesus did not comment on this situation, Paul gave an apostolic ruling: the believing spouse **must not divorce** the unbelieving spouse. The passage also assumes that the unbeliever agrees that there are benefits to continuing the marital relationship **(is willing to live with** him or her).

7:14 A Christian spouse who remains faithful to his or her unbelieving spouse has a "sanctifying effect" on unbelieving family

members. Paul is referring not just to the possible future salvation of unbelievers in the household, but to their present protection from pagan values through the influence of the Christian member's exemplary morals.

7:15–16 Paul gives a qualification to the above ruling: do not hinder a nonbeliever's desire to separate. **Peace** in this context refers to being "at peace" if the unbelieving spouse should decide to **leave,** for in this event the believer has done nothing wrong.

7:17–19 To **undo his circumcision** involved undergoing a painful operation, as some secular-minded Jews did in the first century (Josephus, *Ant.* 12.241).

7:20–23 Paul again states the remain-as-you-are principle and illustrates it with a choice faced by slaves: willingly to remain a **slave** or to seek freedom. **By all means take the opportunity** to become free if it presents itself, he said. But on the other hand, the fact of being a slave should not be a **concern.** In Roman parlance, a **freedman** was an emancipated slave, whereas a **free man** was one who had never been enslaved.

7:25–27 The focus of this entire discussion (vv. 25–27) is cast from the male perspective since ancient culture gave males primary responsibility for marital decisions. **Now about** serves as a marker denoting that

by the Lord's mercy is faithful. [26] Because of the present distress, I think that it is good for a man to remain as he is. [27] Are you bound to a wife? Do not seek to be released. Are you released from a wife? Do not seek a wife. [28] However, if you do get married, you have not sinned, and if a virgin^ marries, she has not sinned. But such people will have trouble in this life, [B] and I am trying to spare you.

[29] This is what I mean, brothers and sisters: The time is limited, so from now on those who have wives should be as though they had none, [30] those who weep as though they did not weep, those who rejoice as though they did not rejoice, those who buy as though they didn't own anything, [31] and those who use the world as though they did not make full use of it. For this world in its current form is passing away.

[32] I want you to be without concerns. The unmarried man is concerned about the things of the Lord — how he may please the Lord. [33] But the married man is concerned about the things of the world — how he may please his wife — [34] and his interests are divided. The unmarried woman or virgin is concerned about the things of the Lord, so that she may be holy both in body and in spirit. But the married woman is concerned about the things of the world — how she may please her husband. [35] I am saying this for your own benefit, not to put a restraint on you, but to promote what is proper and so that you may be devoted to the Lord without distraction.

[36] If any man thinks he is acting improperly toward the virgin he is engaged to, if she is getting beyond the usual age for marriage, and he feels he should marry — he can do what he wants. He is not sinning; they can get married. [37] But he who stands firm in his heart (who is under no compulsion, but has control over his own will) and has decided in his heart to keep her as his fiancée, will do well. [38] So, then, he who marries his fiancée does well, but he who does not marry will do better.^C

[39] A wife is bound^D as long as her husband is living. But if her husband dies, she is free to be married to anyone she wants — only in the Lord. [40] But she is happier if she remains as she is, in my opinion. And I think that I also have the Spirit of God.

Food Offered to Idols

8 Now about food sacrificed to idols: We know that "we all have knowledge." Knowledge puffs up, but love builds up. [2] If anyone thinks he knows anything, he does not yet know it as he ought to know it. [3] But if anyone loves God, he is known by him.

[4] About eating food sacrificed to idols, then, we know that "an idol is nothing in the world,"^E and that "there is no God but one." [5] For even if there are so-called gods, whether in heaven or on earth — as there are many "gods" and many "lords" — [6] yet for us there is one God, the Father. All things are from him, and we exist for him. And there is one Lord, Jesus Christ. All things are through him, and we exist through him.

[7] However, not everyone has this knowledge. Some have been so used to idolatry up until now that when they eat food sacrificed to an idol, their conscience, being weak, is defiled. [8] Food will not bring us close to God.^F We are not worse off if we don't eat, and we are not better if we do eat. [9] But be careful that this right of yours in no way becomes a stumbling block to the weak. [10] For if someone sees you, the one who has knowledge, dining in an idol's

^7:28 Or *betrothed woman* ^B7:28 Lit *in the flesh* ^C7:36–38 Or *36If any man thinks he is acting improperly toward his virgin daughter, if she is getting beyond the usual age for marriage, and he feels she should marry — he can do what he wants. He is not sinning; she can get married. 37But he who stands firm in his heart (who is under no compulsion, but has control over his own will) and has decided in his heart to keep his own virgin daughter will do well. 38So then he who gives his own virgin daughter in marriage does well, but he who does not give his own virgin daughter in marriage will do better.* ^D7:39 Other mss add *by law* ^E8:4 Or *An idol has no real existence* ^F8:8 Or *bring us before* (the judgment seat of) *God*

Paul is now applying the remain-as-you-are principle (vv. 17–24) to the dilemma facing **virgins**. In this case Paul has **no command from the Lord**, but that does not lessen the impact of his teaching (i.e., **it is good for a man to remain as he is**). "Virgins" in this context refers to betrothed, female virgins. Their dilemma was brought about by an unnamed **present distress** (impending hardship). Paul's talk of being **bound** to or **released** from **a wife** in v. 27 can be summarized as follows: (1) The man who was bound by promise to a betrothed virgin (essentially already his wife, given the seriousness of betrothal) was not to seek release from future obligations to consummate the marriage (v. 27a-b), and (2) the man who had already been released from obligation (to a virgin) was not to seek betrothal with another woman (v. 27c-d). In other words, keep your commitments and/or remain as you are.

7:28 Paul does not define **trouble in this life**. Possibly it refers to the responsibilities and hardships that can attend marriage and child-rearing.
7:29–31 Regardless of a person's situation, he or she should live for the Lord. Two realities should heighten our emphasis on such a lifestyle of devotion: **The time is limited** and **the world . . . is passing away**.
7:32–40 In this section Paul shares his motivation for espousing the remain-as-you-are principle for the **unmarried**: the significant change in life status could pose a **distraction** from devotion **to the Lord**.
7:39–40 Newly widowed women were free to marry **in the Lord** (i.e., other believers), but Paul reiterates the virtue of the remain-as-you-are principle. Remaining **as she is** offered the widow the possibility of undistracted devotion to the Lord.
8:1a Now about indicates that Paul is answering a question the Corinthians had asked

him in a previous letter (5:9; 7:1). By custom, Corinthians commonly dined in pagan temples (which were centers for civic activity) or else partook of meat portions that had been offered there. The Corinthian Christians wanted to know if it was permissible to eat **food sacrificed to idols** as they reclined "at banquet" in a pagan temple ("dining in an idol's temple," v. 10) or feasted in a household that had received such things.
8:4–6 Paul's answer that believers technically have the right to eat **food sacrificed to idols** may surprise us, but the logic is sound: idols are a "non-reality" and **there is no God but one**. But his advice on this matter does not stop here (cp. vv. 7–13; and esp. 10:14–22).
8:7–8 Christian freedom should never be flaunted or wielded carelessly. Some in their fellowship could be harmed by seeing Christians partake of food associated with idols.
8:10–12 If a **weak person** saw a knowledgeable believer dining in an **idol's temple**, he

temple, won't his weak conscience be encouraged[A] to eat food offered to idols? [11] So the weak person, the brother or sister for whom Christ died, is ruined[B] by your knowledge. [12] Now when you sin like this against brothers and sisters and wound their weak conscience, you are sinning against Christ. [13] Therefore, if food causes my brother or sister to fall, I will never again eat meat, so that I won't cause my brother or sister to fall.

Paul's Example as an Apostle

9 Am I not free? Am I not an apostle? Have I not seen Jesus our Lord? Are you not my work in the Lord? [2] If I am not an apostle to others, at least I am to you, because you are the seal of my apostleship in the Lord.

[3] My defense to those who examine me is this: [4] Don't we have the right to eat and drink? [5] Don't we have the right to be accompanied by a believing wife[C] like the other apostles, the Lord's brothers, and Cephas? [6] Or do only Barnabas and I have no right to refrain from working? [7] Who serves as a soldier at his own expense? Who plants a vineyard and does not eat its fruit? Or who shepherds a flock and does not drink the milk from the flock? [8] Am I saying this from a human perspective? Doesn't the law also say the same thing? [9] For it is written in the law of Moses, **Do not muzzle an ox while it treads out grain.**[D] Is God really concerned about oxen? [10] Isn't he really saying it for our sake? Yes, this is written for our sake, because he who plows ought to plow in hope, and he who threshes should thresh in hope of sharing the crop. [11] If we have sown spiritual things for you, is it too much if we reap material benefits from you? [12] If others have this right to receive benefits from you, don't we even more? Nevertheless, we have not made use of this right; instead, we endure

everything so that we will not hinder the gospel of Christ.

[13] Don't you know that those who perform the temple services eat the food from the temple, and those who serve at the altar share in the offerings of the altar? [14] In the same way, the Lord has commanded that those who preach the gospel should earn their living by the gospel.

[15] For my part I have used none of these rights, nor have I written these things that they may be applied in my case. For it would be better for me to die than for anyone to deprive me of my boast! [16] For if I preach the gospel, I have no reason to boast, because I am compelled to preach[E] — and woe to me if I do not preach the gospel! [17] For if I do this willingly, I have a reward, but if unwillingly, I am entrusted with a commission. [18] What then is my reward? To preach the gospel and offer it free of charge and not make full use of my rights in the gospel.

[19] Although I am free from all and not anyone's slave, I have made myself a slave to everyone, in order to win more people. [20] To the Jews I became like a Jew, to win Jews; to those under the law, like one under the law — though I myself am not under the law[F] — to win those under the law. [21] To those who are without the law, like one without the law — though I am not without God's law but under the law of Christ — to win those without the law. [22] To the weak I became weak, in order to win the weak. I have become all things to all people, so that I may by every possible means save some. [23] Now I do all this because of the gospel, so that I may share in the blessings.

[24] Don't you know that the runners in a stadium all race, but only one receives the prize? Run in such a way to win the prize. [25] Now everyone who competes exercises self-control in everything. They do it to receive a perishable

---

[A]8:10 Or built up   [B]8:11 Or destroyed   [C]9:5 Lit a sister as a wife   [D]9:9 Dt 25:4   [E]9:16 Lit because necessity is laid upon me
[F]9:20 Other mss omit though I myself am not under the law

---

might attach religious significance to it and become confused about allegiance to Christ.
8:13 Self-limitation by more mature believers safeguards the Christian allegiance of new believers, especially in overtly pagan environments such as Corinth.
9:3–6 Paul's "rights" as an apostle, which were exercised by other apostles, included (1) the right to be compensated for his apostolic service; (2) the right to take a believing wife; and (3) the right to refrain from outside work, devoting himself entirely to ministry.
9:8–11 Paul uses a greater-to-lesser argument to justify his right to an allowance. If he has supplied **spiritual things** (the greater) to the Corinthians, surely he ought to receive **material benefits** (the lesser) from them in return.
9:12 Now Paul uses a lesser-to-greater argument to support his right to a living wage. If those who presently labored among the Corinthians received wages, how much more should the one who had founded the church?

9:13 Paul makes his point here from the Mosaic law.
9:14 The Lord has commanded may refer to Lk 10:4–8, where Jesus says, "The [gospel] worker is worthy of his wages."
9:16–17 I am compelled to preach alludes to Paul's **commission** at Damascus as a "chosen instrument" (Ac 9:15) who had been given a stewardship to discharge the message of the gospel to the nations (1Co 4:1).
9:20–22 The phrase **not without God's law but under the law of Christ** refers to Paul as one who had the right under God's law to receive a wage (cp. 9:8–10), yet among Gentiles he yielded that right.
9:24–27 Like hard-driven runners and boxers, Paul had a single-minded focus. His exercise of **self-control** was aimed at keeping him from being **disqualified**. "Disqualified" does not mean loss of salvation, which Paul elsewhere said is impossible (Rm 8:38–39; cp. Jn 10:28–30), but rather failure to fulfill

crown, but we an imperishable crown. **26** So I do not run like one who runs aimlessly or box like one beating the air. **27** Instead, I discipline my body and bring it under strict control, so that after preaching to others, I myself will not be disqualified.

Warnings from Israel's Past

10 Now I do not want you to be unaware, brothers and sisters, that our ancestors were all under the cloud, all passed through the sea, **2** and all were baptized into Moses in the cloud and in the sea. **3** They all ate the same spiritual food, **4** and all drank the same spiritual drink. For they drank from the spiritual rock that followed them, and that rock was Christ. **5** Nevertheless God was not pleased with most of them, since they were struck down in the wilderness.

6 Now these things took place as examples for us, so that we will not desire evil things as they did.^A **7** Don't become idolaters as some of them were; as it is written, **The people sat down to eat and drink, and got up to party.**^B,C **8** Let us not commit sexual immorality as some of them did,^D and in a single day twenty-three thousand people died. **9** Let us not test Christ as some of them did^E and were destroyed by snakes. **10** And don't grumble as some of them did,^F and were killed by the destroyer.^G **11** These things happened to them as examples, and they were written for our instruction, on whom the ends of the ages^H have come. **12** So, whoever thinks he stands must be careful not to fall. **13** No temptation has come upon you except what is common to humanity. But God is faithful; he will not allow you to be tempted beyond what you are able, but with the temptation he will also provide the way out so that you may be able to bear it.

Warning against Idolatry

14 So then, my dear friends, flee from idolatry. **15** I am speaking as to sensible people. Judge for yourselves what I am saying. **16** The cup of blessing that we bless, is it not a sharing in the blood of Christ? The bread that we break, is it not a sharing in the body of Christ? **17** Because there is one bread, we who are many are one body, since all of us share the one bread. **18** Consider the people of Israel.^I Do not those who eat the sacrifices participate in the altar? **19** What am I saying then? That food sacrificed to idols is anything, or that an idol is anything? **20** No, but I do say that what they^J sacrifice, they sacrifice to demons and not to God. I do not want you to be participants with demons! **21** You cannot drink the cup of the Lord and the cup of demons. You cannot share in the Lord's table and the table of demons. **22** Or are we provoking the Lord to jealousy? Are we stronger than he?

Christian Liberty

23 "Everything is permissible,"^K but not everything is beneficial. "Everything is permissible,"^K but not everything builds up. **24** No one is to seek his own good, but the good of the other person.

25 Eat everything that is sold in the meat market, without raising questions for the sake of conscience, **26** since **the earth is the Lord's, and all that is in it.**^L **27** If any of the unbelievers invites you over and you want to go, eat everything that is set before you, without raising questions for the sake of conscience. **28** But if someone says to you, "This is food from a sacrifice," do not eat it, out of consideration

---

^A **10:6** Lit *they desired*   ^B **10:7** Or *to dance*   ^C **10:7** Ex 32:6   ^D **10:8** Lit *them committed sexual immorality*   ^E **10:9** Lit *them tested*   ^F **10:10** Lit *them grumbled*   ^G **10:10** Or *the destroying angel*   ^H **10:11** Or *goals of the ages*, or *culmination of the ages*   ^I **10:18** Lit *Look at Israel according to the flesh*   ^J **10:20** Other mss read *Gentiles*   ^K **10:23** Other mss add *for me*   ^L **10:26** Ps 24:1

---

his God-given commission to evangelize the nations (Ac 9:15; 13:2; Rm 1:1).
9:26b–27 Paul viewed his boxing opponent as his own **body**. When it resisted giving up rights and liberties, he brought it under **strict control** (lit "I enslave it").
10:1–5 To make vivid the possibility of disqualification, Paul drew on the exodus (Ex 12–17). Those Hebrews enjoyed unique access to God (**were all under the cloud** of God's presence and **were baptized into Moses**), and yet **most of them . . . were struck down**. The phrase **they all ate the same spiritual food** points back to God's daily provision for Israel in the wilderness (Dt 8:14–15).
10:6–10 The phrase **now these things** refers to the idolatrous activity of the wilderness generation that provoked God to cut them down (v. 5). The prohibition **don't become idolaters as some of them were** is emphatic in the Greek and becomes the paradigm for three exhortations: (1) do **not commit sexual immorality** (cp. Nm 25:1–18, esp. v. 9), (2) do **not test Christ** (cp.

Nm 21:5–6), and (3) do not **grumble** (cp. Ex 12:23; Nm 16:41–50). In all three of these OT examples, God judged and destroyed the people for their sins.
10:16–17 Paul wanted the Corinthians to know that participants at the Lord's Supper represent a unified body that is dependent on the death of Christ. The phrase **because there is one bread, we who are many are one body** refers to the individual members who make up one corporate body, the church (12:12–27).
10:18–22 Actual "idolatry" (v. 14) is in view here, not merely partaking of foods offered to idols (8:1–13). Participation in idolatrous rites is a violation of the believer's union with Christ and thus with the one-body relationship that they had with other believers.
10:18–19 People of Israel (lit "Israel according to the flesh") in the present context refers ultimately to the sinful wilderness generation. Likewise, Paul's reference to **the altar** probably alludes to Ex 32:5–6 (cited in 1Co 10:7), which recounts Aaron's building of an altar in front of the idol, the golden calf.

10:20–21 Paul prohibited participation in pagan ritualistic meals because this involved intimacy with **demons**. He continued to affirm the nonreality of idols as deities (8:4–6), but demons are both real and powerful. The word **they** refers back to idolatrous Israel in the wilderness (cp. v. 18, "the people of Israel") when they overlooked demonic presence, just as the Corinthian believers were tempted to do.
10:24–26 In what may seem a surprising twist, Paul said seeking **the good of the other person** (v. 24) meant a believer who objected to buying meat that had been sacrificed to idols should not interrogate the meat sellers in order to certify that the meat had no association with idolatry. Paul offered scriptural support for this position from Ps 24:1: "**The earth is the Lord's, and all that is in it.**" Therefore, partake of the meat out of gratitude and a clear conscience.
10:27 The rule for eating in a pagan home is the same as in the meat market.
10:28–29a Paul prohibited eating meat if someone bothered explicitly to point

for the one who told you, and for the sake of conscience.^A ^29 I do not mean your own conscience, but the other person's. For why is my freedom judged by another person's conscience? ^30 If I partake with thanksgiving, why am I criticized because of something for which I give thanks?

^31 So, whether you eat or drink, or whatever you do, do everything for the glory of God. ^32 Give no offense to Jews or Greeks or the church of God, ^33 just as I also try to please everyone in everything, not seeking my own benefit, but the benefit of many, so that they may be saved. ^1 Imitate me, as I also imitate Christ.

Instructions about Head Coverings

^2 Now I praise you^B because you remember me in everything and hold fast to the traditions just as I delivered them to you. ^3 But I want you to know that Christ is the head of every man, and the man is the head of the woman,^C and God is the head of Christ. ^4 Every man who prays or prophesies with something on his head dishonors his head. ^5 Every woman who prays or prophesies with her head uncovered dishonors her head, since that is one and the same as having her head shaved. ^6 For if a woman doesn't cover her head, she should have her hair cut off. But if it is disgraceful for a woman to have her hair cut off or her head shaved, let her head be covered.

^7 A man should not cover his head, because he is the image and glory of God. So too, woman is the glory of man. ^8 For man did not come from woman, but woman came from man. ^9 Neither was man created for the sake of woman, but woman for the sake of man. ^10 This is why a woman should have a symbol of authority on her head, because of the angels. ^11 In the Lord, however, woman is not independent of man, and man is not independent of woman. ^12 For just as woman came from man, so man comes through woman, and all things come from God.

^13 Judge for yourselves: Is it proper for a woman to pray to God with her head uncovered? ^14 Does not even nature itself teach you that if a man has long hair it is a disgrace to him, ^15 but that if a woman has long hair, it is her glory? For her hair is given to her^D as a covering. ^16 If anyone wants to argue about this, we have no other^E custom, nor do the churches of God.

---

^A 10:28 Other mss add *"For the earth is the Lord's and all that is in it."* ^B 11:2 Other mss add *brothers,* ^C 11:3 Or *the husband is the head of the wife* ^D 11:15 Other mss omit *to her* ^E 11:16 Or *no such*

---

out, **"This is food from a sacrifice"** (Gk *hierothutos*, "meat devoted to a divinity"). This rare Greek term was used by pagans to designate meat devoted to a particular god. In this situation, the food's history did matter because the person who pointed it out (whether he be a nonbelieving Gentile or a Christian of weak conscience) apparently felt that a Christian eating such meat would be compromising his allegiance to Christ.
10:29b–30 After a parenthetical interruption that explains an exception to one's freedom (vv. 28–29a), these rhetorical questions introduce the basis for the believers' freedom to eat whatever is given them without questions of conscience.
10:31–33 People who wish to **do everything for the glory of God** cannot succeed if they act in disregard for others.
11:1 Paul's admonition to **imitate** him was justified insomuch as he was an apt imitator of **Christ** (4:16).
11:2 Paul seems to be giving his readers general praise to prepare them for his criticism for the areas in chaps. 11–14 in which he needs to correct them.
11:3 Paul issued a principle for application in corporate worship—the principle of voluntary submission to authority. The phrase **head of every man** means "authority over." That **the man** (husband) **is the head of the woman** (wife) reflects NT teaching from both Paul (Eph 5:22–33; Col 3:18–19) and Peter (1Pet 3:1–7). **God is the head of Christ** refers to the Father's authority over the incarnate Messiah, who as the God-man voluntarily submitted to God.
11:4 The situation in this verse assumes a public setting where corporate worship was taking place. Paul applied the principle ("Christ is the head of every man") to the

praying man. Outward manifestations of piety should not dishonor a believing man's head ("Christ"). The phrase **with something on his head** is literally "having down alongside the head." This refers not to a hat but to the Roman practice of pulling down the toga over the head while bowing for pagan worship, to prevent distractions. Because of the association of this practice with pagan worship, a male believer dishonored his true head ("Christ") when he covered his physical head with the toga. By imitating pagan practice, he shamed Christ and himself.
11:5a In the first century, a woman would speak **with her head uncovered** only in private settings or at pagan clubs meeting in private homes. Paul did not give a reason why women in the church at Corinth were uncovered. It may be that they brought into the church religious practices that paralleled habits in the pagan meetings.
11:5b–6 Paul explains why a Corinthian woman's uncovered head dishonored her head. A woman who prayed or prophesied with her head uncovered was **one and the same** with the one **having her head shaved**. Paul equated the shame of a "head uncovered" (imitating the practice in pagan private religious clubs) with the shame of a person who publicly expressed pagan dedication (i.e., to have her hair cut off or her head shaved). Pagan women at Corinth sometimes sheared their hair and dedicated their locks as a token of worship or fulfillment of a vow to a god. In the Corinthian setting, the "uncovered head" paralleled practices in pagan clubs and thus blurred the divisions between devotion to the true God and false gods, resulting in dishonor to a believing woman's husband and to Christ.
11:7a A man's uncovered head honored his head because it permitted the immediacy

of his reflection of **the image and glory of God**. Therefore, he **should not cover his head** in imitation of pagan practice.
11:7b–9 Paul's second reason for saying a woman's uncovered head dishonored her head is that the first woman was created from man (Gn 2:21–22). Woman completes man in God's created order in the sense that man mirrors the image of God, and woman reflects **the glory of man**. This does not mean woman is inferior to man. She completes God's creation of man as male and female (Gn 1:27), and brings glory to man (Gn 2:23).
11:10 This third reason why a woman's uncovered head dishonored her head is difficult to interpret. Perhaps the church's witness to the angelic hosts (Eph 3:10) would be adversely affected by an uncovered female head. The phrase **authority on her head** seems to refer to an outward symbol that signified to **the angels** her deference to leadership.
11:11–16 These verses have yielded various interpretations. Though Paul addresses the man's headship role in marriage (v. 3), which is rooted in creation (v. 8), he also acknowledges that men and women are **not independent** of one another. In the beginning, **woman** was formed **from man** (see Gn 2:21–23). But through childbirth, man also **comes through woman**. And **all things come from God**—including gender distinctions. For a woman in Corinth to pray with **her head uncovered** was to deny these distinctions. Regardless of the specific local cultural expressions, to deny male/female differences in worship would be improper (1Co 11:13), contrary to **nature** (vv. 14–15), and in opposition to the practices of all **the churches** (v. 16).

The Lord's Supper

[17] Now in giving this instruction I do not praise you, since you come together not for the better but for the worse. [18] For to begin with, I hear that when you come together as a church there are divisions among you, and in part I believe it. [19] Indeed, it is necessary that there be factions among you, so that those who are approved may be recognized among you. [20] When you come together, then, it is not to eat the Lord's Supper. [21] For at the meal, each one eats his own supper.[A] So one person is hungry while another gets drunk! [22] Don't you have homes in which to eat and drink? Or do you despise the church of God and humiliate those who have nothing? What should I say to you? Should I praise you? I do not praise you in this matter!

[23] For I received from the Lord what I also passed on to you: On the night when he was betrayed, the Lord Jesus took bread, [24] and when he had given thanks, broke it, and said,[B] "This is my body, which is[C] for you. Do this in remembrance of me."

[25] In the same way also he took the cup, after supper, and said, "This cup is the new covenant in my blood. Do this, as often as you drink it, in remembrance of me." [26] For as often as you eat this bread and drink the cup, you proclaim the Lord's death until he comes.

Self-Examination

[27] So, then, whoever eats the bread or drinks the cup of the Lord in an unworthy manner will be guilty of sin against the body[D] and blood of the Lord. [28] Let a person examine himself; in this way let him eat the bread and drink from the cup. [29] For whoever eats and drinks without recognizing the body,[E] eats and drinks judgment on himself. [30] This is why many are sick and ill among you, and many have fallen asleep. [31] If we were properly judging ourselves, we would not be judged, [32] but when we are judged by the Lord, we are disciplined, so that we may not be condemned with the world.

[33] Therefore, my brothers and sisters, when you come together to eat, welcome one another.[F] [34] If anyone is hungry, he should eat at home, so that when you gather together you will not come under judgment. I will give instructions about the other matters whenever I come.

Diversity of Spiritual Gifts

12 Now concerning spiritual gifts:[G] brothers and sisters, I do not want you to be unaware. [2] You know that when you were pagans, you used to be enticed and led astray by mute idols. [3] Therefore I want you to know that no one speaking by the Spirit of God says, "Jesus is cursed," and no one can say, "Jesus is Lord," except by the Holy Spirit.

[4] Now there are different gifts, but the same Spirit. [5] There are different ministries, but the same Lord. [6] And there are different activities, but the same God works all of them in each person. [7] A manifestation of the Spirit is given to each person for the common good: [8] to one is given a message of wisdom through the Spirit, to another, a message of knowledge by the same Spirit, [9] to another, faith by the same Spirit, to another, gifts of healing by the one Spirit, [10] to another, the performing of miracles, to another, prophecy, to another, distinguishing between spirits, to another, different kinds of tongues,[H] to another, interpretation of tongues. [11] One and the same Spirit is active in all these, distributing to each person as he wills.

Unity Yet Diversity in the Body

[12] For just as the body is one and has many parts, and all the parts of that body, though many, are one body — so also is Christ. [13] For we were all baptized by[I] one Spirit into one body — whether Jews or Greeks, whether slaves or free — and we were all given one Spirit to drink. [14] Indeed, the body is not one part but many. [15] If the foot should say, "Because I'm not a hand, I don't belong to the body," it is not for that reason any less a part of the body. [16] And if the ear should say, "Because I'm not an eye, I don't belong to the body," it is not for that reason any less a part of the body. [17] If the whole body were an eye, where would the hearing be? If the whole body were an ear, where would

---

[A]11:21 Or *eats his own supper ahead of others*   [B]11:24 Other mss add *"Take, eat.*   [C]11:24 Other mss add *broken*   [D]11:27 Lit *be guilty of the body*   [E]11:29 Other mss read *drinks unworthily, not discerning the Lord's body*   [F]11:33 Or *wait for one another*   [G]12:1 Or *spiritual things*, or *spiritual people*   [H]12:10 languages   [I]12:13 Or *with*, or *in*

11:17–18 Paul chided the Corinthian believers for their inappropriate, divisive behavior when they came **together as a church** (cp. v. 20). The word *church* refers to their assembly as a unified, corporate body. In the NT, "church" never refers to a building or place of meeting.

11:19 The **approved . . . among you** refers to those who were not the cause of divisions within the body. Their behavior was exemplary during a time of strife.

11:23–25 **I received from the Lord** most likely means Paul was given a special revelation from Jesus about this matter.

11:30–32 Asleep is a term Paul and other biblical authors use for physical death (cp. 15:18; Jn 11:11; Ac 7:60).

12:4–11a The Spirit according to his will distributes a diversity of gifts to the body for its common benefit.

12:4–6 The same triune God brings about a variety of gifts and manifests diverse ministries within the corporate body. The **different gifts . . . ministries**, and **activities** within the unified church reflect the essential unity and unified work of the persons of the Godhead (vv. 6,11,24,27–28)—the same **Spirit**, the same **Lord**, the same **God**.

12:7–10 Each **manifestation of the Spirit** in a believer **is given** by God for the mutual benefit of the whole body of believers (cp. vv. 12–31). "Manifestation of the Spirit" refers to gifts, ministries, and activities made possible by the Spirit's enabling power (vv. 8–10). Similar lists of spiritual gifts are given in v. 28; Rm 12:6–8; Eph 4:11; and 1Pt 4:10–11.

12:12 Christ is compressed language for "the body of Christ," the church (cp. vv. 27–28).

12:15–16 Paul personified body parts as speakers to express the absurdity of envy and self-deprecation among members of the physical human body. Some Corinthians

the sense of smell be? **18** But as it is, God has arranged each one of the parts in the body just as he wanted. **19** And if they were all the same part, where would the body be? **20** As it is, there are many parts, but one body. **21** The eye cannot say to the hand, "I don't need you!" Or again, the head can't say to the feet, "I don't need you!" **22** On the contrary, those parts of the body that are weaker are indispensable. **23** And those parts of the body that we consider less honorable, we clothe these with greater honor, and our unrespectable parts are treated with greater respect, **24** which our respectable parts do not need.

Instead, God has put the body together, giving greater honor to the less honorable, **25** so that there would be no division in the body, but that the members would have the same concern for each other. **26** So if one member suffers, all the members suffer with it; if one member is honored, all the members rejoice with it.

27 Now you are the body of Christ, and individual members of it. **28** And God has appointed these in the church: first apostles, second prophets, third teachers, next miracles, then gifts of healing, helping, leading, various kinds of tongues.^A **29** Are all apostles? Are all prophets? Are all teachers? Do all do miracles? **30** Do all have gifts of healing? Do all speak in tongues? Do all interpret? **31** But desire the greater gifts. And I will show you an even better way.

Love: The Superior Way

13 If I speak human or angelic tongues^B but do not have love, I am a noisy gong or a clanging cymbal. **2** If I have the gift of prophecy and understand all mysteries and all knowledge, and if I have all faith so that I can move mountains but do not have love, I am nothing. **3** And if I give away all my possessions, and if

I give over my body in order to boast^C but do not have love, I gain nothing.

4 Love is patient, love is kind. Love does not envy, is not boastful, is not arrogant, **5** is not rude, is not self-seeking, is not irritable, and does not keep a record of wrongs. **6** Love finds no joy in unrighteousness but rejoices in the truth. **7** It bears all things, believes all things, hopes all things, endures all things.

8 Love never ends. But as for prophecies, they will come to an end; as for tongues, they will cease; as for knowledge, it will come to an end. **9** For we know in part, and we prophesy in part, **10** but when the perfect comes, the partial will come to an end. **11** When I was a child, I spoke like a child, I thought like a child, I reasoned like a child. When I became a man, I put aside childish things. **12** For now we see only a reflection^D as in a mirror, but then face to face. Now I know in part, but then I will know fully, as I am fully known. **13** Now these three remain: faith, hope, and love—but the greatest of these is love.

Prophecy: A Superior Gift

14 Pursue love and desire spiritual gifts, and especially that you may prophesy. **2** For the person who speaks in a tongue^E is not speaking to people but to God, since no one understands him; he speaks mysteries in the Spirit.^F **3** On the other hand, the person who prophesies speaks to people for their strengthening,^G encouragement, and consolation. **4** The person who speaks in a tongue builds himself up, but the one who prophesies builds up the church. **5** I wish all of you spoke in tongues,^H but even more that you prophesied. The person who prophesies is greater than the person who speaks in tongues, unless he interprets so that the church may be built up.

6 So now, brothers and sisters, if I come to you speaking in tongues, how will I benefit

---

^A**12:28** languages, also in v. 30 ^B**13:1** languages, also in v. 8 ^C**13:3** Other mss read *body to be burned* ^D**13:12** Lit *we see indirectly* ^E**14:2** Or *another language*, also in vv. 4,13,14,19,26,27 ^F**14:2** Or *in spirit*, or *in his spirit* ^G**14:3** Lit *building up* ^H**14:5** Or *other languages*, also in vv. 6,18,21,22,23,39

---

apparently fell into grading the gifts, attaching importance to public, showy gifts (such as the gift of utterance), and relative unimportance to less observable gifts.
12:18 The dispersion and diversification of gifts is no accident. God himself has given them **just as he wanted**.
12:19–20 Many parts, but one body encapsulates our identity as individuals enfolded into the corporate body of Christ.
12:23–26 We clothe **unrespectable parts** (private areas) of the human body, which we regard as **less honorable**, thus according them **greater respect**. Similarly, God has arranged the body of Christ in such a way that the "less honorable" members are accorded "greater honor."
12:28 Church here refers not just to the local body of believers at Corinth but to the universal church, composed of all believers everywhere and from every age. **God has**

appointed emphasizes that no one can justly appoint themselves to positions within the body. The appointments are God's prerogative alone. **First . . . second . . . third** gives us a glimpse at the priority of roles during the early church era.
12:29–30 In a series of rhetorical questions, Paul emphasizes that no gift is normative.
12:31a Paul concludes by exhorting the Corinthian church to emphasize the **greater gifts** that have more direct edification for the assembled body.
12:31b–13:3 And I will show you an even better way introduces the discussion about the relationship of love to the exercise of gifts within the corporate body. Paul uses three hyperboles to show that gifts without love are pointless.
13:4–5 Paul personifies love in order to show its daily character and choices. Love is not self-centered but other-focused.

13:6b Contrary to common perception, love is not marked by tolerance for error.
13:8–13 Many aspects of church life will end at the end of this current age, but **love never ends**. This permanence signals love's priority within the church.
13:10 The perfect refers to the next age, the eternal age when Messiah reigns.
13:11 Paul uses the analogy of infancy versus adulthood to explain the contrast between our present understanding and the understanding we will have in the next age.
13:13 Of **faith, hope, and love**, love is the **greatest** because it continues into the next age. Both faith and hope will be fulfilled in eternity, and so will not remain.
14:1–4 Paul valued prophecy over uninterpreted tongues (Gk *glossai;* cp. 12:10). Utterance gifts should be exercised only for the edification and exhortation of others. The phrase **no one understands him** refers to

you unless I speak to you with a revelation or knowledge or prophecy or teaching? [7] Even lifeless instruments that produce sounds — whether flute or harp — if they don't make a distinction in the notes, how will what is played on the flute or harp be recognized? [8] In fact, if the bugle makes an unclear sound, who will prepare for battle? [9] In the same way, unless you use your tongue for intelligible speech, how will what is spoken be known? For you will be speaking into the air. [10] There are doubtless many different kinds of languages in the world, none is without meaning. [11] Therefore, if I do not know the meaning of the language, I will be a foreigner[A] to the speaker, and the speaker will be a foreigner to me. [12] So also you — since you are zealous for spiritual gifts,[B] seek to excel in building up the church.

[13] Therefore the person who speaks in a tongue should pray that he can interpret. [14] For if I pray in a tongue, my spirit prays, but my understanding is unfruitful. [15] What then? I will pray with the spirit, and I will also pray with my understanding. I will sing praise with the spirit, and I will also sing praise with my understanding. [16] Otherwise, if you praise with the spirit,[C] how will the outsider[D] say "Amen" at your giving of thanks, since he does not know what you are saying? [17] For you may very well be giving thanks, but the other person is not being built up. [18] I thank God that I speak in tongues more than all of you; [19] yet in the church I would rather speak five words with my understanding, in order to teach others also, than ten thousand words in a tongue.

[20] Brothers and sisters, don't be childish in your thinking, but be infants in regard to evil and adult in your thinking. [21] It is written in the law,

I will speak to this people
by people of other tongues
and by the lips of foreigners,

and even then, they will not listen to me,[E]

says the Lord. [22] Speaking in tongues, then, is intended as a sign, not for believers but for unbelievers, while prophecy is not for unbelievers but for believers. [23] If, therefore, the whole church assembles together and all are speaking in tongues and people who are outsiders or unbelievers come in, will they not say that you are out of your minds? [24] But if all are prophesying and some unbeliever or outsider comes in, he is convicted by all and is called to account by all. [25] The secrets of his heart will be revealed, and as a result he will fall facedown and worship God, proclaiming, "God is really among you."

Order in Church Meetings

[26] What then, brothers and sisters? Whenever you come together, each one[F] has a hymn, a teaching, a revelation, a tongue, or an interpretation. Everything is to be done for building up. [27] If anyone speaks in a tongue, there are to be only two, or at the most three, each in turn, and let someone interpret. [28] But if there is no interpreter, that person is to keep silent in the church and speak to himself and God. [29] Two or three prophets should speak, and the others should evaluate. [30] But if something has been revealed to another person sitting there, the first prophet should be silent. [31] For you can all prophesy one by one, so that everyone may learn and everyone may be encouraged. [32] And the prophets' spirits are subject to the prophets, [33] since God is not a God of disorder but of peace.

As in all the churches of the saints, [34] the women[G] should be silent in the churches, for they are not permitted to speak, but are to submit themselves, as the law also says. [35] If they want to learn something, let them ask their own husbands at home, since it is disgraceful for a woman to speak in the church. [36] Or did the word of God originate from you, or did it come to you only?

[A]**14:11** Gk *barbaros*, or *barbarian*   [B]**14:12** Lit *zealous of spirits*   [C]**14:16** Or *praise by the Spirit*   [D]**14:16** Lit *the one filling the place of the uninformed*   [E]**14:21** Is 28:11–12   [F]**14:26** Other mss add *of you*   [G]**14:34** Other mss read *your women*

---

the uselessness of uninterpreted tongues for the corporate body.

14:11 Just as the **foreigner** is estranged by those speaking a language he does not know, so too members of the body of Christ become estranged from one another if unintelligible, untranslated tongues are spoken in the church.

14:13–19 This section includes an apostolic ruling in which Paul declares the necessity of intelligibility over untranslated tongues for edification of the church body.

14:15–17 The legitimacy of a person's speech in the midst of the congregation is measured by the edification it brings the body of Christ. Speeches, prayers of blessing, and expressions of thanksgiving cannot edify the body if they are unintelligible. Paul's statement, **I will pray with the spirit, and I will**

also pray with my understanding, means he will pray in a way that is both intelligible to bystanders and drawn from his spirit.

14:18 I thank (Gk *eucharistō*) can express either thanksgiving to God ("I give thanks") or prayer ("I pray with thanksgiving"). **More than all of you** indicates that Paul was not merely speaking from theory in his instructions about **tongues** and their proper practice in the church.

14:21–22 Drawing on Is 28:11–12, Paul states that uninterpreted **tongues** serve as a **sign** of God's impending "strange work" of judgment to unbelievers (Is 28:11,21). In Is 28, the leaders of Judah rejected as unintelligible nonsense Isaiah's message that would have given Jerusalem rest from their enemies.

14:23–25 Paul warned the Corinthians that practicing **tongues** carelessly would

be harmful to **outsiders** and **unbelievers**. Churchwide **prophesying**, however, would serve to convict and convert visitors.

14:29–32 That Paul instructed people with the gift of prophecy to speak in turn and then await evaluation by others in attendance suggests that the kind of "prophecy" in view here is not predictive or a foretelling of future events.

14:34–35 During assemblies of the church at Corinth, **women** were **not permitted to speak** in the process of evaluating prophetic utterances (vv. 29–30,37). For the sake of propriety and order, they were to **ask their own husbands** in private at home about what was spoken. These verses should not be taken as a prohibition against women speaking in church. To say otherwise contradicts Paul elsewhere (e.g., 11:5).

37 If anyone thinks he is a prophet or spiritual, he should recognize that what I write to you is the Lord's command. **38** If anyone ignores this, he will be ignored.^A **39** So then, my brothers and sisters, be eager to prophesy, and do not forbid speaking in tongues. **40** But everything is to be done decently and in order.

Resurrection Essential to the Gospel

15 Now I want to make clear for you, brothers and sisters, the gospel I preached to you, which you received, on which you have taken your stand **2** and by which you are being saved, if you hold to the message I preached to you — unless you believed in vain. **3** For I passed on to you as most important what I also received: that Christ died for our sins according to the Scriptures, **4** that he was buried, that he was raised on the third day according to the Scriptures, **5** and that he appeared to Cephas, then to the Twelve. **6** Then he appeared to over five hundred brothers and sisters at one time; most of them are still alive, but some have fallen asleep. **7** Then he appeared to James, then to all the apostles. **8** Last of all, as to one born at the wrong time,^B he also appeared to me.

9 For I am the least of the apostles, not worthy to be called an apostle, because I persecuted the church of God. **10** But by the grace of God I am what I am, and his grace toward me was not in vain. On the contrary, I worked harder than any of them, yet not I, but the grace of God that was with me. **11** Whether, then, it is I or they, so we proclaim and so you have believed.

Resurrection Essential to the Faith

12 Now if Christ is proclaimed as raised from the dead, how can some of you say, "There is no resurrection of the dead"? **13** If there is no resurrection of the dead, then not even Christ has been raised; **14** and if Christ has not been raised, then our proclamation is in vain, and so is your faith.^C **15** Moreover, we are found to be false witnesses about God, because we have testified wrongly about God that he raised up Christ — whom he did not raise up, if in fact the dead are not raised. **16** For if the dead are not raised, not even Christ has been raised. **17** And if Christ has not been raised, your faith is worthless; you are still in your sins. **18** Those, then, who have fallen asleep in Christ have also perished. **19** If we have put our hope in Christ for this life only, we should be pitied more than anyone.

Christ's Resurrection Guarantees Ours

20 But as it is, Christ has been raised from the dead, the firstfruits of those who have fallen asleep. **21** For since death came through a man, the resurrection of the dead also comes through a man. **22** For just as in Adam all die, so also in Christ all will be made alive.

23 But each in his own order: Christ, the firstfruits; afterward, at his coming, those who belong to Christ. **24** Then comes the end, when he hands over the kingdom to God the Father, when he abolishes all rule and all authority and power. **25** For he must reign until he puts all his enemies under his feet. **26** The last enemy to be abolished is death. **27** For **God has put everything under his feet.**^D Now when it says "everything" is put under him, it is obvious that he who puts everything under him is the exception. **28** When everything is subject to Christ, then the Son himself will also be subject to the one who subjected everything to him, so that God may be all in all.

Resurrection Supported by Christian Experience

29 Otherwise what will they do who are being baptized for the dead?^E If the dead are not

---

^A **14:38** Other mss read *he should be ignored*   ^B **15:8** Or *one whose birth was unusual*   ^C **15:14** Or *proclamation is useless, and your faith also is useless*, or *proclamation is empty, and your faith also is empty*   ^D **15:27** Ps 8:6; 110:1   ^E **15:29** Or *baptized on account of the dead*

14:37–38 Those who were truly prophets would discern that Paul's principles for the orderly exercise of prophetic gifts were consistent with the **Lord's command**. It is unclear exactly what is meant by **will be ignored**. Possibly it means those wishing to conduct services correctly will disregard those clamoring to do otherwise.

15:1–58 This chapter represents the most comprehensive discussion of resurrection in the Bible.

15:1–2 Paul wants to **make clear** in the sense of reminding them. They are **being saved** by **the gospel**. Like the kingdom, salvation has both an "already" and a "not yet" quality to it.

15:3–4 These verses recount the basic gospel message as Paul delivered it in town after town.

15:5–11 Early Christian evangelists validated the certainty of Jesus's resurrection by recounting his post-tomb appearances to authoritative eyewitnesses (e.g., Ac 2:32). Paul refers to himself as **one born at the**

wrong time due to his late arrival in the chain of eyewitnesses to Christ's resurrection (Ac 9:1–6).

15:12 Though it is uncertain what caused some Corinthian believers to deny the **resurrection of the dead**, Greeks viewed bodily death as final, with some saying the spirit survived disembodied. This view likely influenced the church at Corinth.

15:13–15 If Christ were not raised, then apostolic preaching of the resurrection was **in vain**, the Corinthians' **faith** was void, and the apostles were **false witnesses**. "Faith" here refers to the content of the gospel message and is synonymous with "system of beliefs."

15:20 Firstfruits refers to the guarantee that Christ's resurrection is the first-of-a-kind resurrection that promises others will follow in the end time (cp. Rm 8:23, where "firstfruits" can be translated "guarantee," "first installment"). In this instance the phrase **who have fallen asleep** refers specifically to those who have died in Christ.

For more general usage of "fallen asleep," see note at 11:30–32.

15:21–22 Paul presents a parallel of necessary effects. Through one man, **Adam**, death came to humanity. If this is ever to be reversed, it must be done through like kind: a man. God has appointed just such a man: Jesus **Christ**, who is fully divine and fully human. The second occurrence of the word **all** refers to all those who are joined to Christ through faith.

15:24–28 The Son as the resurrected Messiah will conquer and subdue everything, including the last enemy—**death**. By saying **he must reign**, Paul touches on the set-in-stone divine plan assuring us that history will end in just this way: with God triumphant now in just this way: with God triumphant and all evil and God's people reigning with Christ forever (1Tm 2:12).

15:29 Being baptized for the dead probably refers to the practice, apparently unique to the Corinthian church, of someone undergoing baptism on behalf of a believer who

❚ Resurrection and the Christian Worldview

by Josh D. Chatraw

Through the resurrection we encounter God's promise of personal, holistic salvation, a promise that includes a bodily existence redeemed in nature and eternal in scope. It is an alluring doctrine that stands in contrast to a common, recurring view of eternal life: a depersonalized and disembodied soul. Yet despite its centrality to the rapid rise of Christianity and of later theological reflection, the claim of Jesus's resurrection was a surprising development in its historical context.

History

The future resurrection of all those redeemed by Christ is rooted in the claim that Jesus himself was crucified and raised from the dead. This belief was unlikely to gain headway in the first-century Greco-Roman world. On the one hand, pagan philosophers held to a dualistic view of the world that prized the nonmaterial and denigrated the physical. Considering the resurrection of a dead corpse unacceptable, their hope instead was to escape the body, not to see it redeemed. On the other hand, the Jews affirmed a bodily resurrection (though not all Jews did). They looked forward to a corporate resurrection of all the faithful at the end of the world. But by no means were they expecting the resurrection of a single person—after which the present world would continue (see N. T. Wright, *The Resurrection of the Son of God [Minneapolis: Fortress, 2003]*).

Neither first-century Jews nor Gentiles were looking for a dead Messiah to rise again. This explains why, in the Gospels, even Jesus's disciples were confused when he informed them of his coming death and resurrection. Jesus's resurrection was surprising and certainly not something a Jew would have conjured up in hopes of convincing a skeptical first-century world. It was a challenging claim, and the early disciples knew they could not escape its public and outlandish nature.

Evident in the Gospels and throughout the New Testament (e.g., 1Co 15:1–9), eyewitness testimony served as the impetus for the proclamation of resurrection. The public confession "He is risen" has echoed down through history and to the nations, changing not only history itself but also transforming lives and communities throughout the world.

Christology

It is difficult to understand the early devotion to and worship of Jesus if such behavior is separated from a sincere belief that Jesus had risen from the grave. Devout first-century Jews were staunch monotheists. While they believed in a host of heavenly beings (e.g., angels), they only worshiped one God, the Creator and Ruler of the universe (Richard Bauckham, *Jesus and the God of Israel [Grand Rapids: Eerdmans, 2008]*, 1–59). Any change in this central belief, then, would seemingly have had to come through a long, gradual shift. Instead, soon after Jesus's death, this group of conservative Jews began to "define and reverence Jesus with reference to the one God" (Larry Hurtado, *Lord Jesus Christ [Grand Rapids: Eerdmans, 2003]*, 151).

This rapid shift took place for several reasons. Firsthand experiences with Jesus, reflections on his teachings, and careful rereading of the Hebrew Scriptures played an important role. But their rereading of the Scriptures, re-evaluation of Jesus's teachings, and—most importantly—their worship of Jesus are difficult to accept without the presence of a dramatic, paradigm-shifting event: Jesus's resurrection.

Creation, New Creation, and Salvation

Within the biblical storyline, Jesus's resurrection points both backward to creation and forward to the new creation (Oliver O'Donovan, *Resurrection and Moral Order [Grand Rapids: Eerdmans, 1994]*, 56–57). The resurrection of the whole person reaffirms the original goodness of God's created order. Furthermore, although sin has distorted creation, Jesus's resurrection reasserts God's commitment to his world and to the coming of a new creation. Christianity, then, is not bent on escaping the physical world but delighting and finding purpose in God's creation.

In the narratives of Jesus's resurrection, we see a mysterious picture of continuity and discontinuity between our world and the new creation to come. The disciples can touch his resurrected body and see the holes in his side. Jesus eats food and interacts as a

raised at all, then why are people baptized for them?^30 Why are we in danger every hour?^31 I face death every day, as surely as I may boast about you, brothers and sisters, in Christ Jesus our Lord. ^32 If I fought wild beasts in Ephesus as a mere man, what good did that do me? If the dead are not raised, **Let us eat and drink, for tomorrow we die.**^B ^33 Do not be deceived: "Bad company corrupts good morals." ^34 Come to your senses^c and stop sinning; for some people are ignorant about God. I say this to your shame.

The Nature of the Resurrection Body

^35 But someone will ask, "How are the dead raised? What kind of body will they have when they come?" ^36 You fool! What you sow does not come to life unless it dies. ^37 And as for what you sow—you are not sowing the body that will be, but only a seed, perhaps of wheat or another

grain. ^38 But God gives it a body as he wants, and to each of the seeds its own body. ^39 Not all flesh is the same flesh; there is one flesh for humans, another for animals, another for birds, and another for fish. ^40 There are heavenly bodies and earthly bodies, but the splendor of the heavenly bodies is different from that of the earthly ones. ^41 There is a splendor of the sun, another of the moon, and another of the stars; in fact, one star differs from another star in splendor. ^42 So it is with the resurrection of the dead: Sown in corruption, raised in incorruption; ^43 sown in dishonor, raised in glory; sown in weakness, raised in power; ^44 sown a natural body, raised a spiritual body. If there is a natural body, there is also a spiritual body. ^45 So it is written, **The first man Adam became a living being;**^D the last Adam became a life-giving spirit. ^46 However, the spiritual is not first, but the natural, then the spiritual.

^15:29 Other mss read *for the dead*　^B15:32 Is 22:13　^c15:34 Lit *Sober up*　^D15:45 Gn 2:7

had died without undergoing baptism. Paul simply pointed out that it was meaningless for the Corinthians to enact such practices if they disbelieved in the resurrection of the dead.
15:32 Wild beasts is almost certainly metaphorical for struggles Paul faced from human opponents of the gospel (Ac 19; 2Co 1:8–10).
15:33–34 "Bad company corrupts good morals" is a quote from the poet Menander. According to Paul "bad company" refers to those who deny the resurrection.

15:35–38 Paul compares human resurrection to the life-death-life cycle from agriculture. The seed body that **dies** gives rise to a totally different plant body, and yet there is retention of identity. So it is with our present bodies and our future resurrection bodies.
15:42–44 Having reviewed differentiations within the created order (vv. 35–41), Paul turns to differentiations of the resurrected body. It was **sown in corruption** and will be **raised in incorruption**. The body changes from a perishable body (a **natural body**) to

an imperishable body (a **spiritual body**), though one that has physical characteristics (e.g., Lk 24:39). It is sown in **dishonor** and **weakness**, and it will be raised a glorious, imperishable body.
15:45 The first man Adam received the breath of life, a life that would become corruptible and perishable. In contrast, the **last Adam** (Jesus) will impart life, granting believers an incorruptible, imperishable, eternal body.
15:46 Grammatically, the words **the spiritual** (Gk *pneumatikon*) and **the natural**

fully embodied human. Yet Jesus also walks through doors, and at times the disciples have trouble recognizing him.

While not downplaying individual salvation, Paul emphasizes the cosmic salvation that was secured by Jesus's resurrection. What results is a sort of dual emphasis, as seen in Romans 8, where Paul reasons that "if the Spirit of him who raised Jesus from the dead lives in you, then he who raised Christ from the dead will also bring your mortal bodies to life through his Spirit who lives in you" (v. 11). He then adds a cosmic dimension of this future salvation, explaining how "the whole creation has been groaning together with labor pains until now. And not only that, but we ourselves who have the Spirit as the firstfruits—we also groan within ourselves, eagerly waiting for adoption, the redemption of our bodies" (vv. 22–23).

This picture, appropriately applied, gives the Christian reason to care about the physical world (body, culture, and environment) while looking forward to a glorified state beyond our present realities, recognizing that Jesus's resurrection secured a redeemed and transformed new creation.

Meaning and Hope

The resurrection speaks powerfully into universal experiences. Death, for instance, is the universal shadow that hangs over all of life. And a frightening one at that, for we fear being cut off from all those we love. The end of love, relationships, and meaning is what makes death so excruciatingly unbearable, even absurd. People today cope by trying to avoid its reality altogether, but imperfectly so.

But with the resurrection death loses its conclusive sting. The resurrection promises that our loves in this world—that is, the things we love in right relation to God—are not simply meaningful; rather, they will exist forever. In Christ, God has reversed what seems irreversible (Jn 11:25–26; 1Co 15:12–28). Christianity's response to this universal human desire to elude death is that in Christ death is not only not the end of life, love, and community but a door that opens to a deeper experience of all these things. In this life the Spirit offers a foretaste of this coming hope, but the consummation of this joy awaits the world to come.

⁴⁷ The first man was from the earth, a man of dust; the second man is^ from heaven. ⁴⁸ Like the man of dust, so are those who are of the dust; like the man of heaven, so are those who are of heaven. ⁴⁹ And just as we have borne the image of the man of dust, we will also bear the image of the man of heaven.

Victorious Resurrection

⁵⁰ What I am saying, brothers and sisters, is this: Flesh and blood cannot inherit the kingdom of God, nor can corruption inherit incorruption. ⁵¹ Listen, I am telling you a mystery: We will not all fall asleep, but we will all be changed, ⁵² in a moment, in the twinkling of an eye, at the last trumpet. For the trumpet will sound, and the dead will be raised incorruptible, and we will be changed. ⁵³ For this corruptible body must be clothed with incorruptibility, and this mortal body must be clothed with immortality. ⁵⁴ When this corruptible body is clothed with incorruptibility, and this mortal body is clothed with immortality, then the saying that is written will take place:

> Death has been swallowed up in victory.^B

⁵⁵ Where, death, is your victory?
    Where, death, is your sting?^C

⁵⁶ The sting of death is sin, and the power of sin is the law. ⁵⁷ But thanks be to God, who gives us the victory through our Lord Jesus Christ!

⁵⁸ Therefore, my dear brothers and sisters, be steadfast, immovable, always excelling in the Lord's work, because you know that your labor in the Lord is not in vain.

Collection for the Jerusalem Church

16 Now about the collection for the saints: Do the same as I instructed the Galatian churches. ² On the first day of the week, each of you is to set something aside and save in keeping with how he is prospering, so that no

^15:47 Other mss add *the Lord*   ^15:54 Is 25:8   ^15:55 Hs 13:14

(Gk *psuchikon*) are in the neuter gender. They refer to two kinds of bodies (cp. v. 44) and not to Adam or Christ. "Spiritual" (*pneumatikon*) here refers to a body brought to life by the last Adam, Christ.
15:47–49 Paul contrasts **the first man** Adam and those who have borne his **image** with **the second man** and those who will bear his image. The first man was made of **earth** (Gk *choikos*, "earthy"), an expression Paul coined in allusion to Gn 2:7. This language emphasizes the transitory nature of those who are related to the first Adam, with bodies that return to dust. The "second man" **from heaven** refers to Jesus in his glorified humanity, as God-man and Messiah, who is coming from heaven to impart imperishable

eternal bodies to those who have borne the image of the **man of dust**.
15:50 Our earthly condition is such (**flesh and blood** and **corruption**, references to our perishable physical nature) that our Adamic bodies cannot inherit the kingdom, implying that they somehow must be changed.
15:51–53 Paul supports the above implication (v. 50) with an apostolic revelation that though not everyone will die (**fall asleep**; see note at v. 20) before Christ's coming, those who are alive when he comes **will all be changed**. No one is transported to the eternal state unchanged.
15:52 In a moment (Gk *atomos*) signifies the smallest possible division of something, in this case time. **Twinkling of an eye** similarly

implies rapidity. Such will be the swiftness of the transformation of the living when **the last trumpet** sounds at Christ's return (1Th 4:16–17).
15:54–55 Paul conflates Is 25:8 and Hs 13:14 in this citation. The exchange of **corruptible** for **incorruptibility** comes only when death and corruption are **swallowed up** by Jesus Christ.
15:57 Christ brings not only victory over death in the resurrection but also victory over sin that leads to death.
15:58 Almost anything we do in this life is vanity (Ec 1:2–3), but **labor in the Lord** has eternal value.
16:1–4 Now about indicates that Paul is responding to a question, expressed to him

---

Character profile:
Priscilla

I n the book of Acts we learn about Aquilla and Priscilla, a husband and wife who were originally from Pontus (in modern-day Turkey). They lived and worked in Italy until the Roman emperor Claudius expelled all Jews from Rome (see Ac 18:2). Then, relocating to Corinth, Greece, around AD 51, their lives changed dramatically: they crossed paths with the apostle Paul.

Like Paul, Priscilla and Aquila were Jewish tentmakers (Ac 18:3). Moreover, they were fervently devoted to the gospel of Jesus Christ (see Rm 16:3). Not surprisingly, a deep friendship formed. For an unspecified time in Corinth, Paul lived with and worked alongside this couple. Soon he began to minister with them.

When Paul returned to his sending church in Antioch, Priscilla and Aquila accompanied him. When their Syria-bound ship stopped briefly in Ephesus, the couple agreed to stay behind to help minister to the fledgling church there (see Ac 18:18–21).

Aquila and Priscilla's impact in Ephesus was significant. A brilliant Jew named Apollos arrived. He was a powerful communicator with an obvious love for Christ. However, when they heard him teach in the synagogue, they realized his understanding of the gospel needed fine-tuning. So Aquila and Priscilla "took him aside and explained the way of God to him

more accurately" (Ac 18:26). As a result, Apollos became an effective church leader.

For Priscilla and Aquila, such gospel-centered hospitality wasn't a one-time event. Three or four years later (AD 55 or 56), Paul returned to Ephesus. From there, he wrote to the believers in Corinth, "The churches of Asia send you greetings. Aquila and Priscilla send you greetings warmly in the Lord, along with the church that meets in their home" (1Co 16:19). They were a gracious couple who welcomed people into their home with the love of Christ.

A year or so later Paul wrote from Corinth to the church in Rome: "Give my greetings to Prisca [the shortened form of Priscilla's name] and Aquila, my coworkers in Christ Jesus, who risked their own necks for my life. Not only do I thank them, but so do all the Gentile churches. Greet also the church that meets in their home" (Rm 16:3–5). Amazingly, this couple was back in Rome, picking up where they left off years before. Another move, more ministry, greater impact.

Some ten years later Paul wrote to Timothy, who was pastoring in Ephesus. In closing, the old apostle wrote, "Greet Prisca and Aquila" (2Tm 4:19). This faithful couple still wasn't done.

Nothing in the New Testament suggests these two were highly educated, extremely wealthy, or phenomenally gifted. Mostly, they were simply available and hospitable. They helped wherever needed. They opened their lives to others.

Wherever they were, Priscilla and Aquila were on mission for God. They encourage us to do likewise and make an eternal difference.

collections will need to be made when I come. ³ When I arrive, I will send with letters those you recommend to carry your gift to Jerusalem. ⁴ If it is suitable for me to go as well, they will travel with me.

Paul's Travel Plans

⁵ I will come to you after I pass through Macedonia — for I will be traveling through Macedonia — ⁶ and perhaps I will remain with you or even spend the winter, so that you may send me on my way wherever I go. ⁷ I don't want to see you now just in passing, since I hope to spend some time with you, if the Lord allows. ⁸ But I will stay in Ephesus until Pentecost, ⁹ because a wide door for effective ministry has opened for me ᴬ — yet many oppose me. ¹⁰ If Timothy comes, see that he has nothing to fear while with you, because he is doing the Lord's work, just as I am. ¹¹ So let no one look down on him. Send him on his way in peace so that he can come to me, because I am expecting him with the brothers.

¹² Now about our brother Apollos: I strongly urged him to come to you with the brothers, but he was not at all willing to come now. However, he will come when he has an opportunity.

Final Exhortation

¹³ Be alert, stand firm in the faith, be courageous, ᴮ be strong. ¹⁴ Do everything in love.

¹⁵ Brothers and sisters, you know the household of Stephanas: They are the firstfruits of Achaia and have devoted themselves to serving the saints. I urge you ¹⁶ also to submit to such people, and to everyone who works and labors with them. ¹⁷ I am delighted to have Stephanas, Fortunatus, and Achaicus present, because these men have made up for your absence. ¹⁸ For they have refreshed my spirit and yours. Therefore recognize such people.

Conclusion

¹⁹ The churches of Asia send you greetings. Aquila and Priscilla send you greetings warmly in the Lord, along with the church that meets in their home. ²⁰ All the brothers and sisters send you greetings. Greet one another with a holy kiss.

²¹ This greeting is in my own hand — Paul. ²² If anyone does not love the Lord, a curse be on him. Our Lord, come! ᶜ ²³ The grace of the Lord Jesus be with you. ²⁴ My love be with all of you in Christ Jesus.

ᴬ16:9 Lit *door has opened to me, great and effective*　ᴮ16:13 Lit *act like men*　ᶜ16:22 Aramaic *Marana tha*

---

in a previous letter (see 7:1 and note), about how to organize the **collection** for the Jerusalem church (2Co 8–9). The Corinthians had pleaded for the opportunity to contribute to the collection (2Co 8:4). **Each** person was to **set . . . aside** funds regularly for the collection, based on his ability to give. All the funds were eventually to be collected and sent in care of designated couriers. Paul personally would go with the couriers if it seemed advisable and the circumstances permitted.
16:5–9 Paul planned to go through **Macedonia** to Corinth (on his third missionary journey) and possibly to **spend the winter** at Corinth. He then expected the Corinthians to provide supplies for his journey when he left them. In the meantime, he intended to stay in **Ephesus** until May (the Jewish feast of **Pentecost**) because of the favorable response to the gospel in that city.

16:10–11 Paul gave instructions on how the Corinthian believers should receive **Timothy**. The word **if** (Gk *ean*) here is equivalent to "whenever." Paul was certain Timothy was going to Corinth. **Send him on his way in peace** is idiomatic for "supply him with all he needs for the journey."
16:12 Apollos, whose vital role in growing the Corinthian church Paul readily acknowledged (see 3:5–6 and note), was most likely unwilling **to come now** because of gospel duties elsewhere.
16:13–14 Believers must **be alert** about competing traditions of worldly wisdom and **stand firm** as one body **in the faith**. "Faith" here refers to the content of the gospel — Christ's death and resurrection (15:1–5,14).
16:15–16 Paul exhorted the Corinthians to submit to **the household of Stephanas** (1:16). The term **firstfruits** is an honorific title referring to their early reception of the gospel in **Achaia**.

16:17–18 Stephanas, Fortunatus, and Achaicus visited Paul and **made up** for the Corinthians' **absence** (lit "these filled up your lack"). Paul instructed the believers at Corinth to **recognize** them.
16:20 In the context of Paul's letters (Rm 16:16; 2Co 13:12; 1Th 5:26) and the early church, the **holy kiss** was a sign of mutual fellowship within the family of believers.
16:21 Paul concluded the letter in his own handwriting, verifying its authenticity and authority (Gl 6:11; Col 4:18; 2Th 3:16–18; Phm 19).
16:22 The call for judgment on those who were disloyal to the Lord was an uncommon way to end a letter. The Aramaic *Marana tha* can be variously translated. The imperative "Our Lord, come!" seems best.
16:23–24 The letter ends with Paul's formulaic "grace greeting," followed by a personal touch that is unique to this letter.

◤ Introduction to 2 Corinthians

Circumstances of Writing

All biblical scholars agree that Paul wrote this letter (1:1; 10:1). It contains more personal information about him than any other letter, and its Greek style is especially like that of Romans and 1 Corinthians. Proposed chronologies of Paul's life and ministry include a number of variations. Yet for 2 Corinthians, the consensus is that the letter was written about AD 56 (from Ephesus during Paul's third missionary journey).

First Corinthians was not well received by the church at Corinth. Timothy had returned to Paul in Ephesus (1Co 4:17; 16:10). He reported that the church was still greatly troubled. This was partly caused by the arrival in Corinth of "false apostles" (2Co 11:13–15). These were perhaps Judaizers, asking Corinthian believers of Gentile heritage to live according to Mosaic regulations (Gl 2:14).

Paul visited Corinth a second time, the first time being his church-planting visit. He described this visit as sorrowful or "painful" (2Co 2:1; 13:2). Apparently the false apostles agitated the Corinthians to disown Paul. This second visit, not mentioned in Acts 19, occurred sometime during the apostle's long ministry in Ephesus.

Paul then wrote a (now lost) severe letter of stinging rebuke to Corinth from Ephesus (2Co 2:3–4,9). He sent this letter by Titus. Titus came to Paul with the news that most of the Corinthian church had repented. They now accepted Paul's authority (7:5–7). Paul decided to write the Corinthians one more

time, expressing his relief but still pleading with an unrepentant minority. He promised to come to Corinth a third time (12:14; 13:1). This was fulfilled when Paul stayed in Corinth while on his way to Jerusalem with the financial collection from many churches (Ac 20:2–3).

Contribution to the Bible

Second Corinthians contributes to our understanding of ministry. On this subject, we learn four key truths: (1) God was in Christ reconciling the world to himself and has given to us a ministry of reconciliation; (2) true ministry in Christ's name involves both suffering and victory; (3) serving Christ means ministering in his name to every need of the people; and (4) leaders in ministry need support and trust from those to whom they minister.

Structure

This letter follows the standard format found in the other letters bearing Paul's name. The salutation (1:1–2) and thanksgiving (1:3–11) at the beginning are followed by the main body of the letter (1:12–13:10). A final greeting (13:11–13) stands as the conclusion.

The body of 2 Corinthians is the most disjointed of Paul's letters. It is hard to miss Paul's change of tone from chapters 1–9 (which are warm and encouraging) to chapters 10–13 (which are harsh and threatening). Whatever one decides about the original unity of the letter, no doubt the major turning point of 2 Corinthians occurs at 10:1.

AD 33–40

Jesus's trials, death, resurrection, and
   ascension NISAN 14–16 or APRIL 3–5, 33
Pentecost 33
Saul's conversion on the Damascus
   Road OCTOBER 34
Paul returns to his native Tarsus. SUMMER 37–40
Barnabas travels from Antioch of
   Syria to find Paul. SUMMER 40

AD 45–50

Paul, Barnabas, and John Mark make the
   first missionary journey. 47–49
Paul and Silas begin second missionary
   journey by land through Cilicia, Galatia,
   and Asia Minor to Troas. 49–50
Paul, Silas, and Timothy sail from Troas to
   Macedonia and minister in the Macedonian
   cities of Philippi, Thessalonica, and Berea. 50
Paul preaches on Mars Hill in Athens. 50
Paul arrives in Corinth and spends eighteen
   months planting the church. 50–51

2 Corinthians Timeline

Largely because of the change in tone between the first part of the letter and the last part, some interpreters have proposed a different understanding of the original form of 2 Corinthians. They propose that two separate letters of Paul have been joined to make up what is now known as 2 Corinthians.

However, it seems much more plausible that the letter originated in the form in which we now have it. All the ancient Christian writers knew the letter only in its present form, which is to say unified as one single letter. Surely within a single letter an author may address two different sets of issues (a majority concern and a minority concern) and use two different tones (encouraging and threatening).

Outline

I. Special Greetings (1:1–11)
II. Clarification of Paul's Ministry (1:12–7:16)
III. A Collection for Needy Christians (8:1–9:15)
IV. The Case against False Apostles (10:1–13:10)
V. Final Greetings (13:11–13)

AD 50–56

Paul meets Aquila and Priscilla, who had come to Corinth when Emperor Claudius expelled the Jews from Rome six years earlier. 51
Paul writes 1 and 2 Thessalonians from Corinth. 51
Paul's hearing before Corinth's proconsul, Gallio, brother of the Roman philosopher Seneca 51
Paul begins his third missionary journey by land through Asia Minor to Ephesus. 53
Paul spends three years in Ephesus. 54–56

AD 56–70

Paul writes 1 Corinthians from Ephesus. 56
Paul writes 2 Corinthians from Ephesus. 56
Paul spends the winter in Corinth where he writes the letter to the Romans. 57
Paul returns to Jerusalem with funds he had collected from Gentile churches to support the poor in the Jerusalem church. 57
Shortly before his death, Emperor Nero brings six thousand slaves from Judea to build a canal across the Isthmus of Corinth. Following Nero's death the project is abandoned. 67

Greeting

1 Paul, an apostle of Christ Jesus by God's will, and Timothy our[A] brother:

To the church of God at Corinth, with all the saints who are throughout Achaia.

[2] Grace to you and peace from God our Father and the Lord Jesus Christ.

The God of Comfort

[3] Blessed be the God and Father of our Lord Jesus Christ, the Father of mercies and the God of all comfort. [4] He comforts us in all our affliction,[B] so that we may be able to comfort those who are in any kind of affliction, through the comfort we ourselves receive from God. [5] For just as the sufferings of Christ overflow to us, so also through Christ our comfort overflows. [6] If we are afflicted, it is for your comfort and salvation. If we are comforted, it is for your comfort, which produces in you patient endurance of the same sufferings that we suffer. [7] And our hope for you is firm, because we know that as you share in the sufferings, so you will also share in the comfort.

[8] We don't want you to be unaware, brothers and sisters, of our affliction that took place in Asia. We were completely overwhelmed — beyond our strength — so that we even despaired of life itself. [9] Indeed, we felt that we had received the sentence of death, so that we would not trust in ourselves but in God who raises the dead. [10] He has delivered us from such a terrible death, and he will deliver us. We have put our hope in him that he will deliver us again[11] while you join in helping us by your prayers. Then many will give thanks on our[C] behalf for the gift that came to us through the prayers of many.

A Clear Conscience

[12] Indeed, this is our boast: The testimony of our conscience is that we have conducted ourselves in the world, and especially toward you, with godly sincerity and purity, not by human wisdom but by God's grace. [13] For we are writing nothing to you other than what you can read and also understand. I hope you will understand completely — [14] just as you have partially understood us — that we are your reason for pride, just as you also are ours in the day of our[D] Lord Jesus.

A Visit Postponed

[15] Because of this confidence, I planned to come to you first, so that you could have a second benefit,[E] [16] and to visit you on my way to Macedonia, and then come to you again from Macedonia and be helped by you on my journey to Judea. [17] Now when I planned this, was I of two minds? Or what I plan, do I plan in a purely human[F] way so that I say "Yes, yes" and "No, no" at the same time? [18] As God is faithful, our message to you is not "Yes and no." [19] For the Son of God, Jesus Christ, whom we proclaimed among you — Silvanus,[G] Timothy, and I — did not become "Yes and no." On the contrary, in him it is always "Yes." [20] For every one of God's promises is "Yes" in him. Therefore, through him we also say "Amen" to the glory of God. [21] Now it is God who strengthens us together with you in Christ, and who has anointed us. [22] He has also put his seal on us and given us the Spirit in our hearts as a down payment.

[23] I call on God as a witness, on my life, that it was to spare you that I did not come to Corinth. [24] I do not mean that we lord it over your faith, but we are workers with you for your joy, because you stand firm in your faith.

2 [1] In fact, I made up my mind about this: I would not come to you on another painful visit.[H] [2] For if I cause you pain, then who will cheer me other than the one being hurt by me?[I] [3] I wrote this very thing so that when I came I

[A]1:1 Lit *the*   [B]1:4 Or *trouble*, or *tribulation*, or *trials*, or *oppression*   [C]1:11 Other mss read *your*   [D]1:14 Other mss omit *our*
[E]1:15 Other mss read *a second joy*   [F]1:17 Or *a worldly*, or *a fleshly*, or *a selfish*   [G]1:19 Or *Silas*; Ac 15:22–32; 16:19–40; 17:1–16
[H]2:1 Lit *not again in sorrow to come to you*   [I]2:2 Lit *the one pained*

1:1 **Timothy** was perhaps Paul's secretary or scribe who wrote down this letter as it was dictated. **Corinth** was the capital of the Roman province of **Achaia**, the southern part of Greece.
1:2 **Grace** begins and ends every NT letter that contains Paul's name in the greeting. Without grace from God, a person cannot have **peace** with God. The equality of the **Father** and his Son **Jesus Christ** is implicit. Both are givers of grace and peace.
1:6–7 In speaking of affliction, Paul probably had in mind the suffering he had endured from the Corinthian church during his painful visit to them (2:1), which was for their **salvation**. He had recently been **comforted** by news from Titus (7:13). The **sufferings** of the Corinthians probably referred to the "fear and trembling" caused by Titus's visit (7:15).
1:8 Paul's **affliction** in **Asia** was a near-death experience during his Ephesian ministry that is not reported in Ac 19.

1:11 The phrase **the gift** probably refers to God's gracious sparing of Paul's life for further ministry (Php 1:24–26).
1:14 The phrase **partially understood** is a reference to the stormy relations between the church and the apostle. The **day of our Lord Jesus** refers to Christ's return, especially to judge believers' works (1Co 3:12–13).
1:15–16 In 1 Corinthians Paul had expressed his intent to spend time with them (1Co 16:5–6). Later he had revised this and **planned to come** twice—once on the way to **Macedonia** (the province north of Achaia), and again on the way south from Macedonia on his way to **Judea** to deliver the collection for Jerusalem. Seeing the Corinthians twice would have been a double **benefit** for them.
1:17 Instead of his announced plans, Paul made a brief, painful visit from Ephesus to Corinth, and then returned to Ephesus. Some believers in Corinth accused him of being unreliable.

1:18–19 The apostle's defense against the charge of fickleness was to remind his readers of the unwavering gospel message he had preached. **Silvanus** is called Silas in Acts.
1:20 **Amen** means "so be it" or "this is true."
1:21–22 This is a Trinitarian text.
1:23 The phrase **I call on God as a witness** is a solemn pledge to be telling the truth (Rm 1:9; 1Th 2:5,10). Instead of the visits planned under happier circumstances (2Co 1:15–16), Paul had made a painful visit to Corinth (2:1). He therefore canceled his previously announced itinerary. Time was needed for healing the raw emotions raised on both sides.
2:1–2 Even when a Christian is justified in bringing **pain** to errant believers, it is hardly likely that those **hurt** will be in a position to **cheer** the one who caused the pain.
2:3–4 Paul's words **wrote . . . wrote** are probably a reference to the severe letter,

wouldn't have pain from those who ought to give me joy, because I am confident about all of you that my joy will also be yours. ⁴ For I wrote to you with many tears out of an extremely troubled and anguished heart — not to cause you pain, but that you should know the abundant love I have for you.

A Sinner Forgiven

⁵ If anyone has caused pain, he has caused pain not so much to me but to some degree — not to exaggerate — to all of you. ⁶ This punishment by the majority is sufficient for that person. ⁷ As a result, you should instead forgive and comfort him. Otherwise, he may be overwhelmed by excessive grief. ⁸ Therefore I urge you to reaffirm your love to him. ⁹ I wrote for this purpose: to test your character to see if you are obedient in everything. ¹⁰ Anyone you forgive, I do too. For what I have forgiven — if I have forgiven anything — it is for your benefit in the presence of Christ, ¹¹ so that we may not be taken advantage of by Satan. For we are not ignorant of his schemes.

A Trip to Macedonia

¹² When I came to Troas to preach the gospel of Christ, even though the Lord opened a door for me, ¹³ I had no rest in my spirit because I did not find my brother Titus. Instead, I said good-bye to them and left for Macedonia.

A Ministry of Life or Death

¹⁴ But thanks be to God, who always leads us in Christ's triumphal procession and through us spreads the aroma of the knowledge of him in every place. ¹⁵ For to God we are the fragrance of Christ among those who are being saved and among those who are perishing. ¹⁶ To some we are an aroma of death leading to death, but to others, an aroma of life leading to life. Who is adequate for these things? ¹⁷ For we do not market the word of God for profit like so many.ᴬ On the contrary, we speak with sincerity in Christ, as from God and before God.

Living Letters

3 Are we beginning to commend ourselves again? Or do we need, like some, letters of recommendation to you or from you? ² You yourselves are our letter, written on our hearts, known and read by everyone. ³ You show that you are Christ's letter, deliveredᴮ by us, not written with ink but with the Spirit of the living God — not on tablets of stone but on tablets of human hearts.ᶜ

Paul's Competence

⁴ Such is the confidence we have through Christ before God. ⁵ It is not that we are competent inᴰ ourselves to claim anything as coming from ourselves, but our adequacy is from God. ⁶ He has made us competent to be ministers of a new covenant, not of the letter, but of the Spirit. For the letter kills, but the Spirit gives life.

New Covenant Ministry

⁷ Now if the ministry that brought death, chiseled in letters on stones, came with glory, so that the Israelites were not able to gaze steadily at Moses's face because of its glory, which was set aside, ⁸ how will the ministry of the Spirit not be more glorious? ⁹ For if the ministry that brought condemnation had glory, the ministry that brings righteousness overflows with even more glory. ¹⁰ In fact, what had been glorious is not glorious now by comparison because of the glory that surpasses it. ¹¹ For if what was set aside was glorious, what endures will be even more glorious.

ᴬ2:17 Other mss read *like the rest* ᴮ3:3 Lit *ministered to* ᶜ3:3 Lit *fleshly hearts* ᴰ3:5 Lit *from*

---

now lost, written after his painful visit to Corinth and then sent by Titus (7:6–8), but some Bible students believe the reference is to 1 Corinthians.
2:5 This may refer to the incestuous man of 1Co 5:1–5. More likely the reference is to an episode regarding the false apostles (2Co 11:4), because Paul spoke about a sin that he had personally forgiven (2:10).
2:6–8 Although church discipline is experienced as **punishment**, the intention is redemptive. Upon repentance, believers are to **forgive and comfort**. The congregation is to be careful not to overwhelm a returning sinner with **excessive grief**. **Reaffirm your love to him** refers to restoration after repentance.
2:9 On **I wrote**, see note at vv. 3–4.
2:11 Behind the sin and discord in the Corinthian church Paul saw **Satan**. **His schemes** always include thwarting the unity of believers.
2:12–13 Troas was a coastal city in the northern part of the province of Asia. Paul

went there after the riot in Ephesus (Ac 19:23–41) on his way to **Macedonia** (Ac 20:1–2). **Titus** is not mentioned in Acts. Titus was effective as Paul's ambassador in dealing with the Corinthian crisis. Later he represented the apostle to Christians in Crete (Ti 1:4).
2:14 In antiquity, victorious generals paraded into their capital city toward the king's palace with human captives and treasure displayed behind them. Sweet incense was offered.
2:15–16 The same scent produces different results. Those who receive the knowledge of Christ through the gospel message live. All others perish.
2:17 Those who **market the word** refers to the false apostles in Corinth whose motive was primarily financial (11:13).
3:1–3 The false apostles who had upset the Corinthians had produced **letters of recommendation**. Paul had never felt the need to ask for recommendations, as the implied "no" answers the two questions. The

spiritual transformation of the Corinthians was endorsement enough for Paul. Literal letters, written with **ink** on paper or even on **tablets of stone**, could not compare with changed lives.
3:6 The **new covenant** was prophesied in Jr 31:31–33, established by Jesus's death in Lk 22:20, and ministered by Paul. **The letter kills** refers to the law of the old covenant, which was not designed to give life.
3:7 The ministry that brought death refers to the old covenant made at Mount Sinai. This was not the fault of the old covenant but of sinners who were unable to meet its demands (Rm 7:13).
3:8–9 The phrases **ministry that brings righteousness** and **ministry of the Spirit** refer to the new covenant.
3:10–11 One way in which the old and new covenants contrast is in the degree of **glory** connected with each.

¹² Since, then, we have such a hope, we act with great boldness. ¹³ We are not like Moses, who used to put a veil over his face to prevent the Israelites from gazing steadily until the end^A of the glory of what was being set aside, ¹⁴ but their minds were hardened. For to this day, at the reading of the old covenant, the same veil remains; it is not lifted, because it is set aside only in Christ. ¹⁵ Yet still today, whenever Moses is read, a veil lies over their hearts, ¹⁶ but whenever a person turns to the Lord, the veil is removed. ¹⁷ Now the Lord is the Spirit, and where the Spirit of the Lord is, there is freedom. ¹⁸ We all, with unveiled faces, are looking as in a mirror at^B the glory of the Lord and are being transformed into the same image from glory to glory; this is from the Lord who is the Spirit.^C

The Light of the Gospel

4 Therefore, since we have this ministry because we were shown mercy, we do not give up. ² Instead, we have renounced secret and shameful things, not acting deceitfully or distorting the word of God, but commending ourselves before God to everyone's conscience by an open display of the truth. ³ But if our gospel is veiled, it is veiled to those who are perishing. ⁴ In their case, the god of this age has blinded the minds of the unbelievers to keep them from seeing the light of the gospel of the glory of Christ,^D who is the image of God. ⁵ For we are not proclaiming ourselves but Jesus Christ as Lord, and ourselves as your servants

for Jesus's sake. ⁶ For God who said, "Let light shine out of darkness," has shone in our hearts to give the light of the knowledge of God's glory in the face of Jesus Christ.

Treasure in Clay Jars

⁷ Now we have this treasure in clay jars, so that this extraordinary power may be from God and not from us. ⁸ We are afflicted in every way but not crushed; we are perplexed but not in despair; ⁹ we are persecuted but not abandoned; we are struck down but not destroyed. ¹⁰ We always carry the death of Jesus in our body, so that the life of Jesus may also be displayed in our body. ¹¹ For we who live are always being given over to death for Jesus's sake, so that Jesus's life may also be displayed in our mortal flesh. ¹² So then, death is at work in us, but life in you. ¹³ And since we have the same spirit of faith in keeping with what is written, **I believed, therefore I spoke,**^E we also believe, and therefore speak. ¹⁴ For we know that the one who raised the Lord Jesus will also raise us with Jesus and present us with you. ¹⁵ Indeed, everything is for your benefit so that, as grace extends through more and more people, it may cause thanksgiving to increase to the glory of God.

¹⁶ Therefore we do not give up. Even though our outer person is being destroyed, our inner person is being renewed day by day. ¹⁷ For our momentary light affliction is producing for us an absolutely incomparable eternal weight of glory. ¹⁸ So we do not focus on what is seen, but

^A 3:13 Or *at the outcome*   ^B 3:18 Or *are reflecting*   ^C 3:18 Or *from the Spirit of the Lord,* or *from the Lord, the Spirit*   ^D 4:4 Or *the gospel of the glorious Christ,* or *the glorious gospel of Christ*   ^E 4:13 Ps 116:10 LXX

3:12 If the ministry of the Spirit can have greater splendor than Moses's ministry, then its ministers can have greater boldness.
3:13 The main purpose of Moses's **veil** was to prevent the Israelites from observing the fading of the old-covenant glory. The law was designed by God with a built-in obsolescence (Gl 3:24–25; Heb 8:13).
3:14 Another purpose of a **veil** is to keep the veiled person from seeing outside. Paul implies that the first-century Jews who had not believed the gospel were unable to recognize

the fading, temporary nature of **the old covenant**, even when their Scriptures were read.
3:15–16 The phrase **a veil lies over their hearts** refers to a spiritual impairment. The passive verb in **the veil is removed** refers to the sovereign work of God.
3:17 This is an important Trinitarian text emphasizing the close relationship between the Son and the Spirit.
3:18 Paul included all believers among the **unveiled**, whose glory, having begun in the new covenant, can never fade. It moves **from glory** (on earth, in regeneration, justification, and sanctification) **to glory** (in heaven, in glorification).
4:1 Because true **ministry** proceeds only from God's undeserved **mercy**, Paul included with it the strength to persevere despite opposition.
4:2 The false apostles may have pandered to the Corinthians by pretending to have "inside information." False teachers are recognized both by wrong motives (**acting deceitfully**) and the wrong message (**distorting the word**).
4:3 On **gospel is veiled**, see note at 3:15–16.
4:4 Satan has a role in keeping persons from Christ and the gospel, even though they are accountable for their own souls and cannot blame the devil.
4:6 The original creation of **light** out of **darkness** (Gn 1:3) provided the paradigm for God's re-creation of spiritual light in a sinner (2Co 5:17). "Light" given by God results in the human

response to "gospel/knowledge" which in turn results in "glory of Christ/God's glory" being admired. Coupled with the statement in v. 4 that he is "the image of God," the words **in the face of Jesus Christ** are a strong testimony to Paul's belief in the deity of Christ.
4:7 Treasure is the unfading glory that accompanies the new covenant (3:8). **Clay jars** is a metaphor for fragile and mortal human bodies.
4:8–9 These verses contain four pairs of opposites. The first element of each pair characterizes frail humanity, especially humans in service to God. The second element gives evidence of God's power.
4:12 Paul's trials as a minister led ultimately to **death**; however, his trials were instrumental in bringing spiritual **life** to the Corinthians.
4:13 Paul quoted the Septuagint (the ancient Greek translation of the OT) of Ps 116:10. The main point is that trust in the Lord motivates a person to action.
4:14 At Christ's coming, God will raise believers. The words **us with you** show that the resurrection of the saints is not individualistic.
4:15 On **the glory of God**, see vv. 4,6.
4:16 The words **we do not give up** are repeated from v. 1. Between these two statements Paul explains why he was not defeated even in extremely negative circumstances.
4:17–18 These verses remind believers that our focus must remain on the **eternal**.

#74 99 Essential Christian Truths

MIRACLES

A miracle is an event in which God makes an exception to the natural order of things, or supersedes natural laws, for the purpose of demonstrating his glory and/or validating his message. Miracles are recorded throughout Scripture; miraculous signs and wonders were oftentimes evident when a prophet or an apostle was speaking God's message to the people. Because we believe God is all-powerful and personally involved in this world, we believe he can and does perform miracles.

on what is unseen. For what is seen is temporary, but what is unseen is eternal.

Our Future after Death

5 For we know that if our earthly tent we live in is destroyed, we have a building from God, an eternal dwelling in the heavens, not made with hands. ² Indeed, we groan in this tent, desiring to put on our heavenly dwelling, ³ since, when we are clothed,ᴬ we will not be found naked. ⁴ Indeed, we groan while we are in this tent, burdened as we are, because we do not want to be unclothed but clothed, so that mortality may be swallowed up by life. ⁵ Now the one who prepared us for this very purpose is God, who gave us the Spirit as a down payment. ⁶ So we are always confident and know that while we are at home in the body we are away from the Lord. ⁷ For we walk by faith, not by sight. ⁸ In fact, we are confident, and we would prefer to be away from the body and at home with the Lord. ⁹ Therefore, whether we are at home or away, we make it our aim to be pleasing to him. ¹⁰ For we must all appear before the judgment seat of Christ, so that each may be repaid for what he has done in the body, whether good or evil.

¹¹ Therefore, since we know the fear of the Lord, we try to persuade people. What we are is plain to God, and I hope it is also plain to your consciences. ¹² We are not commending ourselves to you again, but giving you an opportunity to be proud of us, so that you may have a reply for those who take pride in outward appearance rather than in the heart. ¹³ For if we are out of our mind, it is for God; if we are in our right mind, it is for you. ¹⁴ For the love of Christ compels us, since we have reached this conclusion, that one died for all, and therefore all died. ¹⁵ And he died for all so that those who live should no longer live for themselves, but for the one who died for them and was raised.

The Ministry of Reconciliation

¹⁶ From now on, then, we do not know anyone from a worldly perspective.ᴮ Even if we have known Christ from a worldly perspective,ᶜ yet now we no longer know him in this way. ¹⁷ Therefore, if anyone is in Christ, he is a new creation; the old has passed away, and see, the new hasᴰ come! ¹⁸ Everything is from God, who has reconciled us to himself through Christ and has given us the ministry of reconciliation. ¹⁹ That is, in Christ, God was reconciling the world to himself, not counting their trespasses against them, and he has committed the message of reconciliation to us.

²⁰ Therefore, we are ambassadors for Christ, since God is making his appeal through us. We plead on Christ's behalf, "Be reconciled to God." ²¹ He made the one who did not know sin to be sinᴱ for us, so that in him we might become the righteousness of God.

6 Working together with him, we also appeal to you, "Don't receive the grace of God in vain." ² For he says:

> At an acceptable time I listened to you,
> and in the day of salvation I helped
> you.ᶠ

See, now is the acceptable time; now is the day of salvation!

ᴬ5:3 Other mss read when we have taken it off　ᴮ5:16 Lit anyone according to the flesh　ᶜ5:16 Lit Christ according to the flesh
ᴰ5:17 Other mss read look, all new things have　ᴱ5:21 Or be a sin offering　ᶠ6:2 Is 49:8

5:1–10 This section contains the most extensive teaching in Scripture on the "intermediate state," or the condition of believers between the death of the body and its resurrection.
5:1 Paul compared our bodily existence to living in an **earthly tent**, and the resurrection body to a palace or other grand **building**.
5:2 The resurrection will be something like putting on new clothes (**put on our heavenly dwelling**).
5:3 The word **naked** is a reference to being disembodied. A human soul or spirit apart from bodily existence—thought of as a desired state in some religious systems—was never considered desirable in the Scriptures.
5:4 Paul's preference was for the final state of the resurrection body rather than the intermediate and apparently bodiless situation of the Christian dead.
5:5 This verse emphasizes God's sovereignty. On **the Spirit as a down payment**, see 1:22 and Eph 1:14 for the other NT instances of "down payment," always connected with the Spirit.
5:6–8 Paul drew three contrasts between this life and the intermediate state: at home in the body/out of the body; by faith/by sight; and away from the Lord/at home with the Lord. As long as the saints still live in the body, they perceive Christ only by faith.
5:9–10 **At home or away** refers to either earthly bodily existence or away from

bodily existence (disembodied). The main way in which the righteous dead may be **pleasing to him** is by receiving a positive verdict before the **judgment seat** of Christ (see also Rm 14:10). Christians are saved by faith, but they will be judged according to the **good or evil** deeds they have done. This is a judgment to determine rewards, not eternal destination. See esp. 1Co 3:10–15.
5:11–12 The **fear of the Lord** is the awe and respect due to Christ as the judge of a believer's works.
5:13–15 Paul's opponents probably had suggested that he was religiously unbalanced (see Ac 26:24). He was "insane" in that **the love of Christ** compelled him into vigorous apostolic ministry. On the other hand, his ministry among the Corinthians had never been that of a madman (1Co 2:1–5). The heart of Paul's message was that the Jewish Messiah had **died** on behalf of **all** kinds of sinners (15:3). In union with Christ, sinners who believe the gospel have died to sin and have been raised to walk in a new way of life.
5:16 The phrase **from a worldly perspective** literally is "according to the flesh." There are always two conflicting perspectives on a situation: the worldly versus the divine. A worldly view of Christ led to his crucifixion and to Paul's persecution of Christ-followers. After the light of divine revelation broke in

on Paul on the Damascus Road, he could **no longer know him in this way** (Ac 9).
5:17–18 The words **in Christ** refer to being in union with him. Genuine conversion begins life transformation, but not by reforming the old nature. The indwelling Spirit creates divine life in believers (Rm 8:8–10), so that **the new has come**. The **ministry of reconciliation**—being an agent of this good news—was Paul's special responsibility, but the task belongs to all who have received this ministry.
5:19–21 What **Christ** did, **God** did. Christ's death mainly affected the world, that is, human sinners. Trespasses were placed on **the one who did not know sin**. In return, **the righteousness of God** is credited (imputed) to all who are **in him**. The **message of reconciliation** is known to others only when **ambassadors for Christ** spread it.
6:1 In vain may refer to (1) falling away from a profession of faith that was apparent but not genuine and therefore going into eternity apart from Christ (1Jn 2:19); or (2) developing neither Christlike character nor doing good works because of a life of "backsliding" and therefore having one's works burned at the judgment seat of Christ (1Co 3:12–14; 2Co 5:10).
6:2 The larger context of Is 49:8 was God's restoration that would come at last to the

The Character of Paul's Ministry

³ We are not giving anyone an occasion for offense, so that the ministry will not be blamed. ⁴ Instead, as God's ministers, we commend ourselves in everything: by great endurance, by afflictions, by hardships, by difficulties, ⁵ by beatings, by imprisonments, by riots, by labors, by sleepless nights, by times of hunger, ⁶ by purity, by knowledge, by patience, by kindness, by the Holy Spirit, by sincere love, ⁷ by the word of truth,ᴬ by the power of God; through weapons of righteousness for the right hand and the left, ⁸ through glory and dishonor, through slander and good report; regarded as deceivers, yet true; ⁹ as unknown, yet recognized; as dying, yet see — we live; as being disciplined, yet not killed; ¹⁰ as grieving, yet always rejoicing; as poor, yet enriching many; as having nothing, yet possessing everything. ¹¹ We have spoken openly to you, Corinthians; our heart has been opened wide. ¹² We are not withholding our affection from you, but you are withholding yours from us. ¹³ I speak as to my children; as a proper response, open your heart to us.

Separation to God

¹⁴ Do not be yoked together with those who do not believe. For what partnership is there between righteousness and lawlessness? Or what fellowship does light have with darkness? ¹⁵ What agreement does Christ have with Belial?ᴮ Or what does a believer have in common with an unbeliever? ¹⁶ And what agreement does the temple of God have with idols? For weᶜ are the temple of the living God, as God said:

I will dwell
and walk among them,
and I will be their God,
and they will be my people.ᴰ
¹⁷ Therefore, come out
from among them
and be separate, says the Lord;
do not touch any unclean thing,
and I will welcome you.ᴱ
¹⁸ And I will be a Father to you,
and you will be sons and daughters
to me,
says the Lord Almighty.ᶠ

7 So then, dear friends, since we have these promises, let us cleanse ourselves from every impurity of the flesh and spirit, bringing holiness to completionᴳ in the fear of God.

Joy and Repentance

² Make room for us in your hearts. We have wronged no one, corrupted no one, taken advantage of no one. ³ I don't say this to condemn you, since I have already said that you are in our hearts, to die together and to live together. ⁴ I am very frank with you; I have great pride in you. I am filled with encouragement; I am overflowing with joy in all our afflictions. ⁵ In fact, when we came into Macedonia, weᴴ had no rest. Instead, we were troubled in every way: conflicts on the outside, fears within. ⁶ But God, who comforts the downcast, comforted us by the arrival of Titus, ⁷ and not only by his arrival but also by the comfort he received from you. He told us about your deep

---

ᴬ 6:7 Or *by truthful speech*   ᴮ 6:15 Or *Beliar*   ᶜ 6:16 Other mss read *you*   ᴰ 6:16 Lv 26:12; Jr 31:33; 32:38; Ezk 37:26   ᴱ 6:17 Is 52:11   ᶠ 6:18 2Sm 7:14; Is 43:6; 49:22; 60:4; Hs 1:10   ᴳ 7:1 Or *spirit, perfecting holiness*   ᴴ 7:5 Lit *our flesh*

---

covenant people, Israel. Paul's citation shows that he believed this time had now arrived with the incarnation, death, and resurrection of Christ. **Now** and **day of salvation** refer to the times between Christ's first and second coming.
6:3 Not giving anyone an occasion for offense is a reference to Paul's character and actions, which were open to observation. The list in vv. 4–13 is not self-commendation (like the false teachers; 3:1) but reflects a survey of Paul's actions as God's appointed minister, demonstrating the character and source of his ministry.
6:4–5 This part of the list includes experiences that were physically painful.
6:6–7 This part of the list focuses on character traits and spiritual realities perceived only with the eye of faith. On **weapons of righteousness**, see Eph 6:10–20 for a full discussion of spiritual armor.
6:8–10 The paradox of genuine Christian ministry is nowhere better stated than in these verses. Paul noted nine contrasts between frail humanity and the evidence of God's power.
6:12–13 Paul perceived the relationship problem to lie with the Corinthians. The false teachers had strangled the Corinthians' love for Paul. He yearned for them to be as **open** and loving toward him as he

had been with them—like a father toward wayward **children**.
6:14 Yoked together with those who do not believe refers to the false apostles, whom Paul considered to be Satan's servants. Paul emphasized spiritual incompatibility by noting the impossibility of literal light and darkness equally existing, and, in v. 15, the impossibility of Christ and Satan being friends.
6:15 Belial is a Hebrew term found elsewhere in an OT phrase, literally "sons of Belial," translated "wicked men" in the CSB (see Dt 13:13).
6:16a The "we" in **we are the temple** points to the corporate entity of the local congregation (or the body of Christ as a whole) rather than to the individual (for which, see 1Co 6:19). Paul had believers in mind, not literal buildings (1Pt 2:5).
6:16b–18 These verses assemble a number of OT texts. Verse 16b is stated first in Lv 26:12 and repeated in Jr 31:33; 32:38. This was God's promise of his presence to his covenant people, now fulfilled in the new covenant instituted by Christ (Heb 8:7–13). Verse 17 cites Is 52:11, referring to Israel's future holiness when they will be restored to the Lord's favor. Verse 18 is found first in 2Sm 7:14 in God's covenant promise to David, but it is echoed in Is 43:6; 49:22; 60:4; Hs 1:10. In

these passages the Lord promised a family relationship between himself and his people.
7:1 The phrase **dear friends** (lit "beloved") is a statement of Paul's strong affection for these believers, despite the tears they had caused him. **Cleanse ourselves** is not a reference to Christian baptism but to the daily spiritual cleansing that believers are to experience (Jn 13:10). **Bringing holiness to completion** indicates that growth in holiness is not optional. Believers are to become as mature and Christlike in this lifetime as they can, but the work will be completed only on the day of Christ (Php 1:6). On **fear of God**, see note at 5:11–12.
7:2–3 The false apostles had persuaded some of the Corinthians that Paul had **wronged** . . . **corrupted**, and **taken advantage of** them. He vigorously denied this.
7:4 Paul broke into an exuberant expression of gratitude for the success of Titus's mission to Corinth. Paul's ministry among them had not been in vain but at last had proven to be successful.
7:5 On **Macedonia**, see notes at 1:15–16; 2:12–13. Paul's **conflicts** and **fears** were because of his anguish over the state of the Corinthian Christians.
7:6–7 God's comfort came to Paul through Titus because of the Corinthians' repentance.

longing, your sorrow, and your zeal for me, so that I rejoiced even more. [8] For even if I grieved you with my letter, I don't regret it. And if I regretted it — since I saw that the letter grieved you, yet only for a while — [9] I now rejoice, not because you were grieved, but because your grief led to repentance. For you were grieved as God willed, so that you didn't experience any loss from us. [10] For godly grief produces a repentance that leads to salvation without regret, but worldly grief produces death. [11] For consider how much diligence this very thing — this grieving as God wills — has produced in you: what a desire to clear yourselves, what indignation, what fear, what deep longing, what zeal, what justice! In every way you showed yourselves to be pure in this matter. [12] So even though I wrote to you, it was not because of the one who did wrong, or because of the one who was wronged, but in order that your devotion to us might be made plain to you in the sight of God. [13] For this reason we have been comforted.

In addition to our own comfort, we rejoiced even more over the joy Titus had, because his spirit was refreshed by all of you. [14] For if I have made any boast to him about you, I have not been disappointed; but as I have spoken everything to you in truth, so our boasting to Titus has also turned out to be the truth. [15] And his affection toward you is even greater as he remembers the obedience of all of you, and how you received him with fear and trembling. [16] I rejoice that I have complete confidence in you.

Appeal to Complete the Collection

8 We want you to know, brothers and sisters, about the grace of God that was given to the churches of Macedonia: [2] During a severe trial brought about by affliction, their abundant joy and their extreme poverty overflowed in a wealth of generosity on their part. [3] I can testify that, according to their ability and even beyond their ability, of their own accord, [4] they begged us earnestly for the privilege of sharing in the ministry to the saints, [5] and not just as we had hoped. Instead, they gave themselves first to the Lord and then to us by God's will. [6] So we urged Titus that just as he had begun, so he should also complete among you this act of grace.

[7] Now as you excel in everything — in faith, speech, knowledge, and in all diligence, and in your love for us[A] — excel also in this act of grace. [8] I am not saying this as a command. Rather, by means of the diligence of others, I am testing the genuineness of your love. [9] For you know the grace of our Lord Jesus Christ: Though he was rich, for your sake he became poor, so that by his poverty you might become rich. [10] And in this matter I am giving advice because it is profitable for you, who began last year not only to do something but also to want to do it. [11] Now also finish the task, so that just as there was an eager desire, there may also be a completion, according to what you have. [12] For if the eagerness is there, the gift is acceptable according to what a person has, not according to what he does not have. [13] It is not that there should be relief for others and hardship for you, but it is a question of equality.[B] [14] At the present time your surplus is available for their need, so that their abundance may in turn meet your need, in order that there may be equality. [15] As it is written: **The person who had much did not have too much, and the person who had little did not have too little.**[C]

Administration of the Collection

[16] Thanks be to God, who put the same concern for you into the heart of Titus. [17] For he

---

[A]8:7 Other mss read *in our love for you*   [B]8:13 Lit *but from equality*   [C]8:15 Ex 16:18

7:8 The letter refers to the severe (and now lost) letter written after 1 Corinthians. See note at 2:3–4.
7:9–10 From us means "because of us," that is, because of Paul's letter. The loss he refers to is probably the same loss as in 1Co 3:14–15.
7:12 On **I wrote**, see note at v. 8.
7:13–16 Verses 5–12 describe the effect of the Corinthians' change of heart toward Paul. These verses report the effect on Titus. Paul had predicted that the Corinthians would eventually repent, and Titus had been overjoyed when this turned out to be true.
8:1 The **churches of Macedonia** were congregations in Philippi, Thessalonica, and Berea (Ac 16–17).
8:2–3 These churches had been born in **affliction** (Ac 16–17). Moreover, they were limited in financial resources; yet these factors had not impeded their giving.
8:4 The same word (**ministry**) previously used to describe Christian service (4:1; 5:18; 6:3) is now used to describe Christian giving. Financial stewardship is ministry.
8:5 When believers offer **themselves** wholly to **the Lord**, they have no difficulty in offering their wallets to him.

8:6 Paul's collection for the Jerusalem Christians had been a long-term project. The Corinthians had "been ready since last year" (9:2) to give, but had not completed the task. Now that the Corinthians were restored, it was time to finish the task, but it would only be done the right way if it was prompted by God's **grace** (v. 1).
8:7 The Corinthians were more affluent than the Macedonians; therefore they could give more generously.
8:9 Jesus's self-sacrifice is an even higher standard of giving. He willingly exchanged all the wealth of his deity for the **poverty** of the incarnation.
8:10–11 On **finish the task**, see note at v. 6.
8:12 God is more concerned with the quality of giving than with the quantity (Lk 21:1–4).
8:13–14 A congregation that has been generous may later find itself in need of help from others.
8:15 The quotation from Ex 16:18 comes from the Israelites' first experience with gathering daily manna. God saw to it that those who gathered **little** had enough and those who gathered **much** did not have a surplus. Paul calls on the Corinthians to be equitable

voluntarily, trusting God that they would have enough.
8:16–17 Titus had volunteered to return to the Corinthians to oversee the collection. **Went out to you** refers to Titus's role as the letter carrier for 2 Corinthians.

#75 **99 Essential Christian Truths**

DEMONS

Demons are angelic beings who sinned against God and now continually work evil in the world today (Jb 1:6; Zch 3:1; Lk 10:18). Demons oppose God and seek to destroy his work, as seen in the Bible's description of Satan, the head of demons, who seeks to "steal and kill and destroy" (Jn 10:10). Though demons have power, they are limited by God's control and can only act within the constraints of what God permits. In the end, all demons will be cast into the eternal fire that God has prepared for them (Mt 25:41).

welcomed our appeal and, being very diligent, went out to you by his own choice. **18** We have sent with him the brother who is praised among all the churches for his gospel ministry.^ **19** And not only that, but he was also appointed by the churches to accompany us with this gracious gift that we are administering for the glory of the Lord himself and to show our eagerness to help. **20** We are taking this precaution so that no one will criticize us about this large sum that we are administering. **21** Indeed, we are giving careful thought to do what is right, not only before the Lord but also before people. **22** We have also sent with them our brother. We have often tested him in many circumstances and found him to be diligent — and now even more diligent because of his great confidence in you. **23** As for Titus, he is my partner and coworker for you; as for our brothers, they are the messengers of the churches, the glory of Christ. **24** Therefore, show them proof before the churches of your love and of our boasting about you.

Motivations for Giving

9 Now concerning the ministry to the saints, it is unnecessary for me to write to you. **2** For I know your eagerness, and I boast about you to the Macedonians, "Achaia has been ready since last year," and your zeal has stirred up most of them. **3** But I am sending the brothers so that our boasting about you in this matter would not prove empty, and so that you would be ready just as I said. **4** Otherwise, if any Macedonians come with me and find you unprepared, we, not to mention you, would be put to shame in that situation.^ **5** Therefore I considered it necessary to urge the brothers

to go on ahead to you and arrange in advance the generous gift you promised, so that it will be ready as a gift and not as an extortion. **6** The point is this:^ The person who sows sparingly will also reap sparingly, and the person who sows generously will also reap generously. **7** Each person should do as he has decided in his heart — not reluctantly or out of compulsion, since God loves a cheerful giver. **8** And God is able to make every grace overflow to you, so that in every way, always having everything you need, you may excel in every good work. **9** As it is written:

He distributed freely;
he gave to the poor;
his righteousness endures forever.^

10 Now the one who provides seed for the sower and bread for food will also provide and multiply your seed and increase the harvest of your righteousness. **11** You will be enriched in every way for all generosity, which produces thanksgiving to God through us. **12** For the ministry of this service is not only supplying the needs of the saints but is also overflowing in many expressions of thanks to God. **13** Because of the proof provided by this ministry, they will glorify God for your obedient confession of the gospel of Christ, and for your generosity in sharing with them and with everyone. **14** And as they pray on your behalf, they will have deep affection for you because of the surpassing grace of God in you. **15** Thanks be to God for his indescribable gift!

Paul's Apostolic Authority

10 Now I, Paul, myself, appeal to you by the meekness and gentleness of Christ — I who am humble among you in person but

---

^ **8:18** Lit *churches, in the gospel* ^ **9:4** Or *in this confidence* ^ **9:6** Lit *And this* ^ **9:9** Ps 112:9

8:18 The **brother who is praised** is not named, but it may have been Luke.
8:19 Acts 20:4 lists all the church messengers that would **accompany** Paul with this **gift**, with Luke included in Ac 20:5–6 by the words "us" or "we."
8:20–21 From the beginning of Christianity, a scrupulous concern for integrity in dealing with money has been important. **Before people** implies public accountability.
8:22 Like the **brother** of v. 18, this one is also unnamed but praised.
8:23 See note at 2:12–13 for more about Titus's credentials.
8:24 This verse is another appeal for the Corinthian believers to complete the offering.
9:1–5 This section explains that Paul wanted to spare the Corinthians the embarrassment that would happen if their pledge went unfulfilled and others learned about it.
9:1 On **ministry to the saints**, see note at 8:4.
9:2 The **Macedonians** lived in the province north of **Achaia**, the province in which Corinth was located (see note at 1:1). Evidently what Paul had written in 1Co 16:1–4 had met with an enthusiastic pledge from the Corinthians. He had learned about this and boasted of the Corinthians' **zeal** to the

Macedonian churches. This had become a factor in the generous offering for Jerusalem that Paul had already received from Macedonia (8:1–4).
9:5 Paul intended to arrive in Corinth after Titus and the two **brothers** arrived, by which time the collection would be **ready** for him to take to Jerusalem. This is in fact what happened, as noted in Rm 15:25–27 (which was written from Corinth). The phrase **a gift and not ... an extortion** may be translated literally as "a blessing and not a [matter of] greed." In other words, the giving was to be done because this would benefit others, without the givers thinking of getting back something material in return.
9:6–15 These verses contain the most explicit passage in the NT on stewardship.
9:6 The words **sparingly ... sparingly generously ... generously** state a principle that is proverbially true, based on common agricultural experience. Here it is applied to financial matters, but see Lk 6:38; Gl 6:7–9.
9:7 Christian stewardship, like other good works, flows ideally from a heart of love for God and others rather than from a sense of duty (Mt 22:37–40).
9:8 A form of the Greek word for "all" is used in four phrases here, translated as **every**.

9:9 This quotation of Ps 112:9 is taken from a song about those who fear the Lord by living lives of righteous obedience to him, extolling them to give to **the poor.**
9:10–11 These verses return to the agricultural metaphor of v. 6, emphasizing God's sovereignty in providing for the material needs of believers (**seed**) as well as for their spiritual needs (**righteousness**).
9:12–13 The impact of the Corinthians' gift to the poor believers in Jerusalem would go far beyond Jerusalem. Other congregations would learn about it and praise God for the **generosity** of the Corinthians. Christian stewardship is one important way to acknowledge the truth of Christ's **gospel** before others.
9:14 An added incentive for giving is that other believers will **pray** for those who give generously, because generous giving is evidence of the **grace of God** already at work in such people.
9:15 His indescribable gift refers to God's Son, Jesus. Giving ought to be an expression of appreciation to God for sending Jesus (Jn 3:16).
10:1 These words (**Now I, Paul**) mark the most important transition in the epistle. The first nine chapters of 2 Corinthians have been

bold toward you when absent. [2] I beg you that when I am present I will not need to be bold with the confidence by which I plan to challenge certain people who think we are living according to the flesh. [3] For although we live in the flesh, we do not wage war according to the flesh, [4] since the weapons of our warfare are not of the flesh, but are powerful through God for the demolition of strongholds. We demolish arguments [5] and every proud thing that is raised up against the knowledge of God, and we take every thought captive to obey Christ. [6] And we are ready to punish any disobedience, once your obedience is complete.

[7] Look at what is obvious.[A] If anyone is confident that he belongs to Christ, let him remind himself of this: Just as he belongs to Christ, so do we. [8] For if I boast a little too much about our authority, which the Lord gave for building you up and not for tearing you down, I will not be put to shame. [9] I don't want to seem as though I am trying to terrify you with my letters. [10] For it is said, "His letters are weighty and powerful, but his physical presence is weak and his public speaking amounts to nothing." [11] Let such a person consider this: What we are in our letters, when we are absent, we will also be in our actions when we are present.

[12] For we don't dare classify or compare ourselves with some who commend themselves. But in measuring themselves by themselves and comparing themselves to themselves, they lack understanding. [13] We, however, will not boast beyond measure but according to

the measure of the area of ministry that God has assigned to us, which reaches even to you. [14] For we are not overextending ourselves, as if we had not reached you, since we have come to you with the gospel of Christ. [15] We are not boasting beyond measure about other people's labors. On the contrary, we have the hope that as your faith increases, our area of ministry will be greatly enlarged, [16] so that we may preach the gospel to the regions beyond you without boasting about what has already been done in someone else's area of ministry. [17] So let the one who boasts, boast in the Lord.[B] [18] For it is not the one commending himself who is approved, but the one the Lord commends.

Paul and the False Apostles

11 I wish you would put up with a little foolishness from me. Yes, do put up with me![C] [2] For I am jealous for you with a godly jealousy, because I have promised you in marriage to one husband — to present a pure virgin to Christ. [3] But I fear that, as the serpent deceived Eve by his cunning, your minds may be seduced from a sincere and pure[D] devotion to Christ. [4] For if a person comes and preaches another Jesus, whom we did not preach, or you receive a different spirit, which you had not received, or a different gospel, which you had not accepted, you put up with it splendidly! [5] Now I consider myself in no way inferior to those "super-apostles." [6] Even if I am untrained in public speaking, I am certainly not untrained

[A]10:7 Or You are looking at things outwardly   [B]10:17 Jr 9:24   [C]11:1 Or Yes, you are putting up with me   [D]11:3 Other mss omit and pure

---

warm and encouraging. Here the language dramatically changes to a harsh, threatening tone, because Paul was on the defensive against charges made by the false apostles (11:13).

10:2 Paul planned to **challenge certain people** who had accused him of **living according to the flesh**—that is, according to human standards.

10:3–4 Paul often used the language of battle and struggle (1Co 14:8; 1Tm 1:18; 4:7), but there is a right way and a wrong way to fight. Christians should resort neither to the literal weapons of warfare nor to the rhetorical weapons of sophisticated philosophical reasoning to advance the gospel. Divine, supernatural power is required to defeat Satan's **strongholds**.

10:5 The **proud thing** refers to arguments made by false teachers. See 1:18–30 for Paul's earlier guidance to the Corinthians on this topic.

10:6 The phrase **your obedience** means the commitment of the Corinthians to Paul's cause in opposing the false apostles. On his intention to deal severely with the troublemakers, see note at 13:2.

10:7 One clique in the Corinthian church—and perhaps the false teachers—had arrogantly claimed, "I belong to **Christ**" (1Co 1:12) to the exclusion of others. Paul had condemned this divisiveness (1Co 1:10–17) because there is no inner circle in Chris-

tianity made up of an especially enlightened group.

10:8 Within the church Christ has given **authority** and leadership responsibility to certain individuals to use **for building . . . up** believers but never for **tearing . . . down**.

10:9–10 Paul's earlier correspondence caused the Corinthians to be "grieved" (7:8), but it was for their own good and it was not done just to frighten them. The false apostles contrasted the **powerful** impact of his letters with the **weak** impact of his presence and his lack of oratorical skill in his **public speaking** (11:6; 1Co 2:1–4), supposing this was proof of a major defect in the apostle.

10:12 The false apostles were good at self-promotion, or commending **themselves**. For people to use themselves as the standard for evaluating their ministry shows that they **lack understanding**.

10:13–16 Paul's standard of self-evaluation was the extent to which he had obeyed God's call on his life, rather than comparing himself to others. The word **area** suggests either an agricultural image (a measured-out field to be planted and harvested) or an athletic image (a marked-out lane in which to run; vv. 15–16). Paul understood his ministry as essentially that of a pioneer church planter.

10:17–18 The phrase **let the one who boasts, boast in the Lord** is a summary of Jr 9:24. Paul's application to the present situation in Corinth implied that he knew

God, but the false apostles did not. **The one the Lord commends** refers to the judgment seat of Christ (5:10).

11:1 Paul felt compelled by circumstances to compare himself with those who had usurped his authority in Corinth. He foresaw that this would seem like **foolishness** or madness to some, for which he begged indulgence.

11:2–3 In the marriage analogy in these verses, four parties may be identified: (1) Paul was the spiritual father of the Corinthians, (2) the Corinthians were a **pure virgin** daughter of marriageable age, (3) **Christ** was the bridegroom to whom the Corinthians were to be given **in marriage** (at his return, Rv 19:7–9), and (4) the **serpent** was the devil working through the false teachers trying to lure the daughter away from **sincere and pure devotion** to her bridegroom (vv. 13–14).

11:5 The word **super-apostles** is a combination of an adjective meaning "superior" and the usual NT word for "apostle." The only other place in the NT where this word appears is 12:11. The quotation marks indicate Paul's disdain for such a designation of those who were troubling the Corinthians.

11:6 On **untrained in public speaking**, see note at 10:9–10. In the battle of style versus substance, Paul claimed to win when it came to **knowledge** of God (see note at 10:17). His ministry concentrated on the clear truth rather than extravagant oratory.

Spiritual Warfare

by Charles E. Lawless

Spiritual warfare is a reality. From Genesis to Revelation, the Scriptures paint a picture of a cosmic battle that is largely unseen. Satan is, in fact, the "roaring lion, looking for anyone he can devour" (1Pt 5:8). Our enemy is an accuser (Rv 12:10), a deceiver (Rv 20:10), a murderer, and a liar (Jn 8:44). He is the "ruler of this world" (Jn 12:31), the "dragon" who dares to fight against the angels of God (Rv 12:7).

As believers, we wrestle against principalities and powers (Eph 6:12) that work to lure us into sin. The powers disguise themselves as "angels of light," seeking to infiltrate the church through false teachings (2Co 11:1–15). The enemy seeks to steal, kill, and destroy (Jn 10:10). Satan is not, however, the focus of the Bible—God is.

Indeed, God put in place the enmity between the seed of the woman and the seed of the serpent that would lead to the enemy's defeat at Christ's cross (Gn 3:15). God is the warrior who led his people across the Red Sea (Ex 15:3). David fought the Philistine giant, not with a sword and a javelin but in the name of the Lord whose battle it was (1Sm 17:45–47). Jahaziel likewise assured Jehoshaphat of God's presence in the midst of battle by saying, "Do not be afraid or discouraged because of this vast number, for the battle is not yours, but God's" (2Ch 20:15).

Moreover, Paul challenged believers to put on God's armor, not human armor (Eph 6:11). God is our shield (Gn 15:1; Ps 28:7), and he wears righteousness as body armor and the helmet of salvation (Is 59:17). This sovereign God even allows spiritual battles to take place in our lives in order to accomplish the greater good of his will (see Jb 1–2).

Because the Bible's story is about the one who will ultimately cast the devil into the lake of fire (Rv 20:10), our task as spiritual warriors is not to know Satan well; it is to know God so intimately that Satan's counterfeit becomes obvious by comparison. To know God and to recognize his sovereignty is to understand that we gain spiritual victory only through Christ, who has been raised above every power and authority (Eph 1:20–23).

Victory in Spiritual Warfare

Believers need not fear the enemy, for we have the sword of the Spirit, the Word of God, as a primary weapon in battle (Eph 6:17). The Word reminds us that Satan has been disarmed by the cross of Christ (Col 2:15), his power is limited by the will of Almighty God (Jb 1:10–12), and he will ultimately be bound (Rv 20:10). Like Jesus in the wilderness temptations, we can defeat our enemy through confidence in the Word (Mt 4:1–11).

Our victory is anchored in the central story of the Scriptures: the event of the cross. Jesus took on himself the sin of the world, paid the penalty for that sin, and conquered death (2Co 5:21; 1Jn 2:2). He ultimately broke Satan's power by his obedience "to the point of death—even to death on a cross" (Php 2:8). Through his shed blood Christ has redeemed us (Eph 1:7) and placed us on the winning side of this spiritual battle. Indeed, we are on the offensive, daily living out the triumph of the cross.

The world sees our victory in spiritual warfare not by our strategies and techniques but by our walking in truth and righteousness. The defeat of the enemy is consequently evident by how we live. And, for many believers who face persecution today, the enemy's defeat will also be seen by how they die. What surely seems a loss from a human perspective will instead be an announcement of mighty victory in heaven.

Cautions in Spiritual Warfare

Interest in the topic of spiritual warfare today has, however, often resulted in faulty understandings of warfare strategies. For example, some "warfare" writers and practitioners emphasize demonic exorcism as a primary tactic. Scholars debate whether demon possession occurs today, but it is difficult to prove that possession never occurs—especially when considering frontier mission fields in animistic cultures. Nevertheless, the Bible does not present exorcism as a chief ministry strategy. Jesus exorcised demons, yet he did so in the context of preaching and teaching ministry (see, e.g., Mk 1:21–28). He did not adopt elaborate exorcism rituals common in his day, nor did he go demon hunting.

Jesus's approaches to exorcism were, in fact, varied. Often he spoke to the demon (e.g., Lk 8:29) but not always (Lk 13:10–17). He was not always physically present with the demon-possessed person (Mt 15:22–28). Only once is there evidence that he asked the name of a demon (Mk 5:9), and that was not to gain authority over the evil spirit. "Rebuking" language is common (e.g., Lk 4:35; 9:42) but not universal. Nowhere in the Bible is there a clear, reproducible exorcism ritual; thus, teaching such a pattern is biblically unwarranted.

Equally problematic are the implications that there are particular symptoms of possession and specific steps in exorcisms; again, such conclusions are not evident in Scripture. Demonic manifestations included, among other things, physical symptoms (e.g., Mt 9:32–33; 12:22), self-inflicted wounds (Mk 5:5), falling (Mk 9:18), and supernatural strength (Mk 5:3–4). Such diverse descriptions, however, are just that: descriptions rather than expectations.

Further, some "exorcists" assert that demons can possess believers. This conclusion is biblically indefensible. The Scriptures teach that believers are indwelt by and sealed by the Spirit of God (2Co 1:22; Eph 1:14), and the one in us is more powerful than the one who rules the world (1Jn 4:4). The Scriptures contain no example of a demon-possessed believer.

Others affirm the existence of "territorial spirits," or demonic beings that inhabit or reside over a region. Some warfare practitioners teach that we must cast down these demons before effectively doing evangelism in an area. The biblical evidence for such demons is weak at best (e.g., Dn 10:1–14), and nowhere is there a mandate for identifying or "praying down" these powers. A process of aggressively attacking territorial demons implies that the air must be cleared before the gospel can be effective. The implication is thus that the word of the cross as "the power of God" (1Co 1:18) apparently needs help in some situations. Such an implication demeans the power of the Word.

Christians and the Armor of God

How, then, should we respond to the issue of spiritual warfare? We must first recognize its reality. Even those who believe exorcisms are unwarranted cannot deny the continued reality of spiritual warfare. The enemy still seeks to destroy God's people, and to deny that is to invite defeat.

Second, we must proclaim the Word of God. Potent and life changing, the message of the cross frees the blinded minds of the unbelieving (2Co 4:3–4) and equips believers for good works (2Tm 3:16–17). The proclamation of the Word is, in fact, an act of warfare against Satan's kingdom. It is no wonder, then, that the enemy so viciously strikes those who stand on the Scriptures—the very Word that promises us victory even in death (Heb 2:14–15).

Third, we must teach believers how to put on the full armor of God and resist the enemy (Eph 6:11; Jms 4:7). Putting on the armor is about learning to walk in truth, righteousness, and faith. It is about reading and proclaiming the Word of God while standing firmly on the gospel. When our strategies for discipleship—a fundamental element of spiritual warfare preparation—are weak, we send new believers into a lethal context unarmed. Defeat is then almost inevitable.

As followers of Christ, we are to wear the full armor of God, proclaim the gospel to unbelievers, and disciple believers. Taking on the enemy is not about a formula or a technique. It is about a lifestyle—a Bible-saturated, God-centered, Jesus-glorifying, Spirit-filled, prayer-driven lifestyle.

in knowledge. Indeed, we have in every way made that clear to you in everything. [7] Or did I commit a sin by humbling myself so that you might be exalted, because I preached the gospel of God to you free of charge? [8] I robbed other churches by taking pay from them to minister to you. [9] When I was present with you and in need, I did not burden anyone, since the brothers who came from Macedonia supplied my needs. I have kept myself, and will keep myself, from burdening you in any way. [10] As the truth of Christ is in me, this boasting of mine will not be stopped[A] in the regions of Achaia. [11] Why? Because I don't love you? God knows I do!

[12] But I will continue to do what I am doing, in order to deny[B] an opportunity to those who want to be regarded as our equals in what they boast about. [13] For such people are false apostles, deceitful workers, disguising themselves as apostles of Christ. [14] And no wonder! For Satan disguises himself as an angel of light. [15] So it is no great surprise if his servants also disguise themselves as servants of righteousness. Their end will be according to their works.

Paul's Sufferings for Christ

[16] I repeat: Let no one consider me a fool. But if you do, at least accept me as a fool so that I can also boast a little. [17] What I am saying in this matter[C] of boasting, I don't speak as the Lord would, but as it were, foolishly. [18] Since many boast according to the flesh, I will also boast. [19] For you, being so wise, gladly put up with fools! [20] In fact, you put up with it if someone enslaves you, if someone exploits you, if someone takes advantage of you, if someone is arrogant toward you, if someone slaps you in the face. [21] I say this to our shame: We have been too weak for that!

But in whatever anyone dares to boast — I am talking foolishly — I also dare: [22] Are they Hebrews? So am I. Are they Israelites? So am I. Are they the descendants of Abraham? So am I. [23] Are they servants of Christ? I'm talking like a madman — I'm a better one: with far more labors, many more imprisonments, far worse beatings, many times near death.

[24] Five times I received the forty lashes minus one from the Jews. [25] Three times I was beaten with rods. Once I received a stoning. Three times I was shipwrecked. I have spent a night and a day in the open sea. [26] On frequent journeys, I faced dangers from rivers, dangers from robbers, dangers from my own people, dangers from Gentiles, dangers in the city, dangers in the wilderness, dangers at sea, and dangers among false brothers; [27] toil and hardship, many sleepless nights, hunger and thirst, often without food, cold, and without clothing. [28] Not to mention[D] other things, there is the daily pressure on me: my concern for all the churches. [29] Who is weak, and I am not weak? Who is made to stumble, and I do not burn with indignation?

[30] If boasting is necessary, I will boast about my weaknesses. [31] The God and Father of the Lord Jesus, who is blessed forever, knows I am not lying. [32] In Damascus, a ruler[E] under King Aretas guarded the city of Damascus in order to arrest me. [33] So I was let down in a basket through a window in the wall and escaped from his hands.

Sufficient Grace

12 Boasting is necessary. It is not profitable, but I will move on to visions and revelations of the Lord. [2] I know a man in Christ who was caught up to the third heaven fourteen

---

[A]11:10 Or *silenced*   [B]11:12 Lit *cut off*   [C]11:17 Or *business*, or *confidence*   [D]11:28 Lit *Apart from*   [E]11:32 Gk *ethnarches*; a leader of an ethnic community

---

11:7–8 The "super-apostles" obviously expected to be paid (see note at 2:17). They had apparently suggested to the Corinthians that it was a sign of Paul's inferiority that he declined financial support.

11:9–11 The **brothers** who came from Macedonia were Silas and Timothy (Ac 18:5). After planting Macedonian churches (in Philippi, Thessalonica, and Berea; Ac 16–17), Paul had traveled to Achaia alone. Following a brief stop in Athens, he had settled in Corinth, supporting himself as a tentmaker (Ac 18:1–4). Some time later, his traveling partners Silas and Timothy came with sufficient funds collected from the Macedonian churches, enabling Paul to devote full attention to his ministry. On his teaching about Christian financial support for ministers in general, see 1Co 9:12–15.

11:12 I will continue is a reference to preaching without pay, which would sharpen the contrast between Paul and the false teachers.

11:13–15 The so-called "super-apostles" were not simply believers who disagreed with Paul in motive or method. They were agents of Satan who had gained a hearing in the church. Verse 13 is the only place in the

NT where the phrase **false apostles** occurs, but see Rv 2:2.

11:16–12:10 Bible interpreters have often identified these verses as Paul's "Fool's Speech." In order to defend himself against the false apostles, he boasted about experiences he had had, many of which would usually be considered evidences of shame or humiliation. Yet the false teachers couldn't come close to matching Paul's record.

11:16 This word for **fool** is from the Greek *aphronos*, meaning "one who is ignorant or unlearned" (vv. 16,19; 12:6,11; Rm 2:20; 1Co 15:36; Eph 5:17). We might translate it as "ignoramus."

11:17 In the Gospels Jesus never spoke the way Paul was about to speak.

11:19 Put up with is the same verb as that in 11:4, expressing the same sarcasm. The Greek word for **so wise** is the opposite of foolish (see note at v. 16).

11:20–21 Tactics of the false teachers included psychological and physical intimidation. Paul responded tongue-in-cheek: **We have been too weak for that!**

11:23 Paul did not concede that these false apostles were **servants of Christ**. He had

just called them Satan's servants (v. 15). But he granted their claim for the sake of argument.

11:24–25 Paul lists five Jewish beatings (thirty-nine lashes; see note at Dt 25:1–3) and three Roman beatings. Of the beatings mentioned here, only the Roman beating at Philippi is reported (Ac 16:22). The stoning occurred in Lystra (Ac 14:19). The shipwreck of Ac 27 occurred after the writing of 2 Corinthians.

11:28 Everything Paul mentioned in vv. 23–27 was endured in the course of church planting or evangelism. After converts were made, he faced the task of cultivating these believers in their faith.

11:32–33 This episode, Paul's first brush with being persecuted, is also reported in Ac 9:23–25. Luke, the Gentile author of Acts, noted that Jews of **Damascus** initiated the plot, while Paul the Jew remembered this as a plot of the Gentile governor of the city. There was probably a coalition of Jews and Nabateans serving under the governor.

12:1 This verse is a continuation of Paul's boasting as a fool, revealing how great he

years ago. Whether he was in the body or out of the body, I don't know; God knows. ³ I know that this man — whether in the body or out of the body I don't know; God knows — ⁴ was caught up into paradise and heard inexpressible words, which a human being is not allowed to speak. ⁵ I will boast about this person, but not about myself, except of my weaknesses.

⁶ For if I want to boast, I wouldn't be a fool, because I would be telling the truth. But I will spare you, so that no one can credit me with something beyond what he sees in me or hears from me, ⁷ especially because of the extraordinary revelations. Therefore, so that I would not exalt myself, a thorn in the flesh was given to me, a messenger of Satan to torment me so that I would not exalt myself. ⁸ Concerning this, I pleaded with the Lord three times that it would leave me. ⁹ But he said to me, "My grace is sufficient for you, for my power is perfected in weakness."

Therefore, I will most gladly boast all the more about my weaknesses, so that Christ's power may reside in me. ¹⁰ So I take pleasure in weaknesses, insults, hardships, persecutions, and in difficulties, for the sake of Christ. For when I am weak, then I am strong.

Signs of an Apostle

¹¹ I have been a fool; you forced it on me. You ought to have commended me, since I am not in any way inferior to those "super-apostles," even though I am nothing. ¹² The signs of an apostle were performed with unfailing endurance among you, including signs and wonders and miracles. ¹³ So in what way are you worse off than the other churches, except that I personally did not burden you? Forgive me for this wrong!

Paul's Concern for the Corinthians

¹⁴ Look, I am ready to come to you this third time. I will not burden you, since I am not seeking what is yours, but you. For children ought not save up for their parents, but parents for their children. ¹⁵ I will most gladly spend and be spent for you.ᴬ If I love you more, am I to be loved less? ¹⁶ Now granted, I did not burden you; yet sly as I am, I took you in by deceit! ¹⁷ Did I take advantage of you by any of those I sent you? ¹⁸ I urged Titus to go, and I sent the brother with him. Titus didn't take advantage of you, did he? Didn't we walk in the same spirit and in the same footsteps?

¹⁹ Have you been thinking all along that we were defending ourselves to you? No, in the sight of God we are speaking in Christ, and everything, dear friends, is for building you up. ²⁰ For I fear that perhaps when I come I will not find you to be what I want, and you may not find me to be what you want. Perhaps there will be quarreling, jealousy, angry outbursts, selfish ambitions, slander, gossip, arrogance, and disorder. ²¹ I fear that when I come my God will againᴮ humiliate me in your presence, and I will grieve for many who sinned before and have not repented of the moral impurity, sexual immorality, and sensuality they practiced.

ᴬ12:15 Lit for your souls, or for your lives　ᴮ12:21 Or come again my God will

was in comparison to the false apostles. Paul's conversion came in response to a vision (see Ac 26:19). As an apostle, he received direct **revelations** from Christ (Gl 1:12; Eph 3:3). The **visions** mentioned here are reported nowhere else.
12:2–3 A **man in Christ** is Paul's euphemism for himself, expressed in the third person for humility's sake. **Third heaven** is the place of God's dwelling. The first heaven is the atmospheric sky, and the second heaven is the planetary sky. The time period, **fourteen years ago**, would have been about AD 42, assuming 2 Corinthians was written in 56. This vision therefore preceded Paul's missionary travels, and he had evidently never spoken of it until now. He was not sure whether his body (**in the body or out of the body**) was taken to heaven or not during the vision.
12:4 The only other place where Paul used this verb **caught up**, other than in v. 2, was to refer to the bodily catching up of living believers to meet the Lord in the air at his return, sometimes called the rapture (1Th 4:17). The word **paradise** expresses the same idea as the third heaven of v. 2. It occurs in two other NT passages, where it also means "heaven" (Lk 23:43; Rv 2:7).
12:7 Paul did not say what his **thorn in the flesh** was, although the Corinthians probably knew. Suggestions about the "thorn" have included physical ailments (poor eyesight or ill health); psychological or spiritual

ailments (depression, demonic oppression, or an ongoing temptation from a bodily desire); and opposition to his ministry (enemies both inside and outside the churches).
12:9 The sufficiency of divine **grace** may be easier to grasp intellectually than through experience, especially for those who are naturally inclined to self-reliance. God ensured that Paul never got away from grace (see note at 1:2). God's glorious **power** is more evident when it is displayed in weak vessels (see note at 4:7).
12:10 All of Paul's sufferings—which he recapped here in five short phrases—became occasions for him to be pleased or delighted (Php 4:13).
12:11 On **fool**, see note at 11:16. On **superapostles**, see note at 11:5.
12:12 The apostles whom Jesus commissioned as his official spokesmen received power from him to do the same mighty **signs and wonders and miracles** he had done. This authenticated their authority and status (Mk 6:7; 1Th 1:5). The "super-apostles" lacked these credentials.
12:13 Paul **did not burden** the Corinthian believers because he did not ask for payment for his ministry (see note at 11:7–8). **Forgive me for this wrong** is a satirical comment.
12:14–15 Paul's first visit to the Corinthians was the long church-planting visit, around AD 50–51 (Ac 18:11). His second visit was the

brief painful experience (2Co 2:1). Earlier in the letter he had promised a **third** visit (see note at 9:5). This was fulfilled, as Rm 15:26 shows. Paul would not burden the Corinthians by asking for money for his personal use. He wanted their hearts and affection, not their money. Paul felt a fatherly **love** for the Corinthians and he yearned for this love to be returned, even though he didn't expect the Corinthians to love him as much as he loved them.
12:16–17 By the phrase **I took you in by deceit**, Paul is either using irony (in which case he meant the opposite) or else he is repeating the slanderous claims made by the false apostles.
12:18 Paul was sending **Titus** and an unnamed **brother** (see 8:6,18,22) along with this letter to oversee the collection for Jerusalem. Paul knew that Titus's behavior in financial matters had been, and would continue to be, above reproach.
12:20 The phrase **I will not find you to be what I want** is another appeal to the unrepentant minority of Corinthian Christians. The eight vices listed in this verse were the "works" of the false apostles, which would result in eternal condemnation (11:15).
12:21 First Corinthians 5 shows that sexual sins had been longstanding challenges in the Corinthian congregation. The false apostles may have added insult to injury by approving of sexual license.

Final Warnings and Exhortations

13 This is the third time I am coming to you. Every matter must be established by the testimony of two or three witnesses.^A ² I gave a warning when I was present the second time, and now I give a warning while I am absent to those who sinned before and to all the rest: If I come again, I will not be lenient, ³ since you seek proof of Christ speaking in me. He is not weak in dealing with you, but powerful among you. ⁴ For he was crucified in weakness, but he lives by the power of God. For we also are weak in him, but in dealing with you we will live with him by God's power.

⁵ Test yourselves to see if you are in the faith. Examine yourselves. Or do you yourselves not recognize that Jesus Christ is in you? — unless you fail the test.^B ⁶ And I hope you will recognize that we ourselves do not fail the test. ⁷ But we pray to God that you do nothing wrong — not that we may appear to pass the test, but that you may do what is right, even though we may appear to fail. ⁸ For we can't do anything against the truth, but only for the truth. ⁹ We rejoice when we are weak and you are strong. We also pray that you become fully mature.^C ¹⁰ This is why I am writing these things while absent, so that when I am there I may not have to deal harshly with you, in keeping with the authority the Lord gave me for building up and not for tearing down.

¹¹ Finally, brothers and sisters, rejoice.^D Become mature, be encouraged,^E be of the same mind, be at peace, and the God of love and peace will be with you. ¹² Greet one another with a holy kiss. All the saints send you greetings.

¹³ The grace of the Lord Jesus Christ, and the love of God, and the fellowship of the Holy Spirit be with you all.^F

---

^A13:1 Dt 17:6; 19:15 ^B13:5 Or you are disqualified, or you are counterfeit ^C13:9 Or become complete, or be restored ^D13:11 Or farewell ^E13:11 Or listen to my appeal ^F13:12-13 Some translations divide these two vv. into three vv. so that v. 13 begins with All the saints... and v. 14 begins with The grace of...

13:1 On **third time**, see note at 12:14–15. The quotation from Dt 19:15 (**testimony of two or three witnesses**) established a pattern for verifying the truth of an accusation.
13:2 Paul would **not be lenient** on his planned third visit to the Corinthian believers. His sense of apostolic authority is nowhere more evident than in this verse.
13:3–4 Christ's crucifixion and Paul's own ministry might be taken as proof that they were weak, but the resurrection showed Christ's power, which Paul shared.

13:5 A believer never gets beyond the need for regular self-examination (1Co 11:28; Gl 6:4).
13:6–7 Profession of faith and possession of faith are two different matters.
13:8 The truth is expressed in 13:4.
13:10 The phrase **when I am there** is a reference to Paul's third visit to the Corinthians. This is the second and last time in the letter that Paul used the term **authority** (10:8). In both cases, he noted that his calling was to build up, not tear down.

13:11 The verb rendered **rejoice** is sometimes translated "farewell," but "rejoice" is better.
13:12 Five NT letters end with an encouragement for Christians to show appropriate affection with a **holy kiss** (v. 12; Rm 16:16; 1Co 16:20; 1Th 5:26; 1Pt 5:14). The exact expression of this practice will vary from culture to culture.
13:13 On **grace**, see note at 1:2. This Trinitarian benediction has been frequently used to conclude worship services. See 1:21–22 and 3:17 for other references in the letter that point to the Trinity.

▼ Introduction to Galatians

Circumstances of Writing

The author's name is stated as Paul, and he claims to be "an apostle" of Christ (Gl 1:1). The autobiographical information in the letter is consistent with what is known about the apostle Paul from Acts and his other letters. Theologically, everything in Galatians agrees with Paul's views elsewhere, notably in Romans.

It is not certain where the Galatian churches were located or when Paul wrote Galatians. The reason is that, during the New Testament era, the term *Galatians* was used both ethnically and politically. If *Galatians* is understood ethnically, the founding of the Galatian churches is only implied in the New Testament. On Paul's second missionary journey, he "went through the region of Phrygia and Galatia" (Ac 16:6) in north-central Asia Minor.

Understood politically, *Galatians* can refer to those living in the southern part of the Roman province of Galatia. That region included the cities of Pisidian Antioch, Iconium, Lystra, and Derbe, where Paul worked to plant churches, as recorded in Acts 13:14–14:23.

The view that Galatians was written to the area where the ethnic Galatians lived is called the North Galatian theory. The possible dates of writing related to this understanding range from AD 52 or 53 (if shortly after the second missionary journey) to AD 56 (if written about the same time as Romans, to which it is similar theologically).

The view that Galatians was sent to churches in the southern portion of the Roman province of Galatia is the South Galatian theory. Some holding this view date Galatians in the early 50s, but others as early as AD 48 or 49, before the Jerusalem Council, which is usually dated to about AD 49.

The key problem addressed in Galatians is that "the works of the law" of Moses (2:16–17; 3:2; cp. 5:4), notably circumcision (5:2; 6:12–13), were added by some teachers to what was required in being justified before God. This is the same issue that Acts records as the reason why the Jerusalem Council met (Ac 15:1,5), supporting the idea that the existing problem in the Galatian churches was part of the reason for the Jerusalem Council.

If Galatians was written after the Jerusalem Council, it is inconceivable that Paul would not have cited the conclusions of the council, which supported his works-free view of the gospel. This strongly implies that the Jerusalem Council had not yet occurred when Paul wrote Galatians.

Contribution to the Bible

There is much about the life and movements of the apostle Paul that is only known—or filled in significantly—from Galatians 1:13–2:14 (and the personal glimpse in 4:13–14). Among these factors are Paul's sojourn in "Arabia" (1:17) and descriptions of two trips to Jerusalem (1:18–19; 2:1–10). Paul described a confrontation with Peter (2:11–14) that is mentioned nowhere else in the New Testament.

In the middle third of Galatians, certain aspects of the gospel's Old Testament

300 BC–AD 33

The Galatians, Celts of European origins, invade Asia Minor. **278 BC**

Mark Antony and Pompey reward the Galatians with additional territory for supporting Rome in its wars against Mithridates. **63–36 BC**

Amyntas, king of Galatia, wills his kingdom to Rome at his death. **25 BC**

Jesus's trials, death, resurrection, and ascension **NISAN 14–16** or **APRIL 3–5, AD 33**

AD 34–46

Saul's conversion on the Damascus Road **OCTOBER 34**

Paul returns to his native Tarsus. **37–40**

Barnabas travels from Antioch of Syria to find Paul. **SUMMER 40**

Barnabas and Paul serve together in Antioch. **41**

Emperor Caligula is murdered by members of his Praetorian Guard. Claudius succeeds him as emperor. **41**

Judea experiences severe famine **46**

background are explained in unique ways. Notable are (1) the curse related to Jesus being crucified, as cited from Deuteronomy 21:23 (Gl 3:13); (2) Jesus's fulfilling the prophecy of the singular physical "seed" of Abraham (3:16; see Gn 22:18); (3) the roles of the law as prison (3:22–23) and guardian (3:24–25) until Christ; and (4) the extended allegory of the slave and free sons of Abraham (4:21–31).

Galatians tells us much about the ministry of the Holy Spirit in relation to the Christian life. After the Spirit's role in the ministry of adoption (4:5–6), believers are commanded to "walk by the Spirit" (5:16), be "led by the Spirit" (5:18), and "keep in step with the Spirit" (5:25), as well as "sow to the Spirit" and "reap" the related eternal harvest (6:8). The moment-by-moment outcome of that kind of sensitivity to the ministry of the Holy Spirit is what is meant by "the fruit of the Spirit" (5:22–23).

Structure

The book of Galatians follows the typical pattern for a first-century letter but lacks the element of thanksgiving: salutation (1:1–5), the main body (1:6–6:15), and a farewell (6:16–18). Contrasting concepts are prominent in the letter: divine revelation versus human insight, grace versus law, justification versus condemnation, Jerusalem versus Mount Sinai, sonship versus slavery, the fruit of the Spirit versus the works of the flesh, and liberty versus bondage.

Outline

I. Introduction (1:1–9)
II. The Authenticity of Paul's Message (1:10–2:21)
III. The Way of Salvation (3:1–4:31)
IV. The Path of Freedom (5:1–6:10)
V. Conclusion: Sacrificial Living vs. Legalism (6:11–18)

Key verses in Galatians

5:13   For you were called to be free, brothers and sisters; only don't use this freedom as an opportunity for the flesh, but serve one another through love.

6:10   Therefore, as we have opportunity, let us work for the good of all, especially for those who belong to the household of faith.

AD 41–49

Paul, Barnabas, and John Mark make their first missionary journey. **47–49**

From Syrian Antioch, Paul writes his letter to the Galatians, assuming the destination of the letter was the churches of southern Galatia: Iconium, Lystra, and Derbe. **49**

Barnabas and Paul travel from Antioch to Jerusalem for the conference dealing with the question of whether Gentiles had to be circumcised in order to be saved. **49**

Paul and Barnabas part ways over the question of whether John Mark should be allowed to join them on a second missionary journey. **49**

AD 49–51

Paul and Silas team up for an overland journey to revisit cities of south Galatia as the first segment of Paul's second missionary journey. **49**

Timothy joins Paul and Silas as they travel through north Galatia to Troas. **49**

Paul, Silas, and Timothy sail from Troas to Macedonia, planting the church in Philippi. **50**

Paul and his companions move from Philippi to Thessalonica and Berea. **50**

As a result of much persecution, Paul and his companions split up, with Paul going to Corinth by way of Athens. **50–51**

Greeting

1 Paul, an apostle — not from men or by man, but by Jesus Christ and God the Father who raised him from the dead — ² and all the brothers who are with me:

To the churches of Galatia.

³ Grace to you and peace from God the Father and our Lord^A Jesus Christ, ⁴ who gave himself for our sins to rescue us from this present evil age, according to the will of our God and Father. ⁵ To him be the glory forever and ever. Amen.

No Other Gospel

⁶ I am amazed that you are so quickly turning away from him who called you by the grace of Christ and are turning to a different gospel — ⁷ not that there is another gospel, but there are some who are troubling you and want to distort the gospel of Christ. ⁸ But even if we or an angel from heaven should preach to you a gospel contrary to what we have preached to you, a curse be on him!^B ⁹ As we have said before, I now say again: If anyone is preaching to you a gospel contrary to what you received, a curse be on him!

¹⁰ For am I now trying to persuade people,^C or God? Or am I striving to please people? If I were still trying to please people, I would not be a servant of Christ.

The Origin of Paul's Gospel

¹¹ For I want you to know, brothers and sisters, that the gospel preached by me is not of human origin. ¹² For I did not receive it from a human source and I was not taught it, but it came by a revelation of Jesus Christ.

¹³ For you have heard about my former way of life in Judaism: I intensely persecuted God's church and tried to destroy it. ¹⁴ I advanced in Judaism beyond many contemporaries among my people, because I was extremely zealous for the traditions of my ancestors. ¹⁵ But when God, who from my mother's womb set me apart and called me by his grace, was pleased ¹⁶ to reveal his Son in me, so that I could preach him among the Gentiles, I did not immediately consult with anyone.^D ¹⁷ I did not go up to Jerusalem to those who had become apostles before me; instead I went to Arabia and came back to Damascus.

¹⁸ Then after three years I did go up to Jerusalem to get to know Cephas,^E and I stayed with him fifteen days. ¹⁹ But I didn't see any of the other apostles except James, the Lord's brother. ²⁰ I declare in the sight of God: I am not lying in what I write to you.

²¹ Afterward, I went to the regions of Syria and Cilicia. ²² I remained personally unknown to the Judean churches that are in Christ. ²³ They simply kept hearing, "He who formerly persecuted us now preaches the faith he once tried to destroy." ²⁴ And they glorified God because of me.^F

Paul Defends His Gospel at Jerusalem

2 Then after fourteen years I went up again to Jerusalem with Barnabas, taking Titus along also. ² I went up according to a revelation

---

^A 1:3 Other mss read *God our Father and the Lord*   ^B 1:8 Or *you, let him be condemned,* or *you, let him be condemned to hell;* Gk *anathema*   ^C 1:10 Or *win the approval of people*   ^D 1:16 Lit *flesh and blood*   ^E 1:18 Other mss read *Peter*   ^F 1:24 Or *in me*

1:1 Paul referred to himself as **an apostle** to assert that his authority for speaking to the problems in the Galatian churches came from **God**, not **men**.
1:2 The churches of Galatia indicates this letter was to be read in multiple congregations.
1:3 Grace begins and ends every one of Paul's NT letters.
1:4 Christ's redemptive death is the heart of the gospel message. Paul emphasized both the death and resurrection of Christ at the beginning of Galatians (1:1) to begin to counteract the message they had recently

#76 99 Essential Christian Truths

IMAGE OF GOD IN HUMANITY

The image of God in humanity is understood as mirroring God's attributes in our nature, actions, and relational capacities. In Jesus, we see the true image of God. He perfectly mirrors God's attributes, fulfills God's will, and enjoys a perfect relationship with the Father. The Bible continues to speak of the image of God in humanity even after our fall into sin, even though our ability to rightly reflect God has been marred.

heard that claimed salvation came through "the works of the law" (2:16).
1:6–7 Verse 6 is abrupt. After Paul left Galatia, the Galatians heard and responded to a **different** gospel they thought was better, but it was actually no true gospel.
1:8–9 The purity of the gospel is so important that even the apostles **or an angel** should be cursed eternally (Gk *anathema*) if they tampered with it.
1:11–12 Paul did not say when his direct **revelation** from **Jesus Christ** came, but it may imply that it was related to his conversion on the Damascus Road (Ac 9:1–9; 22:6–10; 26:12–18).
1:13–14 Paul communicated three things to his readers: (1) he had **advanced** much farther in Judaism than those who had distorted the gospel, (2) he was far more **zealous** for the Jewish traditions than these false teachers, and (3) ironically, Paul's zeal and advancement in Judaism led him to persecute the church before his conversion.
1:15 This verse sounds like Jr 1:5. Paul knew that his callings to salvation and apostleship were both undeserved (Rm 1:5).
1:18 It cannot be known whether the **three years** in this verse speaks of three full calendar years or one full year plus portions of two additional years. It is also not known whether the three years is figured after: (1) Paul's conversion (vv. 15–16), (2) his departure for

Arabia (v. 17), or (3) his return from Arabia to Damascus (v. 17). His trip to Jerusalem was to get to **know** the apostle Peter (the Greek equivalent of the Aramaic **Cephas**, meaning "rock"; Mt 16:18).
1:19 James, the brother of Jesus (Mt 13:55; Jms 1:1), is nowhere else listed as one of the twelve **apostles**. But since he was the senior pastoral figure in the church at Jerusalem (see Ac 15:13; 21:18), James was considered to be virtually an "apostle."
1:21 Paul probably spent most of his time in Antioch and Tarsus.
1:23–24 Since the Judean churches **glorified God** because Paul was preaching the **faith he once tried to destroy**, it is clear that they did not disagree with the gospel as he preached it.
2:1 This reference to **fourteen years** could be to a full fourteen calendar years or twelve full years and fractions of the first and last. The time could look back to: (1) Paul's conversion (1:15–16), (2) Paul's previous trip to **Jerusalem** (1:18–19), or (3) Paul's trip to Syria and Cilicia (1:21). Scholars debate whether this refers to Paul's visit to Jerusalem in Ac 11:29–30 or to his visit for the Jerusalem Council in Ac 15. Paul's relationship with **Barnabas**, whose name means "Son of Encouragement" (Ac 4:36), began in Jerusalem (Ac 9:27). **Titus** was a convert under Paul (Ti 1:4) who became an effective minister (2Co 2:13; 7:13; Ti 1:5).

and presented to them the gospel I preach among the Gentiles, but privately to those recognized as leaders. I wanted to be sure I was not running, and had not been running, in vain. ³ But not even Titus, who was with me, was compelled to be circumcised, even though he was a Greek. ⁴ This matter arose because some false brothers had infiltrated our ranks to spy on the freedom we have in Christ Jesus in order to enslave us. ⁵ But we did not give up and submit to these people for even a moment, so that the truth of the gospel would be preserved for you.

⁶ Now from those recognized as important (what they^A once were makes no difference to me; God does not show favoritism^B) — they added nothing to me. ⁷ On the contrary, they saw that I had been entrusted with the gospel for the uncircumcised, just as Peter was for the circumcised, ⁸ since the one at work in Peter for an apostleship to the circumcised was also at work in me for the Gentiles. ⁹ When James, Cephas,^C and John — those recognized as pillars — acknowledged the grace that had been given to me, they gave the right hand of fellowship to me and Barnabas, agreeing that we should go to the Gentiles and they to the circumcised. ¹⁰ They asked only that we would remember the poor, which I had made every effort to do.

Freedom from the Law

¹¹ But when Cephas^C came to Antioch, I opposed him to his face because he stood condemned.^D ¹² For he regularly ate with the Gentiles before certain men came from James. However, when they came, he withdrew and separated himself, because he feared those from the circumcision party. ¹³ Then the rest of the Jews joined his hypocrisy, so that even Barnabas was led astray by their hypocrisy. ¹⁴ But when I saw

---

^A 2:6 Lit *the recognized ones*   ^B 2:6 Or *God is not a respecter of persons*; lit *God does not receive the face of man*
^C 2:9,11 Other mss read *Peter*   ^D 2:11 Or *he was in the wrong*

2:2 Not running . . . in vain reflects concern over brewing disunity in the church. That Paul met **privately** with the leaders (Gk *dokousin*; lit "the recognized ones") in Jerusalem makes it unlikely he was talking about the Jerusalem Council, which was larger and more public (Ac 15:6,12).
2:3 To make it clear that he had not adjusted his gospel message during this private conference with the church leadership in Jerusalem, Paul used **Titus** (see note at v. 1) as a test case. Had Paul caved in to the view that had recently been preached in the Galatian churches (that it was necessary for a Gentile to be circumcised and keep the Mosaic law to become a Christian; 2:16; 5:2–3),

Titus, a Gentile convert, would have been **compelled to be circumcised**; but he was not, reflecting the fact that Paul's gospel was accepted by the recognized church leaders in Jerusalem.
2:4 False brothers (Gk *pseudadelphoi*) reflects that they were not really Christians. They tried to **enslave** Christians to the law, which was happening in the Galatian churches (5:1).
2:6 What they once were . . . God does not show favoritism was not meant as disparaging to James, Peter, and John.
2:7–8 Paul was not saying in these verses that there are two different **gospel** messages.

2:9 The **right hand of fellowship** was a common sign of friendship and agreement.
2:10 To **remember the poor** was the main reason why Paul and Barnabas had made this trip to Jerusalem (Ac 11:28–30).
2:12–13 Peter's fear-based hypocrisy was even more flagrant because, besides eating **with the Gentiles** in the church at Syrian Antioch, he had been previously instructed by a vision to fellowship with Cornelius, the Gentile (Ac 10). Peter's hypocrisy swayed **the rest of the Jews** in the church at Antioch, including **Barnabas.**
2:14 As soon as Paul determined that **the truth of the gospel** was hanging in the balance, he confronted Peter (Cephas) **in**

Character profile:
Paul

P aul (also known as Saul) was a zealous defender of the Jewish faith. He targeted the disciples of a rabbi named Jesus of Nazareth who were attempting to keep his message alive even after the rabbi himself had been crucified. They spread stories about seeing him risen from the dead. They claimed he was the Son of God and the way to everlasting life.

Saul was determined to stamp out the movement. He led the charge in persecuting these Christians. He participated in the first recorded martyrdom in church history, the stoning of Stephen.

One day Paul set out for Damascus to arrest Christians and take them back to Jerusalem for punishment. His plans were derailed by a bright light from heaven that knocked him to the ground and left him temporarily blind. He heard a voice saying to him, "Saul, Saul, why are you persecuting me?" The voice was that of the Lord Jesus himself who instructed him to go to Damascus (see Ac 9:4–6). There, the Lord sent a believer named Ananias to visit and heal Saul. Then Saul received the Holy Spirit and was baptized.

Shortly thereafter, Saul/Paul started preaching about Jesus in the local synagogues. A devoutly religious Jew, he knew the Scriptures. So once he recognized Jesus as the long-awaited Messiah, he was ready to share the good news. People—including the apostles—were understandably skeptical at first. It didn't take long, though, for most to recognize that his transformation was real.

Thus began a life on the move, as Paul carried the gospel throughout Asia Minor and Europe. The book of Acts records three separate missionary journeys taken by Paul. On his first journey, a group of Jews stoned him and dragged his body outside the city, thinking him dead. On his second journey, he and his fellow missionary Silas were beaten and imprisoned in Philippi. Paul's third journey was marked by stunning miracles, including the healing of a young man thought to be dead. The journey ended in Jerusalem, where Paul was beaten by a Jewish mob, arrested by Roman soldiers, and sent to Rome for trial.

The biblical narrative in Acts ends before Paul stood trial. Most likely the letters of 1–2 Timothy and Titus were written after Paul was released from this first Roman imprisonment. Church tradition indicates that he was arrested (again) in Rome before finally being executed during the reign of the Roman emperor Nero.

The apostle Paul founded or shepherded several different churches during his lifetime. When his journeys took him to a new destination, he maintained contact with congregations through letters. In those letters Paul encouraged, taught, chastised, and challenged Christians. Thirteen of his letters are part of the New Testament canon.

Before his conversion, Paul actively pursued and persecuted God's people and did his best to stamp out Christianity before it could gain a foothold. Yet God chose him to spearhead the spread of Christianity throughout the world. The Lord worked in and through Paul to nurture the development of the church and to spell out the principles of Christian living.

Likewise, God can use you to accomplish extraordinary things in his name and for his kingdom if you make yourself available to him.

that they were deviating from the truth of the gospel, I told Cephas[A] in front of everyone, "If you, who are a Jew, live like a Gentile and not like a Jew, how can you compel Gentiles to live like Jews?"[B]

[15] We are Jews by birth and not "Gentile sinners,"[16] and yet because we know that a person is not justified by the works of the law but by faith in Jesus Christ,[c] even we ourselves have believed in Christ Jesus. This was so that we might be justified by faith in Christ[D] and not by the works of the law, because by the works of the law no human being will[E] be justified. [17] But if we ourselves are also found to be "sinners" while seeking to be justified by Christ, is Christ then a promoter[F] of sin? Absolutely not! [18] If I rebuild those things that I tore down, I show myself to be a lawbreaker. [19] For through the law I died to the law, so that I might live for God. [20] I have been crucified with Christ, and I no longer live, but Christ lives in me. The life I now live in the body,[G] I live by faith in the Son of God, who loved me and gave himself for me. [21] I do not set aside the grace of God, for if righteousness comes through the law, then Christ died for nothing.

Justification through Faith

3 You foolish Galatians! Who has cast a spell on you,[H] before whose eyes Jesus Christ was publicly portrayed[I] as crucified? [2] I only want to learn this from you: Did you receive the Spirit by the works of the law or by believing what you heard?[J] [3] Are you so foolish? After beginning by the Spirit, are you now finishing by the flesh? [4] Did you experience[K] so much for nothing — if in fact it was for nothing? [5] So then, does God give you the Spirit and work miracles among you by your doing the works of the law? Or is it by believing what you heard — [6] just like Abraham who **believed God, and it was credited to him for righteousness?**[L] [7] You know, then, that those who have faith, these are Abraham's sons. [8] Now the Scripture saw in advance that God would justify the Gentiles by faith and proclaimed the gospel ahead of time to Abraham, saying, **All the nations[M] will be blessed through you.**[N] [9] Consequently, those who have faith are blessed with Abraham, who had faith.[O]

Law and Promise

[10] For all who rely on the works of the law are under a curse, because it is written, **Everyone who does not do everything written in the book of the law is cursed.**[P] [11] Now it is clear that no one is justified before God by the law, because **the righteous will live by faith.**[Q] [12] But the law is not based on faith; instead, **the one who does these things will live by them.**[R] [13] Christ redeemed us from the curse of the law by becoming a curse for us, because it is written, **Cursed is everyone who is hung on a tree.**[S] [14] The purpose was that the blessing of Abraham would come to the Gentiles by Christ Jesus, so that we could receive the promised Spirit through faith.

[A]2:14 Other mss read *Peter*   [B]2:14 Some translations continue the quotation through v. 16 or v. 21.   [C]2:16 Or *by the faithfulness of Jesus Christ*   [D]2:16 Or *by the faithfulness of Christ*   [E]2:16 Lit *law all flesh will not*   [F]2:17 Or *servant*   [G]2:20 Lit *flesh*   [H]3:1 Other mss add *not to obey the truth*   [I]3:1 Other mss add *among you*   [J]3:2 Lit *hearing with faith*, also in v. 5   [K]3:4 Or *suffer*   [L]3:6 Gn 15:6   [M]3:8 Or *Gentiles*   [N]3:8 Gn 12:3; 18:18   [O]3:9 Or *with believing Abraham*   [P]3:10 Dt 27:26   [Q]3:11 Hab 2:4   [R]3:12 Lv 18:5   [S]3:13 Dt 21:23

front of everyone (i.e., in a church meeting). Peter's behavior, in eating Gentile meals prior to the group "from James" arriving in Antioch (vv. 11–12), showed he believed it was right to **live like a Gentile** among Gentiles. Thus, his later decision to compel the Gentiles in the church at Antioch to **live like Jews** was seen as inconsistent and hypocritical.

2:15 Gentile sinners likely was a phrase that his opponents, who were **Jews by birth** and apparently conceited about it, used to describe non-Jews.

2:16 Justification is a legal idea, meaning "to be declared (not *made*) righteous." When Paul speaks of the message **we . . . believed**, the plural "we" may refer to: (1) "all the brothers" with Paul at that time (1:2); (2) Paul and the Galatians, who believed when they first heard Paul's preaching (3:2); or (3) both.

2:17 Paul's opponents in Syrian Antioch and Galatia were apparently depicting his message of being **justified** by faith in Jesus **Christ** alone as "lowering" Jews spiritually to the level of being **sinners**, which somehow would make **Christ . . . a promoter of sin**. Paul's response to this preposterous idea was the strongest possible negation—**absolutely not!**

2:18 Having believed a law-free gospel of justification by faith, Paul could not go back and **rebuild** the false gospel message

(salvation through "the works of the law"; v. 16) he previously had torn down. If he did this, he would be a **lawbreaker** in the sense of sinning against grace.

2:19–20 Paul meant by his statement **through the law I died to the law** that because Jesus died under the law (3:13), Paul was now separated from the law. *I died* refers to being **crucified with Christ**, as if the believer died on the cross with Jesus. The Christian continues to live physically, but spiritually this new life is by **faith** in Christ.

2:21 If it were possible to gain God's **righteousness** through keeping **the law**, the death of Christ on the cross would have been **for nothing**, but since salvation via the law is not possible, the only alternative is justification by faith in Christ.

3:2–3 Paul asked questions about: (1) a key aspect of becoming a Christian, and (2) living as a Christian. Paul knew the Galatians would have to admit that the presence of **the Spirit** in their lives began with their **believing** what they heard (Rm 10:17). His second question was whether the Holy Spirit or **the flesh** was God's intended means of sanctification.

3:4 If in fact it was for nothing implies that Paul believed his readers would come to their senses.

3:5 The question here is essentially repeated from v. 2. **Believing what you heard** means faith in the gospel message.

3:6 The example of the faith of **Abraham** and the justification that resulted neutralizes the arguments of those who were teaching justification by the works of the law (2:16).

3:7–9 Those who have faith are **Abraham's** spiritual **sons** and daughters, whether they are Jewish or Gentile by bloodline.

3:10 Not only is it impossible to be justified by the "works of the law" (2:16), but such a perspective actually brings **a curse** on people. According to Dt 27:26, everyone who does not continue observing every detail of the law is cursed.

3:11–12 Paul added Hab 2:4 to the example of Abraham being declared **righteous . . . by faith** (see notes at v. 6; Rm 1:17). Negatively, he quoted Lv 18:5 to show that since Scripture says righteousness is by faith, it is impossible to be righteous by keeping **the law**.

3:13 Since Paul's readers were trying to be justified by the "works of the law" (2:16), they were already under its curse (see note at v. 10). Fortunately, **Christ** had **redeemed** those under such a **curse** by his crucifixion. Paul quoted Dt 21:23 to show that, by his being **hung on a tree** (the cross), Jesus was cursed in our place.

¹⁵ Brothers and sisters, I'm using a human illustration. No one sets aside or makes additions to a validated human will.ᴬ ¹⁶ Now the promises were spoken to Abraham and to his seed. He does not say "and to seeds," as though referring to many, but referring to one, **and to your seed**,ᴮ who is Christ. ¹⁷ My point is this: The law, which came 430 years later, does not invalidate a covenant previously established by Godᶜ and thus cancel the promise. ¹⁸ For if the inheritance is based on the law, it is no longer based on the promise; but God has graciously given it to Abraham through the promise.

The Purpose of the Law

¹⁹ Why, then, was the law given? It was added for the sake of transgressionsᴰ until the Seed to whom the promise was made would come. The law was put into effect through angels by means of a mediator. ²⁰ Now a mediator is not just for one person alone, but God is one. ²¹ Is the law therefore contrary to God's promises? Absolutely not! For if the law had been granted with the ability to give life, then righteousness would certainly be on the basis of the law. ²² But the Scripture imprisoned everything under sin's power,ᴱ so that the promise might be given on the basis of faith in Jesus Christ to those who believe. ²³ Before this faith came, we were confined under the law, imprisoned until the coming faith was revealed. ²⁴ The law,

then, was our guardian until Christ, so that we could be justified by faith. ²⁵ But since that faith has come, we are no longer under a guardian, ²⁶ for through faith you are all sons of God in Christ Jesus.

Sons and Heirs

²⁷ For those of you who were baptized into Christ have been clothed with Christ. ²⁸ There is no Jew or Greek, slave or free, male and female; since you are all one in Christ Jesus. ²⁹ And if you belong to Christ, then you are Abraham's seed, heirs according to the promise. 4 ¹ Now I say that as long as the heir is a child, he differs in no way from a slave, though he is the owner of everything. ² Instead, he is under guardians and trustees until the time set by his father. ³ In the same way we also, when we were children, were in slavery under the elementsᶠ of the world. ⁴ When the time came to completion, God sent his Son, born of a woman, born under the law, ⁵ to redeem those under the law, so that we might receive adoption as sons. ⁶ And because you are sons, God sent the Spirit of his Son into ourᴳ hearts, crying, "*Abba*," Father!" ⁷ So you are no longer a slave but a son, and if a son, then God has made you an heir.

Paul's Concern for the Galatians

⁸ But in the past, since you didn't know God, you were enslaved to thingsᴴ that by nature are not gods. ⁹ But now, since you know God,

---

ᴬ3:15 Or *a human covenant that has been ratified* ᴮ3:16 Gn 12:7; 13:15; 17:8; 24:7 ᶜ3:17 Other mss add *in Christ* ᴰ3:19 Or *because of transgressions* ᴱ3:22 Lit *under sin* ᶠ4:3 Or *spirits*, or *principles* ᴳ4:6 Other mss read *your* ᴴ4:6 Aramaic for *father* ᴵ4:8 Or *beings*

3:16–17 The use of the singular **seed** (Gk *sperma*) is Paul's biblical basis for saying that Christ is the one who fulfilled God's **promises . . . to Abraham**. The Mosaic law—and "the works of the law" (2:16)—cannot override the role of Christ in fulfilling the Abrahamic covenant or Abraham's example of justifying faith.

3:19–20 The divine purpose of **the law** was to clarify sin until Christ (**the Seed**; see note at vv. 16–17) came. Acts 7:38 says that an angel was involved as a **mediator** (a "go-between"), which was needed because the law was a two-party contract, with both **God** and Israel responsible for keeping it. The Abrahamic covenant was a one-party contract, as seen in the way the Lord ratified the covenant as the only active party (Abram was asleep) in Gn 15:9–12. Such a covenant is unconditional.

3:21–23 Paul clarified that the law was never in conflict with **God's promises** to Abraham. The law played the necessary role of convicting people of sin during the almost 1,500 years between Mount Sinai and the gospel of justification by **faith in Jesus Christ**. The **law** is pictured here as a jail cell.

3:24–25 Here the law is portrayed as a **guardian**. A guardian (Gk *paidagōgos*) was a slave who took a young pupil for instruction and protected him from harm until he came of age. When the gospel of Christ came on the scene, the guardian role of the law was no longer needed.

3:27 Paul used the image of a person emerging from the water after being baptized and putting on new clothes. On **baptized into Christ**, see Rm 6:3–4. On **clothed with Christ**, see Eph 4:20–24; Col 3:9–10.

3:29 To be **Abraham's seed** is the same thing as being his "sons" (v. 7).

4:1 In the ancient world, an underage **heir** had no right to his inheritance and was temporarily in the same legal situation as a **slave**, owning nothing.

4:2 Guardians (Gk *paidagōgos*) does not refer to the same idea as in 3:24–25 (see note there). In this case, a "guardian" was a slave who protected the underage heir, while **trustees** were responsible for the heir's other needs until he came of age (**the time set by his father**).

4:3 The **elements of the world** are called "things that by nature are not gods" in v. 8 and "the weak and worthless elements" in v. 9.

4:4 The Greek word translated **completion** is *pleroma*, indicating that Christ came at the perfect time. **God sent his Son, born of a woman** looks back to God's promise in regard to the offspring of the woman in Gn 3:15, and it may allude to Christ's virgin birth (Is 7:14; Mt 1:18–25). **Born under the law** refers to the fact that Jesus knew what it was like to live under the Mosaic law.

4:5–6 One big difference between unbelievers and the underage heir of vv. 1–2 is that, apart from a relationship with Christ,

all people are actually spiritual slaves to sin, which is made clear by **the law**. Thus, it was necessary for Jesus to die; to **redeem** (Gk *exagorazō*, "set free by purchase") sinners out of the slave market. A second great difference is that Christians **receive adoption as sons** instead of being a son of the bloodline. **Abba** means "Father" in Aramaic, but it has a personal tone. On Jesus's use of "Abba," see Mk 14:36.

4:7 Paul's appeal to those in the churches in Galatia was that the person who tries to be justified before God by works is a **slave** to the Mosaic law. But he who is justified by faith in Christ is no longer a slave, but **a son**, with full rights as an heir to God's infinite treasures.

4:8–11 Paul asked how they could **turn back again** and be **enslaved** to a viewpoint of

---

#77 **99 Essential Christian Truths**

CHRIST AS PRIEST

As our great high priest, Jesus accomplishes the work of reconciling us to God. He is the one whose perfect righteousness is presented to the Father for our justification. He is the one who intercedes for us before the Father (Heb 7:25; 9:24) and prays for us to remain faithful (Lk 22:31–32; Jn 17).

or rather have become known by God, how can you turn back again to the weak and worthless elements? Do you want to be enslaved to them all over again? ¹⁰ You are observing special days, months, seasons, and years. ¹¹ I am fearful for you, that perhaps my labor for you has been wasted.

¹² I beg you, brothers and sisters: Become as I am, for I also have become as you are. You have not wronged me; ¹³ you know^A that previously I preached the gospel to you because of a weakness of the flesh. ¹⁴ You did not despise or reject me though my physical condition was a trial for you.^B On the contrary, you received me as an angel of God, as Christ Jesus himself.

¹⁵ Where, then, is your blessing? For I testify to you that, if possible, you would have torn out your eyes and given them to me. ¹⁶ So then, have I become your enemy because I told you the truth? ¹⁷ They court you eagerly, but not for good. They want to exclude you from me, so that you would pursue them. ¹⁸ But it is always good to be pursued^C in a good manner — and not just when I am with you. ¹⁹ My children, I am again suffering labor pains for you until Christ is formed in you. ²⁰ I would like to be with you right now and change my tone of voice, because I don't know what to do about you.

Sarah and Hagar: Two Covenants

²¹ Tell me, you who want to be under the law, don't you hear the law? ²² For it is written that Abraham had two sons, one by a slave and the other by a free woman. ²³ But the one by the slave was born as a result of the flesh, while the one by the free woman was born through promise. ²⁴ These things are being taken figuratively, for the women represent two covenants. One is from Mount Sinai and bears children into slavery — this is Hagar. ²⁵ Now Hagar represents Mount Sinai in Arabia and corresponds to the present Jerusalem, for she is in slavery with her children. ²⁶ But the Jerusalem above is free, and she is our mother. ²⁷ For it is written,

Rejoice, childless woman,
unable to give birth.
Burst into song and shout,
you who are not in labor,
for the children of the desolate
  woman will be many,
more numerous than those
of the woman who has a husband.^D

²⁸ Now you too, brothers and sisters, like Isaac, are children of promise. ²⁹ But just as then the child born as a result of the flesh persecuted the one born as a result of the Spirit, so also now. ³⁰ But what does the Scripture say? "Drive out the slave and her son, for the son of the slave will never be a coheir with the son of the free woman."^E ³¹ Therefore, brothers and sisters, we are not children of a slave but of the free woman.

Freedom of the Christian

5 For freedom, Christ set us free. Stand firm, then, and don't submit again to a yoke of slavery. ² Take note! I, Paul, am telling you that if you get yourselves circumcised, Christ will not benefit you at all. ³ Again I testify to every man who gets himself circumcised that he is obligated to do the entire law. ⁴ You who are trying to be justified by the law are alienated from Christ; you have fallen from grace. ⁵ For

---

^A 4:12–13 Or ¹² Become like I am, because I — inasmuch as you are brothers and sisters — am not requesting anything of you. You wronged me. ¹³ You know   ^B 4:14 Other mss read me   ^C 4:18 Lit zealously courted   ^D 4:27 Is 54:1   ^E 4:30 Gn 21:10

---

justification by works that was as **weak and worthless** as the **elements** they had worshiped before (v. 3). The presence of the Jewish teachers in Galatia makes it likely that the **special days** were Sabbath observances, while **months** and **seasons** had to do with longer seasons of the Jewish calendar (e.g., the time from Passover to Pentecost). **Years** would be sabbatical years or the year of Jubilee.
4:13–15 It is not known what the exact nature of Paul's **physical condition** was. One theory holds that Paul was stoned and left for dead (Ac 14:19) while in the area on his first missionary journey. Some think eye problems were Paul's "thorn in the flesh" (2Co 12:7). Others think Paul contracted malaria in the lowlands of southern Asia Minor (Ac 13:13–14).
4:16 Paul was saddened that the Galatians now viewed him as an **enemy** simply because he told them what they needed to hear (**the truth**), rather than what they wanted to hear.
4:17–18 The only way these teachers could maintain the zeal of the Galatian churches was to **exclude** them from the other Gentile churches who were not trying to be justified by the "works of the law" (2:16).

4:19 Emotionally, Paul felt like a woman in **labor** giving birth to the same baby for the second time (i.e., in trying to bring the Galatians back around to justification by faith).
4:21 The law does not refer specifically to the law of Moses, but to the books of the Law—the Pentateuch (i.e., Genesis–Deuteronomy).
4:22–23 Genesis records the births of these **two sons**—Ishmael, born to Hagar, **a slave**, and Isaac, born to Sarah, **a free woman**. Ishmael was born **as a result of the flesh**, because Sarah and Abraham used Hagar to have a son by their own ingenuity, not through patient trust in God's promise (Gn 16). Isaac was born as God promised (Gn 15:4; 17:16–17; 21:1–3) after many years of waiting by Abraham and Sarah.
4:24–26 Paul declared that he was using **these things ... figuratively** in an elaborate allegory. On one side of the comparison of **covenants** is (a) **Mount Sinai**, where the law of Moses was given, (b) **Hagar**, the mother of Ishmael, and (c) **the present Jerusalem**, from which the false teachers had come to Syrian Antioch (2:11–13) and Galatia. This side of the comparison represents spiritual slavery through the law. On the other side

of the comparison is **the Jerusalem above** (Rv 21:2,9–22:5).
4:27 The quote from Is 54:1 deals with the fact that **the children** born after the exile were more fortunate and greater in number than those righteously judged for breaking the law. The implication is that those who still rely on the law are being replaced by the church and its law-free gospel.
4:28–30 As Ishmael persecuted **Isaac** in Gn 21:9–10, it is to be expected that the Judaizers will persecute true Christians.
5:1 Paul believed that, even though the Galatians had recently moved toward embracing the false gospel (1:6–7) of being justified by "the works of the law" (2:16), they could still **stand firm** and reject the view.
5:2–3 The main issue was whether the Galatians had so completely adopted the Judaizers' perspective that they would now act on this view by being **circumcised** (see note at 2:3). Paul reminded the Galatians that those who are circumcised are obligated to keep the entire law (see more at 5:11–12).
5:4 Alienated means "to be cut off from." By being circumcised and seeking justification before God by the law, the Galatians were cutting themselves off from Christ. In this

we eagerly await through the Spirit, by faith, the hope of righteousness. **⁶** For in Christ Jesus neither circumcision nor uncircumcision accomplishes anything; what matters is faith working through love.

⁷ You were running well. Who prevented you from being persuaded regarding the truth?^ **⁸** This persuasion does not come from the one who calls you. **⁹** A little leaven⁸ leavens the whole batch of dough. **¹⁰** I myself am persuaded in the Lord you will not accept any other view. But whoever it is that is confusing you will pay the penalty. **¹¹** Now brothers and sisters, if I still preach circumcision, why am I still persecuted? In that case the offense of the cross has been abolished. **¹²** I wish those who are disturbing you might also let themselves be mutilated!

¹³ For you were called to be free, brothers and sisters; only don't use this freedom as an opportunity^ for the flesh, but serve one another through love. **¹⁴** For the whole law is fulfilled in one statement: **Love your neighbor as yourself.**^ **¹⁵** But if you bite and devour one another, watch out, or you will be consumed by one another.

The Spirit versus the Flesh

¹⁶ I say, then, walk by the Spirit and you will certainly not carry out the desire of the flesh. **¹⁷** For the flesh desires what is against the Spirit, and the Spirit desires what is against the flesh; these are opposed to each other, so that you don't do what you want. **¹⁸** But if you are led by the Spirit, you are not under the law.

¹⁹ Now the works of the flesh are obvious:^ sexual immorality, moral impurity, promiscuity, **²⁰** idolatry, sorcery, hatreds, strife, jealousy, outbursts of anger, selfish ambitions, dissensions, factions, **²¹** envy,^ drunkenness, carousing, and anything similar. I am warning you about these things — as I warned you before — that those who practice such things will not inherit the kingdom of God.

²² But the fruit of the Spirit is love, joy, peace, patience, kindness, goodness, faithfulness, **²³** gentleness, and self-control. The law is not against such things.^ **²⁴** Now those who belong to Christ Jesus have crucified the flesh with its passions and desires. **²⁵** If we live by the Spirit, let us also keep in step with the Spirit. **²⁶** Let us not become conceited, provoking one another, envying one another.

Carry One Another's Burdens

6 Brothers and sisters, if someone is overtaken in any wrongdoing, you who are spiritual, restore such a person with a gentle spirit,^ watching out for yourselves so that you also won't be tempted. **²** Carry one another's burdens; in this way you will fulfill the law of Christ. **³** For if anyone considers himself to be something when he is nothing, he deceives himself. **⁴** Let each person examine his own work, and then he can take pride in himself alone, and not compare himself with someone else. **⁵** For each person will have to carry his own load.

⁶ Let the one who is taught the word share all his good things with the teacher. **⁷** Don't be deceived: God is not mocked. For whatever a person sows he will also reap, **⁸** because the one who sows to his flesh will reap destruction from the flesh, but the one who sows to the Spirit will reap

---

^5:7 Or *obeying the truth* ⁸5:9 Or *yeast* ^5:13 Lit a *pretext*; a military term for abuse of position ^5:14 Lv 19:18 ^5:19 Other mss add *adultery,* ^5:21 Other mss add *murders,* ^5:23 Or *Against such things there is no law* ^6:1 Or *with the Spirit of gentleness*

---

context, **fallen from grace** refers to falling away from, or forfeiting, the perspective of salvation by grace through faith.
5:7–10 The Galatians had started **running** the race of the Christian life well, but the Jewish teachers **prevented** them from continuing. The implication of the proverbial statement, **A little leaven leavens the whole batch of dough**, is that, even if the teaching of the Judaizers was initially accepted by only a few in the Galatian churches, it would spread quickly.
5:11–12 Apparently, a rumor from the Jewish teachers claimed that Paul still preached **circumcision** in certain circumstances. **Those who are disturbing you** were the Jewish teachers who emphasized circumcision.
5:13–14 Paul expressed concern about the behavioral opposite of bondage: licentiousness (**an opportunity for the flesh**; see note at vv. 19–21). He also expanded his initial reference to **love** (see vv. 5–6).
5:15 The phrase **bite and devour one another** shows Paul apparently had heard that there was serious dissension in the churches of Galatia. He warned them that such attitudes and behavior would consume them.

5:16–18 The ongoing struggle with strong **desires** (Gk *epithumia,* "craving, desire") is why it was necessary to consciously **walk by the Spirit** in faith (v. 5).
5:19–21 The "flesh" is usually understood as the sinful nature of mankind that continues even after a person becomes a Christian. Some interpreters take it to mean mankind in its unsaved state with its sinful thoughts and behavioral patterns continuing after conversion. When the desire of the flesh has the upper hand, **the works of the flesh are obvious** (Gk *phaneros,* "evident, visible"). Some are gross sins, but many are often viewed as "acceptable" behavior. Paul's point is that this type of behavior as a pattern of life (**practice**) is enough to cause a person **not** to inherit **the kingdom of God.** Thus, a legalist cannot be justified by "the works of the law" (Gl 2:16), and a licentious person is excluded from the kingdom of God by the works of the flesh.
5:22–23 The mention of **love** first in the list looks back to Gl 5:6,13–14. Such loving behavior comes through the power of the Holy Spirit by faith. **Self-control** (Gk *egkrateia,* "holding in passions and appetites") is placed

last in the list for emphasis, because all the works of the flesh reflect lack of self-control. There is no need for prohibitive **law** when people's lives exhibit love and self-control.
6:1 A person who falls into sin at a vulnerable point should be spiritually restored in a **gentle** manner (part of "the fruit of the Spirit," 5:23). A danger for those doing such restoration is that they themselves might be pulled into the sin.
6:2 The **law of Christ** is "love your neighbor as yourself" (5:14).
6:3–5 Anyone who **considers himself** superior to a fallen believer is deceiving himself and risks being tempted also (v. 1). We cannot legitimately compare ourselves to **someone else** because each person is assigned a different **load** (Gk *phortion;* not the same word as in v. 2, but meaning "cargo, capacity") by the Lord.
6:6 The principle that **the one who is taught** the Scriptures should support **the teacher** is also stated elsewhere by Paul (1Co 9:11,14; 1Tm 5:17).
6:8 Destruction here may refer to: (1) eternal damnation (5:21) or (2) loss of eternal rewards (1Co 3:12–15). **Eternal life** does not

eternal life from the Spirit. ⁹ Let us not get tired of doing good, for we will reap at the proper time if we don't give up. ¹⁰ Therefore, as we have opportunity, let us work for the good of all, especially for those who belong to the household of faith.

Concluding Exhortation

¹¹ Look at what large letters I use as I write to you in my own handwriting. ¹² Those who want to make a good impression in the flesh are the ones who would compel you to be circumcised — but only to avoid being persecuted for the cross of Christ. ¹³ For even the circumcised don't keep the law themselves, and yet they want you to be circumcised in order to boast about your flesh. ¹⁴ But as for me, I will never boast about anything except the cross of our Lord Jesus Christ. The world has been crucified to me through the cross, and I to the world. ¹⁵ For^A both circumcision and uncircumcision mean nothing; what matters instead is a new creation. ¹⁶ May peace come to all those who follow this standard, and mercy even to the Israel of God!^B ¹⁷ From now on, let no one cause me trouble, because I bear on my body the marks of Jesus. ¹⁸ Brothers and sisters, the grace of our Lord Jesus Christ be with your spirit. Amen.

^A 6:15 Other mss add in Christ Jesus ^B 6:16 Or And for those who follow this standard, may peace and mercy be upon them, even upon the Israel of God, or And as many who will follow this standard, peace be upon them and mercy even upon the Israel of God.

mean earning your salvation since justification before God is through faith (2:16). It refers to life from the Holy Spirit (Rm 6:22). **6:9–10** The Christian life is a marathon race, so **let us not get tired** (i.e., grow weary or lose heart). **Doing good** is not seeking to be justified by works, but living as God has planned for those who have received his gracious salvation through faith (Eph 2:8–10). **6:11** Paul had dictated the earlier part of the letter to an unnamed amanuensis, or secretary, and now he added a postscript in his own handwriting. Some believe that the oversized letters (**large letters**) indicate that Paul was having problems with his eyesight. See also 1Co 16:21; Col 4:18; 2Th 3:17; Phm 19.

6:12–13 The Jewish teachers who were compelling the Galatians to be **circumcised** were doing so for appearance's sake and to avoid being persecuted by unbelieving Jews for the **cross of Christ**, as Paul had been (Ac 14:19). They had no basis for boasting since they could not **keep the law themselves** (see note at 3:10). **6:14–15** The only basis for believers to boast is in the death of **our Lord Jesus Christ**, which makes each of us **a new creation** (see 2Co 5:17). On **the world has been crucified to me**, see 2:19–20; 5:24–26 (cp. 1Jn 2:15–17). On **both circumcision and uncircumcision mean nothing**, see Gl 5:6; 1Co 7:19. **6:16** The **Israel of God** may mean: (1) the Gentile church, which through faith has

inherited the promise God gave to Abraham (3:29) or (2) more likely, the "remnant" of believing Israel "chosen by grace" (Rm 11:5), as opposed to the "false brothers" among the Jews (Gl 2:4), who were seeking to be justified by "the works of the law" (2:16). **6:17** Paul's scars were from injuries he had received through persecution (Ac 14:19; 2Co 11:23–25). He considered these far more significant than the "mark" of circumcision (Gl 6:12–13,15). **6:18** Paul ended Galatians on the same note with which he began—**grace** (see note at 1:3). Although they have been tempted by "another gospel" (Gl 1:7), it is significant that in Paul's last sentence he addresses the Galatians as **brothers and sisters**.

◥ Introduction to Ephesians

Circumstances of Writing

Paul referred to himself by name as the author of the book of Ephesians in two places (1:1; 3:1). Many regard this book as the crown of all of Paul's writings. Today some scholars think the book contains a writing style, vocabulary, and even some teachings that are not typical of the apostle. If that is the case, then it would mean a disciple of Paul had surpassed him in theological insight and spiritual perception. Of such an erudite disciple the early church has no record. Furthermore, pseudonymity (a writer writing under someone else's name) probably was not practiced by early Christians. We can conclude, in line with the undisputable acceptance of Pauline authorship in the early church, that there is no reason to dispute the Pauline authorship of Ephesians.

Paul penned the letter while in prison (3:1; 4:1; 6:20). Disagreement exists concerning whether Paul wrote this letter when he was imprisoned in Caesarea (Ac 24:22) around AD 57–59 or in Rome (Ac 28:30) around 60–62. Paul most likely wrote Colossians, Philemon, and Philippians during the same imprisonment. Tradition suggests that Paul wrote the letter from Rome around 60–61, which would have transpired while Paul was under house arrest in guarded rental quarters (Ac 28:30).

Relatively little is known about the recipients of the letter called Ephesians. Some important and early manuscripts do not contain the words "at Ephesus" (1:1). The letter was carried to its destination by Tychicus, who in Ephesians 6:21 and Colossians 4:7 is identified as Paul's emissary. The Ephesian and Colossian letters probably were delivered at the same time since in both letters the apostle noted that Tychicus would inform the churches concerning Paul's situation.

We can suggest the following possible scenario: While Paul was imprisoned in Rome, the need arose to respond to new religious philosophies influencing the Asia Minor area. The impetus to write the letters came to Paul from Epaphras, who informed him of the threats to Christianity in the Lycus Valley. In response, Paul wrote a letter to the church at Colossae. About the same time (either shortly before or shortly thereafter), he penned a more expansive and general letter intended for churches in Asia Minor, including Laodicea (see Col 4:16) and Ephesus.

Contribution to the Bible

The letter to the Ephesians was probably a circular letter, with Ephesus being the primary church addressed. Paul stayed at Ephesus, the capital city of the province of Asia, for almost three years (see Ac 20:31). The fact that it was a circular letter helps explain the absence of personal names of Ephesian believers. From its inception Paul intended for the letter to gain a wider audience than that which would be found in Ephesus alone. After the Ephesians read it, the letter would have been routed to Colossae, Laodicea, and other churches in the area. Known to be a letter of the apostle

Paul, the letter was readily accepted as Scripture by the recipients.

Structure

The salutation and structure of Ephesians are quite similar to Colossians. Many topics are commonly treated in both letters. The message is strikingly similar. Of the 155 verses in Ephesians, more than half contain identical expressions with those in Colossians.

Colossians, however, is abrupt, argumentative, and seemingly compressed. Ephesians presents a bigger, finished picture that is meditative, instructive, and expansive.

Though Ephesians and Colossians contain many similarities, it is important to observe the distinctives of Ephesians. When the content of Ephesians that is common to Colossians is removed, there remain at least seven units of material unique to Ephesians.

Outline

I. Introduction (1:1–14)
II. Paul's Prayer of Thanksgiving (1:15–23)
III. Salvation by Grace through Faith (2:1–10)
IV. Unity of God's New People (2:11–22)
V. Revelation of the Divine Mystery (3:1–13)
VI. Paul's Prayer for Strength and Love (3:14–21)
VII. Unity of the Body of Christ (4:1–16)
VIII. Exhortations to Holy Living (4:17–5:21)
IX. New Relationships (5:22–6:9)
X. Warfare of the New People (6:10–20)
XI. Conclusion (6:21–24)

Key verses in Ephesians

2:8   For you are saved by grace through faith, and this is not from yourselves; it is God's gift—

4:32   And be kind and compassionate to one another, forgiving one another, just as God also forgave you in Christ.

6:1   Children, obey your parents in the Lord, because this is right.

---

50 BC–AD 54

Mark Antony and Cleopatra reside in Ephesus. **33–32 BC**
Ephesus experiences a destructive earthquake. **AD 17**
Paul travels through Ephesus toward the end of his second missionary journey. **AD 52**
Apollos comes to Ephesus and is mentored by Aquila and Priscilla. **AD 52**
Paul returns to Ephesus for a two-and-a-half-year ministry. **AD 54**

AD 55–110

Paul writes 1 Corinthians from Ephesus. **56**
Paul writes letter to the Ephesians. **61**
Timothy, bishop of Ephesus, receives his first letter from Paul. **62**
Timothy receives second letter from Paul **67**
Paul's death in Rome **67?**
Ignatius of Antioch sends one of his seven letters to the church at Ephesus. **110**

Greeting

1 Paul, an apostle of Christ Jesus by God's will: To the faithful saints in Christ Jesus[A] at Ephesus.[B]

[2] Grace to you and peace from God our Father and the Lord Jesus Christ.

God's Rich Blessings

[3] Blessed is the God and Father of our Lord Jesus Christ, who has blessed us with every spiritual blessing in the heavens in Christ. [4] For he chose us in him, before the foundation of the world, to be holy and blameless in love before him.[C] [5] He predestined us to be adopted as sons through Jesus Christ for himself, according to the good pleasure of his will, [6] to the praise of his glorious grace that he lavished on us in the Beloved One.

[7] In him we have redemption through his blood, the forgiveness of our trespasses, according to the riches of his grace [8] that he richly poured out on us with all wisdom and understanding.[D] [9] He made known to us the mystery of his will, according to his good pleasure that he purposed in Christ [10] as a plan for the right time[E] — to bring everything together in Christ, both things in heaven and things on earth in him.

[11] In him we have also received an inheritance,[F] because we were predestined according to the plan of the one who works out everything in agreement with the purpose of his will, [12] so that we who had already put our hope in Christ might bring praise to his glory.

[13] In him you also were sealed with the promised Holy Spirit when you heard the word of truth, the gospel of your salvation, and when you believed. [14] The Holy Spirit is the down payment of our inheritance, until the redemption of the possession, to the praise of his glory.

Prayer for Spiritual Insight

[15] This is why, since I heard about your faith in the Lord Jesus and your love for all the saints, [16] I never stop giving thanks for you as I remember you in my prayers. [17] I pray that the God of our Lord Jesus Christ, the glorious Father,[G] would give you the Spirit[H] of wisdom and revelation in the knowledge of him. [18] I pray that the eyes of your heart may be enlightened so that you may know what is the hope of his calling, what is the wealth of his glorious inheritance in the saints, [19] and what is the immeasurable greatness of his power toward us who believe, according to the mighty working of his strength.

God's Power in Christ

[20] He exercised this power in Christ by raising him from the dead and seating him at his right hand in the heavens — [21] far above every ruler and authority, power and dominion, and

---

[A]1:1 Or *to the saints, the believers in Christ Jesus* [B]1:1 Other mss omit *at Ephesus* [C]1:4 Or *in his sight. In love* [D]1:8 Or *on us. With all wisdom and understanding* [E]1:10 Or *the fulfillment of times* [F]1:11 Or *In him we are also an inheritance,* [G]1:17 Or *the Father of glory* [H]1:17 Or *a spirit*

1:1 An **apostle** was a person whom the resurrected Christ had commissioned and sent on special service, and who was gifted by the Holy Spirit for that service. **Ephesus** was the most important city in western Asia Minor (present-day Turkey), positioned at an intersection of major trade routes in a significant commercial center. It had a harbor that opened into the Cayster River, which in turn emptied into the Aegean Sea. Ephesus boasted a pagan temple dedicated to the Roman goddess Artemis (Diana, Ac 19:23–41).

1:2 Grace and **peace** are unmerited gifts from God. Paul used the word *grace* twelve times and the word *peace* eight times in Ephesians. On "grace," see note at 2:4.

1:3–14 These twelve verses form one long sentence in the original Greek.

1:3 This often is called "the doxology" because it recites what God has done and is an expression to him of worship, praise, and honor.

1:4 He chose us in him: The idea of divine election flows out of the important theme of spiritual union, for election is "in Christ." The meaning of election is best understood as God's sovereign initiative in bringing persons to faith in Christ. That God chose us in Christ **before the foundation of the world** indicates the centrality of the gospel in God's plan for history. **Holy and blameless** are the results, not the basis, of God's election.

1:5 Predestination refers to the consistent and coherent intention of God's will, an eternal decision rendering certain that which will come to pass. Believers are **adopted** into God's family. Adoption is the legal declaration that we are God's children with all of the rights, privileges, and duties belonging to believers.

1:6 The ultimate purpose of God's redemptive plan is **the praise of his glorious grace**. **The Beloved One** refers to Christ and recalls the Father's declarations at Jesus's baptism and transfiguration (Mt 3:17; 17:5).

1:7 Redemption means that believers have been bought with the price of Christ's blood (1Co 6:20; 1Tm 2:6; 1Pt 1:18–19). The result of redemption is complete forgiveness.

1:8 Wisdom and understanding probably refer to gifts of God's grace.

1:9 By **the mystery of his will** Paul does not mean that God's will is secret in the way that the mystery religions of Asia Minor taught. For Paul, "mystery" meant the revelation of a component of God's plan so that it now can be understood by all (3:2–13). Specifically the mystery involved the fulfillment of God's plan to bring everything together in the Messiah.

1:10 The goal of history is based on God's divine purpose concerning Jesus the Messiah. One day he will establish his kingdom and bring in the new heavens and the new earth, fulfilling and finalizing God's redemptive purpose.

1:12 Those who **had already put our hope in Christ** consist of Paul and all Jewish believers.

1:13–14 The **Holy Spirit** was **promised** by the prophets and by Jesus (Jl 2:28–29; Jn 14:15–26; 16:5–16). The Spirit is described as both a seal showing ownership and a pledge pointing to the future final redemption. On the sealing of the Holy Spirit, see 4:30; 2Co 1:21–22.

1:15 Philemon 5 indicates that Paul recently had received word about the faith of the believers in the region of Asia Minor.

1:16 Paul particularly was thankful for his readers' faith and love.

1:17 Revelation refers to the insight and the discernment the Spirit brings to the mysteries of divine truth. Paul wanted his readers to have a spirit of **wisdom** so that they might get to know God more completely.

1:18 The hope of his calling refers to the assurance of eternal life guaranteed by the possession of the Holy Spirit. The phrase **his glorious inheritance** could mean either God's inheritance or ours, that is, either the inheritance God receives or the inheritance he bestows. The OT consistently taught that God's people were his inheritance.

1:19 God's **power** alone can bring believers safely to the riches of the final glory that will be made available in heaven.

1:20–23 In **raising** Jesus **from the dead**, God raised Jesus to a completely new life, giving him a resurrection body. Not only was Jesus raised, but he was also seated at God's **right hand**, the place of authority from which Christ now reigns. Christ is **above** all, indicating that he is infinitely superior

every title given,^A not only in this age but also in the one to come. ²² And **he subjected everything under his feet**^B and appointed him^C as head over everything for the church, ²³ which is his body, the fullness of the one who fills all things in every way.

From Death to Life

2 And you were dead in your trespasses and sins ² in which you previously walked according to the ways of this world, according to the ruler of the power of the air, the spirit now working in the disobedient.^D ³ We too all previously lived among them in our fleshly desires, carrying out the inclinations of our flesh and thoughts, and we were by nature children under wrath as the others were also. ⁴ But God, who is rich in mercy, because of his great love that he had for us,^E ⁵ made us alive with Christ even though we were dead in trespasses. You are saved by grace! ⁶ He also raised us up with him and seated us with him in the heavens in Christ Jesus, ⁷ so that in the coming ages he might display the immeasurable riches of his grace through his kindness to us in Christ Jesus. ⁸ For you are saved by grace through faith, and this is not from yourselves;

it is God's gift — ⁹ not from works, so that no one can boast. ¹⁰ For we are his workmanship, created in Christ Jesus for good works, which God prepared ahead of time for us to do.

Unity in Christ

¹¹ So, then, remember that at one time you were Gentiles in the flesh — called "the uncircumcised" by those called "the circumcised," which is done in the flesh by human hands. ¹² At that time you were without Christ, excluded from the citizenship of Israel, and foreigners to the covenants of promise, without hope and without God in the world. ¹³ But now in Christ Jesus, you who were far away have been brought near by the blood of Christ. ¹⁴ For he is our peace, who made both groups one and tore down the dividing wall of hostility. In his flesh, ¹⁵ he made of no effect the law consisting of commands and expressed in regulations, so that he might create in himself one new man from the two, resulting in peace. ¹⁶ He did this so that he might reconcile both to God in one body through the cross by which he put the hostility to death.^F ¹⁷ He came and proclaimed the good news of peace to you who were far away and peace to those who were near. ¹⁸ For through him we

---

^A 1:21 Lit *every name named*   ^B 1:22 Ps 8:6   ^C 1:22 Lit *gave him*   ^D 2:2 Lit *sons of disobedience*   ^E 2:4 Lit *love with which he loved us*   ^F 2:16 Or *death in himself*

2:1–6 Paul's point in these verses was to draw contrasts between the human condition described in vv. 1–3 and the new life pictured in vv. 4–6.

2:1 Apart from Christ, people are without authentic spiritual life. They are **dead in . . . trespasses and sins**.

2:2 **This world** is associated with the realm of Satan. The way of life without Christ is in accordance with Satan's ways.

2:3 **Lived** means behaved in accordance with certain principles. Apart from Christ, people are dominated by **fleshly desires**, which refers to an orientation away from God toward selfish concerns. The plural suggests multiple unredeemed urges in **our** life apart from Christ. Sin's entrance brought about a sinful nature in all humanity. Men and women are **by nature** hostile to God and estranged from him. Sin always

negatively influences human decisions and actions.

2:4 Over against the human rejection of God, Paul painted a picture of the new life manifested in God's gracious acceptance of sinners because of Christ. The strong contrast of **but God** points to God's answer to people's dreadful situation. **Mercy** is God's compassion for the helpless that relieves their situation. While grace involves God giving believers what they do not deserve.

2:5 **Made us alive . . . even though we were dead** is Paul's extension of his thoughts in v. 1. Because of God's great love, he "made us alive" **with Christ**.

2:6 **With him** God's loving mercy not only makes new life possible, but by it God has made us alive, **raised us** up, and **seated us** with Christ.

2:7–10 The work of reconciliation in these verses is described with four key terms: kindness . . . grace . . . faith . . . saved.

2:7 The salvation of men and women is to **display the immeasurable riches of his grace**, the exhibition of God's divine favor.

2:8–9 The work of salvation is for God's glory and is not accomplished by human works. The whole process of salvation is not a human achievement, but is an act of God's goodness. We must not portray grace as God's part and faith as our part, for *all* of salvation is a gift from God. This prevents the slightest self-congratulation or boasting in the believer.

2:10 **Good works** are the fruit of our salvation, not the cause of it. Also, good works are not incidental to God's plan; they are instead an essential part of his redemption plan for each believer.

2:11–22 This section of Paul's letter touches on three states of being for the recipients:

(1) their former corporate condition apart from Christ (vv. 11–13); (2) their corporate reconciliation in Christ (vv. 14–18); and (3) their new standing as members of God's new humanity (vv. 19–22).

2:11–12 Not only were the **Gentiles** morally separated from God (vv. 1–3), but they were also separated from God's covenant people. They were without any knowledge of Christ. They had no rights in God's family and were not recipients of God's covenants. They were **without hope** and ultimately without God.

2:13 Paul used the strong transitional phrase **But now in Christ Jesus** to point to the Gentiles' new relationship in Christ.

2:14–16 These verses emphasize the centrality of Jesus Christ in bringing Gentiles and Jews together, not only with one another but also with God. Christ is both our **peace** and our peacemaker. His reconciling death on the cross has made the two—Jews and Gentiles—into one, forming Christ's church. God has torn down **the dividing wall of hostility**. By "dividing wall" Paul likely had in mind the area in the Jerusalem temple that separated the court of the Gentiles from the temple. The outer court of the Gentiles had an inscription on its wall warning Gentiles of their ensuing death if they entered the enclosure around the temple. In Christ this dividing wall was broken down.

2:16 **Reconcile both to God** extends the concept of "peace" and involves the idea of restoration to a unity. The goal was not merely to reconcile two groups but to reconcile them to God. The **one body** is the church.

2:17 **Far away** and **near** refer to Gentiles and Jews and derives from Is 57:19.

2:18 The imagery is of a court official who escorts visitors into the king's presence.

#78 99 Essential Christian Truths

CLARITY OF SCRIPTURE

Because God gave us his Word as authoritative in all matters related to life and faith, we believe his Word was written in a way that can be understood with the help of the Holy Spirit. Believing the Scriptures are clear does not mean that every part is equally easy to interpret, neither does it mean we will never make mistakes in our interpretation. It does mean that with God's help, people are capable of understanding the biblical text for themselves as they employ correct methods of interpretation.

◥ Fall and Redemption

by Anthony L. Chute

The fall of humanity refers to the first act of human disobedience by Adam and Eve recorded in Genesis 3. Prior to their rebellion, our first parents had unbroken fellowship with God, unparalleled intimacy with each other, and undisturbed enjoyment in Eden. There has never been a time such as theirs when humans exercised biblical dominion over creation, complemented one another so completely, and joyously lived every moment under the rule of God. But there will be.

The Bible envisions a day when these broken relationships will be forever restored. God's people will inherit a new earth that is free of the curse (Rv 22:3). They will never feel pain, and their tears will be eternally wiped away (Rv 21:4). Death will no longer haunt the living. Best of all, God will dwell with his people (Rv 22:3). Nothing unclean will be allowed to enter the new creation. Worship, not worry, will characterize the family of God in a world without end.

The Fall and Sin

Currently God's good world is spoiled by human sin (the fall), but sinful humans are made fit to enjoy God forever through placing faith in Jesus Christ (redemption). Critics of the Christian worldview tend to dismiss the idea of the fall by minimizing the reality of human sinfulness. They likewise set aside the doctrine of redemption by maximizing their expectations of human progress. Sin is thus reduced to social constructs, and self-help becomes the means of salvation. In one sense the denial of sin is another manifestation of sin. Just as Adam and Eve tried to hide their wrongs from the God who sees all things (Gn 3:8), humans habitually maintain their innocence in spite of the biblical claim to the contrary (Rm 3:23).

There is another reason why people reject the biblical teaching about the fall. It is because the world continues to work—sort of. After the fall, Adam and Eve's oldest son proved remarkably adept at navigating through life even though he was guilty of murdering his own brother (Gn 4:8). Cain married a woman and loved his son (Gn 4:17). The curse of the ground notwithstanding,

Cain became a farmer and then a city builder (Gn 4:3,17). Cain's descendants were known for their creative prowess, including advancements in shepherding livestock, playing musical instruments, and developing sturdy weaponry (Gn 4:20–22). Put simply, even fallen people in a fallen world manage to contribute to human progress, by the grace of God.

On the other hand, even morally upright people manage to confirm the human predicament. Noah is such a man who, in the midst of a moral sewer, managed to find favor in God's eyes (Gn 6:8). His craftsmanship is demonstrated through his ability to build an ark that withstood the most destructive storm ever. His attention to detail spared not only his life but also that of his family and the entire animal kingdom (Gn 6:14–22). Nevertheless, in spite of God's grace toward him, Noah later became drunk and passed out naked in his tent (Gn 9:20–21). When he awoke, he cursed generations yet to be born (Gn 9:24). This is hardly the behavior one would expect from the man through whom God rescued the world, but Noah's life confirms that "there is no one righteous, not even one" (Rm 3:10).

The doctrine of the fall asserts that while most of us are not as bad as we could be, none of us is as good as we should be either. Humans retain the image of God, which accounts for any semblance of goodness and enables progress (Gn 1:26–27; 9:6). Nevertheless, life is not as it should be in this fallen world.

Theologians have disagreed over the means by which Adam's sin has been passed down to every person, but the reality of death provides sufficient confirmation that no one is exempt (Rm 5:12). Though Charles Manson and Billy Graham took completely different paths with their lives, both are subject to the death sentence—as are we. The Bible thus describes our common plight: we are "dead" in our "trespasses and sins," and we are "by nature children under wrath" (Eph 2:1,3).

Redemption as Reversal

Redemption is the reversal of the fall. In part, this reversal means that those who were spiritually dead are made alive (Eph 2:4), and those who were children of wrath are now children of God (1Jn 3:1).

Though the Bible recognizes that fallen people may make positive contributions to the world as a whole, it is also clear that no one can contribute anything positive to their own redemption (Rm 3:23–28). The only person qualified to undo the effects of the fall is Jesus Christ who, as the eternal Son of God incarnate through the virgin Mary, did not inherit Adam's sin. He was tempted as we are but never sinned (2Co 5:21; Heb 4:15; 1Pt 2:22). Thus, he alone is the one who can make sinful humans fit to worship a holy God (Ac 4:12). The death of Jesus was the most gracious act of love ever displayed: He took upon himself the sins of the world so that all who believe in him would be saved (Rm 5:6–11).

The doctrine of redemption extends even beyond the matter of individual salvation. During his lifetime, Jesus provided abundant proof of his ability to completely restore a fallen world. He demonstrated his lordship over heaven when he calmed the storms on the sea (Mk 4:35–41); he demonstrated his lordship over hell when he exorcised demons from a troubled man (Mk 5:1–20); he demonstrated his lordship over life when he healed a woman of her incurable disease (Mk 5:24–34); and he demonstrated his lordship over death when he raised a young girl from the dead (Mk 5:35–43). With these and countless other miracles (Jn 20:30–31; 21:25), Jesus provided ample reason for us to conclude that this troubled world is not our home. He himself will make all things new (Rv 21:5).

The final book of the Bible is a fitting end to the story of the fall with its triumphant declaration of full redemption:

"Then he showed me the river of the water of life, clear as crystal, flowing from the throne of God and of the Lamb down the middle of the city's main street. The tree of life was on each side of the river, bearing twelve kinds of fruit, producing its fruit every month. The leaves of the tree are for healing the nations, and there will no longer be any curse. The throne of God and of the Lamb will be in the city, and his servants will worship him. They will see his face, and his name will be on their foreheads. Night will be no more; people will not need the light of a lamp or the light of the sun, because the Lord God will give them light, and they will reign forever and ever" (Rv 22:1–5).

Fall and Redemption in the Christian Worldview

The Christian worldview thus includes both fall and redemption. To exclude the former is to deny the reality of sin; to exclude the latter is to deny the ultimate reality of Christ's work. Living in a fallen world means that Christians will experience trials and tribulations, and they will continue to struggle with their own temptations and sin. We are forgiven, but God is not finished with us yet (Phm 1:6). Consequently, longing for a better world, even a perfect world, is not a form of escapism. Rather, it is the Christian's rightful anticipation of a promise made by the one who justly pronounced a curse on this world (Gn 3; Rm 8:20–22) and then lovingly took that curse upon himself in order to redeem people for his glory.

both have access in one Spirit to the Father. ¹⁹ So, then, you are no longer foreigners and strangers, but fellow citizens with the saints, and members of God's household, ²⁰ built on the foundation of the apostles and prophets, with Christ Jesus himself as the cornerstone. ²¹ In him the whole building, being put together, grows into a holy temple in the Lord. ²² In him you are also being built together for God's dwelling in the Spirit.

Paul's Ministry to the Gentiles

3 For this reason, I, Paul, the prisoner of Christ Jesus on behalf of you Gentiles — ² assuming you have heard about the administration of God's grace that he gave me for you. ³ The mystery was made known to me by revelation, as I have briefly written above. ⁴ By reading this you are able to understand my insight into the mystery of Christ. ⁵ This was not made known to people^A in other generations as it is now revealed to his holy apostles and prophets by the Spirit: ⁶ The Gentiles are coheirs, members of the same body, and partners in the promise in Christ Jesus through the gospel. ⁷ I was made a servant of this gospel by the gift of God's grace that was given to me by the working of his power.

⁸ This grace was given to me — the least of all the saints — to proclaim to the Gentiles the incalculable riches of Christ, ⁹ and to shed light for all about the administration of the mystery hidden for ages in God who created all things. ¹⁰ This is so that God's multi-faceted wisdom may now be made known through the church to the rulers and authorities in the heavens. ¹¹ This is according to his eternal purpose accomplished in Christ Jesus our Lord. ¹² In him we have boldness and confident access through faith in him.^B ¹³ So, then, I ask you not to be discouraged over my afflictions on your behalf, for they are your glory.

Prayer for Spiritual Power

¹⁴ For this reason I kneel before the Father^C ¹⁵ from whom every family in heaven and on earth is named. ¹⁶ I pray that he may grant you, according to the riches of his glory, to be strengthened with power in your inner being through his Spirit, ¹⁷ and that Christ may dwell in your hearts through faith. I pray that you, being rooted and firmly established in love, ¹⁸ may be able to comprehend with all the saints what is the length and width, height and depth of God's love, ¹⁹ and to know Christ's love that surpasses knowledge, so that you may be filled with all the fullness of God.

²⁰ Now to him who is able to do above and beyond all that we ask or think according to the power that works in us — ²¹ to him be glory in the church and in Christ Jesus to all generations, forever and ever. Amen.

Unity and Diversity in the Body of Christ

4 Therefore I, the prisoner in the Lord, urge you to walk worthy of the calling you have received, ² with all humility and gentleness,

---

^A 3:5 Lit to the sons of men ^B 3:12 Or through his faithfulness ^C 3:14 Other mss add of our Lord Jesus Christ

---

2:19 Foreigners means short-term transients, nonresidents with no rights. **Strangers** is a similar word, pointing to resident foreigners who had settled permanently in the country of their choice but who nevertheless had only limited rights. These terms described the Gentiles' position before Christ came. **Fellow citizens . . . and members** are terms that picture the Gentiles' new position. Now they enjoy all the privileges of God's **household**, where "household" describes their togetherness and inclusion. **2:20** God's new family is not only a new nation but also a new building with a distinctive foundation. The **apostles and prophets** in their unique relationship to Christ, exemplified by the authoritative teachings they communicated to the church, are the **foundation**. Paul proclaimed Christ Jesus as the **cornerstone** of the foundation. "Cornerstone" holds an entire structure together. **2:21–22** "By virtue of its connection to the **Lord** Jesus Christ, the cornerstone, the universal church as a **whole** is in the process of becoming the **holy** dwelling place of God. The passive **being put together** indicates this is not being accomplished by us, but by God himself" (Peter T. O'Brien, *The Letter to the Ephesians*). The description of a building under construction is indicated by the word **grows**. It conveys the idea of a dynamic church in the process of expansion. **3:1** Paul here initiates a thought that he leaves unfinished until v. 14. The apostle

celebrates his present circumstances in light of God's will and calling for his life. Twice (3:1; 4:1) Paul reminds his readers that while he is a prisoner of Rome, he is also a **prisoner of Christ Jesus**, the Lord (see Php 1:13). **3:2 The administration of God's grace** refers to Paul's unique ministry. Paul's ministry was not of his own making but was given to him as a commission from God (Ac 9). **3:3 Mystery** points to something that once was hidden or secret and now God has revealed (see 1:9). The mystery revealed is that God determined through the person and work of Christ to incorporate the Gentiles into one body of the church as equal partners with Israel (v. 6). **3:4–5 By reading this** refers to what Paul had written in the first two chapters. **3:6** That the Gentiles would have equal footing as **coheirs** with God's covenant people was a new aspect of God's revelation. **3:7** The reference to **God's grace** forms an *inclusio* with v. 2 that brackets the paragraph. **3:8 Least of all the saints** is a combination of a superlative and a comparative in one Greek term. **3:9** The content of what is brought to light is **the administration of the mystery**, or how God intended to fulfill his purpose. **3:10** God's intent was that through the church, his **multi-faceted wisdom** should be made known. "Multi-faceted" means manifold or multicolored like a beautiful jewel. The unfolding drama of redemption

is watched with avid interest by the **rulers and authorities in the heavens**, an apparent reference to angels (cp. 1Pt 1:12). **3:11–13** The church is central to God's working in history. **3:14** Paul resumed the prayer that he began in v. 1. In this prayer, he asked that believers might be blessed with inner strength, insightful understanding, and spiritual excellence. **3:15** The concept and institute of fatherhood (shared with minor variation by all cultures) stems from God's role as Father and Creator of all peoples. **3:16–19** Paul prayed for inner power, which is the result of God dwelling in the hearts of believers. He asked for believers to be **strengthened . . . rooted**, and **filled** via the work of the three persons of the Trinity: Spirit, Christ, and God the Father. **3:20–21** Paul burst into a grand doxology concerning God's majestic abilities. He prayed that God's glory be abundantly manifested in the church and in Christ. Even in the eternal state, the church will bring glory to God **forever and ever**. **4:1** This exhortation serves as a major transition in the letter as it moves from the church's belief statement to the church's mission statement. Paul insisted that a believer's behavior must be worthy of his divine calling. **4:2 Humility . . . gentleness**, and **patience** are absolutely essential if unity is to be maintained.

with patience, bearing with one another in love, ³ making every effort to keep the unity of the Spirit through the bond of peace. ⁴ There is one body and one Spirit — just as you were called to one hope^ at your calling — ⁵ one Lord, one faith, one baptism, ⁶ one God and Father of all, who is above all and through all and in all.

⁷ Now grace was given to each one of us according to the measure of Christ's gift. ⁸ For it says:

> When he ascended on high,
> he took the captives captive;
> he gave gifts to people.ᴮ

⁹ But what does "he ascended" mean except that heᶜ also descended to the lower parts of the earth?ᴰ ¹⁰ The one who descended is also the one who ascended far above all the heavens, to fill all things. ¹¹ And he himself gave some to be apostles, some prophets, some evangelists, some pastors and teachers, ¹² to equip the saints for the work of ministry, to build up the body of Christ, ¹³ until we all reach unity in the faith and in the knowledge of God's Son, growing into maturity with a stature measured by Christ's fullness. ¹⁴ Then we will no longer be little children, tossed by the waves and blown around by every wind of teaching, by human cunning with cleverness in the techniques of deceit. ¹⁵ But speaking the truth in love, let us grow in every way into him who is the head — Christ. ¹⁶ From him the whole body, fitted and knit together by every supporting ligament, promotes the growth of the body for building itself up in love by the proper working of each individual part.

Living the New Life

¹⁷ Therefore, I say this and testify in the Lord: You should no longer walk as the Gentiles do, in the futility of their thoughts. ¹⁸ They are darkened in their understanding, excluded from the life of God, because of the ignorance that is in them and becauseᴱ of the hardness of their hearts. ¹⁹ They became callous and gave themselves over to promiscuity for the practice of every kind of impurity with a desire for more and more.ᶠ

²⁰ But that is not how you came to know Christ, ²¹ assuming you heard about him and were taught by him, as the truth is in Jesus, ²² to take offᴳ your former way of life, the old self that is corrupted by deceitful desires, ²³ to be renewedᴴ in the spirit of your minds, ²⁴ and to put onᴵ the new self, the one created according to God's likeness in righteousness and purity of the truth.

²⁵ Therefore, putting away lying, **speak the truth, each one to his neighbor,**ᴶ because we are members of one another. ²⁶ **Be angry and do not sin.**ᴷ Don't let the sun go down on your anger, ²⁷ and don't give the devil an opportunity. ²⁸ Let the thief no longer steal. Instead, he is to do honest work with his own hands, so that he has something to share with anyone in need. ²⁹ No foul language should come from your mouth, but only what is good for building up someone in need,ᴸ so that it gives grace to those who hear. ³⁰ And don't grieve God's Holy Spirit. You were sealed by himᴹ for the day of redemption. ³¹ Let all bitterness, anger and wrath, shouting and slander be removed from you, along with all malice. ³² And be kind and compassionate to one another, forgiving one another, just as God also forgave youᴺ in Christ.

^**4:4** Lit called in one hope   ᴮ**4:8** Ps 68:18   ᶜ**4:9** Other mss add first   ᴰ**4:9** Or the lower parts, namely, the earth   ᴱ**4:18** Or in them because   ᶠ**4:19** Lit with greediness   ᴳ**4:21–22** Or Jesus. This means: take off (as a command)   ᴴ**4:22–23** Or desires; renew (as a command)   ᴵ**4:23–24** Or minds; and put on (as a command)   ᴶ**4:25** Zch 8:16   ᴷ**4:26** Ps 4:4   ᴸ**4:29** Lit for the building up of the need   ᴹ**4:30** Or Spirit, by whom you were sealed   ᴺ**4:32** Other mss read us

4:3–6 The seven "ones" enumerated in these verses constitute the foundation on which the Trinitarian God creates a oneness in the church.
4:8 This verse is an allusion to Ps 68:18. The essence of the psalm is that a military victor has the right to receive gifts from the people he has conquered and who now are his subjects. Paul suggested that Christ has conquered his enemies and has given gifts to them, with Paul himself being the perfect example. As victor over sin and death, Christ gives gifts to his new devoted followers, his captives.
4:11 The description here is about gifted people. Five groups of gifted people are listed. Apostles and prophets are foundational for the church's work (3:5; see note at 2:20). The term **apostles** primarily refers to people sent with a divine mission or task. **Prophets** revealed God's will to believers for the present (forthtelling) and predicted the future (foretelling). **Evangelists** were gifted to spread the gospel and plant churches. **Pastors** and **teachers** shared similar responsibilities. Pastors provided oversight, comfort, and guidance as the church's shepherds

(Ac 20:28; 1Pt 5:1–4). Teachers instructed and helped apply God's revelation to the life of the church.
4:12 The purpose of the gifted people is to equip others to minister. Like many other long sentences in Ephesians, vv. 11–16 form one long sentence in the original Greek text. The term translated **to equip** was sometimes used to refer to mending or restoring.
4:13 Ministry is intended to move believers toward accomplishing three goals: (1) unity of faith and full knowledge of God's Son, (2) maturity, and (3) the fullness of Christ. Maturity and unity are measured in terms of the relationship of the body to the head, Christ.
4:14 When the gifted people equip the church, the community of faith will evidence stability in precept and practice.
4:15 When a church is faithful to speak **truth in love**, it will have transparent relationships where people edify and benefit one another.
4:16 Ultimately the church will grow up into Christ in all aspects, with each part fitting together and supporting the other. Each member of the body must function properly if the body is to grow. We get our

English word harmony from the Greek term translated **fitted and knit together**.
4:17–19 This section of the letter provides the practical outworking of v. 1. Paul's exhortations denounced the readers' former way of life.
4:20–21 Paul pictures **the truth** totally in terms of the Messiah, who is the way, the truth, and the life (Jn 14:6).
4:22–24 The apostle often described who believers already are, while also pointing to what they should strive to become. The practical paradox is that while freedom from sin's eternal penalty is already ours, freedom from the **former way of life** (a life of sin) comes only through our daily quest for obedience and purity. These are lifestyle commitments that every believer is called to make.
4:25–32 Paul offered five examples of what living the new life means in the context of relationship with others. All of the examples include a negative command, a positive command, and a spiritual principle on which the commands are based. In v. 32 Paul used a play on words to illustrate his point. Believers are urged to be kind (Gk chrestos) because of Christ (Gk Christos).

5 Therefore, be imitators of God, as dearly loved children, ² and walk in love, as Christ also loved us and gave himself for us, a sacrificial and fragrant offering to God. ³ But sexual immorality and any impurity or greed should not even be heard of^ among you, as is proper for saints. ⁴ Obscene and foolish talking or crude joking are not suitable, but rather giving thanks. ⁵ For know and recognize this: Every sexually immoral or impure or greedy person, who is an idolater, does not have an inheritance in the kingdom of Christ and of God.

Light versus Darkness

⁶ Let no one deceive you with empty arguments, for God's wrath is coming on the disobedient⁸ because of these things. ⁷ Therefore, do not become their partners. ⁸ For you were once darkness, but now you are light in the Lord. Walk as children of light — ⁹ for the fruit of the light^c consists of all goodness, righteousness, and truth — ¹⁰ testing what is pleasing to the Lord. ¹¹ Don't participate in the fruitless works of darkness, but instead expose them. ¹² For it is shameful even to mention what is done by them in secret. ¹³ Everything exposed by the light is made visible, ¹⁴ for what makes everything visible is light. Therefore it is said:

Get up, sleeper, and rise up from the dead,
and Christ will shine on you.

Consistency in the Christian Life

¹⁵ Pay careful attention, then, to how you walk — not as unwise people but as wise — ¹⁶ making the most of the time,^D because the days are evil. ¹⁷ So don't be foolish, but understand what the Lord's will is. ¹⁸ And don't get drunk with wine, which leads to reckless living, but be filled by the Spirit: ¹⁹ speaking to one another in psalms, hymns, and spiritual songs, singing and making music with your heart to the Lord, ²⁰ giving thanks always for everything to God the Father in the name of our Lord Jesus Christ, ²¹ submitting to one another in the fear of Christ.

Wives and Husbands

²² Wives, submit^E to your husbands as to the Lord, ²³ because the husband is the head of the wife as Christ is the head of the church. He is the Savior of the body. ²⁴ Now as the church submits to Christ, so also wives are to submit to their husbands in everything. ²⁵ Husbands, love your wives, just as Christ loved the church and gave himself for her ²⁶ to make her holy, cleansing^F her with the washing of water by the word. ²⁷ He did this to present the church to himself in splendor, without spot or wrinkle or anything like that, but holy and blameless. ²⁸ In the same way, husbands are to love their wives as their own bodies. He who loves his wife loves himself. ²⁹ For no one ever hates his own flesh but provides and cares for it, just as Christ does for the church, ³⁰ since we are members of his body.^G ³¹ **For this reason a man will leave his father and mother and be joined to his wife, and the two will become one flesh.**^H ³² This mystery is profound, but I am talking about

---

^A5:3 Or be named   ^B5:6 Lit sons of disobedience   ^C5:9 Other mss read fruit of the Spirit   ^D5:16 Lit buying back the time
^E5:22 Other mss omit submit   ^F5:26 Or having cleansed   ^G5:30 Other mss add and of his flesh and of his bones   ^H5:31 Gn 2:24

5:1–2 Believers are challenged to **be imitators of God**. Being imitators of God means being imitators of Christ in his sacrificial love.
5:3–5 All of God's gifts, including sexuality in the bonds of marriage, are to be subjects for thanksgiving, not of **crude joking**.
5:6–7 Viewed actively, God's **wrath** is his firm, ongoing opposition to evil; he is eternally opposed to everything that is contrary to his design and his holy nature. God's new community is to reflect the character of God.
5:8–9 Walking as **children of light** means adopting values that are the opposite of the surrounding culture.
5:10 Testing what is pleasing to the Lord makes duty and Christian living a delight, and invests service with joy.
5:11–14 Faithful believers do more than abstain from evil; they denounce the deeds of darkness as unfruitful, shameful, and not worthwhile. The material Paul quotes in v. 14 may have been an early Christian hymn.
5:15–16 These words provide a solemn warning that Christians should be wise and careful in all things, including their use of time. Our use of time is not neutral; it can be evil if it is not invested for good (Ps 90).
5:18 Paul's imperatives contrast the differences between being under the influence of wine, which leads to **reckless living**, and being under the influence of the Spirit, which results in joyful living. The commands are plural; thus they refer not merely to

individuals but to the corporate community of faith.
5:19–21 The church that is filled with the Spirit will be characterized by praise and thanksgiving to God.
5:21 This verse serves as a hinge to connect what is prior with what follows. Grammatically, the participial phrase (lit "submitting yourselves") goes with vv. 18–20. The content of vv. 22–33, however, depends on the principle of submission in v. 21.
5:22 Wives, submit directs wives to be submissive to their own (Gk idios, "one's own") husbands (cp. Col 3:18–4:1). The distinctive feature here is that the relationship between husband and wife is compared with that between the church and the church. No verb is in the original language of v. 22. The imperative "submit" is understood from v. 21.
5:22–24 Paul addressed wives first. They are to be voluntarily submissive to their husbands. No external coercion should be involved, nor should submission imply that the wife is a lesser partner in the marital union. The submission is governed by the phrase **as to the Lord**. A Christian wife's submission to her husband is one aspect of her obedience to Christ. Submission is a person's yielding his or her own rights and losing self for another. Submission is patterned after Christ's example (Php 2:5–8) and reflects the essence of the gospel. Submission distinguishes the lifestyle of all Christians.

5:25 Paul turned to the duties of husbands. Paul exhorted husbands to love their wives. Christ's self-sacrificing love for the church is the pattern for the husband's love for his wife.
Husbands are to **love** their wives continually as Christ loves the church. The tense of the Greek word translated "love" indicates a love that continues. Love is more than family affection or sexual passion. Rather it is a deliberate attitude leading to action that concerns itself with another's well-being. A husband should love his wife: (1) as Christ loved the church (vv. 25–27); (2) as his own body (vv. 28–30); and (3) with a love transcending all other human relationships (vv. 31–33).
5:26–27 Christ's atonement for the church makes the church holy and pure. The purpose of Christ's giving himself up for the church is the church's sanctification and cleansing.
5:29–30 On first reading, Paul seems to have descended from the lofty standard of Christ's love to the low standard of self-love when he says **no one ever hates his own flesh**; but he reminded Christian couples of their oneness, their "one-flesh" relationship. For this reason a husband's obligation to cherish his wife as he does his own body is more than a helpful guide. His sacrificial love is an expression of the sacred marital union.
5:31–32 Paul appealed to Gn 2:24, which is God's initial statement regarding marriage.

◄ A Biblical View of Marriage

by Alan B. Terwilleger

God loves marriage. The Bible, after all, begins with a marriage as Adam received his bride, Eve, and celebrated with the world's first love song (Gn 2:22–25). The Bible ends with a marriage as Jesus receives his bride, the church, at the great marriage supper of the Lamb (Rv 19:7). And Jesus, anticipating that final marriage supper, performed his first miracle at a wedding celebration (Jn 2:1–11).

The Bible presents marriage as the sacred, foundational institution designed by God for human flourishing, the well-being of children, and the advancement of his kingdom. While culture today exerts a significant influence on our attitudes and behavior surrounding marriage, Christians should desire to know what God thinks about this most sacred of institutions that he designed and loves. God hasn't left us uninformed about marriage. His revelation in Scripture guides us to his design for marriage. By embracing it, we will see his human creatures flourish.

People Need Companionship

After God created the heavens and the earth, he created man in his own image to rule and manage his creation. He did not create us all the same, but "he created them male and female" (Gn 1:27). In the process of creation, God repeatedly declared his creation *good* (Gn 1:4,10,12,18,21,25,31). But God stated that it was *not good* for man to be alone, to exist as a solitary being (Gn 2:18). Without human companionship, creation was incomplete. If man was alone, there could be no procreation and, more importantly, no possibility for man to experience the kind of intimate relationship that exists within the Godhead. And so God created woman to complement the man and thus complete the good design he had for humanity.

In his delight with Eve, Adam called her "bone of my bone and flesh of my flesh; this one will be called 'woman,' for she was taken from man" (Gn 2:23). In the next verse we read, "This is why a man leaves his father and mother and bonds with his wife, and they become one flesh" (Gn 2:24).

As seventeenth-century Bible commentator Matthew Henry wrote, "Eve was not taken from Adam's head that she should rule over him, nor from his feet, to be trampled under foot, but she was taken from his side that she might be his equal, from under his arm that she might be protected by him, near his heart, that he might cherish and love her."

In this way men and women provide companionship for each other in laboring together interdependently in God's kingdom work and in having children and nurturing families to populate God's creation.

One Man and One Woman

At creation God established marriage as the union of one man and one woman. Since then, our fallen state has created all kinds of distortions in God's design for marriage, including the moral confusion of our day. But God clearly demonstrates his design for one man and one woman to come together in this sacred union.

It is critical to understand that while God made man and woman as equals, he also created them to be different from one another. Men and women are not interchangeable; they are complementary. In marriage they become one flesh (Gn 2:24), one functioning unit, especially in procreation.

In our culture it is vital to remind ourselves that in addition to the joy of husband and wife, sexual intercourse is designed for procreation. Marriage, sex, and children go together. The family, which is central to God's design for his kingdom, is made possible through the procreative act that brings together one man and one woman and defines the one-flesh unity of marriage. "Reproductive technologies" aside, only a man and a woman, complementing one another, can create another human person.

Marriage Is a Covenantal Relationship

Just as God and his bride, the church, are bound together by the new covenant of Christ crucified (Lk 22:19–20; Heb 9:15; 12:22–24), so husband and wife are bound together by the covenant of marriage (Mal 2:14).

Marriage is not a contract. Contracts are agreements of "consideration given for consideration received." They are 50–50 arrangements in which one partner puts something

Christ and the church. **³³** To sum up, each one of you is to love his wife as himself, and the wife is to respect her husband.

Children and Parents

6 Children, obey your parents in the Lord, because this is right. **²** Honor your father and mother, which is the first commandment with a promise, **³** so that it may go well with you and that you may have a long life in the land.^A,B **⁴** Fathers, don't stir up anger in your children, but bring them up in the training and instruction of the Lord.

Slaves and Masters

⁵ Slaves, obey your human^c masters with fear and trembling, in the sincerity of your heart, as you would Christ. **⁶** Don't work only while being watched, as people-pleasers, but as slaves of Christ, do God's will from your heart. **⁷** Serve with a good attitude, as to the Lord and not to people, **⁸** knowing that whatever good each one does, slave or free, he will receive this back from the Lord. **⁹** And masters, treat your slaves the same way, without threatening them, because you know that both their Master and yours is in heaven, and there is no favoritism with him.

Christian Warfare

¹⁰ Finally, be strengthened by the Lord and by his vast strength. **¹¹** Put on the full armor of God so that you can stand against the schemes of the devil. **¹²** For our struggle is not against flesh and blood, but against the rulers, against the authorities, against the cosmic powers of this darkness, against evil, spiritual forces in the heavens. **¹³** For this reason take up the full armor of God, so that you may be able to resist in the evil day, and having prepared

^6:3 Or *life on the earth*   ^6:2–3 Ex 20:12   ^6:5 Lit *according to the flesh*

The marriage commitment takes precedence over every other human relationship. **5:31 One flesh** means closely joined. It hallows the biblical standard of covenantal heterosexual marital relations and excludes polygamy, adultery, and other sexual expressions. What is primarily a divine ordinance is graciously and lovingly designed for mutual satisfaction and delight. **5:33 Love . . . respect** concludes and restates this section's theme. The husband's ultimate responsibility is to love his wife with a Christlike love.

6:1–3 Paul called for **children** to be obedient as taught in natural law, in the Mosaic law, and in the gospel. The word for **obey** is different from the term for "submission". Obedience involves recognition of authority. **6:4** Parents have responsibility both to discipline and to instruct their children. Paul indicated that **fathers** are to take the lead in this responsibility. Parents are not to **stir up anger** in their children. Discipline is not to be arbitrary or something done out of anger. **6:5–9** The NT, as well as the OT, includes guidelines for **slaves** and slavery. Paul's

claim that slaves and masters are equal before God no doubt shocked his contemporaries. Paul's words in this context provided groundwork for a new sense of brotherhood between races, and were later used to help inspire the anti-slavery movement. Paul's words **don't work only while being watched** are good instruction for all Christian employees. **6:10–13** Three times Paul called for believers to **stand** against the devil's schemes, the spiritual battle that takes place **against evil, spiritual forces in the heavens**.

---

in expecting to get something out. And contracts are over once they are fulfilled or when both parties agree to break them. Covenants, then, are radically different. In covenants, both parties are expected to give 100 percent, offering consideration even when none is received in return. Covenants are established by solemn vows invoking the name of God. Those bound together by the covenant of marriage in the name of God through solemn vows witnessed by family and friends are sealed with God's divine blessing in a permanent relationship. "Therefore," as Jesus said, "what God has joined together, let no one separate" (Mk 10:9).

Since marriage is a lifelong commitment, the Christian's goal should not be to have merely a good marriage but to have a godly one. While our fallen nature does not provide for marital bliss all the time, we must remember that where sin abounds, grace abounds (Rm 5:20). And where grace abounds, so does the potential for lifelong, loving marriage. While the Bible acknowledges the concession of divorce under certain circumstances,

this falls short of God's ideal for marriage (Mt 19:1–9; 1Co 7:10–16).

Witness to the World

In their complementarity, married couples represent to the world the beauty and mystery of the love relationship God has with his people. Beginning in the Old Testament, God referred to his people as his bride, bound to him by covenant (Is 54:5–8; Ezk 16:8; Hs 2:19–20). He calls Israel's breaking of the covenant "adultery" and "prostitution" (Ezk 23; Hs 2:2–13). At the same time, he promises a day will come when "as a groom rejoices over his bride, so your God will rejoice over [Israel]" (Is 62:5).

That same promise carries over into the New Testament. Paul concludes his instructions about Christian marriage with this statement: "This mystery is profound, but I am talking about Christ and the church" (Eph 5:32). Christian marriages are to demonstrate the love of God to a world in need of that love, and every wedding day anticipates the day Jesus will return to glorify and honor his bride, the church, and be with her forever (Rv 19:7–9; 21:2,9).

everything, to take your stand. [14] Stand, therefore, with truth like a belt around your waist, righteousness like armor on your chest, [15] and your feet sandaled with readiness for the gospel of peace. [16] In every situation take up the shield of faith with which you can extinguish all the flaming arrows of the evil one. [17] Take the helmet of salvation and the sword of the Spirit — which is the word of God. [18] Pray at all times in the Spirit with every prayer and request, and stay alert with all perseverance and intercession for all the saints. [19] Pray also for me, that the message may be given to me when I open my mouth to make known with boldness the mystery of the gospel. [20] For this I am an ambassador in chains. Pray that I might be bold enough to speak about it as I should.

Paul's Farewell

[21] Tychicus, our dearly loved brother and faithful servant[A] in the Lord, will tell you all the news about me so that you may be informed. [22] I am sending him to you for this very reason, to let you know how we are and to encourage your hearts.

[23] Peace to the brothers and sisters, and love with faith, from God the Father and the Lord Jesus Christ. [24] Grace be with all who have undying love for our Lord Jesus Christ.[B,C]

[A] 6:21 Or *deacon*　[B] 6:24 Other mss add *Amen.*　[C] 6:24 Lit *all who love our Lord Jesus Christ in incorruption*

6:14–16 The defensive armor that Paul describes in these verses includes five components. Paul called for believers to put on the "full armor" (v. 13), which points to its divine nature more than its completeness.

6:17 The offensive armor included only one weapon, a short **sword** used in close combat. The "sword" symbolizes God's Word. **6:18–20** Each piece of armor must be carefully put on with prayer, drawing upon divine resources. Praying in the Spirit is an admission of a believer's dependence on God.

6:21–24 Paul concluded with greetings that lack the personal references usually present in his letters. Such omissions are hard to explain if the letter was intended only for the church at Ephesus, the place where Paul stayed longer than anywhere else in his ministry (Ac 18:19–21; 19; 20:13–31) and presumably had numerous personal relationships. For this reason many conclude that the letter was intended to circulate more broadly among other churches of the region. Most likely **Tychicus** carried the letter, along with the letter to the Colossian church and the personal letter to Philemon.

#79 99 Essential Christian Truths

ANGELS

Besides the creation of humanity and animals, the Bible also speaks of other beings that God created—angels, whom Scripture also refers to as "sons of God," "holy ones," "spirits," "principalities," and "powers." In the original languages of the Bible, the word *angel* carries the meaning of a messenger, which indicates one of their primary reasons for existence. Angels carry out a number of other functions throughout Scripture: bringing God glory, carrying out God's plans and purposes, and reminding humanity that the unseen world is real.

Introduction to Philippians

Circumstances of Writing

Paul the apostle wrote this short letter, a fact that no scholar seriously questions. The traditional date for the writing of Philippians is during Paul's first Roman imprisonment (AD 60–62); few have challenged this conclusion.

Paul planted the church at Philippi during his second missionary journey (AD 51) in response to his "Macedonian vision" (Ac 16:9–10). This was the first church in Europe (Ac 16).

The text of this letter from Paul suggests several characteristics of the church at Philippi. First, Gentiles predominated. Few Jews lived in Philippi, and apparently the church included few. Second, women had a significant role (Ac 16:11–15; Php 4:1–2). Third, the church was generous. Fourth, they remained deeply loyal to Paul.

Philippi, the ancient city of Krenides, had a military significance. It was the capital of Alexander the Great, who renamed it for his father, Philip of Macedon, and it became the capital of the Greek Empire (332 BC). The Romans conquered Greece, and in the civil war after Julius Caesar's death (44 BC), Antony and Octavian repopulated Philippi by allowing the defeated armies (Brutus and Cassius) to settle there (eight hundred miles from Rome). They declared the city a Roman colony. It flourished, proud of its history and entrenched in Roman political and social life. In his epistle to the Philippians, Paul alluded to military and political structures as metaphors for the church.

Paul wanted to thank the church for their financial support (4:10–20). He also addressed disunity and the threat of heresy. Disunity threatened the church, spawned by personal conflicts (4:2) and disagreements over theology (3:1–16). The heresy came from radical Jewish teachers. Paul addressed both issues personally and warmly.

The church at Philippi sent Epaphroditus to help Paul in Rome. While there, he became ill (2:25–28). The church learned of Epaphroditus's illness, and Paul wished to ease their concern for him. Some people possibly blamed Epaphroditus for failing his commission, but Paul commended him and sent him home. Perhaps Epaphroditus carried this letter with him.

Contribution to the Bible

Paul's letter to the Philippians teaches us much about genuine Christianity. Although most of its themes may be found elsewhere in Scripture, it is within this letter that we can see how those themes and messages affect life. Within the New Testament, Philippians contributes to our understanding of Christian commitment and what it means to be Christlike.

Structure

Philippians can be divided into four primary sections. Paul had definite concerns that he wanted to express, and he also wrote to warn about false teachers who threatened

---

Philippians Timeline

500–31 BC

Settlers from Thasos occupy what would later be called Philippi and named it Krenides. **500**

Philip II of Macedon invests in the development of the area and so the city was named in his honor. **358**

The Romans win an overwhelming victory over the Macedonians at the battle of Pydna, after which Philippi came under Roman control. **168**

The battle of Philippi, a strategic turning point in Roman history, is fought between the army of Cassius and Brutus against that of Octavius and Mark Antony. **42**

31 BC–AD 49

A decade later Octavius (Augustus) prevails against Mark Antony in the battle of Actium, after which Philippi became a colony where veterans of the Roman civil war were settled and enjoyed the privileges of those who lived in Rome. **31 BC**

Jesus's trials, death, resurrection **NISAN 14–16** or **APRIL 3–5, AD 33**

Pentecost **AD 33**

Saul's conversion on the Damascus Road **OCTOBER AD 34**

Paul, Barnabas, and John Mark make first missionary journey. **AD 47–49**

Paul and Silas begin second missionary journey overland through Cilicia to Derbe, Lystra, Iconium, and Pisidian Antioch. **AD 49**

the church. Many of Paul's letters can be divided into theological and practical sections, but Philippians does not follow that pattern. Paul's theological instruction is woven throughout the fabric of a highly personal letter.

Outline

I. Salutation (1:1–2)
II. Explanation of Paul's Concerns (1:3–2:30)
   A. Paul's thanksgiving and prayer (1:3–11)
   B. Paul's joy in the progress of the gospel (1:12–26)
   C. Exhortation to Christlike character (1:27–2:18)
   D. Paul's future plans (2:19–30)
III. Exhortations to Christian Living (3:1–4:9)
   A. Exhortations to avoid false teachers (3:1–21)
   B. Miscellaneous exhortations (4:1–9)
IV. Expression of Thanks and Conclusion (4:10–23)
   A. Repeated thanks (4:10–20)
   B. Greetings and benediction (4:21–23)

Key verses in Philippians

4:13   I am able to do all things through him who strengthens me.

4:19   And my God will supply all your needs according to his riches in glory in Christ Jesus.

AD 49–52

Paul, Silas, and Timothy continue through North Galatia to Troas. **49**
Paul and his companions arrive in Philippi and plant the first Christian church in Europe. **50**
Paul's ministry in the Macedonian cities of Thessalonica and Berea **50**
Paul plants the church at Corinth. **50–51**
Paul concludes second missionary journey, returning to Antioch of Syria. **52**

AD 54–140

Paul's third missionary journey takes him to Ephesus. **54**
Paul's extended ministry in Ephesus **54–56**
Paul likely revisits Philippi collecting funds for the church at Jerusalem. **57**
Paul's first imprisonment in Rome **60–62**
Paul writes his letter to the church at Philippi. **62**
Polycarp's letter to the Philippians **110–140**

Greeting

1 Paul and Timothy, servants of Christ Jesus: To all the saints in Christ Jesus who are in Philippi, including the overseers and deacons. ² Grace to you and peace from God our Father and the Lord Jesus Christ.

Thanksgiving and Prayer

³ I give thanks to my God for every remembrance of you,^ ⁴ always praying with joy for all of you in my every prayer, ⁵ because of your partnership in the gospel from the first day until now. ⁶ I am sure of this, that he who started a good work in you⁸ will carry it on to completion until the day of Christ Jesus. ⁷ Indeed, it is right for me to think this way about all of you, because I have you in my heart,ᶜ and you are all partners with me in grace, both in my imprisonment and in the defense and confirmation of the gospel. ⁸ For God is my witness, how deeply I miss all of you with the affection of Christ Jesus. ⁹ And I pray this: that your love will keep on growing in knowledge and every kind of discernment, ¹⁰ so that you may approve the things that are superior and may be pure and blameless in the day of Christ, ¹¹ filled with the fruit of righteousness that comes through Jesus Christ to the glory and praise of God.

Advance of the Gospel

¹² Now I want you to know, brothers and sisters, that what has happened to me has actually advanced the gospel, ¹³ so that it has become known throughout the whole imperial guard, and to everyone else, that my imprisonment is because I am in Christ. ¹⁴ Most of the brothers have gained confidence in the Lord from my imprisonment and dare even more to speak the word⁰ fearlessly. ¹⁵ To be sure, some preach Christ out of envy and rivalry, but others out of good will. ¹⁶ These preach out of love, knowing that I am appointed for the defense of the gospel; ¹⁷ the others proclaim Christ out of selfish ambition, not sincerely, thinking that they will cause me trouble in my imprisonment. ¹⁸ What does it matter? Only that in every way, whether from false motives or true, Christ is proclaimed, and in this I rejoice. Yes, and I will continue to rejoice ¹⁹ because I know this will lead to my salvationᴱ through your prayers and help from the Spirit of Jesus Christ. ²⁰ My eager expectation and hope is that I will not be ashamed about anything, but that now as always, with all courage, Christ will be highly honored in my body, whether by life or by death.

Living Is Christ

²¹ For me, to live is Christ and to die is gain. ²² Now if I live on in the flesh, this means fruitful work for me; and I don't know which one I should choose. ²³ I am torn between the two. I long to depart and be with Christ — which is far better — ²⁴ but to remain in the flesh is more necessary for your sake. ²⁵ Since I am persuaded of this, I know that I will remain and continue with all of you for your progress and joy in the faith, ²⁶ so that, because of my coming to you again, your boasting in Christ Jesus may abound.

²⁷ Just one thing: As citizens of heaven, live your life worthy of the gospel of Christ. Then, whether I come and see you or am absent, I will hear about you that you are standing firm in

^1:3 Or for your every remembrance of me ᴮ1:6 Or work among you ᶜ1:7 Or because you have me in your heart ᴰ1:14 Other mss add of God ᴱ1:19 Or vindication

1:1a Timothy was with Paul and Silas when they planted the church at Philippi (2:19–24; Ac 16). **Servants** expresses humility.
1:1b Saints are believers. On qualifications for **overseers**, see 1Tm 3:1–7; Ti 1:5–9; for **deacons**, see 1Tm 3:8–13.
1:2 Grace and **peace**, jointly from **God** and **Jesus Christ**, attest to the deity and equality of both.
1:5 Partnership (lit "fellowship") expresses participation. **From the first day** shows Paul's continued joy in these believers, in spite of his initial difficulty in the city of Philippi (Ac 16).
1:6–8 Paul's confidence in prayer resulted from the principle that God finishes what he begins, and the fact that the Philippians demonstrated their Christian character by joining in the support of the gospel work.
1:9–10 Paul prayed two petitions: a growing love (v. 9) and complete character (v. 10). **Love** (Gk agapē) is selfless action for another person. **Knowledge** is both intellectual and experiential. **Discernment** occurs only here in the NT and connotes moral sensitivity. The word **pure** emphasizes personal integrity; **blameless** means good character that survives all accusations.

1:11 Filled with the fruit of righteousness expresses how a person attains purity and blamelessness.
1:12 Paul's attitude was that all that had happened to him served to open new opportunities for gospel witness.
1:13 The first opportunity (see v. 12 and note) for gospel witness involved the **imperial guard**, an elite military force charged with protecting the Roman emperor and his concerns. As the soldiers rotated shifts, each heard Paul's message. The guards knew that Paul's commitment to **Christ** had led to his arrest and **imprisonment**.
1:14–18 The second opportunity for gospel witness involved the church itself. Responding to Paul's imprisonment, Christians divided into those who supported him and those who opposed him. Paul's imprisonment spawned renewed enthusiasm for preaching in both groups, but the group that opposed him preached the gospel out of **envy** and **rivalry**. They hoped to cause Paul greater difficulty, perhaps an unfavorable trial verdict. Their motivation was **selfish ambition**, intending to **cause . . . trouble** by social turmoil. Paul does not say what drove the rivalry. The group that supported Paul was motivated by **good will** and **love**. They

realized Paul was **appointed** (lit "set") by God for defending the gospel. Paul accepted the message and work of both groups as long as the end result was **Christ . . . proclaimed**.
1:19 Paul expected exoneration. He hoped for **prayers**, the "human" side, and **help**, divine assistance. "Prayers" implies intense intercession.
1:20 Ashamed implies cowering or embarrassment. Paul expected that **Christ** would **be highly honored** in his **body**. The physical body symbolizes earthly life. Further, Paul hoped Christ would also be glorified in his death.
1:21–24 To live is Christ restates the theme of v. 20. If he carried on living, every aspect of Paul's life would continue to be **fruitful** and worthwhile. Likewise, his death would be **gain** since it would usher him into Christ's presence. Paul felt **torn between the two** (lit "in a dilemma"), acknowledging the benefits of both outcomes. The phrase **is more necessary for your sake** expresses Paul's servant heart.
1:25–26 Paul apparently planned a trip to Philippi following his anticipated release.
1:27–28 Live your life (lit "conduct yourselves as citizens"; cp. Ac 23:1) alludes to Philippi's political history, reminding the

one spirit, in one accord,[A] contending together for the faith of the gospel, **28** not being frightened in any way by your opponents. This is a sign of destruction for them, but of your salvation — and this is from God. **29** For it has been granted to you on Christ's behalf not only to believe in him, but also to suffer for him, **30** since you are engaged in the same struggle that you saw I had and now hear that I have.

Christian Humility

2 If, then, there is any encouragement in Christ, if any consolation of love, if any fellowship with the Spirit, if any affection and mercy, **2** make my joy complete by thinking the same way, having the same love, united in spirit, intent on one purpose. **3** Do nothing out of selfish ambition or conceit, but in humility consider others as more important than yourselves.

4 Everyone should look not to his own interests, but rather to the interests of others.

Christ's Humility and Exaltation

5 Adopt the same attitude as that of Christ Jesus,
6   who, existing in the form of God,
    did not consider equality with God
    as something to be exploited.[B]
7   Instead he emptied himself
    by assuming the form of a servant,
    taking on the likeness of humanity.
    And when he had come as a man,
8   he humbled himself
    by becoming obedient
    to the point of death —
    even to death on a cross.
9   For this reason God highly exalted him
    and gave him the name
    that is above every name,

[A]**1:27** Lit *soul* [B]**2:6** Or *to be grasped,* or *to be held on to*

church of its higher citizenship in **heaven**. Paul's primary concern was that **you are standing firm in one spirit**. "One spirit" expresses the believer's unified attitude. **One accord** (lit "same soul") means that believers share "life." Together they prevent divisiveness. Standing firm involves **contending together**. "Contending" comes from athletics where teams contended for a prize (cp. 4:3). Standing also involves not being **frightened . . . by your opponents**. Soldiers used "frightened" to describe horses that might easily be startled.
1:29–30 Granted (lit "by grace") indicates that God "graces" Christians to **believe** and **suffer** on **Christ's behalf**.
2:1–2 Four **if** statements in v. 1 form the basis of Paul's appeal. These phrases express conditions that are assumed for the sake of argument. Four actions on the Philippians' part in v. 2 explain what Paul meant by **make my joy complete**. Two verbs translate the Greek word *phroneō*—**thinking** and being **intent on**. Beyond mere "thinking," this

addresses values. The Philippians were to value **the same way** and with **one purpose**. Between these two, Paul included shared **love** and **united in spirit**.
2:3–4 Selfish ambition or conceit recalls the problem Paul condemned (1:15,17). **Humility** results in considering **others as more important**. Additionally, humility looks not to one's **own interests, but rather to the interests of others**.
2:5–11 This passage is designed to illustrate Christian humility. Because of its rhythmic character, it is often considered an early hymn.
2:5 The phrase **adopt the same attitude** commands the church to value Christ's character as a model.
2:6 The key thought of this verse is that Jesus **did not consider** (cp. v. 3) his own interests, thus allowing them to dominate his actions. **Form** (Gk *morphē*) suggests his complete deity. **Equality with God** indicates his coequality with God and separate personality (the Second Person of the Trinity). **To be**

exploited is capable of two connotations. It can mean "to grasp" (steal), but because of Jesus's deity it probably means "to clutch" (hang on to at all costs).
2:7–8 Theologians ponder what Christ **emptied** himself of. It is certain that he did not divest himself of deity or its attributes. Two statements accompany the verb. First, **by assuming the form of a servant** indicates that God the Son came to demonstrate true servanthood. Second, **the likeness of humanity** explains both emptying and servanthood. Two further statements explain the second verb **humbled** (cp. v. 3). First, **when he had come as a man** provides the time of his humility. Second, Jesus's humility came through **becoming obedient**. Jesus obeyed God, even to the point of dying on a cross.
2:9–11 God is described as acting in these verses. Again, two verbs organize the thought. First, **God highly exalted him** ("super-exalted," occurring only here) suggests that God gave Jesus a new position, although some take it as superlative ("to

Q & A: Did Jesus claim to be God?

by Robert M. Bowman Jr. and J. Ed Komszewski

J esus spoke and acted as God in the flesh. We can consider the evidence for Jesus being God in five related categories, which you can remember using the mnemonic HANDS:

    Jesus gets God's *Honors*
    Jesus has God's *Attributes*
    Jesus has God's *Names*
    Jesus does God's *Deeds*
    Jesus sits in God's *Seat*

Let's look at a few examples of each of these.

Honors: Jesus expected people to honor him "just as they honor the Father" (Jn 5:23). He accepted worship from his disciples (Mt 14:33; 28:17). He encouraged them to have faith in him as they did in God (Jn 14:1). He invited them to pray to him: "If you ask me anything in my name, I will do it" (14:14).

Attributes: Jesus claimed to be just like God the Father—so much so that if you saw him you had seen the Father (Jn 14:7–10). He revealed himself to be omnipresent when he asserted that he would be present with his disciples wherever they gathered in his name (Mt 18:20). He even said that he had existed before creation (Jn 17:5).

Names: The way Jesus spoke of himself as God's Son implied that he was on a par with God the Father (Mt 11:27; Jn 5:17–18). His "I am" sayings echoed the way God identified himself in the Old Testament (cp. Is 43:10 with Jn 8:24,28,58). Jesus's favorite title for himself, "the Son of Man," refers to Old Testament prophetic visions of a divine yet human figure (Ezk 1:26–28; Dn 7:13–14). Jesus accepted Thomas's reference to him as "my Lord and my God" (Jn 20:28).

Deeds: Jesus did things, and claimed to do things, that only God could do. He calmed a raging storm with a simple word, walked on the sea, and fed thousands of people with one boy's lunch (Mt 8:23–27; 14:13–33). He claimed the right to forgive people of all their sins (Mt 9:1–8; Mk 2:1–12). Jesus said that he would raise the dead (Jn 5:28–29; 11:25–26) and judge all humanity (Mt 25:31–46; Jn 5:22–23).

Seat: Jesus claimed that he would sit on the seat of God's own throne, the place from which God rules over his entire creation (Mt 25:31; Mk 12:36; Lk 20:42–43). That is exactly what Jesus will do there: rule over the entire created order (Mt 11:25–27; 28:18; Lk 10:21–22).

The religious people who rejected Jesus understood that he was claiming to be equal to God (Mk 2:7; Jn 5:17–18; 10:27–33)—they just didn't believe him. We should not only recognize that Jesus claimed to be God but also commit our lives to him as our Lord and Savior.

10 so that at the name of Jesus
    every knee will bow —
    in heaven and on earth
    and under the earth —
11 and every tongue will confess
    that Jesus Christ is Lord,
    to the glory of God the Father.

Lights in the World

12 Therefore, my dear friends, just as you have always obeyed, so now, not only in my presence but even more in my absence, work out your own salvation with fear and trembling. **13** For it is God who is working in you both to will and to work according to his good purpose. **14** Do everything without grumbling and arguing, **15** so that you may be blameless and pure, children of God who are faultless in a crooked and perverted generation, among whom you shine like stars in the world, **16** by holding firm to the word of life. Then I can boast in the day of Christ that I didn't run or labor for nothing. **17** But even if I am poured out as a drink offering on the sacrificial service of your faith, I am glad and rejoice with all of you. **18** In the same way you should also be glad and rejoice with me.

Timothy and Epaphroditus

19 Now I hope in the Lord Jesus to send Timothy to you soon so that I too may be encouraged by news about you. **20** For I have no one else like-minded who will genuinely care about your interests; **21** all seek their own interests, not those of Jesus Christ. **22** But you know his proven character, because he has served with me in the gospel ministry like a son with a father. **23** Therefore, I hope to send him as soon as I see how things go with me.

24 I am confident in the Lord that I myself will also come soon. **25** But I considered it necessary to send you Epaphroditus — my brother, coworker, and fellow soldier, as well as your messenger and minister to my need — **26** since he has been longing for all of you and was distressed because you heard that he was sick. **27** Indeed, he was so sick that he nearly died. However, God had mercy on him, and not only on him but also on me, so that I would not have sorrow upon sorrow. **28** For this reason, I am very eager to send him so that you may rejoice again when you see him and I may be less anxious. **29** Therefore, welcome him in the Lord with great joy and hold people like him in honor, **30** because he came close to death for the work of Christ, risking his life to make up what was lacking in your ministry to me.

Knowing Christ

3 In addition, my brothers and sisters, rejoice in the Lord. To write to you again about this is no trouble for me and is a safeguard for you.

2 Watch out for the dogs, watch out for the evil workers, watch out for those who mutilate the flesh. **3** For we are the circumcision, the ones who worship by the Spirit of God, boast in Christ Jesus, and do not put confidence in the flesh — **4** although I have reasons for confidence in the flesh. If anyone else thinks he has grounds for confidence in the flesh, I have more: **5** circumcised the eighth day; of the nation of Israel, of the tribe of Benjamin, a Hebrew born of Hebrews; regarding the law, a Pharisee; **6** regarding zeal, persecuting the church; regarding the righteousness that is in the law, blameless.

---

the highest"). Second, God **gave him the name**. This name that is **above every name** is **Lord** (*kurios* = *Yahweh*). **Every knee will bow** and **every tongue will confess** state one result of God's exaltation. The posture and the confession imply submissive reverence. "Every" includes spatial dimensions: **heaven** . . . **earth**, and **under the earth**. Together they indicate the living and the dead (blessed and condemned). All bring glory to God. **2:12–13 Work out** means to apply salvation, not to earn it. **Fear and trembling** means to have proper respect in response to God's blessing. True obedience comes from reverence, not fright. **God** . . . **is working** provides the deeper incentive: Christians are recipients of God's initiatives of motivation and empowerment. **2:14–16 Grumbling and arguing** come from selfishness and vainglory (1:15,17; cp. Dt 32:5). **Blameless** (complete Christian character) and **pure** (inoffensive living; cp. 1:10) introduce metaphors. First, believers are to be morally **faultless** in a world **crooked and perverted** by its failure to understand the Word of God. Second, they are to **shine like stars** whose brilliance contrasts with the darkened world.

2:17–18 Drink offering recalls the OT sacrificial system. Paul was the substance being **poured out** for these believers. **2:19–24** On **Timothy**, see note at 1:1a. **Like-minded** (lit "equal souled") means "soul mate or partner" in service. Paul characterized Timothy three ways: he genuinely cared for their interests (cp. vv. 1–4); he valued the things of Jesus Christ and others; and he had **proven character** (lit "tested by fire"), refined in the demands of the **gospel ministry**. **2:25–30 Epaphroditus** shared Paul's ministry (**brother, coworker, and fellow soldier**) and represented the church. **Messenger** and **minister** indicate that the church expected Epaphroditus to care for Paul in Rome. Traveling to Rome, Epaphroditus suffered a near-fatal illness. The words **welcome him** and **hold people like him in honor** reveal that Epaphroditus gave his best for the **work of Christ**. The words **what was lacking** refer to the churches' care for Paul. Epaphroditus took it upon himself to make up that lack. **3:1 About this** refers to Paul's warning about false teachers that follows. He had previously dealt with this subject. **3:2 Dogs** was often used of Gentiles, but in this context it refers to overly zealous Jewish

teachers who were ravenous like scavengers. These **evil workers** attempted to gain salvation by keeping the law. **Mutilate the flesh** refers to their "circumcision." Paul used a play on the Greek words for "circumcision" and "mutilation." **3:3** Those of **the circumcision**—"true Jews" or Christians—have three characteristics. First, they **worship by the Spirit of God**, not the works of the flesh (Gl 5:16–18). Second, they **boast in Christ Jesus**. "Boast" ("take pride in") means their highest treasure is Jesus. Third, they **do not put confidence in the flesh**. "The flesh" describes the values and activities of humanity unaided by the Holy Spirit. **3:4–6** Paul's fleshly **confidence** included heredity and accomplishments. On the issue of his heredity, **circumcised the eighth day** (lit "an eighth-day one") placed him in a special group whose parents scrupulously kept the law. A **Hebrew born of Hebrews** countered those who may have assumed otherwise because Paul was from Tarsus. Regarding achievement, he spoke of zeal and the law. **Pharisee** comes from a word meaning "separation," e.g., to honor the OT law. **Zeal**, evidenced by **persecuting the church**, was unnecessary even for Pharisees.

7 But everything that was a gain to me, I have considered to be a loss because of Christ. **8** More than that, I also consider everything to be a loss in view of the surpassing value of knowing Christ Jesus my Lord. Because of him I have suffered the loss of all things and consider them as dung, so that I may gain Christ **9** and be found in him, not having a righteousness of my own from the law, but one that is through faith in Christ^A — the righteousness from God based on faith. **10** My goal is to know him and the power of his resurrection and the fellowship of his sufferings, being conformed to his death, **11** assuming that I will somehow reach the resurrection from among the dead.

Reaching Forward to God's Goal

12 Not that I have already reached the goal or am already perfect, but I make every effort to take hold of it because I also have been taken hold of by Christ Jesus. **13** Brothers and sisters, I do not^B consider myself to have taken hold of it. But one thing I do: Forgetting what is behind and reaching forward to what is ahead, **14** I pursue as my goal the prize promised by God's heavenly^C call in Christ Jesus. **15** Therefore, let all of us who are mature think this way. And if you think differently about anything, God will reveal this also to you. **16** In any case, we should live up to whatever truth we have attained. **17** Join in imitating me, brothers and sisters, and pay careful attention to those who live according to the example you have in us. **18** For I have often told you, and now say again with tears, that many live as enemies of the cross of Christ. **19** Their end is destruction; their god is their stomach; their glory is in their shame; and they are focused on earthly things. **20** Our citizenship is in heaven, and we eagerly wait for a Savior from there, the Lord Jesus Christ. **21** He will transform the body of our humble condition into the likeness of his glorious body, by the power that enables him to subject everything to himself.

4 So then, my dearly loved and longed for brothers and sisters, my joy and crown, in this manner stand firm in the Lord, dear friends.

Practical Counsel

2 I urge Euodia and I urge Syntyche to agree in the Lord. **3** Yes, I also ask you, true partner,^D to help these women who have contended for the gospel at my side, along with Clement and the rest of my coworkers whose names are in the book of life. **4** Rejoice in the Lord always. I will say it again: Rejoice! **5** Let your graciousness^E be known to everyone. The Lord is near. **6** Don't worry about anything, but in everything, through prayer and petition with thanksgiving, present your requests to God. **7** And the peace of God, which surpasses all understanding, will guard your hearts and minds in Christ Jesus.

^A **3:9** Or *through the faithfulness of Christ*   ^B **3:13** Other mss read *not yet*   ^C **3:14** Or *upward*   ^D **4:3** Or *true Syzygus*, possibly a person's name   ^E **4:5** Or *gentleness*

Righteousness that is in the law means that Paul achieved all the law could promise. **3:7–8** Paul evaluated his former life (vv. 7–8) and expressed his current aspirations (vv. 9–11). The word **loss** and a synonym **dung** are compared with **gain** three times. Paul's loss was for the sake of Christ (v. 7), for the surpassing value of knowing Christ (v. 8), and for gaining Christ (v. 8).

3:9–11 Paul described his new aspirations in three ways: gaining Christ and being found in him, having a Christian righteousness, and attaining resurrection from the dead. **Found** refers to judgment day. Christ brings a **righteousness** through faith in Christ (imputed), not from works of the law (cp. v. 6). **To know him** (personally, experientially) involves experiencing the **power of his resurrection** and knowing the **fellowship** (lit "participation in") **of his sufferings**. Identification with Christ's suffering brings conformity to Jesus's death.

3:12–14 Not **reached the goal** and not **already perfect** indicate the need for growth. **Make every effort** recalls the athlete's discipline and focus. **Pursue** (cp. v. 12), **goal**, and **prize** use athletic imagery of the runner's energy, focus, and reward. "The prize" is **God's heavenly call** (to heaven), like a referee calling a winner to the platform to receive the prize.

3:17–21 Imitating me reveals Paul's confidence that he lived correctly before God and man. Paul often urged believers to imitate him (4:9; 1Co 11:1; 1Th 1:6; 2Th 3:8–9). Paul described the **enemies of the cross** in four ways. First, their **end is destruction** (not annihilation but eternal judgment). Second, their **god is their stomach** reflects their preoccupation with Jewish dietary laws. Third, their **glory is in their shame** means focusing inappropriately on the genitals (circumcision). Fourth, they **focused on**

earthly things, unable to see beyond the present time.

Citizenship was rare and prized, and the Philippians were justifiably proud of their Roman citizenship. "Citizenship" **in heaven** reminded the church of the existence of a greater society and culture. **The body of our humble condition** refers to the body limited by illness, frailty, finiteness, and sin. Christ will change the body into the **likeness of his glorious body**.

4:1 Stand firm recalls Roman soldiers who never retreated for fear of being killed while under assault.

4:2 Euodia and **Syntyche** were influential, like many women in the Philippian church (Ac 16). **Urge** occurs twice, once with each name, avoiding favoritism.

4:3 True partner is singular. Someone in authority would be the mediator. Paul provided reasons to help these women. First, they **contended** with Paul (an athletic term). Second, they worked alongside **Clement** (unknown) and Paul's coworkers. The **book of life** refers to those listed among the saved (cp. Rv 3:5; 20:15; 21:27).

4:5 Graciousness implies selflessness and respect for others (cp. 2:1–4). **Be known** indicates it is part of the church's reputation. **The Lord is near** reminded the Philippian believers of Christ's unseen presence. It also reminded them of his return.

4:6–7 Worry is anxiety (Mt 6:25–34). Prayer is the antidote for worry. Three words express different aspects of prayer: **prayer**, a

---

#80   99 Essential Christian Truths

NEW IDENTITY OF THE BELIEVER

A person who places faith in Christ undergoes a fundamental change of identity. He or she goes from being an enemy under God's wrath (Eph 2:1–3) to being welcomed into God's family as a beloved child (Eph 2:19). The believer in Christ is declared righteous on account of Christ's perfect life, substitutionary death, and resurrection. No longer is the person a slave to sin, defined by past failures or present struggles, but has instead been delivered from the realm of darkness and now belongs to the kingdom of light (Col 1:13). Anyone who is in Christ is a "new creation" in whom the old, sinful self has passed away and the new, redeemed self is alive and becoming more and more like Christ (2Co 5:17).

8 Finally[A] brothers and sisters, whatever is true, whatever is honorable, whatever is just, whatever is pure, whatever is lovely, whatever is commendable — if there is any moral excellence and if there is anything praiseworthy — dwell on these things. **9** Do what you have learned and received and heard from me, and seen in me, and the God of peace will be with you.

Appreciation of Support

10 I rejoiced in the Lord greatly because once again you renewed your care for me. You were, in fact, concerned about me but lacked the opportunity to show it. **11** I don't say this out of need, for I have learned to be content in whatever circumstances I find myself. **12** I know how to make do with little, and I know how to make do with a lot. In any and all circumstances I have learned the secret of being content — whether well fed or hungry, whether in abundance or in need. **13** I am able to do all things through him[B] who strengthens me. **14** Still, you did well by partnering with me in my hardship.

15 And you Philippians know that in the early days of the gospel, when I left Macedonia, no church shared with me in the matter of giving and receiving except you alone. **16** For even in Thessalonica you sent gifts for my need several times. **17** Not that I seek the gift, but I seek the profit[C] that is increasing to your account. **18** But I have received everything in full, and I have an abundance. I am fully supplied,[D] having received from Epaphroditus what you provided — a fragrant offering, an acceptable sacrifice, pleasing to God. **19** And my God will supply all your needs according to his riches in glory in Christ Jesus. **20** Now to our God and Father be glory forever and ever. Amen.

Final Greetings

21 Greet every saint in Christ Jesus. The brothers who are with me send you greetings. **22** All the saints send you greetings, especially those who belong to Caesar's household. **23** The grace of the Lord Jesus Christ be with your spirit.[E]

[A] 4:8 Or *In addition*　[B] 4:13 Other mss read *Christ*　[C] 4:17 Lit *fruit*　[D] 4:18 Or *Here, then, is my receipt for everything, I have an abundance, for I am fully supplied*　[E] 4:23 Other mss add *Amen.*

---

worshipful attitude; **petition**, a need; and **requests**, the specific concern. **Thanksgiving** shapes prayers with gratitude. In response, **the peace of God** brings power to endure. The peace **surpasses** knowledge, calming a troubling situation when explanations fail. Further, peace guards by keeping anxieties from **hearts** (choices) and **minds** (attitudes). **4:8–9** Minds focused on these seven qualities experience the peace of God. **True** is ethical "truthfulness." **Honorable** is "noble," to be respected. **Just** is giving people what they deserve. **Pure** is holy in relation to God. **Lovely**, mentioned only here in the NT, is attractive. **Commendable**, also used only here in the NT, is praiseworthy. **The God of peace** complements "the peace of God" (v. 7) in that life with these characteristics encourages God's presence. **4:10 Once again** indicates that some time had elapsed between the Philippian believers' previous gifts to Paul (cp. 2Co 8) and their sending Epaphroditus to him in Rome (2:25–30).

4:11 Learned (Greek perfect tense) implies a lesson resulting in better knowledge. **Content** (lit "self-reliant") is self-sufficiency that grows out of trust in Christ. **4:12 I know** results from evaluating various circumstances. The difficult circumstances are **to make do with little**, to be **hungry**, and to be **in need**. The contrasting good are **to make do with a lot**, to be **well fed**, and to be **in abundance**. **4:13 All things** refers to the economic fluctuations of life (v. 12). **Through him who strengthens me** teaches that Christ empowers believers to live in God's will. **4:14 Partnering** is the word for "fellowship" (1:5). **Hardship** is "tribulations." Real partners share difficulties. **4:15 The early days of the gospel** refers to Paul's leaving Philippi to continue witnessing in Europe. **You alone** reveals one reason why Paul loved the Philippian church. They did what others did not. **4:16** Paul entered **Thessalonica** after leaving Philippi, and the Philippian believers' gifts

to him began immediately and continued consistently (**several times**). **4:17** Paul did not **seek the gift**. That would abuse his converts and compromise servanthood. With a higher, spiritual motivation, Paul, using financial terms, sought **the profit that is increasing to your account**. "Increasing" is the interest it would bear to the account of the Philippian believers. **4:18** Continuing financial language, Paul had **received everything in full**. Any responsibility to him was paid. What Epaphroditus embodied was **an abundance**. Their material support was **a fragrant offering** and **an acceptable sacrifice** because it met Paul's needs and was **pleasing to God** (cp. Rm 12:1–2). **4:19–20** God bountifully blesses those who give with glorious provision in accord with his glory and for his purposes. Paul's doxology is based on the ultimate purpose of life—to bring **glory** to God now and **forever**. **4:21–22 Caesar's household** probably indicates these Christians were not immediate family but perhaps members of the civil service.

Colossians

Circumstances of Writing

Colossians retains its place among the epistles of Paul, who identified himself as the author (Col 1:1; 4:18). The church fathers unreservedly endorsed Pauline authorship (Irenaeus, *Against Heresies* 3.14.1; Tertullian, *Prescription against Heretics* 7; Clement of Alexandria, *Miscellanies* 1.1; see Justin, *Dialogue with Trypho* 85.2; 138.2). A close reading of Colossians reveals a considerable number of lexical, grammatical, and theological similarities with the other Pauline writings (1:9,26; 2:11–14,16,20–21; 3:1,3,5–17). Also favoring the authenticity of Colossians as a letter of Paul is its close connection with Philemon, an epistle widely regarded as Pauline.

During his ministry in Ephesus (Ac 19:10), Paul sent Epaphras to spread the gospel in the Lycus Valley. Epaphras subsequently established the church at Colossae (1:7; 4:12–13). The city's population consisted mostly of Phrygians and Greeks, but it also included a significant number of Jews. The church, likewise, was mostly composed of Gentiles (1:21,27; 2:13), but it also had Jewish members (2:11,16,18,21; 3:11). When Epaphras (Phm 23) informed Paul of certain heretical teachings that had spread there, Paul wrote the letter to the Colossians as a theological antidote.

Paul wrote Colossians during his first Roman imprisonment (Col 4:3,10,18; see Ac 28:30–31; Eusebius, *Ecclesiastical History* 2.22.1) in the early AD 60s. Together with Philemon, Philippians, and Ephesians, Colossians is commonly classified as a Prison Epistle. All four epistles share several personal links that warrant this conclusion (Col 1:7; 4:7–8,17; Eph 6:21–22; Phm 2,12,23).

Contribution to the Bible

Colossians provides one of the Bible's fullest expressions of the deity and supremacy of Christ. This is most evident in the magnificent hymn of praise (Col 1:15–20) that sets forth Christ as the image of the invisible God, the Creator and sustainer of the universe, and the head of his body, the church. In Christ are all the "treasures of wisdom and knowledge" (2:3), because in him "the entire fullness of God's nature dwells bodily" (2:9). The supremacy of Christ also has implications for believers' salvation (2:10,13,20; 3:1,11–12,17) and conduct (3:5–4:6). Colossians contributes to Scripture a high Christology and a presentation of its implications for the believer's conduct.

Structure

Colossians may be divided into two main parts. The first (1:3–2:23) is a polemic against false teachings. The second (3:1–4:17) is made up of exhortations to proper Christian living. This is typical of Paul's approach, presenting a theology position first, a position on which the practical exhortations are built. The introduction (1:1–2) is in the form of a Hellenistic, personal letter.

430 BC–190 BC

Herodotus describes Colossae as "a great city of Phrygia" strategically located on the main road from Ephesus and Sardis eastward to the Euphrates. **430**
Xenophon describes Colossae as a "populous" city, wealthy and large. **400**
Cyrus and his army spend seven days in Colossae as he moves from Sardis east to take the throne of Persia. **400**
Laodicea founded by Antiochus II who named it for his wife, Laodice **262–246**
The regions of Colossae, Hierapolis, and Laodicea become subject to the Pergamenes after the battle of Magnesia. **190**

130 BC–AD 18

Hierapolis comes under Roman rule after being established earlier in the second century. **129 BC**
A sizeable Jewish population lives in the region of Colossae, Hierapolis, and Laodicea. **62 BC**
Laodicea receives from Rome the title of a free city. **10 BC**
In his *Geography*, Strabo describes Colossae as a small town. Laodicea was then the growing city in the Lycus Valley because of its location, its banking, and its trade of black sheep wool. **AD 7–18**
A destructive earthquake in the region of Colossae, Hierapolis, and Laodicea **AD 17**

Notable in the final section are the mention of Onesimus (4:9), which links this letter with Philemon; the mention of a letter at Laodicea (4:16) that may have been Ephesians; and Paul's concluding signature, which indicates that the letter was prepared by an amanuensis (secretary; see 4:18).

Outline
I. Greeting and Thanksgiving (1:1–12)
II. God's Work in Christ (1:13–23)
III. Paul's Ministry (1:24–2:3)
IV. False Teaching Denounced (2:4–23)
V. The Christian Life (3:1–4:6)
VI. Conclusion (4:7–18)

Key verses in Colossians
3:13b Just as the Lord has forgiven you, so you are also to forgive.
3:23 Whatever you do, do it from the heart, as something done for the Lord and not for people.

AD 33–52

Jesus's trials, death, and resurrection
  NISAN 14–16 or **APRIL 3–5, 33**
Pentecost **33**
Saul's conversion on the Damascus
  Road **OCTOBER 34**
Paul, Barnabas, and John Mark make
  first missionary journey. **47–49**
Paul and Silas take second
  missionary journey. **49–52**

AD 53–62

Paul's third missionary journey **53–57**
Paul's ministry in Ephesus becomes the nucleus of
  church planting throughout Asia Minor. **54–56**
Paul arrives in Rome. **60**
Paul encounters Onesimus, a runaway
  slave from Colossae. **61**
Paul's letter to the Colossians **61**
Paul sends a letter to Philemon,
  Onesimus's master. **61**
Colossae, Laodicea, and Hierapolis experience
  a devastating earthquake. **60** or **64**

Greeting

1 Paul, an apostle of Christ Jesus by God's will, and Timothy our brother: [2] To the saints in Christ at Colossae, who are faithful brothers and sisters.

Grace to you and peace from God our Father.[A]

Thanksgiving

[3] We always thank God, the Father of our Lord Jesus Christ, when we pray for you, [4] for we have heard of your faith in Christ Jesus and of the love you have for all the saints [5] because of the hope reserved for you in heaven. You have already heard about this hope in the word of truth, the gospel [6] that has come to you. It is bearing fruit and growing all over the world, just as it has among you since the day you heard it and came to truly appreciate God's grace.[B] [7] You learned this from Epaphras, our dearly loved fellow servant. He is a faithful minister of Christ on your[C] behalf, [8] and he has told us about your love in the Spirit.

Prayer for Spiritual Growth

[9] For this reason also, since the day we heard this, we haven't stopped praying for you. We are asking that you may be filled with the knowledge of his will in all wisdom and spiritual understanding,[D] [10] so that you may walk worthy of the Lord, fully pleasing to him: bearing fruit in every good work and growing in the knowledge of God, [11] being strengthened with all power, according to his glorious might, so that you may have great endurance and patience, joyfully [12] giving thanks to the Father,

who has enabled you[E] to share in the saints' inheritance in the light. [13] He has rescued us from the domain of darkness and transferred us into the kingdom of the Son he loves. [14] In him we have redemption,[F] the forgiveness of sins.

The Centrality of Christ

[15] He is the image of the invisible God,
the firstborn over all creation.
[16] For everything was created by him,
in heaven and on earth,
the visible and the invisible,
whether thrones or dominions
or rulers or authorities —
all things have been created
through him and for him.
[17] He is before all things,
and by him all things hold together.
[18] He is also the head of the body, the church;
he is the beginning,
the firstborn from the dead,
so that he might come to have
first place in everything.
[19] For God was pleased to have
all his fullness dwell in him,
[20] and through him to reconcile
everything to himself,
whether things on earth or things
in heaven,
by making peace
through his blood, shed on the cross.[G]

[21] Once you were alienated and hostile in your minds as expressed in your evil actions. [22] But now he has reconciled you by his physical body through his death, to present you holy,

[A]1:2 Other mss add *and the Lord Jesus Christ* [B]1:6 Or *and truly recognized God's grace* [C]1:7 Other mss read *our* [D]1:9 Or *all spiritual wisdom and understanding* [E]1:12 Other mss read *us* [F]1:14 Other mss add *through his blood* [G]1:20 Other mss add *through him*

1:3–8 Paul offered a prayer of thanksgiving for the Colossian believers.
1:3 Paul's use of **we** probably included Timothy (v. 1) and possibly others (4:7–14). Paul expressed the frequency of his thanksgiving with the adverb **always**.
1:4 The reason for Paul's thanksgiving is rooted in reports he had heard about the Colossians' **faith in Christ Jesus** and **love . . . for all the saints**.
1:5–6 This **hope** was the result of having heard and received the **word of truth** or more specifically, **the gospel**.
1:7–8 Paul did not start the church at Colossae and had not yet visited there, so it was through **Epaphras** that he had learned of their condition. He endorsed Epaphras as a beloved **fellow servant** and a **faithful minister** (cp. 2:1; 4:12–13; Phm 23).
1:9 **For this reason** harks back to Epaphras's good report about the Colossian believers' faith in Christ. The word **filled** (the passive verb indicates God as causal agent) typically conveys the sense of "completeness" in Colossians (vv. 9,19,25; 2:9–10; 4:17). Paul asked that they receive full **knowledge of his will**. The phrase **in all wisdom and spiritual understanding** expresses the means through which this knowledge comes.

1:10–12 The purpose of Paul's prayer was that the believers at Colossae might **walk worthy of the Lord** so that all their conduct would please him.
1:13–14 The reference to being **rescued** and **transferred** evokes OT imagery of God delivering his people from the grip of hostile oppressors (Ex 6:6; 14:30; Jdg 6:9; 8:34; Pss 18:19; 79:9; 86:14). Believers have been rescued from the realm of Satan's oppression (**domain of darkness**) by having been transferred to the realm of Christ, which is a kingdom "in the light" (v. 12). **Redemption** is the incalculable price paid for this deliverance and transfer. The result is **forgiveness of sins**.
1:15–23 Some scholars think these verses are possibly a poem or an early hymn expressing Christ's supremacy as Creator and Redeemer.
1:15 The word **image** refers to an exact visible representation of something or someone. Thus, Jesus the Son represented the invisible God of the OT (Jn 1:18). The title **firstborn** does not mean that Jesus was created (v. 16), but indicates his priority of rank as supreme over all the created order.
1:16–17 Christ is supreme over creation because he is the Creator. Paul's mention of **thrones . . . dominions . . . rulers**, and **authorities** may refer to four classes of angelic

beings (possibly directing human affairs). This may be a corrective against the false teaching promoting the worship of angels (2:18). Thus Paul asserted the supremacy of Christ over all creation because **all things** were created **through him and for him**. The phrase **by him all things hold together** presents Christ as the one who sustains all creation.
1:18 Christ is the **head** of **the church** because he is **the beginning** and **the firstborn from the dead**. Christ's resurrection resulted in the fulfillment of God's purpose for Christ that **he might come to have first place in everything**.
1:19–20 God was **pleased** that **his fullness**, the entirety of God's being, would **dwell in the Son**. Thus Jesus was fully divine as well as fully human. God took pleasure in this because, through Christ, God would **reconcile** (reestablish a right relationship) all things to himself on the **cross** (cp. Rm 5:11; 2Co 5:19).
1:21 Paul explained the need for reconciliation to God by appealing to the Colossian believers' spiritual condition before their salvation. Before they heard the gospel they were **alienated** from God. Corrupt thinking results in immoral behavior.
1:22 Paul contrasted the Colossian believers' former life with their current salvation. The

Christian Higher Education

by Barry H. Corey

The notion that colleges and universities can be deeply Christian in their mission is hardly a modern concept. Many of today's Christian institutions of higher learning were founded in the middle 1800s, while many European and North American schools were established centuries earlier and have deep roots in Christianity.

Over time, the leaders of many of these institutions untethered their decision-making from the convictions of their forebears. As a result, these schools today do not resemble the Christian intent of their founders. Several reasons account for the drift away from Christ-centeredness and biblical authority. One is that over time faculty no longer were expected to teach from a perspective that all learning is connected to all truth—truth authored and ordered by God, truth that transcends all of life and all disciplines.

Knowledge and the God of Truth

Christians who see life from a biblical worldview understand learning differently. They do not believe scholarship and faith are incompatible. Rather than education disconnected from faith, Christian thinkers believe all knowledge falls within the realm of God's sovereignty and should be studied with that in mind. They believe all matters related to the arts and sciences—in fact, the entirety of life—were created by God as good and contain truth that ultimately points back to him.

In Colossians 1 Paul summarizes Christ's dominion over all of life. It's a passage often cited in advocating for the great Christian intellectual tradition. Notice the repetition of the phrase "all things" in 1:16–17, strengthening the biblical argument that a Trinitarian God is the Creator of all things, the object of all things, and the connector of all things. Regarding Jesus the Son Paul says,

"He is the image of the invisible God, the firstborn over all creation. For everything was created by him, in heaven and on earth, the visible and the invisible, whether thrones or dominions or rulers or authorities—all things have been created through him and for him. He is before all things, and by him all things hold together" (Col 1:15–17).

Integrative Teaching

Christian colleges and universities teach from the perspective that God is the Creator of all things and that God holds all things together. Teaching this way is often referred to as "integrative teaching." In the ideal Christian higher education setting, God's created and connecting truth ought to be evident throughout the entire curriculum and community. Christian higher education is not "Christian" because faculty members sign a faith statement or students are required to attend chapel. Christian higher education is "Christian" when the understanding throughout the institution is that the entirety of knowledge and wisdom comes from God and points toward God.

Being part of a Christian college or university, therefore, means students grapple with the truths within each academic discipline and among all academic disciplines by seeing them as under God's sovereignty. This is what the Dutch theologian Abraham Kuyper meant when he said, "There is not a square inch in the whole domain of our human existence over which Christ, who is Sovereign over all, does not cry, 'Mine!'"

This approach to learning is what characterizes Christian higher education, and it must stay as a distinguishing mark of an exemplary Christian university. In the world's marketplace of ideas, the person and work of Jesus Christ and the implications of a biblical worldview currently hold little sway, yet they are vitally important to the Christian's assessments of and responses to dominant cultural ideologies. The role of Christian higher education is to preserve and advance the Christian intellectual tradition and to glorify God.

Christianity for All of Life

As Christian higher education enables Christians to think from the center of all knowledge—knowing that God is the Author of all truth—students begin asking new questions:

"How do faith and reason intersect in all of life and not run on separate tracks?"

"How should I live in a way that honors Christ and brings glory to God in the world of finance or law, medicine or politics, art or media?"

"What does it mean to think Christianly about the big questions of our times?"

"How does a biblical worldview influence the way I run my business, give away my money, nurture my family, or serve my community?"

Both the curricular programs in Christian higher education and cocurricular activities create a community in which students explore the answers to these and other worldview questions within a theological framework. Christian higher education is far more than sprinkling Christian flavorings on a college degree. Instead, it is an intellectually robust and academically holistic way of thinking.

To get there, scholars at the university need to be intentional about integrative thinking—the idea that academic disciplines are not disconnected from one another but are held together, since all truth is within the realm of God's ordered creation. An integrated faculty in Christian higher education allows professors to set aside time for discussing what God's revealed Word brings to bear on their respective disciplines and on the educational mission of the institution. This notion of integration brings together faculty from the social sciences, theology, the arts, the physical sciences, the humanities, business, education, and so forth into a community with a shared approach to the connectedness of all things. If most of what is taught in the classrooms of a self-identified Christian college is indistinguishable from what is taught in non-Christian schools, then integration is evidently not a priority and a full understanding of a Christian worldview is being shortchanged.

Education and Spiritual Formation

Since a Christian college or university provides a foundation for intellectual development, academic competence will accompany thought leadership in church and society.

Much happens within the life of a university to cultivate this discipline of the mind and soul together. It is the idea Paul writes about to the church in Rome, explaining that spiritual transformation takes place by the renewing of the mind (Rm 12:2).

Colleges or universities that appoint faculty who are first-rate scholars, have a deep love for Christ, and are well-articulated integrators of scholarship and faith will impact generations of students. Such Christian thought leaders shape communities, congregations, and cultures for the advancement of Christ's kingdom.

Because God's Word bears witness to the truth of Christ at the core of all things, a Christ-centered university must be biblically grounded. The cornerstone of the evangelical movement from its starting point was an ineradicable belief in the authority of the Bible, alongside serious scholarship. Such commitment to the revealed Word of God is at the core of exemplary Christian universities. Being a Christian college or university means the Christian Scriptures—as originally intended and as understood through the ages—have a central role in all programs.

Christian Education as Worship

Christian higher education is an act of worship, built on the lordship of Christ over all things—including our lives. Scholarship separated from loving God is a type of idolatry. By seeing all of life and vocation as a holy calling, graduates of Christian higher education should be alive in a way that encourages others to see Christ's redemptive work and to receive God's grace.

Learning this way is not an act of self-enrichment. It is an act of worshiping our Creator God. This is what Jesus meant when he called his followers to love the Lord with all their hearts, souls, strength, and minds (Mt 22:37; Lk 10:27). The purpose of theology is not mere intellectual exercise but doxology, an expression of praise to God. We study all of God's truths so that we may love God more.

faultless, and blameless before him — ²³ if indeed you remain grounded and steadfast in the faith and are not shifted away from the hope of the gospel that you heard. This gospel has been proclaimed in all creation under heaven, and I, Paul, have become a servant of it.

Paul's Ministry

²⁴ Now I rejoice in my sufferings for you, and I am completing in my flesh what is lacking in Christ's afflictions for his body, that is, the church. ²⁵ I have become its servant, according to God's commission that was given to me for you, to make the word of God fully known, ²⁶ the mystery hidden for ages and generations but now revealed to his saints. ²⁷ God wanted to make known among the Gentiles the glorious wealth of this mystery, which is Christ in you, the hope of glory. ²⁸ We proclaim him, warning and teaching everyone with all wisdom, so that we may present everyone mature in Christ. ²⁹ I labor for this, striving with his strength that works powerfully in me.

2 For I want you to know how greatly I am struggling for you, for those in Laodicea, and for all who have not seen me in person. ² I want their hearts to be encouraged and joined together in love, so that they may have all the riches of complete understanding and have the knowledge of God's mystery — Christ.^A ³ In him are hidden all the treasures of wisdom and knowledge.

Christ versus the Colossian Heresy

⁴ I am saying this so that no one will deceive you with arguments that sound reasonable.

⁵ For I may be absent in body, but I am with you in spirit, rejoicing to see how well ordered you are and the strength of your faith in Christ. ⁶ So then, just as you have received Christ Jesus as Lord, continue to walk in him, ⁷ being rooted and built up in him and established in the faith, just as you were taught, and overflowing with gratitude.

⁸ Be careful that no one takes you captive through philosophy and empty deceit based on human tradition, based on the elements of the world, rather than Christ. ⁹ For the entire fullness of God's nature dwells bodily^B in Christ, ¹⁰ and you have been filled by him, who is the head over every ruler and authority. ¹¹ You were also circumcised in him with a circumcision not done with hands, by putting off the body of flesh, in the circumcision of Christ, ¹² when you were buried with him in baptism, in which you were also raised with him through faith in the working of God, who raised him from the dead. ¹³ And when you were dead in trespasses and in the uncircumcision of your flesh, he made you alive with him and forgave us all our trespasses. ¹⁴ He erased the certificate of debt, with its obligations, that was against us and opposed to us, and has taken it away by nailing it to the cross. ¹⁵ He disarmed the rulers and authorities and disgraced them publicly; he triumphed over them in him.^C

¹⁶ Therefore, don't let anyone judge you in regard to food and drink or in the matter of a festival or a new moon or a Sabbath day.^D ¹⁷ These are a shadow of what was to come;

---

^2:2 Other mss read mystery of God, both of the Father and of Christ; other ms variations exist on this v. ^2:9 Or nature lives in a human body ^2:15 Or them through it ^2:16 Or sabbaths

---

reference to Jesus's **physical body** highlights his humanity, whereas v. 19 expresses his divinity. The purpose of this reconciliation is so that believers may be presented **holy, faultless, and blameless** before him.
1:23 Faith refers to the content of the gospel with Jesus as the object (vv. 4,23; 2:5,7,12).
1:24 The enigmatic phrase what is **lacking in Christ's afflictions** cannot mean that something was lacking in Christ's atoning work (v. 20). Rather, Paul's sufferings benefited the church by promoting the spread of the gospel.
1:25 God's **commission** (Eph 1:10; 3:2,9) pertains to his plan for Gentiles.
1:26 The term **mystery** (cp. v. 27; 2:2; 4:3; Rm 11:25; Eph 1:9; 3:3–9) refers to something that was previously **hidden** in God's plan but has now been **revealed**. Here it relates to the inclusion of the Gentiles into people of God.
1:27 In you could mean "among you," or, more likely, refer to Christ's indwelling of believers (Rm 8:10; 2Co 13:5; Gl 2:20; Eph 3:17).
1:28 The words **warning** and **teaching** express the manner of their proclamation, which is further characterized as being in keeping **with all wisdom**. The purpose of this ongoing ministry was to **present everyone mature in Christ** in correspondence with Christ's purpose in reconciliation (v. 22).
2:1 On **have not seen me in person**, see note at 1:7–8.

2:3 Christ is the only source required for **wisdom** and **knowledge**; the Colossians did not need to look to any other philosophy. **Hidden** does not mean secretive (1:26) but plays on the word **treasures**. Jewish writers often used this imagery to encourage seekers to dig deep when looking for truth.
2:4 For the first time in the letter, Paul directly stated his opposition to the false teaching. The words **deceive** and **arguments that sound reasonable** imply the use of misleading or faulty reasoning.
2:6–7 The command to **continue to walk in** him, (cp. 1:10) is followed by expressions of what this involved: (1) being **rooted** (firmness; cp. Eph 3:17); (2) **built up**; (3) **established in the faith** (a legal term meaning "confirmed"); and (4) **overflowing with gratitude** (cp. 1:3,12; 3:15–17; 4:2).
2:8 Be careful is a strong warning to watch out so believers are not taken **captive** and enslaved to false doctrines through **philosophy** and **empty deceit**. **Human tradition** implies human origin (whether Jewish or Gentile) as opposed to the divine nature of the gospel. The **elements of the world** were most likely astral deities, spirits, and/or angels commonly associated with pagan worship, astrology, and magical practices (see vv. 15,20; 1:16; Gl 4:3,9; Eph 1:21; 2:2; 3:10; 6:12).
2:9 On the **fullness** of Christ, see note at 1:19–20.

2:10 You have been filled denotes a completed act with ongoing results.
2:11 The reference to circumcision indicates the Jewish nature of this false philosophy. **The circumcision of Christ** was spiritual and associated with "circumcision of the heart" (Dt 10:16; 30:6; Jr 4:4; Ezk 44:7; Rm 2:29).
2:12 Believer's **baptism** symbolizes union with Christ in death and complete separation from the former way of life.
2:13 Prior to their faith in Christ, the Colossians were spiritually **dead in trespasses** (cp. Eph 2:1–3). However, in Christ, God made them **alive** and **forgave** all their sins (Eph 2:4–8).
2:14 The **certificate of debt** may refer to a handwritten document or to the Mosaic law. God erases the sinner's certificate of debt and removes it by **nailing it to the cross**.
2:15 The phrase **disgraced them publicly** relates to God humiliating these spiritual rulers in a public spectacle of shame and defeat. The word **triumphed** (see note at 2Co 2:14) evokes the imagery of a triumphal procession where a victorious general would lead a parade to display the treasures and prisoners of war from his conquest.
2:16 The Colossian believers were apparently pressured by some in the church to observe Jewish dietary laws and holy days.
2:17 Paul used the words **shadow** and **substance** to contrast the incomplete nature of

the substance is^A Christ. ^18 Let no one condemn^B you by delighting in ascetic practices and the worship of angels, claiming access to a visionary realm. Such people are inflated by empty notions of their unspiritual^C mind. ^19 He doesn't hold on to the head, from whom the whole body, nourished and held together by its ligaments and tendons, grows with growth from God.

^20 If you died with Christ to the elements of this world, why do you live as if you still belonged to the world? Why do you submit to regulations: ^21 "Don't handle, don't taste, don't touch"? ^22 All these regulations refer to what is destined to perish by being used up; they are human commands and doctrines. ^23 Although these have a reputation for wisdom by promoting self-made religion, false humility, and severe treatment of the body, they are not of any value in curbing self-indulgence.^D

The Life of the New Man

3 So if you have been raised with Christ, seek the things above, where Christ is, seated at the right hand of God. ^2 Set your minds on things above, not on earthly things. ^3 For you died, and your life is hidden with Christ in God. ^4 When Christ, who is your^E life, appears, then you also will appear with him in glory.

^5 Therefore, put to death what belongs to your earthly nature: sexual immorality, impurity, lust, evil desire, and greed, which is idolatry. ^6 Because of these, God's wrath is coming upon the disobedient,^F ^7 and you once walked in these things when you were living in them. ^8 But now, put away all the following: anger, wrath, malice, slander, and filthy language from your mouth. ^9 Do not lie to one another, since you have put off the old self with its practices ^10 and have put on the new self. You are being renewed in knowledge according to the image of your^G Creator. ^11 In Christ there is not Greek and Jew, circumcision and uncircumcision, barbarian, Scythian, slave and free; but Christ is all and in all.

The Christian Life

^12 Therefore, as God's chosen ones, holy and dearly loved, put on compassion, kindness,

^A 2:17 Or substance belongs to ^B 2:18 Or disqualify ^C 2:18 Lit fleshly ^D 2:23 Lit value against indulgence of the flesh ^E 3:4 Other mss read our ^F 3:6 Other mss omit upon the disobedient ^G 3:10 Lit his

---

these former obligations with the fullness brought about by **Christ**.
2:18 Ascetic practices refers to harsh treatment of the body (i.e., self-humiliation). The **worship of angels** may be understood as worship improperly rendered to angels, or as worship of God performed by angels. This worship was conducted through entrance into the **visionary realm**. Paul, however, identified these visions as egotistical delusions of a carnal mind.
2:19 On Christ as the **head**, see 1:18 (cp. Eph 4:16).
2:20 Since believers have died with Christ (v. 11) to the **elements of this world** (see note at v. 8), they are liberated from worldly rules. The word **regulations** means literally "obligation" (v. 14).
2:21 Paul quoted some of the purity and dietary laws imposed by the false teachers, who were judging and disqualifying believers.
2:22 These dietary regulations were merely physical and temporal because once food is consumed it is destroyed. Paul identified these false teachers' regulations as **human commands and doctrines** (alluding to Is 29:13; see note at Col 2:8).
2:23 Paul conceded that these regulations had **a reputation for wisdom** in that they appeared to provide enlightened spiritual understanding (1:9), but in reality these practices offered no help in dealing with self-indulgence.
3:1–17 In these verses Paul offered positive advice on true spiritual living that effectively remedies sinful cravings of the flesh.
3:1–2 So if resumes the implications of believers' identification with Christ begun in 2:20. It signals a shift in the letter from doctrinal instruction (chaps. 1–2) to practical application (3:1–4:6). The objects of believers' efforts and thoughts are **Christ** and **things above** rather than **earthly things**.

3:3 Hidden connotes that God fully completed the action in the past with permanent results.
3:5 The command to **put to death** (2:20; Mt 5:29–30; Rm 8:13) refers to the practical outworking of seeking and thinking about heavenly things. Paul offered a fivefold catalog of vices explaining what he meant by **what belongs to your earthly nature**. These vices are listed moving from specific outward behaviors to general inward inclinations and thoughts.
3:6 God's wrath indicates the severe consequences for these sins.
3:7 Once walked emphasizes the discontinuity between believers' new and former ways of life.
3:8–10 Put away literally means to "take off" or "remove" something and may evoke

the familiar Pauline metaphor of changing clothes (Rm 13:12; Eph 4:22). All the vices listed relate to behaviors that disrupt interpersonal relationships. The new self replaces the old but is also continuously being **renewed** to reflect the image of God.
3:11 The old order was characterized by ethnic and social division, but the new order obliterates those distinctions in the body of Christ (see Gl 3:27–28). The phrase **Christ is all and in all** refers to his supremacy (1:17) and indwelling presence in believers (1:27).
3:12 After commanding believers to "put away" worldly behaviors, Paul offered a series of positive commands to **put on** with behavior fitted for God's people. The five virtues are just the opposite of the vices listed in vv. 5 and 8.

#81 99 Essential Christian Truths

FAMILY RELATIONSHIPS

God has ordained the family as the foundational institution of human society. It is composed of persons related to one another by marriage, blood, or adoption. Marriage is the uniting of one man and one woman in covenant commitment for a lifetime. It is God's unique gift to reveal the union between Christ and his church and to provide for the man and the woman in marriage the framework for intimate companionship, the channel of sexual expression according to biblical standards (Heb 13:4), and the means for procreation of the human race. The husband and wife are of equal worth before God, since both are created in God's image. The marriage relationship models the way God relates to his people. A husband is to love his wife as Christ loved the church. He has the God-given responsibility to provide for, to protect, and to lead his family. A wife is to submit herself graciously to the servant leadership of her husband even as the church willingly submits to the headship of Christ. She, being in the image of God as is her husband and thus equal to him, has the God-given responsibility to respect her husband and to serve as his helper in managing the household and nurturing the next generation (Eph 5:22–33; 1Pt 3:1–7). Children, from the moment of conception, are a blessing and heritage from the Lord. Parents are to demonstrate to their children God's pattern for marriage. Parents are to teach their children spiritual and moral values and to lead them, through consistent lifestyle example and loving discipline, to make choices based on biblical truth (Dt 6:4–9). Children are to honor and obey their parents (Eph 6:1–3).

humility, gentleness, and patience, [13] bearing with one another and forgiving one another if anyone has a grievance against another. Just as the Lord has forgiven you, so you are also to forgive. [14] Above all, put on love, which is the perfect bond of unity. [15] And let the peace of Christ, to which you were also called in one body, rule your hearts. And be thankful. [16] Let the word of Christ dwell richly among you, in all wisdom teaching and admonishing one another through psalms, hymns, and spiritual songs,[A] singing to God with gratitude in your hearts. [17] And whatever you do, in word or in deed, do everything in the name of the Lord Jesus, giving thanks to God the Father through him.

Christ in Your Home

[18] Wives, submit yourselves to your husbands, as is fitting in the Lord. [19] Husbands, love your wives and don't be bitter toward them. [20] Children, obey your parents in everything, for this pleases the Lord. [21] Fathers, do not exasperate your children, so that they won't become discouraged. [22] Slaves, obey your human masters in everything. Don't work only while being watched, as people-pleasers, but work wholeheartedly, fearing the Lord. [23] Whatever you do, do it from the heart, as something done for the Lord and not for people, [24] knowing that you will receive the reward of an inheritance from the Lord. You serve the Lord Christ. [25] For the wrongdoer will be paid back for whatever wrong he has done, and there is no favoritism.

4 Masters, deal with your slaves justly and fairly, since you know that you too have a Master in heaven.

Speaking to God and Others

[2] Devote yourselves to prayer; stay alert in it with thanksgiving. [3] At the same time, pray also for us that God may open a door to us for the word, to speak the mystery of Christ, for which I am in chains, [4] so that I may make it known as I should. [5] Act wisely toward outsiders, making the most of the time. [6] Let your speech always be gracious, seasoned with salt, so that you may know how you should answer each person.

Final Greetings

[7] Tychicus, our dearly loved brother, faithful minister, and fellow servant in the Lord, will tell you all the news about me. [8] I have sent him to you for this very purpose, so that you may know how we are[B] and so that he may encourage your hearts. [9] He is coming with Onesimus, a faithful and dearly loved brother, who is one of you. They will tell you about everything here.

[10] Aristarchus, my fellow prisoner, sends you greetings, as does Mark, Barnabas's cousin (concerning whom you have received instructions: if he comes to you, welcome him), [11] and so does Jesus who is called Justus. These alone of the circumcised are my coworkers for the kingdom of God, and they have been a comfort to me. [12] Epaphras, who is one of you, a servant of Christ Jesus, sends you greetings. He is always wrestling for you

---

^3:16 Or *and songs prompted by the Spirit*   B4:8 Other mss read *that he may know how you are*

3:13 The words **bearing with** (cp. Rm 15:7; Eph 4:2) and **forgiving** (cp. Eph 4:32) express the habitual manner in which believers exhibit the stated virtues. Both verbs pertain to interpersonal relationships in the body of Christ. **Just as the Lord has forgiven** echoes Jesus's injunction to forgive because believers are forgiven (Mt 6:12,14–15; 18:23–35; Lk 7:42).
3:16 The words **teaching** and **admonishing** express the means of how the gospel is to dwell among believers. **Singing** and **gratitude** characterize the manner of this teaching and admonishing.
3:17 This verse is similar to 1Co 10:31. Doing everything **in the name of the Lord Jesus** means doing it in obedience to him.
3:18–4:1 In this section Paul showed how doing everything in the name of the Lord applies to every member of a household.
3:18 Paul exhorted **wives** to **submit** themselves to their husbands (Eph 5:21–24). This submission is not subservience but voluntary subordination. This disposition is based on the wife's relationship with Christ and her role within the family (**as is fitting in the Lord**) rather than on a false notion of inferiority (1Co 11:3,7–9; see note at Eph 5:22–24).
3:19 Coupled with his exhortation for wives, Paul admonished **husbands** to **love your wives**, with the additional warning not to

become **bitter toward them.** "Bitterness" pertains to harsh treatment and could be translated as "to cause bitter feelings."
3:20 Children must be obedient to their parents (Ex 20:12; Dt 5:16; Eph 6:1–3); this is how they please the Lord. The word **obey** lacks the voluntary sense found in the command to be submissive.
3:21 Although the term **fathers** could include both parents (Heb 11:23), fathers in particular are warned to not **exasperate** their children (Eph 6:4). "Exasperate" means to cause or provoke someone to harbor feelings of resentment. The reason for this injunction is so that children do not become **discouraged** or disheartened.
3:22–25 Paul offered an extensive rationale for exhorting Christian **slaves** to **obey** their earthly masters in **everything**: (1) slaves are ultimately serving the Lord rather than a human master; (2) their service to the Lord will be gloriously rewarded in eternity; and (3) God does not discriminate when it comes to punishing bad behavior. See also Eph 6:5–8.
4:1 Paul exhorted **masters** to deal justly with their **slaves** because they themselves **have a Master in heaven.** See also Eph 6:9.
4:2 Stay alert or "staying awake" refers to the mental attitude of expectancy and watchfulness.

4:3–4 An "open door" was a common expression for an opportunity for someone to do something (Ac 14:27; 1Co 16:9; 2Co 2:12). Paul asked believers to intercede for him so he could continue to spread the gospel. On **mystery**, see note at 1:26.
4:5–6 Paul's final exhortation to the Colossians was that they would use wisdom in their interaction with unbelievers (1:9–10). The phrase **making the most** comes from a verb meaning "to buy up," as if finding a bargain.
4:7–8 Tychicus, a native of Asia, first joined Paul in Ac 20:4 and continued to serve alongside him (Eph 6:21; 2Tm 4:12; Ti 3:12). He may also have been the person who delivered this letter to the Colossians as well as the letter to the Laodiceans (see note at v. 16).
4:9 Onesimus, a native of Colossae, was a runaway slave (Phm 10). His name means "useful."
4:10–11 Aristarchus, a native of Thessalonica, was one of Paul's companions and his fellow prisoner (Ac 19:29; 20:4). John **Mark**, the Gospel writer, joined Paul and Barnabas on their first missionary journey (Ac 12:12,25). Paul and Barnabas parted ways because Paul did not want Mark along for their second journey (Ac 15:37–39). At some point Paul became convinced again of Mark's usefulness. **Jesus who is called Justus** was a fellow Jewish believer.
4:12–13 On **Epaphras**, see note at 1:7–8.

in his prayers, so that you can stand mature and fully assured[A] in everything God wills. [13] For I testify about him that he works hard[B] for you, for those in Laodicea, and for those in Hierapolis. [14] Luke, the dearly loved physician, and Demas send you greetings. [15] Give my greetings to the brothers and sisters in Laodicea, and to Nympha and the church in her home. [16] After this letter has been read at your gathering, have it read also in the church of the Laodiceans; and see that you also read the letter from Laodicea. [17] And tell Archippus, "Pay attention to the ministry you have received in the Lord, so that you can accomplish it."

[18] I, Paul, am writing this greeting with my own hand. Remember my chains. Grace be with you.[C]

[A]4:12 Other mss read *and complete*   [B]4:13 Other mss read *he has a great zeal*   [C]4:18 Other mss add *Amen.*

4:14 This is the only place in the NT where Luke's profession is identified. **Demas**, one of Paul's companions, later abandoned the gospel ministry because of his love for the world (2Tm 4:10).
4:15 Laodicea, ten miles from Colossae, also had a fledgling congregation of believers.

Paul specifically mentioned **Nympha**, in whose home the Laodicean church met.
4:16 Once this letter had been read among the Colossian believers, they were to send it or a copy of it to Laodicea. Paul apparently wrote a letter to the Laodiceans that was also to be read in Colossae. The letter to

the Laodiceans was either another of Paul's letters (Ephesians?) or a letter that has not been preserved.
4:17 On **Archippus**, see note at Phm 2.
4:18 Paul often signed his letters himself as a mark of their authenticity (1Co 16:21; Gl 6:11; 2Th 3:17; Phm 19).

◥ Introduction to 1 Thessalonians

Circumstances of Writing

No serious objections have been made to dispute that Paul was the author of 1 Thessalonians (1:1). The greeting also mentions Silvanus and Timothy. Sometimes Paul wrote from the team perspective, but he was the primary author (2:18; 3:2).

About AD 50, the missionary team led by Paul and Silas left Philippi and traveled westward on the Roman road known as the *Via Egnatia*. They proceeded toward the strategic capital city of the Roman province of Macedonia—Thessalonica.

Thessalonica was a large port city on the Aegean Sea in modern-day Greece, with a population of about two hundred thousand. The city was filled with pagan worshipers of idols, the full pantheon of Greek and Roman gods, and was well known for its emperor worship. Thessalonica was loyal to Caesar, and he had granted its citizens many privileges.

As was his custom, Paul found the local Jewish synagogue and started teaching there. For three Sabbaths, he reasoned with the Jews from the Scriptures. He explained and demonstrated that the promised Messiah had to suffer and rise from the dead. After explaining the life, death, and resurrection of Jesus, he then stated boldly, "This Jesus I am proclaiming to you is the Messiah" (Ac 17:3). Some of the Jews were persuaded, along with some of the devout Greeks who were worshipers at the synagogue, and some of the prominent women.

They joined Paul and Silas, and the church in Thessalonica was born.

There were Jews in the city who were not persuaded, and they became envious of what Paul and Silas had done. They incited the people into an uproar and attacked Jason's house where the missionary team had been staying. Wanting to drag Paul and Silas out before the crowd, they found only Jason and some new believers. They dragged these out before the city authorities. The rulers, not wanting more unrest, forced Jason and the rest of the brothers to make a financial payment of security to ensure that there would not be a repeat of such a disturbance. That very night the Thessalonian believers sent Paul and Silas away to Berea, where they could continue their ministry (Ac 17:1–9).

From Berea, Paul went to Athens. He wanted to see the Thessalonians again. When he could endure the separation no longer, he sent Timothy to encourage the Thessalonian believers (1Th 3:2). Timothy came back with an encouraging report about the Thessalonian church (3:6). Paul wrote to them from Corinth in response to Timothy's report. Based on the archaeological evidence of a dated inscription mentioning Gallio, proconsul of Achaia, by name (Ac 18:12) and correlating this with Paul's visit to Corinth when Gallio was there, 1 Thessalonians can be reliably dated to AD 50 or 51. This would make 1 Thessalonians the earliest of Paul's letters with the probable exception of the book of Galatians.

---

1 Thessalonians Timeline

2300–150 BC

Prehistoric settlement on the site of Thessalonica **2300**

Founding of Therme at the head of the Thermaic Gulf **600**

Cassander, king of Macedon, establishes Thessalonica at the site where Therme had existed, naming the new city in honor of his wife. **316**

The Romans gain control of Thessalonica when Perseus, king of Macedonia, is defeated at Pydna. **168**

First Jewish community in Thessalonica—emigrants from Alexandria **168–103**

149–42 BC

Construction of the Macedonian leg of the Egnatian Way, a Roman military road connecting Thessalonica with the Adriatic Sea in the west and with Neapolis in the east **147–120**

Thessalonica becomes the capital of the Roman province of Macedonia and is referred to as "the Mother of Macedonia." **146**

The Roman statesman Cicero spends six months of his self-imposed exile in Thessalonica. **58**

Many Roman officials flee Rome and take up residence in Thessalonica during the Roman civil war. **49–48**

Augustus declares Thessalonica a free city following the battle of Philippi. **42**

Contribution to the Bible

First Thessalonians contributes to our understanding of the second coming of Christ. Paul wrote to correct some misunderstandings of this doctrine. In doing so, he showed us that Christ's return gives us true hope. First Thessalonians and 1 Corinthians (chap. 15) are the only books that explicitly mention that Christians who are alive at Christ's return will be changed and will meet Christ in the air without dying.

Structure

First Thessalonians follows the standard form for a first-century letter: greeting (1:1), thanksgiving (1:2–4), body (1:5–5:22), and farewell (5:23–28). The body of the letter does not follow Paul's typical structure of presenting doctrine first, followed by practical exhortation based on that doctrine. Instead, 1 Thessalonians moves back and forth between the doctrinal and the practical.

Outline

Key verse in 1 Thessalonians

5:18 Give thanks in everything; for this is God's will for you in Christ Jesus.

AD 15–45

Tiberius Caesar takes away Thessalonica's status as a free city when her citizens protest increased taxation. **15**
Jesus's trials, death, and resurrection **NISAN 14–16** or **APRIL 3–5, 33**
Pentecost **33**
Saul's conversion on the Damascus Road **OCTOBER 34**
Claudius Caesar restores Thessalonica's status as a free city. **44**

AD 45–52

Paul, Barnabas, and John Mark make their first missionary journey. **47–49**
Paul and Silas begin their second missionary journey. **49**
Paul, Silas, and Timothy preach in Thessalonica. **50**
Paul writes 1 Thessalonians several months after his ministry among the Thessalonians. **51**
Paul concludes his second missionary journey and arrives in Antioch of Syria. **52**

Greeting

1 Paul, Silvanus,[A] and Timothy:
To the church of the Thessalonians in God the Father and the Lord Jesus Christ. Grace to you and peace.[B]

Thanksgiving

[2] We always thank God for all of you, making mention of you constantly in our prayers. [3] We recall, in the presence of our God and Father, your work produced by faith, your labor motivated by love, and your endurance inspired by hope in our Lord Jesus Christ. [4] For we know, brothers and sisters loved by God, that he has chosen you, [5] because our gospel did not come to you in word only, but also in power, in the Holy Spirit, and with full assurance. You know how we lived among you for your benefit, [6] and you yourselves became imitators of us and of the Lord when, in spite of severe persecution, you welcomed the message with joy from the Holy Spirit. [7] As a result, you became an example to all the believers in Macedonia and Achaia. [8] For the word of the Lord rang out from you, not only in Macedonia and Achaia, but in every place that your faith[C] in God has gone out. Therefore, we don't need to say anything, [9] for they themselves report[D] what kind of reception we had from you: how you turned to God from idols to serve the living and true God [10] and to wait for his Son from heaven, whom he raised from the dead — Jesus, who rescues us from the coming wrath.

Paul's Conduct

2 For you yourselves know, brothers and sisters, that our visit with you was not without result. [2] On the contrary, after we had previously suffered and were treated outrageously in Philippi, as you know, we were emboldened by our God to speak the gospel of God to you in spite of great opposition. [3] For our exhortation didn't come from error or impurity or an intent to deceive. [4] Instead, just as we have been approved by God to be entrusted with the gospel, so we speak, not to please people, but rather God, who examines our hearts. [5] For we were never used flattering speech, as you know, or had greedy motives — God is our witness — [6] and we didn't seek glory from people, either from you or from others. [7] Although we could have been a burden as Christ's apostles, instead we were gentle[E] among you, as a nurse[F] nurtures her own children. [8] We cared so much for you that we were pleased to share with you not only the gospel of God but also our own lives, because you had become dear to us. [9] For you remember our labor and hardship, brothers and sisters. Working night and day so that we would not burden any of you, we preached God's gospel to you. [10] You are witnesses, and so is God, of how devoutly, righteously, and blamelessly we conducted ourselves with you believers. [11] As you know, like a father with his own children, [12] we encouraged, comforted, and implored each one of you to walk worthy of God, who calls you into his own kingdom and glory.

[A] 1:1 Or *Silas*; Ac 15:22–32; 16:19–40; 17:1–16   [B] 1:1 Other mss add *from God our Father and the Lord Jesus Christ*   [C] 1:8 Or *in every place news of your faith*   [D] 1:9 Lit *report about us*   [E] 2:7 Many mss read *infants*   [F] 2:7 Or *nursing mother*

1:1 **Silvanus** (2Co 1:19; 2Th 1:1), or Silas (Ac 15:22), was chosen by Paul to accompany him on his second missionary journey, replacing Barnabas (Ac 15:40). Silas participated in the work of planting the Thessalonian church (Ac 17:4) and was with Paul in Corinth at the time of the writing of this letter. Paul may have encountered **Timothy** at Lystra on his first missionary journey (Ac 14:8–18). On the second visit Timothy

SANCTIFICATION

After we are justified by faith, declared to be in right standing with God through the righteousness of Christ, we undergo a lifetime of sanctification where we are continually made more like Christ through the work of the Holy Spirit (Gl 5:16–26; 2Th 2:13). Scripture speaks of sanctification as a present position (we have already been sanctified) and as a continuing process. Sanctification affects the whole of a person, transforming one's heart, mind, and character to reflect that of Jesus.

is described as a disciple who was ready to assist Paul in the missionary efforts (Ac 16:1–3). Paul sent him from Athens to assist the newly formed and persecuted church when Paul realized he could not return to the Thessalonians (1Th 3:1–2). Timothy's encouraging report on the state of the Thessalonian church prompted Paul to write this letter (3:6).
1:3 The Thessalonians' **work** and **labor** were evident in that the gospel had gone throughout not only their province of Macedonia but into the neighboring province of Achaia (vv. 7–8).
1:4 Paul reminded the Thessalonians that God is the one who had **chosen** them and that they were **loved** by him.
1:5–6 The **gospel** is more than a message of words. It is a message that comes in **power** and in the **Holy Spirit**. The basic meaning of "gospel" (Gk *euangelion*) is "good news." Even though the church at Thessalonica was founded in the midst of **severe persecution**, the message was warmly received with **joy** that came from the Holy Spirit. **How we lived among you** is further explained in 2:1–12.
1:7–9 These two Roman provinces — **Macedonia** in the north and **Achaia** in the south — make up a large part of modern-day Greece and included the major cities of Philippi,

Athens, and Corinth. Thessalonica was the capital of Macedonia. The Thessalonians' predominantly Gentile background is evident from the false worship of lifeless **idols**, from which they turned to serve **the living and true God**.
1:10 While the Thessalonians were enduring persecution, they were also waiting for the coming Son from heaven. **The coming wrath** refers to a future time of God's wrath against the unbelieving world.
2:2 At **Philippi** Paul and Silas were beaten and imprisoned for casting a demon out of a slave girl. It was illegal to punish Roman citizens like this without a trial (Ac 16:16–40). In spite of **great opposition**, which continued into Thessalonica, the **gospel of God** was faithfully proclaimed.
2:8 Paul's method of ministry was not only the impartation of the gospel but the sharing of his own life as well.
2:9 Paul **preached God's gospel** without taking any financial support but working so as not to **burden** them. Paul was a tentmaker by trade (Ac 18:3).
2:10–12 Having compared himself to the gentleness of a nursing mother in v. 7, Paul here compares himself to a father who encourages, comforts, and implores his children **to walk worthy of God**.

Reception and Opposition to the Message

[13] This is why we constantly thank God, because when you received the word of God that you heard from us, you welcomed it not as a human message, but as it truly is, the word of God, which also works effectively in you who believe. [14] For you, brothers and sisters, became imitators of God's churches in Christ Jesus that are in Judea, since you have also suffered the same things from people of your own country, just as they did from the Jews [15] who killed the Lord Jesus and the prophets and persecuted us. They displease God and are hostile to everyone, [16] by keeping us from speaking to the Gentiles so that they may be saved. As a result, they are constantly filling up their sins to the limit, and wrath has overtaken them at last.[A]

Paul's Desire to See Them

[17] But as for us, brothers and sisters, after we were forced to leave you[B] for a short time (in person, not in heart), we greatly desired and made every effort to return and see you face to face. [18] So we wanted to come to you — even I, Paul, time and again — but Satan hindered us. [19] For who is our hope or joy or crown of boasting in the presence of our Lord Jesus at his coming? Is it not you? [20] Indeed you are our glory and joy!

Anxiety in Athens

3 Therefore, when we could no longer stand it, we thought it was better to be left alone in Athens. [2] And we sent Timothy, our brother and God's coworker[C] in the gospel of Christ, to strengthen and encourage you concerning your faith, [3] so that no one will be shaken by these afflictions. For you yourselves know that we are appointed to this. [4] In fact, when we were with you, we told you in advance that we were going to experience affliction, and as

you know, it happened. [5] For this reason, when I could no longer stand it, I also sent him to find out about your faith, fearing that the tempter had tempted you and that our labor might be for nothing.

Encouraged by Timothy

[6] But now Timothy has come to us from you and brought us good news about your faith and love. He reported that you always have good memories of us and that you long to see us, as we also long to see you. [7] Therefore, brothers and sisters, in all our distress and affliction, we were encouraged about you through your faith. [8] For now we live, if you stand firm in the Lord. [9] How can we thank God for you in return for all the joy we experience before our God because of you, [10] as we pray very earnestly night and day to see you face to face and to complete what is lacking in your faith?

Prayer for the Church

[11] Now may our God and Father himself, and our Lord Jesus, direct our way to you. [12] And may the Lord cause you to increase and overflow with love for one another and for everyone, just as we do for you. [13] May he make your hearts blameless in holiness before our God and Father at the coming of our Lord Jesus with all his saints. Amen.[D]

The Call to Sanctification

4 Additionally then, brothers and sisters, we ask and encourage you in the Lord Jesus, that as you have received instruction from us on how you should live and please God — as you are doing[E] — do this even more. [2] For you know what commands we gave you through the Lord Jesus.

[3] For this is God's will, your sanctification: that you keep away from sexual immorality,

---

[A]2:16 Or *to the end*   [B]2:17 Lit *orphaned from you*   [C]3:2 Other mss read *servant*   [D]3:13 Other mss omit *Amen.*   [E]4:1 Lit *walking*

2:13 This verse introduces renewed thanksgiving for the Thessalonians, connected to 1:2. Paul thanks God because they received the message preached as the very **word of God**, which it was.
2:14 Though the Thessalonian church was founded in the midst of persecution, Paul pointed out that their sufferings were not unique. Persecution was ever present in the early church.
2:15 **They** refers to the Jews of v. 14. This is the only place in Paul's writings where he identified those who were responsible for Jesus's death. **Prophets** appears to be a reference to the OT prophets who also suffered persecution at the hands of their countrymen (Ac 7:52).
2:16 Some Jews objected to offering the message of the gospel to **Gentiles** (Ac 13:46–50; 14:2; 17:5,13). The phrase **filling up their sins** implies that God will tolerate only a certain number of sins before his judgment falls.
2:17–18 The intensity of Paul's desire to see the Thessalonians again is evident by these

emphatic descriptions: **greatly desired . . . made every effort . . . even I, Paul, time and again**. The phrase **Satan hindered us** probably refers to the persecution Paul was experiencing or possibly an illness (2Co 12:7). The name *Satan* means "adversary," as one who is opposed to God, his plan, and his people.
2:19–20 The reference to a **crown** carries the image of a laurel wreath worn on the head in reward for victory at a Greek athletic contest.
3:1–2 Sent from **Athens** to help the Thessalonian church, **Timothy** could help these believers grow in the faith but would not be as conspicuous as Paul or Silas.
3:3–4 Christians should not be **shaken** by persecution because **we are appointed to this** in God's plan.
3:5 For this reason refers back to the persecution of the Thessalonians mentioned in v. 4. **Tempter** is another reference to Satan as one who entices people to sin (Mt 4:1–11).

3:6–9 Verse 8 expresses strongly the nature of Paul's emotional connection to his converts. His very life depends on their perseverance in the faith.
3:10–13 Paul was praying to see the Thessalonian believers in person in order to **complete** what was **lacking** in their **faith**. Since the missionaries had to leave so suddenly (2:17–18), they did not complete their instruction of the Thessalonians in their new faith. Thus some elements and teaching were lacking—especially concerning Jesus's resurrection and the second coming (4:13–18). Since Paul was not able to personally return, he used this letter to address those matters (4:1–5:22). The prayer's request that the church **overflow with love for one another** and be **blameless in holiness** is addressed in detail in the following two paragraphs (4:1–8,9–12).
4:3 Sanctification refers to the consecration of the believer to God in holy and proper behavior in regard to sexual purity. God's

◥ A Biblical View of Work

by Gregory B. Forster

Work is central to human life. Between work in the home, on the job, in schools, and in neighborhoods, the overwhelming majority of our waking hours is taken up by it. How we work and how we view work are major factors determining the shape of our whole lives. And a culture's understanding of work is one of its most important defining elements, as important to its identity and functioning as its understanding of sexuality, justice, or worship.

When the Holy Spirit changes the way we work, he changes the way we live—all day, every day. This is why throughout history a biblical view of work has been central to Christian spiritual and cultural revival. From Gregory the Great and the scholars of the High Middle Ages to Martin Luther and John Calvin to the Wesleyan movement and twentieth-century heroes like Martin Luther King Jr., it's always the same story: if you look at Christian reformers who had a huge impact on our lives, you always find they had a lot to say about work.

Work presents one of the most central and far-reaching contrasts between the Bible's teaching and the way human cultures naturally tend to think. In the ancient world, a common element among pagan religions was the teaching that the gods don't work; they made people to work so they wouldn't have to. Work is mere toil and drudgery in this view, a curse. In the modern world, as the influence of Christianity on our worldview has receded, we increasingly view work either in similar terms—as a curse, mere toil, and drudgery—or else as an idol, an obsession, what we trust in to provide money, power, status, security, and self-expression.

We certainly do experience pain, frustration, and injustice in our work. Most people aren't going to pay attention to any view of work if it doesn't begin from our lived experience of suffering. Moreover, those who idolize work are right that human work is one of the world's most powerful forces: it can take a pile of sand, a puddle of oil, and a few other basic elements and transform them into a smartphone capable of recording video and beaming it around the world.

God as a Worker

The Bible makes a shocking and outrageous claim that transforms both the suffering of work and the power of work. God is a worker, and work is a primary reason he created humanity, because when we work rightly, we glorify God by loving him and neighbor.

In the Old Testament this claim has a central place in the Ten Commandments (Ex 20:9), the Mosaic law (Lv 19:9–18; Dt 25:13–16), the Wisdom books (Pr 12:11–14; 16:3; 18:9; 22:29; 24:27; 31:1,13–31; Ec 3:22; 5:6; 9:10), the prophetic witness against injustice to the poor (1Sm 8:14; 1Kg 21:1–19; Is 3:13–15; 5:8–10; 10:1–2; Hs 5:10; Mc 2:1–4,8–9), and much more.

In the New Testament it has a central place in the parables (forty-five of the fifty-two parables draw on work and business as images of spiritual life). It also appears in the teachings of Jesus (Mk 10:42–45; Jn 13:1–20), the conflict between Jesus and his enemies (Mt 12:1–8; Mk 2:23–3:6; Lk 6:1–11; 13:10–17; 14:1–6; Jn 5:1–18; 7:23; 9:14–41), and the ethics of the letters (Eph 4:28; Col 3:23–24; 1Th 4:11; 2Th 3:10–12; 1Tm 5:8; 2Tm 2:6; 1Pt 2:18–25).

Because he is love, God works (Gn 2:2–3; Jn 5:17), and so do we. God also rests, appreciating the beauty of the divine work (Gn 1:31–2:3), and so do we. Through our work we exercise stewardship over the world God created. When we work faithfully as God's stewards, we manifest the glory of the holy love of God, and we make the world under our care manifest it as well.

Work as Stewardship

We serve God as stewards of his world individually, and also collectively, as we labor together in households and businesses and trade our work with one another through economic exchange. Thus, we were made as an image of the holy love that is the tri-une God, unity in diversity and diversity in unity.

This claim is shocking and outrageous to our natural sensibilities because it transforms the suffering of work. We experience toil, frustration, and injustice in our work not because work is bad but because we are bad

(Rm 3:23). Work is not a curse, but our work is one of the main places where we experience the curse on our sin that God, in his holy love, has ordained (Gn 3:17–19).

This is also a reason the Bible's shocking claim is necessary if we are to have any hope for joy, peace, and righteousness. If Jesus is in us through our faith in the gospel, we can take comfort that God is using our persistance through the suffering of our work to transform us (cp. Jms 1:2–4; Rm 8:28). Worldly people working in worldly ways are shaping themselves, all day every day, into ever more worldly people. But we, as we make the difficult choice to keep on working faithfully, day in and day out, are shaped into Christlikeness by King Jesus.

The Power of Work

The Bible's claim about work is also shocking and outrageous to our natural sensibilities because it transforms the power of work. The enormous power of our work is indeed breathtaking; even God himself seems amazed at it (Gn 11:6). But this power was given to us to glorify the holy love of God by serving God and neighbor. When we trust in our work rather than in God for identity, security, and provision, we fall into a monstrous evil that will enslave us, turn us against one another, make us miserable, and bring us to ruin.

Doing our daily work with ethical integrity for the love of God and neighbor in Jesus is a high and difficult calling. Moreover, a special responsibility rests on business leaders to order work ethically, as an expression of voluntary stewardship and mutual love. Another responsibility falls on political leaders to protect this ordering of work. The complex challenge of extending the opportunity of gainful work to the poor and the oppressed also weighs on us.

But this too is a reason the Bible's shocking claim is necessary if we are to have any hope for joy, peace, and righteousness. Those who follow God's calling in their work discover a new kind of life. For them, glorifying God by loving God and neighbor as a citizen of God's kingdom is not a special activity they squeeze into a few hours a week. It is their daily routine. Our work, done in this way, is the main way we give God a return on his investment in us (Mt 25:14–30). It allows us to feed the hungry, clothe the naked, and visit the sick (25:31–46). These are among the good works we were saved to do (Eph 2:10), which force even the enemies of God to give him glory (Mt 5:16; 1Pt 2:15).

This is not just one more biblical truth among thousands of others. It is a central pattern in the narrative of Scripture. It is one of the deep, defining elements of the biblical testimony. Work takes up the overwhelming majority of our lives and is central to our understanding of who we are as individuals and as cultures. Why are we surprised that the Bible says God designed us with work at the center? Or that Holy Spirit transformation of our work has always been—and continues to be today—one of the most important paths to spiritual and cultural reformation?

4 that each of you knows how to control his own body^A in holiness and honor, **5** not with lustful passions, like the Gentiles, who don't know God. **6** This means one must not transgress against and take advantage of a brother or sister in this manner, because the Lord is an avenger of all these offenses, as we also previously told and warned you. **7** For God has not called us to impurity but to live in holiness. **8** Consequently, anyone who rejects this does not reject man, but God, who gives you his Holy Spirit.

Loving and Working

9 About brotherly love: You don't need me to write you because you yourselves are taught by God to love one another. **10** In fact, you are doing this toward all the brothers and sisters in the entire region of Macedonia. But we encourage you, brothers and sisters, to do this even more, **11** to seek to lead a quiet life, to mind your own business,^B and to work with your own hands, as we commanded you, **12** so that you may behave properly in the presence of outsiders and not be dependent on anyone.^C

The Comfort of Christ's Coming

13 We do not want you to be uninformed, brothers and sisters, concerning those who are asleep, so that you will not grieve like the rest, who have no hope. **14** For if we believe that Jesus died and rose again, in the same way, through Jesus, God will bring with him those who have fallen asleep. **15** For we say this to you by a word

from the Lord: We who are still alive at the Lord's coming will certainly not precede those who have fallen asleep. **16** For the Lord himself will descend from heaven with a shout,^D with the archangel's voice, and with the trumpet of God, and the dead in Christ will rise first. **17** Then we who are still alive, who are left, will be caught up together with them in the clouds to meet the Lord in the air, and so we will always be with the Lord. **18** Therefore encourage^E one another with these words.

The Day of the Lord

5 About the times and the seasons: Brothers and sisters, you do not need anything to be written to you. **2** For you yourselves know very well that the day of the Lord will come just like a thief in the night. **3** When they say, "Peace and security," then sudden destruction will come upon them, like labor pains on a pregnant woman, and they will not escape. **4** But you, brothers and sisters, are not in the dark, for this day to surprise you like a thief. **5** For you are all children of light and children of the day. We do not belong to the night or the darkness. **6** So then, let us not sleep, like the rest, but let us stay awake and be self-controlled. **7** For those who sleep, sleep at night, and those who get drunk, get drunk at night. **8** But since we belong to the day, let us be self-controlled and put on the armor of faith and love, and a helmet of the hope of salvation. **9** For God did not appoint us to wrath, but to obtain salvation through our Lord Jesus Christ, **10** who died for

^A **4:4** Or *to acquire his own wife*; lit *to possess his own vessel*   ^B **4:11** Lit *to practice one's own things*   ^C **4:12** Or *not need anything*, or *not be in need*   ^D **4:16** Or *command*   ^E **4:18** Or *comfort*

will is clear—to **keep away from sexual immorality**. This includes premarital sex, incest, homosexuality, bestiality, and adultery.
4:4–5 The phrase **control his own body** probably refers to the idea of controlling the body's lustful sexual desires that might lead a Christian to sin. An alternate view is that it refers to obtaining a wife.
4:6–8 Brother or sister is a fellow Christian. A sexual transgression defrauds one's brother in the sense that sexual sin is a form of theft: you take something that does not belong to you. It defrauds both the partner of the illicit relationship as well as a spouse or future spouse who alone has rights in sexual matters. **In this manner** points back to the discussion of sexual purity in vv. 3–5. Paul gave two reasons for Christians to abstain from sexual immorality. First is that **the Lord is an avenger** who will judge the offense. Second is that sexual impurity violates God's call to **live in holiness**.
4:9–12 The reference to **brotherly love** (Gk *philadelphia*) seems to govern the content of these verses in encouraging fellow Christians to **lead a quiet life**, mind one's **own business**, and **work** with one's **hands**.
4:13 The term **asleep** in this context is a metaphorical reference to Christians who have died. Just as a sleeping person expects to rise in the morning, Christians who have died will experience a bodily resurrection and will rise again (v. 16; Jn 11:11). Apparently the

cause of the Thessalonians' grief was related to the misunderstanding that dead Christians would miss the events and subsequent blessings associated with the Lord's coming. Paul corrected this misunderstanding by teaching that the dead in Christ will rise first (1Th 4:16). In contrast to unbelievers who grieve over the loss of loved ones, Christians who grieve over a fellow believer can do so with **hope** because of the future glorious resurrection.
4:14 Jesus's resurrection revealed what resurrection will be like for those who have **fallen asleep** believing in Christ.
4:15–17 The **word** that Paul received relates to what has been called the "rapture." It refers to the event when believers who are alive at the Lord's coming are **caught up** (Gk *harpazo*) in the clouds **to meet the Lord in the air**. The term *rapture* is derived from *rapturo*, the Latin translation of the Greek term. The Greek term means "to snatch or take away suddenly." **We who are still alive** implies that Paul thought the rapture could occur at any moment, even during his lifetime. The "archangel" or chief angel is probably a reference to Michael (Dn 10:13; Jd 9).
5:1 Times and seasons mentioned together refers to the end times (Ac 1:7).
5:2 Here **the day of the Lord** refers specifically to the end-time period of God's judgment on the unbelieving world known as the great tribulation (Mal 4:5; Ac 2:20; 2Th 2:2; 2Pt 3:10). The description of the day of

the Lord coming as **a thief in the night** emphasizes that it will come unexpectedly (1Th 5:4; 2Pt 3:10).
5:3 The comparison of this **sudden destruction** to the **labor pains** of a pregnant woman speaks of the increasing intensity of God's judgment and the certainty of its coming (Mt 24:8).
5:4–6 Paul contrasted **brothers and sisters** in the faith who are **children of light** and **day** with the rest of the world who are of **the night** and **darkness**. Paul issued an encouragement for Christians as sons of light to be **awake**, meaning alert and morally ready. One's readiness is described with the military analogy of a soldier who prepares himself for war.
5:6–7 The Greek word for **sleep** in these verses (see also v. 10) is different from that in 4:13–15. In 5:6–7, "sleep" refers to moral lethargy. Some interpreters take "sleep" in v. 10 as a euphemism for death, but a good case can be made that the same Greek word in this context refers to moral lethargy as well. Thus Paul is saying in v. 10 that whether believers are alert or not for the day of the Lord, we will still "live together" with the Lord.
5:8 Although Christians **belong to the day**, we live in a world of darkness and must be prepared for battle (cp. Eph 6:11–17).
5:9 Paul reminded the Thessalonians that as Christians they were not appointed to God's **wrath** but to **salvation**.

us, so that whether we are awake or asleep, we may live together with him. ¹¹ Therefore encourage one another and build each other up as you are already doing.

Exhortations and Blessings

¹² Now we ask you, brothers and sisters, to give recognition to those who labor among you and lead you^A in the Lord and admonish you, ¹³ and to regard them very highly in love because of their work. Be at peace among yourselves. ¹⁴ And we exhort you, brothers and sisters: warn those who are idle,^B comfort the discouraged, help the weak, be patient with everyone. ¹⁵ See to it that no one repays evil for evil to anyone, but always pursue what is good for one

another and for all. ¹⁶ Rejoice always, ¹⁷ pray constantly, ¹⁸ give thanks in everything; for this is God's will for you in Christ Jesus. ¹⁹ Don't stifle the Spirit. ²⁰ Don't despise prophecies, ²¹ but test all things. Hold on to what is good. ²² Stay away from every kind of evil.

²³ Now may the God of peace himself sanctify you completely. And may your whole spirit, soul, and body be kept sound and blameless at the coming of our Lord Jesus Christ. ²⁴ He who calls you is faithful; he will do it. ²⁵ Brothers and sisters, pray for us also. ²⁶ Greet all the brothers and sisters with a holy kiss. ²⁷ I charge you by the Lord that this letter be read to all the brothers and sisters. ²⁸ The grace of our Lord Jesus Christ be with you.

---

^A 5:12 Or care for you   ^B 5:14 Or who are disorderly, or who are undisciplined

5:12–13 To **give recognition** means respect for the authority and work of church leaders.
5:14 Brothers and sisters elsewhere in the letter refers to the whole church. So it likely does not refer only to the leaders here. All Christians are to **warn . . . comfort . . . help** and **be patient**.
5:15 Not to repay **evil for evil** but to **pursue what is good** reflects back on Jesus's teaching not to follow a retaliatory "eye for an eye" ethic but to give a blessing instead (Mt 5:38–42).
5:16 Verses 16–22 deal with religious duties as opposed to interpersonal behavior. Rejoicing has its source in God. This verse is parallel to Php 4:4; Gl 5:22; Jms 1:2.

5:17 To **pray constantly** does not mean continuous, uninterrupted prayer but humble submission to God in the details of life.
5:18 This verse is closely related to 5:16 (cp. Col 3:17).
5:19 One can **stifle** (lit "quench") **the Spirit** by not submitting to the Holy Spirit's leading or by committing other sins that would grieve the Spirit.
5:20–21a Test all things probably refers to the content of the prophecies that had to be evaluated with God's known truth as expressed by the OT, Jesus, and the apostles (1Jn 4:1–3).
5:21b–22 These two commands are two sides of the same coin.

5:23 The prayer for **spirit, soul, and body** to be kept sound and blameless teaches that God sees the whole person as important in living a life pleasing to God.
5:24 What God will do is not specified. But the context is his sanctifying and his keeping (v. 23).
5:26 Greeting one another with **a holy kiss**, probably on the cheek, was a common first-century greeting that expressed love (Rm 16:16).
5:27 Paul was insistent that **all the brothers and sisters** needed to hear the contents of the letter, even if it entailed reading it several times in different places.
5:28 Paul's closing benediction is almost identical to Rm 16:20 and 1Co 16:23.

▼ Introduction to 2 Thessalonians

Circumstances of Writing

Paul is stated to be the author of 2 Thessalonians (1:1). The greeting also mentions Silvanus (Silas) and Timothy, but Paul was the primary author (3:17).

Although there are few indicators of the date and place of writing of 2 Thessalonians, it was probably written from Corinth around AD 50–51 shortly after 1 Thessalonians. The mention of Paul, Silvanus, and Timothy together in the salutation, as was the case with 1 Thessalonians (1:1), supports this conclusion. An additional support for this view is the mention of a previous letter, which was probably 1 Thessalonians (2Th 2:15).

Contribution to the Bible

Second Thessalonians continues and further amplifies some of the same themes as 1 Thessalonians: persecution, sanctification, and end-time events associated with the second coming of Christ. One important difference is that 2 Thessalonians describes the "man of lawlessness" who will be revealed in the end times and what restrains him from being revealed (2:1–12). The book also contains a lengthy discourse on the need for believers to have a proper work ethic to provide for their own needs (3:6–15).

Structure

The tone of Paul's second letter to the Thessalonians is markedly "cooler" than his first letter. In his first letter, Paul was enthusiastic about the Thessalonians' progress in the gospel, and he offered calm advice about congregational life (1Th 5:12–22). In this second letter, though, Paul expressed grave concern about the spiritual state of the Thessalonian believers. He gave them a sharp rebuke about congregational life (2Th 3:6–15). His style is typical of his other letters—a doctrinal section followed by practical exhortation.

Outline

5 BC–AD 33

Jesus's birth **5 BC**

Paul born in Tarsus of Cilicia **AD 5**

Paul studies with Gamaliel in Jerusalem. **AD 15–20**

Tiberius takes away Thessalonica's status as a free city when opposition to increased taxation is expressed. **AD 15**

Jesus's trials, death, and resurrection **NISAN 14–16** or **APRIL 3–5, AD 33**

Pentecost **AD 33**

AD 34–56

Saul's conversion on the Damascus Road **OCTOBER 34**

Paul, Timothy, and Silas minister in Thessalonica, one of the earliest churches planted in Europe. **50**

Paul writes 1 Thessalonians a few months after being forced to leave Thessalonica. **51**

Paul soon follows up with a second letter to the Thessalonian believers. **51**

Paul likely revisits the Thessalonian Christians as he visits the churches planted in Macedonia. **56**

Greeting

1 Paul, Silvanus,[A] and Timothy:
To the church of the Thessalonians in God our Father and the Lord Jesus Christ. [2] Grace to you and peace from God our Father and the Lord Jesus Christ.

God's Judgment and Glory

[3] We ought to thank God always for you, brothers and sisters, and rightly so, since your faith is flourishing and the love each one of you has for one another is increasing. [4] Therefore, we ourselves boast about you among God's churches — about your perseverance and faith in all the persecutions and afflictions that you are enduring. [5] It is clear evidence of God's righteous judgment that you will be counted worthy of God's kingdom, for which you also are suffering, [6] since it is just for God to repay with affliction those who afflict you [7] and to give relief to you who are afflicted, along with us. This will take place at the revelation of the Lord Jesus from heaven with his powerful angels, [8] when he takes vengeance with flaming fire on those who don't know God and on those who don't obey the gospel of our Lord Jesus. [9] They will pay the penalty of eternal destruction from the Lord's presence and from his glorious strength [10] on that day when he comes to be glorified by his saints and to be marveled at by all those who have believed, because our testimony among you was believed. [11] In view of this, we always pray for you that our God will make you worthy of his calling, and by his power fulfill your every desire to do good[B] and your work produced by faith, [12] so that the name of our Lord Jesus will be glorified by you, and you by him, according to the grace of our God and the Lord Jesus Christ.

The Man of Lawlessness

2 Now concerning the coming of our Lord Jesus Christ and our being gathered to him: We ask you, brothers and sisters, [2] not to be easily upset or troubled, either by a prophecy[C] or by a message or by a letter supposedly from us, alleging that the day of the Lord[D] has come. [3] Don't let anyone deceive you in any way. For that day will not come unless the apostasy[E] comes first and the man of lawlessness[F] is revealed, the man doomed to destruction. [4] He opposes and exalts himself above every so-called god or object of worship, so that he sits[G] in God's temple, proclaiming that he himself is God.

[5] Don't you remember that when I was still with you I used to tell you about this? [6] And you know what currently restrains him, so that he will be revealed in his time. [7] For the mystery of lawlessness is already at work, but the one now restraining will do so until he is

---

[A]1:1 Or Silas; Ac 15:22–32; 16:19–40; 17:1–16   [B]1:11 Or power bring to fruition your desire to do good   [C]2:2 Or spiritual utterance   [D]2:2 Other mss read Christ   [E]2:3 Or rebellion   [F]2:3 Other mss read man of sin   [G]2:4 Other mss add as God

---

1:1–2 On **Silvanus** and **Timothy**, see note at 1Th 1:1.
1:6–7 God will reward his people with rest and repay those who oppose him at the future **revelation of the Lord Jesus from heaven. Angels** are often presented as participating in executing God's awesome judgments and thus are described as **powerful** (cp. Mt 25:31; Mk 8:38).
1:8 The phrase **those who don't know God** is a reference to unbelieving Gentiles (1Th 4:5). **Those who don't obey the gospel** is probably a reference to many Jews who had rejected the witness of the apostles to Jesus as Messiah and Lord.

 # 83 99 Essential Christian Truths

CHURCH AND KINGDOM

The church and the kingdom of God are closely related, though not identical. When the Bible speaks of the kingdom of God, it is referring to the reign of God in the world. The church is the people of God who live under his loving rule now, anticipating the full manifestation of God's kingdom in the future. The church's mission is to witness to God's kingdom, proclaiming God's message of salvation through Christ and demonstrating the power of the gospel through good works so that others may be brought to live under God's reign.

1:9 The **penalty of eternal destruction** is described as being away from **the Lord's presence**. The word **destruction** does not imply ceasing to exist or annihilation but separation from God in a miserable state.
1:10 Saints refers to all of those called in God's plan of salvation (1Co 1:2; 2Co 1:1).
1:11–12 In view of this probably refers to the whole preceding passage about the people's perseverance in persecution.
2:1 Our being gathered to him probably refers to the gathering of believers at the time of the rapture (1Th 4:13–18).
2:3 The word **apostasy** (Gk apostasia) can also be translated "rebellion." It carries the idea of defection or departure from true religion. It probably refers to the widespread religious defection from worship of the true God that will intensify during the day of the Lord through the workings of the man of lawlessness and Satan (vv. 3–9). An alternate view is that "apostasy" refers to the departure of the church from the earth known as the rapture. The **man of lawlessness** is probably the end-time manifestation of the antichrist (1Jn 2:18), or the beast from the sea (Rv 13:1–10). This particular title emphasizes that he is opposed to God and his law. He is also the **man doomed to destruction** (v. 8).
2:4 The man of lawlessness (or "man of sin") is so blasphemous that he takes a seat in God's sanctuary, declaring that he himself is **God** and demanding worship (see Rv 13:4; cp. Dn 9:27 and Mt 24:15). The reference to **God's temple** suggests that a future rebuilt temple will exist during this time in Jerusalem (Rv 11:1–2).

2:5 Paul reminded the Thessalonians that he taught about these things during the short time he was with them (Ac 17:1–13).
2:6–7 The identity of this restrainer has puzzled Bible interpreters for centuries. In v. 6 **what . . . restrains him** is in the neuter in Greek while in v. 7 **the one . . . restraining** is in the masculine. Some things are clear. First, the restrainer is holding back the actual manifestation of the man of lawlessness. Second, at some point the restrainer will cease this activity and the man of lawlessness will be revealed. One common view is that the neuter form refers to government, while the masculine refers to the leader of that government. A more appealing solution is to see the restrainer as God's Holy Spirit. In v. 6 the reference could be to the restraining force of the Holy Spirit while v. 7 may refer to his personage. Another possible variation of this view is that the restrainer is the Holy Spirit working through the church. The phrase **until he is out of the way** would be a removal of the restraining force of the Holy Spirit through the rapture of the church prior to the day of the Lord.
2:7 In Paul's writings, "mystery" refers to something not previously revealed but now made known. Though the man of lawlessness is not currently revealed, the **mystery of lawlessness is already at work**. Satan's opposition to God and his standards of righteousness is a current and ongoing reality.
2:8 The glory of **the lawless one** will be short-lived.

out of the way, **8** and then the lawless one will be revealed. The Lord Jesus will destroy him with the breath of his mouth and will bring him to nothing at the appearance of his coming. **9** The coming of the lawless one is based on Satan's working, with every kind of miracle, both signs and wonders serving the lie, **10** and with every wicked deception among those who are perishing. They perish because they did not accept the love of the truth and so be saved. **11** For this reason God sends them a strong delusion so that they will believe the lie, **12** so that all will be condemned — those who did not believe the truth but delighted in unrighteousness.

Stand Firm

13 But we ought to thank God always for you, brothers and sisters loved by the Lord, because from the beginning^A God has chosen you for salvation through sanctification by the Spirit and through belief in the truth. **14** He called you to this through our gospel,

so that you might obtain the glory of our Lord Jesus Christ. **15** So then, brothers and sisters, stand firm and hold to the traditions you were taught, whether by what we said or what we wrote.

16 May our Lord Jesus Christ himself and God our Father, who has loved us and given us eternal encouragement and good hope by grace, **17** encourage your hearts and strengthen you in every good work and word.

Pray for Us

3 In addition, brothers and sisters, pray for us that the word of the Lord may spread rapidly and be honored, just as it was with you, **2** and that we may be delivered from wicked and evil people, for not all have faith.^B **3** But the Lord is faithful; he will strengthen you and guard you from the evil one. **4** We have confidence in the Lord about you, that you are doing and will continue to do what we command. **5** May the Lord direct your hearts to God's love and Christ's endurance.

^A **2:13** Other mss read *because as a firstfruit*　^B **3:2** Or *for the faith is not in everyone*

2:9 Signs and wonders are not necessarily evidence of God's acts. Satan has the power to perform deceptive supernatural acts. We must examine the source of the act and the content of the message being promoted in order to avoid deception (see Mt 24:24; Rv 13:13–14; 16:14; 19:20).

2:10–12 Satan's activities will result in wide-scale **deception** of the unbelieving world. First, however, Paul pointed out that

unbelievers reject the truth that would save them. Therefore God will send them this **strong delusion** after they have already turned him away. Their condemnation is based on the fact that they did not believe **the truth**.

2:13–14 The **sanctification** Paul referred to here was not the process by which a Christian grows in Christlikeness but the initial work of grace in which the Spirit works in a believer and makes him God's possession.

2:15 The word **traditions** refers to God's truths passed on to the Thessalonians by Paul (1Th 4:1–2). **What we wrote** refers to 1 Thessalonians.

3:1–5 Because **the Lord is faithful** to strengthen and guard them (v. 3), Paul could have **confidence** that the Thessalonians would obey his commands. He then prays that they would have the **love** God has and the **endurance** Christ exhibited.

Q&A: How do we know the Bible includes the right books?

by Jonathan Morrow

Did the Roman emperor Constantine (ca AD 272–337) dictate which books were included in the New Testament, all in an attempt to forge political and religious power alliances? Popular books like *The Da Vinci Code* and documentaries on the History Channel say yes.

But could it be that the books included in the New Testament are there because they accurately report Jesus's life and teachings? Which view best fits with the faith and preaching of the early church as represented in the New Testament? Do early Christian beliefs and practices seem devised for building political power structures and suppressing outsiders, or do they more naturally fit with the sort of teachings one would expect of an expanding, hopefilled movement that drew adherents from every corner of society?

New Testament scholar Darrell Bock points to three kinds of New Testament texts that show what the earliest Christians believed.

Schooling: Passages included within the New Testament contain doctrinal summaries, which Christians would have memorized and read alongside Old Testament texts when they gathered for worship (Rm 1:2–4; 1Co 8:6; 15:1–5).

Singing: The New Testament reveals that early Christians sang their theology in hymns, showing their devotion to the Lord Jesus Christ (Col 1:15–20; Php 2:5–11).

Sacraments: The New Testament shows that baptisms and the Lord's Supper were regularly practiced by the early

church. These pictured the basic elements of the gospel as core theology (Mt 28:19–20; 1Co 11:23–26; Eph 4:4–6).

These verses reflect the earliest realities of Christianity, and it is clear they do not fit with the cynical theory that Constantine teamed up with politicians and priests to invent Christianity. With that in mind, by what process did early Christians identify which books should be included in the New Testament canon?

First, books written by apostles or an associate of an apostle were accepted. Mark was accepted because he was an associate of Peter; Luke was accepted because of his relationship to Paul. If a book was written later than the first century, it was not accepted because it could not be traced to the apostles who were taught and commissioned by the risen Jesus.

Second, to be acceptable, books had to conform to the teachings of other accepted New Testament books. In some cases, this helped non-apostolic books (like Hebrews) gain acceptance.

Third, if a book was widely accepted early among churches that were spread throughout the region, it was likely accepted into the New Testament canon.

Early Christians believed the New Testament books held authority from God since they were inspired. Hence, they did not *decide* which books were Scripture, but, rather, they *recognized* books as Scripture. By the end of the second century—long before Constantine—the four Gospels, Acts, and the letters of Paul were already recognized as authoritative and were used as Scripture in the churches.

Some of the other New Testament books were long debated by representatives of the Eastern and Western churches, but even these were widely embraced as Scripture in the earliest churches. While there was no *universal* declaration concerning the final list of New Testament books, the canon was effectively closed by the time of the Council of Carthage in AD 397.

Warning against Irresponsible Behavior

⁶ Now we command you, brothers and sisters, in the name of our Lord Jesus Christ, to keep away from every brother or sister who is idle and does not live^A according to the tradition received from us. ⁷ For you yourselves know how you should imitate us: We were not idle among you; ⁸ we did not eat anyone's food free of charge; instead, we labored and toiled, working night and day, so that we would not be a burden to any of you. ⁹ It is not that we don't have the right to support, but we did it to make ourselves an example to you so that you would imitate us. ¹⁰ In fact, when we were with you, this is what we commanded you: "If anyone isn't willing to work, he should not eat." ¹¹ For we hear that there are some among you who are idle. They are not busy but busybodies.

¹² Now we command and exhort such people by the Lord Jesus Christ to work quietly and provide for themselves.⁸ ¹³ But as for you, brothers and sisters, do not grow weary in doing good.

¹⁴ If anyone does not obey our instruction in this letter, take note of that person; don't associate with him, so that he may be ashamed. ¹⁵ Yet don't consider him as an enemy, but warn him as a brother.

Final Greetings

¹⁶ May the Lord of peace himself give you peace always in every way. The Lord be with all of you. ¹⁷ I, Paul, am writing this greeting with my own hand, which is an authenticating mark in every letter; this is how I write. ¹⁸ The grace of our Lord Jesus Christ be with you all.

^A 3:6 Lit walk ᴮ 3:12 Lit they may eat their own bread

3:6 The view by some people in the Thessalonian church that they were in the day of the Lord and thus Jesus was coming very soon (2:2) may have led them to stop their normal work activities. Or this may have just been ordinary lazy behavior (1Th 5:14).

3:7–9 Paul set an example for the Thessalonians by **working** to provide for his own needs so he did not **burden** them. He worked when he was with them to show them the importance of work and to set an **example** for them to **imitate**.

3:10 Christian charity is to be directed at true need, not artificial need created by irresponsibility.

3:11 Some Thessalonians were **not busy but busybodies**. This English play on words conveys a play on words in the Greek text.

3:12–15 Paul's solution to this problem was to **command and exhort such people** to work **quietly** and thereby to **provide for themselves**. But for any who refused to listen, Paul wanted the Thessalonian church to not **associate with** this type of person

and to **warn him as a brother**, with a view toward correcting the problem.

3:16 Paul referred to the Lord as the **Lord of peace** and prayed for God's granting of peace to them **in every way**. This was particularly important for a church under persecution.

3:17–18 Paul wrote the final **greeting** in his **own hand** (see also 1Co 16:21; Gl 6:11; Col 4:18; 2Th 3:17; Phm 19). The rest of the letter was written with the help of a skilled scribe.

▼ Introduction to 1 Timothy

Circumstances of Writing

As stated in the opening of each letter, 1 Timothy, 2 Timothy, and Titus were written by Paul (1Tm 1:1; 2Tm 1:1; Ti 1:1). However, many scholars today assume that Paul did not write them. This opinion is based on the differences from his other letters in vocabulary and style, alleged differences in theology, and uncertainties about where these letters fit chronologically in the life of the apostle. But the differences in style and vocabulary are not troublesome when one considers that authors often use different vocabulary when addressing different groups and situations. Rather than addressing churches in these letters, Paul was writing to coworkers who were in unique ministry settings. Hence we would expect different vocabulary. Also, the traditional view of the historical situation in which Paul wrote these letters is reasonable and defensible. Therefore, in spite of significant opposition by some scholars, there is a solid basis for accepting the Pastoral Epistles as Pauline.

Paul most likely wrote these letters after the time covered in the book of Acts. Acts closes with Paul in prison. Traditionally it has been believed that Paul was released from this imprisonment, then continued his work around the Mediterranean, perhaps even reaching Spain (Rm 15:22–29). During this time, he visited Crete and other places. First Timothy and Titus were written during this period of further mission work. Timothy had been left in Ephesus to handle some problems with false teaching there (1Tm 1:3–4). Titus had been left in Crete after the initial work to set up the church there (Ti 1:5). Eventually Paul was imprisoned again, and this led to his execution. During this final imprisonment, Paul wrote 2 Timothy to request another visit from Timothy and to give final exhortations as he anticipated his martyrdom.

Contribution to the Bible

These letters are rich theologically and ethically. One of their key contributions is the clear way they show the connection between doctrine and ethics, belief and behavior.

Although these letters were not intended to provide a detailed account of church government, they do provide some significant insights on this topic. The lists of characteristics for overseers (1Tm 3:1–7; Ti 1:5–9) and deacons (1Tm 3:8–13) are the only such lists in the New Testament.

Structure

All three letters follow the typical pattern of a Greek epistle. Although there are some lexical differences with many of Paul's other letters, keep in mind that these letters were written to specific individuals. One thing unique to the structure of these letters is the focus on church leadership.

Outline

I. Greetings (1:1–2)
II. Introductory Remarks (1:3–20)
III. Instructions for Worship (2:1–15)
IV. Qualifications of Church Leaders (3:1–13)
V. The Minister's Job in Tough Times (3:14–4:16)
VI. Duties toward Others (5:1–6:2)
VII. Conclusion (6:3–21)

Key verse in 1 Timothy

4:12 Don't let anyone despise your youth, but set an example for the believers in speech, in conduct, in love, in faith, and in purity.

AD 56–62

Paul sends Timothy with the 1 Corinthians letter to the troubled church in Corinth. **56**
While ministering in Ephesus, Paul sends Titus to mediate the conflict between Paul and the church at Corinth. **56**
Paul comes to Corinth in person and from there he writes the letter to the Romans. **57**
Upon his release from his first imprisonment, Paul goes to Ephesus and appoints Timothy as chief pastor. **62**

AD 62–67

Paul writes 1 Timothy and Titus. **62–64**
Paul commissions Titus to train leaders for the young Christian congregations on Crete. **62–64**
Major persecution of the Christians in Rome begins following the great fire. **JULY 18–24, 64**
Paul returns to Rome, is arrested, and writes 2 Timothy from the Mamertine Prison. **67?**
Paul's martyrdom in Rome **67?**

Greeting

1 Paul, an apostle of Christ Jesus by the command of God our Savior and of Christ Jesus our hope:

[2] To Timothy, my true son in the faith.

Grace, mercy, and peace from God the^ Father and Christ Jesus our Lord.

False Doctrine and Misuse of the Law

[3] As I urged you when I went to Macedonia, remain in Ephesus so that you may instruct certain people not to teach false doctrine [4] or to pay attention to myths and endless genealogies. These promote empty speculations rather than God's plan, which operates by faith. [5] Now the goal of our instruction is love that comes from a pure heart, a good conscience, and a sincere faith. [6] Some have departed from these and turned aside to fruitless discussion. [7] They want to be teachers of the law, although they don't understand what they are saying or what they are insisting on. [8] But we know that the law is good, provided one uses it legitimately. [9] We know that the law is not meant for a righteous person, but for the lawless and rebellious, for the ungodly and sinful, for the unholy and irreverent, for those who kill their fathers and mothers, for murderers, [10] for the sexually immoral and males who have sex with males, for slave traders, liars, perjurers, and for whatever else is contrary to the sound teaching [11] that conforms to the gospel concerning the glory of the blessed God, which was entrusted to me.

Paul's Testimony

[12] I give thanks to Christ Jesus our Lord who has strengthened me, because he considered me faithful, appointing me to the ministry — [13] even though I was formerly a blasphemer, a persecutor, and an arrogant man. But I received mercy because I acted out of ignorance in unbelief, [14] and the grace of our Lord overflowed, along with the faith and love that are in Christ Jesus. [15] This saying is trustworthy and deserving of full acceptance: "Christ Jesus came into the world to save sinners" — and I am the worst of them. [16] But I received mercy for this reason, so that in me, the worst of them, Christ Jesus might demonstrate his extraordinary patience as an example to those who would believe in him for eternal life. [17] Now to the King eternal, immortal, invisible, the only^ God, be honor and glory forever and ever. Amen.

Engage in Battle

[18] Timothy, my son, I am giving you this instruction in keeping with the prophecies previously made about you, so that by recalling them you may fight the good fight, [19] having faith and a good conscience, which some have rejected and have shipwrecked the faith. [20] Among them are Hymenaeus and Alexander, whom I have delivered to Satan, so that they may be taught not to blaspheme.

Instructions on Prayer

2 First of all, then, I urge that petitions, prayers, intercessions, and thanksgivings be made for everyone, [2] for kings and all those who are in authority, so that we may lead a tranquil and quiet life in all godliness and dignity. [3] This is good, and it pleases God our Savior, [4] who wants everyone to be saved and to come to the knowledge of the truth.

---

^1:2 Other mss read our   ^1:17 Other mss add wise

1:2 Paul's normal greeting in his letters was **grace** and **peace**. The addition of **mercy** here prepares for the discussion of Paul receiving mercy in vv. 13,16.
1:3 At least one of Timothy's purposes in Ephesus was to address the false teaching that was troubling the church.
1:4 Myths is a negative term used to characterize something as fanciful or untrue. **Genealogies** seems to refer to speculative interpretations of the OT.
1:5–7 The goal of all Christian teaching should always be love.
1:8 There is an important contrast here. The false teachers did not know what they were talking about (v. 7), but Paul and his coworkers (**we**) did know the truth about **the law**, which if used properly **is good**.
1:9–10 The law works to expose sin.
1:12 Having just mentioned being entrusted with the gospel (v. 11), Paul gave **thanks** because Christ was willing to appoint him to service in spite of his past sins.
1:13–14 Paul's **ignorance** was not the reason he had been shown mercy, as if ignorance excused sin or warranted mercy. The point is that when Paul opposed Christ and persecuted the church in the past, he had not

yet professed faith. These false teachers professed to follow Christ but still acted to undermine his influence.
1:15–16 The designation of certain sayings as **trustworthy** is a particular distinctive of 1 Timothy, 2 Timothy, and Titus. Paul used this designation for emphasis. The result of the gospel in his life was not idle speculation but transformation.
1:17 Whether Paul's praise here is of the Father or the Son is unclear, but it could be either.
1:18 The point here is that God had spoken through others to set Timothy apart for the task of ministry.
1:19 The phrase **shipwrecked the faith** is strong language. It refers to someone who once professed faith but has now destroyed it, showing they were never truly converted.
1:20 Hymenaeus is mentioned in 2Tm 2:17–18 as teaching false doctrine about the resurrection. **Delivered to Satan** is a typical way of referring to excommunication, or being put out of the church (1Co 5:5).
2:1 Petitions, prayers, intercessions, and thanksgivings are several different terms for prayer.

2:2–3 Paul says that the "everyone" of v. 1 includes even secular authorities. But the purpose of such prayer is clear: so that believers **may lead a tranquil and quiet life in all godliness and dignity**.
2:4 Come to the knowledge of the truth is a way of referring to being converted. This verse implies the universal offer of the gospel.
2:5–6 These verses provide the theological basis for the preceding statement that God wants people to be saved.

⁵ For there is one God and one mediator between God and mankind, the man Christ Jesus, ⁶ who gave himself as a ransom for all, a testimony at the proper time. ⁷ For this I was appointed a herald, an apostle (I am telling the truth;ᴬ I am not lying), and a teacher of the Gentiles in faith and truth.

Instructions to Men and Women

⁸ Therefore, I want the men in every place to pray, lifting up holy hands without anger or argument. ⁹ Also, the women are to dress themselves in modest clothing, with decency and good sense, not with elaborate hairstyles, gold, pearls, or expensive apparel, ¹⁰ but with good works, as is proper for women who profess to worship God. ¹¹ A woman is to learn quietly with full submission. ¹² I do not allow a woman to teach or to have authority over a man; instead, she is to remain quiet. ¹³ For Adam was formed first, then Eve. ¹⁴ And Adam was not deceived, but the woman was deceived and transgressed. ¹⁵ But she will be saved through childbearing, if they continue in faith, love, and holiness, with good sense.

Qualifications for Overseers and Deacons

3 This saying is trustworthy: "If anyone aspires to be an overseer,ᴮ he desires a noble work." ² An overseer, therefore, must be above reproach, the husband of one wife, self-controlled, sensible, respectable, hospitable, able to teach, ³ not an excessive drinker, not a bully

but gentle, not quarrelsome, not greedy. ⁴ He must manage his own household competently and have his children under control with all dignity. ⁵ (If anyone does not know how to manage his own household, how will he take care of God's church?) ⁶ He must not be a new convert, or he might become conceited and incur the same condemnation as the devil. ⁷ Furthermore, he must have a good reputation among outsiders, so that he does not fall into disgrace and the devil's trap.

⁸ Deacons, likewise, should be worthy of respect, not hypocritical, not drinking a lot of wine, not greedy for money, ⁹ holding the mystery of the faith with a clear conscience. ¹⁰ They must also be tested first; if they prove blameless, then they can serve as deacons. ¹¹ Wives,ᶜ likewise, should be worthy of respect, not slanderers, self-controlled, faithful in everything. ¹² Deacons are to be husbands of one wife, managing their children and their own households competently. ¹³ For those who have served well as deacons acquire a good standing for themselves and great boldness in the faith that is in Christ Jesus.

The Mystery of Godliness

¹⁴ I write these things to you, hoping to come to you soon. ¹⁵ But if I should be delayed, I have written so that you will know how people ought to conduct themselves in God's household, which is the church of the living God, the pillar and foundation of the truth. ¹⁶ And most certainly, the mystery of godliness is great:

ᴬ2:7 Other mss add in Christ ᴮ3:1 Or bishop, pastor ᶜ3:11 Or Women

2:8–9 Lifting up . . . hands was a typical posture for prayer in the Bible (Ex 9:29; 1Kg 8:22; Pss 28:2; 63:4; Is 1:15; Lk 24:50).
2:10 Christian women are to be less concerned about their apparel than about pursuing good works.
2:11–12 The phrase **I do not allow** is not simply a statement of Paul's personal wishes but the statement of an authoritative position. This statement prohibits women from providing public teaching for men, but it does not prevent women from speaking in other circumstances.
2:13 The word **for** introduces the biblical basis for the preceding prohibition in regards to women. Gender roles are rooted in creation and God's original purposes. Rooting the command in the order of creation makes this an abiding command rather than something that held only for Paul's culture and era.
2:14 When Paul declared that **Adam was not deceived,** he did not excuse him for his sin. The point here is not blame but deception. That Adam sinned and bore the primary responsibility for the fall of humanity is clear in Rm 5:12–14.
2:15 This is a difficult verse. Paul did not believe people can earn salvation **through childbearing** or any other means. The verse is probably best understood as an affirmation of roles particular to women in contrast to the role prohibited to them in vv. 11–14.
3:1 The terms **overseer** and **elder** are used in the NT to refer to the same office.

3:2–7 These verses describe the character of a person who would serve in this office. The list is not intended to be exhaustive, but it envisions a person of mature Christian character (see also Ti 1:5–9).
3:2 The meaning of **husband of one wife** is widely debated. It probably does not refer to the issue of divorce. It could be a prohibition of polygamy, but most likely it refers to marital faithfulness in general. **Able to teach** is the one requirement in this list that is not necessarily required of all believers. It is also not required of deacons. Thus, it is a distinguishing mark of an overseer or elder (Ti 1:9).
3:3 The requirement of not being **an excessive drinker** here and "not drinking a lot of wine" in v. 8 should probably be taken as synonymous.
3:4–5 The management of one's own **household** is highlighted by the greater amount of discussion given to it. The home is the proving ground of Christian character.
3:6 The point of this verse is that quickly elevating a **new** convert to a leadership position might result in sinful pride.
3:7 A good church leader is one who has demonstrated his character even to those outside the church.
3:8 Deacons are the other office of the NT church, in addition to the overseer or elder. **Likewise** suggests a link between the lists of qualifications.
3:9 The word **mystery** (Gk musterion) is a common Pauline word. It refers to the gospel

(1Co 2:7; 4:1; 15:51; Eph 3:4–13; Col 1:25–26; 2:2; 4:3).
3:10 The testing described here would presumably be done by the church under the leadership of the overseers.
3:11 The Greek word behind **wives** here can mean "women" or "wives." Context (e.g., v. 2) suggests "wives" is the better translation choice.
3:12 On **husbands of one wife,** see note at v. 2.
3:13 This verse highlights two results of good service in the role of deacon. **Good standing** refers to respect and appreciation from the church toward those who serve the church in this way. **Great boldness** probably refers to the increase in confidence in the faith that comes from serving and seeing the truths of the gospel proven in ministry.
3:14 Paul wanted them to know of his interest in coming to see them soon, but he also wanted them to know that might not be possible.
3:15 This verse provides a threefold description of the church's identity and mission. **Household** refers to the church as God's family. The phrase **church of the living God** highlights the church as the gathering where God most clearly shows his presence. The church as **the pillar and foundation of the truth** means that God has entrusted to the church the task of promoting and protecting the gospel.
3:16 Again, the word **mystery** refers to the gospel (v. 9). This verse contains a poetic exposition of the gospel.

He^A was manifested in the flesh,
vindicated in the Spirit,
seen by angels,
preached among the nations,
believed on in the world,
taken up in glory.

Demonic Influence

4 Now the Spirit explicitly says that in later times some will depart from the faith, paying attention to deceitful spirits and the teachings of demons, ² through the hypocrisy of liars whose consciences are seared. ³ They forbid marriage and demand abstinence from foods that God created to be received with gratitude by those who believe and know the truth. ⁴ For everything created by God is good, and nothing is to be rejected if it is received with thanksgiving, ⁵ since it is sanctified by the word of God and by prayer.

A Good Servant of Jesus Christ

⁶ If you point these things out to the brothers and sisters, you will be a good servant of Christ Jesus, nourished by the words of the faith and the good teaching that you have followed. ⁷ But have nothing to do with pointless and silly myths. Rather, train yourself in godliness. ⁸ For the training of the body has limited benefit, but godliness is beneficial in every way, since it holds promise for the present life and also for the life to come. ⁹ This saying is trustworthy and deserves full acceptance. ¹⁰ For this reason we labor and strive,^B because we have put our hope in the living God, who is the Savior of all people, especially of those who believe.

Instructions for Ministry

¹¹ Command and teach these things. ¹² Don't let anyone despise your youth, but set an example for the believers in speech, in conduct, in love,^C in faith, and in purity. ¹³ Until I come, give your attention to public reading, exhortation,

and teaching. ¹⁴ Don't neglect the gift that is in you; it was given to you through prophecy, with the laying on of hands by the council of elders. ¹⁵ Practice these things; be committed to them, so that your progress may be evident to all. ¹⁶ Pay close attention to your life and your teaching; persevere in these things, for in doing this you will save both yourself and your hearers.

5 Don't rebuke an older man, but exhort him as a father, younger men as brothers, ² older women as mothers, and the younger women as sisters with all purity.

The Support of Widows

³ Support^D widows who are genuinely in need. ⁴ But if any widow has children or grandchildren, let them learn to practice godliness toward their own family first and to repay their parents, for this pleases God. ⁵ The widow who is truly in need and left all alone has put her hope in God and continues night and day in her petitions and prayers; ⁶ however, she who is self-indulgent is dead even while she lives. ⁷ Command this also, so that they will be above reproach. ⁸ But if anyone does not provide for his own family, especially for his own household, he has denied the faith and is worse than an unbeliever.

⁹ No widow is to be enrolled on the list for support unless she is at least sixty years old, has been the wife of one husband, ¹⁰ and is well known for good works — that is, if she has brought up children, shown hospitality, washed the saints' feet, helped the afflicted, and devoted herself to every good work. ¹¹ But refuse to enroll younger widows, for when they are drawn away from Christ by desire, they want to marry ¹² and will therefore receive condemnation because they have renounced their original pledge. ¹³ At the same time, they also learn to be idle, going from house to house; they are not only idle, but are also gossips and

---

^A 3:16 Other mss read God   ^B 4:10 Other mss read and suffer reproach   ^C 4:12 Other mss add in spirit,   ^D 5:3 Lit Honor

4:1 Just how the **Spirit explicitly says** is not made clear here. The **later times** in view here included Timothy's day. The last days are considered to have begun with the work of Christ.
4:2–5 Although **everything created by God is good**, the false teachers **forbid marriage** and certain **foods**. But Paul rejected the teachings of these **liars**. The good gifts of God are to be **received with thanksgiving**.
4:7–8 Paul compares **godliness** with athletic prowess. Both require **training**.
4:10 The statement that Jesus is the **Savior of all people, especially of those who believe** may seem to teach universalism, the belief that all persons will eventually go to heaven regardless of whether they accept Christ. The point is not that Jesus saves everybody and then saves believers even more. Rather, Jesus is the Savior for all—all who believe. "All people" pictures the transnational scope of the gospel.

4:11–12 Timothy was to continue to **teach** sound doctrine and to **command** the false teachers to cease. Every one of the five qualities enumerated in verse 12 was missing from the lives of the false teachers.
4:14 Gift probably refers to Timothy's calling and gifting for ministry indicated by God (**through prophecy**) and recognized by the church (laying on of hands by the **elders**).
4:15 These things that Paul called on Timothy to **practice** and **be committed to** are the things commanded in vv. 12–13.
4:16 Ultimately, salvation requires perseverance in faith (cp. Rm 11:22; 1Co 9:27; 15:1–2; Php 2:12; Col 1:23).
5:1–2 Verse 1 does not prohibit the correcting of older men but speaks to the respectful manner in which this should be done.
5:3–7 Care for **widows** has always been a concern of God's and a command for God's people (Ex 22:22; Dt 27:19; Is 1:17). The **widow who is truly in need** and deserves support

from the church is one without family members to support her and who devotes herself to prayer and not to self-indulgence.
5:8 The strong language in this verse indicates that provision for one's **own household** is a spiritual responsibility.
5:9 The phrase **wife of one husband** probably refers to marital faithfulness (see note at 3:2). If it forbids remarriage after the death of a husband, then Paul's advice in v. 14 would make those women ineligible.
5:10 This list reviews the deeds of godly older women. These are examples to which younger women should aspire.
5:11–16 The issue in these verses is either that these **widows** who were being supported by the church had pledged to remain unmarried or that these **younger widows** might be tempted by their desires to marry unbelievers, thus turning away from the faith. It seems likely that Paul's concern was over remarriage to an unbeliever.

◂ Is Gender a Choice?

by Stanton L. Jones

Sex and gender are commonly differentiated, with sex referring to the biological components of maleness and femaleness, and gender referring to their psychological and cultural components.

More precisely, the biological components of sex resolve into four facets:
1. chromosomes, with the prototypical male having one X and one Y chromosome and the female having two X chromosomes;
2. gonads and the hormones they produce, with males having testes and females ovaries;
3. sexual anatomy;
4. secondary sex characteristics, including for males denser, coarser body and facial hair, larger stature, and greater muscle mass, while females manifest enlarged breasts, wider hips, less body hair, and less muscle mass.

The psychological/cultural complements of gender resolve into at least three separate facets:
1. gender identity, the subjective sense of being a man or woman;
2. sexual orientation, with the prototypical male experiencing only erotic attraction to females and the female to males; and
3. gender role, the person's adoption of cultural expectations for maleness/masculinity or femaleness/femininity.

Given the complexity of the seven factors and their development, it is remarkable that so many adults align consistently on all seven factors, thus experiencing a somewhat uncomplicated sense of being a woman or a man. But some individuals deviate from the norms in one or more of the seven areas, as the following examples illustrate:
1. Some individuals inherit extra chromosomes (e.g., XXY and XYY, conditions with attendant complications).
2. Some persons experience incomplete gonadal development, and others develop gonads of mixed testicular and ovarian tissues (e.g., true hermaphroditism).
3. Malfunctioning gonads or a hormonally abnormal uterine environment may result in problematic anatomical development; further, environmental events may create problems.
4. Hormonal problems can result in minimized or exaggerated secondary sex characteristics.
5. Certain individuals report emphatic gender identification in contrast with their biological sex (transgenderism).
6. Three to five percent of the population report consistent, stable erotic attraction (orientation) toward persons of the same sex or to both sexes in varying degrees; others report stable attractions in other directions.
7. Some individuals are drawn to gender-atypical roles; further, cultures vary widely in their prescribed gender roles, including their clarity and rigidity.

Scientific evidence exists for some biological contribution to the three gender variables and for some psychosocial contribution to the four biological aspects of sex, though we are uncertain how determinative these contributions are or how they interact with human choice.

Is Sex or Gender a Choice?

Christians begin by recognizing that God is the Creator and we are not, that humans are of two sexes by creational intent ("he created them male and female," Gn 1:27), and that our sexuality is intended as a gift to be first received with gratitude and humility and then to be formed responsibly by our parents and our choices. God exists eternally in Trinitarian community, and in his divine image we exist as embodied women and men in community and charged under the authority of our Lord with the proper stewardship of these gifts of sex and gender. Given that our sin blinds us at times to understanding what is good, we affirm with gratitude God's moral guidance of this stewardship.

Our sexuality is a gift given for purposes beyond our individual existence: maleness and femaleness typically set the foundation for marriage, a covenantal union of one man and one woman that includes full sexual intimacy often resulting in the procreation of children and the extension of multigenerational families. Sexuality is a gift with relational and community entailments; the husband and wife are gifts to each other.

Christians do not insist that every biological or psychological given is God's eternal will. Because of sin, neither humanity nor the world around us is as God intended. We are disordered. Thus, we cannot take our experience as God's intent. Where cruelty or immorality is a cultural norm (e.g., the practice of female genital mutilation in certain African and Islamic cultures or the Hindu practice of settee, the burning to death of a widow at the cremation of her husband's body), we seek to produce cultural change.

Further, we recognize our finite limitations in interpreting God's special revelation. For example, in the realm of gender roles reasonable Christians recognize that there is room for responsible choice; many would support the young woman who wants to study business leadership or the young father who chooses homemaking in support of his wife's career given her higher earning power. Neither choice, however, denies the unique callings of men and women.

There is legitimacy to seeking to correct disorders in the realm of physical sexual characteristics as well. As we would support surgical correction of a child's cleft palette, so we would support reattachment of a severed penis, surgical breast reduction for a woman whose heavy breasts contribute to muscular and spinal pain, or testosterone-enhancing treatments for a chromosomally and anatomically male teenager with delayed puberty and development of male secondary sex characteristics.

But more radical options are now possible. The question of whether sex or gender is a choice is challenging today because our technological prowess allows us to intervene medically or psychologically in ways once impossible. Such options present us with dilemmas. What of cases like the homosexual transsexual who, though born biologically female, undergoes sexual reassignment surgery to remove her ovaries and construct an artificial penis, takes testosterone, and develops male secondary sex characteristics, reports psychological identification as a man, adopts culturally masculine roles, yet desires sex with other men? In this case, six of the seven dimensions of sex/gender have been deviated from the presumptive norm with only the chromosomes unchanged. What do we make of her/his argument that "LGBT identity is congruent with how I have always felt and how God has made me"?

Biblical Christians in humble and full submission to Christ will accept the gift of their sexuality along with biblical norms for expression of that sexuality. But we live in a secular culture that rejects the Creator and his creational intent. This, in turn, leads to the rejection of any norms governing behavior and of the idea that departures from these norms constitute disorders in any objective sense. In the area of sexuality, we have seen steady shifts in the official mental health diagnostic criteria defining what constitute sexual disorders. Many behavioral or arousal patterns that were once regarded as "deviant" have been normalized; this includes nonheterosexual orientation and "fetishes."

Even more fundamentally, a materialistic worldview that assumes that chance alone determines life outcomes robs us of any deep sense of meaning or the good. With only a vague aspiration of genetic propagation and evolutionary progress as a guide, brute assertion of human will against cruel chance may be all that is left. This can lead to a broad societal embrace of something like the original temptation placed before Adam and Eve at the time of the fall, that through exercising one's choice in violation of norms, "you will be like God, knowing good and evil" (Gn 3:5).

Christians recognize that as a result of our disorder and that of our world due to humanity's choice to sin, we experience discord in many ways: between physical sex and the sexual prototypes, between facets of our sex and gender, between our personal inclinations and cultural standards, between biblical norms and our personal inclinations (or cultural standards), and others. Resolution of such discord may take many forms, requiring us as humble stewards to make complex choices. There are times to intervene medically or psychologically to correct disorders, following Christ's model as healer.

More troubling are cases like transsexualism in which one's gender identity is discordant with the clear testimony of biological sex. Many today reject viewing this condition as a disorder in favor of celebrating it as part of human diversity. But in the Christian perspective incorporating God's creational intent, such conditions must be seen as disorders. Indeed, all human life is disordered because of sin. Our overarching call is to pursue conformity of our lives (body and soul) to God's revealed will (1Tm 4:1–5) and to seek his sovereign healing of our brokenness in confidence of our ultimate healing in eternity.

While it can prove difficult to discern the proper response in complex cases, the simple

busybodies, saying things they shouldn't say. ¹⁴ Therefore, I want younger women to marry, have children, manage their households, and give the adversary no opportunity to accuse us. ¹⁵ For some have already turned away to follow Satan. ¹⁶ If any^ believing woman has widows in her family, let her help them. Let the church not be burdened, so that it can help widows in genuine need.

Honoring the Elders

¹⁷ The elders who are good leaders are to be considered worthy of double honor,ᴮ especially those who work hard at preaching and teaching. ¹⁸ For the Scripture says: **Do not muzzle an ox while it is treading out the grain,**ᶜ and, "The worker is worthy of his wages." ¹⁹ Don't accept an accusation against an elder unless it is supported by two or three witnesses. ²⁰ Publicly rebuke those who sin, so that the rest will be afraid. ²¹ I solemnly charge you before God and Christ Jesus and the elect angels to observe these things without prejudice, doing nothing out of favoritism. ²² Don't be too quick to appointᴰ anyone as an elder, and don't share in the sins of others. Keep yourself pure. ²³ Don't continue drinking only water, but use a little wine because of your stomach and your frequent illnesses. ²⁴ Some people's sins are obvious, preceding them to judgment, but the sins of others surfaceᴱ later. ²⁵ Likewise, good works are obvious, and those that are not obvious cannot remain hidden.

Honoring Masters

6 All who are under the yoke as slaves should regard their own mastersᶠ as worthy of all respect, so that God's name and his teaching will not be blasphemed. ² Let those who have believing masters not be disrespectful to them because they are brothers, but serve them even better, since those who benefit from their service are believers and dearly loved.ᴳ

False Doctrine and Human Greed

Teach and encourage these things. ³ If anyone teaches false doctrine and does not agree with the sound teaching of our Lord Jesus Christ and with the teaching that promotes godliness, ⁴ he is conceited and understands nothing, but has an unhealthy interest in disputes and arguments over words. From these come envy, quarreling, slander, evil suspicions, ⁵ and constant disagreement among people whose minds are depraved and deprived of the truth, who imagine that godliness is a way to material gain.ᴴ ⁶ But godliness with contentment is great gain. ⁷ For we brought nothing into the world, andᴵ we can take nothing out. ⁸ If we have food and clothing,ᴶ we will be content with these. ⁹ But those who want to be rich fall into temptation, a trap, and many foolish and harmful desires, which plunge people into ruin and destruction. ¹⁰ For the love of money is a rootᴷ of all kinds of evil, and by craving it, some have wandered away from the faith and pierced themselves with many griefs.

^5:16 Other mss add *believing man* or   ᴮ5:17 Or *of respect and remuneration*   ᶜ5:18 Dt 25:4   ᴰ5:22 Lit *to lay hands on*   ᴱ5:24 Lit *follow*   ᶠ6:1 Or *owners*   ᴳ6:2 Or *because, as believers who are dearly loved, they are devoted to others' welfare*   ᴴ6:5 Other mss add *From such people withdraw yourself.*   ᴵ6:7 Other mss add *it is clear that*   ᴶ6:8 Or *food and shelter*   ᴷ6:10 Or *is the root*

5:17 The phrase **good leaders** can also be translated as "those who rule well." The role of elder involved authority, particularly in **preaching and teaching**. These elders were to be **considered worthy** of **double honor**. The exact identity of this "double honor" is not clear.
5:18 The command **not** to **muzzle an ox** is a quote from Dt 25:4. The idea is that a person who works for something should be able to benefit from it. **The worker is worthy of his wages** is a direct quote from Lk 10:7. This indicates that Paul was already referring to the recorded statements of Jesus as authoritative Scripture.
5:19 This requirement is based on Dt 19:15 (cp. Mt 18:16; 2Co 13:1).

5:20 The people to be **publicly** rebuked were elders who sinned. **The rest** who would fear to sin as a result of this rebuke included the rest of the elders and probably the rest of the congregation as well.
5:21–22 These things refers back to the instructions in vv. 19–20. God the Father, Christ, and the angels see our actions and care what we do. **Elect angels** are distinguished from fallen angels. They will be involved in the judgment (cp. Mt 13:41–42; 16:27; 24:31; 25:31; 2Th 1:7; Heb 12:22–24; Rv 14:10,14–20).
5:23 How this verse connects to the rest of the paragraph is not clear.
5:24–25 After the aside of v. 23, Paul returned to the issue of appointing elders

to serve the church. These verses illustrate why it is wise to be patient and thorough in assessing potential elders.
6:3–5 This is the third time in the letter that Paul deals with false teachers (1:3–11; 4:1–5). Paul considered his teaching to be in accord with **the sound teaching of our Lord Jesus Christ**.
6:6–8 The opposite of greed is contentment, which means being satisfied with food and clothing.
6:9–10 What is condemned here is **harmful desires**, not the possession of things. The warning is not simply that **love of money** can be harmful, but that this **craving** has led some people to deny the faith and show themselves to be unbelievers.

---

prioritization of the experiential self and a facile manipulation of biological sex must be rejected even as we seek compassionate responses to persons suffering with an objective disorder. We must resist the illusion that the ultimate determination of sex and

gender is ours to make autonomously. There are many choices to be made about how we live out our sexuality in godliness. But in the deepest sense, our choices that shape sex and gender should first reflect humble submission to God's choices for us.

Fight the Good Fight

[11] But you, man of God, flee from these things, and pursue righteousness, godliness, faith, love, endurance, and gentleness. [12] Fight the good fight of the faith. Take hold of eternal life to which you were called and about which you have made a good confession in the presence of many witnesses. [13] In the presence of God, who gives life to all, and of Christ Jesus, who gave a good confession before Pontius Pilate, I charge you [14] to keep this command without fault or failure until the appearing of our Lord Jesus Christ. [15] God will bring this about in his own time. He is the blessed and only Sovereign, the King of kings, and the Lord of lords, [16] who alone is immortal and who lives in unapproachable light, whom no one has seen or can see, to him be honor and eternal power. Amen.

^[6:17] Other mss read *on the living God*

Instructions to the Rich

[17] Instruct those who are rich in the present age not to be arrogant or to set their hope on the uncertainty of wealth, but on God,^ who richly provides us with all things to enjoy. [18] Instruct them to do what is good, to be rich in good works, to be generous and willing to share, [19] storing up treasure for themselves as a good foundation for the coming age, so that they may take hold of what is truly life.

Guard the Heritage

[20] Timothy, guard what has been entrusted to you, avoiding irreverent and empty speech and contradictions from what is falsely called knowledge. [21] By professing it, some people have departed from the faith.

Grace be with you all.

6:11–12 Fleeing sin is paired with chasing down virtue.

6:13 **Pontius Pilate** appears as a backdrop for Jesus's **good confession**, which is the model for the "good confession" of believers (v. 12).

6:14–16 God is the **only Sovereign**. He rules over all **kings** and accomplishes all his purposes. He **alone is immortal** and dwells in **unapproachable light**. The opposition Timothy faces in his ministry is small and weak by comparison.

6:17–19 Those who are rich have a tendency to be **arrogant** and must guard against it. They are also prone to put their hope in their wealth rather than in Christ. Real life consists in doing **what is good** and being **generous**.

6:20–21 The phrase **what has been entrusted to you** refers to the gospel. **What is falsely called knowledge** refers to the false teaching addressed elsewhere in the letter.

◤ Introduction to 2 Timothy

Circumstances of Writing

As stated in the opening of each letter, 1 Timothy, 2 Timothy, and Titus were written by Paul (1Tm 1:1; 2Tm 1:1; Ti 1:1). However, many scholars today assume that Paul did not write them. This opinion is based on the differences from his other letters in vocabulary and style, alleged differences in theology, and uncertainties about where these letters fit chronologically in the life of the apostle. But the differences in style and vocabulary are not troublesome when one considers that authors often use different vocabulary when addressing different groups and situations. Rather than addressing churches in these letters, Paul was writing to coworkers in unique ministry settings. Hence we would expect different vocabulary. Also, the traditional view of the historical situation in which Paul wrote these letters is reasonable and defensible. Therefore, in spite of significant opposition by some scholars, there is a solid basis for accepting the Pastoral Epistles as Pauline.

Paul most likely wrote these letters after the time covered in the book of Acts. Acts closes with Paul in prison. Traditionally it has been believed that Paul was released from this imprisonment, then continued his work around the Mediterranean, perhaps even reaching Spain (Rm 15:22–29). During this time, he visited Crete and other places. First Timothy and Titus were written during this period of further mission work. Timothy had been left in Ephesus to handle some problems with false teaching there (1Tm 1:3–4). Titus had been left in Crete after the initial work to set up the church there (Ti 1:5). Eventually Paul was imprisoned again, and this led to his execution. During this final imprisonment, Paul wrote 2 Timothy to request another visit from Timothy and to give final exhortations as he anticipated his martyrdom.

Contribution to the Bible

These letters are rich theologically and ethically. One of their key contributions is the clear way they show the connection between doctrine and ethics, belief and behavior.

While these letters were not intended to provide a detailed account of church government, they do provide some significant insights on this topic. The lists of characteristics for overseers (1Tm 3:1–7; Ti 1:5–9) and deacons (1Tm 3:8–13) are the only such lists in the New Testament.

Structure

All three letters follow the typical pattern of a Greek epistle. While there are some lexical differences with many of Paul's other letters, keep in mind that these letters were written to specific individuals. One thing unique to the structure of these letters is the focus on church leadership.

See the introduction to 1 Timothy for the timeline.

Outline

I. Greetings and Thanksgiving (1:1–7)
II. Not Ashamed of the Gospel (1:8–12)
III. Loyal to the Faith (1:13–18)
IV. Strong in Grace (2:1–13)
V. An Approved Worker (2:14–26)
VI. Preparation for Difficult Times (3:1–9)
VII. The Sacred Scriptures (3:10–17)
VIII. Fulfilling Your Ministry (4:1–8)
IX. Final Instructions (4:9–18)
X. Benediction (4:19–22)

Key verses in 2 Timothy

1:7 For God has not given us a spirit of fear, but one of power, love, and sound judgment.

2:15 Be diligent to present yourself to God as one approved, a worker who doesn't need to be ashamed, correctly teaching the word of truth.

3:16 All Scripture is inspired by God and is profitable for teaching, for rebuking, for correcting, for training in righteousness, . . .

Greeting

1 Paul, an apostle of Christ Jesus by God's will, for the sake of the promise of life in Christ Jesus:

[2] To Timothy, my dearly loved son.

Grace, mercy, and peace from God the Father and Christ Jesus our Lord.

Thanksgiving

[3] I thank God, whom I serve with a clear conscience as my ancestors did, when I constantly remember you in my prayers night and day. [4] Remembering your tears, I long to see you so that I may be filled with joy. [5] I recall your sincere faith that first lived in your grandmother Lois and in your mother Eunice and now, I am convinced, is in you also.

[6] Therefore, I remind you to rekindle the gift of God that is in you through the laying on of my hands. [7] For God has not given us a spirit of fear, but one of power,[A] love, and sound judgment.

Not Ashamed of the Gospel

[8] So don't be ashamed of the testimony about our Lord, or of me his prisoner. Instead, share in suffering for the gospel, relying on the power of God. [9] He has saved us and called us with a holy calling, not according to our works, but according to his own purpose and grace, which was given to us in Christ Jesus before time began. [10] This has now been made evident through the appearing of our Savior Christ Jesus, who has abolished death and has brought life and immortality to light through the gospel. [11] For this gospel I was appointed a herald, apostle, and teacher,[B] [12] and that is why I suffer these things. But I am not ashamed,

because I know whom I have believed and am persuaded that he is able to guard what has been entrusted to me[C] until that day.

Be Loyal to the Faith

[13] Hold on to the pattern of sound teaching that you have heard from me, in the faith and love that are in Christ Jesus. [14] Guard the good deposit through the Holy Spirit who lives in us. [15] You know that all those in the province of Asia have deserted me, including Phygelus and Hermogenes. [16] May the Lord grant mercy to the household of Onesiphorus, because he often refreshed me and was not ashamed of my chains. [17] On the contrary, when he was in Rome, he diligently searched for me and found me. [18] May the Lord grant that he obtain mercy from him on that day. You know very well how much he ministered at Ephesus.

Be Strong in Grace

2 You, therefore, my son, be strong in the grace that is in Christ Jesus. [2] What you have heard from me in the presence of many witnesses, commit to faithful men[D] who will be able to teach others also.

[3] Share in suffering as a good soldier of Christ Jesus. [4] No one serving as a soldier gets entangled in the concerns of civilian life; he seeks to please the commanding officer. [5] Also, if anyone competes as an athlete, he is not crowned unless he competes according to the rules. [6] The hardworking farmer ought to be the first to get a share of the crops. [7] Consider what I say, for the Lord will give you understanding in everything.

[8] Remember Jesus Christ, risen from the dead and descended from David, according

---

[A]1:7 Or *For the Spirit God gave us does not make us fearful, but gives us power* [B]1:11 Other mss add *of the Gentiles* [C]1:12 Or *guard what I have entrusted to him*, or *guard my deposit* [D]2:2 Or *faithful people*

1:1 As Paul wrote, awaiting death, he reminded Timothy of **the promise of life**.
1:3–5 Paul and Timothy both had a heritage of faith. Timothy had a Greek father (Ac 16:1,3) but a godly Jewish grandmother and mother (Ac 16:1; 2Tm 1:5). When Paul said he prayed for Timothy constantly **night and day**, he used a common expression for continual prayer.

1:6 The phrase **rekindle the gift of God** was a call to action lest sluggishness set in. On "gift of God," see note at 1Tm 4:14. The **laying on of . . . hands** probably refers to Timothy's ordination (1Tm 4:14). This passage focuses on Paul's part in the event while 1Tm 4:14 focuses on the involvement of the full group of elders.
1:7 **Spirit** here probably refers to the Holy Spirit. The Greek word translated **fear** is a strong term for cowardice. Boldness, not cowardice, is a mark of the Holy Spirit (Pr 28:1; Ac 4:31).
1:8 Paul warns Timothy not to be embarrassed by the gospel message about a Jew executed as a criminal or by having a colleague imprisoned by the Romans.
1:9–10 These verses summarize the gospel for which believers suffer.
1:11–12 The phrase **these things** refers to Paul's imprisonment and impending death. He was confident that God would protect, literally, "my entrustment" which is either the gospel (**what has been entrusted to me**) or his own soul ("what I have entrusted to him"). Either way, it was this confidence in God that prevented Paul from being **ashamed**.

1:13 The word for **pattern** could also be rendered "standard." Timothy is to guard the pattern of teaching while he maintains faith in God and exhibits love for others.
1:14 **The good deposit** is the gospel.
1:15 **Asia** was the name of the Roman province in which Ephesus was located. Key people who could have supported Paul had failed to do so. We know nothing about **Phygelus** and **Hermogenes**.
1:16–18 **Onesiphorus** was also an example of faithfulness.
2:2 Those who receive the gospel have a responsibility to faithfully pass it on to others, who pass it on to still others.
2:3–6 In these three analogies, Paul expounded the call to service and suffering. Verse 4 calls for single-minded desire to please God. Verse 5 declares that a person must obey God's rules in order to succeed. Verse 6 encourages hard work by holding out the promise of blessing.
2:7 This verse is a call to contemplation of what has been written, not a promise of complete knowledge or **understanding**.
2:8 The phrase **descended from David** is a reminder of Jesus's messianic credentials.

to my gospel, ⁹ for which I suffer to the point of being bound like a criminal. But the word of God is not bound. ¹⁰ This is why I endure all things for the elect: so that they also may obtain salvation, which is in Christ Jesus, with eternal glory. ¹¹ This saying is trustworthy:

For if we died with him,
we will also live with him;
¹² if we endure, we will also reign
with him;
if we deny him, he will also deny us;
¹³ if we are faithless, he remains faithful,
for he cannot deny himself.

An Approved Worker

¹⁴ Remind them of these things, and charge them before God[A] not to fight about words. This is useless and leads to the ruin of those who listen. ¹⁵ Be diligent to present yourself to God as one approved, a worker who doesn't need to be ashamed, correctly teaching the word of truth. ¹⁶ Avoid irreverent and empty speech, since those who engage in it will produce even more godlessness, ¹⁷ and their teaching will spread like gangrene. Hymenaeus and Philetus are among them. ¹⁸ They have departed from the truth, saying that the resurrection has already taken place, and are ruining the faith of some. ¹⁹ Nevertheless, God's solid foundation stands firm, bearing this inscription: **The Lord knows those who are his**,[B] and let everyone who calls on the name of[C] the Lord turn away from wickedness.

²⁰ Now in a large house there are not only gold and silver vessels, but also those of wood and clay; some for honorable[D] use and some for dishonorable.[E] ²¹ So if anyone purifies himself from anything dishonorable,[F] he will be a special[G] instrument, set apart, useful to the Master, prepared for every good work.

²² Flee from youthful passions, and pursue righteousness, faith, love, and peace, along with those who call on the Lord from a pure heart. ²³ But reject foolish and ignorant disputes, because you know that they breed quarrels. ²⁴ The Lord's servant must not quarrel, but must be gentle to everyone, able to teach,[H] and patient, ²⁵ instructing his opponents with gentleness. Perhaps God will grant them repentance leading them to the knowledge of the truth. ²⁶ Then they may come to their senses and escape the trap of the devil, who has taken them captive to do his will.

Difficult Times Ahead

3 But know this: Hard times will come in the last days. ² For people will be lovers of self, lovers of money, boastful, proud, demeaning, disobedient to parents, ungrateful, unholy, ³ unloving, irreconcilable, slanderers, without self-control, brutal, without love for what is good, ⁴ traitors, reckless, conceited, lovers of pleasure rather than lovers of God, ⁵ holding to the form of godliness but denying its power. Avoid these people.

⁶ For among them are those who worm their way into households and deceive gullible women overwhelmed by sins and led astray by a variety of passions, ⁷ always learning and never able to come to a knowledge of the truth. ⁸ Just as Jannes and Jambres resisted Moses, so these also resist the truth. They are men who are corrupt in mind and worthless in regard to the faith. ⁹ But they will not make further progress, for their foolishness will be clear to all, as was the foolishness of Jannes and Jambres.

Struggles in the Christian Life

¹⁰ But you have followed my teaching, conduct, purpose, faith, patience, love, and endurance,

---

[A]**2:14** Other mss read *before the Lord*   [B]**2:19** Nm 16:5   [C]**2:19** Lit *everyone who names the name of*   [D]**2:20** Or *special*
[E]**2:20** Or *ordinary*   [F]**2:21** Lit *from these*   [G]**2:21** Or *an honorable*   [H]**2:24** Or *everyone, skillful in teaching*

2:9–10 Paul was encouraged by the fact that though God's messenger could be **bound**, the message itself could not be. Paul speaks of the **elect** here as those who had been predestined to be saved.
2:11–13 The **trustworthy** statement moves from comfort to challenge and back to comfort. Verse 12 is a clear statement on the necessity of perseverance (cp. Mt 10:22). Verse 13 is a reminder of God's preserving power and faithfulness. In this context, the **deny him** envisions a more serious offense than being **faithless**. To "deny him" envisions apostasy, whereas "faithless" refers to a lapse in trust.
2:14 What Paul had in mind here was meaningless argument.
2:15 Be diligent could also be translated, "Be zealous." Paul had in mind a zealous pursuit of God's approval. One way to do this is to make sure we handle Scripture correctly.
2:17 Hymenaeus was mentioned as a false teacher previously in 1Tm 1:20, but Philetus is not mentioned elsewhere.

2:18 Apparently some people were teaching that believers had already entered the glorified post-resurrection state.
2:19 In spite of the work of these evildoers and evil teachers, God's church still **stands firm**. The **inscription** emphasizes both divine sovereignty (preserving) and human responsibility (persevering).
2:20–21 The **large house** represents the Christian community; the **vessels** for **dishonorable** use represents the false teachers. The point of v. 21 is that one should try to be an honorable vessel, **useful to** the **Master**.
2:22 The word **passions** in this context refers to sinful desires in general. It is significant that fleeing wrong is combined with pursuing right, **along with** other believers.
2:23 On **ignorant disputes**, see note at v. 14.
2:24–25 The **Lord's servant** must be qualified both in ability (**able to teach**) and in character (not quarrelsome, **gentle . . . patient**). The **knowledge of the truth** is salvation.

2:26 Paul often described humanity as enslaved by the **devil** and in need of rescue (2Co 4:4).
3:2–4 The list here may be compared to that found in Rm 1:29–31.
3:5 These false teachers had the external trappings of **godliness** but not the real essence.
3:6 Because of their guilt from their past, these **women overwhelmed by sins** were particularly susceptible to the asceticism and legalism of these false teachers.
3:7 This verse refers to the women who are **always learning** from the false teachers. Gaining the **knowledge of the truth** is spoken of elsewhere of being saved (cp. 2:25; 1Tm 2:4; Ti 1:1).
3:8 Jannes and Jambres were the names given in early Jewish nonbiblical writings to the Egyptian magicians who opposed Moses (Ex 7:8–13). The names do not appear in the Hebrew Bible.
3:10 The words **but you** set vv. 1–9 in contrast with vv. 10–17.

❮ Biblical Authority

by Stephen J. Wellum

Biblical Christianity has always affirmed that Scripture is authoritative because it is God's Word written, the product of God's mighty action through the Word, Jesus, and by the Holy Spirit whereby human authors freely wrote exactly what God intended to be written and without error. Why has the church affirmed this view? What is meant by the inspiration and inerrancy of Scripture?

Christians have affirmed biblical authority because of Scripture's self-testimony. As one evaluates a worldview, it is crucial to begin with the specific claims of that worldview. Thus, if we are to evaluate Christianity, we must begin with Scripture's self-attestation. We do not confer upon the Bible an authority alien to it. Rather, we let Scripture speak for itself. In doing this, we discover that it makes the staggering claim that it is God's Word written and is thus completely authoritative, sufficient, and reliable.

For example, 2 Timothy 3:16 describes Old Testament Scripture as being "inspired by God" (an allusion to creation, where the sovereign Lord speaks the universe into being) and thus fully authoritative. So, in relation to his Word, the sovereign-personal triune God of the universe has spoken again and given us his Word through the agency of human authors (2Pt 1:20–21). And it is precisely because he stands behind his Word as Creator and Lord—the God who knows and plans all things (Eph 1:11), who cannot lie or change his mind (Nm 23:19; 1Sm 15:29; Heb 6:18)—that we have an authoritative Scripture.

Scripture's view of itself is not found in merely one or two texts; it is found throughout the entire canon. From the opening pages of the Old Testament we are presented with the eternal triune God who speaks with all authority (Gn 1:1–2:3). As he enters into covenant relationship with Israel, he gives them his Word, which is to be believed and obeyed (Dt 5:22,32; 29:9; 30:15–16; Jos 1:7–8). As redemptive history unfolds, the covenant-making and covenant-keeping God continues to disclose himself through the prophets. This ultimately reaches fulfillment in Christ (Heb 1:1–2).

In Christ—God the Son incarnate—God's final word is spoken (Jn 1:1–3,14–18). Our Lord Jesus not only fulfills the Old Testament, but he also views it as God's Word—the standard by which we are to live and evaluate everything, alongside his own spoken words (e.g., Mt 4:4; 5:17–19; Jn 14:6; 10:35; cp. 2Tm 3:15–16). In this way our Lord authenticates the Old Testament as God's Word, and he prepares us for the writing of the New Testament through his apostles by the agency of the Holy Spirit (see Jn 16:5–15; Eph 2:20). This is why, as the New Testament Scripture is being written, New Testament authors already view their own writings as authoritative, parallel to Old Testament Scripture (1Th 1:5; 2:13). Specifically, one thinks of 1 Timothy 5:18 (which quotes from Dt 25:4 and Lk 10:7) and 2 Peter 3:16 (which refers to Paul's writings); these view New Testament writings as "Scripture."

In all these ways Scripture views itself as supremely authoritative precisely because it is God's Word. What Scripture says, God says; what God says, Scripture says. To disbelieve or disobey any point of Scripture is to disbelieve or disobey God. The only proper response to God's Word is to trust and obey (Is 66:2).

It is crucial to affirm biblical authority because without it we would have no basis to affirm that the God of the Bible has spoken definitively and objectively. Without an authoritative and inerrant Scripture, we could hypothesize about God and the world, but none of our hypotheses would be properly grounded. Without biblical authority we have no foundation on which to justify our beliefs since any statement of Scripture may be false. But if this is so, then one would need an independent criterion to justify which statements of Scripture are to be judged true or false. This only compounds the problem. Not only would Scripture not be able to be used as a sufficient ground of justification, but also one must ask what exactly are the independent criteria by which we judge Scripture true or false? Would it be human reason? Religious experience? The problem with all of these so-called solutions to grounding our beliefs is that they require their own independent justification. So, in the end, without a fully authoritative Bible as the foundation for grounding our

[11] along with the persecutions and sufferings that came to me in Antioch, Iconium, and Lystra. What persecutions I endured — and yet the Lord rescued me from them all. [12] In fact, all who want to live a godly life in Christ Jesus will be persecuted. [13] Evil people and impostors will become worse, deceiving and being deceived. [14] But as for you, continue in what you have learned and firmly believed. You know those who taught you, [15] and you know that from infancy you have known the sacred Scriptures, which are able to give you wisdom for salvation through faith in Christ Jesus. [16] All Scripture is inspired by God[A] and is profitable for teaching, for rebuking, for correcting, for training in righteousness, [17] so that the man of God may be complete, equipped for every good work.

Fulfill Your Ministry

4 I solemnly charge you before God and Christ Jesus, who is going to judge the living and the dead, and because of his appearing and his kingdom: [2] Preach the word; be ready in season and out of season; correct, rebuke, and encourage with great patience and teaching. [3] For the time will come when people will not tolerate sound doctrine, but according to their own desires, will multiply teachers for themselves because they have an itch to hear what they want to hear. [4] They will turn away from hearing the truth and will turn aside to myths. [5] But as for you, exercise self-control in everything, endure hardship, do the work of an evangelist, fulfill your ministry.

[6] For I am already being poured out as a drink offering, and the time for my departure is close. [7] I have fought the good fight, I have finished the race, I have kept the faith. [8] There is reserved for me the crown of righteousness, which the Lord, the righteous Judge, will give me on that day, and not only to me, but to all those who have loved his appearing.[B]

Final Instructions

[9] Make every effort to come to me soon, [10] because Demas has deserted me, since he loved this present world, and has gone to Thessalonica. Crescens has gone to Galatia, Titus to Dalmatia. [11] Only Luke is with me. Bring Mark with you, for he is useful to me in the ministry. [12] I have sent Tychicus to Ephesus. [13] When you come, bring the cloak I left in Troas with Carpus, as well as the scrolls, especially the parchments. [14] Alexander the coppersmith

---

[A] 3:16 Lit *breathed out by God*　[B] 4:8 Or *have longed for his appearing*

3:11 Antioch, Iconium, and **Lystra** were the cities that Paul visited on his first missionary journey. Lystra was Timothy's hometown, so he was probably aware of what had happened to Paul there.
3:12–13 All who want to live a godly life are not a special kind of Christian, but it should be true of every believer. The false teachers, who were **evil** and **impostors**, were not being persecuted.
3:14 The phrase **those who taught you** probably refers to Timothy's mother and grandmother (1:5), especially since v. 15 mentions the teaching he received in childhood.
3:15 Scripture has the power to bring people to faith.
3:16–17 Inspired means "breathed out by God." Because Scripture comes from God himself, it is profitable in many ways, ultimately leading us to **righteousness**, maturity, and service. **All Scripture** refers to the OT, but by implication to the writings of the NT as well (1Tm 5:18; 2Pt 3:15–16).

4:1 The solemnity of the charge is heightened by references to living before the gaze of God, to the fact that this God is judge, to Christ's second coming (**appearing**), and to the reality of his present reign over **his kingdom**.
4:2 The word is especially the gospel but includes the entirety of the Christian tradition taught by Paul and the other apostles (2:15). It is equated in 4:3 with "sound doctrine."
4:4 On **myths,** see 1 Tm 1:4.
4:6 By referring to a **drink offering,** Paul used OT sacrificial language to refer to his own death (Gn 35:14; Ex 29:40–41; Lv 23:13; Nm 15:5–10).
4:7 To call his life **the good fight** uses imagery that portrays a struggle (cp. 1Co 9:25–26; 1Tm 1:18; 6:12). On viewing his life as a **race,** see Ac 20:24. And Paul **kept the faith** in that he contended for the faith and he persevered in believing.
4:8 Crown of righteousness probably means "the crown which consists of righteousness,"

referring to the final righteous state of believers. Thus, it will be given not only to Paul but to **all those who have loved his appearing,** a reference to all believers.
4:10 Paul persevered in spite of suffering (1:11–12; 2:8–13) because he had an eternal perspective (4:6–8), but **Demas** abandoned Paul because **he loved this present world.** **Crescens** is otherwise unknown. For **Titus,** see the introduction to the book of Titus.
4:11 In spite of his earlier disapproval of Mark (Ac 15:36–40), Paul now desired Mark's presence and considered him **useful . . . in the ministry.**
4:12–13 Tychicus was a coworker (Ti 3:12) who carried two of Paul's earlier prison letters to churches—Ephesians (Eph 6:21) and Colossians (Col 4:7). The identity of the writings Paul wanted is unknown, but they likely included Scripture.
4:14–15 The **Alexander** mentioned here cannot be identified with certainty. Paul mentioned an Alexander in 1Tm 1:20 as a person

---

theological beliefs, we have lost the ability to do theology and know truth in a universal, objective way.

Today we face an authority crisis in every direction. Whether in issues of morality, philosophy, or religion, we live in a pluralistic age that has no grounds for saying that something is right while something else is wrong or that something is true while something else is false. We have witnessed a massive loss of confidence in the concept of truth in the academy, on the street, and even in the pew. We have lost any sense that "God has spoken" authoritatively and definitively. Nevertheless, Scripture says the opposite. The God who is has spoken, and as such, there are universal, objective grounds for morality, human thought, and theology, rooted in Scripture as God's authoritative written Word.

did great harm to me. The Lord will repay him according to his works. [15] Watch out for him yourself because he strongly opposed our words. [16] At my first defense, no one stood by me, but everyone deserted me. May it not be counted against them. [17] But the Lord stood with me and strengthened me, so that I might fully preach the word and all the Gentiles might hear it. So I was rescued from the lion's mouth. [18] The Lord will rescue me from every evil work and will bring me safely into his heavenly kingdom. To him be the glory forever and ever! Amen.

Benediction

[19] Greet Prisca and Aquila, and the household of Onesiphorus. [20] Erastus has remained at Corinth; I left Trophimus sick at Miletus. [21] Make every effort to come before winter. Eubulus greets you, as do Pudens, Linus, Claudia, and all the brothers and sisters. [22] The Lord be with your spirit. Grace be with you all.

---

who had been excommunicated. He may have still been in Ephesus causing trouble. Or, since he is identified as a **coppersmith**, and there is evidence of a guild of coppersmiths in Troas, this may refer to a different man living in Troas. This would explain his appearance here after Paul asked Timothy to visit Troas (v. 13).
4:16 In his forgiveness of others, Paul followed the teaching and model of Jesus (Lk

23:34), the practice of Stephen whom Paul saw die (Ac 7:60), and his own teaching (1Co 13:5).
4:17 Deliverance from a **lion's mouth** was a common biblical metaphor for rescue from great danger (Ps 22:21).
4:19 Prisca is a variant of Priscilla. This is a reference to the Priscilla and **Aquila** often mentioned in connection with Paul (e.g., Rm 16:3; 1Co 16:19).

4:20 On **Erastus**, see Rm 16:23.
4:21 This verse repeats the essence of v. 9. Travel in the Mediterranean area was usually suspended during **winter** because the weather resulted in dangerous conditions on land and sea.
4:22 Paul used the phrase **be with your spirit** also in his closing in Gl 6:18; Php 4:23; Phm 25.

⃔ Introduction to Titus

Circumstances of Writing

As stated in the opening of the letter, Titus was written by Paul (Ti 1:1). However, many scholars today assume that Paul did not write Titus. This opinion is based on the differences from his other letters in vocabulary and style, alleged differences in theology, and uncertainties about where Titus along with 1 and 2 Timothy fit chronologically in the life of the apostle. But the differences in style and vocabulary are not troublesome when one considers that authors often use different vocabulary when addressing different groups and situations. Rather than addressing churches in these Pastoral Epistles, Paul was writing to coworkers who were in unique ministry settings. Hence we would expect different vocabulary. Also, the traditional view of the historical situation in which Paul wrote Titus is reasonable and defensible. Therefore, in spite of significant opposition by some scholars, there is a solid basis for accepting the Pastoral Epistles as Pauline.

Paul most likely wrote Titus after the time covered in the book of Acts. Acts closes with Paul in prison. Traditionally it has been believed that Paul was released from this imprisonment, then continued his work around the Mediterranean, perhaps even reaching Spain (Rm 15:22–29). During this time, he visited Crete and other places. Titus was written during this period of further mission work. Titus had been left in Crete after the initial work to set up the church there (Ti 1:5). Eventually Paul was imprisoned again, and this led to his execution.

Contribution to the Bible

Titus is rich theologically and ethically. One of the key contributions is the clear way it shows the connection between doctrine and ethics, belief and behavior.

While this letter was not intended to provide a detailed account of church government, it does provide some significant insights on this topic.

Structure

Titus follows the typical pattern of a Greek epistle. Although there are some lexical differences with many of Paul's other letters, keep in mind that this letter is written to a specific individual. One thing unique to the structure of this letter is the focus on church leadership.

See the introduction to 1 Timothy for the timeline.

Outline

Greeting

1 Paul, a servant of God and an apostle of Jesus Christ, for[A] the faith of God's elect and their knowledge of the truth that leads[B] to godliness, [2] in the hope of eternal life that God, who cannot lie, promised before time began. [3] In his own time he has revealed his word in the preaching with which I was entrusted by the command of God our Savior:

[4] To Titus, my true son in our common faith.

Grace and peace from God the Father and Christ Jesus our Savior.

Titus's Ministry in Crete

[5] The reason I left you in Crete was to set right what was left undone and, as I directed you, to appoint elders in every town. [6] An elder must be blameless, the husband of one wife, with faithful[C] children who are not accused of wildness or rebellion. [7] As an overseer of God's household, he must be blameless, not arrogant, not hot-tempered, not an excessive drinker, not a bully, not greedy for money, [8] but hospitable, loving what is good, sensible, righteous, holy, self-controlled, [9] holding to the faithful message as taught, so that he will be able both to encourage with sound teaching and to refute those who contradict it.

[10] For there are many rebellious people, full of empty talk and deception, especially those from the circumcision party. [11] It is necessary to silence them; they are ruining entire households by teaching what they shouldn't in order to get money dishonestly. [12] One of their very own prophets said, "Cretans are always liars, evil beasts, lazy gluttons." [13] This testimony is true. For this reason, rebuke them sharply, so that they may be sound in the faith [14] and may not pay attention to Jewish myths and the commands of people who reject the truth.

[15] To the pure, everything is pure, but to those who are defiled and unbelieving nothing is

---

[A]1:1 Or *according to*   [B]1:1 Or *corresponds*   [C]1:6 Or *believing*

1:1 The word **truth** refers to the gospel specifically, and this gospel leads to **godliness**. **1:2–4** Biblical **hope** is certainty not wishful thinking. It is a vital part of the message of the gospel that Paul preached. The fact that God cannot **lie** is also declared in Nm 23:19 and 1Sm 15:29. Paul identified **Titus** as **my true son**. The words recall what Paul said of Timothy (1Tm 1:2; 2Tm 1:2). **1:5** On **elders**, see notes at 1Tm 3:1,2–7. **1:6** On **husband of one wife**, see note at 1Tm 3:2. **With faithful children** assumes, but does not require, such men will likely have children at home still under their authority. The word "faithful" can also be translated

"believing." The parallel passage in 1Tm 3 speaks only to the children being well behaved, not to their conversion. Thus, Paul was requiring elders to govern the behavior of their children, not allowing them to be characterized with **wildness or rebellion**. **1:7–8** The **overseer** is not a separate office but is another word for elder. The list of characteristics is very similar to that found in 1Tm 3:2–7. **1:9** By placing **teaching** last in his list, Paul emphasized the importance of an "overseer" (v. 7) being able to teach. The reason for this is clear from what follows (vv. 10–16). **1:10–11** The elders were to be equipped and prepared to refute the false teachers.

Paul's description—**they are ruining entire households . . . to get money dishonestly**—recalls his words in 1Tm 6:5 and 2Tm 3:6. **1:14** On **myths**, see note at 1Tm 1:4. The specific content of the "myths" and **commands** Paul had in mind in the present verse is unstated, but the false teaching in Titus is more explicitly tied to a **Jewish** background (v. 10) than that referenced in 1 and 2 Timothy. **1:15** This statement echoes Jesus's teaching (Lk 11:41) and Paul's earlier writing (Rm 14:20). The issue here was probably Jewish food laws. The false teachers seemed to be concerned with this ritual purity, but were nevertheless defiled by their own unbelief and sin.

Q&A: Can something be true for you but not true for me?

by Dillon Burroughs

Have you ever heard someone say, "That might be true for you, but it's not true for me"? This popular expression reflects a philosophy known as *relativism*. Simply put, relativism says objective standards for belief and morality do not exist. All points of view are said to be equally valid. All truths and moral decisions are relative to you as an individual.

Certainly, we can have differing opinions about the best sports teams or styles of music or flavors of ice cream. But what about concrete things like math, science, history, and whether or not murder is wrong?

Two plus two equals four—no matter what we think. Gravity keeps us from flying into space, no matter what we believe about the cause or reality of gravity. As for history, events in the past cannot be altered by our opinions or beliefs. What has happened has happened, *period*. And regarding murder, who would dare to argue that the cold-blooded, unjustified killing of another human being could be wrong for some but right for others?

What about religion? Can religious truth be relative, true for some and not true for others? Keep in mind that religions make fundamental claims about such things as the nature of God, the origin and purpose of the universe, the meaning of human life, and the existence of an afterlife. Are these merely matters of opinion, and can contradictory opinions all count as true? No.

Consider the opening claim of the Bible: "In the beginning God created . . ." This contradicts all religious views that say the world is eternal or else was created by multiple gods or some god other than the biblical God. Is the Bible correct or not in its claim? Either this God made the world, or he did not. There is no third option in which it is true for me that God created the universe but not true for you. There can only be one right answer.

When a person says your religious belief is true for you but not for them, what they really mean is, "You believe that is true, but I believe differently." The two of you hold differing beliefs about questions to which there is only one right answer. Consider these other yes-or-no questions:

· Are human beings born with a sinful nature?

· Is Jesus the Son of God?

· Is there only one way to know God and receive eternal life?

· Did Jesus physically rise to life after his death?

These are foundational beliefs of Christianity. There can only be one correct answer to such questions. The Bible allows for variation of opinion in many areas of life, but some things are true for all people in all places.

So when someone suggests that your religious beliefs can be true for you but not for them, gently point out that some things are either true or not. Jesus really is God's Son, sent to die and rise again on our behalf. This good news is true for *everyone*.

pure; in fact, both their mind and conscience are defiled. [16] They claim to know God, but they deny him by their works. They are detestable, disobedient, and unfit for any good work.

Sound Teaching and Christian Living

2 But you are to proclaim things consistent with sound teaching. [2] Older men are to be self-controlled, worthy of respect, sensible, and sound in faith, love, and endurance. [3] In the same way, older women are to be reverent in behavior, not slanderers, not slaves to excessive drinking. They are to teach what is good, [4] so that they may encourage the young women to love their husbands and to love their children, [5] to be self-controlled, pure, workers at home, kind, and in submission to their husbands, so that God's word will not be slandered. [6] In the same way, encourage the young men to be self-controlled [7] in everything. Make yourself an example of good works with integrity and dignity[A] in your teaching. [8] Your message is to be sound beyond reproach, so that any opponent will be ashamed, because he doesn't have anything bad to say about us. [9] Slaves are to submit to their masters in everything, and to be well-pleasing, not talking back [10] or stealing, but demonstrating utter faithfulness, so that they may adorn the teaching of God our Savior in everything.

[11] For the grace of God has appeared, bringing salvation[B] for all people, [12] instructing us to deny godlessness and worldly lusts and to live in a sensible, righteous, and godly way in the present age, [13] while we wait for the blessed hope, the appearing of the glory of our great God and Savior, Jesus Christ. [14] He gave himself for us to redeem us from all lawlessness and to cleanse for himself a people for his own possession, eager to do good works.

[15] Proclaim these things; encourage and rebuke with all authority. Let no one disregard[C] you.

Christian Living among Outsiders

3 Remind them to submit to rulers and authorities, to obey, to be ready for every good work, [2] to slander no one, to avoid fighting, and to be kind, always showing gentleness to all people. [3] For we too were once foolish, disobedient, deceived, enslaved by various passions and pleasures, living in malice and envy, hateful, detesting one another. [4] But when the kindness of God our Savior and his love for mankind appeared, [5] he saved us — not by works of righteousness that we had done, but according to his mercy — through the washing of regeneration and renewal by the Holy Spirit. [6] He poured out his Spirit on us abundantly through Jesus Christ our Savior [7] so that, having been justified by his grace, we may become heirs with the hope of eternal life. [8] This saying is trustworthy. I want you to insist on these things, so that those who have believed God might be careful to devote themselves to good works. These are good and profitable for

---

[A] 2:7 Other mss add *and incorruptibility*   [B] 2:11 Or *appeared with saving power*   [C] 2:15 Or *despise*

1:16 The actions (**works**) of these people proved conclusively that they were unbelievers, although they claimed to **know God**. The three descriptors at the end of the verse summarize the behavior that proved they did not know God.
2:1 The intentional contrast, **but you**, must not be missed. Titus in contrast to the false teachers was to teach the believers to live in a way **consistent with sound teaching**.
2:2 Older men are to strive toward four characteristics. The fourth characteristic is split into three. They are to aim for soundness in **faith**, in **love** for others, and **endurance** or perseverance.
2:3–5 **Older women** can help model for **young women** what it means to be a wife and mother.
2:6–7 **Young men** are to be **self-controlled**, meaning "prudent" or "sensible." The word is also found in the instructions for older men (v. 2, "sensible") and young women (v. 5, "self-controlled"). Titus was to be an **example** for the young men. Therefore, young men were to exhibit **good works** . . . **integrity**, and **dignity**.
2:9–10 The words used to describe desirable behavior in slaves can apply equally to workers in general (see Eph 6:5–8; Col 3:22–24; 1Tm 6:1–2).
2:11–14 This paragraph provides the theological basis for the lifestyle commended in vv. 1–10. Christians should live sanctified lives because the grace of God that saves us also instructs us to live in a new way.

2:11 This verse has sometimes been misunderstood as saying that all people will be saved. However, such a reading flatly contradicts other portions of Scripture. The force of **all people** is to emphasize the universal offer of the gospel.
2:12 **Godlessness** refers to behavior that is not in accordance with God's ways. **Lusts** refer not only to sexual desires but to sinful desires in general.
2:13 The verb used here for **wait** often carries a connotation of eagerness. The **blessed hope** is **the appearing of** . . . **Christ**. The reference to Jesus as **God and Savior** is a strong affirmation of his deity.
2:14 The phrase **people for his own possession** translates an unusual phrase with intentional echoes from the OT (Ex 19:5; Mal 3:17). The phrase expresses the sense of "prized, treasured possession" (see 1Pt 2:9).
2:15 This verse is an unmistakable call for authoritative teaching in the church.
3:1–2 The phrase **ready for every good work** refers back to 1:16 and 2:14. The false teachers were "unfit for any good work" (1:16). One of the purposes of the cross was to create a people "eager to do good works" (2:14). And here, in contrast to the false teachers, Titus was to teach the people to be "ready for every good work."
3:3–7 These verses provide the doctrinal basis for the teaching in vv. 1–2.

3:4 The words **kindness of God** . . . **and his love for mankind** stand in stark contrast to the description of lost humanity in v. 3.
3:5 Salvation comes **not by works** but through the washing of **regeneration and renewal by the Holy Spirit**. The washing described here is the spiritual cleansing that is symbolized outwardly by water baptism.
3:6–7 Part of our salvation involves receiving the **Spirit** whom Jesus **poured out** . . . **on us**.
3:8 The command **to insist on these things** is similar to 2:15. Note the emphasis on **good works** as a mark of believers (v. 1; 1:16; 2:14).

#86 **99 Essential Christian Truths**

CHRIST'S EXALTATION

Whereas the death of Christ was the ultimate example of his humiliation, his resurrection from the dead is the first and glorious example of his exaltation. Christ was exalted when God raised him from the dead and when he ascended to the Father's right hand. He will be exalted by all creation when he returns. All of these aspects of his exaltation magnify the glory and worth of Christ, resulting in the praise of the glory of his grace in rescuing sinners.

everyone. ⁹ But avoid foolish debates, genealogies, quarrels, and disputes about the law, because they are unprofitable and worthless. ¹⁰ Reject a divisive person after a first and second warning. ¹¹ For you know that such a person has gone astray and is sinning; he is self-condemned.

Final Instructions and Closing

¹² When I send Artemas or Tychicus to you, make every effort to come to me in Nicopolis, because I have decided to spend the winter there. ¹³ Diligently help Zenas the lawyer and Apollos on their journey, so that they will lack nothing.

¹⁴ Let our people learn to devote themselves to good works for pressing needs, so that they will not be unfruitful. ¹⁵ All those who are with me send you greetings. Greet those who love us in the faith. Grace be with all of you.

3:9 As elsewhere in the letters to Timothy and Titus, the exact nature of these **debates** and **quarrels** is not clear (e.g., 1:10–14). The point is that these **disputes** were **worthless**. 3:10–11 A divisive person who refused to repent and change after being confronted showed himself to be twisted by sin; thus, he was **self-condemned**. See Mt 18:15–17 for

Jesus's description of the stages of church discipline.
3:12–13 Apparently Paul had not decided which of the two men to send to Crete to replace Titus, or when. Before that, Paul was sending **Zenas** and **Apollos** through Crete, perhaps with this letter. **Nicopolis** was a port city about two hundred miles northwest of Athens.

3:14 Paul paused once more to emphasize the importance of **good works**.
3:15 The plural greeting **grace be with all of you** appears odd in a letter addressed to an audience of one (Titus), but it shows Paul's awareness (and likely his intention) that the letter would be read to the entire congregation.

◥ Introduction to Philemon

Circumstances of Writing

During Paul's two-year imprisonment in Rome (Ac 28:30), probably during AD 60–61, he wrote four letters called the Prison Epistles, one of which is Philemon (the others are Ephesians, Philippians, and Colossians).

References to Paul's being in prison at the time of writing are found in verses 1,9–10,13, and perhaps 23. Paul was kept under house arrest—what the Romans called "free custody"—in his own rented house as he awaited trial (Ac 28:30).

Although Paul addresses the letter to Apphia, Archippus, and the church that meets in Philemon's house (vv. 1–2), the main addressee is Philemon himself, for "you" or "your" (vv. 2,4–21,23) is singular and refers to Philemon. Apparently he was a prosperous businessman living in Colossae (implied in Col 4:9) whose household included several slaves and whose house was large enough to accommodate meetings of the young church. He had been converted through Paul's ministry, perhaps by Paul himself (vv. 10,19), and had become Paul's "dear friend and coworker" (v. 1) and "partner" (v. 17) in the gospel service. Although the letter is basically Paul's personal appeal to Philemon, the plural "you" (vv. 3,22) and "your" (vv. 22,25) indicate that the whole church would have listened to its reading and thus been witnesses of Philemon's response to Paul's requests.

Onesimus had apparently run away and taken with him some of his master's money or possessions (vv. 15,18). Perhaps attracted by the anonymity of a large, distant city, he traveled to Rome seeking a life of freedom. His path crossed Paul's, and he became a Christian (vv. 10,16) and a useful helper to Paul (v. 11).

An alternative view denies that Onesimus was a runaway looking for freedom. It instead suggests that he left Philemon and looked for Paul so that Paul could become his advocate regarding some serious loss Philemon had experienced. All along Onesimus had intended to return to his master's household. Paul was therefore not guilty of harboring a fugitive slave. But on this view we would expect Paul to reassure Philemon that Onesimus had always intended to return.

Contribution to the Bible

Although it is the shortest and most personal of Paul's letters, Philemon was included in the New Testament canon for several reasons.

First, it illustrates the breaking down of social and cultural barriers that occurred between Christians (see Gl 3:28). Paul, a highly educated Roman citizen, takes up the cause of a poor runaway slave whose life was in danger because of his theft and flight (Phm 18). Social and cultural barriers are eliminated in Christian fellowship.

Second, it reflects early Christian attitudes toward slavery. Although Paul accepts (but does not endorse) slavery as an existing social condition and as a legal fact (v. 12),

---

he emphasizes Onesimus's higher identity as a Christian brother and sets the master-slave relationship on a new footing (v. 16) and so ultimately undermines the institution of slavery. This contrasts with dominant views of the ancient world. For instance, Aristotle defined a slave as "a living tool, just as a tool is an inanimate slave" (*Nicomachean Ethics* 8.11.6).

Third, it shows a skillful pastor at work: Paul gives up his apostolic right to issue commands (vv. 8–9) and prefers to appeal to Philemon's free choice (vv. 10,14) to follow his Christian conscience in deciding how his love should be expressed (vv. 5,7); he identifies with Onesimus, his spiritual son (v. 10), calling him "my very own heart" (v. 12) and guaranteeing to repay his debts (vv. 18–19); and he gives his requests to Philemon in the hearing of the whole local church (vv. 1–3,22–25).

Fourth, it pictures the heart of the gospel (vv. 16–19). When we come to God in repentance and faith, he gives us a new status and welcomes us as if we were Christ. What we owe God, he has debited to Christ's account. Christ assumed personal responsibility for the full repayment of our debt to God.

Outline

I. Address and Greetings (vv. 1–3)
II. Thanksgiving for Philemon's Faith and Love (vv. 4–7)
III. Paul's Appeal for Onesimus (vv. 8–20)
IV. Plans and Hopes for a Visit (vv. 21–22)
V. Final Greeting (vv. 23–25)

---

104 BC–AD 54

Second Roman slave revolt in Sicily **104–101 BC**
Third Roman slave revolt
  led by the gladiator Spartacus **73–71 BC**
By the time Augustus becomes Roman emperor, there are some 3 million slaves of a total population of 7.5 million Romans. **31 BC**
In his *Geographia*, Strabo says there are more than 1,000 temple slaves—prostitutes—in the temple of Aphrodite in 6th-century-BC Corinth. **AD 20**
Roman Emperor Claudius rules that a slave who was old or sick and abandoned by his master should be considered free. **AD 41–54**

AD 60–407

During Nero's rule, slaves gain the right to complain against their masters in court. **54–68**
Paul arrives in Rome. **60**
Paul encounters Onesimus, a runaway slave from Colossae. **61**
Paul writes his letter to Philemon and sends it and the letter to the Colossians by Tychicus and Onesimus. **61**
Gregory of Nyssa **(D. 395)** and Chrysostom **(347–407)** oppose slavery based on Christian theology.

Greeting

P aul, a prisoner of Christ Jesus, and Timothy our brother:

To Philemon our dear friend and coworker, [2] to Apphia our sister,[A] to Archippus our fellow soldier, and to the church that meets in your home.

[3] Grace to you and peace from God our Father and the Lord Jesus Christ.

Philemon's Love and Faith

[4] I always thank my God when I mention you in my prayers, [5] because I hear of your love for all the saints and the faith that you have in the Lord Jesus. [6] I pray that your participation in the faith may become effective through knowing every good thing that is in us[B] for the glory of Christ. [7] For I have great joy and encouragement from your love, because the hearts of the saints have been refreshed through you, brother.

An Appeal for Onesimus

[8] For this reason, although I have great boldness in Christ to command you to do what is right, [9] I appeal to you, instead, on the basis of love. I, Paul, as an elderly man[C] and now also as a prisoner of Christ Jesus, [10] appeal to you for my son, Onesimus.[D] I became his father while I was in chains. [11] Once he was useless to you, but now he is useful both to you and to me. [12] I am sending him back to you — I am sending my very own heart.[E,F] [13] I wanted to keep him with me, so that in my imprisonment for the gospel he might serve me in your place. [14] But I didn't want to do anything without your consent, so that your good deed might not be out of obligation, but of your own free will. [15] For perhaps this is why he was separated from you for a brief time, so that you might get him back permanently, [16] no longer as a slave, but more than a slave — as a dearly loved brother. He is especially so to me, but how much more to you, both in the flesh and in the Lord.

[17] So if you consider me a partner, welcome him as you would me. [18] And if he has wronged you in any way, or owes you anything, charge that to my account. [19] I, Paul, write this with my own hand: I will repay it — not to mention to you that you owe me even your very self. [20] Yes, brother, may I benefit from you in the Lord; refresh my heart in Christ. [21] Since I am confident of your obedience, I am writing to you, knowing that you will do even more than I say. [22] Meanwhile, also prepare a guest room for me, since I hope that through your prayers I will be restored to you.

[A]2 Other mss read our beloved   [B]6 Other mss read in you   [C]9 Or an ambassador   [D]10 In Gk, Onesimus means "useful"   [E]12 Other mss read him back. Receive him, my own heart.   [F]12 Lit you — that is, my own heart

---

1 In the phrase **of Christ Jesus**, "of" may mean "belonging to," "for the sake of," or "because of [my service for]." **Timothy** is associated with Paul as co-author or co-sender, but the letter is primarily Paul's own intercession with Philemon on behalf of Onesimus, for only the singular "I" (not "we") is found in vv. 4–22.
2 Apphia was probably Philemon's wife and **Archippus** their son.
3 This was Paul's standard greeting.
4 Paul's letters usually begin with prayers of thanksgiving for his readers' spiritual life and progress (e.g., Rm 1:8; 1Co 1:4–7; Php 1:3–5).
6–7 Paul prays that Philemon's faith would work out in his intuition of what is **good** and right. Paul goes on to outline what is good in the rest of the letter.
8–11 Paul wants Philemon's consent out of **love** rather than his obedience. That Paul **became** the **father** of Onesimus while **in chains** means somehow Onesimus had been converted during Paul's prison sentence (1Co 4:15). Through the conversion power of the gospel, a person who had previously been **useless** (Gk achrestos) had become **useful** (Gk euchrestos), now living up to his name (Onesimus means "useful" in Greek).
12 A runaway slave who was returned to his rightful owner could face a variety of punishments, including flogging, branding, chains, or even crucifixion.
15–16 Paul implies that Onesimus's separation from Philemon, which was caused by the slave's unlawful departure, was encompassed within the gracious, providential will of God.

Upon his return, Onesimus would be even dearer to Philemon as a Christian brother (**in the Lord**).
17 Here Paul finally specifies what he is asking Philemon. Paul is asking him to treat Onesimus just as Paul would be treated, as a fellow Christian.
18 The wrong that Onesimus had done may have been some misconduct before he ran away, a theft when he disappeared, or the loss Philemon suffered by Onesimus's unlawful absence.
19 Following his usual practice of dictating his letters to a scribe (see Rm 16:22), Paul may have written this short and intensely personal letter by his own hand (see also 1Co 16:21; Gl 6:11; Col 4:18; 2Th 3:17). In any case, Paul here is giving a promissory note, a signed statement of indebtedness (Gk cheirographon in Col 2:14),

by which he formally and legally assumes all of Onesimus's indebtedness toward Philemon. That Philemon owed Paul his **very self** probably means Paul had led Philemon to the Lord.
21 By **your obedience**, Paul could have meant obedience to God's will, obedience to his own requests as a friend and "prisoner of Christ Jesus" (v. 1), or obedience to "what is right" (v. 8). The undefined and climactic **you will do even more** could refer to the forgiveness of Onesimus and his reinstatement as a slave in Philemon's household. More likely it refers to the setting free (manumission) of Onesimus, allowing him to enter Christian service there at Colossae or at Rome with Paul.
22 The request for **a guest room** suggests Paul expected to be released from prison and pay Philemon a visit.

#87 99 Essential Christian Truths

SECOND COMING OF CHRIST

The Bible is clear that one day Christ will return in bodily form (Mt 24–25) to rule and reign over all creation. Scripture gives no timeline as to when it will occur (Ac 1:7), only assuring that it will be unexpected (Mt 25:8–10) and glorious (Mt 24:30). Because of the mystery surrounding these events, several views have emerged through Christians' attempts to understand everything the Bible teaches about this return and his millennial reign. One view holds that, upon his return, Jesus will begin a literal one-thousand-year reign on earth. Another holds that this millennium occurs in this church age, to be followed by his return. Yet another holds that the millennium symbolically represents Christ's reign in heaven and in the hearts of God's people while we wait for his return. Despite these differences, all views agree that the imminent return of Christ is the hope of all Christians, who know that when Christ returns, all things will be made new.

Final Greetings

²³ Epaphras, my fellow prisoner in Christ Jesus, sends you greetings, and so do ²⁴ Mark, Aristarchus, Demas, and Luke, my coworkers.

²⁵ The grace of the Lord^ Jesus Christ be with your spirit.

^25 Other mss read *our Lord*

23–24 For these names, see notes at Col 4:10,12,14.
25 All of Paul's letters begin and end with a reference to **grace** (Gk *charis*), God's unsought and undeserved favor, his free and unmerited saving action.

◥ Introduction to Hebrews

Circumstances of Writing

The text of Hebrews does not identify its author. What we do know is that the author was a second-generation Christian, for he said he received the confirmed message of Christ from "those who heard" Jesus himself (2:3). Because Paul claimed his gospel was revealed directly by the Lord (1Co 15:8; Gl 1:12), it is doubtful that he was the author of Hebrews. The author was familiar with Timothy, but he referred to him as "our brother" (13:23), rather than as "my true son in the faith," as did Paul (1Tm 1:2).

Scholars have also proposed the following people as authors: Luke, Clement of Rome, Barnabas, Apollos, Timothy, Philip, Peter, Silas, Jude, and Aristion. Ultimately it does not matter that the identity of the author is now lost. We should be satisfied with the fact that early Christians received the letter as inspired and authoritative Scripture and that its value for Christian discipleship is unquestioned.

The author of Hebrews knew his recipients well, calling them "brothers and sisters" (3:12; 7:5; 10:19; 13:22) and "dearly loved friends" (6:9). Like the writer, they were converts who had heard the gospel through the earliest followers of Christ (2:3). Scholars have speculated that those to whom the book was written were a breakaway group, such as a house church that had separated from the main church. Another theory holds that the recipients were former Jewish priests who had converted to Christianity and were considering a return to Judaism (at least in conformity to certain practices) to avoid persecution from fellow Jews. Another theory holds that the group was not necessarily Jewish since Gentile Christians also revered the Old Testament as Scripture.

Regarding when the book was written, it is clear that the fall of Jerusalem (AD 70) had not yet occurred. The destruction of the temple would have been mentioned if it had already occurred, for it would have strengthened the letter's argument about Christ's sacrifice spelling the end of the temple sacrificial system. The public persecution mentioned in 10:32–34 implies one of two possibilities for dating the book. We know that Roman Emperors Nero and Domitian (in AD 64–68 and 81–82 respectively) persecuted Christians. Most likely, Hebrews was written during the persecution under Nero, perhaps just before the destruction of the temple.

Contribution to the Bible

No other book in the New Testament ties together Old Testament history and practices with the life of Jesus Christ as thoroughly as the book of Hebrews. Just as Jesus Christ taught that the Old Testament was fulfilled in himself (Mt 5:17–18; Lk 24:27), so the author of Hebrews taught that the old covenant was brought to completion in the new covenant (7:20–8:13). Hebrews also shows that because the old covenant has been fulfilled in the new covenant,

―――――― PREHISTORY–1900 BC ――――――

Abel offers a better sacrifice than Cain.
Abraham moves from Haran to Canaan. **2091**
Sarah conceives at age ninety. **2066**
Abraham offers up Isaac in obedience to God's command. **2046?**
Isaac blesses Jacob and Esau. **1930?**

―――――― 1900–1445 BC ――――――

Jacob blesses Joseph's sons, Ephraim and Manasseh. **1859**
Birth of Moses **1526**
Exodus from Egypt and defeat of Pharaoh at the Red Sea **1446**
God's awesome manifestation and covenant with Israel at Sinai **1446**
Tabernacle is built and dedicated **1445**

the new covenant is "better" (7:22). The new covenant was made superior by the ministry of Jesus Christ.

Structure

In concluding the book of Hebrews, the author wrote, "I urge you to receive this message of exhortation, for I have written to you briefly" (13:22). If the literary style of Hebrews indicates anything, it is that it is a written theological sermon. It is not so much a letter—although it certainly ends like one—because it has no opening subscription, as was the norm with ancient letters. Hebrews instead begins with an introductory essay about the superiority of Jesus Christ (1:1–4). However, its capacity to encounter the reader's soul indicates it is more than just a literary essay. Indeed, it has a definite sermonic character since it expounds the Scriptures at length in order to challenge the reader to faith and faithfulness. The sustained development of a complex, holistic theology of covenant indicates that Hebrews is a written theological sermon that discloses the broad sweep of God's grand redemptive plan for humanity.

Outline

1445–1125 BC

Israel wanders in the wilderness. **1445–1407**
Rahab supports the conquest of Jericho. **1406**
Deborah and Barak defeat the Canaanites. **1320?**
GIDEON 1250–1175?
JEPHTHAH 1200–1150?

1125 BC–AD 95

SAMSON 1120–1060 BC?
SAMUEL 1105–1025 BC?
DAVID 1050–970 BC
Jesus's death, resurrection, and ascension **AD 33**
Hebrews is first quoted by Clement of Rome in his letter to the Corinthians. **AD 96**

The Nature of the Son

1 Long ago God spoke to our ancestors by the prophets at different times and in different ways. ² In these last days, he has spoken to us by his Son. God has appointed him heir of all things and made the universe^A through him. ³ The Son is the radiance^B of God's glory and the exact expression^C of his nature, sustaining all things by his powerful word. After making purification for sins,^D he sat down at the right hand of the Majesty on high.^E ⁴ So he became superior to the angels, just as the name he inherited is more excellent than theirs.

The Son Superior to Angels

⁵ For to which of the angels did he ever say,

You are my Son;
today I have become your Father,^F,G

or again,

I will be his Father,
and he will be my Son?^H

⁶ Again, when he' brings his firstborn into the world, he says,

And let all God's angels worship him.^J

⁷ And about the angels he says:

He makes his angels winds,^K
and his servants^L a fiery flame,^M

⁸ but to^N the Son:

Your throne, God,
is forever and ever,
and the scepter of your kingdom
is a scepter of justice.
⁹ You have loved righteousness
and hated lawlessness;
this is why God, your God,
has anointed you
with the oil of joy
beyond your companions.^O,P

¹⁰ And:

In the beginning, Lord,
you established the earth,
and the heavens are the works
of your hands;

¹¹ they will perish, but you remain.
They will all wear out
like clothing;
¹² you will roll them up like a cloak,^Q
and they will be changed
like clothing.
But you are the same,
and your years will never end.^R

¹³ Now to which of the angels has he ever said:

Sit at my right hand
until I make your enemies
your footstool?^S

¹⁴ Are they not all ministering spirits sent out to serve those who are going to inherit salvation?

Warning against Neglect

2 For this reason, we must pay attention all the more to what we have heard, so that we will not drift away. ² For if the message spoken through angels was legally binding^T and every transgression and disobedience received a just punishment, ³ how will we escape if we neglect such a great salvation? This salvation had its beginning when it was spoken of by the Lord, and it was confirmed to us by those who heard him. ⁴ At the same time, God also testified by signs and wonders, various miracles, and distributions of gifts from the Holy Spirit according to his will.

Jesus and Humanity

⁵ For he has not subjected to angels the world to come that we are talking about. ⁶ But someone somewhere has testified:

What is man that you remember him,
or the son of man that you care
for him?
⁷ You made him lower than the angels
for a short time;
you crowned him with glory
and honor^U
⁸ and subjected everything
under his feet.^V

---

^A 1:2 Lit ages   ^B 1:3 Or reflection   ^C 1:3 Or representation, or copy, or reproduction   ^D 1:3 Other mss read for our sins by himself   ^E 1:3 Or he sat down on high at the right hand of the Majesty   ^F 1:5 Or have begotten you   ^G 1:5 Ps 2:7   ^H 1:5 2Sm 7:14; 1Ch 17:13   ^I 1:6 Or When he again   ^J 1:6 Dt 32:43 LXX; Ps 97:7   ^K 1:7 Or spirits   ^L 1:7 Or ministers   ^M 1:7 Ps 104:4   ^N 1:8 Or about   ^O 1:9 Or associates   ^P 1:8–9 Ps 45:6–7   ^Q 1:12 Other mss omit like a cloak   ^R 1:10–12 Ps 102:25–27   ^S 1:13 Ps 110:1   ^T 2:2 Or valid, or reliable   ^U 2:7 Other mss add and set him over the works of your hands   ^V 2:6–8 Ps 8:4–6 LXX

1:1–2a These verses relate the revelation of Jesus Christ to God's previous revelation to the OT prophets.

1:2b–4 Seven praises start the letter's argument that Jesus Christ and everything connected with him is superior to all that had come before and all that will come after him. (1) Jesus Christ is the **heir** of creation for whom all things have been made. (2) He is the Creator through whom all things have come into existence. (3) He is the **radiance** of the divine glory toward which all of creation looks for fulfillment. (4) He is the **exact expression** of the *nature* of God the Father. (5) He is the "Word" of God, the only prophet of God who is also God himself. (6) He is the priest of God who has provided the perfect sacrifice for all human sins. (7) He is the King

who sits on the throne at the **right hand** of the Father.

1:5–14 Drawing on a series of OT quotations attributed to God, the author demonstrated how God the Father had addressed his Son as divine. God the Father addressed him uniquely as **my Son** (2Sm 7:14; 1Ch 17:13; Ps 2:7), **God** (Ps 45:6–7), and **Lord** (Ps 102:22). Moreover, God the Father attributed divine activities to his Son. He is the **firstborn** and "begotten" Son who was brought into the world so that all the angels must **worship him** (Dt 32:43; Ps 97:7). He is the Son who made the angels **his angels** and **his servants** (Ps 104:4). He is the Son who sits on the divine **throne** and rules with the divine attribute of **righteousness** (Ps 45:6–7). He is the Son who created heaven and earth in the

beginning, and who will remain the same when creation is consummated, because he shares in the divine attribute of the eternal (Ps 102:25–27).

2:1–18 In this chapter the author turned to consider Jesus as a human being. The author uses the fact that the law was **binding** to introduce the first of several strong exhortations in the book (3:7–19; 5:11–6:3; 10:26–31; 12:1–2,14–29). The gospel was verified to its first hearers by **signs and wonders**, various miracles, and distributions of gifts **from the Holy Spirit** as the church was in its foundational stages.

2:5–9 The author demonstrated that the eternal Son entered creation to become a man and thereby temporarily became **lower than the angels**. Psalm 8, on one level taken

A Biblical View of Angels

by Bruce A. Ware

Angels are created spirit beings. Some of them are holy and some are evil. Both in the Old Testament and the New Testament, the terms translated *angel* refer to one sent with a message or one acting as a messenger. The terms are used of human messengers in some instances (e.g., 1Sm 23:27; 1Kg 19:2; Lk 7:24; 9:52) and often in the Old Testament apply particularly to the angel of the Lord (e.g., Gn 16:7–14; Jdg 6:11–14; 2Sm 24:16; Zch 1:12–13). Most often, however, the terms are used for created spiritual beings (e.g., Ex 23:20; Mt 1:20; 4:11; 25:31,41).

The Origin of Angels

Because all that God creates and does is wholly good (Gn 1:31; Jms 1:17), we must understand angels, in their entire class, as created by God as good. Psalm 148:1–6 expresses praise to God for his creation of all things, and among those things specified are "all his angels" and "all his heavenly armies" (Ps 148:2). Furthermore, Colossians 1:16 makes clear that by Christ all things were created, including things "in heaven and on earth, the visible and the invisible" (cp. Rm 8:38–39). Also relevant is God's statement to Job (Jb 38:4–7) indicating that angels ("sons of God") were present and shouted for joy at the creation of the heavens and earth.

A difficult question concerns how some of the good angels God created have become evil. First, we must understand all fallen angels, in their originally created form, to have been wholly good. This was a goodness they forfeited, presumably, because of their rebellion against God. Two passages in particular lead us to think this is the case. Jude 6 and 2 Peter 2:4 both speak of angels who departed from God's purposes and hence received God's judgment and condemnation. When one adds to this the clear implication from Matthew 25:41 and Revelation 12:9 that demons are the followers of Satan, it seems obvious that these evil spirits, though created good, became evil as they followed their leader's enticement to sin against their Creator.

The Character of Holy Angels

Less is said in the Bible about the character of unfallen angels than about their activities, but some aspects of their character are evident.

1. They are personal beings with intelligence, emotions, and volition. We receive insights about their intelligence in 1 Peter 1:12, where they long to know more of God's salvation plan; in Revelation 17:1–18, where they know and communicate God's plans; and in Matthew 24:36, where they know much but not everything. Witness to their emotions is seen in Job 38:7, where they rejoice over God's creation; in Isaiah 6:1–4, where with awe and wonder they cry out "Holy, holy, holy" before God; in Luke 15:10, where they rejoice when sinners repent; and in Revelation 5:11–14, where they worship the Lamb who was slain. The idea that they have their own will is tied to passages such as Hebrews 1:6, where God appeals to their will to worship the Son, and 2 Peter 2:4, with its implication of some angels sinning in their choice to rebel against God.

2. They are spirit beings. Hebrews 1:14 calls angels "ministering spirits." In Luke 8:2 and 11:24 we see that demons are sometimes referred to as "evil spirits" or "unclean spirits," so presumably they are spirits by virtue of their being angels. But they can, for specific purposes, take on human form. We see this in Genesis 19:1, when the angels visit Sodom, and in Hebrews 13:2, which notes that one might unknowingly entertain angels.

3. They apparently are not sexual in that they do not marry and hence do not procreate. According to Matthew 22:30, in heaven people, like angels, will not marry or be given in marriage.

4. They exist forever. Luke 20:36 states that angels cannot die.

5. They are powerful (2Th 1:7). In 2 Kings 19:35 one angel sent by God destroyed 185,000 Assyrian soldiers, and in Daniel 6:22 an angel shut the lions' mouths.

6. They are holy. Angels are called "holy ones" and "holy angels" (Jb 5:1; Ps 89:7; Mk 8:38).

7. Although wondrous beings, they are not to be worshiped. In Colossians 2:18 the "worship of angels" is rejected. In

Revelation 19:10 and 22:8–9, John fell down to worship the angel, but the angel said to worship God.

The Functions and Ministry of Holy Angels

Angels are servants of God who surround his presence (Dn 7:9–10; Rv 5:11–14) and carry out his will in various ways on earth (e.g., Gn 32:1; 2Sm 24:16–17). Hebrews 1:14 calls them "ministering spirits." Specific functions of angels are spoken of throughout the Scriptures.

1. They worship God (e.g., Is 6:1–3; Lk 2:13–14; Rv 5:11–14).
2. They ministered with regard to Jesus during his earthly life. This is seen in Luke 1:11–20, where an angel appeared to Zacharias predicting John's birth; in Luke 2:26–38, where Gabriel appeared to Mary; in Matthew 1:20, where an angel appeared to Joseph; in Luke 2:8–15, where an angel appeared to the shepherds; in Matthew 2:13,19, where an angel told Joseph to go to Egypt and then back to Israel; in Matthew 4:11, where angels ministered to Jesus at his temptation; in Luke 22:43, where an angel strengthened Jesus in the garden; in Matthew 28:2–8, where an angel rolled away the stone and proclaimed Jesus's resurrection; and in Acts 1:10–11, where two angels foretold of Jesus's return.
3. They proclaim God's word and ordain the law. Evidence of their proclamation is in Luke 1:26–38 and Acts 27:23–24. Their work of ordaining appears in Acts 7:53; Galatians 3:19; and Hebrews 2:2.
4. They protect and deliver God's people as he directs. In Exodus 23:20–23 an angel protected Israel on entering the land. In 2 Kings 19:35 an angel killed 185,000 Assyrians. In Daniel 3:28 an angel delivered the three Hebrews in the furnace. In Daniel 6:22 an angel closed the lions' mouths. In Psalm 34:7 the angel of the Lord is said to encamp around those who fear him. In Acts 5:19 and 12:7 an angel delivered the apostles from prison.
5. They bear witness to and long to know more of God's salvific purposes (1Co 4:9; Eph 3:10; 1Pt 1:12; possibly also 1Co 11:10).
6. They will bear witness when Christ will confess or deny people "before the angels of God" (Lk 12:8–9).
7. Even before the final judgment, they play a role in God's reward of the righteous and punishment of the wicked. In Luke 16:22 angels take the poor man to Abraham's bosom. In Acts 12:23 an angel struck Herod dead for not giving glory to God.
8. They will come with Christ at his return to carry out his will—gathering his people and dispensing judgment on the wicked (Mt 13:39–42,49–50; 16:27; 24:30–31; 25:31; 2Th 1:7).
9. They are used by God to defeat evil powers and nations. This is evidenced in Daniel 10 (the intervention of the angel Michael to defeat ungodly forces). It also appears in Daniel 12:1 (Michael will rescue God's people from great distress) and in Revelation 12:7–9 (Michael and his angels defeat the dragon and his angels).
10. An angel binds Satan during the millennium (Rv 20:1–3).
11. They are stationed at the twelve gates of the New Jerusalem (Rv 21:12). In light of their continuous biblical role of ascribing praise to God, it stands to reason that angels will be among the great heavenly choir singing praises to God forevermore.

For in **subjecting everything** to him, he left nothing that is not subject to him. As it is, we do not yet see **everything subjected** to him. [9] But we do see Jesus — **made lower than the angels for a short time** so that by God's grace he might taste death for everyone — **crowned with glory and honor** because he suffered death.

[10] For in bringing many sons and daughters to glory, it was entirely appropriate that God — for whom and through whom all things exist — should make the pioneer[A] of their salvation perfect through sufferings. [11] For the one who sanctifies and those who are sanctified all have one Father.[B] That is why Jesus is not ashamed to call them brothers and sisters, [12] saying:

I will proclaim your name
to my brothers and sisters;
I will sing hymns to you
in the congregation.[C]

[13] Again, I will trust in him.[D] And again, Here I am with the children God gave me.[E]

[14] Now since the children have flesh and blood in common, Jesus also shared in these, so that through his death he might destroy the one holding the power of death — that is, the devil — [15] and free those who were held in slavery all their lives by the fear of death. [16] For it is clear that he does not reach out to help angels, but to help Abraham's offspring. [17] Therefore, he had to be like his brothers and sisters in every way, so that he could become a merciful and faithful high priest in matters[F] pertaining to God, to make atonement[G] for the sins of the people. [18] For since he himself has suffered when he was tempted, he is able to help those who are tempted.

Our Apostle and High Priest

3 Therefore, holy brothers and sisters, who share in a heavenly calling, consider Jesus, the apostle and high priest of our confession. [2] He was faithful to the one who appointed him, just as Moses was in all God's household. [3] For

Jesus is considered worthy of more glory than Moses, just as the builder has more honor than the house. [4] Now every house is built by someone, but the one who built everything is God. [5] Moses was faithful as a servant in all God's household, as a testimony to what would be said in the future. [6] But Christ was faithful as a Son over his household. And we are that household if we hold on to our confidence and the hope in which we boast.[H]

Warning against Unbelief

[7] Therefore, as the Holy Spirit says:

Today, if you hear his voice,
[8]   do not harden your hearts
        as in the rebellion,
    on the day of testing
        in the wilderness,
[9]   where your ancestors tested me,
        tried me,
    and saw my works [10] for forty years.
    Therefore I was provoked to anger
        with that generation
    and said, "They always go astray
        in their hearts,
    and they have not known my ways."
[11]   So I swore in my anger,
        "They will not enter my rest."[I]

[12] Watch out, brothers and sisters, so that there won't be in any of you an evil, unbelieving heart that turns away from the living God. [13] But encourage each other daily, while it is still called **today**, so that none of you is hardened by sin's deception. [14] For we have become participants in Christ if we hold firmly until the end the reality[J] that we had at the start. [15] As it is said:

Today, if you hear his voice,
do not harden your hearts
as in the rebellion.[K]

[16] For who heard and rebelled? Wasn't it all who came out of Egypt under Moses? [17] With whom was God angry for forty years? Wasn't it with those who sinned, whose bodies fell in the

---

[A]2:10 Or *source*, or *leader* [B]2:11 Or *father*, or *origin*; lit *all are of one* [C]2:12 Ps 22:22 [D]2:13 2Sm 22:3 LXX; Is 8:17 LXX; 12:2 LXX [E]2:13 Is 8:18 LXX [F]2:17 Lit *things* [G]2:17 Or *propitiation* [H]3:6 Other mss add *firm to the end* [I]3:7–11 Ps 95:7–11 [J]3:14 Or *confidence* [K]3:15 Ps 95:7–8

---

to be a reference to humankind and the dominion conferred on man by God, also applies to the **son of man** as Jesus Christ. Jesus was **crowned with glory and honor** by God because he suffered death for **everyone**.
2:10–18 In these verses the author showed why it was necessary that the eternal Son became a man. First, it was **appropriate** that the Son should have a ministry completed in suffering, with all human's experience, so that he might identify with us and bring **many sons and daughters** into the presence of God. The author quoted three OT verses to show that the Son is present in the gathered church (Ps 22:22), that the Son trusts the Father (Is 8:17), and that the church can come before the Father because it is united with Christ (Is 8:18). Second, the Son

became a man and suffered death so that he could **destroy the one holding the power of death—that is, the devil**. By virtue of Christ's death on our behalf we are freed from the fear of death. Third, the Son became a man and suffered death so that he could serve as a **faithful high priest** in service to God. The only person who can serve as a mediator between God and man is the one who is both God and man.
3:1–4:16 In these chapters the author turned from demonstrating the Son's superiority over the angels to demonstrating that the Son is superior to Moses, the mediator of the law, and Joshua, the conqueror of the promised land.
3:1–6 God had identified Moses as the one who was uniquely **faithful . . . in all God's**

household (see Nm 12:7). His faithfulness was for the sake of showing the superiority of the faithfulness of Christ, since Christ was faithful as **a Son over his household**. Jesus was faithful "over" the "household" of which Moses was a part. Jesus, who was faithful in his role of bringing the gospel to those under the condemnation of the law, is therefore **worthy of more glory**.
3:7–19 Having established the superiority of the gospel of Christ to the law of Moses, the author proceeded to explain the meaning of Ps 95. His purpose was to warn his readers that if the punishment for disobedience of the law was severe, then punishment for faithlessness to the gospel would be far worse. The result of such unbelief is divine judgment. They would **not enter** God's **rest**.

wilderness? [18] And to whom did he swear that they would not enter his rest, if not to those who disobeyed? [19] So we see that they were unable to enter because of unbelief.

The Promised Rest

4 Therefore, since the promise to enter his rest remains, let us beware^A that none of you be found to have fallen short.^B [2] For we also have received the good news just as they did. But the message they heard did not benefit them, since they were not united with those who heard it in faith.^C [3] For we who have believed enter the rest, in keeping with what^D he has said,

So I swore in my anger,
"They will not enter my rest,"^E

even though his works have been finished since the foundation of the world. [4] For somewhere he has spoken about the seventh day in this way: **And on the seventh day God rested from all his works.**^F [5] Again, in that passage he says, **They will never enter my rest.**^E

[6] Therefore, since it remains for some to enter it, and those who formerly received the good news did not enter because of disobedience, [7] he again specifies a certain day — **today.** He specified this speaking through David after such a long time:

Today, if you hear his voice,
do not harden your hearts.^G

[8] For if Joshua had given them rest, God would not have spoken later about another day. [9] Therefore, a Sabbath rest remains for God's people. [10] For the person who has entered his rest has rested from his own works, just as God did from his. [11] Let us, then, make every effort to enter that rest, so that no one will fall into the same pattern of disobedience.

[12] For the word of God is living and effective and sharper than any double-edged sword, penetrating as far as the separation of soul and spirit, joints and marrow. It is able to judge the thoughts and intentions of the heart. [13] No creature is hidden from him, but all things are naked and exposed to the eyes of him to whom we must give an account.

Our Great High Priest

[14] Therefore, since we have a great high priest who has passed through the heavens — Jesus the Son of God — let us hold fast to our confession. [15] For we do not have a high priest who is unable to sympathize with our weaknesses, but one who has been tempted in every way as we are, yet without sin. [16] Therefore, let us approach the throne of grace with boldness, so that we may receive mercy and find grace to help us in time of need.

Christ, a High Priest

5 For every high priest taken from among men is appointed in matters pertaining to God for the people, to offer both gifts and sacrifices for sins. [2] He is able to deal gently with those who are ignorant and are going astray, since he is also clothed with weakness. [3] Because of this, he must make an offering for his own sins as well as for the people. [4] No one takes this honor on himself; instead, a person is called by God, just as Aaron was. [5] In the same way, Christ did not exalt himself to become a high priest, but God who said to him,

You are my Son;
today I have become your Father,^H,I

[6] also says in another place,

You are a priest forever
according to the order
of Melchizedek.^J

[7] During his earthly life,^K he offered prayers and appeals with loud cries and tears to the one who was able to save him from death, and he was heard because of his reverence. [8] Although he was the Son, he learned obedience from what he suffered. [9] After he was perfected, he became the source of eternal salvation for all who obey him, [10] and he was declared by God a high priest according to the order of Melchizedek.

The Problem of Immaturity

[11] We have a great deal to say about this, and it is difficult to explain, since you have become

---

^A 4:1 Lit *fear*   ^B 4:1 Or *that any of you might seem to have missed it*   ^C 4:2 Other mss read *since it was not united by faith in those who heard*   ^D 4:3 Or *rest, just as*   ^E 4:3,5 Ps 95:11   ^F 4:4 Gn 2:2   ^G 4:7 Ps 95:7–8   ^H 5:5 Lit *I have begotten you*   ^I 5:5 Ps 2:7   ^J 5:6 Gn 14:18–20; Ps 110:4   ^K 5:7 Lit *In the days of his flesh*

4:1–16 If the result of unbelief and disobedience to God is exclusion from divine rest, then the result of true faith and faithfulness to God is entrance into everlasting divine rest. Such a rest was not available through the ministry of **Joshua** in the OT since it was reserved for the ministry of the NT "Joshua," **Jesus.** The ministry of Joshua did not bring people **Sabbath rest.** Only through the superior ministry of Jesus the Son of God may a person enter divine rest. Only through the **great high priest,** who has come from heaven and identified with human beings in their weakness, may we approach the **throne of grace** with **boldness.**

5:1–6:20 In these chapters the author established the superiority of Jesus as priest over Aaron as priest.

5:1–10 Aaron was the high priest of Israel who had been **called by God,** thus establishing his authority. His purpose as a priest was to offer to God **sacrifices for sins** on behalf of the people, and to **deal gently** with the ignorance and waywardness of the people on behalf of God. The problem with Aaron's priesthood was Aaron himself; since he was a sinner, he had to **make an offering for his own sins as well as for the people.**

Like Aaron, Jesus was called by God, but according to Ps 110:4, God gave him a unique

calling as **a high priest . . . according to the order of Melchizedek.** Christ's priesthood was on an entirely different level than that of Aaron. Unlike Aaron, the salvation that Christ brought was eternal.

The author speaks of Jesus as being **perfected** (v. 9; 2:10; 7:28). This is not a reference to *moral* perfection; the author has made clear that Jesus was "without sin" (4:15). Rather, Jesus was perfected in the sense of being qualified for his role as our great high priest.

5:11–6:3 In this section the author paused to consider the theological and moral state of his readers. He expressed concern that they

too lazy to understand. [12] Although by this time you ought to be teachers, you need someone to teach you the basic principles of God's revelation again. You need milk, not solid food. [13] Now everyone who lives on milk is inexperienced with the message about righteousness, because he is an infant. [14] But solid food is for the mature — for those whose senses have been trained to distinguish between good and evil.

Warning against Falling Away

6 Therefore, let us leave the elementary teaching about Christ and go on to maturity, not laying again a foundation of repentance from dead works, faith in God, [2] teaching about ritual washings,[A] laying on of hands, the resurrection of the dead, and eternal judgment. [3] And we will do this if God permits.

[4] For it is impossible to renew to repentance those who were once enlightened, who tasted the heavenly gift, who shared in the Holy Spirit, [5] who tasted God's good word and the powers of the coming age, [6] and who have fallen away. This is because,[B] to their own harm, they are recrucifying the Son of God and holding him up to contempt. [7] For the ground that drinks the rain that often falls on it and that produces vegetation useful to those for whom it is cultivated receives a blessing from God. [8] But if it produces thorns and thistles, it is worthless and about to be cursed, and at the end will be burned.

[9] Even though we are speaking this way, dearly loved friends, in your case we are confident of things that are better and that pertain to salvation. [10] For God is not unjust; he will not forget your work and the love[C] you demonstrated for his name by serving the saints

— and by continuing to serve them. [11] Now we desire each of you to demonstrate the same diligence for the full assurance of your hope until the end, [12] so that you won't become lazy but will be imitators of those who inherit the promises through faith and perseverance.

Inheriting the Promise

[13] For when God made a promise to Abraham, since he had no one greater to swear by, he swore by himself: [14] **I will indeed bless you, and I will greatly multiply you.**[D] [15] And so, after waiting patiently, Abraham obtained the promise. [16] For people swear by something greater than themselves, and for them a confirming oath ends every dispute. [17] Because God wanted to show his unchangeable purpose even more clearly to the heirs of the promise, he guaranteed it with an oath, [18] so that through two unchangeable things, in which it is impossible for God to lie, we who have fled for refuge might have strong encouragement to seize the hope set before us. [19] We have this hope as an anchor for the soul, firm and secure. It enters the inner sanctuary behind the curtain. [20] Jesus has entered there on our behalf as a forerunner, because he has become a high priest forever according to the order of Melchizedek.

The Greatness of Melchizedek

7 For this Melchizedek, king of Salem, priest of God Most High, met Abraham and blessed him as he returned from defeating the kings, [2] and Abraham gave him a tenth of everything. First, his name means king of righteousness, then also, king of Salem, meaning king of peace. [3] Without father, mother, or

---

might not understand the **difficult doctrines** he was explaining (5:11). Because of their immaturity, they needed to be warned about failure and encouraged toward maturity. The author listed six basic principles of the elementary message about Christ that serve as the foundation of the Christian faith and life. These principles may be divided into three groups of two each. (1) **Repentance** from sinful actions and **faith** toward God (6:1) are the two sides of conversion that begin the Christian life. (2) The baptism of new believers who have received the gospel and **laying on of hands** for Christian leaders (6:2) to proclaim the gospel are fundamental components of church life. (3) The good news of the **resurrection** and the prospect of **eternal judgment** (6:2) are essential components in the gospel that the church preaches.

6:4–20 Verses 6–9 have been the subject of much debate. There are several possible interpretations regarding the author's intentions and the identity of those who **have fallen away**. First, some say those who had "fallen away" were genuine Christians who had forsaken Jesus and reverted to Judaism. A second view says they were hearers who

had understood the gospel but had not become true believers. A third interpretation identifies the **things that are better and that pertain to salvation** as sanctification rather than justification. A fourth interpretation holds that the writer is speaking about apostasy as an unfulfilled possibility rather than a concrete reality.

The fourth interpretation seems most acceptable. The author was not defending a doctrine of apostasy; he was calling his readers to progress toward maturity. Like Abraham, who obtained the promise of God after waiting patiently, the readers should **seize the hope** before them because God has **guaranteed** his promise with an oath. And because Jesus has entered the **inner sanctuary** of God's presence, the Christian has a sure and firm **anchor for the soul.**

7:1–10:39 These chapters are an extended discourse on the superiority of the priesthood of Christ as demonstrated by the superiority of his order, his covenant, his ministry, and his sacrifice.

7:1–19 The Levitical priesthood of the Jews was grounded in the **order of Aaron**, but the priesthood of Jesus Christ is grounded in the **order of Melchizedek**. The mysterious

Melchizedek appeared in Gn 14:18–20 and was not mentioned again until the messianic promise was made in Ps 110. The author of Hebrews drew from the OT witness to show that the order of Melchizedek was eternal in origin and scope. Melchizedek was a type of Christ reflecting the divine attributes of eternity, righteousness, peace, and sovereignty. His eternality is evident in that he was a **priest forever**—without record of beginning or end. His righteousness is evident in his name since Melchizedek is Hebrew for **king of righteousness.** His peace is evident in the fact that he was also declared to be the **king of Salem**, which means **king of peace.**

Finally, Melchizedek's sovereignty was recognized by **Abraham**, who paid this priest-king a tithe of all he had when he returned victorious from war. The Levitical priesthood was inferior to that of Melchizedek because **the inferior is blessed by the superior.** The sovereignty of Melchizedek is reflected in the sovereignty of the Son of God, because while the Levitical priesthood was authorized by **a legal regulation**, the priesthood of Christ was authorized by **the power of an indestructible life.**

▼ Christ as Priest

A Priest: Appointed by God to offer gifts and sacrifices to God on behalf of his people for their sins and out of gratitude for God's provision and grace; a mediator between God and his people *(Ex 28–29; Lv 9:7; Heb 5:1)*.

WHO WAS AN OLD TESTAMENT PRIEST?

REQUIREMENTS

- A Levite, a descendant of Levi
- Specifically, a descendant of Aaron
- Holy to the Lord
  - Physically without blemish
  - Ceremonially clean
  - Morally clean by virtue of prescribed sacrifices

DUTIES

- Offer sacrifices to God on behalf of the people
- Bless the people on behalf of God
- Teach the people the law of God

WHO WAS AN OLD TESTAMENT HIGH PRIEST?

- A specific descendant of Aaron
- Appointed by God
- Had the responsibility of entering the most holy place once a year to make atonement for the people's sins on the Day of Atonement

WHO WERE SOME OF THE HIGH PRIESTS?

- **Aaron** *(Ex 28:1; Heb 5:1–4)*
- **Eleazar** *(Nm 20:25–28)*
- **Phinehas** *(Jdg 20:27–28)*
- **Eli** *(1Sm 1:9)*
- **Ahimelech** *(1Sm 21:1)*
- **Abiathar** *(1Sm 23:9; Mk 2:26)*
- **Zadok** *(1Kg 2:35)*
- **Jehoiada** *(2Kg 12:2)*
- **Hilkiah** *(2Kg 22:8)*
- **Joshua** *(Hg 1:1; Zch 3:1)*
- **Eliashib** *(Neh 3:1)*

AARON

Aaron, along with his descendants after him, was appointed by God for the priestly ministry of offering sacrifices to God on behalf of the people and for blessing the people in the name of the Lord.

PHINEHAS

Phinehas was zealous with the Lord's zeal among the Israelites when he put a man and woman to death for blatant disobedience against God *(Nm 25:1–13)*.

REQUIREMENTS

- A Levite, specifically, a descendant of Aaron
- Holy to the Lord: physically without blemish, ceremonially clean, morally clean by virtue of prescribed sacrifices

JESUS

- The Messiah, a descendant of Judah *(Heb 7:14)*
- Holy to the Lord *(Heb 4:15)*: tested in every way as we are, yet without sin
- A priest in the order of Melchizedek, not based on physical genealogy but on the power of his indestructible, resurrection life *(Heb 7:15–17)*

WHO WAS MELCHIZEDEK?

- Genesis 14:17–20; Psalm 110:4; Hebrews 7
- Name means "king of righteousness"; king of Salem means "king of peace"
- A priest of God Most High
- Blessed Abraham and received a tenth of Abraham's possessions

- Appears in Genesis (a book of beginnings, genealogies, births, and deaths) without father, mother, or genealogy, without a beginning of days nor end of life
- A king-priest who remains a priest forever, foreshadowing the Son of God

HOW WAS JESUS THE GREAT HIGH PRIEST?

THE LEVITICAL HIGH PRIEST	JESUS THE GREAT HIGH PRIEST
Mediator of the old covenant *(Heb 9:1–10)*	Mediator of a new, better covenant *(Heb 9:11–28)*
Offered a sacrifice first for his own sin *(Heb 5:3)*	Tempted in every way, yet without sin *(Heb 4:15)*
Appointed by God according to physical descent from Aaron *(Heb 5:4)*	Appointed by God not according to physical descent but in the order of Melchizedek *(Heb 5:5–6)*
Remained a priest until death *(Heb 7:23)*	Remains a priest forever *(Heb 7:24)*
Offered sacrifices daily for the sins of the people and himself *(Heb 7:27)*	Offered himself once for all for the sins of the people *(Heb 7:27)*
Entered the most holy place only once a year with the blood of an animal to make atonement for himself and the people, but this sacrifice could never perfect the worshiper's conscience *(Heb 9:7,9)*	Entered the most holy place in heaven once for all with his own blood to make eternal atonement for the people and to cleanse their consciences from dead works to serve the living God *(Heb 9:14)*
Offered the same yearly sacrifices that could never perfect the worshiper *(Heb 10:1)*	Offered himself once for all to sanctify the worshiper *(Heb 10:10)*
Stood day after day offering the same ineffectual sacrifices *(Heb 10:11)*	Offered himself as the one effectual sacrifice for sins and sat down at the right hand of God *(Heb 10:12)*

The old-covenant priests were appointed by God according to lineage, being descendants of Aaron. They were to be holy and set apart to the Lord. The priesthood of Aaron served its purpose for a time but could never accomplish the ultimate goal of sanctification for the worshiper because of sin in both the priest and the people. Therefore, we need a priest who is holy, innocent, undefiled, separated from sinners, and exalted above the heavens: **Jesus** *(Heb 7:26)*. This sinless Son of God is a priest forever in the order of Melchizedek *(Heb 7:17)*. He is the unblemished Lamb of God *(Jn 1:29,36)* who offers himself once for all as the atoning sacrifice for the worshiper *(Heb 10:10)*. He has sat down at the right hand of the Father in heaven, having completed his sacrificial work *(Heb 10:12)*. As our great high priest, Jesus reconciles us to God. His perfect righteousness is presented to the Father for our justification. He intercedes for us before the Father *(Heb 7:25; 9:24)* and prays for us *(Lk 22:31–32; Jn 17)*. In him we have forgiveness for sin and peace with God.

genealogy, having neither beginning of days nor end of life, but resembling the Son of God, he remains a priest forever.

[4] Now consider how great this man was: even Abraham the patriarch gave a tenth of the plunder to him. [5] The sons of Levi who receive the priestly office have a command according to the law to collect a tenth from the people — that is, from their brothers and sisters — though they have also descended from Abraham. [6] But one without this[A] lineage collected a tenth from Abraham and blessed the one who had the promises. [7] Without a doubt, the inferior is blessed by the superior. [8] In the one case, men who will die receive a tenth, but in the other case, Scripture testifies that he lives. [9] And in a sense Levi himself, who receives a tenth, has paid a tenth through Abraham, [10] for he was still within his ancestor[B] when Melchizedek met him.

A Superior Priesthood

[11] Now if perfection came through the Levitical priesthood (for on the basis of it the people received the law), what further need was there for another priest to appear, said to be according to the order of Melchizedek and not according to the order of Aaron? [12] For when there is a change of the priesthood, there must be a change of law as well. [13] For the one these things are spoken about belonged to a different tribe. No one from it has served at the altar. [14] Now it is evident that our Lord came from Judah, and Moses said nothing about that tribe concerning priests.

[15] And this becomes clearer if another priest like Melchizedek appears, [16] who did not become a priest based on a legal regulation about physical[C] descent but based on the power of an indestructible life. [17] For it has been testified:

You are a priest forever
according to the order
of Melchizedek.[D]

[18] So the previous command is annulled because it was weak and unprofitable [19] (for the law perfected nothing), but a better hope is introduced, through which we draw near to God.

[20] None of this happened without an oath. For others became priests without an oath, [21] but he became a priest with an oath made by the one who said to him:

The Lord has sworn
and will not change his mind,
"You are a priest forever."[D]

[22] Because of this oath, Jesus has also become the guarantee of a better covenant.

[23] Now many have become Levitical priests, since they are prevented by death from remaining in office. [24] But because he remains forever, he holds his priesthood permanently. [25] Therefore, he is able to save completely those who come to God through him, since he always lives to intercede for them.

[26] For this is the kind of high priest we need: holy, innocent, undefiled, separated from sinners, and exalted above the heavens. [27] He doesn't need to offer sacrifices every day, as high priests do — first for their own sins, then for those of the people. He did this once for all time when he offered himself. [28] For the law appoints as high priests men who are weak, but the promise of the oath, which came after the law, appoints a Son, who has been perfected forever.

A Heavenly Priesthood

8 Now the main point of what is being said is this: We have this kind of high priest, who sat down at the right hand of the throne of the Majesty in the heavens, [2] a minister of the sanctuary and the true tabernacle that was set up by the Lord and not man. [3] For every high priest is appointed to offer gifts and sacrifices; therefore, it was necessary for this priest also to have something to offer. [4] Now if he were on earth, he wouldn't be a priest, since there are those[E] offering the gifts prescribed by the law. [5] These serve as a copy and shadow of the heavenly things, as Moses was warned when he was about to complete the tabernacle. For God said, Be careful that you

---

[A]7:6 Lit their   [B]7:10 Lit still in his father's loins   [C]7:16 Or fleshly   [D]7:17,21 Ps 110:4   [E]8:4 Other mss read priests

7:20–8:13 The author addressed next the authorizing sources of the two priesthoods. Citing Jr 31:31–34, the author noted the old covenant between God and Israel was dependent on the oath of man; unfortunately, **they did not continue** in this covenant. But the new covenant promised through Jeremiah was different, because that oath was made entirely by God. Because God swore to the new covenant, it was eternally guaranteed. Because of the divine oath, the new covenant is **a better covenant**. The priesthood based on the old covenant was filled with priests who could not remain in office because they died, but the new covenant priest **always lives to intercede**. The old covenant priesthood was filled with priests who were **weak** (7:28), but the new

covenant priest was **perfected forever** through Jesus's obedient suffering. The old covenant priest had to **offer sacrifices every day**, but the new covenant priest offered a sacrifice **once for all time**. The old covenant priest sacrificed for both himself and his people, but the new covenant priest, being sinless, **offered himself** on behalf of the people.

#88 99 Essential Christian Truths

GOD IS TRANSCENDENT

God's transcendence refers to the fact that he is distinct from and independent of his created world. He is transcendent over us with regard to his greatness and power as well as his goodness and purity. The implication of this doctrine is that God is inherently superior to humanity: His thoughts and ways are higher than ours (Is 55:8–9). When God saves us, he restores us so that we can fulfill our human purpose. This does not mean that we become God or that distinctions between God and humanity are obliterated. Understanding God's transcendence evokes awe and wonder at his goodness and power.

make everything according to the pattern that was shown to you on the mountain.^A ^6 But Jesus has now obtained a superior ministry, and to that degree he is the mediator of a better covenant, which has been established on better promises.

A Superior Covenant

^7 For if that first covenant had been faultless, there would have been no occasion for a second one. ^8 But finding fault with his people,^B he says:^C

See, the days are coming,
    says the Lord,
when I will make a new covenant
    with the house of Israel
    and with the house of Judah —
^9   not like the covenant
    that I made with their ancestors
    on the day I took them by the hand
    to lead them out of the land of Egypt.
I showed no concern for them,
    says the Lord,
because they did not continue
    in my covenant.
^10   For this is the covenant
    that I will make with the house
      of Israel
    after those days, says the Lord:
I will put my laws into their minds
    and write them on their hearts.
I will be their God,
    and they will be my people.
^11   And each person will not teach
    his fellow citizen,^D
    and each his brother or sister, saying,
    "Know the Lord,"
because they will all know me,
    from the least to the greatest of them.
^12   For I will forgive their wrongdoing,
    and I will never again remember
    their sins.^E,F

^13 By saying a new covenant, he has declared that the first is obsolete. And what is obsolete and growing old is about to pass away.

Old Covenant Ministry

9 Now the first covenant also had regulations for ministry and an earthly sanctuary. ^2 For a tabernacle was set up, and in the first room, which is called the holy place, were the lampstand, the table, and the presentation loaves. ^3 Behind the second curtain was a tent

called the most holy place. ^4 It had the gold altar of incense and the ark of the covenant, covered with gold on all sides, in which was a gold jar containing the manna, Aaron's staff that budded, and the tablets of the covenant. ^5 The cherubim of glory were above the ark overshadowing the mercy seat. It is not possible to speak about these things in detail right now.

^6 With these things prepared like this, the priests enter the first room repeatedly, performing their ministry. ^7 But the high priest alone enters the second room, and he does that only once a year, and never without blood, which he offers for himself and for the sins the people had committed in ignorance. ^8 The Holy Spirit was making it clear that the way into the most holy place had not yet been disclosed while the first tabernacle was still standing. ^9 This is a symbol for the present time, during which gifts and sacrifices are offered that cannot perfect the worshiper's conscience. ^10 They are physical regulations and only deal with food, drink, and various washings imposed until the time of the new order.

New Covenant Ministry

^11 But Christ has appeared as a high priest of the good things that have come.^G In the greater and more perfect tabernacle not made with hands (that is, not of this creation), ^12 he entered the most holy place once for all time, not by the blood of goats and calves, but by his own blood, having obtained eternal redemption. ^13 For if the blood of goats and bulls and the ashes of a young cow, sprinkling those who are defiled, sanctify for the purification of the flesh, ^14 how much more will the blood of Christ, who through the eternal Spirit offered himself without blemish to God, cleanse our^H consciences from dead works so that we can serve the living God?

^15 Therefore, he is the mediator of a new covenant,^I so that those who are called might receive the promise of the eternal inheritance, because a death has taken place for redemption from the transgressions committed under the first covenant. ^16 Where a will exists, the death of the one who made it must be established. ^17 For a will is valid only when people die, since it is never in effect while the one who made it is living. ^18 That is why even the first covenant was inaugurated with blood. ^19 For when every command had been proclaimed

^A8:5 Ex 25:40 ^B8:8 Lit with them ^C8:8 Other mss read finding fault, he says to them ^D8:11 Other mss read neighbor ^E8:12 Other mss add and their lawless deeds ^F8:8–12 Jr 31:31–34 ^G9:11 Other mss read that are to come ^H9:14 Other mss read your ^I9:15 The Gk word used here can be translated covenant, will, or testament, also in vv. 16,17,18.

9:1–28 The author turned his attention to a comparison of the ministries of the old and new priesthoods. The **regulations for ministry** given through the old covenant were for an **earthly sanctuary**. The sacrificial ministry of the old priesthood was unable to **perfect the worshiper's** **conscience**. The sacrificial ministry of Christ is able to **cleanse our consciences**. Christ's ministry is superior because he does not enter an earthly sanctuary, but into **heaven itself**. Unlike the high priest who entered annually into the most holy place, Christ entered into the most holy place **once for** **all time**. Unlike the old priesthood that offered the blood of animals, Christ offered **his own blood**. Unlike the old priesthood that offered sacrifices continually without effect, the blood of Christ obtained eternal redemption.

by Moses to all the people according to the law, he took the blood of calves and goats,[A] along with water, scarlet wool, and hyssop, and sprinkled the scroll itself and all the people, [20] saying, This is the blood of the covenant that God has ordained for you.[B] [21] In the same way, he sprinkled the tabernacle and all the articles of worship with blood. [22] According to the law almost everything is purified with blood, and without the shedding of blood there is no forgiveness.

[23] Therefore, it was necessary for the copies of the things in the heavens to be purified with these sacrifices, but the heavenly things themselves to be purified with better sacrifices than these. [24] For Christ did not enter a sanctuary made with hands (only a model[c] of the true one) but into heaven itself, so that he might now appear in the presence of God for us. [25] He did not do this to offer himself many times, as the high priest enters the sanctuary yearly with the blood of another. [26] Otherwise, he would have had to suffer many times since the foundation of the world. But now he has appeared one time, at the end of the ages, for the removal of sin by the sacrifice of himself. [27] And just as it is appointed for people to die once — and after this, judgment — [28] so also Christ, having been offered once to bear the sins of many, will appear a second time, not to bear sin, but[D] to bring salvation to those who are waiting for him.

The Perfect Sacrifice

10 Since the law has only a shadow of the good things to come, and not the reality itself of those things, it can never perfect the worshipers by the same sacrifices they continually offer year after year. [2] Otherwise, wouldn't they have stopped being offered, since the worshipers, purified once and for all, would no longer have any consciousness of sins? [3] But in the sacrifices there is a reminder of sins year after year. [4] For it is impossible for the blood of bulls and goats to take away sins. [5] Therefore, as he was coming into the world, he said:

You did not desire sacrifice
　and offering,
but you prepared a body for me.

[6] You did not delight
　in whole burnt offerings
　and sin offerings.
[7] Then I said, "See —
　it is written about me
　in the scroll —
　I have come to do your will, God."[E]

[8] After he says above, You did not desire or delight in sacrifices and offerings, whole burnt offerings and sin offerings (which are offered according to the law), [9] he then says, See, I have come to do your will.[F] He takes away the first to establish the second. [10] By this will, we have been sanctified through the offering of the body of Jesus Christ once for all time.

[11] Every priest stands day after day ministering and offering the same sacrifices time after time, which can never take away sins. [12] But this man, after offering one sacrifice for sins forever, sat down at the right hand of God.[G] [13] He is now waiting until his enemies are made his footstool. [14] For by one offering he has perfected forever those who are sanctified. [15] The Holy Spirit also testifies to us about this. For after he says:

[16] This is the covenant I will make
　　with them
　after those days,
the Lord says,
　I will put my laws on their hearts
　and write them on their minds,
[17] and I will never again remember
　　their sins and their lawless acts.[H]

[18] Now where there is forgiveness of these, there is no longer an offering for sin.

Exhortations to Godliness

[19] Therefore, brothers and sisters, since we have boldness to enter the sanctuary through the blood of Jesus — [20] he has inaugurated[I] for us a new and living way through the curtain (that is, through his flesh) — [21] and since we have a great high priest over the house of God, [22] let us draw near with a true heart in full assurance of faith, with our hearts sprinkled clean from an evil conscience and our bodies washed in pure water. [23] Let us hold on to the confession of our hope without wavering, since he who promised is faithful. [24] And let us

---

[A]9:19 Some mss omit and goats　[B]9:20 Ex 24:8　[C]9:24 Or antitype, or figure　[D]9:28 Lit time, apart from sin,　[E]10:5–7 Ps 40:6–8　[F]10:9 Other mss add God　[G]10:12 Or offering one sacrifice for sins, sat down forever at the right hand of God　[H]10:16–17 Jr 31:33–34　[I]10:20 Or opened

---

10:1–18 The author in these verses focused on the superiority of the sacrifice of Christ. The old sacrifices were only a **shadow** of the blessed realities that come from the personal sacrifice of Christ. Citing Ps 40:6–8, the author demonstrated that God was no longer interested in the **whole burnt offerings and sin offerings** of the old covenant. The old sacrifices had to be offered continually, and they did not accomplish anything beyond ritual purification because they could not **take away sins**. Jesus offered **one sacrifice for sins forever** by offering himself. Afterward, he sat down at the throne of God. By his blood atonement, he has **perfected forever** those who are sanctified. **10:19–39** The author's exhortation to faithfulness contains commands, a warning, an encouraging reminder, a promise, and an expression of confidence. Due to the **boldness** that believers have to enter the divine presence through the perfect sacrifice of Christ, the author commands his readers to: (1) **draw near** to God with assurance, (2) **hold on** to their confession without wavering, and (3) **consider one another** and not forsake the gathering of the church. The warning is a reminder that there is no effective sacrifice for sin apart from that provided by Christ. If Christians turn their backs on Jesus, they have no hope—only the expectation of terror.

The New Covenant

COVENANTS OF SCRIPTURE	RECIPIENTS	COMMANDS	PROMISES/ CONDITIONS	COVENANT SIGN
Creation Covenant (Gn 1–3)	Adam and Eve	Be fruitful, multiply, fill the earth, and subdue it; do not eat from the tree of the knowledge of good and evil	Eternal life for obedience; death for disobedience (including spiritual alienation, exile from the garden)	
Noahic Covenant (Gn 6–9)	Noah and all his descendants and every living creature	Be fruitful, multiply, fill the earth, and rule it; do not eat meat with its lifeblood in it; do not murder	Never again shall all life be destroyed by a flood **permanent covenant (Gn 9:16)**	Rainbow
Abrahamic Covenant (Gn 12; 15; 17)	Abraham, Isaac, and Jacob and their descendants	Keep the covenant; circumcise every male	Land (Canaan); offspring (nations and kings); blessing (a great name and blessing to others) **permanent covenant (Gn 17:7)**	Circumcision
Mosaic (Old) Covenant (Ex 19–24)	The people of Israel	Keep the covenant; obey the law (Ten Commandments on tablets and other laws)	Blessing for obedience; curse for disobedience (agricultural plight, military defeat, exile from the land)	The Sabbath
Davidic Covenant (2Sm 7; Ps 89)	David and his descendants	Keep the covenant; obey the law	A great name; stability for God's people; an eternal house, kingdom, and throne **permanent covenant (2Sm 23:5)**	
New Covenant (Jr 31:31–34; Ezk 36–37; Lk 22:14–20; Heb 8–10)	Believers in the Messiah; Gentile believers are branches grafted onto the tree of Israel	Repentance and faith	A new heart indwelled by God's Holy Spirit and having God's teaching within, written on hearts instead of tablets; cleansing and forgiveness of sin; a Davidic king forever **permanent covenant (Ezk 37:26)**	The cross (Lord's Supper)

consider one another in order to provoke love and good works, **²⁵** not neglecting to gather together, as some are in the habit of doing, but encouraging each other, and all the more as you see the day approaching.

Warning against Deliberate Sin

²⁶ For if we deliberately go on sinning after receiving the knowledge of the truth, there no longer remains a sacrifice for sins, **²⁷** but a terrifying expectation of judgment and the fury of a fire about to consume the adversaries. **²⁸** Anyone who disregarded the law of Moses died without mercy, based on the testimony of two or three witnesses. **²⁹** How much worse punishment do you think one will deserve who has trampled on the Son of God, who has regarded as profane^A the blood of the covenant by which he was sanctified, and who has insulted the Spirit of grace? **³⁰** For we know the one who has said,

Vengeance belongs to me;
I will repay,^B,^C

and again,

The Lord will judge his people.^D

³¹ It is a terrifying thing to fall into the hands of the living God.

³² Remember the earlier days when, after you had been enlightened, you endured a hard struggle with sufferings. **³³** Sometimes you were publicly exposed to taunts and afflictions, and at other times you were companions of those who were treated that way. **³⁴** For you sympathized with the prisoners^E and accepted with joy the confiscation of your possessions, because you know that you yourselves have a better and enduring possession.^F **³⁵** So don't throw away your confidence, which has a great reward. **³⁶** For you need endurance, so that after you have done God's will, you may receive what was promised.

³⁷   For yet in a very little while,
the Coming One will come
and not delay.
³⁸   But my righteous one^G will live
by faith;
and if he draws back,
I have no pleasure^H in him.^I

³⁹ But we are not those who draw back and are destroyed, but those who have faith and are saved.

Living by Faith

11 Now faith is the reality^J of what is hoped for, the proof^K of what is not seen. **²** For by this our ancestors were approved.

³ By faith we understand that the universe was^L created by the word of God, so that what is seen was made from things that are not visible.^M

⁴ By faith Abel offered to God a better sacrifice than Cain did. By faith he was approved as a righteous man, because God approved his gifts, and even though he is dead, he still speaks through his faith.

⁵ By faith Enoch was taken away, and so he did not experience death. **He was not to be found because God took him away.**^N For before he was taken away, he was approved as one who pleased God. **⁶** Now without faith it is impossible to please God, since the one who draws near to him must believe that he exists and that he rewards those who seek him.

⁷ By faith Noah, after he was warned about what was not yet seen and motivated by godly fear, built an ark to deliver his family. By faith he condemned the world and became an heir of the righteousness that comes by faith.

⁸ By faith Abraham, when he was called, obeyed and set out for a place that he was going to receive as an inheritance. He went out, even though he did not know where he was going. **⁹** By faith he stayed as a foreigner in the land of promise, living in tents as did Isaac and Jacob, coheirs of the same promise. **¹⁰** For he was looking forward to the city that has foundations, whose architect and builder is God.

¹¹ By faith even Sarah herself, when she was unable to have children, received power to conceive offspring, even though she was past the age, since she^O considered that the one who had promised was faithful. **¹²** Therefore, from one man — in fact, from one as good as dead — came offspring as numerous as the stars of the sky and as innumerable as the grains of sand along the seashore.

¹³ These all died in faith, although they had not received the things that were promised. But they saw them from a distance, greeted them, and confessed that they were foreigners and temporary residents on the earth. **¹⁴** Now those who say such things make it clear that

---

^A**10:29** Or *ordinary*   ^B**10:30** Other mss add *says the Lord*   ^C**10:30** Dt 32:35   ^D**10:30** Dt 32:36   ^E**10:34** Other mss read *sympathized with my imprisonment*   ^F**10:34** Other mss add *in heaven*   ^G**10:38** Other mss read *the righteous one*   ^H**10:38** Lit *my soul has no pleasure*   ^I**10:37–38** Is 26:20 LXX; Hab 2:3–4   ^J**11:1** Or *assurance*   ^K**11:1** Or *conviction*   ^L**11:1** Or *the worlds were, or the ages were*   ^M**11:3** Or *so that what is seen was made out of what was not visible*   ^N**11:5** Gn 5:21–24   ^O**11:11** Or *By faith Abraham, even though he was past age — and Sarah herself was barren — received the ability to procreate since he*

11:1–40 This chapter compares the faith of the OT fathers with the faith exercised by Christian believers. Faith is defined as **the reality of what is hoped for** and **the proof of what is not seen**. Faith is not fleeting but substantial enough to generate confidence. The Greek word for "proof" indicates an inner conviction that is not based on visible

matters. **To please God** requires **faith**. One **must believe that he exists and that he rewards those who seek him**. He is there and he responds.

Throughout the chapter, the author provided examples of people in the OT who exercised faith. He focused most heavily on **Abraham** and **Moses**. To complete the list

with a crescendo (vv. 32–40), he recounted an inspiring litany of the fruit of faith displayed in the virtuous life, faithful death, and anticipated resurrection of numerous OT heroes. Although their faith was **approved**, they did not receive what God had **promised**. The purpose of this delay was to ensure that they would not be perfected apart from Jesus Christ.

they are seeking a homeland. ¹⁵ If they were thinking about where they came from, they would have had an opportunity to return. ¹⁶ But they now desire a better place — a heavenly one. Therefore, God is not ashamed to be called their God, for he has prepared a city for them.

¹⁷ By faith Abraham, when he was tested, offered up Isaac. He received the promises and yet he was offering his one and only son, ¹⁸ the one to whom it had been said, **Your offspring^ will be traced through Isaac.**ᴮ ¹⁹ He considered God to be able even to raise someone from the dead; therefore, he received him back, figuratively speaking.ᶜ

²⁰ By faith Isaac blessed Jacob and Esau concerning things to come. ²¹ By faith Jacob, when he was dying, blessed each of the sons of Joseph, and **he worshiped, leaning on the top of his staff.**ᴰ ²² By faith Joseph, as he was nearing the end of his life, mentionedᴱ the exodus of the Israelites and gave instructions concerning his bones.

²³ By faith Moses, after he was born, was hidden by his parents for three months, because they saw that the child was beautiful, and they didn't fear the king's edict. ²⁴ By faith Moses, when he had grown up, refused to be called the son of Pharaoh's daughter ²⁵ and chose to suffer with the people of God rather than to enjoy the fleeting pleasure of sin. ²⁶ For he considered reproach for the sake of Christ to be greater wealth than the treasures of Egypt, since he was looking ahead to the reward.

²⁷ By faith he left Egypt behind, not being afraid of the king's anger, for Moses persevered as one who sees him who is invisible. ²⁸ By faith he instituted the Passover and the sprinkling of the blood, so that the destroyer of the firstborn might not touch the Israelites. ²⁹ By faith they crossed the Red Sea as though they were on dry land. When the Egyptians attempted to do this, they were drowned. ³⁰ By faith the walls of Jericho fell down after being marched around by the Israelites for seven days. ³¹ By faith Rahab the prostitute welcomed the spies in peace and didn't perish with those who disobeyed.

³² And what more can I say? Time is too short for me to tell about Gideon, Barak, Samson, Jephthah, David, Samuel, and the prophets, ³³ who by faith conquered kingdoms, administered justice, obtained promises, shut the mouths of lions, ³⁴ quenched the raging of fire, escaped the edge of the sword, gained strength in weakness, became mighty in battle, and put foreign armies to flight. ³⁵ Women received their dead, raised to life again. Other people were tortured, not accepting release, so that they might gain a better resurrection. ³⁶ Others experienced mockings and scourgings, as well as bonds and imprisonment. ³⁷ They were stoned,ᶠ they were sawed in two, they died by the sword, they wandered about in sheepskins, in goatskins, destitute, afflicted, and mistreated. ³⁸ The world was not worthy of them. They wandered in deserts and on mountains, hiding in caves and holes in the ground.

³⁹ All these were approved through their faith, but they did not receive what was promised, ⁴⁰ since God had provided something better for us, so that they would not be made perfect without us.

The Call to Endurance

12 Therefore, since we also have such a large cloud of witnesses surrounding us, let us lay aside every hindrance and the sin that so easily ensnares us. Let us run with endurance the race that lies before us, ² keeping our eyes on Jesus,ᴳ the pioneer and perfecterᴴ of our faith. For the joy that lay before him,ᴵ he endured the cross, despising the shame, and sat down at the right hand of the throne of God.

Fatherly Discipline

³ For consider him who endured such hostility from sinners against himself, so that you won't grow weary and give up. ⁴ In struggling against sin, you have not yet resisted to the point of shedding your blood. ⁵ And you have forgotten the exhortation that addresses you as sons:

My son, do not take the Lord's
discipline lightly
or lose heart when you are
reproved by him,
⁶ **for the Lord disciplines the one**
he loves
and punishes every son he receives.ᴶ

⁷ Endure suffering as discipline: God is dealing with you as sons. For what son is there that a father does not discipline? ⁸ But if you are without discipline — which all receiveᴷ — then you

---

^11:18 Lit *seed*   ᴮ11:18 Gn 21:12   ᶜ11:19 Or *back, as a foreshadowing,* or *as a type*   ᴰ11:21 Gn 47:31   ᴱ11:22 Or *remembered*
ᶠ11:37 Other mss add *they were tempted,*   ᴳ12:2 Or *us, looking to Jesus*   ᴴ12:2 Or *the founder and completer,* or *the source
and perfecter*   ᴵ12:2 Or *who instead of the joy lying before him*   ᴶ12:6 Pr 3:11–12   ᴷ12:8 Lit *discipline, of which all have
become participants*

12:1–2 Because Jesus Christ is the **pioneer and perfecter** of the Christian faith, the author called on Christians to keep their eyes on Jesus. The Christian who has faith will **lay aside** every sinful weight and **run** toward Christ. Just as Jesus **endured the cross, despising the shame,** in order to attain the joy of rejoicing in the Father on his throne, so should Christians run their race with **endurance**. **12:3–13** The Son became a human being in order to unite himself with his believing brothers and sisters. The Son can then bring believers into the presence of the Father, who will discipline them as **sons**. Citing Pr 3:11–12, the author argued that just as the readers have accepted discipline from their **human fathers**, so too should they receive discipline from the **Father of spirits**. God does not discipline his sons to harm them, but to bless them. The benefit of the Father's discipline is fellowship in his **holiness** and bearing the **peaceful fruit of righteousness**.

are illegitimate children and not sons. [9] Furthermore, we had human fathers discipline us, and we respected them. Shouldn't we submit even more to the Father of spirits and live? [10] For they disciplined us for a short time based on what seemed good to them, but he does it for our benefit, so that we can share his holiness. [11] No discipline seems enjoyable at the time, but painful. Later on, however, it yields the peaceful fruit of righteousness to those who have been trained by it.

[12] Therefore, strengthen your tired hands and weakened knees, [13] and make straight paths for your feet, so that what is lame may not be dislocated[A] but healed instead.

Warning against Rejecting God's Grace

[14] Pursue peace with everyone, and holiness — without it no one will see the Lord. [15] Make sure that no one falls short of the grace of God and that no root of bitterness springs up, causing trouble and defiling many. [16] And make sure that there isn't any immoral[B] or irreverent person like Esau, who sold his birthright in exchange for a single meal. [17] For you know that later, when he wanted to inherit the blessing, he was rejected, even though he sought it with tears, because he didn't find any opportunity for repentance.

[18] For you have not come to what could be touched, to a blazing fire, to darkness, gloom, and storm, [19] to the blast of a trumpet, and the sound of words. Those who heard it begged that not another word be spoken to them, [20] for they could not bear what was commanded: If even an animal touches the mountain, it must be stoned.[C] [21] The appearance was so terrifying that Moses said, I am trembling with fear.[D] [22] Instead, you have come to Mount Zion, to the city of the living God (the heavenly Jerusalem), to myriads of angels, a festive

gathering, [23] to the assembly of the firstborn whose names have been written[E] in heaven, to a Judge, who is God of all, to the spirits of righteous people made perfect, [24] and to Jesus, the mediator of a new covenant, and to the sprinkled blood, which says better things than the blood of Abel.

[25] See to it that you do not reject the one who speaks. For if they did not escape when they rejected him who warned them on earth, even less will we if we turn away from him who warns us from heaven. [26] His voice shook the earth at that time, but now he has promised, Yet once more I will shake not only the earth but also the heavens.[F] [27] This expression, "Yet once more," indicates the removal of what can be shaken — that is, created things — so that what is not shaken might remain. [28] Therefore, since we are receiving a kingdom that cannot be shaken, let us be thankful. By it, we may serve God acceptably, with reverence and awe, [29] for our God is a consuming fire.

Final Exhortations

13 Let brotherly love continue. [2] Don't neglect to show hospitality, for by doing this some have welcomed angels as guests without knowing it. [3] Remember those in prison, as though you were in prison with them, and the mistreated,[G] as though you yourselves were suffering bodily.[H] [4] Marriage is to be honored by all and the marriage bed kept undefiled, because God will judge the sexually immoral and adulterers. [5] Keep your life free from the love of money. Be satisfied with what you have, for he himself has said, I will never leave you or abandon you.[I] [6] Therefore, we may boldly say,

The Lord is my helper;
I will not be afraid.
What can man do to me?[J]

[A]12:13 Or so that the lame will not be turned aside [B]12:16 Or sexually immoral [C]12:20 Ex 19:12 [D]12:21 Dt 9:19 [E]12:23 Or registered [F]12:26 Hg 2:6 [G]13:3 Or tortured [H]13:3 Or mistreated, since you are also in a body [I]13:5 Dt 31:6 [J]13:6 Ps 118:6

12:14–29 The church does not exist on Mount Sinai, **terrifying** to the Israelites in both what they heard and saw. Rather, the church is moving toward **Mount Zion** where it should dwell in the presence of God, Jesus, angels, and the righteous people who have been perfected by the **sprinkled blood** of Christ. The author urges the readers to persevere in faith. Though God will shake heaven and earth, believers can trust they **are receiving a kingdom that cannot be shaken.**
13:1–25 In the final chapter of the book, the author addressed the benefits and responsibilities of life lived in the church.
13:1–6 Under the general theme of allowing **brotherly love** to reign within the church, the author addressed five specific activities in which Christians should engage: (1) **show hospitality** toward strangers, (2) visit **those in prison**, (3) minister to the mistreated, (4) honor **marriage**, and (5) **free** themselves **from the love of money**.

13:7–19 The author addressed seven specific ways in which Christians should revere church leaders. (1) Christians should **observe** the lives of their leaders and imitate their faith. (2) Christians should remember that Christ is always the same and judge every teaching according to the gospel. (3) Christians should recognize their church may not be appreciated by the world because the Christian community is gathered to worship their Lord, whom the world despises. (4) Christians should continually offer their own **sacrifice of praise** in appreciation for the sacrifice of Christ by confessing his name. (5) The church should be active in doing good works and sharing with one another. (6) Christians should **obey** their leaders and **submit** to them, because they are accountable to God for caring for Christian souls. (7) Christians should **pray** for their leaders to have clear consciences, conducting themselves with honor in everything.

#89 99 Essential Christian Truths

RESURRECTION

Both the Old and New Testaments teach that one day believers will experience a resurrection of the body from the dead (Is 26:19; Ezk 37:12–14; Jn 11). The promise of the resurrection is found in the resurrection of Christ from the dead, and it will take place at the future return of Christ. Because Christ is the firstfruits of the resurrection, Christians can be assured that their resurrection will be similar in nature, meaning it will be both bodily and glorious (Rm 8:22–23; Php 3:20–21). The hope of the future resurrection gives Christians confidence that death has been defeated in the death and resurrection of Christ.

⁷ Remember your leaders who have spoken God's word to you. As you carefully observe the outcome of their lives, imitate their faith. **⁸** Jesus Christ is the same yesterday, today, and forever. **⁹** Don't be led astray by various kinds of strange teachings; for it is good for the heart to be established by grace and not by food regulations, since those who observe them have not benefited. **¹⁰** We have an altar from which those who worship at the tabernacle do not have a right to eat. **¹¹** For the bodies of those animals whose blood is brought into the most holy place by the high priest as a sin offering are burned outside the camp. **¹²** Therefore, Jesus also suffered outside the gate, so that he might sanctify^ the people by his own blood. **¹³** Let us, then, go to him outside the camp, bearing his disgrace. **¹⁴** For we do not have an enduring city here; instead, we seek the one to come. **¹⁵** Therefore, through him let us continually offer up to God a sacrifice of praise, that is, the fruit of lips that confess his name. **¹⁶** Don't neglect to do what is good and to share, for God is pleased with such sacrifices. **¹⁷** Obey your leaders⁸ and submit to them, since they keep watch over your souls as those who will give an account, so that they can do this with joy and not with grief, for that would be unprofitable for you. **¹⁸** Pray for us, for we are convinced that we have a clear conscience, wanting to conduct ourselves honorably in everything. **¹⁹** And I urge you all the more to pray^ that I may be restored to you very soon.

Benediction and Farewell

²⁰ Now may the God of peace, who brought up from the dead our Lord Jesus — the great Shepherd of the sheep — through the blood of the everlasting covenant, **²¹** equip^ you with everything good to do his will, working in us what is pleasing in his sight, through Jesus Christ, to whom be glory forever and ever.^ Amen.

²² Brothers and sisters, I urge you to receive this message of exhortation, for I have written to you briefly. **²³** Be aware that our brother Timothy has been released. If he comes soon enough, he will be with me when I see you. **²⁴** Greet all your leaders and all the saints. Those who are from Italy send you greetings. **²⁵** Grace be with you all.

---

^13:12 Or *set apart*, or *consecrate*   ⁸13:17 Or *rulers*   ᶜ13:19 Lit *to do this*   ᴰ13:21 Or *perfect*   ᶠ13:21 Other mss omit *and ever*

13:20–25 Recounting the sacrificial work of Christ, the author prayed that God would **equip** them to do his will. He ended his message with a blessing: **Grace be with you all**.

◥ Introduction to James

Circumstances of Writing

James is named as the author in 1:1. A number of New Testament personalities were named James, but only three are candidates for the authorship of this book. James the son of Zebedee died in AD 44, too early to have been the author. No tradition names James the son of Alphaeus (Mk 3:18) as the author. This leaves James the brother of Jesus, also called James the Just (Mk 6:3; Ac 1:14; 12:17; 15:13; 21:18; 1Co 15:7; Gl 2:9,12), as the most likely candidate.

This James is identified as the brother of Jesus in Matthew 13:55; Mark 6:3; and Galatians 1:19. Though he was not a follower of Christ during his earthly ministry (Jn 7:3–5), a postresurrection appearance convinced James that Jesus is indeed the Christ (Ac 1:14; 1Co 15:7). James later led the Jerusalem church (Gl 2:9,12), exercising great influence there (Ac 1:14; 12:17; 15:13; 21:18; 1Co 15:7; Gl 2:9,12).

James was probably written between AD 48 and 52, though nothing in the epistle suggests a more precise date. James's death in AD 62 or 66 means the epistle was written before this time. Similarities to Gospel traditions and Pauline themes are suggestive. If Mark was written around AD 65 and time is allowed for the events of Acts 15 and 21 to have occurred between Paul's first and second missionary journeys, a date between AD 48 and 52 seems most likely.

James led the Jerusalem church. The reference to "the twelve tribes dispersed abroad" (1:1) suggests the letter was written to Jewish Christians living outside of Israel. The reference to a synagogue (Gk; 2:2) also suggests that his audience was Jewish Christians. References to their circumstances (e.g., oppression by wealthy landowners; 5:1–6) could refer to congregations anywhere in the Roman Empire. However, Semitic word order, quotations from the Septuagint, and the overall dependence of the letter on the Jewish wisdom tradition suggest a specifically Jewish Christian audience.

Contribution to the Bible

James continually called for obedience to the law of God. He never referred to the ceremonial law, but to the moral law. Although some people think James is at odds with Paul about the Christian's relationship to the law, both authors combine to give us a solid understanding of the Old Testament law. Paul showed believers that Christ met the demands of the law and, thus, brings us to salvation. James showed believers that their obedience to God's moral standards is an indication of a living faith, which is a life lived in step with the one who met the demands of the law. Some choose to oversimplify the distinctions between the Old Testament and the New Testament and say the Old Testament is grounded in works and the New Testament is grounded in faith, but James brings both testaments together to show that faith and works are integrally related in both the old and new covenants.

James Timeline

2100–900 BC

JOB 2100–1900?
ABRAHAM 2166–1991
The Mosaic law at Sinai **1446**
Rahab supports the conquest of Jericho. **1406**
Much of Proverbs is written. **970–931**

900 BC–AD 33

Elijah's ministry **862–852 BC**
The Book of Wisdom **220–50 BC?**
The deuterocanonical book of Ecclesiasticus **180 BC**
Jesus's trials, death, and resurrection
  NISAN 14–16 or **APRIL 3–5, AD 33**
Following his resurrection, Jesus appears
  to James his brother. **AD 33**

Structure

The book of James is a letter (an epistle), though only the greeting conforms to the ancient Greek form exemplified in Paul's letters, especially Galatians. The greeting identifies the author as James, includes a title demonstrating the source of his authority ("a servant of God and of the Lord Jesus Christ"), names the recipients ("the twelve tribes dispersed abroad"), and conveys "greetings" (1:1). Epistles were often used as a means of spurring the recipients to a change in behavior or belief based on the authoritative word and guidance of the sender.

The book of James has been compared to Old Testament Wisdom literature. Although there are wisdom elements in James, such as comparing the wisdom of the world with the wisdom that comes from God, it also contains exhortations and prophetic elements not common to Wisdom literature.

Outline

I. Salutation (1:1)
II. Surviving Trials and Temptation (1:2–18)
III. Authentic Religion (1:19–2:26)
IV. The Need for Wise Teachers (3:1–18)
V. Peace with God and One Another (4:1–17)
VI. Discipline in the Christian Life (5:1–20)

Key verses in James

1:19 My dear brothers and sisters, understand this: Everyone should be quick to listen, slow to speak, and slow to anger.

1:22 But be doers of the word and not hearers only, deceiving yourselves.

5:16 Therefore, confess your sins to one another and pray for one another, so that you may be healed. The prayer of a righteous person is very powerful in its effect.

AD 33–44

Pentecost **33**
Saul's conversion on the Damascus
  Road **OCTOBER, 34**
Paul meets with Peter and James on his first visit
  to Jerusalem following his conversion. **37?**
James becomes leader of the
  church at Jerusalem. **44**
Execution of James, son of Zebedee,
  by Herod Agrippa **44**

AD 44–330

The letter of James **48–52**
Martyrdom of James, half brother of Jesus **62**
Destruction of Jerusalem **70**
Origen quotes James in his commentary
  on the Gospel of John. **230**
Eusebius refers to the letter of
  James as Scripture. **330**

Greeting

1 James, a servant of God and of the Lord Jesus Christ:
To the twelve tribes dispersed abroad.[A] Greetings.

Trials and Maturity

[2] Consider it a great joy, my brothers and sisters, whenever you experience various trials, [3] because you know that the testing of your faith produces endurance. [4] And let endurance have its full effect, so that you may be mature and complete, lacking nothing. [5] Now if any of you lacks wisdom, he should ask God — who gives to all generously and ungrudgingly — and it will be given to him. [6] But let him ask in faith without doubting.[B] For the doubter is like the surging sea, driven and tossed by the wind. [7] That person should not expect to receive anything from the Lord, [8] being double-minded and unstable in all his ways.[C]

[9] Let the brother of humble circumstances boast in his exaltation, [10] but let the rich boast in his humiliation because he will pass away like a flower of the field. [11] For the sun rises and, together with the scorching wind, dries up the grass; its flower falls off, and its beautiful appearance perishes. In the same way, the rich person will wither away while pursuing his activities.

[12] Blessed is the one who endures trials, because when he has stood the test he will receive the crown of life that God[D] has promised to those who love him.

[13] No one undergoing a trial should say, "I am being tempted by God," since God is not tempted by evil, and he himself doesn't tempt anyone. [14] But each person is tempted when he is drawn away and enticed by his own evil desire. [15] Then after desire has conceived, it gives birth to sin, and when sin is fully grown, it gives birth to death.

[16] Don't be deceived, my dear brothers and sisters. [17] Every good and perfect gift is from above, coming down from the Father of lights, who does not change like shifting shadows. [18] By his own choice, he gave us birth by the word of truth so that we would be a kind of firstfruits of his creatures.

Hearing and Doing the Word

[19] My dear brothers and sisters, understand this: Everyone should be quick to listen, slow to speak, and slow to anger, [20] for human anger does not accomplish God's righteousness. [21] Therefore, ridding yourselves of all moral filth and the evil that is so prevalent,[E] humbly receive the implanted word, which is able to save your souls.

[22] But be doers of the word and not hearers only, deceiving yourselves. [23] Because if anyone is a hearer of the word and not a doer, he is like someone looking at his own face[F] in a mirror. [24] For he looks at himself, goes away, and immediately forgets what kind of person he was. [25] But the one who looks intently into the perfect law of freedom and perseveres in it, and is not a forgetful hearer but a doer who works — this person will be blessed in what he does.

[26] If anyone[G] thinks he is religious without controlling his tongue, his religion is useless and he deceives himself. [27] Pure and undefiled religion before God the Father is this: to look after orphans and widows in their distress and to keep oneself unstained from the world.

The Sin of Favoritism

2 My brothers and sisters, do not show favoritism as you hold on to the faith in our glorious Lord Jesus Christ. [2] For if someone

---

[A] 1:1 Gk *diaspora*; Jewish people scattered throughout Gentile lands [B] 1:6 Or *without divided loyalties* [C] 1:8 Or *in all his conduct* [D] 1:12 Other mss read *that the Lord* [E] 1:21 Or *the abundance of evil* [F] 1:23 Or *at his natural face* [G] 1:26 Other mss add *among you*

1:1 **Servant** indicates James's humility and total devotion in service to his Lord. The **twelve tribes dispersed abroad** refers to Jewish Christians scattered outside of Israel. 1:2 The phrase **whenever you experience various trials** assumes that trials are a normal part of the Christian life. **Joy** suggests an eschatological (end times) hope of deliverance from trials.
1:3 Knowledge **that the testing of your faith produces endurance** is the basis for joy.
1:4 **Endurance** indicates that further work must be done for the purpose of making the believer **mature and complete, lacking nothing.**
1:6–8 The basis for confidence here is not just the fact that we exercise faith, but the person in whom we place our faith—God.
1:9–11 In relation to eternity, neither the poor nor the wealthy have anything to boast about; they are equals before God.
1:12 **Blessed** reflects the understanding that a person who walks in the paths set by the

Lord sees his plight in terms of the eschatological hope that awaits him.
1:13–18 God's relationship to temptation is made clear by two kinds of statements. On the one hand, there are assertions that clarify what God is not or does not do: **God is not tempted . . . and he himself doesn't tempt.** On the other hand, there are assertions as to what things do come from God: **every good and perfect gift.** The source of temptation is one's **own evil desire.** "Desire" focuses on the immediacy that carnal desire creates, spurring a person to act, to be **drawn away and enticed.**
1:17 **Father of lights** refers to God (v. 5), who created the lights that rule days and seasons (Gn 1:14–19). **Who does not change like shifting shadows** alludes to the fact that God's nature is unchanging and that his promises are secure.
1:18 **Word of truth** refers to the gospel, by which new **birth** comes. **Firstfruits** refers to the best that the harvest produces.

1:21 **Implanted word** refers to the gospel as received by the believer.
1:23–25 In the contrast between the **hearer of the word** who looks at **his own face in a mirror** and yet **forgets,** and the **doer** of the word who looks intently into the perfect law of freedom and perseveres, the distinction is found in whether the one who looks allows "the perfect law of freedom" (the gospel) to shape his life's course. The person who hears and does "the word" puts faith into action and is **blessed.**
1:26–27 James's definition of **pure and undefiled religion** is based on action, not heedless hearing and meaningless lip service. Care for orphans and widows has always been a special concern of God's (e.g., Ex 22:22–24; Dt 10:18; Is 1:17).
2:1 The phrase **show favoritism** is addressed four times in the NT (cp. Rm 2:11; Eph 6:9; Col 3:25), each time indicating that God does not show favoritism. When we sin by showing "favoritism" we imply that God did not make all men and women equal.

◥ Faith and Works

by Mark DeVine

Whenever "faith" is set beside "works" it recalls the theological conflicts that shaped the Reformation of the sixteenth century. To this day these conflicts largely account for the division of the Western church between Roman Catholic and Protestant. Martin Luther's rediscovery of the gospel included a recovery of the apostle Paul's insistence that "no one will be justified in his [God's] sight by the works of the law" (Rm 3:20). Instead, "you are saved by grace through faith, and this is not from yourselves; it is God's gift—not from works, so that no one can boast" (Eph 2:8–9).

The faith that saves, Luther realized from his study of the Bible, is not mere historical faith, a bare belief that what the Bible declares as true is in fact true, a faith that, according to John Calvin, merely "flits in the brain" and saves no one. Of such faith James said, "Even the demons believe—and they shudder" (Jms 2:19). No, the faith that saves the soul is trusting faith, so that salvation comes by grace alone through faith alone in Christ alone. This trusting faith is faith that relies upon the death of Jesus Christ on the cross in the place of sinners. There Jesus bore the punishment of sinners upon himself so that now God promises to treat as righteous those who believe in his name. Just as "Abraham believed God, and it was credited to him for righteousness" (Rm 4:3), so now all who repent of their sins, abandon hope of being made right with God on the basis of their own good works, and trust only in the mercy of God offered in the death of Jesus Christ in their place, will be saved.

Then what of good works? Have they no place in the Christian life? James anticipates and answers this question: "But someone will say, 'You have faith, and I have works.' Show me your faith without works, and I will show you faith by my works" (Jms 2:18). While God's salvation is all of grace, including the faith that saves, which "is not from yourselves; it is God's gift—not from works so that no one can boast" (Eph 2:8–9), Paul follows this assertion with a word about works: "For we are his [God's] workmanship, created in Christ Jesus for good works, which God prepared ahead of time for us to do" (Eph 2:10). So good works follow saving faith. Salvation is not gained through works, but rather good works are the fruit of saving faith in Jesus Christ.

Sinners saved by grace through faith rest their confidence before God neither in their works nor their faith, as if faith itself were a source of pride. Faith derives its saving power from its object, Jesus Christ. A believer's good works are no grounds for boasting, for the works stem from Christ himself. The apostle Paul described this mystery as follows: "I have been crucified with Christ, and I no longer live, but Christ lives in me" (Gl 2:19–20). Good works are performed by believers due to Christ working in them. Thus, a believer's confidence in their salvation is based on Christ, not their performance of good works. With the apostle Paul believers long to "be found in him [Christ], not having a righteousness of my own from the law, but one that is through faith in Christ—the righteousness from God based on faith" (Php 3:9). They know that "without faith it is impossible to please God" (Heb 11:6).

comes into your meeting wearing a gold ring and dressed in fine clothes, and a poor person dressed in filthy clothes also comes in, ³ if you look with favor on the one wearing the fine clothes and say, "Sit here in a good place," and yet you say to the poor person, "Stand over there," or "Sit here on the floor by my footstool," ⁴ haven't you made distinctions among yourselves and become judges with evil thoughts?

⁵ Listen, my dear brothers and sisters: Didn't God choose the poor in this world to be rich in faith and heirs of the kingdom that he has promised to those who love him? ⁶ Yet you have dishonored the poor. Don't the rich oppress you and drag you into court? ⁷ Don't they blaspheme the good name that was invoked over you?

⁸ Indeed, if you fulfill the royal law prescribed in the Scripture, **Love your neighbor as yourself,**ᴬ you are doing well. ⁹ If, however, you show favoritism, you commit sin and are convicted by the law as transgressors. ¹⁰ For whoever keeps the entire law, and yet stumbles at one point, is guilty of breaking it all. ¹¹ For he who said, **Do not commit adultery,**ᴮ also said, **Do not murder.**ᶜ So if you do not commit adultery, but you murder, you are a lawbreaker. ¹² Speak and act as those who are to be judged by the law of freedom. ¹³ For judgment is without mercy to the one who has not shown mercy. Mercy triumphs over judgment.

Faith and Works

¹⁴ What good is it, my brothers and sisters, if someone claims to have faith but does not have works? Can such faith save him?

¹⁵ If a brother or sister is without clothes and lacks daily food ¹⁶ and one of you says to them, "Go in peace, stay warm, and be well fed," but

you don't give them what the body needs, what good is it? ¹⁷ In the same way faith, if it does not have works, is dead by itself.

¹⁸ But someone will say, "You have faith, and I have works."ᴰ Show me your faith without works, and I will show you faith by my works. ¹⁹ You believe that God is one. Good! Even the demons believe — and they shudder.

²⁰ Senseless person! Are you willing to learn that faith without works is useless? ²¹ Wasn't Abraham our father justified by works in offering Isaac his son on the altar? ²² You see that faith was active together with his works, and by works, faith was made complete, ²³ and the Scripture was fulfilled that says, **Abraham believed God, and it was credited to him as righteousness,**ᴱ and he was called God's friend. ²⁴ You see that a person is justified by works and not by faith alone. ²⁵ In the same way, wasn't Rahab the prostitute also justified by works in receiving the messengers and sending them out by a different route? ²⁶ For just as the body without the spirit is dead, so also faith without works is dead.

Controlling the Tongue

3 Not many should become teachers, my brothers,ᶠ because you know that we will receive a stricter judgment. ² For we all stumble in many ways. If anyone does not stumble in what he says, he is mature, able also to control the whole body. ³ Now if we put bits into the mouths of horses so that they obey us, we direct their whole bodies. ⁴ And consider ships: Though very large and driven by fierce winds, they are guided by a very small rudder wherever the will of the pilot directs. ⁵ So too, though the tongue is a small part of the body, it boasts great things. Consider how a small fire sets ablaze a large forest. ⁶ And the

---

ᴬ2:8 Lv 19:18 ᴮ2:11 Ex 20:14; Dt 5:18 ᶜ2:11 Ex 20:13; Dt 5:17 ᴰ2:18 The quotation may end here or after v. 18b or v. 19.
ᴱ2:23 Gn 15:6 ᶠ3:1 Or *brothers and sisters*

2:2–3 James portrayed favoritism by illustrating contrasting attitudes toward a wealthy man and a poor man who enter the **meeting**. The attendance of a wealthy man promises financial advantage since his tithes and offerings may be large, thus the people in the assembly **look with favor** on him. "Look with favor" is related in meaning to "showing favoritism" in v. 1.
2:5 God's choice of **the poor** here is not favoritism because the choice was not based on bias.
2:7 The good name refers to Jesus Christ. **Blaspheme** means that the wealthy blaspheme either by speaking against Christ directly or through their actions against the members of the assembly.
2:8–11 Attitudes among Christians should be based on the **royal law**, which says **Love your neighbor as yourself** (Lv 19:18; Mt 19:19; 22:39; Mk 12:31; Rm 13:9; Gl 5:14). Favoritism violates this command, thus convicting those guilty of its practice as **transgressors** of the law.

2:12–13 The phrase **speak and act** refers to "hearing and doing" and tempered speech, as in 1:19–27. The **law of freedom**, or the gospel, will serve as the basis for eschatological judgment (1:2–12).
2:14 Can such faith save him should be understood to mean, "Can a faith that does not express itself in good works be a saving faith?" The answer is no.
2:18 Beginning in this verse James answered a "straw man" argument (**but someone will say**) against his assertion that faith without works is dead.
2:19–20 The demons believe—and they shudder is an answer to the mistaken assertion that belief in God by itself is sufficient for salvation. Saving faith entails more than mere knowledge. It includes trust and obedience, for **faith without works is useless**.
2:21–23 The example of Abraham and his offer of Isaac as a sacrifice (Gn 22:1–19) affirms James's teachings about faith. Good works prove faith genuine. Abraham's faith was proven genuine by his obedience to

God's command. His faith made his good works possible.
2:24–26 James's declaration that **a person is justified by works and not by faith alone** may seem to contradict Rm 3:28, but note that Paul was writing about "works of the law," meaning the Mosaic law.
3:1 Many people desire to be **teachers** because this is an important role in the church. Yet the proliferation of untrained teachers can allow false teachings to arise within congregations, leading some astray. Teachers receive **a stricter judgment** and should not be appointed carelessly.
3:2 Body carries a dual meaning here. It refers to the physical body and the role the tongue plays in it, but it also refers to the body of believers and the influence that teachers have in it.
3:3–6 Like horse **bits** and ship rudders, the size of **the tongue** is disproportionate to the influence it holds. False teaching (expressed by "the tongue") is **a world of unrighteousness**. It pollutes the whole

tongue is a fire. The tongue, a world of unrighteousness, is placed[A] among our members. It stains the whole body, sets the course of life on fire, and is itself set on fire by hell. [7] Every kind of animal, bird, reptile, and fish is tamed and has been tamed by humankind, [8] but no one can tame the tongue. It is a restless evil, full of deadly poison. [9] With the tongue we bless our Lord and Father, and with it we curse people who are made in God's likeness. [10] Blessing and cursing come out of the same mouth. My brothers and sisters, these things should not be this way. [11] Does a spring pour out sweet and bitter water from the same opening? [12] Can a fig tree produce olives, my brothers and sisters, or a grapevine produce figs? Neither can a saltwater spring yield fresh water.

The Wisdom from Above

[13] Who among you is wise and understanding? By his good conduct he should show that his works are done in the gentleness that comes from wisdom. [14] But if you have bitter envy and selfish ambition in your heart, don't boast and deny the truth. [15] Such wisdom does not come down from above but is earthly, unspiritual, demonic. [16] For where there is envy and selfish ambition, there is disorder and every evil practice. [17] But the wisdom from above is first pure, then peace-loving, gentle, compliant, full of mercy and good fruits, unwavering, without pretense. [18] And the fruit of righteousness is sown in peace by those who cultivate peace.

Proud or Humble

4 What is the source of wars and fights among you? Don't they come from your passions that wage war within you?[B] [2] You desire and do not have. You murder and covet and cannot obtain. You fight and wage war.[C] You do not have because you do not ask. [3] You ask and don't receive because you ask with wrong motives, so that you may spend it on your pleasures.

[4] You adulterous people![D] Don't you know that friendship with the world is hostility toward God? So whoever wants to be the friend of the world becomes the enemy of God. [5] Or do you think it's without reason that the Scripture says: The spirit he made to dwell in us envies intensely?[E]

[6] But he gives greater grace. Therefore he says:

God resists the proud
but gives grace to the humble.[F]

[7] Therefore, submit to God. Resist the devil, and he will flee from you. [8] Draw near to God, and he will draw near to you. Cleanse your hands, sinners, and purify your hearts, you double-minded. [9] Be miserable and mourn and weep. Let your laughter be turned to mourning and your joy to gloom. [10] Humble yourselves before the Lord, and he will exalt you.

[11] Don't criticize one another, brothers and sisters. Anyone who defames or judges a fellow believer[G] defames and judges the law. If you judge the law, you are not a doer of the law

---

[A] 3:6 Or places itself, or appoints itself   [B] 4:1 Or war in your members   [C] 4:2 Or You desire and do not have, so you murder. You covet and cannot obtain, so you fight and wage war.   [D] 4:4 Lit Adulteresses   [E] 4:5 Or Scripture says: He jealously yearns for the spirit he made to live in us?, or Scripture says: The Spirit he made to dwell in us longs jealously?   [F] 4:6 Pr 3:34   [G] 4:11 Or his brother or sister

---

body (an individual or a congregation) and determines the destiny of all who follow it. **3:7–8** James refers to all creatures in four categories (see Gn 9:2). He is probably alluding to Gn 1:26.
3:13–18 In spiritual maturity speech plays a role (**don't boast and deny the truth**), but the larger issues are **envy and selfish ambition**. Far from being minor character flaws, these traits are **earthly, unspiritual, demonic**.
3:13 As faith is demonstrated by **works**, so also **wisdom** is demonstrated by **good conduct** and **gentleness**.

3:14–15 The phrase **envy and selfish ambition** contrasts with "good conduct" and "gentleness that comes from wisdom" in v. 13. Denial of **truth** is a constant threat in churches that tolerate false teachings.
3:16–18 James contrasted the two types of wisdom in terms of their sources. Teachers who teach on the basis of "earthly" wisdom produce **disorder and every evil practice**. Teachers who possess **wisdom from above** produce virtues that fulfill the "royal law" (2:8) and promote unity within the congregation.
4:1 While pride and selfishness are natural to fallen humanity and often serve as a basis for advancement in worldly rank, James names them as the **source of wars and fights** within the congregation. **Passions** refers to the pleasures of life, the pursuit of which leads to conflicts.
4:2–3 Two statements distinguished by paired opposites (**desire** . . . **do not have** and **murder and covet** . . . **cannot obtain**) and two direct assertions (**fight and wage war** and **do not have because you do not ask**) describe the problem to which the circumstances had led. Likely, the murder James speaks of refers to their intense anger (see Mt 5:21–22). Their desires were unappeased because they were asking with **wrong motives**.

4:4–5 **Adulterous people** refers to the congregation's unfaithfulness to God. This charge was common in the OT of Israel's relationship to God (Is 54:5–6; Jr 2:20; 3:6–10,20; Ezk 16:38; 23:45; Hs 1:2; 2:5–7). Self-centeredness is cast as diametric opposition (**hostility**) to God.
4:6 James quoted Proverbs 3:34: **God resists the proud**. "Resist" is a military term used to describe an army arrayed for battle. To remain in sinful pride is to invite God's battle array against you. In contrast to this, God **gives grace to the humble** (1:17).
4:7–9 James issued ten commands needed to resolve the conflict within the congregation. **Submit to God** carries the idea of self-humbling; **resist the devil** suggests an active resistance against temptation. **Sinners** and **double-minded** people are parallel terms. "Double-minded" recalls the doubter of 1:8.
4:10 The words **humble yourselves** . . . **and he will exalt you** summarize the path to having forgiveness from God as well as reconciliation among members of the congregation.
4:11–12 Criticism is malicious, judgmental speech toward others. It violates the "royal law" (2:8) and by extension the Mosaic law.

but a judge. ¹² There is one lawgiver and judge^A who is able to save and to destroy. But who are you to judge your neighbor?

Our Will and God's Will

¹³ Come now, you who say, "Today or tomorrow we will travel to such and such a city and spend a year there and do business and make a profit." ¹⁴ Yet you do not know what tomorrow will bring — what your life will be! For you are like vapor that appears for a little while, then vanishes. ¹⁵ Instead, you should say, "If the Lord wills, we will live and do this or that." ¹⁶ But as it is, you boast in your arrogance. All such boasting is evil. ¹⁷ So it is sin to know the good and yet not do it.

Warning to the Rich

5 Come now, you rich people, weep and wail over the miseries that are coming on you. ² Your wealth has rotted and your clothes are moth-eaten. ³ Your gold and silver are corroded, and their corrosion will be a witness against you and will eat your flesh like fire. You have stored up treasure in the last days. ⁴ Look! The pay that you withheld from the workers who mowed your fields cries out, and the outcry of the harvesters has reached the ears of the Lord of Armies. ⁵ You have lived luxuriously on the earth and have indulged yourselves. You have fattened your hearts in a day of slaughter. ⁶ You have condemned, you have murdered the righteous, who does not resist you.

Waiting for the Lord

⁷ Therefore, brothers and sisters, be patient until the Lord's coming. See how the farmer waits for the precious fruit of the earth and is patient with it until it receives the early and the late rains. ⁸ You also must be patient. Strengthen your hearts, because the Lord's coming is near.

⁹ Brothers and sisters, do not complain about one another, so that you will not be judged. Look, the judge stands at the door! ¹⁰ Brothers and sisters, take the prophets who spoke in the Lord's name as an example of suffering and patience. ¹¹ See, we count as blessed those who have endured.^B You have heard of Job's endurance and have seen the outcome that the Lord brought about — the Lord is compassionate and merciful.

Truthful Speech

¹² Above all, my brothers and sisters, do not swear, either by heaven or by earth or with any other oath. But let your "yes" mean "yes," and your "no" mean "no," so that you won't fall under judgment.^C

Effective Prayer

¹³ Is anyone among you suffering? He should pray. Is anyone cheerful? He should sing praises. ¹⁴ Is anyone among you sick? He should call for the elders of the church, and they are to pray over him, anointing him with oil in the name of the Lord. ¹⁵ The prayer of faith will save the sick person, and the Lord will raise him up; if he has committed sins, he will be forgiven. ¹⁶ Therefore, confess your sins to one another and pray for one another, so that you may be healed. The prayer of a righteous person is very powerful in its effect. ¹⁷ Elijah was a human being as we are, and he prayed earnestly that it would not rain, and for three years and six months it did not rain on the land. ¹⁸ Then he prayed again, and the sky gave rain and the land produced its fruit.

---

^A 4:12 Other mss omit *and judge*   ^B 5:11 Or *persevered*   ^C 5:12 Other mss read *fall into hypocrisy*

4:13–14 In a hypothetical but realistic scenario, James accused a merchant who had big designs on making a profit of leaving God out of his plans. Neglecting to entrust our hopes and plans to God and his counsel is paramount to arrogance and unbelief.
4:15–16 The phrase **you should say** and what follows indicate that it is God's will that conditions the course of life.
5:1–6 Oppressive landowners and people who put their trust in riches were commonly addressed in prophetic speech, including by Jesus himself (e.g., Lk 6:24). People who use their wealth to oppress others may seem to go unpunished in this lifetime, but James warns that **miseries** are **coming** in the future judgment.
5:2–3 Wealth is often measured in terms of quality foods, clothes, and silver and gold. Besides referring to **moth-eaten** clothing, the phrase **wealth has rotted** could indicate that food is perishable and thus not a measure of lasting wealth. James's statement about **gold and silver** corroding is paradoxical, emphasizing that even incorruptible commodities are destined to perish. **Last days** emphasizes the eschatological nature

of the pronouncement against greed. **Stored up** (or hoarded) wealth will become the undoing of greedy persons.
5:4 In ancient times payment for work performed was due at the end of the workday. Greed motivated some landowners to withhold these wages. **Withheld** could be translated "defrauded." **Lord of Armies** is an OT reference to God as a warrior (1Ch 11:4–9; Is 2:12ff). The plight of the poor and oppressed worker is known to God.
5:5 Indulging one's passions is described here as fattening the heart.
5:6 **Condemned** is a legal term suggesting that the wealthy took land and wages through decisions rendered in dishonest courts. **Who does not resist you** indicates the helplessness of the poor.
5:7–8 In light of the certainty of God's coming judgment on their oppressors, James encouraged his audience to **be patient** and to await **the Lord's coming**. The phrase **strengthen your hearts** is an expansion on "be patient," signifying firm resolve.
5:9 To **complain about one another** constitutes being judgmental, already prohibited in 4:11–12. The immediacy of the Lord's return

brings judgment to the person who judges, just as it does for the oppressors.
5:10–11 By **suffering and patience**, James means suffering with patience or patience in hardship.
5:12 **Do not swear** is an exhortation to truthfulness, not a universal prohibition against oath-making.
5:13–18 James used a series of questions followed by commands as an effective way of exhorting the congregation to prayer and worship. **Suffering** in v. 13 is not a reference to physical illness; it is instead a spiritual burden caused by misfortune or poor choices. **Elders** should anoint any **sick** person with **oil** and **pray over him**. Olive oil was considered a cure-all ointment in the ancient world, but for James the real healing power is in prayer.

The **prayer of faith** echoes 1:5–8. **Save** refers to physical healing. **The Lord will raise him up** does not indicate that death is at hand (v. 14), but that once healed by the power of God, the sick person could get up and walk (Mt 9:5–7; Mk 1:31; 2:9–12; 9:27; Ac 3:7). **He will be forgiven** indicates that perhaps the illness was connected with sin,

19 My brothers and sisters, if any among you strays from the truth, and someone turns him back, **20** let that person know that whoever turns a sinner from the error of his way will save his soul from death and cover a multitude of sins.

---

and the prayers of the elders could bring spiritual healing as well.

Pray for one another echoes the prayers of the elders, and these should lead to both physical and spiritual healing (i.e., forgiveness). Prayer is not a magical incantation or a guarantee of healing, but when offered fervently by a righteous person, God will respond in a way that best fits his good purposes.

James cited a biblical personality, **Elijah**, who **prayed** effectively (see 1Kg 17:1; 18:41–46). The illustration is intended to encourage his audience that their prayers could lead to similar results.

5:19–20 Someone turns and **whoever turns** both reflect an effort to bring a straying believer back to an authentic Christian faith and lifestyle. **Cover a multitude of sins** probably refers to God's forgiveness (see Pss 32:1; 85:2).

Circumstances of Writing

The author of 1 Peter identified himself as "Peter, an apostle of Jesus Christ" (1:1). He viewed himself as a divinely ordained, directly commissioned, authoritative representative of the Lord Jesus himself. Several statements in the letter indicate that the Peter who plays a prominent role in the Gospels is the author. For example, he called himself an "elder and witness" to Christ's sufferings (5:1). Further, he described Christ's crucifixion with an intimate knowledge that only a disciple would have of that event (2:21–24).

Several expressions in 1 Peter reflect Peter's experiences with Jesus. For example, the exhortation for elders to "shepherd God's flock" (5:2) evokes the charge that Jesus gave Peter in John 21:15–17. Moreover, the command to "clothe yourselves with humility" (5:5) may recall the episode in John 13:2–17 where Jesus washed the disciples' feet.

Objections to the letter's authorship by Peter are inconclusive and cannot be proven. The claim that someone wrote this letter using the apostle's name as a pseudonym cannot be sustained. A number of early church leaders, including Irenaeus, Tertullian, and Clement of Alexandria, accepted the letter as authentic. Further, the early church soundly rejected the practice of writing under an apostolic pseudonym as forgery. In light of the above, the epistle should be accepted as genuinely written by the apostle Peter. Silvanus (Silas) may have in some fashion helped Peter write the letter while serving as his secretary (amanuensis), but more likely he was merely the letter carrier (5:12).

The recipients of 1 Peter are identified in 1:1. Peter wrote to the "exiles dispersed abroad in Pontus, Galatia, Cappadocia, Asia, and Bithynia." These were Roman provinces located in the northern part of what is now modern Turkey, unless Galatia includes the Galatia in the southern region of Asia Minor. These people were likely persecuted Gentile Christians. They had earlier been involved in idolatry (4:3), were ignorant (1:14) and "empty" (1:18) before they came to Christ, and they formerly were "not a people" but now were "God's people" (2:9–10).

The reference in 1 Peter 5:13—"She who is in Babylon, chosen together with you, sends you greetings"—suggests Rome as the place of the letter's origin. "Babylon" was used cryptically to refer to a place of exile, but specifically for Rome. Other possibilities for Babylon include the cities of Babylon in Mesopotamia and in the Nile Delta in Egypt, but these places are highly unlikely because we have no record of Peter ever being in those places.

First Peter was probably written sometime between AD 62 and 64. While Paul was under house arrest from AD 60 to 62, he did not refer to Peter in Rome. Peter likewise did not mention Paul as being in Rome; only Silvanus and Mark were his companions (5:12–13). These facts suggest that Peter wrote 1 Peter sometime after AD 62 and before the writing of 2 Peter.

The theme of suffering appears throughout 1 Peter. The recipients of the letter are the sufferers in four of its five chapters. Given a

---

1 Peter Timeline

AD 1–29

Simon Peter is born in Galilee, probably in the village of Bethsaida. 1?
Simon, a fisherman by trade, moves to Capernaum. 20?
Simon's brother, Andrew, introduces him to Jesus. 29
Jesus calls Simon Peter "the rock." 29
Jesus calls Peter to be one of his twelve disciples. 29

AD 30–33

Jesus heals Simon Peter's mother-in-law. 30
Peter's confession at Caesarea Philippi that Jesus is the Messiah 32
Peter, James, and John witness Jesus's transfiguration. 32
Peter vows to die with Jesus. 33
Peter denies Jesus in the courtyard of Annas. 33

composition date of about AD 62–64, 1 Peter was written during the persecution of Christians under Nero's reign. The persecution arose in Rome and was spreading into Asia Minor.

Contribution to the Bible

Peter's intent in writing was to strengthen believers in the midst of the suffering and persecution they were facing. His message to them continues to speak to modern believers, reminding us of our heavenly hope and eternal inheritance in the midst of our sufferings. We are called to holiness and a life of love. We are also called to glorify God in our daily lives and to imitate Christ.

Structure

The structure of 1 Peter has been the subject of discussion from the earliest history of the church. The diversity of outlines illustrates that the task of exegesis is not merely a science but also an art. Peter wrote this letter with a typical opening for a letter (1:1–2) and then began the next major section (1:3–2:10) with a blessing (1:3). The two succeeding sections are marked by "dear friends" (2:11; 4:12), and, as noted earlier, the segment from 2:11 to 4:11 concludes with a doxology and "amen." The fourth section of the letter also ends with a doxology and "amen" (5:11) before the closing.

Outline

I. Opening (1:1–2)
II. Called to Salvation as Exiles (1:3–2:10)
III. Living as Strangers in a Hostile World (2:11–4:11)
IV. Persevering in Suffering (4:12–5:11)
V. Concluding Words (5:12–14)

Key verse in 1 Peter

4:19 So then, let those who suffer according to God's will entrust themselves to a faithful Creator while doing what is good.

AD 33–40

Following his resurrection, Jesus appears to Peter and recommissions him. **33**

Three thousand people respond to Peter's sermon at the feast of Pentecost. **33**

Saul's conversion on the Damascus Road **OCTOBER 34**

Paul meets with Peter and James on his first visit to Jerusalem following his conversion. **37?**

AD 40–114

Peter, James, John, Paul, Barnabas, and Titus meet in Jerusalem to deal with the question of whether Gentiles had to be circumcised to become Christians. **49**

At Antioch, Paul confronts Peter's refusal to share meals with Gentile believers. **49**

Peter's martyrdom in Rome during Nero's persecution of Christians **66**

Destruction of Jerusalem **70**

Polycarp's Letter to Philippians shows dependence on 1 Peter. **112–114**

Greeting

1 Peter, an apostle of Jesus Christ:
To those chosen, living as exiles dispersed abroad in Pontus, Galatia, Cappadocia, Asia, and Bithynia, chosen ² according to the foreknowledge of God the Father, through the sanctifying work of the Spirit, to be obedient and to be sprinkled with the blood of Jesus Christ. May grace and peace be multiplied to you.

A Living Hope

³ Blessed be the God and Father of our Lord Jesus Christ. Because of his great mercy he has given us new birth into a living hope through the resurrection of Jesus Christ from the dead ⁴ and into an inheritance that is imperishable, undefiled, and unfading, kept in heaven for you. ⁵ You are being guarded by God's power through faith for a salvation that is ready to be revealed in the last time. ⁶ You rejoice in this, ^ even though now for a short time, if necessary, you suffer grief in various trials ⁷ so that the proven character of your faith — more valuable than gold which, though perishable, is refined by fire — may result in praise, glory, and honor at the revelation of Jesus Christ. ⁸ Though you have not seen him, you love him; though not seeing him now, you believe in him, and you rejoice with inexpressible and glorious joy, ⁹ because you are receiving the goal of your faith, the salvation of your souls.

¹⁰ Concerning this salvation, the prophets, who prophesied about the grace that would come to you, searched and carefully investigated. ¹¹ They inquired into what time or what circumstances the Spirit of Christ within them was indicating when he testified in advance to the sufferings of Christ and the glories that would follow.^ ¹² It was revealed to them that they were not serving themselves but you. These things have now been announced to you through those who preached the gospel to you by the Holy Spirit sent from heaven — angels long to catch a glimpse of these things.

A Call to Holy Living

¹³ Therefore, with your minds ready for action, be sober-minded and set your hope completely

---

^1:6 Or *In this fact rejoice*   ^1:11 Or *the glories after that*

1:1–2 The apostles were Christ's divinely ordained, directly commissioned, authoritative representatives in the early church. **Exiles** (v. 1; 2:11) refers to people living in a region that is not their permanent place of residence—in this case, the five Roman provinces located in what is now modern Turkey. **Dispersed** means a "scattering" and usually refers to God's people scattered outside of their homeland. Divine **foreknowledge** is the basis on which a believer is **chosen** (i.e., "elect"). It is more than just God's prior knowledge of everything; it also includes his predetermination. **Through the sanctifying work of the Spirit** is the means by which being "chosen" is made a reality. The phrase **to be obedient and to be sprinkled with the blood of Jesus Christ** describes the aim and purpose of election (Ex 24:3–8). Christ's blood brings believers into this relationship. **1:3–5** Peter informed his readers that God had given them **new birth** into an inheritance that will never perish, be defiled, or fade—indeed a sure salvation. That salvation is **to be revealed in the last time** reminds us of the future aspect of salvation. **1:6–9** Christians can **rejoice** in this imperishable inheritance and sure salvation even though they are tested by persecution and suffering while in this world. **1:10–12** The good news of salvation that the **prophets** sought and looked forward to had now been **revealed**. Salvation in Christ is so great and the blessings so tremendous that **angels long to catch a glimpse of these things**. The gospel excites their interest so much that they want to study it intently. **1:13** The **grace to be brought to you at the revelation of Jesus Christ** refers to

---

Character profile:
Peter

A s Jesus walked along the Sea of Galilee he saw two brothers, Simon Peter and Andrew, fishermen by trade. "'Follow Me,' he told them, 'and I will make you fish for people.' Immediately they left their nets and followed him" (Mt 4:19–20).

That seaside encounter with Peter is perhaps the only unremarkable reference to him in the Gospels. For better or worse, the man's personality leaps off the page of practically every Bible passage that mentions him.

Peter was a complex man. He proved himself to be courageous and loyal yet capable of stunning lapses in judgment. Yet if Peter seems to be on the receiving end of more than his share of rebukes from Jesus, it may be because he dared to risk more than his fellow disciples.

Along with James and John, Peter was part of Jesus's inner circle—the companions to whom he turned for support at critical times. Even among that trio, Peter stood out. In stories involving the disciples, Peter is often at the center of the action. During a precarious crossing of the Sea of Galilee, only Peter had the courage and desire to step out of the boat in the middle of a raging storm in order to walk on the water to Jesus.

When thoughts and questions occurred to him, Peter didn't spend a lot of time in deep contemplation over them. He simply blurted them out. Sometimes that earned him high praise from the Lord, as when he declared Jesus to be "the Messiah, the Son of the living God" (16:16). At other times it put him in

the proverbial doghouse, such as when Peter dared to object to Jesus's prophecy of his impending death and received Jesus's sharp rebuke: "Get behind me, Satan!" (16:23).

Peter no doubt experienced significant despair and self-loathing after he denied knowing Jesus three times on the night the Lord was arrested and put on trial. Yet Peter didn't stay down for long.

Even before Peter's betrayal, Jesus prayed that his strength would not fail and that he would strengthen his fellow disciples (Lk 22:31–32). After the Lord's resurrection, he restored Peter (Jn 21:15–19). As the early church began, Peter assumed a significant leadership role, preaching a message on the day of Pentecost that led to thousands of conversions (Ac 2:14–41). He fulfilled the destiny Jesus laid out for him: "I also say to you that you are Peter, and on this rock I will build my church, and the gates of Hades will not overpower it" (Mt 16:18).

Peter boldly proclaimed Jesus's message throughout the Jewish world—and later throughout the Gentile world—until his own death. According to church tradition, Peter was crucified upside down because he didn't believe he was worthy to be crucified in the same manner as his Lord.

Peter serves as a mirror for Christians who read the Gospels and the book of Acts. His decisions are relatable. His human nature is all too recognizable. His boldness and his cowardice touch our hearts.

For all his bluster, confusion, wrongheadedness, and mistakes, the man was deemed useful by the Son of God. Jesus looked past his dross and saw the gold, just as he does for anyone who follows him. If you ever feel useless in your walk with Christ, look to the apostle Peter for inspiration.

on the grace to be brought to you at the revelation of Jesus Christ. [14] As obedient children, do not be conformed to the desires of your former ignorance. [15] But as the one who called you is holy, you also are to be holy in all your conduct; [16] for it is written, **Be holy, because I am holy.**[A] [17] If you appeal to the Father who judges impartially according to each one's work, you are to conduct yourselves in reverence during your time living as strangers. [18] For you know that you were redeemed from your empty way of life inherited from your ancestors, not with perishable things like silver or gold, [19] but with the precious blood of Christ, like that of an unblemished and spotless lamb. [20] He was foreknown before the foundation of the world but was revealed in these last times for you. [21] Through him you believe in God, who raised him from the dead and gave him glory, so that your faith and hope are in God.

[22] Since you have purified yourselves by your obedience to the truth,[B] so that you show sincere brotherly love for each other, from a pure[C] heart love one another constantly,[D] [23] because you have been born again — not of perishable seed but of imperishable — through the living and enduring word of God. [24] For

All flesh is like grass,
and all its glory like a flower
    of the grass.
The grass withers,
    and the flower falls,
[25]   but the word of the Lord
    endures forever.[E]

And this word is the gospel that was proclaimed to you.

The Living Stone and a Holy People

2 Therefore, rid yourselves of all malice, all deceit, hypocrisy, envy, and all slander. [2] Like newborn infants, desire the pure milk of the word,[F] so that by it you may grow up into your salvation, [3] if **you have tasted that the Lord is good.**[G] [4] As you come to him, a living stone — rejected by people but chosen and honored by[H] God — [5] you yourselves, as living stones, a spiritual house, are being built to be a holy priesthood[I] to offer spiritual sacrifices acceptable to God through Jesus Christ. [6] For it stands in Scripture:

See, I lay a stone in Zion,
a chosen and honored[J] cornerstone,
and the one who believes in him
    will never be put to shame.[K]

[7] So honor will come to you who believe; but for the unbelieving,

The stone that the builders
    rejected —
this one has become the cornerstone,[L]
[8] and

A stone to stumble over,
and a rock to trip over.[M]

They stumble because they disobey the word; they were destined for this. [9] But you are **a chosen race,**[N,O] **a royal priesthood,**[P] **a holy nation,**[Q] **a people for his possession,**[R] **so that you may proclaim the praises**[S,T] of the one who called you out of darkness into his marvelous light. [10] Once you were not a people, but now you are God's people; you had not received mercy, but now you have received mercy.

A Call to Good Works

[11] Dear friends, I urge you as strangers and exiles to abstain from sinful desires that wage war against the soul. [12] Conduct yourselves honorably among the Gentiles,[U] so that when they slander you as evildoers, they will observe your good works and will glorify God on the day he visits.

[13] Submit to every human authority because of the Lord, whether to the emperor[V] as the supreme authority [14] or to governors as those sent out by him to punish those who do what is evil and to praise those who do what is good. [15] For it is God's will that you silence the ignorance of foolish people by doing good. [16] Submit as free people, not using your freedom as a cover-up for evil, but as God's slaves. [17] Honor

---

[A] 1:16 Lv 11:44–45; 19:2; 20:7   [B] 1:22 Other mss add *through the Spirit*   [C] 1:22 Other mss omit *pure*   [D] 1:22 Or *fervently*   [E] 1:24–25 Is 40:6–8   [F] 2:2 Or *desire pure spiritual milk*   [G] 2:3 Ps 34:8   [H] 2:4 Or *precious to*   [I] 2:5 Or *you yourselves, as living stones, are being built into a spiritual house for a holy priesthood*   [J] 2:6 Or *precious*   [K] 2:6 Is 28:16 LXX   [L] 2:7 Ps 118:22   [M] 2:8 Is 8:14   [N] 2:9 Or *generation, or nation*   [O] 2:9 Dt 7:6; 10:15; Is 43:20 LXX   [P] 2:9 Ex 19:6; 23:22 LXX; Is 61:6   [Q] 2:9 Ex 19:6; 23:22 LXX   [R] 2:9 Ex 19:5; 23:22 LXX; Dt 4:20; 7:6; Is 43:21 LXX   [S] 2:9 Or *the mighty deeds*   [T] 2:9 Is 42:12; 43:21   [U] 2:12 Or *among the nations,* or *among the pagans*   [V] 2:13 Or *king*

---

the culmination of God's redemptive activity in Jesus that will occur at his return (v. 5). **1:14** *Former ignorance* suggests that the recipients of this letter were mostly Gentiles. **1:17** Believers should live with a healthy *reverence* in all their conduct in the world. **1:18–19** The metaphor of an *unblemished and spotless lamb* points to Christ's sinlessness (Lv 22:19–25). He is the sacrificial Lamb of God (Jn 1:29; Rv 5). **1:20** The plan for Christ's sacrifice on behalf of sinners was fixed in eternity past, a sure reality set to unfold at a divinely appointed time in history (Gl 4:4).

1:22–25 Believers are those who are born again through the **living and enduring word of God**, the gospel. **2:1–3** Spiritual **milk** is a metaphor that refers to the divine sustenance drawn from the gospel. The statement **you have tasted that the Lord is good** (cp. Ps 34:8) means they had found God to be gracious. **2:4–10** Jesus is called the **living stone** and **the cornerstone**, but also the **rejected** stone and the **stone to stumble over**. Peter assured his readers that they are God's valuable possession—**living stones** built into **a spiritual house**. **A chosen race**

(v. 9; cp. vv. 4,6; Is 43:20) seems to refer to the corporate unity of believers. They are also **a royal priesthood**—a collective company of priests—who offer up **spiritual sacrifices** to God (v. 5). The transfer from **darkness** to **light** is a common NT description of conversion (Ac 26:18; 2Co 4:6; Eph 5:8). **2:11–12** Peter commanded his readers to live honorably as holy **strangers and exiles** so that even hostile Gentile residents of the earth might come to glorify God. **2:13–17** Peter exhorted his readers to submit to governmental and civil authority, acting

everyone. Love the brothers and sisters. Fear God. Honor the emperor.

Submission of Slaves to Masters

18 Household slaves, submit to your masters with all reverence not only to the good and gentle ones but also to the cruel. **19** For it brings favor if, because of a consciousness of God, someone endures grief from suffering unjustly. **20** For what credit is there if when you do wrong and are beaten, you endure it? But when you do what is good and suffer, if you endure it, this brings favor with God.

21 For you were called to this, because Christ also suffered for you, leaving you an example, that you should follow in his steps. **22** He did not commit sin, **and no deceit was found in his mouth;**[A] **23** when he was insulted, he did not insult in return; when he suffered, he did not threaten but entrusted himself to the one who judges justly. **24** He himself bore our sins in his body on the tree; so that, having died to sins, we might live for righteousness. **By his wounds**[B] **you have been healed. 25** For you were like sheep going astray,[C] but you have now returned to the Shepherd and Overseer[D] of your souls.

Wives and Husbands

3 In the same way, wives, submit yourselves to your own husbands so that, even if some disobey the word, they may be won over without a word by the way their wives live **2** when they observe your pure, reverent lives. **3** Don't let your beauty consist of outward things like elaborate hairstyles and wearing gold jewelry or fine clothes, **4** but rather what is inside the heart[E] — the imperishable quality of a gentle and quiet spirit, which is of great worth in God's sight. **5** For in the past, the holy women who put their hope in God also adorned themselves in this way, submitting to their own husbands, **6** just as Sarah obeyed Abraham, calling him lord. You have become her

children when you do what is good and do not fear any intimidation.

7 Husbands, in the same way, live with your wives in an understanding way, as with a weaker partner, showing them honor as coheirs of the grace of life, so that your prayers will not be hindered.

Do No Evil

8 Finally, all of you be like-minded and sympathetic, love one another, and be compassionate and humble,[F] **9** not paying back evil for evil or insult for insult but, on the contrary, giving a blessing, since you were called for this, so that you may inherit a blessing.

10　For the one who wants to love life
　　　and to see good days,
　　　let him keep his tongue from evil
　　　and his lips from speaking deceit,
11　and let him turn away from evil
　　　and do what is good.
　　　Let him seek peace and pursue it,
12　because the eyes of the Lord are
　　　　on the righteous
　　　and his ears are open to their prayer.
　　　But the face of the Lord is against
　　　those who do what is evil.[G]

Undeserved Suffering

13 Who then will harm you if you are devoted to what is good? **14** But even if you should suffer for righteousness, you are blessed. **Do not fear them**[H] **or be intimidated,**[I] **15** but in your hearts regard[J] Christ[K] the Lord as holy, ready at any time to give a defense to anyone who asks you for a reason for the hope that is in you. **16** Yet do this with gentleness and reverence, keeping a clear conscience, so that when you are accused,[L] those who disparage your good conduct in Christ will be put to shame. **17** For it is better to suffer for doing good, if that should be God's will, than for doing evil. **18** For Christ also suffered for sins once for all, the righteous for the unrighteous, that he

---

[A]**2:22** Is 53:9　[B]**2:24** Is 53:5　[C]**2:25** Is 53:6　[D]**2:25** Or *Guardian*　[E]**3:4** Or *rather, the hidden person of the heart*　[F]**3:8** Other mss read *courteous*　[G]**3:10–12** Ps 34:12–16　[H]**3:14** Or *Do not fear what they fear*　[I]**3:14** Is 8:12　[J]**3:15** Or *sanctify*, or *set apart*　[K]**3:15** Other mss read *set God*　[L]**3:16** Other mss read *when they speak against you as evildoers*

---

as free people. The **foolish people** refers to the Gentiles mentioned in v. 12.
2:18–25 Peter charged **household slaves** to **submit** to their **masters** by doing good, even though they might suffer unjustly. Such behavior **brings favor with God**. While doing so they are to remember the example of Christ, who suffered unjustly while submitting to God's will. The phrase **by his wounds** (cp. Is 53:5) refers to the death of Christ and not to the flogging he suffered at the hands of Roman soldiers (Jn 19:1). By his death believers are **healed** spiritually.
3:1–6 Peter instructed **wives** to **submit** to their **husbands** because they bear distinctive witness to them through their God-honoring lifestyles. The statement **you have become her children** means that Christian

wives in essence show themselves to be Sarah's spiritual children when they **do what is good** and **do not fear any intimidation**.
3:7 Peter enjoined **husbands** to live in harmony with their **wives** and to show them **honor as coheirs of the grace of life**, or to treat them as fellow inheritors of salvation and its privileges. **Weaker partner** denotes physical weakness and should not be taken to mean that wives are morally or intellectually inferior to their husbands.
3:8–12 The apostle's teaching here (v. 9) reflects that of Christ elsewhere (Mt 5:43–44; Lk 6:27–28).
3:13–17 Believers are commanded to suffer only for the doing of good and not for evil among those who call this world their home.

3:13–14 Doing **what is good** will harm no one, though believers may suffer for it—in which case they should count it a privilege to suffer for a lifestyle that pleases God (Jms 1:2).
3:15 Peter urged believers to **regard Christ the Lord as holy** from the center of their being. This inner reverence for Christ should lead believers to be **ready at any time** to give a frank **defense** of the **hope** within them. On "hope," cp. v. 5; 1:3,21.
3:16–17 Christians ought to defend their faith **with gentleness and reverence**, not anger and arrogance. By this means, unbelievers will be humiliated when they malign believers.
3:18–22 Jesus' innocent suffering, death, and resurrection/exaltation are the foundation for the salvation and vindication of believers.

might bring you to God. He was put to death in the flesh^A but made alive by the Spirit,[8] [19] in which^c he also went and made proclamation to the spirits in prison [20] who in the past were disobedient, when God patiently waited in the days of Noah while the ark was being prepared. In it a few — that is, eight people^D — were saved through water. [21] Baptism, which corresponds to this, now saves you (not as the removal of dirt from the body, but the pledge^E of a good conscience toward God) through the resurrection of Jesus Christ, [22] who has gone into heaven and is at the right hand of God with angels, authorities, and powers subject to him.

Following Christ

4 Therefore, since Christ suffered^F in the flesh, arm yourselves also with the same understanding^G — because the one who suffers in the flesh is finished with sin^H — [2] in order to live the remaining time in the flesh no longer for human desires, but for God's will. [3] For there has already been enough time spent in doing what the Gentiles choose to do: carrying on in unrestrained behavior, evil desires, drunkenness, orgies, carousing, and lawless idolatry. [4] They are surprised that you don't join them in the same flood of wild living — and they slander^I you. [5] They will give an account to the one who stands ready to judge the living and the dead. [6] For this reason the gospel was also preached to those who are now dead,^J so that, although they might be judged in the flesh according to human standards, they might live in the spirit according to God's standards.

End-Time Ethics

[7] The end of all things is near; therefore, be alert and sober-minded for prayer. [8] Above all, maintain constant love for one another, since **love covers a multitude of sins.**^K [9] Be hospitable to one another without complaining. [10] Just

as each one has received a gift, use it to serve others, as good stewards of the varied grace of God. [11] If anyone speaks, let it be as one who speaks God's words; if anyone serves, let it be from the strength God provides, so that God may be glorified through Jesus Christ in everything. To him be the glory and the power forever and ever. Amen.

Christian Suffering

[12] Dear friends, don't be surprised when the fiery ordeal comes among you to test you, as if something unusual were happening to you. [13] Instead, rejoice as you share in the sufferings of Christ, so that you may also rejoice with great joy when his glory is revealed. [14] If you are ridiculed for the name of Christ, you are blessed, because the Spirit of glory and of God^L rests on you. [15] Let none of you suffer as a murderer, a thief, an evildoer, or a meddler.^M [16] But if anyone suffers as a Christian, let him not be ashamed but let him glorify God in having that name.^N [17] For the time has come for judgment to begin with God's household, and if it begins with us, what will the outcome be for those who disobey the gospel of God?

[18]   And **if a righteous person is saved**
            with difficulty,
        what will become of the ungodly
            and the sinner?^O

[19] So then, let those who suffer according to God's will entrust themselves to a faithful Creator while doing what is good.

About the Elders

5 I exhort the elders among you as a fellow elder and witness to the sufferings of Christ, as well as one who shares in the glory about to be revealed: [2] Shepherd God's flock among you, not overseeing^P out of compulsion but willingly, as God would have you;^Q not out of greed for money but eagerly; [3] not

---

^A 3:18 Or *By the flesh,* or *in the fleshly realm*   ^B 3:18 Or *in the spirit,* or *in the Spirit,* or *in the spiritual realm*   ^c 3:19 Or *by whom,* or *in whom,* or *at that time*   ^D 3:20 Or *souls*   ^E 3:21 Or *the appeal*   ^F 4:1 Other mss read *suffered for us*   ^G 4:1 Or *perspective,* or *attitude*   ^H 4:1 Or *the one who suffered in the flesh has finished with sin*   ^I 4:4 Or *blaspheme*   ^J 4:6 Or *those who are dead*   ^K 4:8 Pr 10:12   ^L 4:14 Or *God's glorious Spirit*   ^M 4:15 Or *as one who defrauds others*   ^N 4:16 Other mss read *in that case*   ^O 4:18 Pr 11:31 LXX   ^P 5:2 Other mss omit *overseeing*   ^Q 5:2 Other mss omit *as God would have you*

3:19–20a This statement is extremely difficult to interpret. According to one plausible view, the term **spirits** refers to the souls of people who died in the great flood (Gn 6–7). The **proclamation** was made by the pre-incarnate Christ through Noah's preaching to his disobedient contemporaries. Peter could refer to Noah's contemporaries as **the spirits in prison** because when he wrote this letter they had long been dead, were incorporeal spirits, and were under confinement awaiting God's final judgment. The position taken in the text of the CSB is that Christ after his death and resurrection made a proclamation of victory over the demonic spirits. In this view the "spirits" are evil angels.
3:20b–21 Baptism in the NT corresponds to this OT event (Gn 7:22–23) in that both involve breaks from past lives and a fresh

start and entrance into new life. That the act of **baptism** is viewed symbolically and does not actually save us is explained by Peter in the latter half of v. 21 with the words **not as the removal of dirt from the body**.
4:1 Suffering doesn't result in sinless perfection. But to resolve to embrace suffering as a follower of Christ is clear evidence that one has turned from a life of sin.
4:5 The living and the dead means anyone who has ever lived, or people of all generations.
4:6 Those who are now dead seems to refer to deceased believers in Christ. When they were alive, the gospel was preached to them. While on earth they were **judged in the flesh according to human standards,** or condemned and martyred on account of the gospel. But they now **live in the spirit according to God's standards**.

4:8 The phrase **love covers a multitude of sins** means that love repeatedly forgives (Pr 10:12).
4:10 The **gift** that **each one has received** refers to a spiritual gift. Spiritual gifts are divine endowments that God entrusts to believers as **stewards**.
4:15–16 Peter encouraged his readers to live in such a way that their sufferings were caused by their devotion to Christ and not by any evil acts; they would **glorify God** by doing so.
4:17–18 If even believers in Christ will be judged, then what terrible punishment must surely await unbelievers, who pay no heed to the gospel of Christ?
5:1–4 Peter charged **elders** to be exemplary, responsible servants (see 1Tm 3:1–7; Ti 1:5–9). The term *elders* refers to the office

lording it over those entrusted to you, but being examples to the flock. [4] And when the chief Shepherd appears, you will receive the unfading crown of glory. [5] In the same way, you who are younger, be subject to the elders. All of you clothe yourselves with[A] humility toward one another, because

**God resists the proud
but gives grace to the humble.[B]**

Conclusion

[6] Humble yourselves, therefore, under the mighty hand of God, so that he may exalt you at the proper time, [7] casting all your cares on him, because he cares about you. [8] Be sober-minded, be alert. Your adversary the devil is prowling around like a roaring lion, looking for anyone he can devour. [9] Resist him, firm in the faith, knowing that the same kind of sufferings are being experienced by your fellow believers throughout the world.

[10] The God of all grace, who called you to his eternal glory in Christ,[C] will himself restore, establish, strengthen, and support you after you have suffered a little while.[D] [11] To him be dominion[E] forever.[F] Amen.

[12] Through Silvanus,[G] a faithful brother (as I consider him), I have written to you briefly in order to encourage you and to testify that this is the true grace of God. Stand firm in it! [13] She who is in Babylon, chosen together with you, sends you greetings, as does Mark, my son. [14] Greet one another with a kiss of love. Peace to all of you who are in Christ.[H]

[A] 5:5 Or *you tie around yourselves* [B] 5:5 Pr 3:34 LXX [C] 5:10 Other mss read *in Christ Jesus* [D] 5:10 Or *to a small extent*
[E] 5:11 Some mss read *dominion and glory*; other mss read *glory and dominion* [F] 5:11 Other mss read *forever and ever*
[G] 5:12 Or *Silas*; Ac 15:22–32; 16:19–40; 17:1–16 [H] 5:14 Other mss read *Christ Jesus. Amen.*

---

of pastoral leaders in the church. Peter's appeal was based on the fact that he was a **fellow elder and witness** to Christ's sufferings. This helped him identify fully with the "elders" he was addressing and gave added support for his plea. He commanded them to be shepherds of **God's flock**. In other words,

they were to nurture, lead, and protect God's people without **lording it over** them. Elders who have served faithfully, despite suffering while on earth, will receive glory in heaven from Christ, **the chief Shepherd**.
5:5a Here the term **elders** may refer to age, not office.

5:5b–7 Peter reminded all believers to practice **humility** and trust God with their cares.
5:8–9 Peter warned believers to be aware of Satan's deceitful practices and to **resist** him firmly. Peter strengthened his readers with the knowledge that other Christians were also suffering.
5:12–14 Silvanus (or "Silas," Ac 15:22–32; 16:19–40; 17:1–15; 18:5; 2Co 1:19; 1Th 1:1; 2Th 1:1) may have helped Peter write this letter as his secretary (cp. Rm 16:22), but more likely he was the letter carrier. Peter conveyed greetings to his readers from the church in Rome, i.e., from **she who is in Babylon**, and also from **Mark, my son**—Peter's son in the faith, not his biological son. The **kiss of love** was a customary form of greeting in the first-century church. **Peace** is the sense of well-being and blessedness that believers have because of their relationship with Christ.

#91   99 Essential Christian Truths

PEOPLE OF GOD

Scripture describes the church as "the people of God" (2Co 6:16). Comprised of both Jew and Gentile, the church is created by God through the atoning death of Christ. The term *church* is used in two senses in Scripture. Individual *local* churches are composed of people who have covenanted together under the lordship of Christ. The *universal* church is composed of all believers in Christ from all times. As the people of God, the church seeks to live under God's rule while we are protected and cared for by him.

Circumstances of Writing

The author of 2 Peter plainly identified himself as the apostle Peter (1:1). He called himself "Simeon Peter" (1:1), a name not generally used of the apostle (elsewhere only in Ac 15:14). The spelling is Semitic and lends a sense of authenticity to Peter's letter. Moreover, it was natural for Peter, as a Semite, to use the original form of his name. Peter designated himself as "a servant and an apostle of Jesus Christ." He viewed himself as a servant submitted to Christ's lordship and as a divinely ordained, directly commissioned, authoritative representative of the Lord Jesus himself.

The letter contains several personal allusions to Peter's life. He mentioned that his death was close (1:14), described himself as an eyewitness of the transfiguration of Jesus (1:16–18), quoted the words of the voice from heaven at this event (1:17), indicated that he had previously written to the letter's recipients (whom he called "dear friends" in 3:1), and also called Paul "our dear brother" (3:15). This suggests that the author was close to Paul. Such references point to Peter as the author.

Many contemporary scholars, however, reject Peter as the author of this letter. They argue, for example, that (1) the personal references to Peter's life are a literary device used by someone who wrote under the apostle's name to create the appearance of authenticity; (2) the style of Greek in 2 Peter is different from that of 1 Peter; (3) the reference to Paul's letters as a collection (3:15–16) points to a date later than Peter's lifetime; and (4) 2 Peter was

dependent upon Jude. If this is true, Peter's authorship is problematic.

In response to these objections, one should consider that (1) the early church soundly rejected the practice of writing under an apostolic pseudonym, regarding it as outright forgery; (2) Peter may have had help in writing 1 Peter (1Pt 5:12) and not in writing 2 Peter, which would lead to different styles in his Greek; (3) rather than the whole collection, Peter may have referred only to those Pauline letters that were known at the time of writing; and (4) Peter may have borrowed some from Jude, or both may have used a common source. All of these evidences suggest that 2 Peter should be accepted as authentic.

Unlike 1 Peter, 2 Peter does not mention specific recipients or refer to an exact destination. The apostle referred to his epistle as the "second letter" he had written to his readers (3:1). If the letter written prior to 2 Peter is 1 Peter, then he wrote to the same recipients ("exiles dispersed abroad in Pontus, Galatia, Cappadocia, Asia, and Bithynia"; 1Pt 1:1). But if the previous letter is a reference to some other epistle that is now unknown, we cannot determine with certainty to whom or to where 2 Peter was written.

Peter likely wrote 2 Peter from Rome, where church tradition placed the apostle in his latter days. Because he mentioned that his death was near (1:14), it seems the letter was written just before his death. Tradition places the date of Peter's martyrdom at about AD 67 during Nero's reign (AD 54–68).

PREHISTORY–AD 29

Noah, his family, and the animal kingdom are spared in the great flood.
God rescues Lot from the complete destruction of Sodom and Gomorrah. **2085 BC?**
Israel kills every male, including Balaam, in their war against Midian. **1407 BC**
Jesus calls Simon Peter "the rock." **AD 29**
Jesus calls Peter to be one of his twelve disciples. **AD 29**

AD 30–33

Jesus heals Simon Peter's mother-in-law. **30**
Peter's confession at Caesarea Philippi that Jesus is the Messiah. **32**
Peter, James, and John witness Jesus's transfiguration **32**
Peter vows to die with Jesus. **33**
Peter denies Jesus in the courtyard of Annas. **33**

Peter wrote this letter shortly before he died (1:14) and, though not mentioned, possibly while in prison. He wrote to Christian friends confronted with the threat of false teachers who were denying Christ's saving work and second coming. As an eyewitness of Jesus's life (1:16–18), Peter sought to affirm for his readers the reality of Christ's return and to remind them of truths they might otherwise forget (3:1).

Contribution to the Bible

Peter made strong connections with the Old Testament and challenged his audience to live authentic Christian lives. Peter had been with Jesus when Jesus first spoke of his return (Mt 24–25), and he gave emphasis to the surety of the second coming.

It is the word of God that holds the forefront of this short letter. Peter does this in chapter 1 by emphasizing knowledge (vv. 3,5–6,8,12,20–21) and its divine origin; in chapter 2, by showing its historicity (vv. 4–8); in chapter 3, by indicating Paul's letters are equal with "the rest of the Scriptures" (vv. 15–16). Peter insisted on the importance of Scripture for guiding and preserving our faith.

Structure

Second Peter is a general letter with the typical features of a salutation, main body, and farewell. What is missing is an expression of thanksgiving. Its style is that of a pastoral letter, driven by the needs of the recipients, rather than some type of formal treatise.

Outline

AD 33–40

Following his resurrection, Jesus appears to Peter and recommissions him. **33**

Three thousand people respond to Peter's sermon at the feast of Pentecost. **33**

Saul's conversion on the Damascus Road **OCTOBER 34**

Paul meets with Peter and James on his first visit to Jerusalem following his conversion. **37?**

Peter bears witness to and baptizes Cornelius and his family at Caesarea Maritima. **40**

AD 50–SECOND CENTURY

Peter, James, John, Paul, Barnabas, and Titus meet in Jerusalem to deal with the question of whether Gentiles had to be circumcised to become Christians. **49**

At Antioch, Paul confronts Peter's refusal to share meals with Gentile believers. **49**

Peter's martyrdom in Rome during Nero's persecution of Christians **66**

Destruction of Jerusalem **70**

Allusions to 2 Peter may exist in a number of second-century documents, including 1 and 2 Clement, Barnabas, Shepherd of Hermas, the letters of Ignatius of Antioch, and the Martyrdom of Polycarp.

Greeting

1 Simeon^A Peter, a servant and an apostle of Jesus Christ:

To those who have received a faith equal to ours through the righteousness of our God and Savior Jesus Christ.

² May grace and peace be multiplied to you through the knowledge of God and of Jesus our Lord.

Growth in the Faith

³ His^B divine power has given us everything required for life and godliness through the knowledge of him who called us by^c his own glory and goodness. ⁴ By these he has given us very great and precious promises, so that through them you may share in the divine nature, escaping the corruption that is in the world because of evil desire. ⁵ For this very reason, make every effort to supplement your faith with goodness, goodness with knowledge, ⁶ knowledge with self-control, self-control with endurance, endurance with godliness, ⁷ godliness with brotherly affection, and brotherly affection with love. ⁸ For if you possess these qualities in increasing measure, they will keep you from being useless or unfruitful in the knowledge of our Lord Jesus Christ. ⁹ The person who lacks these things is blind and shortsighted and has forgotten the cleansing from his past sins. ¹⁰ Therefore, brothers and sisters, make every effort to confirm your calling and election, because if you do these things you will never stumble. ¹¹ For in this way, entry into the eternal kingdom of our Lord and Savior Jesus Christ will be richly provided for you.

¹² Therefore I will always remind you about these things, even though you know them and are established in the truth you now have. ¹³ I think it is right, as long as I am in this bodily tent, to wake you up with a reminder, ¹⁴ since I know that I will soon lay aside my tent, as our Lord Jesus Christ has indeed made clear to me. ¹⁵ And I will also make every effort so that you are able to recall these things at any time after my departure.^D

The Trustworthy Prophetic Word

¹⁶ For we did not follow cleverly contrived myths when we made known to you the power and coming of our Lord Jesus Christ; instead, we were eyewitnesses of his majesty. ¹⁷ For he received honor and glory from God the Father when the voice came to him from the Majestic Glory, saying "This is my beloved Son,^E with whom I am well-pleased!" ¹⁸ We ourselves heard this voice when it came from heaven while we were with him on the holy mountain. ¹⁹ We also have the prophetic word strongly confirmed, and you will do well to pay attention to it, as to a lamp shining in a dark place, until the day dawns and the morning star rises in your hearts. ²⁰ Above all, you know this: No prophecy of Scripture comes from the prophet's own interpretation, ²¹ because no prophecy ever came by the will of man; instead, men spoke from God as they were carried along by the Holy Spirit.

The Judgment of False Teachers

2 There were indeed false prophets among the people, just as there will be false teachers among you. They will bring in destructive

---

^1:1 Other mss read *Simon* ᴮ1:3 Lit *As his* ᶜ1:3 Or *to* ᴰ1:15 Or *death* ᴱ1:17 Or *my Son, my beloved*

1:1–2 Peter called himself **Simeon Peter**, a name not generally used of him (elsewhere only in Ac 15:14). He further identified himself as **a servant** submitted to Christ's lordship and as one of Christ's divinely appointed, authoritative representatives—**an apostle**. Peter named neither specific recipients in his letter nor their precise geographic location. Peter described Jesus as both **God and Savior**, which is not surprising since elsewhere Jesus is called God (Jn 1:1,18; 20:28; Rm 9:5; Ti 2:13; Heb 1:8). **Grace** is God's unmerited favor displayed toward sinners who trust Christ for salvation. **Peace** is the sense of well-being and the attendant blessings that a person enjoys because of a right relationship with Christ.
1:3–4 Christ provides believers everything they need for **life and godliness**. "Life" is eternal life, whereas "godliness" is godly living; the latter cannot be obtained without the former. **By these**—by Christ's **glory and goodness**—he has given us very great **and precious promises**. The content of these great promises includes sharing in the **divine nature**. Peter did not mean that believers become gods or that they share in the divine nature of God in every way. He meant that they participate in God's moral

excellence and will one day be morally perfected. Participation in the divine nature is possible only after escaping the **corruption** in the world because of **evil desire**.
1:5–7 Because of God's generous provision in Christ, Peter encouraged his readers to build upon their foundation of **faith**—their initial acceptance of God's love—with the Christian virtues of **goodness**, knowledge, **self-control**, endurance, godliness, **brotherly affection**, and **love**. These graces are the fruit of sharing in the divine nature. Each successive quality seems to spring from the previous one.
1:8–9 Those who lack the qualities mentioned in vv. 5–7 are **blind and shortsighted** because they have forgotten the cleansing from their **past sins**. "Past sins" refers to sins committed before professing faith in Christ.
1:10–11 Peter charged his readers to **make every effort** to prove the reality of their **calling and election** to salvation. Two results follow. (1) They **will never stumble**. (2) They will receive a glorious entry into the **eternal kingdom** of our Lord and Savior Jesus Christ.
1:12–13 As long as Peter was **in this bodily tent**—alive in the human body, a temporary dwelling place for this life—he determined always to **remind** his readers of teachings

that they might otherwise lay aside despite his conviction that they were well-grounded in the truths they had been taught.
1:14–15 The apostle knew that his death was near, and he committed to **make every effort** to arrange that his readers would be **able to recall** his teachings **at any time**. This seems to refer to a written witness since it could be consulted "at any time." Peter might have been referring to Mark's Gospel. Mark's Gospel was based on eyewitness information given by Peter.
1:16–18 Peter had been an eyewitness of Jesus's transfiguration (Mt 17:1–7; Mk 9:2–9; Lk 9:28–36).
1:19–21 The metaphor of the prophetic Scriptures as **a lamp shining in a dark place** means that they act as a torch that shines in this dark world. **The day dawns and the morning star rises** seems to refer to Christ's return. **In your hearts** may refer to the glowing hope that occurs in believers' hearts when they see clear signs of the Lord's return. Peter further explained that Scripture is trustworthy because it has a divine origin; men **carried along by the Holy Spirit** wrote the OT.
2:1–3 **False prophets** arose among the people in OT times, just as **false teachers**

The Historical Reliability of the New Testament

by Craig L. Blomberg

The New Testament contains four biographies of Jesus (the Gospels), one history book of the early church (Acts), twenty-one letters (Romans to Jude), and an apocalypse (Revelation). While the letters and the apocalypse contain references to historical events, the Gospels and Acts are written as straightforward historical narratives. These are the New Testament books about which it makes particularly good sense to ask the question, "Are they historically reliable?" Twelve lines of evidence converge to suggest strongly that the answer is "yes":

1. We have more than 5,700 Greek manuscripts representing all, or part, of the New Testament. By examining these manuscripts, more than 99 percent of the original text can be reconstructed beyond reasonable doubt. We also discover that no Christian doctrine or ethic depends solely on one of the doubted texts. These facts do not prove that the New Testament is true, but it does mean we know what the original writers wrote. Without this assurance, the question of historical reliability is pointless.

2. The authors of the Gospels and Acts were in an excellent position to report reliable information. Matthew and John were among the twelve disciples Jesus himself chose; Mark was a close companion of Peter; Luke (who also wrote Acts) traveled extensively with Paul. Even critical scholars who doubt the traditional attributions of authorship affirm that these five books were written by followers of Matthew, Mark, Luke, and John, which still puts them in a good place to tell the stories accurately.

3. These five books were almost certainly written in the first century, within sixty to seventy years of Jesus's death (most likely in AD 30). Conservative evangelical scholars typically date Matthew, Mark, and Luke–Acts to the AD 60s and John to the AD 80s or 90s. Critical liberal scholars suggest slightly later dates, typically placing Mark in the AD 60s or 70s, Matthew and Luke–Acts in the AD 80s, and John in the AD 90s. Even if one accepts the later dates, the amount of time separating the historical events and the composition of the five books is very short as compared to most ancient historical and biographical accounts, where many centuries could intervene between events and the books that narrated them.

4. Ancient Jews and Greeks meticulously cultivated the art of memorization, committing complex oral traditions to memory. Even before the Gospels or any other written sources about Jesus were compiled, Jesus's followers were carefully passing along accounts of his teachings and mighty works by word of mouth. This kept the historical events alive until the time they were written down.

5. The ancient memorization and transference of sacred tradition allowed for some freedoms in retelling the stories. Guardians of the tradition could abbreviate, paraphrase, prioritize, and provide commentary on the subject matter as long as they were true to the gist or meaning of the accounts they passed along. This goes a long way to explaining both the similarities and the differences among the four Gospels. All four authors were true to the gist of Jesus's life, yet they exercised reasonable freedom to shape the accounts in ways they saw fit.

6. The fact that these writers had distinct ideological or theological emphases does not mean they distorted history, as is often alleged. Oftentimes the very cause that a historian or biographer supports requires them to write their accounts accurately, for they know that their cause will be undermined if they are charged with bias or distortion. The first Christians had the uphill battle of promoting a crucified Messiah and his bodily resurrection. Had they been known to have falsified the details of their accounts, their

movement would have been squelched from the outset.

7. Luke's prologue (Lk 1:1–4) closely parallels the form and content of other works of generally reliable historians and biographers of antiquity, most notably Josephus, Herodotus, and Thucydides. The Gospel writers clearly believed that they were writing historically accurate works, not fiction or embellished history.

8. The so-called hard sayings of Jesus support their authenticity. If the Gospel writers felt free to distort what Jesus originally said in order to increase the attractiveness of Christianity, why would they preserve unmodified his difficult and easily misunderstood teachings about hating family members (Lk 14:26) or not knowing when he would return (Mk 13:32)? The fact that they let these teachings stand indicates their faithfulness to recount true history.

9. The fact that the New Testament does not record Jesus speaking about many of the topics that arose after his earthly life, during the time of the early church, supports its historical accuracy. For instance, early Christians were divided over how or whether the laws of Moses applied to Gentile converts (Ac 15). The easiest way to settle the controversy would be to cite Jesus's teachings on the matter, but the Gospels record no such teachings. This silence suggests that the Gospel writers did not feel free to play fast and loose with history by putting on the lips of Jesus teachings that could solve early church controversies.

10. The testimony of non-Christian writers supports the details of the Gospels and Acts. About a dozen ancient Jewish, Greek, and Roman writers mention Jesus. Taken together, their writings attest to the basic contours of Jesus's life. Many names of people and places, as well as the exploits of first-century political and religious leaders, are attested in other writings of the day.

11. Archaeology regularly confirms details about geography, topography, customs, artifacts, buildings, tombs, inscriptions, and graffiti that are mentioned in the New Testament—the Gospels and Acts in particular.

12. The portions of the New Testament that were written before the completion of the Gospels and Acts confirm the historicity of these five books. For instance, Paul, James, and Peter show multiple signs of quoting or alluding to teachings and actions of Jesus in letters they wrote before the Gospels were written. Their quotes and allusions agree with what we find in the Gospels. This indicates that the Gospels are in tune with the very earliest writings about Jesus—the New Testament Letters. These earliest writings were in turn dependent on the authoritative oral traditions that were passed on by eyewitnesses to Jesus's life. Paul expresses this in 1 Corinthians 15:3–8, where he lists the beliefs he had "received" from these eyewitnesses when he became a Christian no more than two years after Jesus's death and resurrection. These are not late, slowly developing legends that he is reporting!

heresies, even denying the Master who bought them, and will bring swift destruction on themselves. ² Many will follow their depraved ways, and the way of truth will be maligned because of them. ³ They will exploit you in their greed with made-up stories. Their condemnation, pronounced long ago, is not idle, and their destruction does not sleep.

⁴ For if God didn't spare the angels who sinned but cast them into hell^ and delivered them in chains⁸ of utter darkness to be kept for judgment; ⁵ and if he didn't spare the ancient world, but protected Noah, a preacher of righteousness, and seven others,ᶜ when he brought the flood on the world of the ungodly; ⁶ and if he reduced the cities of Sodom and Gomorrah to ashes and condemned them to extinction,ᴰ making them an example of what is coming to the ungodly; ⁷ and if he rescued righteous Lot, distressed by the depraved behavior of the immoral ⁸ (for as that righteous man lived among them day by day, his righteous soul was tormented by the lawless deeds he saw and heard) — ⁹ then the Lord knows how to rescue the godly from trials and to keep the unrighteous under punishment for the day of judgment, ¹⁰ especially those who follow the polluting desires of the flesh and despise authority.

Bold, arrogant people! They are not afraid to slander the glorious ones; ¹¹ however, angels, who are greater in might and power, do not bring a slanderous charge against them before the Lord.ᴱ ¹² But these people, like irrational animals — creatures of instinct born to be caught and destroyed — slander what they do not understand, and in their destruction they too will be destroyed. ¹³ They will be paid back with harm for the harm they have done. They consider it a pleasure to carouse in broad daylight. They are spots and blemishes,

delighting in their deceptionsᶠ while they feast with you. ¹⁴ They have eyes full of adultery that never stop looking for sin. They seduce unstable people and have hearts trained in greed. Children under a curse! ¹⁵ They have gone astray by abandoning the straight path and have followed the path of Balaam, the son of Bosor,ᴳ who loved the wages of wickedness ¹⁶ but received a rebuke for his lawlessness: A speechless donkey spoke with a human voice and restrained the prophet's madness.

¹⁷ These people are springs without water, mists driven by a storm. The gloom of darkness has been reserved for them. ¹⁸ For by uttering boastful, empty words, they seduce, with fleshly desires and debauchery, people who have barely escapedᴴ from those who live in error. ¹⁹ They promise them freedom, but they themselves are slaves of corruption, since people are enslaved to whatever defeats them. ²⁰ For if, having escaped the world's impurity through the knowledge of the Lordᴵ and Savior Jesus Christ, they are again entangled in these things and defeated, the last state is worse for them than the first. ²¹ For it would have been better for them not to have known the way of righteousness than, after knowing it, to turn back from the holy command delivered to them. ²² It has happened to them according to the true proverb: A dog returns to its own vomit,ᴶ and, "A washed sow returns to wallowing in the mud."

The Day of the Lord

3 Dear friends, this is now the second letter I have written to you; in both letters, I want to stir up your sincere understanding by way of reminder, ² so that you recall the words previously spoken by the holy prophets and the command of our Lord and Savior given through your apostles. ³ Above all, be aware

^2:4 Gk Tartarus ⁸2:4 Other mss read in pits ᶜ2:5 Lit Noah, the eighth, a preacher of righteousness ᴰ2:6 Other mss omit to extinction ᴱ2:11 Other mss read them from the Lord ᶠ2:13 Other mss read delighting in the love feasts ᴳ2:15 Other mss read Beor ᴴ2:18 Or people who are actually escaping ᴵ2:20 Other mss read our Lord ᴶ2:22 Pr 26:11

---

were present among Peter's readers. Peter's warning describes these "false teachers" as those who spread **destructive heresies**, or teachings destructive to the faith. The effect of their teaching was so far-reaching that they even denied the **Master** ("sovereign Lord"; Gk *despotēs*) who bought them. Though many followed the heretics' shameful immorality and the **way of truth** was **maligned**, little did the false teachers realize that denying the Lord would **bring swift destruction on themselves** (cp. v. 3). Driven by greed, the false teachers invented deceptive stories (the exact opposite of Peter in 1:16) with which they exploited their listeners. **2:4–10a** To warn his readers and urge them to action, Peter recalled three examples of God's judgment and deliverance. (1) God judged **the angels who sinned** (cp. Gn 6:1–4). (2) God also judged the ancient world at the time of the flood (cp. Gn 7:17–23) but **protected Noah and seven others** (cp. Gn 7:13–16). (3) He judged the immoral **cities of Sodom and Gomorrah** (cp. Gn 19:23–29), yet

rescued **righteous Lot**, who was distressed and tormented by the immoral behavior of the ungodly (cp. Gn 19:29). Peter then pointed out to his readers that God was capable of delivering them, **the godly**, from the destructive false teachings of heretics in their midst. Peter further assured his readers that the unrighteous would not escape God's punishment. **2:10b–22** The false teachers were rash, **arrogant**, and slanderously insolent. They were brute-like and **irrational** in their understanding, blasphemous, and ruled by lust and greed. Peter compared the false teachers to **Balaam** (Nm 22–24). Like Balaam, these false teachers had abandoned the straight path, were consumed by greed, and would receive the wages of their unrighteousness. The false teachers are described as **springs without water** and **mists driven by a storm**. They were unsatisfactory and unstable. As punishment, **the gloom of darkness** was reserved for them. These false teachers led their hearers into the same spiritual slavery

and corruption to which they themselves were enslaved. These heretics were worse off in the end with their rejection of Christ than they were at the beginning when in a state of ignorance; indeed, it would be better for them **not to have known the way of righteousness**. Just as a **dog returns to its own vomit** and a pig returns to wallow in the mud, so also these false teachers reverted to the immoral lifestyles they preferred by nature. The immoral behavior of the false teachers shows that they had never been genuinely converted. **3:1–2** Peter referred to this letter as the **second letter** he had written to his readers. Presumably the previous letter was 1 Peter. In both letters Peter reminded his readers not to forget the teachings they had received through the prophets and apostles. **The command** may refer to the revelation of God in Christ through the apostles, or possibly to specific warnings about false teachers. **3:3–4** Peter warned his readers that **scoffers will come in the last days**. The "last days"

of this: Scoffers will come in the last days scoffing and following their own evil desires, **4** saying, "Where is his 'coming' that he promised? Ever since our ancestors fell asleep, all things continue as they have been since the beginning of creation." **5** They deliberately overlook this: By the word of God the heavens came into being long ago and the earth was brought about from water and through water. **6** Through these the world of that time perished when it was flooded. **7** By the same word, the present heavens and earth are stored up for fire, being kept for the day of judgment and destruction of the ungodly.

8 Dear friends, don't overlook this one fact: With the Lord one day is like a thousand years, and a thousand years like one day. **9** The Lord does not delay his promise, as some understand delay, but is patient with you, not wanting any to perish but all to come to repentance. **10** But the day of the Lord will come like a thief;^A on that day the heavens will pass away with a loud noise, the elements will burn and be dissolved, and the earth and the works on it will be disclosed.^B,C **11** Since all these things are to be dissolved in this way, it is clear what sort of people you should be in holy conduct

and godliness **12** as you wait for the day of God and hasten its coming.^D Because of that day, the heavens will be dissolved with fire and the elements will melt with heat. **13** But based on his promise, we wait for new heavens and a new earth, where righteousness dwells.

Conclusion

14 Therefore, dear friends, while you wait for these things, make every effort to be found without spot or blemish in his sight, at peace. **15** Also, regard the patience of our Lord as salvation, just as our dear brother Paul has written to you according to the wisdom given to him. **16** He speaks about these things in all his letters. There are some things hard to understand in them. The untaught and unstable will twist them to their own destruction, as they also do with the rest of the Scriptures.

17 Therefore, dear friends, since you know this in advance, be on your guard, so that you are not led away by the error of lawless people and fall from your own stable position. **18** But grow in the grace and knowledge of our Lord and Savior Jesus Christ. To him be the glory both now and to the day of eternity.^E

^A3:10 Other mss add *in the night* ^B3:10 Other mss read *will be burned up* ^C3:10 Some Syriac and Coptic mss read *will not be found* ^D3:12 Or *and speed the coming* ^E3:18 Other mss add *Amen.*

refers to the period of time between Christ's incarnation and his return. The scoffers mocked Christ's return because many years had passed and it had not yet occurred. **Our**

ancestors probably refers to the OT patriarchs given the mention of **the beginning of creation**.

3:5–7 The heretics argued that the world was unchanging, that it would remain so, and thus that the Lord would not return. To counter this charge, Peter reminded readers that the world had not always been orderly and that the source of the world's order was God. **By the word** means "by God's decree"—he spoke, and creation happened. Peter also reminded his readers of the great flood that took place in Noah's day when the earth was destroyed. So God does demonstrate his power and intervene in judgment in a world that otherwise seems unchanging. **By the same word**, he will do it again when Christ returns.

3:8 What seems like a delay makes the Lord's return no less certain. Peter noted that God views time differently than human beings do. Christ will return in accordance with the divine timetable, not ours.

3:9 You is variously interpreted as a reference to the letter's Christian recipients (identified in 1:1) or else more broadly as all people.

3:10 God's patience toward sinners is not inexhaustible. The **day of the Lord** will be sudden and will catch many people unprepared, as when a burglar sneaks in and robs a house (cp. Mt 24:43–44; Lk 12:39–40).

3:11–14 The anticipation of the Lord's return and its accompanying events of judgment should rouse Christians to **holy** living. Evil will be completely destroyed when Christ returns, and **righteousness** will permanently dwell in **new heavens and a new earth** (cp. Is 32:16).

3:15–16 Peter notes that the teaching in Paul's letters said that the Lord's **patience** provided opportunities for salvation (Rm 2:4). Peter grouped Paul's letters together with **the rest of the Scriptures**, clearly affirming the God-given authority of Paul's writings (2Pt 1:20–21; see note at 1:19–21).

3:17–18 Since Peter's readers had now been warned about the false teachers in their midst, he instructed them to be on their guard and not be led astray. He also encouraged them to grow in the **grace and knowledge** of Jesus Christ (cp. 1:2–11). He closed with a doxology in which he ascribed **glory** to Christ both now and forever.

Introduction to 1 John

Circumstances of Writing

Ancient manuscripts are unanimous in naming John as the author of 1 John. This was understood to be John the son of Zebedee, the "beloved disciple" who was also the author of the Fourth Gospel. The style and vocabulary of 1, 2, and 3 John are so close to that of John's Gospel that they beg to be understood as arising from the same person. Some contemporary scholars theorize that an "elder John" (see 2Jn 1; 3Jn 1), not the apostle, may have written the letters. Others speak of a "Johannine school" or "circle" as the originators of the epistles of John (and perhaps Revelation too). But the view with the best support is that Jesus's disciple John was the author.

Second-century sources reported that around AD 70, the year the Romans destroyed Jerusalem and the temple, John left Jerusalem where he was a church leader and relocated to Ephesus. He continued his pastoral work in that region and lived until nearly AD 100. Ephesus is probably the place where John wrote the three New Testament letters that bear his name. They could have been composed at any time in the last quarter of the first century.

Contribution to the Bible

First John maps out the three main components of a saving knowledge of God: (1) faith in Jesus Christ, (2) obedient response to God's commands, and (3) love for God and others from the heart. This epistle shows how Jesus expects his followers to honor him in practical church life and wherever God calls his people to go and serve.

Structure

It is widely agreed that 1 John does not logically, methodically, or rigorously set forth and develop its arguments. For this reason scholars are divided on the best way to structurally outline the letter. It is the least letter-like of the three Johannine epistles because of its lack of identification of the sender and the recipient. It is more like an unsystematic treatise. It often makes assertions along thematic lines, moves to related or contrasting themes, and then returns to the earlier topic, or perhaps takes up a different subject altogether.

---

1 John Timeline

AD 4–33

John the apostle, son of Zebedee and Salome is born. **8?**
John and his brother James are part of their father's fishing business in Capernaum, on the Sea of Galilee. **25**
Jesus calls James and John to be two of his twelve disciples. **29**
Peter, James, and John witness Jesus's transfiguration. **32**
John and Peter are asked to prepare the Passover meal Jesus shares with his disciples. **33**

AD 33–44

Peter, James, and John are with Jesus as he prays in Gethsemane. **33**
As he dies, Jesus gives the care of his mother, Mary, to John. **33**
John may be the first of the twelve disciples to believe that Jesus rose from death. **33**
Following Pentecost, John and Peter show great courage in Jerusalem by bearing witness to Jesus's acts. **33**
John's brother, James, is the first of the twelve disciples to die a martyr's death. **44**

Key verses in 1 John

1:9 If we confess our sins, he is faithful and righteous to forgive us our sins and to cleanse us from all unrighteousness.

4:14 And we have seen and we testify that the Father has sent his Son as the world's Savior.

4:19 We love because he first loved us.

4:21 And we have this command from him: The one who loves God must also love his brother and sister.

AD 45–65

John is among the pillars of the Jerusalem church who meet with Paul, Barnabas, and Titus in Jerusalem to deal with the question of whether Gentiles had to be circumcised to become Christians. **49**

Paul travels through Ephesus toward the end of his second missionary journey. **52**

Apollos comes to Ephesus and is mentored by Aquila and Priscilla. **52**

Paul returns to Ephesus for a two-and-a-half-year ministry. **54**

Timothy, elder of Ephesus, receives the first letter from Paul. **62**

AD 65–LATE SECOND CENTURY

The Jewish War is started by zealots who drive the Romans out of Jerusalem temporarily. **66**

John leaves Jerusalem for Ephesus. **66–70?**

The Romans crush the Jewish rebellion and destroy Jerusalem and the temple. **70**

John is spiritual leader of the church at Ephesus. **70–100**

Irenaeus (**140–202**) affirms that the body of John's writings were composed in Ephesus.

Prologue: Our Declaration

1 What was from the beginning, what we have heard, what we have seen with our eyes, what we have observed and have touched with our hands, concerning the word of life — ² that life was revealed, and we have seen it and we testify and declare to you the eternal life that was with the Father and was revealed to us — ³ what we have seen and heard we also declare to you, so that you may also have fellowship with us; and indeed our fellowship is with the Father and with his Son, Jesus Christ. ⁴ We are writing these things^A so that our^B joy may be complete.

Fellowship with God

⁵ This is the message we have heard from him and declare to you: God is light, and there is absolutely no darkness in him. ⁶ If we say, "We have fellowship with him," and yet we walk in darkness, we are lying and are not practicing the truth. ⁷ If we walk in the light as he himself is in the light, we have fellowship with one another, and the blood of Jesus his Son cleanses us from all sin. ⁸ If we say, "We have no sin," we are deceiving ourselves, and the truth is not in us. ⁹ If we confess our sins, he is faithful and righteous to forgive us our sins and to cleanse us from all unrighteousness. ¹⁰ If we say, "We have not sinned," we make him a liar, and his word is not in us.

2 My little children, I am writing you these things so that you may not sin. But if anyone does sin, we have an advocate with the Father — Jesus Christ the righteous one. ² He himself is the atoning sacrifice^C for our sins, and not only for ours, but also for those of the whole world.

God's Commands

³ This is how we know that we know him: if we keep his commands. ⁴ The one who says, "I have come to know him," and yet doesn't keep his commands, is a liar, and the truth is not in him. ⁵ But whoever keeps his word, truly in him the love of God is made complete. This is how we know we are in him: ⁶ The one who says he remains in him should walk just as he walked.

^A 1:4 Other mss add *to you*   ^B 1:4 Other mss read *your*   ^C 2:2 Or *the propitiation*

1:1–2 The words **what was from the beginning** echo both Gn 1:1 and Jn 1:1. John wrote as an eyewitness.
1:3 The phrase **we also declare to you** shows that John passed on faithfully to his readers what the apostolic generation had received. **Fellowship** refers to the close ties of kinship that God extends to his people.
1:4 A major reason why John wrote this letter was so **our joy may be complete**.
1:5 John had divine guidance in **the message** he related. John testified to him who is **light**.
1:6 The words **if we say** may indicate that John was paraphrasing false views that

needed to be exposed and corrected. To **walk in darkness** is to persist in sin.
1:7 To **walk in the light** is to live consistent with God's commands and character. **Fellowship**, the shared knowledge of God's light and love, is one of life's deepest satisfactions. With the phrase **the blood of Jesus**, John identified the focal point of Christ's saving work in the cross.
1:9 Confessing **our sins** does not mean a shallow reciting of misdeeds. It means owning up to wrongdoing and bringing our lives into line with God's goodness and commands.
1:10 To claim to be without sin is to claim to be on par with God. If **his word is not**

in us, the saving message of Christ has not taken root.
2:1 Jesus now serves as our **advocate** or helper and mediator at the Father's right hand.
2:2 Jesus's sacrificial death satisfied God's just demand for sin to be punished (**atoning sacrifice**). But his punishment was for others, not for himself. The phrase **for those of the whole world** does not mean the salvation of all people. It does mean that Jesus's saving death extends the offer of salvation to all nations.
2:4 The words **his commands** mean the same thing as "his word" in v. 5.
2:5–6 The life of Jesus Christ is the paradigm or pattern for the believer's life. The love of

Character profile:
John

John wasn't always known as "the disciple Jesus loved" (Jn 13:23; 19:26; 21:7,20). Jesus also called him and his brother the "Sons of Thunder" (Mk 3:17), likely because of their fiery tempers. Fits of temper occasionally landed John in trouble, such as the time he wanted to call down judgment from heaven on a Samaritan village that refused to welcome Jesus (see Lk 9:51–56).

John was a fisherman from Capernaum, was called by Jesus as one of his twelve disciples, and was part of Jesus's inner circle that included Peter and John's brother James. John occasionally struggled to keep his ego in check. He once tried to stop a man from doing the Lord's work simply because the man wasn't an official disciple. He and his brother James earned the ire of the other disciples by requesting exclusive places of honor in Jesus's future kingdom.

But those incidents merely reflected the spiritual growing pains of a man coming to grips with the extraordinary responsibilities that were laid out before him. Through it all, John maintained a fierce loyalty and unshakable closeness to Jesus. As Jesus hung on the cross, he entrusted John with the responsibility of taking care of his mother, Mary, after his death.

When the news of Jesus's resurrection reached the disciples, John was the first one to reach the empty tomb. After Jesus ascended to heaven, John emerged as one of the leaders of first-century Christianity.

The apostle Paul cited John as one of the "pillars" of the Christian church (Gl 2:9). In time, John became an elder statesman of sorts—a trusted adviser to various first-century evangelists and congregations.

John wrote one of the four Gospels. Through his words many people have come to know Jesus Christ. In addition to John's Gospel, three New Testament letters (1–3 John) and the book of Revelation are credited to the faithful fisherman from Capernaum.

Church tradition tells us that John was the only apostle who did not die a martyr's death. Instead, he was banished to the prison island of Patmos, where he lived out his final days—faithful to the end.

John was rough around the edges, as were all of Jesus's disciples. He faced the occasional rebuke from Jesus. But he learned from his mistakes and grew in his faith. He made himself a valuable member of Jesus's ministry team, as well as a trusted confidante of the Lord himself.

In the spirit of Matthew 25:23 ("Well done, good and faithful servant! You were faithful over a few things; I will put you in charge of many things. Share your master's joy."), John's responsibilities increased with his spiritual growth.

The same principle applies today. If you prove yourself faithful to the Lord in your daily decisions, interactions with others, commitments to prayer and Bible study, and efforts to use your spiritual gifts and abilities, you will experience growth in your relationship with him.

7 Dear friends, I am not writing you a new command but an old command that you have had from the beginning. The old command is the word you have heard. **8** Yet I am writing you a new command, which is true in him and in you, because the darkness is passing away and the true light is already shining. **9** The one who says he is in the light but hates his brother or sister is in the darkness until now. **10** The one who loves his brother or sister remains in the light, and there is no cause for stumbling in him.^A **11** But the one who hates his brother or sister is in the darkness, walks in the darkness, and doesn't know where he's going, because the darkness has blinded his eyes.

Reasons for Writing

12 I am writing to you, little children, since your sins have been forgiven on account of his name.

13 I am writing to you, fathers, because you have come to know the one who is from the beginning. I am writing to you, young men, because you have conquered the evil one.

14 I have written to you, children, because you have come to know the Father. I have written to you, fathers, because you have come to know the one who is from the beginning. I have written to you, young men, because you are strong, God's word remains in you, and you have conquered the evil one.

A Warning about the World

15 Do not love the world or the things in the world. If anyone loves the world, the love of the Father is not in him. **16** For everything in the world — the lust of the flesh, the lust of the eyes, and the pride in one's possessions — is not from the Father, but is from the world. **17** And the world with its lust is passing away, but the one who does the will of God remains forever.

The Last Hour

18 Children, it is the last hour. And as you have heard that antichrist is coming, even now many antichrists have come. By this we know that it is the last hour. **19** They went out from us, but they did not belong to us; for if they had belonged to us, they would have remained with us. However, they went out so that it might be made clear that none of them belongs to us. **20** But you have an anointing from the Holy One, and all of you know the truth.^B **21** I have not written to you because you don't know the truth, but because you do know it, and because no lie comes from the truth. **22** Who is the liar, if not the one who denies that Jesus is the Christ? This one is the antichrist: the one who denies the Father and the Son. **23** No one who denies the Son has the Father; he who confesses the Son has the Father as well.

Remaining with God

24 What you have heard from the beginning is to remain in you. If what you have heard from the beginning remains in you, then you will remain in the Son and in the Father. **25** And this is the promise that he himself made to us: eternal life.

26 I have written these things to you concerning those who are trying to deceive you. **27** As for you, the anointing you received from him remains in you, and you don't need anyone to teach you. Instead, his anointing teaches you about all things and is true and is not a lie; just as it has taught you,^C remain in him.

^A **2:10** Or *it* ^B **2:20** Other mss read *and you know all things* ^C **2:27** Or *as he has taught you*

God in v. 5 could be either God's love for us or our love for God. The former is probably correct.
2:7 Dear friends is literally "Beloved." This was a favorite term of address for John (3:2,21; 4:1,7,11). It is a reminder that Christians are what they are—"beloved"—because God has loved them (4:10). The love **command** was intensified and perfected in its expression by Jesus. Yet it is **old**, rooted in God's love and his commands in the OT (Lv 19:18; Dt 6:5).
2:8 That Christ has come into the world means that the gloom of present evil and sin is giving way as the **true light** is **already shining**.
2:9–11 Relationships with fellow believers are key indicators of whether one is walking in the **light** or in **darkness**. **Walks**, here and elsewhere in 1 John, is a metaphor for the course of a person's life.

2:12–14 The author included all readers with the inclusive terms **fathers** and **young men**.
2:13 The **one who is from the beginning** could refer to either the Father or the Son.
2:14 God's word refers to the saving gospel message that Christ brought, now embodied in the Bible.
2:15 Things in the world are not just material objects. They are things that absorb human **love** to an undue degree.
2:16 John warned against what the body desires, what the eyes itch to see, and what people work hard to acquire.
2:17 Like the darkness in v. 8, **the world with its lust is passing away**. This opens the way for doing **the will of God** and establishing fellowship with him forever.
2:18 Many antichrists is probably a reference to misguided or diabolical individuals who were guilty of the sins that he described and condemned.

2:19 The phrase **they went out from us** shows there had been a division among the church members to whom John wrote. Not all who were in the church were authentic believers.
2:20 The **anointing** in this verse could be the Holy Spirit, but it more likely refers to the gospel or the saving message—the teaching that believers had received.
2:22 The error John referred to here was not ethical but theological—false teaching about **the Father** and **the Son**.
2:23 This verse affirms the unity and identity of God **the Father** and **the Son**. Yet it also affirms their distinctiveness.
2:24 The phrase **from the beginning** refers to the earliest exposure of John's readers to gospel teaching.
2:27 On **anointing**, see note at v. 20. John was content to entrust his readers to the powerful message they had received.

God's Children

[28] So now, little children, remain in him so that when he appears we may have confidence and not be ashamed before him at his coming. [29] If you know that he is righteous, you know this as well: Everyone who does what is right has been born of him. [1] See what great love[A] the Father has given us that we should be called God's children — and we are! The reason the world does not know us is that it didn't know him. [2] Dear friends, we are God's children now, and what we will be has not yet been revealed. We know that when he appears,[B] we will be like him because we will see him as he is. [3] And everyone who has this hope in him purifies himself just as he is pure.

[4] Everyone who commits sin practices lawlessness; and sin is lawlessness. [5] You know that he was revealed so that he might take away sins,[C] and there is no sin in him. [6] Everyone who remains in him does not sin;[D] everyone who sins[E] has not seen him or known him.

[7] Little children, let no one deceive you. The one who does what is right is righteous, just as he is righteous. [8] The one who commits[F] sin is of the devil, for the devil has sinned from the beginning. The Son of God was revealed for this purpose: to destroy the devil's works. [9] Everyone who has been born of God does not sin,[G] because his seed remains in him; he is not able to sin,[H] because he has been born of God. [10] This is how God's children and the devil's children become obvious. Whoever does not do what is right is not of God, especially the one who does not love his brother or sister.

Love in Action

[11] For this is the message you have heard from the beginning: We should love one another, [12] unlike Cain, who was of the evil one and murdered his brother. And why did he murder him? Because his deeds were evil, and his brother's were righteous.

[13] Do not be surprised, brothers and sisters, if the world hates you. [14] We know that we have passed from death to life because we love our brothers and sisters. The one who does not love remains in death. [15] Everyone who hates his brother or sister is a murderer, and you know that no murderer has eternal life residing in him. [16] This is how we have come to know love: He laid down his life for us. We should also lay down our lives for our brothers and sisters. [17] If anyone has this world's goods and sees a fellow believer[I] in need but withholds compassion from him — how does God's love reside in him? [18] Little children, let us not love in word or speech, but in action and in truth.

[19] This is how we will know that we belong to the truth and will reassure our hearts before him [20] whenever our hearts condemn us; for God is greater than our hearts, and he knows all things. [21] Dear friends, if our hearts don't condemn us, we have confidence before God [22] and receive whatever we ask from him because we keep his commands and do what is pleasing in his sight. [23] Now this is his command: that we believe in the name of his Son, Jesus Christ, and love one another as he commanded us. [24] The one who keeps his commands remains in him, and he in him. And the way we know that he remains in us is from the Spirit he has given us.

The Spirit of Truth and the Spirit of Error

[1] Dear friends, do not believe every spirit, but test the spirits to see if they are from God, because many false prophets have gone out into the world. [2] This is how you know the Spirit of God: Every spirit that confesses that Jesus Christ has

---

[A]3:1 Or *what sort of love*   [B]3:2 Or *when it appears*   [C]3:5 Other mss read *our sins*   [D]3:6 Or *not keep on sinning*   [E]3:6 Or *who keeps on sinning*   [F]3:8 Or *practices*   [G]3:9 Or *not practice sin*   [H]3:9 Or *to keep on sinning*   [I]3:17 Lit *sees his brother or sister*

2:28 Ashamed refers to the guilt and terror of judgment by God.

2:29 The doctrinal knowledge of John's **if** statement sets up the ethical response implied by **does what is right**, but the response is a function of spiritual rebirth (**born of him**) and not human effort.

3:1 John marveled at God's **love** because of its effect—sinners can be called **God's children**.

3:2 The world may think little of God's children **now**, but at Christ's return things will change. Believers will be transformed because they will **see him as he is**.

3:3 Knowing that the Lord will return is a strong incentive for believers to live in ways that are pleasing to him.

3:4 Sin is a grave matter because God has revealed his moral character in his holy law.

3:5 The purpose of Jesus's incarnation was to **take away sins**. John's statement affirms the sinlessness of Jesus (see 2Co 5:21; Heb 4:15).

3:6 By **everyone who sins has not seen him or known him**, John had in mind flagrant sin by false "believers."

3:9–10 God's **seed** is the gospel message. **Not able to sin** means freedom from bondage to breaking God's law and freedom to live as **God's children**. John spoke of what spiritual rebirth makes **obvious**—a life surrendered fully to God.

3:11 Apostolic preaching emphasized that faith in a God of love moved believers to become people who **love one another**.

3:12 On **Cain**, see Gn 4:1–16.

3:13 Jesus foretold that his followers would not always be well received (Jn 16:2).

3:14 Our assurance of salvation rests in part on the love that God gives us for our **brothers and sisters**—that is, fellow believers. If we have this love, it is a sign of our salvation.

3:15 The person who neglects to love **hates his brother or sister**. This signals absence of **eternal life**. This verse recalls Jesus's teaching in Mt 5:21–22.

3:16 Jesus's death is the yardstick by which believers gauge their own love for other believers.

3:17 Selfishness and God's love are mutually exclusive.

3:18 With the phrase **in action and in truth**, John declared that faith which is only talk is false faith.

3:19 Before him refers to God's observation of our lives. Faithful living results in confident hearts rather than guilt, evasion, or fear.

3:20 Human hearts can be self-deceived, but God who **knows all things** can grant assurance.

3:22 We will receive **whatever we ask** in prayer if our prayer is within God's will (5:14). If we **keep his commands**, we will have no desire to request what God does not wish.

3:23 His command and faith in his **Son, Jesus Christ** are not different things but two aspects of a single, undivided love of God.

3:24 The Holy **Spirit** is mentioned here for the first time.

4:1 Since there are many counterfeits, discernment is a critical characteristic for Christian disciples.

4:2 John insisted that Christ had **come in the flesh**. God was truly and fully incarnate in Jesus of Nazareth.

come in the flesh is from God, ³ but every spirit that does not confess Jesus^ is not from God. This is the spirit of the antichrist, which you have heard is coming; even now it is already in the world. ⁴ You are from God, little children, and you have conquered them, because the one who is in you is greater than the one who is in the world. ⁵ They are from the world. Therefore what they say is from the world, and the world listens to them. ⁶ We are from God. Anyone who knows God listens to us; anyone who is not from God does not listen to us. This is how we know the Spirit of truth and the spirit of deception.

Knowing God through Love

⁷ Dear friends, let us love one another, because love is from God, and everyone who loves has been born of God and knows God. ⁸ The one who does not love does not know God, because God is love. ⁹ God's love was revealed among us⁸ in this way: God sent his one and only Son into the world so that we might live through him. ¹⁰ Love consists in this: not that we loved God, but that he loved us and sent his Son to be the atoning sacrifice^c for our sins. ¹¹ Dear friends, if God loved us in this way, we also must love one another. ¹² No one has ever seen God. If we love one another, God remains in^D us and his love is made complete in us. ¹³ This is how we know that we remain in him and he in us: He has given us of his Spirit. ¹⁴ And we have seen and we testify that the Father has sent his Son as the world's Savior. ¹⁵ Whoever

confesses that Jesus is the Son of God — God remains in him and he in God. ¹⁶ And we have come to know and to believe the love that God has for us.

God is love, and the one who remains in love remains in God, and God remains in him. ¹⁷ In this, love is made complete with us so that we may have confidence in the day of judgment, because as he is, so also are we in this world. ¹⁸ There is no fear in love; instead, perfect love drives out fear, because fear involves punishment.^E So the one who fears is not complete in love. ¹⁹ We love^F because he first loved us. ²⁰ If anyone says, "I love God," and yet hates his brother or sister, he is a liar. For the person who does not love his brother or sister whom he has seen cannot love God whom he has not seen.^G ²¹ And we have this command from him: The one who loves God must also love his brother and sister.

5 Everyone who believes that Jesus is the Christ has been born of God, and everyone who loves the Father^H also loves the one born of him. ² This is how we know that we love God's children: when we love God and obey^I his commands. ³ For this is what love for God is: to keep his commands. And his commands are not a burden, ⁴ because everyone who has been born of God conquers the world. This is the victory that has conquered the world: our faith.

The Certainty of God's Testimony

⁵ Who is the one who conquers the world but the one who believes that Jesus is the Son of God? ⁶ Jesus Christ — he is the one who came

---

^4:3 Other mss read *confess that Jesus has come in the flesh* ^4:9 Or *in us* ^4:10 Or *the propitiation* ^4:12 Or *remains among* ^4:18 Or *fear has its own punishment* or *torment* ^4:19 Other mss add *him* ^4:20 Other mss read *has seen, how is he able to love . . . seen?* (as a question) ^5:1 Or *loves the one who has given birth* ^5:2 Other mss read *keep*

4:3 The words **spirit that does not confess Jesus** show that John was aware of people speaking by the power of spirits other than the Holy Spirit.
4:4 The **one who is in the world** probably refers to the devil, whether in person or as represented by his spiritual and human servants.
4:5 Spiritual deception is more attractive and plausible to non-Christians than the truth of the gospel message.

#93 99 Essential Christian Truths

INSPIRATION OF SCRIPTURE

The inspiration of Scripture refers to God's direction of the human authors of the Bible so that they composed and recorded his message to humankind in their original writings (2Tm 3:16; 2Pt 1:19–21). Occasionally this inspiration was achieved through dictation, where God spoke directly to the original authors. Most of the time, however, this inspiration was achieved through the supernatural influence of the Holy Spirit through the personalities of the authors so that their writings can be considered the very words of God.

4:6 The **we** here consists of John and the apostolic circle and then all who accept their message.
4:7 The appeal here echoes Jesus himself (Jn 13:34) as well as 1Jn 3:11,23; 4:1.
4:8 God is love. Those who truly know him share in this attribute.
4:9 The phrase **live through him** means eternal life.
4:10 On **atoning sacrifice**, see note at 2:2. The standard of love is not what humans feel but what God has revealed in Christ's death on the cross.
4:11 The phrase **God loved us in this way** means that Jesus was obedient to the point of death.
4:12 John used the phrase **no one has ever seen God** to refer to God the Father in his heavenly splendor, but God the Son makes the invisible Father clearly known (Jn 1:18).
4:13 His Spirit plays a crucial role in assuring and convincing believers.
4:14 Like the "we" of the opening verses of 1 John, this **we** refers to John and other apostles.
4:15 Confession of the truth about **the Son** is a condition for a relationship with **God** the Father.
4:16 On **God is love**, see v. 8.
4:17 The "he" in **as he is, so also are we** could refer to either Jesus or God the Father.

If the reference is to Jesus, John was saying that as the Son lived in this world, loved others, and pleased God, so can his followers. If the "he" refers to the Father, John meant that as God dwells with his people and moves them to reflect his love, they have complete confidence in view of the coming judgment.
4:18 With the words **no fear**, John was speaking of the terror of final judgment (v. 17) and eternal **punishment**.
5:1–2 To believe is to have been acted upon in a dynamic, transformative way by God. It is to have been **born of God**. The words **also loves the one born of him** refers to love for a fellow believer.
5:3 Love for God is not separate from keeping **his commands**. God's commands teach his people how to do what God accepts as pleasing (Rm 12:1–2). Knowledge of God transforms the human will, making what was once **a burden** light and easy to carry (Mt 11:30).
5:5 Confessing Jesus as **the Son of God** should be understood as including his status as the Christ and that he has come in the flesh.
5:6 The words **came by water and blood** probably refer to Jesus's baptism and his death. **The Spirit** . . . **testifies** through John's witness to the meaning of these events in Jesus's life. John was present at both the baptism and the crucifixion of Jesus.

by water and blood, not by water only, but by water and by blood. And the Spirit is the one who testifies, because the Spirit is the truth. [7] For there are three that testify:[A] [8] the Spirit, the water, and the blood — and these three are in agreement. [9] If we accept human testimony, God's testimony is greater, because it is God's testimony that he has given about his Son. [10] The one who believes in the Son of God has this testimony within himself. The one who does not believe God has made him a liar, because he has not believed in the testimony God has given about his Son. [11] And this is the testimony: God has given us eternal life, and this life is in his Son. [12] The one who has the Son has life. The one who does not have the Son of God does not have life. [13] I have written these things to you who believe in the name of the Son of God so that you may know that you have eternal life.

Effective Prayer

[14] This is the confidence we have before him: If we ask anything according to his will, he hears us. [15] And if we know that he hears whatever we ask, we know that we have what we have asked of him.

[16] If anyone sees a fellow believer[B] committing a sin that doesn't lead to death, he should ask, and God will give life to him — to those who commit sin that doesn't lead to death. There is sin[C] that leads to death. I am not saying he should pray about that. [17] All unrighteousness is sin, and there is sin that doesn't lead to death.

Conclusion

[18] We know that everyone who has been born of God does not sin, but the one who is born of God keeps him,[D] and the evil one does not touch him. [19] We know that we are of God, and the whole world is under the sway of the evil one. [20] And we know that the Son of God has come and has given us understanding so that we may know the true one.[E] We are in the true one — that is, in his Son, Jesus Christ. He is the true God and eternal life.

[21] Little children, guard yourselves from idols.

[A]5:7–8 A few late Gk mss and some late Vg mss add *testify in heaven: the Father, the Word, and the Holy Spirit, and these three are one.* [B]*And there are three who bear witness on earth:*　[B]5:16 Lit *sees his brother or sister*　[C]5:16 Or *is a sin*　[D]5:18 Other mss read *himself*　[E]5:20 Other mss read *the true God*

5:7–8 By speaking of **three** witnesses, John may have been thinking of Dt 19:15 (also Mt 18:16). **The Spirit** testifies along with **the water** (Jesus's baptism) and **the blood** (Jesus's atoning death).
5:12 There is no salvation outside of faith in Christ.
5:13 Assurance was one of John's major goals in writing this letter.
5:14–15 The deepest answer to prayer is to know that **he hears us**. To know this is to **have what we have asked of him**. For believers, prayer seeks communion with the Father more than the acquisition of favors or the satisfaction of desires.

5:16 A **sin that doesn't lead to death** (cp. v. 17) is a sin for which forgiveness is possible (1:9). **Sin that leads to death** may be the flagrant offenses against God that so much of 1 John warns against. John called on his readers to leave these offenses and offenders in God's hands rather than agonizing in prayer about them. "Death" means spiritual death and eternal separation from God.
5:17 As grave as all sin is, and granting that particular evil deeds can bespeak terminal opposition to God, there is also sin that can be overcome through prayer, repentance, and renewed faith resulting in reform and restoration.

5:18 On **does not sin**, see 3:6.
5:19 **We know** refers both to apostles like John and to his readers. The **whole world** is **under the sway** of Satan, but his reign is fleeting and fading (2:8,17).
5:20 With the phrase **he is the true God**, John clearly affirmed the full divinity of Christ.
5:21 This closing verse of the epistle has puzzled interpreters for centuries. **Idols** may be John's shorthand for all the lies, errors, hate, and rebellion that his letter warned against.

◢ Introduction to 2 John

Circumstances of Writing

"The elder" (v. 1) is a title that the apostle John applied to himself late in life. (The apostle Peter referred to himself the same way; 1Pt 5:1.) No one other than the apostle John was ever suggested by the early church as the writer of 1 John. Since there are so many similarities between 1 and 2 John, it is generally accepted that John also wrote the second letter.

Second John likely was written during the last two decades of the first century. During this era, John gave pastoral leadership to churches in the area of Ephesus. We have no way of precisely dating 2 John, but it is reasonable that it was written around the same time as 1 John or slightly afterward. Its tone reveals it to be a highly personal letter that reflects John's affection for these believers and his deep concern for their welfare.

Contribution to the Bible

It is easy for congregations to get off track. Second John reminds readers of the high priority of the most basic Christian outlook and activity—mutual love. Yet another priority is no less critical—true Christian teaching. This epistle strikes a short but strong blow for steadfastness, assuring that attentive readers would take the right steps to "receive a full reward" (v. 8).

Structure

Second John is an excellent example of hortatory or exhortation discourse, which has the intent of moving readers to action. It follows the normal New Testament pattern for a letter with an opening, main body, and closing. There are only two commands in this short letter: a call to "watch yourselves" (v. 8) and the command, "do not receive" those who plant false teaching (v. 10). There is the reminder to "love one another" in verse 5. This bears the force of an imperative, in part because of the close proximity of the word *command*, which occurs four times in verses 4–6.

AD 17–61

Ephesus experiences a destructive earthquake. **17**
Paul travels through Ephesus toward the end of his second missionary journey. **52**
Apollos comes to Ephesus and is mentored by Aquila and Priscilla. **52**
Paul returns to Ephesus for a two-and-a-half-year ministry. **54**
Paul writes the letter to the Ephesians. **61**

AD 62–67

Timothy, elder of Ephesus, receives the first letter from Paul, 1 Timothy. **62**
Peter's first letter from Rome to Christians in Pontus, Galatia, Cappadocia, Asia, and Bithynia **64**
Peter's second letter from Rome **66**
The Jewish War is started by zealots who drive the Romans out of Jerusalem temporarily. **66**
Timothy receives the second letter from Paul, 2 Timothy. **67?**

Outline

AD 64–70S

Peter and Paul's death in Rome 64–67?
John leaves Jerusalem for Ephesus. 66–70?
The Romans crush the Jewish rebellion and
   destroy Jerusalem and the temple. 70
John is spiritual leader of the
   church at Ephesus 70–100
John's Gospel written 70S

AD 80S–100

John's first letter (1 John) to the
   churches of Asia Minor 80S
John's letter to the elect lady (2 John) 80S
John's letter to Gaius (3 John) 80S
John is exiled to Patmos and writes
   the book of Revelation. 95
Ephesus becomes one of the largest cities
   in the Roman province of Asia after
   Sardis and Alexandria Troas. 100

Greeting

T he elder:
To the elect lady and her children, whom I love in the truth — and not only I, but also all who know the truth — ² because of the truth that remains in us and will be with us forever.

³ Grace, mercy, and peace will be with us from God the Father and from Jesus Christ, the Son of the Father, in truth and love.

Truth and Deception

⁴ I was very glad to find some of your children walking in truth, in keeping with a command we have received from the Father. ⁵ So now I ask you, dear lady — not as if I were writing you a new command, but one we have had from the beginning — that we love one another. ⁶ This is love: that we walk according to his commands. This is the command as you have heard it from the beginning: that you walk in love.^

⁷ Many deceivers have gone out into the world; they do not confess the coming of Jesus Christ in the flesh. This is the deceiver and the antichrist. ⁸ Watch yourselves so that you don't lose what we⁸ have worked for, but that you may receive a full reward. ⁹ Anyone who does not remain in Christ's teaching but goes beyond it does not have God. The one who remains in that teaching, this one has both the Father and the Son. ¹⁰ If anyone comes to you and does not bring this teaching, do not receive him into your home, and do not greet him; ¹¹ for the one who greets him shares in his evil works.

Farewell

¹² Though I have many things to write to you, I don't want to use paper and ink. Instead, I hope to come to you and talk face to face so that our joy may be complete.

¹³ The children of your elect sister send you greetings.

^6 Or in it ⁸8 Other mss read you

---

1 The elder is the self-designation of the aged apostle John. **Elect lady** probably

#94 99 Essential Christian Truths

BODY OF CHRIST

The New Testament describes the church as the body of Christ. The church lives and operates as Christ's representative here on earth, with Christ as its head (Col 1:18). This means that the church is an extension of Christ's ministry, carrying out his work by fulfilling the Great Commission (Mt 28:18–20). In addition, the picture of the church as the body of Christ shows us the interconnectedness of individual Christians, with each member dependent upon one another for growth and sanctification (1Co 12).

refers to a congregation. Early Christians knew themselves to be "elect" or "chosen" by the Lord (Rm 16:13; 1Pt 1:1; 2:9).
2 In John's letters, **truth** frequently refers to the gospel of Jesus Christ and the realm of eternal life that believers have entered through their trust in him.
3 John was confident of the presence of **grace, mercy, and peace** as tokens of God's favor.
4 John had heard good things about the members (**children**) of this congregation.
5 Love in a congregation must be nurtured and protected (**now I ask you**). Jesus declared that love among believers is a primary means of their witness to the world (Jn 13:35).
6 For John, **love** was not sentimental affection but an ethical expectation. The definition and standard for love is found in Scripture's teaching.
7 In Greek this verse begins with the conjunction gar ("because"). Love and obedience are critical because **deceivers** always stand

ready to mislead and disrupt congregations that grow slack or rebellious. Jesus assumed human form and nature to the full (**in the flesh**). Some early false teachers taught that Jesus was fully divine but not fully human.
8 It is dangerous to become lethargic in Christian living.
9 There are always new ways to apply **Christ's teaching**, but the foundations were established by his coming and the instruction he gave to his followers.
10–11 If traveling ministers taught falsity, believers were instructed to withhold support from their destructive mission. Greeting someone involved more than a mere hello. It stood for endorsing their false teaching and helping to further their evil works.
12 On **don't want to use paper and ink**, see note at 3Jn 13.
13 The phrase **children of your elect sister** probably refers to the congregation in which John served when he wrote this letter to a "sister" congregation.

▼ Introduction to 3 John

Circumstances of Writing

"The elder" (v. 1) is a title that the apostle John applied to himself late in life. (The apostle Peter referred to himself the same way; 1Pt 5:1.) No one other than the apostle John was ever suggested by the early church as the writer of 1 John. Since there are so many similarities between 1 and 3 John, it is generally accepted that John also wrote the third letter.

Third John likely was written during the last two decades of the first century. During this era, John gave pastoral leadership to churches in the area of Ephesus. We have no way of precisely dating 3 John, but it is reasonable that it was written around the same time as 1 and 2 John or slightly afterwards. Its tone reveals it to be a highly personal letter that reflects John's affection for these believers and his deep concern for their welfare.

The two short epistles of 2 and 3 John are often described as "twin epistles," though they should be viewed as fraternal and not identical. There are some significant similarities worth noting. In both epistles, the author described himself as "the elder" (2Jn 1; 3Jn 1), and the recipients were those whom he loved "in the truth" (2Jn 1; 3Jn 1). The recipients were a cause for great rejoicing by John (2Jn 4; 3Jn 3). They were "walking in truth" (2Jn 4; 3Jn 3), and the elder has received good reports about them (2Jn 4; 3Jn 3,5). Both letters contain a warning (2Jn 8; 3Jn 9–11), and the elder desired to see the recipients face to face (2Jn 12; 3Jn 14). Finally, both letters convey greetings from others (2Jn 13; 3Jn 15).

Contribution to the Bible

This brief letter of apostolic instruction underscores certain central Christian convictions: love, truth, faithfulness, the church, and witness. It also testifies to the God-centeredness of apostolic faith (vv. 7,11). Jesus and the Spirit are not mentioned specifically (unless "the truth itself" in v. 12 refers to Jesus; see Jn 14:6; 1Jn 5:20). But in the writer's view, Jesus and the Spirit were undoubtedly included in the reference to "God" whose "truth" this epistle appeals to so frequently (3Jn 1,3,4,8,12).

Structure

The letter follows the basic epistolary pattern with an introduction (vv. 1–4), body (vv. 5–12), and a conclusion (vv. 13–15). Though verses 1–4 clearly function as the salutation, it is also possible to outline the letter around the four personalities of the book. Verses 1–8 contain a multifold commendation of Gaius. Verses 9–10 condemn the highhanded and malicious autocracy of Diotrephes. Verses 11–12, taken as a unit, praise the godly Demetrius. Verses 13–15 close with a glimpse into the heart of the elder. Four men and their reputations (growing out of their behavior) are the sum and substance of 3 John's subject matter. John constructed this letter with the building blocks of key-word repetition: "dear friend" (vv. 1,2,5,11); "truth" or "true" (vv. 1,3,4,8,12). Third John provides insight into a personality conflict that arose at the end of the first century and the strategy adopted by the elder to resolve it.

---

3 John Timeline

AD 17–61

Ephesus experiences a destructive earthquake. **17**
Paul travels through Ephesus toward the end of his second missionary journey. **52**
Apollos comes to Ephesus and is mentored by Aquila and Priscilla. **52**
Paul returns to Ephesus for a two-and-a-half-year ministry. **54**
Paul writes the letter to the Ephesians. **61**

AD 62–67

Timothy, elder of Ephesus, receives the first letter from Paul, 1 Timothy. **62**
Peter's first letter from Rome to Christians in Pontus, Galatia, Cappadocia, Asia, and Bithynia **64**
Peter's second letter from Rome **66**
The Jewish War is started by zealots who drive the Romans out of Jerusalem temporarily. **66**
Timothy receives the second letter from Paul, 2 Timothy. **67?**

Outline

AD 64–70S

Peter and Paul's death in Rome **64–67?**
John leaves Jerusalem for Ephesus. **66–70?**
The Romans crush the
  Jewish rebellion and
  destroy Jerusalem and the temple. **70**
John is spiritual leader of the
  church at Ephesus **70–100**
John's Gospel written **70S**

AD 80S–100

John's first letter (1 John) to the
  churches of Asia Minor **80S**
John's letter to the elect lady (2 John) **80S**
John's letter to Gaius (3 John) **80S**
John is exiled to Patmos and writes
  the book of Revelation. **95**
Ephesus becomes one of the largest cities
  in the Roman province of Asia after
  Sardis and Alexandria Troas. **100**

Greeting

The elder:
To my dear friend Gaius, whom I love in the truth.

[2] Dear friend, I pray that you are prospering in every way and are in good health, just as your whole life is going well.^ [3] For I was very glad when fellow believers came and testified to your fidelity to the truth — how you are walking in truth. [4] I have no greater joy than this: to hear that my children are walking in truth.

Gaius Commended

[5] Dear friend, you are acting faithfully in whatever you do for the brothers and sisters, especially when they are strangers. [6] They have testified to your love before the church. You will do well to send them on their journey in a manner worthy of God, [7] since they set out for the sake of the Name, accepting nothing from pagans.^ [8] Therefore, we ought to support such people so that we can be coworkers with the truth.

Diotrephes and Demetrius

[9] I wrote something to the church, but Diotrephes, who loves to have first place among them, does not receive our authority. [10] This is why, if I come, I will remind him of the works he is doing, slandering us with malicious words. And he is not satisfied with that! He not only refuses to welcome fellow believers, but he even stops those who want to do so and expels them from the church.

[11] Dear friend, do not imitate what is evil, but what is good. The one who does good is of God; the one who does evil has not seen God. [12] Everyone speaks well of Demetrius — even the truth itself. And we also speak well of him, and you know that our testimony is true.

Farewell

[13] I have many things to write you, but I don't want to write to you with pen and ink. [14] I hope to see you soon, and we will talk face to face.

[15] Peace to you. The friends send you greetings. Greet the friends by name.

---

^2 Or *as your soul prospers*   ^7 Or *Gentiles*

---

1 Dear friend is literally "beloved." Nothing certain is known about **Gaius**, a common name.
2 On **dear friend**, see note at v. 1. **Good health** was especially valued in ancient times since medical care could be ineffective and life expectancy was low.
3–4 Joy is a feature of the opening of all John's letters (1Jn 1:4; 2Jn 4). **My children** may refer to John's converts, or they may have been believers who were encouraged by his ministry. **Walking in truth** means living in a way that honors and pleases God.
5 On **dear friend**, see note at v. 1. Jesus taught that his followers should be gracious to **strangers** (Mt 5:43–48).
6 Send them on their journey includes physical and monetary provision. These laborers for the Lord deserved to be supported in a manner **worthy of God** because they were doing God's work (Mt 10:10).
7 The Name could refer either to God himself or to Jesus. These workers relied on the Lord and his people, the church, not on **pagans**, or nonbelievers, for their support.
8 A privilege of Christian identity is to be in sync with what God is doing as well as with fellow servants who are giving their all to do God's bidding.
9 Wrote something probably refers to a letter that has not been preserved, although

some think it could refer to 1 John. **Diotrephes** should have deferred to the authority of the apostle John.
10 The phrase **refuses to welcome fellow believers** contrasts with those who did great things "for the brothers and sisters" in v. 5. Diotrephes must have been a person with some power in his congregation.
11 On **dear friend**, see note at v. 1. John did not want Gaius to be like Diotrephes, a person who professes Christian faith but whose profession is bogus (Mt 7:21–23).
12 Possibly **Demetrius** was supposed to deliver this letter.
13 With the words **don't want to write**, John indicated that this letter was a stopgap measure until he could pay a personal visit to his readers.
15 Peace harks back to the Hebrew word *shalom*, indicating God's living presence and blessing. **Greetings** and **greet . . . by name** are reminders that one of the great joys of the household of God is the fellowship of shared commitment to Jesus Christ.

#95 **99 Essential Christian Truths**

THE WORLD OPPOSED TO GOD

There are times in Scripture where the term *world* refers to more than the physical planet Earth or the collective human population. In many instances, the term refers to an active and evil spiritual force that is in direct conflict with God and his kingdom. This evil world force operates under Satan's control (Jn 14:30; Eph 2:2), displaying the same self-centeredness and deceit that is found within his character. Christians are called to overcome this world of spiritual evil by faith in the Son of God (1Jn 5:4–5).

Introduction to Jude

Circumstances of Writing

Jude called himself "a servant of Jesus Christ and a brother of James" (v. 1). The James to whom Jude referred is not the son of Zebedee. He can be ruled out of consideration because he was martyred at an early date (Ac 12:1–2). The James to whom Jude refers is surely the well-known leader of the Jerusalem church (Ac 15:13–21; Gl 2:9). This is significant, for this James was the brother of Jesus (Mk 6:3). If Jude was a brother of James, then he was also a brother of Jesus. Rather than call himself Jesus's brother outright, Jude chose humbly to designate himself as Christ's servant.

Jude wrote to those who are "the called, loved by God the Father and kept for Jesus Christ" (v. 1). This designation is general enough to apply to Christian believers anywhere. But Jude clearly had a specific group in mind because he called them "dear friends" (vv. 3,17,20) and addressed a situation that affected them. The readers were probably Jewish Christians because of Jude's several references to Hebrew history. Beyond this information we do not know exactly who the recipients of the letter were.

Jude is difficult to date precisely. If Jude the brother of Jesus was the author, the letter must be dated sometime within his lifetime. Any date for the letter's writing must also allow time for the false teachings to have developed. Jude may be dated reasonably somewhere between AD 65 and 80. Nothing in the letter points to a date of writing beyond this time. A date within Jude's lifetime rules out the viewpoint that the false teaching in question was second-century Gnosticism.

Contribution to the Bible

Jude is often overlooked because of its brevity. The book is also neglected because of unexpected features such as its quotation of 1 Enoch and its allusion to the Assumption of Moses. Some readers wonder how a canonical book could cite noninspired, nonbiblical writings. Furthermore, the message of Jude is alien to many in today's world because Jude emphasized that the Lord will judge evil intruders who are attempting to corrupt the church. The message of judgment strikes many people today as intolerant, unloving, and contrary to the message of love proclaimed elsewhere in the New Testament.

Nevertheless, some of the Bible's most beautiful statements about God's sustaining grace are found in Jude (vv. 1,24–25), and they shine with a greater brilliance when contrasted with the false teachers who had departed from the Christian faith.

The message of judgment is especially relevant to people today. Jude's letter reminds us that errant teaching and promiscuous living have dire consequences. Jude was written so believers would contend for the faith that was transmitted to them (v. 3) and so they would not abandon God's love at a crucial time in the life of the church.

Structure

The epistle of Jude is a vigorous and pointed piece of writing. Scholars have often

Jude Timeline

2085–1406 BC

Destruction of Sodom and Gomorrah 2085?
The exodus 1446
Korah's rebellion 1420?
Balaam's error 1409?
Moses's death 1406

250 BC–AD 50

Pseudepigraphal books of Enoch
   written 250 BC–AD 50
Jesus's birth WINTER, 5 BC
The Assumption of Moses written 4 BC–AD 30
Birth of Jude, half-brother of Jesus AD 5
Jesus's trials, death,
   resurrection NISAN 14–16
   or APRIL 3–5, AD 33

remarked that its Greek is quite good and that Jude used imagery effectively. The letter bears the marks of a careful and disciplined structure and was directed to specific circumstances in the life of the church. Jude was steeped in the Old Testament and Jewish tradition, and he regularly applied Old Testament types and texts to the false teachers who had invaded the church (vv. 8,12,16).

Pseudepigraphal writings are noncanonical books not written by their purported authors. Jude cited from the pseudepigraphal book of *1 Enoch* (1:9) in verses 14–15. He likely also referred to an event found in the *Assumption of Moses* (v. 9). But this does not mean that Jude viewed these noncanonical books as authoritative Scripture. Under the inspiration of the Holy Spirit, he used them as illustrations.

Outline

I. Greeting and Purpose (vv. 1–4)
II. Description of the False Teachers (vv. 5–19)
III. Exhortation to Faithfulness (vv. 20-23)
IV. Doxology (vv. 24-25)

Greeting

Jude, a servant of Jesus Christ and a brother of James:

To those who are the called, loved^A by God the Father and kept for Jesus Christ. ² May mercy, peace, and love be multiplied to you.

Jude's Purpose in Writing

³ Dear friends, although I was eager to write you about the salvation we share, I found it necessary to write, appealing to you to contend for the faith that was delivered to the saints once for all. ⁴ For some people, who were designated for this judgment long ago,ᴮ have come in by stealth; they are ungodly, turning the grace of our God into sensuality and denying Jesus Christ, our only Master and Lord.

Apostates: Past and Present

⁵ Now I want to remind you, although you came to know all these things once and for all, that Jesusᶜ saved a people out of Egypt and later destroyed those who did not believe; ⁶ and the angels who did not keep their own position but abandoned their proper dwelling, he has kept in eternal chains in deep darkness for the judgment on the great day. ⁷ Likewise, Sodom and Gomorrah and the surrounding towns committed sexual immorality and perversions,ᴰ and serve as an example by undergoing the punishment of eternal fire.

⁸ In the same way these people — relying on their dreams — defile their flesh, reject authority, and slander glorious ones. ⁹ Yet when Michael the archangel was disputing with the devil in an argument about Moses's body, he did not dare utter a slanderous condemnation against him but said, "The Lord rebuke you! " ¹⁰ But these people blaspheme anything they do not understand. And what they do understand by instinct — like irrational animals — by these things they are destroyed. ¹¹ Woe to them! For they have gone the way of Cain, have plunged into Balaam's error for profit, and have perished in Korah's rebellion.

The Apostates' Doom

¹² These people are dangerous reefsᴱ at your love feasts as they eat with you without reverence. They are shepherds who only look after themselves. They are waterless clouds carried along by winds; trees in late autumn — fruitless, twice dead and uprooted. ¹³ They are wild waves of the sea, foaming up their shameful deeds; wandering stars for whom the blackness of darkness is reserved forever.

¹⁴ It was about these that Enoch, in the seventh generation from Adam, prophesied: "Look! The Lord comes with tens of thousands of his holy ones ¹⁵ to execute judgment on all and to convict all the ungodly concerning all the ungodly acts that they have done in an ungodly way, and concerning all the harsh things ungodly sinners have said against him." ¹⁶ These people are discontented grumblers, living according to their desires; their mouths

---

^1 Other mss read *sanctified*　*4 Or *whose judgment was written about long ago*　ᶜ5 Other mss read *the Lord*, or *God*　°7 Or *and went after other flesh*　ᴱ12 Or *are like blemishes*

---

1 The **James** named here was surely the well-known leader of the Jerusalem church (Ac 15:13–21; Gl 2:9). This James was the brother of Jesus (Mk 6:3). **Jude** humbly designated himself as Christ's **servant** rather than mention that he was related to Jesus. The **called** are those who respond in faith to God's initiative in salvation. **Loved by God the Father** is a result of being called. The expression **kept for Jesus Christ** means that believers are preserved until their salvation is consummated at Jesus's return.
2 **Mercy** is God's kindness and compassion toward his people. **Peace** is the well-being

that results from this relationship. **Love** has the best interests of other persons in mind.
3–4 Jude originally meant to write a letter about salvation to his friends, but he changed his plans when he learned about false teachers who had secretly made their way into the church. Because of the influence of false teachers he urged his readers to **contend for the faith**. The faith **delivered** once for all refers to the Christian revelation, or the body of fixed, authoritative, orthodox apostolic teaching.
5–7 Jude wanted to **remind** his readers that God had acted decisively in the past against those who opposed him. He mentioned three examples of God's judgment: (1) the judgment of unbelieving Israel in the wilderness after being delivered **out of Egypt** (Nm 32:10–12), (2) the **angels** who fell (cp. 2Pt 2:4; 1 Enoch 6:19), and (3) the destruction of **Sodom and Gomorrah** for **sexual immorality** (Gn 19:24–29; 2Pt 2:6–7).
8 The false teachers' sins were like those mentioned in vv. 5–7. **Glorious ones** frequently refers to angels.
9 Scholars generally agree that this story was taken from the *Assumption of Moses*, an apocryphal book.
10 Jude compared the false teachers to **irrational animals** that **are destroyed** by the things they instinctively pursued.

11 Jude also compared the heretics to **Cain** (Gn 4:4–5,8–9), **Balaam** (Nm 22:1–24:25; 31:16), and Korah (Nm 16:1–35). These men deceived others and were known for their hatred, greed, and rebellion.
12–13 Jude portrayed the false teachers with several metaphors. He described them as **dangerous reefs at your love feasts**. The faith **delivered** means the false teachers were like submerged rocks, unseen by sailors, that could wreck a ship. "Love feasts" were fellowship meals at which the Lord's Supper was observed. These heretics were shepherds who **only look after themselves** without any concern for others. They were useless and full of empty promises like **waterless clouds carried along by winds**. Jude portrayed them as barren fruit trees and **wild waves of the sea** that deposited their refuse on the shore of people's shameful deeds on the shore of people's lives. The heretics were also like **wandering stars** for whom the **blackness of darkness** was reserved forever.
14–15 Jude emphasized that the heretics would suffer divine retribution. He pictured this judgment by quoting a prophecy from *1 Enoch* 1:9. Their punishment would take place when **the Lord** returns to judge the wicked.
16 The false teachers were self-indulgent, **discontented** complainers. They uttered **arrogant words, flattering people** in order to take what they wanted from them.

him." **16** These people are discontented grumblers, living according to their desires; their mouths utter arrogant words, flattering people for their own advantage.

17 But you, dear friends, remember what was predicted by the apostles of our Lord Jesus Christ. **18** They told you, "In the end time there will be scoffers living according to their own ungodly desires." **19** These people create divisions and are worldly, not having the Spirit.

Exhortation and Benediction

20 But you, dear friends, as you build yourselves up in your most holy faith, praying in the Holy Spirit, **21** keep yourselves in the love of God, waiting expectantly for the mercy of our Lord Jesus Christ for eternal life. **22** Have mercy on those who waver; **23** save others by snatching them from the fire; have mercy on others but with fear, hating even the garment defiled by the flesh.

24 Now to him who is able to protect you from stumbling and to make you stand in the presence of his glory, without blemish and with great joy, **25** to the only God our Savior, through Jesus Christ our Lord,^ be glory, majesty, power, and authority before all time,^ now and forever. Amen.

^**25** Other mss omit *through Jesus Christ our Lord*   ^**25** Other mss omit *before all time*

17–19 The apostles had foretold of such people who scoffed at those who refused to follow them. Jude may have referred to warnings like those in Ac 20:29–30 and 1Tm 4:1–3. The heretics created **divisions** and followed their **ungodly desires**. As people who were **worldly**, they did not have the **Spirit**.

20–23 Jude now exhorted his readers on how to contend for the faith (cp. v. 3). They were to show **mercy** to those who were wavering, reach out to those who had already been taken in and needed to be snatched from the **fire** (cp. Am 4:11; Zch 3:2), and show concern for the wayward heretics, all at the same time.

24–25 Jude ended his letter with a doxology that served as a reminder of the divine power available to believers.

▼ Introduction to Revelation

Circumstances of Writing

The traditional view holds that the author of Revelation is the apostle John, who wrote the Fourth Gospel and the three letters of John. Evidences for this view include the following: (1) the writer referred to himself as John (1:4,9; 22:8); (2) he had personal relationships with the seven churches of Asia Minor (1:4,11; chaps. 2–3); (3) his circumstances at the time of writing (1:9) matched those of John the apostle (who was placed in Asia Minor ca AD 70 to 100 by reliable historical sources from the second century AD); and (4) the saturation of the book with Old Testament imagery and echoes implies a Jewish writer, like John, operating in overwhelmingly Gentile Asia Minor.

The initial audience that received the book of Revelation was a group of seven local churches in southwest Asia Minor (1:11; chaps. 2–3). Some of these congregations were experiencing persecution (2:9–10,13), probably under the Roman Emperor Domitian (reigned AD 81–96). Others had doctrinal and practical problems (2:6,13–15,20–23). Also behind these surface problems was the backdrop of unseen but powerful spiritual warfare (2:10,14,24; 3:9).

Though some scholars have dated the book later and a few have dated it earlier, commonly held dates of Revelation among evangelical scholars are the mid-90s and the late 60s of the first century AD. The mid-90s view is the stronger view, and it is held by majority opinion. Each view gives a different account of the persecution portrayed in the letters to the churches (2:9–10,13).

Substantial historical evidence shows that some of the churches were persecuted intensely by Nero in the late 60s. But the reference in 17:10 to seven kings, five of whom have fallen, supports a date in the mid-90s, during the reign of Domitian.

While a case can be made for a late-60s date based on the Nero-related inferences and a possible reference to the Jerusalem temple in 11:1–2 (which may imply that the temple had not yet been destroyed, as it was by the Romans in AD 70), all other factors favor a date of about AD 95. Most notable among these factors is the tradition that John the apostle was exiled to Patmos during a period of intensifying local persecution of Christians by Emperor Domitian.

Contribution to the Bible

The book of Revelation provides an almost complete overview of theology. There is much in this book about Christ, humankind and sin, the people of God (both the church and Israel), holy angels, and Satan and the demons. There is important material on God's power and tri-unity (i.e., Trinity), plus aspects of the work of the Holy Spirit and the nature of Scripture.

Structure

The book of Revelation previews its sequential structure in 1:19: "Therefore write what you have seen, what is, and what will take place after this." From the apostle John's vantage point in being commanded to "write," he had already seen the vision of the exalted Son of Man (chap. 1). Next, he was told to "write" letters to the seven churches, telling each the state of its spiritual health (chaps. 2–3). Last comes the body of the book (4:1–22:5), which covers all the events that would "take place after this."

Outline

Key verse in Revelation

4:11 Our Lord and God, you are worthy to receive glory and honor and power, because you have created all things, and by your will they exist and were created.

550–5 BC   **AD 30–100**

Persian hegemony **539–331**
Exiles return to Jerusalem **538**
Greek hegemony **331–63**
Roman hegemony **63 BC–AD 476**
Jesus's birth **5 BC**

Jesus's trials, death, and resurrection
    NISAN 14–16 or **APRIL 3–5, 33**
Pentecost **33**
Saul's conversion on the Damascus
    Road **OCTOBER 34**
Fall of Jerusalem to the Romans **70**
John is spiritual leader of the
    church at Ephesus. **70–100**

Prologue

1 The revelation of^A Jesus Christ that God gave him to show his servants what must soon take place. He made it known by sending his angel to his servant John, ² who testified to the word of God and to the testimony^B of Jesus Christ, whatever he saw.^C ³ Blessed is the one who reads aloud the words of this prophecy, and blessed are those who hear the words of this prophecy and keep^D what is written in it, because the time is near.

⁴ John: To the seven churches in Asia. Grace and peace to you from^E the one who is, who was, and who is to come, and from the seven spirits^F before his throne, ⁵ and from Jesus Christ, the faithful witness, the firstborn from the dead and the ruler of the kings of the earth.

To him who loves us and has set us free^G from our sins by his blood, ⁶ and made us a kingdom,^H priests¹ to his God and Father — to him be glory and dominion forever and ever. Amen.

⁷ Look, he is coming with the clouds,
and every eye will see him,
even those who pierced him.
And all the tribes^J of the earth^K
will mourn over him.^L,M
So it is to be. Amen.

⁸ "I am the Alpha and the Omega," says the Lord God, "the one who is, who was, and who is to come, the Almighty."

John's Vision of the Risen Lord

⁹ I, John, your brother and partner in the affliction, kingdom, and endurance that are in Jesus, was on the island called Patmos because of the word of God and the testimony of Jesus. ¹⁰ I was in the Spirit^N on the Lord's day, and I heard a loud voice behind me like a trumpet ¹¹ saying, "Write on a scroll^O what you see and send it to the seven churches: Ephesus, Smyrna, Pergamum, Thyatira, Sardis, Philadelphia, and Laodicea."

¹² Then I turned to see whose voice it was that spoke to me. When I turned I saw seven golden lampstands, ¹³ and among the lampstands was one like the Son of Man,^P dressed in a robe and with a golden sash wrapped around his chest. ¹⁴ The hair of his head was white as wool — white as snow — and his eyes like a fiery flame. ¹⁵ His feet were like fine bronze as it is fired in a furnace, and his voice like the sound of cascading^Q waters. ¹⁶ He had seven stars in his right hand; a sharp double-edged sword came from his mouth, and his face was shining like the sun at full strength.

¹⁷ When I saw him, I fell at his feet like a dead man. He laid his right hand on me and said, "Don't be afraid. I am the First and the Last, ¹⁸ and the Living One. I was dead, but look — I am alive forever and ever, and I hold the keys of

---

^A1:1 Or *Revelation of*, or *A revelation of*   ^B1:2 Or *witness*   ^C1:2 Or *as many as he saw*   ^D1:3 Or *follow*, or *obey*   ^E1:4 Other mss add *God*   ^F1:4 Or *the sevenfold Spirit*   ^G1:5 Other mss read *has washed us*   ^H1:6 Other mss read *kings and*   ^I1:6 Or *made us into* (or *to be*) *a kingdom of priests*; Ex 19:6   ^J1:7 Or *peoples*   ^K1:7 Gn 12:3; 28:14; Zch 14:17   ^L1:7 Or *will wail because of him*   ^M1:7 Dn 7:13; Zch 12:10   ^N1:10 Or *in spirit*; lit *I became in the Spirit*   ^O1:11 Or *book*   ^P1:13 Or *like a son of man*   ^Q1:15 Lit *many*

1:1 Revelation means "unveiling." The revelation of **Jesus Christ** could mean the unveiling *about* Jesus, the unveiling *by* him, or both. **His servants** refers to all Christians. **1:3** The reading of this prophecy carries with it a promise of blessing. The reader must also **keep** (i.e., "take to heart" and apply) **what is written.** This is the first of seven significant "blessing" statements or beatitudes in the book of Revelation (14:13; 16:15; 19:9; 20:6; 22:7,14). **1:4 The one who is, who was, and who is to come** (v. 8) means that God not only exists now but always has existed and always will. The **seven spirits before his throne** may refer to: (1) "the angels of the seven

churches" (v. 20; chaps. 2–3), (2) other angels seen in the book (e.g., 8:2), or (3) the fullness of the Holy Spirit described in Is 11:2. **1:5–6** The **firstborn from the dead** looks back to Jesus's resurrection, the guarantee of the future resurrection. **1:7** This collage of Scripture from Dn 7:13 and Zch 12:10 expresses the theme for Revelation. The reference to **mourn** is sometimes understood as the response of those for whom it is too late to be saved. But the context of Zch 12:10 indicates the mourning will be true saving repentance, even for **those who pierced him** (i.e., the Jews; see 7:4–8; 11:13, and note there). **1:8 Alpha** and **Omega** are the first and last letters of the Greek alphabet, emphasizing that God is the beginning and the end. On **the one who is . . . and who is to come,** see note at v. 4. **1:9** Tradition indicates the apostle **John** was exiled by the Roman emperor Domitian to a penal colony on the **island called Patmos,** about forty miles southwest of Ephesus in the Aegean Sea, in about AD 95. He was released sometime after Domitian's death in AD 96. **1:10 In the Spirit** refers to the exalted spiritual state that John was in as he received the visions. **The Lord's day** is likely a phrase referring to the first day of the week—Sunday, the day of resurrection. **1:11** The **seven** local **churches** (see note at 2:1–3:22) addressed in Revelation were chosen from among all the churches in Asia Minor to serve as examples of the kinds of

realities playing out in church life. These seven were obvious choices since they were located on the roads of a circular postal route. **1:12** The **seven golden lampstands** are the seven churches (v. 11; chaps. 2–3). **1:14** The similes of the Son of Man's head and hair being **white as wool,** depicting wisdom and purity, and his eyes being **like a fiery flame,** picturing piercing holiness, fuse the vision of the "Ancient of Days" (Dn 7:9) and Jesus's appearance on the Mount of Transfiguration (Mt 17:2). **1:15** The **feet . . . like fine bronze . . . fired in a furnace** speaks of strength and stability. A **voice like the sound of cascading waters** would have riveted John's attention as he was imprisoned on an island where powerful waves crashed ashore. **1:16** The **seven stars** are the angels of the seven churches (v. 20). The **sharp double-edged sword** that came from his **mouth** symbolizes the power of the word of God to judge (Heb 4:12). The Son of Man's **face . . . shining like the sun** was another reminder to John of what he saw with his own eyes on the Mount of Transfiguration (Mt 17:2). **1:17** That John **fell at his feet** was an act of fear and awe at the Lord. **1:18** Christ's authority over **the keys of death and Hades** was stated in his declaration that he would found the church (Mt 16:18). This will be exercised when death and Hades are destroyed at the great white throne judgment (Rv 20:11–15).

#97 99 Essential Christian Truths

GLORIFICATION

Glorification is the final stage in the process of salvation. It refers to the future time when a Christian reaches moral and spiritual perfection at the time of death or at Christ's return (Php 1:9–11; Col 1:22). Glorification also involves the physical perfection that we will have once our bodies have been resurrected. When we are glorified, we will have a fuller knowledge and understanding of God and his Word (1Co 13:12; Php 3:20–21).

death and Hades. **¹⁹** Therefore write what you have seen, what is, and what will take place after this. **²⁰** The mystery of the seven stars you saw in my right hand and of the seven golden lampstands is this: The seven stars are the angels^A of the seven churches, and the seven lampstands^B are the seven churches.

THE LETTERS TO THE SEVEN CHURCHES

The Letter to Ephesus

2 "Write to the angel^C of the church in Ephesus: Thus says the one who holds the seven stars in his right hand and who walks among the seven golden lampstands: **²** I know your works, your labor, and your endurance, and that you cannot tolerate evil people. You have tested those who call themselves apostles and are not, and you have found them to be liars. **³** I know that you have persevered and endured hardships for the sake of my name, and you have not grown weary. **⁴** But I have this against you: You have abandoned the love you had at first. **⁵** Remember then how far you have fallen; repent, and do the works you did at first. Otherwise, I will come to you^D and remove your lampstand from its place, unless you repent. **⁶** Yet you do have this: You hate the practices of the Nicolaitans, which I also hate.

⁷ "Let anyone who has ears to hear listen to what the Spirit says to the churches. To the one

who conquers, I will give the right to eat from the tree of life, which is in^E the paradise of God.

The Letter to Smyrna

⁸ "Write to the angel of the church in Smyrna: Thus says the First and the Last, the one who was dead and came to life: **⁹** I know your^F affliction and poverty, but you are rich. I know the slander of those who say they are Jews and are not, but are a synagogue of Satan. **¹⁰** Don't be afraid of what you are about to suffer. Look, the devil is about to throw some of you into prison to test you, and you will experience affliction for ten days. Be faithful to the point of death, and I will give you the crown^G of life.

¹¹ "Let anyone who has ears to hear listen to what the Spirit says to the churches. The one who conquers will never be harmed by the second death.

The Letter to Pergamum

¹² "Write to the angel of the church in Pergamum: Thus says the one who has the sharp, double-edged sword: **¹³** I know^H where you live — where Satan's throne is. Yet you are holding on to my name and did not deny your faith in me,^I even in the days of Antipas, my faithful witness who was put to death among you, where Satan lives. **¹⁴** But I have a few things against you. You have some there who hold to the teaching of Balaam, who taught Balak

---

^A**1:20** Or *messengers*   ^B**1:20** Other mss add *that you saw*   ^C**2:1** Or *messenger*, also in vv. 8,12,18   ^D**2:5** Other mss add *quickly*   ^E**2:7** Other mss read *in the midst of*   ^F**2:9** Other mss add *works and*   ^G**2:10** Or *wreath*   ^H**2:13** Other mss add *your works and*   ^I**2:13** Or *deny my faith*

1:19 What you have seen is the vision of vv. 12–18. **What is** refers to the present state of affairs in the churches in chaps. 2–3. **What will take place after this** refers to the body of the book (chaps. 4–22), which begins with "after this" (4:1).

1:20 The Greek word translated **mystery** speaks of something formerly unknown which has now been revealed. Perhaps the **angels of the seven churches** spoken of here functioned like so-called guardian angels for members of those churches (Heb 1:14).

2:1–3:22 In general, each letter includes: (1) a *characteristic* of the risen Christ drawn from the vision in 1:12–18, (2) *commendation* of the church (though not the churches at Sardis and Laodicea), (3) *criticism* of the church's shortcomings (though not of the churches at Smyrna and Philadelphia) and how to correct them, (4) a *command* to "listen to what the Spirit says to the churches," and (5) a *commitment* to the persevering spiritual "one who conquers."

2:1 On **the angel of the church**, see note at 1:20. **Ephesus** was one of the largest and most powerful cities in the Roman Empire. It was devoted to the worship of the goddess Artemis (Lat *Diana*, Ac 19:28), the fertility goddess, and the emperor of Rome, who was considered a god. The church at Ephesus was apparently planted by Priscilla and Aquila around AD 52. Paul ministered there for two or three years (Ac 20:31), and used the city as a home base for the evangelization of the

region (Ac 19:8–10). On the **seven stars** and the **seven golden lampstands**, see 1:20. **2:2–4** The church at Ephesus did not **tolerate evil people** and was faithful to put false apostles to the test. But they had **abandoned the love** they **had at first**, meaning their love for God.

2:5 Having **fallen** does not mean loss of salvation but indicates a serious spiritual matter requiring soul-searching repentance (i.e., a change of mind and heart, implying a related change of behavior). If they did not **repent**, Christ would cause the church to close (**remove your lampstand**).

2:6 The **practices of the Nicolaitans** are explained in the letter to the church at Pergamum (vv. 14–15).

2:7 Let anyone who has ears to hear listen echoes Jesus's warning to his hearers at the end of the parable of the sower (Mt 13:9). **The one who conquers** refers to faithful and obedient believers. The **paradise of God** is the new heavens and earth (Rv 22:2). **The tree of life** will be there (Gn 3:22–24).

2:8 On **the angel of the church**, see note at 1:20. Like Ephesus, **Smyrna**, thirty-five miles to the north, was a harbor city. Its large Jewish population bitterly opposed Christianity. The church in Smyrna was likely founded during Paul's third missionary journey (Ac 19). On **the First and the Last** and **the one who was dead and came to life**, see notes at 1:5–6,8.

2:9–10 The church at Smyrna, against whom Christ voiced no criticism, was suffering

through spiritual warfare. A local **synagogue** of Jews was engaged in **slander** that resulted in church members being jailed for a short time (**ten days**). The phrase **those who say they are Jews and are not** does not deny the Jewish bloodlines of the persecutors. Rather, it mirrors Paul's assertion that, ultimately, Jewishness is not just outward but inward, related to the "circumcision is of the heart" by faith (Rm 2:28–29). The **crown of life** is also referred to in Jms 1:12, where it is received by those who love the Lord and endure trials.

2:11 On **let anyone who has ears to hear listen**, see note at v. 7. The **second death** is the lake of fire (20:14), the place of eternal torment for the devil, the beast, the false prophet (20:10), and all the non-elect (20:15). On the meaning of **the one who conquers**, see note at v. 7.

2:12–13 On the **angel of the church**, see note at 1:20. In the first century AD, the city of **Pergamum**, fifty miles north of Smyrna, was the leading religious center of Asia Minor. Like Smyrna, Pergamum was a center of emperor worship, and Christians were persecuted harshly for their refusal to engage in such worship. This is why Jesus called Pergamum the place **where Satan's throne is**. The situation for Christians in Pergamum was even worse than at Smyrna. A faithful man named **Antipas** had already been put **to death**. On the **sharp, double-edged sword**, see note at 1:16.

2:14–15 A viewpoint resembling **the teaching of Balaam** in the OT (Nm 22–25), which to place a stumbling block^A in front of the Israelites: to eat meat sacrificed to idols and to commit sexual immorality. ^15 In the same way, you also have those who hold to the teaching of the Nicolaitans.^B ^16 So repent! Otherwise, I will come to you quickly and fight against them with the sword of my mouth.

^17 "Let anyone who has ears to hear listen to what the Spirit says to the churches. To the one who conquers, I will give some of the hidden manna.^C I will also give him a white stone, and on the stone a new name is inscribed that no one knows except the one who receives it.

The Letter to Thyatira

^18 "Write to the angel of the church in Thyatira: Thus says the Son of God, the one whose eyes are like a fiery flame and whose feet are like fine bronze: ^19 I know your works — your love, faithfulness,^D service, and endurance. I know that your last works are greater than the

---

^A 2:14 Or to place a trap   ^B 2:15 Other mss add which I hate   ^C 2:17 Other mss add to eat   ^D 2:19 Or faith

---

is probably linked to **the teaching of the Nicolaitans** (cp. vv. 6,20–23), had a strong foothold in the church.
2:16 The **sword of my mouth** is the sword of v. 12. The clear-cut duty of the church at Pergamum was to combat the false viewpoints in their midst (vv. 14–15) or else they would be judged by the Lord Jesus.
2:17 On **let anyone who has ears to hear listen** see note at v. 7. The reference to **the one who conquers** (see note at v. 7) receiving **hidden manna** is intended to remind readers that Israel's sin in eating food

sacrificed to idols (Nm 25) was that much worse because God was still giving them manna, even as he was still caring for his church in Pergamum. The **white stone** and **new name** may be related to: (1) victory in the ancient Greek athletic games, which allowed an athlete to retire permanently; or (2) entrance to a community feast.
2:18 On **the angel of the church**, see note at 1:20. **Thyatira** was thirty miles southeast of Pergamum on the Lycus River. Each of its trade guilds was devoted to a patron god or goddess, and social events centered on

their worship. The pressure for Christians to participate in this idolatrous lifestyle, both for economic and social reasons, was great. The letter to Thyatira is the longest of the seven messages. This is odd, considering that Thyatira was the smallest and least consequential city of the group. Christ, for the only time in Revelation, is called the **Son of God**. On **eyes . . . like a fiery flame** and **feet . . . like fine bronze**, see notes at 1:14,15.
2:19 Significant spiritual growth was taking place in the church at Thyatira.

CHURCHES OF THE REVELATION
REVELATION 2–3
• City
⛪ Cities of the Seven Churches
— Major road

John writes Revelation encouraging Christians to remain faithful.

THRACE · Heraclea · Byzantium (Istanbul) · Bosporus · Chalcedon · Nicomedia · BITHYNIA AND PONTUS · Nicaea · Prusa · Dorylaeum · Cotiaeum · Ancyra · Appia · Nacolea · MARMARA SEA · Cyzicus · Dardanelles · Abydos · Samothrace · Imbros · Lemnos · Troas · MYSIA · Assos · Adramyttium · Lesbos · Mitylene · Pergamum · Thyatira · A S I A · Temenothyrae/Flaviopolis · Sebaste · PHRYGIA · Apamea · Hierapolis · Laodicea · Hermus R. · Chios · Smyrna · Sardis · Philadelphia · LYDIA · Tripolis · Ephesus · Tralles · Magnesia · Maeander R. · Colossae · PISIDIA · AEGEAN SEA · Skiros · Euboea · Andros · Tinos · Ikaria · Samos · Trogyllium · Alabanda · Aphrodisias · Delos · Miletus · Heraclea · Cyclades · Paros · Naxos · Patmos · CARIA · Halicarnassus · Idyma · Cibyra · PAMPHYLIA · Islands · Cos · Cos · Cnidus · LYCIA · Perga · Santorini · Rhodes · Rhodes · Xanthus · Patara · Myra

MEDITERRANEAN SEA

Crete

first. ²⁰ But I have this against you: You tolerate the woman Jezebel, who calls herself a prophetess and teaches and deceives my servants to commit sexual immorality and to eat meat sacrificed to idols. ²¹ I gave her time to repent, but she does not want to repent of her sexual immorality. ²² Look, I will throw her into a sickbed and those who commit adultery with her into great affliction. Unless they repent of her^ works, ²³ I will strike her children dead.ᴮ Then all the churches will know that I am the one who examines minds and hearts, and I will give to each of you according to your works. ²⁴ I say to the rest of you in Thyatira, who do not hold this teaching, who haven't known "the so-called secretsᶜ of Satan" — as they say — I am not putting any other burden on you. ²⁵ Only hold on to what you have until I come. ²⁶ The one who conquers and who keeps my works to the end: I will give him authority over the nations —

²⁷   and he will ruleᴰ them
    with an iron scepter;
  he will shatter them like potteryᴱ —

²⁸ just as I have received this from my Father. I will also give him the morning star. ²⁹ "Let anyone who has ears to hear listen to what the Spirit says to the churches.

The Letter to Sardis

3 "Write to the angel of the church in Sardis: Thus says the one who has the seven spirits of God and the seven stars: I know your works; you have a reputationᴳ for being alive, but you are dead. ² Be alert and strengthenᴴ what remains, which is about to die,ᴵ for I have not found your works complete before my God.

³ Remember, then, what you have received and heard; keep it, and repent. If you are not alert, I will comeᴶ like a thief, and you have no idea at what hour I will come upon you. ⁴ But you have a few peopleᴷ in Sardis who have not defiledᴸ their clothes, and they will walk with me in white, because they are worthy.

⁵ "In the same way, the one who conquers will be dressed in white clothes, and I will never erase his name from the book of life but will acknowledge his name before my Father and before his angels.

⁶ "Let anyone who has ears to hear listen to what the Spirit says to the churches.

The Letter to Philadelphia

⁷ "Write to the angel of the church in Philadelphia: Thus says the Holy One, the true one, the one who has the key of David, who opens and no one will close, and who closes and no one opens: ⁸ I know your works. Look, I have placed before you an open door that no one can close because you have but little power; yet you have kept my word and have not denied my name. ⁹ Note this: I will make those from the synagogue of Satan, who claim to be Jews and are not, but are lying — I will make them come and bow down at your feet, and they will know that I have loved you. ¹⁰ Because you have kept my command to endure, I will also keep you from the hour of testing that is going to come on the whole world to test those who live on the earth. ¹¹ I am coming soon. Hold on to what you have, so that no one takes your crown.

¹² "The one who conquers I will make a pillar in the temple of my God, and he will never go out again. I will write on him the name

---

^2:22 Other mss read *their* ᴮ2:23 Or *with a plague* ᶜ2:24 Or *The secret things* ᴰ2:27 Or *shepherd* ᴱ2:27 Ps 2:9 ᶠ3:1 Or *messenger*, also in vv. 7,14 ᴳ3:1 Or *have a name* ᴴ3:2 Other mss read *guard* ᴵ3:2 Or *strengthen who remain, who are about to die* ᴶ3:3 Other mss add *upon you* ᴷ3:4 Lit *few names* ᴸ3:4 Or *soiled*

2:20 Jezebel involved her followers in the same sins as those that infected the church at Pergamum (v. 14)—sexual immorality and eating meat sacrificed to idols. "Jezebel" was likely a nickname recalling the idolatrous queen of the northern king of Israel (1Kg 16; 18; 19; 21; 2Kg 9).
2:21–23 Great affliction foreshadows the time of great affliction to come upon the entire earth (Rv 3:10; 7:14). The children of Jezebel are not literal children, but spiritual "children" who have committed themselves to her false teaching.
2:24 The so-called secrets of Satan shows that this false belief and behavior originated with the devil.
2:26–27 By use of a messianic prophecy from Ps 2:9, Christ promises that the victor will have authority over the nations, which means ruling with him after his second coming (20:4,6).
2:28 The morning star is a symbol of the Messiah in Nm 24:17. Christ calls himself the "bright morning star" in Rv 22:16.
3:1 On the angel of the church, see note at 1:20. Sardis, thirty miles southeast of Thyatira, was one of the most ancient cities

in Asia Minor, founded around 1200 BC. In AD 17 an earthquake destroyed Sardis (and Philadelphia, see note at v. 7), but it was later rebuilt with the help of Emperor Tiberius. The people of Sardis were fascinated with death and immortality. On the seven spirits of God, see note at 1:4. On the seven stars, see note at 1:16. There is no praise for the church in Sardis. Spiritually they were as good as dead.
3:3 That Christ would come like a thief was an allusion to the fact that the city had been captured twice in its history because it failed to watch out for its enemies.
3:4–5 To be dressed in white was to wear the garments of the one who conquers (see note at 2:7). The book of life contains the name of each person who is elect (13:8; 20:15).
3:6 On let anyone who has ears to hear listen, see note at 2:7.
3:7 On the angel of the church, see note at 1:20. Philadelphia, forty miles southeast of Sardis, suffered long-term effects from the earthquake of AD 17. The letter indicates a situation similar to that of Smyrna. The phrases the key of David and no one opens echo Is 22:22 and speak of Christ's authority in the household of God.

3:8 Christ commended the faithful works of this small congregation, in spite of their little power.
3:9 On synagogue of Satan and who claim to be Jews and are not, see note at 2:9–10.
3:10 The hour of testing refers to "the great tribulation" (7:14). Those who live on the earth ("earth dwellers" from this point on in the notes) is a phrase used repeatedly in Revelation (6:10; 8:13; 11:10; 13:8) speaking of the non-elect, "whose names have not been written in the book of life" (17:8). To "keep . . . from the hour of testing" has been taken to mean: (1) removed before the time of tribulation, or (2) supernaturally protected within the tribulation. Since the purpose of "the hour of testing" is to test the non-elect "earth dwellers" rather than believers, it seems likely that believers will be removed before the hour of great tribulation begins.
3:11 To hold on to what you have appears to refer to the faithfulness of the church, described in v. 8.
3:12 The one who conquers (see note at 2:7) is promised a permanent place in the temple in God's eternal city, the new Jerusalem. This "temple" is actually the Lord himself

of my God and the name of the city of my God — the new Jerusalem, which comes down out of heaven from my God — and my new name. [13] "Let anyone who has ears to hear listen to what the Spirit says to the churches.

The Letter to Laodicea

[14] "Write to the angel of the church in Laodicea: Thus says the Amen, the faithful and true witness, the originator[A] of God's creation: [15] I know your works, that you are neither cold nor hot. I wish that you were cold or hot. [16] So, because you are lukewarm, and neither hot nor cold, I am going to vomit[B] you out of my mouth. [17] For you say, 'I'm rich; I have become wealthy and need nothing,' and you don't realize that you are wretched, pitiful, poor, blind, and naked. [18] I advise you to buy from me gold refined in the fire so that you may be rich, white clothes so that you may be dressed and your shameful nakedness not be exposed, and ointment to spread on your eyes so that you may see. [19] As many as I love, I rebuke and discipline. So be zealous and repent. [20] See! I stand at the door and knock. If anyone hears my voice and opens the door, I will come in to him and eat with him, and he with me. [21] "To the one who conquers I will give the right to sit with me on my throne, just as I also conquered and sat down with my Father on his throne. [22] "Let anyone who has ears to hear listen to what the Spirit says to the churches."

The Throne Room of Heaven

[4] After this I looked, and there in heaven was an open door. The first voice that I had heard speaking to me like a trumpet said, "Come up here, and I will show you what must take place after this."

[2] Immediately I was in the Spirit, and there was a throne in heaven and someone was seated on it. [3] The one seated[C] there had the appearance of jasper and carnelian stone. A rainbow that had the appearance of an emerald surrounded the throne.

[4] Around the throne were twenty-four thrones, and on the thrones sat twenty-four elders dressed in white clothes, with golden crowns on their heads.

[5] Flashes of lightning and rumblings and peals of thunder came from the throne. Seven fiery torches were burning before the throne, which are the seven spirits of God. [6] Something like a sea of glass, similar to crystal, was also before the throne.

Four living creatures covered with eyes in front and in back were around the throne on each side. [7] The first living creature was like a lion; the second living creature was like an ox; the third living creature had a face like a man; and the fourth living creature was like a flying eagle. [8] Each of the four living creatures had six wings; they were covered with eyes around and inside. Day and night they never stop,[D] saying,

Holy, holy, holy,
Lord God, the Almighty,
who was, who is, and who is to come.

[A]3:14 Or *beginning of God's creation*, or *ruler of God's creation* [B]3:16 Or *spit* [C]4:3 Other mss omit *The one seated* [D]4:8 Or *rest*

---

and the Lamb (21:2,22). Christ's **new name** may refer to "a name . . . that no one knows except himself" (19:12).
3:13 On **let anyone who has ears to hear listen**, see note at 2:7.
3:14 On the **angel of the church**, see note at 1:20. **Laodicea**, forty-five miles southeast of Philadelphia and ninety miles east of Ephesus, was an important trade center. The city had to bring in its water supply through an aqueduct. This made it vulnerable to drought and disruption by enemies. The Laodicean church was probably planted by Epaphras (Col 1:7), along with the churches of Hierapolis and Colossae, during Paul's three-year ministry at Ephesus (Ac 19:8–10; 20:31). **Amen** is a transliteration of the Hebrew word for "truth." Being the **originator of God's creation** means Jesus was the agent of creation (Jn 1:3; Col 1:16).
3:15–16 Because the water in Laodicea was piped in, it was neither **cold** and refreshing nor **hot** and therapeutic. The **lukewarm** water was thus not useful. The spiritual worthlessness of the church in Laodicea was nauseating to Christ (**I am going to vomit you out of my mouth**).
3:17–19 Because many believers in the Laodicean church were **rich** and arrogant, they were completely **blind** to the fact that they were spiritually **wretched** and **naked**. The only way Christ would give them spiritual

sight and make them spiritually rich and properly **dressed** was for them to **repent** (see note at 2:5) and be **zealous** to him. **As many as I love, I . . . discipline** echoes Pr 3:11–12, which is cited in Heb 12:6.
3:20 The Lord had been pushed to the outside of the church at Laodicea, and he was now seeking to reenter through their repentance (**opens the door**).
3:21 On **the one who conquers**, see note at 2:7. The right to **sit** with Christ on his **throne** goes beyond his promise to the apostles in Mt 19:28 and looks to his reign on earth in Rv 20:4–6. The phrase **sat down with my Father on his throne** looks ahead to the heavenly throne room in chaps. 4–5.
3:22 On **let anyone who has ears to hear listen**, see note at 2:7.
4:1–2 The phrases **after this** and **what must take place after this** signal the beginning of the body of the book (4:1–22:5) spoken of in 1:19. Even though John was told to **come up here**, it is not clear whether: (1) he was actually taken up into **heaven** (with the same command in 11:12 the two witnesses were taken to heaven), or (2) he was still "in the Spirit" (see note at 1:10) on the isle of Patmos (1:9–10).
4:3–4 Jasper is an opaque jewel also mentioned in the description of the new Jerusalem (21:11,19). **Carnelian stone** is a vivid red color. A **rainbow** is God's covenant sign

that he will never again judge the earth by destroying every creature in a flood (Gn 9:8–17). The **twenty-four elders** could refer to angels, but since there were elders as leaders in both Israel (Nm 11:16) and the church (Ti 1:5), it is more likely that twelve of the twenty-four represent the tribes of Israel and the other twelve the apostles of Christ, previewing the reference to the twelve tribes and twelve apostles in the new Jerusalem (21:12,14). Elsewhere in Revelation, **white clothes** and **golden crowns** make up the attire of victorious believers (3:5; 6:11; 7:9; 19:8,14).
4:5 Flashes of lightning . . . and thunder coming from God (**the throne**) represent phenomena that intensify and spill over from heaven to earth as part of God's just judgment (8:5; 11:19; 16:18,21). On the **seven spirits of God**, see note at 1:4.
4:6–7 The **four living creatures** resemble the cherubim in Ezk 1 and 10. **Covered with eyes** means that very few things escape the notice of these watchful angelic creatures. The imagery of the **lion . . . ox . . . man . . .** and **eagle** has strong linkage to Ezk 1:5–10 and may represent animate creation.
4:8 The mention of the creatures having **six wings** and the words **holy, holy, holy** echo the description of the seraphim in the heavenly throne room in Is 6:1–3. On **who was, who is, and who is to come**, see note at 1:4.

⁹ Whenever the living creatures give glory, honor, and thanks to the one seated on the throne, the one who lives forever and ever, ¹⁰ the twenty-four elders fall down before the one seated on the throne and worship the one who lives forever and ever. They cast their crowns before the throne and say,

> ¹¹ Our Lord and God,ᴬ
> you are worthy to receive
> glory and honor and power,
> because you have created all things,
> and by your will
> they exist and were created.

The Lamb Takes the Scroll

5 Then I saw in the right hand of the one seated on the throne a scroll with writing on both sides, sealed with seven seals. ² I also saw a mighty angel proclaiming with a loud voice, "Who is worthy to open the scroll and break its seals?" ³ But no one in heaven or on earth or under the earth was able to open the scroll or even to look in it. ⁴ I wept and wept because no one was found worthy to openᴮ the scroll or even to look in it. ⁵ Then one of the elders said to me, "Do not weep. Look, the Lion from the tribe of Judah, the Root of David, has conquered so that he is able to open the scroll andᶜ its seven seals."

⁶ Then I saw one like a slaughtered lamb standing in the midst of the throne and the four living creatures and among the elders. He had seven horns and seven eyes, which are the seven spirits of God sent into all the earth. ⁷ He went and took the scroll out of the right hand of the one seated on the throne.

The Lamb Is Worthy

⁸ When he took the scroll, the four living creatures and the twenty-four elders fell down before the Lamb. Each one had a harp and golden bowls filled with incense, which are the prayers of the saints. ⁹ And they sang a new song:

> You are worthy to take the scroll
> and to open its seals,
> because you were slaughtered,
> and you purchasedᴰ peopleᴱ
> for God by your blood
> from every tribe and language
> and people and nation.
> ¹⁰ You made them a kingdomᶠ
> and priests to our God,
> and they will reign on the earth.

¹¹ Then I looked and heard the voice of many angels around the throne, and also of the living creatures and of the elders. Their number was countless thousands, plus thousands of thousands. ¹² They said with a loud voice,

> Worthy is the Lamb who was
> slaughtered
> to receive power and riches
> and wisdom and strength
> and honor and glory and blessing!

¹³ I heard every creature in heaven, on earth, under the earth, on the sea, and everything in them say,

> Blessing and honor and glory
> and power
> be to the one seated on the throne,
> and to the Lamb, forever and ever!

¹⁴ The four living creatures said, "Amen," and the elders fell down and worshiped.

The First Seal on the Scroll

6 Then I saw the Lamb open one of the sevenᴳ seals, and I heard one of the four living creatures say with a voice like thunder, "Come!" ² I looked, and there was a white horse. Its rider held a bow; a crown was given to him, and he went out as a conqueror in order to conquer.ᴴ

ᴬ4:11 Some mss add the Holy One; other mss read Lord ᴮ5:4 Other mss add and read ᶜ5:5 Other mss add loose
ᴰ5:9 Or redeemed ᴱ5:9 Other mss read us ᶠ5:10 Other mss read them kings ᴳ6:1 Other mss omit seven ᴴ6:2 Or went out conquering and in order to conquer

---

4:11 The beginning point of worship is to recognize that God is completely **worthy** to be recognized for his unrivaled **glory and honor and power**, and his work as Creator and Sustainer of **all things**.
5:1 The **right hand** of God symbolizes power and authority. **With writing on both sides** echoes Ezk 2:9–10. Because the outer edge of the scroll was **sealed**, the contents could be seen only when all seven seals were removed.
5:5–7 Speaking of Jesus as **the Lion from the tribe of Judah** echoes the messianic prophecy in Gn 49:9–10. On the **four living creatures**, see note at 4:6–7. On **the elders**, see note at 4:3–4. In the book of Daniel, **horns** stand for power and authority (Dn 7:8,20,24). On the **seven spirits of God**, see note at 1:4. The Lamb taking the scroll out of the **right hand** of the Father signifies a transfer of authority.

5:8 Believers' prayers are described as filling **golden bowls** before the throne of God. **Saints** means "holy ones." These are not elite and exceptional Christians. The NT uses this term for all believers in Christ (Rm 1:7).
5:9–10 The **new song** sung in heaven about Christ is inspired by his redemptive work, the shedding of his **blood** on the cross. The target group for redemption (described as **every tribe . . . nation**) is the same group that is identified in the Great Commission: "all nations" (Mt 28:19). The promise that **they will reign on the earth** is fulfilled in 20:6.
5:11–14 On the **living creatures**, see note at 4:6–7. On **the elders**, see note at 4:3–4.
6:1–8:1 Some interpreters believe that the description of the unsealing of the scroll is the beginning of the tribulation period. However, the scroll in the Lamb's hand (5:7) is not open for viewing until all seven seals have been removed. Six of the seals are removed in chap. 6. The two scenes in chap. 7 (vv. 1–8,9–17) form an interlude prior to the removal of the seventh seal (8:1). It appears that the "unsealing" sequence in Rv 6:1–8:1 occurs before the tribulation period.
6:1–8 The lifting of the first four seals is portrayed in this section as four horsemen, an image likely drawn from Zch 1:7–11, though the colors of the horses are different.
6:1,3,5,7 It appears that the command **Come!** from each of **the four living creatures** sets in motion the dramatic effects unleashed by removing each of the seals.
6:2 Some have taken the **rider** here as a description of Christ because of its similarity to him at the second coming (19:11). Given the context, this rider symbolizes destructive conquest followed by war, famine, and death.

The Second Seal

3 When he opened the second seal, I heard the second living creature say, "Come!" **4** Then another horse went out, a fiery red one, and its rider was allowed to take peace from the earth, so that people would slaughter one another. And a large sword was given to him.

The Third Seal

5 When he opened the third seal, I heard the third living creature say, "Come!" And I looked, and there was a black horse. Its rider held a set of scales in his hand. **6** Then I heard something like a voice among the four living creatures say, "A quart of wheat for a denarius,^A and three quarts of barley for a denarius, but do not harm the oil and the wine."

The Fourth Seal

7 When he opened the fourth seal, I heard the voice of the fourth living creature say, "Come!" **8** And I looked, and there was a pale green^B horse. Its rider was named Death, and Hades was following after him. They were^C given authority over a fourth of the earth, to kill by the sword, by famine, by plague, and by the wild animals of the earth.

The Fifth Seal

9 When he opened the fifth seal, I saw under the altar the souls of those who had been slaughtered because of the word of God and the testimony they had given.^D **10** They cried out with a loud voice, "Lord,^E the one who is holy and true, how long until you judge those who live on the earth and avenge our blood?" **11** So they were each given a white robe, and they were told to rest a little while longer until the number would be completed of their fellow servants and their brothers and sisters,

who were going to be killed just as they had been.

The Sixth Seal

12 Then I saw him open^F the sixth seal. A violent earthquake occurred; the sun turned black like sackcloth made of hair; the entire moon^G became like blood; **13** the stars^H of heaven fell to the earth as a fig tree drops its unripe figs when shaken by a high wind; **14** the sky was split apart like a scroll being rolled up; and every mountain and island was moved from its place.

15 Then the kings of the earth, the nobles, the generals, the rich, the powerful, and every slave and free person hid in the caves and among the rocks of the mountains. **16** And they said to the mountains and to the rocks, "Fall on us and hide us from the face of the one seated on the throne and from the wrath of the Lamb, **17** because the great day of their^I wrath has come! And who is able to stand?"

The Sealed of Israel

7 After this I saw four angels standing at the four corners of the earth, restraining the four winds of the earth so that no wind could blow on the earth or on the sea or on any tree. **2** Then I saw another angel rising up from the east, who had the seal of the living God. He cried out in a loud voice to the four angels who were allowed to harm the earth and the sea, **3** "Don't harm the earth or the sea or the trees until we seal the servants of our God on their foreheads." **4** And I heard the number of the sealed:

144,000 sealed from every tribe of the Israelites:

5   12,000 sealed from the tribe of Judah,
       12,000 from the tribe of Reuben,
       12,000 from the tribe of Gad,

^A **6:6** A denarius = one day's wage   ^B **6:8** Or *a greenish gray*   ^C **6:8** Other mss read *He was*   ^D **6:9** Other mss add *about the Lamb*   ^E **6:10** Or *"Master*   ^F **6:12** Or *I saw when he opened*   ^G **6:12** Or *the full moon*   ^H **6:13** Perhaps meteors   ^I **6:17** Other mss read *his*

The word for crown (Gk *stephanos*) differs from the many crowns (Gk *diademata*) of Jesus in Rv 19:12.
6:4 The description here strongly parallels Mt 24:6–7.
6:5–6 The apparent descriptions of famine conditions here would naturally follow the state of war portrayed in vv. 2,4. A **quart** of **wheat** or **barley** was enough food for a person for one day. Thus, the greatly inflated cost of these necessities indicates a severe drought, though **oil** and **wine** are plentiful.
6:8 Hades was popularly known as the grave and resting place after **Death** (see note at 20:11–15). The text does not say that **a fourth** of the population of the earth was killed, but only that **authority** was given to "Death" and "Hades" over this proportion of the world, allowing them to kill freely.
6:9–11 The **souls of those who had been slaughtered** may refer to believers killed during the removal of the first four seals (6:2,4,8) or generally to all slaughtered

believers (see 18:24). Their being killed because of **the word of God** and their **testimony** for Christ is the same reason given for John's imprisonment on the island of Patmos (1:9). The delay here (**rest a little while longer**) implies the "hour of testing" has not yet begun. On **white robe,** see note at 3:4–5.
6:12–17 The effects when the sixth seal is lifted from the scroll (**sun turned black** and **moon became like blood**) are very similar to those in Jl 2:28–31, which are said to occur just before the day of the Lord (Jl 2:31). This is the same as the **great day of the wrath** of God the Father and **the Lamb** (vv. 16–17; Zph 1:14–15). The question **and who is able to stand?** is answered in chap. 7.
7:1–17 Two visions make up this interlude between the opening of the sixth (6:12) and seventh (8:1) seals—(1) the sealing of the 144,000 servants of God on earth (7:1–8), and (2) the innumerable multitude arriving in heaven (7:9–17).

7:1–3 The "calm in the midst of the storm" calls attention to the **seal of the living God** being applied to the **foreheads** of the **servants of our God.** In the ancient world, seals were signs of ownership (5:1) or authority (Mt 27:66).
7:4–8 The identity of the **144,000** has been variously interpreted. (1) Jehovah's Witnesses falsely maintain this is the total number of the anointed who will dwell in heaven with the Lord and rule over the inhabitants of a purified earth. (2) Since all Christians are sealed by the Holy Spirit (2Co 1:22; Eph 4:30), and the 144,000 are called "the servants of . . . God" in Rv 7:3, the seal of vv. 2–4 may be placed on all Christians, and this host is generically representative of them. (3) The most literal interpretation is highly plausible. The 144,000 represent Israel following a future conversion of the nation.
7:5–8 The **tribe of Judah** is mentioned first because it was the royal tribe of Israel (Gn 49:9–10) into which Jesus was born

Equality of the Races and Racial Reconciliation

by Robert Smith Jr.

Today talk of *race*, a word referring to ethnic distinctions associated with culture and skin color, is a treacherous matter. But in the beginning, God created all peoples out of one blood to dwell on the face of the earth (Ac 17:26), and in the Bible we see his intentions for humanity: "A vast multitude from every nation, tribe, people, and language, which no one could number, [was] standing before the throne and before the Lamb. They were clothed in white robes with palm branches in their hands" (Rv 7:9). All humans are descended from Adam and Eve (cp. Gn 3:20), and Jesus died so that *all* who would accept him by faith could spend eternity in his presence.

Yet in spite of these biblical realties, the enslavement of peoples from Africa survived the two great religious movements in American history—the first and second Great Awakenings. Western Christianity, in fact, still struggles with conscienceless power and powerless conscience as Christians sit around their Communion tables and worship in segregated church contexts. In adopting racist attitudes and remaining in separate camps as it were, humanity, made in the image of God and after God's likeness (Gn 1:26), has not only attempted to make God in its own image (that is, prone to categorize by appearances) but has also tried to de-theologize the divine DNA within mankind.

The establishment of racial hierarchy has led to apartheid, anti-Semitism, and rampant racism. History records educational exclusion and societal separation, resulting in bloodstained streets. The sacrificial blood of Christ shed at Calvary, however, was offered to cleanse humanity from sin, thus enabling us to move even beyond racial reconciliation to Christo-conciliation—fulfilling the prayer of Jesus in Gethsemane. He wanted his followers to "be one" (Jn 17:11). "As you, Father, are in me and I am in you, may they also be in us," he said (17:21).

Christo-conciliation, then, is better than mere racial reconciliation. Because of the death of the Son of God, Jesus Christ, Christians from all backgrounds are not just members of one biological family; we are one spiritual family, co-heirs with Christ. South African Archbishop Desmond Tutu places strong emphasis on forgiveness with regard to this matter: "Forgiving means abandoning your right to pay back the perpetrator in his own coin" (*No Future without Forgiveness [New York: Image]*, 219). African theologian Allan Aubrey Boesak contends that forgiveness is "taking the sting out of memory" (*Radical Reconciliation [Maryknoll, NY: Orbis]*, 138).

Christ-Centered Reconciliation

If we are to move beyond superficial conversation and onward to true healing with regard to this topic, we must consider three points. First, the evangelical church too often seems more influenced by sociology than by Scripture. Second, the evangelical church must take seriously the oneness of the human race. Third, that the gospel was intended for everyone is clearly understood, but the evangelical church tends to handle the gospel differently as it addresses different people groups. That needs to change.

Evangelicals must not merely assume the equality of the people groups; this truth must be embraced and proclaimed. Evangelicals must think seriously about the topic, drawing on Acts 17:26, and pointing toward the eschatological reality of the beloved community made up of different tribes and nations and tongues and peoples. We all descend from one couple, and as Christians, we have been washed in the blood of Jesus Christ.

Dr. William Holmes Borders, an African American pastor of the Wheat Street Baptist Church in Atlanta, Georgia, once told this story:

> [A Negro] had been denied an education, political and economic opportunity, and was forced to beg for food. He rang the front doorbell of a southern mansion and the owner of the house answered. "I'm hungry," the Negro said. "Go around to the back door," he was told. Food was prepared, and the owner of the house brought it to the Negro. "First we will bless the food," the white man said. "Now

6 12,000 from the tribe of Asher,
12,000 from the tribe of Naphtali,
12,000 from the tribe of Manasseh,
7 12,000 from the tribe of Simeon,
12,000 from the tribe of Levi,
12,000 from the tribe of Issachar,
8 12,000 from the tribe of Zebulun,
12,000 from the tribe of Joseph,
12,000 sealed from the tribe of Benjamin.

A Multitude from the Great Tribulation

9 After this I looked, and there was a vast multitude from every nation, tribe, people, and language, which no one could number, standing before the throne and before the Lamb. They were clothed in white robes with palm branches in their hands. **10** And they cried out in a loud voice:

Salvation belongs to our God,
who is seated on the throne,
and to the Lamb!

11 All the angels stood around the throne, and along with the elders and the four living creatures they fell facedown before the throne and worshiped God, **12** saying,

Amen! Blessing and glory and wisdom
and thanksgiving and honor
and power and strength
be to our God forever and ever. Amen.

13 Then one of the elders asked me, "Who are these people in white robes, and where did they come from?"

14 I said to him, "Sir,^ you know."

Then he told me: These are the ones coming out of the great tribulation. They washed their robes and made them white in the blood of the Lamb.

15 For this reason they are
before the throne of God,
and they serve him day and night
in his temple.
The one seated on the throne
will shelter[8] them:
16 They will no longer hunger;
they will no longer thirst;
the sun will no longer strike them,
nor will any scorching heat.
17 For the Lamb who is at the center
of the throne
will shepherd them;
he will guide them to springs of the
waters of life,
and God will wipe away every tear
from their eyes.

The Seventh Seal

8 When he opened the seventh seal, there was silence in heaven for about half an hour. **2** Then I saw the seven angels who stand in the presence of God; seven trumpets were given to them. **3** Another angel, with a golden incense burner, came and stood at the altar. He was given a large amount of incense to offer with the prayers of all the saints on the golden altar in front of the throne. **4** The smoke of the incense, with the prayers of the saints, went up in the presence of God from the angel's hand. **5** The angel took the incense burner, filled it with fire from the altar, and hurled it to the earth; there were peals of thunder, rumblings, flashes of lightning, and an earthquake.

^7:14 Or *"My lord*　[8]7:15 Or *will spread his tent over*

(Rv 5:5). **Reuben** is next because he was Jacob's firstborn (Gn 49:3). The tribes of Dan and Ephraim are replaced by **Joseph** and **Levi**, neither of which was included in the military encampment of tribes in Nm 2.
7:9–12 This scene is at least a partial fulfillment of the Great Commission (Mt 28:19–20). Some interpreters understand the **vast multitude** to be all martyrs, who arrive in heaven over a period of time. Others see this as the time when the church is raptured (1Th 4:14–17).
7:13–14 The **robes** of the vast multitude (v. 9) being made **white** in the **blood of the Lamb** refers to the redemptive work of Christ (1:5; 5:9). The multitude **coming out of the great tribulation** (Dn 12:1; Mt 24:21) may refer to the rapture of the church before the great tribulation.
8:1 When **the seventh seal** is lifted, the scroll is finally opened (5:1), so that its contents can be released. The **half an hour** of **silence in heaven** echoes Zph 1:7. This implies that the day of the Lord begins with the trumpet judgments.
8:2–6 This pause implies that the "hour of testing" (3:10) begins with the judgment of the **seven trumpets**.

you repeat after me, Our Father . . ." The Negro said, "Your Father . . ." "Why do you insist upon saying, 'Your Father,' when I keep telling you to say, "'Our Father'?" the white man asked. The Negro beggar replied, "Well, boss, if I say, 'Our Father,' that would make you and me brothers, and I'm 'fraid the Lord wouldn't like it, you makin' your brother come to the back porch to get a piece of bread" (James W. English, *Handyman of the Lord: The Life and*

Ministry of the Rev. William Holmes Borders [New York: Meredith Press, 1967], 33–34).

The apostle Paul reminds us that all persons have come into being out of one blood. That one blood makes each individual equal within the human race. The blood of Christ shed for the forgiveness of the sins of humanity, however, makes believing humanity brothers and sisters. May we move forward to embrace the divine design.

The Seven Trumpets

⁶ And the seven angels who had the seven trumpets prepared to blow them.

The First Trumpet

⁷ The first angel blew his trumpet, and hail and fire, mixed with blood, were hurled to the earth. So a third of the earth was burned up, a third of the trees were burned up, and all the green grass was burned up.

The Second Trumpet

⁸ The second angel blew his trumpet, and something like a great mountain ablaze with fire was hurled into the sea. So a third of the sea became blood, ⁹ a third of the living creatures in the sea died, and a third of the ships were destroyed.

The Third Trumpet

¹⁰ The third angel blew his trumpet, and a great star, blazing like a torch, fell from heaven. It fell on a third of the rivers and springs of water. ¹¹ The name of the star is Wormwood, and a third of the waters became wormwood. So, many of the people died from the waters, because they had been made bitter.

The Fourth Trumpet

¹² The fourth angel blew his trumpet, and a third of the sun was struck, a third of the moon, and a third of the stars, so that a third of them were darkened. A third of the day was without light and also a third of the night. ¹³ I looked and heard an eagleᴬ flying high overhead, crying out in a loud voice, "Woe! Woe! Woe to those who live on the earth, because of the remaining trumpet blasts that the three angels are about to sound!"

The Fifth Trumpet

9 The fifth angel blew his trumpet, and I saw a star that had fallen from heaven to earth. The key for the shaft to the abyss was given to him. ² He opened the shaft to the abyss, and smoke came up out of the shaft like smoke from a greatᴮ furnace so that the sun and the air were darkened by the smoke from the shaft. ³ Then locusts came out of the smoke on to the earth, and powerᶜ was given to them like the power that scorpions have on the earth. ⁴ They were told not to harm the grass of the earth, or any green plant, or any tree, but only those people who do not have God's seal on their foreheads. ⁵ They were not permitted to kill them but were to torment them for five months; their torment is like the torment caused by a scorpion when it stings someone. ⁶ In those days people will seek death and will not find it; they will long to die, but death will flee from them.

⁷ The appearance of the locusts was like horses prepared for battle. Something like golden crowns was on their heads; their faces were like human faces; ⁸ they had hair like women's hair; their teeth were like lions' teeth; ⁹ they had chests like iron breastplates; the sound of their wings was like the sound of many chariots with horses rushing into battle; ¹⁰ and they had tails with stingers like scorpions, so that with their tails they had the power to harm people for five months. ¹¹ They had as their kingᴰ the angel of the abyss; his name in Hebrew is Abaddon,ᴱ and in Greek he has the name Apollyon.ᶠ

¹² The first woe has passed. There are still two more woes to come after this.

The Sixth Trumpet

¹³ The sixth angel blew his trumpet. From the fourᴳ horns of the golden altar that is before God, I heard a voice ¹⁴ say to the sixth angel

---

ᴬ8:13 Other mss read *angel* ᴮ9:2 Other mss omit *great* ᶜ9:3 Or *authority*, also in v. 10 ᴰ9:11 Or *as king over them* ᴱ9:11 Or *Destruction* ᶠ9:11 Or *Destroyer* ᴳ9:13 Other mss omit *four*

8:7–12 The first four trumpet judgments in this section mirror the plagues upon Egypt in Ex 7–11.
8:7 The effects of the **first . . . trumpet** are **hail . . . fire**, and **blood**, which combines what happened in the first (Ex 7:19–20) and seventh (Ex 9:22–25) plagues on Egypt.
8:8–9 The description of the **second . . . trumpet** sounds like the eruption of a great island volcano. A **third of the sea** becoming **blood** and a third of the **living creatures** in it dying is similar to what happened to the Nile River and its fish in the first plague on Egypt (Ex 7:17–21), but on a global scale.
8:10–11 The effects of the **third . . . trumpet** are like a meteorite (i.e., a falling **star**) hitting the earth and causing toxic **water** pollution, killing many people. **Wormwood** is a nonpoisonous but bitter plant common to the Middle East.
8:12 It is difficult to understand the exact effects of the **fourth . . . trumpet**, though it clearly echoes the ninth plague on Egypt (Ex 10:21–23). For the **sun . . . moon**, and **stars** to

be darkened by **a third** could mean: (1) These heavenly bodies are visible for "a third" less time than is normal; or (2) the intensity of their light is reduced by "a third," as if by the recent cosmic disturbances.
8:13 The remaining three trumpet judgments will maximize the **woe** upon the "earth dwellers."
9:1 The judgment of the **fifth . . . trumpet** recalls both the eighth plague on Egypt in Ex 10:12–15 and the plague of locusts in Jl 1:2–4; 2:25, which was a foreshadowing of the day of the Lord (Jl 1:15). The **star** here may refer to: (1) the demon mentioned in v. 11, (2) Satan (see notes at 12:4,7–10), or (3) the angel who has the **key** to the **abyss** (the bottomless pit) in 20:1. The last option is most likely.
9:2–10 The **locusts** origin from the abyss, plus the fact that, unlike regular locusts, these are not allowed to harm any **plant** or **tree** on the earth, makes it clear that these creatures are demonic. They target **people** who do not have **God's seal on their foreheads**. Some hold that the span

of the torment for all the unbelievers is **five months** because that is the life span of a locust, while others think it has to do with the time of the year when locust plagues occur with devastating impact—from mid-spring to late summer.
9:11 The **king** of these demonic creatures is called **Abaddon** (Hb) and **Apollyon** (Gk), both of which mean "destruction."
9:12 The **first woe** predicted in 8:13 has now **passed** with the fifth trumpet (vv. 1–11). The two remaining woes are the sixth trumpet (vv. 13–21; 11:14) and the seventh trumpet (11:15–19).
9:13 When the **sixth . . . trumpet** sounds, the authority of the **voice** from the **altar . . . before God** strongly suggests that this is the Lamb (Christ), not the martyrs under the altar (6:9–10), or even the angel whose actions led to the trumpet judgment (8:3–5).
9:14–16 The **four angels** are apparently demons in positions of authority over the demonic army, like Apollyon (v. 11). The **river Euphrates** was the eastern boundary of the land promised to Abraham (Gn 15:18). That

who had the trumpet, "Release the four angels bound at the great river Euphrates." [15] So the four angels who were prepared for the hour, day, month, and year were released to kill a third of the human race. [16] The number of mounted troops was two hundred million;[A] I heard their number. [17] This is how I saw the horses and their riders in the vision: They had breastplates that were fiery red, hyacinth blue, and sulfur yellow. The heads of the horses were like the heads of lions, and from their mouths came fire, smoke, and sulfur. [18] A third of the human race was killed by these three plagues — by the fire, the smoke, and the sulfur that came from their mouths. [19] For the power of the horses is in their mouths and in their tails, because their tails, which resemble snakes, have heads that inflict injury.

[20] The rest of the people, who were not killed by these plagues, did not repent of the works of their hands to stop worshiping demons and idols of gold, silver, bronze, stone, and wood, which cannot see, hear, or walk. [21] And they did not repent of their murders, their sorceries, their sexual immorality, or their thefts.

The Mighty Angel and the Small Scroll

10 Then I saw another mighty angel coming down from heaven, wrapped in a cloud, with a rainbow over his head.[B] His face was like the sun, his legs[C] were like pillars of fire, [2] and he held a little scroll opened in his hand. He put his right foot on the sea, his left on the land, [3] and he called out with a loud voice like a roaring lion. When he cried out, the seven thunders raised their voices. [4] And when the seven thunders spoke, I was about to write, but I heard a voice from heaven, saying, "Seal

up what the seven thunders said, and do not write it down!"

[5] Then the angel that I had seen standing on the sea and on the land raised his right hand to heaven. [6] He swore by the one who lives forever and ever, who created heaven and what is in it, the earth and what is in it, and the sea and what is in it, "There will no longer be a delay, [7] but in the days when the seventh angel will blow his trumpet, then the mystery of God will be completed, as he announced to his servants the prophets."

[8] Then the voice that I heard from heaven spoke to me again and said, "Go, take the scroll that lies open in the hand of the angel who is standing on the sea and on the land." [9] So I went to the angel and asked him to give me the little scroll. He said to me, "Take and eat it; it will be bitter in your stomach, but it will be as sweet as honey in your mouth." [10] Then I took the little scroll from the angel's hand and ate it. It was as sweet as honey in my mouth, but when I ate it, my stomach became bitter. [11] And they said to me, "You must prophesy again about[D] many peoples, nations, languages, and kings."

The Two Witnesses

11 Then I was given a measuring reed like a rod,[E] with these words: "Go[F] and measure the temple of God and the altar, and count those who worship there. [2] But exclude the courtyard outside the temple. Don't measure it, because it is given to the nations,[G] and they will trample the holy city for forty-two months. [3] I will grant[H] my two witnesses authority to prophesy for 1,260 days, dressed in sackcloth." [4] These are the two olive trees and the two lampstands that stand before the

---

^9:16 Other mss read *a hundred million*   ^10:1 Or *a halo on his head*   ^10:1 Or *feet*   ^10:11 Or *prophesy again against*   ^11:1 Other mss add *and the angel stood up*   ^11:1 Lit *"Arise*   ^11:2 Or *Gentiles*   ^11:3 Or *I will give to*

---

these demons are **prepared for the hour, day, month, and year** indicates that all these events are according to God's sovereign plan and timing (Dn 9:24–27). An army of **two hundred million** is large enough to accomplish such a horrific slaughter as killing **a third of the human race.** Some believe this army is human, but more likely it is demonic.

9:17–19 The term **plagues** is used to echo God's plagues on Egypt in Ex 7–11. It is also the first of many uses of "plague" in Revelation, speaking of God's judgment in the end times (11:6; 15:1,6,8; 16:9,21; 18:4,8).

9:20–21 The "earth dwellers" give the same hard-hearted response Pharaoh gave when confronted with the plagues (Ex 7:22; 9:7).

10:1–11:14 This is a second interlude in the book of Revelation (the first is 7:1–17), falling between the sixth and seventh trumpets.

10:1 The **mighty angel** could be: (1) the angel introduced in 5:2, (2) the angel seen in 18:1, or (3) **another** angel altogether. In spite of his impressive appearance and the similarity to the Son of Man in the vision of

1:13–16, it is unlikely this is Christ as Christ is never called an angel elsewhere in the NT.

10:2 The **little scroll** may be: (1) a second scroll in the Apocalypse; or (2) since it is opened, the scroll which was finally **opened** for viewing in 8:1. Perhaps the scroll appears small because the angel holding it is so huge (his **right foot** being on **the sea** and his **left** foot being on **the land**).

10:3–4 The **seven thunders** may be an allusion to Ps 29.

10:5–7 On the **angel . . . standing on the sea,** see note at v. 1. The pace of divine judgment is about to quicken and **be completed,** with the sounding of the seventh trumpet (11:15–19). **The mystery of God** is truth that has not been previously revealed or fulfilled, but is being revealed now (Eph 3:9). The phrase **his servants the prophets** probably refers to both OT and NT prophets.

10:8–11 For John to **eat** the scroll recalls Ezekiel being commanded to do the same thing (Ezk 3:1–3). While the eating was as **sweet as honey,** the digesting was **bitter.** While the intake and preaching of Scripture is

sweet, the calloused rejection of the hearers is bitter indeed.

11:1–2 The mention of a **measuring reed like a rod** and the command to **go and measure the temple of God and the altar** calls to mind Ezk 40:3,5. The statement that the Gentiles will **trample the holy city** (Jerusalem) echoes Jesus's statement about "the times of the Gentiles" (Lk 21:24) just before the second coming of Christ.

11:3–4 The **1,260 days,** in which **two** unnamed **witnesses . . . prophesy** for the Lord, is in stark contrast to the "forty-two months" of v. 2 and 13:5. Since no one can harm the witnesses until "they finish their testimony" (11:7), and since they die in Jerusalem (see note at vv. 8–10)—apparently having ministered there—this period of 1,260 days cannot be the same three and one-half year period as the reign of the beast (13:5). The 1,260 days precede the beast's reign, because part of his rise to worldwide prominence is based on killing the two witnesses (11:7). These witnesses are **dressed in sackcloth,** the garb of mourning and repentance (Jl 1:13; Jnh 3:5–6). The **two olive trees** and the **two**

Lord^A of the earth. ⁵ If anyone wants to harm them, fire comes from their mouths and consumes their enemies; if anyone wants to harm them, he must be killed in this way. ⁶ They have authority to close up the sky so that it does not rain during the days of their prophecy. They also have power over the waters to turn them into blood and to strike the earth with every plague whenever they want.

The Witnesses Martyred

⁷ When they finish their testimony, the beast that comes up out of the abyss will make war on them, conquer them, and kill them. ⁸ Their dead bodies^B will lie in the main street^C of the great city, which figuratively^D is called Sodom and Egypt, where also their Lord was crucified. ⁹ And some of^E the peoples, tribes, languages, and nations will view their bodies for three and a half days and not permit their bodies to be put into a tomb. ¹⁰ Those who live on the earth will gloat over them and celebrate and send gifts to one another because these two prophets had tormented those who live on the earth.

The Witnesses Resurrected

¹¹ But after three and a half days, the breath^F of life from God entered them, and they stood on their feet. Great fear fell on those who saw them. ¹² Then they heard^G a loud voice from heaven saying to them, "Come up here." They went up to heaven in a cloud, while their enemies watched them. ¹³ At that moment a violent earthquake took place, a tenth of the city fell, and seven thousand people were killed in the earthquake. The survivors were terrified and gave glory to the God of heaven.

¹⁴ The second woe has passed. Take note: The third woe is coming soon!

The Seventh Trumpet

¹⁵ The seventh angel blew his trumpet, and there were loud voices in heaven saying,

The kingdom of the world has become
　the kingdom
of our Lord and of his Christ,
　and he will reign forever and ever.

¹⁶ The twenty-four elders, who were seated before God on their thrones, fell facedown and worshiped God, ¹⁷ saying,

We give you thanks, Lord God,
　the Almighty,
who is and who was,^H
because you have taken
　your great power
and have begun to reign.

¹⁸ 　The nations were angry,
but your wrath has come.
The time has come
for the dead to be judged
and to give the reward
to your servants the prophets,
to the saints, and to those who fear
　your name,

---

^A11:4 Other mss read God　^B11:8 Or Their corpse　^C11:8 Or lie on the broad street　^D11:8 Or spiritually　^E11:9 Lit And from　^F11:11 Or spirit　^G11:12 Other mss read Then I heard　^H11:17 Other mss add and who is to come

---

lampstands are imagery from Zch 4, where the two figures appear to be Zerubbabel the governor and Joshua the high priest.
11:5–6 Besides being invulnerable to physical **harm**, the ministry of the two witnesses echoes the great miracles of the ministries of Elijah and Moses. **Fire** that **consumes their enemies** looks back to Elijah's ministry in 2 Kg 1:10–12. No **rain during the days of their prophecy** (which is three and one-half years long, v. 3) echoes the three-year drought that Elijah prophesied (1Kg 17:1; 18:1). Power over the waters **to turn them into blood** and **to strike the earth with every plague** recalls Moses's ministry in Egypt (Ex 7–11).
11:7 The **beast**, the great antichrist figure prophesied elsewhere (Dn 7:20–21,25; 2Th 2:9–11; 1Jn 2:18) and the satanically inspired world ruler in Rv 13 and 17, now makes its initial appearance. Its origin is said to be **the abyss**, from which the demonic locusts came (9:1–10), and where Satan will be imprisoned (20:1–3). It is only because their three and one half-year period of ministry is completed that the beast is able to **make war** on the two witnesses and kill them.
11:8–10 The great city is the usual way of referring to Babylon the Great in Revelation (17:18; 18:10), as well as **Sodom** (infamous for its sexual immorality) and **Egypt** (where God's people had been slaves). This depicts the wickedness of Jerusalem's inhabitants at this time. The brutal death of the two witnesses, the sacrilege of not giving them a proper burial, and the glee of the

non-elect "earth dwellers" at their deaths demonstrate that wickedness. The witnesses are also called **prophets** in the context of their death.
11:11–12 The phrase **after three and a half days** is intended to be compared with Jesus being resurrected on the third day (1Co 15:4). **Great fear** can be a positive thing. The phrase **come up here** (cp. 4:1) is understood by some interpreters to speak of the rapture of the church at the middle of the tribulation, though this passage refers to only two people.
11:13 Everything changes in one **moment**, from rejoicing at the death of the two witnesses (vv. 7–10) to shock at their resurrection, then hanging on for dear life in the devastation of **a violent earthquake**. In the midst of the widespread damage and death, fear turns into faith for many who saw the resurrection and ascension of the two witnesses. Since this takes place in Jerusalem, where most people present would be Jewish, this could be the fulfillment of Paul's prophecy that "all Israel will be saved" (Rm 11:25–26). Others view this as a momentary acknowledgment of the Lord but no authentic faith.
11:14 The **second woe** of the three predicted in 8:13 has now passed. Since **the third woe is coming soon**, it apparently is closely related to the seventh trumpet (vv. 15–19, see note there).
11:15–19 The sense of finality in the wording of the **seventh … trumpet** has caused some

interpreters to think this is the point of the second coming of Christ and that the following chapters double back and retrace the same ground from a different perspective. In a full-blown "recapitulation" view, it is held that the seals, trumpets, and bowls all speak of the same judgments from different perspectives. Such an approach is not necessary since the seventh trumpet overarches the seven bowls of wrath, with the seventh bowl telescoping all the way to the preparation for the second coming of Christ.
11:15 The phrase **the kingdom of the world has become the kingdom of our Lord and of his Christ** can be understood as follows. (1) The earthly reign of Christ (20:4–6) has already begun at this point, and chaps. 12–19 is a déjà vu of the first half of the book. (2) The past tense "has become" speaks of certainty so strong that the future is spoken of in the past tense (i.e., "will certainly become"). (3) What is already true in heaven will come true on earth; or (4) the timeless perspective of heaven is different from that of this world. Any of the last three explanations is more likely than the first.
11:16–18 On the **twenty-four elders**, see note at 4:3–4. **Lord God … who is and who was** means the one who not only exists but has existed eternally. **You … have begun to reign** may mean that: (1) the kingdom of God already exists in this world in some sense (1:9), or (2) God's power to reign in heaven is about to come to earth in the wake of his climactic **wrath** being displayed in the pouring out of

both small and great,
and the time has come to destroy
those who destroy the earth.

19 Then the temple of God in heaven was opened, and the ark of his covenant[A] appeared in his temple. There were flashes of lightning, rumblings and peals of thunder, an earthquake,[B] and severe hail.

The Woman, the Child, and the Dragon

12 A great sign[C] appeared in heaven: a woman clothed with the sun, with the moon under her feet and a crown of twelve stars on her head. **2** She was pregnant and cried out in labor and agony as she was about to give birth. **3** Then another sign[D] appeared in heaven: There was a great fiery red dragon having seven heads and ten horns, and on its heads were seven crowns.[E] **4** Its tail swept away a third of the stars in heaven and hurled them to the earth. And the dragon stood in front of the woman who was about to give birth, so that when she did give birth it might devour her child. **5** She gave birth to a Son, a male who is going to rule[F] all nations with an iron rod. Her child was caught up to God and to his throne. **6** The woman fled into the wilderness, where she had a place prepared by God, to be nourished there[G] for 1,260 days.

The Dragon Thrown Out of Heaven

7 Then war broke out in heaven: Michael and his angels fought against the dragon. The dragon and his angels also fought, **8** but he could not prevail, and there was no place for them in heaven any longer. **9** So the great dragon was thrown out — the ancient serpent, who is called the devil and Satan, the one who deceives the whole world. He was thrown to earth, and his angels with him. **10** Then I heard a loud voice in heaven say,

The salvation and the power
and the kingdom of our God
and the authority of his Christ
have now come,
because the accuser of our brothers and
sisters,
who accuses them
before our God day and night,
has been thrown down.
11 They conquered him
by the blood of the Lamb
and by the word of their testimony;
for they did not love their lives
to the point of death.
12 Therefore rejoice, you heavens,
and you who dwell in them!
Woe to the earth and the sea,
because the devil has come down to you
with great fury,
because he knows his time is short.

[A]**11:19** Other mss read *ark of the covenant of the Lord* [B]**11:19** Other mss omit *an earthquake* [C]**12:1** Or *great symbolic display*; see Rv 12:3 [D]**12:3** Or *another symbolic display* [E]**12:3** Or *diadems* [F]**12:5** Or *shepherd* [G]**12:6** Or *God, that they might feed her there*

---

the bowls of wrath (15:1–19:5), immediately after the prelude to that section (chaps. 12–14). The **time . . . for the dead to be judged . . . , to give the reward** to God's people (2Co 5:10), and **to destroy those who destroy the earth** comes after Christ's return (20:11–15).
11:19 The **ark** of the **covenant** had been in the "holy of holies" in the tabernacle (Ex 40:3) and the temple (1Kg 6:19), which was destroyed by the invading Babylonian army (2Ch 36:19). Now it is seen in the heavenly "holy of holies."
12:1–14:20 This section functions as a prelude to the bowls-of-wrath sequence

#98 **99 Essential Christian Truths**

NEW HEAVEN AND NEW EARTH

When Christ returns and the children of God are revealed, the creation itself will be made new. Like the resurrected bodies that Christians will one day receive, the physical world itself will undergo a similar transformation, so much so that the Scriptures describe it as a new heaven and a new earth (2Pt 3:13). Scripture describes the new earth as a city (Rv 21:10–11,21–26) and as a physical place that will include eating and drinking (Lk 22:18; Rv 19:9). Best of all, Christ will be all and in all, and we shall see him face to face.

(15:1–19:5). During a "time-out" from the progress of the narrative, it provides a midstream orientation to some characters and content that are crucial to understanding the second half of the Apocalypse.
12:1–2 John first used the word **sign** for imagery that echoes Joseph's vision in Gn 37:9. More likely this sign refers to ethnic Israel or a believing remnant of Jews. The woman being **pregnant** and **in labor and agony** recalls Gn 3:15–16. The prophecy of the virgin birth (Is 7:14) of Christ may also be in view.
12:3 The second **sign** (see note at vv. 1–2), a **great . . . dragon**, is interpreted in v. 9 as referring to the devil and Satan. The description of the dragon having **seven heads** and **ten horns** is similar to that of the beast in 13:1, but different enough to make clear that the two are separate characters.
12:4 It is possible that **a third of the stars in heaven** being **swept away** is related to the destruction of one-third during several of the trumpet judgments (8:7–10,12; 9:15,18), but since the **dragon** symbolizes Satan, these "stars" may stand for fallen angels who followed Satan in his rebellion (Mt 25:41). The phrase **the dragon stood in front of the woman . . . so that . . . it might devour her child** indicates that the attempt of King Herod the Great to kill the baby Jesus (Mt 2:1–16) was satanically inspired.
12:5 The words **Son . . . all nations**, and **with an iron rod** are allusions to Ps 2, which is replete with messianic prophecy. The narrative

then leaps ahead all the way from the birth of Christ to his ascension.
12:6 Some time after the ascension of the Son, **the woman** is supernaturally cared for by the Lord for **1,260 days** (three and one-half years)—the exact words that describe the period of protection of the two witnesses (11:3). This probably takes place shortly after the two witnesses have ascended, near the beginning of the second half of a seven-year tribulation period. The woman fleeing likely is representative of Jewish converts who feared God (11:18) and glorified him (11:13) after the witnesses were resurrected and ascended (11:11–13). The **wilderness** was the setting where the nation of Israel was protected by the Lord from Pharaoh's army and was miraculously fed manna and quail (Ex 16).
12:7–10 The **war . . . in heaven** probably also takes place just after the midpoint of the tribulation period. The sense that the "woman" in Rv 12:6 is a believing remnant of Israel (see notes at 11:13; 12:6) is strengthened by the clash of the **dragon** (identified as the devil and Satan) with **Michael** the archangel (Jd 9), who is assigned to protect Israel (Dn 12:1).
12:11 What looks like defeat is victory. Satan has killed them, but they are the ultimate victors.
12:12 **The devil**, having been cast down to earth, is enraged and will take out his great fury on **the earth and the sea**, because **he knows his time is short**.

The Woman Persecuted

[13] When the dragon saw that he had been thrown down to the earth, he persecuted[A] the woman who had given birth to the male child. [14] The woman was given two wings of a great eagle, so that she could fly from the serpent's presence to her place in the wilderness, where she was nourished for a time, times, and half a time. [15] From his mouth the serpent spewed water like a river flowing after the woman, to sweep her away with a flood. [16] But the earth helped the woman. The earth opened its mouth and swallowed up the river that the dragon had spewed from his mouth. [17] So the dragon was furious with the woman and went off to wage war against the rest of her offspring[B] — those who keep the commands of God and hold firmly to the testimony about Jesus.

The Beast from the Sea

[18] The dragon[C] stood on the sand of the sea.[D]

13 And I saw a beast coming up out of the sea. It had ten horns and seven heads. On its horns were ten crowns,[E] and on its heads were blasphemous names.[F] [2] The beast I saw was like a leopard, its feet were like a bear's, and its mouth was like a lion's mouth. The dragon gave the beast his power, his throne, and great authority. [3] One of its heads appeared to be fatally wounded, but its fatal wound was healed.

The whole earth was amazed and followed the beast. [4] They worshiped the dragon because he gave authority to the beast. And they worshiped the beast, saying, "Who is like the beast? Who is able to wage war against it?" [5] The beast was given a mouth to utter boasts and blasphemies. It was allowed to exercise

authority[G,H] for forty-two months. [6] It began to speak[I] blasphemies against God: to blaspheme his name and his dwelling — those who dwell in heaven. [7] And it was permitted to wage war against the saints and to conquer them. It was also given authority over every tribe, people, language, and nation. [8] All those who live on the earth will worship it, everyone whose name was not written from the foundation of the world in the book[J] of life of the Lamb who was slaughtered.[K]

[9] If anyone has ears to hear, let him listen.

[10]   If anyone is to be taken captive,
         into captivity he goes.
     If anyone is to be killed[L] with a sword,
         with a sword he will be killed.

This calls for endurance[M] and faithfulness from the saints.

The Beast from the Earth

[11] Then I saw another beast coming up out of the earth; it had two horns like a lamb,[N] but it spoke like a dragon. [12] It exercises all the authority of the first beast on its behalf and compels the earth and those who live on it to worship the first beast, whose fatal wound was healed. [13] It also performs great signs, even causing fire to come down from heaven to earth in front of people. [14] It deceives those who live on the earth because of the signs that it is permitted to perform in the presence of the beast, telling those who live on the earth to make an image[O] of the beast who was wounded by the sword and yet lived. [15] It was permitted to give breath[P] to the image of the beast, so that the image of the beast could both speak and cause whoever would not worship the image of the beast to be killed. [16] And it makes everyone — small

---

^12:13 Or *pursued*   ^12:17 Or *seed*   ^12:18 Or *he*; other mss read *I*   ^12:18 Some translations put Rv 12:18 either in Rv 12:17 or Rv 13:1.   ^13:1 Or *diadems*   ^13:1 Other mss read *heads was a blasphemous name*   ^13:5 Other mss read *to wage war*   ^13:5 Or *to rule*   ^13:6 Or *He opened his mouth in*   ^13:8 Or *scroll*   ^13:8 Or *written in the book of life of the Lamb who was slaughtered from the foundation of the world*   ^13:10 Other mss read *anyone kills*   ^13:10 Or *Here is the perseverance*   ^13:11 Or *ram*   ^13:14 Or *a statue, or a likeness*   ^13:15 Or *a spirit, or life*

12:13–14 The dragon (Satan) persecuted **the woman** (believing Israel) for a period of three and one-half years. The phrase **time, times, and half a time** is a year, two years, and half a year—three and one-half years total. This phrase is taken from Dn 7:25 and 12:7, where it speaks of a period in which "the holy ones" are persecuted in the end times. That the woman was given **two wings of a great eagle** is the same imagery used of Israel escaping the Egyptian army in the wilderness (Ex 19:4). **12:15–16** There is no way of knowing if the onslaught of the **serpent . . . dragon** (Satan, see note at vv. 7–10) against the woman (believing Israel; see notes at v. 6; 11:13), as well as the description of the Lord's protection (**the earth . . . swallowed up the river**), is meant to be taken literally or metaphorically. **12:17** Unable to get at the woman, the devil (**the dragon**) turns aside to **wage war** against (i.e., kill, 11:7) **the rest of her offspring**, the Gentile "saints" (13:7).

13:1–3 The **beast coming up out of the sea** was first mentioned in 11:7 (where his origin was the abyss). **13:4** The masses worshiped the beast because they believed it to be invincible. **13:5–7** The Lord allows the beast to **speak blasphemies against God** as well as the **authority** to conduct its worldwide reign of terror against Gentile believers (**the saints**; see note at 12:17). This blasphemy takes place for the remaining three and one-half years (**forty-two months**) of the tribulation period, after the witnesses complete their ministry and are taken to heaven (11:3,7,11–12). This is the same forty-two months spoken of in 11:2. **13:8** This verse explains why the "earth dwellers" (see note at 3:10) **worship** the beast—the absence of their names from **the book of life of the Lamb**. **13:9–10** The phrase **if anyone has ears** functions as a call to **endurance** and the **faithfulness from the saints**, even unto death if necessary.

13:11 A second beast (**another** of the same kind, Gk *allos*) that arises is apparently a religious leader because it is called "the false prophet" in 16:13; 19:20; 20:10. Outwardly, it seems gentle like Christ (**like a lamb**), but its prophecies are the voice of Satan (**like a dragon**). **13:12–13** The second beast has full, delegated **authority** from **the first beast** to complete its mission—worldwide **worship** of the first beast. Causing **fire** to come down from **heaven** sounds like a mimicking of the miracles performed by the two witnesses (11:5). **13:14–15** The second beast shows its likeness to Satan as it **deceives** (12:9) the "earth dwellers" through the spectacular **signs** it can perform (see 2Th 2:9). It persuades the "earth dwellers" to erect an **image** of the first beast to worship. This image comes to life. **13:16–18** The **mark** of the beast, a brand of the beast's **name** or its numerical equivalent—the **number** (**666**)—is required for anyone to conduct business in that day.

and great, rich and poor, free and slave — to receive a mark on his right hand or on his forehead, [17] so that no one can buy or sell unless he has the mark: the beast's name or the number of its name.

[18] This calls for wisdom:[A] Let the one who has understanding calculate[B] the number of the beast, because it is the number of a person. Its number is 666.[C]

The Lamb and the 144,000

14 Then I looked, and there was the Lamb, standing on Mount Zion, and with him were 144,000 who had his name and his Father's name written on their foreheads. [2] I heard a sound[D] from heaven like the sound of cascading waters and like the rumbling of loud thunder. The sound I heard was like harpists playing on their harps. [3] They sang[E] a new song before the throne and before the four living creatures and the elders, but no one could learn the song except the 144,000 who had been redeemed from the earth. [4] These are the ones who have not defiled themselves with women, since they remained virgins. These are the ones who follow the Lamb wherever he goes. They were redeemed[F] from humanity as the firstfruits for God and the Lamb. [5] No lie was found in their mouths; they are blameless.

The Proclamation of Three Angels

[6] Then I saw another angel flying high overhead, with the eternal gospel to announce to the inhabitants of the earth — to every nation, tribe, language, and people. [7] He spoke with a loud voice: "Fear God and give him glory, because the hour of his judgment has come. Worship the one who made heaven and earth, the sea and the springs of water."

[8] And another, a second angel, followed, saying, "It has fallen, Babylon the Great has fallen.[G] She made all the nations drink the wine of her sexual immorality,[H] which brings wrath."

[9] And another, a third angel, followed them and spoke with a loud voice: "If anyone

worships the beast and its image and receives a mark on his forehead or on his hand, [10] he will also drink the wine of God's wrath, which is poured full strength into the cup of his anger. He will be tormented with fire and sulfur in the sight of the holy angels and in the sight of the Lamb, [11] and the smoke of their torment will go up forever and ever. There is no rest[I] day or night for those who worship the beast and its image, or anyone who receives the mark of its name. [12] This calls for endurance from the saints, who keep God's commands and their faith in Jesus."[J]

[13] Then I heard a voice from heaven saying, "Write: Blessed are the dead who die in the Lord from now on."

"Yes," says the Spirit, "so they will rest from their labors, since their works follow them."

Reaping the Earth's Harvest

[14] Then I looked, and there was a white cloud, and one like the Son of Man[K] was seated on the cloud, with a golden crown on his head and a sharp sickle in his hand. [15] Another angel came out of the temple, crying out in a loud voice to the one who was seated on the cloud, "Use your sickle and reap, for the time to reap has come, since the harvest of the earth is ripe." [16] So the one seated on the cloud swung his sickle over the earth, and the earth was harvested.

[17] Then another angel who also had a sharp sickle came out of the temple in heaven. [18] Yet another angel, who had authority over fire, came from the altar, and he called with a loud voice to the one who had the sharp sickle, "Use your sharp sickle and gather the clusters of grapes from the vineyard of the earth, because its grapes have ripened." [19] So the angel swung his sickle at the earth and gathered the grapes from the vineyard of the earth, and he threw them into the great winepress of God's wrath. [20] Then the press was trampled outside the city, and blood flowed out of the press up to the horses' bridles for about 180 miles.[L]

[A]13:18 Or *Here is wisdom* [B]13:18 Or *count*, or *figure out* [C]13:18 Other Gk mss read *616* [D]14:2 Or *voice* [E]14:3 Other mss add *as it were* [F]14:4 Other mss add *by Jesus* [G]14:8 Other mss omit the second *has fallen* [H]14:8 Or *wine of her passionate immorality* [I]14:11 Or *They have no rest* [J]14:12 Or *and the faith of Jesus*, or *and faithfulness to Jesus* [K]14:14 Or *like a son of man* [L]14:20 Lit *1,600 stadia*

14:1–5 The 144,000, first seen on earth in 7:4–8 (see note there), are now seen on the heavenly Mount Zion with Christ, the Lamb. The beast cannot touch them, even though they do not have its mark (13:16–17), because they have Christ's and the Father's name on their foreheads. The new song cannot be the same as the one in 5:9–10 because this one can only be learned by the 144,000. On the four living creatures, see note at 4:6–7. On the elders, see note at 4:3–4. In their spiritual purity, they are fitting firstfruits (either the first produce to be harvested, the best of the harvest, or both) of the Lord's final harvest (vv. 14–20).

14:8–11 The fall of Babylon and God's wrath will be expanded in 16:17–21 and 18:1–19:3. 14:12–13 Blessed marks the second beatitude in Revelation (see notes at 1:3; 16:15; 19:9; 20:4–6; 22:6–7; 22:14–15,17). Believers (the saints) who persevere in keeping God's commands and faith in Jesus will be blessed with the reward of their godly works (20:12; 2Co 5:10).

14:14–20 The Son of Man associated with a cloud is a clear allusion to Dn 7:13. This section visualizes the "harvest . . . at the end of the age" (Mt 13:38–43). The wheat harvest apparently gleans those responding positively to the preaching of the gospel. The harvest of grapes leads to the judgment

pictured here as the great winepress of God's wrath. Since the winepress imagery related to divine wrath is seen in connection with the second coming of Christ (19:15), the events of 14:17–20 must occur at that point. If taken literally, when the "grapes of wrath" are trampled in Christ's winepress (19:15) outside the city (Jerusalem, apparently), the blood (from the climactic battle at his second coming in 19:19,21) rises to the height of horses' bridles for some 180 miles. This is roughly the length of Israel from north to south. Some view this horrific description as symbolic of God's righteous judgment resulting in the deaths of many of the unrepentant.

Preparation for the Bowl Judgments

15 Then I saw another great and awe-inspiring sign^A in heaven: seven angels with the seven last plagues; for with them God's wrath will be completed. ² I also saw something like a sea of glass mixed with fire, and those who had won the victory over the beast, its image,^B and the number of its name, were standing on the sea of glass with harps from God. ³ They sang the song of God's servant Moses and the song of the Lamb:

> Great and awe-inspiring are your works,
> Lord God, the Almighty;
> just and true are your ways,
> King of the nations.^C
> ⁴ Lord, who will not fear
> and glorify your name?
> For you alone are holy.
> All the nations will come
> and worship before you
> because your righteous acts
> have been revealed.

⁵ After this I looked, and the heavenly temple — the tabernacle of testimony — was opened. ⁶ Out of the temple came the seven angels with the seven plagues, dressed in pure, bright linen, with golden sashes wrapped around their chests. ⁷ One of the four living creatures gave the seven angels seven golden bowls filled with the wrath of God who lives forever and ever. ⁸ Then the temple was filled with smoke from the glory of God and from his power, and no one could enter the temple until the seven plagues of the seven angels were completed.

The First Bowl

16 Then I heard a loud voice from the temple saying to the seven angels, "Go and pour out the seven^D bowls of God's wrath

on the earth." ² The first went and poured out his bowl on the earth, and severely painful sores broke out on the people who had the mark of the beast and who worshiped its image.

The Second Bowl

³ The second^E poured out his bowl into the sea. It turned to blood like that of a dead person, and all life in the sea died.

The Third Bowl

⁴ The third^E poured out his bowl into the rivers and the springs of water, and they became blood. ⁵ I heard the angel of the waters say,

> You are just,
> the Holy One, who is and who was,
> because you have passed judgment
> on these things.
> ⁶ Because they poured out
> the blood of the saints and the prophets,
> you have given them blood to drink;
> they deserve it!
> ⁷ I heard the altar say,
> Yes, Lord God, the Almighty,
> true and just are your judgments.

The Fourth Bowl

⁸ The fourth^E poured out his bowl on the sun. It was allowed to scorch people with fire, ⁹ and people were scorched by the intense heat. So they blasphemed the name of God, who has the power^F over these plagues, and they did not repent and give him glory.

The Fifth Bowl

¹⁰ The fifth^E poured out his bowl on the throne of the beast, and its kingdom was plunged into darkness. People^G gnawed their tongues because of their pain ¹¹ and blasphemed the God

---

^A15:1 Or *and awesome symbolic display*   ^B15:2 Other mss add *his mark*   ^C15:3 Other mss read *ages*   ^D16:1 Other mss omit *seven*   ^E16:3,4,8,10 Other mss add *angel*   ^F16:9 Or *authority*   ^G16:10 Lit *They*

15:1 This is the third **sign** in the Apocalypse—**seven angels** and their corresponding **plagues** (calling to mind the judgment of the plagues on Egypt). They are called the "last plagues" because they bring **God's wrath** to completion. Since the seventh bowl of wrath (16:17,21) fulfills exactly what appears about to take place in 11:19, the bowls-of-wrath sequence (15:1–19:6) spans from the end of the trumpets sequence all the way to the second coming of Christ (19:11–16). **15:2–4** **Mixed with fire** may preview the fire that engulfed Babylon the Great, the climactic focus of the bowl judgments (16:17–21; 18:8–9,18). Those who had **won the victory over the beast** are martyrs (12:11). The **song of God's servant Moses** appears in Ex 15. Israel sang it when they had escaped their Egyptian pursuers, reaching safety on the other side of the Red Sea. Calling Rv 15:3–4 the song of God's servant **Moses and the song of the Lamb** infers that these martyrs are spiritually "safe on the other side," meaning heaven.

15:5–8 The **heavenly temple** was last seen in 11:19, in connection with the sounding of the last trumpet. The **angels** with the **plagues** are dressed in the garments of OT priests. The **seven golden bowls** are **filled with the wrath of God**. The sanctuary being **filled with smoke from the glory of God** recalls the cloud and the glory of God filling the tabernacle in the wilderness (Ex 40:34), indicating God was present with his people and guiding them. **16:1** The **loud voice** from the sanctuary is probably that of the Lord. **16:2** The **first . . . bowl** is poured out on those who have **the mark of the beast and who worshiped its image**. They are struck with **painful sores**. This recalls the sixth plague on Egypt (Ex 9:8–11). **16:3** The effects of the **second . . . bowl** are like the second trumpet judgment (8:8–9), only all the **sea** and **all life in the sea** are affected by this bowl of God's wrath. This echoes the first plague on Egypt (Ex 7:14–21).

16:4–7 The **third . . . bowl** is like the third trumpet judgment (8:10–11) since it impacts the fresh water sources. On the description of God as **who is and who was**, see note at 11:16–18. The significance of turning the water into blood is now clarified. Those who worshiped the beast (16:2) are being judged by a **true and just** God for the **blood** (6:10) of the martyred **saints** (see note at 5:8) and **prophets** (see note at 10:5–7). Since such vengeance was predicted for the "earth dwellers" (6:10–11), the beast worshipers and the "earth dwellers" must be the same group. **16:8–9** The **fourth . . . bowl** causes people to be burned with **fire** and **intense heat**. The response of the beast worshipers was to blaspheme the Lord, like the beast itself (13:5) refusing to **repent** (see 9:20–21). They also **did not . . . give him glory**, indicating that they rejected the preaching of the gospel in 14:6–7. **16:10–11** The **fifth . . . bowl** is like the fourth trumpet (8:12–13) in that the sun, moon, and stars are darkened, but only by "a third."

of heaven because of their pains and their sores, but they did not repent of their works.

The Sixth Bowl

[12] The sixth[A] poured out his bowl on the great river Euphrates, and its water was dried up to prepare the way for the kings from the east. [13] Then I saw three unclean spirits like frogs coming from the dragon's mouth, from the beast's mouth, and from the mouth of the false prophet. [14] For they are demonic spirits performing signs, who travel to the kings of the whole world to assemble them for the battle on the great day of God, the Almighty. [15] "Look, I am coming like a thief. Blessed is the one who is alert and remains clothed[B] so that he may not go around naked and people see his shame." [16] So they assembled the kings at the place called in Hebrew, Armageddon.[C]

The Seventh Bowl

[17] Then the seventh[A] poured out his bowl into the air,[D] and a loud voice came out of the temple[E] from the throne, saying, "It is done!" [18] There were flashes of lightning, rumblings, and peals of thunder. And a severe earthquake occurred like no other since people have been on the earth, so great was the quake. [19] The great city split into three parts, and the cities of the nations[F] fell. Babylon the Great was remembered

in God's presence; he gave her the cup filled with the wine of his fierce anger. [20] Every island fled, and the mountains disappeared. [21] Enormous hailstones, each weighing about a hundred pounds,[G] fell from the sky on people, and they blasphemed God for the plague of hail because that plague was extremely severe.

The Woman and the Scarlet Beast

17 Then one of the seven angels who had the seven bowls came and spoke with me: "Come, I will show you the judgment of the notorious prostitute[H] who is seated on many[I] waters. [2] The kings of the earth committed sexual immorality with her, and those who live on the earth became drunk with the wine of her sexual immorality." [3] Then he carried me away in the Spirit[J] to a wilderness.

I saw a woman sitting on a scarlet beast that was covered[K] with blasphemous names and had seven heads and ten horns. [4] The woman was dressed in purple and scarlet, adorned with gold, jewels, and pearls. She had a golden cup in her hand filled with everything detestable and with the impurities of her[L] prostitution. [5] On her forehead was written a name, a mystery: BABYLON THE GREAT, THE MOTHER OF PROSTITUTES AND OF THE DETESTABLE THINGS OF THE EARTH. [6] Then I saw that the woman was drunk with the blood of the saints and with

People may have **gnawed their tongues** in **pain** due to: (1) extreme cold caused by the ongoing darkness, (2) the sores from the first bowl judgment (v. 2), (3) the severe burns related to the fourth bowl (vv. 8–9), or (4) all three of these factors. That this bowl was poured out on the **throne of the beast** and its **kingdom** was to show that its worldwide authority (13:7) was about to end. On the people's blasphemy and refusal to **repent**, see 9:20–21. This judgment recalls the ninth plague on Egypt (Ex 10:21–23).

16:12–14 The sixth . . . bowl of wrath is the preparation for the battle of Armageddon (v. 16). The sixth trumpet judgment also mentioned the **great river Euphrates** (see note at 9:14–16). It is possible that the phrase, **its water was dried up**, is intended to recall the parting of the Red Sea. The **frogs** recall the second plague on Egypt (Ex 8:2–13). These armies are moving to join the kings of the **whole world** for the battle of the great day of **God, the Almighty** (the day of the Lord; see note at 6:12–17) to war against God (see note at 16:16). The **demonic spirits** perform deceiving **signs** to influence these kings (see Dn 10:13,20) to do the will of Satan (the dragon, see note at 12:7–10).

16:15 In the midst of the description of the lead-up to Armageddon (see note at v. 16) is the third blessing statement of the Apocalypse (1:3; 14:13; 19:9; 20:6; 22:7,14), warning readers always to be spiritually **alert**. Coming **like a thief** echoes Jesus's parable in Mt 24:43–44 and his earlier threat to the church

at Sardis (Rv 3:3). Spiritual nakedness was one of Christ's indictments of the church at Laodicea (3:17–18).

16:16 Many explanations have been offered for **the place called . . . Armageddon**. In Hebrew, it appears to mean "hill or mount of Megiddo." Some view this as referring to Mount Carmel—located some fifteen miles from Megiddo. Others think Armageddon is not an actual place but a symbol for the concluding battle between good and evil.

16:17–21 The **seventh . . . bowl** of wrath is focused on **Babylon the Great**, introduced in 14:8. The phenomena poured out in judgment (**lightning, rumblings . . . thunder . . . earthquake . . . hailstones**) have been "on hold" since being seen in heaven in 11:19. The **great city** here is not Jerusalem, as in 11:8, but Babylon. In 14:10, the beast worshipers were told they would "drink the wine of God's wrath . . . the cup of his anger." Now, Babylon receives the cup filled with the **wine** of his **fierce anger**. The phrase "Babylon the Great" is taken from Nebuchadnezzar's boast in Dn 4:30. It could speak of a rebuilt end-time city, though Jr 51:26 makes that unlikely. It could be a code name for Rome, or it could picture any proud society.

17:1–19:5 This section is a postscript to the bowls of wrath, expanding the reader's understanding of Babylon the Great, her relationship with the beast, and the scope of her just and final judgment.

17:1–2 On the **seven angels** and **seven bowls**, see note at 15:1. The **notorious**

prostitute is Babylon the Great. The **many waters** in v. 15 are explained as "peoples, multitudes, nations, and languages." Babylon has essentially the same relationship of **sexual immorality** with the **kings of the earth** and the "earth dwellers" (v. 2) as "Jezebel" did with the sinners in the church at Thyatira (2:20).

17:3–6 On **in the Spirit**, see note at 1:10. The **woman**, Babylon, also has a very close relationship with the beast (on the **blasphemous names . . . seven heads and ten**

99 Essential Christian Truths

#99

WORSHIP

While many reduce worship to an event or the singing of worship songs, worship is first and foremost something of the heart and extends to all areas of life. The aim and focus of worship is God, giving him the exact due of praise and adoration that he deserves. Worship should be carried out not only at a personal level within a Christian's life but also in joining with other Christians in the corporate act of worship and stewarding our gifts for the glory of God. Corporate worship serves to edify and strengthen other Christians, but it also serves as a witness to non-believers of the greatness of God.

the blood of the witnesses to Jesus. When I saw her, I was greatly astonished.

The Meaning of the Woman and of the Beast

[7] Then the angel said to me, "Why are you astonished? I will explain to you the mystery of the woman and of the beast, with the seven heads and the ten horns, that carries her. [8] The beast that you saw was, and is not, and is about to come up from the abyss and go to destruction. Those who live on the earth whose names have not been written in the book of life from the foundation of the world will be astonished when they see the beast that was, and is not, and is to come. [9] This calls for a mind that has wisdom.[A]

"The seven heads are seven mountains on which the woman is seated. They are also seven kings: [10] Five have fallen, one is, the other has not yet come, and when he comes, he must remain for only a little while. [11] The beast that was and is not, is itself an eighth king, but it belongs to the seven and is going to destruction. [12] The ten horns you saw are ten kings who have not yet received a kingdom, but they will receive authority as kings with the beast for one hour. [13] These have one purpose, and they give their power and authority to the beast. [14] These will make war against the Lamb, but the Lamb will conquer them because he is Lord of lords and King of kings. Those with him are called, chosen, and faithful."

[15] He also said to me, "The waters you saw, where the prostitute was seated, are peoples, multitudes, nations, and languages. [16] The ten horns you saw, and the beast, will hate the prostitute. They will make her desolate and naked, devour her flesh, and burn her up with fire. [17] For God has put it into their hearts to carry out his plan by having one purpose and to give their kingdom[B] to the beast until the words of God are fulfilled. [18] And the woman you saw is the great city that has royal power over the kings of the earth."

The Fall of Babylon the Great

18 After this I saw another angel with great authority coming down from heaven, and the earth was illuminated by his splendor. [2] He called out in a mighty voice:

It has fallen,[C]
Babylon the Great has fallen!
She has become a home for demons,
a haunt for every unclean spirit,
a haunt for every unclean bird,
and a haunt[D] for every unclean
    and despicable beast.[E]
[3]   For all the nations have drunk[F]
the wine of her sexual immorality,
which brings wrath.
The kings of the earth
have committed sexual immorality
    with her,
and the merchants of the earth
have grown wealthy
    from her sensuality and excess.
[4] Then I heard another voice from heaven:
Come out of her, my people,
so that you will not share in her sins
or receive any of her plagues.
[5]   For her sins are piled up[G] to heaven,
and God has remembered her crimes.

[A]17:9 Or *Here is the mind of wisdom*   [B]17:17 Or *sovereignty*   [C]18:2 Other mss omit *It has fallen*   [D]18:2 Or *prison*   [E]18:2 Other mss omit the words *and a haunt for every unclean beast*. The words *and despicable* then refer to the *bird* of the previous line.   [F]18:3 Some mss read *collapsed*; other mss read *fallen*   [G]18:5 Or *sins have reached up*

---

horns, see 13:1–3). To the casual outward observer, Babylon has all the trappings of wealth and royalty, but in actuality, she is characterized by **everything detestable** and the **impurities of her prostitution**. The name on her **forehead** has to do with her being the source of harlotry (**MOTHER OF PROSTITUTES**) and moral abominations (**THE DETESTABLE THINGS OF THE EARTH**), and killing throughout history.

17:7–8 Another aspect of **the mystery of** Babylon (**the woman**) and the beast is their hold on the "earth dwellers." It is because their **names** were **not . . . written** in the **book of life** (see note at 13:8). On the **seven heads and the ten horns**, see 13:1–3.

17:9–10 The **seven heads** are **seven mountains** (or hills, the Gk can mean either). This seems to be a reference to Rome, which was known in antiquity as "the city on seven hills." The identity of the **seven kings** is highly disputed. Some interpreters understand this to refer to seven historic Roman emperors, but more hold that it refers to seven successive world empires (e.g., Egypt, Assyria, Babylon, Medo-Persia, Greece, Rome, and a yet future empire). The phrase **a little while** would refer to the beast's unrivaled reign of "forty-two months" (13:5).

17:11 On **the beast that was and is not**, see vv. 7–8. The phrase that the beast is an **eighth king** yet **belongs to the seven** is difficult to interpret. The best explanation seems to be that, even though the physical body remains the same, the beast is two different personalities at "before-and-after" points in his career. This dramatic change could happen either: (1) when the beast initially comes to prominence by killing the two witnesses (11:7), or (2) after its "resurrection" from a presumed fatal wound (13:3;12,14). That the beast is **going to destruction** refers to eternal torment in the lake of fire (19:20; 20:10).

17:12–13 The **ten horns** of Dn 7:7,20,24 (see Rv 17:3,7) are **ten kings** who will rule alongside the beast during his unrivaled reign of forty-two months (13:5). This period is referred to here as **one hour**, much as the tribulation period is called "the hour of testing" (3:10).

17:14 The battle here takes place at the second coming of Christ. This verse clarifies that the armies following the Lamb in 19:14 are believers since the combined terms **called, chosen, and faithful** are never used of angels.

17:15–17 The **prostitute** (Babylon the Great) has ingratiated herself to the remaining world population (**peoples . . . languages**). The irony here is that, in the end, the very rulers (**the ten horns . . . and the beast**) with which the pseudo-queen (v. 4; 18:7) Babylon the Great has acted immorally (17:2), will turn on her and destroy her. Most amazing is that, ultimately, this will take place according to God's **purpose** and sovereign **plan**.

17:18–18:3 The **woman** (Babylon the Great, 17:5) is now pictured as the **great city** (see note at 16:17–21), which has secured political influence over the **kings of the earth** (17:18) by sexual immorality (17:2). Babylon could include an actual city in the end times, but it is more likely that **Babylon the Great** (18:2) is the world system (1Jn 2:15–17) organized in arrogant rebellion against God.

18:4 A few interpreters understand the rapture of the church to take place at this point.

18:5–8 Babylon the Great's **sins** and **crimes** are **piled up to heaven** like a growing refuse heap, the stench of which finally becomes unbearable. God will **pay . . . back** (Rm 12:19) Babylon for **her works** in full measure and more so. Babylon may arrogantly **sit as a queen**, with a false sense of security, but the judgment for her manifold sins, including self-glorification and lavish living, is certain and will be strong and swift.

6 Pay her back the way she also paid,
and double it according to her works.
In the cup in which she mixed,
mix a double portion for her.
7 As much as she glorified herself
and indulged her sensual and
excessive ways,
give her that much torment and grief.
For she says in her heart,
"I sit as a queen;
I am not a widow,
and I will never see grief."
8 For this reason her plagues will come
in just one day —
death and grief and famine.
She will be burned up with fire,
because the Lord God who judges her
is mighty.

The World Mourns Babylon's Fall

9 The kings of the earth who have committed
sexual immorality and shared her sensual and
excessive ways will weep and mourn over her
when they see the smoke from her burning.
10 They will stand far off in fear of her torment,
saying,

Woe, woe, the great city,
Babylon, the mighty city!
For in a single hour
your judgment has come.

11 The merchants of the earth will weep and
mourn over her, because no one buys their
cargo any longer — 12 cargo of gold, silver,
jewels, and pearls; fine linen, purple, silk, and
scarlet; all kinds of fragrant wood products;
objects of ivory; objects of expensive wood,
brass,^A iron, and marble; 13 cinnamon, spice,^B
incense, myrrh,^C and frankincense; wine, olive oil, fine flour, and grain; cattle and sheep;
horses and carriages; and slaves — human
lives.
14 The fruit you craved has left you.
All your splendid and glamorous things
are gone;
they will never find them again.

15 The merchants of these things, who became rich from her, will stand far off in fear of
her torment, weeping and mourning, 16 saying,

Woe, woe, the great city,
dressed in fine linen, purple, and scarlet,
adorned with gold, jewels, and pearls;

17 for in a single hour
such fabulous wealth was destroyed!

And every shipmaster, seafarer, the sailors,
and all who do business by sea, stood far off
18 as they watched the smoke from her burning
and kept crying out, "Who was like the great
city?" 19 They threw dust on their heads and
kept crying out, weeping, and mourning,

Woe, woe, the great city,
where all those who have ships
on the sea
became rich from her wealth;
for in a single hour she was destroyed.
20 Rejoice over her, heaven,
and you saints, apostles, and prophets,
because God has pronounced on her the
judgment she passed on you!

The Finality of Babylon's Fall

21 Then a mighty angel picked up a stone like a
large millstone and threw it into the sea, saying,

In this way, Babylon the great city
will be thrown down violently
and never be found again.
22 The sound of harpists, musicians,
flutists, and trumpeters
will never be heard in you again;
no craftsman of any trade
will ever be found in you again;
the sound of a mill
will never be heard in you again;
23 the light of a lamp
will never shine in you again;
and the voice of a groom and bride
will never be heard in you again.
All this will happen
because your merchants
were the nobility of the earth,
because all the nations were deceived
by your sorcery.
24 In her was found the blood of prophets
and saints,
and of all those slaughtered
on the earth.

Celebration in Heaven

19 After this I heard something like the
loud voice of a vast multitude in heav-
en, saying,

Hallelujah!
Salvation, glory, and power belong
to our God,

---

^A18:12 Or bronze, or copper ^B18:13 Other mss omit spice ^C18:13 Or perfume

---

18:11-14 The merchants of the earth . . .
weep and mourn at her demise because of
their loss of business. The inventory of about
thirty items of cargo is similar to the list in
Ezk 27. All these splendid and glamorous
things will disappear.
18:15-16 The merchants do not come to
Babylon's aid but stand far off to protect
themselves.

18:17-19 The next group to lament the loss
of Babylon the Great are those heavily invested in maritime commerce.
18:20 The martyrs in heaven (saints, apostles, and prophets) are urged to rejoice
because God has judged Babylon, largely
because of their shed blood.
18:21 On mighty angel, see note at 10:1. A
large millstone could weigh several tons.

18:22-23 After the judgment of Babylon the
Great, such perversion of God's intention for
beauty will never happen again.
19:1-4 The vast multitude pictured was
taken to heaven in 7:9. They now praise God
for: (1) their salvation, and (2) his righteous
judgments upon Babylon, the notorious
prostitute (17:1), thus avenging the blood
of his servants, the martyrs (see note at

² because his judgments are true^A
　　and righteous,
　　because he has judged
　　the notorious prostitute
　　who corrupted the earth
　　with her sexual immorality;
　　and he has avenged the blood
　　of his servants
　　that was on her hands.
³ A second time they said,
　　Hallelujah!
　　Her smoke ascends forever and ever!
⁴ Then the twenty-four elders and the four living creatures fell down and worshiped God, who is seated on the throne, saying,
　　Amen! Hallelujah!
⁵ A voice came from the throne, saying,
　　Praise our God,
　　all his servants, and the ones
　　who fear him,
　　both small and great!
⁶ Then I heard something like the voice of a vast multitude, like the sound of cascading waters, and like the rumbling of loud thunder, saying,
　　Hallelujah, because our Lord God,
　　the Almighty,
　　reigns!
⁷ 　Let us be glad, rejoice,
　　and give him glory,
　　because the marriage of the Lamb
　　has come,
　　and his bride has prepared herself.
⁸ 　She was given fine linen to wear, bright
　　and pure.
For the fine linen represents the righteous acts of the saints.

⁹ Then he^B said to me, "Write: Blessed are those invited to the marriage feast of the Lamb!" He also said to me, "These words of God are true." ¹⁰ Then I fell at his feet to worship him, but he said to me, "Don't do that! I am a fellow servant with you and your brothers and sisters who hold firmly to the testimony of Jesus. Worship God, because the testimony of Jesus is the spirit^C of prophecy."

The Rider on a White Horse

¹¹ Then I saw heaven opened, and there was a white horse. Its rider is called Faithful and True, and with justice he judges and makes war. ¹² His eyes were like a fiery flame, and many crowns^D were on his head. He had a name written that no one knows except himself. ¹³ He wore a robe dipped in blood, and his name is called the Word of God. ¹⁴ The armies that were in heaven followed him on white horses, wearing pure white linen. ¹⁵ A sharp^E sword came from his mouth, so that he might strike the nations with it. He will rule^F them with an iron rod. He will also trample the winepress of the fierce anger of God, the Almighty. ¹⁶ And he has a name written on his robe and on his thigh: KING OF KINGS AND LORD OF LORDS.

The Beast and Its Armies Defeated

¹⁷ Then I saw an angel standing in the sun, and he called out in a loud voice, saying to all the birds flying high overhead, "Come, gather together for the great supper of God, ¹⁸ so that you may eat the flesh of kings, the flesh of military commanders, the flesh of the mighty, the flesh of horses and of their riders, and the flesh of everyone, both free and slave, small and great." ¹⁹ Then I saw the beast, the kings of the earth, and their armies gathered together to wage war against the rider on the horse and against his army. ²⁰ But the beast was taken prisoner, and along with it the false prophet, who had performed the signs in its presence. He deceived those who accepted the mark of the beast and those who worshiped its image

---

^A19:2 Valid; Jn 8:16; 19:35　^B19:9 Probably an angel; Rv 17:1; 22:8–9　^C19:10 Or *the Spirit*　^D19:12 Or *diadems*　^E19:15 Other mss add *double-edged*　^F19:15 Or *shepherd*

6:9–11). On the **twenty-four elders**, see note at 4:3–4. On the **four living creatures**, see note at 4:6–7.
19:6–8 The praise of the **vast multitude** (see note at vv. 1–4) as a heavenly choir now heralds: (1) the coming reign of the Lord, and (2) the joyful **marriage of the Lamb**. The wife of the Lamb (Christ) is the church (Eph 5:31–32).
19:9 This is the fourth beatitude of the Apocalypse. It concerns **the marriage feast of the Lamb**.
19:10 Overcome with awe, John **fell at the feet** of the angel **to worship him**. The angel immediately corrected him. The phrase **the testimony of Jesus is the spirit of prophecy** apparently means that all biblical prophecy either directly or indirectly testifies about Jesus, the Messiah (Lk 24:27,44–48; 1Pt 1:11–12).
19:11–13 This **rider** on a **white horse** is not the same as the one in 6:2 (see note there). **With justice he judges and makes war.**

This is why he is called **Faithful and True**. On **eyes . . . like a fiery flame**, see note at 1:14. **Many crowns** shows that Christ has more power to rule than Satan (12:3) or the beast (13:1). A **name . . . that no one knows except himself** reminds readers that the Lord has not revealed everything about himself and his plan (Dt 29:29). **A robe dipped in blood** looks backward at Jesus's redemptive death (7:9) and forward to his treading the winepress of God's wrath (19:15; Is 63:1–6). In the Gospel of John (1:1,14), John began by referring to Jesus as **the Word** (Gk *logos*).
19:14 Since the **armies** accompanying the Lord are wearing **pure white linen**, as did the Lamb's wife (v. 8), this is another image for the same group elsewhere called the "vast multitude" (vv. 1,6; 7:9) and the "heaven dwellers" (12:12; 13:6). On why these are not angels, see note at 17:14. **White horses** implies that Christ allows his people to participate in the climactic victory.

19:15–16 God's word pictured as **a sharp sword** looks back to the description of the Son of Man in 1:13–16. **Strike the nations** is reminiscent of Ps 2:9. **Rule . . . with an iron rod** is the end-time fulfillment of what was predicted of the newborn Son in 12:5. On the **winepress of the fierce anger of God**, see note at 14:14–20.
19:17–19,21 The great **armies** of the earth, led by **the beast** and **the kings of the earth**, assemble to make war against the Lamb (apparently at Armageddon; see notes at 16:12–14,16). But they end up being killed by the **sword** that comes out of the **mouth** of the rider on the white horse (Christ) and fed to the birds at the **great supper of God**.
19:20 The **beast** (see note at 13:1–3) and the **false prophet** (see note at 13:11) are captured and **thrown alive** into the **lake of fire**, apparently the first to be sentenced there (Mt 25:41). They are not destroyed, but will suffer torment forever (Rv 20:10).

with these signs. Both of them were thrown alive into the lake of fire that burns with sulfur. ²¹ The rest were killed with the sword that came from the mouth of the rider on the horse, and all the birds ate their fill of their flesh.

Satan Bound

20 Then I saw an angel coming down from heaven holding the key to the abyss and a great chain in his hand. ² He seized the dragon, that ancient serpent who is the devil and Satan,^ and bound him for a thousand years. ³ He threw him into the abyss, closed it, and put a seal on it so that he would no longer deceive the nations until the thousand years were completed. After that, he must be released for a short time.

The Saints Reign with Christ

⁴ Then I saw thrones, and people seated on them who were given authority to judge. I also saw the souls of those who had been beheaded because of their testimony about Jesus and because of the word of God, who had not worshiped the beast or his image, and who had not accepted the mark on their foreheads or their hands. They came to life and reigned with Christ for a thousand years. ⁵ The rest of the dead did not come to life until the thousand years were completed.

This is the first resurrection. ⁶ Blessed and holy is the one who shares in the first resurrection! The second death has no power᷉ over them, but they will be priests of God and of Christ, and they will reign with him for a thousand years.

Satanic Rebellion Crushed

⁷ When the thousand years are completed, Satan will be released from his prison

⁸ and will go out to deceive the nations at the four corners of the earth, Gog and Magog, to gather them for battle. Their number is like the sand of the sea. ⁹ They came up across the breadth of the earth and surrounded the encampment of the saints, the beloved city. Then fire came down from heaven᷉ and consumed them. ¹⁰ The devil who deceived them was thrown into the lake of fire and sulfur where the beast and the false prophet are, and they will be tormented day and night forever and ever.

The Great White Throne Judgment

¹¹ Then I saw a great white throne and one seated on it. Earth and heaven fled from his presence, and no place was found for them. ¹² I also saw the dead, the great and the small, standing before the throne, and books were opened. Another book was opened, which is the book of life, and the dead were judged according to their works by what was written in the books. ¹³ Then the sea gave up the dead that were in it, and death and Hades gave up the dead that were in them; each one was judged according to their works. ¹⁴ Death and Hades were thrown into the lake of fire. This is the second death, the lake of fire. ¹⁵ And anyone whose name was not found written in the book of life was thrown into the lake of fire.

The New Creation

21 Then I saw a new heaven and a new earth; for the first heaven and the first earth had passed away, and the sea was no more. ² I also saw the holy city, the new Jerusalem, coming down out of heaven from God, prepared like a bride adorned for her husband.

---

^20:2 Other mss add *who deceives the whole world*   ᴮ20:6 Or *authority*   ᶜ20:9 Other mss add *from God*

20:1-3 On the **angel . . . holding the key to the abyss**, see note at 9:1. The **great chain** is used to bind **the dragon** (Satan) in the abyss. Some hold that the wording **a thousand years** (vv. 2,3,4,5,6,7) is figurative for a long period of time. Others think it speaks of a literal period of a thousand years. On Satan being **released**, see note at vv. 7-10. **20:4-6** Those who sit on the **thrones** and have **authority to judge** are God's people (Dn 7:18,27; 1Co 6:2). The resurrection of martyrs before Christ's earthly reign is called **the first resurrection**. The fifth beatitude (**blessed**) of the book recognizes the holiness of those in the first resurrection. On the **second death**, see v. 14 and note at vv. 11-15. *Premillennialists* follow the natural order of this passage, taking the thousand years as occurring after the second coming of Christ. Others believe it is a "flashback" (recapitulation) of the time before the second advent. Among those who take the recapitulation approach, *Amillennialists* believe the reign of Christ is being accomplished spiritually even now through the church. This view takes the thousand years figuratively, stretching

over the entire church era. *Postmillennialists* believe the preaching of the gospel will at some future date bring about virtual worldwide conversion and a golden era of biblical values lasting a thousand years (a time taken literally by some, figuratively by others). **20:7-10** Satan's release from the abyss (v. 3) is related to the **Gog and Magog** prophecy in Ezk 38-39. This incident will serve as final proof that, even after an extended, unrivaled reign of Christ (Rv 20:4-6), mankind (those born during the thousand years) will still follow **the devil**. When the rebellion surrounding **the beloved city** (probably Jerusalem, "renovated" for Christ's reign of a thousand years) is put down by fire from heaven, as in Ezk 39:6, the devil is thrown into the lake of fire, to join **the beast and the false prophet** (see note at 19:20) for eternity. **20:11-15** The phrase **great white throne** emphasizes God's purity and holiness in judging and his sovereign right to both rule and judge the earth. The phrases **earth and heaven fled** and **no place was found for them** apparently refer to "the first heaven and the first earth" giving way at the final

judgment to "a new heaven and a new earth" (21:1). **The dead . . . standing before the throne** come to life in the "second resurrection" (implied in v. 5). There are two sets of books at this judgment. The names of all believers are in the **book of life**. The names of the "earth dwellers" are not in the book of life (13:8; 17:8). They are **judged according to their works**, which are recorded in other books. The eternal dwelling place of all unbelievers is the **lake of fire**. As part of the present creation, **Death and Hades** (see note at 1:18) are also thrown into the lake of fire. **21:1** While like the present creation in some ways, the **new heaven and a new earth** will be much different. For example, there will be no **sea**. Some believe that "sea" is symbolic for the wickedness of the current created order. **21:2** The **bride** of the Lamb, introduced in 19:7-9, is now pictured as **the holy city, the new Jerusalem**. The expression **coming down out of heaven** is used in all three references to the new Jerusalem (see note at 3:12). **Prepared . . . adorned** may mean

The Eternal State

by Russell D. Moore

The reigning worldview of contemporary secularism—rooted in Darwinian naturalism—assumes that death is itself natural and that it is a final end. The biblical perspective is startlingly different, revealing that death is an unnatural enemy, a predator stalking a human race meant to live forever. In the crucified and resurrected Jesus of Nazareth, death is undone and the cosmos redeemed.

The biblical story tells us that God imposed the curse of death as a result of the insurrection of the primal human pair, Adam and Eve (Gn 3:8). God had instructed Adam not to partake of "the tree of the knowledge of good and evil" (Gn 2:17), so when Adam and Eve rejected this prohibition and ate, God exiled them from his presence. He placed a fiery sword at the entrance of the garden precisely so that the sinful human race would no longer have access to the tree of life (Gn 3:22–24).

After the fall the entire universe revolted at its created kings and queens, no longer obediently heeding the reign of humanity. Disease, natural disaster, animal attack, and the like seem normal to us now; such is the only reality we've known, but the Bible says this reign of death is not natural and it is not permanent. What seems to be normal is not actually how things are supposed to be.

Some religions have asserted that humans are reincarnated in a cycle of lives. Some have taught that the final goal of human existence is a personality-nullifying absorption into the cosmos itself. Others have envisioned a shadowy, otherworldly existence beyond the grave. Atheistic systems see human consciousness ending, like that of an animal, with the cessation of bodily life. The gospel of Jesus Christ, however, teaches that every human will end up in one of two possible eternal states: that of blessing or that of curse (Mt 13:41–43).

Hell

The Bible speaks of hell as a reality of indescribable torment. This place was not created for humanity but instead, as Jesus puts it, for the devil and his angels (Mt 25:41). Those who choose the headship of Satan as their god and who share in his nature will join the devil in his inheritance. The Bible says that this is the fate of all of us if we are left to ourselves (Eph 2:1–3). It is not possible for us to earn salvation through good works (Gl 2:16).

The Bible uses various images to convey the horror of hell. John sees it as a "lake of fire" (Rv 20:14). Jesus called hell a place of "outer darkness" filled with "weeping and gnashing of teeth" (Mt 8:12) and a place where there is no end to the torment of the damned, for "their worm does not die, and the fire is not quenched" (Mk 9:48).

Those outside of Christ find themselves in punishment immediately upon death, as pictured in Jesus's account of the rich man and Lazarus (Lk 16:19–31). This intermediate state of torment, awful as it is, is not the final accounting, however. At the end of the age, the damned are resurrected and face trial before the great white throne of Christ himself (Rv 20:11–15). The sinner will give an account for every idle word, thought, and deed, as well as his or her response to Jesus himself (e.g., Mt 12:36). Sinners are then sentenced to the judgment they have already pronounced on themselves—exile from the presence of God and into the lake of fire. This eternal curse means suffering that is physical as well as spiritual, emotional, and psychological. Hell is not something that humans create for themselves on this earth. Hell is the reality of God's justice and wrath, and it reflects the dignity of the human: each person must be held accountable for decisions made.

Heaven

The distinction between those who inherit damnation and those who, as the Bible puts it, "inherit the earth," is found in obedience to the will of God, summed up in loving the Lord and loving neighbor (Mk 12:28–31). Nevertheless, the depravity of humanity is such that every human, with the exception of Jesus, is found guilty as a lawbreaker, and is thus deserving of hell (Rm 3:10–18). Unlike the rest of us, Jesus of Nazareth lived a life of obedience to the law of God. He did this for our sake and died under the curse of the law for our sins so that the punishment that was due to us fell on him instead, securing salvation for all who place their faith in him. At his resurrection and ascension, Jesus was crowned the rightful King of the universe. Those who

³ Then I heard a loud voice from the throne:ᴬ Look, God's dwellingᴮ is with humanity, and he will live with them. They will be his peoples,ᶜ and God himself will be with them and will be their God.ᴰ ⁴ He will wipe away every tear from their eyes. Death will be no more; grief, crying, and pain will be no more, because the previous thingsᴱ have passed away.

⁵ Then the one seated on the throne said, "Look, I am making everything new." He also said, "Write, because these wordsᶠ are faithful and true." ⁶ Then he said to me, "It is done! I am the Alpha and the Omega, the beginning and the end. I will freely give to the thirsty from the spring of the water of life. ⁷ The one who conquers will inherit these things, and I will be his God, and he will be my son. ⁸ But the cowards, faithless,ᴳ detestable, murderers, sexually immoral, sorcerers, idolaters, and all liars — their share will be in the lake that burns with fire and sulfur, which is the second death."

The New Jerusalem

⁹ Then one of the seven angels, who had held the seven bowls filled with the seven last plagues, came and spoke with me: "Come, I will show you the bride, the wife of the Lamb." ¹⁰ He then carried me away in the Spiritᴴ to a great, high mountain and showed me the holy city, Jerusalem, coming down out of heaven from God, ¹¹ arrayed with God's glory. Her radiance was like a precious jewel, like a jasper stone, clear as crystal. ¹² The city had a massive high wall, with twelve gates. Twelve angels were at the gates; the names of the twelve tribes of Israel's sons were inscribed on the gates. ¹³ There were three gates on the east, three gates on the north, three gates on the south, and three gates

---

ᴬ21:3 Other mss read *from heaven* ᴮ21:3 Or *tent,* or *tabernacle* ᶜ21:3 Other mss read *people* ᴰ21:3 Other mss omit *and will be their God* ᴱ21:4 Or *the first things* ᶠ21:5 Other mss add *of God* ᴳ21:8 Other mss add *the sinful,* ᴴ21:10 Or *in spirit*

---

that the bride will be just as beautiful—and will be for eternity—as she was during the wedding festivities (19:7–8).
21:3–4 God's presence (**dwelling is with humanity**) will do away with all **death . . . grief, crying, and pain**.
21:5–8 In the new heaven and new earth, the Lord will make **everything new**. The written Word of God is faithful and true (2Tm 3:16), and the living Word of God is also faithful

and true (Rv 19:11). On **the Alpha and the Omega,** see note at 1:8. Living water (22:17) will always be freely available. This pictures the word of grace, received through saving faith, that offers eternal life. But those who remain unrepentant in their sin will experience eternal judgment, **the second death.**
21:9–11a The angel's offer to show John **the bride, the wife of the Lamb,** parallels the angel's offer to show him the judgment of

Babylon in 17:1. On **in the Spirit,** see note at 1:10. On **coming down out of heaven,** see note at v. 2.
21:11b–14,21 On **a jasper stone,** see note at 4:3–4. The **twelve gates** (each made of a massive single pearl) in the great wall of the new Jerusalem have written on them the names of the **twelve tribes** of Israel. The **twelve foundations** of the city wall have the **twelve names** of the **apostles** of Christ.

---

approach God, hidden in Jesus by faith, are already judged righteous; thus, their sentence to hell is cancelled, and God's justice is reconciled to his mercy. Those in Christ also now share in his life, in his resurrection, and in his inheritance.

Immediately after death, believers find themselves in the presence of God, a present reality known by Christians as "heaven" (see Jesus's words to the repentant thief on the cross in Lk 23:43 and Paul's comments about his desires in Php 1:23). This disembodied existence of blessedness is not, however, the eternal state of those in Christ. God did not send Christ into the world to condemn the world, but to save it (Jn 3:17). The final state of redeemed humanity is life in a renewed cosmos, free from the curse and under the reign of Christ and his joint-heirs (Rv 21).

The New Earth

At the resurrection from the dead, believers join Jesus in his resurrection life—including the restoration of their bodies. At the end of time, heaven and earth are joined in a new earth that is transfigured by the presence and glory of God in Christ. This eternal reality is

not merely a restoration of Eden but a glorious civilization with a city in which the glory of the nations redeemed are brought into it. This presumably means that every aspect of culture will be present there. We reasonably may imagine this means music, painting, literature, architecture, commerce, agriculture, and any other worthy aspect of human endeavor will be practiced there and freed from sin, made holy in undiluted service to God.

While the Bible keeps much of the future from us, presumably because our minds at this point could not comprehend it, we know that the eternal state of those in Christ is one that includes work and labor (though freed from the frustration of the curse), personal relationships, worship, and ruling and reigning with Christ. The Bible uses the imagery of a wedding feast to signify the feasting and celebrating of the age to come (Rv 19:6–9).

In this everlasting age, God's covenants will be seen to have come to a climax in the identity and mission of Christ Jesus, and his reign will be all encompassing. The kingdoms of this world will become the kingdom of our Lord and of his Christ, and he shall reign forevermore (Rv 11:15).

on the west. **14** The city wall had twelve foundations, and the twelve names of the twelve apostles of the Lamb were on the foundations. **15** The one who spoke with me had a golden measuring rod to measure the city, its gates, and its wall. **16** The city is laid out in a square; its length and width are the same. He measured the city with the rod at 12,000 *stadia.*^ Its length, width, and height are equal. **17** Then he measured its wall, 144 cubits according to human measurement, which the angel used. **18** The building material of its wall was jasper, and the city was pure gold clear as glass. **19** The foundations of the city wall were adorned with every kind of jewel: the first foundation is jasper, the second sapphire, the third chalcedony, the fourth emerald, **20** the fifth sardonyx, the sixth carnelian, the seventh chrysolite, the eighth beryl, the ninth topaz, the tenth chrysoprase, the eleventh jacinth, the twelfth amethyst. **21** The twelve gates are twelve pearls; each individual gate was made of a single pearl. The main street^ of the city was pure gold, transparent as glass.

22 I did not see a temple in it, because the Lord God the Almighty and the Lamb are its temple. **23** The city does not need the sun or the moon to shine on it, because the glory of God illuminates it, and its lamp is the Lamb. **24** The nations will walk by its light, and the kings of the earth will bring their glory into it.^ **25** Its gates will never close by day because it will never be night there. **26** They will bring the glory and honor of the nations into it.^ **27** Nothing unclean will ever enter it, nor anyone who does what is detestable or false, but only those written in the Lamb's book of life.

The Source of Life

22 Then he showed me the river^ of the water of life, clear as crystal, flowing from the throne of God and of the Lamb **2** down the middle of the city's main street. The tree of life was on each side of the river, bearing twelve kinds of fruit, producing its fruit every month. The leaves of the tree are for healing the nations, **3** and there will no longer be any curse. The throne of God and of the Lamb will be in the city, and his servants will worship him. **4** They will see his face, and his name will be on their foreheads. **5** Night will be no more; people will not need the light of a lamp or the light of the sun, because the Lord God will give them light, and they will reign forever and ever.

The Time Is Near

6 Then he said to me, "These words are faithful^ and true. The Lord, the God of the spirits of the prophets,^ has sent his angel to show his servants what must soon take place."

7 "Look, I am coming soon! Blessed is the one who keeps the words of the prophecy of this book."

8 I, John, am the one who heard and saw these things. When I heard and saw them, I fell down to worship at the feet of the angel who had shown them to me. **9** But he said to me, "Don't do that! I am a fellow servant with you, your brothers the prophets, and those who keep the words of this book. Worship God!"

10 Then he said to me, "Don't seal up the words of the prophecy of this book, because the time is near. **11** Let the unrighteous go on in unrighteousness; let the filthy still be filthy; let the righteous go on in righteousness; let the holy still be holy."

12 "Look, I am coming soon, and my reward is with me to repay each person according to his work. **13** I am the Alpha and the Omega, the first and the last, the beginning and the end.

14 "Blessed are those who wash their robes,^ so that they may have the right to the tree of life and may enter the city by the gates. **15** Outside are the dogs, the sorcerers, the sexually immoral, the murderers, the idolaters, and everyone who loves and practices falsehood.

---

^21:16 A *stadion* (sg) = about 600 feet; 12,000 *stadia* = 1,400 miles. ^21:21 Or *The public square* ^21:24 Other mss read *will bring to him the nations' glory and honor* ^21:26 Other mss add *in order that they might go in* ^22:1 Other mss read *pure river* ^22:6 Or *trustworthy* ^22:6 Other mss read *God of the holy prophets* ^22:14 Other mss read *who keep his commands*

21:15–20 The mention of the **measuring rod** is an allusion to Ezk 40–41 (see note at Rv 11:1–2). For a city to be 1,400 miles square (**12,000 stadia**) with walls over two hundred feet thick (**144 cubits**) is mind-boggling, as are the materials of the wall—**jasper** stone and **gold**.
21:22–27 No temple is needed in the new Jerusalem. God the Father (**the Almighty**) and the **Lamb** (Christ) are its **temple**. There is no need for light (**sun or the moon**) in the new Jerusalem because **the glory of God illuminates it**. There apparently will be national distinctions (**the nations**) and human rulers (**the kings of the earth**) in the eternal state, but since all who will be there are included in the Lamb's book of life (see note at 3:4–5), there is no need for security, and there can be no sin (the **unclean** . . . **detestable** . . . **false**).

22:1–5 The **river of the water of life** looks back to Ezk 47. The **tree of life** was in the center of the garden of Eden (Gn 2:9; 3:3). The wording here pictures the new Jerusalem as the new and permanent "Eden," where **there will no longer be any curse** (see Gn 3:14–19). All inhabitants will have **his name** on **their foreheads**, as was the case with the 144,000 (14:1). On **night will be no more**, see note at 21:22–27.
22:6–7 The sixth beatitude of the book (**blessed**) repeats the emphases on the imminence of the events in Revelation and the need for application of its prophecies seen in the first beatitude in 1:3.
22:8–9 John once again feels compelled to worship an angel. Again, the angel rebukes him, reminding him that they are fellow servants (see 19:10 and note there).

22:10–12 In light of the imminence of the events (**the time is near**) portrayed in Revelation, John was commanded not to **seal up the words of the prophecy of this book**. Until the events of the book are fulfilled, people will continue to act in keeping with their spiritual nature (**filthy** . . . **filthy** or **righteous** . . . **righteousness**), but when the Lord comes, he will render to each person according to his deeds (20:12; 2Co 5:10).
22:13 On **the Alpha and the Omega**, see note at 1:8.
22:14–15,17 The final beatitude (**blessed**) of the Apocalypse is an elegant presentation of the gospel, using the imagery of the "new Eden" ("the tree of life") and the eternal city (**enter the city by the gates**). Wash **their robes** means faith in the shed blood of Christ. **The right to the tree of life** is what

¹⁶ "I, Jesus, have sent my angel to attest these things to you for the churches. I am the Root and descendant of David, the bright morning star."

¹⁷ Both the Spirit and the bride say, "Come!" Let anyone who hears, say, "Come!" Let the one who is thirsty come. Let the one who desires take the water of life freely.

¹⁸ I testify to everyone who hears the words of the prophecy of this book: If anyone adds to them, God will add to him the plagues that are written in this book. ¹⁹ And if anyone takes away from the words of the book of this prophecy, God will take away his share of the tree of life and the holy city, which are written about in this book.

²⁰ He who testifies about these things says, "Yes, I am coming soon."

Amen! Come, Lord Jesus!

²¹ The grace of the Lord Jesus^A be with everyone.^B Amen.^C

---

^A **22:21** Other mss add *Christ*   ^B **22:21** Other mss read *with all the saints*   ^C **22:21** Other mss omit *Amen*.

Adam and Eve were cut off from by their sin. The gates of the city and access to the tree of life are made available to those who believe in Jesus, but all unbelievers, with their various sinful lifestyles, are excluded. With the repeated invitation to **come** and **take the water** of life **freely** (i.e., free grace; see Eph 2:8–9), Revelation ends with passionate

evangelistic appeal. **Dogs** in this case likely refers to false teachers, whatever their ethnicity, as in Php 3:2.
22:16 Jesus is a blood **descendant of David**. On **the bright morning star**, see note at 2:28.
22:18–19 It is doubtful the wording here directly refers to closing the canon of the Bible

(**this book**). The book (Gk *biblion*, "scroll") that is not to be tampered with is the book of Revelation.
22:20 Jesus promised that he is **coming soon**. Believers long for Jesus's return.
22:21 The book of Revelation begins (1:4) and ends with **grace**.

Table
of Weights and Measures

Weights

Biblical Unit	Language	Biblical Measure	U.S. Equivalent	Metric Equivalent	Various Translations
Gerah	Hebrew	1/20 shekel	1/50 ounce	.6 gram	gerah; oboli
Bekah	Hebrew	1/2 shekel or 10 gerahs	1/5 ounce	5.7 grams	bekah; half a shekel; quarter ounce; fifty cents
Pim	Hebrew	2/3 shekel	1/3 ounce	7.6 grams	2/3 of a shekel; quarter
Shekel	Hebrew	2 bekahs	2/5 ounce	11.5 grams	shekel; piece; dollar; fifty dollars
Litra (pound)	Greco-Roman	30 shekels	12 ounces	.4 kilogram	pound; pounds
Mina	Hebrew/Greek	50 shekels	1 1/4 pounds	.6 kilogram	mina; pound
Talent	Hebrew/Greek	3,000 shekels or 60 minas	75 pounds/ 88 pounds	34 kilograms/ 40 kilograms	talent/talents; 100 pounds

Length

Biblical Unit	Language	Biblical Measure	U.S. Equivalent	Metric Equivalent	Various Translations
Handbreadth	Hebrew	1/6 cubit or 1/3 span	3 inches	8 centimeters	handbreadth; three inches; four inches
Span	Hebrew	1/2 cubit or 3 handbreadths	9 inches	23 centimeters	span
Cubit/Pechys	Hebrew/Greek	2 spans	18 inches	.5 meter	cubit/cubits; yard; half a yard; foot
Fathom	Greco-Roman	4 cubits	2 yards	2 meters	fathom; six feet
Kalamos	Greco-Roman	6 cubits	3 yards	3 meters	rod; reed; measuring rod
Stadion	Greco-Roman	1/8 milion or 400 cubits	1/8 mile	185 meters	miles; furlongs; race
Milion	Greco-Roman	8 stadia	1,620 yards	1.5 kilometers	mile

Dry Measure

Biblical Unit	Language	Biblical Measure	U.S. Equivalent	Metric Equivalent	Various Translations
Xestes	Greco-Roman	1/2 cab	1 1/6 pints	.5 liter	pots; pitchers; kettles; copper pots; copper bowls; vessels of bronze
Cab	Hebrew	1/18 ephah	1 quart	1 liter	cab; kab
Choinix	Greco-Roman	1/18 ephah	1 quart	1 liter	measure; quart
Omer	Hebrew	1/10 ephah	2 quarts	2 liters	omer; tenth of a deal; tenth of an ephah; six pints
Seah/Saton	Hebrew/Greek	1/3 ephah	7 quarts	7.3 liters	measures; pecks; large amounts
Modios	Greco-Roman	4 omers	1 peck or 1/4 bushel	9 liters	bushel; bowl; peck

Ephah [Bath]	Hebrew	10 omers	3/5 bushel	22 liters	bushel; peck; deal; part; measure; six pints; seven pints
Lethek	Hebrew	5 ephahs	3 bushels	110 liters	half homer; half sack
Kor [Homer]/ Koros	Hebrew/Greek	10 ephahs	6 bushels or 200 quarts	220 liters/ 525 liters	cor; homer; sack; measures; bushels

Liquid Measure

Log	Hebrew	1/72 bath	1/3 quart	.3 liter	log; pint; cotulus
Xestes	Greco-Roman	1/8 hin	1 1/6 pints	.5 liter	pots; pitchers; kettles; copper bowls; vessels of bronze
Hin	Hebrew	1/6 bath	1 gallon or 4 quarts	4 liters	hin; pints
Bath/Batos	Hebrew/Greek	1 ephah	6 gallons	22 liters	gallon(s); barrels; liquid measures
Metretes	Greco-Roman	10 hins	10 gallons	39 liters	firkins; gallons

◤ CSB
Concordance

- A -

AARON
Levite, brother of Moses (Ex 4:14; 6:16–20). Spokesman for Moses (4:14–16; 7:1–2). Consecrated (Ex 29) and ordained (Lv 8) as priest (Ex 28:1; 1Ch 6:49; Heb 5:1–4; 7). Made golden calf (Ex 32). Died outside the promised land (Nm 20:1–12,22–29; 33:38–39).

ABADDON
your faithfulness in **A**? . . . . Ps 88:11
Sheol and **A** lie open before
the LORD . . . . Pr 15:11
his name in Hebrew is **A**, ... Rv 9:11

ABANDON
I will **a** them and hide my face . . . . Dt 31:17
I will not leave you or **a** you. . . . . . . Jos 1:5
certainly not **a** the LORD . . . . Jos 24:16
the LORD has **a-ed** us . . . . Jdg 6:13
LORD will not **a** his people, ... 1Sm 12:22
but if you **a** him, he will **a** you. 2Ch 15:2
For you will not **a** me to Sheol; . . . . Ps 16:10
my God, why have you **a-ed** me? . . Ps 22:1
or **a** his heritage, ... Ps 94:14
Don't **a** wisdom, ... Pr 4:6
My God, why have you **a-ed**
me? . . . . Mt 27:46
will never leave you or **a** you. . . . . Heb 13:5
a-ed the love you had at first. . . . . . Rv 2:4

ABBA
He said, "**A**, Father! . . . . Mk 14:36
we cry out, "**A**, Father!" . . . . Rm 8:15
crying, "**A**, Father!" . . . . Gl 4:6

ABEL
Shepherd, second son of Adam; brought acceptable sacrifice; was murdered (Gn 4:2–8; Mt 23:35; Heb 11:4).

ABIGAIL
Intelligent wife of the fool Nabal; pled for his life; married David after Nabal died (1Sm 25).

ABIJAH
1. Tragic son of King Jeroboam of Israel (1Kg 14:1,13).
2. Son of Rehoboam, King of Judah (2Ch 13). Also known as Abijam (1Kg 15:1–8).

ABILITY
depending on each one's **a**. . . . . Mt 25:15
according to their **a** 2Co 8:3

ABIMELECH
1. King of Gerar at the time of Abraham (Gn 20:1–18; 21:22–32).
2. King of Gerar at the time of Isaac (Gn 26:1–31).
3. Son of Gideon, tried to become king of Shechem (Jdg 9).

ABLE
count the stars, if you are **a** . . . . Gn 15:5
Moses chose **a** men . . . . Ex 18:25
God is **a** to raise up children. . . . . . . Mt 3:9
Are you **a** to drink the cup . . . . . . Mt 20:22
the Lord is **a** to make him
stand. . . . . Rm 14:4
tempted beyond what you are **a**, . . 1Co 10:13
Now to him who is **a** to do. . . . . . . Eph 3:20
to him who is **a** to protect you . . . . . . Jd 24
a to open the scroll . . . . Rv 5:3

ABNER
Saul's cousin and commander of his army (1Sm 14:50). At first supported Saul's son Ish-bosheth (2Sm 2:8–9) but defected to David (3:6–21). Killed by Joab and mourned by David (3:22–39).

ABOMINATION
and set up the **a** of desolation. . . . . Dn 11:31
see the **a** of desolation, ... Mt 24:15

ABOVE
the LORD is God in heaven **a**. . . . . . . Dt 4:39
the name that is **a** every name, . . . Php 2:9
Set your minds on things **a**, ... Col 3:2

ABRAHAM
Born Abram son of Terah in Ur, Mesopotamia; married Sarai, then lived in Haran (Gn 11:31; Ac 7:2–4). Called to Canaan and given a promise of progeny and prosperity (Gn 12:1–3). Lied to Pharaoh in Egypt about Sarai (12:10–20). Separated from his nephew Lot (Gn 13). Rescued Lot (14:1–16) and was blessed by Melchizedek (14:17–20; Heb 7:1–10). God declared him righteous because of his faith (Gn 15:6; Rm 4:3,20–22; Gl 3:6; Jms 2:23).

Fathered Ishmael by Hagar (Gn 16). Name changed (17:5); circumcised (17:9–27; Rm 4:9–12). Visited by angels (Gn 18); promised a son with Sarah (18:9–14; cp. 17:15–19). Lied to Abimelech in Gerar about Sarah (Gn 20). Fathered Isaac (21:1–7). Sent Hagar away at Sarah's request (21:8–14). Tested by God concerning Isaac (Gn 22; Heb 11:17–19; Jms 2:21–24). Buried Sarah at Machpelah (Gn 23). Sent servant to find wife for Isaac (24:1–9). Died and was buried with Sarah (25:7–11).

God promised a covenant with Abraham, then made it and confirmed it (Gn 12:1–3; 13:14–17; 15; 17; 22:15–18). It was the basis of future blessings for many people (Ex 2:24; Lv 26:42; 2Kg 13:23; Ps 105:6–11; Ac 3:25).

ABSALOM
Son of David by Maacah (2Sm 3:3). Known for his looks and hair (14:25–26). Killed Amnon for raping Tamar and was banished by David (2Sm 13). Reinstated by David at Joab's insistence (2Sm 14). Rebelled, ousted David (2Sm 15–17). Killed by Joab (18:9–15) despite David's warning (18:5). Greatly mourned by David (18:33–19:4).

ABSENT
a in the body, I am present in spirit, . . 1Co 5:3
I may be **a** in body, but . . . . Col 2:5

ABSTAIN
he is to **a** from wine and beer. . . . . . . Nm 6:3
a from food offered to idols, ... Ac 15:29
a from sinful desires 1Pt 2:11

ABUNDANCE
Seven years of great **a** . . . . Gn 41:29
bearing spices, gold in great **a**, ... 1Kg 10:2
have life and have it in **a** . . . . Jn 10:10

ABUNDANTLY
He poured out his Spirit on us **a** . . . . . Ti 3:6

ABUSED
a her all night . . . . Jdg 19:25

ABYSS
not to banish them to the **a**. . . . . Lk 8:31
Who will go down into the **a**? . . . . . Rm 10:7

ACCEPT
Should we **a** only good from God . . . Jb 2:10
the LORD **a-ed** Job's prayer. . . . . Jb 42:9
My son, if you **a** my words . . . . Pr 2:1
A my instruction. . . . . Pr 8:10
Not everyone can **a** this saying, . . . Mt 19:11

ACCEPTABLE
the meditation of my heart be **a** . . Ps 19:14
See, now is the **a** time; 2Co 6:2
spiritual sacrifices **a** to God 1Pt 2:5

ACCEPTANCE
what will their **a** mean . . . . Rm 11:15
and deserving of full **a**: 1Tm 1:15

ACCESS
a through him by faith
into … grace. Rm 5:2
we both have **a** in one Spirit . . . . . Eph 2:18

ACCOMPANY
signs will **a** those who believe: . . . . Mk 16:17

ACCOMPLISH
it will **a** what I please . . . . Is 55:11
I watch over my word to **a** it." . . . . . . Jr 1:12

ACCORDING
be done for you **a** to your
faith! . . . . Mt 9:29
who do not walk **a** to the flesh. . . . . Rm 8:4
ask anything **a** to his will 1Jn 5:14
were judged **a** to their works . . . . . Rv 20:12

ACCOUNT
a for every careless word . . . . Mt 12:36

ACCUSATION
Who can bring an **a** . . . . Rm 8:33
an **a** against an elder. 1Tm 5:19

ACCUSE
He will not always **a** us. . . . . Ps 103:9
standing at his right side to **a** . . . . . . Zch 3:1
in order to be able to **a** him . . . . Mt 12:10; Mk 3:2
They began to **a** him, ... Lk 23:2
Your **a-r** is Moses, ... Jn 5:45
so that when you are **a-d**, ... 1Pt 3:16

ACHAIA
he wanted to cross over to **A**, ... Ac 18:27

ACHAN
Sinned at Jericho; stoned (Jos 7; 1Ch 2:7).

ACHISH
King of Gath before whom David feigned madness (1Sm 21:10–15). Later, he favored David (1Sm 27–29).

ACKNOWLEDGE
Then I **a-d** my sin to you . . . . Ps 32:5
I will also **a** him before my Father in
heaven . . . . Mt 10:32

ACQUIT
I know you will not **a** me. . . . . Jb 9:28

ACT (N)
an outstretched arm and
great **a-s** . . . . Ex 6:6
deeds and mighty **a-s** like yours? . . Dt 3:24
this woman was caught in the **a**. . . . Jn 8:4

ACT (V)
trust in him, and he will **a**, ... Ps 37:5
I **a-ed** for the sake of my name, . . . Ezk 20:9
these words of mine and **a-s** . . . . . . Mt 7:24
a-ed out of ignorance in
unbelief. 1Tm 1:13

ACTION
a-s are weighed by him. 1Sm 2:3
with your minds ready for **a**, ... 1Pt 1:13
word or speech, but in **a** 1Jn 3:18

ACTIVE
You see that faith was **a** . . . . Jms 2:22

ADAM
First man. Created by God (Gn 1:26–27; 2:7). Named animals (2:18–20). Given Eve (2:21–25). Failed to obey and was evicted (1:15–17; 3:6–24; Rm 5:14; 1Co 15:22). Died at 930 years (Gn 5:3–5).

ADD

no **a-ing** to it or taking from it. . . . . Ec 3:14
Can any of you **a** one moment . . . . Mt 6:27
three thousand people were **a-ed** . . Ac 2:41

ADMINISTRATION

the **a** of the mystery . . . . Eph 3:9

ADMONISHING

teaching and **a** one another. . . . . . . Col 3:16

ADONIJAH

Son of David (2Sm 3:4). Conspired for the
throne and was executed by Solomon (1Kg
1–2).

ADOPTION

you received the Spirit of **a**,. . . . . . Rm 8:15
to them belong the **a**, ...Rm 9:4
that we might receive **a** as sons. . . . . . Gl 4:5

ADORN

A yourself with majesty . . . . Jb 40:10
as a bride **a-s** herself. . . . . Is 61:10
it was **a-ed** with beautiful stones . . Lk 21:5
a the teaching of God our Savior . . . Ti 2:10
also **a-ed** themselves in this way,. . . 1Pt 3:5
a-ed with gold, jewels, and
pearls . . . . Rv 17:4
a bride **a-ed** for her husband. . . . . . Rv 21:2

ADORNMENT

life for you and **a** for your neck. . . . . Pr 3:22

ADULTERER

both the **a** and the adulteress. . . . . Lv 20:10
a-'s eye watches for twilight, ... Jb 24:15
you associate with **a-s**. . . . . Ps 50:18
the land is full of **a-s**; . . . . Jr 23:10
idolaters, **a-s**, male who have 1Co 6:9
judge sexually immoral
and **a-s**, ... Heb 13:4

ADULTERESS

both the adulterer and the **a**. . . . . . Lv 20:10
This is the way of an **a**: she eats . . Pr 30:20
they are **a-es** . . . . Ezk 23:45

ADULTEROUS

You **a** wife, ... Ezk 16:32
An evil and **a** generation . . . . Mt 12:39; 16:4
this **a** and sinful generation, ... Mk 8:38
You **a** people! Don't you know . . . . Jms 4:4

ADULTERY

Do not commit **a**. . . . . Ex 20:14; Dt 5:18
If a man commits **a** . . . . Lv 20:10
already committed **a** with her. . . . Mt 5:28
marries another, commits **a**. . . . . . . Mt 19:9
do not commit **a**; do not steal; . . . .Mt 19:18
brought a woman caught in **a**, ...Jn 8:3
who said, Do not commit **a**,
also . . . . .Jms 2:11

ADVANCE (N)

Scripture saw in **a** that God . . . . Gl 3:8

ADVANCE (V)

has actually **a-d** the gospel,. . . . . . .Php 1:12

ADVANTAGE

the **a** of wisdom. . . . . Ec 10:10
So what **a** does the Jew have? . . . . . Rm 3:1

ADVERSARY

I will take vengeance on my **a-ies** . Dt 32:41
You exalt me above my **a-ies**;. . . . . Ps 18:48
give the **a** no opportunity 1Tm 5:14
Your **a** the devil is prowling 1Pt 5:8

ADVERSITY

life and prosperity, death and **a**. . . Dt 30:15
only good from God and not **a**? . . . . Jb 2:10
both **a** and good come from . . . . . . Lm 3:38

ADVICE

rejected the elders' **a**. 2Ch 10:13
walk in the **a** of the wicked . . . . Ps 1:1
should have followed my **a** . . . . Ac 27:21

ADVISERS

with many **a** they succeed. . . . . Pr 15:22

ADVOCATE

we have an **a** with the Father 1Jn 2:1

AFFECTION

not withholding our **a** from you . . .2Co 6:12
with the **a** of Christ Jesus. . . . . .Php 1:8

AFFLICT

the Almighty has **a-ed** me? . . . . .Ru 1:20
He was oppressed and **a-ed**, ...Is 53:7
you who are **a-ed**, along with us. . . . 2Th 1:7
destitute, **a-ed**, and mistreated. . . Heb 11:37

AFFLICTION

fruitful in the land of my **a**. . . . . . . .Gn 41:52
LORD saw that the **a** of Israel. 2Kg 14:26
Consider my **a** and trouble, ... Ps 25:18
He does not enjoy bringing **a** . . . . . Lm 3:33
she was healed of her **a**. . . . . Mk 5:29
a-s are waiting for me. . . . . .Ac 20:23
a produces endurance, ... Rm 5:3
momentary light **a** is producing . . .2Co 4:17

AFRAID

I was **a** because I was naked, ...Gn 3:10
not be **a**, Abram. I am your shield. . . Gn 15:1
he was **a** to look at God. . . . . .Ex 3:6
Do not be **a**, alarmed, or terrified. . .Dt 20:3
Do not be **a** or discouraged,. . . . . . . Jos 1:9
I will not be **a** of the thousands . . . . .Ps 3:6
of whom should I be **a**? . . . . Ps 27:1
When I am **a**, I will trust in you. . . . . Ps 56:3
She is not **a** for her household. . . . . Pr 31:21
I will trust him and not be **a**, ...Is 12:2
Do not be **a** of anyone, for I
will be . . . . .Jr 1:8
don't be **a** to take Mary . . . . Mt 1:20
Jesus told them, "Do not be **a**. . . . . Mt 28:10
Don't be **a**. Only believe. . . . . Mk 5:36
they were **a** of him, ...Mk 11:18
they were **a** of the crowd. . . .Mk 11:32; 12:12
Do not be **a**, Mary, ... Lk 1:30
they were **a** of the people. . . . . Lk 22:2
It is I. Don't be **a**! . . . . .Jn 6:20
they were **a** of the Jews, ... Jn 9:22
I will not be **a**. What can man do . . Heb 13:6

AGABUS

Early church prophet (Ac 11:28; 21:10).

AGAG

Amalekite king spared by Saul, executed by
Samuel (1Sm 15).

AGAINST

who is not with me is **a** me,. . . . . . Mt 12:30
whoever is not **a** us is for us. . . . . . .Mk 9:40
If God is for us, who is **a** us? . . . . . . Rm 8:31

AGE

already existed in the **a-s** before . . . Ec 1:10
the worries of this **a** . . . . .Mt 13:22; Mk 4:19

AGONY

a like a woman in labor. . . . . Jr 22:23
I am in **a** in this flame! . . . . Lk 16:24

AGREE

If two of you on earth **a**. . . . . Mt 18:19
the testimonies did not **a**. . . . . Mk 14:56
Why did you **a** to test the Spirit . . . . .Ac 5:9
Saul **a-d** with putting him to
death. . . . . Ac 8:1
I **a** with the law that it is good . . . . Rm 7:16
does not **a** with the sound
teaching 1Tm 6:3

AGREEMENT

making a binding **a** in writing . . . . Neh 9:38
we have an **a** with Sheol; . . . . .Is 28:15
a does Christ have with Belial? 2Co 6:15
these three are in **a**. 1Jn 5:8

AGRIPPA

Herodian king who heard Paul's testimony
(Ac 25–26).

AHAB

Son of Omri, king of Israel (1Kg 16:28–22:40).
Married Jezebel and promoted baalism
(16:31–33). Killed Naboth (21:1–14). Condemned by Elijah (18:18; 21:17–24) and other
prophets (20:35–43; 22:19–28). Died in disguise in battle (22:29–40).

AHASUERUS

King of Persia, son of Darius and grandson
of Cyrus. Greek name is Xerxes. Dismissed
Vashti and married Esther (Est 1–2). Signed
Haman's decree (Est 3) then was convinced
by Esther to reverse it and hang Haman (Est
4–7) and allow the Jews to defend themselves (Est 8–9).

AHAZ

Idolatrous king of Judah (2Kg 16:2–4). Son
of Jotham. Attacked by Aram and Israel
(16:5–6; 2Ch 28:5–7). Refused Isaiah's advice
and turned to Assyria for help (Is 7). Not
buried among the kings (2Ch 28:27).

AHAZIAH

1. Son of Ahab; king of Israel (1Kg 22:40).
Injured in a fall; condemned by Elijah for
seeking Baal (2Kg 1:2–17).
2. Son of Jehoram; king of Judah (2Kg
8:25–27). Mortally wounded by Jehu
while visiting King Joram of Israel (9:27).

AHEAD

Each creature went
straight **a**. . . . . .Ezk 1:9; 10:22
sending my messenger **a** of you; . . .Mt 11:10
I will go **a** of you to Galilee. . . . . . . Mt 26:32
which God prepared **a** of time. . . . .Eph 2:10
reaching forward to what is **a**, ...Php 3:13

AHIJAH

1. Priest at the time of Saul (1Sm 14:3–4,18).
2. Prophet from Shiloh to Jeroboam (1Kg
4:3; 11:29–39).

AI

Bethel on the west and **A** on the . . .Gn 12:8
they fled from the men of **A**. . . . . . . .Jos 7:4
Joshua burned **A**. . . . . Jos 8:28

AIJALON

moon, over the Valley of **A**. . . . . . . Jos 10:12
A with its pasturelands, ... Jos 21:24

AIMLESSLY

do not run like one who runs **a** 1Co 9:26

AIR

box like one beating the **a**. 1Co 9:26
meet the Lord in the **a** 1Th 4:17
poured out his bowl into the **a**,. . . . Rv 16:17

ALABASTER

an **a** jar. . . . . .Mt 26:7; Mk 14:3

ALARM

sound the **a** on my holy mountain! . . .Jl 2:1

ALARMED

and rumors of wars, don't be **a**; . . . Mk 13:7

ALERT

be **a**, since you don't know . . . . . . Mt 24:42
Be **a**, stand firm in the faith, ... 1Co 16:13

stay **a** with all perseverance . . . . . .Eph 6:18
prayer; stay **a** in it . . . . Col 4:2
Be sober-minded! Be **a**! 1Pt 5:8

ALEXANDER

Hymenaeus and **A** 1Tm 1:20
A the coppersmith 2Tm 4:14

ALIEN

Your offspring will be resident **a-s** . . Gn 15:13
"I have been a resident **a**" . . . . .Ex 2:22
the land they lived in as **a-s**. . . . . . . .Ex 6:4
and resident **a-s** in Canaan, ... Ps 105:12
no longer oppress the resident **a**, ... Jr 7:6

ALIENATED

are **a** from Christ; . . . . Gl 5:4
Once you were **a** and hostile . . . . . .Col 1:21

ALIVE

to keep them **a** with you. . . . . Gn 6:19
when they heard that he was **a** . . .Mk 16:11
he also presented himself **a** . . . . Ac 1:3
dead to sin and **a** to God . . . . Rm 6:11
in Christ all will be made **a**. 1Co 15:22
made us **a** with Christ . . . . Eph 2:5
he made you **a** with him. . . . . Col 2:13
We who are still **a** 1Th 4:17
made **a** by the Spirit, ... 1Pt 3:18
but look—I am **a** forever. . . . . Rv 1:18

ALL

with **a** your heart, with **a** your soul, and
  with **a** your strength. . . . . .Dt 6:5
search for me with **a** your heart. . . . Jr 29:13
love the Lord ... with **a**
  your heart, ... Lk 10:27
a have sinned and fall short. . . . . . . Rm 3:23
He died to sin once for **a** . . . . Rm 6:10
We will not **a** fall asleep, but we
  will **a** be changed, ...1Co 15:51
the one who fills **a** things. . . . . .Eph 1:23
I am able to do **a** things . . . . .Php 4:13
A Scripture is inspired by God 2Tm 3:16
but **a** to come to repentance. 2Pt 3:9

ALLEGIANCE

every tongue will swear **a**. . . . . Is 45:23

ALLIANCE

Solomon made an **a** with Pharaoh . . 1Kg 3:1
they will form an **a**, ...Dn 11:6

ALLOTMENT

Israel according to their tribal **a-s**: . . Jos 12:7

ALLOW

will not **a** your faithful one to see . . Ps 16:10
A it for now, ...Mt 3:15
a your holy one to see decay. . . . . . .Ac 2:27
will not **a** you to be tempted. 1Co 10:13

ALMIGHTY

I am God **A**. . . . . Gn 17:1
Isaac, and Jacob as God **A**, ...Ex 6:3
discover the limits of the **A**? . . . . . . .Jb 11:7
dwells in the shadow of the **A**. . . . . . Ps 91:1
was, and who is coming, the **A**. . . . . .Rv 1:8
Holy, holy, holy, Lord God, the **A**, . . . Rv 4:8
God, the **A**, reigns! . . . . Rv 19:6

ALMOND

the **a** tree blossoms, ... Ec 12:5

ALONE

not good for the man to be **a**. . . . . . .Gn 2:18
man does not live on bread **a** . . . . . .Dt 8:3
I **a** am left, ... 1Kg 19:10
Against you—you **a**— . . . . Ps 51:4
the Lᴏʀᴅ **a** will be exalted . . . . Is 2:11
Man must not live on bread **a** . . . . . .Mt 4:4
to a remote place to be **a**. . . . . .Mt 14:13
Who can forgive sins but God **a**? . . . Mk 2:7
by works and not by faith **a**. . . . . . Jms 2:24

ALPHA

the **A** and the Omega, ... Rv 1:8; 21:6; 22:13

ALREADY

Whatever is, has **a** been, and
  whatever will be, **a** is. . . . . Ec 3:15
has **a** committed adultery . . . . Mt 5:28
how I wish it were **a** set ablaze! . . . Lk 12:49
does not believe is **a** judged, ... Jn 3:18
You are **a** clean . . . . Jn 15:3
You are **a** full! You are **a** rich! 1Co 4:8
Not that I have **a** reached. . . . . .Php 3:12
it is **a** in the world now. 1Jn 4:3

ALTAR

Noah built an **a** to the Lᴏʀᴅ. . . . . . . Gn 8:20
Isaac and placed him on the **a** . . . . . Gn 22:9
construct the **a** of acacia wood. . . . . Ex 27:1
an **a** for the burning of incense; . . . .Ex 30:1
tear down their **a-s**, ... Ex 34:13
take hold of the horns of the **a**. . . .1Kg 1:50
I will come to the **a** of God, ...Ps 43:4
leave your gift ... in front
  of the **a**. Mt 5:24
takes an oath by the **a**, ... Mt 23:18
We have an **a** from which. . . . . . .Heb 13:10
in offering Isaac ... on the **a**? . . . . .Jms 2:21
I saw under the **a** the souls . . . . Rv 6:9

ALTOGETHER

reliable and **a** righteous. . . . . Ps 19:9
righteous and **a** trustworthy. . . . . Ps 119:138

ALWAYS

my sin is **a** before me. . . . . Ps 51:3
You **a** have the poor with you, ...Mt 26:11
I am with you **a**, ... Mt 28:20
Rejoice in the Lord **a**. . . . . Php 4:4
A be ready to give a defense. 1Pt 3:15

AM SEE I AM

AMASA

David's nephew; commander of Absalom's
army (2Sm 17:25). Reinstated by David
(19:13). Killed by Joab (20:10).

AMAZED

a and asked, "What kind of man. . . Mt 8:27
the crowds were **a**, ... Mt 9:33
he was **a** at their unbelief. . . . . .Mk 6:6
they were astounded and **a**, ...Ac 2:7

AMAZIAH

Son of Joash; king of Judah. Defeated Edom
but adopted their gods (2Ch 25:11–14). Rejected God's rebuke, challenged King Jehoash of Israel, and was defeated (26:15–
24). Killed by a conspiracy (26:27).

AMBASSADOR

we are **a-s** for Christ, ...2Co 5:20
For this I am an **a** in chains. . . . . . . Eph 6:20

AMBITION

bitter envy and selfish **a**. . . . . .Jms 3:14

AMBUSH

Set an **a** behind the city. . . . . .Jos 8:2
set up an **a** around Gibeah. . . . . . .Jdg 20:29
Let's set an **a** and kill someone. . . . . .Pr 1:11
forty of them lying in **a**, ... Ac 23:21

AMEN

all the people will reply, 'A!' . . . . . . Dt 27:15
be the Lᴏʀᴅ forever. **A** and **a**. . . . . .Ps 89:52
will the outsider say "**A**" 1Co 14:16
through him we also say "**A**" 2Co 1:20
The **A**, the faithful and true . . . . . . .Rv 3:14
A! Come, Lord Jesus! . . . . Rv 22:20

AMNON

Oldest son of David (2Sm 3:2). Raped his sister Tamar; killed by Absalom (2Sm 13).

AMON

Son of Manasseh; king of Judah; killed by
his servants (2Kg 21:18–26).

AMOS

Prophet against moral decay in Israel under
Jeroboam II (Am 5:24).

ANANIAS

1. Lied about gift to the church at Jerusalem and died (Ac 5:1–6).
2. Disciple in Damascus who visited Paul
(Ac 9:10–19).
3. High priest at Paul's arrest (Ac 23:1–5;
24:1).

ANCESTOR

from the day their **a-s** came out. . 2Kg 21:15
a clear conscience as my **a-s** did, . . 2Tm 1:3

ANCHOR

this hope as an **a** for our lives, ... Heb 6:19

ANCIENT

Will you continue on the **a** path . . . Jb 22:15
Rise up, **a** doors! . . . . .Ps 24:7,9
Ask about the **a** paths, ... Jr 6:16
the **A** of Days took his seat. . . . . Dn 7:9
since **a** times, Moses . . . . Ac 15:21
if he didn't spare the **a** world, ...2Pt 2:5
seized the dragon, that **a** serpent . . Rv 20:2

ANDREW

Apostle; fisherman; Peter's brother (Mt
4:18; 10:2; Mk 1:16,29; 3:18; 13:3; Lk 6:14; Jn
1:35–44; 6:8–9; 12:12; Ac 1:13).

ANGEL

two **a-s** entered Sodom . . . . .Gn 19:1
a of the Lᴏʀᴅ called to him . . . . Gn 22:11
he will send his **a** before you, ... Gn 24:7
a-s were going up and down. . . . . . Gn 28:12
going to send an **a** before you . . . .Ex 23:20
a of the Lᴏʀᴅ took his stand . . . . Nm 22:22
God sent an **a** to Jerusalem 1Ch 21:15
A of the Lᴏʀᴅ encamps around. . . . Ps 34:7
he will give his **a-s** orders. . . . . .Ps 91:11
Bless the Lᴏʀᴅ, all his **a-s** . . . . Ps 103:20
the **a** of the Lᴏʀᴅ ... struck down . . .Is 37:36
He sent his **a** and rescued. . . . . Dn 3:28
My God sent his **a** and shut . . . . . . Dn 6:22
Jacob struggled with the **a** . . . . Hs 12:4
a of the Lord appeared . . . . .Mt 2:13
He will give his **a-s** orders . . . . Mt 4:6
is going to come with his **a-s** . . . . .Mt 16:27
their **a-s** continually view . . . . . . .Mt 18:10
are like **a-s** in heaven. . . . . Mt 22:30
for the devil and his **a-s**! . . . . .Mt 25:41
the **a-s** were serving him.. . . . . . . .Mk 1:13
the **a** Gabriel was sent . . . . Lk 1:26
a said to them, "Don't be afraid . . . . Lk 2:10
the **a-s** of God ascending . . . . .Jn 1:51
face was like the face of an **a**. . . . . . Ac 6:15
we will judge **a-s** 1Co 6:3
If I speak human or **a-ic** tongues . . .1Co 13:1
disguises himself as an **a** of light. . 2Co 11:14
even if we or an **a** from heaven . . . . . Gl 1:8
the worship of **a-s**, ... Col 2:18
some have welcomed **a-s**
  as guests .Heb 13:2
A-s long to catch a glimpse 1Pt 1:12
if God didn't spare the **a-s**. 2Pt 2:4
Write to the **a** of the church in . . . . . Rv 2–3

ANGER

until your brother's **a** subsides . . . Gn 27:44
alone, so that my **a** can burn. . . . . . Ex 32:10
gracious God, slow to **a**. . . . . .Ex 34:6
Lᴏʀᴅ's **a** burned against Israel . . . .Jdg 2:14
his **a** may ignite at any moment. . . Ps 2:12
do not rebuke me in your **a**; . . . . Ps 6:1
For his **a** lasts only a moment, ... Ps 30:5
I swore in my **a**, "They will not . . . . Ps 95:11
A gentle answer turns away **a**, ...Pr 15:1

ANGRY

A fool gives full vent to his **a**, ... Pr 29:11
compassionate, slow to **a**, ...Jl 2:13
slow to **a**, ...Jnh 4:2
jealousy, outbursts of **a**, ... Gl 5:20
sun go down on your **a**, ... Eph 4:26
All bitterness, **a** and wrath, ...Eph 4:31
a, wrath, malice, slander, ... Col 3:8
So I swore in my **a**, ...Heb 3:11
slow to speak, and slow to **a**, . . . Jms 1:19
the cup of his **a**. . . . . .Rv 14:10
winepress of the fierce **a** of God, . . Rv 19:15

ANGRY

the Son or he will be **a** . . . . Ps 2:12
Be **a** and do not sin; . . . . .Ps 4:4
An **a** person stirs up conflict, ... Pr 29:22
Is it right for you to be **a**? . . . . .Jnh 4:4
who is **a** with his brother . . . . Mt 5:22
Be **a** and do not sin. . . . . Eph 4:26

ANGUISH

After his **a**, he will see light, ... Is 53:11
in **a**, he prayed more fervently, . . . Lk 22:44
I wrote to you with ... **a-ed** heart . . 2Co 2:4

ANIMAL

Lord God formed ... every wild **a** . . .Gn 2:19
with an **a** must be put to death. . . Ex 22:19
may eat all these ... land **a-s** . . . . . .Lv 11:2
every **a** of the forest is mine, ... Ps 50:10
cares about his **a-'s** health, ... Pr 12:10
and the fate of **a-s** is the same. . . . Ec 3:19
four-footed **a-s** and reptiles . . . . . Ac 10:12

ANNIHILATE

a all the Jewish people . . . . Est 3:13

ANNOUNCE

I **a** them to you before they occur . . Is 42:9

ANOINT

A Aaron and his sons . . . . Ex 30:30
Lord sent me to **a** you as king 1Sm 15:1
The Lord **a-ed** you king 1Sm 15:17
You **a** my head with oil; . . . . Ps 23:5
a-ed me to bring good news. . . . . . . Is 61:1
a-ed my body in advance . . . . Mk 14:8
a-ed me to preach good news . . . . .Lk 4:18
You didn't **a** my head with ... oil, . . .Lk 7:46
a-ed Jesus's feet, ... Jn 12:3
against ... Jesus, whom you **a-ed**, . . .Ac 4:27
pray over him, **a-ing** him . . . . .Jms 5:14

ANOINTED (ADJ)

If the **a** priest sins, ...Lv 4:3
he will walk before my **a** one. 1Sm 2:35
Do not touch my **a** ones 1Ch 16:22
against the Lord and his **A** One: . . . Ps 2:2
Do not touch my **a** ones, ... Ps 105:15
an **a** guardian cherub, ... Ezk 28:14
until the **A** One, the ruler . . . . Dn 9:25
These are the two **a** ones, ... Zch 4:14

ANOINTED (N)

lift my hand against ... Lord's **a**. . . 1Sm 24:6

ANOINTING (N)

an **a** from the Holy One, ...1Jn 2:20
his **a** teaches you 1Jn 2:27

ANOINTING (ADJ)

spices for the **a** oil . . . . Ex 25:6

ANOTHER

Let **a** praise you, and not your . . . . . Pr 27:2
I will not give my glory to **a**. . . . . . . Is 48:11
he will give you a Counselor . . . Jn 14:16
not that there is **a** gospel, ... Gl 1:7

ANSWER (N)

A gentle **a** turns away anger, ...Pr 15:1
a of the tongue is from the Lord . . . Pr 16:1
who gives an **a** before he
listens . . . . Pr 18:13

money is the **a** for everything. . . . Ec 10:19
were astounded at ... his **a-s**. . . . . . Lk 2:47

ANSWER (V)

he **a-ed** him with fire 1Ch 21:26
but you do not **a** me; . . . . .Jb 30:20
a me, for I am poor and needy . . . . Ps 86:1
Don't **a** a fool according to. . . . . . . Pr 26:4
A a fool according to . . . . Pr 26:5
But Jesus still did not **a** . . . . Mk 15:5

ANT

Go to the **a**, you slacker! . . . . Pr 6:6
a-s are not a strong people, ... Pr 30:25

ANTICHRIST

heard that **a** is coming, even now many
a-s have come. 1Jn 2:18
is the **a**: the one who denies . . . 1Jn 2:22
spirit of the **a**; which you have 1Jn 4:3
This is the deceiver and the **a**. 2Jn 7

ANTIOCH

first called Christians at **A**. . . . . Ac 11:26
reached Pisidian **A**. . . . . Ac 13:14

ANTIQUITY

origin is from **a**, from eternity. . . . Mc 5:2

ANXIETY

A in a person's heart weighs . . . . . . Pr 12:25

ANXIOUS

don't be **a**. . . . . Lk 12:29

ANYTHING

Is **a** impossible for the Lord? . . . . Gn 18:14
Is **a** too difficult for me? . . . . Jr 32:27
A you ask the Father . . . . Jn 16:23

APART

Set **a** for me Barnabas and Saul. . . . . Ac 13:2
a from the law, the
righteousness of . . . . Rm 3:21
my mother's womb set me
a and called . . . . .Gl 1:15

APOLLOS

Alexandrian Jew, became a Christian apologist after being instructed in doctrine by
Priscilla and Aquila in Ephesus (Ac 18:24–28).
Was popular like Paul and Peter (1Co 1:12)
but not a rival (3:5–6,22; 4:6; 16:12; Ti 3:13).

APOSTASY

a-ies will reprimand you. . . . . .Jr 2:19
save them from all their **a-ies** . . . Ezk 37:23
I will heal their **a**; . . . . Hs 14:4
unless the **a** comes first 2Th 2:3

APOSTLE

the names of the twelve **a-s**: . . . . . Mt 10:2
twelve, whom he also named **a-s**, . .Mk 3:14
was added to the eleven **a-s**. . . Ac 1:26
laid it at the **a-s'** feet. . . . . .Ac 5:2
called as an **a** and set apart . . . . Rm 1:1
I am an **a** to the Gentiles, ... Rm 11:13
first **a-s**, second prophets, ... 1Co 12:28
not worthy to be called an **a**, ... 1Co 15:9
such people are false **a-s**, ... 2Co 11:13
signs of an **a** were performed 2Co 12:12
on the foundation of the **a-s** . . . . Eph 2:20
some to be **a-s**, some prophets, . . . Eph 4:11
Jesus, the **a** and high priest . . . . . . .Heb 3:1
twelve names of twelve **a-s** . . . . . Rv 21:14

APOSTLESHIP

We have received grace and **a** . . . . . Rm 1:5
you are the seal of my **a** 1Co 9:2
Peter for an **a** to the circumcised . . . Gl 2:8

APPEAL (N)

God is making his **a**
through us. 2Co 5:20

APPEAL (V)

I **a** to Caesar! . . . . Ac 25:11
I **a**, ... on the basis of love. . . . . Phm 9

APPEAR

the Lord **a-ed** to Abram. . . . . .Gn 12:7
sign of the Son of Man will **a** . . . Mt 24:30
and **a-ed** to many. . . . . Mt 27:53
the third time Jesus **a-ed**. . . . . . Jn 21:14
he **a-ed** to over five hundred 1Co 15:6
all **a** before the judgment seat . . . 2Co 5:10
until the **a-ing** of our Lord. 1Tm 6:14
those who have loved his **a-ing** . . 2Tm 4:8
blessed hope, the **a-ing** of the
glory . . . . .Ti 2:13
will **a** a second time, ... Heb 9:28

APPEARANCE

Do not look at his **a** 1Sm 16:7
no **a** that we should desire him. . . . . .Is 53:2
judging according to outward **a-s**; . . Jn 7:24

APPETITE

A worker's **a** works for him. . . . . Pr 16:26
if you have a big **a**; . . . . Pr 23:2
yet the **a** is never satisfied. . . . . Ec 6:7
He enlarges his **a** like Sheol, ... Hab 2:5
Lord Christ but their own **a-s**. . . . . Rm 16:18

APPLES

is like gold **a** in silver settings. . . . Pr 25:11

APPLY

A yourself to discipline . . . . Pr 23:12
I **a-ied** my mind to seek . . . . .Ec 1:13

APPOINT

These are the Lord's **a-ed** times, . . Lv 23:4
a a king to judge us. 1Sm 8:5
A a king for them. 1Sm 8:22
I will **a** peace as your government . .Is 60:17
A harvest is also **a-ed** for you, ... Hs 6:11
the Lord **a-ed** a great fish . . . . .Jnh 1:17
God **a-ed** a worm. . . . . Jnh 4:7
vision is yet for the **a-ed** time; . . . . Hab 2:3
He **a-ed** twelve, ... Mk 3:14
been **a-ed** for you as the Messiah. Ac 3:20
God did not **a** us to wrath, ...1Th 5:9
For this I was **a-ed** a herald, ...1Tm 2:7
Don't be too quick to **a** anyone. . . 1Tm 5:22
a elders in every town: . . . . Ti 1:5
God has **a-ed** him heir of all things. . Heb 1:2
it is **a-ed** for people to die once . . Heb 9:27

APPROACH

let us **a** the throne of grace . . . . . . Heb 4:16

APPROPRIATE

Luxury is not **a** for a fool . . . . Pr 19:10
made everything **a** in its time. . . . . . Ec 3:11

APPROVAL

I stood there giving **a** . . . . .Ac 22:20
and receives human **a**. . . . . Rm 14:18

APPROVE

just as we have been **a-d** by God . . 1Th 2:4
to present yourself ... as one **a-d**, . .2Tm 2:15
by this our ancestors were **a-d** . . . Heb 11:2

AQUILA

Husband of Priscilla; tentmaker; Jewish
Christian; teacher; coworker with Paul (Ac
18:2,18,26; Rm 16:3; 1Co 16:19; 2Tm 4:19).

ARAB

Geshem the **A** . . . . Neh 2:19; 6:1
Cretans and **A-s** . . . . Ac 2:11

ARABAH

in the **A** opposite Suph, ... Dt 1:1
the Sea of the **A**—the Dead Sea)—. . Jos 3:16
along the route to the **A**, ...2Kg 25:4
and goes down to the **A**. . . . . .Ezk 47:8

ARAM

Son of Shem (Gn 10:22). The nation named for him, perennial enemy of Israel (Jdg 3:8; 2Sm 8:6; 1Kg 11:25; 20; 22; 2Kg 6:8–24; 8:12–13; 13:3,22; 16:7).

ARAMAIC

speak to your servants in **A**, ... 2Kg 18:26
The letter was written in **A** . . . . Ezr 4:7
spoke to the king (**A** begins here): . . Dn 2:4

ARAMEAN

My father was a wandering **A**. . . . . Dt 26:5

ARARAT

on the mountains of **A**. . . . . Gn 8:4

ARAUNAH

Man whose threshing floor David bought (2Sm 24:15–25); also called Ornan (1Ch 21:15–28); threshing floor became site of the temple (1Ch 22:1; 2Ch 3:1).

ARCHANGEL

a shout, with the **a**-'s voice, ... 1Th 4:16
Michael the **a**, ... Jd 9

ARCHER

the **a**-s found him and severely . . 1Sm 31:3
The **a**-s shot King Josiah, ... 2Ch 35:23
like an **a** who wounds everyone . . . Pr 26:10

ARCHITECT

whose **a** and builder is God. . . . . . Heb 11:10

AREOPAGUS

stood in the middle of the **A** . . . . . . Ac 17:22

ARGUE

Let him who **a**-s with God give . . . . Jb 40:2
Pharisees ... began to **a** with him, . . Mk 8:11
What were you **a**-ing about . . . . . . Mk 9:33
don't **a** about disputed matters. . . . Rm 14:1
without grumbling and **a**-ing, ... Php 2:14

ARGUMENT

Hear now my **a**, ... Jb 13:6
An **a** started among them . . . . Lk 9:46
We demolish **a**-s 2Co 10:4
deceive you with empty **a**-s, ... Eph 5:6
deceive you with
   persuasive **a**-s. . . . . Col 2:4
holy hands without anger or **a**. 1Tm 2:8

ARISE

God **a**-s. His enemies scatter, ... Ps 68:1
A, my darling. Come away, ... Sg 2:10
A, shine, for your light has come. . . . Is 60:1
false prophets will **a** . . . . Mt 24:24

ARK

Make ... an **a** of gopher wood. . . . . Gn 6:14
make an **a** of acacia wood, ... Ex 25:10
Put the tablets ... into the **a**. . . . . . Ex 25:16
The **a** of God was captured, ...1Sm 4:11
Nothing was in the **a** except 1Kg 8:9
a place there for the **a**, ...1Kg 8:21
the day Noah boarded the **a**. . . . Mt 24:38
built an **a** to deliver his family. . . . Heb 11:7
while the **a** was being prepared. . . 1Pt 3:20
the **a** of his covenant appeared . . . Rv 11:19

ARM

with an outstretched **a**. . . . . .Ex 6:6
a strong hand and an
   outstretched **a**, ...Dt 4:34
underneath are the
   everlasting **a**-s. . . . . .Dt 33:27
Do you have an **a** like God's? . . . . . .Jb 40:9
a-s can bend a bow of bronze. . . . Ps 18:34
holy **a** have won him victory. . . . . . .Ps 98:1
as a seal on your **a**. . . . . Sg 8:6
taking them in my **a**-s, ... Hs 11:3
taking them in his **a**-s, ... Mk 10:16

to whom has the **a** of the Lord been
   revealed? . . . . Jn 12:38

ARMAGEDDON

place called in Hebrew, **A**. . . . . .Rv 16:16

ARMOR

Saul ... had him put on **a**. 1Sm 17:38
one who puts on his **a** boast 1Kg 20:11
through the joints of his **a**. 1Kg 22:34
penetrate his double layer of **a**? . . . Jb 41:13
put on the **a** of light. . . . . .Rm 13:12
Put on the full **a** of God . . . . Eph 6:11
put on the **a** of faith and love, ... 1Th 5:8

ARMY

chariots and his **a** into the sea; . . . . Ex 15:4
commander of the LORD's **a**. . . . . . . Jos 5:14
defied the **a**-ies of the living
   God 1Sm 17:36
a great **a**, like an **a** of God. 1Ch 12:22
Though an **a** deploys against me, . . Ps 27:3
king is not saved by a large **a**; . . . . Ps 33:16
Jerusalem surrounded by **a**-ies, . . . Lk 21:20
The **a**-ies that were in heaven . . . . Rv 19:14
on the horse and against his **a**. . . . Rv 19:19

ARREST

Herod had **a**-ed John, ... Mt 14:3
looking for a way to **a** him, ... Mt 21:46
hold of Jesus, and **a**-ed him. . . . . . Mt 26:50
they **a**-ed the apostles. . . . . Ac 5:18
he proceeded to **a** Peter too, ... Ac 12:3

ARROGANCE

your **a** have reached my ears, ...2Kg 19:28
A leads to nothing but strife, ... Pr 13:10
gossip, **a**, and disorder. 2Co 12:20
you boast in your **a**. . . . . .Jms 4:16

ARROGANT

For I envied the **a**; . . . . Ps 73:3
a people have attacked me; . . . . . . .Ps 86:14
I hate **a** pride, evil conduct, ... Pr 8:13
an **a** spirit before a fall. . . . . Pr 16:18
Do not be **a**, but beware. . . . . Rm 11:20

ARROW

I will shoot three **a**-s
   beside it 1Sm 20:20
Elisha said, "Take the **a**-s!" 2Kg 13:18
a-s of the Almighty have
   pierced . . . . .Jb 6:4
the **a** that flies by day, ... Ps 91:5
a-s in the hand of a warrior. . . . . . . Ps 127:4
He made me like a sharpened **a**; . . . Is 49:2
Their tongues are deadly **a**-s— . . . . . Jr 9:8
extinguish all the flaming **a**-s . . . . Eph 6:16

ARTAXERXES

King of Persia who allowed Ezra to rebuild the temple (Ezr 6:14; 7:1–26) and Nehemiah to rebuild the wall of Jerusalem (Neh 2:1–6).

ARTEMIS

Greek goddess (Ac 19:24–35).

ASA

Son of Abijam; king of Judah (1Kg 15:8). Instituted reforms (15:13). Rebuked for relying on Aram for military help and on doctors for healing rather than on the Lord (2Ch 16:1–12).

ASCEND

Who may **a** the mountain . . . . Ps 24:3
I will **a** to the heavens; . . . . Is 14:13
No one has **a**-ed into heaven . . . . . Jn 3:13
observe the Son of Man **a**-ing . . . . .Jn 6:62
not yet **a**-ed to the Father. . . . . . . Jn 20:17
is also the one who **a**-ed . . . . .Eph 4:10

ASCENTS

song of **a**. . . . . .Pss 120–134

ASCRIBE

a to the LORD glory and . .1Ch 16:28; Ps 96:7
A power to God. . . . . .Ps 68:34

ASENATH

Wife of Joseph (Gn 41:45,50; 46:20).

ASHAMED

All my enemies will be **a** . . . . Ps 6:10
Jacob will no longer be **a** . . . . Is 29:22
is **a** of me and of my words . . . . . . .Mk 8:38
I am not **a** of the gospel, ... Rm 1:16
don't be **a** of the testimony. 2Tm 1:8
who doesn't need to be **a**, ...2Tm 2:15
not **a** to call them brothers, ...Heb 2:11
is not **a** to be called
   their God, ... Heb 11:16
Christian, let him not be **a** 1Pt 4:16

ASHER

Jacob's eighth son, born of Zilpah (Gn 30:13; 35:26). The tribe's territory was in the northwest on the Phoenician coast (Jos 19:24–31). Also, a town (17:7).

ASHERAH

cut down the **A** pole beside it. . . . Jdg 6:25
and the 400 prophets of **A**. 1Kg 18:19
an obscene image of **A**. 2Ch 15:16

ASHES

even though I am dust and **a**. . . . . Gn 18:27
is to gather up the cow's **a**. . . . . . .Nm 19:9
Tamar put **a** on her head 2Sm 13:19
the **a** poured from the altar, ...1Kg 13:5
put on sackcloth and **a**, ... Est 4:1
he sat among the **a**. . . . . .Jb 2:8
I am dust and **a**. . . . . .Jb 42:6
a crown of beauty instead of **a**, . . . Is 61:3
covered himself with sackcloth,
   and sat in **a**. . . . . .Jnh 3:6
in sackcloth and a long ago! . . . . Mt 11:21
the **a** of a young cow . . . . Heb 9:13

ASIA

forbidden ... to speak the word
   in **A**. . . . . Ac 16:6
first convert to Christ from **A**. . . . . . Rm 16:5
To the seven churches in **A**. . . . . .Rv 1:4

ASIDE

Do not turn **a** to the right or . . . . . Dt 28:14
took the twelve disciples **a** . . . . . . Mt 20:17
set something **a** and save. 1Co 16:2
let us lay **a** every hindrance . . . . . .Heb 12:1

ASK

When your children **a** you, ... Ex 12:26
When your son **a**-s you. . . . . Dt 6:20
A of me, and I will make. . . . . .Ps 2:8
Two things I **a** of you; . . . . Pr 30:7
sought by those who did not **a**; . . . .Is 65:1
Give to the one who **a**-s you, ... Mt 5:42
you need before you **a** him. . . . . . . Mt 6:8
A, and it will be given. . . . . Mt 7:7
you pray and **a** for—believe. . . . . Mk 11:24
Holy Spirit to those who **a** . . . . . . .Lk 11:13
Whatever you **a** in my name, ...Jn 14:13
a whatever you want . . . . Jn 15:7
A and you will receive, ... Jn 16:24
the Jews **a** for signs. 1Co 1:22
lacks wisdom, he should
   a God, ... Jms 1:5
You **a** and don't receive because
   you **a** with wrong motives, ... Jms 4:3
a anything according to his will, . . . 1Jn 5:14

ASLEEP

The child is not dead but **a**. . . . . . Mk 5:39
as they were sailing he fell **a**. . . . . .Lk 8:23
Lazarus has fallen **a**, ...Jn 11:11
We will not all fall **a**, ...1Co 15:51
concerning those who
   are **a**, ... 1Th 4:13

ASSEMBLE

a the whole community . . . . Lv 8:3
A on the mountains of Samaria . . . . Am 3:9
to gather nations, to **a** kingdoms, . . Zph 3:8
a-d together against your holy
   servant Jesus, ... Ac 4:27
to **a** them for the battle . . . . Rv 16:14

ASSEMBLY

sacred **a** on the first day and another
   sacred **a** on the seventh day. . . . . Ex 12:16
the **a** in front of the rock, ... Nm 20:10
his praise in the **a** of the faithful. . . Ps 149:1
the **a** was divided. . . . . Ac 23:7
the **a** of the firstborn . . . . Heb 12:23

ASSOCIATE

you **a** with adulterers. . . . . Ps 50:18
Don't **a** with those who drink . . Pr 23:20
don't **a** with rebels, ... Pr 24:21
a with the humble. . . . . Rm 12:16
not to **a** with anyone who claims
   to be a believer. 1Co 5:11
don't **a** with him, ... 2Th 3:14

ASSURANCE

Holy Spirit, and with full **a**. 1Th 1:5
true heart in full **a** of faith, ... Heb 10:22

ASSURED

stand mature and fully **a** . . . . Col 4:12

ASSYRIA

From that land he went to **A** . . . . . . Gn 10:11
The king of **A** deported the
   Israelites to **A** 2Kg 18:11
Woe to **A**, the rod of my anger . . . . . . Is 10:5

ASTONISHED

crowds were **a** at his teaching, ... Mt 7:28
were **a** and said, "Where did this . . Mt 13:54
they were **a** at his teaching. . . . . . Mt 22:33
were **a**. "Where did this man get . . Mk 6:2
disciples were **a** at his words. . . . . Mk 10:24
parents saw him, they were **a**, . . . Lk 2:48
all **a** at the greatness of God. . . . . Lk 9:43

ASTOUNDED

were **a** at his understanding . . . . Lk 2:47

ASTRAY

led **a** to bow down ... to other
   gods . . . . Dt 30:17
who rejects correction goes **a**. . . . . Pr 10:17
We all want a like sheep; . . . . Is 53:6
their shepherds led them **a**, ... Jr 50:6
and one of them goes **a**, ... Mt 18:12
lead **a**, if possible, the elect. . . . . . Mk 13:22
always go **a** in their hearts, ... Heb 3:10
you were like sheep going **a**, ... 1Pt 2:25

ATHALIAH

Wife of Jehoram and mother of Ahaziah,
kings of Judah; descendant of Omri (2 Kg
8:26). Encouraged Baal worship (8:27). Killed
heirs and ruled after her son's death (2Kg
11:1–3). Jehoiada the priest executed her
and crowned Josiah, the only surviving heir
(11:4–20).

ATHENS

City in Greece (Ac 17; 1Th 3:1).

ATHLETE

if anyone competes as an **a**, ... 2Tm 2:5

ATONE

only you can **a** for our rebellions. . . . Ps 65:3
Rescue us and **a** for our sins, ... Ps 79:9

ATONEMENT

blood of the sin offering for **a**. . . . . Ex 30:10
priest will make **a** on their behalf, . . Lv 4:20
make **a** before the LORD . . . . Lv 14:31

---

is the Day of **A**. . . . . Lv 23:27
he ... made **a** for the Israelites. . . . Nm 25:13
to make **a** for the sins of the . . . . . . Heb 2:17

ATONING SACRIFICE

himself is the **a** for our sins, ... 1Jn 2:2
Son to be the **a** for our sins 1Jn 4:10

ATTACK

he may come and **a** me, ... Gn 32:11
I will **a** him while he is weary. 2Sm 17:2
a worm that **a-ed** the plant, ... Jnh 4:7

ATTEMPTED

a to establish their ...
   righteousness, ... Rm 10:3
When the Egyptians **a** to do this, . . Heb 11:29

ATTENDANT

gave it back to the **a**, and sat . . . . . . Lk 4:20

ATTENTION

to pay **a** is better than the fat. . . . 1Sm 15:22
Pay **a** to the sound of my cry, ... Ps 5:2
The God of Jacob doesn't pay **a**. . . . . Ps 94:7
My son, pay **a** to my words; . . . . Pr 4:20
pay **a** to the words of the wise, ... Pr 22:17
pay **a** to myths and endless 1Tm 1:4
give your **a** to public reading, ... 1Tm 4:13
not pay **a** to Jewish myths. . . . . Ti 1:14
a all the more to what we
   have heard. . . . . Heb 2:1

ATTIRE

attendants' service and their **a**, . . 1Kg 10:5

ATTITUDE

Serve with a good **a**, as to the Lord. . Eph 6:7
Adopt the same **a** as that of Christ . Php 2:5

ATTRIBUTES

For his invisible **a**, ... Rm 1:20

AUTHORITY

Confer some of your **a** on him. . . . Nm 27:20
like one who had **a**, ... Mt 7:29
Son of Man has **a** on earth . . . . Mt 9:6
gave them **a** over unclean spirits . . Mt 10:1
All **a** has been given to me. . . . . . . Mt 28:18
you gave him **a** over all people; . . . . Jn 17:2
You would have no **a** over me . . . . Jn 19:11
submit to the governing **a-ies**, ... Rm 13:1
there is no **a** except from God, ... Rm 13:1
a symbol of **a** on her head, ... 1Co 11:10
far above every ruler and **a**, ... Eph 1:21
rulers, against the **a-ies**, ... Eph 6:12
disarmed the rulers and **a-ies** . . . . . Col 2:15
teach or to have **a** over a man; . . . 1Tm 2:12
submit to rulers and **a-ies**, ... Ti 3:1
Submit to every human **a** 1Pt 2:13
a-ies, and powers subject to him. . . 1Pt 3:22
glory, majesty, power, and **a** . . . . Jd 25
I will give him **a** over the nations . . Rv 2:26
who were given **a** to judge. . . . . Rv 20:4

AVENGE

He will **a** the blood . . . . Dt 32:43
Should I not **a** myself . . . . Jr 5:9
do not **a** yourselves; . . . . Rm 12:19
how long until you ... **a** . . . . Rv 6:10

AVENGER

cities as a refuge from the **a**, ... Nm 35:12
hand him over to the **a** of blood . . . Dt 19:12
to silence the enemy and the **a**. . . . . Ps 8:2
Lord is an **a** of all these offenses, . . 1Th 4:6

AVOID

a irreverent and empty speech . . . 2Tm 2:16
But **a** foolish debates, genealogies, . . Ti 3:9

AWAKE

A! A, Deborah! . . . . Jdg 5:12
when I **a**, I will be satisfied. . . . . Ps 17:15

---

or **a-n** love until . . . . Sg 2:7; 3:5; 8:4
I **a-ned** you under the apricot tree. . Sg 8:5
He **a-ns** me each morning; he
   a-ns my ear to listen . . . . Is 50:4
in the dust of the earth will **a**, ... Dn 12:2
Couldn't you stay **a** one hour? . . . . Mk 14:37
let us stay **a** and be self-controlled. . 1Th 5:6
whether we are **a** or asleep, ... 1Th 5:10

AWAY

All have turned **a**; . . . . Ps 53:3

AWE

of the world stand in **a** of him. . . . . . Ps 33:8
I tremble in **a** of you; . . . . Ps 119:120
so that people will be in **a** of him. . . Ec 3:14
stand in **a** of the God of Israel. . . . . Is 29:23
I stand in **a** of your deeds. . . . . Hab 3:2

AWE-INSPIRING

the great, mighty, and a God, ... Dt 10:17
glorious and **a** name—the LORD, . . Dt 28:58
looked like the **a** Angel of God. . . . Jdg 13:6
the great and **a** God who keeps . . . Neh 1:5
great, mighty, and **a** God . . . . Neh 9:32
right hand show your **a** acts. . . . . . . Ps 45:4
the LORD, the Most High, is **a**, ... Ps 47:2
You answer us ... with **a** works, ... Ps 65:5
his acts for humanity are **a**. . . . . . . Ps 66:5
you are **a** in your sanctuaries. . . . . . Ps 68:35
LORD—the great and **a** God . . . . Dn 9:4
Great and **a** are your works, ... Rv 15:3

AWESOME

What an **a** place this is! . . . . Gn 28:17

AX

iron **a** head fell into the water, ... 2Kg 6:5
Does an **a** exalt itself. . . . . Is 10:15
the **a** is already at the
   root of. . . . . Mt 3:10; Lk 3:9

AZARIAH

1. Prophet (2Ch 15:1–8).
2. King of Judah, also called Uzziah (2Kg
   15:1–7).

- B -

BAAL

Israel aligned itself with **B** of
   Peor, ... Nm 25:3
the 450 prophets of **B** 1Kg 18:19
knee that has not bowed to **B**. . . . 1Kg 19:18
no longer call me, "my **B**." . . . . Hs 2:16
who have not bowed down to **B**. . . Rm 11:4

BAASHA

King of Israel (1Kg 15:16–16:7). Exterminated
Jeroboam's family (15:29).

BABY

Give the living **b** to the first 1Kg 3:27
the **b** leaped inside her, ... Lk 1:41
You will find a **b** wrapped . . . . Lk 2:12
and the **b** who was lying in . . . . Lk 2:16

BABYLON

Mesopotamian city; place of captivity (2Kg
24; Dn 1:1–6); symbol of wickedness (Rv
17:5).
Therefore it is called **B**, ... Gn 11:9
from a distant country,
   from **B**. 2Kg 20:14
went up from **B** to Jerusalem. . . . . . Ezr 1:11
By the rivers of **B**— . . . . Ps 137:1
B has fallen, has fallen. . . . . Is 21:9
the king of **B** for seventy years. . . . Jr 25:11
She who is in **B**, chosen. 1Pt 5:13
It has fallen, **B** the Great. . . . . Rv 14:8

BACK (N)

gave my **b** to those who beat me, . . Is 50:6

BACK (ADV)

looked **b** and became a pillar..... Gn 19:26
ahead ten steps or go **b** ten
  steps?....................... 2Kg 20:9
plow and looks **b** is fit for ....Lk 9:62

BAD

but a **b** tree produces **b** fruit......Mt 7:17
B company corrupts good 1Co 15:33

BAG

in each man's sack was his **b** of... Gn 42:35
different weights in your **b,**....... Dt 25:13
David put his hand in the **b,**......1Sm 17:49
weeping, carrying the **b** of seed, .. Ps 126:6
or **b-s** of deceptive weights?.......Mc 6:11
wages into a **b** with a hole in it..... Hg 1:6

BAKE

b-d unleavened bread for them,....Gn 19:3
b-d the dough they had brought.. Ex 12:39
B what you want to **b**, ... Ex 16:23
a grain offering **b-d** in an oven, ... Lv 2:4

BAKER

king of Egypt's cupbearer and **b**... Gn 40:1

BALAAM

Prophet hired by King Balak of Moab to
curse Israel (Nm 22). His donkey talked
(22:21–30; 2Pt 2:16). He blessed Israel (Nm
23–24; Jos 24:10; Neh 13:2). Executed for
practicing divination (Nm 31:8; Jos 13:22; 2Pt
2:15; Jd 11; Rv 2:14).

BALAK

King of Moab who hired Balaam to curse
Israel (Nm 22–24).

BALANCE

You are to have honest **b-s,**....... Lv 19:36
b-s and scales are the LORD's; ..... Pr 16:11
weighed the mountains on a **b** .... Is 40:12

BALDY

chanting, "Go up, **b**!.............2Kg 2:23

BALM

Is there no **b** in Gilead?............ Jr 8:22

BAN

will **b** you from the synagogues. .... Jn 16:2

BANDAGE

For he wounds but also **b-s**; .... Jb 5:18
and **b-s** their wounds............. Ps 147:3
cleansed, **b-d**, or soothed with oil....Is 1:6
LORD **b-s** his people's injuries...... Is 30:26
Look, it has not been **b-d**....... Ezk 30:21
healed the sick, **b-d** the injured .. Ezk 34:4
and **b-d** his wounds,............. Lk 10:34

BANDIT

your need, like a **b**..........Pr 6:11; 24:34

BANISH

plans so that the one **b-ed** from him does
  not remain **b-ed**............. 2Sm 14:14
not **b** me from your presence ......Ps 51:11
nations where I will **b** them....... Ezk 4:13

BANK

put my money in the **b**?..........Lk 19:23

BANNER

The LORD Is My **B**................. Ex 17:15
lift the **b** in the name of our God ..Ps 20:5
as an army with **b-s**............. Sg 6:4,10

BANQUET

the king held a week-long **b** .... Est 1:5
He brought me to the **b** hall,.......Sg 2:4
love the place of honor at **b-s**, ... Mt 23:6
a **b**, invite those who are poor, ... Lk 14:13

BAPTISM

Sadducees coming to his **b**, ... Mt 3:7
proclaiming a **b** of repentance ..... Mk 1:4
with the **b** I am baptized with?... Mk 10:38
baptized with John's **b**............Lk 7:29
I have a **b** to undergo,...........Lk 12:50
he knew only John's **b**............ Ac 18:25
we were buried with him by **b** .....Rm 6:4
one Lord, one faith, one **b**, ... Eph 4:5
buried with him in **b,**............. Col 2:12
B ... now saves you 1Pt 3:21

BAPTIST

In those days John the **B** came,.....Mt 3:1
Give me John the **B-'s** head...... Mt 14:8
Some say John the **B**; ....Mt 16:14
John the **B** sent us to ask you,.....Lk 7:20

BAPTIZE

I **b** you with water for............Mt 3:11
b-ing them in the name of ...... Mt 28:19
to be **b-d** with the baptism I ..... Mk 10:38
and is **b-d** will be saved,....... Mk 16:16
Tax collectors also came to be **b-d**, .. Lk 3:12
Jesus also was **b-d**................ Lk 3:21
b-ing more disciples than John...... Jn 4:1
will be **b-d** with the Holy Spirit ..... Ac 1:5
Repent and be **b-d**,..............Ac 2:38
there's water. What would keep
  me from being **b-d**?............Ac 8:36
who were **b-d** into Christ Jesus
  were **b-d** into his death?.......Rm 6:3
Christ did not send me to **b**, but ...1Co 1:17
all were **b-d** into Moses 1Co 10:2
we were all **b-d** by one Spirit 1Co 12:13
are being **b-d** for the dead? 1Co 15:29

BARABBAS

Insurrectionist released by Pilate instead
of Jesus (Mt 27:16–26; Mk 15:7–15; Lk 23:18;
Jn 18:40).

BARAK

Reluctantly joined Deborah to fight Canaanites (Jdg 4–5; 1Sm 12:11; Heb 11:32).

BARBARIAN

obligated both to Greeks and **b-s**,...Rm 1:14
b, Scythian, slave and free; ....Col 3:11

BAREFOOT

he did that, going stripped and **b**... Is 20:2

BARK

peeled the **b**, exposing white .... Gn 30:37

BARLEY

a loaf of **b** bread came tumbling .. Jdg 7:13
five **b** loaves and two fish ....Jn 6:9

BARN

sow or reap or gather into **b-s**,.... Mt 6:26
but collect the wheat in my **b**. ... Mt 13:30
I'll tear down my **b-s** and build.... Lk 12:18

BARNABAS

Levite from Cyprus, named Joseph (Ac 4:36).
Introduced Paul to Jerusalem church (9:26–
27). Worked with Paul, initially as leader in
Antioch (11:19–30), then on a journey (Ac
13–14), then in Jerusalem (15:1–21). Separated from Paul over whether to bring John
Mark with them again (15:36–41).

BARTHOLOMEW

Apostle (Mt 10:3; Mk 3:18; Lk 6:14; Ac 1:13),
possibly also called Nathanael (Jn 1:43–51).

BARUCH

Jeremiah's scribe (Jr 36).

BASED

not be **b** on human wisdom........1Co 2:5
the law is not **b** on faith; ....Gl 3:12

righteousness from God **b** on faith. ..Php 3:9
b on the testimony of two...... Heb 10:28
b on what seemed good to
  them...................... .Heb 12:10

BASHAN

the rest of Gilead and all **B**, ... Dt 3:13
strong ones of **B** encircle me. ..... Ps 22:12
against all the oaks of **B**, ... Is 2:13
you cows of **B**................... Am 4:1

BASIN

Make a bronze **b** for washing .... Ex 30:18
he made ten bronze **b-s** 1Kg 7:38
poured water into a **b** and
  began to...................... Jn 13:5

BASKET

Three **b-s** ... were on my head. ... Gn 40:16
she got a papyrus **b** for him........Ex 2:3
LORD showed me two **b-s** of figs ....Jr 24:1
A **b** of summer fruit............... Am 8:1
a woman sitting inside the **b**. ..... Zch 5:7
a lamp and puts it under a **b,**......Mt 5:15
they picked up twelve **b-s** full ... Mt 14:20
lowered him in a large **b**..........Ac 9:25

BATCH

holy, so is the whole **b**...........Rm 11:16
a little leaven leavens the whole **b**. . 1Co 5:6

BATHE

he saw a woman **b-ing**..........2Sm 11:2
One who has **b-d**, ... Jn 13:10

BATHSHEBA

Wife of Uriah the Hethite. David committed
adultery with her, then married her (2Sm
11). Solomon's mother (2Sm 12; 1Kg 1–2).

BATTLE

the **b** is the LORD's............... 1Sm 17:47
the **b** is not yours, but God's......2Ch 20:15
He smells the **b** from a distance .. Jb 39:25
clothed me with strength for **b**; .. Ps 18:39
the LORD, mighty in **b**............Ps 24:8
A horse is prepared for ... **b**, ... Pr 21:31
or the **b** to the strong, ... Ec 9:11
nations against Jerusalem for **b**... Zch 14:2
like horses prepared for **b**..........Rv 9:7
the **b** on the great day of God, ... Rv 16:14
Magog, to gather them for **b**...... Rv 20:8

BEAM

b of wood in your own eye? .... Mt 7:3

BEAR (N)

Whenever a lion or a **b** came 1Sm 17:34
two female **b-s** came out....... 2Kg 2:24
to meet a **b** robbed of her cubs ....Pr 17:12
The cow and the **b** will graze, ... Is 11:7
He is a **b** waiting in ambush, ... Lm 3:10
second one, that looked like a **b**.... Dn 7:5

BEAR (V)

b children with painful effort.......Gn 3:16
punishment is too great to **b**! .....Gn 4:13
wife Sarah will **b** you a son,....... Gn 17:19
that **b-s** its fruit in season .... Ps 1:3
a burden too heavy for me to **b**....Ps 38:4
he **b-s** our burdens;.............. Ps 68:19
They will still **b** fruit in old age,.... Ps 92:14
he himself **bore** our sicknesses, ... Is 53:4
yet he **bore** the sin of many .... Is 53:12
"Blessed is the womb that
  bore you ....Lk 11:27
does not **b** his own cross .... Lk 14:27
but you can't **b** them now......... Jn 16:12
that we may **b** fruit for God....... Rm 7:4
b the weaknesses of those....... Rm 15:1
so that you may be able to **b** it. .. 1Co 10:13
b all things, believes all.......... 1Co 13:7
b-ing with one another .... Eph 4:2; Col 3:13
offered once to **b** the sins of ..... Heb 9:28

He himself **bore** our sins 1Pt 2:24
tree of life ... **b-ing** twelve kinds . . .Rv 22:2

BEARD

shaved off half their **b-s**, ... 2Sm 10:4
on the **b**, running down Aaron's **b**, . . Ps 133:2

BEAST

Four huge **b-s** came up. . . . . Dn 7:3
b that comes up out of the abyss. . . Rv 11:7
a **b** coming up out of the sea. . . . . . Rv 13:1
calculate the number of the **b**, ... Rv 13:18
who had the mark of the **b** . . . . .Rv 16:2
who accepted the mark of the **b**. . .Rv 19:20

BEAT

gave my back to those who **b** me, . . Is 50:6
will **b** their swords into plows, ... Mc 4:3
they spat in his face and **b** him; . . Mt 26:67
to **b** him, saying, "Prophesy!" . . . Mk 14:65
they stopped **b-ing** Paul. . . . . Ac 21:32
or box like one **b-ing** in the air. 1Co 9:26
Three times I was **b-en** 2Co 11:25

BEATING (N)

by **b-s**, by imprisonments, by riots, . .2Co 6:5

BEAUTIFUL

daughters of mankind were **b**, ... Gn 6:2
know what a **b** woman you are. . . Gn 12:11
Now the girl was very **b**, ... Gn 24:16
Rebekah, for she is a **b** woman. . . . Gn 26:7
but Rachel was shapely and **b**. . . .Gn 29:17
when she saw that he was **b**, ...Ex 2:2
woman was intelligent and **b**, . . . 1Sm 25:3
Let a search be made for **b** young . Est 2:2
praise from the upright is **b**. . . . . . . Ps 33:1
How **b** you are, my darling. . . . Sg 1:15; 4:1
How **b** on the mountains are. . . . . . . .Is 52:7
which appear **b** on the outside, . . Mt 23:27
used to sit and beg at the **B** Gate. . . Ac 3:10

BEAUTY

gazing on the **b** of the LORD . . . . . . Ps 27:4
Zion, the perfection of **b**, ...Ps 50:2
Don't lust in your heart for her **b** . . . Pr 6:25
is deceptive and **b** is fleeting, ... Pr 31:30
a crown of **b** instead of ashes, ...Is 61:3
you declared: I am perfect in **b**. . . . Ezk 27:3
b consist of outward things. 1Pt 3:3

BED

on my **b**, I meditate on you . . . . Ps 63:6
if I make my **b** in Sheol, ... Ps 139:8
prepare evil plans on their **b-s**! . . . . . Mc 2:1
under a basket or under a **b**?. . . . . . Mk 4:21
I have gone to **b**. I can't get up . . . . .Lk 11:7
be in one **b**: one will be taken . . . . . Lk 17:34
the marriage **b** kept undefiled, . . . Heb 13:4

BEE

b-s with honey in the carcass. . . . . . Jdg 14:8

BEELZEBUL

if I drive out demons by **B**, ...Mt 12:27

BEER

he is to abstain from wine and **b**. . . . Nm 6:3
eat food or drink wine or **b** . . . . Dt 29:6
Wine is a mocker, **b** is a brawler, ... Pr 20:1
or for rulers to desire **b**. . . . . Pr 31:4
Give **b** to one who is dying . . . . Pr 31:6
in the morning in pursuit of **b**, ... Is 5:11
who are champions at pouring **b**, . . Is 5:22
they stagger, but not with **b**. . . . . . Is 29:9
preach to you about wine and **b**, . . .Mc 2:11
will never drink wine or **b**. . . . . Lk 1:15

BEER-SHEBA

place was called **B** because . . . . . . Gn 21:31
Abraham settled in **B**. . . . . .Gn 22:19
All the Israelites from Dan to **B** . . . .Jdg 20:1
throne of David ... from
Dan to **B**. 2Sm 3:10

BEFORE

B a word is on my tongue, ... Ps 139:4
No god was formed **b** me, ...Is 43:10
Even **b** they call, I will answer; . . . . Is 65:24
messenger ... clear the way **b** me. . . Mal 3:1
Father knows ... **b** you ask him. . . . . . Mt 6:8
B the rooster crows twice, ... Mk 14:72
B Philip called you, ... Jn 1:48
B Abraham was, I am. . . . . .Jn 8:58
For the joy that lay **b** him. . . . . . . .Heb 12:2

BEG

At that time I **b-ged** the LORD: . . .Dt 3:23
or his children **b-ging** for bread . . . Ps 37:25
b-ging him, 'Be patient
  with me . . . . Mt 18:29
I'm ashamed to **b**. . . . . Lk 16:3
the one who used to sit **b-ging**? . . . Jn 9:8

BEGGAR

a blind **b**, was sitting by . . . . Mk 10:46
who had seen him before as a **b** . . . . Jn 9:8

BEGINNING

In the **b** God created the heavens. . . . Gn 1:1
of the LORD is the **b** of wisdom; . . Ps 111:10
of the LORD is the **b** of knowledge; . . Pr 1:7
The LORD acquired me at the **b** . . . . . Pr 8:22
of the LORD is the **b** of wisdom, . . . Pr 9:10
of a matter is better than its **b**; . . . . Ec 7:8
I declare the end from the **b**, ... Is 46:10
The **b** of the gospel of Jesus . . . . . .Mk 1:1
In the **b** was the Word, ... Jn 1:1
What was from the **b**, ...1Jn 1:1
as you have heard it from the **b**: 2Jn 6
Omega, the **b** and the end. . . . . . .Rv 21:6

BEHEADED

had John **b** in the prison. . . . . .Mt 14:10
"I **b** John," Herod said, ...Lk 9:9
b because of their testimony. . . . . . Rv 20:4

BEHEMOTH

Look at **B**, which I made . . . . .Jb 40:15

BEHIND

told Peter, "Get **b** me, Satan! . . . . Mt 16:23
Forgetting what is **b** . . . . Php 3:13

BEING

the man became a living **b**. . . . . . . .Gn 2:7
Adam became a living **b**; 1Co 15:45

BELIEVE

Abram **b-d** the LORD, ...Gn 15:6
they did not **b** God or rely on . . . . Ps 78:22
inexperienced one **b-s** anything, . . Pr 14:15
one who **b-s** will be unshakable. . . .Is 28:16
Who has **b-d** what we have heard? . . Is 53:1
Do you **b** that I can do this?. . . . . . Mt 9:28
of these little ones who **b** in me. . . Mt 18:6
if you **b**, you will receive. . . . . Mt 21:22
or, 'Over here!' do not **b** it!. . . . . . . Mt 24:23
Repent and **b** the good news!. . . . . Mk 1:15
I do **b**; help my unbelief!" . . . . Mk 9:24
not doubt in his heart, but **b-s** . . . .Mk 11:23
Don't be afraid. Only **b**, ...Lk 8:50
slow to **b** all that the prophets . . . Lk 24:25
so that all might **b** through him. . . . Jn 1:7
so that everyone who **b-s** in him . . . Jn 3:16
if you **b-d** Moses, you would **b** . . . Jn 5:46
you **b** in the one he has sent. . . . . .Jn 6:29
b-s in me will ever be thirsty. . . . . . Jn 6:35
who sees the Son and **b-s** in him . . Jn 6:40
Anyone who **b-s** has eternal life. . . Jn 6:47
who **b-s** in me, as the Scripture . . . Jn 7:38
you don't **b** me, **b** the works. . . . . Jn 10:38
b-s in me will never die . . . . Jn 11:26
Lord, who has **b-d** our message? . Jn 12:38
B in God; **b** also in me. . . . . Jn 14:1
B me that I am in the Father . . . . . Jn 14:11
By this we **b** that you came. . . . . . . Jn 16:30
world may **b** you sent me. . . . . Jn 17:21
went in, saw, and **b-d**. . . . . Jn 20:8

seen me, you have **b-d**. Blessed are those
  who have not seen and yet **b**. . . . Jn 20:29
written so that you may **b** . . . . Jn 20:31
by **b-ing** you may have life . . . . . . Jn 20:31
appointed to eternal life **b-d**. . . . . Ac 13:48
B in the Lord Jesus, ... Ac 16:31
but others did not **b**. . . . . .Ac 28:24
salvation to everyone who **b-s**, ... Rm 1:16
in Jesus Christ, to all who **b**, ... Rm 3:22
Abraham **b-d** God, and it was . . . . . . Rm 4:3
the father of all who **b** . . . . Rm 4:11
b in your heart that God raised. . . . Rm 10:9
b-s with the heart, resulting in. . . Rm 10:10
call on him they have not **b-d** in? . Rm 10:14
And how can they **b** without . . . . Rm 10:14
who has **b-d** our message? . . . . . . Rm 10:16
b-s all things, hopes all things, ... 1Co 13:7
unless you **b-d** for no purpose. 1Co 15:2
I **b-d**, therefore I spoke, ... 2Co 4:13
just like Abraham who **b-d** God, ... Gl 3:6
if we **b** that Jesus died and 1Th 4:14
b-d on in the world, taken up 1Tm 3:16
especially of those who **b**. 1Tm 4:10
must **b** that he exists . . . . Heb 11:6
You **b** that God is one, ... Even the
  demons **b**. . . . . Jms 2:19
Abraham **b-d** God, and it was . . . . .Jms 2:23
not seeing him now, you **b**. 1Pt 1:8
do not **b** every spirit, but test 1Jn 4:1
Everyone who **b-s** that Jesus is
  the Christ has been born of God, . . .1Jn 5:1

BELIEVER

intended as a sign, not for **b-s** . . . 1Co 14:22
what does a **b** have in common . . . 2Co 6:15
an example to all the **b-s** 1Th 1:7

BELLY

move on your **b** and eat dust . . . . .Gn 3:14
For as Jonah was in the **b** of . . . . Mt 12:40

BELONG

that **b-s** to your neighbor. . . . . Ex 20:17
hidden things **b** to the LORD our God,
  but the revealed things **b** . . . . Dt 29:29
under heaven **b-s** to me. . . . . Jb 41:11
Salvation **b-s** to the LORD; . . . . Ps 3:8
kingship **b-s** to the LORD; . . . . Ps 22:28
the leaders of the earth **b** to God; . .Ps 47:9
for all the nations **b** to you. . . . . . . Ps 82:8
Look, every life **b-s** to me. . . . . . . Ezk 18:4
forgiveness **b** to the Lord our God . . Dn 9:9
you may **b** to another. . . . . Rm 7:4
to them **b** the adoption, the glory . Rm 9:4
we live or die, we **b** to the Lord. . . . Rm 14:8
you **b** to Christ, and Christ **b-s** to . . 1Co 3:23
I don't **b** to the body, ... 1Co 12:15
if they had **b-ed** to us, they would
  have remained with us. 1Jn 2:19
Salvation **b-s** to our God, ... Rv 7:10

BELOVED

The LORD's **b** rests securely. . . . . . . .Dt 33:12
This is my **b** Son, with whom I am . .Mt 3:17
my **b** in whom my **I** delight; . . . . . .Mt 12:18
I will send my **b** son. . . . . Lk 20:13
This is my **b** Son, with whom. 2Pt 1:17

BELSHAZZAR

King of Babylon (Dn 5; 7:1; 8:1).

BELT

his sword, his bow, and his **b**. 1Sm 18:4
a leather **b** around his waist. 2Kg 1:8
with a leather **b** around his waist, . . Mt 3:4
took Paul's **b**, tied his own feet. . . . .Ac 21:11
with truth like a **b** around your. . . . Eph 6:14

BELTESHAZZAR

Daniel's Babylonian name (Dn 1:7).

BENAIAH

Heroic warrior in charge of David's bodyguard (2Sm 8:18; 20:23; 23:20–23). Loyal to

Solomon (1Kg 1; 4:4); executed Adonijah, Joab, and Shimei (2:25–46).

BENEFICIAL
but godliness is **b** in every way, . . . 1Tm 4:8

BENEFIT
and do not forget all his **b-s**....... Ps 103:2
What will it **b** someone if
  he gains .... Mt 16:26
you have **b-ed** from their labor..... Jn 4:38
It is for your **b** that I go away,...... Jn 16:7
what is the **b** of circumcision?..... Rm 3:1
Christ will not **b** you at all.......... Gl 5:2

BEN-HADAD
1. King of Aram in Asa's time (1Kg 15:18–20; 2Ch 16:2–4).
2. King of Aram from Ahab's time (1Kg 20; 2Kg 6:24; 8:7–13).
3. King of Aram in Jehoash's time (2Kg 13:24–25).

BENJAMIN
Second son of Rachel, twelfth son of Jacob (Gn 35:17–18,24). Tribe with the smallest territory; Jerusalem may have originally been in it (Jos 18:16; Jdg 1:21). Nearly wiped out (Jdg 20–21). Saul and Paul were Benjaminites (1Sm 9:1; Rm 11:1; Php 3:5).

BEREA
sent Paul and Silas away to **B**...... Ac 17:10

BERNICE
Wife of Agrippa (Ac 25:13,23; 26:30).

BESIDES
not have other gods **b** me... .Ex 20:3; Dt 5:7
no Savior exists **b** me............... Hs 13:4

BEST
He chose the **b** part for himself, . . . Dt 33:21
spared ... the **b** of the sheep,......1Sm 15:9

BETHANY
to **B**, and spent the night there....Mt 21:17
He led them to the vicinity of **B**,. .Lk 24:50
in **B** ... where John was baptizing.... Jn 1:28
Lazarus from **B**,.....................Jn 11:1
came to **B** where Lazarus was,...... Jn 12:1

BETHEL
east of **B** and pitched his tent, ...Gn 12:8
and named the place **B**, ... Gn 28:19
He set up one in **B**,.............1Kg 12:29

BETHLEHEM
B Ephrathah, you are small .... Mc 5:2
After Jesus was born in **B**...........Mt 2:1
city of David, which is called **B**,......Lk 2:4
Let's go straight to **B** and see ......Lk 2:15

BETRAY
have finished **b-ing**, they will **b** you...Is 33:1
Brother will **b** brother to death, ...Mt 10:21
a good opportunity to **b** him. ..... Mt 26:16
One of you will **b** me. .... Mt 26:21
that man by whom he is **b-ed**!....Lk 22:22
b-ing the Son of Man with
  a kiss?........................Lk 22:48
He knew who would **b** him.........Jn 13:11
the night when he was **b-ed**, ...1Co 11:23

BETTER
to obey is **b** than sacrifice,.......1Sm 15:22
Your faithful love is **b** than life......Ps 63:3
B a little with the fear of .... Pr 15:16
B a meal of vegetables where.....Pr 15:17
B a dry crust with peace...........Pr 17:1
B a poor person ... with integrity ... Pr 19:1
B to live on the corner of a roof ... Pr 21:9
B to live in a wilderness .... Pr 21:19
B an open reprimand.............. Pr 27:5

b a neighbor nearby .... Pr 27:10
nothing **b** for a person than
  to eat,.........................Ec 2:24
B one handful with rest ....Ec 4:6
Two are **b** than one ....Ec 4:9
B that you do not vow ....Ec 5:5
good name is **b** than fine perfume... Ec 7:1
The end of a matter is **b** than ....Ec 7:8
a live dog is **b** than a dead lion. .....Ec 9:4
Your caresses are much **b** than wine,.. Sg 4:10
it is **b** that you lose one of the
  parts ....Mt 5:29
for him if a heavy millstone ..... Mt 18:6
Are we any **b** off? Not at all!.......Rm 3:9
it is **b** to marry than to burn 1Co 7:9
we are not **b** if we do eat. 1Co 8:8
I will show you an even **b** way. ... 1Co 12:31
be with Christ—which is far **b** ....Php 1:23
confident of things that are **b**.....Heb 6:9
the guarantee of a **b** covenant.....Heb 7:22
to be purified with **b** sacrifices ... Heb 9:23
it is **b** to suffer for doing good,.....1Pt 3:17

BETWEEN
hostility **b** you and the woman, and **b**
  your offspring and her offspring. .Gn 3:15
torch ... **b** the divided animals. .... Gn 15:17
the LORD judge **b** me and you.....Gn 16:5
and to discern **b** good and evil....1Kg 3:9
passed **b** the pieces of the calf .... Jr 34:19
lifted me up **b** earth and heaven .... Ezk 8:3
you murdered **b** the sanctuary ... Mt 23:35
distinction **b** Jew and Greek, ... Rm 10:12
one mediator **b** God and mankind, . . 1Tm 2:5

BEWARE
b of the leaven of the Pharisees ... Mt 16:6
B of the scribes ... in long robes ...Lk 20:46

BEYOND
not too difficult or **b** your reach. . . Dt 30:11
b these, my son, be warned: ...... Ec 12:12
Nothing **b** what is written..........1Co 4:6
tempted **b** what you are able,.....1Co 10:13
able to do above and **b** all .... Eph 3:20
in Christ's teaching, but goes **b** it, ... 2Jn 9

BILHAH
Rachel's slave, mother of Dan and Naphtali (Gn 30:1–7).

BIND
He **bound** his son Isaac............ Gn 22:9
her vows are **b-ing**,................Nm 30:7
B them as a sign on your hand ..... Dt 6:8
b them as a sign on your hands,... Dt 11:18
Always **b** them to your heart; ...... Pr 6:21
B up the testimony.................Is 8:16
and he will **b** up our wounds. ....Hs 6:1
Whatever you **b** on earth is already
  bound in heaven,........ Mt 16:19; 18:18
I am ready not only to be **bound** . . Ac 21:13
A wife is **bound** as long as........1Co 7:39
but the word God is not **bound**.... 2Tm 2:9
and **bound** him for a thousand
  years.. .... Rv 20:2

BIRD
You may eat every clean **b**, ... Dt 14:11
b-s of the sky, and the fish of
  the sea ....Ps 8:8
in its branches the **b-s** of the sky ...Dn 4:21
Consider the **b-s** of the sky:...... Mt 6:26
b-s of the sky have nests, but..... Mt 8:20
the **b-s** came and devoured them... Mt 13:4
worth much more than the **b-s**?... Lk 12:24

BIRTH
the Rock who gave you **b**;........Dt 32:18
a time to give **b** and a time to die;... Ec 3:2
to a stone, "You gave **b** to me.".... Jr 2:27
b of Jesus Christ came about....... Mt 1:18
she gave **b** to her firstborn son, ... Lk 2:7
new **b** into a living hope...........1Pt 1:3

BIRTHDAY
Herod's **b** celebration came,....... Mt 14:6

BIRTHRIGHT
First sell me your **b**................Gn 25:31
b in exchange for a single meal. ..Heb 12:16

BIT
put **b-s** into the mouths of horses. . Jms 3:3

BITE
anyone who is **bitten** looks at it,... Nm 21:8
If the snake **b-s** like a snake ...... Pr 23:32
If the snake **b-s** before it is ....Ec 10:11
if you **b** and devour one another,... Gl 5:15

BITTER
and made their lives **b** .... Ex 1:14
unleavened bread and **b** herbs...... Ex 12:8
water at Marah because it was **b** . . Ex 15:23
in the end she's as **b** as wormwood .. Pr 5:4
woe to one whose life is **b**......... Is 21:6
who substitute **b** for sweet .... Is 5:20
pour out sweet and **b** water ...... Jms 3:11

BITTERNESS
The heart knows its own **b**, ... Pr 14:10
All **b**, anger and wrath, ...Eph 4:31
that no root of **b** springs up, ...Heb 12:15

BLACK
the second chariot **b** horses, ...Zch 6:2
make a single hair white or **b**...... Mt 5:36
I looked, and there was a **b** horse.... Rv 6:5
the sun turned **b** like sackcloth .....Rv 6:12

BLAMELESS
b you prove yourself **b**,........ 2Sm 22:26
happy are those whose way is **b**, ..Ps 119:1
b in the day of our Lord Jesus 1Co 1:8
to be holy and **b** in love before
  him ....Eph 1:4
so that you may be **b** and pure, ...Php 2:15
in the law, **b**.......................Php 3:6
May he make your hearts **b** 1Th 3:13
body be kept sound and **b** 1Th 5:23
b, the husband of one wife,........ Ti 1:6

BLASPHEME
my name is continually **b-d**........Is 52:5
He has **b-d**!..................... Mt 26:65
He's **b-ing**! Who can forgive sins ... Mk 2:7
b-s against the Holy Spirit........ Mk 3:29
tried to make them **b** .... Ac 26:11
God is **b-d** among the Gentiles ....Rm 2:24
they may be taught not to **b**......1Tm 1:20

BLASPHEMER
I was formerly a **b**,................1Tm 1:13

BLASPHEMOUS
We heard him speaking **b** words... Ac 6:11
and on its heads were **b** names..... Rv 13:1

BLASPHEMY
b against the Spirit will not .... Mt 12:31
you've heard the **b**............... Mt 26:65
stoning you ... for **b**,............. Jn 10:33
to utter boasts and **b-ies**..........Rv 13:5

BLAZE
fire from the LORD **b-d** among .....Nm 11:1
mountain was **b-ing** with fire...... Dt 5:23
in the morning it **b-s** like ....Hs 7:6

BLAZING (ADJ)
into the furnace of **b** fire.......... Dn 3:20

BLEMISH
he is to present one without **b** ..... Lv 3:1
offered himself without **b** to
  God,.........................Heb 9:14
b in his sight, at peace, ...2Pt 3:14
b and with great joy,.............. Jd 24

BLESS

God **b-ed** them: "Be fruitful,......Gn 1:22
God **b-ed** the seventh day.........Gn 2:3
I will **b** you, ...Gn 12:2
I will **b** her; indeed, ...Gn 17:16
b you and make your offspring..Gn 22:17
B me too, my father!............Gn 27:34
let you go unless you **b** me.......Gn 32:26
LORD **b-ed** the Sabbath day......Ex 20:11
LORD **b** you and protect you; .....Nm 6:24
since he has **b-ed**, I cannot ......Nm 23:20
they curse, you will **b**...........Ps 109:28
A generous person will be **b-ed**,...Pr 22:9
b-es his neighbor with a loud......Pr 27:14
the nations will be **b-ed** by him ... Jr 4:2
from this day on I will **b** you......Hg 2:19
took bread, **b-ed** and broke it, ...Mt 26:26
he **b-ed** and broke the loaves. ...Mk 6:41
hands on them and **b-ed** them. .. Mk 10:16
b those who curse you,..........Lk 6:28
families of the earth will be **b-ed**...Ac 3:25
B those who persecute you; **b**.. Rm 12:14
When we are reviled, we **b**;.....1Co 4:12
nations will be **b-ed** through you.. Gl 3:8
has **b-ed** us with every spiritual... Eph 1:3
inferior is **b-ed** by the superior. ... Heb 7:7

BLESSED (ADJ)

You will be **b** in the city and **b** in the
country........................Dt 28:3
May you be **b** by the LORD, ...Ps 115:15
He who comes in the name of
the LORD is **b**................Ps 118:26
Let your fountain be **b**,...........Pr 5:18
children rise up and call her **b**......Pr 31:28
who trusts in the LORD... is **b**.....Jr 17:7
B are the poor in spirit,...........Mt 5:3
B is he who comes in the name of.. Mt 21:9
B are you among women, ...Lk 1:42
B are those who have not seen
and ....Jn 20:29
more **b** to give than to receive....Ac 20:35
while we wait for the **b** hope ....Ti 2:13
B is the one who endures trials, ... Jms 1:12
for righteousness, you are **b**......1Pt 3:14
B is the one who reads aloud the words of
this prophecy, and **b** are those..... Rv 1:3
B is the one who keeps the words
of the prophecy of this book. ....Rv 22:7

BLESSING (N)

you will be a **b**..................Gn 12:2
deceitfully and took your **b**. ......Gn 27:35
set before you a **b** and a curse:... Dt 11:26
He turned the curse into a **b** ......Dt 23:5
these **b-s** will come and overtake. .Dt 28:2
God turned the curse into a **b**. ...Neh 13:2
May the LORD's **b** be on you. ......Ps 129:8
B-s are on the head of the
righteous,.....................Pr 10:6
send down ... showers of **b**.....Ezk 34:26
pour out a **b** for you ....Mal 3:10
cup of **b** that we bless, ...1Co 10:16
b of Abraham ... to the Gentiles .. Gl 3:14
blessed us with every spiritual **b** ...Eph 1:3
so that you may inherit a **b** 1Pt 3:9
and honor and glory and **b**!......Rv 5:12

BLIND (ADJ)

mute or deaf, seeing or **b**?........ Ex 4:11
When you present a **b** animal ....Mal 1:8
Woe to you, **b** guides, ...Mt 23:16
a **b** beggar, was sitting ....Mk 10:46
I was **b**, and now I can see! ....Jn 9:25
are wretched, pitiful, poor, **b**, ...Rv 3:17

BLIND (N)

block in front of the **b**, ...Lv 19:14
I was eyes to the **b**...............Jb 29:15
LORD opens the eyes of the **b**......Ps 146:8
the eyes of the **b** will be opened,...Is 35:5
the **b** receive their sight, the lame ..Mt 11:5
Can the **b** guide the **b**?...........Lk 6:39
you are a guide for the **b**,.........Rm 2:19

BLIND (V)

a bribe **b-s** the clear-sighted......Ex 23:8
king of Babylon **b-ed** Zedekiah, ...2Kg 25:7
deafen their ears and **b** their eyes;.. Is 6:10
He has **b-ed** their eyes ....Jn 12:40
the god of this age has **b-ed**......2Co 4:4
the darkness has **b-ed** his eyes. ...1Jn 2:11

BLOCK

I will bow down to a **b** of wood? .. Is 44:19
became a sinful stumbling **b** .....Ezk 44:12
Christ crucified, a stumbling **b**. ...1Co 1:23

BLOOD

Your brother's **b** cries out to me ... Gn 4:10
Whoever sheds human **b**, by humans
his **b** will be shed,..............Gn 9:6
You are a bridegroom of **b** ....Ex 4:25
Nile ... will turn to **b**. ....Ex 7:17
see the **b**, I will pass over you......Ex 12:13
This is the **b** of the covenant......Ex 24:8
must not eat any fat or any **b**. .....Lv 3:17
life of a creature is in the **b**, ...Lv 17:11
a man of war and have shed **b**....1Ch 28:3
or drink the **b** of goats? ....Ps 50:13
land became polluted with **b**.....Ps 106:38
I have no desire for the **b** of bulls, ... Is 1:11
hold you responsible for his **b**, ...Ezk 3:18
moon to **b** before the great........Jl 2:31
flesh and **b** did not reveal this....Mt 16:17
this is my **b** ... the covenant;.....Mt 26:28
field has been called "Field of **B**" .. Mt 27:8
sweat became like drops of **b** ....Lk 22:44
who were born, not of **b**, ...Jn 1:13
and drinks my **b** has eternal life,....Jn 6:54
Hakeldama (that is, "Field of **B**").... Ac 1:19
and the moon to **b** before the
great..........................Ac 2:20
been strangled, and from **b**. ......Ac 15:20
as the mercy seat by his **b**,.......Rm 3:25
justified by his **b**, ...Rm 5:9
is it not a sharing in the **b** 1Co 10:16
covenant in my **b**, ...1Co 11:25
Flesh and **b** cannot inherit 1Co 15:50
redemption through his **b**,........Eph 1:7
brought near by the **b**............Eph 2:13
struggle is not against flesh
and **b**,........................Eph 6:12
by making peace through the **b** ... Col 1:20
not by the **b** of goats and calves,
but by his own **b**, ...Heb 9:12
without ... **b** there is no
forgiveness ....Heb 9:22
with the precious **b** of Christ, ...1Pt 1:19
b of Jesus his Son cleanses us 1Jn 1:7
one who came by water and **b**,....1Jn 5:6
set us free from our sins by his **b**,...Rv 1:5
purchased people ... by your **b** .....Rv 5:9
the entire moon became like **b**;....Rv 6:12
made them white in the **b** ....Rv 7:14
a third of the sea became **b**, ...Rv 8:8
conquered ... by the **b** of the
Lamb ....Rv 12:11
He wore a robe dipped in **b**,......Rv 19:13

BLOODSHED

no one is guilty of **b**...............Ex 22:2
b defiles the land, ...Nm 35:33
responsibility for **b** will be wiped ...Dt 21:8
Save me from the guilt of **b**, ...Ps 51:14

BLOSSOM (N)

cups shaped like almond **b-s**, ...Ex 25:33
has budded, if the **b** has opened,...Sg 7:12
their **b-s** will blow away like dust,.. Is 5:24

BLOSSOM (V)

sprouted, formed buds, **b-ed**,.....Nm 17:8
the almond tree **b-s**,.............Ec 12:5
Jacob will take root. Israel will **b**... Is 27:6

BLOT

I will destroy them and **b** out ......Dt 9:14
b out all my guilt. ....Ps 51:9

BLOW

B the ram's horn in Zion; sound the.. Jl 2:1
blew and pounded that house.... Mt 7:25
The wind **b-s** where it pleases, ...Jn 3:8
b-n around by every wind ....Eph 4:14
seven trumpets prepared to
b them. ....Rv 8:6

BOAST

who puts on his armor **b** like 1Kg 20:11
I will **b** in the LORD; ....Ps 34:2
We **b** in God all day long; ....Ps 44:8
The one who **b-s** about a gift ..... Pr 25:14
Don't **b** about tomorrow, ... Pr 27:1
wise man should not **b** in his
wisdom; ....Jr 9:23
the one who **b-s** should **b** in this:... Jr 9:24
You who **b** in the law, ...Rm 2:23
one who **b-s**, **b** in the Lord. 1Co 1:31
give over my body in order to **b** ...1Co 13:3
gladly **b** ... about my weaknesses, ..2Co 12:9
b about anything except the cross.. Gl 6:14
so that no one can **b**.............Eph 2:9
it **b-s** great things................Jms 3:5

BOASTFUL

b cannot stand in your sight;.......Ps 5:5
Love does not envy, is not **b**, ...1Co 13:4

BOAT

they left the **b** and their father.... Mt 4:22
the **b** was being swamped........Mt 8:24
climbing out of the **b**, Peter......Mt 14:29

BOAZ

Husband of Ruth (Ru 4:13), kinsman redeemer (Ru 2:20; 3:1; 4:3–10,16–17). Ancestor
of David (Ru 4:21–22; 1Ch 2:11–12) and Jesus
(Mt 1:5; Lk 3:32).

BODY

one who comes from your own **b**. ..Gn 15:4
He must not go near a dead **b**......Nm 6:6
The eye is the lamp of the **b**......Mt 6:22
Don't fear those who kill the **b** ... Mt 10:28
Take and eat it; this is my **b**. .....Mt 26:26
the temple of his **b**. ....Jn 2:21
let sin reign in your mortal **b**, ...Rm 6:12
rescue me from this **b** of death?...Rm 7:24
present your **b-ies** as a living ......Rm 12:1
absent in the **b**, I am present.......1Co 5:3
b-ies are a part of Christ's **b**? 1Co 6:15
know that your **b** is a temple 1Co 6:19
This is my **b**, which is for you. 1Co 11:24
the **b** is one and has many parts, ..1Co 12:12
sown a natural **b**, raised a
spiritual **b**. 1Co 15:44
away from the **b** and at home with ..2Co 5:8
I bear on my **b** the marks of Jesus... Gl 6:17
There is one **b** and one Spirit—.... Eph 4:4
to build up the **b** of Christ,........Eph 4:12
their wives as their own **b-ies**. .....Eph 5:28
since we are members of his **b**.....Eph 5:30
control his own **b** in holiness 1Th 4:4
spirit, soul, and **b** be kept sound. ...1Th 5:23
bore our sins in his **b** on 1Pt 2:24

BODILY

God's nature dwells **b** in Christ,.....Col 2:9

BOIL (N)

festering **b-s** on people and
animals.......................Ex 9:9
infected Job with terrible **b-s** ....Jb 2:7

BOIL (V)

not **b** a ... goat in ... milk. .. Ex 23:19; Dt 14:21

BOLD

but **b** toward you when absent.... 2Co 10:1
Pray that I might be **b** enough ... Eph 6:20

BOLDLY

to speak the word of God **b**........Ac 4:31

BOLDNESS

In him we have **b** . . . . Eph 3:12
make known with **b**. . . . . Eph 6:19
approach the throne … with **b**, . . . Heb 4:16

BOND

the perfect **b** of unity. . . . . Col 3:14

BONE

This one, at last, is **b** of my **b**. . . . . . Gn 2:23
not break any of its **b-s**. . . . . .Ex 12:46
Joseph's **b-s**, … were buried. . . . . . Jos 24:32
all my **b-s** are disjointed; . . . . Ps 22:14
b-s; not one of them is broken. . . .Ps 34:20
jealousy is rottenness to the **b-s**. . . Pr 14:30
a gentle tongue can break a **b**. . . . Pr 25:15
shut up in my **b-s**. . . . . Jr 20:9
valley; it was full of **b-s**. . . . . Ezk 37:1
the **b-s** came together, to **b**. . . . . Ezk 37:7
are full of **b-s** of the dead . . . . Mt 23:27
Not one of his **b-s** will be. . . . . .Jn 19:36

BOOK

erase me from the **b** you have . . . .Ex 32:32
this **b** of the law and place it. . . . . .Dt 31:26
b of instruction must not depart . . . Jos 1:8
I have found the **b** of the law 2Kg 22:8
Ezra read out of the **b** of the
  law of God every day, ... Neh 8:18
be erased from the **b** of life. . . . . . .Ps 69:28
no end to the making of many **b-s**, . .Ec 12:12
seal the **b** until the time of . . . . .Dn 12:4
that are not written in this **b**. . . . . .Jn 20:30
could contain the **b-s** that . . . . Jn 21:25
whose names are in the **b** of life. . . Php 4:3
written in the Lamb's **b** of life. . . . .Rv 21:27

BORN

cursed the day he was **b**. . . . . Jb 3:1
I was guilty when I was **b**; . . . . Ps 51:5
I was **b** when there were no . . . . . . .Pr 8:24
a child will be **b** for us, ... Is 9:6
LORD called me before I was **b**. . . . . .Is 49:1
I set you apart before you were **b**. . . .Jr 1:5
who has been **b** King of the Jews. . . Mt 2:2
was **b** for you, who is the Messiah, . . Lk 2:11
you must be **b** again. . . . . Jn 3:7
as to one **b** at the wrong time, ... 1Co 15:8
b of a woman, **b** under the law, ... Gl 4:4
was **b** as a result of the flesh, ... Gl 4:23
because you have been **b** again . . . 1Pt 1:23
who loves has been **b** of God 1Jn 4:7

BORROW

When a man **b-s** an animal . . . . . . .Ex 22:14
You will lend to many nations,
  but you will not **b**. . . . . .Dt 28:12
wicked person **b-s** and does not
  repay. . . . . Ps 37:21
the **b-er** is a slave to the lender. . . . Pr 22:7
one who wants to **b** from you. . . . . Mt 5:42

BOUNDARY

move your neighbor's **b** marker, . . . Dt 19:14
he set the **b-ies** of the peoples. . . . .Dt 32:8
when I determined its **b-ies** . . . . . . Jb 38:10
set all the **b-ies** of the earth; . . . . . Ps 74:17
You set a **b** they cannot cross; . . . . Ps 104:9
set the sand as the **b** of the sea,. . . Jr 5:22

BOW (N)

placed my **b** in the clouds, ...Gn 9:13
arms can bend a **b** of bronze. . . . 2Sm 22:35
I do not trust in my **b**, ...Ps 44:6
bent their tongues like their **b-s**; . . . . Jr 9:3

BOW (V)

May … nations **b** in worship
  to you. . . . . Gn 27:29
and **b-ed** down to my sheaf. . . . . . .Gn 37:7
knee that has not **b-ed** to Baal. . . 1Kg 19:18
Come, let's worship and **b** down; . . . Ps 95:6
Every knee will **b** to me, ... Is 45:23
coast and islands … will **b**. . . . . Zph 2:11

every knee will **b** to me, ...Rm 14:11
name of Jesus every knee will **b** . . Php 2:10

BOWL

the gold **b** is broken, ... Ec 12:6
one who dipped his hand with
  me in the **b** . . . . Mt 26:23
the seven **b-s** of God's wrath . . . . . Rv 16:1

BOX

or **b** like one beating the air. 1Co 9:26

BOY

some small **b-s** came out 2Kg 2:23
b here who has five barley loaves . . .Jn 6:9

BOZRAH

Edomite city (Gn 36:33; 1Ch 1:44; Is 34:6; 63:1;
Jr 49:13,22; Am 1:12).

BRANCH

B of the LORD will be beautiful . . . . . . Is 4:2
a **b** from his roots will bear fruit. . . . . Is 11:1
raise up a Righteous **B** for David. . . . Jr 23:5
about to bring my servant, the **B**. . . .Zch 3:8
a man whose name is **B**; . . . . .Zch 6:12
I am the vine; you are the **b-es**. . . . . Jn 15:5
root is holy, so are the **b-es**. . . . . . .Rm 11:16
a wild olive **b**, were grafted in. . . . .Rm 11:17

BRAWLER

Wine is a mocker, beer is a **b**, ... Pr 20:1

BREAD

eat **b** by the sweat of your brow . . .Gn 3:19
Festival of Unleavened **B** . . . . Ex 12:17
B of the Presence on the table . . . .Ex 25:30
man does not live on **b** alone . . . . . . Dt 8:3
You provided **b** from heaven . . . . . Neh 9:15
I trusted, one who ate my **b**, ... Ps 41:9
b eaten secretly is tasty! . . . . Pr 9:17
b on the surface of the waters,. . . . . Ec 11:1
tell these stones to become **b** . . . . . . Mt 4:3
Man must not live on **b** alone . . . . . . Mt 4:4
Give us today our daily **b**. . . . . Mt 6:11
if his son asks him for **b**, ... Mt 7:9
took **b**, blessed and broke it, ... Mt 26:26
one who is dipping **b** with me. . . . Mk 14:20
I am the **b** of life, ... Jn 6:35
breaking of **b**, and to prayers. . . . . .Ac 2:42
the Lord Jesus took **b**, ... 1Co 11:23

BREAK SEE ALSO BROKEN (ADJ)

I will **b** down your strong pride. . . . Lv 26:19
I will never **b** my covenant. . . . . Jdg 2:1
will **b** them with an iron scepter; . . . .Ps 2:9
a gentle tongue can **b** a bone. . . . . . Pr 25:15
three strands is not easily
  broken. . . . . Ec 4:12
He will not **b** a bruised reed, ... Is 42:3
long ago I **broke** your yoke; . . . . Jr 2:20
where thieves don't **b** in and. . . . . . Mt 6:19
He will not **b** a bruised reed, ... Mt 12:20
bread, blessed and **broke** it, ... Mt 26:26
She **broke** the jar and poured it . . . Mk 14:3
Not only was he **b-ing** the
  Sabbath . . . . Jn 5:18
the Scripture cannot be **broken** . . . Jn 10:35
they did not **b** his legs . . . . Jn 19:33
of his bones will be **broken**. . . . . . . Jn 19:36
broke bread from house to house . .Ac 2:46
Branches were **broken** off
  so that . . . . .Rm 11:19
given thanks, **broke** it, ... 1Co 11:24
is guilty of **b-ing** it all. . . . . Jms 2:10
to open the scroll and its seals?. . . . Rv 5:2
war **broke** out in heaven. . . . . .Rv 12:7

BREAKERS

b and your billows swept over me . .Jnh 2:3

BREAST

let her **b-s** always satisfy you; . . . . . Pr 5:19
Your **b-s** are like two fawns, ... Sg 4:5; 7:3

BREATH

breathed the **b** of life into . . . . .Gn 2:7
Remember that my life is but a **b**. . . . Jb 7:7
the **b** entered them, ... Ezk 37:10
gives everyone life and **b** . . . . Ac 17:25
b of life from God entered them, . . .Rv 11:11

BREATHE

b-d the breath of life into . . . . .Gn 2:7
Let everything that **b-s** praise. . . . . Ps 150:6
b into these slain so that they. . . . . Ezk 37:9
a loud cry and **b-d** his last. . . . . Mk 15:37
He **b-d** on them and said, ...Jn 20:22

BRIBE

not take a **b**, for a **b** blinds. . . . . . . .Ex 23:8
no partiality and taking no **b**. . . . . . Dt 10:17
Do not accept a **b**, for it blinds . . . . Dt 16:19
the one who hates **b-s** will live. . . . . Pr 15:27
a **b** corrupts the mind.. . . . . Ec 7:7
love graft and chase after **b-s**. . . . . . Is 1:23

BRICK

They used **b** for stone. . . . . Gn 11:3
require the same quota of **b-s** . . . . . .Ex 5:8

BRIDE

rejoices over his **b**, so your God. . . . Is 62:5
I will remove … the voices of the
  groom and the **b**, ... Jr 7:34
the **b** her honeymoon chamber. . . . .Jl 2:16
He who has the **b** is the groom. . . . . Jn 3:29
the **b**, the wife of the Lamb. . . . . . . .Rv 21:9

BRIDEGROOM SEE ALSO GROOM

You are a **b** of blood to me! . . . . . . .Ex 4:25

BRIGHT

B eyes cheer the heart; . . . . Pr 15:30
suddenly a **b** cloud covered . . . . . . .Mt 17:5
dressed in pure, **b** linen, ...Rv 15:6
the **b** morning star. . . . . Rv 22:16

BRIGHTER

shining **b** and **b** until midday. . . . . . Pr 4:18

BRILLIANCE

I did not come with **b** of speech . . . 1Co 2:1

BRING

brought each to the man to see . . .Gn 2:19
b into the ark two of all . . . . Gn 6:19
LORD who **brought** you from Ur. . . . Gn 15:7
I **brought** you out of Egypt. . . . . Jdg 2:1
LORD **b-s** death and gives life; 1Sm 2:6
b an offering and enter . . . . Ps 96:8
don't know what a day might **b**. . . . . Pr 27:1
I **brought** you from the ends of . . . .Is 41:9
B my sons from far away, ... Is 43:6
I have spoken; so I will also **b** it. . . . Is 46:11
anointed me to **b** good news . . . . . . Is 61:1
about to **b** a sword against you, ...Ezk 6:3
will **b** you into your own land. . . . . .Ezk 36:24
B the full tenth into the
  storehouse. . . . . Mal 3:10
I did not come to **b** peace,
  but. . . . . Mt 10:34
brought to him all who
  were sick. . . . . Mt 14:35
I came to **b** fire on the earth,. . . . . . Lk 12:49
b in here the poor, maimed,. . . . . . . Lk 14:21
feet of those who **b**
  good news. . . . . Rm 10:15
more will their fullness **b**!. . . . . .Rm 11:12
b them up in the training and. . . . . Eph 6:4
brought nothing into the world, . . . 1Tm 6:7

BROAD

b that leads to destruction, ...Mt 7:13

BROKEN (ADJ) SEE ALSO BREAK

sacrifice pleasing to God is a **b** spirit.
  You will not despise a **b** and
  humbled heart, God. . . . . Ps 51:17

BROKENHEARTED

The LORD is near the **b**; . . . . Ps 34:18
He heals the **b** and bandages . . . . . Ps 147:3
He has sent me to heal the **b**, ... Is 61:1

BRONZE

So Moses made a **b** snake. . . . . Nm 21:9
The sky above you will be **b**, ... Dt 28:23
my arms can bend a bow of **b**. . . 2Sm 22:35
a third kingdom, of **b**, ... Dn 2:39

BROOD

B of vipers! Who warned you . . . . . . Mt 3:7

BROTHER

Am I my **b-'s** guardian?. . . . . Gn 4:9
His **b-s** were jealous of him, ... Gn 37:11
When **b-s** ... and one of them
  dies without a son, ... Dt 25:5
good when **b-s** live together. . . . . . Ps 133:1
a **b** is born for a difficult time. . . . . . Pr 17:17
offended **b** is harder to reach . . . . Pr 18:19
friend who stays closer than a **b**. . . Pr 18:24
be reconciled with your **b**, ... Mt 5:24
B will betray **b** to death, ... Mt 10:21
If your **b** sins against you, ... Mt 18:15
Whoever does the will of God
  is my **b** and sister and mother. . . . Mk 3:35
no one who has left house or **b-s** . . Mk 10:29
b of yours was dead and is alive. . . Lk 15:32
my **b-s** ... my own flesh and blood. . . Rm 9:3
b goes to court against **b**, ... 1Co 6:6
if food causes my **b** to fall, ... 1Co 8:13
but warn him as a **b**. 2Th 3:15
not ashamed to call them **b-s**, ... Heb 2:11
the one who hates his **b** is in
  the darkness, ... 1Jn 2:11
lay down our lives for our **b-s**. 1Jn 3:16

BROTHER-IN-LAW

Perform your duty as her **b** . . . . . . Gn 38:8
Her **b** is to take her as his wife, ... Dt 25:5

BROTHERLY

show sincere **b** love for each , ... 1Pt 1:22

BRUISED

He will not break a **b** reed, . . Is 42:3; Mt 12:20

BUD

let's see if the vine has **b-ded**, ... Sg 7:12
Though the fig tree does not **b**. . . . Hab 3:17

BUILD

let's **b** ourselves a city. . . . . Gn 11:4
cities that you did not **b**, ... Dt 6:10
So he **built** it in seven years. 1Kg 6:38
who will **b** a house for me, ... 1Ch 17:12
began to **b** the LORD's temple 2Ch 3:1
appointed me to **b** him a house . . . . Ezr 1:2
Unless the LORD **b-s** a house, ... Ps 127:1
Wisdom has **built** her house; . . . . . . Pr 9:1
wise woman **b-s** her house, ... Pr 14:1
to tear down and a time to **b**; . . . . . . Ec 3:3
B houses and live in them. . . . . Jr 29:5
who **built** his house on the rock. . . Mt 7:24
on this rock I will **b** my church, ... Mt 16:18
which is able to **b** you up . . . . Ac 20:32
for his good, to **b** him up. . . . . Rm 15:2
be careful how he **b-s** on it. 1Co 3:10
puffs up, but love **b-s** up. 1Co 8:1
but not everything **b-s** up. 1Co 10:23
Lord gave for **b-ing** you up 2Co 10:8
built on the foundation of the
  apostles and prophets, ... Eph 2:20
to **b** up the body of Christ, ... Eph 4:12
rooted and **built** up in him . . . . Col 2:7
and **b** each other up 1Th 5:11

BUILDING (N)

Do you see these great **b-s**? . . . . . . Mk 13:2
You are God's field, God's **b**. 1Co 3:9
we have a **b** from God, ... 2Co 5:1
the whole **b**, being put together, . . Eph 2:21

BUILDER

The stone that the **b-s** rejected . . Ps 118:22
The stone that the **b-s** rejected . . Mt 21:42
whose architect and **b** is God. . . . Heb 11:10
The stone that the **b-s** rejected . . . 1Pt 2:7

BULL

their hands on the **b-'s** head. . . . . Ex 29:10
unblemished **b** as a sin offering . . . . Lv 4:3
Many **b-s** surround me; . . . . Ps 22:12
I will not take a **b** from . . . . Ps 50:9
Do I eat the flesh of **b-s** . . . . Ps 50:13
no desire for the blood of **b-s**, ... Is 1:11
impossible for the blood of **b-s** . . Heb 10:4

BULLY

not a **b** but gentle, ... 1Tm 3:3
not a **b**, not greedy for money, ... Ti 1:7

BURDEN (N)

bear the **b** of the people, ... Nm 11:17
Cast your **b** on the LORD, ... Ps 55:22
Day after day he bears our **b-s**; . . Ps 68:19
They have become a **b** to me; . . . . . . Is 1:14
no longer refer to the **b** of
  the LORD, ... Jr 23:36
yoke is easy and my **b** is light. . . . . Mt 11:30
You load people with **b-s** . . . . Lk 11:46
Carry one another's **b-s**; . . . . Gl 6:2

BURDEN (V)

have **b-ed** me with your sins; . . . . . Is 43:24
you who are weary and **b-ed**, ... Mt 11:28
I will not **b** you, ... 2Co 12:14
Let the church not be **b-ed**, ... 1Tm 5:16

BURIAL

Give me **b** property among you . . . Gn 23:4
does not even have a proper **b**, ... Ec 6:3
she has prepared me for **b**. . . . . . . Mt 26:12

BURN

Why isn't the bush **b-ing** up? . . . . . . Ex 3:3
b for **b**, bruise for bruise, ... Ex 21:25
b-ing on the altar continually; . . . Lv 6:13
Israel did not **b** any of the
  cities . . . . Jos 11:13
to **b** their sons and daughters . . . . . . Jr 7:31
king not to **b** the scroll, ... Jr 36:25
the chaff he will **b** with fire . . . . Mt 3:12
into the fire, and they are **b-ed**. . . . Jn 15:6
If anyone's work is **b-ed** up, ... 1Co 3:15
better to marry than to **b**. 1Co 7:9
a third of the earth was **b-ed** up, . . . Rv 8:7
lake of fire that **b-s** with sulfur. . . Rv 19:20

BURNING (ADJ)

turned from his **b** anger. . . . . Jos 7:26
my insides are full of **b** pain, ... Ps 38:7
in my **b** zeal I speak against . . . . . . Ezk 36:5

BURNT

If his offering is a **b** offering . . . . Lv 1:3

BURST

vast watery depths **b** open, ... Gn 7:11
about to **b** like new wineskins. . . . . Jb 32:19
the new wine will **b** the skins, ... Lk 5:37
He fell headfirst, his body **b** open . . Ac 1:18

BURY

be **b-ied** at a ripe old age. . . . . Gn 15:15
so that I can **b** my dead, ... Gn 23:4
Joseph's bones, ... were **b-ied** . . . Jos 24:32
first let me go **b** my father. . . . . Mt 8:21
let the dead **b** their own dead. . . . . Mt 8:22
were **b-ied** with him by baptism . . . Rm 6:4
was **b-ied**, that he was raised. 1Co 15:4
b-ied with him in baptism, ... Col 2:12

BUSH

the **b** was on fire but was not . . . . . . Ex 3:2
passage about the burning **b**, ... Mk 12:26
in the flame of a burning **b** . . . . Ac 7:30

BUSINESS

to mind your own **b**, ... 1Th 4:11
and do **b** and make a profit. . . . . . . Jms 4:13

BUSYBODIES

are also gossips and **b**, ... 1Tm 5:13

BUTTER

churning of milk produces **b**, ... Pr 30:33

BUY

B—and do not sell—truth, ... Pr 23:23
b wine and milk without silver . . . . Is 55:1
threw out all those **b-ing** and . . . . Mt 21:12
for you were **bought** at a price. . . . 1Co 6:20
denying the Master who **bought**. . . 2Pt 2:1
b from me gold refined . . . . Rv 3:18
no one can **b** or sell unless . . . . Rv 13:17

BUYER

it's worthless!" the **b** says, ... Pr 20:14

- C -

CAESAREA

came to the region of **C** Philippi, . . . Mt 16:13
a man in **C** named Cornelius, ... Ac 10:1
Paul should be kept at **C**, ... Ac 25:4

CAIAPHAS

High priest, along with his father-in-law
Annas, who sentenced Jesus (Mt 23:6; Lk
3:2; Jn 18:13). Spoke prophetically (Jn 11:49–
52). Threatened Peter and John (Ac 4:6).

CAIN

Firstborn of Adam and Eve; crop farmer;
murdered his brother; God marked and
banished him (Gn 4:1–25; Heb 11:4; 1Jn 3:12;
Jd 11).

CALAMITY

will laugh at your **c**. . . . . Pr 1:26
your brother in the day of his **c**; . . . . Ob 12

CALCULATE

first sit down and **c** the cost . . . . . . Lk 14:28
c the number of the beast, ... Rv 13:18

CALEB

Judahite who scouted Canaan and, along
with Joshua, recommended invasion (Nm
13:30–14:38). Entered the promised land (Dt
1:36); received Hebron (Jos 14:13).

CALF

made it into an image of a **c**. . . . . . . Ex 32:4
Then he made two golden **c-ves**, . . 1Kg 12:28
bring the fattened **c** and slaughter. . Lk 15:23
not by the blood of goats and
  c-ves. . . . . Heb 9:12

CALL

people began to **c** on the name . . . Gn 4:26
I **c** heaven and earth as witnesses . . Dt 4:26
Then the LORD **c-ed** Samuel, ... 1Sm 3:4
I **c-ed** to the LORD in my distress; . . 2Sm 22:7
c on the name of your god, and
  I will **c** on the name of LORD, . . . 1Kg 18:24
C on me in a day of trouble; . . . . . . Ps 50:15
I **c** to you from the ends of the earth . Ps 61:2
is near all who **c** out to him, ... Ps 145:18
Doesn't wisdom **c** out? . . . . Pr 8:1
Her children rise up and **c** her
  blessed. . . . . Pr 31:28
Woe to those who **c** evil good. . . . . . Is 5:20
c to him while he is near. . . . . Is 55:6
Even before they **c**, I will answer; . . Is 65:24
everyone who **c-s** on the name of . . Jl 2:32
I didn't come to **c** the righteous, . . Mt 9:13
Why do you **c** me 'Lord, Lord,' . . . . Lk 6:46
He **c-s** his own sheep by name . . . . . Jn 10:3

You **c** me Teacher and Lord. . . . . Jn 13:13
I do not **c** you servants anymore, . . . Jn 15:15
those he **c-ed**, he also justified; . . . Rm 8:30
everyone who **c-s** on the
name of . . . . Rm 10:13
God's heavenly **c** in Christ Jesus. . . . Php 3:14
God has not **c-ed** us to impurity. . . . 1Th 4:7

CALLING (N)

God's ... and **c** are irrevocable. . . . . Rm 11:29
Brothers and sisters, consider
your **c**: 1Co 1:26
walk worthy of the **c** you have . . . . . Eph 4:1
confirm your **c** and election, ... 2Pt 1:10

CALM (N)

And there was a great **c**. . . . . Mt 8:26

CALM (V)

I have **c-ed** and quieted myself . . . Ps 131:2
one slow to anger **c-s** strife. . . . . . . Pr 15:18

CAMEL

she got down from her **c** . . . . Gn 24:64
easier for a **c** to go through the
eye. . . . . Mt 19:24
gnat, but gulp down a **c**! . . . . Mt 23:24

CAMP (N)

Jacob said, "This is God's **c**." . . . . Gn 32:2
outside the **c** and slaughtered. . . . . Nm 19:3
go to him outside the **c**, ... Heb 13:13

CAMP (V)

c around the tent of meeting . . . . . . Nm 2:2

CANA

a wedding took place in **C** of
Galilee. . . . . Jn 2:1

CANAAN

Son of Ham, his descendants, and the land
they populated (Gn 9:18–27; 10:15–19). God
promised the land to Abraham (12:4–7; 17:8;
Ex 6:4; 1Ch 16:15–18).

CANAANITE

"Do not marry a **C** woman." . . . . Gn 28:6
drive out the **C-s**, Amorites, ... Ex 33:2
so the **C-s** have lived among
them. . . . . Jdg 1:30
a **C** woman from that region
came . . . . Mt 15:22

CANAL

among the exiles by the Chebar **C**, . . Ezk 1:1
I was beside the Ulai **C**. . . . . Dn 8:2

CANCEL

seven years you must **c** debts. . . . . . Dt 15:1

CANOPY

made darkness a **c** around him, . . . 2Sm 22:12
spreading out the sky like a **c**, ... Ps 104:2

CAPERNAUM

went to live in **C** by the sea, ... Mt 4:13
teaching in the synagogue in **C**. . . . . Jn 6:59

CAPITALS

made two **c** of cast bronze. 1Kg 7:16
Strike the **c** of the pillars . . . . Am 9:1

CAPTIVE

the king of Babylon took him **c**. . . 2Kg 24:12
took many **c-s** to Damascus. 2Ch 28:5
to the heights, taking away **c-s**; . . . Ps 68:18
to proclaim liberty to the **c-s**. . . . . . Is 61:1
to proclaim freedom to the **c-s** . . . . Lk 4:18
take every thought **c**. 2Co 10:5
took the captives; he gave gifts. . Eph 4:8
Be careful that no one takes
you **c** . . . . Col 2:8
taken **c**, into captivity he goes. . . . . Rv 13:10

CAPTIVITY

returned to Jerusalem from the **c**, . . Ezr 3:8
those destined for **c**, to **c**. . . . . Jr 15:2
taken captive, into **c** he goes. . . . . . Rv 13:10

CARCASS

who touches its **c** will be unclean. . Lv 11:39
honey from the lion's **c**. . . . . Jdg 14:9

CARE (N)

the sheep under his **c**. . . . . Ps 95:7
I was sick and you took **c** of me; . . Mt 25:36
to an inn, and took **c** of him. . . . . . Lk 10:34
casting all your **c-s** on him, ... 1Pt 5:7

CARE (V)

what is a human that you
c for him, ... Ps 144:3
son of man that you **c** for him? . . . Heb 2:6
because he **c-s** about you. 1Pt 5:7

CAREFUL

be **c** not to forget the LORD . . . . Dt 6:12
do all these things . . . . . . Dt 12:28
c not to practice your
righteousness . . . . Mt 6:1
each one is to be **c** how he builds. . 1Co 3:10
But be **c** that this right of yours . . . 1Co 8:9
c attention, then, to how you
walk. . . . . Eph 5:15

CARELESS

to account for every **c** word. . . . . . . Mt 12:36

CARMEL

gathered the prophets at
Mount **C** 1Kg 18:20

CARMI

Son of Reuben (Gn 46:9; Nm 26:6).

CAROUSING

not in **c** and drunkenness; . . . . Rm 13:13

CARPENTER

Isn't this the **c-'s** son? . . . . Mt 13:55
Isn't this the **c**, the son of Mary, . . . Mk 6:3

CARRY

I **c-ied** you on eagles' wings . . . . Ex 19:4
God **c-ied** you as a man **c-ies** his son. . Dt 1:31
No one but the Levites may **c** 1Ch 15:2
shepherd them, and **c** them forever. . Ps 28:9
lambs in his arms and **c-ies** them . . . Is 40:11
and he **c-ied** our pains; . . . . Is 53:4
not **c-ing** a load ... on the
Sabbath day . . . . Jr 17:22
He himself ... **c-ied** our diseases. . . . Mt 8:17
Don't **c** a money-bag, traveling bag, . Lk 10:4
not **c** out the desire of the flesh. . . . Gl 5:16
c one another's burdens; . . . . Gl 6:2

CASE

argue my **c** before God. . . . . Jb 13:3
The first to state his **c** seems right . . Pr 18:17
Let's argue the **c** together. . . . . Is 43:26
the LORD has a **c** against his people, . Mc 6:2

CAST (ADJ)

Do not make **c** images of gods . . . . Ex 34:17
his **c** images are a lie; . . . . Jr 10:14; 51:17

CAST (V)

c spells, consult a medium or . . . . . . Dt 18:11
Joshua **c** lots for them at Shiloh . . Jos 18:10
He **c** the Pur—that is, the lot— . . . . Est 9:24
they **c** lots for my clothing. . . . . Ps 22:18
C your burden on the LORD, ... Ps 55:22
The lot is **c** into the lap, ... Pr 16:33
who comes to me I will never **c** out. . Jn 6:37
they **c** lots for my clothing. . . . . Jn 19:24
Who has **c** a spell on you, ... Gl 3:1
c-ing all your care on him, ... 1Pt 5:7
c their crowns before the throne . . . Rv 4:10

CATCH

your sin will **c** up with you. . . . . . . Nm 32:23
C the foxes for us—the little foxes. . Sg 2:15
now on you will be **c-ing** people! . . . Lk 5:10
brought a woman **caught** in
adultery, ... Jn 8:3
caught up to the third heaven 2Co 12:2
be **caught** up together with
them 1Th 4:17
her child was **caught** up to God . . . Rv 12:5

CATTLE

is mine, the **c** on a thousand hills. . . Ps 50:10

CAUSE (N)

For you have upheld my just **c**; . . . . . Ps 9:4
have persecuted me without **c**, . . . Ps 119:161
upholds the just **c** of the poor, . . . Ps 140:12
Don't accuse anyone without **c**, ... Pr 3:30
he will champion their **c**
against you. . . . . Pr 23:11

CAUSE (V)

and **c-s** grass to grow on the hills. . Ps 147:8
Even if he **c-s** suffering, ... Lm 3:32
c you to follow my statutes. . . . . . Ezk 36:27
whoever **c-s** ... to fall away— . . . . . Mt 18:6
c one of these little ones to stumble. . Lk 17:2

CAVE

give me the **c** of Machpelah . . . . . . Gn 23:9
took refuge in the **c** of Adullam. . . . 1Sm 22:1
Then Saul left the **c** and went on . . 1Sm 24:7
hid them, fifty men to a **c**, ... 1Kg 18:4
hid in the **c-s** and among the rocks. . Rv 6:15

CEASE

and day and night will not **c**. . . . . . Gn 8:22
there will never **c** to be poor people . . Dt 15:11
sin ... by **c-ing** to pray for you 1Sm 12:23
He makes wars **c**. . . . . Ps 46:9
got into the boat, the wind **c-d**. . . . Mt 14:32
otherwise grace **c-s** to be grace. . . . Rm 11:6
as for tongues, they will **c**; 1Co 13:8

CEDAR

I am living in a **c** house while 2Sm 7:2
command that **c-s** from Lebanon be . . 1Kg 5:6
and grow like a **c** tree in Lebanon. . Ps 92:12

CELEBRATE

c it as a festival to the LORD. . . . . . . Lv 23:41

CENSUS

Take a **c** of the entire. . . . . Nm 1:2; 26:2
he had taken a **c** of the troops. . . 2Sm 24:10

CENTURION

a **c** came to him, pleading with him. . Mt 8:5
When the **c** saw what happened, . . Lk 23:47
in Caesarea named Cornelius, a **c** . . . Ac 10:1

CEPHAS

Aramaic for "Rock"; Peter (Jn 1:42; 1Co 1:12;
3:22; 9:5; 15:5; Gl 1:18; 2:9,11,14).

CERTIFICATE

he may write her a divorce **c**, ... Dt 24:1
He erased the **c** of debt, ... Col 2:14

CHAFF

were shattered and became like **c** . . Dn 2:35
But the **c** he will burn up with fire . . Mt 3:12

CHAIN

and broke their **c-s** apart. . . . . Ps 107:14
the **c-s** fell off his wrists. . . . . Ac 12:7
for this I am an ambassador in **c-s**. . Eph 6:20
in **c-s** of utter darkness. 2Pt 2:4
a great **c** in his hand. . . . . Rv 20:1

CHALDEA

Another name for the Babylonian Empire
(Jr 51:24; Ezk 12:13; 23:15).

CHALDEAN

Inhabitants of Chaldea (Gn 11:28). Known as sages or magicians (Dn 2:2; 4:7). Took Judah into exile (2Kg 25; 2Ch 36:17–19; Ezr 5:12; Jr 32).

CHAMBER

the king would bring me to his **c-s**. . . Sg 1:4

CHAMPION

a **c** named Goliath, from Gath, ...1Sm 17:4

CHANCE

time and **c** happen to all of them. . . Ec 9:11

CHANGE

c-d my wages ten times. . . . . .Gn 31:7
or a son of man, that he might **c**
his mind . . . . .Nm 23:19
does not lie or **c** his mind, ...1Sm 15:29
You will **c** them like a garment, . . .Ps 102:26
Can the Cushite **c** his skin, ...Jr 13:23
Because I, the Lord, have not
c-d, ...Mal 3:6
but we will all be **c-d**, ...1Co 15:51
and they will be **c-d** like clothing. .Heb 1:12
and will not **c** his mind, ...Heb 7:21

CHANGERS

overturned the tables of the
money **c** .Mt 21:12

CHANNEL

Who cuts a **c** for the flooding rain . .Jb 38:25

CHARACTER

you are a woman of noble **c**. . . . . Ru 3:11
c, and proven **c** produces hope. . . . . .Rm 5:4
so that the proven **c** of your faith . . .1Pt 1:7

CHARGE (N)

Joseph was in **c** of the country; . . . . Gn 42:6
Above his head they put up
the **c** . . . . .Mt 27:37
that they could find a **c** against him. . Lk 6:7
the gospel and offer it free of **c** . . 1Co 9:18

CHARGE (V)

Do not **c** your brother interest. . . . Dt 23:19
man the Lord will never **c** with sin! . . Rm 4:8
I solemnly **c** you before God 1Tm 5:21
c them before God not to fight. . . 2Tm 2:14
c that to my account. . . . . Phm 18

CHARIOT

came back and covered the **c-s** . . .Ex 14:28
even though they have iron **c-s** . . .Jos 17:18
because those people had iron **c-s**. Jdg 1:19
nine hundred iron **c-s**, ...Jdg 4:3
Solomon accumulated 1,400 **c-s** . . 1Kg 10:26
a **c** of fire with horses of fire 2Kg 2:11
covered with horses and **c-s** of fire. .2Kg 6:17
Some take pride in **c-s**, ...Ps 20:7
God's **c-s** are tens of thousands, . . Ps 68:17
making the clouds his **c**, ...Ps 104:3
saw four **c-s** coming . . . . .Zch 6:1
I will cut off the **c** from Ephraim . .Zch 9:10

CHARITY

doing good works and acts of **c**. . . . .Ac 9:36
your acts of **c** have ascended . . . . . .Ac 10:4

CHARM

C is deceptive and beauty is . . . . . . Pr 31:30

CHARMED

If the snake bites before it is **c**, ...Ec 10:11

CHASE

whoever **c-s** fantasies lacks sense. . .Pr 12:11

CHEAT

c-ed me and changed my wages . . .Gn 31:7
Why not rather be **c-ed**? 1Co 6:7

CHEEK

My **c-s** to those who tore out my . . Is 50:6
Let him offer his **c** to the one . . . . .Lm 3:30
if anyone slaps you on your
right **c**, ...Mt 5:39

CHEERFUL

God loves a **c** giver. 2Co 9:7

CHEMOSH

Moab's god (Jdg 11:24; 1Kg 11:7,33).

CHERUB

Make one **c** at one end and . . . . . . .Ex 25:19
He rode on a **c** and flew, ...2Sm 22:11
The first **c-'s** height was 15 feet . . .1Kg 6:26
one was the face of a **c**, ...Ezk 10:14

CHERUBIM

stationed the **c** and the flaming, . . Gn 3:24
he made two **c** 15 feet high 1Kg 6:23
You who sit enthroned between
the **c**, ...Ps 80:1
four wheels beside the **c**, ...Ezk 10:9

CHEST

righteousness like armor on
your **c**, ...Eph 6:14

CHICKS

as a hen gathers her **c** . . . Mt 23:37; Lk 13:34

CHIEF

the **c-s** of David's warriors 1Ch 11:10
rejected by the elders, the
c priests, ...Mk 8:31
when the **c** Shepherd appears, ... 1Pt 5:4

CHILD

quieted my soul like a weaned **c** . . Ps 131:2
For a **c** will be born for us, ... Is 9:6
and a **c** will lead them. . . . . .Is 11:6
Can a woman forget her nursing **c**, . .Is 49:15
When Israel was a **c**, I loved him, . . . Hs 11:1
He called a small **c** and had him . . . Mt 18:2
When I was a **c**, I spoke like a **c**, . .1Co 13:11
give birth it might devour her **c**. . . .Rv 12:4

CHILDBEARING

But she will be saved through **c**, . . .1Tm 2:15

CHILDISH

a man, I put aside **c** things. 1Co 13:11

CHILDLESS

I am **c** and the heir of my house is . . Gn 15:2
No woman will miscarry or be **c** . . Ex 23:26
who is **c** gives birth to seven, ...1Sm 2:5
Rejoice, **c** one, ...Is 54:1
Rejoice, **c** woman, ... Gl 4:27

CHILDREN

you will bear **c** with painful effort. . . Gn 3:16
When your **c** ask you, ...Ex 12:26
the consequences of the fathers'
iniquity on the **c**, ...Ex 20:5
Teach them to your **c**, ...Dt 11:19
Fathers are not to be put to death for
their **c**, and **c** ... for their fathers; . . Dt 24:16
In the future, when your **c** ask you, . .Jos 4:6
Rachel weeping for her **c**, refusing
to be comforted for her **c** because . .Jr 31:15
and the **c-'s** teeth are set on edge. . .Jr 31:29
and the **c-'s** teeth are set on edge . .Ezk 18:2
c for Abraham from these stones. . . Mt 3:9
how to give good gifts to your **c**, . . Mt 7:11
you turn and become like little **c**, . . Mt 18:3
Let the little **c** come to me. . . . . . . Mk 10:14
C will rise up against parents. . . . . Mk 13:12
women without **c**, ... are
fortunate! . . . . .Lk 23:29
gave them the right to be **c** of God, . .Jn 1:12
testifies ... that we are God's **c**, ...Rm 8:16
C, obey your parents in the Lord, . . Eph 6:1

CHINNERETH

Another name for the Sea of Galilee (Nm 34:11; Jos 13:27) and a city there (Jos 19:35).

CHOICE

I am offering you three **c-s** 2Sm 24:12

CHOOSE SEE ALSO CHOSEN (ADJ)

Lot **chose** the entire plain of the
Jordan. . . . . .Gn 13:11
He will let the one he **c-s** come. . . . Nm 16:5
He **chose** their descendants . . . . . . .Dt 4:37
Lord ... **chose** you, not because . . . . .Dt 7:7
the place the Lord your God **c-s**. . . .Dt 12:5
C life so that you . . . . .Dt 30:19
c for yourselves today; . . . . Jos 24:15
who **chose** me over your father . . 2Sm 6:21
the Lord has **chosen** Zion; . . . . . . Ps 132:13
A good name is to be **chosen** over. . Pr 22:1
servant, Jacob, whom I have
chosen, ...Is 41:8
I **chose** you before I formed you . . . . .Jr 1:5
are invited, but few are **chosen** . . Mt 22:14
and he **chose** twelve of them . . . . . Lk 6:13
You did not **c** me, but I **chose** you. . Jn 15:16
a remnant **chosen** by grace. . . . . . . Rm 11:5
he **chose** us in him, before the . . . . .Eph 1:4
loved by God, that he has
chosen you 1Th 1:4

CHOSEN (ADJ)

this is my **c** one; I delight in him. . . .Is 42:1
This is my Son, the **C** One; . . . . .Lk 9:35
God's **c** ones, holy and dearly . . . . . Col 3:12
a **c** and honored cornerstone, ...1Pt 2:6
you are a **c** race, a royal priesthood, . .1Pt 2:9

CHRIST SEE ALSO MESSIAH

The birth of Jesus **C** came about. . . .Mt 1:18
Messiah is coming" (... called **C**). . . . Jn 4:25
Scriptures that Jesus is the **C**. . . . . .Ac 18:28
through faith in Jesus **C**, to all. . . . . Rm 3:22
we were still sinners, **C** died for us. . . Rm 5:8
if we died with **C**, we believe that . .Rm 6:8
heirs of God and coheirs with **C** . . . Rm 8:17
can separate us from the
love of **C**? . . . . Rm 8:35
For **C** is the end of the law . . . . Rm 10:4
who are many are one body in **C** . . Rm 12:5
But put on the Lord Jesus **C**, ... Rm 13:14
but we preach **C** crucified, ...1Co 1:23
and that rock was **C**. 1Co 10:4
Imitate me, as I also imitate **C**. 1Co 11:1
C is the head of every man, ...1Co 11:3
you are the body of **C**, ...1Co 12:27
C died for our sins according to. . . .1Co 15:3
also in **C** all will be made alive. 1Co 15:22
Jesus **C** as Lord, and ourselves as . . .2Co 4:5
is in **C**, he is a new creation; 2Co 5:17
I no longer live, but **C** lives in me. . . Gl 2:20
except the cross of ... Jesus **C**. . . . . .Gl 6:14
into him who is the head—**C**. . . . . .Eph 4:15
just as **C** loved the church. . . . . .Eph 5:25
to live is **C** and to die is gain. . . . . . .Php 1:21
considered ... a loss because of **C**. . .Php 3:7
C is all and in all. . . . . .Col 3:11
the dead in **C** will rise first. 1Th 4:16
the coming of our Lord Jesus **C** 2Th 2:1
C ... came into the world to save. . . .1Tm 1:15
salvation, which is in **C** Jesus, ...2Tm 2:10
C also suffered for sins once for all, . .1Pt 3:18
ridiculed for the name of **C**, ...1Pt 4:14
who denies that Jesus is the **C**? 1Jn 2:22
with **C** for one thousand years . . . . Rv 20:4

CHRISTIAN

were first called **C-s** at Antioch. . . . Ac 11:26
if anyone suffers as a **C**, ...1Pt 4:16

C, obey your parents in
everything, ... Col 3:20
Fathers, do not exasperate your **c**, . . Col 3:21
managing their **c** and their own . . 1 Tm 3:12
that we should be called God's **c**—. .1Jn 3:1

CHURCH

on this rock I will build my **c**, ... Mt 16:18
pay attention to them, tell the **c**. . . Mt 18:17
as overseers, to shepherd the **c**. . . . Ac 20:28
the **c** that meets in their home. . . . Rm 16:5
one who prophesies builds up
  the **c**. 1Co 14:4
for a woman to speak in the **c**. . . 1Co 14:35
wife as Christ is the head of the **c**. . Eph 5:23
regarding zeal, persecuting the **c**; . . Php 3:6
the head of the body, the **c**; . . . . Col 1:18
are the angels of the seven **c-es**, . . Rv 1:20
to the angel of the **c** in Ephesus . . . . . Rv 2:1

CIRCUMCISE

your males must be **c-d**. . . . . Gn 17:10
Abraham **c-d** him, ... Gn 21:4
Therefore, **c** your hearts . . . . Dt 10:16
God will **c** your heart. . . . . Dt 30:6
C yourselves to the LORD; . . . . Jr 4:4
they came to **c** the child . . . . Lk 1:59
you **c** a man on the Sabbath. . . . . . . Jn 7:22
Unless you are **c-d** according to . . . . Ac 15:1
if ... **c-d**, Christ will not benefit you . . Gl 5:2
c-d the eighth day; . . . . Php 3:5

CIRCUMCISION

and **c** is of the heart . . . . Rm 2:29
c and uncircumcision mean nothing; . . Gl 6:15
we are the **c**, the ones who
  worship. . . . . Php 3:3
with a **c** not done with hands, ... Col 2:11

CIRCUMSTANCES

learned to be content in
  whatever **c**. . . . . Php 4:11

CISTERN

may drink water from his own **c**. . 2Kg 18:31
Drink water from your own **c**, ... Pr 5:15
dug **c-s** for themselves, cracked **c-s**. . Jr 2:13
Jeremiah had been put into the **c**. . . Jr 38:7

CITIZEN

realized Paul was a Roman **c** . . . . . Ac 22:29

CITIZENSHIP

I bought this **c** for a large amount. Ac 22:28
Our **c** is in heaven, ... Php 3:20

CITY

Lot lived in the **c-ies** on the plain . . Gn 13:12
give **c-ies** ... for the Levites . . . . Nm 35:2
will include six **c-ies** of refuge, ... Nm 35:6
Select your **c-ies** of refuge, ... Jos 20:2
gave the Levites these **c-ies**. . . . . . . Jos 21:3
and **c-ies** you did not build, ... Jos 24:13
which he named the **c** of David. . . . 2Sm 5:9
unless the LORD watches over a **c**, . . Ps 127:1
her works praise her at the **c** gates. . . Pr 31:31
Say to the **c-ies** of Judah, "Here is your
  God!". . . . . Is 40:9
c situated on a hill cannot be
  hidden. . . . . Mt 5:14
I have many people in this **c**. . . . . . Ac 18:10
he was looking forward to the **c**. . Heb 11:10
we do not have an enduring **c**. . . . Heb 13:14
saw the holy **c**, the new Jerusalem, . . Rv 21:2

CLAIM

rose up, **c-ing** to be somebody, ... Ac 5:36
while **c-ing** to be somebody great. . . Ac 8:9
C-ing to be wise, ... became fools. . Rm 1:22

CLAN

small among the **c-s** of Judah; . . . . . Mc 5:2

CLANGING

a noisy gong or a **c** cymbal. 1Co 13:1

CLAP

C your hands, all you peoples; . . . . . Ps 47:1
Let the rivers **c** their hands; . . . . Ps 98:8
trees of the field will **c** their . . . . . . Is 55:12

CLAY

strength is dried up like baked **c**; . . Ps 22:15
out of the muddy **c**, and set my
  feet . . . . Ps 40:2
Does **c** say to the one forming it, . . . Is 45:9
we are the **c**, and you are our potter; . . Is 64:8
Just like **c** in the potter's hand, ... Jr 18:6
partly iron and partly fired **c**. . . . . . . Dn 2:33
has the potter no right over the **c**, . . Rm 9:21
Now we have this treasure in **c** jars, . . 2Co 4:7

CLEAN

of all the **c** animals, and two . . . . Gn 7:2
The one who has **c** hands and a . . . Ps 24:4
with hyssop, and I will be **c**; . . . . Ps 51:7
create a **c** heart for me and . . . . Ps 51:10
You can make me **c**. . . . . Mt 8:2
You **c** the outside of the cup and . . Mt 23:25
he declared all foods **c**). . . . . Mk 7:19
You are **c**, but not all of you. . . . . . Jn 13:10
You are already **c** because of the. . . Jn 15:3
God has made **c**, do not call . . . . . . Ac 10:15

CLEANSE

my guilt and **c** me from my sin. . . . . Ps 51:2
holy, **c-ing** her with the washing . . Eph 5:26
to **c** for himself a people. . . . . Ti 2:14
Jesus his Son **c-s** us from all sin. 1Jn 1:7
to **c** us from all unrighteousness. . . . 1Jn 1:9

CLEAR

and he will **c** the way before me. . . . Mal 3:1
and he will **c** his threshing . . . . Mt 3:12
strive to have a **c** conscience. . . . . . Ac 24:16
the faith with a **c** conscience. 1Tm 3:9
keeping a **c** conscience, ... 1Pt 3:16

CLIFF

your nest is set in the **c-s**. . . . . Nm 24:21

CLIMB

I will **c** the palm tree and take . . . . . Sg 7:8
he **c-ed** up a sycamore tree to see . . Lk 19:4
by the door but **c-s** in some other . . Jn 10:1

CLING

"Don't **c** to me," Jesus told her. . . . . Jn 20:17
Detest evil; **c** to what is good. . . . . . Rm 12:9

CLOAK

Put your hand inside your **c**. . . . . Ex 4:6
neighbor's **c** as collateral, ... Ex 22:26
Wrap your **c** around you, ... Ac 12:8
bring the **c** I left in Troas with 2Tm 4:13
You will roll them up like a **c**, ... Heb 1:12

CLOSE (ADV)

who stays **c-r** than a brother. . . . . . . Pr 18:24

CLOSE (V)

what he opens, no one can **c**; . . . . . Is 22:22
who opens and no one will **c**, ... Rv 3:7

CLOTH

of unshrunk **c** on an old garment . . Mk 2:21
him tightly in **c** and laid him . . . . Lk 2:7
he saw the linen **c-s** lying there, . . . Jn 20:5

CLOTHE

and **c-d** me with gladness . . . . Ps 30:11
If that's how God **c-s** the grass of . . Mt 6:30
I was naked and you **c-d** me; . . . . . Mt 25:36
mortal ... is **c-d** with immortality, . . 1Co 15:54
not want to be unclothed but **c-d**, . . 2Co 5:4
All of you **c** yourselves with
  humility 1Pt 5:5
a woman **c-d** with the sun, with the . . Rv 12:1

CLOTHES

your **c** ... did not wear out; . . . . Dt 29:5
anointed himself, changed his **c**, . . 2Sm 12:20
fire and his **c** not be burned?. . . . . . Pr 6:27
Tear your hearts, not just your **c**, ... Jl 2:13

And why do you worry about **c**? . . . Mt 6:28
get in here without wedding **c**? . . Mt 22:12
in fine **c**, and a poor man dressed
  in filthy **c** also comes in . . . . Jms 2:2

CLOTHING

Your **c** did not wear out, and . . . . . . Dt 8:4
and they cast lots for my **c**. . . . . . . Ps 22:18
Strength and honor are her **c**, ... Pr 31:25
and the body more than **c**? . . . . . . Mt 6:25
come to you in sheep's **c**, ... Mt 7:15
they cast lots for my **c**. . . . . Jn 19:24
If we have food and **c**, ... 1Tm 6:8

CLOUD

I have placed my bow in the **c-s**, . . . Gn 9:13
a pillar of **c** to lead them . . . . Ex 13:21
the mountain, the **c** covered it. . . . Ex 24:15
the **c** filled the LORD's temple, ... 1Kg 8:10
a **c** as small as a man's hand. 1Kg 18:44
your faithfulness reaches the **c-s**. . . Ps 57:10
making the **c-s** his chariot, ... Ps 104:3
temple was filled with the **c**, ... Ezk 10:4
coming with the **c-s** of heaven. . . . . Dn 7:13
a bright **c** covered them, and a
  voice from the **c** said, ... Mt 17:5
coming on the **c-s** of heaven with . Mt 24:30
coming in **c-s** with great power . Mk 13:26
of Man coming in a **c** with power . . Lk 21:27
a **c** took him out of their sight. . . . . . Ac 1:9
ancestors were all under the **c**, ... 1Co 10:1
in the **c-s** to meet the Lord in the. . 1Th 4:17
have such a large **c** of witnesses. . . Heb 12:1
he is coming with the **c-s**, ... Rv 1:7

CLOUDLESS

the sun rises on a **c** morning, ... 2Sm 23:4

COAL

rain burning **c-s** and sulfur. . . . . Ps 11:6
will heap burning **c-s** on his head, . Pr 25:22
a glowing **c** that he had taken. . . . . . Is 6:6
be heaping fiery **c-s** on his head. . Rm 12:20

COAT

let him have your **c** as well. . . . . Mt 5:40

COFFIN

and placed him in a **c** in Egypt. . . . Gn 50:26

COHEIRS

heirs of God and **c** with Christ. . . . . Rm 8:17
The Gentiles are **c**, members of. . . . Eph 3:6
them honor as **c** of the grace of 1Pt 3:7

COIN

open its mouth you'll find a **c**. . . . . Mt 17:27
Show me the **c** used for the tax. . . Mt 22:19
if she loses one **c**, ... Lk 15:8
widow dropping in two tiny **c-s**. . . . Lk 21:2

COLD

is like **c** water to a parched throat. . Pr 25:25
even a cup of **c** water to one . . . . . Mt 10:42
the love of many will grow **c**. . . . . Mt 24:12
that you are neither **c** nor hot. . . . . . Rv 3:15

COLLAPSED

a great shout, and the wall **c**. . . . . Jos 6:20
pounded that house, and it **c**. . . . . . Mt 7:27

COLLECTION

Now about the **c** for the saints: . . . 1Co 16:1

COLLECTOR

even the tax **c-s** do the same? . . . Mt 5:46
Thomas and Matthew the tax **c**; . . Mt 10:3
a friend of tax **c-s** and sinners! . . . Mt 11:19
let him be like ... a tax **c** to you. . . Mt 18:17
Tax **c-s** and prostitutes are
  entering . . . . Mt 21:31
Tax **c-s** also came to be baptized, . . Lk 3:12
a Pharisee and the other a tax **c**. . . Lk 18:10
chief tax **c**, and he was rich. . . . . Lk 19:2

COLT

on a donkey, on a **c**, the foal of . . . . .Zch 9:9
a donkey and on a **c**, the foal. . . . . .Mt 21:5
sitting on a donkey's **c**. . . . . .Jn 12:15

COME

Spirit ... **c** powerfully on him,. . .Jdg 14:6,19
Spirit ... **c** powerfully on David . . .1Sm 16:13
who **c-s** in the name of the Lord . .Ps 118:26
Your kingdom **c**. Your will be . . . . . .Mt 6:10
to another, 'C!' and he **c-s** . . . . .Mt 8:9
Are you the one who is to **c**, ...Mt 11:3
who **c-s** in the name of the Lord. . .Mt 21:9
Father gives me will **c** to me,. . . . . . .Jn 6:37
No one **c-s** to the Father except . . . .Jn 14:6
who is, who was, and who is **c-ing**;. . Rv 1:4
Spirit and the bride say, "C! . . . . . .Rv 22:17
Let the one who is thirsty **c**. . . . . .Rv 22:17
Amen! **C**, Lord Jesus! . . . . .Rv 22:20

COMFORT (N)

This is my **c** in my affliction: . . . . .Ps 119:50
it is for your **c** and salvation; 2Co 1:6

COMFORT (V)

rod and your staff—they **c** me. . . . . .Ps 23:4
Lord, have helped and **c-ed** me. . .Ps 86:17
they have no one to **c** them. . . . . .Ec 4:1
"C, **c** my people," says your God . . . .Is 40:1
For the Lord has **c-ed** his people,. . .Is 49:13
I—I am the one who **c-s** you. . . . . . .Is 51:12
refusing to be **c-ed** for her. . . . . .Jr 31:15
mourn, for they will be **c-ed**. . . . . . .Mt 5:4
able to **c** those who are in any kind of
affliction, through the **c** we 2Co 1:4

COMFORTERS

You are all miserable **c**. . . . . .Jb 16:2

COMING

can endure the day of his **c**? . . . . . .Mal 3:2
what is the sign of your **c** and
of the . . . . .Mt 24:3
still alive at the Lord's **c** 1Th 4:15
Now concerning the **c** of our Lord . .2Th 2:1
be patient until the Lord's **c**. . . . . . .Jms 5:7
"Where is his '**c**' that he promised? . .2Pt 3:4

COMMAND (N)

who love him and keep his **c-s**. . . . . .Dt 7:9
the **c** of the Lord is radiant,. . . . . . .Ps 19:8
I love your **c-s** more than gold, . . .Ps 119:127
but let your heart keep my **c-s**;. . . . . .Pr 3:1
who respects a **c** will be rewarded. .Pr 13:13
least of these **c-s** and teaches. . . . .Mt 5:19
teaching as doctrines human **c-s**. . .Mt 15:9
the greatest and most
important **c**. . . . . .Mt 22:38
Abandoning the **c** of God, ...Mk 7:8
I give you a new **c**:. . . . . .Jn 13:34
love me, you will keep my **c-s**. . . . .Jn 14:15
If you keep my **c-s** you will
remain. .Jn 15:10
This is my **c**: Love one another . . . . .Jn 15:12
I write to you is the Lord's **c**. 1Co 14:37
I am not writing you a new **c**. 1Jn 2:7
Now this is his **c**: that we 1Jn 3:23
love for God is: to keep his **c-s**.
And his **c-s** are not a burden, ...1Jn 5:3
saints, who keep God's **c-s**. . . . . . . .Rv 14:12

COMMAND (V)

the tree about which I **c-ed** you, . . .Gn 3:17
everything that God had **c-ed** him. .Gn 6:22
You must say whatever I **c** you;. . . . . .Ex 7:2
not add anything to what I **c** you . . .Dt 4:2
so that you may **c** your children . . .Dt 32:46
you have **c-ed** us we will do, ...Jos 1:16
he **c-ed**, and it came into existence. .Ps 33:9
for he **c-ed**, and they were created. .Ps 148:5
everything I have **c-ed** you. . . . . . .Mt 28:20
I do as the Father **c-ed** me. . . . . . . .Jn 14:31
God ... **c-s** all people everywhere . .Ac 17:30
love one another as he **c-ed** us. . . .1Jn 3:23

COMMANDER

I have ... come as **c** of the Lord's. . . Jos 5:14

COMMANDMENT

He wrote the Ten **C-s**, ...Ex 34:28
follow the Ten **C-s**, which he
wrote . . . . .Dt 4:13
the **c** is holy and just and good. . . . .Rm 7:12
is the first **c** with a promise . . . . . . .Eph 6:2

COMMISSION

and **c** him in their sight. . . . . .Nm 27:19
The Lord **c-ed** Joshua son of Nun,. . .Dt 31:23

COMMIT

Do not **c** adultery.. . . . . . . .Ex 20:14; Dt 5:18
C your way to the Lord; . . . . .Ps 37:5
one who **c-s** adultery lacks sense; . .Pr 6:32
C your activities to the Lord . . . . . . .Pr 16:3
c-ted adultery with her in his
heart. . . . . .Mt 5:28
Everyone who **c-s** sin is a slave of . .Jn 8:34
he has **c-ted** the message ... to us. .2Co 5:19
c to faithful men who will be 2Tm 2:2
He did not **c** sin, and no deceit 1Pt 2:22

COMMON

between the holy and the **c**, ...Lv 10:10
and the poor have this in **c**. . . . . . . .Pr 22:2
the oppressor have this in **c**: . . . . . .Pr 29:13
between the holy and the **c**, . . .Ezk 22:26
and held all things in **c**. . . . . .Ac 2:44
except what is **c** to humanity. 1Co 10:13
believer have in **c** with an 2Co 6:15

COMPANION

but a **c** of fools will suffer harm. . . Pr 13:20
a **c** of gluttons humiliates his father.. Pr 28:7
falls, his **c** can lift him up;. . . . . .Ec 4:10

COMPANY

Bad **c** corrupts good morals. 1Co 15:33

COMPARE

none can **c** with you. . . . . .Ps 40:5
To what should I **c** this generation? . .Mt 11:16
What can I **c** it to? . . . . .Lk 13:20
are not worth **c-ing** with the glory. .Rm 8:18
c-ing themselves to themselves, . .2Co 10:12

COMPASSION

will have **c** on whom I will have **c**. . Ex 33:19
and have **c** on his servants. . . . . . .Dt 32:36
because of your great **c**. . . . . .Neh 9:19
according to your abundant **c**,. . . . . .Ps 51:1
As a father has **c** on his children,. . .Ps 103:13
my **c** is stirred! . . . . .Hs 11:8
crowds, he felt **c** for them . . . . .Mt 9:36
will have **c** on whom I will have **c**. .Rm 9:15
put on **c**, kindness, humility,. . . . . . .Col 3:12

COMPASSIONATE

the Lord your God is a **c** God. . . . . .Dt 4:31
gracious and **c**, slow to anger . . . .Neh 9:17
The Lord is **c** and gracious,. . . . . . .Ps 103:8
you are a gracious and **c** God, ...Jnh 4:2
And be kind and **c** to one another . .Eph 4:32
Lord is **c** and merciful. . . . . .Jms 5:11

COMPELS

love of Christ **c** us, since we 2Co 5:14

COMPETE

Their **c-ing** thoughts either . . . . . . .Rm 2:15
Now everyone who **c-s** exercises . .1Co 9:25
if anyone **c-s** as an athlete, ...2Tm 2:5

COMPETENT

not that we are **c** in ourselves 2Co 3:5
He has made us **c** to be ministers . . .2Co 3:6

COMPLAIN

So the people **c-ed** to Moses, ...Ex 17:2
All the Israelites **c-ed** about Moses. .Nm 14:2

do not **c** about one another, ...Jms 5:9
to one another without **c-ing**. 1Pt 4:9

COMPLAINT

He has heard your **c-s** about him.. . .Ex 16:7
the Israelites' **c-s** that they make. .Nm 14:27
I will give vent to my **c** . . . . .Jb 10:1
I pour out my **c** before him; . . . . . .Ps 142:2
anyone has a **c** against another. . . .Col 3:13

COMPLETE (ADJ)

seventy years for Babylon are **c**,. . . Jr 29:10
So this joy of mine is **c**. . . . . .Jn 3:29
in you and your joy may be **c**. . . . . .Jn 15:11
that your joy may be **c**. . . . . .Jn 16:24
that the man of God may be **c**, ...2Tm 3:17
that you may be mature and **c**,. . . . .Jms 1:4
so that our joy may be **c**. 1Jn 1:4

COMPLETE (V)

God had **c-d** his work that he had
done . . . . .Gn 2:2
When the seventy years are **c-d**, . . .Jr 25:12
When the thousand years are **c-d**, . .Rv 20:7

COMPLETION

carry it on to **c** until the day . . . . . .Php 1:6

COMPREHEND

may be able to **c** with all the . . . . . .Eph 3:18

CONCEAL

I did not **c** your constant love . . . . .Ps 40:10
the glory of God to **c** a matter . . . . . .Pr 25:2
an open reprimand than **c-ed** love . .Pr 27:5
who **c-s** his sins will not prosper, . . Pr 28:13
For nothing is **c-ed** that won't be. . .Lk 8:17
it was **c-ed** from them so that they . .Lk 9:45

CONCEIT

So that you will not be **c-ed**,. . . . . .Rm 11:25
Let us not become **c-ed**, provoking. .Gl 5:26
nothing from selfish ambition or **c**,. .Php 2:3
or he might become **c-ed** and
incur 1Tm 3:6
he is **c-ed** and understands
nothing, ...1Tm 6:4

CONCEIVE

Sarai was unable to **c**; . . . . .Gn 11:30
Rachel was unable to **c**. . . . . .Gn 29:31
Did I **c** all these people? . . . . .Nm 11:12
Manoah; his wife was unable to **c** . .Jdg 13:2
was sinful when my mother **c-d** me.. Ps 51:5
the virgin will **c**, have a son . . . . .Is 7:14
what has been **c-d** in her is by the. . Mt 1:20
You will **c** and give birth to a . . . . . . .Lk 1:31
desire has **c-d**, it gives birth. . . . . .Jms 1:15

CONCERN (N)

Then I had **c** for my holy name,. . . .Ezk 36:21
have the same **c** for each other. . . .1Co 12:25

CONCERN (V)

master does not **c** himself with. . . . .Gn 39:8
married man is **c-ed** about. 1Co 7:33

CONCUBINES

and three hundred **c**,. 1Kg 11:3

CONDEMN

my own mouth would **c** me; . . . . . . .Jb 9:20
God will help me; who will **c** me? . . . Is 50:9
by your words you will be **c-ed**. . . .Mt 12:37
can you escape being **c-ed** to hell?. .Mt 23:33
They all **c-ed** him as deserving . . . .Mk 14:64
does not believe will be **c-ed**. . . . . .Mk 16:16
Do not **c**, and you will not be **c-ed**. .Lk 6:37
"Neither do I **c** you," said Jesus . . . .Jn 8:11
He **c-ed** sin in the flesh by sending. .Rm 8:3
Who is the one who **c-s**? . . . . .Rm 8:34
doubts stands **c-ed** if he eats,. . . . .Rm 14:23
Let no one **c** you by delighting . . . .Col 2:18
whenever our hearts **c** us; 1Jn 3:20

CONDEMNATION

Their **c** is deserved! . . . . Rm 3:8
there is now no **c** for those in . . . . . . Rm 8:1
the same **c** as the devil. 1Tm 3:6

CONDUCT (N)

shameful **c** is pleasure for a fool, . . Pr 10:23
are to be holy in all your **c**; 1Pt 1:15

CONDUCT (V)

knows how to **c** himself before . . . . . . Ec 6:8
you are to **c** yourselves in. 1Pt 1:17
C yourselves honorably among the. .1Pt 2:12

CONFESS

the live goat and **c** over it all. . . . . . Lv 16:21
But if they will **c** their iniquity . . . .Lv 26:40
person is to **c** the sin he has. . . . . . . .Nm 5:7
I will **c** my transgressions to. . . . . Ps 32:5
If you **c** with your mouth, "Jesus. . .Rm 10:9
tongue will **c** that Jesus . . . . .Php 2:11
c your sins to one another and . . .Jms 5:16
If we **c** our sins, he is faithful. 1Jn 1:9
he who **c-es** the Son has the
  Father 1Jn 2:23
Every spirit that **c-es** that Jesus 1Jn 4:2

CONFESSION

good **c** in the presence of many . . .1Tm 6:12
let us hold fast to the **c**. . . . . Heb 4:14

CONFIDENCE

Lord God, my **c** from my youth. . . . . Ps 71:5
will be your **c** and will keep . . . . .Pr 3:26
and do not put **c** in the flesh . . . . . . Php 3:3
So don't throw away your **c**, . . . Heb 10:35

CONFIRM

to **c** the promises to the fathers . . . Rm 15:8
every effort to **c** your calling 2Pt 1:10
the prophetic word strongly **c-ed**,. . 2Pt 1:19

CONFLICT

A hot-tempered person stirs up **c**, . . Pr 15:18

CONFORMED

predestined to be **c** to the image . .Rm 8:29
Do not be **c** to this age, but be . . . . Rm 12:2
being **c** to His death, ...Php 3:10
do not be **c** to the desires of 1Pt 1:14

CONFUSE

down there and **c** their language . . . Gn 11:7

CONFUSION

So the city was filled with **c**, ...Ac 19:29

CONGREGATION

sing hymns to you in the **c**. . . . . . .Heb 2:12

CONQUER

I have **c-ed** the world. . . . . Jn 16:33
Do not be **c-ed** by evil, but **c** evil . .Rm 12:21
victory that has **c-ed** the world:. . . .1Jn 5:4
as a conqueror in order to **c**. . . . . . . Rv 6:2

CONQUEROR

are more than a **c** through him . . . .Rm 8:37
I will give the **c** the right to . . . . .Rv 2:7

CONSCIENCE

a clear **c** toward God and men. . . . . Ac 24:16
Their **c-s** confirm this. . . . . Rm 2:15
but also because of your **c**. . . . . . . Rm 13:5
their **c**, being weak, is defiled. 1Co 8:7
of liars whose **c-s** are seared. 1Tm 4:2
cleanse our **c-s** from dead
  works to . . . . Heb 9:14
sprinkled clean from an evil **c** . . .Heb 10:22
keeping a clear **c**, so that 1Pt 3:16

CONSECRATE

C every firstborn male to me, ... Ex 13:2
c them to serve me as priests. . . . . .Ex 29:1

---

c it along with all its furnishings. . . Ex 40:9
C yourselves and be holy, for I. . . . . .Lv 20:7
Joshua told the people,
  "**C** yourselves . . . . Jos 3:5
I have **c-d** this temple you have 1Kg 9:3

CONSECRATED (ADJ)

However, there is **c** bread, but. 1Sm 21:4

CONSIDER

Have you **c-ed** my servant Job? . . . . . Jb 1:8
Lord; **c** my sighing. . . . . Ps 5:1
Even a fool is **c-ed** wise when he . . Pr 17:28
C how the wildflowers grow:. . . . . . Lk 12:27
you too **c** yourselves dead to sin . . Rm 6:11
Brothers and sisters, **c** your calling:. .1Co 1:26
but in humility **c** others as more . . . Php 2:3
I also **c** everything to be a loss . . . . Php 3:8
she **c-ed** that the one who had. . . . Heb 11:11
C it a great joy, my brothers. . . . . . .Jms 1:2

CONSISTENT

produce fruit **c** with repentance . . . . Mt 3:8

CONSOLATION

Christ, if any **c** of love, if any . . . . . .Php 2:1

CONSOLE

refused to be **c-d**, because they . . . Mt 2:18

CONSPIRE

all of you have **c-d** against me!. . . 1Sm 22:8
and the rulers **c** together . . . . .Ps 2:2
they **c-d** to arrest Jesus . . . . Mt 26:4

CONSTANTLY

Pray **c**. 1Th 5:17

CONSULT

Saul said, "**C** a spirit for me. 1Sm 28:8
Rehoboam **c-ed** with the elders . . .1Kg 12:6
even **c-ed** a medium for guidance. .1Ch 10:13
shouldn't a people **c** their God? . . . . .Is 8:19
not immediately **c** with anyone. . . . . Gl 1:16

CONSUME

bush was on fire but was not **c-d**. . . .Ex 3:2
so I may **c** them instantly. . . . . Nm 16:21
the Lord your God is a **c-ing** fire,. . .Dt 4:24
fire fell and **c-d** the burnt
  offering 1Kg 18:38
zeal for your house has **c-d** me, ...Ps 69:9
For we are **c-d** by your anger; . . . . . Ps 90:7
Zeal for your house will **c** me. . . . . . Jn 2:17
for our God is a **c-ing** fire. . . . . . . Heb 12:29

CONTAIN

heaven, cannot **c** you, much less. . . 1Kg 8:27
highest heaven cannot **c** him?. 2Ch 2:6
itself could **c** the books that . . . . . . Jn 21:25

CONTEMPT

some to disgrace and eternal **c**. . . . .Dn 12:2
things and be treated with **c**? . . . . . Mk 9:12
treated him with **c**, mocked him . . . Lk 23:11
of God and holding him up to **c**. . . . Heb 6:6

CONTEND

Let Baal **c** with him . . . . .Jdg 6:32
Will the one who **c-s** with the. . . . . .Jb 40:2
will **c** with the one who **c-s**
  with you. . . . . Is 49:25
appealing to you to **c** for the faith . . . .Jd 3

CONTENT

have learned to be **c** in whatever. . Php 4:11
we will be **c** with these. 1Tm 6:8

CONTENTMENT

godliness with **c** is a great gain. . . . 1Tm 6:6

CONTINUE

If you **c** in my word, ... Jn 8:31
urging them to **c** in the grace . . . . .Ac 13:43

Should we **c** in sin so that grace . . . . Rm 6:1
c in what you have learned 2Tm 3:14

CONTRARY

a gospel **c** to what you received, ... Gl 1:9
law therefore **c** to God's promises? . .Gl 3:21
whatever else is **c** to the sound. . . .1Tm 1:10

CONTRIVED

we did not follow cleverly **c**
  myths 2Pt 1:16

CONTROL (N)

have his children under **c** 1Tm 3:4

CONTROL (V)

the one who **c-s** his lips is
  prudent. . . . . Pr 10:19
person who does not **c** his
  temper is . . . . .Pr 25:28
able also to **c** the whole body . . . . .Jms 3:2

CONVERT

land and sea to make one **c** . . . . . .Mt 23:15
from Rome (both Jews and **c-s**), ...Ac 2:10
must not be a new **c**, or he might . .1Tm 3:6

CONVICT

Who among you can **c** me of sin?. . .Jn 8:46
He will **c** the world about sin, ... Jn 16:8
he is **c-ed** by all and is
  judged by. 1Co 14:24
c all the ungodly . . . . .Jd 15

CONVICTION

same understanding and the
  same **c**. 1Co 1:10

CONVINCED

fully **c** that what he had promised. . Rm 4:21
be fully **c** in his own mind . . . . Rm 14:5

CONVINCING

alive to them by many **c** proofs, ...Ac 1:3

COPING

from foundation to **c** and from 1Kg 7:9

COPPER

whose hills you will mine **c**. . . . . Dt 8:9
and **c** is smelted from ore. . . . . Jb 28:2
All of them are **c**, tin, iron. . . . . . . Ezk 22:18
gathers silver, **c**, iron, lead . . . . . . Ezk 22:20
it becomes hot and its **c** glows. . . . Ezk 24:11
gold, silver, or **c** for your. . . . . Mt 10:9

COPPERSMITH

blacksmiths and **c-s** to repair the. .2Ch 24:12
Alexander the **c** did great harm. . . 2Tm 4:14

COPY

These serve as a **c** and shadow of. . Heb 8:5
c-ies of the things in the heavens. .Heb 9:23

CORBAN

have received from me is **c**. . . . . . . .Mk 7:11

CORD

A **c** of three strands is not . . . . Ec 4:12
before the silver **c** is snapped, ... Ec 12:6
them with human **c-s**, with ropes . . Hs 11:4

CORINTH

left Athens and went to **C**, ...Ac 18:1

CORNELIUS

Centurion; Christian (Ac 10).

CORNER

cut off the **c** of Saul's robe. 1Sm 24:4
on the street **c-s** to be seen by
  people. . . . . Mt 6:5
since this was not done in a **c**. . . . .Ac 26:26
at the four **c-s** of the earth, ... Rv 7:1; 20:8

CORNERSTONE

rejected has become the **c**....... Ps 118:22
a precious **c**, a sure foundation;.....Is 28:16
The **c**, the tent peg,..............Zch 10:4
builders rejected has become
  the **c**.....................Mt 21:42
This Jesus ... has become the **c**.....Ac 4:11
Christ Jesus himself as the **c**.....Eph 2:20
in Zion, a chosen and honored **c**,....1Pt 2:6

CORPSE

The boy became like a **c**,.........Mk 9:26
he gave the **c** to Joseph..........Mk 15:45
Where the **c** is, there also.........Lk 17:37

CORRECT

The one who **c-s** a mocker will ......Pr 9:7
if you really **c** your ways............Jr 7:5
rebuking, for **c-ing**, for training ..2Tm 3:16
c, rebuke, and encourage 2Tm 4:2

CORRECTION

but one who hates **c** is stupid. ......Pr 12:1

CORRESPONDS

Hagar ... **c** to the present Jerusalem,..Gl 4:25
Baptism, which **c** to this, now saves..1Pt 3:21

CORRUPT (N)

the earth was **c** in God's sight, ...Gn 6:11
all alike have become **c**. ....Ps 14:3
Be saved from this **c** generation! ..Ac 2:40

CORRUPT (V)

splendor you **c-ed** your wisdom. .Ezk 28:17
Bad company **c-s** good morals....1Co 15:33
prostitute who **c-ed** the earth with ..Rv 19:2

CORRUPTIBLE

For this **c** body must be clothed ..1Co 15:53

CORRUPTION

Sown in **c**, raised in 1Co 15:42
escaping the **c** that is in the........2Pt 1:4

COST

offerings that **c** me nothing.....2Sm 24:24
without silver and without **c**! ....Is 55:1
calculate the **c** to see if he has ..Lk 14:28

COUNCIL

praise him in the **c** of the elders. .Ps 107:32
on of hands by the **c** of elders. 1Tm 4:14

COUNSEL

c and understanding are his.......Jb 12:13
with my eye on you, I will give **c**...Ps 32:8
whoever listens to **c** is wise. ....Pr 12:15
Plans fail when there is no **c**,.....Pr 15:22
and no **c** will prevail against ......Pr 21:30
Has **c** perished from the prudent? ..Jr 49:7

COUNSELOR

He leads **c-s** away barefoot and ...Jb 12:17
but with many **c-s** there is ....Pr 11:14
victory comes with many **c-s**......Pr 24:6
He will be named Wonderful **C**,......Is 9:6
you another **C** to be with you ....Jn 14:16
But the **C**, the Holy Spirit,........Jn 14:26
When the **C** comes, the one I ....Jn 15:26
go away the **C** will not come to ...Jn 16:7
Or who has been his **c**?..........Rm 11:34

COUNT

c the stars, if you are able to
  c them....................Gn 15:5
incited David to **c** the people 1Ch 21:1
of your head have all been **c-ed**. .Mt 10:30
we are **c-ed** as sheep to be ....Rm 8:36
not **c-ing** their trespasses against ..2Co 5:19
May it not be **c-ed** against them. .2Tm 4:16

COUNTRY

has no honor in his own **c**..........Jn 4:44

COURAGE

Have **c**, son, your sins ....Mt 9:2
Have **c**! It is I. Don't be afraid......Mt 14:27
stood by him and said, "Have **c**! ...Ac 23:11

COURAGEOUS

Be strong and **c**; don't be ....Dt 31:6
Be strong and **c**, for you will ......Jos 1:6
be strong and let your heart be **c**..Ps 27:14
Be **c**! I have conquered the world. ..Jn 16:33

COURSE

to finish my **c** and the...........Ac 20:24

COURT

If one wanted to take him to **c**,.....Jb 9:3
a day in your **c-s** than a thousand ..Ps 84:10
an offering and enter his **c-s**......Ps 96:8
and his **c-s** with praise...........Ps 100:4
Don't take a matter to **c** hastily. ...Pr 25:8
The **c** was convened, and the
  books ....Dn 7:10
you and drag you into **c**? ....Jms 2:6

COURTYARD

make the **c** for the tabernacle. .....Ex 27:9
Peter was sitting outside in the **c**..Mt 26:69
Jesus into the high priest's **c**.......Jn 18:15

COVENANT

I will establish my **c** with you,.... Gn 6:18
I am establishing my **c** with you ...Gn 9:9
the Lord made a **c** with Abram, ...Gn 15:18
listen to me and keep my **c**,.......Ex 19:5
will remember my **c** with Jacob. ...Lv 26:42
will never break my **c** with you ....Jdg 2:1
book of the **c** that had been found ..2Kg 23:2
Therefore, let's make a **c** before
  our God......................Ezr 10:3
I have made a **c** with my eyes......Jb 31:1
who keep his **c**, who remember ..Ps 103:18
have made a **c** with death ....Is 28:15
I will make a new **c** with..........Jr 31:31
I will establish a permanent **c** ....Ezk 16:60
Messenger of the **c** you desire ....Mal 3:1
This cup is the new **c**............Lk 22:20
the adoption, the glory, the **c-s**,....Rm 9:4
this will be my **c** with them ....Rm 11:27
This cup is the new **c**...........1Co 11:25
to be ministers of a new **c**,........2Co 3:6
the women represent two **c-s**. ....Gl 4:24
the guarantee of a better **c**......Heb 7:22
he is the mediator of a new **c**,....Heb 9:15

COVER (N)

He spread a cloud as a **c-ing** .....Ps 105:39
hair is given to her as a **c-ing**......1Co 11:15

COVER (V)

the rock and **c** you with my hand ..Ex 33:22
is forgiven, whose sin is **c-ed**! .....Ps 32:1
You **c-ed** all their sin..............Ps 85:2
He will **c** you with his feathers;.....Ps 91:4
but love **c-s** all offenses...........Pr 10:12
with two they **c-ed** their faces,.....Is 6:2
as the water **c-s** the sea...........Hab 2:14
and to the hills, 'C us!'.............Lk 23:30
forgiven and whose sins are **c-ed**! ..Rm 4:7
if a woman doesn't **c** her head,....1Co 11:6
man should not **c** his head 1Co 11:7
and **c** a multitude of sins..........1Pt 4:8
since love **c-s** a multitude of sins ..1Pt 4:8

COVER-UP (N)

using your freedom as a **c** for evil ..1Pt 2:16

COVET

Do not **c** your neighbor's ..Ex 20:17; Dt 5:21
quarter, I **c-ed** them and took
  them.........................Jos 7:21
I have not **c-ed** anyone's silver ....Ac 20:33
what it is to **c** if the law had not....Rm 7:7
do not steal; do not **c**;...........Rm 13:9
You murder and **c** and cannot .....Jms 4:2

COW

seven other **c-s**, sickly and thin.....Gn 41:3
you **c-s** of Bashan who are on the ..Am 4:1

COWARDS

But the **c**, faithless, detestable,....Rv 21:8

CRAFTINESS

He traps the wise in their **c** ....Jb 5:13
He catches the wise in their **c** 1Co 3:19

CRAFTSMAN

I was a skilled **c** beside him........Pr 8:30
business for the **c**-men. ....Ac 19:24

CRAVE

by **c-ing** it, some have wandered..1Tm 6:10

CRAZY

the man is **c**," Achish said 1Sm 21:14
He has a demon and he's **c**. ....Jn 10:20

CREATE

In the beginning God **c-d** the
  heavens ....Gn 1:1
God **c-d** man in his own image;....Gn 1:27
c a clean heart for me ....Ps 51:10
You who **c-d** my inward parts;....Ps 139:13
commanded, and they were **c-d**. ..Ps 148:5
who **c-d** the heavens and stretched ..Is 42:5
All things were **c-d** through him, ...Jn 1:3
served what has been **c-d** instead ..Rm 1:25
man was not **c-d** for the sake of
  woman,.......................1Co 11:9
c-d in Christ Jesus for good works. ..Eph 2:10
c in himself one new man from....Eph 2:15
everything was **c-d** by him,........Col 1:16
everything **c-d** by God is good,....1Tm 4:4
you have **c-d** all things, and by
  your will they ... were **c-d**. ......Rv 4:11

CREATION

he rested from all his work of **c**....Gn 2:3
the beginning of **c** God made
  them..........................Mk 10:6
preach the gospel to all **c**. ....Mk 16:15
have been clearly seen since the **c**..Rm 1:20
For the **c** eagerly waits with ......Rm 8:19
is in Christ, he is a new **c**;.........2Co 5:17
the firstborn over all **c**............Col 1:15
been since the beginning of **c**. 2Pt 3:4

CREATOR

God Most High, **C** of heaven and ..Gn 14:22
So remember your **C** in the days....Ec 12:1
created instead of the **C**,..........Rm 1:25
entrust themselves to a faithful **C**. .1Pt 4:19

CREATURE

and every living **c** that moves......Gn 1:21
No **c** is hidden from him, ...Heb 4:13
Four living **c-s** covered with eyes ...Rv 4:6

CREDIT (N)

what **c** is that to you?.............Lk 6:32
what **c** is there if when you do
  wrong........................1Pt 2:20

CREDIT (V)

he **c-ed** it to him as righteousness. ..Gn 15:6
was **c-ed** to him for righteousness. .Ps 106:31
was **c-ed** to him for righteousness. ..Rm 4:3
God **c-s** righteousness apart from ..Rm 4:6
will be **c-ed** to us who believe ....Rm 4:24
was **c-ed** to him for righteousness, ..Gl 3:6
was **c-ed** to him as righteousness. .Jms 2:23

CRETANS

prophets said, **C** are always ....Ti 1:12

CRETE

Island in the Mediterranean Sea. Paul assigned Titus as supervisor there (Ti 1:5) and
moored there on his way to Rome (Ac 27).

CRIMINAL
as if I were a **c**, to capture me . . . . Mt 26:55
Then two **c-s** were crucified with. .Mt 27:38
man weren't a **c**, we wouldn't . . . . .Jn 18:30

CRIMSON
though they are **c** red,. . . . . .Is 1:18
from Edom in **c**-stained garments . . .Is 63:1

CROOKED
with the **c** you prove . . 2Sm 22:27; Ps 18:26
What is **c** cannot be straightened. . . .Ec 1:15
out what he has made **c**? . . . . Ec 7:13
the **c** will become straight,. . . . . .Lk 3:5
faultless in a **c** and perverted . . . . .Php 2:15

CROP
have anywhere to store my **c-s**?. . . .Lk 12:17

CROSS (N)
doesn't take up his **c** and follow . . Mt 10:38
take up his **c** daily, and follow . . . . . .Lk 9:23
so that the **c** of Christ will not. 1Co 1:17
word of the **c** is foolishness 1Co 1:18
except the **c** of our Lord Jesus . . . . . Gl 6:14
death—even to death on a **c** . . . . . Php 2:8
his blood, shed on the **c**. . . . . Col 1:20
joy ... before him, he endured a **c** . .Heb 12:2

CROSS (V)
your God will **c** over ahead of you . . .Dt 9:3

CROUCH
sin is **c-ing** at the door. . . . . Gn 4:7
He **c-es**; he lies down like a lion . . . Gn 49:9

CROW
the rooster **c-s**, you will deny me. .Mt 26:34
Immediately a rooster **c-ed**, ... Mt 26:74

CROWD
Large **c-s** followed him . . . . Mt 4:25
he saw a large **c**, had compassion. .Mt 14:14
I have compassion on the **c**,. . . . . . .Mt 15:32
him to Jesus because of the **c**,. . . . . .Mk 2:4
through the **c** and went on his . . . . .Lk 4:30

CROWN (N)
she will give you a **c** of beauty. . . . . .Pr 4:9
wife ... is her husband's **c**,. . . . . Pr 12:4
Gray hair is a glorious **c**; . . . . Pr 16:31
to give them a **c** of beauty. . . . . .Is 61:3
twisted together a **c** of thorns,. . . Mt 27:29
to receive a perishable **c**, ...1Co 9:25
and longed for ... my joy and **c**,. . . .Php 4:1
the **c** of righteousness, ...2Tm 4:8
receive the **c** of life that God . . . . . Jms 1:12
the unfading **c** of glory. 1Pt 5:4
I will give you the **c** of life. . . . . . . .Rv 2:10
cast their **c-s** before the throne,. . .Rv 4:10
a **c** was given to him, and he . . . . . . Rv 6:2

CROWN (V)
than God and **c-ed** him with glory. . . Ps 8:5
he is not **c-ed** unless he competes. . 2Tm 2:5
you **c-ed** him with glory and honor. .Heb 2:7

CRUCIFY *SEE ALSO* RECRUCIFYING
to be mocked, flogged, and **c-ied**, . .Mt 20:19
they kept shouting ... "**C** him!" . . . Mt 27:23
two criminals were **c-ied** with him. . Mt 27:38
looking for Jesus who was **c-ied**. . . Mt 28:5
be **c-ied**, and rise on the third day . . Lk 24:7
to them, "Should I **c** your king?" . . .Jn 19:15
they **c-ied** him and two others. . . . Jn 19:18
you **c-ied** and whom God raised. . . . .Ac 4:10
our old self was **c-ied** with him in . .Rm 6:6
preach Christ **c-ied**, a stumbling. . . 1Co 1:23
would not have **c-ied** the Lord of . .1Co 2:8
I have been **c-ied** with Christ . . . . . Gl 2:20
Jesus have **c-ied** the flesh with. . . . . Gl 5:24

CRUEL
merciful acts of the wicked are **c**. . . Pr 12:10

CRUSH
he saves those **c-ed** in spirit. . . . . . Ps 34:18
the bones you have **c-ed** rejoice. . . . Ps 51:8
c-ed because of our iniquities; . . . . .Is 53:5
the LORD was pleased to **c** him . . . .Is 53:10
the poor and **c** the needy, ... Am 4:1
will soon **c** Satan under your feet. . Rm 16:20
in every way but not **c-ed**;. 2Co 4:8

CRY
Your brother's blood **c-ies** out . . . . . Gn 4:10
difficult labor, they **c-ied** out;. . . . . .Ex 2:23
Israelites **c-ied** out to the LORD. . . . . Jdg 3:9
attention to the sound of my **c**, ...Ps 5:2
his ears are open to their **c** for help . .Ps 34:15
My eyes are worn out from **c-ing**. . . Ps 88:9
A voice of one **c-ing** out: . . . . .Is 40:3
the stones will **c** out from the wall, . .Hab 2:11
A voice of one **c-ing** out in the . . . . . Mt 3:3
silent, the stones would **c** out! . . . .Lk 19:40
grief, **c-ing**, and pain will be no . . . .Rv 21:4

CRYSTAL
gleamed like awe-inspiring **c**, ...Ezk 1:22
a sea of glass, similar to **c**, ... Rv 4:6

CUP
head with oil; my **c** overflows. . . . . . Ps 23:5
even a **c** of cold water to . . . . Mt 10:42
to drink the **c** that I am about. . . . . Mt 20:22
Then he took a **c**, and after . . . . . . Mt 26:27
let this **c** pass from me. . . . . Mt 26:39
This **c** is the new covenant. . . . . . . .Lk 22:20
This **c** is the new covenant. 1Co 11:25
full strength into the **c** of his
    anger. . . . . .Rv 14:10

CUPBEARER
The king of Egypt's **c** and baker . . . Gn 40:1
I was the king's **c**. . . . . .Neh 1:11

CURE
But he cannot **c** you or heal your . . .Hs 5:13

CURSE (N)
come and put a **c** on these people. .Nm 22:6
before you a blessing and a **c**: . . . . . Dt 11:26
hung on a tree is under God's **c**. . . . Dt 21:23
all these **c-s** will come. . . . . Dt 28:15
an undeserved **c** goes nowhere. . . . . Pr 26:2
preached to you, a **c** be on him! . . . . .Gl 1:8
redeemed us from the **c** of the law by
    becoming a **c** for us, ... Gl 3:13
Blessing and **c-ing** come out of . . .Jms 3:10

CURSE (V)
will never again **c** the ground . . . . .Gn 8:21
I will **c** anyone who treats you . . . . .Gn 12:3
Those who **c** you will be **c-d**, ... Gn 27:29
C God and die! . . . . .Jb 2:9
and **c-d** the day he was born. . . . . . . Jb 3:1
Whoever **c-s** his father or mother . .Pr 20:20
he started to **c** and to swear . . . . . Mt 26:74
fig tree that you **c-d** has withered. . Mk 11:21
bless those who **c** you, pray for. . . . .Lk 6:28
persecute you; bless and do not **c**. . Rm 12:14
with it we **c** people who are . . . . . .Jms 3:9

CURSED (ADJ)
The ground is **c** because of you. . . . .Gn 3:17
I could wish that I myself were **c** . . .Rm 9:3
C is everyone who is hung on a tree. . Gl 3:13

CURTAIN
the **c** of the sanctuary was torn . . .Mt 27:51
inaugurated ... through the **c**. . . . .Heb 10:20

CUSTOM
and are promoting **c-s** that are not. .Ac 16:21
or the **c-s** of our ancestors, ...Ac 28:17

CUT
right hand causes you to sin,
    c it off. . . . . Mt 5:30

servant, and **c** off his right ear. . . . . Jn 18:10
you too will be **c** off. . . . . Rm 11:22

CYMBAL
Praise him with resounding **c-s**; . . . Ps 150:5
noisy gong or a clanging **c**. 1Co 13:1

CYRUS
King of Persia; used by God (Is 44:28; 45:1);
permitted the exiles to return and rebuild
the temple (2Ch 36:22–Ezr 1:8; 3:7; 4:3–5;
5:13–6:14).

- D -

DAGON
Philistine god (Jdg 16:23; 1Sm 5:2–7; 1Ch
10:10).

DAILY
Give us today our **d** bread. . . . . .Mt 6:11
up his cross **d**, and follow me. . . . . . .Lk 9:23

DAMASCUS
he traveled and was nearing **D**,. . . . .Ac 9:3

DAN
Son of Jacob and Bilhah (Gn 30:4–6; 35:25).
Tribe; unable to conquer allotted land west
of Jerusalem and up the coast to Joppa;
took land in the far north (Jos 19:40–48;
Jdg 18). City (Jdg 18:29).

DANCE (N)
You turned my lament into **d-ing**;. . Ps 30:11
Praise him with tambourine
    and **d**;. .Ps 150:4

DANCE (V)
David was **d-ing** with all his
    might 2Sm 6:14
time to mourn and a time to **d**;. . . . . .Ec 3:4
flute for you, but you didn't **d**; . . . . Mt 11:17
Herodias's daughter **d-d**. . . . . Mt 14:6

DANGER
I fear no **d**, for you are with. . . . . . . Ps 23:4
or nakedness or **d** or sword? . . . . . Rm 8:35
d-s in the city, **d-s** in the 2Co 11:26

DANIEL
1. Son of David (1Ch 3:1).
2. Prophet during the exile in Babylon.
Called Belteshazzar (Dn 1:7); refused to
eat the king's food (1:8–20); interpreted
the king's dreams (Dn 3; 4) and the writing on the wall (Dn 5); thrown in the lions'
den (Dn 6). Received visions (Dn 7–12).

DARE
someone might even **d** to die. . . . . . Rm 5:7

DARIUS
1. The Mede, who conquered Babylon (Dn
5:31).
2. Darius I of Persia allowed the rebuilding
of the temple (Ezr 4:5; 5–6; Hg 1:1; Zch 1:1).
3. Darius II of Persia (Neh 12:22).

DARK
the darkness is not **d** to you. . . . . . Ps 139:12
have said in the **d** will be
    heard. . . . . .Lk 12:3

DARKEST
when I go through the **d** valley, ...Ps 23:4

DARKNESS
walking in **d** have seen a great . . . . . .Is 9:2
I form light and create **d**, ...Is 45:7
if the light within you is **d**, how
    deep is that **d**!. . . . . .Mt 6:23
shines in the **d**, and yet the **d** did not . .Jn 1:5

and people loved **d** rather than .... Jn 3:19
fellowship does light have
with **d**?........................2Co 6:14
you were once **d**, but now .... Eph 5:8
called you out of **d** into his 1Pt 2:9
is absolutely no **d** in him. 1Jn 1:5
but hates his brother or sister is
in the **d**. 1Jn 2:9

DAUGHTER

the sons of God came to the **d-s** of ..Gn 6:4
sons and your **d-s** will prophesy, ... Jl 2:28
Rejoice greatly, **D** Zion! ....Zch 9:9
mother against **d**, **d** against
mother .... Lk 12:53

DAVID

Youngest son of Jesse, anointed king by
Samuel (Ru 4:17–22; 1Sm 16:1–13). Sought
God's heart (1Sm 13:14; Ac 13:22). Killed Goliath (1Sm 17). Covenant of friendship with
Jonathan (18:1–4; 19–20; 23:16–18). Spared
Saul's life (1Sm 24; 26). Anointed king of Judah (2Sm 2:1–11) and Israel (5:1–4).
Conquered Jerusalem (5:6–9) and
brought the ark there (2Sm 6). Was promised by God that he would keep his descendant on the throne (2Sm 7). Prepared for
building the temple (1Ch 22–29). Psalmist,
musician (Ps 23:1), and prophet (Mt 22:43;
Ac 1:16; 4:25).
Committed adultery with Bathsheba
and murdered Uriah, then was confronted
by Nathan (2Sm 11–12). Family and political troubles followed: Amnon, Tamar, and
Absalom (2Sm 13–18); Sheba (2Sm 20); punished for military census (2Sm 24; 1Ch 21);
Adonijah and Solomon (1Kg 1–2).
Named Solomon as successor (1Kg 1:29–
30). Died (2Sm 23:1–7; 1Kg 2:10–12). Ancestor
of Jesus (Mt 1:1,6); Jesus is heir to his throne
forever (Mt 12:23; 21:9; Mk 11:10; Lk 1:32; Rv
22:16).

DAWN (N)

righteousness shine like the **d**, ... Ps 37:6
appearance is as sure as the **d**. ..... Hs 6:3

DAWN (V)

a light has **d-ed** on those living in ... Is 9:2
of death, light has **d-ed**. .... Mt 4:16

DAY

God called the light "**d**," ....Gn 1:5
he meditates on it **d** and night. ...... Ps 1:2
pursue me all the **d-s** of my life,.... Ps 23:6
Teach us to number our **d-s** ...... Ps 90:12
This is the **d** the LORD has made .. Ps 118:24
Creator in the **d-s** of your youth: ... Ec 12:1
can endure the **d** of his coming?....Mal 3:2
that **d** and hour no one.......... Mt 24:36
Give us each **d** our daily bread...... Lk 11:3
will raise him up on the last **d**. ..... Jn 6:40
now is the **d** of salvation..........2Co 6:2
time, because the **d-s** are evil. .... Eph 5:16
well that the **d** of the Lord will 1Th 5:2
entrusted to me until that **d**,......2Tm 1:12
one **d** is like a thousand years,......2Pt 3:8

DEACONS

D, likewise, should be 1Tm 3:8

DEAD

and let the **d** bury their own **d**..... Mt 8:22
He is not the God of the **d**, ... Mt 22:32
'He has been raised from the **d**. ... Mt 28:7
looking for the living among
the **d**?..........................Lk 24:5
consider yourselves **d** to sin. ...... Rm 6:11
you were **d** in your trespasses...... Eph 2:1
the firstborn from the **d**, ...Col 1:18
and the **d** in Christ will rise 1Th 4:16
also faith without works is **d**. ..... Jms 2:26

DEAD SEA

The end of the Jordan River, forming the
southeastern border of Canaan (Nm 34:3;
Jos 15:5); also called the Sea of the Arabah
(Dt 3:17; Jos 3:16; 12:3; 2Kg 14:25) and the
Eastern Sea (Ezk 47:18; Zch 14:8).

DEAF

makes him mute or **d**, seeing or .... Ex 4:11
On that day the **d** will hear the..... Is 29:18
the **d** hear, the dead are raised,..... Mt 11:5

DEATH

You put me into the dust of **d**. ...... Ps 22:15
The **d** of his faithful ones is ....Ps 116:15
Rescue those being taken off to **d**, .. Pr 24:11
When he has swallowed up **d**
once and for all.................. Is 25:8
D, where are your barbs? .... Hs 13:14
will not taste **d** until they see .... Mt 16:28
but has passed from **d** to life. ...... Jn 5:24
he will never see **d**. .... Jn 8:51
d reigned from Adam to Moses, ... Rm 5:14
For the wages of sin is **d**, ...Rm 6:23
neither **d** nor life, nor angels nor
rulers, ...Rm 8:38
Where, **d**, is your victory?...... 1Co 15:55
passed from **d** to life because 1Jn 3:14
I hold the keys of **d** and Hades...... Rv 1:18
D and Hades were thrown into the ..Rv 20:14
D will be no more; .... Rv 21:4

DEBATE

Where is the **d-r** of this age?...... 1Co 1:20
But avoid foolish **d-s**, genealogies ... Ti 3:9

DEBORAH

Prophet and judge (Jdg 4–5).

DEBT

forgive us our **d-s**, as we also ..... Mt 6:12
forgive everyone in **d** to us......... Lk 11:4
He erased the certificate of **d**,..... Col 2:14

DEBTORS

as we also have forgiven our **d**..... Mt 6:12

DECAY

allow your faithful one to see **d**.... Ps 16:10
allow your holy one to see **d**. ......Ac 2:27
not allow your holy one to see **d**... Ac 13:35

DECEIT

and in whose spirit is no **d**! ....Ps 32:2
Israelite in whom there is no **d**..... Jn 1:47
quarrels, **d**, and malice........... Rm 1:29
and no **d** was found in his mouth; .. 1Pt 2:22

DECEITFUL

heart is more **d** than anything...... Jr 17:9

DECEIVE

I am he,' and they will **d** many. .... Mk 13:6
Let no one **d** himself............... 1Co 3:18
Don't be **d-d**: God is not mocked .... Gl 6:7
Let no one **d** you with empty ..... Eph 5:6
worse, **d-ing** and being **d-d**.......2Tm 3:13
have no sin," we are **d-ing** ourselves .. 1Jn 1:8

DECENCY

clothing, with **d** and good sense, .. 1Tm 2:9

DECEPTIVE

Charm is **d** and beauty is .... Pr 31:30

DECISION

but its every **d** is from the LORD ... Pr 16:33
multitudes in the valley of **d**! ....Jl 3:14

DECLARE

The heavens **d** the glory of God,.... Ps 19:1

DECREE

In those days a **d** went out from .... Lk 2:1

DEDICATE

the Israelites **d-d** the LORD's 1Kg 8:63
for anyone to **d** something rashly ..Pr 20:25

DEED

whatever you do, in word or in **d**,...Col 3:17

DEEP

D calls to **d** in the roar of ....Ps 42:7

DEER

As a **d** longs for streams of .... Ps 42:1
like those of a **d** and enables me ..Hab 3:19

DEFECT

No man who has any **d** is to come ..Lv 21:18

DEFENSE

At my first **d**, no one stood
by me,.........................2Tm 4:16
ready ... to give a **d** to anyone who.. 1Pt 3:15

DEFILE

that Shechem had **d-d** his
daughter .... Gn 34:5
out of the mouth—this **d-s** a man.. Mt 15:11
These are the things that **d** a
person, ... Mt 15:20
conscience, being weak, is **d-d**...... 1Co 8:7

DELIGHT (N)

his **d** is in the LORD's .... Ps 1:2
Take **d** in the LORD, and he will ..... Ps 37:4
your instruction is my **d**........Ps 119:77,174

DELIGHT (V)

rescued me because he **d-ed**
in me. .... Ps 18:19
disciplines the son in whom he **d-s**... Pr 3:12
my beloved in whom I **d**; ....Mt 12:18

DELILAH

Philistine woman who betrayed Samson
(Jdg 16:4–22).

DELIVER

but **d** us from the evil one........ Mt 6:13
He was **d-ed** up for our trespasses .. Rm 4:25
has **d-ed** us from such a terrible... 2Co 1:10
faith that was **d-ed** to the saints once .. Jd 3

DELIVERANCE

d will come to the Jewish people from
another place,................. Est 4:14
me with joyful shouts of **d**........ Ps 32:7

DELIVERER

the LORD raised up ... a **d** to save ...Jdg 3:9
my fortress, and my **d**, ... 2Sm 22:2; Ps 18:2
You are my help and my **d**;... Ps 40:17; 70:5

DELUSION

them a strong **d** so that they 2Th 2:11

DEMOLISH

We **d** arguments.................2Co 10:4

DEMOLITION

for the **d** of strongholds. 2Co 10:4

DEMON

sacrificed to **d-s**, not God, ... Dt 32:17
drive out **d-s** in your name .... Mt 7:22
and they say, 'He has a **d**!' .... Mt 11:18
spirits and the teachings of **d-s**, ... 1Tm 4:1
Even the **d-s** believe—and they .. Jms 2:19
stop worshiping **d-s** and idols of .. Rv 9:20

DEMON-POSSESSED

brought ... the **d**, the epileptics, ... Mt 4:24
two **d** men met him as they came. Mt 8:28

DEMONSTRATE

to **d** his righteousness......... Rm 3:25,26

DEN

threw him into the lions' **d**. . . . . . . Dn 6:16
are making it a **d** of thieves! . . . . . . Mt 21:13

DENY

But whoever **d-ies** me before others,
  I will also **d** him before my . . . . Mt 10:33
let him **d** himself, take up. . . . . . . Mt 16:24
you will **d** me three times! . . . . . . Mt 26:34
he has **d-ied** the faith and is
  worse 1Tm 5:8
if we **d** him, he will also **d** us; 2Tm 2:12
of godliness but **d-ing** its power. . . 2Tm 3:5
but they **d** him by their works. . . . . . Ti 1:16
d-ing the Master who bought them, . .2Pt 2:1
who **d-ies** ... Jesus is the Christ? . . . 1Jn 2:22

DEPART

scepter will not **d** from Judah . . . . Gn 49:10
is old he will not **d** from it. . . . . Pr 22:6
on the left, 'D from me, you who . .Mt 25:41
I long to **d** and be with. . . . . .Php 1:23

DEPRIVE

Do not **d** one another— 1Co 7:5

DEPTH

height nor **d**, nor any other . . . . . . .Rm 8:39
the **d** of the riches and the
  wisdom. . . . . .Rm 11:33
everything, even the **d-s** of God. . . 1Co 2:10

DESCEND

the Spirit **d-ing** from heaven like . . . Jn 1:32
ascending and **d-ing** on the Son of . . Jn 1:51
the one who **d-ed** from heaven . . . . Jn 3:13
The one who **d-ed** is also the one . . Eph 4:10
himself will **d** from heaven with . . . 1Th 4:16

DESCENDANT

So will your **d-s** be. . . . . Rm 4:18

DESERT (N)

highway for our God in the **d**. . . . . . Is 40:3
rivers in the **d**, to give drink. . . . . . Is 43:20

DESERT (V)

disciples **d-ed** him and ran away . . Mt 26:56

DESERVE

has not dealt with us as our sins **d** . . Ps 103:10
He has done nothing to **d** death. . . . Lk 23:15

DESIRE (N)

Your **d** will be for your husband . . . .Gn 3:16
will give you your heart's **d-s**. . . . . . Ps 37:4
my heart's **d** and prayer to God . . . Rm 10:1
no provision for the flesh to gratify
  its **d-s** . . . . Rm 13:14
to marry than to burn with **d**. 1Co 7:9
carry out the **d** of the flesh. . . . . Gl 5:16
and enticed by his own evil **d**. . . . . .Jms 1:14

DESIRE (V)

or **d** your neighbor's house, ... Dt 5:21
nothing you **d** can equal her. . . . . Pr 3:15
that we should **d** him. . . . . .Is 53:2
For I **d** loyalty and not. . . . . Hs 6:6
I **d** mercy and not sacrifice . . Mt 9:13; 12:7
I have fervently **d-d** to eat this. . . . . Lk 22:15
But **d** the greater gifts 1Co 12:31
d-ing to put on our heavenly
  dwelling 2Co 5:2

DESOLATE

your house is left to you **d**. . . . . . Mt 23:38
the children of the **d** woman, ... Gl 4:27

DESOLATION

set up the abomination of **d**. . . . . . Dn 11:31
the abomination of **d**, ...Mt 24:15
abomination of **d** standing
  where it . . . . .Mk 13:14
that its **d** has come near. . . . . Lk 21:20

DESPAIR (N)

myself over to **d** concerning all . . . . .Ec 2:20
we are perplexed but not in **d**; 2Co 4:8

DESPAIR (V)

so that we even **d-ed** of life 2Co 1:8

DESPISE

So Esau **d-d** his birthright. . . . . Gn 25:34
and she **d-d** him in her heart. 2Sm 6:16
fools **d** wisdom and discipline. . . . . . Pr 1:7
He was **d-d** and rejected by men, ...Is 53:3
devoted to one and **d** the other. . . . Mt 6:24
Don't let anyone **d** your youth, ...1Tm 4:12
endured a cross, **d-ing** the shame. .Heb 12:2

DESTINED

this child is **d** to cause the fall. . . . . .Lk 2:34

DESTITUTE

in goatskins, **d**, afflicted . . . . Heb 11:37

DESTROY

who is able to **d** both soul and . . . Mt 10:28
Have you come to **d** us? . . . . Mk 1:24
to steal and kill and **d**. . . . . Jn 10:10
we are struck down but not **d-ed**. . .2Co 4:9
our outer person is being **d-ed**, . . . 2Co 4:16
if our earthly tent ... is **d-ed**, ... 2Co 5:1
who is able to save and to **d**. . . . . .Jms 4:12

DESTRUCTION

set apart to the LORD for **d**. . . . . . . Jos 6:17
Pride comes before **d**, ... Pr 16:18
road broad that leads to **d**, ...Mt 7:13
objects of wrath prepared for **d**? . .Rm 9:22
Their end is **d**; their god is . . . . Php 3:19
the penalty of eternal **d** 2Th 1:9
twist them to their own **d**, ... 2Pt 3:16

DETERMINE

Since a person's days are **d-d** and . . . Jb 14:5
I have **d-d** that my mouth will . . . Ps 17:3
but the LORD **d-s** his steps. . . . . Pr 16:9
person's steps are **d-d** by the LORD, . .Pr 20:24

DETEST

D evil; cling to what is good. . . . . . . Rm 12:9

DETESTABLE

committed all these **d** acts, ... Lv 18:27
imitating the **d** practices 2Kg 16:3

DEVIL

to be tempted by the **d**. . . . . Mt 4:1
enemy who sowed them is the **d**. . Mt 13:39
for the **d** and his angels! . . . . .Mt 25:41
Yet one of you is the **d**! . . . . Jn 6:70
don't give the **d** an opportunity . . .Eph 4:27
against the schemes of the **d**. . . . . .Eph 6:11
Resist the **d**, and he will . . . . .Jms 4:7
adversary the **d** is prowling 1Pt 5:8
who is called the **d** and Satan, ...Rv 12:9

DEVOTED

be **d** to one and despise the other . . Mt 6:24

DEVOUR

Must the sword **d** forever? 2Sm 2:26
if you bite and **d** one another, ... Gl 5:15
looking for anyone he can **d**. 1Pt 5:8

DEVOUT

This man was righteous and **d**, ...Lk 2:25

DEW

If **d** is only on the fleece, ...Jdg 6:37

DICTATION

At Jeremiah's **d**, Baruch wrote on . . . Jr 36:4

DIE

from it, you will certainly **d**. . . . . . . .Gn 2:17
Where you **d**, I will **d**, and there I . . . Ru 1:17

DISEASE

but fools **d** for lack of sense. . . . . . . Pr 10:21
him with a rod, he will not **d**. . . . . . Pr 23:13
a time to give birth and a time to **d**; . .Ec 3:2
and drink, for tomorrow we **d**! . . . .Is 22:13
Even if I have to **d** with you, ... Mt 26:35
believes in me will never **d**. . . . . . . Jn 11:26
wheat falls to the ground and **d-s**, . .Jn 12:24
time, Christ **d-d** for the ungodly. . . .Rm 5:6
How can we who **d-d** to sin still . . . .Rm 6:2
and if we **d**, we **d** for the Lord. . . . .Rm 14:8
that Christ **d-d** for our sins 1Co 15:3
the law I **d-d** to the law, ...Gl 2:19
to live is Christ and to **d** is gain. . . .Php 1:21
for people to **d** once . . . . Heb 9:27
The dead who **d** in the Lord. . . . . . . Rv 14:13

DIG

cisterns that you did not **d**, ... Dt 6:11
fence around it, **dug** a winepress . .Mt 21:33

DINAH

Daughter of Jacob and Leah (Gn 30:21).
Raped by Shechem; avenged by Simeon
and Levi (Gn 34).

DIP

the one who is **d-ping** bread . . . . Mk 14:20

DIRECT

He **d-s** it wherever he chooses. . . . . . .Pr 21:1
May the Lord **d** your hearts to 2Th 3:5

DISAPPOINT

hope will not **d** us, because God's. . . Rm 5:5

DISARM

He **d-ed** the rulers and authorities . . .Col 2:15

DISASTER

the wicked for the day of **d**. . . . . . . Pr 16:4
I make success and create **d**; . . . . . .Is 45:7
If a **d** occurs in a city, hasn't. . . . . . Am 3:6
No **d** will overtake us. . . . . Mc 3:11

DISCERN

so that you may **d** what is the . . . . Rm 12:2

DISCIPLE

Summoning his twelve **d-s**, he
  gave . . . . .Mt 10:1
A **d** is not above his teacher, ... Mt 10:24
and make **d-s** of all nations, ... Mt 28:19
come after me cannot be my **d**. . . .Lk 14:27
and his **d-s** believed in him. . . . . .Jn 2:11
my word, you really are my **d-s**. . . . Jn 8:31
and the **d** he loved. . . . . Jn 19:26
d-s were first called Christians at . . .Ac 11:26

DISCIPLINE (N)

Apply yourself to **d** and listen to . . Pr 23:12
Don't withhold **d** from a youth; . . . Pr 23:13
No **d** seems enjoyable at the time. .Heb 12:11

DISCIPLINE (V)

your anger or **d** me in your wrath. . Ps 38:1
for the LORD **d-s** the one he loves, . . Pr 3:12
D your son while there is hope; . . . . Pr 19:18
judged ... we are **d-d**, so that we . . 1Co 11:32
for the Lord **d-s** the one he loves . .Heb 12:6

DISCOURAGED

Do not be afraid or **d**, ... Jos 1:9
stopped walking and looked **d**. . . . . Lk 18:1

DISCUSS

And they were **d-ing** among
  themselves, ...Mt 16:7

DISEASE

all the terrible **d-s** of Egypt that. . . . Dt 7:15
he heals all your **d-s**. . . . . Ps 103:3
and healing every **d** and sickness . .Mt 4:23
weaknesses and carried our **d-s**. . . . .Mt 8:17
demons and to heal **d-s**. . . . . Lk 9:1

DISFIGURED

was so **d** that he did not. . . . . Is 52:14

DISGRACE

When arrogance comes, **d** follows, . . .Pr 11:2
but sin is a **d** to any people. . . . . . . Pr 14:34
has long hair it is a **d** to him, ...1Co 11:14

DISGRACEFUL

But if it is **d** for a woman to. 1Co 11:6
for it is **d** for a woman to speak . . 1Co 14:35

DISGUISE

king of Israel **d-d** himself 1Kg 22:30
Satan **d-s** himself as an angel . . 2Co 11:14

DISHONEST

D scales are detestable to the . . . . . . .Pr 11:1
one who hates **d** profit prolongs . . Pr 28:16

DISHONOR (N)

for honor and another for **d**?. . . . . . Rm 9:21
sown in **d**, raised in glory; 1Co 15:43

DISHONOR (V)

her head uncovered **d-s** her head, . . 1Co 11:5

DISMISS

You can **d** your servant in peace, ...Lk 2:29

DISOBEDIENCE

through one man's **d** the many . . . . Rm 5:19
received mercy through their **d**, . . Rm 11:30

DISOBEDIENT

out my hands to a **d** and defiant . .Rm 10:21
spirit now working in the **d**. . . . . . . Eph 2:2

DISORDER

is not a God of **d** but of peace. . . . 1Co 14:33

DISPERSE

Jewish people **d-d** among the. . . . . . Jn 7:35

DISPLAY

I will **d** my glory among the. . . . . . Ezk 39:21
I think God has **d-ed** us, ...1Co 4:9
ages he might **d** the immeasurable. .Eph 2:7

DISPUTE

was **d-ing** with the devil . . . . Jd 9

DISQUALIFY

others, I myself will not be **d-ied** . . .1Co 9:27

DISSENSIONS

selfish ambitions, **d**, factions, ... Gl 5:20

DISTINCTION

They make no **d** between the
  holy. . . . . Ezk 22:26
believe, since there is no **d**. . . . . Rm 3:22
for there is no **d** between Jew. . . . Rm 10:12

DISTINGUISH

You must **d** between the holy and. . Lv 10:10
to another, **d-ing** between spirits . .1Co 12:10

DISTRACTED

But Martha was **d** by her many . . .Lk 10:40

DISTRESS

to be sorrowful and deeply **d-ed**. . Mt 26:37
will be great **d** in the land . . . . Lk 21:23

DISTRIBUTE

d the land as an inheritance. . . . . . .Jos 13:6
This was then **d-d** to each person . . Ac 4:35
d-ing to each person as he wills. . .1Co 12:11

DIVIDE

your hand over the sea, and **d** it . . . Ex 14:16
They **d-d** my garments among . . . . Ps 22:18
Every kingdom **d-d** against itself . .Mt 12:25

---

him, they **d-d** his clothes . . . . . . Mt 27:35
my brother to **d** the inheritance . . . . Lk 12:13
Is Christ **d-d**? Was it Paul who. 1Co 1:13

DIVINATION

not to practice **d** or sorcery. . . . . . . Lv 19:26
rebellion is like the sin of **d**, ...1Sm 15:23

DIVINE

his eternal power and **d** nature, . . . Rm 1:20
His **d** power has given us everything. . 2Pt 1:3
you may share in the **d** nature, ... 2Pt 1:4

DIVISION

No, I tell you, but rather **d**!. . . . . Lk 12:51
that there be no **d-s** among you, . . 1Co 1:10
church there are **d-s** among you, . . 1Co 11:18
would be no **d** in the body, ... 1Co 12:25

DIVORCE

he cannot **d** her as long as he . . . . .Dt 22:19
may write her a **d** certificate, ...Dt 24:1
given her a certificate of **d**. . . . . Jr 3:8
If he hates and **d-s** his wife, ...Mal 2:16
decided to **d** her secretly. . . . . .Mt 1:19
must give her a written notice of **d**. . Mt 5:31
permitted you to **d** your wives . . . . Mt 19:8

DIVORCED (ADJ)

marries a **d** woman commits . . . . . . Mt 5:32

DOCTOR

who are well who need a **d**, ... Mt 9:12
proverb to me: '**D**, heal yourself . . . .Lk 4:23

DOCTRINE

teaching as **d-s** human commands. . Mt 15:9
people not to teach false **d** 1Tm 1:3
they will not tolerate sound **d**, ... 2Tm 4:3

DOER

But be **d-s** of the word and not . . .Jms 1:22

DOG

'The **d-s** will eat Jezebel in the . . . 1Kg 21:23
As a **d** returns to its vomit, ... Pr 26:11
since a live **d** is better than a. . . . . . . Ec 9:4
bread and throw it to the **d-s**. . . . . . Mk 7:27
A **d** returns to its own vomit, ... 2Pt 2:22

DOMAIN

us from the **d** of darkness . . . . .Col 1:13

DOMINION

His **d** is an everlasting **d** . . . . . .Dn 4:34; 7:14
power and **d**, and every title . . . . . Eph 1:21
to him be glory and **d** forever . . . . . .Rv 1:6

DONKEY

the LORD opened the **d-'s** mouth,. . Nm 22:28
riding on a **d**, on a colt, the foal of . .Zch 9:9
mounted on a **d** and on a colt . . . . .Mt 21:5
A speechless **d** spoke with a human. .2Pt 2:16

DOOR

Rise up, ancient **d-s**! Then the King. . Ps 24:7
keep watch at the **d** of my lips. . . . . Ps 141:3
and the **d** will be opened to you. . . . Mt 7:7
to enter through the narrow **d**, ... Lk 13:24
the Lord opened a **d** for me. 2Co 2:12
that God may open a **d** to us for. . . . Col 4:3
you an open **d** that no one can. . . . . Rv 3:8
I stand at the **d** and knock. . . . . Rv 3:20

DOORPOST

blood and put it on the two **d-s**. . . . Ex 12:7
Write them on the **d-s** of
  your house . . . . Dt 6:9

DOUBLE-EDGED

and as sharp as a **d** sword. . . . . Pr 5:4
and sharper than any **d** sword. . . . . Heb 4:12
sharp **d** sword came from his
  mouth, ... Rv 1:16

DOUBT

of little faith, why did you **d**? . . . . .Mt 14:31
If you have faith and do not **d**, ...Mt 21:21
they worshiped, but some **d-ed**. . . .Mt 28:17
whoever **d-s** stands condemned. . Rm 14:23
let him ask in faith without **d-ing**. . .Jms 1:6

DOUGH

took their **d** before it was
  leavened, .Ex 12:34
leavens the whole batch of **d**? 1Co 5:6
leavens the whole batch of **d**. . . . . . .Gl 5:9

DOVE

he sent out a **d** to see whether. . . . . Gn 8:8
Spirit of God descending like a **d** . . Mt 3:16
serpents and as innocent as **d-s**. . . .Mt 10:16

DOWNFALL

Before his **d** a person's heart is
  proud, ... Pr 18:12

DRAGON

And the **d** stood in front of the. . . . .Rv 12:4
He seized the **d**, that ancient
  serpent . . . . Rv 20:2

DRAW

the Father who sent me **d-s** him, . . .Jn 6:44
earth I will **d** all people to . . . . .Jn 12:32
let us **d** near with a true heart . . . Heb 10:22
D near to God, and he will **d** near. .Jms 4:8

DREAM (N)

Joseph had a **d**. . . . . .Gn 37:5
Daniel also understood ... **d-s** . . . . . Dn 1:17
Daniel had a **d** with visions in . . . . .Dn 7:1
your old men will have **d-s**, and . . . . Jl 2:28
appeared to Joseph in a **d**, ...Mt 2:13
terribly in a **d** because of him. . . . . .Mt 27:19
and your old men will dream **d-s**. . . Ac 2:17

DREAM (V)

he **d-ed**: A stairway was set on. . . .Gn 28:12

DRESS

the women are to **d** themselves in. .1Tm 2:9

DRINK

D water from your own cistern, ... Pr 5:15
eat and **d**, for tomorrow we die!. . . .Is 22:13
and you gave me something
  to **d**; . . . . Mt 25:35
and they all **drank** from it. . . . . . . Mk 14:23
Do this, as often as you **d** it, ...1Co 11:25
we were all given one Spirit to **d**. . .1Co 12:13

DRIVE

did not **d** them out completely. . . .Jos 17:13
He **drove** everyone out of the
  temple . . . . .Jn 2:15
perfect love **d-s** out fear, ... 1Jn 4:18

DRUNK (ADJ)

And don't get **d** with wine, ...Eph 5:18

DRUNKARD

a glutton and a **d**, a friend of . . . . .Mt 11:19
abusive, a **d** or a swindler. 1Co 5:11

DRUNKENNESS

not in carousing and **d**; . . . . .Rm 13:13
envy, **d**, carousing, and anything . . . Gl 5:21
evil desires, **d**, orgies. 1Pt 4:3

DRY

and let the **d** land appear. . . . . .Gn 1:9
go through the sea on **d**
  ground. . . . . .Ex 14:16
D bones, hear the word of . . . . . . .Ezk 37:4

DULL

Make the minds of these
  people **d**; . . . . Is 6:10

DUST

man out of the **d** from the ground. . .Gn 2:7
belly and eat **d** all the days . . . . . . .Gn 3:14
offspring like the **d** of the earth, . .Gn 13:16
I am **d** and ashes. . . . . .Jb 42:6
remembering that we are **d**. . . . . Ps 103:14
all come from **d**, and all return
  to **d**. . . . . .Ec 3:20
shake the **d** off your feet when . . .Mt 10:14
The first man was ... a man of **d**; . . 1Co 15:47

DUTY

we've only done our **d**. . . . . Lk 17:10

DWELL

LORD, who can **d** in your tent?. . . . . . Ps 15:1
and I will **d** in the house of the . . . . . Ps 23:6
became flesh and **dwelt** among
  us. . . . . Jn 1:14
that Christ may **d** in your hearts. . . Eph 3:17
praiseworthy—**d** on these things. . Php 4:8
all his fullness **d** in him,. . . . . .Col 1:19
God's nature **d-s** bodily in Christ, . . . Col 2:9

DWELLING

a place for your **d** forever. 1Kg 8:13
a place for your **d** forever. 2Ch 6:2
being built together for God's **d** . . Eph 2:22

- E -

EAGLE

I carried you on **e-s'** wings and. . . . .Ex 19:4
youth is renewed like the **e**. . . . . . .Ps 103:5
they will soar on wings like **e-s**; . . . Is 40:31
the left, and the face of an **e**. . . . . Ezk 1:10
creature like a flying **e**. . . . . .Rv 4:7

EAR

One who shaped the **e** not hear,. . . .Ps 94:9
otherwise they ... hear with
  their **e-s**,. Is 6:10
Let anyone who has **e-s** listen! . . . . Mt 11:15
servant, and cut off his right **e**. . . . Jn 18:10
no eye has seen, no **e** has heard,. . . .1Co 2:9
And if the **e** should say. 1Co 12:16
who has **e-s** to hear listen to. . . . . . .Rv 2:7

EARTH

God created the heavens and the **e**. . Gn 1:1
may know the **e** belongs to LORD. . .Ex 9:29
The **e** and everything in it,. . . . . Ps 24:1
whole **e** sing to the LORD. . . . . Ps 96:1
he is coming to judge the **e**. . . . . . . Ps 96:13
his glory fills the whole **e**. . . . . Is 6:3
they will inherit the **e**. . . . . Mt 5:5
Heaven and **e** will pass away, . . . Mt 24:35
and peace on **e** to people he . . . . . . Lk 2:14
we wait for ... a new **e**, ... 2Pt 3:13

EARTHLY

if our **e** tent we live in. 2Co 5:1
They are focused on **e** things, ...Php 3:19
not ... above but is **e**, unspiritual, . .Jms 3:15

EARTHQUAKE

but the LORD was not in the **e**. 1Kg 19:11
be famines and **e-s** in various . . . . . Mt 24:7
There was a violent **e**,. . . . . Mt 28:2
was such a violent **e** that the . . . . .Ac 16:26
A violent **e** occurred;. . . . . .Rv 6:12

EASIER

For which is **e**: to say, 'Your . . . . Mt 9:5
it is **e** for a camel to go. . . . . Mt 19:24
But it is **e** for heaven and earth . . . Lk 16:17

EAST

As far as the **e** is from the west, . . Ps 103:12
wise men from the **e** arrived . . . . . . .Mt 2:1

EASY

For my yoke is **e** and my burden. . .Mt 11:30

EAT

You are free to **e** from any tree . . . . .Gn 2:16
took some of its fruit and **ate** it; . . . Gn 3:6
words were found, and I **ate** them . . Jr 15:16
E this scroll, then go and speak. . . . . Ezk 3:1
of Man came **e-ing** and
  drinking,. Mt 11:19
Everyone **ate** and was satisfied. . . Mt 14:20
They all **ate** and were satisfied. . . .Mt 15:37
and said, "Take and **e** it; . . . . Mt 26:26
sinners and **e-s** with them! . . . . Lk 15:2
who **e-s** my flesh and drinks . . . . . . .Jn 6:54
Get up, Peter; kill and **e**! . . . . Ac 10:13
believes he may **e** anything, ... Rm 14:2
whether you **e** or drink, or 1Co 10:31
work, he should not **e**. 2Th 3:10
He said to me, "Take and **e** it; . . . . .Rv 10:9

EDEN

LORD God planted a garden in **E**,. . . . Gn 2:8
You were in **E**, the garden of God. . Ezk 28:13

EDOM

is why he was also named **E**. . . . . . Gn 25:30
land of Seir, the territory of **E**. . . . . . Gn 32:3

EFFECTIVE

is living and **e** and sharper than . . Heb 4:12

EFFORT

not depend on human will or **e** . . .Rm 9:16
then, make every **e** to enter that . .Heb 4:11
make every **e** to supplement your . . 2Pt 1:5

EGYPT

Abram went down to **E** to stay . . .Gn 12:10
sold Joseph in **E** to Potiphar, ... Gn 37:36
all his offspring with him came
  to **E**. . . . . .Gn 46:6
lived in **E** was 430 years. . . . . .Ex 12:40
out of **E** I called my son. . . . . Hs 11:1
Out of **E** I called my Son. . . . . .Mt 2:15

EHUD

Benjaminite judge (Jdg 3:12–30).

ELAH

1. Valley where David fought Goliath (1Sm 17:2,19; 21:9).
2. Son of Baasha; king of Israel (1Kg 16:6–14).

ELDER

break the tradition of the **e-s**? . . . . .Mt 15:2
appointed **e-s** ... in every church. . . Ac 14:23
The **e-s** who are good leaders. 1Tm 5:17
accusation against an **e** unless 1Tm 5:19
call for the **e-s** of the church, ...Jms 5:14
thrones sat twenty-four **e-s** . . . . . . Rv 4:4

ELEAZAR

Son of Aaron; high priest (Ex 6:23; Nm 20:25–28). Helped Joshua distribute land (Jos 14:1).

ELECT

if possible, even the **e**. . . . . Mt 24:24
justice to his **e** who cry out to. . . . . Lk 18:7
but the **e** did find it. . . . . .Rm 11:7

ELECTION

purpose according to **e** might stand. . Rm 9:11
to confirm your calling and **e**, ... 2Pt 1:10

ELEMENTS

based on the **e** of the world, ... Col 2:8

ELEVEN

appeared to the **E** themselves as . .Mk 16:14

ELI

High priest at Samuel's birth (1Sm 1–4). Blessed Hannah (1:17; 2:20). Failed to discipline his sons (2:12–17,22–36). Died when the ark was captured (4:11–18).

ELÍ

E, E, lemá sabachtháni?. . . . . Mt 27:46

ELIAKIM

1. Son of Hilkiah; Hezekiah's administrator (2Kg 18:18; Is 22:20; 36:3).
2. Son of Josiah; king of Judah. Called Jehoiakim (2Kg 23:34; 2Ch 36:4).

ELIEZER

1. Abraham's servant (Gn 15:2).
2. Son of Moses (Ex 18:4; 1Ch 23:15).
3. Ancestor of Jesus (Lk 3:29).

ELIJAH

Prophet against Ahab and Ahaziah. Predicted famine (1Kg 17:1; Jms 5:17). Fed by ravens (1Kg 17:2–7); fed by widow (17:8–16; Lk 4:26); raised widow's son (1Kg 17:17–24). Defeated prophets of Baal (18:19–40). Fled Jezebel (19:1–3). Chose Elisha to succeed him (19:16,19–21); taken up into heaven (2Kg 2:1–12).
  Forerunner to the Messiah, embodied in John the Baptist (Mal 4:5; Mt 11:14; 17:10–13; Lk 1:17). Appeared with Jesus (Mt 17:3–4).

ELISHA

Prophet; successor to Elijah (1Kg 19:16–21; 2Kg 2:1–18). Made bad water good (2Kg 2:19–22); called bears to punish boys (2:23–24); provided water for army (3:13–22). Provided miraculous supply of oil for widow (4:1–7); granted son to barren woman and restored him to life (4:8–37). Healed Naaman and punished Gehazi (5:1–27). Made iron ax head float (6:5–7). Blinded Aramean army (6:8–7:20). A man was revived by touching his dead bones (13:20–21).
  Made Hazael king of Aram (2Kg 8:7–15) and Jehu king of Israel (9:1–13).

ELIZABETH

Mother of John the Baptist; Mary's relative (Lk 1).

ELKANAH

Father of Samuel; husband of Hannah (1Sm 1:1).

ELOI

voice, "**E, E, lemá sabachtháni** . . . . Mk 15:34

EMBRACE

Can a man **e** fire and his clothes . . . . Pr 6:27

EMMAUS

on their way to a village called **E**,. . Lk 24:13

EMPTY (ADJ)

mouth will not return to me **e**, ... Is 55:11
deceive you with **e** arguments,. . . . Eph 5:6

EMPTY (V)

cross of Christ will not be **e-ied** 1Co 1:17
he **e-ied** himself by assuming. . . . . Php 2:7

EMPTY-HANDED

No one is to appear before
  me **e**. . . . . .Ex 23:15

ENCAMPS

of the LORD **e** around those
  who. . . . . .Ps 34:7

ENCOURAGE

Therefore **e** one another and. 1Th 4:18

ENCOURAGEMENT

(which is translated Son of **E**),. . . . . .Ac 4:36
through the **e** from the
  Scriptures. . . . . Rm 15:4
then, there is any **e** in Christ,. . . . . .Php 2:1

END (N)

to put an **e** to every creature, ...Gn 6:13
and the **e-s** of the earth your ....Ps 2:8
make me aware of my **e** ....Ps 39:4
but its **e** is the way to death......Pr 14:12
The **e** of a matter is better than .....Ec 7:8
endures to the **e** will be saved....Mt 10:22
endures to the **e** will be saved.....Mt 24:13
and his kingdom will have no **e**.....Lk 1:33
He loved them to the **e**..........Jn 13:1
and to the **e-s** of the earth.........Ac 1:8
Christ is the **e** of the law for ......Rm 10:4
who keeps my works to the **e**: ....Rv 2:26
last, the beginning and the **e**......Rv 22:13

END (V)

Love never **e-s**. But as for.........1Co 13:8

ENDURANCE

that affliction produces **e**, ...Rm 5:3
faith, love, **e**, and gentleness. 1Tm 6:11
Let us run with **e** the race that ....Heb 12:1
the testing of your faith produces **e**..Jms 1:3

ENDURE

of the LORD is pure, **e-ing** forever;..Ps 19:9
May they fear you while the sun **e-s**..Ps 72:5
for he is good. His faithful love **e-s**...Ps 136:1
But who can **e** the day of his......Mal 3:2
the one who **e-s** to the end will ...Mt 10:22
e-d with much patience objects of..Rm 9:22
hopes all things, **e-s** all things.....1Co 13:7
if we **e**, we will also reign with 2Tm 2:12
a better and **e-ing** possession...Heb 10:34
that lay before him, he **e-d** the
    cross ....Heb 12:2
the word of the Lord **e-s** forever...1Pt 1:25

ENEMY

an **e** to your **e-ies** and a foe to ....Ex 23:22
me in the presence of my **e-ies**;....Ps 23:5
do not let my **e-ies** gloat over me...Ps 25:2
I make your **e-ies** your footstool...Ps 110:1
If your **e** is hungry, give him ......Pr 25:21
a man's **e-ies** are the men of his
    own.........................Mc 7:6
love your **e-ies** and pray for those ..Mt 5:44
a man's **e-ies** will be the members..Mt 10:36
e who sowed them is the devil. ..Mt 13:39
I put your **e-ies** under your feet ..Mt 22:44
if, while we were **e-ies**, we were ..Rm 5:10
But if your **e** is hungry, feed him..Rm 12:20
The last **e** he abolishes is death...1Co 15:26
the world becomes the **e** of God...Jms 4:4

ENGAGED

to a virgin **e** to a man named ......Lk 1:27

ENJOY

to eat, drink, and **e** his work........Ec 2:24
provides us with all things to **e**....1Tm 6:17

ENLIGHTENED

eyes of your heart may be **e** ......Eph 1:18
those who were once **e**, ...Heb 6:4

ENOCH

Father of Methuselah (Gn 5:18–21); prophet (Jd 14); walked with God, and God took him (Gn 5:22–24; Heb 11:5).

ENSLAVE

we may no longer be **e-d** to sin,...Rm 6:6
put up with it if someone **e-s** you,..2Co 11:20
want to be **e-d** to them all
    over again? ....Gl 4:9

ENSNARE

the sin that so easily **e-s** us. ......Heb 12:1

ENTANGLE

The ropes of Sheol **e-d** me; 2Sm 22:6
soldier gets **e-d** in the concerns ...2Tm 2:4
they are again **e-d** in these things..2Pt 2:20

ENTER

anger, "They will not **e** my rest."...Ps 95:11
E his gates with thanksgiving.....Ps 100:4
you will never **e** the kingdom of...Mt 5:20
E through the narrow gate.........Mt 7:13
like a little child will never **e** it....Mk 10:15
he cannot **e** the kingdom of God.....Jn 3:5
just as sin **e-ed** the world
    through ....Rm 5:12
anger, "They will not **e** my rest."...Heb 3:11

ENTHRONED

e between the cherubim,........2Kg 19:15
But the LORD sits **e** forever;.........Ps 9:7
e on the praises of Israel...........Ps 22:3

ENTICE

son, if sinners **e** you, don't be ......Pr 1:10
drawn away and **e-d** by his own...Jms 1:14

ENTRUST

Into your hand I **e** my spirit; ....Ps 31:5
into your hands I **e** my spirit......Lk 23:46
what has been **e-ed** to me until...2Tm 1:12

ENVY (N)

They are full of **e**, murder.........Rm 1:29
For where there is **e** and selfish ...Jms 3:16

ENVY (V)

Don't your heart **e** sinners;......Pr 23:17
Don't **e** the evil or desire to be .....Pr 24:1
Love does not **e**, is not boastful,...1Co 13:4

EPHESUS

City in Asia Minor visited by Paul (Ac 18:19; 19:1; 1Co 16:8; Eph 1:1; Rv 2:1).

EPHOD

are to make the **e** of finely spun....Ex 28:6

EPHRAIM

Son of Joseph (Gn 41:52); tribe with territory north and west of Bethel (Gn 48; Jos 14:4; 16:4–5); designation for Israel (Is 11:13; Jr 7:15; Ezk 37:16; Hs 5:13).

EPHRATHAH

Bethlehem **E**, you are small
    among.........................Mc 5:2

EQUAL

making himself **e** to God...........Jn 5:18

EQUALITY

did not consider **e** with God as ....Php 2:6

EQUIP

be complete, **e-ped** for every
    good 2Tm 3:17
e you with everything good to...Heb 13:21

ERASE

Let them be **e-d** from the
    book of.......................Ps 69:28
and I will never **e** his name from.....Rv 3:5

ERROR

appropriate penalty of their **e**.....Rm 1:27
from the **e** of his way will ....Jms 5:20

ESAU

Son of Isaac; elder twin of Jacob (Gn 25:24–26); rejected by God (Mal 1:2–3;Rm 9:13); sold birthright (Gn 25:30–34; Heb 12:16); tricked out of blessing (Gn 27:1–30; Heb 11:20); reconciled with Jacob (33:4–16). Progenitor of Edomites in Seir (Dt 2:4–29).

ESCAPE (V)

can I go to **e** your spirit?..........Ps 139:7
that you will **e** God's judgment?....Rm 2:3
how will we **e** if we neglect such ..Heb 2:3

ESTABLISH

But I will **e** my covenant with .....Gn 6:18
and I will **e** his kingdom..........2Sm 7:12
up in him and **e-ed** in the faith, ...Col 2:7

ESTHER

Persian name of Hadassah, Mordecai's cousin (Est 2:7). Chosen queen of Persia (2:16–18); interceded at great risk to foil a plot to exterminate the Jews (Est 3–9).

ESTIMATION

Do not be wise in your own **e**.....Rm 12:16

ETERNAL

must I do to have **e** life?.........Mt 19:16
will go away into **e** punishment,
    but the righteous into **e** life. ...Mt 25:46
not perish but have **e** life. ....Jn 3:16
that he may give **e** life to everyone . Jn 17:2
gift of God is **e** life in Christ.......Rm 6:23
incomparable **e** weight of glory....2Co 4:17
pay the penalty of **e** destruction,...2Th 1:9
Now to the King **e**, immortal.....1Tm 1:17
may know that you have **e** life.....1Jn 5:13

ETERNITY

from **e** to **e**, you are God...........Ps 90:2
has also put **e** in their hearts........Ec 3:11

ETHIOPIAN

There was an **E** man, a eunuch.....Ac 8:27

EUNUCH

For there are **e-s** who were
    born..........................Mt 19:12
The **e** said to Philip, "I ask.........Ac 8:34

EUPHRATES

And the fourth river is the **E**.......Gn 2:14

EVALUATE

it since it is **e-d** spiritually........1Co 2:14

EVANGELIST

prophets, some **e-s**, some
    pastors.......................Eph 4:11
the work of an **e**, fulfill your 2Tm 4:5

EVE

First woman; wife of Adam (Gn 3:20; 4:1–2,25). Gave in to temptation (3:1; 2Co 11:3; 1Tm 2:13–14).

EVERLASTING

and underneath are the **e** arms....Dt 33:27
The LORD is the **e** God,...........Is 40:28
have loved you with an **e** love;......Jr 31:3

EVERYTHING

you do, do **e** for the glory of God. 1Co 10:31
has given us **e** required for life 2Pt 1:3

EVIL

of the knowledge of good and **e**....Gn 2:9
To fear the LORD is to hate **e**........Pr 8:13
who call **e** good and good **e**,.......Is 5:20
but deliver us from the **e** one....Mt 6:13
then, who are **e**, know how to .....Mt 7:11
an **e** man produces **e** things from . Mt 12:35
protect them from the **e** one......Jn 17:15
Do not repay anyone **e** for **e**......Rm 12:17
Stay away from every kind of **e**...1Th 5:22
is a root of all kinds of **e**......1Tm 6:10
since God is not tempted by **e**,....Jms 1:13

EVILDOER

I tell you, don't resist an **e**........Mt 5:39

EWE

one small **e** lamb that he had 2Sm 12:3

EXACT

the **e** expression of his nature, ...Heb 1:3

EXALT

the rock of my salvation, is
e-ed.........................2Sm 22:47
let us **e** his name together.........Ps 34:3
be **e-ed** above the heavens; ..... Ps 57:5,11
You are **e** above all the gods. ...Ps 97:9
Righteousness **e-s** a nation, but ... Pr 14:34
humbles himself will be **e-ed**.....Mt 23:12
God highly **e-ed** him and gave ....Php 2:9
the Lord, and he will **e** you. ......Jms 4:10

EXAMINE

and **e-d** the Scriptures daily to
see............................Ac 17:11
Let a person **e** himself; 1Co 11:28

EXAMPLE

given you an **e**, that you also .....Jn 13:15
things took place as **e-s** for us, ... 1Co 10:6
to the **e** you have in us. ....Php 3:17
set an **e** for the believers 1Tm 4:12
you, but being **e-s** to the flock. 1Pt 5:3

EXASPERATE

Fathers, do not **e** your children .... Col 3:21

EXCHANGE

anyone give in **e** for his life? ..... Mt 16:26

EXCHANGED

They **e** their glory for the image. .Ps 106:20
and **e** the glory of the immortal ... Rm 1:23

EXCUSE

they have no **e** for their sin....... Jn 15:22
As a result, people are without **e**... Rm 1:20

EXHORT

older man, but **e** him as a father. ...1Tm 5:1

EXHORTATION

with many other **e-s**, he proclaimed. .Lk 3:18

EXILE

went into **e** from its land........2Kg 25:21
the returned **e-s** were building..... Ezr 4:1
I urge you as strangers and **e-s**.....1Pt 2:11

EXILED

So Israel has been **e-d** to Assyria ..2Kg 17:23

EXIST

who, **e-ing** in the form of God,.... Php 2:6
and through whom all things **e** .. Heb 2:10
believe that he **e-s** and that he ... Heb 11:6
your will they **e** and were..........Rv 4:11

EXPECT

coming at an hour you do not **e**... Mt 24:44
and lend, **e-ing** nothing in return. .. Lk 6:35

EXPECTANTLY

the LORD and wait **e** for him; ...... Ps 37:7

EXPECTATION

e of the wicked comes will perish... Pr 10:28
but a terrifying **e** of judgment .. Heb 10:27

EXPLAIN

He will **e** everything to us............Jn 4:25

EXPOSE

so that his deeds may not be **e-d**. .Jn 3:20
darkness, but instead **e** them...... Eph 5:11
Everything **e-d** by the light is .....Eph 5:13

EXPRESSION

the exact **e** of his nature, ...Heb 1:3

EXTEND

would bless me, my border, ...1Ch 4:10

EXTINGUISH

you can **e** all the flaming arrows. ..Eph 6:16

EYE

e for **e**, tooth for tooth...Ex 21:24; Lv 24:20
For the **e-s** of the LORD roam......2Ch 16:9
have made a covenant with my
e-s.............................. Jb 31:1
Protect me as the pupil of your **e**; .. Ps 17:8
I lift my **e-s** toward the ....Ps 121:1
they might see with their **e-s** and .. Is 6:10
Your **e-s** are too pure to look on...Hab 1:13
If your right **e** causes you to ...... Mt 5:29
An **e** for an **e** and a tooth for..... Mt 5:38
The **e** is the lamp of the body...... Mt 6:22
the splinter in your brother's
e but........................... Mt 7:3
And their **e-s** were opened........ Mt 9:30
see with their **e-s** and hear with.. Mt 13:15
and it is wonderful in our **e-s**? ... Mt 21:42
Then their **e-s** were opened, and . . Lk 24:31
keeping our **e-s** on Jesus,........Heb 12:2
what we have seen with our **e-s**, ...1Jn 1:1
clouds, and every **e** will see him ..... Rv 1:7
away every tear from
their **e-s**.....................Rv 7:17; 21:4

EYEWITNESSES

the original **e** ... handed them down ..Lk 1:2
we were **e** of his majesty..........2Pt 1:16

EZEKIEL

Hebrew prophet at the time of the exile,
writing from Babylon (Ezk 1:1; 2Kg 24:14–
16). Wrote about the fall of Jerusalem (Ezk
33:21) and the ultimate restoration of the
city and temple (Ezk 40–48).

EZRA

Priest and teacher of the law; leader of the
returning exiles, sent by King Artaxerxes of
Persia to reestablish worship in the temple
(Ezr 7–8). Nehemiah's colleague (Neh 8:2,6;
12:31–37). Made priests stop intermarriage
with foreigners (Ezr 9–10).

- F -

FACE

I have seen God **f** to **f**,..............Gn 32:30
LORD would speak ... **f** to **f**,........ Ex 33:11
Moses, the skin of his **f** shone! ....Ex 34:30
LORD make his **f** shine on you .....Nm 6:25
LORD, I will seek your **f**............Ps 27:8
I have set my **f** like flint,........... Is 50:7
oil on your head and wash your **f**, ..Mt 6:17
and his **f** shone like the sun.......Mt 17:2
spat in his **f** and beat him; .... Mt 26:67
appearance of his **f** changed,........Lk 9:29
a mirror, but then **f** to **f**..........1Co 13:12
with unveiled **f-s** are looking 2Co 3:18
But the **f** of the Lord is against....1Pt 3:12
and his **f** was shining like the sun. .. Rv 1:16

FACTIONS

it is necessary that there be **f** 1Co 11:19
ambitions, dissensions, **f**,.........Gl 5:20

FADE

the flowers **f**, but the word of .... Is 40:8
a crown that will never **f** away.....1Co 9:25

FAIL

you that your faith may not **f**. .... Lk 22:32
as though the word of God has
f-ed...........................Rm 9:6

FAILURE

and their **f** riches for the ....Rm 11:12

FAINT

my body **f-s** for you in a land that .. Ps 63:1
they will walk and not **f**.......... Is 40:31

FAIR

The Lord's way isn't **f**.. Ezk 18:25,29; 33:17,20

FAIRLY

He judges the peoples **f**..........Ps 96:10
with your slaves justly and **f**,...... Col 4:1

FAITH

righteous one will live by his **f**.... Hab 2:4
Your **f** has saved you. ....Mt 9:22
If you have **f** the size of a mustard. .Mt 17:20
woman, "Your **f** has saved you......Lk 7:50
to the Lord, "Increase our **f**......... Lk 17:5
will he find **f** on earth?............Lk 18:8
that he had **f** to be healed, ...Ac 14:9
is justified by **f** apart from........Rm 3:28
been justified by **f**, ...Rm 5:1
So **f** comes from what is heard,.. .Rm 10:17
that is not from **f** is sin. ....Rm 14:23
if I have all **f** so that I can. 1Co 13:2
three remain: **f**, hope, and love. ...1Co 13:13
stand firm in the **f**, be courageous,. .1Co 16:13
For we walk by **f**, not by sight. 2Co 5:7
I live by **f** in the Son of God, ...Gl 2:20
the righteous will live by **f**.........Gl 3:11
patience, kindness, goodness, **f**, ... Gl 5:22
you are saved by grace through **f**, ..Eph 2:8
one Lord, one **f**, one baptism, ...Eph 4:5
situation take up the shield of **f**, .. Eph 6:16
righteousness from God based on **f** . Php 3:9
the armor of **f** and love, ...1Th 5:8
some will depart from the **f**, ...1Tm 4:1
Fight the good fight of the **f**; 1Tm 6:12
finished the race, I have kept the **f**. . 2Tm 4:7
righteous one will live by **f**; ..... Heb 10:38
Now **f** is the reality of what is..... Heb 11:1
By **f** we understand that the ....Heb 11:3
By **f** Abel offered to God a........Heb 11:4
Now without **f** it is impossible ....Heb 11:6
pioneer and perfecter of our **f**, ...Heb 12:2
f, if it does not have works, is dead. .Jms 2:17
supplement your **f** with goodness,.. 2Pt 1:5

FAITHFUL *SEE ALSO* **FAITHFUL LOVE**

he is **f** in all my household.........Nm 12:7
the **f** God who keeps his gracious....Dt 7:9
With the **f** you prove yourself **f**;. .2Sm 22:26
Love the LORD, all his **f** ones. ...... Ps 31:23
Who then is a **f** and wise servant,. .Mt 24:45
Well done, good and **f** servant!.....Mt 25:21
God is **f**; you were called by him....1Co 1:9
God is **f**, he will not allow you... 1Co 10:13
He who calls you is **f**; he will 1Th 5:24
commit to **f** men who will be able.. 2Tm 2:2
he remains **f**, for he cannot deny ..2Tm 2:13
since he who promised is **f**. ..... Heb 10:23
entrust themselves to a **f** Creator. .1Pt 4:19
he is **f** and righteous to forgive. 1Jn 1:9
Its rider is called **F** and True,...... Rv 19:11

FAITHFUL LOVE

goodness and **f** will pursue ....Ps 23:6
because your **f** is better ....Ps 63:3
will sing about the LORD's **f** forever;. .Ps 89:1
to declare your **f** in the morning....Ps 92:2
so great is his **f** toward those .....Ps 103:11
For I desire **f** and not sacrifice ...... Hs 6:6
slow to anger, abounding in **f**,...... Jnh 4:2
because he delights in **f**...........Mc 7:18

FAITHFULNESS

to heaven, your **f** to the clouds. .... Ps 36:5
Your **f** reaches the clouds.........Ps 57:10
proclaim your **f** to all generations .. Ps 89:1
his **f**, through all generations......Ps 100:5
great is your **f**! ....Lm 3:23
unfaithfulness nullify God's **f**? .....Rm 3:3

FAITHLESS

if we are **f**, he remains faithful,...2Tm 2:13

FALL

How the mighty have **f-en**!.......2Sm 1:19
Though he **f-s**, he will not be .....Ps 37:24
Though a thousand **f** at your side .. Ps 91:7
an arrogant spirit before a **f**....... Pr 16:18
a righteous person **f-s** seven times,.. Pr 24:16

FALSE

you have **f-en** from the heavens . . . Is 14:12
Babylon has **f-en**, has **f-en**. . . . . Is 21:9
some seed **fell** along the path, ... Mt 13:4
to cause the **f** and rise of many . . . . Lk 2:34
I watched Satan **f** from heaven. . . . Lk 10:18
grain of wheat **f-s** to the ground . . Jn 12:24
have sinned and **f** short of the . . . . Rm 3:23
must be careful not to **f**. 1Co 10:12
you have **f-en** from grace. . . . . Gl 5:4
and who have **f-en** away, ... Heb 6:6
thing to **f** into the hands . . . . Heb 10:31
a great star ... **fell** from heaven. . . . . Rv 8:10
f-en, Babylon the Great has **f-en**, . . Rv 14:8

FALSE

Do not give **f** testimony against . . . Ex 20:16
Beware of **f** prophets who come. . . . Mt 7:15
do not bear **f** witness; . . . . Mt 19:18
Many **f** prophets will rise up and . . Mt 24:11
F messiahs and **f** prophets will . . . Mt 24:24
whether from **f** motives or true, . . . Php 1:18
there will be **f** teachers among you. . 2Pt 2:1
the mouth of the **f** prophet. . . . . . . Rv 16:13

FALSEHOOD

I hate and abhor **f**, but I love. . . . . Ps 119:163
Keep **f** and deceitful words far . . . . . Pr 30:8

FALSELY

f say every kind of evil against you. . Mt 5:11
what is **f** called knowledge. 1Tm 6:20

FAMILY

As for me and my **f**, we will . . . . . Jos 24:15
All the **f-ies** of the nations will . . . . Ps 22:27
makes their **f-ies** multiply like . . . Ps 107:41
All the **f-ies** of the earth will be . . . . Ac 3:25
he and all his **f** were baptized. . . . . Ac 16:33
from whom every **f** in heaven
  and . . . . Eph 3:15

FAMINE

There was a **f** in the land, ... Gn 12:10
seven years of **f** will take place. . . . Gn 41:30
by sword, **f**, and plague. . . . . Jr 14:12
not a **f** of bread or a thirst for . . . . . Am 8:11
There will be **f-s** and
  earthquakes. . . . . Mt 24:7
or persecution or **f** or nakedness . . Rm 8:35

FAR

As **f** as the east is from the . . . . . Ps 103:12
yet their hearts are **f** from me, ... Is 29:13
but their heart is **f** from me. . . . . . . Mt 15:8
You are not **f** from the kingdom . . Mk 12:34
you who were **f** away have been . . Eph 2:13

FAST (N)

Will the **f** I choose be like this: . . . . . Is 58:5
Announce a sacred **f**; . . . . Jl 1:14; 2:15

FAST (V)

baby was alive, you **f-ed** 2Sm 12:21
After he had **f-ed** forty days and
  forty . . . . Mt 4:2
Whenever you **f**, don't be
  gloomy . . . . Mt 6:16
but your disciples do not **f**? . . . . . . Mt 9:14
guests cannot **f** while the groom . . Mk 2:19
I **f** twice a week; I give a tenth . . . . Lk 18:12
after they had **f-ed**, prayed, and . . . Ac 13:3

FASTING

so that their **f** is obvious to people. . Mt 6:16

FAT

is better than the **f** of rams.. . . . . 1Sm 15:22

FATAL

but its **f** wound was healed. . . . . . . Rv 13:3

FATE

there is one **f** for everyone. . . . . Ec 9:3
and who considered his **f**? . . . . Is 53:8

FATHER

a man leaves his **f** and mother . . . . Gn 2:24
become the **f** of many nations . . . . . Gn 17:4
Honor your **f** and your mother so . . Ex 20:12
Honor your **f** and your mother . . . . Dt 5:16
F-s are not to be put to death
  for . . . . Dt 24:16
Isn't he your **F** and Creator? . . . . . . Dt 32:6
I will his **f**, and he. 2Sm 7:14
today I have become your **F** . . . . . . Ps 2:7
You are my **F**, my God, the rock. . . . Ps 89:26
Listen, my son, to your **f-'s**
  instruction . . . . Pr 1:8
A wise son brings joy to his **f**, ... Pr 10:1
Eternal **F**, Prince of Peace. . . . . Is 9:6
not die for his **f-'s** iniquity. . . . . . . Ezk 18:17
Our **F** in heaven, your name be . . . . Mt 6:9
who loves a **f** or mother more. . . . Mt 10:37
Honor your **f** and your mother; . . . Mt 15:4
will leave his **f** and mother and. . . . Mt 19:5
you have one **F**, who is in heaven . . Mt 23:9
Abba, **F**! All things are possible . . Mk 14:36
for me to be in my **F-'s** house? . . . . Lk 2:49
What **f** among you, if his son asks . . Lk 11:11
Jesus said, "**F**, forgive them . . . . . . Lk 23:34
Stop turning my **F-'s** house into . . . Jn 2:16
was even calling God his own **F**, . . . Jn 5:18
You are of your **f** the devil, ... Jn 8:44
snatch them out of the **F-'s** hand. . Jn 10:29
I and the **F** are one. . . . . Jn 10:30
the **F** is in me and I in the **F**. . . . . . . Jn 10:38
In my **F-'s** house are many rooms. . Jn 14:2
comes to the **F** except through . . . . Jn 14:6
show us the **F**, and that's enough. . . Jn 14:8
who has seen me has seen the **F**. . . Jn 14:9
you ask the **F** in my name, ... Jn 15:16
by whom we cry out, "Abba, **F**!" . . . Rm 8:15
I will be a **F** to you, and you 2Co 6:18
one God and **F** of all, who is. . . . . . Eph 4:6
Honor your **f** and mother, which . . . Eph 6:2
F-s, don't stir up anger in. . . . . Eph 6:4
F-s, do not exasperate your . . . . . . Col 3:21
I will be his **F**, and he will be . . . . . . Heb 1:5
what son is there that a **f** does not . Heb 12:7
down from the **F** of lights, ... Jms 1:17

FATHERLESS

He executes justice for the **f** and . . Dt 10:18
You are a helper of the **f**. . . . . Ps 10:14
a father of the **f** and a champion . . Ps 68:5
and helps the **f** and the widow, . . . Ps 146:9
don't encroach on the fields of
  the **f** . . . . Pr 23:10

FATTENED

Then bring the **f** calf and . . . . Lk 15:23
You have **f** your hearts . . . . Jms 5:5

FAULT

Cleanse me from my hidden **f-s**. . . . Ps 19:12
Why then does he still find **f**? . . . . . Rm 9:19
without **f** or failure until. 1Tm 6:14

FAULTLESS

who are **f** in a crooked . . . . Php 2:15

FAVOR (N)

Noah ... found **f** with the LORD . . . . Gn 6:8
moment, but his **f**, a lifetime. . . . . . Ps 30:5
and obtains **f** from the LORD, ... Pr 8:35
for you have found **f** with God. . . . Lk 1:30
and in **f** with God and with . . . . . . Lk 2:52
God and enjoying the **f** of all. . . . . Ac 2:47
trying to win the **f** of people, ... Gl 1:10

FAVOR (V)

peace on earth to people he **f-s**! . . Lk 2:14

FAVORITISM

that God doesn't show **f**, ... Ac 10:34
There is no **f** with God. . . . . Rm 2:11
and there is no **f** with him. . . . . . . Eph 6:9
doing nothing out of **f**. 1Tm 5:21
do not show **f** as you hold on to. . . Jms 2:1

FEAR (N)

The **f** of the LORD is pure, ... Ps 19:9
and rescued me from all my **f-s**. . . Ps 34:4
f of the LORD is the beginning. . . . . Ps 111:10
The **f** of the LORD is the beginning. . . Pr 1:7
delight will be in the **f** of the LORD. . Is 11:3
of slavery to fall back into **f**, ... Rm 8:15
salvation with **f** and trembling. . . . Php 2:12
There is no **f** in love; instead,
  perfect love drives out **f**, ... 1Jn 4:18

FEAR (V)

For now I know that you **f** God, . . . Gn 22:12
F the LORD your God ... worship
  him. . . . . Dt 6:13
f-ed the LORD, but they also 2Kg 17:33
He is **f-ed** above all gods. 1Ch 16:25
f-s God and turns away from . . . Jb 1:8; 2:3
darkest valley, I **f** no danger, for . . . Ps 23:4
my salvation—whom should I **f**? . . . Ps 27:1
To **f** the LORD is to hate evil. . . . . Pr 8:13
but a woman who **f-s** the LORD
  will. . . . . Pr 31:30
f God and keep his commands, ... Ec 12:13
Do not **f**, for I am with you; . . . . . . Is 41:10
f him who is able to destroy both. . Mt 10:28
town who didn't **f** God or respect . . Lk 18:2
So the one who **f-s** is not complete . 1Jn 4:18

FEARFULNESS

has not given us a spirit of **f**, ... 2Tm 1:7

FEAST

I hate, I despise your **f-s**! . . . . Am 5:21
us observe the **f**, not with old 1Co 5:8
to the marriage **f** of the Lamb! . . . . Rv 19:9

FEASTING (N)

than a house full of **f** with strife. . . Pr 17:1
than to go to a house of **f**, ... Ec 7:2

FEATHERS

He will cover you with his **f**; . . . . . . Ps 91:4

FEED

He **fed** you in the wilderness with . . Dt 8:16
shepherds **f** themselves rather
  than. . . . . Ezk 34:8
your heavenly Father **f-s** them. . . . . Mt 6:26
so the one who **f-s** on me will live . . Jn 6:57
"**F** my lambs," He told him. . . . . Jn 21:15
If your enemy is hungry, **f** him. . . . Rm 12:20

FEEDING

no oxen, the **f** trough is empty, ... Pr 14:4

FELLOWSHIP

this is the law of the **f** sacrifice . . . . . Lv 7:11
We used to have close **f**; . . . . Ps 55:14
teaching, to the **f**, to the breaking . . Ac 2:42
Or what **f** does light have with 2Co 6:14
and the **f** of the Holy Spirit be . . . 2Co 13:13
we say, "We have **f** with him" 1Jn 1:6

FEMALE

he created them male and **f**. . . . . . . Gn 1:27
new ... a **f** will shelter a man. . . . . . Jr 31:22
beginning made them male and **f**, . Mt 19:4
slave or free, male or **f**; . . . . Gl 3:28

FERVENT

and being **f** in spirit, he was . . . . . . Ac 18:25
be **f** in the Spirit; serve the Lord. . . . Rm 12:11

FESTIVAL

Celebrate a **f** in my honor three . . . Ex 23:14
"Not during the **f**," they said . . . . . . Mk 14:2
the matter of a **f** or a new moon . . Col 2:16

FESTIVE

leading the **f** procession to the . . . . Ps 42:4

FEVER

was lying in bed with a **f**, ... Mk 1:30

FEW

were **f** in number, very **f** indeed .. Ps 105:12
Let his days be **f**; let another...... Ps 109:8
but the workers are **f**.............. Mt 9:37
are invited, but **f** are chosen... Mt 22:14
a **f** people going to be saved?..... Lk 13:23

FEWEST

you were the **f** of all peoples........ Dt 7:7

FIELD

Let the **f-s** and everything in them .. Ps 96:12
blooms like a flower of the **f**; .... Ps 103:15
I went to the **f** of a slacker and ... Pr 24:30
how the wildflowers of the **f** grow:..Mt 6:28
f is the world; and the good seed .. Mt 13:38
out in the **f-s** and keeping watch ...Lk 2:8
your eyes and look at the **f-s**,...... Jn 4:35
You are God's **f**, God's building 1Co 3:9

FIERY

surprised when the **f** ordeal comes ..1Pt 4:12

FIG

so they sewed **f** leaves together..... Gn 3:7
Though the **f** tree does not bud ...Hab 3:17
At once the **f** tree withered. ...... Mt 21:19
F-s aren't gathered from
   thornbushes .... Lk 6:44
Can a **f** tree produce olives, ... Jms 3:12

FIGHT (N)

Fight the good **f** of the faith; 1Tm 6:12
I have fought the good **f**, I have ... 2Tm 4:7

FIGHT (V)

The LORD will **f** for you;............. Ex 14:14
LORD; **f** those who **f** me........... Ps 35:1
F the good fight of the faith; 1Tm 6:12
God not to **f** about words;....... 2Tm 2:14
I have **fought** the good fight,
   I have 2Tm 4:7

FILL

Be fruitful, multiply, **f** the earth,....Gn 1:28
glory of the LORD **f-ed** the temple. .1Kg 8:11
whole earth is **f-ed** with his glory .. Ps 72:19
His glory **f-s** the whole earth........ Is 6:3
Do I not **f** the heavens and the.... Jr 23:24
and I will **f** this house with glory,... Hg 2:7
He will be **f-ed** with the Holy ...... Lk 1:15
"**F** the jars with water," Jesus....... Jn 2:7
you ate the loaves and were **f-ed**...Jn 6:26
they were all **f-ed** with the Holy ....Ac 2:4
Then Peter was **f-ed** with the Holy.. Ac 4:8
sight and be **f-ed** with the Holy.... Ac 9:17
called Paul—**f-ed** with the Holy .... Ac 13:9
the God of hope **f** you with all ....Rm 15:13
who **f-s** all things in every way. ...Eph 1:23
heavens, to **f** all things............Eph 4:10
but be **f-ed** by the Spirit:.........Eph 5:18
f-ed with the fruit of .... Php 1:11

FILTH

of all moral **f** and the evil, ... Jms 1:21
removal of the **f** of the flesh, ... 1Pt 3:21

FILTHY

was dressed with **f** clothes as he ... Zch 3:3
and **f** language from your mouth ... Col 3:8
Let the **f** still be **f**; .... Rv 22:11

FIND

If I **f** fifty righteous people ...... Gn 18:26
you will **f** him when you seek ..... Dt 4:29
those who search for me **f** me....... Pr 8:17
For the one who **f-s** me **f-s** life .... Pr 8:35
who **f-s** a wife **f-s** a good thing ... Pr 18:22
Who can **f** a wife of noble ...... Pr 31:10
the LORD while He may be **found**; .. Is 55:6
will seek me and **f** me when you ... Jr 29:13
Seek, and you will **f**. .... Mt 7:7
and you will **f** rest for..........Mt 11:29
life because of me will **f** it....... Mt 16:25

whom master **f-s** doing his job... Mt 24:46
I have **found** my lost sheep! .... Lk 15:6
he was lost and is **found**!......... Lk 15:24
whose name was not **found**
   written .... Rv 20:15

FINISH

He said, "It is **f-ed**!".............. Jn 19:30
to **f** my course and the ministry ...Ac 20:24
I have **f-ed** the race, I have kept... 2Tm 4:7

FIRE

and the pillar of **f** by night........ Ex 13:22
a chariot of **f** with horses of 2Kg 2:11
their **f** will never go out,.......... Is 66:24
he will be like a refiner's **f** .... Mal 3:2
you with the Holy Spirit and **f**..... Mt 3:11
burn with **f** that never goes out. ...Mt 3:12
into the eternal **f** prepared for ...Mt 25:41
and the **f** is not quenched........Mk 9:44
I came to bring **f** on the earth, ... Lk 12:49
like flames of **f** that separated .....Ac 2:3
the **f** will test the quality of 1Co 3:13
for our God is a consuming **f**.... Heb 12:29
And the tongue is a **f**............. Jms 3:6
second death, the lake of **f**.......Rv 20:14

FIRM

Stand **f** and see the LORD's........ Ex 14:13
If you do not stand **f** in your faith,... Is 7:9
Be alert, stand **f** in the faith...... 1Co 16:13
stand **f** and hold to the.......... 2Th 2:15

FIRMLY

The world is **f** established;...Pss 93:1; 96:10
are like **f** embedded nails. .... Ec 12:11
being rooted and **f** established.....Eph 3:17
if we hold **f** until the end....... Heb 3:14

FIRST

The **f** to state his case seems...Pr 18:17
I and the LORD, the **f** and with the ...Is 41:4
I am the **f** and I am the last......... Is 44:6
But seek the kingdom of God... Mt 6:33
F take the beam ... out of your eye,... Mt 7:5
f will be last, and the last **f**...... Mt 19:30
wants to be **f** among you must be.. Mt 20:27
F clean the inside of the cup,.... Mt 23:26
this, the **f** of his signs, in Cana...... Jn 2:11
were **f** called Christians at
   Antioch. .... Ac 11:26
who does evil, **f** to the Jew, and ....Rm 2:9
The **f** man Adam became a living... 1Co 15:45
the dead in Christ will rise **f** 1Th 4:16
We love because he **f** loved us..... 1Jn 4:19
I am the **F** and the Last,......... Rv 1:17
abandoned the love you had at **f**.. Rv 2:4
for the **f** heaven and the **f** earth
   had .... Rv 21:1

FIRSTBORN

LORD struck every **f** male in ...... Ex 12:29
Consecrate every **f** male to me,..... Ex 13:2
He struck all the **f** in Egypt,...... Ps 78:51
she gave birth to her **f** son, ... Lk 2:7
the **f** from the dead and the ....Rv 1:5

FIRSTFRUITS

the **f** of those who have fallen ... 1Co 15:20

FISH (N)

will rule the **f** of the sea, ...Gn 1:26
Jonah was in ... the **f** three days ...Jnh 1:17
he asks for a **f**, will give him ...... Mt 7:10
have five loaves and two **f** here,... Mt 14:17
the seven loaves and the **f** ...... Mt 15:36
full of large **f**—153 of them........ Jn 21:11

FISH (V)

I will make you **f** for people. ...... Mt 4:19

FISHERMEN

Then the **f** will mourn. ....Is 19:8
the sea—for they were **f**.......... Mk 1:16

FIT

looks back is **f** for the kingdom..... Lk 9:62

FITTING

husbands, as is **f** in the Lord....... Col 3:18

FIVE

hand and chose **f** smooth stones. .1Sm 17:40
For you've had **f** husbands, ... Jn 4:18

FIVE HUNDRED

to over **f** brothers 1Co 15:6

FIVE THOUSAND

who ate were about **f** men, ...Mt 14:21

FIX

great chasm has been **f-ed**
   between.................... Lk 16:26

FIXED (ADJ)

it is firmly **f** in heaven. .... Ps 119:89
If this **f** order departs from before.. Jr 31:36

FLAME

to him in a **f** of fire within .... Ex 3:2
Love's **f-s** are fiery **f-s**............. Sg 8:6
a fire, and its Holy One, a **f**........ Is 10:17

FLAMING

cherubim and the **f**, whirling sword.. Gn 3:24
can extinguish all the **f** arrows of.. Eph 6:16

FLASH

the lightning **f-es** from horizon to. .Lk 17:24

FLATTER

they **f** with their tongues. .... Ps 5:9
A person who **f-s** his neighbor
   spreads..................... Pr 29:5
f-ing people for their own advantage.. Jd 16

FLATTERING (ADJ)

and a **f** mouth causes ruin........ Pr 26:28

FLEE

But Moses **fled** from Pharaoh and.. Ex 2:15
Where can I **f** from your presence? .. Ps 139:7
The wicked **f** when no one is .... Pr 28:1
dear friends, **f** from idolatry...... 1Co 10:14
F from youthful passions, and.... 2Tm 2:22
devil, and he will **f** from you....... Jms 4:7

FLEECE

If dew is only on the **f**, ...Jdg 6:37

FLEETING

is deceptive and beauty is **f**, ... Pr 31:30
all the days of your **f** life,..........Ec 9:9

FLESH

bone of my bone, and **f** of my **f**;... Gn 2:23
wife, and they become one **f**...... Gn 2:24
yet I will see God in my **f**......... Jb 19:26
and give them a heart of **f**, ...Ezk 11:19
and give you a heart of **f**........Ezk 36:26
f and blood did not reveal this ....Mt 16:17
and the two will become one **f**?... Mt 19:5
is willing, but the **f** is weak....... Mt 26:41
Whatever is born of the **f** is **f**,.......Jn 3:6
one who eats my **f** and drinks my ...Jn 6:56
are not in the **f**, but in the Spirit, ...Rm 8:9
sisters, my own **f** and blood....... Rm 9:3
a thorn in the **f** was given to me,.. 2Co 12:7
the works of the **f** are obvious:..... Gl 5:19
is not against **f** and blood,........Eph 6:12

FLOCK

protects his **f** like a shepherd; ..... Is 40:11
You have scattered my **f**, ... Jr 23:2
but you do not tend the **f**........Ezk 34:3
sheep of the **f** will be scattered... Mt 26:31
watch at night over their **f**.......... Lk 2:8
will be one **f**, one shepherd........ Jn 10:16

FLOGGED

having Jesus **f**, handed him over . . Mt 27:26

FLOOD

I am bringing a **f**. . . . . .Gn 6:17
LORD sits enthroned over the **f**; . . . Ps 29:10
They didn't know until the **f**
came . . . . Mt 24:39
When the **f** came, the river . . . . .Lk 6:48

FLOODGATES

the **f** of the sky were opened, ... Gn 7:11
will not open the **f** of heaven . . . . .Mal 3:10

FLOODWATERS

f on the earth to destroy every. . . . .Gn 6:17
Don't let the **f** sweep over me or . . Ps 69:15

FLOW

streams of living water **f** from . . . . .Jn 7:38

FLOWER

blooms like a **f** of the field; . . . . . . Ps 103:15
withers, the **f-s** fade, but the word . . Is 40:8
withers, and the **f** falls, ... 1Pt 1:24

FLUTE

We played the **f** for you, but you . . Mt 11:17

FLY (N)

send swarms of **f-ies** against you, . . Ex 8:21
will whistle to the **f-ies** at the . . . . . .Is 7:18

FLY (V)

the arrow that **f-ies** by day, ... Ps 91:5

FOAL

on a colt, the **f** of a donkey. . . . . . . .Zch 9:9
the **f** of a donkey. . . . . .Mt 21:5

FOCUS

So we do not **f** on what is seen, . . .2Co 4:18
They are **f-ed** on earthly things. . . .Php 3:19

FOLD (V)

little **f-ing** of the arms to rest, . .Pr 6:10; 24:33
but was **f-ed** up in a separate place . .Jn 20:7

FOLLOW

Do not **f** other gods, the gods of . . .Dt 6:14
If the LORD is God, **f** him. 1Kg 18:21
f me, ... and I will make you. . . . . . . Mt 4:19
take up his cross, and **f** me. . . . . . . Mt 16:24
Anyone who **f-s** me will never walk . . Jn 8:12
The sheep **f** him because they. . . . . .Jn 10:4
These are the ones who **f** the Lamb . . Rv 14:4

FOLLY

F is a rowdy woman; . . . . Pr 9:13

FOOD

every green plant for **f**. . . . . .Gn 1:30
Every creature... will be **f** . . . . Gn 9:3
He gives **f** to every creature. . . . . . Ps 136:25
feed me with the **f** I need. . . . . .Pr 30:8
Isn't life more than **f** . . . . Mt 6:25
(thus he declared all **f-s** clean). . . . Mk 7:19
My **f** is to do the will of him . . . . . . .Jn 4:34
Don't work for the **f** that perishes . . Jn 6:27
Now about **f** sacrificed to idols: . . .1Co 8:1

FOOL

The **f** says in his heart,
"... no God." . . . . Pss 14:1; 53:1
f-s despise wisdom and discipline. . . . Pr 1:7
A **f** despises his father's discipline, . . Pr 15:5
Don't answer a **f** according to . . . . . .Pr 26:4
Whoever says, 'You **f**!' will be . . . . . Mt 5:22
to be wise, they became **f-s** . . . . . .Rm 1:22
We are **f-s** for Christ, but you are . . 1Co 4:10

FOOLISH

A **f** son is grief to his father . . . . Pr 17:25
like a **f** man who built his house on . . Mt 7:26

of them were **f** and five were . . . . . Mt 25:2
God made the world's wisdom **f**? . . 1Co 1:20
f Galatians! Who has cast a spell on . . Gl 3:1

FOOLISHNESS

but the **f** of fools produces **f**. . . . . Pr 14:24
a fool according to his **f** . . . . Pr 26:4,5
the word of the cross is **f** 1Co 1:18
of this world is **f** with God, ... 1Co 3:19

FOOT

Remove the sandals from your **feet**, . .Ex 3:5
You put everything under his **feet**: . .Ps 8:6
strike your **f** against a stone. . . . . . Ps 91:12
is a lamp for my **feet** and a
light. . . . . Ps 119:105
on the mountains are the **feet** of. . . .Is 52:7
strike your **f** against a stone. . . . . . . Mt 4:6
f causes you to fall away, cut it off . . Mt 18:8
to wash his **feet** with her tears. . . .Lk 7:38
showed them his hands and **feet**. . Lk 24:40
began to wash his disciples' **feet** . . . Jn 13:5
beautiful are the **feet** of those . . . Rm 10:15
soon crush Satan under your **feet**. . Rm 16:20
If the **f** should say, "Because 1Co 12:15
all his enemies under his **feet**. 1Co 15:25
and your **feet** sandaled with. . . . . . Eph 6:15

FOOTSTOOL

I make your enemies your **f**. . . . . . . .Ps 110:1
and earth is my **f**. . . . . .Is 66:1
is my throne, and earth my **f**. . . . . . Ac 7:49
His enemies are made his **f**. . . . . . .Heb 10:13

FORBID

f-den by the Holy Spirit to speak. . Ac 16:6
do not **f** speaking in tongues 1Co 14:39

FORBIDDEN (ADJ)

the lips of the **f** woman drip . . . . Pr 5:3

FORCE (N)

violent have been seizing it by **f**. . Mt 11:12
take him by **f** to make him king, ... Jn 6:15
the elemental **f-s** of the world. . . . . . Gl 4:3
against evil, spiritual **f-s** in the . . . .Eph 6:12

FORCE (V)

And if anyone **f-s** you to go one . . . .Mt 5:41
They **f-d** him to carry his . . . . Mt 27:32

FORCED (ADJ)

the Canaanites serve as **f** labor . . . .Jdg 1:28

FORDS

captured the **f** of the Jordan . . . . . .Jdg 12:5

FOREHEAD

and as a reminder on your **f**, ... Ex 13:9
hit the Philistine on his **f**. 1Sm 17:49
a mark on the **f-s** of the men who . .Ezk 9:4
servants of our God on their **f-s**. . . . .Rv 7:3
not have God's seal on their **f-s**. . . . . Rv 9:4
on his right hand or on his **f**, ... Rv 13:16
mark on their **f-s** or their hands. . . Rv 20:4

FOREIGN

get rid of the **f** gods that are . . . . .Jos 24:23
must not bow down to a **f** god. . . . . Ps 81:9
sing the LORD's song on **f** soil? . . . . Ps 137:4

FOREIGNER

the land where you live as a **f**, ... Gn 28:4
the Passover: no **f** may eat it. . . . . . Ex 12:43
by the lips of **f-s**, and even then, . 1Co 14:21
are no longer **f-s** and strangers, . . .Eph 2:19
that they were **f-s** and temporary . . Heb 11:13

FOREKNEW

For those he **f** he also . . . . .Rm 8:29
rejected his people whom he **f**. . . . Rm 11:2

FORERUNNER

entered there on our behalf as a **f**, . .Heb 6:20

FORESKIN

circumcise the flesh of your **f** . . . . . Gn 17:11

FOREVER

will not remain with mankind **f**, ... Gn 6:3
your throne will be established **f**. . 2Sm 7:16
But the LORD sits enthroned **f**; . . . . . .Ps 9:7
"You are a priest **f** . . . . Ps 110:4
for wealth is not **f**; . . . . Pr 27:24
of this bread he will live **f**. . . . . Jn 6:51
You are a priest **f** according to. . . . Heb 5:6
same yesterday, today, and **f**. . . . . Heb 13:8
the word of the Lord endures **f**. . . . 1Pt 1:25
and they will reign **f** and ever. . . . . .Rv 22:5

FORFEITS

whole world, and yet loses or **f**
himself? . . . . .Lk 9:25

FORGET

be careful not to **f** the LORD who . . .Dt 6:12
you **f-got** the God who gave birth . Dt 32:18
and do not **f** all his benefits. . . . . . Ps 103:2
If I **f** you, Jerusalem, may my right
hand **f** its skill. . . . . Ps 137:5
My son, don't **f** my teaching, but . . . Pr 3:1
Can a woman **f** her nursing child. . . .Is 49:15
F-ting what is behind. . . . . .Php 3:13
you have **f-gotten** the exhortation .Heb 12:5
and immediately **f-s** what kind of. . Jms 1:24

FORGIVE

if you would only **f** their sin. . . . . .Ex 32:32
f their sin, and heal their land. 2Ch 7:14
one whose transgression is **f-n**, . . . Ps 32:1
For I will **f** their iniquity and . . . . . . .Jr 31:34
And **f** us our debts, as we also
have **f-n** our debtors. . . . . Mt 6:12
Who can **f** sins but God alone? . . . . . Mk 2:7
But the one who is **f-n** little, ... Lk 7:47
and if he repents, **f** him. . . . . Lk 17:3
Father, **f** them, because . . . . .Lk 23:34
f-ing one another, just as God
also **f-gave** you in Christ. . . . . . . Eph 4:32
and **f-gave** us all our trespasses. . . Col 2:13
committed sins, he will be **f-n**. . . . .Jms 5:15
and righteous to **f** us our sins 1Jn 1:9

FORGIVENESS

you there is **f**, so that you may . . . . Ps 130:4
poured out for many for the **f** of
sins. . . . . Mt 26:28
through his blood, the **f** of our . . . . Eph 1:7
have redemption, the **f** of sins. . . . .Col 1:14
shedding of blood there is no **f**. . . Heb 9:22

FORM (N)

He didn't have ... **f** or majesty . . . . . . .Is 53:2
and you haven't seen his **f**. . . . . Jn 5:37
existing in the **f** of God, did not . . . Php 2:6
holding to the **f** of godliness but . . 2Tm 3:5

FORM (V)

Then the LORD God **f-ed** the
man out . . . . .Gn 2:7
when I was **f-ed** in the depths of . .Ps 139:15
Will what is **f-ed** say to the one
who **f-ed** it, ...Rm 9:20
you until Christ is **f-ed** in you. . . . . . Gl 4:19

FORMLESS

Now the earth was **f** and empty, ...Gn 1:2

FORTRESS

The LORD is my rock, my **f**, ... 2Sm 22:2
refuge and my **f**, my God in whom . .Ps 91:2

FORTUNES

LORD restores the **f** of his people, . . . Ps 14:7

FORTY

rain fell ... **f** days and **f** nights. . . . . .Gn 7:12
on the mountain **f** days and **f** . . . . .Ex 24:18
in the wilderness for **f** years . . . . . Nm 14:33

f days to be tempted by the devil.... Lk 4:2
appearing to them during **f** days .... Ac 1:3

FORWARD

and reaching **f** to what is ahead . . . Php 3:13
he was looking **f** to the city...... Heb 11:10

FOUND

The LORD **f-ed** the earth by
wisdom...................... Pr 3:19

FOUNDATION

established the earth on its **f-s**; . . . Ps 104:5
precious cornerstone, a sure **f**;..... Is 28:16
because its **f** was on the rock...... Mt 7:25
builds on the **f** with gold,....... 1Co 3:12
built on the **f** of the apostles. .... Eph 2:20
God's solid **f** stands firm, ... 2Tm 2:19
looking ... to the city that has **f-s**,. Heb 11:10

FOUNTAIN

for with you is life's **f**............. Ps 36:9
abandoned me, the **f** of living water,. Jr 2:13

FOUR HUNDRED

will be ... oppressed **f** years........ Gn 15:13
enslave and oppress them **f** years.... Ac 7:6

FOX

F-es have dens, and birds of the . . Mt 8:20
Go tell that **f**, 'Look! .... Lk 13:32

FRAGRANCE

we are the **f** of Christ among...... 2Co 2:15

FRAGRANT

sacrificial and **f** offering to God..... Eph 5:2

FRANKINCENSE

carry gold and **f** and proclaim ...... Is 60:6
gold, **f**, and myrrh................. Mt 2:11

FREE (ADJ)

and the truth will set you **f**......... Jn 8:32
Jesus has set you **f** from the law . . . Rm 8:2
slave or **f**, male or female; .... Gl 3:28
For freedom, Christ has set us **f**..... Gl 5:1
and has set us **f** from our sins .... Rv 1:5

FREE (V)

The LORD **f-s** prisoners........... Ps 146:7
who has died is **f-d** from sin........ Rm 6:7

FREEDOM

to proclaim ... **f** to the prisoners;.... Is 61:1
Spirit of the Lord is, there is **f**...... 2Co 3:17
For freedom, Christ has set us **f**..... Gl 5:1
don't use this **f** as an opportunity . Gl 5:13
not using your **f** as a cover-up..... 1Pt 2:16

FREELY

our God, for he will **f** forgive. .... Is 55:7
are justified **f** by his grace .... Rm 3:24

FRESH

put new wine into **f** wineskins,.... Mt 9:17
saltwater spring yield **f** water. .... Jms 3:12

FRIEND

as a man speaks with his **f**, ... Ex 33:11
Now when Job's three **f-s**—Eliphaz. Jb 2:11
A **f** loves at all times,............. Pr 17:17
but there is a **f** who stays closer... Pr 18:24
wounds of a **f** are trustworthy ..... Pr 27:6
a **f** of tax collectors and .... Mt 11:19
lay down his life for his **f-s**........ Jn 15:13
and he was called God's **f**........ Jms 2:23
be the **f** the world becomes the ... Jms 4:4

FRIENDSHIP

f with the world is hostility....... Jms 4:4

FRONT

the **f** seats in the synagogues, ... Mt 23:6

FRUIT

that bears its **f** in season .... Ps 1:3
The **f** of the righteous is a tree .... Pr 11:30
produce **f** consistent with .... Mt 3:8
recognize them by their **f**......... Mt 7:16
not drink from this **f** of the vine. . Mt 26:29
that does not produce **f** he
removes,....................... Jn 15:2
But the **f** of the Spirit is love, joy,. . . Gl 5:22
bearing **f** in every good work .... Col 1:10
tree of life ... bearing twelve
kinds of **f**,..................... Rv 22:2

FRUITFUL

blessed them: "Be **f**, multiply, ...Gn 1:22
But the Israelites were **f**, ... Ex 1:7

FULFILL

May the LORD **f** all your requests . . . Ps 20:5
F what you vow................... Ec 5:4
not come to abolish but to **f**...... Mt 5:17
this Scripture has been **f-ed**..... Lk 4:21
and the Psalms must be **f-ed**..... Lk 24:44
loves another has **f-ed** the law. ... Rm 13:8
husband should **f** his marital 1Co 7:3
whole law is **f-ed** in one statement. Gl 5:14
way you will **f** the law of Christ ..... Gl 6:2

FULFILLMENT

therefore, is the **f** of the law...... Rm 13:10

FULL

land will be as **f** of the knowledge . . Is 11:9
whole body will be **f** of light. .... Mt 6:22
from the Father, **f** of grace and..... Jn 1:14
Stephen, **f** of the Holy............. Ac 7:55
You are already **f**!................ 1Co 4:8

FULLNESS

grace upon grace from his **f**, ... Jn 1:16
until the **f** of the Gentiles........ Rm 11:25
the **f** of the one who fills all ...... Eph 1:23
filled with all the **f** of God....... Eph 3:19
have all his **f** dwell in him, ... Col 1:19
entire **f** of God's nature dwells ..... Col 2:9

FULLY

I will know **f**, as I am **f** known..... 1Co 13:12

FURNACE

tested you in the **f** of affliction. ... Is 48:10
thrown into a **f** of blazing fire. .... Dn 3:6
throw them into the blazing **f**..... Mt 13:42

FURY

who have drunk the cup of his **f** .... Is 51:17
and the **f** of a fire about to ..... Heb 10:27

FUTILE

Everything is **f**..................... Ec 1:2

FUTILITY

"Absolute **f**," says the Teacher........ Ec 1:2
For he comes in **f** and he goes in..... Ec 6:4
creation was subjected to **f**....... Rm 8:20
in the **f** of their thoughts. .... Eph 4:17

FUTURE

person of peace will have a **f**. ..... Ps 37:37
For the evil have no **f**;........... Pr 24:20
to give you a **f** and a hope. .... Jr 29:11

- G -

GABRIEL

Angel who explained Daniel's visions (Dn 8:16; 9:21) and announced John's and Jesus's births (Lk 1:19,26).

GAD

1. Son of Jacob by Zilpah (Gn 30:9–11). Tribe with Transjordan territory north of the Dead Sea (Nm 32; Dt 3:16–17; Jos 18:7).

2. Seer at time of David (1Sm 22:5; 2Sm 24:11–19; 1Ch 21:9–19; 29:29; 2Ch 29:25).

GAIN (N)

Ill-gotten **g-s** do not profit .... Pr 10:2
to live is Christ and to die is **g**. .... Php 1:21
with contentment is a great **g**. 1Tm 6:6

GAIN (V)

someone if he **g-s** the whole
world........................ Mt 16:26
benefit someone to **g** the whole
world........................ Mk 8:36
dung, so that I may **g** Christ ...... Php 3:8

GALILEAN

You were with Jesus the **G** too.... Mt 26:69

GALILEE

1. Region in northern Palestine (Jos 20:7; 21:32; 1Kg 9:11); where Jesus lived (Mt 2:22; 3:13; 21:11) and ministered (Is 9:1; Mt 4:12,15,23); where he appeared after the resurrection (Mt 26:32; Ac 1:11).
2. Sea along the Jordan (Mt 4:18; 15:29).

GALL

they gave me **g** for my food,...... Ps 69:21
him wine mixed with **g** to drink... Mt 27:34

GALLOWS

he had the **g** constructed. .... Est 5:14

GAMALIEL

Pharisee (Ac 5:34); Paul's teacher (22:3).

GANG

a **g** of evildoers has closed in...... Ps 22:16

GANGRENE

their teaching will spread like **g**; . . . 2Tm 2:17

GAP

and stand in the **g** before me on . . Ezk 22:30

GARDEN

LORD God planted a **g** in Eden, ... Gn 2:8
A new tomb was in the **g**; .... Jn 19:41

GARDENER

and my Father is the **g**............. Jn 15:1
Supposing he was the **g**, she ...... Jn 20:15

GARMENT

But leaving his **g** in her hand, ...Gn 39:12
They divided my **g-s** among ...... Ps 22:18
You will change them like a **g**,.... Ps 102:26
clothed me with the **g-s** of
salvation...................... Is 61:10
patches an old **g** with unshrunk ... Mt 9:16

GATE

Lift up your heads, you **g-s**!....... Ps 24:7
Enter his **g-s** with thanksgiving ...Ps 100:4
Enter through the narrow **g**. .... Mt 7:13
and the **g-s** of Hades will not ..... Mt 16:18
I am the **g**. If anyone enters by.... Jn 10:9
also suffered outside the **g**,...... Heb 13:12
Its **g-s** will never close by day..... Rv 21:25

GATHER

and **g** enough for that day. .... Ex 16:4
G my faithful ones to me,......... Ps 50:5
and a time to **g** stones;........... Ec 3:5
he **g-s** the lambs in his arms and . Is 40:11
who does not **g** with me scatters. . Mt 12:30
or three are **g-ed** together
in my...................... Mt 18:20
I wanted to **g** your children
together, as a hen **g-s** her
chicks .... Mt 23:37

GAZE (N)

fix your **g** straight ahead........... Pr 4:25

GAZE (V)

So I **g** on you in the sanctuary.......Ps 63:2
they were **g**-ing into heaven ...... Ac 1:10

GEHAZI

Elisha's attendant (2Kg 4:11–37; 5:20–27; 8:4–5).

GENEALOGY

Israel was registered in the **g**-ies ... 1Ch 9:1
to myths and endless **g**-ies. 1Tm 1:4
Without father, mother, or **g**, ... Heb 7:3

GENERATION

to the third and fourth **g**..........Ex 34:7
been our refuge in every **g**. .... Ps 90:1
There is a **g** that.................. Pr 30:11
To what should I compare this **g**?.. Mt 11:16
adulterous **g** demands a sign, ... Mt 12:39
This **g** will certainly not pass ..... Mt 24:34
from now on all **g**-s will call me ... Lk 1:48

GENEROSITY

giving, with **g**; .... Rm 12:8

GENEROUS

A **g** person will be blessed,........ Pr 22:9
to be **g** and willing to share, ...1Tm 6:18

GENEROUSLY

who sows **g** will also reap **g**. 2Co 9:6

GENTILE

Don't even the **G**-s do the same?.. Mt 5:47
They will hand him over to
the **G**-s....................... Mt 20:19
a light for revelation to the **G**-s .... Lk 2:32
trampled by the **G**-s until the
times of the **G**-s are fulfilled..... Lk 21:24
Why do the **G**-s rage................ Ac 4:25
poured out even on the **G**-s....... Ac 10:45
Is he not also the God of **G**-s..... Rm 3:29
fullness of the **G**-s has come ...... Rm 11:25
he regularly ate with the **G**-s
before........................ Gl 2:12

GENTLE

A **g** answer turns away anger,.......Pr 15:1
a **g** tongue can break a bone. ..... Pr 25:15
is coming to you, **g**, and mounted ..Mt 21:5
peace-loving, **g**, compliant, full.. Jms 3:17
quality of a **g** and quiet spirit,...... 1Pt 3:4

GENTLENESS

or in love and a spirit of **g**? 1Co 4:21
appeal to you by the ... **g** of Christ. . 2Co 10:1
goodness, faithfulness, **g**,
self-control..................... Gl 5:23
humility and **g**, with patience ..... Eph 4:2
faith, love, endurance, and **g**. 1Tm 6:11
do this with **g** and reverence, ... 1Pt 3:16

GENUINELY

widows who are **g** in need. 1Tm 5:3

GENUINENESS

am testing the **g** of your love....... 2Co 8:8

GERASENE

sailed to the region of the **G**-s,.....Lk 8:26

GET

G wisdom .... Pr 16:16

GETHSEMANE

with them to a place called **G**,.... Mt 26:36

GHOST

they thought it was a **g** and cried ..Mk 6:49
because a **g** does not have flesh...Lk 24:39

GIBEON

inhabitants of **G** heard what .... Jos 9:3
Sun, stand still over **G**, ... Jos 10:12

GIDEON

Judge (Jdg 6–8; Heb 11:32). The fleece (Jdg 6:36–40). God reduced his army (7:2–8).

GIFT

person's **g** opens doors for him.... Pr 18:16
leave your **g** there in front of ..... Mt 5:24
to give good **g**-s to your children, .. Mt 7:11
will receive the **g** of the Holy ......Ac 2:38
but the **g** of God is eternal life .... Rm 6:23
we have different **g**-s: .... Rm 12:6
each has his own **g** from God,...... 1Co 7:7
Now there are different **g**-s, ... 1Co 12:4
to God for his indescribable **g**! 2Co 9:15
good and perfect **g** is from above, .. Jms 1:17

GILEAD

Region east of the Jordan and north of
Moab, allotted to Reuben, Gad, and half of
Manasseh (Nm 32:40; Dt 3:12–13; Jos 13:8–31;
17:1–6).

GIRL

by the hand, and the **g** got up..... Mt 9:25
"Little **g**, I say to you, get up" ..... Mk 5:41

GIVE

I will **g** this land to your offspring .. Gn 12:7
The LORD **g**-s, and the LORD takes... Jb 1:21
g thanks to the God of gods. ...... Ps 136:2
if he is thirsty, **g** him water .... Pr 25:21
leech has two daughters: "G, G!" .. Pr 30:15
be born for us, a son will be
g-n to us, ... Is 9:6
I will not **g** my glory to another .... Is 48:8
I will **g** you a new heart and .....Ezk 36:26
G us today our daily bread. .... Mt 6:11
Ask, and it will be **g**-n............ Mt 7:7
hungry and you **gave** me....... Mt 25:35
G, and it will be **g**-n to you;.....Lk 6:38
is my body, which is **g**-n for you. .. Lk 22:19
He **gave** them the right to be..... Jn 1:12
He **gave** his one and only Son, ... Jn 3:16
I **g** them eternal life, ... Jn 10:28
not **g** to you as the world **g**-s. .... Jn 14:27
since he himself **g**-s everyone life .. Ac 17:25
blessed to **g** than to receive. ......Ac 20:35
he himself **gave** some to be.... Eph 4:11
gave himself as a ransom for all, .. 1Tm 2:6
ready ... to **g** a defense to......... 1Pt 3:15

GIVER

since God loves a cheerful **g**.......2Co 9:7

GLAD

Let the heavens be **g** and........ 1Ch 16:31
let's rejoice and be **g** in it. ...... Ps 118:24
Be **g** and rejoice, because your ....Mt 5:12

GLADNESS

Let me hear joy and **g**; .... Ps 51:8
Serve the LORD with **g**; .... Ps 100:2

GLASS

Something like a sea of **g**, ... Rv 4:6
city was pure gold clear as **g**. ..... Rv 21:18

GLEAN

do not **g** what is left............. Dt 24:21
saw what she had **g**-ed...........Ru 2:18

GLOAT

not let my enemies **g** over me...... Ps 25:2

GLOOM

a day of darkness and **g**,...........Jl 2:2
to darkness, **g**, and storm, ...Heb 12:18

GLOOMY

don't be **g** like the hypocrites...... Mt 6:16

GLORIFY

I have **g**-ied it, and I will **g** it
again! .... Jn 12:28

the Son of Man is **g**-ied, and God
is **g**-ied in him.................. Jn 13:31
G your Son so that the Son may **g** ... Jn 17:1
those he justified, he also **g**-ied. .. Rm 8:30
So **g** God in your body. 1Co 6:20

GLORIOUS

Who is like you, **g** in holiness.......Ex 15:11
G things are said about you, ... Ps 87:3

GLORY

Please, let me see your **g**.......... Ex 33:18
The **g** has departed from Israel, ...1Sm 4:21
Declare his **g** among the nations .. 1Ch 16:24
crowned him with **g** and honor. ..... Ps 8:5
Then the King of **g** will come in..... Ps 24:7
ascribe to the LORD **g** and strength.. Ps 29:1
the whole earth is filled with his **g**.. Ps 72:19
ascribe to the LORD **g** and strength. .Ps 96:7
His **g** fills the whole earth........... Is 6:3
And the **g** of the LORD will appear,.. Is 40:5
the **g** of the LORD filled...... Ezk 43:5; 44:4
the Son of Man comes in his **g**, ...Mt 25:31
and the **g** of the Lord shone ...... Lk 2:9
G to God in the highest heaven, ... Lk 2:14
We observed his **g**, the **g** as the
one and only Son .... Jn 1:14
exchanged the **g** of the immortal.. Rm 1:23
and fall short of the **g** of God...... Rm 3:23
not worth comparing with the **g** .. Rm 8:18
adoption, the **g**, the covenants.....Rm 9:4
do everything for the **g** of God. .. 1Co 10:31
incomparable eternal weight of **g**.. 2Co 4:17
Christ in you, the hope of **g**. ......Col 1:27
crowned him with **g** and honor.... Heb 2:7
worthy to receive **g** and honor ..... Rv 4:11

GLUTTON

and the **g** will become poor..... Pr 23:21
they say, 'Look, a **g** and a drunkard. .Mt 11:19

GNASH

they **g**-ed their teeth at me....... Ps 35:16
will be weeping and **g**-ing of
teeth. .... Mt 8:12; 13:12; 25:30
and **g**-ed their teeth at him........Ac 7:54

GNAT

strain out a **g**, yet gulp down .... Mt 23:24

GO

Let my people **g**, ... Ex 5:1
For wherever you **g**, I will **g**, ... Ru 1:16
Where can I **g** to escape your ..... Ps 139:7
We all **went** astray like sheep; ..... Is 53:6
I say to this one, 'G!' and he **g**-es;.. Mt 8:9
G, therefore, and make disciples.. Mt 28:19
G into all the world and preach....Mk 16:15
I am **g**-ing to prepare a place ...... Jn 14:2

GOAL

I pursue as my **g** the prize ....Php 3:14
receiving the **g** of your faith,....... 1Pt 1:9

GOAT

put them on the **g**-'s head and
send........................ Lv 16:21
bulls or drink the blood of **g**-s? ... Ps 50:13
separates the sheep from the **g**-s.. Mt 25:32
For if the blood of **g**-s and bulls .. Heb 9:13

GOD

In the beginning **G** created the...... Gn 1:1
you will be like **G**, knowing good ... Gn 3:5
the sons of **G** saw that the ...... Gn 6:2
he was a priest to **G** Most High. ... Gn 14:18
saying, "I am **G** Almighty. .... Gn 17:1
LORD, the Everlasting **G**, ... Gn 21:33
G planned it for good to bring ... Gn 50:20
I am the **G** of your father, the **G**
of Abraham, the **G** of Isaac, and the
G of Jacob.......................Ex 3:6
LORD, the **G** of your ancestors ...... Ex 3:15
LORD, the **G** of the Hebrews, ... Ex 3:18

This is my **G**, and I will praise him, . . Ex 15:2
Do not have other **g-s** besides me. . Ex 20:3
I, Lᴏʀᴅ your **G**, am a jealous **G**, ...Ex 20:5
G is not a man, that he might lie,. .Nm 23:19
G is a consuming fire, a jealous **G**. . .Dt 4:24
the voice of the living **G** speaking . .Dt 5:26
Lᴏʀᴅ your **G** is **G**, the faithful **G** . . . . .Dt 7:9
the Lᴏʀᴅ your **G** is the **G** of **g-s**. . . . Dt 10:17
The **G** of old is your dwelling. . . . . Dt 33:27
and your **G** will be my **G**. . . . . .Ru 1:16
there is no rock like our **G**. 1Sm 2:2
will know that Israel has a **G**,. . . .1Sm 17:46
Lᴏʀᴅ of Armies was with him. . 2Sm 5:10
But will **G** indeed live on earth . . .1Kg 8:27
G who answers with fire, he is **G**. .1Kg 18:24
Their **g-s** are **g-s** of the hill 1Kg 20:23
they had worshiped other **g-s**. 2Kg 17:7
And **G** granted his request. 1Ch 4:10
Save us, **G** of our salvation; 1Ch 16:35
our **G** is greater than any of the **g-s**. . 2Ch 2:5
says in his heart,
　"There's no **G**." . . . . Pss 14:1; 53:1
My **G**, my **G**, why have you . . . . Ps 22:1
the nation whose **G** is the Lᴏʀᴅ— . .Ps 33:12
G is our refuge and strength,. . . . . . .Ps 46:1
Our **G** is a **G** of salvation, ... Ps 68:20
What **g** is great like **G**? . . . . Ps 77:13
For he is our **G**, and we are the . . . . .Ps 95:7
Acknowledge that the Lᴏʀᴅ is **G**. .Ps 100:3
Give thanks to the **G** of **g-s**. . . . . . Ps 136:2
fear **G** and keep his commands, . . .Ec 12:13
Wonderful Counselor, Mighty **G**,. . . Is 9:6
of Judah, "Here is your **G**!" . . . . . . .Is 40:9
The Lᴏʀᴅ is the everlasting **G**, ... Is 40:28
There is no **G** but me. . . . . Is 44:6
I will be their **G**, and they will . . . . . .Jr 31:33
I am the Lᴏʀᴅ, the **G** of every . . . . . Jr 32:27
people, and I will be your **G**. . . . . .Ezk 36:28
Didn't one **G** create us?. . . . . .Mal 2:10
is translated "**G** is with us.". . . . . . .Mt 1:23
heart, for they will see **G**. . . . . .Mt 5:8
Therefore, what **G** has joined. . . . . Mt 19:6
and to **G** the things that are **G-'s**. . .Mt 22:21
that is, "My **G**, My **G**, why have. . . Mt 27:46
Who can forgive sins but **G** alone? . . Mk 2:7
was with **G**, and the Word was **G**. . . .Jn 1:1
For **G** loved the world in this way: . .Jn 3:16
G is spirit, and those who worship . .Jn 4:24
I said, you are **g-s**? . . . . .Jn 10:34
to him, "My Lord and my **G**!" . . . . .Jn 20:28
We must obey **G** rather than
　people. . . . . .Ac 5:29
The **g-s** are come down to us in. . .Ac 14:11
g-s made by hand are not **g-s**! . . . .Ac 19:26
Let **G** be true, even though
　everyone . . . . .Rm 3:4
If **G** is for us, who is against. . . . . . .Rm 8:31
G is the one who justifies. . . . . Rm 8:33
Be reconciled to **G**. 2Co 5:20
I will be their **G**, and they will be . .2Co 6:16
that by nature are not **g-s**. . . . . Gl 4:8
one **G** and Father of all, who is . . . . Eph 4:6
who, existing in the form of **G**, ... Php 2:6
one **G** and one mediator between **G**. .1Tm 2:5
our great **G** and Savior, Jesus. . . . . .Ti 2:13
for our **G** is a consuming fire. . . . Heb 12:29
G is light, and there is 1Jn 1:5
does not know **G**, because **G** is love. .1Jn 4:8
holy, holy, Lord **G**, the Almighty, . . . Rv 4:8
G-'s dwelling is with humanity,. . . . .Rv 21:3

GODDESS

Ashtoreth, the **g** of the Sidonians, . .1Kg 11:5
temple of the great **g** Artemis. . . . . Ac 19:27

GOD-FEARING

centurion, an upright and **G** man,. . Ac 10:22

GODLESS

the hope of the **g** will perish. . . . . . . Jb 8:13

GODLESSNESS

heaven against all **g** and. . . . . Rm 1:18
he will turn **g** away from Jacob. . . Rm 11:26

GODLINESS

life in all **g** and dignity. 1Tm 2:2
but **g** is beneficial in every way 1Tm 4:8
But **g** with contentment is. 1Tm 6:6
holding to the form of **g** but 2Tm 3:5
required for life and **g**. 2Pt 1:3
endurance, endurance with **g**,. 2Pt 1:6

GODLY

is the one seeking? **G** offspring. . . .Mal 2:15
For **g** grief produces a 2Co 7:10
want to live a **g** life in Christ 2Tm 3:12
and **g** way in the present age,. . . . . . .Ti 2:12

GOG

the day when **G** comes against . . . Ezk 38:18
G and Magog, to gather them. . . . . Rv 20:8

GOLD

G cannot be exchanged for it, ... Jb 28:15
They are more desirable than **g**. . . . Ps 19:10
more than **g**, even the purest **g**, . .Ps 119:127
is better than silver and **g**. . . . . .Pr 22:1
is like **g** apples in silver settings. . . .Pr 25:11
street of the city was pure **g**, ... Rv 21:21

GOLGOTHA

they came to a place called **G** . . . . Mt 27:33

GOLIATH

Philistine giant from Gath killed by David
(1Sm 17).

GOMER

Hosea's wife (Hs 1:3,8).

GOOD

And God saw that it was **g**. . . . . .Gn 1:10
God planned it for **g** to bring
　about . . . . Gn 50:20
There is no one who does **g**. . . Pss 14:1; 53:1
Taste and see that the Lᴏʀᴅ is **g**. . . .Ps 34:8
withhold the **g** from those who . . . Ps 84:11
How delightfully **g** when . . . . Ps 133:1
A joyful heart is **g** medicine, ... Pr 17:22
who brings news of **g** things, ... Is 52:7
to do what is **g** on the Sabbath. . . Mt 12:12
Well done, **g** and faithful slave! . . .Mt 25:21
Why do you call me **g**? ... No one
　is **g** except God. . . . . Mk 10:18
I am the **g** shepherd. . . . . .Jn 10:11
together for the **g** of those
　who . . . . .Rm 8:28
by evil, but conquer evil with **g**. . . Rm 12:21
in Christ Jesus for **g** works,. . . . . . . Eph 2:10

GOODNESS

cause all my **g** to pass in front. . . . Ex 33:19
Only **g** and faithful love will . . . . . . Ps 23:6
patience, kindness, **g**, faithfulness,. . Gl 5:22

GOODS

You have many **g** stored up for. . . . Lk 12:19
has this world's **g** and sees 1Jn 3:17

GOSHEN

Region of Egypt where Israel settled (Gn
45:10; 46:28–34); the best part of the land
(47:6,27); excluded from plagues (Ex 8:22;
9:26).

GOSPEL

and preach the **g** to all creation. . .Mk 16:15
For I am not ashamed of the **g**,. . . . Rm 1:16
But if our **g** is veiled,. 2Co 4:3
and are turning to a different **g** . . . . .Gl 1:6
with the eternal **g** to announce . . . .Rv 14:6

GOSSIP

A **g** goes around revealing a . . . . . . .Pr 11:13
but are also **g-s** and busybodies, . .1Tm 5:13

GOVERNMENT

and the **g** will be on his shoulders. . . .Is 9:6

GRACE

g flows from your lips. . . . . Ps 45:2
g and truth came through Jesus. . . .Jn 1:17
sin so that **g** may multiply?. . . . . . . Rm 6:1
My **g** is sufficient for you, ...2Co 12:9
you have fallen from **g**. . . . . .Gl 5:4
you are saved by **g** through faith . . Eph 2:8
For the **g** of God has appeared . . . . .Ti 2:11
having been justified by his **g**, ... Ti 3:7
But he gives greater **g**. . . . . Jms 4:6

GRACIOUS

I will be **g** to whom I will be **g**, ... Ex 33:19
Be **g** to me, God, according to. . . . . .Ps 51:1
are a compassionate and **g** God,. . . Ps 86:15
Let your speech always be **g**,. . . . . . . Col 4:6

GRAFT

wild olive branch, were **g-ed** in . . .Rm 11:17
God has the power to **g** them in. . Rm 11:23

GRANDCHILDREN

G are the crown of the elderly, ... Pr 17:6

GRAPE

not drink any **g** juice or eat . . . . .Nm 6:3
with a single cluster of **g-s**, ...Nm 13:23
The fathers have eaten sour **g-s**, . . Jr 31:29
because its **g-s** have ripened. . . . . . Rv 14:18

GRASP

so that they could not **g** it, ...Lk 9:45
him, but he escaped their **g**. . . . . . Jn 10:39

GRASS

As for man, his days are like **g** . . . . Ps 103:15
All humanity is **g**, and all its. . . . . Is 40:6
The **g** withers, the flowers fade . . . . . Is 40:7
God clothes the **g** of the field, ...Mt 6:30
All flesh is like **g**, and all its 1Pt 1:24
The **g** withers, and the flower. 1Pt 1:24

GRASSHOPPER

To ourselves we seemed like **g-s**,. . Nm 13:33

GRATITUDE

to God with **g** in your hearts. . . . . . Col 3:16

GRAVE

their throat is an open **g**; . . . . Ps 5:9
He was assigned a **g** with the
　wicked . . . . .Is 53:9
You are like unmarked **g-s**;. . . . . . . .Lk 11:44
Their throat is an open **g**; . . . . Rm 3:13

GRAY

G hair is a glorious crown; . . . . .Pr 16:31

GREAT

God made the two **g** lights . . . . .Gn 1:16
will make you into a **g** nation,. . . . . .Gn 12:2
Lᴏʀᴅ is a **g** God, a **g** King above all. .Ps 95:3
g is your faithfulness! . . . . .Lm 3:23
wants to become **g** among you . . .Mt 20:26
because of his **g** love that he. . . . . . . Eph 2:4
with contentment is **g** gain. 1Tm 6:6
we neglect such a **g** salvation? . . . . Heb 2:3
Then I saw a **g** white throne and . . Rv 20:11

GREATER

something **g** than the temple
　is here. . . . . .Mt 12:6
No one has **g** love than this, ... Jn 15:13
But desire the **g** gifts. 1Co 12:31
the one who is in you is **g** than the . .1Jn 4:4

GREATEST

Who is **g** in the kingdom . . . . .Mt 18:1
g among you will be your servant. . .Mt 23:11
But the **g** of these is love. 1Co 13:13

GREED

be on guard against all **g**,. . . . . Lk 12:15

GREEDY

A **g** person stirs up conflict, ... Pr 28:25
thieves, **g** people, drunkards 1Co 6:10

GREEK

to the Jew, and also to the **G**. . . . . . Rm 1:16
signs and the **G-s** seek wisdom, . . . 1Co 1:22
is no Jew or **G**, slave or free, ... Gl 3:28

GREEN

lets me lie down in **g** pastures; . . . . . Ps 23:2

GRIEF

and joy may end in **g**. . . . . .Pr 14:13
because your **g** led to repentance. . .2Co 7:9
this with joy and not with **g**, ... Heb 13:17

GRIEVE

rebelled and **g-d** his Holy Spirit. . . . Is 63:10
Peter was **g-d** that he asked him . . .Jn 21:17
And don't **g** God's Holy Spirit. . . . . Eph 4:30
you will not **g** like the rest, ... 1Th 4:13

GROAN

we also **g** within ourselves, ...Rm 8:23

GROANING

God heard their **g**, ...Ex 2:24
the whole creation has been **g** . . . .Rm 8:22
intercedes for us with inexpressible
  g-s. . . . . .Rm 8:26

GROOM SEE ALSO BRIDEGROOM

as a **g** rejoices over his bride, ... Is 62:5
I will eliminate... the voice of the
  g and the bride, ... Jr 7:34
Let the **g** leave his bedroom, ...Jl 2:16
sad while the **g** is with them? . . . . Mt 9:15
When the **g** was delayed, they . . . . Mt 25:5
He who has the bride is the **g**. . . . . .Jn 3:29

GROUND

The **g** is cursed because of you. . . . . .Gn 3:17
you are standing is holy **g**. . . . . .Ex 3:5
Others fell on rocky **g**, ...Mt 13:5

GROW

He **grew** up before him like a young . .Is 53:2
the wildflowers of the field **g**: . . . . Mt 6:28
boy **grew** up and became strong, . . .Lk 2:40
let us **g** in every way into him. . . . .Eph 4:15
But **g** in the grace and
  knowledge. 2Pt 3:18

GROWTH

but only God who gives the **g**. 1Co 3:7

GUARD (N)

The **g-s** were so shaken by fear . . . Mt 28:4

GUARD (V)

G your heart above all else, ...Pr 4:23
will **g** your hearts and minds . . . . . . Php 4:7
g what has been entrusted
  to you, ...1Tm 6:20

GUARDIAN

Am I my brother's **g**?. . . . . Gn 4:9
law, then, was our **g** until Christ, ...Gl 3:24
Shepherd and **G** of your souls. 1Pt 2:25

GUIDE

And if the blind **g** the blind, ...Mt 15:14
He will **g** you into all the truth . . . .Jn 16:13

GUILT

You forgave the **g** of my sin. . . . . Ps 32:5
my sins and blot out all my **g**. . . . . . Ps 51:9

GUILTY

I will not justify the **g**. . . . . Ex 23:7
I was **g** when I was born; . . . . Ps 51:5
Acquitting the **g** and condemning . .Pr 17:15
but is **g** of an eternal sin". . . . . Mk 3:29

- H -

HABAKKUK

Prophet in Judah before the exile (Hab 1:1).

HADES

You will go down to **H**. . . . . .Mt 11:23
and the gates of **H** will not . . . . . . .Mt 16:18
You will not abandon me in **H** . . . . . .Ac 2:27
I hold the keys of death and **H**. . . . . .Rv 1:18

HAGAR

Sarah's slave; mother of Ishmael (Gn 16; Gl
4:21–31). Sent away by Sarah (Gn 16:5–9;
21:9–21).

HAGGAI

Prophet after the exile, who encouraged
rebuilding the temple (Ezr 5:1; 6:14; Hg 1–2).

HAIL

I will rain down the worst **h** that . . .Ex 9:18
and mocked him: "**H**, king of the . . Mt 27:29

HAILSTONES

LORD threw large **h** on them from. . Jos 10:11
Enormous **h**, each weighing about . .Rv 16:21

HAIR

is to let the **h** of his head grow. . . .Nm 6:5
But his **h** began to grow back . . . .Jdg 16:22
are more than the **h-s** of my head,. . Ps 40:12
make a single **h** white or black. . . . . Mt 5:36
But even the **h-s** of your head
  have . . . . Mt 10:30
and wiped his feet with her **h**, ... Jn 11:2
she should have her **h** cut off. 1Co 11:6

HAIRSTYLES

with elaborate **h**, gold, pearls, ...1Tm 2:9
elaborate **h** and wearing gold 1Pt 3:3

HAIRY

A **h** man with a leather belt 2Kg 1:8

HALF

give you, up to **h** my kingdom. . . . . Mk 6:23

HALLELUJAH

H! My soul, praise the LORD. . . . . . . Ps 146:1
multitude in heaven, saying, **H**! . . . . Rv 19:1

HAM

Son of Noah (Gn 5:32; 9:18–27). Ancestor of
Cushites, Egyptians, and Canaanites (Gn
9:18–27; 10:6; Pss 78:51; 105:23,27; 106:22).

HAMAN

Nobleman of Persia at the time of Esther
(Est 3:1–2); enemy of Jews (3:3–15). Hanged
on his own gallows (7:9–10).

HANANIAH

1. False prophet; opposed Jeremiah (Jr 28).
2. Shadrach's original name (Dn 1:6).

HAND (N)

rock and cover you with my **h**. . . . . Ex 33:22
lay their **h-s** on the bull's head . . . . . Lv 4:15
they pierced my **h-s** and my feet. . .Ps 22:16
Sit at my right **h** until I make. . . . . . .Ps 110:1
even there your **h** will lead me;. . . Ps 139:10
Whatever your **h-s** find to do, ... Ec 9:10
of the field will clap their **h-s**. . . . . .Is 55:12
man's **h** appeared and began
  writing . . . . Dn 5:5
if your right **h** causes you to . . . . . . Mt 5:30
let your left **h** know what your
  right . . . . Mt 6:3
Sit at my right **h** until I put . . . . . . Mt 22:44
into your **h-s** I entrust my spirit. . . .Lk 23:46
he showed them his **h-s** and feet. . .Lk 24:40
will snatch them out of my **h**. . . . . .Jn 10:28

HAND (V)

h-ed him over to be crucified.. . . . Mt 27:26
when he **h-s** over the kingdom to . .1Co 15:24

HANDLE

Don't **h**, don't taste, don't touch"?. .Col 2:21

HANG

anyone **hung** on a tree is under . . . Dt 21:23
Then he went and **h-ed** himself. . . . Mt 27:5
everyone who is **hung** on a tree. . . . Gl 3:13

HANNAH

Wife of Elkanah; mother of Samuel (1Sm
1–2).

HAPPY

How **h** is the one who does not . . . . . Ps 1:1
H is the nation whose God is. . . . . . Ps 33:12
H is the man who has filled his . . . . Ps 127:5
H is a man who finds wisdom and . . Pr 3:13

HARD

It will be **h** for a rich person. . . . . . Mt 19:23
This teaching is **h**! Who can accept . .Jn 6:60
some things **h** to understand. 2Pt 3:16

HARDEN

But I will **h** his heart so that. . . . . . . .Ex 4:21
Do not **h** your hearts as at Meribah,. .Ps 95:8
and he **h-s** whom he wants to **h**. . .Rm 9:18
elect did find it. The rest were **h-ed**. .Rm 11:7
A partial **h-ing** has come upon
  Israel . . . . Rm 11:25
do not **h** your hearts as in the. . . . . Heb 3:8

HAREM

beautiful young women to the **h** . . . Est 2:3

HARM (N)

Don't plan any **h** against your. . . . . . Pr 3:29

HARM (V)

But they were planning to **h** me. . . Neh 6:2

HARP

praise him with **h** and lyre. . . . . Ps 150:3
Each one had a **h** and golden bowls. . Rv 5:8

HARSH

but a **h** word stirs up wrath. . . . . . . .Pr 15:1

HARVEST

earth endures, seedtime and **h**, ... Gn 8:22
observe the Festival of **H** with . . . . Ex 23:16
sleeps during **h** is disgraceful. . . . . . . Pr 10:5
The **h** is abundant, but the workers. .Mt 9:37
because they are ready for **h**. . . . . . .Jn 4:35
since the **h** of the earth is ripe. . . . .Rv 14:15

HASTY

Do not be **h** to speak, ... Ec 5:2

HATE

You who love the LORD, **h** evil!. . . . . Ps 97:10
To fear the LORD is to **h** evil. . . . . Pr 8:13
will not use the rod **h-s** his son, . . . Pr 13:24
a time to love and a time to **h**; . . . . .Ec 3:8
H evil and love good; . . . . Am 5:15
I loved Jacob, but I **h-d** Esau. . . . . . .Mal 1:3
If he **h-s** and divorces . . . . .Mal 2:16
your neighbor and **h** your enemy. . . Mt 5:43
do what is good to those who **h** you. .Lk 6:27
me and does not **h** his own father. . Lk 14:26
want to do, but I do what I **h**. . . . . . Rm 7:15
loved Jacob, but I have **h-d** Esau. . . Rm 9:13

HATRED

not harbor **h** against your brother.. Lv 19:17

HAY

stones, wood, **h**, or straw,. 1Co 3:12

HEAD

will strike your **h**, and you will . . . . .Gn 3:15
lay their hands on the bull's **h** . . . . . . Lv 4:15
You anoint my **h** with oil; . . . . .Ps 23:5
will heap burning coals on his **h**,. . . Pr 25:22
Man has no place to lay his **h**. . . . . Mt 8:20
His **h** was brought on a platter . . . . Mt 14:11
Christ is the **h** of every man, and
   the man is the **h** of the woman, . . 1Co 11:3
her **h** uncovered dishonors her **h**,. . 1Co 11:5
husband is the **h** of the wife as. . . .Eph 5:23

HEAL

For I am the LORD who **h-s** you. . . . Ex 15:26
their sin, and **h** their land. 2Ch 7:14
He **h-s** the brokenhearted . . . . Ps 147:3
a time to kill and a time to **h**; . . . . Ec 3:3
and we are **h-ed** by his wounds.. . . .Is 53:5
H the sick, raise the dead . . . . Mt 10:8
it lawful to **h** on the Sabbath?. . . .Mt 12:10
Doctor, **h** yourself. . . . . .Lk 4:23
turn, and I would **h** them. . . . . .Jn 12:40
so that you may be **h-ed**. . . . . .Jms 5:16
By his wounds you have been
   h-ed. 1Pt 2:24

HEALING

will rise with **h** in its wings, ... Mal 4:2
gifts of **h** by the one Spirit, ... 1Co 12:9
the tree are for **h** the nations, ...Rv 22:2

HEALTHY

The **h** don't need a doctor, ... Lk 5:31

HEAR

may you **h** in heaven and forgive . . 1Kg 8:34
One who shaped the ear not **h**,. . . . .Ps 94:9
with their eyes and **h** with their ears,. . Is 6:10
Have you not **h-d**? Has it not been . . Is 40:21
Dry bones, **h** the word of the LORD. . Ezk 37:4
You have **h-d** that it was said . . . . . .Mt 5:21
longed ... to **h** the things you **h**. . . Mt 13:17
Anyone who **h-s** my word and . . . . .Jn 5:24
My sheep **h** my voice, ... Jn 10:27
And how can they **h** without a . . . Rm 10:14
So faith comes from what is **h-d**,. . Rm 10:17
no eye has seen, no ear has **h-d**,. . . .1Co 2:9
according to his will, he **h-s** us. . . . 1Jn 5:14
If anyone **h-s** my voice and opens . . Rv 3:20

HEARERS

For the **h** of the law are not. . . . . . . Rm 2:13
of the word and not **h** only, ...Jms 1:22

HEARING (N)

works of the law or by **h** with faith? . .Gl 3:2

HEART

I will harden his **h** so that he . . . . . . Ex 4:21
when you seek him with all your **h** . .Dt 4:29
LORD your God with all your **h**, ...Dt 6:5
found a man after his own **h**. 1Sm 13:14
but the LORD sees the **h**. 1Sm 16:7
meditation of my **h** be acceptable . .Ps 19:14
create a clean **h** for me and . . . . Ps 51:10
Your word in my **h** so that I may. . . Ps 119:11
Search me, God, and know my **h**; . .Ps 139:23
Trust in the LORD with all your **h**, ... Pr 3:5
The **h** is more deceitful than . . . . . .Jr 17:9
them and write it on their **h-s**. . . . . .Jr 31:33
I will give you a new **h** . . . . .Ezk 36:26
Blessed are the pure in **h**, ... Mt 5:8
there your **h** will be also. . . . . Mt 6:21
the law is written on their **h-s**. . . . . Rm 2:15
and circumcision is of the **h** . . . . . . Rm 2:29
believe in your **h** that God raised . . Rm 10:9
you do, do it from the **h**, as done . . Col 3:23

HEAVEN

God created the **h-s** and the earth. . . Gn 1:1
Most High, Creator of **h** and earth,. . Gn 14:19

h, the highest **h**, cannot contain. . .1Kg 8:27
When I observe your **h-s**, the work . .Ps 8:3
The **h-s** declare the glory of God,. . . Ps 19:1
Your faithful love reaches to **h**,. . . . Ps 36:5
Who do I have in **h** but you? . . . . . . Ps 73:25
Let the **h-s** be glad and the earth. . Ps 96:11
For as high as the **h-s** are above . . .Ps 103:11
time for every activity under **h**: . . . . . Ec 3:1
create new **h-s** and a new earth; . . . Is 65:17
coming with the clouds of **h**. . . . . . . Dn 7:13
the kingdom of **h** has come near!. . . Mt 3:2
The **h-s** suddenly opened for him,. . Mt 3:16
for yourselves treasures in **h**,. . . . . Mt 6:20
H and earth will pass away, ... Mt 24:35
Who will go up to **h**?. . . . . Rm 10:6
to the third **h** fourteen years ago. . .2Co 12:2
Our citizenship is in **h**, ... Php 3:20
Christ did not enter a sanctuary
   ... but into **h** itself, ... Heb 9:24
that day the **h-s** will pass away . . . 2Pt 3:10
I saw a new **h** and a new earth . . . Rv 21:1

HEAVENLY

and your **h** Father knows that you . .Mt 6:32
a multitude of the **h** host with . . . . Lk 2:13
There are **h** bodies and earthly . . . 1Co 15:40
by God's **h** call in Christ. . . . . .Php 3:14
who share in a **h** calling, ...Heb 3:1

HEBREW

came and told Abram the **H**, ... Gn 14:13
This is one of the **H** boys. . . . . .Ex 2:6
LORD, the God of the **H-s**, ...Ex 3:18
He answered them, "I'm a **H**. . . . . . Jnh 1:9
of Benjamin, a **H** born of **H-s**; . . . . Php 3:5

HEEL

and you will strike his **h**. . . . . .Gn 3:15
Esau's **h** with his hand. . . . . Gn 25:26
has raised his **h** against me. . . . . . . Ps 41:9
has raised his **h** against me. . . . . . . Jn 13:18

HEIGHT

h nor depth, nor any other. . . . . . . .Rm 8:39
length and width, **h** and depth. . . . .Eph 3:18

HEIR SEE ALSO COHEIRS

born in my house will be my **h**. . . . .Gn 15:3
if children, also **h-s—h-s** of God. . . Rm 8:17
h-s according to the promise. . . . . . . Gl 3:29
then God has made you an **h**. . . . . . . Gl 4:7

HELL SEE ALSO HADES, SHEOL

to have two hands and go to **h**. . . .Mk 9:43
authority to throw people into **h** . . . Lk 12:5

HELMET

and a **h** of salvation on his head; . . .Is 59:17
Take the **h** of salvation . . . . Eph 6:17

HELP (N)

He is our **h** and shield. . . . . .Ps 33:20
Where will my **h** come from?. . . . . . Ps 121:1
gifts of healing, **h-ing**, leading, . . 1Co 12:28

HELP (V)

LORD has **h-ed** us to this point 1Sm 7:12
I do believe; **h** my unbelief!. . . . . . .Mk 9:24
He is able to **h** those who are . . . . Heb 2:18

HELPER

I will make a **h** corresponding to
   him. . . . . .Gn 2:18
You are a **h** of the fatherless. . . . . . Ps 10:14
a **h** who is always found in
   times. . . . . .Ps 46:1
Lord is my **h**; I will not be
   afraid. . . . . Heb 13:6

HELPLESS

For while we were still **h**, ...Rm 5:6

HEN

as a **h** gathers her chicks under. . . Mt 23:37

HERALD

are the feet of the **h**, who proclaims. .Is 52:7

HERB

unleavened bread and bitter **h-s**. . . .Ex 12:8

HERE

"**H** I am," he answered. . . . . .Ex 3:4
ran to Eli and said, "**H** I am; 1Sm 3:5
I said: **H** I am. Send me. . . . . Is 6:8

HERITAGE

Sons are indeed a **h** from the LORD,. .Ps 127:3

HEROD

1. The Great; king in Judea at the time
   of Jesus's birth; executed male babies
   (Mt 2).
2. Archelaus; son of 1. (Mt 2:22).
3. Philip; son of 1. (Mk 6:17).
4. Antipas; son of 1.; tetrarch of Galilee; arrested and executed John the Baptist (Mt
   14:1–12).
5. Agrippa I; grandson of 1.; persecuted the
   church; died when he didn't give glory to
   God (Ac 12).
6. Agrippa II; son of 5. (Ac 25:13). Heard Paul's
   defense (25:22–26:32).

HERODIAS

Wife of Herod Antipas, formerly of Herod
Philip; requested head of John the Baptist
(Mt 14:3–11; Mk 6:17–28; Lk 3:19).

HETHITE

Ancient people of the promised land (Gn
10:15–18; 15:20); Abraham lived among them
(Gn 23); Esau married them (26:34; 27:46;
36:2). Formerly lived in the hill country (Nm
13:29; Jos 9:1; 11:3; 12:8); dispossessed by Israel (Ex 23:23; Dt 7:1; 20:17; Jos 3:10); some
remained (Jdg 3:5; 1Kg 9:20–21); fought
alongside Israel (1Sm 26:6).
H-s, Perizzites, Rephaim. . . . . Gn 15:20
and spoke to the **H-s**: . . . . Gn 23:20
daughter of Beeri the **H** . . . . Gn 26:34
wife of Uriah the **H**? 2Sm 11:3
and your mother a **H**. . . . . Ezk 16:3

HEZEKIAH

Son of Ahaz; king of Judah (2Kg 18–20;
2Ch 29–32; Is 36–39). Reformer (2Kg 18:4;
2Ch 29–31). Healed of fatal illness (2Kg
20:1–11); showed treasuries to Babylonians
(20:12–19).

HIDDEN (ADJ)

The **h** things belong to the LORD. . Dt 29:29
Cleanse me from my **h** faults. . . . . . Ps 19:12
and nothing **h** that won't be made. .Mt 10:26

HIDE

they **hid** from the LORD . . . . .Gn 3:8
she **hid** him for three months. . . . . . .Ex 2:2
because she **hid** the messengers . .Jos 6:17
h me in the shadow of your wings. . Ps 17:8
hid me in the shadow of his hand. . . Is 49:2
situated on a hill cannot be **h-den**. . Mt 5:14
and went off and **hid** your talent. . Mt 25:25
your life is **h-den** with Christ . . . . . . Col 3:3
Fall on us and **h** us from the. . . . . . .Rv 6:16

HIDING (ADJ)

You are my **h** place; . . . . Ps 32:7

HIGH SEE ALSO HIGH PLACE, HIGH PRIEST, MOST HIGH

For as **h** as the heavens are . . . . . . .Ps 103:11
took him to a very **h** mountain . . . . . Mt 4:8

HIGH PLACE

people were sacrificing on the **h-s**,. . 1Kg 3:2
LORD at the **h** in Gibeon 1Ch 16:39
They enraged him with their **h-s** . . Ps 78:58

HIGH PRIEST

led him away to Caiaphas the **h**,.. Mt 26:57
become a merciful and faithful **h** ..Heb 2:17
this is the kind of **h** we need: .... Heb 7:26

HIGHER

so my ways are **h** than your ways, .. Is 55:9

HIGHLY

the LORD is great and is **h** praised; ..Ps 145:3
of himself more **h** than he should. . Rm 12:3

HIGHWAY

make a straight **h** for our God in.... Is 40:3
Go out into the **h-s** and hedges
    and .... Lk 14:23

HILL

the cattle on a thousand **h-s**. .....Ps 50:10
mountain and **h** will be leveled; .. Is 40:4
situated on a **h** cannot be hidden.. Mt 5:14
mountain and **h** will be made low ... Lk 3:5
and to the **h-s**, 'Cover us!' ....Lk 23:30

HINDER

your prayers will not be **h-ed**...... 1Pt 3:7

HIP

He struck Jacob's **h** socket .... Gn 32:25

HIRAM

1. King of Tyre; helped David build his palace and Solomon build the temple (2Sm
5:11; 2Kg 5). Manned Solomon's fleet (1Kg
9:27).
2. Craftsman; helped build the temple and
its furnishings (1Kg 7:13–14); also called
Huram (2Ch 4:11) or Huram-abi (2:13; 4:16).

HIRE

the morning to **h** workers for his .. Mt 20:1

HIRED (ADJ)

of my father's **h** workers have
    more ....Lk 15:17
he is a **h** hand and doesn't care.... Jn 10:13

HIT

Who was it that **h** you?...........Lk 22:64

HITTITE

A people group from Asia Minor (modern
Turkey) in contrast to the Hethites, who
were Canaanites.
all the land of the **H-s**............. Jos 1:4
to all the kings of the **H-s** 1Kg 10:29
Solomon loved ... **H** women....... 1 Kg 11:1

HOLD

Your right hand **h-s** on to me.......Ps 63:8
You **h** my right hand.............Ps 73:23
Your heart must **h** on to my words.. Pr 4:4
I will **h** on to you with my ....Is 41:10
h-ing firm to the word of life......Php 2:16
by him all things **h** together........Col 1:17
test all things. **H** on to what is 1Th 5:21
take hold of eternal life 1Tm 6:12
Let us **h** on to the confession of .. Heb 10:23

HOLIDAY

It is a **h** when they send gifts ..... Est 9:19

HOLINESS

Who is like you, glorious in **h**, ...Ex 15:11
in the splendor of his **h**...... Pss 29:2; 96:9
so that we can share his **h**........Heb 12:10

HOLY *SEE ALSO* **HOLY PLACE, HOLY SPIRIT**

you are standing is **h** ground. ....Ex 3:5
and be **h** because I am **h**. ....Lv 11:44
is no one **h** like the LORD. 1Sm 2:2
H, h, h is the LORD of................ Is 6:3
who is my equal?" asks the **H** One...Is 40:25

So then, the law is **h**, and the ..... Rm 7:12
and called us with a **h** calling, ... 2Tm 1:9
is written, Be **h**, because I am **h**....1Pt 1:16
regard Christ the Lord as **h**........1Pt 3:15
H, h, h, Lord God, the .... Rv 4:8
I also saw the **h** city, new ....Rv 21:2

HOLY PLACE

between the **h** and the most **h**. ... Ex 26:33
enter the most **h** in this way: ...... Lv 16:3
Then he made the most **h**; 2Ch 3:8
Who may stand in his **h**? ....Ps 24:3
standing in the **h**" (let the reader ..Mt 24:15
entered the most **h** once for all... Heb 9:12

HOLY SPIRIT

Third person of the Trinity, through whom
God acts, reveals his will, empowers individuals, and discloses his personal presence.
or take your **H** from me. ....Ps 51:11
and grieved his **H**................. Is 63:10
baptize you with the **H** and fire.... Mt 3:11
speaks against the **H**, it will not ...Mt 12:32
Father and of the Son and of
    the **H**, ... Mt 28:19
The **H** will come upon you .... Lk 1:35
and the **H** descended on.......... Lk 3:22
Father give the **H** to those
    who ask ....Lk 11:13
the Counselor, the **H**,............. Jn 14:26
they were all filled with the **H**...... Ac 4:31
H had been poured out even on... Ac 10:45
forbidden by the **H** to speak .... Ac 16:6
Did you receive the **H** when you.... Ac 19:2
your body is a temple of the **H**.... 1Co 6:19
sealed with the promised **H**. ...... Eph 1:13
don't grieve God's **H**,............. Eph 4:30
carried along by the **H**............ 2Pt 1:21

HOME

God provides **h-s** for those who
    are ....Ps 68:6
sparrow finds a **h**, and a swallow ...Ps 84:3
Go back to your **h**, and tell all .....Lk 8:39
to him and make our **h** with him. .. Jn 14:23
is hungry, he should eat at **h**,...... 1Co 11:34
from the body and at **h** with
    the Lord..........................2Co 5:8

HOMEOWNER

If the **h** had known what time the ..Mt 24:43

HOMETOWN

not without honor except in his **h** ..Mt 13:57

HONEST

How painful **h** words can be!.......Jb 6:25
word with an **h** and good heart,.... Lk 8:15

HONEY

land flowing with milk and **h**......Ex 3:8
What is sweeter than **h**?.........Jdg 14:18
sweeter than **h** dripping from a ... Ps 19:10
It is not good to eat too much **h**... Pr 25:27
his food was locusts and wild **h**..... Mt 3:4

HONOR (N)

crowned him with glory and **h**......Ps 8:5
is not without **h** except in his .....Mt 13:57
don't sit in the place of **h**..........Lk 14:8

HONOR (V)

H your father and your mother.... Ex 20:12
H the LORD with your possessions ... Pr 3:9
your name be **h-ed** as holy......... Mt 6:9
H your father and your mother;.... Mt 15:4
This people **h** me with their.......Mt 15:8
if one member is **h-ed**, all the.... 1Co 12:26

HONORABLE

whatever is **h**, whatever is just .... Php 4:8

HONORABLY

ourselves **h** in everything. ....Heb 13:18

HOPE (N)

where then is my **h**? Who can see .. Jb 17:15
Put your **h** in God, for I will ....Ps 42:5
This **h** will not disappoint..........Rm 5:5
Rejoice in **h**; be patient in........ Rm 12:12
three remain: faith, **h**, and love. ..1Co 13:13
what is the **h** of his calling, ... Eph 1:18
Christ in you, the **h** of glory.........Col 1:27
like the rest, who have no **h**....... 1Th 4:13
a helmet of the **h** of salvation......1Th 5:8
birth into a living **h** through 1Pt 1:3
reason for the **h** that is in you.....1Pt 3:15
who has this **h** in him purifies....... 1Jn 3:3

HOPE (V)

He kills me, I will **h** in him. ....Jb 13:15
all things, **h-s** all things 1Co 13:7
the reality of what is **h-d** for, ... Heb 11:1

HORN

caught in the thicket by its **h-s**. ...Gn 22:13
My shield, the **h** of my salvation. . 2Sm 22:3
and it had ten **h-s**................. Dn 7:7
has raised up a **h** of salvation ...... Lk 1:69

HORSE

has thrown the **h** and its rider into . Ex 15:1
chariots, and others in **h-s**, but we.. Ps 20:7
The **h** is a false hope for safety.... Ps 33:17
and there was a white **h**. .... Rv 6:2
and there was a white **h**. .... Rv 19:11

HOSANNA

H in the highest heaven! .... Mt 21:9

HOSEA

Prophet in Israel near the end of the kingdom; his marriage modeled God's love and
Israel's unfaithfulness (Hs 1–3).

HOSHEA

Son of Elah; last king of Israel (2Kg 15:30;
17:1–6).

HOSPITABLE

respectable, **h**, able to teach,...... 1Tm 3:2
Be **h** to one another without....... 1Pt 4:9

HOSPITALITY

in their needs; pursue **h**.......... Rm 12:13
neglect to show **h**, for by doing ...Heb 13:2

HOST

of the heavenly **h** with the angel ... Lk 2:13

HOSTILE

mindset of the flesh is **h** to God.... Rm 8:7

HOSTILITY

I will put **h** between you and the ...Gn 3:15
down the dividing wall of **h**. ...... Eph 2:14
who endured such **h** from sinners ..Heb 12:3
with the world is **h** toward God? .. Jms 4:4

HOT

you are neither cold nor **h**..........Rv 3:15

HOT-TEMPERED

not **h**, not an excessive drinker,...... Ti 1:7

HOUR

that day and **h** no one knows .... Mt 24:36
But an **h** is coming, and is now ....Jn 4:23
The **h** has come for the Son of..... Jn 12:23
Father, the **h** has come.............Jn 17:1
keep you from the **h** of testing.....Rv 3:10

HOUSE

dwell in the **h** of the LORD as.......Ps 23:6
zeal for your **h** has consumed me, ..Ps 69:9
Unless the LORD builds a **h**, ...Ps 127:1
Wisdom has built her **h**; .... Pr 9:1
for my **h** will be called a **h** of prayer.. Is 56:7
who built his **h** on the rock........ Mt 7:24

And everyone who has left **h-s**, .. Mt 19:29
My **h** will be called a **h** of prayer. . .Mt 21:13
he was of the **h** and family line......Lk 2:4
my Father's **h** into a marketplace . . .Jn 2:16
In my Father's **h** are many ....Jn 14:2
builder has more honor than the **h**.. Heb 3:3
a spiritual **h**, are being built.......1Pt 2:5

HOUSEHOLD

will be the members of his **h**. .... Mt 10:36
believed, along with his whole **h**....Jn 4:53
believe God with his entire **h**.....Ac 16:34
manages his own **h** competently . . 1Tm 3:4

HULDAH

Wife of Shallum; prophetess in Josiah's time
(2Kg 22:14).

HUMAN

heaven on the **h** race to see if......Ps 14:2
Even **h** wrath will praise you;.....Ps 76:10
I led them with **h** cords, with......Hs 11:4
is he served by **h** hands, ...Ac 17:25
not depend on **h** will or effort.....Rm 9:16
is wiser than **h** wisdom, ...1Co 1:25
is one flesh for **h-s**, another for .. 1Co 15:39

HUMANITY

and all **h** together will see it ....Is 40:5
pour out my Spirit on all **h**; ....Jl 2:28
you except what is common to **h**...1Co 10:13

HUMBLE (ADJ)

Moses was a very **h** man, ...Nm 12:3
He leads the **h** in what is right .....Ps 25:9
but gives grace to the **h**. ....Pr 3:34
h and riding on a donkey,.........Zch 9:9
Blessed are the **h**, for they ....Mt 5:5
I am lowly and **h** in heart,........Mt 11:29
but gives grace to the **h**. ....Jms 4:6

HUMBLE (V)

that he might **h** you and test you. . . .Dt 8:2
despise a broken and **h-d** heart....Ps 51:17
whoever **h-s** himself like this child . Mt 18:4
who exalts himself will be **h-d**,....Lk 14:11
he **h-d** himself by becoming ......Php 2:8
H yourselves before the Lord, ... Jms 4:10
H yourselves, therefore, under the . 1Pt 5:6

HUMBLY

and to walk **h** with your God. ......Mc 6:8

HUMILIATION

In his **h** justice was denied him.....Ac 8:33

HUMILITY

and **h** comes before honor........ Pr 15:33
but in **h** consider others as more .. Php 2:3
clothe yourselves with **h** toward one . .1Pt 5:5

HUNGER

Those who **h** ... for righteousness... Mt 5:6
They will no longer **h**; ....Rv 7:16

HUNGRY

If I were **h**, I would not tell........Ps 50:12
and giving food to the **h**..........Ps 146:7
your enemy is **h**, give him food.... Pr 25:21
days and forty nights, he was **h**... Mt 4:2
For I was **h** and you gave me.....Mt 25:35
Blessed are you who are **h** now.... Lk 6:21
who comes to me will ever be **h**, .. Jn 6:35
If your enemy is **h**, feed him......Rm 12:20

HURAM *SEE* HIRAM

HURAM-ABI *SEE* HIRAM

HURRY

You are to eat it in a **h**; ....Ex 12:11

HURT

sister is **h** by what you eat.......Rm 14:15

HUSBAND

Your desire will be for your **h**, ...Gn 3:16
"Go call your **h**," he told her,........Jn 4:16
you've had five **h-s**, and the man
   you now have is not your **h**.......Jn 4:18
A **h** should fulfill his marital........1Co 7:3
for the **h** is the head of the wife. ..Eph 5:23
H-s, love your wives, just as......Eph 5:25
the **h** of one wife, ...1Tm 3:2
encourage... women to love their **h-s**. . Ti 2:4
H-s, in the same way, live with 1Pt 3:7

HUSHAI

David's friend and spy in Absalom's court
(2Sm 15:32–17:15).

HYMN

praying and singing **h-s** to God, . . .Ac 16:25
in psalms, **h-s**, and spiritual ....Eph 5:19
psalms, **h-s**, and spiritual songs . . . Col 3:16

HYPOCRISY

are full of **h** and lawlessness ..... Mt 23:28
Let love be without **h**............Rm 12:9

HYPOCRITE

you must not be like the **h-s**, ... Mt 6:5
H! First take the beam of wood .... Mt 7:5
scribes and Pharisees, **h-s**!........Mt 23:13

HYSSOP

Purify me with **h**, and I will be ..... Ps 51:7

– I –

I AM

I WHO I...........................Ex 3:14
I the first and I the last.
   There is no ....Is 44:6
"I," said Jesus, ...Mk 14:62
"I ... **am** he"....................Jn 4:26
Before Abraham was, I.............Jn 8:58
"I he," Jesus told them............Jn 18:6

IDLE

warn those who are **i**, comfort 1Th 5:14

IDOL

Do not make an **i** for yourself,......Ex 20:4
Their **i-s** are silver and gold,....... Ps 115:4
incense, another praises an **i**— .... Is 66:3
abstain from food offered to **i-s**, . .Ac 15:29
about food sacrificed to **i-s**:........1Co 8:1
we know that "an **i** is nothing......1Co 8:4

IDOLATRY

my dear friends, flee from **i**. 1Co 10:14
i, sorcery, hatreds, strife,..........Gl 5:20
desire, and greed, which is **i**. ....Col 3:5

IGNORANCE

overlooked the times of **i**, ...Ac 17:30
silence the **i** of foolish people 1Pt 2:15

IGNORANT

reject foolish and **i** disputes, ... 2Tm 2:23
those who are **i** and are going..... Heb 5:2

ILLEGITIMATE

then you are **i** children and not... Heb 12:8

ILLNESSES

stomach and your frequent **i**. 1Tm 5:23

ILLUMINATE

my God **i-s** my darkness. ....Ps 18:28

IMAGE

Let us make man in our **i**, ...Gn 1:26
Whose **i** and inscription is this? . .. Mt 22:20
he is the **i** and glory of God,.......1Co 11:7
He is the **i** of the invisible God,.....Col 1:15
an **i** of the beast...................Rv 13:14

IMITATE

I urge you to **i** of me............. 1Co 4:16
I me, as I also **i** Christ. 1Co 11:1
of their lives, **i** their faith.........Heb 13:7
do not **i** what is evil, but what is 3Jn 11

IMITATORS

Therefore, be **i** of God, as..........Eph 5:1
but will be **i** of those who
   inherit.........................Heb 6:12

IMMANUEL

have a son, and name him **I**. .....Is 7:14
they will name him **I**, which is......Mt 1:23

IMMORAL

associate with sexually **i** people 1Co 5:9
No sexually **i** person, idolaters,.....1Co 6:9
Every sexually **i** or impure or......Eph 5:5
there isn't any **i** or irreverent.....Heb 12:16
murderers, sexually **i**, sorcerers ....Rv 21:8

IMMORALITY

except in a case of sexual **i**, ... Mt 5:32
except for sexual **i**, and marries.... Mt 19:9
We weren't born of sexual **i**, ...Jn 8:41
abstain ... from sexual **i**, ...Ac 15:20
The body is not for sexual **i** but
   for 1Co 6:13
Flee sexual **i**! Every other sin 1Co 6:18
Let us not commit sexual **i** as some .1Co 10:8
But sexual **i** and any impurity or....Eph 5:3
that you keep away from sexual **i**, . .1Th 4:3

IMMORTAL

glory of the **i** God for images ..... Rm 1:23
the King eternal, **i**, invisible 1Tm 1:17

IMMORTALITY

body must be clothed with **i**. .. 1Co 15:53
the only One who has **i**, dwelling . .1Tm 6:16
brought life and **i** to light........2Tm 1:10

IMPERISHABLE

into an inheritance that is **i**,........ 1Pt 1:4

IMPLANTED

humbly receive the **i** word, ...Jms 1:21

IMPORTANT

have neglected the more **i** matters . .Mt 23:23
on to you as most **i** what I also.... 1Co 15:3
others as more **i** than yourselves .. Php 2:3

IMPOSSIBLE

Is anything **i** for the LORD?.......Gn 18:14
It is **i** for God to do wrong,........Jb 34:10
Nothing will be **i** for you........ Mt 17:20
With man this is **i**, but with God .. Mt 19:26

IMPRISONED

For God has **i** all in disobedience, . . Rm 11:32
Scripture **i** everything under .... Gl 3:22

IMPURE

immoral or **i** or greedy person, ...Eph 5:5

IMPURITY

cleanse you from all your **i-ies** . . .Ezk 36:25
as slaves to moral **i**,..............Rm 6:19
and any **i** or greed should.........Eph 5:3

INCALCULABLE

to the Gentiles the **i** riches of ..... Eph 3:8

INCENSE

an altar for the burning of **i**; ....Ex 30:1
prayer be set before you as **i**, ... Ps 141:2

INCITED

against Israel and **i** David to count. . 1Ch 21:1

INCORRUPTIBLE

and the dead will be raised **i**,..... 1Co 15:52

INCORRUPTION

Sown in corruption, raised in **i**; ... 1Co 15:42

INCREASE

If wealth **i-s**, don't set your heart
on it. . . . . Ps 62:10
said to the Lord, "**I** our faith.". . . . . Lk 17:5
He must **i**, but I must decrease. . . . . Jn 3:30

INDICATING

Christ within them was **i** when he . . 1Pt 1:11

INEXPRESSIBLE

heard **i** words, which a human
being. 2Co 12:4
rejoice with **i** and glorious joy 1Pt 1:8

INFANT

mouths of **i-s** and nursing babies, . . . Ps 8:2
mouths of **i-s** and nursing babies? . . Mt 21:16
Like newborn **i-s**, desire the. 1Pt 2:2

INFERIOR

in no way **i** to those
"super-apostles" 2Co 11:5
the **i** is blessed by the superior. . . . . Heb 7:7

INFINITE

His understanding is **i**. . . . . Ps 147:5

INFLATE

Such people are **i-d** by empty . . . . . Col 2:18

INHERIT

You will **i** their land, since I. . . . . . . Lv 20:24
the humble will **i** the land . . . . Ps 37:11
his household will **i** the wind, ... Pr 11:29
blameless will **i** what is good. . . . . Pr 28:10
humble, for they will **i** the earth. . . . Mt 5:5
must I do to **i** eternal life? . . . Lk 10:25; 18:18
will not **i** God's kingdom?. 1Co 6:9

INHERITANCE

to be a people for his **i**, ... Dt 4:20
Levi has no **i** among his brothers,
the LORD is his **i**, ... Dt 18:2
In him we have also received an **i**, . . Eph 1:11
and into an **i** that is imperishable, . . 1Pt 1:4

INIQUITY

you and did not conceal my **i**. . . . . . Ps 32:5
crushed because of our **i-ies**; . . . . . . Is 53:5
punished him for the **i** of us all. . . . . Is 53:6

INJURY

born prematurely but there is no **i**, . . Ex 21:22

INJUSTICE

Is there **i** with God? . . . . Rm 9:14

INK

don't want to use paper and **i**. 2Jn 12

INN

him to an **i**, and took care. . . . . Lk 10:34

INNER

our **i** person is being renewed 2Co 4:16
strengthened ... in the **i** being . . . . . Eph 3:16

INNKEEPER

two denarii, gave them to the **i**, . . . Lk 10:35

INNOCENCE

wash my hands in **i** and go around. . Ps 26:6
will they be incapable of **i**? . . . . Hs 8:5

INNOCENT

hands that shed **i** blood, ... Pr 6:17
as serpents and as **i** as doves. . . . . Mt 10:16
sinned by betraying **i** blood, ... Mt 27:4

INSANE

pretended to be **i** in their 1Sm 21:13

INSCRIBE

tablets **i-d** by the finger of God. . . . Ex 31:18
I have **i-d** you on the palms of my . . Is 49:16

INSCRIPTION

but none could read the **i**. . . . . Dn 5:8
Whose image and **i** is this?. . . . . . . Mt 22:20

INSENSITIVITY

God gave them a spirit of **i**, ... Rm 11:8

INSIGHT

A man is praised for his **i**, ... Pr 12:8
to understand my **i** into the. . . . . . . Eph 3:4

INSIST

I **i** on paying the full price, ... 1Ch 21:24

INSPIRED

then that David, **i** by the Spirit . . . Mt 22:43
All Scripture is **i** by God and is 2Tm 3:16

INSTALL

I have **i-d** my king on Zion, ... Ps 2:6

INSTITUTED

those that exist are **i** by God. . . . . . . Rm 13:1

INSTRUCT

Your good Spirit to **i** them. . . . . Neh 9:20
I will **i** you and show you the. . . . . . . Ps 32:8
a wise person **i-s** its mouth; . . . . . . Pr 16:23

INSTRUCTION

This book of **i** must not depart . . . . . Jos 1:8
his delight is in the LORD's **i**, ... Ps 1:2
The **i** of the LORD is perfect, ... Ps 19:7
see wondrous things from your **i** . . Ps 119:18
but I delight in your **i**. . . . . Ps 119:70
Listen, my son, to your father's **i**, ... Pr 1:8
Listen to **i** and be wise; . . . . Pr 8:33
who follows divine **i** will be happy. . Pr 29:18
For I will go out of Zion and. . . . . Is 2:3
For I will go out of Zion and. . . . . Mc 4:2
in the past was written for our **i**, . . Rm 15:4
were written for our **i**, ... 1Co 10:11
the goal of our **i** is love 1Tm 1:5

INSTRUCTOR

may have countless **i-s** in Christ, . . . 1Co 4:15

INSULT (N)

whoever ignores an **i** is sensible. . . Pr 12:16
there began to yell **i-s** at him: . . . . . Lk 23:39

INSULT (V)

of those who **i** you have fallen . . . . . Ps 69:9
who mocks the poor **i-s** his Maker, . . Pr 17:5
blessed when they **i** you and. . . . . . Mt 5:11
of those who **i** you have fallen . . . . Rm 15:3
he was **i-ed**, but he did not **i**. 1Pt 2:23

INTEGRITY

if you walk before me ... with ... **i** . . 1Kg 9:4
He still retains his **i**, even though you . . Jb 2:3
You desire **i** in the inner self. . . . . . . Ps 51:6
with **i** and dignity in your teaching. . Ti 2:7

INTELLIGENT

The woman was **i** and beautiful, . . . 1Sm 25:3

INTENSIFY

I will **i** your labor pains; . . . . Gn 3:16

INTENTION

and reveal the **i-s** of the hearts. 1Co 4:5

INTERCEDE

But Moses **i-d** with the LORD his. . . Ex 32:11
sins against the LORD, who can **i**. . . 1Sm 2:25
the Spirit himself **i-s** for us with . . . Rm 8:26
He always lives to **i** for them. . . . . Heb 7:25

INTERCESSION

perseverance and **i** for all the . . . . . Eph 6:18
prayers, **i-s**, and thanksgivings 1Tm 2:1

INTERCOURSE

has sexual **i** with an animal . . . . . . Ex 22:19
You are not to have sexual **i** with . . . Lv 18:9

INTEREST

you must not charge him **i**. . . . . . . Ex 22:25
You may charge a foreigner **i**, ... Dt 23:20
who does not lend his silver at **i** . . . Ps 15:5
received my money back with **i**. . . Mt 25:27
not to his own **i-s**, but rather . . . . . Php 2:4
has an unhealthy **i** in disputes. 1Tm 6:4

INTERMARRY

i with us; give your daughters. . . . . Gn 34:9
You must not **i** with them, ... Dt 7:3
and **i** with the peoples who . . . . . . Ezr 9:14

INTERPRET

a dream, and no one can **i** it. . . . . . Gn 41:15
and the ability to **i** dreams, ... Dn 5:12
in tongues? Do all **i**? 1Co 12:30
unless he **i-s** so that the church . . . 1Co 14:5
and let someone **i**. 1Co 14:27

INTERPRETATION

Don't **i-s** belong to God? . . . . Gn 40:8
tell me the dream and its **i**, ... Dn 2:5
inscription and give me its **i**, ... Dn 5:16
to another, **i** of tongues. 1Co 12:10
from the prophet's own **i**, ... 2Pt 1:20

INTERPRETER

But if there is no **i**, that person . . . 1Co 14:28

INTIMATE

The man was **i** with his wife Eve, . . . Gn 4:1

INVADE

king of Assyria **i-d** the whole land, . . 2Kg 17:5
For a nation has **i-d** my land, ... Jl 1:6

INVALIDATE

fine way of **i-ing** God's command . . Mk 7:9

INVESTIGATE

glory of kings to **i** a matter. . . . . Pr 25:2
I have carefully **i-d** everything . . . . . . Lk 1:3

INVISIBLE

His **i** attributes, that is, his . . . . Rm 1:20
He is the image of the **i** God, ... Col 1:15
immortal, **i**, the only God, ... 1Tm 1:17

INVITE

Then **i** Jesse to the sacrifice, ... 1Sm 16:3
For many are **i-d**, but few are . . . . Mt 22:14
a banquet, **i** those who are poor, . . Lk 14:13

INWARD

was you who created my **i** parts; . . Ps 139:13

INWARDLY

a person is a Jew who is one **i**, ... Rm 2:29

IRON

it there, and made the **i** float. 2Kg 6:6
break them with an **i** scepter; . . . . . . Ps 2:9
i sharpens **i**, and one man. . . . . Pr 27:17
legs were **i**, ... feet were partly **i** and . . Dn 2:33

IRREVERENT

the unholy and **i**, for those who 1Tm 1:9

IRREVOCABLE

gracious gifts and calling are **i**. . . . Rm 11:29

ISAAC

Son of Abraham and Sarah; fulfillment
of a promise (Gn 17:17; 21:5). God tested
Abraham by asking him to sacrifice Isaac

(Gn 22; Heb 11:17–19). Married Rebekah (Gn 24). Heir to Abraham's promise (Gn 25:5,11; Ps 105:9; Rm 9:7). Father of Esau and Jacob (Gn 25:21–26); blessed Jacob (Gn 27). Lied to Abimelech in Gerar about Rebekah (26:7–11). Died in Hebron (35:27–29).

ISAIAH

Son of Amoz; prophet to four kings of Judah (Is 1:1). Called (Is 6). Sons' names were symbolic (7:3; 8:3).

ISH-BOSHETH

Saul's son; tried to become king (2Sm 2:8–17; 3:6–16); was murdered (2Sm 4).

ISHMAEL

Son of Abraham and Hagar (Gn 16:11–15). Received a blessing but not the promise (17:18–21). Descendants are perpetual opponents of Israel (25:18).

ISLAND

the many coasts and **i-s** be glad. . . . Ps 97:1

ISRAEL

Name God gave Jacob (Gn 32:28; 35:10). Also his descendants—God's chosen people—and their land (Ex 3:16; 1Sm 13:19; 15:35; 1Kg 4:1; Mt 2:6,20; Php 3:5). In the divided kingdom, the northern (1Kg 12:20).

ISRAELITE

about him, "Here truly is an **I**. . . . . . Jn 1:47
They are **I-s**, and to them belong. . .Rm 9:4
For I too am an **I**, a descendant . . . . .Rm 11:1
Are they **I-s**? So am I. 2Co 11:22

ISSACHAR

Son of Jacob and Leah (Gn 30:18). Tribe with territory from Jezreel to Tabor (Jos 19:17–23); its troops who rallied to David understood the times (1Ch 12:32).

ITCH

have an **i** to hear what they want . .2Tm 4:3

ITHAMAR

Fourth son of Aaron (Ex 6:23; 28:1; Nm 26:20; 1Ch 6:3; 24:1); took over priesthood when his brothers died (Lv 10:6,12,16; Nm 3:4; 1Ch 24:2); in charge of the Levites (Ex 38:21; Nm 4:28,33; 7:8).

IVORY

from **i** palaces harps bring you . . . . .Ps 45:8
lie on beds inlaid with **i**, ...Am 6:4

- J -

JABEZ

Israelite who asked for and received a blessing (1Ch 4:9–10).

JABIN

A king of Canaan, whose commander Sisera was defeated by Israel (Jdg 4–5).

JACOB

Son of Isaac and Rebekah; younger twin brother of Esau (Gn 25:21–26). Took birthright (25:33); fled Esau (27:41–28:5). Received the promise (28:10–22). Worked for his wives (29:1–30). Wrestled with God (32:22–32); God changed his name to Israel (32:28; 49:2). Reconciled with Esau (33:4–16). Fathered the twelve tribes (29:31–30:24; 35:16–18). Went to Egypt (46:1–7). Died there, buried in Hebron (49:29–50:14). Ancestor of Jesus (Mt 1:2).

Even so, I loved **J**, ...Mal 1:2
J-'s well was there, and Jesus . . . . . . .Jn 4:6
J I have loved, but Esau I have. . . . .Rm 9:13

JAIRUS

Synagogue leader whose daughter Jesus restored (Mk 5:22–43; Lk 8:41–56).

JAMES

1. Apostle; son of Zebedee; brother of John (Mt 4:21; 10:2). At transfiguration (17:1); in Gethsemane (26:36–37). Martyred (Ac 12:2).
2. Apostle; son of Alphaeus (Mt 10:3).
3. Brother of Jesus (Mt 13:55; Gl 1:19). Believed after the resurrection (Jn 7:3; Ac 1:14; 1Co 15:7). Leader of church in Jerusalem (Ac 15; 21:18; Gl 2:9). Author (Jms 1:1).

JAPHETH

Son of Noah (Gn 5:32; 9:18–27).

JAR

in the house except a **j** of oil. 2Kg 4:2
an alabaster **j** of very expensive . . . Mk 14:3
an alabaster **j** of perfume. . . . . Lk 7:37
have this treasure in clay **j-s**, ...2Co 4:7

JAWBONE

He found a fresh **j** of a donkey, . . . Jdg 15:15

JEALOUS

His brothers were **j** of him, ... Gn 37:11
LORD your God, am a **j** God, ...Ex 20:5
another god. He is a **j** God. . . . . .Ex 34:14
is a consuming fire, a **j** God. . . . . . . .Dt 4:24
and I will be **j** for my
holy name . . . . Ezk 39:25
I will make you **j** of those who . . . Rm 10:19
For I am **j** for you with a godly 2Co 11:2

JEALOUSY

provoked his **j** with different
gods . . . . .Dt 32:16
For **j** enrages a husband,
and he. . . . . .Pr 6:34
hatreds, strife, **j**, outbursts of . . . . . .Gl 5:20

JEBUSITES

Descendants of Canaan (Gn 10:16; 15:21; Ex 3:8; Dt 7:1; 20:17), inhabitants of Jebus (1Ch 11:4). Defeated by Judah and Benjamin, but not dispossessed (Jos 15:63; Jdg 1:8,21; 3:5); defeated by David (2Sm 5:6–9) and enslaved by Solomon (1Kg 9:20–21).

JEHOAHAZ

1. Son of Jehu; king of Israel (2Kg 13:1–9).
2. Son of Josiah; king of Judah (2Kg 23:30–34). Called Shallum (Jr 22:11).

JEHOASH

1. Alternate name of Joash son of Ahaziah, king of Judah (2Kg 12).
2. Son of Jehoahaz; king of Israel (2Kg 13:10–14:13).

JEHOIACHIN

Son of Jehoiakim; king of Judah (2Kg 24:6). Also called Jeconiah or Coniah (Jr 22:24; 24:1). Exiled (2Kg 24:10–17) but later favored (25:27–30).

JEHOIAKIM

Son of Josiah; king of Judah. Succeeded his brother Jehoahaz; name changed from Eliakim by Neco (2Kg 23:34). Burned Jeremiah's scroll (Jr 36). Became vassal of Babylon; later rebelled and was defeated (2Kg 24:1–6; Dn 1:2).

JEHORAM

1. Alternate form of Joram, son of Ahab; king of Israel (2Kg 3:1).
2. Son of Jehoshaphat; king of Judah (2Kg 8:16–24; 2Ch 21). Ahab's son-in-law (2Kg 8:18). Edom gained independence during his reign (8:20).

JEHOSHAPHAT

1. Son of Asa; king of Judah (1Kg 15:24). Initially faithful, strong, blessed (2Ch 17). Then married Ahab's daughter Athaliah and formed alliances with Ahab and Joram, kings of Israel (1Kg 22; 2Kg 3; 8:26; 2Ch 18; 20).
2. Valley of judgment (Jl 3:2,12).

JEHU

1. Son of Hanani; prophet against Baasha king of Israel (1Kg 16:1–12).
2. Son of Jehoshaphat; king of Israel. Anointed by Elisha's servant; executed Ahaziah king of Judah, Joram, Jezebel and the house of Ahab in Israel, and the worshipers of Baal (2Kg 9–10; cp. 1Kg 19:16–17).

JEPHTHAH

Gileadite judge who made rash vow affecting his daughter (Jdg 11–12; 1Sm 12:11; Heb 11:32).

JEREMIAH

Prophet to Judah in the time leading up to the exile (Jr 1:1–3). Put in stocks (20:1–3), threatened (Jr 26), opposed (Jr 28), imprisoned (32:2; 37), censured (Jr 36), and thrown into a cistern (Jr 38). Taken to Egypt against his will (Jr 43).

JERICHO

City near the Jordan River north of the Dead Sea (Nm 22:1). Spied out (Jos 2) and conquered (Jos 6; Heb 11:30) by Joshua; rebuilt by Hiel (1Kg 16:34). Visited by Jesus (Mt 20:29–34; Mk 10:46–52; Lk 18:35; 19:1–10).

JEROBOAM

1. Son of Nebat; Solomon's servant; rebelled; first king of Israel (1Kg 11:26–12:20). Judged for notorious idolatry (12:25–14:20).
2. Son of Joash, king of Israel (2Kg 14:23–29).

JERUSALEM

Formerly called Salem (Gn 14:18; Ps 76:2) or Jebus (Jos 18:28); 1Ch 11:4. David conquered it and made it his capital (2Sm 5:5–9); Solomon built temple, palace, and fortifications (1Kg 3:1). Conquered by Babylon (2Kg 24:10–12). Rebuilt and resettled after the exile (Ezr 1; Neh 12:27). Jesus visited (Mt 21:1; Jn 2:13); mourned (Mt 23:37). Important city in early church (Ac 15:4). New Jerusalem promised (Rv 3:12; 21:2,10).

in **J** he reigned thirty-three years . .2Sm 5:5
J, the city I chose for myself to
put my name there. 1Kg 11:36
For a remnant will go out from **J**,. .2Kg 19:31
Pray for the well-being of **J**: . . . . . .Ps 122:6
If I forget you, **J**, may my right . . . .Ps 137:5
Speak tenderly to **J**, and
announce . . . . Is 40:2
From ... rebuild **J** until an Anointed . . Dn 9:25
J! **J** that kills the prophets and . . . Mt 23:37
say that the place to worship is in **J**. . Jn 4:20
you will be my witnesses in **J**, in all . .Ac 1:8
holy city, the new **J**, coming down . . Rv 21:2

JESHUA

Son of Jozadak; high priest; returned with Zerubbabel (Ezr 3:2; Neh 7:7).

JESSE

David's father (Ru 4:17–22; 1Sm 16; 1Ch 2:12–16; Mt 1:5–6; Lk 3:32).

JESUS

Messiah and Lord (Ac 2:36; Eph 3:11; 1Pt 3:15). Born in Bethlehem (Mt 1:18–25; Lk 2:1–7) to a virgin, Mary (Mt 1:20; Lk 1:26–38). Genealogy (Mt 1:1–17; Lk 3:23–38). Raised in

Nazareth (Mt 2:19–23; Lk 2:39–40). Visited the temple at age 12 (Lk 2:41–50).

Baptized by John (Mt 3:13–17; Lk 3:21). Tempted in the wilderness (Mt 4:1–11; Lk 4:1–13). Chose apostles (Lk 5:1–11,27–28; 6:12–16; Jn 1:35–51).

Transformation (Mt 17:1–9; Mk 9:2–10). Triumphal entry into Jerusalem (Mt 21:1–11; Lk 19:28–40). Betrayal and arrest (Mt 26:17–25,47–56; Mk 14:17–21,43–50; Lk 22:1–6,47–54), trial (Mt 26:57–66; 27:11–31; Mk 14:53–65; 15:1–20; Lk 22:66–23:25), crucifixion (Mt 27:32–56; Mk 15:21–39; Lk 23:32–49), and resurrection (Mt 28; Mk 16; Lk 24; Jn 20–21).

JETHRO

Priest of Midian; Moses's father-in-law and adviser (Ex 3:1; 4:18; 18). Also called Reuel (2:18).

JEW

He planned to destroy all ... the **J-s**, . . Est 3:6
has been born king of the **J-s**? . . . . . Mt 2:2
Are you the king of the **J-s**? . . . . . . Mt 27:11
How is it that you, a **J**, ask for a . . . . Jn 4:9
salvation is from the **J-s**. . . . . Jn 4:22
first to the **J**, and also to the . . . . . . Rm 1:16
a person is a **J** who is one inwardly, . . Rm 2:29
the God of **J-s** only? Is he not . . . . . Rm 3:29
To the **J-s** I became like a **J**, ... 1Co 9:20
There is no **J** or Greek, slave or . . . . Gl 3:28

JEWEL

She is far more precious than **j-s**. . . . Pr 3:15

JEZEBEL

Wife of King Ahab of Israel, daughter of the king of Sidon; brought Baal worship to Israel (1Kg 16:31–33). Killed prophets and threatened Elijah (18:4,13; 19:1–2). Killed by Jehu (2Kg 9:30–37) in fulfillment of prophecy (1Kg 21). Name used as a label (Rv 2:20).

JOAB

Son of Zeruiah; David's nephew and commander of his troops (1Ch 2:16; 11:6). Killed Abner (2Sm 3:22–39), Absalom (2Sm 18), Amasa, and Sheba (2Sm 20). Sided with Adonijah (1Kg 1:7,19); David told Solomon to execute him (2:5–6,28–35).

JOASH

1. Son of Ahaziah; king of Judah (2Kg 12). Protected by Jehoiada (2Kg 11). Repaired temple (2Ch 24:4–14).
2. Alternate name of Jehoash son of Jehoahaz, king of Israel (2Kg 13:10).

JOB

Wealthy patriarch. His book tells of his testing (Jb 1–2), perseverance (Jb 3–37), rebuke (Jb 38–41), and vindication (Jb 42; Jms 5:11).

JOEL

1. Dishonest son of Samuel (2Sm 8:2).
2. Son of Pethuel; prophet who urged priests to call Judah to repentance; depicted calamities (Jl 1:1–2:11); predicted the Messiah (2:21–32; Ac 2:16).

JOHANAN

Commander; stayed in Judah and tried to protect Gedaliah (2Kg 25:23); forced Jeremiah to go to Egypt (Jr 40–43).

JOHN

1. The baptizer; Son of Zechariah; prophet. Annunciation and birth (Lk 1:5–25,57–66). Preached repentance, announced the coming Messiah (Mt 3:1–12; Mk 1:1–8; Lk 3:1–18; 7:27–28), and baptized Jesus (Mt 3:13–15; Mk 1:9; Lk 3:21–22). Fulfilled the role of Elijah (Mt 11:13–14; 17:12–13; Mk 9:12–13; Mt 3:4 cp. 2Kg 1:8). Asked Jesus to

verify his identity (Mt 11:2–6; Lk 7:18–23). Beheaded by Herod Antipas (Mt 14:1–12; Mk 6:14–29; Lk 3:19–20; 9:7–9).
2. Apostle; Son of Zebedee; brother of James. Call (Mt 4:21–22; Mk 1:19–20). Among the inner three at special occasions (Mk 9:2; 14:32–33). With James, called "Sons of Thunder" (Mk 3:17); asked for places of honor (Mk 10:35–41). Often with Peter (Ac 1:13; 3:1–11; 4:13–20; 8:14); a leader in Jerusalem (Gl 2:9). In his gospel, called the disciple Jesus loved (Jn 13:23; 19:26; 20:2; 21:7,20); also wrote three letters and Revelation.
3. John Mark *see* MARK, JOHN

JOIN

to house and **j** field to field . . . . Is 5:8
Then **j** them together into a . . . . . Ezk 37:17
what God has **j-ed** together, ... Mt 19:6

JOINTS

soul and spirit, **j** and marrow. . . . . Heb 4:12

JOKING

or crude **j** are not suitable . . . . Eph 5:4

JONAH

Son of Amittai; prophet at the time of Jeroboam II (2Kg 14:23–27). Rejected God's call to preach in Nineveh; swallowed by a great fish (Jnh 1). Prayed (Jnh 2); preached repentance in Nineveh (Jnh 3); scolded by God for his anger (Jnh 4). Used as an example (Mt 12:39–41; 16:4; Lk 11:29–32).

JONATHAN

Son of Saul; friend of David (1Sm 18:1–4; 19:1–7; 20; 23:16–18). Killed in battle (31:1–13); mourned by David (2Sm 1:17–27).

JORAM

1. Son of Ahab; king of Israel (2Kg 3). Succeeded his brother Ahaziah (1:17). Attacked Moab with the help of Judah, Edom, and Elisha (3:4–27). Wounded by Arameans (8:28); killed by Jehu (9:14–26).
2. Alternate form of Jehoram, son of Jehoshaphat; king of Judah (2Kg 8:16–24; 2Ch 21).

JORDAN

Lot chose the entire plain of **J** . . . . . Gn 13:11
the border will go down to the **J** . . Nm 34:12
dry ground in the middle of the **J**, . . Jos 3:17
himself in the **J** seven times, ... 2Kg 5:14
Jesus came ... to John at the **J**, ... Mt 3:13

JOSEPH

1. Son of Jacob and Rachel. Sold into slavery in Egypt (Gn 37); imprisoned on false accusations (Gn 39); became Pharaoh's second in command (41:39–45); sold grain to brothers (Gn 42–45); enabled his father and brothers to move to Egypt (Gn 46–47). Sons Ephraim and Manasseh each became tribes (Gn 48). Died in Egypt, buried in Canaan (50:22–26; Ex 13:19; Jos 24:32; Ac 7:16).
2. Husband of Mary; foster father of Jesus (Mt 1:16,20; Lk 2:4; 3:23; 4:22; Jn 1:45; 6:42). Carpenter (Mt 13:55). Told in a dream not to divorce Mary (Mt 1:18–25); told in a dream to flee to Egypt (2:13–23).
3. Of Arimathea; a righteous member of the Sanhedrin who sought the kingdom of God; put Jesus's body in his tomb (Mt 27:57–60; Mk 15:43–46; Lk 23:50–53; Jn 19:38–42).

JOSHUA

Son of Nun; successor to Moses as leader of Israelites. Leader of Moses's army (Ex 17:8–13); Moses's servant on Mt. Sinai (32:17).

Scouted Canaan and, along with Caleb, recommended invasion (Nm 13:30–14:38). Chosen, commissioned, and encouraged by God (Nm 27:15–23; Dt 31:14–15,23; Jos 1:1–9).

Conquered Canaan (Jos 2–11) and distributed the land (Jos 12–21). Renewed the covenant and charged the people (Jos 23–24).

JOSIAH

Son of Amon; king of Israel. Became king at age eight (2Kg 21:19–22:2). Found the book of the law and instituted reforms (2Kg 22–23; 2Ch 34–35). Died resisting Pharaoh Neco (2Kg 23:29–30; 2Ch 35:20–25).

JOTHAM

1. Son of Gideon (Jdg 9).
2. Son of Uzziah/Azariah; coregent (2Kg 15:5), then king of Judah (15:32–38).

JOURNEY

like a man on a **j**, who left his . . . . Mk 13:34
On frequent **j-s**, I faced dangers . . 2Co 11:26

JOY

altar of God, to God, my greatest **j**. . Ps 43:4
Restore the **j** of your salvation . . . . Ps 51:12
A wise son brings **j** to his father, ... Pr 10:1
crowned with unending **j**. . . . . Is 35:10; 51:11
turn their mourning into **j**, ... Jr 31:13
immediately receives it with **j**. . . . . Mt 13:20
Share your master's **j**!' . . . . Mt 25:21
news of great **j** that will be for . . . . . Lk 2:10
will be more **j** in heaven over. . . . . . Lk 15:7
but your sorrow will turn to **j**. . . . . Jn 16:20
peace, and **j** in the Holy Spirit. . . . . Rm 14:17
fruit of the Spirit is love, **j**, peace . . Gl 5:22
make my **j** complete by thinking
  the same . . . . Php 2:2
For the **j** that lay before him . . . . . Heb 12:2
Consider it a great **j**, my brothers . . . Jms 1:2
inexpressible and glorious **j**, ... 1Pt 1:8
I have no greater **j** than this: 3Jn 4

JOYFUL

come before him with **j** songs. . . . . Ps 100:2
A **j** heart is good medicine, ... Pr 17:22
In the day of prosperity be **j**, ... Ec 7:14
ate their food with a **j** and sincere . . Ac 2:46

JOYFULLY

Let the whole earth shout **j** to God! . . Ps 66:1

JUBILEE

It will be your **J**, when. . . . . Lv 25:10

JUDAH

Son of Jacob and Leah (Gn 29:35); tribe with large territory west and south of Jerusalem (Jos 15:20–63). Tricked by daughter-in-law (Gn 38). Ancestor of David and Jesus (Gn 49:10; 1Sm 17:12; Mt 1:3,6,16; Rv 5:5). Name of the southern part of the divided kingdom (2Kg 12:20; 14:21; 23:27; Ezk 37:15–23) and the Persian province in the restoration (Neh 5:14; Hg 1:1).

JUDAISM

my former way of life in **J**: . . . . Gl 1:13

JUDAS

1. Iscariot; apostle (Mt 10:4); treasurer, miser, thief (Jn 12:4–6). Betrayed Jesus (Mt 26:21–25,44–50; Lk 22:3–6; Jn 13:21–30); committed suicide (Mt 27:3–10; Ac 1:16–20).
2. Son of James; apostle; called Thaddaeus (Mt 10:3; Mk 3:18; Lk 6:16; Jn 14:22).
3. Brother of Jesus (Mt 13:55; Mk 6:3); also called Jude.

JUDE

Brother of Jesus; also called Judas; author (Mt 13:55; Jd 1).

JUDEA

Another name for the territory of Judah.
Jesus was born in Bethlehem of **J**. . . .Mt 2:1
Pontius Pilate was governor of **J**, ... Lk 3:1
in Jerusalem, in all **J** and Samaria,. . . .Ac 1:8

JUDGE (N)

Won't the **J** of the whole earth do . . Gn 18:25
LORD raised up **j-s**, who saved. . . . .Jdg 2:16
a **j** ... who didn't fear God or . . . . Lk 18:2

JUDGE (V)

May the LORD **j** between me and . . .Gn 16:5
He is coming to **j** the earth. 1Ch 16:33
He **j-s** the world with righteousness;. . Ps 9:8
There is a God who **j-s** on earth!. . . Ps 58:11
coming to **j** the earth. He will **j** the . Ps 96:13
Do not **j**, so that you won't be **j-d**. . . .Mt 7:1
rather **j** according to righteous . . . . .Jn 7:24
I did not come to **j** the world but . . Jn 12:47
that the saints will **j** the world? 1Co 6:2
who is going to **j** the living and . . . 2Tm 4:1
who are you to **j** your neighbor?. . . Jms 4:12
the dead were **j-d** according to. . . .Rv 20:12

JUDGMENT

the wicked will not stand up in the **j**,. . Ps 1:5
my mouth, for I hope in your **j-s**. . .Ps 119:43
Teach me good **j** and discernment,. . Ps 119:66
arrived and a **j** was given in. . . . . . . Dn 7:22
Sodom on the day of **j** than for. . . .Mt 11:24
not come under **j** but has passed . . .Jn 5:24
his **j-s** and untraceable . . . . .Rm 11:33
eats and drinks **j** on himself. 1Co 11:29
die once—and after this, **j**— . . . . . Heb 9:27
has come for **j** to begin with 1Pt 4:17
because his **j-s** are true and. . . . . . . .Rv 19:2

JUDGMENT SEAT

will all stand before the **j** of God. . Rm 14:10
all appear before the **j** of Christ,. . .2Co 5:10

JUG

and the oil **j** will not run dry 1Kg 17:14

JUST

Judge of the whole earth do
  what is **j**?. .Gn 18:25
is holy and **j** and good. . . . . Rm 7:12
whatever is **j**, whatever is pure . . . . Php 4:8

JUSTICE

must not deny **j** to a poor person. . .Ex 23:6
but he gives **j** to the oppressed. . . . .Jb 36:6
The evil do not understand **j**,. . . . . . .Pr 28:5
He will bring **j** to the nations. . . . . . . .Is 42:1
the LORD, showing faithful love, **j**, . . Jr 9:24
But let **j** flow like water, ...Am 5:24
will proclaim **j** to the nations. . . . . .Mt 12:18
kind of herb, and you bypass **j** . . . . Lk 11:42

JUSTIFICATION

and raised for our **j**. . . . . Rm 4:25
j leading to life for everyone. . . . . . Rm 5:18

JUSTIFY

he had **j-ied** himself rather than
  God. . . . . .Jb 32:2
righteous servant will **j** many, ...Is 53:11
But wanting to **j** himself, he . . . . . .Lk 10:29
down to his house **j-ied** rather
  than. . . . . Lk 18:14
who believes is **j-ied** through him . Ac 13:39
they are **j-ied** freely by his grace . . Rm 3:24
a person is **j-ied** by faith apart . . . . Rm 3:28
and those he called, he also **j-ied**; . Rm 8:30
God is the one who **j-ies**. . . . . Rm 8:33
no one is **j-ied** by the works of the . Gl 2:16
we might be **j-ied** by faith in Christ . Gl 2:16
that God would **j** the Gentiles by . . . . Gl 3:8
a person is **j-ied** by works and not. . Jms 2:24

JUSTLY

the LORD requires of you: to act **j**,. . .Mc 6:8

- K -

KADESH

Oasis, also called Kadesh-barnea. Where
Abraham fought the Amalekites (Gn 14:7).
Where the Israelites camped, they sent out
spies, and Moses struck the rock (Nm 13:26;
20:1,11; 27:14; 32:8; Dt 1:46; 9:23; Jdg 11:16–17).
Southern limit of Judah (Nm 34:4; Jos 10:41;
15:3).

KEEP

be with me, and **k** me from harm . . 1Ch 4:10
and in **k-ing** them there is an . . . . . .Ps 19:11
K your tongue from evil and your . . Ps 34:13
How can a young man **k** his way
  pure? By **k-ing** your word. . . . . . . Ps 119:9
K my commands and live . . . . Pr 4:4; 7:2
fear God and **k** his commands, ...Ec 12:13
K listening, but do not understand;. . Is 6:9
I have **kept** all these," the young. .Mt 19:20
hates his life in this world will **k** it . . Jn 12:25
loves me, he will **k** my word. . . . . . . Jn 14:23
the race, I have **kept** the faith. 2Tm 4:7
whoever **k-s** the entire law, ...Jms 2:10
and unfading, **kept** in heaven for. . . 1Pt 1:4
and those who **k** the words of . . . . Rv 22:9

KETURAH

Abraham's second wife (Gn 25:1–4).

KEY

give you the **k-s** of the kingdom . .Mt 16:19
and I hold the **k-s** of death and . . . . Rv 1:18
the One who has the **k** of David, ...Rv 3:7

KIDNAP

Whoever **k-s** a person must be put. .Ex 21:16

KILL

his brother Abel and **k-ed** him. . . . . . Gn 4:8
Am I God, **k-ing** and giving life. 2Kg 5:7
a time to **k** and a time to heal; . . . . . . Ec 3:3
Don't fear those who **k** the body
  but are not able to **k** the soul; . . Mt 10:28
k-ed, and be raised the third day. . Mt 16:21
way to arrest Jesus and **k** him. . . . . .Mk 14:1
Why are you trying to **k** me?. . . . . . . Jn 7:19
You **k-ed** the source of life, ... Ac 3:15
For the letter **k-s**, but the Spirit 2Co 3:6

KIND (ADJ)

Love is patient, love is **k**. 1Co 13:4
And be **k** and compassionate to . . Eph 4:32

KIND (N)

seed in it according to their **k-s**. . . . . Gn 1:11
the birds according to their **k-s**, . . . Gn 6:20
asked, "What **k** of man is this? . . . Mt 8:27
is a root of all **k-s** of evil, ...1Tm 6:10

KINDNESS

K to the poor is a loan to the. . . . . .Pr 19:17
God's **k** is intended to lead you to . . Rm 2:4
consider God's **k** and severity:. . . . Rm 11:22
patience, **k**, goodness, faithfulness . . Gl 5:22

KING

days there was no **k** in Israel;. . . . . .Jdg 17:6
said, "Give us a **k** to judge us. 1Sm 8:6
anointed David **k** over the house . . 2Sm 2:4
The **k-s** of the earth take their . . . . . .Ps 2:2
The LORD is **K** forever and ever;. . . . Ps 10:16
Who is this **K** of glory? . . . . .Ps 24:8
It is by me that **k-s** reign and rulers. . Pr 8:15
the glory of **k-s** to investigate . . . . . Pr 25:2
my eyes have seen the **K**, ... Is 6:5
the living God and eternal **K**. . . . . . . Jr 10:10
Look, your **k** is coming to you;. . . . .Zch 9:9
who has been born **k** of the Jews? . . Mt 2:2
See, your **K** is coming to you,. . . . . .Mt 21:5
JESUS, THE **K** OF THE JEWS . . . . .Mt 27:37

Now to the **K** eternal, immortal . . . 1Tm 1:17
for **k-s** and all those who are in . . . 1Tm 2:2
K of **k-s**, and the Lord of lords, ...1Tm 6:15
K OF **K-s** AND LORD OF . . . . .Rv 19:16

KINGDOM *SEE ALSO* KINGDOM OF GOD; KINGDOM OF HEAVEN

you will be my **k** of priests and. . . . .Ex 19:6
Your **k** is an everlasting **k**; . . . . Ps 145:13
showed him all the **k-s** of the world. . Mt 4:8
Your **k** come. Your will be done . . . . Mt 6:10
these are the children of the **k**. . . . Mt 13:38
I will give you the keys of the **k** . . .Mt 16:19
mother, and **k** against **k**. . . . . .Mt 24:7
will give you, up to half my **k**. . . . . .Mk 6:23
But seek his **k**, and these . . . . Lk 12:31
my **k** is not from here." . . . . Jn 18:36
transferred us into the **k** of the Son . Col 1:13
The **k** of the world has become. . . . Rv 11:15

KINGDOM OF GOD (GOD'S KINGDOM)

But seek first the **k** and his . . . . Mt 6:33
for a rich person to enter the **k**. . . Mt 19:24
for the **k** belongs to such as these. . Mk 10:14
You are not far from the **k**. . . . . Mk 12:34
you see, the **k** is in your midst. . . . .Lk 17:21
is born again, he cannot see the **k**. . . Jn 3:3
for the **k** is not eating drinking, . . Rm 14:17
will not inherit God's **k**? 1Co 6:9

KINGDOM OF HEAVEN

Repent, because the **k** has come
  near! . . . . Mt 3:2
poor in spirit, for the **k** is theirs. . . . Mt 5:3
The **k** is like a mustard seed. . . . . . Mt 13:31
I will give you the keys of the **k**,. . .Mt 16:19
k belongs to such as these. . . . . . . .Mt 19:14

KINGSHIP

for **k** belongs to the LORD; . . . . .Ps 22:28

KISS (N)

but the **k-es** of an enemy are . . . . . . Pr 27:6
betraying the Son of Man
  with a **k**? .Lk 22:48
Greet one another with a holy **k**. . Rm 16:16

KISS (V)

mouth that has not **k-ed** him. 1Kg 19:18
that he would **k** me with the. . . . . . . Sg 1:2
The One I **k**, he's the one; . . . . .Mt 26:48

KNEE

Every **k** will bow to me, every . . . . . Is 45:23
the Lord, every **k** will bow to me . Rm 14:11
name of Jesus every **k** will bow . . Php 2:10

KNEEL

let's **k** before the LORD our. . . . . .Ps 95:6
a stone's throw, **knelt** down, ... Lk 22:41
For this reason I **k** before the. . . . . .Eph 3:14

KNIFE

and took the **k** to slaughter his. . . .Gn 22:10

KNIT

k me together in my mother's. . . . Ps 139:13
fitted and **k** together by every . . . .Eph 4:16

KNOCK

K, and the door will be . . . . Mt 7:7
I stand at the door and **k**. . . . . Rv 3:20

KNOW

be like God, **k-ing** good and evil. . . Gn 3:5
For now I **k** that you fear God, . . Gn 22:12
Egyptians will **k** that I am the LORD . . Ex 7:5
But I **k** that my Redeemer lives, . . .Jb 19:25
since he **k-s** the secrets of the. . . . . Ps 44:21
and **k** that I am God, ...Ps 46:10
LORD **k-s** the thoughts of mankind; . Ps 94:11
You have searched me and **k-n** me. . Ps 139:1
You **k** when I sit down and when I . . Ps 139:2

Search me, God, and **k** my heart; . . Ps 139:23
for you don't **k** what a day might. . . Pr 27:1
K the LORD, for they will all **k** me . . Jr 31:34
your left hand **k** what your right . . . Mt 6:3
your Father **k-s** the things you
need . . . . Mt 6:8
I never **knew** you! Depart
from me, ... Mt 7:23
that day and hour no one **k-s** . . . . Mt 24:36
you don't **k** what day your Lord . . Mt 24:42
I **k** my own, and my own **k** me, ... Jn 10:14
We **k** that his testimony is true. . . . Jn 21:24
not for you to **k** times or . . . . Ac 1:7
For though they **knew** God, they. . Rm 1:21
searches our hearts **k-s** the mind . . Rm 8:27
We **k** that all things work. . . . . . . .Rm 8:28
Now I **k** in part, but then I will **k**
fully, as I am fully **k-n**. 1Co 13:12
k Christ's love that surpasses. . . . .Eph 3:19
is not how you came to **k** about. . Eph 4:20
the surpassing value of
k-ing Christ . . . . Php 3:8
to **k** him and the power of his. . . .Php 3:10
I **k** whom I have believed in 2Tm 1:12
The Lord **k-s** those who are his, . . . 2Tm 2:19
who says, "I have come to **k** him," . . . 1Jn 2:4
to **k** love: he laid down his life. 1Jn 3:16

KNOWLEDGE

the tree of the **k** of good and evil. . . Gn 2:9
Can anyone teach God **k**, ... Jb 21:22
wondrous **k** is beyond me. . . . . Ps 139:6
of the LORD is the beginning of **k**; . . . Pr 1:7
The wise store up **k**, ... Pr 10:14
the wisdom and the **k** of God! . . .Rm 11:33
K inflates with pride, but love. 1Co 8:1
all mysteries and all **k**, ... 1Co 13:2
Christ's love that surpasses **k**, ...Eph 3:19
In him are hidden ... wisdom and **k**. . Col 2:3
what is falsely called **k**. 1Tm 6:20
in the grace and **k** of our Lord 2Pt 3:18

KORAH

1. Led rebellion against Moses (Nm 16; Jd 11).
2. Kohathite Levite (Ex 6:21; 1Ch 6:22); ancestor of temple singers (2Ch 20:19; Pss 42;
44–49; 84–85; 87–88).

- L -

LABAN

Rebekah's brother (Gn 24:29); father of Leah
and Rachel (Gn 29:15–30).

LABOR (N)

that your I in the Lord is 1Co 15:58

LABOR (V)

You are to I six days and do all . . . . Ex 20:9
they don't I or spin thread. . . . . Mt 6:28

LACK

but fools die for I of sense. . . . . . . Pr 10:21
You I one thing: Go, sell all . . . . . . Mk 10:21
Now if any of you **I-s** wisdom, ...Jms 1:5

LAKE

were thrown alive into the I of fire.Rv 19:20
second death, the I of fire. . . . . . . .Rv 20:14

LAMB

God himself will provide the I . . . . . Gn 22:8
The wolf will dwell with the I, ...Is 11:6
He gathers the **I-s** in his arms . . . . . .Is 40:11
Like a I led to the slaughter . . . . . . .Is 53:7
you out like **I-s** among wolves. . . . . . Lk 10:3
L of God, who takes away the sin. . . Jn 1:29
"Feed my **I-s**," he told him. . . . . Jn 21:15
an unblemished and spotless I 1Pt 1:19
Worthy is the **L** who was
slaughtered . . . . Rv 5:12
the marriage feast of the **L**! . . . . . . .Rv 19:9
written in the **L-'s** book of life. . . . .Rv 21:27

LAME

Then the I will leap like a deer, ... Is 35:6
receive their sight, the I walk, ...Mt 11:5

LAMENT

the following I for Saul and his 2Sm 1:17
You turned my I into dancing; . . . . . Ps 30:11
heard in Ramah, a I with bitter . . . . Jr 31:15
we sang a I, but you didn't . . . . Mt 11:17

LAMP

LORD, you light my I; . . . . .Ps 18:28
Your word is a I for my feet and . . Ps 119:105
but the I of the wicked is put out. . . Pr 13:9
No one lights a I and puts it. . . . . . .Mt 5:15
The eye is the I of the body. . . . . . . Mt 6:22
like ten virgins who took their **I-s**. . .Mt 25:1
the light of a I will never . . . . .Rv 18:23

LAMPSTAND

a I out of pure, hammered gold. . . . Ex 25:31
but rather on a I, and it gives light. .Mt 5:15
seven **I-s** are the seven churches. . . .Rv 1:20
and remove your I from its place . . . .Rv 2:5

LAND

God called the dry I "earth," . . . . Gn 1:10
I will give this I to your. . . . . Gn 12:7
a I flowing with milk and honey . . . . .Ex 3:8
So Joshua took the entire I, ... Jos 11:23
divide this I as an inheritance . . . . . Jos 13:7
Judah went into exile from its I . . .2Kg 25:21
forgive their sin, and heal their I . . .2Ch 7:14
the humble will inherit the I . . . . . . .Ps 37:11
Woe to you, I, when your king is . . . Ec 10:16
My flock from all the **I-s** where I. . . . Jr 23:3
and strike the I with a curse. . . . . . . Mal 4:6
those who owned **I-s** or houses sold. .Ac 4:34
on the sea, his left on the I, ...Rv 10:2

LANGUAGE

The whole earth had the same I . . . . Gn 11:1
He will speak ... in a foreign I . . . . . .Is 28:11
and filthy I from your mouth. . . . . . . Col 3:8
every tribe and I and people . . . . Rv 5:9

LAPPED

with the three hundred men who I . .Jdg 7:7

LASHES

than a hundred I into a fool. . . . . . . Pr 17:10
Five times I received forty I 2Co 11:24

LAST (ADJ)

These are the I words of David: . . . 2Sm 23:1
In the I days the mountain of . . . . . . .Is 2:2
are first will be I, and the I first. . . Mt 19:30
he must be I and servant of all. . . . . Mk 9:35
The I enemy to be abolished is . . . 1Co 15:26
of an eye, at the I trumpet. 1Co 15:52
In these I days, he has spoken . . . . . .Heb 1:2
Children, it is the I hour. 1Jn 2:18

LAST (N)

I am the first and I am the **I**. . . . . Is 44:6
I am the First and the **L**, ... Rv 1:17

LAST (V)

For his anger **I-s** only a moment, . . .Ps 30:5

LATER

that in I times some will depart 1Tm 4:1

LAUGH

Why did Sarah I, ... Gn 18:13
The one enthroned in heaven **I-s**; . . .Ps 2:4
a time to weep and a time to I; . . . . . .Ec 3:4

LAUGHTER

Even in I a heart may be sad, ...Pr 14:13
Let your I be turned to mourning . . Jms 4:9

LAUNDERER

white as no I on earth could . . . . . . Mk 9:3

LAW

the stone tablets with the **I** . . . . . . .Ex 24:12
Moses wrote down this I and
gave it. . . . . Dt 31:9
L after **I**, **I** after **I**, line after line, . . . Is 28:10
think that I came to abolish the **L**. . .Mt 5:17
All the **L** and the Prophets depend. .Mt 22:40
stroke of a letter in the I to drop . . Lk 16:17
the I was given through Moses; . . . .Jn 1:17
not under the I but under grace . . . Rm 6:14
So then, the I is holy, and the . . . . . Rm 7:12
For Christ is the end of the **I** . . . . . .Rm 10:4
The **I**, then, was our guardian until. . Gl 3:24
For the whole I is fulfilled in . . . . . . Gl 5:14
I will put my **I-s** into their minds . . Heb 8:10
Since the I has only a shadow . . . .Heb 10:1
For whoever keeps the entire **I**, . . .Jms 2:10

LAWBREAKER

Depart from me, you **I-s**! . . . . Mt 7:23

LAWLESS

and then the I one will be 2Th 2:8

LAWLESSNESS

Because I will multiply, ...Mt 24:12
the mystery of I is already at. 2Th 2:7
who commits sin practices I. 1Jn 3:4

LAY

Look, I have **laid** a stone in Zion, . . .Is 28:16
Man has no place to I his head. . . . . Mt 8:20
in cloth and **laid** him in a manger, . . .Lk 2:7
I I down my life for the sheep. . . . . . Jn 10:15
through the **I-ing** of my hands . . 2Tm 1:6
ritual washings, **I-ing** on of hands. . Heb 6:2
let us I aside every weight and . . . .Heb 12:1
He **laid** down his life for us. 1Jn 3:16

LAZARUS

1. Poor man in Jesus's parable (Lk 16:19–31).
2. Brother of Mary and Martha; friend of
Jesus (Jn 11:1–5). Died; revived by Jesus
(11:3–44). Endangered because of fame
(12:9–11,17).

LAZY

A I hunter doesn't roast his game, . . Pr 12:27
and a I person will go hungry. . . . . . Pr 19:15
so that you won't become I . . . . . . Heb 6:12

LEAD

of cloud to I them on their way . . . Ex 13:21
way of the wicked **I-s** to ruin. . . . . . . Ps 1:6
He **I-s** me beside quiet waters. . . . . . Ps 23:2
way, LORD, and I me on a level . . . . Ps 27:11
L me to a rock that is high above me. .Ps 61:2
I me in the everlasting way. . . . . . . Ps 139:24
The fear of the LORD **I-s** to life; . . . . Pr 19:23
and a child will I them. . . . . .Is 11:6
Like a lamb **led** to the slaughter . . . .Is 53:7
I astray, if possible, even the elect. . .Mt 24:24
and **led** him away to crucify him. . .Mt 27:31
sheep by name and **I-s** them out. . . . Jn 10:3
is intended to I you to repentance?. . Rm 2:4
sin **I-ing** to death or of obedience. . Rm 6:16
All those **led** by God's Spirit are . . . Rm 8:14
But if you are **led** by the Spirit, ... Gl 5:18

LEADER

He chose Judah as I, ...1Ch 28:4
For the **I-s** of the earth belong to. . .Ps 47:9
of the synagogue **I-s**, named Jairus. .Mk 5:22
Obey your **I-s** and submit. . . . . . . .Heb 13:17

LEADING (ADJ)

as a number of the I women. . . . . . . Ac 17:4

LEAF

they sewed fig **I-ves** together and . . Gn 3:7
and its I does not wither . . . . Ps 1:3
becomes tender and sprouts
I-ves, ... Mt 24:32
The **I-ves** of the tree are for . . . . . . .Rv 22:2

LEAH

Wife of Jacob; mother of Reuben, Simeon, Levi, Judah, Issachar, Zebulun, and Dinah (Gn 29:16–35; 30:14–21).

LEAN

temple, so I can **I** against them. . .Jdg 16:26
So he **I-ed** back against Jesus
and . . . . .Jn 13:25

LEAP

with my God I can **I** over a wall. . . . Ps 18:29
greeting, the baby **I-ed** inside her . . Lk 1:41
walking, **I-ing**, and praising God. . . . .Ac 3:8

LEARN

will listen and I to fear the LORD . . . Dt 31:13
that I could **I** your statutes. . . . . . . .Ps 119:71
and the inexperienced **I** a lesson; . . Pr 19:25
L to do what is good. . . . . Is 1:17
take up my yoke and I from me, . . . Mt 11:29
for I have **I-ed** to be content in. . . . .Php 4:11
A woman is to **I** quietly. 1Tm 2:11
He **I-ed** obedience through
what he . . . . Heb 5:8

LEASE

He **I-d** it to tenant farmers and. . . .Mt 21:33

LEAST

are by no means **I** among the . . . . . . Mt 2:6
will be called **I** in the kingdom. . . . . Mt 5:19
you did for one of the **I** of these. . Mt 25:40
For I am the **I** of the apostles, ...1Co 15:9

LEATHER

man with a **I** belt around his 2Kg 1:8
garment with a **I** belt around his . . . Mt 3:4

LEAVE

This is why a man **I-s** his father. . . . Gn 2:24
I will not **I** you or abandon you. . . . . Jos 1:5
Spirit of the LORD had **left** Saul, . .1Sm 16:14
I alone am **left**, and they are 1Kg 19:10
do not **I** me or abandon me,. . . . . . . .Ps 27:9
I your gift there in front of . . . . Mt 5:24
won't he **I** the ninety-nine on . . . Mt 18:12
we have **left** everything and. . . . .Mt 19:27
reason a man will **I** his father. . . . . . Mk 10:7
I will not **I** you as orphans; . . . . Jn 14:18
of Hosts had not **left** us
offspring,. . . . . .Rm 9:29
I will never **I** you or abandon . . . . . .Heb 13:5

LEAVEN (N)

of heaven is like **I** that a woman. . .Mt 13:33
beware of the **I** of the Pharisees. . . Mt 16:6
know that a little **I** 1Co 5:6

LEAVEN (V)

A little leaven **I-s** the whole batch . . . Gl 5:9

LEBANON

Mountainous region of northern promised land (Dt 1:7; 11:24). Known for its cedars and lush growth (Jdg 9:15; 1Kg 5:6; 2Ch 2:8,16; Pss 72:16; 92:12; Sg 4:11,15; Is 2:13; Ezk 27:5; 31:3). God is greater (Pss 29:5–6; 104:16).

LEECH

The **I** has two daughters: "Give,. . . . Pr 30:15

LEFT

not to turn aside to the right or
the **I**. . . . . .Dt 5:32
Don't turn to the right or to the **I**; . . Pr 4:27
down on your **I** side and place. . . . . .Ezk 4:4
don't let your **I** hand know what . . . Mt 6:3
right and the other on your **I**, ... Mt 20:21
right and the goats on the **I**. . . . . Mt 25:33

LEFT-HANDED

Ehud son of Gera, a **I**
Benjaminite,. . . . . .Jdg 3:15

LEFTOVER

up twelve baskets full of **I** pieces! . .Mt 14:20
they collected the **I** pieces . . . . .Mt 15:37
Collect the **I-s** so that nothing . . . . . Jn 6:12

LEGAL

It's not **I** for us to put . . . . Jn 18:31
that are not **I** for us as Romans. . . . Ac 16:21
Is it **I** for you to scourge a. . . . . . . .Ac 22:25

LEGION

with more than twelve **I-s** of
angels? . . . . Mt 26:53
"My name is **L**," he answered him, . . Mk 5:9

LEGS

its **I** were iron, and its feet . . . . Dn 2:33
they did not break his **I** since. . . . . . Jn 19:33

LEND

If you **I** silver to my people . . . . . . .Ex 22:25
who does not **I** his silver at . . . . Ps 15:5
come to the one who **I-s**
generously. Ps 112:5
and **I**, expecting nothing in return. . .Lk 6:35

LENDER

borrower is a slave to the **I**. . . . . Pr 22:7

LENGTH

I of days forever and ever. . . . . Ps 21:4
Its **I**, width, and height are equal. . . Rv 21:16

LENGTHENING (ADJ)

I fade away like a **I** shadow; . . . . . .Ps 109:23

LEOPARD

and the **I** will lie down with the . . . . . Is 11:6
his skin, or a **I** his spots? . . . . .Jr 13:23

LEPROSY

a man with **I** came up and knelt . . . . Mt 8:2
cleanse those with **I**, ... Mt 10:8

LESS

punished us **I** than our sins . . . . . . Ezr 9:13
You made him little **I** than God . . . . . Ps 8:5

LESSER

the **I** light to rule over. . . . . .Gn 1:16

LET

L there be light, ...Gn 1:3
L the little children come to me. . . Mk 10:14

LETTER

not the smallest **I** or one stroke . . . Mt 5:18
I kills, but the Spirit gives life. 2Co 3:6
His **I-s** are weighty and powerful,. .2Co 10:10
Look at what large **I-s** I use . . . . .Gl 6:11
these things in all his **I-s**. 2Pt 3:16

LEVEL (ADJ)

My foot stands on **I** ground; . . . . . . Ps 26:12
Spirit lead me on **I** ground. . . . . . . Ps 143:10
The path of the righteous is **I**; . . . . .Is 26:7
and rough places into **I** ground.. . . .Is 42:16

LEVEL (V)

mountain and hill will be **I-ed**; . . . . . Is 40:4

LEVI

1. Son of Jacob and Leah (Gn 29:34). Ancestor of priestly tribe (Ex 32:25–29; Nm 3:11–13; Dt 10:6–9); received no allotment of land, only scattered towns and cities of refuge (Nm 18:20; 35:1–8; Jos 13:14,33); supported by tithes (Nm 18:21; Heb 7:5). Assisted descendants of Aaron in worship (Nm 3:5–9; 1Ch 6:16,31–32,49; 23:24–32; 2Ch 29:12–21); taught the word of God (2Ch 17:7–9; Neh 8:9–12).
2. Apostle, called Matthew (Mk 2:14; Lk 5:27–29; cp. Mt 9:9).

LEVIATHAN

Can you pull in **L** with a hook or . . . . Jb 41:1
You crushed the heads of **L**; . . . . Ps 74:14

LEVITICAL

came through the **I** priesthood . . . .Heb 7:11

LIAR

alarm I said, "Everyone is a **I**." . . . .Ps 116:11
he is a **I** and the father of **I-s**. . . . . .Jn 8:44
be true, even though everyone is
a **I**, ... Rm 3:4
we make him a **I**, and his word is . . .1Jn 1:10
and all **I-s**—their share will . . . . . . .Rv 21:8

LIBERTY

to proclaim **I** to the captives . . . . Is 61:1

LICK

the dogs will also **I** up your
blood!. 1Kg 21:19
The dogs **I-ed** up his blood, ...1Kg 22:38

LIE (N)

one who utters **I-s** will not escape. . Pr 19:9
They are prophesying a **I** to you. . . .Jr 27:10
exchanged the truth of God for a **I**, . .Rm 1:25
because no **I** comes from the truth. . .1Jn 2:21

LIE (V) (DECEIVE) *SEE ALSO* **LYING**

or **I** to one another. . . . . .Lv 19:11
God is not a man, that he might **I**, . .Nm 23:19
your heart to **I** to the Holy Spirit. . . . .Ac 5:3
Do not **I** to one another, since . . . . . Col 3:9

LIE (V) (RECLINE)

when you **I** down and when you get. .Dt 6:7
He lets me **I** down in green . . . . .Ps 23:2
the leopard will **I** down with the. . . . .Is 11:6
in cloth and **I-ing** in a manger. . . . . .Lk 2:12

LIFE

the breath of **I** into his . . . . .Gn 2:7
the tree of **I** in the middle . . . . Gn 2:9
then you must give **I** for **I**, ...Ex 21:23
the **I** of a creature is in the blood,. . . Lv 17:11
Choose **I** so that you and your. . . .Dt 30:19
Remember that my **I** is but a breath. . Jb 7:7
LORD is perfect, renewing one's **I**; . . Ps 19:7
will pursue me all the days of my **I**, .Ps 23:6
the blessing—**I** forevermore. . . . . . .Ps 133:3
preserve my **I** from the anger . . . . . Ps 138:7
Guard it, for it is your **I**. . . . . Pr 4:13
the one who finds me finds **I**. . . . . . . Pr 8:35
setting before you the way of **I**
and the. . . . . .Jr 21:8
awake, some to eternal **I**, and some . .Dn 12:2
Don't worry about your **I**, ... Mt 6:25
gains whole world yet loses his **I**? . .Mt 16:26
to give his **I** as a ransom for many. . Mt 20:28
one's **I** is not in the abundance of . .Lk 12:15
In him was **I**, and that **I** was the light . .Jn 1:4
in him may have eternal **I**. . . . . Jn 3:15
but has passed from death to **I**. . . . . Jn 5:24
"I am the bread of **I**," Jesus told. . . . .Jn 6:35
that they may have **I** and have it . . . .Jn 10:10
I am the resurrection and the **I**. . . . .Jn 11:25
the way, the truth, and the **I**. . . . . . .Jn 14:6
too may walk in newness of **I**. . . . . . .Rm 6:4
but the Spirit gives **I**. 2Co 3:6
The **I** I now live in the body, ...Gl 2:20
and your **I** is hidden with Christ . . . . Col 3:3
required for **I** and godliness. 2Pt 1:3
lay down our **lives** for our brothers. .1Jn 3:16
in the book of **I** of the Lamb who. . .Rv 13:8

LIFEBLOOD

not eat meat with its **I** in it. . . . . Gn 9:4

LIFE-GIVING

last Adam became a **I** Spirit. 1Co 15:45

LIFETIME

only a moment, but his favor, a **I**. . . Ps 30:5

LIFT

and the One who **l-s** up my head. . . . Ps 3:3
L up your heads, you gates! . . . . Ps 24:7
You have **l-ed** me up and have . . . . . . Ps 30:1
so the Son of Man must be **l-ed** up, . . Jn 3:14
When you **l** up the Son of Man, ... Jn 8:28
if I am **l-ed** up from the earth I . . . . Jn 12:32

LIGHT (N)

"Let there be **l**," and there was **l** . . . . . Gn 1:3
The LORD is my **l** and my salvation . . Ps 27:1
for my feet and a **l** on my path. . Ps 119:105
like the **l** of dawn, shining brighter . . Pr 4:18
let's walk in the LORD's **l**. . . . . Is 2:5
in darkness have seen a great **l**; . . . . Is 9:2
people and a **l** to the nations. . . . . . Is 42:6
Arise, shine, for your **l** has come, . . . Is 60:1
live in darkness have seen a
    great **l**, ... Mt 4:16
You are the **l** of the world. . . . . Mt 5:14
a **l** for revelation to the Gentiles. . Lk 2:32
I am the **l** of the world. . . . . Jn 8:12
walk in the **l** as he ... is in the **l** 1Jn 1:7

LIGHT (V)

No one **l-s** a lamp and puts it . . . . . . Mt 5:15
to horizon and **l-s** up the sky, ... Lk 17:24

LIGHTNING

was thunder and **l**, a thick cloud . . . Ex 19:16
he hurled **l** bolts and routed them. . Ps 18:14
For as the **l** comes from the east. . Mt 24:27
His appearance was like **l**, ... Mt 28:3

LIKE

you will be **l** God, knowing good . . . Gn 3:5
I am God, and no one is **l** me. . . . . . . Is 46:9
LORD, there is none **l** you. . . . . Jr 10:6
What is the kingdom of God **l**, . . . Lk 13:18
spoke **l** a child, I thought **l** a child, . . 1Co 13:11
He had to be **l** his brothers. . . . . . . Heb 2:17

LIKE-MINDED

have no one else **l** who will . . . . . . Php 2:20

LIKENESS

our image, according to our **l**. . . . . . Gn 1:26
united with him in the **l** of his
    death . . . . Rm 6:5
servant, taking on the **l** of
    humanity. . . . . Php 2:7
curse people who are made in
    God's **l**. . . . . Jms 3:9

LIMIT

when he set a **l** for the sea so . . . . . . Pr 8:29

LINE

I after **l**, I after **l**, a little here . . . . . . Is 28:10

LINEN

on his **l** robe and **l** undergarments. . . Lv 6:10
body, wrapped it in clean, fine **l**, . . Mt 27:59
tomb and saw the **l** cloths lying . . . . Jn 20:6

LINTEL

and brush the **l** and the two . . . . . . Ex 12:22

LION

Judah is a young **l** . . . . Gn 49:9
and the **l** will eat straw like cattle. . . Is 11:7
will be thrown into the **l-s** den. . . . . Dn 6:7
prowling around like a roaring **l**, . . . 1Pt 5:8
The **l** from the tribe of Judah, ... Rv 5:5

LIPS

His praise will always be on my **l**. . . Ps 34:1
a stranger, and not your own **l**. . . . . Pr 27:2
I am a man of unclean **l**. . . . . Is 6:5
people honors me with their **l**, ... Mt 15:8
and by the **l** of foreigners, ... 1Co 14:21

LIP-SERVICE

honor me with **l**, yet their hearts . . . Is 29:13

LISTEN

L, Israel: The LORD our God; . . . . Dt 6:4
Speak, for your servant is **l-ing**. . . . 1Sm 3:10
LORD, **l** and be gracious to me; . . . . . Dn 9:19
For the LORD **l-s** to the needy and . . Ps 69:33
L, sons, to a father's discipline, ... Pr 4:1
who gives an answer before he **l-s** . . Pr 18:13
Keep **l-ing**, but do not understand; . . Is 6:9
You will **l** and **l**, but never . . . . Mt 13:14
whom I am well-pleased. **L** to him! . .Mt 17:5
But if he won't **l**, take one or. . . . . . Mt 18:16
you cannot **l** to my word. . . . . Jn 8:43
and they will **l** to my voice. . . . . Jn 10:16
Everyone should be quick to **l**, ... Jms 1:19
not from God does not **l** to us. 1Jn 4:6

LITTLE

You made him **l** less than God and . . . Ps 8:5
Better a **l** with the fear of the . . . . . Pr 15:16
are you afraid, you of **l** faith? . . . . . Mt 8:26
the one who is forgiven **l**, loves **l**. . . Lk 7:47
know how to make do with **l**, ... Php 4:12
and he held a **l** scroll opened in. . . . Rv 10:2

LIVE

for humans cannot see me and **l**. . . Ex 33:20
man does not **l** on bread alone . . . . . Dt 8:3
But I know that my Redeemer **l-s**, . . Jb 19:25
The LORD **l-s**—blessed be my. . . . . . Ps 18:46
to my God as long as I **l**. . . . . Ps 146:2
Keep my commands and **l**. . . . . . . Pr 4:4; 7:2
on those **l-ing** in the land of
    darkness. . . . . Is 9:2
listen, so that you will **l**. . . . . Is 55:3
the righteous one will **l** by his
    faith. . . . . Hab 2:4
Man must not **l** on bread alone. . . . . Mt 4:4
in me, even if he dies, will **l**. . . . . . . Jn 11:25
Because I **l**, you will **l** too. . . . . Jn 14:19
in him we **l** and move and . . . . Ac 17:28
The righteous will **l** by faith. . . . . . . Rm 1:17
the life he **l-s**, he **l-s** to God. . . . . . . Rm 6:10
If we **l**, we **l** for the Lord; . . . . Rm 14:8
I no longer **l**, but Christ **l-s** in me. The
    life I now **l** in the body, I **l** by faith. . Gl 2:20
to **l** is Christ and to die is gain. . . . . Php 1:21

LIVING (ADJ)

and the man became a **l** being. . . . . Gn 2:7
the voice of the **l** God speaking . . . . Dt 5:26
flesh cry out for the **l** God. . . . . Ps 84:2
let every **l** thing bless his . . . . Ps 145:21
me, the fountain of **l** water, and dug . . Jr 2:13
On that day **l** water will flow. . . . . . Zch 14:8
Messiah, the Son of the **l** God! . . . . Mt 16:16
and he would give you **l** water. . . . . Jn 4:10
I am the bread that came down . . . Jn 6:51
your bodies as a **l** sacrifice, ... Rm 12:1
word of God is **l** and effective. . . . Heb 4:12
into the hands of the **l** God. . . . . . . Heb 10:31

LIVING (N)

God of the dead, but of the **l**. . . . . Mt 22:32
to judge the **l** and the dead. 1Pt 4:5

LOAD (N)

tie up heavy **l-s** that are hard to. . . Mt 23:4

LOAD (V)

You **l** people with burdens that. . . . Lk 11:46

LOAF

only have five **l-ves** and two fish. . Mt 14:17
took the seven **l-ves** and the fish, . .Mt 15:36

LOAN

to the poor is a **l** to the LORD, ... Pr 19:17
Don't ... put up security for **l-s**. . . . Pr 22:26

LOCUST

I will bring **l-s** into your territory. . . . Ex 10:4
fruit of their labor to the **l**. . . . . Ps 78:46
What the devouring **l** has left, the . . . Jl 1:4
his food was **l-s** and wild honey. . . . Mt 3:4

LOFTY

It is I; I am unable to reach it. . . . . . Ps 139:6
against all that is proud and **l**, ... Is 2:12
Lord seated on a high and **l** throne, . . . Is 6:1

LONG (ADJ)

you may have a **l** life in the land . . . Ex 20:12
How **l** will you waver between . . . 1Kg 18:21
How **l** will you hide your face . . . . . Ps 13:1
How **l**, LORD? Will you hide . . . . . . Ps 89:46
if a man has **l** hair it is a disgrace . . 1Co 11:14

LONG (V)

As a deer **l-s** for flowing
    streams, so. . . . . Ps 42:1
l I **l** for you in the night; . . . . Is 26:9
He **l-ed** to eat his fill from the . . . . Lk 15:16

LOOK

But Lot's wife **l-ed** back and
    became. . . . . Gn 19:26
he was afraid to **l** at God. . . . . Ex 3:6
Do not **l** at his appearance or. 1Sm 16:7
The LORD **l-s** down from heaven on. . Ps 14:2
L down from heaven and see; . . . . . Ps 80:14
Let your eyes **l** forward; . . . . Pr 4:25
keep **l-ing**, but do not perceive. . . . . Is 6:9
that day people will **l** to their Maker. . Is 17:7
that we should **l** at him, ... Is 53:2
eyes are too pure to **l** on evil, ... Hab 1:13
will **l** at me whom they pierced. . . . Zch 12:10
everyone who **l-s** at a woman . . . . . Mt 5:28
because **l-ing** they do not see, ... Mt 13:13
the plow and **l-s** back is fit for . . . . Lk 9:62
L at my hands and my feet, ... Lk 24:39
your eyes and **l** at the fields, ... Jn 4:35
They will **l** at the one they . . . . Jn 19:37
l-ing as in a mirror at the glory. . . . 2Co 3:18

LOOSE

whatever you **l** on earth will have . . Mt 16:19

LORD

LD our God, the **LD** is one. . . . . Dt 6:4
For the **LD** your God is the God of
    gods and **L** of **l-s**, ... Dt 10:17
LD gives, and the **LD** takes away. . . . . Jb 1:21
The **LD** is my shepherd; . . . . Ps 23:1
declaration of the **LD** to my **L**: . . . . . Ps 110:1
Give thanks to the **L** of **l-s**. . . . . . . Ps 136:3
l-s other than you have owned us, . . Is 26:13
who says to me, '**L**, **L**,' will enter . . . Mt 7:21
Son of Man is **L** of the Sabbath. . . . Mt 12:8
The **L** declared to my **L**, ... Mt 22:44
If David calls him '**L**,' how, then . . . Mt 22:45
The **L** our God, the **L** is one. . . . . . . Mk 12:29
you call me '**L**, **L**,' and don't do . . . . Lk 6:46
You call me Teacher and **L**. . . . . Jn 13:13
Thomas ... "My **L** and my God!" . . Jn 20:28
crucified, both **L** and Messiah." . . . . Ac 2:36
with your mouth, "Jesus is **L**," . . . . Rm 10:9
are many "gods" and many "**l-s**" . . 1Co 8:5
one **L**, Jesus Christ. 1Co 8:6
can say, "Jesus is **L**," except by 1Co 12:3
Now the **L** is the Spirit; 2Co 3:17
one **L**, one faith, one baptism, ... Eph 4:5
confess that Jesus Christ is **L**, ... Php 2:11
King of kings, and the **L** of **l-s**, ... 1Tm 6:15
obeyed Abraham, calling him **l**. 1Pt 3:6
but regard Christ the **L** as holy, ... 1Pt 3:15
was in the Spirit on the **L-'s** day, . . . Rv 1:10
KING OF KINGS AND **LD** OF **LD-S** . . . . . Rv 19:16

LORDING

not **l** it over those entrusted to. 1Pt 5:3

LOSE

who finds his life will **l** it, ... Mt 10:39
but whoever **l-s** his life because. . Mt 16:25
a hundred sheep and **l-s** one . . . . . . Lk 15:4
that I should **l** none of those he . . . . Jn 6:39

LOSS

everything to be a **l** in view of . . . . Php 3:8

LOST (ADJ)

I wander like a l sheep; . . . . Ps 119:176
and a time to count as l; . . . . Ec 3:6
My people were l sheep; . . . . Jr 50:6
go to the l sheep of the house . . . . Mt 10:6
sent only to the l sheep of the . . . . Mt 15:24
he was l and is found! . . . . Lk 15:24
them and not one of them is l, ... Jn 17:12

LOST (N)

I will seek the l, bring back . . . . . . Ezk 34:16
will not seek the l or heal the . . . . Zch 11:16
come to seek and to save the l. . . . Lk 19:10

LOT

Abraham's nephew (Gn 11:27). Separated
from Abraham; settled in Sodom (13:1–13).
Rescued from kings (14:1–16); from Sodom (18:16–19:29; Lk 17:28–29; 2Pt 2:7–9).
Fathered Moabites and Ammonites by his
daughters (Gn 19:30–38).

LOT

The land is to be divided by l; . . . .Nm 26:55
Cast the l between me and my . . .1Sm 14:42
pur—that is, the l—was cast . . . . . Est 3:7
and they cast l-s for my clothing . . Ps 22:18
The l is cast into the lap, ... Pr 16:33
cast l-s, and the l singled out
  Jonah . . . . Jnh 1:7
His clothes by casting l-s . . . . Mt 27:35
Let's not tear it, but cast l-s for it, . .Jn 19:24
and the l fell to Matthias . . . . .Ac 1:26

LOUD

neighbor with a l voice early . . . . . . Pr 27:14
Jesus cried out with a l voice, ... Mt 27:46
I heard a l voice behind me like . . . . . Rv 1:10

LOVE (N)

showing faithful l to a thousand . . .Ex 20:6
abounding in faithful l and truth, . . .Ex 34:6
not withdraw my faithful l from . . . Ps 89:33
His faithful l endures forever. . . Ps 136:1–26
but l covers all offenses . . . . Pr 10:12
have loved you with an
  everlasting l; . . . . Jr 31:3
with human cords, with ropes of l . . Hs 11:4
No one has greater l than this: . . . .Jn 15:13
God proves his own l for us in that. . Rm 5:8
Let l must be without hypocrisy . . . Rm 12:9
puffs up, but l builds up. 1Co 8:1
L is patient, l is kind. l does not 1Co 13:4
For the l of money is a root of 1Tm 6:10
God is l, ... 1Jn 4:16
abandoned the l you had at first . . . . Rv 2:4

LOVE (V)

but l your neighbor as yourself; . . . Lv 19:18
L the Lord your God with all . . . . Dt 6:5
Your God l-d Israel enough to 2Ch 9:8
I l you, Lord, my strength . . . . Ps 18:1
He l-s righteousness and justice; . . . Ps 33:5
I l the Lord because he has . . . . Ps 116:1
How I l your instruction! . . . . Ps 119:97
Lord disciplines the one he l-s, ... Pr 3:12
I l those who l me, and those . . . . . . Pr 8:17
A friend l-s at all times, ...Pr 17:17
a time to l and a time to hate; . . . . . .Ec 3:8
I have l-d you with an everlasting . . .Jr 31:3
When Israel was a child, I l-d him, . . Hs 11:1
Hate evil and l good; . . . . Am 5:15
Even so, I l-d Jacob, ... Mal 1:2
l your enemies and pray for . . . . Mt 5:44
will hate one and l the other, ... Mt 6:24
L the Lord your God with all . . . . . . Mt 22:37
L your neighbor as yourself . . . . . . Mt 22:39
is forgiven little, l-s little . . . . Lk 7:47
For God l-d the world in this way: . . .Jn 3:16
a new command: I one another. . . . Jn 13:34
since God l-s a cheerful giver 2Co 9:7
Husbands, l your wives, just as . . . Eph 5:25
He who l-s his wife l-s himself . . . . Eph 5:28
Do not l the world or the things 1Jn 2:15

I one another, because l is
  from God 1Jn 4:7
We l because he first l-d us 1Jn 4:19
As many as I l, I rebuke and . . . . Rv 3:19

LOVELY

How l is your dwelling place, ... Ps 84:1
I am dark … yet l like the
  curtains of . . . . Sg 1:5
whatever is pure, whatever is l, . . . Php 4:8

LOVER

will be l-s of self, l-s of money 2Tm 3:2

LOW

and hill will be made l; . . . . Lk 3:5

LOWER

You made him l than the angels . . . Heb 2:7

LOWLY

He sets the l on high, ... Jb 5:11
thrones and exalted the l. . . . . Lk 1:52

LOYALTY

keeps his gracious covenant l . . . . . . Dt 7:9
He shows l to his anointed, ... 2Sm 22:51
Never let l and faithfulness . . . . Pr 3:3

LUKE

Companion of Paul (2Tm 4:11; Phm 24); physician (Col 4:14); author of Luke and Acts
(note "we" in Ac 16:10; 28:16).

LUKEWARM

because you are l, and neither. . . . . Rv 3:16

LUST (N)

the l of the flesh, the l of the
  eyes 1Jn 2:16

LUST (V)

looks at a woman l has already . . . Mt 5:28

LUXURY

L is not appropriate for a fool— . . . Pr 19:10

LYDIA

First Philippian convert; seller of purple (Ac
16:12–15,40).

LYING (ADJ)

go and become a l spirit 1Kg 22:22
arrogant eyes, a l tongue, hands . . . . Pr 6:17

LYING (N)

Cursing, l, murder, stealing, ...Hs 4:2
Therefore, putting away l,
  speak . . . . Eph 4:25

LYRE

who knows how to play the l 1Sm 16:16
Praise the Lord with the l; . . . . Ps 33:2
we hung up our l-s on the poplar . . Ps 137:2
flute, zither, l, harp, drum . . . . Dn 3:5

- M -

MAACAH

1. David's wife; mother of Absalom (2Sm
   3:3; 1Ch 3:2).
2. Mother of Judah's King Abijam (1Kg 15:2);
   promoted Asherah worship (15:13).

MAD

Too much study is driving you m! . . Ac 26:24

MADMAN

He acted like a m around them, . .1Sm 21:13
I'm talking like a m— 2Co 11:23

MADNESS

and knowledge, m and folly; . . . . . . .Ec 1:17

MAGDALENE see MARY 2.

MAGIC

seems like a m stone to its . . . . Pr 17:8
practiced m collected their books. . Ac 19:19

MAGICIAN

summoned all the m-s of Egypt . . . Gn 41:8
the m-s of Egypt, and they
  also did . . . . Ex 7:11

MAGNIFICENT

our Lord, how m is your name . . . . . . Ps 8:1
m acts of God in our own tongues . . Ac 2:11

MAGOG

Land ruled by Gog, an apocalyptic foe from
the north (Ezk 38:2; 39:6; Rv 20:8).

MAIMED

It is better for you to enter life m . . .Mt 18:8
invite those who are poor, m, lame, . . Lk 14:13

MAJESTIC

All that he does is splendid and m; . .Ps 111:3
came to him from the M Glory: 2Pt 1:17

MAJESTY

Splendor and m are before him; . . 1Ch 16:27
and the splendor and the m 1Ch 29:11
awesome m surrounds him . . . . Jb 37:22
He is robed in m; . . . . Ps 93:1
right hand of the M on high . . . . .Heb 1:3
we were eyewitnesses of his m 2Pt 1:16

MAKE

Let us m man in our image, ... Gn 1:26
The sea is his; he made it. . . . . Ps 95:5
He made us, and we are his . . . . . . Ps 100:3
is the day the Lord has made; . . . . Ps 118:24
I have been … wondrously made . . Ps 139:14
forming it, 'What are you m-ing?' . . Is 45:9
when I will m a new covenant . . . . . Jr 31:31
and I will m you fish for people! . . . Mt 4:19
and m disciples of all nations, ... Mt 28:19
Sabbath was made for man and
  not . . . . Mk 2:27
Why did you m me like this? . . . . . Rm 9:20
made him lower than the angels . . Heb 2:7

MAKER

a man be more pure than his M? . . . Jb 4:17
kneel before the Lord our M. . . . . . . Ps 95:6
Indeed, your husband is your M . . . . Is 54:5

MALACHI

Postexilic prophet (Mal 1:1).

MALE

he created them m and female . . . . Gn 1:27
made them m and female, ... Mt 19:4
m-s who have sex with m-s, ... 1Co 6:9
slave or free, m or female; . . . . Gl 3:28

MALICE

quarrels, deceit, and m . . . . Rm 1:29
anger, wrath, m, slander, ... Col 3:8

MAN SEE ALSO MAN OF GOD

Let us make m in our image, ... Gn 1:26
God formed the m out of the dust . . .Gn 2:7
Egyptians are men, not God; . . . . Is 31:3
that he did not look like a m, ... Is 52:14
One like a son of m was coming
  with . . . . Dn 7:13
I am God and not m, the Holy One . . Hs 11:9
M must not live on bread alone . . . . Mt 4:4
this reason a m will leave his . . . . . Mt 19:5
will see the Son of M coming on . . Mt 24:30
for m and not m for the Sabbath . . Mk 2:27
You—being a m—make yourself . . Jn 10:33
your young men will see visions, . . . Ac 2:17
Men committed shameless acts . . . Rm 1:27
entered the world through one m, . . Rm 5:12

MAN OF GOD

Christ is the head of every **m**,
and the **m** is the head of the
woman,....................... 1Co 11:3
What is **m**, that you remember him. . Heb 2:6
was one like the Son of **M**,......... Rv 1:13

MAN OF GOD

blessing that Moses, the **m**, gave . . . Dt 33:1
She said to Elijah, "**M**, why are . . . 1Kg 17:18
When Elisha the **m** heard 2Kg 5:8
word ... came to Shemaiah, the **m**: . . 2Ch 11:2
as David the **m** had prescribed. . . Neh 12:24
you, **m**, flee from these things,. . . .1Tm 6:11
so that the **m** may be complete,. . .2Tm 3:17

MANAGE

m his own household competently. . 1Tm 3:4

MANASSEH

1. Son of Joseph and Asenath (Gn 41:50–51).
Adopted by Jacob as a tribe (Gn 48); allotted half of its territory east of the
Jordan from Gerasa to Mt. Hermon in the
far north and half west of the Jordan to
the Mediterranean from the Yarkon River
to Mt. Carmel (Nm 32:33–42; Jos 13:29–31;
17).
2. Son of Hezekiah; king of Judah (2Kg
21:1–18). Wickedness brought on God's
judgment (21:10–15; Jr 15:4).

MANGER

in cloth and lying in a **m**. . . . . Lk 2:12

MANIFESTATION

A **m** of the Spirit is given to each . . 1Co 12:7

MANIFESTED

He was **m** in the flesh, vindicated . . 1Tm 3:16

MANNA

Israel named the substance **m**. . . . . Ex 16:31
The **m** resembled coriander seed,. . Nm 11:7
the land, the **m** ceased.. . . . . Jos 5:12
ancestors ate the **m** in the . . . . . .Jn 6:31,49

MANSLAUGHTER

could flee there who committed **m**,. . Dt 4:42
for the one who commits **m**,. . . Jos 21:13–38

MANTLE

him and threw his **m** over him. . . . 1Kg 19:19
picked up the **m** that had fallen . . . 2Kg 2:13

MANY

give his life as a ransom for **m**. . . Mt 20:28
For **m** are invited, but few are. . . . Mt 22:14
way we who are **m** are one body . . Rm 12:5

MARCH

m around the city seven times,. . . . . Jos 6:4

MARITAL

his **m** duty to his wife, ... 1Co 7:3

MARK

he placed a **m** on Cain so that . . . . . .Gn 4:15
If I don't see the **m** of the nails. . . . Jn 20:25
and receives a **m** on his forehead . . .Rv 14:9
who accepted the **m** of the beast . . Rv 19:20

MARK, JOHN

Missionary (Ac 12:12,25); Barnabas's cousin
(Col 4:10); cause of split between Paul and
Barnabas (Ac 15:36–40); later apparently
reconciled to Paul (Col 4:10; 2Tm 4:11; Phm
24). Also close to Peter (1Pt 5:13). Wrote the
Gospel of Mark.

MARKET

that is sold in the meat **m** 1Co 10:25

MARKETPLACE

My Father's house into a **m**!. . . . . . .Jn 2:16

MARRIAGE

nor are given in **m** but are like . . . Mt 22:30
and giving in **m**, until the day . . . . Mt 24:38
M is to be honored by all,. . . . . . . Heb 13:4
the **m** of the Lamb has come, ...Rv 19:7

MARRIED (ADJ)

a **m** man is concerned about 1Co 7:33

MARROW

soul and spirit, joints and **m**. . . . . . Heb 4:12

MARRY

who have **m-ied** foreign women. . Ezr 10:14
divorces ... and **m-ies** another, ... Mt 19:9
For all seven had **m-ied** her. . . . . . .Lk 20:33
the dead neither **m** nor are given. .Lk 20:35
it is better to **m** than to burn 1Co 7:9

MARTHA

Sister of Mary and Lazarus (Lk 10:38–42; Jn
11:1–12:2).

MARVELOUS

of darkness into his **m** light 1Pt 2:9

MARY

1. Mother of Jesus (Mt 1:16; Lk 1:26–56;
2:1–20,34–35). Present at the cross (Jn
19:25–27); among the believers (Ac 1:14).
2. Magdalene; delivered from demons (Lk
8:2); follower and supporter of Jesus (Mk
15:40–41). Witness to the crucifixion and
resurrection (Mt 27:54–28:10; Mk 16:1–10;
Lk 24:10; Jn 19:25–20:18).
3. Mother of James and Joseph/Joses;
follower and supporter of Jesus (Mk
15:40–41). Witness to the crucifixion and
resurrection (Mt 27:54–28:10; Mk 16:1–8;
Lk 24:10).
4. Sister of Martha and Lazarus (Jn 11);
anointed Jesus's feet (12:1–3).

MASSACRE

He gave orders to **m** all the boys . . Mt 2:16

MASTER (N)

And if I am a **m**, where is . . . . .Mal 1:6
No one can serve two **m-s** . . . . Mt 6:24
is not greater than his **m**, ... Jn 13:16
doesn't know what his **m** is
doing. . . . . .Jn 15:15
obey your human **m-s** with fear. . . Eph 6:5
m-s, treat your slaves the same
way . . . . Eph 6:9

MAT

lowered the **m** ... the paralytic . . . . . Mk 2:4
pick up your **m** and walk!. . . . . .Jn 5:8

MATERIAL

godliness is a way to **m** gain. 1Tm 6:5

MATTHEW

Apostle; former tax collector (Mt 9:9; 10:3).
Also called Levi son of Alphaeus (Mk 2:14;
cp. Lk 5:27–32). Wrote a Gospel.

MATTHIAS

Chosen to replace Judas (Ac 1:23–26).

MATURE

speak a wisdom among the **m**,. . . .1Co 2:6
let all of us who are **m** think . . . . . .Php 3:15
But solid food is for the **m**. . . . . . . Heb 5:14

MATURITY

and go on to **m**, not laying. . . . . Heb 6:1

MEAL

in exchange for a single **m**. . . . . . .Heb 12:16

MEANS

by every possible **m** save some. . . .1Co 9:22

MEASURE (N)

a full and honest dry **m**,. . . . . Dt 25:15
by the same **m** you use. . . . . Mt 7:2
a good **m**—pressed down, shaken . .Lk 6:38
he gives the Spirit without **m**. . . . . .Jn 3:34

MEASURE (V)

Who has **m-d** the waters in the . . . Is 40:12
He **m-d** the thickness of the . . . . . .Ezk 40:5
you will be **m-d** by the same. . . . . . . Mt 7:2
He **m-d** the city with the rod at . . . Rv 21:16

MEASUREMENTS

Do not be unfair in **m** . . . . Lv 19:35
These are the city's **m**: . . . . .Ezk 48:16

MEASURING (ADJ)

will make justice the **m** line . . . . .Is 28:17
and a **m** rod in his hand. . . . . .Ezk 40:3
was given a **m** reed like a rod . . . . . . Rv 11:1

MEAT

Lᴏʀᴅ will give you **m** to eat . . . . Ex 16:8
It is a good thing not to eat **m**,. . . Rm 14:21
I will never again eat **m**,
so that I 1Co 8:13

MEDES

People of Media, conquerors of Babylon
(Is 13:17; 21:2; Jr 51:11,28); Darius (Dn 5:31; 9:1;
11:1); present at Pentecost (Ac 2:9).

MEDIA

Country of the Medes, north of Elam and
west of Assyria (Ezr 6:2); ally of Persia (Est
1:3; Dn 5:28; 8:20); cursed by Jeremiah (Jr
25:25).

MEDIATOR

through angels by means of a **m**. . . . Gl 3:19
one God and one **m** between
God 1Tm 2:5
He is the **m** of a better . . . . Heb 8:6

MEDICINE

A joyful heart is good **m**, ... Pr 17:22

MEDITATE

he **m-s** on it day and night. . . . . Ps 1:2
I will **m** on your precepts . . . . .Ps 119:15
in her heart and **m-ing** on them. . . . Lk 2:19

MEDITATION

mouth and the **m** of my heart. . . . . Ps 19:14
It is my **m** all day long. . . . . Ps 119:97

MEDITERRANEAN SEA

Western border of Israel (Ex 23:31; Nm 34:6;
Dt 11:24; 34:2; Jos 1:4; 23:4; Ezk 47:15–20), including several of the tribal territories (Jos
15:4,11,12,47; 16:3,8; 17:9).

MEDIUM

Do not turn to **m-s** or consult . . . . . Lv 19:31
A man or a woman who is a **m** . . . .Lv 20:27
a woman at En-dor who is a **m**. . . .1Sm 28:7

MEET

I will **m** with you there above . . . . .Ex 25:22
faithful God will come to **m** me; . . . Ps 59:10
Israel, prepare to **m** your God!. . . . . Am 4:12
in the clouds to **m** the Lord in 1Th 4:17

MEETING (N)

In the tent of **m** outside the . . . . . . Ex 27:21

MELCHIZEDEK

King of Salem and priest (Gn 14:18); represents undying priesthood (Ps 110:4; Heb
5:6,10; 6:20; 7).

MELT

The mountains **m** like wax at the . . . Ps 97:5
elements will **m** with the heat. 2Pt 3:12

MEMBER

individually **m-s** of one another.... Rm 12:5
one **m** suffers, all the **m-s** suffer .. 1Co 12:26
since we are **m-s** of his body. .... Eph 5:30

MEMORY

All **m** of him perishes from the .... Jb 18:17
let him remove all **m** of them .... Ps 109:15
will also be told in **m** of her....... Mt 26:13

MENAHEM

King of Israel; obtained throne by force
(2Kg 15:10–16). Paid tribute to the king of
Assyria (15:19–20).

MENE

inscribed: **M**, **M**, TEKEL, PARSIN ..... Dn 5:25

MENTION

that I constantly **m** you,........... Rm 1:9
shameful even to **m** what is done .. Eph 5:12
my God when I **m** you in my .... Phm 4

MEPHIBOSHETH

1. Son of Jonathan; granted privilege in David's court (2Sm 4:4; 9; 16; 19).
2. Son of Saul whom David delivered to
   the Gibeonites (2Sm 21:1–9). His mother
   guarded his body until he was buried
   (21:10–14).

MERCIFUL

Blessed are the **m**, for they will be.. Mt 5:7
Be **m**, just as your Father also is **m**. .Lk 6:36
a **m** and faithful high priest....... Heb 2:17
is compassionate and **m**. .... Jms 5:11

MERCY

Make a **m** seat of pure gold, ... Ex 25:17
in the cloud above the **m** seat...... Lv 16:2
from above the **m** seat that was ..Nm 7:89
LORD is waiting to show you **m**.... Is 30:18
for his **m-ies** never end........... Lm 3:22
In your wrath remember **m**!....... Hab 3:2
merciful, for they will be shown **m**.. Mt 5:7
I desire **m** and not sacrifice....... Mt 9:13
of the law—justice, **m**, and faith.. Mt 23:23
him as the **m** seat by his blood .... Rm 3:25
show **m** to whom I will show **m**,... Rm 9:15
in view of the **m-ies** of God,...... Rm 12:1
the Father of **m-ies** and the God of ..2Co 1:3
But God, who is rich in **m**, ... Eph 2:4
ark overshadowing the **m** seat..... Heb 9:5
M triumphs over judgment........Jms 2:13

MESSAGE

Their **m** has gone out to all the..... Ps 19:4
because his **m** had authority........ Lk 4:32
Lord, who has believed our **m**? .... Jn 12:38
committed to us the **m** of reconciliation. .2Co 5:19

MESSENGER

or deaf like my **m** I am sending?.... Is 42:19
See, I am going to send my **m**, ... Mal 3:1
am sending my **m** ahead of you;.. .Mt 11:10
a **m** of Satan to torment me so.... 2Co 12:7

MESSIAH SEE ALSO CHRIST

false **m-s** and false prophets.... Mt 24:24
was born for you, who is the **M**,.... Lk 2:11
M is coming" (... called Christ)....... Jn 4:25
that you may believe
  Jesus is the **M** .... Jn 20:31
been appointed for you as the **M**. ..Ac 3:20

MICAH

1. Ephraimite idolater (Jdg 17–18).
2. Prophet to Israel and Judah in the days
   of kings Jotham, Ahaz, and Hezekiah of
   Judah (Jr 26:18; Mc 1:1).

MICAIAH

Son of Imlah; prophet against Ahab (1Kg 22;
5–28; 2Ch 18:4–27).

MICHAEL

Archangel; guardian of Israel (Dn 10:13,21;
12:1). Disputed with the devil (Jd 9); will
fight the dragon (Rv 12:7).

MICHAL

Daughter of Saul (1Sm 14:49); offered to David to endanger him (18:20–29); warned David of a plot (19:11–17). Given to Palti (25:44);
taken back (2Sm 3:12–16). Despised David
dancing before the Lord (6:14–23; 1Ch 15:29).

MIDDLE

tree in the **m** of the garden, ... Gn 3:3

MIDWIFE

of Egypt said to the Hebrew **m-ves**. .Ex 1:15

MIGHT

and will declare your **m** .... Ps 145:11
Not by strength or by **m**, but
  by my .... Zch 4:6
who are greater in **m** and power, .. 2Pt 2:11

MIGHTY

How the **m** have fallen! 2Sm 1:19
strong and **m**, the LORD, **m** in battle. . Ps 24:8
and will proclaim your **m** acts...... Ps 145:4
Counselor, **M** God, Eternal Father .... Is 9:6
because the **M** One has done great.. Lk 1:49
Lord God who judges her is **m**..... Rv 18:8

MILE

if anyone forces you to go one **m**, ..Mt 5:41

MILK

a land flowing with **m** and honey.... Ex 3:8
churning of **m** produces butter.... Pr 30:33
gave you **m** to drink, not solid food,.. 1Co 3:2
You need **m**, not solid food....... Heb 5:12
desire the pure **m** of the word,..... 1Pt 2:2

MILL

while the sound of the **m** fades;.... Ec 12:4
will be grinding ... with a hand **m**;.. Mt 24:41

MILLSTONE

the upper **m** as security for a ...... Dt 24:6
better for him if a heavy **m** were .. Mt 18:6

MINA

gave them ten **m-s**, and told them. .Lk 19:13

MIND

that he might change his **m**...... Nm 23:19
is not man who changes his **m**.... 1Sm 15:29
wholeheartedly and a willing **m**, .. 1Ch 28:9
or gave the **m** understanding? ....Jb 38:36
examine my heart and **m**. .... Ps 26:2
I applied my **m** to examine .... Ec 1:13
Make the **m-s** of these people dull;.. Is 6:10
will keep the **m** ... in perfect peace,.. Is 26:3
all your soul, and with all your **m**. ..Mt 22:37
them over to a corrupt **m**........ Rm 1:28
by the renewing of your **m**,....... Rm 12:2
But we have the **m** of Christ....... 1Co 2:16
has blinded the **m-s** of the 2Co 4:4
renewed in the spirit of your **m-s**; . Eph 4:23
Set your **m-s** on things above, ... Col 3:2
will put my laws into their **m-s**... Heb 8:10
One who examines **m-s** and hearts,.. Rv 2:23

MINDSET

Now the **m** of the flesh is death, ...Rm 8:6

MINISTER (N)

Levites to be **m-s** before the ark .. 1Ch 16:4
speak of you as **m-s** of our God .... Is 61:6
be a **m** of Christ Jesus to the ..... Rm 15:16
as God's **m-s**, we commend....... 2Co 6:4
a **m** of the sanctuary and the ..... Heb 8:2

MINISTER (V)

worn by Aaron whenever he **m-s** . .Ex 28:35

MINISTERING (N)

Are they not all **m** spirits sent..... Heb 1:14

MINISTRY

prayer and to the **m** of the word.... .Ac 6:4
given us the **m** of reconciliation:.. ..2Co 5:18
the saints for the work of **m** ...... Eph 4:12
an evangelist, fulfill your **m**. 2Tm 4:5
has now obtained a superior **m**.... Heb 8:6

MINT

pay a tenth of **m**, dill, and cumin,.. Mt 23:23

MIRACLE

Pharaoh tells you, 'Perform a **m**,' ....Ex 7:9
and do many **m-s** in your name? .. Mt 7:22
For if the **m-s** that were done in. .. Mt 11:21
was not able to do a **m** there,...... Mk 6:5
extraordinary **m-s** by Paul's hands. Ac 19:11
testified by signs ... various **m-s**, .. Heb 2:4

MIRIAM

Sister of Moses and Aaron; daughter of
Jochebed and Amram (Nm 26:59; 1Ch 6:3).
Watched over baby Moses (Ex 2:4–8).
Prophetess; led dancing at Red Sea (15:20–
21). Struck with skin disease for criticizing
Moses (Nm 12; Dt 24:9); died in Kadesh (Nm
20:1).

MIRROR

as in a **m**, but then face to face. ...1Co 13:12
looking at his own face in a **m**..... Jms 1:23

MISERABLE

You are all **m** comforters........... Jb 16:2
Be **m** and mourn and weep....... Jms 4:9

MISERY

I have observed the **m** of my people . .Ex 3:7

MIST

Your love is like the morning **m**..... Hs 6:4

MISTAKE

do not say ... that it was a **m** .... Ec 5:6

MISTREAT

pray for those who **m** you......... Lk 6:28

MISTRESS

her **m** became contemptible to her. .Gn 16:4

MISUSE

Do not **m** the name of the LORD ....Ex 20:7

MOABITE

No Ammonite or **M** may enter the .. Dt 23:3

MOABITESS

her daughter-in-law Ruth the **M**.... Ru 1:22

MOCK

At noon Elijah **m-ed** them........ 1Kg 18:27
Everyone who sees me **m-s** me;.... Ps 22:7
He **m-s** those who **m** but gives
  grace............................. Pr 3:34
down before him and **m-ed** him:.. Mt 27:29
God is not **m-ed**. For whatever a
  person............................. Gl 6:7

MOCKER

or sit in the company of **m-s**! ...... Ps 1:1
one who corrects a **m** will bring ..... Pr 9:7
Wine is a **m**, beer is a brawler;...... Pr 20:1

MODEST

dress themselves in **m** clothing, ... 1Tm 2:9

MOMENT

For his anger lasts only a **m**, ... Ps 30:5
I deserted you for a brief **m**........ Is 54:7
in a **m**, in the twinkling of an
  eye,............................... 1Co 15:52

MOMENTARY

For our **m** light affliction is 2Co 4:17

MONEY

and **m** is the answer for
  everything. Ec 10:19
cannot serve both God and **m**. . . . Mt 6:24
overturned the tables of the **m** . . . Mt 21:12
no traveling bag, no bread, no **m**;. . . . Lk 9:3
a lot of wine, not greedy for **m**, . . . 1Tm 3:8
For the love of **m** is a root of 1Tm 6:10
free from the love of **m**. . . . . Heb 13:5

MONEY-BAG

Don't carry a **m**, traveling bag, ... Lk 10:4
charge of the **m** and would steal . . . Jn 12:6

MONSTER

all sea **m-s** and ocean depths, ... Ps 148:7

MONTH

it is the first **m** of your year. . . . . Ex 12:2
Each **m** they will bear fresh fruit . . Ezk 47:12
producing its fruit every **m**. . . . . Rv 22:2

MOON

this time the sun, **m**, and eleven
  stars . . . . Gn 37:9
sun stood still and the
  m stopped . . . . Jos 10:13
the **m** and the stars, which you set . . Ps 8:3
you by day or the **m** by night. . . . . . Ps 121:6
the **m** to blood before the great. . . . . Jl 2:31
and the **m** will not shed its light;. . Mt 24:29
the **m** to blood before the great. . . . . Ac 2:20
another of the **m**, and another . . . 1Co 15:41

MORALS

Bad company corrupts good **m**. . . 1Co 15:33

MORDECAI

Cousin and legal guardian of Esther (Est 2:7). Uncovered assassination plot (2:21–23). Offended Haman (3:1–7); Haman sought genocide (3:7–15); Mordecai led Esther to thwart the attempt (Est 4–5). Honored by the king (Est 6); wrote revenge edict (Est 8).

MORNING

and there was **m**: one day. . . . . Gn 1:5
the **m** stars sang together . . . . Jb 38:7
but there is joy in the **m**. . . . . Ps 30:5
a loud voice early in the **m**, ... Pr 27:14
They are new every **m**; . . . . Lm 3:23
Very early in the **m**, on the first day. . Mk 16:2
and the **m** star rises in your hearts. . 2Pt 1:19
of David, the bright **m** star. . . . . . . Rv 22:16

MORON

'You **m**!' will be subject to hellfire. . Mt 5:22

MORTAL

Do not let a mere **m** hinder you. . . 2Ch 14:11
Can a **m** be righteous before . . . . Jb 4:17
What can mere **m-s** do to me? . . . . . Ps 56:4
let sin reign in your **m** body, ... Rm 6:12
and this **m** body must be clothed . . 1Co 15:53

MORTALITY

that **m** may be swallowed up 2Co 5:4

MOSES

Leader of Israel; Levite; brother of Aaron and Miriam (1Ch 6:3). Born under Egyptian oppression (Ex 1); set adrift on Nile; rescued and raised by Pharaoh's daughter (2:1–10). Killed Egyptian; fled to Midian and married Zipporah (2:11–22). Called by God from burning bush (Ex 3–4). Announced ten plagues (Ex 7–11).
  Divided the Red Sea (Ex 14). Brought water from a rock (17:1–7); held up God's staff and defeated Amalek (17:8–13). Delegated judging (18:13–26).

God spoke to him at Sinai: law (Ex 19–23); tabernacle, equipment, and garments (Ex 25–28; 30); consecration of priests (Ex 29). Discovered golden calf and broke tablets (Ex 32). Saw God's glory (33:12–34:28). Ordained Aaron and his sons (Lv 8–9).
  Opposed by Aaron and Miriam (Nm 12); opposed by Korah (Nm 16). Excluded from promised land for striking rock (Nm 20:1–13; 27:12–14; Dt 32:51). Made a bronze snake for healing (Nm 21:4–9; Jn 3:14). Wrote the book of the law (Jos 23:6; 2Ch 34:14). Saw promised land from a distance (Dt 3:23–27; 34:1–4); commissioned Joshua as successor (Nm 27:12–23); buried by God (34:5–8).

MOST

holy place and the **m** holy place. . . Ex 26:33
is the **m** important of all? . . . . Mk 12:28
making the **m** of the time . . . . Eph 5:16

MOST HIGH

he was a priest to God **M**. . . . . Gn 14:18
I call to God **M**, to God who. . . . . . . Ps 57:2
you are all sons of the **M**. . . . . Ps 82:6
under the protection of the **M** . . . . . Ps 91:1
come from the mouth of the **M**? . . Lm 3:38
Jesus, Son of the **M** God? . . . . Mk 5:7
called the Son of the **M**, ... Lk 1:32
the **M** does not dwell in
  sanctuaries. Ac 7:48
of Salem, priest of the God **M**, ... Heb 7:1

MOTH

where **m** and rust destroy and . . . . Mt 6:19

MOTHER

a man leaves his father and **m** . . . . Gn 2:24
she was the **m** of all the living. . . . . Gn 3:20
Honor your father and your **m** so . . Ex 20:12
Naked I came from my **m-'s**
  womb, ... Jb 1:21
the joyful **m** of children. . . . . Ps 113:9
don't reject your **m-'s** teaching, ... Pr 1:8
pronouncement that his **m** taught. . Pr 31:1
As a **m** comforts her son, so I. . . . . . Is 66:13
father or **m** more than me is . . . . . Mt 10:37
Who is my **m** and who are my . . . Mt 12:48
Honor your father and your **m**; . . . .Mt 15:4
leave his father and **m** and be
  joined . . . . Mt 19:5
not hate his own father and **m** . . . Lk 14:26
to the disciple, "Here is your **m**." . . . Jn 19:27

MOTHER-IN-LAW

a daughter-in-law is against
  her **m**; . . . . Mc 7:6
a daughter-in-law against her **m**;. . Mt 10:35
Simon's **m** was suffering from. . . . . . Lk 4:38

MOTIVES

but the Lord weighs **m**. . . . . Pr 16:2
whether from false **m** or . . . . Php 1:18

MOUNT (N) SEE ALSO CARMEL, MOUNT OF OLIVES, SINAI, ZION

The Lord came down on **M** Sinai . . Ex 19:20
the blessing at **M** Gerizim and. . . . . Dt 11:29
M Zion—the summit of Zaphon— . . Ps 48:2
M Zion, which he loved. . . . . Ps 78:68
The **M** of Olives will be split in . . . Zch 14:4
was sitting on the **M** of Olives. . . . Mt 24:3
they went out to the **M** of Olives. . Mt 26:30
Now Hagar represents **M** Sinai . . . Gl 4:25

MOUNT (V)

gentle, and **m-ed** on
  a donkey, ... Mt 21:5

MOUNT OF OLIVES

The **M** will be split in half. . . . . Zch 14:4
psalms, they went out to the **M**. . . Mt 26:30
made his way as usual to the **M**,. . . Lk 22:39
But Jesus went to the **M**. . . . . Jn 8:1

MOUNTAIN

will be provided on the Lord's **m**. . .Gn 22:14
came to Horeb, the **m** of God. . . . . . . Ex 3:1
my king on Zion, my holy **m**. . . . . . . Ps 2:6
The **m-s** melt like wax at the. . . . . . Ps 97:5
I lift my eyes toward the **m**. . . . . . . Ps 121:1
The **m-s** surround Jerusalem . . . . . Ps 125:2
let's go up to the **m** of the Lord, ... Is 2:3
beautiful on the **m** of the one . . . . Is 52:7
became a great **m** and filled the. . . Dn 2:35
to a very high **m** and showed him . . Mt 4:8
up on a high **m** by themselves. . . . Mt 17:1
will tell this **m**, 'Move from . . . . . . Mt 17:20
and every **m** and hill will be. . . . . . . Lk 3:5
all faith so that I can move **m-s** . . . 1Co 13:2

MOURN

a time to **m** and a time to dance; . . . . Ec 3:4
to comfort all who **m**, ... Is 61:2
will **m** for him as one **m-s** for . . . . Zch 12:10
Blessed are those who **m**, for . . . . . . Mt 5:4
Be miserable and **m** and weep. . . . . Jms 4:9
of the earth will **m** over him. . . . . . . Rv 1:7

MOURNING (N)

day long I go around in **m**. . . . . Ps 38:6
festive oil instead of **m**, ... Is 61:3
I will turn their **m** into joy, ... Jr 31:13

MOUTH

Who placed a **m** on . . . . Ex 4:11
from the **m-s** of infants . . . . Ps 8:2
May the words of my **m** and. . . . . . . Ps 19:14
They have **m-s** but cannot speak,. . Ps 115:5
from his **m** come knowledge and . . . . Pr 2:6
praise you, and not your own **m** . . . Pr 27:2
Do not let your **m** bring guilt on. . . . Ec 5:6
yet he did not open his **m**. . . . . Is 53:7
that comes from the **m** of God. . . . . Mt 4:4
If you confess with your **m** . . . . Rm 10:9
cursing come out of the same **m**. . . Jms 3:10

MOVE

M-ed with compassion, Jesus . . . . Mt 20:34
so that I can **m** mountains 1Co 13:2

MUD

made some **m** from the saliva, ... Jn 9:6

MUDDY

out of the **m** clay, and set my feet . . Ps 40:2

MULTIPLY

Be fruitful, **m**, fill the earth, ... Gn 1:28
fruitful, increased rapidly, **m-ied**, ... Ex 1:7
Yet the fool **m-ies** words. . . . . Ec 10:14
The more they **m-ied**, the more
  they. . . . . Hs 4:7
where sin **m-ied**, grace **m-ied** . . . . Rm 5:20
sin so that grace may **m**? . . . . Rm 6:1

MULTITUDE

M-s, m-s in the valley of decision!. . . Jl 3:14
and cover a **m** of sins. . . . . Jms 5:20
since love covers a **m** of sins. 1Pt 4:8
there was a vast **m** from every . . . . . Rv 7:9

MURDER

Do not **m**. . . . . Ex 20:13
Do not **m**, and whoever **m-s** will . . Mt 5:21
whom you had **m-ed** by hanging. . Ac 5:30
adultery, also said, Do not **m**. . . . . Jms 2:11

MURDERER

the **m** must be put to death. . . . . . . Nm 35:16
He was a **m** from the beginning . . . Jn 8:44
hates his brother or sister is a **m**, . . 1Jn 3:15

MUSIC

in charge of the **m** in the Lord's . . . 1Ch 6:31
sing and make **m** to the Lord. . . . . . Ps 27:6
harp and the **m** of a lyre. . . . . Ps 92:3
house, he heard **m** and dancing. . . . Lk 15:25
songs, singing and making **m** . . . . Eph 5:19

MUSICAL
accompanied by **m** instruments . . 1Ch 15:16
the **m** instruments of the LORD, ...2Ch 7:6
the **m** instruments of David. . . . . Neh 12:36

MUSTARD
is like a **m** seed that a man. . . . . . .Mt 13:31
faith the size of a **m** seed, ... Mt 17:20

MUTE
Who makes a person **m** or deaf, ... Ex 4:11

MUTUALLY
to be **m** encouraged by each . . . . . . Rm 1:12

MUZZLE
Do not **m** an ox while it treads . . . . .Dt 25:4
my mouth with a **m** as long as the. . Ps 39:1
Do not **m** an ox while it is 1Tm 5:18

MYRRH
My hands dripped with **m**,. . . . . .Sg 5:5
gold, frankincense, and **m**. . . . . .Mt 2:11

MYSTERY
I will speak **m-ies** from the past. . . . Ps 78:2
The **m** was then revealed to Daniel. . Dn 2:19
I am telling you a **m**: 1Co 15:51
This **m** is profound, but I am . . . . . .Eph 5:32
the **m** hidden for ages and. . . . . Col 1:26
holding the **m** of the faith with . . . 1Tm 3:9
the **m** of godliness is great:. 1Tm 3:16

MYTHS
pay attention to **m** and endless 1Tm 1:4
truth and will turn aside to **m**. 2Tm 4:4
contrived **m** when we made known. . 2Pt 1:16

- N -

NAGGING (ADJ)
share a house with a **n** wife. . . . . . . Pr 21:9
rainy day and a **n** wife are . . . . Pr 27:15

NAGGING (N)
a wife's **n** is an endless . . . . Pr 19:13

NAHUM
Prophet against Nineveh (Nah 1:1).

NAIL (N)
finger into the mark of the **n-s**. . . .Jn 20:25

NAIL (V)
people to **n** him to a cross . . . . .Ac 2:23
away by **n-ing** it to the cross . . . . . Col 2:14

NAKED
the man and his wife were **n** . . . . . . Gn 2:25
Who told you that you were **n**? . . . . . Gn 3:11
N I came from my mother's womb, . .Jb 1:21
I was **n** and you clothed me; . . . . . Mt 25:36
we will not be found **n**. 2Co 5:3

NAKEDNESS
they covered their father's **n**. . . . . . Gn 9:23
or famine or **n** or danger or . . . . . .Rm 8:35

NAME (N)
The man gave **n-s** to all the. . . . . . . Gn 2:20
This is my **n** forever; . . . . Ex 3:15
Do not misuse the **n** of the LORD . . .Ex 20:7
the place to have his **n** dwell. . . . . .Dt 12:11
people, who bear my **n**, ...2Ch 7:14
magnificent is your **n** throughout . . . Ps 8:1
we take pride in the **n** of the LORD. .Ps 20:7
let us exalt his **n** together. . . . . .Ps 34:3
within me, bless his holy **n**. . . . . . . Ps 103:1
who comes in the **n** of the LORD . . Ps 118:26
n of the LORD is a strong tower; . . . Pr 18:10
A good **n** is to be chosen over . . . . . Pr 22:1
I am the LORD. That is my **n**,. . . . . . . Is 42:8
I had concern for my holy **n**, ... Ezk 36:21

Your **n** be honored as holy. . . . . Mt 6:9
These are the **n-s** of the twelve . . . Mt 10:2
that your **n-s** are written in
heaven. . . . . .Lk 10:20
have asked for nothing in my **n**. . . .Jn 16:24
calls on the **n** of the Lord will . . . . . .Ac 2:21
there is no other **n** under heaven . . .Ac 4:12
calls on the **n** of the Lord will . . . . Rm 10:13
the **n** that is above every **n**, ... Php 2:9
whose **n-s** are in the book. . . . . Php 4:3
beast's **n** or the number of its **n**. . . Rv 13:17

NAME (V)
and you are to **n** him Jesus, ...Mt 1:21

NAOMI
Ruth's mother-in-law (Ru 1:2–4).

NAPHTALI
Son of Jacob and Bilhah (Gn 30:1–8). Tribe
with territory north and west of the Sea of
Galilee (Jos 19:32–39); praised by Deborah
(Jdg 5:18); produced Hiram the craftsman
(1Kg 7:13–14).

NARROW
Enter through the **n** gate. . . . . .Mt 7:13

NATHAN
Prophet to David; told David he would never
fail to have a descendant on the throne (2Sm
7:4–17); confronted David about Bathsheba
(2Sm 12:1–15). Anointed Solomon (1Kg 1).

NATHANAEL
Apostle "in whom is no deceit"; invited by
Philip; asked if anything good comes out
of Nazareth (Jn 1:45–49; 21:2); possibly also
called Bartholomew (Mt 10:3).

NATION
I will make you into a great **n** . . . . . .Gn 12:2
kingdom of priests and my holy **n**. . .Ex 19:6
Why do the **n-s** rage and the . . . . Ps 2:1
Happy is the **n** whose God is . . . . . . Ps 33:12
Declare his glory among the **n-s**. . . .Ps 96:3
Righteousness exalts a **n**, but sin . . Pr 14:34
N will not take up the sword. . . . . Is 2:4
proclaim my glory among the **n-s**. . . Is 66:19
For **n** will rise up against **n**, ... Mt 24:7
and make disciples of all **n-s** . . . . . Mt 28:19
a royal priesthood, a holy **n**, ... 1Pt 2:9
and language and people and **n**. . . . Rv 5:9

NATURAL
exchanged **n** sexual relations . . . . . Rm 1:26
did not spare the **n** branches, ...Rm 11:21
sown a **n** body, raised a. 1Co 15:44

NATURE
His eternal power and divine **n** . . . . Rm 1:20
and against **n** were grafted into . . Rm 11:24
Does not even **n** itself teach you . . .1Co 11:14
you may share in the divine **n** 2Pt 1:4

NAZARENE
that he will be called a **N**. . . . . Mt 2:23
of the sect of the **N-s**! . . . . .Ac 24:5

NAZARETH
Hometown of Jesus (Mt 2:23; Lk 2:51; 4:16;
Jn 1:45–46).
"Jesus of **N**," they answered. . . . . . . Jn 18:5

NAZIRITE
a special vow, a **N** vow,. . . . . Nm 6:2
boy will be a **N** to God from . . . . . .Jdg 13:5

NEAR
But the message is very **n** you, ...Dt 30:14
The LORD is to all who call out . . . Ps 145:18
call to him while he is **n**. . . . . Is 55:6
The great day of the LORD is **n**, ...Zph 1:14
kingdom of heaven has come **n**!. . . . Mt 3:2

The message is **n** you, in your . . . . .Rm 10:8
The Lord is **n**. Php 4:5
Draw **n** to God, and he will draw **n** . .Jms 4:8
because the time is **n**. . . . . Rv 22:10

NEARER
our salvation is **n** than when we. . .Rm 13:11

NEBUCHADNEZZAR
King of Babylon; defeated and exiled Judah
(2Kg 24–25; 1Ch 6:15; 2Ch 36; Jr 39). Dreams
interpreted by Daniel (Dn 2; 4); threw
Shadrach, Meshach, and Abednego into the
furnace (Dn 3); temporarily insane (Dn 4);
praised God (2:47; 3:28; 4:34–37).

NECK
you and adornment for your **n**. . . . . . Pr 3:22
Your **n** is like the tower of . . . . .Sg 4:4

NEED (N)
a robber, your **n**, like a bandit. . . . . Pr 24:34
supply all your **n-s** according. . . . . Php 4:19
a fellow believer in **n** but withholds . .1Jn 3:17

NEED (V)
Father knows the things you **n** . . . . . Mt 6:8
not those who are well who **n** a
doctor. . . . . Mt 9:12
say to the hand, "I don't **n** you!". . 1Co 12:21

NEEDLE
the eye of a **n** than for a rich. . . . . . Mt 19:24

NEEDY
and lifts the **n** from the trash 1Sm 2:8
I was a father to the **n**, ...Jb 29:16
He heard the outcry of the **n**. . . . . .Jb 34:28
is kind to the **n** honors him. . . . . . . Pr 14:31

NEGATIVE
a **n** report about the land. . . . . Nm 14:36

NEGLECT
you have **n-ed** the more
important. . . . . Mt 23:23
Don't **n** the gift that is in you; 1Tm 4:14
we escape if we **n** such a great . . . . Heb 2:3
not **n-ing** to gather together . . . Heb 10:25

NEHEMIAH
Cupbearer to King Artaxerxes of Babylon
(Neh 1:11); obtained permission, planned,
and supervised rebuilding Jerusalem's walls
despite opposition (Neh 2–6). Was appointed governor of Judah (5:14). Dedicated wall
(12:27–43). Promoted reforms (Neh 8–10; 13).
Prayed frequently (1:4–11; 2:4; 4:4–5,9; 5:19;
6:9,14; 13:14,22,29,31).

NEIGHBOR
false testimony against your **n**. . . . .Ex 20:16
Do not covet your **n-'s** wife, ...Ex 20:17
but love your **n** as yourself; . . . . Lv 19:18
better a **n** nearby than a brother . . Pr 27:10
one teach his **n** or his brother, ...Jr 31:34
to him who gives his **n-s** drink, ...Hab 2:15
Love your **n** and hate your enemy . . Mt 5:43
and love your **n** as yourself. . . . . . . Mt 19:19
asked Jesus, "And who is my **n**?". . .Lk 10:29
Love your **n** as yourself. . . . . Gl 5:14

NEST (N)
your **n** is set in the cliffs. . . . . Nm 24:21
and make your **n** among the stars . . . .Ob 4
and birds of the sky have **n-s** . . . . Mt 8:20

NEST (V)
sky come and **n** in its branches. . . . .Mt 13:32

NET
They prepared a **n** for my steps; . . . .Ps 57:6
to spread a **n** where any bird can . . . .Pr 1:17
street like an antelope in a **n**. . . . . . .Is 51:20

they left their **n-s** and followed . . . Mt 4:20
Cast the **n** on the right side of . . . . . Jn 21:6

NEVER

and they will **n** perish. . . . . Jn 10:28
Love **n** ends. 1Co 13:8
I will **n** leave you or abandon. . . . . . Heb 13:5

NEW

A **n** king, who did not know. . . . . Ex 1:8
Sing a **n** song to him;. . . . . Ps 33:3
He put a **n** song in my mouth,. . . . . . Ps 40:3
there is nothing **n** under the sun. . . . . Ec 1:9
will create **n** heavens and a **n** earth;. . Is 65:17
I will make a **n** covenant with . . . . . . Jr 31:31
you a **n** heart and put a **n** spirit . . Ezk 36:26
And no one puts **n** wine into old. . . . Mt 9:17
A **n** teaching with authority! . . . . . . Mk 1:27
This cup is the **n** covenant . . . . Lk 22:20
I give you a **n** command: Love . . . . . Jn 13:34
in Christ, he is a **n** creation; 2Co 5:17
and have put on the **n** self. . . . . Col 3:10
wait for **n** heavens and a **n** earth . . 2Pt 3:13
I saw a **n** heaven and a **n** earth; . . . . Rv 21:1
I am making everything **n**." . . . . Rv 21:5

NEWBORN

Like **n** infants, desire the 1Pt 2:2

NEWS

good **n** strengthens the bones. . . . . Pr 15:30
who brings **n** of good things, ... Is 52:7
Then the **n** about him spread . . . . Mt 4:24
the poor are told the good **n**. . . . . . Mt 11:5
Repent and believe in the good **n**! . . Mk 1:15

NICODEMUS

Pharisee and member of the Sanhedrin.
Visited Jesus at night (Jn 3:1–21); defended
Jesus to the Sanhedrin (7:45–52); helped
prepare Jesus's body for burial (19:39).

NIGHT

the darkness he called "**n**." . . . . Gn 1:5
earth forty days and forty **n-s** . . . . . Gn 7:4
you are to meditate on it day and **n**. . Jos 1:8
he meditates on it day and **n**. . . . . . . Ps 1:2
not fear the terror of the **n** . . . . Ps 91:5
fasted forty days and forty **n-s**. . . . . Mt 4:2
watch at **n** over their flock. . . . . Lk 2:8
man came to him at **n** and said, ... Jn 3:2
come just like a thief in the **n**. 1Th 5:2
not belong to the **n** or the darkness. . . 1Th 5:5
N will be no more;. . . . . Rv 22:5

NILE

River of Egypt (Gn 41:1; Ex 1:22; 2:3; Is 7:18;
19:7–8; Ezk 29:3–10; Nah 3:8; Zch 10:11);
floods periodically (Jr 46:7–8; Am 8:8; 9:5);
struck by the plagues (Ex 7:20–21; 8:3).

NINE

He was **n** feet, **n** inches tall 1Sm 17:4
ten cleansed? Where are the **n**? . . . . Lk 17:17
since it's only **n** in the morning. . . . . Ac 2:15

NINETY-NINE

Abraham was **n** years old when . . . Gn 17:24
leave the **n** in the open field . . . . Lk 15:4

NINETY-YEAR-OLD

Can Sarah, a **n** woman, give birth? . . Gn 17:17

NINEVEH

Capital of Assyria (Gn 10:11–12; 2Kg 19:36; Is
37:37); Jonah preached against (Jnh 3:2–4)
and the people repented (3:5–7; Mt 12:41;
Lk 11:30–32); prophets condemned (Nah 1:1;
Zph 2:13).

NOAH

Son of Lamech; descendant of Seth; a
righteous man (Gn 5:28–29; 6:9; Ex 14:14;
2Pt 2:5; Heb 11:7). Built an ark, entered it

with animals and his family, and survived
the flood (Gn 6:14–8:19; 1Pt 3:20). Received
God's promise (Gn 8:20–9:17). Got drunk
and cursed Canaan (9:20–27). Flood a symbol of sudden judgment (Mt 24:37–38; Lk
17:26–27).

NOBLE (ADJ)

you are a woman of **n** character. . . . Ru 3:11
My heart is moved by a **n** theme as I. . Ps 45:1
She has done a **n** thing for me. . . . Mt 26:10
powerful, not many of **n** birth. 1Co 1:26

NOBLE (N)

Do not trust in **n-s**, in man, who. . . Ps 146:3
when your king is a son of **n-s** . . . Ec 10:17
slaughtered all Judah's **n-s**. . . . . Jr 39:6

NOISE

Pharaoh king of Egypt was all **n**; . . Jr 46:17
an end to the **n** of your songs, . . . Ezk 26:13
from me the **n** of your songs! . . . . Am 5:23
will pass away with a loud **n** 2Pt 3:10

NORTH

the king of the **N** will come, ... Dn 11:15

NOSE

and twisting a **n** draws blood,. . . . Pr 30:33

NOSTRILS

the breath of life into his **n** . . . . Gn 2:7
from God remains in my **n** . . . . Jb 27:3
blast of the breath of your **n**. . . . . Ps 18:15

NOTHING

N is too difficult for you! . . . . Jr 32:17
N will be impossible for you. . . . . . Mt 17:20
you can do **n** without me. . . . . Jn 15:5
but do not have love, I am **n**. 1Co 13:2
I didn't run or labor for **n**. . . . . . . Php 2:16
For we brought **n** into the world, . . 1Tm 6:7

NULLIFY

You **n** the word of God by your
tradition. . . . . Mk 7:13

NUMBER (N)

and grew daily in **n**. . . . . Ac 16:5
it is the **n** of a person. Its **n** is 666. . Rv 13:18

NUMBER (V)

Teach us to **n** our days carefully . . . Ps 90:12
God has **n-ed** the days of your . . . Dn 5:26
who was **n-ed** among the Twelve. . Lk 22:3

NURSE

that Sarah would **n** children?. . . . . . Gn 21:7
woman took the boy and **n-d** him. . Ex 2:9

NURSING (ADJ)

mouths of infants and **n** babies, . . . Ps 8:2
a woman forget her **n** child, ... Is 49:15
mouths of infants and **n** babies? . . Mt 21:16

- O -

OAK

live near the **o-s** of Mamre . . . . . . Gn 13:18
and he was as sturdy as the **o-s**; . . . Am 2:9

OATH

The Lord swore an **o** to David, ... Ps 132:11
I tell you, don't take an **o** at all: . . . Mt 5:34
by earth or with any other **o**. . . . . Jms 5:12

OBADIAH

Prophet against Edom (Ob 1).

OBEDIENCE

through the one man's **o** the many . . Rm 5:19
or of **o** leading to righteousness?. . Rm 6:16
He learned **o** through what he . . . . Heb 5:8

OBEDIENT

to Nazareth and was **o** to them. . . . . Lk 2:51
becoming **o** to the point of death—. . Php 2:8

OBEY

to **o** is better than sacrifice, ... 1Sm 15:22
the winds and the sea **o** him! . . . . . Mt 8:27
unclean spirits, and they **o** him. . . Mk 1:27
We must **o** God rather than . . . . Ac 5:29
Children, **o** your parents as . . . . . . Eph 6:1

OBLIGATED

are not **o** to the flesh to . . . . Rm 8:12

OBSCENE

O and foolish talking. . . . . Eph 5:4

OBSERVE

You must **o** my Sabbaths, ... Ex 31:13
When I **o** your heavens, the work . . . Ps 8:3
teaching them to **o** everything I. . Mt 28:20
o-ing special days, months, ... Gl 4:10
they will **o** your good works 1Pt 2:12

OBTAIN

have **o-ed** righteousness . . . . Rm 9:30

OBVIOUS

each one's work will become **o** 1Co 3:13
the works of the flesh are **o**: . . . . . . Gl 5:19
good works are **o**, and those that. . 1Tm 5:25

OFFEND

one who isn't **o-ed** by me. . . . . Mt 11:6

OFFENSE

but love covers all **o-s**. . . . . Pr 10:12
o-s will inevitably come, but
woe to . . . . Mt 18:7
that case the **o** of the cross has . . . . Gl 5:11

OFFENSIVE

if there is any **o** way in me; . . . . . . Ps 139:24

OFFER

o him there as a burnt offering. . . . Gn 22:2
if you are **o-ing** your gift on . . . . . . Mt 5:23
once for all time when he **o-ed**
himself . . . . Heb 7:27
not do this to **o** himself many . . . . Heb 9:25

OFFERING (N)

take pleasure in burnt **o-s** ... as much as in
obeying the Lord? 1Sm 15:22
You do not delight in sacrifice and **o**. . Ps 40:6
You make him a guilt **o**, ... Is 53:10
of God rather than burnt **o-s**. . . . . . Hs 6:6
and fragrant **o** to God. . . . . Eph 5:2
You did not desire sacrifice and **o**, . Heb 10:5

OFFSPRING

and between your **o** and her **o**. . . . Gn 3:15
I will give this land to your **o**. . . . . . Gn 12:7
said, 'For we are also his **o**.' . . . . . . Ac 17:28

OIL

and the **o** jug did not run dry, ... 1Kg 17:16
You anoint my head with **o**; . . . . . . Ps 23:5
wise ones took **o** in their flasks. . . . Mt 25:4

OLD

I have been young and now I am **o**, . . Ps 37:25
even when he is **o** he will not . . . . . Pr 22:6
your **o** men will have dreams, ... Jl 2:28
puts new wine into wineskins. . . . Mt 9:17
and your **o** men will dream dreams. . Ac 2:17
the **o** has passed away, ... 2Co 5:17
have put off the **o** self with its . . . . Col 3:9

OLDER

The **o** will serve the younger. . . . . . Rm 9:12

OLIVE *SEE ALSO* **MOUNT OF OLIVES**

was a plucked **o** leaf in its beak . . . . Gn 8:11

OMEGA

the Alpha and the **O** . . . . . Rv 1:8; 21:6; 22:13

OMRI

Army commander; king of Israel; founded the city of Samaria (1Kg 16:15–28).

ONCE

He died to sin **o** for all; . . . . Rm 6:10
appointed for people to die **o** . . . . Heb 9:27

ONE *SEE ALSO* ONE AND ONLY SON

and then morning: **o** day. . . . . .Gn 1:5
the LORD our God, the LORD is **o**. . . . . .Dt 6:4
Are you the **o** who is to come, ... Mt 11:3
the two will become **o** flesh? . . . . . Mt 19:5
I and the Father are **o**. . . . . .Jn 10:30
they may be **o** as we are **o**. . . . . . . .Jn 17:11
baptized by **o** Spirit into **o** body. . 1Co 12:13
you are all **o** in Christ Jesus. . . . . Gl 3:28
o Lord, **o** faith, **o** baptism, ... Eph 4:5
For there is **o** God and **o** mediator . . 1Tm 2:5
You believe that God is **o**. . . . . .Jms 2:19

ONE AND ONLY SON

glory as the **o** from the Father, ... Jn 1:14
No one has ever seen God. The **o** . . . Jn 1:18
He gave his **o**, so that everyone . . . . Jn 3:16
not believed in the name of the **o** . . Jn 3:18
God sent his **o** into the world 1Jn 4:9

OPEN

eyes will be **o-ed** and you will be. . . Gn 3:5
O my eyes so that I may. . . . . Ps 119:18
what he **o-s**, no one can close; . . . . Is 22:22
yet he did not **o** his mouth. . . . . . . .Is 53:7
and the door will be **o-ed** to you . . . Mt 7:7
hears my voice and **o-s** the door, . . Rv 3:20
Who is worthy to **o** the scroll . . . . . . .Rv 5:2
and books were **o-ed**. . . . . Rv 20:12

OPPORTUNITY

looking for a good **o** to betray
him. . . . . Mt 26:16
and don't give the devil an **o**. . . . . .Eph 4:27

OPPRESS

He was **o-ed** and afflicted, ...Is 53:7
to the blind, to set free the **o-ed**, . . Lk 4:18
Don't the rich **o** you and drag . . . . . Jms 2:6

ORACLE

The **o** of Balaam son of Beor, ...Nm 24:3
received living **o-s** to give to us. . . . .Ac 7:38

ORDAIN

the way you will **o** Aaron and his . . .Ex 29:9
unless the Lord has **o-ed** it?. . . . . . . Lm 3:37

ORDER

Set your house in **o**, ...2Kg 20:1
give his angels **o-s** concerning . . . . .Ps 91:11
give his angels **o-s** concerning . . . . . Mt 4:6
must be done decently and in **o**. . 1Co 14:40
according to the **o** of
Melchizedek. . . . . Heb 5:6

ORDINANCE

the **o-s** of the LORD are reliable. . . . . . Ps 19:9

ORDINATION

the ram of Aaron's **o** . . . . Ex 29:26

ORGIES

drunkenness, **o**, carousing, ...1Pt 4:3

ORIGINATE

Did the word of God **o** from you,. . 1Co 14:36

ORNAN *SEE* ARAUNAH

ORPHANS

I will not leave you as **o**; . . . . Jn 14:18
to look after **o** and widows in . . . .Jms 1:27

OTHER

I am the LORD, and there is no **o**; . . . . Is 45:5
as you want **o-s** to do for you, ... Lk 6:31

OTHNIEL

Judge; defeated Arameans (Jdg 3:7–11); Caleb's nephew (Jos 15:17; Jdg 1:13).

OUTER

though our **o** person is being 2Co 4:16

OUTRAN

other disciple **o** Peter and got. . . . . .Jn 20:4

OUTSIDE

You clean the **o** of the cup and . . Mt 23:25
person commits is **o** the body. 1Co 6:18
Jesus also suffered **o** the gate, . . .Heb 13:12

OUTSIDER

Act wisely toward **o-s**, ... Col 4:5
properly in the presence of **o-s**. . . . 1Th 4:12

OUTSTRETCHED

you with an **o** arm and great acts. . . .Ex 6:6

OUTWARD

Stop judging according to **o**. . . . . . . .Jn 7:24
consist of **o** things like 1Pt 3:3

OUTWARDLY

person is not a Jew who is one **o**,. .Rm 2:28

OVERCOME

yet the darkness did not **o** it. . . . . . . Jn 1:5

OVERFLOW

my cup **o-s**. . . . . Ps 23:5
speaks from the **o** of the heart. . . Mt 12:34
to make every grace **o** to you, ...2Co 9:8

OVERLOOK

having **o-ed** the times of
ignorance .Ac 17:30

OVERPOWER

gates of Hades will not **o** it. . . . . . .Mt 16:18

OVERSEE

not **o-ing** out of compulsion but . . . 1Pt 5:2

OVERSEER

If anyone aspires to be an **o**, ...1Tm 3:1
an **o** of God's household. . . . . .Ti 1:7
Shepherd and **O** of your souls. 1Pt 2:25

OVERSHADOW

of the Most High will **o** you. . . . . . . Lk 1:35

OVERTAKE

so that darkness doesn't **o** you. . . . Jn 12:35

OVERTURN

o-ed tables of the money
changers. .Mt 21:12

OVERWHELM

rivers will not **o** you. . . . . .Is 43:2

OWE

one who **o-d** ten thousand
talents . . . . Mt 18:24
not ... a gift, but as something **o-d**. .Rm 4:4
Do not anyone anything, except . .Rm 13:8
you **o** me even your very self. . . . . . .Phm 19

OWN (ADJ)

rely on your **o** understanding; . . . . . . Pr 3:5
all have turned to our **o** way; . . . . . Is 53:6

OWN (N)

He came to his **o**, ...Jn 1:11
Having loved his **o** who were in . . . .Jn 13:1
You are not your **o**, ... 1Co 6:19

OX

Do not muzzle an **o** while it treads . . Dt 25:4
not muzzle an **o** while it treads. 1Co 9:9

- P -

PAIN

I will intensify your labor **p-s**; . . . . . .Gn 3:16
so that I will not experience **p**. . . . 1Ch 4:10
and he carried our **p-s**; . . . . Is 53:4
if I cause you **p**, then who will. 2Co 2:2
and **p** will be no more, ... Rv 21:4

PALM

you on the **p-s** of my hands; . . . . . . Is 49:16
they took **p** branches and went . . . Jn 12:13

PARABLE

He told them many things in **p-s** . . .Mt 13:3
Why are you speaking ... in **p-s**? . . .Mt 13:10
tell them anything without a **p**, . . . Mt 13:34
I will open my mouth in **p-s**; . . . . . .Mt 13:35
but to the rest it is in **p-s**, so that . . Lk 8:10

PARADISE

you will be with me in **p**. . . . . Lk 23:43
was caught up into **p**. 2Co 12:4

PARALYTIC

brought to him a **p** lying on a . . . . . . Mt 9:2
told the **p**, "Son, your sins are . . . . . . Mk 2:5

PARENT

who sinned, this man or his **p-s**, ...Jn 9:2
evil, disobedient to **p-s**, ... Rm 1:30
Children, obey your **p-s** as . . . . .Eph 6:1
obey your **p-s** in everything, ... Col 3:20
disobedient to **p-s**, ungrateful, ...2Tm 3:2

PART

You who created my inward **p-s**; . Ps 139:13
wash you, you have no **p** with me. . . Jn 13:8
as we have many **p-s** in one body,. . Rm 12:4
your bodies are a **p** of Christ's. 1Co 6:15
body is one and has many **p-s**, . . . 1Co 12:12
know in **p**, and we prophesy in **p**. . 1Co 13:9

PARTIAL

A **p** hardening has come upon
Israel . . . . Rm 11:25

PARTIALITY

Do not show **p** when deciding . . . . . Dt 1:17
not good to show **p**. . . . Pr 18:5; 24:23; 28:21
nor do you show **p** but teach . . . . Mk 12:14

PARTNERSHIP

For what **p** is there between 2Co 6:14
because of your **p** in the gospel . . . .Php 1:5

PASS

see the blood, I will **p** over you. . . . Ex 12:13
When you **p** through the waters, . . . Is 43:2
Heaven and earth will **p** away, but my
words will never **p** away. . . . . Mt 24:35
let this cup **p** from me. . . . . Mt 26:39
he **p-ed** by on the other side. . . . . . Lk 10:31
but has **p-ed** from death to life. . . . .Jn 5:24
God **p-ed** over the sins
previously .Rm 3:25
For I **p-ed** on to you as most 1Co 15:3
the old has **p-ed** away, ...2Co 5:17
we have **p-ed** from death to life . . . 1Jn 3:14

PASSIONS

them over to disgraceful **p**. . . . . . . Rm 1:26
Flee from youthful **p**, and
pursue. 2Tm 2:22

PASSOVER

it is the LORD's **P**. . . . . .Ex 12:11
the **P** lamb had to be sacrificed. . . . .Lk 22:7
eat this **P** with you before I suffer. . Lk 22:15

PAST

Christ our **P** lamb has been
sacrificed...................1Co 5:7

PAST

Do not hold **p** iniquities against us;. . Ps 79:8
the cleansing from his **p** sins. 2Pt 1:9

PASTORS

some **p** and teachers, ... Eph 4:11

PASTURE

lets me lie down in green **p-s**;. . . . . Ps 23:2
His people, the sheep of his **p**. . . . Ps 100:3
come in and go out and find **p**. . . . . Jn 10:9

PATCH

No one sews a **p** of unshrunk . . . . . Mk 2:21

PATH

the right **p-s** for his name's . . . . Ps 23:3
for my feet and a light on my **p**. . Ps 119:105
make his **p-s** straight!. . . . . Mt 3:3
some seeds fell along the **p**, ... Mt 13:4
make straight **p-s** for your feet, . . Heb 12:13

PATIENCE

endured with much **p** objects of. . . Rm 9:22
love, joy, peace, **p**, kindness, ... Gl 5:22

PATIENT

Rejoice in hope; be **p** in affliction;. . Rm 12:12
Love is **p**, love is kind. 1Co 13:4
able to teach, and **p**, ... 2Tm 2:24
but is **p** with you, not wanting any . . 2Pt 3:9

PATIENTLY

I waited **p** for the Lord, ... Ps 40:1

PATTERN

according to the **p** you have been
shown on the mountain. . . . . Ex 25:40
according to the **p** that was
shown. . . . . Heb 8:5

PAUL

Early church missionary, theologian, and writer. Also called Saul (Ac 13:9). Citizen of Tarsus, a Benjaminite, raised in Jerusalem as a rabbinical student and Pharisee (Ac 21:39; 22:3,28; 26:5; Gl 1:14; Php 3:5). Persecuted Christians, including Stephen (Ac 8:1; 26:9–11); converted on the way to Damascus (9:1–19); began preaching Christ in Arabia and Damascus and was threatened (9:20–22; Gl 1:17; 2Co 11:32–33).

Introduced to the church at Jerusalem by Barnabas (Ac 9:26–30); carried money with Barnabas from Antioch to Judea (11:27–30). Set apart with Barnabas to go through Cyprus and Galatia as missionaries (Ac 13–14); stoned (Ac 14:19–20). Focused on Gentile evangelism (Ac 9:15; Gl 2:7; Eph 3:8). Attended Jerusalem council (Ac 15). Split with Barnabas over John Mark (15:36–39).

Traveled with Silas and Timothy through Asia Minor and Greece (15:39–16:3). Hindered by the Spirit from entering Bithynia; called to Macedonia in a vision (16:7–10). Beaten, imprisoned, and released in Philippi (16:16–40). Spoke at Areopagus in Athens (17:19–34). Preached at Corinth and Ephesus (Ac 18–19). Said farewell in Ephesus (20:17–38).

Arrested at riot in Jerusalem (21:26–36); testified before the Sanhedrin (23:1–10), Governors Felix and Festus (24:10–21; 25:1–12), and King Agrippa (Ac 26); appealed to Caesar (25:11). Shipwrecked on the way to Rome (Ac 27); ministered in Malta, then Rome (Ac 28).

PAY

until you have **paid** the last penny. . Mt 5:26
Is it lawful to **p** taxes to Caesar. . . . Mt 22:17

P your obligations to everyone: . . . Rm 13:7
not **p-ing** back evil for evil or 1Pt 3:9

PAYMENT

Spirit in our hearts as a down **p**. . . 2Co 1:22
gave us the Spirit as a down **p**. 2Co 5:5
Spirit is the down **p** of our. . . . . . . Eph 1:14

PEACE

favor on you and give you **p**. . . . . . Nm 6:26
seek **p** and pursue it. . . . . Ps 34:14
time for war and a time for **p**. . . . . . . Ec 3:8
Eternal Father, Prince of **P**. . . . . Is 9:6
You will keep ... in perfect **p**. . . . . . . Is 26:3
who proclaims **p**, who brings news . . Is 52:7
P, p, when there is no **p**. . . . . . . Jr 6:14; 8:11
I did not come to bring **p**,. . . . . Mt 10:34
and **p** on earth to people he favors!. . Lk 2:14
P I leave with you. My **I** give . . . . Jn 14:27
we have **p** with God through our . . . Rm 5:1
fruit of the Spirit is love, joy, **p**,. . . . . Gl 5:22
For he is our **p**, who made both . . Eph 2:14
And the **p** of God, which surpasses . .Php 4:7
by making **p** through the blood . . . . Col 1:20
to take **p** from the earth, ... Rv 6:4

PEACEMAKERS

Blessed are the **p**, for they . . . . Mt 5:9

PEARL

or toss your **p-s** before pigs, ... Mt 7:6
When he found one priceless **p**. . Mt 13:46
gate was made of a single **p**. . . . . . Rv 21:21

PEKAH

King of Israel; assassin (2Kg 15:25–31).

PEKAHIAH

Son of Menahem; king of Israel; assassinated by his captain, Pekah (2Kg 15:22–26).

PENTECOST

When the day of **P** had arrived, ... Ac 2:1

PEOPLE

your **p** will be my **p**,. . . . . Ru 1:16
and my **p**, who bear my name. 2Ch 7:14
his **p**, the sheep of his pasture. . . . . Ps 100:3
but sin is a disgrace to any **p**. . . . . . Pr 14:34
They will be my **p**, and I will be. . . . . Jr 24:7
will save his **p** from their sins. . . . . . Mt 1:21
has God rejected his **p**?. . . . . Rm 11:1
God, and they will be my **p**. 2Co 6:16
God, and they will be my **p**. . . . . . . Heb 8:10
a holy nation, a **p** for his possession, . 1Pt 2:9
and language and **p** and nation. . . . . Rv 5:9
will be his **p**, and God himself . . . . . . Rv 21:3

PEOPLE-PLEASERS

Don't work ... as **p**,. . . . . Eph 6:6

PERCEIVE

keep looking, but do not **p**. . . . . Is 6:9
look and look, but never **p**. . . . . . . .Mt 13:14

PERFECT (ADJ)

The instruction of the Lord is **p**,. . . . Ps 19:7
You will keep ... in **p** peace . . . . Is 26:3
Be **p**, therefore, as your heavenly . . Mt 5:48
pleasing, and **p** will of God. . . . . Rm 12:2
But when the **p** comes,. 1Co 13:10
good and **p** gift is from above, ... Jms 1:17
instead, **p** love drives out fear, ... 1Jn 4:18

PERFECT (V)

for my power is **p-ed** in weakness. . 2Co 12:9

PERFECTER

the pioneer and **p** of our faith. . . . . .Heb 12:2

PERISH

If I **p**, I **p**. . . . . Est 4:16
one of these little ones **p**. . . . . Mt 18:14
in him will not **p** but have . . . . Jn 3:16

Don't work for the food that **p-es**. . Jn 6:27
and they will never **p**. . . . . Jn 10:28
foolishness to those who are **p-ing**. . 1Co 1:18
not wanting any to **p** but all to. 2Pt 3:9

PERISHABLE

not of **p** seed but of 1Pt 1:23

PERMISSIBLE

"Everything is **p** for me,". 1Co 6:12
"Everything is **p**," but not 1Co 10:23

PERPLEXED

we are **p** but not in despair;. 2Co 4:8

PERSECUTE

Princes have **p-d** me without . . . .Ps 119:161
blessed when they insult you
and **p** you. Mt 5:11
and pray for those who **p** you, ... Mt 5:44
they **p-d** me, they will also **p** you. . Jn 15:20
Saul, Saul, why are you **p-ing** me? . . Ac 9:4
Bless those who **p** you;. . . . . Rm 12:14
we are **p-d** but not abandoned; . . . 2Co 4:9
in Christ Jesus will be **p-d**. 2Tm 3:12

PERSECUTION

When distress or **p** comes . . . . .Mt 13:21
a severe **p** broke out against . . . . Ac 8:1
or distress or **p** or famine or. . . . . . . Rm 8:35

PERSEVERE

p in these things, for in doing 1Tm 4:16

PERSISTENT

be **p** in prayer. . . . . Rm 12:12

PERSUADE

Are you going to **p** me to become. . Ac 26:28
For I am **p-d** that neither death . . .Rm 8:38
we seek to **p** people. 2Co 5:11
and am **p-d** that he is able. 2Tm 1:12

PERVERSION

to mate with it; it is a **p**. . . . . Lv 18:23

PERVERT

Does God **p** justice?. . . . . Jb 8:3

PERVERTED (ADJ)

in a crooked and **p** generation, ...Php 2:15

PESTERING

because this widow keeps **p** me, . . . Lk 18:5

PESTILENCE

or the **p** that ravages at noon. . . . . . Ps 91:6

PETER

Apostle; originally named Simon; also called Simeon (Ac 15:14) and Cephas. A fisherman in business with James and John (Lk 5:2–3,10); married, lived in Capernaum (Mk 1:21,29–30).

Walked on water (Mt 14:28–31). Confessed Jesus as Messiah (Mt 16:13–20; Mk 8:27–30; Lk 9:18–21). At transfiguration (Mt 17:1–9; Mk 9:2–8; Lk 9:28–36; 2Pt 1:16–18). Jesus predicted he would deny him (Mt 26:31–35; Mk 14:27–31; Lk 22:31–34; Jn 13:36–38); denial (Mt 26:69–75; Mk 14:66–72; Lk 22:54–62; Jn 18:15–18,25–27); restoration to "feed my sheep" (Jn 21:15–19).

Spoke at Pentecost (Ac 2:14–40). Healed people (3:1–10; 5:15; 9:34); raised Tabitha from the dead (9:36–43). Arrested and forbidden to preach (4:1–31; 5:17–41). Saw vision: sent to Cornelius (Ac 10); reported Gentile conversions (Ac 11; 15); confronted by Paul for inconsistency (Gl 2:11–14). Imprisoned by Herod; freed by angel (Ac 12:1–19).

Focused on Jewish evangelism (Gl 2:7). Wrote two letters (1Pt 1:1; 2Pt 1:1).

PETITION
prayer and **p** with thanksgiving,... Php 4:6
I urge that **p-s**, prayers, ...1Tm 2:1

PHARAOH
Then **P** sent for Joseph, ...Gn 41:14
when I receive glory through **P**, ... Ex 14:18
For the Scripture tells **P**, ...Rm 9:17

PHARISEE
surpasses that of the scribes and
P-s..........................Mt 5:20
Then the **P-s** went and plotted....Mt 22:15
woe to you, scribes and **P-s**, ...Mt 23:13
a **P** asked him to dine with him. ....Lk 11:37
one a **P** and the other a tax.......Lk 18:10
I am a **P**, a son of **P-s**!..........Ac 23:6
regarding the law, a **P**; ....Php 3:5

PHILIP
1. Apostle (Mt 10:3; Jn 12:21–22). Invited
Nathanael to "come and see" (Jn 1:43–51);
questioned how to feed the five thousand (6:5–7); asked Jesus to show them
the Father (14:8–9).
2. One of the first seven deacons (Ac 6:1–6);
evangelized Simon the sorcerer in Samaria (8:5–13) and an Ethiopian eunuch
(8:26–39).

PHILIPPI
City in Macedonia where Paul preached (Ac
16:12; 20:6; 1Th 2:2) and to whom he wrote
(Php 1:1; 4:15).

PHILISTINES
People of Philistia (Gn 10:14; 26:1). Originated in Caphtor (Jr 47:4; Am 9:7) as the Casluh
(Gn 10:14).
　Enemies of Israel: Moses and Joshua
did not defeat them (Ex 13:17; Jos 13:2; Jdg
3:1–3). In conflict with Shamgar (3:31); with
Samson (13–16); with Samuel (1Sm 4–7);
with Saul (13–14; 17; 23:27–28; 28:5,15; 31:1–6);
with David (17:20–57; 18:20–27; 19:8; 23:1–5;
30:16; 2Sm 5:17–25; 8:1; 21:15–22; 23:9–13);
with Jehoram (2Ch 21:16); with Uzziah
(26:6–7); with Ahaz (28:18); and with Hezekiah (2Kg 18:8). David hid among them (1Sm
27:1,7,11; 29:11) but did not fight for them
(27:8–12; 29:9).
　Prophesied against (Is 11:14; 14:29–32; Jr
47; Ezk 25:15–17; Am 1:6–8; Ob 19; Zph 2:4–7;
Zch 9:5–7).

PHILOSOPHY
captive through **p** and empty ......Col 2:8

PHYSICIAN
Luke, the dearly loved **p**, ...Col 4:14

PIECE
weighed out thirty **p-s** of silver .. Mt 26:15

PIERCE
they **p-d** my hands and my feet. .. Ps 22:16
But he was **p-d** because of our...... Is 53:5
will look at me whom they **p-d**. .. Zch 12:10
a sword will **p** your own soul.......Lk 2:35
the soldiers **p-d** his side with ......Jn 19:34
will look at the one they **p-d**. ......Jn 19:37

PIG
like a gold ring in a **p-'s** snout......Pr 11:22
or toss your pearls before **p-s**, ...Mt 7:6
a large herd of **p-s** was feeding....Mt 8:30
him into his fields to feed **p-s**......Lk 15:15

PILATE, PONTIUS
Governor of Judea; presided over Jesus's
trial and sentencing (Mt 27:11–26; Mk 15:1–
15; Lk 23:1–25; Jn 18:28–19:16); warned by his
wife (Mt 27:19); gave Jesus's body to Joseph
of Arimathea (Mt 27:58; Mk 15:45; Lk 23:52;

Jn 19:38); assigned guards to the tomb (Mt
27:65).

PILLAR
back and became a **p** of salt...... Gn 19:26
p of cloud by day and the **p** of
fire............................. Ex 13:22
the **p** and foundation of the
truth...........................1Tm 3:15

PINNACLE
stand on the **p** of the
temple,................... Mt 4:5; Lk 4:9

PIT
redeems your life from the **P**; ..... Ps 103:4
blind, both will fall into a **p**........Mt 15:14

PITIED (ADJ)
we should be **p** more than
anyone...................... 1Co 15:19

PLACE SEE ALSO HIGH PLACE, HOLY PLACE
Surely the LORD is in this **p**, ... Gn 28:16
going to prepare a **p** for you? ...... Jn 14:2
they now desire a better **p**. ......Heb 11:16

PLAGUE
to send all my **p-s** against you,.....Ex 9:14
angels with the seven last **p-s**; .....Rv 15:1
add to him the **p-s** that are.......Rv 22:18

PLAIN
and the rough places, a **p**. ....Is 40:4

PLAN
P-s fail when there is no..........Pr 15:22
A man's heart **p-s** his way, but .....Pr 16:9
Many **p-s** are in a man's heart, ...Pr 19:21
I have **p-ned** it; I will also do it. ...Is 46:11

PLANT (N)
will eat the **p-s** of the field........Gn 3:18
grew up before him like a young **p**...Is 53:2

PLANT (V)
LORD God **p-ed** a garden in Eden,... Gn 2:8
like a tree **p-ed** beside flowing...... Ps 1:3
a time to **p** and a time to uproot;... Ec 3:2
I **p-ed**, Apollos watered, but God ...1Co 3:6

PLATTER
the Baptist's head here on a **p**! .... Mt 14:8

PLAY
p skillfully on the strings,..........Ps 33:3
An infant will **p** beside the..........Is 11:8
p-ed the flute for you, but you ... Mt 11:17
eat and drink, and got up to **p**.....1Co 10:7

PLEAD
We **p** on Christ's behalf, ...2Co 5:20

PLEASANT
have fallen for me in **p** places;......Ps 16:6

PLEASE
heaven and does whatever
he **p-s**. .... Ps 115:3
does whatever he **p-s** in heaven... Ps 135:6
the LORD was **p-d** to crush him.....Is 53:10
it will accomplish what I **p** ....Is 55:11
I give it to anyone I **p**............Jr 27:5
The wind blows where it **p-s**, ...Jn 3:8
in the flesh cannot **p** God.........Rm 8:8
even Christ did not **p** himself. ....Rm 15:3
—how he may **p** his wife— 1Co 7:33
as I also try to **p** everyone in 1Co 10:33
am I striving to **p** people? ....Gl 1:10
God was **p-d** to have all his ....Col 1:19
obey ... for this **p-s** the Lord......Col 3:20
in order to **p** men, but............Col 3:22
it is impossible to **p** God, ...Heb 11:6

PLEASING (ADJ)
The sacrifice **p** to God is a ....Ps 51:17
May my meditation be **p** to
him;........................Ps 104:34
living sacrifice, holy and **p** to God;. Rm 12:1
acceptable sacrifice, **p** to God..... Php 4:18

PLEASURE
at your right hand are eternal **p-s**..Ps 16:11
since he takes **p** in him............Ps 22:8
The one who loves **p** will become..Pr 21:17
I take no **p** in the death of the ... Ezk 18:32
according to his good **p** ....Eph 1:9
lovers of **p** rather than lovers 2Tm 3:4
enjoy the fleeting **p** of sin........Heb 11:25

PLOT
and the peoples **p** in vain?..........Ps 2:1

PLOW (N)
swords into **p-s** and their spears .... Is 2:4
Beat your **p-s** into swords and ......Jl 3:10
his hand to the **p** and looks back ...Lk 9:62

PLOW (V)
If you hadn't **p-ed** with my
young.......................Jdg 14:18
he who **p-s** ought to **p** in hope, ...1Co 9:10

PLUMB LINE
I am setting a **p** among my people. Am 7:8

POINT
obedient to the **p** of death .... Php 2:8
yet stumbles in one **p**, is guilty....Jms 2:10

POISON
evil, full of deadly **p**.............. Jms 3:8

POISONOUS
the LORD sent **p** snakes among ....Nm 21:6

POLLUTED
abstain from things **p** by idols, ...Ac 15:20

POOL
your eyes like **p-s** in Heshbon ....Sg 7:4
there is a **p**, called Bethesda ....Jn 5:2

POOR
there will never cease to be **p** .....Dt 15:11
He raises the **p** from the dust 1Sm 2:8
He raises the **p** from the dust .....Ps 113:7
Idle hands make one **p**,...........Pr 10:4
me to bring good news to the **p**. ....Is 61:1
Blessed are the **p** in spirit, ... Mt 5:3
and the **p** are told the good news ..Mt 11:5
You always have the **p** with you, ..Mt 26:11
for your sake he became **p**, ...2Co 8:9

PORE
You **p** over the Scriptures..........Jn 5:39

PORTION
But the LORD's **p** is his people,.....Dt 32:9
strength of my heart, my
p forever.......................Ps 73:26
Jacob's **P** is not like these........Jr 10:16
The LORD is my **p**, therefore I......Lm 3:24
and brought a **p** of it and laid ......Ac 5:2

POSSESS
to give you this land to **p**..........Gn 15:7
nothing yet **p-ing** everything. 2Co 6:10

POSSESSION
Canaan—as a permanent **p**,.......Gn 17:8
chosen you to be his own **p** .. Dt 7:6; 14:2
the ends of the earth your **p** ....Ps 2:8
Honor the LORD with your **p-s**. ....Pr 3:9
in the abundance of his **p-s**. .... Lk 12:15
sold their **p-s** and property ....Ac 2:45
a people for his own **p**,............Ti 2:14
a holy nation, a people for his **p**, ... 1Pt 2:9

POSSIBLE

but with God all things are **p**..... Mt 19:26
If it is **p**, let this cup pass........ Mt 26:39
Everything is **p** for the one who... Mk 9:23
If **p**, as far as it depends on you,.. Rm 12:18

POTTER

we are the clay, and you are our **p**;.. Is 64:8
Just like clay in the **p-'s** hand,...... Jr 18:6
and bought the **p-'s** field with it .. Mt 27:7
Or has the **p** no right over the
   clay,........................ Rm 9:21

POUR

after day they **p** out speech;....... Ps 19:2
p out your hearts before him....... Ps 62:8
I will **p** out my Spirit on your..... Is 44:3
I will **p** out my Spirit on all........ Jl 2:28
of heaven and **p** out a blessing... Mal 3:10
that I will **p** out my Spirit on .... Ac 2:17
even if I am **p-ed** out as a drink .. Php 2:17

POVERTY

your **p** will come like a .... Pr 6:11; 24:34
Give me neither **p** nor wealth;..... Pr 30:8
but she out of her **p** has put in .. Mk 12:44
so that by his **p** you might....... 2Co 8:9

POWER

this purpose: to show you my **p** ... Ex 9:16
Ascribe **p** to God................ Ps 68:34
life are in the **p** of the tongue,.. Pr 18:21
the Scriptures or the **p** of God.... Mt 22:29
right hand of **P** and coming...... Mt 26:64
the kingdom of God come in **p**..... Mk 9:1
you will receive **p** when the Holy ... Ac 1:8
the Holy Spirit and with **p**,........ Ac 10:38
the **p** of God for salvation to .... Rm 1:16
his eternal **p** and divine nature .... Rm 1:20
or things to come, nor **p-s**,....... Rm 8:38
for **p** is perfected in weakness.... 2Co 12:9
the cosmic **p-s** of this darkness.... Eph 6:12
know him and the **p** of his........ Php 3:10
fear, but one of **p**, love,........... 2Tm 1:7
form of godliness but denying
   its **p**......................... 2Tm 3:5
His divine **p** has given us 2Pt 1:3
glory, and **p** belong to our God, ... Rv 19:1

POWERFUL

many **p**, not many of noble 1Co 1:26
are **p** through God for the........ 2Co 10:4

PRACTICE

they don't **p** what they teach..... Mt 23:3
those who **p** such things ... Rm 1:32; Gl 5:21
and are not **p-ing** the truth........ 1Jn 1:6

PRAISE (N)

enthroned on the **p-s** of Israel...... Ps 22:3
his **p** will always be on my lips ..... Ps 34:1
Sing **p** to God, sing **p**;........... Ps 47:6
and his courts with **p**............. Ps 100:4
have prepared **p** from the mouths. .Mt 21:16
For they loved human **p**
   more than .... Jn 12:43
to the **p** of his glorious grace...... Eph 1:6
up to God a sacrifice of **p**, ... Heb 13:15

PRAISE (V)

This is my God, and I will **p** him, ... Ex 15:2
LORD is great and highly **p-d**; 1Ch 16:25
that breathes the LORD........ Ps 150:6
Let another **p** you, and not your.... Pr 27:2
host with the angel, **p-ing** God .... Lk 2:13

PRAY

against the LORD by ceasing to **p**.. 1Sm 12:23
my name, humble themselves, **p** ..2Ch 7:14
we **p-ed** to our God and stationed .Neh 4:9
P for the well-being of Jerusalem:.. Ps 122:6
and **p** for those who persecute you,.. Mt 5:44
you should **p** like this:........... Mt 6:9
the mountain by himself to **p**..... Mt 14:23

teach us to **p**, just as John .... Lk 11:1
I **p** for them. I am not **p-ing** for ... Jn 17:9
know what to **p** for as we should .. Rm 8:26
Every man who **p-s** or prophesies . 1Co 11:4
P at all times in the Spirit........ Eph 6:18
p constantly.................... 1Th 5:17
suffering? He should **p**.......... Jms 5:13

PRAYER

the LORD accepts my **p**.............. Ps 6:9
a house of **p** for all nations....... Is 56:7
will be called a house of **p**........ Mt 21:13
be persistent in **p**. .... Rm 12:12
everything, through **p** and petition ..Php 4:6
which are the **p-s** of the saints...... Rv 5:8

PREACH

the world and **p** the gospel to.... Mk 16:15
how can they **p** unless they are... Rm 10:15
but we **p** Christ crucified,........ 1Co 1:23
p Christ out of envy and strife .... Php 1:15
seen by angels, **p-ed** among the ..1Tm 3:16

PREACHER

how can they hear without a **p**?.. Rm 10:14

PRECIOUS

their lives are **p** in his sight........ Ps 72:14
She is more **p** than jewels;........ Pr 3:15
She is far more **p** than jewels...... Pr 31:10
a tested stone, a **p** cornerstone... Is 28:16
but with the **p** blood of Christ,..... 1Pt 1:19

PREDESTINED

your will had **p** to take place. ...... Ac 4:28
He also **p** to be conformed....... Rm 8:29
a wisdom God **p** before the ages ... 1Co 2:7
He **p** us to be adopted as sons ... Eph 1:5
p according to the plan of the one. .Eph 1:11

PREGNANT

and hit a **p** woman so that her .... Ex 21:22
that she was **p** from the Holy ...... Mt 1:18
will become **p** and give birth to .... Mt 1:23
was engaged to him and was **p**.... Lk 2:5

PREPARE

You **p** a table before me in the ..... Ps 23:5
P the way of the LORD in the....... Is 40:3
Israel, **p** to meet your God! ...... Am 4:12
P the way for the Lord;............ Mt 3:3
he will **p** your way before you..... Mt 11:10
she has **p-d** me for burial....... Mt 26:12
going to **p** a place for you?...... Jn 14:2
God **p-d** this for those who love.... 1Co 2:9
which God **p-d** ahead of time..... Eph 2:10
but you **p-d** a body for me....... Heb 10:5

PRESENCE

the Bread of the **P** on the table .. Ex 25:30
in the **p** of my enemies;.......... Ps 23:5
Do not banish me from your **p** or .. Ps 51:11
Where can I flee from your **p**?..... Ps 139:7
not only in my **p**, but now even ...Php 2:12
appear in the **p** of God for us.... Heb 9:24

PRESENT (ADJ)

things **p** nor things to come,......Rm 8:38
absent in body, I am **p** in spirit,..... 1Co 5:3

PRESENT (V)

I urge you to **p** your bodies as a ... Rm 12:1
He did this to **p** the church to ......Eph 5:27
Be diligent to **p** yourself.........2Tm 2:15

PRESERVE

loses his life will **p** it.............. Lk 17:33

PRESS

good measure—**p-ed** down, shaken. .Lk 6:38

PREVIOUSLY

over the sins committed. .... Rm 3:25
in which you **p** walked according .. Eph 2:2

PRICE

I insist on paying the full **p**,...... 1Ch 21:24
the **p** of him whose **p** was set by .. Mt 27:9
for you were bought at a **p**....... 1Co 6:20
You were bought at a **p**;......... 1Co 7:23

PRICELESS

When he found one **p** pearl, ... Mt 13:46

PRIDE

P comes before destruction, ... Pr 16:18

PRIEST

he was a **p** to God Most High...... Gn 14:18
be my kingdom of **p-s** and my holy . .Ex 19:6
serve me as **p**—Aaron, his sons..... Ex 28:1
You are a **p** forever according to .. Ps 110:4
A **p** happened to be going ... Lk 10:31
a great high **p** who has passed ... Heb 4:14
You are a **p** forever according to ... Heb 5:6
but they will be **p-s** of God and ... Rv 20:6

PRIESTHOOD

a permanent **p** for them.......... Ex 40:15
he holds his **p** permanently....... Heb 7:24
race, a royal **p**, a holy nation 1Pt 2:9

PRINCE

P-s have persecuted me without. .Ps 119:161
Eternal Father, **P** of Peace....... Is 9:6

PRISON

I was in **p** and you visited me'.... Mt 25:36
Peter was kept in **p**, but the church. .Ac 12:5
saw the doors of the **p** standing... Ac 16:27
to the spirits in **p** 1Pt 3:19

PRISONER

The LORD frees **p-s**. .... Ps 146:7
and freedom to the **p-s**;.......... Is 61:1
p of Christ Jesus on behalf........ Eph 3:1

PRIZE

but only one receives the **p**?...... 1Co 9:24
as my goal the **p** promised by.... Php 3:14

PROCLAIM

and I will **p** the name the LORD .... Ex 33:19
P his salvation from day to day . 1Ch 16:23
and the expanse **p-s** the work of
   his .... Ps 19:1
The heavens **p** his righteousness ...Ps 50:6
to **p** liberty to the captives .... Is 61:1
He has sent me to **p** release....... Lk 4:18
you **p** the Lord's death until he ... 1Co 11:26

PRODUCE

A good tree can't **p** bad fruit; ....Mt 7:18
of your faith **p-s** endurance....... Jms 1:3

PROFANE

Do not **p** the name of your God;... Lv 18:21

PROFIT

who hates dishonest **p** prolongs... Pr 28:16
and do business and make a **p**..... Jms 4:13

PROFITABLE

God and is **p** for teaching........ 2Tm 3:16

PROGRESS

for your **p** and joy in the faith, ...Php 1:25
so that your **p** may be evident to..1Tm 4:15

PROMINENT

number of the **p** Greek women.... Ac 17:12

PROMISCUITY

Go and marry a woman of **p** .... Hs 1:2
moral impurity, **p**,................. Gl 5:19

PROMISE (N)

not one **p** has failed............. Jos 23:14
For the **p** is for you and for .... Ac 2:39

of God's **p-s** is "Yes" in him........2Co 1:20
first commandment with a **p**,.....Eph 6:2
since it holds **p** for the present....1Tm 4:8
The Lord does not delay his **p**....2Pt 3:9

PROMISE (V)
This is the land I **p-d** Abraham,.....Dt 34:4
since he who **p-d** is faithful.....Heb 10:23
did not receive what was **p-d**,....Heb 11:39

PROMISED (ADJ)
from the Father the **p** Holy Spirit,..Ac 2:33

PRONOUNCE
he could not **p** it correctly,.......Jdg 12:6

PROOF
to them by many convincing **p-s**....Ac 1:3
the **p** of what is not seen.........Heb 11:1

PROPER
Is it **p** for a woman to pray to.....1Co 11:13
among you, as is **p** for saints......Eph 5:3

PROPERTY
wife Sapphira, sold a piece of **p**......Ac 5:1

PROPHECY
miracles, to another, **p**,..........1Co 12:10
If I have the gift of **p**...........1Co 13:2
But as for **p-ies**, they will come to..1Co 13:8
it was given to you through **p**,....1Tm 4:14
No **p** of Scripture comes from.....2Pt 1:20

PROPHESY
sons and your daughters will **p**,.....Jl 2:28
Lord, didn't we **p** in your name,...Mt 7:22
P to us, Messiah! Who was it....Mt 26:68
sons and your daughters will **p**.....Ac 2:17
and especially that you may **p**.....1Co 14:1
to **p** for 1,260 days, dressed in......Rv 11:3

PROPHET
God will raise up for you a **p** like...Dt 18:15
A **p** is not without honor except...Mt 13:57
be called a **p** of the Most High,.....Lk 1:76
No **p** is accepted in his hometown...Lk 4:24
"Are you the **P**?" "No,"............Jn 1:21
first apostles, second **p-s**,......1Co 12:28
apostles, some **p-s**, some.........Eph 4:11
the beast and the false **p** are,.....Rv 20:10

PROPHETESS
There was also a **p**, Anna,.........Lk 2:36

PROPHETIC
known through the **p** Scriptures,..Rm 16:26
also have the **p** word strongly.....2Pt 1:19

PROSPER
Whatever he does **p-s**.............Ps 1:3
will **p** in what I send it to do........Is 55:11

PROSPERITY
set before you life and **p**,........Dt 30:15
I saw the **p** of the wicked..........Ps 73:3

PROSTITUTE
a **p** named Rahab, and stayed there..Jos 2:1
p-s are entering the kingdom.....Mt 21:31
and make it part of a **p**?..........1Co 6:15

PROTECT
P me as the pupil of your eye;......Ps 17:8
He **p-s** his flock like a shepherd;....Is 40:11
who is able to **p** you from..........Jd 24

PROTECTION
lives under the **p** of the Most High..Ps 91:1

PROUD
Lord, my heart is not **p**;..........Ps 131:1
downfall a person's heart is **p**,....Pr 18:12
arrogant, **p**, boastful, inventors...Rm 1:30

money, boastful, **p**, demeaning....2Tm 3:2
God resists the **p** but gives.......Jms 4:6

PROVE
But God **p-s** his own love for us....Rm 5:8

PROVEN
endurance produces **p** character,...Rm 5:4

PROVERB
Solomon spoke 3,000 **p-s**,.......1Kg 4:32
The **p-s** of Solomon son of David,...Pr 1:1
you will quote this **p** to me:.......Lk 4:23

PROVIDE
God himself will **p** the lamb.......Gn 22:8
all these things will be **p-d** for you..Mt 6:33
he will also **p** the way out.......1Co 10:13
own flesh but **p-s** and cares for it,..Eph 5:29
if anyone does not **p** for his own..1Tm 5:8
richly **p-s** us with all things.......1Tm 6:17

PROVOKE
tested God and **p-d** the Holy One..Ps 78:41

PROWLING
the devil is **p** around like a........1Pt 5:8

PRUNES
and he **p** every branch that........Jn 15:2

PSALM
and the **P-s** must be fulfilled.....Lk 24:44
speaking to one another in **p-s**,..Eph 5:19

PUBLIC
your attention to **p** reading,......1Tm 4:13

PUBLICLY
not wanting to disgrace her **p**......Mt 1:19
P rebuke those who sin, so that..1Tm 5:20

PUNISH
the Lord has **p-ed** him for the.....Is 53:6
and **p-es** every son he receives....Heb 12:6

PUNISHMENT
My **p** is too great to bear!.......Gn 4:13
p for our peace was on him,......Is 53:5
son won't suffer **p** for the father's..Ezk 18:20
they will go away into eternal **p**,..Mt 25:46
because fear involves **p**.........1Jn 4:18

PUPIL
protected him as the **p** of his eye..Dt 32:10
Protect me as the **p** of your eye;....Ps 17:8

PURCHASED
which he **p** with his own blood....Ac 20:28

PURE
The fear of the Lord is **p**,.........Ps 19:9
can a young man keep his way **p**?..Ps 119:9
eyes are too **p** to look on evil,.....Hab 1:13
Blessed are the **p** in heart,........Mt 5:8
whatever is just, whatever is **p**,...Php 4:8
To the **p**, everything is **p**, but to...Ti 1:15
from a **p** heart love one another..1Pt 1:22

PURIFICATION
After making **p** for sins, he sat.....Heb 1:3

PURIFY
P me with hyssop, and I will be.....Ps 51:7
he will **p** the sons of Levi and.....Mal 3:3

PURIM
reason these days are called **P**,...Est 9:26

PURITY
by **p**, by knowledge, by patience,..2Co 6:6

PURPLE
crown of thorns and the **p** robe.....Jn 19:5

PURPOSE
has prepared everything for his **p**..Pr 16:4
because I was sent for this **p**......Lk 4:43
are called according to his **p**.......Rm 8:28
so that God's **p** according to......Rm 9:11
and to work out his good **p**......Php 2:13

PURSUE
seek peace and **p** it.............Ps 34:14
who did not **p** righteousness,.....Rm 9:30
and **p** righteousness, godliness....1Tm 6:11
P peace with everyone, and......Heb 12:14
Let him seek peace and **p** it,......1Pt 3:11

PURSUIT
futile, a **p** of the wind...........Ec 1:14

PUT
But **p** on the Lord Jesus Christ,....Rm 13:14
P on the full armor of God so.....Eph 6:11

- Q -

QUAIL
So at evening **q** came...........Ex 16:13

QUAKE
earth **q-d**, and the rocks were
  split.....................Mt 27:51

QUALITY
will test the **q** of each one's.......1Co 3:13

QUARREL
The Lord's servant must not **q**,...2Tm 2:24

QUARRELSOME
but gentle, not **q**, not greedy.....1Tm 3:3

QUEEN
The **q** of Sheba heard about......1Kg 10:1
The **q** of the south will rise up....Mt 12:42

QUICK
Everyone must be **q** to listen,.....Jms 1:19

QUICKLY
What you're doing, do **q**.........Jn 13:27
I am coming **q**. Hold on to what....Rv 3:11
Yes, I am coming **q**.............Rv 22:20

QUIET
He leads me beside **q** waters......Ps 23:2
a tranquil and **q** life in all........1Tm 2:2
of a gentle and **q** spirit,..........1Pt 3:4

QUIVER
who has filled his **q** with them.....Ps 127:5

QUOTA
require the same **q** of bricks.......Ex 5:8

- R -

RABBI
do not be called '**R**,' because you..Mt 23:8

RABBONI
she said to him in Aramaic, "**R**!"...Jn 20:16

RACE (N)
the **r** is not to the swift,..........Ec 9:11
I have finished the **r**, I have kept...2Tm 4:7
endurance the **r** that lies before...Heb 12:1
you are a chosen **r**, a royal........1Pt 2:9

RACE (V)
the runners in a stadium all **r**,....1Co 9:24

RACHEL
Daughter of Laban; wife and cousin of
Jacob (Gn 29:10,18-30); mother of Joseph

and Benjamin (30:24; 35:16–20); stole her
father's household idols (31:19).
R weeping for her children; . . . . Mt 2:18

RADIANCE
The Son is the r of God's glory, ... Heb 1:3

RAGE (N)
king's r is like the roaring of a
  lion, ... Pr 19:12

RAGE (V)
Why do the Gentiles r and . . . . Ac 4:25

RAHAB
Prostitute in Jericho who hid the Israelite
spies (Jos 2; Heb 11:31); spared by Joshua
(Jos 6:17,22–25). Mother of Boaz (Mt 1:5).

RAIN (N)
and the r fell on the earth forty . . . . Gn 7:12
and sends r on the righteous and . . Mt 5:45

RAIN (V)
prayed ... that it would not r, ... Jms 5:17

RAISE
I will r up for them a prophet . . . . . Dt 18:18
LORD r-d up judges, who saved . . . . Jdg 2:16
God is able to r up children for . . . . . Mt 3:9
killed, and be r-d the third day . . . . Mt 16:21
and on the third day he will be r . . . Mt 20:19
and I will r it up in three days . . . . . . Jn 2:19
and I will r him up on the last . . . . . Jn 6:40
God has r this Jesus. . . . . Ac 2:32
and r-d for our justification. . . . . . . Rm 4:25
that he was r-d on the third 1Co 15:4
dead will be r-d incorruptible, ... 1Co 15:52
who r-d the Lord Jesus will r us . . . 2Co 4:14
He also r-d us up with him and. . . . Eph 2:6

RAM
and saw a r caught in the thicket . . Gn 22:13

RANSOM (N)
these cannot ... pay his r to God . . . . Ps 49:7
to give his life as a r for many. . . . Mt 20:28
gave himself as a r for all, ... 1Tm 2:6

RANSOM (V)
r-ed of the LORD will return. . . Is 35:10; 51:11
for the LORD has r-ed Jacob and . . . . Jr 31:11

RASHLY
something r and later to
  reconsider . . . . Pr 20:25

RAVEN
he sent out a r. . . . . Gn 8:7
The r-s kept bringing him bread. . . 1Kg 17:6
Consider the r-s: They don't sow . . Lk 12:24

READ
Sabbath day and stood up to r . . . . . . Lk 4:16
you understand what you're
  r-ing? . . . . Ac 8:30
your attention to public r-ing, ... 1Tm 4:13
Blessed is the one who r-s aloud . . . . Rv 1:3

READY
R ... to give a defense 1Pt 3:15

REALITY
faith is the r of what is hoped . . . . Heb 11:1

REALLY
Did God r say, 'You can't eat from . . . Gn 3:1

REAP
sow in tears will r with shouts . . . . Ps 126:5
the wind and r the whirlwind . . . . Hs 8:7
They don't sow or r or gather . . . . . Mt 6:26
a person sows he will also r, ... Gl 6:7
r, for the time to r has come, ... Rv 14:15

REASON (N)
They hated me for no r. . . . . Jn 15:25
asks you for a r for the hope 1Pt 3:15

REASON (V)
So he r-ed in the synagogue with . . Ac 17:17
a child, I r-ed like a child. 1Co 13:11

REBEKAH
Sister of Laban; wife of Isaac (Gn 24); mother of Jacob and Esau (25:21–26). Passed off
as Isaac's sister (26:6–11). Encouraged Jacob
to secure Isaac's blessing (27:1–17).

REBEL
Only don't r against the LORD, ... Nm 14:9
but they have r-led against me . . . . . . Is 1:2

REBELLION
For r is like the sin of divination, . . 1Sm 15:23
the wicked increase, r increases . . . Pr 29:16

REBELLIOUS
a stubborn and r generation, ... Ps 78:8
unbelieving and r generation! . . . . Mt 17:17

REBUILD
to go up and r the LORD's house . . . . Ezr 1:5
Come, let's r Jerusalem's wall. . . . . . Neh 2:17
and the ruins will be rebuilt . . . . . Ezk 36:33
temple of God and r it in three
  days. . . . . Mt 26:61

REBUKE
do not r me in your anger; . . . . Ps 6:1
The LORD r you, Satan! . . . . Zch 3:2
he got up and r-d the winds . . . . . . Mt 8:26
Don't r an older man, ... 1Tm 5:1
Publicly r those who sin, ... 1Tm 5:20
profitable for teaching, for r-ing, . . 2Tm 3:16
correct, r, and encourage with. 2Tm 4:2
him but said, "The Lord r you!" . . . . . . Jd 9
many as I love, I r and discipline . . . Rv 3:19

RECEIVE
who asks r-s, and the one who . . . . . Mt 7:8
But to all who did r him, he gave . . . Jn 1:12
Ask and you will r, ... Jn 16:24
But you will r power when the . . . . . . Ac 1:8
is more blessed to give than to r . . Ac 20:35
What do you have that you
  didn't r? 1Co 4:7
For I r-d from the Lord what I . . . 1Co 11:23
as you have r-d Christ Jesus . . . . Col 2:6

RECOGNIZE
r-d his brothers, they did not r him . . Gn 42:8
opened, and they r-d him, but . . . Lk 24:31
yet the world did not r him . . . . Jn 1:10

RECONCILE
First go and be r-d with your . . . . . Mt 5:24
Christ's behalf, "Be r-d to God." . . . 2Co 5:20
that he might r both to God . . . . . . Eph 2:16
through him to r everything to . . . . Col 1:20

RECONCILIATION
we have now received this r . . . . . . Rm 5:11
if their rejection brings r. . . . . Rm 11:15
has given us the ministry of r; 2Co 5:18

RECONSIDER
rashly and later to r his vows . . . . . Pr 20:25

RECORD
does not keep a r of wrongs 1Co 13:5

RECRUCIFYING
they are r the Son of God . . . . Heb 6:6

RED
Don't gaze at wine because it is r, . . Pr 23:31
they are crimson r, ... Is 1:18
good weather because the sky is r'. . Mt 16:2

another horse went out,
  a fiery r one, ... Rv 6:4

RED SEA
Crossed by Israel (Ex 13:18; 14:15–31; Nm
21:14; Dt 11:4; Jos 2:10; 4:23; 24:6; Neh 9:9;
Pss 106:7,9–11,22; 136:13–15; Ac 7:36; Heb
11:29); southern extent of the promised
land (Ex 23:31); location of Solomon's fleet
(1Kg 9:26).

REDEEM
I will r you with an outstretched
  arm . . . . Ex 6:6
to r a people for himself, ... 2Sm 7:23
the price of r-ing him is too costly, . . Ps 49:8
He r-s your life from the Pit; . . . . . Ps 103:4
Christ r-ed us from the curse . . . . . . Gl 3:13
to r those under the law, ... Gl 4:5

REDEEMED (N)
Let the r of the LORD . . . . Ps 107:2

REDEEMER
I know that my R lives, ... Jb 19:25
LORD, my rock and my R. . . . . Ps 19:14
for their R is strong, ... Pr 23:11
Your R is the Holy One of Israel. . . . Is 41:14

REDEMPTION
because your r is near! . . . . Lk 21:28
adoption, the r of our bodies. . . . . . Rm 8:23
In him we have r through his blood, . . Eph 1:7
We have r, the forgiveness of sins. . Col 1:14
having obtained eternal r. . . . . Heb 9:12

REED
He will not break a bruised r, ... Is 42:3
A r swaying in the wind? . . . . Mt 11:7
He will not break a bruised r . . . . . Mt 12:20

REFINER
For he will be like a r-'s fire . . . . Mal 3:2

REFRESHING (N)
that seasons of r may come . . . . Ac 3:19

REFUGE
will include six cities of r, ... Nm 35:6
whose wings you have come for r. . . Ru 2:12
God is our r and strength, ... Ps 46:1
shield to those who take r in him. . . Pr 30:5
we who have fled for r might . . . . Heb 6:18

REFUTE
For he vigorously r-d the Jews in . . Ac 18:28

REGARD (N)
The LORD had r for Abel and his . . . . Gn 4:4

REGARD (V)
but we in turn r-ed him stricken, . . . Is 53:4

REGENERATION
through the washing of r and . . . . . . Ti 3:5

REGION
In the same r, shepherds were . . . . . . Lk 2:8

REGISTER
that the whole empire should
  be r-ed. . . . . Lk 2:1

REGRET
LORD r-ted that he had made man . . Gn 6:6
I r that I made Saul king, ... 1Sm 15:11

REGULATIONS
Why do you submit to r: . . . . Col 2:20

REHOBOAM
Son of Solomon; king of Judah (1Kg 11:43).
Answered people harshly; the kingdom was
divided (12:1–19; 2Ch 10:1–19).

REIGN

The LORD will **r** forever and ever! . . Ex 15:18
The LORD **r-s**! He is robed in . . . . Ps 93:1
The LORD **r-s** forever; . . . . Ps 146:10
who says to Zion, "Your God **r-s**!" . . . Is 52:7
He will **r** over the house of . . . . Lk 1:33
death **r-ed** from Adam to Moses, . . Rm 5:14
do not let sin **r** in your mortal . . . . . Rm 6:12
For he must **r** until he puts all 1Co 15:25
we will also **r** with him; 2Tm 2:12
and he will **r** forever and ever . . . . . . Rv 11:15
will **r** with him a thousand years. . . Rv 20:6

REJECT

LORD, he has **r-ed** you as king 1Sm 15:23
stone that the builders **r-ed** has . . Ps 118:22
He was despised and **r-ed** by men, . . Is 53:3
the builders **r-ed** has become . . . . Mt 21:42
Whoever **r-s** you **r-s** me . . . . Lk 10:16
but the one who **r-s** the Son . . . . . . Jn 3:36
has God **r-ed** his people? . . . . Rm 11:1
r-ed by men but chosen and 1Pt 2:4

REJOICE

all who take refuge in you **r**; . . . . Ps 5:11
let's **r** and be glad in it . . . . Ps 118:24
R greatly, Daughter Zion! . . . . Zch 9:9
but **r** that your names are written. . Lk 10:20
R with those who **r**; . . . . Rm 12:15
but **r-s** in the truth 1Co 13:6
R in the Lord always. I will say it
again: **R**! . . . . Php 4:4
R always, ... 1Th 5:16

RELATIONS

men ... left natural **r** with women. . Rm 1:27

RELATIVE

The man is a close **r**. . . . . Ru 2:20
in his hometown, among his **r-s**, . . . Mk 6:4

RELEASE

do you want me to **r** for you? . . . . . Mt 27:21

RELENT

and **r** concerning this disaster . . . . . Ex 32:12
but the LORD **r-ed** concerning . . . 2Sm 24:16
may turn and **r** and leave a blessing . . Jl 2:14
so God **r-ed** from the disaster . . . . . Jnh 3:10

RELIGION

and undefiled **r** before God . . . . Jms 1:27

RELIGIOUS

are extremely **r** in every respect. . . Ac 17:22

RELY

He **r-ies** on the LORD; let him . . . . . Ps 22:8
do not rely on your own understanding; . . Pr 3:5
What are you **r-ing** on? . . . . Is 36:4
all who **r** on the works of the law. . Gl 3:10

REMAIN

the word of our God **r-s** forever . . . . Is 40:8
R in me, and I in you . . . . Jn 15:4
three **r**: faith, hope, and love. 1Co 13:13
they would have **r-ed** with us. 1Jn 2:19

REMARKABLE

and look at this **r** sight . . . . Ex 3:3

REMARKABLY

been **r** and wondrously made . . . . . Ps 139:14

REMEMBER

God **r-ed** Noah, ... Gn 8:1
R the Sabbath day, to keep it holy: . . Ex 20:8
human being that you **r** him, ... Ps 8:4
made of, **r-ing** that we are dust. . Ps 103:14
So **r** your Creator in the days . . . . . . Ec 12:1
own sake and **r** your sins no more . . Is 43:25
and never again **r** their sin. . . . . . . Jr 31:34
R Lot's wife! . . . . Lk 17:32
asked only that we would **r** the poor . . Gl 2:10

R my chains. . . . . Col 4:18
I will never again **r** their sins . . . . . Heb 8:12

REMEMBRANCE

there is no **r** of you in death; . . . . . . Ps 6:5
Do this in **r** of me. . . . . . . Lk 22:19; 1Co 11:24

REMIND

r you of everything I have told
you . . . . Jn 14:26

REMINDER

there is a **r** of sins year after
year . . . . Heb 10:3

REMNANT

For a **r** will go out from 2Kg 19:31
our God to preserve a **r** for us . . . . . Ezr 9:8
The **r** will return, the **r** of Jacob, . . . Is 10:21
I will gather the **r** of my flock . . . . . Jr 23:3
only the **r** will be saved; . . . . Rm 9:27

REMOTE

by boat to a **r** place to be alone . . . Mt 14:13

REMOVAL

not as the **r** of the dirt from 1Pt 3:21

REMOVE

R the sandals from your feet, ... Jos 5:15
so far has he **r-d** our . . . . Ps 103:12
I will **r** your heart of stone and . . . Ezk 36:26

RENEW

He **r-s** my life; he leads me along . . . Ps 23:3
and **r** a steadfast spirit within me. . Ps 51:10
youth is **r-ed** like the eagle . . . . . . Ps 103:5
the LORD will **r** their strength; . . . . . Is 40:31
by the **r-ing** of your mind, ... Rm 12:2
person is being **r-ed** day by day . . . 2Co 4:16
is impossible to **r** to repentance . . . Heb 6:4

RENEWAL

regeneration and **r** by the
Holy Spirit. Ti 3:5

REPAY

deserve or **repaid** us according to . . Ps 103:10
Do not **r** anyone evil for evil . . . . . . Rm 12:17
I will **r**, says the Lord . . . . Rm 12:19
that no one **r-s** evil for evil 1Th 5:15

REPEAT

R them to your children . . . . Dt 6:7

REPENT

R, because the kingdom of heaven . . Mt 3:2
who **r-s** than over ninety-nine . . . . Lk 15:7
R and be baptized, ... Ac 2:38
all people everywhere to **r**, ... Ac 17:30

REPENTANCE

fruit consistent with **r**. . . . . Mt 3:8
a baptism of **r** for the forgiveness . . Mk 1:4
righteous, but sinners to **r** . . . . Lk 5:32
r for forgiveness of sins . . . . Lk 24:47
and do works worthy of **r** . . . . Ac 26:20
is intended to lead you to **r**? . . . . . . Rm 2:4
godly grief produces a **r** 2Co 7:10
any to perish but all to come to **r**. . . 2Pt 3:9

REPRIMAND

Better an open **r** than concealed . . . . Pr 27:5

REPROACH

must be above **r**, the husband of . . . 1Tm 3:2
he considered **r** for the sake of . . . Heb 11:26

REPUTATION

have a good **r** among outsiders, ... 1Tm 3:7
you have a **r** for being alive, ... Rv 3:1

REQUEST

your **r-s** be made known to God. . . Php 4:6

REQUIRE

what it is the LORD **r-s** of you: . . . . . Mc 6:8
much will be **r-d**; . . . . Lk 12:48

REQUIREMENT

in order that the law's **r** would . . . . . Rm 8:4

RESCUE

let the LORD **r** him, since he . . . . Ps 22:8
the LORD **r-s** him from them all. . . . Ps 34:19
R those being taken off to death, . . Pr 24:11
He trusts in God; let God **r** him . . . Mt 27:43
has **r-d** us from the domain of . . . . Col 1:13
r-s us from the coming wrath. 1Th 1:10
Lord knows how to **r** the godly 2Pt 2:9

RESIDE

Christ's power may **r** in me 2Co 12:9
has eternal life **r-ing** in him. 1Jn 3:15

RESIDENCE

I will place my **r** among you, ... Lv 26:11

RESIST

tell you, don't **r** an evildoer . . . . Mt 5:39
are always **r-ing** the Holy Spirit . . . . Ac 7:51
For who **r-s** his will? . . . . Rm 9:19
may be able to **r** in the evil day . . . Eph 6:13
have not yet **r-ed** to the point . . . . Heb 12:4
R the devil, and he will flee . . . . Jms 4:7

RESOUND

sea and all that fills it **r**. . . . . Ps 96:11
Praise him with **r-ing** cymbals; . . . Ps 150:5

RESPECT (N)

r to those you owe **r**, ... Rm 13:7
masters as worthy of all **r**, ... 1Tm 6:1
do this with gentleness and **r**, ... 1Pt 3:16

RESPECT (V)

Each of you is to **r** his mother . . . . . Lv 19:3
'They will **r** my son,' he said. . . . . . Mt 21:37
the wife is to **r** her husband . . . . . Eph 5:33

REST (N)

be a Sabbath of complete **r**, ... Ex 31:15
They will not enter my **r**. . . . . Ps 95:11
and find **r** for yourselves . . . . Jr 6:16
and I will give you **r**. . . . . Mt 11:28
Sabbath **r** remains for God's people. . Heb 4:9

REST (V)

he **r-ed** on the seventh day . . . . Gn 2:2

RESTORE

the LORD **r-d** his fortunes and . . . . . Jb 42:10
R the joy of your salvation to me, . . Ps 51:12
is coming and will **r** everything, . . . Mt 17:11
it out, and his hand was **r-d**. . . . . . . Mk 3:5
are you **r-ing** the kingdom to Israel. . Ac 1:6
spiritual, **r** such a person . . . . Gl 6:1

RESTRAIN

know what currently **r-s** him, ... 2Th 2:6

RESTRAINT

because in his **r** God passed over . . Rm 3:25

RESURRECTION

in the **r** ... whose wife will she be. . Mt 22:28
the **r** of life ... the **r** of
condemnation . . . . Jn 5:29
I am the **r** and the life. . . . . Jn 11:25
if there is no **r** of the dead, ... 1Co 15:13
know him and the power of his **r** . . Php 3:10
This is the first **r**. . . . . Rv 20:5

RETAIN

r the sins of any, they are **r-ed** . . . Jn 20:23

RETURN

you are dust, and you will **r** to dust. . Gn 3:19
the spirit **r-s** to God who gave . . . . . Ec 12:7

REUBEN

mouth will not **r** to me empty, ... Is 55:11
Come, let's **r** to the Lord. . . . . Hs 6:1

REUBEN

Son of Jacob and Leah; eldest (Gn 29:32).
Lost birthright for sleeping with father's
concubine (35:22; 49:4; 1Ch 5:1). Tried to rescue Joseph (Gn 37:21–29); offered to protect
Benjamin (42:37). Tribe with territory east
of the Dead Sea, north of the Arnon River
(Nm 32; Jos 13:15–23).

REVEAL

the arm of the Lord been **r-ed**? . . . . . Is 53:1
whom the Son desires to **r** him. . . . Mt 11:27
blood did not **r** this to you, ... Mt 16:17
him and will **r** myself to him. . . . . Jn 14:21
of his heart will be **r-ed**, ... 1Co 14:25

REVELATION

Without **r** people run wild, ... Pr 29:18
light for **r** to the Gentiles . . . . Lk 2:32
eagerly wait for the **r** of
   our Lord 1Co 1:7
has a hymn, a teaching, a **r**, ... 1Co 14:26
it came by a **r** of Jesus. . . . . Gl 1:12
was made known to me by **r**, ... Eph 3:3
at the **r** of the Lord Jesus 2Th 1:7
at the **r** of Jesus Christ 1Pt 1:7
The **r** of Jesus Christ that God gave . . Rv 1:1

REVERE

descendants of Israel, **r** him! . . . . . . Ps 22:23

REVERENCE

a place for your **r** forever. 2Ch 6:2
serve God acceptably, with **r** . . . . Heb 12:28

REVERENT

observe your pure, **r** lives. 1Pt 3:2

REVILE

When we are **r-d**, we bless; 1Co 4:12

REVIVE

Will you not **r** us again so that . . . . . Ps 85:6

REWARD (N)

there is a **r** for the righteous! . . . . . Ps 58:11
from the Lord, offspring, a **r** . . . . . . Ps 127:3
and his **r** accompanies him. . . . . Is 40:10
your **r** is great in heaven. . . . . Mt 5:12
they have their **r**. . . . . Mt 6:2,5,16
survives, he will receive a **r** 1Co 3:14
looking ahead to the **r**. . . . . Heb 11:26

REWARD (V)

that he **r-s** those who seek him. . . . Heb 11:6

RIB

God made the **r** . . . into a woman. . . Gn 2:22

RICH

Don't wear yourself out to get **r**; . . . Pr 23:4
in a hurry to get **r** will not . . . . Pr 28:20
hard for a **r** person to enter . . . . . . Mt 19:23
woe to you who are **r**, ... Lk 6:24
who want to be **r** fall into 1Tm 6:9
r boast in his humiliation . . . . Jms 1:10

RICHES

and you have not requested **r** 2Ch 1:11
in her left, **r** and honor. . . . . Pr 3:16
make known the **r** of his glory . . . Rm 9:23
Oh, the depth of the **r** . . . . Rm 11:33
immeasurable **r** of his grace. . . . . . . Eph 2:7

RIDDLE

directly, openly, and not in **r-s**; . . . . Nm 12:8
"Let me tell you a **r**," Samson said . . Jdg 14:12
words of the wise, and their **r-s**. . . . . Pr 1:6

RIDE

humble and **r-ing** on a donkey, ... Zch 9:9

RIDER

horse and its **r** into the sea. . . . . . . Ex 15:1,21

RIGHT (ADJ)

So you are **r** when you pass . . . . Ps 51:4
Sit at my **r** hand until I make . . . . Ps 110:1
way that seems **r** to a person, . . Pr 14:12; 16:25
one on your **r** and the other on. . . Mt 20:21
Sit at my **r** hand until I put. . . . . . . Mt 22:44
He will put the sheep on his **r** . . . . Mt 25:33
He also is at the **r** hand of God . . . . Rm 8:34
Sit at my **r** hand until I make . . . . . . Heb 1:13
sat down at the **r** hand of God. . . . Heb 10:12

RIGHT (N)

Defend the **r-s** of the fatherless. . . . . Is 1:17
gave them the **r** to be children . . . . Jn 1:12

RIGHTEOUS (ADJ)

no one alive is **r** in your sight. . . . . . Ps 143:2
raise up a **R** Branch of David. . . . . . . Jr 23:5
But the **r** one will live by his faith. . Hab 2:4
Joseph, being a **r** man, and not . . . . . Mt 1:19
saying, "This man really was **r**!" . . . Lk 23:47
the coming of the **R** One, ... Ac 7:52
is no one **r**, not even one. . . . . Rm 3:10
But my **r** one will live by faith; . . Heb 10:38
Jesus Christ the **r** one. 1Jn 2:1

RIGHTEOUS (N)

watches over the way of the **r** . . . . . . Ps 1:6
I have not seen the **r** abandoned . . Ps 37:25
The **r** will never be shaken, ... Pr 10:30
the **r** run to it and are protected. . . Pr 18:10
sends rain on the **r** and the . . . . Mt 5:45
I didn't come to call the **r** . . . . Mk 9:13
The **r** will live by faith. . . . . Rm 1:17
because the **r** will live by faith. . . . . . Gl 3:11

RIGHTEOUSLY

He will judge the world **r** . . . . Ps 98:9

RIGHTEOUSNESS

He credited it to him as **r**. . . . . Gn 15:6
He judges the world with **r**; . . . . Ps 9:8
His **r** endures forever. . . . . . . Pss 111:3; 112:3
R exalts a nation, but sin is . . . . Pr 14:34
will be named: The Lord is Our **R**. . . Jr 23:6
those who hunger and thirst
   for **r**, ... Mt 5:6
kingdom of God and his **r**, ... Mt 6:33
apart from the law, the **r** of God. . . Rm 3:21
it was credited to him for **r**. . . . . Rm 4:3
end of the law for **r** to everyone. . . Rm 10:4
His **r** endures forever. 2Co 9:9
r like armor on your chest, ... Eph 6:14
reserved for me the crown of **r**, . . . 2Tm 4:8
was credited to him as **r** . . . . Jms 2:23

RING

is like a gold **r** in a pig's snout. . . . . . Pr 11:22

RISE

From the **r-ing** of the sun to its . . . Ps 113:3
After three days I will **r** again. . . . . . Mt 27:63
For he has **r-n**, just as he said. . . . . . Mt 28:6
He is **r-n**! He is not here!. . . . . Mk 16:6
A great prophet has **r-n** among us, . Lk 7:16
that Jesus died and **rose** again, ... 1Th 4:14
dead in Christ will **r** first. 1Th 4:16

RIVALRY

that there is **r** among you. 1Co 1:11
proclaim Christ out of **r**. . . . . Php 1:17
Do nothing out of **r** or conceit, ... Php 2:3

RIVER

There is a **r**—its streams . . . . Ps 46:4
By the **r-s** of Babylon—there we . . . Ps 137:1
make peace flow to her like a **r**, . . . Is 66:12
were baptized by him in the
   Jordan **R**. . . . . Mt 3:6
showed me the **r** of the
   water of life, ... Rv 22:1

ROAD

r broad that leads to destruction, . . . Mt 7:13

ROAR

though its water **r-s** and foams . . . . Ps 46:3
The Lord **r-s** from on high; . . . . Jr 25:30
The Lord will **r** from Zion and . . . . . . Jl 3:16

ROARING (ADJ)

prowling around like a **r** lion, ... 1Pt 5:8

ROAST

they should eat it, **r-ed** over
   the fire . . . . Ex 12:8
A lazy hunter doesn't **r** his game, . . Pr 12:27

ROB

to meet a bear **r-bed** of her cubs . . Pr 17:12
Will a man **r** God? Yet you are . . . . . Mal 3:8

ROBBER

this house ... become a den of **r-s**. . . Jr 7:11
and fell into the hands of **r-s**. . . . . . Lk 10:30

ROBE

and he made a long-sleeved **r**. . . . . Gn 37:3
cut off the corner of Saul's **r**. 1Sm 24:4
hem of his **r** filled the temple. . . . . . . Is 6:1
If I can just touch his **r**, ... Mt 9:21
and his **r** was as white as snow. . . . Mt 28:3
crown of thorns and the purple **r**. . . Jn 19:5
He wore a **r** dipped in blood, ... Rv 19:13

ROBED (V)

He is **r** in majesty; . . . . Ps 93:1

ROCK

when you hit the **r**, water will . . . . . Ex 17:6
will put you in the crevice
   of the **r**. Ex 33:22
and struck the **r** twice with his . . . Nm 20:11
The Lord is my **r**, ... Ps 18:2
Lord, my **r** and my Redeemer. . . . . . Ps 19:14
and set my feet on a **r**, ... Ps 40:2
and a **r** to trip over, ... Is 8:14
who built his house on the **r**. . . . . . Mt 7:24
on this **r** I will build my church, . . . Mt 16:18
Other seed fell on the **r**; . . . . Lk 8:6
and a **r** to trip over, ... Rm 9:33
drank from a spiritual **r** that followed
   them, and that **r** was Christ. . . 1Co 10:4
and a **r** to trip over. 1Pt 2:8

ROCKY

Other seed fell on **r** ground, ... Mt 13:5

ROD

your **r** and your staff—they . . . . Ps 23:4
not use the **r** hates his son, ... Pr 13:24
with a **r**, he will not die. . . . . Pr 23:13

ROLL

The sky will **r** up like a scroll, ... Is 34:4
Who will **r** away the stone from . . . Mk 16:3
very large—had been **r-ed** away. . . . Mk 16:4

ROMAN

Tell me, are you a **R** citizen? . . . . . . Ac 22:27

ROME

Italian city, capital of the Roman Empire;
represented at Pentecost (Ac 2:10); Jews expelled (18:2); Paul addressed a letter to the
church there (Rm 1:7,15) and goes there (Ac
19:21; 23:11; 28:14–16; 2Tm 1:17).

ROOF

From the **r** he saw a woman 2Sm 11:2
went up on the **r** and lowered him. . Lk 5:19

ROOM

you pray, go into your private **r**, ... Mt 6:6
there was no guest **r** available . . . . . . Lk 2:7
Father's house are many **r-s**. . . . . . . Jn 14:2

ROOSTER

before the **r** crows, you will . . . . . . Mt 26:34

ROOT

On that day the **r** of Jesse will. . . . . . Is 11:10
and like a **r** out of dry ground. . . . . . . Is 53:2
since it had no **r**, it withered . . . . . . Mt 13:6
And if the **r** is holy, so are the . . . . . Rm 11:16
The **r** of Jesse will appear, ... Rm 15:12
r-ed and firmly established. . . . . . . Eph 3:17
r-ed and built up in him and . . . . . . Col 2:7
of money is a **r** of all kinds. 1Tm 6:10
and that no **r** of bitterness. . . . . Heb 12:15
of Judah, the **R** of David, ... Rv 5:5

ROUGH

and the **r** places, a plain. . . . . Is 40:4
straight, the **r** ways smooth, ... Lk 3:5

ROYAL

if you fulfill the **r** law prescribed. . . Jms 2:8
a chosen race, a **r** priesthood, a 1Pt 2:9

RUIN (N)

his lips invites his own **r**. . . . . Pr 13:3
my house still lies in **r**-s . . . . Hg 1:9
desires, which plunge people
    into **r**. 1Tm 6:9
leads to the **r** of those who
    listen. 2Tm 2:14

RUIN (V)

Woe is me for I am **r**-ed . . . . Is 6:5
and the skins are **r**-ed. . . . . Mt 9:17

RULE (N)

when he abolishes all **r** and all . . . 1Co 15:24
he competes according to the **r**-s. . 2Tm 2:5

RULE (V)

They will **r** the fish of the sea . . . . . . Gn 1:26
He **r**-s forever by his might; . . . . Ps 66:7
For sin will not **r** over you, ... Rm 6:14

RULER

and the **r**-s conspire together
    against . . . . Ps 2:2
one will come from you to be **r** . . . . . Mc 5:2
know that the **r**-s of the
    Gentiles . . . . Mt 20:25
Now the **r** of this world will be . . . . Jn 12:31
death nor life, nor angels nor **r**-s, . Rm 8:38
but against the **r**-s, against . . . . . . Eph 6:12
Remind them to submit to **r**-s. . . . . . . Ti 3:1

RUMOR

to hear of wars and **r**-s of wars. . . . Mt 24:6

RUN

his word **r**-s swiftly. . . . . Ps 147:15
righteous **r** to it and are
    protected. . . . . Pr 18:10
they will **r** and not become weary, . . Is 40:31
R in such a way to win the prize. . 1Co 9:24
was not **r**-ning, and had not been **r**. . Gl 2:2
You were **r**-ning well. . . . . Gl 5:7
Let us **r** with endurance the race. . . Heb 12:1

RUNNER

the **r**-s in a stadium all race, but . . . 1Co 9:24

RUSH

sound … of a violent **r**-ing wind . . . . . Ac 2:2

RUST

where moth and **r** destroy and . . . . Mt 6:19

RUTH

Moabitess; widowed daughter-in-law of
Naomi (Ru 1:1–5); married Boaz; ancestor of
David and Christ (Ru 4:1; Mt 1:5–6,16).

RUTHLESSLY

They worked the Israelites **r** . . . . Ex 1:13

- S -

SABBATH

Remember the **S** day to keep it. . . . Ex 20:8
through the grainfields on the **S**. . . Mt 12:1
The **S** was made for man and not . . Mk 2:27
Son of Man is Lord even of the **S**. . . Mk 2:28
whether he would heal him
    on the **S**. . . . . Mk 3:2
lawful to do good on the **S** or . . . . . Mk 3:4
a **S** rest remains for God's people . . Heb 4:9

SACKCLOTH

with fasting, **s**, and ashes. . . . . Dn 9:3
proclaimed a fast and dressed in **s** . . Jnh 3:5
would have repented in **s**
    and ashes . . . . Mt 11:21

SACRED

you have known the **s** Scriptures, . . 2Tm 3:15

SACRIFICE

is the Passover **s** to the LORD, ... Ex 12:27
to obey is better than **s**, ... 1Sm 15:22
You do not delight in **s** and
    offering; . . . . Ps 40:6
You do not want a **s**, or I would . . . Ps 51:16
The **s** pleasing to God is a broken . . Ps 51:17
faithful love and not **s**, ... Hs 6:6
I desire mercy and not **s**. . . . . Mt 9:13
your bodies as a living **s**, ... Rm 12:1
our Passover lamb has been **s**-d. . . . 1Co 5:7
an acceptable **s**, pleasing to
    God. . . . . Php 4:18
need to offer **s**-s every day, ... Heb 7:27
of sin by the **s** of himself. . . . . Heb 9:26
offer up to God a **s** of praise, ... Heb 13:15
offer spiritual **s**-s acceptable to . . . 1Pt 2:5

SADDUCEES

of the leaven of the Pharisees
    and **S**. . . . . Mt 16:6
S, who say there is no
    resurrection. . . . . Mt 22:23

SAFETY

The horse is a false hope for **s**; . . . . Ps 33:17

SAINT

intercedes for the **s**-s according . . . Rm 8:27
glorious inheritance in the **s**-s, ... Eph 1:18
Greet every **s** in Christ Jesus. . . . . Php 4:21
to the **s**-s once for all. . . . . Jd 3
are the prayers of the **s**-s. . . . . Rv 5:8
the righteous acts of the **s**-s. . . . . . Rv 19:8

SAKE

right paths for his name's **s**. . . . . . . Ps 23:3
not for your **s** that I will act. . . Ezk 36:22,32

SALOME

Wife of Zebedee, mother of James and
John (Mk 15:40; 16:1; cp. Mt 27:56); possibly
Mary's sister (Jn 19:25).

SALT

back and became a pillar of **s**. . . . . Gn 19:26
It is a permanent covenant of **s** . . . Nm 18:19
You are the **s** of the earth. . . . . Mt 5:13
seasoned with **s**, so that you may . . Col 4:6

SALVATION

Stand firm and see the LORD's **s** . . . Ex 14:13
He has become my **s**. . . . . Ex 15:2
Proclaim his **s** from day to day. . . . 1Ch 16:23
The God of my **s** is exalted. . . . . Ps 18:46
The LORD is my light and my **s**. . . . . Ps 27:1
Restore the joy of your **s** to me, . . . Ps 51:12
He has become my **s**. . . . . Ps 118:14
who proclaims **s**, who says to . . . . . . Is 52:7
For my eyes have seen your **s**. . . . . . Lk 2:30
everyone will see the **s** of God. . . . . . Lk 3:6
There is **s** in no one else, ... Ac 4:12

---

now is the day of **s**. 2Co 6:2
the helmet of **s** and the . . . . Eph 6:17
work out your own **s** with fear . . . . Php 2:12
if we neglect such a great **s**? . . . . . . Heb 2:3
S belongs to our God, who is. . . . . . . Rv 7:10

SAMARIA

Capital and namesake of the northern kingdom (1Kg 13:32; 16:24; 2Kg 17:24; Is 7:9; Ezk
16:46; 23:4; Hos 8:5; Ob 19; Mc 1:1); captured
by Assyria (2Kg 17:6).
    In NT times, region of central hill coun-
try between Judah and Galilee (Lk 17:11;
Ac 1:8; 8:1,5,14), often shunned by Jews (Jn
4:4–9); home of Samaritans.

SAMARITAN

But a **S** on his journey came up . . . Lk 10:33
thanking him. And he was a **S**. . . . . Lk 17:16
Jews do not associate with **S**-s. . . . . . Jn 4:9

SAME

Jesus Christ is the **s** yesterday, . . . Heb 13:8

SAMSON

Son of Manoah; Danite judge. Birth announced; to be a Nazirite (Jdg 13). Rashly
married a Philistine; posed a riddle (Jdg
14). Took revenge on Philistines: set fire to
fields; killed one thousand with donkey's
jawbone (Jdg 15). Married Delilah; was betrayed (16:4–21). Slaughter in Dagon's temple (16:23–30; Heb 11:32–34).

SAMUEL

Son of Elkanah and Hannah; Ephraimite
judge, kingmaker, priest, and prophet. Born
in answer to prayer (1Sm 1:1–20); raised at
Shiloh by Eli (1:25–28; 2:11); called (3:1–18).
Served as military and judicial judge (1Sm
7). Warned people about the nature of a
king (8:10–18; 10:25); anointed Saul (10:1);
rejected Saul (13:11–14; 15:10–29). Anointed
David (16:1–13); protected David from Saul
(19:18–24). Death (25:1); appearance to Saul
after death (28:3–19).

SANCTIFICATION

which results in **s** . . . . Rm 6:19,22
For this is God's will, your **s**; 1Th 4:3

SANCTIFY

S them by the truth; . . . . Jn 17:17
washed, you were **s**-ied, you
    were 1Co 6:11
the God of peace himself **s** you. . . . 1Th 5:23

SANCTUARY

They are to make a **s** for me . . . . . . Ex 25:8
up my hands toward your
    holy **s**. . . . . Ps 28:2
Praise God in his **s**. . . . . Ps 150:1
and will set my **s** among them . . . Ezk 37:26
not enter a **s** made with hands . . . Heb 9:24

SAND

offspring like the **s** of the sea, ... Gn 32:12
who built his house on the **s**. . . . . . . Mt 7:26

SANDAL

Remove the **s**-s from your feet, ... Ex 3:5
Remove the **s**-s from your feet, ... Jos 5:15
not worthy to remove his **s**-s. . . . . . Mt 3:11

SARAH

Wife and half sister of Abraham; originally named Sarai (Gn 11:29–31; 20:12); barren
(11:30). Twice passed off as Abraham's
sister (12:10–20; 20). Gave Hagar to Abraham, then sent her away (Gn 16; 21:9–21).
Laughed when she heard the promise of a
son (18:9–15). Bore Isaac (21:1–7; Heb 11:11).
Died; buried at Machpelah (Gn 23; 25:10;
49:31).

SATAN

SATAN

Lord asked S, "Where have you . . . . . Jb 1:7
Jesus told him, "Go away, S!. . . . . . Mt 4:10
If S drives out S, he is divided . . . Mt 12:26
told Peter, "Get behind me, S! . . . Mt 16:23
I watched S fall from heaven. . . . . Lk 10:18
Then S entered Judas, called . . . . Lk 22:3
and from the power of S to God, . . Ac 26:18
S disguises himself as an angel . . 2Co 11:14
messenger of S to torment
me so 2Co 12:7
synagogue of S. . . . . Rv 2:9; 3:9
who is called the devil and S, ... Rv 12:9
S will be released from his . . . . Rv 20:7

SATISFY

your wages on what does not s? . . . . Is 55:2

SAUL

1. First king of united Israel. Son of Kish; tall,
handsome Benjaminite (1Sm 9:1–2). Met
Samuel while looking for donkeys (9:3–
27). Anointed privately (10:1); chosen by
lot and announced publicly (10:17–24); delivered Jabesh–gilead (11:1–11); confirmed
king at Gilgal (11:12–15). Rebuked and
rejected (13:8–15; 15:11–30). Attempted
to kill David (18:11,17,25; 19:10–17; 23:8,25;
24:2; 26:2); spared by David (1Sm 24; 26).
Among the prophets (10:9–13; 19:18–24).
Consulted a medium to inquire of Samuel
(1Sm 28). Killed by Philistines (1Sm 31).
2. Paul's Hebrew name. see PAUL

SAVE

and I was s–d from my enemies. . . . . Ps 18:3
and s those stumbling toward . . . . Pr 24:11
Turn to me and be s–d, all the ends. . Is 45:22
on the name of the Lord will
be s–d, ... Jl 2:32
Jesus, because he will s his people . . Mt 1:21
whoever wants to s his life will. . . Mt 16:25
asked, "Then who can be s–d?" . . . Mt 19:25
cut short, no one would be s–d. . . Mt 24:22
and is baptized will be s–d, ... Mk 16:16
come to seek and to s the lost. . . . Lk 19:10
to s the world through him. . . . . Jn 3:17
name of the Lord will be s–d. . . . . . Ac 2:21
Sirs, what must I do to be s–d? . . . Ac 16:30
on name of the Lord will be s–d. . Rm 10:13
you are s–d by grace through faith, . .Eph 2:8
came into the world to s sinners. . . 1Tm 1:15
wants everyone to be s–d 1Tm 2:4
to this, now s–s you (not as the . . . 1Pt 3:21

SAVIOR

They forgot God their S, ... Ps 106:21
Besides me, there is no S. . . . . Is 43:11
and no S exists besides me. . . . . Hs 13:4
a S ... who is Messiah, the Lord. . . . . . Lk 2:11
God, who is the S of all people, . . . 1Tm 4:10
appearing of our S Christ Jesus, . . 2Tm 1:10
glory of our great God and S, ... Ti 2:13
of our Lord and S Jesus Christ. 2Pt 3:18

SAY

"who do you s that I am?" . . . . Mt 16:15

SCALE

Dishonest s–s are detestable . . . . Pr 11:1
something like s–s fell from his. . . . . Ac 9:18
had a set of s–s in his hand. . . . . Rv 6:5

SCARLET

Though your sins are s, ... Is 1:18
dressed him in a s robe. . . . . Mt 27:28

SCATTER

sheep of the flock will be s–ed. . . . Mt 26:31
A man s–s seed on the ground; . . . . Mk 4:26

SCEPTER

s will not depart from Judah . . . . . Gn 49:10
break them with an iron s; . . . . Ps 2:9

SCHEMES

against the s of the devil. . . . . Eph 6:11

SCOFFERS

S will come in the last days 2Pt 3:3

SCORN

and s–ed the Rock of his salvation. . Dt 32:15
s–ed by mankind and despised by . Ps 22:6

SCORPION

asks for an egg, will give him a s? . . Lk 11:12

SCOUT

Send men to s out the land . . . . Nm 13:2

SCRIBE

authority, and not like their s–s. . . . Mt 7:29
woe to you, s–s and Pharisees, ... Mt 23:13

SCRIPTURE

don't know the S–s or the power . Mt 22:29
Today ... this S has been fulfilled. . . . Lk 4:21
concerning himself in all the S–s. . Lk 24:27
You pore over the S–s
because you. Jn 5:39
and the S cannot be broken. . . . . . . Jn 10:35
you have known the sacred S–s, . . 2Tm 3:15
All S is inspired by God and is 2Tm 3:16
No prophecy of S comes from 2Pt 1:20

SCROLL

Eat this s, then go and speak to . . . . Ezk 3:1
open the s and break its seals? . . . . . Rv 5:2

SEA

through the s on dry ground, ... Ex 14:22
the winds and the s obey him! . . . . Mt 8:27
toward them walking on the s. . . . Mt 14:25
Something like a s of glass, ... Rv 4:6

SEAL (N)

Set me as a s on your heart, ... Sg 8:6
He has also put his s on us and
given. 2Co 1:22
the scroll and break its s–s?' . . . . Rv 5:2

SEAL (V)

s the book until the time of the end. . . Dn
12:4
were s–ed with the promised
Holy. . . . . Eph 1:13
s–ed with seven seals. . . . . Rv 5:1
s the servants ... on their foreheads. . Rv 7:3

SEARCH

You have s–ed me and known me . . Ps 139:1
S me, God, and know my heart; . . Ps 139:23
me when you s for me with all . . . Jr 29:13
And he who s–es our hearts
knows . . . . Rm 8:27
since the Spirit s–es everything, . . . 1Co 2:10

SEASON

that bears its fruit in its s. . . . . Ps 1:3
days, months, s–s, and years. . . . . . . Gl 4:10
About the times and the s–s: 1Th 5:1

SEASONED

be gracious, s with salt, so . . . . Col 4:6

SEAT (N)

Make a mercy s of pure gold, ... Ex 25:17
love the front s in the. . . . . Lk 11:43

SEAT (V)

I saw the Lord s–ed on a high and . . . Is 6:1
s–ed at the right hand of Power. . Mt 26:64
and s–ed us with him in the
heavens, ... Eph 2:6

SECOND

The s is like it: Love your. . . . . Mt 22:39
This is the s death, the lake of. . . . . Rv 20:14

SECRET

He knows the s–s of the heart? . . . . Ps 44:21
Father who sees in s will
reward you. . . . . Mt 6:4
things kept s from the . . . . Mt 13:35
judges what people have kept s, . . . Rm 2:16
The s–s of his heart will be. 1Co 14:25
I have learned the s of being. . . . . . Php 4:12

SECRETLY

decided to divorce her s. . . . . Mt 1:19
but s because of his fear of the . . . Jn 19:38

SECURE

anchor for the soul, firm and s. . . . Heb 6:19

SEE

humans cannot s me and live. . . . . Ex 33:20
They say, "The Lord doesn't s it. . . . Ps 94:7
they might s with their eyes . . . . Is 6:10
darkness have s–n a great light, . . . Mt 4:16
heart, for they will s God. . . . . Mt 5:8
because looking they do not s, . . . Mt 13:13
No one has ever s–n God. . . . . Jn 1:18
I was blind, and now I can s! . . . . . . Jn 9:25
who has s–n me has s–n the Father. Jn 14:9
what we have s–n with our eyes, . . . 1Jn 1:1
because we will s him as he is. 1Jn 3:2

SEED

who sowed good s in his field. . . . Mt 13:24
like a mustard s that a man took . . Mt 13:31
faith the size of a mustard s, ... Mt 17:20
Other s fell on the rock; . . . . Lk 8:6
He does not say "and to s–s," . . . . . Gl 3:16
not of perishable s but of. 1Pt 1:23

SEEK

when you s him with all your . . . . . Dt 4:29
If you s him, he will be found 1Ch 28:9
pray and s my face, and turn. 2Ch 7:14
s peace and pursue it. . . . . Ps 34:14
S the Lord while he may be
found; . . . . Is 55:6
But s first the kingdom of God . . . . Mt 6:33
S, and you will find. . . . . Mt 7:7
come to s and to save the lost. . . . . Lk 19:10
No one is to s his own good, ... 1Co 10:24
he rewards those who s him. . . . . . Heb 11:6

SEEM

a way that s–s right to a
person. . . . . Pr 14:12; 16:25

SEIZE

Then they tried to s him. . . . . Jn 7:30

SELF

put off the old s with its . . . . Col 3:9
For people will be lovers of s, ... 2Tm 3:2

SELF-CONTROL

you because of your lack of s. 1Co 7:5
gentleness, s. The law is not
against . . . . Gl 5:23
knowledge with s, with
endurance, ... 2Pt 1:6

SELF-CONTROLLED

let us stay awake and be s. 1Th 5:6
sensible, righteous, holy, s, ... Ti 1:8

SELF-INDULGENCE

not of any value in curbing s. . . . . . Col 2:23

SELFISH

anger outbursts, s ambitions,
slander 2Co 12:20
envy and s ambition . . . . Jms 3:14,16

SELL

and do not s—truth, wisdom . . . . . Pr 23:23
"You were sold for nothing, and you. . Is 52:3
joy he goes and s–s everything. . . Mt 13:44

s all you have and give to the poor . . Mk 10:21
sold his birthright in exchange . . . Heb 12:16
one can buy or **s** unless he has . . . . Rv 13:17

SEND

I AM has **sent** me to you . . . . Ex 3:14
Who will I **s**? . . . Here I am. **S** me. . . . . . Is 6:8
of the harvest to **s** out workers. . . . Mt 9:38
sent out these twelve after giving . . Mt 10:5
me welcomes him who **sent** me. . . Mt 10:40
has **sent** me to proclaim release . . . . Lk 4:18
For God did not **s** his Son into . . . . . . Jn 3:17
the will of him who **sent** me. . . Jn 5:30; 6:38
If I go, I will **s** him to you. . . . . Jn 16:7
Father has **sent** me, I also **s** you. . . . Jn 20:21
they preach unless they are **sent**? . . Rm 10:15
God **sent** his Son, born of a woman, . . . Gl 4:4
he loved us and **sent** his Son to be . . 1Jn 4:10

SENSE

who commits adultery lacks **s**; . . . . . Pr 6:32

SENSIBLE

who accepts correction is **s** . . . . Pr 15:5

SEPARATE (ADJ)

out from among them and be **s**, . . . 2Co 6:17

SEPARATE (V)

and a gossip **s-s** close friends . . . . . . Pr 16:28
joined together, let no one **s** . . . . . . Mt 19:6
just as a shepherd **s-s** the sheep. . . Mt 25:32
Who can **s** us from the love of . . . . Rm 8:35

SEPARATION

as far as the **s** of soul and spirit, . . Heb 4:12

SERPENT

Now the **s** was the most cunning . . . . Gn 3:1
as shrewd as **s-s** and as innocent . . Mt 10:16
as the **s** deceived Eve by his 2Co 11:3
the ancient **s**, who is called . . . . Rv 12:9

SERVANT

Speak, for your **s** is listening 1Sm 3:10
Give praise, you **s-s** of the LORD . . . . Ps 135:1
"This is my **s**; I strengthen him, ... Is 42:1
See, my **s** will be successful; . . . . Is 52:13
Here is my **s** whom I have chosen, . . Mt 12:18
great among you must be your **s**, . . Mt 20:26
he must be last and **s** of all . . . . Mk 9:35
"I am the Lord's **s**," said Mary. . . . . . . Lk 1:38
s-s; we've only done our duty. . . . . Lk 17:10
Where I am, there my **s** also will be . . Jn 12:26
I do not call you **s-s** anymore,
    because a **s** doesn't know what . . Jn 15:15

SERVE

S the LORD with gladness; . . . . Ps 100:2
No one can **s** two masters, ... Mt 6:24
did not come to be **s-d**, but to **s**, . . Mt 20:28
am among you as the one who **s-s**. . Lk 22:27
but **s** one another through love . . . . . Gl 5:13
S with a good attitude, ... Eph 6:7

SERVICE

if **s**, use it in **s**; if teaching, in
    teaching; . . . . Rm 12:7

SET

S apart for me Barnabas and Saul. . . Ac 13:2
instrument, **s** apart, useful to 2Tm 2:21

SEVEN

march around the city **s** times, ... Jos 6:4
will be **s** weeks and sixty-two
    weeks. . . . . Dn 9:25
sins against me him? As many
    as **s** times? . . . . Mt 18:21
To the **s** churches in Asia. . . . . Rv 1:4
s angels with the **s** last plagues; . . . Rv 15:1

SEVEN HUNDRED

He had **s** wives who were 1Kg 11:3

SEVENTH

On the **s** day God had completed . . . Gn 2:2
the **s** day is a Sabbath to the
    LORD . . . . Ex 20:10
And on the **s** day God rested from. . Heb 4:4

SEVENTY

until **s** years were fulfilled. 2Ch 36:21
When **s** years for Babylon . . . . Jr 29:10
number of years ... would be **s** . . . . . Dn 9:2
S weeks are decreed about your . . . Dn 9:24
but **s** times seven. . . . . Mt 18:22

SEVENTY-TWO

The **s** returned with joy, saying, . . . Lk 10:17

SEVERE

and **s** treatment of the body, ... Col 2:23

SEW

so they **s-ed** fig leaves together. . . . . Gn 3:7
No one **s-s** a patch of unshrunk . . Mk 2:21

SHADE

to provide **s** for his head. . . . . Jnh 4:6
birds of the sky can nest in its **s** . . . Mk 4:32

SHADOW

Our days on earth are like a **s**, ... 1Ch 29:15
hide me in the **s** of your wings . . . . . Ps 17:8
person goes about like a mere **s** . . . . Ps 39:6
dwells in the **s** of the Almighty. . . . . . Ps 91:1
in darkness and the **s** of death, ... Lk 1:79
least his **s** might fall on some . . . . . . Ac 5:15
as a copy and **s** of the heavenly . . . Heb 8:5

SHAKE

established; it cannot be **s-n**. 1Ch 16:30
of the LORD **s-s** the wilderness; . . . . . Ps 29:8
The righteous will never be **s-n**, . . . Pr 10:30
s the dust off your feet when you . . Mt 10:14
pressed down, **s-n** together, ... Lk 6:38
where they were assembled
    was **s-n**, ... Ac 4:31
once more I will **s** not only the . . Heb 12:26

SHALLUM

1. King of Israel; assassinated Zechariah; was
    assassinated by Menahem (2Kg 15:10–15).
2. Alternate name for Jehoahaz (2Kg 23:30–
    34; Jr 22:11). *see* JEHOAHAZ

SHAME

were naked, yet felt no **s** . . . . Gn 2:25
hope in me will not be put to **s**. . . . Is 49:23
some to **s** and eternal contempt. . . Dn 12:2
on him will not be put to **s**. . . . . . Rm 9:33
what is foolish ... to **s** the wise, ... 1Co 1:27
their glory is in their **s**. . . . . Php 3:19
the cross, despising the **s**. . . . . . . Heb 12:2
in him will never be put to **s** 1Pt 2:6

SHAMEFUL

For it is **s** even to mention what . . . Eph 5:12

SHAMELESS

Men committed **s** acts with men . . Rm 1:27

SHAMGAR

Judge; killed six hundred Philistines with a
    cattle prod (Jdg 3:31; 5:6).

SHAPHAN

Josiah's court secretary or scribe (2Kg
    22:3–14); his sons were friends of Jeremiah
    (Jr 26:24; 36:10; 39:14).

SHARE

S your master's joy. . . . . Mt 25:21
two shirts must **s** with someone. . . . Lk 3:11

SHARES

let me inherit two **s** of your
    spirit. 2Kg 2:9

SHARP

They had such a **s** disagreement. . . Ac 15:39

SHARPEN

s-s iron, and one man **s-s** another. . Pr 27:17

SHARPER

s than any double-edged sword, . . Heb 4:12

SHAVE

If I am **s-d**, my strength will leave . . Jdg 16:17
emissaries, **s-d** off half their 2Sm 10:4
for them to get their heads **s-d** . . Ac 21:24
the same as having her head **s-d** . . 1Co 11:5

SHEAF

shouts of joy, carrying his **s-ves** . . . Ps 126:6

SHEARER

a sheep silent before her **s-s**, ... Is 53:7
a lamb is silent before its **s**, ... Ac 8:32

SHEBA

Nation whose queen came to see Solomon
(1Kg 10; 2Ch 9); also called Sabeans (Jb 1:15;
Jl 3:8).

SHECHEM

1. City in the hill country of Ephraim. Sime-
    on and Levi destroyed the city in revenge
    for the rape of Dinah (Gn 34); Joshua re-
    newed the covenant there (Jos 24:1–28);
    served as first capital of the northern
    kingdom (1Kg 12:25).
2. Son of Hamor; raped Dinah (Gn 34).

SHED

Whoever **s-s** human blood. . . . . Gn 9:6
without the **s-ding** of blood
    there . . . . Heb 9:22

SHEEP

hills like **s** without a shepherd. . . . 1Kg 22:17
people, the **s** of his pasture. . . . . . Ps 100:3
We all went astray like **s**; . . . . Is 53:6
and like a **s** silent before her . . . . . . Is 53:7
and the **s** will be scattered; . . . . . . Zch 13:7
like **s** without a shepherd. . . . . Mt 9:36
go to the lost **s** of the house of . . . Mt 10:6
someone has a hundred **s**, and . . . Mt 18:12
separates the **s** from the goats. . . Mt 25:32
He calls his own **s** by name . . . . . . Jn 10:3
I lay down my life for the **s**. . . . . . . Jn 10:15
My **s** hear my voice, I know them, . . Jn 10:27
"Feed my **s**," Jesus said. . . . . Jn 21:17
was led like a **s** to the slaughter, . . . Ac 8:32

SHEET

a large **s** coming down, ... Ac 10:11

SHELTER

The Festival of **S-s** to the LORD . . . . Lv 23:34
dwell in **s-s** during the festival . . . Neh 8:14
under the **s** of your wings. . . . . Ps 61:4
I will set up three **s-s** here: . . . . Mt 17:4
Jewish Festival of **S-s** was near, ... Jn 7:2

SHEOL

You will not abandon me to **S**; . . . . Ps 16:10
make my bed in **S**, you are there. . . Ps 139:8
Her house is the road to **S**, ... Pr 7:27
S and Abaddon lie open before . . . . Pr 15:11
S, where is your sting? . . . . Hs 13:14

SHEPHERD (N)

hills like sheep without a **s**. 1Kg 22:17
The LORD is my **s**; I have what . . . . . . Ps 23:1
He protects his flock like a **s**; . . . . . . Is 40:11
prophesy against the **s-s** of Israel. . Ezk 34:2
establish over them one **s**, ... Ezk 34:23
Strike the **s**, and the sheep will . . . . Zch 13:7
like sheep without a **s**. . . . . Mt 9:36
I will strike the **s**, and the sheep . . Mt 26:31
s-s were staying out in the fields . . . Lk 2:8

SHEPHERD (V)

I am the good **s**. The good **s** lays . . .Jn 10:11
the great **S** of the sheep . . . . Heb 13:20
And when the chief **S** appears, ... 1Pt 5:4

SHEPHERD (V)

You will **s** my people Israel 2Sm 5:2
overseers, to **s** the church of
God, ...Ac 20:28
S God's flock among you, not 1Pt 5:2

SHIELD

He is a **s** to all who take refuge . . 2Sm 22:31
LORD is my strength and my **s**; . . . .Ps 28:7
situation take up the **s** of faith . . . .Eph 6:16

SHINE

LORD make his face **s** on you . . . . . .Nm 6:25
Arise, **s**, for your light has . . . . Is 60:1
let your light **s** before others, . . . Mt 5:16
righteous will **s** like the sun . . . . . .Mt 13:43
and his face **shone** like the sun; . . .Mt 17:2
glory of the Lord **shone**
around them, ...Lk 2:9
That light **s-s** in the darkness, ... Jn 1:5
and Christ will **s** on you. . . . . .Eph 5:14

SHIPWRECK

Three times I was **s-ed** 2Co 11:25
have **s-ed** the faith 1Tm 1:19

SHIRT

to sue you and take away your **s**, . . Mt 5:40

SHOOT

a **s** will grow from the stump . . . . Is 11:1

SHORE

daybreak came, Jesus stood on
the **s** . . . . .Jn 21:4

SHORT

the crowd, since he was a **s** man. . . . Lk 19:3
sinned and fall **s** of the glory . . . . . . Rm 3:23

SHOULDERS

government will be on his **s**. . . . . Is 9:6

SHOUT

until the time I say, '**S**!' Then you . . Jos 6:10
Let the whole earth **s** to the LORD; . .Ps 98:4
s triumphantly to the LORD, ...Ps 100:1
kept **s-ing** all the more, "Crucify
him!" . . . . Mt 27:23
descend from heaven with a **s**, ...1Th 4:16

SHOW

for they will be **s-n** mercy . . . . Mt 5:7
He **s-ed** them his hands and feet. .Lk 24:40
s us the Father, and that's enough . . Jn 14:8
s mercy to whom I will **s** mercy, . . . Rm 9:15
And I will **s** you an even better . . . 1Co 12:31
S me your faith without works, ...Jms 2:18

SHOWERS

s in ... season—**s** of blessing. . . . . .Ezk 34:26

SHREWD

crooked you prove yourself **s** . . . . . . Ps 18:26
Therefore be as **s** as serpents . . . .Mt 10:16

SHUDDER

demons believe—and they **s**. . . . . .Jms 2:19

SHUT

and they have **s** their eyes; . . . . . . .Mt 13:15
that every mouth may be **s** . . . . Rm 3:19

SICK

need a doctor, but those who
are **s**. . . . . Mt 9:12
I was **s** and you took care of
me; . . . . Mt 25:36
is why many are **s** and ill among. . 1Co 11:30
Is anyone among you **s**? . . . . .Jms 5:14

SICKLE

Swing the **s** because the harvest . . . .Jl 3:13
and a sharp **s** in his hand . . . . Rv 14:14

SICKNESS

he himself bore our **s-es**, ... Is 53:4
healing every disease and every **s**. . Mt 9:35

SIDE

Though a thousand fall at your **s** . . . Ps 91:7
the LORD had not been on our **s**— . . Ps 124:1
pierced his **s** with a spear, ...Jn 19:34
showed them his hands and his **s**. . .Jn 20:20

SIFT

has asked to **s** you like wheat . . . . . . Lk 22:31

SIGHT

The blind receive their **s**, ... Lk 7:22
For we walk by faith, not by **s** 2Co 5:7

SIGN

will give you a **s**: See, the virgin . . . . . Is 7:14
demands a **s**, but no **s** will be given
to it except the **s** of ... Jonah. . . Mt 12:39
s of your coming and of the end. . . Mt 24:3
This will be the **s** for you: . . . . Lk 2:12
the first of his **s-s**, in Cana of Galilee. . Jn 2:11
Jesus performed many other **s-s** . . .Jn 20:30
them to do **s-s** and wonders . . . . . . Ac 14:3
Jews ask for **s-s** and the Greeks . . . 1Co 1:22
tongues, then, is intended as a **s**, . .1Co 14:22

SILAS

Early church leader and prophet; also called
Silvanus. Brought news from Jerusalem
to Antioch (Ac 15:22,32); worked with Paul
and Peter in missions and writing letters
(15:40–41; 16:19–40; 17:10–15; 18:5; 2Co 1:19;
1Th 1:1; 2Th 1:1; 1Pt 5:12).

SILENCE (N)

there was **s** in heaven for about . . . . .Rv 8:1

SILENCE (V)

that he had **s-d** the Sadducees, . . Mt 22:34
said to the sea, "**S**! Be still!" . . . . . . .Mk 4:39

SILENT

If you keep **s** at this time, ... Est 4:14
When I kept **s**, my bones became . . .Ps 32:3
considered wise when he keeps **s**, . .Pr 17:28
and like a sheep **s** before her . . . . . .Is 53:7
But Jesus kept **s**. . . . . Mt 26:63
and as a lamb is **s** before its. . . . . . .Ac 8:32
women should be **s** in the 1Co 14:34
instead, she is to be **s** 1Tm 2:12

SILOAM

Pool in Jerusalem (Jn 9:7,11).

SILVER

return each man's **s** to his sack, . . . Gn 42:25
my instruction instead of **s**, ...Pr 8:10
like gold apples in **s** settings . . . . . . .Pr 25:11
loves **s** is never satisfied with **s**, . . . Ec 5:10
you without **s**, come, buy, and eat! . .Is 55:1
thirty pieces of **s** for him. . . . . Mt 26:15
I don't have **s** or gold, but . . . . .Ac 3:6

SIMEON

1. Son of Jacob and Leah (Gn 29:33); with
Levi, avenged Dinah's rape by Shechem
(34:25–31; 49:5); held as hostage by Joseph (42:24). Tribe with territory within
Judah (Jos 19:1–9; Jdg 1:3,17).
2. Devout Jew who blessed the baby Jesus
(Lk 2:25–35).
3. Jewish variation of Simon (Ac 15:14; 2Pt
1:1). see PETER

SIMON

1. Apostle Peter's original name (Mt 4:18).
see PETER

2. Apostle; called the Zealot (Mt 10:4; Mk
3:18; Lk 6:15; Ac 1:13).
3. Leper who hosted Jesus (Mt 26:6–13).
4. Cyrenian forced to carry Jesus's cross (Mk
15:21).
5. Sorcerer who wanted to buy the power of
the Spirit (Ac 8:9–24).
6. Tanner of Joppa who hosted Peter, where
Peter saw the vision (Ac 9:43).

SIN (N)

be sure your **s** will catch up with . .Nm 32:23
forgive their **s**, and heal their land. . 2Ch 7:14
and my **s** is always before me . . . . . . Ps 51:3
but **s** is a disgrace to any people. . . Pr 14:34
yet he bore the **s** of many . . . . .Is 53:12
authority on earth to forgive **s-s** . . Mt 9:6
forgive us our **s-s**, for we . . . . Lk 11:4
takes away the **s** of the world! . . . . . Jn 1:29
The one without **s** among you . . . . . .Jn 8:7
just as **s** entered the world . . . . Rm 5:12
For the wages of **s** is death, ... Rm 6:23
Christ died for our **s-s** according to. .1Co 15:3
who did not know **s** to be **s** for us, . . 2Co 5:21
way as we are, yet without **s**. . . . . Heb 4:15
hindrance and the **s** that so easily. . Heb 12:1
confess our **s-s**, he is faithful. 1Jn 1:9
and **s** is lawlessness. 1Jn 3:4

SIN (V)

you—you alone—I have **s-ned** . . . . Ps 51:4
so that I may not **s** against you . . . .Ps 119:11
your right eye causes you to **s**, ... Mt 5:29
If your brother **s-s** against you, . . .Mt 18:15
If your brother **s-s**, rebuke him, . . . Lk 17:3
And if he **s-s** against you seven . . . . Lk 17:4
from now on do not **s** anymore. . . . Jn 8:11
Rabbi, who **s-ned**, this man or . . . . . .Jn 9:2
For all have **s-ned** and fall short. . . Rm 3:23
say, "We have not **s-ned**," we 1Jn 1:10
so that you may not **s**. 1Jn 2:1

SINAI

Mountain where God revealed the Law (Ex
19:20; 31:18; 34:32; Lv 25:1; Ac 7:38; Gl 4:25).
The wilderness region (Ex 19:1; Lv 7:38).

SINCERE

s brotherly love for each other, ... 1Pt 1:22

SINFUL

I was **s** when my mother conceived. .Ps 51:5
into the hands of **s** men, ...Lk 24:7

SING

I will **s** to the LORD, for he is. . . . . . . .Ex 15:1
Let the whole earth **s** to the LORD. .1Ch 16:23
the morning stars **sang** together . . .Jb 38:7
S praise to God, **s** praise; . . . . .Ps 47:6
S a new song to the LORD . . . . .Pss 96:1; 98:1
After **s-ing** a hymn, they went
out . . . . Mt 26:30
praying and **s-ing** hymns to God, . .Ac 16:25
songs, **s-ing** and making music. . . .Eph 5:19
s-ing to God with gratitude in . . . . Col 3:16
cheerful? He should **s** praises . . . . .Jms 5:13
they **sang** a new song: You are . . . . . Rv 5:9

SINGED

not a hair of their heads was **s**, ... Dn 3:27

SINGER

S-s lead the way, with musicians . .Ps 68:25

SINK

I have **sunk** in deep mud, ...Ps 69:2
And beginning to **s** he cried out, . . Mt 14:30

SINNER

or stand in the pathway of **s-s** . . . . . Ps 1:1
My son, if **s-s** entice you, don't . . . . . Pr 1:10
Don't let your heart envy **s-s**; . . . . Pr 23:17
to call the righteous, but **s-s**. . . . . . Mt 9:13
friend of tax collectors and **s-s**! . . .Mt 11:19

Even **s-s** do that. . . . . .Lk 6:33
in heaven over one **s** who repents . . Lk 15:7
while we were still **s-s**, Christ died. . Rm 5:8
came into the world to save **s-s** . . . 1Tm 1:15

SISTER

say you're my **s**. . . . . Gn 12:13
is my brother and **s** and mother. . . Mt 12:50
the younger women as **s-s**. 1Tm 5:2

SIT

the LORD **s-s** enthroned forever;. . . . .Ps 9:7
S at my right hand until I make. . . . .Ps 110:1
You know when I **s** down and when . .Ps 139:2
But to **s** at my right and left is . . . Mt 20:23
into heaven and **sat** down at the. . Mk 16:19
S at my right hand until I make. . . .Heb 1:13

SIX

are to labor **s** days and do all. . . . . . Ex 20:9

SIX HUNDRED THOUSAND

about **s** soldiers on foot,. . . . . Ex 12:37

SIXTY-TWO

seven weeks and **s** weeks. . . . . Dn 9:25

SKILL

may my right hand forget its **s**. . . . Ps 137:5

SKIN

clothing from **s-s** for the man and . .Gn 3:21
unclean; he has a ... **s** disease. . . . . . Lv 13:8
Naaman ... had a **s** disease. 2Kg 5:1
"**S** for **s**!" Satan answered. . . . . .Jb 2:4
Even after my **s** has been
    destroyed,. . . . . .Jb 19:26
Can the Cushite change his **s**, ...Jr 13:23
Otherwise, the **s-s** burst, ...Mt 9:17

SKULL

Golgotha (which means Place of
    the **S**),. . . . . Mt 27:33

SKY

God called the expanse "**s**." . . . . .Gn 1:8
good weather because the **s** is red. . Mt 16:2
Son of Man will appear in the **s**, . . Mt 24:30
the **s** was split apart like a scroll. . . .Rv 6:14

SLACKER

Go to the ant, you **s**! . . . . .Pr 6:6
by the field of a **s** and by the . . . . .Pr 24:30

SLANDER (N)

and whoever spreads **s** is a fool. . . . Pr 10:18
hypocrisy, envy, and all **s**. 1Pt 2:1

SLANDER (V)

who does not **s** with his tongue,. . . . Ps 15:3
are **s-ed**, we respond graciously. . . . 1Co 4:13
to **s** no one, to avoid fighting,. . . . . . Ti 3:2

SLANDERER

worthy of respect, not **s-s**,. 1Tm 3:11
behavior, not **s-s**, not slaves to . . . . . .Ti 2:3

SLANDEROUSLY

as some people **s** claim we say, ...Rm 3:8

SLAP

if anyone **s-s** you on your right. . . . Mt 5:39

SLAUGHTER

are counted as sheep to be **s-ed**. . .Ps 44:22
save those stumbling toward **s**. . . . .Pr 24:11
Like a lamb led to the **s**. . . . . .Is 53:7
was led like a sheep to the **s**,. . . . . . . .Ac 8:32
are counted as sheep to be **s-ed**. . .Rm 8:36
Worthy is the Lamb who was **s-ed**. . Rv 5:12

SLAVE

Remember that you were a **s** in . . . . Dt 5:15
borrower is a **s** to the lender. . . . . . . Pr 22:7

to my **s**, 'Do this!' and he does it. . . . Mt 8:9
first among you must be your **s**;. . Mt 20:27
Well done, good and faithful **s**!. . . .Mt 25:21
who commits sin is a **s** of sin. . . . . .Jn 8:34
you used to be **s-s** of sin, ... Rm 6:17
no Jew or Greek, **s** or free, male . . . .Gl 3:28
by assuming the form of a **s**,. . . . . . Php 2:7
but as God's **s-s**. Honor everyone. . 1Pt 2:16

SLAVERY

out of Egypt, out of the place of **s**,. . Ex 13:3
you did not receive a spirit of **s**. . . . Rm 8:15
don't submit again to a yoke of **s**. . . . Gl 5:1

SLEEP (N)

God caused a deep **s** to come over. . Gn 2:21
A little **s**, a little slumber, ... Pr 6:10; 24:33

SLEEP (V)

of Israel does not slumber or **s**. . . . . Ps 121:4
disciples and found them **s-ing**. . . Mt 26:40

SLEEPER

Get up, **s**, and rise up from the . . . .Eph 5:14

SLING

Philistine with a **s** and a stone. . . .1Sm 17:50

SLOW

s to anger and abounding in
    faithful . . . . .Ex 34:6
to hear, **s** to speak, and **s** to anger, . . Jms 1:19

SLUMBER

your Protector will not **s**. . . . . Ps 121:3
A little sleep, a little **s**,. . . . . Pr 6:10; 24:33

SMALL

Four things on earth are **s**,. . . . . Pr 30:24
faithful in a very **s** matter, ... Lk 19:17

SMALLEST

It's the **s** of all the seeds, ...Mt 13:32

SMOKE

Sinai was ... enveloped in **s**. . . . . Ex 19:18
the temple was filled with **s**. . . . . Is 6:4

SMOLDERING

He will not put out a **s** wick; . . . . Is 42:3
He will not put out a **s** wick, ... Mt 12:20

SMOOTH

S lips with an evil heart are . . . . . . Pr 26:23
the uneven ground will become **s**. . . Is 40:4
straight, the rough ways **s**, ... Lk 3:5

SNAKE

the ground, it became a **s**, ...Ex 4:3
made a bronze **s** and mounted it . . Nm 21:9
In the end it bites like a **s**. . . . . Pr 23:32
for a fish, will give him a **s**? . . . . . . Mt 7:10
they will pick up **s-s**; . . . . Mk 16:18
the authority to trample on **s-s** . . . Lk 10:19
as Moses lifted up the **s** in the . . . . . Jn 3:14

SNARE

their gods, it will be a **s** for you. . . .Ex 23:33
the **s-s** of death confronted me. . .2Sm 22:6
will keep your foot from a **s**. . . . . . . Pr 3:26
The fear of mankind is a **s**,. . . . . Pr 29:25

SNATCH

one comes and **s-es** away what
    was . . . . .Mt 13:19
No one will **s** them out of my . . . . .Jn 10:28

SNOUT

like a gold ring in a pig's **s**. . . . . . .Pr 11:22

SNOW

and I will be whiter than **s**. . . . . Ps 51:7
they will be as white as **s**; . . . . .Is 1:18
his clothing was as white as **s**. . . . . Mt 28:3

SOAR

s-ing on the wings of the wind. . . . Ps 18:10
will **s** on wings like eagles;. . . . . Is 40:31

SOBER-MINDED

Be **s**! Be on the alert!. 1Pt 5:8

SODOM

City on the plain, where Lot settled (Gn
10:19; 13:10; 14:11–12); destroyed along with
Gomorrah by God (Gn 18:20; 19:24).

SOIL

quickly since the **s** wasn't deep. . . . .Mt 13:5

SOLDIER

The **s-s** also mocked him. . . . . .Lk 23:36
No one serving as a **s** gets
    entangled. 2Tm 2:4

SOLID

gave you milk to drink, not **s**
    food,. 1Co 3:2
But **s** food is for the mature . . . . . Heb 5:14

SOLOMON

Son of David and Bathsheba; third king of
Israel (2Sm 12:24; 1Kg 1:30–40). Asked for
wisdom (1 Kg 3:5–15); knew many proverbs and songs (4:32; Pss 72; 127; Pr 1:1; 10:1;
25:1; Sg 1:1); wisdom demonstrated in child
dispute (1Kg 3:16–28) and the visit of the
Queen of Sheba (10:1–13). Built and dedicated the temple (1Kg 5–8). Accumulated
vast wealth (9:26–28; 10:26–29); had many
wives and concubines, who influenced him
toward idolatry (11:1–8).

SON SEE ALSO SON OF DAVID, SON OF GOD, SON OF MAN, SONS OF GOD

"Take your **s**," he said, "your only . . Gn 22:2
and he will be my **s**. 2Sm 7:14
My **s** Absalom! My **s**, my **s** 2Sm 18:33
He said to me, "You are my **S**; . . . . Ps 2:7
are all **s-s** of the Most High. . . . . .Ps 82:6
S-s are indeed a heritage from . . . . Ps 127:3
the virgin will conceive, have a **s**, ...Is 7:14
born for us, a **s** will be given to us,. . . Is 9:6
be called: **S-s** of the living God. . . . .Hs 1:10
and out of Egypt I called my **s**. . . . . . Hs 11:1
Out of Egypt I called my **S**. . . . . .Mt 2:15
This is my beloved **S**, with whom . . .Mt 3:17
how, then, can he be his **s**?". . . . . . Mt 22:45
Truly this man was the **S** of God! . Mt 27:54
called the **S** of the Most High,. . . . . . Lk 1:32
longer worthy to be called your **s**. . Lk 15:19
He gave his one and only **S**, ... Jn 3:16
believes in the **S** has eternal life,. . . .Jn 3:36
by God's Spirit are God's **s-s**. . . . . . Rm 8:14
conformed to the image of his **S**, . . Rm 8:29
He did not even spare his own **S**. . . Rm 8:32
will be called **s-s** of the living . . . . . Rm 9:26
you will be **s-s** and daughters 2Co 6:18
slave but a **s**, and if a **s**, then God. . . Gl 4:7
He has spoken to us by his **S**. . . . . . .Heb 1:2
that addresses you as **s-s**: . . . . .Heb 12:5
one and only **S** into the world. 1Jn 4:9
loved us and sent his **S** to be 1Jn 4:10
The one who has the **S** has life. 1Jn 5:12

SON OF DAVID

Have mercy on us, **S**! . . . . Mt 9:27
"Could this be the **S**?" . . . . .Mt 12:23
Hosanna to the **S**! . . . . Mt 21:9

SON OF GOD

If You are the **S**, come down . . . . . Mt 27:40
will be called the **S**. . . . . Lk 1:35
Are you, then, the **S**? . . . . .Lk 22:70
that this is the **S**. . . . . Jn 1:34
of the one and only **S**. . . . . Jn 3:18
appointed to be the powerful **S** . . . Rm 1:4
confesses that Jesus is the **S** 1Jn 4:15

one who believes that Jesus is
the **S**? 1Jn 5:5

SON OF MAN

s that you think of him? . . . . .Ps 8:4
He said to me, "**S**, ... Ezk 2:1
one like a **s** was coming . . . . Dn 7:13
S has no place to lay his . . . . Mt 8:20
S coming in his kingdom. . . . . Mt 16:28
When the **S** comes in his glory, . . . Mt 25:31
see the **S** seated at the right
hand . . . . Mk 14:62
so the **S** must be lifted up, ... Jn 3:14
Who is this **S**? .Jn 12:34
S standing at the right hand of
God!. . . . . .Ac 7:56
One like the **S** was seated on. . . . . Rv 14:14

SONG

The LORD is my strength and my **s**; . .Ex 15:2
Sing a new **s** to him; . . . . Ps 33:3
He put a new **s** in my mouth, ...Ps 40:3
psalms, hymns, and spiritual
s-s, ... Eph 5:19; Col 3:16
the **s** of the Lamb: . . . . .Rv 15:3

SONS OF GOD

the **s** saw that the daughters of
mankind . . . . Gn 6:2
peacemakers ... will be called **s**. . . . . Mt 5:9
through faith you are all **s** in Christ . Gl 3:26

SORCERER

But Elymas the **s** ... opposed them . . Ac 13:8

SORCERY

interpret omens, practice **s**, ... Dt 18:10
idolatry, **s**, hatreds, strife, ...Gl 5:20

SORROW

For with much wisdom is much **s**; . . . Ec 1:18
and **s** and sighing will flee... . . Is 35:10; 51:11
but your **s** will turn to joy. . . . . Jn 16:20
I have great **s** and unceasing . . . . . . Rm 9:2

SOUL

with all your **s**, and with all
strength. . . . . .Dt 6:5
to destroy both **s** and body in hell. . Mt 10:28
with all your **s**, and with all . . . . . . Mt 22:37
a sword will pierce your own **s**— . . . Lk 2:35
Now my **s** is troubled. . . . . Jn 12:27
separation of **s** and spirit, joints . . Heb 4:12
the salvation of your **s-s** 1Pt 1:9
Shepherd and Overseer of your **s-s**. . 1Pt 2:25

SOUND (N)

if the bugle makes an unclear **s**, . . . 1Co 14:8
voice like the **s** of cascading waters. . Rv 1:15

SOUND (V)

s the alarm on my holy mountain! . . . .Jl 2:1
the trumpet will **s**, and the dead . . 1Co 15:52

SOUR

The fathers have eaten **s** grapes, . . . Jr 31:29
The fathers eat **s** grapes, and . . . . . Ezk 18:2

SOURCE

You killed the **s** of life, ... Ac 3:15

SOVEREIGN

He is the blessed and only **S**, ... 1Tm 6:15

SOW

those who **s** trouble reap the same. . . Jb 4:8
Those who **s** in tears will reap . . . . . Ps 126:5
who **s-s** injustice will reap disaster, . . Pr 22:8
They don't **s** or reap or gather. . . . . Mt 6:26
As he **s-ed**, some seeds fell . . . . Mt 13:4
a man who **s-ed** good seed . . . . . . Mt 13:24
One **s-s** and another reaps. . . . . Jn 4:37
we have **sown** spiritual things 1Co 9:11
Sown in corruption, raised in 1Co 15:42

person who **s-s** sparingly will 2Co 9:6
whatever a person **s-s** he will also . . . Gl 6:7

SOWER

Consider the **s** who went out to . . . .Mt 13:3
The **s** sows the word.. . . . . Mk 4:14

SPARE

He did not even **s** his own Son . . . . Rm 8:32
if God didn't **s** the angels who 2Pt 2:4

SPARINGLY

person who sows **s** will also reap **s**, . 2Co 9:6

SPARROW

are worth more than many **s-s**. . . . .Mt 10:31

SPEAK

He **spoke**, and it came into being; . . Ps 33:9
to be silent and a time to **s**; . . . . Ec 3:7
the mouth of the LORD has **spoken**. . Is 40:5
worry about ... what you are to **s**. . . Mt 10:19
We **s** what we know . . . . Jn 3:11
began to **s** in different tongues, ... Ac 2:4
If I **s** human or angelic tongues, . . . 1Co 13:1
was a child, I **spoke** like a child, . . . 1Co 13:11
But **s-ing** the truth in love, let . . . Eph 4:15
he has **spoken** to us by his Son. . . . Heb 1:2
instead, men **spoke** from God. 2Pt 1:21

SPEAR

their **s-s** into pruning knives. . Is 2:4; Mc 4:3
your pruning knives into **s-s**. . . . . Jl 3:10
pierced his side with a **s**, ... Jn 19:34

SPECTACLE

We have become a **s** to the world . . 1Co 4:9

SPEECH

Day after day they pour out **s**; . . . . . Ps 19:2
There is no **s**; there are no words; . . . Ps 19:3
Let your **s** always be gracious, ... Col 4:6

SPEND

gladly **s** and be **spent** for you. . . . 2Co 12:15

SPICES

cloths with the fragrant **s**, ... Jn 19:40

SPIN

They don't labor or **s** . . . . . . Mt 6:28; Lk 12:27

SPIRIT SEE ALSO HOLY SPIRIT, SPIRIT OF GOD, SPIRIT OF THE LORD

My **S** will not remain with mankind. . Gn 6:3
an evil **s** sent from the LORD 1Sm 16:14
Into your hand I entrust my **s**; . . . . . Ps 31:5
renew a steadfast **s** within me. . . . Ps 51:10
or take your Holy **S** from me. . . . . . Ps 51:11
pleasing to God is a broken **s** . . . . . Ps 51:17
Where can I go to escape your **S**? . . Ps 139:7
Who knows if the **s** of the children . . Ec 3:21
the **s** returns to God who gave . . . . . Ec 12:7
I have put my **S** on him; . . . . .Is 42:1
and put a new **s** within you; . . . . Ezk 36:26
pour out my **S** on all humanity . . . . Jl 2:28
but by my **S**,' says the LORD . . . . .Zch 4:6
Blessed are the poor in **s**, ... Mt 5:3
them authority over unclean **s-s**, . . . Mt 10:1
I will put my **S** on him, and he . . . . Mt 12:18
against the **S** will not be. . . . . Mt 12:31
The **s** is willing, but the flesh. . . . . . Mt 26:41
open and the **S** descending to him. . Mk 1:10
into your hands I entrust my **s**. . . . . Lk 23:46
God is **s**, and those who worship
him must worship in **S** and truth. . Jn 4:24
He is the **S** of truth. . . . . Jn 14:17
pour out my **S** on all people. . . . . . . Ac 2:17
but the **S** of Jesus did not allow . . . . Ac 16:7
had a **s** by which she predicted. . . . Ac 16:16
are not in the flesh, but in the **S**, . . Rm 8:9
testifies together with our **s**
that we. . . . . Rm 8:16

have the **S** as the firstfruits— . . . . .Rm 8:23
S helps us in our weakness, ...Rm 8:26
different gifts, but the same **S**. . . . 1Co 12:4
distinguishing between **s-s**, ... 1Co 12:10
the **S** ... as a down payment. 2Co 1:22
walk by the **S** and you will. . . . . Gl 5:16
There is one body and one **S** . . . . . . Eph 4:4
but be filled by the **S**: . . . . Eph 5:18
Don't stifle the **S**. 1Th 5:19
And may your whole **s**, soul, and . . 1Th 5:23
separation of soul and **s**, joints . . . Heb 4:12
proclamation to the **s-s** in prison . . 1Pt 3:19
not believe every **s**, but test the **s-s** . 1Jn 4:1

SPIRIT OF GOD

S was hovering over the surface. . . . .Gn 1:2
He saw the **S** descending like a
dove . . . . .Mt 3:16

SPIRIT OF THE LORD

S came powerfully on David
from 1Sm 16:13
The **S** GOD is on me, ... Is 61:1
S is on me ... he has anointed me . . . Lk 4:18
where the **S** is, there is freedom. . . 2Co 3:17

SPIRITIST

not turn to mediums or consult **s-s**, . .Lv 19:31

SPIRITUAL

explaining **s** things to **s** people. . . . 1Co 2:13
a natural body, raised a **s** body. . . . 1Co 15:44
who are **s**, restore such a person. . . . . Gl 6:1
blessed us with every **s** blessing. . . . Eph 1:3
psalms, hymns, and **s**
songs, ... Eph 5:19; Col 3:16

SPIRITUALLY

since it is evaluated **s**. 1Co 2:14

SPIT

Then they **spat** in his face
and beat. . . . . Mt 26:67
He **s** on the ground, made some mud . Jn 9:6

SPLATTER

blood he **s-ed** on the altar. . . . . .Ex 24:8
s it on all sides of the altar. . . . . Ex 29:16
present the blood and **s** it . . . . Lv 1:5

SPLENDOR

S and majesty are before him; 1Ch 16:27
Worship the LORD in the **s** of . . . . Ps 29:2
are clothed with majesty and **s** . . . Ps 104:1
not even Solomon in all his **s** was . . Mt 6:29

SPLINTER

the **s** in your brother's eye . . . . Mt 7:3

SPLIT

He **s** the rock, and water gushed . . . Is 48:21

SPONGE

a **s** full of sour wine on a hyssop. . . Jn 19:29

SPOT

his skin, or a leopard his **s-s**? . . . . . . Jr 13:23
without **s** or wrinkle or anything . . Eph 5:27
without **s** or blemish in his sight. . . 2Pt 3:14

SPRAWL

with ivory, **s-ed** out on their . . . . . . Am 6:4
of those who **s** out will come to . . . . Am 6:7

SPREAD

s-ing out the sky like a canopy, . . . Ps 104:2
word ... may **s** rapidly and 2Th 3:1

SPRING (N)

give ... from the **s** of the water . . . . . Rv 21:6

SPRING (V)

S up, well—sing to it! . . . . Nm 21:17
well of water **s-ing** up in him . . . . . . Jn 4:14

SPRINKLE

so he will **s** many nations. . . . . Is 52:15
will also **s** clean water on you,. . . .Ezk 36:25
hearts **s-d** clean from an evil. . . . Heb 10:22
and to the **s-d** blood, which
  says. . . . . Heb 12:24
s-d with the blood of Jesus Christ.. . 1Pt 1:2

SPROUT

cause ... Branch to **s** up for David,. . .Jr 33:15

SPY

to **s** on the freedom we have . . . . Gl 2:4

SQUANDERED

he **s** his estate in foolish living. . . . . .Lk 15:13

STAFF

threw down his **s** before Pharaoh. . Ex 7:10
s of the man I choose will sprout,. . Nm 17:5
rod and your **s**—they comfort me. . . Ps 23:4
the manna, Aaron's **s** that budded,. . Heb 9:4

STAIRWAY

A **s** was set on the ground with . . .Gn 28:12
the shadow ... on **s** of Ahaz. 2Kg 20:11

STAND

where you are **s-ing** is holy ground. .Ex 3:5
place where you are **s-ing** is holy. . Jos 5:15
And the sun **stood** still and . . . . . . Jos 10:13
s still, and see the salvation. 2Ch 20:17
Who may **s** in his holy place?. . . . . . .Ps 24:3
will be able to **s** when he appears? . .Mal 3:2
against itself, that house cannot **s**. .Mk 3:25
into this grace in which we **s**, ... Rm 5:2
he **s-s** or falls. And he will **s**, because
  the Lord is able to make him **s**. . Rm 14:4
thinks he **s-s** must be careful . . 1Co 10:12
so that you can **s** against the . . . . . Eph 6:11
I **s** at the door and knock. . . . . Rv 3:20

STAR

God made ... as well as the **s-s**. . . . . .Gn 1:16
numerous as the **s-s** of the sky. . . .Gn 22:17
the morning **s-s** sang together. . . . .Jb 38:7
moon and the **s-s**, which you set . . . .Ps 8:3
we saw his **s** in the east . . . . Mt 2:2
you shine like **s-s** in the world. . . .Php 2:15
of David, the bright morning **s**. . . .Rv 22:16

STARTED

He who **s** a good work in you . . . . . .Php 1:6

STATURE

look at his appearance or his **s** 1Sm 16:7
Jesus increased in wisdom and **s**, . . Lk 2:52

STAY

and **s** awake with me. . . . . Mt 26:38

STEADFAST

me and renew a **s** spirit within . . . . Ps 51:10

STEAL

Do not **s**. . . . . .Ex 20:15
or I might have nothing and **s**, . . .Pr 30:9
where thieves break in and **s**. . . . . Mt 6:19
adultery; do not **s**; do not bear . . . .Mt 19:18
comes only to **s** and to kill and . . . .Jn 10:10
the thief no longer **s**. . . . . Eph 4:28

STEP

but the Lord determines his **s-s**. . . Pr 16:9
you should follow in his **s-s**. 1Pt 2:21

STEPHEN

Foremost of the first seven deacons (Ac
6:1–7). First Christian martyr (6:8–7:60); Saul
approved of his death (8:1; 22:20); start of
persecution and dispersion (11:19).

STIFLE

Don't **s** the Spirit. 1Th 5:19

STILL

reflect in your heart while on your
  bed and be **s**. . . . . .Ps 4:4
Silence! Be **s**!" The wind ceased. . . .Mk 4:39

STING

Sheol, where is your **s**? . . . . Hs 13:14
Where, death, is your **s**? 1Co 15:55

STIR

but a harsh word **s-s** up wrath. . . . . .Pr 15:1
my compassion is **s-red**!. . . . . Hs 11:8

STOLEN

S water is sweet, ... Pr 9:17

STOMACH

passes into the **s** and is eliminated?. . Mt 15:17
"Food is for the **s** and the **s** for
  food,". 1Co 6:13
their god is their **s**;. . . . . .Php 3:19
a little wine because of your **s** . . .1Tm 5:23

STONE (N)

s tablets inscribed by ... God. . . . . . .Ex 31:18
five smooth **s-s** from the wadi . .1Sm 17:40
strike your foot against a **s**. . . . . . . Ps 91:12
The **s** that the builders rejected . . Ps 118:22
a time to throw **s-s** and a time to. . . . .Ec 3:5
He will be a **s** to stumble over. . . . .Is 8:14
I have laid a **s** in Zion, a tested **s**, . .Is 28:16
remove your heart of **s** and give. .Ezk 36:26
tell these **s-s** to become bread." . . . . Mt 4:3
strike your foot against a **s**. . . . . . . Mt 4:6
for bread, will give him a **s**?. . . . . Mt 7:9
The **s** that the builders rejected . . Mt 21:42
Who will roll away the **s** from . . . . Mk 16:3
silent, the **s-s** would cry out!. . . . . . Lk 19:40
be the first to throw a **s** at her. . . . . . Jn 8:7
stumbled over the stumbling **s**. . . .Rm 9:32
not on tablets of **s** but on tablets . .2Co 3:3
to him, a living **s**—rejected by. 1Pt 2:4

STONE (V)

were **s-ing** Stephen, he called out, . . Ac 7:59

STORE

Don't **s** up for yourselves treasures. .Mt 6:19
have anywhere to **s** my crops? . . . . .Lk 12:17

STOREHOUSE

brings the wind from his **s-s**. .Jr 10:13; 51:16
Bring the full tenth into the **s** . . . . .Mal 3:10

STOREROOM

brings out of his **s** treasures new . .Mt 13:52

STORM

and shelter from **s** and rain. . . . . Is 4:6
such a great **s** arose on the sea . . . . . Jnh 1:4
a violent **s** arose on the sea, ... Mt 8:24

STRAIGHT

make a **s** highway for our God in . . . Is 40:3
the crooked will become **s**,. . . . . Lk 3:5
Make **s** the way of the Lord . . . . .Jn 1:23

STRAIN

You **s** out a gnat, but gulp down. . Mt 23:24

STRANGER

I was a **s** and you took me in; . . . . Mt 25:35
no longer foreigners and **s-s**,. . . . . .Eph 2:19
I urge you as **s-s** and exiles 1Pt 2:11

STRANGLE

eating anything that has been **s-d**,. . Ac 15:20

STRAP

whose sandal **s** I'm not worthy to . . Jn 1:27

STRAW

go and gather **s** for themselves. . . . . .Ex 5:7
costly stones, wood, hay, or **s**, ... 1Co 3:12

STREAM

planted beside flowing **s-s** . . . . Ps 1:3
its **s-s** delight the city of God,. . . . . .Ps 46:4
s-s of living water flow from. . . . . . .Jn 7:38

STREET

Wisdom calls out in the **s**; . . . . Pr 1:20
on the **s** corners to be seen by
  people. . . . . Mt 6:5
s of the city was pure gold, ... Rv 21:21

STRENGTH

The Lord is my **s** and my song; . . . . . Ex 15:2
all your soul, and with all your **s**. . . .Dt 6:5
does not prevail by his own **s** 1Sm 2:9
I love you, Lord, my **s**. . . . . Ps 18:1
The Lord is my **s** and my shield; . . . .Ps 28:7
God is our refuge and **s**, a helper . .Ps 46:1
ascribe to the Lord glory and **s**. . . . .Ps 96:7
in the Lord will renew their **s**;. . . . . Is 40:31
strong should not boast in his **s**;. . . . Jr 9:23
Not by **s** or by might, but by my . .Zch 4:6
your mind, and with all your **s**. . . . Mk 12:30

STRENGTHEN

have turned back, **s** your brothers. .Lk 22:32
He will also **s** you to the end, ...1Co 1:8
speaks to people for their **s-ing**, . .1Co 14:3
be **s-ed** by the Lord and by his . . . .Eph 6:10
things through him who **s-s** me. . . .Php 4:13
Lord who has **s-ed** me, ...1Tm 1:12
Therefore **s** your tired hands . . . . .Heb 12:12

STRICKEN

but we in turn regarded him **s**, ... Is 53:4

STRIFE

a house full of feasting with **s**. . . . . .Pr 17:1
there is envy and **s** among you, ...1Co 3:3
sorcery, hatreds, **s**, jealousy, ... Gl 5:20

STRIKE

s your head, and you will **s** his heel. .Gn 3:15
and **struck** the rock twice . . . . Nm 20:11
you will not **s** your foot against . . . Ps 91:12
The sun will not **s** you by day . . . . . Ps 121:6
S the shepherd, and the sheep
  will. . . . . Zch 13:7
you will not **s** your foot against . . . . Mt 4:6
I will **s** the shepherd, and the . . . . Mt 26:31
struck down but not destroyed. . . 2Co 4:9

STRIP

They **s-ped** him, beat him up,. . . . . .Lk 10:30

STRIVE

Don't **s** for what you should eat. . . Lk 12:29
s-ing with his strength that works. .Col 1:29

STROKE

or one **s** of a letter will pass from. . Mt 5:18
than for one **s** of a letter ... to drop. . Lk 16:17

STRONG

Be **s** and courageous; . . . . .Dt 31:6
be **s** and very courageous. . . . . Jos 1:7
Lord, **s** and mighty, the Lord, ... Ps 24:8
The name of the Lord is a **s** tower;. .Pr 18:10
Redeemer is **s**, and he will . . . . .Pr 23:11
Their Redeemer is **s**; the Lord . . . . Jr 50:34
can someone enter a **s** man's
  house . . . . Mt 12:29
The boy grew up and became **s**, ...Lk 2:40
Now we who are **s** have an . . . . .Rm 15:1
For when I am weak, then I am **s**. . 2Co 12:10

STRONGER

God's weakness is **s** than human. . . 1Co 1:25

STRONGHOLD

David did capture the **s** of Zion, . . .2Sm 5:7
my salvation, my **s**, my refuge, ... 2Sm 22:3
the God of Jacob is our **s**. . . . . Ps 46:7,11
my rock and my salvation, my **s**;. . . Ps 62:2,6

STRUGGLE

way of the LORD is a **s** for the . . . . . Pr 10:29
for the demolition of **s-s**. 2Co 10:4

STRUGGLE

our **s** is not against flesh and
blood. . . . . .Eph 6:12
s-ing against sin, you have not. . . Heb 12:4

STUBBORN

a **s** and rebellious generation, ...Ps 78:8

STUDY

and much **s** wearies the body. . . . . . Ec 12:12
Too much **s** is driving you mad. . . . .Ac 26:24

STUMBLE

nothing makes them **s**. . . . . .Ps 119:165
when you run, you will not **s**. . . . . . . Pr 4:12
be a stone to **s** over and a rock . . . . . .Is 8:14
cause one of these little ones to **s**. . Lk 17:2
walks during the day, he doesn't **s**, . . Jn 11:9
They **s-d** over the **s-ing** stone. . . . .Rm 9:32
for we all **s** in many ways. . . . . .Jms 3:2
A stone to **s** over, ... 1Pt 2:8
who is able to protect you from
s-ing . . . . Jd 24

STUMBLING BLOCK

instead decide never to put a **s**. . . Rm 14:13
Christ crucified, a **s** to the Jews. . . 1Co 1:23
this right ... in no way becomes a **s** . . 1Co 8:9

STUMP

shoot will grow from the **s** of Jesse,. . Is 11:1

STUPID

one who hates correction is **s**. . . . . . .Pr 12:1

SUBDUE

fill the earth, and **s** it. . . . . .Gn 1:28

SUBJECT

the creation was **s-ed** to futility. . .Rm 8:20
when everything is **s** to Christ, . . . 1Co 15:28
s-ed everything under his feet. . . . Heb 2:8

SUBMISSION

learn quietly with full **s**. 1Tm 2:11

SUBMIT

he willingly **s-ted** to death, ...Is 53:12
s to the governing authorities, ...Rm 13:1
don't **s** again to a yoke of slavery. . . . Gl 5:1
Wives, **s** to your husbands . . . . . . .Eph 5:22
Why do you **s** to regulations: . . . . . .Col 2:20
Remind them **s** to rulers. . . . . Ti 3:1
Therefore, **s** to God. Resist . . . . .Jms 4:7
S to every human authority. 1Pt 2:13
s yourselves to your own husbands. . 1Pt 3:1

SUCCESS

He stores up **s** for the upright; . . . . . . Pr 2:7

SUDDENLY

you seek will **s** come to his temple,. . Mal 3:1

SUE

one who wants to **s** you and take . . Mt 5:40

SUEZ

LORD will divide the Gulf of **S**. . . . . . Is 11:15

SUFFER

Son of Man must **s** many things . . . Mk 8:31
Passover with you before I **s**. . . . . . Lk 22:15
s these things and enter into his . . Lk 24:26
Messiah would **s** and rise from . . . .Lk 24:46
that his Messiah would **s**. . . . . .Ac 3:18
we **s** with him so that we may . . . . Rm 8:17
one member **s-s**, all ... **s** with it; . . 1Co 12:26
share in **s-ing** for the gospel, ... 2Tm 1:8
obedience from what he **s-ed**. . . . . Heb 5:8
Is anyone among you **s-ing**? . . . . . .Jms 5:13
when you do what is good and **s**,. . 1Pt 2:20

Christ also **s-ed** for you, ... 1Pt 2:21
it is better to **s** for doing good,. . . .1Pt 3:17
Christ also **s-ed** for sins once. 1Pt 3:18

SUFFERING (N)

man of **s** who knew what sickness . . .Is 53:3
the **s-s** of this present time are
not. . . . . .Rm 8:18
the fellowship of his **s-s**, ...Php 3:10
share in the **s-s** of Christ. 1Pt 4:13

SUFFICIENT

My grace is **s** for you, ...2Co 12:9

SUMMER

it prepares its provisions in **s**; . . . . . . .Pr 6:8
leaves, you know that **s** is near. . . Mt 24:32

SUN

And the **s** stood still. . . . . Jos 10:13
the LORD God is a **s** and shield. . . . . Ps 84:11
s will not strike you by day . . . . Ps 121:6
there is nothing new under the **s**. . . . Ec 1:9
The **s** will be turned to darkness. . . . .Jl 2:31
the **s** of righteousness will rise . . . . Mal 4:2
For he causes his **s** to rise on . . . . . . Mt 5:45
The **s** will be darkened, ... Mt 24:29
Don't let the **s** go down on your. . Eph 4:26
His face was shining like the **s**. . . . . .Rv 1:16
not need the **s** or the moon to . . . .Rv 21:23

SUNRISE

they went to the tomb at **s**. . . . . . . Mk 16:2

SUPERIOR

became **s** to the angels. . . . . Heb 1:4
inferior is blessed by the **s**. . . . . Heb 7:7

SUPPER

took the cup after **s** and said, ...Lk 22:20
he took the cup after **s**, and said . . 1Co 11:25

SUPPLY

And my God will **s** all your needs . . Php 4:19

SUPPORT

but the LORD was my **s**. 2Sm 22:19

SUPPRESS

unrighteousness **s** the truth, ... Rm 1:18

SURE

be **s** your sin will catch up with. . .Nm 32:23
cornerstone, a **s** foundation; . . . . . . Is 28:16

SURELY

to say to him, "**S** not I, Lord?" . . . . Mt 26:22

SURPASS

deeds, but you **s** them all! . . . . Pr 31:29
unless your righteousness **s-es** . . . . Mt 5:20
love that **s-es** knowledge, ...Eph 3:19
view of the **s-ing** value of knowing. . Php 3:8
peace of God, which **s-es** every . . . Php 4:7

SURROUND

Many bulls **s** me; . . . . .Ps 22:12
large cloud of witnesses **s-ing** us, . . Heb 12:1

SURVIVE

built **s-s**, he will receive a reward. . . 1Co 3:14

SURVIVOR

of Armies had not left us a few **s-s**, . . .Is 1:9

SUSTAIN

wake again because the LORD **s-s** me. .Ps 3:5
establish and **s** it with justice . . . . . . Is 9:7
not **s** the root, but the root
s-s you. . . . . .Rm 11:18
s-ing all things by his powerful . . . .Heb 1:3

SUSTAINER

the Lord is the **s** of my life. . . . . .Ps 54:4

SWALLOW

has been **s-ed** up in victory. 1Co 15:54

SWEAR

By myself I have **sworn**, ...Gn 22:16
swore in my anger, "They
will not . . . . Ps 95:11
LORD **swore** an oath to David, ...Ps 132:11
Do not **s** by your head, ... Mt 5:36
swore in my anger, "They will not. .Heb 3:11
to **s** by, he **swore** by himself: . . . . Heb 6:13
Lord has **sworn** and will not . . . . . .Heb 7:21
do not **s**, either by heaven or . . . .Jms 5:12

SWEAT

eat bread by the **s** of your brow. . . .Gn 3:19
His **s** became like drops of blood . .Lk 22:44

SWEEP

vacant, **swept**, and put in order. . . Mt 12:44
not light a lamp, **s** the house, ... Lk 15:8

SWEET

How **s** your word is to my
taste— . . . . Ps 119:103
Stolen water is **s**, ... Pr 9:17
it was as **s** as honey in my mouth. . . Ezk 3:3
Does a spring pour out **s** and bitter . Jms 3:11

SWIFT

that the race is not to the **s**, ... Ec 9:11
Their feet are **s** to shed blood; . . . . . Rm 3:15

SWINDLER

or **s-s** will inherit God's kingdom. . . 1Co 6:10

SWORD

whirling **s** east of the garden of . . . Gn 3:24
not by **s** ... that the LORD saves, . . 1Sm 17:47
Nation will not take up the **s** against . .Is 2:4
Beat your plows into **s-s**. . . . . Jl 3:10
will beat their **s-s** into plows, ... Mc 4:3
come to bring peace, but a **s**. . . . . Mt 10:34
who take up the **s** will perish by
a **s**. . . . . Mt 26:52
a **s** will pierce your own soul— . . . . . Lk 2:35
does not carry the **s** for no reason. . Rm 13:4
and the **s** of the Spirit, ...Eph 6:17
sharper than any double-edged **s**, . .Heb 4:12
a **s** came from his mouth, ... Rv 1:16

SYCAMORE

he climbed up a **s** tree to see. . . . . . Lk 19:4

SYMBOL

a **s** on your forehead . . . . . . Ex 13:16; Dt 6:8
should have a **s** of authority 1Co 11:10

SYMPATHIZE

a high priest who is unable to **s** . . Heb 4:15

SYNAGOGUE

teaching in their **s-s**, preaching. . . . Mt 4:23
He entered the **s** on the Sabbath . . Lk 4:16
They will ban you from the **s-s**. . . . . Jn 16:2
taught in the **s** and in the temple. . Jn 18:20
reasoned in the **s** every Sabbath. . . .Ac 18:4
but are a **s** of Satan. . . . . Rv 2:9

- T -

TABERNACLE

the pattern of the **t**. . . . . .Ex 25:9
glory of the LORD filled the **t**. . . . . Ex 40:34
more perfect **t** not made with. . . . .Heb 9:11

TABLE

construct a **t** of acacia wood, ...Ex 25:23
You prepare a **t** before me in the . . . Ps 23:5
overturned the **t-s** of the money
changers. . . . . Mt 21:12
and drink at my **t** in my kingdom. . . Lk 22:30
the Lord's **t** and the **t** of demons. . . 1Co 10:21

TABLET

that I may give you the stone **t-s** . . Ex 24:12
them on the **t** of your heart. . . . . Pr 3:3; 7:3
engraved on the **t** of their hearts. . . . Jr 17:1
not on **t-s** of stone but on **t-s**. 2Co 3:3

TAKE

or **t** your Holy Spirit from me. . . . . . Ps 51:11
T up my yoke and learn from me,. . Mt 11:29
deny himself, **t** up his cross, ... Mt 16:24
one will be **taken** and one left. . . . Mt 24:40
T and eat it; this is my body. . . . . . Mt 26:26
who **t-s** away the sin of the world!. . Jn 1:29
they've **taken** away my Lord, ... Jn 20:13
t up the full armor of God,. . . . . . . Eph 6:13

TALENTS

To one he gave five **t**; . . . . Mt 25:15

TALK

T about them when you sit in . . . . . . Dt 6:7

TALL

He was nine feet, nine inches **t** . . . 1Sm 17:4

TAMAR

1. Judah's daughter-in-law; widow of Er and
   Onan; mother of Judah's sons (Gn 38).
2. Daughter of David; raped by Amnon;
   avenged by Absalom (2Sm 13).

TAMBOURINE

Praise him with **t** and dance; . . . . . . Ps 150:4

TARSHISH

Distant Mediterranean port city known for
sea trade (1Kg 10:22; 22:48; Pss 48:7; 72:10; Is
2:16; 23:1,6,10,14; 66:19; Jr 10:9; Ezk 27:12,25;
38:13); Jonah fled toward it (Jnh 1:3).

TASTE

T and see that the LORD is good.. . . Ps 34:8
if the salt should lose its **t**,. . . . . Mt 5:13
who will not **t** death until they. . . Mt 16:28
he will never **t** death—ever!'. . . . . Jn 8:52
handle, don't **t**, don't touch"? . . . . Col 2:21
grace he might **t** death for. . . . . . . Heb 2:9
who **t-d** the heavenly gift,. . . . . Heb 6:4
if you have **t-d** that the Lord. 1Pt 2:3

TATTOO

not ... put **t** marks on yourselves; . . Lv 19:28

TAUNT

crucified with him **t-ed** him. . . . . . Mt 27:44

TAX *SEE ALSO* TAX COLLECTOR

lawful to pay **t-es** to Caesar or
not?. . . . . Mt 22:17
t-es to those you owe **t-es**,. . . . . . Rm 13:7

TAX COLLECTOR

Don't even the **t-s** do the same? . . Mt 5:46
a friend of **t-s** and sinners!. . . . . . . Mt 11:19
like an Gentile and a **t** to you. . . . . Mt 18:17
T-s and prostitutes are entering . . Mt 21:31
one a Pharisee and the other a **t**. . Lk 18:10
Zacchaeus who was a chief **t**, ... Lk 19:2

TEACH

T them to your children . . . . . . Dt 4:9; 11:19
t me your paths. . . . . Ps 25:4
T us to number our days. . . . . Ps 90:12
No longer will one **t** his neighbor. . . Jr 31:34
t-ing them to observe
everything . . . . Mt 28:20
t-ing them as one having
authority. . . . . Mk 1:22
He **taught** them many things in. . . . Mk 4:2
t us to pray, just as John also **taught**. . Lk 11:1
Holy Spirit ... will **t** you all things . . Jn 14:26
allow a woman to **t** or to have 1Tm 2:12
hospitable, able to **t**,. 1Tm 3:2
will be able to **t** others also. 2Tm 2:2

correctly **t-ing** the word of truth. . 2Tm 2:15
able to **t**, and patient,. 2Tm 2:24
you don't need anyone to **t** you. . . 1Jn 2:27

TEACHER

A disciple is not above his **t**,. . . . . . Mt 10:24
you have one **T**, and you are all. . . . Mt 23:8
Are you a **t** of Israel and don't. . . . . Jn 3:10
if I, your Lord and **T**, have washed . . Jn 13:14
some pastors and **t-s**, ... Eph 4:11
will be false **t-s** among you. 2Pt 2:1

TEACHING (N)

I will put my **t** within them . . . . Jr 31:33
were astonished at his **t** . . . . Mt 7:28; 22:33
is contrary to the sound **t**. 1Tm 1:10
and is profitable for **t**,. 2Tm 3:16

TEAR (N)

My **t-s** have been my food day and . . Ps 42:3
Put my **t-s** in your bottle. . . . . Ps 56:8
Those who sow in **t-s** will reap . . . . Ps 126:5
to wash his feet with her **t-s**. . . . . . Lk 7:38
away every **t** from their eyes. . . Rv 7:17; 21:4

TEAR (V)

T your hearts, not just your . . . . Jl 2:13
high priest **tore** his robes and. . . . Mt 26:65

TELL

t about all his wonderful works!. . . Ps 105:2
he has **told** each of you what is
good . . . . Mc 6:8
if it were not so, would I have
told you?. . . . . Jn 14:2
I have **told** you now before it . . . . . Jn 14:29

TEMPLE

The LORD is in his holy **t**;. . . . . Ps 11:4
But the LORD is in his holy **t**; . . . . . Hab 2:20
will suddenly come to his **t**,. . . . . . . Mal 3:1
something greater than the **t** is
here! . . . . Mt 12:6
they found him in the **t** complex . . Lk 2:46
Destroy this **t**, and I will raise . . . . . Jn 2:19
that you are God's **t**. 1Co 3:16
your body is a **t** of the Holy. 1Co 6:19
Almighty and the Lamb are its **t**. . . Rv 21:22

TEMPORARY

what is seen is **t**, but what is. 2Co 4:18

TEMPT

wilderness to be **t-ed** by the devil. . Mt 4:1
allow you to be **t-ed** beyond what . 1Co 10:13
and he himself doesn't **t** anyone. . . Jms 1:13
when he was **t-ed**, he is able. . . . . . Heb 2:18
who has been **t-ed** in every way . . Heb 4:15

TEMPTATION

And do not bring us into **t**,. . . . . Mt 6:13
pray, so that you won't enter
into **t**. . . . . Mt 26:41
No **t** has come upon you except . . 1Co 10:13

TEMPTER

Then the **t** approached him and . . . . Mt 4:3

TEN

He wrote the **T** Commandments, . . Ex 34:28
will be like **t** virgins who took. . . . . Mt 25:1
to the one who has **t** talents. . . . Mt 25:28
Were not **t** cleansed?. . . . . Lk 17:17
The **t** horns you saw are **t** kings . . . Rv 17:12

TEN THOUSAND

one who owed **t** talents was . . . . . Mt 18:24
than **t** words in a tongue. 1Co 14:19

TEND

I will **t** my flock and let them . . . . Ezk 34:15

TENDERLY

Speak **t** to Jerusalem, and . . . . Is 40:2

TENT

ark of God sits inside **t** curtains. . . . 2Sm 7:2
dwell in your **t** forever and . . . . Ps 61:4
Enlarge the site of your **t**,. . . . . Is 54:2

TENTH

Abram gave him a **t** of everything. . . Gn 14:20
give to you a **t** of all that you give. . . Gn 28:22
Bring the full **t** into the storehouse . Mal 3:10
You pay a **t** of mint, dill, and . . . . . Mt 23:23
I give a **t** of everything I get. . . . . . . Lk 18:12

TERRIBLE

great and **t** day of the LORD . . Jl 2:31; Mal 4:5

TERRIFY

around them, and they were **t-ied**. . . Lk 2:9
It is a **t-ing** thing to fall into . . . . . Heb 10:31

TERROR

not fear the **t** of the night, ... Ps 91:5
are not a **t** to good conduct. . . . . . . Rm 13:3

TEST

God **t-ed** Abraham. . . . . Gn 22:1
Do not **t** the LORD your God. . . . . Dt 6:16
The LORD left them to **t** Israel,. . . . . . Jdg 3:4
t me and know my concerns. . . . . . Ps 139:23
but the LORD is the **t-er** of hearts. . . Pr 17:3
stone in Zion, a **t-ed** stone, ... Is 28:16
T me in this way," says the LORD . . . Mal 3:10
Do not **t** the Lord your God. . . . . Mt 4:7
approached him to **t** him. . . . . Mt 19:3
expert in the law stood up to **t** him. . Lk 10:25
asked this to **t** him, for he ... knew . . Jn 6:6
did you agree to **t** the Spirit . . . . . . Ac 5:9
t all things. Hold on to what 1Th 5:21
but **t** the spirits to see 1Jn 4:1

TESTIFY

is another who **t-ies** about me, ... Jn 5:32
the Scriptures ... **t** about me. . . . . . Jn 5:39
the Spirit ... he will **t** about me. . . . Jn 15:26
Spirit himself **t-ies** together . . . . . . Rm 8:16
For there are three that **t**: 1Jn 5:7

TESTIMONY

Do not give false **t** against your . . . Ex 20:16
based on the **t** of one witness. . . . Nm 35:30
the **t** of the LORD is trustworthy, . . . Ps 19:7
Bind up the **t**. Seal up the. . . . . Is 8:16
looking for false **t** against Jesus . . Mt 26:59
We know that his **t** is true. . . . . Jn 21:24

THANKS

Give **t** to the LORD; call on 1Ch 16:8
Give **t** to the LORD, ... he is good. . . 1Ch 16:34
Give **t** to him and bless his name. . . Ps 100:4
Give **t** to the LORD, for he is good. . . Ps 136:1
gave **t**, broke them, and gave . . . . Mt 15:36
and after giving **t**, he gave it. . . . . . Mt 26:27
But **t** be to God, who gives us. 1Co 15:57
Give **t** in everything; for this 1Th 5:18

THANKSGIVING

Let's enter his presence with **t**; . . . . Ps 95:2
Enter his gates with **t** and . . . . Ps 100:4
I will offer you a **t** sacrifice. . . . . . . Ps 116:17
through prayer and petition with **t**, . Php 4:6

THIEF

and where **t-ves** don't break in and. . Mt 6:19
you are making it a den of **t-ves**!. . . Mt 21:13
what time the **t** was coming,. . . . . . Mt 24:43
other way is a **t** and a robber. . . . . . Jn 10:1
Let the **t** no longer steal. . . . . Eph 4:28
come just like a **t** in the night. 1Th 5:2
Look, I am coming like a **t**. . . . . Rv 16:15

THING

all these **t-s** will be provided. . . . . . Mt 6:33
with God all **t-s** are possible. . . . . . Mt 19:26
kept all these **t-s** in her heart. . . . . . Lk 2:51
But one **t** I do: Forgetting. . . . . Php 3:13

THINK

praiseworthy—dwell on
these **t-s**........................Php 4:8
able to do all **t-s** through him.....Php 4:13

THINK *SEE ALSO* **THOUGHT (N)**

son of man, that you **t** of him?....Ps 144:3
not to **t** of himself more
highly than.....................Rm 12:3
a child, I **thought** like a child,....1Co 13:11
beyond all that we ask or **t**.......Eph 3:20

THIRD

and on the **t** day he will raise.......Hs 6:2
killed, and be raised the **t** day.....Mt 16:21
raised on the **t** day according to...1Co 15:4

THIRST

I **t** for God, the living God..........Ps 42:2
who hunger and **t** for
righteousness....................Mt 5:6
they will no longer **t**;..............Rv 7:16

THIRSTY

and if he is **t**, give him water......Pr 25:21
everyone who is **t**, come to the......Is 55:1
was **t** and you gave me something..Mt 25:35
this water will get **t** again..........Jn 4:13
in me will never be **t** again.........Jn 6:35
If anyone is **t**, let him come........Jn 7:37
Let the one who is **t** come.........Rv 22:17

THIRTY

my wages, **t** pieces of silver......Zch 11:12
weighed out **t** pieces of silver....Mt 26:15
Jesus was about **t** years old and...Lk 3:23

THISTLES

produce thorns and **t** for you,......Gn 3:18

THOMAS

Apostle; sought evidence of resurrection; made confession of faith (Jn 20:24–29).

THORN

It will produce **t-s** and thistles.....Gn 3:18
fell among **t-s**, and the **t-s** came up..Mt 13:7
twisted together a crown of **t-s**,..Mt 27:29
t in the flesh was given to me,....2Co 12:7

THOUGHT (N)

The LORD knows the **t-s** of
mankind;.......................Ps 94:11
You understand my **t-s** from far...Ps 139:2
My **t-s** are not your **t-s**,...........Is 55:8
Perceiving their **t-s**, Jesus said,.....Mt 9:4
take every **t** captive to obey......2Co 10:5

THOUSAND

his **t-s**, but David his tens of **t-s**..1Sm 18:7
the cattle on a **t** hills.............Ps 50:10
in your sight a **t** years are like......Ps 90:4
one day is like a **t** years,.........2Pt 3:8
and bound him for a **t** years......Rv 20:2
reign with him for a **t** years.......Rv 20:6

THREATEN

he suffered, he did not **t**..........1Pt 2:23

THREE

cord of **t** strands is not easily......Ec 4:12
the huge fish **t** days and **t** nights..Mt 12:40
For where two or **t** are gathered..Mt 18:20
you will deny me **t** times.".......Mt 26:34
and rebuild it in **t** days..........Mt 26:61
killed, and rise after **t** days.......Mk 8:31
Now these **t** remain: faith, hope,..1Co 13:13
For there are **t** that testify:.......1Jn 5:7

THRESHING FLOOR

David bought the **t**............2Sm 24:24

THROAT

their **t** is an open grave;...........Ps 5:9
Their **t** is an open grave;..........Rm 3:13

THRONE

will establish the **t** of his
kingdom.......................2Sm 7:13
Your **t**, God, is forever and ever;...Ps 45:6
seated on a high and lofty **t**,........Is 6:1
He will reign on the **t** of David...Is 9:7
Heaven is my **t**, and earth is my....Is 66:1
heaven, because it is God's **t**;....Mt 5:34
will also sit on twelve **t-s**,.......Mt 19:28
whether **t-s** or dominions or......Col 1:16
Your **t**, God, is forever and.......Heb 1:8
let us approach the **t** of grace
with..........................Heb 4:16
cast their crowns before the **t**,...Rv 4:10
great white **t** and one seated
on it...........................Rv 20:11

THROW

He has **t-n** the horse and its rider...Ex 15:1
should be the first to **t** a stone
at her.........................Jn 8:7

THUNDERCLOUD

I answered you from the **t**.........Ps 81:7

TIME

for such a **t** as this................Est 4:14
a **t** for every activity under heaven:..Ec 3:1
for a **t**, **t-s**, and half a **t**........Dn 7:25; 12:7
Teacher says: My **t** is near;.......Mt 26:18
you will deny me three **t-s**!.......Mt 26:34
My **t** has not yet fully come,........Jn 7:6
It is not for you to know **t-s**........Ac 1:7
making the most of the **t**.........Col 4:5
About the **t-s** and the seasons:.....1Th 5:1
for a **t**, **t-s**, and half a **t**.........Rv 12:14

TIMOTHY

Companion of Paul (Ac 16–20; Rm 16:21; 2Co 1:1; 1Th 1:1; 2Th 1:1; Php 1:1; Phm 1). Sent by Paul to Corinth (1Co 4:17); to Philippi (Php 2:19); to Thessalonica (1Th 3:2). Pastored Ephesian church (1Tm 1:3). Received two letters from Paul (1Tm 1:2; 2Tm 1:2) and a plea to come (4:9).

TIRED

let us not get **t** of doing good,......Gl 6:9

TITUS

Gentile coworker with Paul (Gl 2:1–3; 2Co 8:23). Sent to Corinth (2:1–4; 7:13–15; 8:16–17); in charge of church in Crete (Ti 1:5); went to Dalmatia (2Tm 4:10).

TOBIAH

Adversary against Nehemiah's efforts to rebuild Jerusalem's walls (Neh 2:10,19; 4:1–9; 6; 13:4–9).

TODAY

T, if you hear his voice:............Ps 95:7
Give us our daily bread..........Mt 6:11
T you will be with me in paradise..Lk 23:43
t I have become your Father,...Heb 1:5; 5:5
while it is still called **t**,...........Heb 3:13
T, if you hear his voice, do not....Heb 3:15
same yesterday, **t**, and forever....Heb 13:8

TOLA

Issacharite judge (Jdg 10:1–2).

TOLERABLE

It will be more **t** on the day of....Mt 10:15

TOLERATE

will not **t** sound doctrine,.........2Tm 4:3
and that you cannot **t** evil people....Rv 2:2

TOMB

You are like whitewashed **t-s**,...Mt 23:27
he laid him in a **t** cut out of......Mk 15:46
stone rolled away from the **t**......Lk 24:2
already been in the **t** four days.....Jn 11:17

TOMORROW

Don't boast about **t**, for you don't..Pr 27:1
Let's eat and drink, for **t** we die!....Is 22:13
Therefore don't worry about **t**,....Mt 6:34
us eat and drink, for **t** we die.....1Co 15:32
do not know what **t** will bring—...Jms 4:14

TONGUE

Before a word is on my **t**, you....Ps 139:4
death are in the power of the **t**,...Pr 18:21
every **t** will swear allegiance.......Is 45:23
t-s like flames of fire that..........Ac 2:3
in **t-s** and declaring..............Ac 10:46
in **t-s** and to prophesy............Ac 19:6
interpretation of **t-s**.............1Co 12:10
If I speak human or angelic **t-s**...1Co 13:1
as for **t-s**, they will cease;.........1Co 13:8
person who speaks in a **t**.........1Co 14:2
not forbid speaking in **t-s**........1Co 14:39
and every **t** will confess that......Php 2:11
but no man can tame the **t**........Jms 3:8

TOOTH

eye for eye,
t for **t**.................Ex 21:24; Lv 24:20; Dt 19:21
for an eye and a **t** for a **t**.........Mt 5:38
weeping and gnashing of **teeth**...Mt 8:12

TOP

was torn in two from **t** to bottom,..Mt 27:51

TORCH

fire pot and a flaming **t** appeared..Gn 15:17

TORMENT

come here to **t** us before the time?..Mt 8:29
those **t-ed** by unclean spirits.......Lk 6:18
they will be **t-ed** day and night...Rv 20:10

TORRENT

the **t** would have swept over us;..Ps 124:4

TOSS

driven and **t-ed** by the wind.......Jms 1:6

TOUCH

You must not eat it or **t** it,.........Gn 3:3
t-ed my mouth with it and said:....Is 6:7
If I can just **t** his robe,...........Mt 9:21
in order that he might **t** them,...Mk 10:13
T me and see, because a ghost....Lk 24:39
Don't handle, don't taste, don't **t**?..Col 2:21
and have **t-ed** with our hands,......1Jn 1:1

TOWEL

took a **t**, and tied it around himself..Jn 13:4

TOWER

a **t** with its top in the sky..........Gn 11:4
name of the LORD is a strong **t**;....Pr 18:10

TOWN

and from the **t** of Bethlehem,......Jn 7:42

TRADERS

When Midianite **t** passed by,.....Gn 37:28

TRADITION

nullify the word of God by your **t**..Mk 7:13
empty deceit based on human **t**,...Col 2:8
hold to the **t-s** you were taught,..2Th 2:15

TRAGEDY

a sickening **t**...................Ec 5:13,16
Here is a **t** I have observed..........Ec 6:1

TRAIN

who **t-s** my hands for battle and..Ps 144:1
will never again **t** for war....Is 2:4; Mc 4:3

TRAINING

them up in the **t** and instruction...Eph 6:4
t of the body has a limited benefit,..1Tm 4:8
correcting, for **t** in righteousness,..2Tm 3:16

TRAITOR

Judas Iscariot, who became a **t**. . . . . Lk 6:16

TRAMPLE

be thrown out and **t-d** under . . . . . . Mt 5:13
pearls before pigs, or they will **t** . . . . Mt 7:6
Jerusalem will be **t-d** by the . . . . . . Lk 21:24
who has **t-d** on the Son of
God, ... Heb 10:29

TRAMPLING (N)

you—this **t** of my courts? . . . . Is 1:12

TRANSFIGURE

He was **t-ed** in front of them, ... Mt 17:2

TRANSFORM

be **t-ed** by the renewing of your . . Rm 12:2
are being **t-ed** into the same
image 2Co 3:18
He will **t** the body of our humble . . Php 3:21

TRANSGRESSION

is the one whose **t** is forgiven, ... Ps 32:1
has he removed our **t-s** from us . . Ps 103:12
I am the one, I sweep away
your **t-s** . . . . Is 43:25
where there is no law, there is no **t** . Rm 4:15

TRANSLATE

law ... **t-ing** and giving the
meaning . . . . Neh 8:8
Immanuel ... **t-d** "God is with us." . . .Mt 1:23

TRAP

their gods will be a **t** for you. . . . . . Jdg 2:3
to **t** him by what he said. . . . . Mt 22:15
into disgrace and the devil's **t**. 1Tm 3:7

TREAD

your foot **t-s** will be yours. . . . . Dt 11:24
ox while it **t-s** out grain. . . . Dt 25:4; 1Co 9:9
ox while it is **t-ing** out the grain, . . 1Tm 5:18

TREASURE (N)

for yourselves **t-s** on earth, ... Mt 6:19
For where your **t** is, there your . . . . Mt 6:21
The kingdom of heaven is like **t**, . . Mt 13:44
and you will have **t** in heaven. . . . . Mt 19:21
Now we have this **t** in clay jars, ... 2Co 4:7
the **t-s** of wisdom and knowledge . . Col 2:3

TREASURE (V)

I have **t-d** your word in my heart . . Ps 119:11
But Mary was **t-ing** up all these . . . . Lk 2:19

TREATY

Make no **t** with them . . . . Dt 7:2
Please make a **t** with us. . . . . Jos 9:6

TREE SEE ALSO TREE OF LIFE

the **t** of the knowledge of good
and . . . . Gn 2:9
hung on it is under God's curse. . . Dt 21:23
He is like a **t** planted beside. . . . . . . Ps 1:3
all the **t-s** of the forest will . . . . Ps 96:12
all the **t-s** of the field will clap . . . . Is 55:12
every **t** that doesn't produce good Mt 3:10
for a **t** is known by its fruit. . . . . . Mt 12:33
At once the fig **t** withered. . . . . Mt 21:19
Cursed is everyone ... hung on a **t**. . . Gl 3:13
our sins in his body on the **t**; 1Pt 2:24

TREE OF LIFE

the **t** in the middle of the garden, . . Gn 2:9
must not ... take from the **t**, eat, . . . Gn 3:22
She is a **t** to those who embrace
her, ... Pr 3:18
The fruit of the righteous is a **t**, . . . Pr 11:30
the right to eat from the **t**, ... Rv 2:7
will take away his share of the **t** . . Rv 22:19

TREMBLE

let the whole earth **t** before him. . . 1Ch 16:30

TREMBLING (N)

your own salvation with fear
and **t**. . . . . Php 2:12

TRESPASS

delivered up for our **t-es** and
raised . . . . Rm 4:25
by the one man's **t** the many
died, ... Rm 5:15
not counting their **t-es** against. . . . 2Co 5:19
you were dead in your **t-es** and
sins . . . . Eph 2:1
when you were dead in **t-es** . . . . . . Col 2:13

TRIAL

you experience various **t-s**, ... Jms 1:2

TRIBE

These are the **t-s** of Israel,
twelve. . . . . Gn 49:28
He chose instead the **t** of Judah, . . . Ps 78:68
judging the twelve **t-s** of Israel. . . Mt 19:28
every **t** and language and people. . . Rv 5:9
the names of the twelve **t-s** . . . . . . Rv 21:12

TRIBULATION

ones coming out of the great **t**. . . . . Rv 7:14

TRIP

over and a rock to **t** over, ... Is 8:14
a rock to **t** over, and the one who . . Rm 9:33
and a rock to **t** over. 1Pt 2:8

TRIUMPH

When the righteous **t**, there is
great . . . . Pr 28:12
He **t-ed** over them in him. . . . . Col 2:15
Mercy **t-s** over judgment. . . . . Jms 2:13

TROPHIMUS

and Tychicus and **T** from Asia. . . . . . Ac 20:4
previously seen **T** the Ephesian . . . Ac 21:29
I left **T** sick at Miletus. 2Tm 4:20

TROUBLE (N)

humans are born for **t** as surely as . . Jb 5:7
a refuge in times of **t**. . . . . Ps 9:9
is always found in times of **t**. . . . . . Ps 46:1
and our salvation in time of **t**. . . . . Is 33:2
Each day has enough **t** of its own. . Mt 6:34

TROUBLE (V)

Now my soul is **t-d**. What should . . Jn 12:27
Don't let your heart be **t-d**. . . . . . . Jn 14:1
your heart be **t-d** or fearful. . . . . . . Jn 14:27

TRUE

He is righteous and **t**. . . . . Dt 32:4
The **t** light that gives light to . . . . . . Jn 1:9
I am the **t** vine, and my Father . . . . . Jn 15:1
you, the only **t** God, and the one . . . Jn 17:3
his testimony is **t** . . . . Jn 19:35; 21:24
Let God be **t**, even though
everyone . . . . Rm 3:4
whatever is **t**, whatever is . . . . Php 4:8
these words are faithful and **t**. . .Rv 21:5; 22:6

TRULY

"**T** you are the Son of God." . . . . . . Mt 14:33

TRUMPET

priests carry seven ram's-horn **t-s** . . Jos 6:4
give ... don't sound a **t** before you, . . Mt 6:2
at the last **t**. For the **t** will sound, . . 1Co 15:52
with the **t** of God, and the dead in . . 1Th 4:16
seven **t-s** were given to them. . . . . . Rv 8:2

TRUST

When I am afraid, I will **t** in you. . . . . Ps 56:3
in God I **t**; ... What can mere. . . Ps 56:4,11
T in the LORD with all your . . . . Pr 3:5
those who **t** in the LORD will renew. . Is 40:31
Again, I will **t** in him. . . . . .Heb 2:13

TRUSTWORTHY

the testimony of the LORD is **t**, ... Ps 19:7
The wounds of a friend are **t**, ... Pr 27:6
This saying is **t** 1Tm 1:15; 3:1; 4:9

TRUTH

The entirety of your word is **t**, . . Ps 119:160
grace and **t** came through Jesus . . . . .Jn 1:17
worship the Father in Spirit and **t**. . .Jn 4:23
the **t**, and the **t** will set you free. . . .Jn 8:32
am the way, the **t**, and the life. . . . . Jn 14:6
exchanged the **t** of God for a lie . . . Rm 1:25
But speaking the **t** in love, ...Eph 4:15
teaching the word of **t**. 2Tm 2:15
and the **t** is not in us. 1Jn 1:8

TUNIC

took the **t**, which was seamless, . . . Jn 19:23

TURMOIL

Why are you in such **t**? . . . . .Pss 42:5,11; 43:5

TURN

All have **t-ed** away; all alike have . . . Ps 14:3
T my heart to your decrees and . . Ps 119:36
A gentle answer **t-s** away anger, ...Pr 15:1
t back, and be healed. . . . . Is 6:10
we all have **t-ed** to our own way; . . . Is 53:6
should **t** from his way and live. . . . Ezk 33:11
t to me with all your heart, ...Jl 2:12
And he will **t** the hearts of fathers. . Mal 4:6
right cheek, **t** the other to him . . . . Mt 5:39
to **t** the hearts of fathers to. . . . . . . .Lk 1:17
All have **t-ed** away, all alike have . . . Rm 3:12
that whoever **t-s** a sinner from. . . Jms 5:20

TURTLEDOVE

may take two **t-s** or two young . . . . Lv 12:8
pair of **t-s** or two young pigeons . . . Lk 2:24

TWELVE

Jacob had **t** sons: . . . . Gn 35:22
the names of the **t** apostles: . . . . . . Mt 10:2
t thrones, judging the **t** tribes. . . . Mt 19:28
He appointed the **T**: . . . . Mk 3:16
When he was **t** years old, they . . . . Lk 2:42
t foundations, and the **t** names of
the **t** apostles of the Lamb . . . . . . Rv 21:14

TWENTY-FOUR

on the thrones sat **t** elders. . . . . Rv 4:4
and the **t** elders fell down . . . . .Rv 5:8

TWIN

were indeed **t-s** in her womb. . . . . Gn 25:24

TWINKLING

in a moment, in the **t** of an eye, . . . 1Co 15:52

TWIST

They **t** my words all day long; . . . . . Ps 56:5
and unstable will **t** them to their . . 2Pt 3:16

TWO

into the ark **t** of all the living . . . . . Gn 6:19
T are better than one because. . . . . . Ec 4:9
No one can serve **t** masters, ... Mt 6:24
where **t** or three are gathered. . . . . Mt 18:20
are no longer **t**, but one flesh. . . . . . Mt 19:6
and the **t** will become one flesh. . . . Eph 5:31

- U -

UNAPPROACHABLE

lives in **u** light, ...1Tm 6:16

UNAUTHORIZED

and presented **u** fire before the . . . . Lv 10:1

UNBELIEF

And he was amazed at their **u**. . . . . .Mk 6:6
I do believe; help my **u**! . . . . .Mk 9:24
He rebuked their **u** and hardness . . Mk 16:14

they were broken off because
of u, ... Rm 11:20

UNBELIEVER

But if the **u** leaves, let him leave. . . 1Co 7:15
not for believers but for **u-s** 1Co 14:22
faith and is worse than an **u** 1Tm 5:8

UNBELIEVING (ADJ)

You **u** and perverse generation, . . . Mt 17:17
If any brother has an **u** wife. 1Co 7:12

UNCIRCUMCISED

house of Israel is **u** in heart. . . . . Jr 9:26
A man who is physically **u**, ... Rm 2:27
called "the **u**" by those called . . . . . Eph 2:11

UNCIRCUMCISION

matter and **u** does not matter, ... 1Co 7:19
circumcision nor **u** accomplishes . . . . . Gl 5:6
circumcision and **u**, barbarian, ... Col 3:11

UNCLEAN

if someone touches anything **u** . . . . . . Lv 5:2
I am a man of **u** lips and live among . . Is 6:5
gave them authority over **u**
spirits, ... Mt 10:1
Whenever the **u** spirits saw him . . . Mk 3:11
I have never eaten anything … **u**! . . Ac 10:14
am persuaded … that nothing
is **u**. . . . . Rm 14:14

UNCLOTHED

do not want to be **u** but clothed, . . 2Co 5:4

UNCOVER

go in and **u** his feet, and lie down. . . Ru 3:4
with her head **u-ed** dishonors
her. 1Co 11:5

UNDEFILED

and the marriage bed kept **u**, ... Heb 13:4

UNDER

no other name **u** heaven given to . . Ac 4:12
you are not **u** the law but **u** grace. . Rm 6:14

UNDERNEATH

and **u** are the everlasting arms. . . . . Dt 33:27

UNDERSTAND

then you will **u** the fear of the LORD . . Pr 2:5
Keep listening, but do not **u**; . . . . Is 6:9
u with their hearts and turn back. . Mt 13:15
holy place" (let the reader **u**), ... Mt 24:15
Then he opened their minds to **u** . . Lk 24:45
but **u** what the Lord's will is. . . . . Eph 5:17
some things hard to **u** in them. 2Pt 3:16

UNDERSTANDING (N)

and do not rely on your own **u**; . . . . . . Pr 3:5

UNEDUCATED

that they were **u** and untrained . . . . Ac 4:13

UNFADING

and **u**, kept in heaven 1Pt 1:4
receive the **u** crown of glory. 1Pt 5:4

UNFRUITFUL

but my understanding is **u**. 1Co 14:14

UNGODLY

time, Christ died for the **u**. . . . . Rm 5:6

UNINFORMED

We do not want you to be **u**, ... 1Th 4:13

UNITED

were continually **u** in prayer, ... Ac 1:14

UNITY

until we all reach **u** in the faith . . . . Eph 4:13
the perfect bond of **u**. . . . . Col 3:14

UNJUST

Listen to what the **u** judge says. . . . . Lk 18:6
For God is not **u**; he will not. . . . . . Heb 6:10

UNKNOWN

'To an **U** God.' . . . . Ac 17:23

UNLEAVENED

observe the Festival of **U** Bread . . . Ex 12:17
On the first day of **U** Bread . . . . . . .Mt 26:17

UNMARRIED

I say to the **u** and to widows: 1Co 7:8

UNNATURAL

natural sexual relations for **u**
ones. . . . . Rm 1:26

UNPUNISHED

will not leave the guilty **u**, ... Ex 34:7
that the wicked will not go **u**, ... Pr 11:21

UNQUENCHABLE

and go to hell, the **u** fire, ... Mk 9:43

UNRIGHTEOUS

rain on the righteous and the **u**. . . . Mt 5:45
whoever is **u** in very little is also. . . . Lk 16:10
the righteous for the **u**, ... 1Pt 3:18

UNRIGHTEOUSNESS

and there is no **u** in him. . . . . Ps 92:15
and to cleanse us from all **u**. 1Jn 1:9

UNSEARCHABLE

How **u** his judgments and . . . . Rm 11:33

UNSEEN

temporary, but what is **u** is eternal. . 2Co 4:18

UNSHRUNK

an old garment with **u** cloth, ... Mt 9:16

UNSTABLE

double-minded and **u** in all his
ways. . . . . Jms 1:8
They seduce **u** people 2Pt 2:14

UNTIE

sandal strap I'm not worthy to **u**. . . . Jn 1:27

UNTRACEABLE

his judgments and **u** his ways! . . . . Rm 11:33

UNVEILED

We all, with **u** faces, are looking . . . 2Co 3:18

UNWORTHY

cup of the Lord in an **u** way 1Co 11:27

UPRIGHT

The **u** will see his face. . . . . Ps 11:7
God made people **u**, but they . . . . . . Ec 7:29

UPROOT

Be **u-ed** and planted in the sea, ... Lk 17:6

UPSTAIRS

He will show you a large room **u**, . . Mk 14:15

UR

City in lower Mesopotamia; birthplace of
Abraham (Gn 11:28,31; 15:7; Neh 9:7).

URIAH

Hethite; husband of Bathsheba. One of David's warriors (2Sm 23:39); David arranged
his death (2Sm 11).

URIM

Place the **U** and Thummim in the . . Ex 28:30

USEFUL

now he is **u** both to you and to me. . Phm 11

USELESS

that faith without works is **u**? . . . . Jms 2:20

UZZIAH

Son of Amaziah; king of Judah; also known
as Azariah (2Kg 15:1–7). Made king by
popular acclaim (2Ch 26:1); expanded and
fortified Judah (26:6–15); struck with skin
disease when he attempted to serve as
priest (26:16–21).

- V -

VAIN

and the peoples plot in **v**? . . . . Ps 2:1
its builders labor over it in **v**; . . . . . . Ps 127:1
They worship me in **v**, ... Mt 15:9
labor in the Lord is not in **v**. 1Co 15:58
and had not been running, in **v**. . . . . . Gl 2:2

VALLEY

when I go through the darkest **v**, . . Ps 23:4
Every **v** will be lifted up, ... Is 40:4
multitudes in the **v** of decision! . . . . . Jl 3:14
Every **v** will be filled, and every . . . . . Lk 3:5

VALUE

despised, and we didn't **v** him. . . . . . Is 53:3
the surpassing **v** of knowing . . . . . . Php 3:8
any **v** in curbing self-indulgence. . . Col 2:23

VANISH

the heavens will **v** like smoke, ... Is 51:6

VEGETABLE

Let us be given **v-s** to eat and. . . . . . Dn 1:12
one who is weak eats only **v-s**. . . . . Rm 14:2

VEIL

he put a **v** over his face. . . . . Ex 34:33
old covenant, the same **v** remains; . . 2Co 3:14

VENGEANCE

V and retribution belong to me. . . Dt 32:35
For the LORD has a day of **v**, ... Is 34:8
it is written: **V** belongs to me; . . . Rm 12:19
who has said, **V** belongs to me,. . Heb 10:30

VICTORY

has been swallowed up in **v**. 1Co 15:54
Where, death, is your **v**? 1Co 15:55
gives us the **v** through our Lord . . 1Co 15:57
This is the **v** that has conquered. . . . 1Jn 5:4

VINDICATE

wisdom is **v-d** by all her children. . . . Lk 7:35

VINE

I am the true **v**, and My Father . . . . . Jn 15:1

VINEGAR

thirst they gave me **v** to drink. . . . . Ps 69:21

VINEYARD

to hire workers for his **v**. . . . . Mt 20:1
who planted a **v**, put a fence. . . . . . .Mt 21:33

VIOLENCE

because he had done no **v** . . . . Is 53:9
of heaven has been suffering **v**, . . . Mt 11:12

VIOLENT

and the **v** have been seizing it . . . . Mt 11:12

VIPER

he said to them, "Brood of **v-s**! . . . . Mt 3:7
Snakes! Brood of **v-s**! How can . . . Mt 23:33

VIRGIN

The **v** will conceive, have a son, ... Is 7:14
the **v** will become pregnant and. . . Mt 1:23
be like ten **v-s** who took their. . . . . . Mt 25:1
The **v-'s** name was Mary. . . . . Lk 1:27

VISIBLE

humans see what is **v**, but the
LORD 1Sm 16:7
made from things that are not **v**. . .Heb 11:3

VISION

and your young men will see **v-s**. . . . Jl 2:28
your young men will see **v-s**, ... Ac 2:17
move on to **v-s** and revelations . . . 2Co 12:1

VISIT

was in prison and you **v-ed** me. . . Mt 25:36
God has **v-ed** his people. . . . . Lk 7:16

VOICE

after the fire there was a **v**, a soft 1Kg 19:12
Today, if you hear his **v**: . . . . Ps 95:7
A **v** of one crying out . . . . Is 40:3
A **v** was heard in Ramah, a lament . . Jr 31:15
A **v** was heard in Ramah, weeping,. Mt 2:18
And a **v** from heaven said: . . . . . . .Mt 3:17
and the sheep hear his **v**. . . . . Jn 10:3
Then a **v** came from heaven: . . . Jn 12:28
Their **v** has gone out to the . . . . . . Rm 10:18
Today, if you hear his **v**, ... Heb 3:7,15; 4:7
If anyone hears my **v** and opens. . . Rv 3:20

VOMIT (N)

As a dog returns to its **v**, ... Pr 26:11
A dog returns to its own **v**, ... 2Pt 2:22

VOMIT (V)

I am going to **v** you out of my . . . . .Rv 3:16

VOW (N)

makes a special **v**, a Nazirite **v**, ...Nm 6:2
Jephthah made this **v** to the LORD: . .Jdg 11:30
I will fulfill my **v-s** before those . . . Ps 22:25
and later to reconsider his **v-s**. . . . . Pr 20:25

VOW (V)

Fulfill what you **v**. . . . . Ec 5:4

- W -

WAGE

the worker is worthy of his **w-s**. . . . Lk 10:7
For the **w-s** of sin is death, ...Rm 6:23
The worker is worthy of his **w-s**. . .1Tm 5:18

WAIST

a leather belt around his **w**, ... Mt 3:4

WAIT

W for the LORD; be strong . . . . Ps 27:14
creation eagerly **w-s** with . . . . Rm 8:19
we eagerly **w** for it with patience. . Rm 8:25
as you eagerly **w** for the revelation . . 1Co 1:7
to **w** for his Son from heaven, ... 1Th 1:10

WALK

Enoch **w-ed** with God; then he was. Gn 5:24
his sons did not **w** in his ways. 1Sm 8:3
to **w** in his ways and to keep. 1Kg 2:3
they will **w** and not faint. . . . . Is 40:31
and to **w** humbly with your God. . . . Mc 6:8
or to say, 'Get up and **w**'?. . . . . Mt 9:5
saw him **w-ing** on the sea, ... Mt 14:26
pick up your mat and **w**. . . . . .Jn 5:8
we too may **w** in newness of life. . . .Rm 6:4
we **w** by faith, not by sight 2Co 5:7
w by the Spirit and you will. . . . . . . Gl 5:16
W as children of light . . . . Eph 5:8
If we **w** in the light as he 1Jn 1:7

WALL

shout, and the **w** collapsed. . . . . . . .Jos 6:20
let's rebuild Jerusalem's **w**, ...Neh 2:17
down the dividing **w** of hostility. . .Eph 2:14
By faith the **w-s** of Jericho fell . . .Heb 11:30

WANDER

have **w-ed** away from the faith . . 1Tm 6:10

WANDERER

will be a restless **w** on the earth. . . .Gn 4:12

WAR

makes **w-s** cease throughout the . . .Ps 46:9
a time for **w** and a time for . . . . .Ec 3:8
will never again train for **w**. . . . . Is 2:4
hear of **w-s** and rumors of **w-s**. . . . Mt 24:6
do not wage **w** according to the
flesh, ...2Co 10:3

WARFARE

weapons of our **w** are not flesh,
but. 2Co 10:4

WARM

lie down together, they can
keep **w**; . . . . Ec 4:11

WARN

if you **w** a wicked person . . . . Ezk 3:19; 33:9
And being **w-ed** in a dream. . . . . Mt 2:12,22
Who **w-ed** you to flee from the . . . . Mt 3:7
w-ing and teaching everyone
with. . . . . Col 1:28

WARRIOR

LORD is a **w**; the LORD is his name. . . Ex 15:3

WASH

Go **w** seven times in the Jordan . . .2Kg 5:10
w me, and I will be whiter than . . . . Ps 51:7
they don't **w** their hands when. . . . .Mt 15:2
began to **w** his feet with her tears. . Lk 7:38
began to **w** his disciples' feet . . . . . Jn 13:5
and **w** away your sins by calling . . . Ac 22:16
But you were **w-ed**, you were. 1Co 6:11
the **w-ing** of water by the word. . Eph 5:26
Blessed . . . who **w** their robes, ...Rv 22:14

WASTE

Why has this perfume been **w-d**? . . Mk 14:4
my labor for you has been **w-d**. . . . . .Gl 4:11

WATCH (N)

keeping **w** at night over their flock. .Lk 2:8
since they keep **w** over your souls . .Heb 13:17

WATCH (V)

the LORD **w-es** over the way of. . . . . . Ps 1:6
unless the LORD **w-es** over a city, . . .Ps 127:1
W! Be alert! For you don't know. . . Mk 13:33

WATCHMAN

the **w** stays alert in vain. . . . . .Ps 127:1
more than **w-men** for the morning. .Ps 130:6
I have made you a **w** . . . . Ezk 3:17; 33:7

WATER (N)

w covered the earth. . . . . Gn 7:6
I am poured out like **w**, ... Ps 22:14
He leads me beside quiet **w-s**. . . . . .Ps 23:2
bread on the surface of the **w**, ... Ec 11:1
who is thirsty, come to the **w**; . . . . .Is 55:1
abandoned . . . fountain of living **w**, . . Jr 2:13
will also sprinkle clean **w** on you, . .Ezk 36:25
that day living **w** will flow out . . . .Zch 14:8
I baptize you with **w** for
repentance, ...Mt 3:11
a cup of cold **w** to one of these . . Mt 10:42
Peter started walking on the **w** . . . Mt 14:29
is born of **w** and the Spirit, ... Jn 3:5
and he would give you living **w**. . . . Jn 4:10
of living **w** flow from deep . . . . .Jn 7:38
the washing of **w** by the word. . . Eph 5:26
the one who came by **w** and blood, . .1Jn 5:6
thirsty, from the spring of the **w**
of life. . . . . .Rv 21:6

WATER (V)

I planted, Apollos **w-ed**, but God . . .1Co 3:6

WATERFALLS

calls to deep in the roar of your **w**; . .Ps 42:7

WAVER

He did not **w** in unbelief at God's. .Rm 4:20
of our hope without **w-ing**, ... Heb 10:23

WAVES

was being swamped by the **w**—. . . Mt 8:24
even the winds and the **w**, ...Lk 8:25

WAX

my heart is like **w**, melting within . . Ps 22:14

WAY

God—his **w** is perfect; 2Sm 22:31
watches over the **w** of the
righteous . . . . Ps 1:6
Commit your **w** to the LORD; . . . . . . .Ps 37:5
can a young man keep his **w** pure? . .Ps 119:9
See if there is any offensive **w** in me; lead
me in the everlasting **w**. . . . . Ps 139:24
There is a **w** that seems right . . . . Pr 14:12
youth out on his **w**; even when he . . Pr 22:6
Prepare the **w** of the LORD in the . . . Is 40:3
we all have turned to our own **w**; . . Is 53:6
and your **w-s** are not my **w-s**. . . . . . Is 55:8
Prepare the **w** for the LORD; . . . . . . Mt 3:3
God loved the world in this **w**: . . . . . Jn 3:16
I am the **w**, the truth, and the life. . . Jn 14:6
found any . . . who belonged to the **W**. . Ac 9:2
will also provide the **w** out 1Co 10:13
will show you an even better **w**. . . 1Co 12:31

WEAK

spirit is willing, but the flesh is **w**. . Mt 26:41
Welcome anyone who is **w** in faith, . .Rm 14:1
God has chosen . . . what is **w** 1Co 1:27
For when I am **w**, then I am 2Co 12:10

WEAKER

as with a **w** partner, ... 1Pt 3:7

WEAKNESS

took our **w-es** and carried our . . . . .Mt 8:17
Spirit also helps us in our **w**, ...Rm 8:26
sown in **w**, raised in power; 1Co 15:43
for power is perfected in **w**. 2Co 12:9
to sympathize with our **w-es** . . . . Heb 4:15

WEALTH

They trust in their **w** . . . . .Ps 49:6
W is not profitable on a day of . . . . . Pr 11:4
Give me neither poverty nor **w**; . . . . Pr 30:8
wealthy should not boast in his **w**. . Jr 9:23
deceitfulness of **w** choke the
word, ...Mt 13:22
hard it is for those who have **w** to . .Mk 10:23

WEAPON

No **w** formed against you will. . . . . . Is 54:17
the **w-s** of our warfare are not 2Co 10:4

WEAR

about your body, what you will **w**. . Mt 6:25
and **w-ing** gold jewelry 1Pt 3:3

WEARISOME

All things are **w**, more than . . . . .Ec 1:8

WEARY

they will run and not become **w**, . . Is 40:31
Come to me, all of you who are **w**. . Mt 11:28
do not grow **w** in doing good. 2Th 3:13

WEDDING

Can the **w** guests be sad while . . . . Mt 9:15
get in here without **w** clothes?' . . .Mt 22:12
a **w** took place in Cana of Galilee. . . . Jn 2:1

WEEDS

w among the wheat, ...Mt 13:25

WEEK

Observe the Festival of **W-s** . . . . . .Ex 34:22
Seventy **w-s** are decreed . . . . Dn 9:24
first day of the **w** was dawning, ... Mt 28:1

WEEP

W-ing may stay overnight, but . . . .Ps 30:5
wept when we remembered Zion. .Ps 137:1
a time to **w** and a time to laugh; . . . .Ec 3:4
Rachel **w-ing** for her children, ...Jr 31:15
Rachel **w-ing** for her children; . . . . . Mt 2:18
there will be **w-ing** and gnashing . Mt 8:12
Jesus **wept**. . . . . .Jn 11:35
who rejoice; **w** with those who **w** . . Rm 12:15

WEIGH

you have been **w-ed** on the
balance . . . . .Dn 5:27

WEIGHT

honest balances, honest **w-s**, ... Lv 19:36
incomparable eternal **w** of glory. . .2Co 4:17

WELCOME

whoever **w-s** one child like this . . . Mt 18:5
w one another, ... Rm 15:7

WELL

and I know this very **w**. . . . . Ps 139:14
master said to him, 'W done, ...Mt 25:21

WELL-BEING

plans for your **w**, not for disaster, . . .Jr 29:11

WENT *SEE* GO

WEST

far as the east is from the **w**, ... Ps 103:12

WHATEVER

W you ask in my name, I will do . . . Jn 14:13
w is true, **w** is honorable, **w** is just, . . Php 4:8

WHEAT

sowed weeds among the **w**, ...Mt 13:25
has asked to sift you like **w**. . . . . . . Lk 22:31
Unless a grain of **w** falls to. . . . . . . Jn 12:24

WHEEL

was like a **w** within a **w**. . . . . Ezk 1:16

WHIPPED

I will have him **w** and . . . . Lk 23:16

WHIRLWIND

Elijah up to heaven in a **w**. 2Kg 2:1
LORD answered Job from the **w**. . . . . Jb 38:1
sow the wind and reap the **w**. . . . . .Hs 8:7

WHISPER

there was a voice, a soft **w**. 1Kg 19:12
What you hear in a **w**, proclaim . . Mt 10:27

WHITE

scarlet, they will be as **w** as snow; . . .Is 1:18
make a single hair **w** or black. . . . . . Mt 5:36
his clothing was as **w** as snow. . . . . Mt 28:3
hair of his head were **w** as wool—. . Rv 1:14
I saw a great **w** throne and one . . . Rv 20:11

WHITER

and I will be **w** than snow. . . . . Ps 51:7

WHITEWASH

You are like **w-ed** tombs, ... Mt 23:27

WHO

w do you say that I am?. . . . . .Mt 16:15

WHOLE

if he gains the **w** world yet loses . . Mt 16:26

WICK

will not put out a smoldering **w**; . . . Is 42:3
will not put out a smoldering **w**, . . Mt 12:20

WICKED

w men of the city surrounded. . . .Jdg 19:22
does not walk in the advice of the **w** . . Ps 1:1

He was assigned a grave with the **w**, . .Is 53:9
no pleasure in the death of the **w**, . . Ezk 33:11

WICKEDNESS

saw that human **w** was widespread. . .Gn 6:5

WIDE

the gate is **w** and the road broad . . .Mt 7:13

WIDOW

Support **w-s** who are genuinely
in need. 1Tm 5:3

WIFE

and mother and bonds with his **w**, . . Gn 2:24
Do not covet your neighbor's **w**, . . . Ex 20:17
seven hundred **w-ves** ... turned
his heart. 1Kg 11:3
pleasure in the **w** of your youth. . . Pr 5:18
A man who finds a **w** finds a good . . Pr 18:22
Who can find a **w** of noble
character?. . . . . Pr 31:10
should have ... with his own **w**, ... 1Co 7:2
W-ves, submit to your . . . . .Eph 5:22
Husbands, love your **w-ves**, ...Eph 5:25
husband of one **w**, ...1Tm 3:2
the bride, the **w** of the Lamb. . . . . . Rv 21:9

WILD

Without revelation people run **w**, . . Pr 29:18
food was locusts and **w** honey. . . . . Mt 3:4
you, though a **w** olive branch, ... Rm 11:17
in the same flood of **w** living. 1Pt 4:4

WILDERNESS

Prepare the way of the LORD in
the **w**; . . . . .Is 40:3
voice of one crying out in the **w**: . . . Mt 3:3
into the **w** to be tempted. . . . . Mt 4:1
ancestors ate the manna in
the **w**, ...Jn 6:31,49

WILDFLOWERS

Consider how the **w** grow: . . . . Lk 12:27

WILL (N)

I delight to do your **w**, my God; . . Ps 40:8
Your **w** be done on earth as it is . . . Mt 6:10
one who does the **w** of my Father . .Mt 7:21
Yet not as I **w**, but as you **w**. . . . . . Mt 26:39
My food is to do the **w** of him . . . . .Jn 4:34
your **w** had predestined to take
place . . . . .Ac 4:28
it does not depend on human **w**. . . Rm 9:16
the good, pleasing, and perfect **w**. . Rm 12:2
See, I have come to do your **w**. . . . Heb 10:9
ask anything according to his **w**, . . 1Jn 5:14

WILL (V)

say, "If the Lord **w-s**, we will . . . . . .Jms 4:15

WILLING (ADJ)

giving me a **w** spirit. . . . . Ps 51:12
her wings, but you were not **w**! . . Mt 23:37
The spirit is **w**, but the flesh . . . . . Mt 26:41
if you are **w**, take this cup away . . Lk 22:42

WIND

but the LORD was not in the **w**. . . .1Kg 19:11
soaring on the wings of the **w**. . . . . Ps 18:10
will inherit the **w**, ... Pr 11:29
they sow the **w** and reap the . . . . . Hs 8:7
the **w-s** and the sea obey him! . . . . Mt 8:27
The **w** blows where it pleases, ...Jn 3:8
around by every **w** of teaching, . . .Eph 4:14

WINDSTORM

A great **w** arose, and the waves . . . Mk 4:37

WINE

W is a mocker, beer is a brawler, ...Pr 20:1
and **w** to one whose life is bitter. . . . Pr 31:6
no one puts new **w** into old. . . . . . . .Mt 9:17
water (after it had become **w**), ...Jn 2:9

said, "They're drunk on new **w**!" . . . . Ac 2:13
And don't get drunk with **w**, ...Eph 5:18
not drinking a lot of **w**, ... 1Tm 3:3; Ti 1:7
a little **w** because of your stomach . . 1Tm 5:23

WINESKIN

no one puts new wine into old **w-s**. . .Mt 9:17

WING

I carried you on eagles' **w-s**. . . . . . . .Ex 19:4
under whose **w-s** you have come. . . .Ru 2:12
soaring on the **w-s** of the wind. . . .2Sm 22:11
hide me in the shadow of your **w-s**. .Ps 17:8
soaring on the **w-s** of the wind. . . . Ps 18:10
will soar on **w-s** like eagles; . . . . . . Is 40:31
rise with healing in its **w-s**, ... Mal 4:2
gathers her chicks under her **w-s**, . .Mt 23:37

WINTER

Pray it won't happen in **w**. . . . . Mk 13:18

WIPE

Lord GOD will **w** away the tears . . . . Is 25:8
She **w-d** his feet with the hair . . . . Lk 7:38
will **w** away every tear . . . . .Rv 7:17; 21:4

WISDOM

God gave Solomon **w**, ...1Kg 4:29
of the LORD is the beginning of **w**, . . Pr 9:10
Yet **w** is vindicated by all her. . . . . . Lk 7:35
the **w** and the knowledge . . . . .Rm 11:33
I will destroy the **w** of the wise, . . . 1Co 1:19
able to give you **w** for salvation . . .2Tm 3:15
Now if any of you lacks **w**, ...Jms 1:5
and riches and **w** and strength . . . . . Rv 5:12

WISE

making the inexperienced **w**. . . . . . . Ps 19:7
is considered **w** when he keeps. . . . Pr 17:28
w men from the east arrived. . . . . . .Mt 2:1
hidden these things from the **w** . . .Mt 11:25
foolish ... to shame the **w**, ... 1Co 1:27

WITHER

and its leaf does not **w**. . . . . Ps 1:3
The grass **w-s**, the flowers fade . . . . Is 40:7
it had no root, it **w-ed** away. . . . . . . Mt 13:6
At once the fig tree **w-ed**. . . . . Mt 21:19
grass **w-s**, and the flower falls, ... 1Pt 1:24

WITHHOLD

have not **w-held** your only son . . Gn 22:12,16

WITNESS

the testimony of two or
three **w-es**. Dt 19:15
two or three **w-es** every fact may. .Mt 18:16
many false **w-es** came forward. . .Mt 26:60
will be my **w-es** in Jerusalem, ... Ac 1:8
a good confession ... many **w-es**. . .1Tm 6:12
large cloud of **w-es** surrounding . .Heb 12:1
from Jesus Christ, the faithful **w**, . . . Rv 1:5
grant my two **w-es** authority . . . . . . Rv 11:3

WOE

W is me for I am ruined . . . . Is 6:5
w to you, scribes and Pharisees, . . .Mt 23:13
W to you who are now full, ...Lk 6:25
And **w** to me if I do not preach 1Co 9:16
W! **W**! **W** to those who live on . . . . .Rv 8:13

WOLF

The **w** will dwell with the lamb, ...Is 11:6
you out like sheep among **w-ves**. . Mt 10:16
savage **w-ves** will come in. . . . . . . .Ac 20:29

WOMAN

this one will be called "w," . . . . Gn 2:23
w who fears the LORD ... praised. . . Pr 31:30
who looks at a **w** lustfully . . . . Mt 5:28
There were also **w-en** watching . . Mk 15:40
Blessed are you among **w-en**, ...Lk 1:42
brought a **w** caught in adultery . . . . .Jn 8:3
for a man not to use a **w** for sex." . . . 1Co 7:1

the man is the head of the **w**, ... 1Co 11:3
w-en should be silent in the 1Co 14:34
God sent his Son, born of a **w**, ... Gl 4:4
I do not allow a **w** to teach 1Tm 2:12

WOMB

Two nations are in your **w**; . . . . Gn 25:23
Naked I came from my mother's **w**, . . Jb 1:21
me together in my mother's **w**. . . . Ps 139:13
me from the **w** to be his servant, . . . Is 49:5
before I formed you in the **w**; . . . . Jr 1:5
his mother's **w** a second time . . . . Jn 3:4

WONDERFUL

He will be named **W** Counselor, ... Is 9:6
and it is **w** in our eyes? . . . . Mt 21:42

WONDERS

God of Israel, who alone does **w** . . Ps 72:18
I will display **w** in the heaven . . . . . . Ac 2:19

WONDROUS

tell about all his **w** works! . . . . Ps 105:2
it is **w** in our sight. . . . . Ps 118:23
w things from your instruction. . . Ps 119:18
Your works are **w**, and I know . . . . Ps 139:14

WONDROUSLY

been remarkably and **w** made. . . . . Ps 139:14

WOOD

I bow down to a block of **w**?" . . . . . Is 44:19
costly stones, **w**, hay, or straw, ... 1Co 3:12

WOOL

made of both **w** and linen. . . . . Dt 22:11
crimson red, they will be like **w**. . . . . . Is 1:18
hair of his head was white as **w**— . . Rv 1:14

WORD

bread alone but on every **w** that . . . Dt 8:3
the **w** of the LORD is pure. . . . . Ps 18:30
May the **w** of my mouth and the . . Ps 19:14
treasured your **w** in my heart so. . . Ps 119:11
Your **w** is a lamp for my feet . . . . Ps 119:105
Before a **w** is on my tongue, ... Ps 139:4
Every **w** of God is pure; . . . . Pr 30:5
w of our God remains forever. . . . . . . Is 40:8
my **w** ... not return to me empty, . . . Is 55:11
bread alone but on every **w** that . . . Mt 4:4
hears these **w-s** of mine and . . . . . Mt 7:24
but my **w-s** will never pass away. . Mt 24:35
The sower sows the **w**. . . . . Mk 4:14
beginning was the **W**, and the **W**
was with God, and the **W** was God. . Jn 1:1
The **W** became flesh and dwelt. . . . . Jn 1:14
You have the **w-s** of eternal life. . . . Jn 6:68
by the truth; your **w** is truth. . . . . . . Jn 17:17
the **w** of the cross is foolishness. . . 1Co 1:18
correctly teaching the **w** of truth. . 2Tm 2:15
For the **w** of God is living and . . . . Heb 4:12
name is called the **W** of God. . . . . . . Rv 19:13
who keeps the **w-s** of this book . . . Rv 22:9

WORK (N)

God had completed his **w**. . . . . Gn 2:2
six days and do all your **w**, ... Ex 20:9
heavens, the **w** of your fingers, ... Ps 8:3
w-s are wondrous, and I know . . . Ps 139:14
There is profit in all hard **w**, ... Pr 14:23
we all are the **w** of your hands. . . . . . Is 64:8
do even greater **w-s** than these, . . . Jn 14:12
faith apart from the **w-s** of the
law. . . . . Rm 3:28
if by grace, then it is not by **w-s**; . . Rm 11:6
test the quality of each one's **w**. . . . 1Co 3:13
because by the **w-s** of the law no . . Gl 2:16
not from **w-s**, so that no one can . . Eph 2:9
in Christ Jesus for good **w-s**, ... Eph 2:10
started a good **w** in you will . . . . Php 1:6
equipped for every good **w**. 2Tm 3:17
have faith but does not have **w-s**? . . Jms 2:14
I know your **w-s**. . . . . Rv 2:2,19; 3:1,8,15
judged according to their **w-s**. . . . . Rv 20:13

WORK (V)

My Father is still **w-ing**, and I . . . . . . Jn 5:17
Don't **w** for the food that . . . . Jn 6:27
that all things **w** together for . . . . . Rm 8:28
w out your own salvation with. . . . Php 2:12
For it is God who is **w-ing** in you . . Php 2:13
isn't willing to **w**, he should not
eat. 2Th 3:10

WORKER

abundant, but the **w-s** are few. . . . Mt 9:37
the **w** is worthy of his wages. . . . . . Lk 10:7
The **w** is worthy of his wages. 1Tm 5:18
a **w** who doesn't need to be 2Tm 2:15

WORKMANSHIP

we are his **w**, created in Christ. . . . . Eph 2:10

WORLD

He judges the **w** with righteousness; . . Ps 9:8
You are the light of the **w**. . . . . Mt 5:14
gains the whole **w** yet loses his . . Mt 16:26
Go into all the **w** and preach the . . Mk 16:15
who takes away the sin of the **w**! . . Jn 1:29
For God loved the **w** in this way: . . . Jn 3:16
I am the light of the **w**. . . . . . . Jn 8:12; 9:5
I have conquered the **w**. . . . . Jn 16:33
Do not love the **w** or the things . . . 1Jn 2:15
greater than the one who is in
the **w**. 1Jn 4:4

WORM

But I am a **w** and not a man, ... Ps 22:6
for their **w** will never die, ... Is 66:24
God appointed a **w** that attacked . . Jnh 4:7

WORMWOOD

The name of the star is **W**, ... Rv 8:11

WORRY

Don't **w** about your life, ... Mt 6:25
don't **w** beforehand what you will. . Mk 13:11
Don't **w** about anything, but in . . . Php 4:6

WORSHIP

W the LORD in the splendor of . . . 1Ch 16:29
Come, let's **w** and bow down; . . . . . Ps 95:6
those who **w** him must **w** in spirit . . Jn 4:24
this is your true **w**. . . . . Rm 12:1

WORSHIPERS

when the true **w** will worship . . . . . . Jn 4:23

WORTHLESS

not been raised, your faith is **w**; . . 1Co 15:17

WORTHY

to the LORD, who is **w** of praise, . . 2Sm 22:4
and follow me is not **w** of me. . . . . Mt 10:38
I am not **w** to untie the strap of . . . . Lk 3:16
not **w** to be called an apostle, ... 1Co 15:9
you to walk of the calling . . . . Eph 4:1
W is the Lamb who was slaughtered . . Rv 5:12

WOUND

and bandages their **w-s**. . . . . Ps 147:3
The **w-s** of a friend are trustworthy, . . Pr 27:6
and we are healed by his **w-s**. . . . . . Is 53:5
By his **w-s** you have been healed. . 1Pt 2:24
but its fatal **w** was healed. . . . . Rv 13:3

WRAP

body, **w-ped** it in clean, fine linen, . . Mt 27:59
and she **w-ped** him tightly in cloth . . Lk 2:7

WRATH

do not discipline me in your **w**. . . . . . Ps 6:1
Even human **w** will praise you; . . . . Ps 76:10
is not profitable on a day of **w**, ... Pr 11:4
but a harsh word stirs up **w**. . . . . . . Pr 15:1
you to flee from the coming **w**? . . . Mt 3:7
For God's **w** is revealed from . . . . . . Rm 1:18
were by nature children under **w**, . . Eph 2:3
and from the **w** of the Lamb, ... Rv 6:16

WRESTLED

man **w** with him until daybreak. . . Gn 32:24

WRETCHED

What a **w** man I am! Who will . . . . . Rm 7:24
you don't realize that you are **w**, . . . Rv 3:17

WRINKLE

without spot or **w** or anything . . . . Eph 5:27

WRITE

Moses **wrote** down all the words. . . Ex 24:4
w them on the tablet of your . . . . Pr 3:3; 7:3
within them and **w** it on their
hearts. . . . . Jr 31:33
hand appeared and began **w-ing**, . . Dn 5:5
because he **wrote** about me. . . . . . . Jn 5:46
are **w-ten** so that you may
believe . . . . Jn 20:31
I will ... **w** them on their hearts. . . Heb 8:10

WRONG

this man has done nothing **w**. . . . . Lk 23:41
Love does no **w** to a neighbor. . . . Rm 13:10
does not keep a record of **w-s**. . . . 1Co 13:5

WRONGDOING

if someone is overtaken in any **w**, . . . Gl 6:1

- Y -

YEAR

The fiftieth **y** will be your Jubilee; . Lv 25:11
a thousand **y-s** are like yesterday. . Ps 90:4
proclaim the **y** of the LORD's favor, . . Is 61:2
proclaim the **y** of the Lord's favor. . Lk 4:19
days, months, seasons, and **y-s**. . . . Gl 4:10
continually offer **y** after **y**. . . . . . . Heb 10:1
one day is like a thousand **y-s**, ... 2Pt 3:8
for a thousand **y-s**. . . . . Rv 20:2,4,6

YES

let your '**y**' mean '**y**,' . . . . Mt 5:37
God's promises is "**Y**" in him. 2Co 1:20
your "**y**" mean "**y**," and your . . . . . . Jms 5:12

YESTERDAY

were born only **y** and know
nothing. . . . . Jb 8:9
Jesus Christ is the same **y**,
today, ... Heb 13:8

YOKE

Your father made our **y** harsh. 1Kg 12:4
take up my **y** and learn from me, . . Mt 11:29
submit again to a **y** of slavery. . . . . . Gl 5:1

YOUNG

How can a **y** man keep his way . . . Ps 119:9
and your **y** men will see visions. . . . Jl 2:28
your **y** men will see visions, ... Ac 2:17

YOUNGER

The older will serve the **y**. . . . . Rm 9:12
y men as brothers, ... 1Tm 5:1

YOUTH

Do not remember the sins of my **y**. . Ps 25:7
y is renewed like the eagle. . . . . . . Ps 103:5
take pleasure in the wife of your **y**. . Pr 5:18
Start a **y** out on his way; . . . . Pr 22:6
your Creator in the days of your **y**: . . Ec 12:1
Don't let anyone despise your **y**, . . 1Tm 4:12

YOUTHFUL

Flee from **y** passions, ... 2Tm 2:22

- Z -

ZACCHAEUS

Tax collector who hosted Jesus and was
converted (Lk 19:2–9).

ZEAL

The **z** of the LORD of Armies will .. 2Kg 19:31
z for your house has consumed
me,............................Ps 69:9
z is not good without knowledge, .. Pr 19:2
The **z** of the LORD of Armies
will........................Is 9:7; 37:32
Z for your house will consume me... Jn 2:17
that they have **z** for God, but ..... Rm 10:2
regarding **z**, persecuting the
church; .... Php 3:6

ZEBULUN

Son of Jacob and Leah (Gn 30:20). Tribe with territory between the Sea of Galilee and Mount Carmel (Jos 19:10–16).

ZECHARIAH

1. Son of Jeroboam II; king of Israel (2Kg 15:8–12).
2. Prophet after the exile; son of Berechiah; descendant of Iddo (Ezr 5:1; Zch 1:1).
3. Father of John the Baptist (Lk 1:5–23,59–79).

ZEDEKIAH

Son of Josiah; last king of Judah; originally called Mattaniah; sons blinded; exiled (2Kg 24:17–25:7).

ZEPHANIAH

Prophet to Josiah; descendant of Hezekiah (Zph 1:1).

ZERUBBABEL

Leader of those returning from exile to rebuild the temple (Ezr 2:2; 4:2; 5:2; Hg 1:1). Descendant of David and Jehoiachin; ancestor of Jesus (1Ch 3:9–19; Mt 1:13; Lk 3:27).

ZIMRI

Chariot commander; killed Elah king of Israel; reigned seven days (1Kg 16:8–20).

ZION

Specifically, the stronghold in Jerusalem; also refers to the temple, hill, city, people, and heavenly city.
did capture the stronghold of Z,... 2Sm 5:7
Mount **Z**—the summit of
Zaphon— ....Ps 48:2
Sing us one of the songs of **Z** ..... Ps 137:3
laid a stone in **Z**, a tested
stone,..........................Is 28:16
Blow the ram's horn in **Z**; sound the
alarm............................Jl 2:1
Rejoice greatly, Daughter **Z**!........Zch 9:9
Tell Daughter **Z**, "See, your King .... Mt 21:5

Do not be afraid,
Daughter **Z**; ....Jn 12:15
a stone in **Z** to stumble over,......Rm 9:33
The Deliverer will come
from **Z**; ....Rm 11:26

- # -

430
lived in Egypt was **430** years......Ex 12:40
which came **430** years later,........Gl 3:17

666
of a person. Its number is **666**..... Rv 13:18

1,260
to prophesy for **1,260** days,........ Rv 11:3

144,000
144,000 sealed from every tribe ....Rv 7:4

Daily Bread
The Word of God in a Year

Compiled by the late Rev. Robert Murray M'Cheyne, MA

January

This is my beloved Son, with whom I am well-pleased. Listen to him! (Mt 17:5)

Genesis	1	Matthew	1	1st	Ezra	1	Acts	1
Genesis	2	Matthew	2	2nd	Ezra	2	Acts	2
Genesis	3	Matthew	3	3rd	Ezra	3	Acts	3
Genesis	4	Matthew	4	4th	Ezra	4	Acts	4
Genesis	5	Matthew	5	5th	Ezra	5	Acts	5
Genesis	6	Matthew	6	6th	Ezra	6	Acts	6
Genesis	7	Matthew	7	7th	Ezra	7	Acts	7
Genesis	8	Matthew	8	8th	Ezra	8	Acts	8
Genesis	9–10	Matthew	9	9th	Ezra	9	Acts	9
Genesis	11	Matthew	10	10th	Ezra	10	Acts	10
Genesis	12	Matthew	11	11th	Nehemiah	1	Acts	11
Genesis	13	Matthew	12	12th	Nehemiah	2	Acts	12
Genesis	14	Matthew	13	13th	Nehemiah	3	Acts	13
Genesis	15	Matthew	14	14th	Nehemiah	4	Acts	14
Genesis	16	Matthew	15	15th	Nehemiah	5	Acts	15
Genesis	17	Matthew	16	16th	Nehemiah	6	Acts	16
Genesis	18	Matthew	17	17th	Nehemiah	7	Acts	17
Genesis	19	Matthew	18	18th	Nehemiah	8	Acts	18
Genesis	20	Matthew	19	19th	Nehemiah	9	Acts	19
Genesis	21	Matthew	20	20th	Nehemiah	10	Acts	20
Genesis	22	Matthew	21	21st	Nehemiah	11	Acts	21
Genesis	23	Matthew	22	22nd	Nehemiah	12	Acts	22
Genesis	24	Matthew	23	23rd	Nehemiah	13	Acts	23
Genesis	25	Matthew	24	24th	Esther	1	Acts	24
Genesis	26	Matthew	25	25th	Esther	2	Acts	25
Genesis	27	Matthew	26	26th	Esther	3	Acts	26
Genesis	28	Matthew	27	27th	Esther	4	Acts	27
Genesis	29	Matthew	28	28th	Esther	5	Acts	28
Genesis	30	Mark	1	29th	Esther	6	Romans	1
Genesis	31	Mark	2	30th	Esther	7	Romans	2
Genesis	32	Mark	3	31st	Esther	8	Romans	3

February

I have treasured the words from his mouth more than my daily food. (Jb 23:12)

Genesis	33	Mark	4	1st	Esther	9–10	Romans	4
Genesis	34	Mark	5	2nd	Job	1	Romans	5
Genesis	35–36	Mark	6	3rd	Job	2	Romans	6
Genesis	37	Mark	7	4th	Job	3	Romans	7
Genesis	38	Mark	8	5th	Job	4	Romans	8
Genesis	39	Mark	9	6th	Job	5	Romans	9
Genesis	40	Mark	10	7th	Job	6	Romans	10
Genesis	41	Mark	11	8th	Job	7	Romans	11
Genesis	42	Mark	12	9th	Job	8	Romans	12
Genesis	43	Mark	13	10th	Job	9	Romans	13
Genesis	44	Mark	14	11th	Job	10	Romans	14
Genesis	45	Mark	15	12th	Job	11	Romans	15
Genesis	46	Mark	16	13th	Job	12	Romans	16
Genesis	47	Luke	1:1-38	14th	Job	13	1 Corinthians	1
Genesis	48	Luke	1:39-80	15th	Job	14	1 Corinthians	2
Genesis	49	Luke	2	16th	Job	15	1 Corinthians	3
Genesis	50	Luke	3	17th	Job	16–17	1 Corinthians	4
Exodus	1	Luke	4	18th	Job	18	1 Corinthians	5
Exodus	2	Luke	5	19th	Job	19	1 Corinthians	6
Exodus	3	Luke	6	20th	Job	20	1 Corinthians	7
Exodus	4	Luke	7	21st	Job	21	1 Corinthians	8
Exodus	5	Luke	8	22nd	Job	22	1 Corinthians	9
Exodus	6	Luke	9	23rd	Job	23	1 Corinthians	10
Exodus	7	Luke	10	24th	Job	24	1 Corinthians	11
Exodus	8	Luke	11	25th	Job	25–26	1 Corinthians	12
Exodus	9	Luke	12	26th	Job	27	1 Corinthians	13
Exodus	10	Luke	13	27th	Job	28	1 Corinthians	14
Exodus	11–12:21	Luke	14	28th	Job	29	1 Corinthians	15

March

But Mary was treasuring up all these things in her heart and meditating on them. (Lk 2:19)

Exodus	12:22ff.	Luke	15	1st	Job	30	1 Corinthians	16
Exodus	13	Luke	16	2nd	Job	31	2 Corinthians	1
Exodus	14	Luke	17	3rd	Job	32	2 Corinthians	2
Exodus	15	Luke	18	4th	Job	33	2 Corinthians	3
Exodus	16	Luke	19	5th	Job	34	2 Corinthians	4
Exodus	17	Luke	20	6th	Job	35	2 Corinthians	5
Exodus	18	Luke	21	7th	Job	36	2 Corinthians	6
Exodus	19	Luke	22	8th	Job	37	2 Corinthians	7
Exodus	20	Luke	23	9th	Job	38	2 Corinthians	8
Exodus	21	Luke	24	10th	Job	39	2 Corinthians	9
Exodus	22	John	1	11th	Job	40	2 Corinthians	10
Exodus	23	John	2	12th	Job	41	2 Corinthians	11
Exodus	24	John	3	13th	Job	42	2 Corinthians	12
Exodus	25	John	4	14th	Proverbs	1	2 Corinthians	13
Exodus	26	John	5	15th	Proverbs	2	Galatians	1
Exodus	27	John	6	16th	Proverbs	3	Galatians	2
Exodus	28	John	7	17th	Proverbs	4	Galatians	3
Exodus	29	John	8	18th	Proverbs	5	Galatians	4
Exodus	30	John	9	19th	Proverbs	6	Galatians	5
Exodus	31	John	10	20th	Proverbs	7	Galatians	6
Exodus	32	John	11	21st	Proverbs	8	Ephesians	1
Exodus	33	John	12	22nd	Proverbs	9	Ephesians	2
Exodus	34	John	13	23rd	Proverbs	10	Ephesians	3
Exodus	35	John	14	24th	Proverbs	11	Ephesians	4
Exodus	36	John	15	25th	Proverbs	12	Ephesians	5
Exodus	37	John	16	26th	Proverbs	13	Ephesians	6
Exodus	38	John	17	27th	Proverbs	14	Philippians	1
Exodus	39	John	18	28th	Proverbs	15	Philippians	2
Exodus	40	John	19	29th	Proverbs	16	Philippians	3
Leviticus	1	John	20	30th	Proverbs	17	Philippians	4
Leviticus	2–3	John	21	31st	Proverbs	18	Colossians	1

April

Send your light and your truth; let them lead me. (Ps 43:3)

Leviticus	4	Psalms	1–2	1st	Proverbs	19	Colossians	2
Leviticus	5	Psalms	3–4	2nd	Proverbs	20	Colossians	3
Leviticus	6	Psalms	5–6	3rd	Proverbs	21	Colossians	4
Leviticus	7	Psalms	7–8	4th	Proverbs	22	1 Thessalonians	1
Leviticus	8	Psalm	9	5th	Proverbs	23	1 Thessalonians	2
Leviticus	9	Psalm	10	6th	Proverbs	24	1 Thessalonians	3
Leviticus	10	Psalms	11–12	7th	Proverbs	25	1 Thessalonians	4
Leviticus	11–12	Psalms	13–14	8th	Proverbs	26	1 Thessalonians	5
Leviticus	13	Psalms	15–16	9th	Proverbs	27	2 Thessalonians	1
Leviticus	14	Psalm	17	10th	Proverbs	28	2 Thessalonians	2
Leviticus	15	Psalm	18	11th	Proverbs	29	2 Thessalonians	3
Leviticus	16	Psalm	19	12th	Proverbs	30	1 Timothy	1
Leviticus	17	Psalms	20–21	13th	Proverbs	31	1 Timothy	2
Leviticus	18	Psalm	22	14th	Ecclesiastes	1	1 Timothy	3
Leviticus	19	Psalms	23–24	15th	Ecclesiastes	2	1 Timothy	4
Leviticus	20	Psalm	25	16th	Ecclesiastes	3	1 Timothy	5
Leviticus	21	Psalms	26–27	17th	Ecclesiastes	4	1 Timothy	6
Leviticus	22	Psalms	28–29	18th	Ecclesiastes	5	2 Timothy	1
Leviticus	23	Psalm	30	19th	Ecclesiastes	6	2 Timothy	2
Leviticus	24	Psalm	31	20th	Ecclesiastes	7	2 Timothy	3
Leviticus	25	Psalm	32	21st	Ecclesiastes	8	2 Timothy	4
Leviticus	26	Psalm	33	22nd	Ecclesiastes	9	Titus	1
Leviticus	27	Psalm	4	23rd	Ecclesiastes	10	Titus	2
Numbers	1	Psalm	35	24th	Ecclesiastes	11	Titus	3
Numbers	2	Psalm	36	25th	Ecclesiastes	12	Philemon	
Numbers	3	Psalm	37	26th	Song of Songs	1	Hebrews	1
Numbers	4	Psalm	38	27th	Song of Songs	2	Hebrews	2
Numbers	5	Psalm	39	28th	Song of Songs	3	Hebrews	3
Numbers	6	Psalms	40–41	29th	Song of Songs	4	Hebrews	4
Numbers	7	Psalms	42–43	30th	Song of Songs	5	Hebrews	5

May

From infancy you have known the sacred Scriptures. (2Tm 3:15)

Numbers	8	Psalm	44	1st	Song of Songs	6	Hebrews	6
Numbers	9	Psalm	45	2nd	Song of Songs	7	Hebrews	7
Numbers	10	Psalms	46–47	3rd	Song of Songs	8	Hebrews	8
Numbers	11	Psalm	48	4th	Isaiah	1	Hebrews	9
Numbers	12-13	Psalm	49	5th	Isaiah	2	Hebrews	10
Numbers	14	Psalm	50	6th	Isaiah	3–4	Hebrews	11
Numbers	15	Psalm	51	7th	Isaiah	5	Hebrews	12
Numbers	16	Psalms	52–54	8th	Isaiah	6	Hebrews	13
Numbers	17–18	Psalm	55	9th	Isaiah	7	James	1

Numbers	19	Psalms	56–57	10th	Isaiah	8–9:7	James	2
Numbers	20	Psalms	58–59	11th	Isaiah	9:8–10:4	James	3
Numbers	21	Psalms	60–61	12th	Isaiah	10:5ff.	James	4
Numbers	22	Psalms	62–63	13th	Isaiah	11–12	James	5
Numbers	23	Psalms	64–65	14th	Isaiah	13	1 Peter	1
Numbers	24	Psalms	66–67	15th	Isaiah	14	1 Peter	2
Numbers	25	Psalm	68	16th	Isaiah	15	1 Peter	3
Numbers	26	Psalm	69	17th	Isaiah	16	1 Peter	4
Numbers	27	Psalms	70–71	18th	Isaiah	17–18	1 Peter	5
Numbers	28	Psalm	72	19th	Isaiah	19–20	2 Peter	1
Numbers	29	Psalm	73	20th	Isaiah	21	2 Peter	2
Numbers	30	Psalm	74	21st	Isaiah	22	2 Peter	3
Numbers	31	Psalms	75–76	22nd	Isaiah	23	1 John	1
Numbers	32	Psalm	77	23rd	Isaiah	24	1 John	2
Numbers	33	Psalm	78:1-37	24th	Isaiah	25	1 John	3
Numbers	34	Psalm	78:38ff.	25th	Isaiah	26	1 John	4
Numbers	35	Psalm	79	26th	Isaiah	27	1 John	5
Numbers	36	Psalm	80	27th	Isaiah	28	2 John	
Deuteronomy	1	Psalms	81–82	28th	Isaiah	29	3 John	
Deuteronomy	2	Psalms	83–84	29th	Isaiah	30	Jude	
Deuteronomy	3	Psalm	85	30th	Isaiah	31	Revelation	1
Deuteronomy	4	Psalms	86–87	31st	Isaiah	32	Revelation	2

June

Blessed is the one who reads aloud the words of this prophecy, and blessed are those who hear the words of this prophecy and keep what is written in it. (Rv 1:3)

Deuteronomy	5	Psalm	88	1st	Isaiah	33	Revelation	3
Deuteronomy	6	Psalm	89	2nd	Isaiah	34	Revelation	4
Deuteronomy	7	Psalm	90	3rd	Isaiah	35	Revelation	5
Deuteronomy	8	Psalm	91	4th	Isaiah	36	Revelation	6
Deuteronomy	9	Psalms	92–93	5th	Isaiah	37	Revelation	7
Deuteronomy	10	Psalm	94	6th	Isaiah	38	Revelation	8
Deuteronomy	11	Psalms	95–96	7th	Isaiah	39	Revelation	9
Deuteronomy	12	Psalms	97–98	8th	Isaiah	40	Revelation	10
Deuteronomy	13–14	Psalms	99–101	9th	Isaiah	41	Revelation	11
Deuteronomy	15	Psalm	102	10th	Isaiah	42	Revelation	12
Deuteronomy	16	Psalm	103	11th	Isaiah	43	Revelation	13
Deuteronomy	17	Psalm	104	12th	Isaiah	44	Revelation	14
Deuteronomy	18	Psalm	105	13th	Isaiah	45	Revelation	15
Deuteronomy	19	Psalm	106	14th	Isaiah	46	Revelation	16
Deuteronomy	20	Psalm	107	15th	Isaiah	47	Revelation	17
Deuteronomy	21	Psalms	108–109	16th	Isaiah	48	Revelation	18
Deuteronomy	22	Psalms	110–111	17th	Isaiah	49	Revelation	19
Deuteronomy	23	Psalms	112–113	18th	Isaiah	50	Revelation	20
Deuteronomy	24	Psalms	114–115	19th	Isaiah	51	Revelation	21
Deuteronomy	25	Psalm	116	20th	Isaiah	52	Revelation	22
Deuteronomy	26	Psalms	117–118	21st	Isaiah	53	Matthew	1
Deuteronomy	27–28:19	Psalm	119:1-24	22nd	Isaiah	54	Matthew	2
Deuteronomy	28:20ff.	Psalm	119:25-48	23rd	Isaiah	55	Matthew	3
Deuteronomy	29	Psalm	119:49-72	24th	Isaiah	56	Matthew	4
Deuteronomy	30	Psalm	119:73-96	25th	Isaiah	57	Matthew	5
Deuteronomy	31	Psalm	119:97-120	26th	Isaiah	58	Matthew	6
Deuteronomy	32	Psalm	119:121-144	27th	Isaiah	59	Matthew	7
Deuteronomy	33–34	Psalm	119:145-176	28th	Isaiah	60	Matthew	8
Joshua	1	Psalms	120–122	29th	Isaiah	61	Matthew	9
Joshua	2	Psalms	123–125	30th	Isaiah	62	Matthew	10

JULY

They received the word with eagerness and examined the Scriptures daily to see if these things were so. (Ac 17:11)

Joshua	3	Psalms	126–128	1st	Isaiah	63	Matthew	11
Joshua	4	Psalms	129–131	2nd	Isaiah	64	Matthew	12
Joshua	5–6:5	Psalms	132–134	3rd	Isaiah	65	Matthew	13
Joshua	6:6ff.	Psalms	135–136	4th	Isaiah	66	Matthew	14
Joshua	7	Psalms	137–138	5th	Jeremiah	1	Matthew	15
Joshua	8	Psalm	139	6th	Jeremiah	2	Matthew	16
Joshua	9	Psalms	140–141	7th	Jeremiah	3	Matthew	17
Joshua	10	Psalms	142–143	8th	Jeremiah	4	Matthew	18
Joshua	11	Psalm	144	9th	Jeremiah	5	Matthew	19
Joshua	12–13	Psalm	145	10th	Jeremiah	6	Matthew	20
Joshua	14–15	Psalms	146–147	11th	Jeremiah	7	Matthew	21
Joshua	16–17	Psalm	148	12th	Jeremiah	8	Matthew	22
Joshua	18–19	Psalms	149–150	13th	Jeremiah	9	Matthew	23
Joshua	20–21	Acts	1	14th	Jeremiah	10	Matthew	24
Joshua	22	Acts	2	15th	Jeremiah	11	Matthew	25
Joshua	23	Acts	3	16th	Jeremiah	12	Matthew	26
Joshua	24	Acts	4	17th	Jeremiah	13	Matthew	27
Judges	1	Acts	5	18th	Jeremiah	14	Matthew	28
Judges	2	Acts	6	19th	Jeremiah	15	Mark	1
Judges	3	Acts	7	20th	Jeremiah	16	Mark	2

Judges	4	Acts	8	21st	Jeremiah	17	Mark	3
Judges	5	Acts	9	22nd	Jeremiah	18	Mark	4
Judges	6	Acts	10	23rd	Jeremiah	19	Mark	5
Judges	7	Acts	11	24th	Jeremiah	20	Mark	6
Judges	8	Acts	12	25th	Jeremiah	21	Mark	7
Judges	9	Acts	13	26th	Jeremiah	22	Mark	8
Judges	10–11:11	Acts	14	27th	Jeremiah	23	Mark	9
Judges	11:12ff.	Acts	15	28th	Jeremiah	24	Mark	10
Judges	12	Acts	16	29th	Jeremiah	25	Mark	11
Judges	13	Acts	17	30th	Jeremiah	26	Mark	12
Judges	14	Acts	18	31st	Jeremiah	27	Mark	13

August

Speak, LORD, for your servant is listening. (1Sm 3:10)

Judges	15	Acts	19	1st	Jeremiah	28	Mark	14
Judges	16	Acts	20	2nd	Jeremiah	29	Mark	15
Judges	17	Acts	21	3rd	Jeremiah	30–31	Mark	16
Judges	18	Acts	22	4th	Jeremiah	32	Psalms	1–2
Judges	19	Acts	23	5th	Jeremiah	33	Psalms	3–4
Judges	20	Acts	24	6th	Jeremiah	34	Psalms	5–6
Judges	21	Acts	25	7th	Jeremiah	35	Psalms	7–8
Ruth	1	Acts	26	8th	Jeremiah	36	Psalm	9
Ruth	2	Acts	27	9th	Jeremiah	37	Psalm	10
Ruth	3–4	Acts	28	10th	Jeremiah	38	Psalms	11–12
1 Samuel	1	Romans	1	11th	Jeremiah	39	Psalms	13–14
1 Samuel	2	Romans	2	12th	Jeremiah	40	Psalms	15–16
1 Samuel	3	Romans	3	13th	Jeremiah	41	Psalm	17
1 Samuel	4	Romans	4	14th	Jeremiah	42	Psalm	18
1 Samuel	5–6	Romans	5	15th	Jeremiah	43	Psalm	19
1 Samuel	7–8	Romans	6	16th	Jeremiah	44	Psalms	20–21
1 Samuel	9	Romans	7	17th	Jeremiah	46	Psalm	22
1 Samuel	10	Romans	8	18th	Jeremiah	47	Psalms	23–24
1 Samuel	11	Romans	9	19th	Jeremiah	48	Psalm	25
1 Samuel	12	Romans	10	20th	Jeremiah	49	Psalms	26–27
1 Samuel	13	Romans	11	21st	Jeremiah	50	Psalms	28–29
1 Samuel	14	Romans	12	22nd	Jeremiah	51	Psalm	30
1 Samuel	15	Romans	13	23rd	Jeremiah	52	Psalm	31
1 Samuel	16	Romans	14	24th	Lamentations	1	Psalm	32
1 Samuel	17	Romans	15	25th	Lamentations	2	Psalm	33
1 Samuel	18	Romans	16	26th	Lamentations	3	Psalm	34
1 Samuel	19	1 Corinthians	1	27th	Lamentations	4	Psalm	35
1 Samuel	20	1 Corinthians	2	28th	Lamentations	5	Psalm	36
1 Samuel	21–22	1 Corinthians	3	29th	Ezekiel	1	Psalm	37
1 Samuel	23	1 Corinthians	4	30th	Ezekiel	2	Psalm	38
1 Samuel	24	1 Corinthians	5	31st	Ezekiel	3	Psalm	39

September

The instruction of the LORD is perfect, renewing one's life. (Ps 19:7)

1 Samuel	25	1 Corinthians	6	1st	Ezekiel	4	Psalms	40–41
1 Samuel	26	1 Corinthians	7	2nd	Ezekiel	5	Psalms	42–43
1 Samuel	27	1 Corinthians	8	3rd	Ezekiel	6	Psalm	44
1 Samuel	28	1 Corinthians	9	4th	Ezekiel	7	Psalm	45
1 Samuel	29–30	1 Corinthians	10	5th	Ezekiel	8	Psalms	46–47
1 Samuel	31	1 Corinthians	11	6th	Ezekiel	9	Psalm	48
2 Samuel	1	1 Corinthians	12	7th	Ezekiel	10	Psalm	49
2 Samuel	2	1 Corinthians	13	8th	Ezekiel	11	Psalm	50
2 Samuel	3	1 Corinthians	14	9th	Ezekiel	12	Psalm	51
2 Samuel	4–5	1 Corinthians	15	10th	Ezekiel	13	Psalms	52–54
2 Samuel	6	1 Corinthians	16	11th	Ezekiel	14	Psalm	55
2 Samuel	7	2 Corinthians	1	12th	Ezekiel	15	Psalms	56–57
2 Samuel	8–9	2 Corinthians	2	13th	Ezekiel	16	Psalms	58–59
2 Samuel	10	2 Corinthians	3	14th	Ezekiel	17	Psalms	60–61
2 Samuel	11	2 Corinthians	4	15th	Ezekiel	18	Psalms	62–63
2 Samuel	12	2 Corinthians	5	16th	Ezekiel	19	Psalms	64–65
2 Samuel	13	2 Corinthians	6	17th	Ezekiel	20	Psalms	66–67
2 Samuel	14	2 Corinthians	7	18th	Ezekiel	21	Psalm	68
2 Samuel	15	2 Corinthians	8	19th	Ezekiel	22	Psalm	69
2 Samuel	16	2 Corinthians	9	20th	Ezekiel	23	Psalms	70–71
2 Samuel	17	2 Corinthians	10	21st	Ezekiel	24	Psalm	72
2 Samuel	18	2 Corinthians	11	22nd	Ezekiel	25	Psalm	73
2 Samuel	19	2 Corinthians	12	23rd	Ezekiel	26	Psalm	74
2 Samuel	20	2 Corinthians	13	24th	Ezekiel	27	Psalms	75–76
2 Samuel	21	Galatians	1	25th	Ezekiel	28	Psalm	77
2 Samuel	22	Galatians	2	26th	Ezekiel	29	Psalm	78:1–37
2 Samuel	23	Galatians	3	27th	Ezekiel	30	Psalm	78:38ff.
2 Samuel	24	Galatians	4	28th	Ezekiel	31	Psalm	79
1 Kings	1	Galatians	5	29th	Ezekiel	32	Psalm	80
1 Kings	2	Galatians	6	30th	Ezekiel	33	Psalms	81–82

October

How I love your instruction! It is my meditation all day long. (Ps 119:97)

1 Kings	3	Ephesians	1	1st	Ezekiel	34	Psalms	83–84
1 Kings	4–5	Ephesians	2	2nd	Ezekiel	35	Psalm	85
1 Kings	6	Ephesians	3	3rd	Ezekiel	36	Psalm	86
1 Kings	7	Ephesians	4	4th	Ezekiel	37	Psalms	87–88
1 Kings	8	Ephesians	5	5th	Ezekiel	38	Psalm	89
1 Kings	9	Ephesians	6	6th	Ezekiel	39	Psalm	90
1 Kings	10	Philippians	1	7th	Ezekiel	40	Psalm	91
1 Kings	11	Philippians	2	8th	Ezekiel	41	Psalms	92–93
1 Kings	12	Philippians	3	9th	Ezekiel	42	Psalm	94
1 Kings	13	Philippians	4	10th	Ezekiel	43	Psalms	95–96
1 Kings	14	Colossians	1	11th	Ezekiel	44	Psalms	97–98
1 Kings	15	Colossians	2	12th	Ezekiel	45	Psalms	99–101
1 Kings	16	Colossians	3	13th	Ezekiel	46	Psalm	102
1 Kings	17	Colossians	4	14th	Ezekiel	47	Psalm	103
1 Kings	18	1 Thessalonians	1	15th	Ezekiel	48	Psalm	104
1 Kings	19	1 Thessalonians	2	16th	Daniel	1	Psalm	105
1 Kings	20	1 Thessalonians	3	17th	Daniel	2	Psalm	106
1 Kings	21	1 Thessalonians	4	18th	Daniel	3	Psalm	107
1 Kings	22	1 Thessalonians	5	19th	Daniel	4	Psalms	108–109
2 Kings	1	2 Thessalonians	1	20th	Daniel	5	Psalms	110–111
2 Kings	2	2 Thessalonians	2	21st	Daniel	6	Psalms	112–113
2 Kings	3	2 Thessalonians	3	22nd	Daniel	7	Psalms	114–115
2 Kings	4	1 Timothy	1	23rd	Daniel	8	Psalm	116
2 Kings	5	1 Timothy	2	24th	Daniel	9	Psalms	117–118
2 Kings	6	1 Timothy	3	25th	Daniel	10	Psalm	119:1-24
2 Kings	7	1 Timothy	4	26th	Daniel	11	Psalm	119:25-48
2 Kings	8	1 Timothy	5	27th	Daniel	12	Psalm	119:49-72
2 Kings	9	1 Timothy	6	28th	Hosea	1	Psalm	119:73-96
2 Kings	10	2 Timothy	1	29th	Hosea	2	Psalm	119:97-120
2 Kings	11–12	2 Timothy	2	30th	Hosea	3–4	Psalm	119:121-144
2 Kings	13	2 Timothy	3	31st	Hosea	5–6	Psalm	119:145-176

November

Like newborn infants, desire the pure milk of the word, so that by it you may grow up into your salvation. (1Pt 2:2)

2 Kings	14	2 Timothy	4	1st	Hosea	7	Psalms	120–122
2 Kings	15	Titus	1	2nd	Hosea	8	Psalms	123–125
2 Kings	16	Titus	2	3rd	Hosea	9	Psalms	126–128
2 Kings	17	Titus	3	4th	Hosea	10	Psalms	129–131
2 Kings	18	Philemon	1	5th	Hosea	11	Psalms	132–134
2 Kings	19	Hebrews	1	6th	Hosea	12	Psalms	135–136
2 Kings	20	Hebrews	2	7th	Hosea	13	Psalms	137–138
2 Kings	21	Hebrews	3	8th	Hosea	14	Psalm	139
2 Kings	22	Hebrews	4	9th	Joel	1	Psalms	140–141
2 Kings	23	Hebrews	5	10th	Joel	2	Psalm	142
2 Kings	24	Hebrews	6	11th	Joel	3	Psalm	143
2 Kings	25	Hebrews	7	12th	Amos	1	Psalm	144
1 Chronicles	1–2	Hebrews	8	13th	Amos	2	Psalm	145
1 Chronicles	3–4	Hebrews	9	14th	Amos	3	Psalms	146–147
1 Chronicles	5–6	Hebrews	10	15th	Amos	4	Psalms	148–150
1 Chronicles	7–8	Hebrews	11	16th	Amos	5	Luke	1:1-38
1 Chronicles	9–10	Hebrews	12	17th	Amos	6	Luke	1:39ff.
1 Chronicles	11–12	Hebrews	13	18th	Amos	7	Luke	2
1 Chronicles	13–14	James	1	19th	Amos	8	Luke	3
1 Chronicles	15	James	2	20th	Amos	9	Luke	4
1 Chronicles	16	James	3	21st	Obadiah		Luke	5
1 Chronicles	17	James	4	22nd	Jonah	1	Luke	6
1 Chronicles	18	James	5	23rd	Jonah	2	Luke	7
1 Chronicles	19–20	1 Peter	1	24th	Jonah	3	Luke	8
1 Chronicles	21	1 Peter	2	25th	Jonah	4	Luke	9
1 Chronicles	22	1 Peter	3	26th	Micah	1	Luke	10
1 Chronicles	23	1 Peter	4	27th	Micah	2	Luke	11
1 Chronicles	24–25	1 Peter	5	28th	Micah	3	Luke	12
1 Chronicles	26–27	2 Peter	1	29th	Micah	4	Luke	13
1 Chronicles	28	2 Peter	2	30th	Micah	5	Luke	14

December

The instruction of his God is in his heart; his steps do not falter. (Ps 37:31)

1 Chronicles	29	2 Peter	3	1st	Micah	6	Luke	15
2 Chronicles	1	1 John	1	2nd	Micah	7	Luke	16
2 Chronicles	2	1 John	2	3rd	Nahum	1	Luke	17
2 Chronicles	3–4	1 John	3	4th	Nahum	2	Luke	18
2 Chronicles	5–6:11	1 John	4	5th	Nahum	3	Luke	19
2 Chronicles	6:12ff.	1 John	5	6th	Habakkuk	1	Luke	20
2 Chronicles	7	2 John		7th	Habakkuk	2	Luke	21
2 Chronicles	8	3 John		8th	Habakkuk	3	Luke	22

2 Chronicles	9	Jude		9th	Zephaniah	1	Luke	23
2 Chronicles	10	Revelation	1	10th	Zephaniah	2	Luke	24
2 Chronicles	11–12	Revelation	2	11th	Zephaniah	3	John	1
2 Chronicles	13	Revelation	3	12th	Haggai	1	John	2
2 Chronicles	14–15	Revelation	4	13th	Haggai	2	John	3
2 Chronicles	16	Revelation	5	14th	Zechariah	1	John	4
2 Chronicles	17	Revelation	6	15th	Zechariah	2	John	5
2 Chronicles	18	Revelation	7	16th	Zechariah	3	John	6
2 Chronicles	19–20	Revelation	8	17th	Zechariah	4	John	7
2 Chronicles	21	Revelation	9	18th	Zechariah	5	John	8
2 Chronicles	22–23	Revelation	10	19th	Zechariah	6	John	9
2 Chronicles	24	Revelation	11	20th	Zechariah	7	John	10
2 Chronicles	25	Revelation	12	21st	Zechariah	8	John	11
2 Chronicles	26	Revelation	13	22nd	Zechariah	9	John	12
2 Chronicles	27–28	Revelation	14	23rd	Zechariah	10	John	13
2 Chronicles	29	Revelation	15	24th	Zechariah	11	John	14
2 Chronicles	30	Revelation	16	25th	Zechariah	12–13:1	John	15
2 Chronicles	31	Revelation	17	26th	Zechariah	13:2ff.	John	16
2 Chronicles	32	Revelation	18	27th	Zechariah	14	John	17
2 Chronicles	33	Revelation	19	28th	Malachi	1	John	18
2 Chronicles	34	Revelation	20	29th	Malachi	2	John	19
2 Chronicles	35	Revelation	21	30th	Malachi	3	John	20
2 Chronicles	36	Revelation	22	31st	Malachi	4	John	21

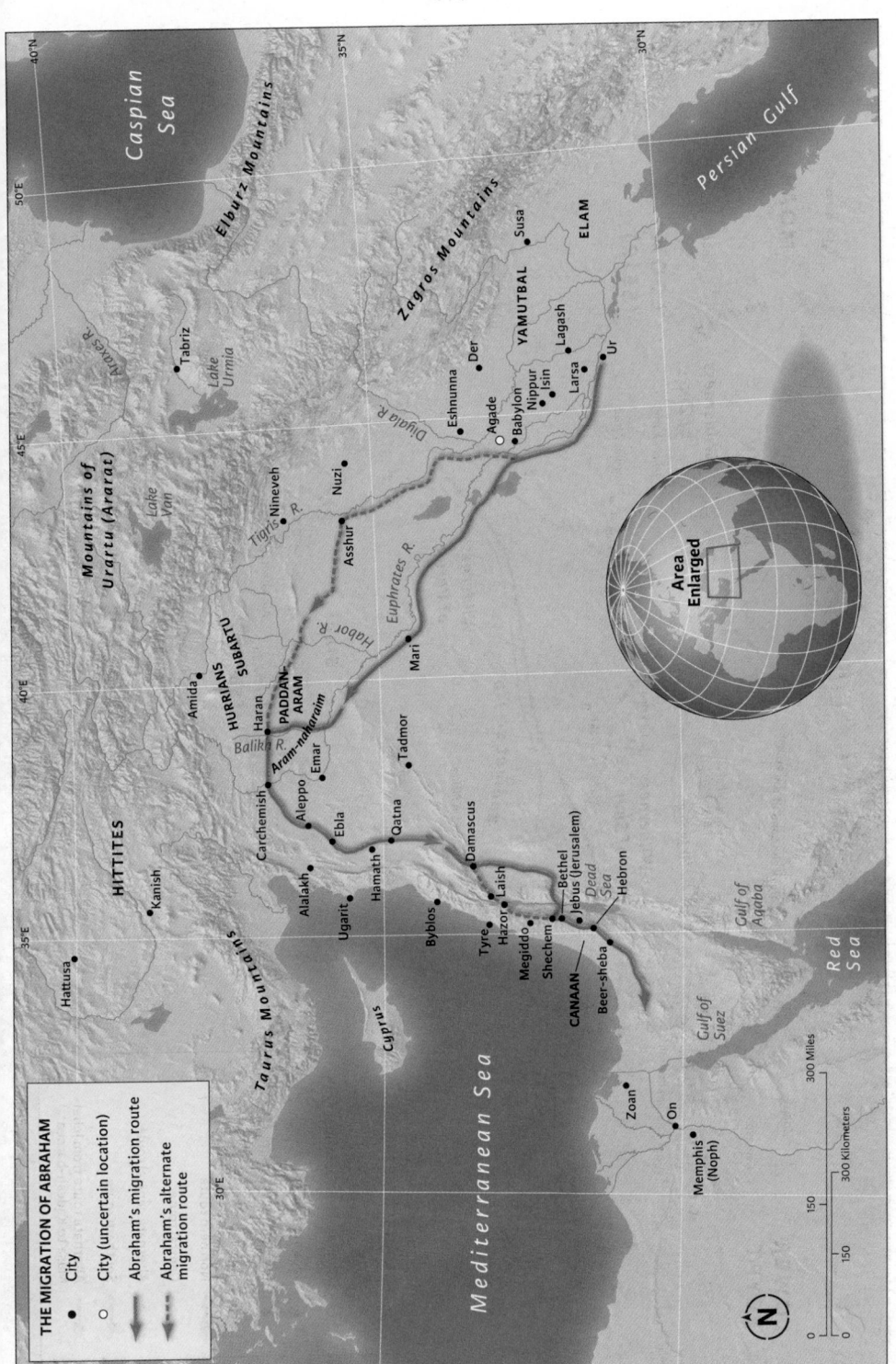

THE MIGRATION OF ABRAHAM

• City
○ City (uncertain location)
Abraham's migration route
Abraham's alternate migration route

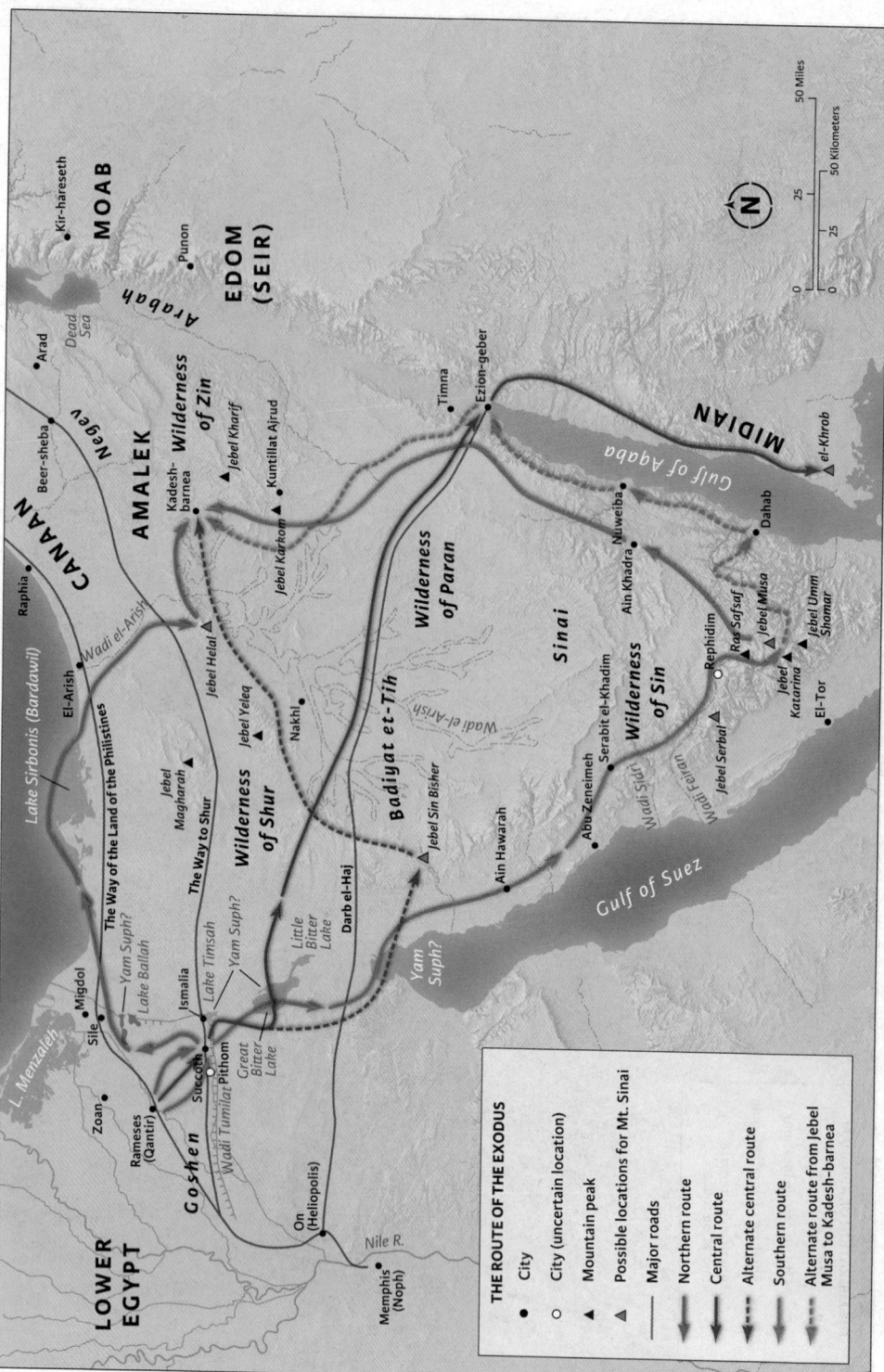

THE ROUTE OF THE EXODUS

- • City
- ○ City (uncertain location)
- ▲ Mountain peak
- ▲ Possible locations for Mt. Sinai
- —— Major roads
- Northern route
- Central route
- Alternate central route
- Southern route
- Alternate route from Jebel Musa to Kadesh-barnea

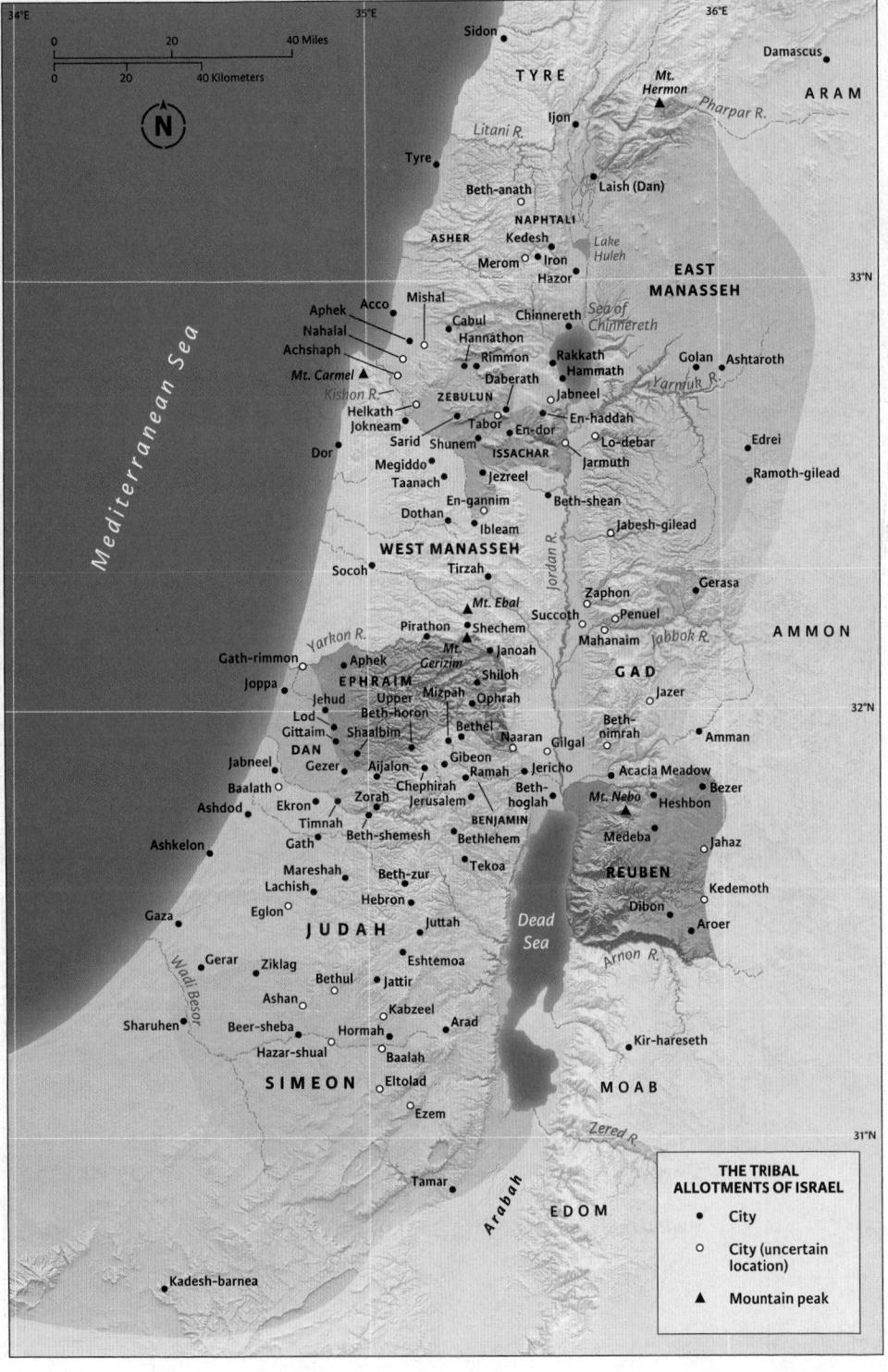

THE TRIBAL
ALLOTMENTS OF ISRAEL

- • City
- ○ City (uncertain location)
- ▲ Mountain peak

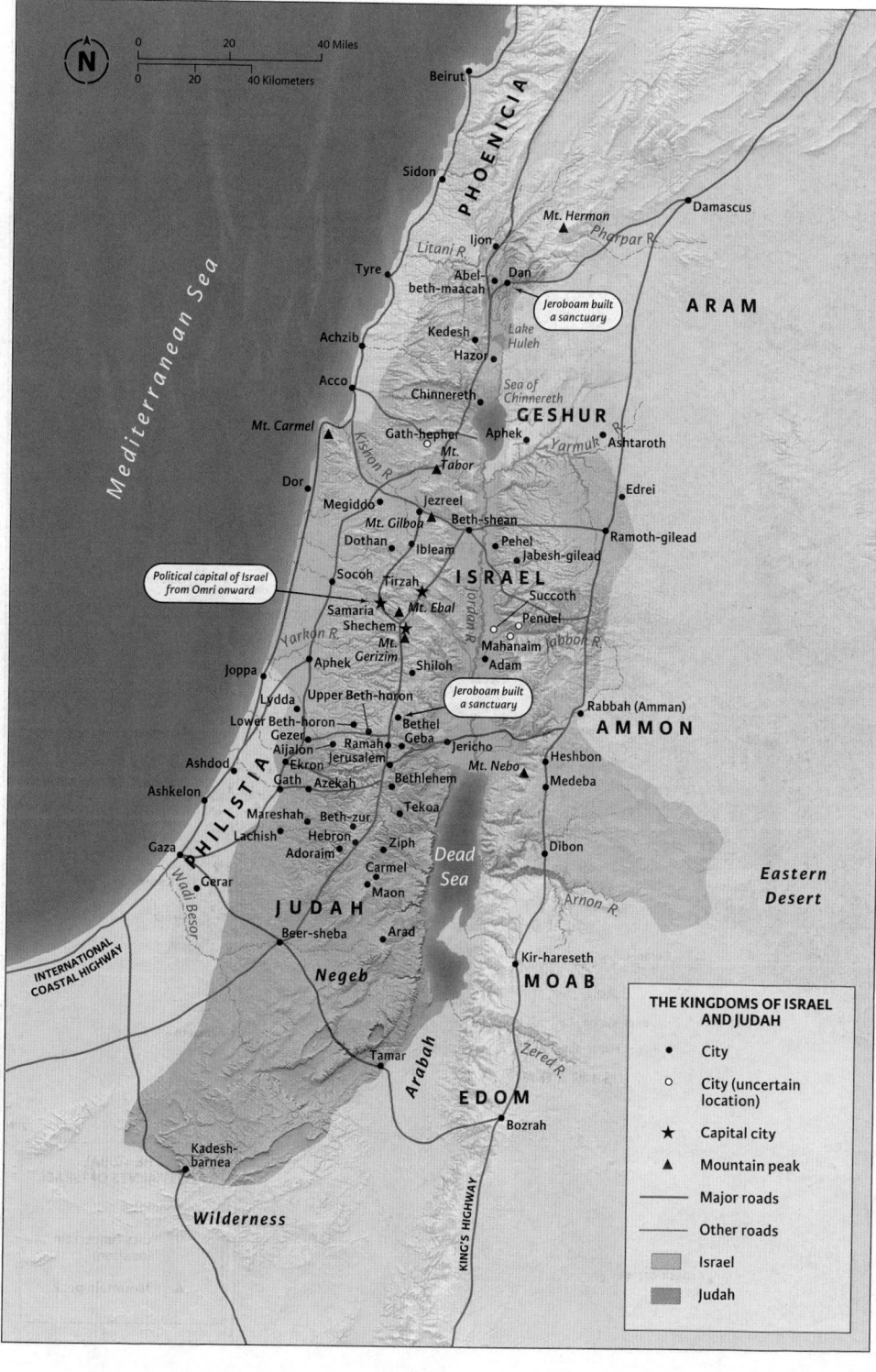

THE KINGDOMS OF ISRAEL
AND JUDAH

- • City
- ○ City (uncertain location)
- ★ Capital city
- ▲ Mountain peak
- —— Major roads
- —— Other roads
- ▮ Israel
- ▮ Judah

Coponius was named the first prefect and established the administrative capital at Caesarea Maritima

ISRAEL IN THE TIME OF JESUS

- • City
- ○ City (uncertain location)
- ◉ Decapolis city
- ○ Decapolis city (uncertain location)
- ★ Administrative capital
- ▲ Mountain peak
- —— Major route
- —— Other route
- ▨ First procuratorship
- ▨ Territory of Antipas
- ▨ Territory of Philip
- ▨ Syrian territory

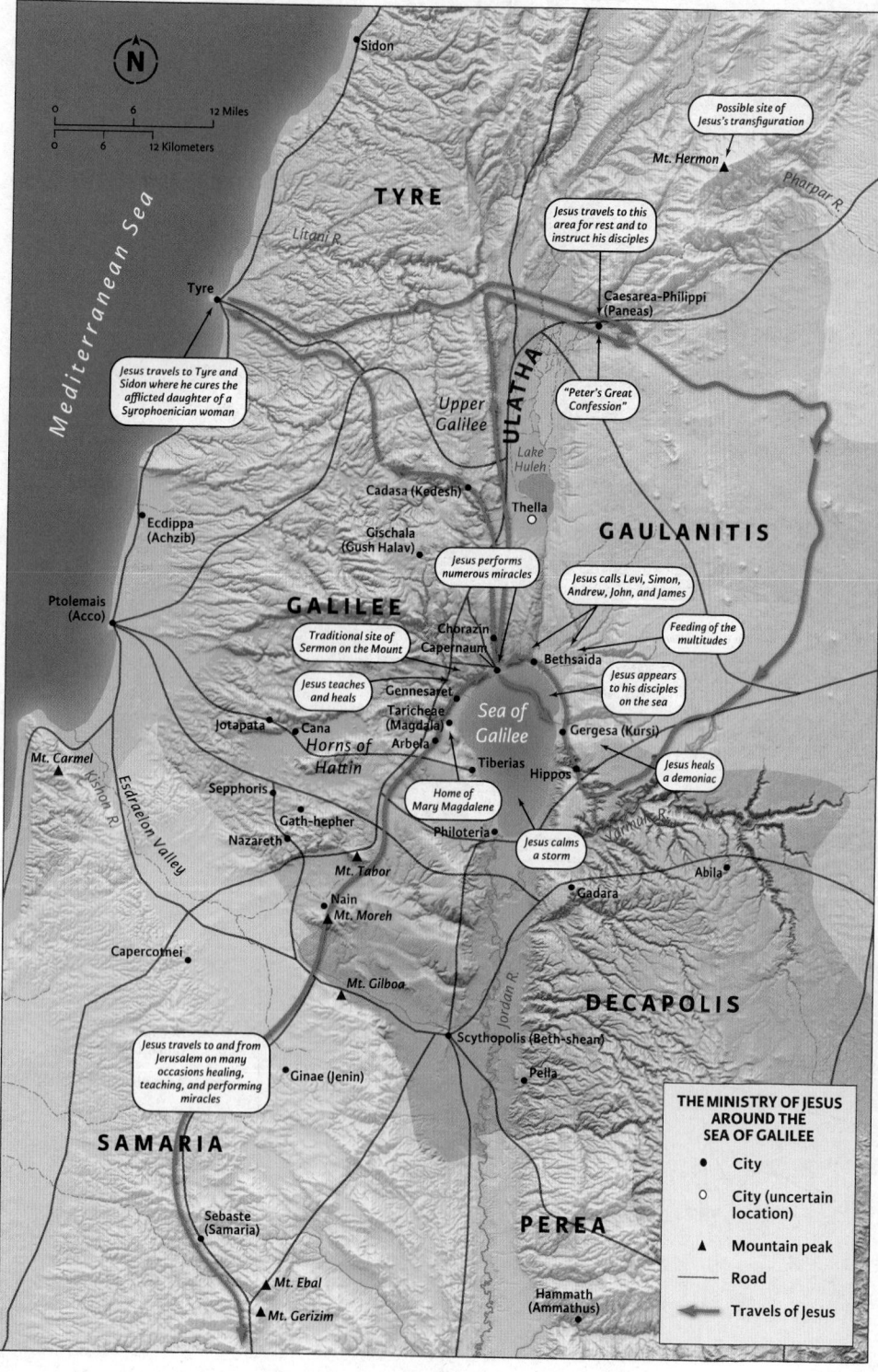

THE MINISTRY OF JESUS
AROUND THE
SEA OF GALILEE

- • City
- ○ City (uncertain location)
- ▲ Mountain peak
- — Road
- ← Travels of Jesus

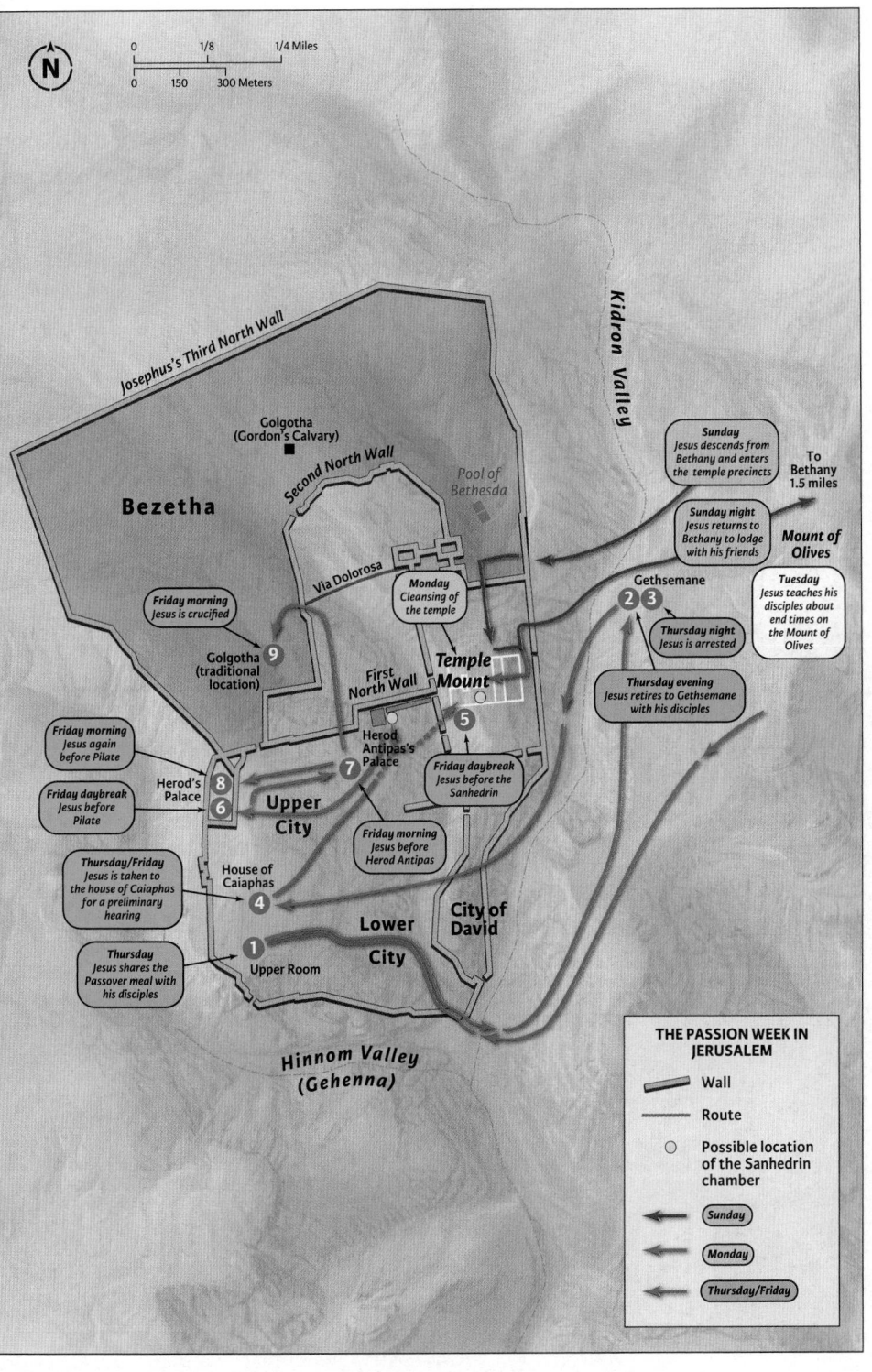

N

| 0 | 1/8 | 1/4 Miles |
| 0 | 150 | 300 Meters |

Josephus's Third North Wall

Golgotha
(Gordon's Calvary)

Second North Wall

Pool of
Bethesda

Bezetha

Via Dolorosa

Friday morning
Jesus is crucified

Monday
Cleansing of
the temple

Golgotha
(traditional
location)   9

First
North Wall

Temple
Mount

Herod
Antipas's
Palace

Friday morning
Jesus again
before Pilate

Herod's
Palace   8

Friday daybreak
Jesus before
Pilate   6

7

Friday daybreak
Jesus before the
Sanhedrin   5

Upper
City

Friday morning
Jesus before
Herod Antipas

Thursday/Friday
Jesus is taken to
the house of Caiaphas
for a preliminary
hearing   4

House of
Caiaphas

Lower
City

City of
David

Thursday
Jesus shares the
Passover meal with
his disciples   1

Upper Room

Hinnom Valley
(Gehenna)

Kidron Valley

Sunday
Jesus descends from
Bethany and enters
the temple precincts

To
Bethany
1.5 miles

Sunday night
Jesus returns to
Bethany to lodge
with his friends

Mount of
Olives

Gethsemane

2 3

Tuesday
Jesus teaches his
disciples about
end times on
the Mount of
Olives

Thursday night
Jesus is arrested

Thursday evening
Jesus retires to Gethsemane
with his disciples

**THE PASSION WEEK IN
JERUSALEM**

Wall

Route

Possible location
of the Sanhedrin
chamber

Sunday

Monday

Thursday/Friday

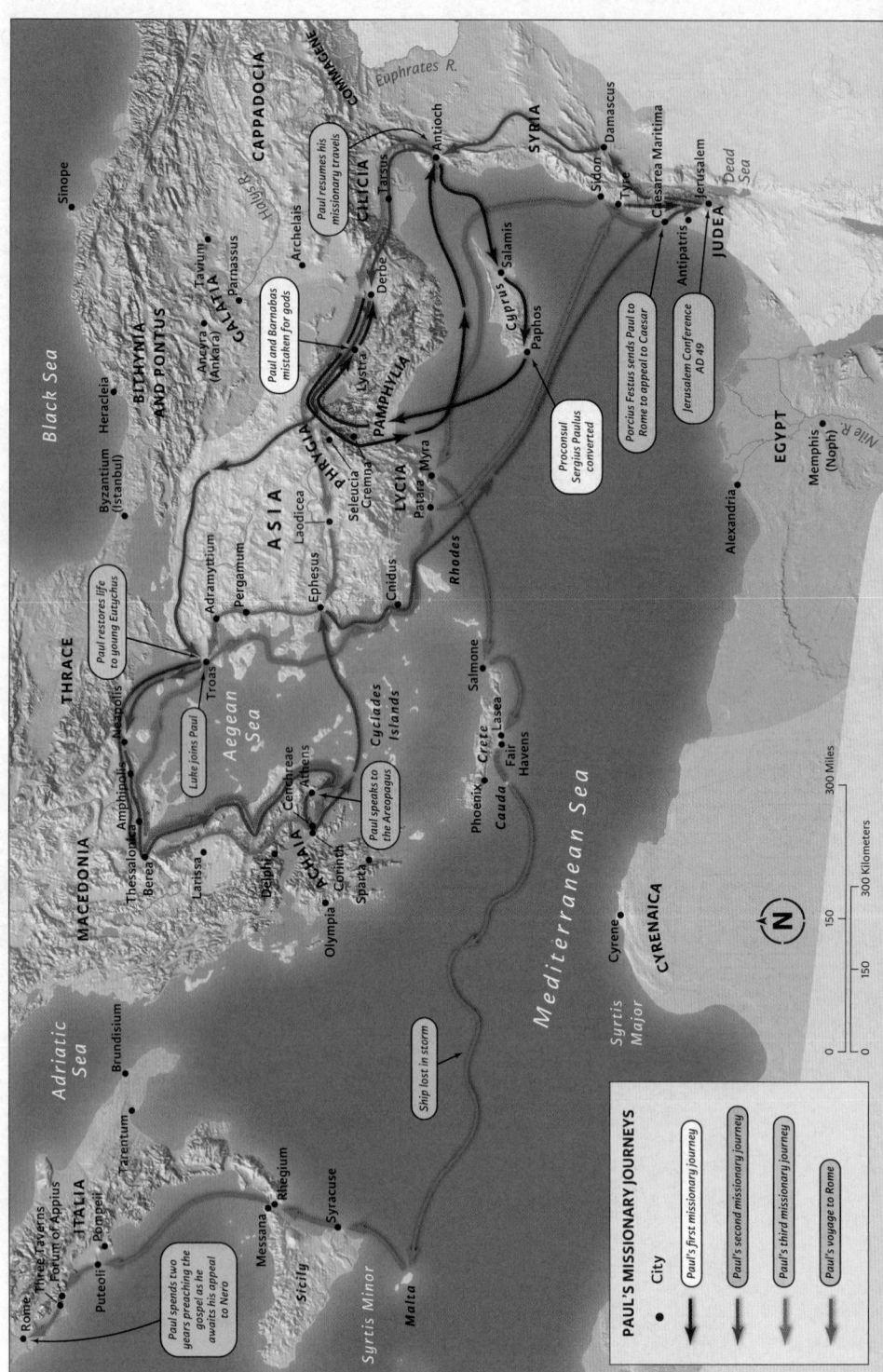

Euphrates R.

CAPPADOCIA

COMMAGENE

HALYS R.

Sinope

Heraclea

Byzantium
(Istanbul)

**BITHYNIA
AND PONTUS**

Ancyra
(Ankara)
Tavium

Parnassus

GALATIA

Archelais

Antioch

Tarsus

CILICIA

Derbe

Lystra

*Paul resumes his
missionary travels*

SYRIA

Damascus

Sidon

Tyre

Caesarea Maritima

Antipatris

Jerusalem

Dead
Sea

JUDEA

*Paul and Barnabas
mistaken for gods*

PAMPHYLIA

Cyprus

Salamis

Paphos

*Proconsul
Sergius Paulus
converted*

*Porcius Festus sends Paul to
Rome to appeal to Caesar*

*Jerusalem Conference
AD 49*

EGYPT

Memphis
(Noph)

Nile R.

Alexandria

THRACE

Adramyttium

Pergamum

ASIA

PHRYGIA

Laodicea

Ephesus

Seleucia
Cremna

LYCIA

Patara
Myra

Cnidus

Rhodes

*Paul restores life
to young Eutychus*

Neapolis

Troas

Luke joins Paul

**Aegean
Sea**

Salmone

*Cyclades
Islands*

MACEDONIA

Amphipolis

Thessalonica

Berea

Larissa

Cenchreae

Athens

Corinth

Sparta

Delphi

ACHAIA

Olympia

*Paul speaks to
the Areopagus*

Phoenix

Cauda

Crete

Lasea

Fair
Havens

Mediterranean Sea

Black Sea

CYRENAICA

Cyrene

Syrtis
Major

Ship lost in storm

N

| 0 | 150 | 300 Miles |
| 0 | 150 | 300 Kilometers |

**Adriatic
Sea**

Brundisium

Tarentum

Rome

Three Taverns
Forum of Appius

Puteoli

Pompeii

ITALIA

Rhegium

Messana

Syracuse

Sicily

Syrtis Minor

Malta

*Paul spends two
years preaching the
gospel as he
awaits his appeal
to Nero*

PAUL'S MISSIONARY JOURNEYS

● City

→ Paul's first missionary journey

→ Paul's second missionary journey

→ Paul's third missionary journey

→ Paul's voyage to Rome